Willings
Press Guide

Volume 2
World News Media
2018

CARDIFF
CAERDYDD

Contents

Volume 2 World News Media ISBN: 978-1-906035-87-7
2-Volume Set   ISBN: 978-1-906035-85-3

Published by: Cision
5 Churchill Place, Canary Wharf E14 5HU

Tel: +44 (0)20 7674 0200
E-mail: Willings@Cision.com
Web: www.cision.com

Willings
Press Guide

Editorial Policy

Willings Press Guide is published in two volumes. The editorial aim of Willings is to be an informative guide to the media industry in the United Kingdom and Ireland (Volume 1) and to provide an overview of news media and broadcast organisations throughout the world (Volume 2).

For the purposes of Willings Press Guide, "media industry" includes: newspapers, freesheets, magazines (business and consumer), journals, newsletters and any other publication appearing on a regular basis, including directories. "News Media" includes: newspapers, television and radio stations and networks, and news services and syndicates.

Willings Press Guide is compiled and edited by Jeffrey Fynes, with additional work by Ronan George, Josh Gray and Thomas Carrington.

Each publication is listed free of charge.

To update entry details
Contact the Research team
Email: ukdata@cision.com

Willings Press Guide 2018

Volume 1 UK & Ireland 2018
ISBN: 978-1-906035-86-0

Volume 2 World News Media 2018
(excl. UK & Ireland)
ISBN: 978-1-906035-87-7

2-Volume-Set
(UK & Ireland 2018 and World News Media 2018)
ISBN: 978-1-906035-85-3

Software and page imaging by Data Standards Ltd, Frome.

Section 1 World Index

Willings Volume 2
Section 1

World Index

Advertising rates: US / Canada

Newspapers show the per-column-inch rate of a full page colour/mono

List of Countries A-Z

List of Countries A-Z

Willings Volume 2
Section 2

World News Media

Newspapers and News Agencies, listed by Country.

Albania

Time Difference: GMT +1
National Telephone Code: 355
Continent: Europe
Capital: Tirana

Newspapers

Gazeta e Tiranes 449324
Owner: SHEKULLI MEDIA GROUP
Editorial: Rr. Aleksander Moisiu, Ish-Kinostudio, Tirane **Tel:** 355 42 51 422
Email: letra@gazetaetiranes.com.al **Web site:** http://www.gazetaetiranes.com.al
Freq: Daily; **Circ:** 10000 Publisher's Statement
Editor In Chief: Elisabeta Ilnica
Profile: Daily newspaper covering news and current affairs from Tirana.
Language (s): Albanian
DAILY NEWSPAPER

Gazeta Metropol 600691
Editorial: Rruga Dull Keta, nr.5, Tirane
Tel: 355 4 233 991
Email: gazetametropol@yahoo.com **Web site:** http://www.gazetametropol.com
Freq: Daily
Profile: National newspaper covering politics, economics, business, social issues, culture and sports.
Language (s): Albanian
DAILY NEWSPAPER

Gazeta TemA 159036
Owner: Media - Enter Sh. p. k.
Editorial: Zayed Business Center, Rr. Sulejman Delvina, Tirane **Tel:** 355 69 20 20 806
Email: info@tema.al **Web site:** http://www.gazetatema.net
Freq: Daily; **Circ:** 10000 Publisher's Statement
Director: Mero Baze
Profile: Newspaper covering politics, economics, social issues, current affairs, culture, entertainment, sport and general news nationally and internationally.
Language (s): Albanian
DAILY NEWSPAPER

Integrimi 600663
Editorial: Rruga "Sami Frashëri", Nr. 20/10, Tirane
Tel: 355 4 270 413
Email: gazetaintegrimi@lsi.al **Web site:** http://www.integrimi.com
Profile: Newspaper in Albania covering general news and political events from the socialist party point of views.
Language (s): Albanian
DAILY NEWSPAPER

Panorama 536098
Owner: Panorama Group
Editorial: Rr "Panorama", Behind Harry Fulltz School, Nd. 3, H. 14, Ap.3, Tirana 1016 **Tel:** 355 42 403 207
Email: info@panorama.com.al **Web site:** http://www.panorama.com.al
Freq: Daily; **Circ:** 25000 Publisher's Statement
Director: Kasem Hysenbelli; **Editor In Chief:** Robert Rakipllari
Profile: Daily newspaper covering general news and current affairs including social, economic, politic and cultural issues.
Language (s): English
Ad Rate: Full Page Mono 450.00
Ad Rate: Full Page Colour 600.00
Currency: Euro
DAILY NEWSPAPER

Shekulli 161211
Owner: Shekulli Media Group
Editorial: Rruga Ismail Qemali, Pallati Abissnet, Tirane **Tel:** 355 4 430 2981
Email: info@shekulli.com.al **Web site:** http://www.shekulli.com.al
Freq: Daily; **Circ:** 25000 Publisher's Statement
Director: Brixhida Kokëdhima; **Director:** Adrian Thano
Profile: Newspaper covering general news and current affairs including politics, economy, health, culture, social events and sport.
Language (s): Albanian
DAILY NEWSPAPER

Sporti Shqiptar 208163
Owner: SHEKULLI MEDIA GROUP
Editorial: Rruga Aleksandër Moisiu, ish-Kinostudio, Tirane **Tel:** 355 43 68 322
Email: www.sportishqiptar@live.com **Web site:** http://www.sportishqiptar.com.al
Freq: Daily; **Circ:** 20000 Not Audited
Publisher: Koço Kokëdhima; **Director:** Alfred Lleshi; **Editor:** Baskhim Tufa
Profile: Newspaper covering sports news from Albania, especially football, international sport news.
Language (s): Albanian
DAILY NEWSPAPER

Standard 658520
Owner: Standard shpk
Editorial: ad. rruga e Kavajes, nr.67, Tirana
Tel: 355 4 2260695
Email: info@standard.al **Web site:** http://www.standard.al
Freq: Daily; **Circ:** 10000 Publisher's Statement
Editor In Chief: Sami Neza
Profile: Newspaper covering daily news, politics, economics, social issues, culture, sports, with special reports and features. Presents right wing political views.
Language (s): Albanian
DAILY NEWSPAPER

Tirana Observer 601230
Editorial: Rruga "Irfan Tomini", pallati "Biorn", Kati i 2-të, Tirane **Tel:** 355 4 2419001
Email: tiranaobserver@gmail.com **Web site:** http://www.tiranaobserver.al
Freq: Daily; **Circ:** 6000 Publisher's Statement
News Editor: Nikoleta Kovaçi; **Editor In Chief:** Altin Sinani
Profile: Informative daily paper distributed on all the territory of the Albanian Republic and Greece.
Language (s): Albanian
Ad Rate: Full Page Mono 40000.00
Ad Rate: Full Page Colour 50000.00
Currency: Albania Leke
DAILY NEWSPAPER

Tirana Times 601236
Owner: Thnegel
Editorial: Rruga "Dëshmorët e 4 shkurtit" No.7/1, Tirane **Tel:** 355 4 274 203
Email: editor@tiranatimes.com **Web site:** http://www.tiranatimes.com
Profile: Weekly newspaper of original news and views devoted to serving the English speaking audience of Albania and abroad.
Language (s): English
DAILY NEWSPAPER

Algeria

Time Difference: GMT +1
National Telephone Code: 213
Continent: Africa
Capital: Algiers

Newspapers

El Ayem El Djazairia 652253
Owner: El Ayem El Djazairia Publishing & Distribution
Editorial: Office 5 & 6, Building 3, Hay 1200 Maskan, Algiers **Tel:** 213 21 634157
Email: watani_ayem@yahoo.fr **Web site:** http://www.elayem.com
Freq: Daily; **Circ:** 100000 Publisher's Statement
News Editor: Siham Ain; **General Manager/ Publisher:** Azzeddine Ben Atteya; **Editor In Chief:** Badreddine Chaa; **PR Manager:** Najat Mezouz
Profile: El Ayem El Djazairia (Algerian Days) is a newspaper covering national and international news, politics, sport, lifestyle and society. It launched in 2004.
Language (s): Arabic
DAILY NEWSPAPER

Le Buteur 417612
Owner: EXA
Editorial: Maison de la Presse, 1, Rue Bachir Attar, Algiers **Tel:** 213 21 731417
Email: lebuteur5@yahoo.fr **Web site:** http://www.lebuteur.com
Freq: Daily; **Circ:** 100000 Rate Card
Advertising Manager: Abderrazak Nabil; **Editor-in-Chief:** Mohamed Saad
Profile: Le Buteur is a daily newspaper covering local and international football. It launched in 2001 and is the French sister title to El Heddaf, which is published in Arabic.
Language (s): French
Ad Rate: Full Page Mono 232500.00
Ad Rate: Full Page Colour 406409.40
Currency: Algeria Dinars
DAILY NEWSPAPER

Compétition 207964
Owner: Top Sport sarl
Editorial: 08 rue Capitaine Mennani, Algiers
Tel: 213 770 929283
Email: contact@competition.dz **Web site:** http://www.competition.dz
Freq: Daily; **Circ:** 65000 Publisher's Statement
Editor: Noureddine Boumali; **Publisher & General Manager:** Djamel Guessoum; **Co-Editor in Chief:** Asma Halimi
Profile: Compétition is a daily newspaper covering local and international sport, particularly football. It launched in 1993, and is aimed at sports fans in Algeria.
Language (s): French
Ad Rate: Full Page Mono 190000.00
Ad Rate: Full Page Colour 350000.00
Currency: Algeria Dinars
DAILY NEWSPAPER

Ech Chaab 328298
Owner: El Chaab Presse
Editorial: PO Box 59, 39, Boulevard des Martyrs, Algiers 16000 **Tel:** 213 21 606783
Email: info@ech-chaab.com **Web site:** http://www.ech-chaab.com
Freq: Daily; **Circ:** 55000 Publisher's Statement
Advertising Manager: Kamel Bouslimane; **General Manager:** Amina Debbache
Profile: Ech Chaab (The People) is a newspaper covering national and international news, politics, business, sport, society, culture and youth issues. It launched in 1962 and is published daily, except Fridays. Sout Al Assir, a supplement covering Palestinian news, history and heritage, is issued with the newspaper on Thursdays.
Language (s): Arabic
Ad Rate: Full Page Mono 181203.75
Ad Rate: Full Page Colour 272665.58
Currency: Algeria Dinars
DAILY NEWSPAPER

Ech-Chorouk El Yaoumi 413470
Owner: Ech-Chorouk Infed SARL
Editorial: Maison de la Presse, 2, Rue Farid Zaouiouech, Algiers **Tel:** 213 23 709368
Email: infos@echoroukonline.com **Web site:** http://www.echoroukonline.com
Freq: Daily; **Circ:** 400000 Publisher's Statement
Head of News: Jamal Alami; **Editor in Chief:** Samira Belamri; **Advertising Manager:** Abdel Ghani Bou Okba; **General Manager & Publisher:** Ali Fodil
Profile: Ech-Chorouk El Yaoumi is a newspaper covering local and international news, business, politics and sport. It launched in 2001.
Language (s): Arabic
Ad Rate: Full Page Mono 165000.00
Ad Rate: Full Page Colour 240900.00
Currency: Algeria Dinars
DAILY NEWSPAPER

Echibek 425818
Owner: Sept Com SARL
Editorial: Office 3, Building 16, Boulevarde Said Hamdine, Algiers **Tel:** 213 21 543464
Email: echibek@yahoo.fr **Web site:** http://sport.ennaharonline.com
Freq: Daily; **Circ:** 87000 Publisher's Statement
Editor In Chief: Walid Medouar
Profile: Echibek (The Goal) is a national newspaper focusing on local and international sport, particularly football. The newspaper launched in 1993 and is published four times a week on Saturdays, Mondays, Tuesdays and Thursdays.
Language (s): Arabic
Ad Rate: Full Page Mono 198900.00
Ad Rate: Full Page Colour 275535.00
Currency: Algeria Dinars
DAILY NEWSPAPER

Ennahar El Djadid 517474
Owner: El Athir Presse sarl
Editorial: PO Box 146, Boulevard Said Hamdine, Algiers **Tel:** 213 23 599292
Email: wataniennahar@gmail.com **Web site:** http://www.ennaharonline.com
Freq: Daily; **Circ:** 364155 Publisher's Statement
National News Editor: Mohamed Bousri; **Editor in Chief:** Ismail Fellah; **General Manager/Publisher:** Anis Rahmani
Profile: Ennahar El Djadid (The New Day) is a newspaper covering news and sport. It is published daily, except Fridays, and launched in 2007.
Language (s): Arabic
Ad Rate: Full Page Mono 275000.00
Ad Rate: Full Page Colour 410000.00
Currency: Algeria Dinars
DAILY NEWSPAPER

Al Fadjr 427181
Owner: Erraid Lilialam S.A.R.L
Editorial: Maison de la Presse, 1 Rue Bachir Attar, Place du 1er Mai, Algiers **Tel:** 213 21 657660
Email: alfadjrwatani@yahoo.fr **Web site:** http://www.al-fadjr.com
Freq: Daily; **Circ:** 65000 Publisher's Statement
Publication Manager: Hadda Hazem; **News Editor:** Amine Lounessi; **Advertising Manager:** Nadra Rahmani; **Editor in Chief:** Malek Reddad
Profile: Al Fadjr is a national newspaper covering local news, current affairs, business and sport. It is published daily, except Fridays, and launched in 2001.
Language (s): Arabic
Ad Rate: Full Page Mono 162393.17
Ad Rate: Full Page Colour 230769.23
Currency: Algeria Dinars
DAILY NEWSPAPER

El Heddaf 409263
Owner: EXA
Editorial: Maison De La Presse, 1 Rue Bachir Attar, Place Du 1er Mai, Algiers **Tel:** 213 21 731417
Email: redaction3@gmail.com **Web site:** http://www.elheddaf.com
Freq: Daily; **Circ:** 400000 Rate Card
Editor in Chief: Redouane Bouhanika; **Advertising Manager:** Abderrazak Nabil
Profile: El Heddaf is a tabloid-sized newspaper covering local and international sport, particularly football. It launched in 1999 and is the Arabic sister title to Le Buteur, which is published in French.
Language (s): Arabic
Ad Rate: Full Page Mono 232500.00
Ad Rate: Full Page Colour 406409.40
Currency: Algeria Dinars
DAILY NEWSPAPER

El Khabar 156735
Owner: El Khabar Spa
Editorial: PO Box 378, 32 Rue Al Fath Ben Khalkan, Algiers 16016 **Tel:** 213 21 484436
Email: redaction@elkhabar.com **Web site:** http://www.elkhabar.com
Freq: Daily; **Circ:** 300000 Publisher's Statement
Editor In Chief: Mohamed Bghali; **General Manager:** Cherif Rezki
Profile: El Khabar (The News) is a 24-page, tabloid-sized newspaper focusing on national and international news. It launched in 1990.
Language (s): Arabic
Ad Rate: Full Page Mono 268000.00
Ad Rate: Full Page Colour 420000.00
Currency: Algeria Dinars
DAILY NEWSPAPER

El Khabar El Riadi 707804
Owner: El Khabar Spa
Editorial: La Maison de la Presse, Zone Industrielle, Constantine **Tel:** 213 31 660587
Email: elkhabarerriadhi@gmail.com **Web site:** http://www.elkhabarerriadhi.com
Freq: Daily; **Circ:** 55000 Publisher's Statement
Editor: Faouzi Zamour; **Editor:** Chouaib Zouazoui
Profile: El Khabar El Riadi (Sports News) is a tabloid-sized newspaper covering national and international football. It launched in 2010.
Language (s): Arabic
DAILY NEWSPAPER

Liberté 161253
Owner: SAEC sarl
Editorial: 37 Larbi Ben M'Hidi, Alger Centre, Algiers
Tel: 213 21 307847
Email: info@liberte-algerie.com **Web site:** http://www.liberte-algerie.com
Freq: Daily; **Circ:** 150000 Publisher's Statement
Advertising Manager: Hamid Abbes; **Picture Editor:** Louiza Ammi; **Co-Editor in Chief:** Omar Ouali; **General Manager:** Abrous Outoudert
Profile: Liberté (Freedom) is a national newspaper focusing on national and international news, business, culture and sport. It is published daily, except Fridays, and launched in 1992. The newspaper includes football supplement Liberté Foot on Mondays.
Language (s): French
Ad Rate: Full Page Mono 268000.00
Ad Rate: Full Page Colour 417500.00
Currency: Algeria Dinars
DAILY NEWSPAPER

Maracana 910174
Owner: La Gazette de L'Omnisports
Editorial: 28, Rue Ali Khodja, Bordj El-Kiffan, Algiers 16000 **Tel:** 213 21 926225
Email: maracanajournal@gmail.com
Freq: Daily; **Circ:** 25000
Publication Manager: Farouk Seba
Profile: Maracana is a daily newspaper covering national and international sport. It launched in February 2005.
Language (s): French
Ad Rate: Full Page Mono 160000.00
Ad Rate: Full Page Colour 320000.00
Currency: Algeria Dinars
DAILY NEWSPAPER

El Massa 156752
Owner: El Massa
Editorial: 51, Rue Arbi Ben Mhidi, Algiers
Tel: 213 21 745799
Email: info@el-massa.com **Web site:** http://www.el-massa.com
Freq: Daily; **Circ:** 50000 Publisher's Statement
News Editor: Malika Khallaf; **Editor In Chief:** Ali Salem
Profile: El Massa is a newspaper focusing on national and international news, current affairs, politics, sports and entertainment. It is published daily, except Fridays, and launched in 1985.
Language (s): Arabic
Ad Rate: Full Page Mono 144000.00
Ad Rate: Full Page Colour 230000.00
Currency: Algeria Dinars
DAILY NEWSPAPER

Al Mawîd Alyaoumi 428984
Owner: Dar Alwaâd
Editorial: Maison de la Presse, Place du 1er Mai, Algiers **Tel:** 213 21 670716
Email: maouidhawa@yahoo.fr **Web site:** http://www.elmaouid.com
Freq: Daily; **Circ:** 50000 Publisher's Statement
News Editor: Hakim Massoudi; **Advertising Manager:** Mohamed Talbi
Profile: Al Mawîd Alyaoumi is a newspaper covering news, culture, society and sport. It is published daily, except Fridays, and launched in 1992.
Language (s): Arabic
DAILY NEWSPAPER

Le Midi Libre 595669
Owner: Midi Libre EURL
Editorial: 26, rue Didouche Mourad, Algiers
Tel: 213 21 638082
Email: redaction@lemidi-dz.com **Web site:** http://www.lemidi-dz.com
Freq: Daily; **Circ:** 50000 Publisher's Statement
News Editor: Sadek Belhocine; **Advertising Manager:** Hind Faras; **Editor in Chief:** Sihem Henine; **Manager:** Réda Mehigueni
Profile: Le Midi Libre is a tabloid-sized newspaper covering local and international news, business and sport. It launched in 2007.
Language (s): French

Ad Rate: Full Page Mono 177000.00
Ad Rate: Full Page Colour 264000.00
Currency: Algeria Dinars
DAILY NEWSPAPER

El Moudjahid 158812
Owner: EPE-SPA El Moudjahid
Editorial: 20 rue de la Liberte, Algiers
Tel: 213 21 737081
Email: elmoudjahid@elmoudjahid.com **Web site:** http://www.elmoudjahid.com
Freq: Daily; **Circ:** 150000 Publisher's Statement
News Editor: Noura Chargui; **Co-Editor in Chief:** Achour Cheurfi; **Editor In Chief:** Kamal Oulman; **Foreign News Editor:** Mourad Termoule
Profile: El Moudjahid is a newspaper focusing on national and international news, current affairs, politics, sports and entertainment. It is published daily, except Fridays, and launched in 1956.
Language (s): French
Ad Rate: Full Page Mono 172500.00
Ad Rate: Full Page Colour 258749.99
Currency: Algeria Dinars
DAILY NEWSPAPER

Le Quotidien D'Oran 318940
Owner: SPA Oran Presse
Editorial: PO Box 110, 1, rue Laid Ould Tayeb, Oran
Tel: 213 41 232522
Email: infos@lequotidien-oran.com **Web site:** http://www.lequotidien-oran.com
Freq: Daily; **Circ:** 155678 Publisher's Statement
Advertising Manager: Chahida Ben Yamina; **CEO & Publisher:** Mohamed Benabbou; **Editor In Chief:** Sid Ahmed Mohamed
Profile: Le Quotidien D'Oran is a newspaper covering national and international news, current affairs, politics, sports and entertainment. It is published daily, except Fridays, and launched in 1994.
Language (s): French
DAILY NEWSPAPER

Le Soir D'Algerie 391145
Owner: Le Soir D'Algerie SARL
Editorial: 1 Rue Bachir Attar, Place du 1er Mai, Algiers 16000 **Tel:** 213 21 670651
Email: info@lesoirdalgerie.com **Web site:** http://www.lesoirdalgerie.com
Freq: Daily; **Circ:** 80000 Publisher's Statement
News Editor: Abderrahmane Bettache; **Publication Manager:** Fouad Boughanem; **Editor In Chief:** Badreddine Manaa
Profile: Le Soir D'Algerie is a daily newspaper focusing on national and international news, business and sport. It launched in 1991.
Language (s): French
Ad Rate: Full Page Mono 225000.00
Ad Rate: Full Page Colour 350000.00
Currency: Algeria Dinars
DAILY NEWSPAPER

Le Temps d'Algérie 611214
Owner: Group Media Temps Nouveaux EURL
Editorial: 20, Saeed Hamdeen Street, Industrial Area, Algiers 9108 **Tel:** 213 23 599163
Email: redaction@letempsdz.com **Web site:** http://www.letempsdz.com
Freq: Daily; **Circ:** 100000 Publisher's Statement
Editor in Chief: Malika Bougherara
Profile: Le Temps d'Algérie is a tabloid-sized newspaper covering local and international news, culture and sport. It is published daily, except Fridays, and launched in 2009.
Language (s): French
Ad Rate: Full Page Mono 1800000.00
Ad Rate: Full Page Colour 400000.00
Currency: Algeria Dinars
DAILY NEWSPAPER

Transaction d'Algerie 429657
Owner: Sedi Eurl
Editorial: 6, Rue du Centenaire, Ruisseau, Algiers
Tel: 213 21 671966
Email: transactiondalgerie@gmail.com **Web site:** http://www.transactiondalgerie.com
Freq: Daily; **Circ:** 45000 Publisher's Statement
News Editor: Hafid Azouz; **Editor in Chief:** Sid-Ahmed Hamache
Profile: Transaction d'Algerie is a daily newspaper covering business and the economy. It is published daily, except Fridays, and launched in 2004.
Language (s): French
Ad Rate: Full Page Mono 240000.00
Ad Rate: Full Page Colour 340418.34
Currency: Algeria Dinars
DAILY NEWSPAPER

El Watan 156755
Owner: El Watan Presse
Editorial: Maison de la Presse Tahar Djaout, 1 rue Bachir Attar, Algiers 16000 **Tel:** 213 21 682183
Email: nationale@elwatan.com **Web site:** http://www.elwatan.com
Freq: Daily; **Circ:** 170000 Publisher's Statement
Picture Editor: Souhil Baghdadi; **Publication Manager:** Omar Belhouchet; **Editor In Chief:** Ali Benyahia; **Head of News:** Nadjia Bouaricha; **Advertising Manager:** Wahiba Gaouaoui; **Co-Editor in Chief:** Mourad Slaimani
Profile: El Watan is a newspaper containing national and international news, business, features and sport. It is published daily, except Fridays when it is replaced by El Watan Week-end. The newspaper includes business supplement El Watan Economie on Mondays, and was first published in 1990.
Language (s): French
Ad Rate: Full Page Mono 270000.00
Ad Rate: Full Page Colour 418000.00
Currency: Algeria Dinars
DAILY NEWSPAPER

El Watan Week-end 537901
Owner: El Watan Presse
Editorial: Maison de la Presse Tahar Djaout, 1 rue Bachir Attar, Algiers 16000 **Tel:** 213 21 653317
Email: mmatarese@elwatan.com **Web site:** http://www.elwatan.com
Freq: Weekly; **Circ:** 100000 Publisher's Statement
Publications Director: Omar Belhouchet; **Advertising Manager:** Wahiba Gaouaoui; **Co-Editor in Chief:** Melanie Matarese; **Editor In Chief:** Adlene Meddi; **News Editor:** Yasmine Said
Profile: El Watan Week-end is the Friday edition of El Watan newspaper, and covers politics, travel, sport, business and culture. The Friday edition was introduced in 2009.
Language (s): French
Ad Rate: Full Page Mono 270000.00
Ad Rate: Full Page Colour 418000.00
Currency: Algeria Dinars
DAILY NEWSPAPER

El Youm 427185
Owner: Group International de Communication
Editorial: Maison de la Presse Tahar Djaout, Place du 1er Mai, Algiers 16000 **Tel:** 213 21 667085
Email: elyoum11@yahoo.fr **Web site:** http://el-youm.info
Freq: Daily; **Circ:** 150000 Publisher's Statement
Publishing Manager: Khaled Lakhdari; **Advertising Manager:** Hadi Mourchidi
Profile: El Youm (The Day) is a daily newspaper covering news, current affairs, business, culture and sport. It launched in 1999.
Language (s): Arabic
Ad Rate: Full Page Mono 150000.00
Ad Rate: Full Page Colour 216000.00
Currency: Algeria Dinars
DAILY NEWSPAPER

News Service/Syndicate

Agence France-Presse - Algiers Bureau 430873
Owner: Agence France-Presse
Editorial: 6 rue Abdelkrim El-Khettabi, Alger Centre, Algiers 16000 **Tel:** 213 21 630781
Email: amer.ouali@afp.com **Web site:** http://www.afp.com
Bureau Chief: Amer Ouali
Profile: Algiers bureau of international news agency supplying news - text, graphics, video and pictures - to subscribers around the world.
Language (s): Arabic
NEWS SERVICE/SYNDICATE

Agence Photo Presse 433891
Owner: Agence Photo Presse
Editorial: 9 Rue Rouiba, Delmonte, Oran 31000
Tel: 213 41 196094
Email: redaction_app@outlook.com
Editor: Ahmed Ben Mohamed; **General Manager:** Sid Ahmed Benzerga
Profile: Agence Photo Presse is a press agency covering news and sport.
Language (s): French
NEWS SERVICE/SYNDICATE

Algérie Presse Service 396487
Owner: Algérie Presse Service
Editorial: PO Box 444, Avenue des Freres Bouadou, Algiers **Tel:** 213 23 569685
Email: dt@aps.dz **Web site:** http://www.aps.dz
Editor in Chief: Leila Benradja; **Editor in Chief:** Haceni Rabeh
Profile: Algérie Presse Service is the national news agency of Algeria and covers news, politics, society, culture, sport, regional news, investigations and business. It was founded in Tunis on 1 December 1961 during the national liberation war and, after independence, its headquarters were transferred to Algiers. The agency produces around 600 news dispatches daily in three languages (Arabic, French and English). It has a staff of nearly 460 employees, including 300 reporters, photographers and translators. As well as the headquarters in Algiers, the agency collects news through a network of four regional directorates with offices in Constantine (East), Oran (West), Ouargla (South) and Blida (Central). It also has overseas representation in Washington, Moscow, Paris, London, Brussels, Rome, Madrid, Cairo, Rabat, Tunis, Amman, and Dakar.
Language (s): Arabic
NEWS SERVICE/SYNDICATE

European Pressphoto Agency - Maghreb Bureau 491399
Owner: European Pressphoto Agency
Editorial: 4, Rue Mohamed Idriss Bay, Algiers 16000
Tel: 213 770 563160
Email: messara@epa.eu **Web site:** http://www.epa.eu
Profile: European Pressphoto Agency is a picture agency representing eleven European news agencies (DPA, ANSA, EFE, Belga, APA, Athens News Agency, PAP, ANP, MTI, Keystone and LUSA). The Maghreb bureau covers news, politics, sports, fashion, economy, conflicts, disasters, features and business from Algeria, Morocco and Tunisia.
Language (s): Arabic
NEWS SERVICE/SYNDICATE

New Press Algerie 458090
Owner: New Press Algerie
Editorial: Maison de la Presse, 1 Rue Bachir Attar, Algiers **Tel:** 213 21 663317
Email: newpress@newpressphoto.com **Web site:** http://www.newpressphoto.com
Photographer: Mohamed Ali; **Photographer:** Anis Belghoul; **Photographer:** Sid Ali Djarboub; **Photographer:** Fethi Khaled
Profile: New Press Algerie is an independent Algerian photo agency.
Language (s): French
NEWS SERVICE/SYNDICATE

American Samoa

Time Difference: GMT -11
National Telephone Code: 1684
Continent: Oceania
Capital: Pago Pago

Newspapers

Samoa News 161270
Editorial: PO Box 909, Pago Pago 96799
Tel: 684 6335599
Email: news.newsroom@samoatelco.com **Web site:** http://www.samoanews.com
Freq: Daily; **Circ:** 4000 Not Audited
Editor in Chief: Rhonda Annesely-Canales
Profile: Samoa News is a local, daily newspaper serving residents of Pago Pago, American Samoa. The paper contains local news, politics, business, community issues and sports, as well as U.S. and world news that affects the readership.
Language (s): Samoan
DAILY NEWSPAPER

Andorra

Time Difference: GMT +1
National Telephone Code: 376
Continent: Europe
Capital: Andorra la Vella

Newspapers

BonDia 395526
Owner: La Veu del Poble S.L.
Editorial: Carre Maria Pla, 28, 1 planta, Andorra La Vella 50500 **Tel:** 376 80 88 88
Email: bondia@bondia.ad **Web site:** http://www.bondia.ad
Freq: Daily; **Circ:** 8000 Publisher's Statement
Editor in Chief: Marta Fernàndez; **Director:** Marc Segalés Dalmau
Profile: Daily newspaper covering regional and national news and current affairs including politics, economics, society, culture and sports.
Language (s): Catalan
Ad Rate: Full Page Colour 985.00
Currency: Euro
DAILY NEWSPAPER

Diari d'Andorra 158738
Owner: Premsa Andorrana SA
Editorial: Calle Bonaventura Riberaygua, 39, 5a planta, Andorra La Vella 50500 **Tel:** 376 87 74 77
Email: redaccio@diariandorra.ad **Web site:** http://www.diariandorra.ad
Freq: Daily; **Circ:** 3200 Publisher's Statement
General Manager: Ignasi de Planell Roda; **Editor in Chief:** David Domingo; **Director:** Ricard Poy
Profile: Daily newspaper covering regional, national and international news and current affairs including politics, economics, culture and sports.
Language (s): Catalan
DAILY NEWSPAPER

El Periòdic d'Andorra 158739
Owner: Andorrana de Publicaciones SA
Editorial: Avinguda Fiter i Rossell, 4, Edifici La Torre d'Escaldes-Engordany, Les Escaldes - Engordany AD700 **Tel:** 376 73 62 00
Email: redaccio@elperiodicdandorra.ad **Web site:** http://www.elperiodic.ad
Freq: Daily; **Circ:** 7700 Publisher's Statement
Director: Joan Ramon Baiges; **Director:** Arnau Colominas
Profile: Daily newspaper covering regional, national and international news and current affairs including politics, economics, society, culture and sports.
Language (s): Catalan
Ad Rate: Full Page Mono 862.93
Ad Rate: Full Page Colour 1188.75
Currency: Euro
DAILY NEWSPAPER

Angola

Time Difference: GMT +1
National Telephone Code: 244
Continent: Africa
Capital: Luanda

Newspapers

Diário da República 460879
Editorial: Cp 1306, Luanda **Tel:** 244 22530
Freq: Daily
Language (s): Portuguese
DAILY NEWSPAPER

Anguilla

Time Difference: GMT -4
National Telephone Code: 1264
Continent: The Americas
Capital: The Valley

Community Newspaper

The Anguillian 224378
Owner: Nat Hodge's Public Relations, Information and Consultancy Se
Tel: 1 264 497-3823
Email: theanguillian@anguillanet.com **Web site:** http://www.anguillian.com
Freq: Fri; **Circ:** 1500 Not Audited
Publisher & Editor: A. Nat Hodge
Profile: The Anguillian is a weekly newspaper providing Local and Community News coverage for the residents of Anguilla.
Language (s): English
COMMUNITY NEWSPAPER

Antigua & Barbuda

Time Difference: GMT -4
National Telephone Code: 1268
Continent: The Americas
Capital: St John's (Antigua), Codrington (Barbuda)

Newspapers

The Daily Observer 160784
Owner: Daily Observer Ltd
Editorial: #15 Pavilion Drive, Coolidge, St John's
Tel: 1 268 480-1750
Email: editor@antiguaobserver.com **Web site:** http://www.antiguaobserver.com
Freq: Daily; **Circ:** 4000 Not Audited
Profile: Serves residents of St. John's, Antigua. Features national and international news, sports, entertainment and leisure.
Language (s): English
Ad Rate: Full Page Mono 40.00
Ad Rate: Full Page Colour 110.00
Currency: United States Dollars
DAILY NEWSPAPER

Argentina

Time Difference: GMT -3
National Telephone Code: 54
Continent: The Americas
Capital: Buenos Aires

Newspapers

Clarín 365430
Owner: Clarín.com - Clarín Digital
Editorial: Tacuari 1840, C.A.B.A, Capital Federal C1140AAN **Tel:** 54 11 5275-6163
Email: lectores@clarin.com **Web site:** http://www.clarin.com
Freq: Daily; **Circ:** 600000

Argentina

Editor: Horacio Convertini; **Director:** Ernestina Herrera de Noble; **Editor:** Pablo Scholz
Profile: Clarín es el principal fuente de información de la Argentina y el mundo. Clarín is the main source of information of Argentina and the world.
Language (s): Spanish
DAILY NEWSPAPER

Crónica 366315
Editorial: Av. Juan de Garay 140, Capital Federal C1063ABO **Tel:** 54 11 43611051
Email: cronica@diariocronica.com.ar **Web site:** http://www.diariocronica.com.ar
Freq: Daily; **Circ:** 160000 Not Audited
Editor: Ricardo Filigueras; **Director:** Eduardo Gonzalez Rouco; **Editor in Chief:** Héctor Lorenzo; **Editor:** Eduardo Marrazzi
Profile: Formato tabloide. No está inscripto al IVC. Es sensacionalista y se destaca por las notas de policiales, de turf y de fútbol. Fecha de Aparición: 29 de julio de 1936
Language (s): Spanish
DAILY NEWSPAPER

Diario Popular 365452
Editorial: Intendente Beguiristain 142, Sarandí B1872CBD **Tel:** 54 1142038091
Email: redaccion@diariopopular.com
Freq: Daily; **Circ:** 70091 Not Audited
Editor: Alberto Calligari; **Editor in Chief:** José Di Mauro; **Editor:** Hugo Iñiguez; **Editor:** Hugo Martinez; **Director:** Luciano Munñoz; **Editor:** Pablo Quiróz; **Editor:** Claudio Rodriguez; **Editor:** Luly Vitcop; **Editor:** Guillermo Vucetich
Profile: Formato tabloide. No está inscripto en el IVC. Es un diario sensacionalista. Fecha de Aparición: 1 de julio de 1974
Language (s): Spanish
DAILY NEWSPAPER

La Nación 366131
Editorial: Bouchard 557, Capital Federal C1106ABG **Tel:** 54 11 6090-5000
Email: exterior@lanacion.com.ar **Web site:** http://www.lanacion.com.ar
Freq: Daily; **Circ:** 160000 Not Audited
Editor: Julio Aguirre Chanetón; **Editor:** Daniel Amiano; **Editor:** Carolina Arenes; **Editor:** Nora Bär; **Editor:** José Luis Brea; **Editor:** Hugo Caligaris; **Editor in Chief:** Ricardo Cárpena; **Editor:** Jesús Cornejo; **Editor in Chief:** Luis Cortina; **Editor:** Diego Cúneo; **Editor:** Alicia de Arteaga; **Editor:** Josefina Giglio; **Editor:** Graciela Guadalupe; **Editor:** Catalina Lanús; **Editor:** Graciela Melgarejo; **Editor:** Cristian Mira; **Director:** Bartolomé Mitre; **Editor:** Javier Navia; **Editor:** Jorge Oviedo; **Editor:** Jorge Pandini; **Editor:** Nicolás Singer; **Editor:** Ariel Torres; **Editor:** Alberto Wainziger
Profile: Since 1870 La Nacion covers national and international news.
Language (s): Spanish
Ad Rate: Full Page Mono 207500.00
Currency: Argentina Pesos
DAILY NEWSPAPER

Página 12 365125
Owner: Editorial La Página S.A.
Editorial: Solis 1525, Capital Federal C1134ADG
Tel: 54 11 6772-4400
Email: redactor@pagina12.com.ar **Web site:** http://www.pagina12.com.ar
Freq: Daily; **Circ:** 125000 Not Audited
Editor: Juan Ignacio Boido; **Editor:** Fernando D'Addario; **Editor:** Eduardo Fabregat; **Editor:** Pedro Lipjobich; **Editor:** Leonardo Moledo; **Editor:** Andrés Osojnik; **Director:** Ernesto Tiffenberg; **Editor:** Nora Veiras; **Editor:** Eduardo Videla; **Editor:** Alfredo Zaiat; **Editor:** Claudio Ariel Zeiger
Profile: Formato tabloide. No está inscripto en el IVC. Es un diario de izquierda. Presenta las noticias con un estilo de revista y realiza trabajos de investigación periodística de denuncia. Fecha de Aparición: 26 de mayo de 1987
Language (s): Spanish
DAILY NEWSPAPER

Tiempo Argentino 692712
Editorial: Unavailable, Buenos Aires
Email: editorial@tiempoargentino.com **Web site:** http://tiempo.infonews.com
Freq: Daily; **Circ:** 50000
Language (s): Spanish
DAILY NEWSPAPER

La Voz del Interior 366275
Editorial: Av. La Voz del Interior 6080, Cordoba 5000
Tel: 54 351 4757100
Email: lavoz@lavozdelinterior.com.ar **Web site:** http://www.lavoz.com.ar
Freq: Daily; **Circ:** 80000 Not Audited
Editor: Eduardo Bocco; **Editor:** Javier Candelero; **Editor:** Alejandra Conti; **Editor:** Mariana Grimaldi; **Editor:** Damián Oroz; **Editor:** Carlos Rodríguez; **Editor:** Carlos Schilling; **Editor:** Juan Turello
Profile: Es el diario de mayor prestigio y tirada en la Provincia de Córdoba. Tiene formato sábana. Fecha de Aparición: La Voz del Interior S.A
Language (s): Spanish
DAILY NEWSPAPER

News Service/Syndicate

Agencia Nosis 370486
Editorial: San Martin 365, Capital Federal C1004AAG
Tel: 54 11 6316-0000
Email: info@nosis.com **Web site:** http://www.nosis.com
Editor in Chief: Marcelo Bottini
Profile: El objetivo de Nosis Laboratorio de investigación y desarrollo es brindar información de antecedentes comerciales, comercio exterior y mercados financieros para apoyar la toma de decisiones en la gestión empresaria. Fecha de Aparición: 3 de marzo de 1988
Language (s): Spanish
NEWS SERVICE/SYNDICATE

Agencia NOVA 370492
Editorial: Calle 13 N 689 4 B (e/ 45 y 46), La Plata 1900 **Tel:** 54 221 421-4958
Email: noticias@agencianova.com **Web site:** http://www.agencianova.com
Editor in Chief: Mario Casalongue; **Director:** Daniel Veloso
Profile: Nova es una agencia que tiene como principal prioridad cubrir la actualidad de la provincia de Buenos Aires, como también del exterior.
Language (s): Spanish
NEWS SERVICE/SYNDICATE

AICA - Agencia Informativa Católica Argentina 370491
Editorial: Bolivar 218 3 Piso, Capital Federal C1066AAF **Tel:** 54 11 4343-4397
Email: info@aica.org **Web site:** http://www.aica.org.ar
Director: Miguel Woites
Profile: Es la agencia de noticias de información católica. Con participación del Arzobispado de Buenos Aires.
Language (s): Spanish
NEWS SERVICE/SYNDICATE

APF Agencia Periodística Federal 370495
Editorial: Tucuman 257, Piso 2, Dpto. 3, Paraná 3100
Tel: 54 343 422-5374
Email: direccion@apfdigital.com.ar **Web site:** http://www.apfdigital.com.ar
General Manager: Juan Bracco
Profile: Agencia de Noticias de Entre Ríos destinada, principalmente, a la parte política de la provincia.
Language (s): Spanish
NEWS SERVICE/SYNDICATE

El Consultor 370496
Editorial: Mendoza 3142 - Piso 1, Santa Fe S3000FTO **Tel:** 54 342 456-6378
Email: correo@elconsultorweb.com **Web site:** http://www.elconsultorweb.com
Editor-in-Charge: José Luis Tepper
Profile: Agencia de Noticias de Santa Fe. Trata temas de actualidad, noticias provinciales y locales principalmente, además de nacionales. Fecha de Aparición: 7 de Septiembre de 2000
Language (s): Spanish
NEWS SERVICE/SYNDICATE

DIB Diarios Bonaerenses 370494
Owner: Diarios Bonaerense S.A.
Editorial: Calle 48 N 726 Piso 4, La Plata 1900
Tel: 54 221 422-0054
Email: editor@dib.com.ar **Web site:** http://www.dib.com.ar
General Manager: Jorge Aníbal Déboli
Profile: Diarios Bonaerenses S.A es una agencia de noticias y publicidad independiente, integrada por 30 diarios locales-regionales, 27 semanarios del interior bonaerense, que con una tirada de 80.000 ejemplares se ha constituido en una de las empresas difusoras m
Language (s): Spanish
NEWS SERVICE/SYNDICATE

DYN – Agencia Diarios y Noticias 370487
Editorial: Julio A. Roca 636, Capital Federal C1067ABO **Tel:** 54 11 43423040
Email: editor@dyn.com.ar **Web site:** http://www.dyn.com.ar
Editor: Gabriela Bersier; **Editor in Chief:** Carmen Coiro; **Editor in Chief:** José Cutello; **Director:** Hugo Grimaldi; **Editor:** Jorge Neri; **President:** Jose Pochat; **Editor in Chief:** Mario Poliak; **Editor:** Miguel Rouco; **Editor:** Walter Schmidt
Profile: Es la agencia de noticias privada más importante. Es de cobertura nacional y en ella tienen participación los diarios Clarín y la Nación. Fecha de Aparición: 15 de marzo 1982
Language (s): Spanish
NEWS SERVICE/SYNDICATE

Noticias Argentinas 370488
Editorial: Moreno 769 3er piso, Capital Federal C1008AAL **Tel:** 54 11 4331-3850
Email: infogral@noticiasargentinas.com **Web site:** http://www.noticiasargentinas.com
President: Fernando Cuello; **Director:** Guillermo Vucetich
Profile: Es una agencia de noticias privada de Cobertura nacional. Pertenece al editor del diario El Día de la ciudad de La Plata, y del diario El Popular. La agencia se proclama a sí misma como "la agencia independiente". Presta servicios fotográficos. Fecha de Aparición: 1 de octubre de 1973
Language (s): Spanish
NEWS SERVICE/SYNDICATE

Télam 370489
Editorial: Bolivar 531, Capital Federal C1066AAK
Tel: 54 11 4339-0300
Email: admperiodistica@telam.com.ar **Web site:** http://www.telam.com.ar
Editor: Marcelo Bianco; **Editor:** Daniel Casas; **Editor:** Mora Cordeau; **Editor:** Eduardo De La Fuente; **Editor:** Eduardo Duschatzky; **Editor:** Mariano Fontella; **Director:** Martín Granovsky
Profile: Es la agencia más importante de noticias. Es propiedad del Estado nacional. Cubre noticias a nivel nacional. Es la única agencia que realiza productos distintos de las noticias diarias, son los llamados "Suplementos", que abarcan distintos temas como: eco Fecha de Aparición: 14 de Abril de 1945
Language (s): Spanish
NEWS SERVICE/SYNDICATE

Armenia

Time Difference: GMT +4
National Telephone Code: 374
Continent: Asia
Capital: Yerevan

Newspapers

168 Hours 518369
Editorial: 3a Pushkin str., Yerevan
Tel: 374 10 584831
Email: 168@168.r.am **Web site:** http://www.168.am
Freq: 2 Times/Week; **Circ:** 5000 Publisher's Statement
Editor-in-Chief: Satik Seyranyan
Profile: Provides information about politics, economics, social issues and society, culture and health, sports.
Language (s): Armenian
DAILY NEWSPAPER

Aravot Daily 161294
Editorial: 2 Arshakuniats, 15th floor, Yerevan 375023
Tel: 374 10 528752
Email: aravotoratert@gmail.com **Web site:** http://www.aravot.am
Freq: Daily; **Circ:** 5000 Publisher's Statement
Editor-in-Chief: Aram Abramyan
Profile: Newspaper covering national and regional news, politics, the economy, culture, sport and entertainment.
Language (s): Armenian
DAILY NEWSPAPER

Argumenty i Fakty Yerevan 970707
Editorial: Yerevan **Tel:** 374 10 527723
Email: aifyerevan@gmail.com **Web site:** http://www.golosarmenii.am
Freq: Weekly
Editor: Ara Meliksetyan
Language (s): Russian
DAILY NEWSPAPER

AZG 161295
Editorial: 47 Hanrapetutian str., Yerevan 375010
Tel: 374 1 52-93-53
Email: azg@azg.am **Web site:** http://www.azg.am
Freq: Daily; **Circ:** 3000 Publisher's Statement
Editor: Hakop Avedikyan
Language (s): Armenian
DAILY NEWSPAPER

Delovoy Express 173490
Owner: EIS Ltd
Editorial: Tigran Metsi, 67a, Yerevan 5
Tel: 374 10 57 33 05
Email: delovoy@express.am **Web site:** http://www.express.am
Freq: Weekly; **Circ:** 3000 Not Audited
Editor-in-Chief: Eduard Naghdalyan
Profile: Newspaper focusing on all aspects of business, finance and banks, real estate market, business investments.
Language (s): Russian
Ad Rate: Full Page Mono 900.00
Currency: United States Dollars
DAILY NEWSPAPER

EFIR 449975
Editorial: 5 Alek Manoukyan street, Yerevan 375025
Tel: 374 10 55 34 13
Email: editor@eter.am **Web site:** http://www.eter.am
Circ: 24000 Publisher's Statement
Editor In Chief: Gor Ghazaryan
Profile: Informative-entertaining newspaper covering TV, cinema, theatre and music.
Language (s): Russian
Ad Rate: Full Page Colour 150000.00
Currency: Armenia Drams
DAILY NEWSPAPER

ETER 449976
Editorial: 5 Alek Manoukyan street, Yerevan 375025
Tel: 374 10 55 34 13
Email: editor@eter.am **Web site:** http://www.eter.am
Circ: 50000 Publisher's Statement
Editor In Chief: Gor Ghazaryan
Profile: Informative-entertaining weekly providing TV guide, cultural and social news, horoscope, humour and crosswords.
Language (s): Armenian
Ad Rate: Full Page Colour 150000.00
Currency: Armenia Drams
DAILY NEWSPAPER

Golos Armenii 161292
Owner: Golos Armenii
Editorial: Arshakuniatz Sq. 2, Floor 7, Yerevan
Tel: 374 1 52 89 28
Email: golosarmenii2013@yandex.com **Web site:** http://www.golosarmenii.am
Freq: 2 Times/Week; **Circ:** 3500 Publisher's Statement
Editor: Flora Nakhshkaryan
Profile: Newspaper covering national and international news, economics, politics, entertainment and sport.
Language (s): Russian
DAILY NEWSPAPER

Hayastany Hanrapetutiun 161297
Owner: Hanrapetutiun
Editorial: Arshakunyats Ave. 2, 13th and 14th Floors, Yerevan 23 **Tel:** 374 1 52 57 56
Email: hh@press.aic.net **Web site:** http://www.hhpress.am
Freq: Daily; **Circ:** 6000 Publisher's Statement
Profile: Newspaper covering national and international news, politics, economy and culture.
Language (s): Armenian
DAILY NEWSPAPER

Haykakan zhamanak 157107
Owner: Haykakan zhamanak
Editorial: Israyelyan St. 37, Yerevan 375015
Tel: 374 10 581175
Email: info@armtimes.com **Web site:** http://armtimes.com
Freq: Daily; **Circ:** 8000 Publisher's Statement
Editor: Anna Hakobyan
Profile: Newspaper covering national and international news, economics, sport and social events.
Language (s): Armenian
DAILY NEWSPAPER

Hayots Ashkharh 161298
Owner: TIGRAN METS
Editorial: 38/ Apt. 41 Tumanyan St., Yerevan 375002
Tel: 374 10 53 88 65
Email: hayashkh@arminco.com **Web site:** http://www.armworld.am
Freq: Daily; **Circ:** 3500 Publisher's Statement
Editor: Gagik Mkrtchyan
Profile: Newspaper covering national and regional news, politics, business, culture and social events.
Language (s): Armenian
DAILY NEWSPAPER

Iravunk 229919
Owner: Iravunk
Editorial: Yeznik Koghbatsu St. 50 A, Yerevan 375002 **Tel:** 374 10 53 27 30
Email: iravunk@narod.ru **Web site:** http://www.iravunk.com
Circ: 60000 Publisher's Statement
Editor: Hovhannes Galajyan
Profile: Newspaper covering national and international news including features on law and legal issues, business and politics.
Language (s): Armenian
Ad Rate: Full Page Mono 200000.00
Currency: Armenia Drams
DAILY NEWSPAPER

Novoye Vremia 161299
Owner: Novoe Vremia Ltd
Editorial: Arshakunyats Ave. 2, 3rd Floor, Yerevan 375023 **Tel:** 374 10 52 69 46
Email: nvremia@arminco.com **Web site:** http://www.nv.am
Freq: 3 Times/Year; **Circ:** 5000 Publisher's Statement
Editor: Ruben Satyan
Profile: Newspaper focusing on national and international news, politics, the economy, culture and social events.
Language (s): Russian
DAILY NEWSPAPER

The Noyan Tapan Highlights 224383
Owner: Noyan Tapan
Editorial: 28 Issahakian Street, Yerevan 375009
Tel: 374 10 56 59 65
Email: contact@nt.am **Web site:** http://www.nt.am
Freq: Weekly; **Circ:** 1500 Publisher's Statement
Editor: Gayaneh Arakelyan; **Director General:** Tigran Harytyunyan
Profile: Weekly newspaper in English language covering politics, economics, society and cultural events in Armenia.
Language (s): English
DAILY NEWSPAPER

Respublica Armenia 161300
Owner: Hayastani Hanrapetutiun-Respublica Armenia CJSC
Editorial: Arshakunyats Prospekt 2, 9 floor, Yerevan 23 **Tel:** 374 10 54 57 00
Email: ra@arminco.am **Web site:** http://www.ra.am
Freq: 2 Times/Week; **Circ:** 3000 Publisher's Statement
Editor In Chief: Yelena Kurdiyan

Profile: Newspaper focusing on national and international news, politics, economics and current affairs.
Language (s): Russian
DAILY NEWSPAPER

Yerkir 229912
Owner: ARF Publication
Editorial: 30 Hanrapetutian Str., Yerevan 10
Tel: 374 10 52 15 01
Email: news@yerkir.am **Web site:** http://www.yerkir.am
Freq: Daily; **Circ:** 2500 Publisher's Statement
Profile: Official newspaper of the Armenian Revolutionary Federation focusing on national and international news, politics, the economy, society, culture, education and sport.
Language (s): Armenian
DAILY NEWSPAPER

News Service/Syndicate

ARKA News Agency 353758
Owner: ARKA News Agency
Editorial: 1/3 Pavstos Byuzand St., Yerevan 375010
Tel: 374 10 52 40 80
Email: arka@arminco.com **Web site:** http://www.arka.am
Language (s): Armenian
NEWS SERVICE/SYNDICATE

Armenpress 353756
Editorial: 22 Sarayan Street, Yerevan 2
Tel: 374 10 539818
Email: contact@armenpress.am **Web site:** http://www.armenpress.am
Editor-in-Chief: Narine Nazaryan; **Editor:** Samvel Sargsyan
Profile: Produces home, international, regional news bulletins, photo news and provides a wide range of analytical stories covering politics, economy, culture and other areas. News items are issued on a daily basis in Armenian, Russian and English.
Language (s): Armenian
NEWS SERVICE/SYNDICATE

De facto 518554
Editorial: 2 Arshakuniats, 9 floor, Yerevan
Tel: 374 10 54 57 99
Web site: http://www.defacto.am
Editor-in-Chief: Karen Zakharyan
Profile: Information Analytical News Agency providing political and economics news in Armenian, Russian and English languages.
Language (s): Russian
NEWS SERVICE/SYNDICATE

Mediamax 353757
Editorial: Abovyan 8, 2nd floor, Yerevan
Tel: 374 10 54 54 31
Email: news@mediamax.am **Web site:** http://www.mediamax.am
Editor-in-Chief: David Alaverdyan; **Editor:** Tatev Hovhannisyan
Profile: Provides news from Armenia, covering important political, economic, public, social and other events - in Russian, English and Armenian languages. Presents qualitative, efficient and reliable source of information about the developments in Armenia and in the region of the South Caucasus.
Language (s): Armenian
NEWS SERVICE/SYNDICATE

NEWS.am 620483
Editorial: 7/1, Verin Shenga vit, 2nd street, Yerevan
Tel: 374 77 26 64 13
Email: editor@news.am **Web site:** https://news.am/arm
Profile: Independent Armenian information-analytic agency, delivering the regular coverage of analyzed current information about politics, lifestyle and culture.
Language (s): Armenian
NEWS SERVICE/SYNDICATE

Yerevan Press Club 353755
Editorial: 9B, Ghazar Parpetsi str, Yerevan 375002
Tel: 374 10 53 00 67
Email: info@ypc.am **Web site:** http://www.ypc.am
President: Boris Navasardian; **Editor:** Elina Poghosbekian
Profile: Informing about the events and the situation of the Armenian media.
Language (s): Armenian
NEWS SERVICE/SYNDICATE

Community Newspaper

Syuniac yerkir 519196
Editorial: 20/32, Kapan **Tel:** 374 285 5 25 63
Email: syuniacyerkir@mail.ru **Web site:** http://www.syuniacyerkir.am
Circ: 2100
Editor-in-Chief: Samvel Aleksanyan
Profile: Regional newspaper covering political and social issues.
Language (s): Armenian
COMMUNITY NEWSPAPER

Aruba

Time Difference: GMT -4
National Telephone Code: 297
Continent: The Americas
Capital: Oranjestad

Newspapers

Aruba Today 158150
Owner: Caribbean Speed Printers
Editorial: Weststraat 22, Oranjestad **Tel:** 297 582-7800
Web site: http://www.arubatoday.com
Freq: Daily; **Circ:** 15000 Not Audited
Director: John Chemaly; **General Manager:** Grace-Mary Maduro; **Editor in Chief:** Julia Renfro
Profile: Newspaper covering national and international news and current affairs, politics, the economy, culture, sport and health.
Language (s): English
Ad Rate: Full Page Mono 2.94
Ad Rate: Full Page Colour 7.15
Currency: United States Dollars
DAILY NEWSPAPER

Bon Dia Aruba 218045
Owner: Caribbean Speed Printers
Editorial: Weststraat 22, Oranjestad
Tel: 297 58 27 800
Email: noticia@bondia.com **Web site:** http://www.bondia.com
Freq: Daily; **Circ:** 25000 Not Audited
Director: John Chemaly; **Manager:** Marijke Croes; **Editor:** Harold Farro; **General Manager:** Grace-Mary Maduro; **Editor:** Benjamin Romero; **Editor:** Oscar Vidal
Profile: Newspaper covering national and international news and current affairs; includes politics, the economy, sports, culture and health.
Language (s): Dutch
Ad Rate: Full Page Mono 2.94
Ad Rate: Full Page Colour 7.15
Currency: United States Dollars
DAILY NEWSPAPER

Australia

Time Difference: GMT +8 (West Coast), GMT +10.5 (East Coast)
National Telephone Code: 61
Continent: Oceania
Capital: Canberra

Newspapers

The Advertiser Adelaide 158949
Owner: News Corp Australia
Editorial: 31 Waymouth St, Adelaide SA 5000
Tel: 61 1300 130 370
Email: newstip@adv.newsltd.com.au **Web site:** http://www.adelaidenow.com.au
Freq: Daily; **Circ:** 90
Profile: Metropolitan daily newspaper first established in 1858. Provides local stories of the day, breaking news from around the world and local discussion.
Language (s): English
DAILY NEWSPAPER

The Age Australia 158938
Owner: Fairfax Media
Editorial: 655 Collins Street, Docklands VIC 3008
Tel: 61 3 8667 2250
Email: newsdesk@theage.com.au **Web site:** http://www.theage.com.au
Freq: Daily; **Circ:** 90
Editor: Margaret Easterbrook; **Picture Editor:** Leigh Henningham; **Editor:** Stephen Nicholls
Profile: Daily newspaper covering regional, national and international news and current affairs including business, finance, economics, politics, sports, technology, entertainment, lifestyle, travel, cars, property and multimedia.
Language (s): English
Ad Rate: Full Page Colour 54400.00
Currency: Australia Dollars
DAILY NEWSPAPER

The Australian 158916
Owner: News Corp Australia
Editorial: 2 Holt Street, Surry Hills NSW 2010
Tel: 61 2 9288 3000
Email: nsw@theaustralian.com.au **Web site:** http://www.theaustralian.com.au
Freq: Daily; **Circ:** 90
Editor at Large: Paul Kelly
Profile: Daily newspaper covering regional, national and international news and current affairs including business, politics, economics, sports, higher education, and information technology.
Language (s): English
DAILY NEWSPAPER

Australian Financial Review 158932
Owner: Fairfax Business Media
Editorial: 1 Darling Island Road, Pyrmont NSW 2009
Tel: 61 2 9282 2833
Email: afrnewsdesk@afr.com.au **Web site:** http://www.afr.com
Freq: Daily; **Circ:** 90
Editor in Chief: Paul Bailey; **Editor:** Kate Cowling; **Melbourne Bureau Chief:** Patrick Durkin; **Editor:** James Eyers
Profile: National daily newspaper covering financial news including business, economics, personal finance, markets and investment.
Language (s): English
Ad Rate: Full Page Colour 19434.00
Currency: Australia Dollars
DAILY NEWSPAPER

The Canberra Times 158937
Owner: Fairfax Media
Editorial: 9 Pirie Street, Fyshwick ACT 2609
Tel: 61 2 6280 2122
Email: letters.editor@canberratimes.com.au **Web site:** http://www.canberratimes.com.au
Freq: Daily; **Circ:** 90
Editor-in-Chief: Rod Quinn
Profile: Provides the latest national and international news. Featuring segments on lifestyle, health, food, wine, fashion etc.
Language (s): English
DAILY NEWSPAPER

The Courier Mail 158930
Owner: News Corp Australia
Editorial: 41 Campbell Street, Bowen Hills QLD 4006
Tel: 61 7 3666 6480
Email: cmonline@qnp.newsltd.com.au **Web site:** http://www.couriermail.com.au
Freq: Daily; **Circ:** 90
Gold Coast Bureau chief: Greg Stolz
Profile: Newspaper covering the latest news issues, sport, food, travel and business.
Language (s): English
DAILY NEWSPAPER

The Daily Telegraph Australia 158924
Owner: News Corp Australia
Editorial: 2 Holt Street, Surry Hills NSW 2010
Tel: 61 2 9288 3000
Email: news@dailytelegraph.com.au **Web site:** http://www.dailytelegraph.com.au
Freq: Daily; **Circ:** 90
Editor: Mark Morri; **Editor at Large:** Jeni O'Dowd; **Editor:** Paul Whittaker; **Editor:** James Wigney
Profile: Daily newspaper covering news and current affairs including politics, economics, business, sport, entertainment and lifestyle.
Language (s): English
Ad Rate: Full Page Colour 38349.00
Currency: Australia Dollars
DAILY NEWSPAPER

The Examiner (TAS) 439466
Owner: Rural Press Limited
Editorial: 113 Cimitiere Street, Launceston TAS 7250
Tel: 61 3 6336 7111
Email: mail@examiner.com.au **Web site:** http://www.examiner.com.au
Freq: Daily; **Circ:** 90
Profile: The Examiner is a daily Australian newspaper covering latest news, sport and business in Launceston and north-eastern Tasmania.
Language (s): English
DAILY NEWSPAPER

Geelong Advertiser 439470
Owner: News Limited
Editorial: 191-195 Ryrie Street, Geelong VIC 3220
Tel: 61 3 5227 4340
Email: journo@geelongadvertiser.com.au **Web site:** http://www.geelongadvertiser.com.au
Freq: Daily; **Circ:** 90
Head of News: Shane Fowles
Profile: Regional daily newspaper. The Geelong Advertiser is the voice of Geelong, Bellarine and Surf Coast. First published in 1840.
Language (s): English
DAILY NEWSPAPER

The Gold Coast Bulletin 436219
Owner: Gold Coast Publications Pty Ltd
Editorial: Seabank 12-14 Marine Parade, Southport QLD 4215 **Tel:** 61 7 5584 2000
Email: editorial@gcb.newsltd.com.au **Web site:** http://www.goldcoast.com.au
Freq: Daily; **Circ:** 90
News Editor: Lendl Ryan
Profile: A newspaper with news and issues relevant to people living on the Gold Coast.
Language (s): English
DAILY NEWSPAPER

The Herald Sun 158923
Owner: News Corp Australia
Editorial: HWT Tower, 40 City Road, Southbank VIC 3006 **Tel:** 61 3 9292 2000
Email: news@heraldsun.com.au **Web site:** http://www.heraldsun.com.au
Freq: Daily; **Circ:** 90
Editor: Zoe Curtis; **News Editor:** Liam Houlihan; **Editor:** Damon Johnston; **Picture Editor:** Wayne Ludbey
Profile: Major daily metropolitan newspaper published in Melbourne. Includes Victorian, national and world news, plus entertainment, sport and business.
Language (s): English
Ad Rate: Full Page Colour 41700.02
Currency: Australia Dollars
DAILY NEWSPAPER

The Mercury 158944
Owner: News Corp Australia
Editorial: Level 1, 2 Salamanca Square, Hobart TAS 7000 **Tel:** 61 3 6230 0760
Email: mercury.news@dbl.newsltd.com.au **Web site:** http://www.themercury.com.au
Freq: Daily; **Circ:** 90
Editor-in-Chief: Matt Deighton
Profile: The Mercury is based in the largest population centre, Hobart, and provides essential reading for Tasmanians. The Mercury features news, sport, business, entertainment and lifestyle.
Language (s): English
DAILY NEWSPAPER

The Newcastle Herald 436221
Owner: Fairfax Media
Editorial: 28 Honeysuckle Drive, Newcastle NSW 2300 **Tel:** 61 2 4979 5000
Email: news@theherald.com.au **Web site:** http://www.theherald.com.au
Freq: Daily; **Circ:** 90
Editor: Chad Watson
Profile: Regional daily newspaper for the Newcastle, Hunter valley and Central coast district.
Language (s): English
Ad Rate: Full Page Mono 9484.80
Currency: Australia Dollars
DAILY NEWSPAPER

The Northern Territory News 158947
Owner: News Corp
Editorial: 1 Printers Place, Darwin NT 0800
Tel: 61 8 8944 9900
Email: news@ntnews.com.au **Web site:** http://www.ntnews.com.au
Circ: 90
Editor: Rachel Hancock
Profile: The Northern Territory News features the latest and local and national news. First published on February 8, 1952. The NT News reaches more than 64,000 people each day Monday – Friday, and the Saturday edition of the NT News is the highest circulating paper of the week. Liftouts in Saturday's NT News such as Property, Career One, Carsguide, Marine Guide and the investigative journalism feature 'Saturday Extra' ensure there is something for everyone.
Language (s): English
DAILY NEWSPAPER

The Saturday Paper 903727
Editorial: 37-39 Langridge Street, Collingwood 3066 Vic **Tel:** 61 3 9486 0288
Email: enquiries@thesaturdaypaper.com.au **Web site:** http://www.thesaturdaypaper.com.au
Freq: Weekly
Editor: Erik Jensen
Profile: The Saturday Paper is a weekly newspaper covering news, culture, and analysis, with a particular focus on Australia. Launched on 1 March 2014.
Language (s): English
Ad Rate: Full Page Colour 8500.00
Currency: Australia Dollars
DAILY NEWSPAPER

Sunday Times Perth Australia 158939
Owner: Seven West Media
Editorial: 50 Hasler Road, Osborne Park, Perth WA 6017 **Tel:** 61 8 9326 9422
Email: news@perthnow.com.au **Web site:** http://www.perthnow.com.au
Freq: Weekly; **Circ:** 90
Editor: Rod Savage
Profile: Metropolitan Sunday newspaper circulating in Perth and Western Australia.
Language (s): English
DAILY NEWSPAPER

Sunshine Coast Daily 158936
Owner: APN News & Media Limited
Editorial: Newspaper Place & Dalton Drive, Maroochydore QLD 4558 **Tel:** 61 7 5430 1012
Email: editorial@scnews.com.au **Web site:** http://www.sunshinecoastdaily.com.au
Freq: Daily; **Circ:** 90
Editor: Damian Bathersby; **News Director:** Bianca Clare; **Editor:** Erle Levey
Profile: Regional newspaper in the Sunshine Coast area. Regular Features: Business, Comics, Crosswords, Letters, Sport, TV and Weather.
Language (s): English
DAILY NEWSPAPER

The Sydney Morning Herald 158920
Owner: Fairfax Media
Editorial: 1 Darling Island Road, Pyrmont NSW 2009
Tel: 61 2 9282 2833
Email: newsdesk@smh.com.au **Web site:** http://www.smh.com.au
Freq: Daily; **Circ:** 90

Australia

Editor: Peter Hannam; **Editor:** Stephen Nicholls; **Morning News Director:** Marcus Strom
Profile: Metropolitan daily broadsheet newspaper in Sydney covering regional, national and international news and current affairs including politics, business, finance, economics, sports, entertainment, lifestyle, travel, cars and property.
Language (s): English
Ad Rate: Full Page Colour 77827.00
Currency: Australia Dollars
DAILY NEWSPAPER

The West Australian 158940
Owner: The West Australian
Editorial: 50 Hasler Road, Osborne Park, Perth WA 6017 **Tel:** 61 8 9482 3111
Email: online@thewest.com.au **Web site:** https://thewest.com.au
Freq: Daily; **Circ:** 90
Editor: Brett McCarthy; **Editor:** Grace Millimaci; **Editor:** Hermione Stott
Profile: Newspaper covering news, weather, employment, real estate, cars, boats, shopping, sport and entertainment.
Language (s): English
Ad Rate: Full Page Colour 13990.72
Currency: Australia Dollars
DAILY NEWSPAPER

News Service/Syndicate

AAP Adelaide 492686
Owner: AAP Information Services Pty Ltd
Editorial: Level 5 West, 50 Grenfell Street, Adelaide SA 5000 **Tel:** 61 8 8238 4300
Email: news.adelaide@aap.com.au **Web site:** http://www.aap.com.au
Bureau Chief: Liza Kappelle
Profile: AAP provides world news and images to our customers through commercial partnerships with major international agencies like Associated Press, Reuters, Agence France-Presse, Agencia EFE, Deutsche Presse-Agentur, The Press Association, Kyodo, Knight-Ridder and New Zealand Press Association.
Language (s): English
NEWS SERVICE/SYNDICATE

AAP Brisbane 492688
Owner: AAP Information Services Pty Ltd
Editorial: Level 2, 200 Mary Street, Brisbane QLD 4000 **Tel:** 61 7 3834 9999
Email: news.brisbane@aap.com.au **Web site:** https://www.aap.com.au
Bureau Chief: Paul Osbourne
Profile: AAP provides world news and images to our customers through commercial partnerships with major international agencies like Associated Press, Reuters, Agence France-Presse, Agencia EFE, Deutsche Presse-Agentur, The Press Association, Kyodo, Knight-Ridder and New Zealand Press Association.
Language (s): English
NEWS SERVICE/SYNDICATE

AAP Canberra 347776
Owner: AAP Information Services Pty Ltd
Editorial: Canberra
Email: news.canberra@aap.com.au **Web site:** http://aap.com.au
Profile: AAP provides world news and images to our customers through commercial partnerships with major international agencies like Associated Press, Reuters, Agence France-Presse, Agencia EFE, Deutsche Presse-Agentur, The Press Association, Kyodo, Knight-Ridder and New Zealand Press Association. PR Accepted in: English
Language (s): English
NEWS SERVICE/SYNDICATE

AAP Darwin 492687
Owner: AAP Information Services Pty Ltd
Editorial: 16-17/24 Cavenagh St, Darwin NT 0800
Tel: 61 8 8942 3388
Email: news.darwin@aap.com.au **Web site:** http://www.aap.com.au
Profile: AAP provides world news and images to our customers through commercial partnerships with major international agencies like Associated Press, Reuters, Agence France-Presse, Agencia EFE, Deutsche Presse-Agentur, The Press Association, Kyodo, Knight-Ridder and New Zealand Press Association.
Language (s): English
NEWS SERVICE/SYNDICATE

AAP Hobart 492690
Owner: AAP Information Services Pty Ltd
Editorial: 97 - 93 Macquarie Street, Hobart TAS 7000
Tel: 61 3 6234 5541
Email: news.hobart@aap.com.au **Web site:** http://www.aap.com.au
Profile: AAP provides world news and images to our customers through commercial partnerships with major international agencies like Associated Press, Reuters, Agence France-Presse, Agencia EFE, Deutsche Presse-Agentur, The Press Association, Kyodo, Knight-Ridder and New Zealand Press Association.
Language (s): English
NEWS SERVICE/SYNDICATE

AAP Melbourne 492689
Owner: AAP Information Services Pty Ltd
Editorial: Level 3, 250 Victoria Parade, East Melbourne VIC 3002 **Tel:** 61 3 9619 9361
Email: news.melbourne@aap.com.au **Web site:** http://www.aap.com.au
Profile: AAP provides world news and images to our customers through commercial partnerships with major international agencies like Associated Press, Reuters, Agence France-Presse, Agencia EFE, Deutsche Presse-Agentur, The Press Association, Kyodo, Knight-Ridder and New Zealand Press Association.
Language (s): English
NEWS SERVICE/SYNDICATE

AAP Perth 492685
Owner: AAP Information Services Pty Ltd
Editorial: Level 7, Septimus Roe Square, 256 Adelaide Terrace, Perth WA 6000 **Tel:** 61 8 9421 2211
Email: news.perth@aap.com.au **Web site:** http://www.aap.com.au
Profile: AAP provides world news and images to our customers through commercial partnerships with major international agencies like Associated Press, Reuters, Agence France-Presse, Agencia EFE, Deutsche Presse-Agentur, The Press Association, Kyodo, Knight-Ridder and New Zealand Press Association.
Language (s): English
NEWS SERVICE/SYNDICATE

AAP Sydney 313574
Owner: AAP Information Services Pty Ltd
Editorial: 3 Rider Boulevard, Rhodes NSW 2138
Tel: 61 2 9322 8000
Email: news.sydney@aap.com.au **Web site:** http://www.aap.com.au
Editor-in-Chief: Tony Gillies; **News Editor:** Bronwyn Walenkamp
Profile: AAP provides world news and images to customers through commercial partnerships with major international agencies like Associated Press, Reuters, Agence France-Presse, Agencia EFE, Deutsche Presse-Agentur, The Press Association, Kyodo, Knight-Ridder and New Zealand Press Association.
Language (s): English
NEWS SERVICE/SYNDICATE

ABC Radio & Television - London Bureau 409969
Owner: ABC Capricornia
Editorial: 4 Millbank Road, London, England
Tel: 44 20 7808 1350
Web site: http://www.abc.net.au
Profile: London bureau for ABC - Australian Broadcasting Corporation.
Language (s): English
NEWS SERVICE/SYNDICATE

Jewish Telegraph Agency Sydney Bureau 313594
Editorial: 34 Rivers Street, Bellevue Hill NSW 2203
Tel: 61 2 9326 2765
Email: dan.goldberg@northonetv.com **Web site:** http://www.jta.org
Profile: Sydney bureau of a Jewish news agency.
Language (s): English
NEWS SERVICE/SYNDICATE

Jiji Press Sydney Bureau 652344
Owner: Jiji Press (Aust) Pty Ltd
Editorial: Suite 1401, 109 Pitt Street, Sydney NSW 2000 **Tel:** 61 2 9230 0020
Email: sydney@jiji.com.au
Bureau Chief: Naoki Odaira
Profile: Nationality: Japan Nabutoshi has taken over the position of bureau chief. He was previously stationed at the Tokyo head office. Preferred method of receiving media releases = email.
Language (s): Japanese
NEWS SERVICE/SYNDICATE

Kyodo News - Sydney Bureau 313591
Owner: Kyodo News Service
Editorial: Level 3, 301B, 46 Market Street, Sydney NSW 2000 **Tel:** 61 2 9262 5400
Email: kyodosyd@bigpond.net.au **Web site:** http://home.kyodo.co.jp
Bureau Chief: Noriko Goi; **Bureau Chief:** Takushi Ohno
Profile: International wire service. Geographical Focus: Japanese
Language (s): English
NEWS SERVICE/SYNDICATE

My Dr 435280
Owner: Cirrus Media
Editorial: Tower 2, Level 3, 475 Victoria Avenue, Chatswood NSW 2067 **Tel:** 61 299027700
Email: editorial@myDr.com.au **Web site:** http://www.mydr.com.au
Freq: Daily
Profile: An online health and medical information site. myDr.com.au is published by Cirrus Media, publishers of the weekly GP newspapers Medical Observer and Australian Doctor.
Language (s): English
NEWS SERVICE/SYNDICATE

RWE Australian Business News 313579
Owner: RWE Australian Business News Pty Ltd
Editorial: 6 Kirpson Street, Berrara NSW 2540
Tel: 61 2 9871 4149
Email: brebase@rweabn.com.au
News Editor: Ben Rebase
Profile: Includes RWE - SNN News Network (video streaming) Distribution: Global
Language (s): English
NEWS SERVICE/SYNDICATE

Xinhua News Agency - Canberra Bureau 689672
Owner: People's Republic of China
Editorial: 50 Russell Street, Hackett ACT 2602
Tel: 61 2 6248 6369
Email: canberraxinhua@gmail.com **Web site:** http://www.xinhuanet.com
Bureau Chief: Yaping Jiang
Profile: Geographical Focus: Chinese
Language (s): English
NEWS SERVICE/SYNDICATE

Community Newspaper

The Advocate Tasmania Newspaper 439056
Owner: Rural Press Limited
Editorial: 54-56 Mount Street, Burnie TAS 7320
Tel: 61 3 6440 7409
Email: news@theadvocate.com.au **Web site:** http://www.theadvocate.com.au
Circ: 21996
Profile: Daily newspaper covering news, sport and current affairs. The Advocate provides news and information for the North-West and West coasts of Tasmania.
Language (s): English
COMMUNITY NEWSPAPER

The Area News 222064
Owner: Fairfax Media
Editorial: 11b Banna Avenue, Griffith NSW 2680
Tel: 61 2 6962 1733
Email: editor@areanews.com.au **Web site:** http://www.areanews.com.au
Circ: 5689
Profile: Weekly regional newspaper that focuses on local issues.
Language (s): English
COMMUNITY NEWSPAPER

The Armidale Express 441251
Owner: Fairfax Media
Editorial: 115 Faulkner Street, Armidale NSW 2350
Tel: 61 2 6776 0500
Email: editor.armexpress@ruralpress.com **Web site:** http://www.armidaleexpress.com.au
Circ: 2320
Profile: The Armidale Express is a bi-weekly newspaper, established in Armidale in northern NSW in 1856, reaching Armidale, Uralla, Guyra and Walcha.
Language (s): English
COMMUNITY NEWSPAPER

The Avon Valley Advocate 230977
Owner: Fairfax Media
Editorial: 146 Fitzgerald Street, Northam WA 6401
Tel: 61 8 9622 5500
Web site: http://www.avonadvocate.com.au
Freq: Weekly; **Circ:** 2188
Profile: Focuses on news, sports and events of the region. Weekly newspaper and circulates 1539. Published every Wednesday.
Language (s): English
COMMUNITY NEWSPAPER

The Border Mail VIC 443723
Owner: Fairfax Media
Editorial: 1 McKoy Street, Wodonga VIC 3690
Tel: 61 2 6024 0555
Email: newsroom@bordermail.com.au **Web site:** http://www.bordermail.com.au
Circ: 24330
Editor: Niall Boyle
Profile: The Border Mail is a community newspaper in the North East of Victoria and Southern NSW.
Language (s): English
COMMUNITY NEWSPAPER

The Bunyip 222107
Owner: Bunyip Press
Editorial: 120-122 Murray Street, Gawler SA 5118
Tel: 61 8 8522 1233
Email: editor@bunyippress.com.au **Web site:** http://www.bunyippress.com.au
Circ: 9500
Advertising Manager: Margaret Betts; **Editor:** Rob McLean
Profile: Weekly regional newspaper covering general news and current affairs in the lower north and Barossa Valley regions of NSW.
Language (s): English
COMMUNITY NEWSPAPER

The Cairns Weekend Post 532952
Owner: The Cairns Post Pty Ltd
Editorial: 22-24 Abbott Street, Cairns QLD 4870
Tel: 61 7 4052 6666
Web site: http://www.cairnspost.com.au
Circ: 41067
Profile: Weekend edition of the regional newspaper covering news and issues that effect the community.
Language (s): English
COMMUNITY NEWSPAPER

The Cessnock Advertiser 221775
Owner: Fairfax Media
Editorial: 155 Vincent Street, Cessnock NSW 2325
Tel: 61 2 4990 1244
Email: manager.cessadvertiser@ruralpress.com **Web site:** http://www.cessnockadvertiser.com.au
Circ: 17866
Manager: Rebecca Gillon; **Editor:** Krystal Sellars
Profile: The Advertiser newspaper, serving the Cessnock City community for over 50 years. The latest local news, sport, real estate, classifieds and more every Wednesday. Geographical Focus: Australia New South Wales
Language (s): English
COMMUNITY NEWSPAPER

The Coastal Rag 445419
Editorial: 1 Captain Cook Drive, Agnes Water QLD 4677 **Tel:** 61 7 4974 7253
Email: coastalrag@bigpond.com **Web site:** http://coastalrag.lcboard.com.au
Circ: 3200
Advertising Manager: Anne Lightfoot; **Editor:** Cheryl Wicks
Profile: The Coastal Rag Community Newspaper, covering the Central Queensland, Discovery Coast, Agnes Water, Miriam Vale, Baffle Creek, Rosedale, Lowmead, Bororen, Turkey Beach and districts to Gladstone & Bundaberg.
Language (s): English
COMMUNITY NEWSPAPER

The Colac Herald 222029
Owner: Gannon Newspapers Pty Ltd
Editorial: 37-41 Bromfield Street, Colac VIC 3250
Tel: 61 3 5231 5322
Email: news@colacherald.com **Web site:** http://www.colacherald.com
Circ: 5167
Advertising Manager: Andrea Graham; **Editor:** David McKenzie
Profile: Produced by a team based in Colac, the Colac Herald arrives each Monday, Wednesday and Friday with the district's up-to-date and in-depth news and sports reports and advertising.
Language (s): English
COMMUNITY NEWSPAPER

The Coonabarabran Times 221779
Owner: Warrumbungle Publications Pty Ltd
Editorial: 44 Dalgarno Street, Coonabarabran NSW 2357 **Tel:** 61 2 6842 1844
Email: cbntimes@tpg.com.au
Circ: 2400
Editor: Richard Duggan
Profile: Independently owned and operated, the Coonabarabran Times is the official newspaper of Warrumbungle Shire. Year First Published: 1885 Target Audience: Local Community.
Language (s): English
COMMUNITY NEWSPAPER

The Dimboola Banner 532179
Owner: Victorian Country Press Association
Editorial: 94 Lloyd St, Dimboola VIC 3414
Tel: 61 3 5389 1440
Email: banner1@iinet.net.au **Web site:** http://dimboolabanner.com.au/newspaper
Circ: 910
Editor: David Ward
Language (s): English
Ad Rate: Full Page Colour 330.00
Currency: Australia Dollars
COMMUNITY NEWSPAPER

The District Reporter 510528
Editorial: PO Box 116, Camden NSW 2570
Tel: 61 2 4655 1234
Email: editor@tdr.com.au **Web site:** http://www.tdr.com.au
Circ: 16900
Editor: Lee Abrahams; **Advertising Manager:** Noel Lowry
Profile: Established 18 years ago, The District Reporter is a family owned, independent country newspaper with a weekly circulation of 16,900 n the local government areas of Camden, Wollondilly - South West of Sydney. The District Reporter targets families on rural properties in this region.Provides articles on financial planning, real estate, community events, sport, politics and local news. It contains the extremely popular historical column on the back page called 'Back Then'.
Language (s): English
Ad Rate: Full Page Mono 792.00
Currency: Australia Dollars
COMMUNITY NEWSPAPER

The Ellenbrook Advocate 230903
Owner: Community Newspaper Group
Editorial: 12 Old Great Northern Highway, Midland WA 6056 **Tel:** 61 8 9237 1900
Email: advocate@communitynews.com.au **Web site:** http://www.communitynews.com.au
Circ: 4272
Profile: he Advocate is a weekly community newspaper delivered to the Swan Valley, Chittering Valley, Gingin and Ellenbrook areas every Wednesday
Language (s): English
Ad Rate: Full Page Colour 2477.42
Currency: Australia Dollars
COMMUNITY NEWSPAPER

The Gazette Warragul & Drouin 222136
Owner: Warragul Regional Newspapers Pty Ltd
Editorial: 97-103 Queen Street, Warragul VIC 3820
Tel: 61 3 5623 5666
Email: editorial@warragulgazette.com.au **Web site:** http://www.warragulgazette.com.au
Circ: 10597
General Manager: Andrew Schreyer
Profile: Regional newspaper covering general news and current affairs in the Warragul and Drouin area.
Language (s): English
COMMUNITY NEWSPAPER

The Gilgandra Weekly 221912
Owner: Rural Press Limited
Editorial: 64 - 66 Miller Street, Gilgandra NSW 2827
Tel: 61 2 6847 2022
Email: editor@gilgandranewspapers.com.au
Freq: Weekly; **Circ:** 1250
Profile: Gilgandra Weekly is the source of local information, news and entertainment.
Language (s): English
COMMUNITY NEWSPAPER

The Greater Springfield Times 510555
Owner: Local News Publications
Editorial: 36 Pradella Street, Richlands QLD 4077
Tel: 61 7 3217 0533
Email: springfieldtimes@lnp.net.au **Web site:** http://lnp.net.au/the-greater-springfield-times/
Circ: 11000
Manager: Graham Friis; **Editor:** Susannah Friis
Profile: Established in 1997, The Greater Springfield Times is a free monthly magazine with distribution reaching the suburbs of Augustine Heights, Bellbird Park, Brookwater, Camira, Gailes, Springfield and Springfield Lakes.
Language (s): English
Ad Rate: Full Page Colour 795.00
Currency: Australia Dollars
COMMUNITY NEWSPAPER

The Hepburn Advocate 222024
Owner: Rural Press Limited
Editorial: 3/32 Vincent Street, Daylesford VIC 3460
Tel: 61 3 5348 1028
Email: theadvocate@fairfaxmedia.com **Web site:** http://www.hepburnadvocate.com.au
Circ: 7718
Profile: Incorporating The Daylesford Advocate and The Creswick Advertiser. Provides news, sport and community information from Daylesford, Creswick and surrounds.
Language (s): English
COMMUNITY NEWSPAPER

The Islander 222229
Owner: Rural Press Limited
Editorial: 20 Osmond Street, Kingscote, Kangaroo Island SA 5223 **Tel:** 61 8 8553 4800
Email: news.theislander@fairfaxmedia.com.au **Web site:** http://www.theislanderonline.com.au
Freq: Weekly; **Circ:** 2067
Profile: The Islander is the local weekly newspaper for Kangaroo Island, South Australia.
Language (s): English
COMMUNITY NEWSPAPER

The Kuranda Paper 773331
Editorial: n/a, Kuranda QLD 4881
Tel: 61 7 4093 8942
Email: mail@kurandapaper.com **Web site:** http://www.kurandapaper.com
Freq: Monthly; **Circ:** 3800
Profile: The community newspaper from the rainforest village of Kuranda, Far North Queensland, Australia.
Language (s): English
COMMUNITY NEWSPAPER

The Lightning Ridge News 221877
Owner: Rural Press Limited
Editorial: 10a Opal Street, Lightning Ridge NSW 2834 **Tel:** 61 2 6829 2150
Email: mail.ridgenews@ruralpress.com **Web site:** http://www.theridgenews.com.au
Circ: 881
Profile: A regional local paper with news and issues relevant to the local community.
Language (s): English
COMMUNITY NEWSPAPER

The Loxton News 222098
Owner: The Loxton News Pty Ltd
Editorial: 54 East Terrace, Loxton SA 5333
Tel: 61 8 8584 7271
Email: editor@loxton-news.com.au **Web site:** http://www.loxton-news.com.au
Circ: 2400
Editor: Paul Mitchell
Profile: Local and regional newspaper in the Mallee region published every Wednesday morning and circulated throughout the Riverland and Northern Mallee. First published: 1960Target readership: Local community Regular features: Finance, Home Improvement, sports coverage, agricultural and horticultural news
Language (s): English
COMMUNITY NEWSPAPER

The Macarthur Chronicle 221780
Owner: Cumberland Newspaper Group
Editorial: Macarthur Place, 1st Floor, Campbelltown NSW 2560 **Tel:** 61 2 4620 1500
Email: editor@macarthurchronicle.com.au **Web site:** http://www.macarthurchronicle.com.au
Circ: 76166
Editor: Mandy Perrin
Profile: A regional newspaper with regular features including travel, finance, sport, news, community notices, food guide and entertainment etc.
Language (s): English
Ad Rate: Full Page Mono 3724.00
Currency: Australia Dollars
COMMUNITY NEWSPAPER

The Monaro Post 539843
Owner: Monaro Media Group Pty Ltd
Editorial: 220-226 Sharp Street, Cooma NSW 2630
Tel: 61 2 6452 0312
Email: editor@monaropost.com.au **Web site:** http://www.monaropost.com.au
Circ: 2200
Editor: Gail Eastaway; **Advertising Manager:** Tracy Frazer
Profile: The Monaro Post, the Monaro's locally owned, independent regional newspaper that covers Monaro region, Cooma, Berridale, Bredbo, Adaminaby, Dalgety, Numeralla, Nimmitabel, Michelago, Delegate, Bombala, Jindabyne, Cabramurra and the Snowy Mountains.
Language (s): English
COMMUNITY NEWSPAPER

The Moorabool News 446175
Owner: Victorian Country Press Association
Editorial: 58a Steiglitz Street, Ballan VIC 3342
Tel: 61 3 5368 1966
Email: news@themooraboolnews.com.au **Web site:** http://themooraboolnews.com.au/
Circ: 11000
Profile: The Moorabool News serves the communities within the bounds of Moorabool Shire with complete focus on all things local.
Language (s): English
COMMUNITY NEWSPAPER

The Morning Bulletin 439465
Owner: APN News & Media Limited
Editorial: 162-164 Quay Street, Rockhampton QLD 4700 **Tel:** 61 7 4930 4222
Web site: http://www.themorningbulletin.com.au
Freq: Daily; **Circ:** 14700
Editor: Frazer Pearce
Profile: Regular Features: Editorial, National, World, Entertainer, Racing, Weddings/Babies, Business, Classifieds and Television.
Language (s): English
COMMUNITY NEWSPAPER

Moruya Examiner 429665
Owner: Fairfax Media
Editorial: Shop 7, 33 Orient Street, Batemans Bay NSW 2536 **Tel:** 61 2 4472 6577
Email: editor.baypost@ruralpress.com **Web site:** https://www.batemansbaypost.com.au
Circ: 3400
Profile: Regional newspaper covering issues and current affairs in Moruya and the surrounding areas.
Language (s): English
COMMUNITY NEWSPAPER

The Moyne Gazette 221716
Owner: Fairfax Media
Editorial: 12 Bank Street, Port Fairy VIC 3284
Tel: 61 3 5568 1982
Email: gazette@fairfaxmedia.com.au **Web site:** http://www.moynegazette.com.au
Circ: 962
Profile: Weekly regional newspaper with issues, sports, gardening etc. news of interest to the wider community. Geographical Focus: South West England
Language (s): English
COMMUNITY NEWSPAPER

Mt Buller News 222177
Owner: North East Newspapers P/L
Editorial: 96 High Street, Mansfield VIC 3722
Tel: 61 3 5775 2115
Email: edit.mcourier@nemedia.com.au **Web site:** https://nemedia.com.au/supplements/mt-buller-news-3
Circ: 6000
Profile: A weekly regional newspaper of particular interest to those living and travelling in the snow region. Distributed through travel and ski outlets on Mountains.Year First Published: 1980 Content Summary: Mount Buller events.Photographic Information: B/W Photographs, Colour Photographs. Preferred Delivery: Email or Post.Preferred Format: TIFF, JPEG, PDF
Language (s): English
COMMUNITY NEWSPAPER

Mudgee Guardian 222084
Owner: Fairfax Media
Editorial: 9 Perry Street, Mudgee NSW 2850
Tel: 61 2 6372 1455
Web site: http://www.mudgeeguardian.com.au
Circ: 3526
Profile: Regional newspaper with news from Mudgee, Gulgong, Kandos, Rylstone, Dunedoo and Coolah. Email is preferred form to receive editorial and advertising.
Language (s): English
COMMUNITY NEWSPAPER

Murray Valley Standard 222103
Owner: Fairfax Media
Editorial: 110-118 Adelaide Road, Murray Bridge SA 5253 **Tel:** 61 8 8532 8000
Email: editor.mvstandard@fairfaxmedia.com.au **Web site:** http://www.murrayvalleystandard.com.au
Freq: 2 Times/Week; **Circ:** 3941
Profile: Regional newspaper with news and issues relevant to people living in the Murray Lands and outer Adelaide. Murray Valley Standard delivers the latest news, including sport, weather, entertainment and lifestyle.
Language (s): English
COMMUNITY NEWSPAPER

Musu Pastoge 221846
Owner: Musu Pastoge
Editorial: 16-20 Meredith Street, Bankstown NSW 2200 **Tel:** 61 2 9782 0080
Email: mpastoge@bigpond.com **Web site:** http://www.slic.org.au/Pastoge
Circ: 800
Editor: Doniela Dalia
Profile: Translation: Our Haven Lithuanian newspaper.
Language (s): Lithuanian
COMMUNITY NEWSPAPER

Namoi Valley Independent 222062
Owner: Gunnedah Publishing Company Pty Ltd
Editorial: 287 Conadilly Street, Gunnedah NSW 2380
Tel: 61 2 6742 0455
Email: editorial@nvi.com.au **Web site:** http://www.nvi.com.au
Circ: 3051
Editor: Kate Ramien
Profile: The Namoi Valley Independent is a rural, bi-weekly community newspaper with 135-year history. It covers the township of Gunnedah and surrounding villages and districts.
Language (s): English
COMMUNITY NEWSPAPER

Naracoorte Herald 222110
Owner: Fairfax Media
Editorial: 93 Smith Street, Naracoorte SA 5271
Tel: 61 8 8762 2555
Email: lee.curnow@fairfaxmedia.com.au **Web site:** http://www.naracoorteherald.com.au
Circ: 2898
Editor: Lee Curnow
Profile: Weekly regional newspaper covering general news and current affairs in the Naracoorte, Lucindale, Padthaway, Penola, Coonawarra and the Victorian border districts.
Language (s): English
COMMUNITY NEWSPAPER

Narooma News 221871
Owner: Fairfax Media
Editorial: Shop 4, Costin Village, Narooma NSW 2546 **Tel:** 61 2 4476 3024
Web site: http://www.naroomanewsonline.com.au
Circ: 2800
Editor: Stan Gorton
Profile: The Narooma News covers the local district from Bodalla to Cobargo and includes Bermagui, Tilba, Potato Point, Dalmeny and Kianga. The focus is on local people, places and events with an emphasis on the community.
Language (s): English
COMMUNITY NEWSPAPER

The Narrabri Courier 221929
Owner: The North Western Courier Pty Ltd
Editorial: 60 Maitland Street, Narrabri NSW 2390
Tel: 61 2 6792 1011
Email: editorial@nwcourier.com.au **Web site:** http://www.thecourier.net.au
Circ: 3500
General Manager: Wanda Dunnet
Profile: Regional weekly newspaper. Covers news, sport and community events in and around Narrabri. Circulates in Narrabri, Wee Waa, Boggabri, Bellata and westward.
Language (s): English
COMMUNITY NEWSPAPER

The Newcastle Star 221933
Owner: Rural Press Limited
Editorial: 28-30 Bolton Street, Newcastle NSW 2300
Tel: 61 2 4979 5000
Email: thestarnews@fairfaxmedia.com.au **Web site:** http://www.newcastlestar.com.au
Circ: 114768
Editor: Kim-Cherie Davidson
Profile: Regional weekly newspaper with the latest community news from Newcastle and Lake Macquarie.
Language (s): English
COMMUNITY NEWSPAPER

North Central News 222120
Owner: Nadalyn Pty Ltd
Editorial: 16-18 Napier Street, St Arnaud VIC 3478
Tel: 61 3 5495 1055
Email: ncn@linet.net.au **Web site:** http://www.northcentralnews.com.au
Circ: 2128
Editor: Peter Marland
Profile: A weekly regional paper with news and issues relevant to the local community.
Language (s): English
COMMUNITY NEWSPAPER

The Northern Argus 222226
Owner: Rural Press Limited
Editorial: 181 Main North Road, Clare SA 5453
Tel: 61 8 8842 2651
Email: northernargus@ruralpress.com **Web site:** http://www.northernargus.com.au
Circ: 4694
Editor: Chelsea Ashmeade
Profile: A regional newspaper with news and issues relevant to the local community in the outer Adelaide and northern region of SA.
Language (s): English
COMMUNITY NEWSPAPER

The Northern Daily Leader 436222
Owner: Rural Press Limited
Editorial: 92 Brisbane Street, Tamworth NSW 2340
Tel: 61 2 6768 1200
Email: mail.ndl@fairfaxmedia.com.au **Web site:** http://www.northerndailyleader.com.au
Circ: 7345
News Editor: Ann Newling
Profile: Regional daily newspaper servicing the entire New England North West region.
Language (s): English
COMMUNITY NEWSPAPER

Northern Guardian 222189
Owner: West Australian Newspapers Holdings Ltd
Editorial: 46 Robinson Street, Cnr Egan Street, Carnarvon WA 6701 **Tel:** 61 8 9941 2222
Email: news@northernguardian.com.au **Web site:** https://au.news.yahoo.com/thewest/regional/gascoyne/
Circ: 4622
Manager: Rachel Johnson
Profile: Regional weekly publication with news and local issues for people living in the Carnarvon - North West area. Alternative email address = amrmail@margaret-river.com.au
Language (s): English
COMMUNITY NEWSPAPER

Numurkah Leader 222163
Owner: Jinki Sixteen Pty Ltd
Editorial: 88 Melville Street, Numurkah VIC 3636
Tel: 61 3 5862 1034
Email: editorial@leader.net.au **Web site:** http://www.vcpa.com.au/vic-members
Circ: 2285
Editor: Beverley Hutchins
Profile: Weekly regional newspaper covering general news and current affairs in the Numurkah, east Cobram, north Strathmerton, south Shepparton and west to Barmah region.
Language (s): English
COMMUNITY NEWSPAPER

The Oakey Champion 222073
Owner: OurNews Pty Ltd
Editorial: 2A Cherry Street, Oakey QLD 4401
Tel: 61 7 4691 1376
Email: editorial@oakeychampion.com.au **Web site:** http://www.themediaworkshop.com.au
Circ: 3000
Managing Director: Jaye Coley
Profile: A regional newspaper with news and issues relevant to local people and surrounds.
Language (s): English
COMMUNITY NEWSPAPER

The Oberon Review 221936
Owner: Rural Press Limited
Editorial: 83 Oberon Street, Oberon NSW 2787
Tel: 61 2 6336 1340
Web site: http://www.oberonreview.com.au
Circ: 1103
Editor: Maureen Lawson
Profile: Central-West NSW regional newspaper. Preferred delivery for media releases: Email
Language (s): English
COMMUNITY NEWSPAPER

On Our Selection News 578821
Owner: OurNews Pty Ltd
Editorial: 60 Clark Street, Clifton QLD 4361
Tel: 61 7 4697 3603
Email: editorial@cliftoncourier.com.au **Web site:** http://www.themediaworkshop.com.au/media-partners/mediapartner/35
Freq: Weekly; **Circ:** 1100
Profile: Weekly newspaper distributed throughout the cambooya district.
Language (s): English
Ad Rate: Full Page Mono 969.00
Currency: Australia Dollars
COMMUNITY NEWSPAPER

Parkes Champion-Post 221802
Owner: Rural Press Limited
Editorial: 7 Court Street, Parkes NSW 2870
Tel: 61 2 6862 2322
Email: editorial.championpost@ruralpress.com **Web site:** http://www.parkeschampionpost.com.au
Freq: 3 Times/Week; **Circ:** 3000
Profile: Regional newspaper covering general news and current affairs . Monday: weekly TV Guide, competitions, Captain Koala kids page and a special series on the Mayors of Parkes since 1883.Wednesday: special four-page Schools Wrap-up liftout covering the news from local schools, Jobs Guide and Super 15s tipping competition. Friday: Domain, NRL preview and tipping competition, jokes, recipes and plenty of local sport.Each edition also

provides comprehensive coverage of local news and sport and now boasts an expanded weather section.
Language (s): English
COMMUNITY NEWSPAPER

Phillip Island & San Remo Advertiser 222023
Owner: Phillip Island & San Remo Advertiser P/L
Editorial: Suite 2, 60 Chapel Street, Cowes VIC 3922
Tel: 61 3 5952 3201
Email: advertiser@pisra.com.au **Web site:** http://www.vcpa.com.au
Freq: Weekly; **Circ:** 2667
Editor: Natasha Crestani; **Advertising Manager:** Annabel Docherty; **Manager:** Anne Oswin
Profile: Regional newspaper covering news and issues relevant to residents and visitors of Phillip Island and San Remo.
Language (s): English
COMMUNITY NEWSPAPER

The Plains Producer 222230
Owner: Papers & Publications Pty Ltd
Editorial: 9 Howe Street, Balaklava SA 5461
Tel: 61 8 8862 1977
Email: editor@plainsproducer.com.au **Web site:** http://www.plainsproducer.com.au
Circ: 2700
Managing Director: Andrew Manuel; **Editor:** Terry Williams
Profile: Weekly newspaper, The Plains Producer, covering the Adelaide Plains and Lower North of South Australia.
Language (s): English
COMMUNITY NEWSPAPER

Port Macquarie Express 442384
Owner: Rural Press Limited
Editorial: 16-20 Milton Circuit, Port Macquarie NSW 2444 **Tel:** 61 2 6581 1622
Email: editor.portnews@ruralpress.com **Web site:** http://www.portnews.com.au
Circ: 23856
Profile: Year First Published: 1986 Regional weekly paper in the Mid-North Coast NSW region.Sister paper: The Port Macquarie News Formats Available: CD-ROM, Other Online.Target Audience: Hastings local government area. Photographic Information: B/W Photographs, Colour Photographs, Colour Transparencies.Preferred Delivery: Email Preferred Fomat: JPEG
Language (s): English
COMMUNITY NEWSPAPER

Port Macquarie News 496826
Owner: Rural Press Limited
Editorial: 16-20 Milton Circuit, Port Macquarie NSW 2444 **Tel:** 61 2 6588 6688
Email: portnews@fairfaxmedia.com.au **Web site:** http://www.portnews.com.au
Circ: 5257
Editor: Tracey Fairhurst
Profile: Regional newspaper in the Mid-North coast NSW region. Sister paper: Port Macquarie ExpressFormats available: CD-ROM Regular features: Youth, Schools, Finance, Business.
Language (s): English
COMMUNITY NEWSPAPER

Port Stephens Examiner 221804
Owner: Fairfax Media
Editorial: 15 William Street, Raymond Terrace NSW 2324 **Tel:** 61 2 4983 8400
Email: news@pse.fairfax.com.au **Web site:** http://www.portstephensexaminer.com.au
Circ: 28355
Editor: Anna Wolf
Profile: Regional weekly paper in the NSW Hunter region. Preferred delivery for media releases: Fax or Email
Language (s): English
COMMUNITY NEWSPAPER

Pyrenees Advocate 222013
Owner: Pyrenees Newspapers
Editorial: 32 Willoby Street, Beaufort VIC 3373
Tel: 61 3 5349 2787
Email: mail@theadvocate.net.au **Web site:** http://theadvocate.net.au
Circ: 1330
Profile: Regional weekly newspaper.
Language (s): English
COMMUNITY NEWSPAPER

The Rural 221706
Owner: Wagga Daily Advertiser Pty Ltd
Editorial: 48 Trail Street, Wagga Wagga NSW 2650
Tel: 61 2 6938 3410
Email: online@dailyadvertiser.com.au **Web site:** http://www.therural.com.au
Circ: 44964
Manager: Thomas Power
Profile: The Rural is one of the largest circulating rural newspapers in Southern NSW. The paper plays a pivotal role in supplying agricultural and farming news to business, industry and farming communities in this part of the State. The Rural offers advertisers a vehicle to target a range of potential customers in the richest and most heavily populated agricultural and grazing areas of the State. The Rural provides agricultural industry news together with national and international news, lifestyle, weather, sport, automotive and property news.
Language (s): English
COMMUNITY NEWSPAPER

Scone Advocate 221817
Owner: Rural Press Limited
Editorial: 152 Kelly Street, Scone NSW 2337
Tel: 61 2 6545 1155
Email: editor.sconeadvocate@ruralpress.com **Web site:** http://www.sconeadvocate.com.au
Circ: 1887
Advertising Manager: Nicole Ward-Pratley
Profile: Regional weekly paper in the Hunter region of NSW. Preferred delivery for media releases: Email
Language (s): English
COMMUNITY NEWSPAPER

The Shepparton Adviser 222119
Owner: Simtru Pty Ltd
Editorial: Newspaper House, 95-97 Welsford Street, Shepparton VIC 3630 **Tel:** 61 3 5822 1522
Email: editorial@sheppartonadviser.com.au **Web site:** http://www.sheppadviser.com.au
Circ: 34739
General Manager: Will Adams; **Editor:** David Lee; **Advertising Manager:** Melanie Spencer
Profile: Weekly regional newspaper with news and issues for the local community. Also distributed in Mooroopna. The Shepparton Car Weekly has combined with the Adviser, they are now a single publication. The car weekly is in the adviser every tuesday.
Language (s): English
COMMUNITY NEWSPAPER

The Singleton Argus 221810
Owner: Fairfax Media Group
Editorial: 6 Campbell Street, Singleton NSW 2330
Tel: 61 2 6572 2611
Email: editor.singletonargus@ruralpress.com **Web site:** http://www.singletonargus.com.au
Circ: 3781
Profile: Regional weekly publication with news and local issues for people living in the Singleton area.
Language (s): English
COMMUNITY NEWSPAPER

South Coast Register 221931
Owner: Rural Press Limited
Editorial: 122 Kinghorne Street, Nowra NSW 2541
Tel: 61 2 4421 9123
Email: editor.scregister@ruralpress.com **Web site:** http://www.southcoastregister.com.au
Circ: 3444
Editor: John Hanscombe
Profile: Year First Published: 1886. Regional newspaper. Preferred delivery for media releases: Email. Target Audience: Residents from Gerringong in the North to Sussex Inlet in the South (South Coast NSW)Regular Features: Property Guide, Auto Guide, Entertainment
Language (s): English
COMMUNITY NEWSPAPER

South Gippsland Sentinel Times 222043
Owner: South-Eastern Newspapers Pty Ltd
Editorial: 8 Radovick Street, Korumburra VIC 3950
Tel: 61 3 5655 1422
Email: news@sgst.com.au **Web site:** http://www.sgst.com.au
Circ: 9800
Advertising Manager: Graham Brookes; **Editor:** Nathan Johnston
Profile: A weekly regional newspaper with news and current issues relevant to the residents of the local community. With coverage north to Warragul, south to Phillip Island, east to Yarram, west to Cranbourne.Formats available: CD-ROM, Disk Photographic information: Colour photos, black & white photosPreferred delivery: e-mail Preferred format: PDF
Language (s): English
COMMUNITY NEWSPAPER

South Western Times 222188
Owner: West Australian Newspapers Holdings Ltd
Editorial: 19 Proffit Street, Bunbury WA 6230
Tel: 61 8 9780 0800
Email: editor@swtimes.com.au **Web site:** https://au.news.yahoo.com/thewest/regional/south-west/
Circ: 12851
Profile: Weekly regional newspaper with news and issues relevant to the local community in south-west WA. Orders can be placed at Proffitt Street or the main Bunbury Herald Office. Newspaper article search also available. Whole back copies of newspapers are not available.PR Accepted in: English
Language (s): English
COMMUNITY NEWSPAPER

The Southern Cross (Junee) 225497
Owner: Rural Press Limited
Editorial: 28 - 34 Lisgar Street, Junee NSW 2650
Tel: 61 2 6924 3861
Email: juneesoutherncross@fairfaxmedia.com.au
Web site: http://www.juneesoutherncross.com.au
Circ: 836
Profile: Published Thursdays, circulates 1,100. The paper offers two sections, special features and business profile. This offers an opportunity for businesses, event organisers, charity groups and industry specific groups, to promote their products and services.
Language (s): English
COMMUNITY NEWSPAPER

The Southern Free Times 230979
Owner: The Victorian Country Press
Editorial: Shop 5, 70 Fitzroy Street, Warwick QLD 4370 **Tel:** 61 7 4661 9800
Email: newsdesk@freetimes.com.au **Web site:** http://freetimes.com.au
Freq: Weekly; **Circ:** 16000
Profile: The Southern Free Times is a newspaper covering grain, fruit, vegetables, dairy, grazing, food processing, transport & distribution and manufacturing.
Language (s): English
COMMUNITY NEWSPAPER

Sunbury Leader 221855
Owner: The Leader Community Newspaper Group
Editorial: 30 Station Street, Sunbury VIC 3429
Tel: 61 3 9744 9303
Email: sunbury@leadernewspapers.com.au **Web site:** http://www.sunburyleader.com.au
Circ: 14727
Language (s): English
Ad Rate: Full Page Mono 3584.00
Currency: Australia Dollars
COMMUNITY NEWSPAPER

Sunbury Star Weekly 221696
Editorial: Shop 3, 342 High Street, Melton
Tel: 61 3 9249 5381
Web site: http://www.macedonranges.starweekly.com.au/
Circ: 23987
Editor: Stephen Linnell
Profile: A weekly regional newspaper with news and issues relevant to residents. Linked with Macedon Ranges TelegraphRegular features: Health, Horse, Dine, Vet care, Home decorating.
Language (s): English
Ad Rate: Full Page Mono 2585.00
Currency: Australia Dollars
COMMUNITY NEWSPAPER

The Tablelander 221948
Owner: North Queensland Newspaper Company Limited
Editorial: 53 Mabel Street, Atherton QLD 4883
Tel: 61 7 4028 5100
Email: editorial@tablelandnewspapers.com.au **Web site:** http://www.newscorpaustralia.com/brand/tablelander
Circ: 16824
Editor: David Anthony
Profile: A regional newspaper with news and issues relevant to the local community.
Language (s): English
COMMUNITY NEWSPAPER

Tamworth Times 442385
Owner: Rural Press Limited
Editorial: 92 Brisbane Street, Tamworth NSW 2340
Tel: 61 2 6768 1245
Email: mail.ndl@ruralpress.com **Web site:** http://www.tamworth.yourguide.com.au
Circ: 16189
Profile: Regional paper in the Tamworth region and satellite townships, including a small part of the Parry Shire. Preferred delivery for media releases: Fax or Email
Language (s): English
COMMUNITY NEWSPAPER

Tennant & District Times 222195
Owner: Tennant & District Times
Editorial: Shop 1, 139 Paterson Street, Tennant Creek NT 0860 **Tel:** 61 8 8962 1040
Email: advertising@tdtimes.com.au **Web site:** http://www.tdtimes.com.au/#folio=1
Circ: 1500
Editor: Jasmin Afianos; **Advertising Manager:** Barry Nattrass
Profile: Regional newspaper.
Language (s): English
COMMUNITY NEWSPAPER

Terang Express 222018
Owner: Western District Newspapers Pty Ltd
Editorial: 126 Manifold Street, Camperdown VIC 3260 **Tel:** 61 3 5593 1888
Email: camperdownchronicle@wdnews.com.au **Web site:** http://www.terangexpress.com.au
Circ: 1100
Profile: A weekly regional newspapers with news and issues relevant to people living in Terang, north to Kolora, south to South Ecklin, east to Boorcan, west to Panmure.
Language (s): English
COMMUNITY NEWSPAPER

The Times (Victor Harbor) 222116
Owner: Fairfax Media
Editorial: 27a Ocean Street, Victor Harbor SA 5211
Tel: 61 8 8552 1488
Email: victortimes@fairfaxmedia.com.au **Web site:** http://www.victorharbortimes.com.au
Circ: 7450
Profile: Regional newspaper with news and issues relevant to people living in outer Adelaide regions. Preferred delivery for media releases: email
Language (s): English
COMMUNITY NEWSPAPER

The Townsville Sun 222213
Owner: The North Queensland Newspaper Company Limited
Editorial: 155 Hanran Street, Townsville QLD 4810
Tel: 61 7 4722 4467
Email: admin@townsvillesun.com.au **Web site:** http://www.townsvillesun.com.au
Circ: 55858
Profile: The Sun, a free weekly newspaper, features news and events affecting the communities of Townsville and Thuringowa, Queensland.
Language (s): English
Ad Rate: Full Page Colour 3840.00
Currency: Australia Dollars
COMMUNITY NEWSPAPER

The Transcontinental 222111
Owner: Rural Press Limited
Editorial: 6 Tassie Street, Port Augusta SA 5700
Tel: 61 8 8642 2688
Web site: http://www.transcontinental.com.au
Circ: 4800
Profile: Regional weekly newspaper in the Northern region of SA.
Language (s): English
COMMUNITY NEWSPAPER

Wagin Argus 221728
Owner: Rural Press Limited
Editorial: 46-48 Tudhoe Street, Wagin WA 6315
Tel: 61 8 9861 1200
Email: waginargus@ruralpress.com **Web site:** http://www.waginargus.com.au
Circ: 743
Profile: Regional weekly publication with news and local issues for people living in the Margaret River area.
Language (s): English
COMMUNITY NEWSPAPER

Walcha News 221822
Owner: Rural Press Limited
Editorial: 16N Derby Street, Walcha NSW 2354
Tel: 61 2 6777 2513
Email: walcha.news@ruralpress.com **Web site:** http://walcha.yourguide.com.au
Circ: 732
Editor: Stephanie van Eyk; **Advertising Manager:** Julie Yates
Profile: Local paper distributed Northern NSW.
Language (s): English
COMMUNITY NEWSPAPER

The Warialda Standard 221824
Owner: DG & PA Wilson
Editorial: 1/38 Hope Street, Warialda NSW 2402
Tel: 61 2 6729 1460
Email: editor@warialdastandard.com.au **Web site:** http://warialdastandard.squarespace.com
Circ: 900
Editor: Rachel Sherman
Profile: Regional paper in the northern NSW region.
Language (s): English
COMMUNITY NEWSPAPER

Warracknabeal Herald 222141
Owner: Warracknabeal Herald Pty Ltd
Editorial: 89 Scott Street, Warracknabeal VIC 3393
Tel: 61 3 5398 2033
Email: news@warrackherald.com.au **Web site:** http://www.warrackherald.com.au
Circ: 1964
Profile: A regional twice-weekly newspaper with news and issues relevant to people living in the area.
Language (s): English
COMMUNITY NEWSPAPER

Warrego Watchman 221969
Owner: Warrego Watchman Pty Ltd
Editorial: 38 John Street, Cunnamulla QLD 4490
Tel: 61 7 4655 1617
Email: editorial@warregowatchman.com.au **Web site:** http://www.warregowatchman.com.au
Circ: 2800
Advertising Manager: James Clark
Profile: A weekly regional newspaper with news and issues for people living in Cunnamulla and Charleville.
Language (s): English
COMMUNITY NEWSPAPER

The Warrnambool Standard 442368
Owner: Fairfax Media
Editorial: 575 Raglan Parade, Warrnambool VIC 3280
Tel: 61 3 5563 1800
Email: editor@thestandard.net.au **Web site:** http://www.standard.net.au
Circ: 12661
Profile: A regional daily paper with news, issues and sport relevant to the local community.
Language (s): English
COMMUNITY NEWSPAPER

Wauchope Gazette 221827
Owner: Fairfax Media
Editorial: 47 Hasting Street, Wauchope NSW 2446
Tel: 61 2 6585 2355
Email: wauchopegazette@fairfaxmedia.com.au **Web site:** http://www.wauchopegazette.com.au
Circ: 2100
Profile: Local newspaper delivering news, sport and events from across the Hastings since 1907.
Language (s): English
COMMUNITY NEWSPAPER

West Coast Sentinel 222100
Owner: Fairfax Media
Editorial: 43B Poynton Street, Ceduna SA 5690
Tel: 61 8 8625 2265

Email: westcoastsentinel@ruralpress.com **Web site:** http://www.westcoastsentinel.com.au
Circ: 3079
Profile: A regional weekly newspaper in the Eyre region of SA. Preferred delivery for media releases: Email.
Language (s): English
COMMUNITY NEWSPAPER

The West Wyalong Advocate 221830
Owner: West Australian Newspapers Holdings Ltd
Editorial: 140-142 Main Street, West Wyalong NSW 2671 **Tel:** 61 2 6972 2033
Email: wwadvoc@bigpond.net.au
Circ: 1402
Advertising Manager: Vicki Glennon; **Editor:** Heatherbelle Vearing
Profile: Regional paper in the central west region of NSW.
Language (s): English
Ad Rate: Full Page Colour 1166.00
Currency: Australia Dollars
COMMUNITY NEWSPAPER

The Western Herald Bourke 221769
Owner: Navoc
Editorial: 36 Mertin Street, Bourke NSW 2840
Tel: 61 2 6872 2035
Email: westernherald@auzzie.net **Web site:** http://www.themediaworkshop.com.au/bourke-western-herald
Circ: 1400
Advertising Manager: Michael Keenan
Profile: Distributed from Bourke, north to Queensland border, south to Nyngan, east to Brewarrina, west to Tibooburra.
Language (s): English
COMMUNITY NEWSPAPER

The Western Times (QLD) 221962
Owner: Western Times
Editorial: 62 Alfred Street, Charleville QLD 4470
Tel: 61 7 4654 1099
Email: editorial@westerntimes.com.au **Web site:** http://www.suratbasin.com.au
Circ: 1742
Advertising Manager: Tracy Saunders; **Advertising Manager:** Donna Wright
Profile: A weekly regional newspaper with news and issues for people living in Western Qld- Charleville, north to Blackall, south to Cunnamulla, east to Mitchell, west to Windorah.
Language (s): English
COMMUNITY NEWSPAPER

The Woolgoolga Advertiser 221730
Owner: Rupak Pty Ltd
Editorial: 53 Moonee Street, Coffs Harbour
Tel: 61 2 6654 2133
Email: editorial@woolgoolgaadvertiser.com.au **Web site:** http://apnarm.com.au/print/community/4684/
Freq: Weekly; **Circ:** 5732
Editor: Matt Deans
Profile: Weekly community newspaper dedicated to Woolgoolga and the Northern Beaches, The Woolgoolga with the coverage of local issues and interests.
Language (s): English
COMMUNITY NEWSPAPER

The Young Witness 618540
Owner: Rural Press Limited
Editorial: 61 Boorowa Street, Young NSW 2594
Tel: 61 2 6382 1477
Web site: http://www.youngwitness.com.au
Circ: 2700
Profile: The Young Witness is a bi-weekly print and daily digital news website in New South Wales, Australia.
Language (s): English
COMMUNITY NEWSPAPER

Austria

Time Difference: GMT +1
National Telephone Code: 43
Continent: Europe
Capital: Vienna

Newspapers

Der Standard 159927
Owner: STANDARD Verlagsgesellschaft m.b.H
Editorial: Vordere Zollamtsstrasse 13, Wien 1030
Tel: 43 1 531 70 0
Email: redaktion@derStandard.at **Web site:** http://derstandard.at/
Freq: Mon thru Fri; **Circ:** 28
Profile: Der Standard ist eine Österreichische Zeitung. Sie ist unabhängig von Institutionen und politischen Parteien. Relevante Themen des Standards sind Kultur, Gesellschaft, Wirtschaft und Politik. Der Standard is an Austrian newspaper. It is independent of institutions and political parties. Relevant topics of the standard culture, society, economy and politics.
Language (s): German
DAILY NEWSPAPER

Die Presse 159822
Owner: "Die Presse" Verlags-Gesellschaft m.b.H. & Co KG
Editorial: "Die Presse" Verlags-Gesellschaft m.b.H. & Co KG, Hainburger Strasse 33, Wien 1030
Tel: 43 1 51414 0
Email: chefredaktion@diepresse.com **Web site:** http://www.diepresse.com
Freq: Daily; **Circ:** 28
Profile: Die Presse ist eine österreichische Tageszeitung mit einer großen Auswahl an Themen. The Austrian daily newspaper Die Presse is a newspaper covering a wide range of news topics.
Language (s): German
DAILY NEWSPAPER

Heute 311193
Owner: AHVV Verlags GmbH
Editorial: AHVV Verlags GmbH, Heiligenstadter Lande 29/Top 6, Wien 1190 **Tel:** 43 50 950 12200
Email: redaktion@heute.at **Web site:** http://www.heute.at
Freq: Daily; **Circ:** 622990
Profile: Heute ist eine kostenlose Tageszeitung in Österreich, welche neben Nachrichten auch Beiträge zu Kultur, Lifestyle, Prominenten, Freizeit und Verbraucherthemen bietet. Heute is a free daily newspaper in Austria, which offers news and reports on culture, lifestyle, celebrities, entertainment, and consumer issues.
Language (s): German
DAILY NEWSPAPER

Kleine Zeitung Kärnten 159568
Owner: Kleine Zeitung GmbH & Co. KG
Editorial: Hasnerstrasse 2, Klagenfurt 9020
Tel: 43 463 5800 0
Email: sekretariat.ktn@kleinezeitung.at **Web site:** http://www.kleinezeitung.at
Freq: Daily; **Circ:** 28
Profile: Die Kleine Zeitung Kärnten ist eine regionale Tageszeitung mit Nachrichten aus Politik, Wirtschaft, Kultur, Sport und Gesellschaft in Kärnten und Umgebung. Die Kleine Zeitung Kärnten ist nur eine der Regionalausgaben der Kleinen Zeitung.The Kleine Zeitung Kärnten is a regional daily newspaper with news from politics, economy, culture, sport and society in Kärnten and the surrounding area. The Kleine Zeitung Kärnten is just one of the regional editions of the Kleine Zeitung.
Language (s): German
DAILY NEWSPAPER

Kleine Zeitung Steiermark 159567
Owner: Kleine Zeitung GmbH & Co. KG
Editorial: Schonaugasse 64, Graz 8010
Tel: 43 316 875 0
Email: redaktion@kleinezeitung.at **Web site:** http://www.kleinezeitung.at
Freq: Daily; **Circ:** 213145
Profile: Die Kleine Zeitung ist eine regionale Tageszeitung für die Steiermark mit Nachrichten aus Politik, Wirtschaft, Kultur, Sport, Reise, Technik und anderen Verbraucherthemen. The Kleine Zeitung is a regional daily newspaper for Styria with news from politics, business, culture, sports, travel, technology and other consumer topics.
Language (s): German
DAILY NEWSPAPER

Kronen Zeitung 318951
Owner: Krone Multimedia GmbH & Co KG
Editorial: Krone Multimedia GmbH & Co KG, Muthgasse 2, Wien 1190 **Tel:** 43 5 70602
Email: chefredaktion@kronenzeitung.at **Web site:** http://www.krone.at
Freq: Daily; **Circ:** 28
Profile: Kronen Zeitung ist eine österreichische Boulevardtageszeitung mit Nachrichten, Sportmeldungen und Boulevardtthemen. Zudem werden auch Verbraucherthemen, wie Freizeit und Gesundheit angesprochen. The newspaper Kronen Zeitung is an Austrian tabloid newspaper with news, sports and society topics. In addition it offers consumer topics, such as leisure and health.
Language (s): German
DAILY NEWSPAPER

KURIER 159587
Owner: Kurier Redaktionsges.m.b.H. & Co.KG
Editorial: Kurier Redaktionsges.m.b.H. & Co.KG, Leopold-Ungar-Platz 1, Wien 1190 **Tel:** 43 1 521 00 0
Email: chefredaktion@kurier.at **Web site:** http://www.kurier.at
Freq: Daily; **Circ:** 28
Profile: KURIER ist eine österreichische Tageszeitung, die über nationale und international Themen, Politik, Wirtschaft und aktuelle Nachrichten berichtet. KURIER is an Austrian daily newspaper which covers national and international news, politics, business and current affairs.
Language (s): German
DAILY NEWSPAPER

Oberösterreichische Nachrichten 159793
Owner: Wimmer Medien GmbH & Co. KG
Editorial: Promenade 23, Linz 4010
Tel: 43 732 7805 410
Email: redaktion@nachrichten.at **Web site:** http://www.nachrichten.at
Freq: Daily; **Circ:** 133324 ÖAK
Profile: Die Oberösterreichischen Nachrichten sind eine regionale Tageszeitung für Oberösterreich mit Nachrichten aus Politik, Wirtschaft, Sport, Kultur, Gesellschaft und Verbraucherthemen. The Oberösterreichische Nachrichten is a regional daily newspaper for Upper Austria with news from politics, economy, sports, culture, society, and consumer issues.
Language (s): German
DAILY NEWSPAPER

ÖSTERREICH 424753
Owner: Mediengruppe,Österreich" GmbH
Editorial: Mediengruppe,osterreich" GmbH, Friedrichstr. 10, Wien 1010 **Tel:** 43 1 58811 1997
Email: redaktion@oe24.at **Web site:** http://www.oe24.at
Freq: Daily; **Circ:** 28
Profile: Österreich ist eine überregionale österreichische Tageszeitung, die durch das Online Portal Oe24.at ergänzt wird. Neben nationalen Nachrichten, bietet die Zeitung auch Unterhaltung, Sport und Ratgeber-Themen wie Reise oder Gesundheit. Österreich is a nationwide Austrian daily newspaper, which is complemented by the online portal Oe24.at. In addition to national news, the newspaper also offers entertainment, sports and consumer topics such as travel or health.
Language (s): German
DAILY NEWSPAPER

Salzburger Nachrichten 159876
Owner: Salzburger Nachrichten Verlagsgesellschaft m.b.H. & Co KG
Editorial: Salzburger Nachrichten Verlagsgesellschaft m.b.H. & Co KG, Karolingerstrasse 40, Salzburg 5021
Tel: 43 662 8373 301
Email: redakt@salzburg.com **Web site:** http://www.salzburg.com
Freq: Daily; **Circ:** 28
Profile: Die Salzburger Nachrichten sind eine regionale Tageszeitung mit Nachrichten zu Politik, Wirtschaft, Kultur, Gesellschaft und Sport, sowie auch mit Ratgeberteil zu Themen wie Reise und Technik. The Salzburger Nachrichten is a regional daily newspaper with news about politics, economy, culture, society and sport, as well as with an advice section on topics such as travel and technology.
Language (s): German
DAILY NEWSPAPER

Tiroler Tageszeitung 159981
Owner: New Media Online GmbH
Editorial: New Media Online GmbH, Brunecker Strasse 3, Innsbruck 6020 **Tel:** 43 50403 1600
Email: redaktion@tt.com **Web site:** http://www.tt.com
Freq: Daily; **Circ:** 28
Profile: Die Tiroler Tageszeitung ist eine regionale Tageszeitung für das Tirol mit 8 Lokalausgaben. Lokale, regionale, nationale und internationale Nachrichten aus Politik, Wirtschaft, gesellschaft und Sport. The Tiroler Daily Newspaper is a regional newspaper for Tirol with 8 local editions covering local, regional, national and international news on politics, business, society and sports.
Language (s): German
DAILY NEWSPAPER

Vorarlberger Nachrichten 160025
Owner: Russmedia Verlag GmbH
Editorial: Gutenbergstr. 1, Schwarzach 6858
Tel: 43 5572 501 500
Email: redaktion@vorarlbergernachrichten.at **Web site:** http://www.vorarlbergernachrichten.at/
Freq: Daily; **Circ:** 28
Profile: Die Vorarlberger Nachrichten sind eine Lokalzeitung für Arlberg und Umgebung. Sie bietet lokale und regionale Berichterstattung, sowie auch Nachrichten aus Politik, Gesellschaft, Wirtschaft, Kultur und Sport. The Vorarlberger Nachrichten is a local newspaper for Arlberg and the surrounding area. It provides local and regional coverage, as well as news from politics, society, economy, culture and sports.
Language (s): German
DAILY NEWSPAPER

WirtschaftsBlatt 173414
Owner: WirtschaftsBlatt Verlag AG
Editorial: Hainburger Str. 33, Wien 1030
Tel: 43 1 60 11 70
Email: online@wirtschaftsblatt.at **Web site:** http://www.wirtschaftsblatt.at
Freq: Mon thru Fri; **Circ:** 28
Profile: Wirtschaftsblatt ist eine überregionale Wirtschaftszeitung in Österreich mit Nachrichten zu Politik und Wirtschaft. Es werden aber auch Themen aus Kultur, Technik u.a. angesprochen. Wirtschaftsblatt is a business newspaper in Austria with news about politics and business. However, topics such as culture, technology and others are also included.
Language (s): German
Ad Rate: Full Page Mono 338.00
Currency: Euro
DAILY NEWSPAPER

Azerbaijan

Time Difference: GMT +4
National Telephone Code: 994
Continent: Asia
Capital: Baku

Newspapers

525-ci qezet 522305
Editorial: S.Mustafayev kuc.27/121, Baku AZ1033
Tel: 994 12 510 28 83
Email: qezet525@mail.ru **Web site:** http://www.525.az
Freq: Daily; **Circ:** 5000 Publisher's Statement
Profile: Newspaper covering national and international news, current affairs, social events, economics and sport.
Language (s): Azeri
DAILY NEWSPAPER

Adalat (Justice) 217969
Owner: Adalat
Editorial: Block 529, Matbuat Avenue, Baku 370146
Tel: 994 12 43 80 550
Email: adalatgezeti@rambler.ru **Web site:** http://www.adalet-az.com
Freq: Daily; **Circ:** 4000 Publisher's Statement
President: Aqil Abbas; **Editor:** Etibar Babayev;
Editor-in-Chief: Irada Tuncay
Profile: Tabloid newspaper covering legal issues and politics.
Language (s): Azeri
DAILY NEWSPAPER

Ayna 217968
Owner: CBS Publishing House
Editorial: ul. Sharif-zadeh 1, Baku Az 1138
Tel: 994 12 49 75 031
Email: gazeta@zerkalo.az **Web site:** http://www.zerkalo.az
Circ: 3000 Publisher's Statement
Editor: Elchin Shikhlintskiy
Profile: Tabloid newspaper covering national and international news, economics, social events and sport.
Language (s): Azeri
DAILY NEWSPAPER

Azat Artsakh 519805
Editorial: Tumanyan 62, Stepanakert
Email: atert@rambler.ru **Web site:** http://www.artsakhtert.com
Freq: Daily; **Circ:** 1000 Publisher's Statement
Editor-in-Chief: Murad Petrossian
Profile: Daily newspaper from Nagorno Karabakh region.
Language (s): Armenian
Ad Rate: Full Page Mono 80000.00
Currency: Armenia Drams
DAILY NEWSPAPER

Azerbaijan 218109
Owner: Azerbaijan Publishing House
Editorial: Matbuat prospekt 529, 4 floor, Baku 3
Tel: 994 12 43 94 920
Email: contact@azerbaijan-news.az **Web site:** http://www.azerbaijan-news.az
Freq: Daily; **Circ:** 12000 Publisher's Statement
Profile: Official government newspaper featuring social and political reviews.
Language (s): Azeri
Ad Rate: Full Page Mono 2000.00
Ad Rate: Full Page Colour 3000.00
Currency: Turkmenistan Manats
DAILY NEWSPAPER

Bakinskiy Rabochiy 218110
Owner: Presidenskiy Aparat
Editorial: Matbuat pr. 529-cu, Baku 370146
Tel: 994 12 43 86 198
Web site: http://www.br.az
Freq: Daily; **Circ:** 3520 Publisher's Statement
Editor-in-Chief: Agabek Askerov
Profile: Tabloid newspaper in Russian language providing political, economical and cultural information on all aspects of life in Azerbaijan.
Language (s): Russian
DAILY NEWSPAPER

Baku Sun 223099
Owner: Boston and Baku Television Communications
Editorial: 2 Inshaatchylar Ave, Baku Az 1073
Tel: 994 12 497 55 31
Email: editor@bakusun.baku.az **Web site:** http://www.bakusun.az
Circ: 4000 Publisher's Statement
Editor: Farid Iskenderov
Profile: English language weekly newspaper which presents latest energy, business and political news of Azerbaijan.
Language (s): English
Ad Rate: Full Page Mono 1200.00
Currency: Turkmenistan Manats
DAILY NEWSPAPER

Azerbaijan

Echo 445602
Owner: AYNA
Editorial: 1 Sharifzadeh str., Baku
Tel: 994 12 447 41 54
Email: gazeta@echo-az.com **Web site:** http://ru.echo.az
Freq: Daily; **Circ:** 6000 Publisher's Statement
Editor In Chief: Rauf Talyshinsky
Profile: Independent social and political newspaper Echo was founded in January 2001. Published five times a week in Russian language, our days on 8 pages, on Saturdays on 20 pages. Publishes current political news and articles on economics, cultural life and recent sports events.
Language (s): Russian
Ad Rate: Full Page Mono 1920.00
Ad Rate: Full Page Colour 2640.00
Currency: Turkmenistan Manats
DAILY NEWSPAPER

Yeni Musavat 564984
Editorial: R.Rüstmov kücsi 2528-ci mhll, 44d, Baku 1000 **Tel:** 994 12 520-01-23
Email: musavat777@gmail.com **Web site:** http://www.musavat.com
Freq: Daily
Profile: Daily newspaper covering general, financial and business news.
Language (s): Azeri
DAILY NEWSPAPER

News Service/Syndicate

Azeri-Press Agency 595615
Editorial: Azerbaijan avenue 27, Baku
Tel: 994 12 5963358
Email: apa@azeurotel.com **Web site:** http://en.apa.az
Editor In Chief: Vugar Huseynov; **Editor:** Shahin Jafarli; **Director General:** Vusala Mahirgizi
Profile: Offers daily news, video footage, bank rankings, weekly and monthly analyses, forecasts and special photo bank in Azerbaijani, Russian, English, French and Arabic.
Language (s): Azeri
NEWS SERVICE/SYNDICATE

AZER-PRESS 564921
Editorial: Baki Iceri Seher, 1-ci Qesr dongesi, 28, Baku Az 1005 **Tel:** 994 12 447 42 88
Email: azerpressmedia@gmail.com **Web site:** http://www.azpress.az
Director/Editor: Sevinc Rzaq?z?
Language (s): Azeri
NEWS SERVICE/SYNDICATE

Bahamas

Time Difference: GMT -5
National Telephone Code: 1242
Continent: The Americas
Capital: Nassau (New Province)

Newspapers

The Bahama Journal 224444
Owner: Wendell Jones Communications
Tel: 1 242 325-3082
Email: jcnnews@gmail.com **Web site:** http://www.jonesbahamas.com
Circ: 7000 Not Audited
Publisher: Wendall Jones; **Editor:** Macushla Pinder
Profile: Daily newspaper focusing on national and international news, business, religion and sports for the residents of The Bahamas.
Language (s): English
DAILY NEWSPAPER

The Freeport News 324938
Owner: Nassau Guardian Ltd.
Tel: 1 242 352-8321
Email: tfneditor@nasguard.com **Web site:** http://freeport.nassauguardian.net
Freq: Daily; **Circ:** 6500 Not Audited
Profile: Freeport News is a daily newspaper focusing on national and local news, business, religion, lifestyle and sports for the residents of Freeport, Grand Bahama.
Language (s): English
Ad Rate: Full Page Mono 6.50
Currency: United States Dollars
DAILY NEWSPAPER

Friday Mirror 156826
Owner: TNT News Centre Ltd
Editorial: 35 Rapsey St, Curepe, Barataria
Tel: 1 868 645-3391
Email: ttnews@tstt.net.tt **Web site:** http://www.tntmirror.com/friday/fridayindex.html
Freq: Weekly; **Circ:** 40000 Not Audited
Profile: Friday Mirror is a daily newspaper covering national and international news, current affairs, business and sports.
Language (s): English
Ad Rate: Full Page Mono 3.64
Ad Rate: Full Page Colour 278.77
Currency: United States Dollars
DAILY NEWSPAPER

The Nassau Guardian 156792
Owner: Nassau Guardian Ltd.
Editorial: No 4 Carter Street, Oakes Field, Nassau
Tel: 1 242 302-2300
Email: editor@nasguard.com **Web site:** http://www.thenassauguardian.com
Freq: Daily; **Circ:** 12000 Not Audited
Profile: The Nassau Guardian is a daily newspaper focusing on national and international news, business, culture, society and sports.
Language (s): English
Ad Rate: Full Page Mono 7.50
Currency: United States Dollars
DAILY NEWSPAPER

Newsday 156820
Owner: Daily News Limited
Editorial: 23A Chacon Street, Port Of Spain
Tel: 1 868 623-4929
Email: newsday@newsday.co.tt **Web site:** http://www.newsday.co.tt
Freq: Daily; **Circ:** 67000 Not Audited
News Editor: Stephon Nicholas
Profile: Newsday is a daily newspaper featuring national and international news, current affairs, business, lifestyle and sports.
Language (s): English
Ad Rate: Full Page Mono 9.86
Currency: United States Dollars
DAILY NEWSPAPER

The Punch 156796
Owner: Punch Publications Ltd
Editorial: Warboys House, Farrington Road, Oakes Field, Nassau **Tel:** 1 242 322-7112-
Email: thepunch@coralwave.com **Web site:** http://nassaupunch.com
Freq: Mon; **Circ:** 40000 Not Audited
Publisher & Editor: Ivan Johnson
Profile: The Punch is a twice-weekly newspaper serving residents of Nassau, Bahamas. Focuses on national and international news, business, culture and sports.
Language (s): English
Ad Rate: Full Page Mono 11.50
Ad Rate: Full Page Colour 100.00
Currency: United States Dollars
DAILY NEWSPAPER

The Tribune (Bahamas) 156797
Owner: The Tribune (Bahamas)
Editorial: PO Box N-3207, Nassau **Tel:** 1 242 322-1986
Email: tips@tribunemedia.net
Freq: Daily; **Circ:** 15000 Not Audited
Publisher: Eileen Dupuch Carron; **News Editor:** Taneka Thompson
Profile: Local newspaper focusing on national and international news, business, culture, social life and sport.
Language (s): English
Ad Rate: Full Page Mono 7.50
Ad Rate: Full Page Colour 1340.10
Currency: United States Dollars
DAILY NEWSPAPER

Trinidad Express 156724
Owner: Trinidad Express Newspapers Ltd
Editorial: 35 Independence Square, Port Of Spain
Tel: 1 868 623-1711
Email: express@trinidadexpress.com **Web site:** http://www.trinidadexpress.com
Freq: Daily; **Circ:** 90000 Not Audited
Editor in Chief: Omatie Lyder
Profile: Trinidad Express is a daily newspaper covering national and international news, politics, sports and current affairs. The Sunday edition is called Sunday Express.
Language (s): English
Ad Rate: Full Page Mono 30.00
Ad Rate: Full Page Colour 1000.00
Currency: United States Dollars
DAILY NEWSPAPER

The Trinidad Guardian 156830
Owner: Trinidad Publishing Co Ltd
Editorial: 22-24 St. Vincent Street, Port Of Spain
Tel: 1 868 623-8871
Email: letters@guardian.co.tt **Web site:** http://www.guardian.co.tt
Freq: Daily; **Circ:** 45000 Not Audited
News Editor: Robert Alonzo; **News Editor:** Debra Wanser
Profile: The Trinidad Guardian is a daily newspaper containing national and international news, business, current affairs and sports. The Saturday and Sunday editions of the paper are called the Sunday Guardian.
Language (s): English
Ad Rate: Full Page Mono 5.30
Ad Rate: Full Page Colour 560.00
Currency: United States Dollars
DAILY NEWSPAPER

Bahrain

Time Difference: GMT +3
National Telephone Code: 973
Continent: Asia
Capital: Manama

Newspapers

4PM News 837161
Owner: Strategic Publicity and Advertising Company WLL
Editorial: PO Box 75538, Office 31 & 32, Ebrahim Plaza, Manama **Tel:** 973 17 579897
Email: 4pmnews@gmail.com **Web site:** http://www.4pmnews.com
Freq: Daily; **Circ:** 10000
Editor: Pradeep Puravankara; **Director:** Latha Unnikrishnan
Profile: 4PM News is a tabloid-sized evening newspaper covering news, business and sport. It launched in June 2012, and is aimed at Indian expatriates in Bahrain.
Language (s): Malayalam
Ad Rate: Full Page Mono 576.00
Ad Rate: Full Page Colour 1152.00
Currency: Bahrain Dinars
DAILY NEWSPAPER

Akhbar Al Khaleej 157019
Owner: Dar Akhbar Al Khaleej Printing & Publishing House WLL
Editorial: PO Box 5300, Building 74, Block 941, Isa Town **Tel:** 973 17 628438
Email: local@aaknews.net **Web site:** http://www.akhbar-alkhaleej.com
Freq: Daily; **Circ:** 36000 Rate Card
News Editor: Abdallah Al Ayoobi; **Head of Foreign News:** Sayed Zahra
Profile: Akhbar Al Khaleej is a daily Arabic newspaper covering national and international news, current affairs, politics, business, culture and sports. It was first published in 1976.
Language (s): Arabic
Ad Rate: Full Page Mono 1777.00
Ad Rate: Full Page Colour 2271.00
Currency: Bahrain Dinars
DAILY NEWSPAPER

Al Ayam 159055
Owner: Al Ayam Publishing Group
Editorial: PO Box 3232, Al Janabia, Manama
Tel: 973 17 617777
Email: localnews@alayam.com **Web site:** http://www.alayam.com
Freq: Daily; **Circ:** 30000 Publisher's Statement
Editor In Chief: Eisa Al Shaiji; **Media Manager:** Elie Maalouf; **Picture Editor:** Abed-Ali Qurban
Profile: Al Ayam (The Days) is a daily newspaper covering national and international news, current affairs, politics, business, culture and sports. The newspaper launched in 1989, and includes a family magazine supplement, Al Osrah, on Fridays.
Language (s): Arabic
DAILY NEWSPAPER

Al Bilad 554828
Owner: Dar Al Bilad for Journalism, Publishing and Distribution BSC
Editorial: PO Box 385, 4th Floor, Mazaya Plaza, Isa Town **Tel:** 973 17 111444
Email: local@albiladpress.com **Web site:** http://www.albiladpress.com
Freq: Daily; **Circ:** 25000 Rate Card
News Editor: Omar Al Jaber; **Editor In Chief:** Moanes Almardi
Profile: Al Bilad is a broadsheet-sized newspaper covering local and international news, politics, business and sport. The daily newspaper launched in October 2008.
Language (s): Arabic
DAILY NEWSPAPER

Daily Tribune 156642
Owner: Strategic Publicity and Advertising Company WLL
Editorial: PO Box 78564, Flat 31, Ebrahim Plaza, Manama **Tel:** 973 17 579911
Email: news@dt.bh **Web site:** http://www.newsofbahrain.com
Freq: Daily; **Circ:** 10000 Rate Card
Director: Latha Unnikrishnan
Profile: Daily Tribune is a tabloid-sized newspaper focusing on national and international news, current affairs, politics, business and sports. The newspaper originally launched as the broadsheet Bahrain Tribune in 1997, but changed its name and size in September 2010.
Language (s): English
Ad Rate: Full Page Mono 1152.00
Ad Rate: Full Page Colour 2304.00
Currency: Bahrain Dinars
DAILY NEWSPAPER

Gulf Daily News 156809
Owner: Al Hilal Publishing and Marketing Group
Editorial: PO Box 5300, Building 74, Block 941, Isa Town **Tel:** 973 17 620222
Email: gdnnews@gdn.com.bh **Web site:** http://www.gdnonline.com
Freq: Daily; **Circ:** 10200 Rate Card
News Editor: Noor Toorani; **Editor-in-Chief:** George Williams
Profile: Gulf Daily News is a tabloid-sized newspaper focusing on national and international news, business, politics, culture and sport. The newspaper launched in 1978, and is aimed at English-speaking locals and expatriates in Bahrain.
Language (s): English
Ad Rate: Full Page Mono 1620.00
Ad Rate: Full Page Colour 2970.00
Currency: Bahrain Dinars
DAILY NEWSPAPER

Gulf Madhyamam - Bahrain edition 683728
Owner: Gulf Madhyamam FZ LLC
Editorial: PO Box 21323, Office 17, Jamiyya Building, Muharraq **Tel:** 973 17 342825
Email: bahrain@gulfmadhyamam.net **Web site:** http://www.gulfmadhyamam.net
Freq: Daily; **Circ:** 22280 Rate Card
Editor-in-Chief: Hamzah Abbas; **General Manager:** Abdul Jalil Abdulla; **Bureau Chief:** A. V. Sherin
Profile: Gulf Madhyamam is an international Indian newspaper covering national and international news, current affairs, politics, business and sport. The newspaper is aimed at Malayalam speakers in the Gulf and publishes separate editions for the UAE, Saudi Arabia (Riyadh, Jeddah, Damam & Abha), Qatar, Oman, Bahrain and Kuwait. The newspaper was first published in 1999.
Language (s): Malayalam
DAILY NEWSPAPER

Al Watan 383377
Owner: Al Watan For Publishing & Distribution Co. (B.S.C.)
Editorial: PO Box 38801, Building No 681, Complex 335, Manama **Tel:** 973 17 496666
Email: alwatan@alwatannews.net **Web site:** http://www.alwatannews.net
Freq: Daily; **Circ:** 27500 Publisher's Statement
Editor in Chief: Yousef Al Binkhalil
Profile: Al Watan is a daily Arabic newspaper focusing on local and international news, business, sport and politics. It was first published in 2005.
Language (s): Arabic
Ad Rate: Full Page Mono 1750.00
Ad Rate: Full Page Colour 2288.00
Currency: Bahrain Dinars
DAILY NEWSPAPER

News Service/Syndicate

Bahrain News Agency 353380
Owner: Bahrain News Agency
Editorial: PO Box 5421, Ministry of Information, Manama **Tel:** 973 17 687007
Email: bna.arabicnews@gmail.com **Web site:** http://www.bna.bh
Editor: Khaled Al Zayani; **Editor In Chief:** Ali El Thawadi; **Editor:** Khaled Ismael; **Director:** Mohanad Sulieman
Profile: Bahrain News Agency is the official news agency of Bahrain. It was founded in 1978 and covers government and royal news, as well as matters of national importance.
Language (s): Arabic
NEWS SERVICE/SYNDICATE

Bangladesh

Time Difference: GMT +6
National Telephone Code: 880
Continent: Asia
Capital: Dhaka

Newspapers

Daily Bhorer Kagoj 460454
Editorial: Karnaphuli Media Point, 2nd Floor, 70 Shahid Sangbadik Selina Parveen, Dhaka 1000
Tel: 880 29360285
Email: bkagoj@yahoo.com **Web site:** http://www.bhorerkagoj.net
Freq: Daily; **Circ:** 82001 Not Audited
Editor: Shaymal Dutta
Profile: Covers of general news.
Language (s): Bengali
DAILY NEWSPAPER

The Daily Inqilab 460427
Editorial: 2/1 R.K. Mission Road, Dhaka 1203
Tel: 880 27122771
Email: inqilab08@dhaka.net **Web site:** http://www.dailyinqilab.com
Freq: Daily; **Circ:** 300003 Not Audited
Editor: A. Bahauddin
Profile: Covers news and general interests.
Language (s): Bengali
DAILY NEWSPAPER

The Daily Ittefaq 460422
Editorial: 40 Kawran Buzar, Dhaka 1215
Tel: 880 2 7122660

Email: dailyittefaq@yahoo.com **Web site:** http://www.ittefaq.com.bd
Freq: Daily; **Circ:** 300003 Not Audited
Editor: Anwar Hossain
Profile: Covers news and general interests.
Language (s): Bengali
DAILY NEWSPAPER

Daily Jaijaidin 460423
Editorial: 446/E Love Road, Tejgaon, Dhaka 1208
Tel: 880 28832222 128
Web site: http://www.jjdin.com
Freq: Weekly; **Circ:** 80003 Not Audited
Editor: Kazi Rukanuddin Ahmed
Profile: A daily newspaper covering local, national, regional and international news.
Language (s): Bengali
DAILY NEWSPAPER

The Daily Jugantor 860745
Editorial: Ka-244, Kuril, Progati, Soroni, Dhaka 1229
Tel: 88 2 84192115
Email: jugantor.newspaper@gmail.com **Web site:** http://www.jugantor.com
Freq: Daily
Publisher: Salma Islam
Profile: Serves as Bangladesh's largest newspaper. Covers national news with a mission of professional journalism, serving as a change catalyst and progressing with innovation and uniqueness.
Language (s): Bangla
DAILY NEWSPAPER

Daily Manab Zamin 460455
Editorial: 21 Kazi Nazrul Islam Avenue, Dhaka 1000
Tel: 880 29661122
Email: manabzamin@yahoo.com **Web site:** http://www.manabzamin.com
Freq: Daily; **Circ:** 50003 Not Audited
Publisher: Mahbuba Chowdhury; **Editor in Chief:** Motiur Chowdhury
Profile: Covers general news.
Language (s): Bangla
DAILY NEWSPAPER

The Daily Nirapekkha 459210
Editorial: 2 R.K Mission Road, Motaled Mansion, Dhaka 1203 **Tel:** 880 29569751
Email: dniro@dhaka.net
Freq: Daily; **Circ:** 50003 Not Audited
Editor: Newaz Shofiqul Rahman
Profile: Covers news and general interests.
Language (s): Bengali
DAILY NEWSPAPER

Daily Prothom Alo 460464
Editorial: 100 Kazi Nazrul Islam Avenue, Kawran Bazar, Dhaka 1215 **Tel:** 880 28110081
Email: info@prothom-alo.com **Web site:** http://www.prothom-alo.com
Freq: Daily; **Circ:** 200003 Not Audited
Editor: Matiur Rahaman
Profile: Provides Bangladesh and International news as well as local and regional perspectives.
Language (s): Bengali
DAILY NEWSPAPER

The Daily Rupali 459211
Editorial: 28/A-3 Toyenbi Circular Road, Motijheel C/A, Dhaka 1000 **Tel:** 880 2 9560080
Freq: Daily; **Circ:** 50003 Not Audited
Editor: S.Q. Quaderi
Profile: An English daily national newspaper.
Language (s): English
DAILY NEWSPAPER

The Daily Star 460429
Editorial: 19, Karwan Bazar, 1st, 2nd & 3rd Floor, Dhaka 1215 **Tel:** 880 28124955
Email: editor@thedailystar.net **Web site:** http://www.thedailystar.net
Freq: Daily; **Circ:** 80000 Not Audited
News Editor: Reaz Ahmad; **Editor:** Mahfuz Anam
Profile: Covers national news and general interest.
Language (s): English
DAILY NEWSPAPER

The Financial Express 460435
Editorial: 45 Topkhana Road, Tropicana Tower, 4th Floor, Dhaka 1000 **Tel:** 880 29553550
Email: tfe@bangla.net **Web site:** http://www.thefinancialexpress-bd.com
Freq: Daily; **Circ:** 13001 Not Audited
Editor: Moazzem Hossain
Profile: Covering financial and business news.
Language (s): English
DAILY NEWSPAPER

The Independent 460432
Editorial: BEL Tower (5th & 6th Floor), 19 Dhanmondi Road No.1, Dhaka 1205 **Tel:** 880 2 9672091
Email: editor@bol-online.com **Web site:** http://www.theindependentbd.com
Freq: Daily; **Circ:** 14503 Not Audited
Editor: Shamsur Rahman
Profile: Covers news and general interests.
Language (s): English
DAILY NEWSPAPER

Janakantha 460428
Editorial: Janakantha Bhaban, 24/A New Eskaton Road, Dhaka 1000 **Tel:** 880 29347780
Email: janakantha@bttb.net.bd **Web site:** https://www.dailyjanakantha.com
Freq: Daily; **Circ:** 160003 Not Audited
Manager: Nazrul Islam; **Editor:** Atiqullah Masud
Profile: Covers news and general interests.
Language (s): Bengali
DAILY NEWSPAPER

New Age 158177
Editorial: Holiday Building, 30 Tejgaon Industrial Area, Dhaka 1208 **Tel:** 880 2 8153034
Email: newagebd@global-bd.net **Web site:** http://newagebd.net
Freq: Daily; **Circ:** 35001 Not Audited
Editor: Nurul Kabir; **Publisher:** Shahidullah Khan
Profile: Covering news and general interests.
Language (s): English
DAILY NEWSPAPER

The New Nation 156864
Editorial: 1 Ramkrishna Mission Road, Dhaka 1203
Tel: 880 2 71 22 660
Email: n_editor@bangla.net
Freq: Daily; **Circ:** 45003 Not Audited
Publisher: Mainul Hosein; **Editor:** A.M. Mufazzal
Profile: Covers news and general interests.
Language (s): English
DAILY NEWSPAPER

Sangram 460456
Editorial: 423 Elephant Road, Bara Magh Bazar, Dhaka 1217 **Tel:** 880 2 8318128
Email: dsangram@gmail.com **Web site:** http://www.dailysangram.com
Freq: Daily; **Circ:** 20003 Not Audited
Editor: Abul Asad
Profile: A daily general newspaper.
Language (s): Bengali
DAILY NEWSPAPER

Weekly 2000 460437
Editorial: 96/97 New Eskaton Road, Dhaka 1000
Tel: 880 29350953
Email: info@shaptahik2000.com **Web site:** http://www.shaptahik2000.com
Freq: Weekly; **Circ:** 35003 Not Audited
Profile: Covers news and general interests.
Language (s): Bengali
DAILY NEWSPAPER

Weekly Holiday 460421
Editorial: Holiday Building, 30 Tejgaon Industrial Area, Dhaka 1208 **Tel:** 880 29110886
Email: holiday@global-bd.net **Web site:** http://www.weeklyholiday.net
Freq: Weekly; **Circ:** 12003 Not Audited
Editor: Syed Kamaluddin
Profile: Covers general news.
Language (s): English
DAILY NEWSPAPER

Young Independent 459489
Editorial: BEL Tower (5th & 6th Floor), 19 Dhanmondi, Road No.1, Dhaka 1205
Tel: 880 2 9672091
Email: editor@bol-online.com **Web site:** http://www.theindependent-bd.com
Freq: Weekly; **Circ:** 25003 Not Audited
Editor: Shamsur Rahman
Profile: Covers lifestyle and general interests.
Language (s): English
DAILY NEWSPAPER

News Service/Syndicate

United News of Bangladesh (UNB) 467632
Editorial: Cosmos Center, 69/1 News Circular Road, Malibagh, Dhaka 1217 **Tel:** 880 29345541
Email: unb_news@yahoo.com **Web site:** http://www.unbnews.org
Freq: Daily
Editor in Chief: Syed Rahman
Profile: Covers news.
Language (s): Bangla
NEWS SERVICE/SYNDICATE

Barbados

Time Difference: GMT -4
National Telephone Code: 1246
Continent: The Americas
Capital: Bridgetown

Newspapers

Barbados Advocate 156793
Owner: Advocate Publishers 2000 Inc
Editorial: Saint Michael **Tel:** 1 246 467-2000
Email: news@barbadosadvocate.com **Web site:** http://www.barbadosadvocate.com
Freq: Daily; **Circ:** 15000 Not Audited
News Editor: Dorian Bryan; **General Manager:** Sandra Clarke
Profile: Daily newspaper that provides the island with local, national and international news, sports, business and politics.
Language (s): English
Ad Rate: Full Page Mono 19.32
Ad Rate: Full Page Colour 250.00
Currency: United States Dollars
DAILY NEWSPAPER

Daily Nation (Barbados) 161013
Owner: Nation Publishing Co. Limited (The)
Tel: 01 246 430-5400
Email: editorial@nationnews.com **Web site:** http://www.nationnews.com
Freq: Daily; **Circ:** 34000 Not Audited
Editor: Barry Alleyne; **News Editor:** Eric Smith
Profile: Newspaper covering breaking news alerts and the most discussed stories in Barbados, as well as national and international news, sports, business and arts & entertainment. Advertising and subscription rates are quoted in Barbados dollars.
Language (s): English
Ad Rate: Full Page Mono 0.78
Ad Rate: Full Page Colour 330.00
Currency: United States Dollars
DAILY NEWSPAPER

Belarus

Time Difference: GMT +3
National Telephone Code: 375
Continent: Europe
Capital: Minsk

Newspapers

BelGazeta 230024
Owner: BelGazeta
Editorial: ul. Kalvariskaya 17 A, office 616A, Minsk 220004 **Tel:** 375 17 200 40 50
Email: bg@bg.org.by **Web site:** http://www.belgazeta.by
Circ: 21300 Publisher's Statement
Advertising Manager: Elena Dubovnik; **Director:** Igor Vysotski
Profile: National newspaper focusing on news in economics, politics and society in Belarus and in the world.
Language (s): Russian
DAILY NEWSPAPER

Belorusy i Rynok 168904
Owner: Mediarynok ZAO
Editorial: pr. Partizanski 6a, office 605, Minsk 220033
Tel: 375 17 246-90-93
Email: info.br.minsk@gmail.com **Web site:** http://www.belmarket.by
Freq: Weekly; **Circ:** 10187 Not Audited
Editor: Irina Krilovich; **News Editor:** Maria Sadovskaya
Profile: Newspaper providing comprehensive and analytical coverage of business events and economic developments in Belarus.
Language (s): Russian
DAILY NEWSPAPER

Ekonomicheskaya Gazeta 230033
Owner: Belbuisnespress
Editorial: ul. Kozyrevskaya 15, Minsk 220028
Tel: 375 17 21 31 800
Email: negrek@neg.by **Web site:** http://www.neg.by
Freq: 2 Times/Week; **Circ:** 13242 Not Audited
Editor-in-Chief: Leonid Fridkin
Profile: Newspaper containing information about economics, civil law, finance and statistics, business news.
Language (s): Russian
Ad Rate: Full Page Mono 2820000.00
Currency: Belarus Rubles
DAILY NEWSPAPER

Express Novosti 446196
Owner: KOMSIS
Editorial: pr. Nezavisimosti 77, Minsk 220013
Tel: 375 17 29 26 405
Email: info@expressnews.by **Web site:** http://www.expressnews.by
Circ: 7000 Publisher's Statement
Editor In Chief: Stanislav Zhuravlevich
Profile: Analytical-informative newspaper.
Language (s): Belarusian
DAILY NEWSPAPER

Gomelskaya pravda 446023
Owner: Gomelskaya pravda
Editorial: ul. Lepeshinskogo 1, Gomel 246015
Tel: 375 232 57 72 78
Email: gp@gp.by **Web site:** http://gp.by
Circ: 21000 Publisher's Statement
Editor In Chief: Sergey Bespaly
Profile: Newspaper focused on regional cultural and political issues and changes in Belarus society.
Language (s): Belarusian
DAILY NEWSPAPER

Komputernaya Gazeta 178314
Owner: Nestor Publishers
Editorial: P. O. Box 563, Minsk 220113
Tel: 375 17 28 93 713
Email: pumpur@nestormedia.com **Web site:** http://www.nestor.minsk.by/kg
Freq: Weekly; **Circ:** 26000 Not Audited
Publishing Director: Anatoly Kiryushkin; **Advertising Manager:** Elena Makarevich; **Editor:** Svetlana Pumpur
Profile: Newspaper containing news, reviews, features general hardware and software information. Places emphasis on details about new and forthcoming products.
Language (s): Russian
Ad Rate: Full Page Mono 2336400.00
Currency: Belarus Rubles
DAILY NEWSPAPER

Komsomolskaya Pravda v Belarusi 564948
Editorial: ul. Platonova 1b, office 401, 4 floor, Minsk 220034 **Tel:** 375 17 294 27 11
Email: kp@phkp.by **Web site:** http://kp.by
Freq: Daily
Profile: Byelorussian edition of Russian daily newspaper covering politics, economics, culture and social issues.
Language (s): Russian
Ad Rate: Full Page Colour 2569151.00
Currency: Belarus Rubles
DAILY NEWSPAPER

Music News Weekly 198833
Owner: Nestor Publishers
Editorial: PO Box 563, Minsk 220113
Tel: 375 17 28 93 713
Email: mg@nestormedia.com **Web site:** http://www.nestor.minsk.by/mg
Freq: Weekly; **Circ:** 3500 Not Audited
Advertising Manager: Anatoly Kiryushkin; **Editor:** Oleg Klimov
Profile: Newspaper containing information about all styles of pop and rock music with emphasis on alternative and recently discovered artists. Includes interviews, features, news, reviews, chart details and classified ads.
Language (s): Russian
DAILY NEWSPAPER

Narodnaya Gazeta 156798
Owner: Narodnaya Gazeta
Editorial: ul. B. Khmelnitskogo 10a, Etazh 7, Minsk 220013 **Tel:** 375 17 28 71 870
Email: infong@sb.by **Web site:** http://ng.sb.by
Freq: Daily; **Circ:** 40000 Publisher's Statement
Profile: Newspaper covering national and international news with features on business and finance, culture, education and lifestyle.
Language (s): Belarusian
DAILY NEWSPAPER

SB Belarus Segodnya 161227
Owner: Administration of the President of the Belarus Republic
Editorial: ul. Khmelnitskogo 10A, Minsk 220013
Tel: 375 17 287-18-03
Email: admin@sb.by **Web site:** http://www.sb.by
Freq: Daily; **Circ:** 417966 Publisher's Statement
Advertising Manager: Anatoliy Litvinski; **Editor In Chief:** Pavel Yakubovich
Profile: Newspaper focusing on financial, economical and social-political issues.
Language (s): Russian
DAILY NEWSPAPER

Vecherny Brest 157240
Owner: Vecherny Brest
Editorial: ul. Pushkinskaya 11, Brest 224005
Tel: 375 162 21 54 00
Email: info@vb.by **Web site:** http://www.vb.by
Circ: 15000 Publisher's Statement
Editor: Vladimir Sergeevich Shparlo
Profile: Regional newspaper containing national and international news, articles on culture, sports and social issues.
Language (s): Belarusian
DAILY NEWSPAPER

Vecherny Minsk 156641
Owner: OOO Izdatelskiy Dom Vecherny Minsk
Editorial: Pr. Fr. Skoriny 44, Minsk 220005
Tel: 375 17 28 45 944
Email: vm@nsys.by **Web site:** http://www.newsvm.com
Freq: Daily; **Circ:** 40000 Publisher's Statement
Advertising Manager: Marina Nesterova; **Editor:** Sergey Sverkunov
Profile: Newspaper focusing on national and international news, politics and the economy, sport, culture and lifestyle.
Language (s): Russian
DAILY NEWSPAPER

Virtual Joys 178901
Owner: Nestor Publishers
Editorial: PO Box 563, Minsk 220113
Tel: 375 17 28 93 713
Email: nestorinfo@nestormedia.com **Web site:** http://www.nestor.minsk.by/vr
Freq: Monthly; **Circ:** 25000 Not Audited
Editor: Marina Biryukova; **Advertising Manager:** Anatoly Kiryushkin
Profile: Newspaper containing information about computer games and related soft- and hardware.
Language (s): Russian
DAILY NEWSPAPER

Belarus

Znamya Yunosti 205931
Owner: Upravlyenye po Delom Maladyozhy Ministerstva Obrozovanya Respspubliki Belarusi
Editorial: ul. Khmelnitskogo 10 A, Minsk 220013
Tel: 375 17 28 71 684
Email: zn@zn.by **Web site:** http://zn.by
Freq: Weekly; **Circ:** 32000 Not Audited
Editor-in-Chief: Evgeniy Meleshko
Profile: Newspaper containing social-political news, articles on history, culture, show business and world-wide youth organisations.
Language (s): Russian
DAILY NEWSPAPER

News Service/Syndicate

AFN 353741
Editorial: ul. Vostochnaya 129-310, Minsk 220113
Tel: 375 17 21 60 111
Email: info@afn.by **Web site:** http://www.afn.by
Profile: Provides financial and economic news, reviews of investments, funds, banking and currency markets.
Language (s): Belarusian
NEWS SERVICE/SYNDICATE

BelaPAN News Agency 353220
Editorial: ul. Akademicheskaya 17, office 3, Minsk 220012 **Tel:** 375 17 29 25 501
Email: redactor@belapan.com **Web site:** http://belapan.by
Language (s): Belarusian
NEWS SERVICE/SYNDICATE

BelTA Belarusian News Agency 353221
Editorial: ul. Kirova 26, Minsk 220030
Tel: 375 17 22 71 992
Email: oper@belta.by **Web site:** http://www.belta.by
Director General: Dmitri Zhuk
Profile: BelTA News Agency is the biggest information agency in the Republic of Belarus and has been official national information provider remaining most authoritative source of up-to-date information on activities of supreme government bodies of Belarus. The agency was founded on December 23, 1918.
Language (s): Belarusian
NEWS SERVICE/SYNDICATE

ECOPRESS Information Agency 457600
Editorial: 21-606 Chicherina Street, Minsk 220029
Tel: 375 17 29 34 020
Email: market@ecopress.by **Web site:** http://www.ecopress.by
Editor In Chief: Pyotr Borovikov
Profile: Financial and economic news agency, provision of current financial and economic information (currency exchange rates, deposit rates, securities quotations, etc.) as well as economic and commercial news of the Republic of Belarus.
Language (s): Belarusian
NEWS SERVICE/SYNDICATE

PRIME-TASS Business News Agency 449852
Editorial: 11-2-412 Nezavisimosti Avenue, Minsk
Tel: 375 17 20 99 500
Email: market@prime-tass.by **Web site:** http://www.prime-tass.by
Editor: Yelena Lazarchuk; **Editor:** Olga Loiko
Profile: Business News Agency dealing with distribution of business news from Belarus, live economic newswire, analysis, market surveys and press clippings. Preparation and distribution of press releases and media monitoring. Coverage of special events, announcements, invitations for media, interviews and accompanying materials.
Language (s): Belarusian
NEWS SERVICE/SYNDICATE

Belgium

Time Difference: GMT +1
National Telephone Code: 32
Continent: Europe
Capital: Brussels

Newspapers

La Dernière Heure / Les Sports 158251
Owner: La Dernière Heure / Les Sports
Editorial: Rue des Francs, 79, Bruxelles 1040
Tel: 32 2 744 44 55
Email: dh.redaction@dhnet.be **Web site:** http://www.dhnet.be
Freq: Daily; **Circ:** 112000 Publisher's Statement
Rédacteur: Antoine Clevers; **Publishing Manager:** Frédéric Vancaster
Profile: Newspaper covering mainly on sports including regional news, media and celebrities Aimed at those with an interest in competitive sport.
Language (s): French
DAILY NEWSPAPER

L' Echo 158253
Owner: mediafin
Editorial: Avenue du port 86C, Boîte 309, Bruxelles 1000 **Tel:** 32 2 423 16 11
Email: redaction@lecho.be **Web site:** http://www.lecho.be
Freq: Daily; **Circ:** 28
Editor in Chief: Joan Condijts; **Rédacteur:** Stéphane Wuille
Profile: Newspaper covering national and international news including politics, economics, business and financial markets.
Language (s): French
Ad Rate: Full Page Mono 9650.00
Ad Rate: Full Page Colour 11750.00
Currency: Euro
DAILY NEWSPAPER

Europolitics 582833
Owner: Europe Information Service s.a
Editorial: Rue d'Arlon, 53, Brussels 1040
Tel: 32 2 737 7722
Email: redaction@europolitics.info **Web site:** http://www.europolitique.info
Freq: Daily
Profile: Newspaper providing in-depth, analytical coverage of the European Union, its institutions and policies as well as the key economic, social and international issues high on the agenda today.
Language (s): English
DAILY NEWSPAPER

De Gentenaar - Nieuwsblad 158256
Owner: CORELIO (EX VUM NV)
Editorial: Gossetlaan 30, Gent 1702
Tel: 32 9 268 72 70
Email: nieuws@gentenaar.be **Web site:** http://www.gentenaar.be
Freq: Daily; **Circ:** 271000 Publisher's Statement
Chief De Gentenaar: Johan Cauwels; **Chief eindredactie:** Nico Vanhee; **Chief News:** Pascal Weiss
Profile: Broadsheet-sized newspaper containing national and international news, business reports and coverage of political events. Read by company directors, managers and senior executives, university students and office personnel, the majority of whom live in Flanders.
Language (s): Flemish
DAILY NEWSPAPER

Het Laatste Nieuws - HLN 158254
Owner: De Persgroep
Editorial: Brusselsesteenweg, 347, Asse/kobbegem 1730 **Tel:** 32 2 454 22 11
Email: info@hln.be **Web site:** http://www.hln.be
Freq: Daily; **Circ:** 300000 Publisher's Statement
Information Director: Dimitri Antonissen; **Chef Nieuws:** Willy Cardon; **Chef eindredactie:** Edwin Ceulebroeck; **Eindredacteur:** An Schoemans
Profile: Broadsheet-sized newspaper covering regional and national news and current affairs including economics, sports and entertainment.
Language (s): Dutch
Ad Rate: Full Page Mono 27450.00
Ad Rate: Full Page Colour 30500.00
Currency: Euro
DAILY NEWSPAPER

La Libre Belgique - Gazette de Liège 306362
Owner: Groupe Multimedia IPM S.A.
Editorial: Rue des Francs, 79, Bruxelles 1040
Tel: 32 2 744 44 44
Email: llb.redaction@saipm.com **Web site:** http://www.lalibre.be
Freq: Daily; **Circ:** 50000 Publisher's Statement
Editor in Chief: Francis Van de Woestyne
Profile: Newspaper covering general news and current affairs including politics, economics, culture, sports, entertainment and lifestyle.
Language (s): French
DAILY NEWSPAPER

Metro 159030
Owner: Mass Transit Media
Editorial: Galerie Ravenstein, 4, Brussels 1000
Tel: 32 2 227 93 43
Email: metro@metrotime.be **Web site:** http://www.metrotime.be
Freq: Daily; **Circ:** 119398 Publisher's Statement
?News Director: Hans Cardyn; **General Manager:** Monique Raaffels; **News Editor:** Jérôme Rombaux
Profile: Tabloid-sized newspaper covering national and international news and current affairs including politics, economy, society, sports, culture and lifestyle.
Language (s): French
Ad Rate: Full Page Mono 12950.00
Ad Rate: Full Page Colour 15450.00
Currency: Euro
DAILY NEWSPAPER

De Morgen 158266
Owner: De Persgroep
Editorial: Brusselsesteenweg 347, Kobbegem 1730
Tel: 32 2 556 68 11
Email: info@demorgen.be **Web site:** http://www.demorgen.be
Freq: Daily; **Circ:** 70000 Publisher's Statement
Rédacteur: Jan Debackere; **Rédacteur:** Agnes Goyvaerts; **Eindredacteur:** Wilfried Poelmans; **Eindredacteur:** Henricus (Rene) Van Munster; **Director General:** Christian Van Thilo
Profile: Newspaper covering news and current affairs including sports, music, opinion, environment, technology, culture and media.
Language (s): Flemish
Ad Rate: Full Page Mono 10620.00
Ad Rate: Full Page Colour 11800.00
Currency: Euro
DAILY NEWSPAPER

New Europe 667844
Editorial: Avenue de Tervuren 96, Bruxelles 1040
Tel: 32 2 539 00 39
Email: info@neurope.eu **Web site:** http://www.neurope.eu
Freq: Weekly; **Circ:** 80000
Editor: Andy Carling; **Editor:** Cillian Donnelly; **Editor:** Kostis Geropoulos; **Director:** Alexandros Koronakis
Profile: Weekly newspaper covering government and politics including current news and analyses on EU institutions and EU-World relations.
Language (s): English
Ad Rate: Full Page Colour 8400.00
Currency: Euro
DAILY NEWSPAPER

Het Nieuwsblad 306896
Owner: CORELIO (EX VUM NV)
Editorial: Katwilgweg 2, Anvers 2050
Tel: 32 2 467 22 23
Email: nieuws@nieuwsblad.be **Web site:** http://www.nieuwsblad.be
Freq: Daily; **Circ:** 270000 Publisher's Statement
Editor: Els Bloemmen; **Editor:** Werner Bourlez; **Editor:** Philippe de Bruin; **Editor:** Mariena Dewulf; **Editor:** Marcel Kumpen; **News Editor:** Peter Mijlemans; **Editor:** Guido Ostyn; **Editor:** Laurens Raskin; **Editor:** Karen Regelbrugge; **Editor:** Kristof Simoens; **eindredacteur:** Marina Tondeleir; **Editor:** Chris Van Geyte; **Chef Oost-Vlaanderen:** Rudi Van Holderbeke; **Editor:** Kathy Vandeportael; **Editor:** Marianne Vanderauwera; **Editor in Chief:** Peter Vandermeersch; **Editor:** Ludo Vandewalle; **Chef eindredactie:** Nico Vanhee; **Editor:** Johan Vercammen; **Editor:** Christine Verlinde; **Editor:** Kurt Vermeersch; **Editor:** Robert Verniers
Profile: Newspaper covering national and international news including sports, politics, economics, business, culture and lifestyle.
Language (s): Flemish
DAILY NEWSPAPER

Le Soir 158257
Owner: Rossel & Cie
Editorial: Rue Royale, 100, Bruxelles 1000
Tel: 32 2 225 54 32
Web site: http://www.lesoir.be
Freq: Daily; **Circ:** 150000 Publisher's Statement
Rédacteur: Fabienne Bradfer; **Rédacteur:** Stéphane Druart; **Publishing Manager:** Philippe Laloux; **Rédacteur:** Catherine Makereel; **Rédacteur:** Olivier Maloteaux; **Rédacteur:** Gisèle Maréchal; **Rédacteur:** Guy Maron; **Publishing Manager:** Olivier Mouton; **Publishing Manager:** Ettore Rizza; **chroniqueur:** Leopold Unger
Profile: Broadsheet-sized evening newspaper covering news and current affairs including business, economics, politics, culture, society, television and sport.
Language (s): French
Ad Rate: Full Page Colour 21700.00
Currency: Euro
DAILY NEWSPAPER

De Standaard 158258
Owner: CORELIO (EX VUM NV)
Editorial: Gossetlaan 28, Groot Bijgaarden 1702
Tel: 32 2 467 27 52
Email: binnenland@standaard.be **Web site:** http://www.standaard.be
Freq: Daily; **Circ:** 100010 Publisher's Statement
Rédacteur: Yves Delepeleire; **Rédacteur:** Nikolas Vanhecke; **Rédacteur:** Sarah Vankersschaever
Profile: National newspaper covering regional, national and international news and current affairs including business, politics, economics, culture, lifestyle, society and sports.
Language (s): Flemish
DAILY NEWSPAPER

De Tijd 306361
Owner: mediafin
Editorial: Havenlaan 86 C, Bus 309, Brussels 1000
Tel: 32 2 423 16 11
Email: persberichten@tijd.be **Web site:** http://www.tijd.be
Freq: Daily; **Circ:** 38582 Publisher's Statement
Hoofdredacteur: Isabel Albers; **Editor:** Bert Broens; **Newsmanager:** Henk Dheedene; **Chef Ondernemingen:** Bas Kurstjens; **New Media Manager:** Roland Legrand; **Newsmanager:** Serge Mampaey; **Multimedia Manager:** Tom Peeters; **News Manager:** Steven Samyn; **Editor:** Michael Sephiha; **Redacteur:** Koen Van Boxem; **Redacteur:** Erik Ziarczyk
Profile: Newspaper covering business and finance including investment, markets, economics, politics and culture.
Language (s): Dutch
Ad Rate: Full Page Mono 14630.00
Ad Rate: Full Page Colour 17150.00
Currency: Euro
DAILY NEWSPAPER

News Service/Syndicate

AGENCE ALTER 581260
Editorial: Rue Coenraets, 64, Bruxelles 1060
Tel: 32 2541 85 20
Email: alter@alter.be **Web site:** http://www.alter.be
Language (s): Dutch
NEWS SERVICE/SYNDICATE

Agence Europe 581262
Editorial: Rue de la Gare, 36, Bruxelles 1040
Tel: 32 2 737 94 94
Email: info@agenceurope.com **Web site:** http://www.agenceurope.com
Editor: Lionel Changeur
Profile: News agency covering European news and current affairs including business, politics, economics, society, culture, agriculture and law.
Language (s): French
NEWS SERVICE/SYNDICATE

AP DOW JONES NEWS SERVICE - BELGIQUE 581267
Editorial: Boulevard Brand Whithlock 87, Bruxelles 1200 **Tel:** 32 2 741 12 11
Email: djnews.brussels@dowjones.com **Web site:** http://www.dowjones.com
Editor: Laurence Norman
Profile: Dow Jones is a leading provider of global business news and information services. Its Consumer Media Group publishes The Wall Street Journal, Barron's, MarketWatch and the Far Eastern Economic Review. Its Enterprise Media Group includes Dow Jones Newswires, Factiva, Dow Jones Client Solutions, Dow Jones Indexes and Dow Jones Financial Information Services. Its Local Media Group operates community-based information franchises. Dow Jones owns 50% of SmartMoney and 33% of Stoxx Ltd. and provides news content to radio stations in the U.S. Since 1882, the Dow Jones name has been synonymous with accuracy, integrity and trust.
Language (s): English
NEWS SERVICE/SYNDICATE

Belga News Agency 581261
Owner: Belga News Agency NV
Editorial: Rue Frederic Pelletier, 8B, Bruxelles 1030
Tel: 32 2 743 23 11
Email: redactie@belga.be **Web site:** http://www.belga.be
Chief News: Lieven De Maertelaere; **Managing Director:** Hans Egbert; **Chief Imagery:** Philippe François; **Newsmanager:** Saskia Laurent; **Chief Politics:** Luc Michiels; **News Manager:** Christian Neyt; **Human Resources Manager:** Mieke Van der Auwera; **Chief Info Resources:** Joris Van Roy
Profile: National News Agency covering news and current affairs including business, politics, economics, sport and culture.
Language (s): Dutch
NEWS SERVICE/SYNDICATE

Euronews - Brussels Bureau 786486
Owner: Euronews
Editorial: 223, rue de la Loi, Bruxelles 1000
Tel: 32 278 819 19
Web site: http://www.euronews.net
Profile: Regional office of the TV cable/satellite channel focussing on national and international news and current affairs.
Language (s): English
NEWS SERVICE/SYNDICATE

MLex 667655
Owner: MLex Belgium SPRL
Editorial: 67 Rue de la Loi, Box 6, Brussels 1140
Tel: 32 2 300 82 50
Email: mcleod@mlex.com **Web site:** http://www.mlex.com
Editor In Chief: Robert Mc Leod; **Merger Analyst:** Dafydd Nelson
Profile: MLex market intelligence is an independent service that provides in-depth intelligence, commentary and analysis, antitrust probes, state-backed bailouts, intellectual property, trade and regulatory issues. aimed at finance, investment and legal professionals.
Language (s): English
NEWS SERVICE/SYNDICATE

ZenithOptimedia Belgium 822040
Owner: ZenithOptimedia
Editorial: Clos Lucien Outers 11-21, Brussels 1160
Tel: 32 2 716 01 20
Web site: http://www.zenithoptimedia.be
Profile: Media agency which is part of the global ZenithOptimedia network with 195 offices in 70 countries and which in itself is part of the Publicis Group. ZenithOptimedia positioning is that of 'the ROI Agency'.
Language (s): English
NEWS SERVICE/SYNDICATE

Belize

Time Difference: GMT -6
National Telephone Code: 501
Continent: The Americas
Capital: Belmopan

Community Newspaper

Amandala 224404
Owner: The Amandala Press
Editorial: 3304 Partridge Street, Belize City
Tel: 1 501 202-4477
Email: amandalapress@gmail.com **Web site:** http://www.amandala.com.bz
Freq: 2 Times/Week; **Circ:** 10000 Not Audited
Publisher: Evan Hyde; **Editor:** Russell Vellos
Profile: Amandala is a newspaper covering national and international news, politics and sports in Belize.
Language (s): English
Ad Rate: Full Page Mono 13.75
Currency: United States Dollars
COMMUNITY NEWSPAPER

The Belize Times 224441
Owner: The Belize Times Press Ltd
Editorial: 3 Queen Street, Belize City **Tel:** 1 501 671-8385
Email: editortimes@yahoo.com **Web site:** http://www.belizetimes.bz
Freq: Weekly; **Circ:** 6000 Not Audited
Editor in Chief: Michael Rudon
Profile: Newspaper covering general news, finance, economic, politics and sport in Belize.
Language (s): English
Ad Rate: Full Page Mono 8.20
Currency: United States Dollars
COMMUNITY NEWSPAPER

The Guardian 230200
Owner: The Guardian Newspaper Ltd
Editorial: Corner Ebony St. & BelChina Bridge, Belize City **Tel:** 1 501 207-5347
Email: guardian@btl.net **Web site:** http://www.guardian.bz
Freq: Weekly; **Circ:** 4000 Not Audited
Editor: Alfonso Noble
Profile: Newspaper focusing on national and international news, politics, business and sport in Belize.
Language (s): English
COMMUNITY NEWSPAPER

The Reporter 225902
Owner: The Reporter Press
Editorial: 147 West Allenby Street, PO Box 707, Belize City **Tel:** 501 227 2503
Web site: http://www.reporter.bz
Freq: Weekly; **Circ:** 7000 Not Audited
Editor: Niell Gillett; **Publisher:** Harry Lawrence
Profile: Newspaper covering national news, business, politics, entertainment and sport.
Language (s): English
Ad Rate: Full Page Mono 15.00
Currency: United States Dollars
COMMUNITY NEWSPAPER

Benin

Time Difference: GMT +1
National Telephone Code: 229
Continent: Africa
Capital: Porto-Novo

Newspapers

Fraternité 969291
Owner: Fraternité
Editorial: Face Station Menontin, Cotonou
Tel: 229 21 38 47 70
Email: contact@fraternitebj.info **Web site:** http://www.fraternitebj.info
Freq: Daily
Editor: Moïse Dossoumou
Profile: Fraternité is a daily newspaper covering national and international news and current affairs including politics, society, sport and culture.
Language (s): French
DAILY NEWSPAPER

La Nation 324937
Owner: ONIP
Editorial: BP 1210, Cotonou **Tel:** 229 21 30 02 99
Email: quotidienlanation@yahoo.fr **Web site:** http://www.lanationbenin.info
Freq: Daily; **Circ:** 5000 Publisher's Statement
Advertising Manager: Marie-Madeleine Akoffodji; **Editor in Chief:** Bruno Sewade
Profile: Newspaper covering national and international news and current affairs including politics, society, economy, sport, culture, health and education.
Language (s): French
Ad Rate: Full Page Colour 281250.00
Currency: Communauté Financière Africaine Francs BCEAO
DAILY NEWSPAPER

News Service/Syndicate

Agence Bénin Presse - ABP 502873
Owner: Agence Bénin Presse
Editorial: Face Agence principale BOA, Cotonou
Tel: 229 21 312655
Email: abpcollecte@yahoo.fr **Web site:** http://www.agencebeninpresse.info
Director: Mathias Léandre Atignon; **News Editor:** Joseph Vodounon Djodo
Profile: Agence Bénin Presse - ABP is the official news agency of Benin covering national and international news and current affairs including politics, economy, science, culture, sports, environment and society.
Language (s): French
NEWS SERVICE/SYNDICATE

Bermuda

Time Difference: GMT -4
National Telephone Code: 1441
Continent: The Americas
Capital: Hamilton

Newspapers

Bermuda Sun 156644
Owner: Bermuda Sun Ltd
Editorial: 19 Elliott Street, Hamilton HM10
Tel: 1 441 295-1944
Email: newsroom@bermudasun.bm **Web site:** http://www.bermudasun.bm
Freq: Fri; **Circ:** 12000 Not Audited
Publisher: Randy French; **Editor in Chief:** Tony McWilliam
Profile: Local newspaper covering business, politics, entertainment and sports.
Language (s): English
Ad Rate: Full Page Mono 21.75
Currency: United States Dollars
DAILY NEWSPAPER

The Royal Gazette 156831
Owner: The Royal Gazette Ltd.
Editorial: 2 Par-la-Ville Rd, Hamilton HM-02
Tel: 1441 295 5881
Email: news@royalgazette.bm **Web site:** http://www.royalgazette.com
Freq: Daily; **Circ:** 9216
Profile: The Royal Gazette is a daily newspaper focusing on national and international news, business and sports for the residents of Bermuda.
Language (s): English
Ad Rate: Full Page Mono 17.76
Ad Rate: Full Page Colour 245.00
Currency: United States Dollars
DAILY NEWSPAPER

Bhutan

Time Difference: GMT +6
National Telephone Code: 975
Continent: Asia
Capital: Thimphu

Newspapers

Kuensel 224386
Owner: Kuensel Corporation
Editorial: PO Box 204, Thimphu **Tel:** 975 2 322483
Email: editor@kuensel.com.bt **Web site:** http://www.kuenselonline.com
Circ: 15000 Publisher's Statement
News Editor: Phuntsho Wangdi
Profile: Newspaper focusing on national news, politics, business, culture, entertainment and sport.
Language (s): Dzongkha
DAILY NEWSPAPER

Bolivia

Time Difference: GMT -4
National Telephone Code: 591
Continent: The Americas
Capital: La Paz

Newspapers

Correo del Sur 160838
Owner: Editorial Canelas del Sur SRL
Editorial: Calle Kilometro 7 N 202, Sucre (chuquisaca) **Tel:** 591 4 64 61 531
Email: correo7@entelnet.bo **Web site:** http://www.correodelsur.com
Freq: Daily; **Circ:** 5000 Not Audited
Editor: Javier Cosulich; **Director:** Marco Antonio Dipp Mukled; **Editor in Chief:** Raykha Flores Cocío; **Editor:** Alberto Guevara; **Editor:** Alvaro Sotomayor; **Editor:** Ernesto Torres
Profile: National newspaper.
Language (s): Spanish
DAILY NEWSPAPER

El Deber 156840
Owner: El Deber SRL
Editorial: Avenida El Trompillo 2 anillo #1144, Santa Cruz **Tel:** 591 3 353 8000
Email: eldeber@eldeber.com.bo **Web site:** http://www.eldeber.com.bo
Freq: Daily; **Circ:** 50000 Not Audited
News Editor: Roberto Aguirre; **Editor in Chief:** Tuffi Aré Vázquez; **International News Editor:** Gerson Rivero; **Director:** Pedro Rivero Mercado; **Editor:** Leopoldo Vegas
Profile: National newspaper containing national and international news, current affairs, business and sport.
Language (s): Spanish
DAILY NEWSPAPER

El Día 378226
Owner: Prisa Internacional
Editorial: Avenida Cristo Redentor 3355, Km 2'5, CP 5344, Santa Cruz **Tel:** 591 33434040
Email: eldia@eldia.com.bo **Web site:** http://www.eldia.com.bo
Freq: Daily; **Circ:** 15000 Not Audited
Director: Eduardo Bowles; **Editor in Chief:** Róger Cuéllar; **Editor:** Carlos Jordan Paz
Profile: Newspaper containing national and international news, current affairs, business and sport.
Language (s): Spanish
DAILY NEWSPAPER

El Diario 156832
Owner: El Diario S.A.
Editorial: Calle Loayza 118, La Paz
Tel: 591 22150900
Email: redinfo@eldiario.net **Web site:** http://www.eldiario.net
Freq: Daily; **Circ:** 70000 Not Audited
Director: Antonio Martín Carrasco Guzmán; **Director:** Jorge Carrasco Gúzman; **Editor:** Susana Gutiérrez; **Manager:** Lourdes Morales; **Editor in Chief:** Rodrigo Ticona
Profile: Newspaper covering national and international news, politics, economics, finance, business, culture and sport.
Language (s): Spanish
DAILY NEWSPAPER

La Estrella del Oriente 378316
Owner: Editorial C.S.S.
Editorial: Calle Republiquetas #353, Santa Cruz
Tel: 591 3 332-9011
Email: laestrelladeloriente@laestrella.bo **Web site:** http://www.laestrelladeloriente.com
Freq: Daily; **Circ:** 5000 Not Audited
Editor: William Guzman
Profile: La Estrella del Oriente is a Bolivian daily newspaper providing Local News, Politics, Editorial Page, Sports, Arts & Entertainment, Economy, National and International coverage.
Language (s): Spanish
DAILY NEWSPAPER

Gente 378225
Owner: Editorial Canelas SA
Editorial: Edificio Los Tiempos, Plaza Quintanilla, Planta baja, Cochabamba **Tel:** 591 4 425 0936
Email: gente@bo.net
Freq: Daily; **Circ:** 16000 Not Audited
Director: Martín Balcazar; **Editor in Chief:** Flavios Ramos
Profile: General news related to criminal justice and policial issues, targeting a low socio-economic status audience.
Language (s): Spanish
DAILY NEWSPAPER

Jornada 157190
Owner: Editorial Aurios SRL
Editorial: Almirante Grau 672, Zona San Pedro, La Paz **Tel:** 591 22407789
Web site: http://www.jornadanet.com
Freq: Daily; **Circ:** 400 Not Audited
Editor: Bernabe López; **Director:** David Ríos Aranda; **Editor in Chief:** Jenny Rodríguez Aranibar
Profile: Newspaper covering national and international news, politics, economics, finance, business, culture and sport.
Language (s): Spanish
DAILY NEWSPAPER

El Mundo 156841
Owner: El Mundo S.A
Editorial: Parque Industrial Manzano 7 Av. perimetral, Santa Cruz **Tel:** 591 3 3-464646
Email: elmundo.bolivia@gmail.com **Web site:** http://www.elmundo.com.bo
Freq: Daily; **Circ:** 13000 Not Audited
News Director: Jesús Benito Espíndola Miranda; **Editor:** Patricia González
Profile: Newspaper focusing on national and international news, politics, business and sport.
Language (s): Spanish
DAILY NEWSPAPER

Opinión 156843
Owner: Editorial Opinión SA
Editorial: Calle General Acha N 0252, Cochabamba
Tel: 591 4 425-4400
Email: redaccion@opinion.com.bo **Web site:** http://www.opinion.com.bo
Freq: Daily; **Circ:** 18000 Not Audited
Editor: Ricardo Becerra; **International News Editor:** Jorge Delgado; **Editor:** Elizabeth Riva Alvarez; **Director:** Edwin Tapia Frontanilla
Profile: Newspaper covering national and international news, politics, economics, finance, business, culture and sport.
Language (s): Spanish
DAILY NEWSPAPER

El País 366234
Owner: El País
Editorial: Calle Colon 968, Tarija **Tel:** 591 4 664 2732
Email: elpais@entelnet.bo **Web site:** http://www.elpaisonline.com
Freq: Daily; **Circ:** 3000 Not Audited
Editor: Gilberto Villarroel
Profile: National newspaper.
Language (s): Spanish
DAILY NEWSPAPER

La Palabra del Beni 157156
Owner: Editorial Tiempo del Beni
Editorial: Calle Nicolas Suarez 693, Trinidad (beni)
Tel: 591 3 462 0808
Email: lpalabra@entelnet.bo **Web site:** http://www.boliviabeni.com/LAPALABRA.htm
Freq: Daily; **Circ:** 1000 Not Audited
Director & CEO: Jorge Melgar Rioja; **Editor:** Emar Schrakman
Profile: National newspaper.
Language (s): Spanish
DAILY NEWSPAPER

La Patria 160840
Owner: Editora SIC Ltda
Editorial: Calle Camacho 1892 Murguia, CP 48, Oruro **Tel:** 591 2 525 0780
Email: direccion@lapatria.com.bo **Web site:** http://www.lapatriaenlinea.com
Freq: Daily; **Circ:** 8000 Not Audited
Editor: Etzhel Llanquel; **Editor:** Estella Miralles; **Director:** Marcelo Miralles Bova; **Editor in Chief:** Jimena Miralles Iporre
Profile: National newspaper.
Language (s): Spanish
DAILY NEWSPAPER

El Potosí 366310
Owner: Editorial Canelas del Sur SRL
Editorial: Calle Cochabamba 35, Potosi
Tel: 591 2 622 7835
Email: elpotosi@entelnet.bo **Web site:** http://www.elpotosi.net
Freq: Daily; **Circ:** 4000 Not Audited
Editor in Chief: Guillermo Bullain Iñiguez; **Editor:** Jaime Menduíña; **Editor:** Luis Subieta; **Editor:** Marvin Valda Angulo
Profile: National newspaper.
Language (s): Spanish
DAILY NEWSPAPER

La Prensa 160830
Owner: Editores Asociados SA
Editorial: Villa Fatima Calle Mayor Lopera 230, La Paz **Tel:** 591 2 2 21 88 21
Email: laprensa@laprensa.com.bo **Web site:** http://www.laprensa.com.bo
Freq: Daily; **Circ:** 15000 Not Audited
Editor: German Aráuz; **Editor:** Marco Belmonte; **Editor in Chief:** Carlos Morales; **Director:** Juan Carlos Rivero; **Editor:** Ramiro Siles
Profile: National newspaper.
Language (s): Spanish
DAILY NEWSPAPER

La Razón 156846
Owner: Prisa Internacional
Editorial: Colinas de Santa Rita, Alto Auquisamana, Zona Sur, La Paz **Tel:** 591 2 277-1415
Email: larazon@la-razon.com **Web site:** http://www.la-razon.com
Freq: Daily; **Circ:** 30000 Not Audited
Editor in Chief: Patricia Cusicanqui; **Director:** Edwin Herrera; **News Director:** Baldwin Montero; **Manager:** Cecilia Tejerina

Bolivia

Profile: Bolivian daily newspaper containing national and international news, current affairs, business and sport.
Language (s): Spanish
DAILY NEWSPAPER

Los Tiempos 156847
Owner: Editorial Canelas SA
Editorial: Edificio Los Tiempos, Plaza Quintanilla Piso 3, Area norte, Casilla 525, Cochabamba
Tel: 591 44254562
Web site: http://www.lostiempos.com
Freq: Daily; **Circ:** 13000 Not Audited
Director: Fernando Canelas; **Editor in Chief:** Alcides Flores; **Editor:** Maria Julia Osório
Profile: Newspaper covering national and international news, politics, economics, finance, business, culture and sport.
Language (s): Spanish
DAILY NEWSPAPER

News Service/Syndicate

ANF - Agencia de Noticias Fides 402877
Editorial: Calle Capitan Castrillo N 409, La Paz
Tel: 591 2 248-2040
Email: anf@noticiasfides.com **Web site:** http://www.noticiasfides.com
Editor: Jaime Loayza Zegarra
Language (s): Spanish
NEWS SERVICE/SYNDICATE

Community Newspaper

Energy Press 381703
Owner: Energy Press.com SRL
Editorial: Equipetrol Norte, Calle F Este 166, CP 3498, Santa Cruz **Tel:** 591 3 345 9095
Email: prensa1@energypress.com.bo **Web site:** http://www.energypress.com.bo
Freq: Weekly; **Circ:** 7000 Not Audited
General Manager: Carmen Hurtado; **Editor:** Vesma Marincovic
Profile: Newspaper focusing on the energetic industry in South America; includes petroleum related news, interviews and statistics.
Language (s): Spanish
COMMUNITY NEWSPAPER

Santa Cruz Económico 381687
Owner: Ilustra
Editorial: Avenida El Trompillo 206, Santa Cruz
Tel: 591 3 353 0944
Email: sceconomico@cotas.com.bo **Web site:** http://www.santacruzeconomico.com.bo
Freq: Weekly; **Circ:** 4000 Not Audited
Editor in Chief: Rudy Ortiz
Profile: National newspaper focusing on financial information.
Language (s): Spanish
COMMUNITY NEWSPAPER

Semanario Pulso 230129
Owner: Pulso SA
Editorial: Avenida 6 de Agosto 2530, CP 9056, La Paz **Tel:** 591 2 212 0330
Email: comunidadboliviana.com.ar@gmail.com **Web site:** http://www.comunidadboliviana.com.ar
Freq: Weekly; **Circ:** 5000 Not Audited
Editor: Daniel Espinoza; **Director:** Fernando Molina
Profile: Covers political and economic news.
Language (s): Spanish
COMMUNITY NEWSPAPER

Bosnia-Herzegovina

Time Difference: GMT +1
National Telephone Code: 387
Continent: Europe
Capital: Sarajevo

Newspapers

Dnevni Avaz 159035
Owner: Aroto Press
Editorial: Tesanjska 24a, Sarajevo 71000
Tel: 387 33 281360
Email: redakcija@avaz.ba **Web site:** http://www.avaz.ba
Freq: Daily; **Circ:** 60000 Publisher's Statement
General Manager: Hasena Hajri?; **Editor-in-Chief:** Fadil Mandal
Profile: Newspaper with news on domestic and international politics, finance, culture, social issues, sport and entertainment.
Language (s): Serbo-Croat
Ad Rate: Full Page Mono 1000.00
Ad Rate: Full Page Colour 1300.00
Currency: Bosnia and Herzegovina Convertible Marka
DAILY NEWSPAPER

Dnevni List 457890
Owner: NATIONAL HOLDING d.o.o.
Editorial: Kralja Petra Kresimira IV br. 66/2, Mostar 88 000 **Tel:** 387 36 31 33 70
Email: mostar@dnevni-list.ba **Web site:** http://www.dnevni-list.ba
Freq: Daily; **Circ:** 5200 Publisher's Statement
Editor: Sanja Bjelica Šagovnovi?; **Editor-in-Chief:** Dario Lukic; **Editor:** Predrag Zvijerac
Language (s): Serbo-Croat
DAILY NEWSPAPER

Glas Srpske 456992
Owner: AD Glas Srpske Banjaluka
Editorial: Brae Pisteljia 1, Banja Luka 78000
Tel: 387 51 21 28 44
Email: dopisnik@glassrpske.com **Web site:** http://www.glassrpske.com
Freq: Daily; **Circ:** 15000 Publisher's Statement
News Editor: Darko Gavrilovi?; **Editor In Chief:** Borjana Radmanovi?-Petrovi?
Language (s): Serbo-Croat
Ad Rate: Full Page Colour 1200.00
Currency: Euro
DAILY NEWSPAPER

Nezavisne Novine 161209
Editorial: Brae Pisteljia 1, Banja Luka 78000
Tel: 387 51 331-840
Email: desk@nezavisne.com **Web site:** http://www.nezavisne.com
Freq: Daily; **Circ:** 20000 Publisher's Statement
Editor-in-Chief: Gordana Milinkovi?
Profile: Newspaper containing national and international news, current affairs and sport.
Language (s): Serbo-Croat
Ad Rate: Full Page Mono 900.00
Ad Rate: Full Page Colour 1170.00
Currency: Bosnia and Herzegovina Convertible Marka
DAILY NEWSPAPER

Oslobo?enje 157097
Owner: Oslobo?enje d.o.o. Sarajevo
Editorial: Dzemala Bijedia 185, Sarajevo 71000
Tel: 387 33 276900
Email: info@oslobodjenje.ba **Web site:** https://www.oslobodjenje.ba
Freq: Daily; **Circ:** 25000 Publisher's Statement
Editor-in-Chief: Vildana Selimbegovi?
Profile: Newspaper focusing on national and international news, business, sport and current affairs.
Language (s): Serbo-Croat
DAILY NEWSPAPER

News Service/Syndicate

Federalna novinska agencija FENA 458091
Editorial: emalusa 1, Sarajevo **Tel:** 387 33 66 37 72
Email: fena@fena.ba **Web site:** http://www.fena.ba
Editor In Chief: Zoran Ili?; **Director:** Zehrudin Isakovi?
Profile: Federal news agency - Fena was founded by the Decree of FBiH Government in November 2000.
Language (s): Serbo-Croat
NEWS SERVICE/SYNDICATE

ONASA News Agency 458092
Editorial: Hamdije Kresevljakovia 12/I, Sarajevo 71000 **Tel:** 387 33 276 595
Email: news@onasa.com.ba **Web site:** http://www.onasa.com.ba
General Manager: Elvira Begovi?; **Editor:** Belma Tabakovi?
Profile: Provides information, news and comments to domestic and foreign public related to relevant events in Bosnia and Herzegovina, countries of the former Yugoslavia and in the whole world.
Language (s): Serbo-Croat
NEWS SERVICE/SYNDICATE

Botswana

Time Difference: GMT +2
National Telephone Code: 267
Continent: Africa
Capital: Gaborone

Newspapers

The Botswana Gazette 229982
Owner: The News Company
Editorial: Plot 125, Sedimosa House, Millennium Park, Gaborone **Tel:** 267 391 2774
Email: info@gazettebw.com **Web site:** http://www.thegazette.news
Freq: Daily; **Circ:** 20000 Publisher's Statement
Editor: Aubrey Lute
Profile: Newspaper focusing on national and international news, politics, business, lifestyle, culture, entertainment and sports.
Language (s): English
DAILY NEWSPAPER

The Botswana Guardian 224417
Owner: CBET (Pty) Ltd
Editorial: Plot 121, Finance Park, Gaborone
Tel: 267 390 84 08
Email: info@guardiansun.co.bw **Web site:** http://www.botswanaguardian.co.bw
Freq: Weekly; **Circ:** 20000 Publisher's Statement
Profile: Newspaper focusing on national and international news, business, politics, entertainment and sports.
Language (s): English
DAILY NEWSPAPER

The Midweek Sun 224416
Owner: CBET (Pty) Ltd
Editorial: Private Bag 00153, Gaborone
Tel: 267 390 8408
Email: info@themidweeksun.co.bw **Web site:** https://www.themidweeksun.co.bw
Circ: 22000 Publisher's Statement
Profile: Newspaper focusing on national and international news, business, politics, entertainment and sports.
Language (s): English
DAILY NEWSPAPER

Mmegi 229981
Owner: Dikgang Publishing Company (DPC)
Editorial: Private Bag BR 50, Gaborone
Tel: 267 397 4784
Email: editor@mmegi.bw **Web site:** http://www.mmegi.bw
Freq: Daily; **Circ:** 9000 Publisher's Statement
Profile: Newspaper covering regional, national and international news and current affairs including business, economics, politics, culture and sports. It is published in Setswana as Mmegi and in English as The Reporter.
Language (s): English
Ad Rate: Full Page Colour 2300.00
Currency: Botswana Pulas
DAILY NEWSPAPER

The Monitor 509602
Owner: Dikgang Publishing Company (DPC)
Editorial: Private Bag BR 50, Gaborone
Tel: 267 397 4784
Email: monitoreditor@mmegi.bw **Web site:** http://www.mmegi.bw
Freq: Weekly; **Circ:** 16000 Publisher's Statement
Profile: Newspaper covering regional and national news and current affairs including business, economics, politics, culture and sport.
Language (s): English
Ad Rate: Full Page Colour 2300.00
Currency: Botswana Pulas
DAILY NEWSPAPER

Brazil

Time Difference: GMT -2 (East Coast), GMT -5 (West Border)
National Telephone Code: 55
Continent: The Americas
Capital: Brasilia

Newspapers

Agora São Paulo 160813
Owner: Empresa Folha da Manhã SA
Editorial: Alameda Barao de Limeira, 425 - 5 Andar, Campos Elíseos, Sao Paulo 01202-900
Tel: 55 11 3224-3141
Web site: http://www.uol.com.br/agora
Freq: Daily; **Circ:** 119892
Editor in Chief: Nilson Camargo; **Editor:** Luiz Carlos Duarte; **Editor, Show!:** Débora Miranda; **Editor:** Adriana Mompean
Language (s): Portuguese
DAILY NEWSPAPER

Amazonas Em Tempo 355765
Owner: Norte Editora Ltda.
Editorial: Rua Dr. Dalmir Câmara, 623, Manaus 69033-070 **Tel:** 55 92 3090-1010
Email: opiniao@emtempo.com.br **Web site:** http://www.emtempo.com.br
Freq: Daily; **Circ:** 25000 Not Audited
Editor, Elenco: Guto Oliveira
Profile: Covers regional, national and international news. Editorial includes politics, sports economy, arts, entertainment, travel and culture.
Language (s): Portuguese
DAILY NEWSPAPER

Amazônia 469966
Editorial: Avenida 25 de Setembro, 2473, Marco, Belém 66093-000 **Tel:** 55 91 3216-1138
Email: redacao@orm.com.br **Web site:** http://www.ormnews.com.br/amazonia
Freq: Daily; **Circ:** 48000
Language (s): Portuguese
DAILY NEWSPAPER

Bom Dia Jundiaí 470646
Editorial: Rua Rangel Pestana, 444, Centro, Jundiaí 13201-000 **Tel:** 55 1145233440
Email: redacao@bomdiajundiai.com.br **Web site:** http://www.bomdiajundiai.com.br
Freq: Daily; **Circ:** 8000
Editor in Chief: Edu Cerioni
Language (s): Portuguese
DAILY NEWSPAPER

Bom Dia Sorocaba 470647
Editorial: Avenida Washington Luiz, 871, Jardim Emília, Sorocaba 18031-000 **Tel:** 55 15 32126001
Email: redacao@bomdiasorocaba.com.br **Web site:** http://www.redebomdia.com.br
Freq: Daily; **Circ:** 29990 Not Audited
Editor in Chief: Djalma Benette; **Editor:** Marcelo Macaus
Language (s): Portuguese
DAILY NEWSPAPER

Bragança Jornal Diário 470000
Editorial: Avenida Antônio Pires Pimentel, 957, Centro, Bragança Paulista 12914-000
Tel: 55 1140340490
Email: jornal@bjd.com.br **Web site:** http://www.bjd.com.br
Freq: Daily; **Circ:** 10000 Not Audited
Editor in Chief: José Omair de Oliveira
Profile: O Bragança Jornal Diário (BJD) passou por sua maior transformação em 10 de Setembro de 1993 com o início da impressão em off-set. A partir dessa data o BJD começou uma nova era e uma grande mudança ocorreu na sua programação visual devido aos recursos fornecidos pela informática. Hoje, o Bragança Jornal Diário entra na era digital com sua Home Page na World Wide Web. Com o grande avanço da Internet em todo o mundo, o BJD abre novas opções para o jornalismo bragantino com a expansão do acesso às notícias provenientes de todo o Brasil e do mundo.
Language (s): Portuguese
DAILY NEWSPAPER

Brasil Econômico 610717
Owner: Empresa Jornalística Econômico S.A.
Editorial: Avenida das Nacões Unidas, 11.633, 8 Andar - Brooklin, Sao Paulo 04578-901
Tel: 55 11 3320-2000
Email: redacao@brasileconomico.com.br **Web site:** http://economia.ig.com.br
Freq: Mon thru Fri; **Circ:** 50000
Publisher: Ramiro Alves; **Editor:** Rita Karam
Profile: Established on October 8, 2009 and it is the second largest Brazilian newspaper dedicated exclusively to cover all topics related to economy and financial markets in Brazil. Editorial includes articles on national and international economy, finance and financial analysis, investments, trade, stock markets, media industry and companies. Also, offers the latest news on politics and society.
Language (s): Portuguese
Ad Rate: Full Page Mono 120582.00
Ad Rate: Full Page Colour 120582.00
Currency: Brazil Reais
DAILY NEWSPAPER

A Cidade 470114
Editorial: Rua Sao Sebastiao, 610, Centro, Ribeirão Preto 14015-040 **Tel:** 55 16 3977-2175
Email: jornalismo@jornalacidade.com.br **Web site:** http://www.jornalacidade.com.br
Freq: Daily; **Circ:** 22000 Not Audited
Editor in Chief: Delcy Cruz; **Editor:** Hélio Pelissari
Language (s): Portuguese
DAILY NEWSPAPER

Comércio da Franca 470003
Editorial: Avenida Eliza Verzola Gosuein, 3103, Jardim Ângela Rosa, Franca 14400-630
Tel: 55 16 3713-8899
Web site: http://gcn.net.br
Freq: Daily; **Circ:** 16000 Not Audited
News Director: Corrêa Neves Júnior; **Editor in Chief:** Joelma Ospedal
Language (s): Portuguese
DAILY NEWSPAPER

Correio 470005
Editorial: Rua Aristides Novis, 123, Federacao, Salvador 40210-630 **Tel:** 55 71 3203-1210
Email: redacao@correio24horas.com.br **Web site:** http://www.correio24horas.com.br
Freq: Daily; **Circ:** 60000 Not Audited
Editor in Chief: Sergio Costa; **Editora, Bazar/Editor, Bazar:** Gabriela Cruz; **Editor:** Jorge Souza
Language (s): Portuguese
DAILY NEWSPAPER

Correio Braziliense 161199
Owner: Fundação Assis Chateaubriand
Editorial: SIG Qd. 02 Lote 340, Brasilia 70610-901
Tel: 55 61 3342-1000
Web site: http://www.correiobraziliense.com.br
Freq: Daily; **Circ:** 53403
Editor: Josemar Dantas; **Editor in Chief:** Ana Dubeux; **Editor, Encontro:** Cristine Gentil; **News Director:** Josemar Gimenez; **Editor:** Luis Carlos Griebeler Tajes; **Editor, Health, Science, Living & Food:** Ana Paula Macedo; **Editor:** Ana Sá; **Editor:** Sandro Silveira; **Editor:** Dad Abi Squarisi
Profile: Newspaper focusing on national and international news, politics, business and sport.
Language (s): Portuguese
Ad Rate: Full Page Mono 20.78
Currency: Brazil Reais
DAILY NEWSPAPER

Correio da Paraíba 469713
Editorial: Avenida Pedro II, 623, Centro, João Pessoa 58013-420 **Tel:** 55 83 3216-5000
Email: redacao@correiodaparaiba.com.br **Web site:** http://www.correiodaparaiba.com.br
Freq: Daily; **Circ:** 20000
Editor: Carlos Aranha; **Editor:** Fábio Cardoso; **Editor:** Ana Maria Felippe; **Editor in Chief:** Walter Galvão; **Editor:** José Magalhães; **Editor:** Lilian Moraes; **Editor:** Jâmarrí Nogueira
Language (s): Portuguese
DAILY NEWSPAPER

Correio de Uberlândia 469923
Editorial: Avenida Jose Andraus Gassani, 4555, Distrito Industrial, Uberlândia 38402-324
Tel: 55 34 3218-7666
Email: correiodeuberlandia@correiodeuberlandia.com.br **Web site:** http://www.jornalcorreio.com.br
Freq: Daily; **Circ:** 12000 Not Audited
Editor in Chief: Roberta Guimarães; **Editor:** Ivan Santos; **Editor:** Selma Silva
Language (s): Portuguese
DAILY NEWSPAPER

Correio do Estado 469714
Owner: Correio do Estado S/A.
Editorial: Avenida Calogeras, 356, Centro, Campo Grande 79004-901 **Tel:** 55 67 3323-6090
Web site: http://www.correiodoestado.com.br
Freq: Daily; **Circ:** 17000 Not Audited
Editor: Hordones Echeverria
Profile: Covers Local, Regional, National and International News.
Language (s): Portuguese
DAILY NEWSPAPER

Correio do Povo 156860
Owner: Correio do Povo
Editorial: Rua dos Andradas, 972 - Centro, Porto Alegre 90019-900 **Tel:** 55 51 3215-6111
Email: pauta@correiodopovo.com.br **Web site:** http://www.cpovo.net
Freq: Daily; **Circ:** 160000
Editor: Eugênio Bortolon; **Editor:** Carlos Brockstedt; **Editor:** Carmem Dóra Chiappetta; **Editor:** Letícia Ferreira; **Editor in Chief:** Paulo Mendes; **Editor:** Maria José Vasconcelos; **Editor, Cidades:** Maria Luiza Velleda
Language (s): Portuguese
DAILY NEWSPAPER

Correio Paranaense 469717
Editorial: Rua Fagundes Varela, 2106, Jardin Social, Curitiba 82520-040 **Tel:** 55 4132632002
Email: geral@jornalcorreioparanaense.com.br **Web site:** http://www.jornalcorreioparanaense.com.br
Freq: Daily; **Circ:** 15000 Not Audited
Editor in Chief: Renato Barroso
Profile: Note: This outlet has the same telephone and fax number. To send a fax, one must call and request that the telephone line be switched to a fax line.
Language (s): Portuguese
DAILY NEWSPAPER

Correio Popular 469697
Owner: Grupo RAC
Editorial: Rua Sete de Setembro, 189, Vila Industrial, Campinas 13035-350 **Tel:** 55 19 3772-8166
Email: faleconosco@rac.com.br **Web site:** http://correio.rac.com.br
Freq: Daily; **Circ:** 4200
Editor: Ricardo Luis Alécio; **Director:** Nelson de Mello; **Editor:** Kátia Fonseca; **Editor:** Rui Motta
Language (s): Portuguese
DAILY NEWSPAPER

A Crítica 469707
Editorial: Avenida Andre Araujo, 1924 A, Bairro Aleixo - Cidade das Comunicacões, Manaus 69060-001 **Tel:** 55 92 3643-1200
Email: jornal@acritica.com.br **Web site:** http://acritica.uol.com.br
Freq: Daily; **Circ:** 55000
Language (s): Portuguese
DAILY NEWSPAPER

Cruzeiro do Sul 470012
Editorial: Avenida Engenheiro Carlos Reinaldo Mendes, 2800, Alto da Boa Vista, Sorocaba 18013-280 **Tel:** 55 15 2102-5100
Email: online@jcruzeiro.com.br **Web site:** http://www.cruzeironet.com.br
Circ: 34848
Editor: Estela Casagrande; **Editor:** Aldo Fogaça; **Editor:** Admir Machado; **Editor:** Adalberto Vieira (Pardal)
Language (s): Portuguese
DAILY NEWSPAPER

O Debate - Diário de Macaé 469767
Editorial: Rua Benedito Peixoto, 90, Centro, Macaé 27916-040 **Tel:** 55 2221066060
Email: odebate@odebateon.com.br **Web site:** http://www.odebateon.com.br
Freq: Daily; **Circ:** 10000
Director: Oscar Pires; **Editor in Chief:** Wesley Radaveri
Profile: Note: This outlet has the same telephone and fax number. To send a fax, one must call and request that the telephone line be switched to a fax line.
Language (s): Portuguese
DAILY NEWSPAPER

Destak 827326
Editorial: Av. Brg. Faria Lima, 2954, 3 Andar, Sao Paulo 01451-000 **Tel:** 55 11 3077-3600
Email: pautadestak@gmail.com **Web site:** http://www.destakjornal.com.br
Freq: Daily; **Circ:** 385000
Editor in Chief: Lúcia Boldrini
Language (s): Portuguese
DAILY NEWSPAPER

O Dia 161008
Owner: Editora O Dia S.A.
Editorial: Rua do Riachuelo 359, 2 andar, Centro, Rio De Janeiro 20230-902 **Tel:** 55 21 2222-8200
Web site: http://odia.ig.com.br
Freq: Daily; **Circ:** 123000
Editor: Alex Campos; **Editor:** Hélio Cícero; **Editor:** Léo Corrêa; **Editor:** Joana Costa; **Editor in Chief:** Alexandre Freeland; **Editor:** Fernanda Portugal
Profile: O Dia covers local, regional, national and international news, as well as business, entertainment, lifestyle and sports.
Language (s): Portuguese
DAILY NEWSPAPER

O Diário 470318
Editorial: Rua Americo Brasiliense, 140, Centro, Ribeirão Preto 14015-050 **Tel:** 55 1639414414
Email: diarioribeirao@netsite.com.br
Freq: Daily; **Circ:** 10000 Not Audited
Editor in Chief: Jubayr Ubyrantan Bispo
Profile: Note: This outlet has the same telephone and fax number. To send a fax, one must call and request that the telephone line be switched to a fax line.
Language (s): Portuguese
DAILY NEWSPAPER

Diário Catarinense 157144
Owner: RBS Zero Hora Editora Jornalística S.A.
Editorial: Rodovia Jose Carlos Daux, 4190, Saco Grande, Florianópolis 88032-005 **Tel:** 55 48 3216-3502
Email: diariodoleitor@diariocatarinense.com.br **Web site:** http://dc.clicrbs.com.br/sc/
Freq: Daily; **Circ:** 38713 Not Audited
Editor: Viviane Araújo; **Editor:** Romi de Liz; **Editor:** Mariju Lima
Language (s): Portuguese
DAILY NEWSPAPER

Diário da Franca 470285
Editorial: Rua dos Pracinhas, 345, Residencial Paraíso, Franca 14403-160
Email: diario@diariodafranca.com.br **Web site:** http://www.diariodafranca.com.br
Freq: Daily; **Circ:** 20000 Not Audited
Editor: Tania Barreto; **Editor in Chief:** René Moreira
Language (s): Portuguese
DAILY NEWSPAPER

Diário da Manhã 469940
Editorial: Avenida Sete de Setembro, 509, Centro, Passo Fundo 99010-121 **Tel:** 55 54 3316-4800
Email: redacao@diariodamanha.net **Web site:** http://www.diariodamanha.com
Freq: Daily; **Circ:** 10000 Not Audited
Editor in Chief: Rosangela Borges Wink
Language (s): Portuguese
DAILY NEWSPAPER

Diário da Manhã 470016
Editorial: Avenida Presidente Vargas, 155, Centro, Erechim 99700-000 **Tel:** 55 54 3522-2711
Email: erechim@diariodamanha.net **Web site:** http://www.diariodamanha.com/erechim
Freq: Daily; **Circ:** 33000 Not Audited
Editor in Chief: Ivanor Oliviecki
Language (s): Portuguese
DAILY NEWSPAPER

Diário da Manhã 470019
Editorial: Av. Anhanguera, 2833, Setor Leste Universitario, Goiânia 74610-010 **Tel:** 55 62 3267-1000
Email: redacao@dm.com.br **Web site:** http://www.dm.com.br
Freq: Daily; **Circ:** 25000 Not Audited
Editor in Chief: Batista Custódio
Language (s): Portuguese
DAILY NEWSPAPER

Diário da Manhã 470020
Editorial: Rua Pedro Vargas 846, Centro, Carazinho 99500-000 **Tel:** 55 54 3329-9666
Email: redacao.carazinho@diariodamanha.net **Web site:** http://www.diariodamanha.com
Freq: Daily; **Circ:** 22000 Not Audited
Editor in Chief: Sérgio Cornélio
Language (s): Portuguese
DAILY NEWSPAPER

Diário da Região 469719
Editorial: Av. Feliciano Sales Cunha, 1515, Distrito Industrial, São José Do Rio Preto 15035
Tel: 55 17 2193-2081
Email: jornalismo@diariodaregiao.com.br **Web site:** http://www.diarioweb.com.br
Freq: Daily; **Circ:** 30000
Editor in Chief: Fabricio Carareto
Language (s): Portuguese
DAILY NEWSPAPER

O Diário da Região 470319
Editorial: Rua Ester Rombenso, 349, Centro, Osasco 06090-120 **Tel:** 55 11 3652-5244
Email: webdiario@webdiario.com.br **Web site:** http://www.webdiario.com.br
Freq: Daily; **Circ:** 25000 Not Audited
Editor In Chief: Simone Perez
Language (s): Portuguese
DAILY NEWSPAPER

Diário de Cuiabá 161001
Owner: Diário de Cuiabá Ltda.
Editorial: Av. Beira Rio, 4435, Bairro Dom Aquino, Cuiabá 78025-190 **Tel:** 55 6536340280
Email: redacao@diariodecuiaba.com.br **Web site:** http://www.diariodecuiaba.com.br
Freq: Daily; **Circ:** 15000
Editor: Jonas Jozino; **Editor:** Noelma Oliveira
Language (s): Portuguese
DAILY NEWSPAPER

Diário de Marília 469721
Editorial: Rua Coronel Galdino de Almeida, 55, Centro, Marília 17500-100 **Tel:** 55 14 3402-5122
Email: diario@diariodemarilia.com.br **Web site:** http://www.diariodemarilia.com.br
Freq: Daily; **Circ:** 15000
Director: Helena Brambilla; **Editor:** Wellington Menon; **Editor in Chief:** José Ursílio
Language (s): Portuguese
DAILY NEWSPAPER

O Diário de Mogi 469768
Editorial: Rua Dr. Ricardo Villela, 568, Centro, Mogi Das Cruzes 08710-150 **Tel:** 55 11 3524-2400
Email: diario@odiariodemogi.com.br **Web site:** http://www.odiariodemogi.com.br
Freq: Daily; **Circ:** 15000 Not Audited
Editor in Chief: Spártaco Da San Biagio; **Director:** Tirreno Da San Biagio; **Editor:** Gerson Lourenço; **Editor in Chief:** Darwin Valente
Language (s): Portuguese
DAILY NEWSPAPER

Diário de Pernambuco 157186
Owner: Diários Associados
Editorial: Rua do Veiga, 600, Santo Amaro, Recife 50040-110 **Tel:** 55 81 2122-7666
Email: faleconosco.pe@dabr.com.br **Web site:** http://www.diariodepernambuco.com.br
Freq: Daily; **Circ:** 30410
Editor, Primeira Página: Fred Figueiroa; **Editor:** Cleide Galdino; **Editor:** Ivana Moura; **Editor, Aurora:** Phelipe Rodrigues; **Editor:** Tatiana Sotero
Language (s): Portuguese
DAILY NEWSPAPER

Diário de S. Paulo 469730
Editorial: R. Rua Ricardo Cavatton, 251, Lapa de Baixo, Sao Paulo 05038-110 **Tel:** 55 11 3279-8500
Web site: http://www.diariosp.com.br
Freq: Daily; **Circ:** 10000
Editor, Viva: Soraia Gama; **Editor in Chief:** Nelson Nunes; **Editor, Dia a Dia:** Fernando Zanelato
Language (s): Portuguese
DAILY NEWSPAPER

Diário de Santa Bárbara 470292
Editorial: Rua Paulo de Moraes, 190, Centro, Santa Bárbara D'oeste 13450-036 **Tel:** 55 1934551062
Email: diariosbo@dglnet.com.br **Web site:** http://www.diariosbo.com.br
Freq: Daily; **Circ:** 11000 Not Audited
Editor in Chief: Maria de Camargo; **Editor:** Marcos Antônio de Oliveira
Language (s): Portuguese
DAILY NEWSPAPER

Diário de Santa Maria 157141
Owner: RBS Zero Hora Editora Jornalística S.A.
Editorial: Av. Mauricio Sirotsky Sobrinho, 25, Patronato, Santa Maria 97020-440 **Tel:** 55 55 3220-1700
Email: leitor@diariosm.com.br **Web site:** http://diariosm.com.br
Freq: Daily; **Circ:** 19000 Not Audited
Editor in Chief: Andreia Fontana
Language (s): Portuguese
DAILY NEWSPAPER

Diário de Sorocaba 470032
Editorial: Rua da Penha, 609, Centro, Sorocaba 18010-900 **Tel:** 55 1532244123
Email: reportagem@diariodesorocaba.com.br **Web site:** http://www.diariodesorocaba.com.br
Freq: Daily; **Circ:** 25000 Not Audited
Editor in Chief: Cláudio Grosso
Language (s): Portuguese
DAILY NEWSPAPER

Diário de Taubaté 469724
Editorial: Rua Engenheiro Fernando de Mattos, 23, Centro, Taubaté 12010-110 **Tel:** 55 1236331527
Email: redacao@diariotaubate.com.br **Web site:** http://www.diariotaubate.com.br
Freq: Daily; **Circ:** 8000
Director: Iara de Carvalho; **Editor in Chief:** Gláucia Moraes
Language (s): Portuguese
DAILY NEWSPAPER

Diário do Aço 470036
Editorial: Av Altina Goncalves, 95, Iguacu, Ipatinga 35160-016 **Tel:** 55 3138228998
Email: jornalismo@diariodoaco.com.br **Web site:** http://www.diariodoaco.com.br
Freq: Daily; **Circ:** 10800 Not Audited
Editor in Chief: João dos Reis
Language (s): Portuguese
DAILY NEWSPAPER

Diário do Alto Tietê 884701
Editorial: Rua Carlos Lacerda, 21, Vila Nova Cintra, Sao Paulo **Tel:** 55 11 4735-8000
Email: redacao@jornaldat.com.br **Web site:** http://www.jornaldat.com.br
Freq: Daily; **Circ:** 15000
Editor: Tiago Pantaleon
Profile: Offers local, regional, national and international news.
Language (s): Portuguese
DAILY NEWSPAPER

Diário do Amazonas 470037
Editorial: Avenida Djalma Batista, 2010, Bairro Chapada, Manaus 69050-010 **Tel:** 55 9236435060
Email: redacao@diarioam.com.br **Web site:** http://www.diarioam.com.br
Freq: Daily; **Circ:** 27000
Language (s): Portuguese
DAILY NEWSPAPER

Diário do Comércio 470013
Owner: Diário do Comércio
Editorial: Rua Boa Vista, 51 - 6 andar, Centro, Sao Paulo 01014-911
Email: editoracao@acsp.com.br **Web site:** http://www.dcomercio.com.br
Freq: Daily; **Circ:** 12000 Not Audited
Contributor: Paulo Brito; **Editor in Chief:** José Guilherme Rodrigues Ferreira
Profile: Covers local, regional, national and international news.
Language (s): Portuguese
DAILY NEWSPAPER

Diário do Comércio 470038
Editorial: Av. Americo Vespucio, 1660, Nova Esperanca, Belo Horizonte 31230-250
Tel: 55 31 3469-2011
Freq: Daily; **Circ:** 10000 Not Audited
Editor: Clério da Silva; **Editor:** Amaury de Pinho; **Editor:** Alexandre Horácio; **Editor:** Márcio Panzera
Language (s): Portuguese
DAILY NEWSPAPER

Diário do Comércio 470294
Editorial: Rua Agenor Paes, 122, Centro, Uberlândia 38400-118 **Tel:** 55 34 3235-4163
Email: contato@jornaldiariodocomercio.com.br **Web site:** http://www.jornaldiariodocomercio.com.br
Freq: Daily; **Circ:** 3000 Not Audited
Editor in Chief: José de Abreu
Language (s): Portuguese
DAILY NEWSPAPER

Diário do Grande ABC 469725
Editorial: Rua Catequese, 562, Centro, Santo André 09090-900 **Tel:** 55 11 4435-8117
Email: dgabconline@gmail.com **Web site:** http://www.dgabc.com.br
Circ: 47000
Editor in Chief: Evaldo Novelini
Language (s): Portuguese
Ad Rate: Full Page Mono 408.94
Ad Rate: Full Page Colour 408.94
Currency: Brazil Reais
DAILY NEWSPAPER

Diário do Litoral 470293
Editorial: Rua General Câmara, 254, Centro, Santos 11010-122 **Tel:** 55 1332262051
Email: editor@diariodolitoral.com.br **Web site:** http://www.diariodolitoral.com.br
Freq: Daily; **Circ:** 32000 Not Audited
Editor in Chief: Tatiane Casemiro
Language (s): Portuguese
DAILY NEWSPAPER

Diário do Litoral Norte 470311
Editorial: Rua Luiz Barreto Barbosa, 359, Centro, Ilha Bela 11630-000 **Tel:** 55 1238961720
Email: diariodolitoralnorte@uol.com.br **Web site:** http://www.oancoradouro.com.br
Freq: Daily; **Circ:** 3000 Not Audited
Editor in Chief: Heloísa Franco
Profile: Note: This outlet has the same telephone and fax number. To send a fax, one must call and request that the telephone line be switched to a fax line.
Language (s): Portuguese
DAILY NEWSPAPER

Diário do Nordeste 469726
Owner: Editora Verdes Mares Ltda.
Editorial: Praca da Imprensa, s/n, Dionísio Torres, Fortaleza 60135-690 **Tel:** 55 85 3266-9773
Web site: http://diariodonordeste.verdesmares.com.br
Freq: Daily; **Circ:** 38857
Cinema Crictic: Pedro Martins Freire; **Editor:** Dellano Rios; **Editor in Chief:** Ildefonso Rodrigues
Language (s): Portuguese
DAILY NEWSPAPER

Diário do Noroeste 470040
Editorial: Av. Parana, 1100, Centro, Paranavaí 87705-190 **Tel:** 55 4434214050

Email: paranavai@diariodonoroeste.com.br **Web site:** http://www.diariodonoroeste.com.br
Freq: Daily; **Circ:** 10600 Not Audited
Editor in Chief: Valdinei Feitosa Dos Santos
Language (s): Portuguese
DAILY NEWSPAPER

O Diário do Norte do Paraná 470321
Editorial: Av. Maua, 1988, Vila Operaria, Maringá 87050-020 **Tel:** 55 4432216055
Email: redacao@odiariomaringa.com.br **Web site:** http://www.odiariomaringa.com.br
Freq: Daily; **Circ:** 18500 Not Audited
Language (s): Portuguese
DAILY NEWSPAPER

Diário do Pará 469728
Editorial: Avenida Almirante Barroso, 2190 - 1 andar, Marco, Belèm 66095-000 **Tel:** 55 91 3084-0100
Web site: http://www.diariodopara.com.br
Freq: Daily; **Circ:** 10000 Not Audited
Editor: Adaucto Couto; **Editor:** Camila Gaia; **Editor, Auto Destaque:** Victor Pinto; **Editor, Brasil:** Carlos Queiroz
Language (s): Portuguese
DAILY NEWSPAPER

Diário do Povo 469729
Editorial: Rua Sete de Setembro, 189, Vila Industrial, Campinas 13035-350 **Tel:** 55 1937728000
Web site: http://www.diariodopovo.com.br
Freq: Daily; **Circ:** 15000 Not Audited
Editor: Roselaine Fontana; **Editor in Chief:** Alayr Ruiz
Profile: <NAIAS> O Diário do Povo faz parte da Rede Anhangüera de Comunicação. Sob administração da RAC, o Diário do Povo cresceu ainda mais, ganhando novo projeto gráfico e uma nova linha editorial que privilegia textos leves, concisos e completos. Seu exemplar tem preço de venda acessível, o que o coloca ao alcance de todas as classes sociais.
Language (s): Portuguese
DAILY NEWSPAPER

Diário do Rio Doce 470042
Editorial: Rua Marechal Deodoro, 715, Centro, Governador Valadares 35010-280
Tel: 55 3321012101
Email: diario@drd.com.br **Web site:** http://www.drd.com.br
Freq: Daily; **Circ:** 14000 Not Audited
Language (s): Portuguese
DAILY NEWSPAPER

Diário do Sudoeste 470625
Editorial: Rua Caramuru, 1267, Centro, Pato Branco 85501-060 **Tel:** 55 46 32202066
Email: redacao@diariodosudoeste.com.br **Web site:** http://www.diariodosudoeste.com.br
Freq: Daily; **Circ:** 15000 Not Audited
Editor in Chief: Rosselani Giordani
Language (s): Portuguese
DAILY NEWSPAPER

Diário do Vale 470044
Editorial: Rue 25A, 23 Vila Santa Cecilia, Volta Redonda 27260 **Tel:** 55 2433408500
Email: redacao@diariodovale.com.br **Web site:** http://www.diariodovale.com.br
Freq: Daily; **Circ:** 15000 Not Audited
Editor: Cláudio Alcântara; **Editor in Chief:** Sônia Paes
Profile: Note: This outlet has the same telephone and fax number. To send a fax, one must call and request that the telephone line be switched to a fax line.
Language (s): Portuguese
DAILY NEWSPAPER

Diário Gaúcho 157138
Owner: RBS Zero Hora Editora Jornalistica S.A.
Editorial: Avenida Ipiranga 1075, Azenha, Porto Alegre 90160-093 **Tel:** 55 51 3218-1685
Email: atendimento@diariogaucho.com.br **Web site:** http://www.diariogaucho.com.br
Freq: Daily; **Circ:** 162778 Not Audited
Editor: Luiz Domingues; **Editor:** Flávia Requião
Language (s): Portuguese
DAILY NEWSPAPER

Diário Popular 470045
Editorial: Rua XV de Novembro, 718, Centro, Pelotas 96015-000 **Tel:** 55 53 3284-7000
Email: diariopopular@diariopopular.com.br **Web site:** http://www.diariopopular.com.br
Freq: Daily; **Circ:** 18000 Not Audited
Editor In Chief: Ivan Rodrigues
Profile: Covers local, regional, national and international news.
Language (s): Portuguese
DAILY NEWSPAPER

Empresas & Negócios 658747
Owner: Jornal Empresas & Negócios Ltda
Editorial: Rua Boa Vista, 84, 9 andar cj. 909, Sao Paulo 01014-000 **Tel:** 55 11 3106-4171
Web site: http://www.jornalempresasenegocios.com.br
Freq: Daily
Advertising Manager: J. L. Lobato; **Editor:** Laura Lobato De Baptisti
Language (s): Portuguese
DAILY NEWSPAPER

Estado de Minas 469731
Owner: Diários Associados
Editorial: Avenida Getulio Vargas, 291, Bairro Funcionarios, Belo Horizonte 30112-020
Tel: 55 31 3263-5800
Email: fale.conosco@em.com.br **Web site:** http://www.em.com.br
Freq: Daily; **Circ:** 130000
Editor: Paulo Eduardo de Queiroz; **Editor:** Ângela Márcia de Barros Faria; **Editor:** Pedro Lobato; **Editor in Chief:** João Bosco Salles; **Editor:** Ney Soares Filho
Language (s): Portuguese
DAILY NEWSPAPER

O Estado de São Paulo 156863
Owner: Grupo Estado
Editorial: Av. Eng. Caetano alvares 55, Sao Paulo 02598-900
Web site: http://www.estadao.com.br
Freq: Daily; **Circ:** 201395
Editor: Roberto Bascchera; **Editor:** Ubiratan Brasil; **Editor, Política:** Conrado Corsalette; **Editor in Chief:** Cida Damasco; **Editor, Divirta-se:** Adriana Del Ré; **Editor, Paladar:** Patrícia Ferraz; **Editor:** Ricardo Grinbaum; **Editor:** Roberto Lameirinhas; **Editor:** Cátia Luz; **Editor, Aliás:** Mônica Manir; **Editor:** Cláudio Marques; **Editor, Viagem:** Adriana Moreira; **Editor, Jornal do Carro:** Tião Oliveira; **Editor:** Cristina Padiglione; **Editor, Casa:** Marina Pauliquevis; **Editor:** Sônia Racy
Profile: Founded in 1875 and has the second largest circulation in the City of São Paulo. Provides regional, national and international news covering politics, economy, sports, culture, education and science.
Language (s): Portuguese
Ad Rate: Full Page Mono 2606.04
Ad Rate: Full Page Colour 2606.04
Currency: Brazil Reais
DAILY NEWSPAPER

O Estado do Maranhão 469976
Editorial: Avenida Ana Jansen, 200, Sao Francisco, São Luís 65076-902 **Tel:** 55 98 3215-5162
Email: redacao@mirante.com.br **Web site:** http://www.oestadoma.com.br
Freq: Daily; **Circ:** 20000 Not Audited
Editor: Ironara Martins
Language (s): Portuguese
DAILY NEWSPAPER

Expresso 470652
Editorial: Rua Irineu Marinho, 70 - 4 andar, Cidade Nova, Rio De Janeiro 20230-901 **Tel:** 55 21 2534-9751
Web site: http://www.infoglobo.com.br
Freq: Daily; **Circ:** 63285
Editor in Chief: Marco Antonio Rocha
Language (s): Portuguese
DAILY NEWSPAPER

Extra 469700
Editorial: Rua Irineu Marinho, 70 - 4 andar, Cidade Nova, Rio De Janeiro 20230-901 **Tel:** 55 21 2534-5900
Web site: http://extra.globo.com
Freq: Daily; **Circ:** 347366
Editor: Roberta Ferraz; **Editor:** Gilmar Ferreira;
Editor in Chief: Octavio Guedes
Language (s): Portuguese
DAILY NEWSPAPER

O Fluminense 469770
Editorial: Rua Visconde de Itaborai, 184, Centro, Niterói 24035-900 **Tel:** 55 21 2125-3057
Email: reportagem@ofluminense.com.br **Web site:** http://www.ofluminense.com.br
Freq: Daily; **Circ:** 55000
Editor in Chief: Sandra Duarte; **Editor:** Fabiana Maia
Language (s): Portuguese
DAILY NEWSPAPER

Folha da Manhã 469704
Editorial: Rua Carlos de Lacerda, 75, Centro, Campos Dos Goytacazes 28013-030
Tel: 55 22 2726-8585
Email: online@fmanha.com.br **Web site:** http://www.folha1.com.br
Freq: Daily; **Circ:** 20000 Not Audited
Editor: Dora Paula Paes
Profile: O Jornal Folha da Manhã circula nas seguintes cidades: Campos dos Goytacazes, Aperibé, Bom Jesus do Itabapoana, Cambuci, Cardoso Moreira, Carapebus, Casimiro de Abreu, Conceição de Macabu, Italva, Itaocara, Macaé, Miracema, Natividade, Porciúncula, Quissamã, Rio das Ostras, Santo Antônio de Pádua, São Fidélis, São Francisco do Itabapoana, São João da Barra e Varre-Sai.
Language (s): Portuguese
DAILY NEWSPAPER

Folha da Manhã 469732
Editorial: Rua 2 de Novembro, 206, Centro, Passos 37900-128 **Tel:** 55 35 35292750
Email: folha@folhadamanha.com.br **Web site:** http://www.folhadamanha.com.br
Freq: Daily; **Circ:** 10000 Not Audited
News Director: Carlos Antônio Parreira; **Editor in Chief:** Marcelo Renato Silva
Language (s): Portuguese
DAILY NEWSPAPER

Folha da Região 470052
Editorial: Rua Joaquim Fernandes, 445, Jardim Nova Iorque, Araçatuba 16018-280 **Tel:** 55 1836367774
Email: redacao@folhadaregiao.com.br **Web site:** http://www.folhadaregiao.com.br
Freq: Daily; **Circ:** 12800 Not Audited
Editor in Chief: Maria Antônio Dario
Profile: Note: This outlet has the same telephone and fax number. To send a fax, one must call and request that the telephone line be switched to a fax line.
Language (s): Portuguese
DAILY NEWSPAPER

Folha de Boa Vista 469733
Editorial: Rua Lobo D'almada, 21, Sao Francisco, Boa Vista 69305-050 **Tel:** 55 95 3623-8806
Email: fale@folhabv.com.br **Web site:** http://www.folhabv.com.br
Freq: Daily; **Circ:** 8000 Not Audited
Director: Nazaré Cruz; **Editor in Chief:** Loide Gomes; **Editor in Chief:** Jessé Souza
Language (s): Portuguese
DAILY NEWSPAPER

Folha de Londrina 469734
Editorial: Rua Piaui, 241, Centro, Londrina 86010-420 **Tel:** 55 43 3374-2020
Email: editoria@folhadelondrina.com.br **Web site:** http://www.folhadelondrina.com.br
Freq: Daily; **Circ:** 37000 Not Audited
Editor in Chief: Fernanda Mazzini
Language (s): Portuguese
DAILY NEWSPAPER

Folha de Pernambuco 469800
Editorial: Avenida Marquês de Olinda, 105, Bairro do Recife Antigo, Recife 50030-000 **Tel:** 55 81 3425-5877
Email: redacao@folhape.com.br **Web site:** http://www.folhape.com.br
Freq: Daily; **Circ:** 30948
Editor: Cynthia Morato; **Editor in Chief:** Patrícia Raposo; **Editor:** Paulo Salgado
Language (s): Portuguese
DAILY NEWSPAPER

Folha de São Paulo 157083
Owner: Folha de S.Paulo
Editorial: Al. Barao de Limeira, 425, Campos Eliseos, Sao Paulo 01202-900 **Tel:** 55 11 3224-3000
Email: lector@grupofolha.com.br **Web site:** http://www.folha.uol.com.br
Freq: Daily; **Circ:** 318872
Editor, Poder: Ricardo Balthazar; **Editor at Large:** Silvio Cioffi; **Editor, Turismo & Comida:** Luiza Fecarotta; **Editor at Large:** Erica Fraga; **Editor, Mercado Aberto:** Cristina Frias; **Editor, Illustrada:** Heloísa Helvécia; **Editor, Painel FC:** Bernardo Itri; **Editor, Folhinha:** Laura Mattos; **Editor at Large:** Fernanda Mena; **Contributor, Mundo:** Luisa Pessoa; **Editor, Mercado:** Ana Estela Pinto; **Editor:** Leticia Sander; **Editor, Equilíbrio, Saúde & Ciência:** Mariana Versolato
Profile: Founded in 1921 and covers local, regional, national and international news, as well as business, politics, economy, entertainment, science, technology, lifestyle and sports.
Language (s): Portuguese
Ad Rate: Full Page Mono 2552.70
Ad Rate: Full Page Colour 2552.70
Currency: Brazil Reais
DAILY NEWSPAPER

Folha do Estado 470054
Editorial: Rua Professora Tereza Lobo, 319, Consil, Cuiabá 78048-670 **Tel:** 55 6533177700
Email: redacao@folhadoestado.com.br **Web site:** http://www.folhadoestado.com.br
Freq: Daily; **Circ:** 28000
Editor in Chief: Marisa Batalha; **Editor:** Janaina Pedrotti
Language (s): Portuguese
DAILY NEWSPAPER

Folha do Povo 469938
Editorial: Rua Pedro Coutinho, 97, Jardim dos Estados, Campo Grande 79020-280 **Tel:** 55 67 3213-0309
Email: redacao@folhadopovo.com.br **Web site:** http://www.folhadopovo.com.br
Freq: Daily; **Circ:** 12000 Not Audited
Editor in Chief: José Roberto Moura Alves
Language (s): Portuguese
DAILY NEWSPAPER

Folha Metropolitana 470057
Editorial: Rua Ipê, 144, Jardim Guarulhos, Guarulhos 07090-130 **Tel:** 55 11 2475-7800
Email: redacao@folhametro.com.br
Freq: Daily; **Circ:** 60000 Not Audited
Editor: Paulo Manso
Language (s): Portuguese
DAILY NEWSPAPER

A Gazeta 161005
Owner: A Gazeta SA
Editorial: Rua Chafic Murad, 902, Ilha De Monte Belo, Vitoria 29050-901 **Tel:** 55 27 3321-8526
Web site: http://www.gazetaonline.com.br
Freq: Daily; **Circ:** 45000
Editor: Cintia Bento Alves; **Editor:** Lúcia Helena Gonçalves; **Editor:** Zainer Rodrigues Silva; **Editor:** Leonel Ximenes
Profile: Offers local, regional, national and international news.
Language (s): Portuguese
DAILY NEWSPAPER

A Gazeta 469986
Editorial: Rua Professora Tereza Lobo, 30, Bairro Concil, Cuiabá 78048-700 **Tel:** 55 6536126000
Email: red.jornal@gazetadigital.com.br **Web site:** http://www.gazetadigital.com.br
Freq: Daily; **Circ:** 16000 Not Audited
Editor in Chief: Margareth Botelho; **Editor:** Oliveira Júnior
Language (s): Portuguese
DAILY NEWSPAPER

Gazeta de Alagoas 469736
Editorial: Rua Saladanha da Gama, Farol, Maceió 57051-020 **Tel:** 55 82 4009-7748
Email: gazeta@gazetaweb.com **Web site:** http://www.gazetaweb.com
Freq: Daily; **Circ:** 18000 Not Audited
Editor: Fernando Coelho; **Editor in Chief:** Célio Gomes; **Editor:** Enio Lins; **Editor, Gazeta Informática:** Valdick Salles
Language (s): Portuguese
DAILY NEWSPAPER

Gazeta de Limeira 470058
Editorial: Rua Senador Vergueiro, 319, Centro, Limeira 13480-000 **Tel:** 55 19 3404-3700
Email: gazeta@gazetadelimeira.com.br **Web site:** http://www.gazetadelimeira.com.br
Freq: Daily; **Circ:** 15000 Not Audited
Editor: José Antônio Encinas; **Editor:** Fabiana Lucato; **Editor in Chief:** Roberto Lucato; **Director:** Eduardo Lucato Neto
Profile: Note: This outlet has the same telephone and fax number. To send a fax, one must call and request that the telephone line be switched to a fax line.
Language (s): Portuguese
DAILY NEWSPAPER

Gazeta de Varginha 469737
Editorial: Av. dos Imigrantes, 445, Santa Maria, Varginha 37022-560 **Tel:** 55 35 3221-4668
Email: gazetavga@varginha.com.br **Web site:** http://www.gazetadevarginha.blogspot.com
Freq: Daily; **Circ:** 15000 Not Audited
Editor: Rodrigo Fernandes; **Editor in Chief:** Ana Maria Silva Piva
Language (s): Portuguese
DAILY NEWSPAPER

Gazeta do Paraná 470061
Editorial: Rua Fortunato Bebber, 868, Cascavel 85808-390 **Tel:** 55 45 3218-2500
Web site: http://www.gazetadoparana.com.br
Freq: Daily; **Circ:** 29000
Editor in Chief: Paulo Alexandre De Oliveira
Language (s): Portuguese
DAILY NEWSPAPER

Gazeta do Povo 469699
Editorial: Rua Pedro Ivo, 459, Centro, Curitiba 80010-020 **Tel:** 55 41 3321-5000
Web site: http://www.gazetadopovo.com.br
Freq: Daily; **Circ:** 100000 Not Audited
Editor: Keyse Caldeira; **Editor:** Deise Campos; **Editor:** José Carlos Fernandes; **Editor in Chief:** Sandra Gonçalves; **Editor:** Célio Martins; **Editor, Automóveis:** Roberto Massignan Filho
Language (s): Portuguese
DAILY NEWSPAPER

Gazeta do Sul 470062
Owner: Gazeta Grupo de Comunicações
Editorial: Rua Ramiro Barcelos, 1206, Santa Cruz Do Sul 96901-900 **Tel:** 55 51 3715-7800
Email: redacao@gazetadosul.com.br **Web site:** http://www.gazetadosul.com.br
Freq: Daily; **Circ:** 18000 Not Audited
Editor in Chief: Maria Roselaine Romero
Language (s): Portuguese
DAILY NEWSPAPER

Gazeta Mundial 469914
Editorial: Rua Largo Sao Vicente de Paulo, 133, Ed. ACIT - Salas 61, 65 e 80, Toledo 85900215
Tel: 55 4530557070
Email: editora@gazetamundial.com.br **Web site:** http://www.gazetamundial.com.br
Freq: Daily; **Circ:** 13000 Not Audited
Editor in Chief: Selma Becker
Language (s): Portuguese
DAILY NEWSPAPER

O Globo 469771
Editorial: Rua Irineu Marinho, 35, Cidade Nova, Rio De Janeiro 20230-901 **Tel:** 55 21 2534-5000
Email: ccr@oglobo.com.br **Web site:** http://oglobo.globo.com
Freq: Daily; **Circ:** 364037
Editor, Ciência & Saúde: Ana Lucia Azevedo; **Editor, Mundo:** Sandra Cohen; **Editor, Morar Bem & Boa Chance:** Léa Cristina; **Editor, Revista da TV:** Valquíria Daher; **Editor, País:** Fernanda Escóssia; **Editor, Revista O Globo:** Gabriela Goulart; **Editor, Informática:** André Machado; **Editor, Opinião:** Aluízio Maranhão; **Editor, Prosa & Verso:** Manya Millen; **Editor, Bairros:** Adriana Oliveira; **Editor, Segundo Caderno:** Fátima Sá; **Editor, Rio:** Gilberto Scofield; **Editor, Carros e Etc.:** Jason Vogel
Profile: Launched in 1925 and offers local, national and international news in Brazil.
Language (s): Portuguese
DAILY NEWSPAPER

Hoje em Dia 469739
Editorial: Rua Padre Rolim, 652, Santa Efigênia, Belo Horizonte 30130-090 **Tel:** 55 31 3236-8000
Web site: http://www.hojeemdia.com.br
Freq: Daily; **Circ:** 54000 Not Audited
Editor: Paulo Leonardo de Carvalho; **Editor in Chief:** Pérsio Fantin; **Editor:** Roberto Mendonça; **Editor:** Ruy José Pales; **Editor:** Leida Reis
Language (s): Portuguese
DAILY NEWSPAPER

Hora de Santa Catarina 470664
Editorial: Avenida Desembargador Pedro Silva, 2958, Itaguacu, Florianópolis 88080-701
Tel: 55 48 3216-3970
Email: redacao@horasc.com.br **Web site:** http://horadesantacatarina.clicrbs.com.br/sc/
Circ: 28398 Not Audited
Editor in Chief: Sergio Negrão
Profile: Daily newspaper of Santa Catarina state, in the southern region of Brazil.
Language (s): Portuguese
DAILY NEWSPAPER

O Imparcial 157184
Owner: Empresa Pacotilha Ltda.
Editorial: Rua Assis Chateaubriand, S/N, Renascenca II, #NAME? 65075-670
Tel: 55 98 3212 2000
Email: redacao@pacotilha.com.br **Web site:** http://www.oimparcial.com.br
Freq: Daily; **Circ:** 15000
Editor in Chief: Marco Aurélio Oliveira; **Editor:** José Ribamar Praseres
Language (s): Portuguese
DAILY NEWSPAPER

O Imparcial 469772
Editorial: Rua Ernesto Rotta, 83, Jardim Novo Bongiovani, Presidente Prudente 19026-900
Tel: 55 18 2104-3737
Email: online@oimparcial.com.br **Web site:** http://www.oimparcial.com.br
Freq: Daily; **Circ:** 12000 Not Audited
Director: Mário Peretti; **Editor in Chief:** Adelmo Santos Rei Vanalli
Language (s): Portuguese
DAILY NEWSPAPER

Imprensa Oficial de Minas Gerais 469797
Owner: Governo de Minas Gerais
Editorial: Avenida Augusto de Lima, 270, Centro, Belo Horizonte 30190-001 **Tel:** 55 3132373453
Email: libertas@iof.mg.gov.br **Web site:** http://www.iof.mg.gov.br
Freq: Daily; **Circ:** 40000 Not Audited
Editor: Afonso de Oliveira
Profile: Minas Gerais é um jornal de caráter oficial para divulgação de atos do governo, decretos e regulamentos que devam ter execução no Estado, compreendendo os cadernos: O Noticiário Diário do Executivo Diário do Legislativo Diário do Judiciário Publicação de Terceiros
Language (s): Portuguese
DAILY NEWSPAPER

Indústria & Comércio 470064
Editorial: Rua Imaculada Conceicao, 205, Reboucas, Curitiba 80215-030 **Tel:** 55 4133339800
Email: pauta@induscom.com.br **Web site:** http://induscom.com.br
Freq: Daily; **Circ:** 10000 Not Audited
Editor in Chief: Eliseu Tisato
Language (s): Portuguese
DAILY NEWSPAPER

Jornal Bom Dia 905874
Editorial: Av. Santo dal Bosco, 97, Erechim 99700-000 **Tel:** 55 54 3520-8500
Email: jornalismo@jornalbomdia.com.br **Web site:** http://www.jornalbomdia.com.br
Circ: 16900
Editora Chefe/Editor in Chief: Rosa Liberman
Profile: Traz informações e notícias de interesse aos habitantes de Erechim e regiões próximas. Provides news for the residents of Erechim and surrounding areas.
Language (s): Portuguese
DAILY NEWSPAPER

Jornal Cidade de Rio Claro 470067
Editorial: Av. Cinco, 283, Centro, Rio Claro 13500-380 **Tel:** 55 1935261000
Email: redacaojc@uol.com.br **Web site:** http://www.journalcidade.net
Freq: Daily; **Circ:** 10000 Not Audited
Editor in Chief: Ludimar Gonzalez
Profile: O Jornal Cidade é expressão viva da imprensa moderna, dinâmica e completa. Pesquisas de mercado revelam a satisfação dos anunciantes pelo retorno garantido a partir de suas veiculações publicitárias. Pioneirismos são as grandes marcas do JC. Sempre presente aos eventos de estímulo ao desenvolvimento empresarial, o JC mantém dinâmica parceria junto a destacadas promoções, como Feira das Noivas, Feira Anual do Comércio e Indústria de Rio Claro (Facirc), ciclo de palestras do grupo empresarial Opção, jogos esportivos do Sesi, serviço de divulgação da Associação dos Corretores de Imóveis de Rio Claro, bem como da rede de supermercados do município.
Language (s): Portuguese
DAILY NEWSPAPER

Jornal Coletivo 470649
Editorial: SIG Quadra 2, Lote 570/590, Brasilia 70610-420 **Tel:** 55 61 3441-0212
Email: redacao@maiscomunidade.com **Web site:** http://www.jornalcoletivo.com.br
Freq: Daily; **Circ:** 90000
Editor in Chief: Ricardo Callado
Language (s): Portuguese
DAILY NEWSPAPER

Jornal da Cidade 469742
Editorial: Rua Xingu, 4-44, Higienopolis, Bauru 17013-510 **Tel:** 55 14 3104-3104
Email: jc@jcnet.com.br **Web site:** http://www.jcnet.com.br
Freq: Daily; **Circ:** 28000 Not Audited
Editor: Eliane Barbosa; **Editor:** Giselle Hilário
Language (s): Portuguese
DAILY NEWSPAPER

Jornal da Cidade 470070
Editorial: Avenida Antônio Cabral, 1069, Bairro Industrial, Aracaju 49065-090 **Tel:** 55 79 3226-4800
Email: redacao@jornaldacidade.net **Web site:** http://www.jornaldacidade.net
Freq: Daily; **Circ:** 20000 Not Audited
Editor: Dilson Ramos; **Editor In Chief:** Acácia Trindade
Language (s): Portuguese
DAILY NEWSPAPER

Jornal da Manhã 470074
Editorial: Avenida Dr. Fidelis Reis, 820, Bairro Boa Vista, Uberaba 38010-030 **Tel:** 55 34 3331-7900
Email: jmonline@jmonline.com.br **Web site:** http://www.jmonline.com.br
Freq: Daily; **Circ:** 15000 Not Audited
Editor in Chief: Marcio Gennari; **Editor:** Marilo Teixeira
Language (s): Portuguese
DAILY NEWSPAPER

Jornal da Manhã 470077
Editorial: Rua 15 de Novembro, 883, Centro, Marília 17500-050 **Tel:** 55 1433115400
Email: jmanha@terra.com.br **Web site:** http://www.jornaldamanhamarilia.com.br
Freq: Daily; **Circ:** 18000 Not Audited
Editor in Chief: Jocelin de Oliveira
Language (s): Portuguese
DAILY NEWSPAPER

Jornal da Mantiqueira 470078
Editorial: Av. Joao Pinheiro, 177, Centro, Poços De Caldas 37701-387 **Tel:** 55 3537290007
Email: redacao@mantiqueira.inf.br **Web site:** http://www.mantiqueira.inf.br
Freq: Daily; **Circ:** 5000
Editor in Chief: Rui Alves
Profile: Note: This outlet has the same telephone and fax number. To send a fax, one must call and request that the telephone line be switched to a fax line.
Language (s): Portuguese
DAILY NEWSPAPER

Jornal de Brasília 470085
Editorial: SIG, Trecho 1, Lotes 585/645, Brasilia 70610-400 **Tel:** 55 61 3343-8070
Email: redacao@jornaldebrasilia.com.br **Web site:** http://www.jornaldebrasilia.com.br
Freq: Daily; **Circ:** 14000 Not Audited
Editor in Chief: Paulo Gusmão
Profile: Offers local, regional, national and international news.
Language (s): Portuguese
DAILY NEWSPAPER

Jornal de Jundiaí 470087
Editorial: Rua Baronesa de Japi, 53, Centro, Jundiaí 13207-000 **Tel:** 55 1121366070
Email: redacao@jj.com.br **Web site:** http://www.portaljj.com.br
Freq: Daily; **Circ:** 25000
Editor: Luciana Alves; **Editor:** Isabel Bueno; **Editor:** Sandra Marques; **Editor in Chief:** Sidney Mazzoni
Language (s): Portuguese
DAILY NEWSPAPER

Jornal de Limeira 470088
Editorial: Av. Comendador Agostinho Prada, 2651, Jardim Florenca, Limeira 13480-220
Tel: 55 19 34045050
Email: redacao@jornaldelimeira.com.br **Web site:** http://www.jlmais.com
Freq: Daily; **Circ:** 14000 Not Audited
Editor in Chief: Carlos Chinellato
Profile: Note: This outlet has the same telephone and fax number. To send a fax, one must call and request that the telephone line be switched to a fax line.
Language (s): Portuguese
DAILY NEWSPAPER

Jornal de Piracicaba 470093
Editorial: Avenida Comendador Luciano Guidotti, 2525, Jardim Pacaembu, Piracicaba 13424-589
Tel: 55 19 3428-4170
Email: jp@jpjornal.com.br **Web site:** http://www.jornaldepiracicaba.com.br
Freq: Daily; **Circ:** 25000 Not Audited
Editor: Simone Cândido; **Editor:** Eleni Destro; **Editor:** Ude Valetim
Language (s): Portuguese
DAILY NEWSPAPER

Jornal de Santa Catarina Newspaper 157143
Owner: RBS Zero Hora Editora Jornalistica S.A.
Editorial: Rua Bahia 2291, Salto, Blumenau 89031-002 **Tel:** 55 47 3221-1555
Web site: http://www.santa.com.br
Freq: Daily; **Circ:** 14798 Not Audited
Editor in Chief: Edgar Gonçalves
Profile: Covers local, regional, national and international news.
Language (s): Portuguese
DAILY NEWSPAPER

Jornal de Uberaba 470094
Editorial: Avenida Leopoldino de Oliveira, 2265, Centro, Uberaba 38015-000 **Tel:** 55 3433184433
Email: jjura@terra.com.br **Web site:** http://www.jornaldeuberaba.com.br
Freq: Daily; **Circ:** 18000
Editor in Chief: Walter Farnezi
Profile: Note: This outlet has the same telephone and fax number. To send a fax, one must call and request that the telephone line be switched to a fax line. O Jornal de Uberaba oferece aos leitores toda informação sobre os acontecimentos políticos, sociais, econômicos, esportivos, classificados e serviços de utilidade pública da região.
Language (s): Portuguese
DAILY NEWSPAPER

Jornal do Comércio 470095
Editorial: Avenida Joao Pessoa, 1282, Cidade Baixa, Porto Alegre 90040-001 **Tel:** 55 51 3213-1300
Web site: http://jcrs.uol.com.br
Freq: Mon thru Fri; **Circ:** 30000 Not Audited
Editor in Chief: Pedro Maciel; **Editor:** Paula Sória
Profile: Jornal do Comércio is a daily newspaper and covers local, regional, national and international news, as well as business, entertainment, lifestyle and sports.
Language (s): Portuguese
DAILY NEWSPAPER

Jornal do Commercio 469743
Editorial: Avenida Tefe, 3025, Japiim, Manaus 69078-000 **Tel:** 55 9221015500
Email: redacao@jcam.com.br **Web site:** http://www.jcam.com.br
Freq: Daily; **Circ:** 11500 Not Audited
Editor: Lilian Araújo
Language (s): Portuguese
DAILY NEWSPAPER

Jornal do Commercio 469746
Editorial: Rua da Fundicao, 257, Santo Amaro, Recife 50040-100 **Tel:** 55 81 3413-6178
Email: jconline@jc.com.br **Web site:** http://jconline.ne10.uol.com.br
Freq: Daily; **Circ:** 53257
Editor, Veículos: Silvio Menezes
Profile: Offers local, regional, national and international news.
Language (s): Portuguese
DAILY NEWSPAPER

Jornal do Dia 469747
Editorial: Rua Mato Grosso, 296, Tacoval, Macapá 68908-350 **Tel:** 55 96 3217-1117
Email: jornaldodia1@uol.com.br **Web site:** http://www.jdia.com.br
Freq: Daily; **Circ:** 10000 Not Audited
Editor in Chief: Janderson Cantanhede; **Editor:** Marcele Correa; **Director:** Lúcia Theresa Pereira; **President:** Maria Inerine Pereira
Language (s): Portuguese
DAILY NEWSPAPER

Jornal do Estado 470097
Editorial: Rua Roberto Barrozo, 22, Centro Cívico, Curitiba 80530-120 **Tel:** 55 41 3350-6600
Email: je@jornaldoestado.com.br **Web site:** http://www.jornaldoestado.com.br
Freq: Daily; **Circ:** 10000 Not Audited
Editor in Chief: Josianne Ritz
Language (s): Portuguese
DAILY NEWSPAPER

Jornal Hora H 470106
Editorial: Rua Alexander Gama Correia, 37, Rancho Novo, Nova Iguaçu 26013-190 **Tel:** 55 2126955360
Email: editoriahorah@ig.com.br **Web site:** http://www.jornalhorah.com.br
Freq: Daily; **Circ:** 20000 Not Audited
News Director: José Roberto de Lemos; **Editor in Chief:** Hélio Sampaio
Profile: Note: This outlet has the same telephone and fax number. To send a fax, one must call and request that the telephone line be switched to a fax line.
Language (s): Portuguese
DAILY NEWSPAPER

Jornal NH 470108
Editorial: Rua Jornal NH, 99, Bairro Ideal, Novo Hamburgo 93334-350 **Tel:** 55 51 3065-4000
Email: redacaomultimidia@gruposinos.com.br **Web site:** http://www.jornalnh.com.br
Freq: Daily; **Circ:** 45248 Not Audited
Editor in Chief: Sérgio Pereira
Language (s): Portuguese
DAILY NEWSPAPER

Jornal VS (Vale dos Sinos) 469945
Editorial: Av. Joao Corrêa, 1017, Centro, São Leopoldo 93020-690 **Tel:** 55 5135912000
Email: redacaovs@gruposinos.com.br **Web site:** http://www.jornalvs.com.br
Freq: Daily; **Circ:** 17405 Not Audited
Editor in Chief: Guilherme Schmidt
Language (s): Portuguese
DAILY NEWSPAPER

Lance! 470011
Editorial: Rua Santa Maria, 47, Cidade Nova, Rio De Janeiro 20211-210 **Tel:** 55 21 3528-5200
Email: redacao-rj@lancenet.com.br **Web site:** http://www.lancenet.com.br
Freq: Daily; **Circ:** 47790 Not Audited
Editor in Chief: Luiz Fernando Gomes
Language (s): Portuguese
DAILY NEWSPAPER

O Liberal 469773
Editorial: Avenida 25 de Setembro, 2473, Marco, Belèm 66093-000 **Tel:** 55 91 3216-1000
Email: redacao@orm.com.br **Web site:** http://www.ormnews.com.br/oliberal
Freq: Daily; **Circ:** 87000
Editor: Orlando Cardoso; **Editor in Chief:** Walmir D' Oliveira; **Editor:** Cary John; **Editor:** Myrian Magalhães; **Editor:** Raimundo Souza
Profile: Offers local, national and international news.
Language (s): Portuguese
DAILY NEWSPAPER

O Liberal 470331
Editorial: Rua Tamoio, 875, Vila Santa Catarina, Americana 13466-250 **Tel:** 55 1934710300
Email: redacao@liberal.com.br **Web site:** http://www.oliberalnet.com.br
Freq: Daily; **Circ:** 15000 Not Audited
Editor: Diógenes Gobbo
Profile: O Jornal O Liberal é publicado pela Empresa Editora O Liberal Ltda., circula em Americana, Santa Bárbara d'Oeste, Nova Odessa e Sumaré.
Language (s): Portuguese
Ad Rate: Full Page Mono 64.77
Ad Rate: Full Page Colour 100.33
Currency: Brazil Reais
DAILY NEWSPAPER

Meia Hora 470653
Editorial: Rua do Riachuelo, 359 - 2 andar, Centro, Rio De Janeiro 20235-902 **Tel:** 55 21 2222-8000
Email: povo@meiahora.com **Web site:** http://www.meiahora.ig.com.br
Freq: Daily; **Circ:** 120000 Not Audited
Editor in Chief: Humberto Tziolas
Language (s): Portuguese
DAILY NEWSPAPER

Meio Norte 469748
Editorial: Rua Professor Alceu Brandao, 2750, Monte Castelo, Teresina 64016-150 **Tel:** 55 86 21073070
Email: meionorte@meionorte.com **Web site:** http://www.meionorte.com
Freq: Daily; **Circ:** 8000
Editor: Tatiara de França
Profile: Meio Norte is a daily newspaper and covers local, regional, national and international news, as well as business, entertainment, lifestyle and sports. The paper was founded in 1995.
Language (s): Portuguese
DAILY NEWSPAPER

Metrô News Newspaper 469778
Editorial: Rua Ipê, 144, Centro, Guarulhos 07090-130
Tel: 55 11 2475-7800
Email: redacao@folhametro.com.br **Web site:** http://www.metronews.com.br
Freq: Daily; **Circ:** 15000 Not Audited
Editor: Wilson Cardoza de Sa; **Editor:** Roberto Iizuka
Language (s): Portuguese
DAILY NEWSPAPER

Metro Rio de Janeiro 881813
Owner: Metro Jornal S/A
Editorial: Rua alvaro Ramos, 350, Botafogo, Rio De Janeiro 22280-110 **Tel:** 55 21 2586-9565
Web site: http://www.metrojornal.com.br
Freq: Mon thru Fri; **Circ:** 105530
Profile: Regional edition for Metro Jornal. Provides news and information on sports, politics, arts, culture and entertainment.
Language (s): Portuguese
DAILY NEWSPAPER

Metro São Paulo 881811
Owner: Metro Jornal S/A
Editorial: Avenida Reboucas, 1585, 1 andar, Jardim América, Sao Paulo 05401-909 **Tel:** 55 11 3528-8522
Email: online@metrojornal.com.br **Web site:** http://www.metrojornal.com.br/
Freq: Mon thru Fri; **Circ:** 151956
Profile: Regional edition for Metro Jornal for Sao Paulo city. Provides news and information on sports, politics, arts, culture and entertainment.
Language (s): Portuguese
DAILY NEWSPAPER

Mogi News 470568
Editorial: Rua Carlos Lacerda, 21, Vilanova Cintra, Mogi Das Cruzes 08745-200 **Tel:** 55 1147358000
Email: moginews@moginews.com.br **Web site:** http://www.moginews.com.br
Freq: Daily; **Circ:** 13000 Not Audited
Editor: Vides Junior; **Editor:** Gisleine Zarbietti
Profile: Com o Jornal Mogi News você terá diariamente notícias completas sobre a situação ecocômica, política, cultural e esportiva da sua

cidade e do resto do mundo. Além de espaço dedicado a lazer informática, educação, saúde e serviços médicos, veículo e transporte, decoração, construção e reforma, imóveis, classificados e muito mais.
Language (s): Portuguese
DAILY NEWSPAPER

Monitor Mercantil 470299
Editorial: Rua Marcilio Dias, 26, Centro, Rio De Janeiro 20221-280 **Tel:** 55 21 25184343
Email: redacao@monitormercantil.com.br **Web site:** http://www.monitormercantil.com.br
Freq: Daily; **Circ:** 26000 Not Audited
Editor in Chief: Marcos de Oliveira; **Editor:** Lauro Freitas
Profile: O Jornal MONITOR MERCANTIL tem distribuição nacional e presença marcante nos mercados de capitais, de seguros e financeiro. Como reconhecimento, recebeu por três vezes o Prêmio ABAMEC- Rio (Associação Brasileira dos Analistas do Mercado de Capitais), na categoria Imprensa e Comunicação, como melhor veículo especializado na opinião dos analistas de mercado, e melhor Profissional de Imprensa. Recebeu um prêmio da Abamec-Nordeste, também como melhor veículo. Em 2002, recebeu o Prêmio Cobertura de Seguros - Melhor Veículo, feito repetido em 2003. Ainda em 2002, um novo passo: a publicação do MONITOR MERCANTIL SÃO PAULO.
Language (s): Portuguese
DAILY NEWSPAPER

Monitor Mercantil São Paulo 157162
Owner: Grupo Monitor Mercantil S/A
Editorial: Avenida Sao Gabriel 149 sala 902, Itaim, Sao Paulo 01435-001 **Tel:** 55 11 3165 6192
Email: monitor.interpress@hipernetelecom.com.br **Web site:** http://www.monitormercantil.com.br
Freq: Daily; **Circ:** 22268 Not Audited
Editor in Chief: Ana Borges; **Director and President:** Acúrcio de Oliveira
Language (s): Portuguese
DAILY NEWSPAPER

O Nacional 470335
Editorial: Rua Silva Jardim, 325 A, Bairro Annes, Passo Fundo 99010-240 **Tel:** 55 5430456266
Email: onacional@onacional.com.br **Web site:** http://www.onacional.com.br
Freq: Daily
Editor in Chief: Zumara Colussi
Profile: O Nacional foi fundado no dia 19 de junho do ano de 1925 pelos Srs. Dr. Herculano A. Annes, Theofilo Guimarães, Americano Araujo Bastos e Hiran Araujo Bastos. Mais tarde foi adquirido por Mucio de Castro, jornalista e ex-Deputado Estadual. Registrar a história, fomentar a intelectualidade de sua gente, abrir espaços para idéias, produzir material literário: assim vem sendo o Jornal O Nacional ao longo destes 77 anos. O Nacional mantém um vínculo permanente com a comunidade de Passo Fundo e região. Não apenas divulgando os fatos, mas também assumindo bandeiras levantadas pelo interesse da própria sociedade. A participação em movimentos de interesse comunitário tiveram nestes anos um engajamento quase compulsório. Foram situações como, por exemplo, a da luta pela formação de uma universidade regional, que é hoje a UPF. Hoje, sob direção de Múcio de Castro Filho, O Nacional permanece ao lado dos interesses maiores da comunidade.
Language (s): Portuguese
DAILY NEWSPAPER

A Notícia 469709
Owner: Grupo RBS
Editorial: Rua Cacador, 112, Atiradores, Joinville 89203-610 **Tel:** 55 47 3419-2100
Email: leitor@an.com.br **Web site:** http://www.an.com.br
Freq: Daily; **Circ:** 23000 Not Audited
Editor: Marina Andrade; **Editor in Chief:** Domingos Aquino; **Editor:** Edenilson de Jesus; **Editor, Variedades & Cultura:** Genara Rigotti; **News Editor:** Raquel Schiavini
Profile: Offers local, regional, national and international news.
Language (s): Portuguese
DAILY NEWSPAPER

Notícia Agora 469753
Editorial: Rua Chafic Murad, 902, Ilha de Monte Belo, Vitoria 29050-901 **Tel:** 55 27 3321-8538
Email: pautana@redegazeta.com.br **Web site:** http://gazetaonline.globo.com
Circ: 28000 Not Audited
Editor: Ana Carolina Passos; **Editor:** Fernanda Zóboli Dalmácio
Language (s): Portuguese
DAILY NEWSPAPER

Oeste Notícias 469776
Editorial: Rua Kametaro Morishita, 95, Cidade Universitaria, Presidente Prudente 19050-700
Tel: 55 1832290304
Email: jornalismo@oestenoticias.com.br **Web site:** http://www.oestenoticias.com.br
Freq: Daily; **Circ:** 12000 Not Audited
Editor in Chief: Cristiano Oliveira
Language (s): Portuguese
DAILY NEWSPAPER

O Paraná 470099
Editorial: Rua Pernambuco, 1600, Centro, Cascavel 85810-021 **Tel:** 55 4533211000
Email: oparana@oparana.com.br **Web site:** http://www.oparana.com.br
Freq: Daily; **Circ:** 24000
Editor in Chief: Antônio Sbadeloto
Language (s): Portuguese
DAILY NEWSPAPER

Pioneiro Newspaper 157139
Owner: RBS Zero Hora Editora Jornalistica S.A.
Editorial: Rua Jacob Luchesi, 2374, Santa Catarina, Caxias Do Sul 95030-000 **Tel:** 55 54 3218-1200
Email: redacao@pioneiro.com **Web site:** http://pioneiro.clicrbs.com.br
Freq: Daily; **Circ:** 34190
Editor: Fábio da Câmara; **Editor in Chief:** Roberto Nielsen; **Director:** Luis Fernando Zanini
Language (s): Portuguese
DAILY NEWSPAPER

O Popular 470338
Editorial: Rua Thomas Edison - Quadra 7, Setor Serrinha, Goiânia 74835-130 **Tel:** 55 62 3250-1471
Web site: http://www.opopular.com.br
Freq: Daily; **Circ:** 42000
News Director: Luis Fernando Lima; **Editor:** Karla Morais
Language (s): Portuguese
DAILY NEWSPAPER

O Povo 161003
Owner: O Povo
Editorial: Av. Aguanambi, 282, Joaquim Tavora, Fortaleza 60055-402 **Tel:** 55 85 3255-6101
Email: centralderelacionamento@opovo.com.br **Web site:** http://www.opovo.com.br
Freq: Daily; **Circ:** 28425 Not Audited
Editor in Chief: Erick Guimarães
Language (s): Portuguese
DAILY NEWSPAPER

Povo do Rio 470662
Editorial: Rua Washington Luis, 54, Centro, Rio De Janeiro 20230-025 **Tel:** 55 21 25092772
Email: povodorio@gmail.com **Web site:** http://www.jornalpovo.com
Freq: Daily
Editor in Chief: Renata Onaindia
Profile: Covers local, regional, national and international news, as well as business, entertainment, lifestyle and sports.
Language (s): Portuguese
DAILY NEWSPAPER

O Progresso 469774
Editorial: Avenida Presidente Vargas, 447, Centro, Dourados 79804-030 **Tel:** 55 6734162600
Email: progresso@progresso.com.br **Web site:** http://www.progresso.com.br
Freq: Daily; **Circ:** 15000 Not Audited
Editor in Chief: Vander Verão
Language (s): Portuguese
DAILY NEWSPAPER

A Razão 469989
Editorial: Rua Serafim Valandro, 1284, Centro, Santa Maria 97015-630 **Tel:** 55 5532202100
Email: redacao@arazao.com.br **Web site:** http://www.arazao.com.br
Freq: Daily; **Circ:** 20000 Not Audited
Editor in Chief: José Mauro Batista
Profile: O jornal A Razão de Santa Maria é um tradicional veículos de comunicação do interior do Rio Grande do Sul. Atinge hoje mais de 40 municípios da região central e fronteira oeste do Rio Grande do Sul, além de cidades importantes como Porto Alegre.
Language (s): Portuguese
DAILY NEWSPAPER

O Rio Branco 470340
Editorial: Avenida Ceara, 2804, Ed. Cristiano M.de Assis - Centro, Rio Branco 69900-460
Tel: 55 6833021313
Email: redacao@oriobranco.com.br **Web site:** http://www.oriobranco.com.br
Freq: Daily; **Circ:** 6943
Director: Liberdade Marques; **Editor in Chief:** Cesar Negreiros
Language (s): Portuguese
DAILY NEWSPAPER

O São Gonçalo 470341
Editorial: Rua Yolanda Saad Abuzaid, 150 - Grupo 917, Alcântara, São Gonçalo 24440-440
Tel: 55 21 26017272
Email: redacao@jornalsg.com.br **Web site:** http://www.osaogoncalo.com.br
Freq: Daily; **Circ:** 15000 Not Audited
Editor in Chief: Ari Lopes
Profile: Covers local, regional, national and international news, as well as business, entertainment, lifestyle and sports.
Language (s): Portuguese
DAILY NEWSPAPER

O Sul 469803
Editorial: Rua Orfanatrofio, 711, Alto Teresopolis, Porto Alegre 90840-440 **Tel:** 55 51 3218-2525
Email: osul@osul.com.br **Web site:** http://www.osul.com.br
Freq: Daily; **Circ:** 64166 Not Audited
Editor: Cristiane Appen; **Editor:** César Bresolin; **Editor:** Fabiola Brites; **Editor:** Renata da Silva; **Editor:** Jacqueline Guedes; **Editor in Chief:** Elton Primaz; **Editor:** Israel Rahal
Profile: Offers local, national and international news.
Language (s): Portuguese
DAILY NEWSPAPER

Super Notícia 883034
Owner: Grupo Editorial Sempre Editora
Editorial: Av. B. Camargos, 1645, Contagem 32210-180 **Tel:** 55 31 2101-3939
Email: falesuper@supernoticias.com.br **Web site:** http://www.otempo.com.br/super-noticia
Freq: Daily; **Circ:** 300000
Editor: Rogério Mauricio
Profile: Provides news and information on sports, politics, entertainment and economy.
Language (s): Portuguese
DAILY NEWSPAPER

A Tarde 469693
Editorial: Rua Professor Milton Cayres de Brito, 204, Caminho das arvores, Salvador 41820-570
Tel: 55 71 3340-8800
Email: redacao-l@grupoatarde.com.br **Web site:** http://www.atarde.com.br
Freq: Daily; **Circ:** 55861 Not Audited
Editor in Chief: Ricardo Mendes; **Editor:** João Mauro Uchôa; **Editor:** Nadja Vladi
Profile: Covers Local, National and International News.
Language (s): Portuguese
DAILY NEWSPAPER

O Tempo 470345
Editorial: Avenida Babita Camargos, 1645, Cidade Industrial, Contagem 32210-180 **Tel:** 55 31 2101-30001
Email: redacao@otempo.com.br **Web site:** http://www.otempo.com.br
Freq: Daily; **Circ:** 72000 Not Audited
Editor, Brasil: Carla Chein; **Editor:** João de Castro
Profile: Covers Local, Regional, National and International News.
Language (s): Portuguese
DAILY NEWSPAPER

TodoDia 469943
Editorial: Avenida Sao Jerônimo, 2210, Bairro Morada do Sol, Americana 13470-310
Tel: 55 1934712700
Email: redacao@tododia.com.br **Web site:** http://www.tododia.com.br
Freq: Daily; **Circ:** 17300 Not Audited
Editor in Chief: Cláudio Giória
Language (s): Portuguese
DAILY NEWSPAPER

A Tribuna 469692
Owner: A Tribuna de Santos Jornal e Editora Ltda.
Editorial: Rua Joao Pessoa, 129, Centro, Santos 11013-900 **Tel:** 55 13 2102-7000
Email: digital@atribuna.com.br **Web site:** http://www.atribuna.com.br
Freq: Daily; **Circ:** 42000
Editor: Giselda Braz; **Editor:** Maria Elizabeth Capelache; **Editor In Chief:** Carlos Conde; **Editor:** Leopoldo Figueiredo; **Editor:** Michella Guijt
Language (s): Portuguese
DAILY NEWSPAPER

A Tribuna 469710
Editorial: Rua Joaquim Placido da Silva, 225, Ilha de Santa Maria, Vitoria 29051-900 **Tel:** 55 27 3331-9000
Email: pauta@redetribuna.com.br **Web site:** http://www.redetribuna.com.br
Freq: Daily; **Circ:** 61000
Editor: Alevi Carneiro
Language (s): Portuguese
DAILY NEWSPAPER

A Tribuna 469990
Editorial: Rua Barao do Amazonas, 31, Ponta D'Areia, Niterói 24030-111 **Tel:** 55 2127191886
Email: jornaldelcarai@urbi.com.br **Web site:** http://atribunarj.com.br
Freq: Daily; **Circ:** 10000 Not Audited
Editor in Chief: José Messias Xavier
Language (s): Portuguese
DAILY NEWSPAPER

O Tribuna 470324
Editorial: Rua Jose Loureiro, 282, Centro, Curitiba 80010-020 **Tel:** 55 41 3321-5000
Email: pauta@parana-online.com.br **Web site:** http://www.parana-online.com.br
Freq: Daily; **Circ:** 20000
Editor: Arlindo Berri
Language (s): Portuguese
DAILY NEWSPAPER

Tribuna 470611
Editorial: Rua Sao Sebastiao, 1380, Centro, Ribeirão Preto 14015-040 **Tel:** 55 16 3632-2200
Email: tribuna@tribunaribeirao.com.br **Web site:** http://www.tribunaribeirao.com.br
Freq: Daily; **Circ:** 16000 Not Audited
Editor: Eduardo Ferrari Batista de Santana; **Editor in Chief:** Hilton Hartmann
Language (s): Portuguese
DAILY NEWSPAPER

Tribuna da Bahia 470492
Editorial: Rua Djalma Dutra, 121, Sete Portas, Salvador 40255-000 **Tel:** 55 71 3321-2161
Email: tribunadabahia@tribunadabahia.com.br **Web site:** http://www.tribunadabahia.com.br
Freq: Daily; **Circ:** 30000 Not Audited
Editor in Chief: Paulo Roberto Sampaio
Language (s): Portuguese
DAILY NEWSPAPER

Tribuna de Minas 469784
Editorial: Rua Espirito Santo, 95, Poco Rico, Juiz De Fora 36020-000 **Tel:** 55 32 2101-4544
Email: redacao@tribunademinas.com.br **Web site:** http://www.tribunademinas.com.br
Freq: Daily; **Circ:** 18000 Not Audited
President: Juracy Azevedo Neves; **Editor in Chief:** Paulo César Magella
Language (s): Portuguese
DAILY NEWSPAPER

Tribuna de Petrópolis 469785
Editorial: Rua Alencar Lima, 26, Centro, Petrópolis 25620-050 **Tel:** 55 24 2244-2440
Email: redacao@e-tribuna.com.br **Web site:** http://www.e-tribuna.com.br
Freq: Daily; **Circ:** 14000 Not Audited
Editor: Alváro Bastos; **Director:** Francisco Bragança; **Editor in Chief:** Douglas Prado
Language (s): Portuguese
DAILY NEWSPAPER

Tribuna do Norte 157187
Owner: Empresa Jornalistica Tribuna do Norte
Editorial: Avenida Duque de Caxias, 06, Ribeira, Natal 59010-200 **Tel:** 55 84 4006-6113
Email: pauta@tribunadonorte.com.br **Web site:** http://www.tribunadonorte.com.br
Freq: Daily; **Circ:** 23000 Not Audited
Editor: Cinthia Lopes; **Editor in Chief:** Vicente Neto; **Editor in Chief:** Carlos Peixoto; **Editor:** Isaac Ribeiro; **Editor:** Ana Silva
Language (s): Portuguese
DAILY NEWSPAPER

Tribuna do Norte 470496
Editorial: Av. Zilda Seixas Amaral, 4.270, Parque Industrial Norte, Apucarana 86806-380
Tel: 55 43 3420-1177
Web site: http://www.tribunadonorte.com
Circ: 15000 Not Audited
Editor: Fernando Klein
Language (s): Portuguese
DAILY NEWSPAPER

Tribuna do Paraná 469968
Editorial: Rua Jose Loureiro, 282, Curitiba 80820-010
Tel: 55 41 3321-5000
Email: geralredacao@tribunadoparana.com.br **Web site:** http://www.parana-online.com.br
Freq: Daily; **Circ:** 15000 Not Audited
Editor in Chief: Rafael Tavares de Mello
Language (s): Portuguese
DAILY NEWSPAPER

A Tribuna Hoje 469993
Editorial: Av. Presidente Castelo Branco, 3815, Umuarama 87501-170 **Tel:** 55 44 3056-6050
Email: tribunahoje@tribunahoje.jor.br **Web site:** http://www.tribunahoje.jor.br
Freq: Daily; **Circ:** 14000 Not Audited
Editor: Jaqueline Mocellin
Profile: Focuses on news, politics, regional, society, sports and local news.
Language (s): Portuguese
DAILY NEWSPAPER

O Vale 470499
Editorial: Avenida Samuel Wainer, 3755, Jardim Augusta, São José Dos Campos 12216-710
Tel: 55 12 3909-3932
Email: editoraexecutiva@ovale.com.br **Web site:** http://www.ovale.com.br
Freq: Daily; **Circ:** 32000
Editor in Chief: Hélcio Costa; **Editor:** Felipe Manoukian
Profile: Vale Paraibano is a daily newspaper and covers local, regional, national and international news, as well as business, entertainment, lifestyle and sports.
Language (s): Portuguese
DAILY NEWSPAPER

Valor Econômico 365822
Owner: Valor Econômico S/A
Editorial: Av. Francisco Matarazzo, 1500, Torre New York, 1, 2, 3 e 8 andares, Sao Paulo 05001-100
Tel: 55 11 3767-1000
Email: redacao@valor.com.br **Web site:** http://www.valor.com.br
Freq: Daily; **Circ:** 53469 Not Audited
Editora/Editor: Alessandra Bellotto; **Editor:** Camila Dias; **Editor S.A.:** Nelson Niero; **Editor, Internacional:** Humberto Saccomandi; **Editora, Brasil/Editor, Brasil:** Catherine Vieira
Profile: Established in May 2000, Valor Econômico is considered the most widely-read finance and business newspaper in Brazil. Dedicated to the financial and investment market in the country.
Language (s): Portuguese
DAILY NEWSPAPER

A Voz da Cidade 469996
Editorial: Rua Michel Wardini, 100, Centro, Barra Mansa 27330-100 **Tel:** 55 2433241879
Email: redacao@avozdacidade.com **Web site:** http://www.avozdacidade.com
Freq: Daily; **Circ:** 12000
Editor: Caroline Macedo; **Editor in Chief:** Antônio Carlos Naves

Profile: Note: This outlet has the same telephone and fax number. To send a fax, one must call and request that the telephone line be switched to a fax line.
Language (s): Portuguese
DAILY NEWSPAPER

Zero Hora 157084
Owner: RBS Zero Hora Editora Jornalistica S.A.
Editorial: Avenida Ipiranga 1075, Azenha, Porto Alegre 90160-093 **Tel:** 55 51 3218-4300
Email: leitor@zerohora.com.br **Web site:** http://zerohora.clicrbs.com.br
Freq: Daily; **Circ:** 184566 Not Audited
Editor, Mundo: Luiz Antônio Araujo; **Editor:** Ricardo Chaves; **Editor:** Bete Duarte; **Editor:** Marcelo Ermel; **Editor:** Gilberto Leal; **Editor:** Leandro Maciel; **Editor:** Clóvis Malta; **Editor, Meu Filho & Viagem:** Priscila Martini; **Editor, Casa & Cia:** Eleone Prestes; **Editor:** Larissa Roso; **Editor:** Nilson Souza; **Editor in Chief:** Nilson Vargas
Profile: Covers local, regional, national and international news.
Language (s): Portuguese
Ad Rate: Full Page Mono 631.44
Currency: Brazil Reais
DAILY NEWSPAPER

News Service/Syndicate

Agência Anhangüera de Notícias 827401
Editorial: Rua Sete de Setembro, 189, Campinas 13035-350 **Tel:** 55 19 3772-8003
Web site: http://www.agenciaanhanguera.com.br
Editor in Chief: Guilherme Busch
Language (s): Portuguese
NEWS SERVICE/SYNDICATE

Agência CMA 880362
Owner: Grupo CMA
Editorial: Rua Professor Filadelfo Azevedo, 712, Vila Nova Conceicao, Sao Paulo 04508-011
Tel: 55 11 3053-2611
Email: socialmedia@cma.com.br **Web site:** http://www.agenciacma.com.br
Profile: Agência CMA is a Brazilian news service providing international financial and stock market information, focusing on major international stock markets and currency exchange markets.
Language (s): Portuguese
NEWS SERVICE/SYNDICATE

Agência Estado 794865
Owner: Grupo Estado
Editorial: Avenida Professor Celestino Bourroul 68 - 1 andar, Bairro do Limao andar, Sao Paulo 02710-000 **Tel:** 55 11 3856-3500
Email: atende.ae@grupoestado.com.br **Web site:** http://institucional.ae.com.br
Editor: Angelo Schincariol
Profile: Agência de notíciasbrasileira na cobertura em tempo real do mercado financeiro. Founded in January 1970, Agência Estado, also known as AE, is the largest and one of the most important vehicles of information in the country. In addition to distributing news and pictures to newspapers and Web sites, is recognized by the dissemination of real-time news, quotes and expert analysis for the financial market.
Language (s): Portuguese
NEWS SERVICE/SYNDICATE

Agência RBS 471531
Editorial: Avenida Ipiranga, 1075 - 4 andar, Azenha, Porto Alegre 90169-900 **Tel:** 55 51 3218-4771
Email: agenciarbs@zerohora.com.br **Web site:** http://www.agenciarbs.com.br
Bureau Chief: Fabiola Bach
Profile: A RBS Online é a unidade de negócio voltada para desenvolvimento de conteúdos multimídia, extensão real time dos veículos/ programas tradicionais e interatividade com a audiência de gaúchos e catarinenses. Todas as ações de internet da RBS convergem para a RBS Online. A empresa investe alto em tecnologia, interatividade, personalização e segmentação para promover a integração dos diferenciais competitivos de cada negócio do grupo. A RBS Online aposta no valor das marcas líderes associadas, no melhor conteúdo regional, na forte relação que estabelece com clientes e comunidades e na distribuição de produtos multimídia personalizados. O principal canal de comunicação é o clicRBS.
Language (s): Portuguese
NEWS SERVICE/SYNDICATE

AutoPress 469889
Owner: Carta Z Notícias Ltda
Editorial: Rua Barao do Flamengo, 32 - 5 andar, Rio De Janeiro 22220-080 **Tel:** 55 21 2286-0020
Email: redacao@autopress.com.br **Web site:** http://www.autopress.com.br
Editor in Chief: Eduardo Rocha
Profile: Offers entertainment and news. Note: This outlet has the same telephone and fax number. To send a fax, one must call and request that the telephone line be switched to a fax line.
Language (s): Portuguese
NEWS SERVICE/SYNDICATE

BR Press 829832
Owner: BR Press
Editorial: Av. Paulista, 2.300 - Andar Pilotis, Sao Paulo 01310-300 **Tel:** 55 11 2847-4958
Email: pauta@brpress.net **Web site:** http://www.brpress.net
Profile: BR Press Agência Jornalística is a Portuguese-language "boutique" news agency that provides News, International News, Sports, Arts & Entertainment, Culture, Style, Business, Health and Wellness coverage. BR Press also provides customized news reports.
Language (s): Portuguese
NEWS SERVICE/SYNDICATE

Folha Press 471524
Editorial: Alameda Barao de Limeira, 401 - 4 andar, Campos Elíseos, Sao Paulo 01290-900
Tel: 55 11 3224-3527
Email: folhapress@folhapress.com.br **Web site:** http://www.folhapress.com.br
General Manager: Raimundo Cunha; **Editor:** Raul Lopes
Profile: A Agência Folha conta com textos de mais de 500 jornalistas da Folha de S.Paulo e do Agora São Paulo em todo o país. A Agência oferece reportagens especiais, serviço fotográfico e excelentes artigos dos colunistas mais renomados, representantes de diversas correntes de opinião. Para quem quer publicar cadernos temáticos, a Agência dispõe de opções para cada dia da semana, com o objetivo de atingir todos os tipos de leitores. Alguns exemplos são os cadernos sobre turismo, comportamento infantil e juvenil, informática, imóveis, veículos e construção. Há também reportagens especiais sobre saúde, literatura, beleza e tecnologia. Você pode contar, ainda, com uma especialidade da Folha Imagem, o Serviço Noticioso Fotográfico, com as fotos mais "quentes" do dia e o melhor arquivo do país.
Language (s): Portuguese
NEWS SERVICE/SYNDICATE

PIA News 471528
Editorial: Rua Guimaraes Natal, 23 - Sala 203, Copacabana, Rio De Janeiro 22011-090
Tel: 55 21 2541-7757
Web site: http://www.pianews.net
Editor in Chief: André Queiroz
Profile: <NAIAS>
Language (s): Portuguese
NEWS SERVICE/SYNDICATE

Brunei

Time Difference: GMT +8
National Telephone Code: 673
Continent: Asia
Capital: Bandar Seri Begawan

Newspapers

Pelita Brunei 668837
Owner: Information Department of Brunei
Tel: 673 2 38 39 41
Email: pelita@brunet.bn **Web site:** http://www.brunet.bn/news/pelita
Freq: Weekly; **Circ:** 25000 Publisher's Statement
Editor: Timbang Bakar
Language (s): Bahasa Malaysia
DAILY NEWSPAPER

Bulgaria

Time Difference: GMT +2
National Telephone Code: 359
Continent: Europe
Capital: Sofia

Newspapers

168 Chasa 434028
Owner: Newspaper Group Bulgaria
Editorial: 47 Tsarigradsko Shose Blvd, Sofia 1504
Tel: 359 2 942 27 32
Email: 168pisma@168chasa.bg **Web site:** http://www.168chasa.bg
Circ: 65000 Publisher's Statement
Editor-in-Chief: Slavi Angelov
Profile: National weekly newspaper including business, political and entertainment news and comments, mainly for intellectuals.
Language (s): Bulgarian
Ad Rate: Full Page Mono 3475.08
Ad Rate: Full Page Colour 4680.72
Currency: Bulgaria Leva
DAILY NEWSPAPER

24 Chasa 433566
Owner: Media Holding
Editorial: 47 Tsarigradsko Shose Blvd, Sofia 1504
Tel: 359 2 942 2514
Email: 24business@24chasa.bg **Web site:** http://www.24chasa.bg
Freq: Daily; **Circ:** 80000 Publisher's Statement
Editor-in-Chief: Borislav Zumbulev
Profile: The second most circulated newspaper mainly for the average Bulgarian reader, strong opinion maker with eight regional editions in Varna, Plovdiv, Burgas, Stara Zagora, etc.
Language (s): Bulgarian
Ad Rate: Full Page Mono 10141.56
Ad Rate: Full Page Colour 13687.56
Currency: Bulgaria Leva
DAILY NEWSPAPER

Banker 224791
Owner: Financial Information Agency
Editorial: bulvar Cerni verekh 25a, Sofia 1421
Tel: 359 2 440 9 440
Email: info@banker.bg **Web site:** http://www.banker.bg
Circ: 6500 Publisher's Statement
Editor-in-Chief: Bistra Georgieva
Profile: National financial weekly mainly for bankers, decision-makers and economists.
Language (s): Bulgarian
Ad Rate: Full Page Colour 8415.00
Currency: Bulgaria Leva
DAILY NEWSPAPER

Capital Daily 167557
Owner: Economedia
Editorial: 20 Ivan Vazov St., Sofia 1000
Tel: 359 2 937 61 22
Email: editors@capital.bg **Web site:** http://www.capital.bg
Freq: Weekly; **Circ:** 24951 Not Audited
Profile: Targets intellectuals, decision-makers and economists. Premier source of financial and business reports and analyses. It's deemed to be the most powerful opinion maker in the country.
Language (s): Bulgarian
Ad Rate: Full Page Mono 4900.00
Ad Rate: Full Page Colour 7350.00
Currency: Bulgaria Leva
DAILY NEWSPAPER

Classa.bg 513695
Owner: MAK Media
Editorial: bulvar Bulgaria 49, Sofia 1404
Tel: 359 2 948 48 00
Web site: http://www.classa.bg
Freq: Daily; **Circ:** 10000 Publisher's Statement
Editor: Stefan Todorov
Profile: Daily newspaper for decision-makers and intellectuals, providing national and international coverage on latest business issues.
Language (s): Bulgarian
Ad Rate: Full Page Mono 3900.00
Ad Rate: Full Page Colour 5850.00
Currency: Bulgaria Leva
DAILY NEWSPAPER

Dnevnik 161200
Owner: Economedia
Editorial: 16 Ivan Vazov St., Sofia 1000
Tel: 359 2 937 63 00
Email: dnevnik@dnevnik.bg **Web site:** http://www.dnevnik.bg
Freq: Daily; **Circ:** 11900 Publisher's Statement
Editor-in-Chief: Velislava Popova
Profile: Daily newspaper published as the only broadsheet in the country. Readership profile: 90% of the readers live in Sofia and big cities and are in their prime. 1/3 of the audience consists of top executives, 1/2 are highly qualified.
Language (s): Bulgarian
Ad Rate: Full Page Mono 3700.00
Ad Rate: Full Page Colour 5500.00
Currency: Bulgaria Leva
DAILY NEWSPAPER

Duma 433569
Owner: PM Press
Editorial: ul. Pozitano 20a, Sofia 1504
Tel: 359 2 97 05 200
Email: duma@duma.bg **Web site:** http://www.duma.bg
Freq: Daily; **Circ:** 9500 Publisher's Statement
Profile: Daily newspaper with leftist orientation, with editorial emphasis on social news and comments. Readers' profile: mainly members and supporters of the Bulgarian Socialist Party.
Language (s): Bulgarian
Ad Rate: Full Page Mono 4095.00
Ad Rate: Full Page Colour 6201.00
Currency: Bulgaria Leva
DAILY NEWSPAPER

Monitor 161220
Owner: New Bulgarian Media Group
Editorial: 113A Tsarigradsko Shose Blvd, Sofia 1784
Tel: 359 2 960 22 37
Email: monitor@monitor.bg **Web site:** http://www.monitor.bg
Freq: Daily; **Circ:** 11500 Publisher's Statement
Profile: Daily newspaper covering general as well as topical news.
Language (s): Bulgarian
Ad Rate: Full Page Mono 9323.42
Ad Rate: Full Page Colour 12619.58
Currency: Bulgaria Leva
DAILY NEWSPAPER

Politika 434031
Owner: New Bulgarian Media Group
Editorial: Elzarkh Yosif 119a, Sofia 1527
Tel: 359 2 960 2251
Email: politika@politika.bg **Web site:** http://www.politika.bg
Circ: 5314 Publisher's Statement
Editor-in-Chief: Kristi Petrova
Profile: Weekly newspaper, published every Saturday, containing mainly politics news, as well as business news over the past week.
Language (s): Bulgarian
Ad Rate: Full Page Mono 5250312.00
Ad Rate: Full Page Colour 7973.28
Currency: Bulgaria Leva
DAILY NEWSPAPER

Sega 161031
Owner: Sega
Editorial: 1 Bulgaria Square, Sofia 1463
Tel: 359 2 915 23 00
Email: economics@segabg.com **Web site:** http://www.segabg.com
Freq: Daily; **Circ:** 10700 Publisher's Statement
Editor-in-Chief: Teodora Peeva
Profile: Daily newspaper mainly for decision-makers and intellectuals, providing national and international coverage and special news features.
Language (s): Bulgarian
Ad Rate: Full Page Mono 4984.20
Ad Rate: Full Page Colour 7137.00
Currency: Bulgaria Leva
DAILY NEWSPAPER

Standart 433567
Owner: Standart News
Editorial: ul. Miziya 23, Sofia 1124
Tel: 359 2 818 23 11
Email: agency@standartnews.com **Web site:** http://www.standartnews.com
Freq: Daily; **Circ:** 68300 Publisher's Statement
Profile: National daily newspaper mainly for decision-makers and intellectuals. Edition of Standart News Ltd. Provides objective and fair view of daily issues in Bulgaria and worldwide. It includes 48 pages with interesting articles about politics, economy, sport, culture, humour and society.
Language (s): Bulgarian
Ad Rate: Full Page Mono 5673.60
Ad Rate: Full Page Colour 8983.20
Currency: Bulgaria Leva
DAILY NEWSPAPER

Telegraf 433568
Owner: Press Group Monitor
Editorial: 113A Tsarigradsko Shose Blvd, Sofia 1784
Tel: 359 2 960 22 12
Email: telegraph@monitor.bg **Web site:** http://www.telegraph.bg
Freq: Daily; **Circ:** 66000 Publisher's Statement
Director: Irena Krasteva; **Editor-in-Chief:** Vladimir Yonchev
Profile: Daily tabloid newspaper covering general news as well as gossip and entertainment.
Language (s): Bulgarian
Ad Rate: Full Page Mono 9687.60
Ad Rate: Full Page Colour 6411.60
Currency: Bulgaria Leva
DAILY NEWSPAPER

Trud 433565
Owner: Media Holding
Editorial: ul. Lachezar Stanchev 7, Sofia 1797
Tel: 359 2 921 41 40
Email: reporteri@trud.bg **Web site:** http://www.trud.bg
Freq: Daily; **Circ:** 105000 Publisher's Statement
Editor-in-Chief: Petyo Bluskov
Profile: The most circulated newspaper mainly for the average Bulgarian reader with eight regional editions in Varna, Plovdiv, Burgas, Stara Zagora, etc.
Language (s): Bulgarian
Ad Rate: Full Page Mono 13663.92
Ad Rate: Full Page Colour 18439.20
Currency: Bulgaria Leva
DAILY NEWSPAPER

Zemya 161032
Owner: Evromedia
Editorial: G. S. Rakovki 99, Sofia 1000
Tel: 359 2 9461902
Email: zemia_core@abv.bg **Web site:** http://zemia-news.bg
Freq: Daily; **Circ:** 12000 Publisher's Statement
Editor-in-Chief: Teofan Germanov; **Publisher:** Svetlana Sharenkova
Profile: Daily newspaper with agricultural orientation but also including news from the economic, political and cultural spheres of Bulgarian life.
Language (s): Bulgarian
Ad Rate: Full Page Mono 2263.20
Ad Rate: Full Page Colour 2902.80
Currency: Bulgaria Leva
DAILY NEWSPAPER

News Service/Syndicate

Forex News 585571
Editorial: 16 Ivan Vazov Street, Sofia 1000
Tel: 359 89994 76 55
Email: info@forexnews.bg **Web site:** http://forexnews.bg
Editor In Chief: Sasho Slavov
Profile: Offers a wide range of business and financial news, updated throughout the day.
Language (s): Bulgarian
NEWS SERVICE/SYNDICATE

Bulgaria

Community Newspaper

100 Vesti 433585
Owner: Publisher House Kolonel - Gabrovo
Editorial: 2 Otets Paisii Str., Gabrovo 5300
Tel: 359 676 810 410
Email: 100vesti@stovesti.info **Web site:** http://www.100vesti.info
Circ: 4000
Editor-in-Chief: Ivan Gospodinov
Profile: 100 Vesti is the private newspaper in the region of Gabrovo. Covers politics, news, sport and public affairs.
Language (s): Bulgarian
COMMUNITY NEWSPAPER

BG Sever 433586
Editorial: D. Popov 18, Pleven 5800
Tel: 359 64 806 891
Email: bg_sever@abv.bg **Web site:** http://www.bgsever.info
Editor: Ivan Dachev; **Editor:** Iliana Tsirovska
Profile: Weekly newspaper focused on northern Bulgaria, issued in Pleven, Lovech, Gabrovo, V.Turnovo, Vraca and Montana.
Language (s): Bulgarian
Ad Rate: Full Page Mono 1442.00
Ad Rate: Full Page Colour 3749.00
Currency: Bulgaria Leva
COMMUNITY NEWSPAPER

Borba 433583
Owner: Borba Publishing House
Editorial: P.O. Box 71, 2 Bulgaria Boulevard, Veliko Tarnovo 5000 **Tel:** 359 62 620 308
Email: borbavt@vali.bg **Web site:** http://www.borbabg.com
Circ: 10000
Profile: Borba is an independent newspaper providing mainly regional news, politics, lifestyle, sports, health and arts.
Language (s): Bulgarian
Ad Rate: Full Page Mono 2160.00
Ad Rate: Full Page Colour 1081.00
Currency: Bulgaria Leva
COMMUNITY NEWSPAPER

Botevgradski Vesti Plus 433588
Editorial: 23 Tzar Osvoboditel Blvd., Botevgrad
Tel: 359 723 2532
Web site: http://bvplus.declera.com
Profile: Informative newspaper with news from the city of Botevgrad and the region.
Language (s): Bulgarian
COMMUNITY NEWSPAPER

Cherno more 433582
Owner: Mustang Holding
Editorial: Chayka 23, Varna 9010
Tel: 359 52 306 000
Email: media@chernomore.bg **Web site:** http://www.chernomore.bg
Freq: Daily; **Circ:** 4000
Editor: Slav Velev
Profile: Daily newspaper with news from Varna and the region, the country and the world.
Language (s): Bulgarian
Ad Rate: Full Page Mono 1000.76
Ad Rate: Full Page Colour 1250.00
Currency: Bulgaria Leva
COMMUNITY NEWSPAPER

Ekip 7 433589
Owner: Ekip 7 Cooperation
Editorial: Grancharska 5, Razgrad 7200
Tel: 359 84 66 16 19
Email: vestnik@ekip7.bg **Web site:** http://ekip7.bg
Freq: 3 Times/Week; **Circ:** 3800
Profile: Regional newspaper for Razgrad city.
Language (s): Bulgarian
Ad Rate: Full Page Mono 655.00
Ad Rate: Full Page Colour 1500.00
Currency: Bulgaria Leva
COMMUNITY NEWSPAPER

Gabrovo Dnes 433587
Editorial: 9 Aprilovska Str., Gabrovo 5300
Tel: 359 878 803 360
Email: gabrovodnes@abv.com **Web site:** http://www.gabrovodnes.info
Editor: Mariana Dimitrova
Profile: The newspaper contains information about the life in Gabrovo Municipality. Gabrovo Dnes offers supplements for culture, healthcare, real estate and business.
Language (s): Bulgarian
COMMUNITY NEWSPAPER

Glasove 434036
Editorial: ul. Chumerna 7, Sofia 1000
Tel: 359 2 988 14 98
Email: glasove@gmail.com **Web site:** http://www.glasove.com
Editor-in-Chief: Yavor Dachkov; **Editor:** Galya Dachkova
Profile: Weekly newspaper with analyses in the social, economic and political spheres.
Language (s): Bulgarian
Ad Rate: Full Page Colour 430.92
Currency: Bulgaria Leva
COMMUNITY NEWSPAPER

Gledishta dnes 434043
Owner: Gledishta JC
Editorial: 10 Tsar Asen Str., Razgrad 7200
Tel: 359 84661350
Email: gledishta@mail.bg
Circ: 5000
Profile: Regional newspaper for Razgrad city.
Language (s): Bulgarian
Ad Rate: Full Page Mono 780.00
Ad Rate: Full Page Colour 975.00
Currency: Bulgaria Leva
COMMUNITY NEWSPAPER

Lovech-pres 434046
Owner: Lovech Press - Miroslav Iliev PC
Editorial: Poschenska Kutia 79, Lovech 5500
Tel: 359 68 623717
Email: lovpress@gmail.com **Web site:** http://www.lovechpress.info
Circ: 3500
Profile: Newspaper for the city of Lovech.
Language (s): Bulgarian
COMMUNITY NEWSPAPER

Maritsa 433574
Owner: Hermes Media
Editorial: 27A Hristo Botev Blvd, Plovdiv 4000
Tel: 359 32 603 450
Email: upravitel@marica.bg **Web site:** http://www.marica.bg
Freq: Daily; **Circ:** 25000
Editor-in-Chief: Rusi Chernev
Profile: Maritsa is the newspaper issued in Plovdiv region.
Language (s): Bulgarian
Ad Rate: Full Page Colour 3440.00
Currency: Bulgaria Leva
COMMUNITY NEWSPAPER

Mont-pres 434045
Editorial: 1 Antim Street, Montana 3400
Tel: 359 96304005
Email: info@mont-press.com **Web site:** http://www.mont-press.com
Circ: 5000
Profile: Regional newspaper for the city of Montana.
Language (s): Bulgarian
Ad Rate: Full Page Mono 1040.00
Ad Rate: Full Page Colour 2080.00
Currency: Bulgaria Leva
COMMUNITY NEWSPAPER

Narodno delo 433579
Editorial: 3 Hristo Botev Boulevard, Varna 9000
Tel: 359 52 222101
Web site: http://www.narodnodelo.bg
Freq: Daily; **Circ:** 5000
Profile: Narodno Delo Daily is a regional newspaper, focusing mainly on news regarding Varna and the region. The newspaper has 20 pages.
Language (s): Bulgarian
COMMUNITY NEWSPAPER

Nov Zhivot 433575
Owner: Rodopi Ltd
Editorial: 2 Bulair St, Kardzhali 6600
Tel: 359 361 6 52 71
Email: novjivotreklama@gmail.com **Web site:** http://www.novjivot.info
Freq: Daily
Profile: Regional issue of Kardzhali - Eastern Rodopi daily. It also includes Perperikon supplement.
Language (s): Bulgarian
Ad Rate: Full Page Mono 336.96
Ad Rate: Full Page Colour 673.92
Currency: Bulgaria Leva
COMMUNITY NEWSPAPER

Nova Dobrudzhanska Tribuna 433593
Editorial: 30 Kiril I Metodi Str; entrance B; floor 1; ap.1, Dobrich 9300 **Tel:** 359 58 602 553
Email: ndt@dobrich.net **Web site:** http://www.ndt1.com
Editor: Velina Vlaykova
Profile: Informative regional newspaper issued in North-East Bulgaria.
Language (s): Bulgarian
COMMUNITY NEWSPAPER

Posrednik Daily 434048
Editorial: 125 Vassil Levski; entrance 3, Pleven 5800
Tel: 359 64 90 05 21
Email: news@posredniknews.com **Web site:** http://www.posredniknews.com
Profile: Regional daily newspaper issued in Pleven region and regarding topics like economics, politics, culture and sports.
Language (s): Bulgarian
COMMUNITY NEWSPAPER

Rositsa 434040
Editorial: 2 Slaveikov Str., Sevlievo
Tel: 359 675 3 44 68
Email: Info@rositza.com **Web site:** http://www.rositza.com
Freq: 3 Times/Week; **Circ:** 3500
Editor-in-Chief: Hristo Hristov
Profile: Special edition for the town of Sevlievo, containing regional news.
Language (s): Bulgarian
COMMUNITY NEWSPAPER

Sapernik 434044
Editorial: 2 A St Kiril I Metodii Street, floor 1, Pernik 2300 **Tel:** 359 76 60-13-72
Email: sapernik_n@yahoo.com **Web site:** http://sapernik.info
Freq: Weekly; **Circ:** 5000
Editor: Lubomira Pelova
Profile: Informative newspaper for Pernik city and the local region.
Language (s): Bulgarian
Ad Rate: Full Page Mono 2001.52
Ad Rate: Full Page Colour 2501.90
Currency: Bulgaria Leva
COMMUNITY NEWSPAPER

Struma 434039
Owner: Pirin Erkul Company
Editorial: 10 Petko D. Petkov Street, Blagoevgrad
Tel: 359 73 885702
Email: struma92@abv.bg **Web site:** http://struma.bg
Freq: Daily; **Circ:** 20000
Profile: Struma is a daily newspaper that is read by Bulgarians living in south-west part of the country. The main topics are news from the region, lifestyle and sports.
Language (s): Bulgarian
Ad Rate: Full Page Mono 1499.62
Ad Rate: Full Page Colour 2155.70
Currency: Bulgaria Leva
COMMUNITY NEWSPAPER

Troyanski glas 433592
Editorial: ul. Opoplchenska 1, Troyan 5500
Email: tr_glas@abv.bg **Web site:** http://www.troyanskiglas.com
Circ: 1000
Editor: Rumyana Mokanova
Profile: Regional newspaper for the city of Troyan.
Language (s): Bulgarian
Ad Rate: Full Page Mono 381.00
Ad Rate: Full Page Colour 381.00
Currency: Bulgaria Leva
COMMUNITY NEWSPAPER

Varna 433580
Editorial: 27 A Russe Str., Varna 9000
Tel: 359 52 650078
Email: reklama_varna@yahoo.com
Circ: 1500
Profile: Varna Weekly is an issue with 36 pages. Varna Weekly publishes mostly analysis, commentaries as well as information about sports, celebrities etc. It is owned by Nedelcho Mihaylov, TV host at MSAT TV.
Language (s): Bulgarian
COMMUNITY NEWSPAPER

Yantra Dnes 433584
Owner: Yantra Press Publishing House
Editorial: 3 Bacho Kiro Street, Veliko Tarnovo 5000
Tel: 359 62 600 793
Email: dnes@vali.bg **Web site:** http://www.dnesbg.com
Circ: 25000
Editor-in-Chief: Mila Milcheva
Profile: Yantra Dnes is the regional newspaper of the city of Veliko Tarnovo. Provides news, analyses and commentaries regarding politics, sports, lifestyle.
Language (s): Bulgarian
Ad Rate: Full Page Mono 1874.52
Ad Rate: Full Page Colour 1218.40
Currency: Bulgaria Leva
COMMUNITY NEWSPAPER

Zname 433576
Owner: Zname Publishing House
Editorial: 22 Bulgaria Blvd, Pazardzhik 4400
Tel: 359 34 44 52 01
Email: znamee@abv.bg **Web site:** http://zname.info
Circ: 2500
Profile: Regional daily paper of Pazardzhik district.
Language (s): Bulgarian
Ad Rate: Full Page Mono 156.00
Ad Rate: Full Page Colour 312.00
Currency: Bulgaria Leva
COMMUNITY NEWSPAPER

Burkina Faso

Time Difference: GMT
National Telephone Code: 226
Continent: Africa
Capital: Ouagadougou

Newspapers

Journal du Jeudi 224418
Owner: Journal du Jeudi
Editorial: 01 BP 3654, Ouagadougou 1
Tel: 226 50 31 41 08
Email: info@journaldujeudi.com **Web site:** http://www.journaldujeudi.com
Freq: Daily; **Circ:** 8000 Publisher's Statement
Publisher: Boubakar Diallo; **Editor in Chief:** Amidou Idogo
Profile: Temporarily suspended (September 2016). Satirical newspaper focusing on national and international news, business, politics, entertainment and sport.
Language (s): French
Ad Rate: Full Page Mono 200000.00
Currency: Communauté Financière Africaine Francs BCEAO
DAILY NEWSPAPER

L' Observateur Paalga 218446
Owner: L'Observateur Paalga
Editorial: 01 BP 584, Ouagadougou 1
Tel: 226 50 33 27 05
Email: lobservateur@lobservateur.bf **Web site:** http://www.lobservateur.bf
Freq: Daily; **Circ:** 9000 Publisher's Statement
Editor in Chief: Boureima Diallo; **Advertising Manager:** Mounir Ky; **Director:** Edouard Ouédraogo
Profile: Newspaper covering regional, national and international news and current affairs including politics, economy, society, technology, arts, culture and sports.
Language (s): French
DAILY NEWSPAPER

Le Pays 318935
Owner: Les Editions Le Pays
Editorial: Cite 1200 Logements, 01 BP 4577, Ouagadougou 1 **Tel:** 226 50 36 20 46
Email: lepays@lepays.bf **Web site:** http://www.lepays.bf
Freq: Daily; **Circ:** 15000 Publisher's Statement
Director: Boureima Jérémie Sigue
Profile: Newspaper covering regional, national and international news and current affairs including business, economics, politics, culture, entertainment and sports.
Language (s): French
Ad Rate: Full Page Mono 150000.00
Ad Rate: Full Page Colour 150000.00
Currency: Communauté Financière Africaine Francs BCEAO
DAILY NEWSPAPER

Sidwaya 217923
Owner: Sidwaya
Editorial: Rue du Nasser, Ouagadougou 1
Tel: 226 25 312289
Email: sidwaya84@yahoo.fr **Web site:** http://www.sidwaya.bf
Freq: Daily; **Circ:** 5000 Publisher's Statement
Editor in Chief: Jean Philippe Tougouma; **Director:** Zakaria Yeye
Profile: Newspaper covering national and international news and current affairs including politics, economy, society, culture and sports.
Language (s): French
DAILY NEWSPAPER

News Service/Syndicate

Agence d'Informations du Burkina - AIB 503658
Owner: Agence d'Information du Burkina - AIB
Editorial: Avenue du Capitaine Thomas SANKARA, Face a l'ambassade du Ghana, Ouagadougou 1
Tel: 226 50 337316
Email: contact@aib.bf **Web site:** http://www.aib.bf
Director: Souleymane Sawadogo
Profile: Official News Agency of the Burkina Faso covering national and international news and current affairs including politics, economy, society and sport.
Language (s): French
NEWS SERVICE/SYNDICATE

Burundi

Time Difference: GMT +2
National Telephone Code: 257
Continent: Africa
Capital: Bujumbura

Newspapers

Le Renouveau du Burundi 156746
Owner: Ministry of Information
Editorial: BP 2573, Bujumbara **Tel:** 257 22 22 54 11
Email: pressequotidienne@yahoo.fr **Web site:** http://ppbdi.com
Freq: Daily; **Circ:** 1000 Publisher's Statement
Directeur Général: Khaddé Siryuyumunsi
Profile: Le Renouveau du Burundi is a national newspaper covering news, current affairs, politics and economics.
Language (s): French
DAILY NEWSPAPER

News Service/Syndicate

Agence Burundaise de Presse (ABP) 353726
Editorial: Avenue Nicolas Mayugi, Bujumbara
Tel: 257 22 21 30 83
Email: abp@cbinf.com **Web site:** http://abpinfos.gov.bi
Directrice: Pascaline Biduda

Profile: National news agency of Burundi, reporting on regional, national and international news.
Language (s): French
NEWS SERVICE/SYNDICATE

Cambodia

Time Difference: GMT +7
National Telephone Code: 855
Continent: Asia
Capital: Phnom Penh

Newspapers

Cambodge Nouveau 459055
Editorial: Cambodge Nouveau, No.58H, Street 302, Phnom Penh **Tel:** 855 23 214610
Email: cambodge.nouveau@forum.org.kh **Web site:** http://www.cambodgenouveau.com
Freq: Monthly; **Circ:** 501 Not Audited
Editor: Alain Gascuel
Profile: Cambodge Nouveau is a daily newspaper which covers the national and international news, business, politics, etc.
Language (s): French
DAILY NEWSPAPER

Cambodge Soir 459706
Editorial: Cambodge Soir Mekong Co Ltd, 26CD, Street 302, BP 627, Phnom Penh **Tel:** 855 23 726804
Email: cambodgesoirpnh@online.com.kh **Web site:** http://www.cambodgesoir.info
Freq: Weekly; **Circ:** 3001 Not Audited
Editor: Frederic Amat; **Editor in Chief:** Bona Pen
Profile: Covers local, national, regional and international news, business, etc.
Language (s): French
DAILY NEWSPAPER

Cambodia Daily 459705
Editorial: #7, Street 228, Samdech Mongkol Em Street, Phnom Penh **Tel:** 855 23 426602
Email: editor@cambodiadaily.com **Web site:** http://www.cambodiadaily.com
Freq: Daily; **Circ:** 5001 Not Audited
Publisher: Bernard Krisher
Profile: Provides unbiased news of Cambodia and the rest of the world to readers in both English and Khmer.
Language (s): English
DAILY NEWSPAPER

Cambodia News 473020
Editorial: Cambodia News, No.15B, Street 612, Phnom Penh 12152 **Tel:** 855 17 535-535
Email: cambodia_news@yahoo.com **Web site:** http://www.cambodia.org/news
Freq: Weekly; **Circ:** 5001 Not Audited
Director: Chhay Sophal
Profile: Covers news topics.
Language (s): English
DAILY NEWSPAPER

Cambodia Sin Chew Daily 459077
Editorial: Sin Chew Media Corp Bhd #1 07ABC Street Joseph214, Sangkat Boeng Prolit Khan 7 Makara Broz Tito Rue, Phnom Penh **Tel:** 855 23 212-628
Email: editorial@camsinchew.com **Web site:** http://www.sinchew-i.com/cambodia
Freq: Daily; **Circ:** 6001 Not Audited
Director: Swee Ping Loh
Profile: Covers news topics.
Language (s): Chinese
DAILY NEWSPAPER

Camgodge Soir (Khmer Version) 459172
Editorial: 26cd, Street 302 Bp627, Phnom Penh
Tel: 855 12 815990
Email: camgodgesoirpnh@online.com.kh **Web site:** http://www.cambodgesoir.info
Freq: Weekly
Editor in Chief: Pierre Gillette
Profile: Covers news topics.
Language (s): Khmer
DAILY NEWSPAPER

Jian Hua Daily 459075
Editorial: Jian Hua Daily, No.116-118, Street 128, Kampuchea Krom, Phnom Penh **Tel:** 855 23 883801
Email: jianhuadaily@jianhuadaily.com **Web site:** http://www.jianhuadaily.com
Freq: Daily; **Circ:** 5001 Not Audited
Editor in Chief: Xeng Zuang Rong
Profile: Jian Hua Daily is a daily newspaper which talks about the Local, National, Regional, International news, Business, Politics, etc.
Language (s): Chinese
DAILY NEWSPAPER

Kampuchea Thmey Daily 473024
Editorial: No.805, Kampuchea Krom Blvd (Street 128), San Gkat Tuk Laak 1, Phnom Penh 12156
Tel: 855 23 882535
Email: kampucheathmey@gmail.com **Web site:** http://www.kampucheathmey.com
Freq: 2 Times/Week; **Circ:** 40001 Not Audited
Editor in Chief: Khieu Navy
Profile: Discusses the Local, National, Regional and International news.
Language (s): Khmer
DAILY NEWSPAPER

Koh Santepheap Daily 395602
Editorial: Koh Santepheap Daily No240 Street 271 Beoung Tum, Meancathey Pun, Phnom Penh
Tel: 855 23 9871119
Email: kohdaily@gmail.com **Web site:** http://kohsantepheapdaily.com.kh
Freq: Daily; **Circ:** 45001 Not Audited
Editor in Chief: Thong Pang; **Editor in Chief:** Saroeun Pol
Profile: Koh Santepheap Daily is a daily newspaper which covers the latest Local, National, Regional and International news, Entertainment, Sports, etc.
Language (s): Khmer
DAILY NEWSPAPER

The Mirror 459954
Editorial: P.O. Box 177, Phnom Penh, Phnom Penh
Email: mirror@gmx.org **Web site:** http://cambodiamirror.wordpress.com
Freq: Weekly; **Circ:** 141 Not Audited
Editor: Norbert Klein
Profile: Published since 1997, it covers news, politics and economics.
Language (s): English
DAILY NEWSPAPER

Phnom Penh Post 157098
Editorial: 888 Building F, 8th fl, Phnom Penh Center, Corner of Sothearos and Sihanouk Blvds, Phnom Penh **Tel:** 855 23 214-311
Email: editors@phnompenhpost.com **Web site:** http://www.phnompenhpost.com
Freq: Daily; **Circ:** 5001 Not Audited
Foreign News Editor: Robin Eberhardt
Profile: Covers national and international news as Cambodia's oldest English-language newspaper.
Language (s): English
DAILY NEWSPAPER

Raksmei Angkor 473023
Editorial: No.25Z, Street 372, Sangkat Beng Salang, Khan Toul Kok, Phnom Penh 12160
Tel: 855 12 922291
Email: raksmeiangkor@yahoo.com
Freq: 2 Times/Week; **Circ:** 5001 Not Audited
Editor in Chief: En Chan Sivutha
Profile: Cover the latest local and international news.
Language (s): Khmer
DAILY NEWSPAPER

Rasmei Kampuchea Daily 459948
Editorial: Rasmei Kampuchea Daily, 476 Monivong Street, Boulevard, Phnom Penh **Tel:** 855 23 362472
Email: rasmei_kampuchea@yahoo.com
Freq: 2 Times/Week; **Circ:** 25001 Not Audited
Editor in Chief: Pen Samitthy
Profile: Covers news topics.
Language (s): English
DAILY NEWSPAPER

Samleng Yuvachun Khmer 459952
Editorial: Khmer Youth News House 24 Road 374 Tuol Svay Prey, Chamkar Mon District 2, Phnom Penh **Tel:** 855 23 997-4701
Email: khmeryouthnews@yahoo.com
Freq: Daily; **Circ:** 6001 Not Audited
Director: Keo Sothea
Profile: Covers news topics.
Language (s): Khmer
DAILY NEWSPAPER

Somne Themey 473021
Editorial: #6, Street 288, Boeng Kengkang 1, Phonm Penh **Tel:** 855 23224303
Email: somnethemey@online.com.kh **Web site:** http://www.mcdcambodia.com
Freq: Weekly; **Circ:** 10001 Not Audited
Editor in Chief: Nhet Pheaktra
Profile: Covers news.
Language (s): Khmer
DAILY NEWSPAPER

News Service/Syndicate

Agence France Presse 467541
Editorial: Agence France Presse (AFP)- Phnom Penh Bureau, Room A2, No.111, Norodom Boulevard, Phnom Penh 12211 **Tel:** 855 23 426-227
Web site: http://www.afp.com
Freq: Daily
Profile: Covers news topics as a bureau for the French-based AFP.
Language (s): English
NEWS SERVICE/SYNDICATE

Agence Kampuchea Presse (AKP) 467607
Editorial: Agence Kampuchea Presse (AKP), 62 Monivong, Phnom Penh 12201 **Tel:** 855 23 430564
Email: akp@camnet.com.kh **Web site:** http://www.camnet.com.kh/akp
Freq: Daily
Profile: Provides a news service in English, French and Cambodian.
Language (s): English
NEWS SERVICE/SYNDICATE

Cameroon

Time Difference: GMT +1
National Telephone Code: 237
Continent: Africa
Capital: Yaoundé

Newspapers

The Cameroon Tribune 224420
Owner: Cameroon news and Editing Corporation SOPECAM
Editorial: Mvan, Yaoundé **Tel:** 237 22 230 41 47
Email: contact-dcm@cameroon-tribune.cm **Web site:** http://www.cameroon-tribune.cm
Freq: Daily; **Circ:** 25000 Publisher's Statement
Directrice Générale: Marie Claire Nnana
Profile: National Daily Newspaper covering general news and current affairs including politics, society, economy, culture and sports.
Language (s): English
Ad Rate: Full Page Mono 1810.00
Ad Rate: Full Page Colour 930.00
Currency: Euro
DAILY NEWSPAPER

Le Messager 161235
Owner: Free Media Group
Editorial: Rue des Ecoles, Douala
Tel: 237 233 420439
Email: lemessager@lemessager.net
Freq: Daily; **Circ:** 7000 Publisher's Statement
Profile: Newspaper covering news and current affairs, politics, business and sports.
Language (s): French
Ad Rate: Full Page Mono 275000.00
Currency: Communauté Financière Africaine Francs BEAC
DAILY NEWSPAPER

Mutations 161236
Owner: Mutations
Editorial: 183 Rue 1.055, Place Repiquet, Yaoundé
Tel: 237 22 22 51 04
Email: jmutations@yahoo.fr
Freq: Daily; **Circ:** 8000 Publisher's Statement
Profile: National daily Newspaper covering news, politics and current affairs.
Language (s): French
Ad Rate: Full Page Mono 350000.00
Currency: Communauté Financière Africaine Francs BEAC
DAILY NEWSPAPER

La Nouvelle Expression 319320
Owner: La Nouvelle Expression
Editorial: 12, rue Prince de Galles, Douala
Tel: 237 33 43 22 27
Email: lanouvelleexpression2005@yahoo.fr
Freq: Daily; **Circ:** 7000 Publisher's Statement
Profile: Newspaper focusing on national and international news, politics, economics, culture and sports.
Language (s): French
Ad Rate: Full Page Mono 500000.00
Currency: Communauté Financière Africaine Francs BEAC
DAILY NEWSPAPER

The Post Newspaper 449329
Editorial: PO Box 91, Buea **Tel:** 237 33 32 32 87
Email: thepostnp@yahoo.com
Freq: 2 Times/Week; **Circ:** 5000 Publisher's Statement
Editor In Chief: Charly Ndi Chia
Profile: The Post is an English-language newspaper with news and current affairs, politics, economics, culture and sports.
Language (s): English
Ad Rate: Full Page Mono 500000.00
Currency: Communauté Financière Africaine Francs BEAC
DAILY NEWSPAPER

Canada

Time Difference: GMT -3.5 (East Coast), GMT -8 (West Coast)
National Telephone Code: 1
Continent: The Americas
Capital: Ottawa

Newspapers

24 Heures Montreal 83666
Owner: Quebecor Communications Inc.
Editorial: 4545 Rue Frontenac, 3e etage, Montreal, Quebec H2H 2R7 **Tel:** 1 514 393-1010
Email: 24h.redaction@quebecormedia.com **Web site:** http://www.journaldemontreal.com/24heures
Freq: Mon thru Fri; **Circ:** 150239 Not Audited
News Director: Cédérick Caron
Profile: 24 Heures Montréal est un quotidien gratuit conçu pour une lecture d'environ 20 minutes ciblant les usagers des transports en commun de Montréal âgés de 25 à 49 ans. Le quotidien présente des actualités locales, nationales et internationales. Cependant, la majeure partie de son contenu présente des nouvelles d'intérêt humain et des histoires de style de vie sur des sujets tels que la santé et la mode.

24 Heures Montréal is a free commuter daily newspaper that is designed for a 20-minute read and targets commuters between the ages of 25 to 49. It features local, national and international headline news. However, the bulk of its content is human interest and lifestyle stories on subjects such as health and fashion.
Language (s): French
Ad Rate: Full Page Mono 92.82
Ad Rate: Full Page Colour 116.06
Currency: Canada Dollars
DAILY NEWSPAPER

24 Hours Toronto 155822
Owner: Postmedia Network Canada Corp
Editorial: 365 Bloor St E, Toronto, Ontario M4W 3L4
Tel: 1 416 947-2222
Web site: http://www.toronto24hours.ca
Freq: Mon thru Fri; **Circ:** 258000 Not Audited
Editor in Chief: Adrienne Batra; **Distribution Manager:** Paul Gault; **Editor in Chief:** Wendy Metcalfe
Profile: 24 Hours Toronto is a commuter daily newspaper that is distributed free of charge to commuters throughout the Toronto area.
Language (s): English
Ad Rate: Full Page Colour 159.58
Currency: Canada Dollars
DAILY NEWSPAPER

24 Hours Vancouver 334261
Owner: Postmedia Network Inc.
Editorial: 1-200 Granville St 1, Vancouver, British Columbia V6C 3N3- **Tel:** 1 604 322-2340
Email: van24news@sunmedia.ca **Web site:** http://vancouver.24hrs.ca/
Freq: Mon thru Fri; **Circ:** 133000 Not Audited
Distribution Manager: Mike MacKichan
Profile: 24 hours Vancouver is a free commuter daily newspaper circulating weekdays throughout the Lower Mainland of British Columbia. It contains an upbeat mix of local and world news, entertainment, lifestyle, fashion, business, sports and feature stories.
Language (s): English
Ad Rate: Full Page Colour 98.22
Currency: Canada Dollars
DAILY NEWSPAPER

L' Acadie Nouvelle 78011
Owner: Éditions de l'Acadie (Les)
Editorial: 476 Boul St-Pierre O, Caraquet, New Brunswick E1W 1A3 **Tel:** 1 800 561-2255
Email: info@acadienouvelle.com **Web site:** http://www.acadienouvelle.com
Freq: Mon thru Fri; **Circ:** 16800 Not Audited
News Editor: Gaëtan Chiasson
Profile: L'Acadie Nouvelle is a daily, French-language newspaper written for the residents of Caraquet, New Brunswick. Its editorial mission is to inform the community about local and national news, including politics, sports, education, arts and weather.
Language (s): French
Ad Rate: Full Page Mono 16.80
Currency: Canada Dollars
DAILY NEWSPAPER

The Brandon Sun 13589
Owner: FP Canadian Newspapers LP
Editorial: 501 Rosser Ave, Brandon, Manitoba R7A 0K4 **Tel:** 1 204 727-2451
Email: opinion@brandonsun.com **Web site:** http://www.brandonsun.com
Freq: Mon thru Fri; **Circ:** 11248
Editor: Colin Corneau; **Editor:** Matt Goerzen;
Publisher: Eric Lawson
Profile: The Brandon Sun is published daily for the residents of Brandon, Manitoba. The newspaper covers local news, business, sports and entertainment. The paper publishes everyday except Sunday.
Language (s): English
DAILY NEWSPAPER

Calgary Herald 15467

Owner: Postmedia Network Inc.
Editorial: 215 16 St SE, Calgary, Alberta T2E 7P5- **Tel:** 1 403 235-7100
Email: submit@calgaryherald.com **Web site:** http://www.calgaryherald.com
Freq: Daily
Profile: Calgary Herald is a broadsheet newspaper established in 1883. The newspaper includes the following sections: Sports, Business, Arts & Style, City and Classifieds. In November 2000, the paper became part of the Southam Publications division of CanWest Global Communications. The Sunday edition ceased publication on July 29, 2012.
Language (s): English
Ad Rate: Full Page Mono 101.08
Ad Rate: Full Page Colour 118.68
Currency: Canada Dollars
DAILY NEWSPAPER

The Calgary Sun 13576

Owner: Postmedia
Editorial: 2615 12 St NE, Calgary, Alberta T2E 7W9- **Tel:** 1 403 410-1010
Email: cal-news@sunmedia.ca **Web site:** http://www.calgarysun.com
Freq: Daily; **Circ:** 49258 Not Audited
Editor in Chief: Jose Rodriguez
Profile: The Calgary Sun is written for residents of Calgary, Alberta. The publication covers local, national and international news on politics, business, homes, entertainment and sports. The publication does not offer reader service cards and does not publish an editorial calendar. Editors do not honor non-disclosure agreements. It debuted in August 1980.
Language (s): English
Ad Rate: Full Page Mono 26.32
Ad Rate: Full Page Colour 148.83
Currency: Canada Dollars
DAILY NEWSPAPER

Canadian Punjabi Post 772605

Editorial: 27 Armthorpe Rd Unit 3, Brampton, Ontario L6T 5M4 **Tel:** 1 905 793-2282
Email: news@punjabipost.ca **Web site:** http://www.punjabipost.ca
Freq: Daily
Editor: Jagdish Grewal
Profile: Canadian Punjabi Post is a daily publication that covers multicultural events and news for the Indian community in Brampton, Canada.
Language (s): English
DAILY NEWSPAPER

Cape Breton Post 13604

Owner: SaltWire Network Inc.
Editorial: 255 George St, Sydney, Nova Scotia B1P 1J7- **Tel:** 1 902 564-5451
Email: comments@cbpost.com **Web site:** http://www.capebretonpost.com
Freq: Daily; **Circ:** 24924 Not Audited
Profile: Cape Breton Post is written for the residents of Cape Breton, Nova Scotia. It covers sports, business, lifestyles, entertainment and local news with specific coverage of the Sydney, Northside, Victoria, Low Point, Little Pond, Port Hawksesbury, Glace Bay and New Waterford regions. The daily deadline is 11:30pm AT. Lead time varies.
Language (s): English
Ad Rate: Full Page Mono 12.04
Ad Rate: Full Page Colour 800.00
Currency: Canada Dollars
DAILY NEWSPAPER

The Chatham Daily News 13611

Owner: Postmedia Network Inc
Editorial: 138 King St W, Chatham, Ontario N7M 1E3- **Tel:** 1 519 354-2000
Email: cdn.newsroom@sunmedia.ca **Web site:** http://www.chathamdailynews.ca
Freq: Fri; **Circ:** 12134 Not Audited
Editor: Peter Epp
Profile: Chatham Daily News serves the Chatham-Kent area in southwestern Ontario.
Language (s): English
Ad Rate: Full Page Mono 13.63
Ad Rate: Full Page Colour 562.74
Currency: Canada Dollars
DAILY NEWSPAPER

The Chronicle Herald 13601

Owner: SaltWire Network Inc.
Editorial: 2717 Joseph Howe Dr, Halifax, Nova Scotia B3L 4T9- **Tel:** 1 902 426-2811
Email: newsroom@herald.ca **Web site:** http://thechronicleherald.ca
Freq: Daily; **Circ:** 74010 Not Audited
Editor, Herald Wheels: Todd Gillis; **Editor in Chief:** Bob Howse; **News Editor:** Christine Soucie; **News Editor:** Pam Sword
Profile: The Chronicle Herald is a broadsheet newspaper targeting Halifax residents. It was established in 1874 and offers to its readers Nova Scotia, National and International News, Business, Sports, Entertainment and more. **The Chronicle Herald's newsroom members associated with Halifax Typographical Union are on strike.
Language (s): English
Ad Rate: Full Page Mono 123.51
Ad Rate: Full Page Colour 442.71
Currency: Canada Dollars
DAILY NEWSPAPER

The Chronicle-Journal 13638

Owner: Continental Newspapers Canada Ltd.
Editorial: 75 Cumberland St S, Thunder Bay, Ontario P7B 1A3 **Tel:** 1 807 343-6200
Email: news@chroniclejournal.com **Web site:** http://www.chroniclejournal.com
Freq: Daily; **Circ:** 21558 Not Audited
Profile: The Chronicle-Journal is written for the Thunder Bay, Ontario vicinity and the Northwestern Ontario general public. The paper covers regional and local news, sports, business, lifestyles and entertainment.
Language (s): English
DAILY NEWSPAPER

Corriere Canadese 80270

Editorial: 2790 Dufferin St, Toronto, Ontario M6B 3R7 **Tel:** 1 416 782-9222
Email: info@corriere.com **Web site:** http://www.corriere.com
Freq: Mon thru Fri; **Circ:** 10000 Not Audited
Editor in Chief: Francesco Veronesi; **Publisher:** Joe Volpe
Profile: Published in Italian, Corriere Canadese serves the Canadian Italian community with articles on culture, arts, entertainment, travel, business and local news, national and international news.
Language (s): Italian
Ad Rate: Full Page Colour 22.40
Currency: Canada Dollars
DAILY NEWSPAPER

The Daily Courier 13578

Owner: Continental Newspapers Canada Ltd.
Editorial: 550 Doyle Ave, Kelowna, British Columbia V1Y 7V1- **Tel:** 1 250 762-4445
Web site: http://www.kelownadailycourier.ca
Freq: Mon thru Fri; **Circ:** 10566 Not Audited
Publisher: Terry Armstrong
Profile: The Daily Courier is a broadsheet newspaper written for the Okanagan Valley, British Columbia general public. It is one of the major newspapers in the region covering news, sports, trends and business. It has won several awards, including the Thomson Award for excellent news, graphics and photography.
Language (s): English
Ad Rate: Full Page Mono 19.40
Ad Rate: Full Page Colour 487.55
Currency: Canada Dollars
DAILY NEWSPAPER

The Daily Gleaner 13594

Owner: Summit Publishing
Editorial: 984 Prospect St, Fredericton, New Brunswick E3B 2T8 **Tel:** 1 506 452-6671
Email: news@dailygleaner.com **Web site:** https://www.telegraphjournal.com/daily-gleaner/
Freq: Daily; **Circ:** 20048 Not Audited
News Editor: Anne Mooers
Profile: The Daily Gleaner is written for residents of Fredericton, New Brunswick and greater residential communities. Aside from the coverage of local and national news, the publication also covers money and economy topics in the business section and local sporting news, statistics and events in sports. There is also a daily entertainment news page, a community calendar, humor and advice columns, television listings and a fitness, nutrition and healthy living page. Weekly sections include the books, lifestyles and Real Estate sections.
Language (s): English
Ad Rate: Full Page Mono 22.96
Ad Rate: Full Page Colour 26.88
Currency: Canada Dollars
DAILY NEWSPAPER

Le Devoir 13647

Owner: Devoir Inc. (Le)
Editorial: 1265 Rue Berri, 8e etage, Montreal, Quebec H2L 4X4 **Tel:** 1 514 985-3333
Email: redaction@ledevoir.com **Web site:** http://www.ledevoir.com
Freq: Daily; **Circ:** 32412 Not Audited
Profile: Le Devoir est un quotidien indépendant prisé par l'élite politique et intellectuelle québécoise. Celui-ci rapporte notamment les nouvelles régionales, nationales et internationales. D'autres sujets incluent également la politique, l'économie, les affaires, la technologie, l'éducation, les sports, le théâtre, le cinéma, la télévision, la critique littéraire et culinaire, la cuisine et le vin.

Le Devoir is an independent French-language newspaper favored by Quebec's political and intellectual elites. It includes regional, national and international news. Other topics include politics, economics, business, health, technology, education, sports, theater, film, television and book reviews, restaurant guides, food recipes and wine tasting.
Language (s): French
Ad Rate: Full Page Mono 31.36
Ad Rate: Full Page Colour 38.64
Currency: Canada Dollars
DAILY NEWSPAPER

Le Droit 13626

Owner: Groupe Capitales Medias
Editorial: 47 Rue Clarence Bureau 222, Ottawa, Ontario K1N 9K1 **Tel:** 1 613 562-0111
Email: nouvelles@ledroit.com **Web site:** http://www.lapresse.ca/le-droit
Freq: Mon thru Fri; **Circ:** 25955
Profile: Founded March 27, 1913, Le Droit is a French-language, daily newspaper covering the Outaouais region of Québec and eastern Ontario. It is the only Francophone daily in Ottawa. National, regional and local information are given the most attention while international news is covered mostly by news wires.
Language (s): French
Ad Rate: Full Page Mono 28.84
Ad Rate: Full Page Colour 33.32
Currency: Canada Dollars
DAILY NEWSPAPER

The Edmonton Journal 13570

Owner: Postmedia Network Inc.
Editorial: 10006 101 St NW, Edmonton, Alberta T5J 0S1- **Tel:** 1 780 429-5100
Email: city@edmontonjournal.com **Web site:** http://www.edmontonjournal.com
Freq: Daily
Profile: The Edmonton Journal is a newspaper written for the Edmonton, Alberta general public. It is one of the major newspapers in the area covering news, sports, business and entertainment. The paper has won several honors, including a National Newspaper Award and an international award for outstanding features. The newspaper is known for quality photography and in-depth coverage.
Language (s): English
Ad Rate: Full Page Mono 69.09
Ad Rate: Full Page Colour 267.08
Currency: Canada Dollars
DAILY NEWSPAPER

The Edmonton Sun 14868

Owner: PostMedia Inc.
Editorial: 10006 101 St NW, Edmonton, Alberta T5J 0S1- **Tel:** 1 780 468-0100
Email: edm-citydesk@sunmedia.ca **Web site:** http://www.edmontonsun.com
Freq: Daily; **Circ:** 51547 Not Audited
Publisher: John Caputo; **Editor in Chief:** Steve Serviss
Profile: The Edmonton Sun covers national and predominantly local news, business, which highlights Alberta or Edmonton specific industries and trends; entertainment and sports. Editors honor non-disclosure agreements. The publication accepts vendor-written articles on a case-by-case basis and does not offer reader-service cards. It was established on April 2, 1978.
Language (s): English
Ad Rate: Full Page Mono 27.09
Ad Rate: Full Page Colour 152.14
Currency: Canada Dollars
DAILY NEWSPAPER

El El Popular 257569

Editorial: 2413 Dundas St W, Toronto, Ontario M6P 1X3 **Tel:** 1 416 531-2495
Email: editor@diarioelpopular.com **Web site:** http://diarioelpopular.com
Freq: Daily; **Circ:** 10500 Not Audited
Profile: El Popular is published for Spanish speaking Canadians. It covers national news, travel, sports, business, arts and lifestyle topics.
Language (s): English
Ad Rate: Full Page Mono 6.02
Ad Rate: Full Page Colour 125.00
Currency: Canada Dollars
DAILY NEWSPAPER

The Expositor 13608

Owner: Postmedia Network Inc
Editorial: 195 Henry St Unit 1, bldg 4, Brantford, Ontario N3S 5C9 **Tel:** 1 519 756-2020
Email: brex.expnews@sunmedia.ca **Web site:** http://www.brantfordexpositor.ca
Freq: Mon thru Fri; **Circ:** 20801 Not Audited
Publisher: Ken Koyama
Profile: The Expositor is written for the residents of Brantford, Ontario. It covers news, sports, business and entertainment. Deadlines are 5pm ET.
Language (s): English
Ad Rate: Full Page Mono 22.26
Ad Rate: Full Page Colour 15.93
Currency: Canada Dollars
DAILY NEWSPAPER

The Gazette 15441

Owner: Postmedia Network Inc.
Editorial: 1010 Sainte-Catherine St W Suite 200, Montreal, Quebec H3B 5L1 **Tel:** 1 514 987-2222
Web site: http://www.montrealgazette.com
Freq: Mon thru Fri
Editor in Chief: Lucinda Chodan; **News Features Editor:** Dave Peters
Profile: The Montreal Gazette is an English-language newspaper written for residents in Montréal. It is one of the oldest newspapers in North America and was founded by Fleury Mesplet in 1778 as a French-language paper. It became bilingual in the late 1700s and ultimately changed to an English-language newspaper in 1822.
Language (s): English
Ad Rate: Full Page Mono 52.99
Ad Rate: Full Page Colour 214.26
Currency: Canada Dollars
DAILY NEWSPAPER

The Globe and Mail 15448

Owner: Woodbridge Company Limited (The)
Editorial: 351 King Street East, Suite 1600, Toronto, Ontario M5A 0N1 **Tel:** 1 416 585-5000
Email: newsroom@globeandmail.com **Web site:** http://www.theglobeandmail.com
Freq: Daily; **Circ:** 347524 Not Audited
Contributor: Chris Atchison; **Market Strategist:** Scott Barlow; **Director, Logistics and Distribution:** Joann Boudreau; **Publisher/CEO:** Phillip Crawley; **Editor:** Hamutal Dotan; **Editor in Chief:** David Walmsley
Profile: The Globe and Mail is a daily, national, Canadian newspaper. Throughout the week, there are various special sections, including Globe Travel, Globe Style, Globe Books, Globe T.O., Globe Drive, Focus and Health and Lifestyle. There is also a Weekend Arts section. Lead times for different departments vary. Attachments to electronic communications are not accepted, so place all information in the body of electronic messages. The publication only wishes to correspond through e-mails or phone calls.
Language (s): English
Ad Rate: Full Page Mono 446.32
Ad Rate: Full Page Colour 499.81
Currency: Canada Dollars
DAILY NEWSPAPER

The Guardian 13643

Owner: SaltWire Network Inc
Editorial: 165 Prince St, Charlottetown, Prince Edward Island C1A 4R7 **Tel:** 1 902 629-6000
Email: newsroom@theguardian.pe.ca **Web site:** http://www.theguardian.pe.ca
Freq: Daily; **Circ:** 20701 Not Audited
Publisher: Don Brander; **Chief Photographer:** Heather Taweel
Profile: The Guardian is a 40+ page broadsheet newspaper serving the Prince Edward Island area. It is one of the area's premier newspapers focusing on all types of business, sports and general news coverage.
Language (s): English
Ad Rate: Full Page Mono 29.57
Ad Rate: Full Page Colour 105.58
Currency: Canada Dollars
DAILY NEWSPAPER

The Hamilton Spectator 13615

Owner: Metroland Media Group Ltd.
Editorial: 44 Frid St, Hamilton, Ontario L8N 3G3 **Tel:** 1 905 526-3333
Web site: http://www.thespec.com
Freq: Daily; **Circ:** 103267 Not Audited
Editor in Chief: Paul Berton
Profile: The Hamilton Spectator is a broadsheet newspaper written for residents of Hamilton, Ontario. It covers local and national news, sports, entertainment and business. The features section focuses on food, gardening, homes and travel. The newspaper has won several honors, including the National Newspaper Award and a Human Rights Award.
Language (s): English
Ad Rate: Full Page Mono 141.10
Ad Rate: Full Page Colour 181.59
Currency: Canada Dollars
DAILY NEWSPAPER

Le Journal de Montréal 13648

Owner: Quebecor Communications Inc.
Editorial: 4545 Rue Frontenac, Montreal, Quebec H2H 2R7- **Tel:** 1 514 521-4545
Email: jdm.transmission@quebecormedia.com **Web site:** http://www.journaldemontreal.com
Freq: Daily; **Circ:** 232137 Not Audited
Editor in Chief: Dany Doucet; **Publisher:** Lyne Robitaille
Profile: Le Journal de Montréal, créé en 1964, est un journal tabloïde quotidien, qui possède l'un des plus grands chiffres de circulation et de lecture dans la province de Québec. Bien que les histoires nationales et internationales soient régulièrement présentées, le contenu de la publication est principalement axé sur les nouvelles locales et spécifiques à Montréal. Les sections quotidiennes individuelles comprennent: les nouvelles locales, habituellement centrées sur le crime et la politique; Société, présentant des arts, du divertissement, de la santé et des informations sur les modes de vie; La politique, y compris les questions liées aux gouvernements provinciaux et fédéraux; Les affaires, qui comprennent également les nouvelles financières, et le sport, qui contient une couverture sportive locale et nationale et des colonnes. Il existe également diverses sections hebdomadaires. Du lundi au samedi, le journal comprend un complément d'affaires. Le complément de fin de semaine est un guide de divertissement basé sur le magazine, axé sur les potins de célébrités, les nouvelles artistiques et de divertissement et les listes d'événements.

Le Journal de Montréal, established in 1964, is a four color, 80+ page, daily, French-language tabloid newspaper which has one of the largest circulation and readership figures in the province of Quebec. Though national and international stories are regularly featured, the publication's content is predominantly focused on local, Montreal-specific news. Individual daily sections include: local news headlines, usually centered on crime and politics; Society, featuring arts, entertainment, health, and lifestyles information; Politics, including Provincial and Federal government-related issues; Business, which also includes financial news, and Sports, which contains local and national sporting coverage and columns. There are also various weekly sections. Monday through Saturday the newspaper comes with a Business supplement. On Wednesdays and Saturdays the business supplement is intertwined with a Careers, Employment, and Training section. Additionally on Saturday's there are the pullout Homes, TV Listings, and Weekend sections. The Travel supplement is available on Tuesdays. And, Entertainment is present as an individual section Mondays through Fridays, and Sundays. On Saturday it is part on a one page Arts, Entertainment and Lifestyles compilation. The Weekend supplement, magazine-style entertainment guide focused on celebrity gossip, arts and entertainment news, and event listings.
Language (s): French
Ad Rate: Full Page Mono 175.00
Ad Rate: Full Page Colour 243.88
Currency: Canada Dollars
DAILY NEWSPAPER

Le Journal de Québec 13654

Owner: Québécor Communications Inc.
Editorial: 450 Av Bechard, Quebec, Quebec G1M 2E9- **Tel:** 1 418 683-1573

Email: jdq-scoop@quebecormedia.com **Web site:** http://www.journaldequebec.com
Freq: Daily; **Circ:** 149635 Not Audited
Publisher: Louise Cordeau; **News Diretcor:** Jean LaRoche; **Editor in Chief:** Sébastien Ménard
Profile: Le Journal de Québec est un quotidien. Il a été fondé en 1967 par Pierre Péladeau. C'est une publication en francophone, qui couvre les Nouvelles Régionales, Nationales et Internationales, en mettant l'accent sur les nouvelles de la ville de Québec. Dans l'est du Québec, il détient la distinction d'avoir la plus grande circulation quotidienne et d'être le premier quotidien à imprimer sept jours par semaine.

Le Journal de Québec is a daily newspaper. It was founded in 1967 by Pierre Péladeau (the founder of Québécor Média itself). It is a French-language publication, which covers regional, national, and international news, with a strong focus on the city news of Québec. In Eastern Québec, it holds the distinction of having the largest circulation for a daily, and being the first daily newspaper to print seven days a week.
Language (s): French
Ad Rate: Full Page Mono 96.32
Ad Rate: Full Page Colour 138.04
Currency: Canada Dollars
DAILY NEWSPAPER

Korea Times Toronto Edition 80510
Editorial: 287 Bridgeland Ave, Toronto, Ontario M6A 1Z6 **Tel:** 1 416 787-1111
Email: public@koreatimes.net **Web site:** http://www.koreatimes.net
Freq: Daily; **Circ:** 16000 Not Audited
Profile: Korea Times Toronto Edition is a daily, Korean-language paper serving the residents of Toronto. It provides local, national and international news.
Language (s): English
Ad Rate: Full Page Mono 36.00
Ad Rate: Full Page Colour 142.88
Currency: Canada Dollars
DAILY NEWSPAPER

La La Tribune 13652
Owner: Groupe Capitales Medias
Editorial: 1950 Rue Roy, Sherbrooke, Quebec J1K 2X8 **Tel:** 1 819 564-5450
Email: redaction@latribune.qc.ca **Web site:** http://www.lapresse.ca/la-tribune
Freq: Daily; **Circ:** 24000
News Editor: Louis-Éric Allard; **Publisher:** Louise Boisvert; **Editor In Chief:** Maurice Cloutier
Profile: La tribune est un quotidien concentrant sa couverture aux nouvelles locales et regionales des Cantons-de-l'est. En plus des informations locales, La tribune inclut les nouvelles nationales ainsi qu'à l'Internaltionales, obtenues principalement de fils de presse.

La Tribune is a daily French-language newspaper with strong coverage of local and regional news in Quebec's Eastern Townships. In addition to local information, La Tribune includes national and international news, obtained primarily from news wires.
Language (s): French/Bilingual
Ad Rate: Full Page Mono 24.78
Ad Rate: Full Page Colour 32.20
Currency: Canada Dollars
DAILY NEWSPAPER

The Leader Post 13657
Owner: Postmedia Network Inc.
Editorial: Regina, Saskatchewan **Tel:** 1 306 781-5211
Email: citydesk@leaderpost.com **Web site:** http://www.leaderpost.com
Freq: Daily
Profile: The Leader Post, established in 1883, is a daily 30+ page, broadsheet newspaper written for residents of Regina, Saskatchewan and its neighboring communities. Every issue of the publication includes six staple sections: Canada & World, Arts & Life, City & Province, Business & Agriculture, Sports and Classifieds. Additionally, on Mondays the paper includes the Minus 20 section, on Tuesdays the paper includes the Fashion section and Wednesday the paper includes the Food section. On Thursdays one will find What's On, Living Spaces and Body & Health. On Fridays, the publication includes the Travel and Driving sections. Saturdays issues include Weekender, Working, Homes and Children's Corner. On Sundays, one will find the Regina Sun Community News. There are two magazine style publications that arrive monthly with the Regina Leader-Post: Home Lifestyles and Kicks.
Language (s): English
Ad Rate: Full Page Mono 30.52
Currency: Canada Dollars
DAILY NEWSPAPER

The Lethbridge Herald 13573
Owner: Alberta Newspaper Group Inc.
Editorial: 504 Seventh St S, Lethbridge, Alberta T1J 2H1 **Tel:** 1 403 328-4411
Email: circulation@lethbridgeherald.com **Web site:** http://www.lethbridgeherald.com
Freq: Daily; **Circ:** 16901 Not Audited
Publisher: Coleen Campbell; **News Editor:** Randy Jensen
Profile: The Lethbridge Herald is a broadsheet newspaper written for the Southern Alberta general public. It is one of the major newspapers in Southern Alberta covering business, agriculture, entertainment, sports and world news.
Language (s): English
Ad Rate: Full Page Mono 11.41
Ad Rate: Full Page Colour 590.00
Currency: Canada Dollars
DAILY NEWSPAPER

The London Free Press 13621
Owner: Postmedia Network Inc.
Editorial: 369 York St, London, Ontario N6B 3R4-
Tel: 1 519 679-1111
Email: lfp.website@sunmedia.ca **Web site:** http://www.lfpress.com
Freq: Mon thru Fri; **Circ:** 73990 Not Audited
News Editor: Howard Burns; **Editor in Chief:** Joe Ruscitti; **News Editor:** Greg Van Moorsel;
Contributor: Janis Wallace
Profile: The London Free Press is a daily newspaper written for the London, Ontario general public. It covers local, national and world news as well as arts & entertainment, lifestyle, food, travel, books, television, art, movies, business, features and sports. There is no dedicated photo editor, but photo inquiries can be directed to the news editor.
Language (s): English
Ad Rate: Full Page Mono 34.44
Ad Rate: Full Page Colour 132.16
Currency: Canada Dollars
DAILY NEWSPAPER

Medicine Hat News 13574
Owner: Alberta Newspaper Group Inc.
Editorial: 3257 Dunmore Rd SE, Medicine Hat, Alberta T1B 3R2 **Tel:** 1 403 527-1101
Web site: http://www.medicinehatnews.com
Freq: Daily; **Circ:** 10557 Not Audited
Photographer: Emma Bennett; **Publisher:** Mike Hertz
Profile: Medicine Hat News is a daily newspaper published for the residents of Medicine Hat, Alberta. The paper focuses on community news and sports, but also includes national news, lifestyle and opinions sections.
Language (s): English
Ad Rate: Full Page Mono 17.92
Ad Rate: Full Page Colour 515.00
Currency: Canada Dollars
DAILY NEWSPAPER

Metro Calgary 450117
Owner: Star Media Group
Editorial: 3030 3 Ave NE Suite 110, Calgary, Alberta T2A 6T7 **Tel:** 1 403 444-0136
Email: calgaryletters@metronews.ca **Web site:** http://www.metronews.ca/calgary
Freq: Daily; **Circ:** 77525 Not Audited
National Advertising Sales Director: Peter Bartrem
Profile: Metro Calgary is a local, commuter daily serving residents of Calgary, Alberta. The paper includes local, national and international news, politics, business, sports, arts & entertainment and pop culture. Sister papers include Metro Vancouver, Metro Edmonton, Metro Toronto, Metro Ottawa, Metro Halifax, Metro Winnipeg, Metro London and Metro Montréal. Combined the newspapers reach around 1.1 million readers.
Language (s): English
Ad Rate: Full Page Colour 83.77
Currency: Canada Dollars
DAILY NEWSPAPER

Metro Edmonton 468897
Owner: Star Media Group
Editorial: 2070-10123 99 St NW 2070, Edmonton, Alberta T5J 3H1 **Tel:** 1 780 702-0592
Email: edmontonletters@metronews.ca **Web site:** http://www.metronews.ca/edmonton
Freq: Daily; **Circ:** 81815 Not Audited
National Advertising Sales Director: Peter Bartrem
Profile: Metro Edmonton is a local, commuter daily written for the residents of Edmonton, Alberta. Sister papers include Metro Vancouver, Metro Calgary, Metro Toronto, Metro Ottawa, Metro Halifax, Metro Winnipeg, Metro London and Metro Montréal. Combined, the papers reach around 1.1 million readers.
Language (s): English
Ad Rate: Full Page Colour 83.77
Currency: Canada Dollars
DAILY NEWSPAPER

Metro Halifax 521777
Owner: Star Media Group
Editorial: 3260 Barrington St Suite 102, Halifax, Nova Scotia B3K 0B5 **Tel:** 1 902 444-4444
Email: halifaxletters@metronews.ca **Web site:** http://www.metronews.ca/halifax
Freq: Mon thru Fri; **Circ:** 43949 Not Audited
National Advertising Sales Director: Peter Bartrem;
Publisher: Greg Lutes
Profile: Metro Halifax is a free newspaper that runs Monday through Friday and serves community, national and international news to the Halifax, Nova Scotia metropolitan population. Sister papers include Metro Vancouver, Metro Edmonton, Metro Toronto, Metro Ottawa, Metro Calgary, Metro Winnipeg, Metro London and Metro Montréal. Combined the newspapers reach around 1.1 million readers.
Language (s): English
Ad Rate: Full Page Colour 48.83
Currency: Canada Dollars
DAILY NEWSPAPER

Métro Montréal 83665
Owner: TC. Transcontinental
Editorial: 1100 Boul Rene-Levesque O, 24e etage, Montreal, Quebec H3B 4N4 **Tel:** 1 514 286-1066
Email: info@journalmetro.com **Web site:** http://www.journalmetro.com
Freq: Mon thru Fri; **Circ:** 175000 Not Audited
Editor in Chief: Éric Aussant; **Publisher:** Nicolas Faucher
Profile: Métro Montréal est un journal quotidien gratuit publié chaque fin de semaine et distribué aux résidents et passagers du réseau de transport du métro de Montréal. Le journal francophone est destiné pour une clientèle jeune, urbaine et bien éduquée. Les nouvelles locales, nationales et internationales sont jumelées avec les dernières actualités sur le divertissement, les critiques et autres. On y trouve également des articles portant sur des sujets comme le sport, la nourriture, la santé, le conditionnement physique, l'éducation, les carrières, les voyages et l'immobilier. Journaux affiliés inlcuent Metro Vancouver, Metro Edmonton, Metro Toronto, Metro Ottawa, Metro Halifax et Metro Calgary. Les publications combinées rejoignent près de 1.1 milions de lecteurs.

Métro Montréal is a free commuter daily newspaper published each weekday and serving residents and commuters in the greater Montreal metro area. The French-language paper is designed and packaged for young, urban and well-educated audiences. Local, national and international news reports are combined with the latest entertainment listings and reviews. It also contains articles on topics such as sports, food, health and fitness, education and careers, travel and real estate.Sister papers include Metro Vancouver, Metro Edmonton, Metro Toronto, Metro Ottawa, Metro Halifax and Metro Calgary. Combined the newspapers reach around 1.1 million readers.
Language (s): French
Ad Rate: Full Page Mono 138.60
Currency: Canada Dollars
DAILY NEWSPAPER

Metro Ottawa 363193
Owner: Star Media Group
Editorial: 130 Slater St, Ottawa, Ontario K1P 6E2
Tel: 1 613 236-5058
Email: ottawaletters@metronews.ca **Web site:** http://www.metronews.ca/ottawa
Freq: Mon thru Fri; **Circ:** 61541 Not Audited
National Advertising Sales Director: Peter Bartrem
Profile: Metro Ottawa is a free commuter daily newspaper distributed each weekday to residents and commuters in the greater Ottawa metro area. It is designed and packaged for young, urban and well-educated audiences and it is available at newstands, restaurants and retailers. Local, national and international news reports are combined with the latest entertainment listings and reviews. It also contains articles on topics such as sports, food, health and fitness, education and careers, travel and real estate. Lead times vary depending on editorial department. Advertising rates include full color. Sister papers include Metro Vancouver, Metro Edmonton, Metro Toronto, Metro Calgary, Metro Halifax, Metro Winnipeg, Metro London and Metro Montréal. Combined the newspapers reach around 1.1 million readers.
Language (s): English
Ad Rate: Full Page Colour 76.97
Currency: Canada Dollars
DAILY NEWSPAPER

Metro Toronto 83662
Owner: Star Media Group
Editorial: 1 Yonge St Fl 2ND, Toronto, Ontario M5E 1E5 **Tel:** 1 416 486-4900
Email: toronto@metronews.ca **Web site:** http://www.metronews.ca/toronto
Freq: Mon thru Fri; **Circ:** 266476 Not Audited
Profile: Metro Toronto is a free, commuter daily newspaper that is distributed to commuters and residents of the Toronto metropolitan area. It targets young professionals and is intended to be read during a 20-minute morning commute. The newspaper has concise articles that focus on local, national and international news, lifestyle, sports and arts & entertainment stories.
Language (s): English
Ad Rate: Full Page Colour 250.17
Currency: Canada Dollars
DAILY NEWSPAPER

Metro Vancouver 334239
Owner: Star Media Group
Editorial: 375 Water St Suite 405, Vancouver, British Columbia V6B 5C6 **Tel:** 1 604 602-1002
Email: vancouverletters@metronews.ca **Web site:** http://www.metronews.ca/vancouver
Freq: Mon thru Fri; **Circ:** 160982 Not Audited
Profile: Metro Vancouver is a free, commuter daily newspaper distributed throughout the Vancouver, British Columbia metropolitan area. It targets young professionals and is intended to be read during a 20-minute morning commute. The newspaper has concise articles that focus on local, national and international news, lifestyle, sports and arts & entertainment stories. Sister papers include Metro Edmonton, Metro Calgary, Metro Toronto, Metro Ottawa, Metro Halifax, Metro Winnipeg, Metro London and Metro Montréal. Combined, the papers reach around 1.1 million readers.
Language (s): English
Ad Rate: Full Page Colour 134.25
Currency: Canada Dollars
DAILY NEWSPAPER

Metro Winnipeg 734459
Owner: Star Media Group
Editorial: 161 Portage Ave E Suite 200, Winnipeg, Manitoba R3B 0Y4 **Tel:** 1 204 943-9300
Email: winnipegletters@metronews.ca **Web site:** http://www.metronews.ca/winnipeg
Freq: Mon thru Fri; **Circ:** 51505
Profile: Metro Winnipeg launched April 4, 2011 as a free, commuter daily newspaper distributed to commuters and residents of the Winnipeg, Manitoba metropolitan area. It targets youthful, active readers between the ages of 18 and 49. The newspaper offers concise articles that focus on local, national and international news, lifestyle, sports and arts & entertainment stories. Sister publications include: Metro Toronto, Metro Montréal, Metro Calgary, Metro Edmonton, Metro Vancouver, Metro Halifax, Metro Ottawa and Metro London.
Language (s): English
Ad Rate: Full Page Colour 49.78
Currency: Canada Dollars
DAILY NEWSPAPER

Ming Pao Daily News 80341
Owner: Ming Pao Holdings (Canada) Ltd
Editorial: 1355 Huntingwood Dr, Scarborough, Ontario M1S 3J1 **Tel:** 1 416 321-0088
Email: information@mingpaotor.com **Web site:** http://www.mingpaotor.com
Freq: Daily; **Circ:** 73390 Not Audited
Editor: Richard Ng
Profile: Ming Pao Daily News is a daily newspaper written for Chinese Canadian readers. The newspaper covers information about news, business and entertainment for Eastern Canada.
Language (s): Chinese
Ad Rate: Full Page Mono 53.00
Ad Rate: Full Page Colour 3856.00
Currency: Canada Dollars
DAILY NEWSPAPER

Ming Pao Daily News 82800
Owner: Ming Pao Holdings (Canada) Ltd
Editorial: 5368 Parkwood Pl, Richmond, British Columbia V6V 2N1 **Tel:** 1 604 231-8998
Web site: http://www.mingpao.com
Freq: Daily; **Circ:** 54000 Not Audited
Publisher: Ka Ming Lui; **Editor in Chief:** Raymond Yeung
Profile: Ming Pao Daily News is daily newspaper written for Chinese Canadians. The publications covers information about news, business and entertainment in western Canada.
Language (s): Chinese
Ad Rate: Full Page Mono 5.00
Ad Rate: Full Page Colour 125.00
Currency: Canada Dollars
DAILY NEWSPAPER

Moncton Times & Transcript 13595
Owner: Moncton Publishing Company Ltd.
Editorial: 939 Main St, Moncton, New Brunswick E1C 8P3 **Tel:** 1 506 859-4900
Email: news@timestranscript.com **Web site:** https://www.telegraphjournal.com/times-transcript/
Freq: Daily; **Circ:** 35050 Not Audited
Profile: Moncton Times & Transcript is a 40+ page broadsheet, daily newspaper written for the New Brunswick general public. The editorial and news content of the publication focuses on Moncton, New Brunswick, but also includes news and events from various parts of northern New Brunswick and eastern Nova Scotia, as well as Albert, Westmoreland and Kent counties. The paper is comprised of four main sections: local and regional news; life and times; sports; and international, national and business news. Special features include national and international commentary, TV Book, What's Up? (a daily list of Moncton events), Saturday Job Market, Leisure Living for weekend reading, Real Estate Tips in the Business section, Homes, and Whatever (a supplement produced by local youths). The publication focuses primarily on issues that have a direct impact on its local readers.
Language (s): English
Ad Rate: Full Page Mono 42.00
Ad Rate: Full Page Colour 1654.00
Currency: Canada Dollars
DAILY NEWSPAPER

National Post 15458
Owner: Postmedia Network Inc.
Editorial: 365 Bloor St E, 3rd fl, Toronto, Ontario M4W 3L4 **Tel:** 1 416 383-2300
Web site: http://www.nationalpost.com
Freq: Daily
Editor: Jodi Lai; **Editor in Chief:** Anne Marie Owens;
National News & Politics Editor: Rob Roberts
Profile: National Post incorporates the former Financial Post Newspaper into its four section national newspaper. They prefer to be contacted by their online form. It is published five times a week, and is organized as follows: The first section delivers comprehensive news, political and health reporting from across the country and around the world; the second section contains the Financial Post business news; the third section covers sports with news on golf, auto racing, hockey and football featured daily; the fourth section titled Arts & Life features news on theater, movies, fine arts and other areas of interest. In addition, the Saturday Post includes a magazine style fifth section. In the words of the publishers, "Incorporating The Financial Post, National Post delivers a comprehensive package of news, arts, life, sports and business coverage the way Canadians say they want it - nationally focused with a window on the world." Technology coverage includes business issues, office technology, computers in the home, consumer issues, financial software, and general computer and communications issues. News content emphasizes "the national outlook of Canada, rather than being Toronto-centric." Types of articles include news briefs, company and personality profiles, trend stories, and occasional product announcements and reviews. Special Reports include the following regular feature topics: Travel & Loyalty and Travel Extras, which cover travel across the country, highlighting services available, travel

planning, and corporate practices; RRSP and Mutual Funds, which cover Canadian investment trends; Legal Post, which covers topics in business law such as pensions, mergers & acquisitions, class action, clean technology and careers; and Luxury Living, which covers the latest in luxury real estate, fashion and goods.
Language (s): English
Ad Rate: Full Page Mono 133.98
Ad Rate: Full Page Colour 608.84
Currency: Canada Dollars
DAILY NEWSPAPER

Niagara Falls Review 13622

Owner: Postmedia Network Inc.
Editorial: 4424 Queen St, Niagara Falls, Ontario L2E 2L3 **Tel:** 1 905 358-5711
Web site: http://www.niagarafallsreview.ca
Freq: Mon thru Fri; **Circ:** 14384 Not Audited
Publisher: Michael Cressman
Profile: The Niagara Falls Review is a daily newspaper tailored for the community in and around Niagara Falls, Ontario.
Language (s): English
Ad Rate: Full Page Mono 12.74
Ad Rate: Full Page Colour 15.29
Currency: Canada Dollars
DAILY NEWSPAPER

North Bay Nugget 13623

Owner: Postmedia Network Inc.
Editorial: 259 Worthington St W, North Bay, Ontario P1B 3B5 **Tel:** 1 705 472-3200
Email: nbay.news@sunmedia.ca **Web site:** http://www.nugget.ca
Freq: Mon thru Fri; **Circ:** 12000 Not Audited
Profile: North Bay Nugget is a 30+ page broadsheet newspaper written for the North Bay, Ontario general public. It is one of the major newspapers in the area covering news, sports and entertainment. Weekly sections include business on Tuesday, technology on Wednesday, entertainment on Thursday, homes on Friday, and lifestyles on Saturday. Lifestyles covers travel, food, gardening and features. The newspaper has won over 20 awards including a Western Ontario Newspaper Award. The newspaper is known for outstanding layout and design. The deadline is 2am ET.
Language (s): English
Ad Rate: Full Page Mono 21.70
Ad Rate: Full Page Colour 887.55
Currency: Canada Dollars
DAILY NEWSPAPER

Le Nouvelliste 13653

Owner: Groupe Capitales Medias
Editorial: 1920 Rue Bellefeuille, Trois-Rivieres, Quebec G9A 3Y2 **Tel:** 1 819 376-2501
Email: information@lenouvelliste.qc.ca **Web site:** http://www.lapresse.ca/le-nouvelliste
Freq: Mon thru Fri; **Circ:** 33000
Editor in Chief: Stéphan Frappier; **News Editor:** Stéphan Ratelle; **President & Publisher:** Alain Turcotte
Profile: Le Nouvelliste est un quotidien quatre couleurs, couvrant les Nouvelles Locales pour les régions de la Mauricie et du Centre-du-Québec. Un accent particulier est mis sur la Politique et les Histoires d'Intérêt général. Des sections supplémentaires sont Commerciales et Sportives. La grande majorité des histoires portant sur la Technologie, les Modes de Vie, les Arts et le Divertissement et les Nouvelles du monde sont obtenues auprès des Services de Nouvelles. Cependant, divers éditeurs locaux et journalistes traitent également de ces sujets uniques.

Le Nouvelliste is four color, daily French-language newspaper, covering local news for the Mauricie and Centre-du-Québec regions of Québec. A particular emphasis is placed on politics and human interest stories. Additional sections are business and sports. The vast majority of stories dealing with technology, lifestyles, arts & entertainment and world news are obtained from news wire services. However, various local editors and journalists also deal with these individual topics.
Language (s): French
Ad Rate: Full Page Mono 24.64
Ad Rate: Full Page Colour 27.58
Currency: Canada Dollars
DAILY NEWSPAPER

Ottawa Citizen 13625

Owner: Postmedia Network Inc.
Editorial: 1101 Baxter Rd, Ottawa, Ontario K2C 3Z3 **Tel:** 1 613 829-9100
Email: copydesk@ottawacitizen.com **Web site:** http://www.ottawacitizen.com
Freq: Daily
Profile: Ottawa Citizen is a 60+ page, four-colour, broadsheet, daily newspaper written for residents of central and greater Ottawa, ON. The publication covers primarily municipal news, as well as provincial, regional, national and international topics that would be of interest to its target audience. The newspaper features information on world news, local news, sports, entertainment, stocks, classifieds, career opportunities, technology and other topics of interests to the citizens of Ottawa, ON. High-technology is featured in every issue of the Ottawa Citizen and looks at technology from the corporate stand-point. Specific daily sections are A, which contains the main headlines, as well as health news and columns; B is arts, which also includes entertainment; sports coverage, columns, and results are in C, and D is the city section, containing municipal news. The regular edition comes with various weekly sections, such as: business and high-technology on Tuesdays, food on Wednesdays, technology news, in the form of TechWeekly on Thursdays, and the style section on Saturdays. Saturday's edition also comes with the Citizen's Weekly lifestyles magazine. The Sunday edition will cease publication in Mid-July, 2012.
Language (s): English
Ad Rate: Full Page Mono 229.00
Ad Rate: Full Page Colour 272.21
Currency: Canada Dollars
DAILY NEWSPAPER

Ottawa Sun 14876

Owner: Postmedia Network Inc.
Editorial: 1101 Baxter Rd, Ottawa, Ontario K2C 3Z3 **Tel:** 1 613 739-7000
Email: ottsun.city@sunmedia.ca **Web site:** http://www.ottawasun.com
Freq: Daily; **Circ:** 49984 Not Audited
Editor in Chief: Wendy Metcalfe
Profile: Ottawa Sun is primarily written for residents in the Ottawa-Carleton region and the neighboring communities of Cornwall, Kingston, Pembroke and Smith Falls, Ontario. There is local, national and international news, as well as extensive sports, business, entertainment, features and technology coverage. Editors honor non-disclosure agreements. The publication does not accept vendor-written articles, offer reader service cards or publish an editorial calendar. It was established in 1988.
Language (s): English
Ad Rate: Full Page Mono 25.55
Ad Rate: Full Page Colour 143.50
Currency: Canada Dollars
DAILY NEWSPAPER

Peterborough Examiner 13629

Owner: Postmedia Network Inc.
Editorial: 60 Hunter St E, Peterborough, Ontario K9H 1G5 **Tel:** 1 705 745-4641
Web site: http://www.thepeterboroughexaminer.com
Freq: Mon thru Fri; **Circ:** 18483 Not Audited
Profile: Peterborough Examiner is a 30+ page newspaper written for the Peterborough, Ontario general public. It covers national and local news, featuring politics, arts & entertainment, technology, business and sports. It is the largest daily in the Peterborough, Ontario region. The daily deadline is 6pm ET.
Language (s): English
Ad Rate: Full Page Mono 6.85
Ad Rate: Full Page Colour 8.22
Currency: Canada Dollars
DAILY NEWSPAPER

The Prince George Citizen 13584

Owner: Glacier Media Inc.
Editorial: 150 Brunswick St, Prince George, British Columbia V2L 2B3 **Tel:** 1 250 562-2441
Email: info@pgcitizen.ca **Web site:** http://www.princegeorgecitizen.com
Freq: Fri; **Circ:** 23634 Not Audited
Publisher: Colleen Sparrow
Profile: The Prince George Citizen is the daily newspaper founded in 1916 for the town of Prince George, British Columbia. The paper covers local, national, world and business news. Effective February 15, 2016, the paper is no longer published on Monday. Send press releases to news@pgcitizen.ca
Language (s): English
Ad Rate: Full Page Mono 22.40
Currency: Canada Dollars
DAILY NEWSPAPER

The Province 14870

Owner: Postmedia Network Inc.
Editorial: 1-200 Granville St 1, Vancouver, British Columbia V6C 3N3- **Tel:** 1 604 605-2030
Email: tabtips@theprovince.com **Web site:** http://www.theprovince.com
Freq: Daily
Contributor: Crystal Kwon; **Editor in Chief:** Wayne Moriarty; **News Editor:** Lorne Smith
Profile: The Province is a tabloid sized newspaper written for the general public of Vancouver, British Columbia and neighboring communities. It is one of the major newspapers in the area covering news specific to Vancouver as well as Canadian national news. It shares offices with the Vancouver Sun but maintains a separate newsroom.
Language (s): English
Ad Rate: Full Page Mono 155.96
Ad Rate: Full Page Colour 362.90
Currency: Canada Dollars
DAILY NEWSPAPER

The Punjabi Daily 772602

Editorial: 44 Canarvan Crt, Brampton, Ontario L6Y 4X5 **Tel:** 1 416 661-7272
Email: newsroom@punjabidaily.com **Web site:** http://punjabidailyonline.com
Freq: Daily; **Circ:** 7500
Editor: Sukhminder Hansra
Profile: The Punjabi Daily is a daily publication that covers multicultural events and news for the Indian community in Brampton, Ontario.
Language (s): English
DAILY NEWSPAPER

Le Quotidien 13645

Owner: Groupe Capitales Medias
Editorial: 1051 Boul Talbot, Chicoutimi, Quebec G7H 5C1 **Tel:** 1 418 545-4474
Email: redaction@lequotidien.com **Web site:** http://www.lapresse.ca/le-quotidien/
Freq: Mon thru Fri; **Circ:** 26410
News Chief: Stéphane Bégin
Profile: Le Quotidien est un journal quotidien francophone. La majorité du contenu éditorial concerne les nouvelles et l'information locales pour la région du Saguenay-Lac-Saint-Jean, Québec. On y couvre également les nouvelles nationales et internationales, principalement dérivées des fils de presse. De plus, on peut y lire les reportages sur le sport, les affaires, la météo, les arts et le divertissement.

Le Quotidien is a daily French-language newspaper. Most editorial content concerns local news and information for the Saguenay-Lac-Saint-Jean region of Québec. It also covers national and international news, mostly derived from news wires. It contains additional reporting on sports, business, weather and arts & entertainment.
Language (s): French
Ad Rate: Full Page Mono 19.32
Ad Rate: Full Page Colour 23.38
Currency: Canada Dollars
DAILY NEWSPAPER

The Recorder & Times 13609

Owner: Postmedia Network Inc.
Editorial: 2479 Parkedale Ave, Brockville, Ontario K6V 3H2 **Tel:** 1 613 342-4441
Web site: http://www.recorder.ca
Freq: Daily; **Circ:** 11689 Not Audited
Profile: The Recorder & Times is a daily newspaper serving the residents of Brockville, Ontario. It covers local and national news, features, sports and weather. It also provides editorial opinion and comment. Contact this outlet through the contact form on their site.
Language (s): English
Ad Rate: Full Page Mono 20.72
Ad Rate: Full Page Colour 525.00
Currency: Canada Dollars
DAILY NEWSPAPER

Red Deer Advocate 13575

Owner: Black Press
Editorial: 2950 Bremner Ave, Red Deer, Alberta T4R 1M9 **Tel:** 1 403 343-2400
Email: editorial@reddeeradvocate.com **Web site:** http://www.reddeeradvocate.com
Freq: Daily; **Circ:** 11639 Not Audited
Profile: Red Deer Advocate is a daily newspaper written for the Red Deer, Alberta general public. It covers local and world news, sports, business, travel, classifieds and entertainment.
Language (s): English
Ad Rate: Full Page Mono 34.72
Ad Rate: Full Page Colour 645.00
Currency: Canada Dollars
DAILY NEWSPAPER

The Sarnia Observer 13631

Owner: Postmedia Network Inc.
Editorial: 140 Front St S, Sarnia, Ontario N7T 7M8 **Tel:** 1 519 344-3641
Web site: http://www.theobserver.ca
Freq: Mon thru Fri; **Circ:** 14348 Not Audited
Editor: Peter Epp; **Publisher:** Linda Leblanc
Profile: The Observer is a daily newspaper tailored for residents of the Sarnia and Lambton region in Ontario.
Language (s): English
Ad Rate: Full Page Mono 14.00
Ad Rate: Full Page Colour 51.72
Currency: Canada Dollars
DAILY NEWSPAPER

The Sault Star 13632

Owner: Postmedia Network
Editorial: 145 Old Garden River Road, Sault Ste. Marie, Ontario P6A 5M5 **Tel:** 1 705 759-3030
Email: sste.star@sunmedia.ca **Web site:** http://www.saultstar.com
Freq: Mon thru Fri; **Circ:** 18353 Not Audited
Profile: The Sault Star is a regional newspaper written for the Sault Sainte Marie, Ontario general public. The publication serves as one of the major newspapers in the area covering a mix of news, sports, business and entertainment. Various news features are included on a weekly basis.
Language (s): English
Ad Rate: Full Page Mono 11.55
Ad Rate: Full Page Colour 821.00
Currency: Canada Dollars
DAILY NEWSPAPER

Sing Tao Daily 80268

Owner: Sing Tao Newspapers Ltd.
Editorial: 8508 Ash St, Vancouver, British Columbia V6P 3M2 **Tel:** 1 604 321-1111
Email: reporter@singtao.ca **Web site:** http://news.singtao.ca/vancouver
Freq: Daily; **Circ:** 31000 Not Audited
Editor in Chief: Victor Ho; **Publisher:** Calvin Wong; **Co-Editor:** Hang-Yee Wong; **Co-Editor:** Xiao Jun Zhang
Profile: Sing Tao Daily is a daily newspaper published for the members of the Chinese speaking community. The newspaper covers local, regional, national and international news as well as entertainment, business and finance and lifestyle issues.
Language (s): Chinese
Ad Rate: Full Page Mono 78.40
Ad Rate: Full Page Colour 94.08
Currency: Canada Dollars
DAILY NEWSPAPER

Sing Tao Daily 80271

Owner: Sing Tao Media Group Canada
Editorial: 221 Whitehall Dr, Markham, Ontario L3R 9T1 **Tel:** 1 416 596-8140
Email: editor_toronto@singtao.ca **Web site:** http://toronto.singtao.ca
Freq: Daily; **Circ:** 38000 Not Audited
Profile: Sing Tao Daily is a daily newspaper published for the members of the Chinese speaking community. The newspaper covers local, regional, national and international news as well as entertainment, business and finance and lifestyle issues.
Language (s): Chinese
Ad Rate: Full Page Mono 35.95
Ad Rate: Full Page Colour 71.68
Currency: Canada Dollars
DAILY NEWSPAPER

Le Soleil 13650

Owner: Groupe Capitales Medias
Editorial: 410 Boul Charest E, Quebec, Quebec G1K 8G3- **Tel:** 1 418 686-3326
Email: nouvelles@lesoleil.com **Web site:** http://www.lapresse.ca/le-soleil
Freq: Daily; **Circ:** 68350
Publisher: Claude Gagnon; **Editor:** Mylène Moisan
Profile: Le Soleil est un quotidien de 52 pages couvrant les nouvelles locales, nationales et internationales. C'est un journal francophone qui met l'accent sur la ville de Québec. En plus des Nouveautés, le journal couvre l'Économie, les Affaires, les Finances, les Marchés Boursiers, le Divertissement, les Modes de vie, le Sport et la Culture.

Le Soleil is a 52-page daily newspaper covering local, national and international news. It is a French-language newspaper with a strong focus on the city of Québec. In addition to news features, the paper covers Economics, Business, Finance, Stock Markets, Entertainment, Lifestyles, Sports and Culture.
Language (s): French
Ad Rate: Full Page Mono 42.42
Ad Rate: Full Page Colour 58.38
Currency: Canada Dollars
DAILY NEWSPAPER

The St. Catharines Standard 13634

Owner: Postmedia Network Corp.
Editorial: 10-1 St. Paul St 10, St Catharines, Ontario L2R 7L4 **Tel:** 1 905 684-7251
Email: stcs.standard@sunmedia.ca **Web site:** http://www.stcatharinesstandard.ca
Freq: Mon thru Fri; **Circ:** 21077
Editor in Chief: Peter Conradi; **Publisher:** Mark Cressman; **Photography Chief:** Bob Tymczyszyn
Profile: The Standard is a 40+ page newspaper written for residents of Niagara, Ontario. It is one of the premier newspapers in the area covering news, business and sports. Spectrum is a daily section including home, film, arts, lifestyles, weather and gardening coverage. The paper has won several honors such as the National Newspaper Award in 2000 for outstanding articles. The daily deadline is 6pm ET.
Language (s): English
Ad Rate: Full Page Mono 16.66
Ad Rate: Full Page Colour 19.99
Currency: Canada Dollars
DAILY NEWSPAPER

Standard-Freeholder 13612

Owner: Postmedia Network Inc.
Editorial: 1150 Montreal Rd, Cornwall, Ontario K6H 1E2 **Tel:** 1 613 933-3160
Email: csf.news@sunmedia.ca **Web site:** http://www.standard-freeholder.com
Freq: Mon thru Fri; **Circ:** 31000 Not Audited
Profile: Standard Freeholder is a daily community newspaper serving Cornwall, ON and the surrounding area. The paper covers local news and events. Press releases can be sent to the assignment editor who will direct them to the appropriate reporter.
Language (s): English
Ad Rate: Full Page Mono 15.68
Ad Rate: Full Page Colour 1.29
Currency: Canada Dollars
DAILY NEWSPAPER

The Star Phoenix 13658

Owner: Postmedia Network Inc.
Editorial: 204 Fifth Ave North, Saskatoon, Saskatchewan S7K 2P1 **Tel:** 1 306 657-6397
Email: citydesk@thestarphoenix.com **Web site:** http://www.thestarphoenix.com
Freq: Daily
Profile: The Star Phoenix is written for the Saskatoon, Saskatchewan general public. It covers local, national and international news, including Aboriginal Canadian affairs.
Language (s): English
Ad Rate: Full Page Mono 29.12
Ad Rate: Full Page Colour 118.56
Currency: Canada Dollars
DAILY NEWSPAPER

The Sudbury Star 13637

Owner: Postmedia Network Inc.Postmedia Network Inc.
Editorial: 128 Pine St, Sudbury, Ontario P3C 1X3 **Tel:** 1 705 674-5271
Email: sud.editorial@sunmedia.ca **Web site:** http://www.thesudburystar.com
Freq: Mon thru Fri; **Circ:** 15643 Not Audited
Profile: The Sudbury Star is a daily newspaper written for the residents of Sudbury, Ontario and neighboring localities. The paper covers local-city events, activities, crime, courts, fires, government, politics and business, lifestyles, arts & entertainment and sports. There are also editorial columns, a community section dealing with events and topics of reader interest and a community events page which

features an activities calendar. Additionally, non-daily sections are the Saturday issued TV listings, the bi-monthly Parenting supplement and the monthly items Vintage Times and the Real Estate Guide. On the weekend, the newspaper publishes a separate entertainment based publication entitled Weekend Alive. Launched in 1909, the publication, which is Northeastern Ontario's largest newspaper, covers Blind River, Sturgeon Falls, Gogama and Britt.
Language (s): English
Ad Rate: Full Page Mono 26.84
Ad Rate: Full Page Colour 30.37
Currency: Canada Dollars
DAILY NEWSPAPER

The Sun Times 13627
Owner: Postmedia Network Inc.
Editorial: 290 Ninth St E, Owen Sound, Ontario N4K 5P2 **Tel:** 1 519 376-2250
Web site: http://www.owensoundsuntimes.com
Freq: Mon thru Fri; **Circ:** 15049 Not Audited
Publisher: Cheryl McMenemy
Profile: The Sun Times is a daily newspaper serving residents of Owen Sound, Ontario. It covers national and regional news, sports, business and entertainment. Weekly sections are also devoted to automotive, lifestyles and health coverage. The lead time varies.
Language (s): English
Ad Rate: Full Page Mono 9.66
Ad Rate: Full Page Colour 559.00
Currency: Canada Dollars
DAILY NEWSPAPER

The Telegram 13599
Owner: SaltWire Network Inc.
Editorial: 36 Austin St, St. John's, Newfoundland A1B 4C2 **Tel:** 1 709 364-2323
Email: telegram@thetelegram.com **Web site:** http://www.thetelegram.com
Freq: Daily; **Circ:** 27412 Not Audited
News Editor: Mark Vaughn Jackson
Profile: The Telegram is a daily newspaper written for the Saint John's, Newfoundland general public. It covers local and national news, business, sports and lifestyles. Deadlines are daily at 6pm AT.
Language (s): English
Ad Rate: Full Page Mono 19.60
Ad Rate: Full Page Colour 877.00
Currency: Canada Dollars
DAILY NEWSPAPER

Telegraph-Journal 83663
Owner: New Brunswick Publishing Company
Editorial: 210 Crown St, Saint John, New Brunswick E2L 2X7 **Tel:** 1 506 632-8888
Email: newsroom@telegraphjournal.com **Web site:** https://www.telegraphjournal.com
Freq: Daily; **Circ:** 28043 Not Audited
Editor in Chief: John Wishart
Profile: The Telegraph-Journal is New Brunswick's provincial newspaper - and also serves as the community newspaper for Saint John. The Telegraph-Journal is the forum for all New Brunswickers to discuss, understand, and debate the big issues.
Language (s): English
Ad Rate: Full Page Mono 3.47
Ad Rate: Full Page Colour 1613.00
Currency: Canada Dollars
DAILY NEWSPAPER

Times Colonist 13587
Owner: Glacier Media Inc.
Editorial: 2621 Douglas St, Victoria, British Columbia V8T 4M2 **Tel:** 1 250 380-5211
Email: localnews@timescolonist.com **Web site:** http://www.timescolonist.com
Freq: Fri; **Circ:** 52017 Not Audited
Editor in Chief: Dave Obee
Profile: Times Colonist is a daily newspaper written for the Victoria, British Columbia general public. It covers local, regional and national news, as well as business, entertainment, health, travel and sports. It is the oldest newspaper in Western Canada.
Language (s): English
Ad Rate: Full Page Mono 3.51
Ad Rate: Full Page Colour 58.13
Currency: Canada Dollars
DAILY NEWSPAPER

Today Commercial News 695975
Editorial: 3375 14th Ave Unit 7, Markham, Ontario L3R 0H2 **Tel:** 1 416 477-2988
Email: editorial@todaycommercialnews.com **Web site:** http://www.todaycommercialnews.com
Circ: 20000
Publisher: Herbert Moon
Profile: Previously titled Today 701 Magazine. Written for the Chinese residents of Scarborough, Ontario and the surrounding communities. It is published every Saturday.
Language (s): Chinese
Ad Rate: Full Page Mono 4.90
Ad Rate: Full Page Colour 7.40
Currency: United States Dollars
DAILY NEWSPAPER

Toronto Star 15350
Owner: Star Media Group
Editorial: 1 Yonge St, 4th fl, Toronto, Ontario M5E 1E5 **Tel:** 1 416 367-2000
Email: city@thestar.ca **Web site:** http://www.thestar.com
Freq: Daily; **Circ:** 361323 Not Audited
Editor In Chief: Michael Cooke; **City Hall Bureau Chief:** David Rider; **News Editor:** Andrew Waugh
Profile: The Toronto Star, established in 1892 and distributed mostly in Ontario, is Canada's highest circulation newspaper. Published seven days a week, this broadsheet newspaper offers provincial, national and international news, as well as opinion columns and editorials, entertainment news, municipal news, sports, business and financial news and trends and more. Optional weekend sections include Starweek, a Saturday TV listings supplement, and on Sundays an abridged version of The New York Times' international section, editorials and book reviews. The paper is a member of the Canadian Press Gallery.
Language (s): English
Ad Rate: Full Page Mono 461.87
Ad Rate: Full Page Colour 563.78
Currency: Canada Dollars
DAILY NEWSPAPER

The Toronto Sun 14925
Owner: Postmedia Network Inc.
Editorial: 365 Bloor St E Fl 6TH, Toronto, Ontario M4W 3L4 **Tel:** 1 416 947-2211
Email: torsun.citydesk@sunmedia.ca **Web site:** http://www.torontosun.com
Freq: Daily; **Circ:** 186904 Not Audited
Queen's Park Bureau Chief: Antonella Artuso; **Editor in Chief:** Adrienne Batra; **Editor in Chief:** Wendy Metcalfe
Profile: The Toronto Sun is written for readers in the greater Toronto area. The publication is also available in Kingston, Windsor, Sault St. Marie and Niagara, Ontario. It centers on Toronto in its reporting. Specific daily sections include: News, which has a national, but mainly local angle; Entertainment; Lifestyles, including such topics as relationships, health, restaurants and nightlife; Money, is the business and finance section with columns and articles on products, trends, personal finance and the economy; and Sports, covering local and national sporting events and athletes. Editors honor non-disclosure agreements. The publication is a member of the Canadian Press Gallery.
Language (s): English
Ad Rate: Full Page Mono 54.88
Ad Rate: Full Page Colour 339.64
Currency: Canada Dollars
DAILY NEWSPAPER

The Vancouver Sun 13586
Owner: Postmedia Network Inc.
Editorial: 1-200 Granville St 1, Vancouver, British Columbia V6C 3N3- **Tel:** 1 604 605-2030
Web site: http://www.vancouversun.com
Freq: Mon thru Fri
Editor in Chief: Harold Munro; **Real Estate Contributor:** Bob Ransford; **News Editor:** Stephen Snelgrove
Profile: The Vancouver Sun, established in 1886, is a broadsheet newspaper containing news, business, arts & entertainment, dining, events and sports. It shares offices with The Province but maintains a separate newsroom.
Language (s): English
Ad Rate: Full Page Mono 75.32
Ad Rate: Full Page Colour 402.63
Currency: Canada Dollars
DAILY NEWSPAPER

La Voix de l'Est 13646
Owner: Groupe Capitales Medias
Editorial: 76 Rue Dufferin, Granby, Quebec J2G 9L4 **Tel:** 1 450 375-4555
Email: redaction@lavoixdelest.ca **Web site:** http://www.lapresse.ca/la-voix-de-lest
Freq: Daily; **Circ:** 10000
News Editor: Marc Gendron; **Editor in Chief:** Marie-France Létourneau
Profile: La Voix de l'Est is a daily French-language publication. It covers news and information pertaining to the municipalities of Ange-Gardien, Bromont, Cowansville, East Farnham, Granby, Roxton Pond, Roxton Falls, Saint-Alphonse, Saint-Césaire, Saint-Joachim-de-Shefford, Saint-Paul-d'Abbotsford, Sainte-Anne-de-la-Rochelle, and Sainte-Cécile-de-Milton, Quebec. Contact the publication by phone, fax, e-mail, or mail.
Language (s): French
Ad Rate: Full Page Mono 13.86
Ad Rate: Full Page Colour 18.20
Currency: Canada Dollars
DAILY NEWSPAPER

Waterloo Region Record 13619
Owner: Metroland Media Group Ltd.
Editorial: 160 King St E, Kitchener, Ontario N2G 4E5 **Tel:** 1 519 894-2231
Web site: http://www.therecord.com
Freq: Daily; **Circ:** 63386 Not Audited
Profile: Waterloo Region Record is a 40+ page broadsheet newspaper written for the residents of Kitchener, Ontario and surrounding communities. It is one of the major newspapers in the region covering business, sports and entertainment. The weekend edition has an expanded entertainment section including event listings and extra entertainment, food, and health coverage.
Language (s): English
Ad Rate: Full Page Mono 98.00
Ad Rate: Full Page Colour 56.11
Currency: Canada Dollars
DAILY NEWSPAPER

The Welland Tribune 13640
Owner: Postmedia Network Inc.
Editorial: 228 E Main St, Welland, Ontario L3B 5P5 **Tel:** 1 905 732-2411
Web site: http://www.wellandtribune.ca
Freq: Mon thru Fri; **Circ:** 13164
Publisher: John Tobon
Profile: The Welland Tribune is a daily newspaper published for the Welland and Port Colborne, Ontario communities.
Language (s): English
Ad Rate: Full Page Mono 17.08
Ad Rate: Full Page Colour 657.00
Currency: Canada Dollars
DAILY NEWSPAPER

The Whig-Standard 13617
Owner: Postmedia Network Inc.
Editorial: 6 Cataraqui St, Kingston, Ontario K7K 1Z7 **Tel:** 1 613 544-5000
Email: whig.local@sunmedia.ca **Web site:** http://www.thewhig.com
Freq: Mon thru Fri; **Circ:** 21880 Not Audited
News Editor: Jan Murphy
Profile: The Whig-Standard is written for the Kingston, Ontario general public. It is the oldest continuously published daily newspaper in Canada and covers predominantly local, but also national and provincial news. The daily deadline is 11pm ET. Press releases should be sent to the main e-mail address.
Language (s): English
Ad Rate: Full Page Mono 23.80
Ad Rate: Full Page Colour 79.81
Currency: Canada Dollars
DAILY NEWSPAPER

The Windsor Star 13641
Owner: Postmedia Network Inc.
Editorial: 300 Ouellette Ave, Windsor, Ontario N9A 7B4- **Tel:** 1 519 255-5711
Email: news@windsorstar.com **Web site:** http://www.windsorstar.com
Freq: Daily
Profile: The Windsor Star, established in 1918, is a 30+ page, four color, broadsheet newspaper. It is the only daily newspaper in Windsor and Essex County, Ontario. The publication covers local, national and international news, business, sports, health, lifestyle, travel, homes and entertainment. The weekend edition comes with a TV Times listing guide. The advertising deadline is 6pm ET two days prior to publication. The lead time varies depending on department.
Language (s): English
Ad Rate: Full Page Mono 97.16
Ad Rate: Full Page Colour 118.62
Currency: Canada Dollars
DAILY NEWSPAPER

Winnipeg Free Press 13592
Owner: FP Canadian Newspapers LP
Editorial: 1355 Mountain Ave, Winnipeg, Manitoba R2X 3B6- **Tel:** 1 204 697-7000
Email: city.desk@freepress.mb.ca **Web site:** http://www.winnipegfreepress.com
Freq: Mon thru Fri; **Circ:** 111338 Not Audited
Photography Director: Mike Aporius; **Publisher:** Bob Cox; **Editor:** Paul Samyn; **Editor:** Jill Wilson; **Contributor:** Shel Zolkewich
Profile: Winnipeg Free Press is a broadsheet newspaper written for the general public of Winnipeg, Manitoba. It is one of the major newspapers in the area covering news, business, entertainment and sports, and having the largest readership in the province.
Language (s): English
Ad Rate: Full Page Mono 49.49
Ad Rate: Full Page Colour 229.22
Currency: Canada Dollars
DAILY NEWSPAPER

Winnipeg Sun 13593
Owner: Postmedia Network Inc.
Editorial: 1700 Church Ave, Winnipeg, Manitoba R2X 3A2 **Tel:** 1 204 694-2022
Email: wpgsun.citydesk@sunmedia.ca **Web site:** http://www.winnipegsun.com
Freq: Daily; **Circ:** 43442 Not Audited
Editor in Chief: Mark Hamm; **Editor:** Darryl Sterdan
Profile: Winnipeg Sun is a daily newspaper written for the Southern Manitoba general public. It covers news, sports, business and entertainment. The newspaper has won several awards. It is known for outstanding news coverage. Deadlines are daily at 6pm CT. Lead time varies.
Language (s): English
Ad Rate: Full Page Mono 19.53
Ad Rate: Full Page Colour 1693.00
Currency: Canada Dollars
DAILY NEWSPAPER

News Service/Syndicate

L' Agence QMI 684420
Owner: Quebecor Communications Inc.
Editorial: 800 Square Victoria, Montreal, Quebec **Tel:** 1 514 380-1997
Email: nouvelles@agenceqmi.ca **Web site:** http://www.agenceqmi.ca
News Editor: Jules Richer; **News Editor:** Patrick White
Profile: Serves as the news service for Quebecor and Sun Media newspapers.
Language (s): French
NEWS SERVICE/SYNDICATE

L' Agence Science-Presse 235021
Editorial: 1124 Rue Marie-Anne E Bureau 12, Montreal, Quebec H2J 2B7 **Tel:** 1 514 844-4388
Email: redaction@sciencepresse.qc.ca **Web site:** http://www.sciencepresse.qc.ca
Publisher & General Manager: Josée Nadia Drouin; **Editor in Chief:** Pascal Lapointe
Profile: Agence Science-Presse is the only scientific press agency in Canada, as well as the only one in all of the French-speaking world.
Language (s): French
NEWS SERVICE/SYNDICATE

Bloomberg News - Calgary Bureau 31338
Editorial: 110 9 Ave SE Fl SUITE, Calgary, Alberta T2G 5A6 **Tel:** 1 587 702-3030
Web site: https://www.bloomberg.com
Editor: Carlos Caminada
Language (s): English
NEWS SERVICE/SYNDICATE

The Canadian Press 31069
Owner: Canadian Press (The)
Editorial: 36 King St E, Toronto, Ontario M5C 1E5- **Tel:** 1 416 507-2159
Email: editorial@thecanadianpress.com **Web site:** http://www.thecanadianpress.com
Editor: Paola Loriggio; **Editor in Chief:** Stephen Meurice
Profile: The Canadian Press, founded in 1917, is a national multimedia Canadian news agency cooperatively owned by more than 100 Canadian newspapers. In addition to enabling news-sharing between these publications, the agency serves more than 500 radio and television broadcasters, as well as a growing number of online publishers, and is a leading supplier of news and information to commercial and government clients. The Canadian Press is also a member of the Canadian Press Gallery.
Language (s): English
NEWS SERVICE/SYNDICATE

The Canadian Press - Calgary Bureau 83318
Editorial: 310-131 9 Ave SW 310, Calgary, Alberta T2P 1K1 **Tel:** 1 403 233-7004
Email: calgary@thecanadianpress.com **Web site:** http://www.thecanadianpress.com
Profile: The Canadian Press is a bilingual news agency, driven by leading-edge technology and the ability to serve multimedia news to multiple platforms. It provides real-time text, photos, audio, graphics, video and online services to newspapers, broadcasters, publishers, websites, wireless carriers, cable companies, government and corporate clients. (source: The Canadian Press)
Language (s): English
NEWS SERVICE/SYNDICATE

The Canadian Press - Edmonton Bureau 83321
Editorial: 10109 106 St NW Suite 504, Edmonton, Alberta T5J 3L7 **Tel:** 1 780 428-6107
Email: edmonton@thecanadianpress.com **Web site:** http://www.thecanadianpress.com
Profile: The Canadian Press is a bilingual news agency, driven by leading-edge technology and the ability to serve multimedia news to multiple platforms. It provides real-time text, photos, audio, graphics, video and online services to newspapers, broadcasters, publishers, websites, wireless carriers, cable companies, government and corporate clients. (Source: The Canadian Press)
Language (s): English
NEWS SERVICE/SYNDICATE

The Canadian Press - Fredericton Bureau 83322
Editorial: 96 St. John St, Fredericton, New Brunswick E3B 5H1 **Tel:** 1 506 457-0746
Email: fredericton@thecanadianpress.com **Web site:** http://www.thecanadianpress.com
Language (s): English
NEWS SERVICE/SYNDICATE

The Canadian Press - Halifax Bureau 83319
Editorial: 1888 Brunswick St, Ste 701, Halifax, Nova Scotia B3J 3J8 **Tel:** 1 902 422-8496
Email: halifax@thecanadianpress.com **Web site:** http://www.thecanadianpress.com
News Editor: Ruth Davenport; **Editor:** Michael Tutton; **Bureau Chief:** Kevin Ward
Language (s): English
NEWS SERVICE/SYNDICATE

The Canadian Press - Montreal Bureau 80319
Editorial: 215 Rue Saint-Jacques Bureau 100, Montreal, Quebec H2Y 1M6 **Tel:** 1 514 849-3212
Email: cpmontreal@cp.org **Web site:** http://www.cp.org
Bureau Chief: Don McKenzie
Profile: The Canadian Press, founded in 1917, is a national multimedia Canadian news agency cooperatively owned by more than 100 Canadian newspapers. In addition to enabling news-sharing between these publications, the agency serves more than 500 radio and television broadcasters, as well as a growing number of online publishers, and is a leading supplier of news and information to commercial and government clients. The Canadian Press is also a member of the Canadian Press Gallery. Canadian Press - Montreal Bureau is based in Montreal.
Language (s): English
NEWS SERVICE/SYNDICATE

The Canadian Press - Ottawa Bureau 83323
Editorial: 56 Sparks St Fl, seventh, Ottawa, Ontario K1P 5A9 **Tel:** 1 613 236-4122
Email: ottawa@thecanadianpress.com **Web site:** http://www.thecanadianpress.com
Bureau Chief: Heather Scoffield
Profile: Please make sure to only send one faxed or e-mailed press release to the bureau, addressed to one contact. They continually receive the same fax addressed to the multiple people at the bureau and find it to be a waste.
Language (s): English
NEWS SERVICE/SYNDICATE

The Canadian Press - Quebec Bureau 83325
Editorial: 1050 Rue des Parlementaires Bureau 207, Quebec, Quebec G1A 1A3 **Tel:** 1 418 646-5377
Email: quebec@thecanadianpress.com **Web site:** http://www.thecanadianpress.com
News Editor: Mario Simard
Profile: The Canadian Press, founded in 1917, is a national multimedia Canadian news agency cooperatively owned by more than 100 Canadian newspapers. In addition to enabling news-sharing between these publications, the agency serves more than 500 radio and television broadcasters, as well as a growing number of online publishers, and is a leading supplier of news and information to commercial and government clients. The Canadian Press is also a member of the Canadian Press Gallery. Canadian Press - Quebec Bureau is based in Quebec.
Language (s): French
NEWS SERVICE/SYNDICATE

The Canadian Press - Regina Bureau 363507
Editorial: Saskatchewan Legislative Bldg, Rm 335, Press Gallery, Regina, Saskatchewan S4S 0B3
Tel: 1 306 585-1011
Email: regina@thecanadianpress.com **Web site:** http://www.thecanadianpress.com
Language (s): English
NEWS SERVICE/SYNDICATE

The Canadian Press - St. John's Bureau 83320
Owner: Canadian Press (The)
Editorial: 139 Water St Bldg SUITE, 901, St. John's, Newfoundland A1C 1B2 **Tel:** 1 709 576-0687
Email: editorial@thecanadianpress.com **Web site:** http://www.thecanadianpress.com
Profile: St. John's Bureau of The Canadian Press.
Language (s): English
NEWS SERVICE/SYNDICATE

The Canadian Press - Vancouver Bureau 83326
Editorial: 840 Howe St Suite 250, Vancouver, British Columbia V6Z 2L2 **Tel:** 1 604 687-1662
Email: vancouver@thecanadianpress.com **Web site:** http://www.thecanadianpress.com
Profile: The Canadian Press, founded in 1917, is a national multimedia Canadian news agency cooperatively owned by more than 100 Canadian newspapers. In addition to enabling news-sharing between these publications, the agency serves more than 500 radio and television broadcasters, as well as a growing number of online publishers, and is a leading supplier of news and information to commercial and government clients. The Canadian Press is also a member of the Canadian Press Gallery.
Language (s): English
NEWS SERVICE/SYNDICATE

The Canadian Press - Victoria Bureau 83327
Editorial: Room 350 Legislative Building, The Press Gallery, Victoria, British Columbia V8V 1X4
Tel: 1 250 384-4912
Email: victoria@thecanadianpress.com **Web site:** http://www.thecanadianpress.com
Profile: The Canadian Press, founded in 1917, is a national multimedia Canadian news agency cooperatively owned by more than 100 Canadian newspapers. In addition to enabling news-sharing between these publications, the agency serves more than 500 radio and television broadcasters, as well as a growing number of online publishers, and is a leading supplier of news and information to commercial and government clients. The Canadian Press is also a member of the Canadian Press Gallery.
Language (s): English
NEWS SERVICE/SYNDICATE

The Canadian Press - Washington Bureau 31225
Editorial: 1100 13th St NW, Washington, District Of Columbia 20005-4051 **Tel:** 1 202 641-9734
Email: washington@thecanadianpress.com
Language (s): English
NEWS SERVICE/SYNDICATE

The Canadian Press - Winnipeg Bureau 83324
Editorial: 386 Broadway Suite 101, Winnipeg, Manitoba R3C 3R6 **Tel:** 1 204 988-1780
Email: winnipeg@thecanadianpress.com **Web site:** http://www.thecanadianpress.com/
Profile: The Canadian Press, founded in 1917, is a national multimedia Canadian news agency cooperatively owned by more than 100 Canadian newspapers. In addition to enabling news-sharing between these publications, the agency serves more than 500 radio and television broadcasters, as well as a growing number of online publishers, and is a leading supplier of news and information to commercial and government clients. The Canadian Press is also a member of the Canadian Press Gallery.
Language (s): English
NEWS SERVICE/SYNDICATE

Média Mosaïque Montréal 722824
Owner: Média Mosaïque Montréal
Editorial: 9071, rue Pie IX, Suites 6A & 5A, Montreal, Quebec H1Z 3V7 **Tel:** 1 514 991-0263
Email: contact@mediamosaique.com **Web site:** http://mediamosaique.com
Editor: Donald Jean
Profile: Founded in 2006, Média Mosaïque Montréal is a French-language news service that provides general and thematic news to meet the interests of different cultural communities in Quebec.
Language (s): French
NEWS SERVICE/SYNDICATE

Parent Previews 153734
Editorial: 83 Midland Cres SE, Calgary, Alberta T2X 1N8 **Tel:** 1 800 565-4661
Web site: http://www.parentpreviews.com
Editor: Donna Gustafson; **Publisher:** Rodney Gustafson
Profile: Since 1993, the columns have appeared in over 50 papers in North America and Canada. It helps take the guess work out of finding appropriate family entertainment. The columns examine popular culture while looking for the good and warning against the dangers. They provide information that will empower individuals to make better choices, enhance their lives and strengthen their families. They help parents discover great movies and entertainment and new ways to use technology effectively. Their geographical focus is the US and Canada with UK, Australia and NZ as secondary.
Language (s): English
NEWS SERVICE/SYNDICATE

Postmedia News 83314
Owner: Postmedia Network Inc.
Editorial: 365 Bloor St E, Toronto, Ontario M4W 3L4
Tel: 1 613 369-4800
Email: pn@postmedia.com **Web site:** https://www.postmedia.com
Profile: Postmedia News has an in-house wire and external field reporters covering national Canadian topics. Stories from Postmedia publications are often picked up by the wire. The news service is a member of the Canadian Press Gallery.
Language (s): English
NEWS SERVICE/SYNDICATE

Postmedia News - Toronto Bureau 83315
Owner: Postmedia Network Inc.
Editorial: Legislative Building, Queens Park Room 354, Toronto, Ontario M7A 1A2 **Tel:** 1 416 325-7833
Email: pn@postmedia.com **Web site:** http://www.postmedia.com/
Profile: Postmedia News Toronto has an in-house wire and external field reporters covering national Canadian topics. Stories from Postmedia publications are often picked up by the wire. The news service is a member of the Canadian Press Gallery.
Language (s): English
NEWS SERVICE/SYNDICATE

Postmedia News - Vancouver Bureau 552204
Editorial: 2875 29th Ave W, Vancouver, British Columbia V6L 1Y2 **Tel:** 1 604 605-2000
Web site: http://www.canada.com/postmedianews
Language (s): English
NEWS SERVICE/SYNDICATE

Reuters - Vancouver Bureau 31364
Editorial: 350-969 Robson St 350, Vancouver, British Columbia V6Z 2V7 **Tel:** 1 604 561-5275
Web site: http://ca.reuters.com
Profile: Designed as a source of online financial commentary for leading investment banks, institutional investors, hedge fund managers, corporations, law firms, public relations advisors and media outlets worldwide. Delivers real-time views on companies, markets and trends, giving clients clear insight into what's happening in business and finance. Features opinions on company events and analysis of big deals.
Language (s): English
NEWS SERVICE/SYNDICATE

Torstar Syndication Services 30734
Owner: Metroland Media Group Ltd.
Editorial: 1 Yonge St, Toronto, Ontario M5E 1E5-
Tel: 1 416 869-4994
Email: syndicationservices@torstar.com **Web site:** http://www.tsscontent.ca
Profile: Offers Columns on Personal Finance, Arts & Entertainment, Business, Home, Food and international travel.
Language (s): English
NEWS SERVICE/SYNDICATE

Young People's Press Group 238376
Editorial: 374 Fraser St, North Bay, Ontario P1B 3W7
Tel: 1 705 495-8887
Email: info@nbdmc.ca **Web site:** http://nbdmc.ca
Profile: Young People's Press empowers a large network of youth and young adult writers to have a voice in the mainstream media and a space at the table of public opinion. It showcases the stuff young people care about, including pop culture, politics and social issues.
Language (s): English
NEWS SERVICE/SYNDICATE

Community Newspaper

100 Mile House Newspaper 531218
Owner: Black Press
Editorial: 2-536 Horse Lake Rd 2, 2 2, 100 Mile House, British Columbia V0K 2E1 **Tel:** 1 250 395-2219
Email: max.winkelman@100milefreepress.net **Web site:** http://www.100milefreepress.net
Freq: Weekly; **Circ:** 10657 Not Audited
Editor: Ken Alexander; **Publisher:** Chris Nickless
Language (s): English
COMMUNITY NEWSPAPER

The Abbotsford News 23362
Owner: Black Press
Editorial: 34375 Gladys Ave, Abbotsford, British Columbia V2S 2H5 **Tel:** 1 604 853-1144
Email: newsroom@abbynews.com **Web site:** http://www.abbynews.com/
Freq: Fri; **Circ:** 44552 Not Audited
Editor: Andrew Holota
Profile: The Abbotsford News is a community newspaper written for the residents of Abbotsford, British Columbia. It covers local news, sports and opinions from the region.
Language (s): English
Ad Rate: Full Page Mono 31.08
Currency: Canada Dollars
COMMUNITY NEWSPAPER

ABC Portuguese Canadian Newspaper 815865
Owner: Portuguese Canadian News Network
Editorial: 725 College St, Toronto, Ontario M6G 1C5
Tel: 1 416 995-9904
Web site: http://abcpcnn.weebly.com/
Freq: Mon
Director: Fernando Cruz Gomes
Profile: ABC Portuguese Canadian Newspaper is a community newspaper serving the Portuguese-Canadian community of Toronto and the greater Toronto area in Ontario, Canada.
Language (s): Portuguese
COMMUNITY NEWSPAPER

Aboriginal Multi-Media Society 80102
Editorial: 13245 146 St NW, Edmonton, Alberta T5L 4S8 **Tel:** 1 780 455-2700
Email: market@ammsa.com **Web site:** http://www.ammsa.com
Circ: 42500 Not Audited
Publisher: Bert Crowfoot; **Editor:** Paul Macedo
Language (s): English
COMMUNITY NEWSPAPER

ACASA 814427
Owner: Goldmark Productions Inc.
Editorial: 35 Longwood Ave, Richmond Hill, Ontario L4E 4A5 **Tel:** 1 905 482-1838
Email: office@acasamedia.com **Web site:** http://www.acasamedia.com
Freq: Bi-Weekly; **Circ:** 20000
Editor in Chief: Mihai Manolache
Profile: ACASA is a biweekly Romanian-language newspaper serving the Romanian community in Toronto and surrounding areas. Outlet offers RSS
Language (s): Romanian
COMMUNITY NEWSPAPER

Accès LE Journal des Pays-d'en-Haut 81733
Owner: Pilotte, Josée
Editorial: 727 Rue Principale, Piedmont, Quebec J0R 1K0 **Tel:** 1 450 227-7999
Email: redaction@journalacces.ca **Web site:** http://www.journalacces.ca
Freq: Wed; **Circ:** 28000
Publisher: Josee Pilotte
Profile: Accès LE Journal des Pays-d'en-Haut is an independent newspaper covering regional news in the Laurentides region of Québec.
Language (s): French
Ad Rate: Full Page Mono 6.93
Currency: Canada Dollars
COMMUNITY NEWSPAPER

Les Actualités Côte-des-Neiges Inc. 257668
Editorial: 6655 Ch de la Côte-Des-Neiges, Montreal, Quebec H3S 2B4 **Tel:** 1 514 945-4650
Email: journal@lesactualites.ca **Web site:** http://www.lesactualites.ca
Freq: Semi-Monthly; **Circ:** 35000 Not Audited
Profile: Les Actualités Côte-des-Neiges Inc. est un journal indépendant bihebdomadaire couvrant les nouvelles des quartiers Côte-des-Neiges (CND), Notre-Dame-de-Grâce (NDG) et Snowdon, à Montréal, Québec.

Les Actualités Côte-des-Neiges Inc. is a independant biweekly newspaper covering news from Côte-des-Neiges (CND), Notre-Dame-de-Grâce (NDG) and Snowdon. The publication is in French.
Language (s): French
Ad Rate: Full Page Mono 7.28
Currency: Canada Dollars
COMMUNITY NEWSPAPER

Actualités-L'Étincelle 24084
Owner: Publidiffusion Inc.
Editorial: 193 Rue Saint-Georges, Windsor, Quebec J1S 1J7 **Tel:** 1 819 845-2705
Email: journal@actualites-letincelle.com **Web site:** http://www.letincelle.qc.ca
Freq: Wed; **Circ:** 10779 Not Audited
Editor in Chief: Ralph Côté; **Publisher:** Claude Frenette
Profile: Actualités-L'Étincelle est un hebdomadaire d'information locale couvrant le territoire des MRC des Sources et du Val-St-François.

Actualités-L'Étincelle is a weekly newspaper covering local news and events covering the territory of des Sources and Val-St-François RCMs.
Language (s): French
Ad Rate: Full Page Mono 10.08
Currency: Canada Dollars
COMMUNITY NEWSPAPER

The Advertiser 387481
Owner: Advertiser 2008
Tel: 1 780 354-2592
Email: beaverlodge.advertiser@gmail.com
Freq: Monthly; **Circ:** 10000 Not Audited
Co-Publisher & Co-Editor: Amber Barclay;
Publisher & Editor: Clayton Barclay
Profile: The Advertiser is a free weekly newspaper serving residents of Beaverlodge, Alberta. It contains community news, events and stories of interest to local readers.
Language (s): English
Ad Rate: Full Page Mono 6.75
Ad Rate: Full Page Colour 90.00
Currency: Canada Dollars
COMMUNITY NEWSPAPER

The Afro News 80201
Owner: Privilege Group Holdings
Editorial: 610-825, Granville Street, Vancouver, British Columbia V6Z 1K9 **Tel:** 1 604 646-0474
Email: info@theafronews.ca **Web site:** http://www.theafronews.ca
Freq: Monthly; **Circ:** 60000 Not Audited
Profile: The Afro News is a weekly newspaper published for the African-American community of Vancouver, British Columbia.
Language (s): English
Ad Rate: Full Page Mono 17.27
Ad Rate: Full Page Colour 24.27
Currency: Canada Dollars
COMMUNITY NEWSPAPER

Airdrie Echo 23383
Owner: Postmedia Network Inc.
Editorial: 112 1 Ave NE, Airdrie, Alberta T4B 0R6
Tel: 1 403 948-7280
Email: airdrie.news@sunmedia.ca **Web site:** http://www.airdrieecho.com
Freq: Wed; **Circ:** 17003 Not Audited
Publisher: Shawn Cornell
Profile: Airdrie Echo is published weekly for the residents of Airdrie, Alberta. The newspaper covers local news, sports and community events.
Language (s): English
Ad Rate: Full Page Mono 8.54
Ad Rate: Full Page Colour 150.00
Currency: Canada Dollars
COMMUNITY NEWSPAPER

Ajax-Pickering News Advertiser 620182
Owner: Metroland Media Group Ltd.
Editorial: 865 Farewell St, Oshawa, Ontario L1H 6N8
Tel: 1 905 579-4400
Email: newsroom@durhamregion.com **Web site:** http://www.newsdurhamregion.com
Circ: 51400
News Editor: Mike Ruta
Language (s): English
COMMUNITY NEWSPAPER

Ajit Weekly 80742
Editorial: 7015-2 Tranmere Dr, Mississauga, Ontario L5S 1T7 **Tel:** 1 905 671-4761
Email: info@ajitweekly.com **Web site:** http://www.ajitweekly.com
Freq: Wed; **Circ:** 39500 Not Audited
Profile: Ajit Weekly is a Punjabi Community Newspaper reporting news to the Punjabis across the world.
Language (s): English
Ad Rate: Full Page Mono 4.00
Currency: Canada Dollars
COMMUNITY NEWSPAPER

Akhbaar-e-Pakistan 815063
Owner: Akhbaar-e-Pakistan
Editorial: 3256 Escada Dr, Mississauga, Ontario L5M 7V5 **Tel:** 1 416 835-1997
Email: akhbaar@gmail.com **Web site:** http://www.akhbaarepakistan.com/
Freq: Weekly; **Circ:** 41000
Editor in Chief: Badar Munir Chaudhary
Profile: Akhbaar-e-Pakistan is a weekly Urdu-language Community newspaper.
Language (s): Urdu
COMMUNITY NEWSPAPER

Alakhbar (An-Nahar) 528253
Editorial: 2086 Av Chartier, Dorval, Quebec H9P 1H2 **Tel:** 1 514 636-4004
Email: info@alakhbar.ca **Web site:** http://www.alakhbar.ca
Freq: Wed; **Circ:** 25000 Not Audited
Publisher & Editor In Chief: Elie Moujaes
Profile: Al-Akhbar est un hebdomadaire de langue arabe desservant la région de Dorval, Québec. Il est associé à An-Nahar.

Alakhbar (An-Nahar) is weekly paper serving the Arabic community in Dorval, Quebec.
Language (s): Arabic
COMMUNITY NEWSPAPER

alAmeen Post 815074
Owner: al-Ameen Media Inc.
Editorial: 7184 120 St Suite 596, Surrey, British Columbia V3W 0M6 **Tel:** 1 604 715-7187
Email: info@alameenpost.com **Web site:** http://www.alameenpost.com
Freq: Bi-Weekly; **Circ:** 3000
Profile: alAmeen Post is a biweekly newspaper, published every other Friday serving the Muslim community in British Columbia, Canada.
Language (s): English
Ad Rate: Full Page Mono 13.72
Currency: Canada Dollars
COMMUNITY NEWSPAPER

Alberni Valley News 417753
Owner: Black Press
Editorial: 4656 Margaret St, Port Alberni, British Columbia V9Y 6H2 **Tel:** 1 250 723-6399
Email: editor@albernivalleynews.com **Web site:** http://www.albernivalleynews.com
Freq: Thu; **Circ:** 9186 Not Audited
Publisher: Teresa Bird; **Editor in Chief:** Susan Quinn
Profile: Alberni Valley News is a weekly newspaper serving residents of Port Alberni, British Columbia. The paper covers local news, events, schools, sports, businesses and features. Advertising deadlines are at 10am PT. The paper launched in August 2006.
Language (s): English
Ad Rate: Full Page Mono 16.24
Currency: Canada Dollars
COMMUNITY NEWSPAPER

Alberta Native News 80109
Owner: Alberta LTD.
Editorial: 11460 Jasper Ave, Ste 207, Edmonton, Alberta T5K 0M1 **Tel:** 1 780 421-7966
Email: editor@albertanativenews.com **Web site:** http://www.albertanativenews.com
Freq: Monthly; **Circ:** 14000 Not Audited
Editor in Chief: Deborah Shatz
Profile: Alberta Native News is a monthly, independent tabloid newspaper that features national and regional news and focuses on issues that are important to the Aboriginal communities across Canada.
Language (s): English
Ad Rate: Full Page Mono 25.06
Currency: Canada Dollars
COMMUNITY NEWSPAPER

Aldergrove Star 23366
Owner: Black Press
Editorial: 27118 Fraser Hwy, Aldergrove, British Columbia V4W 3P6 **Tel:** 1 604 856-8303
Email: newsroom@aldergrovestar.com **Web site:** http://www.aldergrovestar.com
Freq: Thu; **Circ:** 6577 Not Audited
Editor in Chief: Kurt Langmann; **Publisher:** Dwayne Weidendorf
Profile: Aldergrove Star is a weekly newspaper covering local news and information for residents of Aldergrove, British Columbia. Deadlines for the publication are Mondays at 4pm PT.
Language (s): English
Ad Rate: Full Page Mono 13.86
Currency: Canada Dollars
COMMUNITY NEWSPAPER

Alfa 526951
Tel: 1 514 531-1382
Email: journalfa@yahoo.ca **Web site:** http://www.journalfa.ca
Freq: Monthly; **Circ:** 14200 Not Audited
Publisher & Editor in Chief: Mustapha Chelfi
Profile: Alfa is a monthly newspaper that features news and information for the Maghrebi community in Montreal.
Language (s): French
COMMUNITY NEWSPAPER

Al-Mersal 80516
Owner: Malawi (Ziad)
Editorial: 17 Kelfield St, Toronto, Ontario M9W 5A1 **Tel:** 1 416 233-9927
Email: info@canadianarabnetwork.com **Web site:** http://canadianarabnetwork.com/Al_Mersal%20Website/index.html
Freq: Monthly; **Circ:** 15000 Not Audited
Publisher & Editor in Chief: Ziad Malawi
Profile: Al-Mersal is a local community newspaper for the residents of Toronto and the surrounding communities.
Language (s): English
Ad Rate: Full Page Mono 24.50
Currency: Canada Dollars
COMMUNITY NEWSPAPER

Al-Mustakbal 411138
Owner: Centre Canadien pour L'Change Culturel et L'Integration
Editorial: 1305 Rue Mazurette Bureau 200, Montreal, Quebec H4N 1G8 **Tel:** 1 514 334-0909 203
Email: info@almustakbal.com **Web site:** http://www.almustakbal.com
Circ: 60500
Publisher: Joseph Nakhle
Profile: Al-Moustakbal, which means "The Future" in Arabic, is a weekly Arabic-language newspaper serving the Arabic community in Francophone Canada, including Montreal and Halifax, Nova Scotia, and Ottawa, Ontario. It covers local and international news, Arab culture and editorials.
Language (s): Arabic
COMMUNITY NEWSPAPER

Al-Qalam 776801
Editorial: 1010 Richards St., Vancouver, British Columbia V6B 1G??? **Tel:** 1 778 237-4546
Email: info@penlingua.net **Web site:** http://www.penlingua.net
Freq: Weekly
Editor in Chief: B. Abderrazak
Profile: Al-Qalam is a weekly newspaper that provides International and Community News coverage for the Arabic-speaking community in Vancouver, BC.
Language (s): Arabic
COMMUNITY NEWSPAPER

La Alternativa Latina 521140
Editorial: 7203 Papineau Ave, Montreal, Quebec H2E 2G7 **Tel:** 1 514 777-4474
Email: info@elchasquilatino.com **Web site:** http://www.lalternativalatina.com
Freq: Tue; **Circ:** 15000 Not Audited
Editor In Chief: José Ramos
Profile: La Alternativa Latina est un hebdomadaire pour la communauté hispanophone de la grande région de Montréal.

La Alternativa Latina is a weekly newspaper serving the Hispanic community in Montreal.
Language (s): Spanish
Ad Rate: Full Page Mono 7.70
Currency: Canada Dollars
COMMUNITY NEWSPAPER

Alto Media Newspapers 81350
Owner: Altomedia Inc.
Editorial: 99 Professors Lake Pky, Brampton, Ontario L6S 4P8
Circ: 19500 Not Audited
Editor in Chief: Christiane Beaupre; **Editor:** Richard Caumartin; **Publisher:** Denis Poirier
Profile: Alto Media Newspapers cover local news in three weeklies published for the French speaking communities in Toronto, Niagara-Hamilton, London-Sarnia and surrounding communities in Ontario.
Language (s): French
COMMUNITY NEWSPAPER

American Life News 239142
Editorial: 3131 Sheppard Ave E, 2nd fl, Toronto, Ontario M1T 3J7 **Tel:** 1 416 645-0471
Email: nal@skynetinfo.com **Web site:** http://americanlifenews.blogspot.ca/
Freq: Thu; **Circ:** 17000 Not Audited
Editor in Chief: Thomas Lv; **Publisher:** Zhen Xiang Yi
Profile: American Life News is a weekly newspaper that carries news related to up-to-date information, job opportunities, local training, career guide, service provision, global trade, life story and classified advertisements. It is available free of charge in approximately 80 locations in the Greater Toronto Area, which include most Chinese supermarkets, Government sponsored employment service locations, HRDC centers, colleges, training schools, libraries, community plazas, and restaurants.
Language (s): Chinese
COMMUNITY NEWSPAPER

The Anchor Weekly 800875
Tel: 1 403 774-1352
Email: admin@theanchor.ca **Web site:** http://www.theanchor.ca/
Freq: Thu; **Circ:** 10000
Publisher & Editor: Steve Jeffrey
Profile: The Anchor Weekly is a community newspaper serving the residents of Chestermere and surrounding areas near Calgary in Alberta, Canada. Topics include mostly local coverage of news, politics, and events.
Language (s): English
COMMUNITY NEWSPAPER

Anishinabek News 80119
Owner: Union of Ontario Indians
Editorial: 1 Miigizi Mikan, North Bay, Ontario P1B 8J8 **Tel:** 1 705 497-9127
Email: info@anishinabek.ca **Web site:** http://anishinabeknews.ca/
Freq: Monthly; **Circ:** 11000 Not Audited
Publisher & Editor in Chief: Maurice Switzer
Profile: Anishinabek News is a monthly newspaper published in North Bay, Ontario covering news and events of the Anishinabek aboriginals.
Language (s): English
Ad Rate: Full Page Mono 27.30
Currency: Canada Dollars
COMMUNITY NEWSPAPER

Arab News Int'l-Canada Allam Arabic Publishing 80531
Editorial: 602 Millwood Road, Toronto, Ontario M4S 1K8 **Tel:** 1 416 362-0307
Email: arabnews@yahoo.com **Web site:** http://www.arabnews.ca
Circ: 43000 Not Audited
Publisher: Salah Allam; **Editor:** Emad Nafeh; **Director & Media Representative:** Sam Wagdy
Language (s): Arabic
COMMUNITY NEWSPAPER

Asian Connections 773029
Owner: Asian Connections Newspaper
Editorial: 1305 Matheson Blvd E, Mississauga, Ontario L4W 1R1 **Tel:** 1 905 564-6200
Email: theasianconnectionsnewspaper@gmail.com **Web site:** http://www.theasianconnectionsnewspaper.com
Freq: Weekly; **Circ:** 32000
Editor: Sukhpreet Giani; **Publisher:** Rakhee Pbhakar
Profile: Asian Connections is a weekly newspaper providing Community News coverage for the South Asian and Indian Communities in the Greater Toronto area.
Language (s): English
Ad Rate: Full Page Mono 12.94
Currency: Canada Dollars
COMMUNITY NEWSPAPER

Asian Pacific Post 152967
Owner: Asian Post Media Publishing
Tel: 1 778 996 3631
Email: editor@postpeopleinc.com **Web site:** http://www.asianpacificpost.com
Freq: Bi-Weekly; **Circ:** 50000
Publisher: Harbinder Sewak
Profile: Asian Pacific Post, launched in 1993, targets Vancouver, British Columbia Asians and mainstream readers seeking breaking and current news on the island, the Lower Mainland of British Columbia and throughout Asia.
Language (s): English
Ad Rate: Full Page Mono 67.82
Ad Rate: Full Page Colour 350.00
Currency: United States Dollars
COMMUNITY NEWSPAPER

The Asian Star News 831813
Editorial: 7028 120th Street, Surrey, British Columbia V3W 3M8 **Tel:** 1 604 591-5423
Email: editor@theasianstar.com **Web site:** http://www.theasianstar.ca
Freq: Sat; **Circ:** 20000
Publisher: Iftikhar Ahmed; **Editor:** Umendra Singh
Profile: The Asian Star News is a weekly ethnic newspaper written for the Punjabi-speaking and south Asian communities in British Columbia.
Language (s): English
COMMUNITY NEWSPAPER

Auroran 409696
Owner: London Publishing Corp.
Editorial: 15213 Younge Street, Ste 8, Aurora, Ontario L4G 1L8 **Tel:** 1 905 727-3300
Email: cynthia@auroran.com **Web site:** http://www.auroran.com
Freq: Wed; **Circ:** 18500 Not Audited
Editor in Chief & Publisher: Brock Weir
Profile: Auroran is a weekly newspaper serving residents and businesses of Aurora, Ontario. It contains local news, community events and features about local people and places.
Language (s): English
Ad Rate: Full Page Mono 8.40
Currency: Canada Dollars
COMMUNITY NEWSPAPER

L' Autre Voix 527712
Owner: TC. Transcontinental
Editorial: 10989 Boul Sainte-Anne Suite 101, Beaupre, Quebec G0A 1E0 **Tel:** 1 418 840-1472
Email: redaction_quebec@tc.tc **Web site:** http://www.lautrevoix.com
Freq: Wed; **Circ:** 14381 Not Audited
Editor in Chief: Marc Cochrane; **Publisher:** Yvan Rancourt
Profile: L'Autre Voix est un hebdomadaire francophone pour les habitants de la Côte-de-Beaupré et l'Île d'Orléans, au Québec.

L'Autre Voix is a French-language weekly newspaper. It features news for the residents of La Côte-de-Beaupré and l'Île-d'Orléans, Quebec.
Language (s): French
Ad Rate: Full Page Mono 7.00
Currency: Canada Dollars
COMMUNITY NEWSPAPER

L' Avantage Gaspésien 399937
Owner: TC. Transcontinental
Editorial: 310 Rue de la Gare, Matane, Quebec G4W 3J3 **Tel:** 1 418 562-0666
Email: redaction_matane@tc.tc **Web site:** http://www.lavantagegaspesien.com
Freq: Wed; **Circ:** 17622 Not Audited
General Manager & Advertising Sales Manager: Marie-Josee Mailloux
Profile: L'Avantage Gaspesien est un hebdomadaire couvrant les actualités et événements locaux à Matane et en Haute-Gaspésie, au Québec.

L'Avantage Gaspesien is a weekly French newspaper covering local news and events in Matane and Haute-Gaspesie, Quebec.
Language (s): French
Ad Rate: Full Page Mono 6.30
Currency: Canada Dollars
COMMUNITY NEWSPAPER

B.C. Catholic 154537
Owner: Roman Catholic Archdiocese of Vancouver
Editorial: 150 Robson St, Vancouver, British Columbia V6B 2A7 **Tel:** 1 604 683-0281
Email: bccatholic@rcav.org **Web site:** http://bcc.rcav.org
Freq: Fri; **Circ:** 21000 Not Audited
Profile: B.C. Catholic is written for the Catholic community in British Columbia and is the official newspaper of the Archdiocese of Vancouver. It covers international, national and local news of particular interest to Catholics. It also contains editorials, letters, movie and book reviews, saints, liturgy, questions and answers on faith, morals and Catholic theology, announcements and classifieds. Deadlines are on Tuesdays at noon PT.
Language (s): English
Ad Rate: Full Page Mono 16.00
Currency: Canada Dollars
COMMUNITY NEWSPAPER

Bancroft This Week 29960
Owner: White Pine Media Corp.
Editorial: 254 Hastings St North, Bancroft, Ontario K0L 1C0 **Tel:** 1 613 332-2002
Email: jenn@haliburtonpress.com **Web site:** http://www.bancroftthisweek.com
Freq: Fri; **Circ:** 12000 Not Audited
General Manager: John Bauman
Profile: Bancroft This Week is published weekly for the residents of Bancroft, Ontario and its surrounding areas. The newspaper provides information about events, local politics and community news.
Language (s): English
Ad Rate: Full Page Mono 8.33
Ad Rate: Full Page Colour 1185.10
Currency: Canada Dollars
COMMUNITY NEWSPAPER

Barrhaven Independent 23784
Owner: Morris Newspaper Group
Editorial: 1165 Beaverwood Rd, Manotick, Ontario K4M 1A5 **Tel:** 1 613 825-9858
Email: newsfile@bellnet.ca **Web site:** http://www.barrhavenindependent.on.ca
Freq: Fri; **Circ:** 17625 Not Audited
Publisher & Editor in Chief: Jeffrey Morris
Profile: Barrhaven Independent is a publication written for the South Nepean community of Barrhaven, Ontario. The publication covers local news, events, and sports. Deadlines for the publication are two weeks before issue date.
Language (s): English
Ad Rate: Full Page Mono 9.80
Currency: Canada Dollars
COMMUNITY NEWSPAPER

Barrie Advance 23674
Owner: Metroland Media Group Ltd.
Editorial: 21 Patterson Rd, Barrie, Ontario L4N 7W6 **Tel:** 1 705 726-0573
Email: newsroom@simcoe.com **Web site:** http://www.barrieadvance.com
Freq: Thu; **Circ:** 52800 Not Audited

Profile: Barrie Advance is a community newspaper written for the residents of Barrie, Ontario. The paper covers local news, sports and feature stories.
Language (s): English
Ad Rate: Full Page Mono 86.58
Ad Rate: Full Page Colour 335.00
Currency: Canada Dollars
COMMUNITY NEWSPAPER

Battleford Publications 25604
Owner: Glacier Media Inc.
Editorial: 892-104 Street, North Battleford, Saskatchewan S9A 3E6 **Tel:** 1 306 445-7261
Email: newsoptimist.news@sasktel.net **Web site:** http://www.newsoptimist.ca
Circ: 17259 Not Audited
Editor in Chief: Becky Doig; **Publisher:** Alana Schweitzer
Language (s): English
COMMUNITY NEWSPAPER

Bay Observer 623568
Editorial: 140 King St E Suite 14, Hamilton, Ontario L8N 1B2 **Tel:** 1 905 522-6000
Email: john@bayobserver.ca **Web site:** http://bayobserver.ca
Freq: Monthly; **Circ:** 30000
Profile: Bay Observer is written for the residents of Hamilton, Ontario.
Language (s): English
Ad Rate: Full Page Mono 16.96
Currency: Canada Dollars
COMMUNITY NEWSPAPER

Beach Metro Community News 23964
Owner: Ward 9 Community News Inc.
Editorial: 2196 Gerrard St E, Toronto, Ontario M4E 2C7 **Tel:** 1 416 698-1164
Web site: http://www.beachmetro.com
Freq: Bi-Weekly; **Circ:** 30000
Publisher: Sheila Blinoff; **Editor:** Jon Muldoon
Profile: Beach Metro Community News is a non-profit, non-partisan community newspaper covering community news and features in and around Toronto. It was founded in 1972.
Language (s): English
Ad Rate: Full Page Mono 20.72
Ad Rate: Full Page Colour 400.00
Currency: Canada Dollars
COMMUNITY NEWSPAPER

Beauce Média 24056
Owner: TC. Transcontinental
Editorial: 1147, boul. Vachon Nord, Ste-Marie-de-Beauce, Quebec G6E 1M8 **Tel:** 1 418 387-8000
Email: redaction.beaucemedia@tc.tc **Web site:** http://www.beaucemedia.ca/
Freq: Wed; **Circ:** 25156 Not Audited
Editor: André Boutin
Profile: Beauce Média est un hebdomadaire qui couvre les actualités et événements locaux et régionaux pour la population de Sainte-Marie-de-Beauce et ses environs.

Beauce Média is a weekly French-language newspaper that covers local and regional information for the residents of Saint-Marie-de-Beauce, Quebec.
Language (s): French
Ad Rate: Full Page Mono 16.10
Currency: Canada Dollars
COMMUNITY NEWSPAPER

Beseda/The Conversation 80676
Owner: Kolovarsky (Sophie)
Editorial: 662 Sheppards Ave E, Ste 410, Toronto, Ontario M2K 3E6 **Tel:** 1 416 226-5026
Email: beseda@rogers.com
Freq: Fri; **Circ:** 15000 Not Audited
Publisher & Editor: Sophie Kolovarsky
Language (s): English
Ad Rate: Full Page Mono 9.98
Currency: Canada Dollars
COMMUNITY NEWSPAPER

Big and Colourful Print and Publishing 718237
Owner: Big and Colourful Print and Publishing
Editorial: 74 Patterson Drive, Stonewall, Manitoba R0C 2Z0 **Tel:** 1 204 467-5836
Email: news@selkirkrecord.ca **Web site:** http://www.selkirkrecord.com
Circ: 40617
Editor: Donna Maxwell
Language (s): English
COMMUNITY NEWSPAPER

Black Press - Castlegar 450056
Owner: Black Press
Editorial: 1810 8th Ave Unit 2, Castlegar, British Columbia V1N 2Y2 **Tel:** 1 250 365-6397
Email: editor@nelsonstar.com **Web site:** http://www.castlegarnews.com
Circ: 15500 Not Audited
Language (s): English
COMMUNITY NEWSPAPER

Black Press - Victoria 25576
Owner: Black Press
Editorial: 818 Broughton St, Victoria, British Columbia V8W 1E4- **Tel:** 1 250 381-3633
Email: editor@saanichnews.com **Web site:** http://www.blackpress.ca
Circ: 65094 Not Audited
Publisher: Janet Gairdner; **Publisher:** Penny Sakamoto
Language (s): English
COMMUNITY NEWSPAPER

Black Press Publications 25579
Owner: Black Press
Editorial: 2950 Bremner Ave., Red Deer, Alberta T4R 1M9 **Tel:** 1 403 343-2400
Email: editorial@reddeeradvocate.com **Web site:** http://www.reddeeradvocate.com
Circ: 58530 Not Audited
Language (s): English
COMMUNITY NEWSPAPER

Blaue Seiten 525072
Owner: B&Z Vertag Leddin
Tel: 1 519 576-6225
Email: bzv@germanyweb.com **Web site:** http://www.redaktion-blaueseiten.de/kanada.htm
Freq: Monthly; **Circ:** 52000 Not Audited
Editor in Chief: Tom Leddin
Profile: Blaue Seiten is a monthly German-language newspaper.
Language (s): German
Ad Rate: Full Page Mono 43.63
Currency: Canada Dollars
COMMUNITY NEWSPAPER

Bonus 82667
Owner: Newcon Publishing
Editorial: 1183 Finch Ave W Suite 202, Toronto, Ontario M3J 2G2 **Tel:** 1 416 256-4896
Email: bonus@bonus4u.com **Web site:** http://bonus4u.com/
Freq: Fri; **Circ:** 12500 Not Audited
Publisher & Editor: Simon Beker
Language (s): English
Ad Rate: Full Page Mono 35.00
Currency: Canada Dollars
COMMUNITY NEWSPAPER

Boundary Publications 25589
Owner: Glacier Media Inc.
Editorial: 68 Souris Ave N, Estevan, Saskatchewan S4A 2M3 **Tel:** 1 306 634-2654
Email: editor@estevanmercury.ca **Web site:** http://www.estevanmercury.ca
Circ: 12467 Not Audited
Publisher: Peter Ng; **Co-Editor:** Norm Park; **Co-Editor:** Chad Saxon
Language (s): English
COMMUNITY NEWSPAPER

Bracebridge Publications 25621
Owner: Metroland Media Group Ltd.
Editorial: 11 Main St W, Huntsville, Ontario P1H 2C5 **Tel:** 1 705 645-8771
Email: newsroom@muskokaregion.com **Web site:** http://www.muskokaregion.com/muskokaregion/
Circ: 46000 Not Audited
Editor: Kim Good; **News Editor:** Pamela Steel; **Editor in Chief:** Jack Tynan
Profile: Bracebridge Publications is a weekly community newspaper publisher serving the residents of Bracebridge and Muskoka, Ontario.
Language (s): English
COMMUNITY NEWSPAPER

The Bradford Times 23695
Owner: Postmedia Network Inc.
Editorial: 74 John St W, Bradford, Ontario L3Z 2B8 **Tel:** 1 905 775-4471
Email: ntaylor@postmedia.com **Web site:** http://www.bradfordtimes.ca
Freq: Sat; **Circ:** 11992 Not Audited
Editor in Chief: Miriam King
Profile: The Bradford Times covers local news, sports, entertainment, politics, economy, community listings and events for Bradford, Ontario.
Language (s): English
Ad Rate: Full Page Mono 7.49
Ad Rate: Full Page Colour 325.00
Currency: Canada Dollars
COMMUNITY NEWSPAPER

The Brant News 609312
Owner: Metroland Media Group Ltd
Editorial: 111 Easton Rd, Brantford, Ontario N3P 1J4 **Tel:** 1 519 758-1157
Email: editor@brantnews.com **Web site:** http://www.brantnews.com
Freq: Thu; **Circ:** 49000
Profile: The Brant News is a weekly community newspaper that serves the residents of Brantford and Brant County, Ontario.
Language (s): English
Ad Rate: Full Page Mono 16.13
Currency: Canada Dollars
COMMUNITY NEWSPAPER

Brasil News 80578
Owner: Brasil News Publisher Inc.
Editorial: 390 Burnhamthorpe Rd, Toronto, Ontario M9B 2A8 **Tel:** 1 416 538-4298
Email: brasilnews@brasilnews.ca **Web site:** http://www.brasilnews.ca
Freq: Bi-Weekly; **Circ:** 10000 Not Audited
Publisher: Tania Nuttall
Profile: Since 1997, Brasil News has been the only Brazilian newspaper distributed in Toronto, including neighborhoods in the Greater Toronto Area like Brampton and Mississauga. Covers important local news and events. Also publishes articles from the community members about various subjects.
Language (s): English
Ad Rate: Full Page Mono 4.26
Currency: Canada Dollars
COMMUNITY NEWSPAPER

Brome County News 24055
Owner: Glacier Media Inc.
Editorial: 5B Victoria St, Knowlton, Quebec J0E 1V0 **Tel:** 1 450 242-1188
Email: newsroom@sherbrookerecord.com **Web site:** http://www.sherbrookerecord.com
Freq: Tue; **Circ:** 13600 Not Audited
Publisher & Editor: Sharon McCully
Profile: Brome County News est destiné aux habitants de Brome-Missiquoi et des Cantons de l'Est du Québec. Il y est question de nouvelles régionales et locales, des activités sportives, culturelles et familliales, des naissances et réussites scolaires. Brome County News is written for the residents of Brome-Missiquoi and Eastern Townships of Quebec.
Language (s): English, French/Bilingual
Ad Rate: Full Page Mono 16.38
Currency: Canada Dollars
COMMUNITY NEWSPAPER

Brooks Bulletin Newspapers 23485
Owner: Nesbitt Publishing Ltd.
Editorial: 124 3rd St W, Brooks, Alberta T1R 0S3 **Tel:** 1 403 362-5571
Email: editor@brooksbulletin.com **Web site:** http://www.brooksbulletin.com
Circ: 15735 Not Audited
Publisher & Editor in Chief: Jamie Nesbitt
Language (s): English
COMMUNITY NEWSPAPER

Brunswick News Publications - Moncton 493564
Owner: Brunswick News Inc.
Editorial: 939 Main St, Moncton, New Brunswick E1C 8P3 **Tel:** 1 506 859-4900
Email: thisweek@brunswicknews.com **Web site:** https://www.telegraphjournal.com
Freq: Fri; **Circ:** 98000 Not Audited
Editor: Madeleine Leclerc
Profile: Brunswick News Inc. is a Canadian newspaper publishing company based in Moncton, New Brunswick.
Language (s): English
COMMUNITY NEWSPAPER

Brunswick Newspapers - Woodstock 363713
Owner: Brunswick News Inc.
Editorial: 110 Carleton St, Woodstock, New Brunswick E7M 1E4 **Tel:** 1 506 328-8863
Email: news@thebugle.ca **Web site:** http://www.telegraphjournal.com
Circ: 34700 Not Audited
Language (s): English
COMMUNITY NEWSPAPER

Bulgarian Flame 772549
Editorial: 206 – 11 Dervock Cres, Toronto, Ontario M2K 1A6 **Tel:** 1 416 821-9915
Email: info@bulbiz.com **Web site:** http://bulgarianflame.com
Freq: Bi-Weekly
Editor in Chief: Viara Dimitrova
Profile: Bulgarian Flame is a bi-weekly newspaper covering news and cultural events for the Bulgarian community in Canada and Canadians of Bulgarian ancestry.
Language (s): Bulgarian
COMMUNITY NEWSPAPER

The Burlington Post 23705
Owner: Metroland Media Group Ltd.
Editorial: 5046 Mainway Unit 2, Burlington, Ontario L7L 5Z1 **Tel:** 1 905 632-4444
Email: dford@burlingtonpost.com **Web site:** http://www.insidehalton.com/burlington-on
Freq: Fri; **Circ:** 45819 Not Audited
Profile: The Burlington Post is a local newspaper tailored for the community in and around Burlington, Ontario.
Language (s): English
Ad Rate: Full Page Mono 13.58
Ad Rate: Full Page Colour 1160.00
Currency: Canada Dollars
COMMUNITY NEWSPAPER

C.K. News Group 80740
Owner: Charhdi Kala Punjabi Weekly Newspaper International Inc.
Editorial: #6-7743-128th St., Surrey, British Columbia V3W 4E6 **Tel:** 1 604 590-6397
Email: cknewsgroup@telus.net **Web site:** http://cknewsgroup.ca
Circ: 37000 Not Audited
Editor: Gurpreet Sahota
Profile: Publishes two weekly Punjabi newspapers covering local, national and international news. They cover articles regarding religious, political and multicultural issues as well as news events from around the world, sports, business, fiction and non fictional articles and entertainment regarding the Punjabi, Sikh and Indo-Canadian community.
Language (s): English
COMMUNITY NEWSPAPER

Caledon Enterprise 23687
Owner: Metroland Media Group Ltd.
Editorial: 12612 50 Hwy, Bolton, Ontario L7E 1T6 **Tel:** 1 905 857-3433
Email: rwilkinson@caledonenterprise.com **Web site:** http://www.caledonenterprise.com
Freq: Thu; **Circ:** 14685 Not Audited
Editor: Robyn Wilkinson
Profile: Caledon Enterprise is a newspaper published two times a week for the Caledon, Ontario community. The publication covers local news, sports and entertainment.
Language (s): English
Ad Rate: Full Page Mono 21.31
Currency: Canada Dollars
COMMUNITY NEWSPAPER

The Cambridge Times 23713
Owner: Metroland Media Group Ltd.
Editorial: 475 Thompson Dr Unite 1-4, Cambridge, Ontario N1T 2K7 **Tel:** 1 519 623-7395
Email: rvivian@cambridgetimes.ca **Web site:** http://www.cambridgetimes.ca
Freq: Thu; **Circ:** 46525 Not Audited
Editor: Richard Vivian
Profile: Cambridge Times's editorial mission is, "To deliver the community news the readers have come to expect, issue after issue." The newspaper focuses on local issues, special events, what the kids are doing, who won what, and where to find the goods and services they need. The publication is aimed at residents of Cambridge, aged 25 to 40. It is delivered twice weekly, on Tuesday and Friday, free of charge. The lead time is two days. Deadlines for the publication are Monday and Wednesday at 12:00 p.m. ET before issue date.
Language (s): English
Ad Rate: Full Page Mono 31.50
Ad Rate: Full Page Colour 550.00
Currency: Canada Dollars
COMMUNITY NEWSPAPER

Camrose Booster 23508
Owner: Camrose Booster Ltd.
Editorial: 4925 48 St, Camrose, Alberta T4V 1L7 **Tel:** 1 780 672-3142
Email: news@camrosebooster.com **Web site:** http://www.camrosebooster.com
Freq: Tue; **Circ:** 13520 Not Audited
Editor in Chief: B.H. Fowler
Language (s): English
Ad Rate: Full Page Mono 13.30
Ad Rate: Full Page Colour 465.00
Currency: Canada Dollars
COMMUNITY NEWSPAPER

Camrose Canadian 23514
Owner: Postmedia Network Inc.
Editorial: 4610 49 Ave, Camrose, Alberta T4V 0M6 **Tel:** 1 780 672-4421
Email: camcanadian.class@sunmedia.ca **Web site:** http://www.camrosecanadian.com
Freq: Thu; **Circ:** 14500 Not Audited
Editor: Mark Crown; **Publisher:** Nick Goetz
Profile: Camrose Canadian is a weekly newspaper serving the residents of Camrose, Alberta.
Language (s): English
Ad Rate: Full Page Mono 12.32
Currency: Canada Dollars
COMMUNITY NEWSPAPER

Canada China News 556047
Editorial: 1 Cleopatra Dr Suite 208, Nepean, Ontario K2G 3M9 **Tel:** 1 613 233-1034
Email: editor@canadachinanews.com **Web site:** http://www.canadachinanews.com
Freq: Fri; **Circ:** 13000
Editor in Chief: Ming Yang
Profile: Canada China News features local and international news concerning Ottawa's Chinese community. Advertising deadline is Friday before publication. Add 30% for color ads.
Language (s): Chinese
Ad Rate: Full Page Mono 6.66
Currency: Canada Dollars
COMMUNITY NEWSPAPER

The Canadian 491457
Editorial: B.P. 24191, 300 Eagleson Rd., Ottawa, Ontario K2M 2C3 **Tel:** 1 888 377-2222
Email: news@agoracosmopolitan.com **Web site:** http://www.agoracosmopolitan.com
Freq: Tue; **Circ:** 500000 Not Audited
Editor in Chief: Peter Tremblay
Profile: The Canadian is a weekly newpaper featuring national and international news. The paper targets a cross-cultural readership focusing on news, lifestyle, editorial, sexuality, arts & entertainment, travel and health.
Language (s): English
Ad Rate: Full Page Mono 86.87
Currency: Canada Dollars
COMMUNITY NEWSPAPER

Canadian Asian News 155159
Editorial: 852 Preston Manor Dr, Mississauga, Ontario L5V 2L6 **Tel:** 1 905 502-5585
Email: asiannews1@gmail.com **Web site:** http://www.canadianasiannews.com/can.php
Circ: 15000 Not Audited
Publisher & Editor: Latafat Ali Siddiqui
Profile: Canadian Asian News is a community newspaper publisher serving the Asian population of Toronto and Montreal.
Language (s): English
COMMUNITY NEWSPAPER

Canadian Chinese Times - Calgary 874823
Editorial: 1914A Centre St NE, Calgary, Alberta T2E 2S8 **Tel:** 1 403 230-8118
Email: calcct@gmail.com **Web site:** http://2010cctimes.com/main/index.html
Freq: Weekly
General Manager: Harry C
Profile: Covers national news, world news, entertainment, health, and lifestyle.
Language (s): English
COMMUNITY NEWSPAPER

The Canadian Jewish News 80332
Editorial: 1750 Steeles Ave W Suite 218, Concord, Ontario L4K 2L7 **Tel:** 1 416 391-1836
Email: cjninfo@gmail.com **Web site:** http://www.cjnews.com
Freq: Thu; **Circ:** 35000 Not Audited
Editor: Yoni Goldstein
Profile: Canadian Jewish News is Canada's largest Jewish newspaper. Published weekly, the CJN has many traditional news sections, including: sports, arts, travel, health, business, food, seniors, and campus life. It focuses upon Israeli and Jewish Community issues. In addition, the paper also incorporates important news items about Israel as well as other countries' Jewish news stories. There are two editions: the English-only Toronto edition, and the bilingual French-English Montreal edition. The Toronto edition is a national publication (with international subscribers), while the Montreal edition caters to the Quebec region. Press releases, and most news and PR related materials should be directed to the News editor. Deadline for the newspaper is on Wednesday.Contact the publication for advertising rates.
Language (s): English
Ad Rate: Full Page Mono 24.00
Currency: Canada Dollars
COMMUNITY NEWSPAPER

The Canadian Jewish News - Montreal 82685
Editorial: 6900 Decarie Blvd suite 3125, Montreal, Quebec H3X 2T8 **Tel:** 1 514 735-2612
Email: montreal@thecjn.ca **Web site:** http://www.cjnews.com
Freq: Thu; **Circ:** 37187 Not Audited
Editor: Yoni Goldstein
Profile: The Canadian Jewish News s'adresse aux juifs du Canada et il possède un bureau à Montréal et un autre à Toronto. En plus d'un hebdomadaire sur papier, le site web est mis à jour quotidiennement. CJN is in english, some texts are translated in french.

The Canadian Jewish News is for all canadian Jews with an office in Montreal and one in Toronto. A weekly newspaper that have a daily updated web site. CJN is in english, some texts are translated in french.
Language (s): French/Bilingual
Ad Rate: Full Page Mono 27.51
Currency: Canada Dollars
COMMUNITY NEWSPAPER

Canadian Mennonite 82680
Owner: Canadian Mennonite Publishing Service
Editorial: 490 Dutton Dr Unit C, 5, Waterloo, Ontario N2L 6H7 **Tel:** 1 519 884-3810
Email: submit@canadianmennonite.org **Web site:** http://www.canadianmennonite.org
Freq: Bi-Weekly; **Circ:** 13800 Not Audited
Publisher & Editor in Chief: Dick Benner
Profile: Canadian Mennonite contains news, inspirational articles and analysis relating to the Mennonite Church in Canada.
Language (s): English
Ad Rate: Full Page Mono 30.00
Ad Rate: Full Page Colour 175.00
Currency: Canada Dollars
COMMUNITY NEWSPAPER

Can-India News 739680
Owner: World Media Corp (Canada) Inc
Editorial: 365 Watline Ave Unit 3-4, Mississauga, Ontario L4Z 1P3 **Tel:** 1 905 673-6625
Email: office@canindia.com **Web site:** http://www.canindia.com
Freq: Fri; **Circ:** 36213
Publisher: Jaswinder Marjara; **Editor:** Pradip Rodrigues
Profile: Can-India News is a local newspaper for the Indian residents of Mississauga, Ontario and the surrounding communities.
Language (s): English
Ad Rate: Full Page Mono 11.90
Ad Rate: Full Page Colour 14.51
Currency: Canada Dollars
COMMUNITY NEWSPAPER

Canstar Community News 25615
Owner: FP Canadian Newspapers LP
Editorial: 1355 Mountain Ave, Winnipeg, Manitoba R2X 3B6- **Tel:** 1 204 697-7009
Email: letters@canstarnews.com **Web site:** http://www.winnipegfreepress.com/our-communities
Circ: 192357 Not Audited
Language (s): English
COMMUNITY NEWSPAPER

CAPS 727300
Editorial: 201 North St, Port Perry, Ontario L9L 1B7 **Tel:** 1 905 985-9755
Email: deb@scugogcg.com **Web site:** http://www.scugogcg.com
Freq: Monthly; **Circ:** 20000
Co-Publisher: Tony Janssen
Profile: CAPS is a monthly community newspaper for the residents of Port Perry, Ontario and the surrounding communities.
Language (s): English
Ad Rate: Full Page Mono 4.98
Ad Rate: Full Page Colour 5.49
Currency: Canada Dollars
COMMUNITY NEWSPAPER

Cariboo Press Publications - Kitimat 25568
Owner: Black Press
Editorial: 626 Enterprise Ave, Kitimat, British Columbia V8C 2E4 **Tel:** 1 250 632-6144
Email: advertising@northernsentinel.com **Web site:** http://www.northernsentinel.com
Circ: 23200 Not Audited
Editor in Chief: Malcolm Baxter; **Publisher:** Louisa Genzale; **Editor:** Cameron Orr
Profile: The Northern Sentinel has been a part of Kitimat almost from the beginning of the community. Since the first issue hit the muddy, construction-era streets in 1954, it has chronicled the lives and times of this unique town and its people.
Language (s): English
COMMUNITY NEWSPAPER

Cariboo Press Publications - Williams Lake 25577
Owner: Black Press
Editorial: 188 First Ave N, Williams Lake, British Columbia V2G 1Y8 **Tel:** 1 250 392-2331
Email: news@wltribune.com **Web site:** http://www.wltribune.com
Circ: 16070 Not Audited
Language (s): English
COMMUNITY NEWSPAPER

Le Carrefour de Quebec 23973
Owner: Editions du Joyeux-Drille
Editorial: 799 5e Rue, Quebec, Quebec G1J 2S6 **Tel:** 1 418 649-0775
Email: carrefour@webnet.qc.ca **Web site:** http://www.carrefourdequebec.com
Freq: Monthly; **Circ:** 71200
Editor in Chief: Marie-Claude Boileau; **General Manager & Advertising Sales Manager:** Martin Claveau
Profile: Le Carrefour de Quebec is a weekly French-language publication covering two regions with two separate distribution schedules: Week A covers the entire city of Québec, while week B covers only the core of the city of Québec.
Language (s): French
Ad Rate: Full Page Mono 10.15
Currency: Canada Dollars
COMMUNITY NEWSPAPER

Central Plains Herald-Leader 23615
Owner: Postmedia Network Inc.
Editorial: 1941 Saskatchewan Ave W, Portage La Prairie, Manitoba R1N 0R7 **Tel:** 1 204 857-3427
Email: mdumont@postmedia.com **Web site:** http://www.thedailygraphic.com
Freq: Thu; **Circ:** 11500 Not Audited
Publisher: Barry Clayton; **Publisher:** Daria Zmiyiwsky
Profile: Central Plains Herald-Leader is a community newspaper covering local news and information in Portage La Prairie, Manitoba.
Language (s): English
Ad Rate: Full Page Mono 14.98
Currency: Canada Dollars
COMMUNITY NEWSPAPER

The Centretown Buzz 556094
Editorial: 101-210 Gloucester St 101, Ottawa, Ontario K2P 2K4 **Tel:** 1 613 565-6012
Email: editor@centretownbuzz.com **Web site:** http://www.centretownbuzz.com/
Freq: Monthly; **Circ:** 10000
Profile: The Centretown Buzz is a free community newspaper published monthly for residents of the Sommerset Ward, Ontario community. The paper covers neighborhood issues and notable events of community interest. Short notices for not-for-profit community events may be published at no cost. Larger notices and notices for for-profit events will be accepted as advertising.
Language (s): English
Ad Rate: Full Page Mono 10.91
Currency: Canada Dollars
COMMUNITY NEWSPAPER

Le Charlevoisien 24059
Owner: Éditions nordiques 2007 inc. (Les)
Editorial: 53 Rue John-Nairne Suite 100, La Malbaie, Quebec G5A 1L8 **Tel:** 1 418 665-1299
Email: emaltais@lecharlevoisien.com **Web site:** http://www.lecharlevoisien.com
Freq: Wed; **Circ:** 15400 Not Audited
Editor in Chief: Sylvain Desmeules; **Editor:** Charles Warren
Profile: Le Charlevoisien est un hebdo couvrant la grande région de Charlevoix au Québec.

L'Hebdo Charlevoisien is a weekly publication covering local news for the Charlevoix region of Québec. Contact the News Editor.
Language (s): French
Ad Rate: Full Page Mono 9.24
Currency: Canada Dollars
COMMUNITY NEWSPAPER

Chatham Kent This Week 24285
Owner: Postmedia Network
Editorial: 138 King St W, Chatham, Ontario N7M 1E3- **Tel:** 1 519 351-7331
Email: lou.v.pin@gmail.com **Web site:** http://www.chathamthisweek.com
Freq: Wed; **Circ:** 20000 Not Audited
Editor: Peter Epp
Profile: Chatham This Week is a weekly publication written for residents of Chatham, Ontario.
Language (s): English
Ad Rate: Full Page Mono 7.49
Currency: Canada Dollars
COMMUNITY NEWSPAPER

The Chatham Voice 870488
Owner: C-K Media Inc.
Editorial: 84 Dover St, Chatham, Ontario N7L 1T1 **Tel:** 1 519 397-2020
Email: bruce@chathamvoice.com **Web site:** http://www.chathamvoice.com
Freq: Weekly; **Circ:** 21000
General Manager: Jim Blake; **Editor:** Bruce Corcoran
Profile: The Chatham Voice is written for residents of Chatham centering on the community in its reporting. Sections include News, which has a local angle; Arts; Life; Business; and Sports, covering local sporting events and athletes. This outlet offers a free weekly online E-edition. Outlet offers RSS
Language (s): English
Ad Rate: Full Page Colour 1355.00
Currency: Canada Dollars
COMMUNITY NEWSPAPER

Chilliwack Progress 23373
Owner: Black Press
Editorial: 45860 Spadina Ave, Chilliwack, British Columbia V2P 6H9 **Tel:** 1 604 702-5550
Email: editor@theprogress.com **Web site:** http://www.theprogress.com
Freq: Fri; **Circ:** 30374 Not Audited
Publisher: Liz Lynch
Profile: Chilliwack Progress is the oldest weekly newspaper in British Columbia. It covers local news and features for the community of Chilliwack, British Columbia.
Language (s): English
Ad Rate: Full Page Mono 26.32
Ad Rate: Full Page Colour 250.00
Currency: Canada Dollars
COMMUNITY NEWSPAPER

Chinese Canadian Times - Eastern Canada Edition 539298
Editorial: 2528 Bayview Ave, Toronto, Ontario M2L 1A9 **Tel:** 1 416 445-7815
Web site: http://www.cctimes.ca
Freq: Sat; **Circ:** 13000 Not Audited
Publisher: Kathy Lin; **Editor:** Schiller Wang
Profile: Chinese Canadian Times - Eastern Canada Edition is a local, weekly, Mandarin-language newspaper serving primarily Chinese residents of Toronto.
Language (s): Mandarin
Ad Rate: Full Page Mono 17.30
Currency: Canada Dollars
COMMUNITY NEWSPAPER

Chinese News 80245
Owner: Chinese News Group
Editorial: 50 Weybright Crt Unit 11, Scarborough, Ontario M1S 5A8 **Tel:** 1 416 504-0761
Email: cng@096.ca **Web site:** http://www.chinesenewsgroup.com
Freq: Fri; **Circ:** 12000
Editor: Nancy Jin
Profile: Chinese News offers local news and events to the Chinese and Chinese-speaking communities of Toronto.
Language (s): Chinese
Ad Rate: Full Page Mono 23.52
Currency: Canada Dollars
COMMUNITY NEWSPAPER

The Chinese Press/La Presse Chinoise 82891
Owner: Eastern Chinese Press Inc. La Presse Chinoise de l'Est
Editorial: 1123 Clark St Fl 2ND, Montreal, Quebec H2Z 1K3 **Tel:** 1 514 397-9969
Email: cpress@chinesepress.com **Web site:** http://www.chinesepress.com
Freq: Fri; **Circ:** 25000 Not Audited
Publisher & Editor in Chief: Crescent Chau
Profile: The Chinese Press/La Press Chinoise est un hebdomadaire offert en chinois aux membres de la communauté chinoise du Canada francophone. Il y est question de nouvelles internationales, locales, chinoises, communautaires, financières et sur le divertissement.

The Chinese Press/La Presse Chinoise is a Chinese-language publication for members of the Chinese community in Francophone Canada. The paper includes international, local, Chinese, community, financial and entertainment news.
Language (s): Chinese
Ad Rate: Full Page Mono 13.64
Currency: Canada Dollars
COMMUNITY NEWSPAPER

ChristianWeek Papers 506178
Owner: Fellowship for Print Witness Inc.
Editorial: 204-424 Logan Ave., Winnipeg, Manitoba R3A 0R4 **Tel:** 1 204 982-2060
Email: admin@christianweek.org **Web site:** http://www.christianweek.org
Circ: 46000 Not Audited
Publisher: Brian Koldyk; **Editor:** Kelly Rempel
Language (s): English
COMMUNITY NEWSPAPER

Il Cittadino Canadese 80454
Owner: Antonina Mormina
Editorial: 6020 Jean-Talon Est, Suite 710, Montreal, Quebec H1S 3B1 **Tel:** 1 514 253-2332
Email: journal@cittadino.ca **Web site:** http://cittadino.ca/
Freq: Tue; **Circ:** 13000 Not Audited
Publisher: Nina Giordano; **Editor:** Antonina Mormina
Profile: Le journal Cittadino est destiné aux italiens du Québec.

Il Cittadino Canadese is an Italian-language publication for Italians in Quebec.
Language (s): Italian
Ad Rate: Full Page Mono 11.20
Currency: Canada Dollars
COMMUNITY NEWSPAPER

Claridge Community Newspapers 25638
Owner: Claridge Community Newspapers
Editorial: 10 1st St, Orangeville, Ontario L9W 2C4 **Tel:** 1 519 941-2230
Email: mail@citizen.on.ca **Web site:** http://www.citizen.on.ca
Circ: 16612 Not Audited
Publisher: Alan Claridge; **Editor in Chief:** Thomas Claridge
Language (s): English
COMMUNITY NEWSPAPER

Clark's Crossing Gazette 552014
Editorial: 430 D Central St., Warman, Saskatchewan S0K 4S0 **Tel:** 1 306 668-0575
Email: ads@ccgazette.ca **Web site:** http://www.ccgazette.ca
Freq: Thu; **Circ:** 15216
Editor, Publisher & Advertising Sales Manager: Terry Jenson
Profile: Clark's Crossing Gazette is a free, weekly newspaper serving the community of Warman, Saskatchewan. Editorial coverage includes local politics, events and sports. Advertising deadlines fall on Mondays at 5pm and editorial deadlines on Tuesdays at 10am.
Language (s): English
Ad Rate: Full Page Mono 16.24
Currency: Canada Dollars
COMMUNITY NEWSPAPER

Clarkson's Corners 30012
Owner: RJ Publishing
Editorial: 2673 Burnford Trail, Mississauga, Ontario L5M 5E1 **Tel:** 1 905 820-5458
Email: lettersnlines@rogers.com **Web site:** http://rjentpub.com/clarksons-corners/
Freq: Bi-Monthly; **Circ:** 16000 Not Audited
Publisher & Editor in Chief: Julie Donofrio
Profile: Clarkson's Corners is a bi-monthly newspaper serving the community of Mississauga, Ontario and surrounding areas.
Language (s): English
Ad Rate: Full Page Mono 12.57
Currency: Canada Dollars
COMMUNITY NEWSPAPER

The Clipper Weekly 151202
Owner: Clipper Publishing Corp.
Editorial: 27A Third Street South, Beausejour, Manitoba R0E 0C0 **Tel:** 1 204 268-4700
Email: mail@clipper.mb.ca **Web site:** http://www.clipper.mb.ca
Freq: Mon; **Circ:** 10576 Not Audited
Editor in Chief: Mark Buss; **Publisher:** Kim MacAulay
Profile: The Clipper Weekly is a newspaper published for residents of Beausejour, Manitoba. The paper covers local news, weather and events.
Language (s): English
Ad Rate: Full Page Mono 14.00
Currency: Canada Dollars
COMMUNITY NEWSPAPER

Cloverdale Reporter 139375
Owner: Black Press
Editorial: 17586 56A Ave, Surrey, British Columbia V3S 1G3 **Tel:** 1 604 575-2400
Email: editor@cloverdalereporter.com **Web site:** http://www.cloverdalereporter.com
Freq: Wed; **Circ:** 14464 Not Audited
Profile: Cloverdale Reporter is a monthly newspaper serving the residents of Cloverdale, South Surrey and Sullivan, Hazelmere and Fleetwood in British Columbia. It covers local news, sports, events listings and arts & entertainment.
Language (s): English
Ad Rate: Full Page Mono 16.10
Currency: Canada Dollars
COMMUNITY NEWSPAPER

The Coast 70388
Owner: Coast Publishing Ltd.
Editorial: 5567 Cunard St., Halifax, Nova Scotia B3K IC5 **Tel:** 1 902 422-6278
Email: coast@thecoast.ca **Web site:** http://www.thecoast.ca
Freq: Thu; **Circ:** 24000 Not Audited
News Editor: Tim Bousquet; **Publisher:** Christine Oreskovich; **Editor:** Kyle Shaw
Profile: The Coast is local newspaper published every Thursday by Coast Publishing. The newspaper is published for the residents of Halifax, NS. It covers nightlife, entertainment, music, movies, and social events. The newspapers goal is to be provocative, entertaining, and truthful. The lead time is three days.
Language (s): English
Ad Rate: Full Page Mono 35.00
Ad Rate: Full Page Colour 49.80
Currency: Canada Dollars
COMMUNITY NEWSPAPER

Coast Reporter 23408
Owner: Glacier Media Inc.
Editorial: 5485 Wharf Rd 5485 5485, PO Box 1388, Sechelt, British Columbia V0N 3A0 **Tel:** 1 604 885-4811
Email: editor@coastreporter.net **Web site:** http://www.coastreporter.net
Freq: Fri; **Circ:** 12720 Not Audited
Editor: John Gleeson; **Publisher:** Peter Kvarnstrom
Profile: Coast Reporter is a weekly newspaper for the Sunshine Coast of British Columbia. Deadlines are Tuesdays at 5pm.
Language (s): English
Ad Rate: Full Page Mono 15.12
Currency: Canada Dollars
COMMUNITY NEWSPAPER

Cochrane Eagle 152975
Editorial: 126A River Ave, Cochrane, Alberta T4C 2C2 **Tel:** 1 403 932-6588
Email: cpuglia@cochrane.greatwest.ca **Web site:** http://www.cochraneeagle.com
Freq: Wed; **Circ:** 12360 Not Audited
Publisher: Brenda Tennant
Language (s): English
Ad Rate: Full Page Mono 4.13
Currency: Canada Dollars
COMMUNITY NEWSPAPER

Cochrane Times 29871
Owner: Postmedia Network Inc.
Editorial: Bay 8 206 5th Ave. W, Cochrane, Alberta T4C 1X3 **Tel:** 1 403 932-3500
Email: ctimes.editor@sunmedia.ca **Web site:** http://www.cochranetimes.com
Freq: Wed; **Circ:** 11600 Not Audited
Publisher: Shawn Cornell
Profile: Cochrane Times is a weekly newspaper written for the residents of Cochrane, Alberta. The publication prints articles on local news.
Language (s): French/Bilingual
Ad Rate: Full Page Mono 21.00
Ad Rate: Full Page Colour 3207.65
Currency: Canada Dollars
COMMUNITY NEWSPAPER

Colchester Weekly News 750682
Owner: SaltWire Network Inc.
Editorial: 6 Louise St, Truro, Nova Scotia B2N 3K2 **Tel:** 1 902 893-9405
Email: news@trurodaily.com **Web site:** http://www.trurodaily.com
Freq: Thu; **Circ:** 21786
Group Publisher: Richard Russell
Profile: Colchester Weekly News is a community newspaper for the residents of Truro, Nova Scotia and the surrounding communities.
Language (s): English
Ad Rate: Full Page Mono 8.68
Currency: Canada Dollars
COMMUNITY NEWSPAPER

The Collingwood Connection 23736
Owner: Metroland Media Group Ltd.
Editorial: 11 Ronell Cres Unit B, Collingwood, Ontario L9Y 4J6 **Tel:** 1 705 444-1875
Email: connection@simcoe.com **Web site:** http://www.simcoe.com/collingwood-on/
Freq: Fri; **Circ:** 19900 Not Audited
Profile: The Collingwood Connection is a community newspaper written for the Collingwood, ON general public. It covers local news, sports, business and classifieds.
Language (s): English
Ad Rate: Full Page Mono 20.07
Currency: Canada Dollars
COMMUNITY NEWSPAPER

The Collingwood Enterprise-Bulletin 29973
Owner: Postmedia Network Inc.
Editorial: 77 Simcoe St, Collingwood, Ontario L9Y 1H7 **Tel:** 1 705 445-4611
Email: lotw.enterprise@sunmedia.ca **Web site:** http://www.theenterprisebulletin.com
Freq: Fri; **Circ:** 19700 Not Audited
Queen's Park Bureau Chief: Antonella Artuso
Profile: The Enterprise-Bulletin is a weekly community newspaper that covers local news, sports and events for residents of Collingwood, Ontario and its surrounding area.
Language (s): English
Ad Rate: Full Page Mono 8.12
Currency: Canada Dollars
COMMUNITY NEWSPAPER

Community Digest - Calgary 82675
Owner: Community Digest Multicultural Publications
Editorial: 3545 32 Ave NE Suite 660, Calgary, Alberta T1Y 6M6 **Tel:** 1 604 875-8313
Email: digest_news@yahoo.com **Web site:** http://www.communitydigest.ca
Freq: Fri; **Circ:** 25000 Not Audited
Editor in Chief: Steve Bowell; **Publisher:** N. Ebrahim
Profile: Community Digest - Calgary covers multicultural events related to race relations, immigration, diversity and cultural integration in Calgary, Alberta.
Language (s): English
Ad Rate: Full Page Mono 51.03
Currency: Canada Dollars
COMMUNITY NEWSPAPER

Community Digest - Toronto 82696
Owner: Community Digest Multicultural Publications
Editorial: 4261 Hwy 7, Suite 151, Markham, Ontario L3R 3V7 **Tel:** 1 416 283-3373
Email: digest_news@yahoo.com **Web site:** http://www.communitydigest.ca
Freq: Fri; **Circ:** 25000 Not Audited
Editor in Chief: Steve Bowell
Profile: Community Digest - Toronto is a multicultural newspaper published for English-speaking people of Canadian, European, Middle Eastern, East African and Aboriginal origins.
Language (s): English
Ad Rate: Full Page Mono 51.03
Currency: Canada Dollars
COMMUNITY NEWSPAPER

Community Digest - Vancouver 82697
Owner: Community Digest Multicultural Publications
Editorial: 1755 Robson St, Ste 216, Vancouver, British Columbia V6G 3B7 **Tel:** 1 604 875-8313
Email: digest_news@yahoo.com **Web site:** http://www.communitydigest.ca
Freq: Fri; **Circ:** 25000 Not Audited
Editor in Chief: Steve Bowell
Profile: Community Digest - Vancouver is a magazine targeted toward the multicultural community, particularly those of the South Asian descent.

Distributed free of charge in Vancouver, Montreal, and Toronto libraries, each metropolitan area reaches about 25,000 people. The Vancouver issue is contracted out to a language editor, and is the only bilingual issue. Each area includes approximately half the same stories, with the other half tailored to its geographic locale.
Language (s): English
Ad Rate: Full Page Mono 66.99
Currency: Canada Dollars
COMMUNITY NEWSPAPER

Community Herald Newspapers 499885
Owner: Halifax Herald Ltd. (The)
Editorial: 2717 Joseph Howe Dr, Halifax, Nova Scotia B3L 4T9- **Tel:** 1 902 426-2811
Email: newsroom@herald.ca **Web site:** http://thechronicleherald.ca/community
Circ: 145009 Not Audited
Editor: Lindsey Bunin
Profile: Community Herald Newspapers share a staff with The Chronicle-Herald in Halifax, Nova Scotia. Although the staff is shared, all editorial content is different. They are distributed to both subscribers, in their papers, and non-subscribers, in their flyer packages, every Thursday.
Language (s): English
COMMUNITY NEWSPAPER

Community Media Management 74110
Owner: Gleaner Community Press
Tel: 1 416 504-6987
Email: gleanereditor@gmail.com **Web site:** http://gleanernews.ca
Circ: 50000 Not Audited
Editor in Chief: Emina Gamulin
Language (s): English
COMMUNITY NEWSPAPER

Community Press 671226
Owner: Postmedia Network Inc.
Editorial: 199 Front St Suite 535, Belleville, Ontario K8N 5H5 **Tel:** 1 613 962-9171
Email: cp.news@sunmedia.ca
COMMUNITY NEWSPAPER

Community Voice Newspapers 25590
Owner: EJ Lewchuck and Associates Ltd.
Editorial: 15A Albert Avenue, Spruce Grove, Alberta T7X 2Z5 **Tel:** 1 780 962-9228
Email: news@com-voice.com **Web site:** http://www.com-voice.com
Circ: 16000 Not Audited
Publisher & Editor: Elaine Lewchuck
Language (s): English
COMMUNITY NEWSPAPER

Comox Valley Record 23376
Owner: Black Press
Editorial: 765 McPhee Ave, Courtenay, British Columbia V9N 2Z7- **Tel:** 1 250 338-5811
Email: editor@comoxvalleyrecord.com **Web site:** http://www.comoxvalleyrecord.com
Freq: Thu; **Circ:** 21554 Not Audited
Editor: Terry Farrell; **Publisher:** Joanna Ross
Profile: Comox Valley Record is a local newspaper serving the residents of Courtenay, British Columbia. The paper covers breaking news, community events, sports, business and arts & entertainment.
Language (s): English
Ad Rate: Full Page Mono 19.74
Currency: Canada Dollars
COMMUNITY NEWSPAPER

El Contacto Directo 903378
Owner: Colatina International Communications
Editorial: 1259 Kingsway, Vancouver, British Columbia V5V 3E2 **Tel:** 1 604 729-0622
Email: colatina@hotmail.es **Web site:** http://www.elcontactolatino.com
Freq: Fri; **Circ:** 10000
Editor: Victor Alvarado
Profile: A weekly Spanish newspaper in British Columbia that was founded in 1992. It covers National, International and Local news.
Language (s): Spanish/Bilingual
Ad Rate: Full Page Mono 6.93
Ad Rate: Full Page Colour 12.13
Currency: Canada Dollars
COMMUNITY NEWSPAPER

Corriere Italiano 80493
Owner: TC. Transcontinental
Editorial: 8000 Av Blaise Pascal, Montreal, Quebec H1E 2S7 **Tel:** 1 514 643-2300
Email: corriereitaliano@tc.tc **Web site:** http://www.corriereitaliano.com
Freq: Wed; **Circ:** 24500 Not Audited
Editor: Carole Gagliardi; **News Editor:** Farizio Intravaia
Profile: Corriere Italiano est un hebdomadaire destiné aux communautés italiennes de Montréal et du Canada.

Corriere Italiano is a weekly newspaper covering news for the Italian-Canadian communities across Canada. The publication is written in Italian.
Language (s): English
Ad Rate: Full Page Mono 8.00
Currency: Canada Dollars
COMMUNITY NEWSPAPER

The County Weekly News 82898
Owner: Postmedia Network Inc.
Editorial: 252 Main Street, Suite 3, Picton, Ontario K0K 2T0 **Tel:** 1 613 476-4714
Email: cwn.newsroom@sunmedia.ca **Web site:** http://www.countyweeklynews.ca
Freq: Weekly; **Circ:** 13186 Not Audited
Profile: The County Weekly News is written for the residents of Picton and Prince Edward County, Ontario.
Language (s): English
Ad Rate: Full Page Mono 5.04
Ad Rate: Full Page Colour 341.00
Currency: Canada Dollars
COMMUNITY NEWSPAPER

Coup d'œil 23943
Owner: TC. Transcontinental
Editorial: 810-D Rang du Coteau, Napierville, Quebec J0J 1L0 **Tel:** 1 450 245-3344
Email: coupdoeil@tc.tc **Web site:** http://www.coupdoeil.info
Freq: Wed; **Circ:** 15828
Editor: Marc-André Couillard; **Editor in Chief:** Gilles Lévesque; **Publications Director:** Claude Trahan
Profile: Coup d'oeil est un hebdomadaire francophone destiné aux habitants de Napierville et sa région.

Coup d'œil is a weekly French-language newspaper that covers local news and information, including community news, human-interest stories, sports, and education, for Napierville, Quebec.
Language (s): French
Ad Rate: Full Page Mono 15.12
Currency: Canada Dollars
COMMUNITY NEWSPAPER

Courrier De Portneuf 24007
Owner: Cooperative du Courrier de Port Neuf
Editorial: 276 Rue Notre-Dame, Donnacona, Quebec G3M 1G7 **Tel:** 1 418 285-0211
Email: journaliste@courrierdeportneuf.com **Web site:** http://www.courrierdeportneuf.com
Freq: Wed; **Circ:** 35699
Publisher & Advertising Sales Director: Josee-Anne Fiset; **Editor in Chief:** Denise Paquin
Profile: Le Courrier de Portneuf is a local news weekly serving the region of Portneuf, Quebec.
Language (s): French
Ad Rate: Full Page Mono 5.95
Currency: Canada Dollars
COMMUNITY NEWSPAPER

Courrier Laval 86527
Owner: TC. Transcontinental
Tel: 1 450 667-4360
Email: redactionlaval@tc.tc **Web site:** http://www.courrierlaval.com
Freq: Wed; **Circ:** 132833 Not Audited
News Editor: Marc Fradellin; **Editor in Chief:** Diane Hameury
Profile: Courrier Laval est un hebdomadaire, publié le mercredi, destiné à la population de Laval et des environs.

Courrier Laval is a newspaper written exclusively in French. It is one of the largest weekly newspapers in francophone Canada and focuses on reporting local news in the Laval, Quebec area.
Language (s): French
Ad Rate: Full Page Mono 29.26
Currency: Canada Dollars
COMMUNITY NEWSPAPER

Cowichan Valley Citizen   23391
Owner: Black Press
Editorial: 251 Jubilee St, Duncan, British Columbia V9L 1W8 **Tel:** 1 250 748-2666
Web site: http://www.cowichanvalleycitizen.com
Freq: Fri; **Circ:** 23160 Not Audited
Publisher & Advertising Sales Manager: Shirley Skolos
Profile: Cowichan Valley Citizen is a community newspaper written for the residents of Duncan, British Columbia.
Language (s): English
Ad Rate: Full Page Mono 18.06
Currency: Canada Dollars
COMMUNITY NEWSPAPER

Crescent International   82701
Owner: Crescent International Newspaper Inc.
Tel: 1 905 887-8913
Email: crescent@ca.inter.net **Web site:** http://www.crescent-online.net
Freq: Monthly; **Circ:** 32000 Not Audited
Editor in Chief: Zafar Bangash
Profile: Crescent International is a a monthly news-magazine, covers international news, analyses affairs, & discusses issues from an Islamic perspective.
Language (s): English
Ad Rate: Full Page Mono 51.13
Currency: Canada Dollars
COMMUNITY NEWSPAPER

Das Echo   80356
Owner: Independent
Tel: 1 514 335-3653
Email: dasecho@live.ca **Web site:** http://www.dasecho.com
Freq: Monthly; **Circ:** 30000 Not Audited
Publisher & Editor in Chief: Paul Walter
Profile: Das Echo est un mensuel publié en allemand destiné à la communauté germanophone du Canada et à l'étranger.

Das Echo is a German-language publication for members of the German speaking community in Canada. It is published on the first of each month. Contact the publication by phone, fax, or mail.
Language (s): German
Ad Rate: Full Page Mono 18.76
Ad Rate: Full Page Colour 25.07
Currency: Canada Dollars
COMMUNITY NEWSPAPER

The Delta Optimist   23380
Owner: Glacier Media Inc.
Editorial: 207-4840 Delta Street, Delta, British Columbia V4K 2T6 **Tel:** 1 604 946-4451
Email: editor@delta-optimist.com **Web site:** http://www.delta-optimist.com
Freq: Fri; **Circ:** 17250 Not Audited
Publisher: Alvin Brouwer; **Editor in Chief:** Ted Murphy
Profile: The Delta Optimist is a newspaper written for the residents of Delta, British Columbia. The publication covers local news, weather, sports and arts & entertainment.
Language (s): English
Ad Rate: Full Page Mono 16.90
Currency: Canada Dollars
COMMUNITY NEWSPAPER

Desi News   80741
Owner: Easwar (G.A.)
Editorial: 17600 Yonge St, Newmarket, Ontario L3Y 4Z1 **Tel:** 1 416 695-4357
Email: desinews@rogers.com **Web site:** http://www.e-desinews.com
Freq: Monthly; **Circ:** 45000 Not Audited
Editor in Chief: Shagorika Easwar
Profile: Desi News is a monthly publication serving the South Asian community.
Language (s): English

Ad Rate: Full Page Mono 9.47
Currency: Canada Dollars
COMMUNITY NEWSPAPER

Droit de parole   23970
Owner: Communications Basse-ville Inc.
Editorial: 266 Rue Saint-Vallier O, Quebec, Quebec G1K 1K2 **Tel:** 1 418 648-8043
Email: info@droitdeparole.org **Web site:** http://www.droitdeparole.org
Freq: Bi-Monthly; **Circ:** 15000
Profile: Established in 1974, Droit de parole informs people of struggles, concerns and activities in the city of Québec, Québec. Subjects covered include neighborhood living conditions, women, youth, elderly, unemployment, social services and the environment. It is published 8 times a year.
Language (s): French
Ad Rate: Full Page Mono 850.00
Currency: Canada Dollars
COMMUNITY NEWSPAPER

East Central Alberta Review   23530
Owner: Coronation Review Ltd.
Editorial: 4923 Victoria Ave, Coronation, Alberta T0C 1C0 **Tel:** 1 403 578-4111
Email: publisher@ecareview.com **Web site:** http://www.ecareview.com
Freq: Thu; **Circ:** 24062 Not Audited
Publisher & Editor: Joyce Webster
Profile: East Central Alberta Review is a local community newspaper serving residents of Coronation, Alberta. Articles cover local news, weather and travel. Advertising deadlines are at noon MT.
Language (s): English
Ad Rate: Full Page Mono 10.71
Ad Rate: Full Page Colour 80.00
Currency: Canada Dollars
COMMUNITY NEWSPAPER

Eastern News   80806
Owner: Urdu Promotion Board, Canada
Editorial: 119 Royal West Dr, Brampton, Ontario L6X 0V4 **Tel:** 1 416 568.2624
Email: mkhan@theeasternnews.com **Web site:** http://www.easternnews.ca
Freq: Bi-Monthly; **Circ:** 10000 Not Audited
Editor in Chief: Masood Khan; **Publisher:** Alia Sultana
Profile: Eastern News is written for the residents of Mississauga, Brampton, Ontario. It is published in English and Pakistani and is written primarily for South Asians.
Language (s): English
Ad Rate: Full Page Mono 10.74
Currency: Canada Dollars
COMMUNITY NEWSPAPER

L' Écho De La Baie   23951
Owner: Radio du Rocher Percé inc.
Editorial: 143 Boul Perron O, New Richmond, Quebec G0C 2B0 **Tel:** 1 418 392-5083
Email: nrm.redaction@tc.tc **Web site:** http://www.lechodelabaie.ca
Freq: Wed; **Circ:** 14777
Profile: L'Écho de la Baie est une journal hebdomadaire francophone où on couvre les nouvelles et les évènements locaux pour les résidents de la Baie-des-Chaleurs et Restigouche.

L'Écho de la Baie is a French-language weekly newspaper covering local news and events for residents of Baie-des-Chaleurs and Restigouche.
Language (s): French
Ad Rate: Full Page Mono 14.28
Currency: Canada Dollars
COMMUNITY NEWSPAPER

L' Echo de Maskinongé   364575
Owner: TC. Transcontinental
Editorial: 635, rue Pere Daniel, Trois-Rivieres, Quebec G9A 5Z7 **Tel:** 1 819 379-1490
Email: redaction_em@tc.tc **Web site:** http://www.lechodemaskinonge.com
Freq: Wed; **Circ:** 13800 Not Audited
Profile: L'Echo de Maskinongé est un quotidien hebdomadaire couvrant les actualités régionales et locales pour les résidents de Louiseville, D'Autray et Maskinongé, au Québec.

L'Echo de Maskinongé is a weekly, French-language newspaper covering regional and local news for residents of Louiseville, D'Autray and Maskinonge, Quebec.
Language (s): French
Ad Rate: Full Page Mono 6.58
Currency: Canada Dollars
COMMUNITY NEWSPAPER

Echo Germanica   80415
Owner: Echoworld Communications
Editorial: 118 Tyrrel Ave, Toronto, Ontario M6G 2G5 **Tel:** 1 416 652-1332
Email: info@echoworld.com **Web site:** http://www.echoworld.com
Freq: Monthly; **Circ:** 16000 Not Audited
Publisher & Editor in Chief: Sybille Forster-Rentmeister
Profile: Echo Germanica is a community newspaper written for the German residents of Toronto, Ontario.
Language (s): English
Ad Rate: Full Page Mono 21.70
Currency: Canada Dollars
COMMUNITY NEWSPAPER

Échos Montréal   257669
Editorial: 387 Rue Saint-Paul O Bureau 3, Montreal, Quebec H2Y 2A7 **Tel:** 1 514 844-2133
Email: redaction@journalechos.com **Web site:** http://www.echosmontreal.com
Freq: Monthly; **Circ:** 19000 Not Audited
President & Publisher: Vincent Di Candido
Profile: Échos Montréal est un journal mensuel francophone couvrant les nouvelles locales.

Échos Montréal is a monthly newspaper covering local news in French.
Language (s): French
Ad Rate: Full Page Mono 18.41
Ad Rate: Full Page Colour 91.24
Currency: Canada Dollars
COMMUNITY NEWSPAPER

Éditions André Paquette - Hawkesbury   25631
Owner: Cie d'Edition A. Paquette Inc.
Editorial: 1100 Rue Aberdeen, Hawkesbury, Ontario K6A 1K7 **Tel:** 1 613 632-4155
Email: nouvelles@eap.on.ca **Web site:** http://www.editionap.ca/
Freq: Fri; **Circ:** 45045 Not Audited
Publisher: Bertrand Castonguay; **Editor in Chief:** Roger Duplantie
Language (s): English, French
COMMUNITY NEWSPAPER

The Edmonton Examiner   23551
Owner: Postmedia Network Inc.
Editorial: 10006 101 St NW, Edmonton, Alberta T5J 0S1- **Tel:** 1 780 468-0100
Email: dbreakenridge@postmedia.com **Web site:** http://www.edmontonexaminer.com
Freq: Wed; **Circ:** 143157 Not Audited
Publisher: John Caputo; **Editor in Chief:** Steve Serviss
Profile: The Edmonton Examiner is a weekly newspaper published for the Edmonton, Alberta area. The paper covers local news, sports and arts & entertainment.
Language (s): English
Ad Rate: Full Page Mono 27.30
Currency: Canada Dollars
COMMUNITY NEWSPAPER

El Centro News   772581
Editorial: 19-13085 Yonge St., Suite 207, Toronto, Ontario L4E 0K2 **Tel:** 1 416 619-4578
Email: info@elcentro.ca **Web site:** http://www.elcentronews.ca
Freq: Weekly
Director: Susana Donan
Profile: El Centro News is a weekly, bilingual Spanish and English newspaper providing news and local coverage to the Latin American community in the Greater Toronto area. It publishes on Fridays.
Language (s): English
Ad Rate: Full Page Mono 6.50
Ad Rate: Full Page Colour 6.50
Currency: Canada Dollars
COMMUNITY NEWSPAPER

El-Masri Newspaper   80337
Owner: Egyptian Canadian Friendship Association
Editorial: 879 Av Saint-Charles, Laval, Quebec H7V 3T5 **Tel:** 1 450 687-0273
Email: masri.93@hotmail.com **Web site:** http://www.el-masrionline.com
Freq: Bi-Monthly; **Circ:** 12000 Not Audited
Editor in Chief: Adel Iskander; **General Manager:** Nancy Youseff
Profile: El-Masri est un bi-mensuel publié pour la communauté égyptienne du Québec francophone.

El-Masri is a Bi-Monthly newspaper written for the Egyptian community in francophone Québec.
Language (s): Arabic
Ad Rate: Full Page Mono 15.65
Ad Rate: Full Page Colour 17.39
Currency: Canada Dollars
COMMUNITY NEWSPAPER

Elmira Independent Publishers   693896
Owner: Metroland Media Group Ltd.
Editorial: 13A Industrial Dr, Elmira, Ontario N3B 2S1 **Tel:** 1 519 669-5155
Email: editor@elmiraindependent.com **Web site:** http://www.elmiraindependent.com
Circ: 13613
Publisher & General Manager: Bill Huether; **Editor in Chief:** Gail Martin
COMMUNITY NEWSPAPER

Epoch Times - Ottawa Edition   355586
Owner: Epoch Times Media Inc. (The)
Editorial: 2188-A Roberston Road, Ottawa, Ontario K2H 5Z1 **Tel:** 1 613 820-2580
Email: ottawa@epochtimes.com **Web site:** http://printarchive.epochtimes.com/a1/en/region.php?dir=ca/yow
Freq: Fri; **Circ:** 15000 Not Audited
Editor & Publisher: Cindy Gu; **Editor:** Pamela McLennan
Profile: Epoch Times - Ottawa Edition is a free weekly newspaper serving English-speaking residents and businesses in Ottawa. Part of an independent, global media corporation headquarterd in New York, its mission is to enrich local communities with news and perspectives on current events which are often overlooked by mainstream media, especially by outlets inside China.
Language (s): English
Ad Rate: Full Page Mono 9.58
Currency: Canada Dollars
COMMUNITY NEWSPAPER

Epoch Times - Toronto Edition   355585
Owner: Epoch Times Media Inc. (The)
Editorial: 418 Consumers Rd, Toronto, Ontario M2J 1P8 **Tel:** 1 416 298-1933
Email: canada_editor@epochtimes.com **Web site:** http://printarchive.epochtimes.com/a1/en/region.php?dir=ca/yto
Freq: Thu; **Circ:** 40000 Not Audited
Editor & Publisher: Cindy Gu
Profile: Epoch Times - Toronto Edition is a free, weekly newspaper serving English-speaking residents and businesses that are interested in Chinese news globally and in Toronto. Part of an independent, global media corporation headquarterd in New York, its mission is to enrich local communities with news and perspectives on current events which are often overlooked by mainstream media, especially by outlets inside China. It strives to present an alternative and uncensored view to the propaganda generated by the People's Republic of China. It is the most widely-read Chinese newspaper read outside the mainland of China and Taiwan. It is distributed at local newstands, retailers, restaurants, bookstores, apartments and at Chinese community organizations. Contact the editor for lead times.
Language (s): English
Ad Rate: Full Page Mono 5.81
Currency: Canada Dollars
COMMUNITY NEWSPAPER

Equality News   80211
Owner: Equality Group Inc.
Editorial: 206-1560 Brimley Rd 206, Toronto, Ontario M1P 3G9 **Tel:** 1 416 759-6397
Email: equalitygroup@rogers.com **Web site:** http://www.equalitynews.ca
Freq: Monthly; **Circ:** 55000 Not Audited
Profile: Equality News is a 20+ page newspaper written for Caribbean individuals and others interested in local Caribbean news. It covers local Caribbean news, Caribbean sports, and world news. It is published on a monthly basis.
Language (s): English
Ad Rate: Full Page Mono 35.00
Currency: Canada Dollars
COMMUNITY NEWSPAPER

Erin Newspapers   25626
Owner: Metroland Media Group Ltd.
Editorial: 8 Thompson Cr #5, Erin, Ontario N0B 1T0 **Tel:** 1 519 833-9603
Email: editorial@erinadvocate.com **Web site:** http://www.metroland.com
Circ: 18070 Not Audited
Editor in Chief: Joan Murray
Language (s): English
COMMUNITY NEWSPAPER

Essex Free Press   23774
Owner: Essex Free Press Ltd.
Editorial: PO Box 115 Stn Main, Essex, Ontario N8M 2Y1 **Tel:** 1 519 776-4268
Email: essexfreepress@on.aibn.com **Web site:** http://www.sxfreepress.com
Freq: Wed; **Circ:** 11000 Not Audited
Profile: Essex Free Press is a publication written for the members of the Essex, Ontario community. The publication covers local news, weather, sports and entertainment. Deadlines for the publication are one week before issue date.
Language (s): English
Ad Rate: Full Page Mono 7.70
Ad Rate: Full Page Colour 200.00
Currency: Canada Dollars
COMMUNITY NEWSPAPER

Ethnic Media - Montreal   562810
Editorial: 24 Mont-Royal West, #401, Montreal, Quebec H2T 2S2 **Tel:** 1 514 737-0151

Email: marketing@ethnicmedia.ca **Web site:** http://www.ethnicmedia.ca
Circ: 38000
Publisher & Editor: Borislav Nicolov
Language (s): Bulgarian
COMMUNITY NEWSPAPER

L' Etoile du Lac 23985
Owner: Trium Médias
Editorial: 797, boul. St-Joseph, suite 101, Roberval, Quebec G8H 2L4 **Tel:** 1 418 275-2911
Email: redaction_roberval@tc.tc **Web site:** http://www.letoiledulac.com
Freq: Wed; **Circ:** 14829 Not Audited
Editor in Chief: Daniel Migneault
Profile: L'Étoile du Lac est un hebdomadaire francophone qui couvre l'actualité locale pour les habitant de Roberval, du Lac-St-Jean et de la région.

L'Étoile du Lac is a weekly newspaper covering local news of interest to residents of Roberval, Quebec and the Lac Saint-Jean, Quebec region. The editorial deadlines fall at noon ET on Wednesdays before issue date.
Language (s): French
Ad Rate: Full Page Mono 5.88
Currency: Canada Dollars
COMMUNITY NEWSPAPER

Exodus 80675
Owner: Jewish Russian Community Centre
Editorial: 5987 Bathurst St, Ste 3, Toronto, Ontario M2R 1Z3 **Tel:** 1 416 222-7105
Email: exodus@jrcc.org **Web site:** http://www.exodusmagazine.org
Freq: Monthly; **Circ:** 18000 Not Audited
Editor: Izzy Greenberg; **Editor in Chief:** Ella Vorovitch; **Publisher:** Yoseph Zaltzman
Profile: Exodus is a community newspaper written for the Jewish Russian residents of North York, Ontario. The paper is printed in Russian and English.
Language (s): English
Ad Rate: Full Page Mono 6.00
Currency: Canada Dollars
COMMUNITY NEWSPAPER

El Expreso 82714
Editorial: 1233 Nigel Rd, Mississauga, Ontario L5J 3S6 **Tel:** 1 905 823-0602
Email: expreso@interlog.com
Freq: Fri; **Circ:** 55000 Not Audited
Publisher & Editor in Chief: Nabil Saad
Profile: El Expreso: National Spanish Newspaper published in Spanish language.
Language (s): Spanish
Ad Rate: Full Page Mono 12.95
Currency: Canada Dollars
COMMUNITY NEWSPAPER

L' Express Montcalm 375807
Owner: TC. Transcontinental
Editorial: 864, rue St-Isidore Suite 201, St-Lin-Laurentides, Quebec J5M 2V4 **Tel:** 1 450 439-2525
Email: info.montcalm@tc.tc **Web site:** http://www.lexpressmontcalm.com
Freq: Wed; **Circ:** 20300 Not Audited
Editor: Jean Joubert
Profile: L'Express Montcalm est un hebdomadaire francophone s'adressant aux résidents de la région de Montcalm dans Lanaudière, Québec. Il y est question de nouvelles locales et régionales, d'éducation, de sport et de divcertissement.

L'Express Montcalm is a weekly French-language newspaper serving residents of Montcalm region of Lanaudière, Quebec. It covers local news, politics, education, sports and entertainment.
Language (s): French
Ad Rate: Full Page Mono 6.16
Currency: Canada Dollars
COMMUNITY NEWSPAPER

L' Express Newspapers 25652
Owner: L'Express de Toronto Inc.
Editorial: 888 Av Eastern, Toronto, Ontario M4L 1A3 **Tel:** 1 416 465-2107
Email: info@lexpress.to **Web site:** http://www.lexpress.to
Circ: 20000 Not Audited
Profile: News geared toward French-speakers in Toronto.
Language (s): French
COMMUNITY NEWSPAPER

The False Creek News 554086
Editorial: 915 London St, New Westminster, British Columbia V3M 3B5 **Tel:** 1 778 398-2000
Email: news@thefalsecreeknews.com **Web site:** http://www.thefalsecreeknews.com
Freq: Fri; **Circ:** 25000
Editor: Steve Bowell; **Publisher:** M. Juma
Profile: The False Creek News is a weekly community newspaper serving neighborhood news to Vancouver's fast-growing high-income communities including False Creek, Granville Island and Gairview Slopes. Editorial coverage includes news, local issues and arts & entertainment.
Language (s): English
Ad Rate: Full Page Mono 114.94
Currency: Canada Dollars
COMMUNITY NEWSPAPER

Familia Portuguesa 80579
Editorial: 949 Dufferin St, Toronto, Ontario M6H 4B2 **Tel:** 1 416 533-8501
Email: minhaf@ica.net
Freq: Thu; **Circ:** 10000 Not Audited
Publisher & Editor: Alberto Cunha
Profile: Familia Portuguesa is a weekly community newspaper written for the Portuguese speaking resident of Toronto.
Language (s): Portuguese
Ad Rate: Full Page Mono 5.50
Currency: Canada Dollars
COMMUNITY NEWSPAPER

Filipiniana 80416
Editorial: 1531 Queen St W, Toronto, Ontario M6R 1A5 **Tel:** 1 416 534-7836
Email: filipiniananews@rogers.com
Freq: Monthly; **Circ:** 10000 Not Audited
Publisher & Editor: Bin Kon Loo
Profile: Filipiniana is a local community newspaper for the Filipino residents of Toronto.
Language (s): English
Ad Rate: Full Page Mono 7.84
Currency: Canada Dollars
COMMUNITY NEWSPAPER

Filipino Journal 152377
Editorial: 46 Pincarrow Rd, Winnipeg, Manitoba R3Y 1E3 **Tel:** 1 204 489-8894
Email: info@filipinojournal.com **Web site:** http://www.filipinojournal.com
Freq: Bi-Weekly; **Circ:** 10000 Not Audited
Editor in Chief: Ronald Cantiveros
Language (s): English
Ad Rate: Full Page Mono 5.60
Ad Rate: Full Page Colour 985.00
Currency: Canada Dollars
COMMUNITY NEWSPAPER

The Filipino Post 811645
Owner: Asian Post Media Publishing
Editorial: St. 2000 - 1066 West Hastings Street, Vancouver, British Columbia V6E 3X1 **Tel:** 1 778 996-3631
Email: editor@postpeopleinc.com **Web site:** http://www.thefilipinopost.com
Freq: Weekly; **Circ:** 25000
Profile: The Filipino Post is a free weekly newspaper serving the Filipino community in the Vancouver metropolitan area.
Language (s): English
COMMUNITY NEWSPAPER

First Nations Drum 80114
Owner: Totem Publications
Editorial: 101- 1001 West Broadway, Suite 325, Vancouver, British Columbia V6H 4E4 **Tel:** 1 604 669-5582
Email: editor@firstnationsdrum.com **Web site:** http://www.firstnationsdrum.com
Freq: Monthly; **Circ:** 35000 Not Audited
Editor: Rick Littlechild
Profile: First Nations Drum is a monthly publication that serves the native communities in Saskatchewan, Yukon, Northwest Territories, Alberta and throughout British Columbia with news and information relevant to native culture, tradition and lifestyles. Its editorial mission is to "inform and entertain its readers to strengthen understanding between native and non-native residents of Western Canada." The First Nations Drum features profiles on native artists and covers opportunities for educational advancement of native students in special issues.
Language (s): English
Ad Rate: Full Page Mono 30.43
Currency: Canada Dollars
COMMUNITY NEWSPAPER

First Nations Voice 735506
Owner: First Nations Voice
Tel: 1 204 256-0645
Email: rdeagle@mymts.net **Web site:** http://www.firstnationsvoice.com
Freq: Monthly
Editor: Trevor Greyeyes; **Publisher:** Al Isfeld
Profile: First Nations Voice is a monthly newspaper targeting Manitoba's First Nation/Aboriginal population. Features articles on living, the arts, culture, events, politics and more.
Language (s): English
Ad Rate: Full Page Mono 4.50
Currency: Canada Dollars
COMMUNITY NEWSPAPER

The First Perspective/Drum 80118
Owner: Taiga Communications Inc.
Editorial: 703-44 Princess St 703, Winnipeg, Manitoba R3B 1K2 **Tel:** 1 204 943-1500
Email: staff@taiga-communications.com **Web site:** http://www.firstperspective.ca
Freq: Monthly; **Circ:** 15000 Not Audited
Publisher & Editor: James Wastasecoot
Profile: The First Perspective/Drum is published 17 times per year. It is a magazine addressing issues related to indigenous peoples of Canada. The paper includes news, commentary, event listings and discussions related to the community.
Language (s): English
Ad Rate: Full Page Mono 10.43
Ad Rate: Full Page Colour 1640.00
Currency: Canada Dollars
COMMUNITY NEWSPAPER

Flamborough Review 23856
Owner: Metroland Media Group Ltd.
Editorial: 30 Main St, Waterdown, Ontario L9H 2P6
Tel: 1 905 689-4841
Email: editor@flamboroughreview.com **Web site:** http://www.flamboroughreview.com
Freq: Thu; **Circ:** 13313 Not Audited
Editor: Brenda Jefferies
Profile: The Flamborough Review, a community newspaper, brings editorial content, retail information and flyer distribution to Flamborough residents each Thursday. This regional newspaper covers news, sports, weather, and local interest. Their website offers RSS (Really Simple Syndication)
Language (s): English
Ad Rate: Full Page Mono 6.44
Currency: Canada Dollars
COMMUNITY NEWSPAPER

Fort Erie Times Newspapers 364357
Owner: Postmedia Network Inc.
Editorial: 336 Central Ave, Fort Erie, Ontario L2A 3T6
Tel: 1 905 871-3100
Email: sarah.ferguson@sunmedia.ca **Web site:** http://www.forterietimes.ca
Circ: 23500 Not Audited
Publisher: Michael Cressman; **Publisher:** Tim Dundas; **Editor:** Sarah Ferguson
Language (s): English
COMMUNITY NEWSPAPER

Fort McMurray Connect 584627
Owner: Star News Inc.
Editorial: 22-9914 Morrison St 22, Fort McMurray, Alberta T9H 4A4 **Tel:** 1 780 790-6627
Email: info@macmedia.ca **Web site:** http://www.macmedia.ca
Freq: Thu; **Circ:** 25500
Publisher: Andryia Brown
Profile: Fort McMurray Connect offers community news and events to residents in and around Fort McMurray, Alberta.
Language (s): English
Ad Rate: Full Page Mono 13.30
Currency: Canada Dollars
COMMUNITY NEWSPAPER

La Gazette de la Mauricie 24041
Editorial: 942 Rue Sainte-Genevieve, Trois-Rivieres, Quebec G9A 3X6 **Tel:** 1 819 841-4135
Email: info@gazettemauricie.com **Web site:** http://www.gazettemauricie.com/
Freq: Monthly; **Circ:** 75000 Not Audited
Profile: La Gazette de la Mauricie est distribuée mensuellement aux habitants de la Mauricie et offre des nouvelles et de l'information régionale. Son but est de favoriser l'engagement des citoyens.

La Gazette Populaire is a monthly French-language newspaper covering local news and information, especially in the Mauricie region. Its goal is to draw the communities in the region together with news that can help readers form a common regional and political identity.
Language (s): French
Ad Rate: Full Page Mono 11.20
Currency: Canada Dollars
COMMUNITY NEWSPAPER

The Georgia Straight 81253
Owner: Vancouver Free Press
Editorial: 1635 Broadway W, Vancouver, British Columbia V6J 1W9 **Tel:** 1 604 730-7000
Email: contact@straight.com **Web site:** http://www.straight.com
Freq: Thu; **Circ:** 120000 Not Audited
Contributor: Louise Christie; **Publisher:** Dan McLeod; **Editor:** Charlie Smith
Profile: The Georgia Straight is a local urban/city paper written for the residents of Vancouver, British Columbia. It covers features, articles, news, reviews, arts, music, movies, fashion, travel, business, high tech, food and restaurants, plus a comprehensive listing of entertainment activities and special events. Please send press releases to the main e-mail address.
Language (s): English
Ad Rate: Full Page Mono 105.56
Currency: Canada Dollars
COMMUNITY NEWSPAPER

Georgina Advocate 23711
Owner: Metroland Media Group Ltd.
Editorial: 580B Steven Crt, Newmarket, Ontario L3Y 6Z2- **Tel:** 1 905 853-8888
Email: newsroom@yrmg.com **Web site:** http://www.yorkregion.com/georgina-on/
Freq: Thu; **Circ:** 16000 Not Audited
Editor: Ted McFadden
Profile: Georgina Advocate is a weekly community newspaper for the residents of Georgina, Ontario and the surrounding area.
Language (s): English
Ad Rate: Full Page Mono 7.35
Currency: Canada Dollars
COMMUNITY NEWSPAPER

Glacier Media - Tisdale 25606
Owner: Glacier Media Inc.
Editorial: 1004 - 102nd Ave, Tisdale, Saskatchewan S0E 1T0 **Tel:** 1 306 873-4515
Email: t.recorder@sasktel.net
Circ: 10601 Not Audited
Editor: Ivy Wilson
Language (s): English
COMMUNITY NEWSPAPER

Glacier Media Inc. 25614
Owner: Glacier Media Inc.
Editorial: 141 Commercial Pl, Thompson, Manitoba R8N 1T1 **Tel:** 1 204 677-4534
Email: editor@thompsoncitizen.net
Circ: 11500 Not Audited
Editor: John Barker; **General Manager:** Lynn Taylor
Language (s): English
COMMUNITY NEWSPAPER

The Gleaner Company 80213
Editorial: 1390 Eglinton Ave W, Toronto, Ontario M6C 2E4 **Tel:** 1 416 784-3002
Email: feedback@jamaica-gleaner.com **Web site:** http://www.jamaica-gleaner.com
Circ: 90000 Not Audited
Publisher: Sheila Alexander; **Editor:** Neil Armstrong
Profile: Gleaner Company is a weekly community newspaper publisher serving the residents of Toronto.
Language (s): English
COMMUNITY NEWSPAPER

Goldstream News Gazette 23562
Owner: Black Press
Editorial: 117-777 Goldstream Ave 117, Victoria, British Columbia V9B 2X4 **Tel:** 1 250 478-9552
Email: editor@goldstreamgazette.com **Web site:** http://www.goldstreamgazette.com
Freq: Fri; **Circ:** 17895 Not Audited
Publisher: Penny Sakamoto
Profile: Goldstream News Gazette is a publication written for the residents of Victoria, British Columbia. The publication covers local news, sports and arts & entertainment targeted at the West Shore of Greater Victoria, including Langford, Colwood, Metchosin, View Royal and the Highlands.
Language (s): English
Ad Rate: Full Page Mono 22.54
Currency: Canada Dollars
COMMUNITY NEWSPAPER

Grassroots News 395078
Owner: Aborginal Advertising Inc.
Editorial: 150 Henry Ave Rm 107, Winnipeg, Manitoba R3B 0J7 **Tel:** 1 204 589-7495
Email: admin@grassrootsnews.mb.ca **Web site:** http://www.grassrootsnewsmb.com
Freq: Bi-Weekly; **Circ:** 20000 Not Audited
Publisher: Arnold Asham
Profile: Grassroots News is a bi-weekly newspaper that reaches 63 First Nations and Metis communities throughout Manitoba, including Winnipeg, The Pas, Thompson and Flin Flon. It provides major news and events including, assemblies and conferences, politics, arts and culture. Special sections include news from Southern Chiefs Organization, the Manitoba Metis Federation, Manitoba Keewatinook Ininew Okimowin and the Assembly of Manitoba Chiefs. It also features events on education and training, employment, health, economic development and youth.
Language (s): English
Ad Rate: Full Page Mono 16.45
Ad Rate: Full Page Colour 400.00
Currency: Canada Dollars
COMMUNITY NEWSPAPER

Great West Publishing 578915
Owner: Great West Newspapers LP
Editorial: 2903 Kingsview Blvd SE Suite 403, Airdrie, Alberta T4A 0C4 **Tel:** 1 403 948-1885
Email: sales@airdrie.greatwest.ca **Web site:** http://www.greatwest.ca
Circ: 31500

Editor: Allison Chorney; **Publisher & Advertising Sales Manager:** Cam Christianson; **Editor:** Stacie Snow
Language (s): English
COMMUNITY NEWSPAPER

The Greek Canadian Tribune
82732
Owner: Manikis (Christos)
Editorial: 7835 B Wiseman Ave, Montreal, Quebec H3N 2N8 **Tel:** 1 514 272-6873
Email: info@bhma.net **Web site:** http://www.bhma.net
Freq: Sat; **Circ:** 13200 Not Audited
Publisher & Editor: Christos Manikis
Profile: The Greek Canadian Tribune, connu aussi sous les noms la Tribune Grecque Canadienne ou Ellinokanadiko Vimo, est un hebdomadaire pour la communauté grecque canadienne. Plus de 90% de son contenu est en grec avec quelques textes en anglais et parfois en français.

The Greek Canadian Tribune, also known as la Tribune Grecque Canadienne or Ellinokanadiko Vimo, is a French, English and Greek-language newspaper for the Greek community in Francophone, Canada. It covers local news in Quebec, Canadian and Greek politics and events within Hellenic communities and various cultural associations.
Language (s): English
Ad Rate: Full Page Mono 7.73
Currency: Canada Dollars
COMMUNITY NEWSPAPER

The Greek Press
82910
Owner: Olga Management Limited
Editorial: 1033 Pape Ave, Toronto, Ontario M4K 3W1 **Tel:** 1 416 465-3243
Email: greekpress@greekpress.ca **Web site:** http://www.greekpress.ca
Freq: Weekly; **Circ:** 11000 Not Audited
Publisher & Editor: Costas Kranias
Profile: The Greek Press is a Community bilingual Newspaper published weekly that covers Ethnic & Multicultural Greek Canadian community in the Great Toronto Area.
Language (s): English
Ad Rate: Full Page Mono 12.25
Currency: Canada Dollars
COMMUNITY NEWSPAPER

The Grimsby Lincoln News
23800
Owner: Metroland Media Group Ltd.
Editorial: 32 Main St W, Grimsby, Ontario L3M 1R4 **Tel:** 1 905 945-8392
Email: news@niagarathisweek.com **Web site:** https://www.niagarathisweek.com/grimsby-on/
Freq: Thu; **Circ:** 23800 Not Audited
Editor in Chief: Katherine Nadeau
Profile: The Grimsby Lincoln News is a community newspaper written for the residents of Grimsby, Ontario. The paper covers local news, sports and events.
Language (s): English
Ad Rate: Full Page Mono 14.14
Currency: Canada Dollars
COMMUNITY NEWSPAPER

Le Groupe JCL Sainte-Thérèse
25682
Owner: Groupe JCL (Le)
Editorial: 50B Rue Turgeon, Sainte-Therese, Quebec J7E 3H4 **Tel:** 1 450 435-6537
Web site: http://www.groupejcl.com
Editor In Chief: Claude Desjardins
Profile: Le Groupe JCL Sainte-Thérèse publishes two French weeklies, Nord Info (Saturday) and La Voix des Milles-Iles (Wednesday) which cover the local news in the communities of Sainte-Thérèse-De Blainville regional county municipality.
Language (s): French
COMMUNITY NEWSPAPER

Guelph Mercury Tribune
23801
Owner: Metroland Media Group Ltd.
Editorial: 1-27 Woodlawn Rd W 1, Guelph, Ontario N1H 1G8 **Tel:** 1 519 763-3333
Email: info@guelphmercury.com **Web site:** http://www.guelphmercury.com
Freq: Thu; **Circ:** 40607 Not Audited
Profile: Guelph Mercury Tribune is a community newspaper serving the residents of Guelph, Ontario. The paper covers news, weather, travel, sports and entertainment. Formerly known as Guelph Tribune.
Language (s): English
Ad Rate: Full Page Mono 9.49
Ad Rate: Full Page Colour 550.00
Currency: Canada Dollars
COMMUNITY NEWSPAPER

Gujarat Abroad
772679
Owner: Gujarat Abroad Inc.
Editorial: 72 Cadillac Crescen, Brampton, Ontario L7A 3B6 **Tel:** 1 905 846-4988
Email: editorforga@gmail.com **Web site:** http://www.gujaratabroad.ca
Freq: Weekly; **Circ:** 15000
Editor and Publisher: Vipul Jani
Profile: Gujarat Abroad is the largest Gujarati weekly newspaper in the Greater Toronto metropolitan area. It publishes every Friday through over 350 outlets throughout Toronto, Mississauga, Brampton, Markham and Oakville.
Language (s): Gujarati
COMMUNITY NEWSPAPER

Gujarat Express
772689
Editorial: 20 Elderwood Place, Brampton, Ontario L6V 3N3 **Tel:** 1 905 457-7096
Email: abgujaratexpress@yahoo.ca **Web site:** http://www.gujaratexpress.ca
Freq: Weekly
Editor and Publisher: Amit Bhatt
Profile: Gujarat Express is a weekly newspaper written for new immigrants to and South Asian residents of Canada.
Language (s): Gujarati
COMMUNITY NEWSPAPER

Hal-E-Pakistan
736061
Editorial: 2912 Cross Current Dr, Mississauga, Ontario L5N 6K9 **Tel:** 1 905 7850267
Email: halepakistan@gmail.com
Freq: Bi-Monthly
Publisher: Arshad Khan
Profile: Hal-E-Pakistan is a community newspaper written for the Pakistani residents of Mississauga and the surrounding communities.
Language (s): English
Ad Rate: Full Page Mono 7.84
Currency: Canada Dollars
COMMUNITY NEWSPAPER

Hamdard Weekly
80803
Owner: Ontario Ltd.
Editorial: 2-1332 Khalsa Dr 2, Mississauga, Ontario L5S 0A2 **Tel:** 1 905 791-9999
Email: toronto@hamdardweekly.com **Web site:** http://www.hamdardweekly.com
Freq: Thu; **Circ:** 30000 Not Audited
Editor in Chief: Amar Singh Bhullar
Profile: Hamdard Weekly is written for the residents of Mississauga, ON.
Language (s): English
Ad Rate: Full Page Mono 14.64
Currency: Canada Dollars
COMMUNITY NEWSPAPER

The Hamilton Community News Group of Newspapers
76366
Owner: Metroland Media Group Ltd.
Editorial: 333 Arvin Ave, Stoney Creek, Ontario L8E 2M6 **Tel:** 1 905 664-8800
Email: ddowney@hamiltonnews.com **Web site:** http://www.hamiltonnews.com
Freq: Thu; **Circ:** 113489 Not Audited
Editor: Debra Downey; **General Manager:** Jason Pehora
Language (s): English
COMMUNITY NEWSPAPER

Le Haut-Saint-François
23917
Owner: Journal Le Haut-Saint-Francois
Editorial: 57 Rue Craig N Bureau 101, Cookshire-Eaton, Quebec J0B 1M0 **Tel:** 1 819 875-5501
Email: info@journalhsf.com **Web site:** http://www.journalhsf.com
Freq: Bi-Weekly; **Circ:** 11500 Not Audited
General Manager and Editor: Pierre Hebert
Profile: Since April 1986, Le Haut-Saint-François is a French biweekly regional community publication that is delivered, free of charge, by Public-Sac to households in the MRC of Haut-Saint-Francois.
Language (s): French
Ad Rate: Full Page Mono 7.00
Currency: Canada Dollars
COMMUNITY NEWSPAPER

L' Hebdo du St-Maurice
24000
Owner: TC. Transcontinental
Editorial: 1672-A Av Saint-Marc, Shawinigan, Quebec G9N 2H4 **Tel:** 1 819 537-5111
Email: redaction_shawinigan@tc.tc **Web site:** http://www.lhebdodustmaurice.com
Freq: Wed; **Circ:** 36900 Not Audited
Profile: L'Hebdo du St-Maurice est un hebdomadaire qui couvre les actualités locales et régionales pour les habitants de Shawinigan et des environs.

L'Hebdo du St-Maurice is a weekly newspaper that covers local news for the residents of Shawinigan and surrounding areas. It covers local news, sports and education, focusing on human-interest stories.
Language (s): French
Ad Rate: Full Page Mono 8.26
Currency: Canada Dollars
COMMUNITY NEWSPAPER

L' Hebdo Rive-Nord
30104
Owner: TC. Transcontinental
Editorial: 1004 Rue Notre-Dame, Repentigny, Quebec J5Y 1S9 **Tel:** 1 450 581-9082
Email: equiperedaction@transcontinental.ca **Web site:** http://www.hebdorivenord.com
Freq: Tue; **Circ:** 57097 Not Audited
Profile: L'Hebdo Rive-Nord est un hebdomadaire francophone pour les habitants de Repentigny et des environs.

L'Hebdo Rive-Nord is a French-language newspaper that covers local news, including government, education, sports and arts and entertainment for Repentigny, Quebec and surrounding areas.
Language (s): French
Ad Rate: Full Page Mono 7.84
Currency: Canada Dollars
COMMUNITY NEWSPAPER

Herald Monthly
80367
Owner: Chinese Christian Herald Crusades
Editorial: 300 Steelcase Rd W Unit 28, Markham, Ontario L3R 2W2 **Tel:** 1 905 944-1777
Email: toronto@cchc.org **Web site:** http://www.heraldmonthly.ca
Freq: Monthly; **Circ:** 76000 Not Audited
Production Manager: Lucia Chin; **Editor in Chief:** Helena Lee
Profile: Herald Monthly is a local newspaper written for the Chinese community in the greater Toronto area and nearby cities.
Language (s): English
Ad Rate: Full Page Mono 15.06
Ad Rate: Full Page Colour 22.89
Currency: Canada Dollars
COMMUNITY NEWSPAPER

Here's The Scoop
825643
Owner: ADvance Distribution
Editorial: 2903 Kingsview Blvd, Bay 402, Airdrie, Alberta T4A 0C4 **Tel:** 1 403 948-5529
Email: heresthescoop@shaw.ca **Web site:** http://www.heresthescoop.com
Freq: Weekly; **Circ:** 16500
Editor & Publisher: Al Jones
Profile: Here's The Scoop is a weekly newspaper serving the residents of Airdrie in British Columbia, Canada. It focuses on positive news, including community events, heart warming stories and lots of jokes and humor, highlighting the lighter side of life in a small community.
Language (s): English
COMMUNITY NEWSPAPER

Hindi Abroad
772695
Editorial: 7071 Airport Rd Unit 204, Mississauga, Ontario L4T 4J3 **Tel:** 1 905 673-9929
Email: hindiabroad@gmail.com **Web site:** http://www.hindiabroad.com
Freq: Fri; **Circ:** 18000
News Editor: Firoz Khan
Profile: Hindi Abroad is a weekly newspaper covering local and community news for the Hindi-speaking community in the Greater Toronto area.
Language (s): Hindi
COMMUNITY NEWSPAPER

Hi-Rise Community Newspaper
70525
Owner: VAL Publications, Ltd.
Editorial: 121-95 Leeward Glenway 121, Toronto, Ontario M3C 2Z6 **Tel:** 1 416 424-1393
Email: sec.valdunn@vif.com **Web site:** http://www.hi-risenews.com
Freq: Monthly; **Circ:** 60000 Not Audited
Publisher & Editor: Valerie Dunn
Profile: Hi-Rise is a monthly newspaper published for the residents in the Toronto area living in high-rise housing complexes. The editorial mission is to help encourage a sense of community and togetherness in the high-rise community, as well as to encourage creative, positive approaches to life. The lead time for Hi-Rise is six weeks. Contact the publication for details on circulation, deadlines, and advertising rates.
Language (s): English
Ad Rate: Full Page Mono 34.44
Currency: Canada Dollars
COMMUNITY NEWSPAPER

Horizon Armenian Weekly
80369
Owner: Les Publications Armeniennes
Editorial: 3401 Rue Olivar-Asselin, Montreal, Quebec H4J 1L5 **Tel:** 1 514 332-3757
Email: editor@horizonweekly.ca **Web site:** http://www.horizonweekly.ca
Freq: Mon; **Circ:** 15000 Not Audited
Editor: Vahakn Karakashian
Profile: Horizon Armenian Weekly est un hebdomadaire en arménien destiné à la communauté arménienne du Canada francophone.

Horizon Armenian Weekly is a weekly newspaper written for the Armenian community in francophone Canada. It is written in Armenian, French, and English and should be contacted by phone, fax, or mail.
Language (s): Armenian
Ad Rate: Full Page Mono 7.81
Ad Rate: Full Page Colour 62.61
Currency: Canada Dollars
COMMUNITY NEWSPAPER

Humsafar Times
772560
Editorial: 7655 Rue Cordner, Lasalle, Quebec H8N 2X2 **Tel:** 1 514 368-2222
Email: js@radiohumsafar.com **Web site:** http://timesofindia.indiatimes.com/topic/Humsafar
Freq: Weekly
Publisher: Manjeet Singh Atthwal; **Editor in Chief:** Jasvir Singh Sandhu
Profile: Humsafar Times provides local coverage to the Punjabi-speaking community in the Montreal metropolitan area. The newspaper is a 32 pages tabloid with 8 pages full color and 24 pages B&W, and is printed weekly and distributed every Friday. Humsafar Times publishes in English and Punjabi.
Language (s): English
COMMUNITY NEWSPAPER

Immigrant Newsline
490776
Editorial: 3050 Ellesmere Rd, Toronto, Ontario M1E 5E6 **Tel:** 1 647 400-6248
Email: immigrantnews@gmail.com **Web site:** http://www.immigrantnewsline.ca
Freq: Bi-Weekly; **Circ:** 20000 Not Audited
Publisher & Editor: Anjali Soni
Profile: Immigrant Newsline covers local and national South Asian news, immigrant news, international news, sports, science and technology, Bollywood entertainment, health, careers and a popular classified section.
Language (s): English
Ad Rate: Full Page Mono 13.60
Currency: Canada Dollars
COMMUNITY NEWSPAPER

The Independent & Free Press
23792
Owner: Metroland Media Group Ltd.
Editorial: 280 Guelph St Unit 77, Georgetown, Ontario L7G 4B1 **Tel:** 1 905 873-0301
Email: info@theifp.ca **Web site:** http://www.theifp.ca/haltonhills-on
Freq: Thu; **Circ:** 22500 Not Audited
News Editor: Cynthia Gamble
Profile: The Independent & Free Press is a community newspaper written for the residents of Georgetown and Acton, Ontario. The paper is also known as The Georgetown Independent/Acton Free Press.
Language (s): English
Ad Rate: Full Page Mono 28.00
Ad Rate: Full Page Colour 1160.00
Currency: Canada Dollars
COMMUNITY NEWSPAPER

The Independent Newspaper
908548
Editorial: 1201-125 Village Green Sq 1201, Toronto, Ontario M1S 0G3 **Tel:** 1 905 460-6351
Email: independentnewspaper@aol.com
Freq: Bi-Weekly; **Circ:** 15000
Profile: Bi-weekly paper serving minority immigrants in Toronto. It also covers topics like sports, health, business and entertainment.
Language (s): English
Ad Rate: Full Page Mono 8.88
Ad Rate: Full Page Colour 8.88
Currency: Canada Dollars
COMMUNITY NEWSPAPER

India Journal
80807
Editorial: 25 Kingsbridge Garden Cir Suite 1416, Mississauga, Ontario L5R 4B1 **Tel:** 1 905 405-0420
Email: indiajournal@aol.com **Web site:** http://www.ijcanada.com
Freq: Fri; **Circ:** 35000 Not Audited
Profile: India Journal brings information & news for Indian community.
Language (s): English
Ad Rate: Full Page Mono 24.50
Currency: Canada Dollars
COMMUNITY NEWSPAPER

Indo Caribbean World 80777
Editorial: 312 Brownridge Dr, Thornhill, Ontario L4J 5X1 **Tel:** 1 905 738-5005
Email: indocaribbeanworld@gmail.com **Web site:** http://www.indocaribbeanworld.com/main.htm
Freq: Bi-Weekly; **Circ:** 35000 Not Audited
Publisher & Editor: Harry Ramkhelawan
Profile: Indo Caribbean World is published bi-weekly for the residents of Thornhill, Ontario and surrounding areas. The newspaper covers local news and community events.
Language (s): English
Ad Rate: Full Page Mono 16.80
Currency: Canada Dollars
COMMUNITY NEWSPAPER

Indo-Canadian Samay 772705
Editorial: 16 Sled Dog Rd, Brampton, Ontario L6R 0H8 **Tel:** 1 647 707-6100
Email: samay.news@gmail.com
Circ: 38600
Profile: Indo-Canadian Samay is a Hindi weekly newspaper covering Local and Community News for the Indian community Greater Toronto area.
COMMUNITY NEWSPAPER

Indo-Canadian Times 80768
Editorial: 12414 82 Ave Suite 103, Surrey, British Columbia V3W 3E9 **Tel:** 1 604 599-5408
Email: indo@telus.net **Web site:** http://www.indocanadiantimes.com
Freq: Thu; **Circ:** 35000 Not Audited
Editor in Chief: Rupinder Hayer
Profile: Indo-Canadian Times International Inc. is a weekly Punjabi newspaper that covers news from all over the world of interest to the Canadian Punjabi community. Deadlines for the publication are the day before issue date.
Language (s): English
Ad Rate: Full Page Mono 17.89
Currency: Canada Dollars
COMMUNITY NEWSPAPER

Info Dimanche 23981
Owner: Éditions Info Dimanche Inc (Les)
Editorial: 72 Rue Fraser, Riviere-du-Loup, Quebec G5R 1C6 **Tel:** 1 418 862-1911
Email: journal@infodimanche.com **Web site:** http://www.infodimanche.com
Freq: Weekly; **Circ:** 31420
Editor In Chief: Mario Pelletier
Profile: Info Dimanche is a weekly French-language newspaper that covers local news and information in the Rivière-du-Loup region of Québec.
Language (s): French
Ad Rate: Full Page Mono 13.02
Currency: Canada Dollars
COMMUNITY NEWSPAPER

Info Week-end 82745
Owner: Éditions Info Brunswick (Les)
Editorial: 322 Rue Victoria, Edmundston, New Brunswick E3V 2H9 **Tel:** 1 506 739-5025
Email: info@infoweekend.ca **Web site:** http://www.infoweekend.ca
Freq: Weekly; **Circ:** 21700
Profile: Info Week-end covers the local news for the French-speaking residents of Edmundston, NB.
Language (s): French
Ad Rate: Full Page Mono 11.06
Currency: Canada Dollars
COMMUNITY NEWSPAPER

L' Information Sainte-Julie 82761
Editorial: 566 Av Jules-Choquet Loc 2, Ste-Julie, Quebec J3E 1W6 **Tel:** 1 450 641-4844
Email: jul.redaction@tc.tc **Web site:** http://www.infodeste-julie.qc.ca
Freq: Wed; **Circ:** 20525 Not Audited
Editor in Chief: Charline-Eve Pilon
Profile: L'Information de Sainte-Julie est un journal communautaire qui couvre les nouvelles locales de Sainte-Julie et Varennes, QC.

L'Information Sainte-Julie is a French-language newspaper that covers local news and information for Sainte-Julie and Varennes, QC.
Language (s): French
Ad Rate: Full Page Mono 10.36
Currency: Canada Dollars
COMMUNITY NEWSPAPER

Innisfil Examiner 411163
Owner: Postmedia Network Inc.
Editorial: 571 Bayfield St, Barrie, Ontario L4M 4Z9
Tel: 1 705 726-6537
Email: barrie.news@sunmedia.ca **Web site:** http://www.innisfilexaminer.ca
Freq: Fri; **Circ:** 10000 Not Audited
Profile: Innisfil Examiner is a weekly newspaper written for the residents of Innisfil, Ontario.
Language (s): English
Ad Rate: Full Page Mono 3.92
Ad Rate: Full Page Colour 987.84
Currency: Canada Dollars
COMMUNITY NEWSPAPER

Innisfil Journal 525090
Owner: Metroland Media Group Ltd.
Editorial: 21 Patterson Rd, Barrie, Ontario L4N 7W6
Tel: 1 705 726-0573
Email: newsroom@simcoe.com **Web site:** http://www.simcoe.com/innisfil-on/
Freq: Weekly; **Circ:** 10000 Not Audited
Profile: Innisfil Journal is a local community newspaper that serves the residents of Innisfil, Ontario.
Language (s): English
Ad Rate: Full Page Mono 34.63
Currency: Canada Dollars
COMMUNITY NEWSPAPER

InPort News 363670
Owner: Postmedia Network Inc.
Editorial: 10-1 St.Paul St., St Catharines, Ontario
Tel: 1 905 732-2414
Email: welland.tribune@sunmedia.ca **Web site:** http://www.inportnews.ca
Freq: Fri; **Circ:** 12300 Not Audited
Publisher: John Tobon
Profile: InPort News is a free, weekly newspaper serving the residents of Port Colborne, Ontario. It contains stories on community news, events, local politics, schools, sports, businesses and area-specific features. It is based in the same office as the Welland Tribune in Welland, Ontario.
Language (s): English
Ad Rate: Full Page Mono 6.30
Ad Rate: Full Page Colour 1404.00
Currency: Canada Dollars
COMMUNITY NEWSPAPER

Interlake Enterprise 716802
Editorial: Gimli, Manitoba
Email: info@enterprisenews.ca **Web site:** http://www.enterprisenews.ca
Freq: Tue; **Circ:** 10000
Profile: Interlake Enterprise is a community newspaper for the residents of the Interlake Region (Manitoba) including Selkirk, Gimli, Arborg, Riverton, Lockport, Petersfield, Clandeboye, St. Andrews, Fisher Branch, etc.
Language (s): English
Ad Rate: Full Page Mono 13.12
Currency: Canada Dollars
COMMUNITY NEWSPAPER

International Punjabi Tribune Newspaper 80802
Owner: International Punjabi Tribune Inc.
Editorial: 12323 123 st, Surrey, British Columbia
Tel: 1 604 584-5577
Email: info@punjabitribune.ca **Web site:** http://punjabitribune.ca
Freq: Fri; **Circ:** 22000
Editor: Rashpal Sing Gill
Profile: Pubjabi paper that has been printed since 1993 serving most parts of BC including the lower mainland, all major cities of BC and some other provinces of Canada including some of the USA as well. It covers Social, Political, Environmental and Financial issues as well as Sports, Technology, Business, Entertainment, Arts.
Language (s): English
Ad Rate: Full Page Mono 13.28
Ad Rate: Full Page Colour 16.64
Currency: Canada Dollars
COMMUNITY NEWSPAPER

Iran Javan 80514
Owner: Iran Javan Publications
Editorial: 6075 Yonge St Suite 301, Toronto, Ontario M2M 3W2 **Tel:** 1 416 730-0203
Email: info@iranjavan.net **Web site:** http://www.iranjavan.net
Freq: Thu; **Circ:** 15000 Not Audited
Publisher & Editor: Babak Reihanypour
Profile: Iran Javan is a is a free weekly community newspaper written for the residents of North York, Ontario.Outlet offers RSS
Language (s): Arabic
Ad Rate: Full Page Mono 5.11
Currency: Canada Dollars
COMMUNITY NEWSPAPER

Iran Star 82747
Owner: Iran Star Publishing
Editorial: 169 Steeles Ave E, Toronto, Ontario M2M 3Y5 **Tel:** 1 905 763-9770
Email: iranstar@iranstar.com **Web site:** http://www.iranstar.com
Freq: Fri; **Circ:** 12500 Not Audited
Editor in Chief: Bijan Binesh
Profile: Iran Star provides news for Iranians living in Canada.
Language (s): Arabic
Ad Rate: Full Page Mono 30.68
Currency: Canada Dollars
COMMUNITY NEWSPAPER

Island Tides 23481
Owner: Island Tides Publishing Ltd.
Tel: 1 250 629-3660
Email: islandtides@islandtides.com **Web site:** http://www.islandtides.com
Freq: Bi-Weekly; **Circ:** 18000 Not Audited
Profile: Island Tides is a weekly newspaper written for the residents of Pender Island, British Columbia.
Language (s): English
Ad Rate: Full Page Mono 22.26
Currency: Canada Dollars
COMMUNITY NEWSPAPER

Jamac Publications 25596
Owner: Jamac Publishing Ltd.
Editorial: 919 Main St, Kindersley, Saskatchewan S0L 1S0 **Tel:** 1 306 463-4611
Email: editor.jamac@gmail.com
Circ: 22011 Not Audited
Publisher: Stewart Crump; **Editor in Chief:** Kevin McBain
Language (s): English
COMMUNITY NEWSPAPER

The Jewish Tribune 80528
Owner: B'nai Brith Canada
Editorial: 15 Hove St, Toronto, Ontario M3H 4Y8
Tel: 1 416 633-6224
Email: info@jewishtribune.ca **Web site:** http://www.jewishtribune.ca
Freq: Weekly; **Circ:** 60410 Not Audited
Publisher: Frank Dimant; **Editor in Chief:** Norm Gordner
Profile: Jewish Tribune is published by B'Nai Brith of Canada for the nation's Jewish population. It attempts to present a balanced view of the issues facing Jewish Canadians. Deadlines are one week prior to issue date.
Language (s): English
Ad Rate: Full Page Mono 25.00
Currency: Canada Dollars
COMMUNITY NEWSPAPER

Das Journal 798620
Owner: Sol Publishing Group
Editorial: 1278 Dundas Street West, Toronto, Ontario M6J 1X7 **Tel:** 1 416 534-3177
Email: info@dasjournal.com **Web site:** http://dasjournal.ca
Freq: Bi-Weekly; **Circ:** 10000
Publisher: Vasco Evaristo; **Editor:** Mark Liechti
Profile: Das Journal is a bi-weekly German language publication written for German- Autrian and Swiss-Canadians living in Canada. Published out of Toronto, the paper covers local as well as national and international news.
Language (s): German
Ad Rate: Full Page Colour 1215.00
Currency: Canada Dollars
COMMUNITY NEWSPAPER

Le Journal de Chambly 23900
Owner: Versants du Mont-Bruno Inc
Editorial: 1685 Av Bourgogne, Chambly, Quebec J3L 1Y8 **Tel:** 1 450 658-6516
Email: cly.redaction@tc.tc **Web site:** http://www.journaldechambly.com
Freq: Wed; **Circ:** 28712
Profile: Le Journal de Chambly est un hebdomadaire francophone dsetiné aux habitants de ces villes: Chambly, Carignan, Richelieu, St-Mathias-sur-Richelieu, Marieville, Rougemont, Ste-Angèle-de-Monnoir et St-Césaire.

Le Journal de Chambly is a weekly French-language newspaper that covers local news and information for Chambly, Carignan, Richelieu, St-Mathias-sur-Richelieu, Marieville, Rougemont, Ste-Angèle-de-Monnoir and St-Césaire.
Language (s): French
Ad Rate: Full Page Mono 13.02
Currency: Canada Dollars
COMMUNITY NEWSPAPER

Le Journal de Lévis 522074
Editorial: 580, boulevard Alphonse-Desjardins, Levis, Quebec G6V 6R8 **Tel:** 1 418 833-3113
Email: info@journaldelevis.com **Web site:** http://www.journaldelevis.com/fr/accueil.aspx
Freq: Weekly; **Circ:** 69418
General Manager: Sandra Fontaine
Profile: Le Journal de Levis is a French language weekly community newspaper written for the residents of Levis, St-Henri, St-Anselme, Beaumont, St-Michel et St-Lambert.
Language (s): French
Ad Rate: Full Page Mono 14.35
Currency: Canada Dollars
COMMUNITY NEWSPAPER

Journal de St-Michel 23932
Owner: Les Entreprises Leob Inc.
Editorial: C.P. 50, succ. St-Michel, Montreal, Quebec H2A 3L8 **Tel:** 1 514 721-4911
Email: admin@journaldestmichel.com **Web site:** http://www.journaldestmichel.com
Freq: Wed; **Circ:** 24155
Publisher: Claude Bricault
Profile: Journal de Saint-Michel est un hebdomadaire francophone s'adressant aux résident du quartier St-Michel à Montréal.

Journal de Saint-Michel is a weekly, French-language newspaper covering local news and information for the residents of Montreal, Quebec.
Language (s): French
Ad Rate: Full Page Mono 15.12
Currency: Canada Dollars
COMMUNITY NEWSPAPER

Journal Le Courant des Hautes-Laurentides 727204
Editorial: 534 Rue de la Madone, Mont-Laurier, Quebec J9L 1S5 **Tel:** 1 819 623-7374
Email: info@lecourant.ca **Web site:** http://www.lecourant.ca
Freq: Weekly; **Circ:** 18500
Publisher: Sylvain Lacasse
Profile: Le Journal Le Courant des Hautes-Laurentides est un journal communautaire pour les habitants de Mont-Laurier et des environs.

Journal Le Courant des Hautes-Laurentides publishes community news and information for residents of Mont-Laurier, Quebec.
Language (s): French
Ad Rate: Full Page Mono 4.76
Ad Rate: Full Page Colour 514.76
Currency: Canada Dollars
COMMUNITY NEWSPAPER

Journal Le Guide 23933
Owner: TC. Transcontinental
Editorial: 100 Rue Robinson S Suite 127, Granby, Quebec J2G 7L4 **Tel:** 1 450 777-4515
Email: redaction.estrie@tc.tc **Web site:** http://www.journalleguide.com
Freq: Wed; **Circ:** 18283
Editor in Chief: Jean-Philippe Pineault
Profile: Le Guide est un hebdomadaire pour la population de Cowansville où on retrouve de l'information locale et régionale. Le Guide is a weekly newspaper that covers local news and information for residents of Cowansville, Quebec.
Language (s): French/Bilingual
Ad Rate: Full Page Mono 16.94
Currency: Canada Dollars
COMMUNITY NEWSPAPER

Journal Le Nord 24051
Owner: TC. Transcontinental
Editorial: 177 rue Saint-Georges, St-Jerome, Quebec J7Z 4Z8 **Tel:** 1 450 438-8383
Email: editeur@tc.tc **Web site:** http://www.journallenord.com
Freq: Wed; **Circ:** 54914 Not Audited
Profile: Journal Le Nord est un hebdomadaire francophone destiné aux gens de Saint-Jérôme et des environs.

Journal le Nord is a weekly French-language newspaper that covers local news and information in Saint-Jérôme, Quebec and its environs.
Language (s): French
Ad Rate: Full Page Mono 12.88

Ad Rate: Full Page Colour 275.00
Currency: Canada Dollars
COMMUNITY NEWSPAPER

Journal Le Voyageur 23894
Owner: Publications Voyageur Inc.
Editorial: 336 Rue Pine, Sudbury, Ontario P3C 1X8
Tel: 1 705 673-3377
Email: info@lavoixdunord.ca **Web site:** http://www.levoyageur.ca
Freq: Wed; **Circ:** 10000 Not Audited
Profile: Journal le Voyageur is a weekly French-language journal serving the Francophone communities of Sudbury, Sturgeon Falls, Timmins, Cochrane and Kapuskasing, in Ontario.
Language (s): French
Ad Rate: Full Page Mono 8.12
Currency: Canada Dollars
COMMUNITY NEWSPAPER

Journal L'Envol 257658
Editorial: 12 Rue Potvin, Val-des-Monts, Quebec J8N 7B2 **Tel:** 1 819 671-1502
Email: envol.desmonts@sympatico.ca
Freq: Bi-Weekly; **Circ:** 35500 Not Audited
Publisher & Editor: Nicole-Audrey Thibodeau
Profile: L'Envol est un journal bilingue, bi-mensuel dans la région de la MRC des Collines-de-l'Outaouais couvrant Val-des-Monts, La Pêche, Chelsea, Cantley, L'Ange-Gardien.

Journal L'Envol is a bi-weekly publication covering local news for residents of Val-des-Monts, La Pêche, Chelsea, L'Ange-Gardien and Cantley. It also includes columns on various subjects of interest to the community.
Language (s): French/Bilingual
Ad Rate: Full Page Mono 6.02
Currency: Canada Dollars
COMMUNITY NEWSPAPER

Journal MRG 257113
Editorial: 4705 Rue Laval, Lac-Megantic, Quebec G6B 1C4 **Tel:** 1 819 583-2960
Email: info@journalmrg.com **Web site:** http://www.journalmrg.com
Freq: Monthly; **Circ:** 11550
Publisher & Editor: Daniel Poulin
Profile: Journal MRG is a monthly publication covering local news in Saint-Gédéon-de-Beauce, Scotstown and the MRC of Le-Granit, Québec.
Language (s): French
Ad Rate: Full Page Mono 5.42
Currency: Canada Dollars
COMMUNITY NEWSPAPER

Le Journal Saint-François 24048
Owner: TC. Transcontinental
Editorial: 55, rue Jacques-Cartier, Salaberry-de-Valleyfield, Quebec J6T 4R4 **Tel:** 1 450 371-6222
Email: val.redaction@tc.tc **Web site:** http://www.journalsaint-francois.ca
Freq: Wed; **Circ:** 41712 Not Audited
Editor in Chief: Denis Bourbonnais
Profile: Le Journal Saint-François est un hebdomadaire francophone destiné aux habitants de Valleyfield et de la région. On retrouve à l'intérieur du Journal St-François, 4 pages en anglais du journal The Gleaner.

Le Journal St-François is a weekly French-language newspaper that covers local news and information for the residents of Salaberry-de-Valleyfield, Quebec. Inside, you'll find 4 pages of The Gleaner, in english.
Language (s): French
Ad Rate: Full Page Mono 15.96
Currency: Canada Dollars
COMMUNITY NEWSPAPER

Journal.ca Newspapers 882018
Owner: journal.ca inc.
Editorial: 1039 Rue Panneton, L'Ancienne-Lorette, Quebec G2E 6E7 **Tel:** 1 418 780-0999
Email: info@journal-local.ca **Web site:** http://www.journ-al.ca
Freq: Monthly
Editor: Yvon Giroux
Profile: Journal.ca Inc. is a group of community newspapers, which through their local content with photographs present the positive and exclusive local information. It publishes Journal de Sainte-Foy, journal de Saint-Augustin-de-Desmaures, Journal de Val-Bélair, Journal de Sillerie-Saint-Louis-de-France, Journal Des Rivières/Valcartier/Neufchâtel/Loretteville, Journal Des Rivières/Saint-Émile/Neufchâtel/Lebourgneuf, Journal Des Rivières/Les Saules/Duberger/Vanier, Journal de l'Ancienne-Lorette, Journal des Parcs industriels and Nouvelles Économiques, which are all available on its site journ-al.ca.
Language (s): French
COMMUNITY NEWSPAPER

Kamloops This Week 23405
Owner: Black Press Group Ltd.
Editorial: 1365B Dalhousie Dr, Kamloops, British Columbia V2C 5P6 **Tel:** 1 250 374-7467
Email: ktw@kamloopsthisweek.com **Web site:** http://www.kamloopsthisweek.com
Freq: Fri; **Circ:** 30804 Not Audited
Publisher: Kelly Hall
Profile: Kamloops This Week covers local news and events of interest to the residents of Kamloops, British Columbia and the surrounding area. Articles include news, weather, events and travel.
Language (s): English
Ad Rate: Full Page Mono 22.68
Currency: Canada Dollars
COMMUNITY NEWSPAPER

Kawartha Lakes This Week 23731
Owner: Metroland Media Group Ltd.
Editorial: 192 St. David St, Lindsay, Ontario K9V 4Z4
Tel: 1 705 324-8600
Email: lineditor@mykawartha.com **Web site:** http://www.mykawartha.com
Freq: Thu; **Circ:** 29179 Not Audited
News Editor: Mike Lacey
Profile: Kawartha Lakes This Week is a free, bi-weekly newspaper in Kawartha Lakes, Lindsay, Bobcaygeon and Fenelon Falls, Ontario.
Language (s): English
Ad Rate: Full Page Mono 15.40
Ad Rate: Full Page Colour 350.00
Currency: Canada Dollars
COMMUNITY NEWSPAPER

Kelowna Capital News 23416
Owner: Black Press
Editorial: 2495 Enterprise Way, Kelowna, British Columbia V1X 7K2 **Tel:** 1 250 763-3212
Email: edit@kelownacapnews.com **Web site:** http://www.kelownacapnews.com
Freq: Fri; **Circ:** 49297
Profile: Kelowna Capital News is a local newspaper delivering news, arts and entertainment, and sports and weather to the residents of the Central Okanagan region of British Columbia.
Language (s): English
Ad Rate: Full Page Mono 28.00
Ad Rate: Full Page Colour 500.00
Currency: Canada Dollars
COMMUNITY NEWSPAPER

King & Vaughan Weekly Newspapers 412050
Owner: London Publishing Corp.
Editorial: 30 Martha St Suite 205, Bolton, Ontario L7E 5V1 **Tel:** 1 905 729-2287
Email: editor@kingsentinel.com **Web site:** http://kingsentinel.com/
Circ: 30000 Not Audited
Editor: Mark Pavilons
Language (s): English
COMMUNITY NEWSPAPER

Kings County Newspapers 395009
Owner: TC. Transcontinental
Editorial: 28 Aberdeen St Suite 6, Kentville, Nova Scotia B4N 2N1 **Tel:** 1 902 681-0923
Email: events@kentvilleadvertiser.ca **Web site:** http://www.kingscountynews.ca
Circ: 10000 Not Audited
Editor: Jennifer Vardy Little
Language (s): English
COMMUNITY NEWSPAPER

Kings County Weekend 521485
Owner: New Brunswick Publishing Company
Editorial: 593 Main Street, Sussex, New Brunswick E4E 7H5 **Tel:** 1 506 433-1070
Email: news@kingscorecord.com **Web site:** http://www.telegraphjournal.com
Freq: Thu; **Circ:** 12000 Not Audited
Editor in Chief: Patrick Brethour; **Editor:** Tammy Scott-Wallace
Profile: Kings County Weekend is written for the residents of Sussex, New Brunswick.
Language (s): English
Ad Rate: Full Page Mono 8.68
Currency: Canada Dollars
COMMUNITY NEWSPAPER

Kingston This Week 24292
Owner: Postmedia Network Inc.
Editorial: 6 Cataraqui St, Kingston, Ontario K7K 1Z7
Tel: 1 613 389-7400
Email: sserviss@postmedia.com **Web site:** http://www.kingstonthisweek.com
Freq: Thu; **Circ:** 49087 Not Audited
Profile: Kingston This Week is a local newspaper published weekly for the residents of Kingston, Ontario.
Language (s): English
Ad Rate: Full Page Mono 17.12
Currency: Canada Dollars
COMMUNITY NEWSPAPER

Kitchener Citizen 623540
Editorial: 10 Edinburgh Rd, Kitchener, Ontario N2B 1M5 **Tel:** 1 519 578-8228
Email: debrone@sympatico.ca **Web site:** http://www.kitchenercitizen.com
Freq: Monthly; **Circ:** 64000
Publisher & Editor: Carrie Debrone; **Publisher & Editor:** Helen Redgwell Hall
Profile: Independent newspaper started in 1996. Covers community items that bigger organizations seem to miss.
Language (s): English
COMMUNITY NEWSPAPER

Kitchener Post 788595
Owner: Metroland Media Group Lltd.
Editorial: 630 Riverbend Dr Unit 104, Kitchener, Ontario N2K 3S2 **Tel:** 1 519 579-7166
Email: bjackson@kitchenerpost.ca **Web site:** http://www.kitchenerpost.ca
Freq: Weekly; **Circ:** 60000
Editor: Charlotte Prong Parkhill
Profile: Kitchener Post is a weekly community newspaper serving the residents of Kitchener, Ontario, Canada. The paper is released on Fridays. Topics covered include local news, sports, and arts & events.
Language (s): English
Ad Rate: Full Page Mono 59.32
Currency: Canada Dollars
COMMUNITY NEWSPAPER

Kitchissippi Times 545195
Owner: Great River Media Inc.
Tel: 1 613 297-5648
Email: info@kitchissippi.com **Web site:** http://www.kitchissippi.com
Freq: Bi-Weekly; **Circ:** 17600 Not Audited
Profile: Kitchissippi Times, published twenty times each year, is a newspaper serving residents of the Ottawa centre-west neighbourhoods of Westboro, Island Park, West Wellington, Hintonburg, Hampton Park, Highland Park, Carlingwood and Civic Hospital.
Language (s): English
Ad Rate: Full Page Mono 11.12
Ad Rate: Full Page Colour 360.00
Currency: Canada Dollars
COMMUNITY NEWSPAPER

KV Style 363795
Owner: New Brunswick Publishing Company
Editorial: 122 Hampton Rd, Rothesay, New Brunswick E2E 2N5 **Tel:** 1 506 847-5900
Email: dobson.amy@brunswicknews.com **Web site:** http://kvstyle.canadaeast.com
Freq: Fri; **Circ:** 14000 Not Audited
Editor: Cynthia DeKluyver
Profile: KV Style is a free, weekly tabloid-format newspaper that serves residents throughout the Kennebecasis Valley, including Rothesay, New Brunswick. It contains news, events and feature stories. Produced under the umbrella of the Telegraph-Journal in St. Johns, New Brunswick, it is distributed as an insert to the daily paper to area subscribers and as a stand-alone delivered directly to non-subscribers' homes. Advertising deadlines are on Thursdays at noon ET.
Language (s): English
Ad Rate: Full Page Mono 5.10
Currency: Canada Dollars
COMMUNITY NEWSPAPER

La Gatineau 23906
Owner: Éditions La Gatineau Ltee. (Les)
Editorial: 135-B Route 105, Maniwaki, Quebec J9E 3A9 **Tel:** 1 819 449-1725
Email: redaction@lagatineau.com **Web site:** http://www.lagatineau.com
Freq: Thu; **Circ:** 11300
Editor: Jean Lacaille
Profile: La Gatineau est un hebdomadaire francophone offrant des nouvelles régionales et locales aux résidents de la région de Gatineau.

La Gatineau is a weekly newspaper covering local news. It is a French-language publication.
Language (s): French
Ad Rate: Full Page Mono 10.08
Currency: Canada Dollars
COMMUNITY NEWSPAPER

Le Lac-St-Jean 23877
Owner: Trium Médias
Editorial: 100 Rue St-Joseph Suite 1, Alma, Quebec G8B 7A6 **Tel:** 1 418 668-4545
Email: redaction_alma@tc.tc **Web site:** http://www.lelacstjean.com
Freq: Wed; **Circ:** 24464 Not Audited
Profile: Le Lac-Saint-Jean est un hebdomadaire couvrant les nouvealles locales et régionales pour les résidents du Lac_Saint-Jean au Québec.

Le Lac-Saint-Jean is a weekly publication covering local news and events for the residents of Lac-Saint-Jean Est, Québec.
Language (s): French
Ad Rate: Full Page Mono 9.52
Currency: Canada Dollars
COMMUNITY NEWSPAPER

The Langley Advance 23419
Owner: Black Press
Editorial: 112-6375-202 St, Langley, British Columbia V2Y 1N1 **Tel:** 1 604 534-8641
Email: news@langleyadvance.com **Web site:** http://www.langleyadvance.com
Freq: Thu; **Circ:** 28969
Profile: The Langley Advance News is a community newspaper for residents of Langley, British Columbia and the surrounding area. It provides coverage of local news, editorials, sports and special features.
Language (s): English
Ad Rate: Full Page Mono 25.34
Currency: Canada Dollars
COMMUNITY NEWSPAPER

Langley Times 23421
Owner: Black Press
Editorial: 20258 Fraser Hwy Unit 102, Langley, British Columbia V3A 4E6 **Tel:** 1 604 533-4157
Email: newsroom@langleytimes.com **Web site:** http://www.langleytimes.com
Freq: Fri; **Circ:** 36318
Editor in Chief: Frank Bucholtz; **Publisher:** Dwayne Weidendorf
Profile: Langley Times is a local newspaper for residents of Langley, British Columbia and the surrounding areas. The newspaper provides coverage of local news, sports, entertainment, community events, lifestyle topics and feature stories.
Language (s): English
Ad Rate: Full Page Mono 28.98
Currency: Canada Dollars
COMMUNITY NEWSPAPER

L'Annonceur 768524
Owner: MPA Concept
Editorial: 108 Rue Maurault, Pierreville, Quebec J0G 1J0 **Tel:** 1 450 568-3186
Email: lannonceur@lannonceur.ca **Web site:** http://www.lannonceur.ca
Freq: Weekly; **Circ:** 21000
Publisher: Jocelyne Hamel; **Editor:** Sébastien Lacroix
Profile: L'annonceur est un bimensuel francophone qui offre des actualités locales aux habitants de la région du Bas-St-François et des environs.

L'annonceur offers local news and information to residents of Ras-Richelieu, Bas-St-François and Nicolet-Yamaska, Quebec.
Language (s): French
COMMUNITY NEWSPAPER

Last Mountain Times Newspapers 25603
Owner: Last Mountain Times Ltd.
Editorial: 103-1st Ave West, Nokomis, Saskatchewan S0G 3R0 **Tel:** 1 306 528-2020
Email: editor@lastmountaintimes.ca **Web site:** http://www.lastmountaintimes.ca
Freq: Weekly; **Circ:** 11882 Not Audited
Publisher & Editor in Chief: Dave Degenstien
Language (s): English
COMMUNITY NEWSPAPER

The Leader - Niagara This Week
79840
Owner: Metroland Media Group Ltd.
Editorial: 3300 Merrittville HWY, Unit 1B, Thorold, Ontario L2V 4Y6 **Tel:** 1 905 641-1984
Email: letters@niagarathisweek.com **Web site:** http://www.niagarathisweek.com
Freq: Bi-Weekly; **Circ:** 165300 Not Audited
Profile: The Leader-Niagara This Week is a publication for the Port Colborne, Ontario community. Articles deal with the news, weather and local events.
Language (s): English
Ad Rate: Full Page Mono 89.88
Ad Rate: Full Page Colour 111.98
Currency: Canada Dollars
COMMUNITY NEWSPAPER

The Leduc Rep
23655
Owner: Postmedia Network Inc.
Editorial: 4504 61 Ave, Leduc, Alberta T9E 3Z1
Tel: 1 780 986-2271
Email: broy@postmedia.com **Web site:** http://www.leducrep.com
Freq: Fri; **Circ:** 16000 Not Audited
Profile: The Leduc Rep is a weekly newspaper serving Leduc, Alberta and Leduc County, including Calmar, Thorsby, Warburg, and New Sarepta. **All news releases should be sent to Bobby Roy, Regional Editor broy@postmedia.com
Language (s): English
Ad Rate: Full Page Mono 24.36
Currency: Canada Dollars
COMMUNITY NEWSPAPER

The Leduc-Westaskiwin Pipestone Flyer
153036
Editorial: 5025 50th St, Millet, Alberta T0C 1Z0
Tel: 1 780 387-5797
Email: production@pipestoneflyer.com **Web site:** http://www.pipestoneflyer.com
Freq: Thu; **Circ:** 24000 Not Audited
Profile: The Leduc-Westaskiwin Pipestone Flyer is a weekly community newspaper serving the residents of Millet, Alberta.
Language (s): English
Ad Rate: Full Page Mono 14.14
Currency: Canada Dollars
COMMUNITY NEWSPAPER

Lethbridge Journal
693894
Owner: Alberta Newspaper Group Inc.
Editorial: 504 7 St S, Lethbridge, Alberta T1J 2H1
Tel: 1 403 320-8936
Email: rturner@lethbridgeherald.com **Web site:** http://www.lethbridgejournal.ca
Freq: Bi-Weekly; **Circ:** 28000
Editor: Lisa Doerksen
Profile: Lethbridge Journal is a weekly community newspaper published every other Thursday. The paper serves Lethbridge, Alberta and surrounding areas.
Language (s): English
Ad Rate: Full Page Mono 18.00
Currency: United States Dollars
COMMUNITY NEWSPAPER

Lethbridge Newspapers
531220
Owner: Alberta Newspaper Group Inc.
Editorial: 504 7 St S, Lethbridge, Alberta T1J 2H1
Tel: 1 403 328-4411
Email: suntimes@lethbridgeherald.com **Web site:** http://www.lethbridgeherald.com
Circ: 49395 Not Audited
Language (s): English
COMMUNITY NEWSPAPER

L' L'Express
30073
Owner: TC. Transcontinental
Editorial: 1050 Rue Cormier, Drummondville, Quebec J2C 2N6 **Tel:** 1 819 478-8171
Email: redaction_dr@tc.tc **Web site:** http://www.journalexpress.ca
Freq: Sun; **Circ:** 50148 Not Audited
Profile: L'Express est un bi-hebdomadaire francophone pour les gens de Drummondville et des environs.

L'Express is a bi-weekly, French-language newspaper covering local news for Drummondville, Quebec and its surroundings.
Language (s): French
Ad Rate: Full Page Mono 8.82
Currency: Canada Dollars
COMMUNITY NEWSPAPER

Lighthouse Publications
25681
Editorial: 353 York St, Bridgewater, Nova Scotia B4V 3K2 **Tel:** 1 902 543-2457
Email: newstip@lighthousenow.ca **Web site:** http://lighthousenow.ca
Circ: 37169 Not Audited
Publisher: Lynn Hennigar
Language (s): English
COMMUNITY NEWSPAPER

The Link
80769
Owner: Munish (Kaypel)
Editorial: 13463 78 Ave Suite 101, Surrey, British Columbia V3W 0A8 **Tel:** 1 604 591-5160
Email: editor@thelinkpaper.ca **Web site:** http://www.thelinkpaper.ca
Freq: Sat; **Circ:** 25000 Not Audited
Publisher: Sanjiv Batta; **Editor in Chief:** R. Paul Dhillon
Profile: The Link is a weekly newspaper written for the Indo-Canadian community in British Columbia. The paper features regional and national news as well as news on South Asia.
Language (s): English
Ad Rate: Full Page Mono 12.88
Currency: Canada Dollars
COMMUNITY NEWSPAPER

The Lloydminster Source
533391
Owner: The Lloydminster Source
Editorial: 5921 50 Ave, Lloydminster, Saskatchewan S9V 2A4 **Tel:** 1 306 825-5111
Email: editor@lloydminstersource.com **Web site:** http://www.lloydminstersource.com
Freq: Thu; **Circ:** 17300 Not Audited
Publisher: Reid Keebaugh
Profile: The Lloydminster Source is a community newspaper that is published weekly. It covers news and events for the Lloydminster, Saskatchewan area.
Language (s): English
Ad Rate: Full Page Mono 15.26
Currency: Canada Dollars
COMMUNITY NEWSPAPER

The Londoner
151252
Owner: Postmedia Network
Editorial: 369 York St, London, Ontario N6B 3R4-
Tel: 1 519 673-5005
Email: cmontanini@postmedia.com **Web site:** http://www.thelondoner.ca
Freq: Thu; **Circ:** 108000 Not Audited
Publisher: Linda Leblanc
Profile: The Londoner is a local, weekly newspaper written for residents of London, Ontario. It covers local news, events, weather and sports.
Language (s): English
Ad Rate: Full Page Mono 14.46
Currency: Canada Dollars
COMMUNITY NEWSPAPER

Luby Weekly Chinese Newspaper
82789
Owner: Quebec Chinese Information Inc.
Editorial: 1111 Rue Saint-Urbain Suite M-09, Montreal, Quebec H2Z 1Y6 **Tel:** 1 514 875-6806
Email: lubynewsqc@hotmail.com **Web site:** http://www.lubycanada.com
Freq: Fri; **Circ:** 10000 Not Audited
Publisher: Ya-I Chang
Profile: Luby Weekly Chinese Newspaper est un hebdomadaire en chinois (cantonnais?) destiné aux résidents du Grand Montréal, Rive-Sud, Québec, Ottawa.

Luby Weekly Chinese Newspaper is a weekly publication for the residents of Great Montreal, South Shore, Quebec, Ottawa.
Language (s): Chinese
Ad Rate: Full Page Mono 17.50
Currency: Canada Dollars
COMMUNITY NEWSPAPER

Main Street
551969
Owner: Éditions Main Street Inc. (Les)
Editorial: 21 Ch du Mont Oeler, Harrington, Quebec J8G 2S6 **Tel:** 1 819 242-2232
Email: main.street@xplornet.ca **Web site:** http://themainstreet.org/
Freq: Monthly; **Circ:** 12500
Publisher & Editor: Jack Burger
Profile: Main Street est un mensuel gratuit destiné aux anglophones des Laurentides, Québec.

Main Street is a free, monthly newspaper for the English-speaking community of the Laurentians, Quebec. Coverage ranges from local community and cultural events to articles on country living to opinion pieces on local, national and international events.
Language (s): English
Ad Rate: Full Page Mono 21.00
Currency: Canada Dollars
COMMUNITY NEWSPAPER

Le Manic
400077
Owner: Éditions nordiques 2007 inc. (Les)
Editorial: 770 Rue de Bretagne, Baie-Comeau, Quebec G5C 1X5 **Tel:** 1 418 589-2090
Email: info@lemanic.ca **Web site:** http://www.lemanic.ca
Freq: Wed; **Circ:** 16425 Not Audited
Editor: Simon Brisson
Profile: Le Manic est un hebdomadaire couvrant toutes les nouvelles et événements de la région de Baie-Comeau, Québec.

Le Manic is a weekly newspaper covering local news and events of Baie-Comeau Area, Quebec.
Language (s): French
Ad Rate: Full Page Mono 5.18
Currency: Canada Dollars
COMMUNITY NEWSPAPER

Manotick Messenger
23740
Owner: Morris Newspaper Group
Editorial: 1165 Beaverwood, Manotick, Ontario K431A5 **Tel:** 1 613 692-6000
Email: newsfile@bellnet.ca **Web site:** http://www.manotickmessenger.on.ca
Freq: Thu; **Circ:** 15000 Not Audited
Publisher: Jeffrey Morris
Profile: Manotick Messenger is the weekly local newspaper for the residents of the Manotick, Ontario area. The publication covers news from North Gower, the Rideau Township, and from Osgoode Township. The newspaper covers local news and sports.
Language (s): English
Ad Rate: Full Page Mono 6.93
Currency: Canada Dollars
COMMUNITY NEWSPAPER

Maple Ridge & Pitt Meadows THE NEWS
23444
Owner: Black Press
Editorial: 22611 Dewdney Trunk Rd, Maple Ridge, British Columbia V2X 3K1 **Tel:** 1 604 467-1122
Email: newsroom@mapleridgenews.com **Web site:** http://www.mapleridgenews.com
Freq: Fri; **Circ:** 30514 Not Audited
Editor: Michael Hall
Profile: Maple Ridge News is a local newspaper for residents of Meadows, British Columbia, providing readers with local news, business, entertainment, sports and opinion pieces.
Language (s): English
Ad Rate: Full Page Mono 22.26
Currency: Canada Dollars
COMMUNITY NEWSPAPER

Markham Economist & Sun
23746
Owner: Metroland Media Group Ltd.
Editorial: 580B Steven Crt, Newmarket, Ontario L3Y 6Z2- **Tel:** 1 905 294-2200
Email: newsroom@yrmg.com **Web site:** http://www.yorkregion.com/markham-on
Freq: Thu; **Circ:** 67000 Not Audited
Profile: Markham Economist & Sun is a weekly community newspaper for the residents of Markham, Ontario. The publication contains news aimed at local families and businesses, including news, sports, arts & entertainment, educational and economic news, and weather.
Language (s): English
Ad Rate: Full Page Mono 26.25
Ad Rate: Full Page Colour 1160.00
Currency: Canada Dollars
COMMUNITY NEWSPAPER

The Masthead News
151866
Owner: Ocean Breeze Distributions
Editorial: Hubbards, Nova Scotia **Tel:** 1 902 857-9099
Email: themastheadnews@aol.com **Web site:** http://www.themastheadnews.ca
Freq: Monthly; **Circ:** 15500 Not Audited
Publisher & Editor: Ronald Driskill
Profile: The Masthead News is a community newspaper that covers the St. Margaret's Bay area of Nova Scotia including the communities and corridors of Chester, Tantallon, Hammonds Plains Road, the St. Margaret's Bay Road (Hwy #3) to the edge of Bayers Lake in Halifax, and to Indian Harbour along Peggy's Cove Road.
Language (s): English
Ad Rate: Full Page Mono 32.90
Currency: United States Dollars
COMMUNITY NEWSPAPER

The Meridian Booster
23656
Owner: Postmedia Network Inc.
Editorial: 5714 44 St, Lloydminster, Alberta T9V 0B6
Tel: 1 780 875-3362
Email: taylor@meridianbooster.com **Web site:** http://www.meridianbooster.com
Freq: Fri; **Circ:** 15020 Not Audited
Profile: The Meridian Booster is a weekly newspaper that covers local news and events for the residents of Lloydminster, Alberta.
Language (s): English
Ad Rate: Full Page Mono 13.72
Currency: Canada Dollars
COMMUNITY NEWSPAPER

The Metis Voyageur
556988
Owner: Metis Nation
Editorial: 500 Old St. Patrick St, Ottawa, Ontario K1N 9G4 **Tel:** 1 613 798-1488
Web site: http://www.metisnation.org
Freq: Bi-Monthly; **Circ:** 12000
Editor: Linda Lord
Profile: The Metis Voyageur is a community paper published bi-monthly for the Metis Nation and surrounding communities in Ontario. It covers community news and features and is available free with a suggested donation suscription rate.
Language (s): English
Ad Rate: Full Page Mono 24.00
Currency: Canada Dollars
COMMUNITY NEWSPAPER

Metro Life News
773231
Editorial: 100 Dynamic Dr, Toronto, Ontario M1V 5C4
Tel: 1 416 299-8229
Email: adsmetrolife@gmail.com
Freq: Weekly; **Circ:** 10000
Editor: Richard Liu
Profile: Metro News Life is a weekly Chinese newspaper that provides Local and Community News coverage to the Chinese community in Toronto, ON.
Language (s): Chinese
Ad Rate: Full Page Mono 2.02
Currency: Canada Dollars
COMMUNITY NEWSPAPER

Metroland East - Arnprior
25616
Owner: Metroland Media Group Ltd.
Editorial: 80 Colonnade Rd Unit 4, Nepean, Ontario K2E 7L2 **Tel:** 1 613 432-3655
Email: theresa.fritz@metroland.com **Web site:** http://www.insideottawavalley.com
Freq: Thu; **Circ:** 14170 Not Audited
Profile: * Please send press releases to Managing Editor Theresa Fritz theresa.fritz@metroland.com *
Language (s): English
COMMUNITY NEWSPAPER

Metroland East - Belleville
25635
Owner: Metroland Media Group Ltd.
Editorial: 250 Sidney St, Belleville, Ontario K8P 3Z3
Tel: 1 613 966-2034
Email: chris.malette@metroland.com **Web site:** http://www.insidebelleville.com
Circ: 69003 Not Audited
Editor in Chief: Ryland Coyne
Profile: *Please send press releases to Managing Editor Chris Malette chris.malette@metroland.com.*
Language (s): English
COMMUNITY NEWSPAPER

Metroland East - Kingston
73636
Owner: Metroland Media Group
Editorial: 375 Select Dr Unit 14, Kingston, Ontario K7M 8R1 **Tel:** 1 613 546-8885
Email: hpratt-campbell@metroland.com **Web site:** http://www.kingstonregion.com
Circ: 51627 Not Audited
Editor in Chief: Ryland Coyne; **Editor:** Hollie Pratt-Campbell
Language (s): English
COMMUNITY NEWSPAPER

Metroland East - Smiths Falls
25643
Owner: Metroland Media Media Group Ltd.
Editorial: 65 Lorne St, Smiths Falls, Ontario K7A 3K8
Tel: 1 613 283-3182
Email: mdowdall@metroland.com **Web site:** https://www.insideottawavalley.com/smithsfalls-on/
Circ: 73290 Not Audited
Editor in Chief: Ryland Coyne; **News Editor:** Laurie Weir

Profile: "For press releases, please send them to regional Managing Editor Marla Dowdall mdowdall@metroland.com ."
Language (s): English
COMMUNITY NEWSPAPER

Metroland Media - Durham 72450
Owner: Metroland Media Group Ltd.
Editorial: 865 Farewell St, Oshawa, Ontario L1H 6N8 **Tel:** 1 905 579-4400
Email: newsroom@durhamregion.com **Web site:** http://www.durhamregion.com
Circ: 107250 Not Audited
Editor In Chief: Joanne Burghardt; **News Editor:** Ian McMillan
Language (s): English
COMMUNITY NEWSPAPER

Metroland Media Toronto-East 25653
Owner: Metroland Media Group Ltd.
Editorial: 175 Gordon Baker Rd, Toronto, Ontario M2H 2N7 **Tel:** 1 416 493-4400
Email: newsroom@insidetoronto.com **Web site:** http://www.insidetoronto.com
Circ: 296200 Not Audited
Editor in Chief: Ryland Coyne
Language (s): English
COMMUNITY NEWSPAPER

Metroland Media Toronto-West 25651
Owner: Metroland Media Group Ltd.
Editorial: 175 Gordon Baker Rd, Toronto, Ontario M2H 2N7 **Tel:** 1 416 675-4390
Email: newsroom@insidetoronto.com **Web site:** http://www.insidetoronto.com
Circ: 120600 Not Audited
Profile: When sending faxes, please indicate the intended paper in the subject line.
Language (s): English
COMMUNITY NEWSPAPER

The Metropolitain 537866
Editorial: 1470 Rue Peel, tour a, ste. 155, Montreal, Quebec H3A 1T1 **Tel:** 1 514 759-8541
Email: onlineeditor@themetropolitain.ca **Web site:** http://www.themetropolitain.ca
Freq: Bi-Weekly; **Circ:** 40000 Not Audited
Publisher & Editor in Chief: Beryl Wajsman
Profile: The Metropolitain est gratuit, distribué 2 fois par semaine, proposant des idées et commentaires sur les affaires publiques. Le journal bilingue offre des articles et des chroniques concernant la patrie, la place du Canada sur la scène internationale, son économie et des critiques d'arts.

The Metropolitain is a free, bi-weekly tabloid newspaper featuring ideas and public affairs commentary. The bilingual paper includes articles and columns concerning the Canadian homeland, Canada's place in international affairs, its economy, and art and style reviews.
Language (s): French/Bilingual
Ad Rate: Full Page Mono 34.78
Currency: Canada Dollars
COMMUNITY NEWSPAPER

Midland Mirror 23754
Owner: Metroland Media Group Ltd.
Editorial: 174 Pillsbury Drive, Midland, Ontario L4R 4L1 **Tel:** 1 705 527-5500
Email: mirror@simcoe.com **Web site:** http://www.midlandmirror.com
Freq: Thu; **Circ:** 20994 Not Audited
Editor: Travis Mealing
Profile: Midland Mirror is a community newspaper published for Midland, Ontario area local residents. It covers local news, entertainment, lifestyle and community events.
Language (s): English
Ad Rate: Full Page Mono 15.54
Currency: Canada Dollars
COMMUNITY NEWSPAPER

Midweek 903229
Owner: Asian World Today Inc.
Editorial: 1310 Mid-Way Blvd Unit 31, Mississauga, Ontario L5T 2K5 **Tel:** 1 647 272-8182
Email: yudhvir@southasiandaily.com **Web site:** http://www.southasiandaily.com
Freq: Tue; **Circ:** 40000
Editor: Yudhvir Jaswal
Profile: Midweek is a South Asian English Newspaper, Midweek covers news weekly as it relates to the South Asian community and includes international, national and community news. It is delivered across Kitchener, Waterloo, Guelph, Hamilton & Stoney Creek. It includes sections on current news, Analysis, Editorial & Opinion, news from Canada, World, Southasia in the Main section, Sports, Cricket & movies in Entertainment section, Business, Real Estate, Health, Auto and Fashion in the Lifestyle section.
Language (s): English
Ad Rate: Full Page Colour 18.18
Currency: Canada Dollars
COMMUNITY NEWSPAPER

O Milenio 82812
Owner: Lola Investments
Editorial: 2379 Central Park Dr Unit 703, Oakville, Ontario L6H 0E3 **Tel:** 1 905 257-7740
Email: info@mileniostadium.com **Web site:** http://www.mileniostadium.com
Freq: Fri; **Circ:** 40000 Not Audited
Publisher & Editor: Alexandre Franco
Profile: Milénio is a weekly paper serving the Portuguese speaking communities in Mississauga, Ontario. It is published every Friday.
Language (s): English
Ad Rate: Full Page Mono 8.89
Currency: Canada Dollars
COMMUNITY NEWSPAPER

Milton Canadian Champion 82926
Owner: Metroland Media Group Ltd.
Editorial: 555 Industrial Dr, Milton, Ontario L9T 5E1 **Tel:** 1 905 878-2341
Email: editor@miltoncanadianchampion.com **Web site:** http://www.insidehalton.com/milton-on/
Freq: Thu; **Circ:** 25000 Not Audited
Profile: The Milton Canadian Champion serves residents and businesses in Milton, ON. This weekly newspaper contains local news, events, sports, education, business and feature stories.
Language (s): English
Ad Rate: Full Page Mono 7.00
Currency: Canada Dollars
COMMUNITY NEWSPAPER

Miramichi Leader 30122
Owner: Brunswick News Inc.
Editorial: 2428 King George Hwy, Miramichi, New Brunswick E1V 6V9 **Tel:** 1 506 622-2600
Email: news@miramichileader.com **Web site:** http://www.miramichileader.com
Freq: 3 Times/Week; **Circ:** 18641 Not Audited
Editor: Greg Mulock
Profile: Miramichi Leader is a weekly paper, published three times a week that provides coverage of local news to the residents of Miramichi, NB, and its surrounding areas.
Language (s): English
Ad Rate: Full Page Mono 5.25
Ad Rate: Full Page Colour 231.00
Currency: Canada Dollars
COMMUNITY NEWSPAPER

Mission City Record 23446
Owner: Black Press
Editorial: 33047 1st Ave, Mission, British Columbia V2V 1G2 **Tel:** 1 604 826-6221
Email: news@missioncityrecord.com **Web site:** http://www.missioncityrecord.com
Freq: Fri; **Circ:** 11000 Not Audited
Editor: Kevin Mills
Profile: Mission City Record is a weekly newspaper written for the residents of Mission, British Columbia.
Language (s): English
Ad Rate: Full Page Mono 19.88
Currency: Canada Dollars
COMMUNITY NEWSPAPER

The Monday News 498313
Owner: TC. Transcontinental
Editorial: 352 E River Rd, New Glasgow, Nova Scotia B2H 5E2 **Tel:** 1 902 752-3000
Email: news@ngnews.ca
Freq: Mon; **Circ:** 19000 Not Audited
Group Publisher: Richard Russell
Profile: The Monday News is a local newspaper written for the residents of New Glasgow, Truro and Amherst, Nova Scotia. The paper is a weekly combination of The News-New Glasgow (Nova Scotia), Truro (Nova Scotia) Daily News and Amherst (Nova Scotia) Daily News.
Language (s): English
Ad Rate: Full Page Mono 9.80
Currency: Canada Dollars
COMMUNITY NEWSPAPER

Monsoon Journal 773221
Editorial: 3107 Sheppard Ave East, Toronto, Ontario M1T 3J7 **Tel:** 1 416 358-3235
Email: toronto@monsoonjournal.com **Web site:** http://www.monsoonjournal.com
Freq: Monthly; **Circ:** 15000
Profile: Monsoon Journal is a monthly English newspaper that provides Community and International News coverage to the South Asian commnities in the Toronto and the Greater Toronto Area.
Language (s): English
COMMUNITY NEWSPAPER

Montreal Times 257625
Editorial: 3551 Boul Saint-Charles Suite 547, Kirkland, Quebec H9H 3C4 **Tel:** 1 514 457-7656
Email: info@mtltimes.ca **Web site:** http://mtltimes.ca
Freq: Weekly; **Circ:** 72000 Not Audited
Publisher & Editor: Tom West
Profile: Montreal Times est le journal de la communauté anglophone de l'Ile de Montréal et plus particulièrement de l'Ouest de l'Ile. Publié 2 fois semaine, mercredi et samedi, mais la version du mercredi est seulement disponible en ligne.

Montreal Times is a local community newspaper for the residents of Kirkland, Quebec and the surrounding communities. It is published twice weekly on Wednesday and Saturday but the Wednesday edition is only published online.
Language (s): English
Ad Rate: Full Page Mono 11.75
Currency: Canada Dollars
COMMUNITY NEWSPAPER

The Morning Star 23560
Owner: Black Press
Editorial: 4407 25 Ave, Vernon, British Columbia V1T 1P5 **Tel:** 1 250 545-3322
Email: newsroom@vernonmorningstar.com **Web site:** http://www.vernonmorningstar.com
Freq: Fri; **Circ:** 33206 Not Audited
Publisher: Ian Jensen
Profile: The Morning Star is a local newspaper written for the residents of Vernon, British Columbia. The paper covers news, sports, arts & entertainment and community events.
Language (s): English
Ad Rate: Full Page Mono 22.82
Ad Rate: Full Page Colour 371.00
Currency: Canada Dollars
COMMUNITY NEWSPAPER

Mountain View Publishing Inc. 394768
Owner: Great West Newspapers LP
Editorial: 5013-51 Street, Olds, Alberta T4P 1P6 **Tel:** 1 403 556-7510
Email: production@olds.greatwest.ca **Web site:** http://www.oldsalbertan.ca
Circ: 31300 Not Audited
Publisher: Murray Elliott
Language (s): English
COMMUNITY NEWSPAPER

Le Mouton Noir 257664
Owner: Éditions du Berger blanc (Les)
Tel: 1 418 724-6647
Email: mouton@moutonnoir.com **Web site:** http://www.moutonnoir.com
Freq: Bi-Monthly; **Circ:** 10000 Not Audited
Profile: Le Mouton Noir est un journal indépendant publié 6 fois par année, qui offre des opinions et des débats sociaux. Il s'adresse à la population du Bas-Saint-Laurent et de la Gaspésie, mais sa présence sur le web étend son auditoire bien au-delà.

Le Mouton Noir is an independent bi-monthly newspaper offers news and opinion articles to residents of the Bas-Saint-Laurent and Gaspésie regions of Quebec. It is published 6 times a year.
Language (s): French
Ad Rate: Full Page Mono 7.63
Currency: Canada Dollars
COMMUNITY NEWSPAPER

Nanaimo Bulletin 503179
Owner: Black Press
Editorial: 777 Popular St, Nanaimo, British Columbia V9S 2H7 **Tel:** 1 250 753-3707
Email: news@nanaimobulletin.com **Web site:** http://www.nanaimobulletin.com/
Freq: Thu; **Circ:** 31868
Publisher: Maurice Donn; **Editor:** Melissa Fryer
Profile: Nanaimo Bulletin serves the residents of Nanaimo, British Columbia. The publication covers local and regional news, entertainment, education, sports and business. It also includes an editorial page, lifestyle articles and a classifieds section.
Language (s): English
Ad Rate: Full Page Mono 21.84
Ad Rate: Full Page Colour 670.00
Currency: Canada Dollars
COMMUNITY NEWSPAPER

The Napanee Beaver 23778
Owner: Napanee Beaver
Editorial: 72 Dundas St E, Napanee, Ontario K7R 1H9 **Tel:** 1 613 354-6641
Email: beaver@bellnet.ca **Web site:** http://www.napaneebeaver.com
Freq: Thu; **Circ:** 14553 Not Audited
Publisher: Jean Morrison
Profile: The Napanee Beaver is a 12+ page newspaper written for the Napanee, Ontario general public. It covers local news, sports, and business.
Language (s): English
Ad Rate: Full Page Mono 5.99
Currency: Canada Dollars
COMMUNITY NEWSPAPER

Nasha Gazeta 82807
Owner: Russian Canadian Broadcasting
Editorial: 592 Champagne Dr, Toronto, Ontario M3J 2T9 **Tel:** 1 416 725-8337
Email: wfarsalas@sympatico.ca **Web site:** http://rcbcanada.com/broadcasting/nasha-gazeta/
Freq: Tue; **Circ:** 10000 Not Audited
Editor in Chief: T. Toutchinski
Profile: Nasha Gazeta provides news and information to local residents. The newspaper publishes comprehensive analytical articles and interviews with MPs and MPPs, city councillors, police, government representatives, community and spiritual leaders and artists. Leading specialists in finance, real estate, immigration and law regularly publish serious articles with recommendations of interest as for new immigrants as for long term residents of the country.
Language (s): English
Ad Rate: Full Page Mono 13.09
Currency: United States Dollars
COMMUNITY NEWSPAPER

New Canada 80778
Owner: New Canada Publications
Editorial: 120 Eglinton Ave E Suite 500, Toronto, Ontario M4P 1E2 **Tel:** 1 416 481-7793
Email: humanrights@sympatico.ca
Freq: Weekly; **Circ:** 10000 Not Audited
Publisher & Editor in Chief: Hasanat Ahmad Syed
Profile: New Canada is a bilingual, weekly publication written for immigrants. Its objective is to support and promote minorities.
Language (s): English
Ad Rate: Full Page Mono 21.00
Ad Rate: Full Page Colour 800.00
Currency: Canada Dollars
COMMUNITY NEWSPAPER

The Newmarket Era 23799
Owner: Metroland Media Group Ltd.
Editorial: 580B Steven Crt, Newmarket, Ontario L3Y 6Z2- **Tel:** 1 905 853-8888
Email: newsroom@yrmg.com **Web site:** http://www.yorkregion.com/newmarket-on
Freq: Thu; **Circ:** 47879 Not Audited
Profile: The Newmarket Era is a weekly community newspaper published for the residents of Newmarket, Ontario. It features local news, regional sports and classifieds.
Language (s): English
Ad Rate: Full Page Mono 22.89
Currency: Canada Dollars
COMMUNITY NEWSPAPER

The News 29852
Owner: Black Press
Editorial: #4-154 Middleton Ave, Parksville, British Columbia **Tel:** 1 250 248-4341
Email: editor@pqbnews.com **Web site:** http://www.pqbnews.com
Freq: Thu; **Circ:** 15443 Not Audited
Editor in Chief: Steven Heywood; **Publisher & Advertising Sales Manager:** Peter McCully
Profile: The News is a community newspaper that covers the Vancouver Island, British Columbia areas stretching from Deep Bay to the north, Nanoose Bay to the south, and west to Cathedral Grove. This region includes a number of rural communities, including Errington, Coombs, Whiskey Creek, Hilliers, Qualicum Bay, Bowser and Deep Bay, as well as the growing City of Parksville and Town of Qualicum Beach. The paper covers local news, community issues and events.
Language (s): English
Ad Rate: Full Page Mono 18.48
Currency: Canada Dollars
COMMUNITY NEWSPAPER

Niagara This Week 445502
Owner: Metroland Media Group Ltd.
Editorial: 3300 Merrittville Hwy Unit 1B, Thorold, Ontario L2V 4Y6 **Tel:** 1 905 688-2444
Email: letters@niagarathisweek.com **Web site:** http://www.niagarathisweek.com
Freq: Fri; **Circ:** 206500 Not Audited
COMMUNITY NEWSPAPER

Nipawin Newspapers 25602
Owner: Postmedia Network Inc.
Editorial: 220 Centre St, Nipawin, Saskatchewan S0E 1E0 **Tel:** 1 306 862-4618
Email: gwiseman@postmedia.com **Web site:** http://www.nipawinjournal.com
Circ: 27394 Not Audited
Publisher: Ken Sorensen
Language (s): English
COMMUNITY NEWSPAPER

Le Nord-Côtier 476280
Owner: Éditions nordiques 2007 inc. (Les)
Editorial: 719 Boul Laure, Sept-Iles, Quebec G4R 1Y2 **Tel:** 1 418 960-2090
Email: journal@lenord-cotier.com **Web site:** http://www.lenord-cotier.com
Freq: Wed; **Circ:** 19000 Not Audited
Profile: Fondé en mars 2007, le Journal Le Nord-Côtier s'adresse aux résidents de Sept-Îles, au Québec. On y couvre les nouvelles et les événements locaux.

Founded in March 2007, Journal Le Nord-Cotier is written for the residents of Sept-Iles, Quebec. It covers local news and events.
Language (s): French
Ad Rate: Full Page Mono 10.22
Currency: Canada Dollars
COMMUNITY NEWSPAPER

Norfolk News 878032
Owner: Metroland Media Group Ltd.
Editorial: 39 Colborne St S, Simcoe, Ontario N3Y 4H2 **Tel:** 1 519 428-0058
Email: editor@norfolknews.ca **Web site:** http://www.norfolknews.ca
Freq: Weekly; **Circ:** 24000
Profile: Launched on October 3, 2013, Norfolk News is a weekly newspaper for the residents of Norfolk County, Ontario.
Language (s): English
Ad Rate: Full Page Colour 23.79
Currency: Canada Dollars
COMMUNITY NEWSPAPER

North Shore News 23458
Owner: Glacier Media Inc.
Editorial: 100-126 15th St E 100, North Vancouver, British Columbia V7L 2P9 **Tel:** 1 604 985-2131
Email: editor@nsnews.com **Web site:** http://www.nsnews.com
Freq: Fri; **Circ:** 67000 Not Audited
Profile: North Shore News is a weekly newspaper that covers arts & entertainment, business, sports and news for North Vancouver, British Columbia. Their editorial mission is to be the best community paper in Canada. The publication is written in English for residents of North and West Vancouver.
Language (s): English
Ad Rate: Full Page Mono 49.42
Currency: Canada Dollars
COMMUNITY NEWSPAPER

Northern Life 23902
Owner: Laurentian Publishing Group Inc.
Editorial: 158 Elgin St, Sudbury, Ontario P3E 3N5
Tel: 1 705 673-5667
Email: editor@northernlife.ca **Web site:** http://www.sudbury.com
Freq: Thu; **Circ:** 50000 Not Audited
Publisher: Abbas Homayed
Profile: Northern Life is published weekly for the residents of Sudbury, Ontario and surrounding areas. The newspaper covers local news and community events.
Language (s): English
Ad Rate: Full Page Mono 39.46
Ad Rate: Full Page Colour 121.63
Currency: Canada Dollars
COMMUNITY NEWSPAPER

Northern News Services Newspapers 25560
Editorial: 5108 50th St, Yellowknife, Northwest Territories X1A 2R1 **Tel:** 1 867 873-4031
Email: nnsl@nnsl.com **Web site:** http://www.nnsl.com
Circ: 26786 Not Audited
General Manager: Michael Scott; **Publisher:** Jack Sigvaldason; **Editor:** Roxanna Thompson
Language (s): English
COMMUNITY NEWSPAPER

Northumberland News 23727
Owner: Metroland Media Group Ltd.
Editorial: 884 Division St Unit 212, Cobourg, Ontario K9A 5V2 **Tel:** 1 905 373-7355
Email: newsroom@durhamregion.com **Web site:** http://www.northumberlandnews.com
Freq: Fri; **Circ:** 22800 Not Audited
Editor in Chief: Joanne Burghardt
Profile: Northumberland News is a bi-weekly publication written for the residents of Cobourg and Northumberland County, Ontario. The publication includes news, weather, sports and events.
Language (s): English
Ad Rate: Full Page Mono 7.28
Currency: Canada Dollars
COMMUNITY NEWSPAPER

Les Nouvelles Chinoises 82778
Owner: Quebec Culture & Commerce Ltee
Editorial: 200 Boul Rene Levesque W Suite 4, Montreal, Quebec H2Z 1X4 **Tel:** 1 514 842-5689
Email: chinesenewsad@hotmail.com **Web site:** http://montrealchina.com/portal.php
Freq: Fri; **Circ:** 10000 Not Audited
Editor: Larry Thai; **Publisher & Editor:** James Zhang
Profile: Editorials devoted to the Chinese community for its political, social, cultural and economical developments. News coverage of major events happening in Montreal and Quebec.
Language (s): Mandarin
Ad Rate: Full Page Mono 14.56
Currency: Canada Dollars
COMMUNITY NEWSPAPER

Nouvelles Hebdo 24004
Owner: Trium Médias
Editorial: 1741 Rue des Pins, Dolbeau-Mistassini, Quebec G8L 1M9 **Tel:** 1 418 276-6211
Email: redaction.dolbeau@tc.tc **Web site:** http://www.nouvelleshebdo.com/
Freq: Wed; **Circ:** 12819 Not Audited
Publisher: Michel Aube
Profile: Le Journal Nouvelles-Hebdo est distribué dans la MRC de Maria-Chapdelaine, au Lac-Saint-Jean.

Le Journal Nouvelles Hebdo is a French-language newspaper that covers local news for the residents of Maria-Chapdelaine, in Quebec's Saguenay–Lac-Saint-Jean region.
Language (s): French
Ad Rate: Full Page Mono 4.34
Currency: Canada Dollars
COMMUNITY NEWSPAPER

Oakville Beaver 23810
Owner: Metroland Media Group Ltd.
Editorial: 5046 Mainway Unit 2, Burlington, Ontario L7L 5Z1 **Tel:** 1 905 845-3824
Email: editor@oakvillebeaver.com **Web site:** http://www.insidehalton.com/oakville-on
Freq: Fri; **Circ:** 47500 Not Audited
Profile: The Oakville Beaver is a local newspaper published twice a week serving Oakville, ON.
Language (s): English
Ad Rate: Full Page Mono 27.16
Currency: Canada Dollars
COMMUNITY NEWSPAPER

Observer Xtra 23772
Owner: Cathedral Communications Inc.
Editorial: 20B Arthur St N, Elmira, Ontario N3B 1Z9
Tel: 1 519 669-5790
Email: info@observerxtra.com **Web site:** http://www.observerxtra.com
Freq: Thu; **Circ:** 15107 Not Audited
Editor: Steve Kannon; **Publisher:** Joe Merlihan
Profile: Woolwich Observer is a weekly newspaper serving the town of Elmira, ON and the surrounding area. The paper covers local news and events. Deadlines for the publication are one week before issue date.
Language (s): English
Ad Rate: Full Page Mono 14.00
Ad Rate: Full Page Colour 1200.00
Currency: Canada Dollars
COMMUNITY NEWSPAPER

L' Oeil Régional 23889
Owner: DBC Communications Inc.
Editorial: 393 Boul Sir-Wilfrid-Laurier, Beloeil, Quebec J3G 4H6 **Tel:** 1 450 467-1821
Email: bel.redaction@tc.tc **Web site:** http://www.oeilregional.com
Freq: Wed; **Circ:** 34812
Editor in Chief: Vincent Guilbault
Profile: L'Oeil Régional est un journal hebdomadaire couvrant les nouvelles et les informations locales, ce qui inclut l'éducation, les affaires and le divertissement, pour les résidents de la municipalité de Beloeil, Québec.

L'Œil Régional is a weekly newspaper that covers local news and information, including education, business, crime, and entertainment, for residents of Belœil, Québec.
Language (s): French
Ad Rate: Full Page Mono 11.20
Currency: Canada Dollars
COMMUNITY NEWSPAPER

L' Oie Blanche 23924
Owner: Cooperative du Journal L'Oie Blanche
Editorial: 70 Rue de L'Anse, Montmagny, Quebec G5V 1G8 **Tel:** 1 418 248-8820
Email: nouvelles@oieblanc.com **Web site:** http://www.oieblanc.com
Freq: Wed; **Circ:** 24012 Not Audited
Profile: L'Oie blanche est un hebdomadaire coopératif francophone destiné aux habitants de Montmagny, L'Islet et d'une partie de la région de Bellechasse.

L'Oie Blanche is a weekly French-language publication covering local news for Montmagny, L'Islet, and the eastern part of Bellechasse, Quebec.
Language (s): French
Ad Rate: Full Page Mono 4.27
Currency: Canada Dollars
COMMUNITY NEWSPAPER

Orangeville Banner 23813
Owner: Metroland Media Group Ltd.
Editorial: 37 Mill St, Orangeville, Ontario L9W 2M4
Tel: 1 519 941-1350
Email: banner@orangevillebanner.com **Web site:** http://www.orangeville.com
Freq: Thu; **Circ:** 23488 Not Audited
Profile: Orangeville Banner is a weekly community newspaper written for the residents of Orangeville, Ontario. It covers local news, sports, opinions and classifieds.
Language (s): English
Ad Rate: Full Page Mono 10.89
Currency: Canada Dollars
COMMUNITY NEWSPAPER

Oriental Weekly 80241
Owner: Independent
Editorial: 1215-1110 Center Street NE, Room 215, Calgary, Alberta T2E 2R2 **Tel:** 1 403 230-0872
Email: info@trendweekly.com **Web site:** http://www.trendweekly.com
Freq: Fri; **Circ:** 10000 Not Audited
Editor: Paul Wong
Profile: Oriental News is a weekly newspaper providing Local and Community News coverage for the Chinese community in Calgary and Edmonton, AB.
Language (s): Chinese
Ad Rate: Full Page Mono 2.92
Currency: Canada Dollars
COMMUNITY NEWSPAPER

Orillia Today 23814
Owner: Metroland Media Group Ltd.
Editorial: 25 James St W Unit 3, Orillia, Ontario L3V 8A6 **Tel:** 1 705 329-2058
Web site: http://www.simcoe.com
Freq: Thu; **Circ:** 23829 Not Audited
Editor in Chief: Martin Melbourne
Profile: Orillia Today is a local paper written for the residents of Orillia, Ontario. The weekly newspaper covers community news and events.
Language (s): English
Ad Rate: Full Page Mono 13.37
Ad Rate: Full Page Colour 1160.00
Currency: Canada Dollars
COMMUNITY NEWSPAPER

The Oshawa Central 82930
Editorial: 136 Simcoe St N Unit 4, Oshawa, Ontario L1G 4S7 **Tel:** 1 905 432-2657
Email: newspaper@ocentral.com **Web site:** http://www.ocentral.ca/
Freq: Mon; **Circ:** 75000 Not Audited
Publisher & Editor: Joe Ingino
Profile: The Oshawa Central is a local newspaper serving the residents of Oshawa, Ontario. The publication covers local and national news, public affairs, current and community events, sports, lifestyle, arts & entertainment, business and politics.
Language (s): English
Ad Rate: Full Page Mono 42.80
Currency: Canada Dollars
COMMUNITY NEWSPAPER

Oshawa Express 681417
Owner: Dowellman Publishing Corp.
Editorial: 774 Simcoe St S, Oshawa, Ontario L1H 4K6- **Tel:** 1 905 571-7334
Email: newsroom@oshawaexpress.ca **Web site:** http://www.oshawaexpress.ca
Freq: Wed; **Circ:** 35000
Editor: Greg McDowell; **Publisher:** Sandy McDowell
Profile: Oshawa Express is a weekly community newspaper written for the residents of Oshawa, Ontario.
Language (s): English
Ad Rate: Full Page Mono 10.52
Currency: Canada Dollars
COMMUNITY NEWSPAPER

Osprey Media Group-Napanee 559586
Owner: Postmedia Network Inc.
Editorial: 6 Cataraqui St, Kingston, Ontario K7K 1Z7
Tel: 1 613 544-5000
Email: sserviss@postmedia.com **Web site:** http://www.napaneeguide.com
Freq: Weekly; **Circ:** 22326 Not Audited
Editor: Meghan Balogh
Language (s): English
COMMUNITY NEWSPAPER

Ossekeag Publishing 155089
Editorial: 242 Main St, Hampton, New Brunswick E5N 6B8 **Tel:** 1 506 832-5613
Email: info@ossekeag.ca **Web site:** http://www.ossekeag.ca
Circ: 40201 Not Audited
Language (s): English
COMMUNITY NEWSPAPER

Our London 760226
Owner: Metroland Media Group Ltd.
Editorial: 1074 Dearness Dr Unit 80, London, Ontario N6E 1N9 **Tel:** 1 519 451-1500
Web site: https://www.ourlondon.ca/
Circ: 126000
Editor: Scott Taylor
Profile: London Community News offers local news and information to residents of London, Ontario. Local editions are offered to residents in six different neighbourhoods throughout the city.
Language (s): English
COMMUNITY NEWSPAPER

Paivand 903421
Tel: 1 604 921-4726
Web site: http://paivand.com
Freq: 2 Times/Week; **Circ:** 10000
Publisher & Editor: Ramin Mahjouri
Profile: An Iranian community newspaper.
Language (s): Persian
COMMUNITY NEWSPAPER

Parvasi Weekly 773281
Owner: Parvasi Media Group
Editorial: 2980 Drew Rd Unit 221, Mississauga, Ontario L4T 0A7 **Tel:** 1 905 673-0600
Email: office@parvasi.com **Web site:** http://parvasinewspaper.com/
Freq: Weekly; **Circ:** 35000
News Editor: Harinder Jassal; **Publisher and Chief Editor:** Rajinder Saini
Profile: Parvasi Weekly provides Community and Local News to the Punjabi-speaking communities in the Greater Toronto Area, Windsor, Montreal, Vancouver and Calgary. The head office is located in Mississauga, ON and there is also a Vancouver office.
Language (s): Urdu
COMMUNITY NEWSPAPER

Patrides, A North American Review 80452
Owner: Patrides Publications
Editorial: 100 Queen St W, Toronto, Ontario M5H 2N1 **Tel:** 1 416 921-4229
Email: saras@patrides.com **Web site:** http://www.patrides.com
Freq: Monthly; **Circ:** 160000 Not Audited
Publisher: Kathy Saras; **Editor In Chief:** Thomas Saras
Profile: Patrides, A North American Review is a community newspaper written for the Greek community of Toronto, Ontario.
Language (s): English
Ad Rate: Full Page Mono 73.93
Ad Rate: Full Page Colour 350.00
Currency: Canada Dollars
COMMUNITY NEWSPAPER

Peace Country Sun 23460
Owner: Postmedia Network Inc.
Editorial: 10604 100 St, Grande Prairie, Alberta T8V 2M5 **Tel:** 1 780 532-1110
Email: drinne@postmedia.com **Web site:** http://www.peacecountrysun.com
Freq: Fri; **Circ:** 14568 Not Audited
Publisher: Amber Ogilvie; **Editor:** Diana Rinne
Profile: Peace Country Sun is a weekly newspaper published in Grande Prairie, Alberta. It delivers local news and features to rural residents of the Alberta and Northern British Columbia area.
Language (s): English
Ad Rate: Full Page Mono 7.63
Currency: Canada Dollars
COMMUNITY NEWSPAPER

Pembroke/Petawawa News 499874
Owner: Postmedia Network Inc.
Editorial: 186 Alexander St, Pembroke, Ontario K8A 4L9 **Tel:** 1 613 732-3691
Email: pem.editorial@sunmedia.ca
Circ: 37777 Not Audited
Publisher: Jim Kwiatkowski
Language (s): English
COMMUNITY NEWSPAPER

Peninsula News Review 23507
Owner: Black Press
Editorial: 9843 2nd Street, Unit 6, Sidney, British Columbia V8L 3C7 **Tel:** 1 250 656-1151
Email: editor@peninsulanewsreview.com **Web site:** http://www.peninsulanewsreview.com
Freq: Fri; **Circ:** 14132 Not Audited
Editor in Chief: Erin Cardone; **Publisher and Advertising Sales Manager:** Jim Parker
Profile: Peninsula News Review is a local newspaper serving the Sidney Peninsule in British Columbia, include the local communities of Brentwood Bay, Saanichton and Keating. Coverage includes local news and events. The paper was founded in 1912 and was previously known as the Sidney Review.
Language (s): English
Ad Rate: Full Page Mono 24.92
Currency: Canada Dollars
COMMUNITY NEWSPAPER

La Pensée de Bagot 23876
Owner: DBC Communications Inc.
Editorial: 800 Rue de Roxton, Acton Vale, Quebec J0H 1A0 **Tel:** 1 450 546-3271
Web site: http://www.lapensee.qc.ca
Freq: Wed; **Circ:** 14937 Not Audited
Publisher: Benoît Chartier; **Editor:** Michel Dorais
Profile: La Pensée de Bagot est un hebdomadaire francophone couvrant les nouvelles locales et régionales pour les habitants du secteur d'Acton Vale, Québec.

La Pensée de Bagot is a weekly French-language newspaper that covers local news and information for residents of Acton Vale, in Quebec.
Language (s): French
Ad Rate: Full Page Mono 12.88
Currency: Canada Dollars
COMMUNITY NEWSPAPER

Penticton Western News 23466
Owner: Black Press
Editorial: 2250 Camrose St, Penticton, British Columbia V2A 8R1 **Tel:** 1 250 492-3636
Email: editor@pentictonwesternnews.com **Web site:** http://www.pentictonwesternnews.com
Freq: Fri; **Circ:** 21240 Not Audited
Editor in Chief: Dan Ebenal; **Publisher:** Mark Walker
Profile: Penticton Western News is written for the Penticton, British Columbia general public. It covers local news, sports and entertainment.
Language (s): English
Ad Rate: Full Page Mono 16.24
Currency: Canada Dollars
COMMUNITY NEWSPAPER

Peterborough This Week 23829
Owner: Metroland Media Group Ltd.
Editorial: 884 Ford St, Peterborough, Ontario K9J 5V3 **Tel:** 1 705 749-3383
Web site: http://www.mykawartha.com
Freq: Fri; **Circ:** 48484 Not Audited
General Manager: Mary Babcock; **News Editor:** Mike Lacey
Profile: Peterborough This Week is a twice-weekly newspaper tailored for the Peterborough community.
Language (s): English
Ad Rate: Full Page Mono 21.51
Ad Rate: Full Page Colour 350.00
Currency: Canada Dollars
COMMUNITY NEWSPAPER

Philippine Asian Chronicle 903512
Editorial: 152nd St., Ste: 332-151-10090, Surrey, British Columbia V3W 8X8 **Tel:** 1 778 395-6785
Email: philasianchronicle@gmail.com
Freq: Bi-Monthly; **Circ:** 12000
Publisher: Erlinda Juatco; **Publisher & Editor:** Roque Juatco
Profile: A bi-monthly Filipino newspaper in English distributed all over the Vancouver lower mainland.
Language (s): English
Ad Rate: Full Page Mono 24.00
Ad Rate: Full Page Colour 31.00
Currency: Canada Dollars
COMMUNITY NEWSPAPER

Philippine Asian News Today 903521
Owner: Reyfort Media Group
Editorial: 9955 149 St, Surrey, British Columbia V3R 7N2 **Tel:** 1 604 588-6397
Email: info@philippinenewstoday.ca **Web site:** http://www.philippineasiannewstoday.com
Freq: Bi-Weekly; **Circ:** 10000
Publisher: Rey Fortaleza
Profile: A weekly Filipino newspaper distributed all over Vancouver and the Lower Mainland including Delta, Surrey, Langley, New Westminster, Richmond, Burnaby and Coquitlam.
Language (s): English
Ad Rate: Full Page Mono 7.22
Ad Rate: Full Page Colour 9.03
Currency: Canada Dollars
COMMUNITY NEWSPAPER

The Philippine Courier 811696
Owner: Philippine Courier Publishing and Entertainment
Editorial: 419 Alper St, Richmond Hill, Ontario L4C 2Z5 **Tel:** 1 905 780-0114
Email: mondatol@rogers.com **Web site:** http://philippinecourier.com
Freq: Monthly
Publisher & Editor in Chief: Ramon Datol
Profile: The Phillipine Courier is a monthly newspaper serving the Filipino community of the greater Toronto area.
Language (s): English
COMMUNITY NEWSPAPER

The Philippine Journal 80273
Owner: The Philippine Journal Publishing Corporation
Editorial: 201-955 W Broadway Ave, Vancouver, British Columbia V5Z 1K3 **Tel:** 1 604 433-8856
Email: philippinejournal@gmail.com **Web site:** http://www.philippinejournal.com
Freq: Bi-Weekly; **Circ:** 10000 Not Audited
Co-Publisher: Lilia Tiamzon; **Editor in Chief & Co-Publisher:** Irene Yatco
Profile: Philippine Journal is a Filipino-Canadian community newspaper published in Vancouver, British Columbia, Canada. Philippine Journal is a bi-weekly publication featuring RP, Canadian and World News, stimulating editorials, heart tugging human interest stories up-to-date community highlights, light and humorous features and well-written columns that make for interesting, informative and soul lifting reading.
Language (s): English
Ad Rate: Full Page Mono 5.95
Currency: Canada Dollars
COMMUNITY NEWSPAPER

The Philippine Reporter 80335
Editorial: 2682 Eglinton Ave E, Scarborough, Ontario M1K 2S3 **Tel:** 1 416 461-8694
Email: philreporter@gmail.com **Web site:** http://www.philippinereporter.com
Freq: Bi-Weekly; **Circ:** 10000 Not Audited
Publisher & Editor: Hermie Garcia
Profile: Phillippine Reporter is a community newspaper written for the Filipino residents of Toronto. The paper is issued on the 1st and 16th of each month. Please call prior to submitting a fax.
Language (s): English
Ad Rate: Full Page Mono 7.28
Ad Rate: Full Page Colour 11.37
Currency: Canada Dollars
COMMUNITY NEWSPAPER

The Picton Gazette 23832
Owner: Picton Gazette
Editorial: 267 Main St, Picton, Ontario K0K 2T0 **Tel:** 1 613 476-3201
Email: gazette@bellnet.ca **Web site:** http://www.pictongazette.com
Freq: Thu; **Circ:** 11000 Not Audited
Publisher: Jean Morrison
Profile: The Picton Gazette is a local newspaper serving Prince Edward County, Ontario.
Language (s): English
Ad Rate: Full Page Mono 3.85
Currency: Canada Dollars
COMMUNITY NEWSPAPER

Pique News Magazine 82829
Owner: Glacier Media Inc.
Editorial: 103-1390 Alpha Lake Rd 103, Whistler, British Columbia V0N 1B1 **Tel:** 1 604 938-0202
Email: mail@piquenewsmagazine.com **Web site:** http://www.piquenewsmagazine.com
Freq: Fri; **Circ:** 15000 Not Audited
Publisher: Sarah Strother
Profile: Pique News Magazine is published weekly for residents of Whistler, British Columbia. The newspaper covers local news and community events.
Language (s): English
Ad Rate: Full Page Mono 16.80
Currency: Canada Dollars
COMMUNITY NEWSPAPER

Point Sud 82830
Owner: Journal Communautaire de la Rive-Sud de Montreal Inc. (Le)
Editorial: 150 Rue Grant Bureau 110, Longueuil, Quebec J4H 3H6 **Tel:** 1 450 677-2626
Email: info@pointsud.ca **Web site:** http://www.pointsud.ca
Freq: Monthly; **Circ:** 25000 Not Audited
Editor in Chief: Maurice Giroux
Profile: Le journal Point Sud est publié toutes les 3 semaines, sauf en juillet. Il est distribué dans ces agglomérations: Boucherville, Brossard, Greenfield Park, LeMoyne, Longueuil, Saint-Bruno, Saint-Hubert et Saint-Lambert.

Point Sud is French-language newspaper, published every 3 weeks in these agglomarations: Boucherville, Brossard, Greenfield Park, LeMoyne, Longueuil, Saint-Bruno, Saint-Hubert and Saint-Lambert.
Language (s): French
Ad Rate: Full Page Mono 30.24
Currency: Canada Dollars
COMMUNITY NEWSPAPER

Port Perry Star 30025
Owner: Metroland Media Group Ltd.
Editorial: 180 Mary St Unit 11, Port Perry, Ontario L9L 1C4 **Tel:** 1 905 985-7383
Email: newsroom@durhamregion.com **Web site:** http://www.durhamregion.com/scugog-on/
Freq: Thu; **Circ:** 12000 Not Audited
Profile: Port Perry Star is a community newspaper serving the Scugog, Ontario area. It covers news and events for local residents.
Language (s): English
Ad Rate: Full Page Mono 14.00
Currency: Canada Dollars
COMMUNITY NEWSPAPER

Port Rowan Good News 704868
Editorial: 8 Church Street, Port Rowan, Ontario N0E 1M0 **Tel:** 1 519 586-2291
Email: prgn@live.ca **Web site:** http://www.portrowangoodnews.com/
Freq: Monthly
Editor: Pat Finney; **Publisher:** Paul Morris
Profile: Port Rowan Good News is a monthly community newspaper that is published for the residents of Port Rowan, Ontario. Outlet offers RSS (Really Simple Syndication).
Language (s): English
COMMUNITY NEWSPAPER

The Post 25630
Owner: Postmedia Network Inc.
Editorial: 413 18th Ave, Hanover, Ontario N4N 3S5 **Tel:** 1 519 364-2001
Email: jkent@postmedia.com **Web site:** http://www.thepost.on.ca
Freq: Thu; **Circ:** 15106 Not Audited
Profile: The Post is a weekly community newspaper that covers local news, sports and entertainment for the residents of Hanover, Chesley, Durham and South Grey-Bruce, Ontario.
Language (s): English
Ad Rate: Full Page Mono 12.32
Currency: Canada Dollars
COMMUNITY NEWSPAPER

Post City Magazines 25649
Editorial: 30 Lesmill Rd, Toronto, Ontario M3B 2T6 **Tel:** 1 416 250-7979
Email: news@postcity.com **Web site:** http://www.postcitymagazines.com
Circ: 175000 Not Audited
Editor in Chief: Ron Johnson; **Publisher:** Lorne London; **News Editor:** Bree Rody-Mantha
Language (s): English
Ad Rate: Full Page Mono 2.58
Currency: Canada Dollars
COMMUNITY NEWSPAPER

The Post-Gazette 234972
Owner: Brunswick News Inc.
Tel: 1 506 357-9813
Email: oropost@nb.aibn.com
Freq: Thu; **Circ:** 15500 Not Audited
Language (s): English
Ad Rate: Full Page Mono 4.62
Currency: Canada Dollars
COMMUNITY NEWSPAPER

Prairie Newspaper Group 87768
Owner: Glacier Media Inc.
Editorial: 525 Main St, Humboldt, Saskatchewan S0K 2A0 **Tel:** 1 306 682-2561
Email: rzimmer@humboldtjournal.ca **Web site:** http://www.humboldtjournal.ca
Circ: 13390 Not Audited
Editor: Andrea Nicholl
Language (s): English
COMMUNITY NEWSPAPER

Prairie Post East 82835
Owner: Alberta Newspaper Group Inc.
Editorial: 3257 Dunmore Rd SE, Medicine Hat, Alberta T1B 3R2 **Tel:** 1 403 528-5769
Email: ppost@prairiepost.com **Web site:** http://www.prairiepost.com
Freq: Fri; **Circ:** 18071 Not Audited
Publisher: Mike Hertz
Profile: The Prairie Post East covers the community news of Medicine Hat (South East Alberta) and Swift Current (Southwest Saskatchewan) and their surrounding communities.
Language (s): English
Ad Rate: Full Page Mono 16.66
Currency: Canada Dollars
COMMUNITY NEWSPAPER

Prescott-Russell Newspapers 25625
Editorial: 1158 Notre Dame, Embrun, Ontario K0A 1W0 **Tel:** 1 613 443-2753
Circ: 26300 Not Audited
Publisher: Roger Duplantie
Profile: The Prescott-Russell Newspapers are written for the residents of Embrun, ON.
Language (s): French/Bilingual
COMMUNITY NEWSPAPER

La Presse 13649
Owner: Power Corporation of Canada
Editorial: 7 Rue Saint-Jacques, Montreal, Quebec H2Y 1K9- **Tel:** 1 514 285-7000
Email: redaction@lapresse.ca **Web site:** http://www.lapresse.ca
Freq: Sat; **Circ:** 340427
Publisher: Guy Crevier; **Contributor:** Bertrand Gahel; **News Director:** Mario Girard; **International News Editor:** Alexandre Sirois; **Editor in Chief:** Mélanie Thivierge
Profile: La Presse est un journal francophone publié pour les résidents de Montréal, Québec et les villes environnantes. Le journal couvre les nouvelles locales, régionales, nationales ainsi qu'internationales traitant sur différents sujets comme le socioculturel, la finance, l'économie, le style de vie, l'automobile, le sport, les arts et le divertissement. La Presse était auparavant un journal quotidien établie depuis 1884. Le journal a mis un terme à la version papier (lundi au vendredi) en Janvier 2016. L'éditions du samedi est toujours disponibles en format papier.

La Presse is a French-language community newspaper published for residents of Montreal, Quebec and surrounding communities. It covers local, regional, national and international news topics in the aeras of socio-cultural, business, economics, lifestyles, automative, sports, arts and entertainement news.La Presse, formerly a daily newspaper established in 1884, ceased printing its Monday to Friday editions on January 1, 2016. The only printed edition is available on Saturdays.
Language (s): French
Ad Rate: Full Page Mono 133.28
Ad Rate: Full Page Colour 4785.00
Currency: Canada Dollars
COMMUNITY NEWSPAPER

Pride News Magazine 80413
Editorial: 158 Hardwood Avenue South, Suite 204, Ajax, Ontario L1S 2H6 **Tel:** 1 905 686-8868
Email: info@pridenews.ca **Web site:** http://pridenews.ca/
Freq: Tue; **Circ:** 25000 Not Audited
Publisher & Editor: Michael Van Cooten
Profile: Pride News Magazine is a local community newspaper for the residents of Whitby, Ontario and surrounding communities. Outlet offers RSS (Really Simple Syndication).
Language (s): English
Ad Rate: Full Page Mono 20.02
Currency: Canada Dollars
COMMUNITY NEWSPAPER

Progrès-Week-end 23909
Owner: Groupe Capitale Médias
Editorial: 1051 Boul Talbot, Chicoutimi, Quebec G7H 5C1 **Tel:** 1 418 545-4474
Email: redaction@lequotidien.com **Web site:** http://www.lapresse.ca/le-quotidien/progres
Freq: Sun; **Circ:** 29315
Editor in Chief: Denis Bouchard
Profile: Le Progrès Week-end est un journal francophone hebdomadaire de la région de Saguenay, Québec. Ce journal parait chaque samedi et couvre les nouvelles, l'actualité locale, les arts, le divertissement, les sports et des reportages.

Progrès Week-end is a weekly French-language newspaper in Saguenay, Quebec. It is published every Saturday and covers news, arts & entertainment, sports and human-interest stories.
Language (s): French
Ad Rate: Full Page Mono 22.54
Ad Rate: Full Page Colour 26.60
Currency: Canada Dollars
COMMUNITY NEWSPAPER

Przeglad Tygodniowy 772596
Editorial: 6449 Glen Erin Dr Unit 23, Mississauga, Ontario L5N 2T2 **Tel:** 1 905 286-1774
Email: lambroziak@sympatico.ca
Freq: Weekly
Editor: Czeslaw Zacharski
Profile: Przeglad Tygodniowy a weekly publication that covers multicultural events and news for the Polish community in Mississauga, Canada.
Language (s): Polish
COMMUNITY NEWSPAPER

The Punjab Star 772601
Editorial: 203-7035 Maxwell Rd 203, Mississauga, Ontario L5S 1R5 **Tel:** 1 905 673-7666
Email: editor@punjabstar.com **Web site:** http://punjabstar.ca
Freq: Weekly
Editor: Gursimrat Singh Grewal
Profile: Punjab Star is a weekly publication that covers multicultural events and news for the Indian community in Ontario, Canada.
Language (s): English
COMMUNITY NEWSPAPER

Punjabi Haak Canada 772604
Editorial: 3671 Corliss Cres, Mississauga, Ontario L4T 2Z2
Email: punjabihaak@yahoo.ca
Freq: Weekly
Editor: Roman Bawa
Profile: Punjabi Haak Canada is a weekly publication that covers multicultural events and news for the Indian community in Mississauga, Canada.
Language (s): English
COMMUNITY NEWSPAPER

Punjabi National 774289
Editorial: 501-4656 Westwinds Dr NE 501, Calgary, Alberta T3J 3Z5 **Tel:** 1 403 204 0011
Email: punjabinational@gmail.com **Web site:** http://www.punjabinational.com
Editor: Aparjit Singh; **Publisher:** Kuldip Singh
Profile: Punjabi National is a Punjabi-language weekly newspaper providing Local and Community News coverage for the Calgary and Edmonton, AB areas.
COMMUNITY NEWSPAPER

Quebecor Communications - Kapuskasing 25633
Owner: Postmedia Network Inc.
Editorial: 51 Riverside Dr, Kapuskasing, Ontario P5N 1A7 **Tel:** 1 705 335-2283
Email: kaptimes.news@sunmedia.ca **Web site:** http://www.kapuskasingtimes.com
Circ: 15500
Language (s): French/Bilingual
COMMUNITY NEWSPAPER

Quebecor Communications - Sainte-Thérèse 714211
Owner: Quebecor Communications Inc.
Editorial: 214 Boul du Cure-Labelle Bureau 208, Sainte-Therese, Quebec J7E 2X7 **Tel:** 1 450 818-7575
Circ: 124000
Language (s): French
COMMUNITY NEWSPAPER

Red Deer Express 79776
Owner: Black Press
Editorial: #121, 5301-43 St., Red Deer, Alberta T4N 1C8 **Tel:** 1 403 346-3356
Email: express@reddeerexpress.com **Web site:** http://www.reddeerexpress.com
Freq: Wed; **Circ:** 24575 Not Audited
Production Manager: Russ Carr; **Publisher:** Tracey Scheveers; **Editor in Chief:** Mark Weber
Profile: Red Deer Express is a community newspaper that covers hometown news and features for Red Deer, Alberta.
Language (s): English
Ad Rate: Full Page Mono 21.00
Currency: Canada Dollars
COMMUNITY NEWSPAPER

Le Reflet 23993
Owner: TC Transcontinental
Editorial: 11 132 Rte, Delson, Quebec J5B 1G9
Tel: 1 450 635-9146
Email: del.redaction@tc.tc **Web site:** http://www.lereflet.qc.ca
Freq: Wed; **Circ:** 43084 Not Audited
Editor in Chief: Hélène Gingras
Profile: Le Reflet est un hebdomadaire francophone donnant dans les nouvelles et informations locales pour les habitants de Delson, Québec et des environs.

Le Reflet is a weekly French-language newspaper that covers local news and information in Delson, Quebec. Contact the publication by phone, fax, or mail.
Language (s): French
Ad Rate: Full Page Mono 6.86
Currency: Canada Dollars
COMMUNITY NEWSPAPER

Le Reflet du Lac 24002
Owner: TC. Transcontinental
Editorial: 53 Rue du Centre Bureau 300, Magog, Quebec J1X 5B6 **Tel:** 1 819 843-3500
Email: redaction.estrie@tc.tc **Web site:** http://www.lerefletdulac.com
Freq: Wed; **Circ:** 26311 Not Audited
Publisher: Monique Côté; **Editor in Chief:** Dany Jacques
Profile: Le Reflet du Lac est un hebdomadaire francophone destiné aux habitants de Magog et des environs. Le journal s'attarde aux nouvelles locales et régionales.

Le Reflet du Lac is a weekly French-language newspaper published for the residents of Magog, Quebec. The newspaper covers local and regional news.
Language (s): French
Ad Rate: Full Page Mono 7.14
Currency: Canada Dollars
COMMUNITY NEWSPAPER

Le Regional 23682
Owner: Les Publications du Patrimoine B.C.R. Inc.
Editorial: 124 rue Principale E, Hawkesbury, Ontario K6A 1A3 **Tel:** 1 613 632-0112
Email: news@le-regional.ca **Web site:** http://www.le-regional.ca/
Freq: Fri; **Circ:** 34484 Not Audited
Co-Publisher: Andre Cayer; **Editor in Chief:** Jeanette Perrault; **Co-Publisher:** Sylvain Roy
Profile: Le Regional is a community newspaper written for the residents of Hawkesbury, Ontario.
Language (s): French/Bilingual
Ad Rate: Full Page Mono 16.80
Currency: Canada Dollars
COMMUNITY NEWSPAPER

The Renfrew Mercury 30027
Owner: Metroland Media Group Ltd.
Editorial: 35 Opeongo Rd, Renfrew, Ontario K7V 2T2
Tel: 1 613 432-3655
Email: sherry.haaima@metroland.com **Web site:** http://www.insideottawavalley.com/renfrew-on
Freq: Thu; **Circ:** 15600 Not Audited
Profile: The Renfrew Mercury is a weekly newspaper serving residents of Renfrew and all areas between McNab/Braeside and Forrester Falls, Ontario. Coverage includes community news, events, schools, sports, business and features. * Please send press releases to News Editor Sherry Haaima sherry.haaima@metroland.com. *
Language (s): English
Ad Rate: Full Page Mono 3.92
Currency: Canada Dollars
COMMUNITY NEWSPAPER

Le Réseau des Échos 475521
Owner: Réseau des Échos du Nouveau Brunswick (Le)
Editorial: 8217 Rue St-Paul, Bas-Caraquet, New Brunswick E1W 6C4 **Tel:** 1 506 727-4749
Email: textes@echosnb.com **Web site:** http://www.canadamunicipal.ca
Freq: Monthly; **Circ:** 12800 Not Audited
Publisher: Brigitte Cladère; **Editor in Chief:** Gilles Gagné
Profile: Le Réseau des Échos is a French-language publisher in New Brunswick, Canada. It publishes nine community newspapers.
Language (s): French
Ad Rate: Full Page Mono 1890.00
Currency: Canada Dollars
COMMUNITY NEWSPAPER

La Revue 369946
Owner: TC. Transcontinental
Editorial: 1885 Rue Saint-Louis, Gatineau, Quebec J8T 6G4 **Tel:** 1 819 568-7544
Email: redaction.outaouais@tc.tc **Web site:** http://www.journallarevue.com
Freq: Wed; **Circ:** 90789 Not Audited
Publisher: Martin Godcher
Profile: La Revue est un journal hebdomadaire francophone déservant les résidents et les entreprises dans les villes de Hull, Gatineau dans la région de l'Outaouais, au Québec, Le contenu éditorial inclut les nouvelles locales, comprenant la politique locale, les affaires, les évènements, les arts et le divertissement, les sports et les reportages spéciaux.

La Revue is a French-language, weekly newspaper serving residents and businesses in Hull, Aylmer and Gatineau in the region of Outaouasis, QC. Editorial content includes in-depth community news, including local politics, businesses, events, legal news, arts and entertainment, sports and special reports.
Language (s): French
Ad Rate: Full Page Mono 16.52
Currency: Canada Dollars
COMMUNITY NEWSPAPER

Richmond News 23500
Owner: Glacier Media Inc.
Editorial: 5731 No 3 Rd, Richmond, British Columbia V6X 2C9 **Tel:** 1 604 270-8031
Email: editor@richmond-news.com **Web site:** http://www.richmond-news.com
Freq: Fri; **Circ:** 48000 Not Audited
Publisher: Pierre Pelletier
Profile: Richmond News is a weekly newspaper serving the town of Richmond, British Columbia. The publication provides local news, current events, sports, lifestyle and business.
Language (s): English
Ad Rate: Full Page Mono 14.56
Currency: Canada Dollars
COMMUNITY NEWSPAPER

Riverside Neighbours 24098
Owner: Brunswick News Inc.
Editorial: 984 Prospect Street, Fredericton, New Brunswick E3B 2T8 **Tel:** 1 506 452-6671
Email: northside@brunswicknews.com
Freq: Thu; **Circ:** 16000 Not Audited
Profile: Riverside Neighbours is a weekly community newspaper written for the residents of New Brunswick.
Language (s): English
Ad Rate: Full Page Mono 4.20
Currency: Canada Dollars
COMMUNITY NEWSPAPER

Road Today Express 772608
Owner: Road Today Publishing Inc.
Editorial: 1295 Shawson Drive, Ste 201, Mississauga, Ontario L4W 1C4 **Tel:** 1 905 487-1320
Email: contact@roadtodayexpress.com **Web site:** http://www.roadtodayexpress.com
Freq: Bi-Weekly
Editor: Manan Gupta
Profile: Road Today is a bi-weekly publication that covers the trucking industry with a special focus on the South Asian community in Ontario, Canada.
Language (s): English
COMMUNITY NEWSPAPER

Rocky Mountain Outlook 152974
Owner: Black Press
Editorial: 1001 6 Ave Suite 201, Canmore, Alberta T1W 3L8 **Tel:** 1 403 609-0220
Email: info@outlook.greatwest.ca **Web site:** http://www.rmoutlook.com
Freq: Thu; **Circ:** 15000 Not Audited
Publisher: Jason Lyon
Language (s): English
Ad Rate: Full Page Mono 4.70
Currency: Canada Dollars
COMMUNITY NEWSPAPER

Russian Express 82849
Owner: Russian-Canadian Press Inc.
Editorial: 1881 Steeles Ave W Suite 207A, North York, Ontario M3H 5Y4 **Tel:** 1 416 663-3999
Email: russianexpresstoronto@gmail.com **Web site:** http://www.russianexpress.net
Freq: Fri; **Circ:** 14000 Not Audited
Profile: The Russian Express is a Russian newspaper written for the residents of Ontario.
Language (s): English
Ad Rate: Full Page Mono 7.70
Currency: Canada Dollars
COMMUNITY NEWSPAPER

Russian Infotrade Ltd. 80704
Owner: Russian Infotrade Ltd.
Editorial: 5987 Bathurst St, Ste 108, Toronto, Ontario M2R 1Z3 **Tel:** 1 416 226-4777
Email: info@infogazeta.com **Web site:** http://www.russians.ca
Circ: 31300 Not Audited
Publisher & Editor: Boris Nusenbaum
Language (s): English
COMMUNITY NEWSPAPER

Sach Di Awaaz Newspaper 772710
Tel: 1 604 503-0840
Email: info@sachdiawaaz.ca **Web site:** http://www.sachdiawaa.ca
Freq: Fri; **Circ:** 50000
Profile: Sach Di Awaaz Newspaper is a free, weekly South Asian publication. Bi-lingual in Punjabi and English, Sach Di Awaaz is distributed Friday mornings throughout South Asian communities throughout BC and Alberta. Topics covered weekly range from politics and current events, to sports and lifestyle news. Many local and international columnists, journalists and contributors submit their articles for publication in Sach Di Awaaz.
Language (s): English
COMMUNITY NEWSPAPER

Sarnia & Lambton County This Week 23854
Owner: Postmedia Network Inc.
Editorial: 140 Front St N, Sarnia, Ontario N7T 5S3
Tel: 1 519 344-3641
Email: pepp@postmedia.com **Web site:** http://www.sarniathisweek.com
Freq: Thu; **Circ:** 40000 Not Audited
Publisher: Linda Leblanc
Profile: Sarnia & Lambton County This Week is a local newspaper for the residents of Sarnia, Bright's Grove, Point Edward and Corunna, Ontario. It covers local news, sports, features and opinion articles.
Language (s): English
Ad Rate: Full Page Mono 16.52
Currency: Canada Dollars
COMMUNITY NEWSPAPER

Sault This Week 23855
Owner: Postmedia Network Inc.
Editorial: 145 Old Garden River Road, Sault Ste. Marie, Ontario P6A 5M5 **Tel:** 1 705 759-3030
Email: FRupnik@postmedia.com **Web site:** http://www.saultthisweek.com
Freq: Wed; **Circ:** 32000 Not Audited
Profile: Sault This Week is a local community newspaper tailored for the residents of Sault Ste. Marie.
Language (s): English
Ad Rate: Full Page Mono 9.87
Currency: Canada Dollars
COMMUNITY NEWSPAPER

Scugog/Uxbridge Standard 713377
Owner: Scugog Standard Company Limited (The)
Editorial: 94A Water St, Port Perry, Ontario L9L 1J2
Tel: 1 905 985-6985
Email: office-standard@powergate.ca **Web site:** http://www.thestandardnewspaper.ca/
Circ: 14370
General Manager: Colleen Green; **Editor:** Darryl Knight; **General Manager:** Gayle Stapley
Profile: The Scugog/Uxbridge Standard covers news for Scugog, Uxbridge, Brock and Manvers, ON area. This independently owned newspaper offers local coverage of the news, politics, and sports. Their offices are located in Port Perry.
Language (s): English
COMMUNITY NEWSPAPER

Seaway News 23751
Owner: TC. Transcontinental
Editorial: 29 Second St E, Cornwall, Ontario K6H 1Y2
Tel: 1 613 933-0014
Email: editorial@cornwallseawaynews.com **Web site:** http://www.cornwallseawaynews.com
Freq: Thu; **Circ:** 36541 Not Audited
Publisher & Editor in Chief: Rick Shaver
Profile: Seaway News is a weekly newspaper written for the citizens of Cornwall, ON. The paper includes a French-language insert, called the Cornwall Express.
Language (s): English
Ad Rate: Full Page Mono 11.55
Currency: Canada Dollars
COMMUNITY NEWSPAPER

The Senior 652476
Tel: 1 306 525-8988
Email: info@theseniorpaper.com **Web site:** http://www.theseniorpaper.com
Freq: Monthly; **Circ:** 21497
Editor: Clay Stacey
Profile: The Senior is written for the senior citizen residents of Saskatchewan, Canada.
Language (s): English
Ad Rate: Full Page Mono 20.58
Currency: Canada Dollars
COMMUNITY NEWSPAPER

Shahrvand 80525
Owner: Shahrvand Publications Ltd.
Editorial: 505 Hwy. 7 unit 304, Thornhill, Ontario L3T 7T1 **Tel:** 1 905 764-7022
Email: news@shahrvand.com **Web site:** http://www.shahrvand.com
Freq: Thu; **Circ:** 12000 Not Audited
Editor in Chief: Hassan Zerehi
Profile: Shahrvand is written for Iranian residents in Downsview, Ontario. It covers news and events.
Language (s): Arabic
Ad Rate: Full Page Mono 3.00
Currency: Canada Dollars
COMMUNITY NEWSPAPER

Share 80210
Owner: MediaSpawn
Editorial: 658 Vaughan Rd, Toronto, Ontario M6E 2Y5 **Tel:** 1 416 656-3400
Email: share@interlog.com **Web site:** http://www.sharenews.com
Freq: Thu; **Circ:** 40000 Not Audited
Publisher & Editor in Chief: Arnold Auguste
Profile: Share is a weekly community newspaper published for the black and caribbean community of the greater Toronto area of Ontario, Canada.
Language (s): English
Ad Rate: Full Page Mono 33.32
Currency: Canada Dollars
COMMUNITY NEWSPAPER

Sherwood Park/Strathcona County News 23499
Owner: Postmedia Network Inc.
Editorial: 168 Kaska Rd, Sherwood Park, Alberta T8A 4G7 **Tel:** 1 780 464-0033
Email: spn.news@sunmedia.ca **Web site:** http://www.sherwoodparknews.com
Freq: Fri; **Circ:** 28000 Not Audited
Editor: Michael Di Massa; **Publisher:** Jean Figeat
Profile: Sherwood Park/Strathcona County News is written for the residents of Strathcona County, Alberta. It covers local news and events.
Language (s): English
Ad Rate: Full Page Mono 4.62
Currency: Canada Dollars
COMMUNITY NEWSPAPER

The Shoreline News 23960
Owner: Codner Holdings Ltd.
Tel: 1 709 834-2169
Email: tsnews@nf.aibn.com **Web site:** http://www.theshorelinenews.com
Freq: Fri; **Circ:** 16000
Publisher & Editor: Franklin Petten
Profile: Shoreline News provides news and information to the residents of Paradise and Conception Bay South, Newfoundland.
Language (s): English
Ad Rate: Full Page Mono 13.02
Ad Rate: Full Page Colour 700.00
Currency: Canada Dollars
COMMUNITY NEWSPAPER

Simcoe-York Printing & Publishing 25619
Owner: London Publishing Corp.
Editorial: 34 Main St W, Beeton, Ontario L0G 1A0
Tel: 1 905 729-2287
Email: admin.syp@rogers.com
Circ: 22300 Not Audited
News Editor: Breha Bartholet
Language (s): English
COMMUNITY NEWSPAPER

Sol Portugues/Portuguese Sun 80581
Owner: Sol Portugues Publishing Inc.
Editorial: 977 College St, Toronto, Ontario M6H 1A6
Tel: 1 416 538-1788
Email: sol@solnet.com **Web site:** http://www.solnet.com
Freq: Fri; **Circ:** 12000 Not Audited
Editor In Chief: Alice Perinu; **Publisher & Director:** Antonio Perinu
Profile: Sol Portugues is a weekly paper serving the Portugues speaking population in Toronto, Ontario. It is published every Friday.
Language (s): English
Ad Rate: Full Page Mono 11.41
Currency: Canada Dollars
COMMUNITY NEWSPAPER

South Asian Focus 483628
Owner: Metroland Media Group Ltd.
Editorial: 3145 Wolfedale Rd, Mississauga, Ontario L5C 3A9· **Tel:** 1 905 273-8111
Email: newsroom@bramptonguardian.com **Web site:** http://www.southasianfocus.ca/saf/
Freq: Fri; **Circ:** 24000 Not Audited
Profile: South Asian Focus is a weekly newspaper written for the south asian community of Brampton and Mississauga, Ontario.
Language (s): English
Ad Rate: Full Page Mono 9.29
Currency: Canada Dollars
COMMUNITY NEWSPAPER

South Asian Observer   593167

Owner: Global Media Network
Editorial: 29-5160 Explorer Dr 29, Mississauga, Ontario L4W 4T7 **Tel:** 1 905 612-7281
Email: info@southasianobserver.com **Web site:** http://www.southasianobserver.com
Freq: Fri; **Circ:** 32000
Publisher: Jaspal Shetra
Profile: South Asian Observer is a weekly newspaper printed for South Asian Canadians.
Language (s): English
Ad Rate: Full Page Mono 22.40
Currency: Canada Dollars
COMMUNITY NEWSPAPER

South Asian Post   535902

Owner: Post Group Multimedia Inc
Editorial: 2953-349 Georgia St W 2953, Vancouver, British Columbia V6B 0N2 **Tel:** 1 778 996-3631
Email: editor@postpeopleinc.com **Web site:** http://www.southasianpost.com
Freq: Thu; **Circ:** 25000 Not Audited
Editor & Advertising Sales Manager: Jagdeesh Mann; **Publisher:** Harbinder Sewak
Profile: South Asian Post is a weekly newspaper written for the South Asian community in Canada, including Indo-Canadians, East Indians, Punjabis, Pakistanis, Bangladeshis, Fijians and Tamils. It was established in 2005.
Language (s): English
Ad Rate: Full Page Mono 26.59
Ad Rate: Full Page Colour 350.00
Currency: Canada Dollars
COMMUNITY NEWSPAPER

South Asian Star   772718

Editorial: 1295 Shawson Dr Suite 201, Mississauga, Ontario L4W 1C4 **Tel:** 1 905 487-1320
Email: contact@southasianstar.com **Web site:** http://southasianstar.com
Freq: Bi-Weekly
Publisher & Editor: Manan Gupta
Profile: South Asian Star is a bi-weekly publication that covers multicultural events and news for the Indian community in Brampton, Canada.
Language (s): English
COMMUNITY NEWSPAPER

South Asian Vision   772721

Owner: Grewal (Jagdish)
Editorial: 27 Armthorpe Rd., Unit #3, Brampton, Ontario L6T 5M4 **Tel:** 1 905 793-2202
Email: news@punjabipost.ca **Web site:** http://punjabipost.ca
Freq: Weekly; **Circ:** 25000
Editor: Jagdish Grewal
Profile: South Asian Vision is a Weekly publication that covers multicultural events and news for the South Asian community in Brampton, Canada. The Canadian Punjabi Post is distributed throughout GTA particularly at points of interface where South Asian community frequents. The cities of Brampton, Mississauga, Scarborough, Markham, Rexdale, North York and large parts of Toronto city are directly served by the Canadian Punjabi Post. More than 25,000 copies are published six days a week.
Language (s): English
Ad Rate: Full Page Mono 16.80
Currency: Canada Dollars
COMMUNITY NEWSPAPER

South Side Story   23908

Owner: South Side Story Inc.
Editorial: 2140 Regent St Unit 10, Sudbury, Ontario P3E 5S8 **Tel:** 1 705 523-2339
Email: southsidestory@eastlink.ca
Freq: Monthly; **Circ:** 36000 Not Audited
Editor in Chief: Monika Berens; **Publisher:** Colin Firth
Profile: South Side Story is a monthly community newspaper written for the residents of Sudbury, Ontario.
Language (s): English
Ad Rate: Full Page Mono 24.43
Currency: Canada Dollars
COMMUNITY NEWSPAPER

Southern Exposure   23470

Owner: Continental Newspapers Canada Ltd.
Editorial: 186 Nanaimo Ave W Suite 101, Penticton, British Columbia V2A 1N4 **Tel:** 1 250 492-4002
Email: editor@pentictonherald.ca
Freq: Thu; **Circ:** 46885 Not Audited
Publisher: Andre Martin
Profile: Southern Exposure is a free, bi-weekly newspaper serving the residents of the Okanangan region, including Penticton, British Columbia. It contains community news, events, sports, local features and editorials.
Language (s): English
Ad Rate: Full Page Mono 9.10
Currency: Canada Dollars
COMMUNITY NEWSPAPER

Southwest Booster   29928

Owner: TC. Transcontinental
Editorial: 30 4th Ave NW, Swift Current, Saskatchewan S9H 0T5 **Tel:** 1 306 773-9321
Email: boosternews@swbooster.com **Web site:** http://www.swbooster.com
Freq: Thu; **Circ:** 16729 Not Audited
Publisher: Bob Watson
Profile: Southwest Booster is a community newspaper publisher for the residents of Swift Current, Saskatchewan and the surrounding areas. It covers local news, sports and events. Deadlines are on Tuesdays.
Language (s): English

Ad Rate: Full Page Mono 7.84
Ad Rate: Full Page Colour 385.00
Currency: Canada Dollars
COMMUNITY NEWSPAPER

Lo Specchio/The Italian Weekly   80491

Editorial: 160 Woodbridge Ave Suite 101, Woodbridge, Ontario L4L 0B8 **Tel:** 1 905 856-2823
Email: editorial@lospecchio.com **Web site:** http://www.lospecchio.com
Freq: Fri; **Circ:** 20000 Not Audited
Profile: Lo Specchio/The Italian Weekly is written for Canadians of Italian heritage.
Language (s): English
Ad Rate: Full Page Mono 35.70
Currency: Canada Dollars
COMMUNITY NEWSPAPER

Spotlight West Grey   800261

Owner: Metroland Media Group Ltd.
Editorial: 277 Main St., Mount Forest, Ontario N0G 2L0 **Tel:** 1 519 881-1600
Email: jzettel@walkerton.com
Freq: Monthly
Profile: West Grey Progress is a monthly community newspaper saluting the businesses, services and citizens of The Municipality of West Grey. Coverage areas include The Municipality of West Grey including the towns of Ayton, Durham, Elmwood, and Neustadt.
Language (s): English
COMMUNITY NEWSPAPER

Springwater News   375929

Editorial: 9 Glenview Ave, Elmvale, Ontario L0L 1P0 **Tel:** 1 705 322-2249
Email: springwaternews@rogers.com **Web site:** http://www.springwaternews.ca/
Freq: Bi-Weekly; **Circ:** 15400 Not Audited
Publisher & Editor: Michael Jacobs
Profile: Springwater News is a Local Community Newspaper written for the residents of Elmvale, Ontario. It covers local news and events. Deadlines are on Mondays.
Language (s): English
Ad Rate: Full Page Mono 9.85
Currency: Canada Dollars
COMMUNITY NEWSPAPER

St. Albert Gazette   23396

Owner: Great West Newspapers LP
Editorial: 25 Chisholm Ave, Saint Albert, Alberta T8N 5A5 **Tel:** 1 780 460-5500
Email: gazette@stalbert.greatwest.ca **Web site:** http://www.stalbertgazette.com
Freq: Sat; **Circ:** 27093 Not Audited
Publisher: Brian Bachynski
Profile: St. Albert Gazette is written for the residents of St. Albert, Morinville, Bon Accord, Legal and the County of Sturgeon in Alberta. It covers local news and information.
Language (s): English
Ad Rate: Full Page Mono 14.42
Ad Rate: Full Page Colour 300.00
Currency: Canada Dollars
COMMUNITY NEWSPAPER

The St. Thomas/Elgin Weekly News   727493

Owner: Metroland Media Group
Editorial: 15 St. Catharine Street, Saint Thomas, Ontario N5P 2V7 **Tel:** 1 519 633-1640
Email: geoffreyrae@metroland.com **Web site:** http://www.theweeklynews.ca
Freq: Thu; **Circ:** 30565
Editor: Dorothy Gebert
Profile: St. Thomas/Elgin Weekly News is a local community newspaper for the residents of St. Thomas, Ontario and the surrounding communities.
Language (s): English
COMMUNITY NEWSPAPER

Star News Ltd.   25588

Owner: Star News Inc.
Editorial: 1027 3 Ave, Wainwright, Alberta T9W 1T6 **Tel:** 1 780 842-4465
Email: roger@starpress.ca **Web site:** http://www.starnews.ca
Circ: 17918 Not Audited
Editor: Kelly Clemmer; **Publisher:** Roger Holmes
Language (s): English
COMMUNITY NEWSPAPER

StarBuzz Weekly   772732

Editorial: 1022 Zante Cres, Mississauga, Ontario L5J 4M8 **Tel:** 1 647 802-2899
Email: starbuzz.ca@gmail.com **Web site:** http://www.starbuzz.ca
Freq: Weekly; **Circ:** 20000
Publisher: Meena Chopra; **Editor:** Tia Virdi
Profile: StarBuzz is a weekly publication that covers multicultural events, news, entertainment topics and gossip from Bollywood.
Language (s): English
Ad Rate: Full Page Mono 22.66
Currency: Canada Dollars
COMMUNITY NEWSPAPER

Stonewall Newspapers   25613

Owner: Postmedia Network Inc.
Editorial: 486 Main St, Stonewall, Manitoba R0C 2Z0 **Tel:** 1 204 467-2421
Email: bjones@postmedia.com

Circ: 34639 Not Audited
Language (s): English
COMMUNITY NEWSPAPER

Stouffville Free Press   408102

Editorial: 6111 Main St, Stouffville, Ontario L4A 3R4 **Tel:** 1 905 640-3733
Email: info@stouffville.com **Web site:** http://www.stouffville.com/stouffville-free-press/
Freq: Monthly; **Circ:** 11700 Not Audited
Editor in Chief: Kate Gilderdale
Profile: Stouffville Free Press is a free, monthly newspaper serving residents of Whitchurch-Stouffville, Ontario. It covers local news, human interest stories, sports, features and community events.
Language (s): English
Ad Rate: Full Page Mono 9.82
Ad Rate: Full Page Colour 75.00
Currency: Canada Dollars
COMMUNITY NEWSPAPER

Stratford Gazette   82872

Owner: Metroland Media Group Ltd.
Editorial: 10 Downie St Unit 207, Stratford, Ontario N5A 7K4 **Tel:** 1 519 271-8002
Email: news@stratfordgazette.com **Web site:** http://www.ourperth.ca/stratford-on
Freq: Thu; **Circ:** 19000 Not Audited
Profile: The Stratford Gazette is a weekly community newspaper for the residents of Stratford, Ontario and the surrounding communities.
Language (s): English
Ad Rate: Full Page Mono 7.35
Currency: Canada Dollars
COMMUNITY NEWSPAPER

Strathmore Times   735438

Editorial: 202-114 Canal Gdns 202, Strathmore, Alberta T1P 1Y4 **Tel:** 1 403 934-5589
Email: info@strathmoretimes.com **Web site:** http://www.strathmoretimes.com
Freq: Fri; **Circ:** 12000
Publisher & Editor: Mario Prusina
Profile: Strathmore Times is a community newspaper for the residents of Strathmore, Alberta and the surrounding areas.
Ad Rate: Full Page Mono 7.95
Ad Rate: Full Page Colour 9.45
Currency: Canada Dollars
COMMUNITY NEWSPAPER

Streeter Publications   25648

Owner: Streeter Publications
Editorial: 46 St. Clair Ave E Suite 204, Toronto, Ontario M4T 1M9 **Tel:** 1 416 901-8182
Email: news@mytowncrier.ca **Web site:** http://www.mytowncrier.ca
Circ: 327242 Not Audited
Profile: Streeter Publications is a community newspaper publisher servicing the residents of Toronto.
Language (s): English
COMMUNITY NEWSPAPER

The Suburban   364694

Owner: Sochaczevski
Editorial: 7575 Transcanadienne Rte Suite 105, Saint-Laurent, Quebec H4T 1V6 **Tel:** 1 514 484-1107
Email: editor@thesuburban.com **Web site:** http://www.thesuburban.com
Circ: 140000 Not Audited
Publisher: Michael Sochaczevski; **Editor in Chief:** Beryl Wajsman
Profile: The Suburban est le plus grand hebdomadaire anglophone du Québec avec un tirage de 145 000 copies.

_____
_____
_____
_____
_____
_____
_____
_____
_____
_____

The Suburban is the largest English-language weekly newspaper in Quebec with a print circulation of 145,000 copies.
Language (s): English
Ad Rate: Full Page Colour 64.68
Currency: Canada Dollars
COMMUNITY NEWSPAPER

Sunday Post   23579

Owner: Postmedia Network Inc.
Editorial: 1964 Park St, Regina, Saskatchewan S4P 3G4 **Tel:** 1 306 781-5211
Email: citydesk@leaderpost.com **Web site:** http://www.leaderpost.com
Freq: Sun
Profile: Sunday Post is a tabloid sized, total market supplement, highlighting local topics and events within a 70 mile radius of Regina including Moose Jaw, Weyburn and Assiniboia. Deadlines are 4:30pm Tuesdays.
Language (s): English
Ad Rate: Full Page Mono 35.70
Currency: Canada Dollars
COMMUNITY NEWSPAPER

The Surrey Now-Leader   23553

Owner: Black Press
Editorial: 102-5460 152 St 102, Surrey, British Columbia V3S 5J9 **Tel:** 1 604 572-0064
Email: edit@thenownewspaper.com **Web site:** http://www.surreynowleader.com/e-editions
Freq: Fri; **Circ:** 82530 Not Audited
Profile: The Surrey Now-Leader is a twice-weekly newspaper published for residents of the Surrey and North Delta, British Columbia communities. The publication reports local news, events, politics, sports and arts & entertainment.
Language (s): English
Ad Rate: Full Page Mono 41.44
Currency: Canada Dollars
COMMUNITY NEWSPAPER

Suthanthiran   773274

Editorial: 780 Ellesmere Rd, Scarborough, Ontario M1P 2W4 **Tel:** 1 416 840-9752
Email: thesuthanthiran@gmail.com
Freq: Weekly
Editor: Gnanachelvan Chelliah
Profile: Suthanthiran is a weekly publication that covers multicultural events and news for the Indian community in Scarborough, Canada.
Language (s): Tamil
COMMUNITY NEWSPAPER

Swadesh   773033

Editorial: 713 Markham Rd, Scarborough, Ontario M1H 2A8 **Tel:** 1 416 996-7755
Email: info@swadesh.news **Web site:** http://swadesh.news/
Freq: Weekly; **Circ:** 10000
Editor: Manoj Gandhi
Profile: Swadesh is a weekly Gujarati publication that covers multicultural events and news for the Indian community in Canada. Swadesh also has an office in India.
Language (s): Gujarati
COMMUNITY NEWSPAPER

Sylvan Lake Newspapers   25591

Owner: Alberta Newspaper Group Inc.
Editorial: 5020-50A St #103, Sylvan Lake, Alberta T4S 1R2 **Tel:** 1 403 887-2331
Email: admin@sylvanlakenews.com **Web site:** http://www.sylvanlakenews.com
Circ: 75295 Not Audited
Editor in Chief: Steve Dills
Language (s): English
COMMUNITY NEWSPAPER

Take 5 Newsmagazine   82877

Owner: 541806 BC LTD.
Editorial: 622 First Ave, Ladysmith, British Columbia V9G 1A1 **Tel:** 1 250 245-7015
Email: info@take5.ca **Web site:** http://www.take5.ca
Freq: Monthly; **Circ:** 13500 Not Audited
Profile: Publication mailed directly to Central Vancouver Island community's homes.
Language (s): English
Ad Rate: Full Page Mono 5.09
Ad Rate: Full Page Colour 79.00
Currency: Canada Dollars
COMMUNITY NEWSPAPER

TC. Transcontinental - Ottawa   25639

Owner: TC. Transcontinental
Editorial: 5300 Canotek Road, Unit 30, Ottawa, Ontario K1J 8R7 **Tel:** 1 613 744-4800
Email: redaction.ontario@transcontinental.ca **Web site:** http://www.eastottawa.ca
Freq: Weekly; **Circ:** 108096 Not Audited
Editor & Publisher: Madeleine Joanisse
Language (s): English, French
COMMUNITY NEWSPAPER

TC. Transcontinental - Val-d'Or   532498

Owner: TC. Transcontinental
Editorial: 1462 Rue de la Quebecoise, Val-d'Or, Quebec J9P 5H4
Email: redaction.abitibi@tc.tc **Web site:** http://www.lechoabitibien.ca
Freq: Weekly; **Circ:** 35276 Not Audited
News Editor: Marc-André Landry; **Advertising Manager:** Sabrina Lemay
Profile: Transcontinental Val-d'Or publie ces trois hebdomadaires couvrant ainsi toute la région de Val D'Or: L'Écho Abitibien, Le Citoyen de la Vallée-de-l'Or et Le Citoyen de l'Harricana.

_____
_____
_____
_____
_____
_____
_____
_____

Transcontinental - Val-d'Or publishes three French-language weeklies that cover local news for residents of Val-d'Or, a city in northern Quebec: L'Écho Abitibien, Le Citoyen de la Vallée-de-l'Or and Le Citoyen de l'Harricana.
Language (s): French
COMMUNITY NEWSPAPER

Thamilar Senthamarai 82856
Owner: Thamilar Senthamarai Publication Ltd.
Editorial: 3351 Markham Rd, markham east plaza a, Scarborough, Ontario M1X 0A6 **Tel:** 1 416 291-0220
Email: thamilars@aol.com **Web site:** http://senthamarai.ca/
Freq: Fri; **Circ:** 10300 Not Audited
Publisher & Director: Prem Arasaratnam; **Editor:** Ragee Arasaratnam
Profile: Thamilar Senthamarai Formerly "Senthamarai" publishes global news with an emphasis on Sri Lankan, Canadian and South Indian coverage. It also features stories on cinema and sports.
Language (s): English
Ad Rate: Full Page Mono 2.80
Currency: Canada Dollars
COMMUNITY NEWSPAPER

The Chinese Journal - Edmonton 875094
Owner: CC Times
Editorial: #222 9700-105 AVE, Edmonton, Alberta T5H 4J1 **Tel:** 1 780 424-0213
Email: chinesejournal@telusplanet.net **Web site:** http://www.thechinesejournal.com/
General Manager: Harry C
Profile: Covers national news, world news, entertainment, health and lifestyle.
COMMUNITY NEWSPAPER

The The Community Press 693825
Owner: Anderson (Kerry)
Editorial: 4925-47 Street, Sedgewick, Alberta T0B 4C0 **Tel:** 1 780 384-3641
Email: news@thecommunitypress.com **Web site:** http://thecommunitypress.com
Circ: 37900
Publisher: Eric Anderson; **Editor:** Leslie Cholowsky
Profile: The Community Press is the primary newspaper serving Flagstaff County, in East Central Alberta, covering the 10 municipalities within. The Community Press publishes primarily local news, and explores local angles to national and provincial news items.
Language (s): English
COMMUNITY NEWSPAPER

The The Daily Courier 849513
Owner: Postmedia
Editorial: 550 Doyle Ave, Kelowna, British Columbia V1Y 7V1- **Tel:** 1 250 763-4000
Email: csr@ok.bc.ca **Web site:** http://www.kelownadailycourier.ca
Freq: Sat; **Circ:** 20715
Publisher: Terry Armstrong
Profile: The Okanagan Saturday and Okanagan Sunday are distributed Saturday and Sunday to both the Kelowna (The Daily Courier) and Penticton (The Penticton Herald) markets. The papers cover weekend news and entertainment. The circulation for the Saturday edition is 20,715. The circulation for the Sunday edition is 19,419.
Language (s): English
Ad Rate: Full Page Mono 38.54
Ad Rate: Full Page Colour 43.81
Currency: Canada Dollars
COMMUNITY NEWSPAPER

Thoi Bao 82962
Owner: Thoi Bao Inc.
Editorial: 1114 College St, Toronto, Ontario M6H 1B6 **Tel:** 1 416 925-8607
Email: contributions@thoibao.com **Web site:** http://www.thoibao.com
Freq: Thu; **Circ:** 14500 Not Audited
Publisher & Editor in Chief: Dave Nguyen
Profile: Thoi Bao is a community newspaper for the Vietnamese community in Toronto. It features Vietnamese news, stories, poems and entertainment.
Language (s): English
Ad Rate: Full Page Mono 8.09
Currency: Canada Dollars
COMMUNITY NEWSPAPER

The Thornhill Liberal 23844
Owner: Metroland Media Group Ltd.
Editorial: 580B Steven Crt, Newmarket, Ontario L3Y 6Z2- **Tel:** 1 905 294-2200
Email: newsroom@yrmg.com **Web site:** http://www.yorkregion.com/thornhill-on
Freq: Thu; **Circ:** 74850 Not Audited
Profile: The Thornhill Liberal is a weekly community newspaper for the residents of Thornhill, Ontario.
Language (s): English
Ad Rate: Full Page Mono 24.99
Currency: Canada Dollars
COMMUNITY NEWSPAPER

Thunder Bay Source 23945
Owner: Dougall Media
Editorial: 87 Hill St N, Thunder Bay, Ontario P7A 5V6 **Tel:** 1 807 346-2600
Email: ldunick@dougallmedia.com **Web site:** http://www.tbnewswatch.com
Freq: Thu; **Circ:** 44500
Profile: Thunder Bay's Source covers local news, sports and entertainment. It also reports on Northwestern Ontario and Canada.
Language (s): English
Ad Rate: Full Page Mono 20.86
Currency: Canada Dollars
COMMUNITY NEWSPAPER

Timmins Times 23959
Owner: Postmedia Network Inc.
Editorial: 187 Cedar St S, Timmins, Ontario P4N 2G9 **Tel:** 1 705 268-5050
Email: timmins.times@sunmedia.ca **Web site:** http://www.timminstimes.com
Freq: Weekly; **Circ:** 16478
Profile: Timmins Times is a weekly newspaper covering local news and information for Timmins, Ontario and its environs.
Language (s): English
Ad Rate: Full Page Mono 17.36
Currency: Canada Dollars
COMMUNITY NEWSPAPER

Tour of Duty 711869
Tel: 1 902 468-5141
Email: nwpsales@gmail.com
Freq: Bi-Monthly; **Circ:** 18000
Editor: William Harris; **General Manager:** Ross McQuarrie
Profile: Tour of Duty is local newspaper for active duty military personnel, veterans and their families.
Language (s): English
Ad Rate: Full Page Mono 12.39
Currency: Canada Dollars
COMMUNITY NEWSPAPER

Town & Country 29868
Owner: Great West Newspapers LP
Editorial: 9871 - 107 Street, Westlock, Alberta T7P 1R9 **Tel:** 1 780 349-3033
Email: production@westlock.greatwest.ca
Freq: Tue; **Circ:** 16800 Not Audited
Editor in Chief: Kevin Berger; **Publisher:** George Blais
Profile: Town & Country provides news and information to the residents of Westlock, Alberta.
Language (s): English
Ad Rate: Full Page Mono 11.90
Currency: Canada Dollars
COMMUNITY NEWSPAPER

Tremblant Express 774990
Editorial: 2046-2 Chemin du Village, Mont-Tremblant, Quebec J8E 1K4 **Tel:** 1 819 425-7875
Web site: http://www.tremblantexpress.com
Freq: Monthly; **Circ:** 30000
Profile: Tremblant Express is a monthly newspaper providing Local and Community News coverage for Mont-Tremblant, QC.
Language (s): English
COMMUNITY NEWSPAPER

Tri-City News 23536
Owner: Glacier Media Inc.
Editorial: 1405 Broadway St, Port Coquitlam, British Columbia V3C 6L6 **Tel:** 1 604 525-6397
Email: newsroom@tricitynews.com **Web site:** http://www.tricitynews.com
Freq: Fri; **Circ:** 52324 Not Audited
Editor in Chief: Richard Dal Monte; **Publisher:** Nigel Lark
Profile: Tri-City News is written for the tri-city area of Coquitlam Port, Port Moody, Anmore and Belcarra, British Columbia.
Language (s): English
Ad Rate: Full Page Mono 17.15
Ad Rate: Full Page Colour 775.00
Currency: Canada Dollars
COMMUNITY NEWSPAPER

Trident 24108
Owner: Department of National Defense
Editorial: 2740 Barrington St, Halifax, Nova Scotia B3K 2X3 **Tel:** 1 902 427-4235
Email: accounts@tridentnews.ca **Web site:** http://www.tridentnews.ca
Freq: Bi-Weekly; **Circ:** 10000 Not Audited
Editor: Virginia Beaton
Profile: Trident is a bi-weekly publication covering news and issues of interest to the Canadian Navy's East Coast fleet based in Halifax, Nova Scotia. It includes articles and columns from both military and civilian members.
Language (s): French/Bilingual
Ad Rate: Full Page Mono 16.10
Currency: Canada Dollars
COMMUNITY NEWSPAPER

True Buddha News 80274
Owner: True Buddha School
Editorial: 200-357 Hastings St., Vancouver, British Columbia V6A 1P3 **Tel:** 1 604 685-5548
Email: tbnnews@gmail.com **Web site:** http://www.wtbn.org
Freq: Thu
Editor: Marvin Lu; **Publisher:** M.J. Pai
Profile: True Buddha News covers current news including local and international. Features Buddhism Dharma teachings.
Language (s): Chinese
Ad Rate: Full Page Mono 45.00
Currency: Canada Dollars
COMMUNITY NEWSPAPER

Turtle Island News 80166
Owner: Turtle Island News Pub.
Editorial: 2208 Chiefswood Rd, Ohsweken, Ontario N0A 1M0 **Tel:** 1 519 445-0868
Email: news@theturtleislandnews.com **Web site:** http://www.theturtleislandnews.com
Freq: Wed; **Circ:** 10000 Not Audited
Publisher & Editor: Lynda Powless
Profile: Turtle Island News is a community newspaper written for the residents of Ohsweken, Ontario. The paper covers politics, local news, sports, national native news featuring aboriginal headlines from across Canada and a classified section. Deadlines are on Fridays at 5pm ET.
Language (s): English
Ad Rate: Full Page Mono 2.12
Currency: Canada Dollars
COMMUNITY NEWSPAPER

Two Row Times 880501
Editorial: 657 Mohawk Rd, Hagersville, Ontario N0A 1H0 **Tel:** 1 519 900-5535
Email: tworowtimes@gmail.com **Web site:** http://tworowtimes.com
Freq: Weekly; **Circ:** 20000
Publisher: Jonathan Garlow; **Editor in Chief:** Tom Keefer
Profile: The Two Row Times is a weekly print news publication distributed throughout Ontario, Quebec and New York State.
Language (s): English
Ad Rate: Full Page Mono 9.67
Ad Rate: Full Page Colour 12.57
Currency: Canada Dollars
COMMUNITY NEWSPAPER

Ulahathamilar 82971
Owner: World Tamil Movement of Ont.
Editorial: 39 Cosentino Dr, Toronto, Ontario M1P 3A3 **Tel:** 1 416 461-5991
Email: editor@worldtamils.com **Web site:** http://www.worldtamils.com
Freq: Fri; **Circ:** 30000 Not Audited
Publisher & Editor: Kamal Nava
Profile: Ulahathamilar is Community Newspaper based in Toronto that covers Ethnic & Multicultural.
Language (s): English
Ad Rate: Full Page Mono 15.00
Currency: Canada Dollars
COMMUNITY NEWSPAPER

Urdu Post 772967
Email: canurdu@gmail.com **Web site:** http://www.urdupost.info
Freq: Weekly; **Circ:** 22000
Editor-in-Chief: Fayyaz Walana
Profile: Urdu Post is a -weekly publication that covers multicultural events and news for the Indian community in Mississauga, Canada.
Language (s): English
Ad Rate: Full Page Mono 44.44
Currency: Canada Dollars
COMMUNITY NEWSPAPER

Urdu Times Canada 772971
Editorial: 1310 Mid-Way Blvd Unit 28, Mississauga, Ontario L5T 2K5 **Tel:** 1 905 673-7111
Email: urdutimes@gondalbrothers.com **Web site:** http://www.urdutimescanada.com
Freq: Weekly; **Circ:** 18000
Editor: Mohammad Azam Gondal
Profile: Urdu Times Canada is a weekly publication that covers multicultural events and news for the South Asian community in Mississauga, Canada.
Ad Rate: Full Page Mono 8.82
Currency: Canada Dollars
COMMUNITY NEWSPAPER

Uxbridge Times-Journal 23845
Owner: Metroland Media Group Ltd.
Editorial: 16 Bascom St, Uxbridge, Ontario L9P 1J3 **Tel:** 1 905 852-9141
Email: newsroom@durhamregion.com **Web site:** http://www.durhamregion.com/uxbridge-on/
Freq: Thu; **Circ:** 10500 Not Audited
Profile: Uxbridge Times-Journal is a community newspaper for the residents of Uxbridge, Ontario. It covers local news, sports, entertainment and community events.
Language (s): English
Ad Rate: Full Page Mono 8.40
Currency: Canada Dollars
COMMUNITY NEWSPAPER

The Valley Gazette 810915
Owner: Lavigne (Michel)
Editorial: 19574 Opeongo Line, Barry's Bay, Ontario K0J 1B0 **Tel:** 1 613 756-0256
Email: christine@thevalleygazette.ca **Web site:** http://valleygazette.ca/
Freq: Weekly
Publisher & Advertising Sales Manager: Michel Lavigne; **Editor:** Gregory Zawidzki
Profile: The Valley Gazette is a weekly community newspaper serving the residents of Whitney, Pembroke, Barry's Bay, and Bancroft in Ontario, Canada. It covers local and regional news, sports, events and opinion. The publication began printing in May 2010.
Language (s): English
COMMUNITY NEWSPAPER

Vancouver Chinese News 82973
Owner: Chinese News Ltd.
Editorial: 1296 Kingsway, Vancouver, British Columbia V5V 3E1 **Tel:** 1 604 872-6968
Email: vancouverchinesenews@yahoo.ca
Freq: Weekly; **Circ:** 50000 Not Audited
Editor & Publisher: Shing Pao
Language (s): Chinese
COMMUNITY NEWSPAPER

The Vancouver Courier 23556
Owner: Glacier Media Inc.
Editorial: 303 5th Ave W, Vancouver, British Columbia V5Y 1J6 **Tel:** 1 604 738-1411
Email: events@vancourier.com **Web site:** http://www.vancourier.com
Freq: Thu; **Circ:** 103700 Not Audited
Profile: The Vancouver Courier is a weekly, standard sized newspaper for the residents of Vancouver, British Columbia. The publication concentrates specifically on local news and public affairs. The main sections are Local News, Opinions, Entertainment (with a strong focus on theater), Dining - which is mainly local restaurant reviews and Sports. The Vancouver Courier is published in separate editions on Thursday: one edition is for residents of Eastern Vancouver, and one edition is for residents of Western Vancouver. The paper's reporters and editors have individually won numerous local and national journalism awards. Cumulatively, the publication has received two awards for best British Columbia Community newspaper.
Language (s): English
Ad Rate: Full Page Mono 37.94
Currency: Canada Dollars
COMMUNITY NEWSPAPER

Vancouver Express 903601
Owner: Alexander Kulyashov
Editorial: 260 Terminal Ave, Vancouver, British Columbia V6A 2L4 **Tel:** 1 604 729-3590
Email: vancouverexpress@shaw.ca **Web site:** http://www.vancouverexpress.ca
Freq: Bi-Monthly
Publisher & Editor: Alexander Kulyashov
Profile: A Russian language newspaper.
Language (s): Russian
COMMUNITY NEWSPAPER

Vaughan Citizen 82975
Owner: Metroland Media Group Ltd.
Editorial: 580B Steven Crt, Newmarket, Ontario L3Y 6Z2- **Tel:** 1 905 264-8703
Email: newsroom@yrmg.com **Web site:** http://www.yorkregion.com/vaughan-on/
Freq: Thu; **Circ:** 53000 Not Audited
Profile: Vaughan Citizen is a weekly community newspaper published for the residents of Vaughan, Ontario. It covers local news and sales, classifieds, entertainment and community events.
Language (s): English
Ad Rate: Full Page Mono 24.26
Currency: Canada Dollars
COMMUNITY NEWSPAPER

Vegreville News Advertiser 23506
Owner: Vegreville News Advertiser Ltd.
Editorial: 5110 50 Ave, Vegreville, Alberta T9C 1M1 **Tel:** 1 780 632-2861
Email: editor@newsadvertiser.com **Web site:** http://www.newsadvertiser.com
Freq: Weekly; **Circ:** 11717 Not Audited
General Manager: Arthur Beaudette; **Publisher & Editor:** Dan Beaudette; **Production Manager:** Rachel Farr
Profile: Vegreville News Advertiser is a weekly newspaper for the residents of Vegreville, Alberta.
Language (s): English
Ad Rate: Full Page Mono 12.74
Currency: Canada Dollars
COMMUNITY NEWSPAPER

Victoria News 29864
Owner: Black Press
Editorial: 818 Broughton St, Victoria, British Columbia V8W 1E4- **Tel:** 1 250 381-3484
Email: editor@vicnews.com **Web site:** http://www.vicnews.com
Freq: Fri; **Circ:** 23341 Not Audited
Publisher: Penny Sakamoto
Profile: Victoria News is a comprehensive source for Victoria, British Columbia local news, community events and issues. The paper covers breaking news, provincial issues and the law, local sports, classified ads, entertainment and obituaries.
Language (s): English
Ad Rate: Full Page Mono 24.92
Currency: Canada Dollars
COMMUNITY NEWSPAPER

Vision 23849
Owner: Cie d'Édition André Paquette Inc. (La)
Editorial: 1315 Rue Laurier, Rockland, Ontario K4K 1C8 **Tel:** 1 613 446-6456
Email: nouvelles@eap.on.ca **Web site:** http://www.visionrockland.ca
Freq: Fri; **Circ:** 23100 Not Audited
Publisher: Bertrand Castonguay; **General Manager:** Roger Duplantie
Profile: Journal Vision Prescott/Russell is a weekly community newspaper.

Le Journal Vision est un hebdomadaire communautaire bilingue.
Language (s): French/Bilingual
Ad Rate: Full Page Mono 16.38
Ad Rate: Full Page Colour 500.00

Currency: Canada Dollars
COMMUNITY NEWSPAPER

VISTAS 82977
Editorial: 312 Cunningham Avenue, Ottawa, Ontario K1H 6B4 **Tel:** 1 613 737-3835
Email: ctower@sympatico.ca
Freq: Monthly; **Circ:** 12000 Not Audited
Editor in Chief: Celine Tower
Profile: Vistas is a local newspaper written for the residents of Ottawa.
Language (s): English
Ad Rate: Full Page Mono 5.11
Currency: Canada Dollars
COMMUNITY NEWSPAPER

The Voice 23899
Owner: The Voice
Editorial: 26 Erindale Ave, Toronto, Ontario M4K 1R9
Tel: 1 647 838-2126
Email: voclara@yahoo.ca
Freq: Monthly; **Circ:** 28000
Publisher & Editor: Colin Grant
Profile: The Voice is written for the residents of the East Downtown and West Riverdale neighborhoods of Toronto. It covers local news and events. Deadlines for contributions are on the 25th of each month prior to issue date.
Language (s): English
Ad Rate: Full Page Mono 21.98
Currency: Canada Dollars
COMMUNITY NEWSPAPER

Voice 80629
Owner: Voice Portuguese Canadian Newspaper Publishing Inc.
Editorial: 977 College St, Toronto, Ontario M6H 1A6
Tel: 1 416 538-1788
Email: voice@voicenews.ca **Web site:** http://www.voicenews.ca
Freq: Mon; **Circ:** 10000 Not Audited
Editor in Chief: Vasco Evaristo
Profile: Voice is a weekly community newpaper focusing on Canadian Portuguese, Brazilian and community news. The paper also has a Portuguese sports section.
Language (s): English
Ad Rate: Full Page Mono 10.52
Ad Rate: Full Page Colour 450.00
Currency: Canada Dollars
COMMUNITY NEWSPAPER

Voice Group of Publications 903407
Owner: Indo-Canadian Voice Communications LTD.
Editorial: 102-9360 120 St 102, Surrey, British Columbia V3V 4B9 **Tel:** 1 604 502-6100
Email: newsdesk@voiceonline.com **Web site:** http://www.voiceonline.com
Freq: Weekly
Editor: Rattan Mall
Profile: Canada's Largest Group of Indo-Canadian publications catering to the South Asian population with an emphasis on those residing in British Columbia.
Language (s): English
COMMUNITY NEWSPAPER

La Voix Du Sud 24070
Owner: TC. Transcontinental
Editorial: 1516A 277 Rte, Lac-Etchemin, Quebec G0R 1S0 **Tel:** 1 418 625-7471
Email: redaction_lacetchemin@tc.tc **Web site:** http://www.lavoixdusud.com
Freq: Wed; **Circ:** 25612 Not Audited
Profile: La Voix du Sud est un journal francophone hebdomadaire au service des résidentes de Bellechasse, Les Etchemins, la Beauce Nord et Pintendre.

La Voix du Sud is a weekly French-language paper serving residents of Bellechasse, Les Etchemins, Beauce Nord and Pintendre.
Language (s): French
Ad Rate: Full Page Mono 6.86
Currency: Canada Dollars
COMMUNITY NEWSPAPER

A Voz de Portugal 80070
Editorial: 4231 Saint-Laurent Blvd, Montreal, Quebec H2W 1Z4 **Tel:** 1 514 284-1813
Email: jornal@avozdeportugal.com **Web site:** http://www.avozdeportugal.com
Freq: Bi-Weekly; **Circ:** 10000 Not Audited
Publisher & Editor: Eduino Martins; **Editor in Chief:** Sylvio Martins
Profile: A Voz de Portugal est un hebdomadaire publié en portugais et en français pour la communauté portugaise canadienne.

A Voz de Portugal is a weekly newspaper written in Portuguese and French for the Portuguese community in Francophone Canada.
Language (s): English
Ad Rate: Full Page Mono 17.28
Ad Rate: Full Page Colour 328.12
Currency: Canada Dollars
COMMUNITY NEWSPAPER

The Wallaceburg Courier Press 23851
Owner: Postmedia Network Inc.
Editorial: 138 King St W, Chatham, Ontario N7M 1E3- **Tel:** 1 519 628-5719
Email: dgough@postmedia.com **Web site:** http://www.wallaceburgcourierpress.com
Freq: Thu; **Circ:** 11610 Not Audited
Editor: Peter Epp
Profile: The Wallaceburg Courier Press is a weekly newspaper written for the residents of Wallaceburg, Ontario.
Language (s): English
Ad Rate: Full Page Mono 4.83
Currency: Canada Dollars
COMMUNITY NEWSPAPER

Waterloo Chronicle 23858
Owner: Metroland Media Group Ltd.
Editorial: 279 Weber St N Unit 20, Waterloo, Ontario N2J 3H8 **Tel:** 1 519 886-2830
Email: editorial@waterloochronicle.ca **Web site:** http://www.waterloochronicle.ca
Freq: Thu; **Circ:** 32000 Not Audited
Language (s): English
Ad Rate: Full Page Mono 7.00
Currency: Canada Dollars
COMMUNITY NEWSPAPER

Al Wattan 773028
Owner: GQ Multimedia
Editorial: 5004 Timberlea Blvd Suite 201, Mississauga, Ontario L4W 5C5 **Tel:** 1 905 232-8610
Email: info@gqmultimedia.com **Web site:** http://gqmultimedia.com
Freq: Bi-Weekly; **Circ:** 40000
Editor: Jamal Al-Qaryouti
Profile: Al Wattan is a bi-weekly newspaper that provides Local and Community News coverage to the Arabic-speaking community in the Greater Toronto area.
Language (s): Arabic
COMMUNITY NEWSPAPER

Weekly Awam 773038
Editorial: 28-1310 Mid-way Blvd., Mississauga, Ontario L5T 2K5 **Tel:** 1 905 673-7115
Email: weeklyawam@gondalbrothers.com **Web site:** http://www.awam.ca
Freq: Weekly; **Circ:** 18000
Publisher and Editor: M. Nawaf Gondal
Language (s): Urdu
Ad Rate: Full Page Mono 4.05
Currency: Canada Dollars
COMMUNITY NEWSPAPER

Weekly Jogajog 773007
Editorial: 2505 11th Ave Suite 106, Regina, Saskatchewan S4P 0K6 **Tel:** 1 888 884-3777
Email: editor@thejogajog.com **Web site:** http://www.thejogajog.com
Freq: Weekly
Editor: Rafique Bhuiyan
Profile: Weekly Jogajog is a weekly publication that covers multicultural events and news for the South Asian community in Canada.
Language (s): Bangla
COMMUNITY NEWSPAPER

The Weekly Press and Laker Newspapers 238350
Owner: Advocate Media Inc.
Editorial: 287 Hwy #2, Enfield, Nova Scotia B2T 1C9
Tel: 1 902 883-3181
Email: editor@enfieldweeklypress.com **Web site:** http://www.enfieldweeklypress.com
Circ: 10770 Not Audited
Editor: Abby Cameron; **Group Publisher:** Leith Orr
Language (s): English
COMMUNITY NEWSPAPER

Weekly Sunday Times 446394
Editorial: 1662 Bonhill Rd Unit 24, Mississauga, Ontario L5T 1E1 **Tel:** 1 905 276-4048
Email: sundaytimes1@aol.com **Web site:** http://www.sundaytimescanada.com
Freq: Thu; **Circ:** 30000 Not Audited
Editor in Chief: Adnan Hashmi; **Editor:** Zeba Naureen
Profile: Weekly Sunday Times is a local, weekly English and Urdu-language newspaper serving Pakistani, Indian and Bangladeshi residents of Mississauga, Ontario. The paper includes news from Pakistan and India, local community news, Canadian and international news. It covers sports, film, religion, literature, politics, fiction and the arts.
Language (s): English
Ad Rate: Full Page Mono 20.30
Currency: Canada Dollars
COMMUNITY NEWSPAPER

The Weekly Times of India 409775
Editorial: 21 Brisdale Dr, Brampton, Ontario L7A 0H7
Tel: 1 905 256-5630
Email: info@weeklytimesofindia.com **Web site:** http://www.weeklytimesofindia.com
Freq: Fri; **Circ:** 40000 Not Audited
Editor: Sukirdi Chaudhary; **Publisher:** Shashi Malik
Profile: The Weekly Times of India has become a household name among the South-Asian Community since 2001 living in Greater Toronto Area. Maintaining high standards of Journalism with news and articles not just from South Asia and Canada, but also from all around the world on matters that affect our community; News, Opinions, Business, Sports, Entertainment, Leisure, Lifestyle, Health & Wellness, Automotive, Young Times, Real Estates & Classified are the other major sections covered in the Newspaper.
Language (s): English
Ad Rate: Full Page Mono 8.05
Currency: Canada Dollars
COMMUNITY NEWSPAPER

Weekly Voice Newspaper 523555
Owner: Weekly Voice Newspaper
Editorial: 7015 Tranmere Dr Suite 16, Mississauga, Ontario L5S 1T7 **Tel:** 1 905 795-8282
Email: info@weeklyvoice.com **Web site:** http://www.weeklyvoice.com
Freq: 2 Times/Week; **Circ:** 40600 Not Audited
Publisher: Sudhir Anand; **Editor in Chief:** Binoy Thomas
Profile: Reflects the concerns and interests of the South Asian community in the Greater Toronto Area. Emphasis on local coverage of the community as well as international news and features. Includes regular columns on cars, entertainment, women's issues, youth affairs, real estate, home improvement, recipes and sports.
Language (s): English
Ad Rate: Full Page Mono 4.15
Ad Rate: Full Page Colour 350.00
Currency: United States Dollars
COMMUNITY NEWSPAPER

The Wellington Advertiser 23781
Owner: W.H.A. Publications Ltd.
Editorial: 905 Gartshore St., Fergus, Ontario N1M 2W8 **Tel:** 1 519 843-5410
Email: editor@wellingtonadvertiser.com **Web site:** http://www.wellingtonadvertiser.com
Freq: Fri; **Circ:** 39809 Not Audited
Publisher: William Adsett
Profile: The Wellington Advertiser is written for the community of Fergus, Ontario and contains local news, community concerns and editorials.
Language (s): English
Ad Rate: Full Page Mono 8.68
Currency: Canada Dollars
COMMUNITY NEWSPAPER

West East 773265
Editorial: Trans-Island 5120, Montreal, Quebec H3W 2Z9 **Tel:** 1 514 484-9282
Email: allmontreal@gmail.com **Web site:** http://1001news.ca
Profile: West East is a weekly publication that covers multicultural events and news for the Russian community in Canada.
COMMUNITY NEWSPAPER

Western Catholic Reporter 79975
Owner: Great Western Press Ltd.
Editorial: 8421-101st Ave NW, Edmonton, Alberta T6A 0L1 **Tel:** 1 780 465-8030
Email: wcr@wcr.ab.ca **Web site:** http://www.wcr.ab.ca
Freq: Mon; **Circ:** 35000 Not Audited
Profile: Western Catholic Reporter is a weekly newspaper published for Canadian Catholics. It provides Catholic inspiration, news and community updates. Its mission is to serve readers by helping them deepen their faith through accurate information and reflective commentary on events and issues of concern to the Catholic church. Deadlines are Fridays before the print day, Wednesday.
Language (s): English
Ad Rate: Full Page Mono 29.40
Ad Rate: Full Page Colour 33.74
Currency: Canada Dollars
COMMUNITY NEWSPAPER

The Western Sentinel 24444
Owner: Department of National Defence
Editorial: 1 Area Support Group Headquarters, Building 181, Edmonton, Alberta T5J 4J5
Tel: 1 780 973-4011
Email: armywesternsentinel@gmail.com **Web site:** http://www.army.forces.gc.ca/ws
Freq: Bi-Weekly; **Circ:** 10000 Not Audited
Editor in Chief: Grant Cree
Profile: The Western Sentinel is written for all Canadian Army units and bases across the Land Force Western Area from Thunder Bay, Ontario to Vancouver Island.
Language (s): English
Ad Rate: Full Page Mono 5.60
Currency: Canada Dollars
COMMUNITY NEWSPAPER

Westman Journal 153172
Owner: Glacier Media Inc.
Editorial: 315 College Ave., Unit D, Brandon, Manitoba R7A 1E7 **Tel:** 1 204 725-0209
Email: info@wheatcityjournal.ca **Web site:** http://www.westmanjournal.com
Freq: Thu; **Circ:** 35000 Not Audited
Profile: Westman Journal is a weekly newspaper that provides community news to the residents of Brandon, Manitoba.
Language (s): English
Ad Rate: Full Page Mono 5.74
Ad Rate: Full Page Colour 80.00
Currency: Canada Dollars
COMMUNITY NEWSPAPER

Westman This Week 395085
Owner: FP Canadian Newspapers LP
Editorial: 501 Rosser Ave, Brandon, Manitoba R7A 0K4 **Tel:** 1 204 727-2451
Email: opinion@brandonsun.com **Web site:** http://www.brandonsun.com
Freq: Sun; **Circ:** 40158 Not Audited
Editor: Matt Goerzen; **Publisher:** Eric Lawson; **News Editor:** Jim Lewthwaite
Profile: The Brandon Sun Community News is a twice-weekly tabloid providing news for the residents of Brandon and Westman in Western Manitoba, Canada. It features sports, lifestyle, entertainment content and national, world and local news. It is published out of the same office as the Brandon Sun daily newspaper.
Language (s): English
Ad Rate: Full Page Mono 10.50
Ad Rate: Full Page Colour 138.00
Currency: Canada Dollars
COMMUNITY NEWSPAPER

Westside Weekly 23567
Owner: Continental Newspapers Canada Ltd.
Editorial: 550 Doyle Ave, Kelowna, British Columbia V1Y 7V1 **Tel:** 1 250 470-0748
Email: westside@ok.bc.ca **Web site:** http://www.kelownadailycourier.ca
Freq: Thu; **Circ:** 13150 Not Audited
Publisher: Terry Armstrong
Profile: Westside Weekly is a community newspaper written for the residents of Kelowna, British Columbia.
Language (s): English
Ad Rate: Full Page Mono 0.66
Currency: Canada Dollars
COMMUNITY NEWSPAPER

Wetaskiwin Times 23523
Owner: Postmedia Network Inc.
Editorial: 5013 51 St, Wetaskiwin, Alberta T9A 1L4
Tel: 1 780 352-2231
Email: wtimes.editor@sunmedia.ca **Web site:** http://www.wetaskiwintimes.com
Freq: Wed; **Circ:** 11152 Not Audited
Publisher: Jim Clark; **Editor:** Jerold LeBlanc
Profile: Wetaskiwin Times is a community newspaper written for the residents of Wetaskiwin, Alberta.
Language (s): English
Ad Rate: Full Page Mono 6.23
Currency: Canada Dollars
COMMUNITY NEWSPAPER

Weyburn Review & Weyburn This Week Newspapers 25599
Owner: Glacier Media, Inc.
Editorial: 904 East Ave, Weyburn, Saskatchewan S4H 2Y8 **Tel:** 1 306 842-7487
Email: production@weyburnreview.com **Web site:** http://www.weyburnreview.com
Circ: 11267 Not Audited
Publisher: Darryl Ward
Language (s): English
Ad Rate: Full Page Mono 14.32
Currency: Canada Dollars
COMMUNITY NEWSPAPER

Wheatley/Leamington Southpoint Journal Sun 713405
Editorial: 194 Talbot St E, Leamington, Ontario N8H 1M2 **Tel:** 1 519 398-9098
Email: sun@southpointsun.ca **Web site:** http://www.southpointsun.ca
Circ: 12000
Publisher: Jim Heyens; **Editor:** Sheila McBrayne
Profile: Wheatley/Southpoint Journal provides Community News to the Wheatley and Leamington, ON area. It publishes The Wheatley Journal and the Leamington Southpoint Sun.
Language (s): English
COMMUNITY NEWSPAPER

The Whistler Question 23568
Owner: Glacier Media Inc.
Editorial: 103-1390 Alpha Lake Rd 103, Whistler, British Columbia V0N 1B1 **Tel:** 1 604 938-0202
Email: general@whistlerquestion.com **Web site:** http://www.whistlerquestion.com
Freq: Tue; **Circ:** 10480 Not Audited
Editor: Jennifer Miller
Profile: The Whistler Question is a newspaper written for the residents of Whistler and Pemberton, British Columbia. The paper covers local news.
Language (s): English
Ad Rate: Full Page Mono 11.04
Currency: Canada Dollars
COMMUNITY NEWSPAPER

Windsor-Essex Newspapers 588323
Owner: Postmedia Network Inc.
Editorial: 1116 Lesperance Rd, Tecumseh, Ontario N8N 1X2 **Tel:** 1 519 735-2080
Email: WEngland@postmedia.com
Circ: 37700
Editor In Chief: Bill England

Canada

Profile: Windsor-Essex Newspapers publish the Lakeshore News, LaSalle Post and Shoreline Week.
COMMUNITY NEWSPAPER

Yorkton News 87772
Owner: Glacier Media Inc.
Editorial: 18 1st Ave N, Yorkton, Saskatchewan S3N 1J4 **Tel:** 1 306 783-7355
Email: info@yorktonnews.com **Web site:** http://www.yorktonnews.com
Circ: 26700 Not Audited
Profile: Yorkton News publishes The News Review and News Review Extra bi-weekly publication to East-Central Saskatchewan and Western Manitoba. The News Review is published on Thursday; The New Review Extra is published on Saturday.
Language (s): English
COMMUNITY NEWSPAPER

Yorkton Publications 25601
Owner: Glacier Media Inc.
Editorial: 20 Third Ave N, Yorkton, Saskatchewan S3N 1B9 **Tel:** 1 306 782-2465
Email: editorial@yorktonthisweek.com **Web site:** http://www.yorktonthisweek.com
Circ: 24617 Not Audited
Language (s): English
COMMUNITY NEWSPAPER

Your Local Journal 693890
Editorial: 3100 Rte Harwood Suite 201, Vaudreuil-Dorion, Quebec J7V 8P2 **Tel:** 1 450 510-4007
Email: admin@yourlocaljournal.ca **Web site:** http://www.yourlocaljournal.ca
Freq: Thu; **Circ:** 18543
Editor: Carmen Marie Fabio
Profile: Your Local Journal est une hebdomadaire de langue anglaise pour la région de Vaudreuil-Soulange et de l'Ouest de l'Île. Your Local Journal est distribué à Hudson, Saint-Lazare, Vaudreuil-DOrion, RIgaud, Ile Perrot, Pincourt et l'Ouest de l'Île.

Your Local Journal is a weekly English language community newspaper for the Vaudreuil-Soulanges area and the West Island. Your Local Journal is available in Hudson, Saint-Lazare, Vaudreuil-Dorion, Rigaud, Ile Perrot, Pincourt and the West Island.
Language (s): English
Ad Rate: Full Page Mono 19.60
Ad Rate: Full Page Colour 46.20
Currency: United States Dollars
COMMUNITY NEWSPAPER

Cape Verde

Time Difference: GMT -1
National Telephone Code: 238
Continent: Africa
Capital: Praia

Newspapers

Expresso das Ilhas 229998
Owner: Media Comunicações SA
Tel: 238 261 98 07
Email: jornal@expressodasilhas.publ.cv **Web site:** http://www.expressodasilhas.sapo.cv
Circ: 3500 Publisher's Statement
Profile: Newspaper focusing on news and current affairs, politics, economics, society, culture and sports.
Language (s): Portuguese
DAILY NEWSPAPER

A Semana 229997
Owner: Nova Editora, SARL
Tel: 238 262 98 60
Email: asemana@cvtelecom.cv **Web site:** http://www.asemana.publ.cv
Circ: 5000 Publisher's Statement
Chefe de Redação: Jose Vicente Lopes; **Directora:** Filomena Silva
Profile: Newspaper covering news and current affairs, politics, economics, society, culture and sports.
Language (s): Portuguese
DAILY NEWSPAPER

News Service/Syndicate

Inforpress 353732
Tel: 238 2 62 32 69
Email: inforpress@cvtelecom.cv **Web site:** http://www.inforpress.publ.cv
Profile: Inforpress is a news agency reporting on national and regional news, politics, economics, culture, sports, society and environment.
Language (s): Portuguese
NEWS SERVICE/SYNDICATE

Cayman Islands

Time Difference: GMT -5
National Telephone Code: 1345
Continent: The Americas
Capital: George Town (Grand Cayman)

Newspapers

Cayman Compass 156645
Owner: Pinnacle Media Ltd.
Editorial: The Compass Centre, Shedden Road, Grand Cayman KY1-1108 **Tel:** 1 345 949-5111
Email: info@cfp.ky **Web site:** http://www.caymancompass.com
Freq: Daily; **Circ:** 30000 Not Audited
Profile: Cayman Compass formerly Caymanian Compass is a daily newspaper that covers local, national and international news, sports, business and features.
Language (s): English
Ad Rate: Full Page Mono 11.25
Ad Rate: Full Page Colour 524.00
Currency: United States Dollars
DAILY NEWSPAPER

The Cayman Islands Journal 406268
Owner: Cayman Free Press Ltd
Tel: 1345 949 5111
Web site: http://www.caymanfreepress.com
Freq: Monthly; **Circ:** 30000 Not Audited
Publisher: Brian Uzenn
Profile: Focuses on in-depth business news tailored specifically to the Cayman Islands.
Language (s): English
DAILY NEWSPAPER

News Service/Syndicate

Caribbean Net News 476024
Editorial: Miracle Center, 85 North Sound Road., Grand Cayman **Tel:** 345 9466060
Web site: http://caribbeannetnews.com
Editor: Barry Randall
Profile: Provides news and trade information from around the Caribbean.
Language (s): English
NEWS SERVICE/SYNDICATE

Chad

Time Difference: GMT +1
National Telephone Code: 235
Continent: Africa
Capital: N'Djamena

Newspapers

Le Progrès 668445
Owner: Le Progrès
Editorial: Avenue Charles de Gaulle, BP 3055, N'djamena **Tel:** 235 66 23 00 94
Email: quotidienleprogres3@yahoo.fr
Freq: Daily; **Circ:** 3000 Publisher's Statement
Director: Abdéramane Barka
Profile: Newspaper covering regional and national news and current affairs including politics, economics and sport.
Language (s): French
DAILY NEWSPAPER

Chile

Time Difference: GMT -4
National Telephone Code: 56
Continent: The Americas
Capital: Santiago

Newspapers

Diario Estrategia 383387
Editorial: Av. Luis Carrera 1289, Vitacura, Santiago 7650726 **Tel:** 56 2 2655-6200
Email: estrategia@estrategia.cl **Web site:** http://www.estrategia.cl
Freq: Daily
Editor: Rodrigo D'amico N.; **Redactor:** Daniel Gómez Y.; **Editora:** Patricia González M.; **Editor:** Brian Gubbins S.; **Gerente:** Christian L'huissier Villar; **Editor:** Valentin Magallanes H.; **Gerente Comercial:** Francisco Ojeda González; **Presidente Director:** Víctor Manuel Ojeda Méndez; **Editor:** Rodrigo Pacheco C.; **Redactor:** Matías Rodo Y.; **Redactora:** Paulina Rosso V.; **Redactor:** José Pablo Stange C.; **Editora:** Paulina Valenzuela; **Redactor:** César Valenzuela B.
Profile: A newspaper focusing on business and economy news in Chile. Offers analysis of the business world and financial markets. Covers business trends, management issues, marketing, technology, investments and the people who hold power in Chilean business.
Language (s): Spanish
DAILY NEWSPAPER

Diario La Hora 383389
Owner: Copesa S.A.
Editorial: Av. Vicuna Mackenna 1962, nunoa, Santiago
Email: contacto@lahora.cl **Web site:** http://www.lahora.cl
Freq: Daily; **Circ:** 250000
Gerente Comercial: Raúl Cruzat Rioseco; **National News Editor:** Arturo Figueroa; **Presidente:** Jorge Saieh Guzmán
Profile: Diario chileno. Chilean newspaper.
Language (s): Spanish
Ad Rate: Full Page Mono 15875.03
Currency: Chile Pesos
DAILY NEWSPAPER

Diario La Tercera 383583
Owner: Grupo Copesa, S.A.
Editorial: Av. Vicuna Mackenna 1962 9-D, nunoa, Santiago 7780133 **Tel:** 56 22 550-7000
Email: correo@latercera.cl **Web site:** http://diario.latercera.com
Circ: 246207
Editora General: Marialí Bofill García; **Editor:** Victor Cofré Soto; **Editor General:** Felipe Contreras Pedreros; **Editora:** Gabriela De La Maza Palacios; **Editor:** Marcelo Duhalde Casanova; **Editor:** Rodrigo Eyzaguirre Vega; **Director:** Marcelo Godoy Sáez; **Editor:** Juan Pablo Iglesias; **Editor:** Mauricio Jürgensen Roldán; **Editor:** Alejandro Maltés Zárate; **Editor Nocturno:** Sergio Maraboli Triviño; **Editor:** Pablo Marín Castro; **Editor:** Noemí Miranda Gómez; **Editor:** Fernando Ojeda Velozo; **Editor:** Marcelo Palomino Montenegro; **Editor:** José Carlos Pérez Hernández; **Editor:** Juan Andrés Quezada Gómez; **Presidente:** Jorge Saieh Guzmán; **Editor:** Carlos Salvo Callender; **Gerente General:** Max Sichel Dayse; **Editor Nacional:** Gabriel Vargas Espinoza
Profile: Diario La Tercera is a daily newspaper providing Local News, National News, International News, Sports, Arts & Entertainment, Business and Editorial Page coverage in Chile.
Language (s): Spanish
DAILY NEWSPAPER

Diario Publimetro 383528
Owner: Publimetro, S.A.
Editorial: Av Presidente Kennedy 5735 Of 701 Torre Poniente, Las Condes, Santiago **Tel:** 56 22 421-5900
Email: cronica@publimetro.cl **Web site:** http://www.publimetro.cl
Circ: 100000
Editor: Mauricio Ávila; **Editor:** Alexis Cares; **Director Responsable:** Matias Carvajal; **Gerente:** Mario Cruzat; **Editora:** Alejandra Gallagos; **Editora:** Andrea González; **Gerente:** Andrés Israel Abraham; **General Manager:** Pablo Mazzei Pozo
Profile: Diario Publimetro is a free daily newspaper that provides International News, National News, Sports, Arts & Entertainment, Business coverage for the residents of the Santiago, Chile metropolitan area.
Language (s): Spanish
DAILY NEWSPAPER

Pulso 812704
Owner: Grupo Copesa, S.A.
Editorial: El Bosque Sur 90 Piso 4, Las Condes, Santiago 7550248 **Tel:** 56 2 2230-2810
Web site: http://www.pulso.cl
Freq: Daily
Director: Guillermo Turner Olea
Profile: Pulso is a daily financial newspaper providing National and International News coverage on Economy, Finance, Markets, Industry, Technology, Taxes and Politics in Santiago, Chile.
Language (s): Spanish
Ad Rate: Full Page Mono 48219.82
Currency: Chile Pesos
DAILY NEWSPAPER

Revista Wikén 386811
Editorial: Av. Santa Maria 5542, 13-D, Correo Central, Santiago **Tel:** 56 2 2330-1111
Web site: http://www.elmercuriomediacenter.cl/prensa/el-mercurio/revistas/wiken/
Freq: Weekly; **Circ:** 165485
Gerente General: Pablo Dittborn; **Periodista:** Carlos Fernández; **Director:** Juan Andrés Guzmán; **Encargado:** Luis Parraguez; **Diseñador:** Felipe Raveau; **Editor:** Pablo Vergara
Profile: La revista cubre espectáculos y gastronomía. También reporta noticias sobre cine, música, teatro, TV cable, restaurantes y vino. Además ofrece entrevistas con protagonistas del mundo del entretenimiento nacional e internacional, reportajes a los mejores espectáculos, las últimas tendencias culinarias y críticas gastronómicas y cinematográficas. The magazine features entertainment and gastronomy. It covers news on movies, music, theater, cable TV, dining and wine. It also features interviews with stars of the world of national and international entertainment, best entertainment events, the latest culinary trends and dining and movie reviews.
Language (s): Spanish
DAILY NEWSPAPER

Revista Ya 514443
Editorial: Av. Santa Maria 5542, 13-D, Correo Central, Santiago **Tel:** 56 2 330-1111
Web site: http://impresa.elmercurio.com/Pages/SupplementDetail.aspx?dt=2015-04-21&SupplementID=2&BodyID=0
Freq: Weekly
Director: Iván Canales; **Director:** Mariano Feijoo; **Editor:** Raúl Gutiérrez Valenzuela; **Editor:** Cristián Reyes; **Editora General:** María Teresa Villafrade
Profile: Trata temas de estilo de vida, como la moda, la salud, la nutrición, la comida, la gente, entretenimiento y más. Covers lifestyle topics such as fashion, health, nutrition, food, people, entertainment and more.
Language (s): Spanish
DAILY NEWSPAPER

News Service/Syndicate

Agencia Informativa Orbe 385412
Editorial: Av. Presidente Errazuriz 2933, Santiago 7550357 **Tel:** 56 2 2251-7800
Email: prensa@orbe.cl **Web site:** http://www.orbe.cl
Redactor: Andrés Aguilera; **Redactor:** Gabriel Barríos; **Redactor:** Raúl Beltrán; **News Director:** Jorge Díaz S.; **Redactora:** Mariela Espinoza; **Redactor:** Cristián Guzmán; **Redactor:** Raúl Jara; **Redactora:** Marisa Latorre; **Editor:** Francisco Javier Leiva; **Presidente:** Fernando Malatesta García; **Editor:** Cristián Quiriván; **Redactor:** José Ignacio Valenzuela; **Redactor:** Andrés Varas; **Editor:** Andrés Venegas
Language (s): Spanish
NEWS SERVICE/SYNDICATE

Europa Press Chile 385418
Editorial: Av. Americo Vespucio 2900, Vitacura, Santiago 763-0661
Web site: http://www.europapress.cl
Director Gerente: Renato Campodónico; **Director:** José Rios Raggio; **Periodista:** Edmundo Tapia; **Periodista:** Verónica Waissbluth
Language (s): Spanish
NEWS SERVICE/SYNDICATE

China

Time Difference: GMT +8
National Telephone Code: 86
Continent: Asia
Capital: Beijing

Newspapers

21st Century News 460444
Owner: China Daily Newspaper Group
Editorial: China Daily Press Group, 15 Huixin Dongjie, Chaoyangqu, Beijing 100029
Tel: 86 10 64995500
Web site: http://www.i21st.cn
Freq: Weekly; **Circ:** 240000 Not Audited
Editor in Chief: Lisheng Nie
Profile: Founded in 1993 as a guide for learning English, covers current affairs, culture, sports and entertainment. Written primarily for Chinese youth.
Language (s): English
Ad Rate: Full Page Mono 48000.00
Ad Rate: Full Page Colour 72000.00
Currency: China Yuan Renminbi
DAILY NEWSPAPER

21st Century Teens Junior Edition 460055
Owner: China Daily Newspaper Group
Editorial: China Daily Press Group, 15 Huixin Dongjie, Chaoyangqu, Beijing 100029
Tel: 86 1064995500
Web site: http://www.21stcentury.com.cn
Freq: Weekly; **Circ:** 120001 Not Audited
Editor in Chief: Lisheng Nie
Profile: Founded in 2003, focuses on educational and cultural information and English learning materials for junior high schools students.
Language (s): Chinese
DAILY NEWSPAPER

21st Century Teens Senior Edition 404402
Owner: China Daily Newspaper Group
Editorial: China Daily Press Group, 15 Huixin Dongjie, Chaoyangqu, Beijing 100029
Tel: 86 10 64918211
Email: adsales@21stcentury.com.cn **Web site:** http://www.i21st.cn
Freq: Weekly; **Circ:** 120003 Not Audited
Editor in Chief: Lisheng Nie

Profile: A newspaper published in English for senior students in high school. Covers current affairs, culture, sports and entertainment.
Language (s): Chinese
DAILY NEWSPAPER

Agrigoods Herald 460053
Editorial: Agrigoods Herald, Jia 2, Liupukang Beixiaojie, Beijing 100011 **Tel:** 86 1082032080
Web site: http://www.nzdb.com.cn
Freq: 2 Times/Week; **Circ:** 60001 Not Audited
Editor in Chief: Jianqiu Zhang
Profile: Covers topics for those in the agriculture business.
Language (s): Chinese
DAILY NEWSPAPER

Anhui Business News 459041
Editorial: Anhui Daily, 206 Jinzhailu, Hefei 230061
Tel: 86 5515179633
Web site: http://www.ahrb.com.cn
Freq: Daily; **Circ:** 480004 Not Audited
Editor in Chief: Yan Zhao
Profile: It provides latest information on the economy and business in Anhui region.
Language (s): Chinese
Ad Rate: Full Page Mono 140000.00
Ad Rate: Full Page Colour 200000.00
Currency: China Yuan Renminbi
DAILY NEWSPAPER

Anhui Economic News 459028
Editorial: Anhui Economic News Press, 200 Tunxilu, Hefei 230001 **Tel:** 86 5514672920 818
Web site: http://www.ahjjnews.cn
Freq: 2 Times/Week; **Circ:** 100003 Not Audited
Editor in Chief: Shunsheng Ma
Profile: Anhui Economic News mainly contains business and finance news in Anhui region and in China.
Language (s): Chinese
DAILY NEWSPAPER

Anhui Law News 459040
Editorial: Anhui Daily, 1469 Qianshan Road, Hefei 230071 **Tel:** 86 5515179831
Email: ahfzb@ahfzb.com **Web site:** http://www.ahrb.com.cn/
Freq: 2 Times/Week; **Circ:** 66003 Not Audited
Editor in Chief: Youqun Wang
Profile: It covers the law-related issues and cases.
Language (s): Chinese
DAILY NEWSPAPER

Anhui Market News 459037
Editorial: Anhui Market News Press, 10 Yonghonglu, Hefei 230001 **Tel:** 86 5512620110
Web site: http://www.ahscb.com.cn
Freq: Daily; **Circ:** 300003 Not Audited
Editor: Gucheng Ye
Profile: Covers news about finance, business, and economic developments in Anhui and in China.
Language (s): Chinese
Ad Rate: Full Page Mono 88000.00
Currency: China Yuan Renminbi
DAILY NEWSPAPER

Antiquarian Books Weekly 460069
Editorial: Antiquarian Books Weekly, 1 Tianyuan Road, Shijiazhuang 50071 **Tel:** 86 31187732149
Email: cangshubao@126.com
Freq: Weekly; **Circ:** 100002 Not Audited
Editor in Chief: Zhanmin Cheng
Profile: covers historical, cultural and market information of antiques and books information.
Language (s): Chinese
DAILY NEWSPAPER

Asahi Shimbun - Beijing Bureau 459106
Editorial: Asahi Shimbun - Beijing Bureau, Rm 1108 Derun Tower, Beijing 100022 **Tel:** 86 10 58795885
Web site: http://www.asahi.com
Freq: Daily
Profile: A international newspaper covering global issues and news in China.
Language (s): English
DAILY NEWSPAPER

Asahi Shimbun - Shanghai Bureau 459108
Editorial: 1376 Nanjing Road, Shanghai 200040
Web site: http://www.asahi.com
Freq: Daily
Bureau Chief: Okudera Atsushi
Profile: Foreign bureau of Asahi Shimbun newspaper in Japan.
Language (s): English
DAILY NEWSPAPER

Bandao Morning Post 459303
Owner: Liaoning Daily Press Group
Editorial: 360 Changchunlu, Xigangqu, Dalian 116013 **Tel:** 86 41182499922
Web site: http://newspaper.lndaily.com.cn/bdcb
Freq: Daily; **Circ:** 350003 Not Audited
Editor in Chief: Runfu Wang
Profile: Covers news in Dalian.
Language (s): Chinese
Ad Rate: Full Page Mono 90000.00
Currency: China Yuan Renminbi
DAILY NEWSPAPER

Basketball News 459186
Editorial: China Sports Publications Group, 8 Tiyuguanlu, Chongwenqu, Beijing 100061
Tel: 86 10 67110066
Web site: http://www.sportsol.com.cn
Freq: Weekly; **Circ:** 541000
Editor in Chief: Jie Tan
Profile: covers national and international news on basketball competitions and basketball players.
Language (s): Chinese
DAILY NEWSPAPER

Basketball Pioneers 460237
Editorial: 4-1-501, Tiantan Gongguan, 59 Xinfu Dajie, Chongwenqu, Beijing 100061 **Tel:** 86 2081330007
Web site: http://www.goalchina.net
Freq: 2 Times/Week; **Circ:** 200003 Not Audited
Bureau Chief: Huifang Cai; **Editor in Chief:** Qun Su
Profile: Basketball Pioneers is a national newspaper that provides the latest news on basketball.
Language (s): Chinese
DAILY NEWSPAPER

Beijing Broadcasting TV News, People Weekly 460154
Editorial: Beijing Television Weekly, 14 Xizhaosijie, Beijing 100061
Email: zkzggix@vip.sina.com **Web site:** http://www.bgtv.com.cn
Freq: Weekly; **Circ:** 150004 Not Audited
Editor in Chief: Biao Zhang
Profile: covers stories and reports of famous people's lifestyles and their interesting stories.
Language (s): Chinese
DAILY NEWSPAPER

Beijing Business Today 459452
Editorial: Beijing Business Today Press, 21 Hepingli Xijie, Chaoyangqu, Beijing 100013
Tel: 86 10 84276691
Web site: http://www.bbtnews.com.cn
Freq: 2 Times/Week; **Circ:** 150003 Not Audited
Editor: Chen Jie; **Editor in Chief:** Hai Li; **Bureau Chief:** Chengjun Qiu
Profile: reports on business and financial news. It mainly targets Chinese businessmen.
Language (s): Chinese
Ad Rate: Full Page Mono 150000.00
Currency: China Yuan Renminbi
DAILY NEWSPAPER

Beijing Children News 459604
Editorial: Beijing Children News, Room 1802, Beijing Qingnianbao Dasha, Building A, 23 Dongli, Baijiazhuan, Chaoyagqu, Beijing 100026
Tel: 86 10 65902441
Email: bjsnb@ynet.com **Web site:** http://bjsn.ynet.com
Freq: Weekly; **Circ:** 300003 Not Audited
Editor in Chief: Aixue Zhang
Profile: covers educational issues and topics about lifestyle and culture of the youth in China.
Language (s): Chinese
Ad Rate: Full Page Colour 62400.00
Currency: China Yuan Renminbi
DAILY NEWSPAPER

Beijing Entertainment Journal 459620
Editorial: Beijing Entertainment Journal, 10F Guorui Dasha, Chongwenmen WaiDajie, Dongchengqu, Beijing 100062 **Tel:** 86 1087555123
Web site: http://www.stardaily.com.cn/
Freq: Daily; **Circ:** 300000 Not Audited
Bureau Chief: Kun Bi; **Editor:** Bin Chang; **Editor in Chief:** Jinghui Si
Profile: Beijing Entertainment Journal is a metro newspaper which is freely distributed in metro railway stations in Beijing. It mainly covers news and information of entertainment and lifestyle issues.
Language (s): Chinese
Ad Rate: Full Page Colour 201000.00
Currency: China Yuan Renminbi
DAILY NEWSPAPER

Beijing Evening News 404491
Owner: Beijing Daily Press Group
Editorial: Beijing Daily Press Group, 20 Jianguo Mennei Dajie, Beijing 100734 **Tel:** 86 10 8520-1071
Email: jbw@bjd.com.cn **Web site:** http://www.bjd.com.cn
Freq: Daily; **Circ:** 1000000 Not Audited
Editor in Chief: Huanying Ren
Profile: Founded in 1958, covers news, finance, entertainment, sports and social issues.
Language (s): Chinese
Ad Rate: Full Page Mono 218000.00
Ad Rate: Full Page Colour 366000.00
Currency: China Yuan Renminbi
DAILY NEWSPAPER

Beijing Job Market News 459164
Editorial: Beijing Job Market News, 3/F, No. 33 DongwangZhuang, Qinghua East Road, Haidian District, Beijing 100083 **Tel:** 86 1062312502
Email: 2000wujian@163.com **Web site:** http://www.bjrc.com
Freq: 2 Times/Week; **Circ:** 100002 Not Audited
Editor in Chief: Jian Wu
Profile: It provides comprehensive information on job market and career in Beijing area.
Language (s): Chinese
DAILY NEWSPAPER

Beijing Morning Post 404498
Owner: Beijing Daily Group
Editorial: Beijing Daily Group 3rd FlR BlK A Donghuan, #9 Dongzhongjie Dongchengqu Guangchang, Beijing 100027 **Tel:** 86 1064183399
Email: openweek@vip.sina.com **Web site:** http://www.morningpost.com.cn
Freq: Daily; **Circ:** 300000 Not Audited
Profile: It covers news, politics, economy, business, sports, entertainment, lifestyle and social issues.
Language (s): Chinese
Ad Rate: Full Page Mono 240000.00
Ad Rate: Full Page Colour 300000.00
Currency: China Yuan Renminbi
DAILY NEWSPAPER

The Beijing News 404460
Editorial: The Beijing News, 37 Xingfu Beidajie, Beijing 100061 **Tel:** 86 10 67106710
Email: news@thebeijingnews.com **Web site:** http://www.thebeijingnews.com
Freq: Daily; **Circ:** 500003
Profile: A daily newspaper.
Language (s): Chinese
Ad Rate: Full Page Mono 462000.00
Ad Rate: Full Page Colour 359000.00
Currency: China Yuan Renminbi
DAILY NEWSPAPER

Beijing Today 460274
Editorial: Beijing Youth Press, Beijing Qingnianbao Daxia, Dongli, Baijiazhuang, Chaoyangqu, Beijing 100026 **Tel:** 86 10 65902513
Email: info@beijingtoday.com.cn **Web site:** http://bjtoday.ynet.com
Freq: Weekly; **Circ:** 50003 Not Audited
Profile: Launched in 2001, serves Beijing's expat community with news and cultural events.
Language (s): English
DAILY NEWSPAPER

Beijing Youth Daily 404504
Editorial: Beijing Youth Press, Building A, 23 Dongli, Baijiazhuang, Chaoyangqu, Beijing 100026
Tel: 86 10 65902200
Email: jubao@ynet.com **Web site:** http://bjyouth.ynet.com
Freq: Daily; **Circ:** 600003 Not Audited
Editor: Shanshan Yu; **Editor in Chief:** Yabin Zhang
Profile: Covers politics, economy, finance, lifestyle and culture. Beijing Youth Daily has reported a formation of five subnet issue of the publication pattern, the amount of daily published outside the 48 edition, the daily circulation of about 600,000. The next few years, Beijing Youth Daily will be "Three Represents" as guidance, thoroughly implement the party's congress, emancipate our minds, seek truth from facts, insist firmly grasp the correct guidance of public opinion, insisted close reality, life, and the masses, through the growth of the main industry, the integration of resources, innovation system, to build Beijing Media family of brands and core competencies to achieve in the new situation and new opportunities under the leaps and bounds.
Language (s): Chinese
Ad Rate: Full Page Mono 604800.00
Ad Rate: Full Page Colour 342700.00
Currency: China Yuan Renminbi
DAILY NEWSPAPER

Books and Periodicals News 460822
Editorial: Hebei Daily Press Group, 210 Yuhuadonglu, Shijiazhuang 50013
Tel: 86 3118631176
Email: skb186@163.com **Web site:** http://www.hebeidaily.com.cn
Freq: Weekly; **Circ:** 200001 Not Audited
Editor in Chief: Yingchao Zhang
Profile: Covers information on books and journals, as well as historical books and culture.
Language (s): Chinese
DAILY NEWSPAPER

The Bund 460003
Owner: Shanghai The Bund Media Co. Ltd.,
Editorial: 5th Fl, Baoli Dasha, #10 Nong 100, Shanghai 200040 **Tel:** 86 2162480708
Web site: http://www.bundpic.com
Freq: Weekly; **Circ:** 150001 Not Audited
Editor in Chief: Lanni Chen
Profile: Covers cultural and lifestyle information in China and other countries, providing comments and analysis in economic and fashion field. It also includes information on entertainment and business.
Language (s): Chinese
DAILY NEWSPAPER

CAAC Journal 460862
Editorial: Civil Aviation Administration of China Beijing, Chaoyangqu POBox 2264 Shilihe, Beijing 100021 **Tel:** 86 1067301570
Email: news@caacjournal.com **Web site:** http://www.caacjournal.com
Freq: 2 Times/Week; **Circ:** 180000 Not Audited
Editor in Chief: Yue Ding
Profile: covers the latest news and hot issues of Civil Aviation Administration of China, and the latest information of aviation industry.
Language (s): Chinese
Ad Rate: Full Page Mono 120000.00
Currency: China Yuan Renminbi
DAILY NEWSPAPER

CANKAO XIAO XI 404490
Editorial: Xinhua News Agency, 57 Xidajie, Xuanwumen, Beijing 100803 **Tel:** 86 10 63071136
Email: ckxx@xinhua.org **Web site:** http://www.cankaoa.com
Freq: Daily; **Circ:** 3500000 Not Audited
Editor: Jingli Lu
Profile: Provides news and social issues of Chinese society. Can kao xiao xi in early November 1931 in Jiangxi founded, as the Xinhua News Agency's issuance of a unique national mainstream media, newspapers published outside the main current affairs news. China's largest circulation daily newspaper, the daily circulation of 4,000,000 copies, distributed nationally, covering multi-level readers, including 25-34 and 35-44 accounted for a larger proportion of the reader, the reader is relatively mature, rational, is backbone of society, they are in the golden age of business development, has got to have the economic base and decision-making capacity; party and government organs, organizations, business unit leaders of the audience is also a faithful reader of the message reference; Reference News News for the layout are, advertising accounted for less than the version provided the rate 1 / 6, is the launch customer reference information to maximize the advertising effect. Reference information is the most representative of China's political news media, is a favorite of newspaper readers.
Language (s): Chinese
Ad Rate: Full Page Mono 260000.00
Ad Rate: Full Page Colour 350000.00
Currency: China Yuan Renminbi
DAILY NEWSPAPER

Changchun Daily 459122
Editorial: Changchun Daily Press, 10 Xinmin Dajie, Changchun 130021 **Tel:** 86 43185611706
Freq: Daily; **Circ:** 180001 Not Audited
Editor in Chief: Fang Lv
Profile: It covers local and regional news in Jilin province as well as national news.
Language (s): Chinese
DAILY NEWSPAPER

Chengde Daily 459566
Editorial: Chengde Daily, Xinjuzhai, Huochezhanlu, Chengde 67000 **Tel:** 86 31 42152035
Web site: http://www.cddaily.com.cn
Freq: Daily; **Circ:** 50003 Not Audited
Editor: Jianxin Liu
Profile: Chengde Daily is a general newspaper with strong local focus covering news, social issues, lifestyle, society, culture, sports and health.
Language (s): Chinese
DAILY NEWSPAPER

Chengdu Business Daily 460869
Editorial: Chengdu Daily Press Group, 159, 2 Duan, Hongxinlu, Chengdu 610017 **Tel:** 86 28 86612222
Web site: http://www.cdsb.com
Freq: Daily; **Circ:** 600001 Not Audited
Editor in Chief: Shuping Chen
Profile: Covers business and financial news in Chengdu region.
Language (s): Chinese
Ad Rate: Full Page Mono 158000.00
Currency: China Yuan Renminbi
DAILY NEWSPAPER

Chengdu Evening News 405537
Editorial: 159 Hongxinglu Erduan, Chengdu 610017
Tel: 86 28 86746906
Email: cdwb962111@sina.com **Web site:** http://www.cdwb.com.cn
Freq: Daily; **Circ:** 350000 Not Audited
Editor: Yuanhang Ren
Profile: Focuses on news in the Chengdu region of China.
Language (s): Chinese
Ad Rate: Full Page Mono 70000.00
Currency: China Yuan Renminbi
DAILY NEWSPAPER

China Archives News 404547
Editorial: China Archives News Press, 106 Yong'an Road, Xuanwu District, Beijing 100050
Tel: 86 10 63150625
Email: charne@vip.163.com **Web site:** http://www.zgdazxw.com.cn/
Freq: 2 Times/Week; **Circ:** 260003 Not Audited
Editor in Chief: Haiying Guo
Profile: Covers national archives, as well as government, military service and constitutional records.
Language (s): Chinese
DAILY NEWSPAPER

China Art Weekly 460876
Editorial: Zhejiang Daily Press Group, 178 Tiyuchanglu, Hangzhou 310039 **Tel:** 86 57185310158
Web site: http://msb.zjol.com.cn
Freq: Weekly
Editor in Chief: Jingfu Cai
Profile: Covers art trends and art appreciation in China.
Language (s): Chinese
DAILY NEWSPAPER

China Automotive News 459607
Editorial: People Daily Group, 115 Fuchenglu, Haidianqu, Beijing 100036 **Tel:** 86 1088132430
Email: cnautonews@cnautonews.com **Web site:** http://www.cnautonews.com
Freq: Weekly; **Circ:** 110003 Not Audited
Profile: Provides information and news about the Chinese and international auto industries.
Language (s): Chinese
DAILY NEWSPAPER

China Beauty Fashion Newspaper 544769
Editorial: China Beauty Fashion Newspaper, 46 Jiulongxiang, Shudu Dadao, Chengdu 610017
Web site: http://www.cbfmg.com/Index.html
Freq: Weekly; **Circ:** 170000
Editor in Chief: Xiaomei Zhang
Profile: China Beauty Fashion Newspaper is a regional publication which covers the latest news and information of beauty, fashion and cosmetics trends in China.
Language (s): Chinese
DAILY NEWSPAPER

China Book Business Report 459469
Editorial: China Book Business Report, 3F, Waiyan Dasha, 19 Xisanhuan Beilu, Beijing 100089
Tel: 86 10 88817687
Web site: http://www.cbbr.com.cn
Freq: 2 Times/Week; **Circ:** 60003 Not Audited
Editor in Chief: Yuemu Sun
Profile: Provides information, comments and critics about the publications in China.
Language (s): Chinese
DAILY NEWSPAPER

China Business 459615
Editorial: China Business, Building Number 1, Number 6, Xisihuan Beilu, Beijing 100097
Tel: 86 10 88890000
Email: cbweb@cbnet.com.cn **Web site:** http://www.cb.com.cn
Freq: Weekly; **Circ:** 380007 Not Audited
Editor in Chief: Peiyu Li
Profile: Covers corporate management, finance, economics and government regulations. Founded in 1985, the China business newspaper by the Chinese academy of social sciences director, the Chinese academy of social sciences, sponsored by the industrial economy, always adhering to the "lifelong learning and wisdom of good management, social" concept, insight into commercial phenomenon, interpretation of commercial law, thrusting commercial success, to promote the commercial civilization. Is a leading provider of comprehensive financial information provider.Business achievement value, China business newspaper in business management service for readers, to provide comprehensive information product. "The China business news, adhering to the" important and useful, and deeply, can read "news concept, service in the enterprise managers and business people, based on the economic front, capture financial information, mining business value, records and bear witness to China's economic hair. Each issue of 850000, covering the circulation of more than 240 cities. "The China business news readers more concentrated in 25 to 44 years of age, among them 35 to 44 years old rate of 50%, and the male readers rate of 72.1%. High-end consumer spending is strong, brand loyalty is high, consumer focus on quality of life. Focus on finance, investment, automobile, high-end digital electronic products, high-end wines, watches, clothing and the consumption of the EMBA and know how to enjoy life and constantly improve themselves. Pay attention to the physical and mental health, advocates of lohas way.
Language (s): Chinese
Ad Rate: Full Page Mono 352000.00
Ad Rate: Full Page Colour 460000.00
Currency: China Yuan Renminbi
DAILY NEWSPAPER

China Business Herald 459608
Owner: China Business News Press Group
Editorial: China Business News Press Group 1 Baoguosi, Xuanwu District Guang'anmennei, Beijing 100053 **Tel:** 86 1063180875
Email: zhongguoshangbao@yeah.net **Web site:** http://www.cb-h.com
Freq: Daily; **Circ:** 190002 Not Audited
Editor in Chief: Shiyu Fan
Profile: This publication covers news from finance, business, trade and investment to automotive trade, retail market and policy related to the industry.
Language (s): Chinese
DAILY NEWSPAPER

China Chemical Industry News 459599
Editorial: China Chemical Industry News, Jia 2, Liupukang Beixiaojie, Beijing 100011
Tel: 86 1080032707
Email: ccinn@ccin.com.cn **Web site:** http://www.ccin.com.cn
Freq: Daily
Editor in Chief: Shuangxin Liu
Profile: Provides daily news and product updates for professionals in the chemical industry including information on manufacturing, technology, equipment, and supplies.
Language (s): Chinese
DAILY NEWSPAPER

China Coal News 460841
Editorial: China Coal News, Meitan Dasha, Building Number 35, Area 13, Heping Street, Chaoyang District, Beijing 100013 **Tel:** 86 106 4463057
Email: bs@aqb.cn **Web site:** http://www.ccoalnews.com
Freq: 2 Times/Week; **Circ:** 100001 Not Audited
Editor in Chief: Haijin Bai
Profile: Covers coal industry and market news, as well as safety of coal mining industry reports.
Language (s): Chinese
DAILY NEWSPAPER

China Communications News 459645
Editorial: China Communications News, Block 13, Area 3 Anhuaxili, Andingmenwai, Beijing 100011
Tel: 86 10 64250642
Web site: http://www.zgjtb.com
Freq: Weekly; **Circ:** 120001 Not Audited
Editor in Chief: Maichi Du
Profile: Covers news of trucking, shipping, air transport, railroads, traffic control and transportation issues.
Language (s): Chinese
DAILY NEWSPAPER

China Computer Education 459975
Editorial: CCID, 16th Floor, Saidi Dasha, 66 Zizhuyuanlu, Haidianqu, Beijing 100044
Web site: http://www.cce.com.cn
Freq: Weekly; **Circ:** 350003 Not Audited
Profile: China Computer Education is a national newspaper for IT Industry. It reports news on market trends, policies and regulations related to IT industry; it also introduces the latest software and hardware to the readers.
Language (s): Chinese
Ad Rate: Full Page Mono 36000.00
Ad Rate: Full Page Colour 49500.00
Currency: China Yuan Renminbi
DAILY NEWSPAPER

China Computer World 459970
Editorial: China Computer World 3rd FIR bldng 3 16 Cuiwei, Wansinoulu Haidian Dist Zhongli, Beijing 100036 **Tel:** 86 1068130909
Web site: http://www.ccw.com.cn
Freq: Weekly; **Circ:** 258001 Not Audited
Profile: Covers issues about IT products such as computers, phones and softwares.
Language (s): Chinese
DAILY NEWSPAPER

China Construction News 459594
Owner: China Construction News Press
Editorial: Block 40, Zone 12, 188 Nansihuan Xilu, Fengtai District, Beijing 100070 **Tel:** 86 1063703659
Email: thong@newsccn.com **Web site:** http://www.newsccn.com
Freq: 2 Times/Week; **Circ:** 100003 Not Audited
Editor in Chief: Qian Deng
Profile: Covers construction news, projects information and interior decoration issues.
Language (s): Chinese
DAILY NEWSPAPER

China Construction News 460840
Editorial: China Construction News, Room 409, Block B, Xinhong Dasha, 5 Building, 8 Yuan, Chedaogou Xilu, Haidian District, Beijing 100089
Tel: 86 1051555511 8669
Email: xxtgb@chinajsb.cn **Web site:** http://www.chinajsb.cn
Freq: 2 Times/Week; **Circ:** 79002 Not Audited
Bureau Chief: Shijie Liu
Profile: covers news in building design, construction materials and construction industry in China.
Language (s): Chinese
DAILY NEWSPAPER

China Consumer News 460821
Editorial: China Consumer News Press, 8 Beisanjie, Fuchenglu, Haidian District, Beijing 100037
Tel: 86 1068471315
Email: ccn@cen.com.cn **Web site:** http://www.ccn.com.cn
Freq: 2 Times/Week; **Circ:** 150001 Not Audited
Editor in Chief: Xueyin Li
Profile: a national newspaper covering issues about consumer interest, product quality supervision, and national and international regulations on product quality.
Language (s): Chinese
DAILY NEWSPAPER

China Culture Daily 460844
Editorial: China Culture Daily Press, 15 Dongtuchenglu, Chaoyangqu, Beijing 100013
Tel: 86 10 85197805
Email: wenhuanews@ccdy.cn **Web site:** http://www.ccdy.cn
Freq: Daily; **Circ:** 50003 Not Audited
Editor: Biao Jian
Profile: A national newspaper covering news on Chinese modern and traditional cultures, arts, and history.
Language (s): Chinese
DAILY NEWSPAPER

China Daily 460819
Owner: China Daily Newspaper Group
Editorial: 15 Huixindongjie, Chaoyang District, Beijing 100029 **Tel:** 86 10 64995000
Email: cdoffice@chinadaily.com.cn **Web site:** http://www.chinadaily.com.cn
Freq: 2 Times/Week; **Circ:** 300000 Not Audited
Tokyo Bureau Chief: Cai Hong; **Publisher:** Yongzhe Huo; **Editor in Chief:** Ling Zhu
Profile: Founded in 1981, serves as China's national English-language newspaper that has effectively entered Western mainstream society and is the newspaper most quoted by the foreign press. The paper also has published the largest number of supplements for international meetings in China among all media outlets. Aims to provide an important window for "China to understand the world and be understood by the world".
Language (s): English
Ad Rate: Full Page Colour 294000.00
Currency: China Yuan Renminbi
DAILY NEWSPAPER

China Economic Times 404442
Editorial: China Economic Times, Wangfujie, Pingxifu, Changpingqu, Beijing 102209
Tel: 86 1081785100
Email: info@cet.com.cn **Web site:** http://www.cet.com.cn
Freq: 2 Times/Week; **Circ:** 420001 Not Audited
Profile: Covers news about economic development in China.
Language (s): Chinese
Ad Rate: Full Page Mono 180000.00
Ad Rate: Full Page Colour 220000.00
Currency: China Yuan Renminbi
DAILY NEWSPAPER

China Education Daily 408706
Editorial: 10 N WenHuiYuan Road, Haidian District, Beijing **Tel:** 86 10 62257722 245
Email: wlb@edumail.com.cn **Web site:** http://www.jyb.cn/gb/2004/06/07/zy/home.htm
Circ: 400000
Editor in Chief: Bo Di
Profile: Covers education in China. Please note that this outlet is owned by the Chinese government. Often times, these outlets have a set editorial schedule and do not accept press materials or give out staff information. The majority of the staff members speak only Chinese.
Language (s): Chinese
DAILY NEWSPAPER

China Education News 459149
Editorial: China Education Press Agency 10 Wenhuiyuan Beilu, Haidianqu, Beijing 100082
Tel: 86 10 62257722
Web site: http://www.jyb.com.cn
Freq: Daily; **Circ:** 400000 Not Audited
Editor in Chief: Ning Liu; **Editor:** Wen Yu
Profile: Focuses on news and information about education policies and related rules.
Language (s): Chinese
Ad Rate: Full Page Colour 160000.00
Currency: China Yuan Renminbi
DAILY NEWSPAPER

China Electric Power 459598
Editorial: China Power News, 1 Ertiao, Baiguanglu, Xuanwuqu, Beijing 100761 **Tel:** 86 10 63415423
Email: zgdy@cpnn.com.cn **Web site:** http://www.cpnn.com.cn
Freq: 2 Times/Week; **Circ:** 200000 Not Audited
Editor: Zhao Fei
Profile: Covers power engineering information, electrical engineering, electrical power industry, as well as electric power delivery, renewable energy sources, automation, control systems and engineering news issues.
Language (s): Chinese
DAILY NEWSPAPER

China Electronics News 459588
Editorial: 8th Fl, Saidi Daxia, 66 Zizhuyuanlu, Haidianqu, Beijing 100048 **Tel:** 86 10 88558848
Email: zbs@cena.com.cn **Web site:** http://www.cena.com.cn
Freq: 2 Times/Week; **Circ:** 87003 Not Audited
Editor: Ying Li; **Editor in Chief:** Dong Liu; **Editor:** Bo Ma; **Editor in Chief:** Jianzhong Wang; **Editor in Chief:** Xiaobing Wu; **Editor:** Chenbing Xin
Profile: Covers information and news in the IT industry. Aimed at local leaders in charge of electronic information; domestic and foreign investors in electronics and information enterprises; and staff in domestic and foreign securities, finance and consulting.
Language (s): Chinese
DAILY NEWSPAPER

China Environment News 459653
Editorial: China Environment News, 16 Guangqumennei Dajie, Chongwenqu, Beijing 100062
Tel: 86 1067102729
Web site: http://www.cenews.com.cn
Freq: 2 Times/Week; **Circ:** 200003 Not Audited
Bureau Chief: Mingsen Yang
Profile: covers environment protection topics and environment conservation issues.
Language (s): Chinese
DAILY NEWSPAPER

China Fashion Weekly 404446
Editorial: China Fashion Weekly, 2 Baizhifang Dongjie, Xuanwu District, Beijing 100054
Tel: 86 105 8393998
Web site: http://www.cfw.com.cn
Freq: Weekly; **Circ:** 180003 Not Audited
Editor in Chief: Zengjun Chen
Profile: Covers the fashion industry in China.
Language (s): Chinese
Ad Rate: Full Page Mono 45000.00
Currency: China Yuan Renminbi
DAILY NEWSPAPER

China Financial and Economic News 459611
Editorial: China Financial and Economic News, Jia 54, Guang'anlu, Fengtaiqu, Beijing 100161
Tel: 86 10 63812638
Web site: http://www.cfen.com.cn
Freq: 2 Times/Week; **Circ:** 220003 Not Audited
Editor in Chief: Guofu Sun
Profile: covers news on government policies in business, financial sector and accountancy field. Please note that this outlet is owned by the Chinese government. Often times, these outlets have a set editorial schedule and do not accept press materials or give out staff information. The majority of the staff members speak only Chinese.
Language (s): Chinese
DAILY NEWSPAPER

China Flowers & Gardening News 404397
Editorial: China Flower and Gardening News, 19 Hengliutiao, Dongtiejiangying, Fengtai District, Beijing 100079 **Tel:** 86 1087680622
Web site: http://www.china-flower.com
Freq: 2 Times/Week; **Circ:** 50001 Not Audited
Editor in Chief: Xiangrong Wang
Profile: Covers the horticulture and gardening industry.
Language (s): Chinese
DAILY NEWSPAPER

China Food Quality News 459163
Editorial: China Food Industry Association, 19 Xisihuan Zhonglu, Beijing 100143 **Tel:** 86 1051881559
Email: cfqn2009@126.com **Web site:** http://www.cfqn.com.cn
Freq: 2 Times/Week; **Circ:** 100000
Editor in Chief: Changxue Zhu
Profile: China Food Quality News is an official publication of China Food Industry Association that mainly provides the latest news and knowledge about food and health.
Language (s): Chinese
DAILY NEWSPAPER

China Gold News 459472
Editorial: China Gold News 15F BLK B Luoke Shidai Zhongxin, 103 Huizhongli Chaoyang Dist, Beijing 100101 **Tel:** 86 1084871316
Email: zghjbs@163.com **Web site:** http://www.goldnews.com.cn
Freq: 2 Times/Week; **Circ:** 60003 Not Audited
Editor in Chief: Siyuan Rong
Profile: China Gold News is a leading national newspaper that mainly focuses on the latest news on gold industry and gold market in China.
Language (s): Chinese
DAILY NEWSPAPER

China Green Times 460835
Editorial: China Green Times, 18 Dongjie, Hepingli, Beijing 100714 **Tel:** 86 1084238640
Email: yaowenban@sina.com **Web site:** http://www.greentimes.com
Freq: Daily; **Circ:** 50001 Not Audited
Bureau Chief: Fulin Ding; **Editor in Chief:** Jianzhu Li
Profile: Focuses on the news of forestry and lumber in China.
Language (s): Chinese
DAILY NEWSPAPER

China High School Students 459583
Editorial: Building 5, Beili, Zuojiazhuang, Chaoyangqu, Beijing 100028 **Tel:** 86 10 84541086
Web site: http://www.ccppg.com.cn
Freq: 2 Times/Week; **Circ:** 550003 Not Audited
Editor: Wei Si
Profile: focuses on studies and lives of high school students in China.
Language (s): Chinese
Ad Rate: Full Page Mono 100000.00
Currency: China Yuan Renminbi
DAILY NEWSPAPER

China Human Resources News 459162
Editorial: Human Resources Department, PRC, 5 Yuhuili, Chaoyangqu, Beijing 100010
Tel: 86 1084623709
Email: bin2050@163.com **Web site:** http://www.rensb.com
Freq: Weekly; **Circ:** 100004 Not Audited
Editor: Fengxia Chen; **Editor in Chief:** Baozhong Zhang
Profile: It reports and promotes government policies on human resource and labor market.
Language (s): Chinese
DAILY NEWSPAPER

China Industrial and Commerce News 459622
Owner: China Industrial and Commerce News Press
Editorial: China Industrial & Commerce News Press 23 Fangyuan, Jiajimiao Huaxian, Fengtaiqu Dongli, Beijing 100070 **Tel:** 86 1063784486
Email: ykf3601@163.com **Web site:** http://www.cicn.com.cn
Freq: 2 Times/Week; **Circ:** 135003 Not Audited
Bureau Chief: Aifu Liang; **Editor in Chief:** Fengwu Zhao
Profile: provides industrial and commerce news, as well as relevant government policies and regulations issues.
Language (s): Chinese
DAILY NEWSPAPER

China Industrial Economy News 459142
Editorial: China Industrial Information News, 3/F, Block 4, 1 Haoyuan Guanzhuang Shuangliu North

Street, Chaoyang District, Beijing 100024
Tel: 86 1065439061
Email: cjxw1996@vip.163.com **Web site:** http://www.cien.com.cn
Freq: 2 Times/Week; **Circ:** 90003 Not Audited
Bureau Chief: Jun Yao
Profile: Covers news of current affairs ranging from politics, economy, finance, travel and business news with the focus on industrial development and economic growth.
Language (s): Chinese
DAILY NEWSPAPER

China Industry News 459466

Editorial: China Industry News Press, 1 Putaoyuan, Zhanlanlu, Xichengqu, Beijing 100037
Tel: 86 1088378156
Email: zbs@cinn.cn **Web site:** http://www.cinn.cn
Freq: 2 Times/Week; **Circ:** 120003 Not Audited
President: Wei Cheng; **Editor in Chief:** Shiyong He; **News Editor:** Jiusheng Qu
Profile: Covers industry news and relevant government regulations issues.
Language (s): Chinese
DAILY NEWSPAPER

China Information News 460853

Owner: National Bureau of Statistics of China
Editorial: National Bureau of Statistics of China, 57 Yuetan Nanjie, Sanlihe, Xichengqu, Beijing 100826
Tel: 86 1063376756
Email: jrpl@sina.com **Web site:** http://www.zgxxb.com.cn/
Freq: 2 Times/Week; **Circ:** 300002 Not Audited
Profile: China Information News concerns national news, stastistical information and international news.
Language (s): Chinese
DAILY NEWSPAPER

China Inspection and Quarantine Times 459621

Editorial: China Inspection and Quarantine Times, 22 Maizidianjie, Chaoyangqu, Beijing 100026
Tel: 86 10 64194028
Freq: 2 Times/Week; **Circ:** 100003 Not Audited
Editor in Chief: Shunzeng Chen
Profile: reports on inspection and quarantine news, as well as exports and imports supervision issues.
Language (s): Chinese
DAILY NEWSPAPER

China Inspection and Supervision News 691398

Editorial: China Inspection and Supervision News, No. 2, Guang'anmen Nanjiejia, Xuanwu District, Beijing 100053 **Tel:** 86 1059598025
Email: hailong0410@yahoo.cn **Web site:** http://www.mos.gov.cn/csr
Freq: Daily
Editor in Chief: Xiangfeng Meng
Profile: Covers inspection and supervision news, as well as relevant government regulations and policies.
Language (s): Chinese
DAILY NEWSPAPER

China Insurance News 459095

Editorial: China Insurance News Press, 27 Huayuanlu, Haidian District, Beijing 100088
Tel: 86 1063998209
Email: sinoins@sinoins.com **Web site:** http://www.sinoins.com
Freq: 2 Times/Week; **Circ:** 200003 Not Audited
Editor in Chief: Yongsheng Fan
Profile: covers insurance and risk professional news, as well as insurance and protection products issues.
Language (s): Chinese
DAILY NEWSPAPER

China Intellectual Property News 459475

Editorial: China Intellectual Property News, Block 3, No. 8 Yuan, Huayuan Road, Haidianqu, Beijing 100088 **Tel:** 86 1082803936
Web site: http://www.cipnews.com.cn
Freq: 2 Times/Week; **Circ:** 100003 Not Audited
Editor in Chief: Qizhang Li
Profile: covers issues about intellectual property in China.
Language (s): Chinese
DAILY NEWSPAPER

China Land and Resources News 459644

Editorial: China Land and Resources News, Jia 30 Xisi Yangrou Hutong, Xicheng District, Beijing 100011
Tel: 86 1066123059
Email: clr-info@126.com **Web site:** http://www.clr.cn
Freq: Weekly; **Circ:** 75001 Not Audited
Profile: Reports on Chinese land resources news, relevant government regulations and services issues.
Language (s): Chinese
DAILY NEWSPAPER

China Medical Tribune 459999

Editorial: Beijing Lido Plaza Commercial Bldg, Tai Rd, Bldg 5, Beijing 100009 **Tel:** 86 10 64036988 227
Email: web@cmt.com.cn **Web site:** http://www.cmt.com.cn
Freq: Weekly; **Circ:** 160003 Not Audited
Profile: Publishes the latest research reports and academic papers in medicine, as well as analysis of clinical cases.
Language (s): Chinese
DAILY NEWSPAPER

China Medicine News 459527

Owner: China Medicine News Press
Editorial: China Medicine News Press, Jia 2, Wenhuiyuan Nanlu, Haidianqu, Beijing 100088
Tel: 86 1062213355
Email: syw@cnpharm.com **Web site:** http://www.cnpharm.com
Freq: 2 Times/Week; **Circ:** 300002 Not Audited
Editor in Chief: Xianye Fang
Profile: China Medicine News reports on medical and health related news and medicinal technology issues. It also covers the medical development in China.
Language (s): Chinese
DAILY NEWSPAPER

China Metallurgical News 459465

Editorial: China Metallurgical News Press Blk 26 Sanqu, Chaoyangqu Anzhenli, Beijing 100029
Tel: 86 10 64453751
Web site: http://www.csteelnews.com
Freq: 2 Times/Week; **Circ:** 50003 Not Audited
Bureau Chief: Qihua Jiang; **Editor in Chief:** Wenyan Lu
Profile: provides "useful and meaningful" news reports and economic information to serve China's iron and steel industry and other related field in an all-round manner.
Language (s): Chinese
DAILY NEWSPAPER

China Meteorological News 459643

Owner: China Meteorological Administration
Editorial: China Meteorological Administration, 46 Zhongguancun Nandajie, Haidianqu, Beijing 100081
Tel: 86 1068406752
Web site: http://www.zgqxb.com.cn/
Freq: 2 Times/Week; **Circ:** 50002 Not Audited
Bureau Chief: Xin Hu; **Editor in Chief:** Linghui Zeng
Profile: covers meteorology news and weather forecast, as well as climate information collecting and analyzing.
Language (s): Chinese
DAILY NEWSPAPER

China Mining News 459596

Owner: China Mining News Press
Editorial: China Mining News Press, Room 1701, Block 2, Zhiheng Mingyuan, 23 Nanbinghelu, Guang'anmen, Beijing 100055 **Tel:** 86 13718643421
Web site: http://www.chinamining.com.cn
Freq: 2 Times/Week; **Circ:** 80003 Not Audited
Editor in Chief: Jiahua Wang
Profile: provides news and analysis of mining and minerals, it also covers the development of the mining industry, study of environment, geology and management of mining technique.
Language (s): Chinese
DAILY NEWSPAPER

China Modern Enterprises 459652

Editorial: Nongmin Daily Press, 15 Huixin Xijie, Chaoyangqu, Beijing 100029 **Tel:** 86 13401197100
Email: chuan0513@126.com **Web site:** http://www.cmenews.com.cn
Freq: 2 Times/Week; **Circ:** 360003 Not Audited
Editor: Yanling Dong
Profile: Covers news on related rules and regulations, new achievement and development of township enterprises in China. It also focuses on local and national news.
Language (s): Chinese
Ad Rate: Full Page Mono 100000.00
Ad Rate: Full Page Colour 120000.00
Currency: China Yuan Renminbi
DAILY NEWSPAPER

China Network World 459971

Editorial: China Network World, 4th Floor, Block 3, 16 Cuiwei Zhongli, Wanshoulu, Haidianqu, Beijing 100036 **Tel:** 86 10 68130909 8050
Web site: http://www.cnw.com.cn
Freq: Weekly; **Circ:** 120003 Not Audited
Editor in Chief: Hui Gao
Profile: covers the management, security amd development of computers systems and networks.
Language (s): Chinese
DAILY NEWSPAPER

China Nonferrous Metals News 459468

Editorial: China Nonferrous Metals News, 6th Floor, Yi-12, Fuxinglu, Beijing 100814 **Tel:** 86 1063971476
Email: cnmn@cnmn.com.cn **Web site:** http://www.cnmn.com.cn
Freq: 2 Times/Week; **Circ:** 50003 Not Audited
Editor: Yeping Liu; **Editor in Chief:** Yinping Yuan
Profile: Covers nonferrous metals industry news and the latest products prices, company profiles, industry services and products topics.
Language (s): Chinese
DAILY NEWSPAPER

China Ocean News 404391

Editorial: China Ocean News, 1 Fuxingmenwai Dajie, Xicheng District, Beijing 100860 **Tel:** 86 10 68519427
Email: hyb20091104@163.com **Web site:** http://epaper.oceanol.com
Freq: 2 Times/Week; **Circ:** 100003 Not Audited
Editor in Chief: Guangsheng Gai
Profile: Covers national ocean news and environment information, as well as oceanography issues.
Language (s): Chinese
DAILY NEWSPAPER

China Package News 459642

Editorial: PackChina Corporation, 9 Xinghualu, Dongcheng District, Beijing 100013
Tel: 86 10 84271012
Email: bzbz2012@sohu.com **Web site:** http://www.cpackage.com
Freq: 2 Times/Week; **Circ:** 90003 Not Audited
Profile: China Package News is a national newspaper for packaging industry in China, covering package development, market trends, policies and regulation related to the industry; it also introduces new products, materials and equipment to the readers.
Language (s): Chinese
DAILY NEWSPAPER

China Petrochemical News 460842

Editorial: Sinopec News Press, 58 Anwaidajie, Dongchengqu, Beijing 100011 **Tel:** 86 84277215
Web site: http://www.sinopecnews.com.cn
Freq: Daily; **Circ:** 110001 Not Audited
Editor in Chief: Dapeng Lv
Profile: covers market news, tracking the trends and changes in prices that affect the industry, including trade, environmental, and regulatory issues.
Language (s): Chinese
DAILY NEWSPAPER

China Petroleum Daily 459581

Editorial: Jia-3 Anhuali Erqu, Anwai, Chaoyangqu, Beijing 100011 **Tel:** 86 10 64523333
Email: zgsyb@vip.163.com **Web site:** http://www.zgsyb.com
Freq: 2 Times/Week; **Circ:** 110003 Not Audited
Editor in Chief: Ping Tan
Profile: Covers oil and gas news for oil exploration, oil sands, oil drilling, drilling rigs, core drilling, as well as relevant oil industry and engineering issues.
Language (s): Chinese
DAILY NEWSPAPER

China Philanthropy Times 687047

Editorial: China Philanthropy Times, Jia 6 Baijiazhuanglu, Chaoyang District, Beijing 100020
Tel: 86 10 65953695
Web site: http://www.china-lottery.net
Freq: Weekly; **Circ:** 300000
Profile: China Philanthropy Times is a national newspaper which mainly covers the information and latest development in social welfare in China and related news of social lottery, social enterprises, social work and social services in China and overseas.
Language (s): Chinese
DAILY NEWSPAPER

China Philately News 459613

Editorial: People's Posts & Telecommunications News, Office 3F 11 Anyuanlu, Beijing 100029
Tel: 86 1064962938
Web site: http://www.cnjy.com.cn
Freq: 2 Times/Week; **Circ:** 100000
Profile: covers the latest information of stamps collecting.
Language (s): Chinese
DAILY NEWSPAPER

China Police Daily 460843

Editorial: China Police Daily, 9 You'anlu, Fangxingyuan, Fangzhuang, Fengtaiqu, Beijing 100078 **Tel:** 86 108 3731000
Email: wxg@cpd.com.cn **Web site:** http://www.cpd.com.cn
Freq: 2 Times/Week; **Circ:** 300001 Not Audited
Editor in Chief: Huanjing Liu
Profile: Covers current police news, features, training, and relevant policies as well as police services and responsibilities issues.
Language (s): Chinese
DAILY NEWSPAPER

China Population News 404368

Editorial: China Population News, Jia 36 Jiaoda Donglu, Haidian District, Beijing 100044
Tel: 86 1062255622
Freq: 2 Times/Week; **Circ:** 280001 Not Audited
Editor in Chief: Hongwei Yi
Profile: China Population News is a national newspaper which focuses on national population issues, family planning news, reproductive health, gender, gender equality, women empowerment, adolescent, migrants and international cooperation.
Language (s): Chinese
DAILY NEWSPAPER

China Post News 459160

Editorial: China Courier Service Corporation, 173 Yong'anlu, Xuanwuqu, Beijing 100050
Tel: 86 1083162921
Web site: http://www.chinapostnews.com.cn
Freq: 2 Times/Week; **Circ:** 100001 Not Audited
Editor: Jurui Zhang
Profile: Covers the latest news from China State Post Bureau.
Language (s): Chinese
DAILY NEWSPAPER

China Press & Publishing Journal 405538

Editorial: China Press & Publishing Journal, PO Box 2350 Chaoyang District, Beijing 100023
Tel: 86 10 87622075
Email: chinaxwcb@126.com **Web site:** http://www.chinaxwcb.com/index/index.htm
Freq: Daily; **Circ:** 80004 Not Audited
Profile: It covers the latest information on publishing and press industry in China and overseas.It also introduces government policies and regulations.
Language (s): Chinese
DAILY NEWSPAPER

China Quality Daily 460826

Editorial: China Quality Press, 3 Yuhui Nanlu, Chaoyangqu, Beijing 100029 **Tel:** 86 1084639548
Email: lxwm@cqn.com.cn **Web site:** http://www.cqn.com.cn
Freq: 2 Times/Week; **Circ:** 130001 Not Audited
Editor: Dongling Li; **Editor in Chief:** Wei Meng
Profile: covers quality assurance, product improvement issues, and market and technical supervision issues.
Language (s): Chinese
DAILY NEWSPAPER

China Railway Construction News 459591

Owner: China Railroad Construction News Press
Editorial: China Railroad Construction News Press, 40 Fuxinglu, Beijing 100855
Email: zgtdjzb@vip.sina.com **Web site:** http://www.crcn.com.cn/
Freq: 2 Times/Week; **Circ:** 100003 Not Audited
Editor in Chief: Haiyan Zhu
Profile: Covers information and news of railroad construction industry and business, engineering companies, daily rail news, railroad crossings, construction and track removal, as well as railroad evaluations and inspections issues.
Language (s): Chinese
DAILY NEWSPAPER

China Real Estate News 460181

Editorial: China Real Estate News, Jia22 Xiangjun Beili, Chaoyang District, Beijing 100020
Tel: 86 1065079988
Web site: http://www.china-crb.cn
Freq: Weekly; **Circ:** 120001 Not Audited
Editor in Chief: Guozhen Shi
Profile: Covers news, market, property management, policies and regulations, investment, planning and development issues in the property field.
Language (s): Chinese
DAILY NEWSPAPER

China Reform News 404361

Editorial: China Reform News 5 Xiaguangli, Sanyuanqiao Chaoyangqu, Beijing 100027
Tel: 86 1064616555
Web site: http://www.crd.net.cn
Freq: 2 Times/Week; **Circ:** 100000
Editor in Chief: Yijun Ma
Profile: covers the achievements of the economic reform and development in China.
Language (s): Chinese
DAILY NEWSPAPER

China Safety Production News 459171

Editorial: China Safety Production News Press, 4th Floor, Meitan Daxia, Block 35, Area 13, Hepingjie, Chayang District, Beijing 100013 **Tel:** 86 1064463042
Web site: http://www.aqsc.cn
Freq: 2 Times/Week; **Circ:** 140003 Not Audited
Editor in Chief: Haijin Bai
Profile: covers safety production in coal industry, as well as other related safety issues.
Language (s): Chinese
DAILY NEWSPAPER

China Securities Journal 459614

Editorial: China Securities Journal, Jia-97, Xuanwumen Xidajie, Beijing 100031
Tel: 86 10 63070233
Email: csnews@zzb.com.cn **Web site:** http://www.cs.com.cn
Freq: 2 Times/Week; **Circ:** 600003 Not Audited
Editor in Chief: Chen Lin
Profile: A national business and finance newspaper covering the capital markets and financial markets in China and abroad. "China Securities News" is sponsored by the national Xinhua News Agency Securities Daily, China Securities Regulatory Commission is the designated information disclosure of listed companies the newspaper, the China Insurance Regulatory Commission disclosure of insurance information designated newspapers, the China Banking Regulatory Commission disclosed in a trust company designated Information newspaper."China Securities News," the securities, the financial report for the center, reported that domestic and international economic trends, macro-economic policies; reported that the domestic securities market, listed companies and other professional fields; reported in the United States, Europe, Japan and Hong Kong and Taiwan financial and securities markets; concerned about money, insurance, funds, futures, real estate, foreign exchange, gold and other adjacent markets, and in the broader financial field has a greater influence.
Language (s): Chinese
Ad Rate: Full Page Mono 160000.00
Ad Rate: Full Page Colour 320000.00
Currency: China Yuan Renminbi
DAILY NEWSPAPER

China Ship News 459587

Editorial: 5 Yuetan Beijie, Beijing 100861
Tel: 86 10 68058257
Email: news@chinashipnews.com.cn
Freq: 2 Times/Week; **Circ:** 50007 Not Audited

Profile: China Ship News engages in business and information service in the shipbuilding industry. It mainly focuses on information service including updated shipbuilding and shipping information, in-depth analysis on the market trend, shipbuilding forum, supply and demand information, marine equipment, etc.
Language (s): Chinese
DAILY NEWSPAPER

China Society News 459137
Editorial: China Society News Press Group, Xinlong Dasha, 33 Er'long Lu, Xicheng Qu, Beijing 100032
Tel: 86 1066030951
Web site: http://zgsh.ceepa.cn
Freq: Daily; **Circ:** 95003 Not Audited
Editor in Chief: Youlu Mi; **Bureau Chief:** Aiping Wang; **General Manager:** Shujin Wang
Profile: Covers society news and social issues, as well as current government regulations and policies topics.
Language (s): Chinese
DAILY NEWSPAPER

China Space News 692066
Editorial: China Space News, 3.F, Zonghelou, 8 Fuchenglu, Haidian District, Beijing 100830
Tel: 86 1068767232
Web site: http://www.china-spacenews.com
Freq: 2 Times/Week; **Circ:** 40000
Editor in Chief: Xu Shi
Profile: covers information of space science and industry, as well as daily astronomy, star charts, pictures of planets, space missions topics.
Language (s): Chinese
DAILY NEWSPAPER

China Special Product 404409
Editorial: China Special Product Press, No. 16, 4 Qu, Anhui Li, Beijing 100723 **Tel:** 86 1084885778
Email: techanbao6688@163.com **Web site:** http://www.cntcb.com
Freq: 2 Times/Week; **Circ:** 53003 Not Audited
Editor in Chief: Zhen Liu
Profile: provides information about special products in different areas in China, as well as news about agricultural industry, agricultural supply and trade issues.
Language (s): Chinese
DAILY NEWSPAPER

China Sports Daily 460825
Editorial: China Sports Publications Corporation, 8 Tiyuguanlu, Chongwenqu, Beijing 100061
Tel: 86 10 67110066
Web site: http://www.sportsol.com.cn
Freq: Daily; **Circ:** 300003
Profile: Covers both national and international sports news.
Language (s): Chinese
Ad Rate: Full Page Mono 100000.00
Ad Rate: Full Page Colour 120000.00
Currency: China Yuan Renminbi
DAILY NEWSPAPER

China Stock News 829292
Owner: Xinhua News Agency
Editorial: No. A97, West Ave, Xuan Wu Men, Xi Cheng District, Beijing 100031
Email: csnews@zzb.com.cn **Web site:** http://www.cs.com.cn
Profile: Covers China Securities News, financial reports, funds, futures, real estate and foreign exchange. It's hosted by Xinhua News Agency.
DAILY NEWSPAPER

China Taxation News 459600
Editorial: China Taxation News, 21 Huaibaishu Houjie, Xuanwu District, Beijing 100053
Tel: 86 10 83120012
Web site: http://www.ctaxnews.com.cn
Freq: 2 Times/Week; **Circ:** 570003 Not Audited
Editor in Chief: Diken Zhang
Profile: Covers the latest news on the government tax policies and regulations as well as reports related tax issues.
Language (s): Chinese
DAILY NEWSPAPER

China Teacher News 459474
Editorial: China Teacher News, 10 Wenhuiyuan Beilu, Haidian District, Beijing 100082 **Tel:** 86 1082296669
Email: zgjsbtougao@21cn.com **Web site:** http://www.chinateacher.com.cn
Freq: Weekly; **Circ:** 200003 Not Audited
Editor in Chief: Tangjiang Liu
Profile: Covers teaching and education issues in China.
Language (s): Chinese
DAILY NEWSPAPER

China Technology Market News 459289
Editorial: China Technology Market News, 11/F, Jinwan Chuanmei Dasha, No. 358 Nanjing Road, Nankai District, Tianjin 300100 **Tel:** 86 2227509515
Email: zgjsscb@126.com **Web site:** http://www.ctmn.cn
Freq: 2 Times/Week; **Circ:** 160003 Not Audited
Editor in Chief: Qiyuan Miao
Profile: provides information on the national technology market, including funding, contracting and partnership opportunities issues. It also covers the latest development of the technological issues in China.
Language (s): Chinese
DAILY NEWSPAPER

China Television News 459060
Editorial: China Television News, CCTV, Section A, Enfei Keji Dasha, 11 Fuxinglu, Haidian District, Beijing 100859 **Tel:** 86 1068500857
Web site: http://www.cntv.cn
Freq: Weekly; **Circ:** 3650000 Not Audited
Profile: Provides schedules and details on Chinese Central TV Networks (CCTV) programming.
Language (s): Chinese
Ad Rate: Full Page Mono 230000.00
Ad Rate: Full Page Colour 240000.00
Currency: China Yuan Renminbi
DAILY NEWSPAPER

China Textile News 459578
Editorial: China Textile News, Jia 2, 18, Dongsanhuan Zhonglu, Chaoyangqu, Beijing 100022
Tel: 86 10 87751055
Web site: http://www.zgfzb.net.cn
Freq: Daily; **Circ:** 100003 Not Audited
Bureau Chief: Zhiqi Tong
Profile: China Textile News started her initial issue in 1986 and has been a publication of both domestic and international delivery ever since. As a weekday publication Monday to Friday, it is the only the comprehensive and giant newspaper in China specialized in textile industry, China Textile News mirrors the economic performance in the textile and apparel industry in a complete and prompt mannner and timely gives out the governmental policies and regulations with regards to the growth production and performance of the textile industry and provides the readers with textile information from domestic and international markets with the news coverage extended to the three important aspects apparel home textile and industrial applications and to the textile machinery raw materials intermediates and finished products and markets and further all the way to management operation science and technology corporate culture.
Language (s): Chinese
DAILY NEWSPAPER

China Three Gorges Project News 459098
Owner: China Three Gorges Project News Press
Editorial: China Three Gorges Project News Press 80, Dongshanlu, Yichang 443002 **Tel:** 86 7176762587
Email: ctgpn@163.com **Web site:** http://www.ctgpc.com
Freq: Weekly; **Circ:** 50002 Not Audited
Editor: Chengzhang Jin
Profile: It focuses on the development of the three gorges projects.
Language (s): Chinese
DAILY NEWSPAPER

China Tourism News 459623
Editorial: Jia-9, Jianguomennei Dajie, Dongchengqu, Beijing 100740 **Tel:** 86 10 85166219
Email: jzz@ctnews.cn **Web site:** http://www.ctnews.com.cn
Freq: 2 Times/Week; **Circ:** 600003 Not Audited
Editor in Chief: Shunli Gao; **Editor:** Xiuhua Yang
Profile: provides travel news, guide and information, as well as package holidays, touring holidays and overseas travel issues. In early 1979, China travel tour business travel management bureau decided to publish a professional newspaper, "Tourism Newsletter", April 1, 1979 was officially inaugurated, in January 1981 changed its name to "Travel News", January 1985 and further changed its name to "China Tourism News ", which is China's only national tourism industry newspaper.
Language (s): Chinese
Ad Rate: Full Page Mono 65000.00
Ad Rate: Full Page Colour 150000.00
Currency: China Yuan Renminbi
DAILY NEWSPAPER

China Trade News 460830
Editorial: China Trade News, 2, Jin'anxijie, Beisanhuandonglu, Chaoyangqu, Beijing 100028
Tel: 86 10 64667333
Email: lihy@ccpit.org **Web site:** http://www.chinatradenews.com.cn
Freq: 2 Times/Week; **Circ:** 168000 Not Audited
Profile: China Trade News is sponsored by China Council for the Promotion of International Trade (CCPIT) and China Chamber of International Commerce (CCOIC). It reports on the latest international trade news and hot issues, and the updates of market trend.
Language (s): Chinese
Ad Rate: Full Page Mono 120000.00
Ad Rate: Full Page Colour 150000.00
Currency: China Yuan Renminbi
DAILY NEWSPAPER

China Urban-Rural Financial News 459603
Editorial: China Urban-Rural Financial News Press, 32 Babaozhuang, Beijing 100036 **Tel:** 86 1088128486
Web site: http://www.zgcxjrb.com
Freq: 2 Times/Week; **Circ:** 100001 Not Audited
Profile: Reports on Chinese agribusiness, as well as relevant economics and financial information in urban-rural areas.
Language (s): Chinese
DAILY NEWSPAPER

China Water Resources News 459595
Editorial: China Water Resources News Press, 2 Baiguanglu Ertiao, Beijing 100053
Tel: 86 10 63205285
Email: abc@chinawater.com.cn **Web site:** http://www.chinawater.com.cn
Freq: 2 Times/Week; **Circ:** 110003 Not Audited
Manager: Tong Du
Profile: Covers the development of water control, as well as the ecology and tourism issues related to water control.
Language (s): Chinese
DAILY NEWSPAPER

China Women's News 460836
Editorial: China Women's News 103 Xidajie Di'anmen Xichengqu, Beijing 100009
Tel: 86 1066166311
Web site: http://www.china-woman.com
Freq: 2 Times/Week; **Circ:** 100001 Not Audited
Editor in Chief: Xiaofei Lu
Profile: covers politics, social issues, family interest, law, culture, education, healthcare and sports topics centering around women in China.
Language (s): Chinese
DAILY NEWSPAPER

China Youth Daily 459580
Editorial: China Youth Daily, 2 Haiyuncang, Dongzhimennei, Beijing 100702 **Tel:** 86 10 64098000
Email: guojibu@cyd.net.cn **Web site:** http://zqb.cyol.com/html/2011-08/02/nbs.D110000zgqnb_01.htm
Freq: Daily; **Circ:** 600002 Not Audited
Editor in Chief: Xiaochuan Lu
Profile: China Youth Daily focuses on youth interests including news, technology, society, education, culture, sports and society articles. China Youth Daily, founded in April 27, 1951, is a major influence on a comprehensive national daily newspaper. China Youth Daily, the national youth-oriented audience, the scale of tens of millions of readers, the issue effectively in major cities across the country.
Language (s): Chinese
Ad Rate: Full Page Mono 160000.00
Currency: China Yuan Renminbi
DAILY NEWSPAPER

Chinese Business Morning View 460182
Editorial: Chinese Business Morning View, 6th Floor, Guoshi Daxia, 71 Chongshandonglu, Huagnguqu, Shenyang 110032 **Tel:** 86 2496128
Web site: http://www.hscb.com.cn
Freq: Daily; **Circ:** 500001 Not Audited
Editor: Yu Yang; **Editor:** Libin Zhang
Profile: covers local, regional and international news, as well as business and finance issues.
Language (s): Chinese
Ad Rate: Full Page Mono 248000.00
Currency: China Yuan Renminbi
DAILY NEWSPAPER

Chinese Business View 460866
Editorial: Chinese Business View, 156 Hanguangbeilu, Xi'an 710068 **Tel:** 86 2988429016
Web site: http://www.huash.com
Freq: Daily; **Circ:** 500001 Not Audited
Bureau Chief: Huaizhong Zhou
Profile: provides news of business and finance in middle area of China.
Language (s): Chinese
Ad Rate: Full Page Mono 210000.00
Currency: China Yuan Renminbi
DAILY NEWSPAPER

Chinese Children's News 459584
Owner: China Children's Press & Publication Group
Editorial: China Children's Press & Publication Group, Zuojiazhuang Beili Chaoyangqu Building 5, Beijing 100028 **Tel:** 86 1064634863
Web site: http://paper.ccppg.com.cn/zgetb
Freq: Weekly; **Circ:** 400003 Not Audited
Editor in Chief: Renfang Wang
Profile: Chinese Children's News is a national newspaper which focuses on news and information of children's education, study, and school life.
Language (s): Chinese
Ad Rate: Full Page Mono 100000.00
Currency: China Yuan Renminbi
DAILY NEWSPAPER

Chinese People's Political Consultative Conference News 459476
Tel: 86 10 88146900
Email: zxb-tlb@vip.163.com **Web site:** http://www.rmzxb.com.cn
Freq: Daily; **Circ:** 120003 Not Audited
Editor: Xiaohui Geng; **Editor:** Youqiang Wang
Profile: National Committee of the Chinese ppl Political Consultative Conference 69 Xibalizhuanglu Haidian Dist
Language (s): Chinese
DAILY NEWSPAPER

Chinese Photography 459579
Owner: China Photographers Association
Editorial: China Photographers Association, 502, Longjidasha Nanlou, 67 Jinbaojie, Dongdan, Dongchengqu, Beijing 100005 **Tel:** 86 106525189
Email: cphotoeditor@sina.com **Web site:** http://www.cphoto.com.cn
Freq: 2 Times/Week; **Circ:** 100003 Not Audited
Profile: Chinese Photography mainly covers news on different kinds of photograph shows and also reports features on photographers both in China and overseas.
Language (s): Chinese
DAILY NEWSPAPER

Chinese Teenagers News 459609
Editorial: China Children's Press & Publication Group, Building 5, Zuojiazhuang Beili, Chaoyang District, Beijing 100028 **Tel:** 86 10 64634838
Web site: http://www.ccppg.com.cn
Freq: Weekly; **Circ:** 990003 Not Audited
Editor in Chief: Zhenglan Wu
Profile: reports on teenager's interests articles, school and extra-curricular activities issues.
Language (s): Chinese
Ad Rate: Full Page Mono 60000.00
Currency: China Yuan Renminbi
DAILY NEWSPAPER

Chongqing Daily 404486
Editorial: Chongqing Daily Press Group, 85 Jiaochangkou, Yuzhongqu, Chongqing 400010
Tel: 86 236 3907042
Email: cqrb@cqrb.cn **Web site:** http://www.cqnews.net
Freq: Daily; **Circ:** 250003 Not Audited
Editor in Chief: Fengjing Mao
Profile: Covers news in Chongqing area and national news in China.
Language (s): Chinese
DAILY NEWSPAPER

Chongqing Economic Times 404358
Editorial: Chongqing Economic Times, 39 Changjiang Erlu, Yuzhongqu, Chongqing 400042
Tel: 86 2389099677
Web site: http://www.chinacqsb.com
Freq: Daily; **Circ:** 240001 Not Audited
Editor: Zhenghua Zhou
Profile: Chongqing Economic Times is a regional economic and business newspaper centering Chongqing City.
Language (s): Chinese
DAILY NEWSPAPER

Chongqing Evening News 460042
Owner: Chongqing Daily Group
Editorial: Chongqing Daily Group, 85 Jiaochangkou, Yuzhong District, Chongqing 4000010
Tel: 86 2363907399
Web site: http://www.cqwb.com.cn
Freq: Daily; **Circ:** 300004 Not Audited
Editor: Yunming Liu
Profile: covers entertainment, business, news, lifestyles, economy, transportation, education, travel, medical care, sports, culture and art.
Language (s): Chinese
Ad Rate: Full Page Mono 124700.00
Currency: China Yuan Renminbi
DAILY NEWSPAPER

Chongqing Morning Post 460041
Editorial: Chongqing Morning News, 85 Jiaochangkou, Yuzhongqu, Chongqing 400010
Tel: 86 23 63907613
Email: cqcb@cqcb.com **Web site:** http://www.cqcb.com
Freq: Daily; **Circ:** 600001 Not Audited
Editor in Chief: Ainong Fu
Profile: Focuses on local and national news.
Language (s): Chinese
Ad Rate: Full Page Mono 113300.00
Currency: China Yuan Renminbi
DAILY NEWSPAPER

Chuncheng Evening News 460811
Editorial: Yunnan Daily Press Group, 337 Xinwenlu, Kunming 650032 **Tel:** 86 8714161886
Web site: http://www.yndaily.com
Freq: Daily; **Circ:** 300003 Not Audited
Editor in Chief: Jianxiang Zhang
Profile: A daily newspaper mainly focusing on news, lifestyle, social and cultural issues in Kunming.
Language (s): Chinese
Ad Rate: Full Page Mono 86400.00
Ad Rate: Full Page Colour 138900.00
Currency: China Yuan Renminbi
DAILY NEWSPAPER

Communication Information News 459565
Editorial: Communication Info News 13F Xinxi Guangchang, Xiqu 7 Dongjie, Fuzhou 350001
Tel: 86 59187529630
Web site: http://www.txxxb.com
Freq: Weekly; **Circ:** 100003 Not Audited
Profile: Covers the news and information of telecommunication industry.
Language (s): Chinese
DAILY NEWSPAPER

Computer Business Information (East China Edition) 459496
Editorial: Room 1306, No 11 Puhuitanglu, Shanghai 200030 **Tel:** 86 2164412101
Email: shenyao@cbigroup.com **Web site:** http://www.cbinews.com
Freq: Weekly; **Circ:** 120003 Not Audited
Bureau Chief: Xiaoling Lu

Profile: Covers the IT industry.
Language (s): Chinese
DAILY NEWSPAPER

Computer Business Information (Jiangsu Edition)
459498

Editorial: Computer Business Info Jiangsu Edition RM 416 #, Zhujianglu 14 Dongda Yingbi, Nanjing 210018 Tel: 86 2583213831
Web site: http://www.cbinews.com
Freq: Weekly; Circ: 70003 Not Audited
Manager: Gu Xie
Profile: Covers the local computer market.
Language (s): Chinese
DAILY NEWSPAPER

Computer Business Information (Yunnan Edition)
459495

Editorial: Computer Business Information (Yunnan Edition), 1-1 Block C, Shuidian Shuili, Kunming 650031 Tel: 86 87 15111383
Email: xuzw@cbigroup.com Web site: http://www.cbinews.com
Freq: Weekly; Circ: 50003 Not Audited
Profile: Computer Business Information (Yunnan Edition) is a regional edition of Computer Business Information focus on the industry news on Yunnan Province. It covers computer news, Network Communication, information about Hardware, Software and Market Trend.
Language (s): Chinese
DAILY NEWSPAPER

Construction Times
459616

Editorial: Construction Times, 3/F No. 110 E Yan'an Road, Shanghai 200002 Tel: 86 21 63212166
Email: jzsbs@jzsbs.com Web site: http://www.jzsbs.com
Freq: 2 Times/Week; Circ: 80003 Not Audited
Profile: provides information on architecture design, construction project and construction industry in and outside China.
Language (s): Chinese
DAILY NEWSPAPER

Contemporary Health News
460852

Editorial: Jinan Daily Press Group, Number 28-1 Jingqilu, Jinan 250001 Tel: 86 53186695668
Web site: http://jkb.e23.cn
Freq: Weekly; Circ: 100001 Not Audited
Editor: Lu Chen
Profile: Covers information and news about health related issues, and provides consult on health and health care for the public.
Language (s): Chinese
DAILY NEWSPAPER

Cosmetic Newspaper
460358

Editorial: Cosmetic Newspaper, 10 Lihuangpilu, Wuhan 430014 Tel: 86 2782835503
Email: hzpbbjb@126.com Web site: http://www.hzpb.com.cn
Freq: Weekly; Circ: 100003 Not Audited
Editor in Chief: Hongjun Du
Profile: covers issues about beauty, beauty products and brands; perfumes, skincare, cosmetics companies, hair care, cosmetic, professionals, makeup and toiletries market, beauty business news, fragrances and raw materials suppliers topics.
Language (s): Chinese
DAILY NEWSPAPER

Culture and Art Weekly
459134

Editorial: Culture and Art Weekly, 6 Beiguanzhengjie, Xi'an 710014 Tel: 86 2986225811
Email: crx1218@vip.sina.com Web site: http://www.whysb.net
Freq: Weekly; Circ: 80001 Not Audited
Editor in Chief: Ruoxing Chen
Profile: It provides latest information on culture and art in the world. It also covers the current cultural and art events.
Language (s): Chinese
DAILY NEWSPAPER

The Dahe Daily
459187

Editorial: Henan Daily Press Group, 28 Nongye Donglu, Zhengzhou 450008 Tel: 86 37165796171
Email: ygd666@sina.com Web site: http://www.dahe.cn
Freq: Daily; Circ: 1000003 Not Audited
Editor: Guangdao Yan
Profile: Covers local, national and international issues.
Language (s): Chinese
Ad Rate: Full Page Mono 110000.00
Currency: China Yuan Renminbi
DAILY NEWSPAPER

Dalian Daily
459300

Editorial: Liaoning Daily Press Group, 76 Shijijie, Zhongsharqu, Dalian 116001
Email: tuwen-email@163.com Web site: http://www.daliandaily.com.cn
Freq: Daily; Circ: 200000
Bureau Chief: Yikui Wang
Profile: focuses on local, national and international news.
Language (s): Chinese
Ad Rate: Full Page Mono 168000.00
Currency: China Yuan Renminbi
DAILY NEWSPAPER

Datong Daily
460855

Editorial: Datong Daily, 8 Silingbujie, Datong 37004
Tel: 86 3522050994
Web site: http://www.dtnews.cn
Freq: Daily; Circ: 100000
Editor in Chief: Xu Zhang
Profile: Covers news on local, regional, international and financial issues.
Language (s): Chinese
DAILY NEWSPAPER

Datong Evening News
460856

Editorial: Datong Daily, 1 Songzhuang Hanlu, Datong 37006 Tel: 86 3526030991
Email: dtwbzl@sohu.com Web site: http://www.dtwb.com.cn
Freq: Daily; Circ: 50000
Profile: Covers local and regional news.
Language (s): Chinese
DAILY NEWSPAPER

Democracy and Law
459146

Editorial: Democracy and Law, Room 306 Guoji Dasha, 19 Jianguomenwaidajie, Chaoyang District, Beijing 100004 Tel: 86 10 85201155
Email: mzfzsb@163.com Web site: http://www.mzyfz.com
Freq: Weekly; Circ: 530001 Not Audited
Editor in Chief: Hui Feng
Profile: It covers legislation, governmental policies, law, work ethics and social issues.
Language (s): Chinese
DAILY NEWSPAPER

Du Shi Kuai Bao/City Express
595458

Editorial: Hangzhou Daily Press Group, 218 Tiyuchang Rd, Hangzhou 310041
Tel: 86 57185151588
Web site: http://dskb.hangzhou.com.cn
Freq: Daily; Circ: 950000
Editor: Hui Liu; Editor in Chief: Xing Yang
Profile: Provides news in the Hangzhou region of China.
Language (s): Chinese
Ad Rate: Full Page Mono 309000.00
Ad Rate: Full Page Colour 428000.00
Currency: China Yuan Renminbi
DAILY NEWSPAPER

Economic Daily
404506

Editorial: Economic Daily Group, 2 Baizhifangdongjie, Xuanwu District, Beijing 100054
Tel: 86 1058392413
Email: cesnew@163.com Web site: http://paper.ce.cn/jjrb/html/2011-07/28/node_2.htm
Freq: Daily; Circ: 800001 Not Audited
Editor: Xiaoguang Liu; Editor: Wei Wu; Editor in Chief: Xiaoguo Zhang
Profile: A national newspaper reporting issues related to China economic reform and development.
Language (s): Chinese
Ad Rate: Full Page Mono 180000.00
Ad Rate: Full Page Colour 218000.00
Currency: China Yuan Renminbi
DAILY NEWSPAPER

Economic Evening News
459072

Editorial: Economic Evening News, 50 Yuzhang Lu, Nanchang 330006 Tel: 86 13970071515
Web site: http://www.cnjjwb.com
Freq: Daily; Circ: 120001 Not Audited
Editor: Yingying Xiong
Profile: covers economics and business issues.
Language (s): Chinese
DAILY NEWSPAPER

Economic Herald
460032

Editorial: Economic Herald, 46 Jinshilu, Jinan 500014
Tel: 86 10 84990581 323
Web site: http://jjdk.periodicals.net.cn
Freq: Weekly; Circ: 100001 Not Audited
Editor-in-Chief: Hong Ji
Profile: Includes business, economics, finance, insurance and management articles.
Language (s): Chinese
DAILY NEWSPAPER

Economic Information Daily
404507

Editorial: Xinhua News Agency, Jia101 Xuanwumen Xidajie, Beijing 100803 Tel: 86 10 63073790
Web site: http://jjckb.xinhuanet.com
Freq: 2 Times/Week; Circ: 160000 Not Audited
Editor in Chief: Yuejin Du
Profile: Covers China's economic development and national and international economic news and related issues.
Language (s): Chinese
Ad Rate: Full Page Mono 210000.00
Currency: China Yuan Renminbi
DAILY NEWSPAPER

Economic Information Times
459068

Editorial: 100 Xihulu, Guiyang 550002
Tel: 86 8515892169
Web site: http://www.gog.com.cn/jjxxsb
Freq: 2 Times/Week; Circ: 50003 Not Audited
Editor in Chief: Ming Yin
Profile: Mainly focuses on the latest news on financial and economic issues. Readers are mainly the economic and financial professionals in China.
Language (s): Chinese
DAILY NEWSPAPER

Elderly News
459214

Owner: Guangzhou Daily Group
Editorial: Guangzhou Daily Group, Room 508, 92 Dadelu, Guangzhou 510120 Tel: 86 2081881557
Email: gzlrb@gzdaily.com Web site: http://lrb.dayoo.com
Freq: Weekly; Circ: 100003 Not Audited
Editor in Chief: Nancheng Zhao
Profile: Elderly News is a national newspaper targeting senior citizens. It reports on social news, health, healthcare for the elderly.
Language (s): Chinese
DAILY NEWSPAPER

Electronic Newspaper
578421

Owner: Electronic Newspaper Publishing
Editorial: Electronic Newspaper Publishing, 55 Binhe Road, Wanhua, Chengdu 610071 Tel: 86 2886142049
Email: 31409957@qq.com Web site: http://www.netdzb.com
Freq: Weekly; Circ: 800000
Profile: Covers the electronic industry of China. It mainly provides news and information of electronic products and materials.
Language (s): Chinese
DAILY NEWSPAPER

Elite Reference
459167

Editorial: Elite Reference, 2 Dongzhimennei Haiyuncang, Beijing 100702 Tel: 86 10 64682086
Web site: http://www.qnck.net.cn
Freq: 2 Times/Week; Circ: 300003 Not Audited
Editor in Chief: Ping Liang
Profile: covers social news, science, sports, communications and military affairs.
Language (s): Chinese
Ad Rate: Full Page Mono 130000.00
Ad Rate: Full Page Colour 156000.00
Currency: China Yuan Renminbi
DAILY NEWSPAPER

Family Doctor Weekly
460061

Editorial: Family Doctor Weekly, 440 Yangminglu, Nanchang 330006 Tel: 86 7916835702
Email: jthysh@163.com Web site: http://www.jtysb.com.cn
Freq: Weekly; Circ: 400002 Not Audited
Editor in Chief: Hejing Lin
Profile: covers clinical trials, medical consultants, health and medicine issues and family and individual health-related issues.
Language (s): Chinese
Ad Rate: Full Page Mono 80000.00
Currency: China Yuan Renminbi
DAILY NEWSPAPER

Famous Brand Times
459061

Editorial: Famous Brand Times, 33 Fuchenglu, Beijing 100037 Tel: 86 1068981140
Web site: http://www.mpsb.xplus.com
Freq: Weekly; Circ: 100003 Not Audited
Editor in Chief: Xiaowei Wang
Profile: Famous Brand Times is a national newspaper which covers news and issues of famous brands in China.
Language (s): Chinese
DAILY NEWSPAPER

Farmer Daily
404508

Owner: Nongmin Daily Press
Editorial: Nongmin Daily Press 15 Huixinxi, Street, Chaoyang District, Beijing 100025
Tel: 886 10 84395001
Web site: http://www.farmer.com.cn
Freq: 2 Times/Week; Circ: 300004 Not Audited
General Manager: Mei Qu
Profile: It covers the latest news and information on agriculture and agribusiness.
Language (s): Chinese
Ad Rate: Full Page Mono 120000.00
Ad Rate: Full Page Colour 140000.00
Currency: China Yuan Renminbi
DAILY NEWSPAPER

Farmer News
459229

Editorial: Farmer News Press, 181 Donghu Road, Wuchang, Wuhan 430077 Tel: 86 27 88567497
Web site: http://www.cnhubei.com/ncxb/index.htm
Freq: 2 Times/Week; Circ: 400000
Profile: provides information about animal feed, breeding and genetics, agribusiness, agricultural contracting and engineering, machinery and equipment, as well as agricultural shows and supply issues.
Language (s): Chinese
DAILY NEWSPAPER

Farmer's Daily
459096

Editorial: Nongmin Daily Press, 1 Beili Balizhuang, Chaowai, Beijing 100025 Tel: 86 10 85831572
Web site: http://www.farmer.com.cn
Freq: Weekly; Circ: 50001 Not Audited
Publisher: Dexiu Zhang
Profile: It focuses on the development and current trend of the agriculture and agribusiness in China.
Language (s): Chinese
DAILY NEWSPAPER

Fashion News
459352

Editorial: Fashion News Press, 25th Floor, Fangzhi Dasha, 482 Zhongshan donglu, Nanjing 210002
Tel: 86 13851810482
Email: njxzw@163.com
Freq: Weekly; Circ: 110003 Not Audited
Editor in Chief: Jianmin Zhou
Profile: Fashion News is a newspaper of fashion industry focusing on East China fashion market. It reports on fashion, fashion accesoories and trendy products.
Language (s): Chinese
DAILY NEWSPAPER

Financial News
459601

Editorial: Financial News Press, 18/F, Block D, Jia 18, Zhongguancun Nandajie, Haidian District, Beijing 100081 Tel: 86 1082198111
Email: fnweb@126.com Web site: http://www.financialnews.com.cn
Freq: 2 Times/Week; Circ: 370001 Not Audited
Editor in Chief: Fuliang Song
Profile: Covers financial news.
Language (s): Chinese
Ad Rate: Full Page Mono 140000.00
Ad Rate: Full Page Colour 180000.00
Currency: China Yuan Renminbi
DAILY NEWSPAPER

The First
404468

Editorial: No.3 Guangqu Road, Chaoyang District, Beijing 100025 Tel: 86 10 87956000
Web site: http://www.thefirst.cn
Circ: 36000
Editor in Chief: Xing wen Xiw
Profile: Covers information and news of social, cultural and entertainment issues.
Language (s): Chinese
Ad Rate: Full Page Mono 240000.00
Currency: China Yuan Renminbi
DAILY NEWSPAPER

Fortune Times
460066

Editorial: Fortune Times, 22/F, Block D, Shimao Tianjie, 9 Guanghua Road, Chaoyang District, Beijing 100020 Tel: 86 1065873610
Web site: http://www.cftmedia.com/
Freq: Daily; Circ: 270003 Not Audited
Editor in Chief: Hengdai Zhai
Profile: Fortune Times is a national newspaper which includes economics, business, finance, accounting, banking, banks and finance companies, as well as e-commerce, international stock markets, securities, investment and insurance.
Language (s): Chinese
DAILY NEWSPAPER

Friday
460339

Editorial: 223 Longpan Zhonglu, Nanjing 210002
Tel: 86 2584686717
Web site: http://www.njnews.cn
Freq: Weekly
Editor in Chief: Liping Jin
Profile: Covers news of entertainment, lifestyle, and fashion.
Language (s): Chinese
DAILY NEWSPAPER

Friendship News
459127

Editorial: Friendship News, Building 5 Shenfulu, Hangzhou 310007 Tel: 86 571 87055285
Email: lybs@vip.163.com Web site: http://www.lybs.com.cn
Freq: 2 Times/Week; Circ: 100001 Not Audited
Editor in Chief: Weisheng Yuan
Profile: It focuses on the governmental policies and social issues.
Language (s): Chinese
DAILY NEWSPAPER

Fujian Business Times
460030

Editorial: 7th Floor Shangye Daxia, 23 Zhongshanlu, Fuzhou 350003 Tel: 86 59187836149
Email: fjbt@sina.com Web site: http://www.fjbt.net
Freq: 2 Times/Week; Circ: 100004 Not Audited
Profile: Covers China business and financial news with focus on Fujian Province. It also covers marketing, consumer electronics, electrical products and equipment, as well as real estate, travel and health issues.
Language (s): Chinese
DAILY NEWSPAPER

Global Knowledge Weekly
459453

Editorial: Changsha Baoye Zhongxin, 267 Wanbao Dadao, Furongqu, Changsha 410016
Tel: 86 73182205609
Web site: http://www.zsblb.com
Freq: Weekly; Circ: 400000
Bureau Chief: Hanqi Zhao
Profile: Covers current global and regional war affairs and social issues in China.
Language (s): Chinese
DAILY NEWSPAPER

Global Times
404489

Owner: People's Daily Press Group
Editorial: 2 Jintaixilu Chaoyangqu, Beijing 100733
Tel: 86 10 65367574
Email: info@globaltimes.com.cn Web site: http://www.globaltimes.cn
Freq: Daily; Circ: 2000000 Not Audited
Editor in Chief: Xijin Hu
Profile: Global Times is a national newspaper reporting on international news solely reported and edited by Chinese. It contains political, business, economic and current affairs all over the world.
Language (s): Chinese
Ad Rate: Full Page Mono 182000.00
Ad Rate: Full Page Colour 254000.00
Currency: China Yuan Renminbi
DAILY NEWSPAPER

China

Global Times (English Edition) 603630
Owner: People's Daily Press Group
Editorial: People's Daily Press Group, Global Times (English Edition), 7/F Topnew Tower, 15 Guanghua Road, Chaoyang District, Beijing 100026
Tel: 86 10 52937633
Email: info@globaltimes.com.cn **Web site:** http://www.globaltimes.cn
Freq: Daily; **Circ:** 160000
Editor in Chief: Xijin Hu
Profile: Global Times is a national newspaper reporting on international news solely reported and edited by Chinese. It contains political, business, economic and current affairs all over the world.
Language (s): English
DAILY NEWSPAPER

Guangdong Construction News 459228
Editorial: Guangdong Construction News, Yangcheng Wanbao Dayuan, Guangzhou 510085
Tel: 86 2087754527
Web site: http://www.ycwb.com/gdjsb/gdjsb.htm
Freq: 2 Times/Week; **Circ:** 120003 Not Audited
Editor in Chief: Shigong Wu
Profile: Covers information and news concerning city construction, environmental protection, building and construction, residential real estates and building material market.
Language (s): Chinese
DAILY NEWSPAPER

Guangming Daily 404324
Editorial: 5 Dongdajie, Zhushikou, Chongwenqu, Beijing 100062 **Tel:** 86 10 67078755
Email: net@gmw.cn **Web site:** http://en.gmw.cn
Freq: Daily; **Circ:** 330003 Not Audited
Editor in Chief: Zhanfan Hu
Profile: Covers business, computer technology, current affairs, entertainment, finance, government, home affairs, international news, national news and government information and policies.
Language (s): Chinese
Ad Rate: Full Page Mono 160000.00
Currency: China Yuan Renminbi
DAILY NEWSPAPER

Guangxi Daily 459091
Editorial: Guangxi Daily Group, 21 Minzhulu, Nanning 530026 **Tel:** 86 867715690995
Email: newgx@gxrb.com.cn **Web site:** http://www.newgx.com.cn
Freq: Daily; **Circ:** 200001 Not Audited
Editor in Chief: Qirui Li; **Editor:** Jie Yao
Profile: Covers news and information in Guangxi region.
Language (s): Chinese
Ad Rate: Full Page Mono 116000.00
Currency: China Yuan Renminbi
DAILY NEWSPAPER

Guangzhou Daily 404492
Editorial: Guangzhou Daily Press Group, 10 Tonglelu, Renmin Zhonglu, Guangzhou 510121
Tel: 86 20 81919191
Email: dayoo@139.com **Web site:** http://gzdaily.dayoo.com
Freq: Daily; **Circ:** 760000 Not Audited
Editor in Chief: Wanfen Li
Profile: Covers local, national and international news on politics, finance, entertainment and culture.
Language (s): Chinese
Ad Rate: Full Page Mono 542500.00
Ad Rate: Full Page Colour 667700.00
Currency: China Yuan Renminbi
DAILY NEWSPAPER

Guangzhou Morning Post 404367
Editorial: Guangzhou Daily Press Group, 606 Xuri Daxia, 315 Guangfu Zhonglu, Guangzhou 510140
Tel: 86 2081019227
Email: 273346328@qq.com **Web site:** http://www.gzmp.net
Freq: 2 Times/Week; **Circ:** 290001 Not Audited
Profile: Guangzhou Morning Post is an English newspaper for readers who would like to learn English and broaden their scope. The newspaper covers news, social issues, entertainment and English learning.
Language (s): Chinese
DAILY NEWSPAPER

Guiyang Evening News 460817
Editorial: Guiyang Daily Press Group, 25 Zhongshan Donglu, Guiyang 550002 **Tel:** 86 8515870467
Web site: http://www.gywb.cn
Freq: Daily; **Circ:** 280001 Not Audited
Editor in Chief: Xuewu Zhang
Profile: Covers news on finance, lifestyle, entertainment and sports.
Language (s): Chinese
DAILY NEWSPAPER

Guizhou Business News 459070
Editorial: Guizhou Daily Press, 372 Baoshanbeilu, Guiyang 550001 **Tel:** 86 6625075
Email: dsbxwzx@vip.aina.com **Web site:** http://gzsb.gog.com.cn
Freq: Daily; **Circ:** 700001 Not Audited
Editor in Chief: Musong Cheng
Profile: Guizhou Business News is a regional economic newspaper covering economic and market news concerning Guizhou Province.
Language (s): Chinese
Ad Rate: Full Page Mono 70000.00
Ad Rate: Full Page Colour 110000.00
Currency: China Yuan Renminbi
DAILY NEWSPAPER

Haikou Evening News 460815
Editorial: 69 Nansha lu, Haikou 570206
Tel: 86 89866824257
Web site: http://www.hkwb.net
Freq: Daily; **Circ:** 200000
Editor in Chief: Zhili Liu; **Bureau Chief:** Tao Xu
Profile: Covers city news and financial news.
Language (s): Chinese
DAILY NEWSPAPER

Health Consultation News 404426
Editorial: Capital Medical University, Shoudu Yike Daxue, You'anmenwai, Beijing 100054
Tel: 86 1063051195
Web site: http://health.sohu.com
Freq: Weekly; **Circ:** 100003 Not Audited
Editor in Chief: Guozhu Liu
Profile: Health Consultation News deals with health and healthcare, as well as medical consultants and relevant issues.
Language (s): Chinese
DAILY NEWSPAPER

Health News 460827
Editorial: Health News, Jia 6 Xiaojie, Dongzhimenwai, Beijing 100027 **Tel:** 86 1064620055
Email: master@jkb.com.cn **Web site:** http://www.healthnews.com.cn
Freq: 2 Times/Week; **Circ:** 400001 Not Audited
Editor in Chief: Shuo Wang
Profile: Covers the latest news and information on health related issues.
Language (s): Chinese
Ad Rate: Full Page Mono 220000.00
Currency: China Yuan Renminbi
DAILY NEWSPAPER

Health News 906907
Editorial: Beijing Dongzhimen Street No. 6A, Beijing 100027 **Tel:** 86 10 64620055 621
Email: fx@jkb.com.cn **Web site:** http://www.jkb.com.cn
Freq: Daily
Editor: Xue Yan
Profile: Covers public health issues and topics throughout China.
Language (s): Chinese
DAILY NEWSPAPER

Health Times 404455
Editorial: People's Daily Press Group 2, Jintaixilu Chaoyangqu, Beijing 100733 **Tel:** 86 10 65369681
Email: jksbbjb@126.com **Web site:** http://www.jksb.com.cn
Freq: Weekly; **Circ:** 100000 Not Audited
Editor in Chief: Meng Xianli; **Editor in Chief:** Rui Yang
Profile: Covers healthcare issues, such as health problems of all walks of life, the application of Chinese medicine and the government policy on healthcare and public hygiene.
Language (s): Chinese
Ad Rate: Full Page Mono 120000.00
Currency: China Yuan Renminbi
DAILY NEWSPAPER

Healthcare Times 573115
Editorial: Healthcare Times, 154 Gulouxi Dajie, Xicheng District, Beijing 100009 **Tel:** 86 10 64028135
Web site: http://www.baojianshibao.com/
Freq: Weekly; **Circ:** 300000
Bureau Chief: Junpu Gao; **Editor in Chief:** Guofa Zhang
Profile: Covers health related issues.
Language (s): Chinese
DAILY NEWSPAPER

Hebei Law News 459024
Editorial: Hebei Law News, 118 Yuhua Xilu, Shijiazhuang 50051 **Tel:** 86 31183027456
Email: hebfazhi@163.com **Web site:** http://www.hbfzweb.com
Freq: 2 Times/Week; **Circ:** 60003 Not Audited
Editor in Chief: Maokui Liu
Profile: It covers law news, legislation issues and cases.
Language (s): Chinese
DAILY NEWSPAPER

Heilongjiang Labour News 459136
Editorial: Heilongjiang Labour News, 195 Dongdazhijie, Nangangqu, Harbin (ha'erbin) 150001
Tel: 86 45157826898
Email: hljgrb@163.com
Freq: 2 Times/Week; **Circ:** 50000 Not Audited
Editor: Sheng Wang; **Bureau Chief:** Hong Zhang
Profile: It covers the news on labor market, human resources and labor unions in Heilongjiang region.
Language (s): Chinese
DAILY NEWSPAPER

Heilongjiang Morning Post 459569
Editorial: Heilongjiang Morning Post, 101 Changjianglu, Harbin (ha'erbin) 150090
Tel: 86 45188581988
Web site: http://www.hljcb.com
Freq: Daily; **Circ:** 150003 Not Audited
Editor: Huaxing Lin
Profile: Heilongjiang Morning Post focuses on regional news and related issues in Heilongjiang region.
Language (s): Chinese
DAILY NEWSPAPER

Henan Business News 459631
Editorial: 6F Zhongqing Dasha, 16-Fu1 Jinshuilu, Zhengzhou 450003 **Tel:** 86 37165866299
Web site: http://www.shangbw.com
Freq: Daily; **Circ:** 320000 Not Audited
Editor in Chief: Lei Meng
Profile: Provides news in economic and business in and outside of China, and information of finance situation and investment in Henan.
Language (s): Chinese
Ad Rate: Full Page Mono 120000.00
Currency: China Yuan Renminbi
DAILY NEWSPAPER

Henan Daily 459626
Editorial: Henan Daily Press Group, 28 Nongyelu, Zhengzhou 450008 **Tel:** 86 37165796302
Web site: http://www.dahe.cn
Freq: Daily; **Circ:** 400003 Not Audited
Editor: Yining Liu
Profile: Henan Daily is a publication which focuses on the local, regional and national news in Henan and China.
Language (s): Chinese
Ad Rate: Full Page Mono 110000.00
Ad Rate: Full Page Colour 158000.00
Currency: China Yuan Renminbi
DAILY NEWSPAPER

Hohhot Evening News 459317
Editorial: Hohhot Daily Press, 8 Dizhiju Nanjie, Hothot (huhehaote) 10020 **Tel:** 86 47 16914000
Email: hhwb009@163.com **Web site:** http://news.nmgnews.com.cn
Freq: Daily; **Circ:** 300000
Editor in Chief: Li Han; **Bureau Chief:** Guangyi Hang
Profile: covers news in Hohhot region and China.
Language (s): Chinese
DAILY NEWSPAPER

Hubei Daily 460873
Editorial: Hubei Daily Group, 181 Donghu Road, Wuchang, Wuhan 430077 **Tel:** 86 2786770308
Web site: http://www.cnhubei.com
Freq: Daily; **Circ:** 210001 Not Audited
Editor in Chief: Yuantao Tang
Profile: Focuses on political, financial and cultural issues concerning the Hubei province.
Language (s): Chinese
DAILY NEWSPAPER

Huizhou Daily 460062
Editorial: Wenhua Yilu, Jiangbei, Huizhou 516003
Tel: 86 7522831821
Email: hzdaily@hznews.com **Web site:** http://www.hznews.com
Freq: Daily; **Circ:** 40000
Editor in Chief: Zhongchu Hu
Profile: Focuses on political, financial, economic and cultural issues concerning Huizhou.
Language (s): Chinese
DAILY NEWSPAPER

Hunan Daily 460024
Owner: Hunan Daily Press Group
Editorial: Hunan Daily Press Group, 18 Furong Zhonglu, Changsha 410071 **Tel:** 86 73184312999
Web site: http://hunan.voc.com.cn
Freq: Daily; **Circ:** 300001 Not Audited
Editor in Chief: Yuelin Dong
Profile: Covers news on political, financial, cultural and entertainment issues.
Language (s): Chinese
DAILY NEWSPAPER

Hunan Economic Daily 460025
Tel: 86 731 4453570
Freq: 2 Times/Week; **Circ:** 100003 Not Audited
Editor in Chief: Qingsheng Tang
Profile: Research Center of Economics, Hunan Provincial Government, 351 Wuyi Dadao Shengzhengfu, Jiguan Eryuan Wuzi Zhonglu
Language (s): Chinese
DAILY NEWSPAPER

Hygiene and Life News 459103
Editorial: Shenyang Daily Press, 67 Beisanjingjie Shenhequ, Shenyang 110014 **Tel:** 86 24 22855122
Web site: http://www.syd.com.cn
Freq: Weekly; **Circ:** 200001 Not Audited
Editor in Chief: Hongyan He
Profile: It focuses on hygiene, healthcare and medicine issues.
Language (s): Chinese
DAILY NEWSPAPER

Industry and Commercial Guide News 459038
Editorial: Industry and Commercial Guide News, 23F Block C Tianhui Dasha, Hefei 230001
Tel: 86 551 2652215
Email: gsdbs@163.com **Web site:** http://www.gsdbs.com
Freq: 2 Times/Week; **Circ:** 170003 Not Audited
Editor: Huaiyu Chu
Profile: Covers the market information of all kinds of businesses, experience-sharing of successful businesses.
Language (s): Chinese
DAILY NEWSPAPER

Information and Market News 492494
Editorial: Information and Market News, 147-2, Hongqi Dajie, Xiangfang District, Harbin (ha'erbin) 150036 **Tel:** 86 45188869393
Email: xinxiyushichang@126.com
Freq: 2 Times/Week
Editor in Chief: Ling Ma
Profile: Covers mainly the information of market, consumption and the latest business news.
Language (s): Chinese
DAILY NEWSPAPER

Information Daily 404362
Editorial: Jiangxi Daily Press Group, 1326 Hongguzhong Dadao, Nanchang 330006
Tel: 86 791 6849117
Web site: http://jxnews.com.cn/xxrb
Freq: Daily; **Circ:** 350003 Not Audited
Profile: Covers local and national news in Jiangxi region and China.
Language (s): Chinese
Ad Rate: Full Page Mono 106000.00
Ad Rate: Full Page Colour 170000.00
Currency: China Yuan Renminbi
DAILY NEWSPAPER

Inner Mongolia Business Daily 459051
Editorial: Inner Mongolia Business Daily 64 Xing'an North, Road, Hothot (huhehaote) 10050
Tel: 86 4716515902
Email: newhay@126.com
Freq: Daily; **Circ:** 220001 Not Audited
Bureau Chief: Xixiao Li
Profile: covers social news, business news and finance news.
Language (s): Chinese
DAILY NEWSPAPER

Inner Mongolia Daily 459488
Editorial: Inner Mongolia Daily Group, 61 Xinhua Dajie, Hothot (huhehaote) 10010 **Tel:** 86 47 16635761
Email: nmrbybs@163.com **Web site:** http://www.nmgnews.com.cn
Freq: Daily; **Circ:** 100003 Not Audited
Editor in Chief: Xueyi Jia; **Bureau Chief:** Jinghai Liu
Profile: focuses on politics, finance, culture and society.
Language (s): Chinese
DAILY NEWSPAPER

International Business Daily 459582
Editorial: International Business Daily Group Bdng 14 Blk 3, Fangzhuang Fangxingyuan, Beijing 100078
Tel: 86 10 58360000
Email: gjsbzbs@126.com **Web site:** http://ibdaily.mofcom.gov.cn
Freq: Daily; **Circ:** 380005 Not Audited
Editor: Junsheng Liu
Profile: Covers information in market, business, stock and government regulations in and around the world.
Language (s): Chinese
Ad Rate: Full Page Mono 120000.00
Ad Rate: Full Page Colour 168000.00
Currency: China Yuan Renminbi
DAILY NEWSPAPER

Jia jiao zhou bao 460163
Owner: Modern Family Magazine House
Editorial: Modern Family Magazine House, 66 Jianyelu, Nanjing 210004 **Tel:** 86 2584221870
Email: wzm213@126.com **Web site:** http://jjzb.njnews.cn
Freq: Weekly; **Circ:** 800002 Not Audited
Editor in Chief: Mei Fang
Profile: Covers home schooling and other education issues.
Language (s): Chinese
Ad Rate: Full Page Mono 40000.00
Currency: China Yuan Renminbi
DAILY NEWSPAPER

Jiangmen Daily 460848
Editorial: Jiangmen Daily Press, 25 Huayuanzhong Road, Jiangmen 529000 **Tel:** 86 7503502683
Email: info@jmrb.com **Web site:** http://www.jmrb.com.cn
Freq: Daily; **Circ:** 90001 Not Audited
Editor in Chief: Jianguo Zhang
Profile: Focuses on local and regional news in Jiangmen region.
Language (s): Chinese
DAILY NEWSPAPER

Jiangsu Commercial News 459248
Editorial: Nanjing Daily Press Group, 223 Longpan Zhonglu, Nanjing 210016 **Tel:** 86 25 84686611
Web site: http://jssb.njnews.cn
Freq: Daily; **Circ:** 120003 Not Audited
Editor in Chief: Lei Jiang
Profile: covers the news and information of business and finance in Jiangsu.
Language (s): Chinese
DAILY NEWSPAPER

Jiangsu Economic News 459050
Owner: Xinhua Daily Group
Editorial: Xinhua Daily Group, 90 Hujunanlu, Nanjing 210004 **Tel:** 86 2552258319
Email: sxm90@126.com
Freq: 2 Times/Week; **Circ:** 110003 Not Audited
Editor in Chief: Yi Wu
Profile: It focuses on the economic events and news in Jiangsu region as well as China.
Language (s): Chinese
DAILY NEWSPAPER

Jiangsu Law News 459088
Editorial: Jiangsu Law News, Wenhui Dasha, 101 Caochangmen Dajie, Nanjing 210036
Tel: 86 25 86261555
Email: zbb@jslegal.com
Freq: Daily; **Circ:** 100003 Not Audited
Editor in Chief: Yan Li
Profile: It provides news and analysis on law-related issues.
Language (s): Chinese
DAILY NEWSPAPER

Jiangxi Broadcasting & Television News 518210
Editorial: Jiangxi Broadcasting & Television News, 77 Wenjiao Road, Nanchang 330046
Tel: 86 7918521749
Web site: http://jxgdb.jxgdw.com
Freq: Weekly; **Circ:** 90000
Profile: Focuses on entertainment news and television station information in Jiangxi region.
Language (s): Chinese
DAILY NEWSPAPER

Jiaozuo Daily 459647
Editorial: Jiaozuo Daily, 56 Shanyang Road, Jiaozuo 454002 **Tel:** 86 3913924268
Web site: http://www.jzrb.com.cn
Freq: Daily; **Circ:** 90000
Editor: Jianxin Wang
Profile: Covers local, regional, national news.
Language (s): Chinese
DAILY NEWSPAPER

Jinan Daily 460035
Owner: Jinan Daily Press Group
Editorial: Jinan Daily Press Group, Number 28-1, Jinqi Road, Shizhongqu, Jinan 250001
Tel: 86 53182886163
Email: e23bgs@126.com **Web site:** http://www.e23.cn
Freq: Daily; **Circ:** 300002 Not Audited
Profile: Covers regional and national news, health, digital produces, travel, education, sports, entertainment, real estate, cars and social issues.
Language (s): Chinese
DAILY NEWSPAPER

Jinling Evening Post 460022
Editorial: Nanjing Daily Press Group, 223 Longpan Zhonglu, Nanjing 210002 **Tel:** 86 2584687113
Web site: http://www.jlwb.net
Freq: Daily; **Circ:** 1080000 Not Audited
Editor in Chief: Xiaoning Xiang
Profile: Covers the regional news in Nanjing and national news in China.
Language (s): Chinese
Ad Rate: Full Page Mono 243600.00
Ad Rate: Full Page Colour 221800.00
Currency: China Yuan Renminbi
DAILY NEWSPAPER

Jinzhou Evening News 459309
Editorial: Jinzhou Daily Press Group, 2 Nanjinglu Sanduan, Jinzhou 121000 **Tel:** 86 4163705576
Web site: http://www.lm3d.com
Freq: Daily; **Circ:** 80000
Editor: Hui Jiang; **Editor:** Lin Qi
Profile: Jinzhou Evening News is a local publication which covers the local and regional news in Jinzhou.
Language (s): Chinese
DAILY NEWSPAPER

Juvenile Encyclopedia Weekly 460067
Editorial: Sichuan Education Publishing House, 49 Nandajie, Chengdu 610041 **Tel:** 86 2886111802
Email: sbb@mail.sc.cninfo.net
Freq: Weekly
Editor in Chief: Chilin Tang
Profile: Covers popular science knowledge including social science and natural science.
Language (s): Chinese
DAILY NEWSPAPER

Kunming Daily 460023
Owner: Kunming Daily Press Group
Editorial: Kunming Daily Press Group 8F11F, Xinwen, Zhongxin 198 Danxialu, Kunming 650118
Tel: 86 8715391909
Web site: http://www.clzg.cn
Freq: Daily; **Circ:** 100002 Not Audited
Editor in Chief: Xueming Sun
Profile: Covers news on financial, economic, social and cultural issues.
Language (s): Chinese
DAILY NEWSPAPER

Laborers Midday News 812429
Editorial: 53 Taoranting Road, Beijing
Tel: 86 10 83548149
Web site: http://www.ldwb.com.cn
Editor in Chief: Zhaohua Huang
Profile: Covers national news.
DAILY NEWSPAPER

Labour Daily 459560
Editorial: Labour Daily, 700 Changpinglu, Shanghai 200040 **Tel:** 86 2162187286
Email: ldbsgj@online.sh.cn **Web site:** http://www.shzgh.org
Freq: Daily; **Circ:** 200003 Not Audited
Editor in Chief: Bihua Chen
Profile: covers the news, information, and employee's benefits of the labour market. It also includes general news on entertainment and culture.
Language (s): Chinese
DAILY NEWSPAPER

Law and Citizens Daily 459073
Editorial: Law and Citizens Daily, 22 Nanpu Road, Guiyang 550002 **Tel:** 86 8515505030
Web site: http://www.fzshb.cn
Freq: Weekly; **Circ:** 240003 Not Audited
Editor in Chief: Zhu Li
Profile: Covers the law news in local community. It also includes the regional government legislation and the effects on the life of local people.
Language (s): Chinese
DAILY NEWSPAPER

Law Express 459131
Owner: Law Express Press
Editorial: Law Express Press, 15 Jinzhou Road, Nanning 530022 **Tel:** 86 7716119221
Email: gxzfyw@163.com
Freq: Daily; **Circ:** 160002 Not Audited
Profile: It covers law and legal issues.
Language (s): Chinese
DAILY NEWSPAPER

Law News 459054
Editorial: Legal Daily Press Group Jia1 Huajiadi, Chaoyangqu, Beijing 100102
Tel: 86 1064361144 2236
Email: fzwc@sina.com.cn **Web site:** http://www.legaldaily.com.cn
Freq: 2 Times/Week; **Circ:** 500003 Not Audited
Editor in Chief: Guanbin Zhang
Profile: A national newspaper which mainly focuses on law news and social issues related the laws in China.
Language (s): Chinese
Ad Rate: Full Page Mono 160000.00
Currency: China Yuan Renminbi
DAILY NEWSPAPER

Legal Daily 460831
Editorial: Legal Daily Press Group, Jia 1, Huajiadi, Chaoyangqu, Beijing 100102 **Tel:** 86 1084772288
Email: zhengfazongzhi@126.com **Web site:** http://www.legaldaily.com.cn
Freq: Daily; **Circ:** 400001 Not Audited
Editor in Chief: Xiadu Lei
Profile: Legal Daily is a national newspaper which mainly covers national news and international news on law issues in China.
Language (s): Chinese
Ad Rate: Full Page Mono 160000.00
Currency: China Yuan Renminbi
DAILY NEWSPAPER

Legal Mirror 459053
Editorial: Legal Mirror BIK A1 Huitong Shidai Guangchang, 71 Jianguolu, Chaoyangqu, Beijing 100025 **Tel:** 86 10 58635959
Email: fwpl@vip.sohu.com **Web site:** http://www.fawan.com
Freq: Daily; **Circ:** 300001 Not Audited
Editor in Chief: Lin Wang
Profile: Covers news on political, economic and social issues from the perspective of law, ans also provides legal issue consultant.
Language (s): Chinese
Ad Rate: Full Page Mono 175000.00
Ad Rate: Full Page Colour 235000.00
Currency: China Yuan Renminbi
DAILY NEWSPAPER

Liaoning Law News 404482
Editorial: Liaoning Daily Press Group, 38 Bei Sanjingjie, Hepingqu, Shenyang 110003
Tel: 86 2482707000
Email: lnfzb@126.com **Web site:** http://www.lnfzb.com
Freq: 2 Times/Week; **Circ:** 250003 Not Audited
Editor in Chief: Wei Cui
Profile: Mainly focuses on the news related to law, government legislation and policies, as well as legal case analysis from different aspects for the general public.
Language (s): Chinese
DAILY NEWSPAPER

Life News 459045
Editorial: Life News Press 2nd FIR Securities Building 62, Chunchenglu, Kunming 650011
Tel: 86 8713110110
Web site: http://www.shxb.net
Freq: Daily; **Circ:** 200001 Not Audited
Editor: MinFei long
Profile: Focuses on politics, economy and society in Yunnan province.
Language (s): Chinese
Ad Rate: Full Page Mono 72500.00
Currency: China Yuan Renminbi
DAILY NEWSPAPER

Life Style 459349
Editorial: Life Style 7th FIR Haidian Wenhua Yishu Daxia, Jia 28 Zhongguancun Dajie, Beijing 100086
Tel: 86 10 52169000
Web site: http://www.lifestyle.com.cn
Freq: 2 Times/Week; **Circ:** 300003 Not Audited
Editor: Fei Li; **Editor:** Yanzhu Wang; **Editor in Chief:** Shuxin Zhang
Profile: covers information for consumers and shopping guide of different areas in China. It mainly covers the high-end products and services.
Language (s): Chinese
Ad Rate: Full Page Colour 198000.00
Currency: China Yuan Renminbi
DAILY NEWSPAPER

Lighting Weekly 539455
Editorial: Lighting Weekly, China Building Decoration Association, Room 1702, Nanguangchang, Beijing 100055 **Tel:** 86 1083993576
Web site: http://www.lighting-cbda.com
Freq: Weekly; **Circ:** 200001 Not Audited
Profile: covers the information and news on the lighting industry. It also focuses on the interior design of lights.
Language (s): Chinese
DAILY NEWSPAPER

Lingnan Youth News 459206
Editorial: Lingnan Youth News, 602 Xuri Dasha, 315 Guangfu Zhonglu, Guangzhou 510140
Tel: 86 2081019225
Email: lnxjz@126.com **Web site:** http://www.lnsnb.cn
Freq: Weekly; **Circ:** 250003 Not Audited
Editor: Juxing Tang
Profile: Covers different aspects of studies and lives of students.
Language (s): Chinese
DAILY NEWSPAPER

Lingnan Youth News-Modern Child Raising Weekly 459207
Editorial: Lingnan Youth News 601 Xuri Dasha, 315 Guangfu, Zhonglu, Guangzhou 510140
Tel: 86 2081019271
Email: lnsnb@163.com **Web site:** http://xdyeb.dayoo.com/gb/node/2004-02/02/node_491.htm
Freq: Weekly; **Circ:** 350002 Not Audited
Editor in Chief: Zengzhi Zhang
Profile: Covers children's care issues including their lives and studies.
Language (s): Chinese
Ad Rate: Full Page Mono 16000.00
Ad Rate: Full Page Colour 24000.00
Currency: China Yuan Renminbi
DAILY NEWSPAPER

Market Daily Online Version 460872
Editorial: People Daily, No. 1 Block, 2 Jintaixilu, Chaoyangqu, Beijing 100733 **Tel:** 86 1065369460
Email: zhaoyinghua@vip.sohu.net **Web site:** http://www.marketdaily.com.cn
Freq: 2 Times/Week; **Circ:** 300002 Not Audited
Editor: Yinghua Zhao
Profile: Provides latest news and information on markets of different aspects.
Language (s): Chinese
DAILY NEWSPAPER

Market Information 459025
Editorial: Market Information, 229 Yingze Dajie, Taiyuan 30001 **Tel:** 86 3514132553
Email: scxxbcn@263.net **Web site:** http://www.scxxb.com.cn
Freq: Daily; **Circ:** 200001 Not Audited
Editor in Chief: Huiming Jiang
Profile: covers economic news of all main industries in China.
Language (s): Chinese
DAILY NEWSPAPER

Medicine Economic News 459217
Editorial: Institute of Southern Medicine Economic, 6th Floor, West Tower, Tianyu Shangwu Daxia, 753 Dongfeng Donglu, Guangzhou 510405
Tel: 86 20 37886650
Email: yyjjb@21cn.com **Web site:** http://www.yyjjb.com.cn
Freq: 2 Times/Week; **Circ:** 200003 Not Audited
Bureau Chief: Jianning Lin; **Editor in Chief:** Jianhong Tao
Profile: Covers the business and economics of medicine in China. It covers the sales and marketing of medicine, quality assurance, hospital management and other medicine-related issues.
Language (s): Chinese
DAILY NEWSPAPER

Metro Express 460060
Editorial: 25F Meiluo Dasha, 30 Tianyaoqiaolu, Xuhui District, Shanghai 200031 **Tel:** 86 21 60838383
Web site: http://www.jfdaily.com/
Freq: 2 Times/Week; **Circ:** 600000 Not Audited
Editor in Chief: Yefang Niu
Profile: Focuses on local and regional news in Shanghai area, and is distributed through metro. "The Age" by Shanghai Jiefang Daily Newspaper Group, published as "white-collar workers on the road commuting to obtain information of the newspaper," as Shanghai Metro Operation Company licensing of free media in the next seven years there will be no new free media into the Shanghai Metro. Newspaper in Shanghai Metro line 9 total more than 200 sites free of charge. Monday to Friday publication, a series of 7:30 am to 9:30 minutes by subway to work the crowd, the current maturity issue amount of 55 to 60 million copies, and with the increase in subway traffic in the year on year increase. The Age of facilities development with unlimited imagination.
Language (s): Chinese
Ad Rate: Full Page Mono 128000.00
Ad Rate: Full Page Colour 150000.00
Currency: China Yuan Renminbi
DAILY NEWSPAPER

Middle School Current Affair News 459649
Editorial: Beijing Youth Press, Building A, 23 Dongli, Baijiazhuang, Chaoyangqu, Beijing 100026
Tel: 86 1065902448
Email: wunan@ynet.com **Web site:** http://zxss.ynet.com
Freq: 2 Times/Week; **Circ:** 600000
Editor in Chief: Ying Jiang
Profile: Covering important current affairs.
Language (s): Chinese
DAILY NEWSPAPER

Modern Express News 404464
Editorial: Modern Express News, 13th Floor, Dongyu Daxia, 18 Zhenghongjie, Xingjiekou, Nanjing 210005
Tel: 86 84783555
Web site: http://www.dsqq.cn
Freq: Daily; **Circ:** 910000
Editor in Chief: Chen Sha; **Editor:** Yong Xu
Profile: Covers news, current affairs and consumer's hot issues in Nanjing and the surrounding provinces.
Language (s): Chinese
Ad Rate: Full Page Mono 10000.00
Currency: China Yuan Renminbi
DAILY NEWSPAPER

Modern Health News 459226
Editorial: Changjiang Daily Gruop, 2 Changjiang Ribaolu, Hankou, Wuhan 430015 **Tel:** 86 2785719416
Web site: http://www.cnhan.com
Freq: Weekly; **Circ:** 100003 Not Audited
Editor: Li Liu
Profile: Modern Health News is a national newspaper which mainly provides consultant on health problems and medical information to the elderly and the patients.
Language (s): Chinese
DAILY NEWSPAPER

Modern Logistics News 459031
Editorial: Modern Logistics News 25 Yuetan Bejie, Xicheng, District, Beijing 100834 **Tel:** 86 1068391412
Email: yangdaqing@126.com **Web site:** http://www.xd56b.com/
Freq: 2 Times/Week; **Circ:** 120003 Not Audited
Profile: It covers the latest news in the logistics industry in China.
Language (s): Chinese
DAILY NEWSPAPER

Modern Women News 459306
Editorial: Modern Women News, 4 Luxunlu, Zhongshanqu, Dalian 116001 **Tel:** 86 41182650404
Freq: 2 Times/Week
Editor: Yongqian Wu; **Editor in Chief:** Li Zhu
Profile: Modern Women News is a national newspaper that mainly covers women's interest issues such as fashion, lifestyle, food, entertainment and social hotspots.
Language (s): Chinese
DAILY NEWSPAPER

Morning Post 459253
Editorial: 873 Dagu Nanlu, Hexiqu, Tianjin 300211
Tel: 86 22 28201063
Web site: http://www.tianjinwe.com
Freq: Daily; **Circ:** 700001 Not Audited
Profile: covers news on financial, business, social and lifestyle issues in Tianjin Region.
Language (s): Chinese
Ad Rate: Full Page Mono 180000.00
Ad Rate: Full Page Colour 600000.00
Currency: China Yuan Renminbi
DAILY NEWSPAPER

Music Life News 585506
Editorial: Music Life News Press, 115 Dongzhongjie, Dongcheng District, Beijing 100020
Tel: 86 1065519460
Freq: 2 Times/Week; **Circ:** 50000
Editor in Chief: Xinhua Liang
Profile: Provides information and updated news of music industry in China.
Language (s): Chinese
DAILY NEWSPAPER

Nanfang Daily 459209
Editorial: Nanfang Daily Press Group, 289 Guangzhou Dadaozhong, Guangzhou 510601
Tel: 86 20 87373998
Email: contact@nfmedia.com **Web site:** http://www.nanfangdaily.com.cn/southnews/
Freq: Daily; **Circ:** 800003 Not Audited
Profile: Provides news in the southern region of China and national news.
Language (s): Chinese
Ad Rate: Full Page Mono 320000.00
Ad Rate: Full Page Colour 380000.00
Currency: China Yuan Renminbi
DAILY NEWSPAPER

National Business Daily 511057
Editorial: National Buisness Daily, 8/F, Block A, No. 3 Lou, No. 195 Longtian Road, Xuhui District, Shanghai 200235 **Tel:** 86 2160900099

Web site: http://www.nbd.com.cn
Freq: Daily; **Circ:** 100001 Not Audited
Profile: Focuses on business, economic and financial development in China and overseas.
Language (s): Chinese
DAILY NEWSPAPER

New Countryside Commerce 460828
Editorial: International Business Daily Group Bdng 14 Area 3, Fangzhuang Fangxingyuan, Beijing 100078
Tel: 86 1058360188
Email: xncsb2009@163.com **Web site:** http://xncsb.mofcom.gov.cn
Freq: 2 Times/Week; **Circ:** 190001 Not Audited
Editor in Chief: Jishan Sun
Profile: covers the news and issues of agriculture business, supply and policy in China.
Language (s): Chinese
DAILY NEWSPAPER

New Express Newspaper 459215
Editorial: Yangcheng Evening Press Group, 533 Tianhelu, Guangzhou 510630 **Tel:** 86 20 85180888
Web site: http://www.xkb.com.cn
Freq: Daily; **Circ:** 600000
Editor in Chief: Sun Xuan
Profile: reports news in Guangdong region and national news in China. "Express," the editorial team of high quality, young, modern technical means. "Express" in Guangzhou and the Pearl River Delta-based sales market, the core audience is the most dynamic and social spending power of the white-collar and middle class, but also by ordinary readers love the city, with an increasingly wide range of influence and good advertising.
Language (s): Chinese
Ad Rate: Full Page Mono 251700.00
Ad Rate: Full Page Colour 279600.00
Currency: China Yuan Renminbi
DAILY NEWSPAPER

New Legal Report 459121
Owner: Jiangxi Daily Press Group
Editorial: Jiangxi Daily Press Group, 190 Yangming Road, Nanchang 330006 **Tel:** 86 791 6849033
Web site: http://www.jxnews.com.cn/jxfzb
Freq: 2 Times/Week; **Circ:** 200003 Not Audited
Editor in Chief: Jingping Cheng
Profile: It covers news and analysis on law and legal issues.
Language (s): Chinese
DAILY NEWSPAPER

Nihon Keizai Shimbun - Beijing Bureau 459109
Editorial: Diplomatic Compound Chaoyang, 3-13, Jianguomenwai, Beijing 100600 **Tel:** 86 10 65321664
Freq: Daily; **Circ:** 3010558
Bureau Chief: Suguru Shinada
Language (s): Japanese
DAILY NEWSPAPER

Northern Economic News 459062
Editorial: Inner Mongolia Daily Group, 61 Xinhua Dajie, Hothot (huhehaote) 10016 **Tel:** 86 4716266852
Web site: http://news.nmgnews.com.cn
Freq: 2 Times/Week; **Circ:** 70001 Not Audited
Editor in Chief: Jan Lan
Profile: covers regional business and finance news in Inner Mongolia.
Language (s): Chinese
DAILY NEWSPAPER

Oriental City and County News 460047
Owner: Oriental City and County News
Editorial: Oriental City &County News RM 2 Flat 3 779, Xianxia West RD, Shanghai 200335
Tel: 86 2152161710
Web site: http://www.dfcxb.com
Freq: Daily; **Circ:** 100002 Not Audited
Editor in Chief: Xiaowen Xi
Profile: Covers the news of agriculture and other news of the local society in Shanghai region.
Language (s): Chinese
DAILY NEWSPAPER

Oriental Lady 459138
Owner: Jiangxi Women's Association
Editorial: Jiangxi Women's Association, 308 Nanjing Road, Nanchang 330029 **Tel:** 86 7918320090
Email: fnzhshb@hotmail.com **Web site:** http://www.jxwomen.org.cn/newweb/paper/
Freq: Weekly; **Circ:** 60001 Not Audited
Editor in Chief: Liqun Cai
Profile: It covers lifestyle, career, family, relationship and other women's interested issues.
Language (s): Chinese
DAILY NEWSPAPER

Oriental Morning Post 460065
Editorial: Oriental Morning Post, 839 Yan'zhonglu, Shanghai 200040 **Tel:** 86 2162471234
Email: dfzb@wxjt.com.cn **Web site:** http://www.dfdaily.com
Freq: Daily; **Circ:** 400000 Not Audited
Editor: Peng Wang
Profile: Reports on the news of Shanghai City, Jiangsu and Zhejiang Province.
Language (s): Chinese
Ad Rate: Full Page Mono 165000.00
Currency: China Yuan Renminbi
DAILY NEWSPAPER

Oriental Sports Daily 459430
Editorial: Oriental Sports Daily, 839 Yan'an Zhonglu, Shanghai 200040 **Tel:** 86 2162476156
Web site: http://www.sport1.cn
Freq: Daily
Editor in Chief: Min Du
Profile: Oriental Sports Daily is a national newspaper which covers national and overseas sporting events and information.
Language (s): Chinese
DAILY NEWSPAPER

Pearl River Times 460344
Editorial: Pearl River Times, 17 Gangkoulu, Guangzhou 528200 **Tel:** 86 75783000123
Email: times@dadao.net **Web site:** http://dadao.net/php/prtime
Freq: Daily
Editor in Chief: Wanjun Li
Profile: Provides news of Guangzhou region.
Language (s): Chinese
DAILY NEWSPAPER

People's Railway Daily 711908
Editorial: No. 196, Gaoxin Street, Baoji 721013
Tel: 011 86 09172755166
Email: admin@bj-baodeli.com
Freq: Daily
Profile: Focuses on railway development and maintenance in China.
Language (s): Chinese
DAILY NEWSPAPER

People's Court News 459057
Editorial: People's Court News, 22 Beili Xiqu Donghuashi, Chongwenqu, Beijing 100062
Tel: 86 1067550723
Email: xwb@rmfyb.cn **Web site:** http://rmfyb.chinacourt.org/
Freq: Daily; **Circ:** 400000
Editor: Yizhong Yang
Profile: People's Court News is a publication which focuses on the information and news of the courtrooms in China.
Language (s): Chinese
DAILY NEWSPAPER

People's Daily 159010
Editorial: 2 Jintaixilu, Chaoyangqu, Beijing 100733
Tel: 86 10 65363689
Email: englishpd@163.com **Web site:** http://www.peopledaily.com.cn
Freq: Daily; **Circ:** 3000000 Not Audited
Editor: Rujian Chen; **Editor:** Chengliang (Charlie) Wu
Profile: People's Daily is a national newspaper which covers national news in China and international news worldwide.
Language (s): Chinese
Ad Rate: Full Page Mono 280000.00
Ad Rate: Full Page Colour 392000.00
Currency: China Yuan Renminbi
DAILY NEWSPAPER

People's Photography 459624
Owner: People's Photography Press
Editorial: People's Photography Press, 124 Shuangtasijie, Taiyuan 30012 **Tel:** 86 3514297341
Web site: http://www.peoplephoto.com/
Freq: Weekly; **Circ:** 80000
Editor in Chief: Wei Huo
Profile: covers information about different types of photos and the technique and equipment needed when taking these photos.
Language (s): Chinese
DAILY NEWSPAPER

People's Post and Telecommunications 459585
Editorial: People's Posts and Telecommunications News Office, 11 Anyuanlu, Chaoyang District, Beijing 100029 **Tel:** 86 10 64962938
Web site: http://ermyd.cnii.com.cn
Freq: 2 Times/Week; **Circ:** 200000
Editor in Chief: Suoning Wu
Profile: Covers the latest news and development of postal services and telecommunications industry all around the world.
Language (s): Chinese
DAILY NEWSPAPER

People's Railroad News 459618
Editorial: People's Railroad News 3 Beifengwo, Haidian, District, Beijing 100038 **Tel:** 86 1051892022
Email: tougao@peoplerail.com **Web site:** http://www.rmtd.com.cn/
Freq: Daily; **Circ:** 200002 Not Audited
Editor in Chief: Dan Li
Profile: People's Railroad News is a national newspaper circulated on trains and in train stations, covering railway related issues and government regulations.
Language (s): Chinese
DAILY NEWSPAPER

PLA Daily 459343
Editorial: PLA Daily Press, 34 Fuwai Dajie, Beijing 100832 **Tel:** 86 1068586350
Web site: http://www.chinamil.com.cn
Freq: 2 Times/Week; **Circ:** 600000
Editor: Qin Song; **Editor:** Zurong Yang; **Editor:** Feng Zhou
Profile: Provides the latest news and information of The Chinese People's Liberation Army.
Language (s): Chinese
DAILY NEWSPAPER

Popular Life News 586769
Editorial: Popular Life News, 1 Men, Block 4, Youcheng Mingju, 3 Youyi Road, Hexi District, Tianjin 300201 **Tel:** 86 2258586988
Web site: http://www.dzshb.com/
Freq: Weekly
Editor in Chief: Gang Li
Profile: covers social news and entertainment news in China.
Language (s): Chinese
DAILY NEWSPAPER

Popular Network News 460000
Editorial: Joyyang, Kexie Daxia, 3 Shuangganglu, Yuzhong District, Chongqing 400013
Tel: 86 2363658818
Web site: http://www.joyyang.com
Freq: Weekly
Profile: covers issues on internet games such as online games, classic games and sporting & racing games.
Language (s): Chinese
DAILY NEWSPAPER

Popular Science News 459516
Editorial: Popular Science News, 15 Fuxing Road, Beijing 100038 **Tel:** 86 10 58884048
Email: dzkjb@public3.bta.net.cn **Web site:** http://www.stdaily.com/other/dzkj
Freq: 2 Times/Week; **Circ:** 160003 Not Audited
Editor in Chief: Huaying Shu
Profile: reports on latest science development related to people's life covering social issues, health, leisure and consumer affairs.
Language (s): Chinese
DAILY NEWSPAPER

Primary Students Weekly 459179
Editorial: 162 Gupinglu, Fuzhou 350003
Tel: 86 59 187872685
Email: fjedu@fjedu.com.cn **Web site:** http://www.fjedu.com.cn
Freq: 2 Times/Week; **Circ:** 300003 Not Audited
Profile: covers educational and cultural activities and latest information for primary school students.
Language (s): Chinese
DAILY NEWSPAPER

Procuratorial Daily 460839
Editorial: Procuratorial Daily Group 5 Luguxilu Shijingshanqu, Beijing 100040 **Tel:** 86 1068630102
Email: zbs@jcrb.com.cn **Web site:** http://www.jcrb.com/n1
Freq: Daily; **Circ:** 330001 Not Audited
Editor in Chief: Xuehui Li; **Editor in Chief:** Bencai Zhang
Profile: Covers the general law news and social issues in the society of China.
Language (s): Chinese
Ad Rate: Full Page Mono 100000.00
Currency: China Yuan Renminbi
DAILY NEWSPAPER

Qilu Evening News 460816
Editorial: Qilu Evening News, 6 Leyuan Dajie, Jinan 250014 **Tel:** 86 53185193327
Email: qlwbqmt123@163.com **Web site:** http://www.qlwb.com.cn
Freq: Daily; **Circ:** 1700000 Not Audited
Editor: Shinan Han; **Editor in Chief:** Hao Keyaun
Profile: Focuses on both local and regional news.
Language (s): Chinese
Ad Rate: Full Page Mono 165900.00
Ad Rate: Full Page Colour 208000.00
Currency: China Yuan Renminbi
DAILY NEWSPAPER

Qingdao Financial Daily 460036
Editorial: Qingdao Daily Press Group, 77 Xuzhu Lu, Qingdao 266071 **Tel:** 86 53280998776
Web site: http://caijing.qingdaonews.com
Freq: 2 Times/Week; **Circ:** 150001 Not Audited
Editor in Chief: Yachuan Li
Profile: Covers business, economics, finance and securities, as well as financial technology and services issues.
Language (s): Chinese
DAILY NEWSPAPER

Qinghai Law News 459119
Editorial: 18 Nandajie, Xining 810000
Tel: 86 9716312623
Freq: Daily; **Circ:** 37000
Manager: Jun Luo
Profile: It covers law-related news and issues in Qinghai region.
Language (s): Chinese
DAILY NEWSPAPER

Qinzhou Evening News 459365
Editorial: Qinzhou Evening News, Fumin Road, Qinzhou 535000 **Tel:** 86 7773680037
Web site: http://www.qzrb.com.cn
Freq: 2 Times/Week
Profile: Provides news of Qinzhou.
Language (s): Chinese
DAILY NEWSPAPER

Reader's Journal 459238
Editorial: 47 Huaishujie, Chengdu 610041
Tel: 86 2886272070 812
Web site: http://www.duzhebao.com.cn
Freq: 2 Times/Week
Editor in Chief: Shihong Wan
Profile: Reader's Newspaper is a national publication which mainly covers entertainment, lifestyle, news and other related affairs in China.
Language (s): Chinese
DAILY NEWSPAPER

Real Estate Times 459191
Editorial: Jiefang Daily Press Group 25th FlR 300 Hankou Road, Shanghai 200001 **Tel:** 86 21 63521111
Email: lijl047@jfdaily.com **Web site:** http://www.jfdaily.com/gb/jfxww/xlbk/fangdc/index.html
Freq: Weekly; **Circ:** 100000
Editor in Chief: Xinchang Song
Profile: covers news on new houses, second-hand houses, estate management and interior design.
Language (s): Chinese
DAILY NEWSPAPER

Red Scarf News 459247
Editorial: Red Scarf News, 202, 2 Men, 8 Haolou, Xindayuan, Nankaiqu, Tianjin 300192
Freq: Weekly; **Circ:** 300003 Not Audited
Editor in Chief: Shenyong He
Profile: covers stories of excellent youngsters and reports of youth events, student life and educational issues.
Language (s): Chinese
DAILY NEWSPAPER

Reference News 814868
Owner: Xinhua News Agency
Editorial: No. 57 Xi Ave, Xuanwumen, Beijing 100803
Tel: 86 10 63071136
Email: ckxx@xinhua.org **Web site:** http://www.cankaoxiaoxi.com
Circ: 4000000
Editor in Chief: Bing Leng; **Editor:** Li Yang
Profile: Covers news. It's the daily newspaper with largest circulation in China.
DAILY NEWSPAPER

Sangyo Times - Shanghai Bureau 507659
Editorial: Shanghai
Email: kuromasa@sangyo-times-sh.com **Web site:** http://www.sangyo-times.co.jp
Freq: Weekly
Language (s): Japanese
DAILY NEWSPAPER

Sanya Morning Post 459423
Editorial: Sanya Morning Post, 4/F, Zhuoda Dasha, Yingbinlu, Sanya 572000 **Tel:** 86 89831886999
Email: zbs@sycb.com.cn **Web site:** http://www.sycb.com.cn
Freq: Daily; **Circ:** 20000
Editor in Chief: Shuzhen Huang
Profile: Covers national and international news, news of lifestyle, culture and entertainment news.
Language (s): Chinese
DAILY NEWSPAPER

Science & Technology Information News 460273
Editorial: Keji Xinxi Baoshe, 19 Dong'erlu, Qianfoshan, Jinan 250014 **Tel:** 86 53182600789
Freq: 2 Times/Week; **Circ:** 500000
Editor in Chief: Jianyi Wang
Profile: Covers agricultural technology.
Language (s): Chinese
DAILY NEWSPAPER

Science and Technology Daily 460829
Editorial: Science and Technology Daily, 15 Fuxinglu, Haidian District, Beijing 100038 **Tel:** 86 1058884048
Email: gjb@stdaily.com **Web site:** http://www.stdaily.com
Freq: Daily; **Circ:** 300001 Not Audited
Profile: Covers the development and study of science and technology in China and abroad.
Language (s): Chinese
DAILY NEWSPAPER

Science Times 460013
Editorial: Science Times, Yi-3, Zhongguancun Nanyitiao, Haidian District, Beijing 100190
Tel: 86 10 82614607
Email: snnews@stimes.cn **Web site:** http://www.sciencetimes.com.cn
Freq: Daily; **Circ:** 200003 Not Audited
Editor in Chief: Honghai Liu
Profile: Covers science.
Language (s): Chinese
DAILY NEWSPAPER

Securities Times 460834
Editorial: Securities Times, 3F, Zhongyin Mansion, 5015 Caitian Road Futian District, Shenzhen 518026
Tel: 86 75583501827
Email: flyfar@163.com **Web site:** http://www.p5w.net/p5w/home/stime/today/
Freq: 2 Times/Week; **Circ:** 400001 Not Audited
Editor in Chief: Zijian Wen
Profile: Provides information about securities and stock market, financial services, options and futures, personal savings issues.
Language (s): Chinese
Ad Rate: Full Page Mono 100000.00
Ad Rate: Full Page Colour 240000.00
Currency: China Yuan Renminbi
DAILY NEWSPAPER

Shandong Electricity News
460355
Editorial: Shandong Electric Power Corporation, 150 Jing'er lu, Jinan 250001 **Tel:** 86 531 80124762
Email: sddlbs@126.com **Web site:** http://www.sepco.com.cn
Freq: 2 Times/Week
Editor: Mingzhen Xie
Profile: Shandong Electricity News is an industrial newspaper which covers the development and advancement in the electricity industry of Shandong.
Language (s): Chinese
DAILY NEWSPAPER

Shanghai Auto News 460153
Editorial: Shanghai Auto News Rm 10111003 Shanghai Qiche Gongye Dasha, 489 Weihai Road Gongye Dasha, Shanghai 200041
Tel: 86 2122011568
Web site: http://www.shautonews.com
Freq: Weekly; **Circ:** 90003 Not Audited
Editor: Hongwei Du
Profile: Covers news in the car and automobile industry in China.
Language (s): Chinese
DAILY NEWSPAPER

Shanghai Chinese Medicine News 459431
Editorial: Shanghai Chinese Medicine News, 1376 Jiangninglu, Shanghai 200060 **Tel:** 86 21 81874022
Email: shhzyyb@163.com
Freq: Weekly; **Circ:** 50003 Not Audited
Editor in Chief: Changquan Ling
Profile: covers the latest news and development of traditional Chinese medicine and its application in daily life.
Language (s): Chinese
DAILY NEWSPAPER

Shanghai Daily 459180
Editorial: Shanghai Daily Publishing House, 38th Floor, 755 Weihai Road, Shanghai 200041
Tel: 86 215 292-0043
Email: editor@shanghaidaily.com **Web site:** http://www.shanghaidaily.com
Freq: 2 Times/Week; **Circ:** 150000 Not Audited
Editor in Chief: Ciyun Zhang
Profile: Launched in 1999, provides an English window to the news of China. Business-focused, it also reports on social, cultural and diplomatic developments in Shanghai and the surrounding region.
Language (s): English
Ad Rate: Full Page Mono 70000.00
Ad Rate: Full Page Colour 98000.00
Currency: China Yuan Renminbi
DAILY NEWSPAPER

Shanghai Family 459429
Editorial: Wenhui - Xinmin United Press Group, 755 Weihailu, Shanghai 200041 **Tel:** 86 215 2921234
Email: news365@wxjt.com.cn **Web site:** http://shjt.shfamily.com.cn
Freq: Weekly; **Circ:** 80003 Not Audited
Profile: Covers family and lifestyle issues in Shanghai.
Language (s): Chinese
DAILY NEWSPAPER

Shanghai Financial News 459551
Editorial: Shanghai Financial News 18th FIR 1090 Pudong, Shiji Dadao, Shanghai 200120
Tel: 86 2158359626
Web site: http://www.shfinancialnews.com
Freq: 2 Times/Week; **Circ:** 50001 Not Audited
Editor: Guoquan Gu; **Editor in Chief:** Yujun Zheng
Profile: Shanghai Financial News is a regional financial newspaper mainly focusing on business and finance news in East China (incl. Shanghai, Zhejiang Province and Fujian Province). It covers investment, insurance, real estates, business and management, securities news. They also have pages for IT, health and leisure news.
Language (s): Chinese
DAILY NEWSPAPER

Shanghai Law Journal 459147
Editorial: Shanghai Law News, 4th Floor, Number 1, 268 Nong, Xiaomuqiaolu, Shanghai 200032
Tel: 86 2164179999
Web site: http://www.jfdaily.com/gb/jfxww/xlbk/shfzb/node47070/
Freq: Daily; **Circ:** 60000
Editor in Chief: Lemin Jin
Profile: Shanghai Law News is a daily newspaper focusing on legal news in Shanghai region.
Language (s): Chinese
DAILY NEWSPAPER

Shanghai Morning Post 404327
Owner: Jiefang Daily Press Group
Editorial: 300 Hankou Road, Shanghai 200001
Tel: 86 216 3521111
Email: jubao@12377.cn **Web site:** http://www.jfdaily.com
Freq: Daily; **Circ:** 750003 Not Audited
Editor: Xijing Cao; **Editor in Chief:** Yang Wei Zhong
Profile: Launched in 1999, covers mainly news and finance. Focuses on investment, securities, Shanghai news, national news and international news. Also has pages on sports, culture society and entertainment news.
Language (s): Chinese
Ad Rate: Full Page Mono 250000.00
Ad Rate: Full Page Colour 300000.00
Currency: China Yuan Renminbi
DAILY NEWSPAPER

Shanghai Overseas Chinese News 459418
Editorial: Shanghai Overseas Chinese News, 3/F, 847 Yan'an Zhonglu, Changlelu, Shanghai 200040
Tel: 86 2162891010
Web site: http://www.yesqiaobao.com
Freq: Weekly; **Circ:** 100003 Not Audited
Editor: Feiyu Huang; **Editor in Chief:** Ronglin Xie
Profile: Shanghai Overseas Chinese News is a national publication which focuses on the development of Shanghai in business, finance, economics and society and covers the stories and information for oversea Chinese.
Language (s): Chinese
DAILY NEWSPAPER

Shanghai Overseas Information
459433
Editorial: Shanghai Far East Publishers, 357 Xianxialu, Shanghai 200336
Email: shyb2000@online.sh.cn
Freq: Weekly; **Circ:** 100003 Not Audited
Editor: Yuan Sheng
Profile: publishes and translates news and articles about politics and current national and international affairs outside Shanghai.
Language (s): Chinese
DAILY NEWSPAPER

Shanghai Science and Technology Post 459388
Editorial: Shanghai Science & Tech Post 57 Nanchang Road, Shanghai 200020
Tel: 86 21 63866890
Email: newskjb@vip.sina.com **Web site:** http://www.shkp.org.cn
Freq: 2 Times/Week; **Circ:** 100003 Not Audited
Profile: focuses on the information and market development of science and technology in Shanghai.
Language (s): Chinese
DAILY NEWSPAPER

Shanghai Securities News 404570
Editorial: Shanghai Stock Info Service, Corp1100 Yanggao Nanlu, Pudong, Shanghai 200127
Tel: 86 4008200277
Web site: http://www.cnstock.com/
Freq: 2 Times/Week; **Circ:** 400000 Not Audited
Editor in Chief: Wen Gwan; **Editor:** Yi Zhou
Profile: Focuses on the news and information of the securities market in China.
Language (s): Chinese
Ad Rate: Full Page Mono 155000.00
Ad Rate: Full Page Colour 240000.00
Currency: China Yuan Renminbi
DAILY NEWSPAPER

Shanghai Times 459189
Editorial: Jiefang Daily Press Group, 300 Hankou Road, Shanghai 200001 **Tel:** 86 2163521111
Email: shtimes@jfdaily.com **Web site:** http://www.jfdaily.com.cn
Freq: Weekly; **Circ:** 550000 Not Audited
Editor in Chief: Jinjiang Xu
Profile: focuses on the issues of culture and lifestyle, life in Shanghai, and other entertainment information.
Language (s): Chinese
Ad Rate: Full Page Mono 315000.00
Currency: China Yuan Renminbi
DAILY NEWSPAPER

Shantou Te Qu Wan Bao 459327
Editorial: Shantou Jingji Teque Baoshe, 99 Jinxin Road, Shantou 515041 **Tel:** 86 754 8826-0688
Email: sten@stnews.com.cn **Web site:** http://www.stnews.com.cn
Freq: Daily; **Circ:** 150000 Not Audited
Editor in Chief: Qian Cai
Profile: Covers news in Shantou region.
Language (s): Chinese
Ad Rate: Full Page Mono 88200.00
Currency: China Yuan Renminbi
DAILY NEWSPAPER

Shanxi Economic Daily 459089
Editorial: Shanxi Economic Daily 26 Shuixiguanjie Taoyuan, Beilu, Taiyuan 30002 **Tel:** 86 351 4660816
Email: zgsxwz@shanxigov.cn **Web site:** http://www.daynews.com.cn/
Freq: Daily; **Circ:** 100001 Not Audited
Editor in Chief: Jinmin Li
Profile: Focuses on the economical and business issues in Shanxi and in China. "Shanxi Economic Daily News," founded on July 15, 1985, through 20 years of development and growth, from the original version of the four open four tabloid, become off the eighth edition of the Daily News, newspaper staff of several people from the initial development 120 more than the team. "Shanxi Economic Daily" has been revised twice, hit "a social influence economic events and economic figures, in-depth economic observation, insightful Economic Review, there is concern about the economic issues, valuable economic information" which News Category 6 products, reflected in its value, "the lesson of" embodied in the form of "readability" for "economic decision-makers, business managers, marketing and economic researchers," these four categories of target audience services; form reflected in the layout of its fresh, beautiful, generous style. After these two revision, further enhancing the social influence, 20 years, "Shanxi Economic Daily" to become the province's only economic class newspaper.
Language (s): Chinese
DAILY NEWSPAPER

Shenzhen Overseas Chinese News 459048
Editorial: Shenzhen Overseas Chinese News, 8/F, 8 Hongbao Road, Luohu District, Shenzhen 518001
Tel: 86 755 28949558
Email: qbbjb@163.com **Web site:** http://www.sz-qb.com
Freq: Daily; **Circ:** 60000
Profile: It covers local and national news.
Language (s): Chinese
DAILY NEWSPAPER

Shenzhen Special Zone Daily
404462
Editorial: Shenzhen Special Zone Daily, 6008 Shennan Dadao, Shenzhen 518009
Tel: 86 75583510009
Web site: http://sztqb.sznews.com
Freq: Daily; **Circ:** 440000 Not Audited
Editor in Chief: Liangjun Zhun
Profile: covers hotspots on political, financial and cultural issues in Shenzhen.
Language (s): Chinese
Ad Rate: Full Page Mono 339310.00
Ad Rate: Full Page Colour 519140.00
Currency: China Yuan Renminbi
DAILY NEWSPAPER

Shenzhen Television News 459261
Editorial: Shenzhen Television News, Guangdian Dasha, Yijinglu, Shenzhen 518021
Tel: 86 75525160511
Email: sztvdsb@126.com **Web site:** http://www.sztv.com.cn
Freq: Weekly; **Circ:** 200003 Not Audited
Editor in Chief: Zhijiang Pan; **Editor:** Gui Wang
Profile: covers the entertainment news and program list of television stations in Shenzhen.
Language (s): Chinese
DAILY NEWSPAPER

Shenzhen Youth Daily 459262
Editorial: 6008 Shennan Dadao, Shenzhen 518009
Tel: 86 755 83518395
Freq: Weekly; **Circ:** 190000
Editor in Chief: Hongjun Liu
Profile: covers the general interest of youth in Shenzhen region. It also focuses on family life education, popular science knowledge and other aspects related to youth interest.
Language (s): Chinese
DAILY NEWSPAPER

Soccer Fan 459250
Editorial: Tianjin Daily Press Group, 873 Dagu Nanlu, Tianjin 300211 **Tel:** 86 2228202222
Web site: http://www.tianjinwe.com
Freq: 2 Times/Week; **Circ:** 50003 Not Audited
Profile: covers the latest soccer news and information in China and worldwide.
Language (s): Chinese
DAILY NEWSPAPER

Soccer News 404376
Editorial: 97 Haizhuzhonglu, Guangzhou 510120
Tel: 86 20 81330003
Web site: http://www.goalchina.net
Freq: 2 Times/Week; **Circ:** 1600000
Editor in Chief: Xiaoxin Liu
Profile: Covers both national and international news in soccer field.
Language (s): Chinese
DAILY NEWSPAPER

Soccer Winner 460236
Editorial: 97 Haizhuzhonglu, Guangzhou 510120
Tel: 86 208 1330001
Email: soccer-ggb@vip.sina.com **Web site:** http://www.goalchina.net
Freq: 2 Times/Week; **Circ:** 1000003 Not Audited
Editor: Tao Chen; **Editor in Chief:** Xiaoxin Liu;
Editor: Weihua Yin; **Editor:** Yuan Zhao
Profile: Soccer Winner is a national newspaper with information about sports lottery.
Language (s): Chinese
Ad Rate: Full Page Mono 48000.00
Ad Rate: Full Page Colour 90000.00
Currency: China Yuan Renminbi
DAILY NEWSPAPER

South China City News 459463
Editorial: South China City News, Xinwen Daxia, 30 Jinpanlu, Haikou 570216 **Tel:** 86 89866810888
Web site: http://www.ngdsb.com.cn
Freq: Daily
Editor: Chunshan Feng; **Editor in Chief:** Jieyu Yin
Profile: South China City News is a regional publication which focuses on the news and entertainment in Hainan region.
Language (s): Chinese
DAILY NEWSPAPER

Southeast Business 459449
Editorial: Ningbo Daily Press Group, 768 Lingqiaolu, Ningbo 315000 **Tel:** 86 57487270000
Web site: http://dnsb.cnnb.com.cn
Freq: 2 Times/Week; **Circ:** 218000 Not Audited
Editor: Zhiming Wu
Profile: covers financial and business news in southeastern part of China.
Language (s): Chinese
Ad Rate: Full Page Mono 88600.00
Currency: China Yuan Renminbi
DAILY NEWSPAPER

South-East Morning News 459319
Editorial: South-East Morning News, Quanzhou Wanbao Dasha, Citong Nanlu, Quanzhou, Fuzhou 350003 **Tel:** 86 59 122505555
Email: rexian@qzwb.com **Web site:** http://www.dnzb.com.cn
Freq: Daily; **Circ:** 250003 Not Audited
Profile: South-East Morning News is the most popular newspaper in Fujian that mainly covers news on financial, political, cultural and social issues.
Language (s): Chinese
DAILY NEWSPAPER

Southern County 527373
Editorial: Nanfang Daily Press Group, 289 Guangzhou Dadaozhong, Guangzhou 510601
Tel: 86 208 7366121
Email: nfncb@163.com **Web site:** http://www.nfncb.cn/
Freq: 2 Times/Week
Editor in Chief: Yong Chen
Profile: It covers agricultural news in the southern area in China.
Language (s): Chinese
DAILY NEWSPAPER

Sports Review 459216
Editorial: Hubei Daily Press Group, 65 Huanglilu, Wuchang, Wuhan 430077 **Tel:** 86 2786794446
Web site: http://tyzb.cnhubei.com
Freq: 2 Times/Week; **Circ:** 100003 Not Audited
Profile: covers the national sporting events and issues in Hubei province and in China.
Language (s): Chinese
DAILY NEWSPAPER

Stage & Television Screen 460044
Editorial: 8th Floor, Xinwen Zhongxin, 43 Guangyulu, Guangzhou 510121 **Tel:** 86 2081883088 3197
Web site: http://wtyym.dayoo.com
Freq: Weekly
Editor in Chief: Jiangtao Tan
Profile: covers news and information of the entertainment industry in southern regions of China.
Language (s): Chinese
DAILY NEWSPAPER

Strait News 460033
Editorial: Strait News, 1st Floor Fujian Ribao Daxia, 84 Hualinlu, Fuzhou 350003
Tel: 86 0591 5911968111
Web site: http://www.nhaidu.com
Freq: Daily; **Circ:** 750000 Not Audited
Editor in Chief: Dejian Sun
Profile: focuses on the news from Fujian and Taiwan provinces, covering entertainment, business and finance, lifestyle and society news.
Language (s): Chinese
Ad Rate: Full Page Mono 85500.00
Ad Rate: Full Page Colour 119600.00
Currency: China Yuan Renminbi
DAILY NEWSPAPER

Style Weekly 595424
Editorial: Liaoning Daily Press Group, 339 Zhongshan Road, Shenyang 110014
Tel: 86 2462254218
Email: ssshdb@126.com **Web site:** http://newspaper.lndaily.com.cn/styleweekly/
Freq: Weekly; **Circ:** 165000
Editor in Chief: Zhengrong Li
Profile: Provides the latest information and issues on lifestyle, fashions and trends in China and abroad.
Language (s): Chinese
Ad Rate: Full Page Mono 120000.00
Ad Rate: Full Page Colour 180000.00
Currency: China Yuan Renminbi
DAILY NEWSPAPER

Sunshine Daily 460038
Editorial: Sunshine Daily, 6 Beiguanzhengjie, Xi'an 710014 **Tel:** 86 2986232639
Web site: http://www.yangguangbao.com
Freq: 2 Times/Week; **Circ:** 90002 Not Audited
Profile: Covers news in Xi'an and other neighbouring regions.
Language (s): Chinese
DAILY NEWSPAPER

Taiyuan Evening News 459329
Editorial: 15F Xinwen Dasha, 78 Xinjianlu, Taiyuan 30002 **Tel:** 86 3518222191
Web site: http://www.tynews.com.cn
Freq: Daily; **Circ:** 150003 Not Audited
Editor in Chief: Qingfu Wang
Profile: covers news and financial news in Taiyuan region.
Language (s): Chinese
DAILY NEWSPAPER

Tianfu Morning Post 459234
Editorial: Tianfu Morning Post, 70 Erduan, Hongxinglu, Chengdu 610012 **Tel:** 86 28 86969285
Email: tfzb@scol.com.cn **Web site:** http://morning.scol.com.cn
Freq: Daily; **Circ:** 230003 Not Audited
Editor: Wei Zhang

Profile: provides news from Sichuan and China.
Language (s): Chinese
DAILY NEWSPAPER

Tiantian Business News 460235
Owner: Shaoxing Daily Press Group
Editorial: Shaoxing Daily Press Group, 558 Yan'an Donglu, Chengdong Xinqu, Shaoxing 312000
Tel: 86 57588652000
Email: sbtt@263.net **Web site:** http://www.shaoxing.com.cn
Freq: Daily
Profile: Tiantian Business News is a local daily newspaper covering business and finance news in Zhejiang province.
Language (s): Chinese
DAILY NEWSPAPER

Tibet Daily 460838
Editorial: Tibet Daily, 36 Duosenge Road, Lasa 850000 **Tel:** 86 8916323699
Email: xzrbyaowen@163.com **Web site:** http://www.chinatibetnews.com
Freq: Daily; **Circ:** 50001 Not Audited
Editor in Chief: Xiaolin Meng
Profile: covers news in Tibet region and in other areas in China.
Language (s): Chinese
DAILY NEWSPAPER

Time Weekly 608571
Editorial: Time Weekly, 4/F, Yuanyang Mingzhu Dasha Dongta, 19 Huali Road, Zhujiang Xincheng, Guangzhou 510623 **Tel:** 86 2037591420
Web site: http://www.time-weekly.com
Freq: Weekly; **Circ:** 47000
Editor: Xiaolin Wang; **Editor:** Yong Xie
Profile: provides news and latest issues on current affairs and economy in China.
Language (s): Chinese
DAILY NEWSPAPER

Titan Sports 460016
Owner: Titan Media
Editorial: Titan Media Xiduan Blk 22 Beili Xiqu Donghuashi, Chongwenqu, Beijing 100062
Tel: 86 51005876
Email: 24@titan24.com **Web site:** http://www.titansports.cn
Freq: 2 Times/Week; **Circ:** 160000 Not Audited
Profile: Titan Sports is a national newspaper mainly reports the latest news on different sports and different competitions both in China and overseas.
Language (s): Chinese
Ad Rate: Full Page Mono 328000.00
Currency: China Yuan Renminbi
DAILY NEWSPAPER

Today Fortune 460370
Editorial: Room 336 Jibao Dasha, 6426 Ziyou Dalu, Changchun 130033 **Tel:** 86 431886000058
Email: jrcfb@126.com
Freq: 2 Times/Week; **Circ:** 40000
Editor in Chief: Dongsheng Li
Profile: covers information and news of finance and money management targeting the general public.
Language (s): Chinese
DAILY NEWSPAPER

Today Morning Express 459533
Editorial: Zhejiang Daily Press Group, 178 Tiyuchanglu, Hangzhou 310039
Tel: 86 57 188818881
Email: jrzb@zjnews.com.cn **Web site:** http://jrzb.zjol.com.cn
Freq: Daily; **Circ:** 300003 Not Audited
Profile: reports news on finance, economy, culture and lifestyle.
Language (s): Chinese
Ad Rate: Full Page Mono 143000.00
Ad Rate: Full Page Colour 279000.00
Currency: China Yuan Renminbi
DAILY NEWSPAPER

Today Women's News 459534
Editorial: Today Women's News, 1 Xiaoshan Beilu, Changsha 410011 **Tel:** 86 7312333618
Email: fw@fengone.com **Web site:** http://www.fengone.com
Freq: 2 Times/Week; **Circ:** 300002 Not Audited
Editor: Xian Peng; **Editor in Chief:** Fuhu Wang
Profile: focuses on the women's interests and lifestyle. It also covers gender and sexuality studies in China.
Language (s): Chinese
DAILY NEWSPAPER

Travel Times 507128
Editorial: Travel Times, 101 Puhuitang Road, Xuhuiqu, Shanghai 200030 **Tel:** 86 2164642513
Web site: http://www.itraveltimes.com
Freq: Weekly; **Circ:** 150000 Not Audited
Editor: Zhen Chen
Profile: releases the latest travel information and news in China. It also covers news on transportation.
Language (s): Chinese
Ad Rate: Full Page Mono 48000.00
Currency: China Yuan Renminbi
DAILY NEWSPAPER

TV & Life Weekly 459537
Editorial: TV & Life Weekly 4th FlR Guangzhou Dianshitai, 233 Huanshi Zhonglu Zonghe Dalou, Guangzhou 510010 **Tel:** 86 2086191481
Email: shengping@gztv.com **Web site:** http://shengping.gztv.com
Freq: Weekly; **Circ:** 480000
Editor in Chief: Meijin Niu
Profile: Covers entertainment news in Southern regions in China. It also includes TV program listings.
Language (s): Chinese
DAILY NEWSPAPER

Urumqi Evening News 459331
Editorial: Urumqi Evening News, 20 Qingnianlu, Tianshanqu, Urumqi (wulumuqi) 830002
Tel: 86 99 12628292
Email: wlmqzxxw@126.com **Web site:** http://www.wlmqwb.com
Freq: Daily; **Circ:** 140003 Not Audited
Editor in Chief: Weijiang Li
Profile: provides the regional news of Urumqi.
Language (s): Chinese
DAILY NEWSPAPER

The Weekend 459461
Editorial: Nanjing Daily Press Group, 223 Longpan Zhonglu, Nanjing 210002 **Tel:** 86 2584686739
Email: njzmb@126.com **Web site:** http://www.njrb.com.cn/zm
Freq: Weekly; **Circ:** 400000
Editor: Weidong Guan
Profile: The Weekend is a local publication which covers the news and information of culture and lifestyle in Nanjing region and in China.
Language (s): Chinese
DAILY NEWSPAPER

Weekly Guide to Far Eastern Finance and Trade 459039
Editorial: Heilongjiang University, 74 Xuefulu, Nangangqu, Harbin (ha'erbin) 150080
Tel: 86 45186608106
Email: yddb@hlju.edu.cn
Freq: Weekly; **Circ:** 200001 Not Audited
Editor in Chief: Huixin Jin
Profile: Covering trade news and economic situation of China and Russia, as well as related finance, industry, management, trade and news issues.
Language (s): Chinese
DAILY NEWSPAPER

Wenhuibao 459275
Editorial: Wenhui-xinmin United Press Group, 755 Weihailu, Shanghai 200041 **Tel:** 86 2152921234
Email: whb@wxjt.com.cn **Web site:** http://www.whb.cn
Freq: Daily; **Circ:** 400000
Editor in Chief: Jiong Xu
Profile: Wenhuibao is a national newspaper which covers news in China and overseas.
Language (s): Chinese
DAILY NEWSPAPER

Wenzhou Economic Daily 459129
Editorial: Wenzhou Daily Press Group, 202 Liminxilu, Wenzhou 325003 **Tel:** 86 577 88817110
Email: news@wzsee.com **Web site:** http://www.wzsee.com
Freq: Daily; **Circ:** 300001 Not Audited
Editor in Chief: Kesheng Jin
Profile: Covers the latest economic news
Language (s): Chinese
DAILY NEWSPAPER

Women's News Today 459383
Editorial: Shaanxi Daily Group, Room 903, Unit 2, Block A, Jinqiao Guoji, 50 Keji Road, Xi'an 710075
Tel: 86 298114600
Web site: http://www.mladies.com.cn
Freq: Weekly; **Circ:** 100003 Not Audited
Editor: Yongqian Wu
Profile: Women's News Today is a popular fashion newspaper in Xi'an that mainly covers lifestyle, fashion, female healthcare and society issues.
Language (s): Chinese
DAILY NEWSPAPER

Worker's Daily 404503
Editorial: Worker's Daily, 61 Andelujia, Dongcheng District, Beijing 100718 **Tel:** 86 10 84151572
Email: news@workercn.cn **Web site:** http://txzx.workercn.cn
Freq: Daily; **Circ:** 500003 Not Audited
Editor in Chief: Shi Shusi; **Editor:** Mingjiang Zhang
Profile: It covers major news, labor market and governmental policies.
Language (s): Chinese
Ad Rate: Full Page Mono 198000.00
Currency: China Yuan Renminbi
DAILY NEWSPAPER

Wuhan Morning Post 459224
Editorial: Changjiang Daily Press Group, Teyihao Changjiang Ribaolu, Wuhan 430022
Tel: 86 27 85771888 8802
Web site: http://www.cnhan.com
Freq: Daily; **Circ:** 800003 Not Audited
Profile: covers the local and regional news in Wuhan region.
Language (s): Chinese
Ad Rate: Full Page Mono 150000.00
Ad Rate: Full Page Colour 283000.00
Currency: China Yuan Renminbi
DAILY NEWSPAPER

Wuxi Daily 459639
Editorial: Wuxi Daily, Xinwen Daxia, 1 Xueqian Donglu, Wuxi 214002 **Tel:** 86 51082757557
Email: wxrb@wxrb.com **Web site:** http://www.wxrb.com
Freq: Daily; **Circ:** 120000
Editor in Chief: Chuan Liu
Profile: Wuxi Daily is a newspaper covers the local and regional news in Wuxi region.
Language (s): Chinese
DAILY NEWSPAPER

Xiamen Business News 460846
Editorial: Xiamen Daily Press 12th FlR Number 122, Lvninglu, Xiamen 361009 **Tel:** 86 5928080000
Email: 8080000@sunnews.com **Web site:** http://www.xmnn.cn
Freq: Daily; **Circ:** 200000 Not Audited
Editor in Chief: Xingjun Pan
Profile: Economic newspaper which targets people living in Xiamen.
Language (s): Chinese
Ad Rate: Full Page Mono 80000.00
Currency: China Yuan Renminbi
DAILY NEWSPAPER

The xiao xue sheng shi jie 459185
Editorial: Jiaoxue Yuekanshe, 140 Wensanlu, Hangzhou 310012 **Tel:** 86 57188213112
Email: xxssjb@xxssj.com **Web site:** http://www.jxyk.com/oldweb/xxssjb.htm
Freq: Weekly; **Circ:** 760003 Not Audited
Editor in Chief: Jingyao Dong
Profile: The World of Primary Student is a local publication which provides the educational and learning information and knowledge for primary school students.
Language (s): Chinese
Ad Rate: Full Page Mono 50000.00
Currency: China Yuan Renminbi
DAILY NEWSPAPER

Xinhua Daily Telegraph 404439
Editorial: Xinhua Daily Telegraph, 57 Xidajie, Xuanwumen, Xicheng District, Beijing 100803
Tel: 86 106 3072070
Email: xhmrdx@163.com **Web site:** http://www.xinhuanet.com/mrdx
Freq: Daily; **Circ:** 1220000
Profile: Reports news from Xinhua News Agency.
Language (s): Chinese
DAILY NEWSPAPER

Xinjiang Economic News 459117
Editorial: Xinjiang Economic News, Tianji Building, No. 90, Jiefangbei Lu, Urumqi (wulumuqi) 830002
Tel: 86 9912332215
Email: xwmt119@163.com **Web site:** http://epaper.xjjb.com
Freq: Daily; **Circ:** 150003 Not Audited
Editor in Chief: Jishang Su
Profile: It focuses on the economic events and financial news in Xinjiang region.
Language (s): Chinese
DAILY NEWSPAPER

Xinjiang Law News 459082
Editorial: Xinjiang Law News, 6 Wenhuaxiang, Jiefang Beilu, Urumqi (wulumuqi) 830002
Tel: 86 9912826027
Email: xjfzb@xjdaily.com **Web site:** http://www.xjfzb.com/xjfzbindex.asp
Freq: 2 Times/Week; **Circ:** 50001 Not Audited
Editor in Chief: Yuzhi Cai
Profile: Covers law news and law related issues in Xinjiang region.
Language (s): Chinese
DAILY NEWSPAPER

Xinmin Evening News 404497
Editorial: Wenhui - Xinmin United Press Group, 755 Weihailu, Shanghai 200041 **Tel:** 86 21 52921234
Email: xmywn@wxjt.com.cn **Web site:** http://www.xinmin.cn
Freq: Daily; **Circ:** 1000000 Not Audited
Editor: Yinghuan Wu
Profile: Covers the local and national news in Shanghai and China.
Language (s): Chinese
Ad Rate: Full Page Mono 180000.00
Ad Rate: Full Page Colour 264000.00
Currency: China Yuan Renminbi
DAILY NEWSPAPER

Y Weekend 459166
Owner: Y Weekend Publishing
Editorial: Y Weekend Publishing, 12/F, Jintai Guoyi Dasha, 103 Chaoyang Beilu, Chaoyang District, Beijing 100123 **Tel:** 86 1085523009
Email: zhangzhuo@yweekend.com **Web site:** http://www.yweekend.com/
Freq: Weekly; **Circ:** 150002 Not Audited
Editor: Zhuo Zhang
Profile: It covers lifestyle, fashion, entertainment and other youth interested issues.
Language (s): Chinese
DAILY NEWSPAPER

Yanbian Morning Post 459042
Editorial: Yanbian Morning Post, 13A Xingrongshangwu, Yanji 133000 **Tel:** 86 4332900108
Email: ybnews@126.com **Web site:** http://www.ybnews.cn
Freq: Daily
Editor in Chief: Dunliang Lu
Profile: Covers economic and business developments in Northeast Asia and also focuses on social affairs in the area.
Language (s): Chinese
DAILY NEWSPAPER

Yangtse Evening Post 459258
Editorial: 48th Fl Xinhua Dasha 55, Zhongshanlu, Nanjing 210005 **Tel:** 86 25 96096 16096
Email: xwpl@yangtse.com **Web site:** http://www.yangtse.com
Freq: Daily; **Circ:** 2000000 Not Audited
Editor: Jun Li
Profile: Covers news in Jiangsu region.
Language (s): Chinese
Ad Rate: Full Page Mono 221600.00
Ad Rate: Full Page Colour 332400.00
Currency: China Yuan Renminbi
DAILY NEWSPAPER

Yangtze River 459559
Editorial: People's Changjiang News, 1863 Jiefang Dadao, Hankou, Wuhan 430010 **Tel:** 86 2782926362
Email: mcjzz@sina.com **Web site:** http://www.cjw.com.cn
Freq: Weekly
Editor in Chief: Shanzhong Wei
Profile: mainly covers news and latest research development of Changjiang river.
Language (s): Chinese
DAILY NEWSPAPER

Yangzhou Evening News 460345
Editorial: Yangzhou Daily Group, Xinwen Dalou, Xiqu, Wenhui Donglu, Yangzhou 225009
Tel: 86 51485881322
Web site: http://www.yzwb.com
Freq: Daily; **Circ:** 150001 Not Audited
Editor: Gang Zhao
Profile: Focuses on the local and regional news in Yangzhou.
Language (s): Chinese
DAILY NEWSPAPER

Yantai Evening News 460225
Editorial: Yantai Daily Media Group, 54 Bei Dajie, Yantai 264001 **Tel:** 86 53596110
Email: shm535@126.com **Web site:** http://www.shm.com.cn
Freq: Daily; **Circ:** 100002 Not Audited
Profile: Provides local and regional news.
Language (s): Chinese
DAILY NEWSPAPER

Yanzhao Metropolis Daily 460814
Editorial: Hebei Daily News Group, 86 Yuhuadonglu, Shijiazhuang 50013 **Tel:** 86 31188631263
Web site: http://www.yzdsb.com.cn
Freq: Daily; **Circ:** 1000000
Editor in Chief: Bingxiang Li
Profile: Covers news in Shijiazhuang.
Language (s): Chinese
Ad Rate: Full Page Mono 269000.00
Ad Rate: Full Page Colour 376000.00
Currency: China Yuan Renminbi
DAILY NEWSPAPER

Yiwu Business 459029
Owner: Yiwu Business Press
Editorial: Yiwu Business Press, 369 Jiangdongzhonglu, Yiwu, Jinhua 322000
Tel: 86 57985381020
Web site: http://www.ywnews.cn/
Freq: 2 Times/Week; **Circ:** 70003 Not Audited
Profile: It covers the latest business information and market status in Yiwu region.
Language (s): Chinese
DAILY NEWSPAPER

Youth Calligraphy News 459141
Editorial: Qingshaonian Shufa Baoshe, 105 Zhongshan Street, Jiamusi 154002
Tel: 86 454 8225419
Freq: Weekly; **Circ:** 100001 Not Audited
Editor in Chief: Changgui He
Profile: It provides information on Chinese calligraphy as well as features calligraphic works.
Language (s): Chinese
DAILY NEWSPAPER

Youth Real Time News 459168
Editorial: China Youth Press, 2 Haiyuncang, Dongzhimennei, Beijing 100702 **Tel:** 86 10 64098920
Web site: http://qnsx.cyol.com
Freq: Weekly; **Circ:** 220003 Not Audited
Profile: Mainly distributed in the high speed train in China, covering the news about the railway construction and development in China and current social, economic and cultural affairs.
Language (s): Chinese
DAILY NEWSPAPER

Youth Times 460043
Editorial: Youth Times, 69 Zhonghe Beilu, Hangzhou 310003 **Tel:** 86 57185804800
Email: qnsb@vip.sina.com **Web site:** http://www.qnsb.com
Freq: Daily; **Circ:** 420001 Not Audited
Editor in Chief: Feng Zhang
Profile: focuses on the news and information about Youth in China including education, lifestyle and student life.
Language (s): Chinese
Ad Rate: Full Page Mono 172000.00
Ad Rate: Full Page Colour 260000.00
Currency: China Yuan Renminbi
DAILY NEWSPAPER

Yulin Daily 460223
Editorial: Yulin Daily, 6 Minzhu Zhonglu, Yulin 537000
Tel: 86 7752820239

Web site: http://www.gxylnews.com
Freq: Daily; **Circ:** 70000
Editor in Chief: Fuguang Li
Profile: Focuses on news of economic, politics, cultural and social issues.
Language (s): Chinese
DAILY NEWSPAPER

Yunnan Radio & Television Weekly 459481

Editorial: Yunnan Television Station, 182 Renmin Xilu, Kunming 650031 **Tel:** 86 8715385714
Web site: http://paper.yntv.cn
Freq: Weekly; **Circ:** 150003 Not Audited
Editor in Chief: Jianghong Xue
Profile: Covers the entertainment news and broadcasting information in Yunnan region.
Language (s): Chinese
DAILY NEWSPAPER

Yunnan Technology News 459531

Tel: 86 8713126725
Email: ynkjb2006@126.com **Web site:** http://ynkjb.yunnan.cn
Freq: 2 Times/Week; **Circ:** 80003 Not Audited
Editor in Chief: Zhiwei Yue
Profile: Covers news on agricultural business and technological development and application in Yunnan region.
Language (s): Chinese
DAILY NEWSPAPER

Zhaotong Daily 460224

Editorial: Zhaotong Daily, 84 Yingfenglu, Zhaoyang District, Zhaotong 657000 **Tel:** 86 8702158272
Web site: http://www.ztnews.net
Freq: Daily; **Circ:** 40000
Editor in Chief: Zhenghong Tang
Profile: Focuses on news in China.
Language (s): Chinese
DAILY NEWSPAPER

Zhejiang Broadcasting Television News 459321

Editorial: Zhejiang Broadcasting TV News 247 Hushu Nanlu, Hangzhou 310005 **Tel:** 86 57188391055
Freq: Weekly; **Circ:** 280003 Not Audited
Profile: Zhejiang Broadcasting Television News is a local publication which reports the program list and entertainment news in China.
Language (s): Chinese
DAILY NEWSPAPER

Zhengzhou Daily 460027

Editorial: Zhengzhou Daily, Xinwen Dasha, 80 Longhai Xilu, Zhengzhou 450006
Tel: 86 371677655555
Email: zzrbxzxw@sina.com **Web site:** http://www.zynews.com
Freq: Daily; **Circ:** 273001 Not Audited
Editor: Jinxia Wang
Profile: Focuses on political, economic, cultural and social issues.
Language (s): Chinese
DAILY NEWSPAPER

Zhuhai Daily 459341

Editorial: Zhuhai Daily, 566 Yinhualu, Zhuhai 519002
Tel: 86 7562639888
Email: cf@zhuhaidaily.com.cn **Web site:** http://www.zhuhaidaily.com.cn
Freq: Daily; **Circ:** 150000
Editor: Hua Yang
Profile: Covers the news in Zhuhai.
Language (s): Chinese
DAILY NEWSPAPER

Zhujiang Evening News 459342

Editorial: Zhuhaitequ Press, Jiuzhou Dadao, Zhuhai 519000 **Tel:** 86 75639333
Web site: http://www.zhnews.net
Freq: Daily; **Circ:** 100000
Editor: Hua Su
Profile: covers both local and international news and the latest issues related to Zhuhai.
Language (s): Chinese
DAILY NEWSPAPER

Zibo Evening News 459573

Editorial: Zibo Daily Agency, 212 Liuquanlu, Zhangdian Distict, Zibo 255006 **Tel:** 86 53 33182818
Web site: http://www.zbnews.net
Freq: Daily; **Circ:** 250000
Bureau Chief: Gongpin Li
Profile: Zibo Daily has 8 pages in folio, Page 1,2,3,4 are respectively for news in major, local, domestic, international and sports, while page 5,6,7,8 for columns of new life, social science and technology, law, economy and weekend, etc. With intensive information in various fields.
Language (s): Chinese
DAILY NEWSPAPER

News Service/Syndicate

China News Service 490335

Editorial: Beijing Baiwanzhuang St on the 12th, Beijing **Tel:** 86 15699788000
Email: gaojian@chinanews.com.cn **Web site:** http://www.chinanews.com
Freq: Daily
Profile: Established in 1952 as a state-level news agency, spreads news worldwide and serves as a database of information from global Chinese-language media, providing content to overseas Chinese language newspapers and self-running newspapers and journals.
Language (s): Chinese
NEWS SERVICE/SYNDICATE

Interfax China 490347

Editorial: Interfax China., Suite 1601, Wilson House 19-27, Hong Kong **Tel:** 852 25372262
Web site: http://www.interfax.com
Freq: Daily
Profile: covers different news like financial and medical issues.
Language (s): English
NEWS SERVICE/SYNDICATE

Xinhua Financial Network - Shanghai Bureau 467628

Email: ir@xinhuaholdings.com **Web site:** http://www.xfn.com
Freq: Daily
Profile: Xinhua Financial Net Shanghai Bureau 3905 3909 twr 1 Grand gateway 10F bashi Cent Mansion 398 Huaihai Rd M3909 twr 1
Language (s): Chinese
NEWS SERVICE/SYNDICATE

Xinhua News Agency 467575

Editorial: Xinhua News Agency, 57 Xidajie, Xuanwumen, Beijing 100803 **Tel:** 86 1063073741
Email: xinhua381@hotmail.com **Web site:** http://www.xinhuanet.com
Freq: Continuous
Profile: Serves as the official press agency of China, covering news and related topics in the country and beyond, major breaking news events, laws and regulations, appointments and removals of high-ranking officials.
Language (s): Chinese
NEWS SERVICE/SYNDICATE

Colombia

Time Difference: GMT -5
National Telephone Code: 57
Continent: The Americas
Capital: Bogotá

Newspapers

El Colombiano 160819

Owner: El Colombiano S.A. & CIA. S.C.A.
Editorial: Carrera 48 #30 sur 119, Envigado - Antioquia, Medellin **Tel:** 57 4 331-5252
Email: redaccion@elcolombiano.com.co **Web site:** http://www.elcolombiano.com
Freq: Daily; **Circ:** 87000
Editor: Carlos Mario Gómez; **Editor:** Martha Hoyos Franco; **Editor:** Víctor León Zuluaga; **Editor:** Carlos Olimpo Restrepo; **Editor in Chief:** José Guillermo Palacio Patiño; **Editor:** Monica Quintero; **Editor:** Ramiro Velásquez Gómez
Profile: Información y noticias de Colombia, Medellín, Antioquia y el mundo. Information and news from Colombia, Medellin, Antioquia and the world.
Language (s): Spanish
DAILY NEWSPAPER

El Espectador 160103

Editorial: Avenida El Dorado No. 69-76, Bogota
Tel: 57 1 423-2300
Email: servicioalcliente@elespectador.com **Web site:** http://www.elespectador.com
Freq: Daily; **Circ:** 80617
Editor general/Editor in Chief: Jorge Cardona
Profile: News general interest.
Language (s): Spanish
DAILY NEWSPAPER

El Heraldo 160831

Editorial: Calle 53 B #46-25, Barranquilla
Tel: 57 5 3715000
Web site: http://www.elheraldo.com.co
Freq: Daily; **Circ:** 48000
Editor: Rosario Borrero; **Editor:** José Granados; **Editor:** Martha Guarín; **Editor:** Alix López; **Editor:** Zoraida Noriega; **Editor:** Manuel Ortega
Profile: National newspaper covering mostly local and regional news, but also covers national and international news, politics, sports, and entertainment.
Language (s): Spanish
DAILY NEWSPAPER

La Libertad 157151

Owner: Esper Editores
Editorial: Carrera 53 No. 55-166, Barranquilla (atlántico) **Tel:** 57 5 349 1175
Email: lalibertad@lalibertad.com.co **Web site:** http://www.lalibertad.com.co
Freq: Daily; **Circ:** 45000 Not Audited
Editor: Monica Bolaños; **Editor in Chief:** Luis Camacho; **Editor:** Javier de la Oz; **Editor:** Eduardo Esper; **Director:** Roberto Esper Rebaje; **Editor:** Wilder Molina
Profile: National Newspaper.
Language (s): Spanish
DAILY NEWSPAPER

El Mundo 156979

Editorial: Calle 53 #74-50, Los Colores, Medellin
Tel: 57 4 2642800
Email: redaccion@elmundo.com **Web site:** http://www.elmundo.com
Freq: Weekly; **Circ:** 30100
Publisher: Irene Gaviria Correa; **General Manager:** Alberto Gil Valencia; **Editor:** Patricia Giraldo; **Editor:** Carolina Mejía; **Editor:** José Ignacio Mejía; **Editor:** Elkin Pumarejo Daza; **Editor:** Javier Ramírez Uribe; **International News Editor:** Juan Felipe Sierra; **Editor:** Carmen Vasquez Gomez
Profile: Covers national news of Colombia.
Language (s): Spanish
DAILY NEWSPAPER

El Nuevo Diario 157197

Owner: El Espacio J. Ardila C. S.A.
Editorial: Carrera 69 #44-35 Avenida El Dorado, Bogota **Tel:** 57 1 425-1570
Email: nuevodiario.co@gmail.com **Web site:** http://www.nuevodiario.co
Freq: Daily
Editor: Enrique Castañeda; **Editor:** Alejandro Monroy; **Editor in Chief:** Alberto Uribe Gómez
Profile: National newspaper.
Language (s): Spanish
DAILY NEWSPAPER

La Opinión 157257

Editorial: Avenida 4 #16-12, Cúcuta
Tel: 57 75829999
Email: jefederedaccion@laopinion.com.co **Web site:** http://www.laopinion.com.co
Freq: Daily
Director: José Eustorgio Colmenares; **Editor:** Celmira Figueroa; **Editor:** Pedro Jauregui; **Editor in Chief:** Angel Romero; **Editor:** Omar Romero
Profile: Newspaper General interest.
Language (s): Spanish
DAILY NEWSPAPER

El País 160829

Editorial: Carrera 2da #24-46 Barrio San Nicolas, Cali **Tel:** 57 2 898-7000
Email: redesociales@elpais.com.co **Web site:** http://www.elpais.com.co/elpais/
Freq: Daily; **Circ:** 95000
Editor: Judith GOmez; **Editor in Chief:** Paola Gomez;
Editor: Paola Guevara
Profile: Newspaper general news and interest.
Language (s): Spanish
Ad Rate: Full Page Mono 540.93
Currency: Colombia Pesos
DAILY NEWSPAPER

El Tiempo 160827

Owner: Casa Editorial El Tiempo
Editorial: Av. Calle 26 No 68B-70, Bogota 111321
Tel: 57 1 294-0100
Email: redessociales@eltiempo.com **Web site:** http://www.eltiempo.com.co
Freq: Daily; **Circ:** 230000
Editor in Chief/Editor en Jefe: Ernesto Cortés; **Editor/Editora:** Adriana Garzón; **Editor:** Gabriel Meluk; **International News Editor/Editor de Noticias Internacional:** Eduard Soto Guerrero
Profile: A national newspaper in Colombia. Covers national and international news in politics, sciences, technology, travel, health, sports, and more. Principal portal noticioso de Colombia y referente informativo para los hispano parlantes en el mundo. Adicional a una actualización 24/7 en materia noticiosa, el respaldo de los diferentes equipos editoriales de la Casa Editorial El Tiempo garantizan una oferta especializada en temas como viajes, tecnología, salud entre otras.
Language (s): Spanish
Ad Rate: Full Page Mono 24145.30
Currency: Colombia Pesos
DAILY NEWSPAPER

Comoros

Time Difference: GMT +3
National Telephone Code: 269
Continent: Africa
Capital: Moroni

Newspapers

Al-watwan 517701

Owner: Al-watwan
Editorial: BP 984, Moroni **Tel:** 269 773 44 48
Email: direction@alwatwan.net **Web site:** http://www.alwatwan.net
Freq: Weekly; **Circ:** 1000 Publisher's Statement
Directeur de Publication: Djaé Ahamada; **Publicité:** Aminata Mohamed; **Rédacteur en Chef:** Mohamed Soilihi Ahmed
Profile: National newspaper covering regional, national and international news and current affairs including politics, society, economics, sport and education.
Language (s): Arabic
Ad Rate: Full Page Mono 130000.00
Currency: Comoros Francs
DAILY NEWSPAPER

Congo

Time Difference: GMT +1
National Telephone Code: 242
Continent: Africa
Capital: Brazzaville

Newspapers

Les Dépêches de Brazzaville 186050

Owner: ADIAC - Agence d'Information d'Afrique Centrale
Editorial: Immeuble Les Manguiers, 84, boulevard Denis-Sassou-N'Guesso, Brazzaville
Tel: 242 5 532 01 09
Email: lesdepechesdebrazzaville@orange.fr **Web site:** http://www.lesdepechesdebrazzaville.fr
Freq: Daily; **Circ:** 4000 Publisher's Statement
Editor: Gankama N'siah
Profile: Daily newspaper covering general news and current affairs including politics, economics, society, arts, culture and sports. It is published in two national editions, Brazzaville and Kinshasa, and available online.
Language (s): French
Ad Rate: Full Page Mono 250000.00
Currency: Communauté Financière Africaine Francs BEAC
DAILY NEWSPAPER

Cook Islands

Time Difference: GMT -10
National Telephone Code: 682
Continent: Oceania
Capital: Avarua

Newspapers

Cook Islands Herald 539204

Owner: Elijah Communications Ltd
Editorial: PO Box 126, Rarotonga, Cook Islands
Tel: 682 29 460
Email: bestread@ciherald.co.ck **Web site:** http://ciherald.co.ck
Circ: 1300
Editor: Charles Pitt
Profile: Newspaper covering general news and current affairs from the islands.
Language (s): English
DAILY NEWSPAPER

Cook Islands Independent 229970

Owner: Cook Islands Broadcasting & Newspaper Corporation
Editorial: PO Box 126, Rarotonga **Tel:** 682 29 460
Email: bestread@ciherald.co.ck **Web site:** http://www.ciherald.co.ck
Circ: 900 Publisher's Statement
Editor: Trevor Pitt
Profile: Newspaper focusing on local political and social news.
Language (s): English
DAILY NEWSPAPER

Cook Islands News 539109

Owner: Cook Islands News Ltd
Editorial: PO Box 15, Rarotonga, Cook Islands
Tel: 682 22 999
Email: reception@cookislandsnews.com **Web site:** http://www.cookislandsnews.com
Circ: 2500 Publisher's Statement
Editor: John Woods
Profile: Daily newspaper of the Cook Islands covering regional and national news and current affairs.
Language (s): English
DAILY NEWSPAPER

Costa Rica

Time Difference: GMT -6
National Telephone Code: 506
Continent: The Americas
Capital: San José

Newspapers

Al Día 383633
Owner: Grupo Nación GNSA
Editorial: Llorente de Tibas, del cruce 400 metros este y 125 metros norte, Tibás (san José)
Tel: 506 22474647
Email: redaccion@aldia.cr **Web site:** http://www.aldia.cr
Freq: Daily; **Circ:** 82000 Not Audited
Editor: Alexander Ramírez; **Editor:** Gabriela Solano
Profile: Regioanl newspaper covering national and international news, politics, economics, finance, business, culture and sport.
Language (s): Spanish
DAILY NEWSPAPER

Diario Extra 160945
Owner: Sociedad Periodistica Extra Ltda.
Editorial: Edificio de la Prensa Libre, Calle 4 Avenida 4, Aptdo 177 - 1009, San Jose **Tel:** 506 22236666
Email: redaccion@diarioextra.com **Web site:** http://www.diarioextra.com
Freq: Daily; **Circ:** 158100 Not Audited
Editor: Paola Hernandez
Profile: Newspaper focusing on national and international news, politics, business, culture and sport.
Language (s): Spanish
DAILY NEWSPAPER

La Nación 156985
Owner: Grupo Nación GNSA
Editorial: 200 metros al Este del cruce de Llorente de Tibas, Aptdo 10138 - 1000, Llorente De Tibás (san José) **Tel:** 506 2 247-4747
Email: webmaster@nacion.com **Web site:** http://www.nacion.com
Freq: Daily; **Circ:** 120000 Not Audited
Editor: Armando Mayorga; **Editora/Editor in Chief:** Larissa Minsky
Profile: Local newspaper covering national and international news, politics, economics, finance, business, culture and sports relevant to Costa Rica. To contact journalists please us webmaster@nacion.com.For opinion articles use foro@nacion.com. Opinion articles should not exceed 4,000 characters with spaces.
Language (s): Spanish
DAILY NEWSPAPER

La Prensa Libre 156989
Owner: Sociedad Periodistica Extra Ltda.
Editorial: Edificio La Prensa Libre - Calle 4 Avenida 4, Aptdo 10121 - 1000, San Jose **Tel:** 506 2 2236666
Email: plibre@prensalibre.co.cr **Web site:** http://www.prensalibre.co.cr
Freq: Daily; **Circ:** 55000 Not Audited
Editor: Maria Elena Jimenez; **Editor:** Roberto Portuguez
Profile: Newspaper covering national and international news, politics, economics, finance, business, culture and sport.
Language (s): Spanish
DAILY NEWSPAPER

La República 156988
Owner: SRB CR Limitada
Editorial: Barrio Tournon, Contiguo al Hotel Radisson, Aptdo 2130 - 1000, San Jose
Tel: 506 2522 3300
Email: redaccion@larepublica.net **Web site:** http://www.larepublica.net
Freq: Daily; **Circ:** 27300 Not Audited
Editor: Danny Canales; **Editor:** Damaris Ruiz; **Editor in Chief:** Luis Valverde
Profile: National newspaper covering national and international news, politics, economics, finance, business, culture and sport.
Language (s): Spanish
DAILY NEWSPAPER

Cote d'Ivoire

Time Difference: GMT
National Telephone Code: 225
Continent: Africa
Capital: Yamoussoukro

Newspapers

Fraternité Matin 218468
Owner: SNPECI - Société Nouvelle de Presses et d'Edition de Côte d'Ivoire
Editorial: Boulevard du General De Gaulle, Abidjan 1
Tel: 225 20 37 06 66
Email: info@fratmat.info **Web site:** http://www.fratmat.info
Freq: Daily; **Circ:** 25000 Publisher's Statement
Editor in Chief: Moussa Touré
Profile: Newspaper focusing on national and international news and current affairs including politics, economy, society, culture and sports.
Language (s): French
Ad Rate: Full Page Mono 884221.00
Ad Rate: Full Page Colour 1420425.00
Currency: Communauté Financière Africaine Francs BEAC
DAILY NEWSPAPER

L' Intelligent d'Abidjan 488849
Owner: L'Intelligent d'Abidjan
Editorial: 19 BP 1534, Abidjan **Tel:** 225 22 42 71 61
Email: admin@lintelligentdabidjan.info **Web site:** http://www.lintelligentdabidjan.info
Freq: Daily; **Circ:** 10000 Publisher's Statement
Editor in Chief: Joël Touré
Profile: Regional newspaper covering news and current affairs including politics, economics, society, sports, culture and diplomacy.
Language (s): French
Ad Rate: Full Page Mono 400000.00
Ad Rate: Full Page Colour 730000.00
Currency: Communauté Financière Africaine Francs BEAC
DAILY NEWSPAPER

L' Inter 523806
Owner: Groupe Olympe
Editorial: BP 2462, Abidjan 10 **Tel:** 225 21 21 28 00
Email: admin@linfodrome.com **Web site:** http://www.linfodrome.com
Freq: Daily; **Circ:** 22000 Publisher's Statement
Editor in Chief: Jean-Marie Ahoussou
Profile: National daily newspaper covering news and current affairs including economics, politics, society, culture and sport.
Language (s): French
Ad Rate: Full Page Mono 240000.00
Currency: Communauté Financière Africaine Francs BEAC
DAILY NEWSPAPER

Le Patriote 161238
Owner: Mayama Editions et Production
Editorial: 23, rue du Canal - Bietry, Abidjan 22
Tel: 225 20 00 43 42
Email: lepatriote@afnet.net **Web site:** http://www.lepatriote.net
Freq: Daily; **Circ:** 15000 Publisher's Statement
Editor in Chief: Koré Emmanuel
Profile: Newspaper covering regional. national and international news and current affairs including politics, economics, society, culture and sports.
Language (s): French
Ad Rate: Full Page Mono 473000.00
Ad Rate: Full Page Colour 709500.00
Currency: Communauté Financière Africaine Francs BEAC
DAILY NEWSPAPER

Soir Info 523807
Owner: Groupe Olympe
Editorial: BP 2462, Abidjan 10 **Tel:** 225 21 21 28 00
Email: admin@linfodrome.com **Web site:** http://www.linfodrome.com
Freq: Daily; **Circ:** 35000 Publisher's Statement
Editor in Chief: Kikié Nazaire
Profile: National daily newspaper covering general news and current affairs including economy, politics, society, culture and sport.
Language (s): French
Ad Rate: Full Page Mono 280000.00
Currency: Communauté Financière Africaine Francs BEAC
DAILY NEWSPAPER

News Service/Syndicate

Agence Ivoirienne de Presse - AIP 524148
Owner: Agence Ivoirienne de Presse
Editorial: Avenue Chardy, Abidjan 4
Tel: 225 20 22 64 13
Email: aip@aip.ci **Web site:** http://aip.ci
Freq: Daily
Editor in Chief: Pascal Kouao
Profile: National press agency covering general news and current affairs including society, economics, sports, politics, culture and media.
Language (s): French
NEWS SERVICE/SYNDICATE

Croatia

Time Difference: GMT +1
National Telephone Code: 385
Continent: Europe
Capital: Zagreb

Newspapers

24 Sata 378347
Owner: 24sata d.o.o.
Editorial: Oreskovieva 6H/1, Zagreb 10010
Tel: 385 1 6069 500
Email: redakcija@24sata.hr **Web site:** http://www.24sata.hr
Freq: Daily; **Circ:** 110000 Not Audited
Editor: Vesna Blaškovi?; **News Editor:** Ivan Bu?a; **News Editor:** Igor Fejzagi?; **Editor-in-Chief:** Goran Gavranovi?; **Editor:** Renato Ivanuš
Language (s): Serbo-Croat
DAILY NEWSPAPER

Jutarnji list 156788
Owner: Hanza Media d.o.o.
Editorial: Koranska 2, Zagreb 10 000
Tel: 385 1 61 03 100
Email: jutarnji.list@hanzamedia.hr **Web site:** http://www.jutarnji.hr
Freq: Daily; **Circ:** 115000 Publisher's Statement
Editor-in-Chief: Viktor Vresnik
Profile: Newspaper covering national and international news, finance, business, culture, sports and in-depth background information.
Language (s): Serbo-Croat
DAILY NEWSPAPER

Poslovni dnevnik 378931
Owner: Ve?ernji list
Editorial: Oreskovieva 6H/1, Zagreb 10 000
Tel: 385 1 6326-001
Email: redakcija@poslovni.hr **Web site:** http://www.poslovni.hr
Freq: Daily; **Circ:** 8500 Publisher's Statement
Editor-in-Chief: Mislav Šimatovi?
Profile: Business business daily newspaper in Croatia launched in March 2004, and published 5 days a week. Covers stock markets, stocks, economy, capital markets in Croatia and other countries in the region and business.
Language (s): Serbo-Croat
DAILY NEWSPAPER

Slobodna Dalmacija 161233
Owner: Slobodna Dalmacija d.d.
Editorial: Hrvatske mornarice 4, Split 21 000
Tel: 385 21 352-888
Email: redakcija@slobodnadalmacija.hr **Web site:** http://www.slobodnadalmacija.hr
Freq: Daily; **Circ:** 75000 Publisher's Statement
Editor-in-Chief: Ivo Bonkovi?
Profile: Regional newspaper containing national and international news, politics, sports and culture.
Language (s): Serbo-Croat
Ad Rate: Full Page Colour 23100.00
Currency: Croatia Kuna
DAILY NEWSPAPER

Ve?ernji list 161244
Owner: Ve?ernji list d.d.
Editorial: Oreskovieva 6H/1, Zagreb 10 010
Tel: 385 1 6300 605
Email: vecernji@vecernji.hr **Web site:** http://www.vecernji.hr
Freq: Daily
Editor: Gojko Drlja?a; **Editor-in-Chief:** Dražen Klari?; **Editor:** Ana Škilji? Ravenš?ak; **Editor:** Natasa Vlasic-Smrekar
Profile: Evening daily newspaper covering news, politics, culture and sports.
Language (s): Croatian
DAILY NEWSPAPER

News Service/Syndicate

HINA - Croatian News Agency 353226
Editorial: Marulicev trg. 16, Zagreb 10 000
Tel: 385 1 48 08 660
Email: hina@hina.hr **Web site:** http://www.hina.hr
Editor-in-Chief: Ser?o Obratov
Profile: Croatian News Agency HINA is a public national news agency in Croatia.
Language (s): Serbo-Croat
NEWS SERVICE/SYNDICATE

Community Newspaper

Glas Istre 156725
Owner: Glas Istre d.o.o.
Editorial: Riva 10, Pula 52 000 **Tel:** 385 52 591-504
Email: novosti@glasistre.hr **Web site:** http://www.glasistre.hr
Circ: 21500
Editor-In-Chief: Ranko Borove?ki
Profile: Newspaper containing information for people living in the Istrian region.
Language (s): Serbo-Croat
Ad Rate: Full Page Colour 10944.00
Currency: Croatia Kuna
COMMUNITY NEWSPAPER

Glas Slavonije 161257
Owner: Glas Slavonije d.d.
Editorial: Hrvatske Republike 20, Osijek 31 000
Tel: 385 31 223-200
Email: glas@glas-slavonije.hr **Web site:** http://www.glas-slavonije.hr
Circ: 23000
?rna Kronika: Milan Bugari?; **?rna Kronika:** Vera Kova?i?; **Pomo?nica Odgovorne Urednice:** Sanja Marketi?; **Editor-in-Chief:** Mario Mihaljevi?; **News Editor:** Dijana Pavlovi?
Profile: Regional newspaper containing news, politics, economy, sports and culture.
Language (s): Serbo-Croat
Ad Rate: Full Page Colour 9400.00
Currency: Croatia Kuna
COMMUNITY NEWSPAPER

Hrvatsko slovo 225256
Owner: HKZ Hrvatsko slovo d.o.o.
Editorial: Hrvatske bratske zajednice 4, Zagreb 10 000 **Tel:** 385 1 61 90 112
Email: hkz@zg.htnet.hr **Web site:** http://www.hrvatsko-slovo.hr
Freq: Weekly; **Circ:** 15000
Profile: Newspaper featuring current affairs and cultural events in Croatia, also covers cinema and theatre reviews.
Language (s): Serbo-Croat
Ad Rate: Full Page Colour 7200.00
Currency: Croatia Kuna
COMMUNITY NEWSPAPER

Novi List 161254
Owner: Novi list d.d.
Editorial: Zvonimirova 20a, Rijeka 51 000
Tel: 385 51 650-011
Email: novilist.portal@gmail.com **Web site:** http://www.novilist.hr
Circ: 87500
Editor-in-Chief: Branko Mijic
Profile: Newspaper covering news, politics, culture and sports.
Language (s): Serbo-Croat
Ad Rate: Full Page Mono 2508.00
Ad Rate: Full Page Colour 3009.60
Currency: Euro
COMMUNITY NEWSPAPER

Cuba

Time Difference: GMT -5
National Telephone Code: 53
Continent: The Americas
Capital: Habana

Newspapers

Granma 159008
Owner: Combinado Poligráfico Granma
Editorial: Av. General Suarez y Territorial, Plaza de la Revolucion, Habana CP 10699 **Tel:** 53 7 88 13 333
Email: correo@granma.cip.cu **Web site:** http://www.granma.cubaweb.cu
Freq: Daily; **Circ:** 500000 Not Audited
Director: Lázaro Barredo Medina
Profile: Official newspaper of the Central Committee of the communist party of Cuba.
Language (s): Spanish
DAILY NEWSPAPER

News Service/Syndicate

Agencía de Información Nacional 392862
Editorial: Calle 23 no 358 esq.J. Vedado, Plaza de la Revolucion, Habana CP 10400 **Tel:** 53 7 832-5542
Email: editor@ain.cu **Web site:** http://www.ain.cu
Editor in Chief: Carlos Barrueco; **Director:** Esteban Ramírez Alonso
Language (s): Spanish
NEWS SERVICE/SYNDICATE

Prensa Latina 392856
Editorial: Calle 23 esq N. Vedado, Habana CP 10400
Tel: 53 78383496
Email: plchile1@tie.cl **Web site:** http://www.prensa-latina.cu

Profile: Covers national and international news.
Language (s): Spanish
NEWS SERVICE/SYNDICATE

Cyprus

Time Difference: GMT +2
National Telephone Code: 357
Continent: Europe
Capital: Nicosia

Newspapers

Alithia 456990
Owner: Ekdotiki Etaireia Ltd
Editorial: 26A, Corner Pindaros and Androklis Str., Latsia, Nicosia 1512 **Tel:** 357 22 471300
Email: news@alfamedia.press.cy **Web site:** http://www.alfanews.com.cy
Freq: Daily; **Circ:** 7000 Controlled Circulation
Profile: Newspaper covering politics, economics, culture, social events and sports.
Language (s): Greek
DAILY NEWSPAPER

Antilogos 472846
Owner: Drositis Ekdotikes Ltd
Editorial: 24 Elia Papakyriakou, Dafne Building, 1st floor, Acropoli, Nicosia 2081 **Tel:** 357 22 49 14 00
Email: antilogos@cytanet.com.cy
Freq: Weekly; **Circ:** 6500 Publisher's Statement
Director: Andreas Kaouris
Profile: Newspaper covering regional news and current affairs.
Language (s): Greek
DAILY NEWSPAPER

Cyprus Mail 156648
Owner: Cyprus Mail Co Ltd
Editorial: 24, Vassilios Voulgaroktonos St., Nicosia 1502 **Tel:** 357 22 81 85 85
Email: editor@cyprus-mail.com **Web site:** http://www.cyprus-mail.com
Freq: Daily; **Circ:** 10000 ABC-Audit Bureau of Circulations
Managing Director: Kyriacos Iacovides; **Editor in Chief:** Jean Kelly-Christou
Profile: Newspaper covering national and international news, politics, business, culture, entertainment and sports.
Language (s): English
DAILY NEWSPAPER

The Cyprus Weekly 224407
Owner: Phileleftheros Media Group
Editorial: 1 Diogenous Str., Engomi, Nicosia 1501
Tel: 357 22 744400
Email: cynewslive@cyprusweekly.com.cy **Web site:** http://in-cyprus.com
Freq: Weekly; **Circ:** 22000 Publisher's Statement
News Editor: Charlie Charalambous; **Publisher:** Nicos Chr. Pattichis
Profile: Weekly national newspaper covering regional, national and international news and current affairs including politics, economy, culture, events, entertainment, food, travel tips and sport.
Language (s): English
Ad Rate: Full Page Mono 1300.00
Ad Rate: Full Page Colour 1800.00
Currency: Euro
DAILY NEWSPAPER

The Financial Mirror 168684
Owner: Financial Mirror Ltd.
Editorial: P.O.Box 16077, Nicosia 2063
Tel: 357 22 67 86 66
Email: info@financialmirror.com **Web site:** http://www.financialmirror.com
Freq: Weekly; **Circ:** 4000 Not Audited
Advertising Manager: Masis der Parthogh; **Editor:** Angela Komodromou
Profile: Weekly newspaper covering business and financial news and analysis about the Cyprus economy.
Language (s): English
Ad Rate: Full Page Mono 1080.00
Ad Rate: Full Page Colour 1845.00
Currency: Euro
DAILY NEWSPAPER

Foni tis Pafou 537551
Owner: Foni tis Pafou
Editorial: 7 Kiniras Str. and Korivou Corner, Galaxias Building, Pafos 8011 **Tel:** 357 26 953743
Email: paphoni@cytanet.com.cy **Web site:** http://www.foni-pafou.com
Circ: 5000 Publisher's Statement
Director: Michalis Mountis
Profile: Regional newspaper of general interest covering regional political, social and society news.
Language (s): Greek
DAILY NEWSPAPER

Haravgi 157066
Owner: Dialogos Media Group
Editorial: Ezekia Papaioannou 6, Nicosia 1075
Tel: 357 22 76 66 66
Email: haravgi@spidernet.com.cy **Web site:** http://dialogos.com.cy/haravgi
Freq: Daily; **Circ:** 9000 Publisher's Statement
Editor in Chief: Androulla Giourov
Profile: Newspaper covering regional and national news and current affairs including politics, economics and sports.
Language (s): Greek
DAILY NEWSPAPER

I Kathimerini 578211
Owner: NDD Eidikes Ekdoseis
Editorial: 7E NiKou Kranidioti, Nicosia 2411
Tel: 357 22 472472
Email: info@kathimerini.com.cy **Web site:** http://kathimerini.com.cy
Freq: Weekly; **Circ:** 4500
Editor: Yiannis Andoniou; **Publisher:** Demetris Lottides
Profile: Daily newspaper covering regional, national and international news and current affairs including politics, business, economics, lifestyle, sports, culture and entertainment.
Language (s): Greek
Ad Rate: Full Page Colour 3528.00
Currency: Euro
DAILY NEWSPAPER

Kibris Gazetesi 533891
Owner: Kibrisli
Editorial: Dr. Fazıl Kücük Bulvar, Yeni Sanayi Bolgesi, Lefkosa **Tel:** 39 22 252555
Email: kibris@kibrisgazetesi.com **Web site:** http://www.kibrisgazetesi.com
Freq: Daily; **Circ:** 2500 Publisher's Statement
Profile: Turkish newspaper covering news and current affairs including business, politics, economics, culture, lifestyle, entertainment and sports.
Language (s): Turkish
DAILY NEWSPAPER

I Machi 157067
Owner: Nea Elpida Ltd
Editorial: 1 Georgiou Tyrimou, 3rd floor, office 31, Nicosia 1101 **Tel:** 357 22 000012
Email: info@maxh.com.cy **Web site:** http://www.maxhnews.com.cy
Freq: Daily; **Circ:** 5000 Publisher's Statement
Profile: Newspaper covering news and current affairs including business, politics, economy, culture and society.
Language (s): Greek
DAILY NEWSPAPER

The Paphos Post 582300
Owner: Paphos Post & Revival Fashions
Editorial: Shop 1.2.3 & 4, Kissonerga Anenue 71, Paphos 8574 **Tel:** 357 26 632564
Email: paphospost@hotmail.com **Web site:** http://www.thepaphospost.com
Freq: Daily; **Circ:** 20000
Managing Director: Judith Evans
Profile: Free newspaper offering a selection of local interest articles, news and views from around region.
Language (s): English
DAILY NEWSPAPER

O Phileleftheros 156649
Owner: O Phileleftheros Ltd
Editorial: 1 Diogenous Str., Engomi, Nicosia 1501
Tel: 357 22 744000
Email: philenews@phileleftheros.com **Web site:** http://www.philenews.com
Freq: Daily; **Circ:** 17720 Publisher's Statement
General Manager: Michael Karis; **Editor-in-Chief:** Aristos Michaelides
Profile: Newspaper covering regional, national and international news and current affairs including politics, economics, society, entertainment, lifestyle and sports.
Language (s): Greek
Ad Rate: Full Page Mono 4508.00
Ad Rate: Full Page Colour 3315.00
Currency: Euro
DAILY NEWSPAPER

Politis 457393
Owner: Arktinos Publications Ltd
Editorial: 8 Vassileiou Voulgaroktonou Str., Nicosia 1524 **Tel:** 357 22 861861
Email: info@politis-news.com **Web site:** http://politis.com.cy
Freq: Daily; **Circ:** 11000 Publisher's Statement
Publisher: Yiannis Papadopoulos; **Editor:** Sotiris Paroutis
Profile: Newspaper covering regional, national and international news and current affairs including politics, economy and sports.
Language (s): Greek
DAILY NEWSPAPER

I Simerini 156651
Owner: DIAS Media Group
Editorial: 31, Archangelos Avenue, Strovolos, Nicosia 2054 **Tel:** 357 22 580580
Email: mail@simerini.com **Web site:** http://www.sigmalive.com/simerini
Freq: Daily; **Circ:** 13000 Publisher's Statement
Profile: Newspaper covering regional, national and international news and current affairs including business, politics, economics, culture and sports.
Language (s): Greek
Ad Rate: Full Page Mono 714.00
Ad Rate: Full Page Colour 1071.00
Currency: Euro
DAILY NEWSPAPER

Vestnik Kipra 475283
Owner: N.G. Cyprus Advertiser Ltd
Editorial: 14b Byron Str., 1 Park Tower, Limassol 3732 **Tel:** 357 25 58 21 20
Email: editor@vestnikkipra.com **Web site:** http://www.vestnikkipra.com
Circ: 4000 Publisher's Statement
Director: Nataliya Kardash
Profile: Covering political, economical and cultural life of Cyprus, Cyprus and Russian news, interviews with famous politicians, economists, artists, musicians, and TV programmes.
Language (s): Russian
Ad Rate: Full Page Mono 550.00
Ad Rate: Full Page Colour 750.00
Currency: Euro
DAILY NEWSPAPER

YeniDüzen 458256
Owner: YeniDÜZEN Ltd.
Editorial: Yeni Sanayi Bolgesi, Mersin 10, Lefkosa-Kibris **Tel:** 392 225 66 58
Email: web@yeniduzen.com **Web site:** http://www.yeniduzen.com
Freq: Daily; **Circ:** 3500 Publisher's Statement
News Director: Fayka Arseven; **Editor in Chief:** Cenk Mutluyakali; **Editor in Chief:** Mert Özdag
Profile: Newspaper covering regional, national and international news and current affairs including business, politics, economics, culture and sports.
Language (s): Turkish
DAILY NEWSPAPER

News Service/Syndicate

Athens-Macedonian News Agency Cyprus Bureau 578763
Editorial: 12 RIK Avenue, Aglantzia, Nicosia 2120
Tel: 357 22 663110
Email: anacy@cytanet.com.cy **Web site:** http://www.amna.gr
Profile: Cyprus office of the Athens-Macedonian News Agency.
Language (s): Greek
NEWS SERVICE/SYNDICATE

Cyprus News Agency 578760
Owner: Cyprus News Agency
Editorial: 21, Academias Avenue, Aglantzia, Nicosia 2002 **Tel:** 357 22 556009
Email: news@cna.org.cy **Web site:** http://www.cna.org.cy
Editor in Chief: George Penintaex
Profile: National news agency covering news and current affairs including politics, economics, sports and society.
Language (s): English
NEWS SERVICE/SYNDICATE

Community Newspaper

Ergatiki Foni 458736
Owner: Cyprus Workers' Confederation (SEK)
Tel: 357 22 84 98 49
Email: sek@sek.org.cy **Web site:** http://www.sek.org.cy
Freq: Weekly; **Circ:** 12000
Director: Nicos Moyseos; **Editor in Chief:** Xenis Xenophontos
Profile: Newspaper of Cyprus Workers' Confederation covering news and current affairs including politics and social issues.
Language (s): Greek
COMMUNITY NEWSPAPER

Ergatiko Vima 224367
Owner: Cyprus Labour Federation
Editorial: 29 Archemou, Nicosia 1514
Tel: 357 22 866400
Email: info@ergatikovima.com **Web site:** http://www.ergatikovima.com
Freq: Weekly; **Circ:** 14000
Director: Lefteris Georgiades; **Editor in Chief:** Neofitos Papalazarou
Profile: Newspaper of the Cyprus Labour Federation (PEO) providing information on industrial relations, labour legislation, health and welfare funds and trade union news.
Language (s): Greek
COMMUNITY NEWSPAPER

Czech Republic

Time Difference: GMT +1
National Telephone Code: 420
Continent: Europe
Capital: Prague

Newspapers

Hospodá?ské noviny 156633
Owner: Economia
Editorial: Pernerova 673/47, Prague 18600
Tel: 420 233 071 111
Email: hn@economia.cz **Web site:** http://ihned.cz
Freq: Daily; **Circ:** 60848 ABC-Audit Bureau of Circulations
Editor-in-Chief: Martin Jašminský; **Editor:** Luboš Kre?
Profile: Hospodá?ské noviny is the Czech daily newspapers covering news on business, economy, finance, politics and current affairs in the Czech Republic and abroad. The newspapers also provides articles on lifestyle, sports, technology, culture, arts and entertainment, cars and automotive industry.
Language (s): Czech
Ad Rate: Full Page Colour 399000.00
Currency: Czech Republic Koruny
DAILY NEWSPAPER

Lidové noviny 156839
Owner: Mafra
Editorial: Karla Englise 519/11, Prague 15000
Tel: 420 225067111
Email: redakce@lidovky.cz **Web site:** http://www.lidovky.cz
Freq: Daily; **Circ:** 75985 ABC-Audit Bureau of Circulations
Editor: Jan Januš; **Editor-in-Chief:** István Lékó
Profile: National newspaper. Aimed at those interested in current affairs.Local Translation: Celostátní zpravodajský deník.Deník vychází v mutacích: - Praha,- ?echy, - Jižní Morava,- Severní Morava
Language (s): Czech
Ad Rate: Full Page Colour 295974.00
Currency: Czech Republic Koruny
DAILY NEWSPAPER

MF Dnes 156845
Owner: Mafra
Editorial: Karla Englise 519/11, Prague 15000
Tel: 420 225062206
Email: mfdnes@mfdnes.cz **Web site:** http://www.idnes.cz
Freq: Daily; **Circ:** 208000 ABC-Audit Bureau of Circulations
Editor-in-Chief: Jaroslav Plesl
Profile: National newspaper covering world and national news, business, entertainment and society. Aimed at those interested in current affairs.Local Translation: Nejv?tší seriózní noviny v ?R, p?inášejí ?tená??m širokou nabídku rubrik a p?íloh, každodenní zpravodajství z domova a ze zahraní?í, komentá?e a názory, ekonomika, spole?nost, sport, kultura, TV, po?así, aktuální informace z regionu.Deník vychází v regionálních mutacích: Praha-m?sto, St?ední ?echy, Severní ?echy, Liberecký kraj, Hradecký kraj, Pardubický kraj, Vyso?ina, Jižní ?echy, Plze?ský kraj, Karlovarský kraj, Moravskoslezský kraj, St?ední Morava, Východní Morava, Jižní Morava.
Language (s): Czech
DAILY NEWSPAPER

Pravo 156849
Editorial: Slezska 2127/13, Prague 121 50
Tel: 420 221001111
Email: pravo@cpost.cz **Web site:** http://www.pravo.cz
Freq: Daily; **Circ:** 114000 ABC-Audit Bureau of Circulations
Profile: National newspaper. Local Translation:Spole?ensko-politický celostátní deník. Vychází v t?chto mutacích: Praha + St?ední ?echy, Jiho?eský kraj, Plze?ský kraj, Karlovarský kraj, Ústecký kraj, Liberecký kraj, Královehradecký a Pardubický kraj, ?echy mimo ST? a Prahy, celé ?echy, celá Morava, Jihomoravský kraj, Vyso?ina, Olomoucký kraj, Zlínský kraj, Olomoucký a Zlínský kraj, Moravskoslezský kraj.
Language (s): Czech
Ad Rate: Full Page Colour 245800.00
Currency: Czech Republic Koruny
DAILY NEWSPAPER

Democratic Republic of the Congo

Time Difference: GMT +1 (West Coast), GMT +2 (East Border)
National Telephone Code: 243
Continent: Africa
Capital: Kinshasa

Newspapers

Le Phare 668515
Owner: Journal Le Phare
Editorial: Niveau 2, Building du 29 Juin, 3392, Avenue Colonel Lukusa, Kinshasa
Tel: 243 813 33 01 95
Email: lephareonline@gmail.com **Web site:** http://www.lephareonline.net
Freq: Daily; **Circ:** 4000 Publisher's Statement
Advertising Manager: Michel Lungudi; **Editor:** Polydor Muboyayi
Profile: National daily newspaper covering regional, national and international news and current affairs including politics, economics, society, health, culture and sports.
Language (s): French

Democratic Republic of the Congo

Ad Rate: Full Page Mono 600.00
Ad Rate: Full Page Colour 800.00
Currency: United States Dollars
DAILY NEWSPAPER

Le Potentiel   526277
Owner: Le Potentiel
Editorial: 873 Avenue Bas Congo, Gombe, Kinshasa
Tel: 243 998 13 54 83
Email: lepotentiel@yahoo.com **Web site:** https://
www.lepotentielonline.com
Freq: Daily; **Circ:** 3000 Publisher's Statement
Profile: National daily newspaper covering regional,
national and international news and current affairs
including politics, economics, society, sport,
entertainment, culture, science, and media.
Language (s): French
Ad Rate: Full Page Mono 700.00
Ad Rate: Full Page Colour 2500.00
Currency: United States Dollars
DAILY NEWSPAPER

News Service/Syndicate

Agence Congolaise de Presse - ACP   571892
Owner: Agence Congolaise de Presse - ACP
Editorial: Avenue Tombalbaye 44-48, Immeuble
ACP, Kinshasa 1013 **Tel:** 243 81 451 66 56
Email: info@acpcongo.com **Web site:** http://
acpcongo.com
Editor in Chief: Mathieu Yoha
Profile: National press agency focussing on national
and international news and current affairs including
politics, economics, sports, health, education,
culture, society and environment.
Language (s): French
NEWS SERVICE/SYNDICATE

Denmark

Time Difference: GMT +1
National Telephone Code: 45
Continent: Europe
Capital: Copenhagen

Newspapers

Berlingske   158360
Editorial: Pilestræde 34, Copenhagen 1147
Tel: 45 33 75 75 75
Email: redaktionen@berlingske.dk **Web site:** http://
www.b.dk
Freq: Daily; **Circ:** 74948 Dansk Oplagskontrol
Redaktionschef: Jens Grund; **Chefredaktør:** Tom
Jensen
Profile: Berlingske (previously known as Berlingske
Tidende) is a quality newspaper providing in-depth
coverage of national and international news, politics,
events, features, culture, business and sports. First
published on January 3rd in 1749, Berlingske is the
oldest Danish newspaper still published and among
the oldest newspapers in the world.
Language (s): Danish
DAILY NEWSPAPER

Bornholms Tidende   158386
Editorial: Nørregade 11-19, Rønne 3700
Tel: 45 56 90 30 00
Email: redaktion@bornholmstidende.dk **Web site:**
http://www.bornholmstidende.dk
Freq: Daily; **Circ:** 8453 Dansk Oplagskontrol
Nyhedsredaktør/chef: Nanna Krogh
Profile: Bornholms Tidende are the only daily
newspaper on Borhholm. Covers daily news from
Bornholm and the rest of Denmark.
Language (s): Danish
DAILY NEWSPAPER

Børsen   158361
Editorial: Montergade 19, København K 1140
Tel: 45 72 42 33 33
Email: redaktionen@borsen.dk **Web site:** http://
www.borsen.dk
Freq: Daily; **Circ:** 50829 Dansk Oplagskontrol
Editor in Chief: Anders Johansen; **Nyhedschef:**
Trine Kaare Jensen; **Redaktionschef:** Jens Kristian
Lai; **Editor:** Niels Lunde; **Redaktør:** Hakon Redder
Profile: Tabloid-sized quality newspaper covering
business news, finance, economics and politics.
Language (s): Danish
DAILY NEWSPAPER

BT   158359
Editorial: BTMX P/S, Pilestræde 34, Copenhagen
1147 **Tel:** 45 33 75 75 33
Email: bt@bt.dk **Web site:** http://www.bt.dk
Freq: Daily; **Circ:** 47208 Not Audited
News Editor: Casper Hjorth
Profile: BT is a Danish tabloid newspaper owned by
Berlingske media. BT is one of Denmark's biggest
and most popular news and entertainment
newspapers. Covers news, sports, entertainment,
retail and wellness.
Language (s): Danish
DAILY NEWSPAPER

Dagbladet Arbejderen   161388
Editorial: Hillerodgade 30A, Copenhagen 2200
Tel: 45 30 20 55 20
Email: redaktion@arbejderen.dk **Web site:** http://
www.arbejderen.dk
Freq: Daily; **Circ:** 2000 Not Audited
Editor in chief: Birthe Sørensen
Profile: Nationwide left wing newspaper with news
and background from a clear political standpoint.
Language (s): Danish
Ad Rate: Full Page Colour 16170.00
Currency: Denmark Kroner
DAILY NEWSPAPER

Dagbladet Holstebro   158376
Editorial: Kirkestræde 1-3, Holstebro 7500
Tel: 45 99 12 83 00
Email: redaktionen@dagbladetholstebro.dk **Web
site:** http://www.dagbladet-holstebro-struer.dk
Freq: Daily; **Circ:** 20913
Profile: Dagbladet Holstebro is a newspaper
covering local news.
Language (s): Danish
DAILY NEWSPAPER

Dagbladet Information   161373
Editorial: Store Kongensgade 40C, Copenhagen
1264 **Tel:** 45 33 69 60 00
Email: i@information.dk **Web site:** http://www.
information.dk
Freq: Daily; **Circ:** 20307 Not Audited
Nyhedsredaktør: Anders Fjordbak-Trier;
Ansvarshavende chefredaktør: Christian Jensen;
Redaktør: Susan Knorrenborg; **Redaktionschef:**
Rune Lykkeberg; **Redaktionssekretær:** Jens-Arne
Sørensen
Profile: Dagbladet Information is a daily newspaper
in Denmark covering national and international news.
Language (s): Danish
DAILY NEWSPAPER

Dagbladet Køge   435727
Editorial: Torvet 10, Køge 4600 **Tel:** 45 56 65 07 01
Email: koege.red@sn.dk **Web site:** http://sn.dk/
koege
Freq: Daily
Editor in Chief & Director: Torben Dalby Larsen
Profile: Dagbladet Køge is a newspaper covering
local news.
Language (s): Danish
DAILY NEWSPAPER

Dagbladet Ringkøbing-Skjern   435675
Editorial: St. Blichersvej 5, Ringkøbing 6950
Tel: 45 99 75 73 99
Email: redaktion@dagbladetringskjern.dk **Web site:**
http://www.dagbladetringskjern.dk
Freq: Daily
Editor: Mikael Sand; **Advertising Manager:** Kent
Viborg
Profile: Dagbladet Ringkøbing-Skjern is a local
newspaper.
Language (s): Danish
DAILY NEWSPAPER

Dagbladet Ringsted   158385
Editorial: Sogade 4-12, Ringsted 4100
Tel: 45 57 61 25 00
Email: ringsted.red@sn.dk **Web site:** http://www.sn.
dk/ringsted
Freq: Daily
Editor in Chief: Bente Johannessen
Profile: Dagbladet Ringsted is a newspaper covering
local news.
Language (s): Danish
DAILY NEWSPAPER

Dagbladet Roskilde   158387
Editorial: Hersegade 22, Roskilde 4000
Tel: 45 46 35 85 00
Email: roskilde.red@sn.dk **Web site:** http://sn.dk/
roskilde
Freq: Daily; **Circ:** 10222
Editor: Steen Østbjerg
Profile: Dagbladet Roskilde is a newspaper covering
local news.
Language (s): Danish
DAILY NEWSPAPER

Dagbladet Struer   435716
Owner: Berlingske Media
Editorial: Kastaniegarden, ostergade 7, 1. og 2 sal,
Struer 7600 **Tel:** 45 96 84 22 00
Email: redaktionen@dagbladetstruer.dk **Web site:**
http://www.dagbladet-holstebro-struer.dk
Freq: Daily
Profile: Dagbladet Struer is a newspaper covering
local news.
Language (s): Danish
DAILY NEWSPAPER

Der Nordschleswiger   852718
Editorial: Skibbroen 4, Aabenraa 6200
Tel: 45 74 62 38 80
Email: redaktion@nordschleswiger.dk **Web site:**
http://www.nordschleswiger.dk/
Freq: Weekly
Editor in Chief: Cornelius von Tiedemann
Profile: Der Nordschleswiger is a German newspaper
in Denmark, covering news. Der Nordschleswiger is
the only German-language daily newspaper in
Denmark, it is published six times a week. Covering

local news, politics, culture and sport of north
Schleswig, Germany and Denmark.
Language (s): German
DAILY NEWSPAPER

Ekstra Bladet   435501
Editorial: Radhuspladsen 37, Copenhagen 1785
Tel: 45 33 11 13 13
Email: redaktionen@eb.dk **Web site:** http://www.
ekstrabladet.dk
Freq: Daily; **Circ:** 43214
Editor in Chief: Karen Bro; **Nyhedschef:** Mette
Fleckner
Profile: Ekstra Bladet is one of the most read tabloid
newspaper in Denmark.
Language (s): Danish
Ad Rate: Full Page Mono 52500.00
Currency: Denmark Kroner
DAILY NEWSPAPER

Fyens Stiftstidende   158383
Editorial: Banegardspladsen, Odense C 5100
Tel: 45 66 11 11 11
Email: redaktion@fyens.dk **Web site:** http://www.
fyens.dk
Freq: Daily
Editor: Knud Raasthøj; **Redaktør:** Sander Schmidt
Astrup
Profile: Fyens Stiftstidende is a daily newspaper
covering regional news.
Language (s): Danish
DAILY NEWSPAPER

Fyns Amts Avis   158390
Editorial: Sankt Nicolai Gade 3, Svendborg 5700
Tel: 45 62 21 46 21
Email: post@faa.dk **Web site:** http://www.
fynsamtsavis.dk
Freq: Daily; **Circ:** 24591
News Editor: Hans-Henrik Dyssel; **Editor:** Wagn Ivan
Pedersen; **Editor:** Martin Juul Madsen; **Editor in
chief:** Troels Mylenberg
Profile: Fyns Amts Avis is a community newspaper
covering local news in Svendborg, Langeland, Ærø,
Faaborg-Midtfyn and Nyborg.
Language (s): Danish
DAILY NEWSPAPER

Helsingør Dagblad   158372
Editorial: Klostermosevej 101, Helsingør 3000
Tel: 45 49 22 21 10
Email: redaktionen@hdnet.dk **Web site:** http://www.
helsingordagblad.dk
Freq: Daily; **Circ:** 10385
Editor in Chief: Klaus Dalgas
Profile: Helsingør Dagblad is a community
newspaper covering news in the region.
Language (s): Danish
DAILY NEWSPAPER

Jyllands-Posten   158365
Editorial: Grondalsvej 3, Viby J 8260
Tel: 45 87 38 38 38
Email: indland@jp.dk **Web site:** http://jyllands-
posten.dk
Freq: Daily; **Circ:** 75943 Dansk Oplagskontrol
Nyhedsredaktør: Niels Christian Bastholm; **Editor:**
Viggo Lepoutre Ravn; **Redaktør:** Peter Rosendal
Profile: Jyllands-Posten is a daily newspaper
covering national and international news. The
newspaper is not affiliated with any political party,
also free and independent of all economic and
political interests.
Language (s): Danish
Ad Rate: Full Page Mono 111365.00
Currency: Sweden Kronor
DAILY NEWSPAPER

Jyllands-Posten - Aarhus   435558
Editorial: Grondalsvej 3, Viby 8260
Tel: 45 87 38 38 38
Email: jpaarhus@jp.dk **Web site:** http://jyllands-
posten.dk/aarhus
Freq: Daily
Profile: The local editorial board at Jyllands-Posten
covering the region of Aarhus.
Language (s): Danish
DAILY NEWSPAPER

Kristeligt Dagblad   158364
Editorial: Vimmelskaftet 47, Copenhagen 1161
Tel: 45 33 48 05 00
Email: post@k.dk **Web site:** http://www.kristeligt-
dagblad.dk
Freq: Daily; **Circ:** 26756
Editor in Cheif & Publisher: Erik Bjerager; **Editor:**
Kim Schou
Profile: Kristeligt Dagblad is a daily newspaper in
Denmark with a Christian profile.
Language (s): Danish
Ad Rate: Full Page Mono 20384.00
Currency: Denmark Kroner
DAILY NEWSPAPER

Metroxpress   435388
Editorial: Pilestræde 34, København K 1147
Tel: 45 77 30 59 00
Email: news@mx.dk **Web site:** http://www.mx.dk/
Freq: Daily; **Circ:** 325228
Editor-in-Chief: Jonas Rathje; **News Editor:** Allan
Wahlers
Profile: Metroxpress is a national daily newspaper in
Denmark. Covering news, sports, entertainment,
lifestyle, finance and technology.
Language (s): Danish
Ad Rate: Full Page Mono 110660.00

Currency: Denmark Kroner
DAILY NEWSPAPER

Nordschleswiger Tøndern   826858
Editorial: ostergade 3, Tønder 6270
Tel: 45 74 72 19 18
Email: ton@nordschleswiger.dk **Web site:** http://
www.nordschleswiger.dk/
Freq: Daily
EDITOR: Brigitta Lassen
Profile: Local edition for Tønder of Der
Nordschleswiger. Der Nordschleswiger is the only
German-language daily newspaper in Denmark, it is
published six times a week. Covering local news,
politics, culture and sport of north Schleswig,
Germany and Denmark.
Language (s): German
DAILY NEWSPAPER

Politiken   158366
Editorial: Radhuspladsen 37, Copenhagen 1785
Tel: 45 33 11 85 11
Email: nyheder@pol.dk **Web site:** http://www.
politiken.dk
Freq: Daily; **Circ:** 87095
Editor of Analysis: Poul Anders Aarøe Pedersen;
Editor in Cheif: Anne Mette Svane; **Editor:** Annette
Nyvang; **News Editor:** Kathrine Rossau
Profile: Politiken is a daily newspaper covering
national news in Denmark as well as international
news, politics, sports and features.
Language (s): Danish
DAILY NEWSPAPER

Sjællandske   435548
Owner: Sjællandske Medier A/S
Editorial: Dania 38, Næstved 4700
Tel: 45 72 45 11 00
Email: red@sn.dk **Web site:** http://www.sn.dk
Circ: 28615
Profile: Sjællandske is a newspaper, covering
regional news from Sjælland.
Language (s): Danish
DAILY NEWSPAPER

Weekendavisen   161327
Owner: Berlingske Media
Editorial: Pilestræde 34, Copenhagen 1147
Tel: 45 33 75 25 33
Email: bwa@weekendavisen.dk **Web site:** http://
www.weekendavisen.dk
Freq: Weekly
Editor: Ole Nyeng
Profile: Weekendavisen is a democratic newspaper
in Denmark, published every friday.
Language (s): Danish
DAILY NEWSPAPER

News Service/Syndicate

Dagbladenes Bureau   435274
Editorial: Holbergsgade 13, 2. sal, Copenhagen 1057
Tel: 45 33 15 46 01
Email: red@dagbladene.dk **Web site:** http://www.
dagbladene.dk
Profile: Dagbladenes Bureau is a danish news
agency based in Copenhagen, providing national
news, political features, profile interviews, feature
articles on society and culture and background
articles on events and debates as well as various
columns.
Language (s): Danish
NEWS SERVICE/SYNDICATE

Ritzau Finans   435279
Editorial: Store Kongensgade 14, Copenhagen 1264
Tel: 45 33 30 03 35
Email: finans@ritzau.dk **Web site:** http://www.
ritzaufinans.dk/
Nyhedsredaktør/chef: Henning Nielsen
Profile: Ritzau Finans is a news agency focusing on
financial news for companies, primarily within the
financial sector.
Language (s): Danish
NEWS SERVICE/SYNDICATE

Community Newspaper

Aabenraa Ugeavis   222758
Editorial: Skibbroen 4-6, Aabenraa 6200
Tel: 45 74 62 60 00
Email: red.aabenraa@ugeavisen.dk **Web site:** http://
www.ugeavisen.dk/aabenraa
Freq: Weekly; **Circ:** 29226
Profile: Aabenraa Ugeavis is a community
newspaper covering local news.
Language (s): Danish
COMMUNITY NEWSPAPER

Aars Avis   222760
Editorial: Himmerlandsgade 150, Aars 9600
Tel: 45 98 62 17 11
Email: redaktion@aarsavis.dk **Web site:** http://www.
aarsavis.dk
Freq: Weekly; **Circ:** 12663 Publisher's Statement
Editor: Thorkil Christensen
Profile: Aars Avis is a weekly regional newspaper in
Vesthimmerland, Denmark. The paper is published
every Wednesday.
Language (s): Danish
COMMUNITY NEWSPAPER

Adresseavisen Syddjurs 222761
Editorial: Brødgade 4A, Unavailable 8560
Tel: 45 86 99 4511
Email: redaktion.djursland@lokalavisen.dk **Web site:** http://syddjurs.lokalavisen.dk/
Freq: Weekly
Profile: Adresseavisen Syddjurs is a community newspaper covering local news.
Language (s): Danish
COMMUNITY NEWSPAPER

Albertslund Posten 223131
Editorial: Stationstorvet 23, 1. sal, Albertslund 2620
Tel: 45 70 13 11 00
Email: ap@albertslundposten.dk **Web site:** http://www.albertslundposten.dk
Freq: Weekly; **Circ:** 17520 Publisher's Statement
Ansvarshavende redaktør: Jørgen Brieghel
Profile: Albertslund Posten is a community newspaper in Denmark. Covering local news in Albertslund.
Language (s): Danish
COMMUNITY NEWSPAPER

Allerød Nyt 222734
Editorial: Lokesvej 8, 1. sal, Hillerød 3400
Tel: 45 70 13 11 00
Email: redaktion@allerodnyt.dk **Web site:** http://www.allerodnyt.dk
Freq: 2 Times/Week; **Circ:** 15391 Publisher's Statement
Profile: "Allerød Nyt" is a regional newspaper containg news and information from Allerød, Lynge and surrounding areas. Published two times a week with a weekend issue.
Language (s): Danish
COMMUNITY NEWSPAPER

Amager Bladet 435661
Editorial: Ebertsgade 2, 1. sal, Copenhagen 2300
Tel: 45 32 54 21 10
Email: red@amagerbladet.dk **Web site:** http://minby.dk/amagerbladet
Freq: Weekly; **Circ:** 67681
Ansvarshavende redaktør: Jan Jeppesen
Profile: Amagerbladet is a local weekly newspaper covering news and information from the Amager region in Denmark.
Language (s): Danish
COMMUNITY NEWSPAPER

Århus Onsdag 435895
Editorial: P. Hiort-Lorenzens Vej 2A, Århus 8000
Tel: 45 87 90 80 70
Email: red.aarhusonsdag@lokalavisen.dk **Web site:** http://aarhus.lokalavisen.dk/section/aarhusonsdag/2500/
Freq: Weekly; **Circ:** 164930 Publisher's Statement
Redaktør: Helle Holm
Profile: Århus Onsdag is a weekly newspaper containing regional news. Covering Århus Kommune and among others Hornslet, Hinnerup, Galten, Hadsen and Skanderborg.
Language (s): Danish
Ad Rate: Full Page Colour 24621.00
Currency: Denmark Kroner
COMMUNITY NEWSPAPER

Århus Stiftstidende 158369
Owner: Jysk Fynske Medier P/S
Editorial: Banegardspladsen 11, Århus 8000
Tel: 45 87 40 10 10
Email: red@stiften.dk **Web site:** http://www.stiften.dk
Circ: 14468
EDITOR AT LARGE: Dennis Christensen; **EDITOR AT LARGE:** Lilian Dubgaard; **EDITOR AT LARGE:** Henrik Lund; **EDITOR AT LARGE:** Uffe Normand; **Editor in Cheif:** Jan Schouby; **Redaktionschef:** Jens W. Møller
Profile: Århus Stiftstidende is a Danish newspaper published in Aarhus and the surrounding area. Covering news, politics, sports.
Language (s): Danish
COMMUNITY NEWSPAPER

Ballerup Bladet 223133
Editorial: Centrumgaden 2A, Ballerup 2750
Tel: 45 44 60 03 30
Email: red@ballerupbladet.dk **Web site:** http://www.ballerupbladet.dk
Freq: Weekly; **Circ:** 35041
Editor: Mia Thomsen
Profile: Ballerup Bladet is a community newspaper covering local news.
Language (s): Danish
COMMUNITY NEWSPAPER

Billund UgeAvis 222656
Editorial: Hovedgaden 12, 1A, Billund 7190
Tel: 45 75 33 12 18
Email: redaktionen@billund-ugeavis.dk **Web site:** http://vafo.dk/billund
Freq: Weekly; **Circ:** 20247 Publisher's Statement
Redaktør: Keld Stampe; **Redaktionschef:** Morten Theider
Profile: Billund UgeAvis is a weekly newspaper covering local news in Billund. The newspaper is a part of Vejle Amts Folkeblad.
Language (s): Danish
COMMUNITY NEWSPAPER

Bjerringbro Avis 222637
Editorial: Banegardspladsen 3, Bjerringbro 8850
Tel: 45 86 68 17 55
Email: redaktion@gudenaadalens-avis.dk **Web site:** http://bjerringbro-avis.dk/
Freq: Weekly; **Circ:** 11000 Not Audited
Profile: Bjerringbro Avis is a local newspaper covering Bjerringbro, Langå, Ans, Ulstrup, Rødkærsbro and Thorsø.
Language (s): Danish
COMMUNITY NEWSPAPER

Bov Bladet 222746
Editorial: Industrivej 1, Padborg 6330
Tel: 45 72 11 40 20
Email: red.bov@ugeavisen.dk **Web site:** http://ugeavisen.dk/omos/bovbladet
Freq: Weekly; **Circ:** 7450 Not Audited
Profile: Bov Bladet is a weekly newspaper covering the Padborg area in Denmark.
Language (s): Danish
COMMUNITY NEWSPAPER

Brædstrup Avis 222749
Editorial: Sondergade 3b, Brædstrup 8740
Tel: 45 75 75 17 33
Email: br@braedstrup-avis.dk **Web site:** http://hsfo.dk/braedstrup?profile=1297
Freq: Weekly; **Circ:** 14700 Not Audited
EDITOR: Anya Wissendorff
Profile: Brædstrup Avis is a weekly newspaper covering the areas of Brædstrup, Them, Bryrup, Salten, Sepstrup, Hjællund, Hampen, Nørre Snede, Hjortsvang, Åle, Rask Mølle, Flemming, Lund, Sattrup, Østbirk and Tåning. Brædstrup Avis is a part of Horsens Folkeblad and owned by Jysk Fynke Medier.
Language (s): Danish
COMMUNITY NEWSPAPER

Brande Bladet 222748
Editorial: Storegade 25, Brande 7330
Tel: 45 97 18 28 38
Email: post@brandebladet.dk **Web site:** http://www.brandebladet.dk
Freq: Weekly; **Circ:** 16008
Profile: Brande Bladet is a community newspaper covering local news.
Language (s): Danish
COMMUNITY NEWSPAPER

Brønshøj-Husum Avis 223007
Editorial: Soborg Hovedgade 119, Søborg 2860
Tel: 45 38 60 30 03
Email: adm@bha.dk **Web site:** http://www.bha.dk
Freq: Weekly; **Circ:** 28039 Not Audited
Profile: Brønshøj-Husum Avis is a weekly local newspaper covering the Brønshøj-Husum region.
Language (s): Danish
COMMUNITY NEWSPAPER

City Avisen 223008
Owner: Søndagsavisen Lokale Medier
Editorial: Dirch Passers Alle 27, 1. sal, Frederiksberg 2000 **Tel:** 45 33 88 88 88
Email: red@cityavisen.dk **Web site:** http://minby.dk/city-avisen/
Freq: Weekly; **Circ:** 20496
Editor in Chief: Christian Olsen
Profile: City Avisen is a community newspaper covering local news. A part of "Søndagsavisen".
Language (s): Danish
COMMUNITY NEWSPAPER

Dalum-Hjallese Avis 222653
Editorial: Banegardspladsen, Odense 5100
Tel: 45 66 14 14 10
Email: red@dh-avis.dk **Web site:** http://dalumhjalleseavis.dk/
Freq: Weekly; **Circ:** 17693 Publisher's Statement
Profile: Dalum-Hjallese Avis is a local newspaper in Odense.
Language (s): Danish
COMMUNITY NEWSPAPER

Den Lille Avis 435879
Editorial: Korsvangen 15, Ringe 5750
Tel: 45 62 21 31 60
Email: journalist@denlilleavis.dk **Web site:** http://www.denlilleavis.dk
Freq: Weekly; **Circ:** 6700 Not Audited
Profile: 'Den Lille Avis' is a local newspaper in Ringe.
Language (s): Danish
COMMUNITY NEWSPAPER

Det Grønne Område 435663
Editorial: Gammel Lundtoftevej 3 C, Kgs. Lyngby 2800 **Tel:** 45 70 13 11 00
Email: redaktion@dgo.dk **Web site:** http://lyngby-taarbaek.lokalavisen.dk/
Circ: 39757
Profile: "Det Grønne Område" is a local newspaper covering the Lyngby-Taarbæk municipality in Denmark. Published every tuesday and on the weekend.
Language (s): Danish
COMMUNITY NEWSPAPER

Din Avis Randers 435876
Editorial: Brotoften 10, Randers 8940
Tel: 45 86 40 12 22
Email: redaktion@dinavis.dk **Web site:** http://www.dinavis.dk
Freq: Weekly; **Circ:** 39601 Not Audited
Managing Director: Rene Bauer; **Ansvarshavende redaktør:** Ole Søndergaard
Profile: 'Din avis Randers' is a weekly newspaper covering local news in Randers.
Language (s): Danish
COMMUNITY NEWSPAPER

Djurslandsposten 222650
Editorial: osterbrogade 45, Grenaa 8500
Tel: 45 87 58 55 00
Email: redaktion@djurslandsposten.dk **Web site:** http://ugeavisen.dk/omos/djurslandsposten
Freq: Weekly; **Circ:** 28100 Publisher's Statement
Ansvarshavende redaktør: Søren Andersen
Profile: 'Djurslandsposten' is a weekly newspaper covering the region of Djursland.
Language (s): Danish
COMMUNITY NEWSPAPER

Dragør Nyt 223009
Editorial: Sondre Tangvej 22, Dragør 2791
Tel: 45 32 53 08 67
Email: redaktion@dragoer-nyt.dk **Web site:** http://www.dragoer-nyt.dk
Freq: Weekly; **Circ:** 7000 Not Audited
Profile: 'Dragør Nyt' is a weekly newspaper in Dragør, focusing on ads, municipal information and messages to the citizens of Dragør.
Language (s): Danish
Ad Rate: Full Page Mono 12205.00
Currency: Denmark Kroner
COMMUNITY NEWSPAPER

Egtved Posten 222630
Editorial: Aftensang 4, Egtved 6040
Tel: 45 75 55 10 99
Email: redaktionen@egtved-posten.dk **Web site:** http://vafo.dk/egtved
Freq: Weekly; **Circ:** 10740 Not Audited
Profile: "Egtved Posten" is a local newspaper published every tuesday in the region of Egtved.
Language (s): Danish
COMMUNITY NEWSPAPER

ElboBladet 435666
Editorial: Norrebrogade 5, Fredericia 7000
Tel: 45 75 92 12 44
Email: redaktion@elbobladet.dk **Web site:** http://www.elbobladet.dk
Freq: Weekly; **Circ:** 37659
Redaktionel medarbejder: Lisbeth Larsen
Profile: ElboBladet is a weekly newspaper covering local news in the Fredricia region.
Language (s): Danish
COMMUNITY NEWSPAPER

Extra Posten 222643
Editorial: Nygade 30, Nakskov 4900
Tel: 45 54 88 08 20
Email: post@extraposten.dk **Web site:** http://folketidende.dk/extra-posten/
Freq: Weekly; **Circ:** 20792 Not Audited
Profile: Extra Posten is a weekly newspaper in Lolland Falster. It's published at weekends in Nakskov and selected trading places and every Tuesday / Wednesday in the rest of the households at Vestlolland.
Language (s): Danish
COMMUNITY NEWSPAPER

Fanø Ugeblad 222625
Editorial: Willemoesvej 7, Nordby, Fanø 6720
Tel: 45 75 16 20 53
Email: post@fanougeblad.dk **Web site:** http://www.fanougeblad.dk
Freq: Weekly; **Circ:** 2400 Not Audited
Ansvarshavende redaktør: Dorte Hembo; **Ansvarshavende redaktør:** Gedske Vind
Profile: Fanø Ugeblad is a weekly newspaper covering local news from the island of Fanø, in Denmark.
Language (s): Danish
COMMUNITY NEWSPAPER

Farsø Avis 222626
Editorial: Sondergarden 8, Farsø 9640
Tel: 45 98 63 10 61
Email: redaktionen@farso-avis.dk **Web site:** http://www.farsoavis.dk
Freq: Weekly; **Circ:** 8950 Not Audited
Ansvarshavende redaktør: Lars Rabøl
Profile: Farsø Avis is a weekly newspaper covering the Farsø community in Denmark.
Language (s): Danish
COMMUNITY NEWSPAPER

FavrskovAvisen 435950
Editorial: agade 97, Hadsten 8370
Tel: 45 87 61 35 00
Email: redaktion@favrskovavisen.dk **Web site:** http://ugeavisen.dk/omos/favrskovavisen
Freq: Weekly; **Circ:** 26527 Not Audited
Profile: FavrskovAvisen is a regional newspaper covering the Favrskov municipality in Denmark.
Language (s): Danish
COMMUNITY NEWSPAPER

FavrskovPosten 435618
Editorial: P. Hiort-Lorenzens Vej 2A, Aarhus 8000
Tel: 45 86 96 17 66
Web site: http://favrskov.lokalavisen.dk/
Circ: 26461
EDITOR: Claus Krogh
Profile: Wishes not to receive press releases. FavrskovPosten is a weekly regional newspaper published in Hadsten, Trige, Hinnerup, Hammel, Sporupm Sorring, Ulstrup, Thorsø, Fårvang, Gjern as well as parts of Bjerringbro, Langå, Randers and Galten.FavrskovPosten is a part of Lokalaviserne Østjylland A/S and Politikens Lokalaviser A/S.
Language (s): Danish
COMMUNITY NEWSPAPER

Faxe Bugten 222628
Editorial: Ronnedevej 62 B, Faxe, Unavailable 4640
Tel: 45 56 71 32 31
Email: kontor@faxebugten.dk **Web site:** http://www.faxebugten.dk
Freq: Weekly; **Circ:** 15500 Not Audited
Profile: Faxe-Bugten is a weekly newspaper covering regional news. Distributed in Faxe, Hårlev, Karise, Faxe Ladeplads, Tureby, Rønnede, Tappernøje, Haslev, (Dalby, Bråby, Vester Egede, Sdr. Dalby, Ulse og Gisselfeldt). The paper is also published in Haslev by, Store Heddinge and Rødvig last week of the month.
Language (s): Danish
COMMUNITY NEWSPAPER

Fjends Folkeblad 222619
Editorial: Norregade 15, Stoholm Jylland 7850
Tel: 45 97 54 10 02
Email: info@fjendsfolkeblad.dk **Web site:** http://fjendsfolkeblad.dk/
Freq: Weekly; **Circ:** 8300 Not Audited
EDITOR IN CHIEF: Jesper Sørensen
Profile: Fjends Folkeblad is a weekly newspaper covering the Stoholm and Viborg Municipality in Denmark.
Language (s): Danish
COMMUNITY NEWSPAPER

Fjerritslev Ugeavis 435873
Editorial: ostergade 33, Fjerritslev 9690
Tel: 45 99 50 58 00
Email: fjerritslevugeavis@nordjyske.dk **Web site:** http://fjerritslevugeavis.dk/
Freq: Weekly; **Circ:** 7571 Not Audited
Chefredaktør: Lars Jespersen; **Redaktionschef:** Jørgen la Cour-Harbo
Profile: 'Fjerritslev Ugeavis' is a weekly newspaper covering news in Fjerritslev and Jammerbugt Municipality, in Denmark.
Language (s): Danish
COMMUNITY NEWSPAPER

Flensborg Avis 435880
Editorial: Wittenberger Weg 19, Flensburg 24941
Tel: 49 46 15 04 50
Email: red@fla.de **Web site:** http://www.fla.de/
Redaktionssekretær: Trine Flamming
Profile: Flensborg Avis is a Danish and German-language newspaper, published in Flensburg in Southern Schleswig in the German state of Schleswig-Holstein. Aimed for the Danish minority south of the Danish state border, as well as residents in Denmark and Danish citizens with an interest in Germany.
Language (s): Danish
COMMUNITY NEWSPAPER

Folkebladet Djursland 222621
Editorial: Molletorvet 6, Auning 8963
Tel: 45 86 48 34 88
Email: folkebladet@folkebladetdjursland.dk **Web site:** http://ugeavisen.dk/omos/folkebladetdjursland
Freq: Weekly; **Circ:** 13037 Not Audited
Profile: Folkebladet Djursland is a weekly local newspaper covering the region of Djursland in Denmark.
Language (s): Danish
COMMUNITY NEWSPAPER

Folkebladet for Glostrup, Brøndby & Vallensbæk 223011
Editorial: Glostrup Torv 6, Glostrup 2600
Tel: 45 43 96 00 31
Email: folkebladet@folkebladet.dk **Web site:** http://www.folkebladet.dk
Freq: Weekly; **Circ:** 31624 Not Audited
Profile: Folkebladet is a weekly newspaper covering local news in Glostrup, Brøndby and Vallensbæk.
Language (s): Danish
COMMUNITY NEWSPAPER

Folkebladet i Assens kommune 435885
Editorial: Cederfeldsgade 2, Aarup 5560
Tel: 45 64 43 11 78
Email: info@folkebladet.net **Web site:** http://folkebladet.net/
Freq: Weekly; **Circ:** 20953 Not Audited
Profile: Folkebladet i Assens kommune is a weekly regional newspaper for Assens Municipality.
Language (s): Danish
COMMUNITY NEWSPAPER

Folkebladet Lemvig 158885
Editorial: Bredgade 20, Lemvig 7620
Tel: 45 96 63 04 00
Email: lemvig@bergske.dk **Web site:** http://www.lemvig-folkeblad.dk
Freq: Daily; **Circ:** 10658
Profile: Folkebladet Lemvig is a daily newspaper covering local news in the region.
Language (s): Danish
Ad Rate: Full Page Mono 16995.00
Currency: Denmark Kroner
COMMUNITY NEWSPAPER

Fredericia Dagblad 158371
Editorial: Norrebrogade 5-7, Fredericia 7000
Tel: 45 75 92 26 00
Email: fd@frdb.dk **Web site:** http://frdb.dk/
Freq: Daily; **Circ:** 3264
Chefredaktør: Marianne Husted

Profile: Fredericia Dagblad is a regional newspaper covering news, sports and culture from Fredericia and surrounding areas.
Language (s): Danish
COMMUNITY NEWSPAPER

Frederiksberg Bladet 223012

Editorial: Dirch Passers Alle 27, 1. sal, Frederiksberg 2000 **Tel:** 45 33 88 88 88
Email: red@frederiksbergbladet.dk **Web site:** http://minby.dk/frederiksberg-bladet
Freq: Weekly; **Circ:** 58225 Not Audited
Profile: Frederiksberg Bladet is a weekly newspaper covering local news in the region. Frederiksberg Bladet is a part of Søndagsavisen.
Language (s): Danish
Ad Rate: Full Page Colour 24304.00
Currency: Denmark Kroner
COMMUNITY NEWSPAPER

Frederiksborg Amts Avis 435482

Editorial: Slotsgade 1, Ringsted 3400
Tel: 45 48 24 41 00
Email: frederiksborg@sn.dk **Web site:** http://sn.dk/nordsjaelland
Freq: Daily; **Circ:** 19935
Profile: Frederiksborg Amts Avis is a regional newspaper covering Skibby, Allerød, Smørum, Frederiksværk, Hillerød, Jægerspris, Rudersdal, Ølstykke, Hundested, Farum, Slangerup, Stenløse, Helsingør, Veksø, Fredensborg, Frederikssund and all other areas in the Nordsjællandske municipalities. Frederiksborg Amts Avis is part of Sjællandske Medier.
Language (s): Danish
COMMUNITY NEWSPAPER

Fuglebjerg Posten 435917

Editorial: Sogade 4-12, Ringsted 4100
Tel: 45 57 61 25 00
Email: susaalandet.red@sn.dk **Web site:** http://www.susaaavisen.dk
Freq: Weekly; **Circ:** 6683
EDITOR: Britt Nielsen
Profile: Fuglebjerg Posten is a free local newspaper. It is published in Fuglebjerg, Glumsø, Herlufmagle and Sandved. Fuglebjerg Posten and Glumsø Ugeblad share the same editorial team.
Language (s): Danish
COMMUNITY NEWSPAPER

Furesø Avis 514066

Editorial: Lokesvej 8, 1. sal, Hillerød 3400
Tel: 45 70 13 11 00
Email: redaktion@furavis.dk **Web site:** http://www.furesoeavis.dk
Freq: Weekly; **Circ:** 20027
Redaktør: Helene Holm Stolle
Profile: Furesø Avis is a free regional weekly newspaper i Farum Denmark.
Language (s): Danish
COMMUNITY NEWSPAPER

Galten Folkeblad 222667

Editorial: Sondergade 25, Galten 8464
Tel: 45 70 20 09 95
Email: galtenfolkeblad@galtenfolkeblad.dk **Web site:** http://www.galtenfolkeblad.dk
Freq: Weekly; **Circ:** 9103 Not Audited
Profile: Galten og Omegns Folkeblad is a weekly local newspaper published in the town of Galten.
Language (s): Danish
COMMUNITY NEWSPAPER

Give Avis 222738

Editorial: Give - Thyregod Avis, Torvet 12, Give 7323
Tel: 45 75 73 22 00
Email: gb@give-avis.dk **Web site:** http://www.give-avis.dk
Freq: Weekly; **Circ:** 20140 Not Audited
Profile: Give - Thyregod Avis is a weekly local newspaper published in Give.
Language (s): Danish
COMMUNITY NEWSPAPER

Gladsaxe Bladet 223013

Editorial: Soborg Hovedgade 79, stuen, Søborg 2860
Tel: 45 39 56 12 75
Email: gb@gladsaxebladet.dk **Web site:** http://www.gladsaxebladet.dk
Freq: Weekly
Editor in Chief: Mette Hviid Jensen
Profile: Gladsaxe Bladet is a community newspaper covering local news.
Language (s): Danish
Ad Rate: Full Page Colour 18697.50
Currency: Denmark Kroner
COMMUNITY NEWSPAPER

Glumsø Ugeblad 435664

Editorial: Sogade 4 - 12, Ringsted 4100
Tel: 45 57 61 25 00
Email: susaalandet.red@sn.dk **Web site:** http://www.susaaavisen.dk
Freq: Weekly; **Circ:** 3788
Profile: Glumsø Ugeblad is a free weekly newspaper in Glumsø. It is the sister outlet of Fuglebjerg Posten and they share the same editorial team.
Language (s): Danish
COMMUNITY NEWSPAPER

Grenaa Bladet 222703

Editorial: osterbrogade 45, Grenå 8500
Tel: 45 87 58 55 00
Email: redaktion@grenaabladet.dk **Web site:** http://grenaa.lokalavisen.dk/
Freq: Weekly; **Circ:** 22949 Not Audited
Profile: Grenaa Bladet is a weekly local newspaper published in Grenaa.
Language (s): Danish
COMMUNITY NEWSPAPER

Haderslev Ugeavis 222709

Editorial: Posthussvinget 4, Haderslev 6100
Tel: 45 74 52 70 70
Email: red.haderslev@ugeavisen.dk **Web site:** http://www.ugeavisen.dk/haderslev
Freq: Weekly; **Circ:** 30578
Profile: Haderslev Ugeavis is a community newspaper covering local news in the region.
Language (s): Danish
COMMUNITY NEWSPAPER

Hadsund Folkeblad 435871

Editorial: Jens-Erik Bechs Vej 1, Hadsund 9560
Tel: 45 98 57 23 77
Email: tekst@hadsundfolkeblad.dk **Web site:** http://www.hadsundfolkeblad.dk
Freq: Weekly; **Circ:** 19526 Not Audited
Ansvarshavende redaktør: Hans Henrik Rasmussen
Profile: Hadsund Folkeblad is a weekly local newspaper distributed in Hadsund.
Language (s): Danish
COMMUNITY NEWSPAPER

Hals Avis 222723

Owner: Nordjyske
Editorial: Midtergade 34 C, st., Hals, Unavailable 9370
Email: allan.mortensen@nordjyske.dk **Web site:** http://www.nordjyske.dk
Freq: Weekly; **Circ:** 8433 Not Audited
EDITOR: Allan Mortensen
Profile: Hals Avis is a weekly newspaper covering local news.
Language (s): Danish
Ad Rate: Full Page Colour 6628.50
Currency: Denmark Kroner
COMMUNITY NEWSPAPER

Halsnæs Avis 375556

Editorial: Havnevej 1, Frederiksværk 3300
Tel: 45 88 82 65 50
Email: redaktion@halsnaesavis.dk **Web site:** http://halsnaes.lokalavisen.dk/
Freq: Weekly
Profile: Halsnæs Avis is a community newspaper covering local news in the region.
Language (s): Danish
Ad Rate: Full Page Colour 13341.50
Currency: Denmark Kroner
COMMUNITY NEWSPAPER

Hanbo-Bladet 222726

Editorial: Jernbanegade 25C, Brovst 9460
Email: hanbo-bladet@nordjyske.dk
Freq: Weekly; **Circ:** 7526 Not Audited
Chefredaktør: Lars Jespersen
Profile: Hanbo-Bladet is a local newspaper covering the municipality of Brovst.
Language (s): Danish
Ad Rate: Full Page Colour 7206.00
Currency: Denmark Kroner
COMMUNITY NEWSPAPER

Haslev Posten 222624

Editorial: Jernbanegade 12, 1. sal, Haslev 4690
Tel: 45 56 31 11 12
Email: hp@haslev-posten.dk **Web site:** http://www.haslev-posten.dk
Freq: Weekly; **Circ:** 18617 Not Audited
Profile: Haslev Posten is a weekly local newspaper, distributed in Haslev, Fakse, Karise, Rønnede, Tureby and parts of Herflufmagle and Ringsted.
Language (s): Danish
COMMUNITY NEWSPAPER

Heden/Midtsjællands Avis 435943

Editorial: Sovej 1, Borup 4140 **Tel:** 45 57 52 22 88
Email: midtsj@sn.dk **Web site:** http://www.lokalavisen-heden.dk/dk/
Freq: Weekly; **Circ:** 17000 Not Audited
Profile: A weekly local newspaper serving Borup and its surroundings.
Language (s): Danish
COMMUNITY NEWSPAPER

Hedensted / Juelsminde Avis 435660

Editorial: Haralds Plads 10 B, Hedensted 8722
Tel: 45 75 89 13 66
Email: presse@hedensted-avis.dk **Web site:** http://www.hedensted-avis.dk
Freq: Weekly; **Circ:** 23600
Managing Director: Frank Dammand Nielsen
Profile: Local weekly newspaper distributed to the region of Hedensted and Juelsminde.
Language (s): Danish
COMMUNITY NEWSPAPER

Herlev Bladet 375552

Editorial: Herlev Bygade 39, Herlev 2730
Tel: 45 44 94 10 10
Email: herlevbladet@herlevbladet.dk **Web site:** http://www.herlevbladet.dk
Freq: Weekly; **Circ:** 25907 Not Audited
DIRECTOR: Steffen Glaas
Profile: Herlev Bladet is a weekly newspaper covering local news from the municipality Herlev.
Language (s): Danish
Ad Rate: Full Page Colour 26669.00
Currency: Denmark Kroner
COMMUNITY NEWSPAPER

Herning Bladet 222765

Editorial: ostergade 21, Herning 7400
Tel: 45 97 12 15 00
Email: redaktion@herningbladet.dk **Web site:** http://www.herningbladet.dk/
Freq: Weekly; **Circ:** 50000 Not Audited
Profile: Herning Bladet is a weekly newspaper covering local news in the area.
Language (s): Danish
Ad Rate: Full Page Colour 11133.00
Currency: Denmark Kroner
COMMUNITY NEWSPAPER

Herning Folkeblad 158373

Editorial: ostergade 21, Herning 7400
Tel: 45 96 26 37 00
Email: redaktionen@herningfolkeblad.dk **Web site:** http://aoh.dk/
Circ: 10724
Redaktionssekretær: Jette Bentsen; **Chefredaktør:** Vibeke Larsen; **Ansvarshavende redaktør:** Alex Nielsen
Profile: Herning Folkeblad, founded in 1869, is a Danish newspaper based in Herning covering Midtjylland, Herning municipality and cities such as Herning, Brande, Ikast, Vildbjerg among others.
Language (s): Danish
COMMUNITY NEWSPAPER

Hillerød Posten 222767

Editorial: Lokesvej 8, 1. sal, Hillerød 3400
Tel: 45 70 13 11 00
Email: redaktion@hip.dk **Web site:** http://hilleroed.lokalavisen.dk/
Freq: Weekly; **Circ:** 25932
Profile: Hillerød Posten is a community newspaper covering local news in the region.
Language (s): Danish
COMMUNITY NEWSPAPER

Hirtshals Bindslev Avis 222770

Editorial: Jyllandsgade 8, Hirtshals 9850
Tel: 45 99 245060
Email: redaktion.hbavis@nordjyske.dk **Web site:** http://www.hbavis.dk
Freq: Weekly; **Circ:** 11000 Not Audited
Profile: Hirtshals Bindslev Avis is a weekly newspaper covering local news from Hirtshals, Bjergby, Mygdal and Sindal.
Language (s): Danish
Ad Rate: Full Page Colour 5950.00
Currency: Denmark Kroner
COMMUNITY NEWSPAPER

Hjerting Posten 435374

Editorial: Bytoften 2A, Esbjerg V 6710
Tel: 45 75 47 09 99
Email: mail@hjertingposten.dk **Web site:** http://www.hjerting-posten.dk
Circ: 13300
Profile: Hjerting Posten is a monthly newspaper containing local news from Hjerting, Guldager, Ravnsbjergparken, Kokspang, Sjelborg, Sønderris, Ådalen, Sædding, Fovrfeld, Bryndum and Tarp.
Language (s): Danish
Ad Rate: Full Page Colour 7491.00
Currency: Denmark Kroner
COMMUNITY NEWSPAPER

Hobro Avis 222763

Editorial: Adelgade 56, Hobro 9500
Tel: 45 98 52 70 13
Email: hobroavis@nordjyske.dk **Web site:** http://nordjyske.dk/e-avis
Freq: Weekly; **Circ:** 20686 Not Audited
Profile: Hobro Avis is a local weekly newspaper distributed in Hobro.
Language (s): Danish
COMMUNITY NEWSPAPER

Holstebro Onsdag 435949

Editorial: Kirkestræde 1-3, Holstebro 7500
Tel: 45 99 12 83 99
Email: onsdag@bergske.dk **Web site:** http://ugeavisen.dk/omos/holstebroonsdag
Freq: Weekly; **Circ:** 40972 Not Audited
Profile: Holstebro Onsdag is a local weekly newspaper distributed in Holstebro.
Language (s): Danish
COMMUNITY NEWSPAPER

Horsens Folkeblad 158377

Editorial: Sondergade 47, Horsens 8700
Tel: 45 76 27 20 00
Email: redaktionen@hsfo.dk **Web site:** http://hsfo.dk/
Freq: Daily; **Circ:** 10379
Redaktør: Jørgen Hasseriis
Profile: Horsens Folkeblad, founded in 1863, is a Danish regional morning newspapers published Monday-Saturday. The paper covers Horsens, Hedensted, Juelsminde, Nr. Snede, Skanderborg and Odder.
Language (s): Danish
COMMUNITY NEWSPAPER

Horsens Posten 435743

Editorial: Sondergade 47, Horsens 8700
Tel: 45 76 27 21 82
Email: posten@hsfo.dk **Web site:** http://hsfo.dk/horsens?profile=1302
Freq: Weekly; **Circ:** 62715 Not Audited
Redaktør: Jørgen Hasseriis
Profile: Horsens Posten is a weekly newspaper covering local news in the area.
Language (s): Danish
Ad Rate: Full Page Colour 21226.50
Currency: Denmark Kroner
COMMUNITY NEWSPAPER

Hvidovre Avis 223014

Editorial: Hvidovrevej 301, Hvidovre 2650
Tel: 45 36 49 55 55
Email: redaktion@hvidovreavis.dk **Web site:** http://www.hvidovreavis.dk
Freq: Weekly; **Circ:** 22936 Not Audited
Chefredaktør: Niels Erik Madsen
Profile: Hvidovre Avis is a community newspaper covering local news in the region.
Language (s): Danish
COMMUNITY NEWSPAPER

Ikast Avis 435656

Editorial: Stroget 40, Ikast 7430 **Tel:** 45 97 15 18 00
Email: presse@ikastavis.dk **Web site:** http://www.aoib.dk
Circ: 20879
Ansvarshavende redaktør: Steen Hebsgaard
Profile: Ikast Avis is a weekly newspaper providing local news from the region.
Language (s): Danish
COMMUNITY NEWSPAPER

Jyderup Posten 222755

Editorial: Nyvej 14, Jyderup 4450 **Tel:** 45 88 88 44 50
Email: jyderupposten.red@sn.dk **Web site:** http://www.sn.dk/holbaek
Freq: Weekly; **Circ:** 18920 Not Audited
Profile: Jyderup Posten is a weekly newspaper covering local news in the area.
Language (s): Danish
Ad Rate: Full Page Colour 9268.00
Currency: Denmark Kroner
COMMUNITY NEWSPAPER

JydskeVestkysten 160855

Editorial: Norgesgade 1, Esbjerg 6700
Tel: 45 79 12 45 00
Email: jydskevestkysten@jv.dk **Web site:** http://www.jv.dk
Freq: Daily; **Circ:** 45792 Not Audited
Profile: JydskeVestkysten is a daily newspaper covering regional news.
Language (s): Danish
Ad Rate: Full Page Mono 79990.00
Currency: Denmark Kroner
COMMUNITY NEWSPAPER

Kalundborgnyt 222652

Editorial: Skibbrogade 42 B, Kalundborg 4400
Tel: 45 88 88 44 00
Email: kalundborgnyt.red@sn.dk **Web site:** http://sn.dk/kalundborgnyt
Freq: Weekly; **Circ:** 26720
Profile: Kalundborgnyt is a weekly newspaper covering lcoal news in the region.
Language (s): Danish
COMMUNITY NEWSPAPER

Kerteminde Ugeavis 435882

Editorial: Strandgade 1B, Kerteminde 5300
Tel: 45 65 45 54 40
Email: post@faa.dk **Web site:** http://www.kertemindeugeavis.dk
Freq: Weekly; **Circ:** 20616 Not Audited
Profile: Kerteminde Ugeavis is a weekly newspaper covering local news in the area.
Language (s): Danish
Ad Rate: Full Page Colour 13744.50
Currency: Denmark Kroner
COMMUNITY NEWSPAPER

Kjellerup Tidende 222645

Editorial: Papirfabrikken 18, Silkeborg 8620
Tel: 45 86 8620
Email: kjellerup@mja.dk **Web site:** http://www.midtjyllandsavis.dk
Freq: Weekly; **Circ:** 16498 Not Audited
Ansvarshavende redaktør: Rasmus Viuff
Profile: Kjellerup Tidende is a weekly newspaper covering local news in the area.
Language (s): Danish
Ad Rate: Full Page Colour 15534.00
Currency: Denmark Kroner
COMMUNITY NEWSPAPER

Køge Onsdag 222633

Editorial: Torvet 10, Køge 4600 **Tel:** 45 56 65 10 05
Email: ko.red@sn.dk **Web site:** http://sn.dk/koege
Freq: Weekly; **Circ:** 42639 Not Audited
Profile: Køge Onsdag is a weekly newspaper covering local news in the Køge region.
Language (s): Danish
Ad Rate: Full Page Colour 17784.00
Currency: Denmark Kroner
COMMUNITY NEWSPAPER

Liebhaverboligen 230785

Editorial: Mediehuset Hellerup, Henningsens Alle 68, Hellerup 2900 **Tel:** 45 38 88 66 33
Web site: http://www.liebhaverboligen.dk/
Freq: Monthly; **Circ:** 64000 Publisher's Statement
EDITOR: Steen Blendstrup; **EDITOR:** Per Kuskner
Profile: Do not want any press releases. Liebhaverboligen is an exclusive magazine in Denmark focusing on housing, design, lifestyle, cars, travel, gadgets and culture.
Language (s): Danish
Ad Rate: Full Page Colour 13900.00

Currency: Denmark Kroner
COMMUNITY NEWSPAPER

Lokal Nyt Lolland 435577
Editorial: Nebbelundevej 1, Rødby 4970
Tel: 45 54 60 21 08
Email: redaktion@lokalnyt-lolland.dk **Web site:** http://www.lokalnyt-lolland.dk
Circ: 28200
Redaktør: Birthe Christensen
Profile: Lokal Nyt Lolland is a monthly magazine containing local news from the region.
Language (s): Danish
Ad Rate: Full Page Colour 5250.00
Currency: Denmark Kroner
COMMUNITY NEWSPAPER

Lokalavisen Aabenraa 222751
Editorial: Perlegade 4, 1. sal, Aabenraa 6400
Tel: 45 30 38 28 41
Email: red-aab@lokalavisen.dk **Web site:** http://aabenraa.lokalavisen.dk/
Freq: Weekly; **Circ:** 28390
Editor: Betina Skjønnemand
Profile: Lokalavisen Aabenraa is a weekly newspaper covering local news in the region.
Language (s): Danish
COMMUNITY NEWSPAPER

Lokalavisen Assens 435653
Editorial: Provstistræde 16, Assens 5610
Tel: 45 65 45 54 54
Email: redaktion@laa.dk **Web site:** http://www.lokalavisenassens.dk
Circ: 31500
Profile: Lokalavisen Assens is a regional newspaper published every Tuesday in Odense Municipality.
Language (s): Danish
COMMUNITY NEWSPAPER

Lokalavisen Esbjerg 435437
Editorial: Kongensgade 110 - 114, Esbjerg 6700
Tel: 45 75 91 19 11
Email: red-esb@lokalavisen.dk **Web site:** http://esbjerg.lokalavisen.dk
Freq: Weekly; **Circ:** 55463
EDITOR IN CHIEF: Fred Jacobsen
Profile: Lokalavisen Esbjerg is a local newspaper for the area of Esbjerg.
Language (s): Danish
COMMUNITY NEWSPAPER

Lokalavisen Fredericia 435634
Editorial: Fabriksvej 5, Fredericia 7000
Tel: 45 76 20 04 00
Email: red-fre@lokalavisen.dk **Web site:** http://fredericia.lokalavisen.dk/
Freq: Weekly; **Circ:** 39854
Profile: Lokalavisen Fredericia is a local newspaper for the Fredericia region.
Language (s): Danish
COMMUNITY NEWSPAPER

Lokalavisen Frederiksberg 435944
Editorial: Gammel Kongevej 60, 16. sal, Frederiksberg 1850 **Tel:** 45 33 28 88 88
Email: michael@lokalavisen-frb.dk **Web site:** http://www.lokalavisen-frb.dk
Circ: 59043
Redaktør: Finn Edvard
Profile: Lokalavisen Frederiksberg is a weekly newspaper covering local news in the region.
Language (s): Danish
Ad Rate: Full Page Colour 19265.50
Currency: Denmark Kroner
COMMUNITY NEWSPAPER

Lokalavisen Frederikssund 435937
Editorial: Askelundsvej 2, Frederikssund 3600
Tel: 45 70 13 11 00
Email: redaktion.frederikssund@lokalavisen.dk **Web site:** http://frederikssund.lokalavisen.dk/apps/pbcs.dll/forside
Freq: Weekly; **Circ:** 42798 Not Audited
Redaktør: Henrik Gregersen
Profile: Lokalavisen Frederikssund is a weekly newspaper covering local news in the area.
Language (s): Danish
Ad Rate: Full Page Colour 15015.00
Currency: Denmark Kroner
COMMUNITY NEWSPAPER

Lokalavisen Fredrikshavn 222675
Editorial: Tordenskjoldsgade 2, Frederikshavn 9900
Tel: 45 99 20 33 33
Email: redaktion.lokalavisen@nordjyske.dk **Web site:** http://nordjyske.dk
Freq: Weekly; **Circ:** 22927 Not Audited
Redaktionschef: Carl Christian Madsen
Profile: Lokalavisen Fredrikshavn is a weekly newspaper covering local news in the region.
Language (s): Danish
Ad Rate: Full Page Colour 11375.50
Currency: Denmark Kroner
COMMUNITY NEWSPAPER

Lokalavisen Hornsherred 435739
Editorial: Bymidten 6, Skibby 4050
Tel: 45 45 90 83 46
Email: redaktion.hornsherred@lokalavisen.dk **Web site:** http://hornsherred.lokalavisen.dk/
Freq: Weekly; **Circ:** 12366 Not Audited
Redaktør: Henrik Gregersen
Profile: Lokalavisen Hornsherred is a weekly newspaper covering local news in the region.
Language (s): Danish
Ad Rate: Full Page Colour 9868.60
Currency: Denmark Kroner
COMMUNITY NEWSPAPER

Lokalavisen Kaløvig 222678
Editorial: Bredgade 4A, Hornslet 8560
Tel: 45 86 99 45 11
Email: mail@adresseavisen.dk **Web site:** http://kaloevig.lokalavisen.dk
Freq: Weekly; **Circ:** 25130 Not Audited
EDITOR: Claus Krogh; **Redaktør:** Lars Norman Thomsen
Profile: Lokalavisen Kaløvig is a weekly newspaper covering local news in the region.
Language (s): Danish
Ad Rate: Full Page Colour 7161.00
Currency: Denmark Kroner
COMMUNITY NEWSPAPER

Lokalavisen Kolding 222754
Editorial: Rendebanen 13, 1.sal, Kolding 6000
Tel: 45 87 32 48 28
Email: red-kol@lokalavisen.dk **Web site:** http://kolding.lokalavisen.dk/
Freq: Weekly; **Circ:** 42063
Editor: Anne Andersen
Profile: Lokalavisen Kolding is a weekly newspaper covering local news in the region.
Language (s): Danish
COMMUNITY NEWSPAPER

Lokalavisen Norddjurs 435651
Editorial: P. Hiort-Lorenzens Vej 2A, Aarhus 8000
Tel: 45 45 90 80 70
Email: redaktion.djursland@lokalavisen.dk **Web site:** http://norddjurs.lokalavisen.dk/
Circ: 28440
EDITOR: Claus Krogh
Profile: Lokalavisen Norddjurs is a weekly newspaper covering local news in the region.
Language (s): Danish
Ad Rate: Full Page Colour 6352.50
Currency: Denmark Kroner
COMMUNITY NEWSPAPER

Lokalavisen Nordsjælland 222681
Editorial: Klostermosevej 101, Helsingør 3000
Tel: 45 43 33 23 30
Email: redaktionen@nsnet.dk **Web site:** http://www.nsnet.dk
Freq: Weekly; **Circ:** 37451 Not Audited
Editor in chief: Claus Kjærsgaard
Profile: Lokalavisen Nordsjælland is a weekly newspaper covering local news in the region.
Language (s): Danish
Ad Rate: Full Page Colour 16170.00
Currency: Denmark Kroner
COMMUNITY NEWSPAPER

Lokalavisen Nordvest 435905
Editorial: Banegardspladsen, Odense 5100
Tel: 45 66 14 14 10
Email: mail@lokalavisenodense.dk **Web site:** http://lokalavisennordvest.dk
Freq: Weekly; **Circ:** 24177 Not Audited
Profile: Lokalavisen Nordvest is a weekly newspaper covering local news in the region.
Language (s): Danish
Ad Rate: Full Page Colour 13398.00
Currency: Denmark Kroner
COMMUNITY NEWSPAPER

Lokalavisen Nyborg 435649
Editorial: Norrevoldgade 58, Nyborg 5800
Tel: 45 65 45 53 80
Email: nyborg@fyens.dk **Web site:** http://www.lokalavisennyborg.dk
Circ: 20031
EDITOR IN CHIEF: Kasper Riggelsen
Profile: Lokalavisen Nyborg is a weekly newspaper covering local news in the region.
Language (s): Danish
Ad Rate: Full Page Colour 14091.00
Currency: Denmark Kroner
COMMUNITY NEWSPAPER

Lokalavisen Skanderborg 508719
Editorial: P. Hiort-Lorenzens Vej 2A, Aarhus 8000
Tel: 45 45 90 80 70
Email: redaktion.skanderborg@lokalavisen.dk **Web site:** http://skanderborg.lokalavisen.dk/
Circ: 30000
Profile: Lokalavisen Skanderborg is a weekly newspaper covering local news in the region.
Language (s): Danish
Ad Rate: Full Page Colour 8685.50
Currency: Denmark Kroner
COMMUNITY NEWSPAPER

Lokalavisen Sønderborg 222753
Editorial: Perlegade 4, 1. sal, Sønderborg 6400
Email: red-sdb@lokalavisen.dk **Web site:** http://soenderborg.lokalavisen.dk/
Freq: Weekly
Profile: Lokalavisen Sønderborg is a weekly newspaper covering local news.
Language (s): Danish
COMMUNITY NEWSPAPER

Lokalavisen Sydvestvendsyssel / Pandrup Lokalavis 222683
Editorial: Aabybro Centret 4C, Pandrup 9440
Tel: 45 98 24 77 44
Email: redaktion.lokalsyd@nordjyske.dk **Web site:** http://nordjyske.dk/
Freq: Weekly; **Circ:** 7412 Not Audited
EDITOR: Flemming Hansen
Profile: Lokalavisen Sydvestvendsyssel / Pandrup Lokalavis is a weekly newspaper covering local news.
Language (s): Danish
Ad Rate: Full Page Colour 6775.00
Currency: Denmark Kroner
COMMUNITY NEWSPAPER

Lokalavisen Taastrup 435630
Editorial: Marievej 1D, 1. sal, Taastrup 2630
Tel: 45 43 77 26 30
Email: redaktiontaastrup@sn.dk **Web site:** http://sn.dk/taastrup
Circ: 23446
Profile: Lokalavisen Taastrup is a weekly newspaper covering local news.
Language (s): Danish
Ad Rate: Full Page Colour 16489.50
Currency: Denmark Kroner
COMMUNITY NEWSPAPER

Lokalavisen Vanløse 435541
Editorial: Gammel Kongevej 60, 16. sal, Frederiksberg 1850 **Tel:** 45 33 88 88 88
Email: red@lokalavisen-va.dk **Web site:** http://www.lokalavisen-vanlose.dk/
Circ: 26442
Profile: Lokalavisen Vanløse is a weekly newspaper covering local news.
Language (s): Danish
Ad Rate: Full Page Colour 12400.00
Currency: Denmark Kroner
COMMUNITY NEWSPAPER

Lokalavisen Varde 435931
Editorial: Borgergade 38, 2. sal, Esbjerg 6700
Tel: 45 31 75 13 41
Email: red-var@lokalavisen.dk **Web site:** http://varde.lokalavisen.dk/
Freq: Weekly; **Circ:** 23860
Profile: Lokalavisen Varde is a weekly newspaper covering local news in the region.
Language (s): Danish
COMMUNITY NEWSPAPER

Lokalavisen Vejle 435929
Editorial: Roms Hule 8, 1. sal, Vejle 7100
Tel: 45 75 73 57 35
Email: red-vej@lokalavisen.dk **Web site:** http://vejle.lokalavisen.dk/
Freq: Weekly; **Circ:** 55385
Profile: Lokalavisen Vejle is a weekly newspaper covering local news in the region.
Language (s): Danish
COMMUNITY NEWSPAPER

Lokalavsien Lemvig 435652
Editorial: Vestergade 17, Lemvig 7620
Tel: 45 96 63 04 00
Email: apll@bergske.dk **Web site:** http://dinby.dk/lokalavisen-lemvig
Circ: 12982
Profile: Lokalavsien Lemvig is a weekly newspaper covering local news in the region.
Language (s): Danish
Ad Rate: Full Page Colour 8511.00
Currency: Denmark Kroner
COMMUNITY NEWSPAPER

Lokalbladet Ringsted 435575
Editorial: Sogade 4-12, Ringsted 4100
Tel: 45 57 68 22 00
Email: ringsted.red@sn.dk **Web site:** http://sn.dk/
Circ: 22404
Redaktør: Bodil Pinholt
Profile: Lokalbladet Ringsted is a weekly newspaper covering local news.
Language (s): Danish
Ad Rate: Full Page Colour 9816.00
Currency: Denmark Kroner
COMMUNITY NEWSPAPER

Lokalposten Lem Ugeavis 222716
Editorial: Falkevej 4, Videbæk 6920
Tel: 45 97 17 11 22
Email: post@videbaek-bogtrykkeri.dk **Web site:** http://www.danske-lokalaviser.dk/avis/lokalposten-lem-ugeavis
Freq: Weekly; **Circ:** 4000 Not Audited
Profile: Lokalposten Lem Ugeavis is a weekly local newspaper distributed to residents of Lem and its surroundings.
Language (s): Danish
COMMUNITY NEWSPAPER

Løkken Folkeblad 222599
Editorial: Frederikshavnsvej 81, Hjørring 9800
Tel: 45 99 24 50 60
Email: redaktion.loekkenfolkeblad@nordjyske.dk
Web site: http://loekkenfolkeblad.dk/
Freq: Weekly; **Circ:** 9365 Not Audited
Profile: Løkken Folkeblad is a weekly local newspaper distributed throughout Løkken and its surroundings.
Language (s): Danish
COMMUNITY NEWSPAPER

Lolland-Falster Folketidende - Midt & SydLolland 435673
Editorial: Banegardspladsen 2, Maribo 4930
Tel: 45 54 88 08 60
Web site: http://www.folketidende.dk
Circ: 7436
Profile: Lolland-Falster Folketidende's local section covering Midt and SydLolland. No releases!
Language (s): Danish
COMMUNITY NEWSPAPER

Lolland-Falster Folketidende - Vestlolland 435670
Editorial: Nygade 30, Nakskov 4900
Tel: 45 54 88 08 00
Email: nakskov@folketidende.dk **Web site:** http://www.folketidende.dk
Circ: 7436
Profile: Lolland-Falster Folketidende's local section covering Vestlolland.
Language (s): Danish
COMMUNITY NEWSPAPER

Lolland-Falsters Folketidende 222719
Editorial: Tværgade 20, Nykøbing 4800
Tel: 45 54 88 02 00
Email: redaktion@folketidende.dk **Web site:** http://folketidende.dk
Freq: Daily; **Circ:** 14244 Not Audited
Profile: Lolland-Falsters Folketidende is a Danish newspaper covering the Guldborgsund and Lolland municipalities. The main editorial office is in Nykoebing and it also has two local editorial offices in Maribo and Nakskov. The newspaper is published Monday to Saturday and contains local news, sports, debate and entertainment.
Language (s): Danish
COMMUNITY NEWSPAPER

Lørdagsavisen 222722
Editorial: Torvet 15, Køge 4600 **Tel:** 45 56 65 82 00
Email: info@kmc-as.dk **Web site:** http://koege.lokalavisen.dk
Freq: Weekly; **Circ:** 44700 Publisher's Statement
Profile: Lørdagsavisen is a weekly newspaper containing local news from Køge, Solrød, Greve and parts of Stevns.
Language (s): Danish
Ad Rate: Full Page Colour 17784.00
Currency: Denmark Kroner
COMMUNITY NEWSPAPER

Lunderskov og Omegns Folkeblad 222720
Editorial: Torvet 3, Lunderskov 6640
Tel: 45 75 58 59 90
Email: avisen@lhhi.dk **Web site:** http://lhhi.dk/avisen/
Freq: Weekly; **Circ:** 7500 Publisher's Statement
Profile: Lunderskov og Omegns Folkeblad is a weekly local newspaper distributed throughout Lunderskov and Omegns.
Language (s): Danish
Ad Rate: Full Page Colour 6135.50
Currency: Denmark Kroner
COMMUNITY NEWSPAPER

Lyngposten 435574
Editorial: Herningvej 26, Sønder-Omme 7260
Tel: 45 29 44 44 44
Email: post@lyngposten.dk **Web site:** http://www.lyngposten.dk/
Circ: 10037
EDITOR: Henny Eskildsen
Profile: Lyngposten is a weekly newspaper containing local news from Sdr. Omme by, Grindsted, Filskov, Grønbjerg, Blåhøj, Stakroge, Ådum, Sdr. Felding and Skarrild.
Language (s): Danish
Ad Rate: Full Page Colour 7045.50
Currency: Denmark Kroner
COMMUNITY NEWSPAPER

Mariager Avis 222730
Editorial: Kirkegade 13, Mariager 9550
Tel: 45 98 54 26 22
Email: mariageravis@mariageravis.dk **Web site:** http://ugeavisen.dk/omos/mariageravis
Freq: Weekly; **Circ:** 10600 Not Audited
Profile: Mariager Avis is a weekly local newspaper distributed to the residents of Mariager.
Language (s): Danish
COMMUNITY NEWSPAPER

Melfar Posten 222731
Editorial: Havnegade 41, Middelfart 5500
Tel: 45 65 45 55 00
Email: redaktion@melfarposten.dk **Web site:** http://www.melfarposten.dk
Freq: Weekly; **Circ:** 23464 Not Audited
Profile: Melfar Posten is a weekly local newspaper that serve Middelfart and its surroundings.
Language (s): Danish
COMMUNITY NEWSPAPER

Midtfyns Posten 435892
Editorial: ostergade 19, Ringe 5750
Web site: http://www.midtfynsposten.dk
Freq: Weekly; **Circ:** 18028 Not Audited
EDITOR IN CHIEF: Troels Mylenberg; **EDITOR:** Tim Visti
Profile: Midtfyns Posten is a weekly newspaper covering local news in the region. No releases!!
Language (s): Danish
Ad Rate: Full Page Colour 11088.00

Currency: Denmark Kroner
COMMUNITY NEWSPAPER

Midthimmerlands Folkeblad 222736

Editorial: Doktorvænget 6, Støvring 9530
Tel: 45 98 37 24 00
Email: mail@folkebladet.info **Web site:** http://www.folkebladet.info/
Freq: Weekly; **Circ:** 14300 Not Audited
Ansvarshavende redaktør: Henrik Møller
Profile: Midthimmerlands Folkeblad is a weekly local newspaper that serve Støvring and its surroundings.
Language (s): Danish
COMMUNITY NEWSPAPER

Midtjysk Ugeavis 435740

Editorial: Jernbanegade 25, Grindsted 7200
Tel: 45 75 32 05 00
Email: redaktion@midtjyskugeavis.dk **Web site:** http://vafo.dk/Grindsted?profile=1304
Freq: Weekly; **Circ:** 18877
Editor: Jan Kronvold
Profile: Midtjysk Ugeavis is a weekly newspaper covering local news in the region.
Language (s): Danish
COMMUNITY NEWSPAPER

Midtsjællands Folkeblad 222699

Editorial: Kvarmlosevej 36, Tølløse 4340
Tel: 45 59 18 51 57
Email: folkeblad@midttryk.dk **Web site:** http://sn.dk/midtsjaellandsfolkeblad/
Freq: Weekly; **Circ:** 27500 Not Audited
Profile: Midtsjællands Folkeblad is a weekly local newspaper that is distributed throughout Tølløse and its surroundings. Covers a big area between Holbæk, Roskilde, Ringsted and Sorø.
Language (s): Danish
COMMUNITY NEWSPAPER

Midtvendsyssel Avis 222713

Editorial: Jernbanegade 3, Hjallerup 9320
Tel: 45 98 28 11 99
Email: mvavis@mvavis.dk **Web site:** http://www.midtvendsysselavis.dk/?id=46
Freq: Weekly; **Circ:** 8600 Not Audited
Profile: Midtvendsyssel Avis is a weekly local newspaper distributed throughout Hjallerup and its surroundings.
Language (s): Danish
COMMUNITY NEWSPAPER

Midt-Vest Avis 222735

Editorial: Langagervej 1, Aalborg 9220
Tel: 45 99 35 35 35
Email: midtvest@nordjyske.dk **Web site:** http://nordjyske.dk/e-avis
Freq: Weekly; **Circ:** 36901 Not Audited
Profile: Midt-Vest Avis is a weekly local newspaper that is distributed in Aalborg city and the western part of the Aalborg municipality.
Language (s): Danish
COMMUNITY NEWSPAPER

Morsø Folkeblad 158382

Editorial: Elsovej 105, Nykobing Mors, Unavailable 7900 **Tel:** 45 97 72 10 00
Email: redaktion@mf.dk **Web site:** http://www.mf.dk
Circ: 3782
Profile: Morsø Folkeblad is a regional newspaper published in Nykøbing Mors. It is distributed throughout Mors, the northern part of Salling and Thy.
Language (s): Danish
COMMUNITY NEWSPAPER

Morsø Folkeblads Ugeavis 375558

Editorial: Elsovej 105, Nykobing Mors, Nykøbing 7900 **Tel:** 45 97 72 10 00
Email: ugeavis@mf.dk **Web site:** http://www.mf.dk
Freq: Weekly; **Circ:** 18395 Not Audited
Profile: Morsø Folkeblads Ugeavis is a weekly local newspaper that is distributed throughout Mors, the northern part of Salling and Thy.
Language (s): Danish
COMMUNITY NEWSPAPER

Næstved-Bladet 222717

Editorial: Ringstedgade 11, Næstved 4700
Tel: 45 55 73 50 00
Email: redaktion@naestved-bladet.dk **Web site:** http://www.naestved-bladet.dk
Freq: Weekly; **Circ:** 42107 Not Audited
Profile: Næstved-Bladet is a weekly newspaper covering local news.
Language (s): Danish
Ad Rate: Full Page Colour 13609.00
Currency: Denmark Kroner
COMMUNITY NEWSPAPER

Nibe Avis 435891

Editorial: Jacob Petersens Vej 13, Nibe 9240
Tel: 45 98 35 11 45
Email: redaktion@nibeavis.dk **Web site:** http://www.nibeavis.dk
Freq: Weekly; **Circ:** 9500 Not Audited
Redaktør: Jacob Søndergaard
Profile: Nibe Avis is a weekly newspaper covering local news in the region.
Language (s): Danish
Ad Rate: Full Page Colour 7715.40
Currency: Denmark Kroner
COMMUNITY NEWSPAPER

Nørager Avis 435900

Editorial: Holmsvej 3, Nørager 9610
Tel: 45 98 55 17 44
Email: avis@norager-avis.dk **Web site:** http://rebild-avis.dk/
Freq: Weekly; **Circ:** 4000 Not Audited
Ansvarshavende redaktør: Preben Lauritzen
Profile: Nørager Avis is a weekly local newspaper that serve Rebild Syd.
Language (s): Danish
COMMUNITY NEWSPAPER

Nordfalsters Avis 222742

Editorial: Kæpgardsvej 19, Nørre Alslev 4840
Tel: 45 54 43 41 00
Email: redaktion@nordfalstersavis.dk **Web site:** http://www.nordfalstersavis.dk
Freq: Weekly; **Circ:** 8600 Publisher's Statement
Profile: Nordfalsters Avis is a weekly local newspaper distributed throughout Nordfalster.
Language (s): Danish
COMMUNITY NEWSPAPER

Nordjyske Stiftstidende 158368

Editorial: Langagervej 1, Ålborg 9220
Tel: 45 99 35 35 35
Email: nordjyske@nordjyske.dk **Web site:** http://www.nordjyske.dk
Circ: 62075
Chefredaktør: Lars Jespersen;
Redaktionssekretær: Flemming Kristensen;
Redaktionschef: Jørgen la Cour-Harbo;
Ansvarshavende redaktør: Per Lyngby;
Nyhedsredaktør/chef: Karin Pedersen
Profile: Nordjyske Stiftstidende is a daily regional newspaper published in Aalborg, Denmark. It is Denmark's second oldest newspaper.
Language (s): Danish
Ad Rate: Full Page Colour 75936.00
Currency: Denmark Kroner
COMMUNITY NEWSPAPER

Nørresundby Avis 222776

Editorial: Langagervej 1, Aalborg 9220
Tel: 45 99 35 33 80
Email: nsb@nordjyske.dk **Web site:** http://noerresundbyavis.dk/
Freq: Weekly; **Circ:** 30775 Not Audited
Profile: Nørresundby Avis is a weekly newspaper covering local news.
Language (s): Danish
Ad Rate: Full Page Colour 12055.50
Currency: Denmark Kroner
COMMUNITY NEWSPAPER

Ny Tirsdag 222725

Editorial: ostergade 3, Rødding 6630
Tel: 45 78 79 76 00
Email: redaktion@nytirsdag.dk **Web site:** http://ugeavisen.dk/omos/nytirsdag
Freq: Weekly; **Circ:** 18121 Publisher's Statement
Profile: Ny Tirsdag is a weekly local newspaper that serve Rødding and its surroundings.
Language (s): Danish
COMMUNITY NEWSPAPER

Odder Avis 435890

Editorial: Rosengade 15, Odder 8300
Tel: 45 86 54 10 11
Email: odder@hsfo.dk **Web site:** http://hsfo.dk/odder/
Freq: Weekly; **Circ:** 24629 Not Audited
Profile: Odder Avis is a local edition of the newspaper Horsens Folkeblad, covering local news from the region.
Language (s): Danish
COMMUNITY NEWSPAPER

OnsdagsAvisen 222718

Editorial: Norregade 22, Horsens 8700
Tel: 45 75 61 28 77
Email: info@onsdagsavisen.dk **Web site:** http://www.onsdags-avisen.dk
Freq: Weekly
Editor-in-Chief: Torben Rasmussen
Profile: OnsdagsAvisen is a weekly local newspaper in Horsens. News from the town's shops, fashion and everything about the cultural life are some of the topics.
Language (s): Danish
COMMUNITY NEWSPAPER

Oplandsavisen 222721

Editorial: Bredgade 35, Brønderslev 9700
Tel: 45 96 45 55 65
Email: redaktion.oplandsavisen@nordjyske.dk **Web site:** http://oplandsavisen.dk/
Freq: Weekly; **Circ:** 30616 Not Audited
Profile: Oplandsavisen is a weekly newspaper covering local news.
Language (s): Danish
Ad Rate: Full Page Colour 11709.00
Currency: Denmark Kroner
COMMUNITY NEWSPAPER

Østbirk Avis Østjydsk Avis 222691

Editorial: Storegade 14, Østbirk 8752
Tel: 45 75 78 10 11
Email: post@oestbirk-avis.dk **Web site:** http://www.oestbirk-avis.dk
Freq: Weekly; **Circ:** 13228 Publisher's Statement
Ansvarshavende redaktør: Peder Stougaard
Profile: Østbirk Avis Østjydsk Avis is a local weekly newspaper. A merger of Østjydsk Avis (former Hovedgård Avis) and Østbirk Avis. Published every Wednesday and distributed to all households in Gedved Municipality.
Language (s): Danish
Ad Rate: Full Page Colour 7718.00
Currency: Denmark Kroner
COMMUNITY NEWSPAPER

Østerbro Avis 222684

Editorial: Gammel Kongevej 60, 16. sal, Frederiksberg C 1850 **Tel:** 45 35 42 25 15
Email: red@oesterbroavis.dk **Web site:** http://minby.dk/oesterbro-avis/
Freq: Weekly; **Circ:** 50531 Dansk Oplagskontrol
Ansvarshavende redaktør: Thomas Frederiksen
Profile: Østerbro Avis is a local weekly newspaper in Østerbro, Copenhagen.
Language (s): Danish
Ad Rate: Full Page Colour 21480.00
Currency: Denmark Kroner
COMMUNITY NEWSPAPER

Østhimmerlands Folkeblad 222690

Owner: Østhimmerlands Folkeblad
Editorial: Refsnæsvej 8, Kongerslev 9293
Tel: 45 99 35 35 35
Email: avis@oehf.dk **Web site:** http://www.oehf.dk
Freq: Weekly; **Circ:** 14378 Not Audited
Editor: Louise Askou
Profile: Østhimmerlands Folkeblad is a regional newspaper distributed every Tuesday to all households in the former Sejlflod and Skørping municipalities and to the Klarup and Gistrup postal districts.
Language (s): Danish
COMMUNITY NEWSPAPER

Østvendsyssel Avis 375557

Editorial: Bredgade 35, Brønderslev 9700
Tel: 45 98 84 17 00
Email: redaktion.oestvendsysselavis@nordjyske.dk **Web site:** http://oestvendsysselavis.dk/
Freq: Weekly; **Circ:** 13600 Not Audited
Profile: Østvendsyssel Avis is a weekly newspaper covering local news in the region.
Language (s): Danish
Ad Rate: Full Page Colour 6609.50
Currency: Denmark Kroner
COMMUNITY NEWSPAPER

Østvendsyssel Folkeblad 222696

Editorial: Industrivej 12, Østervrå 9750
Tel: 45 98 95 18 81
Email: avis@oestvend.dk **Web site:** http://www.oestvend.dk
Freq: Weekly; **Circ:** 9987 Not Audited
Ansvarshavende redaktør: Søren Ejstrup Brunse
Profile: Østvendsyssel Folkeblad is a local weekly newspaper distributed in Østervrå and its surroundings.
Language (s): Danish
Ad Rate: Full Page Colour 6444.00
Currency: Denmark Kroner
COMMUNITY NEWSPAPER

Randers Amtsavis 158893

Editorial: Norregade 7, Randers 8900
Tel: 45 87 12 20 00
Email: redaktion@amtsavisen.dk **Web site:** http://www.amtsavisen.dk
Circ: 11972
EDITOR ON CHIEF: Bo Hovgaard; **EDITOR:** Niels Mandrup; **EDITOR:** Per Meldgaard; **Redaktionschef:** Axel Præstmark
Profile: Randers Amtsavis is a daily newspaper covering local news in the region.
Language (s): Danish
Ad Rate: Full Page Colour 14692.50
Currency: Denmark Kroner
COMMUNITY NEWSPAPER

Regionalavisen Vestegnen 222567

Editorial: Marievej 1D, Greve 2630
Tel: 45 70 20 64 01
Email: vestegnen.red@sn.dk **Web site:** http://sn.dk/vestegnen
Freq: Weekly; **Circ:** 153147 Not Audited
Profile: Regionalavisen Vestegnen is a weekly newspaper covering local news in the region.
Language (s): Danish
Ad Rate: Full Page Colour 28373.50
Currency: Denmark Kroner
COMMUNITY NEWSPAPER

Rødovre Lokal Nyt 435925

Editorial: Rodovre Centrum 241, Rødovre 2610
Tel: 45 36 36 60 00
Email: rnn@rnn.dk **Web site:** http://www.rnn.dk
Freq: Weekly; **Circ:** 22000 Publisher's Statement
Profile: Rødovre Lokal Nyt is a weekly newspaper covering local news in the region.
Language (s): Danish
Ad Rate: Full Page Colour 13350.00
Currency: Denmark Kroner
COMMUNITY NEWSPAPER

Rold Skov Bladet 490663

Editorial: Jyllandsgade 15, Skørping 9520
Tel: 45 96 82 00 00
Email: rold.tekst@nordjyske.dk **Web site:** http://www.roldskovbladet.dk
Freq: Weekly; **Circ:** 9972 Not Audited
Profile: Rold Skov Bladet is a weekly local newspaper that is distributed in Skørping and its surroundings.
Language (s): Danish
COMMUNITY NEWSPAPER

Roskilde Avis 435458

Editorial: Algade 2, 1. sal., Roskilde 4000
Tel: 45 46 36 20 11
Email: ra.red@sn.dk **Web site:** http://sn.dk/roskilde
Circ: 62076
Lokale / Regionale nyheder: Henrik Brøns
Profile: Roskilde Avis is a regional newspaper published twice a week in Roskilde and surrounding areas.
Language (s): Danish
COMMUNITY NEWSPAPER

Rudersdal Avis 223006

Editorial: Gl. Lundtoftevej 1B, Kongens Lyngby 2800
Tel: 45 45 90 80 70
Email: redaktion@rudersdalavis.dk **Web site:** http://www.birkeroedavis.dk
Freq: 2 Times/Week; **Circ:** 22939 Publisher's Statement
Profile: Rudersdal Avis is a regional newspaper that's published mid-week and at the weekends.
Language (s): Danish
COMMUNITY NEWSPAPER

Ry Ugeavis 435742

Editorial: Klostervej 8 D, Ry 8680 **Tel:** 45 86 82 13 00
Email: ry@mja.dk **Web site:** http://mediehuset-midtjyllandsavis.dk/
Freq: Weekly; **Circ:** 6918 Publisher's Statement
Profile: Ry Ugeavis is a weekly local newspaper based in Ry, Denmark.
Language (s): Danish
COMMUNITY NEWSPAPER

Rytterknægten 222724

Editorial: Norregade 11-19, Rønne 3700
Tel: 45 56 90 30 00
Email: redaktion@bornholmstidende.dk **Web site:** http://tidende.dk/ugeavis/
Freq: Weekly; **Circ:** 22908 Not Audited
Redaktør: Dan Qvitzau
Profile: Rytterknægten is a weekly newspaper covering local news in Bornholm.
Language (s): Danish
Ad Rate: Full Page Colour 12685.00
Currency: Denmark Kroner
COMMUNITY NEWSPAPER

Sæby Folkeblad 222627

Editorial: Gronnegade 24, Sæby 9300
Tel: 45 99 89 14 50
Email: redaktion.folkebladet@nordjyske.dk **Web site:** http://saebyfolkeblad.dk/
Freq: Weekly; **Circ:** 10914 Not Audited
Profile: Sæby Folkeblad is a weekly local newspaper distributed throughout Sæby and its surroundings.
Language (s): Danish
COMMUNITY NEWSPAPER

Salling Avis 222655

Editorial: Norregade 19, Roslev 7870
Tel: 45 97 57 14 00
Email: sallingavis@sallingavis.dk **Web site:** http://sallingavis.dk/
Freq: Weekly; **Circ:** 10200 Not Audited
Profile: Salling Avis is a local newspaper for the Salling region, published Tuesdays and Wednesdays.
Language (s): Danish
Ad Rate: Full Page Colour 8561.00
Currency: Denmark Kroner
COMMUNITY NEWSPAPER

Samsø Posten 222773

Editorial: Industrivej 6A, Samsø 8305
Tel: 45 86 59 13 43
Email: avis@samsoposten.dk **Web site:** http://www.samso.dk/Np.asp
Freq: Daily; **Circ:** 3050 Not Audited
Ansvarshavende redaktør: Morten Christensen
Profile: Samsø Posten is a weekly newspaper covering local news in the region.
Language (s): Danish
Ad Rate: Full Page Colour 5556.00
Currency: Denmark Kroner
COMMUNITY NEWSPAPER

Saxkjøbing Avis 222766

Editorial: Sondergade 2, Sakskøbing 4990
Tel: 45 54 70 47 00
Email: kh@saxkjobing-avis.dk **Web site:** http://folketidende.dk/saxkjoebing-avis
Freq: Weekly; **Circ:** 9667 Not Audited
Profile: Saxkjøbing Avis is a weekly newspaper covering local news in the region.
Language (s): Danish
Ad Rate: Full Page Colour 9804.00
Currency: Denmark Kroner
COMMUNITY NEWSPAPER

Sindal Avis 222768

Editorial: Frederikshavnsvej 81, Hjørring 9800
Tel: 45 99 24 50 60
Email: redaktion.sindalavis@nordjyske.dk **Web site:** http://www.sindalavis.dk
Freq: Weekly; **Circ:** 7763 Not Audited
Redaktør: Martin Nielsen
Profile: Sindal Avis is a weekly local newspaper that is distributed in Sindal and its surroundings.
Language (s): Danish
COMMUNITY NEWSPAPER

Skærbæk Avis
435741

Owner: De Lokale Ugeaviser
Editorial: Ribevej 1, Skærbæk 6780
Tel: 45 74 75 22 70
Email: post@skaerbaek-avis.dk **Web site:** http://ugeavisen.dk/skaerbaek
Freq: Weekly; **Circ:** 17435 Not Audited
Editor in Cheif: Christian Olesen
Profile: Skærbæk Avis is a weekly local newspaper.
Language (s): Danish
COMMUNITY NEWSPAPER

Skagen Onsdag
222769

Editorial: Skolevej 8, Skagen 9990
Tel: 45 96 79 59 00
Email: redaktion.skagenonsdag@nordjyske.dk **Web site:** http://skagenonsdag.dk/
Freq: Weekly; **Circ:** 8749 Not Audited
Profile: Skagen Onsdag is a weekly newspaper covering local news in Skagen.
Language (s): Danish
COMMUNITY NEWSPAPER

Skive Folkeblad
158389

Editorial: Gemsevej 7, Skive 7800
Tel: 45 97 51 34 11
Email: redaktion@skivefolkeblad.dk **Web site:** http://www.skivefolkeblad.dk
Freq: Daily; **Circ:** 31358
Editor in Cheif: Ole Dall; **Editor:** Thue Grum-Schwensen; **Editor:** Merete Just; **Editor:** Hanne Skibsted
Profile: Skive Folkeblad is a newspaper covering local news from Salling, Fjends Herred, Vinderup municipality and Haderup Sogn.
Language (s): Danish
COMMUNITY NEWSPAPER

Skjern-Tarm Ugeblad
222611

Editorial: Trykkerivej 6, Tarm 6880
Tel: 45 97 37 14 44
Email: redaktionen@tarm-bogtryk.dk **Web site:** http://skjerntarm-ugeblad.dk/
Freq: Weekly; **Circ:** 13600 Not Audited
Profile: Skjern-Tarm Ugeblad is a weekly newspaper covering local news in the region.
Language (s): Danish
COMMUNITY NEWSPAPER

Søndagsavisen
222641

Owner: Søndagsavisen a/s
Editorial: Gladsaxe Mollevej 28, Søborg 2860
Tel: 45 39 57 75 00
Email: redaktionen@sondagsavisen.dk **Web site:** http://www.sondagsavisen.dk
Freq: Weekly; **Circ:** 1200000 Not Audited
Profile: Søndagsavisen is a free Danish countrywide weekend newspaper covering news. It is distributed in 23 different regional editions.
Language (s): Danish
COMMUNITY NEWSPAPER

Sønderborg Ugeavis
222623

Editorial: ostergade 3, 1.sal, Sønderborg 6400
Tel: 45 87 54 25 42
Email: redaktion@ugeavisen.dk **Web site:** http://ugeavisen.dk/soenderborg
Freq: Weekly
Editor: Jens Eilertsen
Profile: Sønderborg Ugeavis is a weekly newspaper covering local news in the community. Published by Jysk Fynske Medier.
Language (s): Danish
COMMUNITY NEWSPAPER

Sorø Avis
435915

Editorial: Absalonsgade 1, Sorø 4180
Tel: 45 57 83 47 77
Email: soroe.red@sn.dk **Web site:** http://sn.dk/soroe
Freq: Weekly; **Circ:** 17729 Publisher's Statement
Profile: Sorø Avis is a weekly local newspaper that is distributed throughout Sorø Municipality.
Language (s): Danish
COMMUNITY NEWSPAPER

Spøttrup Ugeavis
222654

Editorial: Norregade 19, Roslev 7870
Tel: 45 97 56 43 30
Email: post@spottrup-ugeavis.dk **Web site:** http://www.spottrup-ugeavis.dk/
Freq: Weekly; **Circ:** 4400 Publisher's Statement
Profile: Spøttrup Ugeavis is a weekly local newspaper distributed in Spøttrup Municipality and its surroundings.
Language (s): Danish
COMMUNITY NEWSPAPER

Sunds-Gjellerup Avis
222651

Editorial: Stroget 40, Ikast 7430 **Tel:** 45 97 15 18 00
Email: redaktion@sgavis.dk **Web site:** http://aoh.dk/sted/sunds
Freq: Weekly; **Circ:** 7100 Publisher's Statement
Profile: Sunds-Gjellerup Avis is a weekly newspaper covering local news in the region.
Language (s): Danish
Ad Rate: Full Page Colour 7738.50
Currency: Denmark Kroner
COMMUNITY NEWSPAPER

Sydkysten
435633

Editorial: Greve Strandvej 24, Greve 2670
Tel: 45 43 90 44 22
Email: sydkysten.red@sj-medier.dk **Web site:** http://sn.dk/sydkysten/
Circ: 64000
EDITOR IN CHIEF: Helle Midskov; **Lokale / Regionale nyheder:** Marianne Pedersen
Profile: Sydkysten is a free regional newspaper distributed to all households, offices and shops in the Køge Bay area. It is published on Fridays and Saturdays and comes out in three editions; Nord, Syd and Weekend.
Language (s): Danish
Ad Rate: Full Page Colour 19592.50
Currency: Denmark Kroner
COMMUNITY NEWSPAPER

Sydsjællands Tidende
222629

Editorial: Torvestræde 4, Vordingborg 4760
Tel: 45 55 37 00 09
Email: redaktion@sydtid.dk **Web site:** http://www.sydtid.dk
Freq: Weekly; **Circ:** 30800 Not Audited
Profile: Sydsjællands Tidende is a weekly newspaper containing news from Sydsjælland, Møn and Nordfalster.
Language (s): Danish
Ad Rate: Full Page Colour 11817.50
Currency: Denmark Kroner
COMMUNITY NEWSPAPER

Thisted Dagblad
158391

Owner: Nordjyske Medier
Editorial: Sydhavnsvej 5, Thisted 7700
Tel: 45 99 19 93 00
Email: thisted@nordjyske.dk **Web site:** http://nordjyske.dk/nyheder/thisted
Freq: Daily; **Circ:** 8900
Redaktør: Jens Fogh Andersen; **Editor in Cheif:** Per Lyngby
Profile: Thisted Dagblad is a local edition of Nordjyske Stiftstidende covering local news from Thisted.
Language (s): Danish
COMMUNITY NEWSPAPER

Thisted Posten
222612

Editorial: Sydhavnsvej 5, Thisted 7700
Tel: 45 99 18 93 00
Email: thisted.posten@nordjyske.dk **Web site:** http://thistedposten.dk/
Freq: Weekly; **Circ:** 22948 Not Audited
Profile: Thisted Posten is a local newspaper distributed every Wednesday to the residents of Thistedt, Hanstholm, Frostrup, Vedslos, Snedsted, Bredsted and parts of Hurup and Erslev Mors.
Language (s): Danish
COMMUNITY NEWSPAPER

Thylands Avis
222615

Editorial: Bredgade 139, Hurup, Thy 7760
Tel: 45 97 95 21 00
Email: thylands.redaktion@nordjyske.dk **Web site:** http://thylandsavis.dk/
Freq: Weekly; **Circ:** 8862 Not Audited
Editor in Cheif: Per Lyngby
Profile: Thylands Avis is a local newspaper covering news from Hurup, Bedsted, Villerslev, Hassing, Koldby, Agger, Vestervig, Ydby, Hvidbjerg, Lyngs, Snedsted, Uglev och Jegindo. It is distributed every Wednesday.
Language (s): Danish
COMMUNITY NEWSPAPER

Tørring Folkeblad
222610

Owner: Tørring Folkeblad A/S
Editorial: Torvegade 17, Tørring 7160
Tel: 45 75 80 22 88
Email: red@folkeblad.net **Web site:** http://www.torring-folkeblad.dk
Freq: Weekly; **Circ:** 14424 Not Audited
Managing Director: Frank Dammand Nielsen
Profile: Tørring Folkeblad is a local weekly newspaper covering news from Tørring.
Language (s): Danish
COMMUNITY NEWSPAPER

Trekantens Folkeblad
222617

Owner: Jysk Fynske Medier
Editorial: Bugattivej 8, Vejle 7100 **Tel:** 45 75 86 51 11
Email: trekantens@trefo.dk **Web site:** http://www.trefo.dk
Freq: Weekly; **Circ:** 7000 Not Audited
Profile: Trekantens Folkeblad is a weekly newspaper covering local news from Trekanten.
Language (s): Danish
COMMUNITY NEWSPAPER

Tyrstrup Herreds Tidende / Christiansfeld Avis
375555

Editorial: Jernbanegade 1, Christiansfeld 6070
Tel: 45 74 56 14 33
Email: info@tht-ugeavis.dk **Web site:** http://www.tht-ugeavis.dk
Freq: Weekly; **Circ:** 5784 Not Audited
Ansvarshavende redaktør: Helle W Ravn
Profile: A weekly local newspaper distributed throughout Christiansfeld and its surroundings.
Language (s): Danish
COMMUNITY NEWSPAPER

Ugeavis Odsherred
435581

Editorial: Gronnehavestræde 1, Nykøbing 4500
Tel: 45 88 88 45 00
Email: ugeavisenodsherred@sn.dk **Web site:** http://sn.dk/
Circ: 22688
Profile: Ugeavis Odsherred is a weekly newspaper covering local news in the region.
Language (s): Danish
Ad Rate: Full Page Colour 10347.00
Currency: Denmark Kroner
COMMUNITY NEWSPAPER

Ugeavisen Ansager Helle
435898

Editorial: Storegade 16-18, Ølgod 6870
Tel: 45 75 24 45 55
Email: red.ansager@ugeavisen.dk **Web site:** http://ugeavisen.dk/omos/ansagerhelle
Freq: Weekly; **Circ:** 7257 Not Audited
Profile: Ugeavisen Ansager Helle is a weekly local newspaper that is distributed in Ansager and its surroundings.
Language (s): Danish
COMMUNITY NEWSPAPER

Ugeavisen Bramming
222577

Editorial: Sct. Knuds Alle 3, Bramming 6740
Tel: 45 75 17 40 00
Email: mawi@ugeavisen.dk **Web site:** http://www.ugeavisen-bramming.dk
Freq: Weekly; **Circ:** 15715 Not Audited
Profile: Ugeavisen Bramming is a weekly local newspaper distributed in Bramming municipality and its surroundings.
Language (s): Danish
COMMUNITY NEWSPAPER

Ugeavisen Digeposten
435877

Editorial: Lillegade 11, 2 sal, Tønder 6270
Tel: 45 74 72 33 42
Email: redaktion@digeposten.dk **Web site:** http://ugeavisen.dk/digeposten
Freq: Weekly
Editor: Holger Ringgaard
Profile: Ugeavisen Digeposten is a newspaper covering local news.
Language (s): Danish
COMMUNITY NEWSPAPER

Ugeavisen Esbjerg
435609

Editorial: Kongensgade 110-114, Esbjerg 6700
Tel: 45 76 11 42 00
Email: red.esbjerg@ugeavisen.dk **Web site:** http://ugeavisen.dk/esbjerg
Circ: 69450
Ansvarshavende redaktør: Erik Haldan
Profile: Ugeavisen Esbjerg is a local weekly newspaper, which is published in Esbjerg and its surroundings.
Language (s): Danish
Ad Rate: Full Page Colour 14346.75
Currency: Denmark Kroner
COMMUNITY NEWSPAPER

UgeAvisen Faaborg
435576

Editorial: Kanneworffs Gaard, Torvet 8b, Faaborg 5600 **Tel:** 45 63 45 22 25
Email: redaktion@ugeavisen-faaborg.dk **Web site:** http://ugeavisenfaaborg.dk
Freq: Weekly; **Circ:** 16745
Profile: UgeAvisen Faaborg is a weekly local newspaper distributed throughout Faaborg, Denmark.
Language (s): Danish
COMMUNITY NEWSPAPER

Ugeavisen Guldborgsund
435622

Editorial: Tværgade 20, Nykøbing 4800
Tel: 45 54 88 02 34
Email: redaktion@ugeavisen-guld.dk **Web site:** http://folketidende.dk/ugeavisen-guldborgsund
Freq: Weekly; **Circ:** 33189
Redaktør: Manfred Sørensen
Profile: Ugeavisen Guldborgsund is a weekly local newspaper that is distributed throughout Guldborgsund municipality.
Language (s): Danish
COMMUNITY NEWSPAPER

Ugeavisen Karup
498224

Editorial: Bredgade 4 F, Karup 7470
Tel: 45 97 10 10 22
Email: presse@ugeavisen-karup.dk **Web site:** http://www.ugeavisen-karup.dk
Freq: Weekly; **Circ:** 7159
Profile: Ugeavisen Karup is a weekly local newspaper distributed in Karup municipality and its surroundings.
Language (s): Danish
Ad Rate: Full Page Mono 8869.00
Currency: Denmark Kroner
COMMUNITY NEWSPAPER

Ugeavisen Kolding
435590

Editorial: Essen 16, Kolding 6000 **Tel:** 45 76 30 80 80
Email: red.kolding@ugeavisen.dk **Web site:** http://ugeavisen.dk/kolding
Circ: 41
Editor: Louise Lauritsen
Profile: Ugeavisen Kolding gives you the latest news from the region.
Language (s): Danish
COMMUNITY NEWSPAPER

Ugeavisen Midtsyd
435935

Editorial: Vestergarde 5, Toftlund 6520
Tel: 45 74 83 22 83
Email: red.midtsyd@ugeavisen.dk **Web site:** http://ugeavisen.dk/midtsyd
Freq: Weekly; **Circ:** 18500 Not Audited
Profile: Ugeavisen Midtsyd is a weekly local newspaper that is distributed in Toftlund and its surroundings.
Language (s): Danish
COMMUNITY NEWSPAPER

Ugeavisen Møsdrup-Aalestrup
435553

Editorial: Vesterbrogade 8, Viborg 8800
Tel: 45 89 27 63 00
Email: uma@bergske.dk **Web site:** http://ugeavisen.dk/kategori/931
Circ: 11856
EDITOR: Dorte Kristensen; **Chefredaktør:** Lars Norup
Profile: Weekly local newspaper about news in local area north of Viborg.
Language (s): Danish
COMMUNITY NEWSPAPER

Ugeavisen Nordfyn
222697

Editorial: Jernbanegade 45, Otterup 5450
Tel: 45 65 45 57 00
Email: redaktion@ua-nordfyn.dk **Web site:** http://www.ugeavisennordfyn.dk
Freq: Weekly; **Circ:** 22447 Not Audited
EDITOR AT LARGE: Thomas Gregersen
Profile: Ugeavisen Nordfyn is a weekly local newspaper distributed in Otterup and Bogense.
Language (s): Danish
COMMUNITY NEWSPAPER

Ugeavisen Øboen
435886

Editorial: orstedsgade 18, Rudkøbing 5900
Tel: 45 63 45 22 38
Email: redaktion@oeboen.dk **Web site:** http://www.oeboen.dk/
Freq: Weekly; **Circ:** 11300 Publisher's Statement
Ansvarshavende redaktør: Bjarne Selvager Hansen
Profile: Ugeavisen Øboen is a local weekly newspaper in Øboen.
Language (s): Danish
Ad Rate: Full Page Colour 11434.50
Currency: Denmark Kroner
COMMUNITY NEWSPAPER

Ugeavisen Odense
222608

Editorial: Banegardspladsen 1, Odense 5100
Tel: 45 66 14 14 10
Email: odense@fyens.dk **Web site:** http://www.ugeavisen-odense.dk
Freq: Weekly; **Circ:** 92200 Not Audited
EDITOR: Jan Bonde
Profile: Ugeavisen Odense is a weekly local newspaper distributed in Odense and its surroundings.
Language (s): Danish
COMMUNITY NEWSPAPER

Ugeavisen Ribe
222570

Editorial: Saltgade 10, 2, Sal, Ribe 6760
Tel: 45 75 42 23 66
Email: red.ribe@ugeavisen.dk **Web site:** http://www.ugeavisen.dk/ribe
Freq: Weekly; **Circ:** 23548 Not Audited
Profile: Ugeavisen Ribe is a weekly local newspaper distributed in Ribe and its surroundings.
Language (s): Danish
COMMUNITY NEWSPAPER

Ugeavisen Ringkøbing
475908

Editorial: St. Blichersvej 5, Ringkøbing 6950
Tel: 45 99 75 73 99
Email: ringkoebing@bergske.dk **Web site:** http://midtjyskemedier.dk/kontakt.html#ugeavisser-ugeavisen%20ringk%C3%B8bing
Freq: Weekly; **Circ:** 15072 Publisher's Statement
Profile: Ugeavisen Ringkøbing is a weekly local newspaper in Ringkøbing.
Language (s): Danish
COMMUNITY NEWSPAPER

Ugeavisen Struer
435624

Editorial: Kastaniegarden, ostergade 7, 1. og 2. sal, Struer 7600 **Tel:** 45 96 84 22 00
Email: struer@bergske.dk **Web site:** http://ugeavisen.dk/omos/ugeavisenstruer
Freq: Weekly; **Circ:** 15023
Profile: Ugeavisen Struer is a weekly local newspaper distributed in Struer and its surroundings.
Language (s): Danish
COMMUNITY NEWSPAPER

Ugeavisen Svendborg
222600

Editorial: Sankt Nicolai Gade 3, Svendborg 5700
Tel: 45 62 21 73 21
Email: red@uas.dk **Web site:** http://ugeavisensvendborg.dk
Freq: Weekly; **Circ:** 32700 Not Audited
EDITOR IN CHIEF: Troels Mylenberg; **Redaktør:** Michael Thorbjørnsen
Profile: Ugeavisen Svendborg is a weekly local newspaper distributed in Svendborg and its surroundings.
Language (s): Danish
COMMUNITY NEWSPAPER

Ugeavisen Svenstrup
222604

Editorial: Godthabsvej 7, Svenstrup 9230
Tel: 45 98 38 14 77
Email: tekst@uge-avisen.net **Web site:** http://ugeavisensvenstrup.dk/
Freq: Weekly; **Circ:** 32695 Publisher's Statement
Profile: Ugeavisen Svenstrup is a weekly local newspaper distributed in Svenstrup and its surroundings.
Language (s): Danish
COMMUNITY NEWSPAPER

Ugeavisen Tistrup - Ølgod 222594
Editorial: Storegade 16-18, Ølgod 6870
Tel: 45 75 24 45 55
Email: red.oelgod@ugeavisen.dk **Web site:** http://ugeavisen.dk/omos/tistrupoelgod
Freq: Weekly; **Circ:** 11489 Not Audited
Profile: Ugeavisen Tistrup - Ølgod is a weekly local newspaper distributed in Ølgod and its surroundings.
Language (s): Danish
COMMUNITY NEWSPAPER

Ugeavisen Tønder 222602
Editorial: Lillegade 11, 1. sal, Tønder 6270
Tel: 45 74 72 47 11
Email: red.toender@ugeavisen.dk **Web site:** http://ugeavisen.dk/toender
Freq: Weekly; **Circ:** 27500 Not Audited
Profile: Ugeavisen Tønder is a local weekly newspaper, covering Tønder municipality.
Language (s): Danish
Ad Rate: Full Page Colour 12236.63
Currency: Denmark Kroner
COMMUNITY NEWSPAPER

Ugeavisen Varde 435559
Editorial: Radhusstræde 5, Varde 6800
Tel: 45 75 22 24 44
Email: red.varde@ugeavisen.dk **Web site:** http://www.ugeavisen.dk/varde
Freq: Weekly; **Circ:** 26304
Profile: Ugeavisen Varde is a weekly local newspaper distributed in Varde and its surroundings.
Language (s): Danish
COMMUNITY NEWSPAPER

Ugeavisen Vejen 435603
Editorial: Vestergade 2D, Vejen 6600
Tel: 45 75 36 00 22
Email: red.vejen@ugeavisen.dk **Web site:** http://ugeavisen.dk/vejen
Freq: Weekly; **Circ:** 26900
Profile: Weekly local newspaper distributed in Vejen, Brørup and Holsted.
Language (s): Danish
COMMUNITY NEWSPAPER

Ugeavisen Vejle 222597
Editorial: Vejle Amts Folkeblad, Bugattivej 8, Vejle 7100 **Tel:** 45 75 83 10 00
Email: redaktion@ugeavisenvejle.dk **Web site:** http://www.ugeavisenvejle.dk
Freq: Weekly; **Circ:** 71843 Not Audited
Profile: Ugeavisen Vejle is a weekly local newspaper distributed in Vejle and its surroundings.
Language (s): Danish
COMMUNITY NEWSPAPER

Ugebladet For Møn 222598
Editorial: Storegade 19B, Stege 4780
Tel: 45 55 81 40 34
Email: redaktion@ugebladet-for-moen.dk **Web site:** http://www.ugebladet-for-moen.dk
Freq: Weekly; **Circ:** 7630 Not Audited
Profile: Ugebladet For Møn is a weekly local newspaper distributed in Møn, Bogø, Nyord, Kalvehave and Langebæk.
Language (s): Danish
COMMUNITY NEWSPAPER

Ugebladet Hørsholm 435617
Owner: Politikens Lokalaviser A/S
Editorial: Horsholm Medie Center, Horsholm Midtpunkt 14, 1, Hørsholm 2970 **Tel:** 45 70 13 11 00
Email: redaktionen@ugebladet.dk **Web site:** http://hoersholm.lokalavisen.dk/
Freq: Weekly
Profile: Ugebladet Hørsholm is a local newspaper covering news from Hørshol, Rungsted, Vedbæk, Kokkedal, Nivå, Fredensborg and Humlebæk.
Language (s): Danish
COMMUNITY NEWSPAPER

Ugebladet Næstved 222601
Owner: Sjællandske Medier A/S
Editorial: Dania 38, Næstved 4700
Tel: 45 72 45 11 00
Email: ugebladet@sn.dk **Web site:** http://ugebladetnaestved.dk/
Freq: Weekly; **Circ:** 38212 Not Audited
Profile: Ugebladet Næstved is a local newspaper covering news from Næstved.
Language (s): Danish
COMMUNITY NEWSPAPER

Uge-Bladet Skanderborg 435887
Owner: Jysk Fynske Medier
Editorial: Adelgade 115, Skanderborg 8660
Tel: 45 86 52 01 44
Email: redaktion@uge-bladet.dk **Web site:** http://dinby.dk/ugebladet-skanderborg
Freq: Weekly; **Circ:** 29916 Not Audited
Profile: Uge-Bladet Skanderborg is a local newspaper covering news from Skanderborg.
Language (s): Danish
COMMUNITY NEWSPAPER

Ugebladet Sydsjælland 222593
Owner: Sjællandske Medier A/S
Editorial: Adelgade 70, Vordingborg 4760
Tel: 45 72 45 12 25
Email: vordingborg.red@sn.dk **Web site:** http://sn.dk/vordingborg
Freq: Weekly; **Circ:** 20115 Publisher's Statement
Profile: Ugebladet Sydsjælland is a local newspaper covering local news from Sydsjælland.
Language (s): Danish
COMMUNITY NEWSPAPER

Ugebladet Tinglev 222603
Editorial: Tværvejen 5, Tinglev 6360
Tel: 45 74 64 40 38
Email: mail@tinglev-bogtrykkeri.dk **Web site:** http://www.tinglev-bogtrykkeri.dk/ugebladet.php
Freq: Weekly; **Circ:** 7500 Not Audited
Profile: Ugebladet Tinglev is a weekly local newspaper distributed in Tinglev and its surroundings.
Language (s): Danish
COMMUNITY NEWSPAPER

Ugebladet Væstsjælland 222591
Owner: Nordvest Nyt
Editorial: Hong Centret, Centervej 33B, Holbæk 4270
Tel: 45 88 88 42 90
Email: hong.red@sn.dk **Web site:** http://sn.dk/ugebladetvestsjaelland
Freq: Weekly; **Circ:** 17347 Not Audited
Profile: Ugebladet Væstsjælland is a local newspaper covering local news from Vestsjælland.
Language (s): Danish
COMMUNITY NEWSPAPER

Uge-Nyt Fredensborg 222616
Owner: Politikens Lokalaviser
Editorial: Horsholm Midtpunkt 14, 1, Hørsholm 2970
Tel: 45 70 13 11 00
Email: redaktion@uge-nyt.dk **Web site:** http://www.uge-nyt.dk
Freq: Weekly; **Circ:** 18722 Publisher's Statement
Profile: Uge-Nyt Fredensborg is a local weekly newspaper in Fredensborg in Nordsjælland.
Language (s): Danish
COMMUNITY NEWSPAPER

Ugeposten Kibæk 222588
Editorial: Falkevej 4, Kibæk 6920 **Tel:** 45 97 17 11 22
Email: ugeposten@vbbt.dk **Web site:** http://videbaekspjaldavis.dk/index.php
Freq: Weekly; **Circ:** 11212 Not Audited
Profile: Ugeposten Kibæk is a weekly newspaper covering local news in the region.
Language (s): Danish
Ad Rate: Full Page Colour 6659.50
Currency: Denmark Kroner
COMMUNITY NEWSPAPER

Ugeposten Skjern 222586
Owner: Jysk Fynske Medier P/S
Editorial: Bergs plads 5, Skjern 6900
Tel: 45 96 81 53 13
Email: redaktion@dagbladetringskjern.dk **Web site:** http://dinby.dk/ugeposten-skjern
Freq: Weekly; **Circ:** 18200 Publisher's Statement
Profile: Ugeposten Skjern is a local newspaper covering Skjern.
Language (s): Danish
COMMUNITY NEWSPAPER

Valby Bladet 222569
Editorial: Gammel Kongevej 60, 16. sal, Frederiksberg C 1850 **Tel:** 45 33 88 88 88
Email: red@valbybladet.dk **Web site:** https://www.valbybladet.dk/
Freq: Weekly; **Circ:** 41000 Not Audited
Profile: Valby Bladet is a weekly newspaper containing local news from Valby and Kgs.
Language (s): Danish
Ad Rate: Full Page Colour 20054.50
Currency: Denmark Kroner
COMMUNITY NEWSPAPER

Vamdrup Ugeblad 222571
Editorial: ostergade 7, Vamdrup 6580
Tel: 45 75 58 12 00
Email: redaktion@vamdrup-ugeblad.dk **Web site:** http://www.vamdrup-ugeblad.dk
Freq: Weekly; **Circ:** 15932 Not Audited
Profile: Vamdrup Ugeblad is a weekly local newspaper distributed in Vamdrup and its suroundings.
Language (s): Danish
COMMUNITY NEWSPAPER

Vanløse Bladet 435602
Editorial: Gammel Kongevej 60, 16. sal, Frederiksberg C 1850 **Tel:** 45 33 88 88 88
Email: red@vanlosebladet.dk **Web site:** https://www.vanlosebladet.dk/
Freq: Weekly; **Circ:** 15038
Profile: Vanløse Bladet is a weekly local newspaper distributed in the district of Vanløse, Copenhagen.
Language (s): Danish
COMMUNITY NEWSPAPER

Vejgaard Avis 222584
Owner: Nordjyske Medier A/S
Editorial: Langagervej 1, Aalborg 9220
Tel: 45 99 35 35 35
Email: vejgaard@nordjyske.dk **Web site:** http://www.vejgaardavis.dk/
Freq: Weekly; **Circ:** 28588 Not Audited
Editor in Chief: Per Lyngby
Profile: Vejgaard Avis is a local newspaper covering news from Vejgaard.
Language (s): Danish
COMMUNITY NEWSPAPER

Vejle Amts Folkeblad 282477
Owner: Jyske Medier A/S
Editorial: Bugattivej 8, Vejle 7100 **Tel:** 45 75 85 77 88
Email: vaf@vafo.dk **Web site:** http://vafo.dk/
Circ: 10650
Redaktionschef: Mogens G. Madsen
Profile: Vejle Amts Folkeblad is a daily newspaper covering local news from Vejle. The main editorial office is in Vejle, but they also have local editorial offices in Billund, Børkop, Egtved, Give, Hedensted, Jelling, Juelsminde, Ikast-Brand and Tørring.
Language (s): Danish
COMMUNITY NEWSPAPER

Vendelbo Posten 222568
Editorial: Frederikshavnvej 81, Hjørring 9800
Tel: 45 99 24 50 60
Email: redaktion.vendelboposten@nordjyske.dk **Web site:** http://vendelboposten.dk/
Freq: Weekly; **Circ:** 32887 Not Audited
Profile: Vendelbo Posten is a weekly local newspaper distributed in Vendelbo and its surroundings.
Language (s): Danish
COMMUNITY NEWSPAPER

Vesthimmerlands Avis 222668
Editorial: Borgergade 17, Aalestrup 9620
Tel: 45 98 64 12 55
Email: redaktionen@vesthimmerland.dk **Web site:** http://www.vesthimmerlandsavis.dk
Freq: Weekly; **Circ:** 10432 Not Audited
Ansvarshavende redaktør: Thorkil Christensen
Profile: Vesthimmerlands Avis is a weekly local newspaper distributed in Aalestrup and its surroundings.
Language (s): Danish
COMMUNITY NEWSPAPER

Vesthimmerlands Folkeblad 222672
Editorial: Blekingevej 13, Løgstør 9670
Tel: 45 98 67 37 11
Email: per.eskildsen@nordjyske.dk **Web site:** http://vesthimmerlandsfolkeblad.dk/
Freq: Weekly; **Circ:** 9600 Not Audited
Profile: Vesthimmerlands Folkeblad is a weekly local newspaper distributed in Løgstør and its surroundings.
Language (s): Danish
COMMUNITY NEWSPAPER

Viborg Nyt 222673
Editorial: Vesterbrogade 8, Viborg 8800
Tel: 45 89 27 63 00
Email: viborgnyt@bergske.dk **Web site:** http://dinby.dk/viborg-nyt
Freq: Weekly; **Circ:** 41630 Not Audited
EDITOR: Jacob Kaas
Profile: Viborg Nyt is a weekly newspaper covering local news in the region.
Language (s): Danish
Ad Rate: Full Page Colour 11352.00
Currency: Denmark Kroner
COMMUNITY NEWSPAPER

Viborg Stifts Folkeblad 158393
Owner: Jysk Fynske Medier P/S
Editorial: Vesterbrogade 8, Viborg 8800
Tel: 45 89 27 63 00
Email: viborg@bergske.dk **Web site:** http://www.viborg-folkeblad.dk
Circ: 7474
Editor in Chief: Lars Norup
Profile: Viborg Stifts Folkeblad is a local newspaper covering news from Viborg.
Language (s): Danish
COMMUNITY NEWSPAPER

Videbæk Spjald Avis 435607
Editorial: Falkevej 4, Videbæk 6920
Tel: 45 97 17 11 22
Email: post@vbbt.dk **Web site:** http://videbaekspjaldavis.dk/
Freq: Weekly; **Circ:** 15900
Profile: Videbæk Spjald Avis is a weekly local newspaper distributed in Videbæk and its surroundings.
Language (s): Danish
Ad Rate: Full Page Colour 7668.00
Currency: Denmark Kroner
COMMUNITY NEWSPAPER

Villabyerne 222674
Owner: Politikens Lokalaviser A/S.
Editorial: Ordrupvej 101 3. sal, Charlottenlund 2920
Tel: 45 70 13 11 00
Email: redaktion@villabyerne.dk **Web site:** http://gentofte.lokalavisen.dk/
Freq: 2 Times/Week; **Circ:** 32285 Not Audited
Profile: Villabyerne is a newspaper covering local and regional news, sports and culture from Gentofte, Hellerup and Charlottenlund.
Language (s): Danish
COMMUNITY NEWSPAPER

Vinderup Avis 222676
Editorial: Sondergade 20, Vinderup 7830
Tel: 45 99 12 83 99
Email: vinderup@bergske.dk **Web site:** http://ugeavisen.dk/omos/vinderupavis
Freq: Weekly; **Circ:** 8600 Publisher's Statement
EDITOR IN CHIEF: Hans Krabbe
Profile: Vinderup Avis is a weekly local newspaper distributed in Vinderup and its surroundings.
Language (s): Danish
COMMUNITY NEWSPAPER

Vollsmose Avisen 597059
Editorial: Vollsmose Sekretariatet, Vollsmose Allé 10, Odense Nø 5240 **Tel:** 45 30 70 29 86
Email: avis@vollsmose.dk **Web site:** http://www.vollsmose.dk/VollsmoseSekretariatet/Vollsmose-Avisen.aspx
Freq: Bi-Weekly; **Circ:** 17000 Publisher's Statement
Profile: Vollsmose Avisen is a newspaper distributed to all households in Vollmose. News and articles about activities and events, competitions and debate from the district.
Language (s): Danish
COMMUNITY NEWSPAPER

Vort Landboblad 222660
Owner: Aars Avis A/S
Editorial: Himmerlandsgade 150, Aars 9600
Tel: 45 98 62 17 11
Email: redaktion@aarsavis.dk **Web site:** http://www.aarsavis.dk/index.php?id=vl
Freq: Weekly; **Circ:** 8000 Not Audited
Editor: Thorkil Christensen
Profile: Vort Landboblad is a newspaper distributed to farms in Vesthimmerland and parts of Han Herred. The paper is a sister newspaper to Aars Avis and is being distributed together in the area where Aars Avis is published. Vort Landboblad is also referred to as Landbrugsnyt.
Language (s): Danish
COMMUNITY NEWSPAPER

Westend & Omegn 435495
Editorial: Verdens Mindste Bladhus, Sondergade 33, Ærøskøbing 5970 **Tel:** 45 25 89 79 43
Email: bladhus@verdensmindste.dk **Web site:** http://www.verdensmindste.dk/Verdens_Mindste_Bladhus.html
Freq: Weekly; **Circ:** 6000
EDITOR IN CHIEF: Rie Holdum
Profile: Westend & Omegn is a local weekly newspaper distributed in Westend and its surroundings. Published by Verdens Mindste Stormagasin.
Language (s): Danish
COMMUNITY NEWSPAPER

Dominica

Time Difference: GMT -4
National Telephone Code: 1 767
Continent: The Americas
Capital: Roseau

Community Newspaper

The Chronicle 224348
Owner: The Chronicle Company
Tel: 767 4486601
Email: thechronicle@cwdom.dm **Web site:** http://www.avirtualdominica.com/thechronicle/index.html
Freq: Weekly; **Circ:** 3300 Not Audited
General Manager: Franklin A. Baron; **Editor:** Gwen Evelyn
Profile: The Chronicle is a weekly newspaper covering business, statistics, travel and tourism, arts, culture and lifestyle, photography, outdoor activities, events, geology, history and maps.
Language (s): English
Ad Rate: Full Page Mono 5.00
Ad Rate: Full Page Colour 645.00
Currency: United States Dollars
COMMUNITY NEWSPAPER

The Sun 230280
Owner: The Sun Inc.
Editorial: 50 Independence Street, Roseau
Tel: 767 4484744
Email: acsun@cwdom.dm **Web site:** http://www.sundominica.com
Freq: Weekly; **Circ:** 35000 Not Audited
Editor: Charles James
Profile: The Sun is a weekly newspaper featuring national and international news.
Language (s): English
Ad Rate: Full Page Mono 6.00
Currency: United States Dollars
COMMUNITY NEWSPAPER

Dominican Republic

Time Difference: GMT -4
National Telephone Code: 1 809
Continent: The Americas
Capital: Santo Domingo

Newspapers

Barrigaverde 400236
Owner: Editora Barrigaverde
Editorial: C/ Thomas F. Reilly No. 45, Villa Alejandra, San Juan De La Maguana **Tel:** 809 5574434
Email: editora@barrigaverde.net **Web site:** http://www.barrigaverde.net
Freq: Daily
Profile: Covers general news of the Dominican Republic. Includes sports, politic, economy and foreign affairs.
Language (s): Spanish
DAILY NEWSPAPER

El Caribe 156990
Owner: Multimedios del Caribe
Editorial: Calle Defillo No. 4, Los Prados, Santo Domingo **Tel:** 809 6838100
Email: redaccionweb@elcaribe.com.do **Web site:** http://www.elcaribe.com.do
Freq: Daily; **Circ:** 50000 Not Audited
Editor in Chief: Hector Marte; **Director:** Manuel Quiroz
Profile: Newspaper covering national and international news, politics, economics, finance, business, culture and sport.
Language (s): Spanish
DAILY NEWSPAPER

El Dia 400231
Owner: Editora Hoy
Editorial: Av. San Martin 236, Distr. Nacional, Santo Domingo **Tel:** 1 809 565-5581
Email: josemonegro@verizon.net.do **Web site:** http://www.eldia.com.do
Freq: Daily; **Circ:** 100000 Not Audited
Director: Rafael Molina Morillo; **Editor in Chief:** Franklin Puello
Profile: Newspaper covering national and international news, includes features on sport, women's interest and entertainment. Distributed Monday through Friday.
Language (s): Spanish
DAILY NEWSPAPER

Diario Libre 161017
Owner: Omnimedia Editorial AA
Editorial: Av. Abraham Lincoln esq, Max Henríquez Urena, Apartado 20313 Piantini, Santo Domingo
Tel: 1 809 476-7200
Web site: http://www.diariolibre.com
Freq: Daily; **Circ:** 115000 Not Audited
Editor in Chief: José Maria Reyes; **Editor:** Bienvenido Rojas
Profile: Newspaper covering national and international news, politics, economics, finance, business, culture and sport.
Language (s): Spanish
DAILY NEWSPAPER

Hoy 400232
Owner: Editora Hoy
Editorial: Av. San Martin 236, Distrito Nacional, Santo Domingo **Tel:** 809 5655581
Email: periodicohoy@hoy.com.do **Web site:** http://www.hoy.com.do
Freq: Daily; **Circ:** 32500 Not Audited
Editor in Chief: Marien Capitán
Profile: National newspaper covering news and current-affairs. Includes economy, business, ecology, sports and health.
Language (s): Spanish
DAILY NEWSPAPER

La Información 156991
Owner: Nueva Editora La Información
Editorial: Calle Del Sol No. 3, Santiago
Tel: 1 809 581-1915
Web site: http://lainformacion.com.do
Freq: Daily; **Circ:** 26500 Not Audited
Editor in Chief: Servio Cepeda; **Director:** Fernando Pérez Memén; **General Manager:** José Souffront
Profile: Daily newspaper in Dominican Republic covering general news and topics related to politics, economics, finance, business, culture and sport.
Language (s): Spanish
DAILY NEWSPAPER

Listín Diario 400235
Owner: Editora Listín Diario
Editorial: Paseo de los Periodistas 52, Ensanche Miraflores, Santo Domingo **Tel:** 809 6866688
Web site: http://www.listindiario.com.do
Freq: Daily; **Circ:** 70000 Not Audited
Director: Antonio Gil; **Editor in Chief:** Marisabel Sol de Vila
Profile: Newspaper covering national and international news and current-affairs, includes sport, events and fashion.
Language (s): Spanish
DAILY NEWSPAPER

El Nacional 400233
Owner: Publicaciones Ahora
Editorial: Av. San Martin 236, Distr. Nacional, Santo Domingo **Tel:** 809 5655581
Email: redaccion@elnacional.com.do **Web site:** http://www.elnacional.com.do
Freq: Daily; **Circ:** 70000 Not Audited
Director: Rhadames Goméz Pepín; **Editor in Chief:** Hector Minaya
Profile: National newspaper covering general news and current-affairs in Dominican Republic.
Language (s): Spanish
DAILY NEWSPAPER

El Nuevo Diario 400234
Owner: Editora El Nuevo Diario
Editorial: Av. Francia No. 41, Santo Domingo
Tel: 1 809 687-7450
Email: redaccionnd@gmail.com **Web site:** http://www.elnuevodiario.com.do/app/frontpage.aspx
Freq: Daily
Director: Cosette Bonnelly; **Editor in Chief:** Ramiro Estrella; **Director:** Persio Maldonado
Profile: Newspaper covering general news and current-affairs. Includes politics, the economy, legal issues, sport and fashion.
Language (s): Spanish
DAILY NEWSPAPER

Ecuador

Time Difference: GMT -5
National Telephone Code: 593
Continent: The Americas
Capital: Quito

Newspapers

El Comercio 156992
Owner: Grupo El Comercio
Editorial: Avenida Pedro Vicente Maldonado 11515, Quito **Tel:** 593 2 267-0999
Email: redaccion@elcomercio.com **Web site:** http://www.elcomercio.com
Freq: Daily; **Circ:** 70000 Not Audited
Editor: Gonzalo Maldonado; **Director:** Guadalupe Mantilla; **Editor:** Martin Pallares
Profile: Periódico nacional se centra en las noticias nacionales e internacionales, la política, los negocios, el entretenimiento y los deportes. National newspaper focusing on national and international news, politics, business, entertainment and sports.
Language (s): Spanish
DAILY NEWSPAPER

Diario El Nacional 734728
Owner: Graficos Orenses C.A.
Editorial: Sucre 1222 entre Guayas y Ayacucho, Ciudad Machala, Quito **Tel:** 593 7 2930375
Email: elnacional@elnacional.ec **Web site:** http://www.elnacional.ec/es
Freq: Daily
Editor: Jacinto Castro; **General Manager:** Jorge Castro; **Editor:** Igna Sanjinés
Language (s): Spanish
DAILY NEWSPAPER

Diario Expreso 734742
Owner: Graficos Nacionales S.A.
Editorial: Av. Carlos Julio Arosemena, Km 2½, frente al Coliseo Granasa, Guayaquil **Tel:** 593 4 2201100
Email: cartas@granasa.com.ec **Web site:** http://www.diario-expreso.com
Editor: Guillermo Lizarzaburo
DAILY NEWSPAPER

Diario Extra 734860
Owner: Graficos Nacionales S.A.
Editorial: Av. Carlos Julio Arosemena Km. 2.5 y Av. Las Monjas, Guayaquil **Tel:** 593 4 2201100
Email: agenciacentenario@granasa.com.ec **Web site:** http://www.diario-extra.com/
Freq: Daily
Editor: Henry Holguin; **Editor in Chief:** Manuel Yepez
Profile: Diario Extra is a national newspaper that covers national news, politics, sports, and entertainment.
Language (s): Spanish
DAILY NEWSPAPER

Diario La Prensa 734873
Editorial: Garcia Moreno 2340 y Primera Constituyente, Riobamba (chimborazo)
Tel: 593 3 2967855
Email: direccion@laprensa.com.ec **Web site:** http://www.laprensa.com.ec/
Freq: Daily
Editor: Carlos Chimborazo; **Editor:** Diego Vallejo
Language (s): Spanish
DAILY NEWSPAPER

Diario Super 734740
Editorial: Av. Domingo Comin, entre calle 11 y Ernesto Alban, Guayaquil **Tel:** 593 4 2324460
Email: redaccion@super.com.ec **Web site:** http://www.super.com.ec
Freq: Daily
News Editor: Monica Camacho; **Editor:** Victor Vera
Language (s): Spanish
DAILY NEWSPAPER

Ecos de Quevedo 734725
Email: diarioecosdequevedo@hotmail.com
Freq: Daily
General Manager: Jose Laborde; **News Editor:** Victor Laborde; **Editor:** Lizzeth Rodriguez
Language (s): Spanish
DAILY NEWSPAPER

La Hora (Edición Nacional) 160832
Owner: Editorial Minotauro SA
Editorial: Panamericana Norte Kilometro 3 1/2 y Nazarett, Quito **Tel:** 593 2 247 5724
Web site: http://www.lahora.com.ec
Freq: Daily; **Circ:** 120000 Not Audited
Director: Nicolas Kingman Riofrio; **General Editor:** Juana López S.; **Editor:** Wilmer Molina; **Editor:** Roque Rivas
Profile: Newspaper covering national and international news, politics, economics, finance, business, culture and sport.
Language (s): Spanish
DAILY NEWSPAPER

El Norte 734729
Editorial: Av. Juan Jose Flores 1155 y Rafael Rosales, Ibarra (imbabura) **Tel:** 593 6 2643873
Web site: http://www.elnorte.ec
Freq: Daily
News Editor: Carla Aguas; **General Manager:** Patricio Perez
Language (s): Spanish
DAILY NEWSPAPER

Opinion 734881
Editorial: Av. 25 de junio Km 1.5 via a pasaje, Machala (el Oro) **Tel:** 593 7 2982732
Email: subdireccion@diariopinion.com **Web site:** http://www.diariopinion.com
Freq: Daily
Editor: Luis Tovar
Language (s): Spanish
DAILY NEWSPAPER

El Telegrafo 734218
Editorial: 10 de Agosto 601 y Boyaca, Guayaquil
Tel: 593 4 2328814
Web site: http://www.telegrafo.com.ec
Freq: Daily
International News Editor: Diana Auz; **Editor:** Nestor Espinoza
Language (s): Spanish
DAILY NEWSPAPER

Ultimas Noticias 735393
Owner: Grupo el Comercio
Editorial: Av. P. Vicente Maldonado 11515 y el Tablon, Quito **Tel:** 593 2 2672870
Email: mivoz@ultimasnoticias.ec **Web site:** http://www.ultimasnoticias.ec
Freq: Daily
Editor in Chief: Carlos Mora
Language (s): Spanish
DAILY NEWSPAPER

El Universo 157200
Owner: El Universo
Editorial: Avenida Domingo Comin y Calle 11, Avenida Ernesto Alban, Guayaguil (guayas)
Tel: 593 4 249-0000
Email: redaccion@eluniverso.com **Web site:** http://www.eluniverso.com
Freq: Daily; **Circ:** 133046 Not Audited
Editor: Gustavo Cortez; **New Media Manager:** Nicolas Pérez
Profile: El Universo is a national newspaper covering national and international news, politics, economics, finance, business, culture and sport.
Language (s): Spanish
DAILY NEWSPAPER

News Service/Syndicate

Agencia Latinoamericana de Información 407763
Editorial: 12 de Octubre N18-24, Oficina 503, Quito
Tel: 593 2 250-5074
Email: info@alainet.org **Web site:** http://www.alainet.org
Editor: Sally Burch; **Director:** Osvaldo León
Language (s): Spanish
NEWS SERVICE/SYNDICATE

Egypt

Time Difference: GMT +2
National Telephone Code: 20
Continent: Africa
Capital: Cairo

Newspapers

Al Ahali 440476
Owner: Al Tajamu Party
Editorial: 1, Karim Al Dawla Street, Talaat Harb Avenue, Cairo **Tel:** 20 2 2579 1628
Email: cairo680@yahoo.com **Web site:** http://www.alahalygate.com
Freq: Weekly; **Circ:** 55000 Publisher's Statement
Editor in Chief: Amina Al Nakash; **Advertising Manager:** Adel Bakr; **Editor:** Abdul Latif Wahba
Profile: Al Ahali is a weekly Arabic newspaper covering national and international news, business and sport. It launched in 1978 and is published on Wednesdays.
Language (s): Arabic
Ad Rate: Full Page Mono 60000.00
Currency: Egypt Pounds
DAILY NEWSPAPER

Al Ahram 156799
Owner: Al Ahram Establishment
Editorial: Al Ahram Building, Al Gala' Street, Cairo 11511 **Tel:** 20 2 2770 3100
Email: websiteahram@hotmail.com **Web site:** http://www.ahram.org.eg
Freq: Daily; **Circ:** 1000000 Rate Card
Head of Foreign News: Sherif Abdeen; **Advertising Manager:** Mohammad Al Najjar; **News Editor:** Hanan Hajaj
Profile: Al Ahram is a broadsheet-sized Arabic newspaper covering local and international news, current affairs, politics, business and sports. The daily newspaper was launched in 1876 and publishes an Egypt edition for domestic distribution and a Pan Arab edition distributed in the rest of the Arab world. Al Sayarat, a tabloid-sized motoring supplement, is issued with the newspaper on Fridays.
Language (s): Arabic
Ad Rate: Full Page Mono 33048.00
Ad Rate: Full Page Colour 41208.00
Currency: United States Dollars
DAILY NEWSPAPER

Al Ahram Al-Masaa'i 360230
Owner: Al Ahram Establishment
Editorial: Al Ahram Building, Al Gala'a Street, Cairo 11511 **Tel:** 20 2 2578 6080
Email: press5555514@yahoo.com **Web site:** http://massai.ahram.org.eg
Freq: Daily; **Circ:** 218541
Advertising Manager: Abdelhamid Abo Al Fadl
Profile: Al Ahram Al-Masaa'i (The Evening Pyramid) is an evening newspaper covering local and international news, current affairs, culture, sport, business and finance. It was first published in January 1991.
Language (s): Arabic
Ad Rate: Full Page Mono 6032.00
Ad Rate: Full Page Colour 7180.00
Currency: United States Dollars
DAILY NEWSPAPER

Al Ahram Hebdo 224307
Owner: Al Ahram Establishment
Editorial: Al Ahram Building, Al Gala'a Street, Cairo 11511 **Tel:** 20 2 2770 4310
Email: hebdo@ahram.org.eg **Web site:** http://hebdo.ahram.org.eg
Freq: Weekly; **Circ:** 79781 Rate Card
Advertising Manager: Mohamed El Dewy; **Editor in Chief:** Fouad Mansour; **Head of Foreign News:** Abeer Taleb
Profile: Al Ahram Hebdo is a weekly, tabloid-sized French newspaper covering news and current affairs. The newspaper launched in September 1994 and aims to communicate the Egyptian view on regional and international affairs. It is published on Wednesdays.
Language (s): French
Ad Rate: Full Page Colour 1532.00
Currency: United States Dollars
DAILY NEWSPAPER

Al Ahram Weekly 225872
Owner: Al Ahram Establishment
Editorial: Al Ahram Building, Al Gala'a Street, Cairo 11511 **Tel:** 20 2 2770 5373
Email: weekly@ahram.org.eg **Web site:** http://weekly.ahram.org.eg
Freq: Weekly; **Circ:** 86850 Rate Card
Editor in Chief: Galal Nassar
Profile: Al Ahram Weekly is an English newspaper covering local and international news, business, sport and culture. It launched in 1991 and is published on Thursdays.
Language (s): English
Ad Rate: Full Page Mono 5550.00
Ad Rate: Full Page Colour 7180.00
Currency: United States Dollars
DAILY NEWSPAPER

Al Akhbar 156800
Owner: Dar Akhbar El Yom
Editorial: 6 & 7 Al Sahafa Street, Cairo
Tel: 20 2 2578 2500
Email: arabicprint_akhbar@yahoo.com **Web site:** http://www.akhbarelyom.com
Freq: Daily; **Circ:** 1319700 Publisher's Statement
PR Manager: Waleed Fawzy
Profile: Al Akhbar (The News) is an Arabic newspaper covering national and international news, current affairs, politics, business and sports. It launched in 1952 and is published daily, except Saturdays.
Language (s): Arabic
Ad Rate: Full Page Mono 35885.00
Ad Rate: Full Page Colour 45159.00
Currency: United States Dollars
DAILY NEWSPAPER

Al Akhbar Al Masae 340718
Owner: Dar Akhbar El Yom
Editorial: Sahafa Street, Cairo **Tel:** 20 2 2794 0266
Email: msaeya2011@yahoo.com **Web site:** http://www.almsaeya.com
Freq: Daily; **Circ:** 80000 Publisher's Statement
Office Manager: Ahmed Fathy; **Advertising Manager:** Ahmad Shawqi; **Head of Foreign News:** Mohammed Yousef
Profile: Al Akhbar Al Masae is a daily newspaper covering national and international news, politics, business, features and sport. It was first published in 2006.
Language (s): Arabic
DAILY NEWSPAPER

Akhbar Al Riada 341329
Owner: Dar Akhbar El Yom
Editorial: 6 Al Sahafa Street, Cairo
Tel: 20 2 2578 2500
Email: akhbarriada@yahoo.com **Web site:** http://reyada.akhbarelyom.com
Freq: Weekly; **Circ:** 316700 Publisher's Statement
Editor in Chief: Ayman Badra
Profile: Akhbar Al Riada (Sports News) is a weekly, tabloid-sized newspaper covering local and international sport. It launched in 1989 and is published on Tuesdays.
Language (s): Arabic
Ad Rate: Full Page Colour 2500.00
Currency: United States Dollars
DAILY NEWSPAPER

Akhbar El-Yom 156801
Owner: Dar Akhbar El Yom
Editorial: 6 & 7 Al Sahafa Street, Cairo
Tel: 20 2 2578 2900
Email: ahmed_mamdouh_83@yahoo.com **Web site:** http://www.akhbarelyom.com
Freq: Weekly; **Circ:** 1622850 Publisher's Statement
Editor in Chief: Sayed Al Naggar; **Head of News:** Ahmad Hashim
Profile: Akhbar El-Yom is a weekly Arabic newspaper covering national and international news, current affairs, politics, business and sport. It was first published in November 1944 and is issued on Saturdays.
Language (s): Arabic
Ad Rate: Full Page Mono 41126.00
Ad Rate: Full Page Colour 51610.00
Currency: United States Dollars
DAILY NEWSPAPER

Alam Al Borsa 559981
Owner: Alam Al Borsa
Editorial: 5th Floor, 39, Ragheb Street, Cairo
Tel: 20 100 692 8075
Email: ebraheem.3ead@gmail.com
Freq: Weekly; **Circ:** 30000 Publisher's Statement
Editor In Chief: Samer Tantawe
Profile: Alam Al Borsa is a weekly Arabic newspaper covering business, investment, finance, banking and stock markets. It launched in 2007 and is published on Sundays.
Language (s): Arabic
DAILY NEWSPAPER

Al Alam Al Youm 362820
Owner: Good News International Corporation
Editorial: 8 Abdul Qawi Shamseddin Street, Dokki, Cairo **Tel:** 20 2 3303 8885
Email: alalamelyoum@alalamelyoum.com **Web site:** http://www.alalamelyoum.com
Freq: Daily; **Circ:** 164070 Rate Card
Advertising Manager: Ayman Al Segeny; **Editor:** Nagwa Taha
Profile: Al Alam Al Youm (The World Today) is a daily newspaper covering the business sector in Egypt, the Middle East and internationally. Coverage includes stock market reports, finance and international business trends. It launched in 1991 and is aimed at business executives in Egypt. Regular features in the newspaper include: Industry & Technology (Sat), Bonouk Al Youm (Sun), Etisalat Al Youm (Mon), Business Al Youm (Tues), Alam El Etisalat (Tues), Tourism (Wed), Medical (Wed), Automotive (Thurs), Real Estate (Thurs), Tele-Business (Thurs) and Computer World (daily, except Mondays).
Language (s): Arabic
Ad Rate: Full Page Mono 77520.00
Ad Rate: Full Page Colour 85680.00
Currency: Egypt Pounds
DAILY NEWSPAPER

Alam Almal 483950
Owner: Alam Almal
Editorial: 3rd Floor, 13, Tobji Street, Giza
Tel: 20 2 3337 3855
Email: a.ali3585@yahoo.com **Web site:** http://www.alamalmal.net
Freq: Weekly; **Circ:** 20000 Publisher's Statement
Advertising Manager: Samia Abdul Fattah; **Editor in Chief:** Ashraf Al Hamdi; **PR Manager:** Abdul Azim Ali; **Public Relations Officer:** Eman Ibrahim; **Editor:** May Saoudi
Profile: Alam Almal (The World of Money) is a weekly Arabic newspaper covering news, politics, business, industry, agriculture, motoring, tourism, telecommunications and aviation. It launched in 2006 and is published on Sundays.
Language (s): Arabic
DAILY NEWSPAPER

Alaqaria 652746
Owner: Al Aqaria
Editorial: 11, Al Mahrousa Street, Al Mohandiseen, Giza **Tel:** 20 2 3302 2891
Email: aleqaria@yahoo.com **Web site:** http://www.aleqaria.com.eg
Freq: Weekly; **Circ:** 100000 Publisher's Statement
Profile: Alaqaria is a 16-page weekly Arabic newspaper focusing on real estate and property in the Arab world, as well as covering business, finance and banking. It launched in 2009 and is published on Sundays.
Language (s): Arabic
Ad Rate: Full Page Mono 80000.00
Ad Rate: Full Page Colour 139000.00
Currency: Egypt Pounds
DAILY NEWSPAPER

Alborsa 542897
Owner: Business News Co
Editorial: 12, Haroun Street, Dokki, Giza, Cairo
Tel: 20 2 3748 6853
Email: news@alborsanews.com **Web site:** http://www.alborsanews.com
Freq: Daily; **Circ:** 90000 Rate Card
Profile: Alborsa is a 16-page daily business newspaper covering economics, real estate, banking, energy, insurance, stock markets, IT, motoring, entertainment and tourism. It launched in May 2008, and is aimed at business executives.
Language (s): Arabic
Ad Rate: Full Page Mono 82500.00
Ad Rate: Full Page Colour 99000.00
Currency: Egypt Pounds
DAILY NEWSPAPER

Al Anbaa Al Dawlia 538146
Owner: Al Anbaa Al Dawlia
Editorial: 97, Al Zomor Street, Cairo
Tel: 20 2 3775 9785
Email: alanbaaaldawliaa@yahoo.com
Freq: Weekly; **Circ:** 200000 Publisher's Statement
PR Manager: Mohamed Abdelkader; **Editor in Chief:** Ahmed Mahfouz
Profile: Al Anbaa Al Dawlia (International News) is a weekly Arabic newspaper covering national and international news, politics, economics, business, society, sport and culture. It launched in 2006 and is published on Tuesdays.
Language (s): Arabic
DAILY NEWSPAPER

Aqidati 375589
Owner: Dar Al Tahrir Publishing & Printing House
Editorial: Al Gomhuriya Building, 111-115 Ramses Street, Cairo **Tel:** 20 2 2578 1777
Email: abnoody@hotmail.com **Web site:** http://www.aqidati.net.eg
Freq: Weekly; **Circ:** 60000 Publisher's Statement
News Editor: Houssam Wahballah
Profile: Aqidati (My Faith) is a weekly Islamic newspaper. It launched in 1992 and is published on Tuesdays.
Language (s): Arabic
DAILY NEWSPAPER

Al Araby 538140
Owner: Al Nasiry Democratic Arab Party
Editorial: PO Box 38, 30 Yaqoub Street, Cairo
Tel: 20 2 2796 1017
Email: alarabyorg@yahoo.com
Freq: Weekly; **Circ:** 40000 Publisher's Statement
Editor In Chief: Magdy Al Basyouni; **Advertising Manager:** Sayed Dimirdash; **General Manager:** Ahmad Hassan
Profile: Al Araby is a weekly Arabic newspaper covering international and national news, politics, sports, business and entertainment. The newspaper is published by the Al Nasiry Democratic Arab Party. It launched in 1993 and is published on Sundays.
Language (s): Arabic
DAILY NEWSPAPER

Arrai 508705
Owner: Dar Al Tahrir Publishing & Printing House
Editorial: Al Gomhuriah Building, 111-115 Ramses Street, Cairo **Tel:** 20 2 2578 3333
Email: arrai8@hotmail.com **Web site:** http://www.arrai.org
Freq: Weekly; **Circ:** 20000 Publisher's Statement
Editor in Chief: Mahmoud Hapsa; **Advertising Manager:** Lotfy Shaker
Profile: Arrai (Point of View) is a weekly Arabic newspaper covering national news and current affairs, politics, business and culture. It launched in 1990 and is published on Sundays.
Language (s): Arabic
Ad Rate: Full Page Mono 20000.00
Currency: Egypt Pounds
DAILY NEWSPAPER

Al Dostour 500516
Owner: Al Dostor Press & Media
Editorial: 9, Rostom Street, Garden City, Cairo
Tel: 20 2 2793 0124
Email: info@dostor.org **Web site:** http://www.dostor.org
Freq: Daily; **Circ:** 220000 Publisher's Statement
Profile: Al Dostour is a daily Arabic newspaper covering news, politics, sports and entertainment. It was first published in 1995.
Language (s): Arabic
Ad Rate: Full Page Mono 133056.00
Ad Rate: Full Page Colour 166320.00
Currency: Egypt Pounds
DAILY NEWSPAPER

The Egyptian Gazette 156625
Owner: Dar Al Tahrir Publishing & Printing House
Editorial: Office 23, 11th Floor, Al Gomhuriya Building, Cairo **Tel:** 20 2 2578 4646
Email: editor.in.chief@hotmail.com
Freq: Daily; **Circ:** 50000 Rate Card
Profile: The Egyptian Gazette is a daily English newspaper covering news, politics, business, sport, health, IT, culture and arts. The newspaper, called the Egyptian Mail on Tuesdays, is aimed at businessmen, foreign residents, members of the diplomatic corps, students and officials. It was first published from Alexandria on 26 January 1880 as a four-page weekly tabloid, before moving to Cairo in February 1938. Just before the Second World War, ownership of the paper passed to Societe Orientale de Publicite, which had launched the daily Egyptian Mail in 1914.Following the end of the war, and the departure of the bulk of British troops, the Egyptian Mail became a weekly, appearing on Tuesdays when The Egyptian Gazette is not published, which continues today. Following the Egyptian Revolution in 1952, ownership of the paper was ceded to its current owners, Dar Al Tahrir.
Language (s): English
Ad Rate: Full Page Mono 18000.00
Ad Rate: Full Page Colour 22400.00
Currency: United States Dollars
DAILY NEWSPAPER

Egyptian Mail 224431
Owner: Dar Al Tahrir Publishing & Printing House
Editorial: Office 23, 11th Floor, Al Gomhuriya Building, Cairo **Tel:** 20 2 2579 2072
Email: editor.in.chief@hotmail.com **Web site:** http://www.egyptiangazette.net
Freq: Weekly; **Circ:** 50000 Publisher's Statement
Editor in Chief: Mohammad Kassim; **Head of News:** Mohamed Salama
Profile: Egyptian Mail is a weekly newspaper covering news, politics, business, sport, health, IT, culture and arts. The newspaper is published on Tuesdays in place of The Egyptian Gazette, and is aimed at businessmen, foreign residents, members of the diplomatic corps, students and officials. The newspaper was launched as a daily in 1914 by Societe Orientale de Publicite, which acquired ownership of The Egyptian Gazette shortly before the Second World War. Following the end of the war, and the departure of the bulk of British troops, the Egyptian Mail became a weekly, appearing on Tuesdays when The Egyptian Gazette is not published, which continues today. Following the Egyptian Revolution in 1952, ownership of the two newspaper was ceded to its current owners, Dar Al Tahrir.
Language (s): English
Ad Rate: Full Page Mono 18000.00
Ad Rate: Full Page Colour 22400.00
Currency: United States Dollars
DAILY NEWSPAPER

Ein 508707
Owner: Sout El Omma for Press & Publishing
Editorial: 9 Education Authority Street, off Michel Bakhoum Street, Cairo **Tel:** 20 2 3761 9856
Email: hameednews@yahoo.com
Freq: Weekly; **Circ:** 122000 Publisher's Statement
Editor In Chief: Abdul Hameed Aleesh
Profile: Ein is a weekly Arabic newspaper covering news, politics and sport. It launched in 2002 and is published on Thursdays. The newspaper was formerly called 3aine.
Language (s): Arabic
Ad Rate: Full Page Mono 50820.00
Ad Rate: Full Page Colour 62700.00
Currency: Egypt Pounds
DAILY NEWSPAPER

Al Ektesadeya 597212
Owner: Alektesadeya Press, Printing and Publishing Company
Editorial: 40, Abdul Khaleq Tharwat Street, Cairo
Tel: 20 2 2396 3228
Email: info@ektesadeya.com
Freq: Weekly; **Circ:** 50000 Publisher's Statement
Advertising Manager: Mahmoud AbdelKarim; **Editor In Chief:** Al Sayed Al Najjar
Profile: Al Ektesadeya is a weekly newspaper covering business, finance, investment, telecommunications, tourism, banking, stock markets and real estate. The newspaper launched in 2007 and is aimed at business executives in Egypt. It is published on Sundays.
Language (s): Arabic
Ad Rate: Full Page Colour 7600.00
Currency: Egypt Pounds
DAILY NEWSPAPER

Elosboa 414033
Owner: Elosboa Press Publishing and Media
Editorial: 45A Champilion Street, Cairo
Tel: 20 2 2577 5592
Email: elaosboa@yahoo.com **Web site:** http://www.elaosboa.com
Freq: Weekly; **Circ:** 150000 Publisher's Statement
Advertising Manager: Abdul Hamid Bakri; **CEO & Editor in Chief:** Mostafa Bakry; **Public Relations Officer:** Walid Zaki
Profile: Elosboa (The Week) is a weekly newspaper covering local and international news, politics, business and sport. It launched in 1997 and is published on Mondays.
Language (s): Arabic
Ad Rate: Full Page Mono 34000.00
Ad Rate: Full Page Colour 40000.00
Currency: Egypt Pounds
DAILY NEWSPAPER

El Fagr 538141
Owner: El Fagr for Press, Printing & Publishing
Editorial: Floor 18, Building 8, Al Sad Al Aali Street, Cairo **Tel:** 20 2 3336 6164
Email: elfagr@elfagr.net **Web site:** http://www.elfagr.org
Freq: Weekly; **Circ:** 200000 Publisher's Statement
PR Manager: Gihan Azmy; **General Manager:** Mohammed Darwish; **Editor in Chief:** Manal Lasheen; **Advertising Manager:** Mohammed Shaheen
Profile: El Fagr is a weekly newspaper covering international and national news, politics, sport, business and entertainment. It launched in 2005 and is published on Thursdays.
Language (s): Arabic
Ad Rate: Full Page Mono 57200.00
Ad Rate: Full Page Colour 71500.00
Currency: Egypt Pounds
DAILY NEWSPAPER

Al Gamaheer 508706
Owner: Sawt Al Gamaheer Press, Printing & Publishing Co.
Editorial: 37 Amman Street, Dokki, Giza
Tel: 20 2 3762 5271
Email: algamaheer@hotmail.com
Freq: Weekly; **Circ:** 30000 Publisher's Statement
Advertising Manager: Abdul Nasser Ali; **Editor In Chief:** Mahmoud Thulathi
Profile: Al Gamaheer (The Audience) is a weekly Arabic newspaper covering news, politics, business, sports, entertainment, culture and society. It was launched in 2004 and published on Wednesdays.
Language (s): Arabic
Ad Rate: Full Page Mono 41126.00
Ad Rate: Full Page Colour 44064.00
Currency: Egypt Pounds
DAILY NEWSPAPER

Al Gomhuriah 378061
Owner: Dar Al Tahrir Publishing & Printing House
Editorial: 9th Floor, Al Gomhuriah Building, 111-115 Ramses Street, Cairo **Tel:** 20 2 2578 3333
Email: itc@gomhuriaonline.com **Web site:** http://www.algomhuria.net.eg
Freq: Daily; **Circ:** 700000 Publisher's Statement
Advertising Manager: Fady El Hosiny; **Editor in Chief:** Fahmy Enaba
Profile: Al Gomhuriah (The Republic) is a broadsheet-sized Arabic newspaper covering local and international news, current affairs, business, finance and sport. A 'weekly' edition is published on Thursdays which includes more features, interviews and photos. The newspaper was first published in 1953.
Language (s): Arabic
Ad Rate: Full Page Mono 50000.00
Currency: Egypt Pounds
DAILY NEWSPAPER

Al Horia We Al Adala 781556
Owner: Freedom & Justice Party
Editorial: 20, Al Malik Al Saleh Street, Al Manyal, Cairo
Email: fjportal2012@gmail.com **Web site:** http://fj-p.com
Freq: Daily; **Circ:** 80000 Publisher's Statement
Editor In Chief: Adel Al Ansari; **News Editor:** Hani Al Makkawi; **Advertising Manager:** Gamal Rashad
Profile: Al Horia We Al Adala (Freedom & Justice) is a daily Arabic newspaper covering local and international news, current affairs, politics, business and sport. It was launched in 2011 by the Freedom & Justice Party.
Language (s): Arabic
DAILY NEWSPAPER

El Khamis 652662
Owner: Pioneer Press, Printing & Publishing Company
Editorial: 3rd Floor, 1, Talaat Harb Square, Cairo
Tel: 20 2 2395 9595
Email: elkhamis_2@yahoo.com **Web site:** http://www.elkhamis.com
Freq: Weekly; **Circ:** 50000 Publisher's Statement
Profile: El Khamis (Thursday) is a weekly newspaper covering news, politics, sport, society and entertainment. It launched in 1998 and is published on Thursdays.
Language (s): Arabic
DAILY NEWSPAPER

Al Koura Wal Mala'eb 207947
Owner: Dar Al Tahrir Publishing & Printing House
Editorial: Office 23, 12th Floor, Al Gomhuriya Building, Cairo **Tel:** 20 2 2578 1919
Email: saadslim@hotmail.com **Web site:** http://www.koura.net.eg
Freq: Weekly; **Circ:** 80000 Publisher's Statement
Advertising Manager: Wageh Bassiony; **Editor in Chief:** Khaled Kamel

Profile: Al Koura Wal Mala'eb is a weekly newspaper covering local and international sport. It launched in 1976, and is published on Sundays.
Language (s): Arabic
DAILY NEWSPAPER

Al Mal 491718
Owner: Egypt Company for Marketing & Distribution
Editorial: 7A Al Sad Al Aali Street, Dokki, Cairo
Tel: 20 2 3748 3104
Email: almalnews@yahoo.com **Web site:** http://www.almalnews.com
Freq: Daily; **Circ:** 55000 Publisher's Statement
Editor In Chief: Hazem Sherif
Profile: Al Mal (The Money) is a daily newspaper covering economics, business, finance, markets, technology, telecommunications, stocks, insurance, banking, tourism, energy, real estate and politics. It launched in 2003 and is aimed at business executives in Egypt.
Language (s): Arabic
DAILY NEWSPAPER

Al Masry Al Youm 413467
Owner: Al-Masry Media Corporation
Editorial: 4th Floor, CIB Bank Building, 49, Mobtadayan Street, Cairo **Tel:** 20 2 2798 0100
Email: website@almasryalyoum.com **Web site:** http://www.almasryalyoum.com
Freq: Daily; **Circ:** 250000 Rate Card
General Manager: Fathy Abou Hatab
Profile: Al Masry Al Youm is an independent Arabic daily newspaper covering local and international news, politics, business and sport. It launched in 2004.
Language (s): Arabic
Ad Rate: Full Page Mono 148920.00
Ad Rate: Full Page Colour 201960.00
Currency: Egypt Pounds
DAILY NEWSPAPER

Al Mesryoon 784060
Owner: Al Mesryoon Press, Publishing, Printing and Distribution LLC
Editorial: 5th Floor, 45 Champillion Street, Cairo
Tel: 20 2 2578 3446
Email: almesryoon.adv@gmail.com **Web site:** http://www.almesryoon.com
Freq: Weekly; **Circ:** 80000 Publisher's Statement
Head of News: Noha Lamloum; **Head of Foreign News:** Gihan Mustafa; **CEO & Editor in Chief:** Gamal Sultan
Profile: Al Mesryoon (The Egyptians) is an Arabic daily newspaper covering national and international news, politics, business, society and sports. It was first published in 2011.
Language (s): Arabic
DAILY NEWSPAPER

Al Messa 156628
Owner: Dar Al Tahrir Publishing & Printing House
Editorial: 10th Floor, Al Gomhuriya Building, 111-115 Ramses Street, Cairo **Tel:** 20 2 2578 7999
Email: askmessa@hotmail.com **Web site:** http://www.almessa.net.eg
Freq: Daily; **Circ:** 450000 Publisher's Statement
Advertising Manager: Iyad Abo-Al-Hagag; **Editor in Chief:** Sami Hamed
Profile: Al Messa is an evening newspaper covering local and international news, politics, society and sport. It was first published in October 1956.
Language (s): Arabic
Ad Rate: Full Page Mono 20000.00
Currency: Egypt Pounds
DAILY NEWSPAPER

The Middle East Observer 354325
Owner: Middle East Observer House
Editorial: 41 Sherif Street, Cairo 11111
Tel: 20 2 2393 9732
Email: info@meobserver.net **Web site:** http://meobserver.org
Freq: Weekly; **Circ:** 25000 Publisher's Statement
Editor In Chief: Hesham Abdel Raouf; **Advertising Manager:** Kamal Mokhtar
Profile: The Middle East Observer is an economic journal focusing on Middle East and international news, economic current affairs, politics, business and development. It launched in 1954 and is published on Wednesdays.
Language (s): English
DAILY NEWSPAPER

Al Mogaz 510524
Owner: Al Mogaz Press Printing and Publishing
Editorial: 4A, Dareeh Saad Zaghlool Street, off Al Qasr Al Aini Street, Cairo **Tel:** 20 2 2793 0055
Email: elmogaz@elmogaz.com **Web site:** http://www.elmogaz.com
Freq: Weekly; **Circ:** 150000 Publisher's Statement
CEO & Editor in Chief: Yasser Barakat; **Office Manager:** Amani Mohamad; **News Editor:** Mohamed Salah
Profile: Al Mogaz is a weekly Arabic newspaper covering local news and current affairs, politics, business, society and sports. It launched in 2002 and is published on Mondays.
Language (s): Arabic
DAILY NEWSPAPER

Al Nabaa Al-Watany 734150
Owner: Dar Al Nabaa Al Watany for Publishing
Editorial: 9 Musician Ali Ismaeel Street, Al Masaha Square, Cairo **Tel:** 20 2 3335 2988
Email: alnaba.alwatany@gmail.com **Web site:** http://www.alnabaa.net
Freq: Weekly; **Circ:** 250000 Publisher's Statement
Profile: Al Nabaa Al-Watany is a broadsheet-sized Arabic newspaper focusing on local and international news, politics, business and sport. It launched in 1989 and is published on Saturdays.
Language (s): Arabic
Ad Rate: Full Page Mono 84000.00
Ad Rate: Full Page Colour 96000.00
Currency: Egypt Pounds
DAILY NEWSPAPER

Al Nahar 507279
Owner: Al Waqai Al Arabiya for Press & Publishing
Editorial: 1065 Corniche El Nil, Garden City, Cairo
Tel: 20 2 2792 6950
Email: alnnhar@yahoo.com **Web site:** http://www.alnaharegypt.com
Freq: Weekly; **Circ:** 50000 Publisher's Statement
Profile: Al Nahar (The Day) is a weekly Arabic newspaper covering news, politics, business, sports, culture and entertainment. It launched in 2007 and is published on Wednesdays.
Language (s): Arabic
Ad Rate: Full Page Mono 64064.00
Ad Rate: Full Page Colour 84864.00
Currency: Egypt Pounds
DAILY NEWSPAPER

Le Progrès Egyptien 156629
Owner: Dar Al Tahrir Publishing & Printing House
Editorial: 10th Floor, Al Gomhuriya Building, 111-115 Ramses Street, Cairo **Tel:** 20 2 2578 3333
Email: leprogresegyptien@yahoo.fr
Freq: Daily; **Circ:** 90000 Rate Card
Editor: Chaimaa Abdel-Illah; **Editor In Chief:** Mohammad Al Azzawi; **Advertising Manager:** Botros Bshay; **News Editor:** Marwa Mourad
Profile: Le Progrès Egyptien is a daily newspaper covering national and international news, business, politics, culture and sport. It was first published in 1893. On Sundays, the newspaper is called Le Progrès Dimanche.
Language (s): French
DAILY NEWSPAPER

Al Rahma 784061
Owner: Al Rahma Establishment
Editorial: PO Box 4, 6th of October City, Cairo 12573
Email: alrahma.press@yahoo.com
Freq: Weekly; **Circ:** 100000 Publisher's Statement
News Editor: Ashraf Al Bahai; **Editor In Chief:** Abdulnasser Al Zouhairy
Profile: Al Rahma is a weekly Arabic newspaper covering national and international news, politics, society, culture and sport. It launched in 2011 and is published on Fridays.
Language (s): Arabic
DAILY NEWSPAPER

Rose Al Youssef 500517
Owner: Rose Al Youssef Group
Editorial: 89A, Al Qasr Al Aini Street, Cairo
Tel: 20 2 2795 8503
Email: rosaelyoussef@yahoo.com **Web site:** http://www.rosaeveryday.com
Freq: Daily; **Circ:** 55000 Publisher's Statement
Advertising Manager: Ahmed Fathy; **Office Manager:** Ibrahim Guishi; **Head of News:** Ahmed Khairy; **Editor in Chief:** Gamal Tayea
Profile: Rose Al Youssef is a daily newspaper covering news, politics, sport and business. It was first published in 2005.
Language (s): Arabic
Ad Rate: Full Page Mono 156000.00
Ad Rate: Full Page Colour 178000.00
Currency: Egypt Pounds
DAILY NEWSPAPER

El Sabah 834188
Owner: El Sabah Establishment For Press
Editorial: 122, Tahrir Street, Giza **Tel:** 20 2 3337 4500
Email: news@elsaba7.com **Web site:** http://www.elsaba7.com
Freq: Weekly; **Circ:** 80000
Editor in Chief: Wael Lotfi; **Advertising Manager:** Su'ad Tahoon
Profile: El Sabah is a weekly newspaper covering news, politics, business and sport. The newspaper launched in September 2012 and is issued on Mondays.
Language (s): Arabic
DAILY NEWSPAPER

Sawt Al Balad 538139
Owner: Arab Press Agency
Editorial: Building 5, Abed Al Moniem Salem Street, Al Wehda Al Arabia, Giza **Tel:** 20 2 3586 7576
Email: balad@apatop.com **Web site:** http://www.baladnews.com
Freq: Weekly; **Circ:** 80000 Publisher's Statement
Advertising Manager: Al Shazly Al Shazly
Profile: Sawt Al Balad (Voice of the Country) is a weekly Arabic newspaper covering international and national news, politics, business, culture, sports, entertainment, youth and family. It launched in 2007 and is published on Thursdays.
Language (s): Arabic
DAILY NEWSPAPER

Al Shorouk 586908
Owner: Egyptian Company For Publishing
Editorial: Building 59, Iran Street, Giza
Tel: 20 2 3748 6383
Email: contactus@shorouknews.com **Web site:** http://www.shorouknews.com
Freq: Daily; **Circ:** 100000 Rate Card
News Editor: Ashraf Al Barbary; **Editor in Chief:** Emadeddine Hussein
Profile: Al Shorouk (The Dawn) is a daily newspaper covering national and international news, business, religion, youth, women's issues and sport. It was first published in 2009.
Language (s): Arabic
Ad Rate: Full Page Mono 108120.00
Ad Rate: Full Page Colour 142800.00
Currency: Egypt Pounds
DAILY NEWSPAPER

Sout El Omma 538142
Owner: Sout El Omma for Press & Publishing
Editorial: 9 Education Authority Street, off Michel Bakhoum Street, Cairo **Tel:** 20 2 3336 3575
Email: soutelomma@yahoo.com **Web site:** http://www.soutalomma.com
Freq: Weekly; **Circ:** 100000 Publisher's Statement
News Editor: Rida Awad; **PR Co-ordinator:** Noha Fathy; **Editor in Chief:** Abdul Haleem Qandeel
Profile: Sout El Omma (Voice of the Nation) is a weekly newspaper covering international and national news, politics, business, sport and entertainment. It launched in 2001 and is published on Saturdays.
Language (s): Arabic
Ad Rate: Full Page Mono 146880.00
Ad Rate: Full Page Colour 183600.00
Currency: Egypt Pounds
DAILY NEWSPAPER

Al Tahrir 761315
Owner: Egyptian Company for Arabic & International Publishing
Editorial: 42, Syria Street, Mohandiseen, Cairo
Tel: 20 2 3760 2339
Email: ta7rir2011@gmail.com **Web site:** http://www.tahrirnews.com
Freq: Daily; **Circ:** 150000 Publisher's Statement
Office Manager: Mona Al-Nahhas
Profile: Al Tahrir (Freedom) is a daily newspaper covering national and international news, politics, business, sport, art, culture and society. It was first published in 2011.
Language (s): Arabic
Ad Rate: Full Page Mono 110160.00
Ad Rate: Full Page Colour 136080.00
Currency: Egypt Pounds
DAILY NEWSPAPER

Veto 788556
Owner: Al Ahrar Press, Printing & Publishing
Editorial: 108, Al Neel Street, Al Dokki, Cairo
Tel: 20 2 3762 0180
Email: info@vetogate.com **Web site:** http://www.vetogate.com
Freq: Weekly; **Circ:** 80000 Publisher's Statement
Picture Editor: Ahmed Farid; **Editor in Chief:** Essam Kamel; **News Editor:** Mokhtar Mahmoud
Profile: Veto is a weekly Arabic newspaper covering politics, business and sport. It launched in 2012 and is published on Tuesdays.
Language (s): Arabic
DAILY NEWSPAPER

Al Wafd 339282
Owner: Wafd Opposition Party
Editorial: PO Box 357, 1 Boulis Hanna Street, Giza
Tel: 20 2 3338 3111
Email: wafdeg@gmail.com **Web site:** http://www.alwafd.org
Freq: Daily; **Circ:** 150000 Publisher's Statement
News Editor: Adel Sabry; **Editor in Chief:** Magdy Sarhan
Profile: Al Wafd is the daily newspaper of the Al Wafd Party and covers national and international news, current affairs, politics, business, sport and arts, as well as the news and activities of the political party. The newspaper launched in 1984.
Language (s): Arabic
DAILY NEWSPAPER

Washwasha 509448
Owner: El Fagr for Press, Printing & Publishing
Editorial: 5 Al Burj Street, Lebanon Square, Cairo
Tel: 20 2 3303 7828
Email: washwashaofficial@gmail.com **Web site:** http://www.washwasha.org
Freq: Weekly; **Circ:** 32500 Publisher's Statement
Advertising Manager: Gamal Abdel Azim; **Editor in Chief:** Ahmad Al Hawari
Profile: Washwasha (Whispers) is a weekly newspaper covering entertainment, cinema, celebrities, culture, sport, women's issues and society. It launched in 2006 and is published on Mondays.
Language (s): Arabic
DAILY NEWSPAPER

El Watan 824426
Owner: Al Mustaqbal Publishing, Distribution & Press Company
Editorial: 27, Mohiey Al Deen Street, Abu El Aizz, Giza **Tel:** 20 2 3333 1000 3
Email: info@elwatannews.com **Web site:** http://www.elwatannews.com
Freq: Daily; **Circ:** 250000 Publisher's Statement
Advertising Manager: Walid El Essawy; **Advertising Manager:** Ehab Farouk
Profile: El Watan is a daily Arabic newspaper covering national and international news, business and sport. It launched in 2012.
Language (s): Arabic
DAILY NEWSPAPER

Watani 343440
Owner: Watani Printing & Publishing Corporation
Editorial: 27 Abdel Khalek Tharwat Street, Downtown, Cairo **Tel:** 20 2 2393 6051
Email: watanipaper@gmail.com **Web site:** http://www.wataninet.com
Freq: Weekly; **Circ:** 60000 Publisher's Statement
Advertising Manager: Milad Ibrahim; **News Editor:** Noura Najib; **PR Manager:** Victor Salameh; **Picture Editor:** Nasser Sobhi
Profile: Watani (My Homeland) is a weekly Arabic newspaper covering national and international news, current affairs, politics, business and sports, as well as Coptic issues, culture, heritage and the Coptic contribution to Egyptian society. It launched in 1958 and is aimed at the Coptic community in Egypt. The newspaper includes English and French supplements and is published on Sundays.
Language (s): Arabic
DAILY NEWSPAPER

Youm7 652735
Owner: Egyptian Company for Press, Publishing & Advertising
Editorial: 5th Floor, Building 6, Al Thawra Street, Dokki, Cairo **Tel:** 20 2 3335 5922
Email: webmaster@youm7.com **Web site:** http://www.youm7.com
Freq: Daily; **Circ:** 100000 Publisher's Statement
Head of News: Shaaban Hedya; **Editor In Chief:** Khaled Salah
Profile: Youm7 (The Seventh Day) is a daily Arabic newspaper covering national and international news, politics, business and sport. It was first published in 2008.
Language (s): Arabic
Ad Rate: Full Page Mono 70000.00
Ad Rate: Full Page Colour 94000.00
Currency: Egypt Pounds
DAILY NEWSPAPER

News Service/Syndicate

Agence France-Presse - Cairo Bureau 370515
Owner: Agence France-Presse
Editorial: PO Box 12612, Orman, Giza 52
Tel: 20 2 3573 8720
Email: afp.lecaire@afp.com **Web site:** http://www.afp.com
Profile: Regional office of the Agence France-Presse covering general news and current affairs.
Language (s): Arabic
NEWS SERVICE/SYNDICATE

APTN Egypt 370513
Owner: Associated Press
Editorial: 4th Floor, 3, Abu Al Fida Street, Cairo 11221 **Tel:** 20 2 2578 4095
Email: aptncairo@gmail.com **Web site:** http://www.aptn.com
Profile: Associated Press Television News (APTN) is the international television arm of the Associated Press - APTN's operations include a main news service, specialised broadcast services, customised coverage for the Middle East, a productions division, weekly and daily entertainment news and an extensive video archive library.
Language (s): Arabic
NEWS SERVICE/SYNDICATE

Arab Press Agency 392860
Owner: Arab Press Agency
Editorial: 5 Abed Al Mounem Salem, Al Wehda Al Arabia, Giza **Tel:** 20 2 3586 7575
Email: news@apatop.com **Web site:** http://www.apatop.com
General Manager: Al Shazli Mohammad
Profile: Arab Press Agency provides news, features and analysis of events in the Arab world, and includes press reports and a photo service.
Language (s): Arabic
NEWS SERVICE/SYNDICATE

Associated Press - Cairo Bureau 370523
Owner: Associated Press
Editorial: 4th Floor, 3, Abu Al Fida Street, Cairo 11211 **Tel:** 20 2 2728 3600
Email: apcairo@ap.org **Web site:** http://www.ap.org
Bureau Chief: Hamza Hendawi
Profile: Cairo bureau of the Associated Press (AP), and also the international wire agency's regional head office for the Middle East. The bureau covers news from Egypt, Libya, Yemen and Sudan.
Language (s): Arabic
NEWS SERVICE/SYNDICATE

Bloomberg - Cairo Bureau 433892
Owner: Bloomberg L.P.
Editorial: 3 Abou El Feda Street, Zamalek, Cairo
Tel: 20 2 2739 6416
Email: egyptnews@bloomberg.net **Web site:** http://www.bloomberg.com
Profile: Financial news wire service.
Language (s): English
NEWS SERVICE/SYNDICATE

Cairo News Company 392858
Owner: Cairo News Company
Editorial: Suite 404, Dohet Maspero Tower, 4 Al-Galaa Street, Cairo 11221 **Tel:** 20 2 2576 2601
Email: info@caironews.tv **Web site:** http://www.caironews.tv
Bureau Chief: Heba Al Qadi
Profile: Cairo News Company (CNC) covers breaking news, sport, business news, social trends, environmental news and human-interest stories from Egypt and the Middle East. The company was co-founded in 2004 by brothers Nader and Hisham

Egypt

Gohar and provides news services to news companies, broadcasters and producers from numerous countries, including the USA, UK, France, Germany, Japan, Israel, Qatar, Saudi Arabia and the UAE via satellite transmission on Nilesat and Eutelsat, and SNG services.
Language (s): Arabic
NEWS SERVICE/SYNDICATE

Deutsche Presse-Agentur - Cairo bureau 492684
Owner: Deutsche Presse-Agentur
Editorial: 20 Gamal El Din Abu El Mahasen Street, Garden City, Cairo **Tel:** 20 2 2795 6842
Email: office.cairo@dpa.com **Web site:** http://www.dpa.com
Editor: Marwa Ghareeb; **Editor In Chief:** Bahai Eldin Taghian
Profile: Cairo bureau of German press agency - covers news, politics, sports, fashion, economy, conflicts, disasters, features and business in the Middle East.
Language (s): Arabic
NEWS SERVICE/SYNDICATE

European Pressphoto Agency - Middle East Head Office 491397
Owner: European Pressphoto Agency
Editorial: 3rd Floor, Building 44, Mohammad Mazhar, Cairo **Tel:** 20 2 2795 6978
Email: epacairo@gmail.com **Web site:** http://www.epa.eu
Profile: European Pressphoto Agency is a picture agency representing eleven European news agencies (DPA, ANSA, EFE, Belga, APA, Athens News Agency, PAP, ANP, MTI, Keystone and LUSA). The Cairo bureau is the head office for the Middle East and also covers news, politics, sports, fashion, economy, conflicts, disasters, features and business from Egypt.
Language (s): Arabic
NEWS SERVICE/SYNDICATE

Middle East News Agency 380841
Owner: Middle East News Agency
Editorial: PO Box 1165, 17 Hoda Sharawi Street, Cairo 11111 **Tel:** 20 2 2393 3000
Email: ticker-1@mena.org.eg **Web site:** http://www.mena.org.eg
Profile: Middle East News Agency is the official Egyptian government news agency and covers issues of national importance. The agency was founded in 1956.
Language (s): Arabic
NEWS SERVICE/SYNDICATE

Reuters - Cairo Bureau 392855
Owner: Thomson Reuters
Editorial: PO Box 2040, 21st Floor, Bank Misr Building, Cairo 11511 **Tel:** 20 2 2394 8000
Email: cairo.newsroom@reuters.com **Web site:** http://www.reuters.com
Head of News: Munir Boweti
Profile: Cairo bureau of international news agency supplying news - text, graphics, video and pictures - to subscribers around the world. Covers Egypt and Sudan from Cairo.
Language (s): Arabic
NEWS SERVICE/SYNDICATE

Reuters TV - Cairo Bureau 370512
Owner: Thomson Reuters
Editorial: PO Box 2040, 21st Floor, Bank Misr Tower, Cairo 11511 **Tel:** 20 2 2394 8000
Email: cairo.reception@thomsonreuters.com **Web site:** http://www.thomsonreuters.com
Producer: Mostafa Saleem
Profile: Cairo Bureau of Thomson Reuters TV providing television broadcasters and internet providers worldwide with international news video, including breaking news stories, human interest items, sport, business and entertainment news.
Language (s): Arabic
NEWS SERVICE/SYNDICATE

Rossiya Segodnya - Egypt & North Africa Bureau 663081
Owner: Rossiya Segodnya
Editorial: 5, Aziz Abaza Street, Zamalek, Cairo
Tel: 20 2 2736 9929
Email: nadim@bk.ru **Web site:** http://ria.ru
Profile: Rossiya Segodnya (Russia Today) is the official Russian government-owned international news agency which has a mandate to 'provide information on Russian state policy and Russian life and society for audiences abroad'. It was founded by presidential decree in December 2013 and incorporates the former RIA Novosti news service and Voice of Russia international radio service. The Egypt & North Africa bureau covers news, political affairs, economics, markets, business and investment.
Language (s): Arabic
NEWS SERVICE/SYNDICATE

Xinhua News Agency - Cairo Bureau 856133
Owner: Xinhua News Agency
Editorial: 27 Corniche El Nile, Maadi, Cairo
Tel: 20 2 2358 7950
Email: terrificln@gmail.com **Web site:** http://www.xinhuanet.com
Profile: Cairo bureau of the Xinhua News Agency, the official press agency of the People's Republic of China. The Cairo bureau is also the Middle East regional office. Correspondence and press releases should be sent in Arabic or Chinese.
Language (s): Arabic
NEWS SERVICE/SYNDICATE

El Salvador

Time Difference: GMT -6
National Telephone Code: 503
Continent: The Americas
Capital: San Salvador

Newspapers

El Diario de Hoy 157006
Owner: El Diario de Hoy
Editorial: 11 Calle Oriente y Avenida, Cuscatancingo No. 271, San Salvador **Tel:** 503 2231-7777
Email: redaccion@elsalvador.com **Web site:** http://www.elsalvador.com
Freq: Daily; **Circ:** 105000 Not Audited
Director: Enrique Altamirano-Madriz; **Editor in Chief:** Ricardo Chacón
Profile: Newspaper covering national and international news, politics, economics, finance, business, culture and sport.
Language (s): Spanish
DAILY NEWSPAPER

La Prensa Gráfica 157007
Owner: La Prensa Grafica
Editorial: Final Bulevar Santa Elena, frente a la embajada USA, Antiguo Cuscatlán (la Libertad)
Tel: 503 2241-2000
Web site: http://www.laprensagrafica.com
Freq: Daily; **Circ:** 109177 Not Audited
President: José Roberto Dutriz; **Editor:** Edguar Gutierrez; **Editor in Chief:** Luis Lainez; **Editor in Chief:** Claudia Ramirez
Profile: Newspaper covering national and international news, politics, economics, finance, business, culture and sport.
Language (s): Spanish
DAILY NEWSPAPER

Estonia

Time Difference: GMT +2
National Telephone Code: 372
Continent: Europe
Capital: Tallinn

Newspapers

Äripäev 156803
Owner: Äripäeva Kirjastuse AS
Editorial: Parnu mnt. 105, Tallinn 19094
Tel: 372 6 6670111
Email: aripaev@aripaev.ee **Web site:** http://www.aripaev.ee
Freq: Daily; **Circ:** 10500 Publisher's Statement
News Editor: Kristi Malmberg; **Editor-In-Chief:** Meelis Mandel; **Foreign News Editor:** Sirje Rank; **Editor:** Rivo Sarapik
Profile: Business newspaper with emphasis on business news from Estonia and news from financial markets. Includes surveys of currency rates, banking services and stock prices. Each issue dedicates two pages for news from abroad and features a selection of interviews, essays, problem stories, reports and personal or corporate profiles.
Language (s): Estonian
Ad Rate: Full Page Colour 2900.00
Currency: Euro
DAILY NEWSPAPER

Delovõje Vedomosti 224371
Owner: Äripäeva Kirjastuse AS
Editorial: Parnu mnt. 105, Tallinn 19094
Tel: 372 66 70 111
Email: dv@aripaev.ee **Web site:** http://www.vedomosti.ee
Freq: Daily; **Circ:** 5900 Publisher's Statement
Profile: Newspaper focusing on business and financial news.
Language (s): Russian
DAILY NEWSPAPER

Eesti Ekspress 224451
Owner: Eesti Ekspressi Kirjatuse AS
Editorial: Narva mnt. 11 E, Tallinn 10151
Tel: 372 66 98 030
Email: ekspress@ekspress.ee **Web site:** http://ekspress.delfi.ee
Circ: 29600 Publisher's Statement
Publisher: Hans Luik
Profile: Newspaper focusing on national and international news, politics, entertainment and sport.
Language (s): Estonian
Ad Rate: Full Page Colour 3771.00
Currency: Euro
DAILY NEWSPAPER

Eesti Päevaleht 156817
Owner: Eesti Päevaleht AS
Editorial: Narva mnt. 13, Tallinn 10151
Tel: 372 6 80 44 00
Email: mail@epl.ee **Web site:** http://epl.delfi.ee
Freq: Daily; **Circ:** 22500 Publisher's Statement
Head of International News: Raimo Poom; **Head of News:** Holger Roonemaa; **Editor-in-Chief:** Urmo Soonvald
Profile: Newspaper covering national and international news, business, finance, culture and sport.
Language (s): Estonian
Ad Rate: Full Page Colour 4200.00
Currency: Euro
DAILY NEWSPAPER

Komsomolskaya Pravda v Severnoi Evrope 668769
Owner: OÜ SKP Media
Editorial: Lembitu 8-2, Tallinn 10114
Tel: 372 6688900
Email: info@kompravda.eu **Web site:** http://kompravda.eu
Freq: Weekly; **Circ:** 12900 Publisher's Statement
Publisher: Igor Teterin
Profile: Newspaper focusing on national and international news, culture, history, social life, tourism and sport.
Language (s): Russian
DAILY NEWSPAPER

MK-Estonia 551314
Owner: Baltic Media Alliance
Editorial: Suur-Karja 21, Tallinn **Tel:** 372 654 1640
Email: sekretar@1bma.ee **Web site:** http://www.mke.ee
Freq: Weekly; **Circ:** 12500 Publisher's Statement
Editor-in-Chief: Andrei Titov
Profile: Newspaper focusing on national and international news, culture, history, social life, tourism and sport.
Language (s): Russian
DAILY NEWSPAPER

Õhtuleht 156653
Owner: SL Õhtuleht AS
Editorial: Narva mnt 13 III korrus, Tallinn 10502
Tel: 372 6 14 40 00
Email: leht@ohtuleht.ee **Web site:** http://www.ohtuleht.ee
Freq: Daily; **Circ:** 49900 Publisher's Statement
Editor: Andres Põld
Profile: Tabloid newspaper focusing on entertainment, sports, national and international news and politics.
Language (s): Estonian
DAILY NEWSPAPER

Postimees 156810
Owner: Eesti Meedia
Editorial: Maakri 23 A, Tallinn 10145
Tel: 372 6 66 22 02
Email: postimees@postimees.ee **Web site:** http://www.postimees.ee
Freq: Daily; **Circ:** 49700 Publisher's Statement
Editor: Marti Aavik; **Editor:** Kadri Hansalu; **Editor:** Mihkel Niglas; **Editor:** Berit Nuka; **Editor:** Linda Pärn; **Editor:** Tõnis Poom; **Editor:** Marko Püüa; **Editor:** Hanneli Rudi; **Editor:** Heili Sibrits
Profile: National newspaper focusing on national and international news, politics, business and sport.
Language (s): Estonian
DAILY NEWSPAPER

News Service/Syndicate

Baltic News Service BNS Estonia 353344
Editorial: Toompuiestee 35, Tallinn 15043
Tel: 372 6 10 88 00
Email: bns@bns.ee **Web site:** http://www.bns.ee
Editor-in-Chief: Toomas Toomsalu
Profile: BNS is the source of information about the Baltic countries.
Language (s): Estonian
NEWS SERVICE/SYNDICATE

Ethiopia

Time Difference: GMT +3
National Telephone Code: 251
Continent: Africa
Capital: Addis Ababa

Newspapers

Addis Fortune 652584
Owner: Independent News & Media plc
Editorial: PO Box 259, Code 1110, Addis Ababa
Tel: 251 11 553 81 40
Email: ad@addisfortune.net **Web site:** http://addisfortune.net
Freq: Weekly
Profile: National weekly newspaper focussing on new and current affairs, business and economic development.
Language (s): English
DAILY NEWSPAPER

Capital Ethiopia 518585
Owner: Crown Publishing P.L.C
Editorial: P.O.Box 95, Code 1110, Addis Ababa
Tel: 251 11 618 32 53
Email: info@capitalethiopia.com **Web site:** http://www.capitalethiopia.com
Freq: Weekly
Editor in Chief: Behailu Desalegn
Profile: Weekly business newspaper focussing on news and current affairs, finance, economics, business development, society, art, culture and sport.
Language (s): English
DAILY NEWSPAPER

News Service/Syndicate

Ethiopian News Agency - ENA 518558
Owner: Ethiopian News Agency
Editorial: PO Box 530, Addis Ababa
Tel: 251 11 155 00 11
Email: ethiopianewsagency@gmail.com **Web site:** http://www.ena.gov.et
Profile: National Ethiopian news agency covering general news and current affairs.
Language (s): English
NEWS SERVICE/SYNDICATE

Falkland Islands

Time Difference: GMT -3
National Telephone Code: 500
Continent: The Americas
Capital: Stanley

Newspapers

Penguin News 157008
Owner: Penguin News
Editorial: Ross Road, Stanley FIQQ 1ZZ
Tel: 500 0050022684
Email: editor@penguinnews.co.fk **Web site:** http://www.penguin-news.com
Freq: Fri; **Circ:** 1500 Not Audited
Profile: Penguin News is a weekly newspaper covering national and international news, business, entertainment, culture and sports.
Language (s): English
Ad Rate: Full Page Mono 10.00
Currency: United States Dollars
DAILY NEWSPAPER

Fiji

Time Difference: GMT +12
National Telephone Code: 679
Continent: Oceania
Capital: Suva

Newspapers

Fiji Sun 538561
Owner: Sun (Fiji) News Ltd
Editorial: 12 Amra Street, Walu Bay, Suva, Fiji Islands **Tel:** 679 330 7555
Email: fijisundigital@gmail.com **Web site:** http://fijisun.com.fj
Freq: Daily
Editor: Leone Cabenatabua; **Advertising Manager:** Ahara Khan; **Publisher:** Peter Lomas
Profile: National daily newspaper covering general news and current affairs including politics, economy entertainment and sports.
Language (s): English
DAILY NEWSPAPER

The Fiji Times 538560
Owner: Fiji Times Limited
Editorial: 177 Victoria Parade, Suva, Fiji Islands
Tel: 679 33 04209
Email: timesnews@fijitimes.com.fj **Web site:** http://www.fijitimes.com
Freq: Daily
Profile: National daily newspaper covering regional, national and international news and current affairs including politics, economy, society and sports.
Language (s): English
Ad Rate: Full Page Mono 1596.00
Currency: United States Dollars
DAILY NEWSPAPER

Wansolwara Online 538679

Owner: Journalism Division, University of the South Pacific
Editorial: Journalism Division, University of the South Pacific, Suva, Fiji Islands **Tel:** 679 323 2680
Email: wansolwara@usp.ac.fj **Web site:** http://usp.ac.fj/journ
Freq: Quarterly; **Circ:** 2000 Not Audited
Profile: South Pacific regional journalism education site with news, newspaper and media freedom links and resources.
Language (s): English
DAILY NEWSPAPER

News Service/Syndicate

PacNews 538697

Owner: Pacific Islands Broadcasting Association
Editorial: Private Mail Bag, Suva, Fiji Islands
Tel: 679 3303 623
Email: pacnews@connect.com.fj **Web site:** http://pinanius.com
Freq: Daily
Editor: Makereta Komai
Profile: Provides full daily coverage of routine, official, for-the-record news from across the region.
Language (s): English
NEWS SERVICE/SYNDICATE

Finland

Time Difference: GMT +2
National Telephone Code: 358
Continent: Europe
Capital: Helsinki

Newspapers

Aamulehti 157057

Owner: Alma Media Oyj
Editorial: Itainenkatu 11, Tampere 33210
Tel: 358 10 66 51 11
Email: al.uutisvinkki@aamulehti.fi **Web site:** http://www.aamulehti.fi
Freq: Daily; **Circ:** 121135
Editor in Chief: Jouko Jokinen; **News Manager:** Vesa Laitinen; **News Manager:** Sari Torvinen
Profile: Regional newspaper mainly for the Tampere region. Editions: Aamulehti Ajankohtaistoimitus, Aamulehti Kulttuuritoimitus, Aamulehti Taloustoimitus, Aamulehti Ulkomaan toimitus, Aamulehti Urheilutoimitus, Aamulehti Uutistoimitus, Asiat ja Ihmiset tabloid on Sundays about current affairs and peopleSupplements: Aamulehti Moro - 52xY, Aamulehti Valo - 52xY
Language (s): Finnish
Ad Rate: Full Page Colour 15000.00
Currency: Euro
DAILY NEWSPAPER

Aamulehti Parkano 161745

Owner: Alma Media Oyj
Editorial: PL 47/ Viinikanrinne 1 A 5, Parkano 39701
Tel: 358 10 665 111
Email: aulis.alatalo@aamulehti.fi **Web site:** http://www.aamulehti.fi
Profile: Parkano regional office of Aamulehti. Aamulehden Parkanon aluetoimisto.
Language (s): Finnish
DAILY NEWSPAPER

Aamulehti Valkeakoski 366412

Owner: Alma Media Oyj
Editorial: Valkeakoski **Tel:** 358 10 665 3313
Email: juha.karilainen@almamedia.fi **Web site:** http://www.aamulehti.fi
Profile: Valkeakoski regional office of Aamulehti. Aamulehden Valkeakosken aluetoimisto.
Language (s): Finnish
DAILY NEWSPAPER

Demokraatti 159042

Owner: Kustannus Oy Demokraatti
Editorial: Haapaniemenkatu 7-9 B, 17-18 krs., Helsinki 530 **Tel:** 358 9 701 041
Email: toimitus@demokraatti.fi **Web site:** https://demokraatti.fi/
Freq: Mon thru Fri; **Circ:** 11243 ABC-Audit Bureau of Circulations
News Manager: Juhani Aro; **News Manager:** Ilkka Yrjä
Profile: Social-democrat newspaper with national news of interest for working-class people. Local Translation: Sosiaalidemokraattinen sanomalehti, jossa on kansallisen tason uutisia lähinnä työväenluokan näkökulmasta.
Language (s): Finnish
Ad Rate: Full Page Colour 5750.00
Currency: Euro
DAILY NEWSPAPER

Etelä-Saimaa 366305

Owner: Sanoma Lehtimedia Oy
Editorial: PL 3/Lauritsalantie 1, Lappeenranta 53501
Tel: 358 5 53 88 13
Email: uutinen@esaimaa.fi **Web site:** http://www.esaimaa.fi
Circ: 25284
Profile: Politically independent newspaper issued mainly in the town of Lappeenranta in southeastern Finland. Local Translation:Poliittisesti sitoutumaton, lähinnä Lappeenrannan alueella ilmestyvä sanomalehti. Regular features: Mondays: Cars and Traffic; Wednesdays: every third week Consumer affairs, every third week Fitness, Health, every third week Nature; Fridays: Youth, Food, Essi weekend magazine; Saturdays: Games.Edition: Etelä-Saimaa Urheilutoimitus Start year: 1885
Language (s): Finnish
DAILY NEWSPAPER

Etelä-Saimaa Imatra 161672

Owner: Kaakon Viestintä Oy
Editorial: Esterinkatu 10, Imatra 55100
Tel: 358 5 538 813
Email: toimitus.imatra@lehtimedia.fi **Web site:** http://www.esaimaa.fi
News Editor: Hannu Ojala
Profile: Imatra regional office of newspaper Etelä-Saimaa. Local Translation:Etelä-Saimaan Imatran aluetoimisto. No e-mails allowed to their address toimitus.imatra@esaimaa.fi or to the personal e-mail addresses.
Language (s): Finnish
DAILY NEWSPAPER

Etelä-Suomen Sanomat 157040

Owner: Esan Kirjapaino Oy
Editorial: PL 80/ Ilmarisentie 7, Lahti 15110
Tel: 358 3 75 751
Email: toimitus@ess.fi **Web site:** http://www.ess.fi
Circ: 53444
News Manager: Mia Miettinen; **Editor:** Esa Rauhanlaakso
Profile: Newspaper mainly issued in Lahti, Hollola, Asikkala, Nastola, Orimattila, Artjärvi, Kärkölä, Hämeenkoski and Padasjoki. Local Translation:Sanomalehti, jonka ilmestymisalueet ovat: Lahti, Hollola, Asikkala, Nastola, Orimattila, Artjärvi, Kärkölä, Hämeenkoski ja Padasjoki. Start year: 1900
Language (s): Finnish
Ad Rate: Full Page Colour 14076.00
Currency: Euro
DAILY NEWSPAPER

Helsingin Sanomat 157020

Owner: Sanoma News Oy
Editorial: PL 75/Toolonlahdenkatu 2, Helsinki 89
Tel: +358 9 12 21
Email: hs.online@hs.fi **Web site:** http://www.hs.fi/
Freq: Daily; **Circ:** 354737 ABC-Audit Bureau of Circulations
Editor in Chief: Antero Mukka; **Editor:** Pekka Mykkänen
Profile: Broadsheet-sized quality newspaper providing in-depth coverage of national and international news, politics, economics, business, events, culture and sport. Read by private households over the whole of Finland. Sanomalehti, joka kattaa kotimaan, ulkomaan, talouden, kulttuurin, urheilun, tapahtumien ja politiikan uutiset.Personnel news (nimitykset) fax number is 00358 9-12 26 56 and its address is PL 75, 00089 SANOMA. Supplements: Helsingin Sanomat Kuukausiliite - 12xY, Helsingin Sanomat Nyt-viikkoliite - 52xY Regular features:Mondays: Elämä (Health and Fitness); Tuesdays: Tiede (Science and Environment);Wednesdays: Kuluttaja (Consumer Affairs); Thursdays: Ruoka (Food);Fridays: Matka (Travel), Saturdays: Auto (Cars and Traffic)Sundays: Talous & Koti (Finance & Home, Housing Ads). See separate listings! Number of pages: 100Start year: 1889
Language (s): Finnish
Ad Rate: Full Page Colour 25338.00
Currency: Euro
DAILY NEWSPAPER

Helsingin Sanomat Kuopio 161678

Owner: Sanoma News Oy
Editorial: Haapaniemenkatu 32 b5, Kuopio 70110
Tel: 358 17 21 13 333
Email: hs.kuopio@hs.fi **Web site:** http://www.hs.fi
Freq: Daily
Profile: Kuopio regional office of national newspaper Helsingin Sanomat. Local Translation:Helsingin Sanomien Kuopion aluetoimisto.
Language (s): Finnish
DAILY NEWSPAPER

Helsingin Sanomat Oulu 161679

Owner: Sanoma News Oy
Editorial: Kauppurienkatu 23, Oulu 90100
Tel: 358 8 31 20 800
Email: hs.oulu@hs.fi **Web site:** http://www.hs.fi
Freq: Daily
Profile: Oulu regional editorial of national newspaper Helsingin Sanomat. Local Translation:Helsingin Sanomien Oulun aluetoimisto.
Language (s): Finnish
DAILY NEWSPAPER

Helsingin Sanomat Tampere 161681

Owner: Sanoma News Oy
Editorial: Tuomiokirkonkatu 17 B 31, Tampere 33100
Tel: 358 3 22 31 257
Email: hs.tampere@hs.fi **Web site:** http://www.hs.fi/kotimaa/aihe/tampere
Freq: Daily
Profile: Tampere regional editorial of national newspaper Helsingin Sanomat. Local Translation:Helsingin Sanomien Tampereen aluetoimisto.
Language (s): Finnish
DAILY NEWSPAPER

Helsingin Sanomat Turku 161760

Owner: Sanoma News Oy
Editorial: Yliopistonkatu 33, Turku 20100
Tel: 358 2 25 16 655
Email: hs.turku@hs.fi **Web site:** http://www.hs.fi
Freq: Daily
Profile: Turku local editorial of national newspaper Helsingin Sanomat. Helsingin Sanomien Turun aluetoimitus.
Language (s): Finnish
DAILY NEWSPAPER

Hufvudstadsbladet 157021

Owner: KSF Media
Editorial: Mannerheimvagen 18, Helsingfors 100
Tel: 358 9 1253 222
Email: nyheter@hbl.fi **Web site:** http://www.hbl.fi
Freq: Daily; **Circ:** 40709 ABC-Audit Bureau of Circulations
Editor: Niclas Lönnqvist
Profile: Tabloid-sized quality newspaper providing national and international news and articles on politics, business, economics, culture, sport and events. Read by Swedish-speaking people throughout Finland.Volt supplement on Saturdays 12/year; Sport on Monday 52/year; Cars and Motoring on Fridays 52/year, Vision (TV and radio) on Thursdays 52/year.
Language (s): Swedish
Ad Rate: Full Page Colour 5676.00
Currency: Euro
DAILY NEWSPAPER

Iltalehti 159011

Owner: Alma Media Suomi Oy
Editorial: Alvar Aallon katu 3 C, Helsinki 100
Tel: 358 10 66 51 00
Email: il.toimitus@ilmedia.fi **Web site:** http://www.iltalehti.fi
Freq: Daily; **Circ:** 73525 ABC-Audit Bureau of Circulations
Editor: Olli Ainola; **News Manager:** Tuukka Matilainen; **News Manager:** Erkki Meriluoto; **Editor:** Juho Rissanen; **News Manager:** Juha Ristamäki
Profile: National evening newspaper with news and celebrity comments. Iltalehti on valtakunnallinen iltapäivälehti, josta löytyy tuoreimmat uutiset kommentoituna sekä julkkisten viimeisimmät tempaukset.Regular features: Women's affairs Ilona; Glamour every day; Tastes and Travel on Weekends; Cars on Fridays. They receive TV and radio programme content information from TV-maailma 50/year.
Language (s): Finnish
Ad Rate: Full Page Colour 4990.00
Currency: Euro
DAILY NEWSPAPER

Iltalehti Turku 161684

Owner: Alma Media Suomi Oy
Editorial: Kuuvuorenkatu 7, Turku 20540
Tel: 358 10 66 52 001
Email: il.toimitus@ilmedia.fi **Web site:** http://www.iltalehti.fi
Freq: Daily
Profile: Turku regional office of national evening newspaper Iltalehti. Local Translation:Iltalehden Turun aluetoimisto.
Language (s): Finnish
DAILY NEWSPAPER

Ilta-Sanomat 157022

Owner: Sanoma News Oy
Editorial: PL 41/ Toolonlahdenkatu 2, Sanoma 89
Tel: 358 9 12 21
Email: uutiset@iltasanomat.fi **Web site:** http://www.is.fi
Freq: Daily; **Circ:** 132253 ABC-Audit Bureau of Circulations
News Editor: Tomi Auremaa; **News Editor:** Simo Holopainen; **News Editor:** Pasi Jaakkonen; **News Editor:** Panu Karhunen; **News Manager:** Riika Kuuskoski; **News Editor:** Timo Myllyniemi; **News Editor:** Kristiina Tolvanen; **Editor:** Kari Ylänne
Profile: Tabloid-sized evening newspaper covering a broad range of national and international news, events, entertainment, sports and features. Read by a broad range of the population.Yleisesti luettu iltapäivälehti, joka sisältää uutisia kotimaasta ja ulkomailta, urheilua, viihdettä ja tapahtumia. Regular features: Monday & Friday: Hyvät Naiset/Women; Tuesdays: Ruokala/Food; Wednesdays: Matka/Travel; Thursdays: Asunto/Home&housing; Fridays: Autot/Cars.Supplements: IS Veikkaaja - 52xY
Language (s): Finnish
Ad Rate: Full Page Colour 6200.00
Currency: Euro
DAILY NEWSPAPER

Kaleva 157045

Owner: Kaleva Kustannus Oy
Editorial: PL 170/ Lekatie 1, Oulu 90401
Tel: 358 8 53 77 111
Email: toimitus@kaleva.fi **Web site:** http://www.kaleva.fi
Circ: 69540
Profile: The biggest newspaper in northern Finland. Pohjois-Suomen suurin sanomalehti.Editions: Kaleva Ajankohtaistoimitus, Kaleva Kulttuuritoimitus, Kaleva Kuntatoimitus, Kaleva Politiikan toimitus, Kaleva Taloustoimitus, Kaleva Ulkomaantoimitus, Kaleva Urheilutoimitus, Kaleva Uutistoimitus, Kaleva Verkkopalvelut Supplement: Peto, weekly supplement on ThursdaysSupplies content from Oulu and Lappi regions for Nelosen uutistoimitus. Regular features: Saturdays Home; Fridays Cars.
Language (s): Finnish
Ad Rate: Full Page Colour 9528.00
Currency: Euro
DAILY NEWSPAPER

Kaleva Raahe 161692

Owner: Kaleva Kustannus Oy
Editorial: Kauppakatu 42, Raahe 92100
Tel: 358 44 79 49 787
Email: timo.myllykoski@kaleva.fi **Web site:** http://www.kaleva.fi
Profile: Raahe regional editorial of newspaper Kaleva. Kalevan Raahen aluetoimitus.
Language (s): Finnish
DAILY NEWSPAPER

Kaleva Vaala 161694

Owner: Kaleva Kustannus Oy
Editorial: Asematie 2 A 8, Vaala 91700
Tel: 358 400 95 60 45
Email: petri.hakkarainen@kaleva.fi **Web site:** http://www.kaleva.fi
Profile: Vaala regional editorial of newspaper Kaleva. Kalevan Vaalan aluetoimitus.
Language (s): Finnish
DAILY NEWSPAPER

Kaleva Ylivieska 161695

Owner: Kaleva Kustannus Oy
Editorial: Kartanontie 1, Ylivieska 84100
Tel: 358 44 79 49 790
Email: toimitus@kaleva.fi **Web site:** http://www.kaleva.fi
Profile: Ylivieska regional editorial of newspaper Kaleva. Kalevan Ylivieskan aluetoimitus.
Language (s): Finnish
DAILY NEWSPAPER

Karjalainen 157031

Owner: Sanomalehti Karjalainen Oy
Editorial: PL 99/ Kosti Aaltosen tie 9, Joensuu 80141
Tel: 358 10 23 08 080
Email: toimitus@karjalainen.fi **Web site:** http://www.karjalainen.fi
Circ: 42396
News Manager: Hanna Käyhkö; **Editor in Chief:** Pasi Koivumaa; **Editor/Theme producer:** Mia Rouvinen; **Editor:** Heli Sallinen
Profile: Karjalainen is a newspaper emphasizing on northern Karelia. Read by people in North Karelia.Local Translation: Suurin sanomiin luokiteltu Karjalainen käsittelee valtakunnan uutisia ja Pohjois-Karjalan alueellisia uutisia.
Language (s): Finnish
DAILY NEWSPAPER

Karjalainen Keski-Suomi 161697

Owner: Sanomalehti Karjalainen Oy
Tel: 358 10 23 08 133
Email: sirpa.suomalainen@karjalainen.fi **Web site:** http://www.karjalainen.fi
Profile: Keski-Karjala regional office of newspaper Karjalainen. Local Translation:Karjalaisen Keski-Karjalan aluetoimisto.
Language (s): Finnish
DAILY NEWSPAPER

Karjalainen Nurmes 161699

Owner: Sanomalehti Karjalainen Oy
Editorial: Pappilansuora 15, Nurmes 75500
Tel: 358 10 230 8130
Email: toimitus@karjalainen.fi **Web site:** http://www.karjalainen.fi
Profile: Nurmes, Valtimo and Juuka regional office of newspaper Karjalainen. Local Translation:Karjalaisen Nurmeksen, Valtimon ja Juuan aluetoimisto.
Language (s): Finnish
DAILY NEWSPAPER

Kauppalehti 157024

Owner: Kauppalehti Oy
Editorial: Alvar Aallon katu 3 C, Helsinki 100
Tel: 358 10 66 51 01
Email: kl.toimitus@kauppalehti.fi **Web site:** http://www.kauppalehti.fi
Freq: Mon thru Fri; **Circ:** 50747 ABC-Audit Bureau of Circulations
News Editor: Tiia Kyynäräinen; **News Editor:** Janne Pöysti
Profile: Tabloid-sized quality newspaper containing financial and business news. Read by the business community, financial executives, business managers and academics.Kauppalehti on merkittävä talousalan lehti. Fax number to be used is 358 10-66 52 424, but generally they do not want any releases. They collect their information from Kauppalehti Online.Kauppalehti is also the producer of MTV3 Talousuutiset. Regular features: Special features on Mondays; Small-business and entrepreneurism on Tuesdays and Thursdays; Wednesdays cover Work and Appointments; Personal-finance and Cars on Fridays.Supplements: Kauppalehti Optio - 26xY. Number of pages: 32Start year: 1898
Language (s): Finnish
Ad Rate: Full Page Colour 12990.00
Currency: Euro
DAILY NEWSPAPER

Keskisuomalainen 157025

Owner: Keskisuomalainen Oyj
Editorial: PL 159/ Aholaidantie 3, Jyväskylä 40101
Tel: 358 14 62 22 71
Email: verkkotoimitus@keskisuomalainen.fi **Web site:** http://www.ksml.fi
Circ: 68163

News Manager: Keijo Lehto
Profile: Broadsheet-sized quality newspaper providing in-depth coverage of national and international news, politics, finance, culture and sport. Supplies regional content to MTV3 Uutistoimitus.Supplements: Sunnuntaisuomalainen - 52xY every Sunday Editions: Keskisuomalainen Kotimaantoimitus, Keskisuomalainen Kulttuuritoimitus, Keskisuomalainen Taloustoimitus, Keskisuomalainen Ulkomaantoimitus, KeskisuomalainenUrheilutoimitusRegular features: fashion, science and outdoor recreation daily, Asuntolehti (Home) every other Saturday and cars and traffic) every Friday.
Language (s): Finnish
Ad Rate: Full Page Colour 12444.00
Currency: Euro
DAILY NEWSPAPER

Keskisuomalainen Äänekoski 161710

Owner: Keskisuomalainen Oyj
Editorial: Kauppakatu 1, Äänekoski 44100
Tel: 358 14 348 9560
Email: Ira.Blomberg-Kantsila@keskisuomalainen.fi
Web site: http://www.ksml.fi
Profile: Äänekoski regional office of newspaper Keskisuomalainen. Local Translation:Keskisuomalaisen Äänekosken aluetoimisto.
Language (s): Finnish
DAILY NEWSPAPER

Keskisuomalainen Jämsä 161706

Owner: Keskisuomalainen Oyj
Editorial: Keskuskatu 4, Jämsä 42100
Web site: http://www.ksml.fi
Profile: Jämsä regional office of newspaper Keskisuomalainen. Local Translation:Keskisuomalaisen Jämsän aluetoimisto.
Language (s): Finnish
DAILY NEWSPAPER

Keskisuomalainen Keuruu 161707

Owner: Keskisuomalainen Oyj
Editorial: Kippavuorentie 7, Keuruu 42700
Tel: 358 50 54 91 824
Email: rainer.liimatainen@keskisuomalainen.fi **Web site:** http://www.ksml.fi
Profile: Keskisuomalainen local editorial covering Keuruu, Multia, Mänttä-Vilppula, Virrat, Ähtäri. Keskisuomalaisen aluetoimittajat Keuruulla, Multialla, Mänttä-Vilppulassa, Virroilla ja Ähtärissä.
Language (s): Finnish
DAILY NEWSPAPER

Keskisuomalainen Saarijärvi 161708

Owner: Keskisuomalainen Oyj
Editorial: Kauppakatu 5, Saarijärvi 43100
Tel: 358 50 37 61 231
Email: maarit.vaaherkumpu@keskisuomalainen.fi
Web site: http://www.ksml.fi
Profile: Keskisuomalainen local editorial covering Saarijärvi, Karstula, Kyyjärvi and Perho regions. Local Translation:Keskisuomalaisen aluetoimisto kattaen Saarijärveb, Karstulan, Kyyjärven ja Perhon alueet.
Language (s): Finnish
DAILY NEWSPAPER

Lännen Media Helsinki 161756

Email: palaute@lannenmedia.fi
Editor: Kirsi Turkki
Profile: Lännen Median Helsingin toimitus.
Language (s): Finnish
DAILY NEWSPAPER

Maaseudun Tulevaisuus 156937

Owner: Viestilehdet Oy
Editorial: PL 440/ Simonkatu 6, Helsinki 101
Tel: 358 20 41 32 100
Email: toimitus@maaseuduntulevaisuus.fi **Web site:** http://www.maaseuduntulevaisuus.fi
Freq: 2 Times/Week; **Circ:** 80754 ABC-Audit Bureau of Circulations
News Director: Janne Impiö
Profile: Official newspaper of the Finnish Farmers' Union. Lehti maa- ja metsätaloudesta sekä yleisestä talouspolitiikasta ja järjestöllisistä asioista.They issue a monthly lifestyle feature called Kantri.
Language (s): Finnish
Ad Rate: Full Page Colour 14390.00
Currency: Euro
DAILY NEWSPAPER

Pohjalainen 157061

Owner: I-Mediat Oy
Editorial: PL 37/ Hietasaarenkatu 19, Vaasa 65101
Tel: 358 6 247 7962
Email: toimitus@pohjalainen.fi **Web site:** http://www.pohjalainen.fi
Circ: 22355
News Manager: Mikko Kallionpää; **Editor/Producer:** Janne Lehtonen; **Editor/Producer:** Jukka-Pekka Porola; **Editor in Chief:** Toni Viljanmaa
Profile: Newspaper distributed mainly in the Vaasa region. Local Translation:Päivittäin ilmestyvä sanomalehti jaetaan lähinnä Vaasan alueella. Start year: 1903Previous title: Pohjalainen (Vaasa)
Language (s): Finnish
DAILY NEWSPAPER

Pohjalainen Härmänmaa 710253

Owner: I-Mediat Oy
Editorial: Nikolaintie 5 B 12, Kauhava 62200
Tel: 358 6 24 77 582
Email: toimitus@pohjalainen.fi **Web site:** http://www.pohjalainen.fi
Profile: Regional editorial of Pohjalainen in Härmänmaa. Local Translation:Pohjalaisen Härmänmaan toimitus.
Language (s): Finnish
DAILY NEWSPAPER

Pohjalainen Pietarsaari 161725

Owner: Vaasa Oy
Editorial: Jaakonkatu 13, Pietarsaari 68600
Tel: 358 6 24 77 581
Email: toimitus@pohjalainen.fi **Web site:** http://www.pohjalainen.fi
Profile: Pietarsaari regional office of newspaper Pohjalainen. Local Translation:Pohjalaisen Pietarsaaren aluetoimisto.
Language (s): Finnish
DAILY NEWSPAPER

Pohjalainen Seinäjoki 161726

Owner: I-Mediat Oy
Editorial: PL 139/ Koulukatu 10, Seinäjoki 60101
Tel: 358 6 24 77 962
Email: toimitus@pohjalainen.fi **Web site:** http://www.pohjalainen.fi
Profile: Seinäjoki regional office of newspaper Pohjalainen. Local Translation:Pohjalaisen Seinäjoen aluetoimisto.
Language (s): Finnish
DAILY NEWSPAPER

Pohjalainen Suomenselän-Järviseudun toimitus 710254

Owner: I-Mediat Oy
Editorial: UNAVAILABLE, Alavus 63300
Tel: 358 6 24 77 576
Email: toimitus@pohjalainen.fi **Web site:** http://www.pohjalainen.fi
Profile: Suomenselkä-Järviseutu local editorial of Pohjalainen. Local Translation:Pohjalaisen Suomenselän-Järviseudun toimitus.
Language (s): Finnish
DAILY NEWSPAPER

Pohjalainen Suupohja 161724

Owner: I-Mediat Oy
Editorial: Topeeka 21, Kauhajoki 61800
Tel: 358 6 247 7579
Email: toimitus@pohjalainen.fi **Web site:** http://www.pohjalainen.fi
Profile: Suupohja regional office of Pohjalainen. Local Translation:Pohjalaisen Suupohjan aluetoimisto.
Language (s): Finnish
DAILY NEWSPAPER

Savon Sanomat 157039

Owner: Savon Mediat Oy
Editorial: PL 68/Vuorikatu 21, Kuopio 70101
Tel: 358 17 30 31 11
Email: uutiset@savonsanomat.fi **Web site:** http://www.savonsanomat.fi
Freq: Daily; **Circ:** 57235
News Manager: Markus Karjalainen; **News Manager:** Marika Löf; **News Manager/Producer:** Pertti Ruohonen
Profile: Newspaper issued mainly in the city of Kuopio and in the Savo region. Sanomalehti, joka julkaistaan lähinnä Kuopiossa ja Savon seudulla.Editions: Savon Sanomat Kulttuuritoimitus, Savon Sanomat Taloustoimitus, Savon Sanomat Urheilutoimitus Regular features: Mondays: Science, Family 2/month, Outdoor and trekking 2/month; Tuesdays: Health; Wednesdays: Fashion and beauty 2/month, Young 2/month; Thursdays: Food and drink; Fridays: Films; Saturdays: Home and housing; Sundays: Travel and Entertainment.Start year: 1908
Language (s): Finnish
Ad Rate: Full Page Colour 7570.00
Currency: Euro
DAILY NEWSPAPER

Savon Sanomat Keski-Savon aluetoimitus 161735

Owner: Savon Mediat Oy
Editorial: PL 197/ Pirnankatu 4, Varkaus 78201
Email: varkaus@savonsanomat.fi **Web site:** http://www.savonsanomat.fi
Profile: Varkaus regional office of newspaper Savon Sanomat. Local Translation:Savon Sanomien Varkauden aluetoimisto.
Language (s): Finnish
DAILY NEWSPAPER

Savon Sanomat Pieksämäki 161669

Owner: Savon Mediat Oy
Editorial: Keskuskatu 15, Pieksämäki 76100
Email: pieksamaki@savonsanomat.fi **Web site:** http://www.savonsanomat.fi
Profile: Pieksämäki regional office of newspaper Savon Sanomat. Local Translation:Savon Sanomien Pieksämäen aluetoimisto.
Language (s): Finnish
DAILY NEWSPAPER

Savon Sanomat Ylä-Savon aluetoimitus 161733

Owner: Savon Mediat Oy
Editorial: Kilpivirrantie 7, 2 krs, Iisalmi 74120
Email: iisalmi@savonsanomat.fi **Web site:** http://www.savonsanomat.fi
Profile: Iisalmi regional office of newspaper Savon Sanomat. Local Translation:Savon Sanomien Iisalmen aluetoimisto.
Language (s): Finnish
DAILY NEWSPAPER

Suomenmaa Helsinki 157047

Owner: Suomenmaan Kustannus Oy
Editorial: Apollonkatu 11 A, Helsinki 100
Tel: 358 44 7370 260
Email: uutiset@suomenmaa.fi **Web site:** http://www.suomenmaa.fi
Freq: 3 Times/Week; **Circ:** 11197 ABC-Audit Bureau of Circulations
Profile: Main newspaper of the Centre Party. Once a month a special issue called Maa- ja metsätalous is distributed to all households of northern Finland, where the Centre Party is strong. Incorporating a monthly suppliment Sentteri. Local Translation: Keskustapuolueen pää-äänenkannattaja. Kerran kuussa ilmestyvä Maa- ja Metsätalousnumero kohdistaa sanomasi tilaajien lisäksi kaikkiin Pohjois-Pohjanmaan maatilatalouksiin. Kuukausittain jaettava kuukausiliite Sentteri.
Language (s): Finnish
DAILY NEWSPAPER

Suomenmaa Oulun toimitus 161761

Owner: Suomenmaan Kustannus Oy
Editorial: Lekatie 4, Oulu 90150
Email: uutiset@suomenmaa.fi **Web site:** http://www.suomenmaa.fi
Freq: 3 Times/Week; **Circ:** 11197 ABC-Audit Bureau of Circulations
News Manager: Katariina Lankinen
Profile: Main newspaper of the Centre Party in Finland. This is the rural edition of the same newspaper that also is issued as a national newspaper from Helsinki. Local Translation:Keskustan pää-äänenkäyttäjä. Maakunta-osio toimitetaan Oulusta.
Language (s): Finnish
DAILY NEWSPAPER

Turun Sanomat 157059

Owner: Turun Sanomat Oy
Editorial: PL 95/ Lansikaari 15, Turku 20101
Tel: 358 2 269 3260
Email: ts.uutiset@ts.fi **Web site:** http://www.ts.fi
Circ: 99220
Editor in Chief: Riitta Monto; **Editor:** Kirsi Turkki
Profile: Newspaper that covers the Turku region, southwest of Finland. Supplements: TS Talous 12xY; Teema-liite weekly features supplement with changing topic; TS. - 52xY every Wednesday; Turun Sanomat Extra - 52xY every Saturday.Desks: Turun Sanomat Kulttuuritoimitus - 365xY, Turun Sanomat Liitteet - 365xY, Turun Sanomat Mielipiteet - 365xY, Turun Sanomat Sunnuntaitoimitus - 365xY, Turun Sanomat Taloustoimitus - 365xY, Turun Sanomat Urheilutoimitus - 365xY, Turun Sanomat Uutistoimitus - 365xY, Turun Sanomat Politiikan toimitus, Turun Sanomat Ulkomaantoimitus Regular features: Cars & Traffic and Consumer Affairs every Monday and Health x2 per month on Mondays; Nature on every Tuesdays and Fitness x2 per month on Tuesdays; Travel on Wednesdays; Food on Thursdays and Style every first Thursday of the month; Home and Housing and Science on Sundays.Start year: 1905
Language (s): Finnish
Ad Rate: Full Page Colour 12449.00
Currency: Euro
DAILY NEWSPAPER

Turun Sanomat Rauma 161739

Owner: Turun Sanomat Oy
Editorial: Rauma
Web site: http://www.ts.fi
Profile: Rauma regional office of Turun Sanomat. Local Translation:Turun Sanomien Rauman aluetoimisto.
Language (s): Finnish
DAILY NEWSPAPER

Turun Sanomat Säkylä 161741

Owner: Turun Sanomat Oy
Editorial: Lehtikallentie 2, Säkylä 27800
Tel: 358 2 86 70 940
Web site: http://www.ts.fi
Profile: Säkylä regional office of Turun Sanomat. Local Translation:Turun Sanomien Säkylän aluetoimisto.
Language (s): Finnish
DAILY NEWSPAPER

Turun Sanomat Salo 161740

Owner: Turun Sanomat Oy
Editorial: Salo
Email: lilli.jokela@turunsanomat.fi **Web site:** http://www.ts.fi
Profile: Salo regional office of Turun Sanomat. Local Translation:Turun Sanomien Salon aluetoimisto.
Language (s): Finnish
DAILY NEWSPAPER

News Service/Syndicate

All Over Press 519927

Owner: Aller Media
Editorial: PL 170/Pursimiehenkatu 29-31 A, 5. krs., Helsinki Helsinki 00151 00101 **Tel:** 358 9 77 77 788
Email: images@alloverpress.fi **Web site:** http://www.alloverpress.fi
Freq: Daily
Profile: Kansainvälinen kuvatoimisto. International Picture Agency.
Language (s): Finnish
NEWS SERVICE/SYNDICATE

AP Associated Press 519910

Editorial: Erottajankatu 9 A, Helsinki 130
Tel: 358 9 68 02 394
Email: aphelsinki@ap.org
Freq: Daily
Profile: The Associated Press correspondent in Helsinki. AP:n kirjeenvaihtaja Suomessa.They wish to only receive information about Finnish companies. Their fax number is 358 9-68 02 310 but generally they want all relevant material sent at aphelsinki@ap.org only covering Finnish stock companies.
Language (s): Finnish
NEWS SERVICE/SYNDICATE

Bloomberg 519933

Editorial: Regus Business Ctre, Off 504, Mannerheimintie 12 B, 5krs, Helsinki 100
Tel: 358 9 25 12 37 32
Email: helsinkinews@bloomberg.net **Web site:** http://www.bloomberg.com
Freq: Daily
Editor: Ville Heiskanen; **Bureau Chief:** Kati Pohjanpalo
Profile: The Finnish office of the international Bloomberg news and finance analysis provider. Bloomberg on uutis- ja finanssitietotoimisto sekä analyysien tarjoaja.
Language (s): English
NEWS SERVICE/SYNDICATE

Kirkon tiedotuskeskus 519943

Editorial: Eteläranta 8, P.O.Box 210, Helsinki 131
Tel: 358 9 18 021
Email: kt@evl.fi **Web site:** http://sakasti.evl.fi/sakasti.nsf/sp?Open&cid=Content866A6
Freq: Daily
Profile: Information center of the Finnish Lutheran Church. Suomen evankelis-luterilainen tiedotuskeskus tekee uutisia, radio- ja tv-ohjelmia, av-materiaaleja, verkkoviestintää ja yhteisöviestintää.
Language (s): Finnish
NEWS SERVICE/SYNDICATE

Nyhetsbyrån FNB 519926

Editorial: PB 550/ Malminkatu 16 A, Helsingfors 101
Tel: 358 9 69 58 11
Email: redaktion@fnb.fi **Web site:** http://www.stt.fi
Freq: Daily
Profile: The Swedish-speaking part of the national news agency Suomen Tietotoimisto (STT). The abbreviation of Finska Notisbyrån is FNB. Previously listed as Finska Notisbyrån.
Language (s): Swedish
NEWS SERVICE/SYNDICATE

STT 519912

Editorial: Malminkatu 16 A, Helsinki 100
Tel: 358 9 69 58 11
Email: toimitus@stt-lehtikuva.fi **Web site:** http://www.stt.fi
Freq: Daily
Editor: Kirsi Aarnula; **Editor in Chief:** Minna Holopainen; **Editor:** Olli Kemppainen; **News Manager:** Laura Kolu; **News Manager:** Merja Könönen; **News Manager:** Mimma Lehtovaara; **News Manager:** Kimmo Mäkilä; **News Manager:** Mia Peltola; **Managing Director:** Mika Pettersson; **News Editor:** Piritta Rautavuori; **Editor:** Tuomas Savonen; **News Manager:** Johanna Vuonokari
Profile: The most important news and photo agency in Finland. Previously listed as Suomen Tietotoimisto Oy.STT-Lehtikuva on Suomen suurin tieto- ja valokuvatoimisto.
Language (s): Finnish
NEWS SERVICE/SYNDICATE

Suomen Tietotoimisto Kuopio 519914

Editorial: Puistokatu 6 as.5, Kuopio 70110
Tel: 358 9 69 58 15 30
Email: kuopio@stt-lehtikuva.fi **Web site:** http://www.stt.fi
Freq: Daily
Profile: Kuopio regional editorial of news agency Suomen Tietotoimisto. Local Translation:STT:n Kuopion alueen toimitus.
Language (s): Finnish
NEWS SERVICE/SYNDICATE

Svensk Presstjänst 519922

Editorial: PB 550/ Malmgatan 16, Helsingfors 101
Tel: 358 9 69 58 12 36
Email: redaktion@svenskpresstjanst.fi **Web site:** http://www.svenskpresstjanst.fi
Freq: Daily
Editor: Heidi Hakala
Profile: Swedish-speaking news coverage from Finland. Finlandssvensk pressbevakning i Finland.
Language (s): Swedish
NEWS SERVICE/SYNDICATE

UP-Uutispalvelu Oy 519919

Editorial: PL 290/Siltasaarenkatu 6, 7. krs., Helsinki 531 **Tel:** 358 9 4780 8800
Email: up@up.fi **Web site:** http://www.up.fi/
Freq: Daily
Editor in Chief: Birgitta Suorsa

Profile: Finnish news service concentrating on finance and political news. Uutispalvelu, joka keskittyy politiikkaan ja talouteen.
Language (s): Finnish
NEWS SERVICE/SYNDICATE

Uutistoimisto Startel 519925
Owner: Sanoma News Oy
Editorial: PL 45/ Toolonlahdenkatu 2, Sanoma 89
Tel: 358 9 12 24 052
Email: uutistoimisto.startel@sanoma.fi **Web site:** http://www.startel.fi
Freq: Daily
News Manager: Martina Ahola; **News Manager:** Johannes Niemeläinen; **News Manager:** Antero Paavonen
Profile: Startel is the first neutral news agency specialized in live finance news in Finland. Startel's finance editors examine domestic and foreign finance events, company news as well as stock and finance markets. About 100-200 news are made daily about Finnish finance markets and companies. An important part of the service is to create prognoses about national economy developments and company results. Uutistoimisto Startel on Suomen ensimmäinen reaaliaikaisiin talousuutisiin erikoistunut puolueeton uutistoimisto. Startelin taloustoimittajat seuraavat koti- ja ulkomaisia taloustapahtumia, yritysuutisia sekä pörssi-, raha- ja valuuttamarkkinoita. Kotimaisista finanssimarkkinoista ja yrityksistä tehdään päivittäin 100-200 uutista. Tärkeä osa palvelua ovat myös ennusteet kansantalouden kehityksestä ja yritysten tuloksista.
Language (s): Finnish
NEWS SERVICE/SYNDICATE

Väli-Suomen Media 519934
Editorial: Aholaidantie 3, Jyväskylä 40320
Tel: 358 14 622 000
Web site: http://www.ksml.fi
Freq: Daily
Managing Director: Tarja Koljonen
Profile: Väli-Suomen Media produces news about politics and finance for newspapers Ilkka, Karjalainen, Keskisuomalainen, Pohjalainen and Savon Sanomat. Local Translation:Väli-Suomen Media tuottaa Ilkalle, Karjalaiselle, Keskisuomalaiselle, Pohjalaiselle ja Savon Sanomille uutisia politiikasta ja taloudesta.
Language (s): Finnish
NEWS SERVICE/SYNDICATE

Xinhua News Agency 519940
Editorial: Hopeasalmentie 14, Helsinki 570
Tel: 358 9 68 47 587
Email: xinhuahelsinki@gmail.com
Freq: Daily
Profile: Finnish correspondent of the Chinese news agency.
Language (s): English
NEWS SERVICE/SYNDICATE

Community Newspaper

Aamuposti 157052
Owner: Etelä-Suomen Media Oy
Editorial: Kauppakatu 12, Riihimaki 11100
Tel: 358 20 770 3461
Email: toimitus.aamuposti@media.fi **Web site:** http://www.aamuposti.fi
Freq: Daily; **Circ:** 17889
Profile: Regional newspaper issued in Riihimäki, Hausjärvi, Loppi, Janakkala, Nurmijärvi, Tuusula, Hyvinkää and Tervakoski. Local Translation:Riihimäellä, Hausjärvellä, Lopissa, Janakkalassa, Nurmijärvellä, Tuusulassa, Hyvinkäällä ja Tervakoskella ilmestyvä aluelehti. Previous title: Riihimäen SanomatThe address to the Hyvinkää office is Kauppalankatu 7-11, 05800 HYVINKÄÄ. Their fax number is 358 19-72 30 83, but e-mails are preferred
Language (s): Finnish
Ad Rate: Full Page Colour 3585.00
Currency: Euro
COMMUNITY NEWSPAPER

Aamuposti Hyvinkää 520644
Owner: Etelä-Suomen Media Oy
Editorial: PL 93/ Kauppalankatu 7-11, Hyvinkää 5801
Tel: 358 20 77 03 461
Email: toimitus.aamuposti@media.fi **Web site:** http://www.aamuposti.fi
Freq: Daily; **Circ:** 17889
Profile: Regional newspaper issued in Riihimäki, Hausjärvi, Loppi, Janakkala, Nurmijärvi, Tuusula, Hyvinkää and Tervakoski. Local Translation:Riihimäellä, Hausjärvellä, Lopissa, Janakkalassa, Nurmijärvellä, Tuusulassa, Hyvinkäällä ja Tervakoskella ilmestyvä aluelehti.
Language (s): Finnish
Ad Rate: Full Page Colour 3585.00
Currency: Euro
COMMUNITY NEWSPAPER

Åbo Underrättelser 157058
Owner: Förlags AB Sydvästkusten
Editorial: LOGOMO Konttori, Hampspinnaregatan 14, Åbo 20100 **Tel:** 358 2 274 9900
Email: nyheter@aumedia.fi **Web site:** http://www.abounderrattelser.fi
Freq: Fri; **Circ:** 7293
Editor: Johan Backas; **News Manager:** Pia Heikkilä; **Editor:** Carina Holm; **News Manager:** Jean Lindén
Profile: Independent newspaper issued in Turku, Kaarina, Naantali, Raisio, Parainen, Nauvo, Korppoo, Houtskari, Iniö, Kemiö, Dragsfjärd, Västanfjärd and Särkisalo. Local Translation:Neutral dagstidning som utkommer främst i Åbo, St Karins, Nådendal, Reso, Pargas, Nagu, Korpo, Houtskär, Iniö, Kimito, Västanfjärd och Särkisalo.
Language (s): Swedish
Ad Rate: Full Page Colour 2750.00
Currency: Euro
COMMUNITY NEWSPAPER

Ähtärinjärven Uutisnuotta 222547
Owner: Suomenselän Sanomat Oy
Editorial: Ostolantie 6, Ähtäri 63700
Tel: 358 6 53 31 362
Email: uutisnuotta.toimitus@sss.inet.fi **Web site:** http://www.ahtarinjarvenuutisnuotta.net
Freq: Weekly; **Circ:** 3998 Publisher's Statement
General Editor: Toimitus
Profile: Newspaper issued in Ähtäri, Lehtimäki and Soini. Local Translation:Description: Newspaper issued in Ähtäri, Lehtimäki and Soini. Ähtärissä, Lehtimäellä ja Soinissa ilmestyvä paikallislehti.Number of pages: 16 Start year: 1987
Language (s): Finnish
Ad Rate: Full Page Colour 2509.00
Currency: Euro
COMMUNITY NEWSPAPER

Akaan Seutu 222392
Owner: Akaan Seutu Lehti Oy
Editorial: PL 60 /Alventie 4, Toijala 37801
Tel: 358 3 54 09 600
Email: toimitus@akaanseutu.fi **Web site:** http://www.akaanseutu.fi
Freq: 2 Times/Week; **Circ:** 5927 ABC-Audit Bureau of Circulations
Editor in Chief: Juha Kosonen
Profile: Newspaper issued in Toijala, Viiala, Kylmäkoski, Saarioispuoli and Kalvola. Local Translation:Toijalassa, Viialassa, Kylmäkoskella, Saarioispuolessa ja Kalvolassa ilmestyvä paikallislehti.
Language (s): Finnish
Ad Rate: Full Page Colour 3049.00
Currency: Euro
COMMUNITY NEWSPAPER

Ålands Sjöfart 723647
Owner: Ålands Tidnings-Tryckeri Ab
Editorial: PB 50/ Strandgatan 16, Åland 22101
Tel: 358 18 26 026
Email: sjofart@alandstidningen.ax **Web site:** http://www.sjofart.ax/sv/nyheter
Freq: Quarterly; **Circ:** 10000 Publisher's Statement
Editor: Malin Henriksson
Profile: Publication covering navigation as an industry as well as sea life in Åland. A news website sjofart.ax will be released. Tidningen med fokus på sjöfart som livsnäring och det åländska sjölivet.Start year: 2011
Language (s): Swedish
COMMUNITY NEWSPAPER

Ålandstidningen 157043
Owner: Ålands Tidnings Tryckeri AB
Editorial: PB 50/ Strandgatan 16, Mariehamn 22101
Tel: 358 18 26 026
Email: 15000@alandstidningen.ax **Web site:** http://www.alandstidningen.ax/
Circ: 8829
News Manager: Malin Henriksson; **Editor in Chief:** Niklas Lampi; **News Manager:** Sandra Widing
Profile: The main newspapers on the Aaland (Ahvenanmaa) Islands. Landskapet Ålands största dagstidning.Number of pages: 32 Start year: 1891Alternative Title: Ålandstidningen
Language (s): Swedish
Ad Rate: Full Page Colour 6329.00
Currency: Euro
COMMUNITY NEWSPAPER

Alasatakunta 222415
Owner: Pyhäjärviseudun Paikallislehti Oy
Editorial: PL 19/ Euruntie 6, Eura 27511
Tel: 358 2 83 87 92 00
Email: toimitus@alasatakunta.fi **Web site:** http://www.alasatakunta.fi
Freq: 2 Times/Week; **Circ:** 10085 ABC-Audit Bureau of Circulations
Profile: Newspaper issued in Kiukainen, Köyliö, Lappi TL, Eura, Yläne and Säkylä. Local Translation:Kiukaisissa, Köyliössä, Lappi TL:ssä, Yläneellä, Eurassa ja Säkylässä ilmestyvä paikallislehti.
Language (s): Finnish
Ad Rate: Full Page Colour 2628.00
Currency: Euro
COMMUNITY NEWSPAPER

Alavieska 222462
Owner: Alavieskan Viri ry
Editorial: Paaskyntie 1, Alavieska 85200
Tel: 358 8 43 01 59
Email: alavieskalehti@gmail.com **Web site:** http://alavieskanviri.sporttisaitti.com/alavieska-lehti
Freq: Weekly
Profile: Newspaper issued in Alavieska. Local Translation:Alavieskassa ilmestyvä paikallislehti.
Email: alavieskalehti@kotinet.com not in use anymore.
Language (s): Finnish
COMMUNITY NEWSPAPER

Alueviesti 222513
Owner: Kustannusliike Aluelehdet Oy
Editorial: PL 101/Hopunkatu 1, Sastamala 38200
Tel: 358 10 22 90 400
Email: toimitus@alueviesti.fi **Web site:** http://www.alueviesti.fi
Freq: Weekly; **Circ:** 32000 Publisher's Statement
Editor in Chief: Maija Latva
Profile: Alueviesti newspaper is distributed in Sastamala, Huittinen, Punkalaidun, Kiikoinen, Lavia, Köyliö, Säkylä, Kokemäki, Yläne, Pöytyä. The first newspaper of the month is distributed also to Nokia. Local Translation:Alueviestin jakelukunnat ovat: Sastamala, Huittinen, Punkalaidun, Kiikoinen, Lavia, Köyliö, Säkylä, Kokemäki, Yläne ja Pöytyä. Joka kuukauden ensimmäinen lehti jaetaan myös Nokialle. Start year: 1983
Language (s): Finnish
COMMUNITY NEWSPAPER

Ankkuri 222510
Owner: Poiju Julkaisut Oy
Editorial: PL 238/ Kymenlaaksonkatu 4, Kotka 48101
Tel: 358 5 21 04 400
Email: toimitus@ankkurilehti.fi **Web site:** http://www.kaupunkilehtiankkuri.fi
Freq: 2 Times/Week; **Circ:** 46200 Publisher's Statement
Editor in Chief: Petri Piipari
Profile: Newspaper issued in Loviisa, Pyhtää, Kotka, Hamina, Miehikkälä and Virolahti. Local Translation: Lehden jakelualueet ovat: Loviisa, Pyhtää, Kotka, Hamina, Miehikkälä ja Virolahti.Incorporating Poiju and previous Kotkansilmä. Number of pages: 20Start year: 1976 Previous title: Kotkansilmä
Language (s): Finnish
Ad Rate: Full Page Colour 2997.00
Currency: Euro
COMMUNITY NEWSPAPER

Annonsbladet-Kemiönseudun Ilmoituslehti 222361
Owner: Förlags Ab Lindan Kustannus Oy
Editorial: PL 18/ Toimittajanpolku, Kemiö 25701
Tel: 358 2 42 17 25
Email: abl@abl-kimito.fi **Web site:** http://www.annonsbladet-kimito.fi
Freq: Weekly; **Circ:** 5238 Publisher's Statement
Editor in Chief: Michael Nurmi
Profile: Lokaltidning i Kimito. Local Translation:Local newspaper issued in Kimito/Kemiö.
Language (s): Finnish
COMMUNITY NEWSPAPER

Auranmaan Viikkolehti 222363
Owner: Priimus Media Oy Auranmaan Viikkolehti
Editorial: PL 15 / Kehityksentie 3, Kyrö 21801
Tel: 358 2 48 64 950
Email: toimitus@avl.fi **Web site:** http://www.auranmaanviikkolehti.fi
Freq: 2 Times/Week; **Circ:** 8730 ABC-Audit Bureau of Circulations
Editor in Chief: Asko Virtanen
Profile: Newspaper issued in Aura, Karinainen, Koski TL, Marttila, Mellilä, Oripää, Pöytyä, Tarvasjoki and Yläne. Local Translation:Aurassa, Karinaisissa, Koski TL:ssä, Marttilassa, Mellilässä, Oripäässä, Pöytyässä, Tarvasjoella ja Yläneellä ilmestyvä paikallislehti.
Language (s): Finnish
Ad Rate: Full Page Colour 3247.00
Currency: Euro
COMMUNITY NEWSPAPER

ByaNytt 222299
Owner: Kustmedia Ab Oy
Editorial: Barkamovagen 3, Solf 65450
Tel: 358 6 34 41 800
Email: info@kustmedia.fi **Web site:** http://www.kustmedia.fi
Freq: Monthly; **Circ:** 3400 Publisher's Statement
Editor-in-Chief: Lisbeth Bäck; **General Editor:** Redaktionen
Profile: Articles about people, companies and events in Korsholm. Local Translation:ByaNytt publicerar artiklar om människor, företag och evenemang i Korsholm. Their fax number is 358 6-34 41 820 but e-mails are preferred.
Language (s): Swedish
COMMUNITY NEWSPAPER

City & Archipelago News 224177
Owner: Förlags Ab Lindan Kustannus Oy
Editorial: PL 18/ Toimittajanpolku, Kemiö 25701
Tel: 358 2 42 17 25
Email: press@canews.fi **Web site:** http://www.canews.fi
Freq: Quarterly; **Circ:** 40000 Publisher's Statement
Editor in Chief: Michael Nurmi
Profile: News and ads from the Swedish-speaking archipelago region in western Uusimaa and southwest of Finland. Local Translation:City & Archipelago News käsittelee uutisia ruotsinkielisellä etelärannikkoseudulla kahdella kielellä. Alternative Title: City & Archipelago NewsAlso known as: Nylands Nyheter Uudenmaan Uutiset, City & Archipelago News.
Language (s): English
Ad Rate: Full Page Colour 1940.00
Currency: Euro
COMMUNITY NEWSPAPER

Dagens Tidning 703819
Owner: Wester Media Group Oy Ab
Editorial: Kanalesplanaden 21, Jakobstad 68600
Tel: 358 6 72 10 245
Web site: http://www.dagenstidning.fi
Freq: Weekly; **Circ:** 20184 Publisher's Statement
News: Nicklas Storbjörk
Profile: Free newspaper distributed in Jakobstad, Pedersöre, Nykarleby, Larsmo and Kronoby. Local Translation:Description: Free newspaper distributed in Jakobstad, Pedersöre, Nykarleby, Larsmo and Kronoby. Gratis tidningen som distribueras i Jakobstad, Pedersöre, Nykarleby, Larsmo och Kronoby.Number of pages: 16 Start year: 2010
Language (s): Finnish
COMMUNITY NEWSPAPER

Elimäen Sanomat 222421
Owner: Elimäen Sanomat Oy
Editorial: PL 10/Vanhamaantie 7, Elimäki 47201
Tel: 358 5 74 00 500
Email: toimitus@elimaensanomat.fi **Web site:** http://www.elimaensanomat.fi
Freq: Weekly; **Circ:** 2777 ABC-Audit Bureau of Circulations
Editor in Chief: Raija Anttila
Profile: Local weekly newspaper issued in Elimäki. Local Translation:Elimäellä ilmestyvä paikallislehti.
Language (s): Finnish
Ad Rate: Full Page Colour 2090.00
Currency: Euro
COMMUNITY NEWSPAPER

Epari 159013
Owner: I-Mediat Oy
Editorial: PL 60/Koulukatu 10, Seinäjoki 60101
Tel: 358 6 24 77 865
Email: toimitus@epari.fi **Web site:** http://www.epari.fi
Freq: Weekly; **Circ:** 46800
Editor in chief: Laura Syväoja
Profile: Epari is a regional newspaper distributed in Seinäjoki, Nurmo and the Finnish speaking region of southern Ostrobothnia. Local Translation:Epari on Seinäjoella, Nurmolla ja suomenkielisellä Etelä-Pohjanmaalla ilmestyvä alueellinen sanomalehti. Incorporating Periskooppi supplement.Also known as: Epari Start year: 1926Alternative Title: Epari
Language (s): Finnish
COMMUNITY NEWSPAPER

Espoo Esbo -lehti 665709
Tel: 358 9 42 42 73 30
Web site: http://www.espoo.fi
Freq: Quarterly; **Circ:** 105000 Publisher's Statement
General Editor: Toimitus
Profile: Magazine for the City of Espoo distributed to all the households.
Language (s): Finnish
COMMUNITY NEWSPAPER

Etelä-Uusimaa 222562
Owner: Länsi-Uusimaa Oy
Editorial: PL 16/ Keskuskatu 76, Karjaa 10301
Tel: 358 19 27 88 66
Email: toimitus@etela.com **Web site:** http://www.etela.com
Freq: 2 Times/Week; **Circ:** 23000 Publisher's Statement
Editor in Chief: Ari Hätönen
Profile: Newspaper issued in Hanko, Inkoo, Karjaa, Pohja and Tammisaari. Local Translation:Description: Newspaper issued in Hanko, Inkoo, Karjaa, Pohja and Tammisaari. Hangossa, Inkoossa, Karjaalla, Pohjassa ja Tammisaaressa ilmesyvä paikallislehti.Their faxnumber is 358 19-23 67 97, but e-mails are preferred. Number of pages: 16Start year: 1979
Language (s): Finnish
Ad Rate: Full Page Colour 2790.00
Currency: Euro
COMMUNITY NEWSPAPER

Forssan Lehti 157027
Owner: Forssan Kirjapaino Oy
Editorial: PL 1000/ Esko Aaltosen katu 2, Forssa 30101 **Tel:** 358 3 41 551
Email: toimitus@forssanlehti.fi **Web site:** http://www.forssanlehti.fi
Freq: Daily; **Circ:** 12111
Editor: Jaakko Leinonen
Profile: Regional newspaper issued in Forssa, Tammela, Jokioinen, Humppila, Ypäjä, Somero and Urjala. Local Translation:Alueellinen Forssassa, Tammelassa, Jokioisissa, Humppilassa, Ypäjällä, Somerossa ja Urjalassa ilmestyvä sanomalehti.
Language (s): Finnish
Ad Rate: Full Page Colour 3589.00
Currency: Euro
COMMUNITY NEWSPAPER

Forum 24 230306
Owner: Kaleva Kustannus Oy
Editorial: Lekatie 6, Oulu 90510
Tel: 358 20 75 45 700
Email: toimitus@forum24.fi **Web site:** http://www.forum24.fi
Freq: 2 Times/Week; **Circ:** 93000 Publisher's Statement
Editor in Chief/Managing Director: Martti Turunen
Profile: Newspaper distributed in Oulu, Haukiputaa, Kempele, Kiiminki, Oulunsalo, Liminga, Muhos, Tupos and Tyrnävä. Local Translation:Oulussa, Haukiputaalla, Kempeleessä, Kiimingissä ja Oulunsalossa, Limingassa, Muhoksella, Tupoksella ja Tyrnävällä jaettava paikallislehti. Start year: 2001
Language (s): Finnish
Ad Rate: Full Page Colour 3148.80
Currency: Euro
COMMUNITY NEWSPAPER

Haagalainen 222564
Owner: Haagalaisen Tuki - Stöd ry.
Editorial: PL 4, Helsinki 321 **Tel:** 358 44 530 0441
Email: toimitus@haagalainen.com **Web site:** http://www.haagalainen.com
Freq: Bi-Monthly; **Circ:** 20000 Publisher's Statement
Editor in Chief: Tuula Salo
Profile: Local newspaper of Helsinki suburb Haaga. Local Translation:Helsingin Haaga-kaupunginosan

uutislehti. No faxes are to be sent to their number 358 9-58 79 135.
Language (s): Finnish
Ad Rate: Full Page Colour 1861.50
Currency: Euro
COMMUNITY NEWSPAPER

Haapavesi-lehti 225019

Owner: Jokilaaksojen Kustannus Oy
Editorial: Tahtelankuja 2, Haapavesi 86600
Tel: 358 20 75 04 640
Email: toimitus@haapavesi-lehti.fi **Web site:** http://www.haapavesi-lehti.fi
Freq: Weekly; **Circ:** 3230 ABC-Audit Bureau of Circulations
Editor in Chief: Katariina Anttila
Profile: Newspaper distributed in the Haapavesi region. Local Translation:Paikallislehti, jota jaetaan Haapavedellä, Kärsämäessä, Piippolassa, Pulkkilassa ja Pyhännässä.
Language (s): Finnish
COMMUNITY NEWSPAPER

Hämeen Sanomat 366149

Owner: Hämeen Sanomat Oy
Editorial: PL 530/ Vanajantie 7, Hämeenlinna 13111
Tel: 358 3 61 511
Email: toimitus@hameensanomat.fi **Web site:** http://www.hameensanomat.fi
Freq: Daily; **Circ:** 27345
Editor in Chief: Pauli Uusi-Kilponen; **News Manager:** Pirjo Vidberg-Pietilä; **News Manager:** Veli-Matti Virtanen
Profile: Newspaper issued in Hämeenlinna, Hattula and Janakkala. Local Translation:Sanomalehti, joka Jaetaan kaikkiin talouksiin Hämeenlinnassa, Hattulassa ja Janakkalassa.
Language (s): Finnish
Ad Rate: Full Page Colour 4665.00
Currency: Euro
COMMUNITY NEWSPAPER

Hämeenkulma 330892

Owner: Victus Oy
Editorial: PL 6/ Keskustie 1, Oitti 12101
Tel: 358 50 36 01 170
Email: toimitus@ehl.fi **Web site:** http://www.ehl.fi
Freq: Weekly; **Circ:** 1531 Publisher's Statement
Editor in Chief/Managing Director: Esa Joensuu
Profile: Newspaper issued in Hausjärvi and Kärkölä. Local Translation:Description: Newspaper issued in Hausjärvi and Kärkölä. Hausjärvellä ja Kärkölässä ilmestyvä paikallislehti.Number of pages: 12 Start year: 2004
Language (s): Finnish
Ad Rate: Full Page Colour 2376.00
Currency: Euro
COMMUNITY NEWSPAPER

Hämeenlinnan Kaupunkiuutiset 375690

Owner: Hämeen Sanomat Oy
Editorial: PL 207/ Vanajantie 7, Hämeenlinna 13110
Tel: 358 3 61 511
Email: ku.toimitus@hameensanomat.fi **Web site:** http://www.hameensanomat.fi/hameenlinnan-kaupunkiuutiset
Freq: 2 Times/Week; **Circ:** 39570 Publisher's Statement
Profile: Newspaper issued in Hämeenlinna. Local Translation:Hämeenlinnassa ilmestyvä paikallislehti. Start year: 1977
Language (s): Finnish
COMMUNITY NEWSPAPER

HangöTidningen - HangonLehti 224354

Owner: Förlags Ab Lindan Kustannus Oy
Editorial: PL 2 / Bulevardi 20, Hanko 10901
Tel: 358 19 21 24 200
Email: newsdesk@hangotidningen.fi **Web site:** http://www.hangotidningen.fi
Freq: Weekly; **Circ:** 2500 Publisher's Statement
Profile: Newspaper both in Swedish and Finnish is mainly issued in Hanko, Tammisaari and Karis. Local Translation:Paikallinen sanomalehti jaetaan Hangossa, Tammisaaressa ja Karjaalla. Previous title: Hangötidningen
Language (s): Finnish
Ad Rate: Full Page Colour 2250.00
Currency: Euro
COMMUNITY NEWSPAPER

Hankasalmen Sanomat 222395

Owner: Maakunnan Sanomat Oy
Editorial: PL 12/Keskustie 32, Hankasalmi 41521
Tel: 358 14 84 11 45
Email: toimitus@hankasalmensanomat.fi **Web site:** http://www.ksml.fi/hankasalmensanomat/
Freq: Weekly; **Circ:** 3324 ABC-Audit Bureau of Circulations
Editor-in-Chief: Arja Korpela
Profile: Local newspaper issued in Hankasalmi. Local Translation:Hankasalmella ilmestyvä paikallislehti.
Language (s): Finnish
COMMUNITY NEWSPAPER

Heinäveden Lehti 222431

Owner: Maakunnan Sanomat Oy
Editorial: PL 23 / Kermantie 24 A, Heinävesi 79701
Tel: 358 17 56 25 71
Email: uutiset@heinavedenlehti.fi **Web site:** http://www.heinavedenlehti.fi
Freq: Weekly; **Circ:** 3485 ABC-Audit Bureau of Circulations
Profile: Newspaper issued in Heinävesi. Local Translation:Heinävedellä ilmestyvä paikallislehti.
Language (s): Finnish
COMMUNITY NEWSPAPER

Helsingin Uutiset 222493

Owner: Etelä-Suomen Media Oy
Editorial: PL 350/ Ralssitie 7a, Vantaa 1511
Tel: 358 20 61 00 110
Email: helsingin.uutiset@media.fi **Web site:** http://www.helsinginuutiset.fi
Freq: 2 Times/Week; **Circ:** 215000 Publisher's Statement
Editor in Chief: Sakari Nupponen; **News Manager:** Kaisa Paastela; **News Manager (Online):** Mikko Välimaa
Profile: Newspaper distributed to households in Helsinki. Local Translation:Helsingissä jaettava ilmaisjakelulehti. Incorporating: Länsi-Helsingin Uutiset, Pohjois- ja Itä-Helsingin UutisetPreviously listed as: Lähilehti Start year: 1981
Language (s): Finnish
Ad Rate: Full Page Colour 5631.00
Currency: Euro
COMMUNITY NEWSPAPER

Helsinki Times 713612

Owner: Helsinki Times Oy
Editorial: Vilhonvuorenkatu 11 B, Helsinki 500
Tel: 358 9 689 67 425
Email: info@helsinkitimes.fi **Web site:** http://www.helsinkitimes.fi
Freq: Weekly; **Circ:** 15000 Publisher's Statement
Editor in Chief: Alexis Kouros
Profile: English language newspaper covering news and events in Finland. Foreign professionals, diplomats and their families as well as people visiting Finland.Local Translation: Englanninkielisiä uutisia Suomesta.
Language (s): English
COMMUNITY NEWSPAPER

Helsinki-info 222304

Owner: Helsingin kaupunki
Editorial: Helsingin Kaupungintalo, Kaupunginkanslia, Viestinta, Helsinki 170
Tel: 358 9 310 1641
Email: helsinki-info.palaute@hel.fi **Web site:** http://www.hel.fi/helsinki-info
Freq: Bi-Monthly; **Circ:** 373475 Publisher's Statement
Editor in Chief: Rita Ekelund
Profile: Magazine about what is going on in Helsinki. Local Translation:Helsingin kaupungin tiedotuslehti kaupungin tapahtumista. Readers: Private households in Helsinki.Start year: 1976 Previous title: Helsingin kaupungin tiedottaa
Language (s): Finnish
COMMUNITY NEWSPAPER

Hervannan Sanomat 222514

Owner: Kustannus Oy Otsikko
Editorial: PL 99/ Insinoorinkatu 30, 2 krs, Tampere 33721 **Tel:** 358 10 66 51 15
Email: hs@hervannansanomat.fi **Web site:** http://www.hervannansanomat.fi
Freq: Weekly; **Circ:** 22000 Publisher's Statement
Editor in Chief: Jari Mylläri
Profile: Local free newspaper distributed in Hallila, Hervanta, Kaukajärvi, Lukonmäki, Messukylä, Finninmäki, Annala, Haihara, Hankkio, Viiala, Turtola, Vuohenoja, Korkinmäki and Muotiala Paikallinen ilmaisjakelulehti jaetaan Hallilaan, Hervantaan, Kaukajärvelle, Lukonmäelle, Messukylään, Finninmäkeen, Annalaan, Haiharaan, Hankkioon, Viialaan, Turtolaan, Vuohenojaan, Korkinmäkeen ja Muotialaan.Number of pages: 12 Start year: 1975
Language (s): Finnish
Ad Rate: Full Page Colour 3438.00
Currency: Euro
COMMUNITY NEWSPAPER

HS Metro 222303

Owner: Sanoma News Oy
Editorial: HS Metro, PL 75, Sanoma 89
Tel: 358 9 1224 362
Email: metro@sanoma.fi **Web site:** http://metro.fi
Freq: Daily; **Circ:** 319000 Publisher's Statement
Profile: Free local newspaper distributed at news stands in Helsinki and its surroundings as well as in Lahti, Hyvinkää, Mäntsälä, Järvenpää, Kerava, Kirkkonummi and Riihimäki. Uutislehti jaetaan ilmaiseksi pääkaupunkiseudun lisäksi Lahden, Hyvinkään, Mäntsälän, Järvenpään, Keravan, Kirkkonummen ja Riihimäen juna-asemilla.
Language (s): Finnish
Ad Rate: Full Page Colour 6352.00
Currency: Euro
COMMUNITY NEWSPAPER

Hyvinkään Viikkouutiset 222482

Owner: Suomen Lehtiyhtymä
Editorial: PL 93 (Kauppalankatu 7-11), Hyvinkää 5810 **Tel:** 358 20 61 00 120
Email: toimitus.rile@lehtiyhtyma.fi **Web site:** http://www.viikkouutiset.fi
Freq: Weekly; **Circ:** 23000 Publisher's Statement
Profile: Newspaper issued in Hyvinkää. Local Translation:Description: Newspaper issued in Hyvinkää. Hyvinkäällä ilmestyvä paikallislehti.Number of pages: 12 Start year: 1953Previous title: Hyvinkään Uutiset
Language (s): Finnish
Ad Rate: Full Page Colour 2504.00
Currency: Euro
COMMUNITY NEWSPAPER

Iijokiseutu 222530

Owner: Pohjois-Suomen Paikallisuutiset Oy
Editorial: PL 24 / Puistotie 2, Pudasjärvi 93100
Tel: 358 8 86 00 715
Email: toimitus@iijokiseutu.fi **Web site:** http://www.iijokiseutu.fi
Freq: 2 Times/Week; **Circ:** 4413 ABC-Audit Bureau of Circulations
Editor in Chief: Martta Oinas-Panuma
Profile: Newspaper issued in Pudasjärvi and Taivalkoski. Local Translation:Pudasjärvellä ja Taivalkoskella ilmestyvä paikallislehti.
Language (s): Finnish
Ad Rate: Full Page Colour 3986.00
Currency: Euro
COMMUNITY NEWSPAPER

Iisalmen Sanomat 157029

Owner: Savon Media Oy
Editorial: Kilpivirrantie 7, Iisalmi 74100
Tel: 358 17 8351 311
Email: toimitus@iisalmensanomat.fi **Web site:** http://www.iisalmensanomat.fi
Freq: Daily; **Circ:** 12214
Editor in Chief: Jarkko Ambrusin; **Editor:** Kai Luttinen
Profile: Newspaper mainly issued in Pyhäntä, Pyhäsalmi, Kiuruvesi, Vieremä, Keitele, Pielavesi, Iisalmi, Sonkajärvi, Lapinlahti, Varpaisjärvi and Rautavaara. Pyhännällä, Pyhäsalmessa, Kiuruvedellä, Vieremällä, Keiteleellä, Pielavedellä, Iisalmessa, Sonkajärvellä, Lapinlahdessa, Varpaisjärvellä ja Rautavaarassa ilmestyvä sanomalehti.Edition: Iisalmen Sanomat Urheilutoimitus Weekly Viisari supplement every second SundayRegular features: Mondays: every second week Nature and Trekking, every second week Consumer Affairs. Tuesdays: Car and Traffic. Wednesdays: every second week Food, every second week Environment. Saturdays: every week Youth pages, every fourth week Health, every fourth week Information Technology, every fourth week Travel, every fourth week Home and Housing Supplement: Salmetar, see separate entry.Number of pages: 20 Start year: 1925
Language (s): Finnish
Ad Rate: Full Page Colour 2205.00
Currency: Euro
COMMUNITY NEWSPAPER

Iitinseutu 222422

Owner: Iitinlehti Oy
Editorial: PL 37/ Kauppakatu 6, Kausala 47401
Tel: 358 5 32 60 355
Email: voitto.ruohonen@iitinseutulehti.fi **Web site:** http://www.iitinseutulehti.fi
Freq: 2 Times/Week; **Circ:** 3436 ABC-Audit Bureau of Circulations
News: Voitto Ruohonen
Profile: Newspaper issued in Iitti and Jaala. Local Translation:Iitissä ja Jaalassa ilmestyvä paikallislehti.
Language (s): Finnish
COMMUNITY NEWSPAPER

Ilmajoki-lehti 222464

Owner: Ilmajoki-lehti
Editorial: PL 12 / Mikontie 3, Ilmajoki 60801
Tel: 358 6 42 44 800
Email: toimitus@ilmajoki-lehti.fi **Web site:** http://www.ilmajoki-lehti.fi
Freq: 2 Times/Week; **Circ:** 4957 ABC-Audit Bureau of Circulations
Profile: Newspaper issued in Ilmajoki. Ilmajoella ilmestyvä paikallislehti.
Language (s): Finnish
Ad Rate: Full Page Colour 1944.00
Currency: Euro
COMMUNITY NEWSPAPER

Imatralainen 222266

Owner: Etelä-Suomen Media Oy
Editorial: Lappeentie 17, Imatra 55100
Tel: 358 20 61 00 113
Email: toimitus.imatra@media.fi **Web site:** http://www.imatralainen.fi
Freq: Weekly
Editor in Chief: Karri Kannala
Profile: Newspaper distributed in Joutseno, Imatra and Ruokolahti. Kaupunkilehti, joka jaetaan ilmaismateriaalina joka talouteen ja yritykseen Joutsenossa, Imatrassa, Ruokolahdessa ja Rautjärvellä.No faxes are allowed to their fax number 358 5-43 66 615.
Language (s): Finnish
COMMUNITY NEWSPAPER

Inarilainen 222557

Owner: Ukko-Media Oy
Editorial: PL 145/ Ivalontie 7, Ivalo 99800
Tel: 358 20 71 09 050
Email: inarilainen@inarilainen.fi **Web site:** http://www.inarilainen.fi
Freq: Weekly; **Circ:** 7500 Publisher's Statement
Editor in Chief: Jaakko Peltomaa
Profile: Newspaper distributed in Inari and Utsjoki. Inarissa ja Utsjoella jaettava ilmaisjakelulehti.No faxes are allowed.
Language (s): Finnish
COMMUNITY NEWSPAPER

Itä-Häme 157028

Owner: Esan Paikallislehdet Oy
Editorial: PL 10/Lampikatu 8, Heinola 18101
Tel: 358 3 75 75 05
Email: iha.toimitus@itahame.fi **Web site:** http://www.itahame.fi
Freq: Daily; **Circ:** 10427
News Manager: Eeva Künnap; **Editor in Chief:** Jari Niemi
Profile: Regional newspaper issued in Heinola, Heinolan mlk, Sysmä, Hartola Luhanka, Pertunmaa and Joutsa. Local Translation:Heinolassa, Hartolassa, Luhangalla, Pertunmaalla ja Joutsassa ilmestyvä sanomalehti. Regular features: Mondays: Consumer-affairs; Tuesdays: Seniors; Wednesdays: Youth; Thursdays: Food; Fridays: Health, Fitness, Hobbies.
Language (s): Finnish
COMMUNITY NEWSPAPER

Itä-Savo 157055

Owner: KAAKON VIESTINTÄ OY
Editorial: PL 101/ Olavinkatu 60, Savonlinna 57101
Tel: 358 15 35 03 400
Email: toimitus@ita-savo.fi **Web site:** http://www.ita-savo.fi
Freq: Daily; **Circ:** 14981
Editor: Riitta-Leena Lempinen-Vesa; **Editor:** Jarmo Pesonen; **Manager:** Janne Tiainen
Profile: Newspaper issued in Savonlinna, Enonkoski, Kerimäki, Punkaharju, Savonranta, Sulkava, Rantasalmi, Parikkala, Saari and Uukuniemi. Local Translation:Description: Newspaper issued in Savonlinna, Enonkoski, Kerimäki, Punkaharju, Savonranta, Sulkava, Rantasalmi, Parikkala, Saari and Uukuniemi. Suomen suuriin sanomiin luokiteltu sanomalehti ilmestyy lähinnä Savonlinnassa, Enonkoskella, Kerimäellä, Punkaharjulla, Savonrannassa, Sulkavassa, Rantasalmella, Parikkalassa, Saaressa ja Uukuniemessä.Regular features: Mondays: Nature and Environment; Tuesdays: Food; Wednesdays: Cars and Traffic, TV; Fridays: Health and fitness; Saturdays: leisure Number of pages: 20Start year: 1907
Language (s): Finnish
COMMUNITY NEWSPAPER

Itäväylä 222274

Owner: Itäväylä Viestintä Oy
Editorial: Rihkamatori A, Porvoo 6100
Tel: 358 19 521 7500
Email: toimitus@itavayla.fi **Web site:** http://www.itavayla.fi
Freq: 2 Times/Week; **Circ:** 49080 Publisher's Statement
Profile: Newspaper distributed in Porvoo, Loviisa, Askola, Lapinjärvi, Liljendal, Myrskylä, Pernaja, Pornainen, Pukkila, Ruotsinpyhtää and Sipoo. Local Translation:Porvoossa, Loviisassa, Askolassa, Lapinjärvellä, Liljendalissa, Myrskylässä, Pernajassa, Pornaisissa, Pukkilassa, Ruotsinpyhtäällä ja Sipoossa ilmestyvä paikallislehti. Previously known as: ItäväyläStart year: 1984 Alternative Title: Palvelulehti ItäväyläPrevious title: Itäväylä
Language (s): Finnish
Ad Rate: Full Page Colour 1250.00
Currency: Euro
COMMUNITY NEWSPAPER

Jämsän Seutu 224355

Owner: Suomen Paikallissanomat Oy
Editorial: Lindemaninkatu 3, Jämsä 42100
Tel: 358 10 66 55 149
Email: toimitus.jamsanseutu@almamedia.fi **Web site:** http://www.jamsanseutu.fi
Freq: Daily; **Circ:** 6922 ABC-Audit Bureau of Circulations
Editor in Chief: Mari Tuohiniemi
Profile: Newspaper issued in Jämsä, Jämsänkoski, Korpilahti, Kuhmoinen, Längelmäki and Kuorevesi. Jämsässä, Jämsänkoskella, Korpilahdessa, Kuhmoisissa, Längelmäellä ja Kuorevedellä ilmestyvä paikallislehti.Previously known as: Koillis-Häme Number of pages: 20Start year: 1921 Previous title: Koillis-Häme
Language (s): Finnish
Ad Rate: Full Page Colour 3019.00
Currency: Euro
COMMUNITY NEWSPAPER

Jämsän Seutu Vekkari 222397

Owner: Suomen Paikallissanomat Oy
Editorial: Lindemaninkatu 3, Jämsä 42100
Tel: 358 10 66 55 149
Email: vekkari@almamedia.fi **Web site:** http://www.jamsanseutu.fi/nakoislehti/vekkari/
Freq: Weekly; **Circ:** 18000 Publisher's Statement
Editor in Chief: Mari Tuohiniemi
Profile: Newspaper distributed every Thursday in Jämsä, Jämsänkoski, Koskenpää, Kuhmoinen, Länkipohja, Kuorevesi-Halli and Korpilahti. Jämsässä, Jämsänkoskella, Koskenpäässä, Kuhmoisissa, Länkipohjassa, Kuorevesi-Hallissa ja Korpilahdessa torstaisin jaettava lehti.Previously known as: Vekkari Number of pages: 20Start year: 1982 Previous title: Vekkari
Language (s): Finnish
Ad Rate: Full Page Colour 2975.00
Currency: Euro
COMMUNITY NEWSPAPER

Janakkalan Sanomat 222403

Owner: Alma Media
Editorial: Harvialantie 7 A, 2. krs, Turenki 14200
Tel: 358 10 66 56 050
Email: toimitus.janakkalansanomat@almamedia.fi **Web site:** http://www.janakkalansanomat.fi
Freq: Weekly; **Circ:** 4484 ABC-Audit Bureau of Circulations
Profile: Newspaper issued in Renko and Janakkala. Local Translation:Rengossa ja Janakkalassa ilmestyvä lehti. Alternative Title: Janakkalan IlvesPrevious title: Kotokulma; Janakkalan-Rengon Sanomat
Language (s): Finnish
Ad Rate: Full Page Colour 2842.00
Currency: Euro
COMMUNITY NEWSPAPER

Järviseudun Sanomat 222467
Owner: Järviseutu-seura ry
Editorial: PL 29/ Maneesintie 4, Lappajärvi 62601
Tel: 358 20 79 40 510
Web site: http://www.jarviseudunsanomat.fi
Freq: Weekly; **Circ:** 7889 ABC-Audit Bureau of Circulations
Profile: Newspaper issued in Evijärvi, Kortesjärvi, Lappajärvi and Vimpeli. Evijärvellä, Kortesjärvellä, Lappajärvellä ja Vimpelissä ilmestyvä paikallislehti.Number of pages: 16 Start year: 1962They do not want press releases into toimitus@jarviseudunsanomat.fi
Language (s): Finnish
COMMUNITY NEWSPAPER

Järviseutu 222468
Owner: Pohjanmaan Lähisanomat Oy
Editorial: PL 33 / Hoiskontie 4, Alajärvi 62901
Tel: 358 6 24 77 890
Email: toimitus@jarviseutu-lehti.fi **Web site:** http://www.jarviseutu-lehti.fi
Freq: Weekly; **Circ:** 5314 ABC-Audit Bureau of Circulations
Profile: Newspaper issued in Alajärvi, Soini, Lehtimäki, Vimpeli and Lappajärvi. Alajärvellä, Soinissa, Lehtimäellä, Vimpelissä ja Lappajärvellä ilmestyvä paikallislehti.Number of pages: 8 Start year: 1937
Language (s): Finnish
COMMUNITY NEWSPAPER

Jokilaakso 222275
Owner: Suomen Paikallissanomat Oy
Editorial: Kilkunkatu 12, Kokemäki 32800
Email: toimitus.jokilaakso@almamedia.fi **Web site:** http://www.jokilaakso.fi
Freq: Weekly
Editor in Chief: Timo Simula
Profile: Newspaper issued in Kokemäki, Harjavalta, Huittinen, Säkylä, Vampula and Köyliö. Local Translation:Description: Newspaper issued in Kokemäki, Harjavalta, Huittinen, Säkylä, Vampula and Köyliö. Kokemäellä, Harjavallassa, Huittisissa, Säkylässä, Vampulassa ja Köyliössä ilmestyvä paikallislehti.Number of pages: 12 Start year: 1994
Language (s): Finnish
Ad Rate: Full Page Colour 1500.00
Currency: Euro
COMMUNITY NEWSPAPER

Joroisten Lehti 222433
Owner: Etelä-Savon Paikallislehdet Oy
Editorial: Joroisniementie 4, Joroinen 79600
Tel: 358 15 35 03 154
Email: toimitus@joroistenlehti.fi **Web site:** http://www.joroistenlehti.fi
Freq: Weekly; **Circ:** 2389 ABC-Audit Bureau of Circulations
Editor in Chief: Päivi Konttinen
Profile: Newspaper issued in Joroinen. Local Translation:Joroisilla ilmestyvä paikallislehti.
Language (s): Finnish
Ad Rate: Full Page Colour 2719.00
Currency: Euro
COMMUNITY NEWSPAPER

Joutsan Seutu 222398
Owner: Joutsan Seutu Oy
Editorial: PL 15/ Jousitie 31, Joutsa 19651
Tel: 358 20 18 76 100
Email: konttori@joutsanseutu.fi **Web site:** http://www.joutsanseutu.fi
Freq: Weekly; **Circ:** 5040 ABC-Audit Bureau of Circulations
Editor in Chief: Markku Parkkonen
Profile: Newspaper issued in Joutsa, Leivonmäki and Luhanka. Local Translation:Description: Newspaper issued in Joutsa, Leivonmäki and Luhanka. Joutsassa, Leivonmäellä ja Luhangalla ilmestyvä paikallislehti.Number of pages: 12 Start year: 1971
Language (s): Finnish
Ad Rate: Full Page Colour 2119.00
Currency: Euro
COMMUNITY NEWSPAPER

Joutseno 222423
Owner: ESV-Paikallismediat Oy
Editorial: Keskuskatu 7, Joutseno 54100
Email: toimitus@joutsenolehti.fi **Web site:** http://www.joutsenolehti.fi
Freq: Weekly; **Circ:** 3240 ABC-Audit Bureau of Circulations
Profile: Newspaper issued in Joutseno. Local Translation:Joutsenon kunnassa ilmestyvä paikallislehti.
Language (s): Finnish
Ad Rate: Full Page Colour 2540.00
Currency: Euro
COMMUNITY NEWSPAPER

JP Kunnallissanomat 222465
Owner: Jalasjärvi Oy
Editorial: PL 53 / Torikuja 9, Jalasjärvi 61601
Tel: 358 6 45 65 100
Email: toimitus@jp-kunnallissanomat.fi **Web site:** http://www.jp-kunnallissanomat.fi
Freq: 2 Times/Week; **Circ:** 6330 ABC-Audit Bureau of Circulations
Editor in Chief/Managing Director: Terhi Rintala
Profile: Newspaper distributed in Jalasjärvi and Peräseinäjoki. Jalasjärvellä ja Peräseinäjoella ilmestyvä kuntalaisten asioista kertova lehti.Ei henkilökohtaisia sähköpostiosoitteita ainoastaan toimituksen yhteinen osoite käytössä. Previous title: Jalasjärven-Peräseinäjoen Kunnallissanomat
Language (s): Finnish
Ad Rate: Full Page Colour 1624.00

Currency: Euro
COMMUNITY NEWSPAPER

Jurvan Sanomat 222466
Owner: Ilkka Oy
Editorial: Hahdonkuja 2, Jurva 66300
Tel: 358 6 24 77 875
Email: toimitus@jurvansanomat.fi **Web site:** http://www.jurvansanomat.fi
Freq: Weekly; **Circ:** 2154 ABC-Audit Bureau of Circulations
Editor in Chief: Jaana Ala-Lahti
Profile: Newspaper issued in Jurva. Local Translation:Jurvalla ilmestyvä sanomalehti.
Language (s): Finnish
Ad Rate: Full Page Colour 3964.00
Currency: Euro
COMMUNITY NEWSPAPER

Juvan Lehti 222434
Owner: Etelä-Savon Paikallislehdet Oy
Editorial: PL 27 / Koulutie 6 A 2, Juva 51901
Tel: 358 15 35 03 172
Email: toimitus@juvanlehti.fi **Web site:** http://www.juvanlehti.fi
Freq: Weekly; **Circ:** 4186 ABC-Audit Bureau of Circulations
Profile: Newspaper issued in Juva. Local Translation:Description: Newspaper issued in Juva. Juvalla ilmestyvä paikallislehti.Number of pages: 8 Start year: 1956
Language (s): Finnish
Ad Rate: Full Page Colour 2686.00
Currency: Euro
COMMUNITY NEWSPAPER

Kaakonkulma 222425
Owner: Sanoma News Oy
Editorial: PL 20/ Makitie 3, Virolahti 49901
Tel: 358 15 35 03 546
Email: toimitus@kaakonkulma.fi **Web site:** http://www.kaakonkulma.fi
Freq: Weekly; **Circ:** 4747 ABC-Audit Bureau of Circulations
Editor in Chief: Jukka Kinnunen
Profile: Newspaper issued in Miehikkälä, Vironlahti and Ylämaa. Miehikkälässä, Vironlahdella ja Ylämaalla ilmestyvä paikallislehti.
Language (s): Finnish
COMMUNITY NEWSPAPER

Kaarina-lehti 222362
Owner: Kaarinan Lehti Oy
Editorial: Pyhan Katariinantie 7, Kaarina 20780
Tel: 358 2 588 8614
Email: toimitus@kaarina-lehti.fi **Web site:** http://www.kaarina-lehti.fi
Freq: Weekly; **Circ:** 4486 ABC-Audit Bureau of Circulations
Editor in Chief: Teija Uurinmäki
Profile: Newspaper issued in Kaarina. Local Translation:Description: Newspaper issued in Kaarina. Kaarinassa ilmestyvä paikallislehti.Supplement: Pointti 12/year Number of pages: 16Start year: 1985 Previous title: Kaarina
Language (s): Finnish
Ad Rate: Full Page Colour 4618.00
Currency: Euro
COMMUNITY NEWSPAPER

Kainuun Sanomat 157033
Owner: Pohjois-Suomen Media Oy
Editorial: PL 150/ Kauppakatu 11, Kajaani 87101
Tel: 358 10 66 50 33
Email: ks.toimitus@kainuunsanomat.fi **Web site:** http://www.kainuunsanomat.fi
Freq: Daily; **Circ:** 16890
Editor in Chief: Markus Pirttijoki; **News Manager:** Seppo Turunen
Profile: Newspaper issued mainly in Kajaani, Vuolijoki, Vaala, Paltamo, Sotkamo, Kuhmo, Ristijärvi, Puolanka, Hyrynsalmi and Suomussalmi. Local Translation:Lähinnä Kajaanilla, Vuolijoella, Vaalassa, Paltamossa, Sotkamossa, Kuhmolla, Ristijärvellä, Puolangassa, Hyrynsalmella ja Suomussalmella ilmestyvä sanomalehti. Editions: Kainuun Sanomat Kulttuuritoimitus, Kainuun Sanomat UrheilutoimitusRegular features: Health every second Monday; Cars and traffic on Wednesdays; Finance and food on Thursdays; Home and housing on Saturdays. Number of pages: 10Start year: 1918
Language (s): Finnish
Ad Rate: Full Page Colour 4710.00
Currency: Euro
COMMUNITY NEWSPAPER

Kalajokilaakso 224359
Owner: Jokilaaksojen Kustannus Oy
Editorial: PL 7/Kartanotie 3, Ylivieska 84101
Tel: 358 20 75 04 600
Email: toimitus@kalajokilaakso.fi **Web site:** http://www.kalajokilaakso-lehti.fi
Freq: Fri
Editor in Chief: Seppo Kangas
Profile: Newspaper issued in Ylivieska. Local Translation:Kalajokilaakso jaetaan Ylivieskan talousalueella.
Language (s): Finnish
COMMUNITY NEWSPAPER

Kalajokiseutu 222515
Owner: Keski-Pohjanmaan Kirjapaino Oyj
Editorial: Kalajoentie 4, Kalajoki 85100
Tel: 358 20 75 04 730
Email: sari.passoja@kalajokiseutu.fi **Web site:** http://www.kalajokilehti.fi
Freq: Weekly; **Circ:** 2147 ABC-Audit Bureau of Circulations
Editor: Sari Passoja
Profile: Newspaper issued in Kalajoki. Local Translation:Kalajoella ilmestyvä paikallislehti.
Language (s): Finnish
COMMUNITY NEWSPAPER

Kallio-lehti 222484
Owner: Karprint Oy
Editorial: Vanha Turuntie 371, Huhmari 3150
Tel: 358 9 413 97 300
Email: juha.ahola@karprint.fi **Web site:** http://www.kalliolehti.fi
Freq: Bi-Weekly; **Circ:** 40000 Publisher's Statement
Editor in Chief: Juha Ahola
Profile: Local newspaper distributed in the Helsinki city centre. Preferred contact method: e-mail. Paikallislehti jonka jakelualueet ovat Merihaka, Siltasaari, Kallio, Torkkelinmäki, Sörnäinen, Alppila, Alppiharju, Harju, Itä-Pasila, Vallila ja Hermanni.Previously listed as: Kallio ja ympäristö Start year: 1969Previous title: Kallio ja ympäristö
Language (s): Finnish
COMMUNITY NEWSPAPER

Kamppi-Eira 222485
Owner: Töölöläinen Oy
Editorial: Temppelikatu 8, Helsinki 100
Tel: 358 9 44 16 58
Email: toimitus@paikallislehdet.com
Freq: Bi-Weekly; **Circ:** 28000 Publisher's Statement
Editor in Chief: Mikko Keski-Vähälä
Profile: Newspaper distributed in the central and southern parts of Helsinki. Local Translation:Description: Newspaper distributed in the central and southern parts of Helsinki. Lehti, jonka jakelualueina toimivat Kamppi, Ruoholahti, Hietalahti, Punavuori, Eira, Kaivopuisto, Ullanlinna, Kaartinkaupunki ja Kluuvi.Number of pages: 16 Start year: 1978
Language (s): Finnish
COMMUNITY NEWSPAPER

Kangasalan Sanomat 222377
Owner: Kangasalan Sanomalehti-Osakeyhtiö
Editorial: Myllystenpohjantie 2, Kangasala 36200
Tel: 358 3 37 76 900
Email: toimitus@kangasalansanomat.fi **Web site:** http://www.kangasalansanomat.fi
Freq: 2 Times/Week; **Circ:** 7000 ABC-Audit Bureau of Circulations
Editor in Chief: Tuula Ruusumaa
Profile: Newspaper issued in Kangasala. Kangasalassa ilmestyvä paikallislehti.toimitus@kangasalansanomat.fi
Language (s): Finnish
COMMUNITY NEWSPAPER

Kangasniemen Kunnallislehti 222435
Owner: Etelä-Savon Paikallislehdet Oy
Editorial: PL 115 / Otto Mannisen tie 13, Kangasniemi 51201 **Tel:** 358 15 35 03 160
Email: toimitus@kangasniemen-kunnallislehti.fi **Web site:** http://www.kangasniemen-kunnallislehti.fi
Freq: Weekly; **Circ:** 4362 ABC-Audit Bureau of Circulations
Profile: Newspaper issued in Kangasniemi. Local Translation:Kangasniemellä ilmestyvä paikallislehti.
Language (s): Finnish
Ad Rate: Full Page Colour 1693.00
Currency: Euro
COMMUNITY NEWSPAPER

Kankaanpään Seutu 222416
Owner: Suomen Paikallissanomat Oy
Editorial: PL 16 / Linnankatu 1, Kankaanpää 38701
Tel: 358 10 66 55 763
Email: toimitus.kankaanpaanseutu@almamedia.fi
Web site: http://www.kankaanpaanseutu.fi
Freq: 2 Times/Week; **Circ:** 9616 ABC-Audit Bureau of Circulations
Profile: Newspaper issued in Honkajoki, Jämijärvi, Kankaanpää, Karvia, Lavia, Pomarkku, Siikainen and Suodenniemi. Honkajoella, Jämijärvellä, Kankaanpäässä, Karviassa, Laviassa, Pomarkussa, Siikaisissa ja Suodenniemellä ilmestyvä paikallislehti.Number of pages: 20 Start year: 1968
Language (s): Finnish
COMMUNITY NEWSPAPER

Kansan Tahto 157046
Owner: Kustannus Oy Kansan Tahto
Editorial: PL 61/Makelininkatu 29, Oulu 90101
Tel: 358 8 53 71 724
Email: toimitus@kansantahto.fi **Web site:** http://www.kansantahto.fi
Freq: Weekly; **Circ:** 6965
Profile: Left-wing regional newspaper issued in Oulu, Lapland and Kainuu in northern Finland. Vasemmistolainen Oulussa, Lapissa ja Kainuussa ilmestyvä sanomalehti.
Language (s): Finnish
Ad Rate: Full Page Colour 5325.00
Currency: Euro
COMMUNITY NEWSPAPER

Käpylä-lehti 222489
Owner: Käpylä-Seura ry
Editorial: Klaneettitie 11, Helsinki 420
Tel: 358 9 53 08 19 90
Email: kapylalehti@eepinen.fi **Web site:** http://www.kaupunginosat.net/kapyla
Freq: Monthly; **Circ:** 18000 Publisher's Statement
Editor in Chief: Alice Karlsson
Profile: Local newspaper distributed in Käpylä, Koskela, Kumpula, Isoniitty, Metsälä, Veräjämäki, Veräjälaakso, Toukola, Arabia, Vanhakaupunki, Viikki and Oulunkylä. Local Translation:Käpylässä, Koskelassa, Kumpulassa, Isoniityssä, Metsälässä, Veräjämäellä, Veräjälaaksossa, Toukolassa, Arabiassa, Vanhakaupungissa, Viikissä ja Oulunkylässä jaettava kaupunkilehti. Their fax number is 358 9-53 08 19 91, but e-mails are preferred.
Language (s): Finnish
COMMUNITY NEWSPAPER

Karjala 222342
Owner: Karjalan Kirjapaino Oy
Editorial: PL 4/ Kauppakatu 41, Lappeenranta 53101
Tel: 358 5 54 14 600
Email: toimitus@karjala-lehti.fi **Web site:** http://www.karjala-lehti.fi
Freq: Weekly; **Circ:** 10246 Publisher's Statement
Editor in Chief: Päivi Parjanen
Profile: Newspaper about events and culture in southern Carelia. Lehti ketoo karjalaisesta kulttuurista, tutkimuksesta ja perinteestä.Number of pages: 12 Start year: 1904
Language (s): Finnish
COMMUNITY NEWSPAPER

Karjalan Heili 222558
Owner: Karelia Viestintä Oy
Editorial: Torikatu 23 E, Joensuu 80100
Tel: 358 10 23 08 500
Email: toimitus@heili.fi **Web site:** http://www.heili.fi
Freq: 2 Times/Week; **Circ:** 49478 Publisher's Statement
Profile: Newspaper distributed in Joensuu, Polvijärvi, Kontiolahti, Eno, Ilomantsi, Outokumpu, Liperi, Pyhäselkä and Kiihtelysvaara. Local Translation:Description: Newspaper distributed in Joensuu, Polvijärvi, Kontiolahti, Eno, Ilomantsi, Outokumpu, Liperi, Pyhäselkä and Kiihtelysvaara. Joensuussa, Polvijärvi, Kontiolahdessa, Enossa, Ilomantsissa, Outokummussa, Liperissä, Pyhäselässä ja Kiihtelysvaarassa ilmestyvä paikallislehti.Number of pages: 16 Start year: 1970Alternative Title: Heili
Language (s): Finnish
Ad Rate: Full Page Colour 2320.00
Currency: Euro
COMMUNITY NEWSPAPER

Karkkilalainen 222294
Owner: SLY-Paikallislehdet Oy
Editorial: Turuntie 2-4, Karkkila 3600
Tel: 358 20 77 03 552
Email: toimitus@karkkilalainen.fi **Web site:** http://www.karkkilalainen.fi
Freq: Weekly; **Circ:** 11500 Publisher's Statement
Profile: Newspaper distributed in Karkkila, Nummi-Pusula, Vihti and Loppi. Karkkilassa, Nummi-Pusulassa, Vihdissä ja Lopeella ilmestyvä paikallislehti.Number of pages: 16 Start year: 1991
Language (s): Finnish
COMMUNITY NEWSPAPER

Karkkilan Tienoo 222355
Owner: Karprint Oy
Editorial: PL 16/ Huhdintie 10-12, Karkkila 3600
Tel: 358 9 22 56 656
Email: kt.toimitus@karprint.fi **Web site:** http://www.karprint.fi/karkkilantienoo
Freq: 2 Times/Week; **Circ:** 15600 Publisher's Statement
Editor in Chief: Mari Ahola-Aalto
Profile: Newspaper distributed in Karkkila and Nummi-Pusula. Karkkilassa ja Nummi-Pusulassa ilmestyvä paikallislehti.Number of pages: 16 Start year: 1962
Language (s): Finnish
COMMUNITY NEWSPAPER

Kauhajoki-lehti 222516
Owner: Kauhajoen Kunnallislehti Oy
Editorial: PL 5 / Puistotie 25, Kauhajoki 61801
Tel: 358 6 23 57 100
Email: toimitus@kauhajoki-lehti.fi **Web site:** http://www.kauhajoki-lehti.fi
Freq: 2 Times/Week; **Circ:** 6960 ABC-Audit Bureau of Circulations
Editor in Chief/Managing Director: Tuomas Koivuniemi
Profile: Newspaper issued in Kauhajoki. Kauhajoella ilmestyvä paikallislehti.Number of pages: 12 Start year: 1925
Language (s): Finnish
COMMUNITY NEWSPAPER

KaupunkiSanomat 222297
Owner: Kaupunkilehdet
Editorial: KaupunkiSanomat viikkolehti, PL 28, Helsinki 421
Email: toimitus@kaupunkisanomat.fi **Web site:** http://www.kaupunkisanomat.fi
Freq: Weekly; **Circ:** 20000 Publisher's Statement
Editor in Chief: Merja Nordbäck-Raunio
Profile: Newspaper distributed in different city parts of Helsinki. 20-45 year old active consumers in the Helsinki region.Local Translation: Pääkaupunkiseudulla jaettava kaupunkilehti.Start year: 1995
Language (s): Finnish
Ad Rate: Full Page Colour 1290.00
Currency: Euro
COMMUNITY NEWSPAPER

Keski-Espoon Sanomat 393895
Owner: Keski-Espoon-seura ry
Editorial: Blominkuja 6, Espoo 2780
Email: pirkko.sillanpaa@espoo.fi **Web site:** http://www.keskiespooseura.fi
Freq: Quarterly; **Circ:** 30000 Publisher's Statement
Editor in Chief: Pirkko Sillanpää

Profile: Newspaper distributed in Espoo, Tuomarila, Mikkelä, Gumböle, Nuuksio, Siikajärvi, Järvenperä, Niipperi, Luukki and Kuuriinniitty. Local Translation:Espoon keskuksessa, Tuomarilassa, Mikkelässä, Gumbölessä, Nuuksiossa, Siikajärvellä, Järvenperässä, Niipperissä, Luukissa ja Kuuriinniityssä jaettava sanomalehti.
Language (s): Finnish
COMMUNITY NEWSPAPER

Keski-Häme 222400
Owner: Hämeen Viestintä Oy
Editorial: Lamminraitti 25, Lammi 16900
Email: toimitus@keski-hame.fi **Web site:** http://www.keski-hame.fi
Freq: Weekly; **Circ:** 5326 ABC-Audit Bureau of Circulations
Editor in Chief: Esa Joensuu
Profile: Local newspaper issued in Hämeenkoski, Lammi, Tuulos and Hauho. Local Translation:Hämeenkosken, Lammin, Tuuloksen ja Hauhon paikallislehti.
Language (s): Finnish
Ad Rate: Full Page Colour 2588.00
Currency: Euro
COMMUNITY NEWSPAPER

Keskilaakso 222420
Owner: Sanoma News Oy
Editorial: PL 20 / Valtatie 12, Inkeroinen 46901
Tel: 358 15 35 03 530
Email: toimitus@keskilaakso.fi **Web site:** http://www.keskilaakso.fi
Freq: 2 Times/Week; **Circ:** 5119 ABC-Audit Bureau of Circulations
Editor in Chief: Stiina Kokkonen
Profile: Newspaper issued in Anjalankoski, Kaipiainen, Myllykoski, Sippola, Inkeroinen and Anjala. Local Translation:Description: Newspaper issued in Anjalankoski, Kaipiainen, Myllykoski, Sippola, Inkeroinen and Anjala. Anjalankoskella, Kaipiaisissa, Myllykoskella, Sippolassa, Inkeroisissa ja Anjalassa ilmestyvä paikallislehti.Number of pages: 16 Start year: 1931Previous title: Anjalankosken Sanomat
Language (s): Finnish
COMMUNITY NEWSPAPER

Keskipohjanmaa 157036
Owner: Keski-Pohjanmaan Kustannus Oy
Editorial: PL 45/ Rantakatu 10, Kokkola 67101
Tel: 358 20 75 04 400
Email: toimitus@kpk.fi **Web site:** http://www.kp24.fi/
Circ: 24126
Editor: Jens Oja
Profile: Newspaper issued mainly in central Ostrobothnia (Pohjanmaa). Local Translation:Keskipohjanmaalla ilmestyvä suuriin sanomiin lukeutuva sanomalehti. Edition: Keskipohjanmaa UrheilutoimitusRegular features: Food 52xY on Saturdays. Start year: 1917
Language (s): Finnish
COMMUNITY NEWSPAPER

Keski-Uusimaa 157060
Owner: Etelä-Suomen Media
Editorial: PL 52/ Klaavolantie 5, Tuusula 4301
Tel: +358 9 273 00202
Email: toimitus.keskiuusimaa@media.fi **Web site:** http://www.keski-uusimaa.fi/
Freq: Weekly; **Circ:** 15658
News Manager: Tomi Backström; **News Editor:** Anu Vertanen
Profile: Newspaper issued mainly in Järvenpää, Kerava, Tuusula, Nurmijärvi, Sipoo and partly in Vantaa and Mäntsälä. Local Translation:Description: Newspaper issued mainly in Järvenpää, Kerava, Tuusula, Nurmijärvi, Sipoo and partly in Vantaa and Mäntsälä. Lähinnä Järvenpäässä, Keravalla, Tuusulassa, Nurmijärvellä ja Sipoossa sekä osin Vantaalla ja Mäntsälässä ilmestyvä suuriin sanomiin lukeutuva lehti.Number of pages: 18 Start year: 1919
Language (s): Finnish
Ad Rate: Full Page Colour 3585.00
Currency: Euro
COMMUNITY NEWSPAPER

Kirkkonummen Sanomat 222488
Owner: Kirkkonummen Sanomat Oy
Editorial: PL 28/ Munkinkuja 4, Kirkkonummi 2401
Tel: 358 9 22 19 200
Email: toimitus@kirkkonummensanomat.fi **Web site:** http://www.kirkkonummensanomat.fi
Freq: 2 Times/Week; **Circ:** 28000 Publisher's Statement
Editor in Chief: Jussi Salo
Profile: Newspaper distributed in Kirkkonummi, Siuntio and Inkoo. Local Translation:Description: Newspaper distributed in Kirkkonummi, Siuntio and Inkoo. Kirkkonummella, Siuntiossa ja Inkoossa ilmestyvä paikallislehti.Number of pages: 20 Start year: 1967
Language (s): Finnish
COMMUNITY NEWSPAPER

Kittilälehti 222565
Owner: Kittilämedia Oy
Editorial: Valtatie 42 A, Kittilä 99100
Tel: 358 16 64 29 63
Email: info@kittilalehti.com **Web site:** http://www.kittilalehti.com
Freq: Weekly; **Circ:** 3120 Publisher's Statement
Editor in Chief: Mari Palomaa
Profile: Newspaper issued in Kittilä in northern Finland. Local Translation:Kittilässä ilmestyvä paikallislehti.
Language (s): Finnish
Ad Rate: Full Page Colour 2109.00
Currency: Euro
COMMUNITY NEWSPAPER

Kiuruvesi 222438
Owner: Kiuruvesi Lehti Oy
Editorial: PL 69/ Hovinpelto 3, Kiuruvesi 74701
Tel: 358 17 77 07 700
Email: toimitus@kiuruvesilehti.fi **Web site:** http://www.kiuruvesilehti.fi/
Freq: Weekly; **Circ:** 6285 ABC-Audit Bureau of Circulations
Editor in Chief: Jaana Selander
Profile: Newspaper issued in Kiuruvesi. Kiuruvedellä ilmestyvä paikallislehti.Number of pages: 12 Start year: 1953
Language (s): Finnish
COMMUNITY NEWSPAPER

KMV-lehti 222379
Owner: Suomen Paikallissanomat Oy
Editorial: PL 33 / Ratakatu 6, Mänttä 35801
Tel: 358 10 66 55 630
Email: toimitus.kmvlehti@almamedia.fi **Web site:** http://www.kmvlehti.fi
Freq: 2 Times/Week; **Circ:** 6800 ABC-Audit Bureau of Circulations
Profile: Local newspaper issued in Kuorevesi, Mänttä, Vilppula and Juupajoki. Local Translation:Kuorevedellä, Mäntässä, Vilppulassa ja Juupajoella ilmestyvä paikallislehti. Previous title: Kuorevesi-Mänttä-Vilppula
Language (s): Finnish
Ad Rate: Full Page Colour 2398.00
Currency: Euro
COMMUNITY NEWSPAPER

Koillismaan Uutiset 222559
Owner: Koillismaan Uutiset Oy
Editorial: Ouluntaival 1, Torikeskus, Kuusamo 93600
Tel: 358 8 54 53 980
Email: toimitus@koillismaanuutiset.fi **Web site:** http://www.koillismaanuutiset.fi
Freq: Weekly; **Circ:** 12726 Publisher's Statement
Editor in Chief: Pasi Määttälä
Profile: Newspaper issued in Koillismaa. Lehti on Koillismaan talousalueen sitoutumaton äänenkannattaja.Number of pages: 16 Start year: 1992
Language (s): Finnish
COMMUNITY NEWSPAPER

Koillissanomat 224356
Owner: Koillissanomat Oy
Editorial: Kitkantie 31-33, Kuusamo 93600
Tel: 358 8 86 00 600
Email: toimitus@koillissanomat.fi **Web site:** http://www.koillissanomat.fi
Freq: Daily; **Circ:** 6936 ABC-Audit Bureau of Circulations
Editor in Chief: Petri Karjalainen
Profile: Newspaper issued in Kuusamo, Posio and Taivalkoski. Kuusamossa, Posiossa ja Taivalkoskella ilmestyvä paikallislehti.Number of pages: 12 Start year: 1950
Language (s): Finnish
COMMUNITY NEWSPAPER

Koillis-Savo 222439
Owner: Maakunnan Sanomat Oy
Editorial: Iso-Oskar, Kaavintie 5 A, Kaavi 73600
Tel: 358 17 28 87 721
Email: uutiset@koillis-savo.fi **Web site:** http://www.koillis-savo.fi
Freq: 2 Times/Week; **Circ:** 5529 ABC-Audit Bureau of Circulations
Editor in Chief: Pirjo Mononen
Profile: Newspaper distributed in Juankoski, Kaavi, Tuusniemi and Riistavesi. Juankoskella, Kaavissa, Tuusniemellä ja Riistavedellä ilmestyvä paikallislehti.Alternative address: Juankoskentie 17, 73500 JUANKOSKI.
Fax: 358 17-28 87 736. Number of pages: 16Start year: 1963
Language (s): Finnish
COMMUNITY NEWSPAPER

Kokkola 222551
Owner: Keski-Pohjanmaan Kustannus Oy
Editorial: PL 45/ Rantakatu 10, Kokkola 67101
Tel: 358 20 75 04 680
Email: toimitus@kokkolalehti.fi **Web site:** http://www.kokkola-lehti.fi
Freq: Weekly; **Circ:** 28800 Publisher's Statement
Profile: Newspaper distributed in Kokkola, Kälviä, Lohtaja and Kruunupyy. Local Translation:Kokkolalehti on Kokkolan, Kälviän, Lohtajan ja Kruunupyyn kuntien alueella ilmestyvä kaupunkilehti. Start year: 1898
Language (s): Finnish
COMMUNITY NEWSPAPER

Komiat 222517
Owner: Pohjanmaan Lähisanomat Oy
Editorial: Nikolaintie 5 B 12, Kauhava 62200
Tel: 358 6 24 77 885
Email: toimitus@komiatlehti.fi **Web site:** http://www.komiatlehti.fi
Freq: Weekly; Circ: 6510 Publisher's Statement
Profile: Newspaper issued in Kauhava, Seinäjoki, Vöyri, Lapua, Kortesjärvi, Ylihärmä and Alahärmä. Kauhavalla, Seinäjoella, Vöyrissä, Lapualla, Kortesjärvellä, Ylihärmässä ja Alahärmässä ilmestyvä paikallislehti.Previously known as: Kauhava Incorporating HärmätNumber of pages: 16 Start year: 1927Alternative Title: Härmänmaan paikallislehti Komiat Previous title: Kauhava
Language (s): Finnish
COMMUNITY NEWSPAPER

Kommunbladet-Kunnallisuutiset 222552
Owner: HSS Media Ab
Editorial: PB 52, Vasa 65101 **Tel:** 358 6 78 48 800
Web site: http://www.vora-maxmo.fi
Freq: Monthly; **Circ:** 4000 Publisher's Statement
News: Karin Sundström
Profile: Newspaper distributed in Vöyriö, Oravainen and Maksamaa. Local Translation:Tidning som delas ut i Vörå, Oravais och Maxmo.
Language (s): Finnish
COMMUNITY NEWSPAPER

Korpilahti 222401
Owner: Korpilahden Paikallislehti Oy
Editorial: Kokkotie 11 C 17, Korpilahti 41800
Tel: 358 40 19 77 400
Email: toimitus@korpilahtilehti.fi **Web site:** http://www.korpilahtilehti.fi
Freq: Weekly; **Circ:** 3030 ABC-Audit Bureau of Circulations
Editor in Chief: Maarit Nurminen
Profile: Newspaper issued in Korpilahti. Local Translation:Description: Newspaper issued in Korpilahti. Korpilahdessa ilmestyvä paikallislehti.Number of pages: 8 Start year: 1971
Language (s): Finnish
Ad Rate: Full Page Colour 1971.00
Currency: Euro
COMMUNITY NEWSPAPER

Koti-Kajaani 222556
Owner: Pohjois-Suomen Media Oy
Editorial: Valikatu 8, Kajaani 87100
Tel: 358 10 66 57 202
Email: simo.hyttinen@koti-kajaani.fi **Web site:** http://www.koti-kajaani.fi
Freq: 2 Times/Week; **Circ:** 28758 Publisher's Statement
Editor in Chief: Simo Hyttinen
Profile: Local newspaper issued in Paltamo, Ristijärvi, Vuolijoki, Kajaani and Sotkamo. A special Kainuu issue is published also in Suomussalmi, Puolanka, Hyrynsalmi and Kuhmo. Paltamolla, Ristijärvellä, Vuolijoella, Kajaanissa ja Sotkamolla ilmestyvä paikallislehti. Kainuun numeron levikkialue on Suomussalmi, Puolanka, Hyrynsalmi ja Kuhmo.Number of pages: 16
Language (s): Finnish
COMMUNITY NEWSPAPER

Koti-Karjala 222437
Owner: Keski-Karjalan Paikallislehti Oy
Editorial: PL 34 / Pokentie 8, Kitee 82501
Tel: 358 13 68 48 411
Email: toimitus@kotikarjala.fi **Web site:** http://www.kotikarjala.fi
Freq: 2 Times/Week; **Circ:** 6477 ABC-Audit Bureau of Circulations
Profile: Newspaper issued in Kitee, Kesälahti, Rääkkylä, Tohmajärvi and Värtsilä. Kiteellä, Kesälahdessa, Rääkkylässä, Tohmajärvellä ja Värtsilässä ilmestyvä paikallislehti.Number of pages: 16 Start year: 1960
Language (s): Finnish
Ad Rate: Full Page Colour 3488.00
Currency: Euro
COMMUNITY NEWSPAPER

Koti-Lappi 222350
Owner: SLP Kustannus Oy
Editorial: PL 19/ Hallituskatu 1, Kemijärvi 98101
Tel: 358 10 665 7920
Email: toimitus.kotilappi@slpmedia.fi **Web site:** http://www.kotilappi.fi/
Freq: Weekly; **Circ:** 3279 ABC-Audit Bureau of Circulations
Editor in Chief: Sami Kasurinen
Profile: Newspaper issued in Kemijärvi, Salla, Savukoski and Pelkosenniemi. Formed when Koillis-Lappi and Kotikymppi merged Local Translation:Koillis-Lapin ja Kotikympin yhdistymisestä syntynyt paikallislehti ilmestyy Kemijärvellä, Sallassa, Savukoskella ja Pelkosenniemellä.
Language (s): Finnish
Ad Rate: Full Page Colour 3066.00
Currency: Euro
COMMUNITY NEWSPAPER

Kotiseudun Sanomat 222402
Owner: Pihtipudas-Seura ry
Editorial: Keskustie 8, Pihtipudas 44800
Tel: 358 20 79 31 620
Email: toimitus@kotiseudunsanomat.fi **Web site:** http://www.kotiseudunsanomat.fi
Freq: Weekly; **Circ:** 5028 ABC-Audit Bureau of Circulations
Editor in Chief: Heikki Jämsén
Profile: Newspaper issued in Pihtipudas and Kinnula. Pihtiputaalla ja Kinnulassa ilmestyvä paikallislehti.Number of pages: 16 Start year: 1961
Language (s): Finnish
COMMUNITY NEWSPAPER

Kotiseutu-uutiset 222440
Owner: Liperin Kotiseutu-Uutiset Ky
Editorial: PL 14 / Keskustie 20, Liperi 83101
Tel: 358 10 66 66 081
Email: toimitus@kotiseutu-uutiset.fi **Web site:** http://www.kotiseutu-uutiset.com
Freq: 2 Times/Week; **Circ:** 3234 ABC-Audit Bureau of Circulations
Profile: Newspaper issued in Liperi and Rääkkylä. Local Translation:Liperissä ja Rääkkylässä ilmestyvä paikallislehti.
Language (s): Finnish
Ad Rate: Full Page Colour 3441.00
Currency: Euro
COMMUNITY NEWSPAPER

Kouvolan Sanomat 157038
Owner: Kaakon Viestintä Oy
Editorial: PL 40/Lehtikaari 1, Kouvola 45101
Tel: 358 5 28 00 14
Email: toimitus@kouvolansanomat.fi **Web site:** http://www.kouvolansanomat.fi
Freq: Daily; **Circ:** 24531
Profile: Newspaper issued mainly in Kouvola in the southeastern part of Finland. Local Translation:Lähinnä Kouvolan alueella ilmestyvä sanomalehti.
Language (s): Finnish
Ad Rate: Full Page Colour 4520.00
Currency: Euro
COMMUNITY NEWSPAPER

Kuhmoisten Sanomat 222404
Owner: Kuhmoisten Sanomat Oy
Editorial: PL 8 / Toritie 52, Kuhmoinen 17801
Tel: 358 3 55 51 437
Email: toimitus@kuhmoistensanomat.fi **Web site:** http://www.kuhmoistensanomat.fi
Freq: Weekly; **Circ:** 2872 ABC-Audit Bureau of Circulations
Profile: Newspaper issued in Kuhmoinen and its surroundings. Local Translation:Lehti, jonka levikkikunnat ovat Kuhmoinen, Lahti, Helsinki, Padasjoki, Asikkala, Hollola, Jämsä, Kuhmalahti, Längelmäki, Tampere.
Language (s): Finnish
Ad Rate: Full Page Colour 2246.00
Currency: Euro
COMMUNITY NEWSPAPER

Kuhmolainen 222531
Owner: Suomen Paikallissanomat Oy
Editorial: Kainuuntie 103, Kuhmo 88900
Tel: 358 44 332 5320
Email: toimitus.kuhmolainen@slpmedia.fi **Web site:** http://www.kainuunsanomat.fi/kuhmolainen
Freq: 2 Times/Week; **Circ:** 5174 ABC-Audit Bureau of Circulations
Profile: Newspaper issued in Kuhmo. Local Translation:Kuhmossa ilmestyvä paikallislehti.
Language (s): Finnish
Ad Rate: Full Page Colour 1100.00
Currency: Euro
COMMUNITY NEWSPAPER

Kunnallislehti Paimio-Sauvo-Kaarina 222364
Owner: Salon Seudun Sanomat Oy
Editorial: PL 29/Vistantie 38, Paimio 21531
Tel: 358 2 58 88 650
Email: toimitus@kunnallislehti.fi **Web site:** http://www.kuntsari.fi
Freq: 2 Times/Week
Editor in Chief: Taina Tukia
Profile: Local newspaper in Piikkiö, Sauvo ja Paimio. Piikkiössä, Sauvossa ja Paimiossa ilmestyvä paikallislehti.Previously known as: Kunnallislehti Paimio-Sauvo-Piikkiö Number of pages: 12Start year: 1916 Previous title: Kunnallislehti Paimio-Sauvo-Piikkiö
Language (s): Finnish
COMMUNITY NEWSPAPER

Kuopion Kaupunkilehti 230956
Owner: Kuopion Kaupunkilehti Oy
Editorial: Tulliportinkatu 8, Kuopio 70100
Tel: 358 44 28 82 801
Email: kuopio.toimitus@kaupunkilehti.fi **Web site:** http://www.kuopionkaupunkilehti.fi
Freq: Weekly; **Circ:** 62670 Publisher's Statement
Editor in Chief: Aija Pirinen
Profile: Newspaper issued in Kuopio, Siilinjärvi, Riistavesi, Karttula, Tervo, Vehmersalmi and Maaninka. Kuopiossa, Siilinjärvellä, Riistavedellä, Karttulassa, Tervossa, Vehmersalmella ja Maaningalla ilmestyvä paikallislehti.Start year: 2001
Language (s): Finnish
Ad Rate: Full Page Colour 1654.00
Currency: Euro
COMMUNITY NEWSPAPER

Kuriiri 222351
Owner: Kuriirilainen Oy
Editorial: Kiertotie 8, Ranua 97700
Tel: 358 10 66 56 333
Email: toimitus@kuriirilehti.fi **Web site:** http://www.kuriirilehti.fi/
Freq: Weekly; **Circ:** 6300 Publisher's Statement
Editor in Chief: Pasi Haarahiltunen
Profile: Newspaper issued in Posio and Ranua. Local Translation:Posiolla ja Ranualla ilmestyvä paikallislehti.
Language (s): Finnish
COMMUNITY NEWSPAPER

Kurikka-Lehti 222519
Owner: Kurikka-lehti Oy
Editorial: PL 50 / Laulajantie 4, Kurikka 61301
Tel: 358 6 45 15 500
Email: toimitus@kurikka-lehti.fi **Web site:** http://www.kurikka-lehti.fi
Freq: 2 Times/Week; **Circ:** 5058 ABC-Audit Bureau of Circulations
Editor in Chief: Jaakko Ujainen
Profile: Local newspaper issued in Kurikka. Kurikan kaupungissa ilmestyvä paikallislehti.Number of pages: 12 Start year: 1928
Language (s): Finnish
COMMUNITY NEWSPAPER

Kurkijokelainen 222366
Owner: Kurkijoki-Säätiö
Editorial: Kuukankuja 1, Loimaa 32200
Tel: 358 50 521 3336
Email: toimitus@kurkijoki.fi **Web site:** http://www.kurkijoki.fi/kurkijokelainen/kj_kjln0.html
Freq: Bi-Weekly; **Circ:** 2000 Publisher's Statement
Profile: Newspaper issued in Kurkijoki. Local Translation:Kurkijoella ilmestyvä paikallislehti.
Language (s): Finnish
COMMUNITY NEWSPAPER

Kurun Lehti 625580
Owner: Kuru-Seura
Tel: 358 44 34 30 031
Email: toimitus@kurunlehti.fi **Web site:** http://www.kurunlehti.fi
Freq: Bi-Weekly; **Circ:** 2800 Publisher's Statement
News: Juhani Latoniemi; **General Editor:** Toimitus
Profile: Newspaper distributed in Kuru and surroundings.
Language (s): Finnish
COMMUNITY NEWSPAPER

KustNytt 222282
Owner: Kustmedia Ab Oy
Editorial: Barkamovagen 3, Solf 65450
Tel: 358 6 34 41 800
Email: info@kustmedia.fi **Web site:** http://www.kustmedia.fi
Freq: Monthly; **Circ:** 2800 Publisher's Statement
News: Lisbeth Bäck; **General Editor:** Redaktionen
Profile: Newspaper with articles about people, companies and events in Malax and Korsnäs. Local Translation:Artiklar om människor, företag och evenemang i Malax och Korsnäs. Their fax number is 358 6-34 41 820, but e-mails are preferred.
Language (s): Swedish
Ad Rate: Full Page Colour 1340.00
Currency: Euro
COMMUNITY NEWSPAPER

Kuukkeli 230973
Owner: Santa Claus Medias Oy
Editorial: Lehontie 2 A, Äkäslompolo 95970
Tel: 358 16 56 95 67
Email: toimitus@kuukkeli.com **Web site:** http://www.kuukkeli.com
Freq: Monthly; **Circ:** 8000 Publisher's Statement
Profile: Local newspaper of ski resort Ylläs and Äkäslompolo. Aimed at ski travellers.Local Translation: Ylläksen ja Äkäslompolon paikallislehti.
Language (s): Finnish
COMMUNITY NEWSPAPER

Kymen Sanomat 157037
Owner: Kaakon Viestintä Oy
Editorial: PL 27/Tornatorintie 3, Kotka 48101
Tel: 358 5 2100 15
Email: uutiset@kymensanomat.fi **Web site:** http://www.kymensanomat.fi
Freq: Daily; **Circ:** 19715
Editor: Pekka Kimpanpää; **Editor:** Markku Kumpunen
Profile: Newspaper distributed mainly in Kotka, Hamina and Vehkalahti. Suuriin sanomiin luokiteltu sanomalehti jaetaan lähinnä Kotkassa, Haminassa ja Vehkalahdessa.Regular features: Mondays: MoneyTuesdays: Well-being Wednesdays: Cars and trafficThursdays: Food Fridays: EntertainmentSaturdays: Youth Sundays: Housing.Number of pages: 28 Start year: 1902
Language (s): Finnish
COMMUNITY NEWSPAPER

Kyrönmaa-lehti 222518
Owner: Kyrönmaa-Laihia Oy
Editorial: PL 61/Ruutintie 2 C, Laihia 66401
Tel: 358 6 47 76 116
Email: toimitus@kyronmaa-lehti.fi **Web site:** http://www.kyronmaa-lehti.fi
Freq: 2 Times/Week; **Circ:** 2975 ABC-Audit Bureau of Circulations
Editor in Chief: Jaakko Ujainen
Profile: Newspaper issued in Laihia, Isokyrö, Vähäkyrö and Ylistaro. Local Translation:Description: Newspaper issued in Laihia, Isokyrö, Vähäkyrö and Ylistaro. Laihialla, Isokyrössä, Vähäkyrössä ja Ylistarossa ilmestyvä paikallislehti.Incorporating: Kranni-Sanomat Number of pages: 16Start year: 1956
Language (s): Finnish
Ad Rate: Full Page Colour 2700.00
Currency: Euro
COMMUNITY NEWSPAPER

LähiLehti - Sysmä, Hartola 222281
Owner: Sysmän Sanomat Oy
Editorial: Sysmantie 30, Sysmä 19700
Tel: 358 3 87 77 60
Email: toimitus@lahilehti.com **Web site:** http://www.lahilehti.com
Freq: Weekly; **Circ:** 5500 Publisher's Statement
Profile: Newspaper issued in Sysmä and Hartola. Sysmässä ja Hartolassa ilmestyvä pitäjälehti.Previously listed as: Sysmän ja Hartolan Pitäjälehti, Lähilehti Number of pages: 12Start year: 1969 Previous title: Sysmän ja Hartolan Pitäjälehti, Lähilehti
Language (s): Finnish
COMMUNITY NEWSPAPER

Laitilan Sanomat 222367
Owner: Plari Oy
Editorial: PL 8/Keskuskatu 2, Laitila 23801
Tel: 358 2 58 88 900
Email: toimitus@laitilansanomat.fi **Web site:** http://www.laitilansanomat.fi
Freq: 2 Times/Week; **Circ:** 4900 ABC-Audit Bureau of Circulations
Editor in Chief: Eija Eskola-Buri
Profile: Newspaper distributed in Laitila, Pyhäranta and Kodisjoki. Laitilassa, Pyhärannassa ja Kodisjoella ilmestyvä paikallislehti.Number of pages: 16 Start year: 1925
Language (s): Finnish
COMMUNITY NEWSPAPER

Längelmävesi-lehti 222302
Owner: Pirkanmaan Viikkokustannus Oy
Editorial: Ellintie 2, Kangasala 36200
Tel: 358 3 35 88 640
Web site: http://www.quu.fi
Freq: Quarterly; **Circ:** 1400 Publisher's Statement
News: Jyrki Jaakkola
Profile: Newspaper distributed in Kangasala and the Längelmävesi region. Local Translation:Kangasalassa ja Längelmävesialueella ilmestyvä paikallislehti. lvesi@quu.fi
Language (s): Finnish
COMMUNITY NEWSPAPER

Länsi-Saimaan Sanomat 375688
Owner: ESV-Paikallismediat Oy
Editorial: Peltoinlahdentie 24, Savitaipale 54800
Email: toimitus@lansisaimaa.fi **Web site:** http://www.lansisaimaa.fi
Freq: 2 Times/Week; **Circ:** 4684 ABC-Audit Bureau of Circulations
News Editor: Timo Sihvo
Profile: Newspaper issued in Savitaipale, Lemi, Suomenniemi and Taipalsaari. Previously listed as Yhteissanomat.Savitaipaleella, Lemissä, Suomenniemellä ja Taipalsaaressa ilmestyvä paikallislehti. Aiemmin nimellä Yhteissanomat.Number of pages: 12 Start year: 1950
Language (s): Finnish
COMMUNITY NEWSPAPER

Länsi-Savo 157044
Owner: Länsi-Savo Oy
Editorial: PL 6/ Teollisuuskatu 2-6, Mikkeli 50101
Tel: 358 15 35 01
Email: toimitus@lansi-savo.fi **Web site:** http://www.lansi-savo.fi
Freq: Daily; **Circ:** 22352
News Manager: Anssi Mehtälä
Profile: Newspaper issued mainly in the Mikkeli region. Local Translation:Lähinnä Mikkelin seudulla ilmestyvä sanomalehti. Their fax number is 015-35 03 337, but e-mails are preferred.Start year: 1889
Language (s): Finnish
COMMUNITY NEWSPAPER

Länsi-Suomi 157051
Owner: Marva Media Oy
Editorial: PL 5/ Susivuorentie 2, Rauma 26101
Tel: 358 10 83 361
Email: toimitus@marvamedia.fi **Web site:** https://ls24.fi
Freq: Daily; **Circ:** 14391
Editor: Elina Helkelä
Profile: Newspaper issued mainly in Rauma and its surroundings in western Finland. Raumalla ja Länsi-Suomessa ilmestyvä Suomen suurin sanomiin lukeutuva sanomalehti.Edition: Länsi-Suomi Urheilutoimitus Number of pages: 18Start year: 1905
Language (s): Finnish
Ad Rate: Full Page Colour 10036.00
Currency: Euro
COMMUNITY NEWSPAPER

Länsi-Uusimaa 157041
Owner: Etelä-Suomen Media Oy
Editorial: Suurlohjankatu 10, Lohja 8100
Tel: 358 20 2730 0203
Email: lu.toimitus@media.fi **Web site:** http://www.lansi-uusimaa.fi
Freq: Fri; **Circ:** 11727
Editor: Maijaliisa Valkonen
Profile: Non-political newspaper issued in Lohja and its neighbouring municipalities. Sitoutumaton sanomalehti, jonka levikkialue on Lohja sekä sen naapurikunnat.Number of pages: 16 Start year: 1915
Language (s): Finnish
Ad Rate: Full Page Colour 3220.00
Currency: Euro
COMMUNITY NEWSPAPER

Länsiväylä 222492
Owner: SLY-Kaupunkilehdet Oy
Editorial: PL 350/ Ralssitie 7 A, Vantaa 1511
Tel: 358 20 61 00 110
Email: lv.toimitus@media.fi **Web site:** http://www.lansivayla.fi
Freq: 2 Times/Week; **Circ:** 114000 Publisher's Statement
News Manager: Minna Airamaa; **Editor in Chief:** Risto Hietanen
Profile: Newspaper distributed in Espoo, Kauniainen and Kirkkonummi. Local Translation:Ilmainen sanomalehti, jonka jakelualueet ovat Espoo, Kauniainen ja Kirkkonummi. Start year: 1954
Language (s): Finnish
Ad Rate: Full Page Colour 4469.00
Currency: Euro
COMMUNITY NEWSPAPER

Lapin Kansa 157053
Owner: Alma Media Oyj
Editorial: Veitikantie 2-8, Rovaniemi 96100
Tel: 358 10 665 022
Email: lktoimitus@lapinkansa.fi **Web site:** http://www.lapinkansa.fi
Freq: Daily; **Circ:** 28735
News Manager: Katja Kärki; **Editor in Chief:** Antti Kokkonen; **News Manager:** Pekka Mauno; **News Manager:** Taru Salo
Profile: Newspaper issued in Lapland, northern Finland. Lapissa ilmestyvä aluelehti.Start year: 1928
Language (s): Finnish
Ad Rate: Full Page Colour 6800.00
Currency: Euro
COMMUNITY NEWSPAPER

Lappeenrannan Uutiset 222284
Owner: SLY Kaupunkilehdet Oy
Editorial: Kauppakeskus Opri 3. krs, Valtakatu 30, Lappeenranta 53100 **Tel:** 358 20 610 0112
Email: toimitus.lpr@lehtiyhtyma.fi **Web site:** http://www.lappeenrannanuutiset.fi
Freq: Weekly; **Circ:** 67000 Publisher's Statement
Editor in Chief: Karri Kannala
Profile: Newspaper issued in southeastern Finland, mainly in the Lappeenranta region. Local Translation:Lappeenrannan talousalueella ilmestyvä paikallislehti. Previously known as: Kaakkois-Suomen Sanomat
Language (s): Finnish
Ad Rate: Full Page Colour 1848.00
Currency: Euro
COMMUNITY NEWSPAPER

Lappilainen 222243
Owner: Teksti- ja Kuvapalvelu Aakkoset Oy
Editorial: Veitikantie 8, Rovaniemi 96100
Tel: 358 40 351 7181
Email: toimitus@lappilainen.fi **Web site:** http://www.lappilainen.fi
Freq: Weekly; **Circ:** 43700 Publisher's Statement
Profile: Newspaper issued in Rovaniemi and surroundings. Previously listed as Roi-Press.Uutislehti, joka ilmestyy Rovaniemellä ja yhdeksän lähikunnan alueella. Their fax number is 358 16-31 61 62, but generally they do not want any releases.
Language (s): Finnish
Ad Rate: Full Page Colour 1525.00
Currency: Euro
COMMUNITY NEWSPAPER

Lapuan Sanomat 222520
Owner: Lapua Säätiö
Editorial: Sanomatie 1, Lapua 62100
Tel: 358 6 43 87 352
Email: toimitus@lapuansanomat.fi **Web site:** http://www.lapuansanomat.fi
Freq: 2 Times/Week; **Circ:** 6495 ABC-Audit Bureau of Circulations
Editor in Chief: Tarja Kojola
Profile: Newspaper issued in Lapua. Local Translation:Description: Newspaper issued in Lapua. Lapualla ilmestyvä paikallislehti.Number of pages: 20 Start year: 1932
Language (s): Finnish
COMMUNITY NEWSPAPER

Laukaa-Konnevesi 222406
Owner: Keski-Suomen Media Oy
Editorial: Laukaantie 26, Laukaa 41340
Tel: 358 14 339 7400
Email: toimitus@laukaa-konnevesi.fi **Web site:** http://www.ksml.fi/laukaa-konnevesi/
Freq: Weekly; **Circ:** 7310 ABC-Audit Bureau of Circulations
Editor in Chief: Arja Korpela
Profile: Local newspaper issued in Laukaa and Konnevesi. Laukkaalla ja Konnevedellä ilmestyvä paikallislehti.Number of pages: 24 Start year: 1964
Language (s): Finnish
COMMUNITY NEWSPAPER

Lauttakylä 222381
Owner: Huittisten Sanomalehti Oy
Editorial: PL 36/Karpintie 13, Huittinen 32701
Tel: 358 2 55 54 200
Email: toimitus@lauttakyla.fi **Web site:** http://www.lauttakyla.fi
Freq: 2 Times/Week; **Circ:** 5230 ABC-Audit Bureau of Circulations
Editor in Chief: Marja-Liisa Hakanen
Profile: Newspaper issued in Huittinen, Vampula and Äetsä. Huittisissa, Vampulassa ja Äetsässä ilmestyvä paikallislehti.Number of pages: 10 Start year: 1913
Language (s): Finnish
COMMUNITY NEWSPAPER

Lauttasaari-lehti 222490
Owner: Lauttasaari-Seura
Editorial: Kauppaneuvoksentie 18, Helsinki 200
Tel: 358 10 38 77 080
Web site: http://www.lauttasaari.fi
Freq: Weekly; **Circ:** 11000 Publisher's Statement
Editor in Chief: Liisa Stjernberg
Profile: Newspaper distributed in the Helsinki suburb of Lauttasaari. Local Translation:Lauttasaari-Seuran äänenkannattaja Helsingin Lauttasaaren asioista. They wish not to receive any material to their generic email address at lehti@lauttasaari.fi.
Language (s): Finnish
Ad Rate: Full Page Colour 1000.00
Currency: Euro
COMMUNITY NEWSPAPER

Lempäälän-Vesilahden Sanomat 222382
Owner: Lempäälän-Vesilahden Sanomat Oy
Editorial: PL 38 / Tampereentie 17, Lempäälä 37501
Tel: 358 3 34 29 000
Email: toimitus@lvs.fi **Web site:** http://www.lvs.fi
Freq: 2 Times/Week; **Circ:** 7020 ABC-Audit Bureau of Circulations
Profile: Newspaper issued in Lempäälä and Vesilahti. Lempäälässä ja Vesilahdessa ilmestyvä paikallislehti.Number of pages: 12 Start year: 1931
Language (s): Finnish
COMMUNITY NEWSPAPER

Lepuski 222491
Owner: Viestintätoimisto Luova Ratkaisu Oy
Editorial: PL 120/ Parkvillanpolku, Espoo 2601
Tel: 358 500 67 53 87
Email: seura@lepuski.fi **Web site:** http://www.lepuski.fi
Freq: Quarterly; **Circ:** 25000 Publisher's Statement
Editor in Chief: Arja Salmi
Profile: Newspaper distributed in Leppävaara, Lintuvaara, Uusimäki, Mäkkylä, Perkkaa, Vermo. Local Translation:Leppävaarassa, Lintuvaarassa, Uusimäellä, Mäkkylässä, Perkkaalla ja Vermossa ilmestyvä paikallislehti.
Language (s): Finnish
Ad Rate: Full Page Colour 1650.00
Currency: Euro
COMMUNITY NEWSPAPER

Lestijoki 222521
Owner: Jokilaaksojen Kustannus Oy
Editorial: PL 1 / Valtakatu 9, Kannus 69101
Tel: 358 20 75 04 650
Email: toimitus@lestijoki-lehti.fi **Web site:** http://www.lestijoki-lehti.fi
Freq: Weekly; **Circ:** 5107 ABC-Audit Bureau of Circulations
Editor in Chief: Marja-Leena Mattila-Numminen
Profile: Newspaper issued in Kannus, Toholampi, Lestijärvi, Himanka and Lohtaja. Kannuksella, Toholammella, Lestijärvellä, Himangassa ja Lohtajassa ilmestyvä paikallislehti.Number of pages: 16 Start year: 1975Previous title: Lestinjoki
Language (s): Finnish
COMMUNITY NEWSPAPER

Lieksan Lehti 222442
Owner: Lieksan Lehti Oy
Editorial: PL 22/ Siltakatu 1, Lieksa 81701
Tel: 358 10 23 08 650
Email: toimitus@lieksanlehti.fi **Web site:** http://www.lieksanlehti.fi
Freq: 2 Times/Week; **Circ:** 6482 ABC-Audit Bureau of Circulations
Editor in Chief: Marja Mölsä
Profile: Newspaper issued in Lieksa. Lieksassa ilmestyvä paikallislehti.Number of pages: 12 Start year: 1954
Language (s): Finnish
COMMUNITY NEWSPAPER

Loimaan Lehti 222368
Owner: Priimus Media Oy
Editorial: Kasityolaiskatu 10, Loimaa 32200
Tel: 358 2 58 88 000
Email: toimitus@loimaanlehti.fi **Web site:** http://www.loimaanlehti.fi
Freq: 2 Times/Week; **Circ:** 8472 ABC-Audit Bureau of Circulations
Editor in Chief: Kati Uusitalo
Profile: Newspaper issued in Loimaa, Alastaro, Mellilä and Oripää. Local Translation:Loimaalla, Alastarossa, Mellilässä ja Oripäässä ilmestyvä paikallislehti.
Language (s): Finnish
COMMUNITY NEWSPAPER

Lopen Lehti 222356
Owner: Karprint Oy
Tel: 358 19 44 00 59
Email: lopen.lehti@karprint.fi **Web site:** http://www.karprint.fi/lopenlehti/
Freq: Weekly; **Circ:** 13860 Publisher's Statement
Editor in Chief: Juha Ahola
Profile: Newspaper issued in Loppi. Local Translation:Lopeella ilmestyvä sanomalehti.
Language (s): Finnish
COMMUNITY NEWSPAPER

Lounais-Lappi 222288
Owner: Alma Media Oyj
Editorial: Sairaalakatu 2, Kemi 94100
Tel: 358 10 665 7760
Email: toimitus@lounaislappi.fi **Web site:** http://www.lounaislappi.fi
Freq: 2 Times/Week; **Circ:** 37000 Publisher's Statement
Editor in Chief: Tiina Nousiainen
Profile: Newspaper distributed in Kemi, Tornio, Keminmaa, Kuivaniemi, Simo, Tervola, Ylitornio and Haaparanta. Local Translation:Kemissä, Torniossa, Keminmaalla, Kuivaniemellä, Simossa, Tervolassa, Ylitorniossa ja Haaparannassa ilmestyvä paikallislehti. Number of pages: 32Start year: 1962
Language (s): Finnish
COMMUNITY NEWSPAPER

Loviisan Sanomat 224360
Owner: Ksf Media Ab
Editorial: Sibeliuksenkatu 10, Loviisa 7900
Tel: 358 19 53 27 01
Email: toimitus@lovari.fi **Web site:** http://www.loviisansanomat.net
Freq: 2 Times/Week; **Circ:** 4368 ABC-Audit Bureau of Circulations
Editor in Chief: Arto Henriksson
Profile: Newspaper issued in Loviisa, Lapinjärvi, Liljendal, Pernaja and Ruotsinpyhtää. Local Translation:Loviisassa, Lapinjärvellä, Liljendalissa,

Pernajassa ja Ruotsinpyhtäällä ilmestyvä paikallislehti.
Language (s): Finnish
Ad Rate: Full Page Colour 2747.00
Currency: Euro
COMMUNITY NEWSPAPER

Luoteis-Lappi 222295
Owner: Heikki Peura Ky
Editorial: Ojapolku 3, Kolari 95900
Tel: 358 16 56 11 81
Email: info@luoteis-lappi.com **Web site:** http://www.luoteis-lappi.com
Freq: Weekly; **Circ:** 5378 Publisher's Statement
Profile: Newspaper issued in Kolari and Muonio. Kolarissa ja Muoniolla ilmestyvä paikallislehti.There is a sister A4-format called Meän Aviisi with the same contact information. Number of pages: 16Start year: 1975 Alternative Title: Meän Aviisi
Language (s): Finnish
COMMUNITY NEWSPAPER

Luoteis-Uusimaa 222357
Owner: Karprint Oy
Editorial: Vanha Turuntie 371, Huhmari 3150
Tel: 358 9 413 97 300
Web site: http://www.luoteis-uusimaa.fi
Freq: 2 Times/Week
Editor in Chief: Mari Ahola-Aalto
Profile: Newspaper issued in Vihti. Vihdissä ilmestyvä paikallislehti.Number of pages: 24 Start year: 1952no generic email-address to the editorial.
Language (s): Finnish
COMMUNITY NEWSPAPER

Luoteisväylä 222417
Owner: Suomen Paikallissanomat Oy
Editorial: Finpyyntie 9, Noormarkku 29600
Tel: 358 10 66 55 640
Email: toimitus.luoteisvayla@almamedia.fi **Web site:** http://www.uutismarkku.fi
Freq: Weekly; **Circ:** 3513 ABC-Audit Bureau of Circulations
Profile: Newspaper issued in Noormarkku and Pomarkku. Newspapers Uutismarkku and Luoteis-Satakunta merged into Luoteisväylä. Noormarkussa ja Pomarkussa ilmestyvä paikallislehti. Uutismarkku ja Luoteis-Satakunta yhdistyivät Luoteisväyläksi.
Language (s): Finnish
Ad Rate: Full Page Colour 2321.00
Currency: Euro
COMMUNITY NEWSPAPER

Luumäen Lehti 222426
Owner: Sanoma News Oy
Editorial: Linnalantie 53, Taavetti 54500
Tel: 358 5 45 72 301
Web site: http://www.luumaenlehti.fi
Freq: Weekly; **Circ:** 3627 ABC-Audit Bureau of Circulations
Editor in Chief: Juhani Partanen
Profile: Newspaper issued in Luumäki. Local Translation:Luumäellä ilmestyvä paikallislehti. No e-mails allowed to their address toimitus@luumaenlehti.fi.
Language (s): Finnish
Ad Rate: Full Page Colour 2786.00
Currency: Euro
COMMUNITY NEWSPAPER

Maaselkä 222532
Owner: Haapajärvi-Seura ry
Editorial: PL 74/ Puistokatu 37, Haapajärvi 85801
Tel: 358 8 77 27 500
Email: toimitus@maaselkalehti.fi **Web site:** http://www.maaselkalehti.fi
Freq: 2 Times/Week; **Circ:** 4206 ABC-Audit Bureau of Circulations
Editor in Chief: Juha Heikkilä
Profile: Newspaper issued in Haapajärvi and Reisjärvi. Local Translation:Haapajärvellä ja Reisjärvellä ilmestyvä paikallislehti.
Language (s): Finnish
Ad Rate: Full Page Colour 2208.00
Currency: Euro
COMMUNITY NEWSPAPER

Matkailulehti Ruka 529500
Owner: Pohjoisen Tunturipalvelut Ky
Editorial: Jokimutkantie 5, Kuusamo 93600
Tel: 358 40 77 20 606
Email: toimitus@matkailulehtiruka.com **Web site:** http://www.matkailulehtiruka.com
Freq: Monthly; **Circ:** 7000 Publisher's Statement
Editor: Rita Uusitalo
Profile: Magazine about travel activities in ski sport center Ruka.
Language (s): Finnish
Ad Rate: Full Page Colour 1200.00
Currency: Euro
COMMUNITY NEWSPAPER

Matti ja Liisa 222443
Owner: Savon Media Oy
Editorial: Juhani Ahontie 2, Lapinlahti 73100
Tel: 358 17 731540
Email: matti.liisa@mattijaliisa.fi **Web site:** http://www.mattijaliisa.fi
Freq: Weekly; **Circ:** 5119 ABC-Audit Bureau of Circulations
Editor in Chief: Tero Joutselainen
Profile: Newspaper issued in Lapinlahti and Varpaisjärvi. Local Translation:Lapinlahdessa ja Varpaisjärvellä ilmestyvä paikallislehti.
Language (s): Finnish
COMMUNITY NEWSPAPER

Meän Tornionlaakso 222353
Owner: Tornionlaakson Kustannus Oy
Editorial: Alkkulanraitti 48, Ylitornio 95600
Tel: 358 40 51 00 213
Web site: http://www.tornionlaakso.net
Freq: Weekly; **Circ:** 4800 Publisher's Statement
Editor in Chief: Minna Siilasvuo
Profile: Newspaper distributed in Ylitornio, Pello, Kolari, Muonio and Enontekiö. Ylitorniossa, Pellossa, Kolarissa, Muoniossa ja Enontekiöllä ilmestyvä ilmaisjakelulehti.Number of pages: 20
Language (s): Finnish
Ad Rate: Full Page Colour 1453.00
Currency: Euro
COMMUNITY NEWSPAPER

Merikarvia-lehti 222369
Owner: Suomen Paikallissanomat Oy
Editorial: PL 3/Kauppatie 36, Merikarvia 29901
Tel: 358 2 55 11 272
Email: toimitus.merikarvialehti@almamedia.fi **Web site:** http://www.merikarvialehti.fi
Freq: Weekly; **Circ:** 3379 ABC-Audit Bureau of Circulations
Profile: Newspaper issued in Merikarvia and Siikainen. Merikarviassa ja Siikaisilla ilmestyvä paikallislehti.Number of pages: 8 Start year: 1982
Language (s): Finnish
Ad Rate: Full Page Colour 1892.00
Currency: Euro
COMMUNITY NEWSPAPER

Miilu 222461
Owner: Maakunnan Sanomat Oy
Editorial: Petterintie 2, Vieremä 74200
Email: miilu@miilu.fi **Web site:** http://www.miilu.fi
Freq: Weekly; **Circ:** 3196 ABC-Audit Bureau of Circulations
Profile: Newspaper issued in Sonkajärvi and Vieremä. Local Translation:Sonkajärvellä ja Vieremällä ilmestyvä paikallislehti. Address to correspondent in Vieremä: Petterintie 2, 74200 VIEREMÄ.
Fax: 358 17-71 48 50.
Language (s): Finnish
COMMUNITY NEWSPAPER

Mikkelin Erikoissanomat 222244
Owner: Mikkelin Erikoissanomat Ky
Editorial: Pulttikatu 2, Mikkeli 50100
Tel: 358 440 21 12 91
Email: toimitus@haumedia.fi **Web site:** http://www.erikoissanomat.fi
Freq: Monthly; **Circ:** 20000 Publisher's Statement
Editor in Chief: Jarno Laatikainen
Profile: Newspaper distributed in Mikkeli, Rantakylä and Otava. Local Translation:Mikkelissä, Rantakylässä ja Otavassa jaettava ilmaisjakelulehti.
Language (s): Finnish
COMMUNITY NEWSPAPER

Mikkelin Kaupunkilehti 222543
Owner: Mikkelin Kaupunkilehti Oy
Editorial: Mikonkatu 8, Mikkeli 50100
Tel: 358 15 22 56 01
Web site: http://www.mikkelinkaupunkilehti.fi/
Freq: Weekly; **Circ:** 35000 Publisher's Statement
Profile: Newspaper issued in Mikkeli. Local Translation:Mikkelissä ilmestyvä paikallislehti. toimitus@mikkelinkaupunkilehti.fi do not want press releases into their generic editorial address
Language (s): Finnish
COMMUNITY NEWSPAPER

MOBILE 230974
Owner: Mobile Kustannus Oy
Editorial: Brahenkatu 14 D 94, Turku 20100
Tel: 358 45 65 67 216
Email: toimitus@mobilekustannus.fi **Web site:** http://mobile-lehti.fi
Freq: Weekly; **Circ:** 5000 Publisher's Statement
Profile: Newspaper about the events in Turku and surroundings. Local Translation:Turun tapahtumista kertova uutislehti.
Language (s): Finnish
Ad Rate: Full Page Colour 1350.00
Currency: Euro
COMMUNITY NEWSPAPER

Munkinseutu 222494
Owner: Karprint Oy
Editorial: Vanha Turuntie 371, Huhmari 3150
Tel: 358 9 41 39 73 00
Email: munkinseutu@karprint.fi **Web site:** http://www.karprint.fi/munkinseutu
Freq: Bi-Weekly; **Circ:** 25000 Publisher's Statement
Editor in Chief: Juha Ahola
Profile: Newspaper distributed in northern Helsinki. Local Translation:Lehti, jonka jakelualueena toimivat Munkkiniemi, Munkkivuori, Niemenmäki, Lehtisaari, Kaskisaari, Kuusisaari, Tali, Pikku Huopalahti, Etelä-Haaga, Pajamäki, Pitäjänmäki, Meilahti ja Töölö. Previous title: Munkinseudun Aluesanomat
Language (s): Finnish
COMMUNITY NEWSPAPER

Muuramelainen 222283
Owner: Muuramen kunta
Editorial: PL 1/ Virastotie 8, Muurame 40951
Tel: 358 14 65 96 11
Email: muuramelainen@muurame.fi **Web site:** http://www.muurame.fi
Freq: Bi-Weekly; **Circ:** 4400 Publisher's Statement
General Editor: Toimitus
Profile: Newspaper issued in Muurame. Local Translation:Muuramen kunnassa ilmestyvä paikallislehti.
Language (s): Finnish
COMMUNITY NEWSPAPER

Nivala-lehti 222522
Owner: Jokilaaksojen Kustannus Oy
Editorial: PL 2/ Kalliontie 30, Nivala 85501
Tel: 358 20 75 04 710
Email: toimitus@nivala-lehti.fi **Web site:** http://www.nivala-lehti.fi
Freq: 2 Times/Week; **Circ:** 5971 ABC-Audit Bureau of Circulations
Editor in Chief: Seija Krapu
Profile: Newspaper issued in Nivala. Nivalassa ilmestyvä paikallislehti.Number of pages: 20 Start year: 1949
Language (s): Finnish
Ad Rate: Full Page Colour 2080.00
Currency: Euro
COMMUNITY NEWSPAPER

Nokian Uutiset 222340
Owner: Suomen Paikallissanomat Oy
Editorial: PL 13/ Valimaenkatu 23, Nokia 37101
Tel: 358 10 66 51 10
Email: toimitus.nokianuutiset@sps.fi **Web site:** http://www.nokianuutiset.fi
Freq: 3 Times/Week; **Circ:** 8479 ABC-Audit Bureau of Circulations
Profile: Newspaper issued in Nokia. Nokialla ilmestyvä paikallislehti.Number of pages: 12 Start year: 1913
Language (s): Finnish
Ad Rate: Full Page Colour 4314.00
Currency: Euro
COMMUNITY NEWSPAPER

Nurmijärven Uutiset 222278
Owner: Medialehdet Oy
Editorial: Kuonomaentie 1, Klaukkala 1800
Tel: 358 20 61 00 151
Email: nurmijarven.uutiset@lehtiyhtyma.fi **Web site:** http://www.nurmijarvenuutiset.fi
Freq: 2 Times/Week; **Circ:** 20200 Publisher's Statement
Editor in Chief: Jan Pippingsköld
Profile: Newspaper issued in Nurmijärvi. Nurmijärvellä ilmestyvä paikallislehti.Previously listed as: Nurmijärven Extra-Uutiset Alternative title: NuutisetNumber of pages: 24 Start year: 1961Alternative Title: Nuutiset Previous title: Nurmijärven Extra-Uutiset
Language (s): Finnish
Ad Rate: Full Page Colour 2060.00
Currency: Euro
COMMUNITY NEWSPAPER

Nya Åland 157065
Owner: Nya Ålands Tidning AB
Editorial: PB 21/Uppgårdsvagen 6, Mariehamn 22101 **Tel:** 358 18 23 444
Email: redaktion@nyan.ax **Web site:** http://www.nyan.ax
Circ: 6683
Editor: Anna Björkroos
Profile: Politically neutral newspaper is issued on the Åland (Ahvenanmaa) Islands. Local Translation:Politiskt neutral tidning utkommer närmast på Åland. They want press releases in Swedish only.Regular features: Every month features for Environment; Crafts; Health; Travel & Leisure; Service; Internet
Language (s): Swedish
Ad Rate: Full Page Colour 5952.00
Currency: Euro
COMMUNITY NEWSPAPER

Nyky-Tampere 222279
Owner: Kokoomuksen Tampereen Aluejärjestö ry
Editorial: Kuninkaankatu 13 B, Tampere 33210
Tel: 358 50 564 5054
Web site: http://www.tamperelainenkokoomus.fi/nykytampere/
Freq: Quarterly; **Circ:** 88000 Publisher's Statement
Profile: Local newspaper issued in Tampere by The Finnish Coalition Party. Kokoomuksen Tampereen paikallislehti.
Language (s): Finnish
COMMUNITY NEWSPAPER

Omalähiö 230089
Owner: Salomaan Kirjapaino Oy
Editorial: Patomaentie 10, Lahti 15610
Tel: 358 3 73 52 016
Email: omalahio@phnet.fi **Web site:** http://www.omalahio.fi
Freq: Weekly; **Circ:** 13000 Publisher's Statement
News: Petri Salomaa
Profile: Newspaper distributed in southern Lahti. Local Translation:Etelä-Lahdessa jaettava paikallislehti.
Language (s): Finnish
COMMUNITY NEWSPAPER

Orimattilan Sanomat 222409
Owner: Pitäjäsanomat Oy
Editorial: PL 5 / Erkontie 17, Orimattila 16301
Tel: 358 3 87 66 78
Email: toimitus@orimattilansanomat.fi **Web site:** http://www.orimattilansanomat.fi
Freq: 2 Times/Week; **Circ:** 4462 ABC-Audit Bureau of Circulations
News: Petri Sipiläinen
Profile: Newspaper issued in Orimattila, Artjärvi, Pukkila and Myrskylä. Local Translation:Orimattilassa, Artjärvellä, Pukkilassa ja Myrskylässä ilmestyvä paikallislehti.
Language (s): Finnish
Ad Rate: Full Page Colour 6674.00
Currency: Euro
COMMUNITY NEWSPAPER

Oriveden Sanomat 222383
Owner: Oriveden Sanomalehti Oy
Editorial: PL 33 / Lehmilaidantie 6, Orivesi 35301
Tel: 358 3 35 89 500
Email: toimitus@orivedensanomat.fi **Web site:** http://www.orivedensanomat.fi
Freq: 2 Times/Week; **Circ:** 5325 ABC-Audit Bureau of Circulations
Editor in Chief/Managing Director: Vesa Kangas
Profile: Newspaper issued in Orivesi, Juupajoki and Längelmä. Local Translation:Description: Newspaper issued in Orivesi, Juupajoki and Längelmä. Orivedellä, Juupajoella ja Längelmässä ilmestyvä paikallislehti.Supplement: Ylä-Pirkanmaa 3/year Number of pages: 12Start year: 1926
Language (s): Finnish
Ad Rate: Full Page Colour 3951.00
Currency: Euro
COMMUNITY NEWSPAPER

Österbottens Tidning 157030
Owner: HSS Media Ab
Editorial: PB 22/Jakobsgatan 13, Jakobstad 68601
Tel: 358 6 784 8803
Email: red@ot.fi **Web site:** http://online.osterbottenstidning.fi/
Circ: 13901
News Manager: Sonja Finholm; **Editor in Chief:** Henrik Othman
Profile: Third biggest Swedish-language newspaper in Finland is issued mainly in northern Ostrobotnia on the west coast. Local Translation:Den tredje största svenska dagstidningen i Finland ges ut främst i Jakobstad, Nykarleby, Pedersöre, Kronoby, Oravais, Karleby och Larsmo. Publiseras om: magasin som utkommer tillsammans med Vasabladet och Österbottens Tidning sex gångar i året.Previous title: Jakobstads Tidning Twitter: http://twitter.com/otwebb.Alternative telephone no: 358 6-78 53 245
Language (s): Swedish
Ad Rate: Full Page Colour 7565.00
Currency: Euro
COMMUNITY NEWSPAPER

Österbottniska posten Öp 429171
Owner: Ab Sidwill OY
Editorial: Kauppapuistikko 10 D, Vaasa 65100
Tel: 358 6 32 05 000
Web site: http://www.webbop.fi/start/
Freq: Monthly; **Circ:** 22300 Publisher's Statement
Profile: Local newspaper distributed in the Pohjanmaa region. Local Translation:Gratistidning som distribueras till hushåll i Österbotten.
Language (s): Swedish
Ad Rate: Full Page Colour 1450.00
Currency: Euro
COMMUNITY NEWSPAPER

Östnyland 157064
Owner: KSF Media
Editorial: Linnankoskigatan 28, Borgå 6100
Tel: 358 20 7569 622
Email: redaktion@ostnyland.fi **Web site:** http://ostnyland.fi
Freq: Fri; **Circ:** 17383
News Editor: Birgitta Ehrstén; **Editor in Chief:** Micaela Röman
Profile: Regional newspaper distributed in Porvoo, Sipoo, Pernaja, Loviisa, Liljendal, Lapinjärvi, Myrskylä and Ruotsinpyhtää. Local Translation:Description: Regional newspaper distributed in Porvoo, Sipoo, Pernaja, Loviisa, Liljendal, Lapinjärvi, Myrskylä and Ruotsinpyhtää. Dagstidning som utkommer i Borgå, Sibbo, Pernå, Lovisa, Liljendal, Lappträsk, Myrskylä och Svenskby.Previous title Borgåbladet & Östra Nyland
Language (s): Swedish
Ad Rate: Full Page Colour 3319.00
Currency: Euro
COMMUNITY NEWSPAPER

Oulu-lehti 222554
Owner: Joutsen Media Oy
Editorial: PL 52 / Lekatie 4, Oulu 90101
Tel: 358 8 53 70 022
Email: toimitus@oululehti.fi **Web site:** http://www.oululehti.fi
Freq: 2 Times/Week; **Circ:** 100000 Publisher's Statement
Editor in Chief: Sauli Pahkasalo
Profile: Newspaper distributed in Oulu. Local Translation:Oulussa jaettava sanomalehti. Number of pages: 8Start year: 1959
Language (s): Finnish
COMMUNITY NEWSPAPER

Oulunkyläinen - Pohjoiset esikaupungit 222325
Owner: Oulunkylä-Seura ry
Editorial: Maanmittarintie 10 B, Helsinki 680
Tel: 358 400 93 44 33
Email: kaija-leena.sinkko@kolumbus.fi **Web site:** http://www.kaupunginosat.net/oulunkyla/oulunkylainen/oulunkylainen_lehti.htm
Freq: Bi-Monthly; **Circ:** 23000 Publisher's Statement
Profile: Newspaper distributed in the Oulunkylä suburb of Helsinki. Local Translation:Helsingin Oulunkylässä jaettava paikallislehti.
Language (s): Finnish
COMMUNITY NEWSPAPER

Outokummun Seutu 222445
Owner: Pohjois-Karjalan Paikallislehdet Oy
Editorial: PL 7 / Koulukatu 2, Outokumpu 83501
Tel: 358 10 23 08 850
Email: toimitus@outokummunseutu.fi **Web site:** http://www.outokummunseutu.fi
Freq: 2 Times/Week; **Circ:** 4571 ABC-Audit Bureau of Circulations
Editor in Chief: Esa Nevalainen
Profile: Newspaper issued in Outokumpu and Polvijärvi. Local Translation:Description: Newspaper issued in Outokumpu and Polvijärvi. Outokummussa ja Polvijärvellä ilmestyvä paikallislehti.Number of pages: 12 Start year: 1968
Language (s): Finnish
Ad Rate: Full Page Colour 2738.00
Currency: Euro
COMMUNITY NEWSPAPER

Padasjoen Sanomat 222408
Owner: Padasjoen Sanomat Oy
Editorial: PL 3/ Koivutie 8, Padasjoki 17501
Tel: 358 3 55 27 500
Email: toimitus@padasjoensanomat.fi **Web site:** http://www.padasjoensanomat.fi
Freq: Weekly; **Circ:** 3675 ABC-Audit Bureau of Circulations
Editor in Chief: Jaana Tanner
Profile: Newspaper issued in Lahti and Padasjoki. Local Translation:Description: Newspaper issued in Lahti and Padasjoki. Lahdessa ja Padasjoella ilmestyvä paikallislehti.No e-mails allowed to their address toimitus@padasjoensanomat.fi Number of pages: 12Start year: 1950
Language (s): Finnish
Ad Rate: Full Page Colour 2622.00
Currency: Euro
COMMUNITY NEWSPAPER

Paikallisuutiset 222399
Owner: Joutsan Seutu Oy
Editorial: PL 40/ Savonmaentie 1, Vaajakoski 40801
Tel: 358 40 54 75 111
Email: toimitus@paikallisuutiset.fi **Web site:** http://www.paikallisuutiset.fi
Freq: Weekly; **Circ:** 1604 ABC-Audit Bureau of Circulations
Profile: Newspaper issued in Toivakka, Uurainen and Jyväskylän maalaiskunta. Local Translation:Description: Newspaper issued in Toivakka, Uurainen and Jyväskylän maalaiskunta. Toivakassa, Uuraisilla ja Jyväskylän maalaiskunnassa ilmestyvä paikallislehti.Number of pages: 12 Start year: 1964
Language (s): Finnish
Ad Rate: Full Page Colour 2964.00
Currency: Euro
COMMUNITY NEWSPAPER

Pargas Kungörelser - Paraisten Kuulutukset 222370
Owner: Förlags AB Sydvästkusten
Editorial: Strandvagen 24, Pargas 21600
Email: leena.lehtonen@fabsy.fi **Web site:** http://www.pku.fi
Freq: Weekly; **Circ:** 6813 ABC-Audit Bureau of Circulations
General Editor: Redaktionen; **News:** Harry Serlo
Profile: Newspaper issued in Parainen/ Pargas. Local Translation:Description: Newspaper issued in Parainen/ Pargas. Tidning som utkommer i Pargas.Incorporating Malmens Marknad - Malmin Markkinat Number of pages: 16Start year: 1913
Language (s): Finnish
Ad Rate: Full Page Colour 3000.00
Currency: Euro
COMMUNITY NEWSPAPER

Parikkalan-Rautjärven Sanomat 222446
Owner: Keski-Karjalan Kustannus Oy
Editorial: Parikkalantie 18, Parikkala 59100
Tel: 358 10 23 08 900
Email: toimitus@parikkalan-rautjarvensanomat.fi
Web site: http://www.parikkalan-rautjarvensanomat.fi
Freq: 2 Times/Week; **Circ:** 5687 ABC-Audit Bureau of Circulations
Editor in Chief: Raine Hämäläinen
Profile: Newspaper issued in Parikkala, Saari, Simpele, Rautjärvi and Uukuniemi. Local Translation:Description: Newspaper issued in Parikkala, Simpele, Saari, Rautjärvi and Uukuniemi. Parikkalassa, Saaressa, Simpeleellä, Rautjärvellä ja Uukuniemellä ilmestyvä paikallislehti.Previously known as: Parikkalan Sanomat Incorporating KaakkoisseutuAlso known as: PARAS Number of pages: 8Start year: 1908 Alternative Title: PARASPrevious title: Parikkalan Sanomat
Language (s): Finnish
Ad Rate: Full Page Colour 3154.00
Currency: Euro
COMMUNITY NEWSPAPER

Perhonjokilaakso 222524
Owner: Jokilaaksojen Kustannus Oy
Editorial: Kirkkotanhua 3, Veteli 69700
Tel: 358 20 75 04 670
Web site: http://www.perhonjokilaakso.fi
Freq: Weekly; **Circ:** 6540 ABC-Audit Bureau of Circulations
Editor in Chief: Mauri Aho
Profile: Newspaper issued in the villages of Halsua, Perho, Veteli and the town of Kaustinen. Local Translation:Description: Newspaper issued in the villages of Halsua, Perho, Veteli and the town of Kaustinen. Perhonjokilaakson levikkialue on Halsua, Kaustinen, Perho ja Veteli.Their e-mail address is toimitus@perhonjokilaakso.fi and their fax number 358 20-75 04 676, but they want local news only. Number of pages: 16Start year: 1970
Language (s): Finnish
Ad Rate: Full Page Colour 2518.00
Currency: Euro
COMMUNITY NEWSPAPER

Perniönseudun Lehti 222371
Owner: Perniönseudun Lehti Oy
Editorial: PL 35 / Salontie 2, Perniö 25501
Tel: 358 2 73 52 301
Email: toimitus@pernionseudunlehti.fi **Web site:** http://www.pernionseudunlehti.fi
Freq: Weekly; **Circ:** 4199 ABC-Audit Bureau of Circulations
Profile: Local newspaper issued in Perniö and Särkisalo. Local Translation:Perniössä ja Särkisalossa ilmestyvä paikallislehti.
Language (s): Finnish
Ad Rate: Full Page Colour 2142.00
Currency: Euro
COMMUNITY NEWSPAPER

Petäjävesi 222396
Owner: Petäjäveden Petäjäiset ry
Editorial: Asematie 6, Petäjävesi 41900
Tel: 358 14 85 42 40
Email: toimitus@petajavesi.net **Web site:** http://www.petajavesi.net
Freq: Weekly; **Circ:** 2046 ABC-Audit Bureau of Circulations
Profile: Newspaper issued in Petäjävesi. Local Translation:Petäjävedellä ilmestyvä paikallislehti.
Language (s): Finnish
COMMUNITY NEWSPAPER

Pieksämäen Lehti 222447
Owner: Maakunnan Sanomat Oy
Editorial: Hallipussi 2, Pieksämäki 76100
Tel: 358 15 34 81 722
Email: toimitus@pieksamaenlehti.fi **Web site:** http://www.pieksamaenlehti.fi
Freq: 2 Times/Week; **Circ:** 6597 ABC-Audit Bureau of Circulations
Editor-In-Chief: Sinikka Hakkarainen
Profile: Newspaper issued in Pieksämäki, Pieksämäen mlk, Haukivuori, Jäppilä and Virtasalmi. Local Translation:Pieksämäellä, Haukivuorella, Jäppilässä ja Virtasalmella ilmestyvä paikallislehti. Regular features: Fridays: Health
Language (s): Finnish
Ad Rate: Full Page Colour 3574.00
Currency: Euro
COMMUNITY NEWSPAPER

Pieksämäen Paikallinen 327515
Editorial: Keskuskatu 14 A, II-krs., Pieksämäki 76100
Tel: 358 40 55 03 035
Email: pmaen.paikallinen@co.inet.fi **Web site:** http://www.pmaenpaikallinen.com
Freq: Weekly; **Circ:** 11500 Publisher's Statement
Editor in Chief: Laila Kimonen
Profile: Newspaper distributed in Pieksämäki. Local Translation:Pieksämäellä jaettava mainoslehti. Ilmestyy keskiviikkoisin.
Language (s): Finnish
COMMUNITY NEWSPAPER

Pielavesi - Keitele 222448
Owner: Maakunnan Sanomat Oy
Editorial: Laaksotie 28, Pielavesi 72400
Tel: 358 17 28 87 781
Email: pieke@pielavesi-keitele.fi **Web site:** http://www.pielavesi-keitele.fi
Freq: Weekly; **Circ:** 5899 ABC-Audit Bureau of Circulations
Editor in Chief: Heli Roivainen
Profile: Newspaper issued in Pielavesi and Keitele. Local Translation:Pielavedellä ja Keiteleessä ilmestyvä paikallislehti.
Language (s): Finnish
COMMUNITY NEWSPAPER

Pielisjokiseutu 222449
Owner: Pohjois-Karjalan Paikallislehdet Oy
Editorial: Liikekeskus, Eno 81200
Tel: 358 10 23 08 700
Email: toimitus@pielisjokiseutu.fi **Web site:** http://www.pielisjokiseutu.fi
Freq: Weekly; **Circ:** 3600 ABC-Audit Bureau of Circulations
Editor in Chief: Sami Tolvanen
Profile: Newspaper issued in Eno and Kontiolahti. Local Translation:Description: Newspaper issued in Eno and Kontiolahti. Enossa ja Kontiolahdella ilmestyvä paikallislehti.Address to the Kontiolahti office: Keskuskatu 14, 81100 KONTIOLAHTI. Number of pages: 12Start year: 1963
Language (s): Finnish
Ad Rate: Full Page Colour 2956.00
Currency: Euro
COMMUNITY NEWSPAPER

Pietarsaaren Sanomat 222523
Owner: HSS Media Ab
Editorial: Runeberginkatu 8, Pietarsaari 68600
Tel: 358 6 750 4740
Email: ps@pietarsaarensanomat.fi **Web site:** http://www.pietarsaarensanomat.fi
Freq: 2 Times/Week
Editor-In-Chief: Osmo Ojala
Profile: Kokkolassa, Kruunupyyssä, Luodossa, Pedersöressä, Pietarsaaressa, Uusikaarlepyyssä ja Oravaisella ilmestyvä paikallislehti. Newspaper issued in Kokkola, Kruunupyy, Luoto, Pedersöre, Pietarsaari, Uusikaarlepyy and Oravainen.
Language (s): Finnish
COMMUNITY NEWSPAPER

Pirkkalainen 222506
Owner: Pirkkala-Seura ry
Editorial: Suupantie 2 A 10, Pirkkala 33960
Tel: 358 3 3143 1900
Email: toimitus@pirkkalainen.com **Web site:** http://www.pirkkalainen.com
Freq: Weekly; **Circ:** 14000 Publisher's Statement
Editor in Chief: Antti Jokinen
Profile: Lehti jaetaan ilmaiseksi kaikkiin Pirkkalan ja Etelä-Tampereen kotitalouksiin, sekä Pirkkalassa myös osaan yrityksistä.
Language (s): Finnish
Ad Rate: Full Page Colour 2344.00
Currency: Euro
COMMUNITY NEWSPAPER

Pitäjäläinen 222444
Owner: Maakunnan Sanomat Oy
Editorial: Nilsiantie 71, Nilsiä 73300
Tel: 358 17 28 87 790
Email: uutiset@pitajalainen.fi **Web site:** http://www.pitajalainen.fi
Freq: 2 Times/Week; **Circ:** 3946 ABC-Audit Bureau of Circulations
Editor-In-Chief: Päivi Laitinen
Profile: Rautavaarassa ja Nilsiässä ilmestyvä paikallislehti. Newspaper issued in Rautavaara and Nilsiä.
Language (s): Finnish
COMMUNITY NEWSPAPER

Pitäjänuutiset 222450
Owner: ESV-Paikallismediat Oy
Editorial: Pentinpolku 1, Mäntyharju 52700
Email: toimitus@pitajanuutiset.fi **Web site:** http://www.pitajanuutiset.fi
Freq: 2 Times/Week; **Circ:** 5540 ABC-Audit Bureau of Circulations
Profile: Mäntyharjulla ja Pertunmaalla ilmestyvä paikallislehti. Newspaper issued in Mäntyharju and Pertunmaa.
Language (s): Finnish
Ad Rate: Full Page Colour 2584.00
Currency: Euro
COMMUNITY NEWSPAPER

Pogostan Sanomat 222451
Owner: Pogostan Sanomat Oy
Editorial: Kauppatie 29, Ilomantsi 82900
Tel: 358 10 23 08 800
Email: toimitus@pogostansanomat.fi **Web site:** http://www.pogostansanomat.fi
Freq: 2 Times/Week; **Circ:** 5623 ABC-Audit Bureau of Circulations
Profile: Ilomantsissa, Kiihtelysvaarassa ja Tuupovaarassa ilmestyvä paikallislehti.
Language (s): Finnish
COMMUNITY NEWSPAPER

Pohjankyrö-lehti 222525
Owner: Pohjakyrön Media Oy
Editorial: Pohjankyrontie 128, Isokyrö 61501
Tel: 358 6 47 15 214
Email: toimitus@pohjankyro-lehti.fi **Web site:** http://www.pohjankyro-lehti.fi
Freq: 2 Times/Week; **Circ:** 5556 ABC-Audit Bureau of Circulations
Editor in Chief: Jaakko Ujainen
Profile: Vähäkyrössä, Isokyrössä, Ylistarossa ja Laihialla ilmestyvä paikallislehti. Newspaper issued in Vähäkyrö, Isokyrö, Ylistaro and Laihia.
Language (s): Finnish
Ad Rate: Full Page Colour 2851.00
Currency: Euro
COMMUNITY NEWSPAPER

Pohjois-Kymenlaakso 222511
Owner: Kaupunkilehti Pohjois-Kymenlaakso Oy
Editorial: Kouvolankatu 21, Kouvola 45100
Tel: 358 5 75 30 500
Email: teija.piipari@pklehti.fi **Web site:** http://www.pklehti.fi
Freq: Weekly; **Circ:** 45000 Publisher's Statement
Editor in Chief: Teija Piipari
Profile: Newspaper issued in Kouvola, Kuusankoski, Anjalankoski, Valkeala, Elimäki, Iitti and Jaala. Kouvolassa, Kuusankoskella, Anjalankoskella, Valkealassa, Elimäellä, Iitissä ja Jaalassa ilmestyvä paikallislehti.Start year: 1968
Language (s): Finnish
COMMUNITY NEWSPAPER

Punkalaitumen Sanomat 222386
Owner: Punkalaitumen Sanomat Oy
Editorial: PL 1 / Lauttakylantie 4, Punkalaidun 31901
Tel: 358 2 76 74 256
Email: toimitus@punkalaitumensanomat.fi **Web site:** http://www.punkalaitumensanomat.fi
Freq: Weekly; **Circ:** 3579 ABC-Audit Bureau of Circulations
Editor in Chief: Juha Aro
Profile: Newspaper issued in Punkalaidun. Local Translation:Description: Newspaper issued in Punkalaidun. Punkalaitumella ilmestyvä paikallislehti.Number of pages: 8 Start year: 1908
Language (s): Finnish
Ad Rate: Full Page Colour 1425.00
Currency: Euro
COMMUNITY NEWSPAPER

Puolanka-lehti 222533
Owner: Kustannus Oy Puolangan DTP
Editorial: PL 15 / Kajaanintie 5, Puolanka 89201
Tel: 358 8 65 32 200
Email: toimitus@puolanka-lehti.fi **Web site:** http://www.puolanka-lehti.fi
Freq: Weekly; **Circ:** 2302 ABC-Audit Bureau of Circulations
Editor in Chief: Tuomo Seppänen
Profile: Newspaper issued in Puolanka. Local Translation:Puolangalla ilmestyvä paikallislehti.
Language (s): Finnish
COMMUNITY NEWSPAPER

Puoli kaupunkia 222469
Owner: Top Contact Oy
Editorial: Sorvaajankatu 15, Helsinki 880
Tel: 358 10 322 1651
Web site: http://www.puolikaupunkia.fi
Freq: Bi-Weekly; **Circ:** 125200 Publisher's Statement
Editor in Chief: Kauko Vanajas
Profile: Newspaper distributed in the Helsinki region. No generic email addressLehdellä on pääkaupunkiseudulla 7 osapainosta, joilla on omat etu- ja takasivunsa sekä keskiaukeamansa. Previously known as: Avaa.Number of pages: 16 Start year: 1989Previous title: Avaa-lehti
Language (s): Finnish
COMMUNITY NEWSPAPER

Puruvesi 222452
Owner: Etelä-Savon Paikallislehdet Oy
Editorial: PL 2 / Kauppatie 16, Punkaharju 58501
Tel: 358 15 35 03 410
Email: uutiset@puruvesi.net **Web site:** http://www.puruvesi.net
Freq: 2 Times/Week; **Circ:** 6483 ABC-Audit Bureau of Circulations
Profile: Newspaper issued in Enonkoski, Kerimäki, Kesälahti, Punkaharju and Savonranta. Local Translation:Description: Newspaper issued in Enonkoski, Kerimäki, Kesälahti, Punkaharju and Savonranta. Enonkoskella, Kerimäellä, Kesälahdessa, Punkaharjulla ja Savonrannassa ilmestyvä paikallislehti.Number of pages: 16 Start year: 1964
Language (s): Finnish
Ad Rate: Full Page Colour 2772.00
Currency: Euro
COMMUNITY NEWSPAPER

Putkilahden uutisia 375691
Owner: Putkilahden Kyläseura ry
Editorial: Putkilahden kylaseura ry, Putkilahti 41870
Tel: 358 14 82 51 10
Web site: http://www.putkilahti.net
Freq: Monthly; **Circ:** 320 Publisher's Statement
News: Aune Turunen
Profile: Newspaper distributed in Putkilahti. Local Translation:Putkilahden kylälehti.
Language (s): Finnish
COMMUNITY NEWSPAPER

Puumala 222427
Owner: Puumala-Seura ry
Editorial: Harkosentie 7, Puumala 52200
Tel: 358 40 1386 332
Email: toimitus@puumalalehti.fi **Web site:** http://www.puumalalehti.fi
Freq: Weekly; **Circ:** 3266 ABC-Audit Bureau of Circulations
News: Elvi Köpman
Profile: Newspaper issued in Puumala. Local Translation:Description: Newspaper issued in Puumala. Puumalassa ilmestyvä paikallislehti.Number of pages: 8 Start year: 1954
Language (s): Finnish
COMMUNITY NEWSPAPER

Pyhäjärven Sanomat 222453
Owner: Pyhäjärven Sanomat Oy
Editorial: PL 41/ Asematie 2, Pyhäsalmi 86801
Tel: 358 8 77 29 000
Email: toimitus@pyhajarvensanomat.fi **Web site:** http://www.pyhajarvensanomat.fi
Freq: Weekly; **Circ:** 4277 ABC-Audit Bureau of Circulations
Profile: Local newspaper in Pyhäjärvi. Local Translation:Description: Local newspaper in Pyhäjärvi. Pyhäjärvellä ilmestyvä paikallislehti.There is a free city edition with the same contact information called Paikallinen, circulation 5300. Number of pages: 16Start year: 1955 Alternative Title: Paikallinen
Language (s): Finnish
Ad Rate: Full Page Colour 1555.00
Currency: Euro
COMMUNITY NEWSPAPER

Pyhäjokiseutu 222534
Owner: Suomen Paikallissanomat Oy
Editorial: PL 1/ Asemakatu 1, Oulainen 86301
Tel: 358 10 66 55 145
Email: toimitus.pyhajokiseutu@almamedia.fi **Web site:** http://www.pyhajokiseutu.fi
Freq: 2 Times/Week; **Circ:** 6211 ABC-Audit Bureau of Circulations
Editor in Chief: Sirpa Kortet
Profile: Newspaper issued in Pyhäjoki, Merijärvi, Haapavesi, Kärsämäki, Vihanti and Oulainen. Local Translation:Pyhäjoella, Merijärvellä, Haapavedellä, Kärsämäellä, Vihannissa ja Oulaisissa ilmestyvä paikallislehti.
Language (s): Finnish
Ad Rate: Full Page Colour 3132.00
Currency: Euro
COMMUNITY NEWSPAPER

Pyhtäänlehti - Pyttisbladet 222428
Owner: KSF Media Ab
Editorial: Sibeliuksenkatu 10, Loviisa 7900
Tel: 358 19 53 27 01
Email: pyhtaanlehti@lovari.fi
Freq: Bi-Weekly; **Circ:** 7600 Publisher's Statement
Editor in Chief: Arto Henriksson
Profile: Newspaper supplement about issues in the municipality of Pyhtää. Local Translation:Pyhtään kunnan asioista kertova liite.
Language (s): Finnish
COMMUNITY NEWSPAPER

Raahelainen 222555
Owner: Alma Media Oy
Editorial: PL 61/ Fellmaninpuistokatu 4, Raahe 92101
Tel: 358 10 66 55 185
Email: rstoimitus@sps.fi **Web site:** http://www.raahenseutu.fi/nakoislehti/raahelainen/
Freq: Weekly; **Circ:** 17020 Publisher's Statement
Editor in Chief: Sanna Keskinen; **News:** Nina Tuomikoski
Profile: Newspaper distributed in Raahe, Pattijoki, Pyhäjoki, Siikajoki, Vihanti and Ruukki. Local Translation:Description: Newspaper distributed in Raahe, Pattijoki, Pyhäjoki, Siikajoki, Vihanti and Ruukki. Kaupunkilehti Raahelaisen jakelualueena toimivat Raahe, Pattijoki, Pyhäjoki, Siikajoki, Vihanti, Ruukki.Number of pages: 12 Start year: 1974
Language (s): Finnish
Ad Rate: Full Page Colour 4205.00
Currency: Euro
COMMUNITY NEWSPAPER

Raahen Seutu 222339
Owner: Alma Media Oy
Editorial: PL 61/ Fellmaninpuistokatu 4, Raahe 92101
Tel: 358 10 66 55 185
Email: toimitus.raahenseutu@almamedia.fi **Web site:** http://www.raahenseutu.fi
Freq: Daily; **Circ:** 8753 ABC-Audit Bureau of Circulations
Editor in Chief: Sanna Keskinen
Profile: Local newspaper issued in Raahe, Pattijoki, Pyhäjoki, Ruukki, Siikajoki and Vihanti. Raahessa, Pattijoella, Pyhäjoella, Ruukissa, Siikajoella ja Vihannissa ilmestyvä paikallislehti.Number of pages: 12 Start year: 1919
Language (s): Finnish
Ad Rate: Full Page Colour 4205.00
Currency: Euro
COMMUNITY NEWSPAPER

Rannikkoseutu 222372
Owner: Alma Media
Editorial: PL 7/ Tornikatu 2, Raisio 21201
Tel: 358 10 66 55 220
Email: toimitus.rannikkoseutu@almamedia.fi **Web site:** http://www.rannikkoseutu.fi
Freq: 2 Times/Week; **Circ:** 7591 ABC-Audit Bureau of Circulations
Profile: Newspaper issued in Raisio, Naantali, Rymättylä, Masku, Merimasku, Askainen and Lemu. Local Translation: Description: Newspaper issued in Raisio, Naantali, Rymättylä, Masku, Merimasku, Askainen and Lemu. Raisiossa, Naantalissa, Rymättylässä, Maskussa, Merimaskussa, Askaisissa ja Lemussa ilmestyvä paikallislehti. Number of pages: 24 Start year: 1932
Language (s): Finnish
Ad Rate: Full Page Colour 2509.00
Currency: Euro
COMMUNITY NEWSPAPER

Rantalakeus 222535
Owner: Pohjois-Suomen Paikallisuutiset Oy
Editorial: PL 21/Limingan Saastokeskus, Liminka 91901 **Tel:** 358 8 38 16 85
Email: toimitus@rantalakeus.fi **Web site:** http://www.rantalakeus.fi
Freq: Weekly; **Circ:** 3303 ABC-Audit Bureau of Circulations
Profile: Newspaper distributed in Hailuoto, Kempele, Liminka. Lumijoki, Oulunsalo, Temmes and Tyrnävä. Local Translation:Hailuodossa, Kempeleessä, Limingalla. Lumijoella, Oulunsalossa, Temmeksessä ja Tyrnävässä ilmestyvä paikallislehti.
Language (s): Finnish
COMMUNITY NEWSPAPER

Rantapohja 222536
Owner: Rantapohja Oy
Editorial: PL 15/Huvipolku 6, Haukipudas 90831
Tel: 358 8 56 37 200
Email: toimitus@rantapohja.fi **Web site:** http://www.rantapohja.fi
Freq: 2 Times/Week; **Circ:** 9578 ABC-Audit Bureau of Circulations
Profile: Newspaper issued in Haukipudas, Kiiminki, Ylikiiminki, Ii, Yli-Ii, Kuivaniemi and Pateniemi. Local Translation:Description: Newspaper issued in Haukipudas, Kiiminki, Ylikiiminki, Ii, Yli-Ii, Kuivaniemi and Pateniemi. Haukiputaalla, Kiimingissä, Ylikiimingissä, Iissä, Yli-Iissä, Kuivaniemellä ja Pateniemellä ilmestyvä paikallislehti.Number of pages: 16 Start year: 1969
Language (s): Finnish
Ad Rate: Full Page Colour 1747.00
Currency: Euro
COMMUNITY NEWSPAPER

Rantasalmen Lehti 222454
Owner: Rantasalmen Lehti Oy
Editorial: PL 4 / Kylatie 37, Rantasalmi 58901
Tel: 358 15 44 07 51
Web site: http://www.rantasalmenlehti.fi
Freq: Weekly; **Circ:** 3122 ABC-Audit Bureau of Circulations
Editor in Chief: Arto Ylhävaara
Profile: Newspaper issued in Rantasalmi. Local Translation:Rantasalmella ilmestyvä paikallislehti.
Language (s): Finnish
Ad Rate: Full Page Colour 1748.00
Currency: Euro
COMMUNITY NEWSPAPER

Raumalainen 222509
Owner: Marva Media Oy
Editorial: Susivuorentie 2, Rauma 26100
Tel: 358 10 83 36 555
Email: toimitus@marvamedia.fi **Web site:** https://ls24.fi/raumalainen
Freq: 2 Times/Week; **Circ:** 38100
Profile: Rauman alueen paikallislehti.
Language (s): Finnish
Ad Rate: Full Page Colour 1825.00
Currency: Euro
COMMUNITY NEWSPAPER

Reimari 625578
Owner: Haminan yrittäjät ry
Editorial: Maariankatu 14, Hamina 49400
Tel: 358 10 42 10 200
Web site: http://www.reimari.fi
Freq: Weekly; **Circ:** 15800 Publisher's Statement
News: Jorma Haapamäki
Profile: Newspaper distributed in Hamina, Miehikkälä, Virolahti, Liikkala and Ruotila. No generic email address for the editorial.
Language (s): Finnish
COMMUNITY NEWSPAPER

Reisjärvi 222352
Owner: Reisjärvi-lehti Oy
Editorial: PL 2/ Kirkkotie 3 H, Reisjärvi 85901
Tel: 358 8 77 70 20
Email: toimitus@reisjarvilehti.fi **Web site:** http://www.reisjarvilehti.fi
Freq: Weekly; **Circ:** 2068 ABC-Audit Bureau of Circulations
Editor in Chief: Leila Lampi; **Editor in Chief:** Merja Tytärniemi
Profile: Newspaper issued in Reisjärvi. Local Translation:Reisjärvellä ja sen ympäristökunnissa ilmestyvä paikallislehti.
Language (s): Finnish
COMMUNITY NEWSPAPER

Riihimäen Seudun Viikkouutiset 222273
Owner: Suomen Lehtiyhtymä
Editorial: PL 14/ Hameenkatu 38, Riihimaki 11101
Tel: 358 20 61 00 121
Email: toimitus.riie@lehtiyhtyma.fi **Web site:** http://www.viikkouutiset.fi
Freq: Weekly; **Circ:** 23000 Publisher's Statement
Editor in Chief: Joonas Romppanen
Profile: Newspaper issued in Janakkala, Loppi, Hausjärvi and Riihimäki. Local Translation:Description: Newspaper issued in Janakkala, Loppi, Hausjärvi and Riihimäki. Janakkalassa, Lopella, Hausjärvellä ja Riihimäellä ilmestyvä paikallislehti.Previously listed as: Riihimäen Viikkouutiset Incorporating: UutisloppiNumber of pages: 12 Start year: 1995Alternative Title: Viikkouutiset Previous title: Riihimäen Viikkouutiset
Language (s): Finnish
Ad Rate: Full Page Colour 4039.00
Currency: Euro
COMMUNITY NEWSPAPER

Ristiinalainen 222285
Owner: Kustannus Janari Oy
Editorial: PL 20/Brahentie 34, Ristiina 52301
Tel: 358 15 33 73 560
Email: toimitus@ristiinalainen.fi **Web site:** http://www.ristiinalainen.fi
Freq: Weekly; **Circ:** 2600 Publisher's Statement
Editor in Chief: Niko Takala
Profile: Newspaper distributed in Ristiina and Suomenniemi. Local Translation:Lehti jaetaan Ristiinassa ja Suomenniemellä joka talouteen sekä liikelaitokseen. Their fax number is 358 15-45 84 61, but e-mails are preferred.
Language (s): Finnish
COMMUNITY NEWSPAPER

Rööperin lehti 704626
Editorial: Vanha Turuntie 371, Huhmari 3150
Tel: 358 9 4139 7300
Email: juha.ahola@karprint.fi **Web site:** http://www.rooperinlehti.fi
Freq: Bi-Weekly; **Circ:** 20000 Publisher's Statement
Editor in Chief: Juha Ahola
Profile: Local newspaper distributed in southern part of Helsinki: Punavuori, Eira, Ullanlinna, Kaartinkaupunki, Munkkisaari and Kamppi. Local Translation:Paikallislehti, joka ilmestyy Punavuoressa, Eirassa, Ullanlinnassa, Kaartinkaupungissa, Munkkisaaressa sekä osassa Kamppia.
Language (s): Finnish
COMMUNITY NEWSPAPER

Ruokolahtelainen 222286
Owner: Ruokolahden Seudun Kustannus Oy
Editorial: Toritie 6, Ruokolahti 56100
Tel: 358 5 26 61 39
Email: toimitus@ruokolahtelainen.com **Web site:** http://www.ruokolahtelainen.com
Freq: Weekly; **Circ:** 1600 Publisher's Statement
News: Airi Ruokonen
Profile: Newspaper issued in Ruokolahti and Vuoksenniska. Local Translation:Ruokolahdessa ja Vuoksenniskassa ilmestyvä paikallislehti. Their fax number is 358 5-26 61 39, but e-mails are preferred.
Language (s): Finnish
COMMUNITY NEWSPAPER

Ruovesi 222387
Owner: Ruoveden Sanomalehti Oy
Editorial: PL 2/ Honkalantie 2, 2 krs, Ruovesi 34601
Tel: 358 3 47 61 400
Email: toimitus@ruovesi-lehti.fi **Web site:** http://www.ruovesi-lehti.fi
Freq: Weekly; **Circ:** 4422 ABC-Audit Bureau of Circulations
Editor in Chief: Anu Kuivasmäki
Profile: Newspaper issued in Ruovesi. Local Translation:Ruovedellä ilmestyvä paikallislehti.
Language (s): Finnish
Ad Rate: Full Page Colour 1998.00
Currency: Euro
COMMUNITY NEWSPAPER

Saarijärveläinen 222410
Owner: Luoteisen Keski-Suomen Viestintä Ky
Editorial: PL 104, Saarijärvi 43101
Tel: 358 14 42 50 67
Email: toimitus@saarijarvelainen.fi **Web site:** http://www.saarijarvelainen.fi
Freq: Bi-Weekly; **Circ:** 12500 Publisher's Statement
Editor in Chief: Hannu Strengell; **General Editor:** Toimitus
Profile: Newspaper issued in Kivijärvi, Kyyjärvi, Karstula, Kannonkoski, Pylkönmäki, Saarijärvi and Uurainen. Local Translation:Kivijärvellä, Kyyjärvellä, Karstulassa, Kannonkoskella, Pylkönmäellä, Saarijärvellä ja Uuraisissa ilmestyvä paikallislehti.
Language (s): Finnish
COMMUNITY NEWSPAPER

Saariselän Sanomat 342070
Editorial: PL 33, Saariselkä 99831
Tel: 358 400 25 26 52
Email: saariselan.sanomat@saariselka.fi **Web site:** http://www.saariselansanomat.fi
Freq: Quarterly; **Circ:** 17000 Publisher's Statement
General Editor: Toimitus
Profile: Newspaper distributed in Saariselkä mainly during the ski season. Local Translation:Saariselällä lähinnä sesongin aikana ilmestyvä paikallislehti.
Language (s): Finnish
COMMUNITY NEWSPAPER

Salon Seudun Sanomat 157054
Owner: Salon Seudun Sanomat Oy
Editorial: PL 117/ orninkatu 14, Salo 24101
Tel: 358 2 77 021
Email: toimitus@sss.fi **Web site:** http://www.sss.fi
Circ: 21459
Editor in Chief: Ville Pohjonen
Profile: Independent newspaper mainly distributed in the Salo-Somero region. Local Translation:Salon talousalueen ykkölehti, levikkialueeseen kuuluu Salon ja Someron kaupunkien lisäksi 16 kuntaa: Salo, Halikko, Perniö, Pertteli, Somero, Kisko, Kiikala, Kuusjoki, Suomusjärvi, Muurla, Koski TL, Paimio, Särkisalo, Kemiö, Marttila, Sauvo, Dragsfjärd ja Västanfjärd. Alternative Title: Salon Seudun Tv-uutisetAlso producer of regional tv and radio news: SSS-radiouutiset; Salon seudun tv-uutiset.
Language (s): Finnish
Ad Rate: Full Page Colour 4600.00
Currency: Euro
COMMUNITY NEWSPAPER

Salonjokilaakso 225869
Owner: Salonjokilaakson Sanoma Oy
Editorial: PL 9/ Turuntie 15, Salo 24101
Tel: 358 2 72 72 983
Email: toimitus@salonjokilaakso.net **Web site:** http://www.salonjokilaakso.net
Freq: Weekly; **Circ:** 28000 Publisher's Statement
Managing Director: Pekka Mäenpää; **General Editor:** Toimitus
Profile: Newspaper issued in the Salo region. Local Translation:Description: Newspaper issued in the Salo region. Somerolla, Kuusjoella, Halikossa, Salossa, Perttelissä, Muurlassa, Perniössä, Kiskossa, Särkisalossa, Suomusjärvellä ja Kiikalassa ilmestyvä paikallislehti.Number of pages: 12
Language (s): Finnish
Ad Rate: Full Page Colour 2497.00
Currency: Euro
COMMUNITY NEWSPAPER

Sampo-lehti 222411
Owner: Maakunnan Sanomat Oy
Editorial: PL 46/ Kauppakatu 5, Saarijärvi 43101
Tel: 358 14 42 14 60
Email: toimitus@sampolehti.fi **Web site:** http://www.sampolehti.fi
Freq: Weekly; **Circ:** 5930 ABC-Audit Bureau of Circulations
Editor in Chief: Hannu Strengell; **General Editor:** Toimitus
Profile: Newspaper issued in Saarijärvi, Kannonkoski and Pylkönmäki. Local Translation:Description: Newspaper issued in Saarijärvi, Kannonkoski and Pylkönmäki. Saarijärvellä, Kannonkoskella ja Pylkönmäellä ilmestyvä paikallislehti.Number of pages: 20 Start year: 1943
Language (s): Finnish
Ad Rate: Full Page Colour 2153.00
Currency: Euro
COMMUNITY NEWSPAPER

Satakunnan Kansa 157048
Owner: Satakunnan Kirjateollisuus Oy
Editorial: PL 58/ Pohjoisranta 11 E, Pori 28101
Tel: 358 10 665 132
Email: sk.toimitus@satakunnankansa.fi **Web site:** http://www.satakunnankansa.fi
Freq: Daily; **Circ:** 44674
News Manager: Marjatta Honkasalo; **Editor:** Marita Lehtojoki; **Editor:** Harri Pullinen; **Manager:** Virve Viitanen
Profile: Newspaper issued in Satakunta, western Finland, mainly around the city of Pori. Satakuntalainen sanomalehti, lähinnä Porin alueella.Editions: Satakunnan Kansa Kulttuuritoimitus, Satakunnan Kansa Urheilutoimitus
Language (s): Finnish
Ad Rate: Full Page Colour 6500.00
Currency: Euro
COMMUNITY NEWSPAPER

Satakunnan Työ 157049
Owner: Kansan Uutiset Oy
Editorial: PL 41/ Etelapuisto 14, Pori 28101
Tel: 358 2 63 03 200
Email: toimitus@satakunnantyo.fi **Web site:** http://www.satakunnantyo.fi
Circ: 2680
Editor in Chief: Sirpa Koskinen
Profile: Workers and employers newspaper distributed in Pori, Ulvila and Noormarkku of Satakunta. Local Translation:Porissa, Ulvilassa ja Noormarkussa jaettava satakuntalainen työväenlehti ja palkansaajien äänenkannattaja.
Language (s): Finnish
Ad Rate: Full Page Colour 4944.00
Currency: Euro
COMMUNITY NEWSPAPER

Satakunnan Viikko 222250
Owner: Lalli Oy
Editorial: Gallen-Kallelankatu 8, Pori 28100
Tel: 358 2 63 44 500
Email: toimitus@satakunnanviikko.fi **Web site:** http://www.satakunnanviikko.fi
Freq: Weekly; **Circ:** 55000 Publisher's Statement
Editor in Chief/Managing Director: Kim Huovinlahti
Profile: Local newspaper distributed in Pori, Ulvila, Luvia and Noormarkku in western Finland. Publishes newspaper with housing ads every other Friday. Porissa, Ulvilassa, Luvialla ja Noormarkussa jaettava paikallinen kaupunkilehti.No e-mails allowed to toimitus@satakunnanviikko.fi Start year: 1999
Language (s): Finnish
Ad Rate: Full Page Colour 2050.00
Currency: Euro
COMMUNITY NEWSPAPER

Savonmaa 222542
Owner: Savonlinnan Mediat Oy
Editorial: Schaumanintie 24, Savonlinna 57230
Email: toimitus@savonmaa.fi **Web site:** http://www.savonmaa.fi
Freq: Weekly; **Circ:** 21000 Publisher's Statement
Profile: Newspaper distributed in Savonlinna, Kerimäki, Punkaharju, Enonkoski, Rantasalmi and Sulkava. Local Translation:Paikallinen ilmaisjakelu jaetaan Savonlinnassa, Kerimäellä, Punkaharjulla, Enonkoskella, Rantasalmella ja Sulkavassa.
Language (s): Finnish
Ad Rate: Full Page Colour 975.00
Currency: Euro
COMMUNITY NEWSPAPER

Säynätsalon Sanomat 222277
Owner: Monexmedia Oy
Editorial: Kirrintie 11, Palokka 40270
Tel: 358 40 51 39 464
Email: toimitus@saynatsalonsanomat.fi **Web site:** http://www.saynatsalonsanomat.fi
Freq: Weekly; **Circ:** 1100 Publisher's Statement
Editor in Chief: Kari Ruuska
Profile: Newspaper issued in Säynätsalo. Local Translation:Säynätsalossa ilmestyvä paikallislehti. Their e-mail address is toimitus@saynatsalonsanomat.fi, but generally they do not want any outside information
Language (s): Finnish
COMMUNITY NEWSPAPER

Seinäjoen Sanomat 554072
Owner: SLY Kaupunkimedia Oy
Editorial: Kauppakatu 20, 2.krs (Torikeskus), Seinäjoki 60100 **Tel:** 358 20 6100 165
Email: sjk.toimitus@seinajoensanomat.fi **Web site:** http://www.seinajoensanomat.fi
Freq: Weekly; **Circ:** 48500 Publisher's Statement
Profile: Newspaper distributed in Seinäjoki. Local Translation:Seinäjoella jaettava ilmaislehti.
Language (s): Finnish
Ad Rate: Full Page Colour 1935.00
Currency: Euro
COMMUNITY NEWSPAPER

Seinäjokinen 230957
Owner: Seinäjokinen Lehti Oy
Editorial: Koulukatu 54 A, Seinäjoki 60100
Email: seinajokinenlehti@gmail.com **Web site:** http://www.seinajokinen.fi
Freq: Weekly; **Circ:** 24912 Publisher's Statement
Profile: Newspaper distributed in the Seinäjoki region. Local Translation:Seinäjoen ja lähiympäristön puolueeton kaupunkilehti.
Language (s): Finnish
COMMUNITY NEWSPAPER

Seutulainen 909683
Editorial: Seutulainen Oy, Kangasalantie 921, Kangasala 36200 **Tel:** 358 3 364 1362
Email: tapio.metsola@seutulainen.fi **Web site:** http://www.seutulainen.fi
Freq: Monthly; **Circ:** 94000

Managing Director/Advertising Contact: Tapio Metsoila
Profile: Seutulainen on Tampereen-seudun paikallismainoslehti. A community paper focusing on adverts published in Tampere region.
Language (s): Finnish
Ad Rate: Full Page Colour 1785.00
Currency: Euro
COMMUNITY NEWSPAPER

SeutuMajakka 665707
Editorial: Rautatienkatu 5 L1, Oulainen 86300
Tel: 358 440 47 01 25
Email: toimitus@seutumajakka.fi **Web site:** http://www.seutumajakka.fi
Circ: 6700
Editor: Ari Vilminko
Profile: Free local newspaper distributed to households in Oulainen, Merijärvi, Vihanti and Haapavesi.
Language (s): Finnish
COMMUNITY NEWSPAPER

Seutuneloset 222407
Owner: Esan Kaupunkilehdet Oy
Editorial: Hameenkatu 5 A 4, Lahti 15110
Tel: 358 3 88 48 00
Email: toimitus@seutuneloset.fi **Web site:** http://www.seutuneloset.fi
Freq: Weekly; **Circ:** 39370 Publisher's Statement
Editor in Chief: Stiina Ikonen
Profile: Newspaper issued in Pyhäntaka, Ruuhijärvi, Nastola, Nastola kk, Villähde, Uusikylä, Asikkala, Orimattila, Hollola, Kärkölä and Hämeenkoski. Local Translation:Asikkalassa, Orimattilassa, Hollolassa, Kärkölässä, Hämeenkoskella, Pyhäntakaassa, Ruuhijärvellä, Nastolassa, Villähteessä ja Uusikylässä ilmestyvä paikallislehti. Alternative Title: SeutuviikkoPrevious title: Seutuviikko
Language (s): Finnish
COMMUNITY NEWSPAPER

Sieviläinen 222526
Owner: Sievi-Seura r.y.
Editorial: Haikolantie 23, Sievi 85410
Tel: 358 8 480 278
Email: toimitus@sievilainenlehti.fi **Web site:** http://www.sievilainenlehti.fi
Freq: Weekly; **Circ:** 2676 ABC-Audit Bureau of Circulations
News: Inke Saviluoto
Profile: Newspaper issued in Sievi, Nivala, Ylivieska, Kannus, Toholampi and Reisjärvi. Local Translation:Sievissä, Nivalassa, Ylivieskassa, Kannuksessa, Toholammella ja Reisjärvellä ilmestyvä paikallislehti.
Language (s): Finnish
COMMUNITY NEWSPAPER

Siikajokilaakso 222537
Owner: Pohjois-Suomen Paikallisuutiset Oy
Editorial: PL 22/Pekkalantie 3, Ruukki 92401
Tel: 358 8 27 07 400
Email: toimitus@siikkis.fi **Web site:** http://www.siikkis.fi
Freq: 2 Times/Week; **Circ:** 4535 ABC-Audit Bureau of Circulations
Editor in Chief: Pekka Kevājärvi
Profile: Newspaper issued in Siikajoki, Ruukki, Rantsila, Kestilä, Pukkila, Piippola and Pyhäntä. Siikajoella, Ruukissa, Rantsilassa, Kestilässä, Pukkilassa, Piippolassa ja Pyhännässä ilmestyvä paikallislehti.Siikajokilaakson toimitus tuottaa myös Raahessa ilmestyvää kaupunkijulkaisu Raahen Pekkaa. Raahen Pekka ilmestyy kerran kuussa keskiviikkoisin ja se levikki on 10.985 kpl.
Language (s): Finnish
Ad Rate: Full Page Colour 3000.00
Currency: Euro
COMMUNITY NEWSPAPER

Sinun Savo 358588
Editorial: Kauppakatu 20, Varkaus 78200
Tel: 358 17 36 69 304
Email: toimitus@sinunsavo.fi **Web site:** http://www.sinunsavo.fi
Freq: 2 Times/Week; **Circ:** 25000 Publisher's Statement
General Editor: Toimitus
Profile: Newspaper distributed in Varkaus, Kangaslampi, Leppävirta, Sorsakoski, Joroinen, Heinävesi, Pieksänmaa and Pieksämäki. Local Translation:Varkaudella, Kangaslammella, Leppävirrassa, Sorsakoskella, Joroisilla, Heinävedellä, Pieksänmaalla ja Pieksämäessä jaettava sanomalehti.
Language (s): Finnish
COMMUNITY NEWSPAPER

Sipoon Sanomat 222359
Owner: Etelä-Suomen Media Oy
Editorial: PL 11/Iso Kylatie 20, Sipoo 4131
Tel: 358 20 61 00 101
Email: sipoon.sanomat@media.fi **Web site:** http://www.sipoonsanomat.fi
Freq: Weekly; **Circ:** 3301 ABC-Audit Bureau of Circulations
Editor in Chief: Riitta Ketola
Profile: Newspaper issued in Sipoo. Local Translation:Description: Newspaper issued in Sipoo. Sipoossa ilmestyvä sanomalehti.Number of pages: 12 Start year: 1980
Language (s): Finnish
Ad Rate: Full Page Colour 2340.00
Currency: Euro
COMMUNITY NEWSPAPER

Sisä-Savo 222298
Owner: Maakunnan Sanomat Oy
Editorial: PL 14/ Iisvedentie 3, Suonenjoki 77601
Tel: 358 17 28 87 700
Email: uutiset@sisa-savolehti.fi **Web site:** http://www.sisa-savonsanomat.fi
Freq: 2 Times/Week; **Circ:** 7039 ABC-Audit Bureau of Circulations
News: Tarja Lappalainen; **General Editor:** Toimitus
Profile: Newspaper issued in Karttula, Rautalampi, Suonenjoki, Tervo and Vesanto. Local Translation:Description: Newspaper issued in Karttula, Rautalampi, Suonenjoki, Tervo and Vesanto. Karttulassa, Rautalammella, Suonenjoella, Tervossa ja Vesannossa ilmestyvä paikallislehti.Previously known as: Sisä-Savon Sanomat Number of pages: 20Start year: 1965 Previous title: Sisä-Savon Sanomat
Language (s): Finnish
Ad Rate: Full Page Colour 2686.00
Currency: Euro
COMMUNITY NEWSPAPER

Sisä-Suomen Lehti 224353
Owner: Maakunnan Sanomat Oy
Editorial: PL 15/ Kauppakatu 1, Äänekoski 44101
Tel: 358 14 34 89 500
Email: toimitus@sisasuomenlehti.fi **Web site:** http://www.ksml.fi/sisis/
Freq: 2 Times/Week; **Circ:** 7222 ABC-Audit Bureau of Circulations
Profile: Local newspaper issued in Äänekoski, Suolahti, Sumiainen and Konnevesi. Local Translation:Description: Local newspaper issued in Äänekoski, Suolahti, Sumiainen and Konnevesi. Äänekoskella, Suolahdessa, Sumiaisella ja Konnevedellä ilmestyvä paikallislehti.Incorporating: Kanavan Seutu Number of pages: 32Start year: 1960
Language (s): Finnish
Ad Rate: Full Page Colour 2531.00
Currency: Euro
COMMUNITY NEWSPAPER

Soisalon Seutu 222441
Owner: Maakunnan Sanomat Oy
Editorial: PL 32 / Savonkatu 32, Leppävirta 79101
Tel: 358 17 28 87 741
Web site: http://www.soisalonseutu.fi
Freq: 2 Times/Week
Editor in Chief: Eeva-Liisa Pennanen
Profile: Leppävirrassa ja Vehmersalmella ilmestyvä paikallislehti. Local Translation:Description: Leppävirrassa ja Vehmersalmella ilmestyvä paikallislehti. Newspaper issued in Leppävirta and Vehmersalmi.No e-mails allowed to uutiset@soisalonseutu.fi Number of pages: 24Start year: 1962
Language (s): Finnish
COMMUNITY NEWSPAPER

Somero 222373
Owner: Salon Seudun Sanomat Oy
Editorial: PL 11/Kiiruuntie 1, Somero 31401
Tel: 358 2 58 88 561
Email: toimitus@somerolehti.fi **Web site:** http://www.somerolehti.fi
Freq: 2 Times/Week; **Circ:** 5333 ABC-Audit Bureau of Circulations
Editor in Chief: Sari Merilä
Profile: Newspaper issued in Ypäjä, Tammela, Nummi-Pusula, Kiikala, Kuusjoki and Koski Tl. Local Translation: Description: Newspaper issued in Ypäjä, Tammela, Nummi-Pusula, Kiikala, Kuusjoki and Koski Tl. Ypäjällä, Tammelassa, Nummi-Pusulassa, Kiikalassa, Kuusjoella ja Koskessa ilmestyvä paikallislehti. Number of pages: 16 Start year: 1924
Language (s): Finnish
Ad Rate: Full Page Colour 2497.00
Currency: Euro
COMMUNITY NEWSPAPER

Sompio 222290
Owner: Fourpress Oy
Editorial: PL 69/ Jaamerentie 4 A, Sodankylä 99601
Tel: 358 10 66 64 140
Email: toimitus@sompio.fi **Web site:** http://www.sompio.fi
Freq: 2 Times/Week; **Circ:** 3482 ABC-Audit Bureau of Circulations
Profile: Newspaper issued in Sodankylä. Local Translation:Sodankylän alueella ilmestyvä paikallislehti.
Language (s): Finnish
COMMUNITY NEWSPAPER

Sotkamo-Lehti 222538
Owner: Suomen Paikallissanomat Oy
Editorial: Akkoniementie 4, Sotkamo 88600
Tel: 358 50 314 5004
Email: toimitus.sotkamolehti@slpmedia.fi **Web site:** http://www.kainuunsanomat.fi/sotkamo-lehti/
Freq: 2 Times/Week; **Circ:** 4639 ABC-Audit Bureau of Circulations
Profile: Local newspaper issued in Sotkamo. Local Translation: Description: Local newspaper issued in Sotkamo. Sotkamossa ilmestyvä paikallislehti. Number of pages: 16 Start year: 1962
Language (s): Finnish
Ad Rate: Full Page Colour 1100.00
Currency: Euro
COMMUNITY NEWSPAPER

Sulkava-lehti 222456
Owner: Sulkavan Kotiseutulehti Oy
Editorial: Uitonrinne 18, Sulkava 58700
Tel: 358 15 47 15 44
Email: sulkava.lehti@co.inet.fi
Freq: Weekly; **Circ:** 2678 ABC-Audit Bureau of Circulations
Editor in Chief: Kalle Keränen; **General Editor:** Toimitus
Profile: Newspaper issued in Sulkava. Local Translation:Sulkavalla ilmestyvä paikallislehti.
Language (s): Finnish
Ad Rate: Full Page Colour 1850.00
Currency: Euro
COMMUNITY NEWSPAPER

Suomenselän Sanomat 222388
Owner: Suomenselän Sanomat Oy
Editorial: PL 11/ Virtaintie 40, Virrat 34801
Tel: 358 3 47 55 320
Email: toimitus@sss.inet.fi **Web site:** http://www.suomenselansanomat.net
Freq: Weekly; **Circ:** 5200 Publisher's Statement
News: Riikka Alalantela
Profile: Newspaper issued in Virrat, Ähtäri, Alavus, Töysä, Soini, Lehtimäki, Ruovesi and Kuru. Local Translation:Virroilla, Ähtärissä, Alavudella, Töysässä, Soinissa, Lehtimäellä, Ruovedellä ja Kurussa ilmestyvä paikallislehti.
Language (s): Finnish
Ad Rate: Full Page Colour 2686.00
Currency: Euro
COMMUNITY NEWSPAPER

Suupohjan Sanomat 222527
Owner: Pohjanmaan Lähisanomat Oy
Editorial: PL 4/Lantinen Pitkakatu 15, Kristiinankaupunki 64101 **Tel:** 358 6 24 77 880
Email: toimitus@suupohjansanomat.fi **Web site:** http://www.suupohjansanomat.fi
Freq: 2 Times/Week; **Circ:** 4092 ABC-Audit Bureau of Circulations
Editor: Tauno Riihiluoma
Profile: Newspaper distributed in Kristiinankaupunki, Isojoki, Karijoki, Kaskinen, Närpiö and Teuva. Local Translation:Kristiinankaupungilla, Isojoella, Karijoella, Kaskisilla, Närpiössä ja Teuvassa ilmestyvä paikallislehti.
Language (s): Finnish
Ad Rate: Full Page Colour 3197.00
Currency: Euro
COMMUNITY NEWSPAPER

Suur-Jyväskylän Lehti 222548
Owner: Keskisuomalainen Oyj
Editorial: PL 115/ Kauppakatu 41 A, Jyväskylä 40101
Tel: 358 44 406 2337
Email: toimitus@sjl.fi **Web site:** http://www.sjl.fi/web/index.php
Freq: 2 Times/Week; **Circ:** 82000 Publisher's Statement
Editor in Chief: Tapani Markkanen
Profile: Newspaper issued in the Jyväskylä, Muurame, Säynätsalo and Laukaan Tiituspohja area. Jyväskylän, Muuramen, Säynätsalon ja Laukaan Tiituspohjan alueella ilmestyvä ilmainen paikallislehti.Start year: 1959
Language (s): Finnish
Ad Rate: Full Page Colour 4884.00
Currency: Euro
COMMUNITY NEWSPAPER

Suur-Keuruu 224357
Owner: Alma Aluemedia
Editorial: Niilontie 1, Keuruu 42701
Tel: 358 10 66 55 186
Email: toimitus.suurkeuruu@almamedia.fi **Web site:** http://www.suurkeuruu.fi
Freq: 2 Times/Week
Editor in Chief: Eija Ruoho
Profile: Newspaper issued in Keuruu, Multia, Mänttä, Vilppula and Petäjävesi. Keuruulla, Multialla, Mäntässä, Vilppulassa ja Petäjävedellä ilmestyvä paikallislehti.Supplement: Keupa-lehti Number of pages: 16Start year: 1922
Language (s): Finnish
Ad Rate: Full Page Colour 1650.00
Currency: Euro
COMMUNITY NEWSPAPER

Suur-Tampere 225909
Owner: Pirkanmaan Sanomat Oy
Editorial: Hameenkatu 27 B 4 krs, Tampere 33200
Tel: 358 10 58 44 222
Email: salli@suurtampere.fi **Web site:** http://suurtampere.fi
Freq: Weekly; **Circ:** 139000 Publisher's Statement
Editor in Chief: Salli Saastamoinen
Profile: Local newspaper issued in Tampere, Ylöjärvi, Hämeenkyrö, Nokia, Pirkkala, Lempäälä, Vesilahti, Viiala, Toijala, Kylmäkoski, Urjala, Valkeakoski, Pälkäne, Kangasala, Sahalahti, Orivesi and Kyröskoski. Tampereella, Ylöjärvellä, Hämeenkyrössä, Nokiassa, Pirkkalassa, Vesilahdessa, Viialassa, Toijalassa, Kylmäkoskella, Urjalassa, Valkeakoskella, Pälkäneellä, Kangasalassa, Sahalahdella, Orivedellä ja Kyröskoskella ilmestyvä paikallislehti.Previously listed as: Pirkanmaan Sanomat Number of pages: 20Start year: 1978 Previous title: PS Viikkolehti
Language (s): Finnish
Ad Rate: Full Page Colour 1990.00
Currency: Euro
COMMUNITY NEWSPAPER

Sydän-Hämeen Lehti 222378
Owner: Sydän-Hämeen Kustannus Oy
Editorial: PL 16 / Onkkaalantie 58, Pälkäne 36601
Tel: 358 3 53 99 800
Email: toimitus@shl.fi **Web site:** http://www.shl.fi
Freq: 2 Times/Week; **Circ:** 5449 ABC-Audit Bureau of Circulations
Editor in Chief: Tommi Liljedahl
Profile: Newspaper issued in Kuhmolahti, Luopioinen, Pälkänen and Sahalahti. Local Translation:Description: Newspaper issued in Kuhmolahti, Luopioinen, Pälkänen and Sahalahti. Kuhmolahdella, Luopioisilla, Pälkäneellä ja Sahalahdessa ilmestyvä paikallislehti.Number of pages: 12 Start year: 1929
Language (s): Finnish
Ad Rate: Full Page Colour 2696.00
Currency: Euro
COMMUNITY NEWSPAPER

Sydän-Satakunta 222321
Owner: Alma Media
Editorial: Kilkunkatu 12, Kokemäki 32800
Email: toimitus.sydansatakunta@almamedia.fi **Web site:** http://www.sydansatakunta.fi
Freq: 2 Times/Week
Editor in Chief: Timo Simula
Profile: Newspaper issued in Harjavalta, Kokemäki, Kiukainen and Nakkila. Local Translation:Description: Newspaper issued in Harjavalta, Kokemäki, Kiukainen and Nakkila. Harjavallassa, Kokemäellä, Kiukaisissa ja Nakkilassa ilmestyvä paikallislehti.Number of pages: 16 Start year: 1999
Language (s): Finnish
Ad Rate: Full Page Colour 1500.00
Currency: Euro
COMMUNITY NEWSPAPER

Syd-Österbotten 159018
Owner: Syd-Österbottens Tidnings Ab
Editorial: PB 6/ Narpesvagen 4, Närpes 64201
Tel: 358 6 78 48 700
Email: redaktion@sydin.fi **Web site:** http://online.sydin.fi/
Circ: 7149
News: Mats Ekman; **News:** Benita Kummel-Erikson; **News:** Lotta Sjöblad
Profile: Regional newspaper distributed in Korsnäs, Närpiö, Kaskinen and Kristiinankaupunki. Local Translation:I Korsnäs, Närpes, Kaskö och Kristinestad utkommande dagstidning.
Language (s): Swedish
Ad Rate: Full Page Colour 3816.00
Currency: Euro
COMMUNITY NEWSPAPER

Tammerfors Aktuellt 230966
Owner: Svenska Sällskapsklubben i Tammerfors rf
Editorial: Satamakatu 19, Tammerfors 33200
Tel: 358 3 22 31 373
Email: tammerfors.aktuellt@elisanet.fi **Web site:** http://www.tammerforsaktuellt.fi
Freq: Bi-Weekly; **Circ:** 600 Publisher's Statement
General Editor: Redaktionen
Profile: Newspaper for the Swedish-speakers in the Tampere region. Local Translation:De svensktalande Tammerfors-bornas egen tidning.
Language (s): Swedish
COMMUNITY NEWSPAPER

Tammerkoski 222319
Owner: Tampere-Seura
Editorial: Kauppakatu 1, Tampere 33200
Tel: 358 3 31 24 14 00
Email: tammerkoski-lehti@tampere-seura.fi **Web site:** http://www.tampere-seura.fi
Freq: Bi-Monthly; **Circ:** 4000 Publisher's Statement
News: Katriina Avonius; **General Editor:** Toimitus
Profile: Magazine about current affairs and the history of Tampere. Local Translation:Tampereen historiasta ja nykypäivästä kertova lehti.
Language (s): Finnish
Ad Rate: Full Page Mono 340.00
Currency: Euro
COMMUNITY NEWSPAPER

Tamperelainen 222507
Owner: Kaupunkilehti Tamperelainen Oy
Editorial: Satakunnankatu 13 B, (2. krs.), Tampere 33100 **Tel:** 358 20 61 00 170
Email: tre.toimitus@lehtiyhtyma.fi **Web site:** http://www.tamperelainen.fi
Freq: 2 Times/Week; **Circ:** 132000 Publisher's Statement
News Manager: Petteri Mäkinen
Profile: Newspaper issued in Tampere, Nokia, Ylöjärvi, Pirkkala, Kangasala and Lempäälä. Tampereella, Nokialla, Ylöjärvellä, Pirkkalassa, Kangasalassa ja Lempäälässä ilmestyvä paikallislehti.Start year: 1957
Language (s): Finnish
Ad Rate: Full Page Colour 4351.00
Currency: Euro
COMMUNITY NEWSPAPER

Tanotorvi 222305
Owner: Kaarela-Seura ry
Editorial: Klaneettitie 11, Helsinki 420
Tel: 358 9 5308 1990
Email: tanotorvi@eepinen.fi **Web site:** http://www.kaarela-seura.com/14
Freq: Monthly; **Circ:** 32000 Publisher's Statement
Profile: Newspaper distributed in Kannelmäki and the northern parts of Helsinki. Lehti, joka jaetaan talouksiin alueella Kannelmäki, Hakuninmaa, Maununeva, Malminkartano, Konala, Reimarla-Marttila, Pitäjänmäki, Pajamäki, Etelä-Haaga, Pohjois-Haaga, Lassila, Kaivoksela, Louhela, Myyrmäki.Start year: 1964
Language (s): Finnish
Ad Rate: Full Page Colour 2300.00
Currency: Euro
COMMUNITY NEWSPAPER

Finland

Tapiolan lähiseudun asiakaslehti 225136
Owner: Oy Quality International QI LtdAb
Editorial: Tapiontori 1, 8. krs, Espoo 2100
Tel: 358 9 46 41 18
Email: tapiolan-lehti@tapiolan.com **Web site:** http://www.tapiolan.com
Freq: Monthly; **Circ:** 50000 Publisher's Statement
Editor in Chief: Eva Kivilaakso-Wellmann
Profile: Advertorial newspaper about company news in the Tapiola suburb of Espoo and Kauniainen. Local Translation:Espoon Tapiolan sekä Kauniaisten, Ruoholahden ja Lauttasaaren paikallisten yritysten tiedotuskanava yksityisille.
Language (s): Finnish
Ad Rate: Full Page Colour 2766.00
Currency: Euro
COMMUNITY NEWSPAPER

Teisko-Aitolahti 222389
Owner: Ruoveden Sanomalehti Oy
Editorial: PL 2/ Runoilijankulma, Honkalantie 2, 2 krs, Ruovesi 34601 **Tel:** 358 3 47 61 400
Email: teisko.aitolahti@ruovesi-lehti.fi **Web site:** http://www.ruovesi-lehti.fi
Freq: Weekly; **Circ:** 1827 ABC-Audit Bureau of Circulations
Editor in Chief: Anu Kuivasmäki
Profile: Newspaper issued in Teisko and Aitolahti. Local Translation:Description: Newspaper issued in Teisko and Aitolahti. Teiskossa ja Aitolahdessa ilmestyvä paikallislehti.Number of pages: 8 Start year: 1926
Language (s): Finnish
Ad Rate: Full Page Colour 1776.00
Currency: Euro
COMMUNITY NEWSPAPER

Tejuka 222528
Owner: Paikallislehti Tejuka Oy
Editorial: PL 16 / Tiilitie 2, Teuva 64701
Tel: 358 6 24 74 300
Email: toimitus@tejuka-lehti.fi **Web site:** http://www.tejuka-lehti.fi
Freq: Weekly; **Circ:** 3988 ABC-Audit Bureau of Circulations
Editor in Chief: Jaakko Ujainen
Profile: Local newspaper in Teuva and Jurva. Local Translation:Jurvalla ja Teuvalla ilmestyvä paikallislehti.
Language (s): Finnish
COMMUNITY NEWSPAPER

Tervareitti 222539
Owner: Tervareitti Oy
Editorial: PL 63/ Aaronkuja 5, Muhos 91501
Tel: 358 8 53 13 700
Email: toimitus@tervareitti.fi **Web site:** http://www.tervareitti.fi
Freq: 2 Times/Week; **Circ:** 5763 ABC-Audit Bureau of Circulations
Editor in Chief: Marianne Ollikainen
Profile: Tervareitti is a local newspaper issued in Muhos, Utajärvi and Vaala. Local Translation:Tervareitti on Muhoksen, Utajärven ja Vaalan paikallinen sanomalehti.
Language (s): Finnish
COMMUNITY NEWSPAPER

Töllötin 230163
Owner: Keskisuomalainen Oyj
Editorial: Riistakatu 5, Iisalmi 74100
Tel: 358 17 81 77 00
Email: ilmoitukset@tollotin.fi **Web site:** http://www.tollotin.fi
Freq: Weekly; **Circ:** 32000 Publisher's Statement
Managing Director: Toni Hujanen
Profile: Newspaper issued in Iisalmi. Containing mainly advertising. Local Translation:Iisalmessa, Vieremällä, Sonkajärvellä, Lapinlahdella, Kiuruvedellä ja Pyhäjärvellä ilmestyvä mainoslehti.
Language (s): Finnish
Ad Rate: Full Page Colour 1350.00
Currency: Euro
COMMUNITY NEWSPAPER

Töölöläinen 222486
Owner: Töölöläinen Oy
Editorial: Temppelikatu 8, Helsinki 100
Tel: 358 9 44 10 51
Email: toimitus@paikallislehdet.com
Freq: Bi-Weekly; **Circ:** 25500 Publisher's Statement
News: Mikko Keski-Vähälä
Profile: Suburban newspaper issued in Töölö and Meilahti in Helsinki. Local Translation:Description: Suburban newspaper issued in Töölö and Meilahti in Helsinki. Töölössä ja Meilahdessa ilmestyvä kaupunkilehti.Incorporating: PASILAlainen; Meri-Helsinki; Siltasaari Number of pages: 20Start year: 1978
Language (s): Finnish
COMMUNITY NEWSPAPER

Torstai -lehti 222326
Owner: Järvi-Pohjanmaan Viestintä Oy
Editorial: PL 85/ Kauppakatu 18, Alajärvi 62901
Tel: 358 6 55 75 900
Email: toimitus@torstai-lehti.fi **Web site:** http://www.torstai-lehti.fi
Freq: Weekly; **Circ:** 14000 Publisher's Statement
Editor in Chief: Tuula Jokiaho
Profile: Newspaper issued in Evijärvi, Lappajärvi, Vimpeli, Perho, Kivijärvi, Kyyjärvi, Alajärvi, Lehtimäki, Soini, Karstula, Lapua and Veteli. Ilmaisjakelulehti Evijärven, Lappajärven, Vimpelin, Perhon, Kivijärven, Kyyjärven, Alajärven, Lehtimäen, Soinin, Karstulan, Lapuan ja Vetelin alueella.Number of pages: 12 Start year: 1998
Language (s): Finnish
COMMUNITY NEWSPAPER

Turkulainen 222512
Owner: Kaupunkilehti Turkulainen Oy
Editorial: PL 396/ Lantinen Pitkakatu 34, 4.krs, Turku 20101 **Tel:** 358 20 6 100 160
Email: tku.toimitus@media.fi **Web site:** http://www.turkulainen.fi
Freq: 2 Times/Week; **Circ:** 118100 Publisher's Statement
News Manager: Teija Uitto
Profile: Newspaper issued in the Turku region. Paikallislehti, jonka vaikutusalueet ovat Nousiainen, Vahto, Masku, Rusko, Lieto, Merimasku, Raisio, Piikkiö, Naantali, Turku, Kaarina, Rymättylä, Parainen.Start year: 1958
Language (s): Finnish
Ad Rate: Full Page Colour 4351.00
Currency: Euro
COMMUNITY NEWSPAPER

Turkuposti 241907
Owner: Turun kaupunki
Editorial: PL 355, Turku 20101 **Tel:** 358 2 33 00 00
Email: turkuposti@turku.fi **Web site:** http://www.turku.fi/turkuposti
Freq: Bi-Monthly; **Circ:** 116000 Publisher's Statement
Editor in Chief: Hannu Waher
Profile: Turku city newspaper distributed to households. Local Translation:Turun kaupungin tiedotuslehti.
Language (s): Finnish
COMMUNITY NEWSPAPER

Turun Tienoo 222374
Owner: Turun Seutu Oy
Editorial: Elotie 26, Lieto As. 21360
Tel: 358 2 48 92 00
Email: toimitus@turuntienoo.fi **Web site:** http://www.turuntienoo.fi
Freq: 2 Times/Week; **Circ:** 5732 ABC-Audit Bureau of Circulations
Editor in Chief: Rauli Ala-Karvia
Profile: Newspaper distributed in Lieto, Maaria, Paattinen, Rusko and Vahto. Local Translation:Description: Newspaper distributed in Lieto, Maaria, Paattinen, Rusko and Vahto. Lieto, Maaria, Paattinen, Rusko ja Vahto ovat lehden ilmestymisalueita.Number of pages: 12 Start year: 1954
Language (s): Finnish
Ad Rate: Full Page Colour 2878.00
Currency: Euro
COMMUNITY NEWSPAPER

Tyrvään Sanomat 222390
Owner: Alma Media
Editorial: Marttilankatu 2, Sastamala 38200
Tel: 358 10 66 55 781
Email: toimitus.tyrvaansanomat@almamedia.fi **Web site:** http://www.tyrvaansanomat.fi
Freq: 2 Times/Week
Profile: Newspaper issued in Vammala, Kiikoinen and Äetsä. Publishes separate pages for news of the areas covered by Paikallissanomat (Lavia, Mouhijärvi ja Suodenniemi) that merged with Tyrvään Sanomat. Vammalan, Äetsän ja Kiikoisten paikallislehti. Tyrvää Sanomiin yhditetyn Paikallissanomien alueen (Lavian, Mouhijärven ja Suodenniemen) uutiset erillisivuina.Number of pages: 12 Start year: 1894
Language (s): Finnish
Ad Rate: Full Page Colour 1600.00
Currency: Euro
COMMUNITY NEWSPAPER

Ulvilan Seutu 222419
Owner: Ulvilan Seutu Oy
Editorial: PL 11/ Friitalantie 13, Ulvila 28401
Tel: 358 2 53 11 721
Email: toimitus@ulvilanseutu.fi **Web site:** http://www.ulvilanseutu.fi
Freq: Weekly; **Circ:** 3072 ABC-Audit Bureau of Circulations
Editor in Chief: Sini Ovaskainen
Profile: Newspaper issued in Ulvila and Kullaa. Local Translation:Ulvilassa ja Kullaassa ilmestyvä paikallislehti.
Language (s): Finnish
COMMUNITY NEWSPAPER

Urjalan Sanomat 222391
Owner: Urjalan Sanomat Oy
Editorial: PL 61/ Urjalantie 26, Urjala 31761
Tel: 358 40 18 13 020
Email: toimitus@urjalansanomat.fi **Web site:** http://www.urjalansanomat.fi
Freq: Weekly; **Circ:** 5192 ABC-Audit Bureau of Circulations
Editor in Chief: Minna Mäkelä; **Editor in Chief:** Olli Ristimäki
Profile: Newspaper issued in Urjala and Kylmäkoski. Local Translation:Urjalan Sanomat on Urjalan ja Kylmäkosken paikallislehti.
Language (s): Finnish
Ad Rate: Full Page Colour 1634.00
Currency: Euro
COMMUNITY NEWSPAPER

Uudenkaupungin Sanomat 159016
Owner: Uudenkaupungin Sanomat Oy
Editorial: PL 68/ Alinenkatu 29, Uusikaupunki 23501
Tel: 358 2 58 88 302
Email: toimitus@uudenkaupunginsanomat.fi **Web site:** http://www.uudenkaupunginsanomat.fi
Circ: 7462
Profile: Newspaper in western Finland issued in Uusikaupunki, Laitila, Vehmaa, Taivalsalo, Pyhätanta and Kustavi. Local Translation:Description: Newspaper in western Finland issued in Uusikaupunki, Laitila, Vehmaa, Taivalsalo, Pyhätanta and Kustavi. Länsisuomalainen sanomalehti, jonka levikkialue on Uusikaupunki, Laitila, Vehmaa, Taivalsalo, Pyhäranta ja Kustavi.Incorporating: Plari 8/year Number of pages: 12Start year: 1890
Language (s): Finnish
COMMUNITY NEWSPAPER

Uusi Aika 159012
Owner: Ajan Sana Oy
Editorial: Itsenaisyydenkatu 39 B, Pori 28100
Tel: 358 44 7300 243
Email: ua.toimitus@uusiaika-lehti.fi **Web site:** http://www.uusiaika-lehti.fi
Circ: 7121
Editor in Chief: Jukka Vilponiemi
Profile: Regional newspaper distributed in the Satakunta region. Local Translation:Satakunnassa ilmestyvä aluelehti.
Language (s): Finnish
COMMUNITY NEWSPAPER

Uusi Lahti 222503
Owner: Esan Paikallislehdet Oy
Editorial: Hameenkatu 5 A 4, 2 krs., Lahti 15110
Tel: 358 3 87 68 76
Email: toimitus@uusilahti.fi **Web site:** http://www.uusilahti.fi
Freq: 2 Times/Week; **Circ:** 54700 Publisher's Statement
Editor in Chief: Tommi Berg
Profile: Newspaper issued in Lahti and Hollola. Uusi Lahti on puolueeton, riippumaton kaupunkilehti Lahdessa ja Hollolassa.Start year: 1982
Language (s): Finnish
COMMUNITY NEWSPAPER

Uusi Pori 222267
Owner: Kustannusosakeyhtiö Uusi-Tuuli
Editorial: Isolinnankatu 28, Pori 28100
Tel: 358 400 788 620
Email: toimitus@uusipori.fi **Web site:** http://www.uusipori.fi
Freq: Weekly; **Circ:** 60000 Publisher's Statement
Profile: Newspaper distributed in Pori, Luvia, Ulvila, Harjavalta, Noormarkku, Merikarvia, Ahlanen, Siikainen and Poomarkku. Porissa, Luvialla, Ulvilassa, Harjavallassa, Noormarkussa, Merikarviassa, Ahlasessa, Siikaisissa ja Poomarkussa ilmestyvä paikallislehti.
Language (s): Finnish
COMMUNITY NEWSPAPER

Uusi Rovaniemi 222560
Owner: Pohjois-Suomen Media Oy
Editorial: Veitikantie 2-8 A, Rovaniemi 96100
Tel: 358 10 66 57 806
Email: ur.toimitus@uusirovaniemi.fi **Web site:** http://www.uusirovaniemi.fi
Freq: 2 Times/Week; **Circ:** 31800 Publisher's Statement
Editor in Chief: Leena Talvensaari
Profile: Newspaper distributed in Rovaniemi. Local Translation:Rovaniemellä ilmestyvä paikallislehti.
Language (s): Finnish
Ad Rate: Full Page Colour 955.28
Currency: Euro
COMMUNITY NEWSPAPER

Uusi Vantaa 222497
Owner: Kokoomuksen Vantaan Kunnallisjärjestö ry
Editorial: Pakkalankuja 5, Vantaa 1510
Tel: 358 20 74 88 523
Email: kim.zilliacus@kokoomus.fi **Web site:** http://www.vantaankokoomus.fi
Freq: Semi-Annual; **Circ:** 85500 Publisher's Statement
Editor in Chief: Kim Zilliacus
Profile: Newspaper distributed by the Coalition Party in Vantaa. Local Translation:Vantaan Kokoomuksen paikallislehti.
Language (s): Finnish
COMMUNITY NEWSPAPER

Uusimaa 157050
Owner: Etelä-Suomen Media Oy
Editorial: PL 15/ Lundinkatu 8, Porvoo 6151
Tel: 358 20 770 3650
Email: toimitus.uusimaa@media.fi **Web site:** http://www.uusimaa.fi
Circ: 10178
News Manager: Veikko Vaniala
Profile: Regional newspaper influencing Porvoo, Askola, Pornainen, Pukkila, Myrskylä, Pernaja, Sipoo, Mäntsälä, Porvoon mlk, Loviisa and Liljendal. Local Translation:Uusimaa on Itä-Uudenmaan sitoutumaton valtalehti, jonka vaikutusalueet ovat Porvoo, Askola, Pornainen, Pukkila, Myrskylä, Pernaja, Sipoo, Mäntsälä, Porvoon mlk, Loviisa ja Liljendal.
Language (s): Finnish
Ad Rate: Full Page Colour 3227.00
Currency: Euro
COMMUNITY NEWSPAPER

Uutis-Jousi 222458
Owner: Maakunnan Sanomat Oy
Editorial: Asematie 2, Siilinjärvi 71800
Tel: 358 17 28 77 800
Email: uutiset@uutis-jousi.fi **Web site:** http://www.uutis-jousi.fi
Freq: 2 Times/Week; **Circ:** 6406 ABC-Audit Bureau of Circulations
Profile: Newspaper issued in Siilinjärvi and Maaninka. Local Translation:Description: Newspaper issued in Siilinjärvi and Maaninka. Siilinjärvellä ja Maaningalla ilmestyvä paikallislehti.Number of pages: 16 Start year: 1967
Language (s): Finnish
Ad Rate: Full Page Colour 3796.00
Currency: Euro
COMMUNITY NEWSPAPER

Uutisvuoksi 222472
Owner: Kaakon Viestintä Oy
Editorial: PL 100/ Esterinkatu 10, Imatra 55101
Tel: 358 5 2100 2600
Email: toimitus@uutisvuoksi.fi **Web site:** http://www.uutisvuoksi.fi
Freq: Daily; **Circ:** 25000 Publisher's Statement
Profile: Newspaper issued in Imatra, Ruokolahti, Rautjärvi, Joutseno, Puumala, Parikkala and Simpele. Imatralla, Ruokolahdella, Rautjärvellä, Joutsenossa, Puumalassa, Parikkalassa ja Simpeléssä ilmestyvä paikallislehti.
Language (s): Finnish
Ad Rate: Full Page Colour 2680.00
Currency: Euro
COMMUNITY NEWSPAPER

Vaarojen Sanomat 222459
Owner: Juuka-seura ry
Editorial: Juuantie 9 A, Juuka 83900
Tel: 358 10 83 54 004
Email: toimitus@vaarojensanomat.fi **Web site:** http://www.vaarojensanomat.fi/etusivu
Freq: 2 Times/Week; **Circ:** 3790 ABC-Audit Bureau of Circulations
Editor in Chief: Pasi Karjalainen
Profile: Newspaper issued in Juuka and Koli. Local Translation:Juukan ja Kolin paikallislehti.
Language (s): Finnish
COMMUNITY NEWSPAPER

Vaasan Ikkuna 222546
Owner: I-Mediat Oy
Editorial: Hietasaarenkatu 19, Vaasa 65100
Tel: 358 6 24 77 966
Email: vaasanikkuna@vaasanikkuna.fi **Web site:** http://www.vaasanikkuna.fi
Freq: Weekly; **Circ:** 52388 Publisher's Statement
Editor in Chief: Vesa Koivumäki
Profile: Newspaper distributed in the Vaasa region. Vaasan alueella jaettava ilmaisjakelulehti.
Language (s): Finnish
Ad Rate: Full Page Colour 3614.00
Currency: Euro
COMMUNITY NEWSPAPER

Vakka-Suomen Sanomat 222502
Owner: Vakka-Suomen Sanomain Kuntayhtymä
Editorial: PL 84/ Rauhankatu 8 A, Uusikaupunki 23501 **Tel:** 358 2 84 26 300
Email: toimitus@vakka.fi **Web site:** http://vakka.fi
Freq: 2 Times/Week; **Circ:** 8380 ABC-Audit Bureau of Circulations
Profile: Newspaper issued in the Uusikaupunki region in southwestern Finland. Local Translation:Vakka-Suomen alueella ilmestyvä paikallislehti.
Language (s): Finnish
Ad Rate: Full Page Colour 4050.00
Currency: Euro
COMMUNITY NEWSPAPER

Valkeakosken Sanomat 224358
Owner: Alma Media
Editorial: Valtakatu 9-11, 4 krs, Valkeakoski 37600
Tel: 358 10 66 55 730
Email: toimitus.valkeakoskensanomat@almamedia.fi **Web site:** http://www.valkeakoskensanomat.fi
Freq: Daily
Editor in Chief: Simo Husso
Profile: Newspaper issued in Valkeakoski. Valkeakoskella ilmestyvä paikallislehti.Number of pages: 12 Start year: 1921
Language (s): Finnish
Ad Rate: Full Page Colour 1700.00
Currency: Euro
COMMUNITY NEWSPAPER

Valkealan Sanomat 222429
Owner: Valkealan Sanomat Oy
Editorial: PL 31 / Vanhatie 3, Valkeala 45371
Tel: 358 10 66 65 466
Email: toimitus@valkealansanomat.fi **Web site:** http://www.valkealansanomat.fi
Freq: Weekly; **Circ:** 4720 Publisher's Statement
Editor in Chief: Auli Kousa
Profile: Local newspaper issued in Valkeala. Local Translation:Description: Local newspaper issued in Valkeala. Valkealassa ilmestyvä paikallislehti.Number of pages: 12 Start year: 1985
Language (s): Finnish
Ad Rate: Full Page Colour 1825.00
Currency: Euro
COMMUNITY NEWSPAPER

Vantaan Sanomat 222354
Owner: SLY-Kaupunkilehdet Oy
Editorial: PL 350/ Ralssitie 7 A, Vantaa 1511
Tel: 358 20 61 00 110
Email: vantaan.sanomat@media.fi **Web site:** http://www.vantaansanomat.fi
Freq: 2 Times/Week; **Circ:** 89600 Publisher's Statement
Editor in Chief: Risto Hietanen
Profile: Newspaper issued in Vantaa. Vantaan Sanomat on Vantaalla ilmestyvä paikallislehti.Regular features: Uusi koti (asunnon välitys ja pankit)/ Home

purchase 12/year; Autoilu/ Cars 12/year Number of pages: 14 Start year: 1967
Language (s): Finnish
Ad Rate: Full Page Colour 3535.00
Currency: Euro
COMMUNITY NEWSPAPER

Vartti Etelä-Karjala 222471
Owner: Sanoma News Oy
Editorial: Lauritsalantie 1, Lappeenranta 53500
Tel: 358 5 53 88 19
Email: toimitus.vartti.ek@sanoma.fi **Web site:** http://www.vartti.fi
Freq: 2 Times/Week; **Circ:** 65000 Publisher's Statement
Editor in Chief: Ari Toivonen
Profile: Local newspaper issued in Lappeenranta, Lemi and Taipalsaari. Local Translation:Description: Local newspaper issued in Lappeenranta, Imatra, Joutseno, Lemi, Ruokolahti and Taipalsaari. Lappeenrannassa, Imatrallla, Joutsenossa, Lemissä, Taipalsaarella ja Ruokolahdella ilmestyvä paikallislehti.Previously listed as: Lappeenrantalainen Also known as: Vartti Lappeenranta
Language (s): Finnish
Ad Rate: Full Page Colour 1950.00
Currency: Euro
COMMUNITY NEWSPAPER

Vartti Kymenlaakso 222280
Owner: Kaakon Viestintä Oy
Editorial: Lehtikaari 1, Kouvola 45130
Email: toimitus.kymenlaakso@vartti.fi **Web site:** http://www.varttikymenlaakso.fi
Freq: Weekly; **Circ:** 48000 Publisher's Statement
Editor in Chief: Hannu Helineva
Profile: Description: Newspaper distributed in Kouvola, Kuusankoski, Anjalankoski, Iitti, Elimäki, Jaala and Valkeala. Kouvolassa, Kuusankoskella, Anjalankoskella, Iittissä, Elimäellä, Jaalassa, Valkealassa ja Jaalassa jaettava kaupunkilehti.Previously known as: Kaupunkilehti Seiska Previous title: Kaupunkilehti Seiska
Language (s): Finnish
Ad Rate: Full Page Colour 1950.00
Currency: Euro
COMMUNITY NEWSPAPER

Vasabladet 157062
Owner: HSS Media Ab
Editorial: PL 52/ Sandogatan 20, Vasa 65101
Tel: 358 6 78 48 200
Email: nyheter@vasabladet.fi **Web site:** http://online.vasabladet.fi/
Freq: Daily; **Circ:** 20696
Editor in Chief: Camilla Berggren; **Editor:** Kaj Enholm; **News Manager:** Björn Nyberg; **Editor:** Lisbeth Rosenback; **News Manager:** Patrik Stenvall
Profile: Regional newspapers for Swedish-speakers mainly in Ostrobotnia on the Finnish western coastline. Local Translation:Regional tidning, som utkommer främst i svenska Österbotten. Publiseras om: magasin som utkommer tillsammans med Vasabladet och Österbottens Tidning sex gångar i året.
Language (s): Swedish
COMMUNITY NEWSPAPER

Västra Nyland 157026
Owner: Ekenäs Tryckeri AB
Editorial: Genvagen 4, Ekenäs 10650
Tel: 358 19 22 28 22
Email: vnred@vastranyland.fi **Web site:** http://www.vastranyland.fi
Freq: Mon thru Fri; **Circ:** 9562
News Manager: Marina Holmberg
Profile: Regional Swedish-language newspaper issued mainly in Western Uusimaa on the south coast of Finland. Local Translation:Description: Regional Swedish-language newspaper issued mainly in Western Uusimaa on the south coast of Finland. Regional dagstidning som utkommer i västra Nyland, främst i Hangö, Ekenäs, Pojo, Karis, Ingå, Lojo, Sjundeå och Kyrkslätt.Number of pages: 16 Start year: 1881
Language (s): Swedish
Ad Rate: Full Page Colour 3946.00
Currency: Euro
COMMUNITY NEWSPAPER

Väylä 222540
Owner: Paltamon Kirjapaino Ky
Editorial: Sairaalatie 8, Paltamo 88300
Tel: 358 8 87 19 99
Email: aineistot@paltamonkirjapaino.fi **Web site:** http://www.paltamonkirjapaino.fi
Freq: Weekly; **Circ:** 1800 Publisher's Statement
General Editor: Toimitus
Profile: Local newspaper issued in Paltamo. Local Translation:Paltamolla ilmestyvä paikallislehti.
Language (s): Finnish
COMMUNITY NEWSPAPER

Vihdin Uutiset 222499
Owner: Etelä-Suomen Media Oy
Editorial: Naaranpajuntie 3, Nummela 3100
Tel: 358 9 273 00 215
Email: viu.toimitus@media.fi **Web site:** http://www.vihdinuutiset.fi
Freq: 2 Times/Week; **Circ:** 16700 Publisher's Statement
Editor in Chief: Vesa Valtonen
Profile: Newspaper distributed in Vihti and Veikkola. Local Translation:Description: Newspaper distributed in Vihti and Veikkola. Vihdissä ja Veikkolassa jaettava paikallislehti.It is distributed 15 times a year to every household in Nummi-Pusula and Karkkila as well and its circulation increases then to 19 250. Number of pages: 12Start year: 1980
Language (s): Finnish
Ad Rate: Full Page Colour 6757.00
Currency: Euro
COMMUNITY NEWSPAPER

Viikko Pohjois-Karjala 222343
Owner: Sanomalehti Uusi Pohjois-Karjala Oy
Editorial: PL 97/ Niskakatu 7, Joensuu 80101
Tel: 358 13 73 75 811
Email: toimitus@viikkopk.fi **Web site:** http://www.viikkopk.fi
Freq: Weekly; **Circ:** 7193 ABC-Audit Bureau of Circulations
General Editor: Toimitus
Profile: Local weekly newspaper issued in Joensuu and its surroundings in northern Carelia. Local Translation:Description: Local weekly newspaper issued in Joensuu and its surroundings in northern Carelia. Pohjois-Karjalassa ilmestyvä paikallislehti.Number of pages: 20 Start year: 1906Alternative Title: Pohjois-Karjala
Language (s): Finnish
Ad Rate: Full Page Colour 5922.00
Currency: Euro
COMMUNITY NEWSPAPER

Viikkosavo 222474
Owner: Viikkosavo Oy
Editorial: PL 8/ Snellmaninkatu 35, Kuopio 70100
Tel: 358 17 288 8300
Email: toimitus.kaupunkilehdet@media.fi **Web site:** http://www.viikkosavo.fi
Freq: Weekly; **Circ:** 62500 Publisher's Statement
Editor in Chief: Aija Pirinen
Profile: Newspaper distributed in Kuopio, Toivola, Vuorela, Riistavesi and Siilinjärvi. Local Translation:Ilmaisjakelulehti Kuopion, Toivolan, Vuorelan, Riistaveden ja Siilinjärven alueella. Start year: 1972
Language (s): Finnish
COMMUNITY NEWSPAPER

Viikkoset 222544
Owner: Kaakon viestintä Oy
Editorial: Teollisuuskatu 2-6, Mikkeli 50130
Tel: 358 440 35 05 22
Email: toimitus.viikkoset@lansi-savo.fi **Web site:** http://www.viikkoset.fi
Freq: Weekly; **Circ:** 26500 Publisher's Statement
General Editor: Toimitus
Profile: Newspaper issued in Mikkeli and Ristiina. Local Translation:Description: Newspaper issued in Mikkeli and Ristiina. Kerran viikossa Mikkelissä ja Ristiinassa ilmestyvä ilmainen lehti.Number of pages: 16 Start year: 1977
Language (s): Finnish
Ad Rate: Full Page Colour 2244.00
Currency: Euro
COMMUNITY NEWSPAPER

Viikkouutiset Keski-Uusimaa 222495
Owner: Suomen Lehtiyhtymä
Editorial: PL 52/Klaavolantie 5, Tuusula 4300
Tel: 358 20 61 00 150
Email: toimitus.keskiuusimaa@media.fi **Web site:** http://www.viikkouutiset.fi
Freq: 2 Times/Week; **Circ:** 50500 Publisher's Statement
Profile: Newspaper issued in Järvenpää and Tuusula. Local Translation:Tuusulassa, Keravalla, Pornaisissa, Pohjois-Sipoossa, Etelä-Mäntsälässä ja Järvenpäässä ilmestyvä paikallislehti. Start year: 1973Previous title: Tuusulanjärven Viikkouutiset
Language (s): Finnish
Ad Rate: Full Page Colour 2507.00
Currency: Euro
COMMUNITY NEWSPAPER

Viiskunta 222529
Owner: Pohjanmaan Lähisanomat Oy
Editorial: PL 11/Kirjapainokuja 2, Alavus 63301
Tel: 358 6 24 77 870
Email: toimitus@viiskunta.fi **Web site:** http://www.viiskunta.fi
Freq: 2 Times/Week; **Circ:** 5987 ABC-Audit Bureau of Circulations
Editor in Chief: Ella Nurmi
Profile: Newspaper issued in Alavus, Kuortane, Lehtimäki, Töysä and Ähtäri. Alavudella, Kuortaneella, Lehtimäellä, Töysässä ja Ähtärissä ilmestyvä paikallislehti.Number of pages: 12 Start year: 1954
Language (s): Finnish
Ad Rate: Full Page Colour 3986.00
Currency: Euro
COMMUNITY NEWSPAPER

Viispiikkinen 222413
Owner: Maakunnan Sanomat Oy
Editorial: PL 41/ Virastotie 3, Karstula 43501
Tel: 358 14 41 77 300
Email: toimitus@viispiikkinen.fi **Web site:** http://www.ksml.fi/viispiikkinen/
Freq: Weekly; **Circ:** 5335 ABC-Audit Bureau of Circulations
Editor in Chief: Ilkka Salonen
Profile: Local newspaper issued in Karstula, Kannonkoski, Kivijärvi, Kyyjärvi and Pylkönmäki. Local Translation:Karstulassa, Kannonkoskella, Kivijärvellä, Kyyjärvellä ja Pylkönmäellä ilmestyvä paikallislehti. Previous title: Viiden Kunnan SanomatFax number is 358 14-41 77 333, but e-mail is preferred.
Language (s): Finnish
COMMUNITY NEWSPAPER

Viitasaaren Seutu 222414
Owner: Maakunnan Sanomat Oy
Editorial: Keskitie 7, Viitasaari 44500
Tel: 358 14 3397 121
Email: seutu.toimitus@keskisuomalainen.fi **Web site:** http://www.ksml.fi/viitasaarenseutu/
Freq: Weekly; **Circ:** 5297 ABC-Audit Bureau of Circulations
Editor in Chief: Esa Kilponen
Profile: Local newspaper issued in the Viitasaari area. Viitasaaren alueella ilmestyvä paikallislehti.Number of pages: 16 Start year: 1934
Language (s): Finnish
COMMUNITY NEWSPAPER

VPL Pyhäjärvi 362899
Editorial: Rautasemantie 375, Lempäälä 37550
Tel: 358 3 37 48 448
Email: marjo.ristila-toikka@kolumbus.fi **Web site:** http://www.vplpyhajarvi.fi
Freq: Monthly; **Circ:** 1900 Publisher's Statement
Editor-in-Chief: Marjo Ristilä-Toikka; **General Editor:** Toimitus
Profile: Newspapers about Russian Carelian town Pyhäjärvi.
Language (s): Finnish
COMMUNITY NEWSPAPER

Vuolijoki -lehti 222248
Owner: Paltamon Kirjapaino Ky
Editorial: Sairaalatie 8, Paltamo 88300
Tel: 358 8 87 19 99
Email: toimisto@paltamonkirjapaino.fi **Web site:** http://www.paltamonkirjapaino.fi/vuolijoki
Freq: Weekly; **Circ:** 1180 ABC-Audit Bureau of Circulations
General Editor: Toimitus
Profile: Local newspaper issued in Vuolijoki. Local Translation:Vuolijoella ilmestyvä paikallislehti.
Language (s): Finnish
COMMUNITY NEWSPAPER

Vuosaari 222500
Owner: Vuopress Ky
Editorial: Merikorttikuja 6 E, Helsinki 960
Tel: 358 9 32 12 556
Web site: http://www.vuosaarilehti.fi
Freq: Weekly; **Circ:** 20000 Publisher's Statement
Editor in Chief: Eero Honkanen
Profile: Newspaper distributed in Vuosaari and Valpakka. Vuosaaressa ja Valpakassa ilmestyvä paikallislehti.They do not want any press releases. Number of pages: 8Start year: 1965
Language (s): Finnish
COMMUNITY NEWSPAPER

Warkauden Lehti 157063
Owner: Warkauden Lehti Oy
Editorial: Pirnankatu 4, Varkaus 78200
Tel: 358 17 778 3635
Email: toimitus@warkaudenlehti.fi **Web site:** http://www.warkaudenlehti.fi
Circ: 10811
Editor in Chief: Sari Ristamäki
Profile: Regional newspaper issued in Joroinen, Kangaslampi, Varkaus, Heinävesi, Jäppilä, Leppävirta and Rantasalmi. Local Translation:Alueellinen sanomalehti, joka ilmestyy Joroisten, Kangaslammen, Varkauden, Heinäveden, Jäppilän, Leppävirran ja Rantasalmen alueella.
Language (s): Finnish
COMMUNITY NEWSPAPER

Wessmanni 222269
Owner: Joutsan Seutu Oy
Editorial: Vision Center, Kirrintie 11, Palokka 40270
Tel: 358 400 757 620
Web site: http://www.wessmanni.fi/
Freq: Bi-Weekly; **Circ:** 8500 Publisher's Statement
Profile: No generic email address to the editorial Newspaper issued in Vaajakoski, Jyskä, Haapaniemi, Kivilampi, Kaunislampi, Nojosniemi, Kanavuori, Oravasaari and Leppälahti.Local Translation: Vaajakoskella, Jyskässä, Haapaniemellä, Kivilammella, Kaunislammella, Nojosniemellä, Kanavuorella, Oravasaaressa ja Leppälahdella ilmestyvä paikallislehti.
Language (s): Finnish
COMMUNITY NEWSPAPER

Wiita-Sanomat 222549
Owner: Maakunnan Sanomat Oy
Editorial: Keskitie 7, Viitasaari 44500
Tel: 358 14 3397 121
Email: seutu.toimitus@keskisuomalainen.fi
Freq: Bi-Weekly; **Circ:** 10450 Publisher's Statement
Editor in Chief: Esa Kilponen
Profile: Local newspaper issued in Viitasaari. Local Translation:Viitasaarella ilmestyvä paikallislehti. Previous title: Viitasaaren Sanomat
Language (s): Finnish
Ad Rate: Full Page Colour 1665.00
Currency: Euro
COMMUNITY NEWSPAPER

Ykköset 230235
Owner: Tuurin Lehti Oy
Editorial: Tuurintie 2, Tuuri 63610
Tel: 358 6 54 27 200
Email: toimitus@ykkoset.fi **Web site:** http://www.ykkoset.fi
Freq: Weekly; **Circ:** 311140 Publisher's Statement
Profile: Newspaper with ads issued in Pohjanmaa. Local Translation:Pohjanmaalla jaettava uutis- ja ilmoituslehti. Start year: 1996
Language (s): Finnish
COMMUNITY NEWSPAPER

Ykkös-Lohja 222287
Owner: JK-Vuokralehdet Oy
Editorial: Vihdinkatu 6, 2. krs., Lohja 8100
Tel: 358 19 37 51 303
Email: toimitus@ykkoslohja.fi **Web site:** http://www.ykkoslohja.fi
Freq: Weekly; **Circ:** 33000 Publisher's Statement
Editor in Chief: Jukka Kuparinen
Profile: Newspaper distributed in Lohja, Karjalohja, Sammatti, Siuntio, Inkoo, Mustio, Vihti and Nummi-Pusula. Local Translation:Ilmaislehti jakelualueena Lohja, Lohjan mlk, Karjalohja, Sammatti, Siuntio, Inkoo, Mustio, Vihti sekä Nummi-Pusula.
Language (s): Finnish
Ad Rate: Full Page Colour 900.00
Currency: Euro
COMMUNITY NEWSPAPER

Ylä-Kainuu 222541
Owner: Suomen Paikallissanomat Oy
Editorial: PL 63 / Kauppakatu 10 A 1, Suomussalmi 89601 **Tel:** 358 8 63 30 00
Email: toimitus.ylakainuu@slpmedia.fi **Web site:** http://www.ylakainuu.fi
Freq: 2 Times/Week; **Circ:** 7746 ABC-Audit Bureau of Circulations
Editor in Chief: Sirkku Rautio
Profile: Newspaper issued in Suomussalmi, Hyrynsalmi and Puolanka. Ylä-Kainuu lehti on Suomussalmen, Hyrynsalmen ja Puolangan alueen paikallislehti.Incorporating monthly Kainuu Plus edition. Number of pages: 16Start year: 1965
Language (s): Finnish
COMMUNITY NEWSPAPER

Ylä-Karjala 222460
Owner: Nurmeksen Kirjapaino Oy
Editorial: PL 5/Pappilansuora 15, Nurmes 75501
Tel: 358 10 23 08 600
Email: toimitus@ylakarjala.fi **Web site:** http://www.ylakarjala.fi
Freq: 3 Times/Week; **Circ:** 5448 ABC-Audit Bureau of Circulations
Profile: Newspaper issued in Nurmes and Valtimo. Nurmeksessa ja Valtimossa ilmestyvä paikallislehti.Number of pages: 6 Start year: 1929
Language (s): Finnish
COMMUNITY NEWSPAPER

Ylä-Satakunta 222393
Owner: Ylä-Satakunnan Sanomalehti Oy
Editorial: Parkanontie 63, Parkano 39700
Tel: 358 3 44 381
Email: toimittajat@ylasatakunta.fi **Web site:** http://www.ylasatakunta.fi
Freq: 2 Times/Week; **Circ:** 6854 ABC-Audit Bureau of Circulations
Editor in Chief/Managing Director: Veli-Matti Heinisuo
Profile: Newspaper issued in Karvia, Parkano and Kihniö. Karvialla, Parkanossa ja Kihniössä ilmestyvä paikallislehti.Number of pages: 16 Start year: 1933
Language (s): Finnish
Ad Rate: Full Page Colour 2141.00
Currency: Euro
COMMUNITY NEWSPAPER

Ylöjärven Uutiset 222394
Owner: Ylöjärven Sanomat Oy
Editorial: PL 26/ Mikkolantie 7, Ylöjärvi 33471
Tel: 358 10 5844570
Web site: http://www.ylojarvenuutiset.fi
Freq: Weekly; **Circ:** 6296 ABC-Audit Bureau of Circulations
Editor in Chief: Matti Pulkkinen
Profile: Newspaper issued in Ylöjärvi. Local Translation:Description: Newspaper issued in Ylöjärvi. Ylöjärvellä ilmestyvä paikallislehti.Number of pages: 24 Start year: 1934
Language (s): Finnish
Ad Rate: Full Page Colour 3828.00
Currency: Euro
COMMUNITY NEWSPAPER

France

Time Difference: GMT +1
National Telephone Code: 33
Continent: Europe
Capital: Paris

Newspapers

Le 1 907699
Owner: Le 1
Editorial: 8 rue Lamennais, Paris 75008
Tel: 33 1 45 61 44 49
Email: redaction@le1hebdo.fr **Web site:** http://le1hebdo.fr
Freq: Weekly; **Circ:** 250000
Editor in Chief: Laurent Greilsamer
Profile: Weekly newspaper covering news and current affairs including politics, economics and society.
Language (s): French
DAILY NEWSPAPER

20 Minutes Bordeaux 306387

Owner: 20 MINUTES FRANCE SAS
Editorial: 22 cours du Chapeau-Rouge, Bordeaux 33000 **Tel:** 33 5 56 56 69 59
Email: bordeaux@20minutes.fr **Web site:** http://www.20minutes.fr
Freq: Daily; **Circ:** 33000 Publisher's Statement
Profile: Daily newspaper of general information on the Bordeaux region. Local Translation:Quotidien d'informations générales de la région de Bordeaux.
Language (s): French
Ad Rate: Full Page Colour 3400.00
Currency: Euro
DAILY NEWSPAPER

20 Minutes Lille 232394

Owner: 20 MINUTES FRANCE SAS
Editorial: 2 rue du Priez, Lille 59800
Tel: 33 3 28 38 16 60
Email: lille@20minutes.fr **Web site:** http://www.20minutes.fr
Freq: Daily; **Circ:** 47800 Publisher's Statement
Profile: Daily newspaper of general information on the Lille region. Local Translation:Quotidien d'informations générales de la région de Lille.
Language (s): French
Ad Rate: Full Page Colour 7850.00
Currency: Euro
DAILY NEWSPAPER

20 Minutes Lyon 232393

Owner: 20 MINUTES FRANCE SAS
Editorial: 32 rue Neuve, Lyon 69002
Tel: 33 4 72 77 01 74
Email: lyon@20minutes.fr **Web site:** http://www.20minutes.fr
Freq: Daily; **Circ:** 52080 Publisher's Statement
Profile: Daily newspaper of general information on the Lyon agglomeration .
Language (s): French
Ad Rate: Full Page Colour 9000.00
Currency: Euro
DAILY NEWSPAPER

20 Minutes Marseille 232395

Owner: 20 MINUTES FRANCE SAS
Editorial: 38 rue Breteuil, Marseille 13006
Tel: 33 4 91 33 59 43
Email: marseille@20minutes.fr **Web site:** http://www.20minutes.fr
Freq: Daily; **Circ:** 39940 Publisher's Statement
Profile: Daily newspaper of general information on the Marseille region. Local Translation:Quotidien d'informations générales de la région de Marseille.
Language (s): French
Ad Rate: Full Page Colour 9000.00
Currency: Euro
DAILY NEWSPAPER

20 Minutes Paris 157265

Owner: 20 Minutes France S.A.S
Editorial: 50-52, Boulevard Haussmann, Paris 75009
Tel: 33 1 53 26 65 65
Email: redaction@20minutes.fr **Web site:** http://www.20minutes.fr
Freq: Daily; **Circ:** 566578 Publisher's Statement
Editor in Chief: Acacio Pereira
Profile: Daily newspaper covering general news and current affairs including society, politics, economics, environment, culture, sports, entertainment, celebrity, sports, technology and multimedia.
Language (s): French
Ad Rate: Full Page Colour 55100.00
Currency: Euro
DAILY NEWSPAPER

20 Minutes Strasbourg 360235

Owner: 20 MINUTES FRANCE SAS
Editorial: 2 rue du Saumon, Strasbourg 67000
Tel: 33 3 88 23 96 36
Email: strasbourg@20minutes.fr **Web site:** http://www.20minutes.fr
Freq: Daily; **Circ:** 27171 Publisher's Statement
Profile: Daily national newspaper of general information including local pages on the Strasbourg region. Local Translation:Quotidien national d'informations générales comportant des pages d'informations locales de la région de Strasbourg.
Language (s): French
Ad Rate: Full Page Colour 3400.00
Currency: Euro
DAILY NEWSPAPER

24 Ore 692519

Editorial: 39 boulevard Paoli, Bastia 20200
Tel: 33 04 95 32 34 63
Email: redaction@24ore.fr **Web site:** http://www.24ore.fr
Freq: Daily; **Circ:** 12000 Publisher's Statement
Directeur de la publication: Frédéric Poletti; **Rédacteur en chef:** Olivier-Jourdan Roulot
Profile: Journal d'informations régionales diffusé en Corse.
Language (s): French
DAILY NEWSPAPER

Les Affiches de Grenoble 414792

Editorial: 6 avenue de l'Europe, Grenoble 38029
Tel: 33 04 76 84 32 07
Email: redaction@affiches.fr
Freq: Weekly; **Circ:** 11437 OJD
PDG - Directeur de la publication: Dominique Verdiel
Profile: Journal isérois d'informations judiciaires, économiques et culturelles. PARUTIONS : vendredi
Language (s): French
Ad Rate: Full Page Colour 1090.00
Currency: Euro
DAILY NEWSPAPER

Les Affiches de la Haute-Saône 665875

Editorial: 29 avenue de la Republique, BP 157, Lure 70204 **Tel:** 33 03 84 30 09 08
Email: fxd.lesaffiches@wanadoo.fr
Freq: Weekly; **Circ:** 15000 Publisher's Statement
Directeur de la publication: Hubert Bobillier; **Rédactrice:** Sylviane Boudou; **Gérant:** Jean-François Royer
Profile: Hebdomadaire régional d'information et de publications légales. PARUTIONS : le vendredi
Language (s): French
DAILY NEWSPAPER

L' Aisne Nouvelle 158800

Editorial: 10 Boulevard Henri Martin, BP 149, Saint-Quentin 2103 **Tel:** 33 03 23 06 36 36
Email: redactionstq@aisnenouvelle.fr **Web site:** http://aisnenouvelle.fr
Freq: 2 Times/Week; **Circ:** 19004 OJD
Profile: Journal d'information régionale et départementale. PARUTIONS : lundi, mardi, jeudi, samedi.
Language (s): French
Ad Rate: Full Page Mono 2714.00
Currency: Euro
DAILY NEWSPAPER

L' Alsace 157284

Owner: SAP L'ALSACE
Editorial: 18 rue de Thann, Mulhouse 68945
Tel: 33 03 89 32 70 00
Email: redaction@lalsace.fr **Web site:** http://www.lalsace.fr
Freq: Daily; **Circ:** 105795 OJD
Editor in Chief: Christian Battesti; **Cinéma Théâtre:** Pierre-Louis Cereja; **Médecine Pharmacie:** Geneviève Daune-Anglard; **Informations générales Politique:** Patrick Fluckiger; **Président du Conseil de Surveillance:** Etienne Pflimlin; **Directeur de la publication:** Jacques Romann
Profile: Utilisation de la quadrichromie - Tous les jours Dans certaines pages. Diffusé à l'Est de la France.
Language (s): French
Ad Rate: Full Page Mono 6797.00
Ad Rate: Full Page Colour 8496.00
Currency: Euro
DAILY NEWSPAPER

L' Alsace Bureau Parisien 157288

Owner: SOCIETE ALSACIENNE DE PUBLICATIONS
Editorial: 3 rue des Petites-Ecuries, Paris 75010
Web site: http://www.lalsace.fr
Freq: Daily; **Circ:** 110000 Publisher's Statement
Profile: Daily regional and current events newspaper. Local Translation:Quotidien d'actualités régionales et d'informations générales.
Language (s): French
DAILY NEWSPAPER

L' Alsace Edition de Colmar 157287

Owner: SOCIETE ALSACIENNE DE PUBLICATIONS
Editorial: 1 route de Rouffach, BP 40087, Colmar 68002 CEDEX **Tel:** 33 3 89 20 50 00
Email: redaction-co@lalsace.fr **Web site:** http://www.lalsace.fr
Freq: Daily; **Circ:** 110000 Publisher's Statement
Chef d'Agence: Patrice Barrère
Profile: Daily regional and current events newspaper. Local Translation:Quotidien régional d'informations générales.
Language (s): French
DAILY NEWSPAPER

L' Alsace Edition de Guebwiller 158789

Owner: SOCIETE ALSACIENNE DE PUBLICATIONS
Editorial: 85-87 rue de la Republique, BP 84, Guebwiller 68502 **Tel:** 33 3 89 76 81 05
Email: redaction-gu@lalsace.fr **Web site:** http://www.lalsace.fr
Freq: Daily
Chef d'Agence: Stéphanie Freedman
Profile: Daily regional newspaper covering general, regional and local current events and sports. 6 to 8 local news pages. Local Translation:Quotidien régional d'informations générales, régionales, locales et sportives. 6 à 8 pages d'informations locales.
Language (s): French
DAILY NEWSPAPER

L' Alsace Edition de Saint-Louis 157290

Owner: SOCIETE ALSACIENNE DE PUBLICATIONS
Editorial: 9 croisee des Lys, Saint-Louis 68300
Tel: +33 3 89 69 13 40
Email: redaction-sl@lalsace.fr **Web site:** http://www.lalsace.fr
Freq: Daily; **Circ:** 142000 Publisher's Statement
Chef d'Agence: Nicole Grentzinger
Profile: Daily regional newspaper covering general, regional and local current events and sports. Local Translation:Quotidien régional d'informations générales, régionales, locales et sportives.
Language (s): French
DAILY NEWSPAPER

L' Alsace Edition du Bas-Rhin 306345

Owner: SOCIETE ALSACIENNE DE PUBLICATIONS
Editorial: 6 place de la Victoire, BP 97, Selestat 67600 **Tel:** +33 3 88 58 88 00
Email: redaction-st@lalsace.fr **Web site:** http://www.lalsace.fr
Freq: Daily; **Circ:** 126500 Publisher's Statement
Chef d'Agence: Jean-Stéphane Arnold; **Chef d'Agence:** Anne Suply
Profile: Daily regional newspaper covering general, regional and local current events and sports. Magazine pages, thematic supplements. Local Translation:Presse quotidienne régionale. Informations générales, régionales, locales et sportives. Pages magazine, suppléments à thèmes.
Language (s): French
DAILY NEWSPAPER

L' Alsace Mulhouse - Redaction Locale 157293

Owner: SOCIETE ALSACIENNE DE PUBLICATIONS
Editorial: 2 C rue Schlumberger, BP 52482, Mulhouse CEDEX 9 **Tel:** +33 3 89 33 40 00
Email: redaction-mu@lalsace.fr **Web site:** http://www.lalsace.fr
Freq: Daily; **Circ:** 120000 Publisher's Statement
Profile: Daily regional newspaper covering general, regional and local current events and sports. Local Translation:Quotidien régional d'informations générales, régionales, locales et sportives.
Language (s): French
DAILY NEWSPAPER

L' Ami Hebdo 224610

Editorial: 30 rue Thomann, Strasbourg 67082
Tel: 33 03 88 22 77 22
Email: direction@ami-hebdo.com
Freq: Weekly; **Circ:** 20969 OJD
Rédacteur: Gérard Banholzer; **PDG - Directeur de la publication:** Bernard Deck; **Rédacteur:** Albert Odouard
Profile: Ceased ER. Hebdomadaire régional d'information, familial et chrétien. PARUTIONS : le vendredi (daté du dimanche)
Language (s): French
Ad Rate: Full Page Mono 3800.00
Ad Rate: Full Page Colour 4905.00
Currency: Euro
DAILY NEWSPAPER

L' Ardennais - Union des Ardennes 157322

Owner: GROUPE HERSANT MEDIA
Editorial: 38-40 cours Aristide Briand, Charleville-Mezieres 8102 **Tel:** 33 03 24 33 78 73
Email: charleville@journal-lunion.fr **Web site:** http://www.lunion.presse.fr
Freq: Daily; **Circ:** 104759 OJD
Faits divers: Bernard Dordonne; **Faits divers:** Gérard Garin-Michaud; **Chef d'agence:** Bernard Giraud
Profile: Zone de diffusion : Ardennes et Arrondissements limitrophes. Utilisation de la quadrichromie - Tous les jours - Dans les pages 1 et dernière - Edition du Dimanche. OJD = L'UNION - L'ARDENNAIS. Pour la REDACTION : voir aussi L'UNION
Language (s): French
Ad Rate: Full Page Mono 8480.00
Currency: Euro
DAILY NEWSPAPER

L' Avenir Cote D'Azur 224612

Owner: RICCOBONO
Editorial: 24 boulevard Carnot, Cannes 6400
Tel: 33 04 93 39 36 87
Email: cletil@riccobono.fr **Web site:** http://www.avenir-cotedazur.com
Freq: Weekly; **Circ:** 10000 Publisher's Statement
Rédacteur en chef NICE: Gérard Cletil; **Directrice de la publication:** Françoise Laveuf; **Directeur de la publication:** Jacques Riccobono
Profile: Informations économiques départementales - Annonces légales. PARUTIONS : vendredi
Language (s): French
Ad Rate: Full Page Colour 700.00
Currency: Euro
DAILY NEWSPAPER

L' Avenir de l'Artois 224613

Editorial: 17 place Clemenceau, BP 21, Bethune 62401 **Tel:** 33 03 21 01 66 00
Email: redaction@avenir-artois.fr
Freq: Weekly; **Circ:** 14457 OJD
Directeur de la publication: Pascal Dejean; **Rédactrice en chef:** Anne Despagne
Profile: PARUTIONS : jeudi - Informations locales
Language (s): French
Ad Rate: Full Page Mono 1043.00
Ad Rate: Full Page Colour 1386.00
Currency: Euro
DAILY NEWSPAPER

Le Berry Republicain 158765

Owner: GROUPE CENTRE FRANCE - LA MONTAGNE
Editorial: 1 rue du General Ferrie, Bourges 18023
Tel: 33 02 48 27 63 63
Email: redaction.berry@centrefrance.com **Web site:** http://www.leberry.fr
Freq: Daily; **Circ:** 30168 OJD
Faits divers: Estelle Bardelot; **Faits divers:** Guillaume Faucheur; **Faits divers:** Geoffroy Jeay; **Politique:** Patrick Martinat; **Editor in Chief:** Philippe Noireaux; **Rédacteur en chef:** Bernard Stephan
Profile: Utilisation de la quadrichromie - Tous les jours - Dans les pages une, trois, antépénultième et dernière - Edition du 7ème jour. Diffusé dans la région berrichonne.
Language (s): French
Ad Rate: Full Page Colour 6519.00
Currency: Euro
DAILY NEWSPAPER

Le Bien Public 158770

Owner: EST BOURGOGNE MEDIA
Editorial: 7 boulevard du Chanoine Kir, Dijon 21000
Tel: 33 3 80 42 42 42
Email: bienpublic@lebienpublic.fr **Web site:** http://www.bienpublic.com
Freq: Daily; **Circ:** 47788 OJD
Enseignement: Vincent Lindeneher; **Médecine Pharmacie:** Catherine Vachon
Profile: Daily newspaper covering regional general interest including community news, politics, public issues and leisure activities.
Language (s): French
Ad Rate: Full Page Mono 4312.00
Ad Rate: Full Page Colour 5217.00
Currency: Euro
DAILY NEWSPAPER

Le Bien Public - Les Depeches Edition Beaune 515247

Owner: EBRA
Editorial: 9 rue de Lorraine, Beaune 21200
Tel: 33 3 80 26 34 50
Email: agc.beaune@lebienpublic.fr **Web site:** http://www.bienpublic.com
Freq: Daily; **Circ:** 46336 OJD
Profile: Regional daily newspaper focussing on news and current affairs. Local Translation:Journal d'actualités régionales et nationales.
Language (s): French
DAILY NEWSPAPER

Le Bien Public - Les Depeches Edition Haute Cote D'or 515248

Owner: EBRA
Editorial: 6 rue Auguste-Carre, Montbard 21500
Tel: 33 3 80 89 91 11
Email: agc.montbard@lebienpublic.fr **Web site:** http://www.bienpublic.com
Freq: Daily; **Circ:** 46336 OJD
Chef d'Agence: David Regazzoni
Profile: Regional daily newspaper focussing on news and current affairs. Local Translation:Journal d'actualités régionales et nationales.
Language (s): French
DAILY NEWSPAPER

Le Canard Enchaîné 185831

Editorial: 173 rue Saint Honore, Paris 75001
Tel: 33 1 42 60 31 26
Email: redaction@lecanardenchaine.fr **Web site:** http://www.lecanardenchaine.fr
Freq: Weekly; **Circ:** 550000 Publisher's Statement
Editor in Chief: Érik Emptaz; **General Manager:** Michel Gaillard; **Editor in Chief:** Louis-Marie Horeau
Profile: Satirical newspaper covering general news and current affairs, politics, society and culture with a satirical view. He prefers to be contacted by email.
Language (s): French
DAILY NEWSPAPER

Centre Presse 158795

Editorial: 5 rue Victor Hugo, BP 299, Poitiers 86007
Tel: 33 05 49 55 55 70
Email: redaction@centre-presse.fr **Web site:** http://www.centre-presse.fr
Freq: Daily; **Circ:** 22350 OJD
Multimédia: Laurence Chegaray; **Education:** Sylvaine Hausseguy; **Rédacteur en chef:** Richard Lavigne; **Politique Religion Informations générales:** Didier Monteil; **Directeur de la publication:** Olivier Saint-Cricq
Profile: Utilisation de la quadrichromie : tous les jours dans les pages 1, 3, 5 et dernière. Diffusé dans la Vienne.
Language (s): French
Ad Rate: Full Page Mono 7777.00
Ad Rate: Full Page Colour 10110.00
Currency: Euro
DAILY NEWSPAPER

Centre Presse Aveyron 157566

Owner: LES JOURNAUX DU MIDI
Editorial: Avenue de la Peyrinie - Bel Air, BP 137, Rodez 12021 **Tel:** 33 05 65 77 78 79
Email: redaction@centrepresse.com
Freq: Daily; **Circ:** 20896 OJD
Directeur de la publication: Joël Canis; **Directeur délégué:** Joël Perreau
Profile: Quotidien d'informations régionales - CENTRE PRESSE AVEYRON DIMANCHE : 10 637ex. Diffusé dans l'Aveyron.
Language (s): French
Ad Rate: Full Page Colour 2277.00
Currency: Euro
DAILY NEWSPAPER

La Charente Libre 365924

Owner: GROUPE SUD OUEST
Editorial: ZI n 3, Angouleme 16903
Tel: 33 05 45 94 16 00
Email: charente@charentelibre.fr **Web site:** http://www.charentelibre.fr
Freq: Daily; **Circ:** 38228 OJD
Directeur de la publication: Jean-Pierre Barjou; **Environnement:** Sylviane Carin; **Editor in Chief:** Jean-Louis Hervois; **Informatique Multimédia Automobile:** Richard Tallet

Profile: Utilisation de la quadrichromie - Tous les jours. EVITEZ D'ENVOYER DES DOSSIERS/ COMMUNIQUES PAR MAIL. Diffusé en Poitou Charentes.
Language (s): French
Ad Rate: Full Page Mono 4533.00
Ad Rate: Full Page Colour 5220.00
Currency: Euro
DAILY NEWSPAPER

Charlie Hebdo 185827
Owner: Les Éditions Rotative
Editorial: 26 rue Serpollet, Paris 75020
Tel: 33 1 76 21 53 00
Email: redaction@charliehebdo.fr **Web site:** http://www.charliehebdo.fr
Freq: Weekly; **Circ:** 130000 Publisher's Statement
Editor in Chief: Gérard Biard
Profile: Satirical newspaper covering news and current affairs including politics, society, religion, secularity, culture, international, ecology and investigation.
Language (s): French
DAILY NEWSPAPER

Chinese Daily News 156737
Owner: Chinese Daily News
Editorial: 32 Remy Ollier Street, PO Box 316, Port Louis **Tel:** 230 240 04 72
Email: cdn@bow.intnet.mu
Freq: Daily; **Circ:** 1000 Publisher's Statement
Advertising Manager: Patricia How; **Editor In Chief:** Wong Yuen Moy
Profile: Newspaper covering politics, economy, culture and social events.
Language (s): Chinese
Ad Rate: Full Page Mono 6200.00
Currency: Mauritius Rupees
DAILY NEWSPAPER

La Chronique Républicaine 224657
Editorial: 39 rue de Nantes, BP 30162, Fougeres 35301 **Tel:** 33 02 99 99 12 15
Web site: http://www.lachroniquerepublicaine.fr
Freq: Weekly; **Circ:** 15202 OJD
Présidente - Directrice de la publication: Martine Cameau
Profile: Journal d'informations régionales et locales paraissant le jeudi. NE SOUHAITENT PAS DE COMMUNICATION PAR MAIL
Language (s): French
Ad Rate: Full Page Mono 2808.00
Ad Rate: Full Page Colour 3900.00
Currency: Euro
DAILY NEWSPAPER

Le Commingeois 224497
Owner: COMMINGEOIS
Editorial: Zac Porte-de-Muret, 23 rue Pierre-de-Fermat, Muret 31600 **Tel:** 33 5 61 51 26 52
Email: lecommingeois@wanadoo.fr **Web site:** http://www.lecommingeois.fr
Freq: Monthly; **Circ:** 40000 Publisher's Statement
Directeur de Publication: Pierre-François Dupin
Profile: Local current events newspaper.
Language (s): French
DAILY NEWSPAPER

Corse-Matin 157266
Owner: GROUPE HERSANT MEDIA
Editorial: 2 rue Sergent Casalonga, Ajaccio 20000
Tel: 33 04 95 51 74 00
Email: redacchef@nicematin.fr **Web site:** http://www.corsematin.com
Freq: Daily; **Circ:** 42312 OJD
Directeur délégué - Rédacteur en chef: Roger Antech; **Directeur de la rédaction:** Olivier Biscaye; **Rédaction Internet:** Nathalie Orvoen
Profile: Edition du Dimanche : 40 546ex.
Language (s): French
Ad Rate: Full Page Mono 2311.00
Ad Rate: Full Page Colour 2889.00
Currency: Euro
DAILY NEWSPAPER

Le Courrier Cauchois 224527
Editorial: 2 rue Edmond Labbe, BP 129, Yvetot 76194 **Tel:** 33 02 35 56 29 64
Email: redaction@lecourriercauchois.fr **Web site:** http://www.lecourriercauchois.fr
Freq: Weekly; **Circ:** 37577
Directeur général - Directeur de la publication: Jean-Michel Maussion
Profile: Hebdomadaire régional d'informations, paraissant le vendredi. 4 Editions Zone de diffusion : de la pointe du Havre à Rouen.
Language (s): French
Ad Rate: Full Page Colour 2028.00
Currency: Euro
DAILY NEWSPAPER

Le Courrier de la Mayenne 224532
Owner: EDIT OUEST
Editorial: 108 rue Victor Boissel, BP 529, Laval 53005
Tel: 33 02 43 59 10 40
Email: redaction@courrierdelamayenne.com **Web site:** http://www.courriermayenne.com
Freq: Weekly; **Circ:** 27726 OJD
Directeur délégué: Jean-Michel Desaunai; **PDG - Directeur de la publication:** Loïk De Guebriant
Profile: Hebdomadaire d'informations locales. PARUTIONS : le jeudi
Language (s): French
Ad Rate: Full Page Mono 3408.00
Currency: Euro
DAILY NEWSPAPER

Le Courrier De L'Ouest 158760
Owner: SIPA
Editorial: Boulevard Albert Blanchoin, BP 10728, Angers 49007 **Tel:** 33 02 41 68 86 88
Email: secretariat.redac-chef.angers@courrier-ouest.com
Freq: Daily; **Circ:** 102225 OJD
Directeur général délégué: Jean-Paul Brunel; **PDG - Directeur de la publication:** Matthieu Fuchs; **Médecine Pharmacie:** Anthony Pasco
Profile: Utilisation de la quadrichromie - Tous les jours - Dans les pages 1, 3 et avant-dernière, dernière, et en pages centrales. OJD Edition du septième jour : 62 570ex.
Language (s): French
Ad Rate: Full Page Mono 12095.00
Ad Rate: Full Page Colour 15893.00
Currency: Euro
DAILY NEWSPAPER

LE Courrier De L'ouest Edition Des Deux-Sevres 157401
Owner: OUEST FRANCE
Editorial: 8 bis rue Paul-Doumer, Bressuire 79300 CEDEX **Tel:** +33 5 49 65 00 27
Email: bressuire@courrier-ouest.com **Web site:** http://www.courrierdelouest.fr
Freq: Daily; **Circ:** 112000 Publisher's Statement
Chef d'Agence: Clotilde Couderc; **Chef d'Agence:** Virginie De Gouveia; **Chef d'Agence:** Christian Desbois; **Manager:** Sonia Gaubeau; **Chef d'Agence:** Jean-Luc Simon
Profile: Deux-Sèvres region news: economy, politics, sport and culture.
Language (s): French
DAILY NEWSPAPER

LE COURRIER DE L'OUEST EDITION DU MAINE-ET-LOIRE 157402
Owner: OUEST FRANCE
Editorial: 16 bis rue Saint-Gilles, BP 38, Beaupreau 49600 **Tel:** 33 2 41 63 19 79
Email: redac.beaupreau@courrier-ouest.com **Web site:** http://www.courrierdelouest.fr
Freq: Daily
Rédacteur en Chef: Pierre-Louis Augereau
Profile: Publication focusing on regional news.
Language (s): French
DAILY NEWSPAPER

Le Courrier Du Pays De Retz 224537
Owner: GROUPE PUBLIHEBDOS
Editorial: 6 rue du Traite de Paris, BP 1529, Pornic 44215 **Tel:** 33 02 51 74 00 30
Email: courrierdupaysderetz@publihebdos.fr
Freq: Weekly; **Circ:** 11276 OJD
Editeur: Eric Lechat; **Rédacteur en chef:** Frédéric Prot
Profile: Hebdomadaire régional d'informations. PARUTIONS : vendredi
Language (s): French
DAILY NEWSPAPER

COURRIER FRANCAIS 224580
Owner: COURRIER FRANCAIS
Editorial: Rue du Docteur Jean Vincent, BP 20238, Bordeaux 33028 **Tel:** 33 05 56 44 72 24
Email: v.david@courrier-francais.fr **Web site:** http://www.courrier-francais.com
Freq: Weekly; **Circ:** 35140 Publisher's Statement
Président - Directeur de la publication: Bernard Cattaneo; **Rédacteur en chef - Directeur des éditions:** Vincent David
Profile: Hebdomadaire régional d'information, d'information catholique et d'annonces légales publiant 15 éditions dans 19 départements. PARUTION : vendredi
Language (s): French
Ad Rate: Full Page Mono 1540.00
Ad Rate: Full Page Colour 2030.00
Currency: Euro
DAILY NEWSPAPER

Le Courrier Picard 158759
Owner: Courrier Picard
Editorial: 29 rue de la Republique, BP 1021, Amiens 80010 **Tel:** 33 3 22 82 60 00
Email: redaction@courrier-picard.fr **Web site:** http://www.courrier-picard.fr
Freq: Daily; **Circ:** 62000 OJD
MONTDIDIER: Fabrice Alves-Teixeira; **Président Directeur Général:** Marien Bonieux; **Editor in Chief:** David Guévard; **NOYON:** Stéphane Le Barber; **CLERMONT:** Sylvie Molines
Profile: Regional and local newspaper.
Language (s): French
Ad Rate: Full Page Mono 6535.00
Ad Rate: Full Page Colour 8169.00
Currency: Euro
DAILY NEWSPAPER

LE Courrier Picard Edition De L'oise 157405
Owner: LE COURRIER PICARD
Editorial: 28 rue des Jacobins, Beauvais 60008 CEDEX **Tel:** 33 3 44 11 41 80
Email: beauvais@courrier-picard.fr **Web site:** http://www.courrier-picard.fr
Freq: Daily; **Circ:** 78000 Publisher's Statement
Chef d'Agence: David Blanchard; **Chef d'Agence:** Olivier Hanquier; **Chef d'Agence:** Sylvie Molinès-Laverdet
Profile: Daily regional and local newspaper. The Oise editorial offices are located in Clermont, Creil, Beauvais, Compiègne and Noyon. Local Translation:Quotidien d'informations régionales et locales. Pour l'édition de l'Oise, bureaux à Clermont, Creil, Beauvais, Compiègne, Noyon.
Language (s): French
Ad Rate: Full Page Mono 1643.00
Ad Rate: Full Page Colour 2054.00
Currency: Euro
DAILY NEWSPAPER

LE Courrier Picard Edition De Picardie Maritime 157403
Owner: LE COURRIER PICARD
Editorial: 47 place Max-Lejeune, Abbeville 80100 CEDEX **Tel:** 33 3 22 20 17 00
Email: abbeville@courrier-picard.fr **Web site:** http://www.courrier-picard.fr
Freq: Daily; **Circ:** 86000 Publisher's Statement
Rédacteur (trice): Karine Galhaut; **Rédacteur (trice):** Fabrice Julien; **Rédacteur (trice):** Hervé Leflond; **Rédacteur (trice):** David Vandevoorde
Profile: Daily regional and local newspaper covering sports, social life. Life at sea pages every Thursday. Local Translation:Quotidien d'informations régionales et locales, sports, social. Page vie maritime tous les jeudis.
Language (s): French
Ad Rate: Full Page Mono 8054.00
Ad Rate: Full Page Colour 10067.00
Currency: Euro
DAILY NEWSPAPER

LE Courrier Picard Edition Saint-Quentin 338976
Owner: LE COURRIER PICARD
Editorial: 21 place de l'Hôtel-de-Ville, Saint-Quentin 2100 **Tel:** 33 3 23 60 39 70
Email: saint-quentin@courrier-picard.fr **Web site:** http://www.courrier-picard.fr
Freq: Daily; **Circ:** 78000 Publisher's Statement
Chef d'Agence: Nicolas Totet
Profile: Daily local current events newspaper. Local Translation: Quotidien d'informations générales et locales.
Language (s): French
Ad Rate: Full Page Mono 1396.00
Ad Rate: Full Page Colour 1745.00
Currency: Euro
DAILY NEWSPAPER

La Croix 158746
Owner: Bayard Presse
Editorial: 18 rue Barbes, Montrouge 92128
Tel: 33 1 74 31 60 60
Email: lecteurs.lacroix@bayard-presse.com **Web site:** http://www.la-croix.com
Freq: Daily; **Circ:** 104901 OJD
Picture Editor: Armelle Canitrot; **Editor in Chief:** Florence Couret; **Editor in Chief:** Guillaume Goubert; **Editor in Chief:** Dominique Greiner; **Director:** Dominique Quinio; **Publisher:** Georges Sanerot
Profile: Newspaper covering a broad range of news and current affairs from a Catholic viewpoint including religion, culture, family, ethics and solidarity.
Language (s): French
Ad Rate: Full Page Mono 17000.00
Ad Rate: Full Page Colour 22300.00
Currency: Euro
DAILY NEWSPAPER

La Croix Du Nord 224660
Editorial: 33 rue Negrier, BP 29, Lille 59009
Tel: 33 03 20 55 42 60
Email: contact@croixdunord.com
Freq: Weekly; **Circ:** 12000 Publisher's Statement
Rédactrice en chef: Véronique Durand; **Directeur de la publication:** Franck Lacroix
Profile: Hebdomadaire régional d'opinion - Diffusion : Nord, Pas-de-Calais PARUTION : Vendredi
Language (s): French
Ad Rate: Full Page Mono 1665.00
Ad Rate: Full Page Colour 2433.00
Currency: Euro
DAILY NEWSPAPER

Le Dauphiné Libéré 158773
Owner: LE DAUPHINE LIBERE
Editorial: 650 route de Valence, Veurey 38913
Tel: 33 4 76 88 71 00
Email: ldlcentreveu@ledauphine.com **Web site:** http://www.ledauphine.com
Freq: Daily; **Circ:** 241867 OJD
Directeur des Informations générales: Guy Abonnenc; **Chef du centre ISERE SUD:** Luis Pedro; **Rédacteur en chef - Informations générales Suppléments:** Jean-Pierre Souchon; **General Manager:** Christophe Tostain
Profile: Regional daily newspaper dedicated to international, national and regional news in Rhone-Alpes and in the north of Provence-Alpes Côtes d'Azur.
Language (s): French
Ad Rate: Full Page Mono 10959.00
Ad Rate: Full Page Colour 14247.00
Currency: Euro
DAILY NEWSPAPER

LE Dauphiné Libéré - Edition Annecy 157409
Owner: LE DAUPHINE LIBERE
Editorial: Centre Bonlieu, 1 rue Jean-Jaures, Annecy 74000 **Tel:** 33 4 50 51 69 69
Email: centre.annecy@ledauphine.com **Web site:** http://www.ledauphine.com
Freq: Daily; **Circ:** 47000 Publisher's Statement
Chef d'Agence: Ludovic Favre
Profile: Daily regional newspaper covering national, regional and local current events. Local Translation:Quotidien régional d'informations nationales, régionales et locales.
Language (s): French
Ad Rate: Full Page Mono 5752.00
Currency: Euro
DAILY NEWSPAPER

LE Dauphiné libéré : Edition Léman et Genevois 157422
Owner: LE DAUPHINE LIBERE
Editorial: 36 avenue de la Gare, Annemasse 74100
Tel: 33 4 50 84 24 01
Email: redaction.annemasse@ledauphine.com **Web site:** http://www.ledauphine.com
Freq: Daily; **Circ:** 26000 Publisher's Statement
Chef d'Agence: Françoise Gruber; **Chef d'Agence:** Catherine Poncet
Profile: Daily regional newspaper covering national, regional and local current events. Local Translation:Quotidien régional d'informations nationales, régionales et locales.
Language (s): French
Ad Rate: Full Page Mono 4927.00
Currency: Euro
DAILY NEWSPAPER

LE Dauphine Libere Edition Chambery-Aix-Les-Bains 157417
Owner: LE DAUPHINE LIBERE
Editorial: 5 avenue Charles-de-Gaulle, Aix-Les-Bains 73100 **Tel:** +33 4 79 35 01 16
Email: redaction.aixlesbains@ledauphine.com **Web site:** http://www.ledauphine.com
Freq: Daily; **Circ:** 303551 Publisher's Statement
Chef d'Agence: Muriel Bernard; **Chef d'Agence:** Clément Debiolles
Profile: Regional news + 1 to 2 local pages. Local Translation:Actualités départementales + 1 à 2 pages locales.
Language (s): French
Ad Rate: Full Page Mono 4927.00
Currency: Euro
DAILY NEWSPAPER

LE DAUPHINE LIBERE EDITION DE GRAND VALENCE 157414
Owner: LE DAUPHINE LIBERE
Editorial: 13 boulevard Maurice-Clerc, BP 931, Valence 26009 **Tel:** 33 4 75 79 78 00
Email: centre.valence@ledauphine.com **Web site:** http://www.ledauphine.com
Freq: Daily
Profile: Regional news, 3 pages covering Valence and 5 to 6 pages of local news. Local Translation:Informations départementales, 3 pages sur Valence et 5-6 pages d'actualités locales.
Language (s): French
Ad Rate: Full Page Mono 5752.00
Currency: Euro
DAILY NEWSPAPER

LE Dauphine libere edition Hautes-Alpes - Vallee de L'Ubaye 157411
Owner: LE DAUPHINE LIBERE
Editorial: Place Frederic-Mistral, Barcelonnette 4400
Tel: 33 4 92 81 30 30
Email: centre.gap@ledauphine.com **Web site:** http://www.ledauphine.com
Freq: Daily; **Circ:** 16000 Publisher's Statement
Chef d'Agence: Luc Chaillot; **Chef d'Agence:** Yohan Gavoille
Profile: Hautes-Alpes, Ubaye valley and Sisteron region news + common pages of the Dauphine Libéré edition. Local Translation:Toute l'actualité des Hautes-Alpes, de la vallée de l'Ubaye et de la région de Sisteron + pages communes à toutes les éditions du Dauphine Libéré.
Language (s): French
Ad Rate: Full Page Mono 3084.00
Currency: Euro
DAILY NEWSPAPER

LE Dauphine Libere Edition Isere Nord Bourgoin - Ville Nouvelle 157408
Owner: LE DAUPHINE LIBERE
Editorial: 19 avenue du Grand-Tissage, Bourgoin-Jallieu 38305 **Tel:** +33 4 74 28 03 00
Email: centre.bourgoin@ledauphine.com **Web site:** http://www.ledauphine.com
Freq: Daily; **Circ:** 330551 Publisher's Statement
Chef du Centre: Bernadette Badin; **Pigiste:** Christiane Botton; **Chef d'Agence:** Myriam Karsenty; **Pigiste:** Pierre Viallet
Profile: Daily regional newspaper covering national, regional and local current events. Local Translation:Quotidien régional d'informations nationales, régionales et locales.
Language (s): French
Ad Rate: Full Page Mono 5453.00
Currency: Euro
DAILY NEWSPAPER

LE DAUPHINE LIBERE EDITION ISERE SUD 157412
Owner: LE DAUPHINE LIBERE
Editorial: 40 avenue Alsace-Lorraine, Grenoble 38040 **Tel:** 33 4 76 88 73 37
Email: centre.grenoble@ledauphine.com **Web site:** http://www.ledauphine.com
Freq: Daily
Chef du Centre: Luis Pedro

Profile: Regional and local news. 5 editions are published in the south Isère region: Grenoble, Romanche & Oisans, Grésivaudan, Chartreuse and south Grésivaudan - Gières. Local Translation:Informations régionales et locales. Dans l'Isère Sud existent 5 éditions :- Grenoble - Romanche & Oisans- Grésivaudan - Chartreuse et sud Grésivaudan- Gières.
Language (s): French
Ad Rate: Full Page Mono 8541.00
Currency: Euro
DAILY NEWSPAPER

LE Dauphine Libere Edition Maurienne-Tarentaise 157407

Owner: LE DAUPHINE LIBERE
Editorial: 51 place de l'Europe, Albertville 73200
Tel: +33 4 79 31 13 70
Email: redaction.albertville@ledauphine.com **Web site:** http://www.ledauphine.com
Freq: Daily; **Circ:** 303551 Publisher's Statement
Chef d'Agence: Jean-François Casanova; **Chef d'Agence:** Mélissa Depeyre; **Chef d'Agence:** Frédéric Thiers
Profile: Daily regional newspaper covering national, regional and local current events. Local Translation:Quotidien régional d'informations nationales, régionales et locales.
Language (s): French
Ad Rate: Full Page Mono 4927.00
Currency: Euro
DAILY NEWSPAPER

LE Dauphine Libere Editions Chambery-Aix-Les-Bains/ Maurienne Et Tarentaise 157426

Owner: LE DAUPHINE LIBERE
Editorial: 8 boulevard du Theâtre, BP 387, Chambery CEDEX **Tel:** +33 4 79 33 46 18
Email: centre.chambery@ledauphine.com **Web site:** http://www.ledauphine.com
Freq: Daily; **Circ:** 303551 Publisher's Statement
Profile: The Chambéry regional office is producing 2 Savoy region edition: Chambéry/Aix-Les-Bains and Maurienne/Tarentaise. Regional news. Local Translation:La direction départementale de Chambéry travaille à deux éditions savoyardes : Chambéry/Aix-Les-Bains et Maurienne/Tarentaise. Actualités départementales.
Language (s): French
Ad Rate: Full Page Mono 5453.00
Currency: Euro
DAILY NEWSPAPER

LE Dauphiné Libéré: Edition Ardèche Nord 157424

Owner: LE DAUPHINE LIBERE
Editorial: 22 rue Montgolfier, Annonay 7100
Tel: 33 4 75 33 31 22
Email: redaction.annonay@ledauphine.com **Web site:** http://www.ledauphine.com
Freq: Daily; **Circ:** 33551 Publisher's Statement
Chef d'Agence: Jean-Xavier Pieri
Profile: Daily regional newspaper covering national, regional and local current events. Local Translation:Quotidien régional d'informations nationales, départementales, locales.
Language (s): French
Ad Rate: Full Page Mono 4927.00
Currency: Euro
DAILY NEWSPAPER

LE Dauphiné Libéré: Edition Isère Nord 157418

Owner: LE DAUPHINE LIBERE
Editorial: 5 rue des Recollets, BP 144, La Tour-Du-Pin 38354 CEDEX **Tel:** 33 4 74 83 56 30
Email: redaction.tourdupin@ledauphine.com **Web site:** http://www.ledauphine.com
Freq: Daily; **Circ:** 33551 Publisher's Statement
Chef d'Agence: François Delestre
Profile: Daily regional newspaper covering national, regional and local current events. Local Translation:Quotidien régional d'informations nationales, régionales et locales.
Language (s): French
Ad Rate: Full Page Mono 4927.00
Currency: Euro
DAILY NEWSPAPER

LE Dauphiné Libéré: Edition Isère Nord Vienne et Roussillon 157419

Owner: LE DAUPHINE LIBERE
Editorial: Place de la Halle, Le Peage De Roussillon 38550 **Tel:** 33 4 74 11 15 70
Email: redaction.peage@ledauphine.com **Web site:** http://www.ledauphine.com
Freq: Daily; **Circ:** 34456 Publisher's Statement
Chef d'Agence: Georges Aubry; **Chef d'Agence:** Benjamin Boutier
Profile: Daily regional newspaper covering national, regional and local current events. Local Translation:Quotidien régional d'informations nationales, régionales et locales.
Language (s): French
Ad Rate: Full Page Mono 4927.00
Currency: Euro
DAILY NEWSPAPER

Le Défi Plus 318941

Owner: Le Defi Plus
Editorial: Route Royale, Grande Riviere, Port Louis
Tel: 230 211 77 66
Email: l.ramdour@defimedia.info **Web site:** http://www.ledefiplus.info
Freq: Weekly; **Circ:** 65000 Publisher's Statement
Profile: Newspaper focusing on national and international news, current events, politics, sports, entertainment and leisure.
Language (s): French
Ad Rate: Full Page Mono 16500.00
Ad Rate: Full Page Colour 19500.00
Currency: Mauritius Rupees
DAILY NEWSPAPER

Depeche de Tahiti (La) 525420

Owner: Groupe Hersant Media Polynesie
Editorial: BP 50, 98713 Papeete, Tahiti
Tel: 689 47 52 83
Email: journal@ladepeche.pf **Web site:** http://ladepeche.pf
Freq: Daily; **Circ:** 15000 Publisher's Statement
Editor: Lara Dupuy
Profile: La Dépêche de Tahiti est le 1er journal d'informations de Polynésie française.
Language (s): French
DAILY NEWSPAPER

La Dépêche d'Evreux 224662

Owner: GROUPE PUBLIHEBDOS
Editorial: 3 rue Jean Jaures, BP 143, Evreux 27001
Tel: 33 2 32 39 85 55
Email: courrier@ladepeche.fr **Web site:** http://www.publihebdos.com
Freq: Weekly; **Circ:** 14447 OJD
Informations générales: David Chapelle; **Rédacteur en chef:** Serge Couasnon; **Publisher:** Denis Lejeune
Profile: Regional newspaper covering news and current affairs.
Language (s): French
Ad Rate: Full Page Mono 2503.00
Ad Rate: Full Page Colour 3004.00
Currency: Euro
DAILY NEWSPAPER

La Dépêche du Midi 158803

Owner: Groupe La Dépêche Du Midi
Editorial: Avenue Jean Baylet, Toulouse 31300
Tel: 33 5 62 11 33 00
Email: redaction@ladepeche.fr **Web site:** http://www.ladepeche.fr
Freq: Daily; **Circ:** 190875 OJD
Directeur de la publication: Jean-Michel Baylet; **Politique:** Jean-Pierre Bedei; **Directeur Général:** José Biosca; **Moto Football:** Patrick Boudreault; **Rédacteur en chef:** Yann Bouffin; **Informations générales:** Dominique Delpiroux; **Rédactrice Agence d'Auch:** Bernadette Faget-Rozes; **Madepeche.com:** Philippe Rioux; **Rédacteur en chef - Dépêche du Dimanche:** Jean-Claude Soulery
Profile: Regional newspaper covering news and current affairs including economics, sports, culture and entertainment.
Language (s): French
Ad Rate: Full Page Mono 6100.00
Ad Rate: Full Page Colour 7625.00
Currency: Euro
DAILY NEWSPAPER

La Dépêche du Midi Edition de Haute-Garonne Comminges 157326

Owner: LA DEPECHE DU MIDI
Editorial: 2 place du Marechal-Juin, Saint-Gaudens 31800 **Tel:** 33 5 61 94 66 31
Email: redaction.saint-gaudens@ladepeche.fr **Web site:** http://www.ladepeche.fr
Freq: Daily; **Circ:** 225114 Publisher's Statement
Chef d'Agence: Jean-Jacques Dard
Profile: Regional and local news. Local Translation:Actualité départementale et régionale.
Language (s): French
DAILY NEWSPAPER

LA Depeche Du Midi Edition De Haute-Garonne Sud-Est 157325

Owner: LA DEPECHE DU MIDI
Editorial: Immeuble Le Stratege - Bât. A, BP 14, Labege CEDEX **Tel:** 33 5 61 39 22 30
Email: contact@ladepeche.com **Web site:** http://www.ladepeche.fr
Freq: Daily; **Circ:** 214445 Publisher's Statement
Profile: Regional and local news. Local Translation:Actualité départementale et régionale.
Language (s): French
DAILY NEWSPAPER

LA Depeche Du Midi Edition De L'aude 160790

Owner: LA DEPECHE DU MIDI
Editorial: 20 place Carnot, Carcassonne 11000
Tel: +33 4 68 11 90 11
Email: redaction.castelnaudary@ladepeche.fr **Web site:** http://www.ladepeche.fr
Freq: Daily; **Circ:** 250000 Publisher's Statement
Pigiste: Walter Desplas; **Chef d'Agence:** Richard Lorente; **Pigiste:** René Mari; **Pigiste:** Lucien Pelofi; **Chef d'Agence:** Françoise Peytavi
Profile: General news covering the Aude region. Local Translation:Actualités générales qui concernent tout le département de l'Aude.
Language (s): French
DAILY NEWSPAPER

LA Depeche Du Midi Edition De L'aveyron 160791

Owner: LA DEPECHE DU MIDI
Editorial: 20 rue Lamartine, Capdenac-Gare 12700
Tel: +33 5 65 63 81 30
Email: redaction.decazeville@ladepeche.fr **Web site:** http://www.ladepeche.fr
Freq: Daily; **Circ:** 223067 Publisher's Statement
Chef d'Agence: Jean-Paul Couffin
Profile: Regional newspaper focussing on news, current affairs, economics, politics, culture and sport. One part general and one regional. Local Translation:Toute l'actualité départementale économique, politique, culturelle, sportive... Une partie générale et une partie départementale.
Language (s): French
DAILY NEWSPAPER

LA Depeche Du Midi Edition Du Lot-Et-Garonne 160796

Owner: LA DEPECHE DU MIDI
Editorial: 109 boulevard Carnot, BP 59, Agen 47003 CEDEX **Tel:** +33 5 53 48 05 10
Email: redaction.villeneuve@ladepeche.fr **Web site:** http://www.ladepeche.fr
Freq: Daily; **Circ:** 255107 Publisher's Statement
Chef d'Agence: Jean-Louis Amella
Profile: Regional and local news covering the Lot-et-Garonne region. Local Translation:Toute l'actualité régionale et départementale du Lot-et-Garonne.
Language (s): French
DAILY NEWSPAPER

LA Depeche Du Midi Edition Du Tarn Sud 160797

Owner: LA DEPECHE DU MIDI
Editorial: 4 quai Miredames, Castres 81100 **Tel:** +33 5 63 51 42 10
Email: redaction.castres@ladepeche.fr **Web site:** http://www.ladepeche.fr
Freq: Daily; **Circ:** 192075 Publisher's Statement
Chef d'Agence: Brian Mendibure
Profile: National, regional and local news. Local Translation:Toute l'actualité départementale, régionale et nationale.
Language (s): French
DAILY NEWSPAPER

LA DEPECHE DU MIDI EDITION DU TARN-ET-GARONNE 160798

Owner: LA DEPECHE DU MIDI
Editorial: 3 rue de la republique, Moissac 82200
Tel: 33 5 63 04 02 24
Email: redaction.moissac@ladepeche.fr **Web site:** http://www.ladepeche.fr
Freq: Daily; **Circ:** 18000 Publisher's Statement
Chef d'Agence: Alain Baute
Profile: National, regional and local news. Local Translation:Toute l'actualité départementale et régionale.
Language (s): French
DAILY NEWSPAPER

LES Dépêches - Le Progrès édition du Jura 157612

Owner: EBRA
Editorial: 59 rue Jean-Jaures, BP 50503, Lons-Le-Saunier 39001 CEDEX **Tel:** 33 3 84 86 07 20
Email: accueillons@leprogres.fr **Web site:** http://www.leprogres.fr
Freq: Daily; **Circ:** 30000 Publisher's Statement
Chef d'Agence: Julien Vandelle
Profile: News covering the Jura region + national and regional current events. Local Translation:Ensemble de l'actualité concernant la région du Jura + informations nationales et régionales.
Language (s): French
Ad Rate: Full Page Mono 3239.00
Ad Rate: Full Page Colour 3580.00
Currency: Euro
DAILY NEWSPAPER

Les Dernieres Nouvelles d'Alsace - DNA 157269

Owner: DNA
Editorial: 17-21 rue de la Nuee-Bleue, BP 406, Strasbourg 67077 CEDEX **Tel:** +33 3 88 21 55 00
Email: a.latham@dna.fr **Web site:** http://www.dna.fr
Freq: Daily; **Circ:** 196301 Publisher's Statement
Directeur Général: Jean-Claude Bonnaud; **Président:** Gérard Lignac; **Rédacteur (trice):** Fabienne Tafani
Profile: Local, regional, national and international information newspaper.
Language (s): French
Ad Rate: Full Page Mono 12510.00
Currency: Euro
DAILY NEWSPAPER

Dimanche Ouest France 157267

Owner: OUEST FRANCE
Editorial: 10 rue du Breil, ZI Sud Est, Rennes 35051 CEDEX 9 **Tel:** +33 2 99 32 67 26
Email: dimanche@ouest-france.fr **Web site:** http://www.ouest-france.fr
Freq: Weekly; **Circ:** 408019
Rédacteur en Chef Délégué: Hervé Bertho; **Pigiste:** Bernadette Bourvon; **Pigiste:** Véronique Couzinou; **Pigiste:** Sarah Gerbouin; **Président Directeur Général:** François Régis Hutin; **Pigiste:** Sébastien Jensonny; **Pigiste:** Fabienne Marais-Pillet; **Pigiste:** Virginie Monvoisin-Moussu
Profile: General, regional and local information newspaper. Divided in 4 parts: News, family, sports and local events guide. Family booklet with 4 pages dedicated to children "Dimoitou" News, comics, games, experiments, DIY, jokes). Local Translation:Journal d'informations générales, régionales et locales. Se divise en quatre cahiers : actualités, famille, sport, guide des événements qui ont lieu dans la région. Dans le cahier Familles, un 4 pages pour les enfants Dimoitou (actu, BD, jeux, expérience, bricolage, blagues).
Language (s): French
Ad Rate: Full Page Mono 1800.00
Ad Rate: Full Page Colour 2340.00
Currency: Euro
DAILY NEWSPAPER

DIRECT BORDEAUX7 239527

Owner: GROUPE SUD OUEST
Editorial: 23 quai de Queyries, Bordeaux 33100
Tel: 33 05 35 31 21 75
Email: info@bordeaux7.com **Web site:** http://www.bordeaux7.com
Freq: Daily; **Circ:** 27196 OJD
Rédactrice en chef: Stella Dubourg
Profile: Quotidien d'informations GRATUIT de la métropole bordelaise. PARUTIONS :du lundi au vendredi. Diffusé en Gironde. POUR L'ENVOI DE COMMUNIQUES : N'UTILISER QUE LE MAIL GENERAL.
Language (s): French
Ad Rate: Full Page Mono 1785.00
Ad Rate: Full Page Colour 2040.00
Currency: Euro
DAILY NEWSPAPER

Direct Matin 449087

Owner: Groupe Bolloré
Editorial: 31-32, quai de Dion-Bouton, Puteaux 92800 **Tel:** 33 1 46 96 31 00
Email: redaction@directmatin.net **Web site:** http://www.directmatin.fr
Freq: Daily; **Circ:** 350000 Publisher's Statement
General Manager: Vincent Bollore; **Editor in Chief:** Ludovic Pompignoli
Profile: Daily newspaper covering general news and current affairs including politics, economics, sports, culture, media, celebrities, technology and environment.
Language (s): French
Ad Rate: Full Page Colour 49500.00
Currency: Euro
DAILY NEWSPAPER

Direct Montpellier Plus 366169

Editorial: Arche Jacques Coeur, Montpellier 34923
Tel: 33 4 99 74 34 38
Email: redaction@montpellier-plus.com **Web site:** http://www.direct-montpellier-plus.com
Freq: Daily; **Circ:** 30000 Publisher's Statement
Education: Fanny Bessiere; **Editor in Chief:** Davy Gounel
Profile: Free regional daily newspaper focussing on general, local, regional, national and international news and current affairs.
Language (s): French
DAILY NEWSPAPER

Direct Strasbourg plus 620523

Owner: GROUPE BOLLORE
Tel: 33 1 46 96 31 00
Email: presse@directmatin.net **Web site:** http://www.directstrasbourg.com
Freq: Daily; **Circ:** 30000 Publisher's Statement
Profile: Local Translation: Edition locale de Direct Matin Plus avec un décryptage de l'actualité nationale puis internationale en collaboration avec Le Monde et Courrier International. 4 à 6 pages dédiées à l'actualité nationale, 4 à l'actualité internationale et 4 àl'actualité régionale.
Language (s): French
DAILY NEWSPAPER

Direct Toulouse Plus 616845

Owner: LE MONDE SA
Editorial: 31 - 32 quai de Dion Bouton, Puteaux 92811 **Tel:** 33 01 46 96 31 00
Email: redaction.direct@ladepeche.fr **Web site:** http://www.directtoulouse.com
Freq: Daily; **Circ:** 29230 Publisher's Statement
Rédacteur en Chef: Ludovic Pompignoli
Profile: Local Translation: Edition locale de Direct Matin Plus avec un décryptage de l'actualité nationale puis internationale en collaboration avec Le Monde et Courrier International. 4 à 6 pages dédiées à l'actualité nationale, 4 à l'actualité internationale et 4 à l'actualité régionale.
Language (s): French
DAILY NEWSPAPER

DNA - Dernieres Nouvelles D'Alsace Edition De Colmar 157271

Owner: DNA
Editorial: 7 rue de la Gare, Colmar 68000
Tel: 33 3 89 20 37 95
Email: redac.colmar@dna.fr **Web site:** http://www.dna.fr
Freq: Daily
Chef d'Agence: Marie-Thérèse Fuchs; **Directeur de la Rédaction:** Jean-Louis Grussenmeyer
Profile: Local, regional, national and international information newspaper. Local Translation:Informations nationales, internationales, régionales et locales.
Language (s): French
DAILY NEWSPAPER

DNA - Dernières Nouvelles d'Alsace Edition de Molsheim 157278

Owner: DNA
Editorial: 14, rue de Saverne BP 28, Molsheim 68061
Tel: 33 3 88 49 70 60

Email: redac.molsheim@dna.fr **Web site:** http://www.dna.fr
Freq: Daily; **Circ:** 35000 Publisher's Statement
Chef d'Agence: Hervé Miclo
Profile: Local, regional, national and international information newspaper. Local Translation:Informations locales, régionales, nationales et internationales.
Language (s): French
DAILY NEWSPAPER

DNA - Dernieres Nouvelles D'alsace Edition De Selestat Centre Alsace 157275
Owner: DNA
Editorial: 119 rue Ml-de-Lattre-de-Tassigny, Sainte-Marie-Aux-Mines 68160 **Tel:** +33 3 89 58 74 75
Email: redac.sainte-marie@dna.fr **Web site:** http://www.dna.fr
Freq: Daily; **Circ:** 195899 Publisher's Statement
Chef d'Agence: Philippe Girard
Profile: Local, regional, national and international information newspaper. Local Translation:Informations locales, régionales, nationales et internationales.
Language (s): French
DAILY NEWSPAPER

DNA - Dernieres Nouvelles D'alsace Editions Guebwiller-Mulhouse Et Guebwiller-Colmar 157274
Owner: DNA
Editorial: 159 rue de la Republique, BP 8, Guebwiller CEDEX **Tel:** 33 3 89 74 93 45
Email: DNAguebwiller@dna.fr **Web site:** http://www.dna.fr
Freq: Daily; **Circ:** 250000 Publisher's Statement
Chef d'Agence: René Bickel
Profile: Local, regional, national and international information newspaper.
Language (s): French
DAILY NEWSPAPER

DNA - Dernières Nouvelles d'Alsace: Edition de Saverne 157279
Owner: DNA
Editorial: 114, Grand'Rue BP 22, BP 22, Saverne 67701 CEDEX **Tel:** 33 3 88 01 83 63
Email: redac.saverne@dna.fr **Web site:** http://www.dna.fr
Freq: Daily; **Circ:** 35000 Publisher's Statement
Profile: Local and regional information newspaper. Local Translation:Informations locales, régionales.
Language (s): French
DAILY NEWSPAPER

L' Echo De La Presqu'Ile 224621
Owner: GROUPE PUBLIHEBDOS
Editorial: La Parc Savary, Route de Bréhadour, Guerande 44351 **Tel:** 33 02 40 15 69 69
Email: echodelapresquile@publihebdos.fr
Freq: Weekly; **Circ:** 16801 OJD
Editeur: Eric Lechat; **Rédacteur en chef:** Christophe Lusseau
Profile: Hebdomadaire d'informations générales, régionales et locales Loire Atlantique Morbihan, paraissant le vendredi.
Language (s): French
DAILY NEWSPAPER

L' Echo de l'Armor et de l'Argoat 224616
Owner: GROUPE PUBLIHEBDOS
Editorial: 8 rue Saint Nicolas, BP 20344, Guingamp 22203 **Tel:** 33 02 96 40 62 40
Email: echo@publihebdos.fr **Web site:** http://www.publihebdos.fr
Freq: Weekly; **Circ:** 11252 OJD
Rédacteur en chef: Jack Malpart
Profile: Hebdomadaire d'informations locales et d'annonces légales paraissant le jeudi
Language (s): French
DAILY NEWSPAPER

L' ECHO DU BERRY 224623
Editorial: 3 rue Ajasson de Grandsagne, BP 318, La Chatre 36400 **Tel:** 33 02 54 06 11 99
Email: echoduberry.dj@orange.fr
Freq: Weekly; **Circ:** 12527
Directeur de la publication: Daniel Juillard
Profile: PARUTION : Jeudi
Language (s): French
Ad Rate: Full Page Mono 1430.00
Ad Rate: Full Page Colour 1715.00
Currency: Euro
DAILY NEWSPAPER

L' Echo Republicain 158768
Owner: GROUPE AMAURY
Editorial: 21 rue Vincent Chevard, BP 50189, Chartres 28004 **Tel:** 33 02 37 88 88 88
Email: lucette.dihars@lechorepublicain.presse.fr **Web site:** http://lechorepublicain.fr
Freq: Daily; **Circ:** 30382 OJD
Rédacteur en chef: Hugues de Lestapis; **PDG - Directeur de la publication:** Richard Metzger
Profile: Informations locales. Diffusé en Eure et Loir.
Language (s): French
Ad Rate: Full Page Mono 4552.00
Ad Rate: Full Page Colour 5684.00
Currency: Euro
DAILY NEWSPAPER

L' Echo Républicain Dreux 157576
Owner: AMAURY
Editorial: 17 Grande-Rue, Dreux 28100 CEDEX
Tel: 33 2 37 62 52 70
Email: dreux@lechorepublicain.presse.fr **Web site:** http://www.lechorepublicain.fr
Freq: Daily; **Circ:** 37400 Publisher's Statement
Chef d'Agence: Martine Pesez
Profile: Regional and local news. Local Translation:Actualités régionales et locales.
Language (s): French
DAILY NEWSPAPER

L' Echo Républicain: Edition Châteaudun - Nogent-le-Rotrou 157575
Owner: AMAURY
Editorial: 36 place du 18-Octobre, BP 49, Chateaudun 28200 CEDEX **Tel:** 33 2 37 45 20 89
Email: chateaudun@lechorepublicain.presse.fr **Web site:** http://www.lechorepublicain.presse.fr
Freq: Daily; **Circ:** 37400 Publisher's Statement
Chef d'Agence: Louis-Marie Martin; **Chef d'Agence:** Emmanuel Tremet
Profile: Regional, national and international news covering sports, leisure, economy... Local Translation:Informations régionales, nationales, internationales, sports, loisirs, économie.
Language (s): French
DAILY NEWSPAPER

Les Echos 158747
Owner: Groupe Les Échos
Editorial: 16 rue du Quatre Septembre, Paris 75002
Tel: 33 1 49 53 65 65
Email: redaction@lesechos.fr **Web site:** http://www.lesechos.fr
Freq: Daily; **Circ:** 125984 OJD
Editor in Chief: David Barroux; **Editor in Chief:** Gilles Denis; **Editor in Chief:** Daniel Fortin; **Editor in Chief:** Etienne Lefebvre; **Editor in Chief:** Guillaume Maujean; **Editor in Chief:** Pascal Pogam
Profile: National newspaper covering all areas of financial and economic news including national and international news, industry, services, technology, media and financial markets.
Language (s): French
Ad Rate: Full Page Mono 41000.00
Ad Rate: Full Page Colour 64000.00
Currency: Euro
DAILY NEWSPAPER

Les Echos Du Touquet - Journal Montreuil 224505
Editorial: 104 rue de Metz, Le Touquet-Paris-Plage 62520 **Tel:** 33 03 21 90 06 60 66
Email: pierre.leduc@lesechosdutouquet.fr
Freq: Weekly; **Circ:** 14249 OJD
Directeur de la publication: Pascal Dejean; **Rédacteur en chef:** Pierre Leduc
Profile: LES ECHOS DU TOUQUET : 2 540ex, LE JOURNAL DE MONTREUIL : 8 063ex, LE REVEIL DE BERCK : 3 646ex. PARUTIONS : mercredi - Informations locales
Language (s): French
Ad Rate: Full Page Mono 799.00
Ad Rate: Full Page Colour 998.00
Currency: Euro
DAILY NEWSPAPER

L' Éclaireur du Gâtinais 224629
Editorial: 48 rue Doree, BP 237, Montargis 45202
Tel: 33 2 38 07 18 81
Email: eclaireur.gatinais@wanadoo.fr **Web site:** http://www.eclaireurdugatinais.fr
Freq: Weekly; **Circ:** 19009 OJD
Directeur - Rédacteur en chef: Francis Bonnet
Profile: Regional newspaper covering local news and current affairs.
Language (s): French
DAILY NEWSPAPER

L' ÉQUIPE 158748
Owner: SNC L'Equipe
Editorial: 145 rue Jean-Jacques Rousseau, Issy-Les-Moulineaux 92138 **Tel:** 33 1 40 93 20 20
Email: courrierdeslecteurs@lequipe.presse.fr **Web site:** http://www.lequipe.fr
Freq: Daily; **Circ:** 311403 OJD
Editor in Chief: Elie Barth; **Editor in Chief:** Pierre Callewaert; **Editor In Chief:** Dominique Issartel;
General Manager: François Moriniere
Profile: Newspaper covering sports including football, tennis, rugby, motor racing and formula 1, basketball, handball, golf, cycling, athletics, swimming, sailing and horse-racing.
Language (s): French
DAILY NEWSPAPER

L' Essor 224636
Editorial: 37-39 avenue de la Liberation, BP 80186, Saint-Etienne 42005 **Tel:** 33 04 77 37 60 60
Email: redaction@lessor.fr **Web site:** http://www.lessor.fr
Freq: Weekly; **Circ:** 12566 OJD
Directeur délégué - Chargé du développement: Fabrice Audouard; **Rédacteur en chef:** Mathieu Ozanam; **Gérant - Directeur de la publication:** Guillaume Riccobono; **Directeur des rédactions:** Denis Tardy
Profile: Hebdomadaire d'informations régionales et locales. PARUTION : Vendredi - 3 éditions : Loire, Rhône, Isère.
Language (s): French
Ad Rate: Full Page Mono 370.00
Ad Rate: Full Page Colour 450.00
Currency: Euro
DAILY NEWSPAPER

L' Est Eclair 282108
Owner: GROUPE HERSANT MEDIA
Editorial: UNAVAILABLE, BP 532, Troyes 10081
Tel: 33 03 25 71 75 75
Email: redaction@lest-eclair.fr **Web site:** http://www.lest-eclair.fr
Freq: Daily; **Circ:** 27821 OJD
Droit - Justice: Valérie Alaniece; **Education - Enseignement:** Aurore Chabaud; **Chef du secrétariat de rédaction:** Sébastien Hebert; **Rédacteur en chef:** Patrick Planchenault
Profile: Edition du 7ème jour - Utilisation de la quadrichromie - Tous les jours. Diffusé dans l'Aube.
Language (s): French
Ad Rate: Full Page Mono 4166.00
Ad Rate: Full Page Colour 5832.00
Currency: Euro
DAILY NEWSPAPER

L' Est Républicain 157302
Owner: L'Est Républicain
Editorial: 5 bis avenue Foch, Nancy 54000
Tel: 33 3 83 59 08 04
Email: lerredacncy@estrepublicain.fr **Web site:** http://www.estrepublicain.fr
Freq: Daily; **Circ:** 60000 Publisher's Statement
Photographer: Alexandre Marchi
Profile: Regional, national and international newspaper. The Nancy agency has only one editorial office for 3 editions: Nancy agglomération (City centre), Banlieue Nord (North suburb), Banlieue Sud (South suburb).
Language (s): French
Ad Rate: Full Page Mono 5490.00
Ad Rate: Full Page Colour 6863.00
Currency: Euro
DAILY NEWSPAPER

L' Est Republicain - Edition Bar-Le-Duc 157295
Owner: L'EST REPUBLICAIN
Editorial: 31 place Reggio, Bar-Le-Duc 55001 CEDEX **Tel:** 33 3 29 79 40 36
Email: lerredacbar@estrepublicain.fr **Web site:** http://www.estrepublicain.fr
Freq: Daily; **Circ:** 80000 Publisher's Statement
Profile: Daily regional and local newspaper. Local Translation:Quotidien d'actualités régionales et locales.
Language (s): French
Ad Rate: Full Page Mono 3443.00
Ad Rate: Full Page Colour 4304.00
Currency: Euro
DAILY NEWSPAPER

L' Est Republicain Edition De Luneville 157308
Owner: L'EST REPUBLICAIN
Editorial: 8 rue Carnot, Luneville 54300
Tel: 33 3 83 73 07 56
Email: lerredaclune@estrepublicain.fr **Web site:** http://www.estrepublicain.fr
Freq: Daily; **Circ:** 60000 Publisher's Statement
Chef d'Agence: Catherine Ambrosi
Profile: Regional and local news. Local Translation:Toute l'actualité régionale et locale.
Language (s): French
Ad Rate: Full Page Mono 3184.00
Ad Rate: Full Page Colour 3980.00
Currency: Euro
DAILY NEWSPAPER

L' Est Republicain Edition De Pont-A-Mousson 157294
Owner: L'EST REPUBLICAIN
Editorial: 46 place Duroc, Pont-A-Mousson 54700
Tel: +33 3 83 81 06 58
Email: lerredacpam@estrepublicain.fr **Web site:** http://www.estrepublicain.fr
Freq: Daily; **Circ:** 207000 Publisher's Statement
Chef d'Agence: Frédéric Plancard
Profile: Daily regional and local newspaper. Local Translation:Quotidien d'actualités régionales et locales.
Language (s): French
Ad Rate: Full Page Mono 2153.00
Ad Rate: Full Page Colour 2691.00
Currency: Euro
DAILY NEWSPAPER

L' Est Republicain edition de Verdun 157299
Owner: L'EST REPUBLICAIN
Editorial: 65 rue Mazel, Verdun 55100
Tel: 33 3 29 86 12 49
Email: redaction.verdun@estrepublicain.fr **Web site:** http://www.estrepublicain.fr
Freq: Daily
Chef d'Agence: Sébastien Georges
Profile: Daily regional and local newspaper. Classified ads supplement every Wednesday: "L'Est Annonces". Local Translation:Quotidien d'actualités régionales et locales. Tous les mercredis, un journal de petites annonces : 'L'Est Annonces'.
Language (s): French
Ad Rate: Full Page Mono 3443.00
Ad Rate: Full Page Colour 4304.00
Currency: Euro
DAILY NEWSPAPER

L' Est Républicain: Edition du Doubs 157300
Owner: L'EST REPUBLICAIN
Editorial: 60 Grande-Rue, BP 149, Besancon 25014 CEDEX **Tel:** 33 3 81 21 15 15
Email: lerredacbes@estrepublicain.fr **Web site:** http://www.estrepublicain.fr
Freq: Daily; **Circ:** 42000 Publisher's Statement
Directeur: Damien Roset
Profile: Regional and local news. International and national news. Weekday price: 0.90 € - Sunday price: 1.60 € - First Wednesday of the month 1 €. Local Translation:Toute l'actualité locale et régionale. Informations internationales et nationales. Prix semaine : 0,90 € - Prix du dimanche : 1,70 € - 1 € le 1er mercredi du mois.
Language (s): French
Ad Rate: Full Page Mono 3227.00
Ad Rate: Full Page Colour 4034.00
Currency: Euro
DAILY NEWSPAPER

L' Est Républicain: Edition Haute-Doubs 468975
Owner: L'EST REPUBLICAIN
Editorial: 50 rue de la Republique, BP 67, Pontarlier 25301 **Tel:** 33 3 81 46 87 88
Email: lerredacpon@estrepublicain.fr **Web site:** http://www.estrepublicain.fr
Freq: Daily; **Circ:** 44000 Publisher's Statement
Profile: Regional and local news. International and national news. Weekday price: 0.90 € - Sunday price: 1.60 € - First Wednesday of the month 1 €. Local Translation:Toute l'actualité locale et régionale. Informations internationales et nationales. Prix semaine : 0,90 € - Prix du dimanche : 1,60 € - 1 € le 1er mercredi du mois.
Language (s): French
DAILY NEWSPAPER

L' Eveil De La Haute Loire 158775
Owner: SUD COMMUNICATION
Editorial: 9 place Michelet, BP 24, Le Puy-En-Velay 43001 **Tel:** 33 04 71 09 32 14
Email: redaction@leveil.fr **Web site:** http://www.leveil.fr
Freq: Daily; **Circ:** 14422 OJD
Photo: Max Barre; **Rédacteur en chef:** Jean-Luc Broc
Profile: Diffusion : Haute-Loire et cantons limitrophes de l'Ardèche, de la Lozère.
Language (s): French
Ad Rate: Full Page Colour 2940.00
Currency: Euro
DAILY NEWSPAPER

L' EVEIL DE PONT AUDEMER 224639
Owner: GROUPE PUBLIHEBDOS
Editorial: 9 Place Louis Gillain, BP 415, Pont Audemer 27504 **Tel:** 33 02 32 41 20 20
Email: eveil.pont-audemer@publihebdos.fr **Web site:** http://www.publihebdos.fr
Freq: Weekly; **Circ:** 10100 OJD
Editeur: Christophe Lemoine; **Rédactrice en chef:** Virginie Veiss
Profile: Journal d'informations locales et régionales - PARUTIONS : le mardi
Language (s): French
Ad Rate: Full Page Mono 2176.00
Ad Rate: Full Page Colour 2831.00
Currency: Euro
DAILY NEWSPAPER

L' EVEIL NORMAND 224640
Owner: GROUPE PUBLIHEBDOS
Editorial: 31 rue Thiers, BP 425, Bernay 27304
Tel: 33 02 32 47 81 00
Email: eveil.normand@publihebdos.fr **Web site:** http://www.publihebdos.fr
Freq: Weekly; **Circ:** 10841 OJD
Rédacteur en chef: Jean-Yves Caruel; **Editeur:** Christophe Lemoine
Profile: Hebdomadaire d'informations paraissant le mercredi.
Language (s): French
Ad Rate: Full Page Mono 2241.00
Ad Rate: Full Page Colour 2916.00
Currency: Euro
DAILY NEWSPAPER

L' Express 156739
Owner: La Sentinelle Ltd (Mauritius)
Editorial: Baie du Tombeau, Pamplemousses, Port Louis 21731 **Tel:** 230 2 06 8200
Email: redaction@lexpress.mu **Web site:** http://www.lexpress.mu
Freq: Daily; **Circ:** 34000 Publisher's Statement
Directeur Général: Denis Hitier; **Rédacteur en Chef:** Raj Meetarbhan
Profile: National daily newspaper focusing on regional, national and international news, current affairs, politics, economics, society, culture and sport.
Language (s): English
Ad Rate: Full Page Mono 35000.00
Ad Rate: Full Page Colour 45000.00
Currency: Mauritius Rupees
DAILY NEWSPAPER

Le Figaro 158749
Owner: Socpresse
Editorial: 14, bd Haussmann, Paris 75009
Tel: 33 1 57 08 50 00
Email: direction.redaction@lefigaro.fr **Web site:** http://www.lefigaro.fr
Freq: Daily; **Circ:** 331022 OJD

Editor in Chief: Bertille Bayart; **Editor in Chief:** Martin Couturie; **General Manager:** Serge Dassault; **Politics:** Jean-Baptiste Garat; **Editor in Chief:** Philippe Goulliaud; **Editor in Chief:** Dominique Guiou; **Editor in Chief:** Bruno Jacquot; **Rédactrice en chef le Figaro Réussir:** Christine Lagoutte; **Editor in Chief:** Jean-Pierre Robin; **Editor in Chief:** Catherine Saint Jean; **Editor in Chief:** Jean-Luc Wachthausen
Profile: Newspaper covering national and international news and current affairs including politics, economic, culture, lifestyle and sport.
Language (s): French
Ad Rate: Full Page Mono 76000.00
Ad Rate: Full Page Colour 102000.00
Currency: Euro
DAILY NEWSPAPER

LE Foot Hebdo 665988
Owner: LAFONT PRESSE
Editorial: 27 bd de Launay, Cedex 9, Nantes 44944
Tel: 33 1 46 10 21 21
Web site: http://www.lafontpresse.fr
Freq: Weekly
Conseiller: Arnaud Bertrande
Profile: Weekly journal about sports Local Translation:Journal hebdomadaire dédié au football national et international.
Language (s): French
DAILY NEWSPAPER

France Dimanche 158756
Owner: Lagardère Active
Editorial: 149 rue Anatole France, Levallois Perret 92534 **Tel:** 33 1 41 34 85 30
Email: contact.francedimanche@lagardere-active.com **Web site:** http://www.francedimanche.fr
Freq: Weekly; **Circ:** 424520 OJD
Publisher: Oscar Becerra; **Editor in Chief:** François Charlonnai
Profile: Sunday newspaper covering gossip news including celebrities and royalty as well as culture and entertainment.
Language (s): French
Ad Rate: Full Page Mono 9200.00
Ad Rate: Full Page Colour 11160.00
Currency: Euro
DAILY NEWSPAPER

FRANCE-ANTILLES GUADELOUPE 343498
Editorial: BP 2241, Jarry Cedex 97197
Tel: 0590 5 90 25 18 88
Web site: http://www.guadeloupe.franceantilles.fr
Freq: Daily; **Circ:** 22000 Publisher's Statement
Rédacteur en Chef: Pascal Le Moal
Profile: Daily regional and local current events newspapers. Local Translation:Quotidien d'actualités régionales et locales.
Language (s): French
Ad Rate: Full Page Mono 2690.00
Ad Rate: Full Page Colour 5170.00
Currency: Euro
DAILY NEWSPAPER

FRANCE-ANTILLES MARTINIQUE 343348
Editorial: Place Francois-Mitterrand, BP 577, Fort-De-France Cedex 97207 **Tel:** 0596 5 96 72 88 00
Email: redaction.fa@media-antilles.fr **Web site:** http://www.martinique.france-antilles.fr
Freq: Daily; **Circ:** 35000 Publisher's Statement
Rédacteur en Chef: Rudi Rabathaly; **Directeur de Publication:** Pierre-Yves Simon
Profile: Daily regional and local current events newspapers. Local Translation:Journal d'informations régionales et locales.
Language (s): French
Ad Rate: Full Page Mono 2650.00
Ad Rate: Full Page Colour 5170.00
Currency: Euro
DAILY NEWSPAPER

FRANCE-GUYANE 360233
Owner: GHM - GROUPE HERSANT MEDIA
Editorial: 17 rue Lallouette, BP 428, Cayenne 97329
Tel: 594 2 97 00 0
Email: france.guyane@media-antilles.fr **Web site:** http://www.franceguyane.fr
Freq: Daily; **Circ:** 10000 Publisher's Statement
Chef du Centre: Kerwin Alcide; **Rédacteur en Chef:** Jérôme Rigolage
Profile: Daily current events newspapers covering the Guyana region. Circulation: 5000 copies per week days and 8000 copies on Saturdays. Local Translation:Quotidien d'informations de la Guyane. Tirage : 5000 exemplaires la semaine et 8000 exemplaires le samedi.
Language (s): French
DAILY NEWSPAPER

La Gazette De Manche 224671
Owner: GROUPE PUBLIHEBDOS
Editorial: UNAVAILABLE, BP 108, Saint-Hilaire-Du-Harcouet 50600 **Tel:** 33 02 33 79 30 80
Email: info@gazette-manche.fr
Freq: Weekly; **Circ:** 10204 OJD
Directeur de la publication: Olivier Bonsart; **Editeur:** Christian Bouzols; **Rédactrice en chef:** Pascale Brassinne
Profile: Informations locales. PARUTIONS : mercredi.
Language (s): French
DAILY NEWSPAPER

La Gazette De Montpellier 224672
Editorial: 13 Place de la Comedie, CS 39530, Montpellier 34960 **Tel:** 33 04 67 06 77 77
Email: laredaction@gazettedemontpellier.fr **Web site:** http://www.lagazettedemontpellier.fr
Freq: Weekly; **Circ:** 19887 OJD
Chroniqueur: Michel Crespy; **Expositions Loisirs - Week-end:** Alice Rolland; **Rédacteur en chef:** Henri-Marc Rossignol; **Directeur de la publication:** Pierre Serre
Profile: City magazine local d'informations sur le Grand Montpellier, accompagné d'un supplément télévision TV GAZETTE. PARUTION : le jeudi.
Language (s): French
Ad Rate: Full Page Mono 1600.00
Ad Rate: Full Page Colour 2600.00
Currency: Euro
DAILY NEWSPAPER

La Gazette Nord Pas De Cais 224460
Editorial: 7 rue Jacquemars Gielee, BP 1380, Lille 59015 **Tel:** 33 03 28 38 45 45
Email: redaction@gazettenpdc.fr **Web site:** http://www.gazettenpdc.fr
Freq: 2 Times/Week; **Circ:** 13700 Publisher's Statement
Directeur d'édition: Antoine Deswarte; **Directeur de la publication:** Arnould Meplon; **Directeur de la rédaction:** Philippe Schroder
Profile: PARUTIONS: mardi (édition Pas-de-Calais) et vendredi (édition Nord). Destiné aux milieux juridiques, industriels, commerciaux et économiques
Language (s): French
Ad Rate: Full Page Mono 1592.00
Ad Rate: Full Page Colour 2229.00
Currency: Euro
DAILY NEWSPAPER

LE HAUT ANJOU 224483
Editorial: 44 avenue du Marechal Joffre, Chateau-Gontier 53200 **Tel:** 33 02 43 07 20 00
Email: hautanjou@hautanjou.fr
Freq: Weekly; **Circ:** 12754
Rédactrice en chef: Typhaine David; **Gérant - Directeur de la publication:** Loïk De Guebriant; **Rédaction Maine et Loire:** Quentin Lanvierge
Profile: Hebdomadaire d'informations générales. PARUTIONS : vendredi. Edite également : LES NOUVELLES D'ANJOU - Mensuel GRATUIT - Renseignements identiques - T.Déclaré : 28 500 ex.
Language (s): French
DAILY NEWSPAPER

LA HAUTE SAINTONGE 224676
Editorial: 12 avenue Gambetta, BP 96, Jonzac 17503
Tel: 33 05 46 48 00 48
Email: hebdo.haute.saintonge@wanadoo.fr
Freq: Weekly; **Circ:** 10512 OJD
Directeur de la publication: Bernard Leveque
Profile: Hebdomadaire d'informations régionales. PARUTIONS : le vendredi Zone de diffusion : moitié sud du département de la Charente Maritime.
Language (s): French
Ad Rate: Full Page Mono 1046.00
Ad Rate: Full Page Colour 1298.00
Currency: Euro
DAILY NEWSPAPER

Le Havre Presse 742165
Owner: GROUPE HERSANT MEDIA
Editorial: 113 boulevard de Strasbourg, Le Havre 76600 **Tel:** 33 02 35 19 17 17
Freq: Daily; **Circ:** 13286 OJD
PDG - Directeur de la publication: Michel Lepinay
Profile: Utilisation de la quadrichromie : tous les jours - Pages couleur en fonction de la pagination. REDACTION : SE REPORTER A HAVRE LIBRE. Diffusé en Seine Maritime.
DAILY NEWSPAPER

L' Hebdo du Vendredi 554989
Owner: B2M
Editorial: 195 rue du Barbâtre, Reims 51100
Tel: 33 3 26 36 50 13
Email: lhebdoduvendredi.redac@orange.fr **Web site:** http://www.lhebdoduvendredi.com
Freq: Weekly; **Circ:** 40000 Publisher's Statement
Directeur de Publication: Frédéric Becquet; **Pigiste:** Aymeric Henniaux; **Rédacteur en Chef:** Olivier Michaux
Profile: Local Translation: Journal gratuit d'information locale (de 16 à 32 pages).3 éditions : Reims, Epernay et Châlons-en-Champagne. Bureau de Châlons : 29 rue Jean Jaurès - 51000 Châlons-en-ChampagneRubriques : société, justice, économie, sport, France, monde, Culture, loisirs, sorties, cinéma.
Language (s): French
DAILY NEWSPAPER

HEBDO+ 545103
Editorial: Pôle Gaston Febus, Quartier Berlanne, Morlaas 64160 **Tel:** 33 05 59 14 01 45
Email: redaction@hebdo-plus.fr **Web site:** http://www.hebdo-plus.fr
Freq: Weekly; **Circ:** 50000 Publisher's Statement
Directeur de la publication: Pierre Lagrave
Profile: Journal d'information locale GRATUIT.
Language (s): French
DAILY NEWSPAPER

L' HERAULT DU JOUR DE LA MARSEILLAISE 157309
Owner: LA MARSEILLAISE
Editorial: 58 allee Paul-Riquet, Beziers 34500
Tel: 33 4 67 49 10 31
Email: agbeziers@lamarseillaise.fr **Web site:** http://www.lamarseillaise.fr
Freq: Daily; **Circ:** 12049 Publisher's Statement
Chef d'Agence: Annie Menras; **Chef d'Agence:** Michel Szewczyk
Profile: Hérault edition of the newspaper "La Marseillaise", the left wing regional community daily newspaper. Current events, 20 local pages (including 3 for Sète and 3 for Béziers). Local Translation:Edition de l'Hérault du journal 'La Marseillaise', quotidien de gauche d'informations régionales de proximité. Informations générales. 20 pages locales (dont 3 pour Sète et 3 pour Béziers).
Language (s): French
Ad Rate: Full Page Mono 5322.00
Ad Rate: Full Page Colour 6919.00
Currency: Euro
DAILY NEWSPAPER

LE HIC 224484
Editorial: 70 rue de Lorraine, BP 1205, Cholet 49312
Tel: 33 02 41 49 02 34
Email: redaction@lehic.com
Freq: Weekly; **Circ:** 90000 Publisher's Statement
Rédactrice (La Flèche/Saumur): Thiphaine David; **Rédactrice (Cholet):** Emmanuelle Echasseriau; **PDG - Directrice de la publication:** Brigitte Rondeau
Profile: Hebdomadaire GRATUIT paraissant le mercredi - Arts - Spectacles - Tourisme Sports - Loisirs.4 Editions : Sablé/La Flèche (lundi), Saumur (mardi) Cholet, Bocage (mercredi)
Language (s): French
Ad Rate: Full Page Mono 1755.00
Ad Rate: Full Page Colour 2094.00
Currency: Euro
DAILY NEWSPAPER

Le Hic Grand Saumur 433743
Owner: HIC GRAND SAUMUROIS
Editorial: 4 place de la Bilange, BP 111, Saumur 49413 CEDEX **Tel:** 33 41 49 02 33
Email: redaction.saumur@lehic.com **Web site:** http://www.lehic.com
Freq: Weekly; **Circ:** 49600 Publisher's Statement
Rédacteur (trice): Typhaine David; **Directeur de Publication:** Brigitte Rondeau; **Directeur de Publication:** Serge Rondeau
Profile: Regional newspaper focussing on local news and current affairs including associations and culture.
Language (s): French
DAILY NEWSPAPER

L' Humanité 158751
Owner: Société nouvelle du journal l'Humanité
Editorial: 164 rue Ambroise Croizat, Saint-Denis 93528 **Tel:** 33 1 49 22 72 72
Email: pam@humanite.fr **Web site:** http://www.humanite.fr
Freq: Daily; **Circ:** 52456 OJD
Editor in Chief: Jean-Emmanuel Ducoin; **Editor in Chief:** Michel Guilloux; **Editor in Chief:** Jean-Paul Pierot
Profile: Newspaper covering national and international news and current affairs including politics, social issues, economics, society, environment, culture, sports and media.
Language (s): French
Ad Rate: Full Page Mono 12650.00
Ad Rate: Full Page Colour 17650.00
Currency: Euro
DAILY NEWSPAPER

L' Humanite Dimanche 396708
Editorial: 164 rue Ambroise Croizat, Saint-Denis 93528 **Tel:** 33 1 49 22 72 72
Web site: http://www.humanite.fr
Freq: Weekly; **Circ:** 200000 Publisher's Statement
Monde: Vadim Kamenka; **Directeur de la publication:** Patrick Le Hyaric
Profile: Vie sociale - Vie quotidienne. PARUTIONS : le jeudi
Language (s): French
DAILY NEWSPAPER

L' Impartial 224644
Owner: GROUPE PUBLIHEBDOS
Editorial: 3/5 rue Sainte Clotilde, BP 507, Les Andelys 27705 **Tel:** 33 02 32 54 00 84
Email: impartial@publihebdos.fr **Web site:** http://www.publihebdos.fr
Freq: Weekly; **Circ:** 12310 OJD
Rédacteur en chef: Jean-Paul Gosselin; **Editeur:** Denis Lejeune
Profile: Informations générales et régionales - Annonces légales. PARUTIONS : le jeudi
Language (s): French
Ad Rate: Full Page Mono 2169.00
Ad Rate: Full Page Colour 2820.00
Currency: Euro
DAILY NEWSPAPER

L' Independant Bureau Parisien 157311
Owner: LES JOURNAUX DU MIDI
Editorial: 80 boulevard Auguste-Blanqui, Paris 75683 CEDEX 14 **Tel:** 33 1 44 71 80 44
Email: redac.paris@midilibre.com **Web site:** http://www.lindependant.com
Freq: Daily; **Circ:** 65523 Publisher's Statement
Rédacteur (trice): Zoé Cadiot
Profile: The Paris office is dedicated to the Indépendant issue of the Midi Libre et Centre Presse. Local Translation:Le Bureau de Paris est celui de l'Indépendant, de Midi Libre et de Centre Presse.
Language (s): French
DAILY NEWSPAPER

L' Independant Du Pas De Calais 224647
Editorial: 14 rue des Clouteries, BP 87, Saint-Omer 62502 **Tel:** 33 03 21 12 22 23
Email: vserbourdin@lindependant.net
Freq: Weekly; **Circ:** 17796 OJD
Rédacteur en chef: Benoît Cailliez; **Directrice de la publication:** Valérie Serbourdin-Devos
Profile: Information régionale et locale - PARUTIONS : Vendredi.
Language (s): French
DAILY NEWSPAPER

L' Independant Rivesaltes 157312
Owner: LES JOURNAUX DU MIDI
Editorial: Mas de la Garrigue, 2 avenue Alfred-Sauvy, Rivesaltes 66605 CEDEX **Tel:** 33 4 68 64 88 88
Email: direction.redaction@lindependant.com **Web site:** http://www.lindependant.com
Freq: Daily; **Circ:** 65523 Publisher's Statement
Editor: Jean-Luc Bobin; **Director:** Thierry Bouldoire; **Rédacteur (trice):** Guillaume Clavaud; **Rédacteur (trice):** Vincent Couture; **Rédacteur (trice):** Estelle Devic; **Rédacteur (trice):** Eric Dubuis; **Rédacteur (trice):** Martine Galonnier; **Rédacteur (trice):** Xavier Hamond; **Rédacteur (trice):** Arnaud Hingray; **Rédacteur (trice):** Valérie Huck; **Rédacteur (trice):** Sylvie Lainé; **Rédacteur (trice):** Martial Mehr; **Rédacteur (trice):** Corinne Sabouraud; **Rédacteur (trice):** Stéphane Sicard; **Rédacteur (trice):** Fabrice Voné
Profile: This daily newspaper was first published in 1846 and covers news.
Language (s): French
Ad Rate: Full Page Colour 8658.00
Currency: Euro
DAILY NEWSPAPER

International New York Times 218052
Owner: The New York Times Company
Editorial: Immeuble le Lavoisier, 4, place des Vosges, Courbevoie 92400 **Tel:** 33 1 41 43 93 00
Email: inytletters@nytimes.com **Web site:** http://international.nytimes.com
Freq: Daily; **Circ:** 219188 OJD
President, International: Stephen Dunbar-Johnson; **Rédactrice en chef:** Katherine Knorr; **Bureau Chief:** Alissa Rubin
Profile: International newspaper covering general news and current affairs including business, politics, sports, culture, society, style, arts and travel.
Language (s): English
Ad Rate: Full Page Mono 59053.00
Currency: Euro
DAILY NEWSPAPER

Investir 168278
Owner: Groupe Les Echos
Editorial: 16, rue du 4 Septembre, Paris 75002
Tel: 33 1 44 88 48 00
Email: rlebailly@investir.fr **Web site:** http://bourse.lesechos.fr
Freq: Weekly; **Circ:** 77639 OJD
Editor in Chief: Rémy Le Bailly
Profile: Newspaper covering investment including stock markets and and financial analysis.
Language (s): French
Ad Rate: Full Page Mono 21200.00
Ad Rate: Full Page Colour 27200.00
Currency: Euro
DAILY NEWSPAPER

Le Journal De Gien 224487
Editorial: 26 rue du General Marcel, BP 65, Gien 45502 **Tel:** 33 02 38 67 19 43
Email: journaldegien@wanadoo.fr
Freq: Weekly; **Circ:** 17957 OJD
Directeur général: Dominique Jatteau; **Président du Conseil de Surveillance:** Jean-Pierre Jatteau; **Rédacteur en chef:** Martial Poncet
Profile: Informations régionales. PARUTIONS : jeudi.
Language (s): French
Ad Rate: Full Page Mono 3460.00
Ad Rate: Full Page Colour 5190.00
Currency: Euro
DAILY NEWSPAPER

JOURNAL DE LA CORSE 416014
Editorial: ZI du Vazzio, Ajaccio 20090
Tel: 33 04 95 21 50 02
Email: redaction@journaldelacorse.net **Web site:** http://www.jdcorse.com
Freq: Weekly; **Circ:** 15000 Publisher's Statement
Collaborateur: Lisandru Bassani; **Directeur Général:** Jean-Michel Emmanuelli; **Collaborateur:** Paul Lucchini; **Collaborateur:** Aristide Nerriere; **Rédactrice en chef:** Caroline Siciliano
Profile: Journal d'informations régionales paraissant le vendredi.
Language (s): French
DAILY NEWSPAPER

Le Journal De La Haute Marne 158769
Editorial: 14 rue du Patronage Laïque, BP 2057, Chaumont 52902 **Tel:** 33 03 25 03 86 40
Email: jhmdir@graphycom.com **Web site:** http://www.jhm.fr
Freq: Daily; **Circ:** 25832 OJD
Président - Directeur de la publication: Jean Bletner
Profile: Informations départementales - Edition du dimanche : 25 650ex. Diffusé en Haute Marne.
Language (s): French
Ad Rate: Full Page Mono 2972.00
Ad Rate: Full Page Colour 3715.00

Currency: Euro
DAILY NEWSPAPER

LE Journal de la Haute-Marne: Edition Nord 157591
Owner: EBRA
Editorial: 45 rue Gambetta, BP 79, Saint-Dizier 52100 **Tel:** 33 3 25 05 20 04
Email: redac@jhmsaint-dizier.com **Web site:** http://www.jhm.fr
Freq: Daily; **Circ:** 31001 OJD
Chef d'Agence: Frédéric Thore
Profile: General and local news. Sunday price: 1,15 € - Subscription including Sunday: 258 € - Subscription without Sunday issues: 199 €. Local Translation:Informations générales et locales. Prix dimanche 1,15 €. Abonnement avec dimanche 258 € - Abonnement sans dimanche 199 €.
Language (s): French
DAILY NEWSPAPER

Le Journal de L'Ile 360234
Owner: GHM - GROUPE HERSANT MEDIA
Editorial: 62 boulevard du Chaudron, BP 40019, Sainte-Clotilde 97491 **Tel:** 33 2 62 48 66 00
Email: societe@jir.fr **Web site:** http://www.clicanoo.re
Freq: Daily; **Circ:** 34000 Publisher's Statement
Rédacteur en chef: Yves Montrouge; **Faits-divers:** Jérôme Talpin
Profile: Quotidien d'informations de la Réunion. Tirage en semaine 33 000 exemplaires.Tirage le samedi 42 000 exemplaires.
Language (s): French
DAILY NEWSPAPER

Le Journal de Saône-et-Loire 158767
Owner: EST REPUBLICAIN
Editorial: 9-15 rue des Tonneliers, BP 30134, Chalon-Sur-Saone 71104 **Tel:** 33 3 85 90 68 00
Email: infos@lejsl.fr **Web site:** http://www.lejsl.com
Freq: Daily; **Circ:** 58036 OJD
Directeur de la publication: Christophe Mahieu
Profile: Zone de diffusion : 7 éditions - Edition du 7ème jour : DIMANCHE SAONE ET LOIRE : 58 617 ex - Utilisation de la quadrichromie : dans l'édition du dimanche + une, trois et dernière en semaine. Diffusé en Saône et Loire.
Language (s): French
Ad Rate: Full Page Mono 4548.00
Ad Rate: Full Page Colour 5504.00
Currency: Euro
DAILY NEWSPAPER

LE Journal De Saone-Et-Loire Edition De Louhans 157431
Owner: EBRA
Editorial: 9 rue d'Alsace, Louhans 71500
Tel: 33 3 85 75 22 49
Email: accueil-louhans@lejsl.fr **Web site:** http://www.lejsl.com
Freq: Daily; **Circ:** 72000 Publisher's Statement
Chef d'Agence: Eric Pellenard
Profile: Regional and local news. Local Translation:Actualités régionales et locales.
Language (s): French
DAILY NEWSPAPER

LE Journal De Saone-Et-Loire Edition De Macon 157432
Owner: EBRA
Editorial: 89 quai Lamartine, Macon 71000
Tel: 33 3 85 39 99 00
Email: redaction-macon@lejsl.fr **Web site:** http://www.lejsl.com
Freq: Daily; **Circ:** 69889 Publisher's Statement
Chef d'Agence: Laurent Bollet
Profile: Regional and local news. Local Translation:Actualités régionales et locales.
Language (s): French
DAILY NEWSPAPER

LE Journal De Saone-Et-Loire Edition Paray-Le-Monial Gueugnon Digoin 157433
Owner: EBRA
Editorial: 49 avenue Charles-de-Gaulle, Digoin 71160
Tel: 33 3 85 53 77 00
Email: text-digoin@lejsl.fr **Web site:** http://www.lejsl.com
Freq: Daily; **Circ:** 65000 Publisher's Statement
Pigiste: Michel Beriard; **Chef d'Agence:** Emmanuel Daligand; **Chef d'Agence:** Eric Dujardin; **Pigiste:** Christian Martel
Profile: Regional and local news. Local Translation:Actualités régionales et locales.
Language (s): French
DAILY NEWSPAPER

Le Journal D'Ici 224475
Editorial: 3 Quai du Carras, BP 309, Castres 81105
Tel: 33 05 63 51 49 49
Email: redaction@lejournaldici.com
Freq: Weekly; **Circ:** 13000 Publisher's Statement
Directeur délégué - Directeur de la rédaction: Pierre Archet; **Gérant - Directeur de la publication:** Eric Ducournau
Profile: Informations générales et régionales. PARUTIONS : jeudi
Language (s): French
DAILY NEWSPAPER

Le Journal Du Centre 158792
Owner: GROUPE CENTRE FRANCE - LA MONTAGNE
Editorial: 3 rue du Chemin de Fer, BP 106, Nevers 58001 **Tel:** 33 03 86 71 45 00
Email: redaction.jdc@centrefrance.com **Web site:** http://www.lejdc.fr
Freq: Daily; **Circ:** 30050 OJD
Directeur de la publication: Jacques Camus
Profile: Utilisation quadri : tous les jours - Dans les pages une, dernière et pages impaires intérieures. Edition du dimanche : JOURNAL DU CENTRE DIMANCHE (12 463 ex). Diffusé en Bourgogne.
Language (s): French
Ad Rate: Full Page Mono 5007.00
Currency: Euro
DAILY NEWSPAPER

Le Journal du Dimanche - JDD 158757
Owner: Hachette Filipacchi Médias
Editorial: 149 rue Anatole France, Levallois Perret 92534 **Tel:** 33 1 41 34 60 00
Email: redaction@lejdd.fr **Web site:** http://www.lejdd.fr
Freq: Weekly; **Circ:** 267659 OJD
Editor in Chief: Bruno Jeudy; **Editor in Chief:** Laurent Valdiguié
Profile: Sunday newspaper covering news and current affairs including politics, world news, society, economics, culture, media, sports, leisure and entertainment.
Language (s): French
Ad Rate: Full Page Mono 52800.00
Ad Rate: Full Page Colour 66000.00
Currency: Euro
DAILY NEWSPAPER

Le Havre - Paris Normandie 157567
Owner: GHM - GROUPE HERSANT MEDIA
Editorial: 113 boulevard de Strasbourg, Le Havre 76600 **Tel:** 33 2 35 19 17 17
Email: redaction.havre@presse-normande.com **Web site:** http://www.paris-normandie.fr
Freq: Daily; **Circ:** 38300 Publisher's Statement
Rédacteur en Chef: Sophie Bloch; **Rédacteur (trice):** Patrick Gobbé; **Président Directeur Général:** Michel Lepinay; **Pigiste:** David Poisnel; **Chef d'Agence:** Stéphane Siret
Profile: Daily current events newspapers covering Le Havre and its region. Only the cover page will be different on each title. Circulation: Havre Libre 12.300 copies, Havre Presse 8.200 copies, Paris Normandie Le Havre 6.000 copies. Local Translation:Quotidiens sur Le Havre et sa région. Seule la une diffère d'un titre à l'autre. Tirages : Havre Libre 12.300 ex., Havre Presse 8.200 ex, Paris Normandie Le Havre 6.000 ex.
Language (s): French
DAILY NEWSPAPER

Libération 158752
Owner: SARL Libération
Editorial: 11, rue Beranger, Paris 75003
Tel: 33 1 42 76 17 89
Email: sergent@liberation.fr **Web site:** http://www.liberation.fr
Freq: Daily; **Circ:** 123339 OJD
Picture Editor: Jany Bianco-Mula; **Editor in Chief:** Gérard Lefort; **Editor in Chief:** Marc Semo; **Editor in Chief:** Béatrice Vallaeys
Profile: Newspaper covering general news and current affairs including politics, society, economics, sports, science, culture, technology, environment and media.
Language (s): French
Ad Rate: Full Page Mono 31600.00
Ad Rate: Full Page Colour 49600.00
Currency: Euro
DAILY NEWSPAPER

LIBERTE - BONHOMME LIBRE 224511
Owner: GROUPE PUBLIHEBDOS
Editorial: 17 rue Commodore Hallet, BP 85341, Caen 14053 **Tel:** 33 02 31 86 03 32
Email: liberte@publihebdos.fr
Freq: Weekly; **Circ:** 17299 OJD
Directeur de la publication: Philippe Rifflet
Profile: Informations générales, régionales et locales, spectacles, enquêtes, sports, annonces légales. PARUTIONS : jeudi.
Language (s): French
Ad Rate: Full Page Mono 2691.00
Ad Rate: Full Page Colour 3510.00
Currency: Euro
DAILY NEWSPAPER

LIBERTE DIMANCHE 158807
Owner: GROUPE HERSANT MEDIA
Editorial: 33 rue des Grosses-Pierres, Deville-Les-Rouen 76250 **Tel:** 33 02 32 08 37 39
Email: redaction.liberte@presse-normande.com
Freq: Weekly; **Circ:** 14491 OJD
Rédacteur en chef: Thierry Delacourt; **PDG - Directeur de la publication:** Michel Lepinay
Profile: PARUTIONS : dimanche - Informations générales, régionales, sportives DIFFUSION : Seine Maritime, Eure.
Language (s): French
Ad Rate: Full Page Mono 8800.00
Ad Rate: Full Page Colour 10560.00
Currency: Euro
DAILY NEWSPAPER

LILLEPLUS 232399
Owner: GROUPE LA VOIX DU NORD
Editorial: PGLM, 29 rue Esquermoise, Lille 59000
Tel: 33 03 20 44 80 00
Email: contact@directlille.com **Web site:** http://www.directlille.com
Freq: Daily; **Circ:** 50853 OJD
Rédaction régionale: Sabrina Alouache; **Rédactrice en chef:** Adeline Boldoduck; **Directeur opérationnel:** Sébastien Duprez; **Rédaction régionale:** Perrine Tiberghien
Profile: Quotidien GRATUIT d'informations générales et locales pour les urbains actifs de 15/35 ans. (Pages internationales et nationales réalisées par DIRECTMATIN)
Language (s): French
Ad Rate: Full Page Colour 2659.00
Currency: Euro
DAILY NEWSPAPER

LA LOZERE NOUVELLE 224514
Editorial: Boulevard des Capucins, BP 17, Mende 48001 **Tel:** 33 04 66 49 65 90
Email: redaction@lozere-nouvelle.com **Web site:** http://www.lozere-nouvelle.com
Freq: Weekly; **Circ:** 22523 OJD
Président: Maurice Buisson; **Directeur de la publication:** Michel Peytavin
Profile: Informations locales et générales.
Language (s): French
Ad Rate: Full Page Mono 1470.00
Currency: Euro
DAILY NEWSPAPER

LYONPLUS 232398
Owner: GROUPE PROGRES
Editorial: 4 rue Montrochet, Lyon 69002
Tel: 33 04 78 14 77 91
Email: info@lyonplus.com **Web site:** http://www.lyonplus.com
Freq: Daily; **Circ:** 62519 OJD
Rédacteur en chef .: Manuel Da Fonseca; **Directeur de la publication:** Pierre Fanneau
Profile: Quotidien GRATUIT d'informations locales, nationales, internationales et culturelles distribué dans les gares, le métro etc... NE SOUHAITENT PAS DE COMMUNICATION PAR FAX
Language (s): French
Ad Rate: Full Page Colour 6000.00
Currency: Euro
DAILY NEWSPAPER

Le Maine Libre 742168
Owner: SIPA
Editorial: 28 Place de l'Eperon, Le Mans 72013
Tel: 33 02 43 83 72 30
Email: redaction@maine-libre.com **Web site:** http://www.lemainelibre.fr
Freq: Daily; **Circ:** 47205 OJD
Directeur des rédactions: Jean-Paul Brunel; **Education:** Bertrand Coudreau; **Président Directeur général:** Matthieu Fuchs; **Rédacteur en chef:** Jérôme Glaize; **Médecine - Santé:** Philippe Lavergne; **Industries Techniques:** Bruno Mortier; **Moto Basket:** Bruno Palmet; **Pêche Chasse:** Hervé Petibon
Profile: Utilisation de la quadrichromie - Tous les jours - Dans les pages une, trois dernière, antépénultième et 4 pages intérieures. Edition du septième jour : 25 704ex. Diffusé dans la Sarthe.
DAILY NEWSPAPER

LE Maine Libre - Edition le Mans 158781
Owner: OUEST FRANCE
Editorial: 28/30 place de l'Eperon, Le Mans 72013 CEDEX 2 **Tel:** 33 2-43-83-72-30
Email: redaction@maine-libre.com **Web site:** http://www.lemainelibre.fr
Freq: Daily; **Circ:** 46117 OJD
Directeur des Rédactions: Jean-Paul Brunel; **Président Directeur Général:** Matthieu Fuchs; **Rédacteur en Chef:** Jérôme Glaize
Profile: Daily general, regional and local newspaper: Saturday price: 0,90 € (including TV guide supplement). Sunday price: 0,90 € (including women supplement Version Fémina).Local Translation: Quotidien d'informations générales, régionales, locales et sportives.Le samedi, prix de 0,90 € (avec supplément TV). Le Dimanche, prix 0,90 € (avec le supplément Femmes Version Fémina).
Language (s): French
Ad Rate: Full Page Mono 10072.00
Ad Rate: Full Page Colour 12590.00
Currency: Euro
DAILY NEWSPAPER

LE Maine Libre - Edition Sarthe Loir 157595
Owner: OUEST FRANCE
Editorial: 28-30, place de l'Eperon, Le Mans 72 013 Cedex 2 **Tel:** 33 2 43 83 72 72
Email: agence.chateauduloir@maine-libre.com **Web site:** http://www.lemainelibre.fr
Freq: Daily; **Circ:** 48000 OJD
Chef d'Agence: Natacha Longeray
Profile: Daily general, regional and local newspaper. Local Translation:Quotidien d'informations générales, régionales, locales.
Language (s): French
DAILY NEWSPAPER

LE Maine Libre Edition Haute Sarthe 157593
Owner: OUEST FRANCE
Editorial: 17 avenue du General-Leclerc, Alencon 61000 **Tel:** 33 2 33 82 64 83
Email: agence.mamers@maine-libre.com **Web site:** http://www.lemainelibre.fr
Freq: Daily; **Circ:** 47000 OJD
Chef d'Agence: Benjamin Nolière
Profile: Daily general, regional and local newspaper: politics, education, magazine... Local Translation:Quotidien d'informations générales, régionales, locales. Politique, éducation, magazine.
Language (s): French
DAILY NEWSPAPER

La Manche Libre 224679
Editorial: Rue de Coutances, Saint-Lo 50950
Tel: 33 02 33 05 10 00
Email: direction@lamanchelibre.com **Web site:** http://www.lamanchelibre.fr
Freq: Weekly; **Circ:** 74836 OJD
Directeur Général - Directeur de la publication: Benoît Leclerc
Profile: Information générale et départementale. PARUTIONS : Jeudi Edition Calvados : Le Bessin Libre - Le Bocage Libre. Diffusion : 7 éditions couvrant la Manche et l'Ouest du Calvados.
Language (s): French
DAILY NEWSPAPER

La Marne 224680
Editorial: 79 avenue de l'Epinette ZI, BP 27, Meaux 77102 **Tel:** 33 01 64 23 35 00
Email: ig@journal-lamarne.fr
Freq: Weekly; **Circ:** 14157 OJD
Editeur: Olivier Bassine
Profile: Hebdomadaire d'informations régionales. PARUTIONS : mercredi
Language (s): French
Ad Rate: Full Page Mono 4318.00
Ad Rate: Full Page Colour 7971.00
Currency: Euro
DAILY NEWSPAPER

La Marseilise 158782
Editorial: 19 cours d'Estienne d'Orves, BP 91862, Marseille 13222 **Tel:** 33 04 91 57 75 00
Email: lamars@lamarseilaise.fr **Web site:** http://www.journal-lamarseillaise.com
Freq: Daily; **Circ:** 139000 Publisher's Statement
Informations générales Politique: Pierre Bastien; **PDG - Directeur de la Publication:** Jean-Louis Bousquet; **Faits divers - Justice:** David Coquille; **Gastronomie - Vins:** Pierre Galaud; **Industries Techniques:** Gerard Lanux; **Rédacteur en chef:** Rolland Martinez; **Faits divers:** Philippe Pujol; **Education - Formation:** Catherine Walgienwtiz
Profile: 7 Titres : l'Hérault du Jour, La Marseillaise du Gard, La Marseillaise Vaucluse, La Marseillaise des Alpes, La Marseillaise Bouches du Rhône, La Marseillaise Marseille, La Marseillaise Le Varois. Diffusé en région PACA.
Language (s): French
Ad Rate: Full Page Mono 5670.00
Ad Rate: Full Page Colour 7371.00
Currency: Euro
DAILY NEWSPAPER

MARSEILLE L'HEBDO 244806
Owner: GROUPE HERSANT MEDIA
Editorial: 248 avenue Roger Salengro, BP 100, Marseille 13326 **Tel:** 33 04 91 84 47 47
Email: redaction@marseillelhebdo.com **Web site:** http://www.marseillelhebdo.com
Freq: Weekly; **Circ:** 12503 OJD
Directeur de la publication: Didier Pillet
Profile: City magazine d'informations sur Marseille. PARUTIONS : le mardi
Language (s): French
DAILY NEWSPAPER

MARSEILLEPLUS 157464
Owner: GROUPE HERSANT MEDIA
Editorial: 248 avenue Roger Salengro, Marseille 13015 **Tel:** 33 04 91 84 80 00
Freq: Daily; **Circ:** 56477 OJD
Rédactrice: Alexanda Cefaï; **Directeur de la publication:** Didier Pillet
Profile: Quotidien régional GRATUIT d'informations générales et locales.
Language (s): French
Ad Rate: Full Page Mono 2900.00
Ad Rate: Full Page Colour 3480.00
Currency: Euro
DAILY NEWSPAPER

Le Mauricien 156682
Owner: Le Mauricien Ltd
Editorial: 8 St Georges Street, Port Louis
Tel: 230 207 8200
Email: redaction@lemauricien.com **Web site:** http://www.lemauricien.com
Freq: Daily; **Circ:** 25000 Publisher's Statement
Directeur de Publication: Bernard Delaitre; **Publicité:** Anick Jean-Louis; **Directeur:** Jacques Rivet
Profile: National daily newspaper covering general news and current affairs including politics, economy, society, culture and sport.
Language (s): French
Ad Rate: Full Page Mono 1303.00
Ad Rate: Full Page Colour 1629.00
Currency: United States Dollars
DAILY NEWSPAPER

Mauritius Times 224399
Owner: Prakash Ramlallah Foundation
Editorial: 23 Bourbon Street, Port Louis
Tel: 230 292 93 01
Email: mtimes@intnet.mu **Web site:** http://www.mauritiustimes.com

Circ: 13500 Publisher's Statement
Advertising Manager: Sultana Kurmaly; **Rédacteur en Chef:** Madhukar Ramlallah
Profile: Newspaper focusing on national and international news and current affairs including, astrology, cookery, fitness, health, education, celebrities, spirituality and women's interest.
Language (s): English
DAILY NEWSPAPER

Le Mensuel de Rennes 665870

Owner: Le Mensuel
Editorial: 1 Quai Lamennais, Rennes 35000
Tel: 33 2 99 79 04 65
Email: rennes@lemensuel.com **Web site:** http://www.rennes.lemensuel.com
Freq: Monthly; **Circ:** 10000 Publisher's Statement
Picture Editor: Romain Joly; **Editor in Chief:** Nicolas Legendre; **News Director:** Killian Tribouillard
Profile: Magazine covering regional news and current affairs.
Language (s): French
DAILY NEWSPAPER

Le Messager 224502

Owner: GROUPE LA VOIX DU NORD
Editorial: 22 avenue du General de Gaulle, BP 102, Thonon-Les-Bains 74201 **Tel:** 33 04 50 71 10 14
Email: sthomas@lemessager.fr **Web site:** http://www.lemessager.fr
Freq: Weekly; **Circ:** 25415 OJD
Président Directeur Général: Alain Bodart; **Rédacteur en chef:** Samuel Thomas
Profile: Journal régional d'informations. PARUTIONS : jeudi. 3 EDITIONS : Chablais - Genevois - Faucigny.
Language (s): French
Ad Rate: Full Page Mono 2225.00
Ad Rate: Full Page Colour 2670.00
Currency: Euro
DAILY NEWSPAPER

Métro - Edition de Lyon 710796

Owner: PUBLICATIONS METRO FRANCE
Editorial: 25 rue Paul-Chenavard, Lyon 69001
Tel: 33 4 72 77 01 90
Web site: http://www.metrofrance.com/info-locale/lyon
Freq: Daily; **Circ:** 46000 Publisher's Statement
Profile: Local Translation: Actualités nationales et locales.
Language (s): French
DAILY NEWSPAPER

Métro: Edition de Lille 711313

Owner: PUBLICATIONS METRO FRANCE
Editorial: 11 rue Masurel, Lille 59000
Tel: 33 3 20 74 66 67
Web site: http://www.metrofrance.com/info-locale/lille
Freq: Daily; **Circ:** 33000 Publisher's Statement
Profile: Local Translation: Actualités nationales et locales.
Language (s): French
DAILY NEWSPAPER

Métro: Edition de Toulouse 710797

Owner: PUBLICATIONS METRO FRANCE
Editorial: 12 rue Gabriel-Peri, Toulouse 31000
Tel: 33 5 34 44 13 00
Web site: http://www.metrofrance.com/info-locale/toulouse
Freq: Daily; **Circ:** 33500 Publisher's Statement
Profile: Local Translation: Actualités nationales et locales.
Language (s): French
DAILY NEWSPAPER

Metronews 157465

Owner: Metro France
Editorial: 35, rue Greneta, Paris 75002
Tel: 33 1 55 34 45 00
Email: metronewsfr@gmail.com **Web site:** http://www.metronews.fr
Freq: Mon thru Fri; **Circ:** 632000 Publisher's Statement
President: Jean-Michel Arnaud; **Public Relation Manager:** Frédéric Henry
Profile: Free regional daily newspaper focussing on general news and current affairs including sports, culture, celebrities, technology, entertainment and video.
Language (s): French
Ad Rate: Full Page Mono 43400.00
Ad Rate: Full Page Colour 62000.00
Currency: Euro
DAILY NEWSPAPER

Midi Libre 366102

Owner: Midi Libre
Editorial: Rue du Mas-de-Grille, Saint-Jean-De-Vedas 34438 **Tel:** 33 4 67 07 67 07
Email: midiloisirs@midilibre.com **Web site:** http://www.midilibre.fr
Freq: Daily; **Circ:** 147392 OJD
Chef de Rédaction: Paul Caraci; **Bureau Chief:** Frédéric Gautier; **Rédacteur en Chef:** François Martin; **Bureau Chief:** Monique Raynaud
Profile: Regional daily newspaper focussing on local, regional and national news and current affairs including entertainment, sports and culture.
Language (s): French
Ad Rate: Full Page Colour 14882.00
Currency: Euro
DAILY NEWSPAPER

MIDI LIBRE EDITION BEZIERS 157473

Owner: MIDI LIBRE
Editorial: 23 rue Jean Roger, Agde 34301
Tel: 33 4 67 94 48 85
Email: redac.agde@midilibre.com **Web site:** http://www.midilibre.com
Freq: Daily; **Circ:** 22450 Publisher's Statement
Chef d'Agence: Arnaud Boucomont; **Rédacteur (trice):** Laurent Vermorel
Profile: Regional daily newspaper focussing on news and current affairs. Local Translation:Quotidien régional d'informations. 6 pages locales + 6 pages villages.
Language (s): French
DAILY NEWSPAPER

Midi Libre Edition Nimes Camargue 157468

Owner: Midi Libre
Editorial: 27 ter quai General-de-Gaulle, Beaucaire 30300 **Tel:** 33 4 66 58 51 98
Email: loisirsgard@midilibre.com **Web site:** http://www.midilibre.com
Freq: Daily
Rédacteur en Chef: François Charcellay; **Rédacteur (trice):** Thierry Montaner; **Pigiste:** Geneviève Oliva
Profile: Regional daily newspaper focusing on regional and local news and current affairs.
Language (s): French
DAILY NEWSPAPER

Le Militant 156740

Owner: Mouvement Militant Mauricien
Editorial: 21 Podriere Street, Port Louis
Tel: 230 212 65 53
Email: lemilitant69@yahoo.fr **Web site:** http://www.lemilitant.com
Circ: 8000 Publisher's Statement
Directeur de Publication: Rajesh Bhagwan; **Rédacteur en Chef:** Ananda Rajoo
Profile: National weekly newspaper focussing on regional and international news, current affairs, politics, economics, society, culture and sport.
Language (s): French
Ad Rate: Full Page Mono 19200.00
Ad Rate: Full Page Colour 24000.00
Currency: Mauritius Rupees
DAILY NEWSPAPER

MINIZOU 544403

Editorial: La Petite Presse, 54 montée des Clarines, Jarrie 38560 **Tel:** 33 04 76 04 98 30
Email: minizou38@free.fr **Web site:** http://www.minizou.fr
Freq: Bi-Monthly; **Circ:** 22000 Publisher's Statement
Directrice de la publication: Hélène Jusselin
Profile: Périodique GRATUIT rassemblant l'actualité jeune public (0-14 ans)en Dauphiné. PARUTIONS : 5 n°/an (23 avril, 1er juillet, 22 septembre, 2 décembre, 13 février).
Language (s): French
DAILY NEWSPAPER

Le Monde 158753

Owner: Le Monde
Editorial: 80, boulevard Auguste Blanqui, Paris 75707 **Tel:** 33 1 57 28 20 00
Email: communication2@lemonde.fr **Web site:** http://www.lemonde.fr
Freq: Daily; **Circ:** 319418 OJD
Editor in Chief: Michel Kajman; **Editor in Chief:** Arnaud Leparmentier; **Editor in Chief:** Franck Nouchi; **Editor in Chief:** Cécile Prieur; **Publisher:** Michel Sfeir; **Nicole Vulser:** Nicole Vulser
Profile: National newspaper covering national and international news and current affairs including politics, society, economy, culture, sports, science, technology and lifestyle.
Language (s): French
Ad Rate: Full Page Mono 89000.00
Ad Rate: Full Page Colour 116800.00
Currency: Euro
DAILY NEWSPAPER

La Montagne 742169

Owner: GROUPE CENTRE FRANCE - LA MONTAGNE
Editorial: 28 rue Morel Ladeuil, Clermont Ferrand 63056 **Tel:** 33 04 73 17 17 17
Email: redaction@centrefrance.com **Web site:** http://www.lamontagne.fr
Freq: Daily; **Circ:** 197424 OJD
ISSOIRE - HAUTE-LOIRE: Olivier Chaperon; **Chef de Rédaction Magazine:** Jack Lamiable; **MONTLUCON:** Jean-Marc Laurent; **MOULINS:** Eric Moine; **GUERET:** Hervé Moisan; **Rédacteur en chef:** Philippe Rousseau
Profile: Edition du dimanche Groupe : 169 907ex.- Quadrichromie : Tous les jours. 8 pages possibles selon configuration. Diffusé en Auvergne et dans le Limousin.
DAILY NEWSPAPER

LA Montagne Clermont-Ferrand 157334

Owner: CENTRE FRANCE
Editorial: 45 rue du Clos-Four, BP 83, Clermont-Ferrand 63056 CEDEX 2 **Tel:** +33 4 73 17 17 17
Email: locale@centrefrance.com **Web site:** http://www.lamontagne.fr
Freq: Daily; **Circ:** 199806
Chef de Rédaction: Jean-Philippe Bertin; **Chef de Rédaction:** Rémi Bouquet des Chaux; **Chef de Rédaction:** Michel Fillière; **Chef de Rédaction:** Didier Lagedamon; **Chef de Rédaction:** Christophe Préault; **Rédacteur en Chef:** Philippe Rousseau; **Rédacteur en Chef Technique:** Philippe Vazeille
Profile: Regional newspaper - Sports - Current events. Local Translation: Quotidien régional - Sports - Informations générales.
Language (s): French
Ad Rate: Full Page Mono 10990.00
Currency: Euro
DAILY NEWSPAPER

LA Montagne Edition De L'allier Montlucon 157343

Owner: CENTRE FRANCE
Editorial: 13 avenue Marx-Dormoy, Montlucon 3100
Tel: +33 4 70 02 21 00
Email: montlucon@centrefrance.com **Web site:** http://www.lamontagne.fr
Freq: Daily; **Circ:** 191639 Publisher's Statement
Pigiste: Jean Chapy; **Chef d'Agence:** Jean-Marc Laurent
Profile: Regional and local news. 1,60 € on Sunday. Local Translation:Informations régionales et locales. 1,60 € le dimanche.
Language (s): French
DAILY NEWSPAPER

LA Montagne Edition Du Puy-De-Dome Issoire 157342

Owner: CENTRE FRANCE
Editorial: 33 boulevard Jules-Cibrand, Issoire 63500
Tel: +33 4 73 55 25 00
Email: issoire@centrefrance.com **Web site:** http://www.lamontagne.fr
Freq: Daily; **Circ:** 191639 Publisher's Statement
Chef d'Agence: Olivier Chapperon
Profile: Regional and local news. Local Translation:Informations régionales et locales.
Language (s): French
DAILY NEWSPAPER

LA Montagne Edition Du Puy-De-Dome Riom 157337

Owner: CENTRE FRANCE
Editorial: 47 rue du Commerce, Riom 63200 **Tel:** +33 4 73 67 10 00
Email: riom@centrefrance.com **Web site:** http://www.lamontagne.fr
Freq: Daily; **Circ:** 191639 Publisher's Statement
Chef d'Agence: Eric Barbier
Profile: Regional and local news.
Language (s): French
DAILY NEWSPAPER

LA Montagne Edition Du Puy-De-Dome Thiers-Ambert 157341

Owner: CENTRE FRANCE
Editorial: 10 rue de la Republique, Ambert 63600
Tel: +33 4 73 82 44 32
Email: ambert@centrefrance.com **Web site:** http://www.lamontagne.fr
Freq: Daily; **Circ:** 191639 Publisher's Statement
Pigiste: Thomas Chastel; **Chef d'Agence:** Michel Conry; **Chef d'Agence:** Laurence Couperier; **Pigiste:** Denis Lorut
Profile: National, regional and local news. TV guide and woman supplement on Sunday.
Language (s): French
DAILY NEWSPAPER

NEUILLY - Journal indépendant 224519

Editorial: 80 avenue Charles de Gaulle, Neuilly Sur Seine 92200 **Tel:** 33 01 46 24 75 06
Email: syham@neuillyjournal.com **Web site:** http://www.neuillyjournal.com
Freq: Monthly; **Circ:** 27000 Publisher's Statement
Rédactrice en chef: Syham Nehab; **Directeur de la publication:** Louis-Robert Porte
Profile: Magazine destiné aux habitants de Neuilly S/ Seine. PARUTIONS : 11 n°/an : 1ère semaine du mois.
Language (s): French
Ad Rate: Full Page Mono 2135.00
Ad Rate: Full Page Colour 3354.00
Currency: Euro
DAILY NEWSPAPER

NICE MATIN 742170

Owner: GROUPE HERSANT MEDIA
Editorial: 214 route de Grenoble, Nice 6290
Tel: 33 04 93 18 28 38
Email: redacchef@nicematin.fr **Web site:** http://www.nicematin.fr
Freq: Daily; **Circ:** 114605 OJD
Directeur des rédactions: Olivier Biscaye; **Médecine - Santé Pharmacie:** Nancy Cattan; **Magazine Cinéma Musique People:** Philippe Dupuy; **Politique:** Eric Neri; **Musique classique (Pigiste régulier):** André Peyregne
Profile: Edition du dimanche : 109 323ex - Utilisation de la quadrichromie - Tous les jours dans environ 16/ 20 pages.
DAILY NEWSPAPER

Nice-Matin - Siege Social 158793

Owner: GHM - GROUPE HERSANT MEDIA
Editorial: 214 route de Grenoble, Nice 06290 CEDEX 3 **Tel:** 33 4 93 18 28 38
Email: redacchef@nicematin.fr **Web site:** http://www.nicematin.com
Freq: Daily; **Circ:** 110224
Président Directeur Général: Dominique Bernard; **Directeur des Rédactions:** Olivier Biscaye; **Rédacteur (trice):** Nancy Cattan; **Président Directeur Général:** Eric Debry; **Chef d'Agence:** Pascale Primi; **Directeur Général Délégué:** frédéric Touraille
Profile: Regional newspaper for Nice and surrounding area, containing four pages devoted specifically to Monaco. Local Translation:Quotidien d'actualités régionales. L'édition du dimanche est réalisée par la même équipe de rédaction.Prix du samedi et du dimanche : 1,10 €.
Language (s): French
Ad Rate: Full Page Colour 33096.00
Currency: Euro
DAILY NEWSPAPER

Nice-Matin Edition De Cagnes-Sur-Mer 157487

Owner: GHM - GROUPE HERSANT MEDIA
Editorial: Le Paris, 8 place Général-de-Gaulle, Cagnes-Sur-Mer 6800 **Tel:** +33 4 92 13 85 10
Email: cagnes-sur-mer@nicematin.fr **Web site:** http://www.nicematin.fr
Freq: Daily; **Circ:** 220000 Publisher's Statement
Chef d'Agence: Thierry Suire
Profile: Regional daily newspaper focussing on news and current affairs. Local Translation:Quotidien régional d'informations.
Language (s): French
DAILY NEWSPAPER

NICE-MATIN EDITION DE NICE 157484

Owner: GHM - GROUPE HERSANT MEDIA
Editorial: 15-17 rue de la Liberte, Nice 6000
Tel: 33 4 97 03 24 50
Email: agencenice@nicematin.fr **Web site:** http://www.nicematin.fr
Freq: Daily; **Circ:** 367000
Chef d'Agence: Pascale Primi
Profile: Regional daily newspaper focussing on local and regional news and current affairs. Local Translation:Quotidien d'actualités régionales.
Language (s): French
DAILY NEWSPAPER

Nord Eclair 742171

Owner: La Voix du Nord
Editorial: 8, Place du General de Gaulle, Lille 59000
Tel: 33 3 20 78 40 40
Email: serviceclients@nordeclair.fr **Web site:** http://www.nordeclair.fr
Freq: Daily; **Circ:** 28622 OJD
Editor in Chief: Arnaud Dujardin; **Président - Directeur de la publication:** Jacques Hardoin
Profile: Regional daily newspaper covering general news and current affairs.
DAILY NEWSPAPER

NORD LITTORAL 158766

Editorial: 91 boulevard Jacquard, BP 108, Calais 62102 **Tel:** 33 03 21 19 12 13 12
Email: courrier@nord-littoral.fr **Web site:** http://www.nordlittoral.fr
Freq: Daily; **Circ:** 10182 OJD
Directeur général - Directeur de la publication: Pascal Dejean; **Rédacteur en chef Automobile:** Henri Desvignes; **Chronique judiciaire Faits divers:** Jean-François Duquene; **Internet - Multimédia Santé:** Laurent Geumetz
Profile: Zone de diffusion : Calais et bande littorale. Informations locales
Language (s): French
Ad Rate: Full Page Mono 1069.00
Ad Rate: Full Page Colour 1437.00
Currency: Euro
DAILY NEWSPAPER

NORMANDIE MAGAZINE 224520

Editorial: 330 rue Valvire, BP 414, Saint-Lo 50004
Tel: 33 02 33 77 32 70
Email: redaction@normandie-magazine.fr **Web site:** http://www.normandie-magazine.fr
Freq: Monthly; **Circ:** 20000 Publisher's Statement
Politique: Michel Boivin; **Politique:** Michel Bussi; **Jardins:** Pamela Currie; **Chroniqueur:** Albert Du Roy; **Directrice de la publication:** Catherine Forestier; **Maquettiste - PAO:** Julie Hec; **Politique:** Jean Quellien; **Maquettiste - PAO:** Régine Quevillon
Profile: Mensuel anglo-normand : Manche, Orne, Calvados, Seine-Maritime, Eure, Hampshire Wessex et Sussex, Jersey et Guernesey. Informations sur les activités économiques, politiques et culturelles de cette Euro-Région.
Language (s): French
Ad Rate: Full Page Colour 3810.00
Currency: Euro
DAILY NEWSPAPER

Le Nouvel Economiste 187005

Owner: Publications du nouvel Economiste
Editorial: 38 bis, rue du Fer à Moulin, Paris 75005
Tel: 33 1 58 30 64 64
Email: patrick.arnoux@nouveleconomiste.fr **Web site:** http://www.nouveleconomiste.fr
Freq: Weekly; **Circ:** 24952 OJD
Editor in Chief: Patrick Arnoux; **Multimédia - Internet Informatique Télécoms - Téléphone Nouvelles technolog:** Edouard Laugier; **Président - Directeur de la publication:** Henri Nijdam
Profile: Magazine covering economy and finance.
Language (s): French
Ad Rate: Full Page Colour 4900.00
Currency: Euro
DAILY NEWSPAPER

La Nouvelle Republique Des Pyrenees 158802
Owner: GROUPE DEPECHE DU MIDI
Editorial: 48 avenue Bertrand Barere, BP 730, Tarbes 65007 **Tel:** 33 05 62 44 05 05
Email: jean-louis.toulouze@nrpyrenees.com **Web site:** http://www.nrpyrenees.com
Freq: Daily; **Circ:** 12867 OJD
Président Directeur Général: Jean-Michel Baylet; **Informations générales:** Philippe Dourthe; **Directeur de la publication:** Bernard Maffre
Profile: Utilisation de la quadrichromie : dans les pages une, trois, avant dernière et & dernière. PARUTIONS : le matin
Language (s): French
Ad Rate: Full Page Mono 2580.00
Currency: Euro
DAILY NEWSPAPER

La Nouvelle République du Centre-Ouest 157353
Editorial: 232 avenue de Grammont, Tours 37048
Tel: 33 2 47 31 70 00
Email: nr.redactionenchef@nrco.fr **Web site:** http://www.lanouvellerepublique.fr
Freq: Daily; **Circ:** 205288 OJD
Rédacteur en chef: Bruno Becard; **News Editor:** Denis Daumin; **Chef du service conseils aux lecteurs:** Yves Mary; **Multimédia:** Chantal Petillat; **Directeur de la publication:** Olivier Saint-Cricq
Profile: Regional daily newspaper covering general news and current affairs including politics, economics, sports and leisure.
Language (s): French
Ad Rate: Full Page Mono 7962.00
Ad Rate: Full Page Colour 10816.00
Currency: Euro
DAILY NEWSPAPER

LA Nouvelle République du Centre-Ouest Dimanche 437631
Owner: LA NOUVELLE REPUBLIQUE DU CENTRE OUEST
Editorial: 232 avenue de Grammont, Tours 37048 CEDEX 1 **Tel:** 33 2 47 31 70 00
Email: nrd@nrco.fr **Web site:** http://www.lanouvellerepublique.fr
Freq: Weekly; **Circ:** 38122 Publisher's Statement
Directeur de Publication: Olivier Saint-Cricq
Profile: National and regional news, sport and leisure sections. Leisure columns: garden, table, health, fashion, decoration, family relationship, travel, new technologies, Internet, your money, new records, books, DVD, comics, and video games. 1 single issue per region. Women over 40 years old.Local Translation: Actualité régionale et nationale, une partie magazine : jardin, à table, nouvelles technologies, Internet, nouveautés disques, livres, dvd, jeux vidéo, consommation.1 édition par département. Femme à partir de 40 ans
Language (s): French
DAILY NEWSPAPER

LA Nouvelle Republique Du Centre-Ouest Edition Sud Deux-Sevres 157347
Owner: LA NOUVELLE REPUBLIQUE DU CENTRE OUEST
Editorial: 10 place de la Comedie, BP 350, Niort 79003 CEDEX **Tel:** 33 5 49 77 27 77
Email: nr.niort@nrco.fr **Web site:** http://www.lanouvellerepublique.fr
Freq: Daily; **Circ:** 52000 Publisher's Statement
Profile: Local, regional and national news: covering politics, finance, art, entertainment, sports, leisure, practical information, and associative life. General news: Sports supplement on Monday – Weekend leisure supplement on Thursday - Weekly TV guide supplement on Saturday - Classified advertisement supplement on Saturday. Local Translation:- Informations locales, régionales, nationales : politique, économie, arts et spectacles, sports, loisirs, informations pratiques, vie associative. - Informations générales.- Cahier des sports le lundi. - 1 supplément loisirs week-end le jeudi.- 1 supplément hebdo TV le samedi. - Cahier petites annonces le samedi.
Language (s): French
Ad Rate: Full Page Mono 5428.00
Ad Rate: Full Page Colour 7726.00
Currency: Euro
DAILY NEWSPAPER

Les Nouvelles Calédoniennes 586950
Owner: GHM - GROUPE HERSANT MEDIA
Editorial: 41, 43 rue de Sebastopol, B.P. G5, Noumea 98848 **Tel:** 687 2 72 58 4
Email: lnc@canl.nc **Web site:** http://www.lnc.nc
Freq: Daily; **Circ:** 21000 Publisher's Statement
Editor in Chief: Patrick Blain; **Directeur Délégué:** François Levassor; **Directeur de Publication:** Thierry Massé; **Rédacteur en Chef:** Xavier Serre
Profile: Regional daily newspaper covering regional, national and international news and current affairs in New Caledonia including politics, economics, society, sport, classifieds, legal ads, leisure, motoring and TV guide.
Language (s): French
DAILY NEWSPAPER

LES NOUVELLES DE MAYOTTE 557304
Owner: NOUVELLES DE MAYOTTE
Editorial: Kaweni, BP 796, Mamoudzou 97600
Tel: 269 6 39 68 65 65
Email: nouvdemay@wanadoo.fr
Freq: Daily
Rédacteur en Chef: Denis Herrmann; **Gérant:** Martine Herrmann
Language (s): French
DAILY NEWSPAPER

L' Opinion 870746
Owner: Bey Médias Presse & Internet
Editorial: 14 rue de Bassano, Paris 75116
Tel: 33 1 47 23 33 33
Email: contact@lopinion.fr **Web site:** http://www.lopinion.fr
Freq: Daily
Editor in Chief: Rémi Godeau
Profile: Daily newspaper covering national and international news and current affairs including business and politics.
Language (s): French
DAILY NEWSPAPER

L' Orne Combattante 224655
Owner: GROUPE PUBLIHEBDOS
Editorial: 24 rue Jules Gevelot, BP 018, Flers 61101
Tel: 33 02 33 62 15 15
Email: didier.gandon@publihebdos.fr
Freq: Weekly; **Circ:** 14729 OJD
Editeur - Directeur: Dominique Lecoq; **Rédacteur en chef:** Frédérick Mace
Profile: Hebdomadaire régional d'informations. PARUTIONS : jeudi.
Language (s): French
Ad Rate: Full Page Mono 2034.00
Ad Rate: Full Page Colour 3036.00
Currency: Euro
DAILY NEWSPAPER

L' Orne Hebdo 224656
Owner: GROUPE PUBLIHEBDOS
Editorial: 9 Place Poulet Malassis, BP 208, Alencon 61006 **Tel:** 33 02 33 82 15 15
Email: orne.hebdo@publihebdos.fr
Freq: Weekly; **Circ:** 10844 OJD
Rédacteur en chef: Jean-Marie Foubert; **Publisher:** Laurent Rebours
Profile: Hebdomadaire d'informations. PARUTIONS : mardi
Language (s): French
DAILY NEWSPAPER

Ouest France 158797
Owner: Ouest-France
Editorial: 10 rue du Breil, ZI Sud Est, Rennes 35051 CEDEX 9 **Tel:** +33 2 99 32 60 00
Email: redaction.multimedia@ouest-france.fr **Web site:** http://www.ouest-france.fr
Freq: Daily; **Circ:** 762233 Publisher's Statement
Director: Cyrille Pitois
Profile: Regional daily newspaper focussing on local and regional news and current affairs.
Language (s): French
Ad Rate: Full Page Mono 14740.00
Ad Rate: Full Page Colour 17688.00
Currency: Euro
DAILY NEWSPAPER

Ouest France Edition Calvados Caen 157515
Owner: OUEST FRANCE
Editorial: 14 place Pierre-Bouchard, BP 174, Caen 14010 CEDEX **Tel:** 33 2 31 38 32 32
Email: redaction.caen@ouest-france.fr **Web site:** http://www.ouest-france.fr
Freq: Daily
Director: Guillaume Ballard; **Publisher:** Josué Lebigre; **Manager:** Xavier Oriot
Profile: This regional newspaper prints daily and covers regional news including sports, culture, society, legal issues, economics, social issues and education.
Language (s): French
Ad Rate: Full Page Mono 5647.00
Ad Rate: Full Page Colour 6776.00
Currency: Euro
DAILY NEWSPAPER

Ouest France Edition De Cotes-D'armor Lannion-Paimpol 157501
Owner: OUEST FRANCE
Editorial: 1 rue de Viarmes, Lannion 22300
Tel: 33 2 96 46 21 20
Email: redaction.lannion@ouest-france.fr **Web site:** http://www.ouest-france.fr
Freq: Daily; **Circ:** 90000 Publisher's Statement
Chef de Rédaction: Loïc Beauverger; **Chef d'Agence:** Malika Meraouri
Profile: Regional daily newspaper focussing on local, regional, national and international news and current affairs. Local Translation:Informations internationales, nationales, régionales et locales.
Language (s): French
Ad Rate: Full Page Mono 4596.00
Ad Rate: Full Page Colour 5515.00
Currency: Euro
DAILY NEWSPAPER

Ouest France Edition de la Mayenne 157517
Owner: OUEST FRANCE
Editorial: 92 avenue Robert-Buron, Laval 53000
Tel: 33 2 43 59 15 59
Email: redaction.chateau-gontier@ouest-france.fr **Web site:** http://www.ouest-france.fr
Freq: Daily; **Circ:** 42000 Publisher's Statement
Chef d'Agence: Julien Belaud; **Chef de Rédaction:** Guillaume Le Du; **Chef d'Agence:** Mickaël Pichard
Profile: Regional daily newspaper focussing on general news and current affairs including politics, society, justice, sport, agriculture, education, training, economics, social and culture. Local Translation:Quotidien régional d'informations générales, avec les rubriques : politique, société, justice, sport, agriculture, éducation, formation, économie, social, culture.
Language (s): French
Ad Rate: Full Page Mono 5975.00
Ad Rate: Full Page Colour 7170.00
Currency: Euro
DAILY NEWSPAPER

OUEST FRANCE EDITION DU FINISTERE BREST 157514
Owner: OUEST FRANCE
Editorial: 24 rue Algesiras, Brest 29200
Tel: 33 2 98 33 22 00
Email: redaction.brest@ouest-france.fr **Web site:** http://www.ouest-france.fr
Freq: Daily
Chef d'Agence: Nelly Cloarec; **Chef de Rédaction:** Olivier Pauly
Profile: Regional daily newspaper focussing on general news and current affairs including culture, society, justice, defence, weapons, sport, health, education, training, economics and social. Local Translation:Quotidien régional d'informations générales, avec les rubriques culture, société, justice, défense, armement, sport, santé, éducation, formation, économie, social.
Language (s): French
Ad Rate: Full Page Mono 4793.00
Ad Rate: Full Page Colour 5752.00
Currency: Euro
DAILY NEWSPAPER

OUEST FRANCE EDITION DU FINISTERE QUIMPER 157503
Owner: OUEST FRANCE
Editorial: 24 boulevard Dupleix, BP 1129, Quimper 29101 **Tel:** 33 2 98 90 93 93
Email: redaction.douarnenez@ouest-france.fr **Web site:** http://www.ouest-france.fr
Freq: Daily
Chef d'Agence: Nicolas Emeriau; **Chef d'Agence:** Renée-Laure Euzen; **Chef de Rédaction:** Christian Gouerou
Profile: Regional daily newspaper focussing on local, regional and national news and current affairs. Local Translation:Informations générales, nationales, régionales et locales. Siège à Rennes.
Language (s): French
Ad Rate: Full Page Mono 6074.00
Ad Rate: Full Page Colour 7288.00
Currency: Euro
DAILY NEWSPAPER

OUEST FRANCE EDITION DU MAINE-ET-LOIRE ANGERS-SEGRE 157497
Owner: OUEST FRANCE
Editorial: 5 bis rue Thiers, BP 65117, Angers 49051
Tel: 33 2 41 25 62 00
Email: redaction.angers@ouest-france.fr **Web site:** http://www.ouest-france.fr
Freq: Daily
Chef de Rédaction: Jean-Philippe Nicoleau; **Chef de Rédaction:** Arnaud Wajdzik
Profile: Regional daily newspaper focussing on regional news and current affairs including cultural heritage, culture, environment, tourism, agriculture, education training, economics, social, sport, justice and professional training. Local Translation:Toute l'actualité du Maine et Loire + pages générales. Rubriques : patrimoine culturel, environnement, tourisme, agriculture, culture, éducation, formation, économie, social, sports, justice, formation professionnelle.
Language (s): French
Ad Rate: Full Page Mono 3874.00
Ad Rate: Full Page Colour 4647.00
Currency: Euro
DAILY NEWSPAPER

Ouest France Edition Du Morbihan Lorient 157510
Owner: OUEST FRANCE
Editorial: 55 rue du Port, Lorient 56100 **Tel:** +33 2 97 84 43 00
Email: redaction.lorient@ouest-france.fr **Web site:** http://www.ouest-france.fr
Freq: Daily; **Circ:** 112000 Publisher's Statement
Chef de Rédaction: Vincent Jarnigon
Profile: Regional daily newspaper focussing on local, regional, national and international news and current affairs. Local Translation:Informations régionales et locales, internationales, nationales, départementales.
Language (s): French
Ad Rate: Full Page Mono 6401.00
Ad Rate: Full Page Colour 7682.00
Currency: Euro
DAILY NEWSPAPER

Ouest France Edition Du Morbihan Vannes 157519
Owner: OUEST FRANCE
Editorial: 15 rue Thomas-de-Closmadeuc, Vannes 56000 **Tel:** +33 2 97 47 42 05
Email: redaction.vannes@ouest-france.fr **Web site:** http://www.ouest-france.fr
Freq: Daily; **Circ:** 112000 Publisher's Statement
Chef de Rédaction: Yves-Marie Robin
Profile: Regional daily newspaper focussing on local, regional, national and international news and current affairs including agriculture.
Language (s): French
Ad Rate: Full Page Mono 6861.00
Ad Rate: Full Page Colour 8234.00
Currency: Euro
DAILY NEWSPAPER

Ouest France Edition Loire-Atlantique 157495
Owner: OUEST FRANCE
Editorial: 2 quai Francois-Mitterrand, BP 80319, Nantes 44203 CEDEX 2 **Tel:** 33 2 40 44 69 69
Email: redaction.nantes@ouest-france.fr **Web site:** http://www.ouest-france.fr
Freq: Daily
Chef de Rédaction: Joël Bigorgne
Profile: Regional daily newspaper focusing on local and regional news and current affairs.
Language (s): French
Ad Rate: Full Page Mono 5220.00
Ad Rate: Full Page Colour 6264.00
Currency: Euro
DAILY NEWSPAPER

Ouest France Editions Sarthe Nord Et Sarthe Sud 157533
Owner: OUEST FRANCE
Editorial: 9-11 quai Ledru-Rollin, Le Mans 72000
Tel: 33 2 43 21 76 76
Email: redaction.lemans@ouest-france.fr **Web site:** http://www.ouest-france.fr
Freq: Daily; **Circ:** 73500 Publisher's Statement
Rédacteur (trice): Stéphane Bois; **Chef de Rédaction:** Matthieu Marin
Profile: Regional daily newspaper focussing on general news and current affairs. Local Translation:Toute l'actualité de la Sarthe et des pages générales.
Language (s): French
Ad Rate: Full Page Mono 4432.00
Ad Rate: Full Page Colour 5318.00
Currency: Euro
DAILY NEWSPAPER

Le Parisien 232392
Owner: Amaury Médias
Editorial: 25 avenue Michelet, Saint-Ouen 93408 CEDEX **Tel:** 33 1 40 10 40 46
Email: edition75@leparisien.presse.fr **Web site:** http://www.leparisien.fr
Freq: Daily; **Circ:** 468576 Publisher's Statement
Editor in Chief: Stéphane Albouy; **Editor in Chief:** Matthieu Croissandeau; **Editor in Chief:** Béatrice Madeline; **Editor in Chief:** François Vey
Profile: Newspaper covering regional, national and international news and current affairs including society, politics, economics, motoring, celebrities, media, technology, science and health.
Language (s): French
Ad Rate: Full Page Mono 11190.00
Ad Rate: Full Page Colour 18240.00
Currency: Euro
DAILY NEWSPAPER

Patrimoines en région 665874
Editorial: Le Passe Muraille Association, 510A, av.de Barcelone-Le Jupiter, Montpellier 34080
Tel: 33 4 67 06 96 04
Email: redaction@lepassemuraille.org **Web site:** http://www.carrefour-des-patrimoines.net
Freq: 3 Times/Year; **Circ:** 30000 Publisher's Statement
Directeur de la Rédaction: René Lechon; **Directeur de Publication:** Pierre Plancheron
Profile: Local Translation: Revue régionale d'éducation au territoire par les patrimoines.Complétée par l'édition (200000 exemplaires) 1 fois par an (en juin) de 'L'Agenda du Patrimoine' qui annonce tous les événements liés aux patrimoines culturel et naturel (balades et visites, concerts et spectacles vivants, gastronomie, vins et terroir, festivités et traditions, expositions...).
Language (s): French
DAILY NEWSPAPER

PATRIOTE COTE D'AZUR - PCA HEBDO 224469
Editorial: 3 passage Macari, Nice 6300
Tel: 33 04 97 00 09 00
Email: redaction@le-patriote.info **Web site:** http://www.le-patriote.info
Freq: Weekly; **Circ:** 12500 Publisher's Statement
Cinéma (Pigiste): Etienne Ballerini; **Cinéma (Pigiste):** Gérard Camy; **Rédacteur en chef .:** Julien Camy; **Directeur de la publication:** Jack-André Clausse; **Directeur Politique:** Jean-Paul Duparc; **Jazz (Pigiste):** Jean-Pierre Lamouroux; **Maquettiste:** Guy Viens
Profile: Hebdomadaire départemental du P.C.F. PARUTIONS : vendredi.
Language (s): French
Ad Rate: Full Page Mono 2350.00
Ad Rate: Full Page Colour 2930.00
Currency: Euro
DAILY NEWSPAPER

Le Pays 157607
Owner: L'ALSACE
Editorial: 10 faubourg de Montbeliard, BP 427, Belfort 90008 **Tel:** 33 3 84 46 67 69
Email: redaction-belfort@lepays.fr **Web site:** http://www.lepays.fr
Freq: Daily; **Circ:** 10000 Publisher's Statement
Chef de Rédaction: Catherine Daudenhan; **Chef d'Agence:** Pascal Lainé; **Président Directeur**

Général: Jean-Dominique Pretet; **Président Directeur Général:** Jacques Romann
Profile: Daily current events newspaper covering the north of the Franche-Conté region with 3 offices: Belfort, Lure, Montbéliard and 3 editions. Local Translation:Quotidien généraliste couvrant le Nord de la Franche-Comté avec 3 agences : Belfort, Lure, Montbéliard et 3 éditions.
Language (s): French
DAILY NEWSPAPER

Le Pays D'Entre Loire Et Rhone 224549

Editorial: 7 avenue Charles de Gaulle, Tarare 69170
Tel: 33 04 74 63 02 68
Email: agence.tarare@le-pays-roannais.com
Freq: Weekly; **Circ:** 10000 Publisher's Statement
Directrice de la publication: Marie-Pierre Bouligaud; **Président du Conseil de Surveillance:** Pierre Bouligaud
Profile: Hebdomadaire régional d'informations. Annonces légales - PARUTIONS : jeudi.
Language (s): French
Ad Rate: Full Page Mono 2925.00
Ad Rate: Full Page Colour 4408.00
Currency: Euro
DAILY NEWSPAPER

Le Pays Malouin 224551

Owner: GROUPE PUBLIHEBDOS
Editorial: 7 rue Emmanuel Le Guen, BP 183, Saint-Malo 35409 **Tel:** 33 02 99 40 27 00
Email: lepaysmalouin@publihebdos.fr **Web site:** http://www.publihebdos.fr
Freq: Weekly; **Circ:** 11389 OJD
Editeur - Rédacteur en chef: Christian Bouzols; **Rédactrice:** Virginie David; **Rédacteur:** Nicolas Evanno; **Rédactrice:** Adélaïde Hasle
Profile: Informations locales et annonces légales. PARUTIONS : jeudi
Language (s): French
DAILY NEWSPAPER

Le Pays Roannais 224552

Editorial: 10/12 rue de Sully, Roanne 42308
Tel: 33 04 77 44 47 47
Email: lepays@le-pays-roannais.com **Web site:** http://www.lepaysroannais.fr
Freq: Weekly; **Circ:** 28101 OJD
Directrice de la publication: Marie-Pierre Bouligaud; **Président du Conseil de Surveillance:** Pierre Bouligaud
Profile: Zone de diffusion : Loire, Rhône, Allier, Saône et Loire. Annonces légales PARUTIONS : jeudi.
Language (s): French
DAILY NEWSPAPER

Le Perche 224554

Owner: GROUPE PUBLIHEBDOS
Editorial: 14/16 Place de la Republique, Mortagne-Au-Perche 61400 **Tel:** 33 02 33 85 20 50
Email: le.perche@publihebdos.fr **Web site:** http://www.publihebdos.fr
Freq: Weekly; **Circ:** 11923 OJD
Informations Régionales: Amine El-Hasnaouy; **Informations Régionales:** Nathtalie Legendre; **Rédacteur en chef:** Luc Moriceau; **Publisher:** Laurent Rebours
Profile: Hebdomadaire régional d'information pour l'Orne, la Sarthe et l'Eure et Loir PARUTIONS : mercredi.
Language (s): French
Ad Rate: Full Page Mono 1856.00
Ad Rate: Full Page Colour 2410.00
Currency: Euro
DAILY NEWSPAPER

Le Petit Journal 224482

Owner: EDITIONS ARC EN CIEL
Editorial: 1300 avenue d'Ardus, BP 386, Montauban 82000 **Tel:** 33 05 63 20 80 00
Email: 82@lepetitjournal.net
Freq: Daily; **Circ:** 10500 Publisher's Statement
Directeur de la publication: Alain Paga
Profile: Journal d'informations locales.
Language (s): French
Ad Rate: Full Page Mono 457.00
Ad Rate: Full Page Colour 594.00
Currency: Euro
DAILY NEWSPAPER

LE Petit journal Pays Toulousain Lauragais 653156

Editorial: 1300 avenue d'Ardus, BP 386, Montauban 82003 CEDEX **Tel:** 33 5 63 20 80 00
Email: 31t@lepetitjournal.net **Web site:** http://www.lepetitjournal.net
Freq: Weekly; **Circ:** 52000 Publisher's Statement
Président: Alain Paga
Profile: Le Petit Journal affiche déjà plusieurs éditions dans le Grand Sud : Comminges-Sud Garonne, Ariège, Gers, Lot, Aveyron... Il existe aussi une édition Pays toulousain/Lauragais très riche en informations sur la ville rose. C'est un hebdomadaire d'informations générales paraissant le vendredi et habilité à publier les annonces légales et commerciales. Toutes les grandes rubriques de l'actualité sont abordées, de la grande ville au plus petit village de la périphérie toulousaine : politique, culture, sports, faits divers.
Language (s): French
DAILY NEWSPAPER

Le Petit Nicois 224556

Owner: EDITION D'AZUR
Editorial: Edition d'Azur, 2 rue Désiré Niel, Nice 6000
Tel: 33 04 93 13 79 89
Email: accueil@editiondazur.fr **Web site:** http://www.lepetitnicois.fr
Freq: Weekly; **Circ:** 10000 Publisher's Statement
Politique: Pascal Gaymard; **Maquettiste:** Nicolas Thomas; **Directeur des Relations Publiques:** Robert Verdoia
Profile: Hebdomadaire généraliste d'informations locales, de Menton à Antibes. PARUTIONS : le jeudi.
Language (s): French
DAILY NEWSPAPER

Le Phare De Re 224557

Editorial: 15 Quai Job Foran, BP 56, Saint-Martin-De-Re 17410 **Tel:** 33 05 46 09 21 09
Email: redaction@pharedere.com
Freq: Weekly; **Circ:** 20000 Publisher's Statement
Directrice Générale: Marie-Pascale Gugger; **Rédacteur en chef:** Yann Werdefroy
Profile: Journal d'intérêt local. PARUTIONS : mercredi + 3 suppléments GRATUITS : 'Guide L'Ile de Ré Pratique' (sortie fin juin, 65 000ex.), 'Bonnes adresses du Phare' (sortie à Pâques, 25 000ex.), 'L'Ile de Ré, à chacun sa saison' (Edition Automne : 20 000ex., Edition Hiver : 20 000ex.) + 1 mensuel GRATUIT 'SORTIR' (60 000ex./mois).
Language (s): French
Ad Rate: Full Page Colour 5000.00
Currency: Euro
DAILY NEWSPAPER

Le Populaire Du Centre 742173

Owner: GROUPE CENTRE FRANCE - LA MONTAGNE
Editorial: Rue du General Catroux, BP 541, Limoges 87011 **Tel:** 33 05 55 58 59 60
Email: lepopulaire@centrefrance.com **Web site:** http://www.lepopulaire.fr
Freq: Daily; **Circ:** 43868 OJD
Rédacteur en chef: Jean-Marc Courbarien; **Directeur délégué:** François Gilardi; **Médecine Pharmacie:** Dominique Pierson; **Directeur de la publication:** Alain Vedrine
Profile: Utilisation de la quadrichromie - Tous les jours dans une page sur deux.
DAILY NEWSPAPER

Les Potins D'Angele 528449

Editorial: 34 rue Tupin, Lyon 69002
Tel: 33 04 78 42 57 97
Email: redac@lespotinsdangele.com
Freq: Weekly; **Circ:** 12000 Publisher's Statement
Directeur de la publication: Gérard Angel
Profile: Hebdomadaire satirique de la vie Lyonnaise. PARUTIONS : le jeudi.
Language (s): French
DAILY NEWSPAPER

La Presse De Manche 157584

Editorial: 9 rue Gambetta, BP 408, Cherbourg 50104
Tel: 33 02 33 97 16 16
Email: redaction.locale@lapressedelamanche.fr
Freq: Daily; **Circ:** 25574 OJD
Faits divers: Ludovic Ameline; **PDG - Directeur de la publication:** Marcel Clairet; **Cuisine (Recettes):** Patricia Lelan-Roussel
Profile: Utilisation de la quadrichromie - Tous les jours - Dans les pages une et dernière. Edition du 7ème jour.
Language (s): French
Ad Rate: Full Page Mono 6640.00
Ad Rate: Full Page Colour 10624.00
Currency: Euro
DAILY NEWSPAPER

PRESSE OCEAN 742174

Owner: SIPA
Editorial: 5 rue Santeuil, BP 22418, Nantes 44024
Tel: 33 02 40 44 24 00
Email: redac.locale.nantes@presse-ocean.com **Web site:** http://www.presseocean.fr
Freq: Daily; **Circ:** 37943
Directeur général délégué: Jean-Paul Brunel; **Rédacteur en chef:** Marc Dejean; **PDG - Directeur de la publication:** Matthieu Fuchs
Profile: Utilisation de la quadrichromie tous les jours. OJD Edition du septième jour : 21 562ex. RENSEIGNEMENTS REDUITS A LA DEMANDE DU JOURNAL. Diffusé en Loire Atlantique.
Language (s): French
DAILY NEWSPAPER

PRESSE OCEAN - L'ECLAIR EDITION ST-NAZAIRE LA BAULE 157615

Owner: OUEST FRANCE
Editorial: 41 avenue du General-de-Gaulle, BP 235, Saint-Nazaire CEDEX **Tel:** 33 2 51 10 11 50
Email: redac.st-nazaire@presse-ocean.com **Web site:** http://www.presseocean.fr
Freq: Daily
Chef d'Agence: Martine Vaillant-Prot
Profile: 2 current affairs regional daily newspapers with the same journalists and columns: covering economy, social, politics, education, training, justice, sports... 1 guide in the summer. Local Translation:2 quotidiens régionaux d'informations générales avec les mêmes journalistes et les mêmes rubriques : économie, social, politique, culture, éducation-formation, justice, sports... 1 guide l'été.
Language (s): French
DAILY NEWSPAPER

Le Progres 742175

Editorial: 4 rue Montrochet, Lyon 69284
Tel: 33 04 72 22 23 23
Email: redactionenchef@leprogres.fr **Web site:** http://www.leprogres.fr
Freq: Daily; **Circ:** 223522 OJD
Rédacteur en chef: Xavier Antoye; **Politique intérieure:** Jacques Boucaud; **PDG - Directeur de la publication:** Gérard Colin; **Rédactrice en chef Bourg en Bresse:** Caroline Daeschler; **Directeur de la rédaction:** Pierre Fanneau; **Education - Enseignement:** Muriel Florin; **Rédacteur en chef Bourg en Bresse:** Hubert Guyon; **Directeur délégué:** Jean-Claude Lassalle; **Directeur d'édition - Ain:** Patrick Maitre; **Concerts:** Thierry Meissirel; **Directeur d'édition Jura:** Fabrice Veysseyre-Redon
Profile: Utilisation de la quadrichromie : tous les jours. OJD = LE PROGRES + LA TRIBUNE - Editions du Dimanche : 239 725ex www.leprogres.fr : 30 000 visiteurs uniques/jour (source éditeur). Diffusé en Rhône Alpes.
DAILY NEWSPAPER

Le Progrès - Edition Lyon-Villeurbanne-Caluire 158779

Owner: LE PROGRES
Editorial: 4 rue Paul-Montrochet, Lyon 69002
Tel: 33 4 72 22 23 23
Email: lprquartiers@leprogres.fr **Web site:** http://www.leprogres.fr
Freq: Daily; **Circ:** 222570 OJD
Directeur de la Rédaction: Xavier Antoyé; **Pigiste:** Julia Beaumet; **Président Directeur Général:** Gérard Colin; **Rédacteur en Chef:** Chantal Danon; **Directeur Général:** Pierre Fanneau; **Rédacteur en Chef:** Pascal Jalabert; **Directeur Délégué:** Jean-Claude Lassalle; **Rédacteur en Chef:** Philippe Pitaud; **Pigiste:** Christel Reynaud
Profile: Daily regional newspaper.
Language (s): French
Ad Rate: Full Page Mono 21812.00
Ad Rate: Full Page Colour 24110.00
Currency: Euro
DAILY NEWSPAPER

LE Progrès -Edition de l'Ain 157436

Owner: LE PROGRES
Editorial: 6 place Joubert, Bourg-En-Bresse 01006 CEDEX **Tel:** 33 4 74 21 66 66
Email: ain@leprogres.fr **Web site:** http://www.leprogres.fr
Freq: Daily; **Circ:** 45000 Publisher's Statement
Chef d'Agence: Karen Chevalier; **Chef d'Agence:** Laurent Jaouen; **Chef d'Agence:** François Le Stir
Profile: Daily regional newspaper including current events pages covering Bourg-en-Bresse, Le Bugey, La Dombes and La Bresse regions. Local Translation:Quotidien régional avec des pages d'actualités Bourg-en-Bresse, Le Bugey, La Dombes, La Bresse... Tirage de 56.000 exemplaires le dimanche.
Language (s): French
Ad Rate: Full Page Mono 3419.00
Currency: Euro
DAILY NEWSPAPER

La Provence 158784

Owner: Groupe Hersant Média
Editorial: 248 avenue Roger Salengro, Marseille 13015 **Tel:** 33 4 91 84 45 45
Email: contact@laprovence.com **Web site:** http://www.laprovence.com
Freq: Daily; **Circ:** 146772 OJD
Directeur Générale: Marc Auburtin; **Informations générales:** Philippe Bougan; **Internet:** Xavier Cherica; **Informations générales Etranger:** Frédéric Cheutin; **Informations générales:** Patrick Coulomb; **Informations générales:** Paule Cournet; **Directeur du développement Internet:** Jean-François Eyraud; **Politique:** Philippe Faner; **Informations générales:** Frédéric Guilledoux; **Internet:** Anthony Jammot; **Faits divers Justice:** Romain Luongo; **Informations générales:** Rémi Mathieu; **Publication Director:** Claude Perrier; **Informations générales:** Sylvain Pignol; **Internet:** Karine Portrait; **Faits divers Justice:** Laétitia Sariroglou; **Internet:** Audrey Savournin; **Informations générales:** Sabrina Testa; **Politique:** François Tonneau; **Informations générales:** Jean-Paul Vespini; **Informations générales:** Chistophe Vial
Profile: Newspaper covering regional and local news.
Language (s): French
Ad Rate: Full Page Mono 11000.00
Ad Rate: Full Page Colour 13750.00
Currency: Euro
DAILY NEWSPAPER

LA Provence: Edition de Carpentras 157368

Owner: GHM - GROUPE HERSANT MEDIA
Editorial: 144 place Aristide-Briand, Carpentras 84200 **Tel:** 33 4 90 67 66 65
Email: carpentras@laprovence-presse.fr **Web site:** http://www.laprovence.com
Freq: Daily; **Circ:** 27616 Publisher's Statement
Chef d'Agence: Christian Gravez
Profile: Regional daily current events newspaper.
Language (s): French
DAILY NEWSPAPER

LA Provence: Edition du Haut Vaucluse Orange 157366

Owner: GHM - GROUPE HERSANT MEDIA
Editorial: 21 rue Caristie, Orange 84100
Tel: 33 4 90 11 33 00
Email: orange@laprovence-presse.fr **Web site:** http://www.laprovence.com
Freq: Daily; **Circ:** 27616 Publisher's Statement
Chef d'Agence: Christine Blanc
Profile: Regional daily current events newspaper.
Language (s): French
DAILY NEWSPAPER

LA Provence: Edition Du Vaucluse 157361

Owner: GHM - GROUPE HERSANT MEDIA
Editorial: 18 rue de la Republique, Avignon 84000
Tel: 33 4 90 80 70 30
Email: avignon@laprovence-presse.fr **Web site:** http://www.laprovence.com
Freq: Daily; **Circ:** 27616 Publisher's Statement
Chef d'Agence: Philippe Thuru
Profile: Regional daily current events newspaper.
Language (s): French
DAILY NEWSPAPER

LA Provence: Edition Vaucluse Sud 157367

Owner: GHM - GROUPE HERSANT MEDIA
Editorial: 83 place de la Bouquerie, Apt 84400
Tel: 33 4 90 74 17 53
Email: apt@laprovence-presse.fr **Web site:** http://www.laprovence.com
Freq: Daily; **Circ:** 27616 Publisher's Statement
Chef d'Agence: Jacques Boudon
Profile: Regional daily current events newspaper. Local Translation:Quotidien régional d'informations générales.
Language (s): French
DAILY NEWSPAPER

Le Quotidien De La Reunion 343154

Editorial: UNAVAILABLE, Saint-Denis 97712
Tel: 33 02 62 92 15 15
Email: laredaction@lequotidien.re
Freq: Daily; **Circ:** 33020 OJD
Magazine: Florence Alavin; **Directeur Général:** Thierry Benbassat; **Magazine:** Stéphanie Buttard; **Directeur de la publication:** Maximin Chane Ki Chune; **Chef d'agence:** Mady Lebeau; **Jardin:** Vincent Pion; **Médecine - Santé:** Hervé Schulz
Profile: Quotidien d'informations générales et locales. Edition du 7ème jour : 31 980ex
Language (s): French
DAILY NEWSPAPER

La Renaissance 224685

Editorial: 13 rue des Deux Ponts, BP 112, Paray-Le-Monial 71603 **Tel:** 33 03 85 81 66 00
Email: journal@la-renaissance.net **Web site:** http://www.la-renaissance.net
Freq: Weekly; **Circ:** 12198 OJD
Directeur de la publication: Yves De La Gorce; **Rédactrice en chef:** Delphine Mignat
Profile: PARUTIONS : Vendredi - Informations générales et régionales du Bourbonnais, Charolais, Brionnais, Clusinois, Mâconnais et Allier.
Language (s): French
Ad Rate: Full Page Mono 1193.00
Ad Rate: Full Page Colour 1475.00
Currency: Euro
DAILY NEWSPAPER

Le Republicain De L'Essonne 224569

Owner: SEMIF Hebdos
Editorial: Boulevard des Champs Elysees, BP 76, Evry 91002 **Tel:** 33 01 69 36 57 09 91
Email: web@le-republicain.fr **Web site:** http://www.le-republicain.fr
Freq: Weekly; **Circ:** 12426 OJD
Dourdan - Etrechy - Etampes - Méréville: Olivia Bazenet; **Dourdan - Etrechy - Etampes - Méréville:** David Berthelem; **Corbeil-Essonnes - Mennecy - La Ferté-Alais - Evry Milly-la-Fôret - Val-de-:** Pauline Chastenet; **De Massy à Longjumeau - Palaiseau - Val-d'Yvette D'Athis Mons à Viry - Evry:** Nolween Cosson; **De Massy à Longjumeau - Palaiseau - Val-d'Yvette d'Athis-Mons à Viry - Evry:** Laura Duret; **Corbeil-Essonnes - Mennecy - La Ferté-Alais - Evry Milly-la-Fôret - Val-de-:** Marine Guillaume; **Directeur de la publication:** Robert Mendibure
Profile: Hebdomadaire d'information régionale et d'annonces paraissant le jeudi matin. PANORAMA : magazine hebdomadaire d'informations GRATUIT distribué sur le département à 100 000ex.
Language (s): French
DAILY NEWSPAPER

Le Republicain Lorrain 742176

Editorial: 3 avenue des Deux Fontaines, Woippy 57140 **Tel:** 33 3 87 34 17 89
Email: lrlinfo@republicain-lorrain.fr **Web site:** http://www.republicain-lorrain.fr
Freq: Daily; **Circ:** 137042 OJD
Chef du service Magazine: Michel Bitzer; **Editor in Chief:** Jean-Marc Lauer; **Musique classique:** Georges Masson; **Chef du service Reportage:** Pierre Roeder; **Magazine Médecine Science:** Didier Romand; **Directeur de la publication:** Pierre Wicker
Profile: Regional newspaper covering news and current affairs.
DAILY NEWSPAPER

Le Republicain Lorrain - Metz Bureau 365758

Owner: LE REPUBLICAIN LORRAIN
Editorial: 24 rue Serpenoise, Metz 57000
Tel: 33 3 87 38 58 00
Email: redaction.metz@republicain-lorrain.fr **Web site:** http://www.republicain-lorrain.fr

Freq: Daily; Circ: 145475 OJD
Rédacteur en Chef: Jean-Marc Lauer; **Directeur de Publication:** Pierre Wicker
Profile: Regional newspaprer newspaper covering international, national, regional and local news. Local Translation:Informations internationales, nationales, régionales, départementales, locales, magazine.
Language (s): French
Ad Rate: Full Page Mono 6240.00
Ad Rate: Full Page Colour 8112.00
Currency: Euro
DAILY NEWSPAPER

LE Républicain Lorrain Nancy 383408

Owner: LE REPUBLICAIN LORRAIN
Editorial: 33 rue des Carmes, Nancy 54000
Tel: 33 3 83 35 50 48
Email: redaction.nancy@republicain-lorrain.fr **Web site:** http://www.republicain-lorrain.fr
Freq: Daily; **Circ:** 40000 Publisher's Statement
Chef d'Agence: Monique Raux
Profile: International, national, regional and local news, magazine. Local Translation:Informations internationales, nationales, régionales, départementales, locale, magazine.
Language (s): French
DAILY NEWSPAPER

La Republique De Seine Et Marne 224688

Owner: GROUPE PUBLIHEBDOS
Editorial: 3 boulevard Victor Hugo, BP 22, Melun 77001 **Tel:** 33 01 64 87 50 00
Email: redaction@larepublique.com **Web site:** http://www.larepublique.com
Freq: Weekly; **Circ:** 22063 OJD
Editeur: Thomas Martin
Profile: Diffusion : arrondissements de Melun, Fontainebleau, Torcy et Provins, sud et centre de la Seine et Marne. 2 éditions : Melun/Val de Seine/Sénart/Melun/Provins/Plaine de Brie - Fontainebleau/Nemours/Montereau. Journal d'informations locales et régionales. PARUTIONS : lundi
Language (s): French
DAILY NEWSPAPER

La Republique Des Pyrenees 157585

Owner: PYRENEES PRESSE
Editorial: 6/8 rue Despourrins, Pau 64002
Tel: 33 05 59 82 20 00
Email: desk@pyrenees.com **Web site:** http://www.pyrenees.com
Freq: Daily; **Circ:** 32465 OJD
Rédacteur en chef: Jean Marziou
Profile: Utilisation de la quadrichromie - Tous les jours
Language (s): French
Ad Rate: Full Page Mono 4347.00
Ad Rate: Full Page Colour 4706.00
Currency: Euro
DAILY NEWSPAPER

La République du Centre 742177

Owner: CENTRE FRANCE LA MONTAGNE
Editorial: 14 avenue des Droits de l'Homme, Orleans 45000 **Tel:** 33 2 38 78 79 80
Email: christine.broudic@centrefrance.com **Web site:** http://www.larep.fr
Freq: Daily; **Circ:** 51029 OJD
Pages Magazine: Katia Beaupetit; **Faits divers - ORLEANS:** Anthony Gautier; **Président délégué:** Michel Habouzit; **EURE ET LOIR - DREUX:** Philippe Marchand; **EURE ET LOIR - CHATEAUDUN:** Gérard Turpin
Profile: Regional newspaper covering regional news and current affairs.
Language (s): French
DAILY NEWSPAPER

LA République du Centre - Edition de Beaugency 410551

Owner: CENTRE FRANCE LA MONTAGNE
Editorial: 28 place du Martroi, Beaugency 45190
Tel: 33 2 38 46 92 10
Email: gb@larep.com **Web site:** http://www.larep.com
Freq: Daily; **Circ:** 51029 OJD
Profile: General, regional and local news. Local Translation:Informations générales, régionales, départementales et locales.
Language (s): French
Ad Rate: Full Page Colour 3838.00
Currency: Euro
DAILY NEWSPAPER

LA République du Centre - Edition de Dreux 157588

Owner: CENTRE FRANCE LA MONTAGNE
Editorial: 7 rue Aux Tanneurs, BP 50126, Dreux 28103 CEDEX **Tel:** 33 2 37 63 03 63
Email: ag.dreux@larep.com **Web site:** http://www.larep.com
Freq: Daily; **Circ:** 51029 Publisher's Statement
Profile: General, regional and local news. Local Translation:Informations générales, régionales, départementales et locales.
Language (s): French
DAILY NEWSPAPER

La République du Centre - Edition de Gien 157589

Owner: CENTRE FRANCE LA MONTAGNE
Editorial: 14 rue Victor-Hugo, Gien 45500
Tel: 33 2 38 29 85 85
Email: loiret.larep@centrefrance.com **Web site:** http://www.larep.com
Freq: Daily; **Circ:** 51029 OJD
Chef d'Agence: François Basley
Profile: Regional newspaper covering general, regional and local news.
Language (s): French
DAILY NEWSPAPER

LA République du Centre - Edition de Montagris 157590

Owner: CENTRE FRANCE LA MONTAGNE
Editorial: 48 rue Doree, Montargis 45200
Tel: 33 2 38 07 18 48
Email: agence.montargis@larep.com **Web site:** http://www.larep.com
Freq: Daily; **Circ:** 51029 Publisher's Statement
Chef d'Agence: Francis Bonnet
Profile: General, regional and local news. Local Translation:Quotidien d'informations générales, régionales et locales.
Language (s): French
DAILY NEWSPAPER

LA République du Centre - Edition de Nogent-Châteaudun 157587

Owner: CENTRE FRANCE LA MONTAGNE
Editorial: 22 place du 18-Octobre, Chateaudun 28200 **Tel:** 33 2 37 94 00 00
Email: ag.chateaudun@larep.com **Web site:** http://www.larep.com
Freq: Daily; **Circ:** 51029 OJD
Chef d'Agence: Philippe Abline
Profile: General and local news. Economy, politics, social life... Local Translation:Informations générales et locales, économie, politique, social.
Language (s): French
DAILY NEWSPAPER

LA République du Centre - Edition de Pithiviers 410550

Owner: CENTRE FRANCE LA MONTAGNE
Editorial: 31 rue de la Couronne, Pithiviers 45300
Tel: 33 2 38 30 22 44
Email: agence.pithiviers@larep.com **Web site:** http://www.larep.com
Freq: Daily; **Circ:** 51029 Publisher's Statement
Chef d'Agence: Stéphane Boutet
Profile: General, regional and local news. Local Translation:Informations générales, régionales, départementales et locales.
Language (s): French
DAILY NEWSPAPER

La République du Centre - Edition du Loiret 158772

Owner: CENTRE FRANCE LA MONTAGNE
Editorial: Rue de la Halte, BP 93035, Fleury-Les-Aubrais 45403 CEDEX **Tel:** 33 2 38 78 79 80
Email: loiret.larep@centrefrance.com **Web site:** http://www.larep.com
Freq: Daily; **Circ:** 51029 OJD
Rédacteur en Chef: Christine Broudic; **Chef d'Agence:** Anne-Marie Dufeu-Coursimault; **Chef de Rédaction:** Matthieu Villeroy
Profile: Regional newspaper covering general, regional and local news.
Language (s): French
DAILY NEWSPAPER

Le Reveil (neufchatel) 224571

Owner: GROUPE PUBLIHEBDOS
Editorial: 11 rue des Tanneurs, BP 100, Neufchatel-En-Bray 76270 **Tel:** 33 02 32 97 53 80
Email: reveil.neufchatel@publihebdos.fr **Web site:** http://www.publihebdos.fr
Freq: Weekly; **Circ:** 12554 OJD
Rédactrice: Sandrine Bossiere; **Rédacteur en chef:** Laurent Hellier; **Rédacteur:** Pierre-Emmanuel Reger; **Rédactrice:** Isabelle Villy; **Editrice:** Catherine Wilmart
Profile: 2 éditions : Pays de Bray, Bresle et Oise Hebdomadaire régional d'informations paraissant le jeudi
Language (s): French
Ad Rate: Full Page Mono 2482.00
Ad Rate: Full Page Colour 3229.00
Currency: Euro
DAILY NEWSPAPER

LE REVEIL DU VIVARAIS 224572

Editorial: 49 avenue de l'Europe, BP 51, Annonay 7102 **Tel:** 33 04 75 69 25 80
Email: contact@reveil-vivarais.fr **Web site:** http://www.reveil-vivarais.fr
Freq: Weekly; **Circ:** 12388 OJD
Rédacteur en chef: Jean-Pierre Bouaffar; **Rédactrice:** Marie-Cécile Chevrier; **Rédacteur:** Jacques Girodet; **Rédacteur:** Gwenaël Pocard; **Directeur Général:** Pierre-Yves Revol; **Rédacteur:** Yves Rivory
Profile: Hebdomadaire politique et d'information. PARUTIONS : jeudi. Zone de diffusion : Ardèche - Drôme - Loire - Isère
Language (s): French
Ad Rate: Full Page Mono 3165.00
Currency: Euro
DAILY NEWSPAPER

LE REVEIL NORMAND 224573

Owner: GROUPE PUBLIHEBDOS
Editorial: 19 bis rue des Emangeards, BP 143, L'aigle 61304 **Tel:** 33 02 33 24 42 33
Email: reveil.normand@publihebdos.fr **Web site:** http://www.publihebdos.fr
Freq: Weekly; **Circ:** 11311 OJD
Publisher: Laurent Rebours
Profile: Hebdomadaire régional d'informations. Zone de diffusion : 12 cantons de la moitié est de l'Orne, 4 cantons de l'Eure, 2 cantons d'Eure et Loir et périphérie. PARUTIONS : mercredi
Language (s): French
Ad Rate: Full Page Mono 1856.00
Ad Rate: Full Page Colour 2410.00
Currency: Euro
DAILY NEWSPAPER

Les Sab-Vendee Journal 224509

Owner: GROUPE PUBLIHEBDOS
Editorial: 16 ter rue de la Caisse d'Epargne, BP 29, Les Sables-D'olonne 85101 **Tel:** 33 02 51 95 42 12
Email: redaction.jds@publihebdos.fr
Freq: Weekly; **Circ:** 12598 OJD
Rédacteur en chef: Gérard Heraud; **Editeur:** Ludovic Robet; **Informations Régionales Loisirs:** Marion Travers
Profile: Hebdomadaire d'informations locales. PARUTIONS : jeudi.
Language (s): French
Ad Rate: Full Page Mono 2059.00
Ad Rate: Full Page Colour 2668.00
Currency: Euro
DAILY NEWSPAPER

Le Saint Affricain 224575

Editorial: 29 Boulevard Emile Borel, Saint-Affrique 12412 **Tel:** 33 05 65 49 25 64
Email: lesaintaffricain@wanadoo.fr **Web site:** http://www.lesaintaffricain.fr
Freq: Weekly; **Circ:** 10380 Publisher's Statement
Rédactrice en chef: Delphine Rouquette; **PDG - Directeur de la publication:** Olivier Rouquette
Profile: Journal local GRATUIT du sud Aveyron paraissant le vendredi.
Language (s): French
Ad Rate: Full Page Colour 500.00
Currency: Euro
DAILY NEWSPAPER

Le Semeur Hebdo 224576

Editorial: 37 rue Montlosier, Clermont Ferrand 63058
Tel: 33 04 73 98 46 00
Email: redaction@semeur.com
Freq: Weekly; **Circ:** 9598
Humanitaire: Jean-Baptiste Botella; **Président - Directeur de la publication:** Williams Captier
Profile: PARUTIONS : vendredi.
Language (s): French
Ad Rate: Full Page Mono 800.00
Currency: Euro
DAILY NEWSPAPER

Sud Ouest 742178

Owner: Groupe Sud Ouest
Editorial: 23 quai de Queyries, Bordeaux 33094
Tel: 33 5 35 31 31 31
Email: s.marraud@sudouest.fr **Web site:** http://www.sudouest.fr
Freq: Daily; **Circ:** 10000 Publisher's Statement
Gastronomie: Jacques Ballarin; **Médiateur:** Patrick Berthomeau; **Education - Emploi Vie quotidienne:** Bruno Beziat; **PYRENEES ATLANTIQUES - Bayonne:** Philippe Campa; **LOT ET GARONNE - Agen:** Maryan Charruau; **Oenologie:** César Compadre; **GIRONDE - Lesparre:** Olivier Delhoumeau; **Politique:** Bruno Dive; **GIRONDE - Arcachon:** Bernadette Dubourg; **PYRENEES ATLANTIQUES - Pau:** Christophe Galichon; **Président du conseil de surveillance:** Pierre Jeantet; **Directeur des informations de la Gironde:** Dominique De Laage De Meux; **Chef du Service Général:** Benoît Lasserre; **Environnement:** Jean-Denis Renard; **GERS:** Pierre Sabathie; **DORDOGNE:** Anne-Marie Simeon; **Pages féminines:** Hélène Valeins-Rouquette; **GIRONDE - Blaye:** Sylvain Viaut
Profile: Regional newspaper covering news and current affairs.
Language (s): French
DAILY NEWSPAPER

Sud Ouest Charente Maritime - Edition la Rochelle-Re 157554

Owner: SUD OUEST
Editorial: Residence Etoile marine, 29 av. Michel Crépeau, La Rochelle 17025 **Tel:** 33 5 46 28 05 05
Email: larochelle@sudouest.fr **Web site:** http://www.sudouest.fr
Freq: Daily; **Circ:** 45000 Publisher's Statement
Profile: Regional daily newspaper focussing on local, regional, national and international news and current affairs. Local Translation:Informations régionales, locales, nationales et internationales.
Language (s): French
Ad Rate: Full Page Mono 2233.00
Ad Rate: Full Page Colour 2532.00
Currency: Euro
DAILY NEWSPAPER

Sud Ouest Charente Maritime - Edition Royan - Jonzac 157540

Owner: SUD OUEST
Editorial: 27 place du Champ-de-Foire, Jonzac 17500 **Tel:** 33 5 46 48 56 31
Email: jonzac@sudouest.fr **Web site:** http://www.sudouest.fr
Freq: Daily; **Circ:** 50000 Publisher's Statement
Chef d'Agence: Philippe Belhache; **Redacteur:** Ronan Chérel
Profile: Regional daily newspaper focussing on local and regional news and current affairs. Local Translation:Journal d'informations générales et régionales.
Language (s): French
Ad Rate: Full Page Mono 2172.00
Ad Rate: Full Page Colour 2480.00
Currency: Euro
DAILY NEWSPAPER

Sud Ouest Charente-Maritime - Edition Rochefort-Oleron 311188

Owner: SUD OUEST
Editorial: 60 rue de la Republique, Rochefort 17300
Tel: +33 5 46 99 89 10
Email: rochefort@sudouest.fr **Web site:** http://www.sudouest.fr
Freq: Daily; **Circ:** 400000 Publisher's Statement
Chef d'Agence: Sylvain Cottin
Profile: Regional daily newspaper focussing on local, regional and national news and current affairs. Local Translation:Informations générales, nationales, régionales et locales.
Language (s): French
Ad Rate: Full Page Mono 2010.00
Ad Rate: Full Page Colour 2314.00
Currency: Euro
DAILY NEWSPAPER

Sud Ouest Dimanche 157558

Owner: SUD OUEST
Editorial: 23, quai de Queyries, Bordeaux 33094 CEDEX **Tel:** +33 5 35 31 31 31
Email: dimanche@sudouest.com **Web site:** http://www.sudouest.com
Freq: Weekly; **Circ:** 278327
Chef de Rédaction: Catherine Debray; **Pigiste:** Anne Pourillou-Journiac
Profile: Sunday edition of the regional daily newspaper focussing on news and current affairs. Local Translation:Edition du dimanche du quotidien Sud-Ouest.
Language (s): French
Ad Rate: Full Page Mono 12631.00
Ad Rate: Full Page Colour 13890.00
Currency: Euro
DAILY NEWSPAPER

Sud Ouest Dordogne - Edition Perigueux 157541

Owner: SUD OUEST
Editorial: 7 bis place Francheville, BP 1054, Perigueux 24001 CEDEX **Tel:** 33 5 53 45 24 52
Email: perigueux@sudouest.fr **Web site:** http://www.sudouest.fr
Freq: Daily; **Circ:** 38000 Publisher's Statement
Chef d'Agence: Anne-Marie Siméon
Profile: Regional daily newspaper focussing on local and regional news and current affairs. Local Translation:Journal d'informations générales et régionales.
Language (s): French
Ad Rate: Full Page Mono 1961.00
Ad Rate: Full Page Colour 2307.00
Currency: Euro
DAILY NEWSPAPER

Sud Ouest Edition Charente 157539

Owner: SUD OUEST
Editorial: 61 bis rue Herge, BP 1219, Angouleme 16006 CEDEX **Tel:** +33 5 45 39 95 95
Email: angouleme@sudouest.fr **Web site:** http://www.sudouest.fr
Freq: Daily; **Circ:** 406726 Publisher's Statement
Chef d'Agence: Patrick Guilloton; **Chef d'Agence:** Olivier Sarazin
Profile: Regional daily newspaper focussing on local and regional news and current affairs. Local Translation:Journal d'informations générales et régionales.
Language (s): French
Ad Rate: Full Page Mono 4720.00
Ad Rate: Full Page Colour 5459.00
Currency: Euro
DAILY NEWSPAPER

Sud Ouest Lot-Et-Garonne - Edition Marmandais 157550

Owner: SUD OUEST
Editorial: 69 rue Charles-de-Gaulle, BP 83, Marmande 47200 **Tel:** +33 5 53 64 96 96
Email: marmande@sudouest.fr **Web site:** http://www.sudouest.fr
Freq: Daily; **Circ:** 390000 Publisher's Statement
Chef d'Agence: Alain Goujon; **Chef d'Agence:** Jean-Marc Lernould
Profile: Regional daily newspaper focussing on local and regional news and current affairs. Local Translation:Journal d'informations générales et régionales.
Language (s): French
Ad Rate: Full Page Mono 795.00
Ad Rate: Full Page Colour 975.00
Currency: Euro
DAILY NEWSPAPER

Sundgau Sans Frontieres 523243

Owner: SUNDGAU SANS FRONTIERES
Editorial: Plume d'Expression, 3C rue du 27-Novembre, Balschwiller 68210 **Tel:** 33 3 89 25 29 72
Email: sundgau-sans-frontieres@neuf.fr **Web site:** http://www.sundgau-sans-frontieres.fr
Freq: Monthly; **Circ:** 60000 Publisher's Statement
Directeur de Publication: Valérie Desjardin

Profile: Regional newspaper focussing on local news and current affairs including cross border information, culture, associations, events, concerts, exhibitions, conferences, sport, history, municipal, society, business, gardening, housing, holidays, motoring, fashion, beauty, well being, shopping and agenda.
Language (s): French
DAILY NEWSPAPER

Le Télégramme 158788
Owner: Le Télégramme
Editorial: 7, voie d'acces au Port, BP 67243, Morlaix 29672 **Tel:** 33 2 98 62 11 33
Email: economie@letelegramme.fr **Web site:** http://www.letelegramme.com
Freq: Daily; **Circ:** 201579 Publisher's Statement
Rédacteur en Chef: Olivier Clech; **Directeur de l'Information:** Hubert Coudurier; **Pigiste:** Alain Joannès; **Editor:** Samuel Petit; **Pigiste:** Gérard Pinguet; **Chef de Rédaction:** Jean-Philippe Quignon
Profile: Magazine covering regional and national news and current affairs including economics, sports and leisure.
Language (s): French
Ad Rate: Full Page Mono 30930.00
Ad Rate: Full Page Colour 37988.00
Currency: Euro
DAILY NEWSPAPER

LE Telegramme Dimanche 157452
Owner: LE TELEGRAMME DE BREST ET DE L'OUEST
Editorial: 7 voie d'Acces-au-Port, BP 67243, Morlaix 29672 **Tel:** +33 2 98 62 11 33
Email: telegramme@letelegramme.fr **Web site:** http://www.letelegramme.com
Freq: Weekly; **Circ:** 155912
Rédacteur en Chef: Olivier Clech; **Directeur de l'Information:** Hubert Coudurier
Profile: 16 sport report removable pages. International, national and regional news, including several special columns on top of the daily national news: games, celebrities, TV guide... The magazine 'Version Fémina' (published by Hachette Filipacchi Médias) is included as supplément.4 editions: Nord Finistère, Sud Finistère, Côtes d'Armor and Morbihan.
Language (s): French
DAILY NEWSPAPER

Temps Libres 696950
Owner: MI TEMPS
Tel: 33 4 74 50 65 66
Email: tempslibre.redaction@wanadoo.fr
Freq: Monthly; **Circ:** 45000 Publisher's Statement
Directeur de Publication: Pacale Mercier
Profile: Local Translation: Journal d'actualité sur le département de l'Ain.Annonces loisirs, publireportage, portraits. Habitants de l'Ain
Language (s): French
DAILY NEWSPAPER

TOULOUSE MAG 224477
Owner: GROUPE DEPECHE DU MIDI
Editorial: Avenue Jean Baylet, Toulouse 31095
Tel: 33 05 62 11 96 00
Email: joelle.porcher@ladepeche.fr **Web site:** http://www.toulousemag.com
Freq: Monthly; **Circ:** 15000
Rédactrice: Manon Haussy; **Directeur de la publication:** Bernard Maffre; **Rédactrice en chef:** Joëlle Porcher; **Maquettiste:** Céline Viguier; **Rédactrice:** Julie Vivier
Profile: Informations régionales Toulouse : culture, voyages, shopping, dossiers, gastronomie.
Language (s): French
Ad Rate: Full Page Colour 3700.00
Currency: Euro
DAILY NEWSPAPER

TOUTES LES NOUVELLES 224479
Owner: S.E.H.P.
Editorial: 4 bis avenue de Sceaux, Versailles 78035
Tel: 33 01 30 97 72 00
Email: s.gauthier@lesnouvelles.fr
Freq: Weekly; **Circ:** 11476 OJD
Rédacteur en chef: Stéphane Gauthier; **Editeur:** Patrick Wassef
Profile: Editions : Versailles et Rambouillet / Chevreuse. PARUTIONS : mercredi
Language (s): French
DAILY NEWSPAPER

Toutes les nouvelles de Rambouillet 224478
Owner: PUBLIHEBDOS
Editorial: 67 rue du General-de-Gaulle, Rambouillet 78120 **Tel:** 33 1 34 83 67 61
Email: redac.rbt@lesnouvelles.fr
Freq: Weekly; **Circ:** 40000 Publisher's Statement
Editeur: Patrick Wassef
Profile: Regional newspaper focussing on local news and current affairs including celebrities.
Language (s): French
DAILY NEWSPAPER

Le Tregor 224578
Owner: GROUPE PUBLIHEBDOS
Editorial: 26 rue Compagnie Roger Barbe, BP 80233, Lannion 22302 **Tel:** 33 02 96 46 67 67
Email: letregor@publihebdos.fr
Freq: Weekly; **Circ:** 21365 OJD
Rédacteur: Philippe Gestin; **Rédacteur en chef:** Erwann Hirel; **Rédacteur:** Etienne Royer; **Rédactrice:** Marion Valee
Profile: Informations régionales, locales - Annonces légales pour tout le département. PARUTIONS : jeudi
Language (s): French
DAILY NEWSPAPER

La Tribune 158755
Owner: La Tribune
Editorial: 18, rue Pasquier, Paris 75008
Tel: 33 1 78 41 40 93
Email: latribunelibre@latribune.fr **Web site:** http://www.latribune.fr
Freq: Daily; **Circ:** 78463 OJD
Editor in Chief: Jean-Louis Alcaide; **Editor in Chief:** Michel Cabirol; **Editor in Chief:** Robert Jules; **Editor at Large:** Isabelle Lefort; **Editor in Chief:** Franck Pauly
Profile: Newspaper covering financial and business news including economics, investment, stock markets, management, related technology and personal finance.
Language (s): French
Ad Rate: Full Page Mono 29800.00
Ad Rate: Full Page Colour 37900.00
Currency: Euro
DAILY NEWSPAPER

La Tribune - Le Progres 742167
Owner: GROUPE PROGRES
Editorial: 24 rue de la Robotique, BP 38, Saint-Etienne 42964 **Tel:** 33 04 77 91 47 47
Email: redactionenchef@leprogres.fr **Web site:** http://www.leprogres.fr
Freq: Daily; **Circ:** 217755 OJD
Rédacteur en chef: Xavier Antoye; **PDG - Directeur de la publication:** Gérard Colin; **Directeur de la rédaction:** Pierre Fanneau; **Politique:** Dominique Goubatian; **Education Faits divers - Société:** Yvette Granger; **Directeur Loire - Haute-Loire:** Patrick Mauge; **Politique:** Véronique Miot; **Rédacteur détaché RIVE DE GIER:** Loïc Todesco
Profile: Utilisation de la quadrichromie : Tous les jours, dans les pages 1, 3, 5, 7 et complémentaires - OJD : LE PROGRES + LA TRIBUNE. Diffusé en Loire et Haute-Loire.
DAILY NEWSPAPER

La Tribune De Montélimar 224697
Editorial: 33 avenue du Gal de Gaulle, Montelimar 26201 **Tel:** 33 04 75 00 84 00
Email: redaction@latribune-montelimar.com **Web site:** http://www.latribune-montelimar.com
Freq: Weekly; **Circ:** 19377 OJD
Rédacteur en chef Justice: Marc Loudin; **Directeur de la publication:** Brice O'Hayon; **Rédactrice en chef:** Laure Ostwalt
Profile: PARUTIONS : le jeudi.
Language (s): French
Ad Rate: Full Page Mono 1011.00
Ad Rate: Full Page Colour 1213.00
Currency: Euro
DAILY NEWSPAPER

La Tribune De Tours 556305
Editorial: 19 rue Mirabeau, Tours 37000
Tel: 33 02 47 61 24 60
Email: tribunetours-redac2@orange.fr **Web site:** http://www.tribune-tours.fr
Freq: Weekly; **Circ:** 28000 Publisher's Statement
Directeur de la publication: Laurent Rouault
Profile: Magazine GRATUIT d'informations locales de l'agglomération tourangelle. PARUTIONS : le jeudi
Language (s): French
DAILY NEWSPAPER

La Tribune D'Orleans 429510
Editorial: 33 boulevard Rocheplatte, Orleans 45000
Tel: 33 02 38 52 95 54
Email: tribuneorleans.redac@orange.fr **Web site:** http://www.tribune-orleans.fr
Freq: Weekly; **Circ:** 26000 Publisher's Statement
Directeur de la publication: Laurent Rouault
Profile: Journal d'informations locales : culture, politique, enquêtes.
Language (s): French
DAILY NEWSPAPER

La Tribune Le Progres Saint-Etienne 158780
Owner: LE PROGRES
Editorial: 2 place Jean-Jaures, Saint-Etienne 42000
Tel: 33 4 77 45 10 10
Email: chefinfo42@leprogres.fr **Web site:** http://www.leprogres.fr
Freq: Daily
Chef d'Agence: Christine Chaumeil; **Chef d'Agence:** Sandrine Kara-Agop
Profile: National, regional and local news. Sunday price: 1,50 € - Full week subscription including Sunday: 327 €. Local Translation:Actualités départementales et locales, régionales et nationales. Prix du dimanche : 1,50 €.Abonnement semaine + dimanche : 327 €
Language (s): French
Ad Rate: Full Page Mono 3717.00
Currency: Euro
DAILY NEWSPAPER

LA Tribune Le Progrès: Edition Haute-Loire 157373
Owner: LE PROGRES
Editorial: 20 boulevard Saint-Pierre, Yssingeaux 43200 **Tel:** 33 4 71 56 06 61
Email: redaction43@leprogres.fr **Web site:** http://www.leprogres.fr
Freq: Daily; **Circ:** 35000 Publisher's Statement
Profile: Regional and local news. Sunday price: 1,05 € and full week subscription including Sunday: 233,60 €. Local Translation:Informations régionales et locales. Prix du dimanche : 1,05 € et abonnement semaine + dimanche : 233,60 €
Language (s): French
Ad Rate: Full Page Mono 1594.00
Currency: Euro
DAILY NEWSPAPER

LA Tribune Valréas 224699
Owner: GROUPE DAUPHINE
Editorial: 18 cours Tivoli, Valreas 84600
Tel: 33 4 90 35 19 76
Email: sblatribune@hotmail.com
Freq: Weekly; **Circ:** 33000 Publisher's Statement
Chef d'Agence: Stéphane Blaise
Profile: Vaucluse, Basse-Drôme and Ardèche regions news.
Language (s): French
Ad Rate: Full Page Mono 1011.00
Ad Rate: Full Page Colour 1213.00
Currency: Euro
DAILY NEWSPAPER

L' Union - L'Ardennais 158796
Owner: L'Union - L'Ardennais
Editorial: 14, rue Edouard Mignot, Reims 51100
Tel: 33 3 26 50 50 50
Email: redac-reims@journal-lunion.fr **Web site:** http://www.lunion.com
Freq: Daily; **Circ:** 106384 OJD
Rédacteur en Chef: Hervé Chabaud; **Chef d'Agence:** Guillaume Flatet; **Pigiste:** Philippe Hervieu; **Rédacteur en Chef:** Sébastien Lacroix; **Editor in Chief:** Didier Louis; **Président Directeur Général:** Jacques Tillier
Profile: Regional daily newspaper covering national, regional and local news and current affairs.
Language (s): French
Ad Rate: Full Page Mono 13059.00
Currency: Euro
DAILY NEWSPAPER

L' Union Edition Chauny - Tergnier - La Fere - St Quentin 157317
Owner: GHM - GROUPE HERSANT MEDIA
Editorial: 4 rue du General-Leclerc, Chauny 2300
Tel: +33 3 23 52 15 84
Email: chauny@journal-lunion.fr **Web site:** http://www.lunion.presse.fr
Freq: Daily; **Circ:** 126325 Publisher's Statement
Chef d'Agence: Ludovic Barbarossa; **Chef d'Agence:** Graziella Basile
Profile: National, regional and local news. Current events.
Language (s): French
DAILY NEWSPAPER

L' Union Edition De Chalons 157319
Owner: GHM - GROUPE HERSANT MEDIA
Editorial: 23 place de la Republique, Chalons-En-Champagne 51000 **Tel:** 33 3 26 68 13 10
Email: chalons@journal-lunion.fr **Web site:** http://www.lunion.presse.fr
Freq: Daily; **Circ:** 126325 Publisher's Statement
Chef d'Agence: Sébastien Laporte; **Chef d'Agence:** Stéphanie Verger
Profile: National, regional and local news. Current events. Local Translation:Actualités locales, départementales, régionales et nationales. Informations générales.
Language (s): French
DAILY NEWSPAPER

L' Union Edition Soissons-Chateau-Thierry 157316
Owner: GHM - GROUPE HERSANT MEDIA
Editorial: 53 rue Carnot, Chateau-Thierry 2400
Tel: +33 3 23 84 11 83
Email: chateau@journal-lunion.fr **Web site:** http://www.lunion.presse.fr
Freq: Daily; **Circ:** 126000 Publisher's Statement
Chef d'Agence: Philippe Robin
Profile: National, regional and local news. Current events.
Language (s): French
DAILY NEWSPAPER

L' Union Editions De L'aisne Direction Departementale De Laon 157315
Owner: GHM - GROUPE HERSANT MEDIA
Editorial: 87, rue Leon Nanquette, Laon 2000
Tel: +33 3 23 27 78 00
Email: dirdep02@journal-lunion.fr **Web site:** http://www.lunion.presse.fr
Freq: Daily; **Circ:** 130000 Publisher's Statement
Profile: Local, regional, national and international news. Current events and sport. Saturday price: 1,50 € (including Fémina and TV guide supplements). Local Translation:Actualités locales, départementales, régionales, nationales et internationales. Informations générales et sportives. *Prix : 1,50 € le samedi (avec suppléments TV et Fémina)
Language (s): French
Ad Rate: Full Page Mono 7759.00
Currency: Euro
DAILY NEWSPAPER

Var Matin 742180
Owner: GROUPE HERSANT MEDIA
Editorial: 26 place Besagne, Toulon 83000
Tel: 33 04 94 93 31 00
Email: redacchef@nicematin.fr **Web site:** http://www.varmatin.com
Freq: Daily; **Circ:** 75473 OJD
PDG - Directeur de la publication: Dominique Bernard; **Directeur des Rédactions:** Olivier Biscaye; **Faits divers:** Gilbert Dasseville; **Faits divers - Reportages:** Eric Marmottans; **Faits divers - Reportages:** Peggy Polleto
Profile: Quadrichromie : tous les jours - Diffusion : 7 éditions sur le Var avec édition du Dimanche - OJD : 74 587ex
DAILY NEWSPAPER

Var-Matin Nice-Matin Edition Brignoles-Le Luc 157563
Owner: GHM - GROUPE HERSANT MEDIA
Editorial: 3 place Saint-Louis, Brignoles 83170
Tel: 33 4 94 69 67 10
Email: brignoles@nicematin.fr **Web site:** http://www.varmatin.com
Freq: Daily; **Circ:** 78965 Publisher's Statement
Chef d'Agence: Alain Revello; **Pigiste:** Gilbert Rinaudo; **Pigiste:** Vincent Tivoli
Profile: Regional daily newspaper focussing on general news and current affairs. Local Translation:Quotidien régional d'informations générales.
Language (s): French
DAILY NEWSPAPER

Var-Matin Nice-Matin Edition Hyeres-Le Lavandou 157562
Owner: GHM - GROUPE HERSANT MEDIA
Editorial: 15 avenue Joseph-Clotis, Hyeres 83400
Tel: 33 4 94 12 81 90
Email: hyeres@nicematin.fr **Web site:** http://www.varmatin.com
Freq: Daily; **Circ:** 70965 Publisher's Statement
Chef d'Agence: Catherine Froget
Profile: Regional daily newspaper focussing on news and current affairs including TV guide and women's interest supplement. Local Translation:Toute l'actualité de la région toulonnaise. Prix : 1,10 € le samedi (avec TV hebdo), 1,10 € le dimanche (avec Version Fémina).
Language (s): French
DAILY NEWSPAPER

VAR-MATIN NICE-MATIN TOULON SIEGE SOCIAL 158794
Owner: GHM - GROUPE HERSANT MEDIA
Editorial: 15 boulevard de Strasbourg, BP 806, Toulon 83051 CEDEX **Tel:** 33 4 94 93 31 50
Email: redacchef@nicematin.fr **Web site:** http://www.varmatin.com
Freq: Daily; **Circ:** 75520 OJD
Directeur des Rédactions: Olivier Biscaye; **Rédacteur (trice):** Catherine Blanchard; **Président Directeur Général:** Eric Debry; **Directeur Général Délégué:** frédéric Touraille
Profile: Regional daily newspaper focussing on news and current affairs. Local Translation:Quotidien régional d'informations. Prix : 1,10 € le samedi, 1,10 € le dimanche.
Language (s): French
Ad Rate: Full Page Colour 19656.00
Currency: Euro
DAILY NEWSPAPER

VAUCLUSE MATIN 157565
Owner: GROUPE DAUPHINE LIBERE
Editorial: 23 rue de la Republique, Avignon 84000
Tel: 33 04 90 16 78 00
Email: centre.avignon@vauclusematin.com
Freq: Daily; **Circ:** 11109 Publisher's Statement
Faits divers: Riad Doua
Profile: Utilisation de la quadrichromie - Tous les jours - Dans les pages une, trois et dernière. Edition du 7ème jour
Language (s): French
Ad Rate: Full Page Mono 4949.00
Ad Rate: Full Page Colour 6434.00
Currency: Euro
DAILY NEWSPAPER

La Vie Correzienne 224703
Owner: COURRIER FRANCAIS
Editorial: 15 rue Fernand Alibert, Brive-La-Gaillarde 19316 **Tel:** 33 05 55 24 11 44
Email: v.david@courrier-francais.fr **Web site:** http://www.lavie-correzienne.com
Freq: Weekly; **Circ:** 11900 Publisher's Statement
Gérant - Directeur de la publication: Bernard Cattaneo; **Rédacteur en chef:** Gérard Dames; **Directeur des rédactions - Rédacteur en chef:** Vincent David
Profile: Hebdomadaire d'informations générales, départementales et d'information catholique. PARUTIONS : vendredi
Language (s): French
Ad Rate: Full Page Mono 1100.00
Ad Rate: Full Page Colour 1440.00
Currency: Euro
DAILY NEWSPAPER

LA VOIX DE L'AIN 224707
Owner: GROUPE HCR
Editorial: 16 rue Lalande, BP 88, Bourg-En-Bresse 1003 **Tel:** 33 04 74 23 80 50
Email: redaction@voixdelain.fr **Web site:** http://www.voixdelain.fr
Freq: Weekly; **Circ:** 22326 OJD
Rédacteur en chef: Nicolas Bernard; **Directeur de la publication:** Bernard Bienvenu
Profile: Hebdomadaire (catholique) départemental d'information paraissant le vendredi.
Language (s): French

Ad Rate: Full Page Mono 1882.00
Ad Rate: Full Page Colour 2356.00
Currency: Euro
DAILY NEWSPAPER

VOIX DU JURA
224481
Editorial: 18 rue de Ronde, BP 173, Lons-Le-Saunier 39005 **Tel:** 33 03 84 87 16 16
Email: redaction@voixdujura.fr
Freq: Weekly; **Circ:** 12187 OJD
Directeur de la publication: Franck Lacroix
Profile: Journal régional d'informations et d'annonces paraissant le jeudi.
Language (s): French
DAILY NEWSPAPER

LA VOIX DU MIDI - GRAND TOULOUSE
414823
Owner: LA VOIX DU MIDI
Editorial: 3 rue Ninau, Toulouse 31000
Tel: 33 05 61 99 44 47
Email: voixdumidi@wanadoo.fr
Freq: Weekly; **Circ:** 12222 Publisher's Statement
Directeur de la publication: Franck Lacroix
Profile: Hebdomadaire régional d'information.
PARUTIONS : le jeudi
Language (s): French
DAILY NEWSPAPER

La Voix du Nord
742181
Owner: La Voix du Nord
Editorial: 8 Place du General de Gaulle, BP 549, Lille 59023 **Tel:** 33 3 20 78 40 40
Email: region@lavoixdunord.fr **Web site:** http://www.lavoixdunord.fr
Freq: Daily; **Circ:** 264348
Directeur de la rédaction - Rédacteur en chef: Jean-Michel Bretonnier; **Musiques:** Virginie Carton; **Magazine - Page 'de vous à nous' Courrier des lecteurs:** Martine Desvaux; **Directeur du bureau parisien Politique:** Hervé Favre; **Directeur de la publication:** Jacques Hardoin; **Cinéma Radio - Télévision:** Philippe Lagouche; **Musique classique:** Christian Larivière; **Magazine - Pages 'de vous à vous':** Béatrice Quintin; **Chef du service Région:** Dominique Serra; **Musiques:** Bruno De Witte
Profile: Regional daily newspaper covering general news and current affairs including politics, economics, culture, sports and leisure.
Language (s): French
Ad Rate: Full Page Mono 4648.00
Ad Rate: Full Page Colour 6275.00
Currency: Euro
DAILY NEWSPAPER

LA Voix du Nord - Edition Dunkerque
157391
Owner: LA VOIX DU NORD
Editorial: 1-3 place de la Republique, Dunkerque CEDEX 1 **Tel:** 33 3 28 59 10 00
Email: dunkerque@lavoixdunord.fr **Web site:** http://www.lavoixdunord.fr
Freq: Daily; **Circ:** 26000 Publisher's Statement
Chef d'Agence: Didier Dupuis
Profile: Daily regional current events and economy newspaper. Local Translation:Quotidien d'informations générales, économiques, régionales.
Language (s): French
DAILY NEWSPAPER

LA Voix Du Nord Bureau Parisien
157378
Owner: LA VOIX DU NORD
Editorial: 14 rue de Bassano, Paris 75116 **Tel:** +33 1 53 83 15 00
Email: paris@lavoixdunord.fr **Web site:** http://www.lavoixdunord.fr
Freq: Daily; **Circ:** 300000 Publisher's Statement
Profile: Daily regional current events newspaper covering the North, Pas-de-Calais, Somme and Aisne regions. Columns: TV, community news, today.
Language (s): French
DAILY NEWSPAPER

LA Voix Du Nord Edition Du Nord Avesnes Fourmies
157380
Owner: LA VOIX DU NORD
Editorial: 2, rue Gambetta, Fourmies 59610
Tel: 33 3 27 61 01 41
Email: avesnes@lavoixdunord.fr **Web site:** http://www.lavoixdunord.fr
Freq: Daily; **Circ:** 389867 Publisher's Statement
Chef d'Agence: Géraldine Beys; **Chef d'Agence:** Lionel Maréchal
Profile: Daily regional current events and economy newspaper. Local Translation:Quotidien d'informations générales, économiques, régionales.
Language (s): French
DAILY NEWSPAPER

LA Voix Du Nord Edition Du Nord Cambrai
157388
Owner: LA VOIX DU NORD
Editorial: 6/8, rue du Marechal-de- Lattre-de-Tassigny, Cambrai 59400 **Tel:** +33 3 27 83 68 32
Email: cambrai@lavoixdunord.fr **Web site:** http://www.lavoixdunord.fr
Freq: Daily; **Circ:** 389267 Publisher's Statement
Chef d'Agence: David Laurence; **Chef d'Agence:** Stéphanie Zorn
Profile: Daily regional current events and economy newspaper. The Cambrai edition includes 1 Caudry page and 1 Cateau page produced by the Caudry office. Local Translation:Quotidien d'informations générales, économiques, régionales... L'édition de

Cambrai contient une page Caudry et 1 page Le Cateau, réalisées par l'agence de Caudry.
Language (s): French
DAILY NEWSPAPER

LA Voix Du Nord Edition Du Nord Lambersart
157399
Owner: LA VOIX DU NORD
Editorial: 2 rue de la Carnoy, Lambersart 59130
Tel: +33 3 20 17 17 17
Email: lambersart@lavoixdunord.fr **Web site:** http://www.lavoixdunord.fr
Freq: Daily; **Circ:** 300000 Publisher's Statement
Chef d'Agence: Benoît Deseure
Profile: Daily regional current events and economy newspaper. 2 editions depend on the Lambersart office: 1 edition for Marcq La Madeleine, Lomme, Lambersart, St-André and another edition for Loos, Haubourdin, Les Weppes. Local Translation:Quotidien d'informations générales, économiques, régionales... 2 éditions dépendent du bureau de Lambersart : une édition pour Marcq La Madeleine, Lomme, Lambersart, St-André ; une autre édition pour Loos, Haubourdin, Les Weppes.
Language (s): French
DAILY NEWSPAPER

LA Voix Du Nord Edition Du Nord Le Melantois
157397
Owner: LA VOIX DU NORD
Editorial: 2 rue Jean-Jaures, Seclin 59113 **Tel:** +33 3 20 90 05 05
Email: seclin@lavoixdunord.fr **Web site:** http://www.lavoixdunord.fr
Freq: Daily; **Circ:** 380000 Publisher's Statement
Chef d'Agence: Stéphane Hubin
Profile: Daily regional current events and economy newspaper. Local Translation:Quotidien d'informations générales, économiques, régionales.
Language (s): French
DAILY NEWSPAPER

LA Voix Du Nord Edition Du Nord Le Pevele - Melantois
157398
Owner: LA VOIX DU NORD
Editorial: 35, boulevard de Valmy, Villeneuve D'ascq 59650 **Tel:** +33 3 20 91 19 05
Email: villeneuvedascq@lavoixdunord.fr **Web site:** http://www.lavoixdunord.fr
Freq: Daily; **Circ:** 340000 Publisher's Statement
Profile: Daily regional international and national current events newspaper. Economy, culture, cinema, news in brief... Local Translation:Quotidien d'informations internationales nationales et régionales. Economie, culture, cinéma, faits divers.
Language (s): French
DAILY NEWSPAPER

LA Voix Du Nord Edition Du Nord Le Quesnoy Maubeuge
157393
Owner: LA VOIX DU NORD
Editorial: 6 rue Thiers, Le Quesnoy 59530 **Tel:** +33 3 27 47 54 00
Email: lequesnoy@lavoixdunord.fr **Web site:** http://www.lavoixdunord.fr
Freq: Daily; **Circ:** 250000 Publisher's Statement
Profile: Daily regional current events and economy newspaper. Local Translation:Quotidien d'informations générales, économiques, régionales.
Language (s): French
DAILY NEWSPAPER

LA Voix Du Nord Edition Pas-De-Calais Bethune Bruay
157386
Owner: LA VOIX DU NORD
Editorial: 23 rue des Treilles, Bethune 62400 **Tel:** +33 3 21 01 14 18
Email: bethune@lavoixdunord.fr **Web site:** http://www.lavoixdunord.fr
Freq: Daily; **Circ:** 380000 Publisher's Statement
Chef d'Agence: Christian Larivière
Profile: Daily regional current events and economy newspaper. Local Translation:Quotidien d'informations générales, économiques, régionales.
Language (s): French
DAILY NEWSPAPER

LA Voix Du Nord Edition Pas-De-Calais Lens Henin Carvin
157400
Owner: LA VOIX DU NORD
Editorial: 35 rue Edouard-Plachez, Carvin 62220
Tel: +33 3 21 74 04 00
Email: henin@lavoixdunord.fr **Web site:** http://www.lavoixdunord.fr
Freq: Daily; **Circ:** 389267 Publisher's Statement
Profile: Daily regional, local, current events, economy, sports, community and leisure newspaper. The Lens pages are common to the Lens Hénin Carvin and the Lens Liévin editions. Local Translation:Quotidien d'informations générales, économiques, régionales, locales. Sports, société, loisirs. Les pages de Lens sont communes aux éditions Lens Hénin Carvin et Lens Liévin.
Language (s): French
DAILY NEWSPAPER

LA Voix Du Nord Edition Pas-De-Calais Lens Lievin
157382
Owner: LA VOIX DU NORD
Editorial: 40 rue de la Gare, Lens 62300 **Tel:** +33 3 21 14 74 74
Email: lens@lavoixdunord.fr **Web site:** http://www.lavoixdunord.fr
Freq: Daily; **Circ:** 350000 Publisher's Statement
Chef d'Agence: Yves Portelli

Profile: Daily regional, local, current events, economy, sports, community and leisure newspaper. The Lens pages are common to the Lens Hénin Carvin and the Lens Liévin editions. Local Translation:Quotidien d'informations générales, économiques, régionales, locales...Sports, société, loisirs. Les pages de Lens sont communes aux éditions Lens Hénin Carvin et Lens Liévin.
Language (s): French
DAILY NEWSPAPER

LA Voix Du Nord Edition Pas-De-Calais St-Omer
157390
Owner: LA VOIX DU NORD
Editorial: 88 rue de Calais, Saint-Omer 62500
Tel: +33 3 21 38 08 33
Email: saintomer@lavoixdunord.fr **Web site:** http://www.lavoixdunord.fr
Freq: Daily; **Circ:** 400000 Publisher's Statement
Chef d'Agence: Isabelle Mathan
Profile: Daily regional current events and economy newspaper. Local Translation:Quotidien d'informations générales, économiques, régionales.
Language (s): French
DAILY NEWSPAPER

VOSGES MATIN
742166
Editorial: 40 quai des Bons Enfants, BP 273, Epinal 88007 **Tel:** 33 03 29 82 98 00
Web site: http://www.vosgesmatin.fr
Freq: Daily; **Circ:** 47965 OJD
Enseignement: Dominique Battini; **Cinéma Vidéo:** Christophe Gobin; **Maison Décoration:** Sophie Maupetit; **Rédacteur en chef:** Gérard Noel; **Médecine - Santé:** Brigitte Tissot
Profile: Utilisation de la quadrichromie - Tous les jours - Dans certaines pages. Edition du dimanche : 45 324ex.
DAILY NEWSPAPER

Vosges Matin Agence de Remiremont
157583
Owner: EBRA
Editorial: 16 rue de la Franche-Pierre, Remiremont 88200 **Tel:** 33 3 29 62 04 03
Email: redaction.remiremont@vosgesmatin.fr **Web site:** http://www.vosgesmatin.fr
Freq: Daily; **Circ:** 50000 OJD
Bureau Chief: Nathalie Bontems
Profile: Regional and local news.
Language (s): French
DAILY NEWSPAPER

Vosges Matin Agence de Saint-Dié
157582
Owner: EBRA
Editorial: 31 rue Thiers, St-Die 88100
Tel: 33 3 29 55 78 10
Email: redaction.saintdie@vosgesmatin.fr **Web site:** http://www.vosgesmatin.fr
Freq: Daily; **Circ:** 32000 OJD
Chef d'Agence: Philippe Cuny
Profile: Regional and local news. Local Translation:Actualités départementales et locales.
Language (s): French
DAILY NEWSPAPER

Vosges Matin Agence d'Epinal
564131
Owner: EBRA
Editorial: 40 quai des Bons-Enfants, Epinal 88000
Tel: 33 3 29 82 98 00
Email: ojorba@vosgesmatin.fr **Web site:** http://www.vosgesmatin.fr
Freq: Daily; **Circ:** 40000 OJD
Profile: Local daily news
Language (s): French
DAILY NEWSPAPER

Week-End (Mauritius)
156636
Owner: Le Mauricien Ltd
Editorial: 8 rue St Georges, BP 7, Port Louis
Tel: 230 207 82 00
Email: redaction@lemauricien.com **Web site:** http://www.lemauricien.com/weekend
Freq: Weekly; **Circ:** 75000 Publisher's Statement
Rédacteur en Chef: Gerard Cateaux; **Advertising Manager:** Stéphanie Foiret; **Directeur:** Jacques Rivet
Profile: National Sunday newspaper focussing on regional, national and international news, current affairs, politics, economics, society, entertainment, culture and TV programmes.
Language (s): French
Ad Rate: Full Page Mono 1303.00
Ad Rate: Full Page Colour 1443.00
Currency: United States Dollars
DAILY NEWSPAPER

L' Yonne Republicaine
742182
Editorial: 8/12 avenue Jean Moulin, Auxerre 89025
Tel: 33 03 86 49 52 00
Email: secretaire.yr@centrefrance.com **Web site:** http://www.lyonne.fr
Freq: Daily; **Circ:** 36472 OJD
Directeur général: Laurent Couronne; **Président délégué:** Gilles Cremillieux; **Rédacteur en chef:** Philippe Noireaux; **Education - Travail - Emploi:** Christian Picardeau; **Magazine (le samedi):** Vincent Roussot; **Faits de société Justice:** Emilie Zaugg
Profile: Utilisation de la quadrichromie - Tous les jours - 64 pages.
DAILY NEWSPAPER

L' Yonne Républicaine - Edition Sud
157579
Owner: YONNE REPUBLICAINE
Editorial: 6 rue de Paris, Avallon 89200
Tel: 33 3 86 34 99 15
Email: secretaire.yr@centrefrance.com **Web site:** http://www.lyonne.fr
Freq: Daily; **Circ:** 36682 Publisher's Statement
Chef d'Agence: Franck Morales; **Chef d'Agence:** Patricia Piquet
Profile: National, regional and local news. Including Version Fémina on Wednesday (1 €) and TV Mag on Saturday (1,50 €) . Local Translation:Actualités nationales, régionales et locales. Avec supplément Fémina le mercredi (1 €) et Mag TV le samedi (1,50 €).
Language (s): French
DAILY NEWSPAPER

L' Yonne Républicaine Agence de Joigny
157580
Owner: YONNE REPUBLICAINE
Editorial: 8, avenue Jean Moulin, Auxerre 89000
Tel: 33 3 86 49 52 15
Email: secretaire.yr@centrefrance.com **Web site:** http://www.lyonne.fr
Freq: Daily; **Circ:** 50000 OJD
Chef d'Agence: François Jaulhac
Profile: Regional news. Local Translation:Actualités régionales.
Language (s): French
DAILY NEWSPAPER

L' Yonne Républicaine Auxerre
158762
Owner: YONNE REPUBLICAINE
Editorial: 8-12 avenue Jean-Moulin, Auxerre 89025 CEDEX **Tel:** 33 3 86 49 52 15
Email: secretaire.yr@centrefrance.com **Web site:** http://www.lyonne.fr
Freq: Daily; **Circ:** 36682 OJD
Directeur Général: Laurent Couronne; **Chef d'Agence:** Yves Durand
Profile: National, regional and local news. Wednesday price: 1 € (including Version Fémina supplement). Saturday price: 1,50 € (including Yonne Mag and TV Magazine supplements). Local Translation:Actualités nationales, régionales et locales. Prix du mercredi : 1 € (avec supplément Version Fémina). Prix du samedi : 1,50 € (avec suppléments Yonne Mag et TV Magazine).
Language (s): French
Ad Rate: Full Page Mono 3330.00
Ad Rate: Full Page Colour 3996.00
Currency: Euro
DAILY NEWSPAPER

L' Yonne Républicaine: Edition Nord
157578
Owner: YONNE REPUBLICAINE
Editorial: 4 bis rue de la Republique, Sens 89100 CEDEX **Tel:** 33 3 86 83 87 50
Email: redaction.sens@centrefrance.com **Web site:** http://www.lyonne-republicaine.fr
Freq: Daily; **Circ:** 36682 OJD
Chef d'Agence: Pascale de Souza
Profile: National, regional and local news. Local Translation:Actualités nationales, régionales et locales. Vendu le mercredi avec Version Fémina (1,10 €) et le samedi avec TV Mag + Cahier annonces classées + cahier Yonne Mag (1,50).
Language (s): French
DAILY NEWSPAPER

News Service/Syndicate

Accroche-press'
876895
Owner: Accroche-press'
Editorial: 8, rue du Delta, Paris 75009
Tel: 33 1 48 78 19 96
Email: florencepuybareau@accroche-press.fr **Web site:** http://www.accroche-press.fr
Profile: News service covering economics and finance.
Language (s): French
NEWS SERVICE/SYNDICATE

AFP - AGENCE FRANCE-PRESSE
353230
Owner: Agence France-Presse
Editorial: 11/13, Place de la Bourse, Paris 75002
Tel: 33 1 40 41 46 46
Email: contact@afp.com **Web site:** http://www.afp.com
Publisher: Paul Defosseux; **Documentation and Print Director:** Yves Gacon; **Havana Bureau Chief:** Alexandre Grosbois; **Project Manager:** Marlowe Hood; **Global News Director:** Michèle Léridon; **France Director:** Bernard Pellegrin; **News Editor:** Adam Plowright; **Marseille Bureaux Chief:** Catherine Rama; **News Editor:** Annie Thomas; **Bogotá Bureau Chief:** Philippe Zygel
Profile: Main office of the international press agency covering regional, national and international news and current affairs including general interest, politics, business, economics, health, science, education and society.
Language (s): Arabic
NEWS SERVICE/SYNDICATE

AFP - AGENCE FRANCE-PRESSE - ABIDJAN BUREAU

870743
Owner: Agence France-Presse
Editorial: 18 avenue du Docteur Crozet, 01 BP 726, Abidjan **Tel:** 225 2 021 9017
Email: joris.fioriti@afp.com **Web site:** http://www.afp.com
Bureau Chief: Joris Fioriti
Profile: Abidjan bureau of international news and picture agency covering general news and current affairs.
Language (s): English
NEWS SERVICE/SYNDICATE

AFP - AGENCE FRANCE-PRESSE - ANKARA BUREAU

879497
Owner: Agence France-Presse
Editorial: 5 rue Milioni, Athina 10673
Tel: 30 210 363 3646
Email: odile.duperry@afp.com **Web site:** http://www.afp.com
Profile: Athens bureau of the international news and picture agency Agence France-Presse covering international news and current affairs.
Language (s): English
NEWS SERVICE/SYNDICATE

AFP - AGENCE FRANCE-PRESSE - ANKARA BUREAU

915543
Owner: Agence France-Presse
Editorial: And Sokak 8/13, Cankaya, Ankara 6680
Tel: 90 312 468 9680
Email: afp.ankara@afp.com **Web site:** http://www.afp.com
Bureau Chief: Michel Sailhan
Profile: Ankara office of the international press agency covering regional, national and international news and current affairs including general interest, politics, business, economics, health, science, education and society.
Language (s): English
NEWS SERVICE/SYNDICATE

AFP - AGENCE FRANCE-PRESSE - BANGKOK BUREAU

870740
Owner: Agence France-Presse
Editorial: 18th Floor, Alma Link Building, 25 Soi Chidlom, Ploenchit, Bangkok 10330
Tel: 66 2 650 3230
Email: bangkok@afp.com **Web site:** http://www.afp.com
Profile: Bangkok bureau of international news and picture agency covering general news and current affairs.
Language (s): English
NEWS SERVICE/SYNDICATE

AFP - AGENCE FRANCE-PRESSE - BEIJING BUREAU

845361
Owner: Agence France-Presse
Editorial: 16, Chao Yang Men Wai Street, China Life Tower, Beijing 100020 **Tel:** 86 10 8525 1757
Email: sebastien.berger@afp.com **Web site:** http://www.afp.com
Profile: Beijing bureau of international news and picture agency covering news and current affairs.
Language (s): Chinese
NEWS SERVICE/SYNDICATE

AFP - AGENCE FRANCE-PRESSE - BERLIN BUREAU 353685

Owner: Agence France-Presse
Editorial: Berliner Freiheit 2, Potsdamer Platz, Berlin 10785 **Tel:** 49 30 308 76 0
Email: post@afp.de **Web site:** http://www.afp.com/de
Profile: Regional office of the Agence France-Presse covering general news and current affairs.
Language (s): German
NEWS SERVICE/SYNDICATE

AFP - AGENCE FRANCE-PRESSE - BRUXELLES BUREAU

581259
Owner: Agence France-Presse
Editorial: Avenue d'Auderghem 22-28, Bruxelles 1040 **Tel:** 32 22 30 83 94
Email: afpbru@afp.com **Web site:** http://www.afp.com
Bureau Chief: Jean-Luc Bardet
Profile: Brussels office of the international news agency covering regional, national and international news and current affairs including general interest, politics, business, economics, health, science, education and society.
Language (s): French
NEWS SERVICE/SYNDICATE

AFP - AGENCE FRANCE-PRESSE - BUCURESTI BUREAU

821119
Owner: AAgence France-Presse
Editorial: 22B Muzeul Zambaccian street, Bucuresti
Tel: 40 21 231 2002
Email: bucarest@afp.com **Web site:** http://www.afp.com
Profile: Romanian bureau of the international news and picture agency Agence France-Presse covering regional and national news and current affairs in Romania.
Language (s): English
NEWS SERVICE/SYNDICATE

AFP - AGENCE FRANCE-PRESSE - COPENHAGEN BUREAU

313504
Owner: AFP
Editorial: Skindergade 7, Copenhagen 1159
Tel: 45 33 974 292
Email: soren.billing@afp.com **Web site:** http://www.afp.com
Freq: Daily
Profile: The Copenhagen branch of AFP. AFP's 200 bureaus cover 150 countries across the world, with 80 nationalities represented among its 2,260 collaborators.
Language (s): Danish
NEWS SERVICE/SYNDICATE

AFP - AGENCE FRANCE-PRESSE - DAKAR BUREAU 845984

Owner: Agence France-Presse
Editorial: 2, Place de l'Independance, Immeuble SDIH - 2eme étage, Dakar **Tel:** 221 33 823 08 17
Web site: http://www.afp.com
Profile: Dakar bureau of the international news and picture agency Agence France-Presse covering international news and current affairs.
Language (s): English
NEWS SERVICE/SYNDICATE

AFP - AGENCE FRANCE-PRESSE - HELSINKI BUREAU

519935
Editorial: Aleksanterinkatu 17, Helsinki 100
Tel: 358 9 68 74 65 46
Web site: http://www.afp.com
Freq: Daily
Profile: French AFP Helsinki office.
Language (s): English
NEWS SERVICE/SYNDICATE

AFP - AGENCE FRANCE-PRESSE - HONG KONG BUREAU

820979
Owner: Agence France-Presse
Editorial: 6201 Central Plaza, 18 Harbour Road, Hong Kong **Tel:** 852 2829 6200
Email: afphkg@afp.com **Web site:** http://www.afp.com
Profile: Hong Kong bureau of the international news and picture agency.
Language (s): English
NEWS SERVICE/SYNDICATE

AFP - AGENCE FRANCE-PRESSE - ISLAMABAD BUREAU

911376
Owner: Agence France-Presse
Editorial: H.9A, Street 24, F-7/2, Islamabad
Tel: 92 51 111 237 475
Email: Islamabad@afp.com **Web site:** http://www.afp.com
Profile: Islamabad bureau of international news and picture agency covering general news and current affairs.
Language (s): English
NEWS SERVICE/SYNDICATE

AFP - AGENCE FRANCE-PRESSE - JERUSALEM BUREAU

736187
Owner: Agence France-Presse
Editorial: Po Box 1507, 206 Jaffa Road, Jerusalem 91014 **Tel:** 972 2 644 0900
Email: hazel.ward@afp.com **Web site:** http://www.afp.com
Profile: Jerusalem Bureau of the Agence France-Presse covering general news and current affairs in the region.
Language (s): English
NEWS SERVICE/SYNDICATE

AFP - AGENCE FRANCE-PRESSE - JOHANNESBU BUREAU

820981
Editorial: 37 Keyes Avenue, Rosebank, Johannesburg 2196 **Tel:** 27 11 530 9900
Email: johannes.myburgh@afp.com **Web site:** http://www.afp.com
Bureau Chief: Christophe Beaudufe
Profile: Johannesburg office of the international press agency covering regional, national and international news and current affairs including general interest, politics, business, economics, health, science, education and society.
Language (s): English
NEWS SERVICE/SYNDICATE

AFP - AGENCE FRANCE-PRESSE - KINSHASA BUREAU

879482
Owner: Agence France-Presse
Editorial: 10, avenue Batetela, Kinshasa
Email: marc.jourdier@afp.com **Web site:** http://www.afp.com
Director: Marc Jourdier
Profile: Kinshasa bureau of the international news and picture agency Agence France-Presse covering international news and current affairs.
Language (s): English
NEWS SERVICE/SYNDICATE

AFP - AGENCE FRANCE-PRESSE - LA HAYE BUREAU

623333
Editorial: Cornelis de Wittlaan 39, Den Haag 2582 AB
Tel: 31 70 350 09 78
Email: afplah@afp.com **Web site:** http://www.afp.com
Language (s): Dutch
NEWS SERVICE/SYNDICATE

AFP - AGENCE FRANCE-PRESSE - LAGOS BUREAU 892893

Owner: Agence France-Presse
Editorial: 11 Awolowo Road, Ikoyi, Lagos
Tel: 234 1 904 1650
Email: afplagos@afp.com **Web site:** http://www.afp.com
Bureau Chief: Phil Hazlewood
Profile: Lagos bureau of the international news and picture agency Agence France-Presse covering international news and current affairs.
Language (s): French
NEWS SERVICE/SYNDICATE

AFP - AGENCE FRANCE-PRESSE - LIBREVILLE BUREAU

870414
Owner: Agence France-Presse
Editorial: Avenue du Colonel Parent, Immeuble Sogapal Les Filaos, Libreville **Tel:** 241 7 44 560
Email: michel.cariou@afp.com **Web site:** http://www.afp.com
Editor in Chief: Michel Cariou
Profile: Libreville bureau of the international news and picture agency Agence France-Presse covering international news and current affairs.
Language (s): English
NEWS SERVICE/SYNDICATE

AFP - AGENCE FRANCE-PRESSE - MADRID BUREAU

773383
Owner: Agence France-Presse
Editorial: Calle Prim, 19, 3 piso, Madrid 28004
Tel: 34 91 435 8740
Email: david.williams@afp.com **Web site:** http://www.afp.com
Bureau Chief: David Williams
Profile: Madrid bureau bureau of international news agency covering news and current affairs.
Language (s): English
NEWS SERVICE/SYNDICATE

AFP - AGENCE FRANCE-PRESSE - MEXICO BUREAU

786686
Editorial: Calle Durango No 183, Colonia Roma Norte, Mexico City, Distrito Federal 6700
Tel: 52 55 5128-1100
Email: redaccion.mexico@afp.com
NEWS SERVICE/SYNDICATE

AFP - AGENCE FRANCE-PRESSE - MIAMI BUREAU 77231

Editorial: 100 Biscayne Blvd Ste 3030, Miami, Florida 33132-2305 **Tel:** 1 305 679-9965
Web site: http://www.afp.com
Profile: This is the Miami office of Agence France-Presse, an international news service.
Language (s): English
NEWS SERVICE/SYNDICATE

AFP - AGENCE FRANCE-PRESSE - MILANO BUREAU

508547
Owner: Agence France Presse
Editorial: Via Vitruvio, 43, Milano Mi 20124
Tel: 39 02 67101283
Email: afp-rome@afp.com **Web site:** http://www.afp.com
Freq: Daily
Profile: Regional office of the international news agency and wire service focussing on news and current affairs.
Language (s): English
NEWS SERVICE/SYNDICATE

AFP - AGENCE FRANCE-PRESSE - MONTREAL BUREAU

870739
Owner: Agence France-Presse
Editorial: 180 Boul Rene-Levesque E, Montreal, Quebec H2X 1N6 **Tel:** 1 514 288 2777
Email: marc.braibant@afp.com **Web site:** http://www.afp.com
Bureau Chief: Marc Braibant
Profile: Montreal bureau of international news and picture agency covering general news and current affairs.
Language (s): English
NEWS SERVICE/SYNDICATE

AFP - AGENCE FRANCE-PRESSE - MOSCOW BUREAU

680938
Editorial: ul. Dolgorukovskaya 18, korpus 3, Moskva 127006 **Tel:** 7 495 7265969
Email: desk.moscou@afp.com **Web site:** http://www.afp.com
Freq: Daily
Profile: Regional office of the national French news agency Agence France Presse (AFP) focusing on regional news and current affairs.
Language (s): English
NEWS SERVICE/SYNDICATE

AFP - AGENCE FRANCE-PRESSE - NAIROBI BUREAU

578176
Owner: Agence France-Presse
Editorial: Lenana Plaza, 4th floor, 197 Lenana Rd, Nairobi 100 **Tel:** 254 203 96 0000
Email: afpnai@afp.com **Web site:** http://www.afp.com
Profile: Nairobi bureau of the international news and picture agency Agence France-Presse covering international news and current affairs.
Language (s): English
NEWS SERVICE/SYNDICATE

AFP - AGENCE FRANCE-PRESSE - NEW DELHI BUREAU

861542
Owner: Agence France-Presse
Editorial: 56 Janpath, 3rd floor, New Delhi 110001
Tel: 91 11 2373 8700
Email: afpdelhi@afp.com **Web site:** http://www.afp.com
Photographer: Prakash Singh
Profile: Regional office covering general news and current affairs.
Language (s): Arabic
NEWS SERVICE/SYNDICATE

AFP - AGENCE FRANCE-PRESSE - NEW YORK BUREAU

87064
Owner: AFP
Editorial: 747 3rd Ave Fl 35, New York, New York 10017-2803 **Tel:** 1 212 735-1750
Email: nyeco@afp.com **Web site:** http://www.afp.com
Profile: AFP is an international news agency delivering fast, in-depth coverage of global events. Discusses wars and conflicts, politics, sports and entertainment, and the latest breakthroughs in health, science and technology.
Language (s): English
NEWS SERVICE/SYNDICATE

AFP - AGENCE FRANCE-PRESSE - RIO DE JANEIRO BUREAU

825299
Owner: Agence France-Presse
Editorial: Avenida Almirante Barroso, N52, Sala 1002, Rio De Janeiro **Tel:** 55 21 2217 0025
Web site: http://www.afp.com
Director: Pierre Ausseil; **Bureau Chief:** Laura Bonilla Cal
Profile: Rio de Janeiro office of the Agence France-Presse covering regional, national and international news and current affairs including general interest, politics, business, economics, health, science, education and society.
Language (s): English
NEWS SERVICE/SYNDICATE

AFP - AGENCE FRANCE-PRESSE - ROME BUREAU 508517

Owner: Agence France Presse
Editorial: Piazza Santi Apostoli, 66, Roma 187
Tel: 39 06 6793588
Email: afp-rome@afp.com **Web site:** http://www.afp.com
Freq: Daily
Bureau Chief: Olivier Baube
Profile: Rome bureau of the international news agency and wire service covering news and current affairs.
Language (s): Arabic
NEWS SERVICE/SYNDICATE

AFP - AGENCE FRANCE-PRESSE - SANTIAGO BUREAU

385406
Editorial: Av.alameda Libertador B.o'higgins 1316, Of.92, Santiago **Tel:** 56 6960559
Web site: http://www.afp.com
Jefe: Paulina Abramovich; **Fotógrafo:** Martín Bernetti; **Jefa:** Patricia Guzmán
Language (s): Spanish
NEWS SERVICE/SYNDICATE

AFP - AGENCE FRANCE-PRESSE - SINGAPORE BUREAU

888933
Editorial: 28 Maxwell Road, #03-06 Red Dot Traffic Building, Singapore 61920 **Tel:** 65 6590 3788
Bureau Chief: Roberto Coloma; **Photographer:** Roslan Rahman
Language (s): English
NEWS SERVICE/SYNDICATE

AFP Relaxnews 897087
Owner: AFP Relaxnews
Email: contact@afprelaxnews.com **Web site:** http://www.afprelaxnews.com
Profile: Press agency covering leisure activities.
Language (s): English
NEWS SERVICE/SYNDICATE

Agence FEP - France Europe Photo 457188
Editorial: 92 rue du Clos de Ville, Sucy-En-Brie 94370 **Tel:** 33 1 45 90 07 55
Email: agence.fep@wanadoo.fr **Web site:** http://www.agencefep.fr
Directeur: Jean Bibard
Profile: Photo agency covering general European news and current affairs.
Language (s): French
NEWS SERVICE/SYNDICATE

Agence France-Presse - Alameda Bureau 503825
Editorial: 753 Central Ave, Alameda, California 94501-3457 **Tel:** 1 510 263-8420
Bureau Chief: Glenn Chapman
NEWS SERVICE/SYNDICATE

Agence France-Presse - Cyprus Bureau 578770
Editorial: 36 Kypranoros str, 7th and 6th floor, Nicosia 1061 **Tel:** 357 22 391391
Email: myrna.luksitch@afp.com
Language (s): Greek
NEWS SERVICE/SYNDICATE

Agence France-Presse - Hollywood Bureau 31324
Editorial: 6430 W Sunset Blvd Ste 702, Hollywood, California 90028-7910 **Tel:** 1 323 463-0675
Email: afpla@afp.com **Web site:** http://www.afp.com
News Editor: Robert Woollard
Language (s): English
NEWS SERVICE/SYNDICATE

Agence France-Presse - Lilles Bureau 353246
Owner: Agence France-Presse
Editorial: 36 rue de l'Hôpital-Militaire, Lille 59800 **Tel:** 33 3 20 74 65 00
Email: afp.lille@afp.com **Web site:** http://www.afp.com
Bureau Chief: Pascal Mallet
Profile: Regional office of the main international press agency in France focussing general interest information.
Language (s): French
NEWS SERVICE/SYNDICATE

Agence France-Presse - Lisbon Bureau 870359
Owner: Agence France-Presse
Editorial: Rua Rosa Araujo, 34, 3, Lisboa 1250-195 **Tel:** 351 21 355 6939
Email: brigitte.hagemann@afp.com **Web site:** http://www.afp.com
Profile: Lisbon bureau of international news and picture agency covering general news and current affairs.
NEWS SERVICE/SYNDICATE

Agence France-Presse - Sydney Bureau 313583
Owner: Agence France-Presse
Editorial: Level 8, 50 Margaret St, Sydney NSW 2000 **Tel:** 61 2 9251 1544
Email: sydney@afp.com **Web site:** http://www.afp.com
Editor: Talek Harris
Profile: Newspaper Service: Wire service for news and photos
Language (s): English
NEWS SERVICE/SYNDICATE

Agence France-Presse - Washington Bureau 31084
Editorial: 1500 K St NW Ste 600, Washington, District Of Columbia 20005-1200 **Tel:** 1 202 414-0600
Email: afp-us@afp.com **Web site:** http://www.afp.com
Bureau Chief: Shafiqul Alam; **Bureau Chief:** Cat Barton
Profile: Founded in 1835, this international news service is headquartered in Paris. It serves thousands of radio, TV, magazine, newspaper and company subscribers around the globe. Journalists are based in 165 countries providing top quality international service tailored for the specific needs of clients in each region.
Language (s): English
NEWS SERVICE/SYNDICATE

AGRA PRESSE 353299
Editorial: 84 boulevard de Sebastopol, Paris 75003 **Tel:** 33 1 42 74 28 00
Web site: http://www.agra-online.com
Rédacteur en Chef: Hervé Plagnol; **Rédacteur en Chef:** François-Xavier Simon
Profile: Press agency focussing on agriculture's economics and politics including business, financial, social, juridical issues. Local Translation:Agence spécialisée dans l'économie et la politique liée à l'agriculture. Les produits :- 'Agra-Presse' : hebdomadaire, rubriques : actualité économique,

financière, sociale, politique, agricole, juridique, - 'Agra-Fil' : quotidien transmis par fax at par e-mail : donne l'essentiel de l'actualité agricole du jour,- 'Agra-Europe' : hebdomadaire qui établit un panorama de la vie européenne agricole, politique et juridique, - 'Agra-Valor' : mensuel de la valorisation industrielle des produits agricoles, fait le point sur les dernières évolutions collectées auprès des industriels, des chercheurs et des producteurs.
NEWS SERVICE/SYNDICATE

AITV - AGENCE INTERNATIONALE D'IMAGES DE TELEVISION 353300
Editorial: 35-37 rue Danton, Malakoff 92240 **Tel:** 33 1 55 22 71 04
Web site: http://www.rfo.fr
Rédacteur en Chef: Didier Gaudermen
Profile: International press agency focussing on general interest information. Aimed at the Middle East and Africa.
Language (s): French
NEWS SERVICE/SYNDICATE

ANDIA 353331
Editorial: 10 rue Charles Croize, ZA de la Teillais, Pace 35740 **Tel:** 33 2 99 83 50 70
Email: photo@andia.fr **Web site:** http://www.andia.fr
Director: Serge Corre
Profile: Photo agency covering regional news and current affairs including economy, tourism, gastronomy, politics and society.
Language (s): French
NEWS SERVICE/SYNDICATE

APM International 353301
Owner: Wilmington Group plc
Editorial: 33 avenue de la Republique, Paris 75011 **Tel:** 33 1 48 06 54 92
Email: redaction@apmnews.com **Web site:** http://www.apmnews.com
Hôpitaux Politique de la santé: Caroline Besnier; **Gynécologie - Reproduction - Cardiologie:** Carole Debray; **Neurologie - Pneumologie - Rhumatologie:** Luu-Ly Do-Quang; **Médecine de ville Assurance Maladie:** Vincent Granier; **Pharmaciens Pneumologie - Douleur - APM SANTE:** Tra-My Ngouanesavanh; **Diabète:** Adelaïde Robert-Geraudel; **Infectiologie - Gastroentérologie:** Valérie Van Den Bos; **Directeur Général:** Alain Vernot
Profile: News agency covering health and medicine.
Language (s): French
NEWS SERVICE/SYNDICATE

COSMOS 741592
Editorial: 56, Boulevard Latour Maubourg, Paris 75007 **Tel:** 33 1 47 05 44 29
Email: info@cosmosphoto.com **Web site:** http://www.cosmosphoto.com
Director: Annie Boulat
Profile: Photography news agency.
Language (s): French
NEWS SERVICE/SYNDICATE

CREDO 741669
Owner: Agence de presse CREDO
Editorial: 30 rue des Acacias, Paris 75017 **Tel:** 33 1 44 09 78 80
Web site: http://info.agencedepresse-credo.fr
Profile: Press agency covering internal security issues, police, justice and investigation.
Language (s): French
NEWS SERVICE/SYNDICATE

ESDPA – European Security and Defence Press Association 916724
Owner: ESDPA
Editorial: 47, rue Erlanger, Paris 75016 **Tel:** 33 1 40 71 00 62
Email: joseph.roukoz@esdpa.org **Web site:** http://www.esdpa.org
Editor: Joseph Roukoz
Profile: News agency covering the defence and security industry.
Language (s): English
NEWS SERVICE/SYNDICATE

Eureka Presse 777027
Owner: S.A.R.L. Eureka Presse
Editorial: Immeuble Antares, Téléport 4, Chasseneuil-Du-Poitou 86962 **Tel:** 33 5 49 50 30 65
Email: redaction@eurekapresse.com **Web site:** http://www.eurekapresse.com
Profile: News service covering sports, automotive and new technologies.
NEWS SERVICE/SYNDICATE

Gamma-Rapho 741584
Owner: Gamma-Rapho
Editorial: 104 Boulevard Arago, Paris 75014 **Tel:** 33 1 73 00 70 70
Email: presse@gamma-rapho.com **Web site:** http://www.gamma-rapho.com
Politique: Sébastien Deslandes; **Directeur de la rédaction:** Alain Frilet; **News - Grands projets:** Rafaële Garnot; **Rédaction - News Internationales:** Daniel Lambert; **People:** Delphine Le Floch; **General Manager:** Stéphane Ledoux
Profile: News and photography agency covering news and current affairs including economics, business, arts, culture, sports and celebrities.
Language (s): French
NEWS SERVICE/SYNDICATE

Groupe AEF 896039
Owner: Groupe AEF
Editorial: 137, rue de l'Universite, Paris 75007 **Tel:** 33 1 53 10 39 39
Email: habitat@aef.info **Web site:** http://www.groupeaef.info
Profile: News service covering employment, education, professional training and HR.
Language (s): French
NEWS SERVICE/SYNDICATE

Infomédia 353310
Owner: Infomédia
Editorial: 58 rue de Châteaudun, Paris 75009 **Tel:** 33 1 48 01 87 35
Email: redaction@infomedia-sas.com **Web site:** http://www.infomediamc.fr
Editor in Chief: Olivier Brunet; **Director:** Jean-Damien Chatelain
Profile: News service covering financial management including asset management, personal finance, retirement, inheritance, life insurance, taxes, investment, property, mortgages, insurance, credits and online banking.
Language (s): French
NEWS SERVICE/SYNDICATE

Objectif Une 605872
Editorial: 172, rue Duguesclin, Lyon 69003 **Tel:** 33 4 72 32 29 01
Email: redaction@objectifune.fr **Web site:** http://www.objectifune.fr
Gastronomie: Pascal Alquier; **Gastronomie Tourisme People:** James Huet; **Développement durable:** Laure Leter; **Gastronomie Tourisme:** Olivier Marie; **Immobilier Aménagement Placement:** Françoise Sigot
Profile: General text and photo agency covering news and current affairs.
Language (s): French
NEWS SERVICE/SYNDICATE

PEOPLE TELEVISION 742844
Editorial: Village de la communication, 44-50, avenue du Capitaine Glarner, Saint Ouen 93400 **Tel:** 33 1 49 48 63 50
Email: benjamin.riffle@people-television.com **Web site:** http://www.people-television.com
Dirigeant: François Baudry; **Editor:** Benjamin Riffle
Profile: Audio visual news agency covering economics.
Language (s): French
NEWS SERVICE/SYNDICATE

Relaxnews 353322
Owner: Relaxnews
Editorial: 34 Quai de La Loire, Paris 75019 **Tel:** 33 1 53 19 89 50
Email: echarpentier@relaxnews.com **Web site:** http://www.relaxnews.com
Editor in Chief: Emmanuelle Charpentier; **President:** Jérôme Doncieux
Profile: Press agency covering leisure activities.
Language (s): English
NEWS SERVICE/SYNDICATE

Sipa Press 488913
Owner: SIPA
Editorial: 101, Boulevard Murat, Paris 75016 **Tel:** 33 1 47 43 47 43
Email: sipa@sipa.com **Web site:** http://www.sipa.com
Director: Miguel Ferro; **Director:** Paul Marnef; **General Manager:** Mete Zihnioglu
Profile: Photo agency covering news and current affairs, entertainment and sports.
Language (s): French
NEWS SERVICE/SYNDICATE

SUNSET Presse 743166
Owner: SUNSET Presse
Editorial: 23, rue Sebastien Mercier, Paris 75015 **Tel:** 33 1 45 75 51 79
Email: sunsetpresse@sunsetpresse.fr **Web site:** http://www.sunsetpresse.fr
Profile: Audio-visual press agency covering general new and current affairs including nature, environment, tourism, leisure, sports, celebrities, industry and lifestyle.
Language (s): French
NEWS SERVICE/SYNDICATE

Technoscope 353325
Editorial: 6 Cite de Trevise, Paris 75009 **Tel:** 33 6 70 39 99 31
Email: redaction@technoscope.fr **Web site:** http://www.technoscope.fr
Rédactrice en chef - Informatique Biotechnologie: Françoise Breton; **Médical - Santé Biotechnologie Environnement:** Corinne Drault; **Directrice:** Marie-Odile Mizier; **Industries et recherche agro-alimentaire:** Paul Tjomb
Profile: Press and photo agency covering applied sciences, technology and environment.
Language (s): French
NEWS SERVICE/SYNDICATE

Gabon
Time Difference: GMT +1
National Telephone Code: 241
Continent: Africa
Capital: Libreville

Newspapers

L' Union 318911
Owner: Sonapresse
Editorial: BP 3849, Libreville **Tel:** 241 1 73 58 60
Email: publicum@sonapresse.com **Web site:** http://www.union.sonapresse.com
Freq: Daily; **Circ:** 22000 Publisher's Statement
Editor In Chief: Leonard Mba Assoume
Profile: National newspaper covering regional, national and international news and current affairs including business, politics, culture and sport.
Language (s): French
Ad Rate: Full Page Mono 810000.00
Currency: Communauté Financière Africaine Francs BEAC
DAILY NEWSPAPER

News Service/Syndicate

Gabonews 518556
Owner: Gabonews
Editorial: Immeuble Papillon Gris, Libreville **Tel:** 241 77 87 44
Email: contact@gabonews.com **Web site:** http://www.gabonews.com
Profile: National news agency focussing on news and current affairs including politics, economics, society, celebrity and sports.
Language (s): French
NEWS SERVICE/SYNDICATE

Gambia
Time Difference: GMT
National Telephone Code: 220
Continent: Africa
Capital: Banjul

Newspapers

The Point Newspaper 156637
Owner: Point Press
Editorial: 2 Garba Jahumpa Road, Bakau, New Town, Banjul **Tel:** 220 4 49 74 41
Email: thepoint13@yahoo.com **Web site:** http://thepoint.gm
Freq: Daily; **Circ:** 2500 Publisher's Statement
Managing Director / Co-Publisher: Pap Saine; **Editor:** Baboucarr Senghore
Profile: Newspaper covering regional, national and international news and current affairs including politics, court news, religion and sport.
Language (s): English
DAILY NEWSPAPER

Georgia
Time Difference: GMT +4
National Telephone Code: 995
Continent: Asia
Capital: Tbilisi

Newspapers

Akhali Taoba 573065
Editorial: 89/24 David Aghmashenebeli Avenue, 11th floor, Tbilisi **Tel:** 995 32 95 25 89
Email: axtaoba@mail.ru **Web site:** http://www.opentext.org.ge/akhalitaoba
Freq: Daily
Editor: Lali Aslanishvili; **Editor In Chief:** Soso Goginashvili
Profile: Newspaper covering general news, politics, public issues, economy, law, international news.
Language (s): Russian
DAILY NEWSPAPER

Argumenty i Fakty Tbilisi 653856
Owner: Planeta LLC
Editorial: 2/7 Sulkhan Saba Street, Tbilisi **Tel:** 995 32 2935563
Web site: http://gazeta.aif.ru/category/external

Georgia

Freq: Weekly; **Circ:** 16000 Publisher's Statement
Editor: Ekaterine Eliava
Profile: Covers politics, economics, culture, education, art, sport and society.
Language (s): Russian
DAILY NEWSPAPER

Gazeti Batumelebi 654245
Owner: Gazeti Batumelebi LLC
Tel: 995 8222 27 45 12
Email: batumelebi@list.ru **Web site:** http://newspaperbatumelebi.blogspot.com
Freq: Weekly; **Circ:** 2400 Publisher's Statement
Profile: Covers politics, education, crime, economy, sport, culture.
Language (s): Russian
DAILY NEWSPAPER

Georgia Today 573062
Editorial: 41 Irakli Abashidze Str., Apt. 45, Tbilisi 179
Tel: 995 32 229 5919
Email: marketing@georgiatoday.ge **Web site:** http://www.georgiatoday.ge
General Manager: George Sharashidze
Profile: Georgia Today is Georgia's independent English-language newspaper, published weekly since 2000 and from November 2015 re-branded and divided into two bi-weekly editions: a Friday Georgia Today newspaper covering Politics, Society and Culture, and a Tuesday GT Business edition focused on Business.
Language (s): English
DAILY NEWSPAPER

Georgian Business Week 653854
Editorial: 87 Paliashvili Street, Tbilisi
Tel: 995 32 22 75 05
Email: gbw@gbc.ge
Freq: Weekly; **Circ:** 4000 Publisher's Statement
Editor-in-Chief: Maia Edilashvili
Profile: Offers a wide range of business news and expert opinions, as well as political stories of specific interest in English language.
Language (s): English
Ad Rate: Full Page Mono 200.00
Ad Rate: Full Page Colour 400.00
Currency: United States Dollars
DAILY NEWSPAPER

The Georgian Times 572922
Owner: Media holding Georgian times
Editorial: 12 Kikodze Street, Tbilisi 38
Tel: 995 32 93 44 05
Email: editor@goetimes.ge **Web site:** http://www.geotimes.ge
Circ: 60000 Publisher's Statement
Publisher: Malkhaz Gulashvili
Profile: Features news on politics, political analysis, business and economics news, religion issues.
Language (s): English
Ad Rate: Full Page Mono 720.00
Currency: United States Dollars
DAILY NEWSPAPER

Komsomolskaya Pravda v Gruzii 653857
Owner: Planeta LLC
Editorial: 2/7 Sulkhan Saba Street, Tbilisi
Tel: 995 32 2921859
Freq: Weekly; **Circ:** 3500 Publisher's Statement
Editor: Nina Argutinskaya
Profile: Georgian edition of Russian national daily that covers politics, economics, culture, art, education, sport, city life and people.
Language (s): Russian
DAILY NEWSPAPER

Kviris Palitra 573066
Owner: Palitra Media Holding
Editorial: Tbilisi **Tel:** 995 32 42 43 40
Email: news@kvirispalitra.com **Web site:** http://www.kvirispalitra.com/palitra/frp_palitra.htm
Freq: Weekly
Profile: Weekly national newspaper covering social and cultural aspects of life.
Language (s): Russian
DAILY NEWSPAPER

The Messenger 653853
Editorial: 43 Belinski Street, Tbilisi
Tel: 995 32 93 91 69
Email: messenger@messenger.com.ge **Web site:** http://www.messenger.com.ge
Freq: Daily; **Circ:** 4000 Publisher's Statement
Editor-in-Chief: Zaza Gachechiladze
Profile: News covered includes market making, banking, investments, marketing surveys, transport, statistics, social issues, currency exchange, tourism, culture, sports and criminal news and provides economic and political analysis of events.
Language (s): English
DAILY NEWSPAPER

Resonance 573064
Editorial: 142 Tsereteli Avenue, 3rd floor, Tbilisi
Tel: 995 32 96 92 60
Email: resonancenewspaper@yahoo.com **Web site:** http://www.resonancedaily.com
Freq: Daily; **Circ:** 4500 Publisher's Statement
Editor In Chief: Lasha Tughushi
Profile: Covers Georgian news, economy, culture, entertainment, sport.
Language (s): Russian
DAILY NEWSPAPER

Version Dossier 653855
Editorial: 7 St. Petersburg St., Tbilisi
Tel: 995 32 45 27 13
Email: dosie@caucasus.net
Freq: 2 Times/Week; **Circ:** 4000 Publisher's Statement
Publisher: Maia Purtseladze; **Editor:** Tamar Rostaishvili
Profile: National informative-analytical newspaper.
Language (s): Russian
DAILY NEWSPAPER

News Service/Syndicate

Prime News Agency 653761
Editorial: 28 Leselidze str., Tbilisi 105
Tel: 995 32 92 32 65
Email: info@primenewsonline.com **Web site:** http://eng.primenewsonline.com
Editor In Chief: Ia Amazashvili
Profile: Provides news on politics, economy, culture, social life and sport in Georgia and abroad.
NEWS SERVICE/SYNDICATE

Community Newspaper

Svobodnaya Gruzia 653837
Editorial: 3 Irakli II street, Tbilisi 108
Freq: Weekly; **Circ:** 5000
Editor In Chief: Tato Lakhishvili
Profile: Newspaper containing general news, digest of Georgian press, news on economy and business, covering political and society aspects.
Language (s): Russian
COMMUNITY NEWSPAPER

Germany

Time Difference: GMT +1
National Telephone Code: 49
Continent: Europe
Capital: Berlin

Newspapers

Aachener Nachrichten 159091
Owner: Zeitungsverlag Aachen GmbH
Editorial: Dresdener Strasse 3, Aachen 52068
Tel: 49 241 5101 310
Email: redaktion@zeitungsverlag-aachen.de **Web site:** http://www.aachener-nachrichten.de/
Freq: Mon thru Fri; **Circ:** 28
Profile: Die Aachener Nachrichten ist eine Tageszeitung für die Region der Stadt Aachen. Sie erscheint zusammen mit der Aachener Zeitung und beide gehören zum Aachener Zeitungsverlag. The Aachener Nachrichten is a daily newspaper for the Aachen city region. It's published together with the Aachener Zeitung and both belong to the Aachener Zeitungsverlag.
Language (s): German
Ad Rate: Full Page Mono 406.95
Currency: Euro
DAILY NEWSPAPER

Aachener Nachrichten, Düren (Dürener Nachrichten) 159353
Owner: Zeitungsverlag Aachen GmbH
Editorial: Lokalredaktion Düren, Pletzergasse 5, Düren 52349 **Tel:** 49 2421 2099870
Email: an-lokales-dueren@zeitungsverlag-aachen.de
Web site: http://www.aachener-nachrichten.de/lokales/dueren
Freq: Mon thru Fri; **Circ:** 28
Profile: Die Aachener Nachrichten, Düren (Dürener Nachrichten) sind eine Lokalausgabe der Aachener Nachrichten und bieten lokale Berichterstattung aus Düren, sowie Nachrichten aus der Umgebung. Die Aachener Nachrichten, Düren (Dürener Nachrichten) are a local edition of the newspaper Aachener Nachrichten and report about local news from Düren and surrounding area.
Language (s): German
DAILY NEWSPAPER

Aachener Nachrichten, Eifel (Eifeler Nachrichten) 159362
Owner: Zeitungsverlag Aachen GmbH
Editorial: Lokalredaktion Eifel, Matthias-Offermann-Strasse 3, Monschau 52156 **Tel:** 49 2472 970030
Email: lokales-eifel@zeitungsverlag-aachen.de **Web site:** http://www.aachener-nachrichten.de/lokales/eifel
Freq: Mon thru Fri; **Circ:** 28
Profile: Die Aachener Nachrichten, Eifel (Eifeler Nachrichten) sind eine Lokalausgabe der Aachener Nachrichten und bieten lokale Berichterstattung aus Monschau und Umgebung, sowie auch regionale Nachrichten. Aachener Nachrichten, Eifel (Eifeler Nachrichten) are a local version of the Aachener Nachrichten and present local news from Monschau and the surrounding area as well as regional news.
Language (s): German
DAILY NEWSPAPER

Aachener Nachrichten, Eschweiler (Eschweiler Nachrichten) 159384
Owner: Zeitungsverlag Aachen GmbH
Editorial: Lokalredaktion Eschweiler, Englerthstrasse 18, Eschweiler 52249 **Tel:** 49 2403 5554930
Email: lokales-eschweiler@zeitungsverlag-aachen.de
Web site: http://www.aachener-nachrichten.de/lokales/eschweiler
Freq: Mon thru Fri; **Circ:** 28
Profile: Die Aachener Nachrichten, Eschweiler (Eschweiler Nachrichten) sind eine Lokalausgabe der Aachener Nachrichten mit lokaler Berichterstattung aus Eschweiler und Nachrichten aus der Umgebung. Aachener Nachrichten, Eschweiler (Eschweiler Nachrichten) are a local version of the Aachener Nachrichten with local news from Eschweiler and news from the sourrounding region.
Language (s): German
DAILY NEWSPAPER

Aachener Nachrichten, Heinsberg (Heinsberger Nachrichten) 159868
Owner: Zeitungsverlag Aachen GmbH
Editorial: Lokalredaktion Heinsberg und Erkelenz, Apfelstrasse 48, Heinsberg 52525
Tel: 49 2452 1571330
Email: lokales-heinsberg@zeitungsverlag-aachen.de
Web site: http://www.aachener-nachrichten.de/lokales/heinsberg
Freq: Mon thru Fri
Profile: Die Aachener Nachrichten, Heinsberg (Heinsberger Nachrichten) ist eine Tageszeitung für die Stadt Region Heinsberg und Umgebung. Sie ist eine Lokalausgabe der Aachener Nachrichten. The Aachener Nachrichten, Heinsberg (Heinsberger Nachrichten) is a daily newspaper for the Heinsberg city region and surroundings. It's a local version of the Aachener Nachrichten.
Language (s): German
DAILY NEWSPAPER

Aachener Nachrichten, Stolberg (Stolberger Nachrichten) 159936
Owner: Zeitungsverlag Aachen GmbH
Editorial: Lokalredaktion Stolberg, Englerthstrasse 18, Stolberg 52222 **Tel:** 49 2402 12600 30
Email: lokales-stolberg@zeitungsverlag-aachen.de
Web site: http://www.aachener-nachrichten.de/lokales/stolberg
Freq: Daily; **Circ:** 28
Profile: Die Aachener Nachrichten, Stolberg (Stolberger Nachrichten) sind eine Lokalausgabe der Aachener Nachrichten mit lokaler Berichterstattung aus Stolberg und Nachrichten aus der Umgebung. Aachener Nachrichten, Stolberg (Stolberger Nachrichten) are a local version of the Aachener Nachrichten with local news from Stolberg and news from the sourrounding region.
Language (s): German
DAILY NEWSPAPER

Aachener Zeitung 159092
Owner: Zeitungsverlag Aachen GmbH
Editorial: Aachener Verlagsgesellschaft mbH, Dresdener Strasse 3, Aachen 52068
Tel: 49 241 5101 0
Email: redaktion@zeitungsverlag-aachen.de **Web site:** http://www.aachener-zeitung.de
Freq: Mon thru Fri; **Circ:** 28
Profile: Die Aachener Zeitung ist eine Tageszeitung für die Stadtregion Aachen, die zusammen mit den Aaachener Nachrichten erscheint. Beide gehören zum Aachener Zeitungsverlag. The Aachener Zeitung is a daily newspaper for the Aachen city region published together with the Aachener Nachrichten. Both belong to the Aachener Zeitungsverlag.
Language (s): German
Ad Rate: Full Page Mono 406.95
Currency: Euro
DAILY NEWSPAPER

Aachener Zeitung, Düren (Dürener Zeitung) 159354
Owner: Zeitungsverlag Aachen GmbH
Editorial: Lokalredaktion Düren, Pletzergasse 5, Düren 52349 **Tel:** 49 2421 2259100
Email: az-lokales-dueren@zeitungsverlag-aachen.de
Web site: http://www.aachener-zeitung.de/lokales/dueren
Freq: Mon thru Fri; **Circ:** 28
Profile: Aachener Zeitung, Düren (Dürener Zeitung) ist eine Lokalausgabe der Aachener Zeitung für Düren und beinhaltet lokale und regionale Berichterstattung, sowie Nachrichten. Aachener Zeitung, Düren (Dürener Zeitung) is a local edition of the Aachener Zeitung for Düren and offers local and regional reporting, as well as news.
Language (s): German
DAILY NEWSPAPER

Aachener Zeitung, Eschweiler (Eschweiler Zeitung) 159385
Owner: Zeitungsverlag Aachen GmbH
Editorial: Lokalredaktion Eschweiler, Englerthstrasse 18, Eschweiler 52249 **Tel:** 49 2403 5554930
Email: lokales-eschweiler@zeitungsverlag-aachen.de
Web site: http://www.aachener-zeitung.de/lokales/eschweiler
Freq: Mon thru Fri; **Circ:** 28
Profile: Die Aachener Zeitung, Eschweiler (Eschweiler Zeitung) sind eine Lokalausgabe der Aachener Zeitung mit lokaler Berichterstattung aus Eschweiler und Nachrichten aus der Umgebung. Aachener Zeitung, Eschweiler (Eschweiler Zeitung) are a local version of the Aachener Zeitung with local news from Eschweiler and news from the sourrounding region.
Language (s): German
DAILY NEWSPAPER

Aachener Zeitung, Jülich (Jülicher Zeitung) 159551
Owner: Zeitungsverlag Aachen GmbH
Editorial: Lokalredaktion Jülich, Bahnhofstrasse 1, Jülich 52428 **Tel:** 49 2461 995730
Email: lokales-juelich@zeitungsverlag-aachen.de
Web site: http://www.aachener-zeitung.de/lokales/juelich
Freq: Mon thru Fri; **Circ:** 28
Profile: Aachener Zeitung, Jülich (Jülicher Zeitung) ist eine Lokalausgabe der Aachener Zeitung für die nördliche Hälfte des Kreises Düren. Aachener Zeitung, Jülich (Jülicher Zeitung) is a local edition of the Aachener Zeitung for the northern half of the Düren region.
Language (s): German
DAILY NEWSPAPER

Aachener Zeitung, Stolberg (Stolberger Zeitung) 159937
Owner: Zeitungsverlag Aachen GmbH
Editorial: Lokalredaktion Stolberg, Englerthstrasse 18, Eschweiler 52249 **Tel:** 49 2402 12600-30
Email: lokales-stolberg@zeitungsverlag-aachen.de
Web site: https://www.aachener-zeitung.de/lokales/stolberg
Freq: Mon thru Fri; **Circ:** 28
Profile: Die Aachener Zeitung, Stolberg (Stolberger Zeitung) sind eine Lokalausgabe der Aachener Zeitung mit lokaler Berichterstattung aus Stolberg und Nachrichten aus der Umgebung. Aachener Zeitung, Stolberg (Stolberger Zeitung) are a local version of the Aachener Zeitung with local news from Stolberg and news from the sourrounding region.
Language (s): German
DAILY NEWSPAPER

Aalener Nachrichten 159093
Owner: Schwäbischer Verlag GmbH & Co. KG
Editorial: Aalener Nachrichten & INFO Ostalb, Marktplatz 15, Aalen 73430 **Tel:** 49 7361 570521
Email: redaktion@aalener-nachrichten.de **Web site:** http://www.schwaebische.de/region/ostalb/aalen/aalen-sz-team.html
Circ: 28
Profile: Aalener Nachrichten ist eine Tageszeitungausgabe der Schwäbischen Zeitung für die Region Aalen. Aalener Nachrichten is a daily newspaper edition of the Schwäbische Zeitung for the region of Aalen.
Language (s): German
DAILY NEWSPAPER

Aar-Bote 159094
Owner: Verlagsgruppe Rhein Main GmbH & Co. KG
Editorial: Verlagsgruppe Rhein Main GmbH & Co. KG, Erich-Dombrowski-Strasse 2, Mainz 55127
Tel: 49 611 3550
Email: impressum@vrm.de **Web site:** http://www.wiesbadener-tagblatt.de
Freq: Daily; **Circ:** 28
Profile: Regionalausgabe des Wiesbadener Tagblatt mit lokalen Themen und Nachrichten. Regionals edition of the Wiesbadener Tagblatt covering local topics and news.
Language (s): German
DAILY NEWSPAPER

Abendzeitung 799062
Owner: Abendzeitung München Verlags-GmbH
Editorial: Abendzeitung München Verlags-GmbH, Garmischer Strasse 35, München 81373
Tel: 49 89 2377 3100
Email: redaktion@abendzeitung.de **Web site:** http://www.abendzeitung-muenchen.de
Freq: Mon thru Fri; **Circ:** 28
Profile: Regionalzeitung für München und Umgebung mit Nachrichten aus Politik, Wirtschaft, Kultur und Sport, Prominente, Veranstaltungen, Reise und Gewinnspiele. Regional newspaper for the Munich area with news from politics, economy, culture and sports, celebrities, events, travel and competitions.
Language (s): German
DAILY NEWSPAPER

Acher-Rench-Zeitung Oberkirch/Achern 159098
Owner: Reiff Verlag KG
Editorial: Lokalredaktion Achern/Oberkirch, Am Marktplatz 4, Oberkirch 77704
Web site: http://www.bo.de/lokales/achern-oberkirch
Freq: Daily; **Circ:** 28
Profile: Lokale Tageszeitung für Orte Achern / Oberkirch in Baden-Württemberg.
Language (s): German
DAILY NEWSPAPER

Aichacher Zeitung 888356
Owner: Verlag Mayer & Söhne Druck- und Mediengruppe GmbH & Co KG
Editorial: Oberbernbacher Weg 7, Aichach 86551
Tel: 49 8251 880140
Email: redaktion@aichacher-zeitung.de **Web site:** http://www.aichacher-zeitung.de/vorort/
Freq: Daily; **Circ:** 28
Profile: Lokalzeitung für Aichach mit Nachrichten aus Politik, Wirtschaft, Sport, Kultur und Gesellschaft.

Local newspaper for Aichach with news from politics, economy, sports, culture and society.
Language (s): German
DAILY NEWSPAPER

Allgäuer Zeitung 159110
Owner: Allgäuer Zeitungsverlag GmbH
Editorial: Allgäuer Zeitungsverlag GmbH / rta.design GmbH, Heisinger Strasse 14, Kempten 87437
Tel: 49 831 206 439
Email: redaktion@azv.de **Web site:** http://www.all-in.de/
Freq: Mon thru Fri; **Circ:** 28
Profile: Die Allgäuer Zeitung ist eine unabhängige, bewusst demokratische Tageszeitung, die vom Allgäuer Zeitungsverlag herausgebracht. Sie stellt die führende Tageszeitung in ihrer Region dar. The Allgäuer Zeitung is an independent and democratic daily newspaper published by the Allgäuer Zeitungsverlag representing the leading daily newspaper in its region.
Language (s): German
DAILY NEWSPAPER

Allgäuer Zeitung, Memmingen (Memminger Zeitung) 159655
Owner: Allgäuer Zeitungsverlag GmbH / rta.design GmbH
Editorial: Memminger Zeitung, Donaustrasse 14, Memmingen 87700 **Tel:** 49 8331 109 170
Email: redaktion@all-in.de **Web site:** http://www.all-in.de/nachrichten/lokales/memmingen/
Freq: Mon thru Fri; **Circ:** 28
Profile: Die Memminger Zeitung ist eine regionale Tageszeitung aus Schwaben. Memminger Zeitung is a regional daily newspaper from Swabia.
Language (s): German
DAILY NEWSPAPER

Allgemeine Zeitung 159115
Owner: Verlagsgruppe Rhein Main GmbH & Co. KG
Editorial: Verlagsgruppe Rhein Main GmbH & Co. KG, Erich-Dombrowski-Strasse 2, Mainz 55127
Tel: 49 6131 485960
Email: az-redaktion@vrm.de **Web site:** http://www.allgemeine-zeitung.de
Freq: Mon thru Fri; **Circ:** 28
Profile: Allgemeine Zeitung ist eine deutsche Tageszeitung mit regionale Nachrichten aus Mainz, Rheinland-Pfalz, Hessen, Rheinhessen und dem westlichen Rhein-Main-Gebiet. Allgemeine Zeitung is a German daily newspaper with regional news from Mainz, Rhineland-Palatinate, Hesse, Rhine-Hesse and the western Rhine-Main area.
Language (s): German
DAILY NEWSPAPER

Allgemeine Zeitung (Coesfeld) 159114
Owner: Verlag J. Fleißig GmbH & Co.
Editorial: Rosenstrasse 2, Coesfeld 48653
Tel: 49 2541 921151
Email: coesfeld@azonline.de **Web site:** http://www.azonline.de
Freq: Mon thru Fri; **Circ:** 28
Profile: Die Allgemeine Zeitung Coesfeld ist eine Lokalzeitung für Coesfeld und Umgebung mit lokaler Berichterstattung zu Politik, Sport, Kultur und Gesellschaft. The Allgemeine Zeitung Coesfeld is a local paper for Coesfeld and surrounding area with local reporting on politics, sports, culture and society.
Language (s): German
DAILY NEWSPAPER

Allgemeine Zeitung der Lüneburger Heide 159116
Owner: C. Beckers Buchdruckerei GmbH & Co. KG
Editorial: C. Beckers Buchdruckerei GmbH & Co. KG, Gross Liederner Strasse 45, Uelzen 29525
Tel: 49 581 808 91 100
Email: redaktion.az@cbeckers.de **Web site:** http://www.az-online.de
Freq: Mon thru Fri; **Circ:** 28
Profile: Die Allgemeine Zeitung der Lüneburger Heide ist eine von der C. Beckers Buchdruckerei GmbH & Co. KG herausgegebene deutsche Tageszeitung, die in der Region der Lüneburger Heide (Niedersachsen) erscheint. The Allgemeine Zeitung der Lüneburger Heide is a German daily newspaper published by C. Beckers Buchdruckerei GmbH & Co. KG appearing in the region of the Lüneburger Heide (Lower Saxony).
Language (s): German
DAILY NEWSPAPER

Anzeiger für Harlingerland 159217
Owner: Brune-Mettcker Druck- und Verlags-GmbH
Editorial: Brune-Mettcker Druck- und Verlags-GmbH, Am Markt 18, Wittmund 26409
Tel: 49 4462 989 180
Email: redaktion@harlinger.de **Web site:** http://www.harlinger.de
Freq: Mon thru Fri; **Circ:** 28
Profile: Der Anzeiger für Harlingerland ist ein regionales Tageblatt für den Ostfriesischen Raum. The Anzeiger für Harlingerland is a regional newspaper of East Frisia.
Language (s): German
DAILY NEWSPAPER

Augsburger Allgemeine 159224
Owner: Presse-Druck- und Verlags-GmbH
Editorial: Augsburger Allgemeine Zeitung, Curt-Frenzel-Str. 2, Augsburg 86167 **Tel:** 49 821 777 0
Email: redaktion@augsburger-allgemeine.de **Web site:** http://www.augsburger-allgemeine.de
Freq: Mon thru Fri; **Circ:** 28
Profile: Die Augsburger Allgemeine ist eine regionale Tageszeitung. Sie gehört zur Mediengruppe Pressedruck. Sie stellt eine der größten bayerischen Tageszeitungen dar. The Augsburger Allgemeine is a regional daily newspaper belonging to the Mediengruppe Pressedruck. It represents one of the biggest Bavarian daily newspapers.
Language (s): German
DAILY NEWSPAPER

Augsburger Allgemeine Nordausgabe 916392
Owner: Presse-Druck- und Verlags-GmbH
Editorial: Augsburger Allgemeine Zeitung, Curt-Frenzel-Str. 2, Augsburg 86167 **Tel:** 49 8217 770
Email: redaktion@augsburger-allgemeine.de **Web site:** http://www.augsburger-allgemeine.de
Freq: Daily; **Circ:** 223010
Profile: Nordausgabe der Augsburger Allgemeinen, einer regionalen Tageszeitung. Sie gehört zur Mediengruppe Pressedruck. Sie stellt eine der größten bayerischen Tageszeitungen dar. Northern edition of the Augsburger Allgemeine, a regional daily newspaper belonging to the Mediengruppe Pressedruck. It represents one of the biggest Bavarian daily newspapers.
Language (s): German
DAILY NEWSPAPER

Augsburger Allgemeine, Dillingen (Donau Zeitung Dillingen) 159348
Owner: Presse-Druck- und Verlags-GmbH
Editorial: Donau Zeitung, Grosse Allee 47, Dillingen 66763 **Tel:** 49 9071 7949 11
Web site: http://www.augsburger-allgemeine.de/dillingen
Freq: Mon thru Fri; **Circ:** 28
Profile: Augsburger Allgemeine, Dillingen (Donau Zeitung Dillingen) ist eine lokale Tageszeitung aus Dillingen., die überwiegend lokale Nachrichten thematisiert. Augsburger Allgemeine, Dillingen (Donau Zeitung Dillingen) is a local daily newspaper for Dillingen covering mostly local news.
Language (s): German
DAILY NEWSPAPER

Augsburger Allgemeine, Donauwörth (Donauwörther Zeitung) 159347
Owner: Presse-Druck- und Verlags-GmbH
Editorial: Donauworther Zeitung, Heilig-Kreuz-Strasse 12, Donauwörth 86609 **Tel:** 49 906 7806 25
Email: redaktion@donauwoerther-zeitung.de **Web site:** http://www.augsburger-allgemeine.de/donauwoerth/
Freq: Mon thru Fri; **Circ:** 28
Profile: Augsburger Allgemeine, Donauwörth (Donauwörther Zeitung) ist eine locale Tageszeitung für die Region um Donauwörth. Augsburger Allgemeine, Donauwörth (Donauwörther Zeitung) is a local daily newspaper for the region of Donauwörth.
Language (s): German
DAILY NEWSPAPER

Augsburger Allgemeine, Friedberg (Friedberger Allgemeine) 159418
Owner: Presse-Druck- und Verlags-GmbH
Editorial: Friedberger Allgemeine, Marienplatz 11a, Friedberg 86316 **Tel:** 49 821 65 07 04 20
Email: redaktion@friedberger-allgemeine.de **Web site:** http://www.augsburger-allgemeine.de/friedberg/
Freq: Mon thru Fri; **Circ:** 28
Profile: Augsburger Allgemeine, Friedberg (Friedberger Allgemeine) ist eine lokale Tageszeitung für Friedberg. Augsburger Allgemeine, Friedberg (Friedberger Allgemeine) is a local daily newspaper for the region of Friedberg.
Language (s): German
DAILY NEWSPAPER

Augsburger Allgemeine, Günzburg (Günzburger Zeitung) 159464
Owner: Presse-Druck- und Verlags-GmbH
Editorial: Günzburger Zeitung, Hofgasse 9, Günzburg 89312 **Tel:** 49 8221 917 40
Email: redaktion@guenzburger-zeitung.de **Web site:** http://www.augsburger-allgemeine.de/guenzburg
Freq: Mon thru Fri; **Circ:** 28
Profile: Augsburger Allgemeine, Günzburg (Günzburger Zeitung) ist eine regionale Tageszeitung in Bayern. Der Mantelteil wird von der Augsburger Allgemeinen Zeitung geliefert. Augsburger Allgemeine, Günzburg (Günzburger Zeitung) is a regional daily newspaper in Bavaria. The cover sections is provided by the Augsburger Allgemeine Zeitung.
Language (s): German
DAILY NEWSPAPER

Augsburger Allgemeine, Landsberg (Landsberger Tagblatt) 159607
Owner: Presse-Druck- und Verlags-GmbH
Editorial: Landsberger Tagblatt, Von-Kühlmann-Strasse 3, Landsberg 86899 **Tel:** 49 8191 326 200
Email: redaktion@landsberger-tagblatt.de **Web site:** http://www.augsburger-allgemeine.de/landsberg/
Freq: Mon thru Fri; **Circ:** 28
Profile: Augsburger Allgemeine, Landsberg (Landsberger Tagblatt) ist eine lokaleTageszeitung für Landsberg. Augsburger Allgemeine, Landsberg (Landsberger Tagblatt) is a local daily newspaper for Landsberg.
Language (s): German
DAILY NEWSPAPER

Augsburger Allgemeine, Mindelheim (Mindelheimer Zeitung) 159660
Owner: Presse-Druck- und Verlags-GmbH
Editorial: Lokalredaktion Mindelheim, Dreerstr. 6, Mindelheim 87719 **Tel:** 49 8261 99 13 20
Email: redaktion@mindelheimer-zeitung.de **Web site:** http://www.augsburger-allgemeine.de/mindelheim/
Freq: Mon thru Fri; **Circ:** 28
Profile: Augsburger Allgemeine, Mindelheim (Mindelheimer Zeitung) ist eine lokale Zeitung mit lokaler Berichterstattung aus Mindelheim, sowie auch Nachrichten aus der Umgebung. Augsburger Allgemeine, Mindelheim (Mindelheimer Zeitung) is a local newspaper with news from Mindelheim and the surrounding region.
Language (s): German
DAILY NEWSPAPER

B.Z. 159318
Owner: B.Z. Ullstein GmbH
Editorial: B.Z. Ullstein GmbH, Axel-Springer-Strasse 65, Berlin 10888 **Tel:** 49 30 2591 73716
Email: redaktion@bz-berlin.de **Web site:** http://www.bz-berlin.de
Freq: Mon thru Fri; **Circ:** 28
Profile: Die deutsche, regionale Boulevardzeitung B.Z. berichtet Nachrichten aus Berlin und Brandenburg und bietet Reportagen, Sport, Kultur, Rätsel und Szene an. B.Z. ist nicht mit der regionalen Zeitschrift Berliner Zeitung zu verwechseln. The German regional tabloid B.Z.'s coverage includes news from Berlin and Brandenburg, features, sports, culture and brainteasers. B.Z. should not be confused the with regional newspaper Berliner Zeitung.
Language (s): German
DAILY NEWSPAPER

Badische Neueste Nachrichten, Bretten (Brettener Nachrichten) 159301
Owner: Badische Neueste Nachrichten Badendruck GmbH
Editorial: Melanchthonstrasse 43, Bretten 75001
Tel: 49 7252 9388 3521
Email: redaktion.bretten@bnn.de **Web site:** http://www.brettener-nachrichten.de/
Freq: Daily
Profile: Die Brettener Nachrichten sind ein Lokalangebot der BNN, mit lokaler und regionaler Berichterstattung, sowie auch Nachrichten für Bretten und Umgebung.
Language (s): German
DAILY NEWSPAPER

Badische Zeitung 159230
Owner: Badischer Verlag GmbH & Co. KG
Editorial: Badischer Verlag GmbH & Co. KG, Lorracher Strasse 3, Freiburg 79115
Tel: 49 761 496 5201
Email: stadtredaktion@badische-zeitung.de **Web site:** http://www.badische-zeitung.de
Freq: Mon thru Fri; **Circ:** 28
Profile: Die Badische Zeitung ist eine Informationszeitung für Freiburg und Südbaden mit Nachrichten, Fotos, Veranstaltungen und Anzeigenmärkten. The Badische Zeitung is an informative newspaper for Freiburg and Südbaden providing information on news, photos, events and the advertising market.
Language (s): German
DAILY NEWSPAPER

Badische Zeitung, Emmendingen 666037
Owner: Badischer Verlag GmbH & Co. KG
Editorial: Badischer Verlag GmbH & Co. KG, Basler Strasse 88, Freiburg 79115 **Tel:** 49 7641 4960
Email: stadtredaktion@badische-zeitung.de **Web site:** http://www.badische-zeitung.de/emmendingen
Freq: Daily; **Circ:** 28
Profile: Badische Zeitung, Emmendingen ist eine Lokalzeitung für den Kreis Emmendingen.
Language (s): German
DAILY NEWSPAPER

Badische Zeitung, Waldkirch 666045
Owner: Badischer Verlag GmbH + Co. KG
Editorial: BADISCHER VERLAG GMBH & CO. KG, Basler Strasse 88, Freiburg 79115
Tel: 49 7681 4779785660
Email: redaktion.waldkirch@badische-zeitung.de
Web site: http://www.badische-zeitung.de
Freq: Daily
Profile: Lokalausgabe für das Waldkirch der Badischen Zeitung, einer Informationszeitung für Freiburg und Südbaden mit Nachrichten, Fotos, Veranstaltungen und Anzeigenmärkten. Local edition for Waldkirch of the Badische Zeitung, an informative newspaper for Freiburg and Südbaden providing information on news, photos, events and the advertising market.
Language (s): German
DAILY NEWSPAPER

Badisches Tagblatt 159229
Owner: Badisches Tagblatt GmbH
Editorial: Badisches Tagblatt GmbH, Stephanienstrasse 1 - 3, Baden-Baden 76530
Tel: 49 7221 2150
Email: redaktion@badisches-tagblatt.de **Web site:** http://www.badisches-tagblatt.de
Freq: Mon thru Fri; **Circ:** 28
Profile: Das Badische Tagblatt ist eine in Baden-Baden erscheinende Tageszeitung für den Landkreis Rastatt und den Stadtkreis Baden-Baden mit lokaler und regionaler Berichterstattung und Nachrichten. Badisches Tagblatt is daily newspaper appearing in Baden-Baden for the rural district of Raststatt and the urban region of Baden-Baden with local and regional reporting, as well as news.
Language (s): German
DAILY NEWSPAPER

Badisches Tagblatt, Bühl 903858
Owner: Badisches Tagblatt GmbH
Editorial: Johannespassage 8, Bühl 77815
Email: redbuehl@badisches-tagblatt.de **Web site:** http://www.badisches-tagblatt.de/buehl/index.html
Freq: Daily; **Circ:** 13425
Profile: Lokalausgabe der Tageszeitung Badisches Tagblatt mit lokalen Nachrichten für Bühl. Local edition of the daily newspaper Badisches Tagblatt covering local news for Bühl.
Language (s): German
DAILY NEWSPAPER

Badisches Tagblatt, Rastatt/Murgtal 666056
Owner: Badisches Tagblatt GmbH
Editorial: Badisches Tagblatt GmbH, Kaiserstrasse 40, Rastatt 76437 **Tel:** 49 7222 767 2221
Email: redmurg@badisches-tagblatt.de **Web site:** http://www.badisches-tagblatt.de/murgtal/index.html
Freq: Daily
Profile: Lokalausgabe der Tageszeitung Badisches Tagblatt mit lokalen Nachrichten für Rastatt/Murgtal. Local edition of the daily newspaper Badisches Tagblatt covering local news for Rastatt/Murgtal.
Language (s): German
DAILY NEWSPAPER

Bayerische Rundschau 159235
Owner: Mediengruppe Oberfranken GmbH & Co. KG
Editorial: Bayerische Rundschau, E.-C.-Baumann-Strasse 5, Kulmbach 95326 **Tel:** 49 9221 949211
Email: redaktion.kulmbach@infranken.de **Web site:** http://www.infranken.de/regional/kulmbach
Freq: Mon thru Fri; **Circ:** 28
Profile: Die Bayerische Rundschau ist eine regionale Tageszeitung für die Stadt und den Landkreis Kulmbach. Sie gehört zur Mediengruppe Oberfranken. Bayerische Rundschau is regional daily newspaper for the urban and rural region of Kulmbach. It belongs to the Mediengruppe Oberfranken.
Language (s): German
DAILY NEWSPAPER

Bayerwald-Echo 159238
Owner: Mittelbayerischer Verlag KG
Editorial: Am Steinmarkt 12, Cham 93413
Tel: 49 9971 8522 0
Email: echo@mittelbayerische.de **Web site:** http://www.mittelbayerische.de/cham
Freq: Mon thru Fri
Profile: Bayerwald-Echo ist eine Lokalzeitung für Cham und Umgebung, welche im Mittelbayerischen Verlag erscheint. Der Fokus der Berichterstattung liegt hierbei auf lokalem Geschehen in der Umgebung, sowie auch auf regionalen Nachrichten.
Language (s): German
DAILY NEWSPAPER

Bergedorfer Zeitung 159242
Owner: Bergedorfer Buchdruckerei von Ed. Wagner (GmbH & Co.)
Editorial: Bergedorfer Buchdruckerei von Ed. Wagner (GmbH & Co.), Curslacker Neuer Deich 50, Hamburg 21029 **Tel:** 49 40 725 66 211
Email: redaktion@bergedorfer-zeitung.de **Web site:** http://www.bergedorfer-zeitung.de
Freq: Mon thru Fri; **Circ:** 28
Profile: Die Bergedorfer Zeitung ist eine regionale Tageszeitung, die in Hamburg veröffentlicht und verlegt wird. Sie bietet lokale und regionale Berichterstattung aus der Region sowie Nachrichten. The Bergedorfer Zeitung is a small regional daily newspaper being distributed and published in Hamburg. It offers local and regional reporting, as well as news.
Language (s): German
DAILY NEWSPAPER

Bergische Landeszeitung - Wipperfürth 159243
Owner: Heinen-Verlag GmbH
Editorial: Marktplatz 2, Wipperfürth 51688
Tel: 49 2267 657000
Email: BLZ.Wipperfuerth@kr-redaktion.de **Web site:** http://www.rundschau-online.de
Freq: Mon thru Fri; **Circ:** 28
Profile: Die Lokalausgabe der Bergischen Landeszeitung für Wipperfürth, bietet vor allem lokale Berichterstattung, sowie auch Nachrichten aus der Umgebung.
Language (s): German
DAILY NEWSPAPER

Berliner Kurier 159245
Owner: Berliner Verlag GmbH
Editorial: Alte Jakobstrasse 105, Berlin 10969
Tel: 49 30 6333 11 0
Email: berlin.chefredaktion@dumont.de **Web site:** http://www.berliner-kurier.de
Freq: Mon thru Fri; **Circ:** 28

Profile: Der Berliner Kurier ist eine fest verankerte Boulevardzeitung der Beliner Region, die neben den Nachrichten aus der Stadt Berlin, Themen aus dem In- und Ausland behandelt. Sie zeichnet sich durch aktuelle, akzeptanzstarke Themen, Serien und Serviceelemente aus. The Berliner Kurier is an anchored bulletin for the region of Berlin besides local news of the city of Berlin also dealing with national and international topics. It's characterized by current and well-received topis, editions and service elements.
Language (s): German
Ad Rate: Full Page Mono 198.00
Currency: Euro
DAILY NEWSPAPER

Berliner Kurier am Sonntag 159246

Owner: Berliner Verlag GmbH
Editorial: Alte Jakobstrasse 105, Berlin 10969
Tel: 49 30 6333 11 0
Email: berlin.chefredaktion@dumont.de **Web site:** http://www.berliner-kurier.de
Freq: Sun
Profile: Der Berliner Kurier am Sonntag ist die Sonntagsausgabe der Berliner Tageszeitung Berliner Kurier. Die Sonntagsausgabe bietet neben Nachrichten und lokaler Berichterstattung auch Sonderthemen, Sportberichte und Beiträge aus Lifestyle, Kultur und Freizeit.
Language (s): German
DAILY NEWSPAPER

Berliner Morgenpost 159247

Owner: Funke Mediengruppe GmbH & Co. KGaA
Editorial: Berliner Morgenpost GmbH, Kurfürstendamm 21 - 22, Berlin 10874
Tel: 49 30 8872 77887
Email: redaktion@morgenpost.de **Web site:** http://www.morgenpost.de
Freq: Mon thru Fri; **Circ:** 28
Profile: Berliner Morgenpost ist eine deutsche Regionalzeitung für Berlin. Sie behandelt regionale, nationale und internationale Themen zu Politik, Wirtschaft und Verbraucherthemen. Berliner Morgenpost is a German regional newspaper for Berlin. It covers regional, national and international news on politics, business and consumer affairs.
Language (s): German
DAILY NEWSPAPER

Berliner Zeitung 159248

Owner: Berliner Verlag GmbH
Editorial: Alte Jakobstrasse 105, Berlin 10969
Tel: 49 30 6333 11 0
Email: berlin.chefredaktion@dumont.de **Web site:** http://www.berliner-zeitung.de
Freq: Mon thru Fri; **Circ:** 28
Profile: Berliner Zeitung ist eine deutsche Tageszeitung für Berlin. Dies beinhaltet regionale, nationale und internationale Nachrichten und Themen wie Politik, Wirtschaft und Kultur. Berliner Zeitung is nicht mit der regionalen Zeitschrift B.Z. zu verwechseln. Berliner Zeitung is a German regional newspaper. It covers regional, national and international news and topics such as politics, economics and culture. Berliner Zeitung should not be confused the with regional newspaper B.Z.
Language (s): German
Ad Rate: Full Page Mono 349.35
Currency: Euro
DAILY NEWSPAPER

Bersenbrücker Kreisblatt 159250

Owner: Neue Osnabrücker Zeitung GmbH & Co. KG
Editorial: Bersenbrücker Kreisblatt, Redaktion, Markt 5, Quakenbrück 49610 **Tel:** 49 54 31 9406 11
Email: redaktion@bersenbruecker-kreisblatt.de **Web site:** http://www.noz.de/bersenbruecker-kreisblatt
Freq: Mon thru Fri; **Circ:** 28
Profile: Das Bersenbrücker Kreisblatt ist eine kleine regionale Tageszeitung. Sie gehört der Neuen Osnabrücker Zeitung an. Bersenbrücker Kreisblatt is a small regional daily newspaper which is part of the Neue Osnabrücker Zeitung.
Language (s): German
DAILY NEWSPAPER

Bietigheimer Zeitung 159255

Owner: Druck- und Verlagsgesellschaft Bietigheim mbH
Editorial: Druck- und Verlagsgesellschaft Bietigheim mbH, Kronenbergstrasse 10, Bietigheim-Bissingen 74321 **Tel:** 49 7142 403 0
Email: info@bietigheimerzeitung.de **Web site:** http://www.swp.de/bietigheim
Freq: Mon thru Fri; **Circ:** 28
Profile: Die Bietigheimer Zeitung ist eine Tageszeitung, die ihren Sitz in Bietigheim-Bissingen hat und mit Ausgaben für Bietigheim, Bönnigheim und Sachsenheim erscheint. Sie gehört zur Redaktionsgruppe der Südwest Presse in Ulm und zur Anzeigengemeinschaft Stuttgart. The Bietigheimer Newspaper is a daily newspaper located in Bietigheim-Bissingen appearing with for editions for Bietigheim, Bönnigheim and Sachsenheim. It is part of the editors group of the Südwest Presse in Ulm as well as to the advertisement community Stuttgart.
Language (s): German
DAILY NEWSPAPER

Bild 159256

Owner: Bild GmbH & Co. KG
Editorial: Bild GmbH & Co. KG, Axel-Springer-Str. 65, Berlin 10888 **Tel:** 49 30 2591 0
Email: info@bild.de **Web site:** http://www.axelspringer.de
Freq: Daily; **Circ:** 28
Profile: BILD ist ein Boulevardblatt. BILD is a German tabloid newspaper.
Language (s): German
DAILY NEWSPAPER

Bild am Sonntag 159257

Owner: Bild GmbH & Co. KG
Editorial: Bild GmbH & Co. KG, Axel-Springer-Strasse 65, Berlin 10888 **Tel:** 49 30 25910
Email: info@bild.de **Web site:** http://www.bild.de/
Freq: Sun; **Circ:** 28
Profile: Die Bild am Sonnatg (BamS) ist eine Boulevardzeitung. Sie stellt eine Sonderauflage der BILD dar, ist im Gegensatz zu dieser aber familienfreundlicher konzipiert und erscheint im kleineren Zeitungsformat. The Bild am Sonntag (BamS) is a bulletin. Being a special edition of the BILD, it's designed more family-friendly and is published in a smaller newspaper format.
Language (s): German
DAILY NEWSPAPER

Bild, Aachen 666651

Owner: Bild GmbH & Co. KG
Editorial: Bild GmbH & Co. KG, Hohenzollernring 16-18, Koln 50672 **Tel:** 49 221 16044 0
Email: INFO@BILD.DE **Web site:** http://www.bild.de/
Freq: Daily; **Circ:** 28
Profile: Lokalausgabe der Bild Zeitung für die Stadt Aachen und Umgebung. Local edition of the Bild newspaper for the city of Aachen and its surroundings.
Language (s): German
DAILY NEWSPAPER

Bild, Münsterland 872166

Owner: Axel Springer SE
Editorial: Dietrich-Oppenberg-Platz 1, Essen 45127
Tel: 49 201 240534 107
Email: mediapilot@axelspringer.de **Web site:** http://www.axelspringer-mediapilot.de/portrait/BILD-MueNSTERLAND-BILD-MueNSTERLAND_673014.html
Freq: Daily; **Circ:** 28
Profile: Die Zeitschrift BILD MÜNSTERLAND ist der regionale Berichterstatter für den Landstrich innerhalb Nordrhein-Westfalens. Aktuelles Tagesgeschehen, Sport, Wirtschaft und Kultur gehört zu den Themengebieten. The magazine BILD MÜNSTERLAND is the regional reporter for the district within North Rhine-Westphalia. Current affairs, sports, business and culture belong to the topics.
Language (s): German
DAILY NEWSPAPER

Bild, Rhein-Main 915893

Owner: Bild GmbH & Co. KG
Editorial: Bild GmbH & Co. KG, Grüneburgweg 2, Frankfurt 60322 **Tel:** 49 69 848484 0
Email: info@bild.de **Web site:** http://www.bild.de
Freq: Daily; **Circ:** 88404
Profile: Regionalausgabe der Bild Zeitung für das Rhein-Main Gebiet. Regional edition of the Bild newspaper for the Rhine Main region.
Language (s): German
DAILY NEWSPAPER

Bild, Ruhr-Ost 915848

Owner: Bild GmbH & Co. KG
Editorial: Bild GmbH & Co. KG, Dietrich-Oppenberg-Platz 1, Essen 45127 **Tel:** 49 231 584439 0
Email: info@bild.de **Web site:** http://www.ruhrgebiet.bild.de
Freq: Daily; **Circ:** 59452
Profile: Regionalausgabe der Bild Zeitung für das östliche Ruhrgebiet. REgional edition of the Bild newspaper for the Eastern Ruhr area.
Language (s): German
DAILY NEWSPAPER

Bild, Ruhr-West 915870

Owner: Bild GmbH & Co. KG
Editorial: Bild GmbH & Co. KG, Dietrich-Oppenberg-Platz 1, Essen 45127 **Tel:** 49 201 2405 340
Email: info@bild.de **Web site:** http://www.ruhrgebiet.bild.de
Freq: Mon thru Fri; **Circ:** 59513
Profile: Regionalausgabe der Bild Zeitung für das westliche Ruhrgebiet. Regional edition of the Bild Zeitung for the Western Ruhr area.
Language (s): German
DAILY NEWSPAPER

Bild, Südwestfalen / Bergisches Land 873788

Owner: Bild GmbH & Co. KG
Editorial: Dietrich-Oppenberg-Platz 1, Essen 45127
Tel: 49 201 240534 107
Email: info@bild.de **Web site:** http://www.bild.de
Freq: Daily; **Circ:** 55803
Profile: Regionalausgabe der Bild Zeitung für Südwestfalen und das Bergische Land. Regional edition of the Bild newspaper for South Westfalia and the the Bergische Land.
Language (s): German
DAILY NEWSPAPER

Bild, Westfalen 890273

Owner: Axel Springer SE
Editorial: Dietrich-Oppenberg-Platz 1, Essen 45127
Tel: 49 231 584439 0
Web site: http://www.bild.de/
Freq: Daily; **Circ:** 28
Profile: Regionalausgabe der Bild Zeitung für die Region Westfalen. Regional edition of the Bild newspaper for the Westfalia region.
Language (s): German
DAILY NEWSPAPER

Billerbecker Anzeiger 159275

Owner: Verlag J. Fleißig GmbH & Co.
Editorial: Billerbecker Anzeiger, Lange Str. 8, Billerbeck 48727 **Tel:** 49 2543 2314 0
Email: billerbeck@azonline.de **Web site:** http://www.azonline.de/Billerbeck
Freq: Mon thru Fri; **Circ:** 28
Profile: Der Billerbecker Anzeiger ist eine lokale Tageszeitung, welche vor allem lokale Berichterstattung aus Billerbeck bietet, sowie auch Nachrichten aus dem Kreis Coesfeld.
Language (s): German
DAILY NEWSPAPER

Böhme-Zeitung 159283

Owner: Mundschenk Nachrichtengesellschaft mbH & Co. KG
Editorial: Mundschenk Nachrichtengesellschaft mbH & Co. KG, Harburger Str. 63, Soltau 29614
Tel: 49 5191 808 0
Email: info@mundschenk.de **Web site:** http://www.boehme-zeitung.de/
Freq: Mon thru Fri; **Circ:** 28
Profile: Die Böhme-Zeitung Zeitung ist eine Tageszeitung. Sie wird im Gebiet Heidekreis verbreitet. The Böhme-Zeitung is a newspaper of the Heidekreis. It's published in the area of Heidekreis.
Language (s): German
DAILY NEWSPAPER

Bönnigheimer Zeitung 159281

Owner: Druck- und Verlagsges. Bietigheim mbH
Editorial: Druck- und Verlagsgesellschaft Bietigheim mbH, Kronenbergstrasse 10, Bietigheim-Bissingen 74321 **Tel:** 49 7142 4030
Email: info@bietigheimerzeitung.de **Web site:** http://www.swp.de/bietigheim/lokales/boennigheim/
Freq: Mon thru Fri; **Circ:** 28
Profile: Die Bönnigheimer Zeitung ist eine lokale Ausgabe der Bietigheimer Zeitung, welche eine Tageszeitung darstellt und zum redaktionellen Manterverbund der Südwest Presse in Ulm sowie zur Anzeigengemeinschaft Stuttgart gehört. Der Fokus liegt hierbei auf lokaler Berichterstattung aus Bönnigheim und Nachrichten aus der Umgebung.
Language (s): German
DAILY NEWSPAPER

Börde Volksstimme 159282

Owner: Magdeburger Verlags- und Druckhaus GmbH
Editorial: Magdeburger Verlags- und Druckhaus GmbH, Bahnhofstrasse 17, Magdeburg 39104
Tel: 49 3949 946923
Email: redaktion.wanzleben@volksstimme.de **Web site:** http://www.volksstimme.de
Freq: Daily
Profile: Die Börde Volksstimme ist eine der 18 Lokalausgaben der Tageszeitung Volksstimme. Diese erscheint für das nördliche und mittlere Sachsen-Anhalt und hat ihren Stammstiz in Magdeburg.

The Börde Volksstimme is one of 18 local editions of the daily newspaper Volksstimme. The Volksstimme appears for the Northern and Middle Saxony-Anhalt and is headquartered in Magdeburg.
Language (s): German
DAILY NEWSPAPER

Borkener Zeitung 159287

Owner: Verlag J. Mergelsberg GmbH & Co. KG
Editorial: Verlag J. Mergelsberg GmbH & Co. KG, Bahnhofstrasse 6, Borken 46325 **Tel:** 49 2861 944 0
Email: redaktion@borkenerzeitung.de **Web site:** http://www.borkenerzeitung.de
Freq: Mon thru Fri; **Circ:** 28
Profile: Die Borkener Zeitung ist eine regionale Tageszeitung, die im Münsterland erscheint. Sie wird vom Verlag Mergelsberg GmbH & Co. KG herausgegeben. The Borkener Zeitung is a regional daily newspaper that is being distributed in the region of Borken (Münsterland) and published by the Verlag Mergelsberg GmbH & Co. KG.
Language (s): German
DAILY NEWSPAPER

Brandenburger Kurier 596201

Owner: Märkische Verlags- und Druck-Gesellschaft mbH Potsdam
Editorial: Friedrich-Engels-Strasse 24, Potsdam 14473 **Tel:** 49 331 28 40 0
Email: kontakt@MAZ-online.de **Web site:** http://www.maerkischeallgemeine.de
Freq: Daily
Profile: Lokalausgabe der Tageszeitung Märkische Allgemeine mit lokalen Themen und Nachrichten für Brandenburg. Local edition of the daily newspaper Märkische Allgemeine covering local news and topics for Brandenburg.
Language (s): German
DAILY NEWSPAPER

Braunschweiger Zeitung 159296

Owner: BZV Medienhaus GmbH
Editorial: BZV Medienhaus GmbH, Hintern Brüdern 23, Braunschweig 38100 **Tel:** 49 531 3900 0
Email: redaktion@bzv.de **Web site:** http://www.braunschweiger-zeitung.de/
Freq: Mon thru Fri; **Circ:** 28
Profile: Die Braunschweiger Zeitung ist eine regionale Tageszeitung. Sie gehört zur Funke Mediengruppe. Die Zeitung hat Lokalausgaben für Braunschweig, Salzgitter, Wolfsburg, Gifthorn, Peine, Helmdtedt und Wolfenbüttel. The Braunschweiger Zeitung is a regional daily newspaper belonging to the Funke Mediengruppe and being published along with six local editions for raunschweig, Salzgitter, Wolfsburg, Gifthom, Peine, Helmdtedt and Wolfenbüttel.
Language (s): German
DAILY NEWSPAPER

Bremer Nachrichten 157640

Owner: Bremer Tageszeitungen AG
Editorial: Martinistr. 43, Bremen 28195
Tel: 49 421 36710
Email: redaktion@bremer-nachrichten.de **Web site:** http://www.bremer-nachrichten.de
Circ: 15228 Not Audited
Profile: Die Bremer Nachrichten sind eine Lokalzeitung für Bremen, die Teil der WESER-KURIER Mediengruppe ist. Sie bietet lokale und regionale Nachrichten und Berichterstattung aus Bremen und Umgebung, sowie auch Informationen zu Kultur, Gesellschaft, Unterhaltung und Verbraucherthemen.
Language (s): German
DAILY NEWSPAPER

Calenberger Zeitung 445222

Owner: Verlagsgesellschaft Madsack GmbH & Co. KG
Editorial: Redaktion Barsinghausen, Marktstrasse 10, Barsinghausen 30890 **Tel:** 49 5105 521310
Email: barsinghausen@calenberger-zeitung.de **Web site:** http://www.haz.de
Freq: Daily; **Circ:** 28
Profile: Die Calenberger Zeitung ist eine Lokalzeitung und liegt montags bis sonnabends der Hannoverschen Allgemeinen Zeitung und der Neuen Presse bei. Berichtet aus den Orten Calenberg, Ronnenberg, Gehrden & Wennigsen in Niedersachsen. The Calenberger newspaper is a local newspaper and published as a supplement, Monday to Saturday, with the Hannover Allgemeine Zeitung and the New Press. Reporting from the towns Calenberg, Ronnenberg, Gehrden & Wennigsen in Lower Saxony.
Language (s): German
DAILY NEWSPAPER

Chamer Zeitung 159321

Owner: Cl. Attenkofer'sche Buch- und Kunstdruckerei
Editorial: Lokalredaktion - Cham, Rindermarkt 9, Cham 93413 **Tel:** 49 9971 8544 99
Email: redaktion@chamer-zeitung.de **Web site:** http://www.chamer-zeitung.de
Freq: Mon thru Fri; **Circ:** 28
Profile: Die Chamer Zeitung ist eine lokale Tageszeitung. Sie erscheint im Gebiet rund um Cham, Straubing und Fürth in Bayern. The Chamer Zeitung is a local daily newspaper that is being distributed in the Bavarian regions of Cham, Straubing and Fürth.
Language (s): German
DAILY NEWSPAPER

Coburger Tageblatt 159324

Owner: Coburger Tageblatt Verlag & Medien GmbH & Co. KG
Editorial: Mediengruppe Oberfranken GmbH & Co. KG, Gutenbergstrasse 1, Bamberg 96050
Tel: 49 9561 888170
Email: stadt.coburg@infranken.de **Web site:** http://www.infranken.de/regional/coburg
Freq: Mon thru Fri; **Circ:** 28
Profile: Das Coburger Tageblatt ist eine regionale Tageszeitung, die in Coburg erscheint. Sie wird vom Coburger Tageblatt Verlag & Medien herausgegeben. Berichtet wird von regionalen Nachrichten aus Coburg. The Coburger Tageblatt is a regional daily newspaper. It covers regional news from Coburg and is published by Coburger Tageblatt Verlag & Medien. The newspaper focuses on regional news from Coburg.
Language (s): German
DAILY NEWSPAPER

Cuxhavener Nachrichten 159326

Owner: Cuxhaven-Niederelbe Verlagsgesellschaft mbH & Co. KG
Editorial: Cuxhaven-Niederelbe Verlagsgesellschaft mbH & Co. KG, Kaemmererplatz 2, Cuxhaven 27472
Tel: 49 4721 585 0
Email: redaktion@cuxonline.de **Web site:** http://www.cn-online.de
Freq: Mon thru Fri; **Circ:** 28
Profile: Die Cuxhavener Nachrichten ist eine regionale Tageszeitung, die im Gebiet um Cuxhaven erscheint. Die Zeitung hat eine Lokalredaktion, alle überregionalen Teile werden von der Nordsee-Zeitung bereitgestellt. The Cuxhavener Nachrichten is a regional daily newspaper that is being distributed in the area of Cuxhaven. It has as local editorial office, an all supra-regional content is provided by the Nordsee-Zeitung.
Language (s): German
DAILY NEWSPAPER

Dachauer Nachrichten 159327

Owner: Zeitungsverlag Oberbayern GmbH & Co. KG
Editorial: Richard-Wagner-Str. 6, Dachau
Email: dah-nachrichten@merkur.de **Web site:** http://www.merkur.de/lokales/dachau/
Freq: Mon thru Fri; **Circ:** 28
Profile: Die Dachauer Nachrichten ist eine Lokalausgabe der bayrischen Tageszeitung Münchner Merkur, die zur Mediengruppe Münchner Merkur/tz gehört. The Dachauer Nachrichten is a local edition of the Bavarian daily newspaper

Münchner Merkur which is part of the Mediengruppe Münchner Merkur/tz.
Language (s): German
DAILY NEWSPAPER

Darmstädter Echo 159328
Owner: Echo Zeitungen GmbH
Editorial: Echo Zeitungen GmbH, Berliner Allee 65, Darmstadt 64295 **Tel:** 49 6151 387 1
Email: echo-zeitungen@darmstaedter-echo.de **Web site:** http://www.echo-online.de
Freq: Mon thru Fri; **Circ:** 28
Profile: Das Darmstädter Echo ist eine regionale Tageszeitung der Stadt Darmstadt. Darmstädter Echo is a regional daily newspaper of the city of Darmstadt.
Language (s): German
DAILY NEWSPAPER

Delmenhorster Kreisblatt 159334
Owner: Neue Osnabrücker Zeitung GmbH & Co. KG
Editorial: DK Medien GmbH & Co. KG, Lange Strasse 122, Delmenhorst 27749
Tel: 49 4221 156 520
Email: verlag@dk-online.de **Web site:** http://www.dk-online.de
Freq: Mon thru Fri; **Circ:** 28
Profile: Das Delmenhorster Kreisblatt ist eine regionale Tageszeitung. Sie berichtet über Neuigkeiten aus Delmenhorst, dem Landkreis Oldenburg und der Metropolregion. The Delmenhorster Kreisblatt is a regional daily newspaper reporting about news from Delmenhorst, the county of Oldenburg and the metropolitan area.
Language (s): German
DAILY NEWSPAPER

Der Bayerwald-Bote 159237
Owner: Neue Presse Verlags-GmbH
Editorial: Medienstrasse 5, München 94036
Tel: 49 851 8020
Email: info@pnp.de **Web site:** http://www.pnp.de
Freq: Daily; **Circ:** 28
Profile: Der Bayerwald-Bote ist eine Lokalausgabe der Passauer neue Presse. Thematischer Schwerpunkt liegt auf allgemeinen Lokalen und Regionalen Nachrichten. The Bayerwald-Bote is a local edition of Passauer neue Presse. The thematic focus is on general Local and Regional News.
Language (s): German
DAILY NEWSPAPER

Der Marktspiegel 893338
Owner: Verlag Der Marktspiegel GmbH
Editorial: Verlag Der Marktspiegel GmbH, Burgschmietstr. 2-4, Nurnberg Nürnberg
Tel: 49 911 399 080
Email: media@marktspiegel.de **Web site:** http://www.marktspiegel.de/
Freq: Daily; **Circ:** 462000
Profile: Lokale Tageszeitung für Nürnberg. Local newspaper for Nürnberg.
Language (s): German
DAILY NEWSPAPER

Der neue Tag 159712
Owner: Der neue Tag Oberpfälzischer Kurier Druck- und Verlagshaus GmbH
Editorial: Medienhaus Der neue Tag, Weigelstrasse 16, Weiden 92637 **Tel:** 49 961 85 0
Email: redaktion@oberpfalznetz.de **Web site:** http://www.oberpfalznetz.de
Freq: Mon thru Fri; **Circ:** 28
Profile: Der Neue Tag ist eine regionale Tageszeitung der Oberpfalz mit Berichterstattung aus der Region. Neue Tag is a regional daily newspaper for the Oberpfalz covering regional news.
Language (s): German
DAILY NEWSPAPER

Der Patriot / Lippstädter Zeitung 159808
Owner: Zeitungsverlag Der Patriot GmbH
Editorial: Zeitungsverlag Der Patriot GmbH, Hansastrasse 2, Lippstadt 59557
Tel: 49 2941 201 257
Email: redaktion@derpatriot.de **Web site:** http://www.derpatriot.de
Freq: Mon thru Fri; **Circ:** 28
Profile: Der Patriot ist eine Lippstädter Zeitung, welche 1848 gegründet wurde. Relevante Themen der Tageszeitung sind Kommunalpolitik, Kultur und Sport. The Patriot is a Lippstädter newspaper, which was established in 1848. Relevant topics of the newspaper are local politics, culture and sport.
Language (s): German
DAILY NEWSPAPER

Der Tagesspiegel 159967
Owner: Verlag Der Tagesspiegel GmbH
Editorial: Verlag Der Tagesspiegel GmbH, Askanischer Platz 3, Berlin 10963 **Tel:** 49 30 29021 0
Email: redaktion@tagesspiegel.de **Web site:** http://www.tagesspiegel.de/
Freq: Daily; **Circ:** 28
Profile: Der Tagesspiegel ist eine Tageszeitung für ganz Deutschland, die vom Verlag Der Tagesspiegel GmbH veröffentlicht wird. Er präsentiert Nachrichten zum aktuellen Tagesgeschehen aus den Bereichen Politik, Wirtschaft, Kultur, Sport, Medien und Wissen. The Tagesspiegel is a daily newspaper for entire Germany that is published by Verlag Der Tagesspiegel GmbH. It presents information about current news from the topics politics, economy, culture, sports, media and knowledge.
Language (s): German
DAILY NEWSPAPER

Die Glocke 159450
Owner: E. Holterdorf GmbH & Co KG
Editorial: E. Holterdorf GmbH & Co KG, Engelbert-Holterdorf-Strasse 4/6, Oelde 59302
Tel: 49 2522 73 0
Email: redaktion@die-glocke.de **Web site:** http://www.die-glocke.de
Freq: Mon thru Fri
Profile: Die Glocke ist eine regionale Tageszeitung aus Oelpe. Der inhaltliche Schwerpunkt liegt auf der Berichterstattung aus dem Gebiet um Oelpe und Nordrhein-Westfalen. Zudem gibt es Nachrichten zu internationalen Themen, wie Wirtschaft, Sport und aktuelle Themen. The Glocke is a regional daily newspaper which focuses on local news from Oelpe and North Rhine-Westfalia. It also features international news such as economics, sports and current topics.
Language (s): German
DAILY NEWSPAPER

Die Glocke, Beckum/Ahlen (Beckumer Zeitung) 913729
Owner: E. Holterdorf GmbH & Co KG
Editorial: Beckumer Zeitung, Oststrasse 2, Beckum 59269 **Tel:** 49 2521 9319 20
Email: be@die-glocke.de **Web site:** http://www.die-glocke.de/lokalnachrichten/kreiswarendorf/ahlen
Freq: Daily; **Circ:** 20113
Profile: Die Glocke Beckum und Ahlen sind lokale Tageszeitungen aus Warendorf. Die inhaltlichen Schwerpunkte sind Neuigkeiten und Nachrichten aus den lokalen mit Themen Wirtschaft, Sport und Politik.
Language (s): German
DAILY NEWSPAPER

Die Glocke, Oelde (Oelder Zeitung) 666129
Owner: E. Holterdorf GmbH & Co KG
Editorial: Engelbert-Holterdorf-Strasse 4/6, Oelde 59302 **Tel:** 49 2522 73 340
Email: oe@die-glocke.de **Web site:** http://www.die-glocke.de/lokalnachrichten/kreiswarendorf/oelde
Freq: Daily; **Circ:** 28
Profile: Die Glocke Oelde ist das Lokalangebot der Zeitung Die Glocke für Oelde. Zusätzlich zum allgemeinen Mantelteil der Zeitung, bietet die Lokalredaktion Nachrichten und Berichterstattung aus Oelde.
Language (s): German
DAILY NEWSPAPER

Die Harke 159481
Owner: J. Hoffmann GmbH & Co. KG
Editorial: J. Hoffmann GmbH und Co. KG, An der Stadtgrenze 2, Nienburg 31582 **Tel:** 49 5021 9661 13
Email: info@dieharke.de **Web site:** http://www.dieharke.de
Freq: Mon thru Fri; **Circ:** 28
Profile: Die Harke ist eine regionale Tageszeitung aus Niedersachsen. Den Mantel bezieht sie von der Hannoverschen Allgemeinen Zeitung. Sonntags erscheint die kostenlose Zeitung Die Harke am Sonntag, die lokale Berichte liefert. Die Harke is a regional newspaper from Lower Saxony. The cover section is being provided by the Hannoversche Allgemeine Zeitung. On Sundays, there is an edition available for free called Die Harke am Sonntag which covers local reports.
Language (s): German
DAILY NEWSPAPER

Die Oberbadische 159772
Owner: Oberbadisches Verlagshaus Georg Jaumann GmbH & Co.KG
Editorial: Oberbadisches Verlagshaus Georg Jaumann GmbH & Co.KG, Am Alten Markt 2, Lörrach 79539 **Tel:** 49 7621 4033 0
Email: info@verlagshaus-jaumann.de **Web site:** http://www.verlagshaus-jaumann.de
Freq: Mon thru Fri; **Circ:** 28
Profile: Die Oberbadische ist eine regionale Tageszeitung mit Hauptsitz in Lörrach, die über lokale Nachrichten in Lörrach und Umgebung berichtet. Die Oberbadische is a regional daily newspaper based in Lörrach. The newspaper offers locale news on the city as well as its surroundings.
Language (s): German
DAILY NEWSPAPER

Die Rheinpfalz 159849
Owner: RHEINPFALZ Verlag und Druckerei GmbH & Co. KG
Editorial: RHEINPFALZ Verlag und Druckerei GmbH & Co. KG, Amtsstrasse 5 - 11, Ludwigshafen 67059
Tel: 49 621 5902 01
Email: redaktion@rheinpfalz.de **Web site:** http://www.rheinpfalz.de
Freq: Mon thru Fri
Profile: Die Rheinpfalz ist eine deutsche Tageszeitung, die Nachrichten aus Deutschland und dem Ausland bietet, sowie Berichterstattungen aus der Region und Sport. Die Rheinpfalz is a German daily newspaper which offers news from Germany and abroad, as well as regional news and sports.
Language (s): German
DAILY NEWSPAPER

Die Rheinpfalz, Kaiserslautern (Pfälzische Volkszeitung) 854234
Owner: RHEINPFALZ Verlag und Druckerei GmbH & Co. KG
Editorial: Geschaftsstelle Kaiserslautern, Pariser Strasse 16, Kaiserslautern 67655 **Tel:** 49 631 3737 0
Email: redkai@rheinpfalz.de **Web site:** http://www.rheinpfalz.de/lokal/kaiserslautern/
Freq: Mon thru Fri; **Circ:** 31910
Profile: Die Rheinpfalz, Kaiserslautern (Pfälzische Volkszeitung) ist eine lokale Tageszeitung. Es werden Themen aus der Region behandelt sowie Sport, Wirtschaft und Politik. Die Rheinpfalz, Kaiserslautern (Pfälzische Volkszeitung) is a local daily newspaper. It deals with topics from the region as well as sports, economy and politics.
Language (s): German
DAILY NEWSPAPER

Die Rheinpfalz, Kusel (Westricher Rundschau) 859878
Owner: RHEINPFALZ Verlag und Druckerei GmbH & Co. KG
Editorial: Geschaftsstelle Kaiserslautern, Pariser Strasse 16, Kaiserslautern 67655 **Tel:** 49 631 3737 0
Email: redkus@rheinpfalz.de **Web site:** http://www.rheinpfalz.de/lokal/kusel/
Freq: Mon thru Fri; **Circ:** 28
Profile: Die Rheinpfalz, Kusel (Westricher Rundschau) ist eine lokale Tageszeitung. Es werden Themen aus der Region behandelt sowie Sport, Wirtschaft und Politik. Die Rheinpfalz, Kusel (Westricher Rundschau) is a local daily newspaper. It deals with topics from the region as well as sports, economy and politics.
Language (s): German
DAILY NEWSPAPER

Die Rheinpfalz, Pirmasens (Pirmasenser Rundschau) 911624
Owner: RHEINPFALZ Verlag und Druckerei GmbH & Co. KG
Editorial: Geschaftsstelle Zweibrücken, Rosengartenstrasse 1 - 3, Zweibrücken 66482
Tel: 49 6322 9221-33
Email: redpir@rheinpfalz.de **Web site:** http://www.rheinpfalz.de/lokal/pirmasens/
Freq: Daily; **Circ:** 11724
Profile: Die Rheinpfalz, Pirmasens (Pirmasenser Rundschau) ist eine lokale Tageszeitung. Es werden Themen aus der Region behandelt sowie Sport, Wirtschaft und Politik. Die Rheinpfalz, Pirmasens (Pirmasenser Rundschau) is a local daily newspaper. It deals with topics from the region as well as sports, economy and politics.
Language (s): German
DAILY NEWSPAPER

Die Rheinpfalz, Speyer (Speyerer Rundschau) 913075
Owner: RHEINPFALZ Verlag und Druckerei GmbH & Co. KG
Editorial: Geschaftsstelle Ludwigshafen, Amtsstrasse 5 - 11, Ludwigshafen 67059 **Tel:** 49 621 5902 01
Email: redspe@rheinpfalz.de **Web site:** http://www.rheinpfalz.de/lokal/speyer/
Freq: Mon thru Fri; **Circ:** 28
Profile: Die Rheinpfalz, Speyer (Speyerer Rundschau) ist eine lokale Tageszeitung. Es werden lokale Themen behandelt sowie Politik, Sport und Wirtschaft. Die Rheinpfalz, Speyer (Speyerer Rundschau) is a local daily newspaper. There are local topics treated and politics, sports and business.
Language (s): German
DAILY NEWSPAPER

DIE WELT 160045
Owner: WeltN24 GmbH
Editorial: WeltN24 GmbH, Axel-Springer-Strasse 65, Berlin 10969 **Tel:** 49 30 2591 0
Email: redaktion@welt.de **Web site:** http://www.welt.de
Freq: Mon thru Fri; **Circ:** 28
Profile: DIE WELT ist eine deutsche überregionale Tageszeitung der Axel Springer SE Die Welt is a German national daily newspaper published by Axel Springer SE.
Language (s): German
DAILY NEWSPAPER

DIE WELT KOMPAKT 311192
Owner: WeltN24 GmbH
Editorial: WeltN24 GmbH, Axel-Springer-Strasse 65, Berlin 10969 **Tel:** 49 30 259 10
Email: kompakt.app@welt.de **Web site:** http://kompakt.welt.de/
Freq: Daily; **Circ:** 28
Profile: DIE WELT KOMPAKT ist die Tabloid Version der deutschen Tageszeitung DIE WELT mit dem Schwerpunkt Internet und Lifestyle. The German daily national DIE WELT's tabloid-sized version
Language (s): German
DAILY NEWSPAPER

DIE WELT Kompakt, Düsseldorf 872295
Owner: WeltN24 GmbH
Editorial: Adersstrasse 12, Dusseldorf 40215
Tel: 49 211 964 88-251
Email: duesseldorf@welt-kompakt.de **Web site:** http://www.welt.de/welt-kompakt
Freq: Mon thru Fri; **Circ:** 28
Profile: Lokalausgabe für Düsseldorf der Tageszeitung WELT Kompakt . Local edition of the daily newspaper WELT Kompakt for Düsseldorf.
Language (s): German
DAILY NEWSPAPER

Die Welt, Hamburg 893143
Owner: Axel Springer SE
Editorial: Axel-Springer-Platz 1, Hamburg 20350
Tel: 49 40 3 472 43 33
Email: hamburg@welt.de **Web site:** http://www.welt.de/regionales/hamburg/
Freq: Daily; **Circ:** 39710
Profile: Regionalausgabe für Hamburg der Tageszeitung Die Welt. Regional edition for Hamburg of the daily newspaper Die Welt.
Language (s): German
DAILY NEWSPAPER

Dill-Post Mittelhessen 159337
Owner: Wetzlardruck GmbH
Editorial: Wetzlardruck GmbH, Elsa-Brandstrom-Strasse 18, Wetzlar 35578
Email: redaktion.dp@mittelhessen.de **Web site:** http://www.mittelhessen.de/lokales/region-dillenburg.html
Circ: 28
Profile: Die Dill-Post ist eine regionale Tageszeitung. Sie gehört zur Zeitungsgruppe Lahn-Dill. Berichtet wird über regionale Nachrichten aus dem Lahn-Dill-Kreis. The Dill-Post is a regional daily newspaper covering local news from the area of the Lahn-Dill-Kreis and being part of the newspaper group Lahn-Dill.
Language (s): German
DAILY NEWSPAPER

Dithmarscher Kurier 607004
Owner: Boyens Medien GmbH & Co. KG
Editorial: Boyens Medien GmbH & Co. KG, Wulf-Isebrand-Platz 1-3, Heide 25746 **Tel:** 49 481 68 86 0
Email: boyens@boyens-medien.de **Web site:** http://zeitungen.boyens-medien.de
Circ: 28
Profile: Lokalausgabe der ""Dithmarscher Landeszeitung"". Mit Nachrichten aus der Region zu Politik, Wirtschaft, Gesellschaft, Sport und Kultur. Local edition of the ""Dithmarsch country newspaper"". With news from the region to politics, economy, society, sports and culture.
Language (s): German
DAILY NEWSPAPER

Dithmarscher Landeszeitung 159340
Owner: Boyens Medien GmbH & Co. KG
Editorial: Boyens Medien GmbH & Co. KG, Wulf-Isebrand-Platz 1-3, Heide 25746 **Tel:** 49 481 68 86 0
Email: redaktion@boyens-medien.de **Web site:** http://zeitungen.boyens-medien.de/
Freq: Mon thru Fri; **Circ:** 28
Profile: Die Dithmarsche Landeszeitung ist eine regionale Tageszeitung mit Sitz in Heide. Sie erscheint im Verlag Boyens Medien. Inhaltlich werden überwiegend regionale Themen behandelt. The Dithmarscher Landeszeitung is a regional daily newspaper published in Heide by the Verlag Boyens Medien. It mainly covers regional topics.
Language (s): German
DAILY NEWSPAPER

Donau-Anzeiger 350449
Owner: Cl. Attenkofer'sche Buch- und Kunstdruckerei
Editorial: Westlicher Stadtgraben 19a, Deggendorf 94469 **Tel:** 49 991 370 170
Email: kontakt@idowa.de **Web site:** http://www.idowa.de
Freq: Daily; **Circ:** 28
Profile: Regionalzeitung für die Region um Isar, Donau und Wald mit aktuellen Nachrichten aus Sport, Wirtschaft, Politik, Kultur und Unterhaltung. Regional newspaper for the regions of Isar, Donau and Wald with news from sports, business, politics, culture and entertainment.
Language (s): German
DAILY NEWSPAPER

DONAUKURIER 159345
Owner: DONAUKURIER Verlagsgesellschaft mbH & Co. KG
Editorial: DONAUKURIER Verlagsgesellschaft mbH & Co. KG, Stauffenbergstrasse 2a, Ingolstadt 85051
Tel: 49 841 96 66 251
Email: redaktion@donaukurier.de **Web site:** http://www.donaukurier.de
Freq: Mon thru Fri; **Circ:** 28
Profile: Der Donaukurier ist eine deutsche regionale Tageszeitung, mit unterschiedlichen Lokalausgaben, welche lokale und regionale Nachrichten und Berichterstattung bietet. The Donaukurier is a German regional daily newspaper, with different local editions, which provides local and regional news and reporting.
Language (s): German
DAILY NEWSPAPER

Dorfener Anzeiger 159344
Owner: Zeitungsverlag Oberbayern GmbH & Co. KG
Editorial: Unterer Markt 10, Dorfen
Email: redaktion@dorfener-anzeiger.de **Web site:** http://www.merkur.de/lokales/erding/dorfen/
Freq: Mon thru Fri; **Circ:** 28
Profile: Der Dorfener Anzeiger ist eine Lokalzeitung des Münchner Merkurs, der zur Mediengruppe Münchner Merkur/tz gehört. Die Zeitung bietet regionale Berichterstattung, sowie auch Nachrichten. The Dorfener Anzeiger is a local edition of the daily newspaper Münchner Merkur which is part of the Mediengruppe Münchner Merkur/tz. The publication offers regional reporting, as well as news.
Language (s): German
DAILY NEWSPAPER

Dreieich-Zeitung 896805
Owner: Günther Medien GmbH
Editorial: Günther Medien GmbH, Ferdinand-Porsche-Ring 17, Rodgau 63110
Tel: 49 6106 2 83 90 00
Email: info@dreieich-zeitung.de **Web site:** http://www.dreieich-zeitung.de/

Freq: Daily; **Circ:** 141025
Profile: Regionale Zeitung für die Region Dreieich. Regional daily newspaper for the region of Dreieich.
Language (s): German
DAILY NEWSPAPER

Dresdner Morgenpost 159350
Owner: Morgenpost Sachsen GmbH
Editorial: Morgenpost Sachsen GmbH, Ostra-Allee 18, Dresden 1067 **Tel:** 49 351 4864 24 24
Email: support@mopo24.de **Web site:** http://www.ddv-mediengruppe.de/produkte_dienstleistungen/produkte/tageszeitungen/morgenpost_sachsen/
Freq: Daily; **Circ:** 28
Profile: Regionale Tagezeitung für die Region Dresden. Regional daily newspaper for the Dortmund region.
Language (s): German
DAILY NEWSPAPER

Ebersberger Zeitung 159357
Owner: Zeitungsverlag Oberbayern GmbH & Co. KG
Editorial: Münchener Zeitungs-Verlag GmbH & Co.KG, Eichthalstrasse 2, Ebersberg 85560
Tel: 49 8092 8282 0
Email: ebe-zeitung@merkur.de **Web site:** http://www.merkur.de/lokales/ebersberg/
Freq: Mon thru Fri; **Circ:** 28
Profile: Die Ebersberger Zeitung ist eine regionale Tageszeitung des Merkur an und bietet lokale und regionale Nachrichten für Ebersberg. The Ebersberger Zeitung is a regional daily newspaper of the Merkur and offers local and regional news for Ebersberg.
Language (s): German
DAILY NEWSPAPER

Eichstätter Kurier 159361
Owner: Donaukurier Verlagsges. mbH & Co. KG
Editorial: DONAUKURIER Verlagsgesellschaft mbH & Co. KG, Stauffenbergstrasse 2a, Ingolstadt 85051
Tel: 49 841 96660
Email: redaktion@donaukurier.de **Web site:** http://www.donaukurier.de/lokales/eichstaett/
Freq: Mon thru Fri; **Circ:** 28
Profile: Der Eichstätter Kurier ist eine Tageszeitung. Sie gehört der Tageszeitung Donaukurier an und berichtet über regionale Themen aus Eichstätt. The Eichstätter Kurier is a regional daily newspaper covering regional topics from the area of Eichstätt. It is part of the newspaper Donaukurier.
Language (s): German
DAILY NEWSPAPER

Elbe-Jeetzel Zeitung 159367
Owner: Druck- und Verlagsges. Köhring GmbH & Co. KG
Editorial: Wallstrasse 22-24, Lüchow
Tel: 49 5841 127 160
Email: redaktion@ejz.de **Web site:** http://www.ejz.de
Freq: Mon thru Fri; **Circ:** 28
Profile: Die Elbe-Jeetzel-Zeitung ist eine regionale Tageszeitung, die im Landkreis Lüchow-Dannenberg erscheint. Den Mantelteil stellt die Landeszeitung für die Lüneburger Heide. Inhaltlich werden sowohl lokale Nachrichten, als auch nationale und internationale Nachrichten aus den Themengebieten Politik, Wirtschaft, Sport, und Technik behandelt. The Elbe-Jeetzel-Zeitung is a regional daily newspaper which is distributed in the area of Lüchow-Dannenberg. Its cover section is produced by the Landeszeitung für die Lüneburger Heide. It covers regional, as well as international and national topics in the fields of politics, economics, sports and technic.
Language (s): German
DAILY NEWSPAPER

Elmshorner Nachrichten 605038
Owner: sh:z Schleswig-Holsteinischer Zeitungsverlag GmbH & Co. KG
Editorial: Elmshorner Nachrichten, Schulstrasse 62-66, Elmshorn 25335 **Tel:** 49 4121 297 1800
Email: redaktion.elmshorn@shz.de **Web site:** http://www.shz.de/lokales/elmshorner-nachrichten/
Freq: Mon thru Fri; **Circ:** 28
Profile: Die Elmshorner Nachrichten ist eine Regionalzeitung des sh:z Schleswig-Holsteinischer Zeitungsverlages für die Region Elmshorn mit lokaler und regionaler Berichterstattung, sowie mit Nachrichten aus Politik, Wirtschaft, Gesellschaft, Kultur und Sport. The Elmshorner Nachrichten is a local newspaper by the sh:z Schleswig-Holsteinischer Zeitungsverlag for the region Elmshorn with local and regional reporting, as well as news in politics, economy, society, culture and sports.
Language (s): German
DAILY NEWSPAPER

Emder Zeitung 159370
Owner: Emder Zeitung GmbH & Co. KG
Editorial: Emder Zeitung GmbH & Co. KG, Ringstrasse 17 a, Emden 26721
Tel: 49 4921 89 00 402
Email: redaktion@emderzeitung.de **Web site:** http://www.emderzeitung.de
Freq: Mon thru Fri; **Circ:** 28
Profile: Die Emder Zeitung ist ein regionale Tageszeitung. Sie berichtet über lokale Nachrichten, Sport, Politik und Wirtschaft im ostfriesischen Emden und Umgebung. The Emder Zeitung is a regional newspaper for the Lower Saxony region Emden. It covers regional news, developments, and events.
Language (s): German
DAILY NEWSPAPER

Erdinger Anzeiger 159379
Owner: Zeitungsverlag Oberbayern GmbH & Co. KG
Editorial: Münchener Zeitungs-Verlag GmbH & Co.KG, Paul-Heyse-Str. 2-4, München 80336
Tel: 49 089 5306 0
Email: info@merkur.de **Web site:** http://www.merkur.de/lokales/erding/
Freq: Mon thru Fri; **Circ:** 28
Profile: Der Erdinger Anzeiger ist eine regionale Tageszeitung in Erding. Sie gehört heute zur Zeitungsgruppe des Münchner Merkurs. The Erdinger Anzeiger is a regional daily newspaper in Ernding. It is part of the newspaper group Münchner Merkur.
Language (s): German
DAILY NEWSPAPER

Erlanger Nachrichten 159383
Owner: Verlag Nürnberger Presse Druckhaus Nürnberg GmbH & Co.
Editorial: Marienstrasse 9/11, Nurnberg 90402
Tel: 49 911 2160
Email: info@pressenetz.de **Web site:** http://www.nordbayern.de/region/erlangen
Freq: Mon thru Fri; **Circ:** 28
Profile: Die Erlanger Nachrichten ist eine Regionalausgabe der Tageszeitung Nürnberger Nachrichten, die ganz Mittelfranken sowie Teile Oberfrankens und der Oberpfalz abdeckt. The Erlanger Nachrichten is a regional edition of the daily newspapaer Nürnberger Nachrichten which covers Middle Franconia and parts of Upper Franconia and Upper Palatinate.
Language (s): German
DAILY NEWSPAPER

Eßlinger Zeitung 159387
Owner: Bechtle Verlag und Eßlinger Zeitung GmbH & Co. KG
Editorial: Esslinger Zeitung, Zeppelinstrasse 116, Esslingen 73730 **Tel:** 49 711 93100
Email: redaktion@ez-online.de **Web site:** http://www.esslinger-zeitung.de
Freq: Mon thru Fri; **Circ:** 28
Profile: Die Eßlinger Zeitung ist eine Tageszeitung der Bechtle Graphische Betriebe und Verlagsgesellschaft mbH & Co. KG in Esslingen mit aktueller regionaler und lokaler Berichterstattung. The Eßlinger Zeitung is a daily newspapaer of the Bechtle Graphische Betriebe und Verlagsgesellschaft mbH & Co. KG in Esslingen with current local and regional reporting.
Language (s): German
DAILY NEWSPAPER

EXPRESS 159388
Owner: DuMont Net GmbH & Co. KG
Editorial: Neven DuMont Haus, Amsterdamer Strasse 192, Koln 50735 **Tel:** 49 221 2240
Email: post@express.de **Web site:** http://www.express.de
Freq: Mon thru Fri; **Circ:** 28
Profile: EXPRESS ist eine lokale Tageszeitung für den Raum Köln mit Nachrichten aus Politik, Wirtschaft, Sport, Gesellschaft und Kultur. EXPRESS is a local daily newspaper for the Cologne area with news from politics, economy, sports, society and culture.
Language (s): German
Ad Rate: Full Page Mono 261.45
Currency: Euro
DAILY NEWSPAPER

EXPRESS Bonn 159286
Owner: M. DuMont Schauberg Expedition der Kölnischen Zeitung GmbH & Co. KG
Editorial: Berliner Freiheit 36, Bonn 53111
Tel: 49 228 729 06 33
Email: bonn@express.de **Web site:** http://www.express.de/bonn/2860,2860.html
Freq: Daily
Profile: Regionalausgabe der EXPRESS für Bonn, einer regionalen Tageszeitung mit Nachrichten aus Politik, Wirtschaft, Sport, Gesellschaft und Kultur. Regional edition of the regional newspaper EXPRESS, a regional daily newspaper with news from politics, economy, sports, society and culture.
Language (s): German
DAILY NEWSPAPER

EXPRESS Düsseldorf 159355
Owner: DuMont Net GmbH & Co. KG
Editorial: Konigsallee 27, Dusseldorf 40212
Tel: 49 211 13930
Email: duesseldorf@express.de **Web site:** http://www.express.de/duesseldorf
Freq: Mon thru Fri; **Circ:** 28
Profile: EXPRESS Düsseldorf ist eine regionale Tageszeitung für den Raum Düsseldorf. Pressemitteilungen bitte an die E-Mail-Adresse senden: duesseldorf@express.de. Je nach Thema werden sie dann in der Redaktion aufgeteilt. EXPRESS Düsseldorf is a regional daily newspaper for the Düsseldorf region. Press communications should be sent to duesseldorf@express.de. Depending on the topic they will then be distributed amongst the editors.
Language (s): German
DAILY NEWSPAPER

Fellbach & Rems-Murr-Kreis 412076
Owner: Stuttgarter Nachrichten Verlagsgesellschaft mbH
Editorial: Cannstatter Strasse 94, Fellbach
Tel: 49 711 9579 670
Email: redaktion@fellbacher-zeitung.zgs.de **Web site:** http://www.fellbacher-zeitung.de
Freq: Mon thru Fri
Profile: Fellbach & Rems-Murr-KreisRegionalzeitung für Fellbach und den Rems-Murr-Kreis mit Nachrichten, Sport, Kultur, Gesellschaft, Wirtschaft und Politik. Fellbach & Rems-Murr-Kreis is a regional newspaper for Fellbach and the Rems-Murr region with news, sports, culture, society, economy and politics.
Language (s): German
DAILY NEWSPAPER

Flensburger Tageblatt 159395
Owner: sh:z Schleswig-Holsteinischer Zeitungsverlag GmbH & Co. KG
Editorial: sh:z Schleswig-Holsteinischer Zeitungsverlag GmbH & Co. KG, Fordestrasse 20, Flensburg 24944 **Tel:** 49 461 8080
Email: redaktion.flensburg@shz.de **Web site:** http://www.shz.de/lokales/flensburger-tageblatt/
Freq: Mon thru Fri; **Circ:** 28
Profile: Das Flensburger Tageblatt ist eine lokale Tageszeitung für die Stadt Flensburg. Sie stellt die Lokalausgabe der Schleswig-Holsteiner Zeitung dar. The Flensburger Tageblatt is a local daily newspaper for the city of Flensburg. It is part of the Schleswig-Holsteiner Zeitung.
Language (s): German
DAILY NEWSPAPER

Frankenpost 159402
Owner: Frankenpost Verlag GmbH
Editorial: Frankenpost Verlag GmbH, Poststrasse 9/11, Hof 95028 **Tel:** 49 9281 816 0
Email: redaktion@frankenpost.de **Web site:** http://www.frankenpost.de
Freq: Mon thru Fri
Profile: Die Frankenpost ist eine regionale Tageszeitung. Zu den Themen gehören Nachrichten aus lokalen, regionale und überregionalen Gebieten, sowie Wirtschaft, Politik, Wissenschaft, Sport und Feuilleton. The Frankenpost is a regional daily newspaper that covers news from local, regional and supra regional areas in the fields of economy, politics, science, sports and feuilleton.
Language (s): German
DAILY NEWSPAPER

Frankenpost Münchberg 159679
Owner: Frankenpost Verlag GmbH
Editorial: Bahnhofstr. 2, Münchberg 95213
Tel: 49 9251 99 54 20
Email: redaktion.mhtz@frankenpost.de **Web site:** http://www.frankenpost.de/lokal/muenchberg/
Freq: Mon thru Fri; **Circ:** 28
Profile: Die Münchberg-Helmbrechtser Tageszeitung ist eine Lokalausgabe der Frankenpost mit lokaler Berichterstattung aus Münchberg und Nachrichten aus der Umgebung.
Language (s): German
DAILY NEWSPAPER

Frankenpost Naila 666146
Owner: Frankenpost Verlag GmbH
Editorial: Frankenpost Verlag GmbH, Poststrasse 9/11, Hof 95028 **Tel:** 49 9282 82280
Email: verlag@frankenpost.de **Web site:** http://www.frankenpost.de/lokal/naila/
Freq: Mon thru Fri; **Circ:** 28
Profile: Frankenpost Naila ist eine lokale Tageszeitung für Naila in Bayern. Sie berichtet über Neuigkeiten aus der Politik, Sport, Wirtschaft und der Gemeinde. Frankenpost Naila is a local daily newspaper for Naila in Bavaria. It offers news and reports on politic, sport, economic and the community.
Language (s): German
DAILY NEWSPAPER

Frankfurter Allgemeine Sonntagszeitung 893127
Owner: Frankfurter Allgemeine Zeitung GmbH
Editorial: Frankfurter Allgemeine Zeitung GmbH, Hellerhofstrasse 2-4, Frankfurt Am Main 60327
Tel: 49 69 759 10
Email: Info@faz.net **Web site:** http://www.faz.net
Freq: Daily; **Circ:** 28
Profile: Die Frankfurter Allgemeine Sonntagszeitung (F.A.S.) ist die Sonntags-Ausgabe der Frankfurter Allgemeinen Zeitung, eine der führenden deutschen Tageszeitungen, die erstmals im Jahre 1949 veröffentlicht wurde. Die F.A.S. wurde bereits zum 5. Mal zur„World's Best Designed Newspaper" von der Society for News Design gewählent events round off the journalistic service. Frankfurter Allgemeine Sonntagszeitung (F.A.S.) is the Sunday edition of the German national newspaper Frankfurter Allgemeine Zeitung, which is a leading national news and business paper and was published for the first time in 1949. F.A.S. was already the 5th time elected as "World's Best Designed Newspaper" by the Society for News Design.
Language (s): German
DAILY NEWSPAPER

Frankfurter Allgemeine Zeitung 801505
Owner: Frankfurter Allgemeine Zeitung GmbH
Editorial: Frankfurter Allgemeine Zeitung GmbH, Hellerhofstrasse 2-4, Frankfurt Am Main 60327
Tel: 49 69 75 9125 20
Email: Info@faz.net **Web site:** http://www.faz.net
Freq: Mon thru Fri; **Circ:** 28
Profile: Die Frankfurter Allgemeine Zeitung ist die führende deutsche Tageszeitung und wurde das erste mal im Jahre 1949 veröffentlicht. Die Publikation wird an sechs Tagen der Woche herausgegeben und erscheint in 145 Ländern. The German national newspaper Frankfurter Allgemeine Zeitung is a leading national news and business paper and was published for the first time in 1949. The newspaper is published six days a week and is available in 145 countries.
Language (s): German
DAILY NEWSPAPER

Frankfurter Neue Presse 159408
Owner: Frankfurter Societäts-Medien GmbH
Editorial: Frankfurter Societats-Medien GmbH, Frankenallee 71–81, Frankfurt Am Main 60327
Tel: 49 6975 010
Email: redaktion@fnp.de **Web site:** http://www.fnp.de
Freq: Daily; **Circ:** 28
Profile: Die Frankfurter Neue Presse ist eine lokale Tageszeitung aus Frankfurt. Es wird über regionale und lokale Themen berichtet, aber auch über internationale Nachrichten. The Frankfurter Neue Presse is a local daily newspaper from Frankfurt covering news on a regional local but also international basis.
Language (s): German
DAILY NEWSPAPER

Frankfurter Rundschau 159409
Owner: Frankfurter Rundschau GmbH
Editorial: Frankfurter Rundschau GmbH, Mainzer Landstrasse 205, Frankfurt Am Main 60326
Tel: 49 69 2199 1
Email: chefredaktion@fr-online.de **Web site:** http://www.fr-online.de
Freq: Mon thru Fri; **Circ:** 28
Profile: Die Frankfurter Rundschau ist eine der führenden überregionalen deutschen Tageszeitungen. Sie liefert Hintergrundberichte, Analysen, Interviews und Kommentare zu den Ressorts Politik, Wirtschaft, Kultur und Sport. . The Frankfurter Rundschau is one of the leading supra regional daily newspapers in Germany. It provides background reporting, analyses, interviews and comments in the fields of politics, economy, culture and sports.
Language (s): German
Ad Rate: Full Page Mono 407.25
Currency: Euro
DAILY NEWSPAPER

Fränkische Landeszeitung - Ansbacher Tagblatt 159398
Owner: Fränkische Landeszeitung GmbH
Editorial: Nürnberger Strasse 9-17, Ansbach 91522
Tel: 49 9 81 95 00-0
Web site: http://www.flz.de
Freq: Mon thru Fri
Profile: Lokalausgabe der Fränkischen Landeszeitung mit lokalen Themen und Nachrichten für Arnsberg. Local edition of the Fränkische Landeszeitung covering local topics and news for Arnsberg.
Language (s): German
DAILY NEWSPAPER

Fränkische Nachrichten, Bad Mergentheim 666217
Owner: Fränkische Nachrichten
Editorial: Fränkische Nachrichten Verlags-GmbH, Kapuzinerstrasse 4, Bad Mergentheim 97980
Tel: 49 7931 5470
Email: fn.info@fraenkische-nachrichten.de **Web site:** http://www.fnweb.de/region/main-tauber/bad-mergentheim
Freq: Daily
Profile: Fränkische Nachrichten Bad Mergentheim ist eine lokale Tageszeitung für Bad Mergentheim in Baden-Württemberg. Sie berichtet über die Gemeinde, Politik, Kultur, Sport und Umwelt. Fränkische Nachrichten Bad Mergentheim is a local daily newspaper for Bad Mergentheim in Baden-Württemberg. It reports on the community, politic, culture, sport and environment.
Language (s): German
DAILY NEWSPAPER

Fränkische Nachrichten, Buchen/Walldürn 666218
Owner: Fränkische Nachrichten
Editorial: Fränkische Nachrichten Verlags GmbH, Marktstr. 16, Buchen 74722 **Tel:** 49 6281 4090
Web site: http://www.fnweb.de/region/neckar-odenwald/buchen
Freq: Daily
Profile: Fränkische Nachrichten Buchen/Walldürn ist eine lokale Tageszeitung für Buchen/Walldürn in Baden-Württemberg. Sie berichtet über die Gemeinde, Politik, Kultur, Sport und Umwelt. Fränkische Nachrichten Buchen/Walldürn is a local daily newspaper for Buchen/Walldürn in Baden-Württemberg. It reports on the community, politic, culture, sport and environment.
Language (s): German
DAILY NEWSPAPER

Fränkische Nachrichten, Wertheim 159399
Owner: Fränkische Nachrichten Verlags-GmbH
Editorial: Maingasse 22, Wertheim 97877
Tel: 49 9342 9010
Email: red.wertheim@fraenkische-nachrichten.de
Web site: http://www.fnweb.de/region/main-tauber/wertheim-freudenberg-kreuzwertheim
Freq: Mon thru Fri
Profile: Die Fränkische Nachrichten - Wertheim sind der Lokalteil der Fränkischen Nachrichten mit lokaler Berichterstattung aus Wertheim.
Language (s): German
DAILY NEWSPAPER

Fränkischer Tag 159401
Owner: Mediengruppe Oberfranken-Mantelredaktion GmbH & Co. KG
Editorial: Mediengruppe Oberfranken GmbH & Co. KG, Gutenbergstrasse 1, Bamberg 96050
Tel: 49 951 188 209
Email: redaktion@infranken.de **Web site:** http://www.infranken.de
Freq: Mon thru Fri; **Circ:** 28
Profile: Der Fränkische Tag ist eine regionale Tageszeitung mit Sitz in Bamberg. Themen umfassen internationale und nationale Nachrichten, Sport, Feuilleton und regionale Berichterstattung. The Fränkische Tag is a regional daily newspaper headquartered in Bamberg covering international and national news, as well as sports and local news.
Language (s): German
DAILY NEWSPAPER

Fränkischer Tag, Bamberg 666091
Owner: Fränkischer Tag GmbH & Co. KG
Editorial: Mediengruppe Oberfranken GmbH & Co. KG, Gutenbergstrasse 1, Bamberg 96050
Tel: 49 951 13296 100
Email: redaktion.bamberg@infranken.de **Web site:** http://www.infranken.de/regional/bamberg/
Freq: Mon thru Fri
Profile: Fränkischer Tag Bamberg ist eine lokale Tageszeitung mit Neuigkeiten und Nachrichten aus der Stadt zu Themen wie Sport, Politik, Kirche, Natur und Gesellschaft.
Language (s): German
DAILY NEWSPAPER

Fränkischer Tag, Forchheim 666086
Owner: Fränkischer Tag GmbH & Co. KG
Editorial: Mediengruppe Oberfranken GmbH & Co. KG, Gutenbergstrasse 1, Bamberg 96050
Tel: 49 9191 708847
Email: redaktion.forchheim@infranken.de **Web site:** http://www.infranken.de/regional/forchheim/
Freq: Mon thru Fri
Profile: Fränkischer Tag Forchheim ist eine lokale Tageszeitung mit Neuigkeiten und Nachrichten aus der Stadt zu Themen wie Sport, Politik, Kirche, Natur und Gesellschaft.
Language (s): German
DAILY NEWSPAPER

Freiberger Zeitung 893858
Owner: Chemnitzer Verlag und Druck GmbH & Co. KG
Editorial: Kirchgasschen 1, Freiberg 9599
Tel: 49 3731 3760
Web site: http://www.freiepresse.de
Freq: Daily; **Circ:** 18240
Profile: Die Freiberger Zeitung ist die Lokalausgabe der regionalen Tageszeitung Freie Presse, deren Verbreitungsgebiet Sachsen ist. Der Schwerpunkt liegt auf lokaler Berichterstattung und Themen aus Politik, Wirtschaft, Kultur und Sport. The Freiberger Zeitung is the local edition of the regional daily newspaper Freie Presse from Saxony. It's main topics are local news and issues such as politics, economics, culture and sports.
Language (s): German
DAILY NEWSPAPER

Freie Presse 159411
Owner: Chemnitzer Verlag und Druck GmbH & Co. KG
Editorial: Chemnitzer Verlag und Druck GmbH & Co. KG, Brückenstrasse 15, Chemnitz 9111
Tel: 49 371 656 0
Email: die.tageszeitung@freiepresse.de **Web site:** http://www.freiepresse.de
Freq: Mon thru Fri; **Circ:** 28
Profile: Die Freie Presse ist eine regionale Tageszeitung aus Sachsen. Es werden die Themen Politik, Wirtschaft, Kultur, Sport, Panorama gedeckt, aber auch lokale und regionale Themen aus Sachsen. Zudem gibt es einen Ratgeber- und Veranstaltungsbereich. The Freie Presse is a regional daily newspaper from Saxony. It covers politics, economics, culture, sports, panorama but also local and regional topics of Saxony. In addition, it provides an advisory and events section.
Language (s): German
DAILY NEWSPAPER

Freie Presse Annaberg 666099
Owner: Chemnitzer Verlag und Druck
Editorial: Annaberger Zeitung, Markt 8, Annaberg-Buchholz 9456 **Tel:** 49 3733 1410
Email: Red.Annaberg@freiepresse.de **Web site:** http://www.freiepresse.de/LOKALES/ERZGEBIRGE/ANNABERG/
Freq: Daily
Profile: Freie Presse Annaberg ist eine lokale Tageszeitung für die Stadt Annaberg in Sachsen. Es werden die Themen Politik, Wirtschaft, Kultur, Sport, Gesundheit und Neuigkeiten aus der Region gedeckt.
Language (s): German
DAILY NEWSPAPER

Freie Presse Aue 666094
Owner: Freie Presse Aue
Editorial: Auer Zeitung, Schneeberger Str. 17, Aue 8280 **Tel:** 49 3771 5940
Email: Red.Aue@freiepresse.de **Web site:** http://www.freiepresse.de/LOKALES/ERZGEBIRGE/AUE/
Freq: Daily
Profile: Freie Presse Aue ist eine lokale Tageszeitung für die Stadt Aue in Sachsen. Es werden die Themen Politik, Wirtschaft, Kultur, Sport, Gesundheit und Neuigkeiten aus der Region gedeckt.
Language (s): German
DAILY NEWSPAPER

Freie Presse Auerbach 666097
Owner: Chemnitzer Verlag und Druck GmbH & Co. KG
Editorial: Auerbacher Zeitung, Nicolaistrasse 3, Auerbach 8209 **Tel:** 49 3744 82760
Email: Red.Auerbach@freiepresse.de **Web site:** http://www.freiepresse.de/LOKALES/VOGTLAND/AUERBACH/
Freq: Daily
Profile: Freie Presse Auerbach ist eine lokale Tageszeitung für die Stadt Auerbach in Sachsen. Es werden die Themen Politik, Wirtschaft, Kultur, Sport, Gesundheit und Neuigkeiten aus der Region gedeckt.
Language (s): German
DAILY NEWSPAPER

Freie Presse Freiberg 666095
Owner: Freie Presse Freiberg
Editorial: Freiberger Zeitung, Kirchgasschen 1, Freiberg 9599 **Tel:** 49 3732 22960
Email: Red.Freiberg@freiepresse.de **Web site:** http://www.freiepresse.de/LOKALES/MITTELSACHSEN/FREIBERG/
Freq: Daily
Profile: Freie Presse Freiberg ist eine lokale Tageszeitung für die Stadt Freiberg in Sachsen. Es werden die Themen Politik, Wirtschaft, Kultur, Sport, Gesundheit und Neuigkeiten aus der Region gedeckt.
Language (s): German
DAILY NEWSPAPER

Freie Presse Oberes Vogtland 666100
Owner: Chemnitzer Verlag und Druck
Editorial: Chemnitzer Verlag und Druck GmbH & Co. KG, Brückenstrasse 15, Chemnitz 9111
Tel: 49 371 656-0
Freq: Mon thru Fri
Profile: Freie Presse Oberes Vogtland ist die Lokalausgabe der Freien Presse für die Region Oberes Vogtland mit dem Schwerpunkt auf lokaler Berichterstattung. Freie Presse Oberes Vogtland is the local edition of Freie Presse for the region Oberes Vogtland with focus on local news.
Language (s): German
DAILY NEWSPAPER

Freie Presse Plauen 666098
Owner: Chemnitzer Verlag und Druck GmbH
Editorial: Plauener Zeitung, Postplatz 7, Plauen 8523
Tel: 49 3741 4080
Email: Red.Plauen@freiepresse.de **Web site:** http://www.freiepresse.de/LOKALES/VOGTLAND/PLAUEN/
Freq: Daily
Profile: Freie Presse Plauen ist eine lokale Tageszeitung für die Stadt Plauen in Sachsen. Es werden die Themen Politik, Wirtschaft, Kultur, Sport, Gesundheit und Neuigkeiten aus der Region gedeckt.
Language (s): German
DAILY NEWSPAPER

Freie Presse Stollberg 666109
Owner: Chemnitzer Verlag und Druck GmbH
Editorial: Stollberger Zeitung, Herrenstrasse 19, Stollberg 9366 **Tel:** 49 3729 669900
Email: Red.Stollberg@freiepresse.de **Web site:** http://www.freiepresse.de/LOKALES/ERZGEBIRGE/STOLLBERG/
Freq: Daily
Profile: Freie Presse Stollberg ist eine lokale Tageszeitung für die Stadt Stollberg in Sachsen. Es werden die Themen Politik, Wirtschaft, Kultur, Sport, Gesundheit und Neuigkeiten aus der Region gedeckt.
Language (s): German
DAILY NEWSPAPER

Freie Presse Zwickau 666096
Owner: Freie Presse Zwickau
Editorial: Zwickauer Zeitung, Hauptstrasse 13, Zwickau 8056 **Tel:** 49 375 5490
Email: Red.Zwickau@freiepresse.de **Web site:** http://www.freiepresse.de/LOKALES/ZWICKAU/ZWICKAU/
Freq: Daily
Profile: Freie Presse Zwickau ist eine regionale Tageszeitung für Zwickau. Es werden die Themen Politik, Wirtschaft, Kultur, Sport, Gesundheit und Neuigkeiten aus der Region gedeckt.
Language (s): German
DAILY NEWSPAPER

Freies Wort 159414
Owner: Suhler Verlagsges. mbH & Co. KG
Editorial: Suhler Verlagsgesellschaft mbH & Co. KG, Schützenstrasse 2, Suhl 98527 **Tel:** 49 3681 851 0
Email: redaktion@freies-wort.de **Web site:** http://www.insuedthueringen.de
Freq: Mon thru Fri
Profile: Das Freie Wort ist eine regionale Tageszeitung aus Südthüringen. Die Berichterstattung umfasst regionale Nachrichten aus Thüringen, sowie Politik, Wirtschaft, Sport, Wissenschaft, Technik. Zudem gibt es das Angebot einer Kinderzeitung und Spiele. The Freie Wort is a regional daily newspaper from South Thüringen. It covers regional news from Thüringen but as well as regional, political, economical news, as well as sports and science. In addition, it features a newspaper for children and games.
Language (s): German
DAILY NEWSPAPER

Freisinger Tagblatt 159417
Owner: Zeitungsverlag Oberbayern GmbH & Co. KG
Editorial: Münchner Strasse 7, Freising 85354
Tel: 49 8161 186 0
Email: info@merkur.de **Web site:** http://www.merkur.de/lokales/freising/
Freq: Mon thru Fri; **Circ:** 28
Profile: Das Freisinger Tagblatt ist eine lokale Tageszeitung aus Freising. Sie ist eine Lokalausgabe des Münchner Merkur und bietet lokale und regionale Berichterstattung, sowie Nachrichten. The Freisinger Tagblatt is a lokale daily newspaper from Freising. It is a local editon of the Münchner Merkur and offers local and regional reporting, as well as news.
Language (s): German
DAILY NEWSPAPER

Fuldaer Zeitung 159424
Owner: Verlag Parzeller GmbH & Co. KG
Editorial: Verlag Parzeller GmbH & Co. KG, Frankfurter Str. 8, Fulda 36043 **Tel:** 49 661 2800
Email: redaktion@fuldaerzeitung.de **Web site:** http://www.fuldaerzeitung.de
Freq: Mon thru Fri; **Circ:** 28
Profile: Die Fuldaer Zeitung ist eine regionale Tageszeitung aus Hessen. Der Fokus liegt auf der regionalen Berichterstattung aus Fulda. The Fuldauer Zeitung is a regional daily newspaper from East Hesse. Its focus is on regional and local news from Fulda.
Language (s): German
DAILY NEWSPAPER

Fürstenfeldbrucker Tagblatt 159422
Owner: Zeitungsverlag Oberbayern GmbH & Co. KG
Editorial: Münchener Zeitungs-Verlag GmbH & Co.KG, Paul-Heyse-Str. 2-4, München 80336
Tel: 49 089 53060
Email: info@merkur.de **Web site:** http://www.merkur.de/lokales/fuerstenfeldbruck/
Freq: Mon thru Fri; **Circ:** 28
Profile: Das Fürstenfeldbrucker Tagblatt ist eine Tageszeitung, die eine Lokalausgabe des Münchner Merkur ist. Schwerpunkte liegen auf der lokalen Berichtersttattung. The Fürstenfeldbrucker Tagblatt is a daily newspaper that is a local edition of the Münchner Merkur. It focuses on local news and events.
Language (s): German
DAILY NEWSPAPER

Fürther Nachrichten 159423
Owner: Verlag Nürnberger Presse Druckhaus Nürnberg GmbH & Co. KG
Editorial: Moststrasse 33, Furth 90762
Tel: 49 911 7798730
Email: fn-redaktion@pressenetz.de **Web site:** http://www.nordbayern.de/region/fuerth
Freq: Mon thru Fri; **Circ:** 28
Profile: Fürther Nachrichten ist eine lokale Tageszeitung. Sie gehört zur Nürnberger Nachrichten. Der Fokus liegt auf der Berichterstattung aus dem Gebiet um Fürth. Fürther Nachrichten is a local daily newspaper that is part of the Nürnberg Nachrichten. It focuses on reporting from the region around Fürth.
Language (s): German
DAILY NEWSPAPER

Garmisch-Partenkirchner Tagblatt 159428
Owner: Zeitungsverlag Oberbayern GmbH & Co. KG
Editorial: Münchener Zeitungs-Verlag GmbH & Co.KG, Alpspitzstrasse 5a, Garmisch-Partenkirchen 82467 **Tel:** 49 8821 75717
Email: info@merkur.de **Web site:** http://www.merkur.de/lokales/garmisch-partenkirchen/
Freq: Mon thru Fri
Profile: Das Garmisch-Partenkirchner Tagblatt ist eine Tageszeitung, die für das Gebiet um Garmisch-Partenkirchen in Bayern berichtet. Die Zeitung gehört dem Münchner Merkur an. The Garmisch-Partenkirchner Tagblatt is a daily newspaper that covers news from the area of Garmisch-Partenkirchen in Bavaria. It is part of the Münchner Merkur.
Language (s): German
DAILY NEWSPAPER

Gäubote 159425
Owner: Theodor Körner GmbH und Co. KG, Druckerei und Verlag
Editorial: Theodor Korner GmbH und Co. KG, Druckerei und Verlag, Horber Strasse 42, Herrenberg 71083 **Tel:** 49 7032 95 25 200
Email: redaktion@gaeubote.de **Web site:** http://www.gaeubote.de
Freq: Mon thru Fri; **Circ:** 28
Profile: Der Gäubote ist eine regionale Tageszeitung aus dem Kreis Böblingen. Den überregionalen Teil der Zeitung stellt die Stuttgarter Nachrichten. The Gäubote is a regional daily newspaper from the area of Böblingen. The supra regional part of the newspapaer is being produced by the Stuttgarter Nachrichten.
Language (s): German
DAILY NEWSPAPER

Geislinger Zeitung 159430
Owner: Geislinger Zeitung Verlagsgesellschaft mbH & Co KG
Editorial: GEISLINGER ZEITUNG Verlagsgesellschaft mbH & Co KG, Hauptstrasse 38, Geislingen 73312
Tel: 49 7331 202 42
Email: geislinger-zeitung.redaktion@swp.de **Web site:** http://www.swp.de/geislingen/
Freq: Mon thru Fri; **Circ:** 28
Profile: Die Geislinger Zeitung ist eine regionale Tageszeitung aus Baden-Württemberg. Sie gehört zur Südwest Presse. Es wird hauptsächlich über lokale Nachrichten berichtet. The Geislinger Zeitung is a regional daily newspaper from Baden-Wuerttemberg and part of Südwest Presse. It mainly covers local news from Geislingen.
Language (s): German
DAILY NEWSPAPER

Gescherer Zeitung 159438
Owner: Verlag J. Fleißig GmbH & Co.
Editorial: Verlag J. Fleissig GmbH & Co., Rosenstrasse 2, Coesfeld 48653 **Tel:** 49 2541 9210
Email: gescher@azonline.de **Web site:** http://www.azonline.de/
Freq: Daily; **Circ:** 28
Profile: Die Gescherer Zeitung ist eine Lokalausgabe der deutschen Tageszeitung Allgemeine Zeitung, die im Verlag J. Fleißig in Coesfeld und Rosendahl erscheint. The Gescherer Zeitung is a local edition of the German daily newspaper Allgemeine Zeitung which is published by the Verlag J. Fleißig in Coesfeld and Rosendahl.
Language (s): German
DAILY NEWSPAPER

Geseker Zeitung 159446
Owner: Zeitungsverlag Der Patriot GmbH
Editorial: Backstrasse 10a, Geseke 59590
Tel: 49 2942 97310
Email: redaktion@derpatriot.de **Web site:** http://www.derpatriot.de/Lokales/Geseke
Freq: Mon thru Fri; **Circ:** 28
Profile: Die Geseker Zeitung ist eine Lokalausgabe der Lippstädter Zeitung Der Patriot und bietet lokale Berichterstattung aus Geseke.
Language (s): German
DAILY NEWSPAPER

Gießener Allgemeine 159447
Owner: Mittelhessische Druck- und Verlagshaus GmbH & Co.KG
Editorial: Mittelhessische Druck- und Verlagshaus GmbH & Co.KG, Marburger Strasse 20, Giessen 35390 **Tel:** 49 6 41 3003 0
Email: redaktion@giessener-allgemeine.de **Web site:** http://www.giessener-allgemeine.de
Freq: Mon thru Fri; **Circ:** 28
Profile: Die Gießener Allgemeine ist eine Regionale Tageszeitung für Gießen und Umgebung mit regionaler und lokaler Berichterstattung und Nachrichten aus Politik, Gesellschaft, Kultur, Wirtschaft und Sport. The Gießener Allgemeine is a regional daily newspaper for Gießen and the surrounding area with regional and local reporting and news on politics, society, culture, business and sports.
Language (s): German
DAILY NEWSPAPER

Gießener Anzeiger 159448
Owner: Gießener Anzeiger Verlags GmbH & Co. KG
Editorial: Giessener Anzeiger Verlags GmbH & Co. KG, Am Urnenfeld 12, Giessen 35396
Tel: 49 641 9504 3405
Email: redaktion@giessener-anzeiger.de **Web site:** http://www.giessener-anzeiger.de
Freq: Mon thru Fri; **Circ:** 28
Profile: Regionale Tageszeitung mit Nachrichten aus der Region. Es gibt u.a. die Rubriken Lokal, Wirtschaft, Sport, Politik und Wissen. Regional daily newspaper with news from the region. There are categories such as business, sports, politics and knowledge.
Language (s): German
DAILY NEWSPAPER

Gmünder Tagespost 159451
Owner: SDZ Druck und Medien GmbH & Co. KG
Editorial: Gmünder Tagespost, Vordere Schmiedgasse 18, Schwäbisch Gmünd 73525
Tel: 49 7171 60010
Email: redaktion@gmuender-tagespost.de **Web site:** http://www.gmuender-tagespost.de
Freq: Mon thru Fri; **Circ:** 28
Profile: Die Gmünder Tagespost ist eine regionale Tageszeitung aus dem Gebiet um Schwäbisch Gmünd. Einen großen Teil der Zeitung macht die lokale Berichterstattung aus. Zudem gibt es auch internationale Berichte aus den Berichen Politik, Wirtschaft, Sport und aktuelle Meldungen. The Gmünder Tagespost is a regional daily newspaper that covers local and international news from the area of Schwäbisch Gmünd. Local reporting represents the main part of the newspaper. In addition, it can be found reports covering politics, economics, sports and current events.
Language (s): German
DAILY NEWSPAPER

Goslarsche Zeitung 159454
Owner: Goslarsche Zeitung Karl Krause GmbH & Co. KG
Editorial: Goslarsche Zeitung Karl Krause GmbH & Co. KG Pressehaus, Backerstrasse 31-35, Goslar 38640 **Tel:** 49 0532 13330
Email: redaktion@goslarsche-zeitung.de **Web site:** http://www.goslarsche.de
Freq: Mon thru Fri; **Circ:** 28
Profile: Die Goslarsche Zeitung ist eine lokale Tageszeitung aus Niedersachsen. Themen: Lokale und regionale Nachrichten, Nachrichten aus aller Welt und Sport. Es gibt zwei weitere Lokalausgaben für Bad-Harzburg und Clausthal-Zellerfeld. The Goslarsche Zeitung is a local daily newspaper from Lower Saxony covering local and regional topics as well as news from all over the world and sports.

There are two local editions for Bad-Harzburg and Clausthal-Zellerfeld.
Language (s): German
DAILY NEWSPAPER

Göttinger Tageblatt 159453
Owner: Göttinger Tageblatt GmbH & Co. KG
Editorial: Göttinger Tageblatt GmbH & Co. KG, Dransfelder Strasse 1, Göttingen 37079
Tel: 49 551 9011
Email: redaktion@goettinger-tageblatt.de **Web site:** http://www.goettinger-tageblatt.de
Freq: Mon thru Fri; **Circ:** 28
Profile: Das Göttinger Tageblatt ist eine Tageszeitung aus Niedersachsen. Die Themen sind vorerst regional geprägt, umfassen aber auch nationale und internationale Nachrichten aus den Gebieten Politik, Wirtschaft, Sport, Kultur, Wissen und Medien. Die Zeitung bietet eine Mediathek und einen Ratgeberbereich an. The Göttinger Tageblatt is a newspaper from Lower Saxony covering mainly local, but also national and international news in the fields of politics, economics, sports, culture, knowledge and media. It features a media archive and a practical guide.
Language (s): German
DAILY NEWSPAPER

Grafenauer Anzeiger 159456
Owner: Neue Presse Verlags-GmbH
Editorial: Buchdruckergasse 4, Grafenau 94481
Tel: 49 8552 408 921
Email: red.grafenau@pnp.de **Web site:** http://www.pnp.de/region_und_lokal/stadt_und_landkreis_passau/
Freq: Mon thru Fri; **Circ:** 28
Profile: Der Grafenauer Anzeiger ist eine Lokalausgabe der Passauer Neuen Presse mit lokaler Berichterstattung aus Grafenau.
Language (s): German
DAILY NEWSPAPER

Gränzbote Tuttlingen 159455
Owner: Schwäbischer Verlag GmbH & Co. KG
Editorial: Schwäbisch Media Digital GmbH & Co. KG, Karlstr. 16, Ravensburg 88212 **Tel:** 49 751 29555555
Email: redaktion@schwaebische.de **Web site:** http://www.schwaebische.de/Gränzbote?
Freq: Mon thru Fri; **Circ:** 28
Profile: Der Gränzbote ist eine regionale Tageszeitung aus Tuttlingen und stellt eine Lokalausgabe der Schwäbischen Zeitung dar. Es werden überwiegend lokale Nachrichten veröffentlicht. The Gränzbote is a regional daily newspaper from Tuttlingen representing a local edition of the Schwäbischen Zeitung. It mainly covers local news.
Language (s): German
DAILY NEWSPAPER

Groß-Gerauer Echo 159494
Owner: Echo Zeitungen GmbH
Editorial: Echo Zeitungen GmbH, Holzhofallee 25-31, Darmstadt 64295 **Tel:** 49 6151 3870
Email: echo-zeitungen@darmstaedter-echo.de **Web site:** http://www.echo-online.de/region/gross-gerau/gross-gerau/?
Freq: Mon thru Fri; **Circ:** 28
Profile: Das Groß-Gerauer Echo ist eine Regionalzeitung für den Landkreis Groß-Gerau. Sie wird von der Echo Zeitungen GmbH herausgebracht, die zur Echo Medien GmbH gehört.

The Groß-Gerauer Echo is a regional daily newspaper for the administrative district of Groß Gerau. It's published by the Echo Zeitungen GmbH which is part of the Echo Medien GmbH.
Language (s): German
DAILY NEWSPAPER

Haigerer Zeitung 159467
Owner: Wetzlardruck GmbH
Editorial: Rathausstrasse 1, Dillenburg 35662
Tel: 49 2771 87 44 00
Email: redaktion.dp@mittelhessen.de **Web site:** http://www.mittelhessen.de
Freq: Mon thru Fri; **Circ:** 28
Profile: Die Haigerer Zeitung ist eine Lokalzeitung, die im Lahn-Dill Kreis erscheint und lokale Berichterstattung und regionale Nachrichten aus der Umgebung bietet. Sie wird von der gleichen Redaktion erstellt wie die Dill-Post, die Dill-Zeitung, das Herborner Tageblatt und das Herborner Echo.
Language (s): German
DAILY NEWSPAPER

Halberstädter Volksstimme 159468
Owner: Magdeburger Verlags- und Druckhaus GmbH
Editorial: Westendorf 6, Halberstadt 38820
Tel: 49 3941 69 92 20
Email: redaktion.halberstadt@volksstimme.de **Web site:** http://www.volksstimme.de/nachrichten/lokal/halberstadt/?
Freq: Mon thru Fri; **Circ:** 28
Profile: Die Halberstädter Volksstimme ist eine Lokalausgabe der Magdeburger Volksstimme und bietet lokale Berichterstattung aus Halberstadt, sowie auch Nachrichten aus der Umgebung.
Language (s): German
DAILY NEWSPAPER

Haller Kreisblatt 159469
Owner: Haller Kreisblatt Verlags GmbH
Editorial: Haller Kreisblatt Verlags-GmbH, Gutenbergstr. 2, Halle 33790
Email: info@haller-kreisblatt.de **Web site:** http://www.haller-kreisblatt.de/
Freq: Mon thru Fri
Profile: Das Haller Kreisblatt ist eine regionale Tageszeitung aus Westfalen. Die Berichterstattung liegt auf lokalen Nachrichten. Haller Kreisblatt is a regional daily newspaper of Westfalia covering local news from Halle.
Language (s): German
DAILY NEWSPAPER

Haller Tagblatt 159470
Owner: SÜDWEST PRESSE Hohenlohe GmbH & Co. KG,
Editorial: SÜDWEST PRESSE Hohenlohe GmbH & Co. KG, Verlagsbetrieb Haller Tagblatt, Haalstrasse 5 und 7, Schwäbisch Hall 74523 **Tel:** 49 791 404 410
Email: redaktion@hallertagblatt.de **Web site:** http://www.swp.de/schwaebisch_hall/
Freq: Mon thru Fri; **Circ:** 28
Profile: Das Haller Tagblatt ist eine regionale Tageszeitung aus Baden-Württemberg. Die überregionalen Nachrichten liefert die Südwest Presse. The Haller Tagblatt is a regional daily newspaper from Baden-Wuerttemberg with local news coverage. National and international news are being provided by the Südwest Presse.
Language (s): German
DAILY NEWSPAPER

Hamburger Abendblatt 159473
Owner: Zeitungsgruppe Hamburg GmbH
Editorial: Zeitungsgruppe Hamburg GmbH, Grosse Burstah 18-32, Hamburg 20457
Tel: 49 40 55 44 71171
Email: hadigital@abendblatt.de **Web site:** http://www.abendblatt.de
Freq: Mon thru Fri; **Circ:** 28
Profile: Das Hamburger Abendblatt ist eine regionale Tageszeitung für Hamburg und Umgebung. The Hamburger Abendblatt is a German regional daily newspaper for news in Hamburg and surroundings.
Language (s): German
DAILY NEWSPAPER

Hamburger Abendblatt, Pinneberg (Pinneberger Zeitung) 666133
Owner: Axel Springer AG
Editorial: Lindenstr. 30, Pinneberg 25421
Tel: 49 4101 510100
Email: pz@abendblatt.de **Web site:** http://www.abendblatt.de/region/pinneberg/
Freq: Daily; **Circ:** 28
Profile: Die Pinneberger Zeitung ist eine Lokalausgabe des Hamburger Abendblatts und bietet lokale Berichterstattung und Nachrichten aus Pinneberg Stadt und Umgebung.
DAILY NEWSPAPER

Hamburger Morgenpost 159474
Owner: Morgenpost Verlag GmbH
Editorial: Morgenpost Verlag GmbH, Griegstrasse 75, Hamburg 22763 **Tel:** 49 40 80 90 57 0
Email: hamburg@mopo.de **Web site:** http://www.mopo.de
Freq: Daily; **Circ:** 28
Profile: Die Hamburger Morgenpost ist eine regionale Hamburger Zeitung. Sie bietet lokale und regionale Berichterstattung, Hintergrundinformationen und Nachrichten aus Politik, Wirtschaft, Sport, Lifestyle, Gesellschaft, Kultur und Unterhaltung aus Hamburg und Umgebung. The Hamburger Morgenpost is regional Hamburg newspaper. It reports local and regional news, background information and current news from politics, economics, sports, lifestyle, society, culture and entertainment from Hamburg and the surrounding regions.
Language (s): German
DAILY NEWSPAPER

Hanauer Anzeiger 159476
Owner: Hanauer Anzeiger GmbH
Editorial: Hanauer Anzeiger GmbH, Donaustrasse 5, Hanau 63452 **Tel:** 49 6181 2903 333
Email: redaktion@hanauer.de **Web site:** http://www.hanauer.de
Freq: Mon thru Fri
Profile: Der Hanauer Anzeiger ist die drittälteste deutsche Tageszeitung (nach der Hildesheimer Allgemeinen Zeitung und dem Pfälzischen Merkur) und die älteste noch existierende mit Vollredaktion (Publizistische Einheit) in Deutschland. Er berichtet über Nachrichten aus der Region Hanau, Hessen. The German daily regional newspaper Hanauer Zeitung, founded in 1725, is the third oldest daily newspaper in Germay and reports about news in the area of Hanau, Hesse.
Language (s): German
DAILY NEWSPAPER

Hanau-Post 159477
Owner: Mediengruppe Offenbach-Post
Editorial: Steinheimer Vorstadt 25, Hanau 63456
Tel: 49 6181 96410 11
Email: red.hanau@op-online.de **Web site:** http://www.op-online.de/lokales/nachrichten/hanau/
Freq: Mon thru Fri; **Circ:** 28
Profile: Die Hanau-Post eine regionale Tageszeitung aus Hessen. Sie stellt eine Lokalausgabe der Offenbach-Post dar. Der inhaltliche Fokus liegt auf der lokalen Berichterstattung aus Hanau und dem Main-Kinzig-Kreis. The Hanau-Post is a regional daily newspaper from Hesse. It is the local edition of the Offenbach-Post and focuses on local news from Hanau and the Main-Kinzig-Kreis.
Language (s): German
DAILY NEWSPAPER

Handelsblatt 159478
Owner: Handelsblatt GmbH
Editorial: Handelsblatt GmbH, Kasernenstr. 67, Dusseldorf 40213 **Tel:** 49 211 887 0
Email: handelsblatt@vhb.de **Web site:** http://www.handelsblatt.com
Freq: Mon thru Fri; **Circ:** 28
Profile: Die deutsche Finanzzeitung Handelsblatt erscheint fünfmal die Woche (von Montag bis Freitag) und informiert zu Unternehmen, Finanzen und Finanzmärkten sowie über Politik und Technologie The German daily national Handelsblatt is a trade newspaper published five times a week (Monday to Friday) and provides information about business, finance and financial markets, politics and technology.
Language (s): German
DAILY NEWSPAPER

Hannoversche Allgemeine Zeitung 159479
Owner: Verlagsgesellschaft Madsack GmbH & Co. KG
Editorial: Verlagsgesellschaft Madsack GmbH & Co. KG, August-Madsack-Strasse 1, Hannover 30559
Tel: 49 511 518 0
Email: redaktion@haz.de **Web site:** http://www.haz.de
Freq: Mon thru Fri; **Circ:** 28
Profile: Die Hannoversche Allgemeine Zeitung ist eine regionale Tageszeitung aus Niedersachsen. Neben der lokalen und regionalen Berichterstattung, gibt es auch Nachrichten aus den Gebieten Politik, Wirtschaft, Sport, Kultur, Medien und Wissen. Zudem gibt es vier Blogs zu verschiedenen Themen. The Hannoversche Allgemeine Zeitung is a regional daily newspaper from Lower Saxony. Besides local and regional reporting, it also covers news in the fields of politics, economics, sports, media and science. In addition, it provides four different blogs.
Language (s): German
DAILY NEWSPAPER

Harzer Volksstimme 159482
Owner: Magdeburger Verlags- und Druckhaus GmbH
Editorial: Breite Strasse 48, Wernigerode 38855
Tel: 49 3943 92 14 20
Email: redaktion.wernigerode@volksstimme.de **Web site:** http://www.volksstimme.de
Circ: 28
Profile: Die Harzer Volksstimme ist eine Lokalteil der Magdeburger Volksstimme mit lokaler Berichterstattung und regionalen Nachrichten aus dem Harz.
Language (s): German
DAILY NEWSPAPER

Havelberger Volksstimme 159486
Owner: Magdeburger Verlags- und Druckhaus GmbH
Editorial: Schulstrasse 8, Havelberg 39539
Tel: 49 39387 7 68 20
Email: redaktion.havelberg@volksstimme.de **Web site:** http://www.volksstimme.de/nachrichten/lokal/havelberg/?
Circ: 28
Profile: Die Havelberger Volksstimme ist ein Lokalteil der Magdeburger Volksstimme und bietet lokale Berichterstattung aus Havelberg.
Language (s): German
DAILY NEWSPAPER

HAZ wirtschaft extra 511317
Owner: Madsack Supplement GmbH & Co. KG
Editorial: August-Madsack-Str. 1, Hannover 30559
Email: haz@madsack.de **Web site:** http://www.haz.de
Freq: Mon thru Fri
Language (s): German
DAILY NEWSPAPER

Heidenheimer Neue Presse 159487
Owner: Heidenheimer Zeitung GmbH & Co. KG
Editorial: Heidenheimer Zeitung GmbH & Co KG, Olgastrasse 15, Heidenheim 89518
Tel: 49 7321 347153
Email: redaktion@hz-online.de **Web site:** http://www.hz-online.de/
Freq: Mon thru Fri
Profile: Die Heidenheimer Neue Presse ist eine regionale Tageszeitung, die über lokale Nachrichten aus Heidenheim und Umgebung berichtet. Sie gehört der Südwest Presse an. The Heidenheimer Neue Presse is a regional daily newspaper covering local news from Heidenheim and its surrounding area. It is part of the Südwest Presse.
Language (s): German
DAILY NEWSPAPER

Heidenheimer Zeitung 159488
Owner: Heidenheimer Zeitung GmbH & Co. KG
Editorial: Heidenheimer Zeitung GmbH & Co KG, Olgastrasse 15, Heidenheim 89518
Tel: 49 7321 347 153
Email: redaktion@hz-online.de **Web site:** http://www.hz-online.de/
Freq: Mon thru Fri; **Circ:** 28
Profile: Die Heidenheimer Zeitung ist eine regionale Tageszeitung. Sie gehört zum Verlag der Südwest Presse. Die Redaktionen der Heidenheimer Zeitung und der Heidenheimer Neuen Presse arbeiten seit 2008 zusammen. The Heidenheimer Zeitung is a regional daily newspaper and part of the publishing house of Südwest Presse. Since 2008, the editors of Heidenheimer Zeitung and Heidenheimer Neue Presse are working in cooperation.
Language (s): German
DAILY NEWSPAPER

Heilbronner Stimme 159489
Owner: Heilbronner Stimme GmbH & Co. KG
Editorial: Heilbronner Stimme GmbH & Co. KG, Allee 2, Heilbronn 74072 **Tel:** 49 7131 615 226
Email: redaktion@stimme.de **Web site:** http://www.stimme.de
Freq: Mon thru Fri; **Circ:** 28
Profile: Die Heilbronner Stimme ist die regionale Tageszeitung der Stadt Heilbronn. Der Schwerpunkt liegt auf der regionalen Berichterstattung aus den Gebieten um Heilbronn, Hohenlohne und Kraichgau. The Heilbronner Stimme is the regional daily newspaper from the city of Heilbronn. Main focus is on regional reporting from the areas around Heilbronn, Hohenlohne and Kraichgau.
Language (s): German
DAILY NEWSPAPER

Heilbronner Stimme, Leintal (Schwaigern) 666143
Owner: Heilbronner Stimme GmbH & Co. KG
Editorial: Allee 2, Heilbronn 74072 **Tel:** 49 7131 6150
Web site: http://www.stimme.de/heilbronn/nachrichten/leintal/
Freq: Daily; **Circ:** 28
Profile: Die Heilbronner Stimme Leintal ist ein Lokalangebot fer Heilbronner Stimme für das Leintal mit Fokus auf lokaler Berichterstattung und Nachrichten aus Schwaigern und Umgebung. Erstellt wird die Publikation in der Redaktion Heilbronn.
Language (s): German
DAILY NEWSPAPER

Heilbronner Stimme, Neckarsulm (Nord-Mitte) 666139
Owner: Heilbronner Stimme GmbH & Co. KG
Editorial: Allee 2, Heilbronn 74072
Tel: 49 7131 615 226
Email: redaktion@stimme.de **Web site:** http://www.stimme.de/heilbronn/nachrichten/neckarsulm-neckartal/
Freq: Daily; **Circ:** 28
Profile: Die Heilbronner Stimme Neckarsulm ist ein Lokalangebot der Heilbronner Stimme mit Fokus auf Berichterstattung und lokalen Nachrichten aus Neckarsulm.
DAILY NEWSPAPER

Heilbronner Stimme, Weinsberger Tal 666138
Owner: Heilbronner Stimme GmbH & Co. KG
Editorial: Allee 2, Heilbronn 74072
Tel: 49 7131 615 226
Email: redaktion@stimme.de **Web site:** http://www.stimme.de/heilbronn/
Freq: Daily; **Circ:** 28
Profile: Die Heilbronner Stimme Weinsberg ist ein Lokalangebot der Heilbronner Stimme mit Nachrichten aus der Region Weinsberg. Erstellt werden die Nachrichten von der Redaktion in Heilbronn.
Language (s): German
DAILY NEWSPAPER

Heiligenhauser Zeitung 159491
Owner: Westdeutsche Allgemeine Zeitungsverlag GmbH
Editorial: Jahnstr. 1, Heiligenhaus 42579
Tel: 49 2056 98530
Email: kontakt@derwesten.de **Web site:** http://www.derwesten.de/staedte/heiligenhaus/
Freq: Daily; **Circ:** 28
Profile: Regionalausgabe für Heiligenhausen der WAZ, Deutschlands größte Regionalzeitung. Untrennbar mit der Entwicklung des Ruhrgebiets verbunden ist die Erfolgsgeschichte der Westdeutsche Allgemeine WAZ. Sie hat seit ihrem Ersterscheinungstag am 3.4.1948 die Region an Ruhr, Emscher und Lippe mitgeprägt wie kein anderes Medium. Lizenznehmer und Herausgeber Erich Brost schuf eine Zeitung nach angelsächsischem Vorbild. Die Ausrichtung war und ist unabhängig und überparteilich. Gemeinsam mit dem Mitherausgeber Jakob Funke realisierte er die erfolgreichste Zeitungsneugründung nach dem Krieg. Heute ist die WAZ Deutschlands größte Regionalzeitung, deren Verbreitungsgebiet vom südlichen Münsterland bis ins Niederbergische, vom Niederrhein bis in den Raum Unna reicht. Die Gesamtfläche beträgt ca. 4.450 qkm. In den Reviermetropolen Essen, Bochum, Gelsenkirchen, Duisburg, Oberhausen und Mülheim an der Ruhr ist die WAZ die jeweils führende Tageszeitung. Die Zeitung des Ruhrgebiets hat immer ein offenes Ohr für die Bürger. In ihr finden sich die Menschen des Reviers wieder. In ihr findet die Stadt statt. Die WAZ berichtet lesernah und kommentiert unbeeinflusst. Die Heiligenhauser Zeitung WAZ ist eine Bezirksausgabe der Westdeutsche Allgemeine WAZ. Regional edition for Heiligenhausenof the WAZ, Germany's largest regional newspaper. Inextricably linked with the development of the Ruhr area is the success story of the Westdeutsche Allgemeine WAZ. Since its first publication on 3.4.1948, it helped shaping the region Ruhr, Emscher and Lippe like no other medium. Licensee and publisher Erich Brost created a newspaper of Anglo-Saxon model. The focus was and is independent and nonpartisan. Together with the co-editor James Funke, he conducted the most successful newspaper start-up after the war. Today, the WAZ is Germany's largest regional newspaper, its range extends from the southern Münsterland to the Niederbergische Region, from the Lower Rhine up to the Region of Unna. The total area is approximately 4450 sq km. In the Ruhr area cities Essen, Bochum, Gelsenkirchen, Duisburg, Oberhausen and Mülheim an der Ruhr, WAZ is the leading daily newspaper. The newspaper of the Ruhr area has always listened to the citizens. In it people

of the territory find themselves. In it the city happens. The WAZ reports and commentes close to its readers and unaffected. The Heiligenhauser Zeitung WAZ is a regional edition of the Westdeutsche Allgemeine WAZ.
Language (s): German
DAILY NEWSPAPER

Hellweger Anzeiger 159496

Owner: Zeitungsverlag Rubens GmbH & Co. KG
Editorial: Zeitungsverlag Rubens GmbH & Co. KG, Wasserstrasse 20, Unna 59423 **Tel:** 49 2303 202 114
Email: verlag@hellwegeranzeiger.de **Web site:** http://www.hellwegeranzeiger.de
Freq: Mon thru Fri; **Circ:** 28
Profile: Der Hellweger Anzeiger ist die regionale Tageszeitung aus Unna. In Zusammenarbeit mit der Ruhr Nachrichten und dem Westfälischen Anzeiger wird der Mantelteil der Zeitung produziert. The Hellweger Anzeiger is the regional daily newspaper in Unna. The cover section of the newspaper is being produced in cooperation with the Rhein Ruhr Nachrichten and the Westfälische Anzeiger.
Language (s): German
DAILY NEWSPAPER

Herborner Tageblatt 159498

Owner: Wetzlardruck GmbH
Editorial: Herborner Tageblatt, Rathausstrasse 1, Dillenburg 35662 **Tel:** 49 2771 874400
Email: redaktion.dp@mittelhessen.de **Web site:** http://www.mittelhessen.de/lokales/region-dillenburg/herborn.html?
Freq: Mon thru Fri; **Circ:** 28
Profile: Das Herborner Tageblatt ist die regionale Tageszeitung für die Stadt Herborn in Mittelhessen. Inhaltlicher Schwerpunkt ist die lokale Berichterstattung. Es wird zusammen mit der Dill-Post und der Haigerer Zeitung produziert. The Herborner Tageblatt is the regional daily newspaper for the city of Herborn in Middle Hesse. It focuses on local reporting and is being produced in cooperation with the Dill-Post and the Haigerer Zeitung.
Language (s): German
DAILY NEWSPAPER

Herforder Kreisanzeiger 666307

Owner: Zeitungsverlag Neue Westfälische GmbH & Co. KG
Editorial: Niedernstrasse 21 - 27, Bielefeld 33602
Tel: 49 521 5550
Email: redaktion@neue-westfaelische.de **Web site:** http://www.westfalen-blatt.de/
Freq: Mon thru Fri
Profile: Nachrichten aus der Stadt Herford und dem Umland. News from the city of Herford and surrounding areas.
Language (s): German
DAILY NEWSPAPER

Herforder Kreisblatt 159499

Owner: WESTFALEN-BLATT Vereinigte Zeitungsverlage GmbH
Editorial: Sudbrackstrasse 14-18, Bielefeld 33611
Tel: 49 521 179413
Email: wb@westfalen-blatt.de **Web site:** http://www.westfalen-blatt.de/
Freq: Daily; **Circ:** 28
Profile: Lokalausgabe des Westfalen-Blatts, mit lokaler Berichterstattung und Themen. Local edition of the Westfalen-Blatt covering local reporting and topics.
Language (s): German
DAILY NEWSPAPER

Heuberger Bote Spaichingen 159502

Owner: Schwäbischer Verlag GmbH & Co. KG
Editorial: Heuberger Bote & INFO - Der Südfinder, Hauptstrasse 90, Spaichingen 78549
Tel: 49 7424 949315
Email: redaktion.spaichingen@schwaebische.de
Web site: http://www.schwaebische.de/region/sigmaringen-tuttlingen/spaichingen.html?
Freq: Mon thru Fri; **Circ:** 28
Profile: Der Heuberger Bote ist eine regionale Tageszeitung, die zur Schwäbischen Zeitung angehört. Es wird überwiegend über lokale Themen aus Spaichingen berichtet. The Heuberger Bote is a regional daily newspaper that is part of the Schwäbischen Zeitungand mainly covers local news from Spaichingen.
Language (s): German
DAILY NEWSPAPER

Hildesheimer Allgemeine Zeitung 159503

Owner: Gebrüder Gerstenberg GmbH & Co. KG
Editorial: Gebrüder Gerstenberg GmbH & Co. KG, Rathausstrasse 18-20, Hildesheim 31134
Tel: 49 5121 106 302
Email: redaktion@hildesheimer-allgemeine.de **Web site:** http://www.hildesheimer-allgemeine.de
Freq: Mon thru Fri; **Circ:** 28
Profile: Die Hildesheimer Allgemeine ist eine regionale Tageszeitung. Die Berichterstattung umfasst weitestgehend lokale Nachrichten, sowie regionale Berichterstattung. The Hildesheimer Allgemeine is a regional daily newspaper which mainly covers local news and regional reporting.
Language (s): German
DAILY NEWSPAPER

HNA Fritzlar/Homberg (Fritzlar-Homberger Allgemeine) 159508

Owner: Dierichs GmbH & Co. KG
Editorial: Ziegenhainer Strasse 10 B, Homberg 34576 **Tel:** 49 5681 993415
Email: homberg@hna.de **Web site:** http://www.hna.de/lokales/fritzlar-homberg/
Freq: Mon thru Fri; **Circ:** 28
Profile: Lokalausgabe für Fritzlar-Homberg der Zeitung Hessische/Niedersächsische Allgemeine. Local edition for Fritzlar-Homberg of the newspaper Hessische/Niedersächsische Allgemeine.
Language (s): German
DAILY NEWSPAPER

HNA Hessische/ Niedersächsische Allgemeine 318950

Owner: Verlag Dierichs GmbH & Co KG
Editorial: Verlag Dierichs GmbH & Co KG, Frankfurter Str. 168, Kassel 34121 **Tel:** 49 561 203 00
Email: info@hna.de **Web site:** http://www.hna.de
Freq: Mon thru Fri
Profile: HNA Hessische/Niedersächsische Allgemeine ist eine regionale Tageszeitung für Nord-Hessen und Süd-Niedersachsen mit 16 lokalen Ausgaben, unter anderem für Göttingen, Hann, Münden, Nordtheim und Solling. Neben Nachrichten und Service-Themen, wird auch lokale und regionale Berichterstattung geboten. RSS (Really Simple Syndication) kann unter http://www.hna.de/media/rssfeeds/ aufgerufen werden.HNA Hessische/ Niedersächsische Allgemeine is a regional daily newspaper for northern Hessen and southern Niedersachsen with 16 local editions, including Göttingen, Hann, Münden, Nordtheim and Solling. In addition to news and consumer topics, local and regional coverage is offered. RSS (Really Simple Syndication) can be accessed at http://www.hna.de/media/rssfeeds/
Language (s): German
DAILY NEWSPAPER

HNA Hofgeismar/Wolfhagen (Hofgeismarer Allgemeine) 159510

Owner: Dierichs GmbH & Co. KG
Editorial: Bahnhofstrasse 6, Hofgeismar 34369
Tel: 49 5671 50 90 13
Email: hofgeismar@hna.de **Web site:** http://www.hna.de/lokales/hofgeismar/
Freq: Mon thru Fri; **Circ:** 28
Profile: Regionalausgabe der Hessisch/Niedersächsische Allgemeine für Hofgeismar mit lokalen Themen und Nachrichten. Regional edition of the newspaper Hessisch/Niedersächsische Allgemeine for Hofgeismar with local topics and news.
Language (s): German
DAILY NEWSPAPER

HNA Northeim (Northeimer Neueste Nachrichten) 159513

Owner: Verlag Dierichs GmbH & Co KG
Editorial: In der Fluth 24, Northeim 37154
Tel: 49 5551 600722
Email: northeim@hna.de **Web site:** http://www.hna.de/lokales/northeim/
Freq: Mon thru Fri; **Circ:** 28
Profile: Die Northeimer Neueste Nachrichten sind eine Lokalausgabe der HNA für Northeim und bieten lokale Berichterstattung und Nachrichten aus der Region.
Language (s): German
DAILY NEWSPAPER

HNA Waldeck/Korbach (Waldeckische Allgemeine) 159517

Owner: Dierichs GmbH & Co. KG
Editorial: Flechtdorfer Strasse 4, Korbach 34497
Tel: 49 5631 974625
Email: korbach@hna.de **Web site:** http://www.hna.de/lokales/korbach-waldeck/
Freq: Daily; **Circ:** 28
Profile: Die Waldeckische Allgemeine ist die Lokalausgabe der HNA für Waldeck und Korbach und bietet lokale Berichterstattung und Nachrichten aus der Umgebung.
Language (s): German
DAILY NEWSPAPER

Höchster Kreisblatt 159522

Owner: Frankfurter Societäts-Medien GmbH
Editorial: Kirschgartenstrasse 4, Hofheim 65719
Tel: 49 6192 96 52 64
Email: hk-hofheim@fnp.de **Web site:** http://www.kreisblatt.de/
Freq: Mon thru Fri; **Circ:** 28
Profile: Das Höchster Kreisblatt ist eine Lokalausgabe der Tageszeitung Frankfurter Neue Presse und bietet lokale Berichterstattung und Nachrichten aus der Umgebung. Die Hauptredaktion befindet sich in Hofheim. Die Lokalredaktion Höchst ist unter der Adresse Albanusstraße 27 65929 Frankfurt-Höchst erreichbar.
Language (s): German
DAILY NEWSPAPER

Hockenheimer Tageszeitung 159521

Owner: Schwetzinger Zeitungsverlag GmbH + Co. KG
Editorial: Karlsruher Strasse 15, Hockenheim 68766
Tel: 49 6205 7035
Email: sz-redaktion@schwetzinger-zeitung.de **Web site:** http://www.morgenweb.de/region/schwetzinger-zeitung-hockenheimer-tageszeitung/hockenheim
Freq: Mon thru Fri; **Circ:** 28
Profile: Die Hockenheimer Tageszeitung ist eine lokale Tageszeitung, die Teil der Schwetzinger Zeitung ist. Sie biete lokale Berichterstattung und Nachrichten aus Hockenheim und Umgebung.
Language (s): German
DAILY NEWSPAPER

Hohenloher Tagblatt 159526

Owner: Wankmüller GmbH & Co. KG
Editorial: SÜDWEST PRESSE Hohenloher Tagblatt, Ludwigstrasse 6-10, Crailsheim 74564
Tel: 49 7951 409321
Email: redaktion.ht@swp.de **Web site:** http://www.swp.de/crailsheim/
Freq: Mon thru Fri; **Circ:** 28
Profile: Das Hohenloher Tagblatt ist eine regionale Tageszeitung. Sie wird im Verlag der Südwest Presse vertrieben. The Hohenloher Tagblatt is a regional daily newspaper covering local news and being published by the Südwest Presse
Language (s): German
DAILY NEWSPAPER

Hohenloher Zeitung 159527

Owner: Heilbronner Stimme GmbH & Co. KG
Editorial: Hohenloher Zeitung, Konsul-Uebele-Strasse 6, Künzelsau 74653 **Tel:** 49 7940 92620
Email: redaktion.kuen@stimme.de **Web site:** http://www.hohenloher-zeitung.de
Freq: Mon thru Fri; **Circ:** 28
Profile: Das Hohenloher Zeitung ist eine regionale Tageszeitung und wird im Verlag der Heilbronner Stimme veröffentlicht. Ihre Berichterstattung konzentriert sich auf den Hohenlohekreis.

The Hohenloher Zeitung is a regional daily newspaper that is being published by the publishing house Heilbronner Stimme.The reporting concentrates on the region of Hohenlohe.
Language (s): German
DAILY NEWSPAPER

Hohenloher Zeitung - Öhringen 666137

Owner: Heilbronner Stimme GmbH & Co. KG
Editorial: Bahnhofstrasse 11, Öhringen 74613
Tel: 49 7941 9161 0
Email: redaktion.oehr@stimme.de **Web site:** http://www.stimme.de/hohenlohe/
Profile: Die Hohenloher Zeitung Öhringen ist der Lokalteil der Hohenloher Zeitung mit Fokus auf lokaler Berichterstattung und Stadtnachrichten.
Language (s): German
DAILY NEWSPAPER

Holsteinischer Courier 159529

Owner: sh:z Schleswig-Holsteinischer Zeitungsverlag GmbH & Co. KG
Editorial: Kuhberg 18, Neumünster 24534
Tel: 49 4321 9461701
Email: redaktion.neumuenster@shz.de **Web site:** http://www.shz.de/lokales/holsteinischer-courier
Freq: Mon thru Fri; **Circ:** 28
Profile: Der Holsteinischer Courier ist eine regionale Tageszeitung, die dem Schleswig-Holsteinischen Zeitungsverlag angehört. Verbreitungsgebiet und Nachrichtenschwerpunkt ist Neumünster und das Umland. The Holsteinischer Courier is a regional daily newspaper and part of the Schleswig-Holsteinische Zeitungsverlag. Its distribution and reporting focuses on the region of Neumünster.
Language (s): German
DAILY NEWSPAPER

Holzkirchner Merkur 159530

Owner: Zeitungsverlag Oberbayern GmbH & Co. KG
Editorial: Thannerstr. 4, Holzkirchen 83607
Tel: 49 8024 9065 0
Email: info@merkur.de **Web site:** https://www.merkur.de/lokales/region-holzkirchen/
Freq: Mon thru Fri; **Circ:** 28
Profile: Holzkirchner Merkur ist eine deutsche, täglich erscheinende Lokalzeitung für Holzkirchen (Bayern). Holzkirchner Merkur is a German daily local newspaper for Holzkirchen (Bavaria).
Language (s): German
DAILY NEWSPAPER

Husumer Nachrichten 159534

Owner: sh:z Schleswig-Holsteinischer Zeitungsverlag GmbH & Co. KG
Editorial: sh:z Schleswig-Holsteinischer Zeitungsverlag GmbH & Co. KG, Fordestrasse 20, Flensburg 24944
Email: redaktion@shz.de **Web site:** http://www.shz.de/lokales/husumer-nachrichten
Freq: Mon thru Fri; **Circ:** 28
Profile: Die Husumer Nachrichten ist eine regionale Tageszeitung aus Norddeutschland. Sie gehört zum Flensburger Zeitungsverlag. The Husumer Nachrichten is a regional daily newspaper from North Germany. It is part of the Flensburger Zeitungsverlag.
Language (s): German
DAILY NEWSPAPER

Ibbenbürener Volkszeitung 159536

Owner: ivz.medien GmbH & Co. KG
Editorial: ivz.medien GmbH & Co. KG, Wilhelmstrasse 240, Ibbenbüren 49475
Tel: 49 5451 933 240
Email: redaktion@ivz-aktuell.de **Web site:** http://www.ivz-aktuell.de
Freq: Mon thru Fri; **Circ:** 28
Profile: Die Ibbenbürener Volkszeitung ist eine regionale Tageszeitung mit Schwerpunkt auf lokaler und regionaler Berichterstattung. The Ibbenbürener Volkszeitung is a regional daily newspaper covering local and regional news.
Language (s): German
DAILY NEWSPAPER

Idsteiner Zeitung 159537

Owner: Verlagsgruppe Rhein Main GmbH & Co. KG
Editorial: Obergasse 16, Idstein 65510
Tel: 49 6126 3221
Email: idstein-lokales@vrm.de **Web site:** http://www.wiesbadener-tagblatt.de/lokales/untertaunus/idstein/index.htm
Circ: 28
Profile: Die Idsteiner Zeitung ist eine Lokalausgabe des Wiesbadener Tagblatts und bietet vor allem lokale Berichterstattung aus Idstein, sowie Nachrichten aus der Region.
Language (s): German
DAILY NEWSPAPER

Ipf- und Jagst-Zeitung Ellwangen 159542

Owner: Schwäbischer Verlag GmbH & Co. KG
Editorial: Ipf- und Jagst-Zeitung & INFO Ostalb, Aalener Strasse 10, Ellwangen 73479
Tel: 49 7961 988867
Email: redaktion@ipf-und-jagst-zeitung.de **Web site:** http://www.schwaebische.de/region/ostalb/ellwangen
Freq: Mon thru Fri; **Circ:** 28
Profile: Die Ipf- und Jagst-Zeitung ist eine regionale Tageszeitung, mit lokaler Berichterstattung und regionalen Nachrichten aus Ellwangen und Umgebung.
Language (s): German
DAILY NEWSPAPER

Iserlohner Kreisanzeiger und Zeitung 159546

Owner: Zeitungsverlag Iserlohn
Editorial: Redaktion Iserlohn, Theodor-Heuss-Ring 4-6, Iserlohn 58636 **Tel:** 49 2371 822 222
Email: red.iserlohn@ikz-online.de **Web site:** http://www.derwesten.de/ikz/ikz-start/
Freq: Mon thru Fri; **Circ:** 28
Profile: Der Iserlohner Kreisanzeiger und Zeitung ist eine Regionalzeitung für Iserlohn und Letmathe im Märkischen Kreis mit lokalen Nachrichten aus Politik, Wirtschaft, Sport, Kultur und Gesellschaft.
Language (s): German
DAILY NEWSPAPER

junge Welt 159552

Owner: Linke Presse Verlags- Förderungs- und Beteiligungsgenossenschaft junge Welt e.G.
Editorial: Linke Presse Verlags- Forderungs- und Beteiligungsgenossenschaft junge Welt e.G., Torstrasse 6, Berlin 10119 **Tel:** 49 30 53 63 55 0
Email: redaktion@jungewelt.de **Web site:** http://www.jungewelt.de
Freq: Daily; **Circ:** 28
Profile: junge Welt ist eine linke Tageszeitung mit Neuigkeiten, Berichten und Meinungen aus Politik, Wirtschaft und Gesellschaft. Sie erscheint im Verlag 8. Mai GmbH. Ihr Fokus liegt auf soziale Frage und Krieg, sie möchte den Protest und die Auseinandersetzung mit Faschismus, Repression und sozialer Demagogie fördern sowie den Dialog und die Vernetzung von linken Strömen unterstützen. Ihre Zielsetzung ist die Aufklärung. junge Welt is a left-wing daily newspaper with news, reports and opinions from politics, economy and society. It is printed by the publisher 8. Mai GmbH. Its focus is set on social issues and war, it wants to promote the protest and confrontation with fascism, repression and social demagogy and to support dialogue and networking between left political trends. Its objective is Enlightenment.
Language (s): German
DAILY NEWSPAPER

Kieler Nachrichten 159563

Owner: Kieler Zeitung Verlags- und Druckerei KG-GmbH & Co.
Editorial: Kieler Nachrichten, Fleethorn 1-7, Kiel 24103 **Tel:** 49 431 9030
Email: redaktion@kieler-nachrichten.de **Web site:** http://www.kn-online.de/
Freq: Mon thru Fri; **Circ:** 28
Profile: Die Kieler Nachrichten ist eine regionale Tageszeitung aus Norddeutschland. Inhaltlich werden lokale und regionale Nachrichten, sowie Politik, Wirtschaft, Kultur, Feuilleton und Sport behandelt. The Kieler Nachrichten is a regional daily newspaper from Northern Germany covering local and regional news, as well as politics, economics, sports and culture.
Language (s): German
DAILY NEWSPAPER

Kölner Rundschau, Rhein-Sieg (Rhein-Sieg Rundschau) 159851

Owner: Heinen-Verlag GmbH
Editorial: Rhein-Sieg Rundschau, Neue Poststrasse 15, (S-Carré), Siegburg 53721 **Tel:** 49 224 1 172 70
Email: Rhein-Sieg.Rundschau@kr-redaktion.de **Web site:** http://www.rundschau-online.de/rhein-sieg/15185860,15185860.html
Freq: Mon thru Fri; **Circ:** 28
Profile: Kölner Rundschau, Rhein-Sieg (Rhein-Sieg Rundschau) ist die Lokalausgabe der Kölnischen Rundschau aus dem Rhein-Sieg-Kreis. Die Zeitung

bietet lokale Nachrichten und Berichte. Kölner Rundschau, Rhein-Sieg (Rhein-Sieg Rundschau) is the local edition of the Kölnische Rundschau covering news and regional news in the area of Rhein-Sieg.
Language (s): German
DAILY NEWSPAPER

Kölner Stadt-Anzeiger 159571
Owner: DuMont Net GmbH & Co. KG
Editorial: Neven DuMont-Haus, Amsterdamer Str.192, Koln 50735 **Tel:** 49 221 224 2297
Email: redaktion-ksta@mds.de **Web site:** http://www.ksta.de
Freq: Mon thru Fri; **Circ:** 28
Profile: Der Kölner Stadt-Anzeiger ist eine regionale Tageszeitung. Berichtet wird über lokale Themen, sowie Politik, Wirtschaft, Sport, Kultur, Medien, Gesundheit. Es gibt außerdem Angebote zu Freizeitaktivitäten. Mit Lokalausgaben für Frechen, Bergheim, Rhein Sieg/Bonn, Euskirchen, Rhein-Erft-Kreis und Bergisches Land. Kölner Stadt-Anzeiger is a regional daily newspaper focusing on local news as well as politics, economics, sports, culture, media and health. In addition, it provides spare time leisure activity offers.
Language (s): German
DAILY NEWSPAPER

Kölner Stadt-Anzeiger, Redaktionsbüro Bergheim 914777
Owner: DuMont Net GmbH & Co. KG
Editorial: Redaktion Bergheim, Hauptstr. 19, Bergheim 50126 **Tel:** 49 2271 47 22 52 20
Email: redaktion.rhein-erft@ksta-kr.de **Web site:** http://www.ksta.de/region/rhein-erft/bergheim
Freq: Mon thru Fri; **Circ:** 15597
Profile: Kölner Stadt-Anzeiger, Bergheim ist eine lokale Tageszeitung. Es werden Themen aus der Region behandelt sowie Sport, Wirtschaft und Politik. The Kölner Stadt-Anzeiger local edition for Bergheim offers regional and local coverage, specifically tailored to the region.
Language (s): German
DAILY NEWSPAPER

Kölner Stadt-Anzeiger, Redaktionsbüro Rhein-Erft Kreis 849892
Owner: DuMont Net GmbH & Co. KG
Editorial: Redaktion Rhein-Erft, Uhlstrasse 19-23, Brühl 50321 **Tel:** 49 2232 50 12 51 40
Email: redaktion.rhein-erft@ksta-kr.de **Web site:** http://www.ksta.de/region/rhein-erft
Freq: Mon thru Fri
Profile: Der Kölner Stadt-Anzeiger Regionalausgabe für den Rhein-Erft Kreis bietet speziell auf die Region ausgerichtete regionale und lokale Berichterstattung. The Kölner Stadt-Anzeiger regional edition for the Rhein-Erft Kreis offers regional and local coverage, specifically tailored to the region.
Language (s): German
DAILY NEWSPAPER

Kölnische Rundschau 159572
Owner: Heinen-Verlag GmbH
Editorial: Zentral-Redaktion Kolnische Rundschau, Stolkgasse 25-45, Koln 50667 **Tel:** 49 221 1632 551
Email: chefredaktion@kr-redaktion.de **Web site:** http://www.rundschau-online.de
Freq: Mon thru Fri; **Circ:** 28
Profile: Die Kölnische Rundschau ist eine regionale Tageszeitung mit Nachrichten, regionaler Berichterstattung und Service-Informationen. Sie wurde vom Kölner Stadt-Anzeiger übernommen, besitzt aber eine eigenständige Redaktion. Kölnische Rundschau is a regional daily newspaper with news, regional reporting and consumer topics. It has been taken over by the Kölner Stadt-Anzeiger but has its own editorial office.
Language (s): German
DAILY NEWSPAPER

Kölnische Rundschau, Bonn (Bonner Rundschau) 159285
Owner: Heinen-Verlag GmbH
Editorial: Bonner Rundschau, Siemensstrasse 38, Bonn 53121 **Tel:** 49 228 9842 0
Email: Bonner.Rundschau@kr-redaktion.de **Web site:** http://www.rundschau-online.de
Freq: Daily; **Circ:** 28
Profile: Kölnische Rundschau, Bonn (Bonner Rundschau) ist eine lokaleTageszeitung. Sie ist Teil der Kölner Rundschau. Kölnische Rundschau, Bonn (Bonner Rundschau) is a daily newspaper published in Bonn and part of the Kölner Rundschau.
Language (s): German
DAILY NEWSPAPER

Kölnische Rundschau, Oberberg (Oberbergische Volkszeitung) 159776
Owner: Heinen-Verlag GmbH
Editorial: Kaiserstr. 1, Gummersbach 51643
Tel: 49 2261 9289-0
Email: OVZ.Gummersbach@kr-redaktion.de **Web site:** http://www.rundschau-online.de/
Freq: Daily; **Circ:** 28
Profile: Regionale Tageszeitung für den Oberbergischen Raum mit regionalen Nachrichten und Themen. Regional daily newspaper for the Oberberg area covering regional news and topics.
Language (s): German
DAILY NEWSPAPER

Kölnische Rundschau, Rhein-Erft Kreis / Köln Land (Rhein-Erft Rundschau) 914792
Owner: Heinen-Verlag GmbH
Editorial: Kolnische Rundschau (Rhein-Erft Rundschau), Redaktion Koln-Land, Brühl 50321
Tel: 49 2232 5012 5140
Email: Rhein-Erft.Rundschau@kr-redaktion.de **Web site:** http://www.rundschau-online.de/
Freq: Mon thru Fri; **Circ:** 37235
Profile: Kölnische Rundschau, Rhein-Erft Rundschau ist eine lokale Tageszeitung. Es werden Themen aus der Region behandelt sowie Sport, Wirtschaft und Politik.
Language (s): German
DAILY NEWSPAPER

Kötztinger Umschau 159573
Owner: Mittelbayerischer Verlag KG
Editorial: Kotztinger Umschau, Müllerstrasse 7, Bad Kötzting 93444 **Tel:** 49 994 194077
Email: umschau@mittelbayerische.de **Web site:** http://www.mittelbayerische.de/unser-haus/redaktion/lokalredaktionen/bad-koetzting/
Freq: Mon thru Fri; **Circ:** 28
Profile: Die Kötztinger Umschau ist eine regionale bayerische Tageszeitung. Sie gehört dem Mittelbayerischen Verlag an und berichtet über lokale Nachrichten aus dem Gebiet um Bad Kötzting. The Kötztinger Umschau is a regional daily newspaper and part of the Mittelbayerische Verlag covering local news from the area of Bad Kötzing.
Language (s): German
DAILY NEWSPAPER

Kreis-Anzeiger 159579
Owner: Gießener Anzeiger Verlags GmbH & Co KG
Editorial: Gabelsbergerstrasse 1, Dillingen 89407
Tel: 49 6043 502 50
Email: redaktion@kreis-anzeiger.de **Web site:** http://www.kreis-anzeiger.de/index.htm
Freq: Daily; **Circ:** 28
Profile: Der Kreis-Anzeiger ist eine Zeitung mit lokaler Berichterstattung aus Büdingen, Nidda und dem Vogelsbergkreis, sowie auch mit regionalen, nationalen und internationalen Nachrichten.
Language (s): German
DAILY NEWSPAPER

Kreiszeitung (Syke) 159583
Owner: Kreiszeitung Verlagsges. mbH & Co. KG
Editorial: Kreiszeitung Verlagsgesellschaft mbH & Co. KG, Am Ristedter Weg 17, Syke 28857
Tel: 49 4242 580
Email: onlineredaktion@kreiszeitung.de **Web site:** http://www.kreiszeitung.de
Freq: Daily
Profile: Die Kreiszeitung ist eine regionale Zeitung für den niedersäsischen Bereich im Süden von Bremen. Sie berichtet über politische, wirtschaftliche und regionale Nachrichten. The Kreiszeitung is a regional newspaper fo the Lower Saxony Region near Bremen. It covers political, business and regional news.
Language (s): German
DAILY NEWSPAPER

Kreiszeitung Syke 666172
Owner: Kreiszeitung Verlagsgesellschaft mbH &Co.KG
Editorial: Hauptstrasse 6, Syke 28857
Tel: 49 4242 934255-0
Email: lokales.syke@kreiszeitung.de **Web site:** http://www.kreiszeitung.de/
Freq: Daily; **Circ:** 28
Profile: Lokale Tageszeitung für Syke mit aktuellen Nachrichten und relevanten Themen. Local daily newspapers for Syke with current news and relevant topics.
Language (s): German
DAILY NEWSPAPER

Landeszeitung für die Lüneburger Heide 159605
Owner: Landeszeitung für die Lüneburger Heide GmbH
Editorial: Landeszeitung für die Lüneburger Heide GmbH, Am Sande 18-20, Lüneburg 21335
Tel: 49 4131 7400
Email: redaktion@landeszeitung.de **Web site:** http://www.landeszeitung.de
Freq: Mon thru Fri; **Circ:** 28
Profile: Die Landeszeitung Lüneburg ist eine Tageszeitung. Der Fokus liegt auf der lokalen Berichterstattung. Landeszeitung Lüneburg is a daily newspaper mainly covering local news
Language (s): German
DAILY NEWSPAPER

Landshuter Zeitung 159606
Owner: Josef Thomann'sche Buchdruckerei Verlag
Editorial: Landshuter Zeitung, Altstadt 89, Landshut 84028 **Tel:** 49 781 850 2184
Email: stadtred@landshuter-zeitung.de **Web site:** http://www.idowa.de/zeitung/landshuter-zeitung
Freq: Mon thru Fri; **Circ:** 28
Profile: Die Landshuter Zeitung ist eine regionale Tageszeitung, die zusammen mit dem Straubinger Tagblatt herausgebracht wird. The Landshuter Zeitung is a regional daily newspaper covering local news and being published together with the Straubinger Tagblatt.
Language (s): German
DAILY NEWSPAPER

Lausitzer Rundschau 159611
Owner: LR Medienverlag und Druckerei GmbH
Editorial: Lausitzer VerlagsService GmbH, Strasse der Jugend 54, Cottbus 3050 **Tel:** 49 355 481 555
Email: redaktion@lr-online.de **Web site:** http://www.lr-online.de
Freq: Mon thru Fri; **Circ:** 28
Profile: Die Lausitzer Rundschau ist die regionale Tageszeitung der Region Lausitz. Sie besitzt mehrere Lokalausgaben in Sachsen und Brandenburg. Lausitzer Rundschau is a regionale daily newspaper of the region of Lausitz. It has several local editions in Saxony and Brandenburg.
Language (s): German
DAILY NEWSPAPER

Lausitzer Rundschau, Finsterwalde 666175
Owner: LR Medienverlag und Druckerei GmbH
Editorial: Strasse der Jugend 54, Cottbus 3050
Tel: 49 355 481555
Email: redaktion@lr-online.de **Web site:** http://www.lr-online.de/regionen/finsterwalde/
Freq: Daily
Profile: Lokale Nachrichten aus der Region Finsterwalde. Local news from Finsterwalde.
Language (s): German
DAILY NEWSPAPER

Lausitzer Rundschau, Guben 666186
Owner: LR Medienverlag und Druckerei GmbH
Editorial: Berliner Strasse 9, Guben 3172
Tel: 49 355 481555
Email: red.guben@lr-online.de **Web site:** http://www.lr-online.de/regionen/guben
Freq: Daily
Profile: Die Lausitzer Rundschau Guben ist eine Lokalausgabe der Lausitzer Rundschau mit Fokus auf lokaler Berichterstattung und Nachrichten aus Guben.
Language (s): German
DAILY NEWSPAPER

Lausitzer Rundschau, Hoyerswerda 666176
Owner: LR Medienverlag und Druckerei GmbH
Editorial: Albert-Einstein-Strasse 47, Hoyerswerda 2977 **Tel:** 49 3571 6055921
Email: red.hoyerswerda@lr-online.de **Web site:** http://www.lr-online.de/regionen/hoyerswerda/
Freq: Daily
Profile: Die Lausitzer Rundschau - Hoyerswerda ist ein Lokalangebot der Lausitzer Rundschau mit Fokus auf lokaler Berichterstattung und Nachrichten aus Hoyerswerda.
Language (s): German
DAILY NEWSPAPER

Lausitzer Rundschau, Lübben 666177
Owner: LR Medienverlag und Druckerei GmbH
Editorial: Hauptstr. 28, Lübben 15907
Tel: 49 3546 2251 22
Email: red.luebbenau@lr-online.de **Web site:** http://www.lr-online.de/regionen/luebbenau-calau/
Freq: Daily
Profile: Die Lausitzer Rundschau Lübbenau ist ein Lokalangebot der Lausitzer Rundschau für Lübbenau mit Fokus auf lokaler Berichterstattung und Nachrichten aus der Umgebung.
Language (s): German
DAILY NEWSPAPER

Lausitzer Rundschau, Luckau/Dahme 666180
Owner: LR Medienverlag und Druckerei GmbH
Editorial: Am Markt 32, Luckau 15926
Tel: 49 3544 55500
Email: red.luckau@lr-online.de **Web site:** http://www.lr-online.de/regionen/luckau/
Freq: Daily
Profile: Die Lausitzer Rundschau Luckau/Dahme ist ein Lokalangebot der Lausitzer Rundschau für Luckau und bietet vor allem lokale Berichterstattung und Nachrichten aus der Umgebung.
Language (s): German
DAILY NEWSPAPER

Lausitzer Rundschau, Senftenberg 666184
Owner: LR Medienverlag und Druckerei GmbH
Editorial: Bahnhofstrasse 28a, Senftenberg 1968
Tel: 49 3573 794540
Email: red.senftenberg@lr-online.de **Web site:** http://www.lr-online.de/regionen/senftenberg/
Freq: Daily
Profile: Die Lausitzer Rundschau Senftenberg ist ein Lokalangebot der Lausitzer Rundschau mit Fokus auf lokaler Berichterstattung und Nachrichten aus Senftenberg und Umgebung.
Language (s): German
DAILY NEWSPAPER

Lausitzer Rundschau, Spremberg 666182
Owner: LR Medienverlag und Druckerei GmbH
Editorial: Badergasse 3, Spremberg 3130
Tel: 49 3563 34590
Email: red.spremberg@lr-online.de **Web site:** http://www.lr-online.de/regionen/spremberg/
Freq: Daily
Profile: Die Lausitzer Rundschau Spremberg ist das Lokalangebot der Lausitzer Rundschau für Spremberg mit Fokus auf lokaler Berichterstattung und Nachrichten.
Language (s): German
DAILY NEWSPAPER

Lausitzer Rundschau, Weißwasser 666183
Owner: LR Medienverlag und Druckerei GmbH
Editorial: Rosa-Luxemburg-Str. 11, Weisswasser 2943
Email: red.weisswasser@lr-online.de **Web site:** http://www.lr-online.de/regionen/weisswasser/
Freq: Daily
Profile: Die Lausitzer Rundschau Weißwasser ist eine sächsische Lokalausgabe der Lausitzer Rundschau mit lokaler Berichterstattung und Nachrichten aus Weißwasser.
Language (s): German
DAILY NEWSPAPER

Leipziger Volkszeitung 159614
Owner: Leipziger Verlags- und Druckereiges. mbH & Co. KG
Editorial: Leipziger Verlags- und Druckereigesellschaft, Peterssteinweg 19, Leipzig 4107 **Tel:** 49 341 2181 0
Email: chefredaktion@lvz.de **Web site:** http://www.lvz.de
Freq: Mon thru Fri; **Circ:** 28
Profile: Die Leipziger Volkszeitung ist eine lokale Tageszeitung für Leipzig. Leipziger Volkszeitung is a local daily newspaper for Leipzig.
Language (s): German
DAILY NEWSPAPER

Leipziger Volkszeitung, Borna/Geithain (Borna-Geithainer Zeitung) 666187
Owner: Leipziger Druck- und Verlagsgesellschaft mbH
Editorial: Brauhausstrasse 3, Borna 4552
Tel: 49 3433 270710
Email: borna.redaktion@lvz.de **Web site:** http://www.lvz.de/region/borna/r-borna.html
Freq: Daily
Profile: Die Borna-Geithainer Zeitung ist eine Lokalausgabe der Leipziger Volkszeitung mit Fokus auf lokaler Berichterstattung und Nachrichten aus Borna und Geithain.
Language (s): German
DAILY NEWSPAPER

Leonberger Kreiszeitung 159615
Owner: Zeitungsverlag Leonberg GmbH
Editorial: Zeitungsverlag Leonberg GmbH, Stuttgarter Strasse 7-9, Leonberg 71229
Tel: 49 7152 937 2 811
Email: redaktion@leonberger-kreiszeitung.zgs.de **Web site:** http://www.leonberger-kreiszeitung.de
Freq: Mon thru Fri; **Circ:** 28
Profile: Die Leonberger Kreiszeitung ist eine regionale Tageszeitung aus der Region Stuttgart. Sie ist eine Regionalausgabe der Stuttgarter Zeitung für Leonberg und berichtet über aktuelle Nachrichten. Leonberger Kreiszeitung is a regional daily newspaper from Stuttgart. It is a reginal edition of the Stuttgarter Zeitung for Leonberg covering local news.
Language (s): German
DAILY NEWSPAPER

Leverkusener Anzeiger (Kölner Stadt-Anzeiger) 159616
Owner: DuMont Net GmbH & Co. KG
Editorial: Redaktion Leverkusen, Friedrich-Ebert-Platz 5, Leverkusen 51373 **Tel:** 49 214 83 10 11
Email: redaktion.leverkusen@ksta.de **Web site:** http://www.ksta.de/region/leverkusen
Freq: Daily; **Circ:** 28
Profile: Kölner Stadt-Anzeiger, Leverkusen (Leverkusener Anzeiger) ist eine Lokalausgabe des Kölner Stadt-Anzeigers und bietet lokale Berichterstattung aus Leverkusen, sowie auch Nachrichten aus der Umgebung. Kölner Stadt-Anzeiger, Leverkusen (Leverkusener Anzeiger) is a local edition of the Kölner Stadt-Anzeiger and provides local news from Leverkusen as well as from the local sourrounding area.
Language (s): German
DAILY NEWSPAPER

Lingener Tagespost 159622
Owner: Neue Osnabrücker Zeitung GmbH & Co. KG
Editorial: Neue Osnabrücker Zeitung GmbH & Co. KG, Breiter Gang 10-16, Osnabrück 49074
Tel: 49 541 310 207
Email: redaktion@lingener-tagespost.de **Web site:** http://www.noz.de/lingener-tagespost?
Freq: Mon thru Fri; **Circ:** 28
Profile: Die Lingener Tagespostist eine Lokalausgabe der Osnabrücker Zeitung. The Lingener Tagespost is a local edition of the Osnabrücker Zeitung.
Language (s): German
DAILY NEWSPAPER

Lippische Landes-Zeitung, Detmold 159624
Owner: Lippischer Zeitungsverlag Giesdorf GmbH & Co. KG
Editorial: Lippischer Zeitungsverlag Giesdorf GmbH & Co. KG, Ohmstrasse 7, Detmold 32758
Tel: 49 523 1911 131
Email: detmold@lz-online.de **Web site:** http://www.lz.de
Freq: Mon thru Fri
Profile: Die Lippische Landeszeitung, Detmold ist eine Lokalausgabe der regionalen Tageszeitung für

den Kreis Lippe. Sie kooperiert mit der Neuen Westfälischen, von der sie den Mantelteil übernimmt. Lippische Landeszeitung is a local daily newspaper for the Lippe region. It cooperates with the Neuen Westfälische for which it provides the cover section.
Language (s): German
DAILY NEWSPAPER

Lüdenscheider Nachrichten
159631
Owner: Märkischer Zeitungsverlag GmbH & Co. KG
Editorial: Markischer Zeitungsverlag GmbH & Co. KG, Schillerstrasse 20, Lüdenscheid 58511
Tel: 49 2351 158 0
Email: ln@mzv.net **Web site:** http://www.come-on.de
Freq: Mon thru Fri; **Circ:** 28
Profile: Die Lüdenscheider Nachrichten ist eine regionale Tageszeitung und gehört zum Märkischen Zeitungsverlag. Lüdenscheider Nachrichten is a regional daily newspaper and part of the Märkische Zeitungsverlag.
Language (s): German
DAILY NEWSPAPER

Ludwigsburger Kreiszeitung
159628
Owner: Ungeheuer + Ulmer KG GmbH + Co.
Editorial: Ludwigsburger Kreiszeitung, Kornerstrasse 14–18, Ludwigsburg 71634 **Tel:** 49 7141 130 240
Email: redaktion@lkz.de **Web site:** http://www.lkz.de
Freq: Mon thru Fri; **Circ:** 28
Profile: Die Ludwigsburger Kreiszeitung ist eine regionale Tageszeitung mit Nachrichten zu Politik, Wirtschaft, Kultur, Sport, Reise und Technik aus Ludwigsburg und Umgebung. The Ludwigsburger Kreiszeitung is a regional daily newspaper covering politics, economics, culture, sports, travel and technology from Ludwigsburg and surroundings.
Language (s): German
DAILY NEWSPAPER

Ludwigsburger Kreiszeitung, Freiberg am Neckar
666196
Owner: Ungeheuer+Ulmer KG GmbH & Co.
Editorial: Kornerstrasse 14–18, Ludwigsburg 71634
Tel: 49 7141 1300
Email: redaktion@lkz.de **Web site:** http://www.lkz.de/lokales/staedte+gemeinden/freiberg-am-neckar.html
Freq: Mon thru Fri
Profile: Die Ludwigsburger Kreiszeitung für Freiberg am Neckar ist ein Lokalangebot der Zeitung und bietet lokale Berichterstattung und Nachrichten aus der Gemeinde Freiberg am Neckar. Erstellt wird der Teil von der Redaktion Ludwigsburg.
Language (s): German
DAILY NEWSPAPER

Ludwigsburger Kreiszeitung, Remseck
666195
Owner: Ungeheuer+Ulmer KG GmbH & Co.
Editorial: Kornerstrasse 14–18, Ludwigsburg 71634
Tel: 49 7141 1300
Email: redaktion@lkz.de **Web site:** http://www.lkz.de/lokales/staedte+gemeinden/remseck-am-neckar.html
Freq: Mon thru Fri
Profile: Die Ludwigsburger Kreiszeitung für Remseck ist ein Lokalangebot der Zeitung und bietet lokale Berichterstattung und Nachrichten aus der Gemeinde Remseck. Erstellt wird der Teil von der Redaktion Ludwigsburg.
Language (s): German
DAILY NEWSPAPER

Ludwigsburger Kreiszeitung, Strohgäu
666197
Owner: Ungeheuer+Ulmer KG GmbH & Co.
Editorial: Kornerstrasse 14–18, Ludwigsburg 71634
Tel: 49 7141 1300
Email: redaktion@lkz.de **Web site:** http://www.lkz.de/lokales/staedte+gemeinden/asperg.html
Freq: Daily
Profile: Die Ludwigsburger Kreiszeitung für Strohgäu ist ein Lokalangebot der Zeitung und bietet lokale Berichterstattung und Nachrichten aus der Gemeinde Asperg und Umgebung. Erstellt wird der Teil von der Redaktion Ludwigsburg.
Language (s): German
DAILY NEWSPAPER

Magdeburger Volksstimme
159635
Owner: Magdeburger Verlags- und Druckhaus GmbH
Editorial: Magdeburger Verlags- und Druckhaus GmbH, Bahnhofstrasse 17, Magdeburg 39104
Tel: 49 391 59 99210
Email: lokalredaktion@volksstimme.de **Web site:** http://www.volksstimme.de/nachrichten/magdeburg/
Freq: Mon thru Fri; **Circ:** 28
Profile: Die Magdeburger Volksstimme ist eine Lokalausgabe der Volkstimme für die Landeshaupstadt von Sachsen-Anhalt und wird bundesweit vertrieben. Die Zeitung bietet lokale und regionale Berichterstattung und Nachrichten. The Magdeburger Volksstimme is a local edition of the Volksstimme for the state capital of Saxony-Anhalt and is being distributed nationwide. The paper offers local and regional reporting and news.
Language (s): German
DAILY NEWSPAPER

Main-Post
159637
Owner: Main-Post GmbH & Co. KG
Editorial: Main-Post GmbH & Co. KG, Berner Str. 2, Würzburg 97084 **Tel:** 49 931 6001 6001
Email: service.center@mainpost.de **Web site:** http://www.mainpost.de
Freq: Mon thru Fri; **Circ:** 28
Profile: Die Main Post ist eine Tageszeitung in der Region Unterfranken und überwiegend in Würzburg und Schweinfurt verbreitet. The Main Post is a daily newspaper in the region Unterfranken (Lower Franconia) and mainly distributed in Würzburg and Schweinfurt.
Language (s): German
DAILY NEWSPAPER

Mainzer Rhein-Zeitung
159640
Owner: Mittelrhein Verlag GmbH
Editorial: Mittelrhein-Verlag GmbH, August-Horch-Str. 28, Koblenz 56070 **Tel:** 49 261 892240
Email: redaktion@rhein-zeitung.net **Web site:** http://www.rhein-zeitung.de/region/lokales/mainzer-rhein-zeitung.html?
Freq: Mon thru Fri
Profile: Die Mainzer Rhein-Zeitung ist die Lokalausgabe der Rhein-Zeitung für die Region Mainz. Nach 26 Jahren des Bestehens wird sie Ende 2013 eingestellt. Mainzer Rhein-Zeitung is the local section for Mainz from the Rhein-Zeitung. It will be discontinued by the end of December 2013.
Language (s): German
DAILY NEWSPAPER

Mangfall-Bote Kolbermoor
159641
Owner: Oberbayerisches Volksblatt GmbH & Co. Medienhaus KG
Editorial: Karlstrasse 1, Kolbermoor 83059
Tel: 49 8031 96032
Email: kolbermoor@mangfall-bote.de **Web site:** http://www.ovb-online.de/rosenheim/kolbermoor/
Freq: Mon thru Fri
Profile: Der Mangfall-Bote Kolbermoor ist eine Lokalzeitung des Oberbayerischen Volksblatts für Kolbermoor und bietet lokale Berichterstattung aus Kolbermoor, sowie Nachrichten aus der Umgebung.
Language (s): German
DAILY NEWSPAPER

Mannheimer Morgen
159642
Owner: Mannheimer Morgen Großdruckerei und Verlag GmbH
Editorial: Mannheimer Morgen Grossdruckerei und Verlag GmbH, Dudenstrasse 12-26, Mannheim 68167
Tel: 49 261 39201
Email: geschaeftsleitung@mamo.de **Web site:** http://www.morgenweb.de/region/mannheimer-morgen
Freq: Mon thru Fri; **Circ:** 28
Profile: Der Mannheimer Morgen ist eine regionale Tageszeitung in Nordbaden und ist in neun Lokalausgaben erhältlich. Die Berichterstattung umfasst Nachrichten aus der Region und überregionale Themen aus Politik, Wirtschaft, Kultur, Wissenschaft, Sport. The Mannheimer Morgen is a regional daily newspaper in Nordbaden and is available in nine local editions. It is covering local and regional news, as well as politics, economics, science, sports and culture.
Language (s): German
DAILY NEWSPAPER

Märkische Allgemeine
159633
Owner: Märkische Verlags- und Druck-GmbH Potsdam
Editorial: Friedrich-Engels-Strasse 24, Potsdam 14473 **Tel:** 49 331 2840 0
Email: kontakt@MAZ-online.de **Web site:** http://www.maz-online.de
Freq: Mon thru Fri; **Circ:** 28
Profile: Die Märkische Allgemeine ist eine regionale Tageszeitung in Brandenburg. Das größte Distributionsgebiet ist Potsdam. Die Märkische Allgemeine erscheint Montag bis Samstag in 15 unterschiedlichen Lokalausgaben. Märkische Allgemeine is a regional daily newspaper in Brandenburg. Mainly distributed in Potsdam. Märkische Allgemeine is published Monday till Saturday in 15 different local editions.
Language (s): German
DAILY NEWSPAPER

Märkische Oderzeitung
159634
Owner: Märkisches Verlags- und Druckhaus GmbH & Co. KG
Editorial: Markisches Verlags- und Druckhaus GmbH & Co. KG, Kellenspring 6, Frankfurt/oder 15230
Tel: 49 335 5530 0
Email: chefredaktion@moz.de **Web site:** http://www.moz.de
Freq: Mon thru Fri; **Circ:** 28
Profile: Die Märkische Oderzeitung ist eine regionale Tageszeitung mit zwölf Lokalausgaben. Die Märkische Oderzeitung berichtet unter anderem über lokale Nachrichten, Wirtschaft, Kultur, Automobil und Sport. Märkische Oderzeitung is a regional daily newspaper with twelve local editions. It reports about local news, business, culture, automotive and sports.
Language (s): German
DAILY NEWSPAPER

Märkische Oderzeitung - Redaktionsbüro Angermünde
666249
Owner: Märkisches Verlags- und Druckhaus GmbH & Co. KG
Editorial: Kellenspring 6, Frankfurt 15230
Tel: 49 3331 260 223
Email: angermuende-red@moz.de
Freq: Daily
Language (s): German
DAILY NEWSPAPER

Märkische Oderzeitung - Redaktionsbüro Eberswalde
666243
Owner: Märkisches Verlags- und Druckhaus GmbH & Co. KG
Editorial: Karl-Marx-Platz 11, Eberswalde
Tel: 49 3334 202950
Email: eberswalde-red@moz.de
Freq: Daily
DAILY NEWSPAPER

Marler Zeitung
159650
Owner: Verlag J. Bauer KG
Editorial: Verlag J. Bauer KG, Kampstr. 84 b, Marl 45772 **Tel:** 49 023 651070
Email: info@medienhaus-bauer.de **Web site:** http://www.marler-zeitung.de/?
Freq: Mon thru Fri; **Circ:** 28
Profile: Die Marler Zeitung ist eine regionale Tageszeitung aus dem Gebiet Recklinghausen. Marler Zeitung is a regional daily newspaper from the area of Recklinghausen.
Language (s): German
DAILY NEWSPAPER

Marner Zeitung
159649
Owner: Boyens Medien GmbH & Co. KG
Editorial: Boyens Medien GmbH & Co. KG, Wulf-Isebrand-Platz 1-3, Heide 25746
Tel: 49 481 68 86 211
Email: redaktion@boyens-medien.de **Web site:** http://zeitungen.boyens-medien.de/tageszeitung/marner-zeitung.html?
Freq: Mon thru Fri; **Circ:** 28
Profile: Die Marner Zeitung ist eine regionale Tageszeitung, die zum Boysens Zeitungen Verlag gehört. Sie ist Teil der Dithmarscher Landeszeitung. Marner Zeitung is a regional daily newspaper belonging to the Dithmarscher Landeszeitung and being part of the Boysens Zeitungen Verlag.
Language (s): German
DAILY NEWSPAPER

Meppener Tagespost
159657
Owner: Neue Osnabrücker Zeitung GmbH & Co. KG
Editorial: Meppener Tagespost, Bahnhofstrasse 4, Meppen 49716 **Tel:** 49 5931 940 111
Email: redaktion@meppener-tagespost.de **Web site:** http://www.noz.de/meppener-tagespost
Freq: Mon thru Fri; **Circ:** 28
Profile: Die Meppener Tagespost ist eine Regionalausgabe der Neuen Osnabrücker Zeitung. Meppener Tagespost is a regional editon of the Neue Osnabrücker Zeitung.
Language (s): German
DAILY NEWSPAPER

Miesbacher Merkur
159659
Owner: Zeitungsverlag Oberbayern GmbH & Co. KG
Editorial: Schlierseer Strasse 4, Miesbach 83714
Tel: 49 8025 285 0
Email: mb-merkur@merkur.de **Web site:** http://www.merkur.de/lokales/miesbach/?
Freq: Mon thru Fri; **Circ:** 28
Profile: Der Miesbacher Merkur ist eine Lokalausgabe des Münchner Merkurs mit lokaler Berichterstattung aus Miesbach, sowie auch mit Nachrichten aus der Umgebung.
Language (s): German
DAILY NEWSPAPER

Mindener Tageblatt
159661
Owner: J. C. C. Bruns Betriebs-GmbH
Editorial: J.C.C.Bruns Betriebs-GmbH, Obermarktstrasse 26-30, Minden 32423
Tel: 49 571 882240
Email: mt@mt-online.de **Web site:** http://www.mt-online.de/?
Freq: Mon thru Fri; **Circ:** 28
Profile: Das Mindener Tageblatt ist eine lokale Tageszeitung. The Mindener Tageblatt is a local daily newspaper.
Language (s): German
DAILY NEWSPAPER

Mittelbayerische Zeitung
804017
Owner: Mittelbayerischer Verlag KG
Editorial: Mittelbayerischer Verlag KG, Kumpfmühler Strasse 15, Regensburg 93047 **Tel:** 49 941 207 0
Email: cr@mittelbayerische.de **Web site:** http://www.mittelbayerische.de
Freq: Mon thru Fri; **Circ:** 28
Profile: Die Mittelbayerische Zeitung mit Sitz in Regensburg berichtet täglich über regionale Nachrichten aus der bayerischen Oberpfalz. Mittelbayerische Zeitung is a daily newspaper based in Regensburg reporting on regional news from the Bavarian region of Oberpfalz.
Language (s): German
DAILY NEWSPAPER

Mittelbayerische Zeitung für Kelheim, Abensberg und Neustadt
159668
Owner: Mittelbayerischer Verlag KG
Editorial: Kumpfmühler Str. 15, Regensburg 93047
Tel: 49 941 20765
Email: mz-redaktion@mittelbayerische.de **Web site:** http://www.mittelbayerische.de
Freq: Mon thru Fri; **Circ:** 28
Profile: Regional daily newspaper with news on politics, economy, culture, sports, travel, technology, etc. What happened in his own front door is the most interesting news! Our Publisher product key is therefore to be the local newspaper. The desire for location-based information has led to our newspaper has become even more "local". The trend is increasingly ecoming the "editorial office" on site. Every city, every region has a permanent place in the newspaper. The Mittelbayerische Zeitung, with its 13 regional editions in the Upper Palatinate and large parts of Lower Bavaria, is the medium number one and reached with a circulation of 130,000 copies around 400,000 daily readers. As one of few newspapers in Germany, it entered against the prevailing trend circulation gains.Facebook: http://www.facebook.com/mittelbayerische Twitter: http://twitter.com/mz_deThis Outlet offers RSS (Really Simple Syndication). Local Translation:Regionale Tageszeitung mit Nachrichten zu Politik, Wirtschaft, Kultur, Sport, Reise, Technik u.a. Was vor der eigenen Haustür passiert, ist die interessanteste Nachricht! Unser zentrales Verlagsprodukt ist deshalb nach wie vor die lokale Tageszeitung. Der Wunsch nach ortsbezogener Information hat dazu geführt, dass unsere Zeitung noch "lokaler" geworden ist. Die Entwicklung geht immer mehr zum "Redaktionsbüro vor Ort". Jedes Stadtgebiet, jede Region hat einen festen Platz in der Zeitung. Die Mittelbayerische Zeitung ist mit ihren 13 regionalen Ausgaben in der Oberpfalz und großen Teilen Niederbayerns das Medium Nummer eins und erreicht mit einer Auflage von über 130.000 Exemplaren täglich rund 400.000 Leser. Als eine von wenigen Tageszeitungen Deutschlands verbucht sie gegen den vorherrschenden Trend Auflagenzugewinne.Facebook: http://www.facebook.com/mittelbayerische Twitter: http://twitter.com/mz_deRSS (Really Simple Syndication) wird angeboten. Hrsg.: Peter Esser.
Language (s): German
DAILY NEWSPAPER

Mitteldeutsche Zeitung
159671
Owner: Mediengruppe Mitteldeutsche Zeitung GmbH & Co. KG
Editorial: Mediengruppe Mitteldeutsche Zeitung GmbH & Co. KG, Delitzscher Strasse 65, Halle 6112
Email: service@mz-web.de **Web site:** http://www.mz-web.de
Freq: Mon thru Fri; **Circ:** 28
Profile: Die Mitteldeutsche Zeitung ist eine regionale Tageszeitung, die täglich aktualisierte Nachrichten aus allen Ressorts von Politik über Sport bis hin zu Kultur in Sachsen-Anhalt bietet. The Mitteldeutsche Zeitung is a regional daily newspaper that provides updated news of Saxony-Anhalt from all departments covering everything from politics to sport and culture.
Language (s): German
DAILY NEWSPAPER

Moosburger Zeitung
159675
Owner: Josef Thomann'sche Buchdruckerei Verlag
Editorial: Auf dem Gries 17, Moosburg 85368
Tel: 49 8761 7410 0
Email: redaktion@moosburger-zeitung.de **Web site:** http://www.idowa.de/zeitung/moosburger-zeitung
Freq: Mon thru Fri; **Circ:** 28
Profile: Die Moosburger Zeitung ist eine Lokalausgabe des Straubinger Tagblatts und der Landshuter Zeitung und berichtet über lokale Nachrichten der Region. Moosburger Zeitung is a local edition of Straubinger Tablatt and Landshuter Zeitung covering local news from this region.
Language (s): German
DAILY NEWSPAPER

Mühldorfer Anzeiger
159678
Owner: Oberbayerisches Volksblatt GmbH & Co. Medienhaus KG
Editorial: Weissgerberstrasse 2-4, Mühldorf 84453
Tel: 49 8631 9878 0
Email: redaktion@muehldorfer-anzeiger.de **Web site:** http://www.ovb-online.de/muehldorf/?
Freq: Mon thru Fri; **Circ:** 28
Profile: Mühldorfer Anzeiger ist eine Lokalausgabe des Oberbayerischen Volksblatts und bietet lokale Berichterstattung aus Mühldorf, sowie auch Nachrichten aus der Umgebung.
Language (s): German
DAILY NEWSPAPER

Münchner Merkur
159680
Owner: Münchener Zeitungs-Verlag GmbH & Co.KG
Editorial: Münchener Zeitungs-Verlag GmbH & Co.KG, Paul-Heyse-Str. 2-4, München 80336
Tel: 49 089 5306 0
Web site: http://www.merkur.de
Freq: Mon thru Fri; **Circ:** 28
Profile: Der Münchner Merkur bietet Nachrichten zu regionalen Themen, Poltitik, Kultur, Boulevard, Reise, Technik und Natur. Der Mantel wird vom Oberbayerischen Volksblatt geliefert. The Münchner Merkur is a daily newspaper covering regional news, as well as politics, culture, technique, travel, entertainment and nature. The cover section is being provided by the Oberbayerische Volksblatt.
Language (s): German
DAILY NEWSPAPER

Münchner Merkur, Würmtal/ Planegg
666273
Owner: Münchener Zeitungs-Verlag GmbH & Co. KG
Tel: 49 89 8597091
Web site: http://www.merkur.de
Freq: Daily; **Circ:** 28
DAILY NEWSPAPER

Münsterland Zeitung
159683
Owner: Verlag Lensing-Wolff GmbH & Co. KG
Editorial: Van-Delden-Strasse 6-8, Ahaus 48683
Tel: 49 2561 697 40
Email: redaktion@muensterlandzeitung.de **Web site:** http://www.muensterlandzeitung.de/
Freq: Mon thru Fri

Profile: Die Münsterland Zeitung ist eine regionale Tageszeitung, die neben überregionalen Nachrichten auch lokale und regionale Berichterstattung bietet. Münsterland Zeitung is a regional daily newspaper covering national as well as local and regional news.
Language (s): German
DAILY NEWSPAPER

Münsterländische Tageszeitung 159681
Owner: Hermann Imsiecke Druck und Verlag GmbH
Editorial: Hermann Imsiecke Druck und Verlag GmbH, Lange Strasse 9/11, Cloppenburg 49661
Tel: 49 4471 178 0
Email: redaktion@mt-friesoythe.de **Web site:** http://www.mt-news.de/
Freq: Mon thru Fri; **Circ:** 28
Profile: Die Münsterländische Tageszeitung ist eine regionale Tageszeitung, die vor allem lokale und regionale Nachrichten aus dem Oldenburger Münsterland bietet. The Münsterländische Tageszeitung is a regional daily newspaper mainly covering local and regional news of the area of Oldenburger Münsterland.
Language (s): German
DAILY NEWSPAPER

Münsterländische Volkszeitung 159682
Owner: Altmeppen Verlag GmbH & Co. KG
Editorial: Altmeppen Verlag GmbH & Co. KG, Bahnhofstrasse 8, Rheine 48431 **Tel:** 49 5971 404 0
Email: redaktion@mv-online.de **Web site:** http://www.mv-online.de
Freq: Mon thru Fri; **Circ:** 28
Profile: Die Münsterländische Volkszeitung ist eine regionale Tageszeitung mit Schwerpunkt auf lokaler Berichterstattung. Münsterländische Volkszeitung is a regional daily newspaper covering local news.
Language (s): German
DAILY NEWSPAPER

Münstersche Zeitung 159684
Owner: MZ Medien Holding Verwaltungsgesellschaft mbH
Editorial: Münstersche Zeitung, Lokalredaktion Münster, Neubrückenstr. 8-11, Munster 48143
Tel: 49 251 592 4051
Email: chefredaktion@zgm-muensterland.de **Web site:** http://www.muensterschezeitung.de
Freq: Daily; **Circ:** 28
Profile: Die Münstersche Zeitung ist eine regionale Tageszeitung, deren Fokus neben den überregionalen Nachrichten aus Poltik, Wirtschaft, Kultur, Sport, auf der lokalen Berichterstattung liegt. Münstersche Zeitung is a regional daily newspaper with main focus on local news but also covering local news, politics, culture, economics, and sports on a national basis.
Language (s): German
DAILY NEWSPAPER

Murnauer Tagblatt 159687
Owner: Münchener Zeitungs-Verlag GmbH & Co.KG
Editorial: Schlossbergstr. 12a, Murnau 82418
Tel: 49 8841 6104 0
Email: mur-tagblatt@merkur.de **Web site:** http://www.merkur.de/lokales/garmisch-partenkirchen/
Circ: 28
Profile: Das Murnauer Tagblatt ist eine Lokalausgabe des Münchner Merkurs und bietet lokale Berichterstattung und Nachrichten aus Murnau und Umgebung.
Language (s): German
DAILY NEWSPAPER

Nahe-Zeitung 159690
Owner: Mittelrhein-Verlag GmbH
Editorial: Nahe-Center 19, Idar-Oberstein 55743
Tel: 49 6781 605 46
Email: idar-oberstein@rhein-zeitung.net **Web site:** http://www.rhein-zeitung.de/region/lokales/nahe.html
Freq: Mon thru Fri
Profile: Die Nahe-Zeitung ist eine Lokalausgabe der Rhein-Zeitung und berichtet über lokale Nachrichten aus der Region Idar-Oberstein. Nahe-Zeitung is a local edition of the daily newspaper Rhein-Zeitung covering local news from the Idar-Oberstein region.
Language (s): German
DAILY NEWSPAPER

Nassauische Neue Presse 159692
Owner: Frankfurter Societäts-Medien GmbH
Editorial: Nassauische Neue Presse, Bahnhofstrasse 9, Limburg 65549 **Tel:** 49 643 1 29 43 0
Email: nnp@fnp.de **Web site:** http://www.nnp.de/
Freq: Mon thru Fri; **Circ:** 28
Profile: Die Nassauische Neue Presse ist eine Lokalausgabe der Frankfurter Neuen Presse und berichtet über lokale Nachrichten aus Limburg. Nassauische Neue Presse is a regional daily newspaper which is a local edition of the Frankfurter Neuen Presse covering news from the Limburg region.
Language (s): German
DAILY NEWSPAPER

Naumburger Tageblatt 159693
Owner: Zeitungsverlag Naumburg Nebra GmbH & Co. KG
Editorial: Zeitungsverlag Naumburg Nebra GmbH & Co. KG, Salzstrasse 8, Naumburg 6618
Tel: 49 34 45 230 78 10
Email: naumburger.tageblatt@mz-web.de **Web site:** http://www.naumburger-tageblatt.de
Freq: Mon thru Fri; **Circ:** 28
Profile: Regionale Ausgabe der Mitteldeutschen Zeitung für den Raum Naumburg mit Fokus auf lokaler Berichterstattung. Regional edition of the Mitteldeutsche Zeitung for the Naumburg region with focus on local reporting.
Language (s): German
DAILY NEWSPAPER

Neue Presse 159704
Owner: Druck- und Verlagsanstalt Neue Presse GmbH
Editorial: Druck- und Verlagsanstalt Neue Presse GmbH, Steinweg 51, Coburg 96450
Tel: 49 9561 850 120
Email: region@np-coburg.de **Web site:** http://www.np-coburg.de/
Freq: Mon thru Fri; **Circ:** 28
Profile: Die Neue Presse ist eine regionale Tageszeitung aus Coburg und bietet regionale und lokale Nachrichten, sowie einen überregionalen Nachrichtenteil. Neue Presse is a regional daily newspaper from Coburg covering local and regional news but also providing an international news section.
Language (s): German
DAILY NEWSPAPER

Neue Presse Hannover 159703
Owner: Verlagsgesellschaft Madsack GmbH & Co. KG
Editorial: Neue Presse Redaktion GmbH & Co. KG, Stiftstrasse 2, Hannover 30159 **Tel:** 49 511 51 01 0
Email: np@neuepresse.de **Web site:** http://www.neuepresse.de
Freq: Daily
Profile: Neue Presse Hannover ist eine lokale Tageszeitung für Hannover und Umgebung mit lokalen und Regionalen Nachrichten, sowie auch mit Unterhaltung und Berichten zu Verbraucherfragen und regionalem Geschehen. Neue Presse Hannover is a local daily newspaper for Hannover and the surrounding area with local and regional news, as well as with entertainment and reporting on consumer issues and regional affairs.
Language (s): German
DAILY NEWSPAPER

Neue Presse, Haßberge/Ebern 666296
Owner: Druck- und Verlagsanstalt Neue Presse GmbH
Editorial: Marktplatz 3, Ebern 96106
Tel: 49 9531 6067
Email: ebern@np-coburg.de **Web site:** http://www.np-coburg.de/lokal/hassberge/
Freq: Daily; **Circ:** 28
Profile: Neue Presse Hassberge Ebern eine lokale Tageszeitung mit dem Neuigkeiten und Nachrichten aus Sport, Politik, Umwelt, Gesellschaft und Literatur. Ein Fokus der Berichterstattung liegt auf lokalen Nachrichten.
Language (s): German
DAILY NEWSPAPER

Neue Presse, Kronach 666298
Owner: Druck- und Verlagsanstalt Neue Presse GmbH
Editorial: Bahnhofstr. 1, Kronach 96317
Tel: 49 9261 601618
Email: kronach@np-coburg.de **Web site:** http://www.np-coburg.de/lokal/kronach/
Freq: Daily; **Circ:** 28
Profile: Neue Presse Kronach ist eine lokale Tageszeitung mit dem Neuigkeiten und Nachrichten aus Sport, Politik, Umwelt, Gesellschaft und Literatur. Ein Fokus der Berichterstattung liegt auf lokalen Nachrichten
Language (s): German
DAILY NEWSPAPER

Neue Westfälische 159714
Owner: Zeitungsverlag Neue Westfälische GmbH & Co. KG
Editorial: Zeitungsverlag Neue Westfälische GmbH & Co. KG, Niedernstrasse 21-27, Bielefeld 33602
Tel: 49 521 555 0
Email: chefredaktion@nw.de **Web site:** http://www.nw.de
Freq: Mon thru Fri; **Circ:** 28
Profile: Die Neue Westfälische ist eine regionale Tageszeitung mit lokaler Berichterstattung, aber auch überregionalen Nachrichten. Neue Westfälische is a regional daily newspaper covering local as well as international news.
Language (s): German
DAILY NEWSPAPER

neues deutschland 159708
Owner: Verlag Neues Deutschland Druckerei und Verlag GmbH
Editorial: Neues Deutschland Druckerei und Verlag GmbH, Franz-Mehring-Platz 1, Berlin 10243
Tel: 49 30 2978 1711
Email: redaktion@nd-online.de **Web site:** http://www.neues-deutschland.de
Freq: Mon thru Fri; **Circ:** 28
Profile: neues deutschland ist eine Tageszeitung, die sozialistisch orientiert ist. Es wird in den Ressorts Meinung, Politik, Gesellschaft, Kultur und Sport berichtet. neues deutschland is a daily socialistic newspaper covering opinions, politics, society, culture and sports.
Language (s): German
DAILY NEWSPAPER

Neumarkter Anzeiger 159717
Owner: Oberbayerisches Volksblatt GmbH & Co. Medienhaus KG
Editorial: Weissgerberstrasse 2-4, Mühldorf 84453
Tel: 49 8631 9878 0
Email: redaktion@muehldorfer-anzeiger.de **Web site:** http://www.ovb-online.de/muehldorf/neumarkt-st-veit/
Freq: Mon thru Fri; **Circ:** 28
Profile: Der Neumarkter Anzeiger ist eine regionale Tageszeitung, die zum Oberbayerischen Volksblatt gehört und im Landkreis Mühldorf erscheint. Erstellt wird die Zeitung von der Redaktion Mühldorf.
Language (s): German
DAILY NEWSPAPER

Neuss-Grevenbroicher Zeitung Dormagen 159720
Owner: Rheinische Post Verlagsges. mbH
Editorial: Zülpicher Str. 10, Dusseldorf 40549
Tel: 49 211 505 2426
Web site: http://www.ngz-online.de
Freq: Mon thru Fri; **Circ:** 28
Profile: Regionale Tageszeitung für den Raum Neuss-Grevenbroich mit aktuellen Nachrichten und Themen aus der Region. Regional daily newspaper for the Neuss-Grevenbroich area covering current news and topics within the region.
Language (s): German
DAILY NEWSPAPER

Neu-Ulmer Zeitung 159721
Owner: Presse-Druck- und Verlags-GmbH
Editorial: Ludwigstr. 10, Neu-Ulm 89231
Tel: 49 731 7071 11
Email: redaktion@nuz.de **Web site:** http://www.augsburger-allgemeine.de/?region=b-nu
Freq: Mon thru Fri; **Circ:** 28
Profile: Die Neu-Ulmer Zeitung ist eine Heimatzeitung für Neu-Ulm, Weißenhorn, Senden, Nersingen und Umgebung. Neu-Ulmer Zeitung is a local newspaper for Neu-Ulm, Weißenhorn, Senden, Nersingen and surrounding regions.
Language (s): German
DAILY NEWSPAPER

Nordbayerische Nachrichten 159754
Owner: Verlag Nürnberger Presse Druckhaus Nürnberg GmbH & Co. KG
Editorial: Marienstrasse 9/11, Nurnberg 90402
Tel: 49 911 2160
Email: info@nordbayern.de **Web site:** http://www.nordbayern.de/
Freq: Daily; **Circ:** 28
Profile: Die deutsche tägliche regionale Zeitung Nordbayerische Nachrichten ist eine Lokalausgabe der Nürnberger Nachrichten. The German daily regional newspaper Nordbayerische Nachrichten is a regional edition of the German daily newspaper Nürnberger Nachrichten.
Language (s): German
DAILY NEWSPAPER

Nordbayerische Nachrichten, Forchheim 666340
Owner: Nürnberger Presse Druckhaus Nürnb. GmbH & Co
Editorial: Nordbayerische Nachrichten Forchheim, Hornschuchallee 7-9, Forchheim 91301
Tel: 49 9191 722020
Email: nn-forchheim-redaktion@pressenetz.de **Web site:** http://www.nordbayern.de/region/forchheim
Freq: Daily
Profile: Nordbayerische Nachrichten Forchheim ist eine lokale Tageszeitung mit dem Neuigkeiten und Nachrichten aus Sport, Politik, Umwelt, Gesellschaft und Literatur. Ein Fokus der Berichterstattung liegt auf lokalen Nachrichten.
Language (s): German
DAILY NEWSPAPER

Nordbayerische Nachrichten, Herzogenaurach 666338
Owner: Verlag Nürnberger Presse Druckhaus Nürnberg GmbH & Co.
Editorial: Nordbayerische Nachrichten Herzogenaurach, An der Schütt 26, Herzogenaurach 91074 **Tel:** 49 9132 780115
Email: nn-herzogenaurach-redaktion@pressenetz.de **Web site:** http://www.nordbayern.de/region/herzogenaurach
Freq: Daily
Profile: Nordbayerische Nachrichten Herzogenaurach ist eine lokale Tageszeitung mit dem Neuigkeiten und Nachrichten aus Sport, Politik, Umwelt, Gesellschaft und Literatur. Ein Fokus der Berichterstattung liegt auf lokalen Nachrichten.
Language (s): German
DAILY NEWSPAPER

Nordbayerische Nachrichten, Pegnitz 666339
Owner: Verlag Nürnberger Presse Druckhaus Nürnberg GmbH & Co.
Editorial: Nordbayerische Nachrichten Pegnitz, Hauptstrasse 20, Pegnitz 91257 **Tel:** 49 9241 97120
Email: nn-pegnitz-redaktion@pressenetz.de **Web site:** http://www.nordbayern.de/region/pegnitz
Freq: Daily
Profile: Nordbayerische Nachrichten Pegnitz ist eine lokale Tageszeitung mit dem Neuigkeiten und Nachrichten aus Sport, Politik, Umwelt, Gesellschaft und Literatur. Ein Fokus der Berichterstattung liegt auf lokalen Nachrichten.
Language (s): German
DAILY NEWSPAPER

Nordbayerischer Kurier 159755
Owner: Nordbayerischer Kurier GmbH & Co. Zeitungsverlag KG
Editorial: Nordbayerischer Kurier GmbH & Co. Zeitungsverlag KG, Maximilianstrasse 58/60, Bayreuth 95444 **Tel:** 49 921 294 163
Email: redaktion@kurier.tmt.de **Web site:** http://www.nordbayerischer-kurier.de
Freq: Mon thru Fri; **Circ:** 28
Profile: Nordbayerische Kurier ist eine regionale Tageszeitung, die über lokale Nachrichten in Nordbayern berichtet. Nordbayerische Kurier is a regional daily newspaper, covering local news in the area of North Bavaria.
Language (s): German
DAILY NEWSPAPER

Nordbayerischer Kurier, Pegnitz 666315
Owner: Nordbayerischer Kurier GmbH & Co. Zeitungsverlag KG
Editorial: Nordbayerischer Kurier Pegnitz, Hauptstrasse 20, Pegnitz 91257 **Tel:** 49 9241 98011
Email: kurier.pegnitz@kurier.tmt.de **Web site:** http://www.nordbayerischer-kurier.de/region/pegnitz
Freq: Mon thru Fri
Profile: Nordbayerischer Kurier Pegnitz ist eine lokale Tageszeitung mit dem Neuigkeiten und Nachrichten aus Sport, Politik, Umwelt, Transport, Gesellschaft und Literatur. Ein Fokus der Berichterstattung liegt auf lokalen Nachrichten und Umgebung.
Language (s): German
DAILY NEWSPAPER

Norddeutsche Rundschau 159757
Owner: sh:z Schleswig-Holsteinischer Zeitungsverlag GmbH & Co. KG
Editorial: Fordestrasse 20, Flensburg 24944
Email: redaktion@shz.de **Web site:** http://www.shz.de
Freq: Daily; **Circ:** 28
Profile: Lokalausgabe der Schleswig-Holsteiner Zeitung mit regionalen Nachrichten und Themen für Norddeutschland. Local edition of the Schleswig-Holsteiner Zeitung covering regional newspapers and topics for Northern Germany.
Language (s): German
DAILY NEWSPAPER

Nordhannoversche Zeitung, Langenhagen 445225
Owner: Madsack Heimatzeitungen GmbH & Co. KG
Editorial: Walsroder Strasse 125, Langenhagen 30853 **Tel:** 49 511 9736618
Email: langenhagen@nordhannoversche.de **Web site:** http://www.haz.de/Hannover/Aus-der-Region/Langenhagen
Profile: Nordhannoverschen Zeitung Langenhagen ist ein Lokalangebot der Zeitung, mit lokaler Berichterstattung und Nachrichten aus der Stadt und Umgebung.
Language (s): German
DAILY NEWSPAPER

Nordsee-Zeitung 159761
Owner: Nordsee-Zeitung GmbH
Editorial: Nordsee-Zeitung GmbH, Hafenstrasse 140, Bremerhaven 27576 **Tel:** 49 471 597 270
Email: redaktion@nordsee-zeitung.de **Web site:** http://www.nordsee-zeitung.de
Freq: Mon thru Fri; **Circ:** 28
Profile: Die Nordsee-Zeitung ist eine regionale Tageszeitung aus Bremerhaven. Nordsee-Zeitung is a regional daily newspaper covering local newsin Bremerhaven
Language (s): German
DAILY NEWSPAPER

Nordwest-Zeitung 159762
Owner: Nordwest-Zeitung Verlagsgesellschaft mbH & Co. KG
Editorial: Nordwest-Zeitung Verlagsgesellschaft mbH & Co. KG, Peterstrasse 28-34, Oldenburg 26121
Tel: 49 441 9988 01
Email: red.online@nordwest-zeitung.de **Web site:** http://www.nwzonline.de
Freq: Mon thru Fri; **Circ:** 28
Profile: Die Nordwest-Zeitung ist die regionale Zeitung für das nordwestliche Niedersachsen, die im Jahr 1946 unter Fritz Bock gegründet wurde. Sie erscheint täglich außer Sonntag. Nordwest-Zeitung is a regional daily newspaper covering news for the north-west region of Niedersachsen. Founded in 1946 by Fritz Bock, the newspaper appears on a daily basis except for Sundays.
Language (s): German
DAILY NEWSPAPER

Nürnberger Nachrichten 159767
Owner: Verlag Nürnberger Presse Druckhaus Nürnberg GmbH & Co. KG
Editorial: Verlag Nürnberger Presse, Marienstrasse 9/11, Nurnberg 90402 **Tel:** 49 911 216 2410
Email: nn-lokales@pressenetz.de **Web site:** http://www.nordbayern.de/
Freq: Mon thru Fri; **Circ:** 28
Profile: Nürnberger Nachrichten ist eine regionale Tageszeitung, die über die Region, Politik, Wirtschaft, Kultur und Sport berichtet. Nürnberger Nachrichten is a regional daily newspaper covering news on the city of Nürnberg and its surroundings. The Newspaper also focuses on politics, business, culture and sport.
Language (s): German
DAILY NEWSPAPER

Nürtinger Zeitung 159768
Owner: Senner Verlag GmbH
Editorial: Senner Verlag GmbH, Carl-Benz-Strasse 1, Nürtingen 72622 **Tel:** 49 7022 9464 294
Email: forum@ntz.de **Web site:** http://www.ntz.de
Freq: Mon thru Fri; **Circ:** 28
Profile: Nürtinger Zeitung ist ein regionale Tageszeitung, die über Nürtingen und Umgebung berichtet. Nürtinger Zeitung is a regional newspaper covering news in the city of Nürtingen and its surroundings.
Language (s): German
DAILY NEWSPAPER

Oberbayerisches Volksblatt 159774
Owner: Oberbayerisches Volksblatt GmbH & Co. Medienhaus KG
Editorial: Oberbayerisches Volksblatt GmbH & Co. Medienhaus KG, Hafnerstrasse 5-13, Rosenheim 83022 **Tel:** 49 8031 213 0
Email: redaktion@ovb.net **Web site:** http://www.ovb-online.de
Freq: Mon thru Fri
Profile: Das Oberbayerische Volksblatt ist eine regionale Tageszeitung in den Stadt- und Landkreisen Rosenheim, Mühldorf am Inn, Chiemsee und Traunstein. Die Zeitschrift bietet lokale Nachrichten über Politik, Wirtschaft und Sport. Oberbayerisches Volksblatt is a regional daily newspaper covering news around the city of Rosenheim as well as its surroundings such as Mühldorf am Inn, Chiemsee und Traunstein. The Newspaper covers news such as politics, business and sports.
Language (s): German
DAILY NEWSPAPER

Oberbergischer Anzeiger (Kölner Stadt-Anzeiger) 159775
Owner: DuMont Net GmbH & Co. KG
Editorial: Redaktion Oberbergischer Anzeiger, Kaiserstrasse 1, Gummersbach 51643
Tel: 49 2261 9289 0
Email: redaktion.oberberg@ksta.de **Web site:** http://www.ksta.de/region/oberberg-ks
Freq: Daily; **Circ:** 28
Profile: Kölner Stadt-Anzeiger, Oberberg (Oberbergischer Anzeiger) ist eine Lokalausgabe des Kölner Stadt-Anzeigers mit Nachrichten aus und für Oberberg. Kölner Stadt-Anzeiger, Oberberg (Oberbergischer Anzeiger) is a local edition of the Kölner Stadt-Anzeiger with news from and for Oberberg.
Language (s): German
DAILY NEWSPAPER

Oberfranken Kombi 670300
Owner: Frankenpost Verlag GmbH
Editorial: Frankenpost Verlag GmbH, Poststr. 9 -11, Hof 95028 **Tel:** 49 9281 8160
Email: verlag@frankenpost.de **Web site:** http://www.frankenpost.de/regional/oberfranken/
Freq: Daily
Profile: Oberfranken Kombi ist eine lokale Tageszeitung mit dem Neuigkeiten und Nachrichten aus Sport, Politik, Umwelt, Gesellschaft und Literatur. Ein Fokus der Berichterstattung liegt auf lokalen Nachrichten.
Language (s): German
DAILY NEWSPAPER

Oberhessische Presse 159779
Owner: HITZEROTH Druck + Medien GmbH & Co. KG
Editorial: HITZEROTH Druck + Medien GmbH & Co. KG, Franz-Tuczek-Weg 1, Marburg 35039
Tel: 49 6421 409 0
Email: redaktion@op-marburg.de **Web site:** http://www.op-marburg.de
Freq: Mon thru Fri; **Circ:** 28
Profile: Die Oberhessische Presse bietet neben der lokalen Berichterstattung, Nachrichten aus den Ressorts Politik, Wirtschaft, Sport, Kultur und Medien. Oberhessische Presse is a regional daily newspaper providing local, as well as political, business cultural and media news.
Language (s): German
DAILY NEWSPAPER

Obermain-Tagblatt 159781
Owner: MPO Medien GmbH
Editorial: MPO Medien GmbH, Bahnhofstrasse 14, Lichtenfels 96215 **Tel:** 49 9571 788 20
Email: redaktion@obermain.de **Web site:** http://www.obermain.de
Freq: Mon thru Fri; **Circ:** 28
Profile: Das Obermain Tagblatt ist eine Regionalzeitung für die Region um Lichtenfels mit Nachrichten, Sport, Kultur, Gesellschaft, Politik und Unterhaltung. The Obermain Tagblatt is a regional newspaper for the region around Lichtenfels with news, sports, culture, society, politics and entertainment.
Language (s): German
DAILY NEWSPAPER

Odenwälder Echo 159785
Owner: Echo Zeitungen GmbH
Editorial: Hauptstrasse 59, Erbach 64711
Tel: 49 606 2 9435 27
Email: odenwald@darmstaedter-echo.de **Web site:** http://www.echo-online.de
Freq: Mon thru Fri; **Circ:** 28
Profile: Odenwälder Echo ist eine regionale Tageszeitung, die über lokale Nachrichten im Odenwaldkreis berichtet. Odenwälder Echo is a regional daily newspaper covering news in the area of Odenwaldkreis.
Language (s): German
DAILY NEWSPAPER

Odenwälder Zeitung 159786
Owner: DiesbachMedien GmbH
Editorial: Friedrichstrasse 24, Weinheim 69469
Tel: 49 62 01 8 11 00
Email: mail@diesbachmedien.de **Web site:** http://www.wnoz.de
Freq: Daily
Profile: Regionale Tageszeitung mit überregionaler und lokaler Berichterstattung für die Odenwald Region. Regional daily newspaper covering national and local reporting for the Odenwald region.
Language (s): German
DAILY NEWSPAPER

Offenbach-Post 159788
Owner: Metac Medien Verlags GmbH
Editorial: Metac Medien Verlags GmbH, Waldstrasse 226, Offenbach 63071 **Tel:** 49 69 85008 0
Email: redaktion@op-online.de **Web site:** http://www.op-online.de
Freq: Mon thru Fri; **Circ:** 28
Profile: Die Offenbach-Post ist eine regionale Tageszeitung, die zudem überregionale Themen bietet. Das Verbreitungsgebiet die Zeitung ist hauptsächlich in der Stadt Offenbach am Main sowie im Landkreis Offenbach. Offenbach-Post is a regional daily newspaper, covering also international topics. The Newspaper is distributed in the city of Offenbach as well as its surroundings.
Language (s): German
DAILY NEWSPAPER

Offenburger Tageblatt - Schwarzwaldzeitung 159789
Owner: Reiff Verlag KG
Editorial: Reiff Verlag KG, Marlener Strasse 9, Offenburg 77656 **Tel:** 49 781 504 0
Email: pr-redaktion@reiff.de **Web site:** http://www.bo.de
Freq: Mon thru Fri; **Circ:** 28
Profile: Offenburger Tageblatt- Schwarzwaldzeitung ist eine regionale Tageszeitung für Offenburg und Umgebung. Das Offenburger Tageblatt-Schwarzwaldzeitung berichtet über lokale Nachrichten und ist gleichzeitig das Amtsblatt der großen Kreisstadt Offenburg. Offenburger Tagesblatt - Schwarzwaldzeitung is a regional daily newspaper for Offenburg and surroundings. Offenburger Tageblatt - Schwarzwaldzeitung reports about local news and serves as official gazette of Offenburg.
Language (s): German
DAILY NEWSPAPER

Oldenburgische Volkszeitung 159791
Owner: Oldenburgische Volkszeitung Druckerei und Verlag KG
Editorial: Oldenburgische Volkszeitung Druckerei und Verlag KG, Neuer Markt 2, Vechta 49377
Tel: 49 4441 9560 300
Email: info@ov-online.de **Web site:** http://www.ov-online.de
Freq: Mon thru Fri
Profile: Oldenburgische Volkszeitung ist eine regionale Tageszeitung, die über lokale Nachrichten in das südliche Oldenburger Münsterland berichtet. Oldenburgische Volkszeitung is a regional daily newspaper covering local news in the southern region of Oldenburger Münsterland.
Language (s): German
DAILY NEWSPAPER

Oranienburger Generalanzeiger 159794
Owner: Märkischer Zeitungsverlag Zweigniederlassung der Westfälischer Anzeiger Verlagsges. mbH & Co. KG
Editorial: Lehnitzstrasse 13, Oranienburg 16515
Tel: 49 330 1 59 63 22
Email: lokales@oranienburger-generalanzeiger.de **Web site:** http://www.die-mark-online.de/heimat/oranienburg/
Freq: Mon thru Fri; **Circ:** 28
Profile: Der Oranienburger Generalanzeiger ist eine regionale Tageszeitung mit dem Fokus auf der lokalen Berichterstattung im Landkreis Oberhavel. Oranienburger Generalanzeiger is a regional daily newspaper covering local news in the area of Oberhavel
Language (s): German
DAILY NEWSPAPER

Oschatzer Allgemeine Zeitung 159795
Owner: Leipziger Verlags- und Druckereiges. mbH & Co. KG
Editorial: Seminarstrasse 2, Oschatz 4758
Tel: 49 3435 9768 0
Email: oschatz.redaktion@lvz.de **Web site:** http://www.oaz-online.de
Circ: 28
Profile: Die Oschatzer Allgemeine ist eine Lokalzeitung für Oschatz in Nordsachsen und bietet lokale Berichterstattung, sowie Nachrichten aus der Umgebung.
Language (s): German
DAILY NEWSPAPER

Osterhofener Zeitung 159797
Owner: Neue Presse Verlags-GmbH
Editorial: Stadtplatz 11, Osterhofen 94486
Tel: 49 993 2 953 821
Email: red.osterhofen@pnp.de **Web site:** http://www.pnp.de/region_und_lokal/landkreis_deggendorf/osterhofen/
Freq: Daily; **Circ:** 28
Profile: Osterhofener Zeitung ist eine Regionlausgabe der Passauer Neuen Presse. Es werden lokale Nachrichten aus Osterhofen berichtet. Osterhofener Zeitung is a regional daily newspaper covering news in the city of Osterhofen.
Language (s): German
DAILY NEWSPAPER

Osterholzer Kreisblatt 666572
Owner: Bremer Tageszeitungen AG
Editorial: Martinistrasse 43, Bremen 28195
Tel: 49 4791 3030
Email: redaktion@osterholzer-kreisblatt.de **Web site:** http://www.weser-kurier.de/
Freq: Daily
Profile: Lokalausgabe des Weser-Kurier für Osterholz mit lokalen Nachrichten und Themen. Local edition of the Weser-Kurier for Osterholz covering local news and topics.
Language (s): German
DAILY NEWSPAPER

Osterländer Volkszeitung 159798
Owner: Leipziger Verlags- und Druckereiges. mbH & Co. KG
Editorial: Kornmarkt 1, Altenburg 4600
Tel: 49 344 7 5749 10
Email: altenburg.redaktion@lvz.de **Web site:** http://www.ovz-online.de
Freq: Mon thru Fri; **Circ:** 28
Profile: Osterländer Volkszeitung ist eine regionale Tageszeitung mit lokalem Fokus auf Altenburg. Osterländer Volkszeitung is a regional daily newspaper covering local news in Altenburg.
Language (s): German
DAILY NEWSPAPER

Ostfriesen-Zeitung 159799
Owner: ZGO Zeitungsgruppe Ostfriesland GmbH
Editorial: ZGO Zeitungsgruppe Ostfriesland GmbH, Maiburger Strasse 8, Leer 26789
Tel: 49 491 97 90 555
Email: redaktion@oz-online.de **Web site:** http://www.oz-online.de/-news/ostfriesland
Freq: Mon thru Fri
Profile: Die Ostfriesen-Zeitung ist eine täglich erscheinende Regionalzeitung für die Region Ostfriesland. Sie wurde 1949 gegründet. Neben dem Hauptsitz der Redaktion in Leer, hat die Zeitung weitere drei Lokalredaktionen in den Städten Weener, Aurich und Emden. Ostfriesen-Zeitung is a daily newspaper for the German region of Ostfriesland, founded in 1949. In addition to its main editorial desk in Leer, the outlet also employs three local editorial teams in the cities of Weener, Aurich and Emden.
Language (s): German
DAILY NEWSPAPER

Ostfriesische Nachrichten 159800
Owner: Ostfriesische Nachrichten GmbH
Editorial: Ostfriesische Nachrichten GmbH, Kirchstrasse 8 - 14, Aurich 26603
Tel: 49 4941 1708 760
Email: redaktion@on-online.de **Web site:** http://www.on-online.de
Freq: Mon thru Fri; **Circ:** 28
Profile: Die Ostfriesische Nachrichten sind eine Regionalzeitung aus Aurich, Ostfriesland. Der redaktionelle Schwerpunkt liegt auf Meldungen und Berichten aus der Stadt Aurich sowie Südbrookmerland, Brookmerland, Ihlow, Großefehn und Wiesmoor. Ostfriesischen Nachrichten is a regional daily newspaper based in Aurich, Ostfriesland. The editorial content mainly focuses on local news and reports from the cities of Aurich, Südbrookmerland, Brookmerland, Ihlow, Großefehn and Wiesmoor.
Language (s): German
DAILY NEWSPAPER

Ostfriesischer Kurier 159801
Owner: Ostfriesischer Kurier GmbH & Co. KG
Editorial: Ostfriesischer Kurier GmbH & Co. KG, Stellmacherstr. 14, Norden 26506
Tel: 49 4931 925 230
Email: ok-redaktion@skn.info **Web site:** https://ostfriesischer-kurier.de
Freq: Mon thru Fri
Profile: Ostfriesischer Kurier ist eine regionale Tageszeitung aus Ostfriesland, die über Nachrichten in der Stadt Norden berichtet. Ostfriesischer Kurier is a regional daily newspaper covering local news in the city of Norden.
Language (s): German
DAILY NEWSPAPER

Ostholsteiner Anzeiger 159803
Owner: sh:z Schleswig-Holsteinischer Zeitungsverlag GmbH & Co. KG
Editorial: Fordestrasse 20, Flensburg 24944
Tel: 49 452 1779 0
Email: redaktion@shz.de **Web site:** http://www.shz.de/lokales/ostholsteiner-anzeiger/
Freq: Mon thru Fri; **Circ:** 28
Profile: Der Ostholsteiner Anzeiger ist die lokale Tageszeitung für Ostholstein. The Ostholsteiner Anzeiger is the regional daily newspaper for the region of Ostholstein.
Language (s): German
DAILY NEWSPAPER

Ostsee-Zeitung 159805
Owner: Ostsee-Zeitung GmbH & Co. KG
Editorial: Ostsee-Zeitung GmbH & Co. KG, Richard-Wagner-Strasse 1a, Rostock 18055 **Tel:** 49 381 365 0
Email: redaktion@ostsee-zeitung.de **Web site:** http://www.ostsee-zeitung.de
Freq: Mon thru Fri; **Circ:** 28
Profile: Die Ostsee-Zeitung ist eine regionale Tageszeitung, die lokale Nachrichten in Mecklenburg-Vorpommern bietet. Ostsee-Zeitung is a daily regional newspaper covering news in the region of Mecklenburg-Vorpommern.
Language (s): German
DAILY NEWSPAPER

Ostthüringer Zeitung 159806
Owner: Mediengruppe Thüringen Verlag GmbH
Editorial: Ostthüringer Zeitung, Bahnhofstrasse 18, Gera 7545 **Tel:** 49 365 77 33 10
Email: redaktion@otz.de **Web site:** http://www.otz.de
Freq: Mon thru Fri; **Circ:** 28
Profile: Die Ostthüringer Zeiting ist die Tageszeitung für Ostthüringen mit aktuellen lokalen, regionalen und nationalen Nachrichten. The Ostthüringer Zeitung is the daily newspaper for Ostthüringen with current local, regional and national news.
Language (s): German
DAILY NEWSPAPER

Ostthüringer Zeitung, Jena 666354
Owner: Ostthüringer Zeitung Verlag GmbH & Co. KG
Editorial: Am Holzmarkt 8, Jena 7743
Tel: 49 3641 5909123
Email: jena@otz.de **Web site:** http://jena.otz.de/
Freq: Mon thru Fri
Profile: Die Lokalredaktion Jena der Ostthüringer Zeitung berichtet über Neuigkeiten in der Region Jena in Thüringen, Deutschland. The German daily regional newspaper for Jena is a regional edition of the German daily newspaper Ostthüringer Zeitung and covers news about the area Jena, a town in Thuringia, Germany.
Language (s): German
DAILY NEWSPAPER

Paderborner Kreiszeitung 911430
Owner: Zeitungsverlag Neue Westfälische GmbH & Co. KG
Editorial: Gertrud-Groninger-Str. 12, Paderborn 33102 **Tel:** 49 5251 29 99 50
Email: redaktion@neue-westfaelische.de **Web site:** http://www.nw-news.de
Freq: Daily; **Circ:** 16026
Profile: Die Paderborner Kreiszeitung ist eine Lokalausgabe der Westfälischen Zeitung. Sie berichtet über das s Tagesgeschehen und Nachrichten aus der Region.The Paderborner Kreiszeitung is a local issue of the Westfälische Zeitung. It reports on the day's events and news from the region.
Language (s): German
DAILY NEWSPAPER

Passauer Neue Presse 159807
Owner: Neue Presse Multimedia GmbH
Editorial: Neue Presse Multimedia GmbH, Medienstrasse 5, Passau 94036 **Tel:** 49 851 802 0
Email: info@pnp.de **Web site:** http://www.pnp.de
Freq: Mon thru Fri; **Circ:** 28
Profile: Die Passauer Neue Presse ist eine regionale Tageszeitung, die neben den überregionalen Ressort, wie Wirtschaft, Politik, Sport und Kultur, auch über lokale Nachrichten berichtet. Passauer Neue Presse is a regional daily newspaper covering regional news, as well as politics, economics, culture and sports.
Language (s): German
DAILY NEWSPAPER

Passauer Neue Presse, Deggendorf (Deggendorfer Zeitung) 159331
Owner: Neue Presse Verlags-GmbH
Editorial: Bahnhofstrasse 28, Deggendorf 94469
Tel: 49 991 370 0 911
Email: red.deggendorf@pnp.de **Web site:** http://www.pnp.de/region_und_lokal/landkreis_deggendorf/deggendorf/
Freq: Mon thru Fri; **Circ:** 28
Profile: Die Deggendorfer Zeitung ist eine lokale Tageszeitung. Sie gehört zur Tageszeitung Passauer Neue Presse. The Deggendorfer Zeitung is a local daily newspaper. It is part of the newspaper Passauer Neue Presse.
Language (s): German
DAILY NEWSPAPER

Passauer Neue Presse, Freyung Grafenau 666366
Owner: Neue Presse Verlags-GmbH
Editorial: Stadtplatz 8-10, Freyung 94078
Tel: 49 8551 57890
Email: red.freyung@pnp.de **Web site:** http://www.pnp.de/region_und_lokal/landkreis_freyung_grafenau/
Freq: Mon thru Fri
Language (s): German
DAILY NEWSPAPER

Passauer Neue Presse, Griesbach 666364
Owner: Neue Presse Verlags-GmbH
Editorial: Neue Presse Multimedia GmbH, Medienstrasse 5, Passau 94036 **Tel:** 49 8532 920641
Email: info@pnp.de
Freq: Daily

Profile: Regionale Tageszeitung. Regional newspaper.
Language (s): German
DAILY NEWSPAPER

Passauer Neue Presse, Pfarrkirchen 666365
Owner: Neue Presse Verlags-GmbH
Editorial: Medienstrasse 5, Passau 94036
Tel: 49 8561 234921
Email: info@pnp.de
Freq: Daily
Profile: Regionale Tageszeitung. Regional newspaper.
Language (s): German
DAILY NEWSPAPER

Passauer Neue Presse, Pocking 666367
Owner: Neue Presse Verlags-GmbH
Editorial: Medienstrasse 5, Passau 94036
Tel: 49 8531 902921
Email: info@pnp.de
Freq: Daily
Profile: Regionale Tageszeitung. Regional newspaper.
Language (s): German
DAILY NEWSPAPER

Pegnitz-Zeitung 893046
Owner: Verlag Hans Fahner GmbH & Co. KG
Editorial: Pegnitz-Zeitung, Nürnberger Str. 19, Lauf 91207 **Tel:** 49 9123 175155
Email: Redaktion@Pegnitz-Zeitung.de **Web site:** http://n-land.de/pegnitz-zeitung/
Freq: Daily; **Circ:** 28
Profile: Die Pegnitz-Zeitung ist eine lokale Tageszeitung für das Nürnberger Land. The Pegnitz-Zeitung is a daily newspaper for the Nuremberg land.
Language (s): German
DAILY NEWSPAPER

Peiner Allgemeine Zeitung 159810
Owner: Peiner Allgemeine Zeitung Verlagsges. mbH & Co. KG
Editorial: Werderstrasse 49, Peine 31224
Tel: 49 517 1 406 131
Email: redaktion@paz-online.de **Web site:** http://www.paz-online.de
Freq: Mon thru Fri; **Circ:** 28
Profile: Die Peiner Allgemeine Zeitung ist eine Tageszeitung, die über regionale Nachrichten und Veranstaltungen berichtet. The Peiner Allgemeine Zeitung is a daily newspaper covers regional news and events.
Language (s): German
DAILY NEWSPAPER

Penzberger Merkur 159812
Owner: Zeitungsverlag Oberbayern GmbH & Co. KG
Editorial: Karlstrasse 7, Penzberg 82377
Tel: 49 885 6 9222 0
Email: penz-merkur@merkur.de **Web site:** http://www.penzberger-merkur.de
Freq: Mon thru Fri; **Circ:** 28
Profile: Die Penzberger Merkur ist die Lokalausgabe des Münchner Merkurs mit regionaler und lokaler Berichterstattung aus Penzberg. The Penzberger Merkur is a local edition of Münchner Merkur covering regional and local news around the city of Penzberg.
Language (s): German
DAILY NEWSPAPER

Pfaffenhofener Kurier 159814
Owner: Donaukurier Verlagsges. mbH & Co. KG
Editorial: Hauptplatz 31, Pfaffenhofen 85276
Tel: 49 844 1 869 33
Email: redaktion@pfaffenhofenerkurier.de **Web site:** http://www.donaukurier.de/lokales/pfaffenhofen/
Freq: Mon thru Fri; **Circ:** 28
Profile: Die Pfaffenhofener Kurier ist die Regionalausgabe des Donaukuriers mit lokaler Berichterstattung aus Pfaffenhofen. The Pfaffenhofener Kurier is a regional edition of Donaukurier covering local news in Pfaffenhofen.
Language (s): German
DAILY NEWSPAPER

Pforzheimer Zeitung 159816
Owner: J. Esslinger GmbH + Co. KG
Editorial: J. Esslinger GmbH & Co. KG, Poststrasse 5, Pforzheim 75172 **Tel:** 49 7231 933 0
Email: redaktion@pz-news.de **Web site:** http://www.pz-news.de
Freq: Mon thru Fri; **Circ:** 28
Profile: Die Pforzheimer Zeitung ist eine regionale Tageszeitung mit Schwerpunkten auf der regionalen Berichterstattung. Daneben gibt es Nachrichten aus Wirtschaft, Kultur und Politik. The Pforzheimer Zeitung is a regional daily newspaper which covers regional news as well as politics, economics, and culture.
Language (s): German
DAILY NEWSPAPER

Potsdamer Tageszeitung 911642
Owner: Märkische Verlags- und Druck-Gesellschaft mbH Potsdam
Editorial: Markische Verlags- und Druck-Gesellschaft mbH Potsdam, Friedrich-Engels-Strasse 24, Potsdam 14473 **Tel:** 49 331 2840 280
Email: potsdam-stadt@MAZ-online.de **Web site:** http://www.maz-online.de/Lokales/Potsdam
Freq: Daily; **Circ:** 24755
Profile: Potsdamer Tageszeitung ist eine Regionalzeitung für Potsdam Stadt und Land. Potsdamer Tageszeitung is a regional newspaper.
Language (s): German
DAILY NEWSPAPER

Recklinghäuser Zeitung 159830
Owner: Verlag J. Bauer KG
Editorial: Breite Strasse 4, Recklinghausen 45657
Tel: 49 236 1 1805 2414
Email: rzredaktion@medienhaus-bauer.de **Web site:** http://www.recklinghaeuser-zeitung.de
Freq: Mon thru Fri; **Circ:** 28
Profile: Die Recklinghäuser Zeitung ist eine Tageszeitung, die über lokale Nachrichten in Recklinghausen berichtet. The Recklinghäuser Zeitung is a daily newspaper which covers local news in the city of Recklinghausen.
Language (s): German
DAILY NEWSPAPER

Regionale Rundschau 159834
Owner: Bremer Tageszeitungen AG
Editorial: Regionale Rundschau, Bassumer Strasse 6a, Brinkum 28816 **Tel:** 49 421 80688 18
Email: redaktion@regionale-rundschau.de **Web site:** http://www.weser-kurier.de
Freq: Mon thru Fri
Profile: Tageszeitung mit regionalem Nachrichten- und Sportteil. Daily newspaper with regional news and a local sports section.
Language (s): German
DAILY NEWSPAPER

Remscheider General-Anzeiger 159838
Owner: Remscheider Medienhaus GmbH & Co. KG
Editorial: Alleestrasse 77-81, Remscheid 42853
Tel: 49 219 1 909 0
Email: rga@rga-online.de **Web site:** http://www.rga-online.de
Freq: Mon thru Fri; **Circ:** 28
Profile: Der Remscheider General-Anzeiger ist eine lokale Tageszeitung mit internationaler und regionaler Berichterstattung. The Remscheider General-Anzeiger is a local daily newspaper which covers international and regional news.
Language (s): German
DAILY NEWSPAPER

Rems-Zeitung 159839
Owner: Remsdruckerei Sigg, Härtel u. Co. KG
Editorial: Paradiesstrasse 12, Schwäbisch Gmünd 73527 **Tel:** 49 717 1 6006 0
Web site: http://remszeitung.de
Freq: Mon thru Fri
Profile: Die Rems-Zeitung ist eine regionale Tageszeitung, die sich auf lokale Nachrichten beschränkt. RSS-Feeds können unter folgendem Link abonniert werden:http://feeds.remszeitung.de/Rems-Zeitung-Lokalnachrichten Rems-Zeitung is a regional daily newspaper that focuses on local news.RSS-feeds are available under the following link: http://feeds.remszeitung.de/Rems-Zeitung-Lokalnachrichten
Language (s): German
DAILY NEWSPAPER

Reutlinger General-Anzeiger 159841
Owner: Reutlinger General-Anzeiger Verlags GmbH & Co. KG
Editorial: Reutlinger General-Anzeiger Verlags-GmbH & Co. KG, Burgstrasse 1-7, Reutlingen 72764
Tel: 49 7121 302 677
Email: redaktion@gea.de **Web site:** http://www.gea.de
Freq: Mon thru Fri; **Circ:** 28
Profile: Der Reutlinger General-Anzeiger ist eine regionale Tageszeitung für Reutlingen, die neben nationalen und internationalen Nachrichten, auch lokale Berichterstattungen veröffentlicht. Reutlinger General-Anzeiger is a regional daily newspaper for the city of Reutlingen, which covers international, national and regional news.
Language (s): German
DAILY NEWSPAPER

Reutlinger Nachrichten 159842
Owner: Georg Hauser GmbH & Co. Zeitungsverlag KG
Editorial: Albstrasse 4, Reutlingen 72764
Tel: 49 7121 9302 0
Email: rn.redaktion@swp.de **Web site:** http://www.swp.de/reutlingen/
Freq: Daily; **Circ:** 28
Profile: Die Reutlingen Nachrichten ist eine regionales Tageszeitung, die Nachrichten über Reutlingen und Umgebung bietet. Reutlingen Nachrichten is a regional daily newspaper covering local news of the city of Reutlingen and its surroundings.
Language (s): German
DAILY NEWSPAPER

Rheiderland Zeitung 159843
Owner: H. Risius KG
Editorial: Risiusstrasse 6 – 10, Weener 26826
Tel: 49 4951 930 117
Email: redaktion@rheiderland.de **Web site:** http://www.rheiderland.de
Freq: Mon thru Fri; **Circ:** 28
Profile: Die Rheiderland-Zeitung ist eine lokale Tageszeitung für die Orte Weender, Bunde, Jemgum und Umgebung. Sie informiert über lokale Nachrichten, Neuigkeiten und Veranstaltungen. The Rheiderland-Zeitung is a local daily newspaper for the places Weender, Bunde, Jemgum and environment. It informs about local news and events.
Language (s): German
DAILY NEWSPAPER

Rhein Main Presse 876422
Owner: Verlagsgruppe Rhein Main GmbH & Co. KG
Editorial: Verlagsgruppe Rhein Main GmbH & Co. KG, Erich-Dombrowski-Strasse 2, Mainz 55127
Tel: 49 6131 4830
Email: impressum@vrm.de **Web site:** http://www.rhein-main-presse.de
Freq: Mon thru Fri
Profile: RHEIN MAIN PRESSE ist eine Tageszeitung aus der Rhein-Main-Region, die sowohl im Print als auch online über Nachrichten, Sport, Politik, Wissenschaft oder Freizeit berichtet. Sie vereint die Zeitungen ALLGEMEINE ZEITUNG, BÜRSTÄDTER ZEITUNG, LAMPERTHEIMER ZEITUNG, MAIN-SPITZE, WIESBADENER KURIER, WIESBADENER TAGBLATT und WORMSER ZEITUNG. RHEIN MAIN PRESSE is a daily newspaper from the Rhine-Main region, which reports both in print and online on news, sports, politics, science or leisure. She combines the newspapers ALLGEMEINE ZEITUNG, BÜRSTÄDTER ZEITUNG, LAMPERTHEIMER ZEITUNG, MAIN-SPITZE, WIESBADENER KURIER, WIESBADENER TAGBLATT and WORMSER ZEITUNG.
Language (s): German
DAILY NEWSPAPER

Rhein-Hunsrück-Zeitung 159845
Owner: Mittelrhein-Verlag GmbH
Editorial: Aulergasse 10, Am Zentralparkplatz, Simmern 55469 **Tel:** 49 676 1 96774 40
Email: simmern@rhein-zeitung.net **Web site:** http://www.rhein-zeitung.de/region/lokales/hunsrueck.html
Freq: Mon thru Fri; **Circ:** 28
Profile: Die Rhein-Hunsrück-Zeitung ist eine regionale Tageszeitung mit Sitz in Simmern, die neben den nationalen und internationalen Nachrichten, auch lokale Berichte druckt. Rhein-Hunsrück-Zeitung is a regional daily newspape based in Simmern which covers national and international news as well as regional news.
Language (s): German
DAILY NEWSPAPER

Rhein-Lahn-Zeitung 159847
Owner: Mittelrhein-Verlag GmbH
Editorial: Rosenstrasse 36, Diez 65582
Tel: 49 6432 9250 23
Email: diez@rhein-zeitung.net **Web site:** http://www.rhein-zeitung.de/region/lokales/diez.html
Circ: 28
Profile: Die Rhein-Lahn-Zeitung ist eine Regionalzeitung für Diez und Umgebung und bietet vor allem lokale und regionale Berichterstattung.
Language (s): German
DAILY NEWSPAPER

Rhein-Main-Presse 912220
Owner: Verlagsgruppe Rhein Main Holding GmbH & Co. KG
Editorial: Erich-Dombrowski-Strasse 2, Mainz 55127
Tel: 49 6131 48 30
Email: impressum@vrm.de **Web site:** http://www.vrm.de
Freq: Mon thru Fri; **Circ:** 170851
Profile: Die Tageszeitung Rhein-Main Presse ist eine Tageszeitung in der Region Rhein Main. Die Schwerpunkte sind Lokalnachrichten sowie Informationen aus der Gegend, desweiteren wird Sport, Lifestyle behandelt. The daily Rhein-Main Press is a daily newspaper in the Rhein Main area. The focus is on local news and information from the area, besides sports is treated lifestyle.
Language (s): German
DAILY NEWSPAPER

Rhein-Main-Presse Alzey 912196
Owner: Verlagsgruppe Rhein Main Holding GmbH & Co. KG
Editorial: Erich-Dombrowski-Str. 2, Mainz 55127
Tel: 49 6131 4848 30
Email: marketing@vrm.de **Web site:** http://www.vrm.de
Freq: Mon thru Fri; **Circ:** 10464
Profile: Zur Tageszeitung Allgemeine Zeitung gehört die Ausgabe Rhein-Main-Presse Alzey. Es werden regionale sowie lokale Nachrichten veröffentlicht.For newspaper Allgemeine Zeitung include the issue Rhein-Main Press Alzey. It will be published regional and local news.
Language (s): German
DAILY NEWSPAPER

Rhein-Main-Presse Bad Kreuznach 912198
Owner: Verlagsgruppe Rhein Main Holding GmbH & Co. KG
Editorial: Erich-Dombrowski-Str. 2, Mainz 55127
Tel: 49 6131 4848 30
Email: impressum@vrm.de **Web site:** http://www.vrm.de/
Freq: Mon thru Fri; **Circ:** 6849
Profile: Die Tageszeitung Allgemeine Zeitung erscheint mit der Ausgabe Rhein-Main-Presse Bad Kreuznach. Die Schwerpunkte sind Lokalnachrichten. The daily newspaper Allgemeine Zeitung appears with the output Rhein-Main Press Bad Kreuznach. The focus is on local news.
Language (s): German
DAILY NEWSPAPER

Rhein-Main-Presse Bingen-Ingelheim 912203
Owner: Verlagsgruppe Rhein Main Holding GmbH & Co. KG
Editorial: Erich-Dombrowski-Str. 2, Mainz 55127
Tel: 49 6131 4848 30
Email: marketing@vrm.de **Web site:** http://www.vrm.de
Freq: Mon thru Fri; **Circ:** 14817
Profile: Die Tageszeitung Allgemeine Zeitung erscheint mit der Ausgabe Rhein-Main-Presse Bingen / Ingelheim. Die Schwerpunkte sind Lokalnachrichten. The daily newspaper Allgemeine Zeitung appears with the output Rhein-Main Press Bingen / Ingelheim. The focus is on local news.
Language (s): German
DAILY NEWSPAPER

Rhein-Main-Presse Mainz 912415
Owner: Verlagsgruppe Rhein Main Holding GmbH & Co. KG
Editorial: Erich-Dombrowski-Str. 2, Mainz 55127
Tel: 49 6131 4848 30
Email: marketing@vrm.de **Web site:** http://www.vrm.de
Freq: Mon thru Fri; **Circ:** 52562
Profile: Die Tageszeitung Rhein Main Presse wird als Lokalausgabe der Allgemeinen Zeitung Mainz veröffentlicht. Die Schwerpunkte sind Lokalnachrichten, Sport und Lifestyle. The daily newspaper Rhein Main Presse is published as a local edition of the Allgemeine Zeitung Mainz. The focus is on local news, sport and lifestyle.
Language (s): German
DAILY NEWSPAPER

Rhein-Main-Presse Worms 912417
Owner: Verlagsgruppe Rhein Main Holding GmbH & Co. KG
Editorial: Erich-Dombrowski-Str. 2, Mainz 55127
Tel: 49 6131 4848 30
Email: impressum@vrm.de **Web site:** http://www.vrm.de
Freq: Mon thru Fri; **Circ:** 16403
Profile: Die Tageszeitung Rhein Main Presse Worms wird als Tageszeitung Wormser Zeitung veröffentlicht. Die Schwerpunkte sind Lokalnachrichten, Sport und Lifestyle. The daily newspaper Rhein Main Presse Worms is published as a daily newspaper Wormser Zeitung. The focus is on local news, sport and lifestyle.
Language (s): German
DAILY NEWSPAPER

Rhein-Neckar-Zeitung 159848
Owner: Rhein-Neckar-Zeitung GmbH
Editorial: Rhein-Neckar-Zeitung GmbH, Neugasse 2, Heidelberg 69117 **Tel:** 49 6221 519 0
Email: online@rnz.de **Web site:** http://www.rnz.de
Freq: Mon thru Fri; **Circ:** 28
Profile: Die Rhein-Neckar-Zeitung ist eine regionale Tageszeitung mit Sitz in Heidelberg. Die Zeitung bietet regionale Nachrichten in Weinheim, Sinsheim, Schwetzingen, Mosbach und Buchen. The Rhein-Neckar-Zeitung is a regional daily newspaper based in Heidelberg. The Newspaper offers regional news in Weinheim, Sinsheim, Schwetzingen, Mosbach and Buchen.
Language (s): German
DAILY NEWSPAPER

Rhein-Sieg-Anzeiger (Kölner Stadt-Anzeiger) 159850
Owner: DuMont Net GmbH & Co. KG
Editorial: Redaktion Rhein-Sieg, Neue Poststrasse 15, (S-Carré), Siegburg 53721 **Tel:** 49 2241 17 49 57 10
Email: redaktion.rheinsieg@ksta.de **Web site:** http://www.ksta.de/region/rhein-sieg-bonn
Freq: Daily; **Circ:** 28
Profile: Kölner Stadt-Anzeiger, Rhein-Sieg (Rhein-Sieg-Anzeiger) ist eine lokale Tageszeitung für den Raum Rhein-Sieg mit aktuellen Nachrichten und Themen für die Region. Kölner Stadt-Anzeiger, Rhein-Sieg (Rhein-Sieg-Anzeiger) is a local daily newspaper for the Rhein-Sieg area covering current news and topics for the region.
Language (s): German
DAILY NEWSPAPER

Rhein-Zeitung 159854
Owner: Mittelrhein-Verlag GmbH
Editorial: Mittelrhein-Verlag GmbH, August-Horch-Str. 28, Koblenz 56070 **Tel:** 49 261 892 00
Email: redaktion@rhein-zeitung.net **Web site:** http://www.rhein-zeitung.de
Freq: Mon thru Fri; **Circ:** 28
Profile: Die Rhein-Zeitung ist eine regionale Tageszeitung mit Berichterstattungen über Politik, Wirtschaft, Sport und Wissenschaft, sowie regionalen Nachrichten. Die Zeitung hat zudem einen Ratgeber- und Netzwelt-Bereich, sowie einen Blog. The Rhein-Zeitung is a daily regional newspaper covering national and international and regional news. The newspaper also offers news on politics, business, sports and science as well as an advice column and a blog.
Language (s): German
DAILY NEWSPAPER

Rhein-Zeitung / Öffentlicher Anzeiger Kirn 159565
Owner: Mittelrhein-Verlag GmbH
Editorial: Nahegasse 10, Kirn 55606
Tel: 49 6752 131 20 20

Email: service-kim@rhein-zeitung.net **Web site:** http://www.rhein-zeitung.de/region/lokales/kirn.html
Circ: 28
Profile: Oeffentlicher Anzeiger Kirn, oder auch Rhein-Zeitung Kirn, ist eine Lokalausgabe der Rhein-Zeitung, mit lokaler Berichterstattung und Nachrichten aus Kirn und Umgebung.
Language (s): German
DAILY NEWSPAPER

Rhein-Zeitung, Mayen-Andernach 666379
Owner: Rhein-Zeitung Mayen
Editorial: August-Horch-Strasse 28, Koblenz 56055
Tel: 49 261 2919215
Email: redaktion-mayen@rhein-zeitung.net **Web site:** http://www.rhein-zeitung.de/
Freq: Mon thru Fri
Profile: Rhein-Zeitung, Mayen - Andernach ist eine Tageszeitung um die Städte Mayen - Andernach. Die Themenschwerpunkte sind lokale Nachrichten, Sport und Lifestyle. Rhein-Zeitung, Mayen - Andernach is a daily newspaper for the cities Mayen - Andernach. The topics include local news, sports and lifestyle.
Language (s): German
DAILY NEWSPAPER

Rhein-Zeitung, Stadt Koblenz 912424
Owner: Mittelrhein-Verlag GmbH
Editorial: August-Horch-Strasse 28, Koblenz 56070
Tel: 49 261 892 347
Email: redaktion-koblenz@rhein-zeitung.net **Web site:** http://www.rhein-zeitung.de/region/lokales/koblenz.html
Freq: Mon thru Fri; **Circ:** 27060
Profile: Rhein-Zeitung Stadt Koblenz ist eine Tageszeitung um die Stadt Koblenz. Die Themenschwerpunkte sind lokale Nachrichten, Sport und Lifestyle. Rhein-Zeitung Stadt Koblenz is a daily newspaper for the city of Koblenz. The topics include local news, sports and lifestyle.
Language (s): German
DAILY NEWSPAPER

Ried Echo 355700
Owner: Echo Zeitungen GmbH
Editorial: Holzhofallee 25-31, Darmstadt 64295
Tel: 49 6151 387 0
Email: echo-zeitungen@darmstaedter-echo.de **Web site:** http://www.echo-online.de/region/gross-gerau/riedstadt/
Freq: Mon thru Fri; **Circ:** 28
Profile: Lokalzeitung des Echo für Riedstadt mit aktuellen Nachrichten aus Sport, Wirtschaft, Politik, Kultur und Unterhaltung. Local Echo newspaper for Riedstadt with news from sports, business, politics, culture and entertainment.
Language (s): German
DAILY NEWSPAPER

Rieser Nachrichten Nördlingen 159858
Owner: Presse-Druck- und Verlags-GmbH
Editorial: Curt-Frenzel-Str. 2, Augsburg 86167
Tel: 49 821 777 0
Email: redaktion@rieser-nachrichten.de **Web site:** http://www.augsburger-allgemeine.de/
Freq: Mon thru Fri; **Circ:** 28
Profile: Die Rieser Nachrichten ist eine Tageszeitung für die Region Nördlingen. Sie erscheint zusammen mit der Augsburger Allgemeinen und beide gehören zur Presse-Druck und Verlags-GmbH. The Rieser Nachrichten is a daily newspaper for the Noerdlingen region. It's published together with the Augsburger Zeitung and both belong to the Presse-Druck und Verlags GmbH.
Language (s): German
DAILY NEWSPAPER

Rottaler Anzeiger 159862
Owner: Neue Presse Verlags-GmbH
Editorial: Medienstrasse 5, Passau 94036
Tel: 49 851 802 0
Email: info@pnp.de **Web site:** http://www.pnp.de/
Freq: Mon thru Fri; **Circ:** 28
Profile: Der Rottaler Anzeiger ist eine Tageszeitung für die Region Eggenfelden. Sie erscheint zusammen mit der Paussauer Neue Presse und beide gehören zur Neue Presse Verlag GmbH. The Rottaler Anzeiger is a daily newspaper for the Eggenfelden region. It's published together with the Passauer Neue Presse and both belong to the Neue Presse Verlag GmbH.
Language (s): German
DAILY NEWSPAPER

Ruhr Nachrichten 159864
Owner: Verlag Lensing-Wolff GmbH & Co. KG
Editorial: Verlag Lensing-Wolff GmbH & Co. KG, Westenhellweg 86-88, Dortmund 44137
Tel: 49 231 9059 48 01
Email: redaktion@ruhrnachrichten.de **Web site:** http://www.ruhrnachrichten.de
Freq: Mon thru Fri; **Circ:** 28
Profile: Die Zeitung Ruhr Nachrichten ist eine Tageszeitung für die Region Ruhr. Sie gehört zum Medienhaus Lensing und erscheint in lokalen Ausgaben für Bochum, Castrop-Rauxel, Dortmund, Lünen, Dorsten, Haltern, Schwerte, Selm und Werne. Ruhr Nachrichten is a daily newspaper for the area of Ruhr. It is published by the Medienhaus Lensing and in local editions for Bochum, Castrop-Rauxel, Dortmund, Lünen, Dorsten, Haltern, Schwerte, Selm and Werne.
Language (s): German
DAILY NEWSPAPER

Ruhr Nachrichten, Dorsten (Dorstener Zeitung) 159349
Owner: Verlag Lensing-Wolff GmbH & Co. KG
Editorial: Lokalredaktion Dorsten, Südwall 27, Dorsten 46282 **Tel:** 49 2362 927710
Email: redaktion@dorstenerzeitung.de **Web site:** http://www.dorstenerzeitung.de
Freq: Mon thru Fri; **Circ:** 28
Profile: Die Dorstener Zeitung ist eine Lokalausgabe der Tageszeitung Ruhr Nachrichten, die zum Medienhaus Lensing gehört. The Dorstener Zeitung is a local edition of the daily newspaper Ruhr Nachrichten which is part of the Medienhaus Lensing.
Language (s): German
DAILY NEWSPAPER

Rüsselsheimer Echo 159863
Owner: Echo Zeitungen GmbH
Editorial: Holzhofallee 25-31, Darmstadt 64295
Tel: 49 615 1 387 0
Email: echo-zeitungen@darmstaedter-echo.de **Web site:** http://www.echo-online.de/region/ruesselsheim/
Freq: Mon thru Fri; **Circ:** 28
Profile: Das Rüsselsheimer Echo ist eine Tageszeitung für die Region Südhessen. Sie gehört zur Echo Medien GmbH. Das Rüsselsheimer Echo berichtet über lokale Nachrichten, Sport, Freizeit, Wirtschaft, Kultur und Gesellschaft. The Rüsselsheimer Echo is a daily newspaper for the Südhessen region. It belongs to the Echo Medien GmbH. The Rüsselsheimer Echo reports on local news, sport, leisure, economy, culture and society.
Language (s): German
DAILY NEWSPAPER

Saale-Zeitung 366111
Owner: Mediengruppe Oberfranken GmbH & Co. KG
Editorial: Redaktion Bad Kissingen, Theresienstrasse 21, Bad Kissingen 97688 **Tel:** 49 971 8040 118
Email: redaktion.badkissingen@infranken.de **Web site:** http://www.infranken.de/regional/bad-kissingen/
Freq: Mon thru Fri
Profile: Regionalzeitung für Bad Kissingen und Umgebung mit Nachrichten, lokaler Berichterstattung, Sport, Gesellschaft und Kultur. Regional newspaper for Bad Kissingen and the surrounding area with news, local coverage, sports, society and culture.
Language (s): German
DAILY NEWSPAPER

Saarbrücker Zeitung 159870
Owner: Saarbrücker Zeitung Verlag und Druckerei GmbH
Editorial: Saarbrücker Zeitung Verlag und Druckerei GmbH, Gutenbergstr 11-23, Saarbrücken 66117
Tel: 49 681 502 0
Email: redaktion@sol.de **Web site:** http://www.saarbruecker-zeitung.de/
Freq: Mon thru Fri; **Circ:** 28
Profile: Die Saarbrücker Zeitung ist eine Tageszeitung für die Region Saarbrücken und für das Saarland. Sie gehört zum Saarbrücker Zeitung Verlag und Druckerei GmbH. The Saarbrücker Zeitung is a daily newspaper for the region Saarbrücken and the State of Saarland. It belongs to the Saarbrücker Zeitung Verlag und Druckerei GmbH.
Language (s): German
DAILY NEWSPAPER

Saarbrücker Zeitung, Merzig/Wadern 666433
Owner: Saarbrücker Zeitung Verlag und Druckerei GmbH
Editorial: Gutenbergstr. 11 - 23, Saarbrücken 66111
Tel: 49 681 502-504
Email: redstv@sz-sb.de
Freq: Mon thru Fri
Profile: Die Saarbrücker Zeitung Merzig - Wadern ist eine lokale Tageszeitung. Es werden lokale Themen behandelt sowie Sport und das Tagesgeschehen. The Saarbrücker Zeitung Merzig - Wadern is a local daily newspaper. There are local topics treated as well as sports and daily events.
Language (s): German
DAILY NEWSPAPER

Saarbrücker Zeitung, Mitte 912545
Owner: Saarbrücker Zeitung Verlag und Druckerei GmbH
Editorial: Gutenbergstr 11-23, Saarbrücken 66117
Freq: Mon thru Fri; **Circ:** 19649
Profile: Die Saarbrücker Zeitung Mitte ist eine lokale Tageszeitung. Es werden lokale Themen behandelt sowie Sport und das Tagesgeschehen. The Saarbrücker Zeitung Mite is a local daily newspaper. There are local topics treated as well as sports and daily events.
Language (s): German
DAILY NEWSPAPER

Saarbrücker Zeitung, Neunkirchen 666429
Owner: Saarbrücker Zeitung Verlag und Druckerei GmbH
Editorial: Gutenbergstr. 11 - 23, Saarbrücken 66111
Tel: 49 681 502504
Email: redstv@sz-sb.de **Web site:** http://www.saarbruecker-zeitung.de/saarland/neunkirchen/
Freq: Mon thru Fri
Profile: Die Saarbrücker Zeitung Neunkirchen ist eine lokale Tageszeitung. Es werden lokale Themen behandelt sowie Sport und das Tagesgeschehen. The Saarbrücker Zeitung Neunkirchen is a local daily newspaper. There are local topics treated as well as sports and daily events.
Language (s): German
DAILY NEWSPAPER

Saarbrücker Zeitung, Saarlouis 666430
Owner: Saarbrücker Zeitung Verlag und Druckerei GmbH
Editorial: Saarlouiser Rundschau, Adlerstrasse 3, Saarlouis 66740 **Tel:** 49 6831 7 68 88 50
Email: redsls@sz-sb.de **Web site:** http://www.saarbruecker-zeitung.de/Saarlouis
Freq: Mon thru Fri
Profile: Die Saarbrücker Zeitung Saarlouis ist eine lokale Tageszeitung. Es werden lokale Themen behandelt sowie Sport und das Tagesgeschehen. The Saarbrücker Zeitung Saarlouis is a local daily newspaper. There are local topics treated as well as sports and daily events.
Language (s): German
DAILY NEWSPAPER

Saarbrücker Zeitung, St. Ingbert 666434
Owner: Saarbrücker Zeitung Verlag und Druckerei GmbH
Editorial: Gutenbergstr. 11 - 23, Saarbrücken 66111
Tel: 49 681 502504
Email: redstv@sz-sb.de **Web site:** http://www.saarbruecker-zeitung.de/saarland/stingbert/
Freq: Mon thru Fri
Profile: Die Saarbrücker Zeitung St. Ingbert ist eine lokale Tageszeitung. Es werden lokale Themen behandelt sowie Sport und das Tagesgeschehen. The Saarbrücker Zeitung St. Ingbert is a local daily newspaper. There are local topics treated as well as sports and daily events.
Language (s): German
DAILY NEWSPAPER

Saarbrücker Zeitung, St. Wendel 666432
Owner: Saarbrücker Zeitung Verlag und Druckerei GmbH
Editorial: Mia-Münster-Strasse 8, St. Wendel 66606
Tel: 49 681 502504
Email: redstv@sz-sb.de **Web site:** http://www.saarbruecker-zeitung.de
Freq: Mon thru Fri
Profile: Die Saarbrücker Zeitung St. Wendel ist eine lokale Tageszeitung. Es werden lokale Themen behandelt sowie Sport und das Tagesgeschehen. The Saarbrücker Zeitung St. Wendel is a local daily newspaper. There are local topics treated as well as sports and daily events.
Language (s): German
DAILY NEWSPAPER

Sachsenheimer Zeitung 890994
Owner: Druck- und Verlagsges. Bietigheim mbH
Editorial: Kronenbergstrasse 10, Bietigheim-Bissingen 74321 **Tel:** 49 7142 403410
Email: redaktion@bietigheimerzeitung.de **Web site:** http://www.swp.de/bietigheim/lokales/sachsenheim/
Freq: Daily; **Circ:** 28
Profile: Lokale Tgeszeitung für den Kreis Sachsenheim. Local daily newspaper for the Sachsenheim region.
Language (s): German
DAILY NEWSPAPER

Sächsische Zeitung 159875
Owner: DD+V Gmbh & Co KG
Editorial: DD+V Gmbh & Co KG, Sachsische Zeitung, Dresden 1067 **Tel:** 49 351 4864 2273
Email: redaktion@dd-v.de **Web site:** http://www.sz-online.de
Freq: Mon thru Fri; **Circ:** 28
Profile: Regionale Tageszeitung für den Raum Sachsen mit regionalen Informationen, Lokalnachrichten und Nachrichten aus Kunst, Unterhaltung, Gesellschaft und Kultur. Regional daily newspaper for the area of ??Saxony with regional information, local news and news from arts, entertainment, society and culture.
Language (s): German
DAILY NEWSPAPER

Sächsische Zeitung, Bautzen 666440
Owner: DD+V Gmbh & Co KG
Editorial: Ostra-Allee 20, Dresden 1067
Tel: 49 351 48640
Email: redaktion@dd-v.de **Web site:** http://www.sz-online.de
Freq: Mon thru Fri
Profile: Sächsische Zeitung Bautzen ist eine regionale Tageszeitung. Es werden Themen behandelt wie Politik, Wirtschaft, Sport und Regionales. Sächsische Zeitung Bautzen is a regional daily newspaper. It deals with themes such as politics, economy, sports and regional.
Language (s): German
DAILY NEWSPAPER

Sächsische Zeitung, Freital 666444
Owner: DD+V Gmbh & Co KG
Editorial: Ostra-Allee 20, Dresden 1067
Tel: 49 351 48640
Email: redaktion@dd-v.de **Web site:** http://www.sz-online.de
Freq: Mon thru Fri
Profile: Sächsische Zeitung Freital ist eine regionale Tageszeitung. Es werden Themen behandelt wie Politik, Wirtschaft, Sport und Regionales. Sächsische Zeitung Freital is a regional daily newspaper. It deals with themes such as politics, economy, sports and Regional.
Language (s): German
DAILY NEWSPAPER

Sächsische Zeitung, Görlitz 666445
Owner: DD+V Gmbh & Co KG
Editorial: Ostra-Allee 20, Dresden 1067
Tel: 49 351 48640
Email: redaktion@dd-v.de **Web site:** http://www.sz-online.de
Freq: Mon thru Fri
Profile: Sächsische Zeitung Görlitz ist eine regionale Tageszeitung. Es werden Themen behandelt wie Politik, Wirtschaft, Sport und Regionales. Sächsische Zeitung Görlitz is a regional daily newspaper. It deals with themes such as politics, economy, sports and Regional.
Language (s): German
DAILY NEWSPAPER

Sächsische Zeitung, Kamenz 666447
Owner: Dresdner Druck- und Verlagshaus GmbH + Co. KG
Editorial: Ostra-Allee 20, Dresden 1067
Tel: 49 351 48640
Email: redaktion@dd-v.de **Web site:** http://www.sz-online.de
Freq: Mon thru Fri
Profile: Sächsische Zeitung Kamenz ist eine regionale Tageszeitung. Es werden Themen behandelt wie Politik, Wirtschaft, Sport und Regionales. Sächsische Zeitung Kamenz is a regional daily newspaper. It deals with themes such as politics, economy, sports and regional.
Language (s): German
DAILY NEWSPAPER

Sächsische Zeitung, Löbau 666450
Owner: Dresdner Druck- und Verlagshaus
Editorial: Ostra-Allee 20, Dresden 1067
Tel: 49 351 48640
Email: redaktion@dd-v.de **Web site:** http://www.sz-online.de
Freq: Mon thru Fri
Profile: Sächsische Zeitung Löbau ist eine regionale Tageszeitung. Es werden Themen behandelt wie Politik, Wirtschaft, Sport und Regionales. Sächsische Zeitung Löbau is a regional daily newspaper. It deals with themes such as politics, economy, sports and regional.
Language (s): German
DAILY NEWSPAPER

Sächsische Zeitung, Meißen 666441
Owner: Sächsische Zeitung
Editorial: Ostra-Allee 20, Dresden 1067
Tel: 49 351 48640
Email: redaktion@dd-v.de **Web site:** http://www.sz-online.de/verlag/kontakt
Freq: Mon thru Fri
Profile: Sächsische Zeitung Meißen ist eine regionale Tageszeitung. Es werden Themen behandelt wie Politik, Wirtschaft, Sport und Regionales. Sächsische Zeitung Meißen is a regional daily newspaper. It deals with themes such as politics, economy, sports and regional.
Language (s): German
DAILY NEWSPAPER

Sächsische Zeitung, Pirna 666442
Owner: DD+V Gmbh & Co KG
Editorial: Ostra-Allee 20, Dresden 1067
Tel: 49 351 48640
Email: redaktion@dd-v.de **Web site:** http://www.sz-online.de
Freq: Mon thru Fri
Profile: Sächsische Zeitung Pirna ist eine regionale Tageszeitung. Es werden Themen behandelt wie Politik, Wirtschaft, Sport und Regionales. Sächsische Zeitung Pirna is a regional daily newspaper. It deals with themes such as politics, economy, sports and regional.
Language (s): German
DAILY NEWSPAPER

Sächsische Zeitung, Riesa 666443
Owner: Sächsische Zeitung
Editorial: Ostra-Allee 20, Dresden 1067
Tel: 49 351 48640
Email: redaktion@dd-v.de **Web site:** http://www.sz-online.de
Freq: Mon thru Fri
Profile: Sächsische Zeitung Riesa ist eine regionale Tageszeitung. Es werden Themen behandelt wie Politik, Wirtschaft, Sport und Regionales. Sächsische Zeitung Riesa is a regional daily newspaper. It deals with themes such as politics, economy, sports and Regional.
Language (s): German
DAILY NEWSPAPER

Sächsische Zeitung, Zittau 666449
Owner: DD+V Gmbh & Co KG
Editorial: Ostra-Allee 20, Dresden 1067
Tel: 49 351 48640
Email: redaktion@dd-v.de **Web site:** http://www.sz-online.de
Freq: Mon thru Fri

Profile: Sächsische Zeitung Zittau ist eine regionale Tageszeitung. Es werden Themen behandelt wie Politik, Wirtschaft, Sport und Regionales. Sächsische Zeitung Zittau is a regional daily newspaper. It deals with themes such as politics, economy, sports and regional.
Language (s): German
DAILY NEWSPAPER

Sauerland Kurier 607780
Owner: Kurier Verlag Lennestadt GmbH
Editorial: Kolner Strasse 18, Lennestadt 57368
Tel: 49 2721 1360
Email: info@sauerlandkurier.de **Web site:** http://www.sauerlandkurier.de
Freq: Sun
Profile: Regionale Tageszeitung mit Lokalnachrichten und Themen aus Kultur, Sport und Unterhaltung. Regional daily newspaper with local news and issues such as culture, sport and entertainment.
Language (s): German
DAILY NEWSPAPER

Schaumburger Nachrichten 159918
Owner: Schaumburger Nachrichten Verlagsges. mbH & Co. KG
Editorial: Vornhager Strasse 44, Stadthagen 31655
Tel: 49 572 1 80 92 30
Email: sn@madsack.de **Web site:** http://www.sn-online.de/
Freq: Mon thru Fri; **Circ:** 28
Profile: Die Schaumburger Nachrichten ist eine Tageszeitung für die Region Schaumburg und Umgebung. Sie gehört zur Verlagsgesellschaft Madsack GmbH & Co. KG The Schaumburger Nachrichten is daily newspaper for the Schaumburger region and surrounding. It belongs to Verlagsgesellschaft Madsack GmbH & Co. KG
Language (s): German
DAILY NEWSPAPER

Schenefelder Tageblatt 159886
Owner: A. Beig Druckerei und Verlag GmbH & Co. KG
Editorial: Damm 9-19, Pinneberg 25421
Tel: 49 4101 535 6121
Email: redaktion@a-beig.de **Web site:** http://www.shz.de/lokales/schenefelder-tageblatt/
Freq: Mon thru Fri; **Circ:** 28
Profile: Das Schenefelder Tageblatt ist eine Tageszeitung für Schenefeld und bietet lokale Berichterstattung, sowie Nachrichten aus der Region Pinneberg. Sie gehört zur Schleswig-Holsteinischer Zeitungsverlag GmbH & Co. KG.
Language (s): German
DAILY NEWSPAPER

Schleswiger Nachrichten 159890
Owner: sh:z Schleswig-Holsteinischer Zeitungsverlag GmbH & Co. KG
Editorial: Stadtweg 54, Schleswig 24837
Tel: 49 4621 808 12 00
Email: redaktion.schleswig@shz.de **Web site:** http://www.shz.de/lokales/schleswiger-nachrichten/
Freq: Mon thru Fri; **Circ:** 28
Profile: Die Schleswiger Nachrichten ist eine Lokalzeitung des Schleswig-Holsteinischen Zeitungsverlags für Schleswig und bietet lokale Berichterstattung, sowie Nachrichten aus der Umgebung.
Language (s): German
DAILY NEWSPAPER

Schleswig-Holsteinische Landeszeitung 159893
Owner: sh:z Schleswig-Holsteinischer Zeitungsverlag GmbH & Co. KG
Editorial: sh:z Schleswig-Holsteinischer Zeitungsverlag GmbH & Co. KG, Fordestrasse 20, Flensburg 24944 **Tel:** 49 800 20507100
Email: redaktion@shz.de **Web site:** http://www.shz.de/lokales/landeszeitung/
Freq: Mon thru Fri; **Circ:** 28
Profile: Die Schleswig-Holsteinische Landeszeitung ist eine Tageszeitung für das Bundesland Schleswig Holstein. Sie gehört zur Schleswig-Holsteinischer Zeitungsverlag GmbH & Co. KG. The Schleswiger-Holsteinische Landeszeitung is a daily newspaper for the Bundesland Schleswig Holstein. It belongs to Schleswig-Holsteinischer Zeitungsverlag GmbH & Co. KG.
Language (s): German
DAILY NEWSPAPER

Schönebecker Volksstimme 159897
Owner: Magdeburger Verlags- und Druckhaus GmbH
Editorial: Wilhelm-Hellge-Strasse 71, Schönebeck 39218
Email: redaktion.schoenebeck@volksstimme.de **Web site:** http://www.volksstimme.de/nachrichten/lokal/schoenebeck/
Freq: Mon thru Fri; **Circ:** 28
Profile: Die Schönebecker Volksstimme ist eine Lokalausgabe der Magdeburger Volksstimme und bietet lokale Berichterstattung aus Schönebeck, sowie Nachrichten aus der Region.
Language (s): German
DAILY NEWSPAPER

Schorndorfer Nachrichten 159899
Owner: Zeitungsverlag GmbH & Co. Waiblingen KG
Editorial: Albrecht-Villinger-Strasse 10, Waiblingen 71332 **Tel:** 49 7151 566 0
Email: schorndorf@zvw.de **Web site:** http://www.zvw.de/schorndorf
Freq: Mon thru Fri; **Circ:** 28
Profile: Die Schorndorfer Nachrichten ist eine Tageszeitung für die Region Schorndorf und Umgebung. Sie gehört zur Zeitungsverlag GmbH & Co Waiblingen KG und bietet lokale und regionale Berichterstattung und Nachrichten. The Schongauer Nachrichten is a daily newspaper for the Schorndorf region and surroundings. It belongs to Zeitungsverlag GmbH & Co Waiblingen KG and offers local and regional reporting and news.
Language (s): German
DAILY NEWSPAPER

Schwabacher Tagblatt 159903
Owner: Verlag Nürnberger Presse Druckhaus Nürnberg GmbH & Co. KG
Editorial: Schwabacher Tagblatt, Spitalberg 3, Schwabach 91126 **Tel:** 49 9122 9380 33
Email: st-redaktion@pressenetz.de **Web site:** http://www.nordbayern.de/region/schwabach
Freq: Mon thru Fri; **Circ:** 28
Profile: Das Schwabacher Tagblatt ist eine Tageszeitung für die Region Schwabach und Umgebung. Sie erscheint zusammen mit dem Nürnberger Nachrichten und bietet lokale und regionale Berichterstattung und Nachrichten. Schwabacher Tagblatt is a daily newspaper for the area of Schwabach. It is published together with the Nürnberger Nachrichten and covers local and regional news.
Language (s): German
DAILY NEWSPAPER

Schwäbische Post 159906
Owner: SDZ Druck und Medien GmbH & Co. KG
Editorial: Bahnhofstrasse 65, Aalen 73430
Tel: 49 7361 5 940
Email: redaktion@schwaebische-post.de **Web site:** http://www.schwaebische-post.de/
Freq: Mon thru Fri; **Circ:** 28
Profile: Die Schwäbische Post ist eine Tageszeitung für die Region Aalen und Umgebung. Sie gehört zur SDZ Druck und Medien GmbH & Co. KG. The Schwaebische Post is a daily newspaper for the Aalen region and surroundings. It belongs to zur SDZ Druck und Medien GmbH & Co. KG.
Language (s): German
DAILY NEWSPAPER

Schwäbische Zeitung 159905
Owner: Schwäbischer Verlag GmbH & Co. KG
Editorial: Schwabischer Verlag GmbH & Co. KG, Karlstr. 16, Ravensburg 88212 **Tel:** 49 751 2955 5555
Email: redaktion@schwaebische.de **Web site:** http://www.schwaebische.de/
Freq: Mon thru Fri
Profile: Das Schwäbische Zeitung ist eine Tageszeitung für die Region Schwaben und Umgebung. Sie gehört zur Schwäbischer Verlag GmbH & Co. KG . The Schwäbische Zeitung is a daily newspaper for the Schwaben region and surroundings. It belongs to Schwäbischer Verlag GmbH & Co. KG .
Language (s): German
DAILY NEWSPAPER

Schwäbische Zeitung, Biberach 666459
Owner: Schwäbischer Verlag GmbH & Co. KG
Editorial: Marktplatz 35, Biberach 88400
Tel: 49 7351 5002 60
Email: redaktion.biberach@schwaebische.de **Web site:** http://www.schwaebische.de
Freq: Mon thru Fri; **Circ:** 28
Profile: Schwäbische Zeitung Biberach ist eine regionale Zeitung. Es werden Themen wie Politik, Wirtschaft und Sport behandelt. Schwäbische Zeitung Biberach is a regional newspaper. It covers basic topics such as politics, economy and sport.
Language (s): German
DAILY NEWSPAPER

Schwäbische Zeitung, Friedrichshafen 666461
Owner: Schwäbischer Verlag GmbH & Co. KG
Editorial: Schanzstrasse 11, Friedrichshafen 88045
Tel: 49 7541 70050
Email: redaktion.friedrichshafen@schwaebische.de **Web site:** http://www.schwaebische.de
Freq: Mon thru Fri; **Circ:** 28
Profile: Schwäbische Zeitung Friedrichshafen ist eine regionale Zeitung. Es werden Themen wie Politik, Wirtschaft und Sport behandelt. Schwäbische Zeitung Friedrichshafen is a regional newspaper. It covers basic topics such as politics, economy and sport.
Language (s): German
DAILY NEWSPAPER

Schwäbische Zeitung, Laichingen 666468
Owner: Schwäbischer Verlag GmbH & Co. KG
Editorial: Marktplatz 25/1, Laichingen 89150
Tel: 49 7333 9657 20
Email: redaktion.laichingen@schwaebische.de **Web site:** http://www.schwaebische.de
Freq: Mon thru Fri
Profile: Schwäbische Zeitung Ulm ist eine regionale Zeitung. Es werden Themen wie Politik, Wirtschaft und Sport behandelt. Schwäbische Zeitung Ulm is a regional newspaper. It covers basic topics such as politics, economy and sport.
Language (s): German
DAILY NEWSPAPER

Schwäbische Zeitung, Ravensburg 666463
Owner: Schwäbischer Verlag GmbH & Co. KG
Editorial: Karlstr.16, Ravensburg 88212
Tel: 49 751 29552222
Email: redaktion.ravensburg@schwaebische.de **Web site:** http://www.schwaebische.de
Freq: Mon thru Fri; **Circ:** 28
Profile: Schwäbische Zeitung Ravensburg ist eine regionale Zeitung. Es werden Themen wie Politik, Wirtschaft und Sport behandelt. Schwäbische Zeitung Ravensburg is a regional newspaper. It covers basic topics such as politics, economy and sport.
Language (s): German
DAILY NEWSPAPER

Schwäbische Zeitung, Tuttlingen 912858
Owner: Schwäbischer Verlag GmbH & Co. KG
Editorial: Jagerhofstrasse 4, Tuttlingen 78532
Tel: 49 7461 7015-53
Email: redaktion.stadt.tuttlingen@schwaebische.de **Web site:** http://www.schwaebische.de
Freq: Mon thru Fri; **Circ:** 20325
Profile: Schwäbische Zeitung Tuttlingen ist eine regionale Zeitung. Es werden Themen wie Politik, Wirtschaft und Sport behandelt. Schwäbische Zeitung Tuttlingen is a regional newspaper. It covers basic topics such as politics, economy and sport.
Language (s): German
DAILY NEWSPAPER

Schwäbisches Tagblatt 159904
Owner: Schwäbisches Tagblatt GmbH
Editorial: Schwabisches Tagblatt GmbH, Uhlandstrasse 2, Tübingen 72072
Tel: 49 7071 934 302
Email: redaktion@tagblatt.de **Web site:** http://www.tagblatt.de
Freq: Mon thru Fri; **Circ:** 28
Profile: Das Schwäbisches Tagblatt ist eine Tageszeitung für die Region Tübingen und Umgebung. Sie gehört zum Verlag SCHWÄBISCHES TAGBLATT GmbH. Berichtet wird über regionale Nachrichten, Nachrichten aus aller Welt, Wirtschaft, Politik, Gesellschaft, Kultur und Kunst. The Schwäbische Tagblatt is a daily newspaper for Tübingen and surroundings. It belongs to the publishing house SCHWÄBISCHES TAGBLATT GmbH. It reports on regional news, world news, business, politics, society, culture and art.
Language (s): German
DAILY NEWSPAPER

Schwabmünchner Allgemeine 607473
Owner: Presse-Druck- und Verlags-GmbH
Editorial: Bahnhofstr. 17, Schwabmünchen 86830
Tel: 49 8232 9677 10
Email: redaktion@schwabmuenchner-allgemeine.de **Web site:** http://www.augsburger-allgemeine.de/schwabmuenchen/lokalnachrichten/
Freq: Mon thru Fri; **Circ:** 28
Profile: Die Schwabmünchner Allgemeine ist eine Lokalausgabe der Augsburger Allgemeinen und bietet lokale Berichterstattung aus Schwabmünchen, sowie Nachrichten aus der Umgebung.
Language (s): German
DAILY NEWSPAPER

Schwarzwälder Bote 159908
Owner: Schwarzwälder Bote Mediengesellschaft mbH
Editorial: Schwarzwalder Bote Mediengesellschaft mbH, Kirchtorstr. 14, Oberndorf am Neckar 78727
Tel: 49 7423 78 132
Email: redaktion@schwarzwaelder-bote.de **Web site:** http://www.schwarzwaelder-bote.de/
Freq: Mon thru Fri; **Circ:** 28
Profile: Der Schwarzwälder Bote ist eine Tageszeitung für die Region Schwarzwald und Umgebung. Sie gehört zur Schwarzwälder Bote Medien GmbH und berichtet über regionales Tagesgeschehen und bietet Informationen aus den Rubriken Politik, Sport, Wirtschaft, Gesellschaft, Kultur und Service. Zusätzlich werden Veranstaltungshinweise geboten. The Schwarzwälder Bote is a daily newspaper for the Schwarzwald region and surroundings. It belongs to Schwarzwälder Bote Medien GmbH and reports on regional affairs and provides information from the categories politics, sports, economy, society, culture and service. In addition, event announcements are available.
Language (s): German
DAILY NEWSPAPER

Schweinfurter Tagblatt 159910
Owner: Mediengruppe Main-Post GmbH & Co. KG
Editorial: Schultesstrasse 19a, Schweinfurt 97421
Tel: 49 9721 548 88 82
Email: red.schweinfurt@mainpost.de **Web site:** http://www.mainpost.de/regional/schweinfurt/
Freq: Mon thru Fri; **Circ:** 28
Profile: Das Schweinfurter Tagblatt ist eine Tageszeitung für die Region Schweinfurt und Umgebung. Sie erscheint gehört zur Main-Post GmbH & Co. KG und bietet lokale und regionale Berichterstattung, sowie auch Nachrichten.
Language (s): German
DAILY NEWSPAPER

Schweriner Volkszeitung 159911
Owner: Zeitungsverlag Schwerin GmbH & Co. KG
Editorial: Zeitungsverlag Schwerin GmbH & Co. KG, Gutenbergstrasse 1, Schwerin 19061
Tel: 49 385 63 78 0
Email: redaktion@svz.de **Web site:** http://www.svz.de/
Freq: Mon thru Fri; **Circ:** 28
Profile: Die Schweriner Volkszeitung ist eine Tageszeitung für die Region Schwerin und Umgebung. Sie gehört zur Zeitungsverlag Schwerin GmbH & Co. KG und berichtet aus Rubriken wie Sport, Freizeit, Politik und Gesellschaft. Die Schweriner Volkszeitung bietet zudem Lokalnachrichten und regionale Informationen. The Schweriner Volkszeitung is daily newspaper for the Schwerin region and surroundings. It belongs to Zeitungsverlag Schwerin GmbH & Co. KG and reports from categories such as sport, leisure, politics and society. The Schweriner Volkszeitung also offers local news and regional information.
Language (s): German
DAILY NEWSPAPER

Schweriner Volkszeitung, Hagenow (Hagenower Kreisblatt) 666491
Owner: Zeitungsverlag Schwerin GmbH & Co. KG
Editorial: Lange Strasse 35, Hagenow 19230
Tel: 49 3883 61 08 8239
Email: lrhag@svz.de **Web site:** http://www.svz.de
Freq: Mon thru Fri
Profile: Die Schweriner Volkszeitung Hagenow ist eine lokale Tageszeitung. Es werden Themen behandelt wie Sport, Wirtschaft und lokale Nachrichten. The Schweriner Volkszeitung Hagenow is a local daily newspaper. It deals with themes such as sports, business, and local news.
Language (s): German
DAILY NEWSPAPER

Schweriner Volkszeitung, Schwerin 912959
Owner: Zeitungsverlag Schwerin GmbH & Co. KG
Editorial: Gutenbergstrasse 1, Schwerin 19061
Tel: 49 385 63 78 8157
Email: lrswh@svz.de **Web site:** http://www.svz.de
Freq: Mon thru Fri; **Circ:** 21457
Profile: Die Schweriner Volkszeitung Schwerin ist eine lokale Tageszeitung. Es werden Themen behandelt wie Sport, Wirtschaft und lokale Nachrichten. The Schweriner Volkszeitung Schwerin is a local daily newspaper. It deals with themes such as sports, business, and local news.
Language (s): German
DAILY NEWSPAPER

Schweriner Volkszeitung, Sternberg 666494
Owner: Zeitungsverlag Schwerin GmbH & Co. KG
Editorial: Am Markt 2, Sternberg 19406
Tel: 49 3847 43028210
Email: sternberg@svz.de **Web site:** http://www.prignitzer.de
Freq: Mon thru Fri
Profile: Die Schweriner Volkszeitung Sternberg ist eine lokale Tageszeitung. Es werden Themen behandelt wie Sport, Wirtschaft und lokale Nachrichten. The Schweriner Volkszeitung Sternberg is a local daily newspaper. It deals with themes such as sports, business, and local news.
Language (s): German
DAILY NEWSPAPER

Schwetzinger Zeitung 159912
Owner: Schwetzinger Zeitungsverlag GmbH + Co. KG
Editorial: Carl-Theodor-Strasse 1, Schwetzingen 68723 **Tel:** 49 621 392 01
Email: geschaeftsleitung@mamo.de **Web site:** http://www.morgenweb.de/region/schwetzinger-zeitung-hockenheimer-tageszeitung
Freq: Mon thru Fri; **Circ:** 28
Profile: Die Schwetzinger Zeitung ist eine Tageszeitung für die Region Schwetzingen und Hockenheim. Sie erscheint zusammen mit dem Mannheimer Morgen und beide gehören zur Mannheimer Morgen Großdruckerei und Verlag GmbH. Die Schwetzinger Zeitung berichtet über regionale Themen und Nachrichten aus Wirtschaft, Politik, Sport und Kultur. The Schwetzinger Zeitung is daily newspaper for the Schwetzinger and Hochenheim region. It's published together with the Mannheimer Morgen and both belong to Mannheimer Morgen Großdruckerei und Verlag GmbH. It reports on local news and issues from economy, politics, sports and culture.
Language (s): German
DAILY NEWSPAPER

Segeberger Zeitung 159960
Owner: C.H. Wäser KG GmbH & Co.
Editorial: Hamburger Strasse 26, Bad Segeberg 23795 **Tel:** 49 455 190430
Email: redaktion@segeberger-zeitung.de **Web site:** http://www.segeberger-zeitung.de/
Freq: Mon thru Fri; **Circ:** 28
Profile: Die Segenberger Zeitung ist eine Tageszeitung für die Region Segenberg und Umgebung. Sie erscheint zusammen mit den Kieler Nachrichten und beide gehören Kieler Zeitung Verlags- und Druckerei KG-GmbH & Co. The Segenberger Zeitung is a daily newspaper for the city region Segenberg and surroundings. It's published together with the Kieler Nachrichten and both belong to the Kieler Zeitung Verlags- und Druckerei KG-GmbH & Co.
Language (s): German
DAILY NEWSPAPER

Siegener Zeitung 159915
Owner: Siegener Zeitung, Vorländer & Rothmaler GmbH & Co. KG
Editorial: Obergraben 39, Siegen 57072
Tel: 49 271 59 400
Email: redaktionssekretariat@siegener-zeitung.de
Web site: http://www.siegener-zeitung.de
Freq: Mon thru Fri; **Circ:** 28
Profile: Die Siegener Zeitung ist eine Tageszeitung für die Region Siegen und Umgebung. Sie gehört zur Vorländer & Rothmaler GmbH & Co. KG. The Siegener Zeitung is daily newspaper for the Siegen region and surrounding. It belongs to Vorländer & Rothmaler GmbH & Co. KG
Language (s): German
DAILY NEWSPAPER

Sindelfinger Zeitung / Böblinger Zeitung 159961
Owner: Röhm Verlag & Medien GmbH & Co. KG
Editorial: Rohm Verlag & Medien GmbH & Co. KG, Boblinger Str. 76, Sindelfingen 71065
Tel: 49 7031 862 210
Email: redaktion@szbz.de **Web site:** http://www.szbz.de
Freq: Mon thru Fri; **Circ:** 28
Profile: Sindelfinger Zeitung / Böblinger Zeitung ist eine regionale Zeitung, die über Nachrichten aus dem Kreis Böblingen berichtet. Sindelfinger Zeitung / Böblinger Zeitung is a regional newspaper covering local news around the city of Böblingen.
Language (s): German
DAILY NEWSPAPER

Soester Anzeiger 159919
Owner: W. Jahn Verlag GmbH & Co. KG
Editorial: Schloitweg 19-21, Soest 59494
Tel: 49 292 1 688 0
Email: internet@soester-anzeiger.de **Web site:** http://www.soester-anzeiger.de/
Freq: Mon thru Fri; **Circ:** 28
Profile: Der Soester Anzeiger ist eine Tageszeitung für die Region Soest und Umgebung. Sie gehört zur Jahn Verlag GmbH & Co. KG . Der Soester Anzeiger berichtet aus Rubriken wie Sport, Service, Leben, Lokales und Nachrichten. The Soester Anzeiger is daily newspaper for the Soest region and surrounding. It belongs to Jahn Verlag GmbH & Co. KG. The Soester Anzeiger reports from categories such as sports, service, lifestyle, local information and news.
Language (s): German
DAILY NEWSPAPER

Solinger Tageblatt 159939
Owner: B. Boll Verlag des Solinger Tageblattes GmbH & Co. KG
Editorial: Mummstr. 9, Solingen 42651
Tel: 49 212 299100
Email: redaktion@solinger-tageblatt.de **Web site:** http://www.solinger-tageblatt.de
Freq: Mon thru Fri
Profile: Lokalzeitung für Solingen mit aktuellen Nachrichten, Sport, Kultur und Veranstaltungshinweisen. RSS-Feeds können unter folgendem Link abonniert werden:http://www.solinger-tageblatt.de/Abo-und-Service/Newsfeeds;jsessionid=BA1F988A047D5FEADAB6210B3B7EAAF8 Local newspaper for Solingen with news, sports, culture and event notes.RSS-Feeds are available under the following link: http://www.solinger-tageblatt.de/Abo-und-Service/Newsfeeds;jsessionid=BA1F988A047D5FEADAB6210B3B7EAAF8
Language (s): German
DAILY NEWSPAPER

Solms-Braunfelser 159921
Owner: Wetzlardruck GmbH
Editorial: Elsa-Brandstrom-Str. 18, Wetzlar 35578
Tel: 49 6441 959595
Email: redaktion.wnz@mittelhessen.de **Web site:** http://www.mittelhessen.de
Freq: Daily; **Circ:** 28
Profile: Tageszeitung mit regionalem Nachrichten- und Sportteil. Daily newspaper with regional news and a local sports section.
Language (s): German
DAILY NEWSPAPER

Stader Tageblatt 159926
Owner: Zeitungsverlag Krause GmbH & Co. KG
Editorial: Zeitungsverlag Krause GmbH & Co KG, Glückstadter Strasse 10, Stade 21682
Tel: 49 414 1 936 333
Email: redaktion-std@tageblatt.de **Web site:** http://www.tageblatt.de/
Freq: Daily; **Circ:** 28
Profile: Das Stader Tageblatt ist eine Tageszeitung für die Stader Region. Sie erscheint zusammen mit anderen Tageszeitungen des Elbe-Weser-Raumes und gehört zur Karl Krause GmbH & Co. KG. The Stader Tageblatt is a daily local newspaper for the Stader region. It's published together with other daily newspaper of the Elbe-Weser region and belongs to the Karl Krause GmbH & Co. KG.
Language (s): German
DAILY NEWSPAPER

Stendaler Volksstimme 159933
Owner: Magdeburger Verlags- und Druckhaus GmbH
Editorial: Hallstr. 51, Stendal 39576
Tel: 49 3931 63899 99
Email: redaktion.stendal@volksstimme.de **Web site:** http://www.volksstimme.de/nachrichten/lokal/stendal/
Freq: Mon thru Fri; **Circ:** 28
Profile: Das Stendaler Volksstimme ist eine Lokalausgabe der Volksstimme für Stendal und bietet lokale Berichterstattung und Nachrichten aus der Umgebung.
Language (s): German
DAILY NEWSPAPER

Straubinger Tagblatt 159935
Owner: Cl. Attenkofer'sche Buch- und Kunstdruckerei
Editorial: Ludwigsplatz 32, Straubing 94315
Tel: 49 942 1 9400
Email: kontakt@idowa.de **Web site:** http://www.idowa.de/zeitung/straubinger-tagblatt
Freq: Mon thru Fri; **Circ:** 28
Profile: Das Straubinger Tagblatt ist eine Tageszeitung für die Region Straubinger-Bogen. Sie gehört der idowaPRO Agentur GmbH & Co. KG. The Straubinger Tagblatt is a daily local newspaper for theStraubbinger-Bogen Region. It belongs to the idowaPRO Agentur GmbH & Co. KG.
Language (s): German
DAILY NEWSPAPER

Stuttgarter Nachrichten 159940
Owner: Stuttgarter Nachrichten Verlagsgesellschaft mbH
Editorial: Stuttgarter Nachrichten Verlagsgesellschaft mbH, Plieninger Strasse 150, Stuttgart 70567
Tel: 49 711 7205 0
Email: cvd@stzn.de **Web site:** http://www.stuttgarter-nachrichten.de/
Freq: Mon thru Fri; **Circ:** 28
Profile: Die Stuttgarter Nachrichten ist eine Tageszeitung für die Stadt-Region Stuttgart und Umgebung. Sie gehört der Stuttgarter Nachrichten Verlagsgesellschaft mbH. The Stuttgarter Nachrichten is a daily newspaper for the city region Stuttgart and surroundings. It belongs to the Stuttgarter Nachrichten Verlagsgesellschaft mbH.
Language (s): German
Ad Rate: Full Page Mono 426.68
Currency: Euro
DAILY NEWSPAPER

Stuttgarter Zeitung 159941
Owner: Stuttgarter Zeitung Verlagsgesellschaft mbH
Editorial: Stuttgarter Zeitung Verlagsgesellschaft mbH, Plieninger Strasse 150, Stuttgart 70567
Tel: 49 711 7205 0
Email: redaktion@stz.zgs.de **Web site:** http://www.stuttgarter-zeitung.de/
Freq: Mon thru Fri; **Circ:** 28
Profile: Die Stuttgarter Zeitung ist eine Tageszeitung für die Stadt und Region Stuttgart und Umgebung. Sie gehört der Stuttgarter Zeitung Verlagsgesellschaft mbH. The Stuttgarter Zeitung is a daily newspaper for the city region Stuttgart and surroundings. It belongs to the Stuttgarter Zeitung Verlagsgesellschaft mbH.
Language (s): German
DAILY NEWSPAPER

Stuttgarter Zeitung Anzeigengemeinschaft Gesamt 913335
Owner: Stuttgarter Zeitung Werbevermarktung GmbH
Editorial: Plieninger Str. 150, Stuttgart 70567
Tel: 49 711 7205 0
Email: info@stzw.zgs.de **Web site:** http://www.stzw.de/
Freq: Mon thru Fri; **Circ:** 434779
Profile: Stuttgarter Zeitung Anzeigengemeinschaft Gesamt ist eine Gemeinschaft an Zeitungen in denen Werbung geschaltet werden kann.
Language (s): German
DAILY NEWSPAPER

Süddeutsche Zeitung 159949
Owner: Süddeutsche Zeitung GmbH
Editorial: Süddeutscher Verlag, Hultschiner Str. 8, München 81677 **Tel:** 49 89 2183 9297
Email: redaktion@sueddeutsche.de **Web site:** http://www.sueddeutsche.de
Freq: Mon thru Fri; **Circ:** 28
Profile: Die Süddeutsche Zeitung ist eine der größten deutschen Tageszeitungen. Sie erscheint im Nordischen Format. Die deutschlandweite Ausgabe enthält Ressorts wie etwa Politik, Kultur, Wirtschaft und Sport. Süddeutsche Zeitung is one of the largest German daily national newspapers and is published in the nordic format. Based in Munich the national edition features several sections such as Politics, Culture, Economy and Sports.
Language (s): German
DAILY NEWSPAPER

Süddeutsche Zeitung, Ebersberg 666502
Owner: Süddeutsche Zeitung GmbH
Editorial: Ebersberger SZ (Redaktion), Ulrichstr. 1, Ebersberg 85560 **Tel:** 49 8092 8266 0
Email: lkr-ebersberg@sueddeutsche.de **Web site:** http://www.sueddeutsche.de/muenchen/ebersberg
Freq: Daily
Profile: Die Süddeutsche Zeitung, Ebersberg ist eine Lokalausgabe für Ebersberg und Umgebung mit einem zusätzlichen Teil mit lokaler und regionaler Berichterstattung. The Süddeutsche Zeitung, Ebersberg is a local issue for Ebersberg and the surrounding area with an additional part with local and regional reporting.
Language (s): German
DAILY NEWSPAPER

Süddeutsche Zeitung, Erding 666505
Owner: Süddeutsche Zeitung GmbH
Editorial: Redaktion Erding, Lange Zeile 10, Erding 85435 **Tel:** 49 8122 9730 0
Email: lkr-erding@sueddeutsche.de **Web site:** http://www.sueddeutsche.de/muenchen/erding
Freq: Daily
Profile: Die Süddeutsche Zeitung, Erding ist eine Lokalausgabe für Erding und Umgebung mit einem zusätzlichen Teil mit lokaler und regionaler Berichterstattung. The Süddeutsche Zeitung, Erding is a local issue for Erding and the surrounding area with an additional part with local and regional reporting.
Language (s): German
DAILY NEWSPAPER

Süddeutsche Zeitung, Freising 666503
Owner: Süddeutsche Zeitung GmbH
Editorial: Redaktion Freising, Johannisstr. 2, Freising 85354 **Tel:** 49 8161 9687 0
Email: lkr-freising@sueddeutsche.de **Web site:** http://www.sueddeutsche.de/muenchen/freising
Freq: Daily
Profile: Die Süddeutsche Zeitung, Freising ist eine Lokalausgabe für Freising und Umgebung mit einem zusätzlichen Teil mit lokaler und regionaler Berichterstattung. The Süddeutsche Zeitung, Freising is a local issue for Freising and the surrounding area with an additional part with local and regional reporting.
Language (s): German
DAILY NEWSPAPER

Süddeutsche Zeitung, Fürstenfeldbruck 666508
Owner: Süddeutsche Zeitung GmbH
Editorial: Schongeisinger Strasse 38 - 40, Fürstenfeldbruck 82256 **Tel:** 49 8141 6114 0
Email: lkr-fuerstenfeldbruck@sueddeutsche.de **Web site:** http://www.sueddeutsche.de/muenchen/fuerstenfeldbruck
Freq: Daily
Profile: Die Süddeutsche Zeitung Fürstenfeldbruck ist eine Lokalausgabe für Fürstenfeldbruck und Umgebung mit einem zusätzlichen Teil mit lokaler und regionaler Berichterstattung. The Süddeutsche Zeitung Fürstenfeldbruck is a local issue for Fürstenfeldbruck and the surrounding area with an additional part with local and regional reporting.
Language (s): German
DAILY NEWSPAPER

Süddeutsche Zeitung, Starnberg (Starnberger SZ) 666501
Owner: Süddeutsche Zeitung GmbH
Editorial: Redaktion Starnberg, Gautinger Str. 9, Starnberg 82319 **Tel:** 49 8151 3605 0
Email: lkr-starnberg@sueddeutsche.de **Web site:** http://www.sueddeutsche.de/muenchen/starnberg
Freq: Mon thru Fri
Profile: Die Süddeutsche Zeitung, Starnberg ist eine Lokalausgabe für Starnberg und Umgebung mit einem zusätzlichen Teil mit lokaler und regionaler Berichterstattung. The Süddeutsche Zeitung, Starnberg is a local issue for Starnberg and the surrounding area with an additional part with local and regional reporting.
Language (s): German
DAILY NEWSPAPER

Süddeutsche Zeitung, Wolfratshausen 666507
Owner: Süddeutsche Zeitung GmbH
Editorial: Redaktion Wolfratshausen, Untermarkt 2, Wolfratshausen 82515 **Tel:** 49 8171 4316 0
Email: lkr-wolfratshausen@sueddeutsche.de **Web site:** http://www.sueddeutsche.de/muenchen/wolfratshausen
Freq: Mon thru Fri
Profile: Die Süddeutsche Zeitung, Wolfratshausen ist eine Lokalausgabe für Wolfratshausen und Umgebung mit einem zusätzlichen Teil mit lokaler und regionaler Berichterstattung. The Süddeutsche Zeitung, Wolfratshausen is a local issue for Wolfratshausen and the surrounding area with an additional part with local and regional reporting.
Language (s): German
DAILY NEWSPAPER

Südkurier 225521
Owner: SÜDKURIER GmbH Medienhaus
Editorial: SÜDKURIER GmbH Medienhaus, Max-Stromeyer-Str. 178, Konstanz 78467
Tel: 49 800 880 8000
Email: kontakt@suedkurier.de **Web site:** http://www.suedkurier.de
Freq: Mon thru Fri
Profile: Der SÜDKURIER ist eine Tageszeitungen in Baden-Württemberg. Er erscheint in einem Gebiet zwischen Rheinfelden vor den Toren Basels und Friedrichshafen am Bodensee sowie in den Schwarzwald hinein bis über Villingen-Schwenningen hinaus - mit 16 Lokalausgaben und dem Alb-Boten.SÜDKURIER is a daily newspaper in Baden-Württemberg. It is distributed in an area between Rheinfelden on the outskirts of Basel and Friedrichshafen at Lake Constance, the Black Forest and Villingen-Schwenningen - with 16 local editions and the Alb-messenger.
Language (s): German
DAILY NEWSPAPER

Südkurier Region Schwarzwald 913372
Owner: SÜDKURIER GmbH, Medienhaus
Editorial: Max-Stromeyer-Str. 178, Konstanz 78467
Tel: 49 800 8808000
Email: info@suedkurier.de **Web site:** http://www.suedkurier.de
Freq: Mon thru Fri; **Circ:** 25307
Profile: Südkurier Region Schwarzwald ist eine regionale Tageszeitung. Es werden lokale Themen behandelt sowie Nachrichten aus Wirtschaft, Sport und Politik.
Language (s): German
DAILY NEWSPAPER

Südkurier, Bodenseekreis 913356
Editorial: Max-Stromeyer-Str. 178, Konstanz 78467
Tel: 49 800 880 8000
Email: info@suedkurier.de **Web site:** http://www.suedkurier.de
Freq: Mon thru Fri; **Circ:** 19947
Profile: Südkurier Bodenseekreis ist eine Tageszeitung. Es werden lokale Themen behandelt sowie Nachrichten aus Wirtschaft, Sport und Politik.
Language (s): German
DAILY NEWSPAPER

Südkurier, Friedrichshafen 159948
Owner: Südkurier GmbH
Editorial: Südkurier Lokalredaktion Friedrichshafen, Karlstrasse 35, Friedrichshafen 88045
Tel: 49 7541 7070 0
Email: friedrichshafen.redaktion@suedkurier.de **Web site:** http://www.suedkurier.de
Freq: Daily; **Circ:** 28
Profile: Regionale Ausgabe für Friedrichshafen der Tageszeitung Südkurier. Regional edition for Friedrichshafen of the daily newspaper Südkurier.
Language (s): German
DAILY NEWSPAPER

Südkurier, Konstanz 904012
Owner: SÜDKURIER GmbH, Medienhaus
Editorial: Max-Stromeyer-Str. 178, Konstanz 78467
Freq: Mon thru Fri; **Circ:** 17089
Profile: Südkurier Konstanz ist eine regionale Tageszeitung. Es werden lokale Themen behandelt sowie Nachrichten aus Wirtschaft, Sport und Politik.
Language (s): German
DAILY NEWSPAPER

Südkurier, Radolfzell/Stockach 913362
Editorial: Max-Stromeyer-Str. 178, Konstanz 78467
Tel: 49 800 8808000
Email: info@suedkurier.de **Web site:** http://www.suedkurier.de
Freq: Mon thru Fri; **Circ:** 28
Profile: Südkurier Radolfzell/Stockach ist eine Tageszeitung. Es werden lokale Themen behandelt sowie Nachrichten aus Wirtschaft, Sport und Politik.
Language (s): German
DAILY NEWSPAPER

Südkurier, Region Bodensee 913364
Owner: SÜDKURIER GmbH, Medienhaus
Editorial: Max-Stromeyer-Str. 178, Konstanz 78467
Tel: 49 800 8808000
Email: info@suedkurier.de **Web site:** http://www.suedkurier.de
Freq: Mon thru Fri; **Circ:** 73663
Profile: Südkurier Region Bodensee ist eine Tageszeitung. Es werden lokale Themen behandelt sowie Nachrichten aus Wirtschaft, Sport und Politik.
Language (s): German
DAILY NEWSPAPER

Südkurier, Region Hochrhein 913369
Owner: SÜDKURIER GmbH, Medienhaus
Editorial: Max-Stromeyer-Str. 178, Konstanz 78467
Tel: 49 800 8808000
Email: info@suedkurier.de **Web site:** http://www.suedkurier.de
Freq: Mon thru Fri; **Circ:** 26457
Profile: Südkurier Region Hochrhein ist eine Tageszeitung. Es werden lokale Themen behandelt sowie Nachrichten aus Wirtschaft, Sport und Politik.
Language (s): German
DAILY NEWSPAPER

Südkurier, Singen 666512
Owner: SÜDKURIER GmbH, Medienhaus
Editorial: Max-Stromeyer-Str. 178, Konstanz 78467
Tel: 49 880 8000
Email: info@suedkurier.de **Web site:** http://www.suedkurier.de
Freq: Mon thru Fri; **Circ:** 28
Profile: Südkurier, Singen ist eine regionale Tageszeitung. Es werden lokale Themen behandelt sowie Nachrichten aus Wirtschaft, Sport und Politik.
Language (s): German
DAILY NEWSPAPER

Südkurier, Villingen-Schwenningen 666517
Owner: SÜDKURIER GmbH, Medienhaus
Editorial: Max-Stromeyer-Str. 178, Konstanz 78467
Tel: 49 800 8808000
Email: info@suedkurier.de **Web site:** http://www.suedkurier.de
Freq: Mon thru Fri; **Circ:** 28

Profile: Südkurier, Villingen-Schwenningen ist eine regionale Tageszeitung. Es werden lokale Themen behandelt sowie Nachrichten aus Wirtschaft, Sport und Politik.
Language (s): German
DAILY NEWSPAPER

Südkurier, Waldshut-Tiengen 666515
Owner: SÜDKURIER GmbH, Medienhaus
Editorial: Max-Stromeyer-Str. 178, Konstanz 78467
Email: info@suedkurier.de **Web site:** http://www.suedkurier.de
Freq: Mon thru Fri; **Circ:** 28
Profile: Südkurier, Waldshut-Tiengen ist eine regionale Tageszeitung. Es werden lokale Themen behandelt sowie Nachrichten aus Wirtschaft, Sport und Politik.
Language (s): German
DAILY NEWSPAPER

Südostbayerische Rundschau 159950
Owner: Neue Presse Multimedia GmbH
Editorial: Gabelsbergerstrasse 4-6, Trostberg 83308
Tel: 49 8621 808 25
Email: red.heimatzeitung@vgp.de **Web site:** http://www.heimatzeitung.de/suedostbayerische_rundschau/
Freq: Mon thru Fri
Profile: Die Südostbayerische Rundschau ist eine Regionalzeitung der Neue Presse Multimedia GmbH und bietet Berichterstattung und Nachrichten aus der Region zwischen Tittmoning, Laufen, Freilassing, Ainring und das Gebiet rund um den Waginger See.
Language (s): German
DAILY NEWSPAPER

Südthüringer Zeitung 159942
Owner: Suhler Verlagsgesellschaft mbH & Co. KG
Editorial: Suhler Verlagsgesellschaft mbH & Co. KG, Andreasstrasse 11, Bad Salzungen 36433
Tel: 49 3695 55 50 50
Email: redaktion@stz-online.de **Web site:** http://www.insuedthueringen.de/
Freq: Mon thru Fri; **Circ:** 28
Profile: Die Südthüringer Zeitung ist eine Tageszeitung für die Region Südthüringen. Sie gehört der Suhler Verlagsgesellschaft mbH & Co. KG und bietet regionale Berichterstattung und Nachrichten The Südthüringer Zeitung is a daily newspaper for the region Südthüringen. It belongs to the Suhler Verlagsgesellschaft mbH & Co. KG and offers regional reporting and news.
Language (s): German
DAILY NEWSPAPER

Südthüringer Zeitung, Schmalkalden 913422
Owner: Suhler Verlagsgesellschaft mbH & Co. KG
Editorial: Hoffnung 26, Schmalkalden 98574
Tel: 49 3683 6976 0
Email: lokal.schmalkalden@stz-online.de **Web site:** http://www.insuedthueringen.de/lokal/schmalkalden/
Freq: Mon thru Fri; **Circ:** 10125
Profile: Die Südthüringer Zeitung Schmalkalden ist eine lokale Tageszeitung. Es werden Themen aus der Region behandelt sowie Sport, Wirtschaft und Politik.
Language (s): German
DAILY NEWSPAPER

SÜDWEST PRESSE 159953
Owner: Neue Pressegesellschaft mbH & Co. KG
Editorial: Neue Pressegesellschaft mbH & Co. KG, Frauenstrasse 77, Ulm 89073 **Tel:** 49 731 156 0
Email: redaktion@swp.de **Web site:** http://www.swp.de/ulm
Freq: Mon thru Fri; **Circ:** 28
Profile: Regionale Tageszeitung für die Region Ulm, Neu-Ulm und Baden-Württemberg. Regional daily newspaper for the region of Ulm, Neu-Ulm and Baden-Württemberg.
Language (s): German
Ad Rate: Full Page Mono 235.71
Currency: Euro
DAILY NEWSPAPER

SWP/Schwäbische Donauzeitung Neu-Ulm 913707
Owner: Neue Pressegesellschaft mbH & Co. KG
Editorial: Frauenstrasse 77, Ulm 89073
Tel: 49 731 156234
Email: regionalredaktion@swp.de **Web site:** http://www.swp.de
Freq: Mon thru Fri; **Circ:** 12443
Profile: SWP/Schwäbische Donauzeitung Neu-Ulm ist eine regionale Tageszeitung. Es werden regionale Themen behandelt sowie Politik und Sport.
Language (s): German
DAILY NEWSPAPER

Taunus Zeitung 159970
Owner: Frankfurter Societäts-Medien GmbH
Editorial: Schwedenpfad 2, Bad Homburg 61348
Tel: 49 6172 92 73 0
Email: tz-badhomburg@fnp.de **Web site:** http://www.taunus-zeitung.de/
Freq: Mon thru Fri; **Circ:** 28
Profile: Die Taunus Zeitung ist eine Tageszeitung für die Taunus und Rhein-Main Region. Sie erscheint zusammen mit der Frankfurter Neuen Presse und wird von der Lokalredaktion Bad Homburg erstellt.
Language (s): German
DAILY NEWSPAPER

taz, Berlin 893542
Owner: taz Verlags- und Vertriebs GmbH
Editorial: taz Verlags- und Vertriebs GmbH, Rudi-Dutschke-Str. 23, Berlin 10969 **Tel:** 49 30 25 902 0
Email: berlin@taz.de **Web site:** http://www.taz.de
Freq: Daily; **Circ:** 8208
Profile: Regionalausgabe für Berlin der Tageszeitung taz. Regional edition for Berlin of the daily newspaper taz.
Language (s): German
DAILY NEWSPAPER

taz.die tageszeitung 159968
Owner: taz Verlags- und Vertriebs GmbH
Editorial: taz Verlags- und Vertriebs GmbH, Rudi-Dutschke-Str. 23, Berlin 10969 **Tel:** 49 30 259 02 0
Email: impressum@taz.de **Web site:** http://www.taz.de
Freq: Mon thru Fri
Profile: die tageszeitung (oft auch taz genannt) ist eine Tageszeitung aus Berlin im Besitz einer Genossenschaft. Sie wurde 1979 gegründet und hat einen starken Fokus auf Umwelt und unterstützt die Grünen. Davon abgesehen bietet sie die gleiche Auswahl von Themen wie die meisten anderen Tageszeitungen (Politik, Wirtschaft, Kultur, Sport etc.) die tageszeitung (referred to commonly as taz) is a daily, cooperative-owned German newspaper based in Berlin. It was founded in 1979 and has a strong focus on ecology and support for the German Green Party. Apart from that, it provides the same range of topics like most other national newspapers (politics, business, culture, sports etc.).
Language (s): German
DAILY NEWSPAPER

Tegernseaktuell 159972
Owner: Hofbuchdruckerei Adalbert Boemmel und Sohn
Editorial: Gasse 22, Gmund 83703
Tel: 49 664 97 34 356
Email: tegernsee@tegernseeaktuell.de **Web site:** http://www.tegernseeaktuell.de
Freq: Mon thru Fri; **Circ:** 28
Profile: Der Tegernseaktuell ist eine Zeitung für das Region Tegernseer. TheTegernseaktuell is a newspaper for the Tegernseer Region.
Language (s): German
DAILY NEWSPAPER

Thüringer Allgemeine, Ilmenau 914847
Owner: ZGT Verlag GmbH
Editorial: August-Bebel-Strasse 3, Ilmenau 99693
Tel: 49 3677 86 39 11
Email: ilmenau@thueringer-allgemeine.de **Web site:** http://www.thueringer-allgemeine.de
Freq: Mon thru Fri; **Circ:** 13373
Profile: Thüringer Allgemeine TA, Ilmenau ist eine regionale Tageszeitung. Es werden Themen aus der Region behandelt sowie Sport, Wirtschaft und Politik.
Language (s): German
DAILY NEWSPAPER

Thüringer Allgemeine, Nordhausen 666535
Owner: ZGT Verlag GmbH
Editorial: Bahnhofstrasse 33, Nordhausen 99734
Tel: 49 3631 605811
Email: nordhausen@thueringer-allgemeine.de **Web site:** http://www.thueringer-allgemeine.de
Freq: Mon thru Fri
Profile: Thüringer Allgemeine, Nordhausen ist eine regionale Tageszeitung. Es werden Themen aus der Region behandelt sowie Sport, Wirtschaft und Politik.
Language (s): German
DAILY NEWSPAPER

Thüringer Allgemeine, Weimar 666536
Owner: Zeitungsgruppe Thüringer Verwaltungsges. mbH
Editorial: Goetheplatz 9a, Weimar 99423
Tel: 49 3643 558130
Email: weimar@thueringer-allgemeine.de **Web site:** http://www.thueringer-allgemeine.de
Freq: Mon thru Fri
Profile: Thüringer Allgemeine, Weimar ist eine regionale Tageszeitung. Es werden Themen aus der Region behandelt sowie Sport, Wirtschaft und Politik.
Language (s): German
DAILY NEWSPAPER

Thüringische Landeszeitung 159984
Owner: Mediengruppe Thüringen Verlag GmbH
Editorial: Mediengruppe Thüringen Verlag GmbH, Marienstrasse 14, Weimar 99423 **Tel:** 49 3643 2063
Email: chefredaktion@tlz.de **Web site:** http://www.tlz.de
Freq: Mon thru Fri
Profile: Die Thüringische Landeszeitung ist eine Tageszeitung für das Bundesland Thüringen. Sie erscheint zusammen mit der Kreiszeitung Syke und beide gehören der ZGT Verlag GmbH. The Thüringer Landeszeitung is a daily newspaper for the federal state of Thüringen. It's published together with the Kreiszeitung Syke and both belong to ZGT Verlag GmbH.
Language (s): German
DAILY NEWSPAPER

Thüringische Landeszeitung, Erfurt 909831
Owner: Mediengruppe Thüringen Verlag GmbH
Editorial: Mediengruppe Thüringen Verlag GmbH, Meyfartstrasse 19, Erfurt 99084 **Tel:** 49 361 55 50 53 3
Email: erfurt@tlz.de **Web site:** http://erfurt.tlz.de
Freq: Mon thru Fri; **Circ:** 31544
Profile: Lokalausgabe der Thüringischen Landeszeitung für Erfurt. Local edition of the THüringische Landeszeitung (Daily regional newspaper) for the town of Erfurt.
Language (s): German
DAILY NEWSPAPER

Thüringische Landeszeitung, Gotha (Gothaer Tagespost) 159986
Owner: Mediengruppe Thüringen Verlag GmbH
Editorial: Mediengruppe Thüringen Verlag GmbH, Gartenstrasse 28, Gotha 99867 **Tel:** 49 3621 354163
Email: gotha@tlz.de **Web site:** http://gotha.tlz.de
Freq: Mon thru Fri
Profile: Die Gothaer Tagespost ist eine Lokalausgabe der Thüringischen Landeszeitung für Gotha und Umgebung, mit lokaler und regionaler Berichterstattung, sowie mit Nachrichten aus Politik, Wirtschaft, Kultur, Gesellschaft und Sport. The Gothaer Tagespost is a local edition of the Thüringische Landeszeitung for Gotha and the surrounding area, with local and regional reporting, as well as with news from politics, business, culture, society and sports.
Language (s): German
DAILY NEWSPAPER

Thüringische Landeszeitung, Heiligenstadt 909828
Owner: Mediengruppe Thüringen Verlag GmbH
Editorial: Mediengruppe Thüringen Verlag GmbH, Wilhelmstrasse 59, Heiligenstadt 37308
Tel: 49 3606 66 95 10
Email: heiligenstadt@tlz.de **Web site:** http://www.tlz.de
Freq: Daily; **Circ:** 267800
Profile: Lokalausgabe der Thüringer Landeszeitung für den Ort Heiligenstadt mit Nachrichten aus Politik, Wirtschaft, Gesellschaft und Sport. Local edition of the Thüringer Landeszeitung for the town of Heiligenstadt with news on polotics, business, society and sports.
Language (s): German
DAILY NEWSPAPER

Traunreuter Anzeiger 159997
Owner: Alois Erdl KG
Editorial: Rathausplatz 7, Traunreut 83301
Tel: 49 8669 4643
Email: red.heimatzeitung@vgp.de **Web site:** http://www.heimatzeitung.de/lokales/landkreis_traunstein/
Freq: Mon thru Fri
Profile: Der Traunreuter Anzeiger ist eine Tageszeitung für Traunreute und Umgebung. Sie gehört der Neue Presse Multimedia GmbH und bietet lokale Berichterstattung und Nachrichten aus der Umgebung.
Language (s): German
DAILY NEWSPAPER

Traunsteiner Tagblatt 159998
Owner: A. Miller, Zeitungsverlag KG
Editorial: Marienstrasse 12, Traunstein 83278
Tel: 49 861 98770
Email: lokales@traunsteiner-tagblatt.de **Web site:** http://www.traunsteiner-tagblatt.de/
Freq: Mon thru Fri
Profile: Das Traunsteiner Tagblatt ist eine Tageszeitung für die Region Traunstein und Umgebung. Sie gehört der A. Miller Zeitungsverlag KG und bietet lokale und regionale Berichterstattung, sowie Nachrichten aus Politik, Sport, Kultur und Gesellschaft.
Language (s): German
DAILY NEWSPAPER

Trierischer Volksfreund 160001
Owner: Volksfreund-Druckerei Nikolaus Koch GmbH
Editorial: Volksfreund-Druckerei Nikolaus Koch GmbH, Hanns-Martin-Schleyer-Strasse 8, Trier 54294
Tel: 49 651 7199 0
Email: redaktion@volksfreund.de **Web site:** http://www.volksfreund.de
Freq: Mon thru Fri; **Circ:** 28
Profile: Der Trierische Volksfreund ist eine Tageszeitung für die Stadtregion Trier und Umgebung. Sie gehört der Volksfreund-Druckerei Nikolaus Koch GmbH. The Trierischer Volksfreund is a daily newspaper for the city region Trier and surroundings. It belongs to Volksfreund-Druckerei Nikolaus Koch GmbH.
Language (s): German
DAILY NEWSPAPER

Trostberger Tagblatt 160003
Owner: Alois Erdl KG
Editorial: Medienstrasse 5, Passau 94036
Tel: 49 851 8020
Email: redaktion@erdl-verlag.de **Web site:** http://www.heimatzeitung.de/
Freq: Mon thru Fri
Profile: Das Trostberger Tagblatt ist eine Tageszeitung für die Region Chiemgau und Umgebung. Sie gehört der Neue Presse Multimedia GmbH. The Trostberger Tagblatt is a daily newspaper for the region Chiemgau and surroundings. It belongs to Neue Presse Multimedia GmbH.
Language (s): German
DAILY NEWSPAPER

Tür-Tor-Fenster-Report 775163
Editorial: VFZ-Verlag für Zielgruppeninformationen GmbH & Co. KG, Hengsener Strasse 14, Dortmund 44309 **Tel:** 49 231 92505550
Email: ttf@vfz-verlag.de **Web site:** http://www.tuer-tor-report.com/
Profile: Fachzeitschrift für die Hersteller von Türen, Toren und Fenstern mit Berichten zu neuen Produkten, Technologie, Veranstaltungen. Messen, Nachrichten aus den Verbänden. Trade magazine for manufacturers of doors, gates and windows with reports on new products, technology, events. Fairs, news from the associations.
Language (s): German
DAILY NEWSPAPER

tz 160004
Owner: Zeitungsverlag tz München GmbH & Co. KG
Editorial: Zeitungsverlag tz München GmbH & Co. KG, Paul-Heyse-Str. 2-4, München 80336
Tel: 49 89 5306 0
Email: sekretariat@tz-online.de **Web site:** http://www.tz.de
Freq: Mon thru Fri; **Circ:** 28
Profile: Die tz ist eine Tageszeitung für das Bundesland Bayern. Sie gehört der Zeitungsverlag tz München GmbH & Co. KG. The tz is a daily newspaper for the federal state of Bayern. It belongs to Zeitungsverlag tz München GmbH & Co. KG.
Language (s): German
DAILY NEWSPAPER

Uckermark Kurier 160005
Owner: Kurierverlags GmbH & Co. KG
Editorial: Friedrich-Engels-Ring 29, Neubrandenburg 17033 **Tel:** 49 800 7036030
Email: red-templin@uckermarkkurier.de **Web site:** http://www.uckermarkkurier.de/
Freq: Daily; **Circ:** 28
Profile: Der Uckermark Kurier ist eine Tageszeitung für die Region Uckermark. Sie gehört der Kurierverlags GmbH & Co.KG.

The Uckermark Kurier is a daily newspaper for the Uckermark region. It belongs to Kurierverlags GmbH & Co.KG.
Language (s): German
DAILY NEWSPAPER

Verdener Aller-Zeitung 160015
Owner: Kreiszeitung Verlagsges. mbH & Co. KG
Editorial: Grosse Strasse 1, Verden 27283
Tel: 49 4231 801 125
Email: redaktion.verden@kreiszeitung.de **Web site:** http://www.kreiszeitung.de/lokales/verden/
Freq: Mon thru Fri; **Circ:** 28
Profile: Die Verdener Aller-Zeitung ist eine Tageszeitung für die Stadtregion Verden und Umgebung. Sie erscheint zusammen mit der Kreiszeitung Syke und bietet vor allem lokale Berichterstattung, sowie auch Nachrichten aus der Umgebung.
Language (s): German
DAILY NEWSPAPER

Viechtacher Bayerwald-Bote 160017
Owner: Neue Presse Verlags-GmbH
Editorial: Monchshofstrasse 9, Viechtach 94234
Tel: 49 9942 947 221
Email: red.viechtach@pnp.de **Web site:** http://www.pnp.de/region_und_lokal/landkreis_regen/viechtach/
Freq: Mon thru Fri; **Circ:** 28
Profile: Der Viechtaler Bayerwald Bote ist eine Tageszeitung für Viechtach und Umgebung und bietet vor allem lokale Berichterstattung, sowie auch Nachrichten aus der Umgebung. Sie erscheint zusammen mit der Neuen Passauer Presse.
Language (s): German
DAILY NEWSPAPER

Volksblatt 160027
Owner: Mediengruppe Main-Post GmbH & Co. KG
Editorial: Berner Str. 2, Würzburg 97084
Tel: 49 931 60010
Web site: http://www.mainpost.de
Freq: Daily; **Circ:** 28
Profile: Regionale Tageszeitung für Würzburg mit regionalen Themen und Nachrichten. Regional daily newspaper for Würzburg covering regional topics and news.
Language (s): German
DAILY NEWSPAPER

Volksstimme Halberstadt 914261
Owner: Magdeburger Verlags- und Druckhaus GmbH
Editorial: Westendorf 6, Halberstadt 38820
Tel: 49 3941 69 92 20
Email: redaktion.halberstadt@volksstimme.de **Web site:** http://www.volksstimme.de
Freq: Mon thru Fri; **Circ:** 12586
Profile: Volksstimme Halberstadt ist eine regionale Tageszeitung. Es werden Themen aus der Region behandelt sowie Sport, Wirtschaft und Politik.
Language (s): German
DAILY NEWSPAPER

Volksstimme Oschersleben/ Wanzleben 666551
Owner: Magdeburger Verlags- und Druckhaus GmbH
Editorial: Hornhauser Strasse 6, Oschersleben 39387
Tel: 49 3949 94 69 20

Email: redaktion.oschersleben@volksstimme.de **Web site:** http://www.volksstimme.de
Freq: Mon thru Fri; **Circ:** 28
Profile: Volksstimme Oschersleben/Wanzleben ist eine regionale Tageszeitung. Es werden Themen aus der Region behandelt sowie Sport, Wirtschaft und Politik.
Language (s): German
DAILY NEWSPAPER

Volksstimme Wernigerode 914288
Owner: Magdeburger Verlags- und Druckhaus GmbH
Editorial: Breite Strasse 48, Wernigerode 38855
Tel: 49 3943 92 14 20
Email: redaktion.wernigerode@volksstimme.de **Web site:** http://www.volksstimme.de
Freq: Mon thru Fri; **Circ:** 16855
Profile: Volksstimme Wernigerode ist eine regionale Tageszeitung. Es werden Themen aus der Region behandelt sowie Sport, Wirtschaft und Politik.
Language (s): German
DAILY NEWSPAPER

Waiblinger Kreiszeitung 914366
Owner: Zeitungsverlag GmbH & Co. Waiblingen KG
Editorial: Albrecht-Villinger-Strasse 10, Waiblingen 71332 **Tel:** 49 7151 5660
Email: kreis@zvw.de **Web site:** http://www.zvw.de
Freq: Mon thru Fri; **Circ:** 14676
Profile: Waiblinger Kreiszeitung ist eine deutsche Regionalzeitung für Waiblingen in Baden-Württemberg. Waiblinger Kreiszeitung is a German regional newspaper for Waiblingen in Baden-Württemberg.
Language (s): German
DAILY NEWSPAPER

Waiblinger Kreiszeitung Gesamt 160031
Owner: Zeitungsverlag GmbH & Co. Waiblingen KG
Editorial: Albrecht-Villinger-Strasse 10, Waiblingen 71332 **Tel:** 49 7151 5660
Email: kreis@zvw.de **Web site:** http://www.zvw.de/
Freq: Mon thru Fri; **Circ:** 28
Profile: Die Waiblinger Kreiszeitung ist eine Tageszeitung für die Stadtregion Stuttgart und Umgebung. Sie gehört der Zeitungsverlag GmbH & Co Waiblingen KG.

The Waiblinger Kreiszeitung is a daily newspaper for the city region Stuttgart and surroundings. It belongs to Zeitungsverlag GmbH & Co Waiblingen KG.
Language (s): German
DAILY NEWSPAPER

Waldeckische Landeszeitung-Frankenberger Zeitung 160032
Owner: Wilhelm Bing Druckerei und Verlag GmbH
Editorial: Lengefelder Strasse 6, Korbach 34497
Tel: 49 5631 56000
Email: info@wlz-fz.de **Web site:** http://www.wlz-fz.de/
Freq: Mon thru Fri; **Circ:** 28
Profile: Die Waldeckische Landeszeitungist eine Tageszeitung für die Region Korbach. Sie gehört der W. Bing Druckerei und Verlag GmbH. The Waldeckische Landeszeitung is a daily newspaper for the region Korbach. It belongs to W. Bing Druckerei und Verlag GmbH.
Language (s): German
DAILY NEWSPAPER

Waldkraiburger Nachrichten 160033
Owner: Oberbayerisches Volksblatt GmbH & Co. Medienhaus KG
Editorial: Berliner Strasse 22, Waldkraiburg 84478
Tel: 49 8638 9818 0
Email: redaktion@waldkraiburger-nachrichten.de **Web site:** http://www.ovb-online.de/muehldorf/waldkraiburg/
Freq: Mon thru Fri; **Circ:** 28
Profile: Die Waldkraiburger Nachrichten ist eine Tageszeitung für Waldkraiburg mit Fokus auf lokaler Berichterstattung. Sie gehört zur Oberbayerischen Volksblatt GmbH & Co. Medienhaus KG.
Language (s): German
DAILY NEWSPAPER

Walsroder Zeitung 160035
Owner: J. Gronemann GmbH & Co. KG
Editorial: J. Gronemann GmbH & Co. KG, Lange Str. 14, Walsrode 29664 **Tel:** 49 5161 6005 0
Email: WalsroderZeitung@wz-net.de **Web site:** http://www.wz-net.de
Freq: Mon thru Fri; **Circ:** 28
Profile: Die Walsroder Zeitung ist eine Tageszeitung für Walsrode in der Region Niedersachsen. Sie gehört der J. Gronemann GmbH & Co. KG und bietet vor allem lokale Berichterstattung und Nachrichten. Walsroder Zeitung is a daily newspaper for Walsrode in the region of Lower Saxony. It belongs to the J. Gronemann GmbH & Co. KG and covers local news.
Language (s): German
DAILY NEWSPAPER

Wasserburger Zeitung 160037
Owner: Oberbayerisches Volksblatt GmbH & Co. Medienhaus KG
Editorial: Marienplatz 16, Wasserburg 83512
Tel: 49 8071 9155 0
Email: redaktion@wasserburger-zeitung.de **Web site:** http://www.ovb-online.de/rosenheim/wasserburg/
Freq: Mon thru Fri; **Circ:** 28
Profile: Wasserburger Zeitung ist eine deutsche Regionalzeitung für Wasserburg in in Bayern. Es werden Nachrichten zu Politik, Wirtschaft und Kultur angeboten. Wasserburger Zeitung is a German regional newspaper for Wasserburg in Bavaria. It covers news on politics, business and culture.
Language (s): German
DAILY NEWSPAPER

WAZ Westdeutsche Allgemeine Zeitung 160057
Owner: FUNKE MEDIEN NRW GmbH
Editorial: FUNKE MEDIEN NRW GmbH, Friedrichstrasse 34 - 38, Essen 45128
Tel: 49 800 60 60 760
Email: zentralredaktion@waz.de **Web site:** http://www.derwesten.de
Freq: Daily
Profile: Die Westdeutsche Allgemeine Zeitung (WAZ) stellt mit ihren 28 Lokalausgaben Deutschlands größte Regionalzeitung dar und konzentriert sich auf das Ruhr-Gebiet. Sie berichtet sowohl auf nationaler als auch auf internationaler Ebene aus den Bereichen Politik, Wirtschaft, Sport und Kultur; deckt aber ebenso regionsspezifische Berichterstattung ab. RSS-Feeds können unter folgendem Link abonniert werden:http://derwesten.dynamic.feedsportal.com/pf/637009/www.derwesten.de/sport/lokalsport/altkreis-brilon/?service=rss Publishing 28 local editions, the Westdeutsche Allgemeine Zeitung (WAZ) represents Germany's biggest regional daily newspaper and focuses on the Ruhr area. Besides reporting on politics, economy, sports and culture on a national and international basis, it also provides region-specific news coverage.RSS-feeds are available under the following link: http://derwesten.dynamic.feedsportal.com/pf/637009/www.derwesten.de/sport/lokalsport/altkreis-brilon/?service=rss
Language (s): German
DAILY NEWSPAPER

WAZ Westdeutsche Allgemeine Zeitung, Bochum 666620
Owner: FUNKE DIGITAL GmbH & Co. KG
Editorial: Westdeutsche Allgemeine, Huestrasse 25, Bochum 44787 **Tel:** 49 234 966 1433
Email: redaktion.bochum@waz.de **Web site:** http://www.derwesten.de/staedte/bochum/
Freq: Daily
Profile: WAZ Westdeutsche Allgemeine Zeitung, Bochum ist die lokale Ausgabe der Regionalzeitung WAZ in Bochum. WAZ Westdeutsche Allgemeine Zeitung, Bochum is the regional edition of the regional newspaper WAZ in Bochum.
Language (s): German
DAILY NEWSPAPER

WAZ Westdeutsche Allgemeine Zeitung, Gladbeck 666635
Owner: FUNKE DIGITAL GmbH & Co. KG
Editorial: Westdeutsche Allgemeine, Horster Strasse 10, Gladbeck 45964 **Tel:** 49 2043 2998 38
Email: redaktion.gladbeck@waz.de **Web site:** http://www.derwesten.de/staedte/gladbeck/
Freq: Daily
Profile: WAZ Gladbeck ist die lokale Ausgabe der Regionalzeitung WAZ für die Stadt Gladbeck und Umgebung. Sie bietet lokale und regionale Berichterstattung und Nachrichten.
Language (s): German
DAILY NEWSPAPER

WAZ Westdeutsche Allgemeine Zeitung, Herne & Wanne-Eickel 666625
Owner: FUNKE DIGITAL GmbH & Co. KG
Editorial: Westdeutsche Allgemeine, Markgrafenstrasse 1, Herne 44623
Tel: 49 2323 9526 31
Email: redaktion.herne@waz.de **Web site:** http://www.derwesten.de/staedte/nachrichten-aus-herne-und-wanne-eickel/
Freq: Daily
Profile: WAZ Westdeutsche Allgemeine Zeitung, Herne ist die lokale Ausgabe der Regionalzeitung WAZ in Herne. WAZ Westdeutsche Allgemeine Zeitung, Herne is the regional edition of the regional newspaper WAZ in Herne.
Language (s): German
DAILY NEWSPAPER

WAZ Westdeutsche Allgemeine Zeitung, Witten 666631
Owner: FUNKE DIGITAL GmbH & Co. KG
Editorial: Westdeutsche Allgemeine, Bahnhofstrasse 62, Witten 58452 **Tel:** 49 2302 91030 30
Email: redaktion.witten@waz.de **Web site:** http://www.derwesten.de/staedte/witten
Freq: Daily
Profile: WAZ Westdeutsche Allgemeine Zeitung, Bochum ist die lokale Ausgabe der Regionalzeitung WAZ in Witten. WAZ Westdeutsche Allgemeine Zeitung, Bochum is the regional edition of the regional newspaper WAZ in Witten.
Language (s): German
DAILY NEWSPAPER

Weiler Zeitung 160040
Owner: Oberbadisches Verlagshaus Georg Jaumann GmbH & Co.KG
Editorial: Redaktion Weiler Zeitung, Hauptstrasse 286, Weil Am Rhein 79576 **Tel:** 49 7621 98 20 10
Email: wzgst@verlagshaus-jaumann.de **Web site:** http://www.verlagshaus-jaumann.de/lokales/weil_am_rhein
Freq: Mon thru Fri; **Circ:** 28
Profile: Die Weiler Zeitung ist eine Tageszeitung für die Region zwischen Basel und Freiburg. Sie erscheint zusammen mit der Die Oberbadische und Markgräfler Tagblatt und gehört der Georg Jaumann GmbH & Co.KG. The Weiler Zeitung is a daily newspaper for the region between Basel and Freiburg. It's published together with the Die Oberbadische and Markgräfler Tagblatt and belongs to the Georg Jaumann GmbH & Co.KG.
Language (s): German
DAILY NEWSPAPER

Weilheimer Tagblatt 160041
Owner: Zeitungsverlag Oberbayern GmbH & Co. KG
Editorial: Münchener Strasse 1, Weilheim 82362
Tel: 49 881 189 0
Email: info@tz-online.de **Web site:** http://www.merkur.de/lokales/weilheim/
Freq: Daily; **Circ:** 28
Profile: Das Weilheimer Tagblatt ist eine Tageszeitung für den Raum Weilheim. Sie gehört zur Münchener Zeitungs-Verlag GmbH & Co.KG . The Weilheimer Tagblatt is a daily newspaper for the Weilheim region. It belongs to Münchener Zeitungs-Verlag GmbH & Co.KG .
Language (s): German
DAILY NEWSPAPER

Weinheimer Nachrichten 160042
Owner: DiesbachMedien GmbH
Editorial: Friedrichstrasse 24, Weinheim 69469
Tel: 49 6201 81 129
Email: online@diesbachmedien.de **Web site:** http://www.wnoz.de/
Freq: Mon thru Fri
Profile: Weinheimer Nachrichten Odenwälder Zeitung ist eine deutsche Regionalzeitung für die Regionen Weinheim und Odenwald. Die Zeitung bietet Themen wie Politik, Wirtschaft, Business, Regional, National – und internationale Nachrichten sowie Sport, Kultur, Freizeit und Entertainment an. Weinheimer Nachrichten Odenwälder Zeitung is a German regional newspaper for Weinheim and Odenwald. It covers topics such as politics, economics, business, regional, national and international news, sports, culture, leisure and entertainment.
Language (s): German
DAILY NEWSPAPER

WELT am SONNTAG 160046
Owner: WeltN24 GmbH
Editorial: WeltN24 GmbH, Axel-Springer-Strasse 65, Berlin 10969 **Tel:** 49 30 2591 0
Email: redaktion@welt.de **Web site:** http://www.welt.de
Freq: Sun; **Circ:** 28
Profile: WELT am SONNTAG ist die Sonntagsausgabe der Zeitung DIE WELT und bietet nationale und internationale Nachrichten, als auch Informationen zu Wirtschaft, Kultur, Gesellschaft und Wissensthemen. WELT am SONNTAG is the Sunday edition of the newspaper DIE WELT and provides national and international news, as well as information on economy, culture, society and science.
Language (s): German
DAILY NEWSPAPER

Wendlinger Zeitung 160048
Owner: Senner Verlag GmbH
Editorial: Carl-Benz-Strasse 1, Nürtingen 72622
Tel: 49 7022 94640
Email: support@ntz.de **Web site:** http://www.ntz.de/nachrichten/wendlingen/
Freq: Daily; **Circ:** 28
Profile: Die Wendlinger Zeitung ist eine Tageszeitung für die Stadtregion Wendlingen und Umgebung. Sie erscheint zusammen mit den Nürtinger Zeitung und gehört der Senner Verlag GmbH.

The Wendlinger Zeitung is a daily newspaper for town region Wendlingen and surroundings. It's published together with the Nürtinger Nachrichten and belongs to the Senner Verlag GmbH.
Language (s): German
DAILY NEWSPAPER

Werra-Rundschau 160051
Owner: Werra Verlag Kluthe GmbH & Co. KG
Editorial: Vor dem Berge 2, Eschwege 37269
Tel: 49 5651 335955
Email: redaktion@werra-rundschau.de **Web site:** http://www.werra-rundschau.de/
Freq: Mon thru Fri; **Circ:** 28
Profile: Die Werra Rundschau ist eine Tageszeitung für die Region Werra. Sie gehört der Werra Verlag Kluthe GmbH & Co. KG und bietet lokale und regionale Berichterstattung aus der Umgebung.
Language (s): German
DAILY NEWSPAPER

WESER-KURIER 159297
Owner: WESER-KURIER Mediengruppe
Editorial: WESER-KURIER Mediengruppe, Martinistrasse 43, Bremen 28195 **Tel:** 49 421 36710
Email: redaktion@weser-kurier.de **Web site:** http://www.weser-kurier.de
Freq: Mon thru Fri; **Circ:** 28
Profile: Die Bremer Nachrichten ist eine regionale Tageszeitung, die in Bremen erscheint. Sie wurde von der Weser-Kurier GmbH übernommen und erscheint nun unter dem Namen Weser Kurier. The Bremer Nachrichten is a regional newspaper that appears in Bremen. It has been taken over by the Weser-Kurier GmbH and is now being published under the name Weser Kurier.
Language (s): German
DAILY NEWSPAPER

Westdeutsche Zeitung 160090
Owner: Westdeutsche Zeitung GmbH & Co. KG
Editorial: Westdeutsche Zeitung GmbH & Co. KG, Otto-Hausmann-Ring 185, Wuppertal 42115
Tel: 49 202 717 0
Email: westdeutsche.zeitung@wz-newsline.de **Web site:** http://www.wz-newsline.de
Freq: Mon thru Fri; **Circ:** 28
Profile: Die Westdeutsche Zeitung ist eine Tageszeitung für das Ruhrgebiet. Sie gehört der W. Girardet GmbH & Co. KG und bietet lokale und regionale Berichterstattung, sowie auch Nachrichten. The Westdeutsche Zeitung is a daily newspaper for the Ruhr region. It belongs to the W. Girardet GmbH & Co. KG and offers local and regional reporting, as well as news.
Language (s): German
DAILY NEWSPAPER

Westdeutsche Zeitung, Krefeld 666569
Owner: Westdeutsche Zeitung GmbH & Co. KG
Editorial: Rheinstrasse 76, Krefeld 47799
Tel: 49 2151 8552830
Email: redaktion.krefeld@wz.de **Web site:** http://www.wz-newsline.de
Freq: Mon thru Fri
Profile: WZ Westdeutsche Zeitung Krefeld ist eine lokale Tageszeitung. Es werden Themen aus der Region behandelt sowie Sport, Wirtschaft und Politik.
Language (s): German
DAILY NEWSPAPER

Westdeutsche Zeitung, Mettmann 666571
Owner: Westdeutsche Zeitung GmbH & Co. KG
Editorial: Otto-Hausmann-Ring 185, Wuppertal 42115 **Tel:** 49 202 7172535
Email: redaktion.kreis-mettmann@wz.de **Web site:** http://www.wz-newsline.de
Freq: Mon thru Fri
Profile: WZ Westdeutsche Zeitung, Mettmann ist eine lokale Tageszeitung. Es werden Themen aus der Region behandelt sowie Sport, Wirtschaft und Politik.
Language (s): German
DAILY NEWSPAPER

Westdeutsche Zeitung, Mönchengladbach 666565
Owner: Westdeutsche Zeitung GmbH & Co. KG
Editorial: Rheinstrasse 76, Krefeld 47799
Tel: 49 2151 855 0
Email: redaktion.moenchengladbach@westdeutsche-zeitung.de **Web site:** http://www.wz-newsline.de/lokales/moenchengladbach
Freq: Daily
Profile: Die Lokalausgabe der Westdeutschen Zeitung für Mönchengladbach und Umgebung bietet regionale und lokale Berichterstattung, sowie Nachrichten aus Politik, Kultur, Wirtschaft, Gesellschaft und Sport. The local edition of the Westdeutsche Zeitung for Mönchengladbach and the surrounding area offers regional and local coverage, as well as news from politics, culture, economy, society and sports.
Language (s): German
DAILY NEWSPAPER

Westerwälder Zeitung 160058
Owner: Mittelrhein-Verlag GmbH
Editorial: Konrad-Adenauer-Platz 3, Montabaur 56410 **Tel:** 49 2602 1604 78
Email: montabaur@rhein-zeitung.net **Web site:** http://www.rhein-zeitung.de
Freq: Mon thru Fri; **Circ:** 28
Profile: Westerwälder Zeitung ist eine deutsche Regionalzeitung für den Westerwald. Sie behandelt Regionalnachrichten zu Politik, Kultur und Wirtschaft. Westerwälder Zeitung is a German regional newspaper for the Westerwald region. It covers regional news on politics, culture and business.
Language (s): German
DAILY NEWSPAPER

Westfalen-Blatt 160062
Owner: WESTFALEN-BLATT Vereinigte Zeitungsverlage GmbH
Editorial: WESTFALEN-BLATT Vereinigte Zeitungsverlage GmbH, Sudbrackstrasse 14-18, Bielefeld 33611 **Tel:** 49 521 585 0
Email: wb@westfalen-blatt.de **Web site:** http://www.westfalen-blatt.de
Freq: Mon thru Fri; **Circ:** 28
Profile: Das Westfalen Blatt ist eine Tageszeitung für die Region Westfalen. Sie erscheint zusammen mit der Augsburger Allgemeinen und gehört der WESTFALEN-BLATT Vereinigte Zeitungsverlage GmbH. The Westfalen Blatt is a daily newspaper for the Westfalen region. It's published together with the Augsburger Allgemeinen and belongs to the WESTFALEN-BLATT Vereinigte Zeitungsverlage GmbH.
Language (s): German
DAILY NEWSPAPER

Westfalen-Blatt, Bünde 159308
Owner: Herforder Kreisblatt Busse GmbH & Co. KG
Editorial: Eschstrasse 17, Bünde 32257
Tel: 49 5223 179 410
Email: redaktion@buender-zeitung.de **Web site:** http://www.westfalen-blatt.de/startseite/
Freq: Daily; **Circ:** 28
Profile: Tageszeitung mit regionalem Nachrichten- und Sportteil. Daily newspaper with regional news and a local sports section.
Language (s): German
DAILY NEWSPAPER

Westfalen-Blatt, Herford 914380

Owner: Westfalen-Blatt Vereinigte Zeitungsverlage GmbH
Editorial: Brüderstrasse 30, Herford 32052
Tel: 49 5221 590 811
Email: herford@westfalen-blatt.de **Web site:** http://www.westfalen-blatt.de
Freq: Mon thru Fri; **Circ:** 16193
Profile: WB Kreis Herford ist eine regionale Tageszeitung. Es werden Themen aus der Region behandelt sowie Sport, Wirtschaft und Politik.
Language (s): German
DAILY NEWSPAPER

Westfalen-Blatt, Paderborn 160061

Owner: Westfalen-Blatt Vereinigte Zeitungsverlage GmbH
Editorial: Westfalisches Volksblatt, Redaktion Paterborn, Senefelderstrasse 13, Paderborn 33100
Tel: 49 5251 896 120
Email: redaktion@westfaelisches-volksblatt.de **Web site:** http://www.westfalen-blatt.de
Freq: Daily; **Circ:** 47058
Profile: Westfalen-Blatt, Kreis Paderborn (Westfälisches Volksblatt) ist eine Tageszeitung für die Region Westfalen. Sie erscheint zusammen mit der Augsburger Allgemeinen und gehört der WESTFALEN-BLATT Vereinigte Zeitungsverlage GmbH. Westfalen-Blatt, Kreis Paderborn (Westfälisches Volksblatt) is a daily newspaper for the Westfalen region. It's published together with the Augsburger Allgemeinen and belongs to the WESTFALEN-BLATT Vereinigte Zeitungsverlage GmbH.
Language (s): German
DAILY NEWSPAPER

Westfalen-Blatt, Schlangen 158187

Owner: Westfalen-Blatt Vereinigte Zeitungsverlage GmbH
Editorial: Ortsmitte 4, Bielefeld 33189
Tel: 49 521 5850
Email: schlangen@westfalen-blatt.de **Web site:** http://www.westfalen-blatt.de
Freq: Daily; **Circ:** 28
Profile: Regional daily newspaper covering local news and topics. Regionale Tageszeitung mit regionalen Nachrichten und Themen.
Language (s): German
DAILY NEWSPAPER

Westfalenpost 402931

Owner: FUNKE Mediengruppe GmbH & Co, KGaA
Editorial: WP-Lokalredaktion Hagen, Schürmannstrasse 4, Hagen 58097
Tel: 49 2331 917 4159
Email: westfalenpost@westfalenpost.de **Web site:** http://www.derwesten.de/wp/
Freq: Daily; **Circ:** 28
Profile: Die Westfalenpost ist eine Regionalzeitung für den Süden von NRW (Südwestfalen) mit Nachrichten, Sport, Gesellschaft, Politik und Kultur. The Westfalenpost is a regional newspaper for the south of North Rhine-Westphalia (South Westalia) with news, sports, society, politics and culture.
Language (s): German
DAILY NEWSPAPER

Westfälische Nachrichten 160059

Owner: Aschendorff Medien GmbH & Co. KG
Editorial: Aschendorff Medien GmbH & Co. KG, An der Hansalinie 1, Munster 48163 **Tel:** 49 251 690 0
Email: redaktion@wn.de **Web site:** http://www.wn.de/
Freq: Mon thru Fri; **Circ:** 28
Profile: Die Westfälischen Nachrichten ist eine Tageszeitung für die Region Westfalen. Sie gehört der Aschendorff Medien GmbH & Co. KG. The Westfaelischen Nachrichten is a daily newspaper for the Westfalen region. It belongs to the Aschendorff Medien GmbH & Co. KG.
Language (s): German
DAILY NEWSPAPER

Westfälische Nachrichten Steinfurt-Burgsteinfurt 914631

Owner: Aschendorff Medien GmbH & Co. KG
Editorial: Wilhelmsplatz 1, Steinfurt 48565
Tel: 49 2551 939470
Email: redaktion.bur@wn.de **Web site:** http://www.wn.de/Muensterland/Kreis-Steinfurt/Steinfurt
Freq: Mon thru Fri; **Circ:** 14515
Profile: Die Westfälischen Nachrichten Steinfurt-Burgsteinfurt sind eine Lokalausgabe der WN und bieten lokale Berichterstattung und Nachrichten aus der Umgebung.
Language (s): German
DAILY NEWSPAPER

Westfälischer Anzeiger, Bönen 666613

Owner: Westfälischer Anzeiger Verlagsges.mbH
Editorial: Westfalischer Anzeiger Verlagsgesellschaft mbH & Co. KG, Gutenbergstr. 1, Hamm 59065
Tel: 49 2381 105 0
Email: internet@wa.de **Web site:** http://www.wa.de
Freq: Daily
Profile: In dieser lokalen Zeitung sind Neuigkeiten von regionalem Interesse aus NRW zu finden. In this local newspaper news of regional interest from NRW are found .
Language (s): German
DAILY NEWSPAPER

Westfälischer Anzeiger, Werne 666614

Owner: Westfälischer Anzeiger Verlagsgesellschaft mbH & Co. KG
Editorial: Westfalischer Anzeiger Verlagsgesellschaft mbH & Co. KG, Gutenbergstr. 1, Hamm 59065
Tel: 49 2381 105 0
Email: internet@wa.de
Freq: Daily
Profile: In dieser regionalen Zeitung sind Neuigkeiten von regionalem Interesse aus NRW zu finden. In this regional newspaper news of regional interest from NRW are found .
DAILY NEWSPAPER

Wetterauer Zeitung 160063

Owner: Mittelhessische Druck- und Verlagsges. mbH
Editorial: Parkstrasse 16, Postfach 10 04 62, Bad Nauheim 61217 **Tel:** 49 6032 9420
Email: redaktion@wetterauer-zeitung.de **Web site:** http://www.wetterauer-zeitung.de
Freq: Mon thru Fri; **Circ:** 28
Profile: Die Wetterauer Zeitung ist eine Tageszeitung für den Wetteraukreis und bietet lokale und regionale Berichterstattung und Nachrichten aus der Umgebung. Sie gehört zur Mittelhessische Druck- und Verlagshaus GmbH & Co.KG.
Language (s): German
DAILY NEWSPAPER

Wetzlarer Neue Zeitung 160064

Owner: Wetzlardruck GmbH
Editorial: Wetzlardruck GmbH, Elsa-Brandstrom-Strasse 18, Wetzlar 35578 **Tel:** 49 6441 959 697
Email: lokalredaktion.wnz@mittelhessen.de **Web site:** http://www.mittelhessen.de/lokales/region-wetzlar.html
Freq: Daily; **Circ:** 28
Profile: Die Wetzlarer Neue Zeitung ist eine Tageszeitung für die Region Mittelhessen. Sie gehört der Wetzlardruck GmbH. The Wetzlarer Neue Zeitung is a daily newspaper for the Mittelhessen region. It belongs to the Wetzlardruck GmbH.
Language (s): German
DAILY NEWSPAPER

Wiesbadener Kurier 160066

Owner: Verlagsgruppe Rhein Main GmbH & Co. KG
Editorial: Verlagsgruppe Rhein Main GmbH & Co. KG, Erich-Dombrowski-Strasse 2, Mainz 552117
Tel: 49 611 3550
Email: impressum@vrm.de **Web site:** http://www.wiesbadener-kurier.de/index.htm
Freq: Mon thru Fri; **Circ:** 28
Profile: Der Wiesbadener Kurier ist eine Tageszeitung für die Region Rhein-Main. Sie gehört der Verlagsgruppe Rhein Main GmbH & Co. KG. The Wiesbadener Kurier is a daily newspaper for the Rhein-Main region. It belongs to the Verlagsgruppe Rhein Main GmbH & Co. KG.
Language (s): German
DAILY NEWSPAPER

Wiesbadener Tagblatt 160067

Owner: Verlagsgruppe Rhein Main GmbH & Co. KG
Editorial: Kleine Schwalbacher Str. 3-7, Wiesbaden 65183 **Tel:** 49 611 355 5380
Email: wiesbaden-lokales@vrm.de **Web site:** http://www.wiesbadener-tagblatt.de/index.htm
Freq: Mon thru Fri; **Circ:** 28
Profile: Das Wiesbadener Tagblatt ist eine deutschsprachige Tageszeitung, die in der hessischen Landeshauptstadt Wiesbaden erscheint. The Wiesbaden Tagblatt is a German regional daily newspaper published in Wiesbaden.
Language (s): German
DAILY NEWSPAPER

Wilhelmshavener Zeitung 160071

Owner: Brune-Mettcker Druck- und Verlagsgesellschaft mbH
Editorial: Brune-Mettcker Druck- und Verlagsgesellschaft mbH, Parkstrasse 8, Wilhelmshaven 26382 **Tel:** 49 4421 488 410
Email: redaktion@WZonline.de **Web site:** http://www.wzonline.de/
Freq: Mon thru Fri; **Circ:** 28
Profile: Die Wilhelmshavener Zeitung ist eine Tageszeitung für die Stadtregion Wilhelmshaven. Sie gehört der Brune-Mettcker Druck- und Verlagsgesellschaft mbH. The Wilhelmshavener Zeitung is a daily newspaper for the Wilhelmshaven city region. It belongs to the Brune-Mettcker Druck- und Verlagsgesellschaft mbH.
Language (s): German
DAILY NEWSPAPER

Wilstersche Zeitung 160073

Owner: sh:z Schleswig-Holsteinischer Zeitungsverlag GmbH & Co. KG
Editorial: Fordestrasse 20, Flensburg 24944
Tel: 49 800 2050 7100
Email: redaktion.wilster@shz.de **Web site:** http://www.shz.de/lokales/wilstersche-zeitung/
Freq: Mon thru Fri; **Circ:** 28
Profile: Die Wilstersche Zeitung ist eine Tageszeitung für die Städte Itzehoe, Glückstadt und den Kreis Steinburg. Sie gehört der Schleswig-Holsteinischen Zeitungsverlag GmbH & Co. KG. The Wilstersche Zeitung is a daily newspaper for the towns Itzehoe, Glueckstadt and the Steinburg region. It belongs to the Schleswig-Holsteinischen Zeitungsverlag GmbH & Co. KG.
Language (s): German
DAILY NEWSPAPER

Wolfsburger Allgemeine 160082

Owner: Adolf Enke GmbH & Co. KG
Editorial: Madsack Medien Ostniedersachsen GmbH & Co. KG, Porschestrasse 74, Wolfsburg 38440
Tel: 49 5361 200-139
Email: redaktion@waz-online.de **Web site:** http://www.waz-online.de/
Freq: Mon thru Fri; **Circ:** 28
Profile: Die Wolfsburger Allgemeine ist eine Tageszeitung für die Stadtregion Wolfsburg und Umgebung. Sie gehört der Madsack Medien Ostniedersachsen GmbH & Co. KG. The Wolfsburger Allgemeine is a daily newspaper for the Wolfsburg city region and surroundings. It belongs to the Madsack Medien Ostniedersachsen GmbH & Co. KG
Language (s): German
DAILY NEWSPAPER

Wolmirstedter Volksstimme 562732

Web site: http://www.volksstimme.de
Language (s): German
DAILY NEWSPAPER

Wolmirstedter Volksstimme 888517

Owner: Magdeburger Verlags- und Druckhaus GmbH
Editorial: Bahnhofstrasse 37, Wolmirstedt 39326
Tel: 49 39201 705 20
Email: redaktion.wolmirstedt@volksstimme.de **Web site:** http://www.volksstimme.de/nachrichten/lokal/wolmirstedt/
Freq: Mon thru Fri; **Circ:** 28
Profile: Die Wolmirstedter Volksstimme ist eine Lokalausgabe der Magdeburger Volksstimme für Wolmirstedt. Sie bietet vor allem lokale Berichterstattung und Stadtnachrichten.
DAILY NEWSPAPER

Wormser Zeitung 160084

Owner: Verlagsgruppe Rhein Main GmbH & Co. KG
Editorial: Adenauerring 2, Worms 67547
Tel: 49 6241 8453231
Email: wz-worms@vrm.de **Web site:** http://www.wormser-zeitung.de/index.htm
Freq: Mon thru Fri; **Circ:** 28
Profile: Die Wormser Zeitung ist eine Tageszeitung für die Stadt und Region Worms. Sie gehört der Verlagsgruppe Rhein Main GmbH & Co. KG und bietet lokale und regionale Berichterstattung und Nachrichten aus der Umgebung.
Language (s): German
DAILY NEWSPAPER

Wörther Anzeiger 160080

Owner: Mittelbayerischer Verlag KG
Editorial: Kumpfmühler Strasse 15, Regensburg 93066 **Tel:** 49 9482 9404 12
Email: woerth@mittelbayerische.de **Web site:** http://www.mittelbayerische.de/regensburg-land/
Circ: 28
Profile: Der Wörther Anzeiger ist eine Tageszeitung für Wörth an der Donau in der Region Regensburg. Sie gehört der Mittelbayerischer Verlag KG und wird von der Redaktion Regensburger Land erstellt.
Language (s): German
DAILY NEWSPAPER

Zaman Almanya 914736

Owner: Zukunft Medien GmbH
Editorial: Zukunft Medien GmbH - Redaktion, Reinhardtstrasse 47a, Berlin 10117
Tel: 49 30 46281 60
Email: info@eurozaman.de **Web site:** http://zaman-online.de
Freq: Daily; **Circ:** 22679
Profile: Zaman Almanya ist die in Deutschland verfügbare Ausgabe der türkischen Tageszeitung. Es werden Nachrichten aus Kultur, Gesellschaft, Sport, Wirtschaft und Politik behandelt. Zaman Almanya is the in Germany published Version of a Turkish Daily Newspaper. It offers articles about news from society, culture, sports, economy and politics.
Language (s): Turkish
DAILY NEWSPAPER

Zeitung für Ganderkesee 606691

Owner: Nordwest-Zeitung Verlagsgesellschaft mbH & Co. KG
Editorial: Mühlenstrasse 1, Ganderkesee 27777
Tel: 49 4222 8077 2742
Email: red.ganderkesee@nordwest-zeitung.de **Web site:** http://www.nwzonline.de/ganderkesee
Profile: Die Zeitung für Ganderkesee ist eine Lokalzeitung für Ganderkesee, welche zur Nordwest-Zeitung Verlagsgesellschaft. Die Lokalredaktion aus der Stadt bietet vor allem lokale Berichterstattung und Nachrichten aus der Umgebung.
Language (s): German
DAILY NEWSPAPER

News Service/Syndicate

Deutsche Presse-Agentur (dpa) 353689

Owner: dpa Deutsche Presse-Agentur GmbH
Editorial: Markgrafenstrasse 20, Berlin 10969
Tel: 49 30 2852 0
Email: themendienst@dpa.com **Web site:** http://www.dpa.com
Profile: Die dpa Deutsche Presse-Agentur ist eine deutsche Nachrichtenagentur mit Sitz in Hamburg, während die Zentralredaktion in Berlin zu finden ist. Die Agentur ist in ca. 100 Ländern vertreten und bietet crossmediale, unparteilsche und unabhängige Nachrichten für alle Mediengattungen. Die Agentur ist hierbei in Ressorts wie Wissenschaft, Technik, Sport, ect aufgeteilt.The dpa German Press Agency is a German news agency based in Hamburg, while the central editorial office can be found in Berlin. The Agency has a presence in approximately 100 countries and provides cross-media, impartial and independent news for all types of media. The Agency is divided into departments such as science, technology, sports, ect.
Language (s): German
NEWS SERVICE/SYNDICATE

Deutsche Presse-Agentur (dpa) - Brussels Bureau 581271

Editorial: Boulevard Charlemagne, 1, Boîte 17, Bruxelles 1041 **Tel:** 32 2230 36 91
Email: dpa@dpa.be **Web site:** http://www.dpa.com
Profile: The German Press Agency dpa is a trusted, accurate and independent provider of news with the digital and multimedia content to power the media at home and abroad. Our customers benefit from the extensive global network of correspondents and editors maintained by Germany's leading news wire. News gathering is completely free of outside influence which in turn guarantees that coverage lives up to the strict requirements of the dpa charter: This document lays down that reporting must be free of bias and unfettered by political, economic or governmental ideologies.Print media, radio stations, online and mobile communication providers in more than 100 countries rely on this journalistic excellence around-the-clock. Among dpa clients are parliaments, governmental and non-governmental organisations as well as businesses and public relations agencies. They all derive news content from the wide range of products and services provided by the dpa group of companies.
Language (s): Dutch
NEWS SERVICE/SYNDICATE

Deutsche Presse-Agentur (dpa) - Cyprus Bureau 578765

Editorial: 4, Valtinou str, Strovolos, Nicosia 2045
Tel: 357 22 320417
Email: masis@financialmirror.com
Language (s): Greek
NEWS SERVICE/SYNDICATE

Deutsche Presse-Agentur (dpa) - Moscow Bureau 815013

Owner: dpa Deutsche Presse-Agentur GmbH
Editorial: Kutuzovsky pr. 7/4, office 210, Moskva 121170
Email: moskau@dpa.com
Profile: dpa editorial bureau based in Moscow. Provides news and political coverage on Russia and CIS countries.
Language (s): English
NEWS SERVICE/SYNDICATE

Deutsche Presse-Agentur (dpa) - Sydney Bureau 313580

Owner: DPA - German Press Agency
Editorial: 10 Terry Street, Tempe NSW 2044
Tel: 61 2 9558 2261
Email: sidastbury@bigpond.com **Web site:** http://www.dpa.de
Profile: Sydney bureau of the German Press Agency
Language (s): English
NEWS SERVICE/SYNDICATE

dpa-AFX Wirtschaftsnachrichten GmbH 353688

Owner: dpa-AFX Wirtschaftsnachrichten GmbH
Editorial: Gutleutstrasse 110, Frankfurt 60327
Tel: 49 69 920 22 400
Email: redaktion@dpa-AFX.de **Web site:** http://www.dpa-afx.de
Circ: 28
Profile: Die dpa-AFX Wirtschaftsnachrichten GmbH ist eine real-time Finanz-Nachrichtenagentur und bietet Neuigkeiten aus der Finanz- und Wirtschaftsbranche. dpa-AFX is a German news agency for German and English language real-time financial and economic news.
Language (s): German
NEWS SERVICE/SYNDICATE

epd - Evangelischer Pressedienst 353690

Owner: epd Evangelischer Pressedienst
Editorial: Emil-von-Behring-Str. 3, Frankfurt Am Main 60439 **Tel:** 49 69 58098 0
Email: info@epd.de **Web site:** http://www.epd.de/
Profile: epd - Evangelischer Pressedienst ist ein Nachrichtendienst der evangelischen Kirche, welcher aktuelle Nachrichten bietet. Zudem ist der epd in weitere Redaktionen unterteilt, die sich unter anderem auf Medien und Gesellschaft spezialisieren. epd - Evangelischer Pressedienst is a news service of the Protestant Church, which offers the latest news. In addition, the EPD is divided into more editorial departments, which specialize, among other things, on the media industy and society.
Language (s): German
NEWS SERVICE/SYNDICATE

Reuters Deutschland 604968

Owner: Thomson Reuters (Markets) Deutschland GmbH
Editorial: Friedrich-Ebert-Anlage 49, Frankfurt 60327
Tel: 49 69 75651000
Web site: http://de.reuters.com
Circ: 28

Profile: Nachrichtenagentur mit Schwerpunkt Wirtschaft und Politik. News agency with main focus on economy and politics.
Language (s): German
NEWS SERVICE/SYNDICATE

teleschau - der mediendienst GmbH 801489
Owner: tele-schau – der medi-en-dienst GmbH
Editorial: Ries-str 17, München 80992
Tel: 49 89 1434190
Email: info@teleschau.de
Circ: 28
Profile: teleschau - der Mediendienst GmbH ist ein Mediendienstleister, der redaktionelle Inhalte zu TV, Kino, Musik, Home Entertainment, Games und Digital anbietet. teleschau - Media Service GmbH is a media service provider, that offers editorial content for TV, movies, music, home entertainment, games and digital.
Language (s): German
NEWS SERVICE/SYNDICATE

Community Newspaper

Grafschafter Nachrichten 666288
Owner: Grafschafter Nachrichten GmbH & Co. KG
Editorial: Grafschafter Nachrichten GmbH & Co. KG, Coesfelder Hof 2, Nordhorn 48527
Tel: 49 5921 707 300
Email: gn@gn-online.de **Web site:** http://www.gn-online.de/
Freq: Mon thru Fri; **Circ:** 28
Profile: Die GN Grafschafter Nachrichten sind eine regionale Tageszeitung für die Grafschaft Bentheim und Umgebung mit lokaler und regionaler Berichterstattung und Nachrichten aus Politik, Kultur, Wirtschaft, Gesellschaft und Sport. The GN Grafschafter Nachrichten is a regional daily newspaper for the county of Bentheim and the surrounding area with local and regional reporting and news from politics, culture, economy, society and sports.
Language (s): German
COMMUNITY NEWSPAPER

Hamburger Abendblatt, Norderstedt (Norderstedter Zeitung) 666132
Owner: Axel Springer SE
Editorial: Regionalausgabe Norderstedt, Rathausallee 64-66, Norderstedt 22846
Tel: 49 40 300 62 00
Email: norderstedt@abendblatt.de **Web site:** http://www.abendblatt.de/region/norderstedt/
Freq: Daily; **Circ:** 34000
Profile: Norderstedter Zeitung ist eine deutsche Regionalzeitung für Norderstedt. Sie bietet Nachrichten zu den Bereichen Politik, Wirtschaft und Kultur. Norderstedter Zeitung is a German regional newspaper for Norderstedt and the surrounding area. It covers news on politics, business and culture.
Language (s): German
COMMUNITY NEWSPAPER

Kölner Stadt-Anzeiger, Redaktionsbüro Euskirchen 914780
Owner: DuMont Net GmbH & Co. KG
Editorial: Redaktion Euskirchen, Wilhelmstr. 10-12, Euskirchen 53879 **Tel:** 49 2251 70 04 54 10
Email: redaktion.euskirchen@ksta.de **Web site:** http://www.ksta.de/region/euskirchen-eifel
Circ: 22872
Profile: Kölner Stadt-Anzeiger, Kreis Euskirchen ist eine lokale Tageszeitung. Es werden Themen aus der Region behandelt sowie Sport, Wirtschaft und Politik. Kölner Stadt-Anzeiger, Kreis Euskirchen is a local newspaper that deals with topics of the region as well as sports, economy and politics.
Language (s): German
COMMUNITY NEWSPAPER

Ghana

Time Difference: GMT
National Telephone Code: 233
Continent: Africa
Capital: Accra

Newspapers

The Chronicle 218472
Owner: General Portfolio Ltd.
Editorial: 37, Bobo Street, Tesano, Accra
Tel: 233 30 223 2713
Email: k2blunt2002@yahoo.com **Web site:** http://thechronicle.com.gh
Freq: Daily; **Circ:** 20000 Publisher's Statement
Editor: Emmanuel Akli
Profile: Newspaper covering national and regional news including politics, business, sports, lifestyle, entertainment, and features.
Language (s): English
DAILY NEWSPAPER

Daily Graphic 217970
Owner: Graphic Communications Group Ltd
Editorial: 3 Graphic Road, Accra
Tel: 233 30 2684001
Email: graphic@graphic.com.gh **Web site:** http://graphic.com.gh
Freq: Daily; **Circ:** 150000 Publisher's Statement
Editor: Ransford Tetteh
Profile: Newspaper covering national and regional news including politics, business, sports, lifestyle, entertainment, and features.
Language (s): English
DAILY NEWSPAPER

The Ghanaian Times 217919
Owner: New Times Corporation
Editorial: Ring Road West, Accra
Tel: 233 302 223285
Email: info@ghanaiantimes.com.gh **Web site:** http://www.ghanaiantimes.com.gh
Freq: Daily; **Circ:** 50000 Publisher's Statement
Editor: Dave Agbenu
Profile: Newspaper covering national and international news and current affairs including business, politics, education, culture, entertainment and sports.
Language (s): English
DAILY NEWSPAPER

The Mirror 224415
Owner: Graphic Communications Group Ltd
Editorial: 3 Graphic Road, Accra
Tel: 233 26 461 0155
Email: mirror@graphic.com.gh **Web site:** http://www.graphic.com.gh
Freq: Weekly; **Circ:** 100000 Publisher's Statement
Editor: Ransford Tetteh
Profile: Newspaper focusing on national and regional news, business, politics, culture and sports.
Language (s): English
DAILY NEWSPAPER

News Service/Syndicate

Ghana News Agency 611195
Editorial: Opposite Registrar Generals Department, Ministries, Accra **Tel:** 233 302 662381
Email: ghnews57@yahoo.com **Web site:** http://www.ghananewsagency.org
Editor: Samuel Osei-Frempong
Profile: News agency acting as a central news collection agent of the state, gathers news from all regional, and some district, capitals. With such national spread, GNA is able to promote a viable, united and cohesive nation by highlighting stories that engender development, integration and peace.
Language (s): English
NEWS SERVICE/SYNDICATE

Gibraltar

Time Difference: GMT +1
National Telephone Code: 350
Continent: Europe
Capital: Gibraltar

Newspapers

Gibraltar Chronicle 217934
Owner: Gibraltar Chronicle
Editorial: Watergate House, Casemates, Gibraltar GX11 1AA **Tel:** 350 200 47063
Email: news@chronicle.gi **Web site:** http://www.chronicle.gi
Freq: Daily; **Circ:** 3000 Publisher's Statement
Profile: Newspaper covering regional, national and international news and current affairs including business, economics, politics and sports.
Language (s): English
DAILY NEWSPAPER

Panorama 217935
Owner: Panorama Publishing
Editorial: 95 Irish Town, Gibraltar GX11 1AA
Tel: 350 200 79797
Email: editorial@panorama.gi **Web site:** http://gibraltarpanorama.gi
Freq: Daily; **Circ:** 4500 Publisher's Statement
Editor: Joe Garcia
Profile: Newspaper covering regional, national and international news and current affairs including business, economics, politics, entertainment and sport.
Language (s): English
DAILY NEWSPAPER

Community Newspaper

The New People 953034
Owner: The New People Publishing Ltd
Editorial: Suite 6/608, Icom House, 1/5 Irish Town, Gibraltar GX11 1AA **Tel:** 350 543 74000
Email: thenewpeople@gibtelecom.net **Web site:** http://www.thenewpeople.net
Profile: Weekly newspaper covering regional news and current affairs and politics.
Language (s): English
COMMUNITY NEWSPAPER

Greece

Time Difference: GMT +2
National Telephone Code: 30
Continent: Europe
Capital: Athens

Newspapers

Dimoprasion & Pleistiriasmon 391214
Editorial: Em. Mpenaki 10 & Panepistemiou 57, Athina 105 64 **Tel:** 30 210 32156922103215688
Email: dimonews@dimoprasion.gr **Web site:** http://www.dimoprasion.gr
Freq: Daily; **Circ:** 7800 Not Audited
Profile: Daily morning financial newspaper covering economics and business. Auction News is published in tabloid size.
Language (s): Greek
Ad Rate: Full Page Colour 3000.00
Currency: Euro
DAILY NEWSPAPER

I Efimerida Ton Syntakton 393567
Editorial: Kolokotroni 8, Athina 115 28
Tel: 30 211 1045000
Email: contact@efsyn.gr **Web site:** http://www.efsyn.gr
Freq: Daily; **Circ:** 9160 Publisher's Statement
News Editor: Dimitris Stathopoulos
Profile: Daily newspaper coming out in the afternoon. Founded on October 20, 2012.
Language (s): Greek
DAILY NEWSPAPER

Eleftheros Typos 217941
Editorial: Agias Lavras 2 & Sarantaporou, Neo Iraklio, Athina 14121 **Tel:** 30 210 8113000
Web site: http://www.e-typos.com
Freq: Daily; **Circ:** 9770
Profile: Eleftheros Typos is a daily newspaper published in Athens, and covers national news, politics and business.
Language (s): Greek
Ad Rate: Full Page Colour 6900.00
Currency: Euro
DAILY NEWSPAPER

Espresso 391219
Editorial: Eratosthenous 1, Athina 11635
Tel: 30 210 2503000
Email: espresso@espressonews.gr **Web site:** http://espressonews.gr
Freq: Daily; **Circ:** 9220 Publisher's Statement
Profile: Tabloid-sized daily with general interest news, celebs, show biz, gossip, sports, high life.
Language (s): Greek
Ad Rate: Full Page Colour 5750.00
Currency: Euro
DAILY NEWSPAPER

Ethnos 350442
Owner: Ethnos Publishing S.A.
Editorial: . Benaki 5, Chalandri, Athina 152 38
Tel: 30 210 6062500
Email: ethnos@pegasus.gr **Web site:** http://www.ethnos.gr
Freq: Daily; **Circ:** 9975 Publisher's Statement
Profile: Newspaper covering national and international news with features on business and finance, lifestyle, entertainment and sport.
Language (s): Greek
Ad Rate: Full Page Mono 6900.00
Ad Rate: Full Page Colour 9600.00
Currency: Euro
DAILY NEWSPAPER

Expres 391165
Editorial: 46th km. Avenue, Lavrion, Athina 190 01
Tel: 30 213 161 700
Email: info@express.gr **Web site:** http://www.express.gr
Freq: Daily
Profile: Provides informative articles, detailed analysis, covering entire spectrum of the Greek economy, news about listed companies and major foreign stock markets.
Language (s): Greek
DAILY NEWSPAPER

Imerisia 391229
Owner: Pegasus Publishing S.A.
Editorial: E. Benaki 5, Chalandri, Athina 152 38
Tel: 30 210 6061000
Email: editor@imerisia.gr **Web site:** http://www.imerisia.gr
Freq: Daily; **Circ:** 1394
Profile: Daily newspaper covering Greek politics, business and economics.
Language (s): Greek
Ad Rate: Full Page Colour 6600.00
Currency: Euro
DAILY NEWSPAPER

Karfitsa 725526
Owner: NK Media Group
Editorial: Politechniou 31 (4th floor), Thessaloniki 546 26 **Tel:** 30 210 3218925
Email: press@karfitsa.gr **Web site:** http://www.karfitsa.gr
Circ: 50000
Publisher: Nikos Karamanlis
Profile: Free newspaper from Thessaloniki. Covers daily events with particular emphasis on facts rather than opinions. Provides comments on the current Greek and international political events, contemporary news in the economy and the market, reviews of cultural and social events and sports news.
Language (s): Greek
DAILY NEWSPAPER

Kathimerini 217948
Owner: IHT - Kathimerini S.A.
Editorial: Ethnarhou Makariou & 2 Falireos, Neo Faliro, Athina 185 47 **Tel:** 30 210 4808000
Email: info@kathimerini.gr **Web site:** http://www.kathimerini.gr
Freq: Daily; **Circ:** 26246 Publisher's Statement
Advertising Manager: Deppie Papazoglou
Profile: Newspaper covering politics, economy, culture and social events.
Language (s): English
Ad Rate: Full Page Mono 5200.00
Ad Rate: Full Page Colour 7400.00
Currency: Euro
DAILY NEWSPAPER

Naftemporiki 217901
Owner: P. Athanassiades & Co S.A
Editorial: Lenorman 205, Kolonos, Athina 104 42
Tel: 30 210 51 98 000
Email: editors@naftemporiki.gr **Web site:** http://www.naftemporiki.gr
Freq: Daily; **Circ:** 658 Publisher's Statement
Profile: Financial newspaper covering all aspects of the economic and business environment.
Language (s): Greek
Ad Rate: Full Page Mono 5700.00
Ad Rate: Full Page Colour 7000.00
Currency: Euro
DAILY NEWSPAPER

Ta Nea 217950
Owner: DIM/KOS Organismos Lambrakis A.E.
Editorial: Michalakopoulou 80, Athina 115 28
Tel: 30 211 36 57 000
Email: epistoles@tanea.gr **Web site:** http://www.tanea.gr
Freq: Daily; **Circ:** 17895 Publisher's Statement
Profile: Newspaper covering politics, economy, current affairs and sport.
Language (s): Greek
Ad Rate: Full Page Colour 10350.00
Currency: Euro
DAILY NEWSPAPER

To Paraskhnio 535109
Editorial: Fidiou 14, Athina 106 78
Tel: 30 210 363 4330
Email: grparaskhnio@gmail.com **Web site:** http://www.paraskhnio.gr
Publisher: Nikos Karamanlis; **Editor:** Chris Konstas; **Editor:** Giannis Parginos; **Editor:** Fotis Sioumpouras; **Editor:** Giannis Vassilakopoulos
Profile: Newspaper providing news and reports from Greece and the world, political, economic and social life in the country, views, reportage and sports, media, lifestyle, health, environment, culture, technology and cars.
Language (s): Greek
DAILY NEWSPAPER

Proto Thema 393746
Owner: Proto Thema S.A.
Editorial: Agrafon 5, Marousi, Athina 151 23
Tel: 30 210 6834444
Email: protothema@protothema.gr **Web site:** http://www.protothema.gr
Freq: Weekly; **Circ:** 100160
Managing Director: Themos Anastasiadis; **News Editor:** Vassilis Anastasopoulos; **Editor/Publisher:** Tasos Karamitsos; **Editor:** Alexandros Kasimatis
Profile: Published every Sunday covering international and domestic political events.
Language (s): Greek
Ad Rate: Full Page Colour 15200.00
Currency: Euro
DAILY NEWSPAPER

Real News 668797
Editorial: Kifissias Av. 215, Maroussi, Athina 15124
Tel: 30 211 2008364
Email: info@realnews.gr **Web site:** http://www.real.gr
Freq: Sun; **Circ:** 62200 Publisher's Statement
Profile: Sunday newspaper with 4 supplements: reallife, realmoney, realplanet and realsports.
Language (s): Greek
Ad Rate: Full Page Colour 13000.00
Currency: Euro
DAILY NEWSPAPER

Greece

News Service/Syndicate

ANA-MPA (Athens News Agency) 519911
Editorial: Tsoha 36, Athina 11521
Tel: 30 210 640 0560
Email: ape@ana-mpa.gr **Web site:** http://www.amna.gr
Freq: Daily
Profile: The Athens News Agency - Macedonian Press Agency (ANA-MPA) was founded on Jan. 1, 1905. ANA merged with Macedonian Press Agency (MPA) in 2008 and formed the Athens Macedonian News Agency (AMNA).
Language (s): English
NEWS SERVICE/SYNDICATE

Independent Balkan News Agency 957161
Editorial: PO D3302, Thermi, Thessaloniki 57 001
Tel: 30 2310 460 344
Email: info@balkaneu.com **Web site:** http://www.balkaneu.com
Editor-in-Chief: Spiros Sideris
Profile: Independent Balkan News Agency provides political, economics, social and cultural news from Balkans region.
Language (s): English
NEWS SERVICE/SYNDICATE

Grenada

Time Difference: GMT -4
National Telephone Code: 1 473
Continent: The Americas
Capital: St George's

Community Newspaper

The Grenada Informer 224347
Owner: Moving Target
Editorial: Market Hill, St George's **Tel:** 473 4405762
Email: grenadainformer@yahoo.com **Web site:** http://www.spicegrenada.com
Freq: Weekly; **Circ:** 5000 Not Audited
Editor: Carla-Rae Briggs
Profile: The Grenada Informer is a weekly newspaper featuring national and international news, politics, entertainment and sports.
Language (s): English
Ad Rate: Full Page Mono 5.20
Currency: United States Dollars
COMMUNITY NEWSPAPER

The Grenadian Voice 224456
Owner: Spice Island Printers Ltd
Editorial: Frequente Industrial Estate, Bldg 1B, St George's **Tel:** 473 4403983
Email: gvoice@spiceisle.com
Freq: Weekly; **Circ:** 3500 Not Audited
Profile: The Grenadian Voice is a weekly newspaper focusing on national and international news, politics, business and sports.
Language (s): English
Ad Rate: Full Page Mono 10.00
Currency: United States Dollars
COMMUNITY NEWSPAPER

Guam

Time Difference: GMT +10
National Telephone Code: 1 671
Continent: Oceania
Capital: Hagatna (Agana)

Newspapers

Pacific Daily News 217937
Owner: Gannett Co., Inc.
Editorial: 244 Archbishop Flores Street, Hagatna 96910 **Tel:** 1 671 472-1736
Email: news@guampdn.com **Web site:** http://www.guampdn.com
Freq: Daily; **Circ:** 19469 Not Audited
Publisher & President: Rindraty Limtiaco; **Photography Chief:** Masako Watanabe
Profile: Pacific Daily News is a newspaper focusing on business, finance, economics, culture, social life, sport and general news for the residents of Guam. The paper won the Robert G. McGruder Award for Diversity Leadership.
Language (s): English
Ad Rate: Full Page Mono 54.60
Ad Rate: Full Page Colour 1350.00
Currency: United States Dollars
DAILY NEWSPAPER

Pacific Sunday News 318913
Editorial: 244 Archbishop Flores St, Hagatna 96910
Tel: 671 4790400
Email: news@guampdn.com **Web site:** http://www.guampdn.com
Freq: Weekly; **Circ:** 24000 Not Audited
Profile: Newspaper focusing on business, finance, economics, culture, social life, sport and general news.
Language (s): English
DAILY NEWSPAPER

Guatemala

Time Difference: GMT -6
National Telephone Code: 502
Continent: The Americas
Capital: Guatemala city

Newspapers

La Hora 217962
Owner: Diario La Hora
Editorial: 9A Calle A 1-56, Zona 1, Guatemala 1001
Tel: 502 2 423 1800
Email: lahora@lahora.com.gt **Web site:** http://lahora.gt/
Freq: Daily; **Circ:** 34000 Not Audited
Profile: Local newspaper in Guatemala covering national news, international news, opinion, culture, sports, economy, and lifestyle.
Language (s): Spanish
DAILY NEWSPAPER

Nuestro Diario 218022
Owner: Diarios Modernos S.A.
Editorial: 15 Avenida 24-27, Zona 13, Guatemala
Tel: 502 2 379 1600
Email: opinion@nuestrodiario.com.gt **Web site:** http://www.nuestrodiario.com.gt
Freq: Daily; **Circ:** 275000 Not Audited
Editor: Giovanni Aldana; **Editor in Chief:** Estuardo Pinto
Profile: Newspaper focusing on economics, culture, social life, sport and general news.
Language (s): Spanish
DAILY NEWSPAPER

El Periódico 218021
Owner: Aldea Global S.A.
Editorial: 15 Avenida 24-51, Zona 13, Guatemala
Tel: 502 2 427 2300
Email: redaccion@elperiodico.com.gt **Web site:** http://www.elperiodico.com.gt
Freq: Daily; **Circ:** 30000 Not Audited
Editor: Ana Isabel Villela
Profile: Local newspaper focusing on national and international news, politics, culture, business and sport.
Language (s): Spanish
DAILY NEWSPAPER

El Quetzalteco 218025
Owner: Ediciones Regionales S. A.
Editorial: Avenida Las Americas 9-50 Ofc.4, Zona 3, Centro Comercial Supercom Delco Quetzaltenango, Quetzaltenango **Tel:** 502 7 767 4331
Web site: http://www.elquetzalteco.com.gt
Freq: 2 Times/Week; **Circ:** 45000 Not Audited
Editor: Ady Albores
Profile: Regional newspaper.
Language (s): Spanish
DAILY NEWSPAPER

Community Newspaper

El Metropolitano (Xela) 396702
Owner: Publicaciones y Acesorías Metropolitanas
Editorial: 3a Calle 15-29, Zona 8 de Mixco, Ciudad San Cristobal, Guatemala **Tel:** 502 2 485 4172
Email: elmetropolitanoxela@gmail.com **Web site:** http://www.elmetropolitano.net
Freq: Bi-Weekly; **Circ:** 145000 Not Audited
Editor: Jorge García; **Director:** José Ramón Hernández Santos
Language (s): Spanish
COMMUNITY NEWSPAPER

Prensa Libre 224342
Owner: Prensa Libre S.A.
Editorial: 13 Calle 9-31, Zona 1, Guatemala 1001
Tel: 502 2 412 5000
Email: redaccion@prensalibre.com.gt **Web site:** http://www.prensalibre.com.gt
Freq: Daily; **Circ:** 160000 Not Audited
Director: Maria Mercedes Girón
Profile: Periódico nacional que cubre noticias, deportes, economía, noticias internacionales, opinión y tecnología. National newspaper covering news, sports, economy, international news, opinion, and technology.
Language (s): Spanish
COMMUNITY NEWSPAPER

Guinea

Time Difference: GMT
National Telephone Code: 224
Continent: Africa
Capital: Conakry

Newspapers

Le Diplomate Guinée 518577
Owner: Afric Vision
Editorial: BP 2222, Conakry **Tel:** 224 624 51 51 51
Email: hawasanouci@yahoo.fr **Web site:** http://www.lediplomateguinee.com
Freq: Weekly; **Circ:** 3000 Publisher's Statement
Editor in Chief: Ibrahima Dieng
Profile: Weekly newspaper covering national and international news and current affairs including politics, economics, diplomacy and regional development.
Language (s): French
Ad Rate: Full Page Mono 1400000.00
Ad Rate: Full Page Colour 1800000.00
Currency: Guinea Francs
DAILY NEWSPAPER

News Service/Syndicate

Agence Guinéenne de Presse - AGP 518557
Owner: Agence Guinéenne de Presse
Editorial: Anciens locaux d'Enelgui, 2eme boulevard, 5eme avenue, Conakry **Tel:** 224 623 232 660
Email: agpguinee70@gmail.com **Web site:** http://agpguinee.com
Advertising Manager: Mamadouba Sylla
Profile: Agence Guinéenne de Presse - AGP is the national press agency of Guinea, focussing on news and current affairs.
Language (s): French
NEWS SERVICE/SYNDICATE

Guyana

Time Difference: GMT -4
National Telephone Code: 592
Continent: The Americas
Capital: Georgetown

Newspapers

Guyana Chronicle 217963
Owner: Guyana National Newspapers Ltd
Editorial: 1 Lama Avenue, Bel Air Park, Georgetown
Tel: 592 227-5216
Email: editorial@guyanachronicle.com **Web site:** http://www.guyanachronicle.com
Freq: Daily; **Circ:** 8500 Not Audited
Profile: Newspaper focusing on national and international news, politics, business, culture and sport. Paper also publishes a Sunday edition of the paper called the Sunday Chronicle.
Language (s): English
Ad Rate: Full Page Mono 8.00
Ad Rate: Full Page Colour 22.22
Currency: United States Dollars
DAILY NEWSPAPER

Guyana Times 536853
Owner: Guyana Times, Inc.
Editorial: Queens Atlantic Inudstrial Estate Ruimveldt, Georgetown **Tel:** 1 592 231-8063
Email: news@guyanatimesgy.com **Web site:** http://www.guyanatimesgy.com
Freq: Daily
Editor in Chief: Nigel Williams
Profile: Guyana Times is an English language, daily newspaper serving the residents of Georgetown, Guyana and surrounding areas.
Ad Rate: Full Page Mono 12.18
Currency: United States Dollars
DAILY NEWSPAPER

Kaieteur News 217973
Owner: National Media & Publishing Co.
Editorial: 24 Saffon Street, Charlestown, Georgetown
Email: kaieteurnews@yahoo.com **Web site:** http://www.kaieteurnewsonline.com
Freq: Daily; **Circ:** 30000 Not Audited
Editor in Chief: Adam Harris; **Publisher:** Glenn Lall; **Editor:** Nigel McKenzie
Profile: Kaieteur News is a daily newspaper focusing on crime, corruption, national and international news, politics, business, culture and sports.
Language (s): English
Ad Rate: Full Page Mono 600.00
Currency: United States Dollars
DAILY NEWSPAPER

Stabroek News 217964
Owner: Guyana Publications Inc.
Editorial: 46-47 Robb Street, Lacytown, Georgetown
Tel: 592 227-4080
Email: stabroeknews@stabroeknews.com **Web site:** http://www.stabroeknews.com
Freq: Daily; **Circ:** 21107 Not Audited
Publisher: David De Caires; **Editor in Chief:** Anand Persaud; **Editor:** Cheryl Stabroek
Profile: Stabroek News is a daily newspaper focusing on national and international news, business, culture and sports. The paper also publishes a Sunday edition called the Sunday Stabroek.
Language (s): English
Ad Rate: Full Page Mono 3.12
Ad Rate: Full Page Colour 3.43
Currency: United States Dollars
DAILY NEWSPAPER

Community Newspaper

Mirror (Guyana) 224351
Owner: New Guyana Co. Ltd
Editorial: 8 Industrial Site, Ruimveldt, Georgetown
Tel: 592 2 26 58 75
Email: weekendmirror@gmail.com **Web site:** http://www.mirrornewsonline.com
Freq: Weekly; **Circ:** 40000 Not Audited
Editor: David DeGroot
Profile: Mirror is a weekly newspaper covering national and international news, politics, economics, finance, business, culture and sports.
Language (s): English
Ad Rate: Full Page Mono 3.68
Currency: United States Dollars
COMMUNITY NEWSPAPER

Haiti

Time Difference: GMT -5
National Telephone Code: 509
Continent: The Americas
Capital: Port-au-Prince

Newspapers

Le Nouvelliste 159090
Owner: Le Nouvelliste
Editorial: 198 Rue du Centre, Port-Au-Prince
Tel: 509 22 24-2054
Email: redaction@lenouvelliste.com **Web site:** http://www.lenouvelliste.com
Freq: Daily; **Circ:** 20000 Not Audited
Director: Max E. Chauvet; **Editor in Chief:** Frantz Duval
Profile: Launched in 1898. Newspaper covering national news, events and sports.
Language (s): French
DAILY NEWSPAPER

News Service/Syndicate

L' Agence Haïtienne de Presse (AHP) 747011
Editorial: 6, rue Fernand, Pont Morin, Port-Au-Prince
Tel: 509 22 45-5055
Email: ahphaiti@yahoo.com **Web site:** http://www.ahphaiti.org/ndujour.html
General Manager: Georges Venel Remarais
Profile: Founded in 1989 L'Agence Haïtienne de Presse is a Haitian news service, which publishes news in English, French and Creole.
Language (s): Creole
NEWS SERVICE/SYNDICATE

Holy See (Vatican City)

Time Difference: GMT +1
National Telephone Code: 379
Continent: Europe
Capital: Vatican City

News Service/Syndicate

Agenzia Fides 527193
Editorial: Palazzo "de Propaganda Fide", Citta Del Vaticano 120 **Tel:** 39 06 69 88 01 15
Email: fides@fides.va **Web site:** http://www.fides.org
Capo redattore: Stefano Lodigiani; **Direttore:** Luca Mata
Profile: News and photo agency of the Holly See focussing on religion, news and current affairs and health.
Language (s): Chinese
NEWS SERVICE/SYNDICATE

Holy See Press Office 527194
Editorial: Unavailable, Citta Del Vaticano 120
Tel: 39 06 698 921
Email: lombardi@pressva.va **Web site:** http://www.vatican.va/news_services/press/index.htm
Direttore: Miguel Castellvi
Profile: Official press agency of the Holy See.
Language (s): English
NEWS SERVICE/SYNDICATE

Community Newspaper

L' Osservatore Romano 217951
Owner: Edizioni Tipografia Vaticana
Editorial: Città Del Vaticano **Tel:** 39 06 69883461
Email: segreteria@ossrom.va **Web site:** http://www.osservatoreromano.va/fr
Circ: 60000
Redattore: Piero di Domenicantonio
Profile: L'Osservatore Romano is a daily community newspaper of the Holy See. It covers all the Pope's public activities, publishes editorials by important churchmen, and runs official documents after being released.
Language (s): English
COMMUNITY NEWSPAPER

Honduras

Time Difference: GMT -6
National Telephone Code: 504
Continent: The Americas
Capital: Tegucigalpa

Newspapers

El Heraldo 157081
Owner: El Heraldo
Editorial: Barrio San Felipe, Av. Los Proceres, Aptdo 1938, Tegucigalpa **Tel:** 504 236-6000
Email: diario@elheraldo.hn **Web site:** http://www.elheraldo.hn
Freq: Daily; **Circ:** 90000 Not Audited
Editor in Chief: Fernando Berrios
Profile: Periódico que cubre noticias nacionales e internacionales, política, economía, finanzas, negocios, cultura y deporte. Newspaper covering national and international news, politics, economics, finance, business, culture and sport.
Language (s): Spanish
DAILY NEWSPAPER

La Prensa 157009
Owner: La Prensa
Editorial: 3 Avenida 6-7 Calle Nor-Oeste No 34, Aptdo Postal 143, Barrio Guamilito, San Pedro Sula
Tel: 504 2236-5454
Web site: http://www.laprensa.hn
Freq: Daily; **Circ:** 65000 Not Audited
Editor in Chief: Nélson García; **Editor in Chief:** Ana Morales; **National News Editor:** Armando Munoz;
Editor: Yesille Ponce
Profile: National newspaper covering national and international news, politics, economics, finance, business, culture and sport.
Language (s): Spanish
DAILY NEWSPAPER

La Tribuna 157068
Owner: La Tribuna
Editorial: Colonia Santa Barbara Carretera al Primer Batallon de la Infanteria, Apdo. 1501, Tegucigalpa
Tel: 504 2343206
Email: tribuna@latribuna.hn **Web site:** http://www.latribunahon.com
Freq: Daily; **Circ:** 50000 Not Audited
Editor: Edgardo Dumes Rodríguez; **Editor:** Daniel Vieda
Profile: Newspaper covering national and international news, politics, economics, finance, business, culture and sport.
Language (s): Spanish
DAILY NEWSPAPER

Hong Kong

Time Difference: GMT +8
National Telephone Code: 852
Continent: Asia
Capital: Hong Kong

Newspapers

am730 489941
Editorial: 10/F, Overseas Trust Bank Building, 160 Gloucester Rd, Hong Kong **Tel:** 852 34083730
Email: info@am730.com.hk **Web site:** http://www.am730.com.hk
Freq: Daily; **Circ:** 272510 Not Audited
Editor: Kusche Cheng; **Editor in Chief:** Kenneth Dai;
Editor: Ceiling Lee; **Publisher:** Alan Lo
Profile: Covers local and international news, finance, sport and entertainment news.
Language (s): Cantonese
Ad Rate: Full Page Mono 167000.00
Ad Rate: Full Page Colour 202000.00
Currency: Hong Kong Dollars
DAILY NEWSPAPER

Apple Daily 489922
Owner: Next Media Limited
Editorial: Next Media Limited, 8 Chun Ying Street, TKO Industrial West, Tseung Kwan O, N.T., Hong Kong **Tel:** 852 29908388
Email: adnews@appledaily.com **Web site:** http://hk.apple.nextmedia.com
Freq: Daily; **Circ:** 318300
Profile: covers latest news of social issues, politics and entertainment.
Language (s): Chinese
Ad Rate: Full Page Mono 159500.00
Ad Rate: Full Page Colour 253000.00
Currency: Hong Kong Dollars
DAILY NEWSPAPER

Asahi Shimbun - Hong Kong Bureau 489923
Editorial: Asahi Shimbun - Hong Kong Bureau., TTG Asia Media Pte Ltd., 11/f, ING Tower, Hong Kong
Tel: 852 22377252
Email: asahihongkong@yahoo.com **Web site:** http://www.asahi.com
Freq: Daily
Bureau Chief: Tetsu Kobayashi
Profile: Covers international and local news in Hong Kong
Language (s): Japanese
DAILY NEWSPAPER

China Daily 489623
Owner: China Daily Newspaper Group
Editorial: Room 1818, Hing Wai Centre, 7 Tin Wan Praya Road, Hong Kong **Tel:** 852 25185111
Email: editor@chinadailyhk.com **Web site:** http://www.chinadaily.com.cn
Freq: 2 Times/Week; **Circ:** 55005
Editor: Albert Au Yeung; **Editor:** Shirley Xiao
Profile: Launched in 1997, provides a local perspective on national and international news for decision-makers, including HKSAR government official, CEOs, senior executives, scholars and academics.
Language (s): English
Ad Rate: Full Page Mono 147000.00
Ad Rate: Full Page Colour 245000.00
Currency: China Yuan Renminbi
DAILY NEWSPAPER

Daily 10 590784
Editorial: Step Max Limited., Unit 1F-1H, Casey Building, 38 Tokku Road, Sheung Wan., Hong Kong
Tel: 852 25438262
Email: editor@daily7-daily10.com **Web site:** http://www.daily7-daily10.com
Freq: 2 Times/Week
Editor: Melanie Holloway
Profile: covers children's interests
Language (s): English
DAILY NEWSPAPER

Daily 7 491098
Editorial: Step Max Limited., Unit 1F-1H, Casey Building, 38 Tokku Road, Sheung Wan., Hong Kong
Tel: 852 25438262
Email: editor@daily7-daily10.com **Web site:** http://www.daily7-daily10.com
Freq: 2 Times/Week
Editor: Melanie Holloway
Profile: covers news for children and children's interests
Language (s): English
DAILY NEWSPAPER

DNA: Daily News & Analysis - Hong Kong Bureau 510029
Owner: Diligent Media Co.
Editorial: 2C, Verdant Court, Discovery Bay, Hong Kong **Tel:** 852 29879169
Freq: 2 Times/Week
Language (s): English
DAILY NEWSPAPER

The Epoch Times 489912
Owner: Epoch Group Limited
Tel: 852 25199881
Email: edt@epochtimes.com.hk **Web site:** http://www.epochtimes.com.hk
Freq: 2 Times/Week; **Circ:** 50009 Not Audited
Editor: Jane Hui
Profile: covers news on culture, social issues and politics. This newspaper has obvious anti-communist tendency towards Chinese government.
Language (s): Chinese
DAILY NEWSPAPER

Headline Daily 489940
Owner: Sing Tao News Corporation Limited
Editorial: Headline Daily Limited, 15th Floor, Sing Tao News Corporation Building, Hong Kong
Tel: 852 3181 3683
Email: info@hkheadline.com **Web site:** http://www.hkheadline.com
Freq: Daily; **Circ:** 790000 Not Audited
Profile: Covers international, local and social news It is a free daily newspaper.
Language (s): Chinese
Ad Rate: Full Page Mono 136000.00
Ad Rate: Full Page Colour 225000.00
Currency: Hong Kong Dollars
DAILY NEWSPAPER

Herald Monthly 489917
Editorial: Chinese Christian Herald Crusades Limited., Room 1602, Hillwood Centre, 17-19 Hillwood Road, Tsimshatsui, Kln, Hong Kong
Tel: 852 21483301
Email: hongkong@cchc.org **Web site:** http://www.cchc.org
Freq: Monthly; **Circ:** 100005 Not Audited
Profile: It is a monthly newspaper published by Headquarters & Herald Mission Center, covers local and national news; religion events and social issues.
Language (s): Cantonese
Ad Rate: Full Page Mono 11520.00
Ad Rate: Full Page Colour 9216.00
Currency: Hong Kong Dollars
DAILY NEWSPAPER

Hong Kong Commercial Daily 489624
Editorial: Hong Kong Commercial Daily, 18th Floor, Number 499, King's Road, Hong Kong
Tel: 852 25640768
Web site: http://www.hkcd.com.hk
Freq: Daily; **Circ:** 307000 Not Audited
Editor: Shirley Wu
Profile: Covers local, international and regional economy and financial news. It also provides information and opportunities of investing in mainland China.
Language (s): Cantonese
Ad Rate: Full Page Mono 75000.00
Ad Rate: Full Page Colour 160000.00
Currency: China Yuan Renminbi
DAILY NEWSPAPER

Hong Kong Economic Journal 489628
Editorial: 8th Floor, Tower B, North Point Industrial Bldg, Hong Kong **Tel:** 852 28567549
Email: editorial@hkej.com **Web site:** http://www.hkej.com
Freq: Daily; **Circ:** 65005 Not Audited
Editor in Chief: King Cheung Chan; **Editor:** Thomas Wong; **News Director:** Chris Yeung
Profile: Covers international and local news, business and economics.
Language (s): Cantonese
Ad Rate: Full Page Mono 67000.00
Ad Rate: Full Page Colour 145000.00
Currency: Hong Kong Dollars
DAILY NEWSPAPER

Hong Kong Economic Times 489933
Owner: Hong Kong Economic Times Limited
Editorial: 6th Fl, Kodak House II, 321 Java Rd, North Point, Hong Kong **Tel:** 852 25654288
Email: info@hket.com **Web site:** http://www.hket.com
Freq: Daily; **Circ:** 90570 Not Audited
Editor: Teddy Au; **Editor in Chief:** Eric Chan;
Director: Andy Ho; **Editor:** Frankie Ho; **Editor:** Oscar Lee; **General Manager:** Salome See; **Editor:** Joann Wong; **Editor:** Man Ki Yeung
Profile: Covers local and international news of business, economic, property and technology.
Language (s): Cantonese
Ad Rate: Full Page Mono 89600.00
Ad Rate: Full Page Colour 192000.00
Currency: Hong Kong Dollars
DAILY NEWSPAPER

Lianhe Zaobao 489919
Editorial: Singapore Press Holding., Room 1308, 13th Floor, Tower II, Lippo Centre, Admiralty, Hong Kong **Tel:** 852 25246191
Web site: http://www.zaobao.com
Freq: Daily
Profile: Covers international and local news.
Language (s): Chinese
DAILY NEWSPAPER

Metro Daily (Hong Kong) 489914
Owner: Wee (Kenny)
Editorial: Metro Publishing HK Ltd, 25th Floor, 148 Electric Road, North Point, Hong Kong
Tel: 852 31961600
Email: news@metrohk.com.hk **Web site:** http://www.metrohk.com.hk
Freq: 2 Times/Week; **Circ:** 380000 Not Audited
Editor: Juan Lam; **Editor in Chief:** Jeff Lee; **Editor:** Ivy Sum
Profile: Launched in 2002, covers international and local news in addition to entertainment news.
Language (s): Chinese
Ad Rate: Full Page Mono 117861.00
Ad Rate: Full Page Colour 202046.00
Currency: Hong Kong Dollars
DAILY NEWSPAPER

Ming Pao Daily News 489926
Editorial: 15F, A Building, Mingpao Enterprise Corporation Ltd., Block A, 15th Floor, Ming Pao Industrial Centre, 18 Ka Yip Street, Chaiwan, Hong Kong **Tel:** 852 25953111
Email: mingpao@mingpao.com **Web site:** http://www.mingpao.com
Freq: Daily; **Circ:** 135006 Not Audited
Manager: Andus Chan; **Editor:** Pui Kuen Chung;
Editor: Bill Ko
Profile: Covers the latest news in politics, entertainment and parenting.
Language (s): Cantonese
Ad Rate: Full Page Mono 233100.00
Ad Rate: Full Page Colour 379100.00
Currency: Hong Kong Dollars
DAILY NEWSPAPER

Nihon Keizai Shimbun - Hong Kong Bureau 489948
Editorial: Suites 1707B-10, Dah Sing, Financial Centre., 108 Gloucester Rd, Hong Kong
Tel: 852 25861863
Email: nikkei@nikkei.com.hk
Freq: Daily
Bureau Chief: Wataru Yoshida
Language (s): Japanese
DAILY NEWSPAPER

NNA 513394
Editorial: NNA (HK) Limited., Unit 401 4/F Kwai Hung Holdings Centre, 89 King's Road, North Point, Hong Kong **Tel:** 852 28026303
Email: nna.sales@nna.hk **Web site:** http://nna.asia.ne.jp
Freq: 2 Times/Week
Editor: Shimizu Miyuki
Profile: Covers financial industry news in of Japan.
Language (s): Japanese
DAILY NEWSPAPER

Oriental Daily News 489928
Editorial: Oriental Daily News, Oriental Press Centre, 23 Dai Cheong Street, Tai Po Industrial Estate, Hong Kong **Tel:** 852 36008811
Email: news@oriental.com.hk **Web site:** http://orientaldaily.on.cc
Freq: Daily; **Circ:** 3440272 Not Audited
Profile: Covers all news including entertainment, lifestyle and social issues.
Language (s): Cantonese
Ad Rate: Full Page Mono 160000.00
Ad Rate: Full Page Colour 297000.00
Currency: Hong Kong Dollars
DAILY NEWSPAPER

People's Daily Overseas Version 489929
Editorial: 160 Connaught Road West, Hong Kong
Tel: 852 23087909
Web site: http://www.peopledaily.com.cn
Freq: Daily; **Circ:** 150000
Bureau Chief: Cao Honglian
Profile: Covers local, international news and current affairs.
Language (s): Chinese
DAILY NEWSPAPER

Sing Pao Daily 489935
Editorial: Sing Pao Daily, 3/F CWG Building, 3A Kung Ngam Village Road, Shaukeiwan, Hong Kong
Tel: 852 25124200
Email: webmaster@singpao.com.hk
Freq: Daily; **Circ:** 75005 Not Audited
Profile: covers local, regional and international news
Language (s): Chinese
Ad Rate: Full Page Mono 238000.00
Currency: Hong Kong Dollars
DAILY NEWSPAPER

Sing Tao Daily 489625
Owner: Sing Tao News Corporation Limited
Editorial: 6/F, Sing Tao Building, 1 Wang Kwong Road, Kowloon Bay, Hong Kong **Tel:** 852 27982323
Email: newspaper@singtaonewscorp.com **Web site:** http://www.singtao.com
Freq: Daily; **Circ:** 80000 Not Audited
Editor: Joey Au; **Manager:** Hak Kong Lau; **Editor:** Joe Mak; **News Editor:** Vemon Sin; **Editor in Chief:** Sai Wo Siu; **Editor:** David Smith
Profile: Covers business, sports, local and international news
Language (s): Cantonese
Ad Rate: Full Page Mono 95200.00
Ad Rate: Full Page Colour 199920.00
Currency: Hong Kong Dollars
DAILY NEWSPAPER

South China Morning Post 489921
Owner: Alibaba
Editorial: Ground Fl, G/F-3/F #1 Leighton Rd, Causeway Bay, Hong Kong **Tel:** 852 25652222
Web site: http://www.scmp.com
Freq: Daily; **Circ:** 104148
Editor, Special Projects: Cliff Buddle; **News Editor:** Chow Chung Yan; **Editor:** Peter Kammerer; **Editor:** Kylie Knott
Profile: Established in 1903 and written for affluent and influential readers, serves as Hong Kong's premier English language newspaper. Provides analysis on news in Hong Kong, China and the rest of Asia. Aims to foster impartial debates on various issues that speak to making the southeast Asian region a better place in which to live and work.
Language (s): English
Ad Rate: Full Page Mono 105462.00
Ad Rate: Full Page Colour 215082.00
Currency: Hong Kong Dollars
DAILY NEWSPAPER

Hong Kong

The Standard
489934

Owner: Sing Tao News Corporation Limited
Editorial: 3/F, Sing Tao News Corporation Building, 3 Tung Wong Road, Shau Kei Wan, Hong Kong
Tel: 852 27982323
Email: editor@thestandard.com.hk **Web site:** http://www.thestandard.com.hk
Freq: Mon thru Fri; **Circ:** 222413 Not Audited
Editor: Marcal Joanilho; **Editor:** Zubair Latif; **Editor in Chief:** Ivan Tong
Profile: Covers international and local news, social issues, culture and arts and so on. The topics are broad and deep. As a free English newspaper. It has evolved into a powerful, influential medium in Hong Kong with a diverse audience and a broad reach.
Language (s): English
Ad Rate: Full Page Mono 49000.00
Ad Rate: Full Page Colour 98000.00
Currency: Hong Kong Dollars
DAILY NEWSPAPER

The Straits Times - Hong Kong Bureau
489936

Editorial: Room 1308, Tower II, Lippo Centre, 89 Queensway, Hong Kong **Tel:** 852 25269018
Freq: Daily
Language (s): English
DAILY NEWSPAPER

Ta Kung Pao
489930

Editorial: Ta Kung Pao, 2nd-3rd Floor, Kodak House II, 39 Healthy Street East, North Point, Hong Kong
Tel: 852 25757181
Email: tkppub@takungpao.com **Web site:** http://www.takungpao.com
Freq: Daily; **Circ:** 235005 Not Audited
Editor: Suk Fun Choi; **Manager:** Han Guang Chu; **News Editor:** Kam Fung Kwok; **Editor:** Man Tung Ma; **Manager:** Kai-Yiu pang; **International News Editor:** Xue Yan
Profile: Covers local, national and international news including technology, sports, politics and social issues.
Language (s): Cantonese
Ad Rate: Full Page Mono 77273.00
Ad Rate: Full Page Colour 205258.00
Currency: Hong Kong Dollars
DAILY NEWSPAPER

Take Me Home
489944

Editorial: 8/F, Kodak House II, 321 Java Road, North Point, Hong Kong **Tel:** 852 28802874
Email: tmh_adv@hket.com **Web site:** http://www.takemehome.com.hk
Freq: Weekly; **Circ:** 300006 Not Audited
Profile: covers lifestyle, health, parenting, and food.
Language (s): Chinese
Ad Rate: Full Page Mono 40000.00
Ad Rate: Full Page Colour 58000.00
Currency: Hong Kong Dollars
DAILY NEWSPAPER

Target Newspaper
603631

Editorial: Target Newspaper Limited., Suite 2901, 29th Floor, Bank of America Tower, Hong Kong
Tel: 852 25730379
Email: info@targetnewspapers.com **Web site:** http://www.targetnewspapers.com
Freq: 2 Times/Week
Manager: Joyce Lee; **Editor:** Raymonde Sacklyn
Profile: covers finance and law industry
Language (s): English
DAILY NEWSPAPER

todaysliving.com
490192

Editorial: Press Mark Media Limited, Room 2207, 22/F, Westland Centre, Hong Kong **Tel:** 852 28822230
Web site: http://www.todaysliving.com
Freq: Monthly; **Circ:** 35005 Not Audited
Profile: covers trendy interior design of houses and apartment
Language (s): Chinese
DAILY NEWSPAPER

True Buddha News Weekly (Hong Kong Edition)
489915

Editorial: True Buddha Infogroup Hong Kong Limited, Flat H, 26th Floor, Shield Industrial Center, Hong Kong **Tel:** 852 21464989
Email: info@tbi.org.hk **Web site:** http://www.tbi.org.hk
Freq: Weekly; **Circ:** 3002 Not Audited
Editor: Ho Shui Lau
Profile: Covers Buddhism international news.
Language (s): Chinese
DAILY NEWSPAPER

United Daily News - Hong Kong Bureau
489937

Editorial: United Daily News - Hong Kong Bureau, 3/F, United Daily Centre, 21 Yuk Yat Street, Tokwawan, Kowloon, Hong Kong **Tel:** 852 27570228
Email: hksit@hkudn.com.hk **Web site:** http://www.udngroup.com.tw
Freq: Daily
Director: Hing Kwok Sit
Profile: Covers daily news
Language (s): Chinese
DAILY NEWSPAPER

The Voice
513393

Editorial: St James' Settlement, 85 Stone Nullah Lane, Wanchai, Hong Kong **Tel:** 852 28313215
Email: thevoice@sjs.org.hk **Web site:** http://www.thevoice.org.hk

Freq: Monthly; **Circ:** 27009 Not Audited
Editor: Ping Lun Chan
Profile: covers of topics that senior citizens' are interesting
Language (s): Chinese
DAILY NEWSPAPER

The Wall Street Journal Asia
788003

Owner: Dow Jones & Company, Inc.
Editorial: 25/F Central Plaza, 18 Harbour Road, Hong Kong **Tel:** 852 2573 7121
Email: wsj.ltrs@wsj.com **Web site:** http://www.wsj.com/asia
Freq: Mon thru Fri; **Circ:** 61024
Profile: Launched in 1976 and covers global business news for Asia. Focuses on news and analysis of regional and global business developments for a pan-Asian audience of corporate and government decision-makers.
Ad Rate: Full Page Mono 45650.50
Ad Rate: Full Page Colour 53684.50
Currency: United States Dollars
DAILY NEWSPAPER

Wednesday Journal
489920

Editorial: Wednesday Journal Limited., Room 2612-2616, The Metropolis Tower, Hong Kong
Tel: 852 28916172
Email: sooyo@wednesdayjournal.net **Web site:** http://www.wednesdayjournal.net
Freq: Weekly
Editor in Chief: Brad Lee
Profile: Covers Korean shops, restaurants and salons, which also focusing on local news, international news, regional news and related Christian community news
Language (s): Korean
DAILY NEWSPAPER

Wen Wei Po
489626

Owner: Wen Wei Po Limited.
Editorial: Fl 2-4, Hing Wai Centre, Number 7, Tin Wan Praya Road, Aberdeen, Hong Kong
Tel: 852 28738288
Web site: http://www.wenweipo.com
Freq: Daily; **Circ:** 200005 Not Audited
Editor: Yuet Kam Leung; **Editor in Chief:** Xiaohui Li
Profile: Covers local and international news, business, current affair, sports and education.
Language (s): Cantonese
Ad Rate: Full Page Mono 59760.00
Ad Rate: Full Page Colour 136080.00
Currency: Hong Kong Dollars
DAILY NEWSPAPER

News Service/Syndicate

Hong Kong China News Agency
490341

Editorial: Hong Kong China News Agency., 22nd Floor, Easter Center Plaza, 3 Yiu Hing Road, Shau Kei Wan, Hong Kong **Tel:** 852 2833-2725
Email: ngaili0072@hotmail.com **Web site:** http://www.hkcna.hk
Freq: Daily
Bureau Chief: Yu Cheung
Profile: Covers local and international news.
Language (s): Chinese
NEWS SERVICE/SYNDICATE

Yonhap News Agency - Hong Kong Bureau
490348

Editorial: Yonhap News Agency - Hong Kong Bureau., 11G Tsui Kung Mansion, Taiwan Road, Taikoo Shing, Hong Kong **Tel:** 852 25138662
Email: ycm@yna.co.kr **Web site:** http://www.yonhapnews.co.kr
Freq: Daily
Profile: covers news and information to its customers in various part of the world
Language (s): Korean
NEWS SERVICE/SYNDICATE

Hungary

Time Difference: GMT +1
National Telephone Code: 36
Continent: Europe
Capital: Budapest

Newspapers

168 óra
158882

Owner: Telegráf Kiadó Kft.
Editorial: Becsi ut 3-5., Budapest 1023
Tel: 36 1 335 1484
Email: online@168ora.hu **Web site:** http://www.168ora.hu
Freq: Weekly; **Circ:** 42294 Publisher's Statement
Profile: Newspaper covering national and international news, focusing on politics.
Language (s): Hungarian
Ad Rate: Full Page Mono 693000.00
Ad Rate: Full Page Colour 1210000.00

Currency: Hungary Forint
DAILY NEWSPAPER

Blikk
158830

Owner: Ringier Kiadó Kft.
Editorial: Futo u. 35-37, Budapest 1082
Tel: 36 1 460 2411
Web site: http://www.blikk.hu
Circ: 305865 Publisher's Statement
Editor: Balázs Kolossváry
Profile: Newspaper focusing on national and international news, politics, business, culture and sport.
Language (s): Hungarian
Ad Rate: Full Page Mono 2745600.00
Ad Rate: Full Page Colour 3706560.00
Currency: Hungary Forint
DAILY NEWSPAPER

The Budapest Times
344468

Owner: BZT Media Kft.
Editorial: Erzsebet krt. 43-49., Budapest 1073
Tel: 36 1 453-0752
Email: editor@bzt.hu **Web site:** http://www.budapesttimes.hu
Circ: 10000 Publisher's Statement
Profile: The Budapest Times provides Hungarian politics, business, economy, news and culture in English language.
Language (s): Hungarian
Ad Rate: Full Page Colour 700000.00
Currency: Hungary Forint
DAILY NEWSPAPER

Budapester Zeitung
187406

Owner: BZT Media Kft.
Editorial: Erzsebet krt. 43-49, Budapest 1073
Tel: 36 1 4530752
Email: redaktion@bzt.hu **Web site:** http://www.bzt.hu
Editor: Elisabeth Katalin Grabow
Profile: Newspaper covering news on politics, economics and social events.
Language (s): German
Ad Rate: Full Page Colour 700000.00
Currency: Hungary Forint
DAILY NEWSPAPER

Délmagyarország
350483

Owner: Lapcom Kft.
Editorial: Szabadkai ut 20, Szeged 6729
Tel: 36 63 567888
Email: online@delmagyar.hu **Web site:** http://www.delmagyar.hu
Circ: 53998 Publisher's Statement
Editor: Csaba Nyerges
Language (s): Hungarian
DAILY NEWSPAPER

Helyi Téma
443098

Owner: Théma Lapkiadó Kft.
Editorial: Prielle Kornelia utca 4, Budapest 1119
Tel: 36 1 814-4755
Email: ertekesites@helyitema.hu **Web site:** http://tema.hu
Freq: Daily; **Circ:** 711850
Language (s): Hungarian
Ad Rate: Full Page Colour 1046760.00
Currency: Hungary Forint
DAILY NEWSPAPER

Magyar Hírlap
156972

Owner: Magyar Hirlap Kiadói Kft.
Editorial: Thokoly ut 105-107., Budapest 1145
Tel: 36 1 8873283
Email: hirdetes@magyarhirlap.hu **Web site:** http://www.magyarhirlap.hu
Freq: Daily
Editor: Lehel Kristály; **Editor-in-Chief:** Péter Petán
Profile: Newspaper concerning politics and economics.
Language (s): Hungarian
Ad Rate: Full Page Mono 1050000.00
Ad Rate: Full Page Colour 1560000.00
Currency: Hungary Forint
DAILY NEWSPAPER

Magyar Nemzet
156632

Owner: Nemzet Lap- és Könyvkiadó Kft.
Editorial: Ülli ut 102., Budapest 1089
Tel: 36 1 4762131
Email: szerk@mno.hu **Web site:** http://mno.hu
Circ: 75696 Publisher's Statement
Profile: Broadsheet-sized quality newspaper containing national and international news, current affairs, culture and in-depth stock market news. Provides Internet recommendations, information about Budapest and political issues worldwide.
Language (s): Hungarian
Ad Rate: Full Page Mono 2200000.00
Ad Rate: Full Page Colour 2950000.00
Currency: Hungary Forint
DAILY NEWSPAPER

Napi Gazdaság
158879

Editorial: Perc utca 8, Budapest 1036
Tel: 36 1 450 9605
Email: szerkesztoseg@napigazdasag.hu **Web site:** http://www.napigazdasag.hu
Freq: Daily; **Circ:** 8000
Editor-in-Chief: György Barcza; **Editor:** Tamás Wiedemann
Profile: Newspaper focusing on national and international economics and finance.
Language (s): Hungarian
Ad Rate: Full Page Mono 629000.00
Ad Rate: Full Page Colour 865000.00

Currency: Hungary Forint
DAILY NEWSPAPER

Népszava
158878

Owner: NÉPSZAVA Lapkiadó Kft.
Editorial: Jokai utca 6., Budapest 1066
Tel: 36 1 4779000
Email: nepszava@nepszava.hu **Web site:** http://nepszava.hu
Circ: 35328 Publisher's Statement
Profile: Newspaper providing national and international news with specific focus on politics.
Language (s): Hungarian
Ad Rate: Full Page Mono 1100000.00
Ad Rate: Full Page Colour 1700000.00
Currency: Hungary Forint
DAILY NEWSPAPER

Neue Zeitung
354177

Owner: Magy.Közl. Lap és könyvkiadó
Editorial: Lendvay u. 22., Budapest 1062
Tel: 36 1 302 68 77
Email: neuezeitung@t-online.hu **Web site:** http://www.neue-zeitung.hu
Circ: 2000 Publisher's Statement
Editor: Angela Korb
Language (s): German
Ad Rate: Full Page Mono 100000.00
Currency: Hungary Forint
DAILY NEWSPAPER

Szabad Föld
158881

Owner: Geomédia Kiadói Zrt.
Editorial: Lajos u. 48-66. B lph II. em., Budapest 1036 **Tel:** 36 1 4898846
Email: info@szabadfold.hu **Web site:** http://www.szabadfold.hu
Circ: 140228 Publisher's Statement
Editor: László Horváth
Profile: Newspaper containing articles on national news, general interest and advice with sections covering various topics.
Language (s): Hungarian
Ad Rate: Full Page Mono 2200000.00
Ad Rate: Full Page Colour 3080000.00
Currency: Hungary Forint
DAILY NEWSPAPER

Vasárnapi Hírek
158894

Owner: VH Kiadó Kft.
Editorial: Lajos u. 48-66. B epület II. emelet, Budapest 1036 **Tel:** 36 1 3192333
Email: szerkesztoseg@vasarnapihirek.hu **Web site:** https://www.vasarnapihirek.hu
Circ: 67564
Editor: Gál Zoltán
Language (s): Hungarian
DAILY NEWSPAPER

Világgazdaság
158877

Owner: MediaWorks
Editorial: Futo u. 35-37, Budapest 1122
Tel: 36 1 4891165
Email: vg@vg.hu **Web site:** http://www.vg.hu
Circ: 13998 Publisher's Statement
Profile: Newspaper covering all aspects of finance and business. Provides in-depth economic, stock market and international share analysis.
Language (s): Hungarian
Ad Rate: Full Page Mono 960000.00
Ad Rate: Full Page Colour 1344000.00
Currency: Hungary Forint
DAILY NEWSPAPER

News Service/Syndicate

Magyar Tavirati Iroda
353202

Editorial: Naphegy ter 8, Budapest 1016
Tel: 36 1 457 7100
Email: info@dunamsz.hu **Web site:** http://www.mti.hu
Editor: Ferenc Gazsó
Language (s): Hungarian
NEWS SERVICE/SYNDICATE

Iceland

Time Difference: GMT
National Telephone Code: 354
Continent: Europe
Capital: Reykjavik

Newspapers

Dagbladid Visir
156982

Owner: Dagbladid-Visir Utgafufelag
Editorial: Editorial dv.is, Tryggvagata 11, Reykjavik 101 **Tel:** 354 512 70 00
Email: ritstjorn@dv.is **Web site:** http://www.dv.is
Freq: Daily; **Circ:** 20000 Publisher's Statement
Editor: Jona Trausti Reynisson; **Editor-in-Chief:** Reynir Traustason
Profile: Newspaper covering news, sports and culture.
Language (s): Icelandic
DAILY NEWSPAPER

Fréttablaðið 653865
Editorial: 365 Skaftahlið, Reykjavik **Tel:** 354 512 5000
Email: ritstjorn@frettabladid.is **Web site:** http://www.visir.is
Íþróttafréttamaður: Sigurður Elvar Þórólfsson; **Fréttastjóri:** Kristján Hjálmarsson; **Blaðamaður:** Álfrún Pálsdóttir; **Fréttastjóri:** Arndís Þorgeirsdóttir
Profile: Newspaper covering international and national news, business, sport and culture.
Language (s): Icelandic
DAILY NEWSPAPER

Fréttatíminn 823398
Editorial: Sætun 8, Reykjavik 105 **Tel:** 354 531 33 00
Email: frettatiminn@frettatiminn.is **Web site:** http://www.frettatiminn.is
Freq: Weekly; **Circ:** 82000
Editor / Ritstjóri: Jónas Haraldsson; **Filmkritiker / kvikmyndagagnrýnandi:** Þórarinn Þórarinsson
Profile: Fréttatíminn is an Icelandic weekend newspaper.The newspaper comes out every Friday, and has a circulation of around 82,000. Around 70,000 copies are distributed in the Reykjavík capital area. Fréttatíminn is free of charge. The paper is owned by the journalists who write for it and the paper does not have any affiliation to vested interest parties. The editor of the paper is Jón Kaldal and the news editor Óskar Hrafn Þorvaldsson.Founded in 2010.
Language (s): Icelandic
DAILY NEWSPAPER

Morgunbladid 156709
Owner: Árvakur nf
Editorial: Hadegismoum 2, Reykjavik 110
Tel: 354 569 11 00
Email: morgunbladid@mbl.is **Web site:** http://www.mbl.is
Freq: Daily; **Circ:** 55000 Publisher's Statement
News Editor / Fréttir: Sunna Ósk Logadóttir; **News Editor / Fréttir:** Sigtryggur Sigtryggsson
Profile: Newspaper covering news, debate and entertainment, sport.
Language (s): Icelandic
Ad Rate: Full Page Mono 187000.00
Currency: Iceland Kronur
DAILY NEWSPAPER

Community Newspaper

Viðskiptablaðið 823410
Editorial: Noatun 17, Reykjavik **Tel:** 354 511 66 22
Email: vb@vb.is **Web site:** http://www.vb.is
Freq: Weekly
Editor / Ritstjór: Björgvin Guðmundsson; **Publisher & CEO / Útgefandi og framkvæmdastjóri:** Pétur Árni Jónsson
Profile: Viðskiptablaðið is the Iceland's principal business-oriented newspaper.
Language (s): Icelandic
COMMUNITY NEWSPAPER

India

Time Difference: GMT +5.5
National Telephone Code: 91
Continent: Asia
Capital: New Dehli

Newspapers

Aaj - Kanpur Edition 460511
Editorial: AaJ Office, 79/75 Bans Mandi, Deputy Ka Parao, Kanpur 208001 **Tel:** 91 512 2342221
Freq: Daily; **Circ:** 186994 Not Audited
Editor: Shardul Gupta; **Editor:** R. Yadav
Profile: Articles focus on local and international news.
Language (s): Hindi
DAILY NEWSPAPER

Aaj - Lucknow Edition 460510
Editorial: AaJ Bhawan, Surajdeep Complex, 1 Jopling Road, Lucknow 226001 **Tel:** 91 522 2209315
Email: aajlucknow@sify.com
Freq: Daily; **Circ:** 66002 Not Audited
Editor in Chief: Shardul Vikram Gupta; **Editor:** R.S. Walia
Profile: Covers local and world news.
Language (s): Hindi
DAILY NEWSPAPER

Aaj Ka Anand 460497
Editorial: Aaj Ka Anand Building, Opposite Shivaji Statue 365/6 Shivajinagar, Pune 411005
Tel: 91 20 25534888
Email: akanand@giaspn01.vsnl.net.in **Web site:** http://www.aajkaanand.com
Freq: Daily; **Circ:** 110002 Not Audited
Profile: Covers local and national news and current events, astrology, health, spirituality and women's interests.
Language (s): Hindi
DAILY NEWSPAPER

Aajkaal 460498
Editorial: BP 5, Sector 5, Sulplex, Kolkata 700921
Tel: 91 33 30110800
Email: aajkaal.net@gmail.com **Web site:** http://www.aajkaal.net
Freq: Daily; **Circ:** 2200002 Not Audited
Editor: Ashok Dasgupta; **Editor:** Rajiv Ghosh; **Editor:** J. Khan
Profile: Covers the latest news in local and international, sports and etc.
Language (s): Bengali
DAILY NEWSPAPER

Aapla Vartahar 460243
Editorial: 220 Narayan Udyog Bhawan, Dr. B A Road, Lal Bagh, Mumbai 400012
Tel: 91 22 24715208
Freq: Daily; **Circ:** 100001 Not Audited
Editor: Anil Joshi
Profile: Aapla Vartahar is a newspaper which covers the news in local and world.
Language (s): Marathi
DAILY NEWSPAPER

Afternoon Despatch & Courier 460501
Editorial: Grace Villa, 125-126, 8th Street, Gandhipuram, Coimbatore 641012
Tel: 91 4222496405
Email: afternoondaily@rediffmail.com **Web site:** http://www.afternoondc.in
Freq: Daily; **Circ:** 68841 Not Audited
Editor: Carol Andrade; **Editor:** M.N. Appadurai
Profile: Covers local and regional news, business, sports, education, leisure and etc.
Language (s): English
DAILY NEWSPAPER

Afternoon Despatch and Courier 157172
Editorial: Afternoon Dispatch & Courier, Tanmabhoomi Bhaban, Mumbai 400001
Tel: 91 22 40768999
Web site: http://www.afternoonele.in
Freq: Daily; **Circ:** 85001 Not Audited
Editor: Behram Contractor
Profile: Afternoon Despatch & Courier is a daily newspaper in Mumbai, India covering local news, sports, business, jobs, and community events.
Language (s): English
DAILY NEWSPAPER

Agrowon 460285
Editorial: 595 Budhwar Peth, Pune 411002
Tel: 91 20 24455500
Email: agrowon@gmail.com **Web site:** http://www.agrowon.com
Freq: Daily; **Circ:** 100002 Not Audited
Profile: Covers Agriculture & Farming news and issues
Language (s): Marathi
DAILY NEWSPAPER

Ahmedabad Mirror 868654
Editorial: 139 Ashram Rd, Ahmedabad 380009
Tel: 91 79 26583758
Web site: http://www.ahmedabadmirror.in
Editor: Bharat Desai
DAILY NEWSPAPER

Aj - Gorakhpur Edition 460505
Editorial: Bank Road, Gorakhpur 273001
Tel: 91 551 2335350
Freq: Daily; **Circ:** 52002 Not Audited
Editor in Chief: Shardul Vikram Gupta; **Editor:** Ratnakar Singh
Profile: Covers news.
Language (s): Hindi
DAILY NEWSPAPER

Aj - Patna Edition 460512
Editorial: AJ Bhawan, Mazharul Haque Path, Fraser Road, Patna 800001 **Tel:** 91 612 2235070
Freq: Daily; **Circ:** 900002 Not Audited
Editor: Deepak Pandey
Profile: Covers the news in local and international.
Language (s): Hindi
DAILY NEWSPAPER

Aj - Ranchi Edition 460507
Editorial: Namkum Industrial Area, Namkum Rd, Ranchi 834002 **Tel:** 91 651 3207938
Freq: Daily; **Circ:** 60301 Not Audited
Manager: Amit Agarwal; **Editor in Chief:** Shardul Vikram Gupta; **Editor:** Dilip Shrivastav
Profile: Aj is a Hindi newspaper published in 13 locations which covers the news in local and international.
Language (s): Hindi
DAILY NEWSPAPER

Aj - Varanasi Edition 460504
Editorial: AJ Bhawan, Sant Kabir Road, Varanasi 221001 **Tel:** 91 542 2393981
Email: neerajvahicam@rediffmail.com
Freq: Daily; **Circ:** 220629 Not Audited
Editor in Chief: Shardul Vikram Gupta
Profile: Covers local and international news.
Language (s): Hindi
DAILY NEWSPAPER

Ajir Asom 460513
Editorial: G S Road, Dispur, Guwahati, Guwahati 781005 **Tel:** 91 361 2529237
Email: thesentinel@satyam.net.in
Freq: Daily; **Circ:** 50002 Not Audited
Editor: Apurva Sharma
Profile: Focuses on regional, local and international news.
Language (s): Assamese
DAILY NEWSPAPER

Ajit 460514
Editorial: Ajit Bhawan, Nehru Garden Road, Jalandhar 144001 **Tel:** 91 181 2458588
Web site: http://www.ajitjalandhar.com
Freq: Daily; **Circ:** 380002 Not Audited
Profile: publishes in Jalandhar punjab with punjab news and international news.
Language (s): Punjabi
DAILY NEWSPAPER

Ajit Samachar 460083
Editorial: Ajit Bhawan, Nehru Garden Road, Jalandhar 144001 **Tel:** 91 1812455961
Web site: http://www.ajitjalandhar.com
Freq: Daily; **Circ:** 120003 Not Audited
Profile: Covers local and world news.
Language (s): Hindi
DAILY NEWSPAPER

Akali Patrika 460515
Editorial: Patrika House 26, Chahar Bagh, Jalandhar 144001 **Tel:** 91 181 2456579
Freq: Daily; **Circ:** 85002 Not Audited
Editor in Chief: Ratnesh Sodhi
Profile: Focuses on local and International news.
Language (s): Punjabi
DAILY NEWSPAPER

Akhbar-E-Mashriq 460516
Editorial: 12 Dargah Road, Kolkata 700017
Tel: 91 33 22815157
Email: mashriq@vsnl.com
Freq: Daily; **Circ:** 60002 Not Audited
Editor: M.W. Haque; **Editor:** Amanullah Mohammed
Profile: Covers local and international news, as well as sports and etc.
Language (s): Urdu
DAILY NEWSPAPER

Akila 459508
Editorial: Moti Taki Chowk, Rajkot 360001
Tel: 91 2812445111
Email: akiladaily@yahoo.com **Web site:** http://www.akilanews.com
Freq: Daily; **Circ:** 67001 Not Audited
Editor: Nimish Ganatra
Profile: Akila is a newspaper which focused on local, regional, and international news.
Language (s): Gujarati
DAILY NEWSPAPER

Akkas 460517
Editorial: 1/A Khetradas Lane 4th Floor, Kolkata 700012 **Tel:** 91 33 22113298
Email: akkasdaily@gmail.com
Freq: Daily; **Circ:** 65001 Not Audited
Editor: Karim Monghyri
Profile: Focuses on the latest news locally and abroad.
Language (s): Urdu
DAILY NEWSPAPER

All India Appointment Gazette 459280
Editorial: 7 Old Court House Street, Kolkata 700001
Tel: 91 033 22435663
Email: uttarbanga@hotmail.com **Web site:** http://www.uttarbangasambad.com
Freq: Weekly; **Circ:** 50003 Not Audited
Editor: S. Talukdar
Profile: All India Appointment Gazette - an English weekly newspaper which covers the news, business, and etc
Language (s): English
DAILY NEWSPAPER

Amar Asom 460499
Owner: G L Publication Ltd.
Editorial: G L Publication Ltd., G S Road, Ulubari, Guwahati 781007 **Tel:** 91 361 2458395
Email: glpghy2009@hotmail.com **Web site:** http://www.amarasom.glpublications.in/#
Freq: Daily; **Circ:** 100002 Not Audited
Editor: Homen Borgohain
Profile: Covers daily, national, and world news, as well as weather, sports, entertainment, business, travel, health, culture, nature and youth.
Language (s): Assamese
DAILY NEWSPAPER

Amar Ujala - Agra Edition 460520
Editorial: Sikandra Road, Agra 282007
Tel: 91 5622601600
Web site: http://www.amarujala.com
Freq: Daily; **Circ:** 150002 Not Audited
Editor in Chief: Ashok Agarwal; **Editor:** Pushpendra Sharma
Profile: Covers society and social issues as well as news.
Language (s): Hindi
DAILY NEWSPAPER

Amar Ujala - Bareilly Edition 460518
Editorial: 19 Civil Lines, Shahjahanpur Road, Bareilly 243005 **Tel:** 91 581 2562843
Web site: http://www.amarujala.com
Freq: Daily; **Circ:** 140002 Not Audited
Editor in Chief: Ashok Agarwal
Profile: Covers society and social issues as well as news.
Language (s): Hindi
DAILY NEWSPAPER

Amar Ujala - Chandigarh Edition 459459
Editorial: 49 Industrial Area, Phase II, Panchkula, Chandigarh 134113 **Tel:** 91 1722591459
Web site: http://www.amarujala.com
Freq: Daily; **Circ:** 80002 Not Audited
Editor in Chief: Ashok Agarwal
Profile: Covers news, sports, business, banking, society and social issues.
Language (s): Hindi
DAILY NEWSPAPER

Amar Ujala - Dehradun Edition 459458
Editorial: Shed No.2, Patel Nagar Industrial Estate, Dehradun 248001 **Tel:** 91 1352720378
Web site: http://www.amarujala.com
Freq: Daily; **Circ:** 125001 Not Audited
Editor: Nisheet Joshi
Profile: Covers society and social issues. The newspaper is known for some ground breaking journalism and even in today's cut throat competition, Amar Ujala is still selling Authenticity, Honesty and Trust.
Language (s): Hindi
DAILY NEWSPAPER

Amar Ujala - Jalandhar Edition 459460
Editorial: A-5, Sports & Surgical Goods Complex, Kapurthala Road, Jalandhar 1440021
Tel: 91 1812650201
Email: editor@jal.amarujala.com **Web site:** http://www.amarujala.com
Freq: Daily; **Circ:** 9848 Not Audited
Editor: Nisheet Joshi
Profile: Covers society and social issues. The newspaper is known for some ground breaking journalism and even in today's cut throat competition, Amar Ujala is still selling Authenticity, Honesty and Trust.
Language (s): Hindi
Ad Rate: Full Page Mono 149787.00
Currency: India Rupees
DAILY NEWSPAPER

Amar Ujala - Meerut Edition 460523
Editorial: 164 Mohkampur, Delhi Road, Meerut 250002 **Tel:** 91 121 2510006
Email: bhawanis@mrt.amarujala.com **Web site:** http://www.amarujala.com
Freq: Daily; **Circ:** 1400002 Not Audited
Editor in Chief: Ashok Agarwal
Profile: Covers society and social issues as well as news.
Language (s): Hindi
DAILY NEWSPAPER

Amar Ujala - Moradabad Edition 460521
Editorial: 588/1 Majhola Delhi Road, Moradabad 24401 **Tel:** 91 591 2484800
Email: editor@amarujala.com **Web site:** http://www.amarujala.com
Freq: Daily; **Circ:** 60003 Not Audited
Editor in Chief: Ashok Agarwal
Profile: Daily Hindi newspaper from Amar Ujala. Jhansi Edition covers news, sports, society and social issues.
Language (s): Hindi
DAILY NEWSPAPER

Amar Ujala - Varanasi Edition 459457
Editorial: A-6 Big Industrial Estate, Chandpur, Lehartara, Varanasi 221106 **Tel:** 91 542 2373921
Email: editor@amarujala.com **Web site:** http://www.amarujala.com
Freq: Daily; **Circ:** 100002 Not Audited
Editor in Chief: Ashok Agarwal
Profile: Covers news, sports, business, banking, society and social issues.
Language (s): Hindi
DAILY NEWSPAPER

Amravati Mandal 460526
Editorial: Behind Irwin Hospital, Khaparde Garden, Amravati 444601 **Tel:** 91 721 2666600
Email: ati_ammandal@sancharnet.in **Web site:** http://www.amravatimandal.com
Freq: Daily; **Circ:** 130002 Not Audited
Editor: Anil Agarwal
Profile: Covers the latest local, regional, international and national news.
Language (s): Hindi
DAILY NEWSPAPER

Amrit Sandesh 460244
Editorial: Amrit Sandesh Bhawan, P B No. 18, Jawaharlal Nehru Marg, Raipur 492001
Tel: 91 771 2535741
Email: amritsandesh@yahoo.co.in
Freq: Daily
Editor: Govindlal Vohra

Profile: Amrit Sandesh is a daily newspaper printed in Hindi covering Local Regional National and International news.
Language (s): Hindi
DAILY NEWSPAPER

Ananda Bazar Patrika 460527
Owner: ABP Pvt. Ltd.
Editorial: 12/4, Ballygunge, Ballygung Park Road, West Bengal, Kolkata 700019 **Tel:** 91 33 22253241
Web site: http://www.anandabazar.com
Freq: Daily; **Circ:** 692359 Not Audited
Editor in Chief: Aveek Sarkar
Profile: Articles cover local and international news.
Language (s): Bengali
Ad Rate: Full Page Colour 2995.00
Currency: India Rupees
DAILY NEWSPAPER

Andhra Bhoomi 460528
Editorial: 36 Sarojini Devi Road, Secunderabad 500003 **Tel:** 91 40 27803930
Email: bhoomi@deccanmail.com **Web site:** http://www.andhrabhoomi.net
Freq: Daily; **Circ:** 110489 Not Audited
Editor: M. Shastri
Profile: Covers the latest news of local, international, national and regional, and etc,
Language (s): Telugu
DAILY NEWSPAPER

Andhra Jyothi 460529
Editorial: Andhra Jyoti Buildings, Plot No:76, HUDA Heights, Ashwani Layout, Road No:70, Journalist Colony, Jubilee Hills, Hyderabad 500033
Tel: 91 40 2355-8233
Email: editor@andhrajyothy.com **Web site:** http://www.andhrajyothy.com
Freq: Daily; **Circ:** 500000 Not Audited
Editor: Vemana Lakshmi; **Editor:** Allam Narayana; **Editor:** K. Srinivas
Profile: Covers the latest news in local and world, sports, and etc.
Language (s): Telugu
Ad Rate: Full Page Colour 43000.00
Currency: India Rupees
DAILY NEWSPAPER

Andhra Prabha 460530
Editorial: Andhra Prabha Publishing Ltd., 6-3-4 Banjara Hills, Road 1, Prem Nager, Hyderabad 500034 **Tel:** 91 4023327178
Web site: http://www.andhraprabha.com
Freq: Daily; **Circ:** 223001 Not Audited
Editor: P. Vijaybabu
Profile: Andhra Prabha is a newspaper which covers the Hyderabad news, current events, politics and business;
Language (s): Telugu
Ad Rate: Full Page Colour 15000.00
Currency: India Rupees
DAILY NEWSPAPER

Around The Times 460209
Editorial: LG-101, Bharat Chambers, 70 Scindia House, Janpath, Connaught Circus, New Delhi 110001 **Tel:** 91 11 23350940
Freq: Daily; **Circ:** 75002 Not Audited
Profile: Around The Times is a newspaper which coves local and world news, sports, business, entertainment and etc.
Language (s): English
DAILY NEWSPAPER

The Asian Age - Kolkata Edition 459152
Editorial: Asian Age Holdings Ltd., 6 Russel Street, Kolkata 700071 **Tel:** 91 33 22890676
Email: kolkatadesk@asianage.com **Web site:** http://www.asianage.com
Freq: Daily; **Circ:** 62002 Not Audited
Bureau Chief: Parwez Hafeez
Profile: Covers local and international news, business, sports, entertainment, and lifestyle. Also has supplements on movies, fashion and lifestyle, education, information and technology, health, and books.
Language (s): English
DAILY NEWSPAPER

Asian Age - Mumbai Edition 459369
Editorial: The Asian Age, 145, Mathura Das Mill Compound, N.M. Joshi Marg, L, Mumbai 400013
Tel: 91 22 24955825
Web site: http://www.asianage.com
Freq: Daily; **Circ:** 94657 Not Audited
Editor in Chief: Venkattram Reddy; **Editor:** Olga Tellis
Profile: Covers local and international news, business, sports, entertainment, and lifestyle. Also has supplements on movies, fashion and lifestyle, education, information and technology, health, and books.
Language (s): Hindi
DAILY NEWSPAPER

Asian Age - New Delhi Edition 879695
Editorial: S - 7, Green Park Main Market, New Delhi 110016 **Tel:** 91 11 26530001 3
Email: delhidesk@asianage.com **Web site:** http://www.asianage.com
Freq: Daily
Profile: Covers local and international news, business, sports, entertainment, and lifestyle. Also has supplements on movies, fashion and lifestyle, education, information and technology, health, and books.
Language (s): English
DAILY NEWSPAPER

Asomiya Pratidin 460535
Editorial: Maniram Dewan Road, Chandmari, Guwahati 781003 **Tel:** 91 3612663647
Web site: http://www.asomiyapratidin.co.in
Freq: Daily; **Circ:** 150002 Not Audited
Editor: Haidar Hussain
Profile: Covers local, regional, international and national news.
Language (s): Assamese
DAILY NEWSPAPER

Assignments Abroad Times 459493
Owner: Aishwarya Publications Pvt Ltd.
Editorial: 401-404 Centre Point, 18th Road, Chembur, E., Mumbai 400071 **Tel:** 91 22 2529-0102
Email: ads@assignmentsabroadtimes.com **Web site:** http://www.assignmentsabroadtimes.com
Freq: 2 Times/Week; **Circ:** 100003 Not Audited
Editor: D. Prasad
Profile: Provides information on careers.
Language (s): English
DAILY NEWSPAPER

Bangalore Mirror 570481
Editorial: SNB Towers, 40/1, Mahatma Gandhi Rd, Shanthala Nagar, Bangalore 560001 **Tel:** 91 80 4220-0000
Web site: http://www.bangaloremirror.com
Freq: Daily
Editor, News Features: Sudha Pillai
Profile: Provides news and analysis on current events, business, finance, economy and sports.
Language (s): English
DAILY NEWSPAPER

Bartaman Patrika 460538
Editorial: 6, J.B.S. Haldane Avenue, Kolkata 700105
Tel: 91 33 23000101
Email: bartamaneast@gmail.com **Web site:** http://www.bartamanpatrika.com
Freq: Daily; **Circ:** 470002 Not Audited
Editor: Subha Dutta
Profile: Covers the latest local and international news.
Language (s): Bengali
DAILY NEWSPAPER

Bharat Tender News (Weekly) 460540
Editorial: LG-101, Bharat Chambers, 70 Scindia House, Janpath Connaught Circus, New Delhi 110001 **Tel:** 91 1123326603
Email: ashbedi@vsnl.net.in **Web site:** http://www.dalitnews.com
Freq: Weekly; **Circ:** 76003 Not Audited
Editor: Ashok Bedi
Profile: Weekly newspaper in the capital of India, paper's main focus is probably politics.
Language (s): Hindi
DAILY NEWSPAPER

Bhor 460541
Editorial: 4/11, Sukhadia Shopping Centre, P.B. No. 81, Sri Ganga Nagar 335001 **Tel:** 91 154 3093337
Email: thebhor@yahoo.com
Freq: Daily; **Circ:** 50002 Not Audited
Profile: Covers the latest news in local and international.
Language (s): Hindi
DAILY NEWSPAPER

Bihar Observer 460542
Editorial: Joraphatak Road, Dhanbad 826001
Tel: 91 326 2301104
Email: dnb_observer@sancharnet.in **Web site:** http://www.biharobserver.tripod.com
Freq: Daily; **Circ:** 69949 Not Audited
Editor: Sushil Bharti; **Editor:** Ganesh Mishra
Profile: Covers local, national and international news.
Language (s): English
DAILY NEWSPAPER

Bijnor Times 460543
Editorial: Bijnor Times Road, Bijnore 246701
Tel: 91 1342 260002
Email: bijnor_times@yahoo.co.in **Web site:** http://www.bijnortimes.com
Freq: Daily; **Circ:** 60002 Not Audited
Editor in Chief: Chanrdramani Raghuvanshi
Profile: Focuses on the latest news in local and world.
Language (s): Hindi
DAILY NEWSPAPER

Bombay Basanti Ank 460545
Editorial: Red House Opposite Dena Bank, Horniman Circle, Sayed Adbulla Brelvi Road, Fort, Mumbai 400001 **Tel:** 91 2222045531
Email: samachar.bombay@gmail.com **Web site:** http://www.bombaysamachar.com
Freq: Weekly; **Circ:** 150003 Not Audited
Profile: Local Newspaper.
Language (s): Gujarati
DAILY NEWSPAPER

The Bombay Samachar 460544
Editorial: Red House, Abdulla Brelvi Road, Horniman Circle Sayed Fort, Mumbai 400001
Tel: 91 22 22045531
Email: samachar.bombay@gmail.com **Web site:** http://www.bombaysamachar.com
Freq: 2 Times/Week; **Circ:** 100002 Not Audited
Profile: Covers the latest in local and national news.
Language (s): Gujarati
DAILY NEWSPAPER

Business Deepika 459282
Editorial: Rashtra Deepika Publications, P.O. Box 2252, Cochin 686025 **Tel:** 91 4813012001
Email: editor@deepika.com **Web site:** http://www.deepika.com
Freq: Weekly; **Circ:** 53003 Not Audited
Profile: Business newspaper.
Language (s): Malayalam
DAILY NEWSPAPER

Business Standard - Ahmedabad Edition 400028
Editorial: Room No. 211 & 212 Sakar II, 2nd Fl, Near Ellise Bridge, Ahmedabad **Tel:** 91 79 26577772
Web site: http://www.business-standard.com
Freq: Daily
Profile: Covers banking, finance markets and business.
Language (s): English
DAILY NEWSPAPER

Business Standard- Hyderabad Edition 499774
Editorial: Business Standard Ltd., 3rd Floor, PTA Building, A C Guards, Hyderabad 500004
Tel: 91 4023303158
Web site: http://www.business-standard.com
Freq: Daily
Bureau Chief: Prashanth Reddy Chintala
Profile: Business Standard is India's premium business daily newspaper (Mumbai Bangalore Delhi Chennai Kolkata Hyderabad and Ahmedabad) which covers the corporate sector banking and finance markets and business apart from the most influential group of editorial writers and columnists.
Language (s): Hindi
DAILY NEWSPAPER

Central Chronicle 460550
Editorial: Nava Bharat Bhavan, 2, Indira Press Complex, Maharana Pratap Nagar, Zone 1, Bhopal 462011 **Tel:** 91 755 4282765
Web site: http://www.centralchronicle.com
Freq: Daily; **Circ:** 50001 Not Audited
Editor in Chief: P.K. Maheshwari; **Editor:** Aneel Pande
Profile: Coves local news, sports, business, jobs, and community events.
Language (s): English
DAILY NEWSPAPER

Chandigarh Tribune 460789
Editorial: The Tribune House, Sector 29-C, Chandigarh 160030 **Tel:** 91 172 2655066
Email: news@tribuneindia.com **Web site:** http://www.tribuneindia.com
Freq: Daily; **Circ:** 110001 Not Audited
Editor in Chief: H. Dua
Profile: Chandigarh Tribune is a newspaper which covers the news in local and international, business, and sports.
Language (s): English
DAILY NEWSPAPER

Charhdikala 460553
Editorial: Charhdikala Group of Publications, Private Ltd., 593, SST Nagar Rajpura Road, Punjab 147003
Tel: 91 17 52370301
Email: cppl@charhdikala.com **Web site:** http://www.charhdikala.com
Freq: Daily; **Circ:** 52003 Not Audited
Editor in Chief: Jagjit Dardi
Profile: Punjabi Family newspaper
Language (s): Punjabi
DAILY NEWSPAPER

Daily Excelsior 161288
Editorial: Excelsior House Excelsior Lane, Janipura, Jammu 180007 **Tel:** 91 191 2537055
Email: editor@dailyexcelsior.com **Web site:** http://www.dailyexcelsior.com
Freq: Daily; **Circ:** 190001 Not Audited
Editor in Chief: S.D. Rohmetra
Profile: Covers local and world news, sports and entertainment.
Language (s): English
DAILY NEWSPAPER

Daily Punjab Kesari 460562
Editorial: Hind Samachar Building, Civil Lines, Jalandhar 144001 **Tel:** 91 181 2280104
Web site: http://www.punjabkesari.com
Freq: Daily; **Circ:** 620044 Not Audited
Co-Editor: Avinash Chopra
Profile: Covers local news, sports, business, jobs, and community events.
Language (s): Hindi
Ad Rate: Full Page Colour 574000.00
Currency: India Rupees
DAILY NEWSPAPER

Daily Taskeen 460564
Editorial: Tasken Complex Dalpatian Wazarat Road, Jammu 180001 **Tel:** 91 191 2543336
Freq: Daily; **Circ:** 60003 Not Audited
Editor in Chief: Maqbool Kazmi
Profile: Covers local and international news.
Language (s): Urdu
DAILY NEWSPAPER

Daily Thanthi 459284
Editorial: Daily Thanthi, 86 E. V. K. Sampath Road, Chennai 600007 **Tel:** 91 4426618661
Email: editor@dt.co.in **Web site:** http://www.dailythanthi.com
Freq: Daily; **Circ:** 10000003 Not Audited
Editor: M. Dhanasekaran; **Publisher:** V. Sundaresan
Profile: Covers international and national news.
Language (s): Tamil
DAILY NEWSPAPER

Dainik Agradoot 460565
Editorial: Agradoot Bhavan, Kalipara Road, Dispur, Guwahati 781006 **Tel:** 91 361 2261923
Web site: http://www.dainikagradoot.com
Freq: Daily; **Circ:** 92001 Not Audited
Editor: Naresh Kalita
Profile: Provides city news, city guides, latest news, current event, current news and entertainment guide.
Language (s): Assamese
DAILY NEWSPAPER

Dainik Bhaskar - Bhopal Edition 460567
Editorial: 6 Dwarka Sadan, Press Complex, M P Nagar, Bhopal 462011 **Tel:** 91 755 3988884
Web site: http://www.bhaskar.com
Freq: Daily; **Circ:** 3500002 Not Audited
Editor in Chief: R. Agarwal; **Editor:** Rajesh Upadhyay
Profile: Dainik Bhaskar is a newspaper which provides the latest local, regional, international and national news, business, lifestyle, sports and etc.
Language (s): Hindi
DAILY NEWSPAPER

Dainik Bhaskar - Gwalior Edition 460566
Editorial: 6 Dwarka Sadan, Press Complex, M.P. Nagar, Bhopal 462011 **Tel:** 91 755 3988884
Web site: http://www.bhaskar.com
Freq: Daily; **Circ:** 3500002 Not Audited
General Manager: Modit Gulati; **Editor:** Hari Mohan Sharma
Profile: Provides the latest local, regional, international and national news, business, lifestyle, sports and etc.
Language (s): Hindi
DAILY NEWSPAPER

Dainik Bhaskar - Jabalpur Edition 460568
Editorial: 581 South Civil Lines, Denning Road, Jabalpur 482001 **Tel:** 91 761 2601352
Email: dbjsn@rediffmail.com **Web site:** http://www.bhaskar.com
Freq: Daily; **Circ:** 3500002 Not Audited
Editor in Chief: R. Agarwal; **Editor:** Manish Gupta; **General Manager:** K.C. Sharma
Profile: Covers local, regional, international and national news, business, lifestyle, sports and etc.
Language (s): Hindi
DAILY NEWSPAPER

Dainik Divya Himachal 460570
Editorial: Pathan Court Road, Purana Mataur, Kangra 176001 **Tel:** 91 1892 264713
Email: edit.dshala@divyahimachal.com **Web site:** http://www.divyahimachal.com
Freq: Daily; **Circ:** 91436 Not Audited
Editor in Chief: Anil Soni
Profile: Covers local and world news, sports, lifestyle and economy
Language (s): Hindi
DAILY NEWSPAPER

Dainik Jagran - Agra Edition 460577
Editorial: Laxmi Hall, Jeevan Mandi, Agra 282004
Tel: 91 5622621662
Web site: http://www.jagran.com
Freq: Daily; **Circ:** 95002 Not Audited
News Editor: Anand Sharma
Profile: Covers Local National Regional And International News.
Language (s): Hindi
DAILY NEWSPAPER

Dainik Jagran - Bareilly Edition 460576
Editorial: 130 Civil Lines, Bareilly 243001
Tel: 91 5812427556
Email: bareilly@brl.jagran.com **Web site:** http://in.Jagran.yahoo.com
Freq: Daily; **Circ:** 100001 Not Audited
Editor in Chief: Sanjay Gupta
Profile: Local reading for anyone in Barielly edition of Dainik Jagran newspaper.
Language (s): Hindi
DAILY NEWSPAPER

Dainik Jagran - Gorakhpur Edition 460578
Editorial: 23 Civil Lines, Gorakhpur 273001
Tel: 91 551 2337137
Web site: http://www.jagran.com
Freq: Daily; **Circ:** 100003 Not Audited

Section 2 World News Media
126

Editor in Chief: Sanjay Gupta; **Editor:** Shailendra Mani Tripathi
Profile: Covers Local National Regional And International News.
Language (s): Hindi
DAILY NEWSPAPER

Dainik Jagran - Kanpur Edition 460575
Editorial: Jagran Building, 2 Sarvodaya Nagar, Kanpur 208005 **Tel:** 91 5122216161
Web site: http://www.jagran.com
Freq: Daily; **Circ:** 175727 Not Audited
Editor: Sandeep Gupta
Profile: Covers Local National Regional And International News.
Language (s): Hindi
DAILY NEWSPAPER

Dainik Jagran - Lucknow Edition 460580
Editorial: 57 A-3 Meera Bai Marg, Lucknow 226001
Tel: 91 5222209484
Web site: http://www.jagran.com
Freq: Daily; **Circ:** 220002 Not Audited
Editor: Shekhar Tripathi
Profile: Covers Local National Regional And International News.
Language (s): Hindi
DAILY NEWSPAPER

Dainik Jagran - Meerut Edition 460581
Editorial: Jagran Bhawan, 140-D Saket, Meerut 250006 **Tel:** 91 1212662245
Web site: http://www.jagran.com
Freq: Daily; **Circ:** 106298 Not Audited
Editor: Dhirendra Mohan Gupta; **Editor:** Prabhat Gupta
Profile: Covers Local, National, Regional and International News.
Language (s): Hindi
DAILY NEWSPAPER

Dainik Jagran - New Delhi Edition 460582
Editorial: 501 INS Building, Rafi Marg, New Delhi 110001 **Tel:** 91 1123359960
Email: mmiadvt@gmail.com **Web site:** http://www.jagran.com
Freq: Daily; **Circ:** 132131 Not Audited
Editor: Vikas Dwivedi; **Editor:** Sanjay Gupta; **National Bureau Chief:** Niti Pradhan
Profile: Covers Local National Regional And International News.
Language (s): Hindi
DAILY NEWSPAPER

Dainik Jagran - Varanasi Edition 156657
Editorial: Andhra Pul, Varanasi 221002
Tel: 91 542 3061000
Email: varanasi@vns.jagran.com **Web site:** http://www.jagran.com
Freq: Daily; **Circ:** 114167 Not Audited
Editor: Sanjav Gupta; **Editor:** Virendra Gupta; **Editor:** Rajeev Sachan
Profile: publishes in all languages (including English) and covers local national and international news.
Language (s): Hindi
DAILY NEWSPAPER

Dainik Kashmir Times 460084
Editorial: Kashmir Times Building, Residency Road, Jammu 180001 **Tel:** 91 1912543676
Web site: http://www.kashmirtimes.com
Freq: Daily; **Circ:** 160003 Not Audited
Editor in Chief: Prabodh Jamwal
Profile: Covers the latest local, regional, international and national news, business, sports and etc.
Language (s): Hindi
DAILY NEWSPAPER

Dainik Lokmat - Ahmednagar Edition 460585
Editorial: 2nd Floor Nirlon, A;B Road, Worli, Mumbai 400018 **Tel:** 91 241 2429902
Web site: http://www.lokmat.net
Freq: Daily; **Circ:** 1000003 Not Audited
Editor in Chief: Rajendra Darda; **General Manager:** Omprakash Kela
Profile: Covers the latest local and international news.
Language (s): English
DAILY NEWSPAPER

Dainik Mahalaxmi Bhagyodaya 460664
Editorial: 184 Patparganj Industrial Area, Delhi 110092 **Tel:** 91 11 22140796
Email: mahalaxmigroup@hotmail.com **Web site:** http://www.mahalaxmigroup.com
Freq: Daily; **Circ:** 53002 Not Audited
Editor: Praveen Jain
Profile: Covers the local and world news.
Language (s): Hindi
DAILY NEWSPAPER

Dainik Navajyoti 460588
Editorial: Dainik Navajyoti Complex, P.O. Box 72, Kaisarganj, Lucknow 305001 **Tel:** 91 145 2426636
Email: jaipur@dainiknavajyoti.com **Web site:** http://www.dainiknavajyoti.com
Freq: Daily; **Circ:** 591002 Not Audited
Profile: Covers local and world news and sports.
Language (s): Hindi
DAILY NEWSPAPER

Dainik Rajpath 460589
Editorial: Mitra Nagar, Gular Road, Aligarh 202001
Tel: 91 571 2521104
Freq: Daily; **Circ:** 50002 Not Audited
Profile: Covers local and world news.
Language (s): Hindi
DAILY NEWSPAPER

Dainik Sambad 459410
Editorial: Jagannath Bari Road, Agartala 799001
Tel: 91 3812326676
Email: dainiksambad@yahoo.com **Web site:** http://www.dainiksambad.net
Freq: Daily; **Circ:** 60003 Not Audited
Editor: Pradeep Bhowmick
Profile: Dainik Sambad is the leading Bengali Daily of Tripura and the largest circulated Bengali newspaper in the North-East India. Dainik Sambad newspaper is also published in Agartala and Tripura.
Language (s): Bengali
DAILY NEWSPAPER

Dainik Udyog Aas-Pass 460592
Editorial: Pujari Bhavan, Tabela Gate, Sikar 332001
Tel: 91 1572-250703
Freq: Daily; **Circ:** 50002 Not Audited
Profile: Covers Local, National And International News.
Language (s): Hindi
DAILY NEWSPAPER

Deccan Chronicle - Bangalore Edition 588570
Editorial: Deccan Chronicle Holdings Ltd., 58, HM Towers, Brigade Road, Bangalore 560025
Tel: 91 80 22226049
Email: editor@deccanmail.com **Web site:** http://www.deccanchronicle.com/
Freq: Daily
Editor: Goutam Das
Profile: Covers the news in local, regional, international and national, business, sports, art, and etc.
Language (s): Hindi
DAILY NEWSPAPER

Deccan Chronicle - Hyderabad Edition 157171
Editorial: Deccan Chronicle Holdings Ltd, 36, Sarojini Devi Road, Secunderabad 500003
Tel: 91 40 27803930
Email: editor@deccanmail.com **Web site:** http://www.deccanchronicle.com/
Freq: Daily; **Circ:** 552855 Not Audited
Editor: A. Jayanti; **Manager:** Pradeep Kumar; **Manager:** K. Rondaswamy
Profile: Covers the news in local, regional, international and national, business, sports, art, and etc.
Language (s): English
DAILY NEWSPAPER

Deccan Herald 156944
Editorial: The Printers (Mysore) Private Limited, 75 Mahatma Gandhi Road P.O. Box 31, Bangalore 560001 **Tel:** 91 80 25 88 0000
Web site: http://www.deccanherald.com
Freq: Daily; **Circ:** 200003 Not Audited
Editor: K.N. Tilak Kumar; **Editor:** K. N. Shanth Kumar
Profile: A general daily newspaper.
Language (s): English
DAILY NEWSPAPER

Deepika Daily 158154
Owner: Rashtra Deepika Publications
Editorial: Rashtra Deepika Publications, P.O. Box 2252, Cochin 686025 **Tel:** 91 481 301 2001
Email: editor@deepika.com **Web site:** http://www.deepikaglobal.com
Freq: Daily; **Circ:** 200002 Not Audited
Editor in Chief: Alexander Paikada; **Editor in Chief:** Jose Panthaplamthottiyil; **Managing Director:** Jose Thomas Pattara; **Managing Director:** P.P. Sunny
Profile: Covers local, regional, international and national news, and sports.
Language (s): Malayalam
DAILY NEWSPAPER

Desh Sewak Daily 460266
Editorial: Bhakna Bhawan, Sector 29 D, Opposite Tribune Colony, Chandigarh 160020
Tel: 91 172 2657256
Email: news@deshsewak.com **Web site:** http://www.deshsewak.com
Freq: Daily
Editor: Prem Gorkhi; **Editor:** Jaspal Singh; **Editor:** Prem Singh; **Editor:** Tejwant Singh Gill; **Editor:** Harbhajan Singh Halwarvi; **Editor:** Joginder Singh Paur; **Editor:** Gulzar Singh Sandhu
Profile: Focuses on well-known literary and social figures as well as local and international news.
Language (s): Punjabi
DAILY NEWSPAPER

Deshabhimani 460596
Editorial: Deshabhimani, Kaloor, Kochi 682017
Tel: 91 4842530739
Web site: http://www.deshabhimani.com
Freq: Daily; **Circ:** 500002 Not Audited
Editor in Chief: V. Dakshinamurthy
Profile: Desabhimani is a Malayalam newspaper which covers the news in local and world, and etc.
Language (s): Malayalam
DAILY NEWSPAPER

Deshbandhu 460597
Editorial: Deshbandhu Ramsagar Para, Raipur 492001 **Tel:** 91 7714288888
Email: deshbandhuraipur@gmail.com **Web site:** http://www.deshbandhu.co.in
Freq: Daily; **Circ:** 60001 Not Audited
Editor: Prabhaker Choubey; **Editor in Chief:** Lalit Surjan
Profile: Covers news.
Language (s): Hindi
DAILY NEWSPAPER

Deshonnati - Akola Edition 460599
Editorial: Nishant Towers, M.G. Road, Akola 444001
Tel: 91 724 2424404
Web site: http://www.deshonnati.com
Freq: Daily; **Circ:** 215002 Not Audited
Bureau Chief: Vikrant Patil; **Editor in Chief:** Prakash Pohare
Profile: Covers local news, sports, business, jobs, and community events.
Language (s): Marathi
DAILY NEWSPAPER

Dharitri 460600
Editorial: B-26 Industrial Estate, Bhubaneshwar 751010 **Tel:** 91 674 2580101
Email: dharitri@sancharnet.in **Web site:** http://www.dharitri.com
Freq: Daily; **Circ:** 200002 Not Audited
Editor: Tathagata Satpathy
Profile: Covers local and world news, sports, education and science.
Language (s): Oriya
DAILY NEWSPAPER

Dinakaran 460601
Editorial: No. 229, Kutchery Road, Mylapore, Chennai 600004 **Tel:** 91 44 42209191
Email: dotcom@dinakaran.com **Web site:** http://www.dinakaran.com
Freq: Daily; **Circ:** 940002 Not Audited
Editor: Kathir Vel
Profile: Covers local and world news, business, sports, entertainment, etc.
Language (s): Tamil
DAILY NEWSPAPER

Dinamalar 460602
Editorial: TVR House, Dinamalar Avenue, Madurai 625016 **Tel:** 91 4522380903
Email: dmrmdu@dinamalar.in **Web site:** http://www.dinamalar.com
Freq: Daily; **Circ:** 600001 Not Audited
Editor: R. Krishnamurthy; **Publisher:** R. Lakshmipathy
Profile: World Number one Tamil daily newspaper.
Language (s): Tamil
Ad Rate: Full Page Colour 1869450.00
Currency: India Rupees
DAILY NEWSPAPER

Dinamani 460603
Editorial: Club House Road, Chennai 600002
Tel: 91 44 28461818
Web site: http://www.dinamani.com
Freq: Daily; **Circ:** 200001 Not Audited
Editor: R.T. Sambandan
Profile: Covers local and world news, sports, business, economy, entertainment, etc.
Language (s): Tamil
DAILY NEWSPAPER

Divya Bhaskar 460357
Editorial: 280, Sarkhej-Gandhinagar Highway, Near YMCA Club, Ahmedabad 380051
Tel: 91 79 39888850
Email: contact@imcl.co.in **Web site:** http://www.divyabhaskar.co.in
Freq: Daily
Editor: Ajay Umat
Profile: Covers the local, regional, international and national news, sports, entertainments, lifestyle, religion, and business.
Language (s): Gujarati
Ad Rate: Full Page Colour 541.00
Currency: India Rupees
DAILY NEWSPAPER

The DQ Week 460763
Editorial: Cyber House, B-35, Sector 32 Institutional, Gurgaon 122001 **Tel:** 91 124 4822222
Web site: http://www.dqweek.com
Freq: Weekly; **Circ:** 60001 Not Audited
Profile: Provides information relating to all areas of information technology.
Language (s): English
DAILY NEWSPAPER

The Economic Times - Ahmedabad Edition 460767
Owner: Bennett, Coleman & Co. Ltd.
Editorial: 139 Ashram Road, Ahmedabad 380009
Tel: 91 79 6560123
Web site: http://www.economictimes.com
Freq: Daily; **Circ:** 6000003 Not Audited
Editor: Ashwin Walunjkr
Profile: Extensively covers the Indian economy, shares prices of commodities and other financial news. Regular topics include personal finance, mutual funds, markets and IPOs.
Language (s): English
Ad Rate: Full Page Colour 12090.00
Currency: United States Dollars
DAILY NEWSPAPER

The Economic Times - Chennai Edition 460766
Owner: Bennett, Coleman & Co. Ltd.
Editorial: Times House, 126/127, Chaimers Road, Nandanam, Chennai 600035 **Tel:** 91 44 24342121
Email: viswanathan.balasubramanian@timesgroup.com **Web site:** http://www.economictimes.com
Freq: Daily; **Circ:** 50002 Not Audited
Profile: Extensively covers the Indian economy, shares prices of commodities and other financial news. Regular topics include personal finance, mutual funds, markets and IPOs.
Language (s): English
DAILY NEWSPAPER

The Economic Times - Kolkata Edition 460765
Owner: Bennett, Coleman & Co. Ltd.
Editorial: 105/7A, S.N.Banerjee Road, Kolkata 700014 **Tel:** 91 3322492222
Web site: http://www.economictimes.com
Freq: Daily; **Circ:** 80003 Not Audited
Editor: Basistha Basu
Profile: Extensively covers the Indian economy, shares prices of commodities and other financial news. Regular topics include personal finance, mutual funds, markets and IPOs.
Language (s): English
DAILY NEWSPAPER

The Economic Times - Mumbai Edition 460764
Owner: Bennett, Coleman & Co. Ltd.
Editorial: 3rd Floor, The Times of India Building, Dr. D N Road, Mumbai 400001 **Tel:** 91 22 66353535
Web site: http://www.economictimes.com
Freq: Daily; **Circ:** 170002 Not Audited
Profile: Extensively covers the Indian economy, shares prices of commodities and other financial news. Regular topics include personal finance, mutual funds, markets and IPOs.
Language (s): Hindi
Ad Rate: Full Page Colour 88652.00
Currency: United States Dollars
DAILY NEWSPAPER

The Economic Times - New Delhi Edition 460769
Owner: Bennett, Coleman & Co. Ltd.
Editorial: 7 Bahadur Shah Zafar Marg, New Delhi 110002 **Tel:** 91 11 2331775
Web site: http://www.economictimes.com
Freq: Daily; **Circ:** 200003 Not Audited
Editor: Bodhisatva Ganguli; **Editor:** Javed Sayed; **Editor:** Amit Tyagi; **Editor, Energy and Infrastructure:** Himangshu Watts
Profile: Extensively covers the Indian economy, shares prices of commodities and other financial news. Regular topics include personal finance, mutual funds, markets and IPOs.
Language (s): English
Ad Rate: Full Page Colour 88652.00
Currency: United States Dollars
DAILY NEWSPAPER

Eenadu 460607
Editorial: Eenadu Complex, Somajiguda, Hyderabad 500482 **Tel:** 91 4023318181
Email: editor@eenadu.net **Web site:** http://www.eenadu.net
Freq: Daily; **Circ:** 100002 Not Audited
Editor: Rahul Kumar
Profile: Covers local and world news, sports and etc.
Language (s): Telugu
Ad Rate: Full Page Colour 3940.00
Currency: India Rupees
DAILY NEWSPAPER

Ei Samay 837876
Editorial: 8 Camac St, Shantiniketan Bldg, Fl 15, Kolkata 700017
Web site: http://eisamay.indiatimes.com
Freq: Daily
Editor: Suman Chattopadhyay
Profile: Launched in October 2012 and published in the Adda language, covers the Bengali region of India. Aims to enlighten readers with dialogue on social, economic and political life by providing context and perspective, nuance and texture. Also known as Eyi Shomoy.
Language (s): Bengali
DAILY NEWSPAPER

Employment & NRI Times 523009
Editorial: 704 Gateway Plaza, Hiranandani Gardens, Powai, Mumbai 400076 **Tel:** 91 2267341770
Email: editorial@enritimes.com **Web site:** http://www.enritimes.com
Freq: Weekly
Editor: E. Vaidyanatyhan
Profile: A weekly newspaper focusing on career advancement, both in India and abroad.
Language (s): Hindi
DAILY NEWSPAPER

Employment News 460363
Editorial: Employment News, East Block IV, Level 5, R K Puram, New Delhi 110066 **Tel:** 91 11 26174975

Email: director.employmentnews@gmail.com **Web site:** http://www.employmentnews.gov.in
Freq: Weekly; **Circ:** 700001 Not Audited
Editor in Chief: Rakesh Jha; **Editor:** Nalini Rani
Profile: Provides information about employment opportunities for young people.
Language (s): English
DAILY NEWSPAPER

Financial Chronicle 535945
Owner: Deccan Chronicle Holdings Limited
Editorial: Financial Chronicle, S-7/8 Free Park, Main Market, New Delhi 110016 **Tel:** 91 1126530001
Email: mymind@mydigitalfc.com **Web site:** http://www.mydigitalfc.com
Freq: Mon thru Fri; **Circ:** 14344 Not Audited
Editor in Chief: Shubhrangshu Roy
Profile: Launched in April 2008 and shares business news.
Language (s): English
Ad Rate: Full Page Colour 27091.00
Currency: United States Dollars
DAILY NEWSPAPER

Financial Express - Mumbai Edition 157165
Editorial: Express Tower 2nd Floor, Nariman Point, Mumbai 400021 **Tel:** 91 22 22022627
Email: editor@expressindia.com **Web site:** http://www.financialexpress.com
Freq: Daily; **Circ:** 150003 Not Audited
Publisher: Prashant Raman
Profile: Mumbai's daily feed on the financial world.
Language (s): English
DAILY NEWSPAPER

Financial Express - New Delhi Edition 586780
Owner: The Indian Express Limited.
Editorial: 9&10, Bhadur Shah Zafar Marg, Express Building, ITO, New Delhi 110002 **Tel:** 91 11 23702100
Web site: http://www.financialexpress.com
Freq: Daily
Editor: Alokananda Chakraborty
Profile: Covers news within business, finance and the stock market with a particular focus on the New Delhi area.
Language (s): English
DAILY NEWSPAPER

Ganashakti 460610
Editorial: 74A Acharya Jagdish Chandra Bose Road, Kolkata 700016 **Tel:** 91 33 2227-8950
Email: mail@ganashakti.co.in **Web site:** http://www.ganashakti.co.in
Freq: Daily; **Circ:** 145002 Not Audited
Editor: Narayan Dutta
Profile: Covers local and world news, travel, literature, science, and technology.
Language (s): Bengali
DAILY NEWSPAPER

Gavakari 460611
Editorial: M/s. Gavakari Prakashan, 'Gavakari, Bhavan 430 H, Tilak Path, Nashik 422001
Tel: 91 25 32305080
Email: dhlgav@yahoo.com
Freq: Daily; **Circ:** 90002 Not Audited
Editor: Vandan Potnis
Profile: Covers local and world news.
Language (s): Marathi
DAILY NEWSPAPER

Glimpses Of Future 460612
Editorial: 63 Padha Street, Purani Mandi, Jammu 180001 **Tel:** 91 191 2546079
Freq: Daily; **Circ:** 85002 Not Audited
Editor in Chief: Prem Nath Sharma
Profile: Covers local and world news.
Language (s): English
DAILY NEWSPAPER

Grameen Duniya 460613
Editorial: 199 C.M.-1, Jhandewalan Extention, New Delhi 110055 **Tel:** 91 11 23626465
Freq: Weekly; **Circ:** 1600002 Not Audited
Editor: Sanjay Gupta
Profile: Focuses on farming and agriculture.
Language (s): Gujarati
DAILY NEWSPAPER

Greater Kashmir 460614
Editorial: 6 Pratap Park, Residency Road, Srinagar 190001 **Tel:** 91 194 2455435
Email: editor@greaterkashmir.com **Web site:** http://www.greaterkashmir.com
Freq: Daily; **Circ:** 70824 Not Audited
Editor: Fayaz Ahmed Kaloo
Profile: Covers the latest local, regional, international and national news, business, sports and etc.
Language (s): English
DAILY NEWSPAPER

Gujarat Samachar 460615
Editorial: Gujarat Samachar Bhavan, Khanpur, Ahmedabad 380001 **Tel:** 91 79 30410000
Web site: http://www.gujaratsamachar.com
Freq: Daily; **Circ:** 380002 Not Audited
Profile: Covers local and world news, sports, business, entertainment, etc.
Language (s): Gujarati
Ad Rate: Full Page Colour 2160.00
Currency: India Rupees
DAILY NEWSPAPER

Gujarat Today Daily 460616
Editorial: Gujarat Today, 33/A, Shah-e-Alam, Ahmedabad 380028 **Tel:** 91 79 25320330
Email: gujarattoday@yahoo.com **Web site:** http://www.gujarattodaydaily.com
Freq: Daily; **Circ:** 61001 Not Audited
Editor: Yunus Patel; **Publisher:** S. Tirmizi
Profile: Covers the latest news in local, regional, international and national, sports.
Language (s): Gujarati
DAILY NEWSPAPER

Gujarat Vaibhav 460617
Editorial: 6 Mill Officers Colony, Ashram Road, Post Bag No. 9, Ahmedabad 380009 **Tel:** 91 79 2658-9474
Email: gvd@icenet.net
Freq: Daily; **Circ:** 182617 Not Audited
Editor: V. V. Videh
Profile: Covers local and world news, sports and etc.
Language (s): Hindi
DAILY NEWSPAPER

Halat-E-Watan 459379
Editorial: B-2/31, 3rd Floor, Taksal Theaters Building, Nadesar, Varanasi 221002 **Tel:** 91 5422500887
Freq: Daily; **Circ:** 62003 Not Audited
Editor: Sandeep Gupta
Profile: Daily Urdu newspaper.
Language (s): Urdu
DAILY NEWSPAPER

Haribhoomi 847462
Editorial: 330 Vinay Nagar, Bypass Road, Rohtak 124001 **Tel:** 91 1262295801
Email: rohtak@haribhoomi.com **Web site:** http://www.haribhoomi.com
Freq: Daily
Profile: One of the most read Hindi newspapers, covers national news.
Language (s): Hindi
DAILY NEWSPAPER

Herald Young Leader 460618
Editorial: C-101, B.G. Tower, O/S Delhi Gate, Ahmedabad 380004 **Tel:** 91 7925625000
Freq: Daily; **Circ:** 347002 Not Audited
Editor in Chief: Bharat Bhushan Chhajjer
Profile: Covers local and world news, analytical articles, film news and views, sports, commercial views.
Language (s): Hindi
DAILY NEWSPAPER

Himachal Times 460622
Editorial: Himachal Times Complex, 21 Rajpur Road, Dehradun 248001 **Tel:** 91 1352651487
Web site: http://www.theimachaltimes.com
Freq: Daily; **Circ:** 54002 Not Audited
Editor: Ashok Pandhi; **Editor in Chief:** Vijay Pandhi
Profile: Covers the local, national and international news.
Language (s): Hindi
DAILY NEWSPAPER

The Hindu 156660
Owner: Hindu Group (The)
Editorial: The Hindu Group, Kasturi Buildings, 859/860, Anna Salai, Chennai 600002 **Tel:** 91 44 2857-6300
Email: epaperth@thehindu.co.in **Web site:** http://www.thehindu.com
Freq: Daily; **Circ:** 1400000 Not Audited
Profile: Established in 1878, covers the latest local and world news, with features on business, sports and the arts.
Language (s): English
Ad Rate: Full Page Mono 112761.00
Ad Rate: Full Page Colour 178398.00
Currency: United States Dollars
DAILY NEWSPAPER

Hindu Business Line - Bangalore Edition 593278
Editorial: The Hindu Group, 19 & 21 Bhagwan Mahaveer Road (Infantry Road), Bangalore 560001
Tel: 91 8022864240
Web site: http://www.thehindubusinessline.com
Freq: Daily
Profile: Covers the latest in local and world, money, banking, marketing, technology, economics and government.
Language (s): Hindi
DAILY NEWSPAPER

The Hindu Business Line - Chennai Edition 460624
Owner: The Hindu Group
Editorial: Kasturi Buildings, 859/860, Anna Salai, Chennai 600002 **Tel:** 91 44 28413344
Email: bleditor@thehindu.co.in **Web site:** http://www.thehindubusinessline.com
Freq: Daily; **Circ:** 195000 Not Audited
Profile: Established in 1994 and covers the latest in local and world, money, banking, marketing, technology, economics, industry, logistic and government.
Language (s): English
Ad Rate: Full Page Mono 33660.00
Ad Rate: Full Page Colour 48807.00
Currency: United States Dollars
DAILY NEWSPAPER

The Hindu Business Line - Hyderabad Edition 499772
Editorial: 6-3-879b, Begumpet, Hyderabad 500016
Tel: 91 22 22885593
Web site: http://www.thehindubusinessline.com
Freq: Daily
Editor: K. Venugopal
Profile: Covers business topics.
Language (s): English
DAILY NEWSPAPER

The Hindu Business Line - New Delhi Edition 592563
Editorial: The Hindu Group, 3rd Floor, PTI Building, 4 Parliament Street, New Delhi 110001
Tel: 91 1143579797
Web site: http://www.thehindubusinessline.com
Freq: Daily
Profile: Covers the latest in local and world, money, banking, marketing, technology and economics.
Language (s): English
DAILY NEWSPAPER

The Hindu- Hyderabad Edition 502089
Editorial: 6-3-879b, Begumpet, Hyderabad 500016
Tel: 91 44 28576300
Freq: Daily
Editor: S. Sreevatsan
Profile: Covers the latest local, regional, international, and national news.
Language (s): Hindi
DAILY NEWSPAPER

Hindustan - Lucknow Edition 460626
Editorial: The Hindustan Times House, 25 Ashok Marg, Lucknow 226001 **Tel:** 91 5222205717
Email: naveenjoshi@hindustantimes.com **Web site:** http://www.hindustantimes.com
Freq: Daily; **Circ:** 292698 Not Audited
Editor: Naveen Joshi
Profile: Covers local and world news, sports, business, entertainment, lifestyle, travel, events and etc.
Language (s): English
Ad Rate: Full Page Colour 5600.00
Currency: India Rupees
DAILY NEWSPAPER

Hindustan - Patna Edition 460627
Owner: Hindustan Times Media Ltd.
Editorial: Hindustan Times Media Ltd., Searchlight Building, Budh Marg, Patna 800001
Tel: 91 6122223434
Web site: http://www.hindustantimes.com
Freq: Daily; **Circ:** 292698 Not Audited
Editor in Chief: Akku Shrivastav
Profile: Covers local, National, Regional and International news.
Language (s): Hindi
DAILY NEWSPAPER

The Hindustan Times - Bhopal Edition 523008
Owner: HT Media Ltd
Editorial: Park Centra Bldg, 7th Floor, Sector 30, Delhi-Jaipur Highway, Bhopal 122001
Tel: 91 124 3954700
Web site: http://www.htmedia.in
Freq: Daily
Profile: Established in 1924, serves as one of India's most widely read newspapers with news, information, analysis and entertainment.
Language (s): Hindi
DAILY NEWSPAPER

The Hindustan Times - Kolkata Edition 460773
Owner: HT Media Ltd
Editorial: HT Media Ltd., 50 Chowringhee Road, Kolkata 700071 **Tel:** 91 3322827315
Email: feedback@hindustantimes.com **Web site:** http://www.hindustantimes.com
Freq: Daily; **Circ:** 117001 Not Audited
Editor: Rajiv Bagchi
Profile: Established in 1924, serves as one of India's most widely read newspapers with news, information, analysis and entertainment.
Language (s): English
Ad Rate: Full Page Colour 390000.00
Currency: India Rupees
DAILY NEWSPAPER

Hindustan Times - Mumbai Edition 723219
Owner: HT Media Ltd
Editorial: HT Media Ltd, LJ Cross Rd, No. 1, Mahim, Mumbai 400016 **Tel:** 91 22 43519500
Web site: http://www.hindustantimes.com
Freq: Daily
Editor: Soumya Bhattacharya
Profile: Established in 1924, serves as one of India's most widely read newspapers with news, information, analysis and entertainment.
Language (s): English
Ad Rate: Full Page Colour 1440000.00
Currency: India Rupees
DAILY NEWSPAPER

The Hindustan Times - New Delhi Edition 460775
Owner: HT Media Ltd
Editorial: Hindustan Times House, 18-20, K.G. Marg, New Delhi 110001 **Tel:** 91 11 2336-1234
Web site: http://www.hindustantimes.com
Freq: Daily; **Circ:** 566585 Not Audited
Editor: Sonal Kalra; **Editor:** Poonam Saxena
Profile: Established in 1924, serves as one of India's most widely read newspapers with news, information, analysis and entertainment.
Language (s): English
Ad Rate: Full Page Colour 540960.00
Currency: India Rupees
DAILY NEWSPAPER

The Hindustan Times - Patna Edition 157167
Owner: HT Media Ltd
Editorial: Searchlight Building, Budh Marg, Patna 800001 **Tel:** 91 6122223314
Email: ashokmishra@hindustantimes.com **Web site:** http://www.hindustantimes.com
Freq: Daily; **Circ:** 500002 Not Audited
Editor: Sonal Kalra; **Editor:** Poonam Saxena
Profile: Established in 1924, serves as one of India's most widely read newspapers with news, information, analysis and entertainment.
Language (s): English
Ad Rate: Full Page Colour 425.00
Currency: India Rupees
DAILY NEWSPAPER

The Hitavada 460628
Editorial: Pandit Jawaharlal Nehru Marg, Wardha Road, Nagpur 440012 **Tel:** 91 7122435737
Email: editor@thehitavada.com **Web site:** http://www.ehitavada.com
Freq: Daily; **Circ:** 60001 Not Audited
Editor: Vijay Phanshikar
Profile: Covers news in the Nagpur metropolitan area.
Language (s): English
DAILY NEWSPAPER

HT Mumbai 460326
Owner: HT Media Ltd.
Editorial: HT Media Ltd., 2nd Floor, Mahalaxmi Engineering Estate, Lady Jamshedji First Cross Road, Mahim (W), Mumbai 400016 **Tel:** 91 2266539200
Web site: http://www.hindustantimes.com
Freq: Daily; **Circ:** 200002 Not Audited
Editor: Soumya Bhattacharya; **Editor:** Akshay Sawai
Profile: Covers the news in local and international, business, sports, travel, entertainment and etc.
Language (s): English
DAILY NEWSPAPER

Humara Awam 459394
Editorial: Awam, Public Garden Road, Nampally, Hyderabad 500001 **Tel:** 91 4055612734
Freq: Daily; **Circ:** 50001 Not Audited
Editor: K.M. Arifuddin
Profile: Covers local, regional, international and national news.
Language (s): Urdu
DAILY NEWSPAPER

Indian Express - Chandigarh Edition 459156
Editorial: Plot No. C-5, Institutional Area, Sector-6, Chandigarh 134109 **Tel:** 91 1725024400
Email: expresschd@gmail.com **Web site:** http://indianexpress.com
Freq: Daily; **Circ:** 80001 Not Audited
Editor: Vipin Pubby
Profile: Established in 1932, covers the latest news from India with exclusive current headlines on hot topics, breaking news, business, sports, politics and entertainment.
Language (s): English
Ad Rate: Full Page Colour 170.00
Currency: India Rupees
DAILY NEWSPAPER

Indian Express - New Delhi Edition 157163
Editorial: The Indian Express Limited, 9&10, Bhadur Shah Zafar Marg, Express Building, ITO, New Delhi 110002 **Tel:** 91 11 23702100
Web site: http://indianexpress.com
Freq: Daily; **Circ:** 100002 Not Audited
Editor: Seema Chishti; **Editor:** Vandana Kalra;
Editor: Coomi Kapoor; **Editor:** Unni Rajan Shanker;
Bureau Chief: P. Vaidyanathan
Profile: Established in 1932, covers the latest news from India with exclusive current headlines on hot topics, breaking news, business, sports, politics and entertainment.
Language (s): English
Ad Rate: Full Page Colour 360.00
Currency: India Rupees
DAILY NEWSPAPER

Indian Punch 460631
Editorial: Upper Bilasi Town, Jharkhand, Deoghar 814117 **Tel:** 91 6432 246216
Email: indianpunch2000@yahoo.com
Freq: Daily; **Circ:** 65002 Not Audited
Profile: This Is The Only Newspaper Represents The People Of Santhal Pargana. It Publishes The Current News Related To Political Affairs Sports And

Education Crime Culture General Human Interest Stories And Many Others Fields.
Language (s): Hindi
DAILY NEWSPAPER

Indinon
460249
Editorial: I-91, Lubna House, Batla House, Okhla, New Delhi 110025 **Tel:** 91 11 2379-2121
Email: editor@thesedaysindia.com
Freq: Daily
Editor in Chief: S. Asif
Profile: Indinon is a newspaper which covers the news in local and world.
Language (s): Hindi
DAILY NEWSPAPER

Ingredients South Asia
544738
Editorial: Saffron Media Private Limited, 2nd Floor, Laura Building, 1st Dhobi Talao Lane, Dhobi Talao, Mumbai 400002 **Tel:** 91 22 42202800
Email: isa@saffronmedia.in **Web site:** http://www.saffronmedia.in
Freq: Weekly
Editor: P. Francis
Profile: Devoted to three key ingredients sectors of pharma, food and cosmetics. Includes news, interviews, guest articles, features and updates on R&D, processing, manufacturing and use of ingredients in pharma, food, functional food, cosmetics, cosmeceuticals, nutraceuticals, ayurveda and herbals, and dietary supplements industry.
Language (s): Hindi
DAILY NEWSPAPER

International Business Times
845440
Editorial: 248, 3rd floor, Defence Colony, 80 Ft. Rd, Bangalore 560008 **Tel:** 91 80 43100900
Email: info@ibtimes.co.in **Web site:** http://www.ibtimes.co.in
Freq: Daily
Profile: Covers the latest headlines pertaining to international and national news.
Language (s): English
DAILY NEWSPAPER

Iris Business Services
586791
Editorial: T-131, Tower 1, 3rd Floor, International Infotech Park, Vashi, Navi Mumbai, Mumbai 400703 **Tel:** 91 22 27814436
Profile: IRIS owns and manages one of India's most comprehensive financial information databases, covering the universe of publicly traded companies, mutual funds, markets reference data to a live news service on Indian business, markets and the economy.
Language (s): English
DAILY NEWSPAPER

Jadeed Indinon
460250
Editorial: I-91, Lubna House, Batla House, Okhla, New Delhi 110001 **Tel:** 91 1123792121
Email: editor@thesedaysindia.com
Freq: Daily
Editor in Chief: S. Asif; **Editor:** R. Singh
Profile: Covers national and international news.
Language (s): Urdu
DAILY NEWSPAPER

Jag Bani, Jalandhar
460634
Editorial: Hind Samachar Building, Civil Lines, Jalandhar 144001 **Tel:** 91 1812280104
Freq: Daily; **Circ:** 300001 Not Audited
Co-Editor: Avinash Chopra; **Editor in Chief:** Vijay Kumar Chopra
Profile: Jag Bani is a daily newspaper in Jalandhar, India covering local news, sports, business, jobs, and community events. The web site is presented in the Punjabi language.
Language (s): Punjabi
DAILY NEWSPAPER

Jai Hind
460635
Editorial: Jai Hind Press Building, Babubhai Shah Marg, Rajkot 360001 **Tel:** 91 2813048684
Email: editor@jaihinddaily.com **Web site:** http://www.jaihinddaily.com
Freq: Daily; **Circ:** 50001 Not Audited
Editor in Chief: Pradeep Shah
Profile: Daily Gujarati newspaper
Language (s): Gujarati
DAILY NEWSPAPER

Jalte Deep
460637
Editorial: Jalte Deep Building, Jalori Gate, Jodhpur 342003 **Tel:** 91 291 2435896
Email: jaltedeep@sancharnet.in **Web site:** http://www.manak.org
Freq: Daily; **Circ:** 50001 Not Audited
Editor in Chief: Padam Mehta
Profile: Covers the news, culture lifestyle and etc.
Language (s): Hindi
DAILY NEWSPAPER

Jam-E-Jamshed
460638
Editorial: 2nd Fl, Arya Samaj Bhavan, 232 Perin Nariman St, Maharashtra, Mumbai 400001 **Tel:** 91 22 2222692572
Email: jame1832@rediffmail.com
Freq: Weekly; **Circ:** 50003 Not Audited
Editor: Rusi Dhondy
Profile: Covers local and world news.
Language (s): English
DAILY NEWSPAPER

Janmabhoomi
460642
Editorial: Janmabhoomi Bhavan, Janmabhoomi Marg, Fort, Mumbai 400001 **Tel:** 91 22 22570831
Email: jbhoomi@yahoo.com **Web site:** http://pravasi.janmabhoominewspapers.com/
Freq: 2 Times/Week; **Circ:** 62001 Not Audited
Editor: Yogesh Pandya; **Editor in Chief:** Kundan Vyas
Profile: Janma bhoomi Newspaper (epaper) is a Gujarati evening Daily newspaper from Inida which focused on the latest news in local and international.
Language (s): Gujarati
DAILY NEWSPAPER

Janmabhoomi Pravasi
460643
Editorial: Janmabhoomi Bhavan, Janmabhoomi Marg, Fort, Mumbai 400001 **Tel:** 91 22 22870831
Email: jbhoomi@yahoo.com **Web site:** http://pravasi.janmabhoominewspapers.com/
Freq: Weekly; **Circ:** 107001 Not Audited
Editor in Chief: Kundan Vyas
Profile: Covers local and world news.
Language (s): Gujarati
DAILY NEWSPAPER

Janmabhumi
460644
Editorial: 34/114 Perandoor Road, Elamakkara, P.O., Cochin 682026 **Tel:** 91 484 3219925
Email: janmabhumi@vsnl.in **Web site:** http://www.janmabhumidaily.com
Freq: Daily; **Circ:** 120003 Not Audited
Editor in Chief: Hari Kartha; **Editor:** Leela Menon
Profile: Covers Cultural topics, Sports, Karshikam (Agriculture), Samakalikam (Recent Events Valuations), Garhikam (House) etc.
Language (s): Malayalam
DAILY NEWSPAPER

Janpath Samachar
460646
Editorial: Janpath House, Seth Srilal Market, Siliguri 734401 **Tel:** 91 353 22544130
Email: janpath_samachar@bsnl.in **Web site:** http://www.janpathsamachar.com
Freq: Daily; **Circ:** 51002 Not Audited
Editor in Chief: Rajendra Baid
Profile: Covers news and related topics.
Language (s): Hindi
DAILY NEWSPAPER

Jharkhand Classified Weekly
460187
Editorial: 55 Baralal Street, Upper Bazar, Ranchi 834001 **Tel:** 91 651 2206320
Email: news@ranchiexpress.com **Web site:** http://www.ranchiexpress.com
Freq: Weekly; **Circ:** 55002 Not Audited
Editor: Balbir Dutt; **Editor:** Manish Maroo; **Editor:** Chandreshwar Singh
Profile: Covers the variety of topics such a the latest news in local and international, regional, automobile, business, career, and entertainments
Language (s): English
DAILY NEWSPAPER

Kannada Prabha
460649
Editorial: Express Building, 1 Queen's Road, Bangalore 560001 **Tel:** 91 80 22866893
Email: bexpress@bgl.vsnl.net.in **Web site:** http://www.kannadaprabha.com
Freq: Daily; **Circ:** 114808 Not Audited
Editor: Shiva Subramanyam
Profile: Covers the latest news in local, regional, international and national, and etc.
Language (s): Kannada
DAILY NEWSPAPER

Karmakshetra
460650
Editorial: 29/1-A, Old Ballygunge, 2nd Lane, Kolkata 700019 **Tel:** 91 33 22835526
Email: swarna@cal2.vsnl.net.in **Web site:** http://www.bhraman.com
Freq: Weekly; **Circ:** 115002 Not Audited
Editor in Chief: Amarendra Chakravorty
Profile: Provides information on business, economics, labor and industrial relations.
Language (s): Bengali
Ad Rate: Full Page Colour 4580.00
Currency: United States Dollars
DAILY NEWSPAPER

The Kashmir Times
460651
Editorial: Kashmir Times Building, Residency Road, Jammu 180001 **Tel:** 91 191 5247379
Email: editor@kashmirtimes.com
Freq: Daily; **Circ:** 160003 Not Audited
Editor in Chief: Prabodh Jamwal
Profile: Covers the latest local, regional, international and national news.
Language (s): English
DAILY NEWSPAPER

Kerala Kaumudi
460653
Editorial: P.O. Box No. 77, Pettah, Thiruvananthapuram 695024 **Tel:** 91 4712461010
Email: editor@ekaumudi.com **Web site:** http://www.kaumudi.com
Freq: Daily; **Circ:** 141193 Not Audited
Editor in Chief: M. Mani
Profile: Covers business, the latest news, sports, automobile, entertainment, etc.
Language (s): Malayalam
DAILY NEWSPAPER

Krishak Jagat - Bhopal Edition
460655
Editorial: 14 Indira Press Complex, M.P. Nagar, Bhopal 462011 **Tel:** 91 755 2768452
Email: info@krishakjagat.org **Web site:** http://www.krishakjagat.org
Freq: Weekly; **Circ:** 1500003 Not Audited
Editor in Chief: Vijay Bondriya; **Editor:** Sunil Gangrade
Profile: Krishak Jagat - Bhopal Edition is a newspaper which covers the news, Agribusiness, Engineering, Agriculture & Farming and Gardening.
Language (s): Hindi
Ad Rate: Full Page Colour 189000.00
Currency: India Rupees
DAILY NEWSPAPER

Kutchmitra
460656
Editorial: Chief of News Bureau, Kutchmitra Bhavan, Near Indira Park, Bhuj 370001 **Tel:** 91 2832 252090
Email: kutchmitra@yahoo.com **Web site:** http://www.kutchmitradaily.com
Freq: Daily; **Circ:** 50002 Not Audited
Editor: Kirti Khatri
Profile: Covers the latest news in local, regional, national and international and lifestyle.
Language (s): Gujarati
DAILY NEWSPAPER

Lokmat - Aurangabad
460658
Editorial: Lokmat Bhavan, Jalna Road, Aurangabad 431210 **Tel:** 91 242 2477264
Web site: http://onlinenews1.lokmat.com
Freq: Daily; **Circ:** 300002 Not Audited
Editor in Chief: Vijay Darda; **General Manager:** Omprakash Kela; **Editor:** Dinakar Raikar
Profile: Discusses news in local, regional, international and national, etc.
Language (s): Hindi
DAILY NEWSPAPER

Lokmat Times - Nagpur Edition
460659
Editorial: Lokmat Bhavan, Pt. J. Nehru Marg, Nagpur 440012 **Tel:** 91 7122523527
Email: lokmat@bom2.vsnl.net.in
Freq: Daily; **Circ:** 166971 Not Audited
Editor in Chief: Vijay Darda
Profile: Lokmat was conceptualized and started by Loknayak Bapuji Aney as a weapon to fight the British imperialism during the freedom movement of India. The name 'Lokmat' was given by the great freedom fighter and literary person Bal Gangadhar Tilak ("Freedom is my birth right and I shall have it") when the publication was first started as a handwritten newspaper from Yavatmal, then a little known town in Maharashtra. Inspired by the great luminaries of the freedom movement, Late Shri Jawaharlal Darda took over this fortnightly published newspaper in 1953. The former Prime Minister of India, Pt. Jawaharlal Nehru formally inaugurated Lokmat as a daily publication in 1958 at Yavatmal and on December 15th 1971, the first full fledge edition was started from Nagpur, the winter capital of one of India's largest and most affluent states - Maharashtra. From its humble beginning in 1971, the publication eventually emerged as the No.1 circulated and read daily of Maharashtra reaching every corner of the state and catering to the news and entertainment needs of millions of its readers everyday.
Language (s): English
DAILY NEWSPAPER

Lokmat, Jalgaon
460660
Editorial: Lokmat Bhavan, C-19, MIDC Area, Aurangabad Road, Jalgaon 425003 **Tel:** 91 257 2273013
Web site: http://www.lokmat.com
Freq: Daily; **Circ:** 76751 Not Audited
Editor: Vijay Bawiskar; **Editor in Chief:** Vijay Darda; **General Manager:** Omprakash Kela; **Editor:** Sudhir Mahajan
Profile: Covers the latest news in local, regional, International and national, business, and etc.
Language (s): Marathi
DAILY NEWSPAPER

Loksatta
460657
Editorial: Express Towers, Nariman Point, Mumbai 400021 **Tel:** 91 22 22022627
Email: loksatta@expressindia.com **Web site:** http://www.loksatta.com
Freq: Daily; **Circ:** 500002 Not Audited
Editor: Kumar Ketkar
Profile: Covers the latest local and world news, sports, industry and etc.
Language (s): Marathi
Ad Rate: Full Page Mono 316800.00
Ad Rate: Full Page Colour 332160.00
Currency: India Rupees
DAILY NEWSPAPER

Maalai Malar
460662
Editorial: Rani Buildings, 1091 Periyar EVR High Road, Chennai 600007 **Tel:** 91 44 25321184
Email: malareditor@yahoo.co.in **Web site:** http://www.maalaimalar.com
Freq: Daily; **Circ:** 160002 Not Audited
Editor in Chief: K. Chandragopal
Profile: Covers local and world news, sports, business and etc.
Language (s): Hindi
DAILY NEWSPAPER

Madhyamam
460663
Editorial: P.O. Box No. 1708, Silver Hills, Calicut/kozhikode 673012 **Tel:** 91 4952731500
Web site: http://www.madhyamam.com
Freq: Daily; **Circ:** 1161621 Not Audited
Editor: O. Rahman
Profile: Covers the latest news in local, regional, international and national, business, sports, and etc
Language (s): Malayalam
DAILY NEWSPAPER

Maharashtra Times
460666
Editorial: Dr D N Road, Fort Mumbai, Dr D N Road, Fort Mumbai, Mumbai 400001 **Tel:** 91 22 66354245
Email: colourmt@gmail.com **Web site:** http://www.maharashtratimes.com
Freq: Daily; **Circ:** 200001 Not Audited
Editor: Meenal Baghel; **Editor:** Chandrima Pal; **Editor in Chief:** Abhijit Pradhan; **Editor:** Bharat Raut; **Editor:** Mayank Shekhar; **Bureau Chief:** C. Unnikrishnan
Profile: Provides the latest news in Marathi about the Maharashtra state of India.
Language (s): Marathi
Ad Rate: Full Page Colour 5950.00
Currency: India Rupees
DAILY NEWSPAPER

Mail Today
531757
Editorial: Mediaplex FC-8, Sector - 16A, New Delhi 110001 **Tel:** 91 11 43530800
Web site: http://www.mailtoday.in
Freq: Daily; **Circ:** 120002 Not Audited
Editor: Bharat Bhushan
Profile: Covers the latest local and world news, and a variety of topics through a wide range of sections, including Money Mail, Good Health, Femail and Travel Mail.
Language (s): English
DAILY NEWSPAPER

Malayala Manorama
460671
Editorial: Manorama Bldgs, K.K. Rd, P.B. #26, Kottayam 686001 **Tel:** 91 4812563646
Email: editorial@mm.co.in **Web site:** http://www.manoramaonline.com
Freq: Daily; **Circ:** 1296361 Not Audited
Profile: Covers international and national news.
Language (s): Malayalam
Ad Rate: Full Page Colour 2500.00
Currency: India Rupees
DAILY NEWSPAPER

Mathrubhumi Daily
460672
Editorial: M.J. Krishnamohan Building, K.P. Kesavamenon Road, Calicut/kozhikode 673001 **Tel:** 91 49 52367744
Email: mbiclt@mpp.co.in **Web site:** http://www.mathrubhumi.com
Freq: Daily; **Circ:** 880003 Not Audited
Editor: K. Sreedharan Nair
Profile: Covers the latest news in local, regional, international and national, business, sports, entertainment, education, health and etc.
Language (s): Malayalam
Ad Rate: Full Page Colour 701460.00
Currency: India Rupees
DAILY NEWSPAPER

Mid Day
157168
Editorial: Mid-day Multimedia Limited, Dr. S.S. Rao Road, Opposite Mahatma Gandhi Hospital, Parel, Mumbai 400012 **Tel:** 91 22 67017171
Email: cs@mid-day.com **Web site:** http://www.mid-day.com
Freq: Daily; **Circ:** 140003 Not Audited
Editor: Dhiman Chattopadhyay
Profile: Focuses on general news, entertainments, relationships, lifestyle, sports and health.
Language (s): English
DAILY NEWSPAPER

mint
499775
Owner: HT Media Ltd.
Editorial: 16th Fl, 18-20 Kasturba Gandhi Marg, New Delhi 110001 **Tel:** 91 11 66561234
Email: newsroom@livemint.com **Web site:** http://www.livemint.com
Freq: Daily; **Circ:** 85003 Not Audited
Editor: Natasha Badhwar; **Editor:** Leslie D'Monte; **Editor, Mint Money:** Monika Halan; **Editor:** Sukumar Ranganathan
Profile: Launched in February 2007, covers breaking news & analyses of Indian and world business, economy & politics. Targets readers in Delhi, Mumbai, Chennai, Bengaluru, Chandigarh, Pune, Kolkata and Ahmedabad.
Language (s): English
Ad Rate: Full Page Colour 58938.00
Currency: United States Dollars
DAILY NEWSPAPER

Mumbai Mirror
460288
Editorial: 4th Floor, The Times of India Building, Dr. D N Road, Mumbai 400001 **Tel:** 91 022 66353535
Email: meenal.baghel@timesgroup.com **Web site:** http://www.mumbaimirror.com
Freq: Daily; **Circ:** 558437 Not Audited
Editor: Meenal Baghel; **Editor:** Dinesh Narayanan; **Editor:** Sudharak Olwe; **Editor:** Chandrima Pal; **Editor:** Kunal Pradhan; **Editor:** Bharat Raut; **Editor:** Mayank Shekhar; **Bureau Chief:** C. Unnikrishnan
Profile: Serves as the largest compact newspaper in Mumbai, featuring local news, sports, entertainment, tech, health and business topics.
Language (s): English
DAILY NEWSPAPER

Munsif Daily 460675
Editorial: 5-9-62, Khan Lateef Khan Estate, FMC Road, Hyderabad 500001 **Tel:** 91 40 66660005
Email: munsifdaily@eth.net **Web site:** http://www.munsifdaily.com
Freq: Daily; **Circ:** 59002 Not Audited
Editor in Chief: Lateef Khan
Profile: Covers the latest local, regional, international and national news, sports and etc.
Language (s): Urdu
DAILY NEWSPAPER

My Mobile Infomedia Pvt. Ltd. 586787
Editorial: #25 Shankar Market, Connaught Palace, New Delhi 110001 **Tel:** 91 11 46206161
Web site: http://www.mymobile.co.in
Freq: Weekly
Profile: Offers news, reviews and views on mobile phones, mobile phone prices, value added services, cellular services, tariff plans and reviews of mobile applications and games.
Language (s): English
DAILY NEWSPAPER

Mysooru Mithra 460253
Editorial: 15C, Industrial A-Layout, Bannimantap, Mysore 570015 **Tel:** 91 821 2496520
Email: voice@starofmysore.com **Web site:** http://www.starofmysore.com
Freq: Daily; **Circ:** 85002 Not Audited
Editor: K. Ganapathy
Profile: Mysooru Mithra is a newspaper which covers the latest news in local and world, sports and etc.
Language (s): Kannada
DAILY NEWSPAPER

Nai Dunia 460677
Owner: NaiDuna Media Put Ltd.
Editorial: 60/1 Babu Labhchand Chhajlani Marg, Indore, New Delhi 452009 **Tel:** 91 731 2763111
Email: delhi@naidunia.com **Web site:** http://www.naidunia.com
Freq: Weekly; **Circ:** 59001 Not Audited
Editor: Shravan Garg; **Editor in Chief:** Shahid Siddiqui
Profile: Discusses news.
Language (s): Urdu
DAILY NEWSPAPER

Nava Bharat - Bhopal 460681
Editorial: 3 Indira Press Complex, Maharana Pratap Nagar, Zone 1, Bhopal 462001 **Tel:** 91 755 2551411
Email: navabharatbhopal@gmail.com **Web site:** http://www.navbharattimes.indiatimes.com
Freq: Daily; **Circ:** 75614 Not Audited
Editor in Chief: P.K. Maheshwari; **Editor:** Nishant Sharma
Profile: Brings news in Hindi from India and international news headlines, with top stories on business, politics, sports and entertainment.
Language (s): Hindi
DAILY NEWSPAPER

Nava Bharat - Jabalpur 460680
Editorial: Nava Bharat Bhavan, Opp. Bus Stand, Napier Town, Jabalpur 482001 **Tel:** 91 761 4005111
Email: navabharatbhopal@gmail.com **Web site:** http://www.navbharattimes.indiatimes.com
Freq: Daily; **Circ:** 84867 Not Audited
Editor in Chief: P.K. Maheshwari; **Editor:** Abhi Manoj
Profile: Brings news in Hindi from India and international news headlines, with top stories on business, politics, sports and entertainment.
Language (s): Hindi
DAILY NEWSPAPER

Nava Bharat - Nagpur 460682
Editorial: Nava Bharat, Chhatrapati Chowk, Vardha Road, Nagpur 440025 **Tel:** 91 712 2726677
Email: navabharatbhopal@gmail.com **Web site:** http://www.navabharat.net
Freq: Daily; **Circ:** 111083 Not Audited
General Manager: Anil Bajpai; **Publisher:** Vinod Maheshwari
Profile: Brings news in Hindi from India and international news headlines, with top stories on business, politics, sports and entertainment.
Language (s): Hindi
DAILY NEWSPAPER

Nava Bharat - Raipur 460683
Editorial: Nava Bharat Bhavan Press Complex, G E Road, Raipur 492001 **Tel:** 91 771 2535544
Email: navabharatbhopal@gmail.com **Web site:** http://www.navabharat.net
Freq: Daily; **Circ:** 89099 Not Audited
Director: Sumeet Maheshwari; **Editor:** Anal Shukla
Profile: Brings news in Hindi from India and international news headlines, with top stories on business, politics, sports and entertainment.
Language (s): Hindi
DAILY NEWSPAPER

Navashakti 460689
Editorial: 215, Free Press House Journal Marg, Nariman Point, Mumbai 400021 **Tel:** 91 22 2287-4566
Email: fpj@vsnl.com
Freq: Daily; **Circ:** 60004 Not Audited
Editor: Prakash Kulkarni; **Editor:** Mahesh Mahatare
Profile: Discusses the latest local, regional, national and international news.
Language (s): Marathi
DAILY NEWSPAPER

Navbharat Times - New Delhi Edition 460685
Editorial: Navbharat Times, Indian Express Building, IInd Floor, Bahadur Shah Zafar Marg, New Delhi 110003 **Tel:** 91 1143505340
Web site: http://www.navbharattimes.com
Freq: Daily; **Circ:** 400001 Not Audited
Profile: Covers local and international, business, sports, entertainment, technology, lifestyle news and etc.
Language (s): Hindi
DAILY NEWSPAPER

Navbharat Times- Mumbai Edition 460686
Editorial: P.O. Box No. 213, Dr. D.N. Road, Mumbai 400001 **Tel:** 91 22 66353535
Web site: http://www.timesofindia.com
Freq: Daily; **Circ:** 166165 Not Audited
Publisher: Sam Dastoor; **Editor:** Sachindra Tripathi
Profile: Covers news and related topics.
Language (s): Hindi
DAILY NEWSPAPER

Neighbourhood Flash 459401
Owner: TEJ Bandhu Group
Editorial: TEJ Bandhu Group, 8-B Bahadur Shah Zafar Marg, New Delhi 110002 **Tel:** 91 11 52225111
Freq: Daily; **Circ:** 125002 Not Audited
Editor: Poonam Singh
Profile: Covers news topics.
Language (s): English
DAILY NEWSPAPER

The New Indian Express - Bangalore Edition 460195
Owner: Express Network Private Limited
Editorial: Express Network Private Limited, Express Building, No. 1 Queen's Road, Bangalore 560001
Tel: 91 8022866893
Email: writetous@newindianexpress.com **Web site:** http://www.newindpress.com
Freq: Daily; **Circ:** 500002 Not Audited
Profile: Covers local and international news.
Language (s): English
DAILY NEWSPAPER

The New Indian Express - Chennai Edition 460779
Editorial: 29 second Main Rd, Ampattur Industrial Estate, Chennai 600058 **Tel:** 91 4423457601
Email: writetous@newindianexpress.com **Web site:** http://www.indian-express.com
Freq: Daily; **Circ:** 310786 Not Audited
Editor: Babu Jayakumar; **Editor:** Shiv Kumar
Profile: Covers the news in local and world, business, lifestyle, sports and technology with a focus on Chennai.
Language (s): English
DAILY NEWSPAPER

Nijukti Khabar 460693
Editorial: TS 3/193, Zone B, Mancheswar Industrial Estate, Bhubaneshwar 700010 **Tel:** 91 674 2582532
Email: nijuktikhabar@gmail.com **Web site:** http://www.nijuktikhabar.net
Freq: Weekly; **Circ:** 97102 Not Audited
Editor: Manoranjan Das
Profile: Covers employment information.
Language (s): English
DAILY NEWSPAPER

Nishpaksh Samachar Jyoti - Varanasi 460694
Editorial: 3rd Floor Taksal Theaters Building, Nadesar, Varanasi 221002 **Tel:** 91 542 2504676
Freq: Daily; **Circ:** 65003 Not Audited
Editor: Suman Gupta
Profile: Covers general news.
Language (s): Hindi
DAILY NEWSPAPER

Nyaydhish 460697
Editorial: 1A, Patrika Marg, Civil lines, Allahabad 211001 **Tel:** 91 5322606194
Email: nyaydhish@sancharnet.in
Freq: Daily; **Circ:** 140001 Not Audited
Editor: R. Jindal; **General Manager:** A. N. Shrivastava
Profile: Covers news.
Language (s): Hindi
DAILY NEWSPAPER

Orissa Times 460699
Editorial: Orissa Times, A-114 Unit-III, Kharvelanagar, Bhubaneshwar 751001
Tel: 91 674 2380686
Email: orissatimes@rediffmail.com
Freq: Daily; **Circ:** 98701 Not Audited
Editor: R. Shastry
Profile: Covers the latest local and international news.
Language (s): English
DAILY NEWSPAPER

Panchjanya 460700
Editorial: Sanskriti Bhawan, D B Gupta Marg, Jhandawala, New Delhi 110055 **Tel:** 91 11 23514244
Email: editor.panchjanya@gmail.com **Web site:** http://www.panchjanya.com
Freq: Weekly; **Circ:** 70003 Not Audited
Editor in Chief: Baldev Sharma
Profile: Covers the latest news in local and world, politics and etc.
Language (s): Hindi
DAILY NEWSPAPER

Parivartan Bharti 460701
Editorial: LG-101 Bharat Chamber, 70 Scindia House, Connaught Circus, New Delhi 110001
Tel: 91 11 23350940
Freq: Daily; **Circ:** 75002 Not Audited
Profile: Covers local news, international, entertainment and etc.
Language (s): Hindi
DAILY NEWSPAPER

Phulchhab 460702
Editorial: Phulchhab Bhavan, Mahatma Gandhi Road, Near Parsi Agyari, Rajkot 360001
Tel: 91 281 2444611
Freq: Daily; **Circ:** 66009 Not Audited
Editor: Kaushik Mehta
Profile: Covering local news, sports, business, jobs, and community events. The web site is presented in the Gujarati language.
Language (s): Gujarati
DAILY NEWSPAPER

The Pioneer 156662
Editorial: 3 Bahadur Shah Zafar Marg, Link House, 2nd Floor, New Delhi 110002
Tel: 91 011 23755271 74
Web site: http://www.dailypioneer.com
Freq: Daily; **Circ:** 83007 Not Audited
Editor in Chief: Chandan Mitra
Profile: Founded in 1865, covers the latest news in local and world, business and sports. Notable historic staff include Winston Churchill as a war correspondent during the second Boer War and Rudyard Kipling as an assistant editor.
Language (s): English
DAILY NEWSPAPER

Prabhat Khabar 459507
Editorial: 15-P, Kokar Industrial Area, Ranchi 834001
Tel: 91 651 3053100
Email: ranchi@prabhatkhabar.in **Web site:** http://www.prabhatkhabar.com
Freq: Daily; **Circ:** 350002 Not Audited
Editor in Chief: Harivansh Singh
Profile: Covers local and world news, sports, business, cinema, etc.
Language (s): Hindi
Ad Rate: Full Page Colour 520.00
Currency: India Rupees
DAILY NEWSPAPER

Prajashakti 460707
Editorial: House No. 1-8-664,21/1 Near RTC, Kalayan Mandapan, Azamabad Industria Area, Hyderabad 500020 **Tel:** 91 40 27665420
Email: editor@indiapress.org **Web site:** http://www.indiapress.org
Freq: Daily; **Circ:** 100002 Not Audited
Publisher: V. Krishnaiah; **Editor:** S. Vinaykumar
Profile: Covers the latest news in local and world, business, sprots and etc.
Language (s): Telugu
DAILY NEWSPAPER

The Prajatantra 460782
Editorial: Prajatantra Buildings, Bihari Bag, Cuttack 753002 **Tel:** 91 6712607183
Freq: Daily; **Circ:** 106233 Not Audited
Editor: Bhartruhari Mahtab
Profile: Covers the latest local, regional, international and national news.
Language (s): Oriya
DAILY NEWSPAPER

Prajavani 460708
Owner: The Printers (Mysore) Private, Ltd.
Editorial: The Printers (Mysore) Private, Ltd.,75 Mahatma Gandhi Road, Bangalore 560001
Tel: 91 80 25880000
Web site: http://www.prajavani.net
Freq: Daily; **Circ:** 315583 Not Audited
Editor: Shanth Kumar
Profile: Covers variety of topics such as the latest news in regional, local, national and international, and etc.
Language (s): Kannada
DAILY NEWSPAPER

Pratah Kamal 460709
Editorial: Sahu Road, Muzaffarpur 242633
Tel: 91 621 2246433
Email: pratahkamal@rediffmail.com
Freq: Daily; **Circ:** 65001 Not Audited
Editor: Brajesh Kumar; **Editor in Chief:** Radhamohan Thakur
Profile: Covers local and international news.
Language (s): Hindi
DAILY NEWSPAPER

Pratahkal 460710
Editorial: 108 Inside Surajpole, Udaipur 313001
Tel: 91 294 2417417
Email: pratahudr@gmail.com **Web site:** http://www.pratahkal.com
Freq: Daily; **Circ:** 70002 Not Audited
Editor in Chief: Suresh Goyal
Profile: Discusses the latest local, regional, international and national news, etc.
Language (s): Hindi
DAILY NEWSPAPER

Pratahkal Mumbai 460372
Editorial: Pratahkal, 543 Laxmi Plaza, Laxmi Industrial Estate, SAB TV Lane, New Link Road, Andheri (W), Mumbai 400053 **Tel:** 91 22 23659926
Email: pratahkal@gmail.com **Web site:** http://www.pratahkal.com
Freq: Daily; **Circ:** 100001 Not Audited
Editor: Mahip Goyal
Profile: Covers the local news, sports, business, jobs, and community events.
Language (s): Hindi
DAILY NEWSPAPER

Pratidin 460072
Editorial: TS3/193, Zone B, Mancheshwar Industrial Estate, Bhubaneshwar 751010 **Tel:** 91 674 2587533
Freq: Daily; **Circ:** 75003 Not Audited
Editor: Gaurang Samantray
Profile: Covers local and world news, sports and entertainment.
Language (s): Oriya
DAILY NEWSPAPER

Pratidin Akhbar 460711
Editorial: Devika, Rajapeth, Amravati 444606
Tel: 91 7212560155
Email: pratidin@indiatimes.com
Freq: Daily; **Circ:** 58001 Not Audited
Editor: Nanak Ahuja
Profile: Daily Hindi newspaper.
Language (s): Hindi
DAILY NEWSPAPER

Punjabi Tribune 460712
Editorial: The Tribune House, Sector 29-C, Chandigarh 160030 **Tel:** 91 172 2655066
Email: editorinchief@tribunemedia.com **Web site:** http://www.tribuneindia.com
Freq: Daily; **Circ:** 70001 Not Audited
Editor in Chief: H.K. Dua; **Editor:** Varinder Walia
Profile: Covers the latest news in local, regional, international and national, sports, entertainment, business and etc.
Language (s): Punjabi
DAILY NEWSPAPER

Punya Nagri 460317
Editorial: Ground Floor, Gala No. 22, Lalbaug, Industrial Estate, Parel, Mumbai 400012
Tel: 91 2224715208
Freq: Daily; **Circ:** 495002 Not Audited
Editor: Subhash Harchekar; **Editor:** Sanjay Malme
Profile: Marathi Mumbai daily Newspaper
Language (s): Marathi
DAILY NEWSPAPER

Purvanchal Prahari 460713
Editorial: G.S. Road, Ulubari, Guwahati 781007
Tel: 91 361 252-1556
Web site: http://www.glpublication.com
Freq: Daily; **Circ:** 135002 Not Audited
Editor: G. Agarwalla
Profile: Covers the latest news in local, regional, international and national news.
Language (s): Hindi
DAILY NEWSPAPER

Rajasthan Patrika - Ahmedabad 460350
Editorial: Sri Krishna Center, 2nd Floor No. 18, Mithakhali, Near Pizza Hut, Navrangpura, Ahmedabad 380009 **Tel:** 91 79 30611566
Web site: http://rajasthanpatrika.patrika.com
Freq: Daily; **Circ:** 130001 Not Audited
Editor: Rajendra Naruka
Profile: Rajasthan Patrika is a newspaper which covers the local, regional, national and international news, and etc.
Language (s): Hindi
DAILY NEWSPAPER

Rajasthan Patrika - Bikaner 460715
Editorial: 21 Gajner Road, Bikaner 334001
Tel: 91 25 23982
Email: info@rajasthanpatrika.com **Web site:** http://rajasthanpatrika.patrika.com
Freq: Daily; **Circ:** 63117 Not Audited
Editor: Santosh Jain
Profile: Covers the local, regional, national and international news, and etc.
Language (s): Hindi
DAILY NEWSPAPER

Rajasthan Patrika - Chennai 460351
Editorial: 2A, Wellington Estate, 24 Commander-in-Chief Road, Egmore, Chennai 600105
Tel: 91 44 28239859
Web site: http://rajasthanpatrika.patrika.com
Freq: Daily; **Circ:** 1100002 Not Audited
Editor: Dileep Chari
Profile: Covers the local, regional, national and international news, sports, business and etc.
Language (s): Hindi
DAILY NEWSPAPER

Rajasthan Patrika - Jaipur 460717
Editorial: Kesargarh, J.L.N. Marg, Jaipur 302004
Tel: 91 141 39404142
Web site: http://rajasthanpatrika.patrika.com
Freq: Daily; **Circ:** 157594 Not Audited
Editor: Santosh Jain; **Editor:** Ajit Maindola

Profile: Covers the local, regional, national and international news, and etc.
Language (s): Hindi
DAILY NEWSPAPER

Rajasthan Patrika - Jodhpur
460716
Editorial: Patrikayan, Manji Ka Hatha, Paota, Jodhpur 342006 **Tel:** 91 2915109911
Web site: http://rajasthanpatrika.patrika.com
Freq: Daily; **Circ:** 92071 Not Audited
Editor: Daulat Chauhan
Profile: Covers the local, regional, national and international news, and etc.
Language (s): Hindi
DAILY NEWSPAPER

Rajasthan Patrika - Kolkata
460307
Editorial: Near Yogayog Bhawan, 19, Kinderdine Lane, Kolkata 700012 **Tel:** 91 33 3299 8041
Web site: http://rajasthanpatrika.patrika.com
Freq: Daily
Editor: Tarkeshwar Mishra
Profile: Daily newspaper, covering news, sports & business.
Language (s): Hindi
DAILY NEWSPAPER

Rajasthan Patrika - Kota
460718
Editorial: 25 Small Scale Industrial Area, Kota 324007 **Tel:** 91 74 42363601
Email: info@rajasthanpatrika.com **Web site:** http://rajasthanpatrika.patrika.com
Freq: Daily; **Circ:** 125003 Not Audited
Editor: Siddharth Bhatt
Profile: Covers News Sports & Business.
Language (s): Hindi
DAILY NEWSPAPER

Ranchi Express
156658
Editorial: 55 Baralal Street, Upper Bazar, Ranchi 834001 **Tel:** 91 651 2206320
Email: news@ranchiexpress.com **Web site:** http://www.ranchiexpress.com
Freq: Daily; **Circ:** 82157 Not Audited
Editor: Balbir Dutt; **Publisher:** Raul Maroo; **Editor:** Chandreshwar Singh
Profile: Covers the news in local and world, sports, health and education.
Language (s): Hindi
DAILY NEWSPAPER

Rashtradeepika
459281
Owner: Rashtra Deepika Publications
Editorial: Rashtra Deepika Publications, P.O. Box 2252, Cochin 686025 **Tel:** 91 481 3012001
Email: editor@deepika.com **Web site:** http://www.deepika.com
Freq: Daily; **Circ:** 300002 Not Audited
Profile: Covers local, regional, international and world news.
Language (s): Malayalam
DAILY NEWSPAPER

Rashtriya Sahara Hindi Daily
460722
Editorial: 1216-1220, 12th Floor, Navrang House 21, Kasturba Gandhi Marg, Aliganj, New Delhi 226024 **Tel:** 91 11 43596017
Freq: Daily; **Circ:** 62003 Not Audited
Editor: Manoj Kumar
Profile: Covers international, national and local news.
Language (s): Hindi
DAILY NEWSPAPER

Rastradoot
460723
Editorial: Sudharma, M.I. Road, Jaipur 302001 **Tel:** 91 141 2361613
Freq: Daily; **Circ:** 350001 Not Audited
Profile: Covers local news and international news.
Language (s): Hindi
DAILY NEWSPAPER

Rastriya Naveen Mail
460724
Editorial: J.J. Road Upper Bazaar, Ranchi 834001 **Tel:** 91 6512306999
Freq: Daily; **Circ:** 63001 Not Audited
Editor: Jyoti Bajaj; **Editor in Chief:** Suresh Bajaj; **Bureau Chief:** Devendra Sharma
Profile: Rastriya Naveen Mail is A Daily Newspaper Covering Local National Regional And International News.
Language (s): Hindi
DAILY NEWSPAPER

Rozana Safeer-E-Nau
460263
Editorial: 18 Tulsipor, Rasoolpor, Allahabad 211003 **Tel:** 91 532 2658114
Freq: Daily; **Circ:** 50002 Not Audited
Editor: Mohammad Hafeezullah Khan
Profile: Covers the news in local and world, and etc.
Language (s): Urdu
DAILY NEWSPAPER

Saamana (Hindi)
459366
Owner: Prabodhankar Prakashan
Editorial: Sadguru Darshan, Nagu Sayaji Wadi, Dainik Saamana Marg, Prabhadevi, Mumbai 400025 **Tel:** 91 2224370160
Email: saamana89@gmail.com **Web site:** http://www.saamana.com
Freq: Daily; **Circ:** 81002 Not Audited

Publisher: Subhash Desai; **Editor:** Uddhav Thackeray
Profile: Launched in February 1993 to reach north Indians settled in Maharashtra. Covers local and international news and government and reflects the views of the Shiv Sena political party.
Language (s): Hindi
DAILY NEWSPAPER

Saamana (Marathi)
460725
Owner: Prabodhankar Prakashan
Editorial: Sadguru Darshan, Nagu Sayaji Wadi, Dainik Saamana Marg, Prabhadevi, Mumbai 400025 **Tel:** 91 22 24370592
Web site: http://www.saamana.com
Freq: Daily; **Circ:** 80650 Not Audited
Publisher: Subhash Desai; **Editor:** Uddhav Thackeray
Profile: Launched in January 1988 to convey the views of the Shiv Sena political party to the Marathi masses. Covers local and international news and government.
Language (s): Marathi
DAILY NEWSPAPER

Sadin
460726
Editorial: M.R.D. Road, Chandmari, Guwahati 781003 **Tel:** 91 361 2660420
Email: sadin@pratidinassam.com **Web site:** http://www.pratidinassam.com/sadin
Freq: Weekly; **Circ:** 50003 Not Audited
General Manager: Mrinmoy De; **Editor:** Anuradha Pujari
Profile: Covers the latest news in local and world.
Language (s): Assamese
DAILY NEWSPAPER

Sahafat
460264
Editorial: Sahafat Daily, 25 Salempur House, Kaisar Bagh, Lucknow 226018 **Tel:** 91 522 4155330
Email: sahafatdaily@yahoo.co.uk
Freq: Daily; **Circ:** 70002 Not Audited
Editor: Amaan Abbas
Profile: Covers local, regional, international and national news.
Language (s): Urdu
DAILY NEWSPAPER

Sakaal Kolhapur
460728
Editorial: D-4, MIDC Shiroli, Kolhapur 416422 **Tel:** 91 2312468383
Email: webeditor@esakal.com **Web site:** http://www.esakal.com
Freq: Daily; **Circ:** 60003 Not Audited
Editor: Vasant Bhosale
Profile: Covers general news.
Language (s): Marathi
DAILY NEWSPAPER

Sakaal Pune
460727
Editorial: Sakal Paper Limited, 595 Budhwar Peth, Pune 411002 **Tel:** 91 20 24405500
Email: webeditor@esakal.com **Web site:** http://www.esakal.com
Freq: Daily; **Circ:** 1000001 Not Audited
Editor: Suresh Padhe
Profile: Sakaal Pune is a newspaper which provides the news in local and international, entertainment, politics, sports, and etc.
Language (s): Marathi
DAILY NEWSPAPER

Sakal Mumbai
460729
Editorial: Sakal Bhavan, Plot No. 42, Sector No. 11, CBD Belapur, Navi Mumbai, Mumbai 400614 **Tel:** 91 2227572960
Email: sakal@vsnl.in **Web site:** http://www.esakal.com
Freq: Daily; **Circ:** 80001 Not Audited
Editor in Chief: Uttam Kamble
Profile: Sukal Mumbai is a newspaper which writes about the news in local and international, sports, entertainment, politics and etc.
Language (s): Marathi
DAILY NEWSPAPER

Sakal Nagpur
459386
Editorial: 5 East High Court Road, Ramdas Estate, Nagpur 44001 **Tel:** 91 7122531482
Email: sakalnagpur@esakal.com **Web site:** http://www.esakal.com
Circ: 75003 Not Audited
Editor: Shreepad Aprajit
Profile: Covers news.
Language (s): Marathi
DAILY NEWSPAPER

Samachar Jagat
460731
Editorial: Opp. Prem Prakash Cinema, Jaipur Hotel, Room No. 9 & 10, S.M.S. Highway, Jaipur 302001 **Tel:** 91 141 2377044
Email: samacharjagat@rediffmail.com **Web site:** http://www.samacharjagat.in
Freq: Daily; **Circ:** 230001 Not Audited
Editor in Chief: Rajendra Godha
Profile: Samachar Jagat is a newspaper which covers the headline, business, sports and entertainment.
Language (s): Hindi
DAILY NEWSPAPER

Samaya
460734
Editorial: Plot No. 44 & 54 Sector A, Zone D, Mancheswar Industrial Estate, Bhubaneshwar 751017 **Tel:** 91 6742585740

Email: thesamaya@yahoo.com **Web site:** http://www.orissasamaya.com
Freq: Daily; **Circ:** 100001 Not Audited
Editor in Chief: Satakadi Hota
Profile: Covers local, national and international news.
Language (s): Oriya
DAILY NEWSPAPER

Sambhaav Daily
460735
Editorial: Sambhaav House Opposite Chief Justice's Bungalow, Bodakdev, Ahmedabad 380015 **Tel:** 91 7926873914
Email: metro@sambhaav.com **Web site:** http://www.sambhaav.com
Freq: Daily; **Circ:** 69003 Not Audited
Editor: Deepal Trevedi
Profile: Covers general news.
Language (s): Gujarati
DAILY NEWSPAPER

Sambhaav Metro
460284
Owner: Sambhaav Media Ltd.
Editorial: Sambhaav Media Ltd., Sambhaav House Opposite Judges Bungalow, Premchandnagar, Bodakdev Satellite, Vastrapur, Ahmedabad 380054 **Tel:** 91 7926873914
Email: metro@sambhaav.com **Web site:** http://www.sambhaav.com
Freq: Daily
Editor: Deepal Trevedi
Profile: Gujarati daily newspaper
Language (s): Gujarati
DAILY NEWSPAPER

Samyukta Karnataka
460736
Editorial: 2 Residency Road, Bangalore 560025 **Tel:** 91 80 22214392
Email: samkarnataka@rediffmail.com
Freq: Daily; **Circ:** 200003 Not Audited
Manager: R. Rajeshwari
Profile: Covers general news.
Language (s): Kannada
DAILY NEWSPAPER

Sandesh
460738
Editorial: Sandesh Ltd. Sandesh Bhavan, Lad Society Road, Badakdev, Ahmedabad 380054 **Tel:** 91 79 40004000
Web site: http://www.sandesh.com
Freq: Daily; **Circ:** 800002 Not Audited
Editor: Falgunbhai Patel
Profile: Covers the latest news in local and world, business, sports and etc.
Language (s): Gujarati
Ad Rate: Full Page Colour 1778400.00
Currency: India Rupees
DAILY NEWSPAPER

Sandhya Jyoti Darpan
460740
Editorial: 3-A, Vidhya Aashram Institutional Area, Jawahar Lal Nehru Marg, Jaipur 302017 **Tel:** 91 141 2709102
Email: vin2.sharma@gmail.com
Freq: Daily; **Circ:** 50002 Not Audited
Editor in Chief: Brij Sharma; **Editor in Chief:** Brij Mohan Sharma; **Editor:** Mahendra Yadav
Profile: Covers the latest news in local and world.
Language (s): Hindi
DAILY NEWSPAPER

Sandhya Mahalaxmi Bhagyodaya
460741
Editorial: 184 Patparganj Industrial Area, New Delhi 110092 **Tel:** 91 11 22410716
Email: mahalaxmigroup@hotmail.com **Web site:** http://www.mahalaxmigroup.com
Freq: Daily; **Circ:** 51001 Not Audited
Editor: Sharad Jain
Profile: Covers the local, regional, international and national news.
Language (s): Hindi
DAILY NEWSPAPER

Sandhya Times
460198
Editorial: Sandhya Times, 7 Bahadur Shah Zafar Marg, New Delhi 110002 **Tel:** 91 1123302000
Email: madhurendra.sinha@timesgroup.com **Web site:** http://www.sandhyatimes.indiatimes.com
Freq: 2 Times/Week; **Circ:** 100001 Not Audited
Editor: Sushma Jagmohan; **Editor in Chief:** Sat Soni
Profile: One of the largest tabloids in India, serves as a popular information and entertainment source for the commuting reader in Delhi.
Language (s): Hindi
DAILY NEWSPAPER

Sandhya Veer Arjun
459416
Editorial: Pratap Bhawan, 5 Bahadur Shah Zafar Marg, New Delhi 110002 **Tel:** 91 11 23312507
Freq: Daily; **Circ:** 52002 Not Audited
Editor: Anil Narendra
Profile: Covers local and world news, sports, etc.
Language (s): Hindi
DAILY NEWSPAPER

Sandhyanand
460743
Editorial: Aaj Ka Anand Building, 365/6 Shivajinagar, Pune 411005 **Tel:** 91 20 25534888
Web site: http://www.sandhyanand.com
Freq: Daily; **Circ:** 350002 Not Audited
Profile: Covers news topics.
Language (s): Marathi
DAILY NEWSPAPER

Sanjevani
460247
Editorial: Sanjevani, 11/2, Queen's Road, Bangalore 560052 **Tel:** 91 80 22866260
Email: sanjevani@gmail.com **Web site:** http://www.sanjevani.com
Freq: Daily; **Circ:** 300002 Not Audited
Editor: B. Amuthan
Profile: Covers local and world news.
Language (s): Kannada
DAILY NEWSPAPER

Sanjh Samachar
460056
Editorial: Babubhai Shah Marg, Jai Hind Press Building, Rajkot 360001 **Tel:** 91 2813048684
Email: sanjhsamachar@gmail.com **Web site:** http://www.jaihinddaily.com
Freq: Daily; **Circ:** 50003 Not Audited
Profile: Covers news.
Language (s): Gujarati
DAILY NEWSPAPER

Sanmarg
460744
Editorial: 160/B, Chittaranjan Avenue, Kolkata 700007 **Tel:** 91 33 30615020
Email: sanmarghindi@gmail.com **Web site:** http://www.sanmarg.in
Freq: Daily; **Circ:** 125003 Not Audited
Editor: Hari Pande
Profile: Covers the latest local, regional, national and international news.
Language (s): Hindi
DAILY NEWSPAPER

Saurashtra Bhoomi
460747
Editorial: Saurashtra Bhoomi Karyalaya, Jail Road, Junagadh 362001 **Tel:** 91 285 2621000
Email: saurashtrabhoomi@gmail.com **Web site:** http://www.saurashtrabhoomi.com
Freq: Daily; **Circ:** 75002 Not Audited
Editor in Chief: Kartik Upadhyay
Profile: Covers the latest news in local and world, business, sports and etc.
Language (s): Gujarati
DAILY NEWSPAPER

Seema Sandesh
460749
Editorial: Sandesh Sadan, Chak 7E Chotti, Hanuman Garh Road, Sri Ganga Nagar 335001 **Tel:** 91 141 4015552
Email: editor@seemasandesh.com
Freq: Daily; **Circ:** 50000 Not Audited
Editor: Lalit Sharma
Profile: Covers the latest news in local and world, business, sports, movie, religion and etc.
Language (s): Hindi
DAILY NEWSPAPER

The Sentinel
157166
Editorial: G.S. Road, Dispur, Guwahati 781005 **Tel:** 91 361 2529237
Email: bikash@sentinelassam.com **Web site:** http://www.sentinelassam.com
Freq: Daily; **Circ:** 50002 Not Audited
Managing Director: Indira Rajkhewa; **Editor:** Shankar Rajkhewa; **Manager:** Loona Sindhiya
Profile: Covers of news and general interests.
Language (s): English
DAILY NEWSPAPER

The Siasat Daily
460750
Editorial: Jawaharlal Nehru Road, Opposite Ram Krishna Theatre, Abids, Hyderabad 500001 **Tel:** 91 40 24744114
Email: siasat.daily@yahoo.com **Web site:** http://www.siasat.com
Freq: Daily; **Circ:** 50003 Not Audited
Manager: Aslam Ali; **Editor:** Aamer Khan; **Editor in Chief:** Zahid Khan
Profile: A daily newspaper which covers the latest local, regional, international and national news, business, politics, sports and entertainment.
Language (s): English
DAILY NEWSPAPER

Star of Mysore
460254
Editorial: 15-C, Industrial A Layout, Bannimantap, Mysore 570015 **Tel:** 91 821 2496520
Email: voice@starofmysore.com **Web site:** http://www.starofmysore.com
Freq: Daily; **Circ:** 75002 Not Audited
Editor: K. Ganapathy
Profile: Star of Mysore is a newspaper which covers the international and local newspapers and articles.
Language (s): English
DAILY NEWSPAPER

The Statesman
157153
Editorial: The Statesman Ltd, Statesman House, 4 Chowringhee Square, Kolkata 700001 **Tel:** 91 33 22127070
Email: thestatesman@vsnl.com **Web site:** http://www.thestatesman.net
Freq: Daily; **Circ:** 200003 Not Audited
Bureau Chief: Manoj Chaurasia; **Editor in Chief:** Ravindra Kumar
Profile: Founded in 1875 and a founding member of Asia News Network, provides objective coverage of national and international news and current events.
Language (s): English
Ad Rate: Full Page Colour 800.00
Currency: India Rupees
DAILY NEWSPAPER

Section 2 World News Media

Sunday Guardian
854200
Owner: ITV Network
Editorial: B-4, 2nd fl, Sector-3, Near Rajnigandha Chowk, New Delhi 20131 Tel: 91 120 4369500
Email: mail@sunday-guardian.com Web site: http://www.sunday-guardian.com
Freq: Daily
Editor in Chief: M. Akbar
Profile: Launched in 2010, covers national news and published simultaneously as India on Sunday out of London.
Language (s): English
DAILY NEWSPAPER

Sunday Mid-Day
460753
Editorial: Peninsula Centre; Dr. S.S. Rao Road, Opposite Mahatma Gandhi Hospital; Parel, Mumbai 400011 Tel: 91 22 67017171
Email: cs@mid-day.com Web site: http://www.mid-day.com
Freq: Weekly; Circ: 120003 Not Audited
Editor: Alpana Sawai
Profile: Covers the latest news in local and international, business, sports, automotive, entertainment, lifestyle and etc.
Language (s): English
DAILY NEWSPAPER

Sunday Times
460742
Editorial: S & B Towers, 2nd Floor, 40 Mahatma Road, Bangalore 560001 Tel: 91 80 25550000
Email: toiblr.reporter@timesgroup.com Web site: http://timesofindia.indiatimes.com/home/sunday-times/articlelist/1945062111.cms
Freq: Weekly; Circ: 302001 Not Audited
Editor: Naheed Ataullah; Editor: Shirish Koyal
Profile: Shares the latest news in local and international, sports, entertainment, and market.
Language (s): English
Ad Rate: Full Page Mono 652.17
Currency: United States Dollars
DAILY NEWSPAPER

Swadesh
460754
Editorial: Swadesh Bhavan, 26-A, Press Complex, Maharana Pratap Nagar, Bhopal 462011
Tel: 91 0755 2556189
Email: swadeshbhopal@gmail.com
Freq: Daily; Circ: 50001 Not Audited
Editor in Chief: Rajendra Sharma
Profile: Swadesh is a newspaper which focused on the latest news in local, regional, international, and national.
Language (s): Hindi
DAILY NEWSPAPER

Swatantra Bharat
460756
Editorial: SurajDeep Complex, 2nd Floor, 1 Jopling Road, Lucknow 226001 Tel: 91 05222204306
Email: sbharats@satyam.net.in Web site: http://www.swatantrabharat.com
Freq: Daily; Circ: 120001 Not Audited
Profile: Covers news topics.
Language (s): Hindi
DAILY NEWSPAPER

Swatantra Chetna
460256
Owner: D A Chetna Prakashan Pvt Ltd.
Editorial: D A Chetna Prakashan Pvt Ltd., Shahmaroof, Hindi Bazar, Gorakhpur 273001
Tel: 91 5512332248
Web site: http://www.swatantrachetna.com
Freq: Daily; Circ: 75002 Not Audited
Editor in Chief: R. Gupta
Profile: Swatantra Chetnat is a daily newspaper which covers the Local Regional National and International news as well as sports and etc.
Language (s): Hindi
DAILY NEWSPAPER

Syandan Patrika
460757
Editorial: 41 Sakuntala Road, Agartala 799001
Tel: 91 381 2386684
Email: syandan@patrikaindia.com Web site: http://www.patrikaindia.com
Freq: Daily; Circ: 70002 Not Audited
Editor in Chief: Subal Dey; Editor: Animesh Dutta; Manager: Tapan Roy; Manager: Tapan Kumar Roy
Profile: Covers the news in local and world.
Language (s): Bengali
DAILY NEWSPAPER

Tehelka, The People's Paper
460194
Editorial: M-76, M-Block Market, First Floor, Greater Kailash II, New Delhi 110048 Tel: 91 11 40575757
Email: editor@tehelka.com Web site: http://www.tehelka.com
Freq: Weekly
Editor: Harinder Baweja
Profile: Covers the latest news locally and internationally, as well as economics, politics, etc.
Language (s): English
DAILY NEWSPAPER

The Telegraph
157158
Owner: ABP Ltd.
Editorial: ABP Ltd, 6 Prafulla Sarkar Street, Kolkata 700001 Tel: 91 33 22345374
Email: ttedit@abpmail.com Web site: http://www.telegraphindia.com
Freq: Daily; Circ: 389549 Not Audited
Editor: Rudrankshu Mukherjee; Editor in Chief: Aveek Sarkar

Profile: Launched in July 1982, covers national, international, and business news, sports, entertainment and travel and publishes in English.
Language (s): English
DAILY NEWSPAPER

Tender World
515147
Editorial: Four Square Media Pvt. Ltd., 202 Jaina Extn., Dr. Mukherjee Nagar, Comml.Complex, New Delhi 110009 Tel: 91 11 27655127
Web site: http://www.businessnewspapers.net
Freq: Weekly
Editor in Chief: Dev Joshi
Profile: Covers more than 3000 industrial products of all trades from all over India & abroad.
Language (s): Hindi
DAILY NEWSPAPER

These Days
460251
Editorial: I-91, Lubna House, Batla House, Okhla, New Delhi 110001 Tel: 91 1123792121
Email: thesedaysindia@gmail.com Web site: http://www.thesedaysindia.com
Freq: Daily
Editor in Chief: S. Asif
Profile: These Days is a newspaper which covers the latest news in local and world.
Language (s): English
DAILY NEWSPAPER

The Times of India - Ahmedabad Edition
460788
Owner: Bennett, Coleman & Co. Ltd.
Editorial: 139 Ashram Road, Ahmedabad 380009
Tel: 91 79 26553300
Web site: http://www.timesofindia.com
Freq: Daily; Circ: 158002 Not Audited
Editor: Bharat Desai
Profile: Covers the latest local, regional, international and national news, with regular sections including business, sports, entertainment, lifestyle and women's interest.
Language (s): English
Ad Rate: Full Page Colour 795.00
Currency: India Rupees
DAILY NEWSPAPER

Times of India - Bangalore Edition
460787
Owner: Bennett, Coleman & Co. Ltd.
Editorial: Times Internet Ltd., #17 Du Park Trinity, Bangalore 560001 Tel: 91 80 40876709
Web site: http://www.timesofindia.indiatimes.com
Freq: Daily; Circ: 4000001 Not Audited
Profile: Covers the latest local, regional, international and national news, with regular sections including business, sports, entertainment, lifestyle and women's interest.
Language (s): English
Ad Rate: Full Page Colour 3390.00
Currency: India Rupees
DAILY NEWSPAPER

Times of India - Chennai Edition
725124
Owner: Bennett, Coleman & Co. Ltd.
Editorial: Times House, 126/127, Chamlers Road, Chennai 600035 Tel: 91 44 40401234
Web site: http://timesofindia.indiatimes.com
Freq: Daily
Profile: Covers local, national and international news.
Language (s): English
Ad Rate: Full Page Colour 1900.00
Currency: India Rupees
DAILY NEWSPAPER

The Times of India - Lucknow Edition
460786
Owner: Bennett, Coleman & Co. Ltd.
Editorial: 16 Rana Pratap Marg, Lucknow 226001
Tel: 91 522 2209484
Web site: http://www.timesofindia.com
Freq: Daily; Circ: 74003 Not Audited
Profile: Covers the latest local, regional, international and national news, with regular sections including business, sports, entertainment, lifestyle and women's interest.
Language (s): English
Ad Rate: Full Page Colour 850.00
Currency: India Rupees
DAILY NEWSPAPER

The Times of India - Mumbai edition
431010
Owner: Bennett, Coleman & Co. Ltd.
Editorial: The Times of India Bldg, 1st Floor, Dr. D. N. Rd, Mumbai 400001 Tel: 011 911 22735610
Email: info.tbsl@timesgroup.com
Freq: Daily; Circ: 776632 Not Audited
Editor: Meena Iyer
Profile: Covers the latest local, regional, international and national news, with regular sections including business, sports, entertainment, lifestyle and women's interest.
Language (s): English
Ad Rate: Full Page Mono 6630.00
Currency: India Rupees
DAILY NEWSPAPER

The Times of India - New Delhi Edition
157154
Owner: Bennett, Coleman & Co. Ltd.
Editorial: 7 Bahadur Shah Zafar Marg, New Delhi 110002 Tel: 91 11 23302000

Web site: http://timesofindia.indiatimes.com/Cities/Delhi/articlelist/-2128839596.cms
Freq: Daily; Circ: 1141846 Not Audited
Profile: Covers the latest local, regional, international and national news, with regular sections including business, sports, entertainment, lifestyle and women's interest.
Language (s): English
Ad Rate: Full Page Colour 5210.00
Currency: India Rupees
DAILY NEWSPAPER

Times of Money
586786
Editorial: 4th Floor, Times Tower, Kamala Mills Compound, Senapati Bapat Marg, Lower Parel (W), Mumbai 400013 Tel: 91 2222731263
Web site: http://www.timesofmoney.com
Editor: Sheena Kapoor
Profile: Covers money topics.
Language (s): English
DAILY NEWSPAPER

The Tribune
157157
Editorial: The Tribune House, Sector 29-C, Chandigarh 160030 Tel: 91 172 26 55 066
Email: advt@tribuneindia.com Web site: http://www.tribuneindia.com
Freq: Daily; Circ: 300003 Not Audited
Profile: A daily newspaper which covers the latest local, regional, international and national news, business, politics, sports and etc.
Language (s): English
DAILY NEWSPAPER

Trinity Mirror
460791
Editorial: No. 1, First Main Road, United India Colony, Kodambakkam, Chennai 600024
Tel: 91 44 24734800
Freq: Daily; Circ: 72001 Not Audited
Publisher: R Muthukumar
Profile: Focuses on news in local and international.
Language (s): English
DAILY NEWSPAPER

Udayavani
156663
Editorial: New Udayavani Building, Manipal 576119
Tel: 91 820 2571159
Email: udayavani@manipalmedia.com Web site: http://www.udayavani.com
Freq: Daily; Circ: 189355 Not Audited
Profile: Covers the latest news in local and world and politics.
Language (s): Kannada
DAILY NEWSPAPER

Utkal Mel
460796
Editorial: C-231 Industrial Estate, Dist Sundargarh, Rourkela 769004 Tel: 91 6612401332
Email: bbsr_utkalmel@rediffmail.com Web site: http://www.utkal
Freq: Daily; Circ: 81953 Not Audited
Editor in Chief: Pitabasa Mishra
Profile: A local newspaper covering local and national news.
Language (s): Hindi
DAILY NEWSPAPER

Uttar Banga Sambad
460797
Editorial: 7 Old Court House Street, Kolkata 700001
Tel: 91 3322435663
Web site: http://www.uttarbangasambad.com
Freq: Daily; Circ: 140002 Not Audited
Editor: S. Talukdar
Profile: Covering local news, sports, business, jobs, and community events. The web site is presented in the Bengali language.
Language (s): Bengali
DAILY NEWSPAPER

Uttar Ujala
460799
Editorial: Ujala Nagar, Bareilly Road, Haldwani 263139 Tel: 91 5946252129
Email: uttarujala@rediffmail.com
Freq: Daily; Circ: 55003 Not Audited
Editor: Snehlata Bhandari
Profile: A daily newspaper in Haldwani India.
Language (s): Hindi
DAILY NEWSPAPER

Vaartha (Hindi)
459367
Editorial: 396 Lower Tank Bund, Hyderabad 500080
Tel: 91 40 66654999
Email: editor@vaartha.com Web site: http://www.vaartha.com
Freq: Daily; Circ: 50002 Not Audited
Editor: Radheshyam Shukla
Profile: Covers news.
Language (s): Hindi
Ad Rate: Full Page Colour 1200.00
Currency: India Rupees
DAILY NEWSPAPER

Vaartha (Telugu)
460800
Editorial: 396 Lower Tank Bund, Hyderabad 500080
Tel: 91 40 66654999
Email: editor@vaartha.com Web site: http://www.vaartha.com
Freq: Daily; Circ: 500001 Not Audited
Editor: Ashok Tankshla
Profile: Covers news.
Language (s): Telugu
DAILY NEWSPAPER

Vacancies For You
460283
Editorial: 401-404 Centre Point Road, 18th Road, Chembur, E., Mumbai 400071 Tel: 91 22 2529 0102
Web site: http://www.vacanciesforyou.com
Freq: Weekly
Editor: D. Prasad
Profile: Focuses on job hunting.
Language (s): English
DAILY NEWSPAPER

Veer Arjun
460801
Editorial: Pratap Bhawan, 5 Bahadurshah Zafar Marg, New Delhi 110002 Tel: 91 11 23318276
Email: dailyvirarjun@gmail.com Web site: http://www.virarjun.com
Freq: Daily; Circ: 82991 Not Audited
Editor: Seema Kiran; Editor: Anil Narendra
Profile: Veer Arjun is a newspaper which covers the news in local and international, business, education, sports, culture, and etc.
Language (s): Hindi
DAILY NEWSPAPER

Vijay Karnataka
459407
Editorial: No 40 KCCF Compound, Pampa Mahakavi Road, Pampa Mahakavi Road, Bangalore 560018
Tel: 91 8040877666
Web site: http://vijaykarnataka.indiatimes.com
Freq: Daily; Circ: 640003 Not Audited
Editor: Vishveshwar Bhatt; News Director: Anand Shankeshwar; Editor: Sugata Srinivasaraju
Profile: Covers local news, sports, business, jobs, and community events in the Kannada language.
Language (s): Kannada
DAILY NEWSPAPER

Vishwa Manav
460804
Editorial: Vishwa Manav Bhawan, 103 Civil Lines, Behind Hind Talkies, Bareilly 243001
Tel: 91 581 2473967
Freq: Daily; Circ: 58641 Not Audited
Profile: Vishwa Manav is a newspaper which covers the news in local, regional, international and national and etc.
Language (s): Hindi
DAILY NEWSPAPER

Vyapar - Rajkot Edition
459400
Editorial: Phulchhab Bhavan, Mahatma Gandhi Road, Near Parsi Agyari, Rajkot 360001
Tel: 91 281 2478317
Web site: http://www.vyapar.com
Freq: 2 Times/Week; Circ: 60003 Not Audited
Editor: Madhusudan Barbhaya
Profile: Covers local and world news within the agriculture industry.
Language (s): Gujarati
DAILY NEWSPAPER

Vyapar Bharati
460806
Editorial: K 37, Udyog Nagar, Industrial Area, Rohtak Road, New Delhi 110085 Tel: 91 114 2380000
Email: info@vyaparbharati.net Web site: http://www.vyaparbharati.net
Freq: Daily; Circ: 60003 Not Audited
Editor: Yyarpar Bharti
Profile: A daily newspaper about India and international news.
Language (s): Hindi
DAILY NEWSPAPER

Yashobhumi
460315
Editorial: 220 Narayan Udyog Bhawan, Dr. B A Road, Lal Bagh, Mumbai 400012
Tel: 91 22 24715208
Freq: Daily; Circ: 130003 Not Audited
Editor: Anand Shukla
Profile: Covers the latest news in local and world.
Language (s): Hindi
DAILY NEWSPAPER

News Service/Syndicate

Cartographic News Service
467640
Editorial: KBK News Graphic Network, 1st Floor 13 Todarmal Lane, New Delhi 110001
Tel: 91 1123315555
Email: vijay@kbknewsgraphics.com Web site: http://www.kbknewsgraphics.com
Freq: Daily
Profile: KBK is India's pioneering and leading daily News Graphics agency providing comprehensive coverage of news through graphics. Through an independent reliable and exclusive network the agency has been producing quality infographics for almost half-a-century. With a mix of accredited correspondents creative graphic artists and researchers as its key editorial resource base KBK has carved a niche for itself as a highly professional setup.
Language (s): English
NEWS SERVICE/SYNDICATE

Global Features
829427
Editorial: B-701, Customs Colony, Military Rd, Marol Naka, Mumbai 400059 Tel: 011 91 9223419060
Editor: Chandragupta Amritkar
Profile: Distributes local, national and international news feature stories throughout India.
Language (s): English
NEWS SERVICE/SYNDICATE

India News and Feature Alliance (INFA) 467644
Editorial: Jeevan Deep, 10 Parliament Street, New Delhi 110001 **Tel:** 91 1123743330
Email: infaservice@infapublications.com **Web site:** http://www.infa.in
Freq: Daily
Editor in Chief: Inder Jit
Profile: Covers news and general interests.
Language (s): English
NEWS SERVICE/SYNDICATE

India Press Agency (IPA) 467646
Tel: 91 1123354648
Email: indiapressagency@gmail.com **Web site:** http://www.ipanewspack.com
Freq: Daily
Profile: Provides constant news coverage of politics, defense, oil & gas and business.
Language (s): English
NEWS SERVICE/SYNDICATE

Indo-Asian News Service (IANS) 467643
Editorial: A-45-50 Right Wing, 1st Fl, Sector-16, Noida 201301 **Tel:** 91 120 4822400
Email: feedback@ians.in **Web site:** http://www.ians.in
Freq: Daily
Editor in Chief: Tarun Basu; **Contributor:** Jacob Puliyel
Profile: Covers news and general interests.
Language (s): English
NEWS SERVICE/SYNDICATE

National News Service 467648
Editorial: 25/10 East Punjabi Bagh, New Delhi 110026 **Tel:** 91 1146867500
Email: Support@nnscommoditynews.com **Web site:** http://www.nnscommoditynews.com/commoditynews/
Freq: Daily
Editor: Kesar Gupta; **Editor:** Rajesh Gupta
Profile: Covers news and general interests.
Language (s): English
NEWS SERVICE/SYNDICATE

News From Non Aligned World 467650
Editorial: A-2/59 Safdarjung Enclave, New Delhi 110029 **Tel:** 91 1146867500
Email: ndt@newsdelhitimes.com
Freq: Weekly
Editor: Vikas Pande
Profile: Covers news and general interests.
Language (s): English
NEWS SERVICE/SYNDICATE

Press Trust of India/PTI 467653
Editorial: 4 Parliament Street, New Delhi 100001
Tel: 91 112316621
Email: trans@pti.in **Web site:** http://www.ptinews.com
Freq: Daily
General Manager: Mohammed Shakeel
Profile: Serves as India's premier news agency, with a reach as vast as the Indian Railways. Correspondents are based in leading capitals and important business and administrative centers around the world.
Language (s): Hindi
NEWS SERVICE/SYNDICATE

Syndicated Journalist 467656
Editorial: C-2-2073, Vasant Kunj, New Delhi 110070
Tel: 91 1126892295
Freq: Daily
Editor in Chief: Narayan Venkat
Profile: It is a news feature agency which has had its features aired across several countries of the world.
Language (s): English
NEWS SERVICE/SYNDICATE

United News of India (UNI) 467657
Editorial: United News of India (UNI), 9 Rafi Marg, New Delhi 110001 **Tel:** 91 011 23718861
Email: desk@uniindia.com **Web site:** http://www.uniindia.com
Freq: Daily
Bureau Chief: Pradeep Kashyap
Profile: Covers news about politics, economics, business, sports, entertainment and stock markets.
Language (s): English
NEWS SERVICE/SYNDICATE

Univarta 467658
Editorial: 9 Rafi Marg, New Delhi 110001
Tel: 91 1123355838
Email: varta@uniindia.com **Web site:** http://www.uniindia.com
Freq: Daily
Editor: Mahabir Singh
Profile: Provides news features on a wide variety of topics, including Art and Culture, Science, Agriculture, Economy, Heritage and India's neighbors.
Language (s): Hindi
NEWS SERVICE/SYNDICATE

Indonesia

Time Difference: GMT +7 to +9
National Telephone Code: 62
Continent: Asia
Capital: Jakarta

Newspapers

Bangka Pos 459988
Editorial: PT Bangka Media Grafika, Jl. Abdulrahman Sidik No.1B, Pangkal Pinang 33127
Tel: 62 717437084
Email: redaksi@bangkapos.com **Web site:** http://www.bangkapos.com
Freq: Daily; **Circ:** 15002 Not Audited
Editor in Chief: Agus Ismunarno
Profile: Covers local, national, international news, as well as entertainment, business, politics, etc.
Language (s): Bahasa Indonesia
DAILY NEWSPAPER

Banjarmasin Post 459961
Editorial: Banjasmasin Post, Gedung HJ Djok Mentaya, Jl AS Musyaffa No16, Banjarmasin 70111
Tel: 62 5113354370
Email: redaksi@banjarmasinpost.co.id **Web site:** http://www.banjarmasinpost.co.id
Freq: Daily; **Circ:** 40001 Not Audited
Profile: Newspaper covering regional, national, and international news, as well as entertainment, sports, politics, etc.
Language (s): Bahasa Indonesia
DAILY NEWSPAPER

Batam Pos 460231
Editorial: PT Ripos Bintana Press, Gedung Graha Pena Lt.1-2, Jl. Raya Batam Center, Batam 29461
Tel: 62 778460000
Email: redaksi@batampos.co.id **Web site:** http://www.batampos.co.id
Freq: Daily; **Circ:** 50003 Not Audited
Profile: Newspaper focusing on national, international, and regional news, as well as politics, economy, entertainment, sports, etc.
Language (s): Bahasa Indonesia
DAILY NEWSPAPER

Bisnis Bali 459456
Editorial: Gedung Pers Balik, Jl. Kebo Iwa 63A, Denpasar - **Tel:** 62 361416676
Web site: http://www.bisnisbali.com
Freq: Daily; **Circ:** 3501 Not Audited
Profile: Daily newspaper focusing on business and finance.
Language (s): Bahasa Indonesia
DAILY NEWSPAPER

Bisnis Indonesia 792979
Editorial: Wisma Bisnis Indonesia Lt. 5-8, Jl KH Mas Mansyur Kav 12A Karet Tengsin, Jakarta 10220
Tel: 62 21 5790-1023
Web site: http://en.bisnis.com
Freq: Daily
Editor in Chief: Arief Budisusilo; **Editor:** Syahran Lubis; **Editor:** Rochmat Purboyo; **News Editor:** Sutarno Subagong; **Editor:** Setyardi Widodo; **Editor:** Inria Zulfikar
Profile: Launched in December 1985 and covers business and economic news in Indonesia.
Language (s): Indonesian
DAILY NEWSPAPER

Galamedia 460071
Editorial: PT Galamedia Bandung Perkasa, Jln. Blk. Factory No. 2B-2C, Bandung 40111
Tel: 62 224210063
Email: surga.galamedia@gmail.com **Web site:** http://www.klik-galamedia.com
Freq: Daily; **Circ:** 40001 Not Audited
Profile: Covers local, national, and international news, as well as business, economy, entertainment, sports, etc.
Language (s): Bahasa Indonesia
DAILY NEWSPAPER

Harian Berita Sore 459923
Editorial: Jl. Letjen Supsapto N.1, Medan 20151
Tel: 62 614150858
Email: redaksi@beritasore.com **Web site:** http://www.beritasore.com
Freq: Daily; **Circ:** 8001 Not Audited
Editor in Chief: H. Teruna Said
Profile: Daily newspaper covering national, regional, and international news, as well as politics, entertainment, business, etc.
Language (s): Bahasa Indonesia
DAILY NEWSPAPER

Harian Bernas 459951
Editorial: Redaksi Hassan Bernas Jogja, Jl. IKIP PGRI - Sonosewu, Yogyakarta 55162
Tel: 62 274377559
Email: redaksi@harianbernas.com **Web site:** http://www.bernas.co.id
Freq: Daily; **Circ:** 25006 Not Audited
Editor in Chief: Bimo Sukarno
Profile: Daily newspaper focusing on national, international, and regional news, as well as politics, economy, entertainment, sports, etc.
Language (s): Bahasa Indonesia
DAILY NEWSPAPER

Harian Cenderawasih Pos 459181
Owner: PT. Cenderawasih Arena Intim Press
Editorial: PT. Cenderawasih Arena Intim Press, Jl. Cenderawasih No. 10, Kelapa Dua Entrop, Jayapura 99013
Email: cepos_jpr@yahoo.com **Web site:** http://www.cenderawasihpos.com
Freq: Daily; **Circ:** 12502 Not Audited
Editor in Chief: Lucky Ireeuw
Profile: Covers local, national, international news, as well as business, entertainment, politics, sports, etc.
Language (s): Bahasa Indonesia
DAILY NEWSPAPER

Harian Ekonomi Neraca 459949
Editorial: PT Daya Cipta Aksara, Jl.Teuku Cik Di Tiro No.68B, Jakarta Pusat **Tel:** 62 21 31931991
Email: neracadaily@yahoo.com **Web site:** http://www.neracaonline.com
Freq: 2 Times/Week; **Circ:** 26004 Not Audited
Editor in Chief: Firdaus Baderi
Profile: Covers business and financial news.
Language (s): Bahasa Indonesia
DAILY NEWSPAPER

Harian Fajar 460232
Editorial: Gedung Graha Pena, Lt. 4, Jl. Urip Sumoharjo No. 21, Jl. Racing Centre 101, Makassar 90231 **Tel:** 62 411441441
Email: redaksi@fajar.co.id **Web site:** http://www.fajar.co.id
Freq: Daily; **Circ:** 65002 Not Audited
Editor in Chief: Sukriansyah Latief
Profile: Covers local, national, and international news, as well as business, entertainment, politics, sports, etc.
Language (s): Bahasa Indonesia
DAILY NEWSPAPER

Harian Indonesia 459006
Editorial: Jl. Gajah Mada No.96-97, Jakarta Pusat 11140 **Tel:** 62 2163868348
Web site: http://www.harian-indonesia.com
Freq: Daily; **Circ:** 50007 Not Audited
Profile: Daily newspaper focusing on business and financial issues.
Language (s): Chinese
DAILY NEWSPAPER

Harian Komentar 460230
Editorial: PT Azravi, Kompleks Ruko Megamas, Blok IB No. 38, Manado - **Tel:** 62 431879799
Email: redaksi@hariankomentar.com **Web site:** http://www.hariankomentar.com
Freq: Daily; **Circ:** 20001 Not Audited
Editor in Chief: Friko S. Poli; **Editor:** Ricky Tulalo
Profile: Newspaper covering regional, national, and international news, as well as entertainment, sports, politics, etc.
Language (s): Bahasa Indonesia
DAILY NEWSPAPER

Harian Olahraga GOSport 466495
Editorial: Media GO, Jl. Kramat Pela No. 17A, Rt. 08/04 Pulo, Jakarta **Tel:** 62 21 98294963
Email: redaksi@mediago.or.id **Web site:** http://www.mediago.or.id
Freq: Daily; **Circ:** 250001 Not Audited
Editor in Chief: Rahmi Aries Nova
Profile: Covers sports news, especially soccer.
Language (s): Bahasa Indonesia
DAILY NEWSPAPER

Indopos 460229
Editorial: Jawa Pos Group, Graha Pena Lantai 10, Jalan Kebayoran Lama No.12, Jakarta Selatan 12210
Tel: 62 2153699556
Email: editor@indopos.co.id **Web site:** http://www.indopos.co.id
Freq: Daily; **Circ:** 110002 Not Audited
Profile: Covers local, national, international news, as well as business, entertainment, politics, sports, etc.
Language (s): Bahasa Indonesia
DAILY NEWSPAPER

Investor Daily Indonesia 459338
Editorial: PT Koran Media Investor Indonesia, Aryaduta Suite, Tower A, Lt. 1, Jl. Gamisun Dalam No.8, Karet Semanggi, Jakarta 12930
Tel: 62 2157901350
Email: koraninvestor@investor.co.id **Web site:** http://www.investorindonesia.com
Freq: Daily; **Circ:** 40002 Not Audited
Editor: Abdul Aziz; **Editor in Chief:** Primus Dorimulu; **Editor:** Euis Rita Hartati; **Manager:** Inne Kuntjaraningrum; **Editor:** Imelda Rahmawati
Profile: Covers investor issues in Indonesia.
Language (s): Bahasa Indonesia
DAILY NEWSPAPER

The Jakarta Globe 578696
Owner: PT Jakarta Globe Media
Editorial: Kawasan Bisnis Granadha, Plz Semanggi 9th Fl, Jl. Jend. Sudirman Kav. 50, Karet Semanggi, Jakarta 12930 **Tel:** 62 2125535053
Web site: http://www.thejakartaglobe.com
Freq: Daily
Editor at Large: John Riady; **President:** Theo L. Sambuaga
Profile: Daily newspaper focusing on national, international, and regional news, as well as politics, economy, entertainment, sports, etc.
Language (s): English
DAILY NEWSPAPER

The Jakarta Post 159050
Owner: PT. Niskala Media Tenggara
Editorial: Jl. Palmerah Barat 142-143, Jakarta 10270
Tel: 62 21 530 04 76
Email: editorial@thejakartapost.com **Web site:** http://www.thejakartapost.com
Freq: Daily; **Circ:** 40000 Not Audited
Editor: Hendrasyah Tarmizi
Profile: Covers national, international and local news.
Language (s): English
Ad Rate: Full Page Colour 22333.00
Currency: United States Dollars
DAILY NEWSPAPER

Jambi Independent 459150
Owner: PT Jambi Independent Press
Editorial: PT Jambi Independent Press, Jl. Jenderal Sudirman No.100, Thekok, Jambi City
Tel: 62 74135272
Email: redaksi@jambi-independent.co.id **Web site:** http://www.jambi-independent.co.id
Freq: Daily; **Circ:** 20002 Not Audited
Editor in Chief: Joni Rizal
Profile: Covers local, national, international news, as well as business, entertainment, politics, sports, etc.
Language (s): Bahasa Indonesia
DAILY NEWSPAPER

Jawa Pos 159051
Editorial: PT Jawa Pos, Graha Pena Building Lt. 4, Surabaya 60234 **Tel:** 62 38283333
Email: info@jawapos.co.id **Web site:** http://www.jawapos.co.id
Freq: Daily; **Circ:** 380001 Not Audited
Editor in Chief: Leak Koestiya
Profile: Newspaper covering regional, national, and international news, as well as entertainment, sports, politics, etc.
Language (s): Bahasa Indonesia
Ad Rate: Full Page Colour 101000.00
Currency: Indonesia Rupiahs
DAILY NEWSPAPER

Kedaulatan Rakyat 459959
Editorial: Kedaulatan Rakyat, Jl. P. Mangkubumi No. 40-44, Yogyakarta 55232 **Tel:** 62 274565685
Web site: http://www.kr.co.id
Freq: Daily; **Circ:** 100001 Not Audited
Profile: Newspaper covering regional, national, and international news, as well as entertainment, sports, politics, etc.
Language (s): Bahasa Indonesia
DAILY NEWSPAPER

Kompas 161289
Owner: PT Kompas Cyber Media
Editorial: PT Kompas Cyber Media, Gedung Kompas Gramedia, Unit 2 Lt. 5, Jl. Palmerah Selatan No. 22-28, Jakarta 10270 **Tel:** 62 215350377
Email: redaksikcm@kompas.co.id **Web site:** http://www.kompas.com
Freq: Daily; **Circ:** 2191988 Not Audited
Profile: Covers news, politics, science, travel, entertainment, etc.
Language (s): Bahasa Indonesia
Ad Rate: Full Page Mono 43.47
Ad Rate: Full Page Colour 64.26
Currency: United States Dollars
DAILY NEWSPAPER

Kontan 491607
Editorial: PT. Grahanusa Mediatama, Jl. Kebayoran Lama No.3119, Jakarta 12210 **Tel:** 62 21 5357636
Email: red@kontan.co.id **Web site:** http://www.kontan.co.id
Freq: Daily; **Circ:** 75004 Not Audited
Editor in Chief: Ardian Taufik Gesuri; **Editor:** Gloria Haraito; **Editor:** Hasbi Maulana; **Editor:** Rumanus Cipta Wahyana
Profile: Covers business and industry news, personal finance, investments, the economy, etc.
Language (s): Bahasa Indonesia
DAILY NEWSPAPER

Kontan Mingguan 459916
Editorial: Gedung Kontan, Jl. Kebayoran Lama No.3119, Jakarta 12210 **Tel:** 62 215357636
Email: red@kontan.co.id **Web site:** http://www.kontan.co.id
Freq: Weekly; **Circ:** 90001 Not Audited
Editor in Chief: Ardian Taufik Gesuri; **Editor:** Harris Hadinata; **Manager:** Diana Eka P; **Editor:** YN Djumyati Partawidjaja
Profile: Daily newspaper focusing on business, finance, economy, and investments.
Language (s): Bahasa Indonesia
DAILY NEWSPAPER

Koran Tempo 460440
Editorial: Redaksi Tempo Interakrif, Kebayoran Center Blok A 11- A 15, Jalan Kebayoran Baru - Mayestik, Jakarta 12440 **Tel:** 62 217255625
Email: interaktif@tempo.co.in **Web site:** http://www.korantempo.com
Freq: Daily; **Circ:** 200002 Not Audited
Editor in Chief: Malela Mahargesari
Profile: Newspaper focusing on national, international, and regional news, as well as politics, economy, entertainment, sports, etc.
Language (s): Bahasa Indonesia
DAILY NEWSPAPER

Lampung Post 460412
Editorial: Media Indonesia Group, Jl. Soekarno Hatta No.108, Rajabasa, Bandar Lampung
Tel: 62 721783693
Email: redaksi@lampung.co.id **Web site:** http://www.lampungpost.com
Freq: Daily; **Circ:** 30001 Not Audited
Editor in Chief: Djadjat Sudradjat
Profile: Daily newspaper covering national, international, regional news, as well as entertainment, politics, etc.
Language (s): Bahasa Indonesia
DAILY NEWSPAPER

Malang Post 459960
Editorial: Malang Post, Jl. Sriwijaya 1-9, Malang
Tel: 62 341340081
Email: redaksi@malang-post.com **Web site:** http://www.malang-post.com
Freq: Daily; **Circ:** 35007 Not Audited
Manager: Edi Iswanto; **Editor in Chief:** Sunavip Ra Indrata
Profile: Newspaper focusing on national, international, and regional news, as well as politics, economy, entertainment, sports, etc.
Language (s): Bahasa Indonesia
DAILY NEWSPAPER

Manado Post 459957
Owner: Jawa Post Group
Editorial: Jawa Post Group, Manado Post Center, Jl. Babe Palar No.62, Manado **Tel:** 62 431855558
Email: infor@jpnn.com **Web site:** http://www.manadopost.com
Freq: Daily; **Circ:** 35002 Not Audited
Editor in Chief: Suhendro Boroma
Profile: Covers local, national, and international news, as well as sports, entertainment, politics, business, etc.
Language (s): Bahasa Indonesia
DAILY NEWSPAPER

Media Indonesia 412085
Editorial: Komplek Delta Kedoya, Jl. Pilar Raya, Kav. A-D Kedoya Selatan, Kebon Jeruk, Jakarta Barat 11520 **Tel:** 62 215812088
Email: redaksi@mediaindonesia.com **Web site:** http://www.mediaindonesia.com
Freq: Daily; **Circ:** 220001 Not Audited
Editor in Chief: Toeti Adhitama; **Editor:** Sadyo Kristianto; **Editor:** Andy Noya; **President:** Surya Paloh; **Editor:** Rosmery Sihombing
Profile: Newspaper covering regional, national, and international news, as well as entertainment, sports, politics, etc.
Language (s): Bahasa Indonesia
DAILY NEWSPAPER

Metro Banjar 459012
Editorial: PT Grafika Wangi Kalimantan, Gedung HJ Djok Mentaya, Jl AS Musyaffa No16, Banjarmasin 70111 **Tel:** 62 5113354370
Email: redaksi@banjarmasinpost.co.id **Web site:** http://www.banjarmasinpost.co.id
Freq: Daily; **Circ:** 20001 Not Audited
Production Manager: M Taufik
Profile: Covers local and international news, as well as entertainment, business, sports, etc.
Language (s): Bahasa Indonesia
DAILY NEWSPAPER

Metro Riau 460414
Editorial: PT Metro Riau, Metro Graha Pena, Jl. Soekarno Hatta No.20-28, Pekanbaru
Email: redaksi@metroriau.com **Web site:** http://www.metroriau.com
Freq: Daily
Editor: Saparudin Koto; **Editor:** Adlis Pitrajaya
Profile: Covers local, national, and international news, as well as entertainment, politics, finance, etc.
Language (s): Bahasa Indonesia
DAILY NEWSPAPER

Padang Ekspres (Daily Morning Express Padang) 836659
Editorial: Jln. By Pass KM., No. 7, Padang
Tel: 0751 841254
Email: redaksi@padangekspres.co.id **Web site:** http://padangekspres.co.id
Freq: Daily
Editor: Nashrian Bahzein; **Editor:** Heri Sugiarto
Profile: Daily coverage of Indonesian and international news.
Language (s): Indonesian
Ad Rate: Full Page Colour 40500.00
Currency: Indonesia Rupiahs
DAILY NEWSPAPER

Pekanbaru Pos 460379
Owner: Riau Pos Group
Editorial: Riau Pos Group, Gedung Pekanbaru Pos, Jl. Soekarno Hatta No. 132, Pekanbaru
Freq: Daily; **Circ:** 15002 Not Audited
Profile: Covers local, national, and international news, as well as business, health, sports. etc.
Language (s): Bahasa Indonesia
DAILY NEWSPAPER

Pikiran Rakyat 459966
Editorial: PT Pikiran Rakyat, Jl. Soekarno Hatta No. 147, Bandung 40223 **Tel:** 62 226037755
Email: redaksi@pikiran-rakyat.com **Web site:** http://www.pikiran-rakyat.com
Freq: Daily; **Circ:** 180002 Not Audited
Editor in Chief: Budiana Kartawijaya
Profile: Covers local, national, and international news, as well as entertainment, business, sports, politics, etc.
Language (s): Bahasa Indonesia
DAILY NEWSPAPER

Pontianak Post 459956
Owner: PT.Akcaya Utama Press Pontianak
Editorial: PT.Akcaya Utama Press Pontianak, Jl. Gajahmada 2-4, Pontianak 78121 **Tel:** 62 561735071
Email: redaksi@pontianakpost.com **Web site:** http://www.pontianakpost.com
Freq: Daily; **Circ:** 40002 Not Audited
Editor in Chief: B. Salman
Profile: Covers local, national, international news, as well as business, entertainment, politics, sports, etc.
Language (s): Bahasa Indonesia
DAILY NEWSPAPER

Pos Kota 459915
Editorial: Yayasan Antar Kota, Jl. Gajah Mada 98-100, Jakarta 11140 **Tel:** 62 216340874
Web site: http://www.poskota.co.id
Freq: Daily; **Circ:** 300000 Not Audited
Editor in Chief: Joko Lestasi
Profile: Daily newspaper focusing on national, international, and regional news, as well as politics, economy, entertainment, sports, etc.
Language (s): Bahasa Indonesia
DAILY NEWSPAPER

Pos Kupang 459921
Editorial: PT Timor Media Grafika, Jl. Kenari No. 1, Naikoten I, Kupang 85115 **Tel:** 62 380 833820
Email: poskpg@yahoo.com **Web site:** http://www.pos-kupang.com
Freq: Daily; **Circ:** 15003 Not Audited
Editor: Benny Dasman; **Editor:** Damyan Godho; **Editor:** Tony Kleden; **Editor in Chief:** Dion Putra
Profile: Covers local and international news, as well as entertainment, business, sports, etc.
Language (s): Bahasa Indonesia
DAILY NEWSPAPER

Radar Bogor 559027
Editorial: Pena Graha Bogor, Jl. KH.R. Abdullah Bin. Muhammad Nuh No. 30, Taman Yasmin, Bogor 16310 **Tel:** 62 2517544001
Email: editorial@radar.bogor.com **Web site:** http://www.radar-bogor.co.id
Freq: Daily
Managing Director: Aswan Achmad; **Manager:** Rieke Fauziah
Profile: Daily newspaper focusing on national, international, and regional news, as well as politics, economy, entertainment, sports, etc.
Language (s): Bahasa Indonesia
DAILY NEWSPAPER

Rakyat Merdeka 460415
Editorial: Gedung, Graha Pena, Lt. 8, Jalan Raya Kebayoran Lama No. 12, Jakarta Selatan 12210
Tel: 62 2153699507
Web site: http://www.rakyatmerdeka.co.id
Freq: Daily; **Circ:** 350001 Not Audited
Editor in Chief: Teguh Santosa
Profile: Newspaper covering local, national, and international news, as well as politics, entertainment, economy, etc.
Language (s): Bahasa Indonesia
DAILY NEWSPAPER

Republika 412073
Editorial: PT Republika Media Mandiri, Jl. Warung Buncit Raya, No. 37, Jakarta 12510
Tel: 62 21 7803747
Email: sekretariat@republika.co.id **Web site:** http://www.republika.co.id
Freq: Daily; **Circ:** 150001 Not Audited
Editor in Chief: Ikhwanul Kiram Mashuri
Profile: Newspaper covering regional, national, and international news, as well as entertainment, sports, politics, etc.
Language (s): Bahasa Indonesia
DAILY NEWSPAPER

Riau Pos 459933
Owner: PT Riau Pos Intermedia
Editorial: PT Riau Pos Intermedia, Gedung Riau Pos Group, Jalan HR Soebrantas KM 10.5, Pekanbaru 28282
Email: redaksi@riaupos.co.id **Web site:** http://www.riaupos.com
Freq: Daily; **Circ:** 35002 Not Audited
Editor in Chief: Raja Isyam Azwar
Profile: Covers local, national, and international news, as well as entertainment, business, sports, politics, etc.
Language (s): Bahasa Indonesia
DAILY NEWSPAPER

Seputar Indonesia 493585
Editorial: MNC Tower Lt.22, Jl. Kebon Sirih Raya No. 17-19, Jakarta 10340 **Tel:** 62 213926955
Email: redaksi@seputar-indonesia.com **Web site:** http://www.seputar-indonesia.com
Freq: Daily; **Circ:** 364537 Not Audited
Director: Priscilla Airin; **Editor in Chief:** Sururi Alfaruq
Profile: Daily newspaper focusing on national, international, and regional news, as well as politics, economy, entertainment, sports, etc.
Language (s): Bahasa Indonesia
DAILY NEWSPAPER

Serambi Indonesia 460290
Editorial: PT Serambi Prima Grafika, Desa Meunasah, 5 Tanjung Permai, Manyang PA, Ingin Jaya, Aceh Besar, Banda Aceh **Tel:** 62 651635544
Email: redaksi@serambinews.com **Web site:** http://www.serambinews.com
Circ: 30002 Not Audited
Editor in Chief: Mawardi Ibrahim
Profile: Covers local, national, and international news, as well as business, economy, entertainment, sports, etc.
Language (s): Bahasa Indonesia
DAILY NEWSPAPER

Solo Pos 460349
Editorial: PT Aksara Solo Pos, Griya Solo Pos, Jl. Adisucipto No.190, Surakarta 57145
Tel: 62 27 1724811
Web site: http://www.solopos.co.id
Freq: Daily; **Circ:** 50003 Not Audited
Manager: Danie H. Soe'oed; **Editor in Chief:** Ya Sunyoto
Profile: Covers local, national, and international news, as well as business, economy, entertainment, sports, etc.
Language (s): Bahasa Indonesia
DAILY NEWSPAPER

Spirit NTT 517361
Editorial: PT Timor Media Grafika, Jl. Kenari No. 1, Kelurahan Naikoten I, Kupang 85118
Tel: 62 380828993
Email: spirit_ntt@yahoo.com **Web site:** http://spiritentete.blogspot.com/
Freq: Weekly; **Circ:** 5001 Not Audited
Editor in Chief: Dion Putra
Profile: Focuses on news in Kupang and surrounding areas.
Language (s): Bahasa Indonesia
DAILY NEWSPAPER

Sriwijaya Post 459918
Editorial: PT Sriwijaya Perdana, Jl. Jend. Basuki Rahmat No.1608 B-D, Palembang 30135
Tel: 62 711310088
Web site: http://www.palembang.tribunenews.com
Freq: Daily; **Circ:** 42001 Not Audited
Profile: Covers national, regional, and international news, politics, entertainment, and other current affairs.
Language (s): Bahasa Indonesia
DAILY NEWSPAPER

Suara Karya 459955
Editorial: PT Suara Karya Membangun, Gedung AKA, Jl. Bangka Raya No. 2, Kebayoran Baru, Jakarta 12720 **Tel:** 62 217191352
Email: redaksi@suarakarya-online.com **Web site:** http://www.suarakarya-online.com
Freq: Daily; **Circ:** 85001 Not Audited
Editor in Chief: Ricky Rachmadi
Profile: Newspaper covering regional, national, and international news, as well as entertainment, sports, politics, etc.
Language (s): Bahasa Indonesia
DAILY NEWSPAPER

Suara Merdeka 412070
Editorial: Jl. Pandanasan 30, Semarang
Tel: 62 248412600
Email: redaksi@suaramerdeka.com **Web site:** http://www.suaramerdeka.com
Freq: Daily; **Circ:** 170006 Not Audited
Editor in chief: Hendra Setiawan Kelana
Profile: Daily newspaper focusing on national, international, and regional news, as well as politics, economy, entertainment, sports, etc.
Language (s): Bahasa Indonesia
DAILY NEWSPAPER

Suara NTB 490676
Editorial: Global FM Lombok, Jalan Bangau No.15, Cakra Negara, Mataram **Tel:** 62 370639543
Email: hariansuarantb@yahoo.com **Web site:** http://www.suarantb.com
Freq: Daily; **Circ:** 6001 Not Audited
Profile: Covers local news.
Language (s): Bahasa Indonesia
DAILY NEWSPAPER

Suara Pembaruan 412069
Editorial: The Aryaduta Suites, Tower A, Lt 1, Jl. Garnisun Dalam No. 8 Karet Semanggi, Jakarta 13630 **Tel:** 62 2157851555
Email: koransp@suarapembaruan.com **Web site:** http://www.suarapembaruan.com
Freq: Daily; **Circ:** 200001 Not Audited
Profile: Daily newspaper covering news, entertainment, politics, etc.
Language (s): Bahasa Indonesia
DAILY NEWSPAPER

Sumatera Ekspres 459958
Editorial: PT Citsa Bumi Sumatera, Jl. kol. Haji Barlian, No.773, KM 6,5 Palembang, Palembang 30152 **Tel:** 62 711411768
Web site: http://www.sumeks.co.id
Freq: Daily; **Circ:** 75006 Not Audited
Profile: Daily newspaper focusing on national, international, and regional news, as well as politics, economy, entertainment, sports, etc.
Language (s): Bahasa Indonesia
DAILY NEWSPAPER

Sumut Pos 492974
Editorial: PT Media Medan Pers, Graha Pena Medan Lt.3, Jl. Sisinga Maharaja KM 8,5 No.134, Amplas, Medan 20148 **Tel:** 62 617881661
Email: redaksi@hariansumutpos.com **Web site:** http://www.hariansumutpos.com
Freq: Daily
Editor: Faliruddin Lubis
Profile: Covers local, national, and international news, as well as politics, entertainment and economy.
Language (s): Bahasa Indonesia
DAILY NEWSPAPER

Surya 459919
Editorial: Jl. Rungkut Industry III No. 68 & 70 S, SIER, Surabaya 60239 **Tel:** 62 318419000
Email: redaksi@surya.co.id **Web site:** http://www.surya.co.id
Freq: Daily; **Circ:** 140001 Not Audited
Editor in Chief: Rusdi Amral; **Editor:** Sigit Sugiharto
Profile: Newspaper covering regional, national, and international news, as well as entertainment, sports, politics, etc.
Language (s): Bahasa Indonesia
DAILY NEWSPAPER

Tribun Batam 460410
Editorial: PT Tribun Media Grafika, Komplek MCP Jl Kerapu, Batu Ampar, Batam 29433
Tel: 62 77 8414326
Email: redaksi@tribunnews.com **Web site:** http://www.tribunnewsbatam.com
Freq: Daily; **Circ:** 30004 Not Audited
Editor: Febby Mahendra Putra; **Editor:** Dedy Suwadha
Profile: Covers local, national, regional, and international news, as well as business, entertainment, sports, etc.
Language (s): Bahasa Indonesia
DAILY NEWSPAPER

Tribun Jabar 459355
Editorial: PT Bandung Media Grafika, Jl Sekelimus Utara No. 2-4, Bandung 40266 **Tel:** 62 227530666
Email: redaksi@tribunjabar.co.id **Web site:** http://tribunjabar.co.id
Freq: Daily; **Circ:** 75001 Not Audited
Editor: Adityas Annas Azhari; **Editor in Chief:** Cecep Bundansyah
Profile: Newspaper covering regional, national, and international news, as well as entertainment, sports, politics, etc.
Language (s): Bahasa Indonesia
DAILY NEWSPAPER

Tribun Kaltim 460408
Editorial: PT Mahakam Media Grafika, Jl., Rt 52 No. 1 Kampun Timus, Balikpapan 76125
Tel: 62 542735015
Email: redaksi@tribunkaltim.co.id **Web site:** http://www.tribunkaltim.co.id
Freq: Daily; **Circ:** 25002 Not Audited
Director: Uki Kurdi; **Editor in Chief:** Achmad Subechi
Profile: Covers local, national, and international news, as well as business, health, sports. etc.
Language (s): Bahasa Indonesia
DAILY NEWSPAPER

Tribun Pekanbaru 520240
Editorial: Kompas Group, Jl. Imam Munandar No.383, RT01/RW04 Bukit Raya, Pekanbaru 28281
Email: tribunpekanbaru@yahoo.co.id **Web site:** http://www.tribunpekanbaru.com
Freq: Daily
Editor in Chief: RHR Dodi Sarjana
Profile: Daily newspaper focusing on national, international, and regional news, as well as politics, economy, entertainment, sports, etc.
Language (s): Bahasa Indonesia
DAILY NEWSPAPER

Tribun Timur 460409
Editorial: PT Bosowa Media Grafika, Jl. Cendsawasih No.430, Makassar 90134
Tel: 62 4118115555
Email: redaksi@tribun-timur.com **Web site:** http://www.tribun-timur.com
Freq: Daily; **Circ:** 40006 Not Audited
Manager: Anny Rahimah Arman; **Editor in Chief:** Dahlan Iskan
Profile: Newspaper focusing on national, international, and regional news, as well as politics, economy, entertainment, sports, etc.
Language (s): Bahasa Indonesia
DAILY NEWSPAPER

Ujung Pandang Ekspres 460378
Editorial: PT Fajar UjungPandang Intermedia, Fajar Graha Pena Makassar LT1, Jl. Urip Sumoharjo No.20, Makassar **Tel:** 62 411457457
Email: redaksi_upeks@yahoo.co.id **Web site:** http://upeks.co.id
Freq: Daily; **Circ:** 12003 Not Audited
Commissioner: H. Mappiar H.S
Profile: Newspaper focusing on national, international, and regional news, as well as politics, economy, entertainment, sports, etc.
Language (s): Bahasa Indonesia
DAILY NEWSPAPER

Waspada 459950
Editorial: Bumi Warta Waspada, Jl Letjen Suprapto/ Brigjen Katamso 1, Medan 20151 **Tel:** 62 614150858

Email: redaksi.online@waspada.co.id **Web site:** http://www.waspada.co.id
Freq: Daily; **Circ:** 55001 Not Audited
Editor in Chief: Avian E Tumengkol
Profile: Covers regional, national, and international news, as well as entertainment.
Language (s): Bahasa Indonesia
DAILY NEWSPAPER

News Service/Syndicate

Agence France-Presse - Jakarta Bureau 896850
Editorial: 17/F, Deutsche Bank Building, 80 Jalan Imam Bonjol, Jakarta 10310 **Tel:** 62 21 193 6082
Email: olivia.rondonuwu@afp.com **Web site:** http://www.afp.com
Profile: Jakarta bureau of the international news and picture agency.
Language (s): English
NEWS SERVICE/SYNDICATE

Antara 467605
Editorial: Wisma ANTARA, Lt.18-20, Jl. Medan Merdeka Selatan 17, P.O.Box 10012, Jakarta 10112
Tel: 62 21 3802383
Email: seksetariatsedaksi@antara.co.id **Web site:** http://www.antara.co.id
Freq: Daily
News Director: M. Saiful Hadi; **Managing Director:** Ahmad Mukhlis Yusuf
Profile: Distributes local, national, and international news.
Language (s): Bahasa Indonesia
NEWS SERVICE/SYNDICATE

Antara - Indonesian News Agency 689639
Editorial: Jalan Merdeka Selatan No. 17, Jakarta
Email: newsroom@antaranews.com **Web site:** http://www.antaranews.com/en
Profile: ANTARA has been officially serving as a National News Agency since 1962. It was declared as a public corporation in July, 2007. With 32 bureaus nationwide, a number of representative offices and correspondents abroad, ANTARA is now trusted to be the president of the Organization of Asia-Pacific News Agency (OANA) for the 2007-2010 period. As a national information emissary, ANTARA remains on the front line to strive for the national development and maintain the national dignity through dissemination of news on Indonesia throughout the country andabroad. Geographical Focus: Indonesia
Language (s): English
NEWS SERVICE/SYNDICATE

Iran

Time Difference: GMT +3.5
National Telephone Code: 98
Continent: Asia
Capital: Tehran

Newspapers

Abrar 542859
Owner: Abrar Publications Group
Editorial: Block 17, Shaheed Beheshti Street, Qaem Maqam Farahani, Tehran **Tel:** 98 21 8870 0804
Email: abrar1388@yahoo.com **Web site:** http://home.abrarnews.com
Freq: Daily
Advertising Manager: Afsheen Mansouri; **Publisher & Editor in Chief:** Mohammad Safizadeh
Profile: Abrar is a daily Persian newspaper covering news, politics, business, cinema, culture and sports. It launched in 1993.
Language (s): Persian
DAILY NEWSPAPER

Abrar Eghtesadi 542898
Owner: Abrar Publications Group
Editorial: Block 17, Shaheed Beheshti Street, Qaem Maqam Farahani, Tehran **Tel:** 98 21 8870 0804
Email: abrar1388@yahoo.com **Web site:** http://www.abrarnews.com
Freq: Daily
Advertising Manager: Afsheen Mansouri; **Publisher & Editor in Chief:** Mohammad Safizadeh
Profile: Abrar Eghtesadi (Daily Economic News) is a Persian newspaper covering business, economics, energy, banking, stocks and information technology. The newspaper launched in 2000 and is aimed at business executives in Iran.
Language (s): Persian
DAILY NEWSPAPER

Abrar Varzeshi 543013
Owner: Abrar Publications Group
Editorial: Block 17, Shaheed Beheshti Steet, Qaem Maqam Farahani, Tehran **Tel:** 98 21 8870 0804
Email: varzeshi_abrar@yahoo.com **Web site:** http://www.abrarnews.com
Freq: Daily
Advertising Manager: Afsheen Mansouri; **Publisher & Editor in Chief:** Mohammad Safizadeh
Profile: Abrar Varzeshi is a daily sports newspaper focusing on the latest football news worldwide. The newspaper launched in 1997, and is aimed at Iranian football fans.
Language (s): Persian
DAILY NEWSPAPER

Aftab Yazd 544062
Owner: Chap-e Golriz
Editorial: PO Box 13145-1134, Unit 1, 1st Floor, No 10, 26th Street, Tehran 1513614714
Tel: 98 21 8832 1397
Email: aftab.yz@gmail.com **Web site:** http://www.aftab-yazd.ir
Freq: Daily; **Circ:** 50000 Publisher's Statement
PR Manager: Safideh Haidarabadi; **Publisher & Managing Director:** Mansour Mozafari
Profile: Aftab Yazd is a daily Persian newspaper covering local and international news, business and sport. It launched in 2001.
Language (s): Persian
DAILY NEWSPAPER

Asia 537894
Owner: Asia
Editorial: Seoul Shopping Center, Sheikh Bahayi Square, Tehran **Tel:** 98 21 8806 6537
Email: info@asianews.ir **Web site:** http://www.asianews.ir
Freq: Daily; **Circ:** 180000 Publisher's Statement
Publisher and Managing Director: Saghi Baghernia; **Editor In Chief:** Iraj Jamshidi; **Advertising Manager:** Mazdak Jamshidi
Profile: Asia is a tabloid-sized Persian newspaper covering local and international business news, IT, health and entertainment. It launched in 2002 and is aimed at business executives in Iran.
Language (s): Persian
Ad Rate: Full Page Colour 12000000.00
Currency: Iran Rials
DAILY NEWSPAPER

Asr-e Eghtesad 537896
Owner: Seifollah Yazdani Publication
Editorial: Unit 2, 1st Floor, Block 11, Dameshq Street, Tehran 14167-83863 **Tel:** 98 21 8894 8104
Email: eghtesad1@yahoo.com
Freq: Daily; **Circ:** 15000 Publisher's Statement
Advertising Manager: Shabnam Bahramian; **Publisher and Managing Director:** Seifollah Yazdani
Profile: Asr-e Eghtesad is a daily newspaper covering economic, social, cultural and sports news. It launched in 2003 and is mostly written in Persian, with two pages in English.
Language (s): English
Ad Rate: Full Page Mono 56000000.00
Ad Rate: Full Page Colour 106400000.00
Currency: Iran Rials
DAILY NEWSPAPER

Donya-e-Eqtesad 526411
Owner: Donya Eqtesad Taban
Editorial: PO Box 141-5744-344, No. 370, Between Mirzaye Shirazi and Sana'i Streets, Tehran
Tel: 98 21 8776 2511
Email: info@donya-e-eqtesad.com **Web site:** http://www.donya-e-eqtesad.com
Freq: Daily
Managing Director: Alireza Bakhtyari; **Advertising Manager:** Parviz Bakhtyari; **Editor In Chief:** Ali Mirzakhani; **PR Manager:** Mohsin Tarvan
Profile: Donya-e-Eqtesad (Economy World) is a daily Persian newspaper covering national and international economic and business news. It launched in 2002, and is aimed at business executives in Iran.
Language (s): Persian
Ad Rate: Full Page Mono 312000000.00
Currency: Iran Rials
DAILY NEWSPAPER

Ebtekar 544066
Owner: Kar-e Karghar
Editorial: Ground Floor, Block 56, Zartesht Gharbi, Tehran **Tel:** 98 21 8897 5710
Email: ebtekarnews@gmail.com **Web site:** http://www.ebtekarnews.com
Freq: Daily; **Circ:** 30000 Publisher's Statement
Advertising Manager: Mahdi Vakili; **Publisher and Managing Director:** Mohammad-Ali Vakili; **Editor In Chief:** Farzola Yari
Profile: Ebtekar is a Persian daily newspaper covering local and international news, politics, business and sport. It launched in 2003.
Language (s): Persian
DAILY NEWSPAPER

Eghtesad Pooya 537979
Owner: Eghtesad Pooya Publication Co.
Editorial: PO Box 14155-8356, Block 44, 21st Street, Kurdestan Street, Tehran **Tel:** 98 21 8833 1615
Email: eghtesadpooya@yahoo.com
Freq: Daily; **Circ:** 100000 Publisher's Statement
Advertising Manager: Masoumeh Akhlaqi; **Editor In Chief:** Afshin Larijani; **Publisher and Managing Director:** Habib-allah Qelishli
Profile: Eghtesad Pooya is a daily newspaper covering business, finance and economics. It launched in 2004 and is aimed at Iranian business executives.
Language (s): Persian
DAILY NEWSPAPER

Esfahan Emrooz 542861
Owner: Esfahan Emrooz Publication
Editorial: No. 5, Naderi Road, Daneshgah Street, Isfahan **Tel:** 98 311 662 6566
Email: esfahanemrooz@gmail.com **Web site:** http://www.esfahanemrooz.ir/fa
Freq: Daily; **Circ:** 17500 Publisher's Statement
Publisher and Managing Director: Abdulmohamad Akbary; **Editor In Chief:** Amir Akbary; **Advertising Manager:** Maryam Eshraqi
Profile: Esfahan Emrooz is a daily newspaper covering news, politics, business and culture. It launched in 2004.
Language (s): Persian
DAILY NEWSPAPER

Etemaad 538554
Owner: Etemaad
Editorial: Block 16, Road No. 8, Khajeh Abdulla Ansari Street, Tehran **Tel:** 98 21 2286 4761
Email: lastpage.etemad@gmail.com **Web site:** http://www.etemaad.ir
Freq: Daily
Editor in Chief: Javad Deliri; **Advertising Manager:** Ali Hazrati; **Publisher and Managing Director:** Elias Hazrati
Profile: Etemaad is a Persian daily newspaper covering local and international news, business, politics and sport. It launched in 2001.
Language (s): Persian
DAILY NEWSPAPER

Iran 350460
Owner: Islamic Republic News Agency
Editorial: PO Box 15875-5388, 208 Khoramshahr Street, Tehran **Tel:** 98 21 8876 1721
Email: editorial@iran-newspaper.com **Web site:** http://www.iran-newspaper.com
Freq: Daily; **Circ:** 360000 Publisher's Statement
Editor In Chief: Mohammad Nouri
Profile: Iran is a daily Persian newspaper covering national and international news, current affairs, politics, business and sports. It was first published in 1994.
Language (s): Persian
DAILY NEWSPAPER

Iran Daily 350466
Owner: Islamic Republic News Agency
Editorial: PO Box 15875-5388, Block 208, Khorramshahr Avenue, Tehran **Tel:** 98 21 8875 5762
Email: irandaily@icpi.com **Web site:** http://www.iran-daily.com
Freq: Daily; **Circ:** 12000 Publisher's Statement
Editor: Mohammad Karimi; **Advertising Manager:** Akebar Mohammadi
Profile: Iran Daily is a tabloid-sized English newspaper covering national and international news, current affairs, politics, business and sports. It launched in 1997, and is aimed at English speakers in Iran.
Language (s): English
DAILY NEWSPAPER

Iran News 157099
Owner: Sokhan Gostar Institute
Editorial: PO Box 15875-8551, No. 13, Pajouhesh Str., Golestan II Street, Tehran 1463777745
Tel: 98 21 4425 3401
Email: info@irannewsdaily.com **Web site:** http://www.irannewsdaily.com
Freq: Daily; **Circ:** 15000 Publisher's Statement
News Editor: Kianoush Amiri; **Managing Director:** Majid Aqazadeh; **Advertising Manager:** Abbas Ghari; **Advertising Manager:** Ali-Akbar Shamshirgaran; **Editor in Chief:** Fereydoon Taherpoor
Profile: Iran News is an English newspaper covering news, politics, economics, society and sports. It is published daily, except Fridays, and launched in 1994.
Language (s): English
Ad Rate: Full Page Mono 1224.00
Currency: Euro
DAILY NEWSPAPER

Jahane Sanat 538613
Owner: Iranchap Company
Editorial: No. 60, Arak Street, Ostad Najatalahi Street, Tehran **Tel:** 98 21 8893 4806
Email: jahan1383@yahoo.com **Web site:** http://www.jahanesanat.ir
Freq: Daily; **Circ:** 40000 Publisher's Statement
Advertising Manager: Masoumeh Fathi; **PR Manager:** Gholamreza Ghafarzadeh; **Publisher & Editor in Chief:** Mohamadreza Sa'adi
Profile: Jahane Sanat (World of Industry) is a daily Persian newspaper covering business and economics. It launched in 2004.
Language (s): Persian
DAILY NEWSPAPER

Jam-e-Jam 537893
Owner: Islamic Republic Of Iran Broadcasting (IRIB)
Editorial: No. 129, Mirdamad Street, Tehran
Tel: 98 21 2222 2511
Email: info@jamejamonline.ir **Web site:** http://www.jamejamonline.ir
Freq: Daily; **Circ:** 450000 Publisher's Statement
Advertising Manager: Morteza Faghani; **Editor In Chief:** Mohsen Mandegari; **Managing Director:** Bijan Moghadam
Profile: Jam-e-Jam is a daily Persian newspaper focusing on national and international news, current affairs, politics, business and sports. The newspaper was launched in 2001.
Language (s): Persian
Ad Rate: Full Page Mono 345600000.00
Currency: Iran Rials
DAILY NEWSPAPER

Javan Newspaper 350461
Owner: Payam Avaran Publishing
Editorial: No. 384, Shahid Motahari Street, Tehran
Tel: 98 21 8849 8449
Email: info@javanonline.ir **Web site:** http://www.javanonline.ir
Freq: Daily; **Circ:** 120000 Publisher's Statement
Managing Director: Mohammad Haidari; **Advertising Manager:** Bahram Honarparvar; **PR Manager:** Ali Mohammed; **Editor In Chief:** Seyed Nezamddine Mosavi
Profile: Javan Newspaper is a Persian daily covering local and international news, politics, business and sport. It was first published in 1999.
Language (s): Persian
DAILY NEWSPAPER

Khorasan 543464
Owner: Khorasan
Editorial: PO Box 91735-511, Shaheed Sadeqi Blvd., Mashhad **Tel:** 98 511 763 4000
Email: info@khorasannews.com **Web site:** http://www.khorasannews.com
Freq: Daily
Editor In Chief: Mohammad Ahadian; **Advertising Manager:** Mir Hossaini; **Publisher and Managing Director:** Koorosh Shojaie
Profile: Khorasan is a Persian daily newspaper covering national & international news, politics, business, culture and arts. It was first published in 1948.
Language (s): Persian
DAILY NEWSPAPER

Quds 355712
Owner: Astan Quds Radwi Publishing
Editorial: PO Box 91735-577, 14 Khayyam Square, Mashhad **Tel:** 98 511 768 5011
Email: info@qudsonline.ir **Web site:** http://www.qudsonline.ir
Freq: Daily; **Circ:** 80000 Publisher's Statement
Advertising Manager: Mahdi Husseini; **Managing Director:** Ghulamreza Kalandarian; **Editor In Chief:** Hamza Vaqaei
Profile: Quds is a daily Persian newspaper covering national and international news, current affairs, politics, business and sports. It was first published in 1987.
Language (s): Persian
DAILY NEWSPAPER

Resalat 350462
Owner: Resalat Publication
Editorial: No. 1, Shaheed Ismail Mohamadi Street, Tehran 1599976711 **Tel:** 98 21 8891 0806
Email: tadrisi60@gmail.com **Web site:** http://www.resalat-news.com
Freq: Daily; **Circ:** 900000 Publisher's Statement
Editor In Chief: Mohammad-Kazem Ambarlaie; **Advertising Manager:** Rasool Fatemi; **Managing Director:** Morteza Nabavi
Profile: Resalat is a daily Persian newspaper covering national and international news, current affairs, politics, business and sports. It launched in 1985.
Language (s): Persian
DAILY NEWSPAPER

Sobhe Eghtesad 564022
Owner: Sokhan Gostar Institute
Editorial: PO Box 15875-8551, No. 13, Pazhuhesh Alley, 2nd Golestan Alley, Tehran 1463777746
Tel: 98 21 4425 3335
Email: info@sobheco.com
Freq: Daily; **Circ:** 45000 Publisher's Statement
Managing Director: Majid Aqazadeh; **Editor In Chief:** Mariam Behnam-Rad; **Advertising Manager:** Shamshir Garan; **Public Relations Manager:** Fatemeh Lashkari; **Advertising Manager:** Ali-Akbar Shamshirgaran
Profile: Sobhe Eghtesad (Morning Economy) is a daily Persian newspaper covering social, economic and political issues. It was first published in 1995.
Language (s): Persian
Ad Rate: Full Page Colour 144000000.00
Currency: Iran Rials
DAILY NEWSPAPER

Tehran Times 350467
Owner: Islamic Ideology Dissemination Organisation
Editorial: PO Box 14155-4843, 18 Bimeh Lane, Tehran 1599814713 **Tel:** 98 21 8889 5450
Email: info@tehrantimes.com **Web site:** http://www.tehrantimes.com
Freq: Daily; **Circ:** 10000 Publisher's Statement
Managing Director: Ali Asgari; **Editor In Chief:** Morad Enadi; **Advertising Manager:** Nasser Najari
Profile: Tehran Times is a daily 16-page English newspaper covering national and international news, current affairs, politics, business and sports. It launched in 1979 and is aimed at English speakers in Iran.
Language (s): English
Ad Rate: Full Page Mono 5760.00
Ad Rate: Full Page Colour 6000.00
Currency: Euro
DAILY NEWSPAPER

Vatan-e Emrooz 668803
Owner: Vatan-e Emrooz
Editorial: PO Box 159163-6587, Block 9, Saeed Street, Tehran 1213027200 **Tel:** 98 21 6641 3783
Email: vatanemrooz1387@gmail.com **Web site:** http://www.vatanemrooz.ir
Freq: Daily
Managing Director: Mohamed Akhondi; **Editor In Chief:** Reza Shakibaei

Iran

Profile: Vatan-e Emrooz is a daily Persian newspaper covering current affairs, politics, business, culture & sports. It launched in 2008.
Language (s): Persian
DAILY NEWSPAPER

Al Vefagh 350465
Owner: Islamic Republic News Agency
Editorial: PO Box 15875-5388, 208 Khoramshahr, Tehran **Tel:** 98 21 8847 1207
Email: al-vefagh@al-vefagh.com **Web site:** http://www.al-vefagh.com
Freq: Daily; **Circ:** 19000 Publisher's Statement
Head of News: Shahla Abshenas; **Advertising Manager:** Ruqaya Marzooqi
Profile: Al Vefagh is a daily Arabic newspaper covering national and international news, current affairs, politics, business and sports. It launched in 1996.
Language (s): Arabic
DAILY NEWSPAPER

News Service/Syndicate

Agence France-Presse - Tehran Bureau 867812
Owner: Agence France-Presse
Editorial: Tehran **Tel:** 98 21 8872 3382
Email: newsroom.tehran@afp.com **Web site:** http://www.afp.com
Profile: Tehran bureau of international news and picture agency covering general news and current affairs.
Language (s): English
NEWS SERVICE/SYNDICATE

APTN Iran 370534
Owner: Associated Press
Editorial: Unit 1, 6th Floor, Jam-e Jam Building, Tehran 1966843168 **Tel:** 98 21 2202 3788
Email: tehranaptn@yahoo.com **Web site:** http://www.aptn.com
Producer: Chivan Bakiri; **Producer:** Mohammad Nasiri
Profile: Associated Press Television News (APTN) is the international television arm of the Associated Press - APTN's operations include a main news service, specialised broadcast services, customised coverage for the Middle East, a productions division, weekly and daily entertainment news and an extensive video archive library.
Language (s): English
NEWS SERVICE/SYNDICATE

Fars News Agency 370519
Owner: Fars News Agency
Editorial: PO Box 10815-3614, Block 1, Alley Shahid Saeidi, Tehran **Tel:** 98 21 8891 1660
Email: info@farsnews.com **Web site:** http://www.farsnews.com
Editor In Chief: Abbas Darvish-Tavangar; **General Director:** Sayed Nizam Al Deen
Profile: Fars News Agency is an independent news agency covering Iranian news, politics, economics, culture, society, law, sports, and military news in Persian and English.
Language (s): Arabic
NEWS SERVICE/SYNDICATE

Iranian Students' News Agency 370520
Owner: Iranian Students' News Agency
Editorial: Shohadaye Jandarmeri Alley, Fakhrerazi Alley, Tehran 1314744951 **Tel:** 98 21 6641 7324
Email: info@isna.ir **Web site:** http://www.isna.ir
Managing Director: Saeed Pourali
Profile: Iranian Students' News Agency is an independent news agency run by university students.
Language (s): Arabic
NEWS SERVICE/SYNDICATE

Islamic Republic News Agency 370499
Owner: Islamic Republic News Agency
Editorial: PO Box 15875-4566, 873 Vali Asr Avenue, Tehran 1595633319 **Tel:** 98 21 8890 5066
Email: irna@irna.ir **Web site:** http://www.irna.ir
Profile: Islamic Republic News Agency is an official government news agency founded in 1934.
Language (s): Arabic
NEWS SERVICE/SYNDICATE

Mehr News Agency 370521
Owner: Mehr News Agency
Editorial: 18 Bimeh Lane, Nejatollahi Street, Tehran 1599814713 **Tel:** 98 21 8880 0789
Email: president@mehrnews.com **Web site:** http://www.mehrnews.com
Director General: Reza Moghadasi
Profile: Mehr News Agency is a semi-official news agency - transmits news and photos in 7 languages (Persian, English, Russian, German, Arabic, Turkish, and Urdu) - coverage includes culture and art, literature, religion, technology, society, economics, politics, international news, sport, energy and defence.
Language (s): Arabic
NEWS SERVICE/SYNDICATE

Iraq

Time Difference: GMT +3
National Telephone Code: 964
Continent: Asia
Capital: Baghdad

Newspapers

Al Adala 395596
Owner: Al Adala Est. for Press Printing and Publishing
Editorial: Al Nobal Street, Baghdad
Tel: 964 770 316 9999
Email: aladalaeditor@yahoo.com **Web site:** http://www.aladalanews.net
Freq: Daily; **Circ:** 6000 Publisher's Statement
Publisher: Adel Abdel Mahdi; **Advertising Manager:** Ali Al Gadban; **News Editor:** Morteza Al Jashami; **PR Manager:** Abdul Karim Al Taweel; **Editor In Chief:** Ali Khleif
Profile: Al Adala (Justice) is an Arabic newspaper covering local and international news, politics, business, culture and sport. It launched in 2003 and is published daily, except Fridays.
Language (s): Arabic
DAILY NEWSPAPER

Al Amal 402280
Owner: Al Amal Publishing
Editorial: 2nd Floor, Roz Building, Salim Street, Sulaimaniyah **Tel:** 964 770 156 4353
Email: shelalgedo@yahoo.com
Freq: Weekly; **Circ:** 2000 Publisher's Statement
Editor in Chief: Shelal Gedo; **News Editor:** Fethulla Huseyni
Profile: Al Amal (Hope) is a weekly newspaper covering national and international news, business and politics. It launched in 2005 and is published on Mondays.
Language (s): Arabic
DAILY NEWSPAPER

Azzaman 395546
Owner: Azzaman International Ltd
Editorial: Al Bataween Area, Baghdad
Tel: 964 790 133 4075
Email: info@azzaman.com **Web site:** http://www.azzaman.com
Freq: Daily; **Circ:** 50000 Publisher's Statement
Editor In Chief: Ahmed Abdulmajeed; **Managing Director & Publisher:** Saad Bazzaz
Profile: Azzaman (The Time) is an Arabic newspaper covering local and international news, current affairs, business, culture and sport. The newspaper was founded in London in 1997 and is printed in Baghdad, London and Beirut. It is published daily, except Fridays.
Language (s): Arabic
DAILY NEWSPAPER

Dar Al-Salam 791483
Owner: Iraqi Islamic Party
Editorial: Al Yarmouk Area, Baghdad
Tel: 964 770 251 9999
Email: basam_f_80@yahoo.com **Web site:** http://www.iraqiparty.com
Freq: Daily; **Circ:** 10000 Rate Card
PR & Media Manager: Bassam Al-Tamimi; **News Editor:** Bahauddin Naqshabandi
Profile: Dar Al-Salam is the newspaper of the Iraqi Islamic Party and covers national and international news, business and sport. The daily newspaper launched in 2004.
Language (s): Arabic
DAILY NEWSPAPER

Al Hoda Newspaper 413469
Owner: Dar Al Hoda for Culture & Media
Editorial: PO Box 155, Al Hussein Street, Karbala
Tel: 964 780 388 9050
Email: al-hodaonline@al-hodaonline.com **Web site:** http://www.al-hodaonline.com/np
Freq: Weekly; **Circ:** 6000 Publisher's Statement
News Editor: Muzaffar Abbas; **Public Relations Director:** Ahmed Al Shakarchi; **Editor In Chief:** Nohman Al Tamimi; **General Manager:** Mohammad-Ali Jawad; **News Editor:** Nabeel Mohsen
Profile: Al Hoda Newspaper is a weekly Arabic newspaper covering local and international news. It launched in 2005 and is published on Wednesdays.
Language (s): Arabic
DAILY NEWSPAPER

Al Ittihad 378283
Owner: Patriotic Union of Kurdistan (PUK)
Editorial: PO Box 5436, Al Qadsiyah, Baghdad
Email: ittihadpress@hotmail.com **Web site:** http://www.alitthad.com
Freq: Daily; **Circ:** 5000 Publisher's Statement
News Editor: Satea Raji; **Editor-in-Chief:** Fryad Rwandzy; **Advertising Manager:** Zeina Saeb
Profile: Al Ittihad (The Union) is a national newspaper covering news, business and sport. It was launched in 1992 by the Patriotic Union of Kurdistan (PUK).
Language (s): Arabic
DAILY NEWSPAPER

The Kurdish Globe 402279
Owner: Mukiryani Establishment for Research & Publication
Editorial: Media Center, Massif Road, Erbil
Tel: 964 750 774 7784
Email: info.kurdishglobe@gmail.com **Web site:** http://www.kurdishglobe.net
Freq: Weekly; **Circ:** 3000
Editor in Chief: Gazi Hassan
Profile: The Kurdish Globe is a 16-page, regional weekly newspaper covering Kurdish and Middle East-related issues, including news, politics, business and culture. The newspaper is aimed at English speakers in Iraqi Kurdistan. Formerly called Hewler Globe, it launched in 2005 and is published on Mondays.
Language (s): English
DAILY NEWSPAPER

Al Mada 391206
Owner: Al Mada Est. For Mass Media, Culture and Arts
Editorial: House no. 141, Abi Nouass Street, Baghdad **Tel:** 964 1 717 8859
Email: info@almadapaper.net **Web site:** http://www.almadapaper.net
Freq: Daily; **Circ:** 20000 Publisher's Statement
General Manager: Ghada Al-Amily; **CEO & Editor in Chief:** Fakhri Kareem; **Advertising Manager:** Ammar Sabah
Profile: Al Mada is a regional newspaper covering local and international news, politics, business and sport. It launched in 2003, and is aimed at people living in central Iraq. The newspaper is published daily, except Fridays.
Language (s): Arabic
DAILY NEWSPAPER

Al Mannarah 378097
Owner: South Press & Publishing Est.
Editorial: Okba Ben Nafea Square, Baghdad
Tel: 962 799 141371
Email: almannarah@almannarah.com
Freq: 2 Times/Week; **Circ:** 25000 Publisher's Statement
News Editor: Abdulwadood Al Diwan; **Media Consultant:** Laith Al Tamimi
Profile: Al Mannarah is a broadsheet-sized newspaper covering local and international news, politics, business and sport. It launched in 2003 and is published twice a week, on Saturdays and Wednesdays.
Language (s): Arabic
Ad Rate: Full Page Mono 1200.00
Currency: United States Dollars
DAILY NEWSPAPER

Al Sabah 404319
Owner: Iraqi Media Network
Editorial: Waziriya, Qahira District, Baghdad
Tel: 964 790 192 9423
Email: al_sabaaah@yahoo.com **Web site:** http://www.alsabaah.iq
Freq: Daily; **Circ:** 55000 Publisher's Statement
Advertising Manager: Nidhal Ibrahim; **Editor In Chief:** Halim Salman
Profile: Al Sabah (The Morning) is an Arabic newspaper covering local and international news, politics, business and sport. It launched in 2003 and is published daily, except Fridays.
Language (s): Arabic
DAILY NEWSPAPER

Al Sabah Al Jadeed 395620
Owner: Al Neel Al Akhdar
Editorial: Al Maghreb Street, Al Waziriya, Baghdad
Tel: 964 770 971 9712
Email: assabahaljaded@yahoo.com **Web site:** http://www.newsabah.com
Freq: Daily; **Circ:** 15000 Publisher's Statement
News Editor: Sami Al Obady; **Advertising Manager:** Feryal Al-Bakry
Profile: Al Sabah Al Jadeed (The New Morning) is a daily Arabic newspaper featuring local and international news, current affairs, culture, sport, business and finance. It launched in 2004.
Language (s): Arabic
DAILY NEWSPAPER

Tareek Alshaab 395529
Owner: Dar Al Rouwad Al Mozdahira Printing Publishing and Advertising
Editorial: PO Box 55429, Sahat Al Andalus, Baghdad
Tel: 964 770 980 7363
Email: tareekalshaab@gmail.com
Freq: Daily; **Circ:** 9000 Publisher's Statement
Managing Director: Jawad Al Taie; **Editor in Chief:** Yasser Khadir; **Advertising Manager:** Nabeel Tawfiq
Profile: Tareek Alshaab is a daily newspaper covering local and international news, politics, business and sport. It was launched by the Iraqi Communist Party in 1961.
Language (s): Arabic
DAILY NEWSPAPER

News Service/Syndicate

Agence France-Presse - Baghdad Bureau 815012
Owner: Agence France-Presse
Editorial: Karrada, Baghdad **Tel:** 964 790 191 3984
Email: newsroom.baghdad@afp.com **Web site:** http://www.afp.com
Bureau Chief: Jean-Marc Mojon
Profile: Baghdad bureau of the international news and picture agency.
Language (s): Arabic
NEWS SERVICE/SYNDICATE

All Iraq News Agency 823616
Owner: All Iraq News Agency
Editorial: 3rd Floor, Al Forat Apartments, Karada, Baghdad **Tel:** 964 780 916 1774
Email: alliraqnews@yahoo.com **Web site:** http://www.alliraqnews.com
Editor In Chief: Kazim Alatwany
Profile: All Iraq News Agency (AIN) covers news and current affairs, business, politics and sport from Iraq.
Language (s): Arabic
NEWS SERVICE/SYNDICATE

National Iraqi News Agency 396490
Owner: National Iraqi News Agency
Editorial: G Floor, Al Safeer Hotel, Abunuas Street, Baghdad **Tel:** 964 1 717 2251
Email: news@ninanews.com **Web site:** http://www.ninanews.com
Editor In Chief: Hafidh Al Rawi; **Managing Director:** Shafeek Alobaidy; **Editor:** Mohammad Hameed; **Editor:** Omar Hisham; **Editor:** Hiba Hussein; **Editor:** Eiad Zaid
Profile: National Iraqi News Agency is an independent news agency supplying newspapers, radio and television stations, Internet sites, international media, non-governmental and governmental organisations and diplomatic representatives.
Language (s): Arabic
NEWS SERVICE/SYNDICATE

Reuters - Iraq Bureau 739084
Owner: Thomson Reuters
Editorial: House 22, 102 Karada Abu Rawda, Baghdad **Tel:** 964 790 191 7052
Email: reuters@fastmail.fm **Web site:** http://www.reuters.com
Profile: Iraq bureau of international news agency supplying news - text, graphics, video and pictures - to subscribers around the world.
Language (s): Arabic
NEWS SERVICE/SYNDICATE

Israel

Time Difference: GMT +2
National Telephone Code: 972
Continent: Asia
Capital: Jerusalem

Newspapers

Globes 156664
Owner: Globes Publisher Itonut (1983) Ltd
Editorial: 53 Etzel Street, Rishon Le Zion 75150
Tel: 972 3 953 8611
Email: mailbox@globes.co.il **Web site:** http://www.globes.co.il
Freq: Daily; **Circ:** 45000 Publisher's Statement
Editor in Chief: Haggai Golan; **News Editor:** Eli Tsipori
Profile: National daily newspaper focussing on business and financial news in Israel including, economics, investment and management.
Language (s): English
DAILY NEWSPAPER

Haaretz 156665
Owner: Haaretz Daily Newspaper Ltd.
Editorial: 21 Schocken Street, Tel Aviv 61001
Tel: 972 3 512 12 04
Email: contact@haaretz.co.il **Web site:** http://www.haaretz.com
Freq: Daily; **Circ:** 75000 Publisher's Statement
Editor in Chief: Aluf Benn; **News Editor:** Noa Landau; **Publisher:** Amos Schocken
Profile: National daily newspaper covering general news and current affairs in Israel and around the world including business, economics, politics and culture.
Language (s): English
DAILY NEWSPAPER

The Jerusalem Post 156789
Owner: Jerusalem Post Group
Editorial: The Jerusalem Post Building, Jerusalem 91000 **Tel:** 972 2 531 5666
Email: letters@jpost.com **Web site:** http://www.jpost.com
Freq: Daily; **Circ:** 50000 Publisher's Statement
News Editor: Ilan Evyatar; **Editor in Chief:** Steve Linde
Profile: National daily newspaper focussing on national and international news, current affairs, politics, economics, business, regional interest, Jewish interest, arts, culture, travel, sports, health, science and technology.
Language (s): English
DAILY NEWSPAPER

Jerusalem Post - New York Bureau 342423
Owner: Jerusalem Post Group
Editorial: 80 Wall St, New York, New York 10005-3601 **Tel:** 1 212 742-0505
Email: editors@jpost.com **Web site:** http://www.jpost.com
Profile: Local bureau of the national daily newspaper focussing on national and international news, current affairs, politics, economics, business, regional interest, Jewish interest, arts, culture, travel, sports, health, science and technology. Aimed at the general public.
Language (s): English
DAILY NEWSPAPER

Jerusalem Post - Washington Bureau 850569
Owner: Jerusalem Post Group
Email: editors@jpost.com **Web site:** http://www.jpost.com
Bureau Chief: Hilary Leila Krieger
Profile: Local bureau of the national daily newspaper focussing on national and international news, current affairs, politics, economics, business, regional interest, Jewish interest, arts, culture, travel, sports, health, science and technology. Aimed at the general public.
DAILY NEWSPAPER

Maariv 156790
Owner: Modin Publishing House
Editorial: 2 Carlebach Street, Tel Aviv 67132
Tel: 972 3 769 1020
Email: deskmaariv@gmail.com **Web site:** http://www.maariv.co.il
Freq: Daily; **Circ:** 250000 Publisher's Statement
Profile: National daily newspaper focusing on national and international news and current affairs including politics, economics, business, culture and society.
Language (s): Hebrew
Ad Rate: Full Page Mono 90924.00
Ad Rate: Full Page Colour 158472.00
Currency: Israel New Shekels
DAILY NEWSPAPER

Makor Rishon 156666
Owner: Makor Rishon
Editorial: 116 Menahen Begin Street, Beth Kalka, Tel Aviv 61570 **Tel:** 972 77 7277700
Email: menuim@makorrishon.co.il **Web site:** http://www.makorrishon.co.il
Circ: 60000 Publisher's Statement
Editor: Amnon Lord
Profile: National daily newspaper covering news and current affairs including politics, economics, culture and general information.
Language (s): Hebrew
DAILY NEWSPAPER

Sawt Al Haq Wal Horriya 327509
Owner: Al Balagh Institution for Communication
Editorial: PO Box: 134, Um Al Fahm 30010
Tel: 972 4 631 7890
Email: sawt@sawt-alhaq.com **Web site:** http://www.sawt-alhaq.com
Circ: 15000 Publisher's Statement
Editor: Tawfeeq Jebareen
Profile: Weekly newspaper focusing on national and international news, current affairs, politics and economics.
Language (s): Arabic
DAILY NEWSPAPER

Yedioth Ahronoth 490492
Owner: Yedioth Tikshoret
Editorial: 127 Yigal Allon Street, Tel Aviv 67433
Tel: 972 3 608 2222
Email: news@ynetnews.com **Web site:** http://www.ynetnews.com
Freq: Daily
Head of News: Gido Ran; **Editor in Chief:** Eran Tiefenbrunn
Profile: National daily newspaper covering regional, national and international news and current affairs including business, politics, economics, Jewish world, art, culture and travel.
Language (s): English
DAILY NEWSPAPER

News Service/Syndicate

Bloomberg - Jerusalem Bureau 509579
Editorial: 23, Hillel Street, 10th Floor, Jerusalem 94582 **Tel:** 972 2 625 0061
Email: israelnews@bloomberg.net **Web site:** http://www.bloomberg.com
Profile: Jerusalem bureau of international financial news wire service.
Language (s): Hebrew
NEWS SERVICE/SYNDICATE

Cursorinfo.co.il 583786
Editorial: P.O. Box 552656, Tel Aviv
Email: sales@cursorinfo.co.il **Web site:** http://cursorinfo.co.il
Freq: Daily
Editor: Ilya Kazachkov; **Editor in Chief:** Maks Lurie; **Director:** Anatoliy Motkin; **Editor:** Ilya Naimark; **Editor:** Gabriel Wolfson
Profile: Web news service providing information on life in Israel and former Soviet Union, with political, economic, sports and cultural news.
Language (s): Russian
NEWS SERVICE/SYNDICATE

ISRA.com 583785
Web site: http://www.isra.com
Freq: Daily
Profile: Online resource providing political, economic, technologies, cultural, sports news.
Language (s): Russian
NEWS SERVICE/SYNDICATE

IsraLife.com 583800
Email: admin@isralife.com **Web site:** http://www.isralife.com
Freq: Daily
Profile: Online resource covering politics, daily news, culture, sports and entertainment.
Language (s): Russian
NEWS SERVICE/SYNDICATE

Izrus.co.il 583788
Email: chief@izrus.co.il **Web site:** http://www.izrus.co.il
Freq: Daily
Director: Mikhail Falkov; **Director:** Alexander Goldenstein; **Editor:** Boris Khotinsky; **Editor:** Alexander Kogan; **Editor:** Galina Malamant
Profile: Online resource providing news and useful information for Russian-speaking community of Israel.
Language (s): Russian
NEWS SERVICE/SYNDICATE

MIGnews.com 583596
Owner: Media International Group
Editorial: Kaufmann 2, Tel Aviv 61500
Tel: 972 54 47 97 074
Email: editor@mignews.com **Web site:** http://www.mignews.com
Editor in Chief: Michael Grizotsky; **Editor:** Boris Kovalev; **Editor:** Elena Sklyarova
Profile: Online publication focusing on politics, economics, society, social, science and culture in Russian language.
Language (s): Russian
NEWS SERVICE/SYNDICATE

mnenia.zahav.ru 583790
Tel: 972 72 2003823
Web site: http://mnenia.zahav.ru
Freq: Weekly
Editor: Alexander Kogan
Profile: Informative-analytical blog providing forum for exchange of political opinions.
Language (s): Russian
NEWS SERVICE/SYNDICATE

NEWS.israelinfo.co.il 583791
Owner: InterLink Info Ltd
Tel: 972 3 9673467
Email: briker@israelinfo.ru **Web site:** http://news.israelinfo.co.il
Freq: Daily
Profile: Online newswire resource with most updated news on Israel in Russian language.
Language (s): Russian
NEWS SERVICE/SYNDICATE

NEWSru.co.il 583784
Editorial: Menahem Begin 48B, Tel - Aviv 66184
Tel: 972 3 6890202
Email: newsru_israel@newsru.co.il **Web site:** http://www.newsru.co.il
Freq: Daily
Editor: Elena Berson; **Editor in Chief:** Evgeniy Finkel; **Editor:** Alexander Pechenkin; **Editor:** Anna Rozina; **Editor:** Mikhail Shafranov; **Editor:** Masha Tamir
Profile: Popular website for Russians living in Israel which reports latest news from Israel, Middle East and all over the world.
Language (s): Russian
NEWS SERVICE/SYNDICATE

Ru.local.co.il 583793
Email: info@localru.co.il **Web site:** http://ru.local.co.il
Freq: Daily
Profile: Provided information and news on Israeli cities and towns.
Language (s): Russian
NEWS SERVICE/SYNDICATE

Vestnik Izraela 583646
Email: info@vestnik.co.il **Web site:** http://www.vestnik.co.il
Freq: Daily
Profile: Online resource providing political, economical, science, technologies, health, cultural news and covering recent events.
Language (s): Russian
NEWS SERVICE/SYNDICATE

Zman.com 583789
Tel: 972 506560108
Email: info@zman.com **Web site:** http://www.zman.com
Freq: Daily
Profile: Online resource providing political, economic, tourist, cultural, sports news and entertainment.
Language (s): Russian
NEWS SERVICE/SYNDICATE

Italy

Time Difference: GMT +1
National Telephone Code: 39
Continent: Europe
Capital: Rome

Newspapers

Avvenire 156935
Owner: Avvenire Nuova Ed.It. SpA
Editorial: Piazza Carbonari, 3, Milano 20125
Tel: 39 02 67801
Email: segreteria.redazione@avvenire.it **Web site:** http://www.avvenire.it
Freq: Daily; **Circ:** 144818
Editor in Chief: Massimo Calvi; **Editor in Chief:** Umberto Folena; **Editor in Chief:** Marco Girardo; **Editor in Chief:** Andrea Lavazza; **Editor in Chief:** Riccardo Maccioni; **Editor in Chief:** Luciano Moia; **Editor in Chief:** Francesco Riccardi; **Director:** Marco Tarquinio
Profile: Caholic newspaper founded in 1968, which covers regional, national and international news and current affairs including politics, economics, culture, entertainment, sports, science and technology.
Language (s): Italian
Ad Rate: Full Page Colour 81664.00
Currency: Euro
DAILY NEWSPAPER

Avvenire - Rome Bureau 436918
Owner: Avvenire Nuova Ed.It. SpA
Editorial: Piazza Indipendenza, 11/B, Roma 185
Tel: 39 06 688231
Email: desk.roma@avvenire.it **Web site:** http://www.avvenire.it
Freq: Daily; **Circ:** 126000 Publisher's Statement
Editor in Chief: Antonio Maria Mira; **Director:** Marco Tarquinio
Profile: Rome bureau of the national newspaper covering local and regional news and current affairs including politics, economics, culture, entertainment, sports, science and technology from a Catholic viewpoint.
Language (s): Italian
DAILY NEWSPAPER

Corriere della Sera 437620
Owner: RCS MediaGroup SpA
Editorial: Via Solferino, 28, Milano 20121
Tel: 39 02 62821
Email: segretcor@rcs.it **Web site:** http://www.corriere.it
Freq: Daily; **Circ:** 405864 Publisher's Statement
Editor in Chief: Marco Ascione; **Editor in Chief:** Antonio Bozzo; **Editor in Chief:** Alessandro Cannavò; **Editor in Chief:** Giovanni Caprara; **Editor in Chief:** Daniele Dallera; **Editor in Chief:** Vito D'Angelo; **Editor in Chief:** Maurizio Donelli; **Editor in Chief:** Luciano Ferraro; **Editor in Chief:** Mario Garofalo; **Editor in Chief:** Luigi Ippolito; **Editor in Chief:** Dino Messina; **Editor in Chief:** Venanzio Postiglione; **Editor in Chief:** Luigi Ripamonti; **Editor in Chief:** Maria Laura Rodotà; **Editor in Chief:** Nicola Saldutti; **Beijing Bureau Chief:** Guido Santevecchi; **Editor in Chief:** Maria Luisa Villa
Profile: Newspaper covering regional, national and international news and current affairs including business, politics, economics, society, sports, culture, entertainment, health, education, science, technology, motoring, travel, home and lifestyle.
Language (s): Italian
Ad Rate: Full Page Mono 113400.00
Ad Rate: Full Page Colour 147420.00
Currency: Euro
DAILY NEWSPAPER

Corriere dello Sport - Stadio 156902
Owner: Corriere dello Sport srl
Editorial: Piazza Indipendenza, 11/B, Roma 185
Tel: 39 06 49921
Email: redazione@corsport.it **Web site:** http://www.corrieredellosport.it
Freq: Daily; **Circ:** 534000 Publisher's Statement
Editor in Chief: Alberto Dalla Palma; **Director:** Paolo De Paola; **Editor in Chief:** Giuliano Riva
Profile: Newspaper covering regional, national and international sports news including football, basketball, motorsports, formula 1, cycling, tennis, volleyball, winter sports, water-sports, competition and events.
Language (s): Italian
DAILY NEWSPAPER

Il Foglio 436928
Owner: Gruppo Sorgente
Editorial: Via Carroccio, 12, Milano 20123
Tel: 39 02 7712951
Email: lettere@ilfoglio.it **Web site:** http://www.ilfoglio.it
Circ: 47000
Director: Claudio Cerasa
Profile: Il Foglio is an Italian centre-right daily newspaper. It covers the most important news of the day with comment and analysis on them.
Language (s): Italian
DAILY NEWSPAPER

La Gazzetta dello Sport 156904
Owner: RCS MediaGroup SpA
Editorial: Via Solferino, 28, Milano 20121
Tel: 39 02 62821
Email: segretgaz@rcs.it **Web site:** http://www.gazzetta.it
Freq: Daily; **Circ:** 297867 Publisher's Statement
Capo redattore Centrale: Pier Battista Bergonzi; **Editor in Chief:** Manlio Gasparotto; **Director:** Andrea Monti
Profile: Newspaper covering all areas of sports including football, basketball, volleyball, motorsports, cycling, tennis, athletics, golf, rugby and sports events.
Language (s): Italian
Ad Rate: Full Page Mono 44100.00
Ad Rate: Full Page Colour 63000.00
Currency: Euro
DAILY NEWSPAPER

Il Gazzettino 596410
Owner: Caltagirone Editore
Editorial: Via Torino, 110, Mestre Ve 30172
Tel: 39 041 665111
Email: segredazione@gazzettino.it **Web site:** http://www.gazzettino.it
Freq: Daily; **Circ:** 74038 Publisher's Statement
Editor in Chief: Vittorino Franchin; **Editor in Chief:** Giorgio Gasco; **Editor in Chief:** Maurizio Paglialunga; **Director:** Roberto Papetti; **Director:** Vittorio Pierobon
Profile: Regional newspaper covering news from Venice, the North-East of Italy and the world.
Language (s): Italian
DAILY NEWSPAPER

Il Giornale 156905
Owner: Soc. Europea Di Edizioni
Editorial: Via Gaetano Negri, 4, Milano 20123
Tel: 39 02 85661
Email: segreteria@ilgiornale.it **Web site:** http://www.ilgiornale.it
Freq: Daily; **Circ:** 143225 Publisher's Statement
Editor in Chief: Angelo Allegri; **Editor in Chief:** Gabriele Barberis; **Editor in Chief:** Pierluigi Bonora; **Editor in Chief:** Alessandro Gnocchi; **Editor in Chef:** Marco Pietro Lombardo; **Editor in Chief:** Giuseppe Marino; **Editor in Chief:** Elia Pagnoni; **Editor in Chief:** Riccardo Pelliccetti; **Director:** Alessandro Sallusti; **Editor in Chief:** Marcello Zacché
Profile: National newspaper covering regional, national and international news and current affairs including business, politics, economics, sports, culture, entertainment, health, education, science, technology, motoring, travel, home and lifestyle.
Language (s): Italian
DAILY NEWSPAPER

Il Giornale - Rome Bureau 436914
Owner: Soc. Europea Di Edizioni
Editorial: Via Terenzio, 35, Roma 193
Tel: 39 06 690031
Email: segreteria.rm@ilgiornale.it **Web site:** http://www.ilgiornale.it
Freq: Daily; **Circ:** 300000 Publisher's Statement
Editor in Chief: Vittorio Macioce
Profile: Rome bureau of Il Giornale covering regional news and current affairs including business, politics, economics, sports, culture, entertainment, health, education, science, technology, motoring, travel, home and lifestyle.
Language (s): Italian
DAILY NEWSPAPER

Il Giorno 156906
Owner: Riffeser Monti
Editorial: Corso Buenos Aires, 54, Milano 20129
Tel: 39 02 277991
Email: segreteria.redazione.milano@monrif.net **Web site:** http://www.ilgiorno.it
Circ: 70345
Direttore responsabile: Ugo Cennamo; **Capo redattore:** Luisa Ciuni; **Capo redattore:** Barbara Consarino; **Capo redattore:** Ivano Costa; **Caporedattore:** Piero Fachin
Profile: Newspaper covering regional news and current affairs in the Milan and the Lombard region including politics, economics, sports, culture and entertainment.
Language (s): Italian
Ad Rate: Full Page Mono 42000.00
Ad Rate: Full Page Colour 58800.00
Currency: Euro
DAILY NEWSPAPER

Italia Oggi 156907
Owner: Class Editori SpA
Editorial: Via Burigozzo, 8, Milano 20122
Tel: 39 02 58219207
Email: italiaoggi@class.it **Web site:** http://www.italiaoggi.it
Freq: Daily; **Circ:** 72280 Publisher's Statement
Magazine Director: Marino Longoni; **Editor in Chief:** Gianni Macheda; **Director:** Pierluigi Magnaschi; **Director:** Paolo Panerai
Profile: Newspaper covering national and international politics, business, finance, economics and legal affairs.
Language (s): Italian
Ad Rate: Full Page Mono 25500.00
Ad Rate: Full Page Colour 35700.00
Currency: Euro
DAILY NEWSPAPER

Leggo 507815
Owner: Caltagirone Editore
Editorial: Via Nazionale, 87, Roma 184
Tel: 39 06 4620731

Email: leggo@leggoposta.it **Web site:** http://www.leggo.it
Freq: Daily; **Circ:** 1424000 Publisher's Statement
Editor in Chief: Carlo Fiorini; **Director:** Alvaro Moretti; **Editor:** Franco Pasqualetti
Profile: Newspaper covering general news including lifestyle, society, celebrities, entertainment, sport, technology, travel, health and motoring.
Language (s): Italian
Ad Rate: Full Page Colour 148560.00
Currency: Euro
DAILY NEWSPAPER

Libero 427234

Owner: Gruppo Angelucci
Editorial: Viale Luigi Majno, 42, Milano 20129
Tel: 39 02 999 666
Email: redazione@liberoquotidiano.it **Web site:** http://www.liberoquotidiano.it
Freq: Daily; **Circ:** 100146
Direttore Responsabile: Maurizio Belpietro; **Caporedattore:** Simona Bertuzzi; **Caporedattore:** Francesco Specchia; **Caporedattore Centrale:** Giuliano Zulin
Profile: Newspaper covering international and national news including politics, economy and entertainment.
Language (s): Italian
DAILY NEWSPAPER

Il Manifesto 156909

Owner: Il Manifesto Coop. Ed.
Editorial: Via Angelo Bargoni, 8, Roma 153
Tel: 39 06 687191
Email: redazione@ilmanifesto.it **Web site:** http://www.ilmanifesto.it
Freq: Daily; **Circ:** 39079
Caporedattore: Marco Boccitto; **Caporedattore:** Michela Bongi; **Caporedattore:** Giulia Sbarigia
Profile: Communist newspaper covering general news and current affairs including politics, finance, economics, culture, sport and entertainment.
Language (s): Italian
DAILY NEWSPAPER

Il Mattino 773110

Owner: Caltagirone Editore
Editorial: Via Chiatamone, 65, Napoli 80121
Tel: 39 081 7947111
Email: redazioneinternet@ilmattino.it **Web site:** http://www.ilmattino.it
Freq: Daily; **Circ:** 56521
Profile: Newspaper covering regional, national and international news and current affairs including business, politics, economics, sports, culture, entertainment, health, education, science, technology, motoring, travel, home and lifestyle.
Language (s): Italian
DAILY NEWSPAPER

Il Messaggero 156910

Owner: Caltagirone Editore
Editorial: Via del Tritone, 152, Rome 187
Tel: 39 06 472070
Email: segreteria.redazione@ilmessaggero.it **Web site:** http://www.ilmessaggero.it
Freq: Daily; **Circ:** 152668 Publisher's Statement
Editor in Chief: Raffaele Alliegro; **Editor in Chief:** Alessandro Di Lellis; **Editor in Chief:** Alberto Gentili; **Editor in Chief:** Franca Giansoldati; **Editor in Chief:** Massimo Pedretti; **Editor in Chief:** Roberto Stigliano; **Editor in Chief:** Giorgio Ursicino
Profile: Newspaper covering regional, national and international news and current affairs including business, politics, economics, sports, culture, entertainment, health, education, science, technology, motoring, travel, home and lifestyle.
Language (s): Italian
Ad Rate: Full Page Mono 129248.00
Ad Rate: Full Page Colour 193872.00
Currency: Euro
DAILY NEWSPAPER

Metro 507820

Owner: New Media Enterprise Srl
Editorial: Via Carlo Pesenti, 130, Roma 156
Tel: 39 06 49241200
Email: roma@metroitaly.it **Web site:** http://www.metronews.it
Freq: Daily; **Circ:** 800000 Publisher's Statement
Editor in chief: Paola Rizzi
Profile: Free newspaper distributed in 8 Italian cities: Roma, Milano, Torino, Genova, Bologna, Firenze, Cagliari and Sassari covering regional, national and international news and current affairs including politics, economy, sports, entertainment, lifestyle, culture and environment.
Language (s): Italian
DAILY NEWSPAPER

La Nazione 156911

Owner: Riffeser Monti
Editorial: Viale Giovine Italia, 17, Firenze 50122
Tel: 39 055 24951
Email: redazione.cronaca@lanazione.net **Web site:** http://www.lanazione.it
Freq: Daily; **Circ:** 111816 Publisher's Statement
Director: Marcello Mancini; **Capo redattore:** Laura Pacciani
Profile: Newspaper covering regional, national and international news and current affairs including politics, economics, sport, cars, lifestyle, fashion, technology and entertainment. Read predominantly by people living in the Tuscany and Umbria regions.
Language (s): Italian
Ad Rate: Full Page Colour 105000.00
Currency: Euro
DAILY NEWSPAPER

QN - Quotidiano Nazionale 427232

Owner: Riffeser Monti
Editorial: Via Enrico Mattei, 106, Bologna 40138
Tel: 39 051 6006111
Email: redazione@quotidiano.net **Web site:** http://www.quotidiano.net
Freq: Daily; **Circ:** 321663 Publisher's Statement
Caporedattore: Sergio Gioli; **Caporedattore:** Gianluigi Schiavon
Profile: Newspapers group covering regional, national and international news and current affairs including economics, politics, sports, cars, lifestyle, entertainment, culture and technology. It gathers the ediorial teams of Il Resto del Carlino, La Nazione and Il Giorno.
Language (s): Italian
DAILY NEWSPAPER

QN - Quotidiano Nazionale - Rome Bureau 436925

Owner: Riffeser Monti
Editorial: Piazza San Silvestro, 13, Roma 187
Tel: 39 06 699541
Email: roma@quotidiano.net **Web site:** http://www.quotidiano.net
Freq: Daily; **Circ:** 597087 Publisher's Statement
Caporedattore: Andrea Cangini
Profile: Rome bureau of QN - Quotidiano Nazionale covering regional and national news and current affairs including economics, politics, sports, cars, lifestyle, entertainment, culture and technology.
Language (s): Italian
DAILY NEWSPAPER

La Repubblica 156912

Owner: Gruppo Ed. L'Espresso SpA
Editorial: Via Cristoforo Colombo, 90, Roma 147
Tel: 39 06 49821
Email: larepubblica@repubblica.it **Web site:** http://www.repubblica.it
Freq: Daily; **Circ:** 336211 Publisher's Statement
Collaboratore: Federica Angeli; **Capo redattore:** Ernesto Assante; **Capo redattore:** Valerio Berruti; **Editor in Chief:** Fabio Bogo; **Editor in Chief:** Giuseppe Casciaro; **Capo redattore:** Giuseppe Cerasa; **Editor:** Arturo Cocchi; **Capo redattore:** Stefania Di Lellis; **Direttore responsabile:** Gabriele Di Matteo; **Editor in Chief:** Fabrizio Filosa; **Editor in Chief:** Aurelio Magistà; **Capo redattore:** Giancarlo Mola; **Editor:** Vincenzo Nigro; **Collaboratore:** Fabio Orecchini; **Redattore:** Carlo Picozza; **Editor in Chief:** Aligi Pontani; **Capo redattore:** Marco Ruffolo; **Editore:** Barbara Spinelli; **Collaboratore:** Alberto Stabile; **Capo redattore:** Claudio Tito
Profile: Newspaper covering regional, national and international news and current affairs including politics, economics, sport, culture, technology, motoring and entertainment.
Language (s): Italian
DAILY NEWSPAPER

Il Resto del Carlino 156913

Owner: Riffeser Monti
Editorial: Via Enrico Mattei, 106, Bologna 40138
Tel: 39 051 6006111
Email: segreteria.redazione.bologna@monrif.net **Web site:** http://www.ilrestodelcarlino.it
Freq: Daily; **Circ:** 139502 Publisher's Statement
Online Director: Andrea Cangini; **Editor in Chief:** Franco Caniato; **Editor in Chief:** Massimiliano Pandolfi
Profile: Newspaper covering regional, national and international news and current affairs including politics, economics, sport, lifestyle, culture and entertainment.
Language (s): Italian
DAILY NEWSPAPER

Il Secolo XIX 156887

Owner: Italiana Editrice SpA
Editorial: Piazza Piccapietra, 21, Genova 16121
Tel: 39 010 53881
Email: redazione@ilsecoloxix.it **Web site:** http://www.ilsecoloxix.it
Circ: 64670
Caporedattore: Eugenio Agosti; **Director:** Alessandro Cassinis; **Giornalista:** Andrea Castanini; **Caporedattore:** Marco Menduni; **Caporedattore:** Roberto Onofrio; **Caporedattore:** Marco Perchiera; **Capo Redattore Centrale:** Massimo Righi; **Editor:** Simone Traverso
Profile: Newspaper covering international, national and regional news, with a special emphasis on news in the Liguria region including politics, economics, sport, culture and entertainment.
Language (s): Italian
DAILY NEWSPAPER

Il Sole 24 Ore 156915

Owner: Gruppo 24 ORE
Editorial: Via Monte Rosa, 91, Milano 20149
Tel: 39 02 30221
Email: segr.redazione@ilsole24ore.com **Web site:** http://www.ilsole24ore.com
Freq: Daily; **Circ:** 213091 Publisher's Statement
Editor in Chief: Daniele Bellasio; **Editor:** Luca De Biase; **Capo redattore:** Jean Marie Del Bo; **Caporedattore:** Laura La Posta; **Editor in Chief:** Christian Martino; **Capo redattore:** Lello Naso; **Capo redattore:** Luca Orlando; **Capo redattore centrale:** Salvatore Padula; **Editor:** Fabio Pavesi; **Editor in Chief:** Christian Rocca; **Editor in Chief:** Fernanda Roggero; **Editor:** Pierangelo Soldavini
Profile: Newspaper covering regional, national and international news and current affairs including business, economics, finance, politics, technology, sport, culture and entertainment.
Language (s): Italian

Ad Rate: Full Page Colour 226560.00
Currency: Euro
DAILY NEWSPAPER

La Stampa 156916

Owner: Italiana Editrice SpA
Editorial: Via Lugaro, 15, Torino 10126
Tel: 39 011 6568111
Email: stampaweb@lastampa.it **Web site:** http://www.lastampa.it
Freq: Daily; **Circ:** 244598 Publisher's Statement
Collaboratore: Luca Bergamin; **Capo redattore:** Guido Boffo; **Director:** Mario Calabresi; **Editor in Chief:** Gabriele Ferraris; **Caporedattore:** Luca Ferrua; **Corrispondente Brazil:** Paolo Manzo; **Inviato/New York:** Paolo Mastrolilli; **Capo redattore:** Gianluca Paolucci; **Capo redattore:** Francesca Sforza; **Capo redattore:** Guido Tiberga; **Redattore:** Raphael Zanotti
Profile: Newspaper covering regional, national and international news and current affairs including politics, economics, society, health, culture, entertainment and sport.
Language (s): Italian
Ad Rate: Full Page Mono 2000.00
Ad Rate: Full Page Colour 228660.00
Currency: Euro
DAILY NEWSPAPER

La Stampa - New York Bureau 620061

Owner: Italiana Editrice SpA
Editorial: 7 Times Sq Ste 4307, New York, New York 10036-6508 **Tel:** 1 212 207-0908
Web site: http://www.lastampa.it
Profile: New York Bureau for La Stampa newspaper covering regional and national news and current affairs including politics, economics, society, health, culture, entertainment and sport.
Language (s): Italian
DAILY NEWSPAPER

Il Tirreno 800133

Owner: Gruppo Ed. L'Espresso SpA
Editorial: Viale Vittorio Alfieri, 9, Livorno 57124
Tel: 39 0586 220111
Email: redazione.@iltirreno.it **Web site:** http://www.iltirreno.it
Circ: 58000
Direttore Responsabile: Roberto Bernabò
Profile: Newspaper covering regional news and current affairs in the Tuscany region including politics, economics and culture.
Language (s): Italian
DAILY NEWSPAPER

Tuttosport 156918

Owner: Nuova Editoriale Sportiva
Editorial: Corso Svizzera, 185, Torino 10149
Tel: 39 011 77731
Email: posta@tuttosport.com **Web site:** http://www.tuttosport.com
Freq: Daily; **Circ:** 132780 Publisher's Statement
Caporedattore Centrale: Gianni De Pace; **Director:** Vittorio Oreggia
Profile: Newspaper covering competitive sport in Italy and throughout the world, with particular emphasis on events in the Turin area.
Language (s): Italian
Ad Rate: Full Page Mono 26768.00
Ad Rate: Full Page Colour 37475.20
Currency: Euro
DAILY NEWSPAPER

Tuttosport - Milan Bureau 427223

Owner: Nuova Editoriale Sportiva
Editorial: Corso Sempione, 8, Milano 20154
Tel: 39 02 316308
Email: posta@tuttosport.com **Web site:** http://www.tuttosport.com
Freq: Daily; **Circ:** 205000 Publisher's Statement
Redattore: Stefano Pasquino; **Redattore:** Alberto Pastorella
Profile: Milan bureau of Tuttosport covering competitive sport in Italy and throughout the world, with particular emphasis on events in the Milan area.
Language (s): Italian
DAILY NEWSPAPER

Tuttosport - Rome Bureau 436919

Owner: Nuova Editoriale Sportiva
Editorial: Via Calderini, 68, Rome 196
Tel: 39 06 3236584
Email: posta@tuttosport.com **Web site:** http://www.tuttosport.com
Freq: Daily; **Circ:** 205000 Publisher's Statement
Director: Vittorio Oreggia
Profile: Rome bureau of Tuttosport covering competitive sport in Italy and throughout the world, with particular emphasis on events in the Rome area.
Language (s): Italian
DAILY NEWSPAPER

News Service/Syndicate

Adnkronos 437131

Owner: Giuseppe Marra Communications
Editorial: Piazza Mastai, 9, Roma 153
Tel: 39 06 58071
Email: segreteria.redazione@adnkronos.com **Web site:** http://www.adnkronos.com
Freq: Daily
Director: Alessia Lautone; **Director:** Giuseppe Marra
Profile: News agency covering regional, national and international news and current affairs including politics, sports, finance, health, culture and entertainment.
Language (s): Arabic
NEWS SERVICE/SYNDICATE

Agenparl 535005

Owner: Agenparl
Editorial: Via del Labaro, 66, Roma 188
Tel: 39 06 93579408
Email: redazione@agenparl.it **Web site:** http://www.agenparl.com
Freq: Daily
Director: Luigi Camilloni
Profile: National news agency covering parliamentary news including politics, economics and social issues.
Language (s): Italian
NEWS SERVICE/SYNDICATE

Agenzia Omniapress 428625

Owner: Agenzia Omniapress
Editorial: Via Mons. Biraghi, 6, Milano 20163
Tel: 39 335 7184166
Email: omniapress1@libero.it **Web site:** http://www.agenziaomniapress.com
Freq: Daily
Direttore responsabile: Pietro COBOR; **Capo redattore:** Maria Grazia SIRTORI
Profile: News agency covering regional and national news and current affairs.
Language (s): Italian
NEWS SERVICE/SYNDICATE

ANSA - Agenzia Nazionale Stampa Associata 437134

Owner: Agenzia Nazionale Stampa Associata
Editorial: Via della Dataria, 94, Roma 187
Tel: 39 06 6774 1
Email: redazione.internet@ansa.it **Web site:** http://www.ansa.it
Freq: Daily
Editor in Chief: Angela Coarelli; **Director:** Luigi Contu; **Editor in Chief:** Paolo Dallorso; **Capo redattore:** Fabrizio FINZI; **Capo redattore:** Andrea LINARES; **Capo redattore:** Massimo LOMONACO; **Capo redattore:** Angela MAJOLI; **Capo redattore centrale:** Andrea MORELLI; **Capo redattore:** Piercarlo PRESUTTI; **Capo redattore centrale:** Vincenzo QUARATINO; **Capo redattore centrale:** Massimo SEBASTIANI; **Capo redattore:** Vincenzo SINAPI; **Capo redattore:** Elisabetta STEFANELLI; **Capo redattore:** Giorgio SVALDUZ; **Capo redattore:** Giuseppe TITO; **Capo redattore:** Gianluca VANNUCCHI
Profile: National news agency covering regional, national and international news and current affairs including politics, business, economics, society, culture, technology and sports.
Language (s): English
NEWS SERVICE/SYNDICATE

ANSA - New York Bureau 730473

Owner: Agenzia Nazionale Stampa Associata
Editorial: 21 W 46th St, 14th Floor, Suite 1406, New York, New York 10036-4119
Email: ansa.newyork@ansa.it **Web site:** http://www.ansa.it
Profile: International bureau of the Italian national news agency covering news in the USA.
Language (s): English
NEWS SERVICE/SYNDICATE

ASAPRESS 428627

Owner: HUB Comunicazione
Editorial: Viale Partigiani, 118/c, Cinisello Balsamo 20092 **Tel:** 39 02 22472162
Email: redazione@hubcomunicazione.it **Web site:** http://www.hubcomunicazione.it
Freq: Monthly
Director: Cristina Altieri
Profile: News service specialising in automotive news.
Language (s): Italian
NEWS SERVICE/SYNDICATE

Inter Press Service - North America Bureau 31046

Owner: Inter Press Service
Editorial: 777 United Nations Plz Rm S-407, New York, New York 10017-3521
Email: thalifdeen@aol.com **Web site:** http://www.ipsnews.net
Profile: International bureau of the news agency, covering sustainable development including social and environmental issues.
Language (s): English
NEWS SERVICE/SYNDICATE

Italpress 428629

Owner: Italpress
Editorial: Via Dante, 69, Palermo 90141
Tel: 39 091 589674
Email: info@italpress.com **Web site:** http://www.italpress.com
Freq: Daily
Direttore responsabile: Gaspare BORSELLINO
Profile: News agency covering regional news including entertainment, economy, energy, tourism, cars, environment, national politics and law.
Language (s): Italian
NEWS SERVICE/SYNDICATE

MF Dow Jones 428633

Owner: Class Editori SpA
Editorial: Via Burigozzo, 5, Milano 20122
Tel: 39 02 582191

Email: redazionemfdj@mfdowjones.it **Web site:** http://mfdowjones.it
Freq: Daily
Direttore: Danilo CASELLI; **Capo redattore:** Gabriele LA MONICA; **Redattore:** Alessandro MOCENNI
Profile: News service covering the stock market.
Language (s): Italian
NEWS SERVICE/SYNDICATE

Radiocor 428622

Owner: Gruppo 24 ORE
Editorial: Via Monte Rosa, 91, Milano 20149
Tel: 39 02 30221
Email: radiocordesk.mi@ilsole24ore.com **Web site:** http://www.radiocor.ilsole24ore.com
Freq: Daily
Capo redattore: Lorenzo LANFRANCONE; **Inviato:** Giuliana LICINI; **Capo redattore:** Isabella TASSO
Profile: News agency owned by the daily newspaper Il Sole 24 Ore, it covers economy and finance.
Language (s): Italian
NEWS SERVICE/SYNDICATE

Community Newspaper

L' Arena 769261

Owner: Athesis SpA
Editorial: Corso Porta Nuova, 67, Verona 37122
Tel: 39 045 9600111
Email: redazione@larena.it **Web site:** http://www.larena.it
Freq: Daily; **Circ:** 61191
Direttore responsabile: Maurizio Cattaneo
Profile: Newspaper covering regional news and current affairs in the Verona region.
Language (s): Italian
COMMUNITY NEWSPAPER

Il Corriere del Sud 429143

Owner: D'Ettoris Editori
Editorial: Via Lucifero, 40, Crotone 88900
Tel: 39 0962 905192
Email: redazione@corrieredelsud.it **Web site:** http://www.corrieredelsud.it
Freq: Semi-Monthly; **Circ:** 52000
Direttore Responsabile: Tina D'Ettoris
Profile: Newspaper mainly distributed in South Italy (Calabria and Sicily), Il Corriere del Sud covers investigative news on politics, economy, international and regional news, with a special emphasis on arts, society and culture.
Language (s): Italian
Ad Rate: Full Page Mono 900.00
Ad Rate: Full Page Colour 1600.00
Currency: Euro
COMMUNITY NEWSPAPER

Corriere del Veneto 427237

Owner: RCS MediaGroup SpA
Editorial: Via Rismondo, 2/E, Padova 35131
Tel: 39 049 8238811
Email: corriereveneto@corriereveneto.it **Web site:** http://www.corrieredelveneto.it
Circ: 40434
Caporedattore: Alessandro Baschieri; **Direttore Responsabile:** Alessandro Russello; **Redattore:** Alessandro Zuin
Profile: Newspaper covering regional news and current affairs from Veneto region including politics, economics, sports culture and entertainment.
Language (s): Italian
COMMUNITY NEWSPAPER

Corriere di Bologna 473179

Owner: RCS MediaGroup SpA
Editorial: Via Cincinnato Baruzzi, 1/2, Bologna 40138
Tel: 39 051 3951201
Email: redazione@corrieredibologna.it **Web site:** http://corrieredibologna.corriere.it
Freq: Daily; **Circ:** 12136
Editor in Chief: Gianmaria Canè; **Redattore:** Luciana Cavina; **Director:** Armando Nanni; **Editor in Chief:** Simone Sabattini
Profile: Corriere di Bologna is the regional edition of the daily newspaper Corriere della Sera. It is dedicated to regional news and current affairs in Bologna including politics, economics, sports, entertainment and culture.
Language (s): Italian
COMMUNITY NEWSPAPER

Corriere Fiorentino 800135

Owner: Editoriale Fiorentina Srl
Editorial: Lungarno delle Grazie, 22, Firenze 50122
Tel: 39 05 524825
Email: cronaca@corrierefiorentino.it **Web site:** http://www.corrierefiorentino.it
Freq: Daily
Director: Paolo Ermini
Profile: Regional edition of Corriere della Sera covering regional, national and international news and current affairs including business, politics, economics, sports, culture, entertainment, health, education, science, technology, motoring, travel, home and lifestyle.
Language (s): Italian
COMMUNITY NEWSPAPER

Corriere Nazionale 473172

Owner: Editrice Grafic Coop Spa di Giornalisti
Editorial: Via Pietro Soriano, 63, Perugia 6132
Tel: 39 075 5280069
Email: redazione@cornaz.it **Web site:** http://www.corrierenazionale.it
Freq: Daily
Profile: National newspaper covering national news, international news, sport, culture and current affairs.
Language (s): Italian
COMMUNITY NEWSPAPER

Corriere Padano 536403

Owner: Corpad Editore Srl
Editorial: Via Trieste, 39, Piacenza 29121
Tel: 39 345 8004819
Email: redazione@corrierepadano.it **Web site:** http://www.corrierepadano.it
Freq: Daily
Director: Giuseppe De Petro
Profile: Newspaper covering regional news and current affairs including politics, economics, sports, culture, entertainment and lifestyle.
Language (s): Italian
COMMUNITY NEWSPAPER

CronacaQui 668825

Owner: Editoriale Argo Srl
Editorial: Via Principe Tommaso, 30, Torino 10125
Tel: 39 011 6669
Email: redazione.to@cronacaqui.it **Web site:** http://www.cronacaqui.it
Freq: Daily
Direttore responsabile: Beppe FOSSATI
Profile: Newspaper covering regional news and current affairs in the Turin area including politics, economics, sports, culture and entertainment.
Language (s): Italian
COMMUNITY NEWSPAPER

Dolomiten 623357

Owner: Athesia SpA
Editorial: Via Del Vigneto, 7, Bolzano 39100
Tel: 39 0471 925544
Email: redaktion@stol.it **Web site:** http://www.stol.it
Circ: 44127
Direttore Responsabile: Toni Ebner
Profile: German speaking local newspaper covering Bolzano area.
Language (s): Italian
COMMUNITY NEWSPAPER

L' Eco di Bergamo 769259

Owner: Editor S.E.S.A.A.B. SpA
Editorial: Viale Papa Giovanni XXIII, 118, Bergamo 24121 **Tel:** 39 035 386111
Email: redazione@eco.bg.it **Web site:** http://www.ecodibergamo.it
Freq: Daily; **Circ:** 45000
Direttore responsabile: Giorgio Gandola
Profile: Newspaper covering regional news and current affairs in the town of Bergamo and vicinity.
Language (s): Italian
COMMUNITY NEWSPAPER

La Gazzetta del Mezzogiorno 536104

Owner: Edisud SpA
Editorial: Piazza Aldo Moro, 37, Bari 70122
Tel: 39 080 5470200
Email: segreteria.redazione@gazzettamezzogiorno.it **Web site:** http://www.lagazzettadelmezzogiorno.it
Freq: Daily; **Circ:** 22841 Publisher's Statement
Director: Giuseppe De Tomaso; **Capo Redattore Centrale:** Michele Partipilo
Profile: Newspaper covering regional, national and international news and current affairs including politics, economy, business and finance as well as sport, culture and entertainment.
Language (s): Italian
COMMUNITY NEWSPAPER

Gazzetta del Sud 605642

Owner: S.E.S. Società Editrice Sud
Editorial: Via Uberto Bonino, 15/C, Messina 98124
Tel: 39 090 2261
Email: segreteriadiredazione@gazzettadelsud.it **Web site:** http://www.gazzettadelsud.it
Circ: 60000
Profile: Newspaper covering regional news and current affairs in Southern Italy including politics, economics, sports, culture and entertainment.
Language (s): Italian
COMMUNITY NEWSPAPER

Gazzetta di Parma 156898

Owner: Gazzetta di Parma Srl
Editorial: Via Mantova, 68, Parma 43100
Tel: 39 0521 2251
Email: segreteria@gazzettadiparma.net **Web site:** http://www.gazzettadiparma.it
Circ: 35542
Profile: Newspaper covering regional and local news and current affairs in the province of Emilia-Romagna and Parma.
Language (s): Italian
COMMUNITY NEWSPAPER

Il Giornale del Lazio 436927

Editorial: Via delle Pietre Piane, 8, Monteleone Sabino Ri 2033 **Tel:** 39 392 5063750
Email: redazionegdlazio@gmail.com **Web site:** http://www.ilgiornaledellazio.it
Profile: Newspaper covering regional news and current affairs in the Lazio region including politics, economics, sports, culture and entertainment.
Language (s): Italian
COMMUNITY NEWSPAPER

Il Giornale di Brescia 605839

Owner: Editoriale Bresciana SpA
Editorial: Via Solferino, 22, Brescia 25121
Tel: 39 030 37901
Email: redazione@giornaledibrescia.it **Web site:** http://www.giornaledibrescia.it
Circ: 37862
Profile: Newspaper covering local and regional news and current affairs in the city of Brescia and vicinity including politics, economics, sports, culture and entertainment.
Language (s): Italian
COMMUNITY NEWSPAPER

Giornale di Erba 230085

Owner: Dmedia Group SpA
Editorial: Corso XXV Aprile, 74/b, Erba Co 22036
Tel: 39 031 646300
Email: giornale.erba@giornaledierba.it **Web site:** http://www.giornaledierba.it
Freq: Weekly
Direttore responsabile: Giancarlo FERRARIO
Profile: Newspaper covering regional news and current affairs including politics, economics, sports, culture and entertainment.
Language (s): Italian
COMMUNITY NEWSPAPER

Giornale di Sicilia 156897

Owner: Giornali di Sicilia Editoriele Poligrafica
Editorial: Via Lincoln, 21, Palermo 90133
Tel: 39 091 6627111
Email: redazioneweb@gds.it **Web site:** http://www.gds.it
Freq: Daily; **Circ:** 89000
Direttore responsabile: Antonio Ardizzone; **Editor:** Giacinto Pipitone
Profile: Newspaper based in Palermo covering regional news and current affairs in Sicily including politics, economics, sports, culture and entertainment.
Language (s): Italian
Ad Rate: Full Page Mono 1900.00
Currency: Euro
COMMUNITY NEWSPAPER

Messaggero Veneto 536107

Owner: Gruppo Ed. L'Espresso SpA
Editorial: Viale Palmanova, 290, Udine 33100
Tel: 39 0432 5271
Email: ufficio.centrale@messaggeroveneto.it **Web site:** http://messaggeroveneto.gelocal.it/udine
Freq: Daily; **Circ:** 49406
Direttore: Omar Monestier
Profile: Newspaper covering regional news and current affairs in the Udine region.
Language (s): Italian
COMMUNITY NEWSPAPER

Metropolis 913788

Owner: Citypress
Editorial: Via Varo, 1, Castellammare di Stabia, Napoli 80053 **Tel:** 39 081 19143850
Email: redazione@metropolisweb.it **Web site:** http://www.metropolisweb.it
Freq: Weekly
Profile: Newspaper covering local and regional news and current affairs.
Language (s): Italian
COMMUNITY NEWSPAPER

Il Nostro Tempo 429138

Owner: Prelum Srl
Editorial: Via Val della Torre, 3, Torino To 10149
Tel: 39 011 5156391
Email: redazione@ilnostrotempo.it **Web site:** http://www.ilnostrotempo.it
Freq: Weekly
Profile: Newspaper covering international, national and regional news in the diocese of Torino.
Language (s): Italian
COMMUNITY NEWSPAPER

La Nuova Sardegna 783887

Owner: DBInformation
Editorial: Predda Niedda, Strada 31, Sassari 7100
Tel: 39 079 222400
Email: redazione@lanuovasardegna.it **Web site:** http://lanuovasardegna.gelocal.it
Freq: Daily; **Circ:** 42956
Profile: Newspaper covering regional news and current affairs in the Sassari region.
Language (s): Italian
COMMUNITY NEWSPAPER

Pagina99 900073

Owner: Editore News 3.0 Spa
Editorial: Viale Bruno Buozzi, 60, Roma 197
Tel: 39 06 8880 2801
Email: segreteria@pagina99.it **Web site:** http://www.pagina99.it
Freq: Weekly
Director: Emanuele Bevilacqua
Profile: Ad free newspaper covering regional, national and international news and current affairs including economics, politics, society, science and culture.
Language (s): Italian
COMMUNITY NEWSPAPER

La Provincia di Lecco 769260

Owner: La Provincia di Como Editoriale SpA
Editorial: Via Raffaello Sanzio, 21, Lecco 23900
Tel: 39 0341 357411
Email: redlecco@laprovincia.it **Web site:** http://www.laprovinciadilecco.it
Freq: Daily; **Circ:** 50000
Profile: La Provincia di Lecco is a daily local newspaper covering the town of Lecco and vicinity (Lecco, Como, Cantu').
Language (s): Italian
COMMUNITY NEWSPAPER

La Provincia di Sondrio 769262

Owner: La Provincia di Como Editoriale SpA
Editorial: Via N. Sauro, 13, Sondrio 23100
Tel: 39 0342 535 511
Email: redsondrio@laprovincia.it **Web site:** http://www.laprovinciadisondrio.it
Freq: Daily
Profile: Newspaper covering regional news and current affairs in Sondrio and vicinity.
Language (s): Italian
COMMUNITY NEWSPAPER

La Provincia di Varese 427240

Owner: La Provincia Editoriale di Varese Srl
Editorial: Via Walter Marcobi, 4, Varese 21100
Tel: 39 0332 836611
Email: redazione@laprovinciadivarese.it **Web site:** http://www.laprovinciadivarese.it
Freq: Daily
Profile: Newspaper covering regional news and current affairs in the Varese region.
Language (s): Italian
COMMUNITY NEWSPAPER

PZ - Pustertaler Zeitung 624177

Owner: Pustertaler Medien
Editorial: Oberragen, 18, Brunico, Bruneck 39031
Tel: 39 0474 550830
Email: info@pz-media.it **Web site:** http://www.pz-media.it
Freq: Daily
Profile: Newspaper covering regional news and current affairs in the Bruneck region.
Language (s): German
COMMUNITY NEWSPAPER

Il Quotidiano della Basilicata 427239

Owner: Luedi Srl
Editorial: Via Nazario Sauro, 102, Potenza 85100
Tel: 39 0971 69309
Email: ilquotidiano.pz@finedit.com **Web site:** http://www.ilquotidianodellabasilicata.it
Freq: Daily
Profile: Newspaper covering regional news and current affairs in the Calabra region.
Language (s): Italian
COMMUNITY NEWSPAPER

Quotidiano di Foggia 536097

Owner: Area Sud Comunicazione e Immagine Soc. Coop.
Editorial: 1 Trav. Viale Fortore, Località Salnitro, Foggia 71100 **Tel:** 39 0881 773633
Email: redazione@quotidianodifoggia.it **Web site:** http://quotidianodifoggia.it
Freq: Daily
Direttore responsabile: Matteo TATARELLA
Profile: Newspaper covering regional news and current affairs including politics, economics, sports, culture and entertainment.
Language (s): Italian
COMMUNITY NEWSPAPER

Il Tempo 156917

Owner: Gruppo Angelucci
Editorial: Piazza Colonna, 366, Roma 187
Tel: 39 06 675881
Email: segreteria@iltempo.it **Web site:** http://www.iltempo.it
Freq: Daily; **Circ:** 33111
Direttore Responsabile: Sarina Biraghi; **Caporedattore Centrale:** Stefano Mannucci
Profile: Newspaper covering regional news and current affairs in the Lazio and Abruzzi regions including politics, economics, sport, culture and entertainment.
Language (s): Italian
COMMUNITY NEWSPAPER

Today 427369

Owner: TVN Media Group Srl
Editorial: Corso Magenta, 85, Milano 20123
Tel: 39 02 4300001
Email: comunicati@pubblicitaitalia.it **Web site:** http://www.pubblicitaitalia.it/il-today-di-pubblicita-italia
Freq: Daily
Profile: Digital daily newspaper covering the advertising industry including marketing, media and internet communication including news, business opportunities, market, events and appointments. It is distributed via e-mail and mobile device.
Language (s): Italian
COMMUNITY NEWSPAPER

Jamaica

Jamaica

Time Difference: GMT -5
National Telephone Code: 1 876
Continent: The Americas
Capital: Kingston

Newspapers

The Daily Star 157001
Owner: The Gleaner Co Ltd
Editorial: 7 North Street, Kingston W.I.
Tel: 876 9223400
Email: editorial@gleanerjm.com **Web site:** http://www.jamaica-star.com
Freq: Daily; **Circ:** 46000 Not Audited
Editor: Sheena Gayle; **Editor in Chief:** Garfield Grandison
Profile: The Star is a daily newspaper covering national and international news, politics, economics, finance, business, culture and sports. Subscription and advertising rates are quoted in Jamaican dollars.
Language (s): English
Ad Rate: Full Page Mono 8.21
Ad Rate: Full Page Colour 241.37
Currency: United States Dollars
DAILY NEWSPAPER

The Gleaner 156999
Owner: The Gleaner Co Ltd
Editorial: 7 North Street, Kingston **Tel:** 876 9223400
Email: feedback@jamaica-gleaner.com **Web site:** http://www.jamaica-gleaner.com
Freq: Daily; **Circ:** 50000 Not Audited
Editor in Chief: Garfield Grandison
Profile: The Gleaner is a daily newspaper containing news, views, sports and in-depth reports for Kingston, Jamaica.
Language (s): English
Ad Rate: Full Page Mono 11.70
Ad Rate: Full Page Colour 438.85
Currency: United States Dollars
DAILY NEWSPAPER

The Jamaica Observer 159009
Owner: Jamaica Observer
Editorial: 40-42 Beechwood Avenue, Kingston 5
Tel: 876 9208136
Email: editorial@jamaicaobserver.com **Web site:** http://www.jamaicaobserver.com
Freq: Daily; **Circ:** 35000 Not Audited
Editor: Vernon Davidson; **Editor:** Oliver Hill
Profile: The Jamaica Observer is a daily newspaper covering national and international news, politics, economics, finance, business, culture and sports.
Language (s): English
Ad Rate: Full Page Mono 11.70
Ad Rate: Full Page Colour 774.14
Currency: United States Dollars
DAILY NEWSPAPER

The Sunday Gleaner 157000
Owner: The Gleaner Co Ltd
Editorial: 7 North Street, Kingston **Tel:** 876 9223400
Email: editorial@gleanerjm.com **Web site:** http://www.jamaica-gleaner.com
Freq: Sun; **Circ:** 100000 Not Audited
Editor: Lavern Clarke; **Editor in Chief:** Garfield Grandison
Profile: The Sunday Gleaner covers national and international news, politics, economics, finance, business, culture and sports. Subscription and advertising rates are quoted in Jamaican dollars.
Language (s): English
Ad Rate: Full Page Mono 20.88
Ad Rate: Full Page Colour 438.85
Currency: United States Dollars
DAILY NEWSPAPER

Community Newspaper

Weekend Star 224412
Owner: The Gleaner Co Ltd
Editorial: 7 North Street, Kingston W.I.
Tel: 876 9223400
Email: star@gleanerjm.com **Web site:** http://www.jamaica-star.com
Freq: Weekly; **Circ:** 85000 Not Audited
Editor: Sheena Gayle; **Editor in Chief:** Garfield Grandison
Profile: Covers national and international news, politics, economics, finance, business, culture and sports.
Language (s): English
COMMUNITY NEWSPAPER

Japan

Time Difference: GMT +9
National Telephone Code: 81
Continent: Asia
Capital: Tokyo

Newspapers

AdverTimes 578692
Editorial: SENDENKAIGI Co., Ltd., 4F, NBF Alliance Building, 5-2-1 Minami Aoyama, Minato-ku, Tokyo 107-8550 **Tel:** 81 334 453033
Email: adti@sendenkaigi.co.jp **Web site:** http://www.sendenkaigi.com/hanbai/magazine/newspaper/
Freq: Weekly; **Circ:** 50000
Editor in Chief: Risa Tanaka
Profile: AdverTimes is a newspaper which reports weekly news of advertising industry such as new campaigns, personnel relocation of campanies, competitions, legislation changes regarding media.
Language (s): Japanese
DAILY NEWSPAPER

Akita Sakigake Shimpo 459829
Editorial: Akita Sakigake Shimpo, 1-1, San-no-rinkai-cho, Akita 010-8601 **Tel:** 81 18 8881800
Web site: http://www.sakigake.co.jp
Freq: Daily; **Circ:** 240000 Not Audited
President & Publisher: Naoki Ogasawara; **News Director:** Yoshihiro Sasaki; **Bureau Chief:** Masanori Waga
Profile: Akita Sakigake Shimpo is a newspaper which writes about the latest news in Akita district and nation wide.
Language (s): Japanese
DAILY NEWSPAPER

The Apparel Industrial Times 558998
Editorial: The Apparel Industrial Times, 731 Iidabashi Hightown, 2-28, Shimomiyabi-Cho, Shinjuku-ku, Tokyo 162-0822 **Tel:** 81 335 137931
Web site: http://www.apako-news.com/
Freq: Monthly
Editor in Chief: Toru Honda
Profile: The Apparel Industrial Times provides all the information about current fashion industry needs, such as textiles, patterning, sewing technique, and Point Of Production.
Language (s): Japanese
DAILY NEWSPAPER

Asahi Shimbun 771230
Editorial: 529 14th St NW Ste 1022, Washington, District Of Columbia 20045-2001 **Tel:** 1 202 783-1000
Email: asahidc@asahiam.com
Freq: Daily
Bureau Chief: Takeshi Yamawaki
Profile: Provides domestic and international news.
Language (s): Japanese
DAILY NEWSPAPER

Asahi Shimbun - New York Bureau 619615
Editorial: 628 8th Ave, New York, New York 10018-1618 **Tel:** 1 212 398-0257
Freq: Daily
Bureau Chief: Hiroki Manabe
Profile: This is the New York bureau for Asahi Shimbun in Tokyo, Japan.
Language (s): English
DAILY NEWSPAPER

Asahi Shimbun (Tokyo) 156667
Editorial: 5-3-2, Tsukiji, Chuo-ku, Tokyo 104-8011
Tel: 81 335 450131
Email: tokyo@asahi.com **Web site:** http://www.asahi.com
Freq: Daily; **Circ:** 3357950
Editor: Wataru Sawamura
Profile: Launching its first edition on January 25, 1879, dedicated to the freedom of speech and democracy in Japan. Provides domestic and international news with up-to-the-minute headlines and updates.
Language (s): Japanese
Ad Rate: Full Page Mono 39855000.00
Ad Rate: Full Page Colour 47435000.00
Currency: Japan Yen
DAILY NEWSPAPER

Asahi Shimbun (Hokkaido) 459783
Editorial: The Asahi Shimbun Company, 1-1-1, Kita 2-jo-nishi, Chuo-ku, Sapporo 060-8602
Tel: 81 112 812131
Email: hokkaido@asahi.com **Web site:** http://www.mytown.asahi.com/hokkaido
Freq: Daily; **Circ:** 162863 Not Audited
News Director: Masatoshi Mikami
Profile: Asahi Shimbun (Hokkaido) is a daily newspaper for Sapporo district which mainly reports on regional news.
Language (s): Japanese
DAILY NEWSPAPER

Asahi Shimbun (Osaka) 459784
Editorial: The Asahi Shimbun Company, 3-2-4, Nakanoshima, Kita-ku, Osaka 530-8211
Tel: 81 662 310131
Email: dai-koe@asahi.com **Web site:** http://www.asahi.com/kansai/
Freq: Daily; **Circ:** 3843985 Not Audited
President: Kotaro Akiyama
Profile: Asahi Shimbun (Osaka) is a newspaper for Osaka district which mainly reports on regional news.
Language (s): Japanese
Ad Rate: Full Page Mono 11250000.00
Ad Rate: Full Page Colour 13600000.00
Currency: Japan Yen
DAILY NEWSPAPER

Cargo News 460094
Editorial: Cargo Japan Co., Ltd., 4-5-10, Roppongi, Minato-ku, Tokyo 106-0032 **Tel:** 81 35 7712101
Email: info@cargo-news.co.jp **Web site:** http://www.cargo-news.co.jp
Freq: 2 Times/Week; **Circ:** 30722 Not Audited
Editor in Chief: Kouichi Matsuzaki; **Publisher:** Kuninori Nishimura
Profile: Reports the latest news on logistics, news of shipping companies, legislations, new trucks, information of warehouses, railways, marine transport, air freight, etc.
Language (s): Japanese
DAILY NEWSPAPER

Chiba Nippo 459843
Editorial: Chiba Nippo Co., Ltd., 4-14-10 Chuo, Chuo-ku, Chiba 260-0013 **Tel:** 81 43 2229215
Email: c-nippo@chibanippo.co.jp **Web site:** http://www.chibanippo.co.jp
Freq: Daily; **Circ:** 188285 Not Audited
President: Yasuhide Akada
Profile: Chiba Nippo is a newspaper which reports regional news in Chiba district.
Language (s): Japanese
DAILY NEWSPAPER

Chubu Keizai Shimbun 459850
Editorial: The Mid-Japan Economist, Aichi-ken Sangyo Roudou Centre 16F, 4-4-38 Meieki, Namamura-ku, Nagoya 450-8561 **Tel:** 81 52 5615212
Web site: http://www.chukei-news.co.jp
Freq: Daily; **Circ:** 94703 Not Audited
President: Wataru Kato; **News Director:** Hiroshi Shimizu
Profile: Chubu Keizai Shimbun is a newspaper which reports financial information in Nagoya district. Articles also cover general financial news.
Language (s): Japanese
DAILY NEWSPAPER

Chugoku Shimbun 459885
Editorial: The Chugoku Shimbun, 7-1, Dobashi-cho, Naka-ku, Hiroshima 730-8677 **Tel:** 81 822 362111
Email: denshi@chugoku-np.co.jp **Web site:** http://www.chugoku-np.co.jp
Freq: Daily; **Circ:** 645988 Not Audited
Profile: The Chugoku Shimbun is a daily local newspaper which covers local and national news.
Language (s): Japanese
DAILY NEWSPAPER

Chunichi Shimbun - Hokuriku 459912
Editorial: The Chunichi Shimbun, 2-12-30 Nishihonmachi, Kanazawa-city, Ishikawa 920-8573
Tel: 81 762 613111
Email: hokuchu@chunichi.co.jp **Web site:** http://www.chunichi.co.jp/hokuriku/
Freq: Daily; **Circ:** 110823 Not Audited
President: Toshiaki Furutani
Profile: Chunichi Shimbun - Hokuriku is a daily regional news paper in Ishikawa district which mainly reports regional news.
Language (s): Japanese
DAILY NEWSPAPER

Daily Aviation News 460330
Editorial: Japan Aviation News Co., Ltd., 2-7-7 Kanda-Sukasamachi, Chiyoda-ku, Tokyo 101-0048
Tel: 81 332 927712
Email: da@da-news.co.jp **Web site:** http://www.da-news.co.jp
Freq: Daily
Editor in Chief: Tsutomu Honda
Profile: Daily Aviation News is a daily newspaper focused on aviation and engineering.
Language (s): Japanese
DAILY NEWSPAPER

Daily Cargo 167035
Editorial: Kaiji Press, 2-1-15, Iwamoto-cho, Chiyoda-ku, Tokyo 101-0032 **Tel:** 81 35 8354184
Web site: http://www.kaiji-press.co.jp
Freq: Daily; **Circ:** 25003 Not Audited
Editor in Chief: Takuya Nishi
Profile: Reports on a wide scope of air-cargo sector including aviation policy and airliners' business performance are reported with details from inside and ouside of the industry. Articles also cover logistic news, industry trend, analysis, and feature articles of Shippers, Logistics Providers and Carriers.
Language (s): Japanese
DAILY NEWSPAPER

Daily Engineering & Construction News 460221
Editorial: The Nikkan Kensetsu Kogyo Shimbun, 2-2-10, Higashi Shinbashi, Minato-ku, Tokyo 105-0021
Tel: 81 33 4337161
Web site: http://www.decn.co.jp
Freq: Daily; **Circ:** 338000
Publisher: Hideki Iizuka
Profile: Daily Engineering & Construction News is a newspaper which reports logistics, building construction and environmental engineering.
Language (s): Japanese
DAILY NEWSPAPER

Daily Sports (Kobe) 459883
Editorial: Daily Sports, 1-5-7, Higashikawasaki-cho, Chuo-ku, Kobe 650-0044 **Tel:** 81 783 627298
Web site: http://www.daily.co.jp
Freq: Daily; **Circ:** 576517 Not Audited
Editor: Yuichiro Matsushita
Profile: Daily Sports reports the latest sports news such as baseball, football, golf as well as entertainment news and horse racing.
Language (s): Japanese
DAILY NEWSPAPER

Daily Sports (Tokyo) 459786
Editorial: 2-14-8 Kiba Koto-Ku, Tokyo 135-8566
Tel: 81 03 36415042
Web site: http://www.daily.co.jp
Freq: Daily; **Circ:** 414473 Not Audited
Profile: DAILY SPORTS (TOKYO) is a daily newspaper which covers sports, gossip, and national news.
Language (s): Japanese
DAILY NEWSPAPER

Dempa Shimbun 180155
Editorial: Dempa Newspaper Co., Ltd., 1-11-15, Higashi Gotanda, Shinagawa-ku, Tokyo 141-8715
Tel: 81 334 456116
Web site: http://www.dempa.co.jp
Freq: Daily; **Circ:** 300003 Not Audited
Editor: Masaharu Hasegawa; **Editor:** Masashige Nishiyama
Profile: Focused on engineering and electrical news.
Language (s): Japanese
DAILY NEWSPAPER

Denkei Shimbun 491174
Editorial: DENKEI-SHIMBUN. 7/F Yamaki-Daini Bldg, 3-4-2 Nishi-Shimbashi, Minato-ku, Tokyo 105-0003
Tel: 81 334 376600
Email: info@denkeishimbun.co.jp **Web site:** http://www.denkeishimbun.co.jp/
Freq: Weekly; **Circ:** 20000
Editor: Naoto Nakayama; **Editor in Chief:** Toshihiko Tanaka
Profile: Denkei Shimbun is a weekly newspaper which reports news of information and communication industry despite it initially reported news of electronics industry.
Language (s): Japanese
DAILY NEWSPAPER

Doshin Sports 459824
Editorial: The Hokkaido Shimbun Press, 3-6, Odori-nishi, Chuo-ku, Sapporo 060-8711
Tel: 81 11 2411230
Email: dou-spo@douspo.com **Web site:** http://www.hokkaido-np.co.jp
Freq: Daily; **Circ:** 132355 Not Audited
President: Takeshi Hama
Profile: Doshin Sports is a regional daily sports newspaper in Sapporo district which writes about daily news on sports, leisure and entertainment.
Language (s): Japanese
DAILY NEWSPAPER

Eizo Shimbun 460359
Editorial: Eizo Shimbun Inc., Eizo Building, 1-24-8 Kohinata, Bunkyo-ku, Tokyo 112-0006
Tel: 81 339 422161
Email: press@eizoshimbun.com **Web site:** http://www.eizoshimbun.com
Freq: Weekly; **Circ:** 30003 Not Audited
Editor in Chief: Satoru Fuse; **Editor:** Koji Suginuma
Profile: The Eizo Shimbun publishes once a week which provides a professional communicative link for educators and industry personnel associated with design, presentation, management, and reproduction of graphic forms of communication.
Language (s): Japanese
DAILY NEWSPAPER

Fuji Sankei Business i (Tokyo) 459798
Editorial: Nihon Kogyo Shimbun Sha, 1-7-2, Otemachi, Chiyoda-ku, Tokyo 100-8125
Tel: 81 33 2317111
Web site: http://www.sankeibiz.jp
Freq: Daily; **Circ:** 153000 Not Audited
President & Publisher: Ryouji Agata; **Editor:** Yuki Suenaga
Profile: Covers industry-specific business news in Japan and throughout the world, with additional lifestyle feature stories.
Language (s): Japanese
DAILY NEWSPAPER

Fukui Shimbun 459875
Editorial: Fukui Shimbun, 56, Oowada-cho, Fukui, Fukui 910-8552 **Tel:** 81 776 575110
Web site: http://www.fukuishimbun.co.jp
Freq: Daily; **Circ:** 2060336 Not Audited

Editor: Yoichiro Adachi
Profile: Fukui Shimbun is a daily newspaper in Fukui district which provides the latest regional news, current affairs happening in the region including coverage on economic and regional activities.
Language (s): Japanese
Ad Rate: Full Page Mono 661500.00
Currency: Japan Yen
DAILY NEWSPAPER

Fukushima Minpo 459831
Editorial: Fukushima-Minpo Co., Ltd., 13-17, Ota-machi, Fukushima 960-8602 **Tel:** 81 245 314111
Web site: http://www.minpo.jp/
Freq: Daily; **Circ:** 310003 Not Audited
News Director: Shinji Yasuda
Profile: Fukushima Mimpo is a daily newspaper in the Fukushima district which reports on local news happening around the neighborhood.
Language (s): Japanese
DAILY NEWSPAPER

Health Industry News 459294
Editorial: UBM Media Co., Ltd., Kanda 91 Bldg. 1-8-3 Kaji-cho, Tokyo 101-0044 **Tel:** 81 3 5296-1020
Web site: http://www.kenko-media.com
Freq: Weekly; **Circ:** 65003 Not Audited
Profile: Covers news for the health products industry, including manufacturing information, trends and legislation.
Language (s): Japanese
DAILY NEWSPAPER

Higashi-Aichi Shimbun 459852
Editorial: The Higashi-Aichi Shimbun, 62, Torinawate, Shinsakae-machi, Toyohashi 441-8666
Tel: 81 532 323111
Email: hensyu@higashiaichi.co.jp **Web site:** http://www.higashiaichi.co.jp
Freq: Daily; **Circ:** 50000 Not Audited
News Director: Akira Honda
Profile: Higashi-Aichi Shimbun is a newspaper that reports on all aspects of news including economical, political, social and cultural on the Toyohashi district.
Language (s): Japanese
DAILY NEWSPAPER

Hoken Mainichi Shimbun 506791
Editorial: Hokenmainichi.Co. 1-4-7 Iwamoto-cho, Chiyoda-ku, Tokyo 101-0032 **Tel:** 81 338 651401
Web site: http://www.homai.co.jp/
Freq: Daily; **Circ:** 18000
Editor: Tokuo Inaba; **Publisher:** Yukimitsu Manabe
Profile: Hoken Mainichi Shimbun reports life, health, property and casual, reinsurance and multiline insurance companies can use technology to maximize productivity and achieve a clear competitive advantage.
Language (s): Japanese
DAILY NEWSPAPER

Hokkaido Shimbun 157119
Editorial: The Hokkaido Shimbun Press, 3-6, Odori-nishi, Chuo-ku, Sapporo 060-8711
Tel: 81 11 2105597
Web site: http://www.hokkaido-np.co.jp
Freq: Daily; **Circ:** 1232913 Not Audited
President: Masatoshi Murata; **Managing Director:** Nobuaki Suga
Profile: Hokkaido Shimbun is a daily newspaper in the morning and evening which writes about the news in japan and the world, as well as hokkaido district.
Language (s): Japanese
Ad Rate: Full Page Mono 505575.00
Ad Rate: Full Page Colour 758363.00
Currency: Japan Yen
DAILY NEWSPAPER

Hokkoku Shimbun 459876
Editorial: The Hokkoku Shimbun, 2-1 Minamimachi, Kanazawa 920-8588 **Tel:** 81 76 2603532
Web site: http://www.hokkoku.co.jp
Freq: Daily; **Circ:** 335826 Not Audited
Director: Takihiro Sunazuka; **President:** Hidekazu Tobita; **News Director:** Kazuo Tsukida
Profile: Hokkoku Shimbun is a daily newspaper in Kanazawa district which reports mainly regional news, national and international news.
Language (s): Japanese
DAILY NEWSPAPER

Hokuu Shimpo 460238
Editorial: Hokuu Shimpo Sha. 3-2 Nishidori-machi, Noshiro 016-0891 **Tel:** 81 18 5543150
Email: hokuupost@hokuu.jp **Web site:** http://www.hokuu.co.jp
Freq: Daily; **Circ:** 32423 Not Audited
Publisher: Yasumasa Yamaki
Profile: Hokuu Shimpo is local newspaper in Northern Akita area which reports mainly local news and useful information in the area.
Language (s): Japanese
DAILY NEWSPAPER

Hoso Times 460436
Editorial: The Hoso Times, 3-1-5, Kanda, Misaki-cho, Chiyoda-ku, Tokyo 101-0061 **Tel:** 81 332 623463
Web site: http://www.nippo.co.jp/ht
Freq: Weekly; **Circ:** 55003 Not Audited
Editor in Chief: Yasuyoshi Asami
Profile: Hoso Times is a weekly newspaper which specialized the packaging industry and it centers around issues related to the environment.
Language (s): Japanese
DAILY NEWSPAPER

Ibaraki Shimbun 459844
Editorial: The Ibaraki Shimbun Co., Ltd., 2-15, Kitami-cho, Mito 310-8686 **Tel:** 81 292 485500
Email: houdou@mail2.ibaraki-np.co.jp **Web site:** http://www.ibaraki-np.co.jp
Freq: Daily; **Circ:** 118003 Not Audited
Editor: Yasuhiro Numata
Profile: Ibaraki Shimbun is a newspaper for the Ibaraki-Ken district which mainly reports on local news happening around the neighborhood.
Language (s): Japanese
DAILY NEWSPAPER

Igakukai Shinbun 460001
Editorial: Igaku-Shoin Ltd., 1-282-3 Hongo, Bunkyo-ku, Tokyo 113-8414 **Tel:** 81 246 175694
Email: shinbun@igaku-shoin.co.jp **Web site:** http://www.igaku-shoin.co.jp
Freq: Weekly; **Circ:** 55003 Not Audited
Editor in Chief: Yoshiyuki Nakajima
Profile: Igakukai Shimbun is a weekly news paper which reviews developments of Japan's medical breakthroughs, improvements and technology. Articles also include industrial medicine, managed medical care, vocational rehabilitation, risk management and related businesses.
Language (s): Japanese
DAILY NEWSPAPER

International Press - Portuguese Edition 459021
Editorial: IPCWORLD, INC., 2-1-9 Minamiazabu, Minato-ku, Tokyo 106-0047 **Tel:** 81 35 4204581
Email: redaccion@ipcjapan.com **Web site:** http://www.ipcdigital.com
Freq: Weekly; **Circ:** 60003 Not Audited
Editor in Chief: Luis Álvarez; **Publisher:** Leonardo Takuya Muranaga; **Publisher:** Yuji Muranaga
Profile: International Press (Portuguese Edition) reports news and information of Japan for Brazilians living in Japan. It is written in Portuguese.
Language (s): Portuguese
DAILY NEWSPAPER

Iwaki Minpo 460220
Editorial: Iwaki Minpo Company, 63-7 HirajiTamachi, Fukushima 970-8026 **Tel:** 81 246 231666
Email: news@iwaki-minpo.co.jp **Web site:** http://www.iwaki-minpo.co.jp
Freq: Daily; **Circ:** 17103 Not Audited
News Director: Tatsuya Ito; **Publisher:** Tatsuya Nozawa
Profile: IWAKI MINPO is a local news paper in Fukushima district, which writes about local news and events.
Language (s): Japanese
DAILY NEWSPAPER

Iwate Nichinichi Shimbun 459835
Editorial: Iwate Nichinichi Shimbun, 60, Minamishin-machi, Ichinoseki 021-8686 **Tel:** 81 191 264204
Email: henshu@iwanichi.co.jp **Web site:** http://www.iwanichi.co.jp
Freq: Daily; **Circ:** 55600 Not Audited
Profile: Iwate Nichinichi Shimbun is a daily regional news paper in the Ichinoseki area of Iwate district which writes about the latest regional news, current affairs happenings in Ichinoseki area, economic and regional activities.
Language (s): Japanese
DAILY NEWSPAPER

Iwate Nippo 459833
Editorial: Iwate Nippo Co., Ltd, 3-7, Uchimaru, Morioka 020-8622 **Tel:** 81 196 535311
Email: houdou@iwate-np.co.jp **Web site:** http://www.iwate-np.co.jp
Freq: Daily; **Circ:** 230003 Not Audited
Profile: Iwate Nippo is a regional daily newspaper in Iwate prefecture which writes about local news and event, as well as international top news.
Language (s): Japanese
DAILY NEWSPAPER

Japan Agricultural News 459799
Editorial: The Japan Agricultural News, 2-3, Akihabara, Taito-ku, Tokyo 110-8722
Tel: 81 352 957411
Web site: http://www.nougyou-shimbun.ne.jp
Freq: Daily; **Circ:** 420003 Not Audited
President & Publisher: Toshio Yasuda
Profile: Japan Agricultural Newspaper is the daily newspaper about agriculture. Articles include agribusiness, general merchandising as well as local autonomous entities.
Language (s): Japanese
DAILY NEWSPAPER

Japan Maritime Daily 459793
Owner: The Japan Maritime Daily Co., Ltd.
Editorial: 5-19-2, Shimbashi, Minato-ku, Tokyo 105-0004 **Tel:** 81 33 4363221
Email: kaiji@jmd.co.jp **Web site:** http://www.jmd.co.jp
Freq: Daily; **Circ:** 55303 Not Audited
Editor in Chief: Itsuro Fujimoto; **President:** Takaaki Oyama
Profile: Reports maritime affairs, as well as information on marine transportation and shipbuilding.
Language (s): Japanese
DAILY NEWSPAPER

Japan Medicine 459414
Editorial: Jiho, inc.5th Floor, Hitotsubashi Building, 2-6-3 Hitotsubashi, Chiyoda-ku, Tokyo 101-8421
Tel: 81 332 659351
Web site: http://www.jiho.co.jp
Freq: 2 Times/Week; **Circ:** 240003 Not Audited
Editor in Chief: Yoshiyuki Numata
Profile: Japan Medicine is a newspaper which provides the latest medical information.
Language (s): Japanese
DAILY NEWSPAPER

The Japan Times (Tokyo) 158811
Owner: Japan Times Ltd. (The)
Editorial: Shibaura 4-chome, Minato-ku, Tokyo 108-8071 **Tel:** 81 3 34535312
Web site: http://www.japantimes.co.jp
Freq: Daily; **Circ:** 61929 Not Audited
Profile: Established in 1897 and serves as Japan's oldest English-language daily. Covers world events and various features.
Language (s): English
Ad Rate: Full Page Mono 2400000.00
Ad Rate: Full Page Colour 2520000.00
Currency: Japan Yen
DAILY NEWSPAPER

The Japan Times Weekly 459375
Owner: Japan Times Ltd. (The)
Editorial: 4-5-4 Shibaura, Minato-ku, Tokyo 108-8071 **Tel:** 81 33 4524099
Email: jtweekly@japantimes.co.jp **Web site:** http://www.japantimes.co.jp
Freq: Weekly; **Circ:** 20003 Not Audited
Profile: Contains editorials and commentary of The Japan Times and leading newspapers in the U.S., Europe and Asia and more.
Language (s): English
DAILY NEWSPAPER

Joho Sangyo Shimbun 475994
Editorial: Johosangyo Shinbunsha Co., Ltd., 3/F Tokyo Tower, 4-2-8 Shiba Park, Minato-ku, Tokyo 105-0011 **Tel:** 81 3 34344911
Email: info@josan.jp **Web site:** http://www.josan.jp/
Freq: Weekly; **Circ:** 36003 Not Audited
Editor in Chief: Toshihiro Sato; **Editor:** Satoru Sugita; **Publisher:** Yugo Tabe
Profile: Focuses on general IT information and the latest news on IT business.
Language (s): Japanese
DAILY NEWSPAPER

Joyo Shimbun 459846
Editorial: The Joyo Shimbun, 2-7-6, Manabe, Tsuchiura 300-0051 **Tel:** 81 29 8211780
Web site: http://www.joyo-net.com
Freq: Daily; **Circ:** 85003 Not Audited
Profile: Joyo Shimbun is a daily regional newspaper in Tsuchiura district which mainly reports on regional news happening around the neighborhood.
Language (s): Japanese
DAILY NEWSPAPER

Kagaku Kogyo Nippo/Chemical Daily 459886
Owner: Chemical Daily Co., Ltd. (The)
Editorial: 3-16-8, Nihonbashi Hamacho, Chuo-ku, Tokyo 103-8485 **Tel:** 81 33 6637934
Email: cd_desk@chemicaldaily.co.jp **Web site:** http://www.chemicaldaily.co.jp
Freq: Daily; **Circ:** 130003 Not Audited
President: Osamu Odajima
Language (s): Japanese
DAILY NEWSPAPER

Kaiji Press 460101
Editorial: Kaiji Press Co., Ltd., Kaiji Press, 2-1-15, Iwamoto-cho, Chiyoda-ku, Tokyo 101-0032
Tel: 81 35 8354182
Email: desk@kaiji-press.co.jp **Web site:** http://www.kaiji-press.co.jp
Freq: Daily; **Circ:** 25003 Not Audited
Editor in Chief: Naoki Nakamura; **Editor:** Kazuhiro Tsushima
Profile: Reports on shipping, shipbuilding, logistics, ports, marine equipment and administrative issues.
Language (s): Japanese
DAILY NEWSPAPER

Kanagawa Shimbun 459847
Editorial: The Kanagawa Shimbun, 2-23. Ota-cho, Naka-ku, Yokohama 231-8445 **Tel:** 81 45 2270100
Email: media@kanaloco.jp **Web site:** http://www.kanagawa-shimbun.jp
Freq: Daily; **Circ:** 224654 Not Audited
President: Kenji Hotta
Profile: Kanagawa Shimbun is a daily regional nespaper in Kanagawa district which provides the latest regional news and current affairs happening in Yokohama district. Articles include economic and regional activities and national news and international news.
Language (s): Japanese
DAILY NEWSPAPER

Koureisha-Jutaku Shimbun 586779
Editorial: Koreisha-Jutaku Shimbun Co., Ltd. 8-12-15, Ginza, Chuo-ku, Tokyo 104-0061
Tel: 81 335 436852
Email: info@koureisha-jutaku.com **Web site:** http://www.koureisha-jutaku.com/
Freq: Daily; **Circ:** 30000
Publisher: Toshikazu Amiya; **Editor:** Ritomo Tanabe
Profile: Koreisha-Jutaku Shimbun is a newspaper which issued three times a month. Articles cover housing for elderly and eldercare facilities as well as elderly's health care and tips for enriching elderly's living.
Language (s): Japanese
DAILY NEWSPAPER

Kumamoto Nichinichi Shimbun 459899
Editorial: Kumamoto Nichinichi Shimbun, 172, Yoyasu-machi, Kumamoto 860-8506
Tel: 81 96 3613111
Web site: http://kumanichi.com/index.cfm
Freq: Daily; **Circ:** 34861 Not Audited
Editor in Chief: Kensei Tagawa
Profile: Kumamoto Nichinichi Shimbun is a regional daily newspaper in Kumamoto district in Kyusyu island which reports local news.
Language (s): Japanese
DAILY NEWSPAPER

Kyoto Shimbun 459882
Editorial: The Kyoto Shimbun Co., Ltd., 239, Ebisugawa-agaru, Karasuma-dori, Chukyo-Ku, Kyoto 604-8577 **Tel:** 81 75 2416119
Email: shakaibu@mb.kyoto-np.co.jp **Web site:** http://www.kyoto-np.co.jp
Freq: Daily; **Circ:** 292417
Publisher: Michikazu Shiraishi
Profile: KYOTO SHIMBUN is a local newspaper which reports regional and national news in Kyoto district.
Language (s): Japanese
DAILY NEWSPAPER

Label Shimbun 459153
Editorial: Label Shimbun, Kanda Asakusabashi Building, 3-1-13, Higashi Kanda, Chiyoda-ku, Tokyo 101-0031 **Tel:** 81 33 8666577
Email: info@labelshimbun.com **Web site:** http://www.labelshimbun.com
Freq: Semi-Monthly; **Circ:** 18753 Not Audited
Editor: Yukiko Suzuki; **Manager:** Sora Yoshinaga
Profile: Label Shimbun is a newspaper which provides information about Label converters, Label materials, Printing Press, die ink, electronic pre-press systems and so on.
Language (s): Japanese
DAILY NEWSPAPER

Logistics Nippon 460090
Editorial: Logistics Nippon News Network Co., Ltd., Hirakawa-cho Building, 1-7-20 Hirakawa-cho, Chiyoda-ku, Tokyo 102-0093 **Tel:** 81 33 2212345
Email: tokyo@logistics.jp **Web site:** http://www.logistics.jp
Freq: 2 Times/Week; **Circ:** 158003 Not Audited
Editor: Hidenori Kitahara; **Editor in Chief:** Akira Yamada
Profile: Provides a wealth of information on the latest technology, services and processes needed in the logistics industry.
Language (s): Japanese
DAILY NEWSPAPER

Mainichi Shimbun - New York Bureau 503940
Editorial: 757 3rd Ave Ste 1902, New York, New York 10017-2048 **Tel:** 1 212 765-1240
Bureau Chief: Kazuhiko Kusano
Language (s): Japanese
DAILY NEWSPAPER

Mainichi Shimbun - Washington Bureau 507760
Editorial: 529 14th St NW Ste 340, Washington, District Of Columbia 20045-1301 **Tel:** 1 202 737-2817
Freq: Daily
Profile: This is the Washington, D.C. bureau of the Mainichi Shimbun in Japan.
Language (s): Japanese
DAILY NEWSPAPER

Mainichi Shimbun (Fukuoka) 459790
Editorial: The Mainichi Newspapers, Mainichi Shimbun Fukuoka, 16-1 Tenjin, Chuo-ku, Fukuoka 810-8551 **Tel:** 81 927 813100
Web site: http://www.mainichi.co.jp
Freq: Daily; **Circ:** 660003 Not Audited
Editor: Ryo Iwamatsu
Profile: Covers Kyushu island, Yamaguchi, Okinawa, and Shimane district in Japan.
Language (s): Japanese
DAILY NEWSPAPER

Mainichi Shimbun (Nagoya) 459788
Editorial: The Mainichi Newspapers, 4-7-1 Meieki, Nakamura-ku, Nagoya 450-8651 **Tel:** 81 525 278010
Web site: http://mainichi.jp/chubu
Freq: Daily; **Circ:** 173893 Not Audited
President: Yutaka Asahira
Profile: Reports local news on the Chubu region and beyond.
Language (s): Japanese
DAILY NEWSPAPER

Mainichi Shimbun (Osaka) 459789
Editorial: The Mainichi Newspapers, 3-4-5, Umeda, Kita-ku, Osaka 530-8251 **Tel:** 81 663 451551
Web site: http://www.mainichi.co.jp
Freq: Daily; **Circ:** 1427193 Not Audited

Profile: Covers news happened in Japan and Osaka region, and national.
Language (s): Japanese
DAILY NEWSPAPER

Mainichi Shimbun (Sapporo) 459791

Editorial: The Mainichi Newspapers, 6-1, Kita 4-jo-nishi, Chuo-ku, Sapporo 060-8643
Tel: 81 112 214141
Web site: http://mainichi.jp/hokkaido
Freq: Daily; **Circ:** 74003 Not Audited
News Director: Masaharu Watanabe
Profile: Covers regional news in Hokkaido Area and domestic in Japan.
Language (s): Japanese
DAILY NEWSPAPER

Mainichi Shimbun (Tokyo) 161286

Editorial: The Mainichi Newspapers, 1-1-1, Hitotsubashi, Chiyoda-ku, Tokyo 100-8051
Tel: 81 332 120321
Web site: http://www.mainichi.co.jp
Freq: Daily; **Circ:** 376124
President: Yutaka Asahina
Profile: Reports daily news in Japan and throughout the world.
Language (s): Japanese
Ad Rate: Full Page Mono 25920000.00
Currency: Japan Yen
DAILY NEWSPAPER

Mainichi Weekly 459076

Editorial: The Mainichi Newspapers, 1-1-1, Hitotsubashi, Chiyoda-ku, Tokyo 100-8051
Tel: 81 332 123265
Email: gaishinbu@mainichi.co.jp **Web site:** http://mainichi.jp/life/weekly
Freq: Weekly; **Circ:** 53003 Not Audited
Editor in Chief: Kaori Oowada
Profile: English publication reports news and events in Japan and throughout the world.
Language (s): English
DAILY NEWSPAPER

Material & Industry News 460088

Editorial: Sangyo Shimbun, Chichibu building 5F, 1-8-6, Shinkawa, Chuo-ku, Tokyo 104-0033
Tel: 81 355 668770
Web site: http://www.japanmetal.com
Freq: Daily
Editor: Toshio Masakiyo; **Publisher:** Toshio Yamamoto
Profile: Material & Industry News covers the domestic and international trends of metal industry. Articles cover specialised information on iron-steel and non-ferrous metal, scrap yard operators as well as electric furnace steel and integrated steel manufacturers.
Language (s): Japanese
DAILY NEWSPAPER

Minato Shimbun 459193

Editorial: Minato-Yamaguchi Co., Ltd. 1-1-7, Higashi-Yamato-machi, Shimonoseki, Yamaguchi 750-8506 **Tel:** 81 832 663214
Web site: http://www.minato-yamaguchi.co.jp/
Freq: Daily; **Circ:** 58003 Not Audited
Profile: Minato Shimbun is a daily newspaper which features information on fishery industry such as the latest news of the industry, economics, trends logiscitcs etc.
Language (s): Japanese
DAILY NEWSPAPER

Miyazaki Nichinichi Shimbun 459902

Editorial: Miyazaki Nichinichi Shinbun, 1-1-33, Takachiho-dori, Miyazaki 880-8570
Tel: 81 985 244201
Email: houdou@the-miyanichi.co.jp **Web site:** http://www.the-miyanichi.co.jp
Freq: Daily; **Circ:** 216700 Not Audited
News Director: Kozuyuki Kasube; **President:** Yasuhisa Machikawa
Profile: Miyazaki Nichinichi Shimbun is a newspaper for Miyazaki district which reports on regional news happening around the Miyazaki area.
Language (s): Japanese
DAILY NEWSPAPER

Nara Shimbun 459884

Editorial: Nara newspaper, 2-4, Hokkeji-machi, Nara 630-8686 **Tel:** 81 74 2322113
Email: edit@nara-np.co.jp **Web site:** http://www.nara-np.co.jp
Freq: Daily; **Circ:** 126324 Not Audited
President: Haruo Amari; **Editor in Chief:** Tadahiro Kokubo; **Editor:** Eiji Yamashita
Profile: Reports local and regional news within the Nara District, with a focus on business and the economy.
Language (s): Japanese
DAILY NEWSPAPER

Nihon Keizai Shimbun - Chicago Bureau 539397

Editorial: 1 S Wacker Dr, Ste 1150, Chicago, Illinois 60606-4616 **Tel:** 1 312 726-9478
Bureau Chief: Yasuko Mouri
Profile: This is the Chicago bureau of the Japan-based financial paper Nihon Keizai Shimbun.
Language (s): English
DAILY NEWSPAPER

Nihon Keizai Shimbun - New York Bureau 394547

Editorial: 1325 Avenue of the Americas Ste 2500, New York, New York 10019-6055 **Tel:** 1 212 261-6323
Language (s): English
DAILY NEWSPAPER

Nihon Keizai Shimbun - Palo Alto, CA Bureau 503934

Editorial: 575 High St, Palo Alto, California 94301
Tel: 1 650 470-7400
Web site: http://www.nni.nikkei.co.jp
Bureau Chief: Nobuyuki Okada
Profile: This is the California bureau of the Japan-based financial paper Nihon Keizai Shimbun.
Language (s): English
DAILY NEWSPAPER

Nihon Keizai Shimbun (Tokyo) 161208

Editorial: 1-9-5 Otemachi, Chiyoda-ku, Tokyo 100-8066 **Tel:** 81 352552196
Web site: http://www.nikkei.com
Freq: Daily; **Circ:** 3027000 Not Audited
Managing Director: Junichi Arai; **Manager:** Hideki Kume
Profile: Also known as the Nikkei (a combination of Nihon and Keizai), serves as one of the world's largest financial newspapers. Covers market and industry news throughout Asia and the world.
Language (s): Japanese
Ad Rate: Full Page Mono 20400000.00
Ad Rate: Full Page Colour 25300000.00
Currency: Japan Yen
DAILY NEWSPAPER

Nihon Ryutsu Shinbun 460097

Editorial: Nihon Ryutsu Newspaper, 19, Tsukiji-machi, Shinzuku-ku, Tokyo 162-0818
Tel: 81 35 2062615
Email: ryu-tsu@luck.ocn.ne.jp **Web site:** http://www.ryu-tsu.com
Freq: Weekly; **Circ:** 10003 Not Audited
Editor in Chief: Shinichi Hori; **President & Publisher:** Shizuo Kasahara; **Editor:** Tadashi Machida
Profile: Focuses on transportation issues in Japan. Topics include news on road and air transport, logistics, vehicle management and local traffic industry.
Language (s): Japanese
DAILY NEWSPAPER

Nihon Securities Journal 601871

Editorial: Nihon Securities Journal Inc, 16-6 Koami-cho, Nihonbashi, Chuo-ku, Tokyo 103-0016
Tel: 81 33 6637279
Email: news@nsjournal.jp **Web site:** http://www.nsjournal.jp
Freq: Daily; **Circ:** 113000
President: Hideo Amano; **Editor in Chief:** Kaoru Suzuki
Profile: Nihon Securities Journal is the newspaper specialized for Securities.
Language (s): Japanese
DAILY NEWSPAPER

Nihon Shokuryo Shimbun 459296

Editorial: Japan Food Journal Co., Ltd., 1-9-9-5F Yaesu, Tokyo 105-0028 **Tel:** 81 334 323103
Web site: http://www.nissyoku.co.jp
Freq: 2 Times/Week; **Circ:** 101303 Not Audited
Publisher: Masayoshi Konno
Profile: Nihon Shokuryo Shimbun is a news paper every other day. Articles cover the latest news in the food industry such as product development, reducing costs of production process and other related critical issues.
Language (s): Japanese
DAILY NEWSPAPER

Niigata Nippo 459878

Editorial: The Niigata Nippo, 772-2 Zen-ku, Niigata-shi, Niigata 950-1189 **Tel:** 81 25 3789400
Web site: http://www.niigata-nippo.co.jp
Freq: Daily; **Circ:** 500000 Not Audited
President: Michiei Takahashi
Profile: Niigata Nippo is a regional daily newspaper which reports the latest regional news in Niigata district.
Language (s): Japanese
DAILY NEWSPAPER

Nikkan Gendai (Tokyo) 459299

Editorial: Nikkan Gendai Co., Ltd., Nakagawa-Tsukiji Bldg., 3-5-4 Tsukiji, Chuo-ku, Tokyo 104-8007
Tel: 81 33 5430531
Web site: http://www.gendai.net
Freq: Daily; **Circ:** 1600003 Not Audited
Profile: Nikkan Gendai, a tabloid newspaper which provides readers with information about various local and national events.
Language (s): Japanese
DAILY NEWSPAPER

Nikkan Jidosha Shimbun (Daily Automotive News) 460336

Editorial: Nikkan Jidosha Shimbun, 2-1-25, Kaigan, Minato-ku, Tokyo 105-0022 **Tel:** 81 33 4555321
Email: desk@njd.jp **Web site:** http://www.njd.jp
Freq: Daily; **Circ:** 143004 Not Audited
Profile: Covers the auto manufacturing, engineering, design, production and suppliers with equal emphasis on the retail side of the auto industry.
Language (s): Japanese
DAILY NEWSPAPER

Nikkan Kenmin Fukui 459868

Editorial: The Chunichi Shimbun, 3-1-8, Ohte, Fukui 910-8567 **Tel:** 81 776 288611
Email: henshu@kenmin-fukui.co.jp **Web site:** http://www.chunichi.co.jp/kenmin-fukui/
Freq: Daily; **Circ:** 40083 Not Audited
President: Tamotsu Okawara; **News Director:** Kazuhiro Tada
Profile: Nikkan Kenmin Fukui is a general daily newspapers in the Fukui district of Japan which mainly reports on regional news and happenings in the area.
Language (s): Japanese
DAILY NEWSPAPER

Nikkan Ryutsu Journal 460099

Editorial: Ryutsu Journal Co., Ltd., 6F/7F Oizumi Higashiueno Bulding, 1-8-2 Higashiueno, Taito-ku, Tokyo 110-0015 **Tel:** 81 33 8346771
Email: rj@ryutsu-j.co.jp **Web site:** http://www.ryutsu-j.co.jp
Freq: Daily
Publisher: Hideo Katou
Profile: Provides readers with information on distribution networks and channels, rail and ship transport including chain management and automation.
Language (s): Japanese
DAILY NEWSPAPER

Nikkan Sports (Tokyo) 459802

Editorial: Nikkan Sports News, 3-5-10, Tsukiji, Chuo-ku, Tokyo 104-8055 **Tel:** 81 35 5508888
Email: webmast@nikkansports.co.jp **Web site:** http://www.nikkansports.com
Freq: Daily; **Circ:** 1965000 Not Audited
Editor in Chief: Hitoshi Aihara; **President:** Motohiro Miura; **Editor:** Fumihiko Sasamori
Profile: Nikkan Sports is a sports newspaper which writes about daily news on sports and on popular celebrities in Japan.
Language (s): Japanese
Ad Rate: Full Page Mono 375000.00
Currency: Japan Yen
DAILY NEWSPAPER

The Nikkei 459794

Editorial: Nikkei Inc., 1-3-7 Otemachi, Chiyoda-ku, Tokyo 100-8066 **Tel:** 81 332 700251
Web site: http://www.nikkei.co.jp
Freq: Daily; **Circ:** 3013563 Not Audited
President: Tsuneo Kita
Profile: Provides the latest news and current affairs happening in Japan and World including coverage on economic and politics.
Language (s): Japanese
DAILY NEWSPAPER

Nikkei - New York Bureau 620638

Editorial: 1325 Avenue Of The Americas Suite 2404, New York, New York 10019-6026 **Tel:** 1 212 261-6450
Web site: http://www.nikkei.com
Profile: This is the New York bureau of Nikkei, which is based in Tokyo, Japan.
Language (s): Japanese
DAILY NEWSPAPER

The Nikkei MJ 460438

Editorial: Nikkei Inc. 1-3-7, Otemachi, Chiyoda-ku, Tokyo 100-8066 **Tel:** 81 332 700251
Web site: http://www.nikkei.co.jp/mj/
Freq: 2 Times/Week; **Circ:** 248440 Not Audited
President: Tsuneo Kita; **Editor in Chief:** Shoji Shinohara
Profile: Provides sources of reliable information on Japanese distribution, retail markets and marketing.
Language (s): Japanese
DAILY NEWSPAPER

Nikkei Sangyo Shimbun/Nikkei Business Daily (Tokyo) 459795

Editorial: 1-3-7, Otemachi, Chiyoda-ku, Tokyo 100-8065 **Tel:** 81 332 700251
Web site: http://netplus.nikkei.co.jp/ssbiz
Freq: Daily; **Circ:** 173763 Not Audited
Editor: Seiji Munakata
Profile: One of Japan's largest industrial information journals, covers local business news, innovative industries and enterprises.
Language (s): Japanese
DAILY NEWSPAPER

Nikkei Veritas 520237

Editorial: Nikkei Inc., 1-3-7 Otemachi Chiyoda-ku, Tokyo 100-8065 **Tel:** 81 3 62562062
Web site: http://veritas.nikkei.co.jp/
Freq: Weekly; **Circ:** 60000
President & Publisher: Tsuneo Kita; **Editor in Chief:** Hiroshi Yamasaki
Profile: NIKKEI VERITAS is a newspaper which focused on finance, banking, and technology.
Language (s): Japanese
DAILY NEWSPAPER

Nikkin 499773

Editorial: The Japan Financial News Co., Ltd., 4-3-15, Kudan-Minami, Chiyoda-ku, Tokyo 102-8677
Tel: 81 33 2619971
Web site: http://www.nikkin.co.jp
Freq: Weekly; **Circ:** 100000
Publisher: Sumio Kinoshita; **Editor:** Gen Nishikawa
Profile: Nikkin is a financial journal which provides banking, financing, and money related news.
Language (s): Japanese
DAILY NEWSPAPER

Nishi Nippon Shimbun 459905

Editorial: The Nishinippon Shimbun, 1-4-1, Tenjin, Chuo-ku, Fukuoka 810-8721 **Tel:** 81 92 7115555
Web site: http://www.nishinippon.co.jp
Freq: Daily; **Circ:** 120455
News Director: Hiroyuki Inoue; **President:** Takao Kawasaki; **Editor:** Akira Kojima; **Editor:** Takeshi Kokubu
Profile: Nishi Nippon Shimbun is a newspaper which reports local news in Tenjin district in Fukuoka. Articles also cover general news in Japan and national.
Language (s): Japanese
Ad Rate: Full Page Mono 180000.00
Ad Rate: Full Page Colour 300000.00
Currency: Japan Yen
DAILY NEWSPAPER

The Noki Shinbun 460057

Editorial: Shinnorinsha CO., Ltd. 2-7-22, Kanda Nishi-cho, Chiyoda-ku, Tokyo 101-0054
Tel: 81 332 913671
Web site: http://www.shin-norin.co.jp
Freq: Weekly
Editor in Chief: Nobuharu Mori
Profile: Noki Shinbun is a weekly newspaper which specialized in agriculture and agricultural machinery and agribusiness and research.
Language (s): Japanese
DAILY NEWSPAPER

Okayama Nichi-Nichi Shimbun 459897

Owner: The Okayama Nichinichi Shimbun Company
Editorial: The Okayama Nichinichi Shimbun Company, 3-30 Banzan-cho, Okayama 700-8678
Tel: 81 862220601
Web site: http://www.okanichi.co.jp
Freq: Daily; **Circ:** 45002 Not Audited
President: Katsuya Harada; **Editor in Chief:** Yasuhiro Inoue
Profile: Okayama Nichi-Nichi Shimbun is a daily regional news paper which provides readers with the latest regional news and current affairs happening in Okayama district including coverage on economic and regional activities.
Language (s): Japanese
DAILY NEWSPAPER

Osaka Nichi-Nichi Shimbun 459818

Editorial: Osaka Nichi-Nichi Shimbun, 2-6-8, Bakuroucho, Chuo-ku, Osaka 541-0059
Tel: 81 661 201800
Email: dainichi@nnn.co.jp **Web site:** http://www.nnn.co.jp/dainichi
Freq: Daily; **Circ:** 110003 Not Audited
President & Publisher: Toshikata Yoshioka
Profile: Osaka Nichi-Nichi Shimbun is a daily regional news paper which provides the latest regional news, current affairs happening in Osaka district including coverage on economic and regional activities.
Language (s): Japanese
DAILY NEWSPAPER

Reitou Shokuhin Shimbun 460106

Editorial: Reitou Shokuhin Shimbunsha, 9 Sanei-cho, Shinjyuku-ku, Tokyo 160-0008 **Tel:** 81 333 599191
Email: edi@reishoku.co.jp **Web site:** http://www.reishoku.co.jp
Freq: Weekly; **Circ:** 25000
Profile: Reitou Shokuhin Shimbun is a weekly newspaper which is specialized in frozen food. Articles include the latest news of the industry such as new products, corporate news etc.
Language (s): Japanese
DAILY NEWSPAPER

Ryukyu Shimpo 459908

Editorial: The Ryukyu Shimpo, 905 Ameku, Naha 900-8525 **Tel:** 81 988655158
Email: shakai@ryukyushimpo.co.jp **Web site:** http://www.ryukyushimpo.co.jp
Freq: Daily; **Circ:** 203778 Not Audited
Editor: Osamu Miyagi; **President & Publisher:** Jyunichi Tomita
Profile: Ryukyu Shimpo is a newspaper which reports the latest news in Ryukyu district in Okinawa.
Language (s): Japanese
DAILY NEWSPAPER

Ryutsu Journal 460100

Editorial: Ryutsu Journal Co., Ltd., 6F/7F Oizumi Higashiueno Bulding, 1-8-2 Higashiueno, Taito-ku, Tokyo 110-0015 **Tel:** 81 33 8346771
Email: rj@ryutsu-j.co.jp **Web site:** http://www.ryutsu-j.co.jp
Freq: Weekly; **Circ:** 28003 Not Audited
Publisher: Hideo Katou
Profile: Discusses chain management and automation industry news.
Language (s): Japanese
DAILY NEWSPAPER

Saga Shimbun 459909

Editorial: Saga Shimbun Co., Ltd., 3-2-23, Tenjin, Saga 840-8585 **Tel:** 81 952 282111

Email: houdou@saga-s.co.jp **Web site:** http://www.saga-s.co.jp
Freq: Daily; **Circ:** 135233 Not Audited
News Director: Yoshifumi Sawano
Profile: Saga Shimbun is a daily regional news paper which writes about regional and lifestyle news in Saga district.
Language (s): Japanese
DAILY NEWSPAPER

Saitama Shimbun 459848
Editorial: 2-282-3, Yoshino-cho, Kita-ku, Saitama 331-8686 **Tel:** 81 48 795-9930
Email: desk@saitama-np.co.jp **Web site:** http://www.saitama-np.co.jp
Freq: Daily; **Circ:** 164003 Not Audited
President: Akira Maruyama
Profile: Reports daily news on business, sports, entertainment and technology.
Language (s): Japanese
DAILY NEWSPAPER

San-In Chuo Shimpo 459889
Editorial: The San-in Chuo Shimpo, Sanin Chuo Building, 383, Tono-machi, Matsue 690-8668
Tel: 81 85 2323320
Web site: http://www.sanin-chuo.co.jp
Freq: Daily; **Circ:** 181000 Not Audited
Editor: Yasufumi Fukumaru; **Director:** Toshinori Makino; **President & Publisher:** Tsunemasa Yamane
Profile: San-In Chuo Shimpo is a daily newspaper in Shimane and Tottori district which mainly reports on regional news happening around the neighborhood.
Language (s): Japanese
DAILY NEWSPAPER

Sankei Shimbun - New York Bureau 503936
Editorial: United Nations Headquarters, Room S-400, New York, New York 10017 **Tel:** 1 212 702-0454
Freq: Daily
Profile: This is the New York bureau of Sankei Shimbun, which is based in Tokyo.
Language (s): Japanese
DAILY NEWSPAPER

Sankei Shimbun (Tokyo) 161287
Editorial: The Sankei Shimbun, 1-7-2, Otemachi, Chiyoda-ku, Tokyo 100-8077 **Tel:** 81 33 2758742
Web site: http://sankei.jp.msn.com
Freq: Daily; **Circ:** 2746203 Not Audited
President: Yoshitaka Sumida
Profile: Sankei Shimbun is a newspaper which writes about the latest daily news on business, sports, entertainment and technology, etc.
Language (s): Japanese
Ad Rate: Full Page Mono 30000000.00
Currency: Japan Yen
DAILY NEWSPAPER

Sankei Sports (Tokyo) 459805
Editorial: Sankei Sports, 13rd Floor, Sankei Building, 1-7-2, Otemachi, Chiyoda-Ku, Tokyo 100-8077
Tel: 81 332 758830
Email: reader@sanspo.com **Web site:** http://www.sanspo.com
Freq: Daily; **Circ:** 815223 Not Audited
President & Publisher: Ryoichi Munechika
Profile: Sankei Sports writes about the latest in sports, leisure and entertainment.
Language (s): Japanese
DAILY NEWSPAPER

The Sekai Nippo 459276
Editorial: 2-6-25 Idabashi-ku, Tokyo 174-0041
Tel: 81 335 583412
Email: voice@worldtimes.co.jp **Web site:** http://www.worldtimes.co.jp
Freq: Daily
President & Publisher: Yoshiaki Kinoshita; **Editor in Chief:** Masahiro Kuroki
Profile: Sekai Nippo is a daily newspaper which reports mainly international news such as the latest news which is provided by more than 20 overseas correspondents. Articles includes current affairs, economics, social affairs and cultural articles.
Language (s): English
DAILY NEWSPAPER

Shimane Nichi-Nichi Shimbun 459891
Editorial: Shimane NichiNichi Shinbun, 545, Satogata-cho, Izumo 693-0064 **Tel:** 81 853 236766
Email: henshu@shimanenichinichi.co.jp **Web site:** http://www.shimanenichinichi.co.jp
Freq: Daily; **Circ:** 25000 Not Audited
Editor in Chief: Toyomi Hino
Profile: Shimane Nichi-Nichi Shimbun is a regional daily newspaper in Shimane district which reports local news, national and international news.
Language (s): Japanese
DAILY NEWSPAPER

Shimbun Quint 491608
Editorial: Quintessence Publishing Co., Ltd., Quint House Bldg., 3-2-6 Hongo, Bunkyo-ku, Tokyo 113-0033 **Tel:** 81 358 422280
Email: news-q@quint-j.co.jp **Web site:** http://www.quint-j.co.jp/
Freq: Monthly; **Circ:** 21000
Editor in Chief: Yushi Kimiya
Profile: SHIMBUN QUINT is a monthly newspaper which focused on dental and medical news and knowledges.
Language (s): Japanese
DAILY NEWSPAPER

Shinano Mainichi Shimbun 459872
Editorial: 657, Minami-agata-machi, Nagano 380-8546 **Tel:** 81 26 2363130
Email: houdo@shinmai.co.jp **Web site:** http://www.shinmai.co.jp
Freq: Daily; **Circ:** 484100 Not Audited
News Director: Kouji Hataya; **President & Publisher:** Kensuke Kosaka
Profile: Covers news amd current affairs in Nagano district including coverage on economic and regional activities.
Language (s): Japanese
DAILY NEWSPAPER

Shonai Nippo 459839
Owner: The Shonai Nippo Press Co., Ltd.
Editorial: The Shonai Nippo Press Co., Ltd., 8-29, Baba-cho, Tsuruoka 997-8691 **Tel:** 81 235221482
Web site: http://www.shonai-nippo.co.jp
Freq: Daily; **Circ:** 22502 Not Audited
President & Publisher: Masayuki Hashimoto; **News Director:** Makoto Togashi
Profile: Shonai Nippo is a newspaper which writes about the latest news and happenings around Tsuruoka district in Yamagata.
Language (s): Japanese
DAILY NEWSPAPER

Shukan Josei 797998
Owner: SHUFU TO SEIKATSU SHA CO., LTD
Editorial: No. 7, No. five, 3-chome, Kyobashi, Chuo-ku, Tokyo **Tel:** 81 3 35635120
Email: webmaster@mb.shufu.co.jp **Web site:** http://www.shufu.co.jp/magazine/woman
Circ: 700000
Profile: Focuses on women's issues.
Language (s): Japanese
DAILY NEWSPAPER

Sports Hochi (Tokyo) 459787
Editorial: The Hochi Shimbun, 4-6-49, Kohnan, Minato-ku, Tokyo 108-8485 **Tel:** 81 35 4791111
Web site: http://hochi.yomiuri.co.jp
Freq: Daily; **Circ:** 1500003 Not Audited
Profile: Newspaper covering sports, leisure and entertainment.
Language (s): Japanese
Ad Rate: Full Page Mono 89119000.00
Ad Rate: Full Page Colour 101929000.00
Currency: Japan Yen
DAILY NEWSPAPER

Sports Nippon (Osaka) 459807
Editorial: Sports Nippon Newspaper, 3-4-5, Umeda, Kita-ku, Osaka 530-8278 **Tel:** 81 66 3468500
Web site: http://www.sponichi.co.jp
Freq: Daily; **Circ:** 610003 Not Audited
President & Publisher: Ken Fujiwara; **General Manager:** Yukio Morito; **Editor:** Haruo Nakagawa
Profile: Sports Nippon (Osaka) is a sports newspaper which writes about daily news on sports and popular celebrities around Osaka district.
Language (s): Japanese
DAILY NEWSPAPER

Sports Nippon (Tokyo) 207946
Editorial: Sports Nippon Newspapers, 2-1-30, Ecchujima, Koto-ku, Tokyo 135-8517
Tel: 81 33 8200700
Email: customer@sponichi.co.jp **Web site:** http://www.sponichi.co.jp
Freq: Daily; **Circ:** 879742 Not Audited
President & Publisher: Yukio Morito
Profile: Sports Nippon is a sports newspaper which writes about daily news on sports and on popular celebrities.
Language (s): Japanese
DAILY NEWSPAPER

Suisan Keizai Shimbun 459808
Owner: The Suisan-Keizai
Editorial: The Suisan-Keizai, 6-8-19, Roppongi, Minato-ku, Tokyo 106-0032 **Tel:** 81 334046531
Web site: http://www.suikei.co.jp
Freq: Daily; **Circ:** 610002 Not Audited
Profile: The Suisan Keizai is a daily newspaper which delivers information on the marine products industry in Japan.
Language (s): Japanese
DAILY NEWSPAPER

Tages-Anzeiger - Tokyo Bureau 489163
Owner: Tamedia AG
Editorial: Tamedia AG, 4-29-13 Kyoto, Setagaya-ku, Tokyo 156-0052 **Tel:** 81 354501162
Web site: http://www.tagesanzeiger.ch
Freq: Daily
Profile: The Tages-Anzeiger is a national daily newspaper that focusses on news in politics, economy, culture and sports.
Language (s): German
DAILY NEWSPAPER

Tokachi Mainichi Shimbun 459827
Editorial: Tokachi Mainichi Newspaper Inc., 8-2, Higashi 1-jo-minami, Obihiro 080-8688
Tel: 81 155 222121
Email: info@kachimai.co.jp **Web site:** http://www.tokachi.co.jp
Freq: Daily; **Circ:** 91023 Not Audited
Managing Director: Hajimi Ito
Profile: Tokachi Mainichi Shimbun is a daily newspaper which delivers the latest regional and lifestyle news on the Obihiro district.
Language (s): Japanese
DAILY NEWSPAPER

Tokushima Shimbun 459896
Editorial: Tokushima Shimbun, 2-5-2, Naka-Tokushima-cho, Tokushima 770-8572
Tel: 81 335 557373
Web site: http://www.topics.or.jp
Freq: Daily; **Circ:** 260663 Not Audited
Editor: Satoru Funakoshi
Profile: TOKUSHIMA SHIMBUN is a daily newspaper which reports regional news in Tokushima district and national news.
Language (s): Japanese
DAILY NEWSPAPER

Tokyo Chunichi Sports 459809
Editorial: The Chunichi Shimbun, 2-1-4 Uchisaiwai-cyo, Chiyoda-ku, Tokyo 100-8505
Tel: 81 369 102211
Email: tochu@tokyo-np.co.jp **Web site:** http://www.chunichi.co.jp/chuspo/
Freq: Daily; **Circ:** 573013 Not Audited
President: Torao Ojima
Profile: Tokyo Chunichi Sports writes about news in sports, leisure, news and entertainment.
Language (s): Japanese
DAILY NEWSPAPER

Tokyo Shimbun (Tokyo) 459810
Editorial: 2-1-4, Uchisaiwai-cho, Chiyoda-ku, Tokyo 100-8505 **Tel:** 81 369 102258
Email: shakai@tokyo-np.co.jp **Web site:** http://www.chunichi.co.jp
Freq: Daily; **Circ:** 620133 Not Audited
President: Torao Tajima
Profile: Covers news throughout the Tokyo metropolitan area.
Language (s): Japanese
DAILY NEWSPAPER

Tokyo Shimbun/Chunichi Shimbun - United Nations Bureau 620308
Editorial: 1 Rockefeller Plz Rm 1714, New York, New York 10020-2044 **Tel:** 1 212 969-1870
Freq: Daily
Bureau Chief: Tomotoshi Aoyagi
Profile: This is the United Nations Bureau for the Tokyo Shimbun in Tokyo and the Chunichi Shimbun in Nagoya, Japan daily newspapers.
Language (s): Japanese
DAILY NEWSPAPER

Tokyo Sports 459811
Editorial: Tokyo Sports, 4/F 6/F ST Building, 2-1-30, Ecchujima, Koto-ku, Tokyo 135-8721
Tel: 81 338 200831
Web site: http://www.tokyo-sports.co.jp
Freq: Daily; **Circ:** 1173203 Not Audited
President & Publisher: Yoshinobu Ebata; **Editor:** Osamu Sakai
Profile: Tokyo Sports is a daily sports newspaper which writes about daily news on sports and on popular celebrities.
Language (s): Japanese
DAILY NEWSPAPER

Transportation & Logistics 460087
Owner: Unyu Shimbun
Editorial: Unyu Shimbun, 3/F, Sasaki Building, 3-6-10, Nishinippori, Arakawa-ku, Tokyo 116-0013
Tel: 81 3 56850035
Web site: http://www.unyu.co.jp
Freq: 2 Times/Week; **Circ:** 45702 Not Audited
Profile: Reports on all aspects of logistics, such as efficiency and effectiveness, cost evaluation and information systems. Articles also cover stories of ministries which are related to the logistics industry.
Language (s): Japanese
DAILY NEWSPAPER

Tsuhan Shimbun 460103
Editorial: Koubun Publishing, 2-14-3 Hongo, Bunkyo-Ku, Tokyo 113-0033 **Tel:** 81 3 38151903
Email: tsuhan@kbns.co.jp **Web site:** http://www.tsuhanshinbun.com/
Freq: Weekly; **Circ:** 29000 Not Audited
Profile: Provides a guide for e-business and electronic commerce.
Language (s): Japanese
DAILY NEWSPAPER

Weekly Logistics News 460089
Editorial: The Weekly Logistics News, 4-15-14, Yamasaka, Higashisumiyoshi-ku, Osaka
Tel: 81 666080501
Email: buturyu@weekly-net.co.jp **Web site:** http://www.weekly-net.co.jp
Freq: Weekly; **Circ:** 165002 Not Audited
Editor in Chief: Hidekazu Nakano; **Publisher:** Naoki Takata
Profile: Includes coverage on the latest trends of the industry, issues in cost management, maintenance, safety, labor and legislation as well as technical reports on vehicles and component developments.
Language (s): Japanese
DAILY NEWSPAPER

Yaeyama Mainichi Shimbun 459910
Editorial: Yaeyama Mainichi Shimbun, 614, Tonoshiro, Ishigaki 907-0004 **Tel:** 81 980822122
Web site: http://www.y-mainichi.co.jp
Freq: Daily; **Circ:** 14801 Not Audited
Editor: Yoshio Kamichi; **Editor:** Yoshitaka Matsuda; **President:** Kiyotaka Nakama
Profile: Yaeyama Mainichi Shimbun is a newspaper which reports on all aspects of news ranging from economical, political, social and cultural in the Ishigaki district in Okinawa.
Language (s): Japanese
DAILY NEWSPAPER

Yakuji Nippo 459413
Owner: Yakuji Nippo Ltd.
Editorial: Yakuji Nippo Ltd.,1 Izumicho, Kanda, Chiyota-ku, Tokyo 101-8648 **Tel:** 81 338622141
Email: henshu@yakuji.co.jp **Web site:** http://www.yakuji.co.jp
Freq: 2 Times/Week; **Circ:** 53002 Not Audited
Editor in Chief: Norio Koyama
Profile: Yakuji Nippo is a journal which provides characteristic of newly approved drug, results of clinical studies, post-approval clinical studies now underway or planned; cautions for use and rationale for their establishment, adverse reaction, clinical pharmacology, pharmacokinetics in humans; chemical structure; pharmacology, toxicology, etc
Language (s): Japanese
DAILY NEWSPAPER

Yamagata Shimbun 459841
Editorial: Yamagata Shimbun, 2-5-12, Hatagomachi, Yamagata 990-8550 **Tel:** 81 236224546
Email: info@yamagata-np.jp **Web site:** http://yamagata-np.jp
Freq: Daily; **Circ:** 217767 Not Audited
President & Publisher: Yosuke Kurosawa; **Editor in Chief:** Hiroji Sagae
Profile: Covers regional and national news.
Language (s): Japanese
DAILY NEWSPAPER

Yamanashi Nichinichi Shimbun 459874
Editorial: The Yamanashi Nichinichi Shimbun, 2-6-10, Kitaguchi, Kofu 400-8515 **Tel:** 81 552313111
Web site: http://www.sannichi.co.jp
Freq: Daily; **Circ:** 207244 Not Audited
News Director: Hirohide Kobayashi; **President & Publisher:** Eiichi Noguchi
Profile: Yamanashi Nichinichi Shimbun is a newspaper which reports the reader with the latest news and current affairs happening in Kofu district in Yamanashi.
Language (s): Japanese
DAILY NEWSPAPER

Yomiuri Shimbun - Los Angeles Bureau 687592
Editorial: 601 S Figueroa St Ste 3540, Los Angeles, California 90017-5740 **Tel:** 1 213 623-7699
Web site: http://www.yomiuri.co.jp
Freq: Daily
Profile: Yomiuri Shimbun - Los Angeles Bureau is the Los Angeles bureau of the Tokyo daily newspaper.
Language (s): Japanese
DAILY NEWSPAPER

Yomiuri Shimbun - New York Bureau 79991
Editorial: 747 3rd Ave, 28th Fl, New York, New York 10017 **Tel:** 1 212 752-2196
Web site: http://www.yomiuri.co.jp
Freq: Daily; **Circ:** 20400 Not Audited
Bureau Chief: Yoshitoshi Sasaki
Profile: Yomiuri Shimbun - New York Bureau is the New York bureau of a Toyko daily newspaper.
Language (s): English
Ad Rate: Full Page Mono 68.89
Currency: United States Dollars
DAILY NEWSPAPER

Yomiuri Shimbun - Singapore Bureau 520236
Editorial: International Plaza, #21-04, 10 Anson Road, Singapore 79903 **Tel:** 65 62223029
Web site: http://www.yomiuri.co.jp
Bureau Chief: Akihiro Ito
Profile: Covers local and international news.
Language (s): Japanese
DAILY NEWSPAPER

The Yomiuri Shimbun - United Nations Bureau 620665
Editorial: 747 3rd Ave Fl 28, New York, New York 10017-2803 **Tel:** 1 212 752-2196
Email: dy@yomiuri.com **Web site:** http://www.yomiuri.co.jp/dy/
Freq: Daily
Profile: This is the United Nations bureau for The Daily Yomiuri, the English-language sister publication of Yomirui Shimbun in Tokyo.
Language (s): English
DAILY NEWSPAPER

Yomiuri Shimbun - Washington, DC Bureau 409725
Editorial: 529 14th St NW, Ste 802, Washington, District Of Columbia 20045 **Tel:** 1 202 783-0186
Bureau Chief: Michiro Okamoto

Profile: The Yomiuri Shimbun is Japan's largest daily newspaper. It has roughly 60 reporters stationed at general bureaus in Washington, D.C., London, Bangkok and 29 branches around the world. Daily sections offer national and international news, politics, business, city news, sports, lifestyle and television listings. Weekly features include education, economics. science, book reviews and fairy tales. Syndication with the Washington Post provides readers with a broad range of international perspectives.
Language (s): Japanese
DAILY NEWSPAPER

Yomiuri Shimbun (Chubu) 459814
Editorial: The Yomiuri Shimbun, 1-17-6, Sakae, Naka-ku, Nagoya 460-8470 **Tel:** 81 522 111151
Web site: http://chubu.yomiuri.co.jp
Freq: Daily; **Circ:** 173503 Not Audited
Editor: Shigekatsu Matsunaga; **President:** Shoichi Oikawa; **Editor:** Toru Takahashi; **News Director:** Shigeru Watanabe
Profile: Provides the latest regional news and current affairs happening in Aichi, Gihu and Mie district including coverage on economic and regional activities.
Language (s): Japanese
DAILY NEWSPAPER

Yomiuri Shimbun (Hokuriku) 459816
Editorial: The Yomiuri Shimbun, 4-5, Shimonoseki-machi, Takaoka 933-8543 **Tel:** 81 766 266833
Web site: http://hokuriku.yomiuri.co.jp
Freq: Daily; **Circ:** 119773 Not Audited
President & Publisher: Shoichi Oikawa
Profile: Yomiuri Shimbun (Hokuriku) is a daily newspaper which provides the latest regional news and current affairs happening in Hokuriku district including coverage on economic and regional activities.
Language (s): Japanese
DAILY NEWSPAPER

Yomiuri Shimbun (Osaka) 459812
Editorial: The Yomiuri Shimbun, 5-9, Nozaki-cho, Kita-ku, Osaka 530-8551 **Tel:** 81 663 611111
Web site: http://osaka.yomiuri.co.jp
Freq: Daily; **Circ:** 1329842
Profile: Yomiuri Shimbun (Osaka) is a daily newspaper which provides the latest regional news and current affairs happening in Osaka district including coverage on economic and regional activities.
Language (s): Japanese
Ad Rate: Full Page Mono 14535000.00
Ad Rate: Full Page Colour 16715000.00
Currency: Japan Yen
DAILY NEWSPAPER

Yomiuri Shimbun (Seibu) 459813
Editorial: The Yomiuri Shimbun, 1-16-5, Akasaka, Chuo-ku, Fukuoka 810-0042 **Tel:** 81 927 155641
Email: tousho@yomiuri.com **Web site:** http://kyushu.yomiuri.co.jp
Freq: Daily; **Circ:** 925323 Not Audited
President & Publisher: Hiroshi Ota; **Editor:** Ikushi Yoshizuka
Profile: Yomiuri Shimbun (Seibu) is a daily newspaper which provides the latest regional news and current affairs happening in Kyushu Island and Yamaguchi district including coverage on economic and regional activities.
Language (s): Japanese
Ad Rate: Full Page Mono 89119000.00
Ad Rate: Full Page Colour 101929000.00
Currency: Japan Yen
DAILY NEWSPAPER

Yomiuri Shimbun (Tokyo) 161285
Editorial: 1-7-1, Otemachi, Chiyoda-ku, Tokyo 104-0061 **Tel:** 81 332 421111
Email: shakai@yomiuri.com **Web site:** http://www.yomiuri.co.jp
Freq: Daily; **Circ:** 2930366
Editor: Kazuyuki Kondo; **News Director:** Jyunichi Maruyama; **Editor:** Takeshi Mizoguchi; **News Director:** Akitoshi Muraoka; **Publisher:** Hitoshi Uchiyama
Profile: Reports all aspects of news ranging from economical, political, social and cultural.
Language (s): Japanese
Ad Rate: Full Page Mono 28003500.00
Ad Rate: Full Page Colour 31703500.00
Currency: Japan Yen
DAILY NEWSPAPER

Yukan Fuji (Tokyo) 459806
Editorial: The Sankei Shimbun, 1-7-2, Otemachi, Chiyoda-ku, Tokyo 100-004 **Tel:** 81 332 317111
Email: desk@zakzak.co.jp **Web site:** http://www.zakzak.co.jp
Freq: Daily; **Circ:** 15590003 Not Audited
Editor: Yoshifumi Ejiri; **Editor:** Takeshi Kubo; **News Director:** Shuji Takami
Profile: YUKAN FUJI is a newspaper only publishes evening daily. Articles cover news, event, sports and gossip.
Language (s): Japanese
DAILY NEWSPAPER

Yuso Keizai 460091
Editorial: Yuso Keizai Shimbunsha, 2-22-4, Shinkawa, Chuo-ku, Tokyo 104-0033
Tel: 81 332 060713
Email: hanbai@yuso.co.jp **Web site:** http://www.yuso.co.jp
Freq: Weekly; **Circ:** 80003 Not Audited
Publisher: Toru Kodaira; **Editor:** Takuya Matsuzaki
Profile: Covers industry news for international logistics executives.
Language (s): Japanese
DAILY NEWSPAPER

News Service/Syndicate

Jiji Press 353209
Owner: JIJI PRESS LTD.
Editorial: JIJI PRESS LTD., 5-15-8, Ginza, Chuo-ku, Tokyo 104-8178 **Tel:** 81 3 68001111
Email: webmaster@jiji.com **Web site:** http://www.jiji.com
Freq: Daily
Editor: Kenji Hattori; **News Director:** Junichi Hoshida
Profile: JIJI PRESS is a news service source which reports the latest news in Japan and around the world.
Language (s): Japanese
NEWS SERVICE/SYNDICATE

Kyodo News 353716
Editorial: 1-71-1 Higashi-Shimbashi, Minato-ku, Tokyo 105-7201 **Tel:** 81 355738000
Email: kni@kyodonews.com **Web site:** http://www.kyodo.co.jp
Editor: Tomohide Okuno
Profile: Founded in 1945, Kyodo is based in Japan and has bureaus all over the world. It is a Japanese news agency independent of government, political and commercial interests. It provides a Japanese-language news service that is distributed to virtually all newspapers and broadcast networks in Japan, as well as English and Chinese language services that reach news agencies, newspapers, and radio and television broadcasters in various parts of the world.
Language (s): English
NEWS SERVICE/SYNDICATE

Kyodo News - Hong Kong Bureau 514553
Editorial: Kyodo News - Hong Kong Bureau., 9 Queen's Road C, Central District, Hong Kong
Tel: 852 25249750
Email: kyodohk@kyodonews.jp **Web site:** http://kyodonews.jp
Freq: Daily
Bureau Chief: Takahashi Shinsuke
Profile: covers political, financial, business and also Asian Culture
Language (s): English
NEWS SERVICE/SYNDICATE

Kyodo News - New Delhi Bureau 467647
Editorial: 201, Silver Arch Apartments, 22 Ferozshah Road, New Delhi 110001 **Tel:** 91 1141503738
Email: tanabe.hiroshi@kyodonews.jp **Web site:** http://home.kyodo.co.jp
Freq: Daily
Publisher: Tanabe Hiroshi
Language (s): Chinese
NEWS SERVICE/SYNDICATE

Kyodo News - Singapore Bureau 888191
Editorial: 8 Eu Tong Sen Street #14-88, The Central Singapore, Singapore 59818 **Tel:** 65 6223 3371
Bureau Chief: Toyoda Yukiko
Language (s): English
NEWS SERVICE/SYNDICATE

Kyodo Tsushin 467599
Editorial: Kyodo News, 18th Floor, Shiodome Media Tower, 1-7-1, Higashi-Shimbashi, Minato-ku, Tokyo 105-7201 **Tel:** 81 362 528101
Web site: http://www.kyodo.co.jp
Freq: Daily
News Director: Kunihiro Hashizume; **Editor:** Kiyoshi Nakagawa
Profile: Kyodo News is a portal site which reports the latest news, entertainments, sports, economics, and so on.
Language (s): English
NEWS SERVICE/SYNDICATE

Nihon Denpa News (NDN) 467603
Editorial: Nihon Denpa News, 3/F., Koike Building 1-5-10 Minamiazabu, Minato-ku, Tokyo 106-0032
Tel: 81 357 656810
Email: info@ndn-news.co.jp **Web site:** http://www.ndn-news.co.jp
Freq: Daily
Editor: Naoki Shima
Profile: Nihon Denpa News is a portal site which cover the latest news of Asian countries, Africa, Europe, the Americas, Iraq and Afghanistan and similar turbulent places.
Language (s): Japanese
NEWS SERVICE/SYNDICATE

NNA Asia - Sydney Bureau 313596
Editorial: 19 & 20, Level 5, 58 Pitt Street, Sydney NSW 2000 **Tel:** 61 2 92640998
Profile: Sydney bureau of the Japanese news agency, News Net Asia.
Language (s): Japanese
NEWS SERVICE/SYNDICATE

Sun Telephoto 467600
Editorial: 1-1-1, Hitotsubashi, Chiyoda-ku, Tokyo 100-0003 **Tel:** 81 332136771
Freq: Daily
Profile: Sun Telephoto is a photo source which deliver photos from Reuters. It also delivers the latest news photo from China and Hong Kong.
Language (s): Japanese
NEWS SERVICE/SYNDICATE

Jordan

Time Difference: GMT +2
National Telephone Code: 962
Continent: Asia
Capital: Amman

Newspapers

Ad-Dustour 159076
Owner: Jordan Press & Publishing Company
Editorial: PO Box 591, Addustour Building, Amman 11118 **Tel:** 962 6 560 8000
Email: dustour@addustour.com.jo **Web site:** http://www.addustour.com
Freq: Daily; **Circ:** 80000 Publisher's Statement
Head of News: Sultan Abdullah; **Editor In Chief:** Mohammed Al Tall; **Office Manager:** Louai Al Wehidi; **Advertising Manager:** Nibal Hindawi
Profile: Ad-Dustour is a daily Arabic newspaper covering national and international news, economics, politics, entertainment and sport. It was first published in 1967, and includes youth supplement Shabab on Wednesdays, and cultural supplement Al Thaqafi on Fridays.
Language (s): Arabic
Ad Rate: Full Page Mono 7.00
Ad Rate: Full Page Colour 10.00
Currency: Jordan Dinars
DAILY NEWSPAPER

Ahali 354397
Owner: Jordanian People's Democratic Party (Hashd)
Editorial: PO Box 9966, Building 116, Amman 11191
Tel: 962 6 562 1827
Email: ahali@go.com.jo **Web site:** http://www.hashd-ahali.org
Freq: Weekly; **Circ:** 5000 Publisher's Statement
Editor In Chief: Adnan Abu Khalifa; **News Editor:** Ahmad Abu Shawer; **Picture Editor:** Yousef Al Ghazawi; **Advertising Manager:** Khalil Al Sayyed
Profile: Ahali is the official newspaper of the The Jordanian People's Democratic Party (Hashd) and covers national and international news, current affairs, politics and business. The weekly newspaper launched in 1989 and is published on Thursdays.
Language (s): Arabic
Ad Rate: Full Page Mono 1597.00
Ad Rate: Full Page Colour 2211.00
Currency: Jordan Dinars
DAILY NEWSPAPER

Akhbar Alnas 491820
Owner: Akhbar Al Nas Newspaper
Editorial: PO Box 795, Princess Haya Street, Amman 11910 **Tel:** 962 6 535 0133
Email: khayyampress@orange.jo
Freq: Bi-Weekly; **Circ:** 6000 Publisher's Statement
Advertising Manager: Basil Hawamdah; **Editor in Chief:** Mamdouh Hawamdah
Profile: Akhbar Alnas (People's News) is a 16-page, fortnightly newspaper covering local and international news, sports and society. It launched in 2007 and is published on alternate Sundays.
Language (s): Arabic
DAILY NEWSPAPER

Alanbat 413471
Owner: Al Anbat Corporation For Media and Press
Editorial: PO Box 962556, Building 66, Al Jaheth Street, Amman 11196 **Tel:** 962 6 520 0100
Email: kazem_jag3@yahoo.com **Web site:** http://www.alanbatnews.net
Freq: Daily; **Circ:** 13000 Publisher's Statement
Photographer: Saad Al Awayesheh; **General Manager:** Hussein Al Jaghbeer; **Publisher & CEO:** Riyad Alhroob; **Editor In Chief:** Fares Shara'an
Profile: Alanbat is a daily Arabic newspaper covering local and international news, politics, business and sport. It launched in 2005.
Language (s): Arabic
DAILY NEWSPAPER

Asharq Al-Awsat - Amman office 383655
Owner: Saudi Research & Publishing Co.
Editorial: PO Box 616, Office 406, Building 118, Jad Center, Amman 11821 **Tel:** 962 6 551 7102
Email: jordan@srpc.com **Web site:** http://www.aawsat.com
Freq: Daily
News Editor: Mohammad Al Daameh; **Office Manager:** Ali Bilal
Profile: Amman bureau of Asharq Al-Awsat newspaper. The Amman office covers news, business and sport from Jordan for the London-based newspaper which is distributed across the Arab world.
Language (s): Arabic
DAILY NEWSPAPER

Assabeel 354396
Owner: Dar Assabeel for Press & Distribution
Editorial: PO Box 213545, Al Hussein Al Sharqi, Amman 11121 **Tel:** 962 6 569 2852
Email: assabeel@assabeel.net **Web site:** http://www.assabeel.net
Freq: Daily; **Circ:** 20000 Publisher's Statement
Advertising Manager: Ikramah Abdul Hameed; **News Editor:** Ayman Al-Fdeilat; **Editor-in-Chief:** Atef Jolani
Profile: Assabeel is a daily newspaper covering national and international news, current affairs, politics, business and sport. It was first published in 1993.
Language (s): Arabic
DAILY NEWSPAPER

Al Bayda 491678
Owner: Al Bayda Group
Editorial: 2nd Floor, Jabr Complex, Makkah Street, Amman **Tel:** 962 79 686 3461
Email: reemash81@yahoo.com
Freq: Weekly; **Circ:** 27000 Publisher's Statement
News Editor: Reema Al Sharbati
Profile: Al Bayda (The Desert) is a weekly newspaper covering local and international news, business and society. It launched in 2004 and is published on Sundays.
Language (s): Arabic
DAILY NEWSPAPER

Al Deyar 430652
Owner: Al Batraa Media Services
Editorial: PO Box 961239, Building 29, Amman 11196 **Tel:** 962 6 562 6588
Email: aldeyar2003@yahoo.com **Web site:** http://www.aldeyarjo.com
Freq: Daily; **Circ:** 15000 Publisher's Statement
Editor In Chief: Mohammad Salama; **Advertising Manager:** Rami Wishah
Profile: Al Deyar is an independent daily newspaper covering local and international news, business & economy, art & culture, food, health and sport. The newspaper launched as a weekly in 2003, and went daily in 2004.
Language (s): Arabic
DAILY NEWSPAPER

Al Ekhbarya 491818
Owner: Al Ekhbarya
Editorial: Islamic Bank Complex, Jabal Al Hussein, Amman **Tel:** 962 5 374 5433
Email: fayezajrashe@yahoo.com **Web site:** http://www.jordnews.com
Freq: Weekly; **Circ:** 50000 Publisher's Statement
PR Manager: Jalal Aghwat; **Editor in Chief:** Fayez Al Ajrashe; **General Manager:** Mohammad Al Ajrashe
Profile: Al Ekhbarya is a weekly newspaper covering national news, business and politics. It launched in 2006 and is published on Wednesdays.
Language (s): Arabic
DAILY NEWSPAPER

Al Ghad 350447
Owner: United Jordan Press Company
Editorial: PO Box 3535, 59 Zaal Abu Tayeh Street, Amman 11821 **Tel:** 962 6 554 4000
Email: editorial@alghad.jo **Web site:** http://www.alghad.com
Freq: Daily; **Circ:** 57000 Publisher's Statement
Profile: Al Ghad (Tomorrow) is a broadsheet-sized Arabic newspaper covering national and international news, current affairs, politics, business and sports. It launched in August 2004 and includes a monthly motoring supplement, Sayyarat Al-Ghad.
Language (s): Arabic
DAILY NEWSPAPER

Al Hayat Weekly 521046
Owner: Dar Al Hayat for Printing & Publishing
Editorial: PO Box 961457, Office 2, 1st Floor, Al Arab Al Youm Building, Amman 11196 **Tel:** 962 6 539 9955
Email: info@alhayatnews.com **Web site:** http://www.alhayatnews.com
Freq: Weekly; **Circ:** 50000
General Manager: Mohammad Daygham; **Editor In Chief:** Diya Khureisat; **Advertising Manager:** Mohammad Khureisat
Profile: Al Hayat Weekly is an Arabic newspaper covering national & international news, business, sports, women's issues and humanitarian issues. It launched in 2006 and is published on Thursdays.
Language (s): Arabic
DAILY NEWSPAPER

The Jordan Times 156807
Owner: Jordan Press Foundation
Editorial: PO Box 6710, Queen Rania Al Abdullah Street, Amman 11118 **Tel:** 962 6 560 0800 2392
Email: editor@jordantimes.com **Web site:** http://www.jordantimes.com
Freq: Daily; **Circ:** 24000 Publisher's Statement
Editor In Chief: Samir Barhoum
Profile: The Jordan Times is a newspaper covering national and international news, business, politics, culture and sport. The newspaper launched in 1975 and is published daily, except Saturdays.
Language (s): English
DAILY NEWSPAPER

Al Majd 351917
Owner: Al Majd Press
Editorial: PO Box 926856, 3rd Floor, Ata Building, Amman 11190 **Tel:** 962 6 553 0553
Email: almajd@almajd.net **Web site:** http://www.almajd.net
Freq: Weekly; **Circ:** 5000 Publisher's Statement
Advertising Manager: Ahed Al Rimawi; **Editor-in-Chief:** Fahd Al Rimawi; **Managing Director:** Mohammad Al Rimawi
Profile: Al Majd (The Glory) is a weekly newspaper focusing on current affairs and politics. It launched in 1994 and is published on Mondays.
Language (s): Arabic
DAILY NEWSPAPER

Al Mannarah - Jordan office 770698
Owner: South Press & Publishing Est.
Editorial: PO Box 963666, Sarh Al Shaheed Street, Amman 11196 **Tel:** 962 78 896 3694
Email: muwaffaq2005@yahoo.com
Freq: 2 Times/Week
Profile: Jordan office of Iraq-based Al Mannarah newspaper. The bureau covers news, politics, culture, business and sport from Jordan.
Language (s): Arabic
DAILY NEWSPAPER

Al Mashhad 521702
Owner: Al Mashhad for Publishing & Distribution
Editorial: Building 7, Khalda, Amman
Tel: 962 6 539 9056
Email: hanni0789@yahoo.com
Freq: Weekly; **Circ:** 35000 Publisher's Statement
Owner & General Manager: Tarek Bani Amer; **News Editor:** Hani Shboul
Profile: Al Mashhad (The Spectacle) is a weekly newspaper covering news, politics, culture, health, business and sport. It launched in 2006 and is published on Sundays.
Language (s): Arabic
Ad Rate: Full Page Colour 2200.00
Currency: Jordan Dinars
DAILY NEWSPAPER

Al Mira'a 673500
Owner: Gerasa News
Editorial: PO Box 928404, Shaheed Wasf El Tal Street, Amman 11110 **Tel:** 962 6 567 5725
Email: info@gerasanews.com
Freq: Weekly; **Circ:** 30000 Publisher's Statement
Publisher & General Manager: Jamal Al Muhtasab; **Editor in Chief:** Mohammed Al Muhtasab
Profile: Al Mira'a (The Mirror) is a weekly newspaper covering politics, business, sport and culture. It launched in 1985 and is published on Mondays.
Language (s): Arabic
DAILY NEWSPAPER

Al Mowajaha 491817
Owner: Al Mowajaha Media & Publishing
Editorial: PO Box 940337, 4th Floor, Building 33, Sultan Center, Amman 11194 **Tel:** 962 6 586 6279
Email: shahenko2001@hotmail.com
Freq: Weekly; **Circ:** 32000 Publisher's Statement
News Editor: Younes Aatiti; **Editor In Chief:** Bassam Al Yassine; **News Editor:** Fadl Sawaeer
Profile: Al Mowajaha is a weekly Arabic newspaper covering international and national news, society, business, sports and politics. It launched in 2007 and is published on Wednesdays.
Language (s): Arabic
Ad Rate: Full Page Colour 600.00
Currency: Jordan Dinars
DAILY NEWSPAPER

Al Rai 156805
Owner: Jordan Press Foundation
Editorial: PO Box 6710, Queen Rania Al Abdullah Street, Amman 11118 **Tel:** 962 6 560 0800
Email: ce@alrai.com **Web site:** http://www.alrai.com
Freq: Daily; **Circ:** 65000 Publisher's Statement
News Editor: Tayel Al Damin; **Head of News:** Ziyad Al Rabaei; **Picture Editor:** Abdullah Ayoub; **General Manager:** Fareed Selwani
Profile: Al Rai (The Opinion) is an Arabic daily newspaper covering local and international news, finance, politics, culture and sport. It was first published in 1971.
Language (s): Arabic
DAILY NEWSPAPER

Al Shahed 491815
Owner: Al Namozajiyah Press
Editorial: PO Box 922859, Next to Comodore Hotel, Amman 11196 **Tel:** 962 6 565 6433
Email: nalsyeed2008@hotmail.com **Web site:** http://www.alshahidonline.net
Freq: Weekly; **Circ:** 18000 Publisher's Statement
News Editor: Abdulla Al Adem; **Editor In Chief:** Nazeera Al Said
Profile: Al Shahed (The Witness) is a weekly Arabic newspaper covering national and international news, politics, sports and society. It was first published in 2000 and is issued on Wednesdays.
Language (s): Arabic
DAILY NEWSPAPER

Al Watan Al Eqtisadi 491719
Owner: Olayan Publishing
Editorial: PO Box 622, Queen Rania Abdulla Street, Amman 11941 **Tel:** 962 6 535 6606
Email: watan.newspaper99@gmail.com **Web site:** http://www.anbaalwatan.com
Freq: Weekly; **Circ:** 25000 Publisher's Statement
Public Relations Manager: Dana Al Ramahi; **Editor In Chief:** Reda Elayyan
Profile: Al Watan Al Eqtisadi is a weekly newspaper covering economics, tourism, investment and business. The newspaper launched in 1997 and is aimed at business executives in Jordan. It is published on Wednesdays.
Language (s): Arabic
Ad Rate: Full Page Mono 1000.00
Ad Rate: Full Page Colour 2000.00
Currency: Jordan Dinars
DAILY NEWSPAPER

News Service/Syndicate

Agence France-Presse - Amman Bureau 370524
Owner: Agence France-Presse
Editorial: PO Box 3340, 22, Ibrahim El Mouelhi Street, Amman 11181 **Tel:** 962 6 464 4978
Email: afp.amman@afp.com **Web site:** http://www.afp.com
Bureau Chief: Imed Lamloum; **Office Manager:** Rebecca Seleme
Profile: Amman bureau of international news agency supplying news - text, graphics, video and pictures - to subscribers around the world.
Language (s): Arabic
NEWS SERVICE/SYNDICATE

APTN Jordan 370510
Owner: Associated Press
Editorial: PO Box 840742, 2nd Floor, Building 46, Amman 11181 **Tel:** 962 6 569 9396
Email: aptn_mes@yahoo.com **Web site:** http://www.aptn.com
Bureau Chief: Mahmoud Naghawi; **News Producer:** Ahed Rabab'a
Profile: Associated Press Television News (APTN) is the international television arm of the Associated Press - APTN's operations include a main news service, specialised broadcast services, customised coverage for the Middle East, a productions division, weekly and daily entertainment news and an extensive video archive library.
Language (s): Arabic
NEWS SERVICE/SYNDICATE

Associated Press - Amman Bureau 370526
Owner: Associated Press
Editorial: PO Box 35111, Office 1, Floor 3, Insurance Building, Amman 11180 **Tel:** 962 6 461 4660
Email: apamman@ap.org **Web site:** http://www.ap.org
Bureau Chief: Karin Laub
Profile: International wire agency - Amman bureau covers Jordan.
Language (s): English
NEWS SERVICE/SYNDICATE

Jordan News Agency 380842
Owner: Jordan News Agency
Editorial: PO Box 6845, Al-Dakhleyeh Circle, Amman 11118 **Tel:** 962 6 560 9700
Email: petra@petra.gov.jo **Web site:** http://www.petra.gov.jo
Editor: Mohamed Abu Oulba; **General Manager:** Faisal Alshboul; **Editor:** Feras Qutaitan
Profile: Jordan News Agency, also known as Petra News Agency, is the official news agency of Jordan. It was founded in 1969 and covers royal and government news, as well as matters of national importance.
Language (s): Arabic
NEWS SERVICE/SYNDICATE

Reuters - Amman Bureau 491400
Owner: Thomson Reuters
Editorial: PO Box 667, Building 1, Amman 11118
Tel: 962 6 465 7937
Email: suleiman.al-khalidi@thomsonreuters.com **Web site:** http://www.reuters.com
Photographer: Mohammad Abu Qutay
Profile: Amman bureau of international news and picture agency.
Language (s): Arabic
NEWS SERVICE/SYNDICATE

Reuters TV - Amman Bureau 370509
Owner: Thomson Reuters
Editorial: PO Box 667, Building 1, Amman 11118
Tel: 962 6 465 7937
Email: suleiman.al-khalidi@thomsonreuters.com **Web site:** http://www.thomsonreuters.com
Producer: Mohammad Al-Ramahi; **Producer:** Bushra Shakhshir
Profile: Amman bureau of Reuters TV, which provides television broadcasters and internet providers worldwide with international news video, including breaking news stories, human interest items, sport, business and entertainment news.
Language (s): Arabic
NEWS SERVICE/SYNDICATE

Kazakhstan

Time Difference: GMT +5 to +6
National Telephone Code: 7
Continent: Asia
Capital: Astana

Newspapers

Biznes i vlast 484000
Owner: Isker Media
Editorial: ul. Djandosova 2, Almaty 50057
Tel: 7 727 3527388
Email: and@and.kz **Web site:** http://www.and.kz
Freq: Weekly; **Circ:** 8000 Not Audited
Editor In Chief: Oleg Khe
Profile: A business and financial weekly paper with 4 supplements.
Language (s): Russian
DAILY NEWSPAPER

Caravan 229874
Owner: Alma Media
Editorial: Ploshad Respubliki 13, Almaty 50013
Tel: 7 727 258-36-00
Email: info@caravan.kz **Web site:** http://www.caravan.kz
Circ: 220000 Publisher's Statement
News Editor: Alexandra Myskina
Profile: Newspaper focusing on national and international news, politics, economics, culture and sport.
Language (s): Russian
Ad Rate: Full Page Mono 968000.00
Ad Rate: Full Page Colour 968000.00
Currency: Kazakhstan Tenge
DAILY NEWSPAPER

Express K 476047
Owner: TOO Express K
Editorial: Kabantai batyry 30a, Almaty 10000
Tel: 7 717 259242
Email: daily@express-k.kz **Web site:** http://www.express-k.kz
Freq: Daily; **Circ:** 25000 Publisher's Statement
Editor In Chief: Tlepbergen Bekmaganbetov
Profile: A daily newspaper covering news on politics, society, social issues and sports.
Language (s): Russian
Ad Rate: Full Page Mono 6000.00
Ad Rate: Full Page Colour 7000.00
Currency: United States Dollars
DAILY NEWSPAPER

Kazakhstanskaya Pravda 218490
Editorial: pr. Pobyedy 18, Astana 473000
Tel: 7 7172 44-53-55
Email: astana@kazpravda.kz **Web site:** http://www.kazpravda.kz
Freq: Daily; **Circ:** 100485 Publisher's Statement
Profile: Newspaper focusing on politics, economics, culture, society, sport and general news.
Language (s): Russian
Ad Rate: Full Page Mono 1400000.00
Currency: Kazakhstan Tenge
DAILY NEWSPAPER

Kursiv 537327
Editorial: pl. Respubliki 15, office 152, Almaty
Tel: 7 727 25 01 384
Email: kursiv@kursiv.kz **Web site:** http://www.kursiv.kz
Freq: Weekly; **Circ:** 28500 Not Audited
Editor: Elena Britskaya; **Editor-in-Chief:** Irina Dorokhova
Profile: National newspaper on finance and banking, financial markets, politics and economics.
Language (s): Russian
DAILY NEWSPAPER

Panorama 476234
Owner: TOO Gazeta Panorama
Editorial: Pl. Respubliki 15, 6 Floor, office 647, 658, 659, 665, Almaty 50013 **Tel:** 7 727 27 21 632
Email: panadv@intelsoft.kz **Web site:** http://www.panoramakz.com
Freq: Weekly; **Circ:** 12500 Publisher's Statement
Editor-in-Chief: Lera Tsoy
Profile: Business weekly specializing in serious analytical information on politics, economics, business and international relations.
Language (s): Russian
DAILY NEWSPAPER

Vremya 529320
Editorial: pr. Raiymbeka 117, office 107, Almaty
Tel: 7 727 258-10-04
Email: info@time.kz **Web site:** http://www.time.kz
Freq: Daily; **Circ:** 30000
Editor-in-Chief: Lev Tarakov
Profile: Daily political newspaper covering general and economic news and events in Kazakhstan.
Language (s): Russian
DAILY NEWSPAPER

Community Newspaper

Megapolis 484069
Owner: Mediaholding 31 Kanal
Editorial: Ul. Tazhibayevoy 155, Almaty 50060
Tel: 7 727 25 00 987
Email: info@megapolis.kz **Web site:** http://www.megapolis.kz
Freq: Weekly; **Circ:** 10000
Director General: Rinat Askarov; **Editor In Chief:** Igor Shakhnovich
Profile: National social and political weekly newspaper.
Language (s): Russian
COMMUNITY NEWSPAPER

Novoye Pokolenye 476227
Editorial: Ul. Bogenbai batyra 156a, office 1-2, Almaty 50098 **Tel:** 7 727 26 13 106
Email: np@np.kz **Web site:** http://www.np.kz
Circ: 35000
Editor In Chief: Sergey Aparin
Profile: Covers political, economical, social and cultural aspects of life of modern Kazakhstan.
Language (s): Russian
COMMUNITY NEWSPAPER

Vecherny Almaty 553676
Editorial: pr. Abylai Khana 2, Almaty 50016
Tel: 7 727 2792890
Email: info@vecher.kz **Web site:** http://www.vecher.kz
Freq: 2 Times/Week; **Circ:** 12000 Publisher's Statement
Editor-in-Chief: Nikolai Zhorov
Profile: Evening city newspaper covering social, cultural events and entertainment.
Language (s): Russian
COMMUNITY NEWSPAPER

Kenya

Time Difference: GMT +3
National Telephone Code: 254
Continent: Africa
Capital: Nairobi

Newspapers

Coastweek 230968
Owner: Coastweek Newspapers Ltd
Editorial: Nkrumah Road / Mwenye Aboud Rd, Oriental Building, 2nd Floor, Mombasa
Tel: 254 41 2230130
Email: info@coastweek.com **Web site:** http://www.coastweek.com
Freq: Weekly; **Circ:** 12000 Publisher's Statement
Editor: Gulshan Jivraj
Profile: Newspaper covering local and national news including politics, economics, entertainment, culture and sports.
Language (s): English
DAILY NEWSPAPER

The Daily Nation 156631
Owner: Nation Media Group Limited
Editorial: Nation Centre, Kimathi Street, Nairobi
Tel: 254 20 3288000
Email: newsdesk@ke.nationmedia.com **Web site:** http://www.nation.co.ke
Freq: Daily; **Circ:** 220000 Publisher's Statement
Profile: Newspaper covering national and international news including politics, business, economics, opinion, culture and sport.
Language (s): English
Ad Rate: Full Page Mono 192765.00
Ad Rate: Full Page Colour 256765.00
Currency: Kenya Shillings
DAILY NEWSPAPER

The East African 224429
Owner: Nation Media Group Limited
Editorial: Nation Centre, Kimithi Street, Nairobi 100
Tel: 254 20 328 8020
Email: eastafrican@ke.nationmedia.com **Web site:** http://www.theeastafrican.co.ke
Freq: Weekly; **Circ:** 35000 Publisher's Statement
Profile: Newspaper covering news and current affairs including features, stories and in-depth analysis from each country in the region, in addition to international stories, business news and opinion. Distributed in Kenya and the other countries of the African Great Lakes region, including Tanzania, Uganda and Rwanda.
Language (s): English
Ad Rate: Full Page Mono 169560.00
Ad Rate: Full Page Colour 217560.00
Currency: Kenya Shillings
DAILY NEWSPAPER

The Standard 156759
Owner: The Standard Group Limited
Editorial: Mombasa Rd, Nairobi 100
Tel: 254 20 32 22 111
Email: online@standardmedia.co.ke **Web site:** http://www.standardmedia.co.ke

Kenya

Freq: Daily; **Circ:** 60000 Publisher's Statement
Profile: Newspaper covering national and international news and current affairs including business, politics, economics, sports and entertainment.
Language (s): English
Ad Rate: Full Page Mono 169560.00
Ad Rate: Full Page Colour 217560.00
Currency: Kenya Shillings
DAILY NEWSPAPER

The Star Kenya 842000
Owner: Radio Africa Group
Editorial: Lion Place, 2nd Floor, Waiyaki Way, Nairobi **Tel:** 254 20 4244000
Email: letters@the-star.co.ke **Web site:** http://www.the-star.co.ke
Freq: Daily; **Circ:** 20000
Editor: Charles Kerich
Profile: National newspaper covering regional and national news and current affairs including business, economics, opinion, sports, lifestyle and society. It was launched in July 2007 as the Nairobi Star, a 32 page tabloid style newspaper concentrating on human interest stories in Nairobi and Kenya.
Language (s): English
Ad Rate: Full Page Colour 453600.00
Currency: Kenya Shillings
DAILY NEWSPAPER

Taifa Leo 875807
Owner: Nation Media Group
Editorial: Nation Centre, Kimathi Street, Nairobi 100 **Tel:** 254 20 3288000
Email: swahilihub@ke.nationmedia.com **Web site:** http://www.swahilihub.com
Freq: Daily
News Editor: Gilbert Mogire
Profile: Daily newspaper in Kenya, published in Swahili language, reporting on national and regional news, politics, economics, sports and entertainment.
Language (s): Swahili
DAILY NEWSPAPER

Community Newspaper

Kass Weekly 875799
Owner: Kass Media Group
Editorial: APA Acarde, 2nd flr, room 24, Floor 138, Nairobi 200 **Tel:** 254 20 28 75 220
Email: marketing@kassfm.co.ke **Web site:** http://kassweekly.co.ke/KW
Freq: Weekly; **Circ:** 20000
Profile: Publication covering news, politics, business, economics, education, tourism, sports, politics, history and culture.
Language (s): English
COMMUNITY NEWSPAPER

Kiribati

Time Difference: GMT +12, GMT +13, GMT +14
National Telephone Code: 686
Continent: Oceania
Capital: Tarawa

Community Newspaper

Kiribati Newstar 538731
Editorial: PO Box 10, Bairiki, Kiribati **Tel:** 686 21652
Freq: Weekly
Profile: Independent weekly newspaper published every Friday and distributed throughout country to many different islands.
Language (s): English
COMMUNITY NEWSPAPER

Te Uekera 538732
Owner: Broadcasting & Publications Authority
Editorial: Te Uekera Printing Services, PO Box 78, Bairiki, Kiribati **Tel:** 686 21162
Freq: Weekly; **Circ:** 3000 Publisher's Statement
Editor: Tearinibeia Eno Teabo
Profile: State-owned weekly covering national news.
Language (s): English
COMMUNITY NEWSPAPER

Korea (South)

Time Difference: GMT +9
National Telephone Code: 82
Continent: Asia
Capital: Seoul

Newspapers

AM 7 460173
Editorial: Munhwa Ilbo, Munhwa Ilbosa, 68 Chungjeongno 1-ga, Seoul 100-723
Tel: 82 2 37015960
Email: am7@munhwa.co.kr **Web site:** http://www.am7.co.kr
Freq: Daily; **Circ:** 600009 Not Audited
Publisher: Byung-Kyu Lee; **Editor in Chief:** Seung-Hun Oh
Profile: Provides news on sports, economy, business, lifestyle, celebrities, etc.
Language (s): Korean
DAILY NEWSPAPER

Asahi Shimbun - Seoul Bureau 460272
Editorial: Asahi Shimbun, 9/F Dong-A Media Center, 139 Sejongno, Jongno-gu, Seoul 110-015
Tel: 82 23 139865
Web site: http://www.asahi.com
Freq: Daily
Bureau Chief: Tetsuya Hakoda
Profile: Covers information for Japanese news readers, both nationally and internationally.
Language (s): Japanese
DAILY NEWSPAPER

Asia Economy 459699
Editorial: 10-11 Floor, Asia Media Tower, Cho-dong, Jung-gu, Seoul 150-890 **Tel:** 82 2 22002114
Email: rlgh9586@asiae.co.kr **Web site:** http://www.asiae.co.kr
Freq: Daily; **Circ:** 100008 Not Audited
News Director: Young-Hoon Cho; **Editor:** Sook-Hye Hwang; **Editor:** Kyung-Tap Lee; **Editor:** Kyu-Sung Lee; **News Director:** Sung-Cheol Oh
Profile: Provides news on finance, economics, real estate, stock market, investment, etc.
Language (s): Korean
Ad Rate: Full Page Mono 100000.00
Currency: South Korea Won
DAILY NEWSPAPER

Busan Ilbo 459721
Editorial: Busan Ilbosa, 1-10, Sujeong-dong, Dong-gu, Busan 601-738 **Tel:** 82 51 4614114
Web site: http://www.busan.com
Freq: Daily; **Circ:** 189019 Not Audited
Editor: Byung-Kil Ahn; **Editor:** Bong-Ijn Choi; **News Director:** Sang-Seop Jeong; **Publisher:** Jong-Ryol Kim
Profile: Provides news on business, sports, entertainment, technology, current issues, etc.
Language (s): Korean
Ad Rate: Full Page Colour 17982000.00
Currency: South Korea Won
DAILY NEWSPAPER

Chosun Ilbo 156993
Editorial: Chosun Ilbosa, 61 Taepyeongro 1-ga, Jung-gu, Seoul 100-756 **Tel:** 82 2 7245114
Email: webmaster@chosun.com **Web site:** http://www.chosun.com
Freq: Daily; **Circ:** 2400009 Not Audited
Publisher: Sang-Hun Bang; **Editor:** Yong Shik Byeon; **Editor:** Heup Choi; **Editor:** Cheol-Joong Kim; **Editor:** Chul-Min Lee; **News Director:** Jeong-Hoon Park
Profile: Provides news on current issues of politics, economy, finance, sports, entertainment, etc.
Language (s): Korean
DAILY NEWSPAPER

Chosun Ilbo - United Nations Bureau 504158
Editorial: 405 E 42nd St, United Nations Rm 453-A, New York, New York 10317-3507 **Tel:** 1 212 963-8921
Web site: http://www.chosun.com
Profile: Chosun Ilbo, established in 1920, first started to promote the freedom of speech in Korea. Standing for justice, building culture, industrial development and impartiality wavering soul, as a paper that "says what needs to be said". The praise given the Chosun Ilbo - accurate, fair and NO.1 - have not changed, either.
Language (s): Korean
DAILY NEWSPAPER

Chungbuk Ilbo 460343
Editorial: Chungbuk Media Co., Limited., 4/F Hyunjeong Building, 2868, Cheongju 361-300
Tel: 82 43 2772114
Web site: http://inews365.com
Freq: Daily
Publisher: Sang-Hun Lee
Profile: Provides news on current issues and local news in Chungbuk province.
Language (s): Korean
DAILY NEWSPAPER

Chungcheong Maeil 460200
Editorial: Chungcheong Daily Newspaper, 962 Uncheon-dong, Heungdeok-gu, Cheongju 361-842
Tel: 82 43 2775555
Email: okok916@ccdn.co.kr **Web site:** http://www.ccdn.co.kr
Freq: Daily
Publisher: Ju-Yeon Byun; **Editor:** Woo-Seok Ham; **Editor:** Byung-Gap Jang; **News Director:** Ho-Sang Lee
Profile: Provides news on current issues.
Language (s): Korean
DAILY NEWSPAPER

Chungcheong Times 460338
Editorial: 8/F, Inseung Building, Garosu-gil, 80 Heungdeok-gu, Cheongju-sil, Cheongju 361-270
Tel: 82 43 2795000
Email: webmaster@ccilbo.com **Web site:** http://www.ccilbo.com
Freq: Daily
Editor: In-Seop Han; **Editor:** Woon-Ki Kim; **Editor:** Sang-Hoon Lee; **Editor in Chief:** Baek-Su Lim; **News Director:** Kyung-Hoon Nam; **President & Publisher:** Jae-Gyu Park
Profile: Provides news on current issues.
Language (s): Korean
DAILY NEWSPAPER

ChungCheong Today 459865
Editorial: Chungcheong Today, Dunwon 1-gil, 50 Galma 1-dong, Seo-gu, Daejeon 302-172
Tel: 82 42 3807101
Email: cctoday@cctoday.co.kr **Web site:** http://www.cctoday.co.kr
Freq: Daily
Editor: In-Seok Choi; **Publisher:** Nam-Jin Jeong; **News Director:** Hyun-Jin Kim; **News Director:** Jang-Sik Kim; **Editor:** Won-Seop Lee
Profile: Provides news on current issues.
Language (s): Korean
DAILY NEWSPAPER

The City 475995
Editorial: City Media, Inc., 3F, Gusegun Building., Seoul 110-061 **Tel:** 82 2 20132095
Email: webmaster@clubcity.kr **Web site:** http://clubcity.kr
Freq: Daily; **Circ:** 400008 Not Audited
Publisher: Choong-Yeon Cho
Profile: Provides news on current issues, politics, economy, government, society, entertainment and sports.
Language (s): Korean
DAILY NEWSPAPER

Daegu Ilbo 459298
Editorial: Daegu Ilbo, 177-10, Beome 2-dong, Suseong-gu, Daegu 706-820 **Tel:** 82 53 7575700
Email: admin@mail.idaegu.com **Web site:** http://www.idaegu.com
Freq: Daily; **Circ:** 87009 Not Audited
News Director: Jong-Yeop Kim; **President & Publisher:** Tae-Yeol Lee; **News Director:** Jeong-Hwa Moon
Profile: Provides news on current issues.
Language (s): Korean
DAILY NEWSPAPER

Daegu Shinmun 459729
Editorial: The Daegu Newspaper, 283-8 Sincheon 3-dong, Dong-gu, Daegu 701-823 **Tel:** 82 53 4240004
Email: webmaster@idaegu.co.kr **Web site:** http://www.idaegu.co.kr
Freq: Daily; **Circ:** 118008 Not Audited
News Director: Sang-Seop Kim; **Publisher:** Deok-Chi Lim
Profile: Provides local news and current affairs that are happening in Daegu.
Language (s): Korean
DAILY NEWSPAPER

Daejon Ilbo 459867
Editorial: Daejonilbosa, 1-135, Munhwa-dong, Jung-gu, Daejeon 301-715 **Tel:** 82 42 2513311
Email: ibiz@daejonilbo.com **Web site:** http://www.daejonilbo.com
Freq: Daily; **Circ:** 200008 Not Audited
Editor in Chief: Jae-Sook Gu; **Bureau Chief:** Jae-Keun Kim; **Editor:** Yong-Kyu Ryu; **Publisher:** Sue-Yong Shin
Profile: Provides news on current issues.
Language (s): Korean
DAILY NEWSPAPER

Daily e-Logistics Times 459748
Editorial: Korea Logistics News Co., Limited., 3/F, Sungsan Building, Seoul 121-876 **Tel:** 82 2 7495445
Web site: http://www.klnews.co.kr
Freq: Daily; **Circ:** 28008 Not Audited
Publisher: Dae-Yong Jang
Profile: Provides news on trading on both local and international levels.
Language (s): Korean
DAILY NEWSPAPER

The Daily Focus 460174
Editorial: 3/F, Solbone Building, 1549-7 Seocho-dong, Seocho-gu, Seoul 137-070 **Tel:** 82 2 5802900
Web site: http://focus.fnn.co.kr
Freq: Daily; **Circ:** 662352 Not Audited
Publisher: Hye-Sook Lee
Profile: Provides news on advertising and printing.
Language (s): Korean
DAILY NEWSPAPER

Digital Times 459709
Editorial: Digital Times, 8/F, Munhwa Ilbo Building, 68, Seoul 100-723 **Tel:** 82 2 37015500
Email: report@dt.co.kr **Web site:** http://www.dt.co.kr
Freq: Daily; **Circ:** 120008 Not Audited
Editor: Myung-Ho Hong; **Editor:** Wook-Won Kim; **Director:** Jae-Kwon Park; **Editor:** Nak-Young Seo; **Editor:** Won-Jun Song
Profile: Provides news mainly on technology, business, economy, communications, culture, social issues, etc.
Language (s): Korean
Ad Rate: Full Page Mono 22200000.00
Currency: South Korea Won
DAILY NEWSPAPER

Dong-A Ilbo 157003
Editorial: The Dong-A Ilbo, 139 Sejongno, Jongno-gu, Seoul 110-715 **Tel:** 82 2 20201310
Web site: http://www.donga.com
Freq: Daily; **Circ:** 2000007 Not Audited
Editor in Chief: Kyou Chul Choi; **Editor:** Young-Hoon Choi; **Publisher:** Il-Heung Kim; **President:** Jae-Ho Kim; **Director:** Sang-Young Kim; **News Director:** Soon-Hwal Kwon; **Editor:** Kang-Woon Lee
Profile: Provides news on current issues.
Language (s): Korean
Ad Rate: Full Page Colour 66600000.00
Currency: South Korea Won
DAILY NEWSPAPER

Dongyang Ilbo 459733
Editorial: Dongyang Ilbo, Dongyang Daily News Building, Cheongju 360-716 **Tel:** 82 43 2187337
Email: webmaster@dynews.co.kr **Web site:** http://www.dynews.co.kr
Freq: Daily; **Circ:** 93009 Not Audited
Publisher: Seong-Hoon Cho; **Editor in Chief:** Dong-Seok Kim
Profile: Provides news about current issues.
Language (s): Korean
DAILY NEWSPAPER

Eorinyi Dong-A 459713
Editorial: Donga Ilbosa, Dong-A Media Centre, Seoul 110-715 **Tel:** 82 2 20201390
Email: kidsroom@donga.com **Web site:** http://kids.donga.com
Freq: Daily
Editor: Hyuk-Joong Choi; **Editor in Chief:** Ho-Pyo Hong; **Publisher:** Hak-Jun Kim
Profile: Provides academic information for children.
Language (s): Korean
DAILY NEWSPAPER

Financial News 331624
Editorial: The Financial News, 6, 7/F Financial News Building, Seoul 150-877 **Tel:** 82 2 20037114
Web site: http://www.fnnews.com
Freq: Daily; **Circ:** 100008 Not Audited
President & Publisher: Jae-Ho Jeon; **Editor:** Hoon-Sik Jeong; **Editor in Chief:** Min-Ku Kang; **Editor:** Jang-Gyu Lee; **Editor:** Jong-Taek Lee; **Editor:** Jung-Hyo Lim; **Editor:** Kye-Shin Song; **Editor:** Lee Won-du; **Editor in Chief:** Lee Yong-kyu
Profile: Provides news on current issues, finance, and real estate.
Language (s): Korean
DAILY NEWSPAPER

Gwangju Dream 489575
Editorial: GJDream.Korea Corp, 4/F Jutaek Hoigwan, 501-15, Gwangju 500-060 **Tel:** 82 62 5208000
Email: webmaster@gjdream.com **Web site:** http://www.gjdream.com
Freq: Daily
President: Tae-Hyung Jeong; **Editor in Chief:** Jeong-Hee Lim; **Director:** Woo-Ki Park
Profile: Provides the latest news on government, culture, social issues, celebrities, etc.
Language (s): Korean
DAILY NEWSPAPER

Gwangnam Ilbo 459743
Editorial: The Gwangnamilbo Co., Limited., 986-12, Ssangchon-dong, Seo-gu, Gwangju 502-260
Tel: 82 62 3702300
Email: webmaster@gwangnam.co.kr **Web site:** http://www.gwangnam.co.kr
Freq: Daily; **Circ:** 67008 Not Audited
Publisher: Haeng-Hwan Park; **Editor in Chief:** Sang-Woo Seo
Profile: Provides news on current issues including business, sports, entertainment, technology, etc.
Language (s): Korean
DAILY NEWSPAPER

Gyeongnam Ilbo 459725
Editorial: Gyeongnam Domin Ilbo Co., Limited., 151-25, Yangdeok 2-dong, Masan 630-811
Tel: 82 55 2500141
Web site: http://www.idomin.com
Freq: Daily; **Circ:** 75008 Not Audited
Publisher: Jung-Do Huh; **News Director:** Woo-Young Jeong
Profile: Provides news on business, sports, entertainment, technology, social issues, etc.
Language (s): Korean
DAILY NEWSPAPER

Halla Ilbo 459862
Editorial: The Hallailbo, 568-1, Samdo 1-dong, Jeju 690-711 **Tel:** 82 64 7502214
Email: webmaster@hallailbo.co.kr **Web site:** http://www.hallailbo.co.kr
Freq: Daily
President & Publisher: Man-Saeng Kang; **Editor in Chief:** Byung-Jun Kim; **Editor:** Chi-Hoon Kim; **Editor:** Tae-Hyun Oh; **Editor:** Bo-Seok Yoon
Profile: Provides news on current issues.
Language (s): Korean
DAILY NEWSPAPER

Hankook Ilbo 459689
Owner: Hankook Ilbo Co., Limited
Editorial: 15/F, Hanjin Bldg, 118 Namdaemunno 2-ga, Jung-gu, Seoul 100-770 **Tel:** 82 2 7242114
Email: webmaster@hankooki.com **Web site:** http://www.hankooki.com
Freq: Daily; **Circ:** 2121540 Not Audited
News Director: Jae-Woo Cho; **Editor:** Jong-Oh Ha; **Editor:** Kwang-Duck Kim; **Editor:** Tae-Sung Ko; **President & Publisher:** Jong-Seung Lee; **News Director:** Sung-Chul Lee
Profile: Provides news on current issues.
Language (s): Korean
DAILY NEWSPAPER

Hankyoreh Shinmun 459690
Editorial: The Hankyoreh, 116-25, Gongdeok 1-dong, Mapo-gu, Seoul 121-750 **Tel:** 82 2 7100114
Web site: http://www.hani.co.kr
Freq: Daily; **Circ:** 1500007 Not Audited
Editor: Seung-Dong Han; **Editor in Chief:** In-Hyun Kim; **President:** Kwang-Heon Ko; **Director:** No-Pil Kwak; **Publisher:** Hyung-Su Seo
Profile: Provides news on current issues including politics, economy, government and social issues.
Language (s): Korean
Ad Rate: Full Page Mono 38850000.00
Currency: South Korea Won
DAILY NEWSPAPER

Hankyung/Hankuk Kyungje (Korea Economic Daily) 160788
Editorial: Hankook Kyungje Shinmunsa Building, 441 Jungnim-dong, Jung-gu, Seoul 100-791
Tel: 82 2 3604114
Email: heeju@hankyung.net **Web site:** http://www.hankyung.com
Freq: Daily; **Circ:** 1000008 Not Audited
Editor: Kim Gi-ung; **Editor in Chief:** Young-Min Jeong; **Editor:** Hong-Jo Kim; **News Director:** Hyung-Bae Kim; **Editor:** Jeong-Ho Kim; **Editor:** Kwang-Cheol Ko; **Editor:** Jeong-Hwan Lee; **Editor:** Hee-Soo Moon; **Editor:** Ki-Seol Yun
Profile: Provides news on current issues, economy, politics, government and business.
Language (s): Korean
Ad Rate: Full Page Mono 44400000.00
Currency: South Korea Won
DAILY NEWSPAPER

Herald Business 459701
Editorial: Herald Media Inc., 3~5/F, 1-17 Jeong-dong, Jung-gu, Seoul 100-120 **Tel:** 82 2 7270114
Email: webeditor@heraldcorp.com **Web site:** http://www.heraldbiz.com
Freq: Daily; **Circ:** 700009 Not Audited
News Director: Young-Hoon Ham; **Editor:** Hae-Chang Hwang; **Editor:** Hwa-Kyun Kim; **News Director:** Choong-Won Kwon; **Editor in Chief:** Beom-Rok Lee; **News Director:** Hae-Jun Lee; **Publisher:** Hang-Hwan Park
Profile: Provides news on current issues, politics, economy and entertainment.
Language (s): Korean
DAILY NEWSPAPER

Hwankyung Kunsul Ilbo 459774
Editorial: Hwankyung Kunsul Ilbo Co., Limited., 43 Seogye-dong, Yongsan-gu, Seoul 140-827
Tel: 82 2 7355558
Email: master@hwankyungdaily.com **Web site:** http://www.hwankyungdaily.com
Freq: Daily; **Circ:** 90008 Not Audited
Publisher: Yong-Hee Cho
Profile: Provides news on social and economic changes.
Language (s): Korean
DAILY NEWSPAPER

Ilgan Sports 459703
Editorial: Joongang Entertainment and Sports Inc., 16/, Korea Economic Daily News Building., Seoul 100-791 **Tel:** 82 2 63631334
Web site: http://isplus.joinsmsn.com
Freq: Daily; **Circ:** 614197 Not Audited
Editor in Chief: Jun-Won Park; **Editor:** Tae-Hoon Park
Profile: Provides news in sports, leisure, entertainment, etc.
Language (s): Korean
DAILY NEWSPAPER

Incheon Ilbo 459714
Editorial: Incheon Ilbo Co., Limted., 222 Joongbongno, Incheon 400-750 **Tel:** 82 32 4520114
Email: webmaster@itimes.co.kr **Web site:** http://news.itimes.co.kr
Freq: Daily
News Director: Jong-Hwan Baek; **Editor:** Tae-Hyun Cho; **Publisher:** Sa-In Jang
Profile: Provides news on the current issues that happens in Incheon, South Korea.
Language (s): Korean
DAILY NEWSPAPER

Jeju Ilbo 459860
Editorial: Jeju Ilbo, 2324-6, Yeon-dong, Jeju 690-713
Tel: 82 64 7406114
Email: ksn@jejunews.com **Web site:** http://www.jejunews.com
Freq: Daily; **Circ:** 60008 Not Audited
Publisher: Dae-Seong Kim
Profile: Provides news on current issues.
Language (s): Korean
DAILY NEWSPAPER

Jeju Times 489576
Editorial: Jeju Times, 1473-1 Ora-dong, Jeju-si, Jeju 690-160 **Tel:** 82 64 7424502
Email: webmaster@jejutimes.co.kr **Web site:** http://www.jejutimes.co.kr
Freq: Daily
Editor in Chief: Heung-Nam Jeong; **President:** Chun-Jong Kang
Profile: Provides news on business, economy, politics, lifestyle, society, etc.
Language (s): Korean
DAILY NEWSPAPER

Jemin Ilbo 459861
Editorial: Jemin Ilbo, 2627-5 Dodu 1-dong, Jeju 690-241 **Tel:** 82 64 7413365
Email: jemin@jemin.com **Web site:** http://www.jemin.com
Freq: Daily
Publisher: Seong-Beom Jin
Profile: Provides news on current issues including politics and sports.
Language (s): Korean
DAILY NEWSPAPER

Jeolla Ilbo 459859
Editorial: The Jeollailbo, 140-1, Jeon-dong, Wansan-gu, Jeonju 560-040 **Tel:** 82 63 2323131
Email: editcont@jeollailbo.com **Web site:** http://www.jeollailbo.com
Freq: Daily
News Director: Jong-Yoon Bae; **Editor:** Byung-Woon Jang; **Editor:** Hee-Sung Kwon; **Editor:** Sang-Deok Lee
Profile: Provides news on the current issues.
Language (s): Korean
DAILY NEWSPAPER

Jeonbuk Domin Ilbo 459857
Editorial: The Jeonbuk Dominilbo, 417-62, Jinbuk 2-dong, Deokjin-gu, Jeonju 561-706
Tel: 82 63 2517111
Email: domin2@chol.com **Web site:** http://www.domin.co.kr
Freq: Daily
Editor in Chief: Dae-Seong Ha; **Editor:** Sung-Cheon Han; **Editor:** Jae-Keun Jeong; **Editor:** Bang-Hee Lee; **News Director:** Bo-Won Lee; **News Director:** Byung-Ju Lee; **Publisher:** Byung-Chan Lim
Profile: Provides news on current issues, lifestyle, etc.
Language (s): Korean
DAILY NEWSPAPER

Jeonbuk Ilbo 459858
Editorial: Jeonbuk Ilbo, Wooseok Building, 710-5, Jeonju 561-762 **Tel:** 82 63 2505500
Email: desk@jjan.kr **Web site:** http://www.jjan.kr
Freq: Daily; **Circ:** 120008 Not Audited
Editor in Chief: Ju-Yeon Hwang; **News Director:** Jae-Ho Kim; **President:** Nam-Gon Kim; **News Director:** Sung-Joong Kim; **Editor in Chief:** Soon-Taek Kwon; **Editor:** Seong-Won Lee; **Publisher:** Chang-Hun Seo
Profile: Provides news on current issues.
Language (s): Korean
DAILY NEWSPAPER

Jeonmin Ilbo 460276
Editorial: Jeonmin Daily Paper, 590 Ua-dong 3-ga, Jeonju 561-823 **Tel:** 82 63 9013000
Email: jmib3000@hanmail.net **Web site:** http://www.jeonminilbo.co.kr
Freq: Daily
President: Joong-Ho Lee; **Publisher:** Yong-Beom Lee; **News Director:** Jong-Duck Park
Profile: Provides news on current issues.
Language (s): Korean
DAILY NEWSPAPER

Jeonnam Ilbo 459853
Editorial: Jeonnam IlboJeonnam Ilbo.com, 700-5, Jungheung-dong, Buk-gu, Gwangju 500-758
Tel: 82 62 5270015
Web site: http://www.jnilbo.com
Freq: Daily; **Circ:** 36006 Not Audited
Editor: Kwang-Mi Jeon; **News Director:** Deok-Gyun Kang; **News Editor:** Kun-Sang Lee; **Editor in Chief:** Jae-Sung Lim; **Editor:** Il-Jong Oh; **Publisher:** Ki-Jeong Park
Profile: Provides news on current issues, business, sports, entertainment, technology, etc.
Language (s): Korean
DAILY NEWSPAPER

Jeonnam Maeil 459742
Editorial: Jeonnam Maeil, Samsan Building, 704-9, Gwangju 500-878 **Tel:** 82 62 7201000
Email: jndn@chol.com **Web site:** http://www.jndn.com
Freq: Daily; **Circ:** 36008 Not Audited
Editor: Rae-Sung Kim; **Editor:** Woo-Kwan Kim; **Editor:** Gyu-Ho Kwak; **Publisher:** Yong-Ho Shin
Profile: Provides news on current issues.
Language (s): Korean
DAILY NEWSPAPER

JoongAng Daily 459382
Owner: JoongAng Media Network
Editorial: Joongang Ilbo, 7 Sunhwa-dong, Jung-gu, Seoul 100-759 **Tel:** 82 2 7519215
Email: eopinion@joongang.co.kr **Web site:** http://koreajoongangdaily.joins.com
Freq: Daily; **Circ:** 150008 Not Audited
Editor: Byung-Gee Hong; **Editor in Chief:** Kilzer Lou; **President & Publisher:** Pil-Ho Song; **Editor:** Si-Yoon Sung
Profile: Provides national and international news in English.
Language (s): English
Ad Rate: Full Page Mono 16650000.00
Ad Rate: Full Page Colour 27750000.00
Currency: South Korea Won
DAILY NEWSPAPER

Joongang Ilbo 459691
Owner: JoongAng Media Network
Editorial: Joongang Ilbo, 7 Sunhwa-dong, Jung-gu, Seoul 100-759 **Tel:** 82 2 7515114
Email: comment@joongang.co.kr **Web site:** http://koreajoongangdaily.joins.com
Freq: Daily
Editor: Sung-Kyu Ahn; **Editor in Chief:** Young-Tae Choi; **Editor:** Byung-Ki Hong; **Editor:** Dong-Sup Kim; **Editor:** Day-Young Oh; **Editor:** Chan-Young Park; **Editor:** Jae-Yong Pyo; **Editor:** Jang-Hwan Son; **Publisher:** Pil-Ho Song
Profile: Provides news on current issues. Its English edition is titled Korea JoongAng Daily.
Language (s): Korean
Ad Rate: Full Page Mono 16650000.00
Ad Rate: Full Page Colour 27750000.00
Currency: South Korea Won
DAILY NEWSPAPER

Joongang Ilbo - Ridgeview, NJ Bureau 503823
Editorial: 154 Hope St, Ridgewood, New Jersey 7450 **Tel:** 1 201 444-2931
Web site: http://joongangdaily.joins.com
Freq: Daily
Profile: This is the New Jersey bureau of Joongang Ilbo in Seoul, South Korea.
Language (s): English
DAILY NEWSPAPER

Joong-Boo Ilbo 459716
Editorial: The Joongbooilbo, 1010, Gwonseon-dong, Suwon 441-390 **Tel:** 82 31 2302114
Email: webmaster@joongboo.com **Web site:** http://www.joongboo.com
Freq: Daily; **Circ:** 75804 Not Audited
Editor: Deuk-Ho Eom; **Editor:** Kyung-Mook Kang; **Publisher:** Jae-Yul Lim
Profile: Provides news on the current issues in Joong-Boo district.
Language (s): Korean
DAILY NEWSPAPER

Joongbu Maeil 459741
Editorial: Joongbu Maeil Shinmun, 150-1, Sinbong-dong, Cheongju 361-111 **Tel:** 82 43 2752001
Email: jb@jbnews.com **Web site:** http://www.jbnews.com
Freq: Daily
Publisher: Seong-Kyu Park; **Editor in Chief:** Chang-Hee Song; **News Director:** Seung-Kap Yang
Profile: Provides news on current issues.
Language (s): Korean
DAILY NEWSPAPER

Joongdo Ilbo 459866
Editorial: Joongdo Ilbo, 175-3 Oryu-dong, Jung-gu, Daejeon 301-829 **Tel:** 82 42 2201114
Web site: http://www.joongdoilbo.co.kr
Freq: Daily; **Circ:** 102554 Not Audited
News Director: Woon-Suk Baek; **Editor:** Jae-Heon Choi; **Editor in Chief:** Hyung-Joong Kim; **Publisher:** Won-Sik Kim; **News Director:** Eun-Nam Kwon; **Editor:** Seung-Gyu Lee; **Editor in Chief:** Ki-Sung Park
Profile: Provides news on current issues.
Language (s): Korean
DAILY NEWSPAPER

Kangwon Domin Ilbo 459863
Editorial: Kangwon Dominilbo, 257-27 Hupyeong 1-dong, Chuncheon 200-707 **Tel:** 82 33 2609000
Email: namoo@kado.net **Web site:** http://www.kado.net
Freq: Daily; **Circ:** 122807 Not Audited
Publisher: Hyung-Soon Ahn; **Editor in Chief:** Nam-Woo Heo; **News Director:** Jong-In Jin; **News Director:** In-Ho Kim; **Editor:** Chang-Sung Namgung; **Director:** Mi-Hyun Park
Profile: Provides news on current issues.
Language (s): Korean
DAILY NEWSPAPER

Kangwon Ilbo 459864
Editorial: Kwnews Corporation, 53 Jungang-no, 1-ga, Chuncheon 200-705 **Tel:** 82 33 2581114
Email: webmaster@kwnews.co.kr **Web site:** http://www.kwnews.co.kr
Freq: Daily; **Circ:** 128008 Not Audited
Publisher: Seung-Ik Choi; **Editor:** Seok-Mahn Kim; **Editor:** Hyun Namgung
Profile: Provides news on current issues.
Language (s): Korean
DAILY NEWSPAPER

Kids Hankook Ilbo 460176
Editorial: Hankooki.com, 15/F, Hanjin Building., Seoul 100-770 **Tel:** 82 2 7242402
Web site: http://kids.hankooki.com
Freq: 2 Times/Week
Editor in Chief: Hoon-Ku Im
Profile: Provides news on games, sports, entertainment, education, etc for children.
Language (s): Korean
DAILY NEWSPAPER

Kiho Ilbo 459715
Editorial: Kiho Ilbo, Jungsan Building, 343-1, Icheon 402-816 **Tel:** 82 32 7610004
Email: webmaster@kihoilbo.co.kr **Web site:** http://www.kihoilbo.co.kr
Freq: Daily
Editor in Chief: Myung-Byung Chae; **Publisher:** Kang-Hun Seo
Profile: Provides news on current issues.
Language (s): Korean
DAILY NEWSPAPER

Kookje Shinmun 459720
Editorial: Kookje Shinmun, 4~7/F, Kookje Shinmun Building, Busan 611-071 **Tel:** 82 51 5005114
Email: webmaster@kookje.co.kr **Web site:** http://www.kookje.co.kr
Freq: Daily
Editor in Chief: In-Suk Ahn; **News Director:** Song-Hyun Cho; **Editor:** Sang-Do Jung; **News Director:** Moon-Seok Song; **Publisher:** Suk-Koo Song
Profile: Provides news on current issues.
Language (s): Korean
DAILY NEWSPAPER

Korea Daily Labor News 460196
Editorial: Labor Today, 607 Byucksan Digital Valley 5-cha, Seoul 153-788 **Tel:** 82 2 3646900
Email: seok@labortoday.co.kr **Web site:** http://www.labortoday.co.kr
Freq: Daily
Publisher: Seong-Guk Bak
Profile: Provides news on current issues, including politics, economy, government and labor.
Language (s): Korean
DAILY NEWSPAPER

Korea Financial Times 459767
Editorial: The Korea Financial Times, 6/F, Dadong Building, Seoul 100-180 **Tel:** 82 2 7736300
Email: webmaster@fntimes.com **Web site:** http://www.fntimes.com
Freq: 2 Times/Week; **Circ:** 50006 Not Audited
Profile: Provides news on finance.
Language (s): Korean
DAILY NEWSPAPER

Korea Herald 160104
Editorial: Herald Media Inc., 3-5Fl, 1-17 Jeong-dong, Jung-gu, Seoul 100-120 **Tel:** 82 2 7270205
Email: khnews@heraldcorp.com **Web site:** http://www.koreaherald.com
Freq: Daily; **Circ:** 210000
News Director: Si-Young Cheon; **Editor in Chief:** Sung-Woo Cheon; **Editor:** Min-Hee Kim; **Editor:** Dong-hyun Min
Profile: Provides news on current issues, politics, economy, business and finance.
Language (s): English
DAILY NEWSPAPER

Korea Medical News 459752
Editorial: Medical Newspaper Co. Limited., 610-1, Jungkok-dong, Kwangjin-gu, Seoul 143-220
Tel: 82 2 4675671
Email: webmaster@bosa.co.kr **Web site:** http://www.bosa.co.kr
Freq: 2 Times/Week; **Circ:** 40009 Not Audited
Editor: Jeong-Yoon Lee; **Publisher:** Yeon-Jun Park; **Editor:** Young-Jin Yoon
Profile: Provides news on medical manufacturing resources, medical technology, and medical equipment.
Language (s): Korean
DAILY NEWSPAPER

Korea Taxation Times 459359
Editorial: Korea Taxation Times, 201-33, Dongkyo-dong, Mapo-gu, Seoul 100-042 **Tel:** 82 2 3381132
Email: chg@taxtimes.co.kr **Web site:** http://www.taxtimes.co.kr
Freq: 2 Times/Week; **Circ:** 15008 Not Audited
President & Publisher: Jeong-Ho Kim
Profile: Provides news on taxation.
Language (s): Korean
DAILY NEWSPAPER

Korea Textile News 459771
Editorial: 440-15 Seogyo-dong, Mapo-gu, Seoul 121-841 **Tel:** 82 2 3263600
Email: yhlee@ktnews.com **Web site:** http://www.ktnews.co.kr
Freq: 2 Times/Week
Publisher: Si-Joong Kim
Profile: Provides news about textile industry in Korea.
Language (s): Korean
DAILY NEWSPAPER

Korea Times 161277
Editorial: 8th Fl., Imgwang Bldg, 81, Tongilro, (Migeun-dong) Seodaemun-gu, Seoul 120-705
Tel: 82 2 724-2359
Email: webmaster@koreatimes.co.kr **Web site:** http://www.koreatimes.co.kr
Freq: Daily; **Circ:** 30000
Editor: Jae-Hyun Cho; **Editor:** Ji-Su Kim; **Editor:** Jong-Chan Kim; **Chief of Industrial News Division:** Yoo-Cheol Kim; **Editor in Chief:** Hee-Soon Lee; **Chief of Political News Division:** Hwan-Woo Lee; **Editor:** Kap-Su Lee; **News Director:** Young-Jin Oh; **Editor:** Charles Sherman
Profile: Established in 1950, provides news on current issues and politics, economy, finance and more.
Language (s): English
Ad Rate: Full Page Colour 12000.00
Currency: United States Dollars
DAILY NEWSPAPER

Korea Times - New York Bureau 620284
Editorial: United Nations, Room S-342, New York, New York 10017 **Tel:** 1 212 869-8484
Profile: This is the New York bureau of Korea Times, based in Seoul, South Korea.
Language (s): Korean
DAILY NEWSPAPER

Kukmin Ilbo 459692
Editorial: Kukminilbo, 5/F, Kookmin Daily News Building., Seoul 150-968 **Tel:** 82 2 7819341
Web site: http://www.kukinews.com
Freq: Daily
Profile: Provides news on current issues.
Language (s): Korean
Ad Rate: Full Page Mono 51800000.00
Ad Rate: Full Page Colour 61050000.00
Currency: South Korea Won
DAILY NEWSPAPER

Kunsul Kyungje 459764
Editorial: The Builders Daily, 12/F, Construction Center, Seoul 135-010 **Tel:** 82 2 5475081
Web site: http://www.cnews.co.kr
Freq: Daily
President & Publisher: Hong-Sa Kwon
Profile: Provides news on current issues focusing on business, technology, social issues, economy and politics.
Language (s): Korean
DAILY NEWSPAPER

Kwangju Daily 459854
Editorial: Kwangju Daily, 1-21 Ku-dong, Nam-gu, Gwangju 503-020 **Tel:** 82 62 3610100
Web site: http://www.kjdaily.com
Freq: Daily; **Circ:** 10657 Not Audited
Publisher: Won-Wook Kim; **Editor:** Young-Soon Kim; **Editor:** Kyung-Su Lee; **Editor:** Sung-Soo Oh; **News Director:** Sang-Won Park
Profile: Provides news on current issues focusing on politics and economy.
Language (s): Korean
DAILY NEWSPAPER

Kwangju Ilbo 459744
Editorial: Kwangju Ilbosa, Mudeung Building., Gwangju 501-711 **Tel:** 82 62 2228111
Email: kwangju@kwangju.co.kr **Web site:** http://www.kwangju.co.kr
Freq: Daily; **Circ:** 200008 Not Audited
Publisher: Jin-Young Kim; **News Director:** Ju-Jung Kim; **Editor:** Jong-Tae Lee; **News Director:** Chi-Kyung Park
Profile: Provides news on current issues.
Language (s): Korean
DAILY NEWSPAPER

Kyeonggi Ilbo 459717
Editorial: Kyeonggiilbo Co., Limited., Gyeonggi Daily News Building., Suwon 440-703 **Tel:** 82 31 2503300
Email: mylee@kgib.co.kr **Web site:** http://www.kgib.co.kr
Freq: Daily
News Director: Jong-Sik Choi; **Editor:** Haeng-Yun Heo; **Editor:** Geun-Ho Jeong; **News Editor:** Il-Hyung Jeong; **President & Publisher:** Hyun-Rak Lee; **News Editor:** Jong-Hyun Lee; **Publisher:** Chang-Ki Shin
Profile: Provides news on current issues.
Language (s): Korean
DAILY NEWSPAPER

Kyeongin Ilbo 459718
Editorial: Kyeongin Ilbo, Gyeongin Daily News Building., Suwon 442-702 **Tel:** 82 31 2315114
Email: ehkim@kyeongin.com **Web site:** http://www.kyeongin.com
Freq: Daily
Editor: Sang-Rok Bae; **Editor:** Woo-Young Choi; **General Manager:** Seok-Cheol Lee; **Editor in Chief:** Min-Young Oh; **Editor:** Young-Mi Shim; **Publisher:** Kwang-Seok Song; **Editor:** Jae-Jun Yun
Profile: Provides news on current issues.
Language (s): Korean
DAILY NEWSPAPER

Kyeongin Maeil 459719
Editorial: Kyeongin Maeil, 201 Shinpoong-dong, Paldal-gu, Suwon 442-040 **Tel:** 82 31 2580114
Email: webmster@kmaeil.com **Web site:** http://www.kmaeil.com
Freq: Daily
Editor in Chief: Cha-Ju Cho; **Publisher:** Kye-Jung Lee
Profile: Provides news on current issues.
Language (s): Korean
DAILY NEWSPAPER

Kyongbuk Ilbo 459731
Editorial: The Kyongbuk Ilbo, 579-12 Sangdo-dong, Nam-gu, Pohang 790-828 **Tel:** 82 54 2892262
Email: kb@kyongbuk.co.kr **Web site:** http://www.kyongbuk.co.kr
Freq: Daily; **Circ:** 135007 Not Audited
News Director: Jae-Yoon Hwang; **Publisher:** Jeong-Hwa Jeong
Profile: Provides news that are happening its region.
Language (s): Korean
DAILY NEWSPAPER

Kyongbuk Maeil 459732
Editorial: Kyongbuk Maeil Co., Limited., 60-14, 1-ga, Dongbin-dong, Pohang 791-060 **Tel:** 82 54 2417112
Email: jtlee@kbmaeil.com **Web site:** http://www.kbmaeil.com
Freq: Daily; **Circ:** 45007 Not Audited
Publisher: Ki-Ho Kim; **News Director:** Jong-Rak Kwon; **Editor:** Chang-Hyung Lee; **Editor:** Jun-Taek Lee
Profile: Provides news on business, sports, social issues, etc.
Language (s): Korean
DAILY NEWSPAPER

Kyongnam Ilbo 459724
Editorial: Kyongnam Ilbo, 237-4 Sangpyeong-dong, Jinju 660-729 **Tel:** 82 55 7511044
Email: gnnews@gnnews.co.kr **Web site:** http://www.gnnews.co.kr
Freq: Daily
Editor: Joong-Ki Han; **Publisher:** In-Tae Hwang; **Editor in Chief:** Mahn-Seok Jeong; **Editor:** Young-Hyo Jung
Profile: Provides news on current issues on politics, social issues, economiy, etc.
Language (s): Korean
DAILY NEWSPAPER

Kyongnam Shinmun 459726
Editorial: The Kyongnam Shinmun, 100-5, Sinwol-dong, Changwon 641-701 **Tel:** 82 55 2832211
Email: knnews@knnews.co.kr **Web site:** http://www.knnews.co.kr
Freq: Daily
Editor: Yoon-Je Cho; **Editor:** Choong-Ho Heo; **News Director:** Seung-Do Huh; **News Director:** Ki-Hong Jeong; **Editor:** Jae-Ik Kim; **Editor:** Myung-Hyun Kim; **Publisher:** Soon-Bok Lee
Profile: Provides news on current issues, politics, economy, entertainment, sports, etc.
Language (s): Korean
DAILY NEWSPAPER

Kyunggi Shinmun 460333
Editorial: Kyunggi Shinmun, 255-19 Yeonmu-dong, Jangan-gu, Suwon 440-814 **Tel:** 82 31 2688114
Email: lkj1@kgnews.co.kr **Web site:** http://www.kgnews.co.kr
Freq: Daily
Editor: Min-Soo Jeong; **News Director:** Ju-Yong Kim; **Editor in Chief:** Kyung-Jae Lee; **News Director:** Dae-Joon Park; **Publisher:** Se-Ho Park; **Editor:** Kye-Tack Yum
Profile: Provides news on current issues.
Language (s): Korean
DAILY NEWSPAPER

Kyunghyang Shinmun 459694
Editorial: Kyunghyang.com, Kyunghyang Shinmun Building., Seoul 100-702 **Tel:** 82 2 37011114
Email: webmaster@khan.co.kr **Web site:** http://www.khan.co.kr
Freq: Daily; **Circ:** 1800007 Not Audited
Editor: Ho-Yeon Cho; **Editor in Chief:** Ki-Seong Kang; **Editor:** Bu-Won Kwon; **Editor:** Hak-Soo Moon; **News Director:** Gu-Jae Park; **Editor:** Jong-Sung Park; **News Director:** Kwon-Mo Yang
Profile: Provides news on current issues on politics, economy, business, sports, etc.
Language (s): Korean
DAILY NEWSPAPER

Kyungsang Ilbo 459722
Editorial: Kyungsang Ilbo, 299-10, Mugeo-dong, Nam-gu, Ulsan 680-190 **Tel:** 82 52 2200530
Email: webmaster@ksilbo.co.kr **Web site:** http://www.ksilbo.co.kr
Freq: Daily
News Director: Sung-Tae Choo; **Editor:** Chang-Sik Kim; **Editor in Chief:** Sung-Kil Kim; **Editor in Chief:** Ae-Jung Lee; **Editor:** Jae-Myung Lee; **News Director:** Chan-Soo Seo; **Publisher:** Won-Ho Shin
Profile: Provides news on current issues.
Language (s): Korean
DAILY NEWSPAPER

Law Times 459750
Editorial: The Lawtimes Co., Limited., 14/F, Gangnam Building, 1321-1, Seoul 137-070
Tel: 82 2 34720604
Email: webadmin@lawtimes.co.kr **Web site:** http://www.lawtimes.co.kr
Freq: 2 Times/Week
President & Publisher: Hyung-Su Seo; **Editor in Chief:** Yeon-Su Shin
Profile: Provides news about laws.
Language (s): Korean
DAILY NEWSPAPER

Maeil Business Newspaper 459700
Editorial: Maeil Business Newspaper, 190 Pil-dong 1-ga, Jung-gu, Seoul 100-728 **Tel:** 82 2 20002114
Email: mkmaster@mk.co.kr **Web site:** http://www.mk.co.kr
Freq: Daily; **Circ:** 877752
Publisher: Dae-Hwan Jang; **Editor:** Jong-Young Kim; **Editor:** Gyu-Jun Lim; **Editor:** Jae-Hyun Park; **Editor:** Im-Ho Shin; **Editor:** Hyung-Sik Yoon; **Editor:** Ku-Hyun Yoon
Profile: Provides news on investing, stocks and savings.
Language (s): Korean
Ad Rate: Full Page Mono 61050000.00
Currency: South Korea Won
DAILY NEWSPAPER

Maeil Shinmun 459728
Editorial: Maeil Shinmunsa, 26 Seosungro, Jung-gu (71 Kyesan 2 ga), Daegu 700-715 **Tel:** 82 53 2555001
Email: edit@imaeil.com **Web site:** http://www.imaeil.com
Freq: Daily; **Circ:** 350008 Not Audited
Editor: Hyang-Rae Cho; **News Director:** Jae-Wang Choi; **News Director:** Jung-Am Choi; **Editor:** Byung-Seon Park
Profile: Provides news on general issues.
Language (s): Korean
DAILY NEWSPAPER

Metro Daily 459278
Editorial: Metro Seoul Holdings Inc., 1-141 Sinmunno 2-ga, Jongno-gu, Seoul 110-062 **Tel:** 82 2 7219822
Web site: http://www.metroseoul.co.kr
Freq: Daily; **Circ:** 400008 Not Audited
Publisher: Seung-Jong Kim; **Editor in Chief:** Young-Do Seo
Profile: Provides news on current issues.
Language (s): Korean
DAILY NEWSPAPER

Money Today 331623
Editorial: Money Today, 3/F, Cheongkye 11 Building, Seoul 110-726 **Tel:** 82 2 7247700
Web site: http://stock.mt.co.kr
Freq: Daily
Editor: Won-Bae Chae; **Publisher:** Seon-Keun Hong; **Editor:** Ho-Byung Kang; **Editor:** Seung-Je Lee
Profile: Provides news on investing, money and the stock market.
Language (s): Korean
DAILY NEWSPAPER

Moodeung Ilbo 459855
Editorial: The Moodeung Ilbo, 7/F, BYC Building., 1180, Gwangju 502-827 **Tel:** 82 62 6067760
Email: zmd@chol.com **Web site:** http://www.honam.co.kr
Freq: Daily
Publisher: Young-Jun Jeon; **Editor:** Jong-Seok Kim; **Editor in Chief:** Seung-Yong Kim; **News Director:** Young-Tae Kim; **Editor:** Jong-Ju Lee
Profile: Provides current news on economy, politics, business, sports, etc.
Language (s): Korean
DAILY NEWSPAPER

Munhwa Ilbo 459697
Editorial: Munhwa Ilbo, Munhwa Ilbosa, Seoul 100-723 **Tel:** 82 2 37015114
Email: opinion@munhwa.co.kr **Web site:** http://www.munhwa.com
Freq: Daily; **Circ:** 500008 Not Audited
Editor in Chief: Joong-Hong Choi; **News Director:** Young-Beom Choi; **Editor:** Byung-Jik Kim; **Editor:** Seung-Hyun Kim; **Publisher:** Byung-Kyu Lee; **Editor:** Hyun-Jong Lee; **Editor:** Ae-Ri Oh
Profile: Provides news on current issues.
Language (s): Korean
DAILY NEWSPAPER

Naeil Shinmun 459746
Editorial: Naeil Shinmoon, Naeil Shinmoon Building, Seoul 110-062 **Tel:** 82 2 22872300
Email: tech@naeil.com **Web site:** http://www.naeil.com
Freq: Daily; **Circ:** 2170009 Not Audited
Editor: Chan-Su Ahn; **Publisher:** Myung-Kook Jang; **News Director:** Ho-Sung Jeon; **News Director:** Seon-Woo Lee; **Editor:** Jin-Beom Park
Profile: Provides news on current issues of politics, government, economy, business, finance, etc.
Language (s): Korean
DAILY NEWSPAPER

Namdo Ilbo 459727
Editorial: The Namdo Ilbo, Namdo Ilbosa, 541-4, Gwangju 503-774 **Tel:** 82 62 6701023
Email: webmaster@namdonews.com **Web site:** http://www.namdonews.com
Freq: Daily; **Circ:** 100007 Not Audited
Editor: Ik-Hee Kim; **Publisher:** Seong-Ho Park; **Editor:** Kwang-Ho Shin
Profile: Provides news on current issues.
Language (s): Korean
DAILY NEWSPAPER

Nodong Ilbo 490674
Editorial: Nodong Ilbo, 30-2 Yeouido-dong, Yeongdeungpo-gu, Seoul 150-010 **Tel:** 82 2 7820204
Email: kim@nodongilbo.com **Web site:** http://www.nodongilbo.com
Freq: Daily; **Circ:** 150007 Not Audited
Profile: Provides news on domestic and international events, especially in the field of labor.
Language (s): Korean
DAILY NEWSPAPER

Nongmin Shinmun 459747
Editorial: The Farmers Newspaper, National Agricultural Cooperative Federation, Seoul 110-121
Tel: 82 2 37036114
Email: master@nongmin.com **Web site:** http://www.nongmin.com
Freq: 2 Times/Week; **Circ:** 330007 Not Audited
Publisher: Won-Byung Choi; **Editor in Chief:** Myung-Han Kim; **Editor:** Jun-Keol Ryu
Profile: Provides news about agriculture.
Language (s): Korean
Ad Rate: Full Page Mono 3570000.00
Ad Rate: Full Page Colour 9280000.00
Currency: South Korea Won
DAILY NEWSPAPER

Pharmaceutical Industry News 459757
Editorial: Yakup Shinmun Inc., 98-1 Chongpa-dong, 2-ga, Seoul 140-734 **Tel:** 82 2 32700144
Web site: http://www.yakup.com
Freq: 2 Times/Week; **Circ:** 38006 Not Audited
Publisher: Yong-Heon Hahm
Profile: Provides news on pharmaceutical industry.
Language (s): Korean
DAILY NEWSPAPER

Segye Ilbo 459698
Editorial: Saegye Ilbo, Saegye Ilbo, 63-1, Seoul 140-740 **Tel:** 82 2 20001234
Email: webmaster@segye.com **Web site:** http://www.segye.com
Freq: Daily; **Circ:** 600009 Not Audited
News Director: Yeon-Kook Bae; **News Director:** Jung-Mi Hwang; **Editor:** Hyun-Cheol Park; **News Director:** Ho-Sang Yeom
Profile: Provides news on politics, economy, finance, current issues, etc.
Language (s): Korean
Ad Rate: Full Page Mono 5500000.00
Ad Rate: Full Page Colour 6500000.00
Currency: South Korea Won
DAILY NEWSPAPER

Seoul Economic Daily/Kyungje Shinmun 459702
Editorial: 9~11/F, Chungmuro Tower, 43 Chungmuro 3-ga, Jung-gu, Seoul 100-013 **Tel:** 82 2 7242114
Email: webmaster@sedaily.com **Web site:** http://economy.hankooki.com
Freq: Daily; **Circ:** 316000
Editor: Hee-Jae Cho; **Publisher:** Lee Jong-whan; **Editor:** Keum-Hee Kang; **Editor in Chief:** Jong-Seo Kim; **Editor in Chief:** Jeong-Beop Lee
Profile: Provides news on economics, politics, technology, current issues, sports and entertainment.
Language (s): Korean
DAILY NEWSPAPER

Seoul Shinmun 459693
Editorial: Seoul Shinmunsa, 33 Taepyung-ro, Jung-gu, Seoul 100-745 **Tel:** 82 2 20009000
Email: webmaster@seoul.co.kr **Web site:** http://www.seoul.co.kr
Freq: Daily; **Circ:** 700007 Not Audited
Editor: Byung-Cheol Joo; **Manager:** Seok-Jin Kang; **Editor:** Tae-Heon Kwak; **Manager:** Yong-Won Lee; **President & Publisher:** Jin-Hwan Noh; **News Director:** Seung-Ho Oh; **Editor:** Chan-Hee Ryu
Profile: Provides the news on the current issues.
Language (s): Korean
Ad Rate: Full Page Mono 9000000.00
Ad Rate: Full Page Colour 10000000.00
Currency: South Korea Won
DAILY NEWSPAPER

Sports Chosun 459080
Editorial: 923-14 Mok 1-dong, Yangchon-gu, Seoul 158-178 **Tel:** 82 2 32198114
Web site: http://www.sportschosun.com
Freq: Daily; **Circ:** 443008 Not Audited
Editor: Yong-Pyo Kim; **Editor in Chief:** Yeo-Kwang Yoon
Profile: Provides news on current issues and sports.
Language (s): Korean
DAILY NEWSPAPER

Sports Hankook 460341
Editorial: Hankook Ilbo, 6/F, Hanjin Bldg Bonkwan, Seoul 100-770 **Tel:** 82 2 7321001
Web site: http://sports.hankooki.com
Freq: Daily
Editor in Chief: Byung-Chang Choi; **Editor:** Jeong-Sik Kwon; **Publisher:** Jin-Yeol Park
Profile: Provides news on sports and celebrities.
Language (s): Korean
DAILY NEWSPAPER

Sports Khan 492972
Editorial: Kyunghyang Shinmunsa, Kyunghyang Shinmun Building., Seoul 100-702
Tel: 82 2 37011271
Web site: http://sports.khan.co.kr
Freq: Daily
Publisher: Young-Jae Ko; **Editor in Chief:** In-Seok Shim
Profile: Provides news on sports, celebrities, etc.
Language (s): Korean
DAILY NEWSPAPER

Sports Seoul Daily 459704
Editorial: Sports Seoul Daily Co., Limited., 5/F, Block 1, ACE hitech city, 55-20, Seoul 150-972
Tel: 82 2 20010021
Email: woosdad@sportsseoul.com **Web site:** http://www.sportsseoul.com
Freq: Daily
Editor: Hee-Young Kim; **Editor in Chief:** Sung-Jin Kim; **Editor:** Jeong-Eun Seong; **President & Publisher:** Dae-Soo Song
Profile: Provides news on sports and celebrities.
Language (s): Korean
DAILY NEWSPAPER

Sports Today 459707
Editorial: 8~9/F Kaya Venture Building, 28~130, Youngdeungpo-dong-2-ga, Seoul 150-900
Tel: 82 2 20020305
Email: stoon@stoo.com **Web site:** http://www.stoo.com
Freq: Daily; **Circ:** 500007 Not Audited
Editor: Dong-Hoi Ku; **Publisher:** Jeong-Woo Lee; **Editor in Chief:** Yong-Hwan Yun
Profile: Provides news on entertainment including celebrities, games and sports.
Language (s): Korean
DAILY NEWSPAPER

Sports World 521475
Editorial: Saegye Ilbo, The Segye Times, 63-1, Seoul 140-740 **Tel:** 82 2 20001829
Web site: http://www.sportsworldi.com
Freq: Daily
Editor: Won-Ik Cho; **Editor:** Yong-Mo Kang
Profile: Provides news on sports and entertainment.
Language (s): Korean
DAILY NEWSPAPER

Standup Korea Times 828955
Editorial: Hankook Ilbo Co, Ltd, 15/F, Hanjin Bldg, Seoul 100-770 **Tel:** 011 82 27242114
Freq: Daily
News Director: Jae-Woo Cho; **News Director:** Sung-Chul Lee
Profile: Covers politics, the economy, society and international news.
Language (s): English
DAILY NEWSPAPER

Steel & Metal News 459773
Editorial: The Korea Metal Journal Co., Limited., 5~7/F KMJ Building, Seoul 137-870 **Tel:** 82 2 5834161
Email: webmaster@kmj.co.kr **Web site:** http://www.snmnews.com/
Freq: 2 Times/Week; **Circ:** 45000
Publisher: Jeong-Woon Bae
Profile: Provides news on metal industry.
Language (s): Korean
DAILY NEWSPAPER

Transportation News 460219
Editorial: The Transportation News, 6/F, Gyotongshinmunsa Building, Seoul 137-803
Tel: 82 2 5952982
Web site: http://www.gyotongn.com
Freq: 2 Times/Week; **Circ:** 10009 Not Audited
Editor in Chief: Young-Seok Lee; **Publisher:** Young-Rak Yoon
Profile: Provides news on transportation and traffic industry.
Language (s): Korean
DAILY NEWSPAPER

Travel Times 459762
Editorial: The Korea Travel Times Co., Limited., 5/F, Daehan Cheyukhoi Building., Seoul 100-170
Tel: 82 2 7578980
Email: tktt@traveltimes.co.kr **Web site:** http://www.traveltimes.co.kr
Freq: 2 Times/Week; **Circ:** 55008 Not Audited
President: Byung-Tae Kim; **Editor in Chief:** Ki-Nam Kim
Profile: Provides news on traveling.
Language (s): Korean
DAILY NEWSPAPER

Ulsan Maeil 459723
Editorial: Ulsan Maeil Shinmunsa, 2/F, Rivertown Building., Ulsan 680-814 **Tel:** 82 52 2431001
Email: hoon9632@hanmail.net **Web site:** http://www.ulsanmaeil.co.kr
Freq: Daily
Publisher: Kil-Nam Jeong; **Editor:** Young-Soo Kim; **News Director:** Hong-Gwan Lee; **News Director:** Yeon-Ok Lee
Profile: Provides news on current issues that are happening in both locally and internationally.
Language (s): Korean
DAILY NEWSPAPER

Yeongnam Ilbo 459730
Editorial: Yeongnam Ilbo, 111 Sincheon-dong, Dong-gu, Daegu 701-750 **Tel:** 82 53 7568001
Email: master@yeongnam.com **Web site:** http://www.yeongnam.com
Freq: Daily
Publisher: Seong-Ro Bae; **Editor in Chief:** Jeong-Rae Cho; **Editor:** Jong-Chul Choi; **Editor:** Do-Hyuk Won
Profile: Provides news on current issues.
Language (s): Korean
DAILY NEWSPAPER

News Service/Syndicate

Newsis 467556
Editorial: 7/F, Seowon Building, 91-1 Gyeongun-dong, Jongno-gu, Seoul 110-310 **Tel:** 82 2 7217400
Email: news@newsis.com **Web site:** http://www.newsis.com
Editor: Young-Ki Park; **Editor:** Se-Jin Yu
Profile: Covers national and international news.
Language (s): Korean
NEWS SERVICE/SYNDICATE

Yonhap English News 467622
Editorial: Yonhap News, 85-1, Susong-dong, Jongno-gu, Seoul 110-140 **Tel:** 82 2 3983114
Email: english@yonhapnews.co.kr **Web site:** http://english.yonhapnews.co.kr
Freq: Daily
Editor: In-Chol Kim; **Editor:** Seung-Ji Kwok
Profile: covers international and national news.
Language (s): English
NEWS SERVICE/SYNDICATE

Yonhap News Agency 353753
Editorial: Yonhap News, 85-1, Susong-dong, Jongno-gu, Seoul 110-140 **Tel:** 82 2 3983114
Email: master@yonhapnews.co.kr **Web site:** http://www.yonhapnews.co.kr
Freq: Daily
President: Young-Sub Chang; **Editor:** Kyung-Sook Hyun; **Editor:** Oh-Yeon Kwon; **Editor:** Byung-Hoon Moon; **Director:** Byung-Chul Yu
Profile: Articles cover international and local news.
Language (s): Korean
NEWS SERVICE/SYNDICATE

Kuwait

Time Difference: GMT +3
National Telephone Code: 965
Continent: Asia
Capital: Kuwait City

Newspapers

Al Anba 159067
Owner: Bab Al-Kuwait Press Company
Editorial: PO Box 23915, Main Building, Press Street, Safat 13100 **Tel:** 965 2227 2727
Email: editorial@alanba.com.kw **Web site:** http://www.alanba.com.kw
Freq: Daily; **Circ:** 92817 Rate Card
Editor In Chief: Yousef Al-Marzouk; **Head of News:** Afaf Mokhtar
Profile: Al Anba (The News) is a daily Arabic newspaper covering local and international news, business, finance, sport and features. It launched in 1976.
Language (s): Arabic
Ad Rate: Full Page Mono 2400.00
Ad Rate: Full Page Colour 3600.00
Currency: Kuwait Dinars
DAILY NEWSPAPER

Annahar 496825
Owner: Dar Annahar for Publishing & Distribution
Editorial: PO Box 900, Ahmed Al Jaber Street, Safat 15251 **Tel:** 965 183 2020
Email: annahar@annaharkw.com **Web site:** http://www.annaharkw.com
Freq: Daily; **Circ:** 35000 Publisher's Statement
Profile: Annahar is a daily newspaper covering local and international news, politics, business, society and sport. It launched in 2007.
Language (s): Arabic
DAILY NEWSPAPER

Arab Times 156727
Owner: Dar Al Seyassah Press Printing & Publishing (WLL)
Editorial: PO Box 2270, Airport Road, Safat 13023
Tel: 965 2481 3566
Email: arabtimes@arabtimesonline.com **Web site:** http://www.arabtimesonline.com
Freq: Daily; **Circ:** 82659 Publisher's Statement
Editor-in-Chief: Ahmed Al Jarallah; **News Editor:** Yacoub Zubrim
Profile: Arab Times is a daily, broadsheet-sized newspaper covering local and international news, business, finance, features and sport. It launched in 1977.
Language (s): English
Ad Rate: Full Page Mono 3200.00
Ad Rate: Full Page Colour 4200.00
Currency: Kuwait Dinars
DAILY NEWSPAPER

Gulf Madhyamam - Kuwait edition 707847
Owner: Gulf Madhyamam FZ LLC
Editorial: PO Box 20867, Office 10, Al Rawda Al Tijariya Complex, Safat 13069 **Tel:** 965 97 957790
Email: kuwait@gulfmadhyamam.net **Web site:** http://www.gulfmadhyamam.net
Freq: Daily; **Circ:** 20100 Rate Card
Profile: Gulf Madhyamam is an international Indian newspaper covering national and international news, current affairs, politics, business and sport. The newspaper is aimed at Malayalam speakers in the Gulf and publishes separate editions for the UAE, Saudi Arabia (Riyadh, Jeddah, Damam & Abha), Qatar, Oman, Bahrain and Kuwait. The newspaper was first published in 1999.
Language (s): Malayalam
DAILY NEWSPAPER

Al Jarida 483643
Owner: Al Jarida for Printing and Publishing
Editorial: PO Box 29846, Souad Commercial Complex, Safat 13159 **Tel:** 965 2225 7030
Email: mail@aljarida.com **Web site:** http://www.aljarida.com
Freq: Daily; **Circ:** 39100 Publisher's Statement
Editor In Chief: Khaled Al Mutairi
Profile: Al Jarida is a daily newspaper covering local and international news, sport, business and politics. It was first published in 2007.
Language (s): Arabic
Ad Rate: Full Page Mono 2400.00
Ad Rate: Full Page Colour 3600.00
Currency: Kuwait Dinars
DAILY NEWSPAPER

Al Khaleej Newspaper 589878
Owner: Al Jabriya Kuwaiti Group for Journalism & Publishing
Editorial: PO Box 25725, 21 Behbehani Building, Street 65, Safat 13118 **Tel:** 965 2243 3765
Email: alkhaleej-newspaper@hotmail.com **Web site:** http://alkhaleej-kw.com
Freq: Weekly; **Circ:** 45000 Publisher's Statement
Picture Editor: Widad Alsheikh
Profile: Al Khaleej Newspaper (The Gulf Newspaper) is a weekly newspaper covering local and international news, business, sports and culture. It launched in 2009 and is published on Tuesdays.
Language (s): Arabic
Ad Rate: Full Page Mono 1800.00
Ad Rate: Full Page Colour 3000.00
Currency: Kuwait Dinars
DAILY NEWSPAPER

Kuwait Times 156668
Owner: Kuwait Times Publishing House
Editorial: PO Box 1301, Kuwait Times Building, Safat 13014 **Tel:** 965 2483 3199
Email: info@kuwaittimes.com **Web site:** http://news.kuwaittimes.net
Freq: Daily; **Circ:** 68000 Publisher's Statement
Editor In Chief: Abd Al-Rahman Alyan; **General Manager:** Badrya Darwish
Profile: Kuwait Times is a daily, broadsheet-sized English newspaper covering local news, business, finance, sport and features. It was first published in 1961.
Language (s): English
Ad Rate: Full Page Mono 3200.00
Ad Rate: Full Page Colour 4800.00
Currency: Kuwait Dinars
DAILY NEWSPAPER

Al Kuwaityah 762272
Owner: Kuwaiti Awraq Company For Advertising Services
Editorial: PO Box 42444, Sahafa Street, Shuwaikh
Tel: 965 2496 1103
Email: info@alkuwaityah.com **Web site:** http://www.alkuwaityah.com
Freq: Daily; **Circ:** 40000
Profile: Al Kuwaityah is a daily Arabic newspaper covering national and international news, business, culture and sport. It was first published in June 2011.
Language (s): Arabic
DAILY NEWSPAPER

Al Qabas 156729
Owner: Dar Al Qabas Press, Printing and Publishing
Editorial: PO Box 21800, Press Street, Safat 13078
Tel: 965 2481 2822
Email: info@alqabas.com.kw **Web site:** http://www.alqabas.com.kw
Freq: Daily; **Circ:** 81000 Publisher's Statement
Editor-in-Chief: Waleed Al Nusuf; **Information Manager:** Hamza Alayan
Profile: Al Qabas is a daily newspaper covering national and international news, business, finance, politics, culture and sport. It was first published in 1972.
Language (s): Arabic
Ad Rate: Full Page Mono 2400.00
Ad Rate: Full Page Colour 3600.00
Currency: Kuwait Dinars
DAILY NEWSPAPER

Al Rai 156731
Owner: Al Rai Media Group Company K.S.C.
Editorial: PO Box 761, Airport Road, Safat 13008
Tel: 965 2481 7777
Email: editor@alraimedia.com **Web site:** http://www.alraimedia.com
Freq: Daily; **Circ:** 93000 Publisher's Statement
Editor In Chief: Majed Al Ali; **Advertising Manager:** Ramzi Khaddaj; **Head of News:** Ahmed Makki
Profile: Al Rai is a daily Arabic newspaper covering news, business, finance, sports, features and classified advertisements. The newspaper launched in 1961, and was previously called Al Rai Al Aam.
Language (s): Arabic
Ad Rate: Full Page Mono 2600.00
Ad Rate: Full Page Colour 3600.00
Currency: Kuwait Dinars
DAILY NEWSPAPER

Al Resala 438015
Owner: Dar Al Resala for Press, Printing & Publishing
Editorial: PO Box 2490, Safat 13025
Tel: 965 2483 4201
Email: info@al-resalapress.com
Freq: Weekly; **Circ:** 23750 Publisher's Statement
Editor in Chief: Sohair Jasem
Profile: Al Resala is a weekly newspaper covering culture, entertainment, politics and economics. It launched in 1961 and is published on Mondays.
Language (s): Arabic
Ad Rate: Full Page Mono 1400.00
Ad Rate: Full Page Colour 1800.00
Currency: Kuwait Dinars
DAILY NEWSPAPER

Al Sabah 532945
Owner: Assabah for Press, Publishing & Distribution
Editorial: PO Box 588, Wara Center, Safat 13006
Tel: 965 2455 4950
Email: editorial@alsabahpress.com **Web site:** http://www.alsabahpress.com
Freq: Daily; **Circ:** 28000 Publisher's Statement
Editor In Chief: Barakat Al-Hedeiban
Profile: Al Sabah (The Morning) is a daily, broadsheet-sized Arabic newspaper covering national and international news, politics, sports and business. It launched in 2006.
Language (s): Arabic
DAILY NEWSPAPER

Al Seyassah 156730
Owner: Dar Al Seyassah Press Printing & Publishing (WLL)
Editorial: PO Box 2270, Airport Road, Safat 13023
Tel: 965 2481 3566
Email: alseyassah@alseyassah.com **Web site:** http://al-seyassah.com
Freq: Daily; **Circ:** 112856 Publisher's Statement
Editor In Chief: Ahmed Al Jarallah; **Office Manager:** Khadija Benisaad
Profile: Al Seyassah (Politics) is a daily Arabic newspaper covering news, business, finance, sports, features and classified advertisements. It was first published in 1968.
Language (s): Arabic
Ad Rate: Full Page Mono 2600.00
Ad Rate: Full Page Colour 3400.00
Currency: Kuwait Dinars
DAILY NEWSPAPER

Al Shahed 507814
Owner: Dar Al Kuwaitiya for Media
Editorial: PO Box 4856, 11th & 12th Floor, Hussein Makki Al Jumaa Building, Safat 2568
Tel: 965 2245 7300
Email: contact@alshahedkw.com **Web site:** http://www.alshahedkw.com
Freq: Daily; **Circ:** 45000 Publisher's Statement
Editor In Chief: Sabah Al-Sabah
Profile: Al Shahed (The Witness) is a daily newspaper covering news, politics, business and sport. It launched in 2001.
Language (s): Arabic
Ad Rate: Full Page Mono 2200.00
Ad Rate: Full Page Colour 3400.00
Currency: Kuwait Dinars
DAILY NEWSPAPER

Al Shahed Al-Isbouya 887651
Owner: Dar Al Kuwaitiya for Media
Editorial: PO Box 4856, 11th & 12th Floor, Hussein Makki Jumaa Building, Safat 70652
Tel: 965 2245 7300
Email: contact@alshahedkw.com **Web site:** http://www.alshahed.com.kw
Freq: Weekly; **Circ:** 45000
Editor In Chief: Sabah Al-Sabah
Profile: Al Shahed Al-Isbouya is the Friday edition of Al Shahed newspaper and covers news, politics, business and sport. It launched in 2001.
Language (s): Arabic
Ad Rate: Full Page Mono 2200.00
Ad Rate: Full Page Colour 3400.00
Currency: Kuwait Dinars
DAILY NEWSPAPER

Al Taleea 354328
Owner: Al Taleea for Printing & Publishing
Editorial: PO Box 1082, Press Street, Airport Road, Safat 13011 **Tel:** 965 2484 7207
Email: editor@altaleea.com **Web site:** http://altaleea.com
Freq: Weekly; **Circ:** 7000 Publisher's Statement
Editor In Chief: Abdallah Al Nibari
Profile: Al Taleea is a weekly newspaper covering national and international news, current affairs, politics and business. It launched in 1962 and is published on Wednesdays.
Language (s): Arabic
Ad Rate: Full Page Mono 1500.00
Ad Rate: Full Page Colour 2250.00
Currency: Kuwait Dinars
DAILY NEWSPAPER

Al Wasat 476046
Owner: Dar Al-Akhbar Printing, Publishing and Distribution
Editorial: PO Box 26541, 3rd Floor, Medical Clinic Tower, Salmiya 13126 **Tel:** 965 2464 5100
Email: editorial@alwasat.com.kw **Web site:** http://www.alwasat.com.kw
Freq: Daily; **Circ:** 40000 Publisher's Statement
Editor In Chief: Adnan Al Wazan
Profile: Al Wasat is a daily Arabic newspaper covering local and international news, politics, business and sport. It launched in 2007.
Language (s): Arabic

Kuwait

Ad Rate: Full Page Mono 2000.00
Ad Rate: Full Page Colour 3000.00
Currency: Kuwait Dinars
DAILY NEWSPAPER

News Service/Syndicate

Kuwait News Agency 370500
Owner: Kuwait News Agency
Editorial: PO Box 24063, Shuwaikh, Safat 13101
Tel: 965 2227 1800
Email: sources@kuna.net.kw **Web site:** http://www.kuna.net.kw
Editor in Chief: Saeed Al-Ali; **Photographer:** Noori Al-Ostath
Profile: Kuwait News Agency is the official news agency of Kuwait and covers government news and issues of national importance. It was founded in 1976.
Language (s): Arabic
NEWS SERVICE/SYNDICATE

Reuters - Kuwait Bureau 436530
Owner: Thomson Reuters
Editorial: PO Box 5616, 4th Floor, Kuwait Stock Exchange Building, Safat 13057 **Tel:** 965 2228 3660
Email: ahmed.hagagy@thomsonreuters.com **Web site:** http://www.reuters.com
Profile: Kuwait bureau of International news agency supplying news - text, graphics, video and pictures - to subscribers around the world.
Language (s): Arabic
NEWS SERVICE/SYNDICATE

Kyrgyzstan

Time Difference: GMT +5
National Telephone Code: 996
Continent: Asia
Capital: Bishkek

Newspapers

Delo No 224390
Owner: Delo No
Editorial: 12 m-n, Bishkek **Tel:** 996 312 90-10-32
Email: delonom@ktnet.kg **Web site:** http://www.delo.kg
Circ: 21000 Publisher's Statement
Editor: Viktor Michaylovich Zapolskiy
Profile: Newspaper focusing on national and international news, politics, social events and legal issues, lifestyle issues.
Language (s): Russian
Ad Rate: Full Page Mono 2000.00
Currency: United States Dollars
DAILY NEWSPAPER

MK Asia 489450
Owner: Inter pressa
Editorial: pr. Chui 34/10, Bishkek 720065
Tel: 996 312 43-78-13
Email: mk@elcat.kg **Web site:** http://www.mk.kg
Circ: 7000 Publisher's Statement
Profile: National newspaper with socio-political news.
Language (s): Russian
Ad Rate: Full Page Mono 36000.00
Currency: Kyrgyzstan Soms
DAILY NEWSPAPER

Slovo Kyrgyzstana 483949
Owner: Slovo Kyrgyzstana
Editorial: ul. Abdumomunova 193, Bishkek 720040
Tel: 996 312 66-45-78
Email: info@slovo.kg **Web site:** http://slovo.kg
Freq: 2 Times/Week; **Circ:** 5000 Publisher's Statement
Profile: National informative and analytical newspaper covering politics, economy, social events, culture, education and sport.
Language (s): Russian
Ad Rate: Full Page Mono 20000.00
Currency: Kyrgyzstan Soms
DAILY NEWSPAPER

Vecherniy Bishkek 157108
Owner: Publishing house Vecherniy Bishkek
Editorial: Ul. Usenbaeva 2, Bishkek 720021
Tel: 996 312 29 88 35
Email: info@vb.kg **Web site:** http://www.vb.kg
Freq: Daily; **Circ:** 8000 Publisher's Statement
Editor-in-Chief: Gennadiy Kuzmin
Profile: Newspaper covering national and international news, politics, economy, culture, social events and sport.
Language (s): Russian
Ad Rate: Full Page Mono 2424.00
Ad Rate: Full Page Colour 2908.00
Currency: United States Dollars
DAILY NEWSPAPER

News Service/Syndicate

Kabar 385421
Editorial: ul. Abrakhmanova 175, Bishkek
Tel: 996 312 960 528
Email: kabar@kabar.kg **Web site:** http://www.kabar.kg
Editor In Chief: Boris Arabayev
Profile: Providing daily updated news in Russian, English, Turkish and Kyrgyz languages.
Language (s): Kyrgyz
NEWS SERVICE/SYNDICATE

Community Newspaper

MSN 488729
Editorial: Ul. Usenbayeva 2, Bishkek 720021
Tel: 996 312 38-64-10
Email: city@msn.kg **Web site:** http://www.msn.kg
Circ: 3000
Profile: Social-political and informative-entertaining newspaper.
Language (s): Russian
COMMUNITY NEWSPAPER

Laos

Time Difference: GMT +7
National Telephone Code: 856
Continent: Asia
Capital: Vientiane

Newspapers

Khao Kila 459822
Owner: Lao National Sports Committee
Editorial: Lao National Sports Committee, National Stadium, Vientiane **Tel:** 856 21 252909
Email: khaokila@hotmail.com **Web site:** http://www.laosportnsc.com
Freq: Daily; **Circ:** 3002 Not Audited
Editor in Chief: Suksakhone Sipraseuth
Profile: Sports and Entertainment related issues.
Language (s): Lao
DAILY NEWSPAPER

Lao Patthana 473088
Editorial: Lao News Agency, 80 Setthatirath Road, P.O. Box 3770, Vientiane **Tel:** 856 21 251090
Email: kplnews@yahoo.com **Web site:** http://www.kpl.net.la
Freq: Daily
Editor in Chief: Khemthong Sanoubane
Profile: Focuses on local and national news.
Language (s): Lao
DAILY NEWSPAPER

Pasaxon Newspaper 459817
Editorial: Pasaxon Newspaper, 66 Sethathirath Road, P.O. Box 1110, Vientiane **Tel:** 856 21212466
Email: infonews@pasaxou.org.la **Web site:** http://www.pasaxon.org.la
Freq: Daily; **Circ:** 7502 Not Audited
News Director: Panee Manithip
Profile: Covers news.
Language (s): Lao
DAILY NEWSPAPER

Pasaxon Van Ar-thit 459819
Editorial: Pasaxon Newspaper, 66 Setthatirath Road, P.O. Box 1110, Vientiane **Tel:** 856 21212466
Email: infonews@pasaxon.org.la **Web site:** http://www.pasaxon.org.la
Freq: Weekly; **Circ:** 2002 Not Audited
Profile: Covering news and general interests.
Language (s): Lao
DAILY NEWSPAPER

Le Renovateur 459856
Editorial: Vientiane Times, Pangkham Street, P.O. Box 8706, Vientiane **Tel:** 856 21217872
Email: lerenovateur@hotmail.com **Web site:** http://www.lerenovateur.org.la
Freq: Weekly; **Circ:** 2002 Not Audited
Editor: Khamphout Xayasomroth
Profile: Covers social issues, culture and related details.
Language (s): French
DAILY NEWSPAPER

Vientiane Mai 459820
Editorial: Setthatirath Road, Baan Chungyin, P.O. Box 989, Vientiane **Tel:** 856 21212623
Email: webmaster@vientianemai.net **Web site:** http://www.vientianemai.net
Freq: Daily; **Circ:** 3502 Not Audited
Editor: Somphet Inthisane
Profile: Covers government and private companies.
Language (s): Lao
DAILY NEWSPAPER

Vientiane Times 157100
Editorial: Vientiane Times, Pangkham Street, P.O. Box 5723, Vientiane **Tel:** 856 21 21 63 64
Email: info@vientianetimes.org.la **Web site:** http://www.vientianetimes.org.la
Freq: 2 Times/Week; **Circ:** 3002 Not Audited
Editor: Panyasith Thammavongsa
Profile: Covers news topics.
Language (s): English
DAILY NEWSPAPER

News Service/Syndicate

Khaosan Pathet Lao (KPL) 467597
Owner: Lao News Agency
Tel: 856 21215402
Email: kplcab@laonet.net **Web site:** http://kpl.gov.la
Freq: Daily
General Manager: Khamsene Phongsa; **Editor in Chief:** Sinhpangna Rattanavong
Profile: Covers news.
Language (s): Lao
NEWS SERVICE/SYNDICATE

Latvia

Time Difference: GMT +2
National Telephone Code: 371
Continent: Europe
Capital: Riga

Newspapers

The Baltic Times Latvia 224408
Owner: Baltic News Ltd
Editorial: Rupniecibas 1-5, Riga 1050
Tel: 371 6 722 99 78
Email: editor@baltictimes.com **Web site:** http://www.baltictimes.com
Circ: 12000 Publisher's Statement
Profile: Newspaper focusing on current political and social events, business, finance and culture in Estonia, Latvia and Lithuania.
Language (s): English
Ad Rate: Full Page Mono 3078.00
Currency: Euro
DAILY NEWSPAPER

Bizness & Baltija 161020
Owner: SIA B&B Redakcija
Editorial: Kr. Valdemara 149, Riga 1013
Tel: 371 6 70 33 047
Web site: http://ru.bb.vesti.lv
Freq: Daily; **Circ:** 12000 Publisher's Statement
Editor-in-Chief: Andrey Svedov
Profile: Full colour broadsheet-sized newspaper focusing on business and finance in the Baltics.
Language (s): Russian
DAILY NEWSPAPER

Diena 157004
Owner: SIA Laikraksts Diena
Editorial: Andrejostas iela 2, Riga LV-1045
Tel: 371 67063145
Email: diena@diena.lv **Web site:** http://www.diena.lv
Freq: Daily; **Circ:** 31500 Publisher's Statement
Editor-in-Chief: Gatis Madži?š
Profile: Broadsheet-sized newspaper focusing on national and international news, politics, business, culture and sport.
Language (s): Latvian
Ad Rate: Full Page Mono 1944.00
Ad Rate: Full Page Colour 2592.00
Currency: Latvia Lati
DAILY NEWSPAPER

Dienas Bizness 161021
Owner: SIA Dienas bizness
Editorial: Mkusalas iel 15, Riga 1004
Tel: 371 6 7063090
Email: redakcija@db.lv **Web site:** http://www.db.lv
Freq: Daily; **Circ:** 12000 Publisher's Statement
Editor-in-Chief: Gatis Madži?š
Profile: Tabloid-sized newspaper focusing on business, finance and economics. In addition to daily business news and commentary, it publishes regular supplements on construction and real estate, new technologies, education, employment market and cars.
Language (s): Latvian
Ad Rate: Full Page Colour 2650.00
Currency: Latvia Lati
DAILY NEWSPAPER

Latvijas Avize 239202
Owner: A/S Lauku Avize
Editorial: AS Lauku Avize, Dzirnavu iela 21, Riga 1010 **Tel:** 371 67096600
Email: redakcija@la.lv **Web site:** http://www.la.lv
Freq: Daily; **Circ:** 23000 Publisher's Statement
Editor In Chief: Linda Rasa; **News Editor:** Guntis Šžerbinskis
Profile: National conservative newspaper focusing on national and international news, business and economics, politics, culture and sport.
Language (s): Latvian

Ad Rate: Full Page Mono 480.19
Ad Rate: Full Page Colour 525.21
Currency: Latvia Lati
DAILY NEWSPAPER

Neatkariga Rita Avize 161036
Owner: SIA Mediju Nams
Editorial: Csu iela 31 - 2, Riga **Tel:** 371 78 86 801
Email: redakcija@nra.lv **Web site:** http://www.nra.lv
Freq: Daily; **Circ:** 35000 Publisher's Statement
Editor-in-Chief: Anita Daukšte
Profile: Broadsheet-sized newspaper focusing on national and international news, politics, business and sport.
Language (s): Latvian
DAILY NEWSPAPER

Vesti Segodnya 161040
Owner: SIA Media Nams Vesti
Editorial: ul. Dzirnavu 37, Riga LV-1050
Tel: 371 6 7088698
Email: redakcija@vesti.lv **Web site:** http://vesti.lv
Freq: Daily; **Circ:** 74000 Publisher's Statement
Profile: Broadsheet-sized newspaper focusing on national and international news, politics, business and sport.
Language (s): Russian
Ad Rate: Full Page Mono 2042.70
Ad Rate: Full Page Colour 3832.69
Currency: Latvia Lati
DAILY NEWSPAPER

News Service/Syndicate

LETA News Agency 503657
Editorial: Marijas 2, Riga 1050 **Tel:** 371 67222509
Email: pr@leta.lv **Web site:** http://www.leta.lv
News Editor: Peteris Rugainis
Profile: LETA is a full service information agency, offering current information about developments in Latvia, the Baltic States and the world, and furnishes informative services for the mass media, state institutions, business organizations and companies.
Language (s): English
NEWS SERVICE/SYNDICATE

Lebanon

Time Difference: GMT +2
National Telephone Code: 961
Continent: Asia
Capital: Beirut

Newspapers

Ad Diyar 159071
Owner: Al Nahdah Publishing
Editorial: PO Box 40-300, Al Diyar Building, Yarze, Beirut **Tel:** 961 5 923830
Email: info@addiyaronline.com **Web site:** http://www.addiyar.com
Freq: Daily; **Circ:** 14000 Publisher's Statement
Editor-in-Chief: Charles Ayoub; **General Manager:** Imad Maalouf; **Head of News:** Najwa Maroun
Profile: Ad Diyar is a daily Arabic newspaper covering national and international news, current affairs, politics, business, sport and entertainment. It launched in 1988.
Language (s): Arabic
DAILY NEWSPAPER

Al Akhbar 433564
Owner: Akhbar Beyrouth S.A.L
Editorial: PO Box 113-5963, 6th Floor, Concorde Centre, Beirut **Tel:** 961 1 759500
Email: mail@al-akhbar.com **Web site:** http://www.al-akhbar.com
Freq: Daily; **Circ:** 16500 Publisher's Statement
Profile: Al Akhbar (The News) is a tabloid-sized Arabic newspaper covering local and international news, business, culture and sport. It launched in 2006 and is published daily, except Sundays.
Language (s): Arabic
Ad Rate: Full Page Mono 4000.00
Ad Rate: Full Page Colour 8000.00
Currency: United States Dollars
DAILY NEWSPAPER

Albalad 343328
Owner: Integra Publishing & Marketing Solutions s.a.l.
Editorial: PO Box 116-5360, 2nd Floor, Freeway Centre, Beirut 2058 **Tel:** 961 1 695695
Email: albaladnews@albaladonline.com **Web site:** http://www.albaladonline.com
Freq: Daily; **Circ:** 60000 Rate Card
Managing Director: Ghada Halawi
Profile: Albalad (The Country) is a tabloid-sized Arabic newspaper covering national and international news, current affairs, politics, business, lifestyle, sport and entertainment. It launched in 2003 and is published daily, except Sundays.
Language (s): Arabic
Ad Rate: Full Page Mono 4600.00
Ad Rate: Full Page Colour 6360.00
Currency: United States Dollars
DAILY NEWSPAPER

An-Nahar 156733
Owner: An Nahar s.a.l
Editorial: PO Box 11226, An Nahar Building, Beirut 2014 **Tel:** 961 1 994888
Email: annahar@annahar.com.lb **Web site:** http://www.annahar.com
Freq: Daily; **Circ:** 45000 Publisher's Statement
Editor: Ali Hamade; **CEO & Editor in Chief:** Nayla Tueni
Profile: An-Nahar is a daily Arabic newspaper covering national and international news, current affairs, politics, business, economy, sport and entertainment. It was first published in 1933.
Language (s): Arabic
DAILY NEWSPAPER

Al Anwar 159073
Owner: Dar Assayad S.A.L
Editorial: PO Box 11-1038, Al Sayyad Building, Beirut **Tel:** 961 5 456374
Email: art.dept@dm.net.lb **Web site:** http://www.alanwar.com
Freq: Daily; **Circ:** 51277 Rate Card
News Editor: George Berberi; **Picture Editor:** Joseph Faddoul; **General Manager:** Elham Freiha; **Editor In Chief:** Michel Raad
Profile: Al Anwar (The Lights) is a daily Arabic newspaper covering national and international news, current affairs, politics, business, sport and entertainment. It was first published in 1959.
Language (s): Arabic
Ad Rate: Full Page Mono 4800.00
Ad Rate: Full Page Colour 7200.00
Currency: United States Dollars
DAILY NEWSPAPER

Asharq Al-Awsat - Beirut office 383657
Owner: Saudi Research & Publishing Co.
Editorial: 11th Floor, Bourj El Ghazal Building, Achrafieh, Beirut **Tel:** 961 1 218701
Email: beirut@aawsat.com **Web site:** http://www.aawsat.com
Freq: Daily
Bureau Chief: Thaer Abbas
Profile: Beirut bureau of Asharq Al-Awsat newspaper. The Beirut office covers news, business and sport from Lebanon for the London-based newspaper which is distributed across the Arab world.
Language (s): Arabic
DAILY NEWSPAPER

Attamaddon 418401
Owner: Dar Al-Bilad Printing and Media
Editorial: PO Box 90, Al Awkaf Building, Tripoli **Tel:** 961 6 441164
Email: attamaddon@hotmail.com **Web site:** http://www.attamaddon.com
Freq: Weekly; **Circ:** 5000 Publisher's Statement
News Editor: Khidir Al Sabeen; **Managing Director:** Rasha Sankari
Profile: Attamaddon is a weekly newspaper focusing on local politics, news and current affairs. It launched in 1933 and is published on Wednesdays.
Language (s): Arabic
Ad Rate: Full Page Mono 600.00
Ad Rate: Full Page Colour 800.00
Currency: United States Dollars
DAILY NEWSPAPER

Aztag Daily 343330
Owner: AZTAG Armenian Daily Company
Editorial: PO Box 80-860, Shaghzoyan Cultural Centre, Beirut **Tel:** 961 1 258526
Email: info@aztagdaily.com **Web site:** http://www.aztagdaily.com
Freq: Daily; **Circ:** 8000 Publisher's Statement
News Editor: Arsho Balain; **Advertising Manager:** Hrair Fermanian; **Editor-in-Chief:** Shahan Kandaharian; **News Editor:** Nora Parseghian
Profile: Aztag Daily is an Armenian newspaper covering national and international news, current affairs, politics, business, sports and entertainment. It launched in 1927, and is aimed at the Armenian community in Lebanon. The newspaper also includes Aztag Magazine, a monthly magazine supplement covering lifestyle and family issues.
Language (s): Armenian
Ad Rate: Full Page Mono 3000.00
Ad Rate: Full Page Colour 3900.00
Currency: United States Dollars
DAILY NEWSPAPER

Aztag Daily - New York Bureau 619613
Owner: AZTAG Armenian Daily Company
Editorial: 315 E 70th St, 3a 3a, New York, New York 10021-8657 **Tel:** 1 212 737-7809
Language (s): English
DAILY NEWSPAPER

Al Binaa 597211
Owner: Al Qawmiyah Media Company
Editorial: 8th floor, Estral Building, Al Hamra Street, Beirut **Tel:** 961 1 748920
Email: info@al-binaa.com **Web site:** http://www.al-binaa.com
Freq: Daily; **Circ:** 4000 Publisher's Statement
Head of News: Ramzi Abdul Khaliq; **Advertising Manager:** Ziad Al Hajj; **Editor in Chief:** Naser Andel
Profile: Al Binaa is a daily Arabic newspaper covering national and international news, politics, business, society and sport. It was first published in 1958.
Language (s): Arabic
Ad Rate: Full Page Mono 4400.00
Ad Rate: Full Page Colour 6000.00
Currency: United States Dollars
DAILY NEWSPAPER

The Daily Star 157090
Owner: The Daily Star
Editorial: PO Box 11-987, 3rd Floor, Markaziah Building, Beirut **Tel:** 961 1 985311
Email: editorial@dailystar.com.lb **Web site:** http://www.dailystar.com.lb
Freq: Daily; **Circ:** 12500 Rate Card
Editor In Chief: Nadim Ladki
Profile: The Daily Star is an English newspaper covering national, regional and international news, current affairs, politics, business, arts and culture, sport and entertainment. It launched in 1952 and is published daily, except Sundays.
Language (s): English
DAILY NEWSPAPER

Al Hayat - International edition 343385
Owner: Dar Al Hayat
Editorial: PO Box 11-1242, Dar Al Hayat Building, Al Maarad Street, Beirut **Tel:** 961 1 987990
Email: information@alhayat.com **Web site:** http://www.alhayat.com
Freq: Daily; **Circ:** 107370 Rate Card
News Editor: Najia Al Hussari; **Editor in Chief:** Ghassan Charbel; **Beirut Bureau Chief:** Zouheir Kseibati
Profile: The International edition of Al Hayat covers national and international news, current affairs, politics, business, sports and entertainment. The newspaper is based in London and Beirut, and also publishes separate editions in Saudi Arabia. It was first published in 1946.
Language (s): Arabic
DAILY NEWSPAPER

Immar Wa Iktissad 426471
Owner: Lebanese Company for Information & Studies
Editorial: PO Box 6517/113, Al Sanobra Building, Beirut **Tel:** 961 1 392444
Email: info@immarwaiktissad.com **Web site:** http://immarwaiktissad.com
Freq: Monthly; **Circ:** 15000 Publisher's Statement
Editor in Chief: Hassan Moukalled
Profile: Immar Wa Iktissad is a fortnightly Arabic business newspaper covering economics and trade. The 16-page tabloid-sized newspaper launched in 1993 and is issued on alternate Fridays.
Language (s): Arabic
Ad Rate: Full Page Colour 2600.00
Currency: United States Dollars
DAILY NEWSPAPER

Al Joumhouria 725508
Owner: Al Joumhouria News Corp Company S.A.L
Editorial: PO Box 90152-1202, 5th & 6th Floor, Al Amara Building, Metn 2020 **Tel:** 961 1 888051
Email: info@aljoumhouria.com **Web site:** http://www.aljoumhouria.com
Freq: Daily; **Circ:** 15000 Publisher's Statement
General Manager: Khalil Abu Antoine; **Editor In Chief:** Georges Soulage
Profile: Al Joumhouria (The Republic) is a tabloid-sized Arabic newspaper covering national and international news, politics, business, sport, entertainment and society. It launched in 2011.
Language (s): Arabic
Ad Rate: Full Page Mono 4000.00
Ad Rate: Full Page Colour 8000.00
Currency: United States Dollars
DAILY NEWSPAPER

El Kalima 354370
Owner: Al Zahliya for Advertising & Publishing Est.
Editorial: 3rd Floor, Al Riyachi and Chouwairi Building, Hay Al Midan, Zahle **Tel:** 961 8 805750
Email: info@el-kalima.com **Web site:** http://www.el-kalima.com
Freq: Weekly; **Circ:** 2000 Publisher's Statement
Editor in Chief: Eid Al Ashkar; **Advertising Manager:** Tony Al Ashqar
Profile: El Kalima (The Word) is a weekly, tabloid-sized newspaper covering national and international news, current affairs, politics, business and sport. It launched in 2000 and is published on Fridays.
Language (s): Arabic
DAILY NEWSPAPER

Al Liwaa 159075
Owner: Dar Al Liwaa for Press & Publishing s.a.r.l
Editorial: PO Box 11-2402, 2nd Floor, Saredar Building, Beirut **Tel:** 961 1 751000
Email: aliwaanewspaper@gmail.com **Web site:** http://www.aliwaa.com
Freq: Daily; **Circ:** 20000 Publisher's Statement
Picture Editor: Jamal Al Shamaa; **Head of News:** Tarek Domloj; **Advertising Manager:** Adnan Ghalayini
Profile: Al Liwaa is an Arabic newspaper covering national and international news, current affairs, business, politics, social issues, entertainment and sport. It launched in 1963 and is published daily, except Sundays.
Language (s): Arabic
DAILY NEWSPAPER

L'Orient Le Jour 159074
Owner: Société Générale de Presse et d'Edition SAL
Editorial: PO Box 45-254, L'Orient le Jour Building, Baabda **Tel:** 961 5 956444
Email: redaction@lorientlejour.com **Web site:** http://www.lorientlejour.com
Freq: Daily; **Circ:** 18000 Publisher's Statement
News Editor: Elie Fayad
Profile: L'Orient Le Jour is a French newspaper covering national and international news, current affairs, business and politics. It was founded as L'Orient in 1925 and Le Jour in 1934 before merging in 1971 to become L'Orient-Le Jour. It is published daily, except Sundays. The newspaper includes L'Orient Littéraire, a monthly literary supplement; L'Orient Le Jour Junior, a monthly youth supplement; and bi-monthly health and beauty supplement Santé Beauté.
Language (s): French
DAILY NEWSPAPER

Al Mustaqbal 343144
Owner: Arab United Press s.a.l.
Editorial: PO Box 14-5426, Al Hamra, Beirut **Tel:** 961 1 746301
Email: almustaqbal@almustaqbal.com.lb **Web site:** http://www.almustaqbal.com
Freq: Daily; **Circ:** 26000 Rate Card
Managing Director: George Bkassini; **Editor In Chief:** Hani Hammoud; **Picture Editor:** Nabil Ismail; **Advertising Manager:** Issam Rahhil
Profile: Al Mustaqbal is a daily Arabic newspaper covering national and international news, current affairs, politics, business and sports. It launched in 1995.
Language (s): Arabic
DAILY NEWSPAPER

Al Raasmal Al Arabi 775007
Owner: Al Raasmal Al Arabi
Editorial: PO Box 11-124, 4th Floor, Tina Center, Beirut **Tel:** 961 1 737271
Email: info@raasmalarabi.com
Freq: Bi-Weekly; **Circ:** 20000 Publisher's Statement
General Manager & Editor in Chief: Hisham Al Yafawi; **Managing Director:** Rita Sfeir
Profile: Al Raasmal Al Arabi (Arab Capital) is a fortnightly Arabic newspaper covering business, economics, investment, finance, banking and stock markets in the Arab world. The newspaper was first published in 1965 and is aimed at business executives.
Language (s): Arabic
Ad Rate: Full Page Colour 5000.00
Currency: United States Dollars
DAILY NEWSPAPER

El Shark 378150
Owner: Dar El Shark
Editorial: PO Box 11-838, 1st Floor, Centre Assaf, Beirut **Tel:** 961 1 810820
Email: info@elshark.com **Web site:** http://www.elsharkonline.com
Freq: Daily; **Circ:** 34000 Rate Card
Publisher: Aouni Al Kaaki; **Managing Director:** Albeir Freiha; **News Editor:** Tareq Osseibi
Profile: El Shark (The East) is an Arabic newspaper featuring news, current affairs, cultural and financial news. It launched in 1926 and is published daily, except Sundays.
Language (s): Arabic
Ad Rate: Full Page Mono 4000.00
Ad Rate: Full Page Colour 5000.00
Currency: United States Dollars
DAILY NEWSPAPER

News Service/Syndicate

Agence France-Presse - Beirut Bureau 370531
Owner: Agence France-Presse
Editorial: PO Box 11-1461, Building Immobiliere 209, Beirut **Tel:** 961 1 730162
Email: newsroom.beirut@afp.com **Web site:** http://www.afp.com
Bureau Chief: Sammy Ketz
Profile: Beirut bureau of international news and picture agency covering general news and current affairs.
Language (s): Arabic
NEWS SERVICE/SYNDICATE

APTN Lebanon 370506
Owner: Associated Press
Editorial: 4th Floor, Shakir Wa Ouani Building, Riyadh Al Solh Square, Beirut **Tel:** 961 1 988889
Email: bhatoum@ap.org **Web site:** http://www.aptn.com
Producer: Moustafa Al Najjar
Profile: Associated Press Television News (APTN) is the international television arm of the Associated Press - APTN's operations include a main news service, specialised broadcast services, customised coverage for the Middle East, a productions division, weekly and daily entertainment news and an extensive video archive library.
Language (s): Arabic
NEWS SERVICE/SYNDICATE

Associated Press - Beirut Bureau 370527
Owner: Associated Press
Editorial: PO Box 11-3780, 4th Floor, Shaker Oueini Building, Beirut **Tel:** 961 1 985190
Email: zkaram@ap.org **Web site:** http://www.ap.org
Bureau Chief: Zeina Karam
Profile: Beirut bureau of international news and photo agency - covers Lebanon and Syria from Beirut. It is aimed at AP subscribers around the world.
Language (s): English
NEWS SERVICE/SYNDICATE

National News Agency 380843
Owner: Ministry of Information, Lebanon
Editorial: Ministry of Information, Hamra, Beirut **Tel:** 961 1 754400
Email: news@nna-leb.gov.lb **Web site:** http://www.nna-leb.gov.lb
Editor in Chief: Ali Laham; **Director:** Laure Saab
Profile: National News Agency is the official government news agency of Lebanon.
Language (s): Arabic
NEWS SERVICE/SYNDICATE

Reuters - Beirut Bureau 370525
Owner: Thomson Reuters
Editorial: PO Box 11-1006, 3rd Floor, Hibat Al Maarad Building, Beirut **Tel:** 961 1 983885
Email: lebanon.news@thomsonreuters.com **Web site:** http://www.reuters.com
Bureau Chief: Thomas Perry
Profile: Beirut bureau of international news and picture agency.
Language (s): English
NEWS SERVICE/SYNDICATE

United Press International - Beirut Bureau 370508
Owner: United Press International
Editorial: 6th Floor, Hyundai Building, Hamra, Beirut **Tel:** 961 1 745971
Email: media@upi.com **Web site:** http://www.upi.com
Profile: United Press International licences content directly to print outlets, online media and institutions of all types.
Language (s): Arabic
NEWS SERVICE/SYNDICATE

Lesotho

Time Difference: GMT +2
National Telephone Code: 266
Continent: Africa
Capital: Maseru

Newspapers

Public Eye 472849
Editorial: Princess Margarett Road, Old Europa, Maseru 100 **Tel:** 266 22 32 14 14
Email: editor@publiceye.co.ls **Web site:** http://www.publiceye.co.ls/
Circ: 22565 Publisher's Statement
Profile: The Public Eye is an independent forum for sharing of opinions; to understand and express popular feelings; to raise awareness of public issues; to provide information regarding development plans and methods; to aid the growth of literacy; to report development news, successes and failures; to act as watchdog on government and public organizations and to promote and protect the freedom of expression.
Language (s): English
DAILY NEWSPAPER

Liberia

Time Difference: GMT
National Telephone Code: 231
Continent: Africa
Capital: Monrovia

Newspapers

The Analyst 493056
Owner: The Analyst Newspaper
Editorial: Broad Street, Opposite First International Bank, Monrovia
Email: analystliberia@yahoo.com
Freq: Daily; **Circ:** 3750 Publisher's Statement
Publisher: Stanley Seakor
Profile: The Analyst is a national daily newspaper focussing on news, current affairs, politics, education, society and sports.
Language (s): English
Ad Rate: Full Page Colour 200.00
Currency: United States Dollars
DAILY NEWSPAPER

Daily Observer 533892
Owner: Liberian Observer Corporation (LOC)
Editorial: 23 McDonald Street, Monrovia **Tel:** 231 88 647 2772
Email: editor@liberianobserver.com **Web site:** http://www.liberianobserver.com
Freq: Daily; **Circ:** 5000 Publisher's Statement
Director: Kenneth Best

Liberia

Profile: Daily newspaper covering regional and national news and current affairs including business and politics.
Language (s): English
Ad Rate: Full Page Mono 300.00
Currency: Liberia Dollars
DAILY NEWSPAPER

The Evidence 535093
Editorial: Carrery Street, Captown Building, Monrovia
Tel: 231 6 532 309
Email: evidenceliberia@islandmix.com
Freq: 2 Times/Week; **Circ:** 2500 Publisher's Statement
Profile: The Evidence is a twice-weekly newspaper focussing on news, current affairs, politics and sports.
Language (s): English
Ad Rate: Full Page Mono 350.00
Ad Rate: Full Page Colour 350.00
Currency: United States Dollars
DAILY NEWSPAPER

The New Democrat 492547
Owner: New Democrat Corporation
Editorial: Bushord Island, (Old Peugeot Garage), Monrovia **Tel:** 231 88 667 0117
Email: editor@thenewdemocrat.info **Web site:** https://thenewdemocrat.info
Freq: Daily; **Circ:** 3500 Publisher's Statement
News Editor: Othello Garblah
Profile: National daily newspaper providing investigative, human interest and feature articles as well as analysis.
Language (s): English
Ad Rate: Full Page Mono 300.00
Ad Rate: Full Page Colour 600.00
Currency: United States Dollars
DAILY NEWSPAPER

Libya

Time Difference: GMT +2
National Telephone Code: 218
Continent: Africa
Capital: Tripoli

Newspapers

Akhbar Al Aan 824323
Owner: Tower Media Middle East FZLLC
Editorial: Al Khiam Hotel, Tripoli
Tel: 218 91 387 7988
Email: libya@alaan.tv **Web site:** http://www.alaan.tv
Freq: Weekly; **Circ:** 10000 Publisher's Statement
General Manager: Sami Albrke; **President:** Alaeddin Mgariaf
Profile: Akhbar Al Aan is a weekly Arabic newspaper covering news and politics in Libya. It was launched in 2011 by the Dubai-based owners of Al Aan TV, and is published on Fridays.
Language (s): Arabic
Ad Rate: Full Page Mono 600.00
Ad Rate: Full Page Colour 800.00
Currency: Libya Dinars
DAILY NEWSPAPER

Brnieq 784058
Owner: Brnieq Establishment
Editorial: 1st Floor, Military Accounts Complex, Shuab Mekka Road, Benghazi **Tel:** 218 91 209 0770
Email: brnieq@yahoo.com **Web site:** http://brnieq.ly
Freq: 3 Times/Week; **Circ:** 5500 Publisher's Statement
Head of News: Moutaz Al Majdari; **News Editor:** Ibrahim Al-Majdali
Profile: Brnieq is an Arabic weekly newspaper covering news, sports and political issues in Libya. It launched in 2011 and is published on Mondays.
Language (s): Arabic
Ad Rate: Full Page Mono 1500.00
Ad Rate: Full Page Colour 2000.00
Currency: Libya Dinars
DAILY NEWSPAPER

Quryna Al Jadida 909802
Owner: Quryna Al Jadida
Editorial: North Benghazi Investment Club Building, Al Sahli Road, Benghazi **Tel:** 218 91 663 3286
Email: qurynan@gmail.com
Freq: Weekly; **Circ:** 6000
News Editor: Rajaa Al Shaikhy; **Editor in Chief:** Fateh Elkhashmi; **Advertising Manager:** Hassan Salem
Profile: Quryna Al Jadida is a weekly newspaper covering news, business and sport. It launched in 2011 and is published on Thursdays.
Language (s): Arabic
Ad Rate: Full Page Mono 1500.00
Ad Rate: Full Page Colour 2000.00
Currency: Libya Dinars
DAILY NEWSPAPER

The Tripoli Post 414032
Owner: Trade, Publishing & Distribution (TPD) Ltd
Editorial: Office 32, 2nd Floor, Tripoli Tower, Tripoli
Tel: 218 21 336 2069
Email: editor@tripolipost.com **Web site:** http://www.tripolipost.com
Freq: Weekly; **Circ:** 7000 Publisher's Statement
News Editor: Al-Adlah Al-Tomi; **Editor In Chief:** Said Laswad
Profile: The Tripoli Post is a weekly English newspaper covering Libya's politics, news, business, culture, sports and history. It launched in 1999 and is published on Saturdays.
Language (s): English
Ad Rate: Full Page Mono 653.00
Ad Rate: Full Page Colour 902.00
Currency: Euro
DAILY NEWSPAPER

News Service/Syndicate

Libya News Agency 353733
Owner: Libya News Agency
Editorial: PO Box 2303, Zaweed Al Dahmany Street, Tripoli **Tel:** 218 21 340 2611
Email: info@lana-news.ly **Web site:** http://www.lana-news.ly
PR Manager: Mohamed Abujaafar
Profile: Libya News Agency (LANA) is the national news agency of Libya and covers news of national importance. The Agency was found in October 1964.
Language (s): Arabic
NEWS SERVICE/SYNDICATE

Liechtenstein

Time Difference: GMT +1
National Telephone Code: 423
Continent: Europe
Capital: Vaduz

Newspapers

auto frühling 527514
Owner: Vaduzer Medienhaus AG
Editorial: Fürst-Franz-Josef-Str. 13, Vaduz 9490
Tel: 42 3 2361616
Email: redaktion@vaterland.li **Web site:** http://www.vaterland.li
Freq: Annual; **Circ:** 11000 Not Audited
Chefredaktion: Niki Eder
Profile: Car magazine.
Language (s): German
Ad Rate: Full Page Mono 1900.00
Ad Rate: Full Page Colour 2035.00
Currency: Switzerland Francs
DAILY NEWSPAPER

Liechtensteiner Vaterland 159618
Owner: Vaduzer Medienhaus AG
Editorial: Austrasse 81, Vaduz 9490
Tel: 423 236 1616
Email: redaktion@vaterland.li **Web site:** http://www.vaterland.li
Freq: Daily; **Circ:** 10373 Publisher's Statement
Musikredaktion: Bettina Frick; **Redaktion Außenpolitik:** Günther Fritz; **Chefredaktion:** Günther Fritz; **Innenpolitik:** Günther Fritz; **Red. Medizin + Gesundheit:** Shusha Meier; **Medizin / Gesundheit:** Manuela Schädler; **Ratgeber:** Manuela Schädler
Profile: Das Liechtensteiner Vaterland ist eine überregionale Tageszeitung in Liechtenstein mit Nachrichten zu Politik, Wirtschaft, Kultur, Sport, Reise, Technik und weiteren Verbraucherthemen. The Liechtensteiner Vaterland is a national daily newspaper in Liechtenstein with news about politics, business, culture, sports, travel, technology and other consumer topics.
Language (s): German
DAILY NEWSPAPER

Liechtensteiner Volksblatt 159619
Owner: Liechtensteiner Volksblatt AG
Editorial: Im alten Riet 103, Schaan 9494
Tel: 42 3 2375161
Email: redaktion@volksblatt.li **Web site:** http://www.volksblatt.li
Freq: Daily; **Circ:** 9000 Publisher's Statement
EDV-Redaktion: Fritz Gauer; **Innenpolitik:** Hubert Hasler; **Innenpolitik:** Franke Holger; **Innenpolitik:** Christian Alexander Koutecky; **Innenpolitik:** Jan Miara; **Lokalredaktion Schaan:** Markus Roth; **Bildredaktion:** Michael Zanghellini; **Managing Director:** Heinz Zöchbauer
Profile: National daily covering politics, economics, sport, travel and the arts. Local Translation:Überregionale Tageszeitung mit Nachrichten zu Politik, Wirtschaft, Kultur, Sport, Reise, Technik u.a.
Language (s): German
DAILY NEWSPAPER

Lithuania

Time Difference: GMT +2
National Telephone Code: 370
Continent: Europe
Capital: Vilnius

Newspapers

15 min (Vilnius) 585360
Owner: UAB 15 minu?i?
Editorial: A. Gostauto 40b, Vilnius
Tel: 370 5 21 05 896
Email: redakcija@15min.lt **Web site:** http://www.15min.lt
Circ: 50000
Director General: Tomas Balžekas; **Editor:** Audrius Ožalas; **Editor-in-Chief:** Žilvinas Pekarskas
Profile: Daily regional newspaper with political, economical, cultural and regional news.
Language (s): Lithuanian
Ad Rate: Full Page Colour 10000.00
Currency: Lithuania Litai
DAILY NEWSPAPER

The Baltic Times Lithuania 224725
Owner: Baltic News Ltd
Editorial: Raugyklos 15, Room 302, Vilnius LT-2001
Tel: 370 5 212 15 45
Email: lithuania@baltictimes.com **Web site:** http://www.baltictimes.com
Profile: Newspaper covering national and international news, business, cultural events and sport.
Language (s): English
Ad Rate: Full Page Colour 3078.00
Currency: Euro
DAILY NEWSPAPER

Ekspress-nedelia 240543
Owner: UAB Savait?s ekspresas
Editorial: Laisvs pr. 60-917, Vilnius LT-2056
Tel: 370 5 24 00 816
Email: ekspres@savaite.lt **Web site:** http://www.nedelia.lt/express_nedelia
Freq: Weekly; **Circ:** 50000 Publisher's Statement
Profile: Features entertainment and social events' articles in Russian language.
Language (s): Russian
DAILY NEWSPAPER

Kauno diena 157010
Owner: UAB Diena Media News
Editorial: Vytauto pr 27, Kaunas LT- 44352
Tel: 370 37 30 22 50
Email: portalas@kaunodiena.lt **Web site:** http://kauno.diena.lt
Freq: Daily; **Circ:** 21900
Editor: J?rat? Kuzmickait?
Profile: Regional newspaper featuring current affairs, finance, culture and sport.
Language (s): Lithuanian
DAILY NEWSPAPER

Laisvas laikrastis 241901
Editorial: Konstitucijos pr 23B, Vilnius
Tel: 370 5 26 24 203
Email: llredakcija@gmail.com **Web site:** http://www.laisvaslaikrastis.lt
Freq: Weekly; **Circ:** 32400 Publisher's Statement
Editor-in-Chief: Aurimas Drizius
Profile: Weekly newspaper covering politics, economics and entertainment.
Language (s): Lithuanian
DAILY NEWSPAPER

Lietuvos Aidas 157245
Owner: Lietuvos Aidas UAB
Editorial: B.Radvilaits g. 9, Vilnius LT-01124
Tel: 370 5 26 10 544
Email: fondas@aidas.lt **Web site:** http://www.aidas.lt
Freq: Daily; **Circ:** 16000 Publisher's Statement
Director: Algirdas Pilvelis
Profile: Newspaper covering national and international current affairs, also features cultural and sport events.
Language (s): Lithuanian
DAILY NEWSPAPER

Lietuvos Rytas 156784
Owner: Lrytas
Editorial: Gedimino pr 12 A, Vilnius LT- 01103
Tel: 370 5 27 43 600
Email: daily@lrytas.lt **Web site:** http://www.lrytas.lt
Freq: Daily; **Circ:** 165000 Publisher's Statement
Editor: Jurgita Noreikien?
Profile: Newspaper featuring national news, lifestyle, gardening, sports, medicine, home, world news, travel, ecology, art and culture.
Language (s): Lithuanian
DAILY NEWSPAPER

Lietuvos Zinios 157251
Owner: UAB Lietuvos Zinios
Editorial: Vykinto g. 14, Vilnius LT- 08117
Tel: 370 5 249 21 52
Email: portalas@lzinios.lt **Web site:** http://www.lzinios.lt
Freq: Daily; **Circ:** 26900 Publisher's Statement
Editor in Chief: Marijus Girša; **News Editor:** Raimonda Ramelien?
Profile: Newspaper featuring news, current affairs, finance, sport and cultural events. It has got two supplement magazines: LŽ žurnalas and LŽ gidas.
Language (s): Lithuanian
DAILY NEWSPAPER

Litovskij Kurjer 224726
Owner: Litovskij Kurjer
Editorial: seskins g. 35, Vilnius LT-0715
Tel: 370 5 212 03 20
Email: info@kurier.lt **Web site:** http://www.kurier.lt
Circ: 30000 Publisher's Statement
Editor-in-Chief: V. Tretyakov
Profile: Newspaper featuring national and regional news, covers current affairs, politics, economics, social issues, culture and sport.
Language (s): Russian
Ad Rate: Full Page Mono 4751.00
Ad Rate: Full Page Colour 6651.00
Currency: Lithuania Litai
DAILY NEWSPAPER

Obzor 241885
Owner: UAB Flobis
Editorial: Konstitucijos pr. 12, Vilnius
Tel: 370 5 27 53 153
Email: info@obzor.lt **Web site:** http://www.obzor.lt
Circ: 36000 Publisher's Statement
Director: Vladimir Farberov; **Editor-in-Chief:** Alexander Shakhov
Profile: A weekly independent newspaper covering international and domestic political, social and business news.
Language (s): Russian
DAILY NEWSPAPER

Respublika 157088
Owner: Respublikos leidiniai
Editorial: A. Smetonos g. 2, Vilnius LT-01115
Tel: 370 5 21 21 574
Email: press@respublika.lt **Web site:** http://www.respublika.lt
Freq: Daily; **Circ:** 37600 Publisher's Statement
Director: Diana Veleckien?; **Editor:** Alfredas Zdramys
Profile: National daily newspaper covering politics, economics, business, social issues and entertainment.
Language (s): Lithuanian
Ad Rate: Full Page Mono 6000.00
Ad Rate: Full Page Colour 6400.00
Currency: Lithuania Litai
DAILY NEWSPAPER

Vakaro zinios 306360
Owner: Naujasis Aitvaras
Editorial: Jogailos g. 11/2 -11, Vilnius LT- 01116
Tel: 370 5 26 11 544
Email: redakcija@vakarozinios.lt **Web site:** http://www.vakarozinios.lt
Freq: Daily; **Circ:** 65000 Publisher's Statement
Editor In Chief: Alfredas Zdramys
Profile: A tabloid covering politics, news and entertainment.
Language (s): Lithuanian
DAILY NEWSPAPER

Verslo zinios 239971
Owner: UAB Verslo Žinios
Editorial: Jasinskio 16 a, Vilnius LT-01112
Tel: 370 5 25 26 300
Email: info@vz.lt **Web site:** http://vz.lt
Freq: Daily; **Circ:** 12600 Publisher's Statement
Editor-in-Chief: Rolandas Barysas; **Managing Director:** Ugnius Jankauskas
Profile: A business daily newspaper in Lithuania which reports on major national economic and business processes and publishes foreign business news. Publishes analyses of markets and companies, covers business and political news, introduces and comments on the latest legislation.
Language (s): Lithuanian
Ad Rate: Full Page Colour 3250.00
Currency: Euro
DAILY NEWSPAPER

News Service/Syndicate

BNS Baltic News Service Lietuva 353705
Editorial: Jogailos g. 9/1, Vilnius LT- 01116
Tel: 370 5 20 58 501
Email: politika@bns.lt **Web site:** http://www.bns.lt
Editor In Chief: Jurat? Damulyt?; **Editor:** Ingrida Gumbyt?; **Editor:** Aloyzas Knabikas; **Editor:** Džolita Mikulskait?; **Editor:** Donata Motuzait?; **Manager:** Monika Zinevi?i?t?
Profile: National and international news agency providing news used by the media, private businesses, banks and the government press office. With its staff of 160 BNS distributes daily around 1,000 news items in five languages (Lithuanian, Latvian, Estonian, Russian and English).
Language (s): English
NEWS SERVICE/SYNDICATE

Luxembourg

Time Difference: GMT +1
National Telephone Code: 352
Continent: Europe
Capital: Luxembourg

Newspapers

d'Letzebuerger Land 218922
Owner: EDITIONS D' LETZEBURGER LAND SARL
Editorial: 59 rue Glesener, Luxembourg L-1020
Tel: 352 48 57 57 1
Email: land@land.lu **Web site:** http://www.land.lu
Freq: Weekly; **Circ:** 7500 Publisher's Statement
Director: Romain Hilgert
Profile: Newspaper covering news and current-affairs, politics, economics and culture for Luxembourg and Europe.
Language (s): English
DAILY NEWSPAPER

Express (Ardener Express & Lokal Express) 668785
Editorial: 42, route de Diekirch, Luxembourg L-7220
Tel: 352 2633 05 85
Email: info@express.lu **Web site:** http://www.express.lu
Freq: Monthly; **Circ:** 52000 Publisher's Statement
Editor In Chief: Sully Prudhomme
Profile: Local Translation: L'express est un journal gratuit qui paraît chaque mois et est distribué directement par voie postale. Son contenu rédactionnel traite de l'actualité locale.Il se décline en deux éditions distinctes : - Ardenner Express : diffusé dans les cantons de Vianden, Diekirch, Wiltz, Clervaux. (Communes de St Vith, Burg Reuland en zone frontalière belge).- Lokal Express : diffusé dans les cantons de dDiekirch, Mersch et Redange. (Communes de Steinsel, Walferdangeet Bereldange).
Language (s): French
DAILY NEWSPAPER

Lëtzebuerger Journal 218065
Owner: EDITIONS LËTZEBURGER JOURNAL SA
Editorial: BP 2101, Luxembourg L-1021
Tel: 352 49 30 331
Email: journal@journal.lu **Web site:** http://www.journal.lu
Freq: Daily; **Circ:** 8500 Publisher's Statement
Editor In Chief: Claude Karger
Profile: Tabloid-sized quality newspaper providing political, financial and economic coverage. Read by decision-makers within business and industry, managers, civil servants, university students and investors.Local Translation: Quotidien traitant d'économie, de finance et politique.
Language (s): English
DAILY NEWSPAPER

Luxemburger Wort 218066
Owner: SAINT-PAUL LUXEMBOURG SA
Editorial: 2, rue Christophe Plantin, Luxembourg L-2988 **Tel:** 352 49 93 1
Email: wort@wort.lu **Web site:** http://www.wort.lu
Freq: Daily; **Circ:** 82327 Publisher's Statement
Managing Director: Paul Lenert; **Editor-in-Chief:** Jean-Lou Siweck
Profile: Broadsheet-sized quality newspaper containing national and international news, political, economic and financial information. Read by decision-makers and business executives, civil servants and university students.Local Translation: Actualité nationale, informations économiques, financières, politiques, culturelles. régionales, locales, internationales.Prix du n° : lundi-vendredi : 1,10 €, samedi : 1,30 €.
Language (s): French
Ad Rate: Full Page Mono 6823.00
Ad Rate: Full Page Colour 9613.00
Currency: Euro
DAILY NEWSPAPER

Tageblatt - Zeitung fir Letzebuerg 158261
Owner: EDITPRESS SA
Editorial: 44, rue du Canal, Esch Sur Alzette L-4050
Tel: 352 54 08 84 680
Email: redaktion@tageblatt.lu **Web site:** http://www.tageblatt.lu
Freq: Daily; **Circ:** 27000 Publisher's Statement
General Manager: Emmanuel Fleig; **Editor in Chief:** Danièle Fonck; **General Manager:** Roland Kayser;
Editor in Chief: Alvin Sold
Profile: Tabloid-sized quality newspaper providing local, national and international news. Includes articles concerning politics, economics and the stock exchange and coverage of sporting events. Aimed at senior executives, managers, university students and office personnel.Local Translation: Actualité nationale, information économique, politique et financière.
Language (s): French
DAILY NEWSPAPER

ZLV - Zeitung vum Lëtzebuerger Vollek 218067
Owner: ZEITUNG
Editorial: 3 rue Zenon Bernard, Esch-Sur-Alzette L-4030 **Tel:** 352 44 60 66 1
Email: info@zlv.lu **Web site:** http://www.zlv.lu
Freq: Daily; **Circ:** 9000 Publisher's Statement
Editor In Chief: Ali Ruckert
Profile: Tabloid-sized newspaper providing local, national and international news; includes information on politics and sport. Political outlook: Left wing.
Language (s): French
DAILY NEWSPAPER

Macau

Time Difference: GMT +8
National Telephone Code: 853
Continent: Asia
Capital: Macau

Newspapers

Macau Daily Times 583938
Editorial: 2nd Floor 62 Av. Infante D., Macau
Tel: 853 2871 6081
Web site: http://www.macaudailytimes.com.mo
Freq: Daily; **Circ:** 12500
Editor in Chief: Paulo Coutinho
Profile: Founded in 2007, covers local, national and regional news. Caters to the constant needs of today's society, keeping in mind new social, economic and political realities that Macau faces on a day-to-day basis.
Language (s): English
Ad Rate: Full Page Mono 15750.00
Ad Rate: Full Page Colour 23100.00
Currency: Hong Kong Dollars
DAILY NEWSPAPER

Macedonia

Time Difference: GMT +1
National Telephone Code: 389
Continent: Europe
Capital: Skopje

Newspapers

Dnevnik 157011
Owner: Media Print Macedonia
Editorial: Bul. Oktomvri 25, Skopje 1000
Tel: 389 2 30 89 201
Email: dnevnik@dnevnik.com.mk **Web site:** http://www.dnevnik.mk
Freq: Daily; **Circ:** 55000 Publisher's Statement
Editor: Liljana Damovska; **Editor-in-Chief:** Darko Janevski
Profile: Newspaper focusing on national and international news, business, politics, culture and sport.
Language (s): Macedonian
Ad Rate: Full Page Mono 560.00
Ad Rate: Full Page Colour 770.00
Currency: Euro
DAILY NEWSPAPER

Makedonski Sport 457891
Owner: Media Print Macedonia
Editorial: Vasil Gjorgov 16, Skopje 1000
Tel: 389 2 323 6870
Email: makedosnkisport@t-home.mk **Web site:** http://www.sport.com.mk
Freq: Daily; **Circ:** 12000 Publisher's Statement
Editor-in-Chief: Igor Ivanovski; **General Manager:** Joze Olevski; **Editor:** Boban Radulovik
Profile: Newspaper featuring articles on all types of sport.
Language (s): Macedonian
DAILY NEWSPAPER

Nova Makedonija 157012
Owner: ZONIK DOOEL-Skopje
Editorial: Your Gagarin 15, Skopje 1000
Tel: 389 2 551 1711
Email: nm@novamakedonija.com.mk **Web site:** http://www.novamakedonija.com.mk
Freq: Daily; **Circ:** 15000 Publisher's Statement
Editor-in-Chief: Aleksandar Dimkovski
Profile: Newspaper focusing on national and international news, politics, business and sport.
Language (s): Macedonian
Ad Rate: Full Page Mono 350.00
Ad Rate: Full Page Colour 500.00
Currency: Euro
DAILY NEWSPAPER

Utrinski Vesnik 161205
Owner: Media Print Macedonia
Editorial: Vasil Gjorgov 16, Skopje 1000
Tel: 389 2 3236 900
Email: vesnik@utrinski.com.mk **Web site:** http://www.utrinski.mk
Freq: Daily; **Circ:** 25000 Publisher's Statement
Editor-in-Chief: Sonja Kramarska
Profile: Newspaper focusing on national and international news, business, politics, sport and entertainment and supplements.
Language (s): Macedonian
Ad Rate: Full Page Mono 27666.00
Ad Rate: Full Page Colour 36403.00
Currency: Macedonia Denars
DAILY NEWSPAPER

Vecer 157013
Owner: Vecer Press
Editorial: Ulica Mito Hatsivasilev Yasmin 66, Skopje 1000 **Tel:** 389 2 321 9650
Email: vecer@vecer.com.mk **Web site:** http://vecer.mk
Freq: Daily; **Circ:** 10000 Publisher's Statement
Editor-in-Chief: Ivona Talevska
Profile: Newspaper focusing on national and international news, politics, business and sport.
Language (s): Macedonian
Ad Rate: Full Page Mono 660.00
Ad Rate: Full Page Colour 830.00
Currency: Euro
DAILY NEWSPAPER

News Service/Syndicate

Macedonian Information Centre 353227
Editorial: Naum Naumovski Borce 73, Skopje 1000
Tel: 389 2 31 17 876
Email: contact@micnews.com.mk **Web site:** http://micnews.com.mk
Director: Dragan Antonov
Profile: Macedonian Information Centre is an independent news agency. MIC's primary task is providing news, information and analyses to the international community, mainly to foreign governments, foreign embassies, governmental organizations, institutes, international businesses, libraries, various research organizations, news agencies and media abroad about Macedonian politics, economy, society, religion, culture, etc.
Language (s): Macedonian
NEWS SERVICE/SYNDICATE

MIA news agency 458093
Editorial: Bojmija K-2, Skopje 1000
Tel: 389 2 24 61 600
Email: mia@mia.com.mk **Web site:** http://www.mia.com.mk
Editor In Chief: Ljupco Jakimoski
Profile: Macedonian Information Agency. MIA launched the first news on September 30, 1998.
Language (s): Macedonian
NEWS SERVICE/SYNDICATE

Madagascar

Time Difference: GMT +3
National Telephone Code: 261
Continent: Africa
Capital: Antananarivo

Newspapers

L' Express de Madagascar 218470
Owner: L'Express de Madagascar S.A
Editorial: ZI Nord route des Hydrocarbures, Ankorondrano, Antananarivo **Tel:** 261 20 22 21 934
Email: lexpress@malagasy.com **Web site:** http://www.lexpressmada.com
Freq: Daily; **Circ:** 11000 Publisher's Statement
Editor in Chief: Lova Rabary-Rakotondravony
Profile: National daily newspaper covering regional, national and international news and current affairs including politics, economy, society, culture and sport.
Language (s): French
Ad Rate: Full Page Mono 400000.00
Ad Rate: Full Page Colour 800000.00
Currency: Madagascar Ariary
DAILY NEWSPAPER

La Gazette de la Grande Ile 324963
Owner: Groupe MPE
Editorial: Lot II W 23 L, Ankorahotra, Antananarivo 101 **Tel:** 261 20 22 61 377
Email: redaction@lagazette-dgi.com **Web site:** http://www.lagazette-dgi.com
Freq: Daily; **Circ:** 60000 Publisher's Statement
Directeur des Rédactions: Franck Raharison
Profile: Newspaper covering regional, national and international news and current affairs including politics, business, culture, health, sports and entertainment.
Language (s): French
DAILY NEWSPAPER

Inona no Vaovao 530956
Editorial: Rue Rainivoninahitriniarivo, Antananarivo 101 **Tel:** 261 20 22 329 94
Email: redaction@madagascar-tribune.com
Freq: Daily; **Circ:** 5000 Publisher's Statement
Directeur de Publication: Daddy Ramanankasina;
Directeur Général: Anselme Randriakoto
Profile: Inona no Vaovao (Malagasy for 'what's new') is a newspaper focusing on national and international news, politics, finance, culture and sport as well as local issues and concerns.
Language (s): Malagasy
Ad Rate: Full Page Mono 264000.00
Ad Rate: Full Page Colour 552000.00
Currency: Madagascar Ariary
DAILY NEWSPAPER

Madagascar Tribune 217915
Owner: Societe Malgache d'Edition
Editorial: Rue Rainivoninahitriniarivo, Ankorodrano, Antananarivo 101 **Tel:** 261 20 22 226 35
Email: redaction@madagascar-tribune.com **Web site:** http://www.madagascar-tribune.com
Freq: Daily; **Circ:** 6500 Publisher's Statement
Rédacteur en Chef: Anselme Randriakoto
Profile: Newspaper covering regional, national and international news and current affairs including politics and economy.
Language (s): French
Ad Rate: Full Page Mono 264000.00
Ad Rate: Full Page Colour 552000.00
Currency: Madagascar Ariary
DAILY NEWSPAPER

Midi Madagasikara 217916
Owner: Ialana Ravoninahitriniarivo
Editorial: Rue Ravoninahitriniarivo, Ankorondrano, Antananarivo 101 **Tel:** 261 33 11 697 79
Email: contact@midi-madagasikara.mg **Web site:** http://www.midi-madagasikara.mg
Freq: Daily; **Circ:** 35000 Publisher's Statement
Editor in Chief: Zo Rakotoseheno
Profile: Newspaper covering regional, national and international news and current affairs including politics, economy, society, sports and culture.
Language (s): French
DAILY NEWSPAPER

Weekly 531209
Editorial: Rue Rainivoninahitriniarivo, Antananarivo 101 **Tel:** 261 20 22 329 94
Email: redaction@madagascar-tribune.com
Circ: 5000 Publisher's Statement
Directeur de Publication: Anselme Randriakoto
Profile: Newspaper focusing on national and international news, politics, finance, culture and sport as well as local issues and concerns.
Language (s): French
Ad Rate: Full Page Mono 264000.00
Ad Rate: Full Page Colour 552000.00
Currency: Madagascar Ariary
DAILY NEWSPAPER

Malawi

Time Difference: GMT +2
National Telephone Code: 265
Continent: Africa
Capital: Lilongwe

Newspapers

The Nation 771904
Owner: Nation Publications Ltd
Editorial: PO Box 30408, Chichiri, Blantyre 3
Tel: 265 111 61 18 89
Email: nationonline@mwnation.com **Web site:** http://mwnation.com
Freq: Weekly; **Circ:** 15000 Publisher's Statement
Editor in Chief: Alfred Ntonga
Profile: National newspaper covering news and current affairs including business, economy, politics, entertainment, lifestyle, society and sport.
Language (s): English
Ad Rate: Full Page Colour 297950.87
Currency: Malawi Kwachas
DAILY NEWSPAPER

Malaysia

Time Difference: GMT +8
National Telephone Code: 60
Continent: Asia
Capital: Kuala Lumpur

Newspapers

Bacaria 425271
Editorial: Kumpulan Karangkraf Sdn Bhd, Lot 2, Jln. Sepana 15/3, Off Persiaran Selangor, Seksyen 15, Selangor Darul Ehsan, Shah Alam 40200
Tel: 60 3 51 01 38 88
Email: editor.bacaria@karangkraf.com.my **Web site:** http://www.karangkraf.com.my
Freq: Weekly; **Circ:** 99001 Not Audited
Editor: Meen Tahrin
Profile: Covers Entertainment, News, Women, Health, etc.
Language (s): Bahasa Malaysia
DAILY NEWSPAPER

Berita Harian 400276
Editorial: Berita Harian Sdn Bhd, Balai Berita, 31 Jln. Riong, Bangsar, Kuala Lumpur 59100
Tel: 60 322822323
Email: bhnews@bharian.com.my **Web site:** http://www.bharian.com.my
Freq: Daily; **Circ:** 192917 Not Audited
Editor: Mohammad Khaidir Abd. Majid; **Editor:** Azhar Abu Samah; **Editor:** Saidon Idris; **Editor:** Fadzlena Jafar; **Editor:** Badrulhisham Othman
Profile: Daily newspaper published in Malaysia. Covers general news, current events and lifestyle.
Language (s): Bahasa Malaysia
Ad Rate: Full Page Mono 12672.00
Ad Rate: Full Page Colour 26172.00
Currency: Malaysia Ringgits
DAILY NEWSPAPER

Berita Minggu 400277
Editorial: Berita Harian Sdn Bhd, Balai Berita, 31 Jln Riong, Kuala Lumpur 59100 **Tel:** 60 322822323
Email: bminggu@bharian.com.my **Web site:** http://www.bharian.com.my
Freq: Daily; **Circ:** 305256 Not Audited
Editor: Norhayati Said
Profile: Daily newspaper published in Malay. General news, current events, lifestyle
Language (s): Bahasa Malaysia
Ad Rate: Full Page Mono 12672.00
Ad Rate: Full Page Colour 26172.00
Currency: Malaysia Ringgits
DAILY NEWSPAPER

The Borneo Post 459926
Editorial: Borneo Post Sdn Bhd, 2nd Floor, Crown Tower, 88 Jln. Pending, Sarawak, Kuching 93450
Tel: 60 82485118
Email: reporters@theborneopost.com **Web site:** http://www.theborneopost.com
Freq: Daily; **Circ:** 84392 Not Audited
Editor: Jimmy Adit; **Manager:** Sing Seng Wong
Profile: Daily newspaper published in Malay. Current events, news and lifestyle with a focus on the Sarawak/Borneo region.
Language (s): English
Ad Rate: Full Page Mono 2200.00
Ad Rate: Full Page Colour 4400.00
Currency: Malaysia Ringgits
DAILY NEWSPAPER

The Borneo Post (Sabah) 460445
Editorial: No.1301 1st Floor Jalan Sri Dgans, Miri Waterfront, Wisma KTS, Jalan Pantai, Sabah, Kota Kinabalu 98000 **Tel:** 60 854277700
Email: borneopostkk@yahoo.com **Web site:** http://www.theborneopost.com
Freq: Daily; **Circ:** 22098 Not Audited
Editor in Chief: Nai Wen Chiu; **Manager:** Lee Ngik Long
Profile: Daily newspaper covering the Sabah area. Current & Local News, International News, Sports, Business, Entertainment, Features, Technology, War, Politics, etc.
Language (s): English
DAILY NEWSPAPER

China Press 400249
Editorial: The China Press Berhad, 80 Jalan Riong, Off Jln Bangsar, Kuala Lumpur 59100
Tel: 603 22896363
Email: enews@chinapress.com.my **Web site:** http://www.chinapress.com.my
Freq: Daily; **Circ:** 240002 Not Audited
Editor: Soong Yoke Chai; **Editor:** Yee Wei Loh; **Editor in Chief:** Yang Khoon Teoh
Profile: Covers local and international news, sports, business, entertainment, economy, etc.
Language (s): Chinese
Ad Rate: Full Page Colour 30800.00
Currency: Malaysia Ringgits
DAILY NEWSPAPER

Daily Express 400268
Editorial: Sabah Publishing House Sdn. Bhd., P.O. Box 10139, Sabah, Kota Kinabalu 88801
Tel: 60 88256422
Email: forum@dailyexpress.com.my **Web site:** http://www.dailyexpress.com.my
Freq: Daily; **Circ:** 30002 Not Audited
Editor in Chief: James Sardahthisa
Profile: Covers a wide range of topics including international, national and local news, financial and business pages, sports, entertainment and leisure.
Language (s): English
Ad Rate: Full Page Mono 3784.20
Ad Rate: Full Page Colour 9460.50
Currency: Malaysia Ringgits
DAILY NEWSPAPER

The Edge 459925
Owner: Edge Communications Sdn Bhd (The)
Editorial: Level 3 Monara KLK, #1, Jalan Pju 7/6, Mutiara Damansara, Petaling Jaya 47810
Tel: 60 377218000
Email: dteoh@bizedge.com **Web site:** http://www.theedgemarkets.com
Freq: Weekly; **Circ:** 24043 Not Audited
Editor in Chief: Kay Tat Ho; **Manager:** Chandran Ravi
Profile: Daily newspaper covering business, general news, current events, international news, sports, etc.
Language (s): English
Ad Rate: Full Page Mono 10878.00
Ad Rate: Full Page Colour 14878.00
Currency: Malaysia Ringgits
DAILY NEWSPAPER

The Edge Financial Daily 172675
Owner: Edge Communications Sdn Bhd (The)
Editorial: Level 3, Menara KLK, #1 Jalan PJU 7/6, Mutiara Damansara, Petaling Jaya 47810
Tel: 603 77218000
Email: info@bizedge.com **Web site:** http://www.theedgemarkets.com
Freq: 2 Times/Week; **Circ:** 15001 Not Audited
Profile: Covers business and finance, assessing stocks with the most momentum.
Language (s): English
DAILY NEWSPAPER

Guang Ming Daily 400250
Editorial: Guang Ming Ribao Sdn Bhd, 19 Jalan Semangat, Selangor, Petaling Jaya 46200
Tel: 60 3 7965 8888
Email: gmkl@guangming.com.my **Web site:** http://www.guangming.com.my
Freq: Daily; **Circ:** 99706 Not Audited
Profile: daily newspaper published in Chinese. Covers general news, current events and lifestyle news for the Chinese community
Language (s): Chinese
Ad Rate: Full Page Colour 65000.00
Currency: Malaysia Ringgits
DAILY NEWSPAPER

Guang Ming Daily (Penang) 459000
Editorial: No.19 Jalan, Semongat, Petaling Jaya Selangor, Penang 96200 **Tel:** 60 379658888
Email: editorial-pg@guangming.com.my **Web site:** http://www.guangming.com.my
Freq: Daily; **Circ:** 70003 Not Audited
Manager: Chin Wah Cheah
Profile: Malaysian Chinese Community in Penang. Local, National, Regional and International News.
Language (s): Chinese
DAILY NEWSPAPER

Harakah 402352
Editorial: Parti Islam SeMalaysia (PAS), No. 22 Jalan Pahang Barat, Pekiling Business Centre, Kuala Lumpur 53000 **Tel:** 60 340233270
Email: editor.harakahdaily@gmail.com **Web site:** http://www.harakahdaily.net
Freq: Daily; **Circ:** 250003 Not Audited
Editor: Roslan Hamid; **Editor:** Tarmizi Mohd Jam; **Editor:** Taufek Yahaya
Profile: Daily newspaper published in Malay. Covers general news, current events & lifestyle.
Language (s): Bahasa Malaysia
DAILY NEWSPAPER

Harian Metro 402433
Editorial: The News Straits Times Press (M) Bhd, Balai Berita, 31 Jln. Riong, Bangsar, Kuala Lumpur 59100
Email: am@hmetro.com.my **Web site:** http://www.hmetro.com.my
Freq: Daily; **Circ:** 331003 Not Audited
Editor: Roslan Ibrahim; **Editor:** Othman Mamat; **Editor in Chief:** Sharifuddin Mohamad; **Editor:** Abdul Khalid Mohd Yasin; **Editor:** Adam Salleh
Profile: Daily newspaper published in Malay. Covers news, current events & lifestyle
Language (s): Bahasa Malaysia
Ad Rate: Full Page Mono 12672.00
Ad Rate: Full Page Colour 26172.00
Currency: Malaysia Ringgits
DAILY NEWSPAPER

International Times 400244
Editorial: International Times Sdn Bhd, Lot 2215, Jalan Bengkel, Pending Industrial Estate, Serawak, Kuching 93450 **Tel:** 60 82487778
Email: kuching@intimes.com.my **Web site:** http://www.intimes.com.my
Freq: Daily; **Circ:** 36001 Not Audited
Editor in Chief: Fook Onn Lee
Profile: Covers local, national, regional and international news, sports, entertainment, economy and politics, etc.
Language (s): Chinese
DAILY NEWSPAPER

Kosmo! 400247
Editorial: Utusan Melayu (Malaysia) Berhad, 46M, Jalan Lima, Off Jalan Chan Sow Lin, Kuala Lumpur 55200 **Tel:** 60 3 922-14001
Web site: http://www.kosmo.com.my
Freq: Daily; **Circ:** 108798 Not Audited
Editor: Badrul Azhar Abdul Rahman; **Editor:** Asan Ahmad; **Editor:** Baharom Mahusin
Profile: Daily newspaper published in Malay targeted at a younger audience
Language (s): Bahasa Malaysia
DAILY NEWSPAPER

Kosmo!Ahad 511056
Editorial: Utusan Melayu (Malaysia) Berhad, 46M, Jalan Lima, Off Jalan Chan Sow Lin, Kuala Lumpur 55200 **Tel:** 60 392217055
Email: berita@kosmo.com.my **Web site:** http://www.kosmo.com.my
Freq: Weekly; **Circ:** 109897 Not Audited
Editor: Zuki Pileh
Profile: Sunday edition of Kosmo! News lifestyle and entertainment for young adults published in Malay
Language (s): Bahasa Malaysia
DAILY NEWSPAPER

Kwong Wah Yit Poh 400251
Owner: Kwong Wah Yit Poh Press Berhad
Editorial: Kwong Wah Yit Poh Press Berhad, 19, Lebuh Presgrave, Pulau Pinang, Penang 10300
Tel: 60 4 261 2312
Email: editor@kwongwah.com.my **Web site:** http://www.kwongwah.com.my
Freq: Daily; **Circ:** 74002 Not Audited
Editor in Chief: Kam Cheong Voo
Profile: Covers Local, National, Regional and International news.
Language (s): Chinese
Ad Rate: Full Page Mono 7314.00
Ad Rate: Full Page Colour 18550.00
Currency: Malaysia Ringgits
DAILY NEWSPAPER

Makkal Osai 402351
Editorial: Makkal Osai Sdn Bhd, 19M, Jalan Murai Dua, Batu Complex, Off Jalan Ipoh, 3 1/4 Mile, Kuala Lumpur 51200 **Tel:** 60 3 6250-4500
Email: news@makkalosai.com
Freq: Daily; **Circ:** 27002 Not Audited
General Manager: M. Periasamy; **Editor:** B. Rajan
Profile: Daily newspaper published in Tamil. Provides local news, national news, regional news and international news for the Malaysian community.
Language (s): Tamil
DAILY NEWSPAPER

The Malay Mail 400226
Editorial: B-3A-02, Dataran 3 Dua, #2, Jalan 19/1, Petaling Jaya 46300 **Tel:** 60 379472288
Email: mmnews@mmail.com.my **Web site:** http://www.themalaymailonline.com
Freq: Daily; **Circ:** 20816 Not Audited
Editor: Yushaimi Yahaya
Profile: Daily newspaper covers general news, current events and lifestyle. The Malay Mail is widely read in the Klang Valley conurbation consisting of the nation's capital Kuala Lumpur, Petaling Jaya and heading west towards Klang and Port Klang; Sungai Buluh and Rawang to the north; and the Multimedia Supercorridor extending towards Kajang, Cyberjaya and Putrajaya, the administrative capital of Malaysia.
Language (s): English
Ad Rate: Full Page Mono 7128.00
Ad Rate: Full Page Colour 7920.00
Currency: Malaysia Ringgits
DAILY NEWSPAPER

Malaysia Nanban 400245
Editorial: Penerbitan Sahabat (M) Sdn Bhd, 544-3, Batu Complex, Kuala Lumpur 51100
Tel: 60 3 6251 5981
Email: news@nanban.com.my **Web site:** http://nanban2u.com.my
Freq: Daily; **Circ:** 60007 Not Audited
Editor: Malayandi M.
Profile: Daily newspaper published in Tamil. Focus on Malaysian Indian Community. General news, Tamil news, Sports and Entertainment. Circulation for Sunday newspaper is 120000 copies.
Language (s): Tamil
DAILY NEWSPAPER

The Malaysian Reserve 483600
Editorial: Unit 23A-1 Menara 1MK, Jalan Kiara, Mont Kiara, Kuala Lumpur 50480 **Tel:** 60 3 62111851
Email: news@themalaysianreserve.com **Web site:** http://www.themalaysianreserve.com
Freq: 2 Times/Week; **Circ:** 12000 Not Audited
Manager: Ching Yin Ng
Profile: Associated with the International New York Times, covers business and financial news.
Language (s): Bahasa Malaysia
Ad Rate: Full Page Mono 7084.00
Ad Rate: Full Page Colour 10584.00
Currency: Malaysia Ringgits
DAILY NEWSPAPER

Melaka Hari Ini 459942
Editorial: Penerbitan IKSEP Sdn Bhd, Bangunan Rumah Media Melaka, Jalan Lingkaran MITC, Ayer Keroh, Melaka 75450 **Tel:** 60 62519315
Email: editorial@melakahariini.com.my **Web site:** http://www.melakahariini.com.my
Freq: Daily; **Circ:** 4006 Not Audited
Editor in Chief: Ishak Dalib
Profile: Daily newspaper published in Malay 90% local & National news :Economy, Business, Politic, State Development, Entertainment, etc.
Language (s): Bahasa Malaysia
DAILY NEWSPAPER

Merdeka Daily News 400261
Editorial: Merdeka Daily News Sdn Bhd, No. 64 Jalan Utara Batu 3 1/2, Sandakan 90000
Tel: 60 89213704
Email: merkk@tm.net.my
Freq: Daily; **Circ:** 12003 Not Audited
Editor in Chief: Kon Shing Fung
Profile: Daily newspaper published in Chinese. Covers general news and current events
Language (s): Chinese
DAILY NEWSPAPER

Metro Ahad 400278
Editorial: The New Straits Times Press (M) Berhad, Balai Berita, Jln. Riong, Bangsar, Kuala Lumpur 59100
Web site: http://www.hmetro.com.my
Freq: Weekly; **Circ:** 370007 Not Audited
Editor: Sharifuddin Mohamad; **Editor:** Tuan Asri Tuan Hussin
Profile: Daily paper for Malay readers covers current and Social Affairs, People news, Entertainment, Sports, etc. Published by New Straits Times
Language (s): Bahasa Malaysia
DAILY NEWSPAPER

Mingguan Malaysia 400248
Editorial: Utusan Melayu (M) Bhd, 46M Jalan Lima, Off Jalan Chan Sow Lin, P.O. Box 671, Kuala Lumpur 55200 **Tel:** 60 392217055
Web site: http://www.utusan.com.my
Freq: Daily; **Circ:** 459793 Not Audited
Editor: Jamliah Abdullah; **Editor:** Zin Mahmud; **Editor:** Mohd Hassan Mohd Noor
Profile: Covers regional, national, and international news, as well as entertainment, business, politics, etc.
Language (s): Bahasa Malaysia
Ad Rate: Full Page Colour 13000.00
Currency: Malaysia Ringgits
DAILY NEWSPAPER

Nanyang Siang Pau 400252
Editorial: Nanyang Siang Pau Sdn Bhd, 1st Floor, No.1, Jalan SS 7/2, Selangor, Petaling Jaya 47301
Tel: 60 3 7872 6888
Email: editor@nanyang.com.my **Web site:** http://www.nanyang.com
Freq: Daily; **Circ:** 105847 Not Audited
editor in chief: Chan Aun Kuang Chen; **Editor:** Siok Ching Tong
Profile: Chinese language daily newspaper covers general news, current events and lifestyle
Language (s): Chinese
DAILY NEWSPAPER

New Sabah Times 157118
Editorial: Inna Kinabalu Sdn Bhd., Jalan Pusat Pembangunan Masyarakat/ Lorong Selungsung D, Off Jalan Mat Salleh, Sembulan, Sabah, Kota Kinabalu 88100 **Tel:** 60 88230055
Web site: http://www.newsabahtimes.com.my
Freq: Daily; **Circ:** 23926 Not Audited
Editor in Chief: Boon Heng Ch'ng; **Editor:** Michael De La Harpe; **Manager:** Foong Yee Hee; **Editor:** Mohd Amin Muin
Profile: Covers regional, national, and international news, as well as entertainment, business, politics, etc.
Language (s): English
DAILY NEWSPAPER

New Sarawak Tribune 845280
Editorial: Lot 231, Jalan Nipah, Off Jalan, Abell Utara, Kuching 93050 **Tel:** 60 82 424411
Web site: http://www.newsarawaktribune.com
Freq: Daily
Editor: William Chan
Profile: Covers local and national news.
Language (s): Bahasa Malaysia
DAILY NEWSPAPER

New Straits Times 158857
Editorial: Balai Berita, 31 Jalan Riong, Kuala Lumpur 59100 **Tel:** 60 322823322
Email: news@nstp.com.my **Web site:** http://www.nst.com.my
Freq: Daily; **Circ:** 139767 Not Audited
Editor: Melanie Proctor; **Editor:** Kamarulzaman Salleh
Profile: Covers general news, current events and lifestyle issues.
Language (s): English
Ad Rate: Full Page Colour 11352.00
Currency: Malaysia Ringgits
DAILY NEWSPAPER

New Sunday Times 158858
Editorial: The New Straits Times Press (M) Berhad, Balai Berita, 31 Jalan Riong, Kuala Lumpur 59100
Tel: 60 322823131
Email: news@nstp.com.my **Web site:** http://www.nst.com.my
Freq: Weekly; **Circ:** 153409 Not Audited
Editor: Hamidah Atan; **Edtior:** Syed Nadzri SyedHarum
Profile: This is the Sunday edition of New Straits Times. Covers news, analyses of issues, features,

informative articles and a variety of leisure reading and entertainment updates.
Language (s): English
Ad Rate: Full Page Colour 11352.00
Currency: Malaysia Ringgits
DAILY NEWSPAPER

Nichi-Ma Press 400265
Owner: Multi Valiant
Editorial: Multi Valiant Sdn. Bhd, 4D, Jalan Petaling Utama 8 (PJS1/29), Batu 7, Jalan Klang Lama, Petaling Jaya 46000 **Tel:** 60 377842317
Email: editor@nichimapress.com **Web site:** http://www.nichimapress.com
Freq: Semi-Monthly; **Circ:** 21002 Not Audited
Editor in Chief: A. Watanabe
Profile: Provides news for the Japanese community living in Malaysia.
Language (s): Japanese
DAILY NEWSPAPER

Oriental Daily News 400253
Editorial: Oriental Daily Sdn Bhd, Wisma Dang Wangi, Jalan Dang Wangi 38, Kuala Lumpur 50100
Tel: 60 326916336
Email: news@orientaldaily.com.my **Web site:** http://www2.orientaldaily.com.my
Freq: Daily; **Circ:** 102502 Not Audited
Editor: Chooi Hor Chen; **Editor:** Chai Yoke Ho; **Editor in Chief:** Keak Hock Ko
Profile: Covers general news, current events & lifestyle
Language (s): Chinese
DAILY NEWSPAPER

Overseas Chinese Daily News 459967
Editorial: Sabah Publishing House Sdn Bhd., P.O. Box 10139, Sabah, Kota Kinabalu 88801
Tel: 60 88256422
Email: sph@dailyexpress.com **Web site:** http://www.ocdn.com.my
Freq: Daily; **Circ:** 20006 Not Audited
Editor in Chief: Yuk Seng Hii; **Publisher:** Clement Yeh Chang
Profile: Covers local, regional, national, and international news.
Language (s): Chinese
DAILY NEWSPAPER

See Hua Daily News 460446
Editorial: See Hua Daily News Bhd, Lot 7705 Jalan Pending, Kuching 93450 **Tel:** 60 843297777
Freq: Daily; **Circ:** 52323 Not Audited
Editor in Chief: Kuok Kiong Ling; **Manager:** Sing Seng Wong
Profile: Daily newspaper published in Chinese. Covers general news, current events and lifestyle
Language (s): Chinese
DAILY NEWSPAPER

See Hua Daily News (Sabah) 400264
Editorial: TB 2097 1st Floor Jln Aps, Hw Dat Lijht Industrial Est, Kota Kinabalu 91000 **Tel:** 60 89912568
Email: seehuasbh@yahoo.com **Web site:** http://seehua.com
Freq: Daily; **Circ:** 22217 Not Audited
Editor in Chief: Chee Kong Toh; **Manager:** Wah Hin Yii
Profile: Daily newspaper for Malaysian Chinese Community in Sabah area. Current & Local News, International News, Business and Politic, Sports, Entertainment, etc.
Language (s): Chinese
DAILY NEWSPAPER

Sin Chew Daily 400254
Editorial: Pemandangan Sinar Sdn Bhd, 19 Jalan Semangat, Petaling Jaya 46200 **Tel:** 60 3 79658888
Email: info@sinchew-i.com **Web site:** http://www.mysinchew.com
Freq: Daily; **Circ:** 336401 Not Audited
Editor: Yoke Loong Lee; **Editor in Chief:** Ah Lek Pook
Profile: Covers national and international news, as well as entertainment, business, sports, etc.
Language (s): Chinese
Ad Rate: Full Page Colour 48000.00
Currency: Malaysia Ringgits
DAILY NEWSPAPER

Sinar Harian 541465
Owner: Akhbar Cabaran
Editorial: Akhbar Cabaran Sdn Bhd, Lot 2 Jalan Sepana 15/3, Off Persiaran Selangor, Seksyen 15, Selangor, Shah Alam 40200 **Tel:** 603 51013888
Email: editor.web@sinarharian.com.my **Web site:** http://www.sinarharian.com.my
Freq: Daily; **Circ:** 150002 Not Audited
Editor: Wan Normi Hasan; **Editor:** Muhamad Mat Yakim; **Editor:** Boon Teck Ong; **Editor:** Azmi Tarmizi
Profile: Covers news, current events and lifestyle.
Language (s): Bahasa Malaysia
DAILY NEWSPAPER

The Star Malaysia 156670
Owner: Star Publications (M) Bhd.
Editorial: Menara Star, 15 Jalan 16/11, Selangor, Petaling Jaya 46350 **Tel:** 60 3 79671388
Email: editor@thestar.com.my **Web site:** http://www.thestar.com.my
Freq: Daily; **Circ:** 309181 Not Audited
Editor, Environment: Tan Cheng Li; **News Editor:** Esther Ng; **News Editor:** Foong Pek Yee; **News Editor:** Devid Rajah
Profile: Covers general news, current events and lifestyle.
Language (s): English
Ad Rate: Full Page Colour 20424.00
Currency: Malaysia Ringgits
DAILY NEWSPAPER

The Sun 400256
Editorial: Sun Media Corporation Sdn Bhd, 4th Flr, Lt 6, Jln 51/217, Sect 51, Selangor Darul Ehsan, Petaling Jaya 46050 **Tel:** 60 3 7784 6688
Web site: http://www.thesundaily.my
Freq: Daily; **Circ:** 275003 Not Audited
Managing Director: Chan Kien Sing; **Editor:** Sebastian Lim; **Editor:** Navjeet Singh; **Editor:** Peter Yap
Profile: Daily newspaper published in English. Covers general news, current events, lifestyle
Language (s): English
Ad Rate: Full Page Mono 13320.00
Ad Rate: Full Page Colour 22320.00
Currency: Malaysia Ringgits
DAILY NEWSPAPER

Sunday Nesan 459928
Editorial: Tamil Nesan (M) Sdn Bhd, No. 23, Jalan SBC 5, Taman Sri Batu Caves, Selangor, Batu Caves 68100 **Tel:** 60 361841818
Email: mytamilnesan@yahoo.com **Web site:** http://www.tamilnewsan.com.my
Freq: Weekly; **Circ:** 95002 Not Audited
Editor: K. Padmanathan
Profile: Covers general news, sports, politics, economy, entertainment, etc.
Language (s): Tamil
DAILY NEWSPAPER

The Sunday Post 460405
Editorial: The Borneo Post, 2nd Floor, Crown Tower, 88 Jalan Pending, Serawak, Kuching 93450
Tel: 60 82485111
Email: bp_editors@yahoo.com **Web site:** http://www.theborneopost.com
Freq: Weekly; **Circ:** 60006 Not Audited
Editor: Aden Nagrace; **Manager:** Sing Seng Wong
Profile: The Sunday Post is the Sunday Edition of The Borneo Post. It covers local and international neews, Entertainment, Sports, and etc. Focus on Sarawak
Language (s): Bahasa Malaysia
DAILY NEWSPAPER

Sunday Star 158856
Owner: Star Publications (Malaysia) Berhad
Editorial: Star Publications (Malaysia) Berhad, Menara Star, 15 Jln. 16/11, Selangor, Petaling Jaya 46350 **Tel:** 60 3 7967 1388
Email: sunday@thestar.com.my **Web site:** http://www.thestar.com.my
Freq: Weekly; **Circ:** 295552 Not Audited
Editor: Asatha Mataayun
Profile: Covers National and International News, Sports and Entertainment, Economic and Politics, Features, etc.
Language (s): English
Ad Rate: Full Page Colour 27000.00
Currency: Malaysia Ringgits
DAILY NEWSPAPER

Tamil Nesan 400246
Editorial: Tamil Nesan (M) Sdn Bhd, No. 23, Jalan SBC 5, Taman Sri Batu Caves, Selangor, Batu Caves 68100 **Tel:** 60 361841818
Email: mytamilnesan@yahoo.com **Web site:** http://www.tamilnesan.com.my
Freq: Daily; **Circ:** 45001 Not Audited
Editor in Chief: K. Padmanathan
Profile: Covers general news, politics, economy, entertainment, sports, etc.
Language (s): Tamil
DAILY NEWSPAPER

Tech & U 460430
Editorial: Tech&U, New Straits Times Sdn.Bhd, 2nd Floor, Balai Berita, Anjung Liku, Kuala Lumpur 59100
Tel: 60 3 2282-3322
Web site: http://technu.nst.com.my
Freq: Weekly; **Circ:** 139763 Not Audited
Editor: Ahmad Kushairi; **Manager:** Kobu Suppayah
Profile: A pullout from New Strait Times newspaper, publishing twice a week (Mondays and Thursdays). Covers tech news, reviews and information. Formerly Computimes.
Language (s): English
DAILY NEWSPAPER

United Daily News 400241
Editorial: Lot 2597, Block 3, MCLD, Wisma United Borneo Press, Jalan Piasau, Sarawak, Miri 98000
Tel: 60 85 656666
Email: miri@uniteddaily.com.my **Web site:** http://www.uniteddaily.com.my
Freq: Daily; **Circ:** 35007 Not Audited
Profile: Chinese language daily newspaper. Covers news locally and internationally. Also offers information on finance and entertainment and offers readers comics and horoscopes.
Language (s): Mandarin
DAILY NEWSPAPER

Utusan Borneo 400240
Editorial: The Borneo Post Sdn Bhd, No.88, Jalan Pending, Level 2 Crown Tower, Kuching 93450
Tel: 60 82 485 118
Web site: http://www.theborneopost.com
Freq: Daily; **Circ:** 10003 Not Audited
Manager: Sing Seng Wong
Profile: Daily newspaper published in Malay, targeting Sarawak region. General news, current events, lifestyle
Language (s): Bahasa Malaysia
DAILY NEWSPAPER

Utusan Borneo (Sabah) 539007
Editorial: Borneo Post (Sabah) Sdn Bhd, Jln. Tuaran Batu 5 1/2, Kota Kinabalu 88450 **Tel:** 60 88421717
Email: utusanborneokk@yahoo.com.my
Freq: Daily
Editor: Samsul Bin Ali Maran
Profile: Daily newspaper published in Malay. Covers general news current events, lifestyle in the Sabah/ Borneo region
Language (s): Bahasa Malaysia
DAILY NEWSPAPER

Utusan Malaysia 400279
Owner: Utusan Melayu (M) Sdn Bhd
Editorial: 46M Jalan Lima, Off Jalan Chan Sow Lin, Kuala Lumpur 55200 **Tel:** 60 392217055
Email: pengarang@utusangroup.com.my **Web site:** http://www.utusan.com.my
Freq: Daily; **Circ:** 197033 Not Audited
Editor: Zulkefli Hamzah; **Editor:** Mustapha Kamal; **Editor:** Mowardi Mahmud; **Editor:** Baharom Mahusin; **Editor:** Othman Mohamad; **Editor:** Gamal Nasir Mohd. Ali; **Editor:** Zaharuddin Mustafa
Profile: Covers general news, current events and lifestyle.
Language (s): Bahasa Malaysia
Ad Rate: Full Page Colour 12000.00
Currency: Malaysia Ringgits
DAILY NEWSPAPER

News Service/Syndicate

Bernama 353208
Owner: Malaysian National News Agency
Editorial: #28, Jalan 1/65A, Off Jalan Tun Razak, Kuala Lumpur 50400 **Tel:** 60 326939933
Email: bgns@bernama.com **Web site:** http://www.bernama.com/bernama/v8/index.php
Freq: Daily
Editor: Mikhail Raj Abdullah; **General Manager:** Hasnul Hassan; **Editor:** Mokhtar Hussain; **Manager:** Zarina Rozali; **Editor in Chief:** Zulkefli Salleh
Profile: News service providing news and information to news papers, radio and television.
Language (s): English
NEWS SERVICE/SYNDICATE

Maldives

Time Difference: GMT +5
National Telephone Code: 960
Continent: Asia
Capital: Malé

Newspapers

Haveeru Daily 157101
Owner: Haveeru Daily
Editorial: PO Box 20103, Ameenee Magu, Male
Tel: 960 332 56 71
Email: haveeru@haveeru.com.mv **Web site:** http://www.haveeru.com.mv
Freq: Daily; **Circ:** 4500 Publisher's Statement
Editor: Ali Rafeeq
Profile: Newspaper focusing on national and international news, politics, economics, culture and sport.
Language (s): English
DAILY NEWSPAPER

Mali

Time Difference: GMT
National Telephone Code: 223
Continent: Africa
Capital: Bamako

Newspapers

Les Echos 529199
Owner: Jamana
Editorial: Av. Cheick Zayed, Porte 2694, Bamako
Tel: 223 229 62 89
Email: lesechos@jamana.org **Web site:** http://www.lesechos.ml
Freq: Daily; **Circ:** 5000 Publisher's Statement
Director: Adama Coulibaly; **Editor:** Alexis Kalambry
Profile: Daily national newspaper focussing on news, current affairs, regional culture, education and humanitarian issues.
Language (s): French
DAILY NEWSPAPER

L' Essor 156736
Owner: Agence Malienne de Presse et de Publicité (AMAP)
Editorial: Square Patrice Lumumba, BP 141, Bamako
Tel: 223 20 22 36 83
Email: info@essor.ml **Web site:** http://www.essor.ml
Freq: Daily; **Circ:** 13000 Publisher's Statement
Director: Souleymane Drabo; **Editor in Chief:** Salim Togola; **Director:** Mahambé Touré
Profile: Newspaper covering national and international news and current affairs including politics, economy, society, culture and sports.
Language (s): French
Ad Rate: Full Page Mono 259750.00
Ad Rate: Full Page Colour 500000.00
Currency: Communauté Financière Africaine Francs BCEAO
DAILY NEWSPAPER

L' Indépendant 529204
Owner: Aci 2000
Editorial: Aci 2000, Immeuble Mamadou Diabira, Bamako **Tel:** 223 20 29 37 27
Email: lindependant2004@yahoo.fr
Freq: Daily; **Circ:** 5000 Publisher's Statement
Director: Saouti Haïdara; **Editor:** Yaya Sidibé
Profile: Newspaper covering national and international news and current affairs including politics, economy, society, culture and sports.
Language (s): French
Ad Rate: Full Page Mono 250000.00
Ad Rate: Full Page Colour 400000.00
Currency: Communauté Financière Africaine Francs BCEAO
DAILY NEWSPAPER

Info-Matin 529203
Owner: A2M SARL
Editorial: 350 Rue 56, Bamako-Coura, Bamako
Tel: 223 20 238209
Email: sambitoure01@yahoo.fr **Web site:** http://info-matin.ml
Freq: Daily; **Circ:** 1400 Publisher's Statement
Director: Sambi Touré
Profile: National daily newspaper covering national and international news and current affairs including politics, economics, society, education, art, culture and sport.
Language (s): French
Ad Rate: Full Page Mono 300000.00
Currency: Communauté Financière Africaine Francs BCEAO
DAILY NEWSPAPER

Le Nouvel Horizon 529205
Editorial: Rue 608, Porte 21, Banankabougou, Bamako **Tel:** 223 220 06 91
Email: zerelani2001@yahoo.fr
Freq: Daily; **Circ:** 1000 Publisher's Statement
Editor: Daba Balla Keita; **Advertising Manager:** Haïdara Kadida Touré
Profile: National daily newspaper focussing on news, current affairs, politics, economics, culture and sport.
Language (s): French
DAILY NEWSPAPER

La Nouvelle Tribune 529321
Editorial: 635 rue Djoukamady Sissoko, Darsalam
Tel: 223 641 71 34
Email: lanouvelletribune2005@yahoo.fr
Circ: 5000 Publisher's Statement
Director: Ibrahima Coulibaly
Profile: National weekly newspaper focussing on news, current affairs, politics, economics, culture and sport.
Language (s): French
Ad Rate: Full Page Mono 250000.00
Currency: Communauté Financière Africaine Francs BCEAO
DAILY NEWSPAPER

Le Soir de Bamako 529206
Editorial: Rue 608, Porte 21, Banankabougou, Bamako **Tel:** 223 220 06 91
Email: zerelani2001@yahoo.fr
Freq: Daily; **Circ:** 1000 Publisher's Statement
Editor: Oumar Sidibe; **Advertising manager:** Haïdara Kadida Touré
Profile: Regional daily evening newspaper focussing on news, current affairs, politics, economics, culture and sport.
Language (s): French
DAILY NEWSPAPER

News Service/Syndicate

Agence Malienne de Presse et de Publicité (AMAP) 529306
Editorial: Square Patrice Lumumba, BP 141, Bamako
Tel: 223 222 23 46
Email: amap@essor.gov.ml
Profile: National and international news and advertising agency.
Language (s): French
NEWS SERVICE/SYNDICATE

Malta

Malta

Time Difference: GMT +1
National Telephone Code: 356
Continent: Europe
Capital: Valletta

Newspapers

Illum 834699
Owner: MediaToday Co. Ltd
Editorial: Vjal ir-Rihan, San Gwann SGN 9016
Tel: 356 21 382741
Email: illum@mediatoday.com.mt Web site: http://www.illum.com.mt
Freq: Weekly
Managing Director: Saviour Balzan
Profile: Newspaper covering regional, national and international news and current affairs including business, politics, economics, sports, lifestyle and culture.
Language (s): Maltese
DAILY NEWSPAPER

In-Nazzjon 217957
Owner: Media.Link Communications Ltd.
Editorial: Triq Herbert Ganado, Pieta HMR 08
Tel: 356 21 24 3641
Email: news@netmedia.com.mt Web site: http://netnews.com.mt
Freq: Daily; Circ: 22000 Publisher's Statement
Editor: Alex Attard
Profile: Newspaper focusing on national and international news, business, politics, culture and sport.
Language (s): Maltese
DAILY NEWSPAPER

KullHadd 218463
Owner: ONE Group
Editorial: One Complex, A 28 B, Industrial Estate, Marsa MRS 3000 Tel: 356 25 68 2500
Email: editorial@kullhadd.com Web site: http://www.kullhadd.com
Freq: Sun; Circ: 20000 Publisher's Statement
Advertising Manager: Alan Saliba
Profile: Tabloid-sized newspaper focusing on regional, national and international news and current affairs including politics, economics, culture, entertainment and sport.
Language (s): Maltese
Ad Rate: Full Page Mono 690.05
Ad Rate: Full Page Colour 947.20
Currency: Euro
DAILY NEWSPAPER

The Malta Business Weekly 218814
Owner: Standard Publications Ltd
Editorial: Standard House, Birkirkara Hill, St Julians STJ 11 Tel: 356 21 34 58 88
Email: tmbw@independent.com.mt Web site: http://www.independent.com.mt
Freq: Weekly; Circ: 5000 Publisher's Statement
Managing Director: Noel Azzopardi; Editor: Noel Grima
Profile: Magazine covering national and international business and finance issues.
Language (s): English
Ad Rate: Full Page Mono 200.00
Ad Rate: Full Page Colour 370.00
Currency: Malta Liri
DAILY NEWSPAPER

The Malta Independent 217972
Owner: MBR Publications Ltd
Editorial: Highland Apartment, Flat 1, Naxxar Road, Birkirkara STJ 11 Tel: 356 21 345 888
Email: tmid@independent.com.mt Web site: http://www.independent.com.mt
Freq: Daily; Circ: 11000 Publisher's Statement
News Editor: Rachel Attard; Managing Director: Noel Azzopardi
Profile: Newspaper covering regional, national and international news and current affairs including politics, economics, business, lifestyle, arts, entertainment and sport.
Language (s): English
Ad Rate: Full Page Mono 512.46
Ad Rate: Full Page Colour 931.75
Currency: Euro
DAILY NEWSPAPER

The Malta Independent on Sunday 217914
Owner: Standard Publications Ltd
Editorial: Standard House, Birkirkara Hill, St Julians STJ 11 Tel: 356 21 345 888
Email: tmis@independent.com.mt Web site: http://www.independent.com.mt
Freq: Weekly; Circ: 20000 Publisher's Statement
Managing Director: Noel Azzopardi
Profile: Sunday version of the newspaper covering regional, national and international news and current affairs including politics, economics, business, lifestyle, arts, entertainment and sport.
Language (s): English
Ad Rate: Full Page Mono 722.11
Ad Rate: Full Page Colour 1153.04

Currency: Euro
DAILY NEWSPAPER

MaltaToday Midweek 578799
Owner: MediaToday Co. Ltd
Editorial: Vjal ir-Rihan, San Gwann SGN 9016
Tel: 356 21 382 741
Email: midweek@mediatoday.com.mt Web site: http://www.maltatoday.com.mt
Freq: Weekly
Managing Director: Saviour Balzan
Profile: Newspaper covering regional, national and international news and current affairs including business, politics, sports, lifestyle and arts.
Language (s): English
DAILY NEWSPAPER

MaltaToday on Sunday 218464
Owner: MediaToday Co. Ltd
Editorial: Vjal ir-Rihan, San Gwann SGN 9016
Tel: 356 21 382741
Email: maltatoday@mediatoday.com.mt Web site: http://www.maltatoday.com.mt
Freq: Weekly; Circ: 10000 Publisher's Statement
Managing Director: Saviour Balzan
Profile: Newspaper covering regional, national and international news and current affairs including business, politics, culture, lifestyle and sports.
Language (s): English
Ad Rate: Full Page Colour 1165.00
Currency: Euro
DAILY NEWSPAPER

L- Orizzont 217959
Owner: Union Press Co. Ltd.
Editorial: A41 Marsa Industrial Estate, Marsa LQA 06
Tel: 356 25 90 0214
Email: orizzont@unionprint.com.mt Web site: http://inewsmalta.com
Freq: Daily; Circ: 20000 Publisher's Statement
Advertising Manager: Alfred Anastasi; Editor: Josef Caruana
Profile: Newspaper covering regional, national and international news and current affairs including, business, economics, politics and sport.
Language (s): Maltese
Ad Rate: Full Page Mono 231.00
Ad Rate: Full Page Colour 431.00
Currency: Malta Liri
DAILY NEWSPAPER

The Sunday Times 217960
Owner: Allied Newspapers Ltd
Editorial: 341, Strickland House, Triq San Pawl, Valletta VLT 1211 Tel: 356 25 59 41 00
Email: sunday@timesofmalta.com Web site: http://www.timesofmalta.com
Freq: Weekly; Circ: 40000 Publisher's Statement
Editor in Chief: Steve Mallia; Advertising Manager: Etienne Portelli
Profile: Newspaper focusing on national and international news, politics, business and sport.
Language (s): English
Ad Rate: Full Page Mono 403.00
Ad Rate: Full Page Colour 617.00
Currency: Malta Liri
DAILY NEWSPAPER

Times of Malta 217961
Owner: Allied Newspapers Ltd
Editorial: Strickland House, 341 St Paul Street, Valletta VLT 1211 Tel: 356 255 94 100
Email: daily@timesofmalta.com Web site: http://www.timesofmalta.com
Freq: Daily; Circ: 21000 Publisher's Statement
Editor: Raymond Bugeja; Advertising Manager: Etienne Portelli
Profile: Newspaper covering regional, national and international news and current affairs including politics, economics, business and sport.
Language (s): English
Ad Rate: Full Page Mono 980.00
Ad Rate: Full Page Colour 1515.00
Currency: Euro
DAILY NEWSPAPER

Marshall Islands

Time Difference: GMT +12
National Telephone Code: 692
Continent: Oceania
Capital: Majuro

Newspapers

The Marshall Islands Journal 668761
Owner: Marshall Islands Journal
Tel: 692 625 8146
Email: marshallislandsjournal@gmail.com Web site: http://marshallislandsjournal.com
Freq: Weekly; Circ: 15000 Publisher's Statement
Editor: Giff Johnson
Profile: Weekly tabloid-size publication is datelined Friday, but printed on Wednesday and distributed in Majuro on Thursday.
Language (s): English
Ad Rate: Full Page Mono 426.00

Currency: United States Dollars
DAILY NEWSPAPER

Mauritania

Time Difference: GMT
National Telephone Code: 222
Continent: Africa
Capital: Nouakchott

Newspapers

Akhbar Nouakchott 529902
Owner: MAPECI
Editorial: BP 1905, Nouakchott Tel: 222 525 02 71
Email: nouakchottinfo@yahoo.fr Web site: http://www.mapeci.com
Freq: Daily; Circ: 3500 Publisher's Statement
Profile: National daily newspaper focussing on news, current affairs, politics, economics, culture and sports.
Language (s): Arabic
DAILY NEWSPAPER

Chaab 529901
Editorial: Ksar 1540, Rue 22-006 Habib Bourguiba, Nouakchott Tel: 222 45 25 29 16
Email: ami@ami.mr Web site: http://www.ami.mr
Freq: Daily; Circ: 3000 Publisher's Statement
Profile: National daily newspaper covering national and international news and current affairs including politics, economy, society, culture and sports.
Language (s): Arabic
DAILY NEWSPAPER

Horizons 529900
Owner: Agence Mauritanienne d'Information
Editorial: Ksar 1540, Rue 22-006 Habib Bourguiba, Nouakchott Tel: 222 45 25 29 16
Email: ami@ami.mr Web site: http://fr.ami.mr
Freq: Daily; Circ: 2000 Publisher's Statement
Profile: National daily newspaper covering national and international news and current affairs including politics, economy, society, culture and sports.
Language (s): French
DAILY NEWSPAPER

Nouakchott Info 529899
Owner: MAPECI
Editorial: BP 1905, Nouakchott Tel: 222 525 02 71
Email: nouakchottinfo@yahoo.fr Web site: http://www.mapeci.com
Freq: Daily; Circ: 2000 Publisher's Statement
Profile: National newspaper focussing on news, current affairs, politics, economics, culture and sports.
Language (s): Arabic
DAILY NEWSPAPER

News Service/Syndicate

Agence Mauritanienne d'Information - AMI 530300
Owner: Agence Mauritanienne d'Information
Editorial: Ksar 1540, Rue 22-006 Habib Bourguiba, Nouakchott Tel: 222 45 25 29 16
Email: amiakhbar@gmail.com Web site: http://www.ami.mr
Profile: National news service covering national and international news and current affairs including politics, economy, society, culture and sports.
Language (s): Arabic
NEWS SERVICE/SYNDICATE

Mexico

Time Difference: GMT -8 (West Coast), GMT -5 (East Coast)
National Telephone Code: 52
Continent: The Americas
Capital: Mexico City

Newspapers

A.m. De La Piedad 15246
Owner: Reforma
Editorial: Av. Mexico Coyoacan No. 40, Sta. Cruz Atoyac, Michoacan, La Piedad, Michoacan C.P. 03310 Tel: 52 55 56287878
Email: guillermo.oropeza@reforma.com Web site: http://www.reforma.com.mx
Manager: Antonia Leon; Editor: Sergio Pedroza Gomez

Profile: The newspaper features national news, entertainment, and sports. It focuses on local news relevant to La Piedad, Michocan, Mexico.
Language (s): Spanish
Ad Rate: Full Page Mono 1.66
Currency: United States Dollars
DAILY NEWSPAPER

A.m. De Querétaro 383462
Owner: Reforma
Editorial: Av. Mexico Coyoacan No. 40, Sta. Cruz Atoyac, Querétaro, Queretaro, Queretaro C.P. 03310
Tel: 52 55 56287878
Email: guillermo.oropeza@reforma.com Web site: http://www.reforma.com.mx
Profile: The newspaper features national news, entertainment, and sports. It focuses on local news relevant to Queretaro, Queretaro, Mexico.
Language (s): Spanish
Ad Rate: Full Page Mono 2.77
Currency: United States Dollars
DAILY NEWSPAPER

a.m. De San Francisco 383522
Owner: Compañía Periodística Meridiano S.A de C.V
Email: web@periodico.am Web site: http://www.am.com.mx/sanfrancisco
Profile: The newspaper features national news, entertainment, and sports. It focuses on local news relevant to San Francisco del Rincon, Guanajuato, Mexico.
Language (s): Spanish
Ad Rate: Full Page Mono 2.03
Currency: United States Dollars
DAILY NEWSPAPER

a.m. Guanajuato 383460
Owner: Reforma
Editorial: Cantarranas #5, Int #1, Numero 16 Interior 3, Guanajuato, Guanajuato C.P. 36000
Tel: 52 73 732-7727
Web site: http://www.periodico.am/guanajuato
Editor: Catalina Reyes
Profile: a.m. Guanajuato is a daily newspaper features national news, entertainment, and sports. It focuses on local news relevant to Guanajuato, Guanajuato, Mexico.
Language (s): Spanish
Ad Rate: Full Page Mono 1.66
Currency: United States Dollars
DAILY NEWSPAPER

El Agora 736560
Editorial: Calle 9 Av. 3 y 5 #311 Col. Centro, Cordoba, Veracruz 94500 Tel: 52 271 7122750
Email: redaccion@elagora.com.mx Web site: http://www.elagora.com.mx
Freq: Daily
Editor: Alfredo Rios
Language (s): Spanish
DAILY NEWSPAPER

El Bravo 15153
Owner: Medios Masivos M.
Editorial: Luz Savinon No. 13, Del Valle, Tamaulipas, Matamoros, Tamaulipas C.P. 03100
Tel: 52 55 53402450
Email: alfredo.ramirez@mediosmasivos.com.mx Web site: http://www.mediosmasivos.com.mx
Freq: Daily; Circ: 60000 Not Audited
Editor: Oscar Aldape; Publisher: Jose Carretero Balboa; Editor: Alda Guerra; Editor: Daniel Lopez; Editor: Jose Pedroza; Gerente De Ventas: José Alfredo Ramírez
Profile: El Bravo is a daily newspaper serving residents of Matamoros, Mexico. It covers national, regional and international news, sports, business and entertainment.
Language (s): Spanish
Ad Rate: Full Page Mono 27.03
Currency: United States Dollars
DAILY NEWSPAPER

Contexto De Durango 395495
Owner: Directo
Editorial: Blvd. Luia D. Colosio No. 860, Industrial Korian, Durango, Durango, Durango
Web site: http://www.contextodedurango.com.mx
Freq: No Frequency Established
Publicidad: Francisco Marquez
Profile: Cover local, national, and international news, sports, crime, culture and entertainment.
Language (s): Spanish
DAILY NEWSPAPER

La Crítica 476352
Owner: La Crisis
Editorial: Durango No. 233, Roma, Hidalgo, Pachuca, Hidalgo C.P. 06700 Tel: 52 311 4560559
Email: critica-nay@hotmail.com Web site: http://www.diariocritica.com.mx/
Freq: No Frequency Established
Editor: Juan Carlos Guzman
Profile: La Critica delivers local and national news, sports, entertainment, and crime. It also has a women and family section.
Language (s): Spanish
DAILY NEWSPAPER

La Crónica De Hoy 14994
Owner: La Crónica
Editorial: Londres No. 38, Ciudad Juarez, Mexico City, Distrito Federal C.P. 06600 Tel: 52 55 1084-5800
Email: publicidad@cronica.com.mx Web site: http://www.cronica.com.mx/noticias.php
Freq: Daily; Circ: 54372 Not Audited

Editor: Adrian Castillo; **Editor:** Nancy Escobar; **Publisher:** Jorge Kahwagi Gastine; **Editor:** Lizbeth Pasillas; **Ejecutivo De Ventas:** Jorge Zeron Medina
Profile: La Crónica De Hoy ofrece noticias locales, nacionales e internacionales, negocios y economía, opinión, entretenimiento, deportes y académicos. La Crónica De Hoy delivers local, national and international news, business and economy, opinion, entertainment, sports and academics.
Language (s): Spanish
Ad Rate: Full Page Mono 49.44
Currency: United States Dollars
DAILY NEWSPAPER

De Peso 383634
Owner: Medios Masivos M.
Editorial: Luz Savinon No. 13, Del Valle, Yucatan, Merida, Yucatan C.P. 03100 **Tel:** 52 55 53402450
Email: alfredo.ramirez@mediosmasivos.com.mx **Web site:** http://www.mediosmasivos.com.mx
Freq: No Frequency Established
Gerente De Ventas: José Alfredo Ramírez
Profile: Delivers national and international news, sports and society.
Language (s): Spanish
Ad Rate: Full Page Mono 6.37
Currency: United States Dollars
DAILY NEWSPAPER

De Peso 426963
Owner: Medios Masivos M.
Editorial: Luz Savinon No. 13, Del Valle, Quintana Roo, Cancun, Quintana Roo C.P. 03100
Tel: 52 55 53402450
Email: alfredo.ramirez@mediosmasivos.com.mx **Web site:** http://www.mediosmasivos.com.mx
Freq: No Frequency Established; **Circ:** 60000 Not Audited
Gerente De Ventas: José Alfredo Ramírez
Profile: Delivers national and international news, sports and society.
Language (s): Spanish
Ad Rate: Full Page Mono 6.37
Currency: United States Dollars
DAILY NEWSPAPER

De Peso 525971
Owner: Medios Masivos M.
Editorial: Luz Savinon No. 13, Del Valle, Quintana Roo, Chetumal, Quintana Roo C.P. 03100
Tel: 52 55 53402450
Email: alfredo.ramirez@mediosmasivos.com.mx **Web site:** http://www.mediosmasivos.com.mx
Freq: No Frequency Established
Gerente De Ventas: José Alfredo Ramírez
Profile: Delivers national and international news, sports and society.
Language (s): Spanish
Ad Rate: Full Page Mono 4.80
Currency: United States Dollars
DAILY NEWSPAPER

Debate 15225
Editorial: Pungarabato Pte No 37, Ciudad Altamirano, Guerrero 40660 **Tel:** 52 76 76722684
Web site: http://ww.eldebatedeloscalentanos.com
Freq: Daily; **Circ:** 150000 Not Audited
Publisher: Juan Cuevas Roman
Profile: El Debate mostly local news and has an opinion section.
Language (s): Spanish
DAILY NEWSPAPER

Diario Amanecer De México 383551
Owner: Uno Mas Uno
Editorial: Gabino Barreda No. 86, San Rafael, Mexico State, Toluca, Mexico State C.P. 06351
Tel: 52 55 10555500
Email: diario_amanecer@yahoo.com.mx **Web site:** http://www.diarioamanecer.com.mx
Freq: Daily; **Circ:** 50000 Not Audited
Profile: Diario Amanecer De México is a newspaper written for the general public in the Toluca, Mexico area. It offers regional, national, and international news and provides its readers with information on business, politics, and sports.
Language (s): Spanish
Ad Rate: Full Page Mono 1.20
Currency: United States Dollars
DAILY NEWSPAPER

DIARIO BASTA 854921
Owner: Editorial Prosperidad S.A. de C.V.
Editorial: Mexico City, Distrito Federal
Tel: 52 55 5254-5244
Web site: http://www.diariobasta.com.mx/index2.php
Freq: Mon thru Fri; **Circ:** 75000
Editor in Chief: David Casco
Profile: The newspaper focuses on celebrity and entertainment news along with some sport and politics.
Language (s): Spanish
DAILY NEWSPAPER

Diario De México 14984
Owner: Diario De México
Editorial: Chimalpopoca No. 38, Obrera, Distrito Federal, Mexico City, Distrito Federal C.P. 06800
Tel: 52 55 54426500
Email: edictos@diariodemexico.com.mx **Web site:** http://www.diariodemexico.com.mx
Freq: Daily; **Circ:** 3600 Not Audited
Manager: Alfonso Atriada; **Publisher:** Federico Bracamontes Baz; **Editor:** Rosa Colin; **President:** Federico Galvez; **Gerente:** Jesús Ruvalcaba Rios; **Editor:** Abraham Sheimberg
Profile: Diario de Juarez is written for the general public in the Mexico City, Mexico area. It offers regional, national, and international news and provides its readers with information on the economy, politics, sports, and entertainment.
Language (s): Spanish
Ad Rate: Full Page Mono 29.12
Currency: United States Dollars
DAILY NEWSPAPER

Diario de Yucatán 15199
Owner: Grupo Megamedia
Editorial: Calle 60 #521, Merida, Yucatan C.P. 97000
Tel: 52 999 942-2222
Email: diario@megamedia.com.mx **Web site:** http://www.yucatan.com.mx
Freq: Sun; **Circ:** 58586 Not Audited
Editor: Luis Luna Cetina; **Editor:** Jorge Munoz Menendez; **Editor:** Ruben Menendez Antuniano; **Publisher:** Carlos Menendez Navarrete; **Editor:** Gaspar Povera; **National News Editor:** Jorge Valan
Profile: Diario De Yucatán is a daily newspaper providing Local, Regional, National and Internation for the residents of the Merida, Yucatan, Mexico area. It offers regional, national, and international news and provides its readers with information on the economy, politics, sports, culture, society, entertainment.
Language (s): Spanish
Ad Rate: Full Page Mono 47.97
Currency: United States Dollars
DAILY NEWSPAPER

El Economista 14986
Owner: Periódico El Economista S.A. de C.V.
Editorial: Avenida Coyoacan, 515 colonial del Valle, Benito Juarez, Mexico City, Distrito Federal 3100
Tel: 52 55 5326-5454 2195
Email: internet@eleconomista.com.mx **Web site:** http://www.eleconomista.com.mx
Freq: Mon thru Fri; **Circ:** 37459 Not Audited
Editor: Alberto Aguirre; **International News Editor:** Jorge Camarena; **Editor:** Daniel Esparza; **Editor:** Manuel Lino; **Publisher:** Luis Enrique Mercado Sanchez; **Editor:** Armando Torres
Profile: El Economista es un periódico económico de México que se especializa en finanzas, empresas, dinero y mas. El Economista is an economic newspaper of Mexico that specializes in finance, business, money and more.
Language (s): Spanish
DAILY NEWSPAPER

Enfoque Diario 728909
Editorial: Calle Guadalupe Victoria #5, Salina Cruz, Oaxaca 70610 **Tel:** 01 97 1716-3492
Email: diarioenfoqued@yahoo.com.mx **Web site:** http://enfoquediario.com
Freq: Daily
Editor: Diana Manzo
Profile: Enfoque Diario is a daily newspaper written for the general public in the Salina Cruz, Oaxaca, Mexico area. It offers regional, national, and international news and provides its readers with information on the economy, politics, science, technology, culture, sports, and entertainment.
Language (s): Spanish
DAILY NEWSPAPER

Esto 14998
Owner: Organización Editorial Mexicana S.A. de C.V.
Editorial: Guillermo Prieto No. 7, Col. San Rafael, Mexico City, Distrito Federal C.P. 06470
Tel: 52 55 5566-1511
Web site: http://estoenlinea.oem.com.mx
Freq: Mon; **Circ:** 403000 Not Audited
Editor in Chief: Carlos Gabino Cu Uc; **Publisher:** Mario Vázquez Raña
Profile: Esto is a daily sports newspaper written for sports fanatics in the Mexico City, Mexico area. It offers regional, national, and international sports news and provides its readers with information on Mexican soccer, boxing, basketball, baseball, wrestling, statistics and more.
Language (s): Spanish
Ad Rate: Full Page Mono 9.96
Currency: United States Dollars
DAILY NEWSPAPER

Excélsior 14991
Owner: Grupo Imagen Multimedia
Editorial: Bucareli No. 1, Col. Centro, Mexico City, Distrito Federal C.P. 06600 **Tel:** 52 55 5128-3600
Email: nacional@nuevoexcelsior.com.mx **Web site:** http://www.excelsior.com.mx
Freq: Daily; **Circ:** 90000 Not Audited
Editor: Juan Pablo Estrada; **Publisher:** Marco Gonsen; **Editora en Jefe RSVP/Editor in Chief:** Jessica Pacheco; **Editor:** Ernesto Rivera Aguilar; **Editor:** Uriel Trejo; **Contributor:** Jose Yuste
Profile: Primero publicado en 1917, Excélsior es un diario que cubre todos los aspectos de la vida mexicana. La publicación proporciona noticias locales, nacionales e internacionales, política, economía, finanzas, tecnología de la información, deportes y entretenimiento. First published in 1917, Excélsior is a daily newspaper covering all aspects of Mexican life. The publication provides local, national and international news, politics, economics, finance, information technology, sports and entertainment.
Language (s): Spanish
Ad Rate: Full Page Mono 729.86
Currency: United States Dollars
DAILY NEWSPAPER

El Financiero 14987
Owner: Grupo Multimedia Lauman, SAPI de CV
Editorial: Lago Bolsena No. 176, Anahuac, Mexico City, Distrito Federal C.P. 11320 **Tel:** 52 55 5449-8600
Email: material@elfinanciero.com.mx **Web site:** http://www.elfinanciero.com.mx
Freq: Mon thru Fri; **Circ:** 72000 Not Audited
Editor: Antonio Armendarez; **Editor:** Rogelio Barela; **Manager:** Humberto Caldos; **Director Comercial:** Ivan Camargo; **Editor:** Araceli Damian; **Group Publisher:** Pilar E. de Cardenas; **Editor:** Lourdes Gonzalez; **Editor:** Alejandro Ramos; **Editor:** Piro Villamil
Profile: El Financiero is a newspaper written for the general public in the Mexico City, Distrito Federal, Mexico area. It offers regional, national, and international news and provides its readers with information on finance, the economy, business, politics, society, culture, sports, and entertainment.
Language (s): Spanish
Ad Rate: Full Page Mono 63.47
Currency: United States Dollars
DAILY NEWSPAPER

La I Laguna 426975
Owner: A.e.e.
Editorial: Av. De Las Palmas No. 239, Desp. 203 Y 204, Lomas De Chapultepec, Coahuila, Torreon, Coahuila C.P. 11000 **Tel:** 52 55 52938240
Email: lai@lailaguna.com.mx **Web site:** http://www.elsiglodetorreon.com.mx/lailaguna/
Freq: Daily; **Circ:** 54600 Not Audited
Profile: La I Laguna is a daily newspaper written for the general public in the Torreon, Coahuila, Mexico area. It offers regional, national, and international news and provides its readers with information on the economy, finance, politics, sports, society, and entertainment.
Language (s): Spanish
DAILY NEWSPAPER

La I Mérida 426976
Owner: A.e.e.
Editorial: Av. De Las Palmas No. 239, Desp. 203 Y 204, Lomas De Chapultepec, Yucatan, Merida, Yucatan C.P. 11000 **Tel:** 52 55 52938240
Email: diario@megamedia.com.mx **Web site:** http://laisureste.com
Freq: Daily; **Circ:** 54600 Not Audited
Profile: La I Mérida is a daily newspaper written for the general public in the Merida, Yucatan, Mexico area. It offers regional, national, and international news and provides its readers with information on the economy, politics, sports, society, family, and entertainment.
Language (s): Spanish
DAILY NEWSPAPER

La I Tijuana 426977
Owner: A.e.e.
Editorial: Av. De Las Palmas No. 239, Desp. 203 Y 204, Lomas De Chapultepec, Baja California, Tijuana, Baja California C.P. 11000 **Tel:** 52 55 52938240
Web site: http://www.aee.com.mx
Freq: Daily; **Circ:** 54600 Not Audited
Profile: La I Tijuana is a daily newspaper written for the general public in the Tijuana, Baja California, Mexico area. It offers regional, national, and international news and provides its readers with information on the economy, politics, sports, society, family, and entertainment.
Language (s): Spanish
DAILY NEWSPAPER

El Informador 15071
Owner: Unión Editorialista, S.A. de C.V.
Editorial: Independencia 300, Col. Centro, Guadalajara, Jalisco 44100 **Tel:** 52 33 3678-7700
Email: eltema@informador.com.mx **Web site:** http://www.informador.com.mx
Freq: Weekly
Editor: Alejandro Cabanillas; **Editor:** Laura Castro; **Publisher:** Carlos Alvarez del Castillo; **President:** Jorge del Castillo Zuloaga; **Manager:** Carlos Flores de la Torre; **Editor:** Carlos Fonseca; **Editor:** Ana Guerrero Santos; **Editor:** Antonio Flores Pozos; **Editor:** Jorge Verea
Profile: El Informador es un diario escrito para el público en general en el área de Guadalajara, Jalisco, México. Ofrece noticias regionales, nacionales e internacionales y proporciona a sus lectores información sobre economía, tecnología, cultura, deportes y entretenimiento. El Informador is a daily newspaper written for the general public in the Guadalajara, Jalisco, Mexico area. It offers regional, national, and international news and provides its readers with information on the economy, technology, culture, sports, and entertainment.
Language (s): Spanish
DAILY NEWSPAPER

La Jornada 14995
Owner: La Jornada
Editorial: Av. Cuauhtemoc No. 1236, Sta Cruz Atoyac, Distrito Federal, Mexico City, Distrito Federal C.P. 03310 **Tel:** 52 55 91830300
Web site: http://www.jornada.unam.mx
Freq: Daily; **Circ:** 110236 Not Audited
News Editor: Elena Gallegos; **Editor:** Julie Hernandez; **Editor:** Fabrizio Leon; **Editor:** Emilio Loman Maldonado; **Gerente De Publicidad:** Manuel Meneses; **Editor:** Julio Reyna Quiroz Quiroz; **Editor:** Ivan Restrepo; **Publisher:** Carmen Lira Saade; **Editor:** Miguel Velasquez; **Editor:** Jose Zaldua
Profile: La Jornada is a daily newspaper written for the general public in the Mexico City, Distrito Federal, Mexico area. It offers regional, national, and international news and provides its readers with information on the economy, politics, society & justice, science, technology, culture, sports, and entertainment.
Language (s): Spanish
Ad Rate: Full Page Mono 70.26
Currency: United States Dollars
DAILY NEWSPAPER

El M 383527
Owner: El M
Editorial: Bucareli No. 8, CentroDistrito Federal, Mexico City, Distrito Federal C.P. 06040
Tel: 52 55 57091313
Freq: Mon thru Fri
Profile: El M cover national and international news, sports and entertainment.
Language (s): Spanish
DAILY NEWSPAPER

El Mañana De Matamoros 15163
Owner: Editora Demar
Editorial: Av. La Rioja No. 119, San Pedro Zacatengo, Tamaulipas, Matamoros, Tamaulipas C.P. 07360 **Tel:** 52 55 55863008
Email: ingantoniovera@prodigy.net.mx **Web site:** http://www.elmananarey.com/diario/seccion/matamoros
Freq: Daily; **Circ:** 70000 Not Audited
Publisher: Heriberto Deandar Martinez; **Editor:** Augustin Lozano Delgado; **Ejecutivo De Ventas:** Antonio Vera Cazares
Profile: El Mañana de Matamoros offers local news in different sections as well as national and international news, sports, entertainment, opinion and society.
Language (s): Spanish
Ad Rate: Full Page Mono 10.26
Currency: United States Dollars
DAILY NEWSPAPER

El Mañana De Reynosa 15169
Owner: Editora Demar
Editorial: Av. La Rioja No. 119, San Pedro Zacatengo, Tamaulipas, Reynosa, Tamaulipas C.P. 07360 **Tel:** 52 55 55863008
Email: ingantoniovera@prodigy.net.mx **Web site:** http://www.elmanana.com/
Freq: Daily; **Circ:** 65000 Not Audited
General Manager: Orlando Ayala; **Publisher:** Heriberto Martinez; **President:** Orlando Martinez; **Editor:** Heriberto Robinson; **Editor:** Erasmo Salinas Perez; **Editor:** Arturo Soto; **Ejecutivo De Ventas:** Antonio Vera Cazares
Profile: El Mañana de Reynosa covers national and international news, sports, opinion, society, entertainment, and culture.
Language (s): Spanish
Ad Rate: Full Page Mono 11.11
Currency: United States Dollars
DAILY NEWSPAPER

El Martinense 733258
Editorial: Blvd Rafael Martinez de la Torre - No. 168 esquina 22 de Noviembre, Col. San Manuel Martinez de la Torre, Veracruz, Veracruz **Tel:** 52 232 3248546
Email: ilha19@hotmail.com **Web site:** http://www.elmartinense.com.mx
Freq: Mon thru Fri
General Manager: Eduardo Sanchez
Language (s): Spanish
DAILY NEWSPAPER

El Mexicano (Tijuana) 816486
Owner: Editorial Kino, S.A., de C.V.
Editorial: Gral. Lazaro Cardenas #3743, Fracc. Los Pirules, Tijuana, Baja California 22540
Tel: 52 664 104-2400
Web site: http://www.el-mexicano.com.mx
Freq: Daily; **Circ:** 451556
Publisher & Editor: Enrique Sánchez Díaz
Profile: El Mexicano is the leading Spanish language daily newspaper in Tijuana, Mexicali in Baja California, Mexico. It serves the region with coverage of current events, entertainment, real estate, sports and business.
Language (s): Spanish
DAILY NEWSPAPER

El Mexicano (Tijuana) - Mexicali Bureau 15215
Editorial: Ave Pioneros #1283, Centro Civico, Mexicali, Baja California 21000 **Tel:** 52 526 557-1078
Email: mexmex@el-mexicano.con.mx
Freq: Daily
Bureau Chief: Alfredo García Amaya
Language (s): Spanish
DAILY NEWSPAPER

El Mexicano (Tijuana) - Mexico City Bureau 15221
Owner: Medios Masivos M.
Editorial: Luz Savinon No. 13, Piso 6, Colonia del Valle, Mexico City, Distrito Federal C.P. 03100
Tel: 52 55 5340-2450
Web site: http://www.el-mexicano.com.mx
Freq: Daily; **Circ:** 57000 Not Audited
Editor: Sergio Anzures
Language (s): Spanish
Ad Rate: Full Page Mono 20.95
Currency: United States Dollars
DAILY NEWSPAPER

Milenio Novedades 426986
Owner: Grupo SIPSE
Editorial: Calle 62 No. 514-A, Col. Centro, Merida, Yucatan C.P. 97000

Email: milenionovedades@yahoo.com.mx **Web site:** http://sipse.com/milenio
Freq: Daily
Profile: Milenio Novedades cubre noticias de Mérida, Yucatán, México y el mundo, deportes, entretenimiento, viajes, tecnología y más. Milenio Novedades covers news from Merida, Yucatan, Mexico and the world, sports, entertainment, travel, technology and more.
Language (s): Spanish
Ad Rate: Full Page Mono 8.58
Currency: United States Dollars
DAILY NEWSPAPER

Mundo De Xalapa 383628
Owner: R. Lemus
Editorial: Londres No. 239, Juarez, Veracruz, Xalapa, Veracruz C.P. 06600 **Tel:** 52 55 55252018
Web site: http://www.mundodexalapa.com/noticias/
Freq: 2 Times/Week
Direccion Comercial: Rodrigo Lemus Novelo
Profile: El Mundo De Xalapa cover local and national news, sports, economy, politics and entertainment.
Language (s): Spanish
DAILY NEWSPAPER

Mundo Uvm 383526
Owner: S/r
Editorial: Av. De Las Palmas No. 731-1003, Lomas De Barrilaco, Distrito Federal, Mexico City, Distrito Federal C.P. 11010 **Tel:** 52 55 52021166
Email: israel.granda@uvmnet.edu **Web site:** http://www.uvmnet.edu/uvm/
Freq: Monthly; **Circ:** 50000 Not Audited
Director Ejecutivo: Javier Chávez De Icaza
Profile: This is the official publication for Universidad del Valle de Mexico. It covers university news, and events.
Language (s): Spanish
DAILY NEWSPAPER

Mural 281830
Owner: Grupo Reforma, S.A. de C.V.
Editorial: Av Mariano Otero #4047, Col La Calma, Guadalajara, Jalisco 45070 **Tel:** 52 33 31343800
Email: staff@mural.com **Web site:** http://www.mural.com
Freq: Daily; **Circ:** 51000 Not Audited
National News Editor: Roberto Castañeda;
Publisher: Alejandro Junco de la Vega; **International News Editor:** Leonardo Valero
Profile: Ofrece variedad de noticias locales, nacionales e internacionales. Mural covers national and international news, business, sports, style, cars, entertainment, politics, crime, social scene and activities.
Language (s): Spanish
DAILY NEWSPAPER

Ovaciones 15001
Owner: Ovaciones
Editorial: Lago Zirahuen No. 279, Anahuac, Distrito Federal, Mexico City, Distrito Federal C.P. 11320
Tel: 52 55 5328-0700
Email: ovaciones@hotmail.com **Web site:** http://www.ovaciones.com
Freq: Daily; **Circ:** 82082 Not Audited
Publisher: Miguel Couchonnal; **News Editor:** Rita Magaña; **Editor:** Ignacio Matos; **Editor:** Leopoldo Meraz; **Ejecutivo De Ventas:** Daniel Molina;
Manager: Jose Ortiz; **Editor:** Enrique Sanchez Marquez
Profile: Ovaciones is a Spanish-language daily newspaper that covers national and international soccer news.
Language (s): Spanish
Ad Rate: Full Page Mono 12.53
Currency: United States Dollars
DAILY NEWSPAPER

Periódico ABC de Monterrey 383456
Owner: Grupo Radio Alegria
Editorial: Platon Sanchez Sur 411, Centro, Monterrey, Nuevo Leon C.P. 64000 **Tel:** 52 81 8344-2510
Email: contacto@periodicoabc.mx **Web site:** http://www.periodicoabc.com.mx
Freq: Daily; **Circ:** 80000 Not Audited
Editor: Gonzalo Estrada Torres
Profile: The newspaper features local, national and international news. It also has sections dedicated to sports, women, and celebrities. The company also has radio stations in Mexico.
Language (s): Spanish
DAILY NEWSPAPER

El Periodico de Mexico 728919
Editorial: Insurgentes sur #800 Piso 8, Col. Del Valle, Distrito Federal CP 03100 **Tel:** 52 55 3300-5616
Email: contacto@elperiodicodemexico.com **Web site:** http://www.elperiodicodemexico.com
Freq: Daily
Editor: Karen Flores; **Editor:** Edwin Mejia; **Editor:** Iliana Vargas
Profile: El Periodico de Mexico is a daily newspaper written for the general public in the Mexico City, Distrito Federal, Mexico area. It offers regional, national, and international news and provides its readers with information on the economy, politics, science, technology, culture, sports, and entertainment.
Language (s): Spanish
DAILY NEWSPAPER

El Periodico de Quintana Roo 735633
Editorial: Bonampak 77 Interior 404, SMZ 3, Cancun, Quintana Roo C.P. 77500 **Tel:** 52 998 884-1004
Web site: http://www.elperiodico.com.mx/
Freq: Daily
Editor in Chief: Gabriela Cruz
Language (s): Spanish
DAILY NEWSPAPER

Periodico Del Centro 476359
Owner: Notmusa
Editorial: Periferico Sur No. 4293, Jardines De La Montana, Distrito Federal, Mexico City, Distrito Federal C.P. 14210 **Tel:** 52 55 50896114
Email: garredondo@notmusa.com.mx **Web site:** http://www.notmusa.com.mx
Freq: Mon thru Fri; **Circ:** 175000 Not Audited
Editor: Guadalupe Arredondo
Profile: El Periodico Del Centro cover national and international news, politics, crime and sports.
Language (s): Spanish
DAILY NEWSPAPER

El Porvenir 15134
Owner: Medios Masivos M.
Editorial: Galeana 344 Sur, Monterrey, Nuevo Leon C.P. 64000 **Tel:** 52 81 8345-4080
Email: publicidad.elporvenir@prodigy.net.mx **Web site:** http://www.elporvenir.mx
Freq: Daily; **Circ:** 75000 Not Audited
Publisher: Jose Gerardo Cantu Escalante; **Editor:** Rogelio Cantu Escalante; **Gerente De Ventas:** José Alfredo Ramírez; **News Editor:** Jose Rodriguez Arroyo
Profile: El Porvenir is a daily newspaper written for the general public in the Monterrey, Nuevo Leon, Mexico area. It offers regional, national, and international news and provides its readers with information on the economy, politics, society, culture, sports, and entertainment.
Language (s): Spanish
Ad Rate: Full Page Mono 7.84
Currency: United States Dollars
DAILY NEWSPAPER

La Prensa 14999
Owner: Organización Editorial Mexicana S.A. de C.V.
Editorial: Basilio Vadillo No. 40, Tabacalera, Distrito Federal, Mexico City, Distrito Federal C.P. 06030
Tel: 52 55 5228-9977
Email: redaccion@la-prensa.com.mx **Web site:** https://www.la-prensa.com.mx
Freq: Daily; **Circ:** 315000 Not Audited
Manager: Juan Hernandez; **General Manager:** Ignacio Ibarra Pescador; **Editor:** Mauricio Ortega Camberos; **Editor:** Jesus Sanchez Ramirez;
Publisher: Mario Vázquez Raña
Profile: La Prensa is a daily newspaper written for the general public in the Mexico City, Distrito Federal, Mexico area. It offers regional, national, and international news and provides its readers with information on the economy, finance, politics, health, science, technology, culture, sports, and entertainment.
Language (s): Spanish
Ad Rate: Full Page Mono 14.02
Currency: United States Dollars
DAILY NEWSPAPER

Prensa De Reynosa 15171
Owner: Gpo. Lemus R.
Editorial: Durango No. 353, Roma, Tamaulipas, Reynosa, Tamaulipas C.P. 06700
Tel: 52 55 52860222
Email: ventas@grupo-lemus.com.mx **Web site:** http://www.laprensa.mx
Freq: Daily; **Circ:** 60000 Not Audited
Editor: Enrique Coronado; **Editor:** Felix Garza Elizondo; **Editor:** Luis Triana
Profile: Prensa De Reynosa is a daily newspaper written for the general public in the Reynosa, Tamaulipas, Mexico area. It offers regional, national, and international news and provides its readers with information on politics, society, culture, sports, and entertainment.
Language (s): Spanish
Ad Rate: Full Page Mono 5.04
Currency: United States Dollars
DAILY NEWSPAPER

Publimetro México 426957
Owner: Metro International
Editorial: Av. Insurgentes Sur No. 716, Piso 10, Col. Del Valle, Mexico City, Distrito Federal 3100
Tel: 52 55 5340-0700
Email: cartas@publimetro.com.mx **Web site:** http://www.publimetro.com.mx
Circ: 17000 Not Audited
Editor: Juan Pablo; **Contributir:** Rodrigo Ponce de Leon
Profile: Publimetro México es un diario que ofrece noticias nacionales e internacionales y proporciona a sus lectores información sobre la economía, los deportes, el entretenimiento, el estilo de vida y más. Publimetro México is a daily newspaper that offers national and international news and provides its readers with information on the economy, sports, entertainment, lifestyle and more.
Language (s): Spanish
DAILY NEWSPAPER

Pueblo 15061
Editorial: Calle Ruben Mora #4, Col Guerrero 2000, Chilpancingo, Guerrero 39000 **Tel:** 52 74 74728070
Email: puebloguerrero@yahoo.com.mx **Web site:** http://www.puebloguerrero.com.mx
Freq: Daily
Manager: Jorge Martinez Zamudio; **Editor:** Roberto Carlos Rosa; **Publisher:** Gustavo Salazar Adame
Profile: Pueblo is a daily newspaper written for the general public in the Chilpancingo, Guerrero, Mexico area. It offers regional, national, and international news and provides its readers with information on the economy, politics, education, culture, and sports.
Language (s): Spanish
DAILY NEWSPAPER

El Pueblo 734258
Tel: 52 614 4103006
Email: reporteros2005@yahoo.com.mx **Web site:** http://www.elpueblo.com
Freq: Daily
Editor: Laura Alba; **News Editor:** Enrique Corte;
Editor in Chief: Hector Garcia
Language (s): Spanish
DAILY NEWSPAPER

Pulso 15157
Owner: Editora Mival S.A. de C.V.
Editorial: Galeana No 485, Centro, San Luis Potosi, San Luis Potosi 78000 **Tel:** 52 44 48127575
Email: pulso@pulsoslp.com.mx **Web site:** http://www.pulsoslp.com.mx
Freq: Daily; **Circ:** 60000 Not Audited
General Manager: Juan Mireles Calderon;
Publisher: Pablo Vallardes Garcia
Profile: Pulso is a daily newspaper written for the general public in the San Luis Potosi, San Luis Potosi, Mexico area. It offers regional, national, and international news and provides its readers with information on the economy, politics, security, sports, and entertainment.
Language (s): Spanish
DAILY NEWSPAPER

Puntual 383430
Owner: Difusa
Editorial: Calle De La Barra No. 57, Casi Esq. Blvd. Temoluco, Fracc. Acueducto De Guadalupe, Mexico State, Toluca, Mexico State C.P. 07279
Tel: 52 55 53919243
Email: difusadivprensa@aol.com
Freq: Daily; **Circ:** 60000 Not Audited
Gerente De Ventas: Saúl Oscar Palomar
Profile: Puntual is a daily newspaper written for the general public in the Toluca, Mexico, Mexico area. It offers regional, national, and international news and provides its readers with information on the economy, politics, education, science, culture, and entertainment.
Language (s): Spanish
Ad Rate: Full Page Mono 11.07
Currency: United States Dollars
DAILY NEWSPAPER

Puras Ofertas 476362
Owner: Bizcom
Editorial: Av. Paseo De Las Palmas No. 731, Piso 10, Desp. 1003, Lomas De Barrilaco, Guanajuato, Leon, Guanajuato C.P. 11010 **Tel:** 52 55 52021166
Email: informes@purasofertas.com.mx **Web site:** http://www.purasofertas.com.mx
Freq: Weekly; **Circ:** 100000 Not Audited
Director Ejecutivo: Javier Chávez De Icaza
Profile: A daily newspaper offering promotions and deals written for the general public in the Leon, Guanajuato, Mexico area.
Language (s): Spanish
DAILY NEWSPAPER

El Quiosco 736164
Owner: Editorial Fundadores S.A. de C.V.
Editorial: Simon Bolivar 1730, Col. Zaragoza, Nuevo Laredo, Tamaulipas 88160 **Tel:** 52 867 711-2222
Web site: http://elquiosco.mx
Freq: Daily
News Editor: Ricardo Flores Alvarez; **Editor:** David Dorantes; **Bureau Chief:** Marco Martinez; **News Editor:** Michelle Piedras
Profile: Covers local, national and international news, as well as sports and entertainment.
Language (s): Spanish
DAILY NEWSPAPER

Récord Guadalajara 383556
Owner: Notmusa
Editorial: Periferico Sur No. 4293, Jardines En La Montana, Jalisco, Guadalajara, Jalisco C.P. 14210
Tel: 52 55 91409500
Email: garredondo@notmusa.com.mx **Web site:** http://www.notmusa.com.mx
Freq: Mon; **Circ:** 146000 Not Audited
Editor: Guadalupe Arredondo
Profile: A sports newspaper on Guadalajara, Jalisco, Mexico sports, including soccer, basketball, football, and baseball. Editorial includes news, sport and team statistics, player biographies, and major sporting events.
Language (s): Spanish
Ad Rate: Full Page Mono 20.85
Currency: United States Dollars
DAILY NEWSPAPER

Récord Monterrey 426988
Owner: Notmusa
Editorial: Periferico Sur No. 4293, Jardines En La Montana, Nuevo Leon, Monterrey, Nuevo Leon C.P. 14210 **Tel:** 52 55 91409500
Email: garredondo@notmusa.com.mx **Web site:** http://www.notmusa.com.mx
Freq: Mon; **Circ:** 146000 Not Audited
Editor: Guadalupe Arredondo
Profile: Récord Monterrey is a sports newspaper written for the general public in the Monterrey, Nuevo Leon, Mexico area. It provides its readers with information on soccer news, statistics, player biographies, and major events.
Language (s): Spanish
Ad Rate: Full Page Mono 20.85
Currency: United States Dollars
DAILY NEWSPAPER

REFORMA 15002
Owner: Consorcio Interamericano de Comunicación S.A. de C.V.
Editorial: Av. Mexico Coyoacan No. 40, Del. Benito Juarez, Mexico City, Distrito Federal C.P. 03310
Tel: 52 55 5628-7100
Web site: http://www.reforma.com
Freq: Daily; **Circ:** 142086
Editor: Roberto Castañeda; **Editor:** Rene Delgado; **Editor:** Adriana Garay; **Editor:** Rodolfo Gerschman; **Director:** Miguel Gonzalez; **Editor:** Raul Huitron; **Publisher:** Alejandro Junco de la Vega; **Editor:** Raul Munoz; **Editor:** Jaime Rubio; **Editor:** Judith Segura; **Editor:** Martha Trejo; **Editor:** Juan Zamora
Profile: Reforma is a daily newspaper written for the general public in the Mexico City, Distrito Federal, Mexico area. It offers regional, national, and international news and provides its readers with information on the economy, politics, society, lifestyle, science, justice, culture, sports, and entertainment.
Language (s): Spanish
Ad Rate: Full Page Mono 2980.00
Currency: Mexico Pesos
DAILY NEWSPAPER

Reforma - Los Angeles Bureau 664374
Owner: Reforma
Editorial: 14014 Nw Passage Apt 224, Marina del Rey, California 90292-7420 **Tel:** 1 310 403-3562
Web site: http://www.reforma.com
Freq: Daily; **Circ:** 150569
Profile: This is the Los Angeles bureau for Reforma, a daily newspaper serving Mexico City.
Language (s): Spanish
Ad Rate: Full Page Mono 686.32
Currency: United States Dollars
DAILY NEWSPAPER

El Regio 728675
Owner: EDITORA REGIO, S.A. DE C.V.
Editorial: Jeronimo Trevino 1702 Poniente, Colonia Centro, Monterrey, Nuevo Leon CP 64000
Tel: 52 81 8372-0597
Email: director@elregio.com **Web site:** http://www.elregio.com
Freq: Daily
Editor: Gloria González Solís
Profile: El Regio is a daily newspaper written for the general public in the Monterrey, Nuevo Leon, Mexico area. It offers regional, national, and international news and provides its readers with information on the economy, politics, science, technology, culture, sports, and entertainment.
Language (s): Spanish
DAILY NEWSPAPER

Rumbo De México 383523
Owner: Grupo Mac
Editorial: Montes Urales No. 425, Lomas De Chapultepec, Distrito Federal, Mexico City, Distrito Federal C.P. 11000 **Tel:** 52 55 3099-3000
Web site: http://www.rumbodemexico.com.mx
Freq: Daily; **Circ:** 63391 Not Audited
Director Comercial: Eduardo Alberto Romero Suárez
Profile: Rumbo de Mexico is a daily newspaper written for the general public in the Mexico City, Distrito Federal, Mexico area. It offers regional, national, and international news and provides its readers with information on the economy, politics, society & justice, sports, and entertainment.
Language (s): Spanish
Ad Rate: Full Page Mono 40.00
Currency: United States Dollars
DAILY NEWSPAPER

San Luis Hoy 15158
Owner: Medios Masivos M.
Editorial: Luz Savinon No. 13, Del Valle, San Luis Potosi, San Luis Potosi, San Luis Potosi C.P. 03100
Tel: 52 55 53402450
Email: alfredo.ramirez@mediosmasivos.com.mx **Web site:** http://www.sanluishoy.com.mx
Freq: Daily
Editor: Eduardo Chavez Aguilar; **Gerente De Ventas:** José Alfredo Ramírez; **Publisher:** Pablo Vallardes Garcia
Profile: San Luis Hoy is a daily newspaper written for the general public in the San Luis Potosi, San Luis Potosi, Mexico area. It offers regional and national news and provides its readers with information on politics, culture, sports, and entertainment.
Language (s): Spanish
Ad Rate: Full Page Mono 2.71
Currency: United States Dollars
DAILY NEWSPAPER

Síntesis 15116
Owner: ASOCIACIÓN PERIODÍSTICA SÍNTESIS SA DE CV
Editorial: Calle 23 Sur 2504, Los Volcanes, Puebla, Puebla 72410 **Tel:** 52 222 709 4579
Email: sintesisweb@gmail.com **Web site:** http://www.sintesisdigital.com.mx
Freq: Daily
Editor: Luis Benitez Armas; **Editor:** Claudio Cisneros; **Editor:** Adolfo Duran; **President:** Armando Prida Huerta; **Publisher:** Mariano Morales Corona

Profile: Síntesis ofrece vanguardia en la información. Síntesis provides cutting edge information.
Language (s): Spanish
Ad Rate: Full Page Mono 2.00
Currency: United States Dollars
DAILY NEWSPAPER

Síntesis De Hidalgo 383419
Owner: Síntesis
Editorial: Calle 23 No. 33, San Pedro De Los Pinos, Hidalgo, Pachuca, Hidalgo C.P. 03800
Tel: 52 55 56150088
Email: sintesisweb@gmail.com **Web site:** http://sintesis.mx/
Freq: Daily
Profile: Síntesis de Hidalgo is a daily newspaper written for the general public in the Pachuca, Hidalgo, Mexico area. It offers regional, national, and international news and provides its readers with information on the economy, politics, science, society, sports, weather and entertainment.
Language (s): Spanish
Ad Rate: Full Page Mono 2.00
Currency: United States Dollars
DAILY NEWSPAPER

Síntesis De Tlaxcala 15180
Owner: Síntesis
Editorial: Calle 23 No. 33, San Pedro De Los Pinos, Tlaxcala, Tlaxcala, Tlaxcala C.P. 03800
Tel: 52 55 56150088
Email: sintesisweb@gmail.com **Web site:** http://www.sintesisdigital.com.mx
Freq: Daily
Manager: Enrique Barella Perez; **Editor:** Isabel Gomez Macias; **Editor:** Jose Mendez; **Publisher:** Mariano Morales Corona; **President:** Armando Prida Huerta
Profile: Síntesis De Tlaxcala is a daily newspaper written for the general public in the Tlaxcala, Tlaxcala, Mexico area. It offers regional, national, and international news and provides its readers with information on the economy, politics, science, society, sports, weather and entertainment.
Language (s): Spanish
Ad Rate: Full Page Mono 2.00
Currency: United States Dollars
DAILY NEWSPAPER

El Sol de Mazatlán 383605
Owner: Organización Editorial Mexicana S.A. de C.V.
Editorial: Av. Miguel Aleman 312, Fracc . Playa sur, Mazatlan, Sinaloa C.P. 82040 **Tel:** 52 669 915-5600
Email: dirmaz@oem.com.mx **Web site:** http://www.oem.com.mx/elsoldemazatlan
Freq: Daily
Editor: Sergio Ontiveros Salas; **President:** Mario Vázquez Raña
Profile: El Sol de Mazatlán is a daily newspaper written for the general public in the Mazatlan, Sinaloa, Mexico area. It offers regional, national, and international news and provides its readers with information on the economy, finance, politics, health, tourism, science, technology, culture, sports, and entertainment.
Language (s): Spanish
Ad Rate: Full Page Mono 4.61
Currency: United States Dollars
DAILY NEWSPAPER

El Sol de México 14989
Owner: El Sol De México
Editorial: Guillermo Prieto No. 9, San Rafael, Distrito Federal, Mexico City, Distrito Federal C.P. 06470
Tel: 52 55 5566-1511
Web site: https://www.elsoldemexico.com.mx
Freq: Daily; **Circ:** 60500 Not Audited
Editor: Eduardo Correa Platan; **Editor:** Benjamin Cruz; **Manager:** Pedro De La O; **Editor:** Edgar Gonzalez Martinez; **Editor:** Gabriel Jantomila; **Editor:** Mario Leyva; **Editor:** Cristina Roman; **President:** Mario Vázquez Raña; **Directora:** Isabel Zamorano Ramos
Profile: El Sol De México is a daily newspaper written for the general public in the Mexico City, Distrito Federal, Mexico area. It offers regional, national, and international news and provides its readers with information on the economy, finance, politics, health, tourism, science, technology, culture, sports, and entertainment.
Language (s): Spanish
Ad Rate: Full Page Mono 10.14
Currency: United States Dollars
DAILY NEWSPAPER

El Sol De Puebla 15113
Owner: Organización Editorial Mexicana S.A. de C.V.
Editorial: Av. 3 Oriente 201, Col. Centro, Puebla, Puebla C.P. 72000 **Tel:** 52 222 514-3300
Email: soldepuebla@yahoo.com.mx **Web site:** https://www.elsoldepuebla.com.mx/
Freq: Daily; **Circ:** 67000 Not Audited
Editor: Candelario Castillo; **Editor:** Jorge Corona; **Editor:** Marco de Leon; **Manager:** Hector Espinoza; **Editor:** Jose Martinez; **Publisher:** Marco Ponce de Leon; **News Editor:** Wendy Sanchez; **Editor:** Maria Sarniza de Meyes; **Director General:** Mario Vázquez; **Editor:** Jorge Zamora
Profile: El Sol De Puebla is a daily newspaper written for the general public in the Puebla, Morelos, Mexico area. It offers regional, national, and international news and provides its readers with information on the economy, finance, politics, health, tourism, science, technology, culture, sports, and entertainment.
Language (s): Spanish
Ad Rate: Full Page Mono 1.90
Currency: United States Dollars
DAILY NEWSPAPER

Super Ofertas 383502
Owner: Sólo Ofertas
Editorial: Av. Lopez Mateos Sur No. 5142, La Calma Zapopan, Jalisco, Guadalajara, Jalisco C.P. 45071
Web site: http://www.nuevosiglo.com.mx
Freq: Weekly; **Circ:** 180000 Not Audited
Profile: Super Ofertas is a daily newspaper written for the general public in the Guadalajara, Jalisco, Mexico area. It offers promotions and deals in various grocery and retail stores in Guadalajara.
Language (s): Spanish
DAILY NEWSPAPER

Tabasco Hoy 15145
Owner: Organización Editorial Acuario S.A. de C.V.
Editorial: Luz Savinon No. 13, Del Valle, Tabasco, Villahermosa, Tabasco C.P. 03100
Tel: 52 99 33100229
Web site: http://www.tabascohoy.com.mx
Freq: Daily; **Circ:** 50000 Not Audited
Editor: Raul Cortes Alamilla; **Editor:** Hector Martinez de Esobar; **Gerente De Ventas:** José Alfredo Ramírez; **Publisher:** Miguel Canton Zetina
Profile: Tabasco Hoy is a daily newspaper written for the general public in the Villahermosa, Tabasco, Mexico area. It offers regional, national, and international news and provides its readers with information on the economy, finance, politics, culture, sports, and entertainment.
Language (s): Spanish
Ad Rate: Full Page Mono 430.34
Currency: Mexico Pesos
DAILY NEWSPAPER

La Tarde 476356
Owner: Medios Masivos M.
Editorial: Luz Savinon No. 13, Del Valle, Tamaulipas, Nvo. Laredo, Tamaulipas C.P. 03100
Tel: 52 55 53402450
Email: alfredo.ramirez@mediosmasivos.com.mx **Web site:** http://www.mediosmasivos.com.mx
Freq: Daily
Gerente De Ventas: José Alfredo Ramírez
Profile: La Tarde is a daily newspaper written for the general public in the Nuevo Laredo, Tamaulipas, Mexico area. It offers regional, national, and international news and provides its readers with information on the economy, politics, culture, sports, and entertainment.
Language (s): Spanish
Ad Rate: Full Page Mono 2.77
Currency: United States Dollars
DAILY NEWSPAPER

El Tren De Guadalajara 438364
Owner: Grupo Unión Editorial, S.A. de C.V.
Editorial: Juan Manuel No. 77, Centro, Jalisco, Guadalajara, Jalisco C.P. 44100
Email: eltren@informador.com.mx **Web site:** http://www.periodicoeltren.com.mx
Freq: Mon thru Fri; **Circ:** 148802 Not Audited
Editor: Ricardo Barba Rabago
Profile: El Tren De Guadalajara is a daily newspaper written for the general public in the Guadalajara, Jalisco, Mexico area. It offers regional, national, and international news and provides its readers with information on the economy, politics, health, culture, sports, and entertainment.
Language (s): Spanish
DAILY NEWSPAPER

El Universal 14996
Owner: EL UNIVERSAL
Editorial: Bucareli No. 8, Centro, Distrito Federal, Mexico City, Distrito Federal C.P. 06040
Tel: 52 55 5709-1313
Email: contacto@eluniversal.com.mx **Web site:** http://www.eluniversal.com.mx
Freq: Daily; **Circ:** 120000 Not Audited
Gerente de Operaciones/Operations Manager: Juan Carlos Ealy; **President:** Juan Francisco Ealy Ortiz; **Photographer:** Crisanto Rodriguez
Profile: El Universal is a daily newspaper written for the general public in the Mexico City, Distrito Federal, Mexico area. It offers regional, national, and international news and provides its readers with information on the economy, politics, society & justice, science, technology, culture, sports, and entertainment.
Language (s): Spanish
Ad Rate: Full Page Mono 221.39
Currency: United States Dollars
DAILY NEWSPAPER

El Universal Gráfico 14997
Owner: El Universal Gráfico
Editorial: Bucareli No. 8, Centro, Distrito Federal, Mexico City, Distrito Federal C.P. 06040
Tel: 52 55 5709-1313
Web site: http://www.eluniversal.com.mx/grafico
Freq: Mon thru Fri; **Circ:** 300000 Not Audited
President: Juan Francisco Ealy Ortiz; **World News Editor:** Eduardo Mora Tavares; **Editor:** Rosalinda Palomeque; **National News Editor:** Araceli Pulido; **Co-Editor:** Sonia Valencia
Profile: El Universal Gráfico is a daily newspaper written for men in the Mexico City, Distrito Federal, Mexico area. It offers news on celebrities and models.
Language (s): Spanish
Ad Rate: Full Page Mono 31.00
Currency: United States Dollars
DAILY NEWSPAPER

Unomasuno 15005
Owner: Impulsora de Periodismo Mexicano, S.A. de C.V.
Editorial: Gabino Barreda 86 Delegacion Cuauhtemoc, Col. San Rafael, Mexico City, Distrito Federal 6470 **Tel:** 52 55 1055-5500
Email: unomasuno@naim.com.mx **Web site:** http://www.unomasuno.com.mx
Freq: Daily; **Circ:** 70000 Not Audited
Manager: Felipe Cen Quintal; **Editor in Chief:** Esteban Duran; **Editor:** Sergio Martinez Estrada; **News Editor:** Jose Montana; **Publisher:** Karina Rocha Priego; **Editor:** Raul Ruiz; **Editor:** Luis Carlos Silva Rodriguez; **Editor:** Raul Tavera Arias
Language (s): Spanish
DAILY NEWSPAPER

Valle del Norte 15173
Editorial: Chihuahua No 1245 Sur, Reynosa, Tamaulipas 88630 **Tel:** 52 89 99238800
Email: editorial@valledelnorte.com.mx **Web site:** http://www.valledelnorte.com.mx
Freq: Daily
Publisher: Fernando De Luna Sanchez; **Editor:** Martin Hernandez Martinez
Profile: La Jornada is a daily newspaper written for the general public in the Reynosa, Tamaulipas, Mexico area. It offers regional, national, and international news and provides its readers with information on the economy, politics, society, security, sports, and entertainment.
Language (s): Spanish
DAILY NEWSPAPER

La Voz de Michoacan 736387
Tel: 52 434 3422058
Web site: http://www.vozdemichoacan.com.mx
Freq: Daily
Editor: Alvaro Medina; **Editor in Chief:** Miguel Medina
Language (s): Spanish
DAILY NEWSPAPER

La Voz de Zihuatanejo 738556
Editorial: Calle Pesquera s/n Col Los Reyes, Zihuatanejo, Guerrero 40880 **Tel:** 52 755 5536172
Email: vozihuatanejo@hotmail.com **Web site:** http://www.vozihuatanejo.com.mx
Freq: Daily
Editor: Alejandro Alvarado; **Editor in Chief:** Hector Alvarado
Language (s): Spanish
DAILY NEWSPAPER

Zacatecas en Imagen 15207
Owner: Grupo Editorial Zacatecas S.A. de C.V.
Editorial: Calzada Revolucion 24, Col Tierra y Libertad, Zacatecas, Zacatecas 98600
Tel: 52 49 29238898
Email: capital@imagenzac.com.mx **Web site:** http://www.imagenzac.com.mx
Freq: Daily; **Circ:** 60000 Not Audited
General Manager: Jesus Amero; **Publisher:** Eugenio Mercado Sanchez; **Editor:** Francisco Reynoso
Profile: Zacatecas en Imagen is a daily newspaper written for the general public in the Zacatecas, Zacatecas, Mexico area. It offers regional, national, and international news and provides its readers with information on the economy, politics, society & justice, science, technology, culture, sports, and entertainment.
Language (s): Spanish
DAILY NEWSPAPER

News Service/Syndicate

Agencia de Información Integral Periodísticas 721799
Editorial: Tabasco 263, Mexico City, Distrito Federal
Tel: 52 55 5514-7389
Email: webmaster@grupoaiip.com.mx **Web site:** http://www.grupoaiip.com.mx
Language (s): Spanish
NEWS SERVICE/SYNDICATE

Notiempo 721791
Owner: Agencia de Noticias Empresariales
Editorial: Ave. de las Americas 1600, 2 Piso, Col. Country Club, Zona Financiera, Guadalajara, Jalisco C.P. 44680 **Tel:** 52 33 3678-9207
Email: noticias@notiemp.com **Web site:** http://www.notiemp.com/sys/index.php
Profile: Notiemp is a Mexican News Agency that covers the most recent developments in economy and business news affecting Latin America and the rest of the world. Notiemp offers its subscribers in Mexico and throughout the world, a wide array of services such as text news, digital news, digital audio, TV and audio production, strategic analysis, monitoring, among others, either via satellite or Internet.
Language (s): Spanish
NEWS SERVICE/SYNDICATE

Notimex 409097
Owner: Notimex México
Editorial: Avenida Baja California #200, Colonia Roma Sur, Delegacion Cuauhtémoc, Mexico City, Distrito Federal 6760 **Tel:** 52 55 5420-1100
Email: atencioncliente@notimex.com.mx **Web site:** http://www.notimex.gob.mx
Publisher: Aurelio Bueno Hernández; **International News Editor:** Olga Ojeda Lajud
Profile: Agencia de Noticias con cobertura nacional e internacional. News agency with national and international news coverage.
Language (s): Spanish
NEWS SERVICE/SYNDICATE

Notimex - Los Angeles Bureau 409101
Editorial: 3600 Wilshire Blvd, Ste 2028, Los Angeles, California 90010-2624 **Tel:** 1 213 483-7088
Email: romerontx9@aol.com
Editor: Jose Romero
Profile: This is the Los Angeles bureau of Notimex in Mexico City, Mexico.
Language (s): Spanish
NEWS SERVICE/SYNDICATE

Notimex - New York Bureau 503990
Editorial: 405 E 42nd St, New York, New York 10017-3507 **Tel:** 1 212 371-1289
Profile: This is the New York bureau of Notimex in Mexico City.
Language (s): Spanish
NEWS SERVICE/SYNDICATE

Notimex - Washington Bureau 409102
Editorial: 529 14th St NW Ste 975, Washington, District Of Columbia 20045-1906 **Tel:** 1 202 347-5227
Profile: This is the Washington, D.C. bureau of Notimex in Mexico City, Mexico.
Language (s): Spanish
NEWS SERVICE/SYNDICATE

Moldova

Time Difference: GMT +2
National Telephone Code: 373
Continent: Europe
Capital: Chi?inau

Newspapers

Comersant Plus 224721
Owner: Comersant Plus Ltd.
Editorial: str. Puskin 22, Chisinau 2012
Tel: 373 22 23 33 18
Email: inform@commert.press.md **Web site:** http://www.km.press.md/
Circ: 3000 Publisher's Statement
Director: Svetlana Burlak; **Editor:** Artem Varenita
Profile: Newspaper focusing on politics, economy and finance.
Language (s): Russian
DAILY NEWSPAPER

Jurnal de Chi?in?u 158158
Owner: SRL "Jurnal de Chichinel"
Editorial: str. Vlaicu Pârclab 63, etaj 3, Centrul Skytower, Chisinau 2012 **Tel:** 373 22 237645
Email: cotidian@jurnal.md **Web site:** http://jc.md
Freq: 2 Times/Week; **Circ:** 13489 Publisher's Statement
Editor/Director: Rodica Mahu
Profile: Newspaper containing news and reportages, political, economic, cultural and social commentaries, sports and general interest articles.
Language (s): Romanian
DAILY NEWSPAPER

Kommersant Plus 655533
Editorial: Puskin str., 22, Casa Presei, of. 601, Chisinau **Tel:** 373 22 233696
Email: inform@commert.press.md **Web site:** http://www.km.press.md
Freq: Weekly; **Circ:** 5000 Publisher's Statement
Editor/Director: Burlac Svetlana
Profile: Newspaper focusing on politics, economy and finance.
Language (s): Russian
DAILY NEWSPAPER

Komsomolskaya Pravda v Moldove 573203
Editorial: V.Pircalab str., 45, 5 floor, Chisinau
Tel: 373 22 220713
Email: kp@kp.md **Web site:** http://www.kp.md
Freq: Daily; **Circ:** 9000 Publisher's Statement
Profile: Komsomolskaya Pravda v Moldove is the Moldova edition of Russian daily national newspaper covering national news, business, economics and society.
Language (s): Russian
DAILY NEWSPAPER

Moldavskie Vedomosti 230025
Owner: Moldavskie Vedomosti
Editorial: Stefan chel mare 182, Chisinau 2012
Tel: 373 22 23 86 18
Email: editor@vedomosti.md **Web site:** http://www.vedomosti.md
Freq: 3 Times/Week; **Circ:** 7500 Publisher's Statement

Moldova

Profile: Newspaper focusing on politics, business, sport, culture and general news.
Language (s): Russian
DAILY NEWSPAPER

Nezavisimaya Moldova 161228
Owner: Pravidelstvo Respubliki Moldova
Editorial: str. Puskin 22, Chisinau 2012
Tel: 373 22 233141
Email: nezavisimaia.moldova@gmail.com **Web site:** http://www.nm.md
Freq: Daily; **Circ:** 17000 Publisher's Statement
Editor-in-Chief: Corneliu Mihalache
Profile: Newspaper focusing on national and international news, politics, business and sport.
Language (s): Russian
DAILY NEWSPAPER

Timpul de diminea?a 230021
Owner: Timpul De Diminatea
Editorial: Alexei ciusev 98, Chisinau MD-2005
Tel: 373 22 225670
Email: secretariat@timpul.md **Web site:** http://www.timpul.md
Freq: Daily; **Circ:** 19227 Publisher's Statement
Editor/Director: Constantin Tanase
Profile: Newspaper focusing on national and international news, culture, society, politics, economics and sport.
Language (s): Romanian
DAILY NEWSPAPER

News Service/Syndicate

INTERLIC News Agency 654823
Tel: 373 22 3 20 67
Email: info@interlic.md **Web site:** http://www.interlic.md
Office Manager: Ludmila Rusnac
NEWS SERVICE/SYNDICATE

MS-PUBLICITATE 655742
Editorial: Columna str., 146/1, Chisinau
Tel: 373 22 29 47 07
Email: plescasimion@mail.md
Editor/Director: Simion Ple?ca
Language (s): Romanian
NEWS SERVICE/SYNDICATE

Monaco

Time Difference: GMT +1
National Telephone Code: 377
Continent: Europe
Capital: Monaco

Newspapers

MONACO-MATIN EDITION MONEGASQUE DE NICE-MATIN 157480
Owner: NICE MATIN
Editorial: 41 rue Grimaldi, Monaco 98000
Tel: 377 9 31 04 39 0
Email: monaco@nicematin.fr **Web site:** http://www.nicematin.fr
Freq: Daily
Pigiste: Jean-Mary Rizza
Profile: Monaco edition of the regional daily newspaper focussing on news and current affairs including TV guide, sport, real estate, economics and women's interest magazine supplement. Local Translation:Edition monégasque de Nice-Matin. Actualités régionales et internationales - Programmes TV. Suppléments : sport le lundi, immobilier le mardi, sortir le mercredi, éco le jeudi, TV le samedi, féminin le dimanche.
Language (s): French
DAILY NEWSPAPER

L' Observateur de Monaco 521708
Owner: EDITIONS MINERVE
Editorial: 27 boulevard d'Italie, Monaco 98000
Tel: 377 9 79 75 95 9
Email: gok@lobservateurdemonaco.mc **Web site:** http://www.lobservateurdemonaco.mc
Freq: Monthly; **Circ:** 1600 Publisher's Statement
Directeur de Publication: Frédéric Bernascon;
Directeur de Publication: Georges-Olivier Kalifa
Profile: Regional newspaper focussing on local news and current affairs including regional interest, health, economics, culture, leisure and cinema. Local Translation: Journal d'actualités monégasques, régionales et nationales : santé, économie, culture, loisirs, cinéma.
Language (s): French
DAILY NEWSPAPER

Community Newspaper

MONACO HEBDO 230122
Owner: MONACO HEBDO
Editorial: 27 boulevard d'Italie, Monaco 98000
Tel: 377 9 35 05 65 2
Web site: http://www.monacohebdo.mc
Freq: Weekly; **Circ:** 6000 Publisher's Statement
Pigiste: Etson Anumu; **Pigiste:** Laurence Carré;
Pigiste: Régis de Closets; **Pigiste:** Yves Majorel;
Rédacteur en Chef: Milena Radoman; **Directeur de Publication:** Roberto Testa
Profile: Regional publication focussing on local news and current affairs including economics, society, culture and sport. Local Translation:Toute l'actualité monégasque : économie, société, culture, sport.
Language (s): French
COMMUNITY NEWSPAPER

Mongolia

Time Difference: GMT +7, +8
National Telephone Code: 976
Continent: Asia
Capital: Ulaanbaatar

Newspapers

The UB Post 387113
Owner: Mongol News Media Group
Editorial: Mongol News Building, Juulchni Street, Ulaanbaatar 15172 **Tel:** 976 88067337
Email: ubpost@mongolnews.mn **Web site:** http://theubpost.mn
Freq: 3 Times/Week; **Circ:** 5000 Publisher's Statement
Profile: Independent newspaper in English focussing on news, current affairs, politics, economics and sport.
Language (s): English
DAILY NEWSPAPER

News Service/Syndicate

Montsame News Agency 534992
Editorial: Jigjidjav 8, Chingeltei, Ulaanbaatar 15160
Tel: 976 11 263 692
Email: technical@montsame.mn **Web site:** http://www.montsame.mn
Editor: Ganzorig Gonda
Profile: National news agency focussing on news, current affairs, politics, business, culture and sport.
Language (s): Chinese
NEWS SERVICE/SYNDICATE

Montenegro

Time Difference: GMT +1
National Telephone Code: 382
Continent: Europe
Capital: Podgorica

Newspapers

Pobjeda 161231
Owner: Pobjeda d o o
Editorial: ul.19. decembra br. 5, Podgorica 81000
Tel: 382 20 246-777
Email: desk@pobjeda.me **Web site:** http://www.pobjeda.net
Freq: Daily; **Circ:** 30000 Publisher's Statement
Editor In Chief: Andrija Rackovi?; **Director:** Dragoljub Šarovi?
Profile: Newspaper covering international and domestic news, business, economics, sports and culture.
Language (s): Serbo-Croat
Ad Rate: Full Page Mono 380.00
Currency: Euro
DAILY NEWSPAPER

Montserrat

Time Difference: GMT -4
National Telephone Code: 1 664
Continent: The Americas
Capital: Plymouth

Community Newspaper

The Montserrat Reporter 224379
Owner: Montserrat Printing & Publishing
Tel: 664 4914715
Email: editor@themontserratreporter.com **Web site:** http://www.themontserratreporter.com
Freq: Weekly; **Circ:** 2000 Not Audited
Publisher & Editor: Bennette Roach
Profile: Focuses on national and international news, politics, business, culture and sports.
Language (s): English
Ad Rate: Full Page Mono 22.50
Ad Rate: Full Page Colour 630.00
Currency: United States Dollars
COMMUNITY NEWSPAPER

Morocco

Time Difference: GMT
National Telephone Code: 212
Continent: Africa
Capital: Rabat

Newspapers

Akhbar Alyoum 673648
Owner: Groupe Media 21
Editorial: 8th Floor, Al Habsi Commercial Center, Avenue Des F.A.R., Casablanca **Tel:** 212 522 545850
Email: akhbartahrir@gmail.com **Web site:** http://www.alyaoum24.com
Freq: Daily; **Circ:** 20006 OJD Maroc
Publisher: Taoufik Bouachrine
Profile: Akhbar Alyoum is a broadsheet-sized newspaper covering national and international news, business, culture, society, art, politics and sport. It launched in 2009 and was previously called Akhbar Al Youm Maghribiya.
Language (s): Arabic
Ad Rate: Full Page Mono 22500.00
Ad Rate: Full Page Colour 30000.00
Currency: Morocco Dirhams
DAILY NEWSPAPER

Annoukhba 472208
Owner: Selection Presse
Editorial: Appt. 7, 4eme Etage, Al Rizk Building, 73, Avenue de la Resistance, Rabat **Tel:** 212 537 731984
Email: naim2759@yahoo.fr **Web site:** http://www.annoukhba.info
Freq: 2 Times/Week; **Circ:** 100000 Publisher's Statement
Profile: Annoukhba (The Elite) is an Arabic sports newspaper covering football. It launched in 1993 and is published twice a week on Mondays and Thursdays.
Language (s): Arabic
DAILY NEWSPAPER

Assabah 328299
Owner: Groupe Eco-Media
Editorial: 70 Boulevard Al Massira Khadra, Casablanca **Tel:** 212 522 953660
Email: assabah.info@gmail.com **Web site:** http://www.assabah.press.ma
Freq: Daily; **Circ:** 45538 OJD Maroc
Editor In Chief: Khaled El Horri
Profile: Assabah (The Morning) is a broadsheet-sized newspaper covering national and international news, current affairs and politics. It launched in 2000 and is published daily, except Sundays.
Language (s): Arabic
Ad Rate: Full Page Mono 29000.00
Ad Rate: Full Page Colour 32000.00
Currency: Morocco Dirhams
DAILY NEWSPAPER

Assiassi 828840
Owner: Selection Presse
Editorial: Office 7, 4eme Etage, Al Rizk Building, 73, Avenue de La Resistance, Rabat **Tel:** 212 537 731984
Email: siyassimaroc20@gmail.com
Freq: Bi-Weekly; **Circ:** 75000 Publisher's Statement
Profile: Assiassi is a fortnightly newspaper covering news and current affairs, business, politics, art, culture and sport. It was first published in 1991.
Language (s): Arabic
DAILY NEWSPAPER

Al Bayane 157071
Owner: Bayane SA
Editorial: PO Box 13152, 2830, rue Benzert, Casablanca 23000 **Tel:** 212 522 467676
Email: albayane@albayane.press.ma **Web site:** http://www.albayane.press.ma
Freq: Daily; **Circ:** 25000 Publisher's Statement
News Editor: Khalid Darfaf; **Publication Manager:** Mahtat Rakas
Profile: Al Bayane is a French newspaper covering national and international news, current affairs and politics. It launched in 1972 and is published daily, except Saturdays.
Language (s): French
Ad Rate: Full Page Mono 25000.00
Ad Rate: Full Page Colour 32500.00
Currency: Morocco Dirhams
DAILY NEWSPAPER

Bayane Al Yaoume 157078
Owner: Bayane SA
Editorial: PO Box 13152, 2830, rue Benzert, Casablanca 23000 **Tel:** 212 522 467676
Email: bayanealyaoume@bayanealyaoume.press.ma
Web site: http://www.bayanealyaoume.press.ma
Freq: Daily; **Circ:** 20000 Publisher's Statement
News Editor: Hassan Arabi; **Editor in Chief:** Hussein Chaabi; **Publication Manager:** Mahtat Rakas
Profile: Bayane Al Yaoume is an Arabic newspaper covering national and international news, current affairs and politics. It launched in 1991 and is published daily, except Sundays.
Language (s): Arabic
Ad Rate: Full Page Mono 25000.00
Ad Rate: Full Page Colour 32500.00
Currency: Morocco Dirhams
DAILY NEWSPAPER

L'Observateur Du Maroc 657113
Owner: Medi Edition
Editorial: App 5, Tilila Building, Rue De Berne, Casablanca **Tel:** 212 522 465950
Email: lobsmaroc@gmail.com **Web site:** http://www.lobservateurdumaroc.info
Freq: Weekly; **Circ:** 20000 Publisher's Statement
General Manager: Hakim Arif; **Publishing Director:** Ahmed Charai; **Editor in Chief:** Mohammed Zainabi
Profile: L'Observateur Du Maroc is a weekly newspaper covering news, economics, society, culture, sport, culture and arts. It launched in 2008 and is published on Fridays.
Language (s): French
Ad Rate: Full Page Colour 33500.00
Currency: Morocco Dirhams
DAILY NEWSPAPER

Al Massae 499950
Owner: Massae Média Groupe
Editorial: 2eme etage, Centre Commercial Diwane, Angle Place Aknoul, Casablanca **Tel:** 212 522 200666
Email: almassae@almassaepress.com **Web site:** http://www.almassaepress.com
Freq: Daily; **Circ:** 75064 OJD Maroc
Publication Manager: Abdallah Damoune
Profile: Al Massae is a daily newspaper covering news and current affairs, culture, society, business and sport. It launched in September 2006.
Language (s): Arabic
Ad Rate: Full Page Mono 26250.00
Ad Rate: Full Page Colour 35000.00
Currency: Morocco Dirhams
DAILY NEWSPAPER

Le Matin 156758
Owner: Groupe Le Matin
Editorial: 17, Rue Othmane Ben Affane, ex Lafuente, Casablanca **Tel:** 212 522 489100
Email: lematin@lematin.ma **Web site:** http://www.lematin.ma
Freq: Daily; **Circ:** 20947 OJD Maroc
News Editor: Mohamed Akisra; **Publication Manager:** Mohamed Haithami; **Editor in Chief:** Lmahjoube Rouane; **Picture Editor:** Issa Saouri
Profile: Le Matin, also known as Le Matin du Sahara et du Maghreb, is a French newspaper focusing on national and international news, business, politics and sport. It launched in 1971 and is published daily, except Sundays.
Language (s): French
Ad Rate: Full Page Colour 37000.00
Currency: Morocco Dirhams
DAILY NEWSPAPER

Rissalat Al Oumma 544815
Owner: Union Constitutionnel
Editorial: 158, Avenue des FAR, Casablanca 20005
Tel: 212 522 907180
Email: aloumma@yahoo.fr **Web site:** http://www.rissalatalomma.press.ma
Freq: Daily; **Circ:** 30000 Publisher's Statement
News Editor: Youssef Boukhari; **Advertising Manager:** Mohamed Inflasse
Profile: Rissalat Al Oumma (The Nation's Message) is a daily newspaper covering national and international news, politics, business, society and sport. It launched in 1983.
Language (s): Arabic
Ad Rate: Full Page Mono 20000.00
Ad Rate: Full Page Colour 40000.00
Currency: Morocco Dirhams
DAILY NEWSPAPER

Al Watan Al An 655386
Owner: Al Mouahed Establishment LLC
Editorial: 33 Rue Mohamed Bahi, Quartier Palmier, Casablanca **Tel:** 212 522 251285
Email: aririabderrahim@gmail.com **Web site:** http://www.anfasspress.com
Freq: Weekly; **Circ:** 20000 OJD Maroc
Editor in Chief: Boujemaa Achefri; **Publication Manager:** Abderrahim Ariri; **News Editor:** Mounir Elktaoui; **Advertising Manager:** Saida Lamkhannet
Profile: Al Watan Al An is a weekly Arabic newspaper covering news, society, politics, business and sport. It launched in 2001 and is published on Thursdays.
Language (s): Arabic
Ad Rate: Full Page Mono 12000.00
Ad Rate: Full Page Colour 16000.00
Currency: Morocco Dirhams
DAILY NEWSPAPER

News Service/Syndicate

Agence France-Presse - Rabat Bureau 407761
Owner: Agence France-Presse
Editorial: PO Box 118, 2 Bis, Rue Al Khahira, Rabat
Tel: 212 537 706940
Email: afp.rabat@afp.com **Web site:** http://www.afp.com

Profile: Rabat bureau of international news agency supplying news - text, graphics, video and pictures - to subscribers around the world.
Language (s): Arabic
NEWS SERVICE/SYNDICATE

Maghreb Arabe Presse 654829
Owner: Maghreb Arabe Presse
Editorial: PO Box 1049, 122 Avenue Allal Ben Abdellah, Rabat 10000 **Tel:** 212 537 279400
Email: com@map.co.ma **Web site:** http://www.map.ma
General Director: Khalil Idrissi
Profile: Maghreb Arabe Presse is the national news agency of Morocco and covers government and royal news, as well as issues of national importance.
Language (s): Arabic
NEWS SERVICE/SYNDICATE

Reuters - Rabat bureau 406377
Owner: Thomson Reuters
Editorial: Bab El Had, Avenue Hassan II, Rabat
Tel: 212 537 720065
Email: maghreb.newsroom@thomsonreuters.com
Web site: http://www.reuters.com
Profile: Rabat bureau of international news agency supplying news - text, graphics, video and pictures - to subscribers around the world.
Language (s): Arabic
NEWS SERVICE/SYNDICATE

Mozambique

Time Difference: GMT +2
National Telephone Code: 258
Continent: Africa
Capital: Maputo

Newspapers

Savana 396709
Editorial: Mediacoop, Caixa Postal 73, Maputo
Tel: 258 82 327 6670
Email: editorsav@mediacoop.co.mz
Freq: Weekly
Editor: Fernando Andre; **Editor:** Fernando Gonçalves; **Director:** Kok Nam
Profile: Cost: Paid. Savana is Mozambique's leading independent weekly newspaper. The Maputo-based Portuguese language publication is published by Mediacoop, the country's principal independent mediahouse. Mediacoop also published the daily mediaFAX. Savana and mediaFAX are the only independent print media being distributed all over Mozambique and Mediacoop operates a network of correspondents throughout the extensive country.
Language (s): Portuguese
DAILY NEWSPAPER

Namibia

Time Difference: GMT +1
National Telephone Code: 264
Continent: Africa
Capital: Windhoel

Newspapers

The Namibian 159062
Owner: The Namibian
Editorial: 42 John Meinert Street, Windhoek
Tel: 264 61 279 600
Email: info@namibian.com.na **Web site:** http://www.namibian.com.na
Freq: Daily; **Circ:** 40000
Editor-in-Chief: Tangeni Amupadhi
Profile: National daily newspaper covering regional, national and international news and current affairs including business, politics, entertainment and sports.
Language (s): English
DAILY NEWSPAPER

Die Republikein 156748
Owner: Namibia Media Holdings
Editorial: PO Box 3436, Windhoek
Tel: 264 61 297 2000
Email: republikein@republikein.com.na **Web site:** http://www.republikein.com.na
Freq: Daily
Profile: Namibia's only Afrikaans daily newspaper. Distributed nationally, Republikein maintains a balance between hard news coverage that is complemented by politics, economics, agriculture, entertainment and sports coverage.
Language (s): Afrikaans
DAILY NEWSPAPER

Nepal

Time Difference: GMT +5.75
National Telephone Code: 977
Continent: Asia
Capital: Kathmandu

Newspapers

Adarsha Samaj 473090
Owner: Adarsh Samaj Bahumukhi Prakashan Pvt Ltd.
Editorial: Adarsh Samaj Bahumukhi Prakashan Pvt Ltd, Bhakti Marg, Newroad, Pokhara
Tel: 977 61531200
Email: adrsamaj@gmail.com **Web site:** http://www.eadarsha.com/
Freq: Daily; **Circ:** 10001 Not Audited
Editor in Chief: Krishna Prasad Bastola
Profile: Covers of news and general interests.
Language (s): Nepali
DAILY NEWSPAPER

Annapurna Post 473096
Owner: News Media Pvt Ltd.
Editorial: News Media Pvt Ltd., PO Box 23781, Anamnagar-32, Kathmandu **Tel:** 977 14770629
Email: editorial@annapost.com **Web site:** http://www.annapurnapost.com
Freq: Daily; **Circ:** 75003 Not Audited
Editor in Chief: Guna Raj Luitel
Profile: Covers national and international news, in addition to general interests.
Language (s): Nepali
DAILY NEWSPAPER

Butwal Today 473091
Editorial: Butwal Media Prakashan Pvt Ltd., Tilottama Path, Butwal-8, Lumbini **Tel:** 977 71551345
Email: info@butwaltoday.com **Web site:** http://www.butwaltoday.com
Freq: Daily; **Circ:** 10003 Not Audited
Editor in Chief: Jiblal Sapkota
Profile: Covers local and national news.
Language (s): Nepali
DAILY NEWSPAPER

City Post 473097
Editorial: CityPost National Daily, Po Box 19155, Dillibazaar, Kathmandu **Tel:** 977 14416961
Email: info@citypostdaily.com.np **Web site:** http://www.citypostdaily.com.np
Freq: Daily; **Circ:** 10003 Not Audited
Editor: Lilanath Gautam
Profile: Covers of news and general interests.
Language (s): Nepali
DAILY NEWSPAPER

Gorkhapatra 156939
Editorial: Gorkhapatra Sansthan, Dharmapath, P.O. Box 23, Kathmandu - **Tel:** 977 14222921
Email: news.gorkhapatra@gmail.com **Web site:** http://www.gorkhapatra.org.np
Freq: Daily; **Circ:** 30003 Not Audited
Profile: Covers of local, national and international news.
Language (s): Nepali
DAILY NEWSPAPER

The Himalayan Times 473095
Owner: Intl Media Network Nepal Pvt. Ltd.
Editorial: APCA House, Baidya Khana Rd, Anam Nagar, Kathmandu **Tel:** 977 14771489
Email: editorial@thehimalayantimes.com **Web site:** http://www.thehimalayantimes.com
Freq: Daily; **Circ:** 45003 Not Audited
Profile: Covers local, national, regional and international news.
Language (s): Nepali
Ad Rate: Full Page Mono 1400.00
Currency: Nepal Rupees
DAILY NEWSPAPER

Janmabhoomi 460487
Editorial: Janmabhoomi, P.O. Box 3244, Tahachal, Kathmandu **Tel:** 977 14271485
Email: sbpti@mos.com.np
Freq: Weekly; **Circ:** 10002 Not Audited
Editor in Chief: Ganesh Pradhan
Profile: Covering local news, sports, business, jobs, and community events.
Language (s): Nepali
DAILY NEWSPAPER

Kantipur 156940
Owner: Kantipur Publications Pvt. Ltd.
Editorial: Kantipur Complex, Subidhanagar, Kathmandu **Tel:** 977 1 44 80 100
Email: kanti@kantipur.com.np **Web site:** http://www.ekantipur.com
Freq: Daily; **Circ:** 210002 Not Audited
Editor: Sudheer Sharma; **Editor:** Hari Bahadur Thapa
Profile: Covers of Local and International News, Sports, Entertainment, Features, etc.
Language (s): Nepali
DAILY NEWSPAPER

The Kathmandu Post 156941
Owner: Kantipur Publications Pvt. Ltd.
Editorial: Kantipur Complex, Subidhanagar, P.O.Box 8559, Kathmandu **Tel:** 977 14480100
Email: kpost@kmg.com.np **Web site:** http://www.ekantipur.com
Freq: Daily; **Circ:** 40003 Not Audited
Editor in Chief: Akhilesh Upadhyay
Profile: Covers of Local and International News, Sports, Entertainment, etc.
Language (s): English
DAILY NEWSPAPER

Madhyanha 473098
Editorial: Madhyanha Daily, PO Box 21934, Bag Bazaar, Kathmandu **Tel:** 977 14226366
Email: madhyanhadaily@enet.com.np **Web site:** http://www.madhyanhadaily.com.np
Freq: Daily; **Circ:** 5002 Not Audited
Editor: Madan Kumar Shrastha
Profile: Local news and foreign employment news (news about nepali who works overseas).
Language (s): Nepali
DAILY NEWSPAPER

Majdoor 473099
Editorial: Majdoor Daily, Golmadi, Bhaktapur-7, Bhaktapur **Tel:** 977 16610921
Email: majdurdaily@gmail.com **Web site:** http://www.majdoor.com.np
Freq: Daily; **Circ:** 10003 Not Audited
Editor: Vishnu Gopal Kushi
Profile: Local and National News.
Language (s): Nepali
DAILY NEWSPAPER

Nagarik Daily 862406
Editorial: JDA Complex, Kathmandu
Tel: 97 71 4265100
Email: news@nagariknews.com **Web site:** http://www.nagariknews.com
Freq: Daily
Editor in Chief: Prateek Pradhan
Profile: One of the most comprehensive and up-to-date news portals in Nepal for national and international news.
Language (s): Nepali
DAILY NEWSPAPER

Nepali Times 460465
Editorial: Himalmedia Pvt. Ltd, G.P.O. Box 7251, Kathmandu **Tel:** 977 15250333
Email: editors@nepalitimes.com **Web site:** http://www.nepalitimes.com
Freq: Weekly; **Circ:** 26003 Not Audited
Publisher & Editor: Kunda Dixit
Profile: Covers general news.
Language (s): English
DAILY NEWSPAPER

Rajdhani 473094
Owner: Utsarga Prakashan Pvt Ltd.
Editorial: Utsarga Prakashan Pvt Ltd, PO Box 20503, Chabhil, Kathmandu **Tel:** 997 1 4260752
Email: rajdhaninews@yahoo.com **Web site:** http://www.rajdhani.com.np
Freq: Daily; **Circ:** 10002 Not Audited
Editor: Jivendra Simkhada
Profile: Local and World News.
Language (s): Nepali
DAILY NEWSPAPER

The Rising Nepal 156942
Editorial: Gorkhapatra Sanstan, Dharmapath, New Road, Kathmandu **Tel:** 977 1 4244435
Email: trn@gorkhapatra.org.np **Web site:** http://www.gorkhapatra.org.np
Freq: Daily; **Circ:** 25003 Not Audited
Profile: Covers local and international news.
Language (s): English
DAILY NEWSPAPER

Sanghu Vernacular Weekly 460175
Editorial: Sanghu Vernacular Weekly, Bagbazar, G.P.O. Box No. 2984, Kathmandu **Tel:** 977 14230748
Email: sanghuweekly@gmail.com **Web site:** http://www.weeklynepal.com/sanghu
Freq: Weekly; **Circ:** 15002 Not Audited
Editor: Gopal Budhathoki
Profile: Covers of news and general interests.
Language (s): Nepali
DAILY NEWSPAPER

The Telegraph Weekly 459563
Owner: Telegraph Pvt. Ltd.
Editorial: Telegraph Pvt. Ltd., P.O. Box 4063, Laligurans Marg-87, Ghattekulo, Kathmandu 32
Tel: 977 14770370
Web site: http://www.telegraphnepal.com
Freq: Weekly; **Circ:** 15002 Not Audited
Profile: Covers of National and International News, Sports, Business, Entertainment, etc.
Language (s): English
DAILY NEWSPAPER

Yugasambad National Weekly 459242
Editorial: Yugasambad Weekly, P.O. Box 5331, New Plaza, Ram Shah Path, Kathmandu -
Tel: 977 14421454
Email: yugasambad@hons.com.np **Web site:** http://www.yugasambad.com.np
Freq: Weekly; **Circ:** 10001 Not Audited
Profile: Comments on contemporary issues on political, economic, social and environmental as well as gender aspects, interviews, entertainment, etc.
Language (s): Nepali
DAILY NEWSPAPER

News Service/Syndicate

Agence France-Presse - Kathmandu Bureau 878906
Editorial: Bhote Bahal South, GPO Box 402, Kathmandu **Tel:** 977 1 253 861
Email: ammu.kannampilly@afp.com **Web site:** http://www.afp.com
Bureau Chief: Ammu Kannampilly
Profile: Kathmandu bureau of international news and picture agency covering general news and current affairs.
Language (s): English
NEWS SERVICE/SYNDICATE

Community Newspaper

People's Review 224458
Owner: People's Review
Editorial: Pipalbot, Dillibazar, P.O. Box 3052, Kathmandu **Tel:** 977 1 4417352
Email: peoplesreview.com@gmail.com **Web site:** http://www.peoplesreview.com.np
Freq: Weekly; **Circ:** 15001 Not Audited
Editor in Chief: Pushpa Raj Pradhan
Profile: Covers news and related topics.
Language (s): English
COMMUNITY NEWSPAPER

Netherlands

Time Difference: GMT +1
National Telephone Code: 31
Continent: Europe
Capital: Amsterdam

Newspapers

AD Algemeen Dagblad 158233
Owner: AD NieuwsMedia B.V.
Tel: 31 10 406 72 11
Email: redactie@ad.nl **Web site:** http://www.ad.nl
Freq: Daily; **Circ:** 320000 HOI
Profile: AD Algemeen Dagblad is een landelijk dagblad gericht op het brengen van landelijk, algemeen nieuws. Het verschijnt van maandag tot en met zondag. AD Algemeen Dagblad is a National Dutch newspaper. It is published daily from Monday to Saturday.
Language (s): Dutch
DAILY NEWSPAPER

De Telegraaf 158237
Owner: Telegraaf Media Groep NV
Editorial: Postbus 376, Amsterdam 1000 EB
Tel: 31 88 824 0000
Email: nieuwsdienst@telegraaf.nl **Web site:** http://www.telegraaf.nl
Freq: Daily; **Circ:** 648958 HOI
Profile: De Telegraaf is de meest gelezen krant van Nederland. De krant kenmerkt zich door uitgebreide verslaggeving in de Nederlandse misdaad en Nederlands showbiz nieuws. De zaterdagbijlages hebben ook tijdschrift varianten op de markt zoals Vrouw en Story. De Telegraaf is the most read newspaper of the Netherlands. The newspaper is most known for its detailed reporting of Dutch crime news and Dutch showbiz news, with journalists frequently appearing as pundits by other media about their topics. The Saturday topics also have their own magazines, like Vrouw and Story.
Language (s): Dutch
DAILY NEWSPAPER

de Volkskrant 158239
Owner: de Persgroep Nederland B.V.
Tel: 31 20 562 92 22
Email: redactie@volkskrant.nl **Web site:** http://www.volkskrant.nl
Freq: Daily; **Circ:** 262183 HOI
Profile: De Volkskrant is een kwaliteitskrant van Nederland. De volkskrant brengt nieuws uit, in de krant, magazine, mobiel en op tablet. Ze brengen kwaliteitsnieuws, opinie, scherpe interviews en fotografie uit. De Volkskrant is gericht op de hoogopgeleide en welstandige lezers. De Volkskrant wordt dagelijks gepubliceerd van maandag tot zaterdag.The Volkskrant is a quality newspaper of the Netherlands. De Volkskrant brings news on, newspaper, magazine, mobile, and tablet. They report on quality news, opinion, sharp interviews and photography. De Volkskrant is focused on highly educated and well-off readers. The Volkskrant is published daily from Monday to Saturday.
Language (s): Dutch
Ad Rate: Full Page Colour 44663.00
Currency: Euro
DAILY NEWSPAPER

Netherlands

Den Haag Centraal 472848
Owner: Den Haag Centraal
Editorial: Juffrouw Idastraat 11, Den Haag 2513 BE
Tel: 31 70 3644040
Email: redactie@denhaagcentraal.net **Web site:** http://www.denhaagcentraal.net
Freq: Weekly; **Circ:** 12500 Publisher's Statement
Profile: Newspaper covering regional news and current affairs.
Language (s): Dutch
DAILY NEWSPAPER

Het Financieele Dagblad 158234
Owner: Het Financieele Dagblad B.V.
Editorial: Postbus 216, Amsterdam 1000 AE
Tel: 31 20 592 88 88
Email: persbericht@fd.nl **Web site:** http://www.fd.nl
Freq: Daily; **Circ:** 50782 HOI
Profile: Het Financieele Dagblad is een ochtendkrant en brengt dagelijks nieuws met een redactionele focus op Economie & Politiek, Ondernemen en Beurs. Het Financieele Dagblad is a Dutch daily that focusses on Finance & Politics, Enterpreneurs and Listed companies.
Language (s): Dutch
DAILY NEWSPAPER

Nederlands Dagblad 158236
Owner: Nederlands Dagblad B.V.
Tel: 31 342 41 17 11
Email: redactie@nd.nl **Web site:** http://www.nd.nl
Freq: Daily; **Circ:** 27000 HOI
Profile: Het Nederlands Dagblad biedt lezers een dagelijks venster op de werkelijkheid, en duiding daarvan in het licht van de Bijbel. Voortdurend doen we verslag van wat we waarnemen en opmerken; we analyseren, duiden en becommentariëren het nieuws vanuit een herkenbare christelijke identiteit. Het Nederlandse Dagblad offers readers a daily view on reality and interpreting them in the light of the Bible. Constantly we report what we observe and note. We analyze, interpret and comment on the news from a recognizable Christian identity.
Language (s): Dutch
DAILY NEWSPAPER

NRC Handelsblad 158235
Owner: NRC Media
Editorial: Nes 76, Amsterdam 1012 KE
Tel: 31 20 755 30 00
Email: nrc@nrc.nl **Web site:** http://www.nrc.nl
Freq: Daily; **Circ:** 187614 HOI
Profile: NRC Handelsblad concentreert zich op berichtgeving over het buitenland, politiek, economie, opinie en kunst (waaronder literatuur). NRC Handelsblad focuses on coverage of countries, politics, economics, opinion and arts (including literature).
Language (s): Dutch
DAILY NEWSPAPER

Trouw 158238
Owner: de Persgroep Nederland B.V.
Editorial: Postbus 859, Amsterdam 1000 AW
Tel: 31 20 562 94 44
Email: internet@trouw.nl **Web site:** http://www.trouw.nl
Freq: Daily; **Circ:** 106440 HOI
Profile: Trouw is een landelijke krant die zich onderscheidt van de andere kwaliteitskranten door een nadrukkelijke aandacht voor nieuws en beschouwingen uit de wereld van religie en filosofie. Trouw wordt gepubliceerd van maandag tot en met zaterdag.Trouw Trouw is considered one of the Dutch national quality newspapers next to NRC Next and Volkskrant. Partly due to its history, and more than those other two, it pays specific attention to religion: Christianity, Islam and all the other world religions. Trouw is published daily from Monday to Friday.
Language (s): Dutch
DAILY NEWSPAPER

News Service/Syndicate

ANP Algemeen Nederlands Persbureau 623323
Owner: Algemeen Nederlands Persbureau ANP
Editorial: Verrijn Stuartlaan 7, Rijswijk 2288 EK
Tel: 31 70 414 14 01
Email: nieuwsdienst@anp.nl **Web site:** http://www.anp.nl
Profile: Algemeen Nederlands Persbureau ANP is the most important news supplier in The Netherlands. It provides news coverage for the Dutch daily newspapers, radio, television and the internet. ANP's general news service supplies a steady flow of news stories, info graphics and photographs from across the country and around the world, 24 hours a day, 7 days a week.
Language (s): Dutch
NEWS SERVICE/SYNDICATE

ANP Amsterdam 623324
Editorial: Vijzelstraat 72, Amsterdam 1017 HL
Tel: 31 20 560 60 60
Email: amsterdam@anp.nl **Web site:** http://www.anp.nl
Profile: Amsterdam bureau of ANP.
Language (s): Dutch
NEWS SERVICE/SYNDICATE

BNO News 623336
Editorial: Pastoor Duchampsstraat 2, Tilburg 5046HV
Email: info@bnonews.com **Web site:** http://www.bnonews.com
Profile: BNO News is a news agency with offices in the Netherlands, Mexico and the United States. Founded in late 2009, BNO News provides content to media organizations – both local and national – in the United States and around the world.
Language (s): Dutch
NEWS SERVICE/SYNDICATE

Netherlands Antilles

Time Difference: GMT -4
National Telephone Code: 599
Continent: The Americas
Capital: Willemstad

Newspapers

Amigoe 156829
Owner: Uitgeverij Amigoe NV
Editorial: Uitgeverij Amigoe NV, Kaya Fraternan di Skerpene z/n, Curacao **Tel:** 599 97672744
Email: management@amigoe.com **Web site:** http://www.amigoe.com
Freq: Daily; **Circ:** 10000 Not Audited
Editor in Chief: Marius Noort; **Editor in Chief:** Linda Van Eekeres
Profile: Amigoe is a newspaper covering national and international news, politics, culture and sports.
Language (s): Dutch
Ad Rate: Full Page Mono 3.50
Ad Rate: Full Page Colour 175.00
Currency: United States Dollars
DAILY NEWSPAPER

The Daily Herald 161016
Owner: The Caribbean Herald NV
Editorial: Bush Road 22, Philipsburg, Sint Maarten
Tel: 599 5 425 253
Email: editorial@thedailyherald.com **Web site:** http://www.thedailyherald.com
Freq: Daily; **Circ:** 9000 Not Audited
Publisher: Paul Dewindt; **Editor in Chief:** Courtney Gibson
Profile: Local newspaper distributed in the Caribbean region.
Language (s): English
Ad Rate: Full Page Mono 7.05
Currency: United States Dollars
DAILY NEWSPAPER

La Prensa 218030
Owner: Uitgeverij de Pers NV
Editorial: West Indische Compagniestraat 41, Curacao **Tel:** 599 9 462 4086
Email: laprensa@laprensacur.com **Web site:** http://www.laprensacur.com
Freq: Daily; **Circ:** 11000 Not Audited
Editor in Chief: Mariano Heyden; **Director:** Romulo Irausquin
Profile: Local newspaper covering regional, national and international news and current-affairs; includes politics, finance, sport and culture.
Language (s): Dutch
Ad Rate: Full Page Mono 3.00
Currency: United States Dollars
DAILY NEWSPAPER

Ultimo Noticia 217943
Owner: Ultimo Noticia NV
Editorial: Frederikstraat 96, Willemstad, Curacao
Tel: 599 9 462 3466
Email: redakshon@ultimo.an
Freq: Daily; **Circ:** 19000 Not Audited
Manager: Jessy Hamilton; **Editor:** Angel Kirchner
Profile: Local newspaper focusing in the native Papiamento language.
Language (s): Dutch
Ad Rate: Full Page Mono 7.61
Currency: United States Dollars
DAILY NEWSPAPER

Community Newspaper

The Bonaire Reporter 225248
Owner: Bonaire Reporter
Tel: 599 7866125
Email: info@bonairereporter.com **Web site:** http://www.bonairereporter.com
Freq: Bi-Monthly; **Circ:** 3000 Not Audited
Publisher: George De Salvo; **Editor in Chief:** Laura De Salvo
Profile: The Bonaire Reporter is a bi-monthly newspaper containing information on and analysis of the events on the Bonaire island.
Language (s): English
Ad Rate: Full Page Mono 3.85
Ad Rate: Full Page Colour 5.19
Currency: United States Dollars
COMMUNITY NEWSPAPER

New Zealand

Time Difference: GMT +12
National Telephone Code: 64
Continent: Oceania
Capital: Wellington

Newspapers

The Dominion Post 156672
Owner: Fairfax Media
Editorial: PO Box 3740, Wellington 6140
Tel: 64 4 474 0196
Email: news@dompost.co.nz **Web site:** http://stuff.co.nz/dominion-post
Freq: Daily; **Circ:** 68912 ABC-Audit Bureau of Circulations
Editor: Bernadette Courtney; **Coumnist:** Vernon Small
Profile: The Dominion Post is a metropolitan broadsheet newspaper published in Wellington, New Zealand.
Language (s): English
Ad Rate: Full Page Colour 13091.06
Currency: New Zealand Dollars
DAILY NEWSPAPER

New Zealand Herald 156719
Owner: NZME
Editorial: 46 Albert Street, Auckland 1010
Tel: 64 9 379 5050
Email: newsdesk@nzherald.co.nz **Web site:** http://www.nzherald.co.nz
Freq: Daily; **Circ:** 30000 ABC-Audit Bureau of Circulations
Editor: Michele Crawshaw; **Editor:** Andrew Laxon; **Editor:** Amanda Linnell; **Contributor:** Tapu Misa
Profile: The New Zealand Herald provides news and current events from around New Zealand and around the world. Awards: Canon Newspaper of the Year and Best Website 2015. Asia-Pacific Newspaper of the Year 2015.
Language (s): English
Ad Rate: Full Page Colour 13468.00
Currency: New Zealand Dollars
DAILY NEWSPAPER

Sunday News 343331
Owner: Fairfax Media
Editorial: PO Box 1327, Shortland Street, Auckland 1140 **Tel:** 64 9 925 9700
Email: editor@sunday-news.co.nz **Web site:** http://stuff.co.nz/sunday-news
Freq: Weekly; **Circ:** 28624 ABC-Audit Bureau of Circulations
News Editor: David Eames; **Editor:** Jonathan Milne
Profile: The Sunday News is published by Fairfax Media. Provides weekend round-up in news, sports and entertainment.
Language (s): English
Ad Rate: Full Page Colour 59544.00
Currency: New Zealand Dollars
DAILY NEWSPAPER

Sunday Star-Times 343137
Owner: Fairfax Media
Editorial: PO Box 1327, Shortland Street, Auckland 1140 **Tel:** 64 9 925 9700
Email: news@star-times.co.nz **Web site:** http://stuff.co.nz/sunday-star-times
Freq: Weekly; **Circ:** 115730 ABC-Audit Bureau of Circulations
News Editor: David Eames; **Editor:** Jonathan Milne
Profile: Sunday Star Times provides latest national news, including breaking sports, entertainment and event news.
Language (s): English
Ad Rate: Full Page Colour 20462.00
Currency: New Zealand Dollars
DAILY NEWSPAPER

Waikato Times 161296
Owner: Fairfax Media
Editorial: 70 Foreman Road, Te Rapa, Hamilton 3240
Tel: 64 7 8499 666
Email: news@waikatotimes.co.nz **Web site:** http://www.stuff.co.nz/waikato-times
Circ: 40096
Editor: Jonathan MacKenzie
Profile: The Waikato Times, a metropolitan daily, forms the core brand within the Fairfax Media Waikato Division. With an average issue readership of 96,000, the Waikato Times has the fifth largest readership of any daily newspaper in New Zealand.
Language (s): English
Ad Rate: Full Page Colour 6730.40
Currency: New Zealand Dollars
DAILY NEWSPAPER

News Service/Syndicate

Appita NZ 688963
Editorial: PO Box 6042, Whakarewarewa, Rotorua 3043 **Tel:** 64 7 350 2252
Email: appita.nz@xtra.co.nz **Web site:** http://appita.com
Profile: Appita is a non-profit technical association serving the New Zealand and Australian pulp and paper industry. Its main purpose is to facilitate the industry's technical network involving all stakeholders to advance the technical capability and expertise. Alternative Co. Name: Australian Pulp and Paper Industry Technical Association
NEWS SERVICE/SYNDICATE

infonews.co.nz 503660
Owner: Citizen Media Ltd
Editorial: 27 Littlejohn St, Hillsborough, Auckland 1042 **Tel:** 64 21 045 5634
Email: news@infonews.co.nz **Web site:** http://infonews.co.nz
Profile: infonews.co.nz is a nation-wide local news website for New Zealand which allows any member of the community to publish news, photos and events.
Language (s): English
NEWS SERVICE/SYNDICATE

MSN New Zealand 528440
Owner: Tasman NineMSN
Editorial: PO Box 8998, Symonds St, Auckland 1150
Tel: 64 9 362 5628
Web site: http://www.msn.com/en-nz
Profile: Provides Latest News, Sports, Entertainment, Money, Weather, Travel, Health, and Lifestyle.
Language (s): English
NEWS SERVICE/SYNDICATE

NewsRoom 347771
Editorial: Wellington
Email: editor@newsroom.co.nz **Web site:** http://newsroom.co.nz
Profile: NewsRoom delivers news feeds and related services to a cross-section of New Zealand's professional services firms, large and medium-sized companies, industry bodies, educational and community-based organisations, government agencies and parliament.
Language (s): English
NEWS SERVICE/SYNDICATE

Pacific Media Centre 714467
Owner: AUT University
Editorial: 10th Floor, Sir Paul Reeves Building, 2 Governor Fitzroy Place, Auckland **Tel:** 64 9 9219388
Email: pmc@aut.ac.nz **Web site:** http://www.pmc.aut.ac.nz
Director: David Robie
Profile: Media research and community resource centre focusing on Maori, Pasifika and ethnic diversity media and community development Director David Robie. Geographical Focus: Maori
Language (s): English
NEWS SERVICE/SYNDICATE

Pacific Media Watch 362367
Owner: Pacific Media Centre, AUT University
Editorial: School of Communication Studies, Private Bag 92006, Auckland 1142 **Tel:** 64 9219388
Email: pmediawa@aut.ac.nz **Web site:** http://www.pacmediawatch.aut.ac.nz
Freq: Daily
Language (s): English
NEWS SERVICE/SYNDICATE

Scoop.co.nz 347770
Owner: Scoop Media Ltd
Editorial: Level 3- 354, Lambton Quay, Wellington 6142 **Tel:** 64 4 910 1844
Email: editor@scoop.co.nz **Web site:** http://www.scoop.co.nz
Co-Editor: Alastair Thompson
Profile: Provides political, business, science, biotechnology, education, health, IT arts/culture, sports, international news.
Language (s): English
NEWS SERVICE/SYNDICATE

Stuff.co.nz 347765
Owner: Fairfax Media
Editorial: PO Box 2595, Wellington 6140
Tel: 64 4 474 0090
Email: newsroom@stuff.co.nz **Web site:** http://stuff.co.nz
Editor: Mark Stevens
Profile: Stuff.co.nz is New Zealand's news and information website. Covers every aspect of news and information, from breaking national and international crises through to in-depth features, sports, business, entertainment and technology articles, weather reports, travel services, movie reviews, rural news.
Language (s): English
Ad Rate: Full Page Colour 7000.00
Currency: New Zealand Dollars
NEWS SERVICE/SYNDICATE

Community Newspaper

Bay of Plenty Times 156675
Owner: NZME
Editorial: 405 Cameron Road, Tauranga
Tel: 64 7 577 7770
Email: editor@bayofplentytimes.co.nz **Web site:** http://www.nzherald.co.nz/bay-of-plenty-times/news/headlines.cfm?c_id=1503343
Circ: 20352
Chief Photographer: John Borren; **Editor:** Scott Inglis
Profile: Read by residents of the Western Bay of Plenty. Covers all aspects of news from local,

national and international events to a full round-up of sporting results and a wide range of reader interests.
Language (s): English
COMMUNITY NEWSPAPER

Hawke's Bay Today
156671
Owner: APN News
Editorial: 301 Heretaunga Street, East Hastings, Hastings 4156 **Tel:** 64 6 873 0800
Email: news@hbtoday.co.nz **Web site:** http://www.nzherald.co.nz/hawkes-bay-today/news/headlines.cfm?c_id=1503462
Circ: 24775
Chief Photographer: Warren Buckland; **Regional Bureau Chief:** Roger Moroney
Profile: Hawke's Bay Today is the principal news media service within the Hawke's Bay Region.
Language (s): English
Ad Rate: Full Page Colour 7661.00
Currency: New Zealand Dollars
COMMUNITY NEWSPAPER

Manawatu Standard
156698
Owner: Fairfax Media
Editorial: PO Box 3, 51 The Square, Palmerston North 4440 **Tel:** 64 6 356 9009
Email: editor@msl.co.nz **Web site:** http://stuff.co.nz/manawatu-standard
Freq: Daily; **Circ:** 12357
Editor: Rob Mitchell
Profile: Newspaper focusing on local, national and world news, sport and entertainment. Aimed at general public in Central North Island, New Zealand.Manawatu, Tararua, Rangitikei, Northern Horowhenua Afternoon Mon-Sat Photo col pref PR txt to round by email; pics to ed.
Language (s): English
COMMUNITY NEWSPAPER

Nelson Mail
343356
Owner: Fairfax Media
Editorial: PO Box 244, Nelson 7040
Tel: 64 3 548 7079
Email: chiefreporter@nelsonmail.co.nz **Web site:** http://www.stuff.co.nz/nelson-mail
Freq: Daily; **Circ:** 11734
Chief Photographer: Martin de Ruyter; **Editor:** Alastair Paulin
Profile: The Nelson Mail has served the Nelson region with a daily newspaper continuously since 1866 and is one of New Zealand's oldest and most respected regional newspapers.
Language (s): English
COMMUNITY NEWSPAPER

Otago Daily Times
156720
Owner: Allied Press Ltd
Editorial: 52 Stuart Street, Dunedin 9054
Tel: 64 3 477 4760
Email: newstips@alliedpress.co.nz **Web site:** http://www.odt.co.nz
Circ: 39097
Music Reviewer: Shane Gilchrist
Profile: A daily regional newspaper covering news, sport, entertainment, lifestyle and opinion for the Otago region. News Tips: newstips@alliedpress.co.nz, Press Releases: press.releases@alliedpress.co.nz.PR Accepted in: English
Language (s): English
Ad Rate: Full Page Colour 6036.80
Currency: New Zealand Dollars
COMMUNITY NEWSPAPER

The Press
343140
Owner: Fairfax Media
Editorial: Private Bag 4722, Christchurch 8140
Tel: 64 3 379 0940
Email: reporters@press.co.nz **Web site:** http://stuff.co.nz/the-press
Circ: 81017
Head of News: Keith Lynch; **Editor - Drive:** Dave Moore; **Editor:** Joanna Norris
Profile: Provides latest Christchurch and South Island news, including breaking sports.
Language (s): English
COMMUNITY NEWSPAPER

The Southland Times
156677
Owner: Fairfax Media
Editorial: 67 Esk Street, Invercargill 9840
Tel: 64 3 211 1130
Email: news@stl.co.nz **Web site:** http://stuff.co.nz/southland-times
Freq: Daily; **Circ:** 23231
Chief Photographer: Robyn Edie; **Photographer:** Nicole Johnstone
Profile: Provides news and current events from around Southland, New Zealand and around the world. Awards:Regional Newspaper of the Year - 2011 Canon Media Award
Language (s): English
COMMUNITY NEWSPAPER

The Taranaki Daily News
156676
Owner: Fairfax Media
Editorial: 49-65 Currie Street, New Plymouth 4310
Tel: 64 6 759 0808
Email: editor@dailynews.co.nz **Web site:** http://www.stuff.co.nz/taranaki-daily-news
Freq: Daily; **Circ:** 18928
Profile: The Taranaki Daily News is one of New Zealand's provincial newspapers. Established in 1857, the Taranaki Daily News provides its readers with in-depth coverage of local, national and

international news, as well as special features that inform, educate and entertain its readers.
Language (s): English
Ad Rate: Full Page Colour 2622.00
Currency: New Zealand Dollars
COMMUNITY NEWSPAPER

Nicaragua

Time Difference: GMT -6
National Telephone Code: 505
Continent: The Americas
Capital: Managua

Newspapers

Bolsa de Noticias
160811
Owner: Grupo Emigdio Suárez Ediciones
Editorial: Colonia Centroamerica de la Iglesia de Fatima 3 cuadras al sur, Casa L#852, Managua
Tel: 505 22700546
Email: prensa@bolsadenoticias.com.ni **Web site:** http://www.bolsadenoticias.com.ni
Freq: Daily; **Circ:** 3500 Not Audited
Editor in Chief: María Elena Palacios; **Director:** María Elsa Suárez García
Profile: Regional newspaper focusing on national and international news, politics, business and sport.
Language (s): Spanish
DAILY NEWSPAPER

El Nuevo Diario
160805
Owner: El Nuevo Diario
Editorial: Kilometro 4.5, Carretera Norte, Managua
Tel: 505 22490499
Email: web@elnuevodiario.com.ni **Web site:** http://www.elnuevodiario.com.ni
Freq: Daily; **Circ:** 46000 Not Audited
Editor: Gustavo Alvarez; **Editor:** Juan Ramón Huerta; **Editor:** Edgar Tijerino
Profile: National newspaper covering national and international news, sport, politics and culture.
Language (s): Spanish
DAILY NEWSPAPER

La Prensa
156838
Owner: Editora La Prensa SA
Editorial: Kilometro 4 1/2 Carretera Norte, Managua 192 **Tel:** 505 22556767
Email: info@laprensa.com.ni **Web site:** http://www.laprensa.com.ni
Freq: Daily; **Circ:** 42600 Not Audited
Editor in Chief: Eduardo Enríquez; **National News Editor:** Nohelia González; **Editor:** Freddy Potoy; **Editor:** Edgar Rodríguez; **Editor:** Luis Sánchez
Profile: Newspaper focusing on national and international news, politics and economics.
Language (s): Spanish
DAILY NEWSPAPER

Niger

Time Difference: GMT +1
National Telephone Code: 227
Continent: Africa
Capital: Niamey

Newspapers

Le Démocrate
522424
Owner: Nouvelles Imprimeries du Niger
Editorial: 21 Rue 067 NB Terminus, Niamey
Tel: 227 94 85 50 90
Email: le_democrate@caramail.com **Web site:** http://www.tamtaminfo.com
Freq: Weekly; **Circ:** 1000 Publisher's Statement
Profile: Regional weekly newspaper focussing on news and current affairs, politics and culture.
Language (s): French
Ad Rate: Full Page Mono 200000.00
Currency: Communauté Financière Africaine Francs BCEAO
DAILY NEWSPAPER

L' Evénement
522432
Owner: Nouvelles Imprimeries du Niger
Editorial: Zabarkan, Rue de L'Entente, Porte: 654, Niamey **Tel:** 227 20 74 15 75
Email: levenement@netcourrier.com **Web site:** http://levenementniger.com
Freq: Weekly; **Circ:** 1000 Publisher's Statement
Editor in Chief: Garé Amadou; **Director:** Moussa Askar
Profile: Bi-weekly newspaper covering general news and current affairs, politics and economics.
Language (s): French
Ad Rate: Full Page Mono 200000.00
Currency: Communauté Financière Africaine Francs BCEAO
DAILY NEWSPAPER

Le Républicain
230969
Owner: Nouvelles Imprimeries du Niger
Editorial: Quartier terminus, Face pharmacie de l'espoir, Niamey **Tel:** 227 20 33 03 03
Email: nin@intnet.ne
Freq: Weekly; **Circ:** 2500 Publisher's Statement
Editor: Maman Abou
Profile: Newspaper covering national and international news and current affairs including politics, business, entertainment and sport.
Language (s): French
DAILY NEWSPAPER

Le Sahel
218469
Owner: Le Sahel Dimanche
Editorial: BP 13182, Niamey **Tel:** 227 20 73 34 87
Email: onep@intnet.ne **Web site:** http://www.lesahel.org
Freq: Daily; **Circ:** 3500 Publisher's Statement
Director: Saidou Daoura; **Editor:** Assane Soumana
Profile: Newspaper covering national and international news and current affairs including economics, politics, business and sport.
Language (s): French
Ad Rate: Full Page Mono 300000.00
Ad Rate: Full Page Colour 500000.00
Currency: Communauté Financière Africaine Francs BCEAO
DAILY NEWSPAPER

Sahel Dimanche
217971
Owner: Le Sahel
Editorial: BP 13182, Niamey **Tel:** 227 20 73 34 87
Email: onep@intnet.ne **Web site:** http://www.lesahel.org
Freq: Weekly; **Circ:** 4000 Publisher's Statement
Director: Saidou Daoura; **Editor:** Dubois Touraoua
Profile: Sunday newspaper focusing on national and international news and current affairs including economics, politics, business, entertainment and sport.
Language (s): French
Ad Rate: Full Page Mono 300000.00
Ad Rate: Full Page Colour 500000.00
Currency: Communauté Financière Africaine Francs BCEAO
DAILY NEWSPAPER

Nigeria

Time Difference: GMT +1
National Telephone Code: 234
Continent: Africa
Capital: Abuja

Newspapers

BusinessDay
318948
Owner: Business Day Ltd.
Editorial: The Brook, 6 Point Road, Apapa, Lagos
Tel: 234 1 34 54 501
Email: mail@businessdayonline.com **Web site:** http://www.businessdayonline.com
Freq: Daily
Editor: Phillip Isakpa; **Editor in Chief:** Onwuchekwa Jemie
Profile: Newspaper covering national and international business news including finance, markets, enterprise, banking, economy, business intelligence and personal finance.
Language (s): English
Ad Rate: Full Page Colour 237000.00
Currency: Nigeria Nairas
DAILY NEWSPAPER

Daily Champion
156750
Owner: Champion Newspapers Limited
Editorial: PO Box 2276, Oshodi, Lagos
Tel: 234 1 4800872
Email: championmails@gmail.com **Web site:** http://www.championnews.com.ng
Freq: Daily; **Circ:** 80000 Publisher's Statement
Editor in Chief: Nwadiuto Iheakanwa; **Publisher:** Emmanuel Iwuanyanwu
Profile: Newspaper covering national and international news and current affairs including business, politics, economy and finance.
Language (s): English
DAILY NEWSPAPER

Daily Independent
318949
Owner: Independent Newspapers Limited
Editorial: Block 5, Plot 8, Wempco Road, Ogba, Ikeja, Lagos **Tel:** 234 803 568 1104
Email: info@independentnig.com **Web site:** http://independentnig.com
Freq: Daily
Editor: Kingsley Ighomwengian; **Advertising Manager:** Emeka Opara
Profile: Newspaper covering national and international news and current affairs including politics, business, economics, lifestyle and sports.
Language (s): English
Ad Rate: Full Page Mono 130000.00
Ad Rate: Full Page Colour 175000.00
Currency: Nigeria Nairas
DAILY NEWSPAPER

Daily Trust
161243
Owner: Media Trust Nigeria Limited
Editorial: No. 20 P.O.W. Mafemi Crescent, Utako District, Abuja **Tel:** 234 700 1777577
Email: dailytrust@yahoo.co.uk **Web site:** http://www.dailytrust.com.ng
Freq: Daily; **Circ:** 20000 Publisher's Statement
Managing Director: Isiaq Ajibola; **Editor in Chief:** Mannir Dan Ali; **Advertising Manager:** Akeem Mustapha
Profile: Newspaper covering national and international news including politics, business, economics, sport, agriculture, education, environment, religion and health.
Language (s): English
DAILY NEWSPAPER

The Guardian
156756
Owner: Guardian Newspapers Limited
Editorial: Rutam House, Km 4 Apapa-Oshodi Expressway, Isolo, Lagos **Tel:** 234 1 44 89 600
Email: letters@ngrguardiannews.com **Web site:** http://guardian.ng
Freq: Daily; **Circ:** 50000 Publisher's Statement
Editor in Chief: Debo Adesina; **Advertising Manager:** Kola Arigbede; **Managing Director:** Emeka Izeze; **News Editor:** Marcel Mbamalu; **Editor (Sunday):** Abraham Ogbodo
Profile: Independent newspaper covering national and international news and current affairs including politics, business, economics, sports, arts and culture.
Language (s): English
Ad Rate: Full Page Mono 3528.00
Currency: United Kingdom Pounds
DAILY NEWSPAPER

Al Mizan
230970
Owner: IM Publications
Editorial: PO Box 686, Babban Dodo, Zariya
Tel: 234 80 37023343
Email: almizanzariya@yahoo.com **Web site:** http://www.almizan.info
Freq: Weekly; **Circ:** 25000 Publisher's Statement
Advertising Manager: Abubaker Abdullahi; **Managing Director:** Hamidu Danlami; **Editor in Chief:** Ibrahim Musa
Profile: Newspaper covering national and international news, politics, religion and sport.
Language (s): Hausa
DAILY NEWSPAPER

The National Mirror
873256
Owner: Global Media Mirror Limited
Editorial: Mirror House, 155/161, Broad Street, Lagos 101001 **Tel:** 234 702 710 7407
Email: mail@nationalmirroronline.net **Web site:** http://nationalmirroronline.net
Freq: Daily
Editor: Segun Fatuase; **Editor:** Callistus Oke
Profile: Newspaper covering the latest news from Nigeria including politics, business, arts, lifestyle, sports, education and health.
Language (s): English
DAILY NEWSPAPER

Nigerian Tribune
156763
Owner: African Newspapers of Nigeria Ltd
Editorial: Tribune House, Imalefalafia Street, Oke-Ado, Ibadan **Tel:** 234 803 806 4581
Email: editornigeriantribune@yahoo.com **Web site:** http://tribuneonlineng.com
Freq: Daily; **Circ:** 45000 Publisher's Statement
Profile: Newspaper covering the latest news from Nigeria including politics, business, community news, lifestyle, sports, education and health.
Language (s): English
Ad Rate: Full Page Mono 222000.00
Ad Rate: Full Page Colour 280000.00
Currency: Nigeria Nairas
DAILY NEWSPAPER

Peoples Daily
875223
Owner: Peoples Media Ltd
Editorial: 35, Ajose Adeogun Street, 1st Floor, Abuja
Tel: 234 9 873 4478
Email: contact@peoplesdailyng.com **Web site:** http://www.peoplesdailyng.com
Freq: Daily
Editor in Chief: Rufai Ibrahim
Profile: Newspaper covering news and current affairs including business, politics, economics, lifestyle and sports.
Language (s): English
DAILY NEWSPAPER

The Punch
318945
Owner: Punch (Nigeria) Limited
Editorial: Km 14 Lagos-Ibadan expressway, Magboro, Ogun, Lagos
Email: info@punchng.com **Web site:** http://www.punchng.com
Freq: Daily; **Circ:** 100000 Publisher's Statement
Profile: Newspaper covering national and international news and current affairs including politics, business, entertainment, sports and opinion.
Language (s): English
Ad Rate: Full Page Mono 272250.00
Ad Rate: Full Page Colour 378000.00
Currency: Nigeria Nairas
DAILY NEWSPAPER

The Sun
318947
Owner: The Sun Publishing Limited
Editorial: 2 Coscharis Street, Kirikiri Industrial Layout, Apapa, P.M.B., Ikeja, Lagos 21776
Tel: 234 805 633 4351

Nigeria

Email: editor@sunnewsonline.com **Web site:** http://www.sunnewsonline.com
Freq: Daily; **Circ:** 80000 Publisher's Statement
Editor in Chief: Femi Adesina; **Director:** Mike Awoyinfa
Profile: Newspaper covering national and international news and current affairs including politics, business, sports and entertainment.
Language (s): English
Ad Rate: Full Page Mono 427805.00
Ad Rate: Full Page Colour 551000.00
Currency: Nigeria Nairas
DAILY NEWSPAPER

THISDAY 161246
Owner: THISDAY Newspapers Limited
Editorial: 35, Creek Road, Apapa, Lagos
Tel: 234 80 22 92 47 21
Email: hello@thisdaylive.com **Web site:** http://www.thisdaylive.com
Freq: Daily; **Circ:** 100000 Publisher's Statement
Managing Director: Eniola Bello; **Editor:** Ijeoma Nwogwugwu; **Editor in Chief:** Nduka Obaigbena
Profile: Newspaper covering regional, national and international news including politics, business, health, education, sport, entertainment and lifestyle.
Language (s): English
Ad Rate: Full Page Mono 290000.00
Ad Rate: Full Page Colour 358000.00
Currency: Nigeria Nairas
DAILY NEWSPAPER

Vanguard 318944
Owner: Vanguard Media Limited
Editorial: 2 Vanguard Avenue, Kirikiri Canal, Apapa, Lagos **Tel:** 234 70 61078412
Email: citizenreport@vanguardngr.com **Web site:** http://www.vanguardngr.com
Freq: Daily; **Circ:** 120000 Publisher's Statement
Advertising Manager: Emeka Nkwocha
Profile: Newspaper covering regional, national and international news including politics, business, sport, entertainment, technology and lifestyle.
Language (s): English
Ad Rate: Full Page Mono 430500.00
Ad Rate: Full Page Colour 567500.00
Currency: Nigeria Nairas
DAILY NEWSPAPER

Weekly Trust 229992
Owner: Media Trust Nigeria Limited
Editorial: No. 20 P.O.W. Mafemi Crescent, Utako District, Abuja **Tel:** 234 9 1777577
Email: dailytrust@yahoo.co.uk **Web site:** http://www.dailytrust.com.ng
Freq: Weekly; **Circ:** 25000 Publisher's Statement
Managing Director: Isiaq Ajibola; **Editor in Chief:** Mannir Dan Ali; **Advertising Manager:** Akeem Mustapha
Profile: Newspaper covering national and international news including politics, business, economics, sport, agriculture, education, environment, religion and health.
Language (s): English
DAILY NEWSPAPER

Norfolk Island

Time Difference: GMT +11
National Telephone Code: 672
Continent: Oceania
Capital: Kingston

Newspapers

The Norfolk Islander 229834
Owner: Greenways Press Pty Ltd.
Editorial: PO Box 248, Norfolk Island
Tel: 672 23 22159
Email: news@islander.nf **Web site:** http://norfolkislander.com
Circ: 1400 Publisher's Statement
Editor: Tom Lloyd; **Editor:** Jonathan Snell
Profile: Newspaper focusing on local and regional news, community issues and sport.
Language (s): English
Ad Rate: Full Page Mono 114.45
Currency: Australia Dollars
DAILY NEWSPAPER

Northern Mariana Islands

Time Difference: GMT +10
National Telephone Code: 1 670
Continent: Oceania
Capital: Saipan

Newspapers

Marianas Variety News & Views 472320
Owner: Younis Art Studio Inc.
Editorial: Alaihai Avenue, Garapan, Saipan
Tel: 1 6702349797
Web site: http://www.mvariety.com
Freq: Daily
Editor: Zaldy Dandan; **President & Publisher:** Abed Younis; **Co-Publisher:** Maria Paz Younis
Profile: Covers local news, sports, business and Pacific Islands news.
Language (s): Chamorro
Ad Rate: Full Page Mono 7.00
Ad Rate: Full Page Colour 788.00
Currency: United States Dollars
DAILY NEWSPAPER

Saipan Tribune 472312
Owner: Pacific Publications & Printing Inc.
Editorial: 2nd Floor CIC Centre, Beach Road, Garapan, Saipan 96950 **Tel:** 1 6702356397
Email: editor@saipantribune.com **Web site:** http://www.saipantribune.com
Freq: Daily; **Circ:** 2500 Not Audited
Editor in Chief: Jayvee Vallejera
Profile: Saipan Tribune is a daily newspaper serving the Northern Mariana Islands. It was the Commonwealth's first daily newspaper. It provides local news, sports, business, entertainment and features. The national and international news is provided by news services.
Language (s): English
Ad Rate: Full Page Mono 6.00
Ad Rate: Full Page Colour 558.00
Currency: United States Dollars
DAILY NEWSPAPER

Norway

Time Difference: GMT +1
National Telephone Code: 47
Continent: Europe
Capital: Oslo

Newspapers

Adresseavisen 158356
Editorial: Ferjemannsveien 10, Trondheim 7042
Tel: 47 07 200
Email: redaksjon@adresseavisen.no **Web site:** http://www.adressa.no
Circ: 61086
Editor-in-Chief: Tor Olav Mørseth
Profile: Adresseavisen is a regional newspaper in Norway published daily, except Sundays, in Trondheim. Adresseavisen is the oldest existing newspaper and published for the first time in 1767.
Language (s): Norwegian
Ad Rate: Full Page Mono 76040.00
Currency: Norway Kroner
DAILY NEWSPAPER

Aftenposten 157837
Editorial: Akersgata 55, Oslo 180 **Tel:** 47 22 86 30 00
Email: 2286@aftenposten.no **Web site:** http://www.aftenposten.no
Freq: Daily; **Circ:** 187694 Not Audited
Editor-in-Chief: Espen Egil Hansen
Profile: Aftenposten is a Norwegian National newspaper based in Oslo. It covers domestic news, international news, finance, sports, travel and culture.
Language (s): Norwegian
Ad Rate: Full Page Mono 171615.00
Currency: Norway Kroner
DAILY NEWSPAPER

Bergens Tidende 158313
Editorial: Krinkelkroken 1, Bergen 5020
Tel: 47 55 21 45 00
Email: 2211@bt.no **Web site:** http://www.bt.no
Freq: Daily; **Circ:** 70209 MBL (Mediebedriftenes Landsforening)
Profile: Bergens Tidende is a Norwegian daily newspaper based in Bergen. It is the fifth largest newspaper in the country and the largest newspaper outside Oslo.
Language (s): Norwegian
Ad Rate: Full Page Mono 119065.00
Currency: Norway Kroner
DAILY NEWSPAPER

Dagbladet 157840
Owner: AS Dagbladet
Editorial: Karvesvingen 1, Oslo 579
Tel: 47 24 00 10 00
Email: 2400@db.no **Web site:** http://www.dagbladet.no
Freq: Daily; **Circ:** 73647 MBL (Mediebedriftenes Landsforening)
Editor-in-Chief: John Arne Markussen
Profile: Dagbladet is a Norwegian national newspaper, covering domestic news, international news, sports, culture and travel. It is Norway's second largest tabloid newspaper.
Language (s): Norwegian
Ad Rate: Full Page Mono 167000.00
Currency: Norway Kroner
DAILY NEWSPAPER

Dagens Næringsliv 158305
Owner: Dagens Næringsliv AS
Editorial: Christian Krohgs gate 16, Oslo 186
Tel: 47 22 00 10 00
Email: redaksjonen@dn.no **Web site:** http://www.dn.no
Freq: Daily; **Circ:** 69916 Not Audited
Editor: Arve Ditmansen; **Editor-in-Chief & Managing Director:** Amund Djuve; **News Editor:** Tor Magne Nondal
Profile: Dagens Næringsliv is a tabloid-sized quality newspaper providing in-depth coverage of national and international business news, politics, finance and economics. Read by the business community, academics, politicians, business managers and financial executives.
Language (s): Norwegian
Ad Rate: Full Page Mono 191000.00
Currency: Norway Kroner
DAILY NEWSPAPER

Dagsavisen 158306
Editorial: Grubbegata 6, Oslo 107
Tel: 47 22 99 80 00
Email: samfunn@dagsavisen.no **Web site:** http://www.dagsavisen.no
Freq: Daily; **Circ:** 21920 MBL (Mediebedriftenes Landsforening)
Sjefsredaktør: Arne Strand; **Helgeredaktør:** Lars West Johnsen
Profile: Dagsavisen is a Norwegian daily newspaper published in Oslo. The paper is politically fully independent, but was historically the party organ of the Norwegian Labour Party.
Language (s): Norwegian
Ad Rate: Full Page Mono 36500.00
Currency: Norway Kroner
DAILY NEWSPAPER

Finansavisen 168499
Editorial: Hoffsveien 70 A, Oslo 214
Tel: 47 23 29 63 00
Email: vaktsjef@finansavisen.no **Web site:** http://finansavisen.no/
Freq: Daily; **Circ:** 21853
Profile: Finansavisen is a daily newspaper covering business and finance in Norway.
Language (s): Norwegian
Ad Rate: Full Page Mono 60118.00
Currency: Norway Kroner
DAILY NEWSPAPER

Klar Tale 157866
Owner: Stiftelsen Klar Tale
Editorial: Pb 1180 Sentrum, Oslo 107
Tel: 47 22 31 02 60
Email: tips@klartale.no **Web site:** http://www.klartale.no
Freq: Weekly; **Circ:** 11920 MBL (Mediebedriftenes Landsforening)
Redaksjonsjef: Gøril Huse; **Redaktør:** Kristin Steien Bratlie
Profile: Klar Tale is the only easy-read newspaper in Norway. Larger fonts and simple language makes paper easier to read than other newspapers. Clear Voice comes out weekly as print, as sound newspaper on CD and podcast, and as Braille edition.
Language (s): Norwegian
DAILY NEWSPAPER

Klassekampen 187201
Editorial: Gronland 4, Oslo 188 **Tel:** 47 21 09 30 00
Email: innenriks@klassekampen.no **Web site:** http://www.klassekampen.no
Freq: Daily; **Circ:** 19025 MBL (Mediebedriftenes Landsforening)
Editor: Bjørgulv Braanen; **Editor:** Velaug Hobbelstad; **News Editor:** Kjell-Erik Kallset
Profile: Klassekampen is a left-wing political daily newspaper in Norway.
Language (s): Norwegian
Ad Rate: Full Page Mono 47500.00
Currency: Norway Kroner
DAILY NEWSPAPER

Morgenbladet 187181
Editorial: Christian Krohgs gate 16, Oslo 186
Tel: 47 21 00 63 00
Email: redaksjon@morgenbladet.no **Web site:** http://www.morgenbladet.no
Freq: Weekly; **Circ:** 29104
Editor & Managing Director: Anna Jenssen
Profile: Morgenbladet is an independent weekly newspaper in Norway focusing on politics, culture and research.
Language (s): Norwegian
Ad Rate: Full Page Mono 45510.00
Currency: Norway Kroner
DAILY NEWSPAPER

Nationen 158307
Editorial: Schweigaardsgate 34 E, Oslo 191
Tel: 47 94 00 86 50
Email: tips@nationen.no **Web site:** http://www.nationen.no
Freq: Daily
Nyhetsredaktør: Rino Andersen
Profile: Nationen is a newspaper covering national news, politics and finance. Nationen has a particular focus on areas such as districs, politics, agriculture, transport and EU.
Language (s): Norwegian
DAILY NEWSPAPER

Stavanger Aftenblad 158351
Editorial: Mediehuset Stavanger Aftenblad, Nykirkebakken 2, Stavanger 4001 **Tel:** 47 51 93 89 00
Email: nyhet@aftenbladet.no **Web site:** http://www.aftenbladet.no
Freq: Daily; **Circ:** 50001 Not Audited
Redaktør: Tarald Aano; **Nyhetsredaktør:** Carl Gunnar Gundersen; **Sjefredaktør:** Lars Helle
Profile: Stavanger Aftenblad is a Norwegian daily newspaper covering regional news in Sør-Rogaland.
Language (s): Norwegian
DAILY NEWSPAPER

Vårt Land 158309
Editorial: Grubbegata 6, Oslo 107
Tel: 47 22 31 03 10
Email: tips@vl.no **Web site:** http://www.vl.no
Freq: Daily; **Circ:** 20678 MBL (Mediebedriftenes Landsforening)
Profile: "Vårt Land" is a national newspaper covering news, features, sports and finance from a Christian viewpoint.
Language (s): Norwegian
DAILY NEWSPAPER

VG 158308
Editorial: Akersgata 55, Oslo 180 **Tel:** 47 22 00 00 00
Email: pressemeldinger@vg.no **Web site:** http://www.vg.no
Freq: Daily; **Circ:** 138188 MBL (Mediebedriftenes Landsforening)
News Editor: Andreas Nielsen; **Redaksjonsjef:** Audun Solberg; **Redaktør:** Helje Solberg; **Redaktionschef:** Rolf Sønstelie; **News Editor:** Leif Welhaven
Profile: VG (Verdens Gang) is a daily newspaper in Norway. Covering national and international news, events, sports, entertainment, politics and culture. Read by a broad range of the population.
Language (s): Norwegian
Ad Rate: Full Page Mono 199804.00
Currency: Norway Kroner
DAILY NEWSPAPER

News Service/Syndicate

ANB - Avisenes Nyhetsbyrå 313568
Editorial: Storgata 33A (9. etasje), Oslo 184
Tel: 47 22 99 84 40
Email: pm@anb.no **Web site:** http://www.anb.no
Profile: ANB - Avisenes Nyhetsbyrå is a News Agency in Norway.
Language (s): Norwegian
NEWS SERVICE/SYNDICATE

Kristelig Pressekontor - KPK 489433
Editorial: Storgt. 10B, Oslo 155 **Tel:** 47 48 17 42 39
Email: kpk@kpk.no **Web site:** http://www.kpk.no
Profile: Kristelig Pressekontor/ Christian Press Office is a Christian news agency in Norway.
Language (s): Norwegian
NEWS SERVICE/SYNDICATE

Newswire 362360
Editorial: Nedre Vollgate 1, Oslo 104
Tel: 47 24 15 50 60
Email: newswire@newswire.no **Web site:** http://www.newswire.no
Dagligleder: Christopher Hoelfeldt-Lund
Profile: Newswire is a mission funded news agency. Delivering news articles and news videos to Norwegian media. The cases created, edited and distributed by editorial Newswires. Issues are newsworthy in areas that are of interest to the Newswire clients.
Language (s): Norwegian
NEWS SERVICE/SYNDICATE

NPK - Nynorsk Pressekontor 313571
Editorial: Langkaia 1, Oslo 130 **Tel:** 47 22 03 46 48
Email: npk@npk.no **Web site:** http://www.npk.no
Ansvarlig redaktør: Karoline Riise Kristiansen
Profile: Nynorsk Pressekontor (NPK) is a Norwegian news agency.
Language (s): Norwegian
NEWS SERVICE/SYNDICATE

NTB Norsk Telegrambyrå 313564
Editorial: Langkaia (Havnelageret), Oslo 150
Tel: 47 22 03 45 45
Email: vaktsjef@ntb.no **Web site:** http://www.ntb.no
Nyhetsredaktør: Ole Kristian Bjellaanes
Profile: NTB is Norway's largest provider of content in the form of text, images, video and graphics to Norwegian media.
Language (s): Norwegian
NEWS SERVICE/SYNDICATE

NTB Norsk Telegrambyrå - Culture 449855
Editorial: Langkaia (Havnelageret), Oslo 150
Tel: 47 22 03 44 22
Email: kultur@ntb.no **Web site:** http://www.ntb.no
Profile: The culture section at NTB Norsk Telegrambyrå .
Language (s): Norwegian
NEWS SERVICE/SYNDICATE

NTB Norsk Telegrambyrå - Foreign News 449854
Editorial: Langkaia (Havnelageret), Oslo 130
Tel: 47 22 03 45 50
Email: utenriks@ntb.no **Web site:** http://www.ntb.no
Profile: The foreign news section at Norsk Telegrambyrå.
Language (s): Norwegian
NEWS SERVICE/SYNDICATE

NTB Norsk Telegrambyrå - Sports 449853
Editorial: Langkaia (Havnelageret), Oslo OSLO
Tel: 47 22 03 45 55
Email: sporten@ntb.no **Web site:** http://www.ntb.no
Profile: The sports section at NTB Norsk Telegrambyrå.
Language (s): Norwegian
NEWS SERVICE/SYNDICATE

TDN Finans 313586
Editorial: Christian Krohgs gate 16, Oslo 107
Tel: 47 22 00 10 00
Email: einar.melberg@tdn.no **Web site:** http://www.nhst.no/business-areas/dn/tdn-nyhetsbyra
Profile: TDN Finans is a real-time supplier of news about and for the Norwegian share and interest-rate markets, providing Norwegian brokers, management companies, listed companies, private individuals and the media with price-driving, leading news.
Language (s): Norwegian
NEWS SERVICE/SYNDICATE

Community Newspaper

Agder 225180
Editorial: Strandgten 34, Flekkefjord 4400
Tel: 47 38 32 03 00
Email: administrasjon@avisenagder.no **Web site:** http://www.avisenagder.no
Freq: 3 Times/Week
Redaktør: Kristen Munksgaard; **Redaksjonssjef:** Erik Thime
Profile: Agder is a local newspaper covering Flekkefjord, Kvinesdal, Sirdal, Lund and Sokndal.
Language (s): Norwegian
COMMUNITY NEWSPAPER

Altaposten 158311
Owner: Nordavis AS
Editorial: Labyrinten 5, Alta 9510 **Tel:** 47 78 45 67 00
Email: redaksjonen@altaposten.no **Web site:** http://www.altaposten.no
Circ: 3935
Profile: Altaposten is a daily newspaper published in Alta in Finnmark. Altaposten was established in 1969 and operates in addition to the print edition with local radio (Radio Alta) and television (TV Nord).
Language (s): Norwegian
COMMUNITY NEWSPAPER

Åmliavisa 579186
Owner: Åmliavisa AS
Editorial: Postboks 41, Åmli 4864 **Tel:** 47 37 08 10 60
Email: post@amliavisa.no **Web site:** http://www.amliavisa.no
Circ: 1264
Profile: Åmliavisa is a local newspaper covering Åmli municipality in Aust-Agder.
Language (s): Norwegian
COMMUNITY NEWSPAPER

Åndalsnes Avis 225223
Owner: Nye Åndalsnes Avis AS
Editorial: Romsdalsvegen 2, Åndalsnes 6300
Tel: 47 71 22 22 22
Email: redaksjon@andalsnes-avis.no **Web site:** http://www.andalsnes-avis.no
Freq: 3 Times/Week; **Circ:** 3444 Not Audited
Profile: Åndalsnes Avis is a local newspaper for Rauma municipality.
Language (s): Norwegian
COMMUNITY NEWSPAPER

Andøyposten 225182
Owner: Andøyposten AS
Editorial: Pb. 143, Andenes 8483 **Tel:** 47 76 11 58 70
Email: redaksjonen@andoyposten.no **Web site:** http://www.andoyposten.no
Freq: 2 Times/Week; **Circ:** 1657
Profile: Andøyposten is Andøyas local newspaper, supplying regional and local news.
Language (s): Norwegian
COMMUNITY NEWSPAPER

Arbeidets Rett 225192
Owner: Arbeidets Rett AS
Editorial: Kjerkgata 2, Røros 7374
Tel: 47 72 40 64 00
Email: redaksjonen@retten.no **Web site:** http://www.retten.no
Freq: 2 Times/Week; **Circ:** 6857 Not Audited
Profile: Arbeidets Rett is a newspaper that comes out on Røros i Sør-Trøndelag.
Language (s): Norwegian
COMMUNITY NEWSPAPER

Arendals Tidende 489439
Owner: Arendals Tidende AS
Editorial: Havnegaten 4b, Arendal 4841 **Tel:** +47 40 69 22 22
Email: post@arendalstidende.no **Web site:** http://www.arendalstidende.no/
Circ: 1623
Profile: Arendals Tidende is a local newspaper in Arendal which comes out twice a week, Monday and Friday. Mondays as a newspaper as usual, while every Friday it comes out as a magazine.
Language (s): Norwegian
COMMUNITY NEWSPAPER

Åsane Tidende 158051
Owner: Åsane Tidende AS
Editorial: Kong Christian Frederiks plass 3, Bergen 5006 **Tel:** 47 55 18 50 00
Email: red@aasanetidende.no **Web site:** http://www.aasanetidende.no
Freq: 2 Times/Week; **Circ:** 1797
Profile: Åsane Tidende is a local newspaper for Åsane in the Bergen municipality.
Language (s): Norwegian
COMMUNITY NEWSPAPER

Askøyværingen 225183
Owner: Askøyværingen AS
Editorial: Pb. 4, Kleppestø 5321 **Tel:** 47 56 15 28 00
Email: redaksjonen@av-avis.no **Web site:** http://www.askoyv.no
Freq: 2 Times/Week; **Circ:** 4310 MBL (Mediebedriftenes Landsforening)
Profile: Askøyværingen is a local newspaper in Bergen.
Language (s): Norwegian
COMMUNITY NEWSPAPER

Aura Avis 225184
Owner: Mediehus Nordmøre AS
Editorial: Pb. 43, Sunndalsøra 6601
Tel: 47 71 58 98 00
Email: redaksjonen@auraavis.no **Web site:** http://www.auraavis.no
Freq: 3 Times/Week; **Circ:** 2718 Not Audited
Profile: Aura Avis is a newspaper published in Sunndalsøra Nordmøre. It comes out three days a week and covers the municipalities Sunndal and Tingvoll.
Language (s): Norwegian
Ad Rate: Full Page Colour 31518.00
Currency: Norway Kroner
COMMUNITY NEWSPAPER

Aust Agder Blad 225185
Owner: Aust Agder Blad AS
Editorial: Pb. 40, Risør 4951 **Tel:** 47 37 14 91 00
Email: redaksjonen@austagderblad.no **Web site:** http://www.austagderblad.no
Freq: 3 Times/Week; **Circ:** 3213 MBL (Mediebedriftenes Landsforening)
Profile: Aust Agder Blad is a newspaper published in Risør in Aust-Agder. It comes out three days a week; Tuesday, Thursday and Saturday and covers municipalities Risør (and Søndeled) and Gjerstad.
Language (s): Norwegian
COMMUNITY NEWSPAPER

Avisa Nordland 157850
Editorial: Dronningens gt 18, Bodø 8002
Tel: 47 75 50 00 00
Email: redaksjonen@an.no **Web site:** http://www.an.no
Circ: 23716
Sjefredaktør: Jan-Eirik Hanssen; **Redaktør:** Børje Klæboe Eidissen; **Redaktør:** Vibeke Madsen
Profile: Avisa Nordland is a regional newspaper covering Salten in Nordland.
Language (s): Norwegian
Ad Rate: Full Page Colour 30675.00
Currency: Norway Kroner
COMMUNITY NEWSPAPER

Ávvir 225188
Owner: Sami Aviisa AS
Editorial: Suomageaidnu 14, Karasjok 9730
Tel: 47 934 40 700
Email: redaksjonen@avvir.no **Web site:** http://www.avvir.no
Freq: 2 Times/Week; **Circ:** 1024 MBL (Mediebedriftenes Landsforening)
Redaksjonsjef: Josef Isak Utsi
Profile: Ávvir is a Sami newspaper that was first published in 2007. The newspaper is the result of a merger of the former Sami newspapers My Ágí (Karasjok) and Áššu (Kautokeino)
Language (s): Norwegian
COMMUNITY NEWSPAPER

Bæringen 362898
Editorial: Bærum kommune, Kommunikasjonsenheten, Sandvika 1304
Tel: 47 67 50 38 11
Email: baeringen@baerum.kommune.no **Web site:** https://www.baerum.kommune.no/om-barum-kommune/baringen/
Freq: Bi-Monthly
Profile: Bæringen is Bærum municipality's information newspaper.
Language (s): Norwegian
COMMUNITY NEWSPAPER

Bergensavisen 158314
Owner: Bergensavisen AS
Editorial: Chr. Michelsens gate 4, Bergen 5807
Tel: 47 55 23 50 00
Email: nyhet@ba.no **Web site:** http://www.ba.no
Freq: Daily; **Circ:** 14671
Profile: Bergensavisen is the second largest newspaper in Bergen, Norway.
Language (s): Norwegian
COMMUNITY NEWSPAPER

Bladet Vesterålen 157863
Owner: Bladet Vesterålen AS
Editorial: Pb. 33, Sortland 8401 **Tel:** 47 76 11 09 00
Email: red@blv.no **Web site:** http://www.blv.no
Freq: Daily; **Circ:** 8698
Profile: Bladet Vesterålen is a regional newspaper published in Sortland Nordland. The newspaper covers the municipalities in Vesterålen (Sortland, Hadsel, Bo, Øksnes and Andoya) and Lødingen and Kvæfjord.
Language (s): Norwegian
COMMUNITY NEWSPAPER

Bø blad 223110
Owner: Bø Blad AS
Editorial: Pb. 104, Bø I Telemark 3833
Tel: 47 35 95 19 45
Email: redaksjon@boblad.no **Web site:** http://www.boblad.no
Freq: Weekly; **Circ:** 2622 Not Audited
Profile: Bø Blad is a local newspaper that is published in Bo I Telemark.
Language (s): Norwegian
COMMUNITY NEWSPAPER

Bømlo-nytt 225166
Owner: A/S Bømlo-nytt
Editorial: Bankbrekko 14, Bremnes 5430
Tel: 47 53 42 53 33
Email: redaksjon@bomlo-nytt.no **Web site:** http://www.bomlo-nytt.no
Freq: 2 Times/Week; **Circ:** 3188 MBL (Mediebedriftenes Landsforening)
Profile: Bømlo-nytt is a local newspaper that is published in Bømlo in Hordaland.
Language (s): Norwegian
COMMUNITY NEWSPAPER

Brønnøysunds Avis 225186
Owner: Brønnøysunds Avis AS
Editorial: Pb. 38, Brønnøysund 8901
Tel: 47 75 01 84 00
Email: desk@ba-avis.no **Web site:** http://www.banett.no
Freq: 3 Times/Week; **Circ:** 3597 MBL (Mediebedriftenes Landsforening)
Nyhetsredaktør: Bård Pedersen
Profile: Brønnøysunds Avis is a local newspaper published in Brønnøysund in Nordland.
Language (s): Norwegian
Ad Rate: Full Page Colour 20632.00
Currency: Norway Kroner
COMMUNITY NEWSPAPER

Budstikka 158316
Editorial: Billingstadsletta 17, Billingstad 1396
Tel: 47 66 77 00 00
Email: post@budstikka.com **Web site:** http://www.budstikka.no
Editor: Nils Harnes; **Nettredaktør:** Dag Otter Johansen
Profile: Budstikka is a local newspaper covering Asker and Bærum.
Language (s): Norwegian
COMMUNITY NEWSPAPER

Byavisa Tønsberg 527214
Owner: Lundquist Media AS
Editorial: Torvgaten 1, Tønsberg 3110
Tel: 47 33 30 88 60
Email: red@byavisatonsberg.no **Web site:** http://www.byavisatonsberg.no
Freq: Weekly; **Circ:** 28000
Profile: Byavisa Tønsberg is a free weekly local newspaper in the municipalities Tønsberg and Nøtterøy. The papers gets distributed every wednesday.
Language (s): Norwegian
COMMUNITY NEWSPAPER

Bygdanytt 157838
Editorial: oyrane Torg, adnavegen 63, Indre Arna 5260 **Tel:** 47 55 53 57 70
Email: bn@bygdanytt.no **Web site:** http://www.bygdanytt.no
Circ: 15000
Redaktør: Nils-Ove Støbakk
Profile: Bygdanytt is a local newspaper covering Arna (community in Bergen) and Osterøy.
Language (s): Norwegian
COMMUNITY NEWSPAPER

Bygdebladet 157961
Owner: Bygdebladet AS
Editorial: Pb. 120, Ørskog 6249 **Tel:** 47 70 27 08 00
Email: post@bygdebladet.com **Web site:** http://www.bygdebladet.com
Freq: 3 Times/Week; **Circ:** 2439
Profile: Local newspaper for Vestnes, Ørskog, Skodje, Haram and Skodje municipalities in Møre og Romsdal.
Language (s): Norwegian
COMMUNITY NEWSPAPER

Bygdebladet Randaberg og Rennesøy 157962
Owner: Randaberg og Rennesøy Bygdeblad AS
Editorial: Pb. 94, Randaberg 4096
Tel: 47 51 41 46 66
Email: tips@bygdebladet.no **Web site:** http://www.bygdebladet.no
Freq: Weekly; **Circ:** 3453
Dagligleder: Marianne A. L. Randeberg; **Ansvarlig redaktør:** Kirsti K. Sømme
Profile: Bygdebladet Randaberg og Rennesøy is a local newspaper published in Randaberg Rogaland. The newspaper is published once a week for municipalities Randaberg, Rennesøy and Kvitsøy.
Language (s): Norwegian
COMMUNITY NEWSPAPER

Bygdeposten 705108
Owner: Bygdeposten AS
Editorial: Pb. 53, Vikersund 3371 **Tel:** 47 85 23 32 78
Email: redaksjon@bygdeposten.no **Web site:** http://www.bygdeposten.no
Circ: 5955
Ansvarlig redaktør: Knut Bråthen
Profile: Bygdeposten is a local newspaper that is published in Modum in Buskerud. It covers the municipalities Modum, Sigdal, and Krødsherad Øvre Eiker.
Language (s): Norwegian
COMMUNITY NEWSPAPER

Dagen 158315
Owner: Dagbladet Dagen AS
Editorial: Fjosangerveien 45, Bergen 5054
Tel: 47 47 77 37 78
Email: redaksjonen@dagen.no **Web site:** http://www.dagen.no
Freq: Daily; **Circ:** 9742
Redaktør: Kari Fure; **Redaktør:** Tarjei Gilje; **Nettredaktør:** Svend Ole Kvilesjø; **Sjefredaktør:** Vebjørn Selbekk
Profile: Dagen is a conservative Protestant Norwegian newspaper established in 1919. Between 2008-2011 the paper was named DagenMagazinet due to a merge.
Language (s): Norwegian
COMMUNITY NEWSPAPER

Dalane Tidende 158321
Owner: Dalane Tidende og Egersunds Avis AS
Editorial: Lindoyveien 2, Egersund 4373
Tel: 47 51 46 11 00
Email: redaksjon@dalane-tidende.no **Web site:** http://www.dalane-tidende.no
Freq: 3 Times/Week; **Circ:** 7853
Profile: Dalane Tidende is a local newspaper for Dalane region published in Egersund.
Language (s): Norwegian
COMMUNITY NEWSPAPER

Demokraten 225206
Owner: Demokraten AS
Editorial: Pb. 83, Fredrikstad 1601
Tel: 47 69 36 80 00
Email: demokraten@demokraten.no **Web site:** http://www.demokraten.no
Freq: 2 Times/Week; **Circ:** 5460 MBL (Mediebedriftenes Landsforening)
Profile: Demokraten is a local newspaper published in Fredrikstad in Østfold.
Language (s): Norwegian
COMMUNITY NEWSPAPER

Dølen 223126
Owner: Dølen AS
Editorial: Næringsvegen 4, Vinstra 2640
Tel: 47 61 29 24 80
Email: post@dolen.no **Web site:** http://www.dolen.no
Freq: Weekly; **Circ:** 3830 Not Audited
Profile: Dølen is a politically independent local newspaper that comes out on Vinstra. The newspaper covers the Middle Gudbrandsdalen Ringebu municipalities, South Fron and Nord-Fron.
Language (s): Norwegian
COMMUNITY NEWSPAPER

Drammens Tidende 157841
Editorial: Stromso Torg 9, Drammen 3044
Tel: 47 32 20 40 00
Email: tips@dt.no **Web site:** http://www.dt.no
Circ: 23579
Nyhetsredaktør: Alf Petter Øverli
Profile: Drammens Tidende is a Norwegian daily newspaper published in Drammen.
Language (s): Norwegian
Ad Rate: Full Page Mono 52250.00
Currency: Norway Kroner
COMMUNITY NEWSPAPER

Drangedalsposten 225340
Owner: Drangedalsposten AS
Editorial: Strandgt. 11, Drangedal 3750
Tel: 47 35 99 69 90
Email: post@drangedalsposten.no **Web site:** http://www.drangedalsposten.no
Freq: Weekly; **Circ:** 1952 Not Audited
Profile: Drangedalsposten is a local newspaper published in Drangedal Telemark.
Language (s): Norwegian
Ad Rate: Full Page Colour 37822.00
Currency: Norway Kroner
COMMUNITY NEWSPAPER

Driva 157842
Owner: Driva-Trykk AS
Editorial: Pb. 143, Sunndalsøra 6601
Tel: 47 71 68 97 40
Email: redaksjon@driva.no **Web site:** http://www.driva.no
Circ: 3495
Profile: Driva is a local newspaper published in Sunndalsøra. Covering Surnadal, Sunndal, Rindal, Halsa, Tingvoll og Nesset
Language (s): Norwegian
Ad Rate: Full Page Colour 16991.00
Currency: Norway Kroner
COMMUNITY NEWSPAPER

Eidsvoll Ullensaker Blad 225178
Owner: Eidsvoll Ullensaker Blad AS
Editorial: Pb. 130, Eidsvoll 2081 **Tel:** 47 63 92 27 00
Email: redaksjon@eub.no **Web site:** http://www.eub.no
Freq: Daily; **Circ:** 7032 MBL (Mediebedriftenes Landsforening)
Profile: Eidsvoll Ullensaker Blad (EUB) is a newspaper that comes out at Eidsvold in Akershus.
Language (s): Norwegian
COMMUNITY NEWSPAPER

Eikerbladet 225342
Owner: Eiker Bladet A/S
Editorial: Pb. 302, Mjøndalen 3051
Tel: 47 32 87 20 23
Email: redaksjonen@eikerbladet.no **Web site:** http://www.eikerbladet.no/
Freq: 2 Times/Week; **Circ:** 3179 MBL (Mediebedriftenes Landsforening)
Profile: Eikerbladet is a local newspaper that is published in Mjøndalen in Buskerud.
Language (s): Norwegian
COMMUNITY NEWSPAPER

Enebakk Avis 225343
Editorial: Lillestromveien 671, Enebakk 1912
Tel: 47 64 92 37 00
Email: post@enebakkavis.no **Web site:** http://www.enebakkavis.no
Freq: Weekly
Profile: Enebakk Avis is a newspaper covering local news.
Language (s): Norwegian
COMMUNITY NEWSPAPER

Fædrelandsvennen 158337
Editorial: Henrik Wergelands gate 16, Kristiansand 4612 **Tel:** 47 38 11 30 00
Email: nyheter@fvn.no **Web site:** http://www.fedrelandsvennen.no
Circ: 30499
Sjefsredaktør: Eivind Ljøstad; **Medieutvikler:** Sondre Zachariassen
Profile: Fædrelandsvennen is a Norwegian regional newspaper published in Kristiansand. The paper covers the southernmost part of the country (Aust-Agder and Vest-Agder), focusing especially on the area between Mandal and Lillesand (west and east of Kristiansand).
Language (s): Norwegian
Ad Rate: Full Page Mono 44603.00
Currency: Norway Kroner
COMMUNITY NEWSPAPER

Fanaposten 225179
Owner: Fanaposten AS
Editorial: Kong Christian Frederiks plass 3, Bergen 5006 **Tel:** 47 55 11 80 10
Email: post@fanaposten.no **Web site:** http://www.fanaposten.no
Freq: 2 Times/Week; **Circ:** 4148 Not Audited
Redaktør: Terje Bringsvor Nilsen; **Ansvarlig redaktør:** Ståle Melhus
Profile: Fanaposten are local newspaper for Fana and Ytrebygda in the southern part of the municipality of Bergen, the former municipality of Fana.
Language (s): Norwegian
COMMUNITY NEWSPAPER

Finnmark Dagblad 365564
Owner: Finnmark Dagblad AS
Editorial: Salsgt. 16, Hammerfest 9600
Tel: 47 78 42 86 00
Email: tips@ifinnmark.no **Web site:** http://www.ifinnmark.no/
Freq: Daily; **Circ:** 5269
Redaktør: Svein G. Jørstad; **Nyhetsredaktør:** Helle Østvik
Profile: Finnmark Dagblad is a daily newspaper covering ten municipalities of West Finnmark and published in Hammerfest in Finnmark.
Language (s): Norwegian
COMMUNITY NEWSPAPER

Finnmarken 158357
Owner: Dagbladet Finnmarken AS
Editorial: Pb. 616, Vadsø 9811 **Tel:** 47 78 95 55 00
Email: desk@finnmarken.no **Web site:** http://www.ifinnmark.no/
Freq: Daily; **Circ:** 5492
Profile: Finnmarken is a daily newspaper published in Vadsø in Finnmark, and is a regional newspaper for East Finnmark.
Language (s): Norwegian
COMMUNITY NEWSPAPER

Finnmarksposten 225187
Editorial: Pb. 44, Honningsvåg 9751
Tel: 47 78 47 19 60
Web site: http://www.finnmarksposten.no/
Freq: Weekly; **Circ:** 1238 MBL (Mediebedriftenes Landsforening)
Profile: Finnmarksposten is a local newspaper published once a week in Finnmark, Honningsvåg.
Language (s): Norwegian
COMMUNITY NEWSPAPER

Firda 158325
Editorial: Firda Media AS, Firdavegen 12, Førde 6801
Tel: 47 57 83 33 00
Email: redaksjon@firda.no **Web site:** http://www.firda.no
Freq: Daily; **Circ:** 35000
Sjefredaktør: Yngve Årdal; **Nyhetssjef:** Trond Jan Grimeland
Profile: Firda is a daily newspaper covering Førde, Sogn and Fjordane.
Language (s): Norwegian
COMMUNITY NEWSPAPER

Firda Tidend 157843
Owner: Avisdrift Gloppen A/S
Editorial: Pb. 38, Sandane 6821 **Tel:** 47 57 86 87 90
Email: redaksjon@firdatidend.no **Web site:** http://www.firdatidend.no
Freq: 3 Times/Week; **Circ:** 2977
Ansvarlig Redaktør: Bjørn Grov
Profile: Firda Tidend is a local newspaper covering Gloppen and Jølster.
Language (s): Norwegian
COMMUNITY NEWSPAPER

Firdaposten 157844
Editorial: Markegata 65, Florø 6900
Tel: 47 57 75 73 00
Web site: http://www.firdaposten.no
Freq: Daily
Nyhetsredaktør: Arve Solbakken
Profile: Do not want to receive any press releases. Firdaposten is a localnewspaper covering Flora and Bremanger (in Sogn og Fjordane).
Language (s): Norwegian
COMMUNITY NEWSPAPER

Fjell-Ljom 223127
Owner: Avisdrift AS
Editorial: Peder Hiorts gate 7, Røros 7374
Tel: 47 72 40 65 90
Email: redaksjon@fjell-ljom.no **Web site:** http://www.fjell-ljom.no
Freq: Weekly; **Circ:** 2272 LLA (Landslaget for Lokalaviser)
Profile: Fjell-Ljom is a Norwegian weekly newspaper that comes out every week in Røros in Sør-Trøndelag
Language (s): Norwegian
Ad Rate: Full Page Colour 29417.00
Currency: Norway Kroner
COMMUNITY NEWSPAPER

Fjordabladet 225175
Owner: Fjordabladet AS
Editorial: Radhusvegen 6, Nordfjordeid 6770
Tel: 47 57 88 53 10
Email: redaksjonen@fjordabladet.no **Web site:** http://www.fjordabladet.no
Freq: 2 Times/Week; **Circ:** 2579 MBL (Mediebedriftenes Landsforening)
Profile: Fjordabladet is the local newspaper for Nordfjord, located at Nordfjordeid in Eid Municipality.
Language (s): Norwegian
COMMUNITY NEWSPAPER

Fjordenes Tidende 225176
Owner: Fjordenes Tidende AS
Editorial: Pb. 55, Måløy 6701 **Tel:** 47 57 84 90 00
Email: fjt@fjt.no **Web site:** http://www.fjt.no
Freq: 2 Times/Week; **Circ:** 4648 MBL (Mediebedriftenes Landsforening)
Profile: Local newspaper covering the municipalities Vågsøy, Selje, Bremanger, Eid and Vanylve.
Language (s): Norwegian
COMMUNITY NEWSPAPER

Fjordingen 225177
Owner: Fjordingen AS
Editorial: Pb. 248, Stryn 6781 **Tel:** 47 57 87 45 00
Email: redaksjon@fjordingen.no **Web site:** http://www.fjordingen.no
Freq: 2 Times/Week; **Circ:** 3863 MBL (Mediebedriftenes Landsforening)
Ansvarlig redaktør: Bengt Flaten
Profile: Local newspaper for Inner Nordfjord with municipalities Stryn and Hornindal primary area.
Language (s): Norwegian
COMMUNITY NEWSPAPER

Fjuken 223128
Owner: Skjåk Mediautvikling AS
Editorial: Bisvoll, Skjåk 2690 **Tel:** 47 61 21 38 60
Email: redaksjon@fjuken.no **Web site:** http://www.fjuken.no
Freq: Weekly
Ansvarlig redaktør: Asta Brimi
Profile: Local newspaper for Ottadalen.
Language (s): Norwegian
COMMUNITY NEWSPAPER

Fosna-Folket 158319
Owner: Fosna-Folket AS
Editorial: Pb. 205, Brekstad 7129 **Tel:** 47 72 51 57 00
Email: redaksjonen@fosna-folket.no **Web site:** http://www.fosna-folket.no
Circ: 6358
Profile: Fosna-people are local newspapers for seven municipalities in Fosenhalvøya Trondelag: Orland, Bjugn, Rissa, Leksvik, Åfjord, Roan and Osen.
Language (s): Norwegian
COMMUNITY NEWSPAPER

Framtid i nord 225201
Owner: Mediaselskapet Nord-Norge Samkjøringen AS
Editorial: Pb 331, Storslett 9156 **Tel:** 47 77 76 69 00
Email: nyhet@framtidinord.no **Web site:** http://www.framtidinord.no
Freq: 3 Times/Week; **Circ:** 3632 Not Audited
Profile: Local newspaper for Northern Troms. Nordreisa, Lyngen, Skjervøy, Kåfjord, Storfjord and Kvænangen.
Language (s): Norwegian
COMMUNITY NEWSPAPER

Fredriksstad Blad 158326
Editorial: Stortorvet 3, Fredrikstad 1601
Tel: 47 46 80 77 77
Email: tips@f-b.no **Web site:** http://www.f-b.no
Freq: Daily
Redaksjonsjef: Geir Ola Eggen; **Nettredaktør:** Espen Normann
Profile: Fredriksstad Blad is a local newspaper.
Language (s): Norwegian
COMMUNITY NEWSPAPER

Fremover 158346
Owner: Fremover AS
Editorial: Pb. 324, Narvik 8504 **Tel:** 47 76 95 00 00
Email: redaksjon@fremover.no **Web site:** http://www.fremover.no
Freq: Daily; **Circ:** 7083
Nyhetssjef: Anders Horne
Profile: Fremover is a local newspaper published in Narvik in Nordland. The newspaper covers news from municipalities Tysfjord, Ballarat, Narvik Evenes, Tjeldsund, Skånland, Bardu, Gratangen, Lavangen and Salangen.
Language (s): Norwegian
COMMUNITY NEWSPAPER

Friheten 157845
Editorial: Norges Kommunistiske Parti, Helgesensgate 21, Oslo 553 **Tel:** 47 920 20 793
Web site: http://www.friheten.no
Redaktør: Harald Øystein Reppesgaard
Profile: Do not want to receive any press releases. Friheten is a Marxist, national newspaper covering politics, economy and culture all over the world.Published two times a month.
Language (s): Norwegian
COMMUNITY NEWSPAPER

Frolendingen 489111
Owner: Ca. 100 lokale bedrifter og privar personer
Editorial: Frolandssenteret 4A, Froland 4820
Tel: 47 37 23 65 00
Email: post@frolendingen.no **Web site:** http://www.frolendingen.no
Freq: Weekly; **Circ:** 1405 Not Audited
Profile: Frolendingen is an independent local newspaper for residents of Froland Municipality.
Language (s): Norwegian
Ad Rate: Full Page Mono 8200.00
Currency: Norway Kroner
COMMUNITY NEWSPAPER

Frostingen 327479
Owner: Frostingen AS
Editorial: Banken, Frosta 7633 **Tel:** 47 74 80 88 35
Email: frostingen@frostingen.no **Web site:** http://frostingen.no
Freq: Weekly; **Circ:** 1679 Not Audited
Profile: Frostingen is a local online and print newspaper in published in Frosta, Norway. It covers the municipality of Frosta and the area of Åsen in Levanger.
Language (s): Norwegian
COMMUNITY NEWSPAPER

Gaula 355708
Editorial: Radhusvegen 3, Melhus 7224
Tel: 47 72 87 24 11
Email: snoefugl@online.no **Web site:** http://www.melhusporten.no
Forlagssjef: Åsmund Snøfugl
Profile: Gaula is a local newspaper covering Melhus, Midtre-Gauldal and Byneset in Trondheim.
Language (s): Norwegian
Ad Rate: Full Page Colour 11400.00
Currency: Norway Kroner
COMMUNITY NEWSPAPER

Gauldalsposten 527020
Owner: Gauldalsposten AS
Editorial: UNAVAILABLE, Støren 7290
Tel: 47 928 08 222
Email: redaksjon@gposten.no **Web site:** http://www.gposten.no
Circ: 1730
Profile: Gauldalsposten is a newspaper that is published in Midtre Gauldal municipality in Rogaland.
Language (s): Norwegian
COMMUNITY NEWSPAPER

Gausdøl'n - Lokalavis for Gausdal 415428
Owner: Gausdal Informasjon
Editorial: UNAVAILABLE, Vestre Gausdal 2653
Tel: 47 61 22 34 23
Email: firmapost@gausdolen.no **Web site:** http://www.gausdolen.no
Freq: Monthly
Redaktør: Olav Iverslien
Profile: Gausdøl'n is a local newspaper in Gausdal. They cover political life in the village and present companies and businesses in Gausdal. Covering the agricultural industry and tourismthat are the two major industrial branches in Gausdal.
Language (s): Norwegian
COMMUNITY NEWSPAPER

Gjengangeren 158333
Owner: Edda Vestfold AS
Editorial: Pb. 85, Horten 3191 **Tel:** 47 33 02 00 00
Email: redaksjonen@gjengangeren.no **Web site:** http://www.gjengangeren.no
Freq: Daily; **Circ:** 6278
Markedssjef: Else-Lill Andresen; **Nyhetssredaktør:** Audun Bårdseth
Profile: Local newspaper covering Horten.
Language (s): Norwegian
COMMUNITY NEWSPAPER

Gjesdalbuen 225353
Owner: Gjesdalbuen AS
Editorial: Pb. 13, Ålgård 4330 **Tel:** 47 51 61 28 51
Email: redaksjonen@gjesdalbuen.no **Web site:** http://gbnett.no/
Freq: Weekly; **Circ:** 3294 MBL (Mediebedriftenes Landsforening)
Profile: Gjesdalbuen is a political independent local newspaper for Gjesdal and Figgjo.
Language (s): Norwegian
COMMUNITY NEWSPAPER

Gjøviks Blad 527236
Editorial: Ringvegen 3, Gjøvik 2804
Tel: 47 61 13 03 00
Email: post@gjoviks-blad.no **Web site:** http://www.gjoviks-blad.no
Profile: Gjøviks Blad is a local newspaper covering Gjøvik since 2002.
Language (s): Norwegian
COMMUNITY NEWSPAPER

Glåmdalen 366312
Editorial: Markensvegen 1 B, Kongsvinger 2204
Tel: 47 62 88 25 00
Email: redaksjon@glomdalen.no **Web site:** http://www.glomdalen.no
Dagvaktsjef: Per Håkon Pettersen
Profile: Glåmdalen is a local newspaper covering Kongsvinger, Sør-Odal, Nord-Odal, Eidskog, Grue, Åsnes, Våler and Nes in Akershus.
Language (s): Norwegian
COMMUNITY NEWSPAPER

Grannar 225226
Owner: Grannar AS
Editorial: Etne Senter, Etne 5590 **Tel:** 47 53 77 11 00
Email: redaksjon@grannar.no **Web site:** http://www.grannar.no
Freq: 2 Times/Week; **Circ:** 3575 Not Audited
Profile: Local newspaper covering Etne and Vindafjord.
Language (s): Norwegian
COMMUNITY NEWSPAPER

Grenda 225164
Owner: Grenda AS
Editorial: Skalagato 36, Rosendal 5470
Tel: 47 53 47 71 00
Email: post@grenda.no **Web site:** http://www.grenda.no
Freq: 2 Times/Week; **Circ:** 2277 LLA (Landslaget for Lokalaviser)
Profile: Local newspaper covering Kvinnherad
Language (s): Norwegian
COMMUNITY NEWSPAPER

Grimstad Adressetidende 225165
Owner: Grimstad Adressetidende AS
Editorial: Storgaten 39, Grimstad 4891
Tel: 47 37 25 80 00
Email: red@gat.no **Web site:** http://www.gat.no
Freq: 3 Times/Week; **Circ:** 6013 MBL (Mediebedriftenes Landsforening)
Profile: Local newspaper covering Grimstad.
Language (s): Norwegian
COMMUNITY NEWSPAPER

Gudbrandsdølen Dagningen 158339
Editorial: Jernbanegata 13, Lillehammer 2609
Tel: 47 61 22 10 00
Email: redaksjonen@gd.no **Web site:** http://www.gd.no
Freq: Daily
Redaksjonssekretær: Kjell Haugerud; **Redaksjonssekretær:** Jostein Hernæs; **Nettansvarlig:** Arnfinn Skinlo; **Ansvarlig redaktør:** Kristian Skullerud; **Nyhetsredaktør:** Anne Stokke; **Redaktør:** Kari Utgaard
Profile: Gudbrandsdølen Dagningen is a regional newspaper covering Lillehammer, Gudbrandsdalen and Ringsaker.
Language (s): Norwegian
COMMUNITY NEWSPAPER

Hadeland 158318
Owner: Hadeland AS
Editorial: Pb. 227, Gran 2711 **Tel:** 47 61 31 31 31
Email: desken@hadeland.net **Web site:** http://www.hadeland.net
Freq: Daily; **Circ:** 6731

Profile: Online version of the local newspaper Hadeland.
Language (s): Norwegian
COMMUNITY NEWSPAPER

Halden Arbeiderblad 158328
Owner: Halden Arbeiderblad AS
Editorial: Storgata 2A, Halden 1751
Tel: 47 69 21 56 00
Web site: http://www.ha-halden.no
Freq: Daily; **Circ:** 6848
Profile: Halden Arbeiderblad is a daily newspaper that is published in Halden Østfold.
Language (s): Norwegian
COMMUNITY NEWSPAPER

Hallingdølen 157846
Owner: Hallingdølen AS
Editorial: Pb. 193, Ål 3571 **Tel:** 47 32 08 65 00
Email: redaksjonen@hallingdolen.no **Web site:** http://www.hallingdolen.no
Freq: 3 Times/Week; **Circ:** 9127
Profile: Hallingdølen is a newspaper published in Hallingdal in Buskerud. The editors are placed in Ål Municipality.
Language (s): Norwegian
COMMUNITY NEWSPAPER

Hamar Arbeiderblad 158329
Editorial: Gronnegata 64, Hamar 2317 **Tel:** 47 02 318
Email: red@h-a.no **Web site:** http://www.h-a.no
Sjefredaktør: Carsten Bleness; **Debattredaktør:** Anne Ekornholmen; **Hovedvaktsjef:** Marianne Thoresen
Profile: Hamar Arbeiderblad is a local newspaper covering Hamar, Ringsaker, Stange and Løten.
Language (s): Norwegian
COMMUNITY NEWSPAPER

Hamar Dagblad 158062
Editorial: Torggata 22, Hamar 2317
Tel: 47 62 54 31 40
Email: redaksjonen@hamar-dagblad.no **Web site:** http://www.hamar-dagblad.no
Freq: Daily
Profile: Hamar Dagblad is a free regional newspaper covering Hamar municipality, Stavsberg and Bekkelaget.
Language (s): Norwegian
COMMUNITY NEWSPAPER

Hardanger Folkeblad 225163
Owner: Hardanger Folkeblad AS
Editorial: Pb. 374, Odda 5750 **Tel:** 47 53 65 06 00
Email: redaksjon@hardanger-folkeblad.no **Web site:** http://www.hardanger-folkeblad.no
Freq: 3 Times/Week; **Circ:** 4422 MBL (Mediebedriftenes Landsforening)
Profile: Hardanger Folkeblad is a local newspaper that is published in Odda Hordaland.
Language (s): Norwegian
COMMUNITY NEWSPAPER

Harstad Tidende 158331
Editorial: Storgata 11, Harstad 9405
Tel: 47 77 01 80 00
Email: redaksjonen@ht.no **Web site:** http://www.ht.no
Redaktør: Odd Leif Andreassen; **Redaktør:** Kjell Magne Angelsen; **Sjefredaktør:** Kjell Rune Henriksen; **Redaktør:** Turid Ingebrigtsen; **Redaktør:** Tore Skadal
Profile: Harstad Tidende is a regional newspaper covering Harstad and Hålogaland.
Language (s): Norwegian
COMMUNITY NEWSPAPER

Haugesunds Avis 158332
Editorial: Karmsundsgata 72, Haugesund 5529
Tel: 47 52 72 00 00
Email: redaksjonen@haugesunds-avis.no **Web site:** http://www.h-avis.no/
Ansvarlig redaktør: Elisiv Hauge Nilsen; **Nyhetsleder:** Torstein Nymoen
Profile: Haugesunds Avis is a newspaper covering Haugalandet and Sunnhordland.
Language (s): Norwegian
COMMUNITY NEWSPAPER

Helgelands Blad 157847
Owner: Helgelands Blad AS
Editorial: Pb. 174, Sandnessjøen 8801
Tel: 47 75 07 03 00
Email: redaksjonen@hblad.no **Web site:** http://www.hblad.no
Freq: 3 Times/Week; **Circ:** 4589
Profile: Helgelands Blad is a politically independent local newspaper for outer Helgeland.
Language (s): Norwegian
COMMUNITY NEWSPAPER

Helgelendingen 158343
Owner: AS Helgeland Arbeiderblad
Editorial: Vefsnvegen 7, Mosjøen 8654
Tel: 47 75 11 36 00
Email: tips@helg.no **Web site:** http://www.helg.no/
Freq: Daily; **Circ:** 7828
Profile: Helgelendingen, until 2014 Helgeland Arbeiderblad, is a daily newspaper published in Mosjoen in Nordland.
Language (s): Norwegian
COMMUNITY NEWSPAPER

Hitra-Frøya 225167
Owner: Hitra-Frøya Lokalavis AS
Editorial: Mediehuset, Fillan, Sandstad 7240
Tel: 47 72 44 04 00
Email: post@hitra-froya.no **Web site:** http://www.hitra-froya.no
Freq: 2 Times/Week; **Circ:** 4105 MBL (Mediebedriftenes Landsforening)
Profile: Hitra-Frøya is a local newspaper published in Fillan in Hitra municipality in Rogaland covering the municipalities Hitra and Frøya.
Language (s): Norwegian
COMMUNITY NEWSPAPER

Hordaland 225168
Owner: Hordaland bladdrift AS
Editorial: Evangervegen 32, Voss 5701
Tel: 47 56 53 03 00
Email: tips@avisa-hordaland.no **Web site:** http://www.avisa-hordaland.no
Freq: 3 Times/Week; **Circ:** 8342 MBL (Mediebedriftenes Landsforening)
Profile: Hordaland is a newspaper published in Voss in Hordaland. The coverage area is the municipalities Voss, Ulvik, Granvin, Vaksdal and Modalen
Language (s): Norwegian
COMMUNITY NEWSPAPER

Hordaland Folkeblad 225169
Owner: Hordaland Folkeblad AS
Editorial: Pb. 94, Norheimsund 5601
Tel: 47 56 55 00 20
Email: redaksjon@hf.no **Web site:** http://www.hf.no
Freq: 2 Times/Week; **Circ:** 5520 Not Audited
Profile: Hardanger Folkeblad is a local newspaper that is published in Odda Hordaland.
Language (s): Norwegian
COMMUNITY NEWSPAPER

Inderøyningen 225354
Owner: Inderøyningen AS
Editorial: Pb. 19, Inderøy 7671 **Tel:** 47 40 00 67 45
Email: avisa@inderoyningen.no **Web site:** http://www.inderoyningen.no
Freq: Weekly; **Circ:** 2047 Not Audited
Profile: Inderøyningen is a local newspaper for the rural municipality of Inderøy in Norway
Language (s): Norwegian
COMMUNITY NEWSPAPER

Indre Akershus Blad 158317
Owner: Indre Akershus Blad AS
Editorial: Pb. 68, Bjørkelangen 1941
Tel: 47 63 85 48 00
Email: redaksjon@iablad.no **Web site:** http://www.indre.no
Freq: 3 Times/Week; **Circ:** 7915
Profile: Indre Akershus Blad has its headquarters on Bjørkelangen. The local newspaper covering the municipalities Aurskog-Holand, Sørum and Bold in Akershus and Østfold Rømskog.
Language (s): Norwegian
COMMUNITY NEWSPAPER

Innherred 225173
Owner: Levanger-Avisa AS
Editorial: Kirkegata 50, Levanger 7600
Email: redaksjon@innherred.no **Web site:** http://www.innherred.no/
Freq: 3 Times/Week; **Circ:** 7991 MBL (Mediebedriftenes Landsforening)
Profile: Innherred is a local newspaper published in Levanger and Verdal municipalities in Nord-Trondelag. In 2015 the newspapers Levanger-Avisa, Innherreds Folkeblad and Verdalingen went together to form the newspaper Innherred.
Language (s): Norwegian
COMMUNITY NEWSPAPER

iTromsø 157859
Owner: Bladet Tromsø AS
Editorial: Pb. 1028, Tromsø 9260 **Tel:** 47 77 64 06 00
Email: tips@itromso.no **Web site:** http://www.itromso.no
Freq: Daily; **Circ:** 6533
Nyhetssjef: Carina Hansen
Profile: iTromsø is an independent local newspaper in Tromsø.
Language (s): Norwegian
COMMUNITY NEWSPAPER

Jærbladet 225171
Editorial: Meierigata 22, Bryne 4340
Tel: 47 40 00 79 00
Email: redaksjon@jbl.no **Web site:** http://www.jbl.no
Freq: 3 Times/Week
Profile: Jærbladet is a local newspaper covering Jæren.
Language (s): Norwegian
COMMUNITY NEWSPAPER

Jarlsberg Avis 225203
Owner: Jarlsberg Avis AS
Editorial: Pb. 303, Holmestrand 3081
Tel: 47 33 09 90 00
Email: redaksjonen@jarlsbergavis.no **Web site:** http://www.jarlsbergavis.no
Freq: 3 Times/Week; **Circ:** 3881 MBL (Mediebedriftenes Landsforening)
Profile: Jarlsberg Avis is a local newspaper for Holmestrand and Hof.
Language (s): Norwegian
COMMUNITY NEWSPAPER

Kanalen 327492
Editorial: Ringsevja 11, Ulefoss 3830
Tel: 47 35 94 35 80
Email: redaktor@kanalen.no **Web site:** http://www.kanalen.no
Freq: Weekly
Redaktør: Tor Espen Simonsen
Profile: Kanalen is a local newspaper covering Nome.
Language (s): Norwegian
Ad Rate: Full Page Colour 12100.00
Currency: Norway Kroner
COMMUNITY NEWSPAPER

Kragerø Blad Vestmar 225365
Owner: Kragerø Blad AS
Editorial: Pb. 55, Kragerø 3791 **Tel:** 47 35 98 67 00
Email: redaksjonen@kv.no **Web site:** http://kv.no/
Freq: 3 Times/Week; **Circ:** 4003 Not Audited
Profile: Kragerø Blad Vestmar is a daily newspaper published in Kragerø in Telemark.
Language (s): Norwegian
COMMUNITY NEWSPAPER

Kristiansand Avis 504345
Editorial: Tordenskjoldsgate 9, Kristiansand 4612
Tel: 47 38 69 99 99
Email: tips@kristiansandavis.no **Web site:** http://www.kristiansandavis.no
Freq: Weekly; **Circ:** 50000 Publisher's Statement
Profile: Kristiansand Avis is a local newspaper covering Kristiansand, Søgne, Songdalen and Vennesla.
Language (s): Norwegian
COMMUNITY NEWSPAPER

Kvinnheringen 241832
Owner: Kvinnheringen AS
Editorial: Lonabratet, Husnes 5460
Tel: 47 53 48 21 45
Email: redaksjon@kvinnheringen.no **Web site:** http://www.kvinnheringen.no
Freq: 3 Times/Week; **Circ:** 4143 MBL (Mediebedriftenes Landsforening)
Profile: Kvinnheringen is a newspaper published in Hordaland. The newspaper is the local newspaper for Kvinnherad and headquartered in Husnes.
Language (s): Norwegian
COMMUNITY NEWSPAPER

Laagendalsposten 158334
Editorial: Stasjonsbakken 3, Kongsberg 3611
Tel: 47 32 77 10 00
Email: redaksjonen@laagendalsposten.no **Web site:** http://www.laagendalsposten.no
Freq: Weekly
Ansvarlig redaktør: Jørn Steinmoen
Profile: Laagendalsposten is a local newspaper covering Kongsberg and Numedal.
Language (s): Norwegian
COMMUNITY NEWSPAPER

Lierposten 225355
Owner: Lierposten AS
Editorial: Vestsideveien 9c, Lier 3400
Tel: 47 32 24 07 60
Email: redaksjonen@lierposten.no **Web site:** http://www.lierposten.no
Freq: Weekly; **Circ:** 3332 MBL (Mediebedriftenes Landsforening)
Profile: Lierposten is a local newspaper that is published in Lier Buskerud.
Language (s): Norwegian
COMMUNITY NEWSPAPER

Lillehammer ByAvis 527221
Editorial: Jernbanegata 13, Lillehammer 2609
Tel: 47 965 02 222
Email: redaksjon@byavis.no **Web site:** http://www.byavis.no
Freq: Weekly; **Circ:** 22365
Redaktør: Tore Feiring
Profile: Lillehammer ByAvis is a local newspaper, distributed as a free newspapers to all households in the municipalities of Lillehammer, Gausdal, Øyer and northern parts of Ringsaker and Gjøvik.
Language (s): Norwegian
Ad Rate: Full Page Colour 15500.00
Currency: Norway Kroner
COMMUNITY NEWSPAPER

Lillesands-Posten 225174
Owner: Lillesandspostens driftsselskap AS
Editorial: ovregate 8, Lillesand 4792
Tel: 47 37 26 95 00
Email: redaksjon@lp.no **Web site:** http://www.lp.no
Freq: 2 Times/Week; **Circ:** 3667 MBL (Mediebedriftenes Landsforening)
Profile: Lillesands-Posten is a local newspaper published in Lillesand and Birkenes municipalities in Aust-Agder.
Language (s): Norwegian
COMMUNITY NEWSPAPER

Lister 158324
Owner: Farsunds Avis
Editorial: Pb. 23, Farsund 4551 **Tel:** 47 38 39 20 86
Email: redaksjon@lister24.no **Web site:** http://www.lister24.no
Circ: 5405
Profile: Lister is a regional newspaper covering municipalities Farsund, Lyngdal, Kvinesdal, Flekkefjord and Hægebostad.
Language (s): Norwegian
COMMUNITY NEWSPAPER

Lofotposten 158353
Owner: Lofotposten AS
Editorial: Torget, Svolvær 8305 **Tel:** 47 76 06 78 00
Email: red@lofotposten.no **Web site:** http://www.lofotposten.no
Freq: Daily; **Circ:** 5243
Profile: Lofotposten is a daily newspaper published in Svolvær Nordland.
Language (s): Norwegian
COMMUNITY NEWSPAPER

Lofot-Tidende 157873
Owner: Lofoten Kommunikasjon AS
Editorial: Storgata 105, Leknes 8370
Tel: 47 76 05 40 00
Email: redaksjon@lofot-tidende.no **Web site:** http://www.lofot-tidende.no
Circ: 3604
Profile: Local newspaper covering Vest-Lofoten.
Language (s): Norwegian
COMMUNITY NEWSPAPER

Lokalavisa - Trysil/Engerdal 375586
Editorial: Storvegen 3, Trysil 2420 **Tel:** 47 02 418
Web site: http://www.lokal-avisa.no/
Freq: 2 Times/Week; **Circ:** 2530 MBL (Mediebedriftenes Landsforening)
Profile: Do not want to receive any press releases. Lokalavisa Trysil-Engerdal is a local newspaper. Previous name was Lokalavisa Sør-Østerdal.
Language (s): Norwegian
COMMUNITY NEWSPAPER

Lokalavisa NordSalten 158042
Owner: Lokalavisa Nordsalten AS
Editorial: Pb. 94, Innhavet 8260 **Tel:** 47 75 77 24 50
Email: lokalavisa@nord-salten.no **Web site:** http://www.nord-salten.no
Circ: 2771
Nettredaktør: Gunnar Grytøyr; **Ansvarlig redaktør:** Børge Strandskog
Profile: Lokalavisa NordSalten (with the Sami name Bájkkeavijssa NuorttaSáltto) is a local newspaper that covers Steigen, Hamarøy and Tysfjord municipalities in Nordland. Headquartered in Innhavet in Hamarøy
Language (s): Norwegian
COMMUNITY NEWSPAPER

Lokalavisen Akers Avis Groruddalen 225181
Editorial: Trondheimsveien 459, Grorud torg, Oslo 905 **Tel:** 47 22918820
Email: redaksjonen@groruddalen.no **Web site:** http://www.groruddalen.no
Freq: 2 Times/Week
Profile: Akers Avis Groruddalen is a local newspaper covering Groruddalen, in the districts Grorud, Bjerke, Alna and Stovner in Oslo.
Language (s): Norwegian
COMMUNITY NEWSPAPER

Malvik-Bladet 225213
Owner: Malvik Bladet AS
Editorial: Pb. 130, Hommelvik 7551
Tel: 47 73 98 00 80
Email: redaksjonen@mb.no **Web site:** http://www.mb.no
Freq: 2 Times/Week; **Circ:** 2965 Not Audited
Profile: Malvik-Bladet is a local newspaper published in Malvik in Sør-Trøndelag.
Language (s): Norwegian
COMMUNITY NEWSPAPER

Marsteinen 375678
Owner: Austevoll Forlag AS
Editorial: Gamle Prestagarde, Storebø 5392
Tel: 47 55 08 21 00
Email: redaksjonen@marsteinen.no **Web site:** http://www.marsteinen.no
Freq: Weekly; **Circ:** 2215 Not Audited
Profile: Marsteinen is a local newspaper published in Austevoll in Hordaland.
Language (s): Norwegian
COMMUNITY NEWSPAPER

Meløyavisa 225208
Owner: Meløyavisa
Editorial: Havneveien 15b, Ørnes 8150
Tel: 47 41 68 66 82
Email: post@meloyavisa.no **Web site:** http://www.meloyavisa.no
Freq: Weekly; **Circ:** 1989 Not Audited
Profile: Local newspaper for the district Meløy, Gildeskål and Rødøy
Language (s): Norwegian
COMMUNITY NEWSPAPER

Møre 157848
Owner: Aarflots Prenteverk AS
Editorial: Storgata 7, Volda 6100 **Tel:** 47 70 07 44 21
Email: red@mre.no **Web site:** http://www.mre.no
Freq: 3 Times/Week; **Circ:** 3373
Redaktør: Tore Aarflot
Profile: Local newspaper published in Volda with Volda and Ørsta as key areas.
Language (s): Norwegian
COMMUNITY NEWSPAPER

Møre-Nytt 157849
Editorial: Parkvegen 2, Ørsta 6153
Tel: 47 70 04 19 00
Email: redaksjon@morenytt.no **Web site:** http://www.morenytt.no
Circ: 4955

Ansvarlig redaktør: Rune Sæbønes
Profile: Møre-Nytt is a local newspaper in Ørsta in the Volda regionen.
Language (s): Norwegian
COMMUNITY NEWSPAPER

Moss Avis 158344
Editorial: Dronningens gate 11, Moss 1530
Tel: 47 958 96 248
Email: desken@moss-avis.no **Web site:** http://www.moss-avis.no
Ansvarlig redaktør: Pål Enghaug; **Redaksjonssjef:** Helge Kjøniksen
Profile: Moss Avis is a daily newspaper covering local news in Moss.
Language (s): Norwegian
COMMUNITY NEWSPAPER

Namdalsavisa 311167
Editorial: Soren R Thornæs veg 10, Namsos 7800
Tel: 47 74 21 21 00
Email: redaksjon@namdalsavisa.no **Web site:** http://www.namdalsavisa.no
Freq: Daily
Nyhetsredaktør: Lars Mørkved
Profile: Namdalsavisa is a local newspaper covering Nord-Trøndelag.
Language (s): Norwegian
COMMUNITY NEWSPAPER

Norddalen 527216
Editorial: Storgata 19, Otta 2670 **Tel:** 47 61 23 48 00
Email: post@norddalen.no **Web site:** http://www.norddalen.no
Circ: 2745
Profile: Norddalen is a newspaper that comes out at Otta, covering municipalities Sel, Vågå and Dovre.
Language (s): Norwegian
COMMUNITY NEWSPAPER

Nordhordland 489849
Editorial: Kvernhusmyrane 29, Isdalstø 5914
Tel: 47 916 20 916
Email: redaksjonen@nordhordland.no **Web site:** http://www.nordhordland.no
Freq: 2 Times/Week
Ansvarlig redaktør: Randi Bjørlo
Profile: Nordhordland is a regional newspaper covering Knarvik, Lindås, Meland, Radøy, Austrheim, Masfjorden, Fedje and Gulen.
Language (s): Norwegian
COMMUNITY NEWSPAPER

Nordlys 158355
Editorial: Radhusgata 3, Tromsø 9008
Email: nyheter@nordlys.no **Web site:** http://www.nordlys.no
Nyhetsredaktør: Helge Nitteberg; **Redaktør:** Stian Saur
Profile: Nordlys is a daily newspaper covering regional news.
Language (s): Norwegian
COMMUNITY NEWSPAPER

Nordre 225162
Owner: Haramsnytt AS
Editorial: Skjelt-Ole bakken 26, Brattvåg 6270
Tel: 47 70 20 84 80
Email: robin@nordrenett.no **Web site:** http://nordrenett.no/
Freq: 2 Times/Week; **Circ:** 2329 MBL (Mediebedriftenes Landsforening)
Profile: Nordre is a local newspaper covering Haram, Sandøy and Skodje.
Language (s): Norwegian
COMMUNITY NEWSPAPER

Nordstrands Blad 223136
Owner: Nordstrands Blad AS
Editorial: Jernbaneveien 5-7, Ski 1400
Tel: 47 22 63 91 00
Email: tips@noblad.no **Web site:** http://www.noblad.no
Freq: 2 Times/Week; **Circ:** 3765 Not Audited
Profile: Nordstrands Blad is a daily newspaper published in Nordstrand, Søndre Nordstrand and Østensjø.
Language (s): Norwegian
COMMUNITY NEWSPAPER

Nye Troms 225207
Editorial: Pb. 44, Moen 9329 **Tel:** 47 77 83 79 00
Email: redaksjon@nye-troms.no **Web site:** http://www.nye-troms.no
Freq: 3 Times/Week
Redaksjonssjef: Morten Kasbergsen; **Redaktør:** Gjermund Nilssen
Profile: Nye Troms is a local newspaper covering i Målselv, Bardu and Balsfjord in Troms.
Language (s): Norwegian
COMMUNITY NEWSPAPER

Nytt i Uka 225363
Editorial: Kongens gate 13, Ålesund 6001
Tel: 47 70 16 19 19
Email: redaksjon@nyttiuka.no **Web site:** http://www.nyttiuka.no
Freq: Weekly; **Circ:** 404000 Publisher's Statement
Profile: Nytt i Uka is a regional newspaper distributed through Edda to all households in the municipalities of Ålesund, Sula, Giske, Skodje, Haram, Hareid, Ørskog, Sykkylven and Stordal. In addition distributed the newspaper to post offices Tomrefjord and Vestnes, and to subscribers at home and abroad.
Language (s): Norwegian
COMMUNITY NEWSPAPER

Øksnesavisa 225368
Owner: Ingress Media & Reklame AS
Editorial: Storgata 50, Myre 8439 **Tel:** 47 76 11 99 40
Email: post@oksnesavisa.no **Web site:** http://www.oksnesavisa.no
Freq: Weekly; **Circ:** 1619 Not Audited
Profile: Øksnesavisa is a local newspaper published in Myre in Nordland, and covers the Øksnes municipality.
Language (s): Norwegian
COMMUNITY NEWSPAPER

Opdalingen 225244
Owner: Opdalingen AS
Editorial: Inge Krokanns vei 3, Oppdal 7340
Tel: 47 99 27 59 00
Email: redaksjon@opdalingen.no **Web site:** http://www.opdalingen.no
Freq: 3 Times/Week; **Circ:** 2089 Not Audited
Profile: Opdalingen is a regional newspaper published in Oppdal in Sør-Trøndelag. The newspaper comes out every Tuesday, Thursday and Saturday.
Language (s): Norwegian
COMMUNITY NEWSPAPER

Oppland Arbeiderblad 158327
Editorial: Sommerroveien 1, Gjøvik 2816
Tel: 47 61 18 93 00
Email: redaksjonen@oa.no **Web site:** http://www.oa.no
Profile: Oppland Arbeiderblad is a regional newspaper covering Vestoppland.
Language (s): Norwegian
COMMUNITY NEWSPAPER

Os & Fusaposten 225228
Owner: Os og Fusaposten AS
Editorial: oyro 31, Os 5203 **Tel:** 47 56 30 29 50
Email: post@osogfusa.no **Web site:** http://www.osogfusa.no
Freq: 2 Times/Week; **Circ:** 5090 Not Audited
Profile: Os & Fusaposten is a politically unfettered local newspaper published in Os and Fusa. The paper comes out every Wednesday and Saturday.
Language (s): Norwegian
COMMUNITY NEWSPAPER

Østfoldavisen 416200
Editorial: Greakerveien 126, Greåker 1718
Tel: 47 69 12 75 00
Email: post@o-a.no **Web site:** http://www.ostfoldavisen.no
Freq: Monthly; **Circ:** 100000 Not Audited
Profile: Østfoldavisen is a community newspaper containing news and information about the region of Østfold.
Language (s): Norwegian
Ad Rate: Full Page Mono 47880.00
Currency: Norway Kroner
COMMUNITY NEWSPAPER

Østhavet 225357
Owner: Østhavet AS
Editorial: Kaigata 14, Vardø 9950 **Tel:** 47 78 98 85 88
Email: redaksjon@osthavet.as **Web site:** http://www.osthavet.as
Freq: Weekly; **Circ:** 1797 Not Audited
Profile: Østhavet is a local newspaper published in Vardø in Finnmark.
Language (s): Norwegian
COMMUNITY NEWSPAPER

Østlandets Blad 157864
Editorial: Jernbaneveien 5-7, Ski 1400
Tel: 47 64 85 50 00
Email: tips@oblad.no **Web site:** http://www.oblad.no
Redaksjonssjef: Rolf-Otto Eriksen; **Ansvarlig redaktør / daglig leder:** Martin Gray
Profile: Østlandets Blad is a daily newspaper covering Follo.
Language (s): Norwegian
COMMUNITY NEWSPAPER

Østlands-Posten 158338
Editorial: Fritzoe Brygge, Larvik 3264
Tel: 47 33 16 30 00
Email: redaksjonen@op.no **Web site:** http://www.op.no
Nyhetsredaktør: Gry R. Nordvik; **Ansvarlig redaktør:** Terje Svendsen; **Redaktør:** Per Marvin Tennum
Profile: Østlands-Posten is a daily newspaper covering Larvik and Lardal.
Language (s): Norwegian
COMMUNITY NEWSPAPER

Østlendingen 158322
Editorial: Gaarderbakken 3, Elverum 2406
Tel: 47 62 40 00 00
Email: redaksjonen@ostlendingen.no **Web site:** http://www.ostlendingen.no
Nyhetsleder: Ola Thorset
Profile: Østlendingen is a regional newspaper covering Østerdalen, Solør, Glåmdalen, Trysil and Engerdal. Published six times a week.
Language (s): Norwegian
COMMUNITY NEWSPAPER

Øy-Blikk 241834
Owner: Øy-Blikk AS
Editorial: oy-Blikk AS, oysenteret, Pettervegen 2, Valderøy 6050 **Tel:** 47 70 18 63 80
Email: redaksjon@oyblikk.no **Web site:** http://www.oyblikk.no
Freq: Weekly; **Circ:** 1548 Not Audited
Profile: Øy-Blikk is a local newspaper for Giske municipality. The paper covers the islands Valderøya, Vigra, Godøya and Giske.
Language (s): Norwegian
COMMUNITY NEWSPAPER

Øyene 225346
Owner: Mediehuset Østlands-Posten AS
Editorial: Teigegarden, 2. etasje, Nøtterøy 3106
Tel: 47 33 34 57 77
Email: red@oyene.no **Web site:** http://www.oyene.no
Freq: Weekly; **Circ:** 3582 Not Audited
Profile: Øyene is a local newspaper that's published weekly in Nøtterøy and Tjøme in Vestfold.
Language (s): Norwegian
COMMUNITY NEWSPAPER

Øyposten 225225
Editorial: Rygjabovegen 4, Finnøy 4160
Tel: 47 51 71 46 60
Email: bladstova@oyposten.no **Web site:** http://www.oyposten.no
Freq: Weekly
Profile: Øyposten is a local newspaper covering Ryfylkeøyane. Primarily covers the islands belonging to Finnøy municipality.
Language (s): Norwegian
COMMUNITY NEWSPAPER

Porsgrunns Dagblad 225235
Owner: Porsgrunns Dagblad AS
Editorial: Jernbanegata 12, Porsgrunn 3901
Tel: 47 35 51 65 00
Email: redaksjon@pd.no **Web site:** http://www.pd.no
Freq: Daily; **Circ:** 3961 MBL (Mediebedriftenes Landsforening)
Profile: Porsgrunns Dagblad is a Norwegian newspaper, published in Porsgrunn in the Telemark county, Norway.
Language (s): Norwegian
COMMUNITY NEWSPAPER

Rakkestad Avis 157851
Owner: Rakkestad Avis AS
Editorial: Storgata 8, Rakkestad 1890
Tel: 47 69 22 25 55
Email: ra@r-a.no **Web site:** http://www.r-a.no/
Freq: 3 Times/Week; **Circ:** 2664
Profile: Rakkestad Avis is a local newspaper published in Rakkestad, Norway.
Language (s): Norwegian
COMMUNITY NEWSPAPER

Rana Blad 157852
Owner: AS Rana Blad
Editorial: Ole Tobias Olsens Gate 2, Mo I Rana 8622
Tel: 47 75 12 55 00
Email: redaksjonen@ranablad.no **Web site:** http://www.ranablad.no
Circ: 8146
Profile: Rana Blad is a regional newspaper in Mo i Rana covering local news, domestic and international news provided by ANB, sports, culture and opinion page.
Language (s): Norwegian
COMMUNITY NEWSPAPER

Raumnes 225358
Owner: Raumnes AS
Editorial: Raumnes AS, Silovegen 12c, Årnes 2150
Tel: 47 63 91 18 14
Email: redaksjon@raumnes.no **Web site:** http://www.raumnes.no
Freq: 3 Times/Week; **Circ:** 5293 Not Audited
Profile: Raumnes is the local newspaper for Nes in Romerike.
Language (s): Norwegian
COMMUNITY NEWSPAPER

Regionavisa 225347
Editorial: Stalhaugen 10, Ulsteinvik 6065
Tel: 47 70 00 96 60
Email: tips@regionavisa.no **Web site:** http://www.regionavisa.no
Freq: Weekly; **Circ:** 33100 Publisher's Statement
Ansvarlig redaktør: Hugo Antonsen
Profile: Regionavisa is a regional newspaper covering Hareid, Ulstein, Herøy, Sande, Vanylven, Ørsta, Volda, Hornindal, Eid, Stryn, Selje and Vågsøy.
Language (s): Norwegian
COMMUNITY NEWSPAPER

Ringerikes Blad 773395
Owner: A-pressen
Editorial: Honefoss Bru 1d, Hønefoss 3502
Tel: 47 32 17 95 00
Email: redaksjonen@ringblad.no **Web site:** http://www.ringblad.no
Freq: Daily; **Circ:** 10303
Nyhetsredaktør: Øyvind Lien
Profile: Ringerikes Blad is a local newspaper published in Hønefoss, Norway. It covers Ringerike, Hole and Jevnaker.
Language (s): Norwegian
COMMUNITY NEWSPAPER

Ringsaker Blad 225246
Owner: Ringsaker Blad AS
Editorial: Storgata 106, Moelv 2390
Tel: 47 62 34 77 00
Email: redaksjonen@ringsaker-blad.no **Web site:** http://www.ringsaker-blad.no
Freq: 3 Times/Week; **Circ:** 6200 MBL (Mediebedriftenes Landsforening)
Profile: Ringsaker Blad is a local newspaper for Ringsaker and Brummundal.
Language (s): Norwegian
COMMUNITY NEWSPAPER

Rjukan Arbeiderblad 225247
Editorial: Storgata 20, Rjukan 3660
Tel: 47 35 08 00 50
Email: ra@rablad.no **Web site:** http://www.rablad.no
Freq: Daily
Profile: Rjukan Arbeiderblad is a local newspaper in Tinn. Published five times a week, Tuesday to Saturday.
Language (s): Norwegian
COMMUNITY NEWSPAPER

Rogalands Avis 158350
Owner: Rogalands Avis AS
Editorial: Klubbgata 1, 6. etasje, Stavanger 4001
Tel: 47 51 82 20 00
Email: redaksjon@rogalandsavis.no **Web site:** http://www.rogalandsavis.no
Circ: 5953
Sjefredaktør: Bjørn Sæbø
Profile: Rogalands Avis is a local newspaper published in Stavanger, Norway.
Language (s): Norwegian
COMMUNITY NEWSPAPER

Romerikes Blad 158340
Editorial: Roseveien 1, Kjeller 2007
Tel: 47 63 80 50 50
Email: redaksjonen@rb.no **Web site:** http://www.rb.no
Freq: Daily; **Circ:** 100000
Redaksjonssjef: Trine Kjus
Profile: Romerikes Blad is a local newspaper in Skedsmo, Akershus.
Language (s): Norwegian
COMMUNITY NEWSPAPER

Romsdals Budstikke 158342
Editorial: Romsdalsgata 9, Molde 6415
Tel: 47 71 25 00 00
Email: redaksjon@r-b.no **Web site:** http://www.rbnett.no
Freq: Daily
Profile: Romsdals Budstikke is a daily newspaper covering Molde, Fræna, Vestnes, Rauma, Nesset, Midsund, Aukra, Sandøy, Gjemnes and Eide.
Language (s): Norwegian
COMMUNITY NEWSPAPER

Ryfylke 157869
Owner: LL Ryfylke
Editorial: Radhusgata 1, Sauda 4200
Tel: 47 52 78 68 00
Email: ryfylke@ryfylke.net **Web site:** http://www.ryfylke.net
Freq: 2 Times/Week; **Circ:** 2452
Profile: Ryfylke is a local newspaper published in Sauda municipality in the Rogaland county. The newspaper is published every Tuesday and Friday.
Language (s): Norwegian
COMMUNITY NEWSPAPER

Ságat 157853
Editorial: Laatasveien, Lakselv 9700
Tel: 47 78 46 59 00
Email: avisa@sagat.no **Web site:** http://www.sagat.no
Freq: 3 Times/Week
Redaksjonssekretær: Oddgeir Johansen; **Redaksjonssekretær:** Lars Birger Persen;
Sjefsredaktør: Geir Wulff
Profile: Ságat is a newspaper aimed at the Sami population. Published five days a week, Tuesday to Saturday.
Language (s): Norwegian
COMMUNITY NEWSPAPER

Saltenposten 225369
Owner: Saltenposten AS
Editorial: Vollgata 16, Fauske 8201
Tel: 47 75 60 24 60
Email: redaksjonen@saltenposten.no **Web site:** http://www.saltenposten.no
Freq: 3 Times/Week; **Circ:** 4612 MBL (Mediebedriftenes Landsforening)
Profile: Saltenposten is a local newspaper in Indre Salten. Sørfold, Fauske, Saltdal, Skjerstad and Beiarn.
Language (s): Norwegian
COMMUNITY NEWSPAPER

Samningen 225229
Owner: Samnanger Bladlag AS
Editorial: Reistadliane 22, Årland 5652
Tel: 47 56 58 77 05
Email: post@samningen.no **Web site:** http://www.samningen.no
Freq: Weekly; **Circ:** 1438 Not Audited
Profile: Samningen is a local newspaper in Samnanger, Hordaland.
Language (s): Norwegian
COMMUNITY NEWSPAPER

Sande Avis 158043
Owner: Sande Avis AS
Editorial: Revaveien 14, Sande I Vestfold 3070
Tel: 47 33 77 84 45
Email: redaksjonen@sandeavis.no **Web site:** http://www.sandeavis.no
Circ: 2227

Profile: Sande Avis is a local newspaper in Sande in Vestfold.
Language (s): Norwegian
COMMUNITY NEWSPAPER

Sandefjords Blad 158347
Editorial: Storgata 4, Sandefjord 3210
Tel: 47 33 42 20 00
Email: redaksjonen@sb.no **Web site:** http://www.sb.no
Profile: Sandefjords Blad is a daily newspaper covering local news. Published six times a week.
Language (s): Norwegian
COMMUNITY NEWSPAPER

Sandnesposten 157868
Owner: Sandnesposten AS
Editorial: Langgata 59, Sandnes 4306
Tel: 47 41 60 70 00
Email: redaksjonen@sandnesposten.no **Web site:** http://www.sandnesposten.no
Circ: 3988
Redaksjonsleder: Trond Erik Olsen
Profile: Sandnesposten is a local newspaper published in Sandnes.
Language (s): Norwegian
COMMUNITY NEWSPAPER

Sarpsborg Arbeiderblad 158348
Editorial: St. Marie gate 68, Sarpsborg 1701
Tel: 47 69 11 11 11
Email: redaksjonen@sa.no **Web site:** http://www.sa.no
Freq: Daily
Profile: Sarpsborg Arbeiderblad is a daily newspaper covering local news.
Language (s): Norwegian
COMMUNITY NEWSPAPER

Selbyggen 225214
Owner: Selbyggen AS
Editorial: Selbyggen, Selbu 7580 **Tel:** 47 73 81 08 80
Email: firmapost@selbyggen.no **Web site:** http://www.selbyggen.no
Freq: Weekly; **Circ:** 2958 LLA (Landslaget for Lokalaviser)
Redaktør: Bodil Uthus
Profile: Selbyggen is a local newspaper covering the municipalities Tydal and Selbu in Sør-Trøndelag. It is published every Friday.
Language (s): Norwegian
COMMUNITY NEWSPAPER

Setesdølen 225242
Editorial: Setesdolen AS, Postboks 40, Bygland 4745
Tel: 47 37 93 45 00
Email: avis@setesdolen.no **Web site:** http://www.setesdolen.no
Freq: 2 Times/Week
Redaktør: Sigurd Haugsgjerd
Profile: Setesdølen is a Norwegian newspaper, issued in the municipality of Bygland, and covering the valley of Setesdal. Published on Tuesdays and Fridays.
Language (s): Norwegian
COMMUNITY NEWSPAPER

Smaalenenes Avis 225349
Editorial: Torget 12, Askim 1830 **Tel:** 47 69 81 61 00
Email: redaksjon@smaalenene.no **Web site:** http://www.smaalenene.no
Nyhetsredaktør: Anne Sterri Harestad
Profile: Smaalenenes Avis is a daily newspaper covering Askim, Eidsberg, Trøgstad, Spydeberg, Marker, Skiptvet and Hobøl.
Language (s): Norwegian
COMMUNITY NEWSPAPER

Snåsningen 225205
Owner: Snåsningen AS
Editorial: Viosen, Snåsa 7760 **Tel:** 47 74 15 15 10
Email: firmapost@snasningen.no **Web site:** http://www.snasningen.no
Freq: Weekly; **Circ:** 1628 LLA (Landslaget for Lokalaviser)
Profile: Snåsningen is a local newspaper in Snåsa in Nord-Trøndelag, Norway.
Language (s): Norwegian
COMMUNITY NEWSPAPER

Sogn Avis 225243
Owner: Sogningen/Sogns Avis AS
Editorial: Riverdalen 5, Leikanger 6863
Tel: 47 57 65 60 00
Email: redaksjon@sognavis.no **Web site:** http://www.sognavis.no
Freq: Daily; **Circ:** 8884 MBL (Mediebedriftenes Landsforening)
Profile: Sogn Avis is a local newspaper in the inner Sogn, covering the municipalities Sogndal, Leikanger, Luster, Årdal, Lærdal, Aurland, Balestrand and Vik.
Language (s): Norwegian
COMMUNITY NEWSPAPER

Solabladet 225362
Owner: Solabladet AS
Editorial: Soltunvegen 1, Sola 4097
Tel: 47 51 64 64 64
Email: tips@solabladet.no **Web site:** http://www.solabladet.no
Freq: Weekly; **Circ:** 3655 MBL (Mediebedriftenes Landsforening)
Profile: Solabladet is a local newspaper covering the Sola municipality. the newspaper is part of the Jæren Avis-group and is published on Thursdays.
Language (s): Norwegian
COMMUNITY NEWSPAPER

Sortlandsavisa 527239
Owner: Sortlandsavisa
Editorial: Strandgata 24, Sortland 8400
Tel: 47 99 15 55 66
Email: red@sortlandsavisa.no **Web site:** http://www.sortlandsavisa.no
Freq: Weekly; **Circ:** 1411
Profile: Sortlandsavisa is a local newspaper for Sortland in Nordland.
Language (s): Norwegian
COMMUNITY NEWSPAPER

Sør-Trøndelag 157856
Owner: Sør-Trøndelag AS
Editorial: Orkedalsveien 57, Orkanger 7300
Tel: 47 72 48 75 00
Email: nyhets.redaksjonen@avisa-st.no **Web site:** http://www.avisa-st.no
Circ: 6366
Ansvarlig redaktør: Anders Aa. Morken
Profile: Sør-Trøndelag is a regional newspaper covering the municipalities Orkdal, Skaun, Meldal, Rennebu, Hemne, Snillfjord, Agdenes and Rindal. The paper is published five days a week.
Language (s): Norwegian
COMMUNITY NEWSPAPER

Sør-Varanger Avis 225240
Owner: Sør-Varanger Avis AS
Editorial: Pasvikveien 1, Kirkenes 9900
Tel: 47 78 97 07 00
Email: redaksjon@sva.no **Web site:** http://www.sva.no
Freq: 3 Times/Week; **Circ:** 3500 Not Audited
Profile: Sør-Varanger Avis is a local newspaper for Sør-Varanger.
Language (s): Norwegian
COMMUNITY NEWSPAPER

Søvesten 225204
Owner: Søvesten Media AS
Editorial: oragata 13, Kyrksæterøra 7200
Tel: 47 72 45 00 50
Email: redaksjon@sovesten.no **Web site:** http://www.sovesten.no
Freq: Weekly; **Circ:** 1317 Not Audited
Profile: Søvesten is a local newspaper for the Hemne and Aure municipalities.
Language (s): Norwegian
COMMUNITY NEWSPAPER

Stangeavisa 489092
Editorial: Kongsvegen 1, Stange 2335 **Tel:** 47 02 519
Email: post@stangeavisa.no **Web site:** http://www.stangeavisa.no
Freq: Weekly
Profile: Stangeavisa is a weekly newspaper covering local news.
Language (s): Norwegian
COMMUNITY NEWSPAPER

Steinkjer-Avisa 225216
Owner: Steinkjer-Avisa AS
Editorial: Elvegata 1, Steinkjer 7715
Tel: 47 74 10 01 30
Email: post@steinkjer-avisa.no **Web site:** http://www.steinkjer-avisa.no
Freq: Weekly; **Circ:** 4943 Not Audited
Profile: Steinkjer-Avisa is a local weekly newspaper in Steinkjer, Norway.
Language (s): Norwegian
COMMUNITY NEWSPAPER

Stjørdalens Blad 157854
Owner: Stjørdalens Blad AS
Editorial: Stokmoveien 2, Stjørdal 7500
Tel: 47 74 83 95 00
Email: redaksjonen@bladet.no **Web site:** http://www.bladet.no
Freq: 3 Times/Week; **Circ:** 6486
Profile: Stjørdalens Blad is a local newspaper covering Stjørdal and Meråker.
Language (s): Norwegian
COMMUNITY NEWSPAPER

Storfjordnytt 225218
Tel: 47 70 25 78 50
Email: post@storfjordnytt.no **Web site:** http://www.storfjordnytt.no/
Freq: Weekly; **Circ:** 1405 Not Audited
Profile: "Storfjordnytt" is a local weekly newspaper in Valldal in Møre and Romsdal.
Language (s): Norwegian
COMMUNITY NEWSPAPER

Strandbuen 223135
Owner: Strandbuen AS
Editorial: Kvalshaugv. 5, Jørpeland 4126
Tel: 47 51 74 47 50
Email: redaksjon@strandbuen.no **Web site:** http://www.strandbuen.no
Freq: 2 Times/Week; **Circ:** 5029 Not Audited
Profile: Strandbuen is a local newspaper for Ryfylke municipalities Strand, Hjelmeland and Forsand.
Language (s): Norwegian
COMMUNITY NEWSPAPER

Strilen 225241
Editorial: Kvassnesvegen 23, Isdalstø 5914
Tel: 47 56 34 30 30
Email: redaksjonen@strilen.no **Web site:** http://www.strilen.no
Freq: 2 Times/Week
Profile: Strilen is a regional newspaper covering Lindås, Meland, Radøy, Austrheim, Fedje, Masfjorden, Gulen and Modalen.
Language (s): Norwegian
COMMUNITY NEWSPAPER

Sulaposten 225219
Owner: Sulaposten AS
Editorial: Geilneset 16, Langevåg 6030
Tel: 47 70 19 86 50
Email: redaksjon@sulaposten.no **Web site:** http://www.sulaposten.no
Freq: Weekly; **Circ:** 2294 Not Audited
Profile: Sulaposten is a local newspaper in the Sula municipality of Møre og Romsdal.
Language (s): Norwegian
COMMUNITY NEWSPAPER

Suldalsposten 225224
Owner: Suldalsposten AS
Editorial: Nordenden 2, Sand 4230
Tel: 47 52 79 05 90
Email: redaksjon@suldalsposten.no **Web site:** http://www.suldalsposten.no
Freq: 2 Times/Week; **Circ:** 2341 LLA (Landslaget for Lokalaviser)
Profile: Suldalsposten is a local newspaper in the Suldal municipality of Rogaland.
Language (s): Norwegian
COMMUNITY NEWSPAPER

Sunnhordland 157855
Owner: Bladet Sunnhordland AS
Editorial: Borggata 15, Stord 5401
Tel: 47 53 45 00 00
Email: redaksjonen@sunnhordland.com **Web site:** http://www.sunnhordland.com
Freq: Daily; **Circ:** 6571
Profile: Sunnhordland is a local newspaper for the municipalities Stord, Fitjar, Bømlo, Tysnes and Kvinnherad.
Language (s): Norwegian
COMMUNITY NEWSPAPER

Sunnmøringen 157871
Owner: Sunnmøringen AS
Editorial: Sjogata 13, Stranda 6200
Tel: 47 70 26 11 22
Email: sunnmoringen@sunnmoringen.no **Web site:** http://www.sunnmoringen.no
Freq: 2 Times/Week; **Circ:** 1779
Profile: Sunnmøringen is a local newspaper for the Stranda municipality, with the surrounding areas Stranda, Geiranger, Hellesylt and Liabygda.
Language (s): Norwegian
COMMUNITY NEWSPAPER

Sunnmørsposten 158310
Editorial: Roysegata 10, Ålesund 6003
Tel: 47 70 12 00 00
Email: redaksjonen@smp.no **Web site:** http://www.smp.no
Ansvarlig redaktør: Hanna Relling Berg;
Markedssjef: Ingrid Sperre
Profile: Sunnmørsposten is a daily newspaper covering regional news.
Language (s): Norwegian
COMMUNITY NEWSPAPER

Svalbardposten 223137
Owner: Stiftelsen Svalbardposten
Editorial: Postboks 503, Longyearbyen 9171
Tel: 47 79 02 47 00
Email: post@svalbardposten.no **Web site:** http://www.svalbardposten.no
Freq: Weekly; **Circ:** 2457 LLA (Landslaget for Lokalaviser)
Profile: Svalbardposten is a local newspaper for Longyearbyen, Ny-Ålesund and Svea as well as for people with a connection to Svalbard.
Language (s): Norwegian
COMMUNITY NEWSPAPER

Svelviksposten 223138
Owner: Svelviksposten AS
Editorial: Storgaten 74, Svelvik 3061
Tel: 47 33 77 30 10
Email: redaksjon@svelviksposten.no **Web site:** http://www.svelviksposten.no
Freq: Weekly; **Circ:** 2226 MBL (Mediebedriftenes Landsforening)
Profile: Svelviksposten is a local newspaper covering the Svelvik, Berger and Nesbygda municipalities.
Language (s): Norwegian
COMMUNITY NEWSPAPER

Sydvesten 365521
Owner: Grieg Lokalaviser AS
Editorial: Kong Christian Frederiks plass 3, Bergen 5006 **Tel:** 47 55 16 47 50
Email: red@sydvesten.no **Web site:** http://www.sydvesten.no
Freq: Weekly; **Circ:** 1180
Redaktør: Mette L. Skulstad
Profile: Sydvesten is a local newspaper for Fyllingsdalen and Laksevågs in Hordaland.
Language (s): Norwegian
COMMUNITY NEWSPAPER

Sykkylvsbladet 225220
Owner: Frank Kjøde og Åge Eikrem
Editorial: Storgata 16, Sykkylven 6230
Tel: 47 70 25 48 48
Email: redaksjonen@sykkylvsbladet.no **Web site:** http://www.sykkylvsbladet.no
Freq: 2 Times/Week; **Circ:** 2856 LLA (Landslaget for Lokalaviser)
Ansvarlig redaktør: Frank Kjøde
Profile: Sykkylvsbladet is a local newspaper for Sykkylven municipality. It is published twice a week, on Wednesdays and Fridays.
Language (s): Norwegian
COMMUNITY NEWSPAPER

Synste Møre 225221
Owner: Synste Møre AS
Editorial: Postboks 53, Fiskåbygd 6139
Tel: 47 70 02 08 20
Email: redaksjonen@synste.no **Web site:** http://www.synste.no
Freq: Weekly; **Circ:** 2167 LLA (Landslaget for Lokalaviser)
Ansvarlig redaktør: Vidar Parr
Profile: Synste Møre is a local newspaper in the Vanylen municipality in Møre og Romsdal.
Language (s): Norwegian
COMMUNITY NEWSPAPER

Telemarksavisa 157857
Editorial: Torggata 8, Skien 3724 **Tel:** 47 35 58 55 00
Email: desken@ta.no **Web site:** http://www.ta.no
Nettredaktør: Tom Erik Holland; **Nyhetsleder:** Ørjan Madsen; **Ansvarlig redaktør:** Ove Mellingen
Profile: Telemarksavisa is a regional newspaper covering Skien in Telemark.
Language (s): Norwegian
COMMUNITY NEWSPAPER

Telen 157858
Owner: Telen AS
Editorial: Heddalsveien 40, Notodden 3674
Tel: 47 93 23 42 00
Email: telen@telen.no **Web site:** http://www.telen.no
Freq: Daily; **Circ:** 4276
Ansvarlig redaktør: Jens Marius Hammer
Profile: Telen is a local newspaper for the municipalities Notodden, Sauherad and Hjartdal in Øst-Telemark.
Language (s): Norwegian
COMMUNITY NEWSPAPER

Tidens Krav 158336
Editorial: Postboks 8, Kristiansund N 6501
Tel: 47 71 57 00 00
Email: redaksjonen@tk.no **Web site:** http://www.tk.no
Circ: 11924
Profile: Tidens Krav is a local newspaper covering Kristiansund and the 10 other municipalities in Nordmøre.
Language (s): Norwegian
COMMUNITY NEWSPAPER

Tønsbergs Blad 158354
Editorial: Nedre Langgate 20, Tønsberg 3126
Tel: 47 33 37 30 00
Email: redaksjonen@tb.no **Web site:** http://www.tb.no
Redaksjonssjef nyheter: Kristin Monstad Lund; **Redaktør:** Morten Wang; **Redaksjonssjef:** Erik Wold Aunemo
Profile: Tønsbergs Blad is a daily newspaper covering Vestfold.
Language (s): Norwegian
COMMUNITY NEWSPAPER

Totens Blad 489441
Editorial: Hauggata 10, Lena 2850
Tel: 47 61 16 87 50
Email: post@totens-blad.no **Web site:** http://www.totens-blad.no
Freq: Weekly
Profile: Totens Blad is a local newspaper covering Toten and distributed to all households in Toten.
Language (s): Norwegian
COMMUNITY NEWSPAPER

Troms Folkeblad 225238
Owner: Troms Folkeblad AS
Editorial: Ringveien 25, Finnsnes 9300
Tel: 47 77 85 20 00
Email: tips@folkebladet.no **Web site:** http://www.folkebladet.no
Circ: 5696
Profile: Troms Folkeblad is a local newspaper covering the municipalities Lenvik, Berg, Torsken, Tranøy, Målselv, Bardu, Sørreisa, Dyrøy, Salangen and Lavangen in Midt-Troms.
Language (s): Norwegian
COMMUNITY NEWSPAPER

TS-Avisen 489107
Owner: TS-Avisen AS
Editorial: Havnegata 4, Arendal 4836
Tel: 47 37 06 39 00
Email: redaksjonen@ts-avisen.no **Web site:** http://www.ts-avisen.no
Freq: Weekly; **Circ:** 25000
Profile: TS-Avisen is a free newspaper distributed in Aust-Agder. The newspaper is published weekly.
Language (s): Norwegian
COMMUNITY NEWSPAPER

Norway

Tvedestrandsposten
157861
Owner: Tvedestrandsposten AS
Editorial: Hovedgata 54, Tvedestrand 4900
Tel: 47 37 16 49 00
Email: redaksjonen@tvedestrandsposten.no **Web site:** http://www.tvedestrandsposten.no
Freq: 3 Times/Week; **Circ:** 3318
Profile: Tvedestrandsposten is a local newspaper for Tvedestrand.
Language (s): Norwegian
COMMUNITY NEWSPAPER

Tysnes
330880
Owner: Bladet Tysnes AS
Editorial: Bladet Tysnes AS, Teiglandsvegen 5, Unavailable 5680 **Tel:** 47 53 43 22 20
Email: redaksjonen@tysnesbladet.no **Web site:** http://www.tysnesbladet.no
Freq: Weekly; **Circ:** 2315 Not Audited
Ansvarlig redaktør: Ole M. Skaten
Profile: Tysnes is a local newspaper in Norway covering Tysnes Hordaland.
Language (s): Norwegian
COMMUNITY NEWSPAPER

Tysvær Bygdeblad
223139
Owner: Tysvær Bygdeblad AS
Editorial: Postboks 13, Aksdal 5575
Tel: 47 52 75 74 00
Email: post@tysver-bygdeblad.no **Web site:** http://www.tysver-bygdeblad.no
Freq: Weekly; **Circ:** 2192 LLA (Landslaget for Lokalaviser)
Profile: Tysvær Bygdeblad is a Norwegian weekly newspaper, published in Aksdal, Norway, and covering the municipality of Tysvær.
Language (s): Norwegian
COMMUNITY NEWSPAPER

Ukeavisen Ledelse
414816
Owner: Magne Lerø
Editorial: Mariboes gate 8, Oslo 183
Tel: 47 24 07 70 07
Email: red@medierogledelse.no **Web site:** http://www.dagensperspektiv.no/
Freq: Weekly; **Circ:** 5286 MBL (Mediebedriftenes Landsforening)
Profile: Ukeavisen Ledelse is a weekly newspaper published in Oslo. The paper focuses on the most important developments in leadership, politics, economics and business. The website is called Dagens perspektiv.
Language (s): Norwegian
COMMUNITY NEWSPAPER

Utrop
489100
Owner: Utrop AS
Editorial: Postboks 8962, Youngstorget, Oslo 28
Tel: 47 22 04 14 60
Email: utrop@utrop.no **Web site:** http://www.utrop.no
Circ: 2478
Profile: Utrop is a newspaper, web portal and TV offering news, entertainment and current affairs about the multicultural Norway.
Language (s): Norwegian
COMMUNITY NEWSPAPER

Våganavisa
489105
Editorial: Torget 2, Svolvær 8301
Email: redaksjon@vaganavisa.no **Web site:** http://www.vaganavisa.no
Freq: Weekly; **Circ:** 2465 Not Audited
Profile: Våganavisa is a weekly local newspaper published in Vågan in Nordland.
Language (s): Norwegian
COMMUNITY NEWSPAPER

Vaksdalposten
225231
Owner: Vaksdal Posten AS
Editorial: Konsul Jebsengt. 3, Dale, Unavailable
Tel: 47 56 59 40 00
Email: post@vp.no **Web site:** http://www.vaksdalposten.no
Freq: Weekly; **Circ:** 2257 Not Audited
Profile: Vaksdalposten is a local newspaper covering the municipalities Vaksdal and Modalen.
Language (s): Norwegian
COMMUNITY NEWSPAPER

Varden
158349
Editorial: Prinsessegate 10-12, Skien 3724
Tel: 47 35 54 30 00
Email: redaksjonen@varden.no **Web site:** http://www.varden.no
Redaksjonssjef: Lasse Johannessen; **Ansvarlig redaktør:** Lars Kise; **Nyhetsredaktør:** Tom Erik Thorsen; **Nett- og utviklingsleder:** Birte Ulveseth
Profile: Varden is a local newspaper published in Skien, Norway.
Language (s): Norwegian
COMMUNITY NEWSPAPER

Vennesla Tidende
225222
Editorial: Torsbyvegen 20, Vennesla 4702
Tel: 47 38 15 25 90
Email: red@venneslatidende.no **Web site:** http://www.venneslatidende.no/
Freq: 2 Times/Week
Profile: Vennesla Tidende is a local newspaper.
Language (s): Norwegian
COMMUNITY NEWSPAPER

Vestby Avis
527357
Owner: Vestby Avis AS
Editorial: Pb. 17, Vestby 1514 **Tel:** 47 64 98 38 88

Email: post@vestbyavis.no **Web site:** http://www.vestbyavis.no
Freq: Weekly; **Circ:** 1973
Profile: Vestby Avis is a local newspaper covering all Vestby municipality (Vestby, Garder, Hvitsten, Son and Hølen).
Language (s): Norwegian
COMMUNITY NEWSPAPER

Vestby Nytt
489104
Editorial: Mediasenteret AS, Kleverveien 3, Vestby 1540 **Tel:** 47 64 98 52 80
Email: post@mediasenteret.no **Web site:** http://www.mediasenteret.no/Vestby-Nytt-201212
Freq: Monthly; **Circ:** 16300
Daglig leder: Ronny Nermo
Profile: Vestby Nytt is a local newspaper containing information about the municipality.
Language (s): Norwegian
COMMUNITY NEWSPAPER

Vesterålen Avis
225236
Owner: Vesterålens Avis AS
Editorial: Markedsgata 12, Stokmarknes 8450
Tel: 47 91 89 88 85
Email: red@vesteraalensavis.no **Web site:** http://www.vesteraalensavis.no
Freq: Daily; **Circ:** 6898 MBL (Mediebedriftenes Landsforening)
Profile: Vesterålen Avis is a regional newspaper published in Sortland i Nordland. The newspaper covers the municipalities in Vesterålen (Sortland, Hadsel, Bo, Øksnes and Andoya) as well as Lødingen and Kvæfjord. The newspaper comes out Tuesday - Saturday.
Language (s): Norwegian
COMMUNITY NEWSPAPER

Vestnesavisa
157872
Owner: Reklamebyrået Vestnesavisa AS
Editorial: Vestnes Brygge, Helland, Vestnes 6399
Tel: 47 71 18 00 00
Email: redaksjon@vestnesavisa.no **Web site:** http://www.vestnesavisa.no
Freq: Weekly; **Circ:** 1846
Profile: Vestnesavisa is a local newspaper for Vestnes Municipality.
Language (s): Norwegian
COMMUNITY NEWSPAPER

Vestnytt
157883
Owner: Vestnytt AS
Editorial: Skjenet 2, Straume 5353
Tel: 47 56 33 65 00
Email: redaksjon@vestnytt.no **Web site:** http://www.vestnytt.no
Circ: 5713
Profile: Vestnytt is a local newspaper for Sund, Fjell and Øygarden.
Language (s): Norwegian
COMMUNITY NEWSPAPER

Vest-Telemark blad
157867
Owner: Vest-Telemark Blad AS
Editorial: Kviteseidgata 18, Kviteseid 3850
Tel: 47 35 06 88 00
Email: redaksjon@vtb.no **Web site:** http://www.vtb.no
Freq: 3 Times/Week; **Circ:** 5713
Profile: Vest-Telemark blad is a local newspaper covering the municipalities Vinje, Kvitseid, Seljord, Fyresdal, Nissedal and Tokke in Vest-Telemark.
Language (s): Norwegian
COMMUNITY NEWSPAPER

Vigga
225233
Owner: Dombås Informasjonssenter AS
Editorial: Postboks 79, Dombås 2659
Tel: 47 61 21 50 10
Email: post@vigga.no **Web site:** http://www.vigga.no
Freq: Weekly; **Circ:** 2189 Not Audited
Profile: Vigga is a local newspaper in Dombås.
Language (s): Norwegian
COMMUNITY NEWSPAPER

Vikebladet Vestposten
225237
Editorial: Sjogata 29, Ulsteinvik 6065
Tel: 47 70 01 85 00
Email: redaksjon@vikebladet.no **Web site:** http://www.vikebladet.no
Freq: 3 Times/Week
Profile: Vikebladet Vestposten is a local newspaper covering Ullstein and Hareid.
Language (s): Norwegian
COMMUNITY NEWSPAPER

Ytre Sogn Avis
225348
Owner: Avisforetaket Ytre Sogn AS
Editorial: Marcus Thranesgt.5, Høyanger 6995
Tel: 47 57 71 45 90
Email: redaksjon@ytresogn.no **Web site:** http://www.ytresogn.no
Freq: 2 Times/Week; **Circ:** 1556 Not Audited
Profile: Ytre Sogn Avis is a local newspaper for outer Sogn.
Language (s): Norwegian
COMMUNITY NEWSPAPER

Ytringen Avis
225217
Owner: Ytringen Avis AS
Editorial: Postboks 100, Kolvereid 7971
Tel: 47 74 39 60 50
Email: ytringen@ytringen.no **Web site:** http://www.ytringen.no
Freq: 2 Times/Week; **Circ:** 2787 Not Audited

Dagligleder/Redaktør: Tor Ludvigsen;
Redaksjonssjef: Morten Wengstad
Profile: Ytringen Avis is a local newspaper for outer Namdal and Bindal in Nord-Trøndelag.
Language (s): Norwegian
COMMUNITY NEWSPAPER

Oman

Time Difference: GMT +4
National Telephone Code: 968
Continent: Asia
Capital: Muscat

Newspapers

Gulf Madhyamam - Oman edition
689589
Owner: Gulf Madhyamam FZ LLC
Editorial: PO Box 331, NBD Area, Ruwi 411
Tel: 968 24 811085
Email: oman@gulfmadhyamam.net **Web site:** http://www.gulfmadhyamam.net
Freq: Daily; **Circ:** 21350 Rate Card
Bureau Chief: Rafeeq Muhammed
Profile: Gulf Madhyamam is an international Indian newspaper covering national and international news, current affairs, politics, business and sport. The newspaper is aimed at Malayalam speakers in the Gulf and publishes separate editions for the UAE, Saudi Arabia (Riyadh, Jeddah, Damam & Abha), Qatar, Oman, Bahrain and Kuwait. The newspaper was first published in 1999.
Language (s): Malayalam
Ad Rate: Full Page Mono 3000.00
Ad Rate: Full Page Colour 4500.00
Currency: Oman Rials
DAILY NEWSPAPER

Hi
475906
Owner: Muscat Media Group
Editorial: PO Box 770, Ruwi 112 **Tel:** 968 24 726666
Email: editor@timesofoman.com **Web site:** http://timesofoman.com/HiWeekend
Freq: Weekly; **Circ:** 54536 Publisher's Statement
Editor: Hubert Vaz
Profile: Hi is a tabloid-sized, weekly newspaper covering news, views, lifestyle features, information, games and puzzles. It is distributed free to Times of Oman subscribers and available free from various outlets and locations in Oman. It launched in 2007 and is published on Fridays.
Language (s): English
Ad Rate: Full Page Colour 1680.00
Currency: Oman Rials
DAILY NEWSPAPER

Koooora Wa Bas
902276
Owner: Sabco Group
Editorial: PO Box 3779, Building 413, Street 5204, Ruwi 112 **Tel:** 968 24 426900
Email: editor@onlykoooora.com **Web site:** http://www.kooorawabas.com
Freq: Weekly; **Circ:** 61000
Editor in Chief: Said Al Baraami; **Editor:** Maan Naddaf
Profile: Koooora Wa Bas (Only Football) is a free weekly newspaper covering national and international football. It launched in December 2008 and is published on Wednesdays.
Language (s): Arabic
Ad Rate: Full Page Colour 1595.00
Currency: Oman Rials
DAILY NEWSPAPER

Al Malaib
581303
Owner: Omani Establishment for Press, Printing, Publishing & Distribution LLC
Editorial: PO Box 463, Al Watan Building, Muscat 100 **Tel:** 968 24 491919
Email: editorial@almalaib.com **Web site:** http://www.almalaib.com
Freq: Weekly; **Circ:** 36030 Publisher's Statement
Editor In Chief: Sulaiman Al Taei; **Group Advertising Manager:** Mohan Pillai
Profile: Al Malaib is a tabloid-sized newspaper covering local and international sport. The weekly newspaper launched in 2006 and is published on Saturdays.
Language (s): Arabic
Ad Rate: Full Page Colour 1200.00
Currency: Oman Rials
DAILY NEWSPAPER

Muscat Daily
608719
Owner: Apex Press and Publishing
Editorial: PO Box 2616, Office A1, 1st Floor, Muscat 112 **Tel:** 968 24 799388
Email: muscatdaily@apexmedia.co.om **Web site:** http://www.muscatdaily.com
Freq: Daily; **Circ:** 30000 Publisher's Statement
Profile: Muscat Daily is a broadsheet newspaper covering local and international news, politics, business and sport. It launched in October 2009 and is published daily (Sat-Wed).
Language (s): English
DAILY NEWSPAPER

Oman Arabic Daily
156765
Owner: Oman Establishment for Press, Publication and Advertising
Editorial: PO Box 974, Madinat Al Ilam, Muscat 100
Tel: 968 24 649444
Email: local@omandaily.om **Web site:** http://omandaily.om
Freq: Daily; **Circ:** 41721 Publisher's Statement
Editor In Chief: Saif Al Mahruqi
Profile: Oman Arabic Daily is a newspaper covering news, business, politics, economics, culture and sport. It launched in 1972.
Language (s): Arabic
DAILY NEWSPAPER

Oman Daily Observer
156766
Owner: Oman Establishment for Press, Publication and Advertising
Editorial: PO Box 974, Madinat Al Ilam, Muscat 100
Tel: 968 24 649444
Email: editorobserver@gmail.com **Web site:** http://omanobserver.om
Freq: Daily; **Circ:** 55000 Publisher's Statement
Editor in Chief: Abdullah Al Shueili
Profile: Oman Daily Observer is a broadsheet-sized newspaper covering local, regional and international news, features, sport and business. It launched in 1981.
Language (s): English
DAILY NEWSPAPER

Oman Tribune
350450
Owner: Omani Establishment for Press, Printing, Publishing & Distribution LLC
Editorial: PO Box 463, Al Watan Building, Muscat 100 **Tel:** 968 24 491919
Email: editor@omantribune.com **Web site:** http://www.omantribune.com
Freq: Daily; **Circ:** 36030 Rate Card
Editor In Chief: Abdul Hamied Al Taie; **Editor:** Ajith Das; **Bureau Chief:** Ajay Kumar
Profile: Oman Tribune is a broadsheet-sized newspaper covering national and international news, current affairs, politics, business and sport. The daily newspaper launched in 2004.
Language (s): English
Ad Rate: Full Page Mono 1620.00
Ad Rate: Full Page Colour 3240.00
Currency: Oman Rials
DAILY NEWSPAPER

Al Roya Newspaper
620493
Owner: Al Roya Press and Publishing
Editorial: PO Box 343, Qurum, Muscat 118
Tel: 968 24 652400
Email: info@alroya.info **Web site:** http://alroya.om/ar
Freq: Daily; **Circ:** 25000 Publisher's Statement
CEO & Editor in Chief: Hatim Al Taie
Profile: Al Roya (The Vision) is a business newspaper covering economics, finance, investment, real estate, culture, sports, politics and arts. It launched in 2009 and is published daily, except Fridays.
Language (s): Arabic
Ad Rate: Full Page Mono 2080.00
Ad Rate: Full Page Colour 3744.00
Currency: Oman Rials
DAILY NEWSPAPER

Sabat Ayam
475905
Owner: Muscat Media Group
Editorial: PO Box 770, Ruwi 112 **Tel:** 968 24 726601
Email: 7ayam@shabiba.com
Freq: Weekly; **Circ:** 29985 Publisher's Statement
Editor In Chief: Mariam Al Zedjali
Profile: Sabat Ayam (7 Days) is a tabloid-sized, weekly newspaper covering local and international news, politics, sport, business, travel, cinema, entertainment, competitions, fashion, beauty, culture, health and medicine, art, relationships, food, home, parenting, religion and women's interests. Formerly called Al Youm Al Sabe, the newspaper launched in 2007 and is published on Fridays.
Language (s): Arabic
Ad Rate: Full Page Colour 1680.00
Currency: Oman Rials
DAILY NEWSPAPER

Al Shabiba
156767
Owner: Muscat Media Group
Editorial: PO Box 770, Ruwi 112 **Tel:** 968 24 726666
Email: editor@shabiba.com **Web site:** http://shabiba.com
Freq: Daily; **Circ:** 45000 Publisher's Statement
News Editor: Khalid Al Shami; **CEO & Editor In Chief:** Ahmed Al Zedjali
Profile: Al Shabiba is a newspaper covering local and international news, business, sports, culture and society. It launched in 1993 and is published daily, except Fridays.
Language (s): Arabic
Ad Rate: Full Page Mono 2700.00
Ad Rate: Full Page Colour 3600.00
Currency: Oman Rials
DAILY NEWSPAPER

Times of Oman
156768
Owner: Muscat Media Group
Editorial: PO Box 770, Ruwi 112 **Tel:** 968 24 726666
Email: editor@timesofoman.com **Web site:** http://www.timesofoman.com
Freq: Daily; **Circ:** 40000 Publisher's Statement
Profile: Times of Oman is a broadsheet-sized newspaper covering local and international news, politics, business and sport, as well as a section of news and features from India. It launched in 1975 and is published daily, except Fridays. The newspaper

includes a monthly magazine, Faces, in the last week of every month.
Language (s): English
Ad Rate: Full Page Mono 2700.00
Ad Rate: Full Page Colour 3600.00
Currency: Oman Rials
DAILY NEWSPAPER

Al Watan
156769
Owner: Omani Establishment for Press, Printing, Publishing & Distribution LLC
Editorial: PO Box 463, Al Watan Building, Muscat 100 **Tel:** 968 24 491919
Email: local@alwatan.com.om **Web site:** http://www.alwatan.com
Freq: Daily; **Circ:** 62000 Publisher's Statement
News Editor: Abdullah Al Jahouri; **Picture Editor:** Ibrahim Al Shukeili; **Editor In Chief:** Mohammed Al Taie; **Group Advertising Manager:** Mohan Pillai
Profile: Al Watan is a daily newspaper covering news, economy, sports and culture. It was first published in 1971, and includes a weekly health supplement - Sehatuna - on Tuesdays.
Language (s): Arabic
Ad Rate: Full Page Mono 2160.00
Ad Rate: Full Page Colour 4320.00
Currency: Oman Rials
DAILY NEWSPAPER

The Week
351831
Owner: Apex Press and Publishing
Editorial: PO Box 2616, Office A1, 1st Floor, Muscat 112 **Tel:** 968 24 799388
Email: theweek@apexmedia.co.om **Web site:** http://www.theweek.co.om
Freq: Weekly; **Circ:** 51000 BPA Worldwide
Editor In Chief: Sameer Zakwani
Profile: The Week is a free, tabloid-sized weekly newspaper covering local news, entertainment, motoring, sports, leisure, design and food. It launched in March 2003 and is published on Thursdays.
Language (s): English
Ad Rate: Full Page Colour 1945.00
Currency: Oman Rials
DAILY NEWSPAPER

News Service/Syndicate

Oman News Agency
370501
Owner: Ministry of Information, Oman
Editorial: PO Box 3659, Ministry of Information Building, Muscat 112 **Tel:** 968 24 944700
Email: onaarabic@hotmail.com **Web site:** http://www.omannews.gov.om
General Manager & Editor in Chief: Mohammed Al Araimi
Profile: Oman News Agency is the official news agency of the Sultanate of Oman. It was founded in 1987 and covers government news and issues of national importance.
Language (s): Arabic
NEWS SERVICE/SYNDICATE

Pakistan

Time Difference: GMT +5
National Telephone Code: 92
Continent: Asia
Capital: Islamabad

Newspapers

Aaj
460461
Editorial: Sikandar Pura, G.T. Road, Peshawar 25000 **Tel:** 92 912570501
Email: dailyaaj@brain.net.pk **Web site:** http://dailyaaj.com.pk
Freq: Daily; **Circ:** 50001 Not Audited
Editor in Chief: Abdul Wahid Yousafi
Profile: Daily newspaper published in Urdu. Covers general news and current events
Language (s): Urdu
DAILY NEWSPAPER

Aghaz
460494
Editorial: 11-Japan Mansion, Preedy Street, Saddar, Karachi 74200 **Tel:** 92 212721688
Email: bilal_aghaz@yahoo.com
Freq: Daily; **Circ:** 64001 Not Audited
Editor in Chief: Muhammad Farooqui
Profile: Daily newspaper published in Urdu. Covers general news and current events
Language (s): Urdu
DAILY NEWSPAPER

Business Recorder
360224
Editorial: Recorder House, 531 Business Recorder Road, Karachi 74550 **Tel:** 92 212250071
Email: ed.khi@br-mail.com **Web site:** http://www.brecorder.com
Freq: Daily; **Circ:** 115251 Not Audited
Publisher: Asif Zuberi; **Editor:** Wamiq Zuberi
Profile: Daily newspaper published in English. Covers business and financial news.
Language (s): English
DAILY NEWSPAPER

Daily Express
460449
Editorial: Korangi Creak Road, Plot No. 5, Expressway Off Korangi Road, Karachi 75500
Tel: 92 21 580-0051
Web site: http://www.express.com.pk
Freq: Daily; **Circ:** 145003 Not Audited
Profile: Daily newspaper published in Urdu. Covers general news and current.
Language (s): Urdu
DAILY NEWSPAPER

Daily Jang
460451
Editorial: Jang Press Building, I.I. Chundrigar Road, Karachi 74200 **Tel:** 92 212637111
Web site: http://www.jang.com.pk
Freq: Daily; **Circ:** 800001 Not Audited
Profile: Covers news topics.
Language (s): Urdu
DAILY NEWSPAPER

Daily Kawish
460477
Owner: Kawish Group of Publications (The)
Editorial: B/2 Civil Lines, Hyderabad 71000
Tel: 92 222780026
Email: kawish12@gmail.com **Web site:** http://www.dailykawish.com
Freq: Daily; **Circ:** 80001 Not Audited
Editor: Ali Kazi
Profile: Daily newspaper published in Urdu. Covers general news and current events
Language (s): Sindhi
DAILY NEWSPAPER

Daily Messenger
915341
Editorial: Office No. 1, 2nd Floor, Abdullah Chamber, Dr. Billimoria Street, Off I.I Chundrigar Road, Karachi
Email: messengerdaily@yahoo.com
Freq: Daily
Editor: Taqi Alvi
Profile: Covers national and international news.
Language (s): English
DAILY NEWSPAPER

Daily Nawa-i-Waqt
460450
Owner: Nipco House
Editorial: Nipco House, 4 Shaarey Fatima Jinnah, Lahore 54000 **Tel:** 92 42 6367580
Email: editor@nawaiwaqt.com.pk **Web site:** http://www.nawaiwaqt.com.pk
Freq: Daily; **Circ:** 350002 Not Audited
Editor in Chief: Majeed Nizami
Profile: Provides national and international news.
Language (s): Urdu
DAILY NEWSPAPER

Daily News
460442
Editorial: I.I. Chundrigar Road, Karachi 74200
Tel: 92 212637111
Email: editorjang@jang.com.pk **Web site:** http://www.jang-group.com
Freq: Daily; **Circ:** 80002 Not Audited
Editor in Chief: Mir Shakil-ur-Rahman
Profile: It is a daily newspaper printed in English covering Local Regional National and International news.
Language (s): English
DAILY NEWSPAPER

Daily Wahdat
459009
Tel: 92 912214154
Email: editorwahdat@gmail.com **Web site:** http://dailywahdat.com.pk
Freq: Daily; **Circ:** 60002 Not Audited
Editor: Syed Shah
Profile: Daily newspaper printed in Pashto and founded in 1976. Appears to cover general news and current events
Language (s): Pashto (Eastern)
DAILY NEWSPAPER

Dawn
360225
Owner: Dawn Group of Newspapers
Editorial: Haroon House, Dr. Zia Uddin Ahmed Rd, Karachi 74200 **Tel:** 92 21 111-444-7777
Email: editor@dawn.com **Web site:** http://www.dawn.com
Freq: Daily; **Circ:** 140002 Not Audited
Editor: Jahanzaib Haque; **Editor:** Abbas Nasier
Profile: Founded in 1941, covers general news and current events.
Language (s): English
DAILY NEWSPAPER

The Express Tribune
830700
Editorial: 5 Expressway, Off Korangi Road, Karachi 75500 **Tel:** 92 21 111397737
Email: editorial@tribune.com.pk **Web site:** http://tribune.com.pk
Freq: Daily
Editor: Vaqas Asghar
Profile: Partnering with the International Herald Tribune, launched as the first internationally affiliated newspaper of Pakistan. Covers national news, politics, the economy, foreign policy, investment, sports and culture.
Language (s): English
DAILY NEWSPAPER

Ibrat Hyderabad
460493
Editorial: Ibrat Building Gadi Khata, P.O. Box 91, Hyderabad 73000 **Tel:** 92 22 2781574
Email: ibrat@yahoo.com **Web site:** http://www.dailyibrat.com
Freq: Daily; **Circ:** 50003 Not Audited
Editor in Chief: Kazi Asad Abid

Profile: Covers current events, news and lifestyle
Language (s): Sindhi
DAILY NEWSPAPER

Juraat
460474
Editorial: Juraat House, Aril Jiyeja Street, II Chundrigar Road, Karachi 74000 **Tel:** 92 212637641-44
Email: juraat@juraat.com **Web site:** http://www.juraat.com
Freq: Daily; **Circ:** 72003 Not Audited
Editor in Chief: Mukhtar Aaqil
Profile: Daily newspaper published in Urdu. Appears to cover general news and current events
Language (s): Urdu
DAILY NEWSPAPER

Khadim-e-Watan
460478
Editorial: B/2 Civil Lines, Hyderabad 71000
Tel: 92 222780026
Web site: http://www.dailykawish.com
Freq: Daily; **Circ:** 50002 Not Audited
Profile: Daily newspaper published in Sindhi. Covers general news and current events
Language (s): Sindhi
DAILY NEWSPAPER

The Nation
360223
Owner: Nawa-e-Waqt Group
Editorial: Nipco House, 4 Shaarey Fatima, Jinnah, Lahore 54000 **Tel:** 92 42 6367580
Email: editor@nation.com.pk **Web site:** http://www.nation.com.pk
Freq: Daily; **Circ:** 85002 Not Audited
Editor in Chief: Majeed Nizami
Profile: Daily newspaper published in English. Covers city, national, sports, foreign and commerce news.
Language (s): English
DAILY NEWSPAPER

The News International
460441
Editorial: Al Rehman Building, I.I Chundrigar Road, Karachi 74200 **Tel:** 92 212637111
Web site: http://www.thenews.com.pk
Freq: Daily; **Circ:** 140002 Not Audited
Editor: Talat Aslam; **Editor in Chief:** Mir Shakil-ur-Rahman
Profile: Daily newspaper published In English Covering All Types Of News.
Language (s): English
DAILY NEWSPAPER

Pakistan Observer
460453
Editorial: Ali Akbar House, Markaz G-8, Islambad 143001 **Tel:** 92 512852027 8
Email: observer@pakobserver.net **Web site:** http://www.pakobserver.net
Freq: Daily; **Circ:** 53002 Not Audited
Editor in Chief: Zahid Malik
Profile: Daily newspaper published in English. Covers general news and current events
Language (s): English
DAILY NEWSPAPER

Qaumi Akhbar
460490
Editorial: 14 Ramzan Chambers, Dr. Billimoria Street, Off Chundrigar Road, Karachi 74200
Tel: 92 21 111778899
Email: qaumi@hotmail.com
Freq: Daily; **Circ:** 90003 Not Audited
Editor in Chief: Ilyas Shakir
Profile: Newspaper published in Urdu. Covers general news and current events
Language (s): Urdu
DAILY NEWSPAPER

News Service/Syndicate

Associated Press of Pakistan (APP)
467634
Editorial: 18, Mauve Area G- 7/1, Islamabad
Tel: 92 512203064
Email: news@app.com.pk **Web site:** http://www.app.com.pk
Freq: Daily
Bureau Chief: Farooq Ahmad
Profile: Covers the latest international and domestic news.
Language (s): Urdu
NEWS SERVICE/SYNDICATE

Bloomberg News - Islamabad Bureau
911190
Owner: Bloomberg News
Editorial: Unavailable, Islamabad
Tel: 92 51 843 0430
Profile: Bloomberg News is an international wire service, including print, television, radio and Internet, that provides news, data and analysis to business and media professionals around the world. Bloomberg publishes over 6,000 stories on an average day, syndicating to over 450 newspapers worldwide with a combined circulation of 80 million people. The service is part of Bloomberg Financial Markets and covers business, financial and economic issues, as well as technology, international, national, political, entertainment and sports news. In 2010, it launched a government platform, Bloomberg Government and breaking news platform, Bloomberg First Word. In 2011, it launched its first opinion section, Bloomberg View. In 2015, Bloomberg Gadfly was formed, which is described as a fast business commentary team.
Language (s): English
NEWS SERVICE/SYNDICATE

Online International News Network
467625
Editorial: House 69 Bhittai Road, F-714, Islamabad 143001 **Tel:** 92 51 8435137
Email: online@dsl.net.pk **Web site:** http://www.onlinenews.com.pk
Freq: Daily
Editor in Chief: Mohsin Baig; **Editor:** Sohail Iqbal; **Editor:** Zia Islam; **Editor:** Aneela ud Din
Profile: Online news service covering international, political, financial, political and sports news
Language (s): English
NEWS SERVICE/SYNDICATE

Pak Tribune
467635
Editorial: 30 Kurshid Alam Rood, Westridge 1, Rawalpindi 46000 **Tel:** 92 515475907
Email: editor@paktribune.com **Web site:** http://www.paktribune.com
Editor: Riaz Jafri
Profile: General news and current events in Pakistan and the surrounding region
Language (s): Urdu
NEWS SERVICE/SYNDICATE

Pakistan Press International (PPI)
467633
Editorial: Press Centre, 1st Floor Shahrah-e-Kamal Attaturk, Karachi 75400 **Tel:** 92 21 2630562
Email: pressrelease@ppinewsagency.com **Web site:** http://www.ppinewsagency.com
Editor: Nasir Aijaz; **Editor in Chief:** Farooq Moin
Profile: Covers general news and current events in Pakistan and the surrounding region
Language (s): Urdu
NEWS SERVICE/SYNDICATE

South Asian News Agency (SANA)
467623
Editorial: 1st Floor Chinar Chamber, Street No. 48, G-6/ 1-1, Islamabad **Tel:** 92 51 2870134
Email: info@sananews.com.pk **Web site:** http://www.sananews.net
Editor in Chief: Shakeel Ahmed Turabi
Profile: Covers news topics.
Language (s): English
NEWS SERVICE/SYNDICATE

Palestine

Time Difference: GMT +2
National Telephone Code: 970
Continent: Asia
Capital: Ramallah

Newspapers

Al Ayyam
324967
Owner: Al Ayyam Printing & Publishing
Editorial: PO Box 1987, Building 39, Betunia, Ramallah **Tel:** 970 2 298 7341
Email: news@al-ayyam.ps **Web site:** http://www.al-ayyam.ps
Freq: Daily; **Circ:** 18000 Publisher's Statement
News Editor: Abed-Rahman Abu-Shamalah; **General Manager:** Mahdi Al Masri; **Editor In Chief:** Akram Haniah
Profile: Al Ayyam (The Days) is a daily newspaper covering national and international news, current affairs, politics and business. It was first published in 1995.
Language (s): Arabic
DAILY NEWSPAPER

Al Hayat Al-Jadedah
431750
Owner: Al Hayat Al-Jadeda Company
Editorial: PO Box 1882, Noor Street, Ramallah
Tel: 970 2 240 7252
Email: alhayat@p-ol.com **Web site:** http://www.alhaya.ps
Freq: Daily; **Circ:** 10623 Publisher's Statement
Editor in Chief: Mahmmoud Abu Elheja; **News Editor:** Wael Barghouthi; **General Manager:** Majed Rimawi
Profile: Al Hayat Al-Jadedah (The New Life) is a daily newspaper covering news, current affairs, politics and sport. It includes weekly business supplement Hayat Wa Souq on Sundays, and was first published in 1995.
Language (s):
Ad Rate: Full Page Mono 3000.00
Ad Rate: Full Page Colour 5000.00
Currency: United States Dollars
DAILY NEWSPAPER

Kul Al Arab
324968
Owner: Kul Al Arab
Editorial: PO Box 430, Al Namsawi Street, Nazareth
Tel: 970 4 655 8000
Email: kul@alarab.net **Web site:** http://www.alarab.com
Freq: Weekly; **Circ:** 40000 Publisher's Statement
Advertising Manager: Mohamad Hassan; **Editor:** Saeed Hassanein
Profile: Kul Al Arab is a weekly Arabic newspaper covering national, regional and international news, current affairs, politics, entertainment and events in

Palestine

the Arab world. It launched in 1987 and is published on Fridays.
Language (s): Arabic
DAILY NEWSPAPER

Al Quds 326111
Owner: Al Quds
Editorial: PO Box 19788, Salah El Din Street, East Jerusalem **Tel:** 972 2 627 2663
Email: contact@alquds.com **Web site:** http://www.alquds.com
Freq: Daily; **Circ:** 70000 Publisher's Statement
News Editor: Mohammad Abu Libdeh; **Publisher:** Walid Abu Zalaf; **Head of News:** Ziad Abu Zalaf; **Advertising Manager:** Hani Al Abbassi; **News Editor:** Amjad Omari
Profile: Al Quds is a daily Arabic newspaper covering news, politics, current affairs, business and sport. It was first published in 1951.
Language (s): Arabic
DAILY NEWSPAPER

News Service/Syndicate

Agence France-Presse - Gaza Bureau 432690
Owner: Agence France-Presse
Editorial: PO Box 1133, Gaza **Tel:** 970 8 282 1533
Email: sakher.abueloun@afp.com **Web site:** http://www.afp.com
Bureau Chief: Sakher Abu El Oun
Profile: Gaza bureau of the AFP news agency - covers the Palestinian territories.
Language (s): Arabic
NEWS SERVICE/SYNDICATE

Associated Press - Gaza Bureau 432693
Owner: Associated Press
Editorial: 11th Floor, Al Jalaa Tower, Al Jalaa Street, Gaza **Tel:** 970 8 284 1583
Email: wshurafa@ap.org **Web site:** http://www.ap.org
Producer: Wafaa Shurafa
Profile: Gaza bureau of international wire agency - covers Gaza and the West Bank.
Language (s): Arabic
NEWS SERVICE/SYNDICATE

Associated Press - Ramallah Bureau 432692
Owner: Associated Press
Editorial: El-Bireh Commercial Tower, Ramallah, West Bank **Tel:** 970 2 240 8255
Email: jhassan@ap.org **Web site:** http://www.ap.org
News Producer: Jalal Al-Bwaitel
Profile: Ramallah Bureau of the Associated Press and APTN.
Language (s): English
NEWS SERVICE/SYNDICATE

Palestine News & Info Agency 432688
Owner: Palestine News & Info Agency
Editorial: Al Masayef, Ramallah **Tel:** 970 2 298 7767
Email: edit@wafa.ps **Web site:** http://www.wafa.ps
Editor: Fadel Atwana; **Editor:** Atlal Darwich; **Editor:** Bilal Ghaith
Profile: Official government news agency.
Language (s): Arabic
NEWS SERVICE/SYNDICATE

Palestine News Network 432694
Owner: Palestine News Network
Editorial: Murra Building, Jerusalem-Hebron Road, Bethlehem **Tel:** 970 2 276 6068
Email: monjed@pnn.ps **Web site:** http://www.pnn.ps
Editor in Chief: Monjed Jadou
Profile: Palestine News Network is a news agency supplying news bulletins to over 13 local Palestinian radio stations in the West Bank and Gaza. Also provides a 24-hour updated news ticker to 10 Palestinian TV stations.
Language (s): Arabic
NEWS SERVICE/SYNDICATE

Palestinian Media and Communications Company 432689
Owner: Palestinian Media and Communications Company
Editorial: PO Box 909, Al Shikh Tower, Ramallah **Tel:** 970 2 298 4858
Email: booking@alfalstiniah.tv **Web site:** http://alfalstiniah.tv
Photographer: Dawood Akealeh; **Office Manager:** Khawla Shalabi; **General Manager:** Maher Shalabi
Profile: Palestinian Media and Communications Company provides news correspondence and production services to television stations throughout the region using the latest satellite technology and equipment. Located in Ramallah in the West Bank, with studios in East Jerusalem and Gaza City.
Language (s): Arabic
NEWS SERVICE/SYNDICATE

Reuters - Ramallah Bureau 432691
Owner: Thomson Reuters
Editorial: PO Box 1079, 5th Floor, Ibn Khaldoun Building, Ramallah **Tel:** 970 2 295 0430
Email: jerusalem.newsroom@thomsonreuters.com
Web site: http://www.reuters.com
Photographer: Saad Hawari
Profile: Ramallah bureau of international news wire service.
Language (s): Arabic
NEWS SERVICE/SYNDICATE

Panama

Time Difference: GMT -5
National Telephone Code: 507
Continent: The Americas
Capital: Panama City

Newspapers

Crítica (Panamá) 156844
Owner: Editora Panamá América SA
Editorial: Av. Ricardo J. Alfaro, al lado de la USMA, Apdo. 0834-02787, Panama **Tel:** 507 2307777 7647
Email: redaccion.critica@epasa.com **Web site:** http://www.critica.com.pa
Freq: Daily; **Circ:** 65000 Not Audited
National News Editor: Mayra Montenegro
Profile: Newspaper containing national and international news, business, sports and events.
Language (s): Spanish
DAILY NEWSPAPER

Día a Día 416977
Owner: Editora Panamá América SA
Editorial: Av. Ricardo J. Alfaro, Apdo. 0834-02787, Panama **Tel:** 507 230-7777
Email: redaccion-diaadia@epasa.com **Web site:** http://www.diaadia.com.pa
Freq: Daily
Editor in Chief: Joyce Baloyes; **Editor:** Diamar Diaz; **Editor:** Elizabeth Muñoz de Lao; **Editor:** Evidelia Velazquez
Profile: Newspaper covering national and international news, politics, the economy, society, sport and culture.
Language (s): Spanish
DAILY NEWSPAPER

Diario Panamá América 156853
Owner: Editora Panamá América SA
Editorial: Av. Ricardo J. Alfaro, al lado de la USMA, Apdo. B-4, zona 9-A, Panama **Tel:** 507 2307777 7612
Email: redaccion.digital@epasa.com **Web site:** http://www.panamaamerica.com.pa
Freq: Daily; **Circ:** 30000 Not Audited
Editor: Rosa Guizado; **Editor:** Guido Rodríguez
Profile: Newspaper covering national and international news and current events; includes finance, business, politics, sport and entertainment.
Language (s): Spanish
DAILY NEWSPAPER

La Estrella de Panamá 156852
Owner: La Estrella de Panamá
Editorial: Calle Alejandro A. Duque y Av. Frangipany, Apdo. 0815-00507, zona 4, Panama
Tel: 507 2040964
Email: online@laestrella.com.pa **Web site:** http://www.laestrella.com.pa
Freq: Daily; **Circ:** 21080 Not Audited
Editor: Carlos Castillo
Profile: Newspaper covering national and international news, politics, economics, finance, business, culture and sport.
Language (s): Spanish
DAILY NEWSPAPER

Panamá América 883821
Owner: Editora Panamá América S.A.
Editorial: Ave. Ricardo J. Alfaro, Apartado B4, Zona 9A, Panama **Tel:** 507 230-7704
Email: redaccion.digital@epasa.com **Web site:** http://www.panamaamerica.com.pa
Freq: Daily
Chief of Information: Leonardo Flores; **Editor:** Alberto Pinto
Profile: Established in 1925 and provides information and news on politics, economics, national and international articles.
Language (s): Spanish
DAILY NEWSPAPER

La Prensa (Panamá) 156854
Owner: Corporación La Prensa
Editorial: Av. 12 de octubre, Apdo. 0819-05620, El Dorado, Hato Pintado Panama **Tel:** 507 222-1222
Email: redaccion@prensa.com **Web site:** http://www.prensa.com
Freq: Daily; **Circ:** 44000 Not Audited
Editor in Chief: Juan Luis Batista; **Editor:** Elizabeth Garrido
Profile: Newspaper covering national and international news, politics, lifestyle, food, cinema and sport.
Language (s): Spanish
DAILY NEWSPAPER

El Siglo 156686
Owner: Geo-Media SA
Tel: 507 2040000
Email: redaccion@elsiglo.com **Web site:** http://elsiglo.com.pa
Freq: Daily; **Circ:** 35000 Not Audited
Editor in Chief: Magaly Montilla
Profile: Regional newspaper covering national, international and regional news and current affairs; includes politics, the economy, sport and society.
Language (s): Spanish
DAILY NEWSPAPER

Papua New Guinea

Time Difference: GMT +10
National Telephone Code: 675
Continent: Oceania
Capital: Port Moresby (New Guinea)

Newspapers

The National 539105
Owner: Pacific Star Limited
Editorial: PO Box 6817, Boroko, Papua New Guinea
Email: editorial@thenational.com.pg **Web site:** http://www.thenational.com.pg
Freq: Daily
Profile: National English daily, published out of Port Moresby, providing analysis of national and international news.
Language (s): English
DAILY NEWSPAPER

Post-Courier 539108
Owner: South Pacific Post Pty Ltdf
Editorial: Lawes Road, Konedobu, National Capital District, Port Moresby **Tel:** 675 309 1000
Email: postcourier@spp.com.pg **Web site:** http://www.postcourier.com.pg
Freq: Daily; **Circ:** 26262 Publisher's Statement
Editor: Alexander Rheeney
Profile: Newspaper covering national news and current affairs. The Post-Courier is the oldest selling newspaper in Papua New Guinea and is published Monday to Friday in English. The newspaper is distributed mostly by air throughout Papua New Guinea.
Language (s): English
DAILY NEWSPAPER

Community Newspaper

Wantok Niuspepa 539202
Owner: Word Publishing Co Ltd
Editorial: Office 02, Section 58 Allotment, 3 Waigani Drive, Papua New Guinea
Web site: http://www.wantokniuspepa.com
Freq: Weekly; **Circ:** 12000 Not Audited
Profile: Newspaper in Papua New Guinea published weekly in Port Moresby and is sold and distributed throughout the country.
Language (s): English
COMMUNITY NEWSPAPER

Paraguay

Time Difference: GMT -4
National Telephone Code: 595
Continent: The Americas
Capital: Asunción

Newspapers

ABC Color 156856
Owner: Editorial AZETA SA
Editorial: Yegros 745, Aptdo. 1421, Asuncion
Tel: 595 21 4151000
Email: azeta@abc.com.py **Web site:** http://www.abc.com.py
Freq: Daily; **Circ:** 46000 Not Audited
Manager: Rufo Medina; **Production Manager:** Marcial Sanchez; **Director:** Aldo Zuccolillo
Profile: Newspaper providing national and international news, includes politics, finance, economics and law.
Language (s): Spanish
DAILY NEWSPAPER

Crónica 410549
Owner: Grafica y Editorial Intersudamericana S.A.
Editorial: Av. Zavala Cue entre 1 y 2, Zona Sur, Fernando De La Mora (central) **Tel:** 595 21 512520
Email: digital@cronica.com.py **Web site:** http://www.cronica.com.py
Freq: Daily; **Circ:** 30000 Not Audited
Editor: Neri Insfran; **Editor in Chief:** Nestor Izaurralde
Profile: National newspaper.
Language (s): Spanish
DAILY NEWSPAPER

Diario Popular 156688
Owner: Grupo Multimedia SA
Editorial: Avenida Mariscal Lopez 2948, Aptdo. 1805, Asuncion **Tel:** 595 21 603400
Email: popular@mm.com.py **Web site:** http://www.diariopopular.com.py
Freq: Daily; **Circ:** 52000 Not Audited
Editor: Adolfo Jiménez; **Director:** Amanda Pedrozo;
Editor in Chief: Carlos Sosa
Profile: Newspaper covering national and international news, includes politics, sport and culture.
Language (s): Spanish
Ad Rate: Full Page Mono 2.67
Currency: United States Dollars
DAILY NEWSPAPER

Diario Vanguardia 156687
Owner: Editora del Este S.A.
Editorial: Avenida San Blas Km. 8 Acaray, Ciudad Del Este (alto Paraná) **Tel:** 595 61 575530
Email: diariovanguardia@diariovanguardia.com.py
Web site: http://www.diariovanguardia.com.py
Freq: Daily; **Circ:** 110000 Not Audited
Editor in Chief: Thomas Beck; **Director:** Héctor Guerín
Profile: Regional newspaper focusing on business, economics, politics, education, tourism and union news from the Departamento de Alto Paraná, Canindeyu, and Itapua. Includes financial statistics and interviews.
Language (s): Spanish
DAILY NEWSPAPER

La Nación 160997
Owner: Grafica y Editorial Intersudamericana S.A.
Editorial: Av Zavala Cue entre 1 y 2, Zona Sur, Fernando De La Mora (central) **Tel:** 595 21 512520
Email: redaccion@lanacion.com.py **Web site:** http://www.lanacion.com.py
Freq: Daily; **Circ:** 23580 Not Audited
Director: Alejandro Dominguez Wilson Smith; **Editor in Chief:** Ricardo Nestor Inzaurralde; **General Manager:** Gabriel Taboada; **International News Editor:** Enrique Vargas Peña
Profile: Newspaper covering national and international news, politics, economics and sport.
Language (s): Spanish
DAILY NEWSPAPER

Ultima Hora 156859
Owner: Editorial El País SA
Editorial: Benjamin Constant 658, Asuncion
Tel: 595 21 496261
Email: ultimahora@uhora.com.py **Web site:** http://www.ultimahora.com.py
Freq: Daily; **Circ:** 14000 Not Audited
Editor in Chief: Miguel Ortíz; **Editor:** Alejandro Peralta
Profile: National newspaper.
Language (s): Spanish
DAILY NEWSPAPER

Peru

Time Difference: GMT -5
National Telephone Code: 51
Continent: The Americas
Capital: Lima

Newspapers

Aja 365339
Owner: Empresa Periodistica Nacional SA
Editorial: Jr Jorge Salazar Araoz 171, Urb. Santa Catalina, La Victoria, Lima **Tel:** 51 1 690 8080
Web site: http://www.aja.com.pe
Freq: Daily
Profile: Newspaper covering news and current-affairs, politics, culture, events and sports.
Language (s): Spanish
DAILY NEWSPAPER

El Comercio (Perú) 156957
Owner: Grupo El Comercio SA
Editorial: Jr. Miro Quesada #300, Lima 1
Tel: 51 1 311-6310
Email: editorweb@comercio.com.pe **Web site:** http://elcomercio.pe
Freq: Daily; **Circ:** 185000 Not Audited
News Director: Mario Cortijo; **Editor in Chief:** Hugo Guerra; **Director:** Francisco Miro Quesada;
Manager: Gabriel Miro Quesada Cisneros
Profile: Te informa lo que sucede en el Perú y el Mundo. Informs you what's happening in Peru and the world.
Language (s): Spanish
DAILY NEWSPAPER

Correo 365256
Owner: Empresa Periodistica Nacional SA
Editorial: Jr Jorge Salazar Araoz 171, Urb. Santa Catalina, La Victoria, Lima **Tel:** 51 1 690-8080
Web site: http://www.correoperu.com.pe
Freq: Daily
Editor: Sileña Cisneros; **Editor in Chief:** Marlene Huamanlazo

Profile: Newspaper containing national and international news and current-affairs, politics, the economy, culture and sports.
Language (s): Spanish
DAILY NEWSPAPER

Diario Correo 157183
Owner: EPENSA
Editorial: Jorge Salazar Araoz 171, Santa Catalina La Victoria, Lima **Tel:** 51 1 631-1111
Email: diariocorreo@grupoepensa.pe **Web site:** http://www.correoperu.com.pe
Freq: Daily; **Circ:** 280000 Not Audited
Director: Iván Slocovich Pardo
Profile: Periódico centrándose en la política, la economía, la cultura, el deporte, gastronomía, noticias de la ciudad y del mundo. Newspaper focusing on politics, economics, culture, sports, community and world news.
Language (s): Spanish
DAILY NEWSPAPER

El Expreso 160835
Owner: Editora Sindesa SA
Editorial: Giron Antonio de Elizalde 753, Altura quadra 8, Av. Argentina, Lima **Tel:** 51 1 612 4000
Email: israel.fernandez@expreso.com.pe **Web site:** http://www.expreso.com.pe
Freq: Daily; **Circ:** 60000 Not Audited
Director: Luis García Miró; **Editor:** Jose Giles; **Editor in Chief:** Ivan Pisua
Profile: Newspaper focusing on national and international news, sport, politics and culture.
Language (s): Spanish
DAILY NEWSPAPER

Extra 365237
Owner: Editora Sindesa SA
Editorial: Giron Antonio de Elizalde 753, Altura quadra 8, Av. Argentina, Lima **Tel:** 51 1 612 4000
Freq: Daily
Editor in Chief: Richard Romero
Profile: National newspaper covering news and current-affairs.
Language (s): Spanish
DAILY NEWSPAPER

Gestión 156955
Owner: Grupo El Comercio S.A
Editorial: Jiron Miro Quesada 247, Piso 8, Lima 1 **Tel:** 51 1 311-6500
Email: gestion2@diariogestion.com.pe **Web site:** http://www.gestion.pe
Freq: Daily; **Circ:** 25000 Not Audited
Profile: National newspaper focusing on business, economics and finance.
Language (s): Spanish
Ad Rate: Full Page Mono 368.53
Currency: Peru Nuevos Soles
DAILY NEWSPAPER

El Men 365619
Owner: Montecristo Editores SAC
Editorial: Jiron Yungay 820-840, Magdalena del Mar, Lima **Tel:** 51 13366465
Email: elmen@elmen.pe **Web site:** http://elmen.pe
Freq: Daily
Editor in Chief: Pascual Fretel Gutierrez; **Editor:** Danilo Riveros
Profile: Newspaper covering news and current-affairs.
Language (s): Spanish
DAILY NEWSPAPER

Ojo 156958
Owner: Familia Agois Banchero
Editorial: Jorge Salazar Araoz 171, Urbanizacion Santa Catalina la Victoria, altura de la cuadra 11 de Nicolas de Ariola, Lima **Tel:** 51 1 690 8080
Email: optativos@epensa.com.pe **Web site:** http://www.ojo.com.pe
Freq: Daily; **Circ:** 90000 Not Audited
Editor in Chief: Carlos Basurto; **Editor:** Luis Angeles Laynes; **Director:** Victor Ramirez Canales
Profile: Newspaper covering national news, culture, entertainment and sport.
Language (s): Spanish
DAILY NEWSPAPER

El Peruano 160834
Owner: Editora Perú
Editorial: Av. Alfonso Ugarte 873, Lima **Tel:** 51 1 315-0400
Web site: http://www.elperuano.com.pe
Freq: Daily; **Circ:** 21000 Not Audited
Editor in Chief: Cesar Chaman
Profile: Newspaper covering national and international news, politics, sport and culture.
Language (s): Spanish
DAILY NEWSPAPER

El Popular 366227
Owner: Grupo la Republica SA
Editorial: Jiron Camana 320, Cercado de Lima, Lima **Tel:** 51 17116010
Web site: http://www.elpopular.com.pe
Freq: Daily
Editor: Dennis Alvaro; **News Editor:** Jorge Paucar
Profile: Newspaper covering news and current-affairs, politics, sports and culture.
Language (s): Spanish
DAILY NEWSPAPER

La Razon 365717
Owner: Montecristo Editores SAC
Editorial: Jiron Yungay 820-840, Magdalena del Mar, Lima **Tel:** 51 (511)336-6465
Email: larazon@larazon.pe **Web site:** http://www.larazon.com.pe
Freq: Daily
Profile: Newspaper covering news and current-affairs and politics.
Language (s): Spanish
DAILY NEWSPAPER

La República 156961
Owner: Grupo La República SA
Editorial: Jiron Camana 320, Cercado de Lima, Lima **Tel:** 51 1 711-6000
Email: director@larepublica.pe **Web site:** http://larepublica.pe
Freq: Daily; **Circ:** 125000 Not Audited
Director: Gustavo Mohme; **Editor:** Percy Ruiz
Profile: Newspaper covering national and international news, politics, economics, finance, business, culture and sport.
Language (s): Spanish
DAILY NEWSPAPER

Todo Sport 160823
Owner: Montecristo Editores SAC
Editorial: Jiron Yungay 820-840, Magdalena del Mar, Lima **Tel:** 51 13366465
Web site: http://www.todosport.com.pe
Freq: Daily; **Circ:** 18000 Not Audited
Editor: Walter Arana
Profile: Newspaper focusing on sports; includes previews, reports and results.
Language (s): Spanish
DAILY NEWSPAPER

News Service/Syndicate

Andina 353228
Editorial: Av. Alfonso Ugarte 873, Lima 1 **Tel:** 51 1 315-0400
Email: andina@editoraperu.com.pe **Web site:** http://www.andina.com.pe
Editor in Chief: Rodolfo Espinal
Profile: Covers news related to politics, economy, culture and entertainment.
Language (s): Spanish
NEWS SERVICE/SYNDICATE

Philippines

Time Difference: GMT +8
National Telephone Code: 63
Continent: Asia
Capital: Manila

Newspapers

Abante 156823
Owner: Monica Publishing Corporation
Editorial: #167 Liberty Bldg. Roberto S. Oca St, Port Area, Manila 1002 **Tel:** 63 2 52 73 355
Email: abante@abante-tonite.com **Web site:** http://www.abante.com.ph
Freq: Daily; **Circ:** 420000 Not Audited
Manager: Ron Tamayo
Profile: VISION AND MISSION "To be the leading and trend setting tabloid in the newspaper industry, ran by highly and technologically creative and innovative Filipino workers, committed and dedicated to serve it's readers by providing credible and accurate news reports and stories that will satisfy the newspaper buying public."
Language (s): English
DAILY NEWSPAPER

Abante Tonite 459924
Owner: Monica Publishing Corporation
Editorial: #167 Liberty Building, Roberto S. Oca St, Port Area, Manila **Tel:** 63 25276722
Email: tonite@abante-tonite.com **Web site:** http://www.abante-tonite.com
Freq: Daily; **Circ:** 278000 Not Audited
Manager: Ron Tamayo
Profile: Covers news topics.
Language (s): English
DAILY NEWSPAPER

Bulgar 459930
Owner: MVRS Publication Inc
Editorial: 538 Quezon Avenue, Quezon City, Manila 1100 **Tel:** 63 327490091
Web site: http://www.bulgar.com.ph
Freq: Daily; **Circ:** 350000 Not Audited
Manager: Tessie Estaban
Profile: Tagalog newspaper published in the Philippines.
Language (s): Tagalog
DAILY NEWSPAPER

BusinessMirror 460360
Owner: Philippine Business Daily Mirror Publishing, Inc.
Editorial: 2113 Chino Roces Avenue corner De La Rosa Street, 2nd Floor, Dominga Building (Annex), Makati City **Tel:** 63 28178407
Email: news@businessmirror.com.ph **Web site:** http://www.businessmirror.com.ph
Freq: Daily; **Circ:** 62000 Not Audited
Publisher: T. Anthony Cabangon; **Editor:** Lorenzo Lombao; **Editor in Chief:** Lourdes Molina-Fernandez; **Editor:** Dionisio Pelayo; **Editor:** Gerard Ramos; **Editor:** Lyn Resurreccion
Profile: Provides readers with a broader look at Filipino business, economy, industries, companies and markets.
Language (s): English
DAILY NEWSPAPER

BusinessWorld 161280
Owner: BusinessWorld Publishing
Editorial: 95 Balete Drive Extension, New Manila, Quezon City 1112 **Tel:** 63 253599117
Email: editor@bworldonline.com **Web site:** http://www.bworldonline.com/
Freq: Daily; **Circ:** 65000 Not Audited
Editor: Fransisco P. Baltazar; **Editor:** Ronnie Romero
Profile: Covers business and news.
Language (s): English
Ad Rate: Full Page Mono 336571.20
Currency: Philippines Pesos
DAILY NEWSPAPER

BusinessWorld Online 792965
Tel: 632 535 9901 405
Web site: http://www.bworldonline.com
Editor: Judy Gulane
Profile: Philippines' leading business newspaper covering business news. The business paper comes out Monday through Friday, with a Saturday exclusive online edition, with national and foreign circulation totalling 54,000.
DAILY NEWSPAPER

Ilonggo Star 460389
Owner: Sun Star Publishing Inc.
Editorial: 3rd floor, Sun.Star Building, P. del Rosario cor. P. Cui Sts., Cebu City 6000 **Tel:** 63 3322546100
Email: sunnex@sunstar.com.ph **Web site:** http://www.sunstar.com.ph/iloilo
Freq: Weekly; **Circ:** 60000 Not Audited
Editor in Chief: Nini Cabaero
Profile: Covers international and national news.
Language (s): English
DAILY NEWSPAPER

Inquirer Libre 459174
Owner: Philippine Daily Inquirer Inc.
Editorial: Chino Roches Avenue, Yague Cor. Mascardo Sts, Makati City 1220 **Tel:** 63 28978808
Email: libre_pdi@inquirer.com.ph **Web site:** http://www.libre.com.ph
Freq: Daily; **Circ:** 100000 Not Audited
Editor: Armin Adina; **Director:** Jesesina Adorable; **Editor in Chief:** Chito Dela Vega; **Editor:** Dennis Eroa; **Editor:** Romel Lalata
Profile: Covers international and local news.
Language (s): Tagalog
DAILY NEWSPAPER

Malaya Business Insight 459929
Owner: People's Independent Media Inc.
Editorial: Leyland Bldg, 20th cor. Railroad St, Port Area, Manila **Tel:** 63 23393329
Email: malayanews@yahoo.com **Web site:** http://www.malaya.com.ph
Freq: Daily; **Circ:** 60000 Not Audited
Editor: Minnie Advincula; **Editor:** Jimmy Cantor; **Publisher:** Amado Macasaep; **Director:** Robert Sombillo; **Editor:** Gie Triallana; **Editor:** Winnie Valaquez
Profile: Malaya means "free" in the Filipino language.Founded in 1981 as a Tagalog newspaper by Jose Burgos Jr., Malaya shifted to English when its sister publication, We Forum, was closed down by the Marcos government in 1983 after it came out with a story exposing the fake medals of former strongman. During the politically Marcos troubled years of 1983 to 1986, Malaya was at the forefront of giving the public the truth.The end of the Marcos regime in February 1986 brought changes to the ownership of Malaya. Burgos sold the newspaper to veteran journalist Amado "Jake" P. Macasaet, who was then Malaya's business editor. Throughout all these changes, Malaya has adhered its mission of giving the public the truth fairly and responsibly. The commitment continues.
Language (s): English
Ad Rate: Full Page Mono 117028.00
Ad Rate: Full Page Colour 210651.00
Currency: Malaysia Ringgits
DAILY NEWSPAPER

Manila Bulletin 158740
Owner: Manila Bulletin Publishing Corp.
Editorial: Manila Bulletin, Muralla Corner Recoletos Street, Intramuros, Manila 1002 **Tel:** 63 2527812135
Email: manila.bulletin@gmail.com **Web site:** http://www.mb.com.ph
Freq: Daily; **Circ:** 260000 Not Audited
Editor: Loreto Cabañes; **Editor:** Isabel De Leon; **Editor in Chief:** Cris Icban; **Editor:** Cris J. Icban Jr.; **Editor:** Ding Marcelo; **Editor:** Crispina Martinez-Belen; **Publisher:** Hermogenes Pobre; **Publisher:** Napoleon G. Rama
Profile: Established in 1900, covers the latest news in the Philippines and abroad.
Language (s): English
Ad Rate: Full Page Mono 150225.00
Currency: Philippines Pesos
DAILY NEWSPAPER

Manila Shimbun 460810
Owner: Bisuku Company Ltd.
Editorial: Manila Shimbun Building, 1037 Teresa Street, Rizal Village, Makati City - **Tel:** 63 28973731
Web site: http://www.manila-shimbun.com
Freq: Daily; **Circ:** 6000 Not Audited
Manager: Nobuhiko Hashimoto; **Editor in Chief:** Yoshihiko Sakai
Profile: Covers international and national news.
Language (s): Japanese
DAILY NEWSPAPER

Manila Standard Today 158741
Owner: Kamahalan Publishing Corporation
Editorial: Leyland Building, Railroad corner 21st Street, Port Area, Manila **Tel:** 63 25278351
Email: info@manilastandardtoday.com **Web site:** http://www.manilastandardtoday.com
Freq: Daily; **Circ:** 150000 Not Audited
Editor: Leo Estonito; **Editor:** Riera Mallari; **Editor:** Isah Red; **Manager:** Gina Versoza
Profile: Covers national and international news.
Language (s): English
Ad Rate: Full Page Colour 121986.00
Currency: Philippines Pesos
DAILY NEWSPAPER

The Manila Times 156691
Owner: The Manila Times Publishing Corp.
Editorial: 371 A. Bonifacio Drive, Port Area, Manila 1018 **Tel:** 63 2524566467
Email: newsdesk@manilatimes.net **Web site:** http://www.manilatimes.net
Freq: Daily; **Circ:** 50000 Not Audited
Editor in Chief: Rene Bas; **Editor:** Conrad M. Carino; **Manager:** Bezz Zamora
Profile: Covers local, international news and lifestyle.
Language (s): English
Ad Rate: Full Page Mono 10303.20
Currency: United States Dollars
DAILY NEWSPAPER

Mindanao Times 459931
Owner: Mindanao Publishers Inc.
Editorial: UMBN Building - Ponciano Reyes St., Mindanao, Davao City 8000 **Tel:** 63 822250309
Email: editorial.mtimes@gmail.com **Web site:** http://www.mindanaotimes.com.ph
Freq: Daily; **Circ:** 11000 Not Audited
Editor in Chief: Amalia Cabusao; **Manager:** Jingo Camomot; **Manager:** Dominic Carpio; **Editor:** Jon Develos; **Manager:** Levis Dingal; **Editor:** Christopher Fabian
Profile: Covers international and national news.
Language (s): English
DAILY NEWSPAPER

Mount Samat Weekly Forum 459937
Owner: Mount Samat Weekly Forum
Editorial: Capitol Drive, G/F Santiago Building, San Jose, Balanga, Bataan 2100 **Tel:** 63 472375988
Freq: Weekly; **Circ:** 2500 Not Audited
Editor: Maricel Galura
Language (s): Tagalog
DAILY NEWSPAPER

The Negros Chronicle 522155
Owner: The Negros Chronicle
Editorial: 106 EJ Blanco Road Piapi, Dumaguete City 6200 **Tel:** 63 352254760
Email: elmarjay@yahoo.com **Web site:** http://www.negroschronicle.com
Freq: Weekly; **Circ:** 4000 Not Audited
Editor: Ely P. Dejaresco
Profile: Covers international and national news.
Language (s): English
DAILY NEWSPAPER

News Express 459962
Owner: Malones Printing Press
Editorial: E. Lopez Street, Jaro, Door 31, Lopez Arcade, Iloilo City 5000 **Tel:** 63 335088725
Freq: 2 Times/Week; **Circ:** 2000 Not Audited
Manager: Remetio Castor; **Publisher:** Teresita Malones; **Editor:** Jun Tillaslor
Language (s): English
DAILY NEWSPAPER

Palawan Sun 460433
Owner: Palawan Sun Publishing Corp.
Editorial: 2/Fl Lustre Building, Malver Street, Puerto Princesa City, Palawan 5300 **Tel:** 63 484334249
Email: palawan.sun@gmail.com **Web site:** http://palawansun.wordpress.com
Freq: Weekly; **Circ:** 1700 Not Audited
Editor in Chief: Redempto Anda
Profile: Covers international and national news.
Language (s): English
DAILY NEWSPAPER

Panay News 459943
Owner: Panay News Inc.
Editorial: 3rd Floor, La Salette Building, Valeria Street, Iloilo City 5000 **Tel:** 63 333212749
Email: editorial.panaynews@gmail.com **Web site:** http://www.panaynewsphilippines.com
Freq: Daily; **Circ:** 65000 Not Audited
Editor in Chief: Danny Fajardo; **Editor:** David Sinay

Philippines

Profile: The Valeria address is for the Marketing office, while the Editorial department is located at Mandurriao.
Language (s): English
DAILY NEWSPAPER

People's Taliba 409273
Owner: Journal Group
Editorial: 6th Floor Universal-Re Building, 106 Paseo de Roxas corner Perea & Gallardo Sts, Legaspi Village, Makati City **Tel:** 63 2892305258
Email: peoples@journal.com.ph **Web site:** http://www.journal.com.ph
Freq: Daily; **Circ:** 230000 Not Audited
Editor in Chief: Jun Abad; **Manager:** Susan Bunyi; **Editor:** Anna Federigan; **Editor:** Marita Pascual Nuque; **Editor in Chief:** Augusto B. Villanueva; **Manager:** Sanaida Viscara
Profile: Covers lifestyle and society.
Language (s): Tagalog
DAILY NEWSPAPER

People's Tonight 409272
Owner: Journal Group
Editorial: 6th Floor Universal-Re Building, 106 Paseo de Roxas Corner Perea & Gallardo Sts, Legaspi Village, Makati City **Tel:** 63 2892305258
Email: tonight@journal.com.ph **Web site:** http://www.journal.com.ph
Freq: Daily; **Circ:** 370000 Not Audited
Editor: Eduardo Andaya; **Manager:** Susan Bunyi; **Editor:** Ian Farrinas; **Editor:** Marita Pascual Nuque; **Editor:** Jun Pisco; **Editor in Chief:** Augusto B. Villanueva; **Manager:** Sanaida Viscara
Profile: Covers lifestyle and entertainment news.
Language (s): English
DAILY NEWSPAPER

Philippine Daily Inquirer 158743
Owner: Inquirer Company
Editorial: Yague Cor. Mascardo Sts., Pasong Tamo, Makati City 1220 **Tel:** 63 28978808
Email: daydesk@inquirer.com.ph **Web site:** https://www.inquirer.net
Freq: Daily; **Circ:** 270000 Not Audited
Editor: Jorge V. Aruta; **Editor:** Pergentino Bandayrel; **Editor:** Artemio Engracia; **Editor:** Chelo Formoso; **Editor:** Raul Marcelo; **Editor:** Teddyvic Melendres; **Editor:** Thelma San Juan; **Editor:** Emmie Velarde
Profile: Covers International and national news.
Language (s): English
Ad Rate: Full Page Mono 168381.00
Ad Rate: Full Page Colour 303085.00
Currency: Philippines Pesos
DAILY NEWSPAPER

The Philippine STAR 282754
Owner: Star Group of Publications
Editorial: 13 Corner Railroad St., Port Area, Manila 1016 **Tel:** 63 2 5277901
Email: editor@philstar.com **Web site:** http://www.philstar.com
Freq: Daily; **Circ:** 300003 Not Audited
Editor, YStyle: Regina Belmonte
Profile: Offers news, entertainment and details on related topics.
Language (s): English
Ad Rate: Full Page Mono 200000.00
Currency: Philippines Pesos
DAILY NEWSPAPER

Pilipino Star Ngayon 156827
Owner: Star Group Publications
Editorial: 202 Roberto Oca Street, Port Area, Manila 1018 **Tel:** 63 2527790115 155
Email: psngayon@philstar.net.ph **Web site:** http://www.philstar.com
Freq: Daily; **Circ:** 350000 Not Audited
Editor: Jo Abelgas; **Editor:** Salve Asis; **Editor:** Mario Basco; **Editor:** Jojo Cruz; **Editor:** Rowena Del Prado; **Editor:** Ronnie Halos; **Manager:** Bonnie Lachica; **Editor in Chief:** Alfonso Pedroche; **Editor:** Dina Villena
Profile: Covers news.
Language (s): Tagalog
DAILY NEWSPAPER

Quirino Quest 459347
Owner: City Star
Editorial: Malvar Highway, Santiago City, Isabela 3311 **Tel:** 63 786827449
Freq: Weekly; **Circ:** 7300 Not Audited
Editor in Chief: Melvin Gascon
Language (s): English
DAILY NEWSPAPER

Sun.Star Bacolod 460387
Owner: Sun Star Publishing Inc.
Editorial: M13Annex Building, Lopues, Lacson Street, Bacolod City **Tel:** 63 347081776
Email: sunnex@sunstar.com.ph **Web site:** http://www.sunstar.com.ph/bacolod
Freq: Daily; **Circ:** 2500 Not Audited
Editor in Chief: Cheryl Cruz; **Manager:** Caesar Sison
Profile: Covers social issues, local and society news.
Language (s): English
DAILY NEWSPAPER

Sun.Star Baguio 460258
Owner: Sun Star Publishing Inc.
Editorial: 110 Wong Buildin, Magsaysay Avenue, Baguio 2600 **Tel:** 63 744438362
Email: sunnex@sunstar.com.ph **Web site:** http://www.sunstar.com.ph/baguio/
Freq: Daily; **Circ:** 8000 Not Audited
Editor in Chief: Renato Samuel Bautista
Profile: Covers local news.
Language (s): English
DAILY NEWSPAPER

Sun.Star Davao 459740
Owner: Sun.Star Publishing Inc.
Editorial: R. Castillo Street, Agdao, Davao City 8000 **Tel:** 63 822351009
Email: sunnex@sunstar.com.ph **Web site:** http://www.sunstar.com.ph/davao/index.html
Freq: Daily; **Circ:** 20000 Not Audited
Editor in Chief: Stella Estremera
Profile: Covers national and international news.
Language (s): English
DAILY NEWSPAPER

Sun.Star Gensan 459553
Owner: Sun Star Publishing Inc.
Editorial: Safi 2 Building, Mansanitas Street, Corner Magsaysay Avenue, General Santos 9500 **Tel:** 63 822351009
Email: sunnex@sunstar.com.ph **Web site:** http://www.sunstar.com.ph/davao/index.html
Freq: Daily; **Circ:** 10000 Not Audited
Editor in Chief: Stella Estremera
Profile: Covers international and national news.
Language (s): English
DAILY NEWSPAPER

Sun.Star Pampanga 460390
Owner: Sun Star Publishing Inc.
Editorial: Tire City Compound, McArthur Highway, Dolores, San Fernando **Tel:** 63 458600517
Email: sunnex@sunstar.com.ph **Web site:** http://www.sunstar.com.ph/pampanga
Freq: Daily; **Circ:** 10000 Not Audited
Editor in Chief: Jun Malik
Profile: Covers national and local news.
Language (s): English
DAILY NEWSPAPER

Sun.Star People's Courier 459964
Owner: Sun Star Publishing Inc.
Editorial: 157 D. Silang Street, Batangas City 4200 **Tel:** 63 437238416
Email: sunnex@sunstar.com.ph
Freq: 2 Times/Week; **Circ:** 10000 Not Audited
Editor in Chief: Vicky Florendo
Language (s): English
DAILY NEWSPAPER

Sun.Star People's Courier - Oriental Mindoro Edition 459523
Owner: Sun Star Publishing Inc.
Editorial: 157 D Silang Street, Batangas City 4200 **Tel:** 63 437238416
Email: sunnex@sunstar.com.ph
Freq: Weekly; **Circ:** 10000 Not Audited
Editor in Chief: Vicky Florendo
Language (s): Tagalog
DAILY NEWSPAPER

Sunday Punch 404318
Owner: Sunday Punch, Inc.
Editorial: 2nd Floor, Tuque Tiongson Building, A.B. Fernandez Avenue, Dagupan City, Pangasinan **Tel:** 63 755155601
Email: punch.sunday@gmail.com **Web site:** http://www.dagupan.com/punch
Freq: Weekly; **Circ:** 8000 Not Audited
Editor: Ermin Garcia; **Editor in Chief:** Ermin F Garcia Jr
Profile: Covers international and local news.
Language (s): English
DAILY NEWSPAPER

Super Balita 460079
Owner: Sun.Star Publishing Inc.
Editorial: R. Castillo Street, Agdao, Davao City 8000 **Tel:** 63 822351009
Email: sunnex@sunstar.com.ph **Web site:** http://www.sunstar.com.ph/superbalitadavao
Freq: Daily; **Circ:** 30000 Not Audited
Profile: Covers news of international and regional.
Language (s): Tagalog
DAILY NEWSPAPER

Il Tempo 459770
Owner: Manila Bulletin Publishing Corp.
Editorial: Manila Bulletin Building, Muralla corner Recoletos Street, Intramuros, Manila 1002 **Tel:** 63 2527812135
Email: tempo@mb.com.ph **Web site:** http://www.tempo.com.ph
Freq: Daily; **Circ:** 200000 Not Audited
Editor in Chief: Cris Icban; **Publisher:** Hermogenes Pobre; **Editor:** Nestor Quartero; **Editor:** Robert Roque
Profile: Covers sports and entertainment news.
Language (s): English
DAILY NEWSPAPER

United Daily News 459735
Owner: United Daily News Group
Editorial: 812 - 818 Benavides Street, Binondo, Metro Manila 1006 **Tel:** 63 22447171
Web site: http://www.udn.com
Freq: Daily; **Circ:** 20000 Not Audited
Editor: Virginia Cheng; **Editor in Chief:** Thua Kee
Profile: Covers international and national news.
Language (s): Chinese
DAILY NEWSPAPER

Visayan Daily Star 459963
Owner: The Visayan Daily Star Publications Inc.
Editorial: Araneta Singcang Street, Daily Star Building, Bacolod City 6100 **Tel:** 63 344330455
Email: visayandailystar@yahoo.com **Web site:** http://www.visayandailystar.com
Freq: 2 Times/Week; **Circ:** 18000 Not Audited
Editor: Nida Buenafe; **Manager:** Maja Dely; **Editor in Chief:** Ninfa Leonardia; **Editor:** Patrick Pangilinan
Profile: Covers nternational and local news.
Language (s): English
DAILY NEWSPAPER

Vizcaya Vanguard 459346
Owner: City Star Inc.
Editorial: Malvar Highway, Santiago City, Isabela 3311 **Tel:** 63 786827449
Freq: Weekly; **Circ:** 11763 Not Audited
Editor in Chief: Melvin Gascon; **Manager:** Julie Rivera; **Publisher:** Francisco Taguinod
Language (s): Filipino
DAILY NEWSPAPER

News Service/Syndicate

The Philippine News Agency 467613
Owner: Republic of the Philippines
Editorial: 2nd Floor, PIA Building, Visayas Avenue, Quezon City 1104
Email: pnadesk@yahoo.com **Web site:** http://www.pna.gov.ph
Freq: Daily
General Manager: Vittorio Vitug
Profile: Established in 1973, serves as the official news agency in the Philippines.
Language (s): English
NEWS SERVICE/SYNDICATE

Pitcairn Islands

Time Difference: GMT -8
National Telephone Code: 64
Continent: Oceania
Capital: Adamstown

Community Newspaper

Pitcairn Miscellany 538729
Editorial: Pitcairn Island, South Pacific Ocean, Via New Zealand
Email: miscellany@pitcairn.pn **Web site:** http://miscellany.pn
Freq: Monthly
Profile: Covers island news, stories of trips to Oeno and Henderson Island, monthly fish catch, ship arrivals, local gossip, birthdays, articles written by visitors, local events and activities.
Language (s): English
COMMUNITY NEWSPAPER

Poland

Time Difference: GMT +1
National Telephone Code: 48
Continent: Europe
Capital: Warsaw

Newspapers

Dziennik Gazeta Prawna 443714
Owner: Infor Biznes sp. z o.o.
Editorial: ul.Okopowa 58/72, Warszawa 01-042 **Tel:** 48 22 531 48 00
Email: gp@infor.pl **Web site:** http://www.gazetaprawna.pl
Freq: Daily; **Circ:** 46973 Publisher's Statement
Profile: A serious opinion creating daily newspaper covering politics, economics, business, law and social issues.
Language (s): Polish
Ad Rate: Full Page Mono 39330.00
Ad Rate: Full Page Colour 51130.00
Currency: Poland Zlotych
DAILY NEWSPAPER

Fakt 383404
Owner: Ringier Axel Springer Polska
Editorial: ul. Domaniewska 52, Warszawa 02-672 **Tel:** 48 22 232 02 00
Email: redakcja@efakt.pl **Web site:** http://www.fakt.pl
Freq: Daily; **Circ:** 310075 Publisher's Statement
Profile: National newspaper covering current affairs, national and international news, politics and economy.
Language (s): Polish
DAILY NEWSPAPER

Gazeta Wyborcza 157002
Owner: Agora SA
Editorial: ul. Czerska 8/10, Warszawa 00-732 **Tel:** 48 22 555 52 38
Email: listy@wyborcza.pl **Web site:** http://www.wyborcza.pl
Freq: Daily; **Circ:** 163255 Publisher's Statement
Profile: Tabloid-sized newspaper covering national and international news with features on business and finance, education, appointments, lifestyle, entertainment and sport.
Language (s): Polish
Ad Rate: Full Page Mono 129900.00
Ad Rate: Full Page Colour 129900.00
Currency: Poland Zlotych
DAILY NEWSPAPER

Gazeta Wyborcza - Washington, DC Bureau 504725
Owner: Agora SA
Editorial: 400 N Capitol St NW Ste 750, Washington, District Of Columbia 20001-1536 **Tel:** 1 202 887-8330
Web site: http://www.wyborcza.pl
Freq: Daily
Profile: This is the Washington, D.C. bureau of Gazeta Wyborcza in Warszawa, Poland.
Language (s): Polish
DAILY NEWSPAPER

Parkiet - Gazeta Gie?dy 218819
Owner: Gremi Media. Sp. z o.o.
Editorial: ul. Prosta 51, Warszawa 00-838 **Tel:** 48 22 46 30 618
Email: redakcja@parkiet.com **Web site:** http://www.parkiet.com
Freq: Daily; **Circ:** 4919 Publisher's Statement
Profile: Newspaper focusing on political and legal issues, information on the stock exchange, business and economic reports and also in-depth analysis of the financial markets.
Language (s): Polish
Ad Rate: Full Page Mono 13300.00
Ad Rate: Full Page Colour 15600.00
Currency: Poland Zlotych
DAILY NEWSPAPER

Polska The Times 555444
Owner: Polskapresse Sp. z o.o.
Editorial: Domaniewska 41, Warszawa 02-672 **Tel:** 48 22 201 42 00
Email: redakcja@polskatimes.pl **Web site:** http://www.polskatimes.pl
Freq: Daily; **Circ:** 13958
Profile: Provides international and national news, covers sports, culture, politics, social issues and economics.
Language (s): Polish
Ad Rate: Full Page Colour 73400.00
Currency: Poland Zlotych
DAILY NEWSPAPER

Puls Biznesu 217975
Owner: Bonnier Business (Polska)
Editorial: ul. Kijowska 1, Warszawa 03-738 **Tel:** 48 22 333 99 99
Email: puls@pb.pl **Web site:** http://www.pb.pl
Freq: Daily; **Circ:** 17941 Publisher's Statement
Profile: National newspaper containing detailed coverage of national and international financial, banking and corporate news.
Language (s): Polish
Ad Rate: Full Page Colour 27500.00
Currency: Poland Zlotych
DAILY NEWSPAPER

Rzeczpospolita 156683
Owner: Gremi Business Communication Sp. z o.o.
Editorial: ul. Prosta 51, Warszawa 00-838 **Tel:** 48 22 6283401
Web site: http://www.rp.pl
Freq: Daily; **Circ:** 56639 Publisher's Statement
Profile: Broadsheet-sized quality newspaper providing in-depth national and international news, with political and financial coverage, social issues, media, education, IT, travel, arts, sport and entertainment. Also includes features on legislation and personal finance.
Language (s): Polish
Ad Rate: Full Page Mono 69600.00
Ad Rate: Full Page Colour 108710.00
Currency: Poland Zlotych
DAILY NEWSPAPER

Super Express 159037
Owner: ZPR Media S.A.
Editorial: ul. Jubilerska 10, Warszawa 00-939 **Tel:** 48 22 515 91 00
Email: listy@superexpress.pl **Web site:** http://www.se.pl
Freq: Daily; **Circ:** 157444 Publisher's Statement
Profile: Newspaper concentrating on national and international politics, finance, business, public issues, culture and entertainment.
Language (s): English
Ad Rate: Full Page Colour 75000.00
Currency: Poland Zlotych
DAILY NEWSPAPER

The Warsaw Voice 224811
Owner: Warsaw Voice SA
Editorial: ul. Ksicia Janusza 64, Warszawa 01-452
Tel: 48 22 3359700
Email: voice@warsawvoice.pl **Web site:** http://www.warsawvoice.pl
Freq: Daily; **Circ:** 10500 Publisher's Statement
Profile: Newspaper focusing on national and international news, politics, business, culture and entertainment.
Language (s): English
DAILY NEWSPAPER

Portugal

Time Difference: GMT
National Telephone Code: 351
Continent: Europe
Capital: Lisbon

Newspapers

Acção Socialista 495210
Owner: Partido Socialista Português - PS
Editorial: Largo do Rato, 2, Lisboa 1269-143
Tel: 351 213 822 000
Email: accaosocialista@ps.pt **Web site:** http://www.accaosocialista.net
Freq: Weekly
Managing Director: Jorge Filipe Teixeira Seguro Sanches
Profile: Official periodical of the national Social Political Party. The events, opinions and political national news. National.Local Translation: Jornal nacional do Partido Socialista. Novidades, opiniões, eventos e notícias sobre a política nacional.
Language (s): Portuguese
DAILY NEWSPAPER

Açoriano Oriental 158290
Owner: Açormedia - Comunicação Multimédia e Edição de Publicações, S.A.
Editorial: R. Dr. Bruno Tavares Carreiro, 34/36, Ponta Delgada 9500-055 **Tel:** 351 296 202 800
Email: acorianooriental@acorianooriental.pt **Web site:** www.acorianooriental.pt
Freq: Daily; **Circ:** 5034 APCT
Editor: Rui Jorge Cabral; **Editor:** Paulo Amaral Faustino; **Director Comercial:** Luís Ferreira; **Director adjunto:** Pedro Nunes Lagarto; **Managing Director:** João Marcelino; **Editor:** Ana Carvalho Melo; **Editor:** Arthur Melo; **Editor:** Luís Pedro Silva
Profile: Daily regional newspaper containing information about Açores' island. Current affairs, politics, society, sport, entertainment and events are some of the main themes. Read by the population of Açores.Local Translation: Jornal diário com informação relativa à ilha dos Açores. Política, actualidade, sociedade, desporto, entretenimento e eventos são alguns dos temas abordados.Phone: +351 296 202 832
Language (s): Portuguese
Ad Rate: Full Page Mono 1290.00
Currency: Euro
DAILY NEWSPAPER

Adega de Pegões (DN + JN) 764997
Owner: Global Notícias, Publicações, S.A.
Editorial: Edificio Diario de Noticias, Av. da Liberdade, 266, Lisboa 1250-149
Tel: 351 213 187 500
Email: dnot@dn.pt
Circ: 168106 Publisher's Statement
Profile: National. Local Translation:Suplemento dedicado à Adega de Pegões, produtora de vinho português.
Language (s): Portuguese
DAILY NEWSPAPER

Agências Funerárias 536485
Owner: Global Notícias, Publicações, S.A.
Editorial: R. de Goncalo Cristovao 195-219, Porto 4049-011 **Tel:** 351 222 096 100
Email: dpe@jn.pt **Web site:** http://www.jn.pt
Circ: 107777 Publisher's Statement
Profile: National. Local Translation:Suplemento sobre o sector funerário.
Email: secdir@jn.pt; roteiro@jn.pt.Phone: +351 213 187 300
Language (s): Portuguese
Ad Rate: Full Page Colour 1500.00
Currency: Euro
DAILY NEWSPAPER

Ágora 495724
Editorial: Instituto Superior da Maia, Av. Carlos Oliveira Campos, Avioso S. Pedro 4475-690
Tel: 351 229 825 319
Email: info@ismai.pt **Web site:** www.ismai.pt
Circ: 122218 Publisher's Statement
Profile: National. Local Translation:Jornal universitário do Laboratório do curso de jornalismo do ISMAI, Instituto Superior da Maia.
Language (s): Portuguese
Ad Rate: Full Page Mono 2700.00
Ad Rate: Full Page Colour 3780.00
Currency: Euro
DAILY NEWSPAPER

Águas 690695
Owner: Global Notícias, Publicações, S.A.
Tel: 351 222 096 100
Email: secdir@jn.pt **Web site:** http://www.jn.pt
Circ: 121713 Publisher's Statement
Profile: National. Local Translation:Suplemento que destaca assuntos relacionados com a água e sua importância. Destaque para empresas de distribuição de água, tratamento e saneamento. Phone: +351 213 187 300
Language (s): Portuguese
DAILY NEWSPAPER

Algarve 495270
Owner: Presselivre - Imprensa Livre, S.A.
Editorial: Arruamento D à R. Jose Maria Nicolau, 3, Lisboa 1549-023 **Tel:** 351 213 185 200
Email: direccao@cmjornal.pt **Web site:** www.cmjornal.pt
Freq: Daily; **Circ:** 161374 APCT
Profile: Algarve edition. Aimed at south Portugal population.Local Translation: Edição local do Correio da Manhã Algarve.Phone: +351 213 540 382; +351 213 540 386
Fax: +351 213 540 386
Language (s): Portuguese
Ad Rate: Full Page Mono 2020.00
Ad Rate: Full Page Colour 3030.00
Currency: Euro
DAILY NEWSPAPER

Ambiente (DN + JN) 619472
Owner: Global Notícias, Publicações, S.A.
Editorial: Edificio Diario de Noticias, Av. da Liberdade, 266, Lisboa 1250-149
Tel: 351 213 187 500
Email: dnot@dn.pt **Web site:** http://www.dn.pt
Circ: 148762 Publisher's Statement
Profile: Published with: Jornal de Notícias; Diário de Notícias. National.Local Translation: Edições especiais sobre o ambiente: a eficiência energética, a energia eólica e as novidades no sector ambiental.Publicado com: Jornal de Notícias; Diário de Notícias
Language (s): Portuguese
DAILY NEWSPAPER

Angola 691610
Owner: Sojornal - Sociedade Jornalística e Editorial, S.A.
Editorial: Edificio S. Francisco de Sales, R. Calvet de Magalhaes, 242, Paço De Arcos 2770-022
Tel: 351 214 544 000
Email: ipublishing@impresa.pt **Web site:** http://www.expresso.pt
Circ: 126575 Publisher's Statement
Profile: National. Local Translation:A Angola enquanto espaço privilegiado para empreendedores ibéricos e de oportunidades de negócio.
Geographical Focus: Africa
Language (s): Portuguese
DAILY NEWSPAPER

Aniversário 523967
Owner: Presselivre - Imprensa Livre, S.A.
Editorial: Av. Joao Crisostomo, 72, Lisboa 1069-043
Tel: 351 213 185 200
Email: direccao@cmjornal.pt **Web site:** http://www.cmjornal.pt
Circ: 166701 APCT
Profile: Special anniversary issue. National.Local Translation: Edição especial de aniversário com entrevistas, informações e curiosidades relativas ao jornal.Phone: +351 213 540 382; +351 213 540 386
Fax: +351 213 540 386
Language (s): Portuguese
Ad Rate: Full Page Mono 2020.00
Ad Rate: Full Page Colour 3030.00
Currency: Euro
DAILY NEWSPAPER

Aqui, Pevidém 425611
Owner: Fábrica da Igreja Paroquial de São Jorge de Selho
Editorial: Paroquia de Selho - R. do Bairro, 2, Pevidém, Guimarães 4810-000 **Tel:** 351 253 532 162
Freq: Weekly
Language (s): Portuguese
DAILY NEWSPAPER

Arte 765796
Owner: Transjornal Edição de Publicações, S.A.
Editorial: Estrada da Outurela, 118, Parque Holanda - Edifício Holanda, Carnaxide 2790-114
Tel: 351 214 169 210
Email: metro@metroportugal.com **Web site:** http://www.readmetro.com
Circ: 130000 Publisher's Statement
Profile: Special edition about art. Aimed for Aveiro, Braga, Coimbra, Évora, Faro, Leiria, Lisboa and Porto regions.Local Translation: Suplemento especial sobre arte: exposições e eventos.Phone: +351 214 241 430
Fax: +351 214 174 206
Language (s): Portuguese
DAILY NEWSPAPER

Atual 516669
Owner: Sojornal - Sociedade Jornalística e Editorial, S.A.
Editorial: Edificio S. Francisco de Sales, R. Calvet de Magalhaes, 242, Paço De Arcos 2770-022
Tel: 351 214 544 000
Email: atual@expresso.impresa.pt **Web site:** http://www.expresso.pt
Freq: Weekly; **Circ:** 132175 Publisher's Statement
Editor: Jorge Araújo
Profile: National. Local Translation:Suplemento dedicado ao mundo das artes e do espectáculo. Cinema, dança, teatro, música, exposições, livros e entrevistas. Url: http://aeiou.escape.expresso.pt
Email: ipublishing@impresa.pt.
Language (s): Portuguese
Ad Rate: Full Page Mono 2520.00
Ad Rate: Full Page Colour 3360.00
Currency: Euro
DAILY NEWSPAPER

Auto 617694
Owner: Global Notícias, Publicações, S.A.
Editorial: R. de Goncalo Cristovao 195-219, Porto 4049-011 **Tel:** 351 222 096 100
Email: dpe@jn.pt **Web site:** http://www.jn.pt
Circ: 106688 Publisher's Statement
Profile: Publication dedicated to the mobile industry and market.
Language (s): Portuguese
Ad Rate: Full Page Mono 2700.00
Ad Rate: Full Page Colour 3780.00
Currency: Euro
DAILY NEWSPAPER

Autódromo do Algarve 556510
Owner: Sociedade Vicra Desportiva, S.A.
Editorial: Travessa da Queimada, 23 - R/C, 1 e 2, Lisboa 1249-113 **Tel:** 351 213 463 981
Web site: http://www.abola.pt
Circ: 120901 Publisher's Statement
Language (s): Portuguese
DAILY NEWSPAPER

Autódromo do Algarve 696704
Owner: Presselivre - Imprensa Livre, S.A.
Editorial: Av. Joao Crisostomo, 72, Lisboa 1069-043
Tel: 351 213 185 462
Email: geral@correiomanha.pt **Web site:** http://www.cmjornal.pt
Circ: 184677 Publisher's Statement
Profile: National. Local Translation:Suplemento sobre o Autódromo Internacional do Algarve: história, o circuito, calendário, entre outros dados.
Language (s): Portuguese
DAILY NEWSPAPER

Badaladas 238034
Owner: Fábrica da Igreja Paroquial da Freguesia de São Pedro e Santiago de Torres Vedras
Editorial: Praca 25 Abril, 6 - 1 Esq., Torres Vedras 2561-311 **Tel:** 351 261 335 476
Email: noticias@badaladas.pt **Web site:** http://www.badaladas.pt
Freq: Weekly; **Circ:** 10000 APCT
Managing Director: Fernando Miguel Silva
Profile: Tabloid-sized newspaper featuring the latest news, entertainment and sport from the region. Read in Lisboa region.Local Translation: Jornal de inspiração cristã, em formato tablóide com notícias, actualidade, entretenimento e desporto relativos principalmente à região de Lisboa.Phone: +351 261 335 470
Language (s): Portuguese
Ad Rate: Full Page Mono 700.00
Ad Rate: Full Page Colour 895.00
Currency: Euro
DAILY NEWSPAPER

Baixo Mondego 424775
Owner: Pixel - Imagem e Comunicação
Editorial: R. da Cadeia Velha, Montemor-O-Velho 3140-853 **Tel:** 351 239 687 530
Email: baixo.mondego@mail.telepac.pt
Freq: Bi-Weekly; **Circ:** 5000 Not Audited
Language (s): Portuguese
DAILY NEWSPAPER

Balada da União 424776
Owner: Convívios Fraternos
Editorial: R. Antonio Maria Pinho, 20, Apartado 12, Avanca 3860-130 **Tel:** 351 234 884 474
Email: convivios_fraternos@hotmail.com
Freq: Monthly
Language (s): Portuguese
DAILY NEWSPAPER

Bandeira Azul 696705
Owner: Global Notícias, Publicações, S.A.
Tel: 351 222 096 100
Email: secdir@jn.pt **Web site:** http://www.jn.pt
Circ: 116688 Publisher's Statement
Profile: National. Local Translation:As praias e marinas classificadas com qualidade e segurança máxima. Phone: +351 213 187 300
Language (s): Portuguese
DAILY NEWSPAPER

Barcelos Popular 235461
Owner: Milho Rei - Cooperativa Popular de Informação e Cultura de Barcelos, C.R.L.
Editorial: Av. Joao Paulo II, 355, Barcelos 4750-304
Tel: 351 253 813 585
Email: geral@barcelos-popular.pt **Web site:** http://www.barcelos-popular.pt
Freq: Weekly; **Circ:** 9000 APCT
Managing Director: José Santos Alves
Profile: Read in Barcelos region. Local Translation:Semanário de informação regional acerca de Barcelos. Política, Concelho, Cultura e Desporto são as secções habituais deste jornal. Phone: +351 917 461 939
Language (s): Portuguese
Ad Rate: Full Page Mono 502.00
Ad Rate: Full Page Colour 552.00
Currency: Euro
DAILY NEWSPAPER

A Bola 158817
Owner: Sociedade Vicra Desportiva, S.A.
Editorial: Travessa da Queimada, 23 - R/C, 1 e 2, Lisboa 1249-113 **Tel:** 351 213 463 981
Email: publicidvd@abola.pt **Web site:** http://www.abola.pt
Freq: Daily; **Circ:** 120000 Publisher's Statement
Director adjunto: José Manuel Delgado; **Editor:** Nélson Marquez Feiteirona; **Director adjunto:** Fernando Guerra; **Editor:** Nuno Perestrelo; **Editor:** João Pimpim; **Managing Director:** Vítor Hugo dos Santos Serpa; **Editor:** Hugo Vasconcelos
Profile: Tabloid-sized newspaper focusing on all aspects of competitive sport in Portugal and throughout the world. Sold in Portugal and in some cities in Brazil, USA and Canada. Read by a broad range of the population, mainly man, with a particular interest in sporting events.Local Translation: Diário em formato tablóide, contendo notícias nacionais e internacionais sobre as mais variadas modalidades de desporto, mas com especial destaque para o futebol.
Language (s): Portuguese
Ad Rate: Full Page Colour 8980.00
Currency: Euro
DAILY NEWSPAPER

Boletim Cultural 425633
Owner: Câmara Municipal de Vila Nova de Famalicão
Editorial: R. Augusto Correia, 38 - 2 Dto., Vila Nova De Famalição 4760
Email: camaramunicipal@vilanovadefamalicao.org
Language (s): Portuguese
DAILY NEWSPAPER

Boletim da Freguesia de Nogueira 425634
Owner: Junta de Freguesia de Nogueira
Editorial: R. do Agrelo, Braga 4700
Freq: Bi-Monthly
Language (s): Portuguese
DAILY NEWSPAPER

Boletim Informativo (Vale de Cambra) 424784
Owner: Câmara Municipal de Vale de Cambra
Editorial: Edificio da Câmara Municipal, Vale De Cambra 3730
Freq: Monthly
Language (s): Portuguese
DAILY NEWSPAPER

Boletim Informativo Câmara Municipal VN Famalicão 425637
Owner: Câmara Municipal de Vila Nova de Famalicão
Editorial: Edificio da Câmara Municipal, Vila Nova De Famalição 4760-000
Freq: Quarterly
Language (s): Portuguese
DAILY NEWSPAPER

Boletim Informativo de Cavez - B I C 425638
Owner: Grupo Desportivo de Cavez
Editorial: Fojo, 71, Cavez, Cabeceiras De Basto 4860
Freq: Monthly
Language (s): Portuguese
DAILY NEWSPAPER

Boletim Municipal - Braga 425640
Owner: Câmara Municipal de Braga
Editorial: Edificio da Câmara Municipal, Braga 4700
Freq: Quarterly
Language (s): Portuguese
DAILY NEWSPAPER

Boletim Municipal - Castelo de Paiva 424785
Owner: Câmara Municipal de Castelo de Paiva
Editorial: Largo do Conde, Castelo De Paiva 4550-000
Freq: Bi-Monthly
Language (s): Portuguese
DAILY NEWSPAPER

Boletim Municipal - Guimarães 425641
Owner: Câmara Municipal de Guimarães
Editorial: Edificio da Câmara Municipal, Guimarães 4800
Freq: Monthly
Language (s): Portuguese
DAILY NEWSPAPER

Boletim Municipal - Santa Maria da Feira 424786
Owner: Câmara Municipal de Santa Maria da Feira
Editorial: Câmara Municipal de Santa Maria da Feira, Santa Maria Da Feira
Freq: Monthly
Language (s): Portuguese
DAILY NEWSPAPER

Boletim Municipal - Vagos 424787
Owner: Câmara Municipal de Vagos
Editorial: Edificio da Câmara Municipal, Vagos 3840-000 **Tel:** 351 234 793 754
Freq: Quarterly
Language (s): Portuguese
DAILY NEWSPAPER

O Bom Samaritano 424788
Owner: Centro Social do Distrito de Aveiro
Editorial: Lugar do Paco, Esgueira, Aveiro 3800
Tel: 351 234 311 459
Email: csdivinaprovidencia@sapo.pt
Freq: Quarterly
Language (s): Portuguese
DAILY NEWSPAPER

Cabra 549713
Owner: Universidade de Coimbra
Editorial: Seccao de Jornalismo da Associacao Academica de Coimbra, R. Padre Antonio Vieira, Coimbra 3000-000 **Tel:** 351 239 821 554
Email: acabra@gmail.com **Web site:** http://www.acabra.net
Freq: Bi-Weekly
Profile: Local Translation: Jornal universitário de Coimbra de interesse geral. Conta com as secções "Ensino Superior", "Cidade", "Nacional", "Internacional", "Ciência", "Cultura", "Desporto", "Media", "Reportagens" e "Economia". É o mais antigo dos jornais académicos ainda activo. No site está disponível a versão em PDF deste jornal.Phone: +351 239 821 554 +351 239 821 554
Language (s): Portuguese
Ad Rate: Full Page Mono 220.00
Ad Rate: Full Page Colour 270.00
Currency: Euro
DAILY NEWSPAPER

Campeão 687338
Owner: Sociedade Vicra Desportiva, S.A.
Editorial: Travessa da Queimada, 23 - R/C, 1 e 2, Lisboa 1249-113 **Tel:** 351 213 463 981
Email: publicidvd@abola.pt **Web site:** http://www.abola.pt
Circ: 120000 Publisher's Statement
Profile: Special issue devoted to the winner of the National Football League. Mainland.Local Translation: Edição especial dedicada ao vencedor do campeonato nacional de futebol.
Language (s): Portuguese
DAILY NEWSPAPER

Campeão Nacional 687340
Owner: Global Notícias, Publicações, S.A.
Tel: 351 222 096 100
Email: secdir@jn.pt **Web site:** http://www.jn.pt
Circ: 106871 Publisher's Statement
Profile: National. Local Translation:Edição especial dedicada ao vencedor do campeonato nacional. Phone: +351 213 187 300
Language (s): Portuguese
DAILY NEWSPAPER

O Campo 425649
Owner: Jota CBS - Comunicação e Imagem, Lda.
Editorial: R. Sanches de Miranda, 12 A, Castro Verde 7780 **Tel:** 351 286 915 473
Freq: Weekly
Language (s): Portuguese
DAILY NEWSPAPER

Carta do Amigo 425652
Owner: Fraternidade Cristã dos Doentes e Limitados Físicos
Editorial: R. de S. Barnabe, 42, Braga 4710-309
Email: avila-cha@facfil.ucp.pt
Freq: Bi-Monthly
Language (s): Portuguese
DAILY NEWSPAPER

Cascais Oeiras 765400
Owner: Grupo Lanjet
Editorial: Apartado 165, Carcavelos 2775-321
Tel: 351 968 051 982
Email: cascaisoeiras@netcabo.pt
Freq: Bi-Weekly
Profile: Local Translation: Jornal regional com informação geral dos concelhos de Cascais e Oeiras.Phone: +351 309 890 691
Language (s): Portuguese
DAILY NEWSPAPER

Ciclismo 597366
Owner: Edisport - Sociedade de Publicações Desportivas, S.A.
Editorial: Av. Conde de Valbom, 30 - 4/5, Lisboa 1050-068 **Tel:** 351 210 124 900
Email: antoniomagalhaes@record.pt **Web site:** http://www.record.xl.pt
Circ: 109613 Publisher's Statement
Language (s): Portuguese
DAILY NEWSPAPER

Cinco Quinas 585023
Owner: Graficôa - Sociedade de Artes Gráficas e Publicações, Lda.
Editorial: Jornal Cinco Quinas, Lote 36, Zona Industrial, Sabugal 6320-317 **Tel:** 351 271 615 054
Email: cincoquinas@gmail.com **Web site:** http://www.cincoquinas.com
Freq: Monthly
Language (s): Portuguese
Ad Rate: Full Page Mono 100.00
Ad Rate: Full Page Colour 200.00
Currency: Euro
DAILY NEWSPAPER

Classificados 425338
Owner: Presselivre - Imprensa Livre, S.A.
Editorial: Av. Joao Crisostomo, 72, Lisboa 1069-043
Tel: 351 213 185 200
Email: direccao@cmjornal.pt **Web site:** http://www.cmjornal.pt
Freq: Daily; **Circ:** 156337 APCT
Profile: Newspaper supplement with classified advertisement, arranged according to specific categories or classifications. The three major headings are employment, real estate, and automotive, although there are additional categories (e.g., business opportunities, pets, personal ads and legal notices). National. Read predominantly by public sector employees and those seeking employment of northern Portugal.Local Translation: Caderno de oportunidades com as seguintes categorias: mercado imobiliário, contactos, diversos, automóveis e emprego.Phone: +351 213 540 382; +351 213 540 386
Fax: +351 213 540 386
Language (s): Portuguese
Ad Rate: Full Page Mono 2160.00
Ad Rate: Full Page Colour 3240.00
Currency: Euro
DAILY NEWSPAPER

Classificados 578281
Owner: Edisport - Sociedade de Publicações Desportivas, S.A.
Editorial: Av. Conde de Valbom, 30 - 4/5, Lisboa 1050-068 **Tel:** 351 210 124 900
Email: antoniomagalhaes@record.pt **Web site:** http://www.record.xl.pt
Freq: Daily; **Circ:** 115568 APCT
Profile: Real estate, cars and jobs. Mainland.Local Translation: Caderno de oportunidades nas seguintes categorias: mercado imobiliário, automóveis e emprego.
Language (s): Portuguese
Ad Rate: Full Page Mono 2160.00
Ad Rate: Full Page Colour 3240.00
Currency: Euro
DAILY NEWSPAPER

Classificados Tuti 425430
Owner: Global Notícias, Publicações, S.A.
Editorial: Av. da Liberdade, 266 - 1, Lisboa 1250-149
Tel: 351 213 187 500
Email: master@tuti.pt **Web site:** www.tuti.pt
Freq: Daily; **Circ:** 106993 Publisher's Statement
Profile: Newspaper supplement with classified advertisement. The three major headings are employment, real estate, and automotive, although there are additional categories (e.g., business opportunities, personals, and legal notices). National. General population.Local Translation: Caderno de compra, venda, alguer, arrendamento e troca, com os seguintes sectores: mercado imobiliário, veículos, emprego e diversos.
Language (s): Portuguese
Ad Rate: Full Page Mono 2400.00
Ad Rate: Full Page Colour 3360.00
Currency: Euro
DAILY NEWSPAPER

Classificados Tuti Casas 765839
Owner: Global Notícias, Publicações, S.A.
Editorial: R. de Goncalo Cristovao, 195, Porto 4049-011 **Tel:** 351 213 187 500
Email: secdir@jn.pt **Web site:** http://www.jn.pt
Circ: 122218 Publisher's Statement
Profile: National. Local Translation:Caderno de compra, venda, alguer, arrendamento e troca no sector do mercado imobiliário.
Language (s): Portuguese
DAILY NEWSPAPER

Classificados Tuti Emprego 765840
Owner: Global Notícias, Publicações, S.A.
Editorial: R. de Goncalo Cristovao, 195, Porto 4049-011 **Tel:** 351 213 187 500
Email: secdir@jn.pt **Web site:** http://www.jn.pt
Circ: 112110 Publisher's Statement
Profile: National. Local Translation:Caderno de divulgação de procura e oferta de emprego.
Language (s): Portuguese
DAILY NEWSPAPER

Classificados Tuti Veículos 765843
Owner: Global Notícias, Publicações, S.A.
Editorial: R. de Goncalo Cristovao, 195, Porto 4049-011 **Tel:** 351 213 187 500
Email: secdir@jn.pt **Web site:** http://www.jn.pt
Circ: 112110 Publisher's Statement
Profile: National. Local Translation:Caderno de compra, venda e aluguer de automóveis.
Language (s): Portuguese
DAILY NEWSPAPER

Concelhos 595665
Owner: Edisport - Sociedade de Publicações Desportivas, S.A.
Editorial: Av. Conde de Valbom, 30 - 4/5, Lisboa 1050-068 **Tel:** 351 210 124 900
Email: antoniomagalhaes@record.pt **Web site:** http://www.record.xl.pt
Circ: 110831 APCT
Language (s): Portuguese
DAILY NEWSPAPER

Conferência 765853
Owner: Presselivre - Imprensa Livre, S.A.
Editorial: Av. Joao Crisostomo, 72, Lisboa 1069-043
Tel: 351 213 185 462
Email: sede@cofina.pt **Web site:** http://www.cmjornal.pt
Circ: 164141 Publisher's Statement
Profile: National. Local Translation:Edição especial relativa às Conferências Correio da Manhã, sobre o Estado da Nação.
Language (s): Portuguese
DAILY NEWSPAPER

Congressos 778800
Owner: Global Notícias, Publicações, S.A.
Editorial: R. de Goncalo Cristovao, 195, Porto 4049-011 **Tel:** 351 213 187 500
Email: secdir@jn.pt **Web site:** http://www.jn.pt
Circ: 107777 APCT
Profile: National. Local Translation:Suplemento dedicado a variados congressos que têm como mote o património e desenvolvimento do território.
Language (s): Portuguese
DAILY NEWSPAPER

Construção Civil & Obras Públicas 425342
Owner: Global Notícias, Publicações, S.A.
Editorial: R. de Goncalo Cristovao 195-219, Porto 4049-011 **Tel:** 351 222 096 100
Email: dpe@jn.pt **Web site:** http://www.jn.pt
Circ: 107589 APCT
Profile: National. Local Translation:Suplemento sobre o sector da construção.
Email: secdir@jn.pt; roteiro@jn.pt.Phone: +351 213 187 300
Language (s): Portuguese
Ad Rate: Full Page Mono 2700.00
Ad Rate: Full Page Colour 3780.00
Currency: Euro
DAILY NEWSPAPER

Cooperativas de Habitação 494487
Owner: Presselivre - Imprensa Livre, S.A.
Editorial: Av. Joao Crisostomo, N 72, Lisboa 1069-043 **Tel:** 351 213 185 462
Email: geral@correiomanha.pt **Web site:** http://www.cmjornal.pt
Circ: 151203 Not Audited
Language (s): Portuguese
Ad Rate: Full Page Mono 2020.00
Ad Rate: Full Page Colour 3030.00
Currency: Euro
DAILY NEWSPAPER

Correio da Manhã 158281
Owner: Presselivre - Imprensa Livre, S.A.
Editorial: Arruamento D à R. Jose Maria Nicolau, 3, Lisboa 1549-023 **Tel:** 351 213 185 200
Email: direccao@cmjornal.pt **Web site:** www.cmjornal.pt
Freq: Daily; **Circ:** 161374 APCT
Editor: Carlos Ferreira; **Editor Chefe:** Paulo Fonte; **Editor:** João Mira Godinho; **Photographer:** Rui Miguel Pedrosa; **Editor:** Marco Pereira; **Editor:** Mário Pereira; **Editor:** Ricardo Ramos; **Editor:** Hugo Real; **Editor:** Rui Pedro Vieira
Profile: Tabloid-sized newspaper providing coverage of national news, events and current affairs. Contains political, economical and international news, interviews and information concerning the environment and current events. Particular emphasis is placed upon advertising, recruitment, entertainment, motoring and sport. National.Local Translation: Diário generalista em formato tablóide com informação nacional e internacional. Actualidade, sociedade, economia, política, desporto, cultura, media, celebridades, agenda e programação televisiva são alguns dos temas focados. "Vidas" é o suplemento fixo deste jornal.Fax: +351 213 540 386
Language (s): Portuguese
Ad Rate: Full Page Mono 6795.00
Ad Rate: Full Page Colour 10170.00
Currency: Euro
DAILY NEWSPAPER

Correio da Murtosa 424818
Owner: Litoral Texto - Sociedade de Comunicação, Lda.
Editorial: R. 29 de Outubro, 8 - 1 A, Pardelhas - Murtosa 3870-206 **Tel:** 351 234 838 054
Email: correio.murtosa@sapo.pt
Freq: Monthly
Profile: Monthly regional newspaper with information about Murtosa (Aveiro). Politics, current affairs, society, religion, sport, entertainment and events.
Language (s): Portuguese
DAILY NEWSPAPER

Correio do Ribatejo 238204
Owner: João Arruda Sucessores, Lda.
Editorial: R. Serpa Pinto, 98/104, Apartado 323, Santarem 2000-046 **Tel:** 351 243 333 116
Email: geral@correiodoribatejo.com **Web site:** http://www.correiodoribatejo.com
Freq: Weekly; **Circ:** 6000 APCT
Managing Director: João Paulo Narciso
Profile: Weekly regional newspaper with information about Ribatejo region. Politics, current affairs, society, religion, sport, entertainment and events. Read in Santarém region.Local Translation: Jornal semanal com informação relativa à região do Ribatejo. Política, actualidade, sociedade, religião, desporto, entretenimento e eventos.
Language (s): Portuguese
Ad Rate: Full Page Mono 800.00
Ad Rate: Full Page Colour 1000.00
Currency: Euro
DAILY NEWSPAPER

Criança 428538
Owner: Global Notícias, Publicações, S.A.
Editorial: Parque Biologico de Gaia, E.M., Estrada Nacional 222, Avintes 4430-757 **Tel:** 351 227 878 120
Email: revista@parquebiologico.pt **Web site:** http://www.parquebiologico.pt
Circ: 111762 Publisher's Statement
Profile: National. Local Translation:Edição especial com informações e dicas de saúde, alimentação, moda e produtos para crianças.
Language (s): Portuguese
DAILY NEWSPAPER

O Crime 415168
Owner: Letra de Forma
Editorial: R. Alexandre Herculano, N 1 - 2 Dto., Lisboa 1150-005 **Tel:** 351 210 962 060
Email: jornalcrime@gmail.com
Freq: Weekly; **Circ:** 25000 APCT
Managing Director: Carlos Saraiva
Profile: Weekly national newspaper covering crime stories. National.Local Translation: Jornal que foca essencialmente a vida das celebridades e casos policiais e judiciais.
Language (s): Portuguese
Ad Rate: Full Page Mono 1200.00
Ad Rate: Full Page Colour 1500.00
Currency: Euro
DAILY NEWSPAPER

Cultura 425414
Owner: Global Notícias, Publicações, S.A.
Editorial: Av. da Liberdade, 266 - 4, Lisboa 1250-149
Tel: 351 213 187 500
Email: secdir@jn.pt **Web site:** http://www.jn.pt
Circ: 107777 APCT
Profile: National.
Language (s): Portuguese
DAILY NEWSPAPER

Cultura 691615
Owner: Sojornal - Sociedade Jornalística e Editorial, S.A.
Tel: 351 214 544 000
Email: expresso@expresso.pt **Web site:** http://www.expresso.pt
Circ: 134400 Publisher's Statement
Profile: National. Local Translation:Edição especial ocasional com informações e curiosidades sobre cultura e artes.
Language (s): Portuguese
DAILY NEWSPAPER

D'Angeja - Mensário Informativo e Cultural 424825
Owner: Associação Os Amigos do Jornal D'Angeja
Editorial: R. Antonio Castilho, Angeja 3850-406
Tel: 351 234 911 163
Email: d.angeja@mail.pt
Freq: Monthly
Language (s): Portuguese
DAILY NEWSPAPER

Datas Festivas 667949
Owner: Transjornal Edição de Publicações, S.A.
Tel: 351 214 169 210
Email: metro@metroportugal.com **Web site:** http://www.readmetro.com
Circ: 130000 Publisher's Statement
Language (s): Portuguese
DAILY NEWSPAPER

Desporto 425351
Owner: Global Notícias, Publicações, S.A.
Editorial: R. de Goncalo Cristovao, 195-219, Porto 4049-011 **Tel:** 351 222 096 100
Email: desporto@jn.pt **Web site:** http://www.jn.pt
Circ: 112136 APCT
Profile: Supplement about sports, specially about the national football championship. Sports news, events and interviews. National.Local Translation: Suplemento com especial destaque para o mundo do futebol, com particular incidência no campeonato português de futebol. Composto por notícias do desporto-rei, de eventos a ter lugar e entrevistas com figuras e intervenientes desta modalidade.Phone: +351 213 187 300
Language (s): Portuguese
Ad Rate: Full Page Mono 2700.00
Ad Rate: Full Page Colour 3780.00
Currency: Euro
DAILY NEWSPAPER

Desporto 690699
Owner: R/com
Editorial: R. Ivens, 14, Lisboa 1249-108
Tel: 351 213 239 239
Email: jornalonline@pagina1.pt **Web site:** http://www.pagina1.pt
Profile: Sports. National.Local Translation: Edição especial com as principais informações desportivas da actualidade, com especial destaque para o futebol.Phone: +351 213 239 200 Geographical Focus: Sport
Language (s): Portuguese
DAILY NEWSPAPER

Destak 237595
Owner: Cofina Media Internet
Editorial: Arruamento D à R. Jose Maria Nicolau, 3, Lisboa 1549-023 **Tel:** 351 214 169 210
Email: destak@destak.pt **Web site:** http://www.destak.pt
Freq: Daily; **Circ:** 135000 Publisher's Statement
Managing Director: Isabel Stilwell

Profile: Daily free newspaper. Read in Aveiro, Braga, Coimbra, Leiria, Lisboa, Porto and Setúbal districts.Local Translation: O Destak é um jornal diário, de distribuição gratuita. Apresenta notícias curtas e directas, essencialmente sobre actualidade, notícias locais, nacionais e internacionais, desporto, lazer, bem-estar e cultura.
Language (s): Portuguese
Ad Rate: Full Page Mono 9200.00
Ad Rate: Full Page Colour 9200.00
Currency: Euro
DAILY NEWSPAPER

Dia Mundial 592216
Owner: Presselivre - Imprensa Livre, S.A.
Editorial: Av. Joao Crisostomo, N 72, Lisboa 1069-043 **Tel:** 351 213 185 462
Email: geral@correiomanha.pt **Web site:** http://www.cmjornal.pt
Circ: 163496 APCT
Profile: National. Local Translation:Suplemento dedicado à comemoração de dias especiais como o Dia Mundial da Alimentação, da Saúde, do Ambiente, entre muitos outros.
Language (s): Portuguese
DAILY NEWSPAPER

Dia Mundial (DN + JN) 671023
Owner: Global Notícias, Publicações, S.A.
Tel: 351 213 187 500
Email: dnot@dn.pt
Circ: 165912 Publisher's Statement
Profile: Published with: Diário de Notícias; Jornal de Notícias. National.Local Translation: Suplemento dedicado à comemoração de dias especiais como o Dia Mundial da Alimentação, da Saúde, do Ambiente, entre muitos outros.Publicado com: Diário de Notícias; Jornal de Notícias
Language (s): Portuguese
DAILY NEWSPAPER

Diário As Beiras 235460
Owner: Sojormedia Beiras, S.A.
Editorial: R. Abel Dias Urbano, 4, 2, Coimbra 3000-001 **Tel:** 351 239 980 280
Email: beirastexto@asbeiras.pt **Web site:** www.asbeiras.pt
Freq: Daily; **Circ:** 12000 APCT
Director Comercial: Luís Filipe Figueiredo; **Managing Director:** Agostinho Franklin; **Editor Chefe:** Dora Loureiro; **Director adjunto:** Eduarda Macário
Profile: Daily newspaper with information about Aveiro, Coimbra, Leiria, Viseu, Guarda and Castelo Branco regions. Politics, current affairs, society, religion, sport, entertainment and events. Read in Aveiro, Castelo Branco, Coimbra, Guarda, Leiria and Viseu but also in Lisboa and Porto regions.Local Translation: Diário com informação relativa à região centro. Política, actualidade, sociedade, desporto, entretenimento e eventos são alguns dos temas abordados. Apresenta os conteúdos em quatro grandes áreas: Essencial, Pensar, Agir e Viver. Primeiro jornal português com Certificação de Qualidade Serviço.Email: redaccao@asbeiras.pt. Phone: +351 962 107 671
Language (s): Portuguese
Ad Rate: Full Page Mono 1500.00
Ad Rate: Full Page Colour 1850.00
Currency: Euro
DAILY NEWSPAPER

Diário Cidade 511422
Owner: Liberal - Empresa de Artes Gráficas, Lda.
Editorial: PEZO - Parque Industrial Zona Oeste, Lote 7, Socorridos, Câmara De Lobos/madeira 9304-006 **Tel:** 351 291 623 499
Email: diariocidade@diariocidade.pt **Web site:** http://www.diariocidade.pt
Freq: Daily; **Circ:** 22219 Publisher's Statement
Managing Director: Edgar R. de Aguiar; **Advertising Manager:** José Manuel Gomes
Profile: Free daily newspaper with information regarding Madeira. Local Translation:Diário gratuito de informação regional com informação relativa à Madeira. Actualidade regional, cultura, economia e sociedade são os temas centrais.
Email: edgaraguiar-35m@adv.oa.pt; hvalente@diariocidade.pt.Phone: +351 291 623 696
Language (s): Portuguese
Ad Rate: Full Page Mono 900.00
Ad Rate: Full Page Colour 1100.00
Currency: Euro
DAILY NEWSPAPER

Diário de Aveiro 158288
Owner: Adriano Lucas - Gestão e Comunicação Social, Lda.
Editorial: Av. Dr. Lourenco Peixinho, 15 - 1 G, Aveiro 3800-801 **Tel:** 351 234 000 030
Email: diarioaveiro@diarioaveiro.pt **Web site:** www.diarioaveiro.pt
Freq: Daily; **Circ:** 7014 APCT
Director adjunto: Miguel Callé Lucas; **Director adjunto:** J. C. Galiano Pinheiro; **Editor Chefe:** José Manuel Rodrigues Silva; **Director adjunto:** Arménio Travassos
Profile: Daily magazine with information about Aveiro region. Politics, current affairs, society, sport, entertainment and events. Read by the population of Aveiro.Local Translation: Diário regional com informação relativa a Aveiro. Actualidade, política, sociedade, desporto, eventos e entretenimento.
Language (s): Portuguese
Ad Rate: Full Page Mono 181253.00
Ad Rate: Full Page Colour 235629.00
Currency: Euro
DAILY NEWSPAPER

Diário de Coimbra 158297
Owner: Adriano Lucas - Gestão e Comunicação Social, Lda.
Editorial: R. Adriano Lucas, Apartado 542, Coimbra 3020-264 **Tel:** 351 239 499 900
Email: redac@diariocoimbra.pt **Web site:** www.diariocoimbra.pt
Freq: Daily; **Circ:** 10321 APCT
Director adjunto: João Luís Campos; **Director adjunto:** J. C. Galiano Pinheiro; **Advertising Manager:** Mário Rasteiro; **Editor Chefe:** António Manuel Rodrigues; **Director adjunto:** Arménio Travassos
Profile: Daily regional newspaper with information about the center region of Portugal. Politics, current affairs, society, religion, sport, entertainment and events. Aimed mainly for Coimbra population, but also distributed in Aveiro, Castelo Branco, Guarda, Lisboa, Porto and Viseu.Local Translation: Jornal regional diário que destaca a informação relativa ao distrito de Coimbra. Política, actualidade, sociedade, desporto, entretenimento e eventos são alguns dos temas abordados.Phone: +351 239 499 930
Language (s): Portuguese
Ad Rate: Full Page Mono 1600.00
Ad Rate: Full Page Colour 2080.00
Currency: Euro
DAILY NEWSPAPER

Diário de Leiria 158296
Owner: Adriano Lucas - Gestão e Comunicação Social, Lda.
Editorial: Edifício Maringa, R. S. Francisco, 7 - 4 Esq., Leiria 2400-000 **Tel:** 351 244 000 030
Email: diarioleiria@diarioleiria.pt **Web site:** www.diarioleiria.pt
Freq: Daily; **Circ:** 36413 APCT
Director adjunto: João Luís Campos; **Director adjunto:** Miguel Callé Lucas; **Director adjunto:** J. C. Galiano Pinheiro; **Editor Chefe:** José Carlos Salgueiro; **Director adjunto:** João Paulo Silva; **Director adjunto:** Arménio Travassos
Profile: Daily regional newspaper with information about Leiria. Politics, current affairs, society, religion, sport, entertainment and events. Read in Leiria region.Local Translation: Jornal reginal com informação sobre Leiria. Política, actualidade, sociedade, religião, desporto, entretenimento e eventos são assuntos habituais.
Language (s): Portuguese
Ad Rate: Full Page Mono 998.80
Currency: Euro
DAILY NEWSPAPER

Diário de Notícias da Madeira 158298
Owner: Empresa Diário de Notícias, Lda.
Editorial: R. Dr. Fernao de Ornelas, 56 - 3, Funchal 9054-514 **Tel:** 351 291 202 300
Email: secretariado@dnoticias.pt **Web site:** www.dnoticias.pt
Freq: Daily; **Circ:** 12972 APCT
Director Comercial: Luís Ferreira; **Photographer:** Teresa Gonçalves; **Advertising Manager:** Luís Carlos Gouveia; **Managing Director:** João Marcelino; **Managing Director:** Ricardo Miguel de Oliveira; **Director Comercial:** Roberto Passos; **Advertising Manager:** Gonçalo Pimenta; **Photographer:** Agostinho Spínola
Profile: Read by Madeira population. Local Translation:Diário de informação regional relativa à ilha da Madeira. Política, Regional, Desporto, Cultura, Casos do Dia e Dê Notícias são algumas das secções que fazem parte deste jornal. Em 2010 foi considerado o Jornal Europeu do Ano, na edição do European Newspaper Award. O título ganhou na categoria de jornal local. Alternative Title: DN MadeiraEmail: lgouveia@dnoticias.pt.
Language (s): Portuguese
Ad Rate: Full Page Mono 1122.00
Ad Rate: Full Page Colour 1683.00
Currency: Euro
DAILY NEWSPAPER

Diário do Minho 158295
Owner: Empresa Diário do Minho, Lda.
Editorial: R. de Santa Margarida, 4 A, Braga 4710-306 **Tel:** 351 253 609 460
Email: redaccao@diariodominho.pt **Web site:** www.diariodominho.pt
Freq: Daily; **Circ:** 8500 APCT
Editor Chefe: Damião Pereira; **Managing Director:** Luís da Silva Pereira
Profile: Daily regional newspaper with information about the north region of Portugal. Politics, current affairs, society, religion, sport, entertainment and events. Read in Braga and Viana do Castelo regions.Local Translation: Diário regional com informação sobre a região Norte de Portugal, em particular sobre política, actualidade, sociedade, religião, desporto, entretenimento e eventos.
Language (s): Portuguese
Ad Rate: Full Page Mono 550.00
Currency: Euro
DAILY NEWSPAPER

Diário do Sul 235794
Owner: Piçarra & Companhia, Lda.
Editorial: Travessa de Santo Andre, 6 - 8, Apartado 2037, Evora 7000-951 **Tel:** 351 266 744 444
Email: administracao@diariodosul.com.pt **Web site:** http://www.diariodosul.com.pt
Freq: Daily; **Circ:** 6000 APCT
Director adjunto: Manuel Piçarra; **Managing Director:** Manuel Madeira Piçarra
Profile: Daily regional newspaper with information about the south region of Portugal. Politics, current affairs, society, religion, sport, entertainment and events. Read in Beja, Évora, Faro, Lisboa, Portalegre and Setúbal.Local Translation: Jornal diário com informação relativa à região do Alentejo. Política, actualidade, sociedade, religião, desporto, entretenimento e eventos são alguns dos temas abordados. Recebeu o Prémio Gazeta Imprensa Regional 2008 atribuído pelo Clube de Jornalistas.Email: redacao@diariodosul.com.pt.
Language (s): Portuguese
Ad Rate: Full Page Mono 700.00
Ad Rate: Full Page Colour 2000.00
Currency: Euro
DAILY NEWSPAPER

Dica da Semana 238199
Owner: Lidl & Cia - Lojas Alimentares
Editorial: Av. 25 de Abril de 1974, 21A, Linda-A-Velha 2795-197
Web site: http://www.lidl.pt
Freq: Weekly; **Circ:** 2800770 APCT
Managing Director: Ana Frazão
Profile: Mainland. Local Translation:Publicação grátis do hipermercado Lidl. Contém os preços de alguns dos produtos do Lidl, sugestões de limpeza e manutenção para a casa.
Language (s): Portuguese
Ad Rate: Full Page Colour 1800.00
Currency: Euro
DAILY NEWSPAPER

Dinheiro 613678
Owner: Sojornal - Sociedade Jornalística e Editorial, S.A.
Editorial: Edifício S. Francisco de Sales, R. Calvet de Magalhaes, 242, Paço De Arcos 2770-022
Tel: 351 214 544 000
Email: ipublishing@impresa.pt **Web site:** http://www.expresso.pt
Circ: 126575 APCT
Profile: National. Local Translation:Suplemento sobre poupança: a poupança em Portugal, a educação financeira, os bancos e fundos de investimento.
Language (s): Portuguese
DAILY NEWSPAPER

Dinheiro Vivo (DN + JN) 772774
Owner: Controlinveste SGPS, S.A.
Editorial: Av. da Liberdade, 266 - 5 Piso, Lisboa 1250-149 **Tel:** 351 213 187 500
Email: dinheirovivo@dinheirovivo.pt **Web site:** www.dinheirovivo.pt
Freq: Weekly; **Circ:** 178238 Publisher's Statement
Editor: Gouveia de Albuquerque; **Editor:** Pedro Araújo; **Editor:** Teresa Costa; **Editor:** Armando Fonseca Júnior; **Managing Director:** André Macedo; **Editor:** Vítor Martins; **Editor Chefe:** Silvia de Oliveira; **Director adjunto:** Miguel Pacheco; **Editor Chefe:** Joana Petiz; **Editor:** Helena Santareno
Profile: Published with: Diário de Notícias; Jornal de Notícias. National.Local Translation: Suplemento com base no portal Dinheiro Vivo, dedicado a áreas específicas, como Economia, Estado, Empresas e Mercados. Contém ainda um espaço dedicado ao Marketing, Publicidade e Media, o Buzz.Publicado com: Diário de Notícias; Jornal de Notícias Geographical Focus: Wirtschaft
Language (s): Portuguese
Ad Rate: Full Page Colour 11250.00
Currency: Euro
DAILY NEWSPAPER

Domingo 597368
Owner: Global Notícias, Publicações, S.A.
Editorial: R. de Goncalo Cristovao 195-219, Porto 4049-011 **Tel:** 351 222 096 100
Email: dpe@jn.pt **Web site:** http://www.jn.pt
Freq: Weekly; **Circ:** 116459 Publisher's Statement
Profile: National. Local Translation:Suplemento semanal com notícias nacionais e internacionais. Inclui várias temáticas: política, economia, sociedade, desporto, saúde e cultura.
Email: secdir@jn.pt.Phone: +351 213 187 300
Language (s): Portuguese
Ad Rate: Full Page Mono 2700.00
Ad Rate: Full Page Colour 3780.00
Currency: Euro
DAILY NEWSPAPER

O Eco 415170
Owner: Sojormedia - Comunicação Social, S.A.
Editorial: Largo do Carmo, 20 - R/C Esq., Apartado 1, Pombal 3100-464 **Tel:** 351 236 209 930
Email: ecoregional@sapo.pt **Web site:** http://www.oeco.pt
Freq: Monthly; **Circ:** 10000 Publisher's Statement
Advertising Manager: João Agrela
Profile: Weekly newspaper. Politics, current affairs, society, sport, entertainment and events. Read by Pombal and northern Leiria district locals.Local Translation: Gratuito de informação regional relativa aos concelhos situados a norte do distrito de Leiria. Actualidade, política, sociedade, negócios e desporto são alguns dos temas habituais neste jornal.Email: adriana.afonso@oeco.pt; info@oeco.pt. Phone: +351 962 108 736
Language (s): Portuguese
Ad Rate: Full Page Mono 700.00
Ad Rate: Full Page Colour 800.00
Currency: Euro
DAILY NEWSPAPER

Eco de Vagos 424835
Owner: João dos Santos Ferreira
Editorial: R. Dr. Francisco de Almeida Brito, 65, Soza, Vagos 3840-347 **Tel:** 351 234 791 984
Web site: http://www.ecodevagos.com
Freq: Monthly
Language (s): Portuguese
DAILY NEWSPAPER

Econews 592879
Owner: Publiregiões - Sociedade Jornalística e Editorial, Lda.
Editorial: Al. Antonio Sergio, 7 - 1 D, Linda-A-Velha 2799-531 **Tel:** 351 214 157 200
Email: jr-editor@jornaldaregiao.pt **Web site:** http://www.jornaldaregiao.pt
Circ: 225000 Publisher's Statement
Profile: Read in Cascais, Oeiras, Amadora e Almada. Local Translation:Suplemento dedicado ao ambiente. Publicado com: Jornal da Região - Cascais; Jornal da Região - Almada; Jornal da Região - Oeiras; Jornal da Região - Amadora; Jornal da Região - Sintra
Language (s): Portuguese
DAILY NEWSPAPER

Economia 425012
Owner: Sojornal - Sociedade Jornalística e Editorial, S.A.
Editorial: Edifício S. Francisco de Sales, R. Calvet de Magalhaes, 242, Paço De Arcos 2770-022
Tel: 351 214 544 000
Email: economia@expresso.impresa.pt **Web site:** http://www.expresso.pt
Freq: Weekly; **Circ:** 132175 Publisher's Statement
Profile: Magazine containing the latest news about national and international economy. Interviews and opinions of famous economists or business people. National.Local Translation: As últimas notícias relativas à economia nacional e internacional. Contém entrevistas e artigos de opinião de economistas e de pessoas ligadas ao mundo dos negócios.Email: ipublishing@impresa.pt.
Language (s): Portuguese
Ad Rate: Full Page Mono 13005.00
Ad Rate: Full Page Colour 17340.00
Currency: Euro
DAILY NEWSPAPER

Ecos da Ria 424838
Owner: Fábrica da Igreja Paroquial de Beduido
Editorial: Residência Paroquial de Beduido, Estarreja 3860-329 **Tel:** 351 234 843 788
Email: ecosdaria@netvisao.pt
Freq: Monthly
Language (s): Portuguese
DAILY NEWSPAPER

Ecos do Sameiro 425683
Owner: Confraria de Nossa Senhora da Conceição do Monte Sameiro
Editorial: Sameiro - Espinho, Braga 4710-023
Tel: 351 253 675 521
Email: sameiro@diocese-braga.pt **Web site:** http://www.diocese-braga.pt/sameiro
Freq: Monthly
Language (s): Portuguese
DAILY NEWSPAPER

Eleições 594011
Owner: Sociedade Vicra Desportiva, S.A.
Editorial: Travessa da Queimada, 23 - R/C, 1 e 2, Lisboa 1249-113 **Tel:** 351 213 463 981
Web site: http://www.abola.pt
Circ: 120901 Publisher's Statement
Language (s): Portuguese
DAILY NEWSPAPER

Emprego 516702
Owner: Sojornal - Sociedade Jornalística e Editorial, S.A.
Editorial: Edifício S. Francisco de Sales, R. Calvet de Magalhaes, 242, Paço De Arcos 2770-022
Tel: 351 214 544 000
Email: ipublishing@impresa.pt **Web site:** http://www.expresso.pt
Freq: Weekly; **Circ:** 132175 Publisher's Statement
Profile: National. Local Translation:Jornal onde se pode procurar ou divulgar emprego. Informa ainda acerca de formações/especializações que se podem cursar.
Language (s): Portuguese
Ad Rate: Full Page Colour 6000.00
Currency: Euro
DAILY NEWSPAPER

Ensino 541713
Owner: Global Notícias, Publicações, S.A.
Editorial: R. de Goncalo Cristovao 195-219, Porto 4049-011 **Tel:** 351 222 096 100
Email: dpe@jn.pt **Web site:** http://www.jn.pt
Circ: 112136 APCT
Profile: National. Local Translation:Suplemento sobre o ensino, desde o básico ao superior.
Email: secdir@jn.pt.Phone: +351 213 187 300
Language (s): Portuguese
Ad Rate: Full Page Colour 1500.00
Currency: Euro
DAILY NEWSPAPER

Ensino Superior 516722
Owner: Sojornal - Sociedade Jornalística e Editorial, S.A.
Editorial: R. Calvet de Magalhaes, 242, Laveiras, Paço De Arcos 2770-022 **Tel:** 351 214 544 000
Email: guiadoestudante@expresso.pt **Web site:** http://www.expresso.pt
Circ: 160400 Not Audited
Profile: National. Local Translation:Suplemento sobre o Instituto Superior Técnico.
Language (s): Portuguese
Ad Rate: Full Page Colour 3600.00
Currency: Euro
DAILY NEWSPAPER

Ensino Superior 549799
Owner: Presselivre - Imprensa Livre, S.A.
Editorial: Av. Joao Crisostomo, 72, Lisboa 1069-043 **Tel:** 351 213 185 462
Email: geral@correiomanha.pt **Web site:** http://www.cmjornal.pt
Circ: 184677 APCT
Profile: National. Local Translation:Suplemento sobre o ensino superior, que contém informação relativa ao concurso nacional de acesso.
Language (s): Portuguese
Ad Rate: Full Page Mono 2020.00
Ad Rate: Full Page Colour 3030.00
Currency: Euro
DAILY NEWSPAPER

Espaços & Casas 516707
Owner: Sojornal - Sociedade Jornalistica e Editorial, S.A.
Editorial: Edificio S. Francisco de Sales, R. Calvet de Magalhaes, 242, Paço De Arcos 2770-022 **Tel:** 351 214 544 000
Email: ipublishing@impresa.pt **Web site:** http://www.expresso.pt
Freq: Weekly; **Circ:** 132175 Publisher's Statement
Profile: National. Local Translation:Suplemento onde se podem encontrar anúncios relativos à compra e venda de apartamentos, armazéns, escritórios, lojas, moradias e terrenos. Inclui desde a edição de 1 de Outubro de 2007 duas páginas dedicadas às principais peças do programa Magazine Imobiliário, uma vez que foi estabelecida uma perceria de partilha de conteúdos entre O Magazine Imobiliário, na SIC Notícias, o caderno Espaços & Casas do Expresso e o site Expressoimobiliario.pt.
Language (s): Portuguese
Ad Rate: Full Page Mono 5350.00
Ad Rate: Full Page Colour 7490.00
Currency: Euro
DAILY NEWSPAPER

Exame - Melhores Empresas para Trabalhar em Portugal 624259
Owner: Sojornal - Sociedade Jornalistica e Editorial, S.A.
Editorial: Edificio S. Francisco de Sales, R. Calvet de Magalhaes, 242, Paço De Arcos 2770-022 **Tel:** 351 214 544 000
Email: expresso@expresso.pt **Web site:** http://www.expresso.pt
Circ: 133460 Publisher's Statement
Language (s): Portuguese
DAILY NEWSPAPER

Exponor News 175265
Owner: Exponor - Feira Internacional do Porto
Editorial: Exponor - Feira Internacional do Porto, Leça Da Palmeira 4450-617 **Tel:** 351 229 981 400
Email: info@exponor.pt **Web site:** http://www.exponor.pt
Circ: 100000 Publisher's Statement
Profile: Journal focusing on professional exhibitions covering all aspects of trade and industry. Published with: Público.Aimed at conference organisers, exhibitors, marketing personnel, events organisers and managers. Local Translation:Publicação periódica sobre exposições profissionais, cobrindo todos os aspectos do comércio e da indústria. Publicado com: PúblicoEmail: elsa.fernandes@exponor.pt; olivia.morais@exponor.pt.
Language (s): Portuguese
DAILY NEWSPAPER

Expressinho 770681
Owner: Sojornal - Sociedade Jornalistica e Editorial, S.A.
Editorial: Edificio S. Francisco de Sales, R. Calvet de Magalhaes, 242, Paço De Arcos 2770-022 **Tel:** 351 214 544 000
Email: ipublishing@impresa.pt **Web site:** http://www.expresso.pt
Circ: 138380 Publisher's Statement
Profile: National. Aimed for children. Local Translation:Jornal que conta com uma secção noticiosa e outra lúdica, de modo a incentivar os mais novos a iniciarem o hábito de leitura de um jornal.
Language (s): Portuguese
DAILY NEWSPAPER

Expresso 185761
Owner: Sojornal - Sociedade Jornalistica e Editorial, S.A.
Editorial: Edificio S. Francisco de Sales, R. Calvet de Magalhaes, 242, Paço De Arcos 2770-022 **Tel:** 351 214 544 000
Email: ipublishing@impresa.pt **Web site:** http://www.expresso.pt
Freq: Weekly; **Circ:** 132175 APCT
Director adjunto: Miguel Francisco Cadete; **Editor:** Rui Cardoso; **Managing Director:** Ricardo Costa; **Director Comercial:** Maria João Peixe Dias; **Advertising Manager:** Manuela Batle Y Font; **Director adjunto:** João Carlos Garcia; **Editor:** Pedro Lima; **Editor:** Miguel Martins; **Director adjunto:** João Vieira Pereira; **Director adjunto:** Nicolau Santos; **Editor:** Martim Silva; **Editor:** Bárbara Simões; **Director Comercial:** Miguel Simões
Profile: Berliner-sized national newspaper providing coverage of national and international current affairs and in-depth information concerning finance, economics, business and industry. Also covers society, culture, media, sports, fashion, lifestyle and television. National.Local Translation: Semanário de informação em formato berliner. Composto essencialmente por notícias, artigos de opinião e reportagens. Contém artigos relativos à actualidade, política, sociedade, desporto e cultura. Como suplementos fixos tem: "Única", "Actual", "Economia", "Emprego" e "Espaços & Casas". Em 2010, o seu grafismofoi premiado pela European Newspaper Award recebendo cinco menções honrosas. Em 2011 vai estar disponivel nos tablets.Email: site@expresso.impresa.pt.
Language (s): Portuguese
Ad Rate: Full Page Mono 13545.00
Ad Rate: Full Page Colour 18060.00
Currency: Euro
DAILY NEWSPAPER

Expresso de Felgueiras 538033
Owner: Carvalho & Mendes - Edições Gráficas e Audiovisuais, Lda.
Editorial: Edificio Seculo XXI, R. Padre Manuel Lopes Dias Rocha, Lixa 4615-656 **Tel:** 351 255 495 751
Email: geral@expressofelgueiras.com **Web site:** http://www.expressofelgueiras.com
Freq: Bi-Weekly
Language (s): Portuguese
DAILY NEWSPAPER

Farpas 667928
Owner: Miguel Fonseca Ferreira Alvarenga
Email: jornalfarpas@hotmail.com **Web site:** http://farpasblogue.blogspot.com
Freq: Weekly
Managing Director: Miguel da Fonseca Ferreira Alvarenga; **Director adjunto:** Solange Pinto
Language (s): Portuguese
DAILY NEWSPAPER

FC Porto 496036
Owner: Sociedade Vicra Desportiva, S.A.
Editorial: Travessa da Queimada, 23 - R/C, 1 e 2, Lisboa 1249-113 **Tel:** 351 213 463 981
Web site: http://www.abola.pt
Circ: 126895 Not Audited
Language (s): Portuguese
Ad Rate: Full Page Mono 4860.00
Currency: Euro
DAILY NEWSPAPER

Feiras 764977
Owner: Global Notícias, Publicações, S.A.
Editorial: R. de Goncalo Cristovao, 195, Porto 4049-011 **Tel:** 351 222 096 100
Email: secdir@jn.pt **Web site:** http://www.jn.pt
Circ: 110608 APCT
Profile: National. Local Translation:Suplemento com informação relativa a diversas feiras e exposições. Phone: +351 213 187 300
Language (s): Portuguese
DAILY NEWSPAPER

Feiras (JN+DN) 705463
Owner: Global Notícias, Publicações, S.A.
Editorial: R. de Goncalo Cristovao, 195, Porto 4049-011 **Tel:** 351 222 096 100
Email: secdir@jn.pt
Circ: 167926 Publisher's Statement
Profile: National. Local Translation:Suplemento dedicado às feiras realizadas em determinadas regiões do país. Distribuído com: Jornal de Notícias; Diário de NotíciasPhone: +351 213 187 300
Language (s): Portuguese
DAILY NEWSPAPER

Feiras e Festas 538044
Owner: Presselivre - Imprensa Livre, S.A.
Editorial: Av. Joao Crisostomo, 72, Lisboa 1069-043 **Tel:** 351 213 185 200
Email: direccao@cmjornal.pt **Web site:** http://www.cmjornal.pt
Circ: 160521 APCT
Profile: Fairs and Festivals. National.Local Translation: Suplemento com informação relativa a diversas feiras, festas e exposições.Phone: +351 213 540 382; +351 213 540 386
Fax: +351 213 540 386
Language (s): Portuguese
Ad Rate: Full Page Mono 2020.00
Ad Rate: Full Page Colour 3030.00
Currency: Euro
DAILY NEWSPAPER

Festa das Cruzes 531047
Owner: Global Notícias, Publicações, S.A.
Editorial: R. de Goncalo Cristovao 195-219, Porto 4049-011 **Tel:** 351 222 096 100
Email: roteiro@jn.pt **Web site:** http://www.jn.pt
Circ: 120759 Not Audited
Language (s): Portuguese
Ad Rate: Full Page Mono 2700.00
Ad Rate: Full Page Colour 3780.00
Currency: Euro
DAILY NEWSPAPER

Festas 495085
Owner: Presselivre - Imprensa Livre, S.A.
Editorial: Av. Joao Crisostomo, 72, Lisboa 1069-043 **Tel:** 351 213 185 462
Email: geral@correiomanha.pt **Web site:** http://www.cmjornal.pt
Circ: 171395 APCT
Language (s): Portuguese
Ad Rate: Full Page Mono 2020.00
Ad Rate: Full Page Colour 3030.00
Currency: Euro
DAILY NEWSPAPER

Festas 539675
Owner: Global Notícias, Publicações, S.A.
Editorial: R. de Goncalo Cristovao 195-219, Porto 4049-011 **Tel:** 351 222 096 100
Email: dpe@jn.pt **Web site:** http://www.jn.pt
Circ: 107589 APCT
Profile: National. Local Translation:Suplemento dedicado a eventos festivos da região e a festividades anuais tais como: Páscoa, Natal, Carnaval, entre outros.
Email: secdir@jn.pt; roteiro@jn.pt.Phone: +351 213 187 300
Language (s): Portuguese
Ad Rate: Full Page Mono 2700.00
Ad Rate: Full Page Colour 3780.00
Currency: Euro
DAILY NEWSPAPER

Festival (DN + JN) 772776
Editorial: Edificio Diario de Noticias, Av. da Liberdade, 266, Lisboa 1250-149
Tel: 351 213 187 500
Email: dnot@dn.pt
Circ: 168106 Publisher's Statement
Profile: National. Local Translation:Suplemento dedicado ao concelho de Manteigas e ao Festival Serra da Estrela.
Language (s): Portuguese
DAILY NEWSPAPER

Finanças 765953
Owner: Presselivre - Imprensa Livre, S.A.
Editorial: Av. Joao Crisostomo, 72, Lisboa 1069-043 **Tel:** 351 213 185 462
Email: geral@correiomanha.pt **Web site:** http://www.cmjornal.pt
Circ: 164141 Publisher's Statement
Profile: National. Local Translation:Edição especial dedicada às finanças nacionais.
Language (s): Portuguese
DAILY NEWSPAPER

Flor do Tâmega 307999
Owner: Empresa Gráfica e Jornalistica Flor do Tâmega, Lda.
Editorial: Freixo de Cima, Apartado 47, Amarante 4900 **Tel:** 351 255 496 224
Email: flordotamega@sapo.pt
Freq: Monthly
Language (s): Portuguese
DAILY NEWSPAPER

Florestas 765957
Owner: Global Notícias, Publicações, S.A.
Editorial: R. de Goncalo Cristovao, 195, Porto 4049-011 **Tel:** 351 213 187 500
Email: secdir@jn.pt **Web site:** http://www.jn.pt
Circ: 106540 Publisher's Statement
Profile: National. Local Translation:Suplemento dedicado às florestas e sua protecção.
Language (s): Portuguese
DAILY NEWSPAPER

Formação Profissional 495743
Owner: Presselivre - Imprensa Livre, S.A.
Editorial: Av. Joao Crisostomo, 72, Lisboa 1069-043 **Tel:** 351 213 185 200
Email: direccao@cmjornal.pt **Web site:** http://www.cmjornal.pt
Circ: 165562 Publisher's Statement
Profile: Vocational Training. National.Local Translation: Suplemento com informação relativa a novas oportunidades e formação profissional.Phone: +351 213 540 382; +351 213 540 386
Fax: +351 213 540 386
Language (s): Portuguese
DAILY NEWSPAPER

Formação Profissional (DN + JN) 689055
Owner: Global Notícias, Publicações, S.A.
Editorial: Edificio Diario de Noticias, Av. da Liberdade, 266, Lisboa 1250-149
Tel: 351 213 187 500
Email: dnot@dn.pt **Web site:** http://www.dn.pt
Circ: 158416 Publisher's Statement
Profile: Published with: Diário de Notícias; Jornal de Notícias. National.Local Translation: Suplemento sobre Formação Profissional em Portugal.Publicado com: Diário de Notícias; Jornal de Notícias
Email: dn@dn.pt.
Language (s): Portuguese
DAILY NEWSPAPER

Franchising (DN + JN) 673736
Owner: Global Notícias, Publicações, S.A.
Editorial: Edificio Diario de Noticias, Av. da Liberdade, 266, Lisboa 1250-149
Tel: 351 213 187 500
Email: dnot@dn.pt **Web site:** http://www.dn.pt
Circ: 165912 Publisher's Statement
Profile: Published with: Diário de Notícias; Jornal de Notícias. National.Local Translation: Edição especial sobre franchising e negócios. Aborda e expõe casos de sucesso, oportunidades de negócio, exemplos práticos e fornece informação sobre como iniciar um negócio.Publicado com: Diário de Notícias; Jornal de Notícias
Language (s): Portuguese
DAILY NEWSPAPER

Fundação Benfica 765967
Owner: Sociedade Vicra Desportiva, S.A.
Editorial: Travessa da Queimada, 23 - R/C, 1 e 2, Lisboa 1249-113 **Tel:** 351 213 463 981
Web site: http://www.abola.pt
Circ: 120000 Publisher's Statement
Profile: Mainland. Local Translation:Suplemento sobre as iniciativas e eventos da Fundação Benfica. Geographical Focus: Sport
Language (s): Portuguese
DAILY NEWSPAPER

Futebol 526610
Owner: Edisport - Sociedade de Publicações Desportivas, S.A.
Editorial: Av. Conde de Valbom, 30 - 4/5, Lisboa 1050-068 **Tel:** 351 210 124 900
Email: antoniomagalhaes@record.pt **Web site:** http://www.record.xl.pt
Circ: 102718 APCT
Profile: Football. Mainland.Local Translation: Caderno dedicado ao futebol em geral.
Language (s): Portuguese
DAILY NEWSPAPER

Futebol 531168
Owner: Presselivre - Imprensa Livre, S.A.
Editorial: Av. Joao Crisostomo, 72, Lisboa 1069-043 **Tel:** 351 213 185 200
Email: direccao@cmjornal.pt **Web site:** http://www.cmjornal.pt
Circ: 165562 APCT
Profile: Football. National.Local Translation: Suplemento dedicado à modalidade que é o futebol.Phone: +351 213 540 382; +351 213 540 386
Fax: +351 213 540 386
Language (s): Portuguese
DAILY NEWSPAPER

Futuro 778802
Owner: Transjornal Edição de Publicações, S.A.
Editorial: Estrada da Outurela, 118, Parque Holanda - Edificio Holanda, Carnaxide 2790-114
Tel: 351 214 169 210
Email: metro@metroportugal.com **Web site:** http://www.readmetro.com
Circ: 130000 Publisher's Statement
Profile: Aimed for Aveiro, Braga, Coimbra, Évora, Faro, Leiria, Lisboa and Porto regions. Local Translation:Secção com notícias falsas pois são relativas a anos futuros. Phone: +351 214 241 430
Fax: +351 214 174 206
Language (s): Portuguese
DAILY NEWSPAPER

Futuro - Revista da Associação Industrial do Minho 425724
Owner: Associação Industrial do Minho
Editorial: Av. Dr. Francisco Pires Goncalves, 45, Braga 4711-954 **Tel:** 351 253 613 357
Email: aiminho@aiminho.pt
Freq: Quarterly
Language (s): Portuguese
DAILY NEWSPAPER

Gadgets 765971
Owner: Transjornal Edição de Publicações, S.A.
Editorial: Estrada da Outurela, 118, Parque Holanda - Edificio Holanda, Carnaxide 2790-114
Tel: 351 214 169 210
Email: metro@metroportugal.com **Web site:** http://www.readmetro.com
Circ: 130000 Publisher's Statement
Profile: Aimed for Aveiro, Braga, Coimbra, Évora, Faro, Leiria, Lisboa and Porto regions. Local Translation:Edição especial com sugestões de compra de material tecnológico para variadas ocasiões. Phone: +351 214 241 430
Fax: +351 214 174 206
Language (s): Portuguese
DAILY NEWSPAPER

Gazeta de Sátão 617692
Owner: Isabel Maria Rodrigues dos Santos Figueiredo
Editorial: Praca Paulo VI, Lote 6 - 1 Esq., Satão 3560-154 **Tel:** 351 232 982 689
Email: gazetadesatao@sapo.pt **Web site:** http://www.gazetadesatao.pt
Freq: Monthly
Editor: Carlos Andrade; **Managing Director:** Vítor Miguel do Amaral Figueiredo
Language (s): Portuguese
Ad Rate: Full Page Mono 250.00
Currency: Euro
DAILY NEWSPAPER

Gazeta Lusófona 424875
Owner: Jornal Gazeta Lusófona Unipessoal, Lda.
Tel: 41 41 310 06 30
Email: a_sa@gazetalusofona.ch **Web site:** http://www.gazetalusofona.ch
Freq: Monthly
Profile: Newspaper for the Portuguese community in Switzerland. Read by portuguese people living in Switzerland.Local Translation: Jornal mensal dirigido à comunidade portuguesa da Suiça.
Language (s): Portuguese
Ad Rate: Full Page Colour 800.00
Currency: Euro
DAILY NEWSPAPER

Gestão de Condomínios 765980
Owner: Global Notícias, Publicações, S.A.
Editorial: R. de Goncalo Cristovao, 195, Porto 4049-011 **Tel:** 351 213 187 500
Email: secdir@jn.pt **Web site:** http://www.jn.pt
Circ: 106540 APCT
Profile: National. Local Translation:Suplemento dedicado à Gestão de Condomínios.
Language (s): Portuguese
DAILY NEWSPAPER

Global Challenge 494522
Owner: Sojornal - Sociedade Jornalística e Editorial, S.A.
Editorial: Edificio S. Francisco de Sales, R. Calvet de Magalhaes, 242, Paço De Arcos 2770-022
Tel: 351 214 544 000
Email: ipublishing@impresa.pt **Web site:** http://www.expresso.pt
Circ: 132175 Publisher's Statement
Profile: National. Local Translation:Competição Internacional do Global Challenge: Management e Investment.
Language (s): Portuguese
DAILY NEWSPAPER

Golfe 611196
Owner: Sojornal - Sociedade Jornalística e Editorial, S.A.
Editorial: Alameda das Linhas de Torres, 179, Lisboa 1750-142 **Tel:** 351 217 541 450
Email: geral@mediagolf.pt **Web site:** http://www.mediagolf.pt
Circ: 132175 APCT
Profile: Special supplement about golf. National.Local Translation: Suplemento especial sobre golfe.Url: http://www.expresso.pt
Email: ipublishing@impresa.pt.
Language (s): Portuguese
DAILY NEWSPAPER

Guia do Estudante 530236
Owner: Sojornal - Sociedade Jornalística e Editorial, S.A.
Editorial: Edificio S. Francisco de Sales, R. Calvet de Magalhaes, 242, Paço De Arcos 2770-022
Tel: 351 214 544 000
Email: guiadoestudante@expresso.pt **Web site:** http://www.guiadoestudante.pt
Circ: 126575 APCT
Profile: National. Local Translation:Directório de cursos e propostas de formação e pós-graduação.
Language (s): Portuguese
Ad Rate: Full Page Colour 6650.00
Currency: Euro
DAILY NEWSPAPER

Inovação & Tecnologia 494563
Owner: Sojornal - Sociedade Jornalística e Editorial, S.A.
Editorial: Eficio S. Francisco de Sales, R. Calvet de Magalhaes, 242, Paço De Arcos 2770-022
Tel: 351 214 544 000
Email: ipublishing@impresa.pt **Web site:** http://www.expresso.pt
Circ: 127500 Publisher's Statement
Profile: National. Local Translation:Edição especial que contém as últimas inovações a nível tecnológico.
Language (s): Portuguese
Ad Rate: Full Page Colour 5800.00
Currency: Euro
DAILY NEWSPAPER

O Interior 424886
Owner: Jorinterior - Jornal do Interior, Lda.
Editorial: R. da Corredoura, 80 - R/C Direito C, Guarda 6300-584 **Tel:** 351 271 212 153
Email: ointerior@ointerior.pt **Web site:** www.ointerior.pt
Freq: Weekly; **Circ:** 8960 APCT
Managing Director: Luís Baptista-Martins; **Editor Chefe:** Luís Martins
Profile: Weekly newspaper with information about Guarda and Castelo Branco regions. Politics, current affairs, society, religion, sport, entertainment and events. Aimed for Guarda and Castelo Branco locals.Local Translation: Semanário regional com informação sobre as regiões da Guarda e de Castelo Branco, abrangendo temas como política, actualidade, sociedade, religião, desporto, entretenimento e eventos.
Language (s): Portuguese
Ad Rate: Full Page Mono 360.00
Ad Rate: Full Page Colour 535.00
Currency: Euro
DAILY NEWSPAPER

Isolamentos (DN + JN) 668427
Owner: Global Notícias, Publicações, S.A.
Tel: 351 213 187 500
Email: dnot@dn.pt **Web site:** http://dn.sapo.pt
Circ: 167565 Publisher's Statement
Profile: National.
Language (s): Portuguese
DAILY NEWSPAPER

JN Cidades 766037
Owner: Global Notícias, Publicações, S.A.
Editorial: R. de Goncalo Cristovao, 195, Porto 4049-011 **Tel:** 351 213 187 500
Email: secdir@jn.pt **Web site:** http://www.jn.pt
Freq: Weekly; **Circ:** 112110 Publisher's Statement
Profile: Local Translation: Suplemento sobre o desenvolvimento de várias cidades do país: retrato regional de questões relativas a toda a população como transportes, economia ou ambiente; acompanhamento das equipas desportivas locais e respectivos resultados das competições; eventos culturais de cada região e sugestões de momentos lúdicos e culturais perto de casa; os restaurantes e bares que estão na moda, as lojas novas ou remodeladas e descrição da vida académica de cada cidade.Geographical Focus: Sport; Wirtschaft
Language (s): Portuguese
DAILY NEWSPAPER

JN Concelhos 523992
Owner: Global Notícias, Publicações, S.A.
Editorial: R. de Goncalo Cristovao, 195, Porto 4049-011 **Tel:** 351 222 096 100
Email: dpe@jn.pt **Web site:** http://www.jn.pt
Circ: 110603 Publisher's Statement
Profile: National. Local Translation:Suplemento sobre o desenvolvimento de variados concelhos do país.
Email: secdir@jn.pt; roteiro@jn.pt.Phone: +351 213 187 300
Language (s): Portuguese
Ad Rate: Full Page Mono 2700.00
Ad Rate: Full Page Colour 3780.00
Currency: Euro
DAILY NEWSPAPER

JN Gente 494252
Owner: Global Notícias, Publicações, S.A.
Editorial: Av. da Liberdade, 266 - 4, Lisboa 1250-149
Tel: 351 213 187 500
Email: secdir@jn.pt **Web site:** http://www.jn.pt
Circ: 106993 APCT
Profile: National. Local Translation:Suplemento com artigos e reportagens acerca das celebridades portuguesas e internacionais.
Email: agenda@jn.pt.
Language (s): Portuguese
DAILY NEWSPAPER

JN Negócios 425433
Owner: Global Notícias, Publicações, S.A.
Editorial: R. de Goncalo Cristovao, 195-219, Porto 4049-011 **Tel:** 351 222 096 100
Email: dpe@jn.pt **Web site:** http://www.jn.pt
Freq: Weekly; **Circ:** 112738 Publisher's Statement
Profile: Newspaper supplement containing a Portuguese adaptation of the Wall Street Journal. National. Individuals with special interest in the economical and financial business areas.Local Translation: Suplemento semanal sobre economia editado em colaboração com a revista Carteira. Emprego, empresários, salários, produtos e consumidores são alguns dos temas abordados.Email: secdir@jn.pt; economia@jn.pt. Phone: +351 213 187 300
Language (s): Portuguese
Ad Rate: Full Page Mono 8000.00
Ad Rate: Full Page Colour 11200.00
Currency: Euro
DAILY NEWSPAPER

Jornal da Praia 424899
Owner: Grupo de Amigos da Praia da Vitória
Editorial: R. Padre Rocha de Sousa, 28, Apartado 45, Praia Da Vitória 9760-000 **Tel:** 351 295 543 101
Email: jornaldapraia@portugalmail.com **Web site:** http://www.jornaldapraia.com/index.php
Freq: Bi-Weekly
Profile: Fortnightly regional newspaper with information about Praia da Vitória (Açores). Politics, current affairs, society, religion, sport, entertainment and events.
Language (s): Portuguese
Ad Rate: Full Page Mono 150.00
Ad Rate: Full Page Colour 250.00
Currency: Euro
DAILY NEWSPAPER

Jornal da Região 224183
Owner: Publiregiões - Sociedade Jornalística e Editorial, Lda.
Editorial: Al. Antonio Sergio, 7 - 1 D, Linda-A-Velha 2799-531 **Tel:** 351 214 157 200
Email: jr-editor@jornaldaregiao.pt **Web site:** http://www.jornaldaregiao.pt
Freq: Weekly; **Circ:** 225000 Publisher's Statement
Editor Chefe: João Carlos Sebastião
Profile: Free weekly regional newspaper with information about Lisboa. Politics, current affairs, society, religion, sport, entertainment and events. Read in Cascais, Sintra, Oeiras, Amadora e Almada.Local Translation: Semanário regional gratuito com informação relativa a seis diferentes concelhos de Lisboa. Política, assuntos actuais, sociedade, desporto, entretenimento e eventos.
Language (s): Portuguese
Ad Rate: Full Page Mono 4990.00
Ad Rate: Full Page Colour 6487.00
Currency: Euro
DAILY NEWSPAPER

Jornal de Alferrarede 238195
Owner: Manuel Martinho da Conceição Francisco Unipessoal, Lda.
Editorial: R. Fonte de S. Jose, 64 - 1, Abrantes 2204-906 **Tel:** 351 241 361 282
Email: jornalferrarede@clix.pt **Web site:** http://jornalferrarede.blogspot.com
Freq: Monthly
Profile: Regional newspaper with information about Abrantes (Santarém). Politics, current affairs, society, religion, sport, entertainment and events. Read in Santerém region.Local Translation: Mensário regional com informação relativa a Abrantes (Santarém). Política, actualidade, sociedade, desporto e cultura são temas habituais.
Language (s): Portuguese
Ad Rate: Full Page Mono 200.00
Currency: Euro
DAILY NEWSPAPER

Jornal de Beja 425751
Owner: Jaime Casimiro Perianes Palma
Editorial: Largo Escritor Manuel Ribeiro, 10 - 2 B, Beja 7802-421 **Tel:** 351 284 329 866
Email: sonia.calvario-1448e@adv.oa.pt
Freq: Weekly
Profile: Weekly regional newspaper with information about Beja. Politics, current affairs, society, religion, sport, entertainment and events.
Language (s): Portuguese
DAILY NEWSPAPER

Jornal de Ferreira 425752
Owner: Câmara Municipal de Ferreira do Alentejo
Editorial: Edificio da Câmara Municipal, Ferreira Do Alentejo 7900-571 **Tel:** 351 284 738 700
Email: geral@cm-ferreira-alentejo.pt **Web site:** http://www.cm-ferreira-alentejo.pt/index.php
Freq: Bi-Monthly
Profile: Regional newspaper with information about Ferreira do Alentejo (Beja). Politics, current affairs, society, religion, sport, entertainment and events.
Language (s): Portuguese
DAILY NEWSPAPER

Jornal de Notícias 425436
Owner: Global Notícias, Publicações, S.A.
Editorial: R. de Goncalo Cristovao, 195-219, Porto 4049-011 **Tel:** 351 222 096 111
Email: secdir@jn.pt **Web site:** www.jn.pt
Freq: Daily; **Circ:** 106993 Publisher's Statement
Editor in Chief: Rute Araújo; **Editor Chefe:** Rafael Barbosa; **Editor:** Vítor Pinto Basto; **Editor:** Teresa Costa; **Editor:** Miguel Conde Coutinho; **Director Comercial:** Luís Ferreira; **Director adjunto:** Paulo Ferreira; **Director adjunto:** Jorge Fiel; **Editor:** Margarida Fonseca; **Editor:** José Miguel Gaspar; **Director adjunto:** Alfredo Leite; **Photographer:** Artur Machado; **Editor:** Elmano Madaíl; **Managing Director:** João Marcelino; **Photographer:** Adelino Meireles; **Editor:** Manuel Molinos; **Editor:** Dora Mota; **Editor:** Jorge Pinto; **Photographer:** César Santos; **Director adjunto:** Fernando Santos; **Photographer:** Ana Luísa Silva; **Director Comercial:** Paulo Pereira da Silva; **Editor:** António Soares; **Managing Director:** Manuel Tavares
Profile: National newspaper providing regional, national and international news, political coverage and in-depth information concerning finance, economics and new technologies. Also covers society, culture, the media, sport and television. Contains comic strips, game puzzles and fait-divers. National.Local Translation: Jornal de carácter generalista, caracterizado por notícias e acontecimentos que marcam a actualidade do país de do mundo. Composto por suplementos das mais variadas áreas (política, sociedade, economia, cultura, lazer, desporto, entre outros). Ao fim-de-semana a última página é dedicada a histórias e entrevistas. Distinguido, em 2008 e 2011, com marca de excelência pela Superbrand.Phone: +351 213 187 500
Language (s): Portuguese
Ad Rate: Full Page Mono 7740.00
Ad Rate: Full Page Colour 10836.00
Currency: Euro
DAILY NEWSPAPER

Jornal de Notícias - Norte 425429
Owner: Global Notícias, Publicações, S.A.
Editorial: R. Goncalo Cristovao, 195-219, Porto 4049-011 **Tel:** 351 222 096 100
Email: dpe@jn.pt **Web site:** http://www.jn.pt
Freq: Daily; **Circ:** 109520 Publisher's Statement
Photographer: Nuno Alegria; **Editor Chefe:** Rafael Barbosa; **Editor:** Margarida Fonseca; **Editor Chefe:** Paulo Martins; **Editor:** Dora Mota; **Editor:** António Soares; **Photographer:** Lisa Soares
Profile: National newspaper providing regional, national and international news, political coverage and in-depth information concerning finance, economics and new technologies. Also covers society, culture, the media, sport and television. Contains comic strips, game puzzles and fait-divers. Local news regarding the north region of Portugal. Publication that is a part of the newspaper Jornal de Notícias.Aimed at northern Portugal readers. Local Translation:Jornal generalista, especialmente concebido para o segmento em que se insere - zona norte de Portugal (essencialmente Aveiro, Guarda, Viseu, Vila Real, Bragança, Braga e Viana do Castelo). Com notícias de cariz nacional e internacional, comporta ainda a vertente local e regionalista da área a que se destina nas mais variadas temáticas (desporto, economia, novas tecnologias ou o social local). Publicação integrante do Jornal de Notícias.Email: secdir@jn.pt. Phone: +351 213 187 500
Language (s): Portuguese
Ad Rate: Full Page Mono 2340.00
Ad Rate: Full Page Colour 3276.00
Currency: Euro
DAILY NEWSPAPER

Jornal do Centro 309735
Owner: Centro - Produção e Edição de Conteúdos, Lda.
Editorial: Bairro S. Joao da Carreira, R. D. Maria Gracinda Torres Vasconcelos, Lote 10 - R/C, Viseu 3500-187 **Tel:** 351 232 437 461
Email: redaccao@jornaldocentro.pt **Web site:** http://www.jornaldocentro.pt
Freq: Weekly; **Circ:** 6000 APCT
Managing Director: Paulo Neto
Profile: Weekly regional newspaper with information about Viseu. Politics, current affairs, society, religion, sport, entertainment and events. Read by Viseu locals.Local Translation: Jornal semanal com informação relativa a Viseu. Política, actualidade, sociedade, religião, desporto, entretenimento e eventos. Recebeu em 2003 o Prémio Gazeta Imprensa Regional. Desde Março de 2010 é distribuído gratuitamente com o Expresso na região de Viseu.
Language (s): Portuguese
Ad Rate: Full Page Mono 900.00
Ad Rate: Full Page Colour 1050.00
Currency: Euro
DAILY NEWSPAPER

Jornal do Centro de Saúde 495372
Owner: Marketing For You, Lda.
Editorial: Beloura Office Park, Edifício 4, Escritorio 1.2, Sintra 2710-693 **Tel:** 351 219 247 670
Email: redaccao@jornaldocentrodesaude.pt **Web site:** http://www.jornaldocentrodesaude.pt
Freq: Monthly; **Circ:** 46000 Publisher's Statement
Director de Produção: Louis Silva Bouclon; **Editor:** Sofia Filipe; **Advertising Manager:** Carla Gonçalves; **Managing Director:** Rui Moreira de Sá
Profile: Elaborated by the Carnaxide health center, Jornal do Centro de Saúde is a free newspaper foccused on public health and the connection between health center professionals and the patients. National.Local Translation: Elaborado pelo Centro de Saúde de Carnaxide, o Jornal do Centro de Saúde é um mensário gratuito sobre os mais variados campos da saúde pública. Tem como objectivo aumentar a qualidade de vida e criar uma interacção entre o cidadão utente e os profissionais do Centro de Saúde.Email: barbara.tavares@jornaldocentrodesaude.pt.
Language (s): Portuguese
Ad Rate: Full Page Colour 2950.00
Currency: Euro
DAILY NEWSPAPER

Jornal do Ténis 425754
Owner: Edisport - Sociedade de Publicações Desportivas, S.A.
Editorial: Av. Conde de Valbom, 30 - 4/5, Lisboa 1050-068 **Tel:** 351 210 124 900
Email: antoniomagalhaes@record.pt **Web site:** http://www.record.xl.pt
Freq: Monthly; **Circ:** 102718 APCT
Profile: Newspaper containing national and international news regarding tennis. Mainland.Local Translation: Jornal com notícias nacionais e internacionais sobre ténis.Email: jornaldotenis@lagossports.com.
Language (s): Portuguese
DAILY NEWSPAPER

Jornal Raiano 238125
Owner: Jornal Raiano
Editorial: Largo do Adro, 11, Idanha-A-Nova 6060-109 **Tel:** 351 277 202 169
Freq: Monthly
Language (s): Portuguese
DAILY NEWSPAPER

Jornal Veris 595945
Owner: Fábrica da Igreja Paroquial da Freguesia de S. Veríssimo de Paranhos
Editorial: Igreja paroquial de S. Verissimo de Paranhos, Porto 4200-325 **Tel:** 351 225 020 729
Email: jornal.veris@gmail.com
Freq: Monthly
Managing Director: André Ricardo Rubim Guimarães
Profile: Regional newspaper regarding Paranhos. Aimed at Paranhos' population.Local Translation: Mensário de informação regional relativa a Paranhos e de cariz religioso.
Language (s): Portuguese
DAILY NEWSPAPER

Le Mans Series 696720
Owner: Edisport - Sociedade de Publicações Desportivas, S.A.
Tel: 351 210 124 900
Email: antoniomagalhaes@record.pt **Web site:** http://www.record.xl.pt
Circ: 115409 APCT
Profile: Mainland. Local Translation:Suplemento sobre o campeonato Le Mans Series.
Language (s): Portuguese
DAILY NEWSPAPER

Manancial 56 - Pequenos Anúncios, Grandes Negócios 424929
Editorial: Gândara - Cesar, Oliveira De Azeméis 3720-000 **Tel:** 351 256412648
Freq: Monthly
Language (s): Portuguese
DAILY NEWSPAPER

Margens do Vouga 424932
Owner: Tavares & Pereira Publicações Periódicas, Lda.
Editorial: Edifício da Torre, Loja 1, Sever Do Vouga 3740-000
Email: margensdovouga@sapo.pt
Freq: Bi-Weekly
Language (s): Portuguese
DAILY NEWSPAPER

Meios & Publicidade 162376
Owner: Workmedia - Comunicação, S.A.
Editorial: R. General Firmino Miguel, 3 - Torre 2, 3, Lisboa 1600-100 **Tel:** 351 210 410 300
Email: geral@workmedia.pt **Web site:** http://www.meiosepublicidade.pt
Freq: Weekly; **Circ:** 2500 APCT
Managing Director: Carla Borges Ferreira; **Editor:** Maria João Lima; **Director Comercial:** Margarida Magalhães; **Director adjunto:** Rui Oliveira Marques; **Advertising Manager:** João Paulo Pereira
Profile: Publication providing information on communications, marketing strategies, studies of trends and advertising especially relating to the

media. National. Aimed at people working in the advertising and media sectors.Local Translation: Publicação sobre o sector de comunicação e publicidade. As novidades e destaques sobre meios de comunicação sociais, jornalistas, marketeers, estratégias de marketing e publicidade, relações públicas, estudos de marca e todos os assuntos relativos a este sector.Email: igarcez@meiosepublicidade.workmedia.pt.
Language (s): Portuguese
Ad Rate: Full Page Colour 1315.00
Currency: Euro
DAILY NEWSPAPER

Mestrados (DN + JN) 668421
Owner: Global Notícias, Publicações, S.A.
Tel: 351 222 096 100
Email: secdir@jn.pt **Web site:** http://www.jn.pt
Circ: 167564 Publisher's Statement
Profile: Published with: Diário de Notícias; Jornal de Notícias. National.Local Translation: Edição especial com informação relativa aos mestrados da época pós-bolonha e quais as ofertas.Publicado com: Diário de Notícias; Jornal de Notícias Phone: +351 213 187 300
Language (s): Portuguese
DAILY NEWSPAPER

Metro Casa 516746
Owner: Transjornal Edição de Publicações, S.A.
Editorial: Estrada da Outurela, 118, Parque Holanda - Edifício Holanda, Carnaxide 2790-114
Tel: 351 214 169 210
Email: metrocasa@metroportugal.com **Web site:** http://www.readmetro.com
Circ: 130000 Publisher's Statement
Profile: Tips on home decorating, the latest style on home fashion tendencies, articles and interviews with well-known interior designers, news on the real estate market and the suggested best places where can acquire a property.
Language (s): Portuguese
Ad Rate: Full Page Colour 4500.00
Currency: Euro
DAILY NEWSPAPER

Metro do Porto 766083
Owner: Global Notícias, Publicações, S.A.
Editorial: R. de Goncalo Cristovao, 195, Porto 4049-011 **Tel:** 351 213 187 500
Email: secdir@jn.pt **Web site:** http://www.jn.pt
Circ: 110393 APCT
Profile: National. Local Translation:Suplemento dedicado ao Metro do Porto.
Language (s): Portuguese
DAILY NEWSPAPER

Metro Portugal 424936
Owner: Transjornal Edição de Publicações, S.A.
Editorial: Arruamento D à R. Jose Maria Nicolau, 3, Lisboa 1549-023 **Tel:** 351 214 169 210
Email: geral@metroportugal.com **Web site:** www.readmetro.com
Freq: Daily; **Circ:** 130000 Publisher's Statement
Director Comercial: Ricardo Branco; **Managing Director:** Diogo Torgal Ferreira
Profile: Free newspaper concerning national and international news and current affairs. Aimed for Aveiro, Braga, Coimbra, Évora, Faro, Leiria, Lisboa and Porto regions.Local Translation: Diário gratuito com notícias sobre a actualidade. Actualidade local, nacional e internacional, Desporto e Entretenimento são algumas das secções. Regularmente convida personalidades dos mais variados sectores para reunir, seleccionar e editar os conteúdos do jornal. Este projecto é uma parceria entre a Metro Internacional, presente em mais de 23 países, e a Media Capital.Phone: +351 214 241 430
Fax: +351 214 174 206
Language (s): Portuguese
Ad Rate: Full Page Mono 9240.00
Ad Rate: Full Page Colour 9240.00
Currency: Euro
DAILY NEWSPAPER

Metro Verão 496000
Owner: Transjornal Edição de Publicações, S.A.
Editorial: Arruamento D à R. Jose Maria Nicolau, 3, Lisboa 1549-023 **Tel:** 351 214 169 210
Email: metro@metroportugal.com **Web site:** http://www.readmetro.com
Freq: 2 Times/Week; **Circ:** 150000 Publisher's Statement
Profile: Special summer edition. Aimed for Faro, Lisboa and Porto regions and in the coast region, mainly in the beaches.Local Translation: Edição especial de Verão que aborda temas como saúde, viagens, cuidados com o Sol, entre outros.Phone: +351 214 241 430
Fax: +351 214 174 206
Language (s): Portuguese
DAILY NEWSPAPER

Minha Revista 425084
Owner: Empresa Diário do Minho, Lda.
Editorial: R. Dr. Justino Cruz, 110 - 2 - Sala 13, Braga 4700-314 **Tel:** 351 253613350
Freq: Monthly
Managing Director: José Miguel Torres Pereira
Profile: Local Translation: Revista regional gratuita, produzida pelos jornalistas do Diário do Minho, que tem como objectivo apresentar a realidade quotidiana do Minho, sobretudo através de histórias de vida (ou institucionais) marcantes.
Language (s): Portuguese
DAILY NEWSPAPER

Modalidades 586393
Owner: Sociedade Vicra Desportiva, S.A.
Editorial: Travessa da Queimada, 23 - R/C, 1 e 2, Lisboa 1249-113 **Tel:** 351 213 463 981
Email: publicidvd@abola.pt **Web site:** http://www.abola.pt
Circ: 120000 Publisher's Statement
Profile: Provides special information about sports in general. Mainland.Local Translation: Suplemento dedicado às várias modalidades desportivas existentes nacionais ou internacionais.
Language (s): Portuguese
DAILY NEWSPAPER

Modalidades 601419
Owner: Edisport - Sociedade de Publicações Desportivas, S.A.
Editorial: Av. Conde de Valbom, 30 - 4/5, Lisboa 1050-068 **Tel:** 351 210 124 900
Email: antoniomagalhaes@record.pt **Web site:** http://www.record.xl.pt
Circ: 115296 Publisher's Statement
Language (s): Portuguese
DAILY NEWSPAPER

Mudar de Vida 572427
Editorial: R. Joao Ortigao Ramos, 19, Lisboa 1500-362
Email: jornalmudardevida@gmail.com **Web site:** http://www.jornalmudardevida.net
Freq: Monthly
Profile: Popular political newspaper, which has as main topics the conditions of life, the aspirations and struggles of workers and popular classes.
Language (s): Portuguese
DAILY NEWSPAPER

Mundo Sénior 668422
Owner: Mundo Sénior
Tel: 351 214 685 361
Email: geral@mundosenior.pt **Web site:** http://www.mundosenior.pt
Freq: Monthly
Language (s): Portuguese
Ad Rate: Full Page Colour 900.00
Currency: Euro
DAILY NEWSPAPER

Mundo Universitário 425215
Owner: Moving Media, Publicações, Lda.
Editorial: Arruamento D à R. Jose Maria Nicolau, 3, Lisboa 1549-023 **Tel:** 351 926 726 060
Email: info@mundouniversitario.pt **Web site:** http://www.mundouniversitario.pt
Freq: Bi-Weekly; **Circ:** 35000 APCT
Advertising Manager: Gisela Correia; **Editor:** Luís Magalhães; **Advertising Manager:** Paula Cristina Reis; **Editor:** Nuno Saraiva
Profile: Free magazine about the university students' lifestyle. Mainland. Distributed in Portuguese universities and Lusomundo cinemas.Local Translation: Quinzenal gratuito com uma secção noticiosa e outra centrada em actividades do interesse dos estudantes fora do recinto universitário. Lifestyle, música (Jukebox), cinema (Sétima Arte), desporto, mundo laboral e a sexualidade dos universitários, numa secção apelidada de Jardim do Éden são algumas das secções habituais.Alternative Title: MU
Language (s): Portuguese
Ad Rate: Full Page Colour 3580.00
Currency: Euro
DAILY NEWSPAPER

Museus 698194
Owner: Presselivre - Imprensa Livre, S.A.
Tel: 351 213 185 462
Email: geral@correiomanha.pt **Web site:** http://www.cmjornal.pt
Circ: 158546 APCT
Profile: National. Local Translation:Suplemento dedicado aos museus, com especial destaque para os museus de Vila Nova de Cerveira.
Language (s): Portuguese
DAILY NEWSPAPER

Norte 497306
Owner: Presselivre - Imprensa Livre, S.A.
Editorial: R. Manuel Pinto de Azevedo, 80 - 1, Porto 4100-320 **Tel:** 351 213 185 200
Email: direccao@cmjornal.pt **Web site:** http://www.cmjornal.pt
Freq: Daily; **Circ:** 158796 APCT
Profile: North edition. Local Translation:Diário generalista em formato tablóide com informação nacional e internacional. Actualidade, sociedade, economia, política, desporto, cultura, media, celebridades, agenda e programação televisiva são alguns dos temas focados. "TV", "Vidas" e "Domingo" são alguns dos suplementos fixos deste jornal. Phone: +351 213 540 382; +351 213 540 386
Fax: +351 213 540 386
Language (s): Portuguese
Ad Rate: Full Page Mono 2020.00
Ad Rate: Full Page Colour 3030.00
Currency: Euro
DAILY NEWSPAPER

Notícias CPLP 500653
Editorial: R. de S. Caetano, 32, Lisboa 1200-829
Tel: 351 21 392 85 60
Email: afpi@afpi.eu.com **Web site:** http://www.cplp.org
Circ: 195000 Publisher's Statement
Language (s): Portuguese
DAILY NEWSPAPER

Notícias de Avanca 428315
Owner: Fábrica da Igreja Paroquial de Avanca
Editorial: Residência Paroquial de Avanca, Estarreja 3860-000 **Tel:** 351 234 884 671
Freq: Monthly
Profile: Regional newspaper of religious tone with information and interest articles about Aveiro.
Language (s): Portuguese
DAILY NEWSPAPER

Notícias de Basto 429000
Owner: Associação Acção Jovem
Editorial: Edifício da Antiga Escola C+S - Sala 15, R. 5 de Outubro, Celorico De Basto 4890-033
Tel: 351 255 323 444
Email: noticiasdebasto@gmail.com **Web site:** http://www.noticiasdebasto.com/index.php
Freq: Bi-Weekly
Profile: Fortnightly regional newspaper with information about Celorico de Basto (Braga). Politics, current affairs, society, religion, sport, entertainment and events.
Language (s): Portuguese
DAILY NEWSPAPER

Notícias de Fafe 429002
Owner: João Paulo Couto Pinto
Editorial: R. dos Combatentes da Grande Guerra, 338, Fafe 4820
Freq: Weekly
Profile: Weekly regional newspaper with information about Braga. Politics, current affairs, society, religion, sport, entertainment and events.
Language (s): Portuguese
DAILY NEWSPAPER

Notícias de Mirandela 238151
Owner: Tipografia Pinto, Lda.
Editorial: R. Alexandre Herculano, 68, Mirandela 5370-299 **Tel:** 351 278 265 904
Email: noticiasdemirandela@tugamail.com
Freq: Bi-Weekly
Profile: Regional newspaper with information about Bragança. Politics, current affairs, society, religion, sport, entertainment and events.
Language (s): Portuguese
Ad Rate: Full Page Mono 200.00
Ad Rate: Full Page Colour 475.00
Currency: Euro
DAILY NEWSPAPER

Notícias de Nariz & Fátima 428318
Owner: Fábrica da Igreja Paroquial de Nossa Senhora de Fátima
Editorial: Paroquia de Nossa Senhora de Fatima, Nossa Senhora De Fátima 3810 **Tel:** 351 234 941 241
Email: jnnarizefatima@gmail.com **Web site:** http://noticiasdenarizefatima.blogspot.com
Freq: Monthly
Profile: Regional newspaper of religious tone with information and interest articles about Santarém.
Language (s): Portuguese
DAILY NEWSPAPER

Notícias de Valongo 309737
Owner: Empresa Jornalistica Notícias de Valongo, Lda.
Editorial: Praca Manuel Guedes, 242 - 2 Fte., Apartado 78, Gondomar 4420-000
Profile: Regional newspaper with information about Porto. Politics, current affairs, society, sport, entertainment and events.
Language (s): Portuguese
Ad Rate: Full Page Mono 270.00
Ad Rate: Full Page Colour 300.00
Currency: Euro
DAILY NEWSPAPER

Notícias de Vendas Novas 309738
Owner: Igreja Paroquial de Vendas Novas
Editorial: Igreja Paroquial de Vendas Novas, Apartado 41, Vendas Novas 7080-000
Tel: 351 265 892 370
Profile: Regional newspaper of religious tone with information and interest articles about Évora.
Language (s): Portuguese
DAILY NEWSPAPER

Notícias de Vila Verde 429017
Owner: Empresa Editorial Vilaverdense, Lda.
Editorial: Praca do Municipio, 48 - 1, Vila Verde 4730-000
Freq: Bi-Weekly
Profile: Fortnightly regional newspaper with information about Braga. Politics, current affairs, society, religion, sport, entertainment and events.
Language (s): Portuguese
DAILY NEWSPAPER

Notícias de Vouzela 238153
Owner: Grupo Media Centro
Editorial: Praca da Republica, 17, Vouzela 3670-245
Tel: 351 232 772 026
Email: jnoticiasdevouzela@sapo.pt **Web site:** http://www.noticiasdevouzela.com
Freq: Weekly; **Circ:** 4990 APCT
Director adjunto: Salete Costa; **Managing Director:** Lino Augusto Vinhal
Profile: Weekly regional newspaper with information about Viseu. Politics, current affairs, society, religion, sport, entertainment and events. Aimed for Viseu region, mainly for Vouzela population.Local Translation: Semanário de informação regional relativa a Viseu. Política, actualidade, sociedade, religião, desporto, entretenimento e eventos.
Language (s): Portuguese
Ad Rate: Full Page Mono 385.00
Ad Rate: Full Page Colour 577.50
Currency: Euro
DAILY NEWSPAPER

Notícias do Comércio 238130
Owner: Active, Lda.
Editorial: R. da Palma, 284 - 2 D, Lisboa 1100-394
Tel: 351 218 860 650
Email: maria.joao@ative.pt
Profile: Occasional newspaper concerning the nourishing industry.
Language (s): Portuguese
DAILY NEWSPAPER

Notícias do Condomínio 683876
Owner: Franquiger, S.A.
Editorial: Sintra Business Park, 1, 2B, Sintra 2710-089 **Tel:** 351 219 112 720
Email: noticias@ldc.pt **Web site:** http://noticiasdocondominio.wordpress.com
Freq: Quarterly; **Circ:** 250000 Publisher's Statement
Managing Director: Helena Portugal
Profile: National. Local Translation:Jornal com notícias relacionadas com o condomínio.
Language (s): Portuguese
DAILY NEWSPAPER

Novas Oportunidades 605640
Owner: Global Notícias, Publicações, S.A.
Editorial: Av. da Liberdade, 266, Lisboa 1250-149
Tel: 351 213 180 000
Email: geral@globalnoticias.pt **Web site:** http://www.globalnoticias.pt
Circ: 166341 Publisher's Statement
Language (s): Portuguese
Ad Rate: Full Page Colour 1649.00
Currency: Euro
DAILY NEWSPAPER

Ofereço-me para Trabalhar 784047
Owner: Global Notícias, Publicações, S.A.
Editorial: R. de Goncalo Cristovao, 195-219, Porto 4049-011 **Tel:** 351 222 096 111
Email: iniciativasolidaria@jn.pt **Web site:** www.jn.pt
Freq: Weekly; **Circ:** 106993 Publisher's Statement
Profile: National. Local Translation:Suplemento semanal para divulgação de quem procura trabalho ou tem um serviço específico que fornece como trabalhador por conta própria. Phone: +351 213 187 500
Language (s): Portuguese
DAILY NEWSPAPER

O Olhanense 238072
Owner: Sporting Clube Olhanense
Editorial: Praca da Restauracao, 18, Olhão 8700-350
Tel: 351 289 703 168
Email: jornalolhanense@iol.pt
Language (s): Portuguese
Ad Rate: Full Page Mono 600.00
Currency: Euro
DAILY NEWSPAPER

Página 1 495267
Owner: R/com
Editorial: R. Ivens, 14, Lisboa 1249-108
Tel: 351 213 239 239
Email: jornalonline@pagina1.pt **Web site:** www.pagina1.pt
Freq: Daily
Editor: Paulo Ribeiro Pinto
Profile: National daily newspaper produced by Rádio Renascença. National.Local Translation: Diário nacional produzido pela Rádio Renascença. Publicação exclusivamente online, com notícias do panorama nacional e internacional, entrevistas e temáticas que marcam a actualidade, como política, sociedade, economia, desporto, entre outros. Lançado às 17h00. Disponível na Internet em formato PDF.Phone: +351 213 239 200
Language (s): Portuguese
DAILY NEWSPAPER

Pauta 765612
Owner: Banda de Alcobaça
Editorial: R. Frei Antonio Brandao, 50-52, Alcobaça 2460-047 **Tel:** 351 262 597 611
Email: press@academiamalcobaca.com **Web site:** http://www.academiamalcobaca.com
Editor: David Mariano; **Managing Director:** Rui Morais
Profile: Local Translation: Publicação electrónica da Academia de Música de Alcobaça com notas, estórias e apontamentos musicais. Edições gratuitamente disponíveis no Issuu.
Language (s): Portuguese
DAILY NEWSPAPER

PEC 667958
Owner: Sojornal - Sociedade Jornalística e Editorial, S.A.
Editorial: Edificio S. Francisco de Sales, R. Calvet de Magalhaes, 242, Paço De Arcos 2770-022
Tel: 351 214 544 000
Email: ipublishing@impresa.pt **Web site:** http://www.expresso.pt
Circ: 136650 Publisher's Statement
Profile: National. Local Translation:Suplemento sobre o PEC: Programa de Estabilidade e Crescimento.
Language (s): Portuguese
DAILY NEWSPAPER

Política 766183
Owner: R/com
Editorial: R. Ivens, 14, Lisboa 1249-108
Tel: 351 213 239 239
Email: jornalonline@pagina1.pt **Web site:** http://www.pagina1.pt
Profile: National. Local Translation:Edição especial com artigos sobre a vida política nacional. Phone: +351 213 239 200
Language (s): Portuguese
DAILY NEWSPAPER

Ponto Final 608834
Owner: Títulos & Parágrafos, Lda.
Editorial: Travessa à R. Direita, 5 - Escritorio 3, Aveiro 3810-093 **Tel:** 351 234 181 105
Email: redaccao@jornalpontofinal.com
Language (s): Portuguese
DAILY NEWSPAPER

Porto 497322
Owner: Global Notícias, Publicações, S.A.
Editorial: R. de Goncalo Cristovao, 195 - 219, Porto 4049-011 **Tel:** 351 222 096 100
Email: dpe@jn.pt **Web site:** http://www.jn.pt
Freq: Daily; **Circ:** 106688 Publisher's Statement
Profile: Distributed in Oporto. Local Translation:Jornal generalista, especialmente concebido para o segmento em que se insere - distrito do Porto. Com notícias de cariz nacional e internacional, comporta ainda a vertente local e regionalista da área a que se destina nas mais variadas temáticas (desporto, economia, novas tecnologias ou o social local). Publicação integrante do Jornal de Notícias.Email: secdir@jn.pt; grandeporto@jn.pt. Phone: +351 213 187 300
Language (s): Portuguese
Ad Rate: Full Page Mono 2340.00
Ad Rate: Full Page Colour 3276.00
Currency: Euro
DAILY NEWSPAPER

Portugal - Angola (DN + JN) 673743
Owner: Global Notícias, Publicações, S.A.
Tel: 351 213 187 500
Email: dnot@dn.pt **Web site:** http://dn.sapo.pt
Circ: 165912 Publisher's Statement
Profile: National. Local Translation:As relações empresariais entre Portugal e Angola - a internacionalização nacional.
Language (s): Portuguese
DAILY NEWSPAPER

Portugal Ano a Ano 781121
Owner: Sojornal - Sociedade Jornalística e Editorial, S.A.
Editorial: Edificio S. Francisco de Sales, R. Calvet de Magalhaes, 242, Paço De Arcos 2770-022
Tel: 351 214 544 000
Email: ipublishing@impresa.pt **Web site:** http://www.expresso.pt
Circ: 127500 Publisher's Statement
Profile: National. Local Translation:Suplemento que indica as medidas políticas e económicas a adoptar no país.
Email: site@expresso.impresa.pt.
Language (s): Portuguese
DAILY NEWSPAPER

The Portugal News 427948
Owner: Anglopress - Edições e Publicidade, Lda.
Editorial: ANGLOPRESS Edicões e Publicidade, Lda., Apartado 13, Lagoa 8400-901
Tel: 351 282 341 100
Email: newsdesk@theportugalnews.com **Web site:** http://www.theportugalnews.com
Freq: Weekly; **Circ:** 19096 APCT
Editor: Brendan de Beer
Profile: Newspaper containing Portuguese news dedicated to the English population in Portugal. National. Aimed at English imigrants living in Portugal.Local Translation: Semanário de informação geral, dedicado à comunidade inglesa residente em Portugal. Contém notícias da actualidade portuguesa, política internacional, notícias de África, guia semanal de TV e satélite, guia de eventos, arte, viagens, desporto, jardinagem, golfe, motores e anúncios de imóveis.Alternative Title: Portugal News (The) Url: http://www.the-news.net.
Language (s): English
Ad Rate: Full Page Mono 1500.00
Ad Rate: Full Page Colour 2250.00
Currency: Euro
DAILY NEWSPAPER

Poupança 613679
Owner: Presselivre - Imprensa Livre, S.A.
Editorial: Av. Joao Crisostomo, N 72, Lisboa 1069-043 **Tel:** 351 213 185 462
Email: geral@correiomanha.pt **Web site:** http://www.cmjornal.pt
Circ: 166385 Publisher's Statement
Language (s): Portuguese
DAILY NEWSPAPER

O Povo do Cartaxo 238065
Owner: Artnews - Sociedade de Comunicações e Arte, Lda.
Editorial: Largo do Valverde, 27, Cartaxo 2070-040
Tel: 351 243 702 154
Email: opovodocartaxo@gmail.com
Freq: Bi-Weekly; **Circ:** 4000 APCT
Profile: Newspaper with information about Cartaxo. Politics, current affairs, society, sport, entertainment and events. Read by Cartaxo locals.Local Translation: Quinzenário regional com informação relativa ao Cartaxo.
Language (s): Portuguese
Ad Rate: Full Page Mono 700.00
Ad Rate: Full Page Colour 950.00
Currency: Euro
DAILY NEWSPAPER

Prazer de Consumir 766199
Owner: Metro News Publicações, S.A.
Editorial: Estrada da Outurela, 118, Parque Holanda - Edifício Holanda, Carnaxide 2790-114
Tel: 351 214 169 210
Email: destak@destak.pt **Web site:** http://www.destak.pt
Circ: 120000 Publisher's Statement
Profile: Local Translation: Suplemento sobre consumo.Email: mjvaz@destak.pt; lfilipe@destak.pt.
Language (s): Portuguese
DAILY NEWSPAPER

Prémio Mulher Activa 667960
Owner: Sojornal - Sociedade Jornalística e Editorial, S.A.
Tel: 351 214 544 000
Email: expresso@expresso.pt **Web site:** http://www.expresso.pt
Circ: 136650 Publisher's Statement
Language (s): Portuguese
DAILY NEWSPAPER

Primeiro Emprego 497021
Owner: Presselivre - Imprensa Livre, S.A.
Editorial: Arruamento D à R. Jose Maria Nicolau, 3, Lisboa 1549-023 **Tel:** 351 213 185 200
Email: direccao@cmjornal.pt **Web site:** www.cmjornal.pt
Freq: Weekly; **Circ:** 161374 APCT
Profile: Employment. National.Local Translation: O Primeiro Emprego divulga as ofertas de emprego disponíveis.Phone: +351 213 540 382; +351 213 540 386
Fax: +351 213 540 386
Language (s): Portuguese
Ad Rate: Full Page Colour 3240.00
Currency: Euro
DAILY NEWSPAPER

Produtos Biológicos (DN + JN) 777447
Owner: Global Notícias, Publicações, S.A.
Editorial: Edificio Diario de Noticias, Av. da Liberdade, 266, Lisboa 1250-149
Tel: 351 213 187 500
Email: dnot@dn.pt
Circ: 168106 Publisher's Statement
Profile: National. Local Translation:Suplemento sobre alimentação saudável: qualidade e segurança alimentar.
Language (s): Portuguese
DAILY NEWSPAPER

Publicidade 511932
Owner: Transjornal Edição de Publicações, S.A.
Editorial: Estrada da Outurela, 118, Parque Holanda - Edifício Holanda, Carnaxide 2790-114
Tel: 351 214 169 210
Email: metro@metroportugal.com **Web site:** http://www.readmetro.com
Circ: 130000 Publisher's Statement
Profile: Distributed in public transports concerning the most populous areas of Aveiro, Braga, Coimbra, Évora, Faro, Leiria, Lisboa and Porto. Phone: +351 214 241 430
Fax: +351 214 174 206
Language (s): Portuguese
DAILY NEWSPAPER

Rally de Portugal - Reis da Condução 494292
Editorial: Av. Conde Valbom, 30 - 4/5, Lisboa 1050-068 **Tel:** 351 210 124 900
Circ: 276095 Not Audited
Profile: Published with: Correio da Manhã; Record.
Language (s): Portuguese
DAILY NEWSPAPER

Reciclagem 495653
Owner: Presselivre - Imprensa Livre, S.A.
Editorial: Av. Joao Crisostomo, N 72, Lisboa 1069-043 **Tel:** 351 213 185 462
Email: geral@correiomanha.pt **Web site:** http://www.cmjornal.pt
Circ: 170737 Publisher's Statement
Language (s): Portuguese
Ad Rate: Full Page Mono 2020.00
Ad Rate: Full Page Colour 3030.00
Currency: Euro
DAILY NEWSPAPER

Revista Portuguesa de Educação 428168
Owner: Universidade do Minho - Ciências da Educação
Editorial: Instituto de Educacao e Psicologia, Campus de Gualtar, Braga 4710
Tel: 351 253 604 249
Email: rpe@iep.uminho.pt **Web site:** http://www.scielo.oces.mctes.pt/scielo.php/script_sci_serial/pid_0871-9187/lng_p
Freq: Semi-Annual
Language (s): Portuguese
Ad Rate: Full Page Colour 600.00
Currency: Euro
DAILY NEWSPAPER

O Ribatejo 416195
Owner: Jortejo Jornais, Rádio e Televisão, Lda.
Editorial: Centro Nacional de Exposicões - Quinta das Cegonhas, Apartado 355, Santarem 2000-471
Tel: 351 243 309 600
Email: info@oribatejo.pt **Web site:** www.oribatejo.pt
Freq: Weekly; **Circ:** 15000 APCT
Editor Chefe: João Baptista; **Managing Director:** Joaquim Duarte; **Director Comercial:** Rita Duarte
Profile: Newspaper featuring economic, business and general news about the Ribatejo region. Read in Santarém region.Local Translation: Jornal regional de informação relativa à região ribatejana.
Language (s): Portuguese
Ad Rate: Full Page Mono 1100.00
Ad Rate: Full Page Colour 1200.00
Currency: Euro
DAILY NEWSPAPER

Rostos 707195
Owner: António de Jesus Sousa Pereira
Editorial: R. Miguel Bombarda, 74, Loja 24 - C. Comercial Bombarda, Barreiro 2830-355
Tel: 351 212 066 758
Email: jornal@rostos.pt **Web site:** http://www.rostos.pt
Freq: Monthly
Managing Director: António Sousa Pereira
Profile: Local Translation: Jornal de cariz local e regional relativo às diversas áreas (empresarial, institucional, política ou ambiental), que caracterizam o distrito de Setúbal.Phone: +351 +351 212 066 779
Language (s): Portuguese
Ad Rate: Full Page Mono 600.00
Ad Rate: Full Page Colour 750.00
Currency: Euro
DAILY NEWSPAPER

Santarém 497220
Owner: Presselivre - Imprensa Livre, S.A.
Editorial: Av. Joao Crisostomo, N 72, Lisboa 1069-043 **Tel:** 351 213 185 462
Email: geral@correiomanha.pt **Web site:** http://www.cmjornal.pt
Circ: 151203 Not Audited
Language (s): Portuguese
Ad Rate: Full Page Mono 2020.00
Ad Rate: Full Page Colour 3030.00
Currency: Euro
DAILY NEWSPAPER

Saúde 511637
Owner: Cofina Media Internet
Editorial: Arruamento D à R. Jose Maria Nicolau, 3, Lisboa 1549-023 **Tel:** 351 214 169 210
Email: destak@destak.pt **Web site:** http://www.destak.pt
Freq: Monthly; **Circ:** 135000 Publisher's Statement
Profile: Health. Read in Lisboa and Setúbal districts.Local Translation: Edição especial dedicada a diferentes assuntos do sector saúde.
Language (s): Portuguese
Ad Rate: Full Page Colour 5390.00
Currency: Euro
DAILY NEWSPAPER

Saúde & Bem-estar (CO + CC) 765689
Owner: Lançar Ideias, Lda.
Editorial: Av. dos Bombeiros Voluntarios, 19, Loja 1, Martins 2725-592 MEM **Tel:** 351 219 205 525
Email: correiocascais@gmail.com
Circ: 110000 Publisher's Statement
Profile: Local Translation: Suplemento sobre sáude e bem-estar e actividades relacionadas.
Language (s): Portuguese
DAILY NEWSPAPER

Saúde Pública 516775
Owner: Sojornal - Sociedade Jornalística e Editorial, S.A.
Editorial: Edificio Lisboa Oriente Office, Av. Infante D. Henrique, 333 H - 5, Lisboa 1800-282
Tel: 351 218 504 000
Email: saudepublica@saudepublica.pt **Web site:** http://www.jasfarma.com
Freq: Monthly; **Circ:** 132175 Publisher's Statement
Director Comercial: José Maria Vilar Gomes
Profile: National. Local Translation:Dossier que pretende promover e divulgar informação na área da saúde, com o apoio de especialistas. Phone: +351 964 041 260
Language (s): Portuguese
Ad Rate: Full Page Mono 11000.00
Ad Rate: Full Page Colour 13000.00
Currency: Euro
DAILY NEWSPAPER

Segurança Infantil (DN + JN) 619469
Owner: Global Notícias, Publicações, S.A.
Editorial: Av. da Liberdade, 266 - 4, Lisboa 1250-149
Tel: 351 213 187 500
Email: agenda@jn.pt **Web site:** http://www.jn.pt
Circ: 156833 Publisher's Statement
Profile: Special edition about child safety.Published with: Diário de Notícias; Jornal de Notícias.
Language (s): Portuguese
Ad Rate: Full Page Mono 2700.00
Ad Rate: Full Page Colour 3780.00
Currency: Euro
DAILY NEWSPAPER

Soberania do Povo 238111
Owner: Soberania do Povo Editora, S.A.
Editorial: Av. Dr. Eugenio Ribeiro, 89, 3, Apartado 145, Agueda 3754-909 **Tel:** 351 234 622 626
Email: geral@soberaniadopovo.pt **Web site:** http://www.soberaniadopovo.pt
Freq: Weekly; **Circ:** 11000 APCT
Profile: Weekly newspaper with information about Águeda region. Politics, current affairs, society, sport, entertainment and events. Aimed for Águeda locals.Local Translation: Semanário de informação regional relativa a Águeda.Phone: +351 234 625 013
Language (s): Portuguese
Ad Rate: Full Page Mono 538.00
Currency: Euro
DAILY NEWSPAPER

Sport 497735
Owner: Presselivre - Imprensa Livre, S.A.
Editorial: Arruamento D à R. Jose Maria Nicolau, 3, Lisboa 1549-023 **Tel:** 351 213 185 200
Email: direccao@cmjornal.pt **Web site:** www.cmjornal.pt
Freq: Weekly; **Circ:** 161374 APCT
Profile: Sport. National.Local Translation: Jornal semanal dedicado ao desporto.Phone: +351 213 540 382; +351 213 540 386
Fax: +351 213 540 386
Language (s): Portuguese
Ad Rate: Full Page Colour 5400.00
Currency: Euro
DAILY NEWSPAPER

Sport 687475
Owner: Metro News Publicações, S.A.
Tel: 351 214 169 210
Email: destak@destak.pt **Web site:** http://www.destak.pt
Circ: 135000 Publisher's Statement
Profile: Local Translation: Edição especial dedicada a diferentes assuntos do sector desportivo.
Language (s): Portuguese
DAILY NEWSPAPER

Superstars Series 689114
Owner: Presselivre - Imprensa Livre, S.A.
Tel: 351 213 185 462
Email: geral@correiomanha.pt **Web site:** http://www.cmjornal.pt
Circ: 158785 Publisher's Statement
Profile: National. Local Translation:Edição especial da Superstars Series, com lugar no Autódromo do Algarve.
Language (s): Portuguese
DAILY NEWSPAPER

Terras do Homem 238126
Owner: Terraimagem - Edição de Publicações Periódicas, Lda.
Editorial: Av. Professor Machado Vilela, 18 - 3 Dto., Vila Verde 4730-721 **Tel:** 351 253 321 450
Email: terrasdohomem@gmail.com **Web site:** www.terrasdohomem.com
Freq: Bi-Weekly
Managing Director: Hélder Manuel de Sá Fernandes
Profile: Local Translation: Jornal dedicado à actualidade da região de Vila Verde, caracterizando-se por secção noticiosa local/regional, desporto, acontecimentos de ordem nacional e internacional, bem como índice noticioso de cariz regionalista, (nomeadamente sobre Terras de Bouro, Amares e/ou Vale do Homem).
Language (s): Portuguese
Ad Rate: Full Page Mono 400.00
Ad Rate: Full Page Colour 600.00
Currency: Euro
DAILY NEWSPAPER

Timoneiro 238014
Owner: Fábrica da Igreja Paroquial da Gafanha da Nazaré
Editorial: Av. Jose Estevao, Cartorio Paroquial, Gafanha Da Nazaré 3830-908 **Tel:** 351 234 365 803
Email: j.timoneiro@gmail.com
Freq: Monthly
Language (s): Portuguese
Ad Rate: Full Page Mono 250.00
Ad Rate: Full Page Colour 275.00
Currency: Euro
DAILY NEWSPAPER

Universidades 597378
Owner: Transjornal Edição de Publicações, S.A.
Editorial: Estrada da Outurela, 118, Parque Holanda - Edifício Holanda, Carnaxide 2790-114
Tel: 351 214 169 210
Email: metro@metroportugal.com **Web site:** http://www.readmetro.com
Circ: 130000 Publisher's Statement
Language (s): Portuguese
DAILY NEWSPAPER

Verão 497709
Owner: Cofina Media Internet
Editorial: Arruamento D à R. Jose Maria Nicolau, 3, Lisboa 1549-023 **Tel:** 351 214 169 210
Email: destak@destak.pt **Web site:** http://www.destak.pt
Freq: Weekly; **Circ:** 200000 Publisher's Statement
Profile: Summer. Distributed on the coast region of Portugal.Local Translation: Edição especial de Verão com sugestões de locais para as férias, alimentação, eventos, lazer, cinema e ainda sobre celebridades.
Language (s): Portuguese
Ad Rate: Full Page Colour 8980.00
Currency: Euro
DAILY NEWSPAPER

Portugal

Vida Saudável (DN + JN) 614171
Owner: Global Notícias, Publicações, S.A.
Editorial: Edifício Diario de Noticias, Av. da Liberdade, 266, Lisboa 1250-149
Tel: 351 213 187 500
Email: dnot@dn.pt **Web site:** http://dn.sapo.pt
Circ: 149901 Publisher's Statement
Profile: Published with: Jornal de Notícias; Diário de Notícias.
Language (s): Portuguese
DAILY NEWSPAPER

Vila Nova de Gaia 497268
Owner: Global Notícias, Publicações, S.A.
Editorial: Av. da Liberdade, 266 - 4, Lisboa 1250-149
Tel: 351 213 187 500
Email: secdir@jn.pt **Web site:** http://www.jn.pt
Circ: 106854 APCT
Profile: Aimed for Vila Nova de Gaia locals. Local Translation:Suplemento dedicado ao Concelho de Vila Nova de Gaia.
Email: agenda@jn.pt.
Language (s): Portuguese
Ad Rate: Full Page Mono 2700.00
Currency: Euro
DAILY NEWSPAPER

Viver Azeméis 765751
Owner: Câmara Municipal de Oliveira de Azeméis
Editorial: Largo da Republica, Oliveira De Azeméis 3720-240 **Tel:** 351 256 674 694
Email: geral@cm-oaz.pt **Web site:** http://www.cm-oaz.pt
Freq: Weekly
Profile: Local Translation: Boletim de eventos do Município de Oliveira de Azeméis. Disponível no site da Câmara e no Issuu.
Language (s): Portuguese
DAILY NEWSPAPER

Voz da Verdade 609194
Owner: Nova Terra - Empresa Editorial, Lda.
Editorial: Mosteiro de S. Vicente de Fora, Lisboa 1100-473 **Tel:** 351 218 810 558
Email: vozverdade@gmail.com **Web site:** http://www.jornalw.org
Freq: Weekly
Profile: Local Translation: Jornal diocesano de Lisboa.Alternative Title: Jornal W - Voz da Verdade
Language (s): Portuguese
Ad Rate: Full Page Colour 325.00
Currency: Euro
DAILY NEWSPAPER

A Voz de Freixianda 415185
Owner: Fábrica da Igreja Paroquial de Freixianda
Editorial: R. Padre Faustino, 1, Freixianda-Ourém 2435-283 **Tel:** 351 249 551 526
Freq: Monthly
Language (s): Portuguese
DAILY NEWSPAPER

A Voz de Trás-os-Montes 238210
Owner: Conferências de S. Vicente de Paulo de Vila Real
Editorial: R. D. Antonio Valente da Fonseca, 22, Apartado 212, Vila Real 5001-911
Tel: 351 259 340 290
Web site: http://www.avozdetrasosmontes.com
Freq: Weekly; **Circ:** 6500 APCT
Profile: Weekly newspaper with information about Trás-os-Montes region. Politics, current affairs, society, sport, entertainment and events. Read in Trás-os-Montes region.Local Translation: Semanário de informação regional relativa à região de Trás-os-Montes.Email: assinaturas@avozdetrasosmontes.com. Phone: +351 914 803 266
Language (s): Portuguese
Ad Rate: Full Page Mono 403.00
Ad Rate: Full Page Colour 564.20
Currency: Euro
DAILY NEWSPAPER

Voz do Mar 415129
Owner: Fábrica da Igreja Paroquial da Freguesia de Ajuda da Cidade de Peniche
Editorial: R. D. Luis Ataide, 19 - 1 D, Peniche 2520-408 **Tel:** 351 262 783 900
Email: avozdomar@sapo.pt
Freq: Bi-Weekly
Language (s): Portuguese
Ad Rate: Full Page Mono 300.00
Ad Rate: Full Page Colour 500.00
Currency: Euro
DAILY NEWSPAPER

Zoom 783576
Owner: Global Notícias, Publicações, S.A.
Editorial: R. de Goncalo Cristovao, 195-219, Porto 4049-011 **Tel:** 351 222 096 111
Email: secdir@jn.pt **Web site:** http://www.jn.pt
Circ: 107777 Publisher's Statement
Profile: National. Local Translation:Publicação com edições temáticas diferentes. Phone: +351 213 187 500
Language (s): Portuguese
DAILY NEWSPAPER

Zoom (DN + JN) 765767
Owner: Global Notícias, Publicações, S.A.
Editorial: Edifício Diario de Noticias, Av. da Liberdade, 266, Lisboa 1250-149
Tel: 351 213 187 500
Email: dnot@dn.pt **Web site:** http://www.dn.pt
Circ: 157478 Publisher's Statement

Profile: Different themes. National.Local Translation: Publicação com edições temáticas diferentes.
Language (s): Portuguese
DAILY NEWSPAPER

News Service/Syndicate

1/2 Formato - Agência de Fotografia, Lda. 496150
Editorial: R. Paraíso, 184 - 3 D, Porto 4000-375
Tel: 351 222 033 087
Web site: http://www.meioformato.com
Freq: Daily
Language (s): Portuguese
NEWS SERVICE/SYNDICATE

ADS Press 496151
Owner: Agência de Representações Dias da Silva, Lda.
Editorial: R. Gil Vicente, 26 B, Cotovia, Sesimbra 2970-305 **Tel:** 351 218 110 270
Email: adspress@ads-press.com
Freq: Daily
Language (s): Portuguese
NEWS SERVICE/SYNDICATE

AEI - Agência Europeia de Imprensa 496152
Owner: Agência Europeia de Imprensa, Lda.
Editorial: Largo Rosa, 6, Lisboa 1100-457
Tel: 351 210 307 860
Email: aei@mail.aei.pt **Web site:** http://www.aei.pt
Freq: Daily
Language (s): Portuguese
NEWS SERVICE/SYNDICATE

Agência Ecclesia 496154
Editorial: Campo dos Martires da Patria, 43, Lisboa 1150-225 **Tel:** 351 218 855 472
Email: agencia@ecclesia.pt **Web site:** http://www.agencia.ecclesia.pt
Freq: Daily
Editor Chefe: Octávio Carmo; **Managing Director:** Paulo Rocha
Profile: News agency regarding the catholic world. Local Translation:Agência noticiosa com informação relativa à religião católica e assuntos relacionados.
Language (s): Portuguese
NEWS SERVICE/SYNDICATE

Agência Feriaque 496156
Owner: Fernando Maia Henrique, Herdeiros
Editorial: R. Chagas, 17 CV - D, Lisboa 1249-195
Tel: 351 213 219 310
Email: feriaque@agenciaferiaque.pt
Freq: Daily
Language (s): Portuguese
NEWS SERVICE/SYNDICATE

Agência Noticiosa Nova China 496157
Owner: Agência Noticiosa Nova China
Editorial: R. Goncalo Velho Cabral, 11 A, Lisboa 1400-188 **Tel:** 351 213 015 783
Email: xinhua@mail.telepac.pt
Freq: Daily
Language (s): Portuguese
NEWS SERVICE/SYNDICATE

AIC Banco de Imagens 765000
Owner: AIC Arquivo Internacional de Cor - Comunicação pela Imagem, Lda.
Editorial: R. Brito Capelo, 822 R/C, Matosinhos 4450-068 **Tel:** 351 229 397 507
Email: info@aic.pt **Web site:** http://www.aic.pt
Managing Director: Conceição Guimarães;
Managing Director: Maria Guimarães
Profile: National. Local Translation:Banco de imagens português, especializado em áreas como a Alimentação, Decoração, Arquitectura e Interiores, Viagens e Destinos. Dispõem também de ofertas em imagens de Obras de Arte. Alternative Title: AIC - Arquivo Internacional de CorPhone: +351 229 397 508
Language (s): Portuguese
NEWS SERVICE/SYNDICATE

Algarsat 496158
Editorial: Quinta Estradas Celões, S. Sebastiao, Loulé 8100-287 **Tel:** 351 289 399 742
Email: vista@mail.telepac.pt
Freq: Daily
Language (s): Portuguese
NEWS SERVICE/SYNDICATE

ASF - Agência de Serviços Fotográficos 496159
Owner: Sociedade Vicra Desportiva, S.A.
Editorial: Travessa da Queimada, 23 -3, Lisboa 1249-113 **Tel:** 351 213 431 565
Email: asf@abola.pt **Web site:** http://www.abola.pt/asf
Freq: Daily
Profile: Coverage of national sport events.
Language (s): Portuguese
NEWS SERVICE/SYNDICATE

Atlânticopress - Comunicação e Imagem, Lda. 496162
Editorial: Av. Luis Bivar, 73 - 1 D, Lisboa 1050-142
Tel: 351 213 570 786

Freq: Daily
Language (s): Portuguese
NEWS SERVICE/SYNDICATE

Bloomberg News 496163
Owner: Regus Business Center, Lda.
Editorial: Av. da Liberdade, 110, Lisboa 1250-146
Tel: 351 213 404 545
Web site: http://www.bloomberg.com
Freq: Daily
Language (s): Portuguese
NEWS SERVICE/SYNDICATE

Brainpix 496164
Owner: Brainpix, Lda.
Editorial: Av. da Republica, 41 - 6 D, Lisboa 1050-187 **Tel:** 351 217 931 886
Email: info@brainpix.com **Web site:** http://www.brainpix.pt
Language (s): Portuguese
NEWS SERVICE/SYNDICATE

Carlos Afonso Augusto de Sousa Barros 496165
Editorial: Av. Fernao de Magalhaes, 858 - 1 E, Porto 4350-152 **Tel:** 351 225 107 132
Freq: Daily
Language (s): Portuguese
NEWS SERVICE/SYNDICATE

Dow Jones Newswires 496166
Owner: Dow Jones & Company, Inc.
Editorial: Praca Duque de Saldanha, 1 - 10 B, Lisboa 1050-094 **Tel:** 351 213 191 863
Web site: http://www.djnewswires.com
Freq: Daily
Language (s): Portuguese
NEWS SERVICE/SYNDICATE

Fórmula Press - Agência Noticiosa Editorial, Lda. 496167
Owner: Fórmula Press - Agência Noticiosa e Editorial, Lda.
Editorial: Praceta Inglaterra 30, 3-D, Carcavelos, Carcavelos 2775-414 **Tel:** 351 214 574 008
Freq: Daily
Language (s): Portuguese
NEWS SERVICE/SYNDICATE

Image Market Place - Agência Noticiosa, Lda. 496168
Owner: Image Market Place - Agência Noticiosa, Lda.
Editorial: R. Bartolomeu Dias, 71, Caxias 2760-013
Tel: 351 214 412 647
Email: info@impagency.com **Web site:** http://www.impagency.com
Freq: Daily
Language (s): Portuguese
NEWS SERVICE/SYNDICATE

João Carreira Bom - Consultores de Comunicação, Lda. 496169
Owner: João Carreira Bom - Consultores de Comunicação, Lda.
Editorial: Praceta Maestro Ivo Cruz, 12 - 5 A, Lisboa 1500-401 **Tel:** 351 217 111 584
Email: jcb@mail.telepac.pt
Freq: Daily
Language (s): Portuguese
NEWS SERVICE/SYNDICATE

Kameraphoto 765544
Editorial: R. da Vinha, 43 A, Lisboa 1200-475
Tel: 351 213 431 676
Email: editorial@kameraphoto.com **Web site:** http://www.kameraphoto.com
Photographer: Nelson D'Aires
Profile: National. Local Translation:Agência de fotografia que tem como um dos objectivos divulgar e representar o trabalho de fotógrafos freelancer.
Language (s): Portuguese
NEWS SERVICE/SYNDICATE

Lusa 496170
Owner: Lusa - Agência de Notícias de Portugal, S.A.
Editorial: R. Dr. Joao Couto, Lote C, Lisboa 1503-809 **Tel:** 351 217 116 500
Email: agencialusa@lusa.pt **Web site:** http://www.lusa.pt
Freq: Daily
Photographer: Manuel de Almeida; **Editor:** Henrique Botequilha; **Managing Director:** Fernando Paula Brito; **Editor:** Cristina Cardoso; **Editor:** Vitor Costa; **Photographer:** Nuno André Ferreira; **Editor:** Francisco J. Marques; **Director Comercial:** Luis Rodrigues Martins; **Director adjunto:** Ricardo Jorge Pinto; **Photographer:** João Relvas; **Director adjunto:** Nuno Simas
Profile: National and international. Local Translation:Agência de notícias portuguesa que fornece informação sobre as mais diversas áreas, nomeadamente actualidade nacional e internacional, economia, política, desporto, cultura, artes, etc. Em Portugal, dispõe de delegações ou correspondentes em todas as capitais de distrito e nos concelhos das áreas metropolitanas de Lisboa e Porto. Tem também delegações e correspondentes em Bruxelas, Madrid, Berlim, Londres, Roma, Paris, Luxemburgo, Moscovo e Estónia (Europa); Bissau, Praia, Luanda e Maputo, S. Tomé, Joanesburgo e Argel (África); Dili, Macau e Pequim (Ásia); S. Paulo, Brasília, Porto Alegre, Caracas (América do Sul); Nova Iorque,

Newark, Rhode Island, New Bedford, Washington e Quebeque, (América do Norte) e em Sidney (Austrália). É uma das agências de notícias, da Europa e dos EUA, que fundaram a rede internacional de cooperação designada Minds International que tem como objectivo partilhar sistemas, processos e práticas tecnológicas. Tem parceria com a agência noticiosa espanhola EFE.
Alternative Title: Lusa - Agência de Notícias de Portugal, S.A.Email: agenda@lusa.pt.
Language (s): Portuguese
NEWS SERVICE/SYNDICATE

Magazine 24 496171
Editorial: R. Victor Cordon, 37 - 6 Dto., Lisboa 1200-482
Freq: Daily
Language (s): Portuguese
NEWS SERVICE/SYNDICATE

Maghreb Arabe Press 496172
Editorial: R. Chagas, 20 - 2 D, Lisboa 1200-107
Tel: 351 213 257 982
Web site: http://www.map.com.ma
Freq: Daily
Language (s): Portuguese
NEWS SERVICE/SYNDICATE

NFactos 765590
Editorial: Estrada Exterior da Circunvalacao, 14618, Matosinhos 4450-097 **Tel:** 351 935 440 440
Email: jornalistas@nfactos.pt **Web site:** http://www.nfactos.pt
Profile: National. Local Translation:A nFACTOS é uma empresa noticiosa que se dedica à produção de trabalhos jornalísticos para a imprensa, rádio, televisão e conteúdos informativos para a internet, especialmente na área da imagem.
Language (s): Portuguese
NEWS SERVICE/SYNDICATE

PNN - Portuguese News Network 496173
Editorial: R. Cândido Oliveira, 5 - Sala 1, Braga 4715-012 **Tel:** 351 253 265 047
Email: press@pnn.com.pt **Web site:** http://www.interpnn.com
Freq: Daily
Language (s): Portuguese
NEWS SERVICE/SYNDICATE

Público Online 583592
Owner: Público - Comunicação Social, S.A.
Editorial: R. do Viriato, 17 - 3, Lisboa 1069-315
Tel: 351 210 111 000
Email: publico@publico.pt **Web site:** http://www.publico.clix.pt
Freq: Daily
Editor: Luís Afonso; **Editor:** José Manuel Tavares Almeida Fernandes; **Editor:** Sérgio B. Gomes; **Editor:** António Granado; **Editor:** Alexandre Martins; **Editor:** José Manuel Rocha
Profile: Web site focused on the latest Portuguese and international breaking news. Headlines on international events, sports, stock markets, Tv and leisure, special editions to collect, blog section, cultural events and art, travelling and auctions galleries are some of the many online services available. General population.Local Translation: Site de cáracter generalista, reflexo da edição impressa, incide e destaca-se pelo índice noticioso de última hora, bem como por diversas temáticas que caracterizam as sociedades modernas, das quais destacamos política, ciências, desporto, cultura, economia, educação, media e tecnologia ou sociedade, lazer ou entretenimento, bem como informação por vídeo, (resultante da parceria entre a Reuters, Lusa e France24), com transmissões em directo dos principais temas que caracterizam a actualidade nacional e internacional.Phone: +351 210 111 102
Language (s): Portuguese
NEWS SERVICE/SYNDICATE

Radimprensa, Lda. 496174
Editorial: R. Barros Lima, 761 - 1, Porto 4300-063
Tel: 351 225 107 137
Email: radimprensa@netc.pt
Freq: Daily
Language (s): Portuguese
NEWS SERVICE/SYNDICATE

Reuters 496177
Editorial: Av. da Liberdade, 190 - 2 A, Lisboa 1250-147 **Tel:** 351 213 509 200
Email: reception.lisbon@thomsonreuters.com **Web site:** http://reuters.com
Freq: Daily
Photographer: Nacho Doce; **Editor:** Sérgio Gonçalves
Profile: Alternative Title: Reuters Europe, S.A. - Sucursal em Portugal
Language (s): Portuguese
NEWS SERVICE/SYNDICATE

RIA - Agência Noticiosa da Rússia 496175
Editorial: Praca Andrade Caminha, 3, Lisboa 1700-039 **Tel:** 351 217 934 700
Freq: Daily
Language (s): Portuguese
NEWS SERVICE/SYNDICATE

SJS - Sociedade Jornalística do Sul, Lda. 496176
Owner: SJS - Sociedade Jornalística do Sul, Lda.
Editorial: Av. 25 de Abril, Lote C 3 - 3 P, Loulé 8100
Tel: 351 289 411 913
Email: sjsul@clix.pt
Freq: Daily
Language (s): Portuguese
NEWS SERVICE/SYNDICATE

Teletráfego - Prestação de Serviços de Informação, Lda. 496178
Editorial: Praca da Republica, 63 - S 5, Montijo 2870-235 **Tel:** 351 212 306 820
Email: teletrafego@netcabo.pt
Freq: Daily
Language (s): Portuguese
NEWS SERVICE/SYNDICATE

Zeta - Fotografia, Media e Comunicação, Lda. 496179
Editorial: R. Damiao Gois, 28 - 4 E, Alges 1495
Tel: 351 214 112 210
Email: zeta.sil.com@mail.telepac.pt
Freq: Daily
Language (s): Portuguese
NEWS SERVICE/SYNDICATE

Puerto Rico

Time Difference: GMT -4
National Telephone Code: 1 787
Continent: The Americas
Capital: San Juan

Newspapers

Claridad 355168
Editorial: Urb. Santa Rita No. 57, Calle Borinquena, San Juan 00925-2732 **Tel:** 1 787 777-0534
Email: info@claridadpuertorico.com **Web site:** http://www.claridadpuertorico.com
Freq: Weekly; **Circ:** 30000 Not Audited
Publisher & Editor: Manuel González; **News Director:** Gervacio Morales Rodriguez
Language (s): Spanish
Ad Rate: Full Page Mono 20.80
Ad Rate: Full Page Colour 33.50
Currency: United States Dollars
DAILY NEWSPAPER

El Nuevo Día 15264
Owner: El Día Inc.
Editorial: Carretera 165 Sector Buchanan, Parque Industrial Amalia, Guaynabo 934 **Tel:** 1 787 641-8000
Email: opinion@elnuevodia.com **Web site:** http://www.elnuevodia.com
Freq: Daily; **Circ:** 168379 Not Audited
Publisher: Maria Ferré
Profile: El Nuevo Dia is a daily newspaper which is distributed throughout the San Juan, PR area. The newspaper provides readers with local and national news. Other features include business, education, politics, health, lifestyle, and classifieds. Deadlines are at 4pm ET.
Language (s): Spanish
Ad Rate: Full Page Mono 47.84
Ad Rate: Full Page Colour 189.51
Currency: United States Dollars
DAILY NEWSPAPER

Primera Hora 15266
Owner: El Dia Inc.
Editorial: Calle Genova A16, Guaynabo 966
Tel: 1 787 641-5454
Email: correo@primerahora.com **Web site:** http://www.primerahora.com
Freq: Fri; **Circ:** 76948
Profile: Primera Hora is written for the general public in Puerto Rico. It covers sports, weather, business, local and national news.
Language (s): Spanish
Ad Rate: Full Page Mono 92.24
Ad Rate: Full Page Colour 1700.00
Currency: United States Dollars
DAILY NEWSPAPER

El Visitante Catolico 355070
Owner: Conferencia Episcopal Puertorriquena
Editorial: Pumarada 1704, Santurce 912
Tel: 1 787 728-3710
Email: director@elvisitante.net **Web site:** http://www.elvisitante.net
Freq: Weekly; **Circ:** 65000 Not Audited
Editor: Verónica Cruz; **Editor:** Efrain Zabala
Language (s): Spanish
Ad Rate: Full Page Mono 25.00
Ad Rate: Full Page Colour 30.00
Currency: United States Dollars
DAILY NEWSPAPER

El Vocero 15265
Editorial: Ave Ponce de Leon 206, Puerta de Tierra, San Juan 901 **Tel:** 1 787 721-2300
Email: opinion@vocero.com **Web site:** http://www.vocero.com
Freq: Daily; **Circ:** 104676 Not Audited
Editor in Chief: Rafael Rivera
Profile: El Vocero is written for Puerto Ricans interested in timely news and covers local news, community, business, sports and other relevant topics.
Language (s): Spanish
Ad Rate: Full Page Mono 70.00
Ad Rate: Full Page Colour 128.00
Currency: United States Dollars
DAILY NEWSPAPER

Qatar

Time Difference: GMT +3
National Telephone Code: 974
Continent: Asia
Capital: Doha

Newspapers

Al Arab 507142
Owner: Dar Al Arab Est.
Editorial: PO Box 22612, Al Arab Newspaper Building, Doha **Tel:** 974 4499 7333
Email: alarab@alarab.qa **Web site:** http://www.alarab.qa
Freq: Daily; **Circ:** 22000 Publisher's Statement
General Manager & Editor in Chief: Abdullah Al Athbah
Profile: Al Arab is a daily Arabic newspaper covering news, culture, business and sport. It was first published in 2007 and includes a monthly lifestyle supplement, Lamsa, and a monthly children's supplement, Abnaa Alarab.
Language (s): Arabic
Ad Rate: Full Page Mono 25000.00
Ad Rate: Full Page Colour 37500.00
Currency: Qatar Riyals
DAILY NEWSPAPER

Doha Stadium Plus 406341
Owner: Aspire Printing, Publishing and Distribution
Editorial: PO Box 24598, 1st Floor, Aspire Press Building, Doha **Tel:** 974 4413 8522
Email: editor@dohastadiumplusqatar.com **Web site:** http://www.dohastadiumplusqatar.com
Freq: Weekly; **Circ:** 15000 Publisher's Statement
Editor In Chief: Ahmed Al Mohannadi; **Advertising Manager:** Ahmed Obeid
Profile: Doha Stadium Plus is a weekly newspaper covering local and international sport, as well as sports-related issues. It launched in 2006 and is published on Wednesdays.
Language (s): English
Ad Rate: Full Page Colour 8000.00
Currency: Qatar Riyals
DAILY NEWSPAPER

Estad Aldoha 406339
Owner: Aspire Printing, Publishing and Distribution
Editorial: PO Box 96204, Aspire Building, Doha
Tel: 974 4499 9626
Email: estad-aldoha4@hotmail.com **Web site:** http://www.estadaldoha.com
Freq: 2 Times/Week; **Circ:** 10000 Publisher's Statement
Editor: Abdel-Majeed Al Kazzar; **Editor In Chief:** Majed Al Khulaifi; **Editor:** Fouad Ben Ajmia
Profile: Estad Aldoha is a sports newspaper, with particular emphasis on football. It launched in 2005 and is published twice a week on Mondays and Thursdays.
Language (s): Arabic
Ad Rate: Full Page Colour 8000.00
Currency: Qatar Riyals
DAILY NEWSPAPER

Gulf Madhyamam - Qatar edition 689588
Owner: Gulf Madhyamam FZ LLC
Editorial: PO Box 19850, Villa 12, Al Hilal Area, Doha
Tel: 974 4436 2122
Email: qatar@gulfmadhyamam.net **Web site:** http://www.gulfmadhyamam.net
Freq: Daily; **Circ:** 23100 Rate Card
Editor-in-Chief: Hamzah Abbas
Profile: Gulf Madhyamam is an international Indian newspaper covering national and international news, current affairs, politics, business and sport. The newspaper is aimed at Malayalam speakers in the Gulf and publishes separate editions for the UAE, Saudi Arabia (Riyadh, Jeddah, Damam & Abha), Qatar, Oman, Bahrain and Kuwait. The newspaper was first published in 1999.
Language (s): Malayalam
DAILY NEWSPAPER

Gulf Times 156781
Owner: Gulf Publishing and Printing Company
Editorial: PO Box 2888, 2nd & 3rd Floor, Gulf Times Building, Doha **Tel:** 974 4435 0478
Email: editor@gulf-times.com **Web site:** http://www.gulf-times.com
Freq: Daily; **Circ:** 40000 Publisher's Statement
Profile: Gulf Times is a broadsheet-sized newspaper covering national and international news, business, politics, entertainment, culture and sport. It was first published in 1978.
Language (s): English
Ad Rate: Full Page Mono 26500.00
Ad Rate: Full Page Colour 39750.00
Currency: Qatar Riyals
DAILY NEWSPAPER

The Peninsula 159079
Owner: Dar Al Sharq Press, Printing & Distribution
Editorial: PO Box 3488, D-Ring Road, Doha
Tel: 974 4455 7741
Email: editor@pen.com.qa **Web site:** http://www.thepeninsulaqatar.com
Freq: Daily; **Circ:** 18000 Publisher's Statement
Advertising Manager: Ali Wahba
Profile: The Peninsula is a daily, broadsheet-sized English newspaper covering national and international news, politics, business, entertainment and sport. It was first published in March 1996.
Language (s): English
Ad Rate: Full Page Mono 26000.00
Ad Rate: Full Page Colour 39000.00
Currency: Qatar Riyals
DAILY NEWSPAPER

Qatar Tribune 395603
Owner: Qatar Information & Marketing
Editorial: PO Box 23493, Villa 57, Street 999, Doha
Tel: 974 4442 2077
Email: qatar.editor@gmail.com **Web site:** http://www.qatar-tribune.com
Freq: Daily; **Circ:** 13000 Publisher's Statement
Editor In Chief: Hassan Al Ansari; **News Editor:** Falak Kabir
Profile: Qatar Tribune is a daily, broadsheet-sized English newspaper covering local and international news, business, entertainment and sport. It was first published in 2006.
Language (s): English
Ad Rate: Full Page Mono 25000.00
Ad Rate: Full Page Colour 37500.00
Currency: Qatar Riyals
DAILY NEWSPAPER

Al Raya 156780
Owner: Gulf Publishing and Printing Company
Editorial: PO Box 533, 2nd & 3rd Floor, Gulf Times Building, Doha **Tel:** 974 4446 6555
Email: edit@raya.com **Web site:** http://www.raya.com
Freq: Daily; **Circ:** 41500 Publisher's Statement
Editor In Chief: Saleh Al Kowary; **Head of News:** Hussni Al Minshawi
Profile: Al Raya is a daily Arabic newspaper covering national and international news, politics, business, culture and sport. It was first published in May 1979 and includes Al Tebbiya, a monthly health supplement, and Hia Wa Houwa, a monthly lifestyle magazine supplement.
Language (s): Arabic
Ad Rate: Full Page Mono 26000.00
Ad Rate: Full Page Colour 39000.00
Currency: Qatar Riyals
DAILY NEWSPAPER

Al Sharq 159078
Owner: Dar Al Sharq Press, Printing & Distribution
Editorial: PO Box 3488, D-Ring Road, Doha
Tel: 974 4455 7777
Email: alsharq@al-sharq.com **Web site:** http://www.al-sharq.com
Freq: Daily; **Circ:** 42000 Publisher's Statement
News Editor: Mosaed Abdel Azeem; **Editor In Chief:** Jaber Al Harmi; **General Manager:** Abdullatif Al Mahmoud; **News Editor:** Yehia Askar; **Head of News:** Alaa Fathi; **Advertising Manager:** Ali Wahba
Profile: Al Sharq (The East) is a daily newspaper covering national and international news, politics, business, culture and sport. It was first published in 1987.
Language (s): Arabic
Ad Rate: Full Page Mono 28000.00
Ad Rate: Full Page Colour 42000.00
Currency: Qatar Riyals
DAILY NEWSPAPER

Varthamanam - Qatar edition 692135
Owner: Dar Al Sharq Press, Printing & Distribution
Editorial: PO Box 246, 6th Floor, Al Mana Tower, Doha **Tel:** 974 4431 6977
Email: qatarvarthamanam@gmail.com **Web site:** http://www.varthamanam.com
Freq: Daily; **Circ:** 24500 Publisher's Statement
Bureau Chief: Mujeeb Kariyaden
Profile: Qatar edition of Kerala-based Varthamanam newspaper. The Qatar edition was first published in 2003 and is aimed at Malayalam speakers. It focuses on national and international news, current affairs, politics, business and sport.
Language (s): Malayalam
Ad Rate: Full Page Mono 8000.00
Ad Rate: Full Page Colour 12000.00
Currency: Qatar Riyals
DAILY NEWSPAPER

Al Watan 156710
Owner: Qatar Information & Marketing
Editorial: PO Box 22345, Salwa Road, Doha
Tel: 974 4465 2244
Email: news@al-watan.com **Web site:** http://www.al-watan.com
Freq: Daily; **Circ:** 25000 Publisher's Statement
General Manager: Ahmed Abdallah; **Editor in Chief:** Mohammad Al Marri; **Head of News:** Abdullah Al Mohannadi; **Picture Editor:** Khalid Moftah
Profile: Al Watan is a daily Arabic newspaper covering national and international news, politics, business, entertainment and sport. It was first published in 1995.
Language (s): Arabic
Ad Rate: Full Page Mono 25000.00
Ad Rate: Full Page Colour 37500.00
Currency: Qatar Riyals
DAILY NEWSPAPER

News Service/Syndicate

Bloomberg - Qatar Bureau 823615
Owner: Bloomberg L.P.
Editorial: PO Box 27111, 14th Floor, Commercial Bank Tower, Doha **Tel:** 974 4452 8148
Email: msergie@bloomberg.net **Web site:** http://www.bloomberg.net
Profile: Qatar bureau of financial news wire service.
Language (s): English
NEWS SERVICE/SYNDICATE

Qatar News Agency 370502
Owner: Qatar News Agency
Editorial: PO Box 3299, Al Sadd, Doha
Tel: 974 4445 0205
Email: qatarnews@qna.org.qa **Web site:** http://www.qna.org.qa
News Manager: Abdullah Al Muzaffar; **Editor:** Samy Al Sayed; **General Manager:** Ahmed Saad
Profile: Qatar News Agency is the official news agency of Qatar. It was founded in 1975.
Language (s): Arabic
NEWS SERVICE/SYNDICATE

Reuters - Doha Bureau 406375
Owner: Thomson Reuters
Editorial: PO Box 23245, Doha **Tel:** 974 4496 7619
Email: tom.finn@thomsonreuters.com **Web site:** http://www.reuters.com
Profile: Doha bureau of International news agency supplying news - text, graphics, video and pictures - to subscribers around the world.
Language (s): English
NEWS SERVICE/SYNDICATE

Romania

Time Difference: GMT +2
National Telephone Code: 40
Continent: Europe
Capital: Bucharest

Newspapers

Adevarul 156953
Owner: SC Adevarul SA
Editorial: Sos. Fabrica de Glucoza, nr 21, Sector 2, Bucuresti **Tel:** 40 21 40 77 609
Email: contact@adevarul.ro **Web site:** http://adevarul.ro
Freq: Daily; **Circ:** 14692 Publisher's Statement
Profile: Independent newspaper containing news and background information. Covers national and international politics, economics, finance, society information, culture and sports.
Language (s): Romanian
Ad Rate: Full Page Mono 17000.00
Ad Rate: Full Page Colour 26000.00
Currency: Moldova Lei
DAILY NEWSPAPER

Azi 156962
Owner: Cicero SA
Editorial: Calea Victoriei 39 A, O.P. 49, C.P. 45, Sector 1, Bucuresti 10062 **Tel:** 40 21 314 19 98
Email: redactia@azi.ro **Web site:** http://www.eazi.ro
Freq: Daily; **Circ:** 20000 Publisher's Statement
Editor-in-Chief: Ruxandra Negrea
Profile: Newspaper covering general news and current affairs business, economics, politics, society, science, sports, lifestyle, arts and entertainment.
Language (s): Romanian
Ad Rate: Full Page Colour 1700.00
Currency: Euro
DAILY NEWSPAPER

Bursa 161039
Owner: SC Ring Press SRL
Editorial: Popa Tatu Str. Nr. 71, Sector 1, Bucuresti 10804 **Tel:** 40 21 315 4356
Email: redactia@bursa.ro **Web site:** http://www.bursa.ro
Freq: Daily; **Circ:** 23000 Publisher's Statement
Editor-in-Chief: Ancu?a Stanciu
Profile: Newspaper providing extensive financial, economical and business cover.
Language (s): English
Ad Rate: Full Page Mono 3450.00
Currency: Euro
DAILY NEWSPAPER

Curierul National 156964
Owner: SC. Curierul National SA
Editorial: Str. Cristian Popisteanu 2-4, Sector 1, Bucuresti 10024 **Tel:** 40 21 59 95 500

Romania

Email: office@curierulnational.ro **Web site:** http://www.curierulnational.ro
Freq: Daily; **Circ:** 35000 Publisher's Statement
News Editor: Valentin Bolocan; **Editor-in-Chief:** Stefan Radeanu
Profile: Newspaper covering news and background information on politics, economics, finance, sports and culture.
Language (s): Romanian
DAILY NEWSPAPER

Gandul 526274
Owner: Mediafax Group
Editorial: Strada Nerva Traian, 3, Sector 3, Bucuresti
Tel: 40 31 8257125
Email: publicitate@gandul.info **Web site:** http://www.gandul.info
Freq: Daily; **Circ:** 16000 Publisher's Statement
Profile: National newspaper covering general news and current affairs including politics, economics, business, society, entertainment, lifestyle and social issues.
Language (s): Romanian
Ad Rate: Full Page Colour 5500.00
Currency: Euro
DAILY NEWSPAPER

Libertatea 156786
Owner: Ringier Romania
Editorial: Bulevardul Dimitrie Pompeiu nr. 6, Sector 2, Bucuresti 20337 **Tel:** 40 21 2030804
Email: subiecte@libertatea.ro **Web site:** http://www.libertatea.ro
Freq: Daily; **Circ:** 320000 Publisher's Statement
Editor-in-Chief: Catalin Alistari; **Editor:** Rodica Dirzu
Profile: Tabloid sized newspaper covering women's interest including lifestyle, fashion, beauty, celebrity, family, health, relationship, sexuality, entertainment, food and culture.
Language (s): Romanian
Ad Rate: Full Page Mono 21000.00
Ad Rate: Full Page Colour 30100.00
Currency: Moldova Lei
DAILY NEWSPAPER

Nine O'Clock 156983
Owner: Casa Editura Nine O'Clock
Editorial: 5, Intrarea Armasului, 1 st district, Bucuresti **Tel:** 40 21 31 77 135
Email: redactia@nineoclock.ro **Web site:** http://www.nineoclock.ro
Freq: Daily; **Circ:** 5000 Publisher's Statement
Profile: English-language Newspaper covering general news and current affairs including business, politics, economy, technology, society, health, sport and culture.
Language (s): English
DAILY NEWSPAPER

Puterea 696595
Owner: Ziarul PUTEREA
Editorial: Casa Presei Libere, nr. 1, Corp B2, Etaj 2, Bucuresti **Tel:** 40 31 413 2776
Email: office@puterea.ro **Web site:** http://www.puterea.ro
Freq: Daily
Editor-in-Chief: Roland Catalin Pena
Profile: National newspaper focused on investigations and analysis of political, economic, social, international events, culture, sport, society.
Language (s): Romanian
Ad Rate: Full Page Colour 4500.00
Currency: Euro
DAILY NEWSPAPER

Romania Libera 156970
Owner: Societatea "R" SA
Editorial: Bd. Theodor Pallady, 54-56, Sector 3, Bucuresti **Tel:** 40 21 2028290
Email: redactia@romanialibera.ro **Web site:** http://www.romanialibera.ro
Freq: Daily; **Circ:** 14228 Publisher's Statement
Profile: Newspaper covering general news and current affairs including politics, economics, society, sports and culture.
Language (s): Romanian
Ad Rate: Full Page Mono 2500.00
Ad Rate: Full Page Colour 4500.00
Currency: Euro
DAILY NEWSPAPER

Ziarul Financiar 161042
Owner: Publimedia International SA
Editorial: Bulevardul Nerva Traian, Nr. 3, sector 3, Bucuresti **Tel:** 40 318 256288
Email: zf@zf.ro **Web site:** http://www.zf.ro
Freq: Daily; **Circ:** 6126 Publisher's Statement
Editor: Bogdan Cojocaru; **Publisher:** Nicoleta Nedea; **Editor-in-Chief:** Sorin Pislaru
Profile: Newspaper covering business and finance including economy, stock market, investment, banking, insurance, money and industry.
Language (s): Romanian
Ad Rate: Full Page Mono 4350.00
Ad Rate: Full Page Colour 6500.00
Currency: Euro
DAILY NEWSPAPER

Community Newspaper

Ziarul de Iasi 157236
Owner: Sc Grupul de Presa Medianet SRL
Editorial: Bulevardul Nicolae Iorga 35, Iasi 700399
Tel: 40 232 271 333
Email: redactie@ziaruldeiasi.ro **Web site:** http://www.ziaruldeiasi.ro
Circ: 9000
Editor-in-Chief: Toni Hritac
Profile: Regional paper offering daily news, as well as weather, sports, entertainment, business, and travel coverage.
Language (s): Romanian
Ad Rate: Full Page Mono 5655.00
Ad Rate: Full Page Colour 13530.00
Currency: Moldova Lei
COMMUNITY NEWSPAPER

Russia

Time Difference: GMT +2 (west), GMT +12 (east)
National Telephone Code: 7
Continent: Europe
Capital: Moscow

Newspapers

Argumenti nedeli 679449
Editorial: Aviatsionny per. 4a, Moskva 125167
Tel: 7 495 638-52-63
Email: anonline@argumenti.ru **Web site:** http://argumenti.ru
Freq: Weekly; **Circ:** 587000 Publisher's Statement
Editor: Andrey Uglanov
Profile: Publication focused political analysis and social issues, business and economical developments.
Language (s): Russian
Ad Rate: Full Page Colour 360000.00
Currency: Russia Rubles
DAILY NEWSPAPER

Izvestia 156726
Editorial: per. Partiynyi 1, korp. 57, str. 3, Moskva 115093 **Tel:** 7 495 645-36-10
Email: info@izvestia.ru **Web site:** http://izvestia.ru
Freq: Daily; **Circ:** 150950 Not Audited
Editor: Alexander Potapov
Profile: National newspaper covering all aspects of Russian politics and economy.
Language (s): Russian
DAILY NEWSPAPER

Kommersant 167770
Owner: Izdatelskiy Dom Kommersant
Editorial: Rublevskoye shosse 28, Moskva 121609
Tel: 7 495 797-69-70
Email: kommersant@kommersant.ru **Web site:** http://www.kommersant.ru
Freq: Daily; **Circ:** 120000
Editor-in-Chief: Sergey Yakovlev
Profile: Newspaper dedicated to the problems of economics and economic processes of Russian and international markets. Includes analyses of Russian micro- and macroeconomics, monetary and stock exchange markets and investments.
Language (s): Russian
Ad Rate: Full Page Colour 1480000.00
Currency: Russia Rubles
DAILY NEWSPAPER

Komsomolskaya Pravda 157232
Owner: ZAO ID Komsomolskaya Pravda
Editorial: Stary Petrovsko-Rozumovsky proyezd 1/23, str.1, Moskva 125993 **Tel:** 7 495 777-02-82
Email: kp@kp.ru **Web site:** http://www.kp.ru
Freq: Daily; **Circ:** 550000 Not Audited
Editor-in-Chief: Vladimir Sungorkin
Profile: Daily newspaper covering politics, economics and social news.
Language (s): Russian
DAILY NEWSPAPER

Metro Moskva 680730
Editorial: ul. Skakovaya 36, Moskva 125040
Tel: 7 495 787-1211
Email: metro@gazetametro.ru **Web site:** http://www.metronews.ru
Freq: Daily; **Circ:** 500000 Publisher's Statement
PR Director: Anna Ivanova; **Director General:** Boris Konoshenko; **Editor In Chief:** Anna Sirota
Profile: Entertainment newspaper with city news distributed for free in Moscow.
Language (s): Russian
Ad Rate: Full Page Colour 425000.00
Currency: Russia Rubles
DAILY NEWSPAPER

Metro Peterburg 680731
Editorial: ul. Avtovskaya 2, Sankt Peterburg 198096
Tel: 7 812 783 27 06
Web site: http://www.metronews.ru
Freq: Daily; **Circ:** 500000 Publisher's Statement
Editor In Chief: Anna Sirota
Profile: City entertainment morning newspaper distributed for free in St. Petersburg.
Language (s): English
DAILY NEWSPAPER

Moskovskaya Pravda 157149
Owner: ZAO Redaktsia Gazety Moskovskaya Pravda
Editorial: ul. 1905 goda, d. 7, D-22, GSP-5, Moskva 123995 **Tel:** 7 499 259-82-33
Email: newspaper@mospravda.ru **Web site:** http://mospravda.ru
Freq: Daily; **Circ:** 95000 Not Audited
Editor-in-Chief: Shod Muladzhanov
Profile: Newspaper covering national and international news, politics, economics, culture and social issues.
Language (s): Russian
Ad Rate: Full Page Colour 295000.00
Currency: Russia Rubles
DAILY NEWSPAPER

Moskovsky Komsomolets 157248
Owner: Moskovsky Komsomolets
Editorial: ul. 1905 goda, d. 7, D-22, Moskva 123995
Tel: 7 495 6094444
Email: info@mk.ru **Web site:** http://www.mk.ru
Freq: Daily; **Circ:** 1600000 Not Audited
Editor: Pavel Gusev; **Editor:** Olga Kochetkova
Profile: Newspaper focusing on national and international affairs, politics, scientific news, culture and arts.
Language (s): Russian
DAILY NEWSPAPER

Moy raion - Sankt Peterburg 679604
Editorial: ul. Odoevskogo 27, lit. A, 4 floor, Sankt Peterburg 199155 **Tel:** 7 812 325 25 15
Email: info@mr7.ru **Web site:** http://www.mr7.ru
Freq: Weekly; **Circ:** 350000 Publisher's Statement
Editor-in-Chief: Vladislav Bachaurov
Profile: Entertainment newspaper with information on holidays, shopping, relaxation, local news and practical advice.
Language (s): Russian
Ad Rate: Full Page Mono 44462.00
Currency: Russia Rubles
DAILY NEWSPAPER

Nezavisimaya Gazeta 157252
Owner: Redaktsiya Nezavisimaya Gazeta
Editorial: ul. Myasnitskaya, d. 13, Moskva 101000
Tel: 7 495 981 61 54
Email: net@ng.ru **Web site:** http://www.ng.ru
Freq: Daily; **Circ:** 40000 Not Audited
Editor: Svetlana Gamova; **Editor in Chief:** Konstantin Remchukov
Profile: Newspaper covering national and international news, politics, business and economy.
Language (s): Russian
DAILY NEWSPAPER

Novaya gazeta 679427
Editorial: Potapovsky per. 3, korp. 1, Moskva 101990
Tel: 7 495 623 68 88
Email: 2017@novayagazeta.ru **Web site:** http://www.novayagazeta.ru
Freq: 2 Times/Week; **Circ:** 535000 Publisher's Statement
Director General: Sergey Kozheurov; **Editor-in-Chief:** Dmitri Muratov; **PR Manager:** Nadezhda Prusenkova
Profile: National newspaper with regional inserts covering politics, economics, society, culture, sports and investigations. Alternative Title: ????? ??????
Language (s): Russian
Ad Rate: Full Page Mono 180000.00
Ad Rate: Full Page Colour 220000.00
Currency: Russia Rubles
DAILY NEWSPAPER

Novye izvestiya 679617
Owner: Novye izvestiya
Editorial: ul. Novoostapovskaya 5, korpus 14, Moskva 107076 **Tel:** 7 495 783-06-36
Web site: http://www.newizv.ru
Freq: Daily; **Circ:** 108200 Publisher's Statement
Editor-in-Chief: Valery Yakov
Profile: Fully colour daily newspaper covering political, social and economical news.
Language (s): Russian
Ad Rate: Full Page Mono 247500.00
Ad Rate: Full Page Colour 264000.00
Currency: Russia Rubles
DAILY NEWSPAPER

Rossiyskaya Gazeta 360221
Editorial: Ul. Pravdy 24, Moskva 125993
Tel: 7 495 257 52 52
Email: economic@rg.ru **Web site:** http://www.rg.ru
Freq: Daily; **Circ:** 400000 Not Audited
Editor-in-Chief: Vladislav Fronin; **Director:** Pavel Negoitsa
Profile: Newspaper covering national and international news, politics, economy, special reports and interview with government officials.
Language (s): Russian
DAILY NEWSPAPER

Sovietskaya Rossiya 679478
Editorial: ul. Pravdy 24, Moskva 125993
Tel: 7 499 257 53 00
Email: sovross@aha.ru **Web site:** http://www.sovross.ru
Freq: Daily; **Circ:** 300000 Publisher's Statement
Editor-in-Chief: Valentin Chikin
Profile: Independent socialist political newspaper covering Russian issues.
Language (s): Russian
DAILY NEWSPAPER

Trud 156998
Owner: Trud Publishing
Editorial: ul. Bolshaya Dmitorvka 9, str. 1, Moskva 125 009 **Tel:** 7 495 221-58-18
Email: letter@trud.ru **Web site:** http://www.trud.ru
Freq: Daily; **Circ:** 612000 Not Audited
Editor-in-Chief: Valeriy Simonov
Profile: National newspaper covering national and international news.
Language (s): Russian
DAILY NEWSPAPER

Vechernyaya Moskva morning edition 157231
Editorial: Bunazhny proyezd 14, str. 2, Moskva 127015 **Tel:** 7 499 557-04-24
Email: news@vm.ru **Web site:** http://www.vm.ru
Freq: Daily; **Circ:** 135000 Not Audited
Editor-in-Chief: Alexander Kupriyanov
Profile: Newspaper focusing on national and international news, politics, the economy, business and society.
Language (s): Russian
DAILY NEWSPAPER

Vedomosti 157102
Owner: Business News Media
Editorial: ul. Polkovaya 3, str.1, Moskva 127018
Tel: 7 495 9563458
Email: info@vedomosti.ru **Web site:** http://www.vedomosti.ru
Freq: Daily; **Circ:** 75000 Not Audited
Editor in Chief: Tatiana Lysova
Profile: The business daily Vedomosti was established with the cooperation of business newspapers Financial Times and The Wall Street Journal. Together with the largest Russian publishing house Independent Media, they released Vedomosti since 1999. The main task of the newspaper Vedomosti is to give readers the most prompt, detailed and objective business information. More than 100 journalists in Moscow and Russian regions with the support of the global network of correspondents Financial Times and The Wall Street Journal inform about the most important economic, financial, corporate and political developments, offering analysis and forecasts.
Language (s): Russian
DAILY NEWSPAPER

Zavtra 679409
Editorial: Frunzenskaya nab. 18-60, Moskva 119146
Tel: 7 495 726 54 83
Email: zavtra@zavtra.ru **Web site:** http://zavtra.ru
Freq: Weekly; **Circ:** 46000 Publisher's Statement
Profile: Daily newspaper writing about political, economic and cultural events in Russia.
Language (s): Russian
Ad Rate: Full Page Mono 3500.00
Currency: United States Dollars
DAILY NEWSPAPER

Zhizn 680888
Editorial: Bumazhny proyezd 14, kopr. 2, Moskva 27015 **Tel:** 7 495 510 29 84
Email: info@zhizn.ru **Web site:** http://www.zhizn.ru
Freq: Weekly; **Circ:** 2200000 Publisher's Statement
PR Director: Nataliaya Abramochkina; **Editor In Chief:** Ruslan Sagaev
Profile: Tabloid-size newspaper covering news, entertainment and gossip.
Language (s): Russian
Ad Rate: Full Page Mono 2400000.00
Currency: Russia Rubles
DAILY NEWSPAPER

News Service/Syndicate

Interfax 353223
Editorial: ul. 1ya Tverskaya-Yamskaya, d. 2, Moskva 127006 **Tel:** 7 499 250-98-40
Email: business@interfax.ru **Web site:** http://www.interfax.ru
Director: Mikhail Komissar
Profile: News agency providing political, business and financial information from Russia, the CIS, Central and Eastern Europe.
Language (s): Russian
NEWS SERVICE/SYNDICATE

Interfax Russia 680056
Editorial: Pervaya Tverskaya-Yamskaya 2, str. 1, Moskva 127006 **Tel:** 7 495 250 98 40
Email: info@interfax-russia.ru **Web site:** http://www.interfax-russia.ru
Freq: Daily
Profile: 24-hour information channel that prioritizes Russian breaking news. Covers political and economic events in Russia as well as sport and culture.
Language (s): Russian
NEWS SERVICE/SYNDICATE

NIA - Novoye Informatsionnoye Agentstvo 353204
Editorial: ul. Mironovskaya 10 A, Moskva 105318
Tel: 7 495 369 03 59
Email: nia@okbprogress.ru
Director: Vitaliy Skorohodov
Language (s): Russian
NEWS SERVICE/SYNDICATE

Rossiya Segodnya - Rome Bureau 508519
Owner: Rossiya Segodnya
Editorial: Via Elio Vittorini, 78, Roma 144
Tel: 39 06 5015840
Web site: https://ria.ru

Freq: Daily
Profile: Regional office of the international Russian news agency and wire service focussing on news and current affairs.
Language (s): English
NEWS SERVICE/SYNDICATE

Rossiya Segodnya - Russia Today 353222
Owner: Rossiya Segodnya
Editorial: Zubovskiy Bulvar, d. 4, Moskva 119021
Tel: 7 495 2012424
Email: pressclub@rian.ru **Web site:** http://ria.ru
Environment News Group Head: Olga Dobrovidova; **Director:** Dmitry Kiselyov; **Editor-in-Chief:** Margarita Simonyan
Profile: News agency providing socio-political, economic, scientific and financial information.
Language (s): Russian
NEWS SERVICE/SYNDICATE

TASS - Helsinki Bureau 519931
Editorial: Ratakatu 1 a, B 10, Helsinki 120
Tel: 358 9 60 18 77
Web site: http://tass.ru/en
Freq: Daily
Profile: Russian news agency in Finland. Venäjän uutistoimisto Suomessa.
Language (s): English
NEWS SERVICE/SYNDICATE

TASS - Informatsionnoye agentstvo Rossii 353203
Editorial: Tverskoy Bulvar 10-12, Moskva 103009
Tel: 7 499 791 0018
Email: glav@tass.ru **Web site:** http://tass.ru
Editor-in-Chief: Maxim Filimonov
Profile: TASS is a news agency with more than 130 bureaus and offices in Russia and abroad. TASS also cooperates with more than 80 foreign news agencies. TASS' editorial and other desks process information from correspondents, check and analyze facts, and translate into five foreign languages.
Language (s): Russian
NEWS SERVICE/SYNDICATE

TASS - New York Bureau 506291
Editorial: 780 3rd Ave Fl 19, New York, New York 10017-2024 **Tel:** 1 212 245-4250
Email: itar@aol.com **Web site:** http://tass.ru/en
NEWS SERVICE/SYNDICATE

TASS - Sydney Bureau 313593
Editorial: Sydney **Tel:** 61 2 9398 2321
Email: australiatass@gmail.com **Web site:** http://tass.ru/en
Profile: Sydney bureau of the Russian news agency.
Language (s): English
NEWS SERVICE/SYNDICATE

TASS - United Nations Bureau 506294
Editorial: 405 E 42nd St Rm C-312, New York, New York 10017-3507 **Tel:** 1 212 688-6764
Web site: http://tass.ru/en
Profile: TASS United Nations bureau.
Language (s): English
NEWS SERVICE/SYNDICATE

TASS - Washington Bureau 155539
Editorial: 529 14th St NW Ste 1004, Washington, District Of Columbia 20045-2001 **Tel:** 1 202 662-7080
Email: washtass@gmail.com **Web site:** http://tass.ru/en
Bureau Chief: Andrei Sitov
Profile: TASS (Information Telegraph Agency of Russia) is the successor to the Soviet era TASS news service. It was originally formed in 1904 as the official news agency of the Russian state. The service has 74 bureaus within Russia and the CIS, with another 65 offices in 62 countries abroad.
Language (s): English
NEWS SERVICE/SYNDICATE

Community Newspaper

Belgorodskaya pravda 679119
Editorial: pr. Slavy 100, Belgorod 308800
Tel: 7 4722 32 05 62
Email: Belpravda31@yandex.ru **Web site:** http://www.belpravda.ru
Circ: 50000
Profile: Covers all aspects of life in Belgorod region.
Language (s): Russian
COMMUNITY NEWSPAPER

Novosti Yugry 679723
Editorial: ul. Mira 46, Khanty-Mansiysk 628011
Tel: 7 34671 36-37-41
Email: gazeta@ugra-news.ru **Web site:** http://ugra-news.ru
Freq: Daily; **Circ:** 52000
Editor-in-Chief: Tatiana Terekhina
Profile: Socio-political newspaper focused on economic, cultural issues of the Siberian region.
Language (s): Russian
Ad Rate: Full Page Mono 55800.00
Ad Rate: Full Page Colour 66960.00
Currency: Russia Rubles
COMMUNITY NEWSPAPER

Podmoskoviye 679431
Owner: Moscovia
Editorial: ul. 5 Magistralnaya 5/12, Moskva 123007
Tel: 7 495 707-29-94
Email: mosregtoday@yandex.ru **Web site:** http://mosregtoday.ru
Circ: 65000
Editor-in-Chief: Natalia Chernysheva
Profile: Provides informative analytical materials society, economics, social issues, culture and sports in Moscow region.
Language (s): Russian
COMMUNITY NEWSPAPER

Slavyanka segodnya 679614
Owner: Nevskaya Storona
Editorial: ul. Karovaevskaya 30, Sankt Peterburg 92177 **Tel:** 7 812 700 42 57
Email: l.az@mail.ru **Web site:** http://www.nslav.spb.ru
Circ: 50000
Director: Irina Grabko; **Editor:** Aleksandr Seleznev
Profile: Provides general and city council news on life in St. Petersburg.
Language (s): Russian
COMMUNITY NEWSPAPER

Rwanda

Time Difference: GMT +2
National Telephone Code: 250
Continent: Africa
Capital: Kigali

Newspapers

Imvaho Nshya 225713
Editorial: Nyarugenge, Kigali **Tel:** 250 783 125 993
Email: info@imvahonshya.rw **Web site:** http://imvahonshya.co.rw
Circ: 12000 Publisher's Statement
Director General: Oscar Kimanuka; **Editor In Chief:** Frank Ndamage
Profile: Newspaper covering regional, national and international news including politics and economy.
Language (s): English
Ad Rate: Full Page Mono 236000.00
Ad Rate: Full Page Colour 320000.00
Currency: Rwanda Francs
DAILY NEWSPAPER

The New Times 229991
Owner: The New Times Publications
Editorial: Immeuble Aigle Blanc, Opposite MINIJUST Kimihurura, Kigali **Tel:** 250 55 10 69 17
Email: editorial@newtimes.co.rw **Web site:** http://www.newtimes.co.rw
Freq: Daily; **Circ:** 3000 Publisher's Statement
News Editor: James Tasamba
Profile: Newspaper covering regional, national and international news and current affairs including politics, business, culture and sport.
Language (s): English
DAILY NEWSPAPER

La Nouvelle Relève 186058
Owner: Orinfor Pecipho
Editorial: ORINFOR, 50, Boulevard de la Révolution, Kigali **Tel:** 250 08 57 57 35
Email: lnr2020@yahoo.fr **Web site:** http://www.orinfor.gov.rw
Circ: 3000 Publisher's Statement
Directeur: Oscar Kimanuka; **Rédacteur en Chef:** Jean-Claude Rwabulindi
Profile: Newspaper containing national and international news, current affairs, business and sport.
Language (s): French
Ad Rate: Full Page Mono 100000.00
Ad Rate: Full Page Colour 190000.00
Currency: Rwanda Francs
DAILY NEWSPAPER

News Service/Syndicate

Rwanda News Agency - RNA 362372
Owner: Rwanda News Agency
Editorial: BP 453, Kigali **Tel:** 250 58 7215
Email: rwandanewsagency@gmail.com **Web site:** http://www.rnanews.com
Director: André Gakwaya
Profile: National news agency of Rwanda covering regional and national news and current affairs including politics, economy, culture, health and sport.
Language (s): French
NEWS SERVICE/SYNDICATE

Saint Helena

Time Difference: GMT
National Telephone Code: 290
Continent: Africa
Capital: Jamestown

Newspapers

St. Helena Independent 537285
Owner: St. Helena Media Productions Ltd.
Editorial: 2nd Floor, Association Hall, Main Street, South Atlantic Ocean STHL 1ZZ **Tel:** 290 26 60
Email: fm@cwimail.sh **Web site:** http://www.saint.fm
Publisher: Mike Olsson
Language (s): English
DAILY NEWSPAPER

Saint Lucia

Time Difference: GMT -4
National Telephone Code: 1 758
Continent: The Americas
Capital: Castries

Newspapers

The Voice 156806
Owner: Voice Publishing Co Ltd
Editorial: Odessa Building, Darling Road, Castries
Tel: 1758 45 22 590
Email: voice@candw.lc
Freq: 3 Times/Week; **Circ:** 8000 Not Audited
Publisher & Editor: Victor Marquis
Profile: The Voice is a daily newspaper covering news and sports.
Language (s): English
Ad Rate: Full Page Mono 7.68
Currency: United States Dollars
DAILY NEWSPAPER

Community Newspaper

The St. Lucia Mirror 411784
Owner: Mirror Publishing Co.
Tel: 1 7584516186
Email: mirror@candw.lc
Freq: Weekly; **Circ:** 5000 Not Audited
Publisher & Editor: Guy Ellis
Profile: The St. Lucia Mirror is a weekly newspaper focusing on politics, business news, community news, sports and entertainment.
Language (s): English
Ad Rate: Full Page Mono 6.74
Ad Rate: Full Page Colour 823.97
Currency: United States Dollars
COMMUNITY NEWSPAPER

Saint Vincent and the Grenadines

Time Difference: GMT -4
National Telephone Code: 1 784
Continent: The Americas
Capital: Kingstown

Community Newspaper

The News 224454
Tel: 1 784 456-2942
Email: thenews@vincysurf.com
Freq: Weekly; **Circ:** 14000 Not Audited
Editor: Shelley Clarke
Profile: The News is a weekly newspaper covering news and current affairs.
Language (s): English
Ad Rate: Full Page Mono 5.00
Ad Rate: Full Page Colour 599.00
Currency: United States Dollars
COMMUNITY NEWSPAPER

The Vincentian 224446
Owner: The Vincentian Publishing Co Ltd
Editorial: Paul Avenue, Kingstown **Tel:** 1 784 456-1123
Email: vinpub@yahoo.com **Web site:** http://www.thevincentian.com
Freq: Weekly; **Circ:** 9000 Not Audited

Editor in Chief: Cytrian Neehall
Profile: The Vincentian is daily newspaper covering national and international news, politics, economics, finance, business, culture and sports.
Language (s): English
Ad Rate: Full Page Mono 11.99
Ad Rate: Full Page Colour 1035.51
Currency: United States Dollars
COMMUNITY NEWSPAPER

Samoa

Time Difference: GMT +11
National Telephone Code: 685
Continent: Oceania
Capital: Apia (Upolu)

Newspapers

Samoa Observer 538566
Owner: Samoa Observer Newspapers Ltd
Editorial: PO Box 1572, Apia, Samoa **Tel:** 685 23 078
Email: news@sobserver.ws **Web site:** http://www.samoaobserver.ws
Freq: Daily
Publisher: Muliaga Jean Ash Malifa; **Editor-in-Chief:** Savea Sano Malifa
Profile: Newspaper covering general news and current affairs in the whole of Samoa including politics, economy, international relations, sports, entertainment and technology.
Language (s): English
DAILY NEWSPAPER

Community Newspaper

Newsline 538737
Owner: Pio Sioa
Editorial: PO Box 2441, Malifa, Western Samoa
Email: sunlinesamoa@gmail.com **Web site:** http://newslinesamoa.com
Editor-in-Chief: Cherelle Jackson
Profile: Provides latest news on Samoa.
Language (s): English
COMMUNITY NEWSPAPER

Savali Newspaper 538734
Owner: Ministry of the Prime Minister and Cabinet
Editorial: Government Building, PO Box 1861, Samoa
Email: terrytavita@yahoo.com
Freq: Bi-Weekly
Editor-in-Chief: Tupuola Terry Tavita
Language (s): English
COMMUNITY NEWSPAPER

San Marino

Time Difference: GMT +1
National Telephone Code: 378
Continent: Europe
Capital: San Marino

Newspapers

La Tribuna Sammarinese 529904
Tel: 378 0549 990420
Email: redazione@latribunasammarinese.net **Web site:** http://www.latribunasammarinese.net
Freq: Daily
Capo redattore: Riccardo Geminiani; **Direttore:** Davide Graziosi; **Redattore:** Alessia Pieroni
Profile: National daily newspaper focussing on news, current affairs, politics, economics, culture and sport.
Language (s): Italian
DAILY NEWSPAPER

Sao Tome & Principe

Time Difference: GMT
National Telephone Code: 239
Continent: Africa
Capital: São Tomé

Newspapers

Correio da Semana 387093
Owner: Impressões e Brindas Publicitarias
Editorial: Avenida Amilcar Cabral 382, São Tomé
Tel: 239 225 299
Email: correiodasemana@cstome.net
Freq: Weekly; **Circ:** 3000 Publisher's Statement
Editor: Rafael Branco; **Director:** Josenau Rodrigues; **Director de Publicidade:** Antonio Suárez
Profile: Newspaper including national and international information: covering economics, politics, society, culture and current affairs.
Language (s): Portuguese
DAILY NEWSPAPER

Vitrina 386968
Owner: PRESCO Lda
Editorial: Rua de Mozambique, Caixa Postal 628, São Tomé **Tel:** 239 227 904
Email: diario_vitrina@cstome.net **Web site:** http://www.vitrina.st
Freq: Weekly; **Circ:** 1500 Publisher's Statement
Chefe de Redacção: Herlânder Aguiar; **Director:** Manuel Barros
Profile: National newspaper providing political coverage and articles covering international affairs, finance, economics, society and culture.
Language (s): Portuguese
DAILY NEWSPAPER

Saudi Arabia

Time Difference: GMT +3
National Telephone Code: 966
Continent: Asia
Capital: Riyadh

Newspapers

Alyaum 156785
Owner: Dar Alyaum Press & Publishing
Editorial: PO Box 565, Dammam 31421
Tel: 966 13 858 0800
Email: edit@alyaum.com **Web site:** http://www.alyaum.com
Freq: Daily; **Circ:** 126000 Publisher's Statement
Editor in Chief: Abdulwahab Al Fayez; **Editor:** Waleed Al Nahdi
Profile: Alyaum (Today) is a daily Arabic newspaper covering local and international news, society, politics, business and sport. It was first published in 1964.
Language (s): Arabic
Ad Rate: Full Page Mono 42400.00
Ad Rate: Full Page Colour 78440.00
Currency: Saudi Arabia Riyals
DAILY NEWSPAPER

Arab News 156795
Owner: Saudi Research & Publishing Co.
Editorial: PO Box 10452, 3rd Floor, Omniya Center, Jeddah 21433 **Tel:** 966 12 283 6200
Email: edit@arabnews.com **Web site:** http://www.arabnews.com
Freq: Daily; **Circ:** 72799 Publisher's Statement
Editor In Chief: Mohammed Al-Harthi
Profile: Arab News is a daily, broadsheet-sized English newspaper covering national and international news, politics, economics, sport and social issues. It was first published in 1975.
Language (s): English
Ad Rate: Full Page Mono 49000.00
Ad Rate: Full Page Colour 75950.00
Currency: Saudi Arabia Riyals
DAILY NEWSPAPER

Arreyadi 160804
Owner: Sab Media FZ LLC
Editorial: PO Box 112193, 9th Floor, Adex Tower, Jeddah 21371 **Tel:** 966 12 639 5713
Email: email@arreyadi.com.sa **Web site:** http://www.arreyadi.com.sa
Freq: Daily; **Circ:** 162770 Rate Card
Profile: Arreyadi (The Sportsman) is a daily Arabic newspaper covering local and international sport, as well as sections covering youth activities, arts and culture, poetry, gadgets, information technology, cars and motoring. The newspaper was first published in 1994 and is aimed at sports enthusiasts in Saudi Arabia.
Language (s): Arabic
Ad Rate: Full Page Mono 48000.00
Ad Rate: Full Page Colour 70000.00
Currency: Saudi Arabia Riyals
DAILY NEWSPAPER

Arriyadiyah 208188
Owner: Saudi Research & Publishing Co.
Editorial: PO Box 478, Conferences Area, Riyadh 11411 **Tel:** 966 11 212 8000 1538
Email: editorial4@arriyadiyah.com **Web site:** http://www.arriyadiyah.com
Freq: Daily; **Circ:** 167357 Rate Card
Office Manager: Saad Al Ghanem
Profile: Arriyadiyah is a daily newspaper covering national and international sport, including cycling, boxing, athletics, tennis, horse racing, basketball, handball and soccer. It launched in 1987 and is aimed at sports enthusiasts.
Language (s): Arabic
Ad Rate: Full Page Mono 48000.00
Ad Rate: Full Page Colour 74400.00
Currency: Saudi Arabia Riyals
DAILY NEWSPAPER

Asharq Al-Awsat 160105
Owner: Saudi Research & Publishing Co.
Editorial: PO Box 14744, 3rd Floor, Omniya Center, Jeddah 21434 **Tel:** 966 11 212 8000
Email: editorial@asharqalawsat.com **Web site:** http://www.aawsat.com
Freq: Daily; **Circ:** 263121 Publisher's Statement
National News Editor: Asmaa Al Ghabri; **News Editor:** Ahmad Azouz
Profile: Asharq Al-Awsat is a daily newspaper covering regional and international news, politics, business and sport. The London-based newspaper was launched in 1978, and is distributed across the Arab world.
Language (s): Arabic
Ad Rate: Full Page Mono 73600.00
Ad Rate: Full Page Colour 114400.00
Currency: Saudi Arabia Riyals
DAILY NEWSPAPER

Al Bilad 156775
Owner: Al Bilad Establishment for Journalism & Publishing
Editorial: PO Box 7095, 2nd Floor, Jeraisy Riyadh House Building, Jeddah 21462 **Tel:** 966 12 275 0020
Email: wr@albiladdaily.com **Web site:** http://www.albiladdaily.com
Freq: Daily; **Circ:** 74472 Publisher's Statement
General Manager: Abdel Hafeez Kari; **Editor:** Ibrahim Madani
Profile: Al Bilad is a daily, broadsheet-sized Arabic newspaper covering local and international news, politics, business and sport. It was first published in 1932.
Language (s): Arabic
Ad Rate: Full Page Mono 38160.00
Ad Rate: Full Page Colour 59360.00
Currency: Saudi Arabia Riyals
DAILY NEWSPAPER

Al Eqtisadiah 160106
Owner: Saudi Research & Publishing Co.
Editorial: PO Box 478, Conferences Area, Riyadh 11411 **Tel:** 966 11 212 8000 1003
Email: edit@aleqt.com **Web site:** http://www.aleqt.com
Freq: Daily; **Circ:** 110713 Publisher's Statement
Editor in Chief: Abdul Rahman Mansour
Profile: Al Eqtisadiah is a daily Arabic business newspaper covering finance, business, investment, economics and sport. It was first published in 1992 and is aimed at Arab business executives.
Language (s): Arabic
Ad Rate: Full Page Mono 54000.00
Ad Rate: Full Page Colour 83600.00
Currency: Saudi Arabia Riyals
DAILY NEWSPAPER

Gulf Madhyamam - Saudi edition 688966
Owner: Gulf Madhyamam FZ LLC
Editorial: PO Box 380169, Office 1106, 11th Floor, Riyadh 11345 **Tel:** 966 11 414 3132
Email: riyadh@gulfmadhyamam.net **Web site:** http://www.gulfmadhyamam.net
Freq: Daily; **Circ:** 96350 Rate Card
Bureau Chief: V. M. Ibrahim
Profile: Gulf Madhyamam is an international Indian newspaper covering national and international news, current affairs, politics, business and sport. The newspaper is aimed at Malayalam speakers in the Gulf and publishes separate editions for the UAE, Saudi Arabia (Riyadh, Jeddah, Damam & Abha), Qatar, Oman, Bahrain and Kuwait. The newspaper was first published in 1999.
Language (s): Malayalam
DAILY NEWSPAPER

Al Hayat - Saudi edition 159063
Owner: Dar Al Hayat
Editorial: PO Box 68907, Prince Mohammed Bin Abdulaziz Street, Riyadh 11537 **Tel:** 966 11 461 2626
Email: editing@alhayat.com **Web site:** http://www.alhayat.com
Freq: Daily; **Circ:** 160000 Rate Card
Head of News: Ali Al Ayed
Profile: The Saudi Arabia editions (Riyadh, Jeddah and Dammam) of Al Hayat cover national and international news, current affairs, politics, business, sports and entertainment. The newspaper is based in London and Beirut and also publishes an International edition distributed outside Saudi Arabia. The newspaper was first published in 1946.
Language (s): Arabic
DAILY NEWSPAPER

Al Jazirah 159065
Owner: Al Jazirah Corporation Press, Printing & Publishing
Editorial: PO Box 354, Press District, Riyadh 11411
Tel: 966 11 487 0000
Email: ccs@al-jazirah.com.sa **Web site:** http://www.al-jazirah.com
Freq: Daily; **Circ:** 91403 BPA Worldwide
Editor In Chief: Khaled Al Malik; **Head of News:** Mansour Al Zahrani; **General Manager:** Abdullatif Al-Ateeq
Profile: Al Jazirah is a daily newspaper covering national, regional and international news, politics, business, culture and sport. It was first published in 1960 and includes Al Jazirah Cultural Magazine, an arts and culture supplement, issued daily.
Language (s): Arabic
Ad Rate: Full Page Mono 41600.00
Ad Rate: Full Page Colour 75960.00
Currency: Saudi Arabia Riyals
DAILY NEWSPAPER

Al Madina 156779
Owner: Al Madina Press Group
Editorial: PO Box 807, Press Street, Jeddah 21421
Tel: 966 12 671 2100
Email: reporters@al-madina.com **Web site:** http://www.al-madina.com
Freq: Daily; **Circ:** 120000 Publisher's Statement
Editor In Chief: Fahed Al Aqran; **News Editor:** Mohammad Al Muheisen; **General Manager:** Mohamed Safeed
Profile: Al Madina (The City) is a daily Arabic newspaper covering news, politics, business and sport. It was first published in 1936. The newspaper includes a weekly arts supplement, Alarbaa, on Wednesdays, and a weekly religious supplement, Alresalah, on Fridays.
Language (s): Arabic
Ad Rate: Full Page Mono 50880.00
Ad Rate: Full Page Colour 82680.00
Currency: Saudi Arabia Riyals
DAILY NEWSPAPER

Makkah Al Mukarramah 156700
Owner: Makkah for Printing and Media Est.
Editorial: PO Box 5803, Makkah Press Building, Makkah 21995 **Tel:** 966 12 520 1733
Email: domestic@makkahnp.com **Web site:** http://www.makkahnewspaper.com
Freq: Daily; **Circ:** 178000
General Manager: Luai Mtabaqani
Profile: Makkah Al Mukarramah is a daily newspaper covering national and international news, culture, business, features and sport. The newspaper launched in January 2013.
Language (s): Arabic
Ad Rate: Full Page Mono 54080.00
Ad Rate: Full Page Colour 95680.00
Currency: Saudi Arabia Riyals
DAILY NEWSPAPER

Malayalam News 350456
Owner: Saudi Research & Publishing Co.
Editorial: PO Box 13443, 3rd Floor, Omniya Center, Jeddah 21493 **Tel:** 966 12 283 6200
Email: malnews@srpc.com **Web site:** http://www.srpc.com
Freq: Daily; **Circ:** 58303 Publisher's Statement
Editor: Sajith Abdulmajeed; **Editor:** Rafeeq Abdurahman; **Editor in Chief:** Tarek Mishkhas; **Editor:** Mohamed Shawkat; **Editor:** Kunjammed Vanimel
Profile: Malayalam News is a daily newspaper covering national and international news, current affairs, politics, business and sport. It was first published in 1999 and is aimed at Malayalam speakers in the Gulf.
Language (s): Malayalam
Ad Rate: Full Page Mono 15000.00
Ad Rate: Full Page Colour 23400.00
Currency: Saudi Arabia Riyals
DAILY NEWSPAPER

Al Nadi 330100
Owner: Okaz Organization for Press & Publication
Editorial: PO Box 55297, Jeddah 21534
Tel: 966 12 676 0000
Email: mahzzi@hotmail.com **Web site:** http://www.al-nadi.com.sa
Freq: Daily; **Circ:** 60000 Publisher's Statement
Editor: Maher Abdulwahab; **Editor:** Saleh Al Eryani; **Editor in Chief:** Mohammad Al Ghamdi; **International Advertising Director:** Tarek El Sharif; **Editor:** Abdullah Gayed; **General Manager:** Walid Kattan; **Editor:** Ibrahim Mousa; **Picture Editor:** Ahmed Rached; **Editor:** Helal Salman
Profile: Al Nadi is a daily, broadsheet-sized Arabic newspaper covering local and international sport. It launched in 1996 and is aimed at sports enthusiasts in Saudi Arabia.
Language (s): Arabic
Ad Rate: Full Page Mono 33280.00
Ad Rate: Full Page Colour 41600.00
Currency: Saudi Arabia Riyals
DAILY NEWSPAPER

Okaz 156782
Owner: Okaz Organization for Press & Publication
Editorial: PO Box 1508, Jeddah 21441
Tel: 966 12 676 0000
Email: okazjed@okaz.com.sa **Web site:** http://www.okaz.com.sa
Freq: Daily; **Circ:** 170000 Publisher's Statement
PR & Advertising Specialist: Ahmed Abdul Wasey; **Head of Foreign News:** Fahim Al Hamed; **Head of News:** Samir Al Himaid; **Editor in Chief:** Jameel Al Theyabi; **International Advertising Director:** Tarek El Sharif; **General Manager:** Walid Kattan
Profile: Okaz is a daily Arabic newspaper covering news, politics, business and sport. It was first published in 1958.
Language (s): Arabic
Ad Rate: Full Page Mono 67840.00
Ad Rate: Full Page Colour 114480.00
Currency: Saudi Arabia Riyals
DAILY NEWSPAPER

Al Riyadh 156783
Owner: Al Yamamah Press Est.
Editorial: PO Box 851, King Fahad Street, Sahafa Area, Riyadh 11421 **Tel:** 966 11 299 6000
Email: rb-localdesk@alriyadh.com **Web site:** http://www.alriyadh.com
Freq: Daily; **Circ:** 180000 Publisher's Statement
PR Manager: Majed Al Breki
Profile: Al Riyadh is a daily Arabic newspaper covering local and international news, politics, society, business and sport. It was first published in 1965.
Language (s): Arabic
Ad Rate: Full Page Mono 41600.00
Ad Rate: Full Page Colour 76960.00
Currency: Saudi Arabia Riyals
DAILY NEWSPAPER

Saudi Gazette 156702
Owner: Okaz Organization for Press & Publication
Editorial: PO Box 5576, Dallah Street, Jeddah 21432
Tel: 966 12 676 0000
Email: news@saudigazette.com.sa **Web site:** http://www.saudigazette.com.sa
Freq: Daily; **Circ:** 60000 Publisher's Statement
PR & Advertising Specialist: Ahmed Abdul Wasey; **International Advertising Director:** Tarek El Sharif; **Editor in Chief:** Somayya Jabarti; **News Editor:** Sayed Rizvi
Profile: Saudi Gazette is a broadsheet-sized, daily English newspaper covering local and international news, politics, opinion, business and sport. It was first published in 1976.
Language (s): English
Ad Rate: Full Page Mono 34320.00
Ad Rate: Full Page Colour 46800.00
Currency: Saudi Arabia Riyals
DAILY NEWSPAPER

Urdu News 159064
Owner: Saudi Research & Publishing Co.
Editorial: PO Box 13402, 3rd Floor, Omniya Center, Jeddah 21493 **Tel:** 966 12 283 6200
Email: editorial3@urdunews.com **Web site:** http://www.urdunews.com
Freq: Daily; **Circ:** 67321 Publisher's Statement
News Editor: Syed Absar Ali; **Foreign News Editor:** Shahzad Azam; **Editor:** Khalid Khursheed; **Picture Editor:** Ghazi Mehdi; **Editor in Chief:** Tarek Mishkhas
Profile: Urdu News is a daily newspaper covering news, politics and business. It launched in 1994 and is aimed at Urdu speakers in the Gulf.
Language (s): Urdu
Ad Rate: Full Page Mono 23100.00
Ad Rate: Full Page Colour 36000.00
Currency: Saudi Arabia Riyals
DAILY NEWSPAPER

Al Watan 328303
Owner: Assir Est. for Press & Publishing
Editorial: PO Box 15155, Airport Road, Abha
Tel: 966 17 227 3333
Email: editorial@alwatan.com.sa **Web site:** http://www.alwatan.com.sa
Freq: Daily; **Circ:** 235000 Publisher's Statement
News Editor: Riyadh Al Missallim
Profile: Al Watan is a daily Arabic newspaper covering national and international news, current affairs, politics, economy, culture, society and sports. It was first published in 2000.
Language (s): Arabic
Ad Rate: Full Page Mono 58240.00
Ad Rate: Full Page Colour 89440.00
Currency: Saudi Arabia Riyals
DAILY NEWSPAPER

News Service/Syndicate

Bloomberg - Riyadh Bureau 823614
Owner: Bloomberg L.P.
Editorial: c/o Regus Kingdom Center, PO Box 230888, Riyadh 11321 **Tel:** 966 11 211 8033
Email: gcarey8@bloomberg.net **Web site:** http://www.bloomberg.com
Profile: Riyadh bureau of global financial news wire service.
Language (s): English
NEWS SERVICE/SYNDICATE

Dow Jones Newswires - Saudi bureau 768568
Owner: Dow Jones
Editorial: PO Box 8953, 2nd Floor, Bahrain Tower, Riyadh 12214-2393 **Tel:** 966 50 691 6123
Email: ahmed.alomran@wsj.com **Web site:** http://www.dowjones.com
Profile: Saudi bureau of US-based financial newswire service.
Language (s): English
NEWS SERVICE/SYNDICATE

International Islamic News Agency 353377
Owner: International Islamic News Agency
Editorial: PO Box 5054, IINA Building, Jeddah 21422
Tel: 966 12 665 8561

Email: iina@islamicnews.org **Web site:** http://www.iinanews.com
Editor: Saad Al Herbash; **News Director - French Section:** Amani Harouna
Profile: International Islamic News Agency (IINA) covers news about the Muslim world, minorities and communities in various fields, including religion, Islamic education, culture, Islamic organizations, charity and dawa. IINA also welcomes reports, press releases and any other material on the above mentioned subjects in Arabic, English and French.
Language (s): Arabic
NEWS SERVICE/SYNDICATE

Reuters - Riyadh Bureau 370532
Owner: Thomson Reuters
Editorial: PO Box 62422, 2nd floor, 30th Commerial Center, Riyadh 11585 **Tel:** 966 11 463 2603
Email: marwa.rashad@thomsonreuters.com **Web site:** http://www.reuters.com
Bureau Chief: Angus McDowall; **Producer:** Nael Shyoukhi
Profile: Saudi bureau of international news agency supplying news - text, graphics, video and pictures - to subscribers around the world.
Language (s): Arabic
NEWS SERVICE/SYNDICATE

Saudi Press Agency 353376
Owner: Saudi Press Agency
Editorial: PO Box 7186, King Fahd Road, Riyadh 11171 **Tel:** 966 11 419 3333
Email: wass2@spa.gov.sa **Web site:** http://www.spa.gov.sa
Head of News: Ahmad Al Awad; **General Manager:** Abdullah Al Hussein; **News Editor:** Mahdi Al Rasheedi
Profile: Saudi Press Agency (SPA) is the official news agency of Saudi Arabia and serves as a central body to collect and distribute local and international news in the Kingdom and abroad.
Language (s): Arabic
NEWS SERVICE/SYNDICATE

Senegal

Time Difference: GMT
National Telephone Code: 221
Continent: Africa
Capital: Dakar

Newspapers

Nouvel Horizon 529202
Owner: Panafrican Systems Production
Editorial: Sicap Liberte 2, Villa N 1589, BP 10037 liberté, Dakar **Tel:** 221 33 864 64 15
Email: nouvelhorizon@nouvelhorizon.sn **Web site:** http://nouvelhorizon.sn
Freq: Daily; **Circ:** 30000 Publisher's Statement
Editor in Chief: Mandiaye Thiombane
Profile: National weekly newspaper focusing on general news and current affairs including politics, economics, culture and sports.
Language (s): French
Ad Rate: Full Page Colour 500000.00
Currency: Communauté Financière Africaine Francs BCEAO
DAILY NEWSPAPER

Le Quotidien 158178
Owner: Groupe Avenir Communication SA
Editorial: 269, Cite Djily Mbaye, Pres du Cimetiere, Dakar Fann **Tel:** 221 33 869 84 84
Email: lequotidien@lequotidien.sn **Web site:** http://www.lequotidien.sn
Freq: Daily; **Circ:** 8000 Publisher's Statement
Advertising Manager: Doudou Dieng
Profile: Newspaper covering national and international news and current affairs including politics, economics, society, culture and sport.
Language (s): French
Ad Rate: Full Page Mono 450000.00
Currency: Communauté Financière Africaine Francs BCEAO
DAILY NEWSPAPER

Le Soleil 156770
Owner: SSPP Le Soleil SA
Editorial: Route du Service Geographique, Hann, Dakar **Tel:** 221 33 859 59 59
Email: lesoleil@lesoleil.sn **Web site:** http://www.lesoleil.sn
Freq: Daily; **Circ:** 25000 Publisher's Statement
Profile: Newspaper focusing on national and international news and current affairs including business, politics, economy, society, culture and sport.
Language (s): French
DAILY NEWSPAPER

Sud Quotidien 156771
Owner: Groupe Sudcommunication
Editorial: Amitie II x Burguiba, BP 4130, Dakar
Tel: 221 33 824 33 06
Email: sudquotidien@yahoo.fr **Web site:** http://www.sudonline.sn
Freq: Daily; **Circ:** 7000 Publisher's Statement
General Manager: Abdoulaye Ndiaga Sylla
Profile: Newspaper covering national and international news and current affairs including politics, economics, business, society, culture and sport.
Language (s): French
DAILY NEWSPAPER

Walfadjri 158179
Owner: Groupe Wal Fadjri
Editorial: 12 Route du front de terre, B.P 576, Dakar
Tel: 221 33 869 10 71
Email: quotidien@walf-groupe.com **Web site:** http://www.walf-groupe.com
Freq: Daily; **Circ:** 7000 Publisher's Statement
Advertising Manager: Sammy Chopin; **General Manager:** Sidy Lamin Niasse
Profile: Newspaper covering national and international news and current affairs including business, politics, economics, sport, health, celebrity and society.
Language (s): French
DAILY NEWSPAPER

News Service/Syndicate

Agence de Presse Africaine - APA 529307
Owner: Agence de Presse Africaine
Editorial: Residence AYA 3eme Etage A24, Rue MZ 81 * 96 Mermoz, Pyrotechnie, Dakar
Tel: 221 33 869 87 87
Email: afeassist@apanews.net **Web site:** http://www.apanews.net
Director: Fernand Tona
Profile: International press agency focusing on news and current affairs in Africa including politics, economics, business, finance, environment, sport and culture.
Language (s): English
NEWS SERVICE/SYNDICATE

PanaPress 353731
Owner: PanaPress
Editorial: Avenue Bourguiba x Sodida, BP 4056, Dakar **Tel:** 221 33 869 12 34
Email: feedback@panapress.com **Web site:** http://www.panapress.com
Profile: Pan African news agency focusing on regional, national and international news and current affairs including agriculture, culture, economy, environment, health, politics, science, society and sports.
Language (s): Arabic
NEWS SERVICE/SYNDICATE

Serbia

Time Difference: GMT +1
National Telephone Code: 381
Continent: Europe
Capital: Belgrade

Newspapers

24 sata 520632
Owner: Ringier Axel Springer d.o.o.
Editorial: zorza Klemansoa 19, Beograd
Tel: 381 11 333 4 555
Email: redakcija@24sata.rs **Web site:** http://www.24sata.rs
Freq: Daily; **Circ:** 120000 Not Audited
Director: Jelena Drakuli?-Petrovi?
Profile: Full colour daily newspaper distributed free of charge in Beograd and in Serbian second biggest city Novi Sad.
Language (s): Serbo-Croat
Ad Rate: Full Page Mono 125000.00
Ad Rate: Full Page Colour 186000.00
Currency: Serbia Dinars
DAILY NEWSPAPER

Alo! 911117
Owner: Ringier Axel Springer d.o.o.
Editorial: zorza Klemansoa 19, Beograd
Email: redakcija_alo@ringieraxelspringer.rs **Web site:** http://www.alo.rs
Freq: Daily
Editor-in-Chief: Dejan Vukeli?
Profile: Serbian daily tabloid covering national news and gossip.
Language (s): Serbian
DAILY NEWSPAPER

Blic Serbia 844063
Owner: Ringier Axel Springer d.o.o.
Editorial: zorza Klemansoa 19, Beograd 11 000
Tel: 381 11 333-4-555
Email: redakcija@blic.rs **Web site:** http://www.blic.rs
Freq: Daily
Publishing Director: Tijana Bajovi?
Profile: Tabloid Newspaper in Serbia covering national news and gossip.
Language (s): Serbian
DAILY NEWSPAPER

Danas 159034
Owner: DAN GRAF d o o
Editorial: Alekse Nenadovia 19-23, Beograd 11000
Tel: 381 11 344-11 86
Email: gl.urednik@danas.rs **Web site:** http://www.danas.rs
Freq: Daily; **Circ:** 30000 Not Audited
Director: Dušan Mitrovi?; **Editor in Chief:** Zoran Panovi?; **Advertising Manager:** Snežana Stojakov
Profile: Newspaper featuring domestic and international news, politics, economics, finance, culture and entertainment.
Language (s): Serbo-Croat
DAILY NEWSPAPER

Dnevnik 161222
Owner: Dnevnik d o o
Editorial: Bulevar oslobodenja 81, Novi Sad 21000
Tel: 381 21 66 14 374
Email: redakcija@dnevnik.rs **Web site:** http://www.dnevnik.rs
Freq: Daily; **Circ:** 20000 Not Audited
Editor-in-Chief: Miroljub Mijuskovic; **Director:** Dušan Vlaovic
Profile: Newspaper focusing on politics, economics, culture, sport and general news.
Language (s): Serbo-Croat
DAILY NEWSPAPER

Informer Serbia 911112
Editorial: Terazije 5/7, Beograd 11000
Tel: 381 11 6555261
Email: redakcija@informer.rs **Web site:** http://www.informer.rs
Freq: Daily; **Circ:** 115000
Editor-in-Chief: Dragan Vucicevic
Profile: Tabloid newspaper published in Belgrade and covering politics, national news, gossip and culture, sport.
Language (s): Serbian
DAILY NEWSPAPER

Kurir 585596
Owner: Adria Media Serbia d.o.o.
Editorial: Vlajkoviceva 8, Beograd 11000
Tel: 381 11 6357 100
Email: redakcija@kurir-info.rs **Web site:** http://www.kurir-info.rs
Freq: Daily; **Circ:** 165000
Profile: A high-circulation daily tabloid published in Belgrade.
Language (s): Serbo-Croat
DAILY NEWSPAPER

Politika Serbia 524688
Owner: Politika a.d.
Editorial: Makedonska 29, Beograd 11000
Tel: 381 11 330-1682
Email: redakcija@politika.rs **Web site:** http://www.politika.rs
Freq: Daily; **Circ:** 85000 Not Audited
Editor in Chief: Ljiljana Smajlovi?
Profile: Oldest daily on the Balkans covering politics, economics, social and cultural issues.
Language (s): Serbo-Croat
DAILY NEWSPAPER

Vecernje Novosti 161226
Owner: Novosti d o o
Editorial: Trg Nikole Pasica 7, Beograd 11000
Tel: 381 11 3028000
Email: redakcija@novosti.rs **Web site:** http://www.novosti.rs
Freq: Daily; **Circ:** 200000 Not Audited
Editor-in-Chief: Ratko Dmitrovic
Profile: Newspaper covering general news, politics, economics, culture and sport.
Language (s): Serbo-Croat
Ad Rate: Full Page Colour 3665.00
Currency: Euro
DAILY NEWSPAPER

News Service/Syndicate

Kosovapress News Agency 353229
Editorial: Rruga, Hamëz Jashari nr. 28, Kati 7, Prishtinë 10000 **Tel:** 381 38 249721
Email: editori@kosovapress.com **Web site:** http://www.kosovapress.com
Director General: Skënder Krasniqi; **Editor:** Nezir Rama
Profile: News Agency Kosova Press was established on January 4, 1999. Provides news in Albanian and English languages.
Language (s): Albanian
NEWS SERVICE/SYNDICATE

Tanjug 818288
Editorial: Ulica Marsala Birjuzova 38, Beograd 11000
Tel: 381 11 3288 284
Email: office@tanjug.rs **Web site:** http://www.tanjug.rs
Editor-in-Chief: Jadranka Žujovi?
Profile: Tanjug is a news agency which broadcasts around 400 pieces of information and over 100 photographs, video and audio recordings every day. Tanjug is a member of AMAN (the Alliance of Mediterranean News Agencies), ABNA (the Association of the Balkan News Agencies), and BSANNA (the Black Sea Association of National News Agencies).
Language (s): English
NEWS SERVICE/SYNDICATE

Seychelles

Time Difference: GMT +4
National Telephone Code: 248
Continent: Africa
Capital: Victoria

Newspapers

Nation Weekend 158183
Owner: Nation Publishing Services
Editorial: Laurier Road, PO Box 800, Victoria
Tel: 248 43 85775
Email: nation@seychelles.net **Web site:** http://www.nation.sc
Freq: Weekly; **Circ:** 4000 Publisher's Statement
Profile: Weekend version of the newspaper covering regional, national and international news and current affairs including politics, economics, tourism, business, environment, culture and sport.
Language (s): Creole
DAILY NEWSPAPER

Seychelles Nation 156772
Owner: National Information Services Agency
Editorial: Laurier Road, PO Box 800, Victoria
Tel: 248 43 85775
Email: nation@seychelles.net **Web site:** http://www.nation.sc
Freq: Daily; **Circ:** 2500 Publisher's Statement
Profile: Newspaper covering regional, national and international news and current affairs including politics, economics, tourism, business, environment, culture and sport.
Language (s): Creole
Ad Rate: Full Page Mono 2365.00
Ad Rate: Full Page Colour 3850.00
Currency: Seychelles Rupees
DAILY NEWSPAPER

Sierra Leone

Time Difference: GMT
National Telephone Code: 232
Continent: Africa
Capital: Freetown

Newspapers

Awoko 655398
Owner: Awoko Newspaper
Tel: 232 76 881 075
Email: awoko71@hotmail.com **Web site:** http://www.awoko.org
Editor: Kelvin Lewis
Profile: Newspaper covering regional and national news and current affairs including politics, business and economy.
DAILY NEWSPAPER

Concord Times 161258
Owner: Concord Times Communications Ltd.
Editorial: 44 Edward Street, Freetown
Tel: 232 22 22 91 99
Email: concordtimes100@yahoo.com **Web site:** http://slconcordtimes.com
Freq: Daily; **Circ:** 1750 Publisher's Statement
Editor: Tanu Jalloh
Profile: Newspaper focusing on national and regional news, business, politics, culture and sports.
Language (s): English
Ad Rate: Full Page Mono 300000.00
Ad Rate: Full Page Colour 1000000.00
Currency: Sierra Leone Leones
DAILY NEWSPAPER

Standard Times Press 161259
Owner: Standard Times
Editorial: 2 A Ascension Town Road, Kingtom Bridge, Freetown **Tel:** 232 22 22 96 34
Email: standardtimes@justice.com **Web site:** http://standardtimespress.org
Freq: Daily; **Circ:** 2000 Publisher's Statement
Editor: Santigie Kamara; **Editor:** Abubakarr Kargbo
Profile: Newspaper covering regional and national news and current affairs including business, politics, entertainment and gossip.
Language (s): English
Ad Rate: Full Page Mono 350000.00
Currency: Sierra Leone Leones
DAILY NEWSPAPER

Singapore

Singapore

Time Difference: GMT +8
National Telephone Code: 65
Continent: Asia
Capital: Singapore City

Newspapers

Asahi Shimbun- Singapore Bureau 459107
Editorial: Asahi Shimbun- Singapore Bureau, 72 Bendemeer Road #2-20 Luzerne, Singapore 339941
Tel: 65 62203315
Email: asahisin@singnet.com.sg **Web site:** http://www.asahi.com
Bureau Chief: Tsuru Etsushi
Profile: Covers news, entertainment, lifestyle and sports.
Language (s): Japanese
DAILY NEWSPAPER

Berita Harian 217908
Owner: Singapore Press Holdings Ltd (SPH)
Editorial: Level 3, Annexe Block, 1000, Toa Payoh North, Singapore 318994 **Tel:** 65 63196319
Email: aadeska@sph.com.sg **Web site:** http://berita.mediacorp.sg
Freq: Daily; **Circ:** 60007 Not Audited
Editor: Mohd. Saat Abdul Rahman
Profile: Covers international and local news.
Language (s): Bahasa Malaysia
DAILY NEWSPAPER

Berita Minggu 217966
Editorial: Singapore Press Holdings Ltd (SPH), Level 3, Annexe Block, 1000, Toa Payoh North, Singapore 318994 **Tel:** 65 63195665
Web site: http://cyberita.asia1.com.sg
Freq: Weekly; **Circ:** 72105 Not Audited
Profile: Covers international and local news.
Language (s): Bahasa Malaysia
DAILY NEWSPAPER

The Business Times 217906
Editorial: SPH 1000 Toa Payoh North, Podium Level 3, Singapore 318994 **Tel:** 65 63195318
Email: btnews@sph.com.sg **Web site:** http://www.businesstimes.com.sg
Freq: Daily; **Circ:** 38000 Not Audited
Editor: Lilian Ang; **Editor:** Amit Choudhury; **Editor:** Jaime Ee; **Manager:** Barbara Lee; **Copy Chief:** Dexter Lee; **Editor:** Edmund Loh; **Editor:** Suresh Menon; **Editor in Chief:** Alvin Tay
Profile: Covers business and economic industry news.
Language (s): English
Ad Rate: Full Page Mono 6264.00
Ad Rate: Full Page Colour 8864.00
Currency: Singapore Dollars
DAILY NEWSPAPER

Die Welt - Singapore Bureau 535948
Editorial: Die Welt - Singapore Bureau, 33E Barker Road, Lotus at Barker, Singapore 309911
Tel: 65 62530358
Profile: Covers international and local news.
Language (s): Japanese
DAILY NEWSPAPER

Economic Daily (China) - Singapore Bureau 459199
Editorial: Economic Daily (China) - Singapore Bureau, 121 Meyer Road, #15-09 The Makena, Singapore 437932 **Tel:** 65 63459056
Web site: http://www.economicdaily.com.cn
Freq: Daily
Profile: Covers major news and economic news reports.
Language (s): Chinese
DAILY NEWSPAPER

The Edge Singapore 460228
Owner: The Edge Publishing Pte Ltd
Editorial: 150 Cecil Street, 13th Fl, Singapore 69543
Tel: 65 62328622
Email: theedgespore@bizedge.com **Web site:** http://www.theedgemarkets.com/sg
Freq: Weekly; **Circ:** 26769 Not Audited
Editor: Cecilia Chow; **Editor:** Audrey Simon
Profile: Launched in 2014, aims to make better business and investment decision by empowering them with the latest news, data and financial analytics.
Language (s): English
DAILY NEWSPAPER

The Hindu 459198
Editorial: 245 Balestier Road, #06-01 Scenic Heights, Singapore 329929 **Tel:** 65 62513635
Web site: http://www.hinduonnet.com
Freq: Daily
Profile: Covers major news.
Language (s): English
DAILY NEWSPAPER

Kwong Wah Yit Poh - Singapore Bureau 535950
Editorial: Kwong Wah Yit Poh - Singapore Bureau, Blk 92, Bedok North Ave 4, #09-1481, Singapore 460092 **Tel:** 65 64443012
Web site: http://www.kwongwah.com.my
Profile: Covers major news daily.
Language (s): Japanese
DAILY NEWSPAPER

Lianhe Zaobao 217911
Editorial: Singapore Press Holdings Ltd (SPH), SPH 1000, Toa Payoh North, Singapore 318994
Tel: 65 6319 6319
Email: zblocal@sph.com.sg **Web site:** http://www.zaobao.com
Freq: Daily; **Circ:** 184477 Not Audited
Editor: Sin Hwee Goh; **Editor:** Maureen Shueh Fern Ho; **News Editor:** Han May; **Editor:** Tee Ming San; **Editor:** Ming San Tee; **Editor:** Pow Ang Yong
Profile: Lianhe Zaobao highlights Local & International News, Lifestyle, Culture, Business, and more.
Language (s): Chinese
DAILY NEWSPAPER

My Paper - Wo Bao 460383
Editorial: Singapore Press Holdings Ltd (SPH), 1000 Toa Payoh North, News Centre, Podium, Level 2, Singapore 318994 **Tel:** 65 63196319
Email: mypaper@sph.com.sg **Web site:** http://www.mypaper.sg
Freq: 2 Times/Week; **Circ:** 300007 Not Audited
Editor: Jill Alphonso; **Editor:** Han Keong Chia; **News Editor:** Hui Chieh Lee; **Editor:** Glenn Low; **Editor:** April Pung; **Editor:** Kai Chai Yeow
Profile: Covers major news, international and local news.
Language (s): Chinese
DAILY NEWSPAPER

NNA - Singapore Bureau 459515
Editorial: NNA - Singapore Bureau, Shenton House #19-01, Singapore 68805 **Tel:** 65 67383333
Web site: http://nna.asia.ne.jp
Freq: Daily
Editor in Chief: Fujino Hidenori
Profile: Covers local and international news.
Language (s): English
DAILY NEWSPAPER

Property Report Singapore-Malaysia-Indonesia 562407
Owner: Ensign Media
Editorial: Ensign Media Co. Ltd., 120 Telok Ayer Street, Singapore 685859
Email: editorial@property-report.com **Web site:** http://www.ensign-media.com
Freq: Monthly
Profile: Focuses on real estate sectors in Singapore, Malaysia and Indonesia. Includes keys interview with an important industry figure and regular sections on finance, legal issues, interiors and architecture.
Language (s): Thai
DAILY NEWSPAPER

Sankei Shimbun - Singapore Bureau 459200
Editorial: Sankei Shimbun - Singapore Bureau, 6 Eu Tong Sen Street #10-02 The central, Singapore 59817 **Tel:** 65 62216894
Web site: http://sankei.jp.msn.com
Freq: Daily
Bureau Chief: Hiroyuki Miyano
Profile: Covers local, national and international news.
Language (s): Japanese
DAILY NEWSPAPER

Shin Min Daily News 217913
Editorial: Singapore Press Holdings Ltd (SPH), News Centre, SPH 1000, Toa Payoh North, Singapore 318994 **Tel:** 65 63192269
Email: shinmin@sph.com.sg
Freq: Daily; **Circ:** 121007 Not Audited
Editor: Kean Huat Chua; **Editor:** Tan Lye Chwee; **Editor:** Toh Lam Huat; **Manager:** Lawrence Loh; **Editor:** Ning Yin Chyun
Profile: Covers international and national news.
Language (s): Chinese
DAILY NEWSPAPER

Singapore American Newspaper 460426
Editorial: American Association of Singapore, 21 Scotts Rd., Singapore 229573 **Tel:** 65 67344811
Email: communications@aasingapore.com **Web site:** http://www.aasingapore.com
Freq: Monthly; **Circ:** 8007 Not Audited
Editor: Brett Gold; **Manager:** Valarie Tietjen
Profile: Covers American community in Singapore.
Language (s): English
DAILY NEWSPAPER

The Straits Times 217910
Owner: Singapore Press Holdings (SPH)
Editorial: SPH 1000, Toa Payoh North, Level 2, Podium Block, Singapore 318994 **Tel:** 65 6319 5397
Web site: http://www.straitstimes.com/global
Freq: Daily; **Circ:** 352100 Not Audited
Editor: Serene Goh; **Editor:** Eugene Leow; **Editor:** Marc Lim; **Editor:** Dominic Nathan; **Editor:** Carl Skadian; **Editor:** Sumiko Tan; **Editor:** Koon Hong Yap; **Editor:** Ah Seng Yeong
Profile: Founded July 15, 1845, serves as the flagship publication of the Singapore Press Holdings group. Strives to be an authoritative provider of news and views, with special focus on Singapore and the Asian region.
Language (s): English
Ad Rate: Full Page Colour 27828.00
Currency: Singapore Dollars
DAILY NEWSPAPER

The Straits Times - Taipei Bureau 459114
Owner: Singapore Press Holdings (SPH)
Editorial: 2nd Fl, Number 130 Bo Ai Rd, Taipei 100
Tel: 886 223703727
Freq: Daily
Language (s): English
DAILY NEWSPAPER

The Sunday Times 217909
Editorial: Singapore Press Holdings (SPH), SPH 1000, Toa Payoh North, Singapore 318994
Tel: 65 63196319
Web site: http://www.sph.com.sg
Freq: Weekly; **Circ:** 399007 Not Audited
Editor: Sumiko Tan
Profile: Covers major international and local news.
Language (s): English
DAILY NEWSPAPER

Tamil Murasu 406674
Editorial: Singapore Press Holdings Ltd (SPH), 82 Genting Lane, Singapore 349567 **Tel:** 65 6319 6319
Web site: http://tamilmurasu.com.sg
Freq: Daily; **Circ:** 10607 Not Audited
Editor: K. Kanagalatha; **Editor:** G. Krishnan; **News Editor:** V. Palanisamy; **Editor:** Chitra Rajaram; **Manager:** Koh Say Kionj
Profile: Tamil Murasu highlights Local and International News, as well as Sports, Technology, and more.
Language (s): Tamil
DAILY NEWSPAPER

Thanh Nien- Singapore Bureau 535947
Editorial: Thanh Nien- Singapore Bureau, 1 Pearl Bank, #26-09, Singapore 169016 **Tel:** 65 62240810
Web site: http://www.thanhniennews.com
Bureau Chief: Thi Thuc Nguyen
Language (s): Japanese
DAILY NEWSPAPER

Thumbs Up 459344
Editorial: Singapore Press Holdings Ltd (SPH), 1000, Toa Payoh Nort, Singapore 318994 **Tel:** 65 63191892
Email: ThumbsUp@sph.com.sg **Web site:** http://youth.zaobao.com/tu.html
Freq: Weekly; **Circ:** 38407 Not Audited
Editor: Soon Lan Lim
Profile: Covers news that interests to young people/students.
Language (s): Chinese
DAILY NEWSPAPER

Today 459662
Editorial: MediaCorp Press Pte Ltd, Caldecott Broadcast Centre, Annex Building, Level 1, Andrew Road, Singapore 299939 **Tel:** 65 62364888
Email: news@newstoday.com.sg **Web site:** http://www.todayonline.com
Freq: Daily; **Circ:** 300007 Not Audited
Editor: Walter Fernandez; **Editor:** Agatha Koh Brazil; **Editor:** Yvonne Lim; **Manager:** Joni Ng; **Editor at Large:** Conrad Raj; **Manager:** Doreen Sabai; **Editor:** Ariel Tam; **Editor:** Leonard Thomas; **Editor:** Phin Wong
Profile: Covers International, regional, national and local news, lifestyle, features, sports for most of the business people.
Language (s): English
DAILY NEWSPAPER

News Service/Syndicate

Bernama - Singapore Bureau 888975
Editorial: 6, Eu Tong Sen Street, The Central #10-04, Singapore 59817 **Tel:** 65 62356521
Email: bernama_spore@singnet.com.sg
Bureau Chief: Tengku Noor Shamsiah Abdullah
Language (s): English
NEWS SERVICE/SYNDICATE

Platts 520292
Editorial: The McGraw-Hill Companies, 30 Cecil Street, #13-00 Prudential Tower, Singapore 49712
Tel: 65 65322800
Web site: http://www.platts.com
Editor: Calvin Lee; **Editor:** Deepa Vijiyasingam
Profile: Covers energy topics, industry news and prices for oil and natural gas.
Language (s): English
NEWS SERVICE/SYNDICATE

Slovakia

Time Difference: GMT +1
National Telephone Code: 421
Continent: Europe
Capital: Bratislava

Newspapers

Hospodárske Noviny 157105
Owner: MAFRA Slovakia
Editorial: Nobelova 34, Bratislava 836 05
Tel: 421 2 48238111
Email: redaktori@mafraslovakia.sk **Web site:** http://hnonline.sk
Freq: Daily; **Circ:** 32000 Publisher's Statement
Editor: Marcela Šimková
Profile: Slovakia's daily broadsheet-sized newspaper Hospodárske Noviny focusing on economics, politics, finances, national and international news, culture, sport, and entertainment. Aimed at business executives, government members and the general public.Local Translation: Slovenské Hospodárske Noviny zam??ené na ekonomiku, politiku, národní a mezinárodní zprávy, finance, politiku, kulturu a sport a zábavu.
Language (s): English
Ad Rate: Full Page Mono 99750.00
Currency: Slovakia Koruny
DAILY NEWSPAPER

Pravda 159027
Owner: Perex
Editorial: Trnavska cesta 39/A, Bratislava 831 04
Tel: 421 2 49596959
Email: pravda@pravda.sk **Web site:** http://www.pravda.sk
Freq: Daily; **Circ:** 90000 Publisher's Statement
Editor: Tomáš Švec
Profile: Newspaper focusing on national and international news, finance, the economy, culture, entertainment and sport.
Language (s): English
Ad Rate: Full Page Mono 4149.00
Ad Rate: Full Page Colour 5145.00
Currency: Euro
DAILY NEWSPAPER

The Slovak Spectator 187309
Owner: The Rock spol. s.r.o.
Editorial: Lazaretska 12, Bratislava 811 08
Tel: 421 2 59233300
Email: spectator@spectator.sk **Web site:** http://spectator.sme.sk
Freq: Bi-Weekly; **Circ:** 5000 Publisher's Statement
Publisher: Jan Pallo; **Editor-in-Chief:** Michaela Terenzani
Profile: Newspaper focusing on general news, business issues, culture, opinion and features.
Language (s): English
Ad Rate: Full Page Mono 2250.00
Ad Rate: Full Page Colour 2800.00
Currency: Euro
DAILY NEWSPAPER

SME 161202
Owner: Petit Press a s
Editorial: Lazaretska 12, P.O.Box 77, Bratislava 811 08 **Tel:** 421 2 59233500
Email: redakcia@sme.sk **Web site:** http://www.sme.sk
Freq: Daily; **Circ:** 92369 Publisher's Statement
Editor-in-Chief: Beata Balogova; **Editor:** Milan Gigel; **Editor:** Kristína Kúdelová; **Editor:** Katarína Lešková
Profile: Slovakia's daily newspaper SME focusing on national and international news, business, politics, culture and sport. Local Translation:Slovenské noviny SME píšou o národních a mezinárodních zprávách, podnikání, politice, kultu?e a sportu.
Language (s): English
Ad Rate: Full Page Mono 3800.00
Ad Rate: Full Page Colour 5400.00
Currency: Euro
DAILY NEWSPAPER

Új Szó 411263
Owner: Petit Press a s
Editorial: Lazaretska 12, Bratislava 811 08
Tel: 421 2 59233421
Email: redakcia@ujszo.com **Web site:** http://ujszo.com
Freq: Daily; **Circ:** 35500 Publisher's Statement
Profile: National newspaper for Hungarian speaking residents in Slovakia. Features home affairs, regional news, international affairs, culture, economics, sports, commentaries and supplements.
Language (s): Hungarian
Ad Rate: Full Page Mono 2290.00
Ad Rate: Full Page Colour 2987.50
Currency: Euro
DAILY NEWSPAPER

News Service/Syndicate

Teraz.sk 654830
Owner: Tasr
Editorial: Dubravska cesta 14, Bratislava 84104
Tel: 421 2 59210130

Email: teraz@tasr.sk **Web site:** http://www.tasr.sk
Director: Marián Kolár; **Editor-in-Chief:** Richard Kvas?ovský
Profile: The News Agency of the Slovak Republic (TASR) is a public-service agency that provides national and international news. Launched in 2008.
NEWS SERVICE/SYNDICATE

Slovenia

Time Difference: GMT +1
National Telephone Code: 386
Continent: Europe
Capital: Ljubljana

Newspapers

Delo   156794
Owner: Delo d.d.
Editorial: Dunajska 5, Ljubljana 1509
Tel: 386 1 4737-400
Email: tuditi@delo.si **Web site:** http://www.delo.si
Freq: Daily; **Circ:** 93000 Publisher's Statement
Editor-in-Chief: Mateja Babi? Stermecki; **Editor:** Tanja Jakli?
Profile: Newspaper focusing on national and international news, economics, finance, culture, entertainment and sport.
Language (s): Slovene
Ad Rate: Full Page Colour 10500.00
Currency: Euro
DAILY NEWSPAPER

Dnevnik   159028
Owner: Dnevnik, ?asopisna družba d.d.
Editorial: Kopitarjeva 2 in 4, Ljubljana 1510
Tel: 386 1 3082-100
Email: info@dnevnik.si **Web site:** http://www.dnevnik.si
Freq: Daily; **Circ:** 38000 Publisher's Statement
Editor: Jana Petkovšek Štakul
Profile: Newspaper providing information on national and international politics, news, economics, finance, culture and entertainment.
Language (s): Slovene
DAILY NEWSPAPER

The Slovenia Times   364920
Owner: DOMUS, založba in trgovina d.o.o.
Editorial: Dunajska cesta 5, Ljubljana 1000
Email: editor@sloveniatimes.com **Web site:** http://www.sloveniatimes.com
Freq: Bi-Weekly; **Circ:** 10000 Publisher's Statement
Profile: The Slovenia Times is the newspaper in the English language in Slovenia since 2003. Offers analysis of the social and economic situation in this country, and covers tourism, culture, sports, recreation and other lifestyle topics.
Language (s): English
DAILY NEWSPAPER

Ve?er   311196
Owner: ?ZP Ve?er, d.d.
Editorial: Ulica slovenske osamosvojitve 2, Maribor 2504 **Tel:** 386 2 2353500
Email: desk@vecer.com **Web site:** http://www.vecer.com
Freq: Daily; **Circ:** 65000 Publisher's Statement
News Editor: Sre?ko Klapš; **Editor-in-Chief:** Katja Šeruga
Profile: Newspaper focusing on national and international news, economics, culture and sport.
Language (s): Slovene
DAILY NEWSPAPER

Solomon Islands

Time Difference: GMT +11
National Telephone Code: 677
Continent: Oceania
Capital: Honiara

Newspapers

Solomon Star   538559
Owner: Solomon Star Newspaper
Editorial: 1st Floor, Tongs Building, Pt. Cruz, Solomon Islands **Tel:** 677 22 062
Email: customerservices@solomonstarnews.com
Web site: http://www.solomonstarnews.com
Freq: Daily
Editor: Robert Iroga
Profile: Solomon Islands' leading daily newspaper covering general news and current affairs including business, politics, economy, sports and entertainment.
Language (s): English
DAILY NEWSPAPER

Community Newspaper

Island Sun   538735
Owner: Trade Wind Company
Editorial: PO Box 1170, Honiara, Solomon Islands
Tel: 677 28070
Email: islandsun@solomon.com.sb
Editor: Richard Toke
Language (s): English
COMMUNITY NEWSPAPER

South Africa

Time Difference: GMT +2
National Telephone Code: 27
Continent: Africa
Capital: Pretoria (Administrative), Cape Town (Legislative)

Newspapers

Beeld   161247
Owner: Media 24: Newspapers
Editorial: PO Box 333, Auckland Park 2006
Tel: 27 11 7139000
Email: nuus@beeld.com **Web site:** http://www.netwerk24.com
Freq: Daily; **Circ:** 70070 ABC-Audit Bureau of Circulations
Editor: Adriaan Basson; **News Editor:** Erika de Beer; **Editor:** Tim du Plessis; **News Editor:** Virginia Keppler; **Editor In Chief:** Peet Kruger; **Editor:** Andre Le Roux; **Editor:** Liesl Louw; **Editor:** Andriette Stofberg; **Editor:** Mariska van Rooyen
Profile: Major daily newspaper full mix of editorial. See separate listings for regional editions Beeld Johannesburg, Beeld Pretoria, Plus, and business section Sake 24. Afrikaans speaking adults, predominantly in and around the PWV area. See separate listing for Sake Beeld, Beeld Pretoria and Beeld Johannesburg.
Language (s): Afrikaans
DAILY NEWSPAPER

Die Burger, Cape Town   156706
Owner: Media 24: Newspapers
Editorial: PO Box 692, Cape Town 8000
Tel: 27 21 406 2815
Email: dbnred@dieburger.com **Web site:** http://www.netwerk24.com
Freq: Daily; **Circ:** 53483 ABC-Audit Bureau of Circulations
Editor: Hendrik Coetzee; **News Editor:** Michele O'Connor; **News Editor:** Michelle O'Connor
Profile: Major daily newspaper with full mix of editorial. The W. Cape editorial edition of Die Burger (combined). Afrikaans speaking adults in the Western Cape.
Language (s): Afrikaans
DAILY NEWSPAPER

Die Burger, Port Elizabeth 161242
Owner: Media 24: Newspapers
Editorial: PO Box 525, Port Elizabeth 6000
Tel: 27 41 5036111
Email: oos@dieburger.com **Web site:** http://www.netwerk24.com
Freq: Daily; **Circ:** 18628 ABC-Audit Bureau of Circulations
Editor: Riana de Lange; **Chief Photographer:** Deon Ferreira; **Editor:** Jo-Ann Floris; **News Editor:** Reint Grobler; **PA to Publisher:** Yvonne Jacobs; **Classifieds Manager:** Rene Olivier
Profile: Regional daily edition of Die Burger, adapting news of regional interest. Afrikaans speaking adults in the Eastern Cape.Alternative Title: BURGER E. Cape
Language (s): Afrikaans
DAILY NEWSPAPER

Business Day   156705
Owner: Times Media (Pty) Ltd
Editorial: PO Box 1745, Saxonwold 2132
Tel: 27 11 2803000
Web site: http://www.bdlive.co.za
Freq: Daily; **Circ:** 36087 ABC-Audit Bureau of Circulations
Editor-in-Chief/Publisher: Peter Bruce; **Editor-at-Large:** Hilary Joffe; **News Editor:** Johwa Wilson; **Editor:** Songezo Zibi
Profile: Business Day is South Africa's daily business newspaper. With daily reports on stock prices, commodities and current affairs as well as in-depth analysis of local and global trends and how they affect your business activity. Previous title: Rand Daily Mail
Language (s): English
DAILY NEWSPAPER

Cape Argus   156728
Tel: 27 214884911
Email: argusnews@inl.co.za **Web site:** http://www.capeargus.co.za
Freq: Daily

Editor: Gasant Abarder; **Editor in Chief:** Chris Whitfield
Language (s): English
DAILY NEWSPAPER

The Cape Argus   699109
Owner: Independent Newspapers: Cape
Editorial: PO Box 56, Cape Town 8000
Tel: 27 21 4884911
Email: argusnews@inl.co.za **Web site:** http://www.iol.co.za/capeargus
Freq: Daily; **Circ:** 43114
Picture Editor: Ian Landsberg
Profile: Major afternoon daily with full editorial mix. Includes 3 zoned editions per day. English speaking adults in the Western Cape.Previous title: The Argus
Language (s): English
Ad Rate: Full Page Mono 74649.60
Ad Rate: Full Page Colour 104509.60
Currency: South Africa Rand
DAILY NEWSPAPER

Cape Times   156734
Owner: Independent Newspapers: Cape
Editorial: PO Box 11, Cape Town 8000
Tel: 27 21 488 4911
Email: ctletters@inl.co.za **Web site:** http://www.iol.co.za/capetimes
Freq: Daily; **Circ:** 63854 ABC-Audit Bureau of Circulations
News Editor: A'Eysha Kassiem; **Promotions Co-ordinator:** Di MacMahon; **Editor:** Aneez Salie
Profile: Newspaper covering regional and national news and current affairs including business, politics, entertainment, sports, motoring, lifestyle, travel, science and technology.
Language (s): English
Ad Rate: Full Page Mono 75249.00
Ad Rate: Full Page Colour 105348.60
Currency: South Africa Rand
DAILY NEWSPAPER

Citizen   460890
Editorial: 9 Wright Street, Industria West, Johannesburg **Tel:** 27 11 2486000
Email: editor@citizen.co.za **Web site:** http://www.citizen.co.za
Freq: Daily; **Circ:** 70112 Not Audited
Editor: Steven Motale
Profile: The Citizen is a tabloid daily newspaper focused on news, sport, business, politics, entertainment and leisure, motoring, health, analysis, auctions and horse racing.
Language (s): English
DAILY NEWSPAPER

City Press   156693
Owner: RCP Media
Editorial: 69 Kingsway, PO Box 3413, Johannesburg 2000 **Tel:** 27 11 713 9001
Email: news@citypress.co.za **Web site:** http://city-press.news24.com
Freq: Weekly; **Circ:** 149586 ABC-Audit Bureau of Circulations
Profile: Sunday newspaper which offers cutting-edge journalism and meaningful content to a diverse demographic. The newspaper's principal target market is the black middle class: urban, young, well-educated and upwardly mobile.
Language (s): English
DAILY NEWSPAPER

Daily Dispatch   156694
Owner: Avusa Media Ltd: Eastern Cape
Editorial: PO Box 131, East London 5200
Tel: 27 43 7022000
Email: letters@dispatch.co.za **Web site:** http://www.dispatchlive.co.za
Circ: 30741
Editor: Barbara Hollands; **Editor in Chief:** Bongani Siqoko
Profile: Daily newspaper with full mix of editorial. English speaking adults in East London, Border, Transkei and Ciskei.
Language (s): English
Ad Rate: Full Page Colour 44080.00
Currency: South Africa Rand
DAILY NEWSPAPER

Daily News   460887
Owner: Independent Newspapers: KwaZulu-Natal
Editorial: 18 Osborne Street, Durban
Tel: 27 31 3082911
Email: DNnews@inl.co.za **Web site:** http://www.iol.co.za/dailynews
Freq: Daily; **Circ:** 32002 ABC-Audit Bureau of Circulations
Photographer: Puri Devjee; **Editor:** Alan Dunn; **Bureau Chief:** Sherlissa Peters
Profile: Major Durban daily newspaper covering regional and national news and current affairs including business, politics, entertainment, sports, motoring, lifestyle, travel, science and technology.
Language (s): English
Ad Rate: Full Page Mono 71031.60
Ad Rate: Full Page Colour 113648.40
Currency: South Africa Rand
DAILY NEWSPAPER

Daily Sun   699496
Owner: Media 24: Newspapers
Editorial: PO Box 121, Media Park, 69 Kingsway Ave, Auckland Park 2006 **Tel:** 27 11 8776000
Email: news@dailysun.co.za **Web site:** http://www.dailysun.co.za
Freq: Daily; **Circ:** 381127 ABC-Audit Bureau of Circulations

General Manager: Minette Ferreira; **Editor-in-Chief:** Reggy Moalusi
Profile: National daily newspaper covering regional, national and international news and current affairs including sports and entertainment.
Language (s): English
Ad Rate: Full Page Colour 93639.00
Currency: South Africa Rand
DAILY NEWSPAPER

Mail & Guardian   224398
Owner: M&G Media Limited
Editorial: PO Box 91667, Auckland Park, Johannesburg 2006 **Tel:** 27 11 2507300
Email: newsdesk@mg.co.za **Web site:** http://mg.co.za
Freq: Weekly; **Circ:** 48016 ABC-Audit Bureau of Circulations
Editor, Education: Prim Gower; **Editor:** Angela Quintal; **Production Manager:** Steve Ramushu
Profile: Newspaper focusing on analysis and comment on current news, social affairs, economics, the arts and sports. Includes distillation of articles from UK Guardian, Washington Post and Le Monde. Aimed at English speaking adults with an enquiring mind and an active interest in SA current affairs.Previous title: Weekly Mail and Guardian
Language (s): English
Ad Rate: Full Page Colour 60424.00
Currency: South Africa Rand
DAILY NEWSPAPER

The Mercury SA   699112
Owner: Independent Newspapers: KwaZulu-Natal
Editorial: 18 Osborne Street, Greyville, Durban 4023
Tel: 27 31 3082911
Email: mercnews@inl.co.za **Web site:** http://www.iol.co.za/mercury
Freq: Daily; **Circ:** 32920 ABC-Audit Bureau of Circulations
Editor: David Canning; **News Editor:** Philani Makhanya; **Editor:** Fikile Ntsikelelo Moya
Profile: Major newspaper with full mix of editorial. English speaking adults, Durban bias.Previous title: The Mercury (Natal)
Language (s): English
Ad Rate: Full Page Colour 68871.60
Currency: South Africa Rand
DAILY NEWSPAPER

The New Age   723958
Owner: TNA Media
Editorial: 52 Lechwe Street, Corporate Park, Midrand 1685 **Tel:** 27 11 5421222
Email: info@thenewage.co.za **Web site:** http://www.thenewage.co.za
Freq: Daily; **Circ:** 680000
Editor: Moegsien Williams
Profile: Newspaper covering regional, national and international news and current affairs including politics, economy, society and sports.
Language (s): English
DAILY NEWSPAPER

The Post   224438
Owner: Independent Newspapers: KwaZulu-Natal
Editorial: PO Box 733, Durban 4000
Tel: 27 31 308 2413
Email: post@inl.co.za **Web site:** http://www.iol.co.za/thepost
Freq: Weekly; **Circ:** 43798 ABC-Audit Bureau of Circulations
News Editor: Khalil Aniff
Profile: The Post is the Independent Media's niche weekly publication for the Indian community in Kwazulu-Natal.
Language (s): English
DAILY NEWSPAPER

Rapport   701081
Owner: RCP Media
Editorial: PO Box 8422, Johannesburg 2000
Tel: 27 11 7139002
Email: nuus@rapport.co.za **Web site:** http://www.rapport.co.za
Freq: Weekly; **Circ:** 275388 ABC-Audit Bureau of Circulations
Photographer: Lisa Hnatowicz; **News Editor:** Inge Kuhne; **Photographer:** Craig Nieuwenhuizen
Profile: Major newspaper containing full mix of editorial. See separate entries for supplements: Sake Rapport, Rapport Tydskrif, Kaap Rapport and Gauteng Rapport. Afrikaans speaking population nationally.
Language (s): Afrikaans
DAILY NEWSPAPER

Son Cape Town   700476
Owner: Media 24: Newspapers
Editorial: PO Box 692, Cape Town 8000
Tel: 27 21 4062121
Web site: http://www.son.co.za
Circ: 92213
Editor: Andrew Koopman; **News Editor:** Neil Scott; **General Manager:** Paul Siguqa
Profile: Son is the tabloid to be published in Afrikaans.The newspaper is based on the British tabloids such as The Sun and focuses on news, scandal, gossip, entertainment, sport and exposés. Son is distributed daily from Monday to Friday in the Western Cape and Eastern Cape.
Language (s): Afrikaans
DAILY NEWSPAPER

Sowetan   700496
Owner: Times Media
Editorial: 4 Biermann Avenue, Rosebank, Johannesburg 2196 **Tel:** 27 11 280 3000

South Africa

Email: newsdesk@sowetan.co.za **Web site:** http://www.sowetanlive.co.za
Freq: Daily; **Circ:** 125490 ABC-Audit Bureau of Circulations
Editor: Lesley Mofokeng
Profile: Newspaper covering regional and national news and current affairs.
Language (s): English
DAILY NEWSPAPER

The Star 156699
Owner: Independent Newspapers: Gauteng
Editorial: 47 Sauer Street, Johannesburg 2000
Tel: 27 11 633 2410
Email: starnews@inl.co.za **Web site:** http://www.iol.co.za/the-star
Freq: Daily; **Circ:** 106484 Not Audited
Editor: Justin Brown; **Editor:** Dennis Droppa; **Editor-in-Chief:** Kevin Ritchie
Profile: Daily newspaper covering regional, national and international news and current affairs including economy, politics and sports.
Language (s): English
Ad Rate: Full Page Mono 157642.20
Ad Rate: Full Page Colour 252228.60
Currency: South Africa Rand
DAILY NEWSPAPER

The Sunday Independent 156703
Owner: Independent Newspapers: Gauteng
Editorial: PO Box 1014, Johannesburg 2000
Tel: 27 11 6339111
Email: scribe@sunday.independent.co.za **Web site:** http://www.iol.co.za/sundayindependent
Freq: Weekly; **Circ:** 40041 ABC-Audit Bureau of Circulations
Foreign News Editor: Peter Fabricius; **Editor:** Jovial Rantao
Profile: Aims to provide top-drawer local & international editorial in two sections. Section one carries news & opinion from SA and overseas. Section two called Sunday Dispatches features politics, review section, international correspondents, the arts, culture, books, sport & business. English speakers aimed at in Gauteng area. Printed also in Cape Town, and distributed in Durban and Port Elizabeth.PR Accepted in: English
Language (s): English
DAILY NEWSPAPER

Sunday Tribune 460888
Owner: Independent Newspapers: KwaZulu-Natal
Editorial: 18 Osborne Street, Greyville, Durban 4023
Tel: 27 31 308 2316
Email: tribunenews@inl.co.za **Web site:** http://www.iol.co.za/sunday-tribune
Freq: Weekly; **Circ:** 109451 ABC-Audit Bureau of Circulations
News Editor: Liz Clarke
Profile: The Sunday Tribune is a weekend paper that is based in Durban in KwaZulu-Natal, South Africa.
Language (s): English
DAILY NEWSPAPER

Sunday World 700549
Owner: Avusa Media Ltd: Newspapers
Editorial: PO Box 6663, Johannesburg 2000
Tel: 27 11 4714000
Email: tellus@sundayworld.co.za **Web site:** http://www.sundayworld.co.za
Freq: Weekly; **Circ:** 160482 ABC-Audit Bureau of Circulations
News Editor: Amos Mananyetso; **Editor:** Abdul Milazi; **News Editor:** Xolile Mtshazo
Profile: Major black interest newspaper with full mix of editorial. Gauteng, Mpumalanga, Northern Province, North West Province, Free State, Kimberley.Previous title: Sowetan Sunday World
Language (s): English
DAILY NEWSPAPER

The Times 531758
Owner: Avusa Media Ltd: Newspapers
Editorial: 4 Biermann Avenue, Rosebank 2196
Tel: 27 11 2803000
Email: newsbreak@timeslive.co.za **Web site:** http://www.timeslive.co.za/thetimes
Freq: Daily; **Circ:** 137457 VFD
Editor-at-Large: Ray Hartley; **Office Manager:** Sandy Hattingh; **Office Manager:** Bongi Khumalo
Profile: Times provides breaking SA and international news and leading opinion.
Language (s): English
DAILY NEWSPAPER

Volksblad 460889
Owner: Media 24: Newspapers
Editorial: PO Box 267, Bloemfontein 9300
Tel: 27 51 4047600
Email: nuus@volksblad.com **Web site:** http://www.netwerk24.com
Freq: Daily; **Circ:** 27233 ABC-Audit Bureau of Circulations
Editor: Jonathan Crowther; **News Editor:** Cathy Dlodla; **Editor:** Clarissa Grobler; **Editor:** Jannie Hennop; **Editor:** Siska Martin; **Editor:** Braam Muller; **Editor:** Marleen Smith; **Editor:** Johanna van Eeden; **Editor:** Betta van Huyssteen
Profile: Major daily newspaper with full editorial mix. Afrikaans speaking adults in Free State and Northern Cape.Previous title: Die Volksblad
Language (s): Afrikaans
Ad Rate: Full Page Colour 45823.60
Currency: South Africa Rand
DAILY NEWSPAPER

News Service/Syndicate

South African Press Association 832765
Owner: South African Press Association
Editorial: Cotswold House, Greenacres Office Park, Victory Park, Johannesburg 2000 **Tel:** 27 11 782 1600
Email: news@sapa.org.za
News Editor: Hannes de Wet
Profile: The South African Press Association, commonly known as SAPA, is the national news agency of South Africa.
Language (s): English
NEWS SERVICE/SYNDICATE

Spain

Time Difference: GMT +1
National Telephone Code: 34
Continent: Europe
Capital: Madrid

Newspapers

AS 158629
Owner: PRISA
Editorial: C/ Valentin Beato, 44, 1 planta, Madrid 28037 **Tel:** 34 91 375 25 00
Email: redaccion@diarioas.es **Web site:** http://www.as.com
Freq: Daily; **Circ:** 185488
Editor in Chief: Tomás Roncero
Profile: Newspaper covering regional, national and international sports news including football, basketball, motorsports, tennis, cycling as well as results, interviews and sporting personalities.
Language (s): Spanish
DAILY NEWSPAPER

El Diario Vasco 158677
Owner: Sociedad Vascongada de Publicaciones SA
Editorial: Camino de Portuetxe, 2, San Sebastian 20018 **Tel:** 34 943 41 07 00
Email: redaccion@diariovasco.com **Web site:** http://www.diariovasco.com
Freq: Daily; **Circ:** 64774 Not Audited
Editor in Chief: Iñigo Beltrán de Heredia Oyarzabal; **Director:** José Gabriel Mujika Migueliz
Profile: Newspaper covering regional, national and international news and current affairs including business, politics, economics, society, culture, celebrity, entertainment and sports.
Language (s): Spanish
DAILY NEWSPAPER

Europa Sur 158709
Owner: Joly Digital
Editorial: Calle Muro, 3, Algeciras, Cádiz 11201
Tel: 34 956 58 82 50
Email: redaccion@europasur.com **Web site:** http://www.europasur.es
Circ: 3258
Director: Alberto Grimaldi
Profile: Regional daily newspaper focussing on news and current affairs.
Language (s): Spanish
Ad Rate: Full Page Colour 1490.00
Currency: Euro
DAILY NEWSPAPER

Expansión 158632
Owner: Unidad Editorial S.A.
Editorial: Avenida de San Luis, 25, Madrid 28033
Tel: 34 91 443 50 00
Email: expansion.com@expansion.com **Web site:** http://www.expansion.com
Freq: Daily; **Circ:** 44504 OJD
Editor in Chief: Tino Fernández Arias; **Director:** Ana Pereda; **Editor in Chief:** Clara Ruiz de Gauna
Profile: Daily newspaper covering business and finance including economics, society, personal finance, investment, markets and law.
Language (s): Spanish
Ad Rate: Full Page Mono 7140.00
Ad Rate: Full Page Colour 9967.00
Currency: Euro
DAILY NEWSPAPER

Gente 159043
Owner: Grupo de Información Gente
Editorial: Calle Conde de Penalver, 17, Primera planta, Local 2, Madrid 28006 **Tel:** 34 91 369 77 88
Email: contacto@gentedigital.es **Web site:** http://www.gentedigital.es
Freq: Daily; **Circ:** 50000 Publisher's Statement
Profile: Regional daily newspaper focussing on news and current affairs.
Language (s): Spanish
DAILY NEWSPAPER

MARCA 158634
Owner: Unidad Editorial S.A.
Editorial: Avenida de San Luis, 25-27, 1 planta, Madrid 28033 **Tel:** 34 91 443 50 00
Web site: http://www.marca.com
Freq: Daily; **Circ:** 252423 Not Audited
Editor in Chief: Emilio Contreras; **Editor in Chief:** Javier Domínguez; **Editor in Chief:** Roberto Palomar; **Editor in Chief:** Germán Pizarro; **Editor in Chief:** José María Rodríguez; **Editor in Chief:** Bruno Sáez
Profile: Newspaper covering regional, national and international sports news including football, basketball, motor racing, tennis, cycling, golf, athletics and handball.
Language (s): Spanish
Ad Rate: Full Page Mono 31880.00
Ad Rate: Full Page Colour 41410.00
Currency: Euro
DAILY NEWSPAPER

EL MUNDO 161177
Owner: Unidad Editorial S.A.
Editorial: Avenida de San Luis, 25, Madrid 28033
Tel: 34 91 443 50 00
Web site: http://www.elmundo.es
Freq: Daily; **Circ:** 217959 Not Audited
Editor in Chief: Ferran Boiza; **Editor in Chief:** Carlos Cuesta; **Director:** Casimiro García-Abardillo; **Magazine Director:** Javier Gómez; **Editor in Chief:** Miguel Gómez Vázquez; **Editor in Chief:** Vicente Lozano
Profile: Newspaper covering regional, national and international news and current affairs including politics, economics, society, culture, sports, motoring, travel, lifestyle, celebrities, science, health, technology and multimedia.
Language (s): Spanish
Ad Rate: Full Page Mono 29600.00
Ad Rate: Full Page Colour 39000.00
Currency: Euro
DAILY NEWSPAPER

El MUNDO - Andalucia Bureau 161179
Owner: Unidad Editorial S.A.
Editorial: Avenida Republica Argentina, 25, 8 planta, Sevilla 41011 **Tel:** 34 95 499 07 10
Email: recepcion@unidadeditorial.es **Web site:** http://www.elmundo.es/elmundo/andalucia.html
Freq: Daily; **Circ:** 286685 Not Audited
Director: Francisco Rosell
Profile: Regional bureau of the daily newspaper focussing on news and current affairs including economics, politics and sport.
Language (s): Spanish
Ad Rate: Full Page Mono 2900.00
Ad Rate: Full Page Colour 3700.00
Currency: Euro
DAILY NEWSPAPER

Mundo Deportivo 158635
Owner: El Mundo Deportivo SA
Editorial: Avda. Diagonal, 477, 5 planta, Barcelona 8036 **Tel:** 34 93 344 100
Email: redaccion@mundodeportivo.com **Web site:** http://www.mundodeportivo.com
Freq: Daily; **Circ:** 95642 Not Audited
Editor in Chief: Hector Coca; **Director:** Cristina Cubero Alcalde
Profile: National daily newspaper covering sports news including football, basketball, tennis, cycling, handball, swimming and motor racing in Spain and throughout the world.
Language (s): Spanish
Ad Rate: Full Page Mono 13800.00
Ad Rate: Full Page Colour 20400.00
Currency: Euro
DAILY NEWSPAPER

El País 158637
Owner: Ediciones El País S.L.
Editorial: C/ Miguel Yuste, 40, Madrid 28037
Tel: 34 91 337 82 00
Web site: http://www.elpais.com
Freq: Daily; **Circ:** 322214 Not Audited
Editor in Chief: Guillermo Altares; **Director:** Antonio Caño; **Porrespondent:** Fernando Garea; **Editor in Chief:** Miguel Jiménez; **Mexico Bureau Chief:** Jan Martínez Ahrens; **Foreign News Editor:** Andrea Rizzi; **Editor in Chief:** José Sámano
Profile: National newspaper covering regional, national and international news and current affairs including business, politics, economy, culture, society and sports.
Language (s): Spanish
Ad Rate: Full Page Mono 18610.00
Ad Rate: Full Page Colour 26010.00
Currency: Euro
DAILY NEWSPAPER

El Periódico de Catalunya 158638
Owner: Grupo Zeta
Editorial: C/ Consell de Cent, 425-427, Barcelona 8009 **Tel:** 34 93 265 53 53
Web site: http://www.elperiodico.com
Freq: Daily; **Circ:** 117500 Publisher's Statement
Editor in Chief: Joan Cañete Bayle; **Editor in Chief:** Teresa Cendrós; **Editor in Chief:** Olga Grau; **Director:** Enric Hernández; **News Editor:** Marta López; **Editor in Chief:** Luis Mauri; **Editor in Chief:** Neus Tomás; **Editor in Chief:** David Torras
Profile: Newspaper covering regional, national and international news and current affairs including politics, business, economics, society, sports, entertainment, culture, lifestyle and television.
Language (s): Spanish
Ad Rate: Full Page Mono 14331.00
Ad Rate: Full Page Colour 21389.00
Currency: Euro
DAILY NEWSPAPER

La Razón 158639
Owner: Audiovisual Española 2000 SA
Editorial: C/ Josefa Valcarcel, 42, Madrid 28027
Tel: 34 91 324 70 00
Email: internacional@larazon.es **Web site:** http://www.larazon.es
Freq: Daily; **Circ:** 110629 Not Audited
Editor in Chief: Sergio Alonso Puente; **Editor in Chief:** Alejandra Clements; **Editor in Chef:** Carlos de Miguel; **Editor in Chief:** Eva Estival; **Director:** Francisco Marhuenda; **Editor in Chief:** Julián Redondo
Profile: National newspaper covering regional, national and international news and current affairs including politics, economics, business, opinion, society, health, culture, religion, sport, motoring, entertainment, travel and lifestyle.
Language (s): Spanish
Ad Rate: Full Page Mono 16226.00
Ad Rate: Full Page Colour 23172.00
Currency: Euro
DAILY NEWSPAPER

La Vanguardia 158640
Owner: La Vanguardia Ediciones, SL
Editorial: Avenida Diagonal, 477, 3 planta, Barcelona 8036 **Tel:** 34 93 481 22 00
Email: redaccion@lavanguardia.es **Web site:** http://www.lavanguardia.es
Freq: Daily; **Circ:** 164700 Not Audited
Editor in Chief: Mariángel Alcázar; **Editor in Chief:** Ramon Aymerich; **Director:** Màrius Carol Pañella; **Editor in Chief:** Dagoberto Escorcia; **General Manager:** Javier Godó; **Editor in Chief:** Celeste López; **Editor in Chief:** Ignacio Orovio; **Editor in Chief:** Susana Quadrado; **Editor in Chief:** Lluís Uría
Profile: National newspaper covering regional, national and international news and current affairs including politics, economics, society, opinion, sports, lifestyle, technology, culture, entertainment and leisure activities.
Language (s): Spanish
Ad Rate: Full Page Mono 17500.00
Ad Rate: Full Page Colour 25000.00
Currency: Euro
DAILY NEWSPAPER

La Voz de Galicia 158716
Owner: La Voz de Galicia SA
Editorial: Avenida de la Prensa, 84-85, Polígono Industrial de Sabon, A Coruña 15142
Tel: 34 98 118 01 80
Email: redac@lavoz.es **Web site:** http://www.lavozdegalicia.es
Freq: Daily; **Circ:** 86604 Not Audited
Director: Xosé Luís Vilela Conde
Profile: Daily newspaper covering local, regional and national news and current affairs including politics, economics, society, culture and sports.
Language (s): Spanish
Ad Rate: Full Page Mono 8589.00
Ad Rate: Full Page Colour 10886.00
Currency: Euro
DAILY NEWSPAPER

News Service/Syndicate

Agencia EFE 353612
Owner: Agencia EFE, S.A.
Editorial: Avenida de Burgos, 8-B, Madrid 28036
Tel: 34 91 346 71 00
Email: efe@efe.com **Web site:** http://www.efe.com
Editor in Chief: Carmen del Portillo; **Editor in Chief:** Carlos Gosch; **Bureau Chief:** Jordi Kuhs; **Bureau Chief:** Noelia López; **Editor in Chief:** Carlos Mínguez; **Editor in Chief:** Javier Muñoz; **Bureau Chief:** José María Rodríguez; **Bureau Chief:** Isabel Saco
Profile: National Spanish news agency covering national and international news and current affairs including politics, economics and culture.
Language (s): Spanish
NEWS SERVICE/SYNDICATE

Agencia EFE - Athens Bureau 871367
Owner: Agencia EFE, S.A.
Editorial: Agiou Konstantinou, 12, 1 4, Athens 10431
Tel: 30 210 520 00 10
Email: atenas@efe.es **Web site:** http://www.efe.com
Bureau Chief: Ingrid Haack
Profile: Bureau in Athens of national Spanish news agency covering national news and current affairs including politics, economics and culture.
Language (s): English
NEWS SERVICE/SYNDICATE

Agencia EFE - Bogotá Bureau 467620
Owner: Agencia EFE
Editorial: Calle 67 N 7-35, Torre C, Of. 301, Bogota
Tel: 57 1 321 48 55
Email: efecol@efebogota.com.co **Web site:** http://www.efe.com
Director: Esther Rebollo
Profile: Regional bureau of the international news agency covering regional and national news and current affairs.
Language (s): English
NEWS SERVICE/SYNDICATE

Agencia EFE - Brussels Bureau 831299
Owner: Agencia EFE
Editorial: Residence Palace, Rue de la Loi 155 7th Fl., Brussels 1040 **Tel:** 32 2 285 48 30

Email: bruselas@efe.com **Web site:** http://www.efe.com
Bureau Chief: Elena Moreno
Profile: Regional bureau of the international news agency covering regional and national news and current affairs.
Language (s): Spanish
NEWS SERVICE/SYNDICATE

Agencia EFE - Caracas Bureau
406374
Owner: Agencia EFE, S.A.
Editorial: Avenida Francisco de Miranda, Edif. Parque Cristal, Torre Este, Piso 5. Oficina 5-7, Caracas 1060 **Tel:** 58 212 284 05 42
Email: eferedcar@efe.com **Web site:** http://www.efe.com
Bureau Chief: Javier García
Profile: Bureau in Caracas of national Spanish news agency covering national news and current affairs including politics, economics and culture.
Language (s): Spanish
NEWS SERVICE/SYNDICATE

Agencia EFE - La Paz Bureau
406373
Owner: Agencia EFE, S.A.
Editorial: Edificio Hilda, 5 Oficina 501, Avenida 6 de Agosto, 2455, La Paz 7403 **Tel:** 591 2 244 57 70
Email: jaliaga@efe.es **Web site:** http://www.efe.com
Profile: Bureau in Bolivia of national Spanish news agency covering national and international news and current affairs including politics, economics and culture.
Language (s): Spanish
NEWS SERVICE/SYNDICATE

Agencia EFE - Mexico Bureau
733698
Owner: Agencia EFE
Editorial: Lafayette, 69. Colonia Nueva Anzures, Mexico City, Distrito Federal 11590
Tel: 52 55 5255 4025
Email: mexico@efe.com **Web site:** http://www.efe.com
Bureau Chief: Raúl Cortés
Profile: Regional bureau of the international news agency covering regional and national news and current affairs.
Language (s): Spanish
NEWS SERVICE/SYNDICATE

Agencia EFE - Montevideo Bureau
380832
Owner: Agencia EFE
Editorial: 25 de Mayo, 741, Ofic. 502, Montevideo 11000 **Tel:** 598 2 902 03 38
Email: redaccion@efe.com.uy **Web site:** http://www.efe.com
Bureau Chief: Pedro Damián Diego Pérez
Profile: Regional bureau of the international news agency covering regional and national news and current affairs.
Language (s): Spanish
NEWS SERVICE/SYNDICATE

Agencia EFE - Moscow Bureau
815019
Owner: Agencia EFE
Editorial: Zubovski blvr 4, Ria Novosti International Press Center, Moskva 119021 **Tel:** 7 495 637 51 07
Email: efemos@gmail.com **Web site:** http://www.efe.com
Bureau Chief: Virginia Hebrero
Profile: Regional bureau of the international news agency covering regional and national news and current affairs.
Language (s): Russian
NEWS SERVICE/SYNDICATE

Agencia EFE - Paris Bureau
742962
Owner: Agencia EFE
Editorial: 10, rue Saint Marc, 4 bureau 165, Paris 75002 **Tel:** 33 1 44 82 65 40
Email: paris@elfe.com **Web site:** http://www.efe.com
Director: Enrique Rubio
Profile: Regional bureau of the international news agency covering regional and national news and current affairs.
Language (s): English
NEWS SERVICE/SYNDICATE

Europa Press
353613
Owner: Europa Press Noticias S.A.
Editorial: Paseo de la Castellana, 210, 2 Planta, Madrid 28046 **Tel:** 34 91 359 26 00
Email: noticias@europapress.es **Web site:** http://www.europapress.es
Editor in Chief: Loli Muriel; **Director:** Marcial Rodríguez Gacio; **Director:** Javier Garcia Vila
Profile: Agencia Europa Press is an international news agency with news covering economy, sports, television, culture, and society from several different regions in Spain.
Language (s): Spanish
NEWS SERVICE/SYNDICATE

Servimedia
408617
Owner: Servimedia S.A.
Editorial: C/ Almansa, 66, Madrid 28039
Tel: 34 91 545 01 00
Email: servimedia@servimedia.es **Web site:** http://www.servimedia.es
Director: Pablo Iglesias
Profile: News service covering national news and current affairs including politics, economics and society.
Language (s): Spanish
NEWS SERVICE/SYNDICATE

SOONimage
907375
Owner: SOONimage
Tel: 34 93 2691962
Email: editorial@soonimage.com **Web site:** https://soonimage.com
Editor: Lino De Vallier
Profile: Press photo agency covering news and current affairs.
Language (s): Spanish
NEWS SERVICE/SYNDICATE

Community Newspaper

El 9 Nou d'Osona i del Ripollès
161150
Owner: Premsa d'Osona SA
Editorial: Placa de la Catedral, 2, Barcelona 8500
Tel: 34 93 88 94 949
Email: direccio@vic.el9nou.com **Web site:** http://www.el9nou.com
Freq: Daily; **Circ:** 9127
Editor in Chief: Jaume Espuny; **Director:** Jordi Molet
Profile: Regional daily newspaper covering news and current affairs.
Language (s): Catalan
Ad Rate: Full Page Mono 2800.00
Ad Rate: Full Page Colour 4100.00
Currency: Euro
COMMUNITY NEWSPAPER

El 9 Nou Valles Oriental
161151
Owner: Premsa d'Osona SA
Editorial: Carrer Girona, 34, 1er. pis, Granollers 8400
Tel: 34 938 60 30 20
Email: recepcio@gra.el9nou.com **Web site:** http://www.el9nou.com
Freq: Daily; **Circ:** 4295
Editor in Chief: Josep Mas
Profile: Regional daily newspaper covering news and current affairs.
Language (s): Catalan
Ad Rate: Full Page Mono 2800.00
Ad Rate: Full Page Colour 4100.00
Currency: Euro
COMMUNITY NEWSPAPER

El Adelantado de Segovia
158681
Owner: El Adelantado de Segovia
Editorial: Calle Morillo, 7, Junto Jardín Botanico, Segovia 40002 **Tel:** 34 921 43 72 61
Email: adelantado@eladelantado.com **Web site:** http://www.eladelantado.com
Freq: Daily; **Circ:** 3511
Director: Carlos Herranz Cano
Profile: Newspaper covering current regional news and current affairs.
Language (s): Spanish
Ad Rate: Full Page Mono 1585.00
Currency: Euro
COMMUNITY NEWSPAPER

ARA
725901
Owner: Premsa Periòdica Ara
Editorial: Diputacio, 119, Barcelona 8015
Tel: 34 93 202 95 95
Email: cartes@ara.cat **Web site:** http://www.ara.cat
Freq: Daily; **Circ:** 29930
Director: Carles Capdevila
Profile: Newspaper covering regional, national and international news and current affairs including politics, society, culture, economics, sports and entertainment.
Language (s): Catalan
COMMUNITY NEWSPAPER

Atlántico Diario
158693
Owner: Rías Baixas Comunicación SA
Editorial: Avenida Camelias, 104, Bajo, Vigo 36211
Tel: 34 986 20 86 86
Email: redaccionad@atlantico.net **Web site:** http://www.atlantico.net
Circ: 3899
Editor in Chief: Ana Fuentes Crego; **Director:** Julio Rodríguez Gonzales
Profile: Newspaper covering regional news and current affairs including politics, economics, sports, society, culture, technology and lifestyle.
Language (s): Spanish
Ad Rate: Full Page Colour 2895.50
Currency: Euro
COMMUNITY NEWSPAPER

Canarias7
158731
Owner: Informaciones Canarias SA
Editorial: Calle Profesor Lozano 7, Urbanizacion El Sebadal, Las Palmas De Gran Canaria 35008
Tel: 34 928 30 13 00
Email: redaccion@canarias7.es **Web site:** http://www.canarias7.es
Circ: 16357
Editor in Chief: Rebeca Chacón; **Director:** Francisco Suárez Alamo
Profile: Newspaper covering regional news and current affairs including politics, economics, society, sports, technology and lifestyle.
Language (s): Spanish
Ad Rate: Full Page Colour 3352.00
Currency: Euro
COMMUNITY NEWSPAPER

El Comercio
158718
Owner: El Comercio SA
Editorial: Calle del Diario El Comercio 1, Gijón 22307
Tel: 34 98 51 79 800
Email: elcomercio@elcomercio.es **Web site:** http://www.elcomercio.es
Freq: Daily; **Circ:** 21894
Director: Julio Maese
Profile: Newspaper covering regional business, economy and commerce.
Language (s): Spanish
Ad Rate: Full Page Colour 2660.00
Currency: Euro
COMMUNITY NEWSPAPER

El Correo
158701
Owner: Diario El Correo, S.A.
Editorial: C/ Pintor Losada, 7, Bilbao 48004
Tel: 34 94 487 01 00
Email: redaccion@elcorreo.com **Web site:** http://www.elcorreo.com
Freq: Daily; **Circ:** 89228
Online News Director: Mikel Iturralde Lázaro
Profile: Newspaper covering local and regional news including politics, economics, sports, society, culture and entertainment.
Language (s): Spanish
Ad Rate: Full Page Colour 9454.00
Currency: Euro
COMMUNITY NEWSPAPER

El Correo de Andalucía
158682
Owner: El Correo de Andalucia SL
Editorial: Parque Empresarial Morera & Vallejo, Calle Aviacion, 14, Sevilla 41007 **Tel:** 34 95 448 8500
Email: redaccion@correoandalucia.es **Web site:** http://www.correoandalucia.es
Freq: Daily; **Circ:** 9150
Director: David López Royo; **Editor in Chief:** Ana Trujillo
Profile: Regional daily newspaper focussing on news and current affairs.
Language (s): Spanish
Ad Rate: Full Page Colour 2650.00
Currency: Euro
COMMUNITY NEWSPAPER

Deia
158702
Owner: Editorial Iparraguirre SA
Editorial: Camino de Capuchinos, 6, 5-C, Bilbao 48004 **Tel:** 34 944 59 91 00
Email: cartas@deia.com **Web site:** http://www.deia.com
Circ: 17013
Editor: Idoia Alonso; **Director:** Bingen Zupiria
Profile: Newspaper covering regional news and current affairs including politics, economics and sports. Circulation number is 20 000 from monday to friday, and between 25 000 and 30 000 during the weekend.
Language (s): Spanish
Ad Rate: Full Page Colour 3625.00
Currency: Euro
COMMUNITY NEWSPAPER

El Día
161095
Owner: Editorial Leoncio Rodríguez SA
Editorial: Avenida Buenos Aires, 71, Santa Cruz De Tenerife 38005 **Tel:** 34 922 23 83 00
Email: norte@eldia.es **Web site:** http://www.eldia.es
Freq: Daily; **Circ:** 22352
Profile: Regional daily newspaper focussing on news and current affairs.
Language (s): Spanish
Ad Rate: Full Page Colour 1515.15
Currency: Euro
COMMUNITY NEWSPAPER

El Día de Córdoba
161097
Owner: Joly Digital
Editorial: Calle Jose Cruz Conde, 12, Cordoba 14008
Tel: 34 95 72 22 050
Email: eldia@eldiadecordoba.com **Web site:** http://www.eldiadecordoba.com
Freq: Daily; **Circ:** 2068
Editor in Chief: Ramón Villar
Profile: Regional daily newspaper focussing on news and current affairs.
Language (s): Spanish
COMMUNITY NEWSPAPER

El Día de Valladolid
161098
Owner: PROMECAL, S. L.
Editorial: Edificio PROMECAL, Calle los Astros s/n, Valladolid 47009 **Tel:** 34 983 32 50 45
Email: redaccion@diavalladolid.es **Web site:** http://www.eldiadevalladolid.com
Freq: Daily; **Circ:** 4876
Director: Juanjo Fernández Corral
Profile: Newspaper covering regional news and current affairs.
Language (s): Spanish
Ad Rate: Full Page Mono 1655.00
Ad Rate: Full Page Colour 2462.00
Currency: Euro
COMMUNITY NEWSPAPER

Diari de Terrassa
158698
Owner: Julián Sanz Soria SL
Editorial: Vinyals, 61, Terrassa, Barcelona 8221
Tel: 34 937 28 37 00
Email: ciudad@diarideterrassa.es **Web site:** http://www.diarideterrassa.es
Freq: Daily; **Circ:** 4345
Editor in Chief: Josep Arnero Argüello; **Director:** Ana Muñoz Núñez
Profile: Newspaper covering regional news and current affairs.
Language (s): Spanish
Ad Rate: Full Page Mono 700.00
Ad Rate: Full Page Colour 900.00
Currency: Euro
COMMUNITY NEWSPAPER

Diario de Avisos
158732
Owner: Canaria de Avisos
Editorial: Calle Salamanca, 5, Santa Cruz De Tenerife 38006 **Tel:** 34 922 27 23 50
Email: lop@diariodeavisos.com **Web site:** http://www.diariodeavisos.com
Circ: 12361
Profile: Newspaper covering regional news and current affairs including politics, economics and sports.
Language (s): Spanish
Ad Rate: Full Page Colour 2440.00
Currency: Euro
COMMUNITY NEWSPAPER

Diario de Burgos
158704
Owner: Diario de Burgos SA
Editorial: Edificio PROMECAL Burgos, Avda. Castilla y Leon, 62-64, Burgos 9006 **Tel:** 34 947 26 72 80
Email: redaccion@diariodeburgos.es **Web site:** http://www.diariodeburgos.es
Circ: 11598
Editor in Chief: Martin Serrano
Profile: Newspaper covering regional news and current affairs including politics, economics and sports.
Language (s): Spanish
Ad Rate: Full Page Mono 1985.00
Ad Rate: Full Page Colour 2571.00
Currency: Euro
COMMUNITY NEWSPAPER

Diario de Cádiz
158707
Owner: Joly Digital
Editorial: Avda de El Puerto, 2, Ed. Fénix, Cádiz 11007 **Tel:** 34 956 29 79 00
Email: redaccion@diariodecadiz.com **Web site:** http://www.diariodecadiz.es
Freq: Daily; **Circ:** 26890
Editor in Chief: Francisco Sanchez Zambrano
Profile: Newspaper covering regional news and current affairs including politics, economics, sports, technology, culture, television entertainment and health.
Language (s): Spanish
Ad Rate: Full Page Colour 3784.00
Currency: Euro
COMMUNITY NEWSPAPER

Diario de Ibiza
158726
Owner: Diario de Ibiza SA
Editorial: Avda. de la Paz, esquina C/ Aubarca, Ibiza 7800 **Tel:** 34 971 19 00 00
Email: diariodeibiza@epi.es **Web site:** http://www.diariodeibiza.es
Freq: Daily; **Circ:** 5780
Editor in Chief: Cristina Martin
Profile: Newspaper covering regional news and current affairs including politics, economics, entertainment, lifestyle and sports.
Language (s): Spanish
Ad Rate: Full Page Mono 1775.00
Ad Rate: Full Page Colour 2663.00
Currency: Euro
COMMUNITY NEWSPAPER

Diario de Jerez
158708
Owner: Grupo Joly
Editorial: Patricio Garvey s/n, Jerez de la Frontera, Cádiz 11402 **Tel:** 34 95 63 21 411
Email: redaccion@diariodejerez.com **Web site:** http://www.diariodejerez.com
Freq: Daily; **Circ:** 6267
Editor in Chief: Luis Gonzaga Díaz del Río
Profile: Newspaper covering regional news and current affairs.
Language (s): Spanish
Ad Rate: Full Page Colour 1710.00
Currency: Euro
COMMUNITY NEWSPAPER

Diario de León
158655
Owner: Diario de León S.A.
Editorial: Carretera Leon-Astorga, Km. 4,5, Trobajo del Camino, León 24010 **Tel:** 34 98 784 03 00
Email: diariodeleon@diariodeleon.es **Web site:** http://www.diariodeleon.es
Freq: Daily; **Circ:** 12914
Editor: Ana Gaitero Alonso
Profile: Newspaper covering regional news and current affairs including politics, economics and sports.
Language (s): Spanish
Ad Rate: Full Page Colour 2195.00
Currency: Euro
COMMUNITY NEWSPAPER

Diario de Mallorca
158727
Owner: Editora Balear SA
Editorial: Calle Puerto Rico 15, Polígono de Levante, Palma De Mallorca 7006 **Tel:** 34 971 17 03 00
Email: secretaria.diariodemallorca@epi.es **Web site:** http://www.diariodemallorca.es
Freq: Daily; **Circ:** 19145
Editor in Chief: Pilar Garces
Profile: Newspaper covering regional news and current affairs including politics, economics and sports.
Language (s): Spanish

Ad Rate: Full Page Mono 2455.00
Ad Rate: Full Page Colour 3685.00
Currency: Euro
COMMUNITY NEWSPAPER

Diario de Navarra 158670
Owner: Diario de Navarra SA
Editorial: Ctra. Zaragoza 23, Pamplona 31191
Tel: 34 948 23 60 50
Email: edicion.digital@diariodenavarra.es **Web site:** http://www.diariodenavarra.es
Circ: 44924
Director: Luis Colina Lorda; **Editor in Chief:** Fernando Hernández Morondo
Profile: Newspaper covering regional news and current affairs including politics, economics, sports, society, culture and entertainment.
Language (s): Spanish
Ad Rate: Full Page Mono 3225.00
Ad Rate: Full Page Colour 4837.00
Currency: Euro
COMMUNITY NEWSPAPER

Diario de Noticias de Navarra 158649
Owner: Zeroa Multimedia S.A.
Editorial: C/ Altzutzate, 8, Poligono Industrial Areta, Pamplona 31620 **Tel:** 34 94 833 25 33
Email: redaccion@noticiasdenavarra.com **Web site:** http://www.noticiasdenavarra.com
Circ: 44924
Director: Joseba Santamaria
Profile: Newspaper covering regional news and current affairs including politics, economics and sports.
Language (s): Spanish
Ad Rate: Full Page Colour 2300.00
Currency: Euro
COMMUNITY NEWSPAPER

Diario de Pontevedra 158671
Owner: El Progreso de Lugo SL
Editorial: Rua Lepanto 5, Pontevedra 36001
Tel: 34 986 01 11 00
Email: diario@diariodepontevedra.com **Web site:** http://www.diariodepontevedra.com
Circ: 6867
Profile: Newspaper covering regional news and current affairs.
Language (s): Spanish
Ad Rate: Full Page Mono 1335.00
Ad Rate: Full Page Colour 1730.00
Currency: Euro
COMMUNITY NEWSPAPER

Diario de Sevilla 161096
Owner: Editorial Andaluza de Periodicos Independientes SA
Editorial: Calle Rioja, 14, Sevilla 41001
Tel: 34 954 50 62 00
Email: secretaria@diariodesevilla.es **Web site:** http://www.diariodesevilla.es
Freq: Daily; **Circ:** 17641
Profile: Newspaper covering regional news and current affairs including politics, economics and sports.
Language (s): Spanish
COMMUNITY NEWSPAPER

Diario del AltoAragón 158651
Owner: Publicaciones y Ediciones del Alto Aragón S.A.
Editorial: C/ Ronda Estacion, 4, Huesca 22005
Tel: 34 97 421 56 57
Web site: http://www.diariodelaltoaragon.es
Freq: Daily; **Circ:** 5942
Director: Javier García Antón; **Editor in Chief:** Jorge Naya
Profile: Newspaper covering regional news and current affairs including politics, economics and sports.
Language (s): Spanish
COMMUNITY NEWSPAPER

Diario Jaén 158653
Owner: Diario Jaén SA
Editorial: C/ Torredonjimeno, 1, Jaén 23009
Tel: 34 953 21 11 11
Email: diariojaen@diariojaen.es **Web site:** http://www.diariojaen.es
Freq: Daily; **Circ:** 7272
Director: Juan Espejo González; **Editor in Chief:** Juana González Cerezo; **Editor in Chief:** José Manuel Serrano Alba
Profile: Newspaper covering regional news and current affairs.
Language (s): Spanish
Ad Rate: Full Page Mono 1176.00
Ad Rate: Full Page Colour 1647.00
Currency: Euro
COMMUNITY NEWSPAPER

El Diario Montañés 158679
Owner: Editorial Cantábria SA
Editorial: Avenida Parayas, 38, Santander 39011
Tel: 34 94 235 40 00
Email: redaccion@eldiariomontanes.es **Web site:** http://www.eldiariomontanes.es
Freq: Daily; **Circ:** 30614
Editor in Chief: Miguel Angel Perez Jorrin
Profile: Regional daily newspaper focussing on news and current affairs including sports, economics, celebrity, media and regional events.
Language (s): Spanish
Ad Rate: Full Page Colour 3300.00
Currency: Euro
COMMUNITY NEWSPAPER

El Diario Palentino 158669
Owner: Grupo Promecal
Editorial: Calle Mayor, 52, Palencia 34001
Tel: 34 979 70 63 08
Email: dp_local@diariopalentino.es **Web site:** http://www.diariopalentino.es
Freq: Daily; **Circ:** 3833
Editor in Chief: Jorge Cancho González; **Director:** Carlos Martin Santoyo
Profile: Regional daily newspaper focussing on news and current affairs.
Language (s): Spanish
COMMUNITY NEWSPAPER

Faro de Vigo 158720
Owner: Faro de Vigo SA
Editorial: Garcia Barbon, 87, bajos, Vigo 36201
Tel: 34 986 81 46 00
Email: contenidos@farodevigomedia.es **Web site:** http://www.farodevigo.es
Circ: 41044
Director: Jaime Abella
Profile: Regional daily newspaper focussing on news and current affairs including economics, politics and sport.
Language (s): Spanish
Ad Rate: Full Page Mono 3510.00
Ad Rate: Full Page Colour 5270.00
Currency: Euro
COMMUNITY NEWSPAPER

La Gaceta de Salamanca 158675
Owner: Grupo Promotor Salmantino SA
Editorial: Avda. de los Cipreses, 81, Salamanca 37004 **Tel:** 34 923 12 52 52
Email: local@lagacetadesalamanca.com **Web site:** http://www.lagacetadesalamanca.com
Circ: 14913
Director: Julian Ballestero Chillon
Profile: Regional daily newspaper focussing on news and current affairs.
Language (s): Spanish
COMMUNITY NEWSPAPER

Heraldo de Aragón 158723
Owner: Heraldo de Aragón SA
Editorial: Paseo de la Independencia, 29, Apdo. 175, Zaragoza 50001 **Tel:** 34 976 76 50 00
Email: heraldo@heraldo.es **Web site:** http://www.heraldo.es
Freq: Daily; **Circ:** 55626
Director: Miguel Iturbe; **Editor in Chief:** Enrique Mored Raluy
Profile: Newspaper covering local, regional and national news and current affairs including politics, economics, sports, society, culture and entertainment.
Language (s): Spanish
Ad Rate: Full Page Mono 3740.00
Ad Rate: Full Page Colour 5236.00
Currency: Euro
COMMUNITY NEWSPAPER

Heraldo de Soria 158685
Owner: Soria Impresión SA
Editorial: El Collado, 17, Soria 42002
Tel: 34 975 23 36 07
Email: soriaredaccion@heraldo.es **Web site:** http://www.heraldodesoria.es
Freq: Daily; **Circ:** 3202
Editor: Luis Casado
Profile: Regional daily newspaper focussing on news and current affairs.
Language (s): Spanish
COMMUNITY NEWSPAPER

HOY 158695
Owner: Corporación de Medios de Extremadura SA
Editorial: Avenida del Diario HOY, Antigua carretera Madrid - Lisboa, 22, Badajoz 6008
Tel: 34 924 214 300
Email: redaccion@hoy.es **Web site:** http://www.hoy.es
Freq: Daily; **Circ:** 23935
Editor in Chief: José Orantos
Profile: Regional daily newspaper focussing on news and current affairs including economics, politics and sport.
Language (s): Spanish
Ad Rate: Full Page Mono 3158.00
Ad Rate: Full Page Colour 3790.00
Currency: Euro
COMMUNITY NEWSPAPER

Huelva Información 158650
Owner: Grupo Joly
Editorial: C/ Alcalde Mora Claros, 1, 1 Planta, Huelva 21001 **Tel:** 34 95 954 11 80
Email: redaccion@huelvainformacion.es **Web site:** http://www.huelvainformacion.es
Freq: Daily; **Circ:** 6131
Profile: Regional daily newspaper focussing on news and current affairs.
Language (s): Spanish
Ad Rate: Full Page Colour 1660.00
Currency: Euro
COMMUNITY NEWSPAPER

Ideal 158648
Owner: Vocento
Editorial: C/ Huelva, 2, Polígono Industrial Asegra, Granada 18210 **Tel:** 34 95 880 98 09
Email: redaccion@ideal.es **Web site:** http://www.ideal.es
Freq: Daily; **Circ:** 33955
Director: Eduardo Peralta de Ana
Profile: Regional daily newspaper focussing on news and current affairs including economics, politics and sports.
Language (s): Spanish
Ad Rate: Full Page Mono 2450.00
Ad Rate: Full Page Colour 3675.00
Currency: Euro
COMMUNITY NEWSPAPER

Información 158644
Owner: Editorial Prensa Alicantina, S.A.
Editorial: Avenida del Doctor Rico, 17, Alicante 3005
Tel: 34 96 598 91 00
Email: informacion.alicante@epi.es **Web site:** http://www.diarioinformacion.com
Freq: Daily; **Circ:** 33821
Director: Juan Gil
Profile: Regional daily newspaper focussing on news and current affairs including economics, politics and sport.
Language (s): Spanish
Ad Rate: Full Page Mono 3155.00
Ad Rate: Full Page Colour 4733.00
Currency: Euro
COMMUNITY NEWSPAPER

Levante - El Mercantil Valenciano 158690
Owner: Editorial Prensa Valenciana SA
Editorial: Calle Traginers, 7, Valencia 46014
Tel: 34 963 992 200
Email: levante-emv@epi.es **Web site:** http://www.levante-emv.com
Freq: Daily; **Circ:** 46079
General Manager: Vicente Pérez
Profile: Regional daily newspaper focussing on news and current affairs including politics, economics and sports.
Language (s): Spanish
COMMUNITY NEWSPAPER

Majorca Daily Bulletin 158728
Owner: Hora Nova SA
Editorial: Passeig de Mallorca, 9A, Palma De Mallorca 7011 **Tel:** 34 971 78 84 00
Email: editorial@majorcadailybulletin.es **Web site:** http://www.majorcadailybulletin.es
Freq: Daily; **Circ:** 2994
Editor in Chief: Humphrey Carter; **Director:** Jason Moore
Profile: Regional daily newspaper focussing on news and current affairs in English.
Language (s): English
Ad Rate: Full Page Mono 916.00
Ad Rate: Full Page Colour 1374.00
Currency: Euro
COMMUNITY NEWSPAPER

La Mañana 161100
Owner: Diari de Ponent SA
Editorial: Poligono industrial El Segre 118, Apdo. de Correus 11, Lleida 25080 **Tel:** 34 973 001 140
Email: redaccio@lamanyana.es **Web site:** http://www.lamanyana.cat
Freq: Daily; **Circ:** 4089
Editor in Chief: Xavier Manau
Profile: Newspaper covering local, regional and national news and current affairs including politics, economics, sports, society, culture and entertainment.
Language (s): Spanish
Ad Rate: Full Page Mono 1498.00
Ad Rate: Full Page Colour 1994.00
Currency: Euro
COMMUNITY NEWSPAPER

Menorca 158729
Owner: Editorial Menorca SA
Editorial: Cap de Cavalleria, 5, Polígono industrial, Mahón 7714 **Tel:** 34 971 351 600
Email: redaccion@menorca.info **Web site:** http://menorca.info
Freq: Daily; **Circ:** 6476
Editor in Chief: Pere Melis Nebot
Profile: Regional daily newspaper focussing on news and current affairs.
Language (s): Spanish
COMMUNITY NEWSPAPER

El Norte de Castilla 158692
Owner: El Norte de Castilla
Editorial: Vazquez de Menchaca, 10, Polígono de Argales, Valladolid 47008 **Tel:** 34 983 412 100
Email: redaccion.nc@elnortedecastilla.es **Web site:** http://www.elnortedecastilla.es
Freq: Daily; **Circ:** 24451
News Editor: Eloy de la Pisa; **Editor in Chief:** Carmen Diez
Profile: Newspaper covering regional news and current affairs.
Language (s): Spanish
COMMUNITY NEWSPAPER

Nueva Alcarria 161141
Owner: Editorial Nueva Alcarria, SA
Editorial: Calle de Francisco Aritio, 76, Guadalajara 19004 **Tel:** 34 949 24 74 70
Email: redaccion@nuevaalcarria.com **Web site:** http://www.nuevaalcarria.com
Circ: 1413
Director: Geles López Valle
Profile: Regional daily newspaper focussing on news and current affairs.
Language (s): Spanish
COMMUNITY NEWSPAPER

La Nueva España 158668
Owner: Editorial Prensa Asturiana, S.A.
Editorial: C/ Calvo Sotelo, 7, Oviedo 33007
Tel: 34 98 527 97 00
Email: pam@lne.es **Web site:** http://www.lne.es
Freq: Daily; **Circ:** 51360
Director: Ángeles Rivero Velasco
Profile: Newspaper covering local, regional and national news and current affairs including politics, economics, sports, society, culture and entertainment.
Language (s): Spanish
Ad Rate: Full Page Colour 3510.00
Currency: Euro
COMMUNITY NEWSPAPER

La Opinión de Málaga 161117
Owner: Editorial Prensa Ibérica
Editorial: Calle Granada, 42, Málaga 29015
Tel: 34 95 21 26 200
Email: redaccion@opinionmalaga.com **Web site:** http://www.laopiniondemalaga.es
Circ: 6866
Editor in Chief: Emilio Fernandez; **Director:** Aurelio Romero Fornelio
Profile: Regional daily newspaper focussing on news and current affairs.
Language (s): Spanish
Ad Rate: Full Page Colour 1935.00
Currency: Euro
COMMUNITY NEWSPAPER

La Opinión de Zamora 158721
Owner: Editorial Prensa Ibérica
Editorial: Rua de los Francos, 20, Zamora 49001
Tel: 34 980 53 47 59
Email: laopinionzamora.rdc@epi.es **Web site:** http://www.laopiniondezamora.es
Freq: Daily; **Circ:** 6789
Director: Francisco García Alonso
Profile: Regional daily newspaper focussing on news, current affairs, economics, politics and sport.
Language (s): Spanish
COMMUNITY NEWSPAPER

El Periódico Extremadura 158705
Owner: Grupo Zeta
Editorial: Calle Doctor Maranon, 2, Local 7, Caceres 10002 **Tel:** 34 92 762 06 00
Email: epextremadura@elperiodico.es **Web site:** http://www.elperiodicoextremadura.com
Freq: Daily; **Circ:** 8281
Editor in Chief: José Luis Guerra; **Director:** Miguel Ángel Muñoz
Profile: Newspaper covering regional news and current affairs.
Language (s): Spanish
COMMUNITY NEWSPAPER

El Periodico Mediterráneo 158712
Owner: Promociones y Ediciones Culturales SA
Editorial: Carretera Almassora s/n, Castellón 12005
Tel: 34 964 34 95 00
Email: redaccion@epmediterraneo.com **Web site:** http://www.elperiodicomediterraneo.com
Freq: Daily; **Circ:** 10895
Editor in Chief: Javier Abad Meliá; **Editor in Chief:** Javier Navarro Cantavella; **Editor in Chief:** Julio Sánchez Isarria; **Director:** Jose Luis Valencia Larrañeta
Profile: Newspaper covering regional news and current affairs.
Language (s): Spanish
COMMUNITY NEWSPAPER

El Progreso 158659
Owner: El Progreso de Lugo SL
Editorial: Rua Ribadeo s/n, Lugo 27002
Tel: 34 98 229 81 00
Email: redaccion@galiciae.com **Web site:** http://elprogreso.galiciae.com/
Freq: Daily; **Circ:** 15614
Editor: Ana Rodil
Profile: Newspaper covering regional news and current affairs.
Language (s): Spanish
Ad Rate: Full Page Mono 2950.00
Ad Rate: Full Page Colour 3600.00
Currency: Euro
COMMUNITY NEWSPAPER

La Provincia 158736
Owner: Editorial Prensa Canaria SA
Editorial: Avda. Alcalde Ramirez Bethencourt, 8, Las Palmas De Gran Canaria 35003 **Tel:** 34 928 47 94 00
Email: laprovincia@epi.es **Web site:** http://www.laprovincia.es
Freq: Daily; **Circ:** 33414
Editor in Chief: Javier Durán; **Advertising Manager:** Vanessa Merino; **Editor in Chief:** Cristobal Rodriguez
Profile: Regional daily newspaper covering news and current affairs including politics, economics and sports.
Language (s): Spanish
COMMUNITY NEWSPAPER

Las Provincias 225912
Owner: Federico Domenech SA
Editorial: Calle Gremis, 4, Valencia 46014
Tel: 34 96 35 02 211
Email: redaccion@lasprovinciasdigital.es **Web site:** http://www.lasprovincias.es
Freq: Daily; **Circ:** 42049
Director: Julián Quirós

Profile: Daily regional newspaper covering news and current affairs including politics, economics and sport.
Language (s): Spanish
COMMUNITY NEWSPAPER

Regió7 158700
Owner: Ediciones Intercomarcales SA
Editorial: Sant Antoni M Claret, 32, Manresa, Barcelona 8243 **Tel:** 34 938 77 22 33
Email: regio7@regio7.cat **Web site:** http://www.regio7.com
Circ: 8559
Director: Marc Marcè i Casaponsa
Profile: Regional daily newspaper covering news and current affairs.
Language (s): Catalan
Ad Rate: Full Page Mono 1398.00
Ad Rate: Full Page Colour 2097.00
Currency: Euro
COMMUNITY NEWSPAPER

La Región 158667
Owner: La Región, S.A.
Editorial: Poligono de San Cibrao das Vinas, "David Ferrer", Calle 4, Ourense 32901 **Tel:** 34 98 851 12 60
Email: info@laregion.es **Web site:** http://www.laregion.es
Freq: Daily; **Circ:** 10683
Editor in Chief: Manuel Fernández Gallego; **Director:** Xosé Pastoriza Martínez
Profile: Regional daily newspaper covering news and current affairs.
Language (s): Spanish
COMMUNITY NEWSPAPER

La Rioja 158658
Owner: Vocento
Editorial: C/ Vara de Rey, 74 Bajos, Logroño 26002
Tel: 34 94 127 91 00
Email: local@larioja.com **Web site:** http://www.larioja.com
Freq: Daily; **Circ:** 11916
Editor in Chief: María Jóse Zapata Rico
Profile: Regional daily newspaper covering news and current affairs including politics, economics and sports.
Language (s): Spanish
COMMUNITY NEWSPAPER

Segre 158657
Owner: Prensa Leridana SAL
Editorial: Carrer del Riu, 6, Lerida 25007
Tel: 34 97 324 80 00
Email: redaccio@segre.com **Web site:** http://www.segre.com
Freq: Daily; **Circ:** 12121
Director: Santiago Costa Miranda
Profile: Regional daily newspaper covering news and current affairs.
Language (s): Catalan
Ad Rate: Full Page Mono 2380.00
Ad Rate: Full Page Colour 3090.00
Currency: Euro
COMMUNITY NEWSPAPER

Sport 160808
Owner: Ediciones Deportivas Catalanes SA
Editorial: Consell de Cent, 425-427, Barcelona 8009
Tel: 34 93 265 53 53
Email: redaccion@diariosport.com **Web site:** http://www.sport.es
Freq: Daily; **Circ:** 118098
Editor: Joaquím Beltran; **Editor in Chief:** Carlos Galindo Ayllon; **Director:** Joan Vehils
Profile: Tabloid-sized daily newspaper covering regional, national and international sports news including football, basketball and motor racing.
Language (s): Spanish
COMMUNITY NEWSPAPER

SUR 158663
Owner: Prensa Malagueña, S.A.
Editorial: Avenida Dr Maranon, 48, Apdo. 98, Málaga 29009 **Tel:** 34 95 264 96 00
Email: redaccion@diariosur.es **Web site:** http://www.diariosur.es
Freq: Daily; **Circ:** 22659
Editor in Chief: José Vicente Astorga
Profile: Regional daily newspaper covering news and current affairs including politics, economics and sports.
Language (s): Spanish
Ad Rate: Full Page Mono 4512.00
Ad Rate: Full Page Colour 6770.00
Currency: Euro
COMMUNITY NEWSPAPER

La Tribuna de Albacete 158641
Owner: Pubalsa
Editorial: Paseo de la Cuba 14, Albacete 2005
Tel: 34 967 19 10 00
Email: albacete@latribunadealbacete.es **Web site:** http://www.latribunadealbacete.es
Freq: Daily; **Circ:** 3581
Editor in Chief: Adolfo Giménez
Profile: Newspaper covering local, regional and national news and current affairs including politics, economics, sports, society, culture and entertainment.
Language (s): Spanish
COMMUNITY NEWSPAPER

La Tribuna de Ciudad Real 158713
Owner: Promecam
Editorial: Calle Alarcos, 4, 4, Ciudad Real 13001
Tel: 34 926 21 53 01
Email: redaccioncr@diariolatribuna.com **Web site:** http://www.latribunadeciudadreal.es
Freq: Daily; **Circ:** 3435
Director: Diego Murillo Herrera
Profile: Regional daily newspaper covering news and current affairs.
Language (s): Spanish
COMMUNITY NEWSPAPER

La Tribuna de Cuenca 408645
Owner: Promecal editorial group
Editorial: Calle Carreteria, 32, 1, Cuenca 16002
Tel: 34 969 23 58 37
Email: redaccion.cuenca@diariolatribuna.com **Web site:** http://www.latribunadecuenca.es
Freq: Daily
Director: Francisco Javier Martínez
Profile: Regional daily newspaper covering news and current affairs.
Language (s): Spanish
COMMUNITY NEWSPAPER

La Verdad 158666
Owner: La Verdad Multimedia, S.A.
Editorial: Camino Viejo de Monteagudo, S/N, Edificio "La Verdad", Murcia 30160 **Tel:** 34 96 836 91 00
Email: local@laverdad.es **Web site:** http://www.laverdad.es
Freq: Daily; **Circ:** 22732
Editor: Manuel Herrero Carcelen
Profile: Regional daily newspaper covering news and current affairs including politics, economics and sports.
Language (s): Spanish
COMMUNITY NEWSPAPER

Viva Cádiz 158706
Owner: Publicaciones del Sur SA
Editorial: Parque Empresarial, C/ de la Investigacion, Jerez De La Frontera 11407 **Tel:** 34 956 167 300
Email: cadiz@publicacionesdelsur.net **Web site:** http://andaluciainformacion.es/cadiz/
Freq: Daily
Editor: José Antonio Mallou Díaz
Profile: Newspaper covering regional news and current affairs including sports, politics and economics.
Language (s): Spanish
COMMUNITY NEWSPAPER

La Voz de Almería 158646
Owner: Novotécnica SA
Editorial: Avenida del Mediterraneo, 159, Almeria 4007 **Tel:** 34 95 018 18 18
Email: lavoz@lavozdealmeria.com **Web site:** http://www.lavozdealmeria.com
Freq: Daily; **Circ:** 6302
Director: Pedro Manuel de la Cruz Alonso
Profile: Newspaper covering local, regional and national news and current affairs including politics, economics, sports, society, culture and entertainment.
Language (s): Spanish
COMMUNITY NEWSPAPER

Sri Lanka

Time Difference: GMT +5.5
National Telephone Code: 94
Continent: Asia
Capital: Colombo

Newspapers

The Bottom Line 502564
Editorial: Rivira Media Corporation Ltd., 742, Maradana Road, Colombo 10 **Tel:** 94 114708888
Email: thebottomline@rivira.lk **Web site:** http://www.thebottomline.lk
Freq: Weekly; **Circ:** 22003 Not Audited
Editor: Nisthar Cassim
Profile: The Bottom Line is a newspaper which covers Business, Economics, Finance, National News, Money, Management, etc.
Language (s): Sinhala
DAILY NEWSPAPER

Daily Mirror 156828
Editorial: Wijeya Newspapers Ltd, No.8, Hunupitiya Cross Road, P.O. Box 1136, Colombo 2
Tel: 94 112 436998
Email: editorial@dailymirror.wnl.lk **Web site:** http://www.dailymirror.lk
Freq: Daily; **Circ:** 32003 Not Audited
Editor: Channaka de Silva; **Editor:** Sanath Dehmond; **Editor in Chief:** Champika Liyanaarachchi
Profile: A daily newspaper.
Language (s): English
DAILY NEWSPAPER

Daily News 156812
Owner: The Associated Newspapers of Ceylon Ltd
Editorial: 35, D.R. Wijewardana Mawatha, Colombo 10 **Tel:** 94 112429211
Email: editor@dailynews.lk **Web site:** http://www.dailynews.lk
Freq: Daily; **Circ:** 65002 Not Audited
Editor: Ranil Wijayapala
Profile: Daily News is a daily newspaper which covers the News, Foreign news, Financial news, Business news, Sports news, Features classified.
Language (s): English
DAILY NEWSPAPER

Dinamina 156821
Owner: The Associated Newspapers of Ceylon Ltd
Editorial: The Associated Newspapers of Ceylon Ltd, No. 35, D.R. Wijewardene Mawatha, Colombo 10
Tel: 94 112429241
Email: editor@dinamina.lk **Web site:** http://www.dinamina.lk
Freq: Daily; **Circ:** 60002 Not Audited
Editor: C. Dodawatta; **Editor:** Vernon Gunasekara; **Editor:** Chandrani Marasinghe
Profile: DINAMINA is a daily newspaper which covers the Political, Cultural, Sports & day to day happen Economics/Foreign/Religion affairs in Sri Lanka & also other countries.
Language (s): Sinhala
DAILY NEWSPAPER

Lankadeepa 156822
Editorial: Wijeya Newspapers Ltd, No.8, Hunupitiya Cross Road, P.O. Box 1136, Colombo 2
Tel: 94 115 383438
Email: epaper@wijeya.lk **Web site:** http://www.lankadeepa.lk
Freq: Daily; **Circ:** 200003 Not Audited
Editor in Chief: Siri Ranasinghe
Profile: Newspaper covering Local, National, Regional and International News, Sports, Features, Entertainment, Business, etc.
Language (s): Sinhala
DAILY NEWSPAPER

Metro News Daily 523708
Editorial: Express Newspapers (Ceylon) Limited, 185, Grandpass Road, Colombo 14 **Tel:** 94 112320927
Email: kesari22@virakesari.lk
Freq: Daily; **Circ:** 30003 Not Audited
Editor in Chief: V. Thevaraj
Profile: Metro News Daily is a radio station targeted for young people. Station covers news and ntertainment.
Language (s): Sinhala
DAILY NEWSPAPER

Metro News Weekly 523707
Editorial: Express Newspapers (Ceylon) Limited, 185, Grandpass Road, Colombo 14 **Tel:** 94 112320927
Email: Kesarizl@virakesari.lk **Web site:** http://www.virakesari.lk
Freq: Weekly; **Circ:** 45003 Not Audited
Editor in Chief: V. Thevaraj
Profile: Metro News Weekly is a newspaper for Young people that covers the Local, National, International News and Entertainment.
Language (s): Sinhala
DAILY NEWSPAPER

The Nation 525276
Editorial: Rivira Media Corporation Pvt Ltd, 742, Maradana Road, Colombo 10 **Tel:** 94 114708888
Email: editor@nation.lk **Web site:** http://www.nation.lk
Freq: Weekly; **Circ:** 97003 Not Audited
Editor in Chief: Gamini Abeywardane
Profile: The Nation is a newspaper which covers politics, defense, national conflicts, business and sports.
Language (s): Sinhala
DAILY NEWSPAPER

Ravaya 843730
Editorial: 83, Piliyandal Rd, Colombo
Email: ravaya@gmail.com **Web site:** http://www.ravaya.lk
Freq: Weekly
Editor: Viktor Ivan
Profile: Provides a nontraditional analysis of social, political, cultural and judicial views of Sri Lanka.
Language (s): Sinhala
DAILY NEWSPAPER

Rivira 502565
Editorial: Rivira Media Corporation Pvt Ltd, 742, Maradana Road, Colombo 10 **Tel:** 94 114708888
Web site: http://www.rivira.lk
Freq: Weekly; **Circ:** 195003 Not Audited
Editor: Upali Tennakoon
Profile: Rivira is a daily newspaper which offers readers news, information, Education, Business, political comments and satire.
Language (s): Sinhala
DAILY NEWSPAPER

Silumina 156834
Owner: The Associated Newspapers of Ceylon Ltd
Editorial: The Associated Newspapers of Ceylon Ltd, No.35, D.R. Wijewardene Mawatha, Colombo 10
Tel: 94 112429261
Email: editor@silumina.lk **Web site:** http://www.silumina.lk/2017/01/01
Freq: Weekly; **Circ:** 250003 Not Audited
Editor: Vajira Palpipa
Profile: SILUMINA is a weekly newspaper which covers the Local News, Foreign news, Financial news, Business news, Sports news, Features classified.
Language (s): Sinhala
DAILY NEWSPAPER

Sunday Lankadeepa 459994
Editorial: Wijeya Newspapers Ltd, No 8, Hunupitiya Cross Road, P.O.Box 1136, Colombo 2
Tel: 94 112423919
Email: epaper@wijeya.lk **Web site:** http://www.lankadeepa.lk
Freq: Weekly; **Circ:** 325003 Not Audited
Editor: Ariyananda Dombagahawatte; **Editor in Chief:** Siri Ranasinghe; **Editor:** Premakeerthi Ranathunga
Profile: Sunday Lankadeepa is a news paper which covers News, Sports, Entertainment, Features, etc.
Language (s): Sinhala
DAILY NEWSPAPER

Sunday Observer 156837
Owner: The Associated Newspapers of Ceylon Ltd
Editorial: The Associated Newspapers of Ceylon Ltd, No.35, D.R. Wijewardene Mawatha, Colombo 10
Tel: 94 11 24 29 231
Email: editor@sundayobserver.lk **Web site:** http://www.sundayobserver.lk
Freq: Weekly; **Circ:** 200003 Not Audited
Editor in Chief: Dinesh Weerawansa
Profile: Sunday Observer is a weekly magazine which covers the Local News, Foreign news, Financial news, Business news, Sports news, Features classifide.
Language (s): English
DAILY NEWSPAPER

The Sunday Times 156690
Editorial: Wijeya Newspapers Ltd, No.8, Hunupitiya Cross Road, Colombo 2 **Tel:** 94 112326247
Email: editor@sundaytimes.wnl.lk **Web site:** http://www.sundaytimes.lk
Freq: Weekly; **Circ:** 100003 Not Audited
Editor in Chief: Sinha Ratnatunga; **Editor:** Faizal Samath
Profile: Covers the local, national, regional and international news, sports and entertainment.
Language (s): English
DAILY NEWSPAPER

Thinakaran 156850
Owner: The Associated Newspapers of Ceylon Ltd.
Editorial: The Associated Newspapers of Ceylon Ltd, No. 35, D.R. Wijewardene Mawatha, Colombo 10
Tel: 94 11 24 29 271
Email: editor.tkn@lakehouse.lk **Web site:** http://www.lakehouse.lk/main
Freq: Daily; **Circ:** 50002 Not Audited
Editor: K. Kunarasha; **Editor:** K. V. Sivasubramanjam
Profile: THINAKARAN is a daily newspaper which covers the Political, Cultural, Sports & day to day incidents, Economics/ Religious affairs.
Language (s): Tamil
DAILY NEWSPAPER

Thinakaran Vara Manjari 156842
Owner: The Associated Newspapers of Ceylon Ltd.
Editorial: The Associated Newspapers of Ceylon Ltd, No 35, D.R. Wijewardene Mawatha, Colombo 10
Tel: 94 112429271
Email: editor.tkn@lakehouse.lk **Web site:** http://www.lakehouse.lk/main
Freq: Weekly; **Circ:** 70002 Not Audited
Editor: K. Kunarasha; **Editor:** Arul Sathyanathan
Profile: Thinakaran Vara Manjari is a weekly magazine which covers the Local and International News, Entertainment, Movies, Sports, etc.
Language (s): Tamil
DAILY NEWSPAPER

Thinakkural 473129
Editorial: Thinakkural, No. 68 Ellie House Road, Colombo 15 **Tel:** 94 11 252-3216
Freq: Daily; **Circ:** 25003 Not Audited
Editor in Chief: V. Thanabalasingham
Profile: Thinakkural is a Tamil language newspaper published in Sri Lanka which talks about the Local, National, Regional and International News. Also publishes a Sunday edition.
Language (s): Sinhala
DAILY NEWSPAPER

Uthayan 473102
Owner: New Uthayan Publications (Pvt) Ltd.
Editorial: 361, Kasturiyar Road, Jaffna
Tel: 94 212229944
Email: editorial@uthayan.com **Web site:** http://www.uthayan.com
Freq: Daily; **Circ:** 16001 Not Audited
Editor in Chief: MV Kanamylnathan; **Managing Director:** E. Saravanapavan
Profile: Covers news.
Language (s): Tamil
DAILY NEWSPAPER

Virakesari Weekly 459996
Editorial: Express Newspapers (Ceylon) Limited, 185, Grandpass Road, Colombo 14 **Tel:** 94 112320927
Email: kesari22@virakesari.lk **Web site:** http://www.virakesari.lk
Freq: Weekly; **Circ:** 150003 Not Audited
Editor: V. Thevaraj
Profile: A radio station which covers the latest News, Politics, Current Affairs, etc.
Language (s): Tamil
DAILY NEWSPAPER

Suriname

Suriname

Time Difference: GMT -3
National Telephone Code: 597
Continent: The Americas
Capital: Paramaribo

Newspapers

Dagblad Suriname 328301
Owner: FaFam Publishing NV
Editorial: Zwartenhovenbrugstraat 154, Paramaribo
Tel: 597 011597426336
Email: general@dbsuriname.com **Web site:** http://www.dbsuriname.com
Freq: Daily; **Circ:** 15000 Not Audited
Editor: James Lal'Mohammad
Profile: Daily newspaper written for the residents of Suriname. It covers national and international news, current-affairs, sport, entertainment and culture.
Language (s): Dutch
Ad Rate: Full Page Mono 6.50
Ad Rate: Full Page Colour 14.50
Currency: United States Dollars
DAILY NEWSPAPER

De Ware Tijd 156811
Owner: Erven C.J. Jong Tjien Fa
Editorial: Malebatrumstraat No 9, Paramaribo
Tel: 597 011597472823
Email: dwt@dwt.net **Web site:** http://dwtdatabase-com.web5.tempwebsite.net
Freq: Daily; **Circ:** 26500 Not Audited
Editor in Chief: Meredith Helstone; **Director:** Steve Jong Tjien Fa; **Editor:** Julian Paneux; **Editor in Chief:** Indra Toelsie
Profile: De Ware Tijd is a daily newspaper covering national news, including politics, economy, culture and sports.
Language (s): Dutch
Ad Rate: Full Page Mono 7.00
Currency: United States Dollars
DAILY NEWSPAPER

De West 156814
Owner: De West
Editorial: Mr. Dr. J.C. de Mirandastr 2-6, Paramaribo
Tel: 597 011597473327
Email: dewest@sr.net **Web site:** http://dagbladdewest.com/
Freq: Daily; **Circ:** 7000 Not Audited
Editor in Chief: George Findlay; **Manager:** Thea Findlay; **Manager:** B. Kasimbeg
Profile: Newspaper covering news and current-affairs; includes politics, economy, sport and culture.
Language (s): Dutch
DAILY NEWSPAPER

Swaziland

Time Difference: GMT +2
National Telephone Code: 268
Continent: Africa
Capital: Mbabane

Newspapers

The Swazi Observer 156954
Owner: Swazi Observer (Pty) Ltd
Editorial: Observer House, 3 West Street, Mbabane
Tel: 268 2 40 49 600
Email: info@observer.org.sz **Web site:** http://www.observer.org.sz
Freq: Daily; **Circ:** 25000 Publisher's Statement
Editor: Alec Lushaba
Profile: Newspaper focusing on national and international news, business, politics, culture and sport.
Language (s): English
DAILY NEWSPAPER

Times of Swaziland 156956
Owner: African Echo (Pty) Ltd.
Editorial: PO Box 156, Mbabane **Tel:** 268 40 42 211
Email: editor@times.co.sz **Web site:** http://www.times.co.sz
Freq: Daily; **Circ:** 25000 Publisher's Statement
Editor: Martin Dlamini; **Advertising Manager:** Ivor Masher
Profile: Newspaper focusing on national and international news, politics, business, entertainment and sport.
Language (s): English
Ad Rate: Full Page Mono 8611.24
Ad Rate: Full Page Colour 12916.80
Currency: Swaziland Emalangeni
DAILY NEWSPAPER

Sweden

Time Difference: GMT +1
National Telephone Code: 46
Continent: Europe
Capital: Stockholm

Newspapers

Aftonbladet 355137
Editorial: Vastra Jarnvagsgatan 21, Stockholm 111 64 **Tel:** 46 8 72 52 000
Email: tipsa@aftonbladet.se **Web site:** http://www.aftonbladet.se
Freq: Daily; **Circ:** 132500 TS
Redaktionschef: Håkan Andreasson; **Chefredaktör, Ansvarig utgivare & VD:** Jan Helin; **Redaktionell Pluschef:** Ted Kudinoff; **Redaktionschef:** Sofia Olsson Olsén
Profile: Aftonbladet är Nordens största, mest lästa dagstidning. Täcker nationella samt internationella aktuella nyheter, evenemang och specialartiklar. Tidningen läses av en bred läsarkrets, varav de flesta bor i och runt Stockholm.
Language (s): Swedish
Ad Rate: Full Page Mono 192200.00
Currency: Sweden Kronor
DAILY NEWSPAPER

Dagen 366443
Owner: Dagen
Editorial: Kungsholmstorg 5, Stockholm 105 33
Tel: 46 8 619 24 00
Email: redaktionen@dagen.se **Web site:** http://www.dagen.se
Freq: 3 Times/Week; **Circ:** 17400 Publisher's Statement
Redaktör: Inger Alestig; **Redaktör:** Therése Alhult; **Nyhetschef:** Rickard Alvarsson; **Redaktionschef:** Thomas Österberg; **Chefredaktör, Ansvarig utgivare & VD:** Felicia Svaeren Ferreira; **Redaktör:** Urban Thoms; **Nyhetschef:** David Wingren; **Redaktör:** Daniel Wistrand
Profile: "Dagen är en politiskt oberoende dagstidning på kristen grund. Visionen är ett samhälle som är genomsyrat av kristen tro och kristna värderingar. Dagen ges ut av Tidnings AB Nya Dagen, som ägs av den nordiska medieföretaget Mentor Media, med huvudkontor i Oslo. Dagen bevakar det som händer inom svensk kristenhet och följer samhällsfrågor utifrån ett kristet perspektiv".Format: Tabloid. Etableringsår: 1945.
Language (s): Swedish
Ad Rate: Full Page Colour 28500.00
Currency: Sweden Kronor
DAILY NEWSPAPER

Dagens ETC 329405
Editorial: Stockholm **Tel:** 46 8 41 03 57 00
Email: dagens@etc.se **Web site:** http://www.etc.se
Freq: Daily; **Circ:** 3900 TS
Nyhetschef: Eigil Söderin
Profile: Dagens ETC är en oberoende dagstidning, utan kopplingar till partier eller intresseorganisationer. Tidningen innehåller politisk debatt, initierad nyhetsjournalistik, kulturbevakning, ekonomimaterial, profilintervjuer och ledande klimatrapportering. Tidningen startades 2005, då som en veckotidning, men sedan 2014 är Dagens ETC en hemburen rikstäckande dagstidning (mån-fre).
Language (s): Swedish
Ad Rate: Full Page Mono 50000.00
Currency: Sweden Kronor
DAILY NEWSPAPER

Dagens Industri 365128
Editorial: Gjorwellsgatan 30, Stockholm 112 60
Tel: 46 8 57 36 50 00
Email: red@di.se **Web site:** http://www.di.se
Freq: Daily; **Circ:** 89100 TS
Redaktör: Mats Brohagen; **Redaktionschef:** Lotta Edling
Profile: Dagens Industri är Sveriges största Näringslivsdagstidning. Tidningen berättar om det svenska och internationella näringslivet på ett kvalificerat, men samtidigt lättillgängligt sätt. Dagens Industri utges av Bonnier Business Press och finns även på webben i form av di.se. För redaktionella medarbetare - se respektive redaktion.
Language (s): Swedish
Ad Rate: Full Page Mono 144300.00
Currency: Sweden Kronor
DAILY NEWSPAPER

Dagens Nyheter 365022
Editorial: Gjorwellsgatan 30, Stockholm 105 15
Tel: 46 8 73 81 000
Email: centralred@dn.se **Web site:** http://www.dn.se
Freq: Daily; **Circ:** 282800
Redaktionschef: Fredrik Björnsson; **Chefredaktör & Ansvarig utgivare:** Peter Wolodarski
Profile: Dagens Nyheter är Sveriges största morgontidning som ges ut i hela landet men med ett fokus framförallt på Stockholmsområdet. Tidningen anser sig vara politiskt "oberoende liberal". DN ingår i Bonnier koncernen. För redaktionella medarbetare - se respektive redaktion.Broadsheet-sized quality newspaper providing in-depth coverage of national and international news, politics, economics, finance, business, culture, sports and events.
Language (s): Swedish
Ad Rate: Full Page Mono 306290.00
Currency: Sweden Kronor
DAILY NEWSPAPER

Expressen 365380
Editorial: Gjorwellsgatan 30, Stockholm 105 16
Tel: 46 8 73 83 000
Email: redaktion@expressen.se **Web site:** http://www.expressen.se
Freq: Daily; **Circ:** 164600 Publisher's Statement
Redaktionschef - Nyheter & Samhälle: Magnus Alselind; **Redaktör:** Christina Lundell; **Chefredaktör & Ansvarig utgivare:** Thomas Mattsson
Profile: Expressen är en av Sveriges största kvällstidningar och täcker en bred mängd ämnen så som nationella samt internationella nyheter, evenemang och artiklar. Expressen säljs i hela landet, men dess största mängd läsare bor i Stockholmsområdet. AB Kvällstidningen Expressen ger ut tre liberala kvällstidningar: Expressen, GT och Kvällsposten.
Language (s): Swedish
Ad Rate: Full Page Mono 189000.00
Currency: Sweden Kronor
DAILY NEWSPAPER

Göteborgs-Posten 355420
Owner: Stampen Media Group
Editorial: Polhemsplatsen 5, Goteborg 405 02
Tel: 46 31 62 40 00
Email: nyheter@gp.se **Web site:** http://www.gp.se
Freq: Daily
Redaktionschef: Ninni Jonzon
Profile: Göteborgs-Posten är Västsveriges största morgontidning, som skriver om det senaste nytt från hela världen men med fokus på Göteborg och Västsverige.
Language (s): Swedish
DAILY NEWSPAPER

GT 158897
Owner: AB Kvällstidningen Expressen
Editorial: Postadress: Box 417, Besoksadress: Kungstorget 2, Goteborg 401 26 **Tel:** 46 31 725 90 01
Email: redaktionen@gt.se **Web site:** http://www.gt.se
Freq: Daily
Chefredaktör/ Ansvarig utgivare: Thomas Mattsson; **Biträdande Nyhetschef:** Johan Sköld
Profile: GT (Göteborgs Tidning) är en daglig kvällstidning som rapporterar regionalt med fokus på nyheter, nöje och sport.
Language (s): Swedish
Ad Rate: Full Page Mono 38400.00
Currency: Sweden Kronor
DAILY NEWSPAPER

Kvällsposten 158818
Owner: AB Kvällstidningen Expressen
Editorial: AB kvallstidningen Expressen, Sodergatan 24, Malmo 205 26 **Tel:** 46 40 602 01 00
Email: redaktionen@kvp.se **Web site:** http://www.expressen.se/kvp
Freq: Daily; **Circ:** 127000
Redaktionschef: Susanne Lindén
Profile: Kvällsposten är en kvällstidning i Sydsverige som handlar om det som berör skåningar, hallänningar, blekingebor och smålänningar. Tidningen har redaktioner i Malmö och Helsingborg. Kvällsposten is a newspaper in southern Sweden which covers news, sports, entertainment & culture in the regions of Skåne, Halland and Småland. The newspaper has editorial offices in Malmö and Helsingborg.
Language (s): Swedish
Ad Rate: Full Page Mono 39650.00
Currency: Sweden Kronor
DAILY NEWSPAPER

Metro 158819
Editorial: Regeringsgatan 105, Stockholm 118 67
Tel: 46 8 402 20 40
Email: redaktionen@metro.se **Web site:** http://www.metro.se
Freq: Daily
Chefredaktör: Christofer Ahlqvist; **Chefredaktör & Ansvarig utgivare:** Linnéa Jonjons; **Nyhetschef:** Karolina Skoglund
Profile: Metro är en gratistidning som delas ut varje morgon i kollektivtrafiken.Tidningen är politiskt obunden och har ca 1,5 miljoner läsare varje dag. Utgivningen i Sverige började i Stockholms tunnelbana 1995 och tidningen finns nu i ett 20-tal länder. Sedan 2014 finns ej längre redaktionerna i Göteborg och Skåne utan verksamheten har koncentrerats till Stockholm. Värmlandsupplagan ges ut av Värmlands folkblad på en franchise-basis.ALLA pressmeddelanden ska skickas till redaktionen@metro.se, INTE till enskilda nyhetschefers mejl. Metro is a free newspaper which is distributed every morning to commuters. The newspaper is politically independent and has around 1,5 million readers every day. Metro was first distributed in the Stockholm underground in 1995, and now exists in just over 20 countries. Metro is owned by Metro International S.A. and publish editions in Stockholm, Gothenburg & Skåne and Värmland (on a franchise-basis by regional newspaper Värmlands folkblad). As the newspaper is free, it is funded by advertising. Metro's articles are written in a simple and concise way, so that its readers can embrace the news.
Language (s): Swedish
Ad Rate: Full Page Mono 208679.00
Currency: Sweden Kronor
DAILY NEWSPAPER

Metro Värmland 498350
Editorial: Varmlands Folkblad, Saterivagen 7, Karlstad 651 03 **Tel:** 46 54 17 55 00
Email: redaktion@metrovarmland.se **Web site:** http://www.metro.se
Circ: 8000
Chefredaktör: Christofer Ahlqvist
Profile: Metro Värmland (fd Riksupplagan fram till maj 2012) ges ut av Värmlands folkblad på en franchise-basis. Gratistidning som distribueras med 100 ställ i Karlstad, Hammarö, Kristinehamn och Kil med omkring 45 000 läsare.
Language (s): Swedish
Ad Rate: Full Page Mono 25000.00
Currency: Sweden Kronor
DAILY NEWSPAPER

Svenska Dagbladet 365295
Owner: Schibsted Sverige AB
Editorial: Vastra jarnvagsgatan 21, Stockholm 105 17
Tel: 46 8 13 50 00
Email: nyheter@svd.se **Web site:** http://www.svd.se
Freq: Daily
Redaktionschef: Niklas Kierkegaard; **Redaktionschef:** Olle Zachrison
Profile: Svenska Dagbladet, SvD, eller "Svenskan" som den även kallas, är en av Sveriges största morgontidningar. Tidningen är baserad i Stockholm och ägs av norska Schibstedt koncernen. Tidningen delas ut med bud i större delen va landet och dess politiska ståndpunkt är "obunden moderat". Svenska Dagbladet or "Svenskan" as it is commonly known as, is one of Sweden's largest morning papers.
Language (s): Swedish
Ad Rate: Full Page Mono 165800.00
Currency: Sweden Kronor
DAILY NEWSPAPER

Sydsvenskan 365359
Owner: Bonnier AB
Editorial: Radmansgatan 16, Malmo 205 05
Tel: 46 40 712 34
Email: 71234@sydsvenskan.se **Web site:** http://www.sydsvenskan.se
Freq: Daily
Redaktör: Malena Henriksson; **Bitr. chef:** Jonas Nyrén; **Chefredaktör & Tf. Ansvarig utgivare:** Pia Rehnquist
Profile: Sydsvenskan är den ledande nyhetstidningen i Skåne. Tidningen grundades 1848 och betecknar sig som oberoende liberal. Sydsvenskan is the biggest news paper in Skåne.
Language (s): Swedish
DAILY NEWSPAPER

News Service/Syndicate

Liberala nyhetsbyrån 313553
Owner: Liberala Landsortstidningar
Editorial: Pressvaningen, RV 7, Riksdagen, Stockholm 100 12 **Tel:** 46 8 786 41 25
Email: redaktionen@lnb.se **Web site:** http://www.lnb.se
Freq: Daily
Profile: Vi förser liberala tidningar över hela Sverige med texter till opinionssidorna. Inkluderar kultur, Media, Ekonomi, Samhälle, Politik, inrikes- och utrikesfrågor.
Language (s): Swedish
NEWS SERVICE/SYNDICATE

LTF Feature 313560
Editorial: Box 2033, Stockholm 103 11
Tel: 46 8 20 70 38
Email: info@ltffeature.com **Web site:** http://www.ltffeature.com
Redaktionschef & Ansvarig utgivare: Ylva Berlin
Profile: LTF - Landsortstidningarnas Featurebyrå. Här kan tidningsredaktioner och medieföretag köpa artiklar, reportage, krönikor och bilder inom jord & skog, djur & natur, politik och miljö.
Language (s): Swedish
NEWS SERVICE/SYNDICATE

News Øresund 823345
Editorial: oresund Media Platform, oresundsinstitutet - ostergatan 9B, Malmo 211 25
Tel: 46 40 30 56 30
Email: redaktion@newsoresund.org **Web site:** http://www.newsoresund.se/
Chefredaktör: Johan Wessman
Profile: Nyhetsbyrån News Øresund är en oberoende dansk-svensk nyhetsbyrå som bevakar av Öresundsregionen. News Øresund bygger på ett nytt open sourcekoncept med en samhällsfinansierad nyhetsbyrå för oberoende journalistik som fritt kommer att erbjuda sitt nyhetsmaterial till media i Sverige och Danmark. Nyhetsbyrån kommer att fokusera på egna nyheter och researchbaserade journalistiska översikter.
Language (s): Danish
NEWS SERVICE/SYNDICATE

Nyheter i Norr - Arjeplog 362356
Editorial: Storgatan 6, Arjeplog 930 90
Tel: 46 961 10 630
Email: info@nyheterinorr.se **Web site:** http://www.nyheterinorr.se
Profile: Nyheter i Norr AB är en nyhetsbyrå som är verksam inom främst Arjeplogs och Arvidsjaurs kommuner. Nyhetsbyrån är ung, verksamheten startade i januari 2005. Nyhetsbyrån tog vid när dagstidningarna Norra Västerbotten och Piteå-Tidningen lade ned sina respektive lokalredaktioner i Arjeplog och Arvidsjaur.
Language (s): Swedish
NEWS SERVICE/SYNDICATE

Nyheter i Norr - Arvidsjaur 362357
Editorial: Domangatan 4 bv, Arvidsjaur 933 31
Tel: 46 960 47 270
Email: info@nyheterinorr.se **Web site:** http://www.nyheterinorr.se
Profile: Nyheter i Norr AB är en nyhetsbyrå som är verksam inom främst Arjeplogs och Arvidsjaurs kommuner.Nyhetsbyrån är ung, verksamheten startade i januari 2005. Nyhetsbyrån tog vid när dagstidningarna Norra Västerbotten och Piteå-Tidningen lade ned sina respektive lokalredaktioner i Arjeplog och Arvidsjaur.
Language (s): Swedish
NEWS SERVICE/SYNDICATE

Nyhetsbyrån Direkt 370553
Editorial: Jakobsbergsgatan 13 plan 6, Stockholm 111 44 **Tel:** 46 8 51 91 79 00
Email: br@direkt.se **Web site:** http://www.direkt.se
Nyhetschef: Mikael Sandbladh; **Nyhetschef:** Kristine Trapp
Profile: Nyhetsbyrån Direkt är Sveriges ledande finansiella nyhetsbyrå med ett trettiotal ledande ekonomijournalister. Nyheterna distribueras elektroniskt via realtidssystem, Internet och intranät. Nyhetsbyrån bevakar nyheter som påverkar kapitalmarknader, tex nyheter om börsföretag, konjunkturstatistik, ekonomisk politik och penningpolitik.De konkurrerande nyhetsbyråerna Direkt och Six gick samman i Norden 31/10 2016. Som en följd av det upphörde SIX News och ersattes av nyheter från Direkt.
Language (s): Swedish
NEWS SERVICE/SYNDICATE

Nyhetsbyrån Direkt - SME Direkt 370548
Editorial: Jakobsbergsgatan 13 plan 6, Stockholm
Tel: 46 8 51 91 79 00
Email: sme@direkt.se **Web site:** http://www.direkt.se
Chefredaktör: Lars Östlund
Profile: SME Direkt är nyhetsbyrån Direkts prognos- och analystjänst med ett 30-tal banker och fondkommissionärer som källor.
Language (s): Swedish
NEWS SERVICE/SYNDICATE

Nyhetsbyrån Siren 889854
Editorial: Bjorns Tradgardsgrand 1, Stockholm 116 21 **Tel:** 46 8 40 88 02 00
Web site: http://www.siren.se
Nyhetschef: Emma Boëthius
Profile: Nyhetsbyrån Siren är en svensk nyhetsbyrån med fokus på myndighetsbevakning. Önskar ej motta pressutskick.
Language (s): Swedish
NEWS SERVICE/SYNDICATE

Nytt från Öresund - NFÖ 313538
Editorial: Malmo **Tel:** 46 40 30 17 90
Email: red@nfo.nu **Web site:** http://www.nfo.nu
Freq: Daily
Profile: Nytt från Öresund är en regional nyhetstjänst som publicerar artiklar, notiser och debattinlägg om Öresundsregionen. Nytt från Öresund ägs och drivs av Rapidus AB.
Language (s): Swedish
NEWS SERVICE/SYNDICATE

Rapidus Nyhetstjänst 313511
Editorial: Box 4140, Stora Nygatan 59, Malmo 203 12 **Tel:** 46 40 30 17 90
Email: rapidus@rapidus.se **Web site:** http://www.rapidus.se
Freq: 2 Times/Week
Chefredaktör: Erik Olausson
Profile: Rapidus är en oberoende nyhetstjänst som bevakar tillväxtbranscherna i Skåne och Köpenhamnsområdet.
Language (s): Swedish
NEWS SERVICE/SYNDICATE

Svenska Nyhetsbyrån 313540
Owner: Svenska Nyhetsbyrån
Editorial: Box 3553, Stockholm 103 69
Tel: 46 8 14 07 50
Email: red@snb.se **Web site:** http://www.snb.se
Chefredaktör: Per Selstam
Profile: Svenska Nyhetsbyrån bevakar svensk inrikespolitik, den offentliga debatten och internationella händelser. De producerar och förmedlar opinionsjournalistik. Svenska Nyhetsbyrån grundades 1948 och har sitt säte i Stockholm. Den nuvarande kundkretsen består huvudsakligen av konservativa, moderata, liberala, borgerliga och obundna tidningar, men även ett par socialdemokratiska finns bland abonnenterna. Byrån är partipolitiskt oberoende.
Language (s): Swedish
NEWS SERVICE/SYNDICATE

TT Nyhetsbyrån 370552
Owner: Tidningarnas Telegrambyrå AB
Editorial: Tidningarnas Telegrambyra, Katarinavagen 15, Stockholm 105 12 **Tel:** 46 8 692 26 00
Email: redaktionen@tt.se **Web site:** http://www.tt.se
Nyhetschef: Lisa Abrahamsson; **Redaktör:** Sara Haldert; **Redaktionschef:** Mats Johansson; **Avdelningschef:** Marc Löfgren; **Redigerare:** Daniel Martinsson; **Btr. Redaktionschef:** Marie Sundström; **Redaktör:** Lisa Wallström
Profile: Tidningarnas Telegrambyrå AB (TT), är en rikstäckande nyhetsbyrå i Sverige. TT bildades 1921 av en grupp storstadstidningar som tog över telegrambyrån De förenade byråerna (DFB), tidigare Svenska Telegrambyrån. År 1922 uppgick även Presstelegrambolaget i TT.
Language (s): Swedish
NEWS SERVICE/SYNDICATE

TT Nyhetsbyrån - Göteborg 313547
Editorial: Box 11901, ostra Hamngatan 30, Goteborg 404 39 **Tel:** 46 31 755 16 00
Email: goteborg@tt.se **Web site:** http://www.tt.se
Profile: TT – Göteborg är en del av Tidningarnas Telegrambyrå AB. TT är en rikstäckande nyhetsbyrå i Sverige som bildades 1921 av en grupp storstadstidningar som tog över telegrambyrån De förenade byråerna (DFB), tidigare Svenska Telegrambyrån. År 1922 uppgick även Presstelegrambolaget i TT.
Language (s): Swedish
NEWS SERVICE/SYNDICATE

TT Nyhetsbyrån - Malmö 313548
Editorial: Radmansgatan 16, 6 tr, Malmo 211 46
Tel: 46 40 10 05 00
Email: malmo@tt.se **Web site:** http://www.tt.se
Profile: TT – Malmö är Tidningarnas Telegrambyrås lokalredaktion. TT är en rikstäckande nyhetsbyrå i Sverige som bildades 1921 av en grupp storstadstidningar som tog över telegrambyrån De förenade byråerna (DFB), tidigare Svenska Telegrambyrån. År 1922 uppgick även Presstelegrambolaget i TT.
Language (s): Swedish
NEWS SERVICE/SYNDICATE

Wighsnews 313555
Editorial: Vrinnevi Hollstad Udde 8, Norrköping 605 95 **Tel:** 46 11 34 33 22
Web site: http://www.wighsnews.se
Profile: Wighsnews är en hemsida som levererar blåljusnyheter till Svensk massmedia. Önskar ej motta pressutskick.
Language (s): Swedish
NEWS SERVICE/SYNDICATE

Community Newspaper

100% Östersund 579073
Editorial: Kyrkgatan 54, Östersund 831 34
Tel: 46 63 13 42 42
Web site: http://www.100procentostersund.se
Freq: Weekly; **Circ:** 32000 Publisher's Statement
Profile: 100% Östersund är stans gratistidning. Vi kommer varje onsdag till alla hushåll i kommunen. Redaktionen önskar endast motta pressutskick gällande Östersund. Epostadress: tidning@100procentostersund.se
Language (s): Swedish
COMMUNITY NEWSPAPER

8 Sidor 158845
Editorial: Palmfeltsvagen 5, Johanneshov 121 17
Tel: 46 8 58 00 28 67
Email: 8sidor@8sidor.se **Web site:** http://www.8sidor.se
Freq: Weekly
Profile: 8 Sidor är en lättläst nyhetstidning som innehåller utrikes/inrikesnyheter, kultur och sport.
Language (s): Swedish
COMMUNITY NEWSPAPER

Alekuriren 222832
Owner: Alekuriren
Editorial: Goteborgsvagen 94, Älvängen 446 33
Tel: 46 30 37 49 940
Email: info@alekuriren.se **Web site:** http://www.alekuriren.se
Freq: Weekly; **Circ:** 13550 Publisher's Statement
Redaktör: Jonas Andersson; **Chefredaktör & Ansvarig utgivare:** Per-Anders Klöversjö
Profile: Alekuriren är en tidning med lokala nyheter, underhållning, sport. Samt kommunpolitik, kommunala nyheter. Tidningen ges ut i Ale kommun samt Lödöse och Nygård varje vecka, och i hela Lilla Edet kommun, sista veckan varje månad.
Language (s): Swedish
Ad Rate: Full Page Mono 14300.00
Ad Rate: Full Page Colour 14300.00
Currency: Sweden Kronor
COMMUNITY NEWSPAPER

Alingsås Tidning 366130
Owner: AB William Michelsens Boktryckeri
Editorial: Sodra Ringgatan 14, Alingsås 441 85
Tel: 46 32 26 70 000
Email: red@alingtid.se **Web site:** http://www.alingsastidning.se
Freq: 3 Times/Week; **Circ:** 12700
Redigerare: Kerstin Brandqvist; **Bitr redaktionschef:** Urban Kärvling
Profile: Lokaltidning med tredagarsutgivning, ägd sedan starten 1865 av familjen Michelsen. Dagsaktuell nyhetstidning på strikt lokal marknad, bevakar kommunala nyheter i Alingsås, Vårgårda och Herrljunga. Sjukvårdsfrågor när de berör dessa tre kommuner. Industri/företags-nyheter när de har lokalt nyhetsvärde.Lokal sport. Lokalt kulturliv
Language (s): Swedish
Ad Rate: Full Page Colour 31700.00
Currency: Sweden Kronor
COMMUNITY NEWSPAPER

AlingsåsKuriren 285922
Owner: AlingsåsKuriren Förvaltnings AB
Editorial: AlingsasKuriren AB, Sodra Ringgatan 13, Alingsås 441 30 **Tel:** 46 32 26 68 300
Email: redaktion@alingsaskuriren.se **Web site:** http://www.alingsaskuriren.se
Freq: Weekly; **Circ:** 26100
Profile: Alingsås Kuriren är en gratisutdelad tidning som delas ut till hushållen i Alingsås, Vårgårda och Sollebrunn. En gång per månad kommer tidningen också ut i Lerums kommun, Herrljunga kommun och Nossebro.
Language (s): Swedish
Ad Rate: Full Page Mono 25200.00
Currency: Sweden Kronor
COMMUNITY NEWSPAPER

Annons-Markna'n 416821
Editorial: Goteborgsv. 15, Bollebygd 517 36
Tel: 46 33 28 41 20
Email: annons@annonsmarknan.se **Web site:** http://www.annonsmarknan.se
Freq: Bi-Weekly
Redaktör: Johanna Molin
Profile: AnnonsMarknan är en lokal tidning i Bollebygd som utkommer var 14:e dag, på onsdagar varannan vecka.
Language (s): Swedish
COMMUNITY NEWSPAPER

Arbetarbladet 158558
Owner: Arbetarbladet AB
Editorial: Hattmakargatan 12, Gävle 801 04
Tel: 46 26 15 93 02
Email: redaktionen@arbetarbladet.se **Web site:** http://www.arbetarbladet.se
Circ: 17100
Nyhetschef: Evelina Davidsson; **Ansvarig utgivare:** Daniel Nordström
Profile: Arbetarbladet är en lokaltidning som ges ut i Gävle samt närliggande kommuner.
Language (s): Swedish
COMMUNITY NEWSPAPER

Arvika Nyheter 158544
Editorial: Box 925, Magasinsgatan 5, Arvika 671 29
Tel: 46 570 71 44 00
Email: redaktion@arvikanyheter.se **Web site:** http://nwt.se/arvika/
Freq: 3 Times/Week
Profile: Arvika Nyheter är en tidning som bevakar lokala nyheter i Arvika och Eda kommun.
Language (s): Swedish
Ad Rate: Full Page Colour 24480.00
Currency: Sweden Kronor
COMMUNITY NEWSPAPER

Backa/Kärra 915911
Editorial: Burggrevegatan 15, Goteborg 411 03
Web site: http://www.litelokalt.se/
Freq: Monthly; **Circ:** 20000
Redaktionschef: Ulf Jörnvik
Profile: Backa/Kärra är en gratistidning som delas ut via VTD och tidningsställ till hushåll i området. Kan kontaktas via formulär på hemsidan: http://www.litelokalt.se/kontakta-oss/
Language (s): Swedish
COMMUNITY NEWSPAPER

Bålsta Upplands-Bro Bladet 222831
Editorial: ostra Jarnvagsgatan 8, Enköping 745 21
Tel: 46 171 15 31 50
Email: manus.balstabladet@direktpress.se **Web site:** http://www.stockholmdirekt.se/balupp/balsta/
Freq: Weekly
Ansvarig Utgivare / VD: Ove Rickardsson
Profile: Bålsta Upplands-Bro Bladet är en gratistidning som distribueras varje vecka till samtliga hushåll i Håbo och Upplands-Bro.
Language (s): Swedish
COMMUNITY NEWSPAPER

Barometern - OT 365930
Owner: Gota Media AB
Editorial: Sodra Langgatan 33, Kalmar 391 88
Tel: 46 48 05 91 00
Email: nyhetschefen@barometern.se **Web site:** http://www.barometern.se
Circ: 39500
Chefredaktör & Ansvarig utgivare: Anders Enström
Profile: Barometern - OT (Oskarshamns- Tidningen) är en lokaltidning som täcker Emmaboda, Hultsfred, Högsby, Kalmar, Mönsterås, Nybro, Oskarshamn, Torsås och Öland. Tidningen kommer ut 6 gånger per vecka.
Language (s): Swedish
Ad Rate: Full Page Mono 66000.00
Currency: Sweden Kronor
COMMUNITY NEWSPAPER

Barometern - OT - Oskarshamns-Tidningen 161401
Owner: Gota Media AB
Editorial: Box 922, Oskarshamn 572 29
Tel: 46 49 15 75 00
Email: redaktion@ot.se **Web site:** http://www.oskarshamnstidningen.se
Circ: 39500
Profile: Oskarshamns redaktion. Vill ej ha pressmedd till enskilda medarbetare.
Language (s): Swedish
Ad Rate: Full Page Mono 66000.00
Currency: Sweden Kronor
COMMUNITY NEWSPAPER

Blekinge Läns Tidning 365931
Owner: Blekinge Läns Tidning AB
Editorial: Ronnebygatan 26, Karlskrona 371 89
Tel: 46 45 57 70 00
Email: nyhetschef@blt.se **Web site:** http://www.blt.se
Freq: Daily; **Circ:** 31800
Profile: Blekinge Läns Tidning (BLT), är en oberoende liberal morgontidning som främst bevakar Blekinge läns lokalnyheter. Tidningen utkommer i västra länsdelen under namnen Karlshamns Allehanda och Sölvesborgs-Tidningen. Sedan 2011 delar Blekinge Läns Tidning webbplats med den andra blekingska tidningen, Sydöstran.
Language (s): Swedish
Ad Rate: Full Page Mono 52560.00
Currency: Sweden Kronor
COMMUNITY NEWSPAPER

Bohusläningen 366074
Owner: Stampen Media Group
Editorial: ostergatan 18, Uddevalla 451 83
Tel: 46 52 29 90 99
Email: redaktionen@bohuslaningen.se **Web site:** http://www.bohuslaningen.se
Freq: Daily; **Circ:** 24500
Profile: Bohusläningen är en lokaltidning i Bohuslän som kommer ut 6 gånger per vecka.
Language (s): Swedish
Ad Rate: Full Page Mono 53148.00
Currency: Sweden Kronor
COMMUNITY NEWSPAPER

BollnäsNytt 222830
Owner: MittMedia AB
Editorial: Box 1059, Stationsgatan 8, Bollnäs 821 12
Tel: 46 27 82 75 50
Email: redaktion@helahalsingland.se **Web site:** http://www.bollnasnytt.se/
Freq: Weekly; **Circ:** 17400 Publisher's Statement
Redaktör: Kristian Westin
Profile: Bollnäs gratistidning, delas ut perioden lördag-måndag varje vecka till samtliga hushåll i kommunen.
Language (s): Swedish
Ad Rate: Full Page Mono 26688.00
Currency: Sweden Kronor
COMMUNITY NEWSPAPER

Borås Tidning 365001
Editorial: Allegatan 67, Borås 501 85
Tel: 46 33 70 00 700
Email: bt.se@bt.se **Web site:** http://www.bt.se
Freq: Daily
Chefredaktör & Ansvarig utgivare: Stefan Eklund; **Nyhetschef:** Hanna Grahn Strömbom; **Redaktionschef / stf ansvarig utgivare::** Anneli Johannisson
Profile: Borås Tidning är en lokal morgontidning som ges ut dagligen i Borås och Sjuhäradsbygden.
Language (s): Swedish
Ad Rate: Full Page Mono 63360.00
Currency: Sweden Kronor
COMMUNITY NEWSPAPER

Borlänge Tidning 158549
Owner: Dalarnas Tidningar
Editorial: Box 29, Borlänge 781 21
Tel: 46 24 36 44 01
Email: bt.red@dt.se **Web site:** http://www.dt.se
Freq: Daily; **Circ:** 15000
Chefredaktör & Ansvarig utgivare: Carl-Johan Bergman; **Nyhetschef:** Maria Svensson
Profile: Borlänge Tidning är en sexdagarstidning inom medieföretaget Dalarnas Tidningar. Tidningen har spridning i Borlänge, Hedemora och Säter. Tidningen är opolitisk men delar ledar- och debattsida med liberala Falu-Kuriren.
Language (s): Swedish
Ad Rate: Full Page Mono 39360.00
Currency: Sweden Kronor
COMMUNITY NEWSPAPER

Dala-Demokraten 158556
Editorial: Zettergrens vag 7-9, Falun 791 29
Tel: 46 23 475 00
Web site: http://www.dalademokraten.se/
Circ: 12800
Chefredaktör: Göran Greider
Profile: Dala-Demokraten (DD) har funnits sedan 1917 och är en fristående socialdemokratisk dagstidning som ges ut i Dalarna. Tidningen är erkänd som en viktig opinionsbildare och ledarsidan är ofta i opposition mot den politik det socialdemokratiska partiet för. Chefredaktör är poeten, författaren och debattören Göran Greider. OBS! Vill ej motta pressreleaser! Skriver enbart om lokala och regionala nyheter.
Language (s): Swedish
Ad Rate: Full Page Colour 40176.00
Currency: Sweden Kronor
COMMUNITY NEWSPAPER

Din Lokaltidning 222829
Editorial: Gavlevagen 76, Sandviken 811 23
Tel: 46 26 24 84 84
Web site: http://www.dinlt.se/
Freq: Weekly; **Circ:** 25000
Ansvarig utgivare: Ann-Louise Kleen
Profile: Redaktionen önskar ej motta pressutskick. Din Lokaltidning bevakar nyheter i Sandvikens och Hofors kommuner med omnejd.
Language (s): Swedish
Ad Rate: Full Page Colour 24500.00
Currency: Sweden Kronor
COMMUNITY NEWSPAPER

Emmaboda Tidning 416260
Editorial: Jenny Nystroms grand 2, Kalmar 392 33
Tel: 46 471 72 02 00
Web site: http://www.emmabodatidning.se
Freq: Monthly; **Circ:** 10100 Not Audited
Ansvarig utgivare: Per-Olof Persson

Profile: Lokal nyhetstidning som täcker området runt Emmaboda. Kommer ut 17 gånger per år. Tidningen önskar ej motta pressutskick.
Language (s): Swedish
Ad Rate: Full Page Colour 15330.00
Currency: Sweden Kronor
COMMUNITY NEWSPAPER

Ena-Håbo Tidningen 577767

Editorial: ostra Jarnvagsgatan 8, Enköping 745 37
Tel: 46 171 338 35
Email: redaktionen.enahabo@direktpress.se **Web site:** http://www.stockholmdirekt.se/enahabo/
Freq: Bi-Weekly; **Circ:** 30000
Ansvarig Utgivare/ VD: Ove Rickardsson
Profile: Ena-Håbo Tidningen är en lokal nyhetstidning som kommer ut en gång i veckan till invånare i Enköping och Håbo.
Language (s): Swedish
Ad Rate: Full Page Colour 15575.00
Currency: Sweden Kronor
COMMUNITY NEWSPAPER

Eskilstuna-Kuriren 158551

Owner: Sörmlands Media AB
Editorial: Rademachergatan 16, Box 120, Eskilstuna 631 02 **Tel:** 46 16 15 61 56
Email: redaktion@ekuriren.se **Web site:** http://www.ekuriren.se
Freq: Daily; **Circ:** 28200
Nyhetschef: Lars Skärlund
Profile: Eskilstuna-Kuriren är Sörmlands största dagstidning, utkommer sex dagar i veckan.
Language (s): Swedish
Ad Rate: Full Page Mono 79056.00
Currency: Sweden Kronor
COMMUNITY NEWSPAPER

Eskilstuna-Kuriren - Strengnäs Tidning 161559

Owner: Sörmlands Media AB
Editorial: Storgatan 14, Strängnäs 645 21
Tel: 46 152 474 00
Email: strangnas@ekuriren.se **Web site:** http://ekuriren.se/nyheter/strangnas
Freq: Daily; **Circ:** 28900
Profile: Strengnäs Tidning är en avläggare till Eskilstuna-Kuriren. Tidningen delar i huvudsak innehåll med Eskilstuna-Kuriren, men har en separat förstasida samt några lokala insidor. Strengnäs tidning ges ut sex dagar i veckan.
Language (s): Swedish
COMMUNITY NEWSPAPER

Extra EK / Extra ST 222801

Editorial: Rademachergatan 16, Eskilstuna 632 20
Tel: 46 16 15 60 00
Email: extra@ekuriren.se **Web site:** http://ekuriren.se/extra
Freq: Weekly; **Circ:** 46120 Publisher's Statement
Profile: Extra EK / Extra ST (fd. Smëjournalen och Strängnäsjournalen) är lokala gratistidningar i Eskilstuna och Strängnäs innehållande gediget innehåll om aktiviteter i stan, föreningsliv, människor i vimlet, studenter och unga familjer. Extra EK och Extra ST ges ut av Eskilstuna-Kuriren.
Language (s): Swedish
Ad Rate: Full Page Colour 19000.00
Currency: Sweden Kronor
COMMUNITY NEWSPAPER

Extra Östergötland 324969

Editorial: Stohagsgatan 6a, Norrköping 601 83
Tel: 46 11 495 88 80
Email: extra@extraostergotland.se **Web site:** http://www.extraostergotland.se
Freq: 3 Times/Week
Redaktionschef / ansvarig utgivare: Mikael Sundgren
Profile: Extra Östergötland är en lokal nyhetstidning i Östergötland som ges ut tre gånger per vecka.
Language (s): Swedish
COMMUNITY NEWSPAPER

Falu Kuriren 158557

Owner: Mittmedia
Editorial: Zettergrens vag 7, Falun 79177
Tel: 46 23 936 00
Email: fk.red@dt.se **Web site:** http://www.dt.se
Freq: Daily
Nyhetschef: Jenny Andreasson; **Chefredaktör & Ansvarig utgivare:** Carl-Johan Bergman;
Nyhetschef: Inger Wallin
Profile: Falu Kuriren är en dagstidning som ges ut 6 gånger per vecka av medieföretaget Dalarnas Tidningar. Tidningen innehåller regionala- & riksnyheter, sport, nöje & kultur, politik och familjesidor. DT Falu kuriren is a newspaper that is published six times per week by the media company Dalarna Newspapers. The newspaper contains regional & national news, sports, entertainment & culture, politics and family pages.
Language (s): Swedish
Ad Rate: Full Page Mono 39744.00
Currency: Sweden Kronor
COMMUNITY NEWSPAPER

Finnveden Nu 218054

Editorial: Storgatsbacken 13, Värnamo 331 30
Tel: 46 370 69 16 40
Email: redaktion@finnveden.nu **Web site:** http://www.finnveden.nu
Freq: Weekly
Redaktionschef & Ansvarig utgivare: Inger Abram Ohlsson
Profile: Finnveden Nu är en gratistidning som ges ut i Värnamo.
Language (s): Swedish
COMMUNITY NEWSPAPER

Folkbladet Västerbotten 158604

Owner: Nya Västerbottens Folkblad AB
Editorial: Box 3164, Forradsvagen 9, Umeå 903 04
Tel: 46 90 17 59 40
Email: redaktionen@folkbladet.nu **Web site:** http://www.folkbladet.nu
Freq: Daily; **Circ:** 8700
Chefredaktör: Anna Lith
Profile: Västerbottens folkblad är en svensk socialdemokratisk dagstidning grundad 1917 som ges ut i Umeåområdet. Tidningens nyhetsbevakning täcker huvudsakligen Västerbottens län.
Language (s): Swedish
Ad Rate: Full Page Mono 27323.00
Currency: Sweden Kronor
COMMUNITY NEWSPAPER

Gefle Dagblad 158559

Owner: MittMedia
Editorial: Hattmakargatan 14, Gävle 801 05
Tel: 46 26 15 96 00
Email: gefle.dagblad@gd.se **Web site:** http://www.gd.se
Freq: Daily
Chefredaktör & Ansvarig utgivare: Anna Gullberg;
Nyhetschef: Magnus Lundquist
Profile: Gefle Dagblad är en nyhetstidning i Gästrikland som kommer ut sju dagar i veckan. Tidningen bevakar områdena runt Gävle, Sandviken, Hofors, Ockelbo och Älvkarleby.
Language (s): Swedish
COMMUNITY NEWSPAPER

Gefle Dagblad - Sandviken 161567

Owner: MittMedia
Editorial: Hyttgatan 14, Sandviken 811 30
Tel: 46 26 15 96 39
Email: sandviken@gd.se **Web site:** http://www.gd.se
Freq: Daily
Profile: Gefle Dagblads nyhetsredaktion i Sandviken. (Bevakar även Hofors och Ockelbo.)
Language (s): Swedish
COMMUNITY NEWSPAPER

Göteborg Direkt - Tidningen Hisingen 573195

Owner: DirektPress Tidningsförlag AB
Editorial: Britta Sahlgrens gata 8 c, Västra Frölunda 421 31 **Tel:** 46 31 7205591
Email: hisingen@gbg.direktpress.se **Web site:** http://www.direktpress.se/goteborg/Hisingen/
Freq: Bi-Weekly; **Circ:** 51000
Chefredaktör & Ansvarig utgivare: Magnus Johansson
Profile: Tidningen Hisingen är en gratis lokaltidning för områdena Säve, Kärra, Tuve, Backa, Lundby, Norra Älvstranden och Torslanda. Ämnesområden: Lokala nyheter, Lokal sport, Lokalt nöje, Lokala människor, Lokala evenemang.
Language (s): Swedish
COMMUNITY NEWSPAPER

Göteborgs Manhattan 915907

Editorial: Burggrevegatan 15, Goteborg 411 03
Web site: http://www.litelokalt.se/
Freq: Monthly
Redaktionschef: Ulf Jörnvik
Profile: Göteborgs Manhattan är en gratistidning som delas ut till hushåll i Kvillebäcken, runt Backaplan, Lindholmen, Eriksberg och Sannegårdshamnen. Nås via kontaktformulär: http://www.litelokalt.se/kontakta-oss/
Language (s): Swedish
COMMUNITY NEWSPAPER

Gotlands Allehanda 158620

Editorial: Visborgsallen 39-41, Box 1284, Visby 621 25 **Tel:** 46 498 20 25 50
Email: redaktion@gotlandsallehanda.se **Web site:** http://www.helagotland.se
Freq: Daily
Redaktionschef & Ansvarig utgivare: Ulrica Fransson Ingelmark
Profile: Gotlands Allehanda är en nyhetstidning som utges på Gotland från måndag till lördag.
Language (s): Swedish
COMMUNITY NEWSPAPER

Gotlands Tidningar 158621

Owner: Gotlandspress AB
Editorial: Visborgsallen 39-41, Box 1284, Visby 621 23 **Tel:** 46 498 20 24 60
Email: redaktion@helagotland.se **Web site:** http://www.helagotland.se
Freq: Daily; **Circ:** 21800
Redaktör: Magnus Ihreskog
Profile: Gotlands Tidningar är en dagstidning som täcker nyheter på lokala nyheter. De två tidningarna Gotlands Folkblad och Gotlänningen slogs ihop till Gotlands Tidningar under början av 80-talet.
Language (s): Swedish
COMMUNITY NEWSPAPER

Hallå Helsingborg 881072

Editorial: Vasatorpsvagen 1, Helsingborg 251 83
Tel: 46 42 489 90 00
Email: redaktion@tidningenhalla.se **Web site:** http://tidningenhalla.se/helsingborg/
Freq: Weekly
Profile: Hallå! Helsingborg är en gratis veckotidningen för invånare i Helsingborgsområdet. Tidningen kommer ut varje onsdag, hem i brevlådan till alla hushåll i kommunen.
Language (s): Swedish
COMMUNITY NEWSPAPER

Hallands Nyheter 366192

Owner: Stampen Media Group
Editorial: UNAVAILABLE, Falkenberg 311 81
Tel: 46 10 471 52 00
Email: redaktionen@hn.se **Web site:** http://www.hn.se
Circ: 27300
Chefredaktör & Ansvarig utgivare: Malin Henrikson;
Nyhetschef: Lena Strömberg
Profile: Hallands Nyheter är din lokaltidning i mellersta Halland. Tidningen kommer ut 6 dagar i veckan.
Language (s): Swedish
Ad Rate: Full Page Colour 47907.00
Currency: Sweden Kronor
COMMUNITY NEWSPAPER

Hallandsposten 365929

Owner: Stampen Media Group
Editorial: Fiskaregatan 21, Halmstad 301 81
Tel: 46 10 471 51 00
Email: redaktionen@hallandsposten.se **Web site:** http://www.hallandsposten.se
Freq: Daily; **Circ:** 29000
Ansvarig utgivare / chefredaktör: Viveka Hedbjörk;
Nyhetschef: Hanna Sjöberg
Profile: Hallandsposten är Hallands största dagstidning med fokus på Halmstad, Laholm och Hylte.
Language (s): Swedish
Ad Rate: Full Page Colour 59350.00
Currency: Sweden Kronor
COMMUNITY NEWSPAPER

Halmstad 7 dagar 770700

Owner: Gratistidningar i Väst AB
Editorial: Nassjogatan 6, Halmstad
Tel: 46 35 219990
Email: redaktion@hstd7dagar.se **Web site:** http://hstd7dagar.se/
Freq: Weekly; **Circ:** 46000
Profile: Den 17:e augusti 2011 lanserades Halmstads nya veckotidning. Halmstad 7 Dagar. En morgontidning för alla Halmstadbor, med ett starkt redaktionellt innehåll, som kommer ut varje onsdag. Tidningen fokuserar på händelser inom Halmstad kommun och på frågor som berör de boende i kommunen.
Language (s): Swedish
COMMUNITY NEWSPAPER

Handelsstaden 731196

Editorial: Nabbtorgsgatan 2, Orebro 701 47
Email: info@hkm.se **Web site:** http://hkm.se/tidningar/handelsstaden/
Freq: Monthly
CEO & Chefredaktör: Stefan Hallenius
Profile: Handelsstaden är en månadstidning som kommer ut i Örebro län. Innehåller kultur, mode, shopping och mycket mer.
Language (s): Swedish
COMMUNITY NEWSPAPER

Helsingborgs Dagblad 366177

Owner: Sydsvenska Dagbladet AB
Editorial: Vasatorpsvagen1, Helsingborg 254 57
Tel: 46 42 489 90 00
Email: redaktionen@hd.se **Web site:** http://www.hd.se
Freq: Daily; **Circ:** 64000
Redaktionschef: Anna Bergenström; **Redigerare:** Hedvig Juhasz-Toth; **Redigerare:** Cilla Nilsson;
Nyhetschef: Sofia Nilsson
Profile: Helsingborgs Dagblad är en regional tidning i Helsingborg. Tidningen utkommer 7 gånger i veckan och innehåller lokala- & regionala nyheter, opinion, inrikes, utrikes, kultur, nöje, sport och ekonomi. 2001 sammanslogs Helsingborgs Dagblad och Nordvästra Skånes Tidningar & då skapades en gemensam nordvästskånsk tidning i tre editioner: Helsingborgs Dagblad, Nordvästra Skånes Tidningar och Landskrona Posten. De är tillsammans idag landets femte största morgontidning. Tidningarna har en spridning över Hässleholm, Ängelholm, Helsingborg/ Landskrona, Halmstad, Halland & Skåne.Helsingborg Dagblad is a regional newspaper in Helsingborg. The newspaper is published seven days a week and includes local & regional news, opinion page, domestic- & foreign affairs, culture, entertainment, sports and finance.
Language (s): Swedish
Ad Rate: Full Page Mono 43856.00
Currency: Sweden Kronor
COMMUNITY NEWSPAPER

Hemmets Vän 158626

Editorial: Hagmarksgatan 12, Orebro 702 02
Tel: 46 19 16 54 20
Email: redaktion@hemmetsvan.se **Web site:** http://www.hemmetsvan.se
Freq: Weekly
Chefredaktör/ Ansvarig Utgivare: Åke Hällzon
Profile: Hemmets Vän är en oberoende kristdemokratisk nyhetstidning som kommer ut en gång i veckan.
Language (s): Swedish
COMMUNITY NEWSPAPER

Höglandet Nu 498334

Editorial: Nybrogatan 8, Eksjö 575 31
Tel: 46 36 30 94 90
Email: redaktion@hogland.nu **Web site:** http://www.nutidningen.nu
Freq: Bi-Weekly
Profile: Höglandet Nu är en lokal gratis nyhetstidning.
Language (s): Swedish
COMMUNITY NEWSPAPER

Hudiksvalls Tidning 158565

Owner: Hälsingetidningar AB
Editorial: Box 1201, Vastra Tullgatan 18-20, Hudiksvall 824 15 **Tel:** 46 650 355 00
Email: redaktion@ht.se **Web site:** http://www.helahalsingland.se
Freq: Daily; **Circ:** 12600
Bilageredaktör: Torkel Bohjort; **Nyhetschef:** Lisa Hall; **Redigerare:** Pia Trybom
Profile: Hudiksvall Tidning är en lokal nyhetstidning som kommer ut sex gånger per vecka.
Language (s): Swedish
Ad Rate: Full Page Colour 42720.00
Currency: Sweden Kronor
COMMUNITY NEWSPAPER

Jönköping Nu 395593

Owner: Lokalmedia Nu i Sverige AB
Editorial: Kapellgatan 1, Jönköping 551 14
Tel: 46 36 30 94 90
Email: redaktion@jonkoping.nu **Web site:** http://www.nutidningen.nu
Freq: Weekly
Profile: Jönköping Nu är en lokal veckotidning som kommer ut varje torsdag i Jönköping, Habo och Mullsjö kommuner.
Language (s): Swedish
COMMUNITY NEWSPAPER

Jönköpings-Posten 365209

Owner: Jönköpings-Posten
Editorial: UNAVAILABLE, Jönköping 551 80
Tel: 46 36 30 40 50
Web site: http://www.jp.se/
Freq: Daily; **Circ:** 31400
Redaktör: Janne Johansson; **Biträdande redaktionschef:** Marie Johansson Flyckt;
Redaktionschef: Patricia Svensson
Profile: Jönköpings-Posten är en lokal nyhetstidning som täcker Jönköping, Mullsjö. Habo, Huskvarna och Vaggeryd kommun. Tidningen kommer ut sex dagar i veckan.
Language (s): Swedish
COMMUNITY NEWSPAPER

KalmarPosten 416262

Owner: Gota Media AB
Editorial: Jenny Nystroms grand 2, Kalmar 392 33
Tel: 46 480 72 02 00
Email: tidningen@kalmarposten.se **Web site:** http://www.kalmarposten.se
Freq: Weekly; **Circ:** 76700 Publisher's Statement
Profile: KalmarPosten är en gratis veckotidning som kommer ut på onsdagar till alla hushåll & företag i Kalmar, Torsås, Nybro kommuner och hela Öland. KalmarPosten is a free weekly newspaper that comes out to all households and businesses in Kalmar, Torsås, Nybro municipalities and Öland every Thursday.
Language (s): Swedish
Ad Rate: Full Page Mono 38873.00
Currency: Sweden Kronor
COMMUNITY NEWSPAPER

Katrineholms-Kuriren 158573

Owner: Katrineholms-Kuriren AB
Editorial: Kopmangatan 2, Katrineholm 641 22
Tel: 46 150 728 00
Email: redaktion@kkuriren.se **Web site:** http://www.kkuriren.se
Freq: Daily; **Circ:** 10400
Chefredaktör: Elisabet Bäck; **Redaktör:** Ingela Gustafsson; **Nyhetschef:** Henrik Wising
Profile: Lokal dagstidning för Katrineholms, Vingåkers och delar av Flens och Finspångs kommuner. Utkommer 6 gånger per vecka.
Language (s): Swedish
Ad Rate: Full Page Colour 37000.00
Currency: Sweden Kronor
COMMUNITY NEWSPAPER

Katrineholms-Kuriren - Vingåker 160335

Owner: Katrineholms-Kuriren
Editorial: Bondegatan 8, Vingåker 643 30
Tel: 46 151 120 50
Email: vingaker@kkuriren.se **Web site:** http://www.kkuriren.se
Circ: 12900
Profile: Katrineholms-Kurirens lokalredaktion i Vingåker.
Language (s): Swedish
COMMUNITY NEWSPAPER

KHaktuellt 416817

Owner: Svensk Mediakonsult AB
Editorial: Ilanda Gard 120, Karlstad 653 50
Tel: 46 54 18 77 18
Email: redaktionen@svenskmediakonsult.se **Web site:** http://www.khaktuellt.com/
Freq: Monthly
Profile: KHaktuellt är södra Värmlands största reklamfinansierade lokaltidning. Tidningen innehåller lokala nyheter och aktualiteter i första hand samt annat featurematerial som anses höja läsvärdet i tidningen.
Language (s): Swedish
COMMUNITY NEWSPAPER

Kristianstadsbladet 365351
Owner: Skånemedia AB
Editorial: Nya Boulevarden 4, Kristianstad 291 84
Tel: 46 44 18 55 00
Email: nyheter@kristianstadsbladet.se **Web site:** http://www.kristianstadsbladet.se
Freq: Daily; **Circ:** 25900
Redigerare: Helena Heliosson; **Nyhetschef:** Bengt-Inge Schölin; **Chefredaktör & Ansvarig Utgivare:** Jörgen Svensson; **Redaktör:** Lotta Tholin
Profile: Kristianstadsbladet är en lokal dagstidning i Kristianstad som kommer ut 6 dagar i veckan.
Language (s): Swedish
Ad Rate: Full Page Colour 54480.00
Currency: Sweden Kronor
COMMUNITY NEWSPAPER

Kristinehamns-Aktuellt 416263
Editorial: Kungsgatan 46, Box 158, Kristinehamn 681 23 **Tel:** 46 550 19 900
Email: redaktion@kristinehamnsaktuellt.se **Web site:** http://www.kristinehamnsaktuellt.se
Freq: Monthly
Chefredaktör & Ansvarig utgivare: Roland Thomas
Profile: Kristinehamns-Aktuellt är en lokal nyhetstidning som delas ut varje månad till alla hushåll och företag i Kristinehamns, Storfors och Gullspångs kommuner.
Language (s): Swedish
Ad Rate: Full Page Colour 14500.00
Currency: Sweden Kronor
COMMUNITY NEWSPAPER

Kungälvs-Posten 223116
Editorial: Nytorget 1, Kungälv 442 15
Tel: 46 303 20 68 00
Email: redaktion@kungalvsposten.se **Web site:** http://www.kungalvsposten.se
Freq: 2 Times/Week
Chefredaktör: Karin Henriksson
Profile: Kungälvs-Posten är en lokal nyhetstidning som kommer två i veckan i Kungälvs kommun.
Language (s): Swedish
Ad Rate: Full Page Colour 22150.00
Currency: Sweden Kronor
COMMUNITY NEWSPAPER

Kvibergs-Staden 915913
Editorial: Burggrevegatan 15, Goteborg 411 03
Email: mats@litelokalt.se **Web site:** http://www.kvibergs-staden.se/
Freq: Monthly; **Circ:** 20000
Redaktionschef: Ulf Jörnvik
Profile: Kvibergs-Staden är en gratistidning som delas ut via VTD och tidningsställ till hushåll i området.
Language (s): Swedish
COMMUNITY NEWSPAPER

Länstidningen Östersund 350401
Editorial: Kyrkgatan 52, Östersund 831 89
Tel: 46 63 15 55 30
Email: redaktionen@ltz.se **Web site:** http://www.ltz.se
Circ: 14300
Nyhetschef: Lasse Ljungmark; **Nyhetschef:** Alexandra Westerlund Karlsson
Profile: Länstidningen Östersund är en lokalt ägd morgontidning med huvudsakligt spridning i Jämtlands län. Huvudredaktionen finns i Östersund och tidningen har även lokalredaktioner i Bräcke och Ragunda. Partibeteckningen är oberoende socialdemokratisk. LT kommer ut sex dagar i veckan. Förutom papperstidningen finns en nätversion av tidningen på webbadressen www.ltz.se.
Language (s): Swedish
Ad Rate: Full Page Colour 25056.00
Currency: Sweden Kronor
COMMUNITY NEWSPAPER

Länstidningen Södertälje 366058
Editorial: Storgatan 3-5, Södertälje 151 82
Tel: 46 8 55 09 21 00
Email: redaktion@lt.se **Web site:** http://www.lt.se
Freq: Daily; **Circ:** 11600
Redigerare: Gert Fundin; **Nyhetschef:** Monika Nilsson Lysell
Profile: Länstidningen Södertälje är en lokaltidning som kommer ut sex dagar i veckan i printformat och som e-tidning på söndagar.
Language (s): Swedish
Ad Rate: Full Page Colour 39936.00
Currency: Sweden Kronor
COMMUNITY NEWSPAPER

Länstidningen Södertälje - Nykvarn & Järna 158141
Editorial: Järna **Tel:** 46 8 550 921 45
Email: mathias.jonsson@lt.se **Web site:** http://lt.se/nyheter/jarna
Freq: Daily
Redaktör: Mathias Jonsson
Profile: Länstidningen Södertäljes lokalredaktion för Nykvarn och Järna.
Language (s): Swedish
COMMUNITY NEWSPAPER

Lerums Tidning 161613
Editorial: Goteborgsvagen 3, Lerum 443 30
Tel: 46 302 51 050
Web site: http://www.lerumstidning.se
Freq: Weekly; **Circ:** 18300
Profile: Lerums lokaltidning är en lokaltidning som utkommer varje torsdag morgon till alla hushåll i kommunen tillsammans med andra morgontidningar av Västsvensk Tidningsdistribution. Redaktionen önskar ej motta pressutskick.
Language (s): Swedish
Ad Rate: Full Page Mono 22600.00
Currency: Sweden Kronor
COMMUNITY NEWSPAPER

Limhamns-Tidningen 416266
Editorial: Jarnvagsgatan 74, Limhamn 216 16
Tel: 46 40 15 74 77
Web site: http://www.limhamnstidningen.se/
Freq: Bi-Weekly
Profile: Limhamns-Tidningen är en lokal nyhetstidning som ges ut till de boende i regionerna Limhamn, Bunkeflostrand, Klagshamn och Vintrie.
Language (s): Swedish
COMMUNITY NEWSPAPER

Linköpings Tidning/Kinda-Posten 335002
Editorial: Torggatan 1, Kisa 590 37
Tel: 46 492 16 000
Email: redaktion@kindaposten.se **Web site:** http://www.linkopingstidning.se
Freq: Daily
Ansvarig utgivare & VD: Bengt Ingemarsson
Profile: Linköpings Tidning/Kinda-Posten är en edition av Vimmerby Tidning. Tidningen utkommer måndag-lördag och är en prenumererad dagstidning innehållande lokala nyheter. Linköpings Tidning/Kinda-Posten har redaktioner i Linköping respektive Kisa. Tidningsgruppen Swepress som Linköpings Tidning/Kinda-Posten tillhör innehåller även Vimmerby Tidning, Ölandsbladet, Växjöbladet, Kalmar Läns Tidning och LinköpingsPosten. Detta gör att redaktionerna tillsammans täcker ett område som omfattar i stort sett hela Småland och Öland, samt Östergötland till Linköping. Textutbyte sker dagligen mellan alla redaktioner.
Language (s): Swedish
COMMUNITY NEWSPAPER

Linköpings-Posten 416825
Editorial: Roxviksgatan 14, Linköping 582 73
Tel: 46 13 25 32 00
Email: redaktion@linkopingsposten.se **Web site:** http://www.linkopingsposten.se
Freq: Weekly; **Circ:** 77400
Redaktionschef: Alf Wesik
Profile: Linköpings-Posten är en gratis veckotidning för invånarna i Linköpings kommun. Tidningen har cirka 50% redaktionellt innehåll och täcker lokala nyheter, samhälle, familj & sport.
Language (s): Swedish
Ad Rate: Full Page Mono 38160.00
Currency: Sweden Kronor
COMMUNITY NEWSPAPER

Ljusnan 158546
Owner: Hälsingetidningar AB
Editorial: Box 1059, Bollnäs 821 12 **Tel:** 46 278- 275 40
Email: nyhetschefen@ljusnan.se **Web site:** http://www.helahalsingland.se/bollnas
Circ: 13000
Bilageredaktör: Torkel Bohjort; **Nyhetschef:** Sofia Rohlin
Profile: Ljusnan är en dagstidning för södra Hälsingland med utgivningsort Bollnäs och primärt utgivningsområde Bollnäs och Ovanåker. Tidningens politiska inriktning är oberoende liberal.
Language (s): Swedish
Ad Rate: Full Page Colour 20160.00
Currency: Sweden Kronor
COMMUNITY NEWSPAPER

Lokaltidningen Alvesta 578955
Editorial: Linnegatan 6B, Växjo 352 33
Tel: 46 10 20 64 532
Email: redaktion.alvesta@lokaltidningen.se **Web site:** http://alvesta.lokaltidningen.se/
Circ: 12285
Profile: Lokaltidningen Alvesta med lokala reportage inom sport, kultur och nyheter.
Language (s): Swedish
Ad Rate: Full Page Colour 17827.00
Currency: Sweden Kronor
COMMUNITY NEWSPAPER

Lokaltidningen Ängelholm 158211
Editorial: Garnisonsgatan 25C, Helsingborg 254 66
Tel: 46 10 20 64 526
Email: redaktion.angelholm@lokaltidningen.se **Web site:** http://angelholm.lokaltidningen.se
Circ: 20200
Nyhetschef: Anders Sjölin; **Redaktör:** Lotta Venhagen
Profile: Lokaltidningen Ängelholm med lokala reportage inom sport, kultur och nyheter.
Language (s): Swedish
Ad Rate: Full Page Colour 21500.00
Currency: Sweden Kronor
COMMUNITY NEWSPAPER

Lokaltidningen Backa/Kärra 343439
Editorial: Martinsson Saljmedia, Box 87, Hisings Kärra 425 02
Email: leif@tidningenbk.se **Web site:** http://www.tidningenbk.se
Freq: Monthly
Ansvarig utgivare: Leif Martinsson
Profile: Lokaltidning som täcker stadsdelarna Backa och Kärra i Göteborg.
Language (s): Swedish
COMMUNITY NEWSPAPER

Lokaltidningen Hässleholm 158202
Editorial: Tredalagatan 3, Kristianstad 291 34
Tel: 46 10 20 64 529
Email: redaktion.hassleholm@lokaltidningen.se **Web site:** http://hassleholm.lokaltidningen.se/
Circ: 25600
Profile: Lokaltidningen Hässleholm med lokala reportage inom sport, kultur och nyheter.
Language (s): Swedish
Ad Rate: Full Page Colour 21500.00
Currency: Sweden Kronor
COMMUNITY NEWSPAPER

Lokaltidningen Helsingborg 158144
Owner: Politikens Lokalaviser
Editorial: Garnisonsgatan 25C, Helsingborg 254 66
Tel: 46 42 19 47 09
Email: redaktion.hbg@lokaltidningen.se **Web site:** http://helsingborg.lokaltidningen.se
Freq: Weekly; **Circ:** 64000
Nyhetschef: Anders Sjölin
Profile: Lokaltidningen Helsingborg är en lokal gratistidning som riktar sig till gammal som ung. Tidningen innehåller lokala reportage, nöje, kultur, samhällsdebatt samt allt som är intressant för de lokala läsarna. Redaktionen skriver även både barn- & ungdomssidor.
Language (s): Swedish
Ad Rate: Full Page Mono 44256.00
Currency: Sweden Kronor
COMMUNITY NEWSPAPER

Lokaltidningen Höganäs 158208
Editorial: Garnisonsgatan 25C, Helsingborg 254 66
Tel: 46 10 20 64 525
Email: redaktion.hoganas@lokaltidningen.se **Web site:** http://hoganas.lokaltidningen.se/
Circ: 13100
Profile: Lokaltidningen Höganäs med lokala reportage inom sport, kultur och nyheter.
Language (s): Swedish
Ad Rate: Full Page Colour 16490.00
Currency: Sweden Kronor
COMMUNITY NEWSPAPER

Lokaltidningen Kävlinge Nya 416265
Editorial: Hantverkaregatan 18, Arlov, Unavailable 232 34 **Tel:** 46 10 20 64 522
Email: redaktion.kavlingenya@lokaltidningen.se **Web site:** http://kavlinge.lokaltidningen.se/
Freq: Bi-Weekly; **Circ:** 30000 Publisher's Statement
Nyhetschef: Marek Stefaniak
Profile: Lokaltidningen Kävlinge Nya med lokala reportage inom sport, kultur och nyheter.
Language (s): Swedish
Ad Rate: Full Page Colour 20700.00
Currency: Sweden Kronor
COMMUNITY NEWSPAPER

Lokaltidningen Kristianstad 158199
Editorial: Karlsgatan 12, Kristianstad 291 59
Tel: 46 10 20 64 528
Email: redaktion.kristianstad@lokaltidningen.se **Web site:** http://kristianstad.lokaltidningen.se/
Circ: 50200
Redaktör: Paola Nordgren
Profile: Lokaltidningen Kristianstad är en lokal gratistidning som riktar sig till boende i Kristianstad, Bromöllas och Östra Göinges kommuner.
Language (s): Swedish
Ad Rate: Full Page Mono 32448.00
Currency: Sweden Kronor
COMMUNITY NEWSPAPER

Lokaltidningen Landskrona & Svalöv 158209
Editorial: Hantverkaregatan 18, Arlov, Unavailable 232 34 **Tel:** 46 10 20 64 525
Email: nyhetsdesk@lokaltidningen.se **Web site:** http://landskrona.lokaltidningen.se/
Freq: Weekly; **Circ:** 6500
Nyhetschef: Anders Sjölin
Profile: Lokaltidningen för Landskrona och Svalöv. Utkommer en gång i veckan.
Language (s): Swedish
Ad Rate: Full Page Colour 12400.00
Currency: Sweden Kronor
COMMUNITY NEWSPAPER

Lokaltidningen Limhamn/Bunkeflo 578958
Editorial: Hantverkargatan 18, Arlov, Unavailable 232 34 **Tel:** 46 10 20 64 520
Email: redaktion.malmo@lokaltidningen.se **Web site:** http://malmo.lokaltidningen.se/
Freq: Weekly; **Circ:** 13642 Publisher's Statement
Redaktör: Markus Celander
Profile: Lokaltidningen Limhamn/Bunkeflo med lokala reportage inom sport, kultur och nyheter.
Language (s): Swedish
Ad Rate: Full Page Colour 28500.00
Currency: Sweden Kronor
COMMUNITY NEWSPAPER

Lokaltidningen Ljungby 578954
Editorial: Linnegatan 6B, Växjo 352 33
Tel: 46 10 20 64 531
Email: redaktion.ljungby@lokaltidningen.se **Web site:** http://ljungby.lokaltidningen.se/
Circ: 13900
Profile: Lokaltidningen Ljungby med lokala reportage inom sport, kultur och nyheter.
Language (s): Swedish
Ad Rate: Full Page Colour 17827.00
Currency: Sweden Kronor
COMMUNITY NEWSPAPER

Lokaltidningen LommaBladet 416267
Editorial: Hantverkaregatan 18, Arlov, Unavailable 232 34 **Tel:** 46 10 20 64 522
Email: redaktion.lommabladet@lokaltidningen.se **Web site:** http://lommabladet.lokaltidningen.se/
Freq: Bi-Weekly; **Circ:** 28100 Not Audited
Nyhetschef: Marek Stefaniak
Profile: Lokaltidningen LommaBladet med lokala reportage inom sport, kultur och nyheter.
Language (s): Swedish
Ad Rate: Full Page Colour 20104.00
Currency: Sweden Kronor
COMMUNITY NEWSPAPER

Lokaltidningen Lund 158200
Editorial: Hantverkaregatan 18, Lund 232 34
Tel: 46 46 20 64 521
Email: nyhetsdesk@lokaltidningen.se **Web site:** http://lund.lokaltidningen.se
Freq: Weekly; **Circ:** 52700
Profile: Lokaltidningen Lund är en gratistidning som bevakar av nyheter, sport, kultur och bostad i Lunds kommun. Tidningen delas ut till samtliga hushåll i Lunds kommun.
Language (s): Swedish
Ad Rate: Full Page Mono 43584.00
Currency: Sweden Kronor
COMMUNITY NEWSPAPER

Lokaltidningen Malmö 579052
Editorial: Hantverkaregatan 18, Malmo 232 34
Tel: 46 40 25 44 50
Email: redaktion.malmo@lokaltidningen.se **Web site:** http://malmo.lokaltidningen.se
Freq: Weekly; **Circ:** 124150
Profile: Lokaltidningen Malmö är en gratis veckotidning som delas ut till invånare i Malmöområdet. Tidningen innehåller lokala nyheter, nöje, kultur & samhälle.
Language (s): Swedish
COMMUNITY NEWSPAPER

Lokaltidningen Mellanskåne 158201
Editorial: Sodergatan 5, Eslöv 241 30
Tel: 46 10 20 64 523
Email: redaktion.mellanskane@lokaltidningen.se **Web site:** http://mellanskane.lokaltidningen.se
Circ: 29100
Nyhetschef: Marek Stefaniak
Profile: Lokaltidningen Mellanskåne med lokala reportage inom sport, kultur och nyheter.
Language (s): Swedish
Ad Rate: Full Page Colour 21000.00
Currency: Sweden Kronor
COMMUNITY NEWSPAPER

Lokaltidningen Söderåsen 335010
Editorial: Garnisonsgatan 25C, Helsingborg 254 66
Tel: 46 431 881 22
Email: nyhetsdesk@lokaltidningen.se **Web site:** http://bjuv.lokaltidningen.se/
Freq: Weekly
Profile: Lokaltidningen Söderåsen bevakar Klippan, Perstorp, Bjuv, Åstorp samt Örkelljunga kommun och ges ut varje onsdag.
Language (s): Swedish
COMMUNITY NEWSPAPER

Lokaltidningen Stenungsund Tjörn Orust 285924
Editorial: Strandvagen 54, Stenungsund 444 21
Tel: 46 303 72 82 30
Email: redaktion@lokaltidningensto.se **Web site:** http://lokaltidningensto.se/
Freq: Weekly
Profile: Lokaltidningen Stenungsund Tjörn Orust är en prenumererad lokal morgontidning. Tidningen innehåller nyheter, sport och de senaste inläggen i den lokala debatten. Lokaltidningen Stenungsund Tjörn Orust utkommer varje tisdag och lördag.
Language (s): Swedish
Ad Rate: Full Page Mono 31000.00
Ad Rate: Full Page Colour 26400.00
Currency: Sweden Kronor
COMMUNITY NEWSPAPER

Lokaltidningen Tomelilla-Simrishamn 579081
Editorial: Hantverkaregatan 18, Arlov, Unavailable 232 34 **Tel:** 46 10 20 64 527
Email: redaktion.ystad@lokaltidningen.se **Web site:** http://ystad.lokaltidningen.se/
Circ: 10000
Profile: Lokaltidningen Tomelilla- Simrishamn med lokala reportage inom sport, kultur och nyheter.
Language (s): Swedish
COMMUNITY NEWSPAPER

Lokaltidningen Trelleborg 498343
Owner: Politikens Lokalaviser
Editorial: Hantverkaregatan 18, Arlov, Unavailable 232 34 **Tel:** 46 10 20 64 520
Email: redaktion.trelleborg@lokaltidningen.se **Web site:** http://trelleborg.lokaltidningen.se
Circ: 34600

Sweden

Profile: Lokaltidningen Trelleborg med lokala reportage inom sport, kultur och nyheter.
Language (s): Swedish
Ad Rate: Full Page Colour 16600.00
Currency: Sweden Kronor
COMMUNITY NEWSPAPER

Lokaltidningen Västbo Andan
222789

Editorial: Torggatan 10, Gislaved 332 30
Tel: 46 10 20 64 533
Email: redaktion.gislaved@lokaltidningen.se Web site: http://vastboandan.lokaltidningen.se/
Freq: Weekly; Circ: 24400 RS
Profile: Lokaltidningen Västbo Andan är en lokal veckoutdelad gratistidning med en ambition belysa positiva nyheter i regionen. Tidningen ges ut till samtliga hushåll och företag i Gislaved- och Gnosjö kommuner, det vill säga Gislaved, Smålandsstenar, Anderstorp, Hestra, Reftele, Gnosjö, Hillerstorp, Kulltorp. Dessutom Mossebo med flera orter.
Language (s): Swedish
Ad Rate: Full Page Colour 18720.00
Currency: Sweden Kronor
COMMUNITY NEWSPAPER

Lokaltidningen Vellinge - Näset
578962

Editorial: Hantverkaregatan 18, Arlov, Unavailable 232 34 Tel: 46 10 20 64 520
Email: redaktion.vellinge@lokaltidningen.se Web site: http://vellinge.lokaltidningen.se/
Circ: 13200
Profile: Lokaltidningen Vellinge - Näset med lokala reportage inom sport, kultur och nyheter.
Language (s): Swedish
Ad Rate: Full Page Colour 14235.00
Currency: Sweden Kronor
COMMUNITY NEWSPAPER

Lokaltidningen Ystad
579083

Owner: Politikens Lokalaviser
Editorial: Hantverkaregatan 18, Arlov, Unavailable 232 34 Tel: 46 10 20 64 527
Email: redaktion.ystad@lokaltidningen.se Web site: http://ystad.lokaltidningen.se/
Circ: 13813
Profile: Lokaltidningen Ystad med lokala reportage inom sport, kultur och nyheter.
Language (s): Swedish
COMMUNITY NEWSPAPER

Magazinet
158139

Editorial: Storgatan 1, Växjö 352 33
Tel: 46 470 71 99 50
Email: lena.olofsson@magazinet.nu Web site: http://www.magazinet.nu
Freq: Weekly; Circ: 62000
Redkationschef: Lena Olofsson
Profile: Magazinet är Kronobergs största nyhetstidning. Magazinet är en annonstidning som ges ut en gång i veckan till alla hushåll i Växjö, Alvesta, Lessebo och Tingsryds kommuner.
Language (s): Swedish
Ad Rate: Full Page Mono 31200.00
Currency: Sweden Kronor
COMMUNITY NEWSPAPER

Mälaröarnas Nyheter
416269

Tel: 46 8 56 03 58 00
Email: red@malaroarnasnyheter.se Web site: http://www.malaroarnasnyheter.se/
Freq: Bi-Weekly
Redaktör: Lo Bäcklinder; Redaktör: Ewa Linnros; Ansvarig utgivare: Laila Westerberg
Profile: Mälaröarnas Nyheter är en lokal tidning med nyheter som rör Ekerö kommun.
Language (s): Swedish
COMMUNITY NEWSPAPER

Malmö-Tidningen
416268

Editorial: Jarnvagsgatan 74, Limhamn 216 16
Tel: 46 40 15 74 77
Web site: http://malmotidningen.se/
Freq: Bi-Monthly
Ansvarig utgivare: Karl-Heinz Forsberg
Profile: Malmö-Tidningen är en tidning med lokalnyheter för Malmö. Redaktionen önskar ej motta pressutskick.
Language (s): Swedish
COMMUNITY NEWSPAPER

Mariestads-Tidningen
158586

Editorial: Stockholmsvagen 21, Mariestad 542 23
Tel: 46 501 68 700
Email: redaktion@mariestadstidningen.se Web site: http://www.mariestadstidningen.se
Circ: 11500
Ansvarig utgivare, Chefredaktör: Karin Eriksson; Nyhetschef: Stefan Östman
Profile: Mariestads-Tidningen är en lokal morgontidning med primärt utgivningsområde i Mariestads, Töreboda och Gullspångs kommuner.
Language (s): Swedish
Ad Rate: Full Page Mono 31800.00
Currency: Sweden Kronor
COMMUNITY NEWSPAPER

Markbladet
222823

Editorial: Box 113, Kinna 511 21
Tel: 46 320 20 91 40
Email: redaktion@markbladet.se Web site: http://www.markbladet.se
Freq: Weekly; Circ: 23500 Publisher's Statement

Profile: Markbladet är en gratistidning i Mark, utgiven sedan 1967. Markbladet bevakar lokala nyheter inom politik, sport och nöje.
Language (s): Swedish
COMMUNITY NEWSPAPER

Mera Linköping
880409

Editorial: Badhusgatan 5, Linköping 581 89
Tel: 46 13 28 02 54
Email: redaktion@meralinkoping.se Web site: http://www.meralinkoping.se
Freq: Weekly; Circ: 73400
Redaktionschef & Ansvarig utgivare: Mikael Sundgren
Profile: Mera Linköping är en veckodistribuerad gratistidning som kommer hem till alla hushåll i Linköpings kommun. Tidningen innehåller artiklar om intressanta händelser och personer.
Language (s): Swedish
Ad Rate: Full Page Mono 24500.00
Currency: Sweden Kronor
COMMUNITY NEWSPAPER

Mitt i Botkyrka Salem
222238

Editorial: Box 47309, Stockholm 100 74
Tel: 46 8 55 05 50 00
Email: botkyrka@mitti.se Web site: http://mitti.se/botkyrkasalem/
Freq: Weekly; Circ: 39700 Not Audited
Profile: Mitt i Botkyrka Salem är en gratis veckotidning som levererar lokalnyheter.
Language (s): Swedish
Ad Rate: Full Page Mono 28968.00
Currency: Sweden Kronor
COMMUNITY NEWSPAPER

Mitt i Bromma
222336

Editorial: Stockholm Tel: 46 8 55 05 50 00
Email: bromma@mitti.se Web site: http://mitti.se/bromma/
Freq: Weekly; Circ: 33600 Not Audited
Nyhetschef: Jakob Larsson
Profile: Mitt i Bromma är en gratis veckotidning med lokala nyheter.
Language (s): Swedish
Ad Rate: Full Page Mono 28152.00
Currency: Sweden Kronor
COMMUNITY NEWSPAPER

Mitt i Danderyd
222333

Editorial: arstaangsvagen 11, 6 tr, Stockholm 100 74
Tel: 46 8 55 05 50 00
Email: danderyd@mitti.se Web site: http://mitti.se/danderyd/
Freq: Weekly
Profile: Mitt i Danderyd är en gratis veckotidning som bevakar lokala nyheter i området.
Language (s): Swedish
Ad Rate: Full Page Colour 33660.00
Currency: Sweden Kronor
COMMUNITY NEWSPAPER

Mitt i Haninge
222817

Editorial: Stockholm Tel: 46 8 55 05 50 00
Email: haninge@mitti.se Web site: http://mitti.se/haninge/
Freq: Weekly; Circ: 34400 Not Audited
Profile: Lokaltidningen Mitt i Haninge är en gratis veckotidning som delas ut till invånare i området varje Tisdag. Tidningen varvar lokala nyheter med erbjudanden från lokala handlare.
Language (s): Swedish
Ad Rate: Full Page Mono 30192.00
Currency: Sweden Kronor
COMMUNITY NEWSPAPER

Mitt i Huddinge
222816

Editorial: Stockholm Tel: 46 8 55 05 500
Email: huddinge@mitti.se Web site: http://mitti.se/huddinge/
Freq: Weekly; Circ: 41700 Not Audited
Profile: Mitt i Huddinge är en gratistidning som innehåller lokala nyheter.
Language (s): Swedish
Ad Rate: Full Page Mono 33211.00
Currency: Sweden Kronor
COMMUNITY NEWSPAPER

Mitt i Järfälla
222334

Owner: Lokaltidningen Mitt i Stockholm AB
Editorial: Box 47309, Stockholm 100 74
Tel: 46 8 55 05 50 00
Email: jarfalla@mitti.se Web site: http://mitti.se/jarfalla/
Freq: Weekly; Circ: 29200 Not Audited
Profile: Mitt i Järfälla är en gratis lokaltidning som utkommer en gång i veckan till samtliga hushåll i området.
Language (s): Swedish
Ad Rate: Full Page Mono 29376.00
Currency: Sweden Kronor
COMMUNITY NEWSPAPER

Mitt i Kista
222335

Editorial: arstaangsvagen 11, 6 tr, Stockholm 100 74
Tel: 46 8 550 550 44
Email: kista@mitti.se Web site: http://mitti.se/kista/
Freq: Weekly; Circ: 15000 Not Audited
Profile: Mitt i Kista är en gratis veckotidning som bevakar lokala nyheter i området.
Language (s): Swedish
Ad Rate: Full Page Colour 18386.00
Currency: Sweden Kronor
COMMUNITY NEWSPAPER

Mitt i Kungsholmen
158126

Editorial: Stockholm Tel: 46 8 550 550 00
Email: kungsholmen@mitti.se Web site: http://mitti.se/kungsholmen/
Circ: 37100
Nyhetschef: Jakob Larsson
Profile: Mitt i Kungsholmen är en gratistidning som innehåller lokala nyheter.
Language (s): Swedish
Ad Rate: Full Page Mono 25010.00
Currency: Sweden Kronor
COMMUNITY NEWSPAPER

Mitt i Lidingö
498333

Editorial: Stockholm Tel: 46 8 55 05 50 00
Email: lidingo@mitti.se Web site: http://mitti.se/lidingo/
Circ: 20400
Nyhetschef: Jakob Larsson
Profile: Mitt i Lidingö är en gratis lokaltidning som utkommer en gång i veckan till samtliga hushåll i området.
Language (s): Swedish
Ad Rate: Full Page Mono 31717.00
Currency: Sweden Kronor
COMMUNITY NEWSPAPER

Mitt i Nacka
230290

Editorial: Stockholm Tel: 46 8 550 550 00
Email: nacka@mitti.se Web site: http://mitti.se/nacka/
Freq: Weekly; Circ: 39500 Not Audited
Profile: Lokaltidningen Mitt i Nacka bevakar allt som händer i Nacka och Värmdö kommun.
Language (s): Swedish
Ad Rate: Full Page Mono 25622.00
Currency: Sweden Kronor
COMMUNITY NEWSPAPER

Mitt i Östermalm
222784

Editorial: Stockholm Tel: 46 8 55 05 50 00
Email: ostermalm@mitti.se Web site: http://mitti.se/ostermalm/
Freq: Weekly; Circ: 38000 RS
Nyhetschef: Jakob Larsson
Profile: Lokaltidning som bevakar allt som händer på Östermalm.
Language (s): Swedish
Ad Rate: Full Page Mono 23950.00
Currency: Sweden Kronor
COMMUNITY NEWSPAPER

Mitt i Södermalm
158094

Editorial: Stockholm Tel: 46 8 550 550 00
Email: sodermalm@mitti.se Web site: http://mitti.se/sodermalm/
Freq: Weekly; Circ: 64100
Nyhetschef: Jakob Larsson
Profile: Lokaltidningen Mitt i Södermalm är en lokal gratistidning. Tidningen innehåller lokala nyheter, kultur, nöje och sport.
Language (s): Swedish
Ad Rate: Full Page Mono 32558.00
Currency: Sweden Kronor
COMMUNITY NEWSPAPER

Mitt i Söderort Bandhagen, Årsta, Enskede, Högdalen
222808

Editorial: Stockholm Tel: 46 8 55 05 50 00
Email: soderort@mitti.se Web site: http://mitti.se/bandhagenarsta/
Freq: Weekly; Circ: 45600
Profile: Lokaltidningen Mitt i Söderort täcker Bandhagen, Årsta, Enskede och Högdalen.
Language (s): Swedish
Ad Rate: Full Page Mono 33089.00
Currency: Sweden Kronor
COMMUNITY NEWSPAPER

Mitt i Söderort Farsta/Sköndal
222815

Editorial: Box 47309, Stockholm 100 74
Tel: 46 8 55 05 50 00
Email: soderort@mitti.se Web site: http://mitti.se/farstaskondal/
Freq: Weekly; Circ: 25700 Not Audited
Nyhetschef: Katarina Linde
Profile: Mitt i Söderort Farsta/Sköndal är en gratis lokaltidning som utges en gång i veckan till samtliga hushåll i området.
Language (s): Swedish
Ad Rate: Full Page Mono 26887.00
Currency: Sweden Kronor
COMMUNITY NEWSPAPER

Mitt i Söderort Hammarby/ Skarpnäck
578966

Editorial: Stockholm Tel: 46 8 55 05 50 00
Email: soderort@mitti.se Web site: http://mitti.se/hammarbyskarpnack/
Circ: 21800
Profile: Mitt i Söderort Hammarby/Skarpnäck är en gratis lokaltidning som utkommer en gång i veckan till samtliga hushåll i området.
Language (s): Swedish
Ad Rate: Full Page Mono 24562.00
Currency: Sweden Kronor
COMMUNITY NEWSPAPER

Mitt i Söderort Liljeholmen, Älvsjö, Gröndal, Hägersten
222813

Editorial: Stockholm Tel: 46 8 55 05 50 00
Email: soderort@mitti.se Web site: http://mitti.se/liljeholmenalvsjo/
Freq: Weekly; Circ: 52200 Not Audited

Profile: Lokaltidningen Mitt i Söderort täcker Liljeholmen, Älvsjö, Gröndal, Hägersten.
Language (s): Swedish
Ad Rate: Full Page Mono 33538.00
Currency: Sweden Kronor
COMMUNITY NEWSPAPER

Mitt i Söderort Skärholmen
222814

Editorial: Stockholm Tel: 46 8 55 05 50 00
Email: soderort@mitti.se Web site: http://mitti.se/skarholmen/
Freq: Weekly; Circ: 14000 Not Audited
Profile: Mitt i Söderort Skärholmen är en gratis lokaltidning som utkommer en gång i veckan till samtliga hushåll i området.
Language (s): Swedish
Ad Rate: Full Page Mono 18972.00
Currency: Sweden Kronor
COMMUNITY NEWSPAPER

Mitt i Södra Roslagen
222821

Editorial: Stockholm Tel: 46 8 55 05 50 00
Email: sodraroslagen@mitti.se Web site: http://mitti.se/sodraroslagen/
Freq: Weekly; Circ: 21400 Not Audited
Profile: Denna tidning skriver om lokala och regionala nyheter för Södra Roslagen. Läses av invånare i regionen.
Language (s): Swedish
Ad Rate: Full Page Mono 23378.00
Currency: Sweden Kronor
COMMUNITY NEWSPAPER

Mitt i Sollentuna
222337

Editorial: Stockholm Tel: 46 8 55 05 50 00
Email: sollentuna@mitti.se Web site: http://mitti.se/sollentuna/
Freq: Weekly; Circ: 27100 Not Audited
Nyhetschef: Erica Lascelles
Profile: Mitt i Sollentuna är en gratis lokaltidning som utkommer en gång i veckan till samtliga hushåll i området.
Language (s): Swedish
Ad Rate: Full Page Mono 30141.00
Currency: Sweden Kronor
COMMUNITY NEWSPAPER

Mitt i Solna
222338

Editorial: Stockholm Tel: 46 8 55 05 50 00
Email: solna@mitti.se Web site: http://mitti.se/solna/
Freq: Weekly; Circ: 36200 Not Audited
Profile: Mitt i Solna är en gratis lokaltidning som utkommer en gång i veckan till samtliga hushåll i området.
Language (s): Swedish
Ad Rate: Full Page Mono 31416.00
Currency: Sweden Kronor
COMMUNITY NEWSPAPER

Mitt i Sundbyberg
222327

Editorial: Stockholm Tel: 46 8 55 05 50 00
Email: sundbyberg@mitti.se Web site: http://mitti.se/sundbyberg/
Freq: Weekly; Circ: 21000 Not Audited
Nyhetschef: Jakob Larsson
Profile: Mitt i Sundbyberg är en gratis lokaltidning som utkommer en gång i veckan till samtliga hushåll i området.
Language (s): Swedish
Ad Rate: Full Page Mono 23664.00
Currency: Sweden Kronor
COMMUNITY NEWSPAPER

Mitt i Täby
222332

Editorial: Stockholm Tel: 46 8 55 05 50 00
Email: taby@mitti.se Web site: http://mitti.se/taby/
Freq: Weekly; Circ: 27600 Not Audited
Profile: Mitt i Täby är en gratis lokaltidning som utkommer en gång i veckan till samtliga hushåll i området.
Language (s): Swedish
Ad Rate: Full Page Mono 25908.00
Currency: Sweden Kronor
COMMUNITY NEWSPAPER

Mitt i Tensta-Rinkeby
218062

Editorial: Box 47309, arstaangsvagen 11, 6 tr, Stockholm 100 74 Tel: 46 8 55 05 50 00
Email: tenstarinkeby@mitti.se Web site: http://mitti.se/tenstarinkeby/
Freq: Weekly
Nyhetschef: Jakob Larsson
Profile: Lokaltidningen Tensta-Rinkeby är en gratis veckotidning som bevakar lokala nyheter i området.
Language (s): Swedish
COMMUNITY NEWSPAPER

Mitt i Tyresö
222811

Editorial: Box 47309, Stockholm 100 74
Tel: 46 8 55 05 50 00
Email: tyreso@mitti.se Web site: http://mitti.se/tyreso/
Freq: Weekly; Circ: 18200 Not Audited
Profile: Mitt i Tyresö är en gratis lokaltidning som utkommer en gång i veckan till samtliga hushåll i området.
Language (s): Swedish
Ad Rate: Full Page Mono 24888.00
Currency: Sweden Kronor
COMMUNITY NEWSPAPER

Mitt i Upplands Väsby
222331

Editorial: Stockholm Tel: 46 8 55 05 50 00
Email: upplandsvasby@mitti.se Web site: http://mitti.se/upplandsvasby/

Freq: Weekly; **Circ:** 18100 Not Audited
Profile: Mitt i Upplands Väsby är en gratis lokaltidning som utkommer en gång i veckan till samtliga hushåll i området.
Language (s): Swedish
Ad Rate: Full Page Mono 20196.00
Currency: Sweden Kronor
COMMUNITY NEWSPAPER

Mitt i Upplands-Bro 222330

Editorial: Box 47309, arstaangvagen 11, Stockholm 100 74 **Tel:** 46 8 55 05 50 00
Email: upplandsbro@mitti.se **Web site:** http://mitti.se/upplandsbro/
Freq: Weekly
Profile: Mitt i Upplands- Bro är gratis veckotidning som bevakar lokala nyheter i området.
Language (s): Swedish
Ad Rate: Full Page Colour 29376.00
Currency: Sweden Kronor
COMMUNITY NEWSPAPER

Mitt i Vallentuna 222328

Editorial: Stockholm **Tel:** 46 8 55 05 50 00
Email: vallentuna@mitti.se **Web site:** http://mitti.se/vallentuna/
Freq: Weekly; **Circ:** 13700 RS
Profile: Mitt i Vallentuna är en gratis lokaltidning som utkommer en gång i veckan till samtliga hushåll i området.
Language (s): Swedish
Ad Rate: Full Page Mono 20196.00
Currency: Sweden Kronor
COMMUNITY NEWSPAPER

Mitt i Värmdö 222810

Editorial: Stockholm **Tel:** 46 8 55 05 50 00
Email: varmdo@mitti.se **Web site:** http://mitti.se/varmdo/
Freq: Weekly; **Circ:** 16600 Not Audited
Profile: Mitt i Värmdö är en gratis lokaltidning som ges ut en gång i veckan till samtliga hushåll i området.
Language (s): Swedish
Ad Rate: Full Page Mono 15300.00
Currency: Sweden Kronor
COMMUNITY NEWSPAPER

Mitt i Vasastan 158125

Editorial: Stockholm **Tel:** 46 8 55 05 50 00
Email: vasastan@mitti.se **Web site:** http://mitti.se/vasastan/
Circ: 35900
Profile: Mitt i Vasastan är en gratis lokaltidning som ges ut en gång i veckan till samtliga hushåll i området.
Language (s): Swedish
Ad Rate: Full Page Mono 22032.00
Currency: Sweden Kronor
COMMUNITY NEWSPAPER

Mitt i Västerort 222329

Editorial: Stockholm **Tel:** 46 8 55 05 50 00
Email: vasterort@mitti.se **Web site:** http://mitti.se/vasterort/
Freq: Weekly; **Circ:** 30000 Not Audited
Nyhetschef: Jakob Larsson
Profile: Mitt i Västerort är en gratis lokaltidning som utkommer en gång i veckan till samtliga hushåll i Hässelby och Vällingby.
Language (s): Swedish
Ad Rate: Full Page Mono 29784.00
Ad Rate: Full Page Colour 24837.00
Currency: Sweden Kronor
COMMUNITY NEWSPAPER

Mora Tidning 158587

Editorial: Strandgatan 28, Mora 792 30
Tel: 46 250 59 24 00
Email: mt.red@dt.se **Web site:** http://www.dt.se/mora
Circ: 11100
Chefredaktör & Ansvarig utgivare: Carl-Johan Bergman
Profile: Mora Tidning är en tredagars tidning (må-on-fr), med inriktning på regionala nyheter i norra Dalarna och Mora med omnejd. Huvudredaktionen finns i Mora och tidningen har även lokalredaktioner i Orsa, Älvdalen och Malung. Tidningen ingår i Dalarnas Tidningar, som i din tur ingår i Mittmedia.
Language (s): Swedish
Ad Rate: Full Page Mono 38976.00
Currency: Sweden Kronor
COMMUNITY NEWSPAPER

Nacka Värmdö Posten 222812

Editorial: Varmdovagen 205, Box 735, Nacka 131 24
Tel: 46 8 55 52 66 20
Email: red@nvp.se **Web site:** http://www.nvp.se
Freq: Weekly; **Circ:** 72100 RS
Chefredaktör & Ansvarig utgivare: Anders Milde
Profile: Nacka Värmdö Posten startades i april 1989 och har sedan dess levererat lokala nyheter, kommunal information & evenemangstips mm. varje vecka till invånarna i Nacka och Värmdö.
Language (s): Swedish
Ad Rate: Full Page Mono 31615.00
Currency: Sweden Kronor
COMMUNITY NEWSPAPER

Nerikes Allehanda 364908

Editorial: Klostergatan 23, Orebro 701 92
Tel: 46 19 15 50 00
Email: nyhet@na.se **Web site:** http://www.na.se
Freq: Daily
Nyhetschef: Ida Johansson
Profile: Nerikes Allehanda är Sveriges tredje största landsortstidning. Dagstidningen täcker nyheter i Örebro med omnejd. Tidningsredaktionen önskar endast motta information angående relevanta regionala nyheter: nyhet@na.se.The editorial office does not wish to receive press releases to the editorial mail. Only information regarding relevant regional news may be of interest: nyhet@na.se. Nerikes Allehanda is a daily newspaper covering regional news.
Language (s): Swedish
COMMUNITY NEWSPAPER

Norra Halland 218113

Editorial: Kyrkogatan 2-4, Kungsbacka 434 24
Tel: 46 300 10 795
Email: redaktionen@norrahalland.se **Web site:** http://www.norrahalland.se
Freq: 2 Times/Week; **Circ:** 9700
Nyhetschef: Christina Forlin
Profile: Norra Halland är en tvådagars nyhetstidning som funnits sedan 1921. Den bevakar det som händer i Kungsbacka kommun.
Language (s): Swedish
Ad Rate: Full Page Mono 19850.00
Currency: Sweden Kronor
COMMUNITY NEWSPAPER

Norra Skåne 366322

Editorial: Vapnaregatan 6, Hässleholm 281 50
Tel: 46 451 74 50 00
Email: nyhetschefen@nsk.se **Web site:** http://www.nsk.se
Freq: Daily; **Circ:** 14500
Redaktör: Hans Bryngelson; **Chefredaktör & Ansvarig utgivare:** Mimmi Karlsson-Bernfalk; **Redaktör:** Marie Strömberg-Andersson
Profile: Dagstidningen Norra Skåne förser dagligen läsare i 5 kommuner i norra Skåne med lokalnyheter. Norra Skåne är en tidningen för familjehushållet. Förutom de lokala nyheterna från kommunerna bjuder de på inrikes, utrikes, regionala nyheter, sport, kultur, nöje, opinion, debatt, radio och teve samt förströelseläsning – sex dagar i veckan.
Language (s): Swedish
Ad Rate: Full Page Mono 40416.00
Currency: Sweden Kronor
COMMUNITY NEWSPAPER

Norran 158593

Editorial: Kanalgatan 59, Skellefteå 931 32
Tel: 46 910 57 700
Email: redaktion@norran.se **Web site:** http://www.norran.se
Circ: 21700
Chefredaktör & Ansvarig utgivare: Lars Andersson
Profile: Norran är en dagstidning för Västerbotten, med lokala nyheter, evenemang, debatt, kultur och webbsida. Tidningen har lokalredaktioner i Norsjö och Malå.
Language (s): Swedish
Ad Rate: Full Page Mono 50688.00
Currency: Sweden Kronor
COMMUNITY NEWSPAPER

Norrbottens-Kuriren 365810

Owner: Norrbottens-Kuriren AB
Editorial: Robertsviksgatan 5, Luleå 971 81
Tel: 46 920 26 29 00
Email: redaktionen@kuriren.com **Web site:** http://www.kuriren.nu
Circ: 17400
Chefredaktör & Ansvarig utgivare: Mats Ehnbom; **Nyhetschef:** Lotta Sandhammar
Profile: Norrbottens-Kuriren är Luleås största och Norrbottens äldsta dagstidning, grundad 1861. Den bevakar framför allt det som händer i Norrbottens län.
Language (s): Swedish
COMMUNITY NEWSPAPER

Norrköpings Tidningar 365828

Editorial: Stohagsgatan 2, Norrköping 601 83
Tel: 46 11 20 00 00
Email: tipsa@nt.se **Web site:** http://www.nt.se
Freq: Daily; **Circ:** 35900
Chefredaktör & Ansvarig utgivare: Anders Nilsson; **Nyhetschef:** Mikael Pihlblad
Profile: Norrköpings Tidningar är Sveriges äldsta nu utkommande nyhetstidning, grundad 1758 och därmed en av världens tio äldsta tidningar. Norrköpings Tidningar, NT skriver främst om regionala nyheter från Östergötland.
Language (s): Swedish
Ad Rate: Full Page Mono 67624.00
Currency: Sweden Kronor
COMMUNITY NEWSPAPER

Norrländska Socialdemokraten 365934

Editorial: Robertsviksgatan 5, Luleå 971 83
Tel: 46 920 26 30 01
Email: redaktion@nsd.se **Web site:** http://www.nsd.se
Freq: Daily; **Circ:** 29400
Redaktionschef: Lenitha Andersson-Junkka; **Nyhetschef:** Ida Folkesson; **Nyhetschef:** Bodil Resare; **Chefredaktör & Ansvarig utgivare:** Kalle Sandhammar; **Redaktör:** Jonny Vikström
Profile: Norrländska Socialdemokraten (NSD), eller Norrländskan som den också kallas lokalt, är en svensk dagstidning som grundades år 1918. Tidningen utkommer i Norrbotten.
Language (s): Swedish
COMMUNITY NEWSPAPER

Norrtelje Tidning 365935

Editorial: Tibeliusgatan 1, Norrtälje 761 84
Tel: 46 176 79 500
Email: redaktionen@norrteljetidning.se **Web site:** http://www.norrteljetidning.se
Freq: Daily; **Circ:** 13300
Profile: Norrtelje tidning skriver om lokala och regionala nyheter och läses av invånare i regionen.
Language (s): Swedish
Ad Rate: Full Page Mono 39680.00
Currency: Sweden Kronor
COMMUNITY NEWSPAPER

Nya Lidköpings-Tidningen 366340

Editorial: Stenportsgatan 14, Lidköping 531 81
Tel: 46 510 89 700
Email: redaktion@nlt.se **Web site:** http://www.nlt.se
Freq: 3 Times/Week; **Circ:** 23500
Redigerare: Christoffer Dunälv; **Chefredaktör och ansvarig utgivare:** Anders Hörling; **Redaktör:** Anders Järnebrand; **Nyhetschef:** Håkan Johansson; **Nyhetschef:** Mats Österman; **Redigerare:** Monica Weihard
Profile: Nya Lidköpings-Tidningen (NLT) är en oberoende liberal morgontidning som utges i Lidköping med omnejd.
Language (s): Swedish
Ad Rate: Full Page Mono 35400.00
Currency: Sweden Kronor
COMMUNITY NEWSPAPER

Nya Wermlands-Tidningen 158571

Editorial: Vaxnasgatan 20, Karlstad 651 02
Tel: 46 54 19 90 00
Email: redaktion@nwt.se **Web site:** http://www.nwt.se
Circ: 44100
Chefredaktör: Staffan Ander; **Redigerare:** Kent Andersson; **Redigerare:** Claes Bonde; **Nyhetschef:** Olov Öström; **Redaktionschef & Ansvarig utgivare:** Mikael Rothsten
Profile: Nya Wermlands-Tidningen är Värmlands största morgontidning. Tidningen ges ut 6 dagar i veckan till utgivningsområdet som sträcker sig från Malung i norr till Dalsland i söder.
Language (s): Swedish
Ad Rate: Full Page Mono 62590.00
Currency: Sweden Kronor
COMMUNITY NEWSPAPER

Nybro-Extra 579170

Editorial: Box 119, Storgatan 20, Nybro 382 22
Tel: 46 481 17 395
Email: info@nybroextra.se **Web site:** http://www.nybroextra.se
Freq: Monthly
Profile: Nybro-Extra är en gratistidning som skriver om lokala och regionala nyheter. Tidningen ges ut till samtliga hushåll och företag i Nybro och Emmaboda, samt Trekanten, Älghult och Fröseke en gång i månaden.
Language (s): Swedish
COMMUNITY NEWSPAPER

Offensiv 158905

Tel: 46 8 60 59 403
Email: rs@socialisterna.org **Web site:** http://offensiv.socialisterna.org/
Freq: Weekly
Chefredaktör & Ansvarig utgivare: Arne Johansson
Profile: Rättvisepartiet Socialisternas Veckotidning. Veckotidning för rättvisa och socialism, allmänpolitisk. Tidskriften speglar kampen mot nedskämingspolitiken, privatiseringar, rasism, den fackliga kampen med mera.
Language (s): Swedish
COMMUNITY NEWSPAPER

Örebroar'n 222782

Owner: GISAB (Gratis tidningar i Sverige AB)
Editorial: Klostergatan 23, Orebro 701 92
Tel: 46 19 15 53 70
Email: redaktion@orebroarn.se **Web site:** http://www.orebroarn.se
Freq: Weekly; **Circ:** 69200
Profile: Örebroar'n är en lokal gratistidning i Örebro.
Language (s): Swedish
Ad Rate: Full Page Mono 33504.00
Currency: Sweden Kronor
COMMUNITY NEWSPAPER

Örgryte & Härlanda Posten 416276

Editorial: C/o Vibergs Foto, Olskrokstorget 6, Goteborg 416 65
Email: redaktionen@ohposten.se **Web site:** http://www.ohposten.se
Freq: Monthly
Profile: Örgryte & Härlanda Posten är en lokal tidning i Göteborgsområdena Härlanda och Örgryte. Tidningen direktutdelas till hushåll, företag, föreningar och publika platser i regionen.
Language (s): Swedish
Ad Rate: Full Page Colour 12000.00
Currency: Sweden Kronor
COMMUNITY NEWSPAPER

Örnsköldsviks Allehanda 158614

Owner: Örnsköldsviks Allehanda
Editorial: Centralesplanaden 18, Örnsköldsvik 891 33
Tel: 46 10 709 70 00
Email: oaredaktion@allehanda.se **Web site:** http://www.allehanda.se/ornskoldsvik
Freq: Daily; **Circ:** 13600
Redigerare: Tommy Ehlin; **Chefredaktör & Ansvarig utgivare:** Anders Ingvarsson
Profile: Örnsköldsviks Allehanda är en regional dagstidning som utkommer 6 dagar i veckan. Tidningens ledarsida är liberal. Sedan 2007 ingår tidningen i bolaget Allehanda Media AB där också Tidningen Ångermanland ingår. De två tidningarna har separata nyhetsdelar, men en gemensam andra del som innehåller nöje, kultur och sport.Tidningen har även en gemensam hemsida, Allehanda.se, tillsammans med Tidningen Ångermanland.
Language (s): Swedish
Ad Rate: Full Page Mono 36720.00
Currency: Sweden Kronor
COMMUNITY NEWSPAPER

ÖsterlenMagasinet 222783

Editorial: Storgatan 23, Simrishamn 272 31
Web site: http://www.osterlenmagasinet.se
Freq: Weekly
Redaktör: Hannah Andersson
Profile: Önskar ej motta pressutskick. ÖsterlenMagasinet är en reklamfinansierad tidning som distribueras med Tidningsbärarna varje torsdag till samtliga hushåll i Simrishamn, Tomelilla och de östra delarna av Ystad.
Language (s): Swedish
Ad Rate: Full Page Colour 40000.00
Currency: Sweden Kronor
COMMUNITY NEWSPAPER

Östermalmsnytt 222785

Owner: Direktpress AB
Editorial: Vallhallavagen 184, Stockholm 102 46
Tel: 46 8 545 870 70
Email: on@direktpress.se **Web site:** http://www.ostermalmsnytt.se
Freq: Weekly; **Circ:** 40800 RS
Profile: Östermalmsnytt är en svensk lokaltidning som ges ut på Östermalm, Gärdet och Djurgården i Stockholm. Östermalmsnytt grundades 1968.
Language (s): Swedish
Ad Rate: Full Page Mono 22280.00
Currency: Sweden Kronor
COMMUNITY NEWSPAPER

Östersunds-Posten 158615

Owner: Östersunds-Postens Tryckeri AB
Editorial: Kyrkgatan 52, Box 720, Östersund 831 28
Tel: 46 10 709 70 00
Email: redaktion@op.se **Web site:** http://www.op.se
Circ: 19700
Nyhetschef: Gabrielle Bäckström; **Nyhetschef:** Olof Ekerlid; **Chefredaktör & Ansvarig utgivare:** Hans Lindeberg; **Nyhetschef:** Karin Wallström
Profile: Östersunds-Posten är Jämtlands läns största dagstidning och ges ut sedan 1877. Tidningen utkommer 6 gånger i veckan. Ledarsidan för tidningen är centerpartistisk.
Language (s): Swedish
Ad Rate: Full Page Mono 46992.00
Currency: Sweden Kronor
COMMUNITY NEWSPAPER

Östgöta Correspondenten 365933

Editorial: Badhusgatan 5, Linköping 581 89
Tel: 46 13 280 000
Email: tipsa@corren.se **Web site:** http://www.corren.se/
Circ: 43000
Redaktionschef & Stf. Ansvarig utgivare: Christer Kustvik; **Nyhetschef:** Maria Kustvik; **Nyhetschef:** Nils Olauson
Profile: Östgöta Correspondenten är en svensk oberoende borgerlig morgontidning som ges ut i Linköping. Tidningen startades 1838.
Language (s): Swedish
Ad Rate: Full Page Mono 71120.00
Currency: Sweden Kronor
COMMUNITY NEWSPAPER

Östgötatidningen 498330

Editorial: Kungsvagen 37, Mjölby 595 24
Tel: 46 142 48 27 00
Email: redaktion@ostgotatidningen.se **Web site:** http://www.ostgotatidningen.se
Freq: Weekly
Profile: Östgötatidningen är en gratis lokaltidning som distribueras med egna bud till alla hushåll och Posten till företag inför varje veckoslut i kommunerna Mjölby, Motala, Vadstena, Ödeshög och Boxholm. Tidningen ges ut i 2 editioner: Östgötatidningen Motala, Östgötatidningen Mjölby Boxholm Vadstena Ödeshög.
Language (s): Swedish
Ad Rate: Full Page Colour 28512.00
Currency: Sweden Kronor
COMMUNITY NEWSPAPER

Östra Småland/Nyheterna 158205

Owner: Östra Småland AB
Editorial: Box 830, Vastra Sjogatan 7, Kalmar 391 28
Tel: 46 480 42 93 00
Email: nyhetschefen@ostrasmaland.se **Web site:** http://www.ostrasmaland.se/
Circ: 8800
Chefredaktör, Redaktionschef & Ansvarig utgivare: Gunilla Persson
Profile: Östran (Östra Småland och Nyheterna) är en svensk socialdemokratisk dagstidning i Kalmar med täckningsområde i södra Kalmar län. I Oskarshamns kommun ges en lokaledition under namnet Nyheterna ut. Nyheternas spridningsområde är den norra delen av Kalmar län.
Language (s): Swedish
Ad Rate: Full Page Mono 48960.00
Currency: Sweden Kronor
COMMUNITY NEWSPAPER

Partille Tidning 239204

Editorial: Kyrktorget 19-21, Partille 443 33
Tel: 46 31 34 02 430

Web site: http://www.partilletidning.se
Freq: Weekly
Profile: Partille Tidning är en gratisutdelad veckotidning som når samtliga hushåll i Partille kommun och dess tätorter Partille, Sävedalen, Jonsered och Öjersjö. Önskar ej motta pressutskick.
Language (s): Swedish
Ad Rate: Full Page Colour 22600.00
Currency: Sweden Kronor
COMMUNITY NEWSPAPER

Piteå-Tidningen 158616

Editorial: Hamnplan 5, Piteå 941 24
Tel: 46 911 64 500
Email: redaktionen@pt.se **Web site:** http://www.pt.se
Circ: 14300
Nyhetschef: Annika Lahti; **Redaktionschef:** Bengt Larsson; **Ansvarig utgivare:** Matti Lilja
Profile: Piteå-Tidningen är en lokal dagstidning i Piteå med omnejd grundad 1915.
Language (s): Swedish
Ad Rate: Full Page Mono 40320.00
Currency: Sweden Kronor
COMMUNITY NEWSPAPER

Skånska Dagbladet 158584

Owner: Skånska Dagbladet, AB
Editorial: St. Gertrudsgatan 3, Malmo 211 25
Tel: 46 40 660 55 00
Email: red.malmo@skd.se **Web site:** http://www.skanskan.se
Circ: 23200
Chefredaktör & Ansvarig utgivare: Lars Eriksson; **Redaktionschef:** Pia Lobell; **Btr. Redaktionschef:** Mats Svensson
Profile: Skånska Dagbladet är mellanskånes största lokaltidning. De skriver om lokala nyheter, inrikes, utrikes, regionala nyheter, sport, kultur, nöje, opinion, debatt, radio och tv samt förströelseläsning. Tidningen täcker dagligen följande kommuner: Malmö, Lund, Eslöv, Höör, Hörby, Svalöv, Landskrona, Lomma, Burlöv, Staffanstorp, Kävlinge, Trelleborg, Vellinge, Skurup, Svedala, Sjöbo och Ystad.
Language (s): Swedish
Ad Rate: Full Page Mono 64560.00
Currency: Sweden Kronor
COMMUNITY NEWSPAPER

Skaraborgs Allehanda 158594

Editorial: Garpastigen 3, Skövde 541 28
Tel: 46 500 46 75 00
Email: redaktion@sla.se **Web site:** http://www.sla.se
Circ: 21000
Nyhetschef: Peter Henriksson; **Redigerare:** Linus Wennblom
Profile: Skaraborgs Allehandas är en dagstidning som utges i Skövde sedan 1884. Tidningen har lokalredaktioner i Tibro, Karlsborg och Hjo.
Language (s): Swedish
Ad Rate: Full Page Mono 34800.00
Currency: Sweden Kronor
COMMUNITY NEWSPAPER

Skaraborgsbygden 223121

Editorial: Jarnvagsgatan 20, Skara 532 30
Tel: 46 511 30 250
Email: redaktion@skaraborgsbygden.se **Web site:** http://www.skaraborgsbygden.se
Circ: 9800
Profile: Skaraborgsbygden är en lokaltidning som utkommer varje fredag. Utgivningsområdet är främst Skaraborg.
Language (s): Swedish
Ad Rate: Full Page Mono 21000.00
Currency: Sweden Kronor
COMMUNITY NEWSPAPER

Skövde Nyheter 158595

Owner: Västgöta-Tidningar AB
Editorial: Storgatan 17, Skövde 541 30
Tel: 46 500 78 48 50
Email: red.sn@vgt.se **Web site:** http://www.skovdenyheter.se/
Circ: 27700
Nyhetschef: Leif Claesson
Profile: Skövde Nyheter bevakar lokala nyheter i Skövde med omnejd.
Language (s): Swedish
Ad Rate: Full Page Mono 24960.00
Currency: Sweden Kronor
COMMUNITY NEWSPAPER

Smålandsposten 365282

Owner: Smålandsposten AB
Editorial: Linnegatan 2B, Växjo 351 70
Tel: 46 470 77 05 00
Email: nyheter@smp.se **Web site:** http://www.smp.se
Freq: Daily; **Circ:** 34200
Redaktionschef: Åsa Carlsson; **Ansvarig utgivare:** Magnus Karlsson; **Redaktör:** Berne Persson; **Nyhetschef:** Johan Persson
Profile: Smålandspostens huvudredaktion bevakar regionala nyheter, sport och kultur.
Language (s): Swedish
Ad Rate: Full Page Mono 55920.00
Currency: Sweden Kronor
COMMUNITY NEWSPAPER

Smålands-Tidningen 160733

Owner: Smålandstidningens Tryckeri AB
Editorial: Nybrogatan 8, Eksjö 575 31
Tel: 46 381 63 85 00
Email: centralred@smt.se **Web site:** http://www.smalandstidningen.se
Circ: 5000
Redaktionschef & Ansvarig utgivare: Johan Hedberg
Profile: Smålandsposten är en dagstidning som ges ut i Kronobergs län med huvudkontor i Växjö
Language (s): Swedish
COMMUNITY NEWSPAPER

Smålands-Tidningen - Eksjö 161425

Editorial: Nybrogatan 8, Eksjö 575 31
Tel: 46 381 63 85 70
Email: eksjored@smt.se **Web site:** http://www.smt.se/eksjo/
Circ: 5000
Redaktionschef & Ansvarig utgivare: Johan Hedberg
Profile: Lokalredaktion av Smålands-Tidningen som täcker Eksjö.
Language (s): Swedish
COMMUNITY NEWSPAPER

Smålänningen 158578

Owner: Herenco AB
Editorial: Foreningsgatan 8B, Ljungby 341 30
Tel: 46 372 692 00
Email: redax@smalanningen.se **Web site:** http://www.smalanningen.se
Freq: Mon thru Fri; **Circ:** 10900
Redaktionschef & Ansvarig utgivare: Inger Abram Ohlsson; **Nyhetschef:** Lars Davidsson
Profile: Lokal nyhetstidning med huvudsakligt spridningsområde Ljungby, Älmhult och Markaryds kommuner. Läses av boende inom spridningsområdetLocal Newspaper in Ljungby, Älmhult och Markaryd.
Language (s): Swedish
Ad Rate: Full Page Mono 34176.00
Currency: Sweden Kronor
COMMUNITY NEWSPAPER

SöderhamnsNytt 222805

Owner: Hälsingetidningar AB
Editorial: Box 514, Bradgardsgatan 6, Söderhamn 826 27 **Tel:** 46 270 26 53 50
Email: stina.gunnarsson@mittmedia.se **Web site:** http://www.soderhamnsnytt.se/
Freq: Weekly; **Circ:** 14700 Publisher's Statement
Profile: Söderhamnsnytt är en veckotidning med fokus på att spegla det som kommer att hända den kommande veckan, istället för att vara en nyhetstidning, och därtill bidra med reportage om intressanta personer och företeelser.
Language (s): Swedish
COMMUNITY NEWSPAPER

Södermalmsnytt 158129

Owner: Direktpress
Editorial: Box 5290, Vallhallavagen 184, Stockholm 102 46 **Tel:** 46 8 545 870 70
Email: info@direktpress.se **Web site:** http://www.sodermalmsnytt.se
Freq: Weekly; **Circ:** 70700
Chefredaktör: Helene Claesson; **Redigerare:** Lotta Waller
Profile: Södermalmsnytt är en gratis lokaltidning med tyngdpunkt på lokala nyheter som vänder sig till boende i alla åldrar på Södermalm.
Language (s): Swedish
Ad Rate: Full Page Mono 27930.00
Currency: Sweden Kronor
COMMUNITY NEWSPAPER

Södermanlands Nyheter 365936

Owner: Södermanlands Nyheter AB
Editorial: Fruangsgatan 4A, Nyköping 611 79
Tel: 46 155 767 70
Email: redaktionen@sn.se **Web site:** http://www.sn.se
Freq: Weekly; **Circ:** 21500
Barnfrågor / Ungdomsfrågor: Sven Rydén
Profile: Södermanlands Nyheter är en dagstidning i östra Södermanlands län. Tidningen ges ut i Nyköping, Oxelösund, Gnesta och Trosa kommuner. Utgivningsorten är Nyköping.
Language (s): Swedish
Ad Rate: Full Page Mono 45036.00
Currency: Sweden Kronor
COMMUNITY NEWSPAPER

Södermanlands Nyheter - Trosa 161640

Editorial: Busstorget 5, Trosa 619 30
Tel: 46 156 137 10
Web site: http://www.sn.se/nyheter/trosa
Circ: 21500
Profile: Södermanlands Nyheters lokalredaktion i Trosa. Vill ej ha utskick Does not want press releases
Language (s): Swedish
Ad Rate: Full Page Mono 45036.00
Currency: Sweden Kronor
COMMUNITY NEWSPAPER

Södertäljeposten 222807

Owner: Tidningsbolaget Promedia i Mellansverige AB
Editorial: Storgatan 3-5, Södertälje 151 82
Tel: 46 8 550 921 61
Email: redaktion@sodertaljeposten.se **Web site:** http://www.sodertaljeposten.se
Freq: Weekly; **Circ:** 52300 Publisher's Statement
Profile: Södertälje-Posten är en gratis postutburen lokaltidning som delas ut till samtliga hushåll i Södertälje, Gnesta och Nykvarn. Tidningen innehåller nyheter, reportage och lokala personporträtt. Södertälje-Posten is a free weekly newspaper featuring news for Södertälje, Gnesta and Nykvarn.
Language (s): Swedish
Ad Rate: Full Page Mono 30912.00
Currency: Sweden Kronor
COMMUNITY NEWSPAPER

Södra Sidan 498332

Owner: Direktpress
Editorial: Bredholmsgatan 3, 1tr, Skärholmen 127 48
Tel: 46 8 740 07 82
Email: redaktion@sodrasidan.se **Web site:** http://www.stockholmdirekt.se/sodrasidan/
Freq: Weekly; **Circ:** 61100
Chefredaktör/ vd: Petter Beckman
Profile: Södra Sidan är en gratis lokaltidning i Stockholm som utkommer en gång i veckan till allla hushåll längs röda linjen mellan Bredäng och Norsborg, i Segeltorp, Tumba, Vårsta, Grödinge och Tullinge. Sedan 2015 utkommer tidningen även i Huddinge.
Language (s): Swedish
COMMUNITY NEWSPAPER

Spegeln Staffanstorp 318937

Tel: 46 46 25 02 02
Email: info@spegeln.se **Web site:** http://www.spegeln.se
Freq: Semi-Monthly
Ansvarig utgivare: Stefan Svensson
Profile: Spegeln Staffanstorp skriver om lokala händelser i området som rör invånare i regionen.
Language (s): Swedish
COMMUNITY NEWSPAPER

Sundsvalls Nyheter 579064

Owner: Sundsvalls Nyheter
Editorial: Badhusparken 1, Sundsvall 851 72
Tel: 46 10 709 84 80
Email: redaktion@sn24.se **Web site:** http://www.sn24.se
Freq: Weekly; **Circ:** 63900
Redaktionsansvarig: Sanna Berglund
Profile: Sundsvalls Nyheter är en politiskt oberoende nyhetstidning. Den utkommer varje fredag gratis till samtliga hushåll och kontor i Sundsvall, Timrå, Härnösand och Ånge kommuner.
Language (s): Swedish
Ad Rate: Full Page Mono 45216.00
Currency: Sweden Kronor
COMMUNITY NEWSPAPER

Sundsvalls Tidning 365026

Owner: Sundsvall Tidning AB
Editorial: Badhusparken 1, Sundsvall 851 72
Tel: 46 60 19 70 00
Web site: http://www.st.nu
Freq: Daily; **Circ:** 23800
Chefredaktör & Ansvarig utgivare: Anders Ingvarsson; **Redaktör:** Tommy Lindberg
Profile: Sundsvalls Tidning är en liberal morgontidning som ges ut i Sundsvall med omnejd.
Language (s): Swedish
Ad Rate: Full Page Mono 71376.00
Currency: Sweden Kronor
COMMUNITY NEWSPAPER

Svenljunga & Tranemo Tidning 222804

Editorial: Hantverksgatan 6, Tranemo 514 23
Tel: 46 325 40 000
Email: redaktion@stthuset.com **Web site:** http://www.stthuset.com
Freq: Weekly
Profile: Svenljunga & Tranemo Tidning är en gratis lokaltidning som når hushåll, kontor och företag i Svenljunga och Tranemo kommuner samt södra delen av Ulricehamns kommun.
Language (s): Swedish
COMMUNITY NEWSPAPER

Sydöstran 365932

Owner: Sydöstran AB
Editorial: Ronnebygatan 26-28, Karlskrona 371 89
Tel: 46 455 33 46 00
Email: redaktion@sydostran.se **Web site:** http://www.sydostran.se/
Circ: 10500
Nyhetschef: Anders Nilsson
Profile: Sydöstran är en svensk dagstidning med täckningsområde i hela Blekinge län. Centralredaktionen ligger i Karlskrona och tidningen har lokalredaktioner i Karlshamn, Ronneby, Sölvesborg och Olofström. Ledarsidan är socialdemokratisk.
Language (s): Swedish
Ad Rate: Full Page Mono 40560.00
Currency: Sweden Kronor
COMMUNITY NEWSPAPER

Tidningen Ångermanland 365382

Owner: MittMedia Förvaltnings AB
Editorial: Nybrogatan 2, Härnösand 871 30
Tel: 46 611 55 48 00
Email: taredaktion@allehanda.se **Web site:** http://www.allehanda.se
Circ: 15600
Chefredaktör & Ansvarig utgivare: Anders Ingvarsson; **Nyhetschef:** Marcus Melinder; **Nyhetschef:** Ulf Westman
Profile: Tidningen Ångermanland är en svensk lokaltidning för Härnösands, Kramfors och Sollefteå kommuner. Tidningen lanserades år 2000 när Nya Norrland och Västernorrlands Allehanda slogs ihop. Tidningen Ångermanland har på grund av detta två ledarsidor, en socialdemokratisk och en liberal. Sedan 2007 ingår tidningen i bolaget Allehanda Media AB där också tidningen Örnsköldsviks Allehanda ingår. De två tidningarna har separata nyhetsdelar, men en gemensam andra del som innehåller nöje, kultur och sport.
Language (s): Swedish
Ad Rate: Full Page Mono 46080.00
Currency: Sweden Kronor
COMMUNITY NEWSPAPER

Tidningen Extra 625573

Editorial: Robertsviksgatan 5, Luleå 972 41
Tel: 46 920 26 28 20
Email: redaktionen@tidningenextra.se **Web site:** http://lulea.tidningenextra.se
Freq: Weekly
Profile: Tidningen Extra är en gratistidning för Boden och Luleå.Tidningen Extra är en lokaltidning i Norrbotten som distribueras till samtliga hushåll och företag i regionen. Tidningen kommer i tre editioner; Luleå, Boden och Malmfälten. Luleå- och Boden-editionerna utkommer en gång i veckan och Malmfälts-editionen en gång i månaden. Redaktionen är densamma för alla editioner och de är baserade i Luleå.
Language (s): Swedish
COMMUNITY NEWSPAPER

Tidningen Nordost 578965

Owner: DirektPress Tidningsförlag AB
Editorial: Britta Sahlgrens gata 8 c, Västra Frölunda 421 31 **Tel:** 46 31 72 05 510
Email: nordost@gbg.direktpress.se **Web site:** http://www.tidningennordost.se/
Freq: Bi-Weekly
Chefredaktör & Ansvarig utgivare: Magnus Johansson
Profile: Tidningen Nordost är en lokaltidning som utkommer två gånger i månaden till hushåll i Bergsjön, Kortedala, Lärjedalen och Gunnared. Utöver det så har tidningen även ställdistribution på flera platser så att tidningen finns tillgänglig för läsaren på språng.
Language (s): Swedish
COMMUNITY NEWSPAPER

Tidningen Sydväst 578137

Editorial: Britta Sahlgrens gata 8 c, Västra Frölunda 421 31 **Tel:** 46 31 72 05 510
Email: sydvast@gbg.direktpress.se **Web site:** http://www.tidningensydvast.se
Freq: Weekly; **Circ:** 15300
Profile: Tidningen Sydväst delas ut i brevlådorna i Eklanda, Sisjön, Askim, Hult, Hovås, Brottkärr, Billdal, Lindås, Malevik, Kullavik och Särö – och områdena däremellan. I tidningen hittar man alltid lokala nyheter - såväl stort till smått. Redaktionen gör egna undersökningar, bevakar kommun- och stadsdelsbeslut och gör regelrätta reportage om sådant som anses intressera läsarna.
Language (s): Swedish
COMMUNITY NEWSPAPER

Torslanda Tidningen 222796

Editorial: Flygmotorvagen 3, Torslanda 423 37
Tel: 46 31 92 45 80
Web site: http://www.tidningen.se
Freq: Weekly
Redaktionsansvarig: Therese Sjöqvist; **Ansvarig utgivare:** Bengt Wester
Profile: Önskar ej motta pressutskick. Torslanda Tidningen är en gratis lokaltidning som når alla hushåll och företag i Torslanda, Björlanda, Säve samt hela Öckerö kommun.
Language (s): Swedish
Ad Rate: Full Page Colour 14900.00
Currency: Sweden Kronor
COMMUNITY NEWSPAPER

Totalt Umeå 840666

Owner: VK-koncernen
Editorial: Forradsvagen 9, Umeå 901 70
Tel: 46 90 70 28 30
Email: redaktion@totaltumea.se **Web site:** http://totaltumea.se
Freq: Weekly; **Circ:** 63900
Chefredaktör & Ansvarig utgivare: Hampus Råde
Profile: Totalt Umeå är en gratistidning som kommer ut en gång i veckan. Hela upplagan distribueras med posten direkt hem till hushållen och till företagen i kommunen i såväl stad som land, tätorter och byar. I tidningen kan man läsa om allt som handlar om Umeå. Den innehåller artiklar och reportage om det som är på gång i kommunen.
Language (s): Swedish
Ad Rate: Full Page Mono 24000.00
Currency: Sweden Kronor
COMMUNITY NEWSPAPER

TTELA 158899

Owner: Stampen Media Group
Editorial: Drottninggatan 12, Box 111, Vänersborg 462 22 **Tel:** 46 521 57 59 00
Email: redaktionen@ttela.se **Web site:** http://www.ttela.se
Freq: Daily; **Circ:** 22200
Redaktör: Karin Engqvist; **Nyhetschef:** Marita Engqvist; **Redaktör:** Suzanne Werner
Profile: TTELA är en lokaltidning för Trollhättans, Vänersborgs, Melleruds och Lilla Edets kommuner. Första utgivningsår för denna tidning var 2004 efter en sammanslagning av de två tidigare dagstidningarna Trollhättans Tidning och Elfsborgs Läns Allehanda. Tidningen utkommer sex dagar i veckan.Newspaper covering local news in the Trollhättans, Vänersborgs, Mellerud and Lilla Edets municipalities.
Language (s): Swedish
Ad Rate: Full Page Mono 53148.00
Currency: Sweden Kronor
COMMUNITY NEWSPAPER

Tyresö Nyheter 416273
Editorial: Bjorkbacksvagen 37, Tyresö 135 40
Web site: http://www.tyresonyheter.nu
Freq: Bi-Monthly
Chefredaktör & Ansvarig utgivare: Anders Linder
Profile: Tyresö Nyheter är en lokaltidning med socialdemokratiska inriktning. Tidningen etablerades 1972 och utkommer med 8 nummer per år. Tyresö Nyheter delas ut gratis till alla fasta hushåll i Tyresö. Önskar ej motta pressutskick.
Language (s): Swedish
COMMUNITY NEWSPAPER

Uppsalatidningen 331621
Owner: DirektPress
Editorial: Danmarksgatan 30, Uppsala 751 45
Tel: 46 18 418 11 11
Email: redaktion@uppsalatidningen.se **Web site:** http://www.uppsalatidningen.se/
Freq: Weekly; **Circ:** 92000
Redigerare: Tone Gellerstedt; **Redaktionsansvarig:** Inger Nilsson
Profile: Uppsalatidningen är politiskt oberoende lokaltidning som eftersträvar en stark lokal förankring. Redaktion bevakar aktuella nyheter, händelser och personer inom samhälle, näringsliv, sport, nöje, kultur och utbildning. De eftersträvar att ge Uppsala- och Knivstabor en aktuell bild av det som händer i Uppsala län.
Language (s): Swedish
Ad Rate: Full Page Mono 36000.00
Currency: Sweden Kronor
COMMUNITY NEWSPAPER

Upsala Nya Tidning 158606
Owner: Upsala Nya Tidning
Editorial: Dragarbrunns torg 2, Uppsala 751 03
Tel: 46 18 47 80 000
Email: 72018@unt.se **Web site:** http://www.unt.se
Freq: Daily; **Circ:** 41100
Chefredaktör, VD & Ansvarig utgivare: Charlotta Friborg; **Nyhetschef:** Lotta Frithiof; **Redaktionschef:** Åsa Pallarp Beckman
Profile: Upsala Nya Tidning (UNT) är en morgontidning som ges ut i Uppsala. UNT är liberal och Sveriges åttonde största landsortstidning.
Language (s): Swedish
Ad Rate: Full Page Mono 65400.00
Currency: Sweden Kronor
COMMUNITY NEWSPAPER

Vallentuna Nya 721404
Editorial: Takpannevagen 109, Vallentuna 186 36
Tel: 46 8 51 17 11 77
Email: info@vallentunanya.se **Web site:** http://www.vallentunanya.se
Freq: Weekly
Chefredaktör: Peter Palmqvist
Profile: Vallentuna Nya är en lokal nyhetstidning i Vallentuna Kommun som utkommer en gång i veckan.
Language (s): Swedish
Ad Rate: Full Page Colour 9000.00
Currency: Sweden Kronor
COMMUNITY NEWSPAPER

VarbergsPosten 222793
Editorial: Backgatan 32, Varberg 432 44
Email: redaktion@varbergsposten.se **Web site:** http://www.varbergsposten.se
Freq: Weekly
Profile: VarbergsPosten är en lokaltidning med siktet inställt på den egna kommunen.
Language (s): Swedish
Ad Rate: Full Page Colour 31000.00
Currency: Sweden Kronor
COMMUNITY NEWSPAPER

Värmlands Folkblad 158572
Owner: Värmlands Folkblad AB
Editorial: Box 67, Saterivagen 7, Karlstad 651 03
Tel: 46 54 17 55 00
Email: redaktion@vf.se **Web site:** http://www.vf.se
Freq: Daily; **Circ:** 14100
Chefredaktör & Ansvarig utgivare: Peter Franke; **Nyhetschef:** Björn Stefanson
Profile: Värmlands Folkblad är en svensk dagstidning som utkommer i Värmland med sex nummer i veckan. Tidningen etablerades 1918 och är socialdemokratikt.
Language (s): Swedish
COMMUNITY NEWSPAPER

Värnamo Nyheter 365107
Owner: Hallpressen AB
Editorial: Storgatsbacken 13, Värnamo 331 30
Tel: 46 370 30 06 00
Email: redaktion@varnamonyheter.se **Web site:** http://www.varnamonyheter.se
Circ: 15300
Nyhetschef: Christer Nordmark
Profile: Värnamo Nyheter är en politiskt obunden lokaltidning som förutom i Värnamo även har redaktioner i Gislaved, Gnosjö, Skillingaryd och Vaggeryd. Tidningen utkommer varje helgfri måndag, tisdag, torsdag och lördag.
Language (s): Swedish
COMMUNITY NEWSPAPER

Vårt Kungsholmen 285925
Owner: Direktpress AB
Editorial: Box 5290, Valhallavagen 184, Stockholm 102 46 **Tel:** 46 8 545 870 70
Email: vk@direktpress.se **Web site:** http://www.vartkungsholmen.se
Freq: Weekly; **Circ:** 41200
Chefredaktör: Helene Claesson
Profile: Vårt Kungsholmen är en gratis lokaltidning för alla hushåll i Kungsholmen samt Lilla och Stora Essingen. Tidningen innehåller lokala nyheter samt bevakning av stans nöjesliv och bostadsmarknad.
Language (s): Swedish
Ad Rate: Full Page Mono 22280.00
Currency: Sweden Kronor
COMMUNITY NEWSPAPER

Vårt Malmö 164063
Owner: Malmö Stad
Editorial: Giv Akt Skane AB, Sodra Forstadsgatan 2, Malmo 211 43 **Tel:** 46 40 34 10 00
Email: info.malmo@givakt.se **Web site:** http://www.malmo.se/vartmalmo
Freq: Monthly; **Circ:** 157000 Publisher's Statement
Ansvarig utgivare: Anders Mellberg
Profile: Vårt Malmö är Malmö stads tidning med samhällsinformation som delas ut gratis till alla hushåll och företag i staden. Tidningen ska spegla samhället Malmö i ett brett perspektiv, inte enbart handla om kommunal verksamhet utan även om annat som kan intressera, som näringsliv, regionala frågor, föreningsverksamhet och mycket annat. Newspaper featuring entertainment and news for Malmö.
Language (s): Swedish
COMMUNITY NEWSPAPER

Västerås Tidning 222781
Owner: DirektPress
Editorial: Norra Kallgatan 17, Västerås 722 11
Tel: 46 21 30 46 00
Email: redaktion@vasterastidning.se **Web site:** http://www.vasterastidning.se
Freq: 2 Times/Week; **Circ:** 87700 RS
Ansvarig utgivare: Lasse Blom; **Redaktionschef:** Jonas Edberg
Profile: Västerås Tidning är en gratistidning med lokalnyheter som delas ut gratis till alla hushåll inom Västerås kommun, Hallstahammar kommun och Surahammar, Ramnäs och Virsbo region A48 samt till tidningsställ i hela Västmanland.
Language (s): Swedish
COMMUNITY NEWSPAPER

Västerbottens-Kuriren 364925
Owner: Västerbottens Kuriren AB
Editorial: Forradsvagen 9, Umeå 901 70
Tel: 46 90 17 60 00
Email: redaktion@vk.se **Web site:** http://www.vk.se
Freq: Daily; **Circ:** 30700
Redaktör: Roland Edlund; **Redaktionschef:** Gunnar Falck; **Nyhetschef:** Patrik Krainer; **Chefredaktör & Ansvarig utgivare:** Ingvar Näslund; **Redaktionschef:** Jessica Wennberg
Profile: Västerbottens-Kuriren är Norrlands största dagstidning. Tidningen utkommer i Umeå med omnejd inklusive södra Lappland bort till norska gränsen.
Language (s): Swedish
COMMUNITY NEWSPAPER

Västerviks-Tidningen 365378
Owner: Norrköpings Tidningar
Editorial: Stora Torget 2, Västervik 593 82
Tel: 46 490 666 00
Email: tipsa@vt.se **Web site:** http://www.vt.se
Freq: Daily; **Circ:** 10200
Nyhetschef: Christoffer Nielsen
Profile: Västerviks-Tidningen är en svensk dagstidning som ges ut i Västervik. Tidningen grundades år 1834.
Language (s): Swedish
Ad Rate: Full Page Mono 24346.00
Currency: Sweden Kronor
COMMUNITY NEWSPAPER

Vestmanlands Läns Tidning 158607
Owner: Vestmanlands Läns Tidning AB
Editorial: Box 3, Slottsgatan 27, Västerås 721 03
Tel: 46 21 19 90 00
Email: nyheter@vlt.se **Web site:** http://www.vlt.se
Freq: Daily; **Circ:** 31300
Redaktionschef: Mårten Enberg; **Nyhetschef:** Karin Thornberg
Profile: Vestmanlands Läns Tidning, VLT, är en lokal morgontidning i Västerås, Hallstahammar och Surahammar som utkommer sex gånger i veckan.
Language (s): Swedish
Ad Rate: Full Page Mono 69408.00
Currency: Sweden Kronor
COMMUNITY NEWSPAPER

Vi i Vasastan 222794
Owner: Direktpress AB
Editorial: Vallhallavagen 184, Box 5290, Stockholm 102 46 **Tel:** 46 8 545 870 70
Email: viv@direktpress.se **Web site:** http://www.viivasastan.se
Freq: Weekly; **Circ:** 37800 RS
Chefredaktör & Ansvarig utgivare: Helene Claesson
Profile: Vi i Vasastan är en gratis lokaltidning som varje lördag delas den ut till alla hushåll i Vasastan och på Norrmalm. Tidningen innehåller lokala nyheter och bevakning av stans nöjesliv och bostadsmarknad.
Language (s): Swedish
Ad Rate: Full Page Mono 22280.00
Currency: Sweden Kronor
COMMUNITY NEWSPAPER

Vi i Väsby 770805
Owner: Direktpress AB
Editorial: Kanalvagen 1 A 2 tr, Upplands Väsby 194 61
Email: redaktion@viivasby.se **Web site:** http://www.viivasby.se
Freq: Weekly; **Circ:** 20300
Nyhetschef: Mats Hedström
Profile: Vi i Väsby är en lokal gratistidning som delas ut till hushållen i Väsby och har flera tidningsställ på olika platser i kommunen.
Language (s): Swedish
COMMUNITY NEWSPAPER

Ystads Allehanda 366231
Owner: Skånemedia AB
Editorial: Lilla Norregatan 9, Ystad 271 81
Tel: 46 411 55 78 00
Email: red@ystadsallehanda.se **Web site:** http://www.ystadsallehanda.se
Freq: Daily; **Circ:** 21100
Nyhetschef: Peter Hellemarck; **Chefredaktör:** Lars Mohlin; **Chefredaktör & Ansvarig Utgivare:** Jörgen Svensson
Profile: Ystads Allehanda är en lokal dagstidning för Ystad, Simrishamn, Sjöbo, Tomelilla och Skurup. Tidningen innehåller regionala nyheter, debatt, sport, ekonomi, kultur och nöje.
Language (s): Swedish
Ad Rate: Full Page Mono 53904.00
Currency: Sweden Kronor
COMMUNITY NEWSPAPER

Switzerland

Time Difference: GMT +1
National Telephone Code: 41
Continent: Europe
Capital: Bern

Newspapers

20 Minuten, Basel 306393
Owner: Tamedia AG
Editorial: 20 Minuten Basel, Marktgasse 8, Basel 4001 **Tel:** 41 61 269 80 20
Web site: http://www.20min.ch
Freq: Daily; **Circ:** 80001 Publisher's Statement
Profile: 20 Minuten bzw. französisch 20 minutes und italienisch 20 minuti ist eine kostenlose Schweizer Pendlerzeitung. Sie erscheint im Tabloidformat und präsentiert Nachrichten in kürzester Form. Einen grösseren Stellenwert haben boulevardeske Geschichten und der Serviceteil. Die Zeitung wird in Zeitungsboxen an Bahnhöfen in den Kernstädten nach dem Selbstbedienungsprinzip vertrieben. Zu den Lokalausgaben zählen Zürich, Bern, St. Gallen, Luzern und Basel.
Language (s): German
DAILY NEWSPAPER

24 heures 160021
Owner: Tamedia Publications romandes SA
Editorial: Avenue de la Gare 33, Lausanne 1001
Tel: 41 21 349 44 44
Email: 24heures@24heures.ch **Web site:** http://www.24heures.ch
Freq: Mon thru Fri; **Circ:** 65505 Publisher's Statement
Profile: 24 heures ist eine Tageszeitung für den französischen Teil der Schweiz, die Nachrichten und aktuelle Themen abdeckt. Hierzu gehören regionale, nationale und internationale Nachrichten, Politik, Wirtschaft, Märktem Kultur, Prominente, Lifestyle, Autos, Technologie, Wissenschaft, Reise und Kunst. 24 heures is a daily newspaper for the french part of Switzerland, covering news and current affairs including regional, national and international news, politics, economics, markets, sport, culture, celebrities, lifestyle, cars, technology, science, travel and the arts.
Language (s): French
Ad Rate: Full Page Mono 13420.00
Ad Rate: Full Page Colour 23580.00
Currency: Switzerland Francs
DAILY NEWSPAPER

az nordwestschweiz 923393
Owner: AZ Zeitungen AG
Editorial: AZ Zeitungen AG, Neumattstrasse 1, Aarau 5001 **Tel:** 41 58 200 58 58
Email: verlag@azmedien.ch **Web site:** http://www.azwerbung.ch/zeitungen/print/az-nordwestschweiz
Freq: Daily; **Circ:** 165489
Profile: Die az nordwestschweiz ist eine überregionale Zeitung, welche den Mantelteil der regionalen Tageszeitungen az Aargauer Zeitung, bz Basellandschaftliche Zeitung, bz Basel, az Limmattaler Zeitung, az Solothurner Zeitung, az Grenchner Tagblatt, Oltner Tagblatt und Zofinger Tagblatt bildet. Die Zentrale liegt hierbei in Aargau. Der Mantelteil bietet hierbei überregionale Nachrichten aus Politik, Wirtschaft, Gesellschaft und Kultur, während jede Regionalausgabe ihre eigenen Regionalteile verwaltet. The az nordwestschweiz is a national newspaper, which forms the mantle part of the national daily newspapers az Aargauer Zeitung, bz Basellandschaftliche Zeitung, bz Basel, az Limmattaler Zeitung, az Solothurner Zeitung, az Grenchner Tagblatt, Oltner Tagblatt and Zofinger Tagblatt. The headquarters are located in Aargau. The mantle part provides national news from politics, economy, society and culture, while each regional edition manages its own regional sections.
Language (s): German
DAILY NEWSPAPER

Blick (Switzerland) 159277
Owner: Ringier AG
Editorial: Redaktion Blick, Dufourstr. 23, Zurich 8008
Tel: 41 44 259 62 62
Email: redaktion@blick.ch **Web site:** http://www.blick.ch
Freq: Daily; **Circ:** 163627
Profile: Blick ist eine Abendzeitung für die deutschsprachige Schweiz, mit regionalen und überregionalen Nachrichten zu Politik, Wirtschaft, Kultur, Gesellschaft und Sport. Zudem bietet sie einen Ratgeberteil mit Themen wie Reise und Technik, als auch Unterhaltung. Blick is a daily newspaper for the German-speaking Swiss, with covering regional, national and international news on politics, economy, culture, society and sports. Additionally, it offers consumer information on topics such as travel and technology, as well as entertainment.
Language (s): German
DAILY NEWSPAPER

BZ Berner Zeitung 159249
Owner: Espace Media AG
Editorial: Hauptredaktion Berner Zeitung BZ, Dammweg 9, Bern 3001 **Tel:** 41 31 330 33 33
Email: redaktion@bernerzeitung.ch **Web site:** http://www.bernerzeitung.ch
Freq: Daily; **Circ:** 28
Profile: Die Berner Zeitung ist eine regionale Tageszeitung mit Nachrichten zu Politik, Wirtschaft, Kultur, Sport, Reise, Technik u.a. The Berner Zeitung is a regional daily newspaper covering politics, economics, sport, travel, technology and the arts.
Language (s): German
DAILY NEWSPAPER

Die Südostschweiz 159955
Owner: Somedia Publishing AG
Editorial: Südostschweiz Zentralredaktion, Sommeraustrasse 32, Chur 7007
Tel: 41 81 255 50 50
Email: nachrichten@suedostschweiz.ch **Web site:** http://www.suedostschweiz.ch
Freq: Daily; **Circ:** 81302
Profile: Die Südostschweiz ist eine regionale Tageszeitung mit Nachrichten zu Politik, Wirtschaft, Kultur, Gesellschaft und Sport für den Südosten der Schweiz. Sie bietet den Mantelteil der Regionalzeitungen Südostschweiz Graubünden, Bündner Tagblatt, La Quotidiana, Südostschweiz Glarus, Südostschweiz Gaster & See, March-Anzeiger, Höfner Volksblatt und Sarganserländer. Großauflage lt. WEMF 2015: Verbreitete Auflage 88.953 ExemplareThe Südostschweiz is a regional daily newspaper with news about politics, economy, culture, society and sports for the south-east of Switzerland. It offers the main portion of the regional papers Südostschweiz Graubünden, Bündner Tagblatt, La Quotidiana, Südostschweiz Glarus, Südostschweiz Gaster & See, March-Anzeiger, Höfner Volksblatt and Sarganserländer.
Language (s): German
DAILY NEWSPAPER

Luzerner Zeitung 159699
Owner: Neue Luzerner Zeitung AG
Editorial: Neue Luzerner Zeitung AG, Luzern 6002
Tel: 41 41 429 52 52
Email: wirtschaft@luzernerzeitung.ch **Web site:** http://www.luzernerzeitung.ch
Freq: Daily; **Circ:** 73088
Profile: Regionale Tageszeitung mit Nachrichten aus Politik, Wirtschaft, Kultur, Sport, Reise, Technik. Regional daily newspaper covering politics, economics, sport, travel, technology and the arts.
Language (s): German
DAILY NEWSPAPER

NZZ Neue Zürcher Zeitung 159715
Owner: Neue Zürcher Zeitung AG
Editorial: Neue Zürcher Zeitung, Falkenstr. 11, Zurich 8021 **Tel:** 41 44 258 11 11
Email: redaktion@nzz.ch **Web site:** http://www.nzz.ch
Freq: Mon thru Fri; **Circ:** 28
Profile: Die Neue Zürcher Zeitung ist eine überregionale Tageszeitung für regionale, nationale und internationale Nachrichten, sowie Politik, Finanzen, Wirtschaft, Sport, Kultur und Freizeit. The Neue Zürcher Zeitung is a national daily newspaper covering regional, national and international news, as well as politics, finance, economics, sport, culture and leisure.
Language (s): German
DAILY NEWSPAPER

Tages-Anzeiger 159965
Owner: Tamedia AG
Editorial: Tamedia AG, Werdstrasse 21, Zurich 8004
Tel: 41 44 248 44 11
Email: redaktion@tagesanzeiger.ch **Web site:** http://www.tagesanzeiger.ch
Freq: Daily; **Circ:** 172920
Profile: Der Tages-Anzeiger ist eine nationale Schweizer Tageszeitung, deren Orientierung mittelinks ist. Er deckt den Großraum Zürich ab und gliedert sich in vier Faszikel: Der erste Faszikel enthält Nachrichten und Kommentare aus der Schweiz und dem Ausland, eine Analyse-Seite, das Wetter, das Leserforum.Der zweite Teil trägt den Titel "Zürich" und enthält regionale Nachrichten aus Stadt und Kanton Zürich, amtliche Anzeigen, einen Veranstaltungskalender sowie die Seite "Bellevue" für

jungere Leser mit einem Comic und ähnlichem. Der dritte Teil nennt sich "Kultur und Gesellschaft" und enthält unter anderem Kulturnachrichten, das Kino-, Theater- und Fernsehprogramm sowie die Seite "Wissen".Im letzten Faszikel sind der Wirtschafts- und Sportteil miteinander vereinigt. Der Wirtschaftsteil enthält einerseits Wirtschaftsnachrichten und andererseits Börsen- und Devisendaten; der Sport untergliedert sich in allgemeine Sportnews sowie Regionalsport. Tages-Anzeiger is a Swiss daily national with a center-left orientation.
Language (s): German
DAILY NEWSPAPER

Community Newspaper

Le Matin Dimanche 574122
Owner: Tamedia SA
Editorial: Avenue de la Gare, 33, Lausanne 1001
Tel: 41 21 349 49 49
Email: info@lematin.ch **Web site:** http://www.lematin.ch
Freq: Weekly; **Circ:** 203838 Publisher's Statement
Profile: Sunday edition of the daily newspaper Le Matin, covering lifestyle, society, culture, science and women's interests. Regionalzeitung für Lausanne mit aktuellen Nachrichten und relevanten Themen im Bereich, Kultur, Sport, Wirtschaft, Politik.
Language (s): French
COMMUNITY NEWSPAPER

SonntagsBlick 228521
Owner: Ringier AG
Editorial: Redaktion SonntagsBlick, Dufourstr. 23, Zurich 8008 **Tel:** 41 44 259 62 62
Email: redaktion@blick.ch **Web site:** http://www.blick.ch/sonntagsblick
Freq: Weekly; **Circ:** 188302
Profile: SonntagsBlick ist eine Schweizer Sonntagszeitung. Sie berichtet über nationale und regionale Nachrichten und Entwicklungen. SonntagsBlick is the weekly Sunday edition of Blick. It covers national and regional news.
Language (s): German
COMMUNITY NEWSPAPER

SonntagsZeitung 228547
Owner: Tamedia AG
Editorial: SonntagsZeitung, Werdstr. 21, Zurich 8021
Tel: 41 44 248 40 40
Email: redaktion@sonntagszeitung.ch **Web site:** http://www.sonntagszeitung.ch
Freq: Weekly; **Circ:** 194764 WEMF
Profile: Die SonntagsZeitung ist eine wöchentliche Zeitung für die deutschsprachige Schweiz. Sie wird in neun unterschiedliche Themenbereiche gegliedert, welche Nachrichten, Sport, Kultur, Wirtschaft, Reisen, Trends und Wissenschaft beinhalten. Dadurch bietet die SonntagsZeitung eine Mischung aus Nachrichten und Unterhaltung. The SonntagsZeitung is a weekly newspaper for the German-speaking part of Switzerland. It is divided into nine different subject areas, which include news, sports, culture, business, travel, trends and science. Thus, the Sunday newspaper offers a mix of news and entertainment.
Language (s): German
COMMUNITY NEWSPAPER

Syria

Time Difference: GMT +2
National Telephone Code: 963
Continent: Asia
Capital: Damascus

Newspapers

An-nour 414034
Owner: Syrian Communist Party
Editorial: PO Box 7394, The White Bridge, Omar Ben Mokhtar Street, Damascus **Tel:** 963 11 332 4914
Email: info@an-nour.com **Web site:** http://www.an-nour.com
Freq: Weekly; **Circ:** 9500 Publisher's Statement
PR Manager: Riman Haddad
Profile: An-nour is the weekly newspaper of the Syrian Communist Party and covers news, politics, current affairs, social issues and cultural activities. It launched in 1955 and is published on Wednesdays.
Language (s): Arabic
DAILY NEWSPAPER

Al Baath 157015
Owner: Dar Al Baath for Press, Printing, Publishing and Distribution
Editorial: PO Box 9389, Al Mazzeh Highway, Damascus **Tel:** 963 11 662 2141
Email: baath-n@net.sy **Web site:** http://albaath.news.sy
Freq: Daily; **Circ:** 56000 Publisher's Statement
Editor In Chief: Mohammad Kanaissi; **Managing Director:** Abdul Latif Omran
Profile: Al Baath is a daily Arabic newspaper covering news, politics, business and sport. It was first published in 1946.
Language (s): Arabic
DAILY NEWSPAPER

Baladna 444559
Owner: United Group for Publishing, Advertising & Marketing
Editorial: PO Box 1999, Huda Building, 5 Iskandaria Street, Damascus **Tel:** 963 11 202 5141
Email: ali.hassoun@ewaseet.net **Web site:** http://baladnaonline.net
Freq: Daily; **Circ:** 90000 Publisher's Statement
General Manager: Fadi Al Zehr; **Editor in Chief:** Ali Hassoun
Profile: Baladna (Our Country) is a daily Arabic newspaper covering local and international news, politics, business and sport. It was first published in 2006.
Language (s): Arabic
Ad Rate: Full Page Mono 95000.00
Ad Rate: Full Page Colour 110000.00
Currency: Syria Pounds
DAILY NEWSPAPER

Bourses and Markets 445249
Owner: Al Marsad Syrian Company for Media and Business
Editorial: PO Box 16545, Damascus
Tel: 963 11 662 5315
Email: info@syriandays.com **Web site:** http://www.syriandays.com
Freq: Weekly; **Circ:** 10000 Publisher's Statement
Advertising Manager: Essam Al Safytle; **Publisher & Editor in Chief:** Youssef Saad
Profile: Bourses and Markets is a weekly Arabic business newspaper covering local and international business news, stocks and stock markets. It launched in 2004 and is published on Sundays.
Language (s): Arabic
Ad Rate: Full Page Mono 90000.00
Currency: Syria Pounds
DAILY NEWSPAPER

Al Fedaa 413476
Owner: Al Wahda Foundation For Press, Printing and Publishing
Editorial: PO Box 395, Al Andalus Street, Hamah
Tel: 963 33 360501
Email: slmas_750@yahoo.com **Web site:** http://fedaa.alwehda.gov.sy
Freq: Daily; **Circ:** 16000 Publisher's Statement
Editor in Chief: Hussein Abbas; **Editor:** Ali Adelah; **Head of News:** Hassan Awaichy; **Investigative News Chief:** Mohammad Khabbazi
Profile: Al Fedaa is a regional newspaper distributed in the Hamah area of Syria. It launched in 1963 and focuses on local news, politics, culture and sport. It is published daily, except Fridays and Saturdays.
Language (s): Arabic
DAILY NEWSPAPER

Al Jamahir 413473
Owner: Al Wahda Foundation For Press, Printing and Publishing
Editorial: Beside Jamea Al Abara, Al Abara Area, Aleppo **Tel:** 963 21 212 9321
Email: malsheesh@gmail.com **Web site:** http://jamahir.alwehda.gov.sy
Freq: Daily; **Circ:** 18000 Publisher's Statement
Head of News: Mohammad Ahmad; **Advertising Manager:** Ahmad Kurdi; **Editor in Chief:** Jihad Steif
Profile: Al Jamahir (Audiences) is a regional newspaper distributed in the Aleppo area of Syria focusing on local news and current affairs. It launchedin 1963 and is published daily, except Fridays and Saturdays.
Language (s): Arabic
DAILY NEWSPAPER

Al Mawkef Al-Riadi 207949
Owner: Al Wahda Foundation For Press, Printing and Publishing
Editorial: PO Box 2448, Kafar Souseh, Damascus
Tel: 963 11 219 3291
Email: riadi@thawra.com **Web site:** http://riadi.alwehda.gov.sy
Freq: Weekly; **Circ:** 30000 Publisher's Statement
Advertising Manager: Ruwaida Maria
Profile: Al Mawkef Al-Riadi is a weekly Arabic newspaper covering local, regional and international sport. It was launched in 1963 and is published on Saturdays.
Language (s): Arabic
DAILY NEWSPAPER

Teshreen Daily 350454
Owner: Al Wahda Foundation For Press, Printing and Publishing
Editorial: PO Box 5452, Corniche Al Medan, Damascus **Tel:** 963 11 213 1100
Email: tnp@mail.sy **Web site:** http://tishreen.news.sy
Freq: Daily; **Circ:** 60000 Publisher's Statement
Picture Editor: Tareq Al Hossneyah
Profile: Teshreen Daily is an Arabic newspaper covering national and international news, current affairs, politics, business and sport. It was first published in 1975.
Language (s): Arabic
DAILY NEWSPAPER

Al Thawra 157016
Owner: Al Wahda Foundation For Press, Printing and Publishing
Editorial: PO Box 2448, Kafar Sosah, Damascus
Tel: 963 11 222 2399
Email: mail@thawraonline.sy **Web site:** http://thawra.sy
Freq: Daily; **Circ:** 80000 Publisher's Statement
News Editor: Ahmed Al Wadi; **Picture Editor:** Mayssoun Eissa; **Office Manager:** Yaser Hamze; **Editor in Chief:** Ali Kasem; **Public Relations Manager:** Amal Maarouf; **Advertising Manager:** Ruwaida Maria
Profile: Al Thawra (The Revolution) is an Arabic newspaper covering local and international news, politics, current affairs, business and sport. The newspaper launched in 1963 and is published daily, except Fridays.
Language (s): Arabic
DAILY NEWSPAPER

Al Watan 433595
Owner: Al A'amal Al Iqtisady Group
Editorial: Al Watan Building, Damascus Free Zone, Damascus **Tel:** 963 11 213 7400
Email: edc@alwatan.sy **Web site:** http://www.alwatan.sy
Freq: Daily; **Circ:** 28000 Publisher's Statement
Editor in Chief: Waddah Abd Rabbo; **News Editor:** Jambulat Shtay
Profile: Al Watan is a newspaper covering local, regional and international news, politics, business and sport. It launched in 2006 and is published daily, except Fridays and Saturdays.
Language (s): Arabic
DAILY NEWSPAPER

News Service/Syndicate

Agence France-Presse - Damascus Bureau 370529
Owner: Agence France-Presse
Editorial: PO Box 2400, 2nd Floor, Sharaf Building, Damascus **Tel:** 963 11 231 8200
Email: afp.damascus@afp.com **Web site:** http://www.afp.com
Photographer: Louai Bechara; **Bureau Chief:** Roueida Mabardi
Profile: Damascus bureau of the French international news agency.
Language (s): Arabic
NEWS SERVICE/SYNDICATE

APTN Syria 370504
Owner: Associated Press
Editorial: 7th Floor, Tabaae Building, Damascus
Tel: 963 11 213 9768
Email: g-saliba7@hotmail.com **Web site:** http://www.aptn.com
Bureau Chief: George Saliba
Profile: Associated Press Television News (APTN) is the international television arm of the Associated Press - APTN's operations include a main news service, specialised broadcast services, customised coverage for the Middle East, a productions division, weekly and daily entertainment news and an extensive video archive library.
Language (s): Arabic
NEWS SERVICE/SYNDICATE

Syrian Arab News Agency 380844
Owner: Ministry of Information, Syria
Editorial: PO Box 2661, Baramka, Damascus
Tel: 963 11 212 9702
Email: sana@sana.sy **Web site:** http://www.sana.sy
Editor: Nezha Al Kouzi; **General Manager:** Ahmad Douwa; **Editor:** Yara Ismaeel
Profile: Syrian Arab News Agency (SANA) is the official government news agency of Syria. It was founded in 1965.
Language (s): Arabic
NEWS SERVICE/SYNDICATE

Taiwan

Time Difference: GMT +8
National Telephone Code: 886
Continent: Asia
Capital: Taipei

Newspapers

Apple Daily 459420
Owner: Next Media Ltd.
Editorial: Number 38, Lane 141, Xing-Ai Road, Neihu District, Taipei 114 **Tel:** 886 266013456
Email: news@appledaily.com.tw **Web site:** http://www.appledaily.com.tw
Freq: Daily; **Circ:** 750003 Not Audited
Editor in Chief: Wei-Ming Ma
Profile: Covers local news and social issues.
Language (s): Chinese
DAILY NEWSPAPER

China Daily News 459986
Editorial: China Daily News., Number 57, Xinhua Street, Tainan 704 **Tel:** 886 62296381
Email: cdn@ms1.hinet.net **Web site:** http://www.cdns.com.tw
Freq: Daily; **Circ:** 250003 Not Audited
Editor in Chief: Xiong Huang
Profile: It covers local news, politics and social issues.
Language (s): Chinese
DAILY NEWSPAPER

The China Post 156646
Editorial: The China Post., Number 8, Fu Shun Street, Taipei 104 **Tel:** 886 2 25969971
Email: editor@mail.chinapost.com.tw **Web site:** http://www.chinapost.com.tw
Freq: Daily; **Circ:** 300003 Not Audited
Manager: Heidi Chan; **Editor in Chief:** Jack Huang
Profile: It covers local and international news.
Language (s): English
DAILY NEWSPAPER

China Times 156855
Editorial: B3, Number 303, Meng Jia Da Dao, Taipei 10801 **Tel:** 886 223087111 5550
Email: editorplan@mail.chinatimes.com.tw **Web site:** http://www.chinatimes.com
Freq: Daily; **Circ:** 1000003 Not Audited
Editor: Chi-Chin Chang; **Manager:** Theresa Pan; **Editor in Chief:** Yu-Lin Tang; **Publisher:** Albert Yu
Profile: Covers politics, economy, society, business, culture, local news and international news.
Language (s): Chinese
DAILY NEWSPAPER

Commercial Times 459972
Editorial: 5th Floor, Number 303, Mengjia Da Dao, Taipei 108 **Tel:** 886 223087111 5727
Email: editor@ctee.com.tw **Web site:** http://news.chinatimes.com
Freq: Daily; **Circ:** 350003 Not Audited
Profile: Covers the economy, financial news, business and investment information.
Language (s): Chinese
DAILY NEWSPAPER

The Commons Daily 459987
Editorial: The Commons Daily., 31st Floor -3, Number 38, Xing Guang Road, Linya District, Kaohsiung - **Tel:** 886 72692121
Email: commons911@gmail.com
Freq: Daily
Editor in Chief: Fu-Lai Chou; **Manager:** Xiang-Ren Liu
Profile: It covers politics, economy and social issues.
Language (s): Chinese
DAILY NEWSPAPER

Dempa Shimbun 623220
Editorial: Dempa Publications, Inc - Taiwan Branch., 7f-1, No. 36 Nanking West Road, Taipei -
Tel: 886 225581817
Web site: http://www.dempa.net
Freq: Daily
Editor: Tricia Huang
Profile: Covers the electrical industry, electrical equipment and products as well as electronic materials.
Language (s): Japanese
DAILY NEWSPAPER

Economic Daily News 459973
Editorial: United Daily News Group, Number 369, Section 1, Da Tong Road, Shijr 22161
Tel: 886 286925588
Web site: http://www.udn.com
Freq: Daily; **Circ:** 400003 Not Audited
Editor: Tian-Liang Lin; **Editor in Chief:** Hank Weng
Profile: It covers economy, finance, business, investment and stock markets.
Language (s): Chinese
DAILY NEWSPAPER

The Epoch Times 460218
Editorial: The Epoch Times., 5th Floor-1, Number 9, Aiguo West Road, Taipei 100 **Tel:** 886 222697097
Email: editor_tw@epochtimes.com **Web site:** http://www.epochtimes.com.tw
Freq: 2 Times/Week; **Circ:** 50003 Not Audited
Editor in Chief: Yi-Ching Lui; **Bureau Chief:** Hui-Ling Zhao
Profile: It covers news, politics, economy and social issues in Taiwan.
Language (s): Chinese
DAILY NEWSPAPER

Investor Weekly 596354
Editorial: Invest Ment Media Ltd., 7th Floor, Number 52, Section 1, Nanjing East Road, Taipei 104
Tel: 886 22544548
Email: wstock@invest.com.tw **Web site:** http://www.investor.com.tw
Freq: Weekly
Editor in Chief: Rong-Chuan Guo
Profile: It focuses on investment news.
Language (s): Chinese
DAILY NEWSPAPER

Keng Sheng Daily News 459977
Editorial: Keng Sheng Daily News., Number 36, Wuchuan Street, Hualien 970 **Tel:** 886 38340131
Email: kengshen@ms6.hinet.net **Web site:** http://www.ksnews.com.tw
Freq: Daily; **Circ:** 100003 Not Audited
Profile: It focuses on the local news and events in Taidong and Hualian.
Language (s): Chinese
DAILY NEWSPAPER

Lianhe Zaobao 459992
Editorial: Lian He Zao Bao - Singapore Press Holding., 2nd Floor, Number 130, Bo-Ai Road, Taipei 100 **Tel:** 886 223832732
Web site: http://www.zaobao.com
Freq: 2 Times/Week

Profile: It covers local and international news.
Language (s): Chinese
DAILY NEWSPAPER

Liberty Times 459979
Editorial: Liberty Square Plaza No. 399 Ruiguang Road, Neihu District, Taipei 114 Tel: 886 2 2656-2828
Web site: http://www.libertytimes.com.tw
Freq: Daily; Circ: 1200003 Not Audited
Editor in Chief: Chin-Rung Chen
Profile: Covers local and international news, entertainment, technology and travel.
Language (s): Taiwanese
DAILY NEWSPAPER

Mandarin Daily News 459980
Editorial: Mandarin Daily News., 3rd Floor, Number 2, Fuzhou Street, Taipei 100 Tel: 886 223921133
Email: mdnnews@email.mdnkids.com Web site: http://www.mdnkids.com.tw
Freq: Daily; Circ: 180003 Not Audited
Editor in Chief: Zhi-Mei Feng
Profile: It focuses on the education in Taiwan.
Language (s): Chinese
DAILY NEWSPAPER

Merit Times 459998
Editorial: Merit Times Daily News, 2nd Floor, Section 1, No. 369, Da-Tong Road., Taipei Xian, Shijr 221
Tel: 886 226919448
Email: newsmaster@merit-times.com.tw Web site: http://www.merit-times.com.tw
Freq: Daily; Circ: 20003 Not Audited
Profile: It focuses on the latest news of the Buddhism religion.
Language (s): Chinese
DAILY NEWSPAPER

Metro Times 602650
Editorial: Metro Times., 10th Floor-4., Number 23, Section 1, Heng Zhou Nan Road, Taipei 100
Tel: 886 223217759
Email: metro.times@msa.hinet.net Web site: http://www.metrotimes.com.tw
Freq: 2 Times/Week
Publisher: Zhong-Yi Chow
Profile: It covers local, regional and international news in Taiwan.
Language (s): Chinese
DAILY NEWSPAPER

Pots Weekly 459993
Editorial: Lihpao Daily., 1st Floor, Number 43, Fu-Xing Road, Xin-Dian City, Taipei Hsien, Taipei 231
Tel: 886 286676655 243
Email: pots@pots.tw Web site: http://www.pots.tw
Freq: Weekly; Circ: 80003 Not Audited
Editor in Chief: Sun-Quan Huang; Manager: Pansy Lin
Profile: It covers culture, society, entertainment, movies, literatures, lifestyle, and arts.
Language (s): Chinese
DAILY NEWSPAPER

Taipei Times 459574
Editorial: 14th Fl, #399, Ruiguang Rd, Neihu District, Taipei 114 Tel: 886 226561000
Email: newsdesk@taipeitimes.com Web site: http://www.taipeitimes.com
Freq: Daily; Circ: 300003 Not Audited
Editor: Kevin Chen
Profile: Launched in June 1999 with the mission of presenting an English-language journal of record for national and international readers, presented from a Taiwanese perspective. Showcases three main sections of local and international news, features and sports.
Language (s): English
DAILY NEWSPAPER

Taiwan Lih Pao 460877
Editorial: Lih Pao., 1st Floor, Number 43, Fu-Xing Road, Xin-Dian City, Taipei Hsien, Taipei 231
Tel: 886 286676655
Email: johann@lihpao.com Web site: http://www.lihpao.com
Freq: 2 Times/Week; Circ: 30001 Not Audited
Profile: It focuses on the education issues in Taiwan.
Language (s): Chinese
DAILY NEWSPAPER

Taiwan News 459974
Editorial: Taiwan News, 7th Floor, Number 88, Section 2, Xinyi Road, Taipei 106 Tel: 886 223517666
Email: editor@etaiwannews.com Web site: http://www.etaiwannews.com
Freq: Daily; Circ: 250003 Not Audited
Director: Emily Lee; Bureau Chief: Jack Ong
Profile: Established in 1949 as the first English newspaper in Taiwan. Written for stakeholders in trade, foreign affairs, tourism and other areas of government. Also covers local and national news.
Language (s): English
DAILY NEWSPAPER

Taiwan Pacific Daily News 460425
Editorial: Pacific Daily News., 6th Floor, Number 8, Ruiguang Road, Neihu District, Taipei 114
Tel: 886 287911588
Email: tpdn@ms23.hinet.net Web site: http://www.pacificnews.com.tw
Freq: 2 Times/Week; Circ: 60003 Not Audited
Manager: Yin-Jing Huang; Editor: Jia-Min Lin
Profile: It covers politics, economy, finance, and social issues.
Language (s): Chinese
DAILY NEWSPAPER

Taiwan Shin Sheng Daily News 459984
Editorial: Taiwan Shin Sheng Daily News., 9th Floor, Number 40, FuHsin North Road, Taipei 104
Tel: 886 287723058
Email: tss.ad@msa.hinet.net Web site: http://www.tssdnews.com.tw
Freq: Daily; Circ: 150003 Not Audited
Profile: It covers politics, economy, social issues, and healthcare.
Language (s): Chinese
DAILY NEWSPAPER

Taiwan Times 459982
Editorial: Taiwan Times., Number 32, Gau-Nan-Guang Road, Ren-Wu Xiang, Kaohsiung 814
Tel: 886 73428666
Email: smart@twtimes.com.tw Web site: http://www.twtimes.com.tw
Freq: Daily; Circ: 200003 Not Audited
Bureau Chief: Shih-Ying Lin
Profile: It covers local news, politics, economy, culture and social issues.
Language (s): Chinese
DAILY NEWSPAPER

T-ynews Online Newspaper 459104
Editorial: Tian Yan News International Corporation, Limited., 1st Floor, Number 60, Alley 30, Lane 53, Gongye South Road, Taoyuan 32460
Tel: 886 323885335
Email: ty.news@msa.hinet.net Web site: http://www.t-ynews.com.tw
Freq: Daily
Director: Zhao-Bin Huang
Profile: It covers politics, legal news and social issues.
Language (s): Chinese
DAILY NEWSPAPER

U Paper 602655
Editorial: U Paper., Number 369, Section 1, Da Tong Road, Shijr 22161 Tel: 886 286925588
Email: upaper@udngroup.com
Freq: 2 Times/Week
Profile: Readership/Audience Profile:Targets: General Public. U Paper is a local newspaper which covers on society, social issues, current affairs, politics and national news.
Language (s): Chinese
DAILY NEWSPAPER

United Daily News 156713
Editorial: United Daily News Group, Number 369, Section 1, Da Tong Road, Shijr 22161
Tel: 886 28 6925588
Email: u9036@udngroup.com Web site: http://udn.com
Freq: Daily; Circ: 1000003 Not Audited
Editor in Chief: Guo-Jun Luo
Profile: Covers local and international news and entertainment.
Language (s): Mandarin
DAILY NEWSPAPER

United Evening News 459990
Editorial: United Evening News, No.369, Section 1, Da Tong Road, Shijr 22161 Tel: 886 286925588
Email: abc002@udngroup.com Web site: http://udnnews.com
Freq: Daily; Circ: 500003 Not Audited
Bureau Chief: Kuo-Ning Hsiang; Editor in Chief: Mei-Yue You; Editor: Shun-Xiong Zhuang
Profile: It covers local news, international news, economy, entertainment, sports and lifestyle.
Language (s): Chinese
DAILY NEWSPAPER

Wealth News 459989
Editorial: 7th Floor, Number 52, Section 1, Nanjing East Road, Taipei 104 Tel: 886 225512561 210
Email: service1@wealthgrp.com.tw Web site: http://www.wealth.com.tw
Freq: Daily; Circ: 150003 Not Audited
Editor in Chief: Hui-Min, Sarah Guo; General Manager: Ming-Mei Qiu
Profile: It focuses on finance, business and investment.
Language (s): Chinese
DAILY NEWSPAPER

Wonder Daily 602660
Editorial: China Times Inc., B3, Number 303, Meng Jia Da Dao, Taipei 108 Tel: 886 223087111
Web site: http://news.chinatimes.com
Freq: Daily
Editor in Chief: Qing-Long Huang
Profile: It covers politics, economy, travel and social issues.
Language (s): Chinese
DAILY NEWSPAPER

World Journal - Taipei Bureau 459555
Editorial: World Journal - Taipei Bureau., Number 369, Section 1, Da Tong Road, Shijr 22161
Tel: 886 286925588 2343
Email: wjtpe1@udngroup.com Web site: http://www.worldjournal.com
Freq: Daily
Profile: It covers international, national and local news on politics, economy and social issues.
Language (s): Chinese
DAILY NEWSPAPER

News Service/Syndicate

The Central News Agency 467609
Editorial: Number 209, Songjiang Rd, Taipei 104
Tel: 886 225051180
Email: services@mail.cna.com.tw Web site: http://www.cna.com.tw
Freq: Daily
Bureau Chief: Sheng-Qing Chen
Profile: It is a Taiwan-wide news agency focusing on local news and international news.
Language (s): Chinese
NEWS SERVICE/SYNDICATE

Chiao Kwang News Agency 467631
Owner: Federation Of Overseas Chinese Associations
Editorial: Federation Of Overseas Chinese Associations -, Chiao Kwang News Agency., 7th Floor-16, Number 121, Section 1, Chongqing South Road, Taipei 100 Tel: 886 223759675
Email: focat@ms51.hinet.net Web site: http://www.focat.org.tw
Freq: Daily
President: He Huang
Profile: It is a local news agency providing major news in Taiwan and overseas.
Language (s): Chinese
NEWS SERVICE/SYNDICATE

China Economic News Service (CENS) 467608
Editorial: China Economic News Service (CENS)., No. 369, section 1, Da Tong Road, Shijr 22161
Tel: 886 2 86925588
Email: webmaster@cens.com Web site: http://cens.com/cens/html/en/news/news_home.html
Freq: Daily
Profile: China Economic News Service provides a variety of economic-related publications.
Language (s): English
NEWS SERVICE/SYNDICATE

Tajikistan

Time Difference: GMT +5
National Telephone Code: 992
Continent: Asia
Capital: Dushanbe

Newspapers

Charkhi Gardun 655128
Owner: Charkhi Gardun
Editorial: pr. S. Sherozi 16, Dushanbe 734018
Tel: 992 372 23 85 384
Email: chg@gazeta.tj Web site: http://www.gazeta.tj/chg
Freq: Weekly; Circ: 15000 Publisher's Statement
Director General: Akbarali Sattorov
Profile: The newspaper providing business and political news, culture and arts, medicine and sports, education, celebrities, live stories of readers and letters to editors.
Language (s): Tajik
Ad Rate: Full Page Mono 1500.00
Currency: United States Dollars
DAILY NEWSPAPER

Digest press 655126
Owner: Charkhi Gardun
Editorial: pr. S. Sherozi 16, Dushanbe
Tel: 992 372 23 85 346
Email: dp@gazeta.tj Web site: http://www.gazeta.tj
Freq: Weekly; Circ: 9750 Publisher's Statement
Editor In Chief: Ravshan Melikshoev; Director General: Akbarali Sattorov
Profile: Covers political news, business, education, sports, celebrities, and provides practical advice in health issues.
Language (s): Russian
Ad Rate: Full Page Mono 1500.00
Currency: United States Dollars
DAILY NEWSPAPER

Jumhuriyat 157124
Owner: Jumkhuriat
Editorial: Saadi Sherozi 16, 5 etazh, Dushanbe
Tel: 992 372 21 73 66
Web site: http://www.jumhuriyat.tj
Freq: Daily; Circ: 22000 Publisher's Statement
Profile: Government newspaper containing news on politics, economics and current affairs.
Language (s): Tajik
Ad Rate: Full Page Mono 250.00
Currency: Tajikistan Somoni
DAILY NEWSPAPER

Sadoi mardum 654835
Editorial: pr. S. Sherozi 16, Dushanbe
Tel: 992 372 385371
Email: info@sadoimardum.tj Web site: http://sadoimardum.tj
Freq: Daily; Circ: 8256 Publisher's Statement
Editor: Khairulloi Abdulavakhob
Profile: Presents political and governmental news.
Language (s): Tajik
Ad Rate: Full Page Mono 1300.00
Currency: Tajikistan Somoni
DAILY NEWSPAPER

Vecherniy Dushanbe 573063
Owner: Charkhi Gardun
Editorial: pr. S. Sherozi 16, Dushanbe 734018
Tel: 992 372 23 85 364
Email: vd@tojikiston.com Web site: http://www.gazeta.tj
Freq: Daily; Circ: 2230 Publisher's Statement
Editor-in-Chief: Ravshan Makhsumov; Editor/ Director: Akbarali Sattorov
Profile: Daily evening newspaper covering city news, analytic political and economical materials, health, society, etc.
Language (s): Russian
Ad Rate: Full Page Mono 1500.00
Currency: United States Dollars
DAILY NEWSPAPER

News Service/Syndicate

Asia-Plus 353211
Owner: Asia-Plus Information Agency
Editorial: prospekt Saadi Sherozi 16, Dushanbe
Tel: 992 372 217220
Email: agency@asiaplus.tj Web site: http://news.tj
Director: Zebo Tadjibaeva
Profile: Provides information and analytic news in English and Russian languages aiming foreign embassies accredited in Tajikistan and majority of international organizations.
Language (s): English
NEWS SERVICE/SYNDICATE

Avesta Information Agency 564922
Editorial: Sherozi Ave.16, 1 floor, Dushanbe
Tel: 992 372 27 14 44
Email: info@avesta.tj Web site: http://www.avesta.tj
News Director: Bakhtier Musoev
Profile: News agency providing current news in Russian language.
Language (s): Tajik
NEWS SERVICE/SYNDICATE

Khovar news agency 573061
Editorial: prospekt Rudaki 40, Dushanbe 734025
Tel: 992 372 273552
Email: info@khovar.tj Web site: http://www.khovar.tj
Director General: Sadriddin Shamsuddinov
Profile: National official news agency at the Government of Tajikistan. Provides news in Russian, Tajik, English, Farsi, Arabic and Uzbek languages.
Language (s): Tajik
NEWS SERVICE/SYNDICATE

Tanzania

Time Difference: GMT +3
National Telephone Code: 255
Continent: Africa
Capital: Dar es Salaam

Newspapers

Daily News 156723
Owner: Tanzania Standard (Newspapers) Ltd
Tel: 255 22 2110595
Email: info@dailynews.co.tz Web site: http://www.dailynews.co.tz
Freq: Daily; Circ: 15000 Publisher's Statement
Editor: Tuma Abdallah; Advertising Manager: Felix Mushi
Profile: Newspaper covering regional, national and international news and current affairs including politics, economy, finance, business, culture and sport.
Language (s): English
DAILY NEWSPAPER

The Guardian 157128
Owner: The Guardian Limited
Tel: 255 22 2700735
Email: info@guardian.co.tz Web site: http://www.guardian.co.tz
Freq: Daily; Circ: 25000 Publisher's Statement
Profile: Newspaper covering national and international news and current affairs including economics, politics, business, culture and sport.
Language (s): English
DAILY NEWSPAPER

Nipashe 318955
Owner: The Guardian Ltd
Tel: 255 22 2700735

Email: info@guardian.co.tz **Web site:** http://www.ippmedia.com
Freq: Daily; **Circ:** 7000 Publisher's Statement
Editor: Wilson Kaigarula
Profile: Daily newspaper covering national and international news and current affairs including politics, business, economy, sports and entertainment.
Language (s): Swahili
DAILY NEWSPAPER

Sunday News 318958
Owner: Tanzania Standard (Newspapers) Ltd
Tel: 255 22 286 4864
Email: info@tsn.go.tz **Web site:** http://www.tsn.go.tz
Freq: Weekly; **Circ:** 12000 Publisher's Statement
Advertising Manager: Felix Mushi
Profile: Sunday newspaper covering national and international news, current affairs, politics, business, sports and entertainment.
Language (s): English
Ad Rate: Full Page Mono 1408900.00
Currency: Tanzania Shillings
DAILY NEWSPAPER

Uwazi 324013
Owner: Global Publishers and General Enterprises Ltd
Tel: 255 22 277 33 57
Email: contact@globalpublishers.info **Web site:** http://www.globalpublishers.info
Freq: Weekly; **Circ:** 35000
Profile: Newspaper covering regional, national and international news and current affairs including politics, society and investigative news.
Language (s): Swahili
DAILY NEWSPAPER

Community Newspaper

The Arusha Times 539102
Owner: FM Arusha Ltd.
Tel: 255 27 250 6438
Email: arushatimes@habari.co.tz **Web site:** http://www.arushatimes.co.tz
Freq: Weekly
Editor: William Lobulu
Profile: Newspaper covering regional news and current affairs.
Language (s): English
COMMUNITY NEWSPAPER

Risasi Jumamosi 498221
Owner: Global Publishers and General Enterprises Ltd
Tel: 255 22 277 33 57
Email: contact@globalpublishers.info **Web site:** http://globalpublishers.co.tz/category/risasi
Freq: Weekly; **Circ:** 60000
Profile: Newspaper covering regional news and current affairs including politics and entertainment.
Language (s): Swahili
COMMUNITY NEWSPAPER

Risasi Mchanganyiko 324015
Owner: Global Publishers and General Enterprises Ltd
Tel: 255 22 277 33 57
Email: contact@globalpublishers.info **Web site:** http://globalpublishers.co.tz/category/risasi
Freq: Weekly; **Circ:** 80000
Profile: Newspaper covering regional news and current affairs including politics and entertainment.
Language (s): Swahili
COMMUNITY NEWSPAPER

Thailand

Time Difference: GMT +7
National Telephone Code: 66
Continent: Asia
Capital: Bangkok (Krung Thep Maha Nakhon)

Newspapers

A Day Bulletin 584931
Editorial: Day Poets, 3 Ekamai 10, Sukhumvit 63, North Klongtan, Wattana, Bangkok 10110
Tel: 66 220 31040 815
Email: adaybulletin@daypoets.com **Web site:** http://www.daypoets.com
Freq: Weekly
Editor: Wilairat Ame-lam
Profile: Covers of lifestyle, social issue, and business.
Language (s): English
DAILY NEWSPAPER

The Andaman 513567
Editorial: Mittraphap Media, 314, Moo 1, Thepkrasatri Rd., Thalang, Phuket 83110
Tel: 66 7622 5873
Freq: Monthly; **Circ:** 5003 Not Audited
Editor: Nualnoi Hitopakorn
Profile: Covers local news, visitor's guide.
Language (s): English
DAILY NEWSPAPER

Andaman Times 460308
Editorial: Andaman Times, 28/4 Moo 4, Thaphaya, Palian, Trang 92140 **Tel:** 66 75268124
Email: andamantimes@thai.com
Freq: Semi-Monthly; **Circ:** 1503 Not Audited
Editor: Phonchai Nakponl
Profile: Covers news and general interest.
Language (s): Thai
DAILY NEWSPAPER

Awol 542781
Editorial: Awol, 136/229 Emerald Hill, Soi 6, Borfai, Hua Hin 77110 **Tel:** 66 816 498361
Email: info@awolonline.net **Web site:** http://www.awolonline.net
Freq: Weekly
Editor: Steve James
Profile: Covers the latest news on travel
Language (s): English
DAILY NEWSPAPER

Bangkok Post 157095
Editorial: 136 Na Ranong Rd, off Sunthorn Kosa Rd, Klong Toey, Bangkok 10110 **Tel:** 662 6164000
Web site: http://www.bangkokpost.com
Freq: Daily; **Circ:** 33142 ABC-Audit Bureau of Circulations
News Editor: Soonruth Bunyamanee; **Editor:** Pattnapong Chantraonontwong; **Editor in Chief:** Pichai Chuensuksawadi; **Editor:** Pitsinee Jitpleecheep; **Manager:** Siriwan Manmak; **Editor:** Saritdet Marukatat; **Editor:** Pongpet Mekloy; **Editor:** Wanchai Rujawongsanti; **Editor:** Borisuthiboun Tasaneeyavej
Profile: Provides breaking local, national and international news as the leading English-language daily newspaper in Thailand and has the longest history of any newspaper in existence in the country. Targets well-educated decision makers, including top executives and high-ranking government officials.
Language (s): English
DAILY NEWSPAPER

Bangkok Shuho 381709
Editorial: Bangkok Shuho, R.S. Tower Bldg. 19/F, 121/64-65 Rajadapisek Rd., Dindaeng, Bangkok 10400 **Tel:** 66 2247 8991
Email: bkkshuho@loxinfo.co.th **Web site:** http://www.bangkokshuho.com
Freq: Weekly; **Circ:** 12603 Not Audited
Editor: Kazuko Otsuka
Profile: Japanese newspaper.
Language (s): English
DAILY NEWSPAPER

Bangkok Times 460211
Editorial: Sachino, 138/157 Moo 4, Kannayao, Kannayao, Bangkok 10230 **Tel:** 66 2919 7308
Email: bangkoktimes@hotmail.com **Web site:** http://www.bangkok.co.jp
Freq: Monthly; **Circ:** 8003 Not Audited
Editor: Wichart Hampisalpipat
Profile: Newspaper which targets Thai people living in Japan Promotion of Relations between Thailand and Japan by providing information to the Thai people in Japan. And dissemination of knowledge about the culture to the public.
Language (s): Thai
DAILY NEWSPAPER

Banmuang 378075
Editorial: Nawakit Banmuang, 1 Soi Pleummanee, Vibhavadee-Rangsit Road, Lardyao, Chatuchak, Bangkok 10900 **Tel:** 66 2513 0230 3
Email: presscenter@banmuang.co.th **Web site:** http://www.banmuang.co.th
Freq: Daily; **Circ:** 380003 Not Audited
Editor in Chief: Polathit Phookphiboon; **Editor:** Chutimol Srikham
Profile: Covers the economy, politics, environment, culture, and business news.
Language (s): Thai
DAILY NEWSPAPER

Builder News 460186
Editorial: TTF International, 200/12-14 6/F., A.E. House, Ramkamhaeng 4, Ramkamhaeng, Suanluang, Bangkok 10250 **Tel:** 66 27172477
Email: editor@buildernews.in.th **Web site:** http://www.buildernews.in.th
Freq: Semi-Monthly; **Circ:** 50001 Not Audited
Editor in Chief: Tommy Jensen; **Editor:** Wimolwal Piboonvech
Profile: Focuses on the business information industry, construction, materials, construction equipment, technology, design, and real estate.
Language (s): Thai
DAILY NEWSPAPER

Bus & Truck 460185
Editorial: TTF International, 200/12-14 7/F., A.E. House, Ramkamhaeng 4, Ramkamhaeng, Suanluang, Bangkok 10250 **Tel:** 66 27172477 171
Email: info@ttfintl.com **Web site:** http://www.busandtrucks.com
Freq: Semi-Monthly; **Circ:** 30001 Not Audited
Editor: Seksan Chaiyaphuak
Profile: Focuses on commercial vehicles.
Language (s): Thai
DAILY NEWSPAPER

Business News Centre (Soon Ruam Khao Thurakij) 459568
Editorial: Business News Centre, 124, 126 Jaransanitwong 36, Janransanitwong Rd., Arun-ammarin, Bangkok 10700 **Tel:** 66 28860800
Email: pooky@ksc.th.com **Web site:** http://www.bnc.co.th
Freq: Daily; **Circ:** 10001 Not Audited
Editor: Jaran Inthakaliaya
Profile: Covers the latest in business news.
Language (s): Thai
DAILY NEWSPAPER

Champ 460009
Editorial: Central Express, 28/39 Soi Kehabangbua 4, Viphawadee 60 Rd., Taladbangken, Laksi, Bangkok 10210 **Tel:** 66 25 6148635
Email: centralexpress@hotmail.com
Freq: Weekly; **Circ:** 150003 Not Audited
Editor: Suwanna Srisongkram
Profile: Publishes twice a week Covers of sports, boxing.
Language (s): Thai
DAILY NEWSPAPER

Chiangmai Business 620458
Editorial: Chiang Mai Raiwan, 164, Rachchiangsaen Rd., Haiya, Muang, Chiangmai 50100
Tel: 66 532796867 201
Email: cmnews@chiangmainews.co.th **Web site:** http://www.chiangmainews.co.th
Freq: Weekly
Editor in Chief: Krailas Jatuwattanakul
Profile: Covers business.
Language (s): Thai
DAILY NEWSPAPER

Chiangmai Mail 381720
Editorial: Chiengmai Mail Publishing, 209/5 Moo 6, Faham, Muang, Chiangmai 50000 **Tel:** 66 53 852557
Email: editor@chiangmai-mail.com **Web site:** http://www.chiangmai-mail.com
Freq: Weekly; **Circ:** 5001 Not Audited
Profile: Covers of local news in Chiangmai area.
Language (s): English
DAILY NEWSPAPER

ChiangmaiNews 517360
Editorial: Chiang Mai Rai Wan, 164 Rachchiangsaen Rd., Haiya, Muang, Chiangmai 50100
Tel: 66 5327 9686 201
Email: cmnews@chiangmainews.co.th **Web site:** http://www.chiangmainews.co.th
Freq: Daily; **Circ:** 30003 Not Audited
Editor: Sunthad Suksoong
Profile: Covers local news.
Language (s): Thai
DAILY NEWSPAPER

Co-op News 460275
Editorial: The Coorperative League of Thailand, 4 Phichai Rd., Dusit, Bangkok 10310 **Tel:** 662 669 3254
Email: clt@clt.or.th **Web site:** http://www.clt.or.th
Circ: 10003 Not Audited
Editor: Sitthidej Attakrit
Profile: Publishes on the 10th & 22nd of every month providing business news for members of cooperation.
Language (s): Thai
DAILY NEWSPAPER

CTV News 608568
Editorial: Cable TV Chantaburi, 49/1, Thachalab Rd., Muang, Chantaburi 22000 **Tel:** 66 393 11749 3
Email: ctv@ctv.co.th **Web site:** http://www.ctv.co.th
Freq: Semi-Monthly
Editor: Ponvit Swatdekant
Profile: The 1st and 16th of every month Covers of business, politics, and local news., etc.
Language (s): Thai
DAILY NEWSPAPER

Dailynews 459734
Editorial: Siphraya Karnphim, 1/4 Moo 2, Viphawadee-Rangsit Rd., Bangkok 10210
Tel: 66 25611456 9
Email: editor@dailynews.co.th **Web site:** http://www.dailynews.co.th
Freq: Daily; **Circ:** 600001 Not Audited
Editor: Suphorn Numnoi
Profile: Covers of local, sports, social issues, politics, and international news.
Language (s): Thai
DAILY NEWSPAPER

Dara Daily 460362
Editorial: Idea Power, 48/18, Soi Ladphrao 15, Ladphrao Rd., Jomphol, Jatujak, Bangkok 10900
Tel: 66 293856478 34
Email: daradaily@gmail.com
Freq: Daily; **Circ:** 300000 Not Audited
Editor in Chief: Chalermkiat Somwang; **Manager:** Narin Yatjantuek
Profile: Covers of celebrities, gossip.
Language (s): Thai
DAILY NEWSPAPER

Dokbia Turakij (The Interest Business) 459736
Editorial: Dokbia, 61/33-34 Park Ploenchit Building, 8th Floor, Sukhumvit 1, Wattana, Bangkok 10110
Tel: 66 26552401
Email: dokbia@hotmail.com
Freq: Weekly; **Circ:** 135001 Not Audited
Profile: Publishes Every Monday Copy Deadline: One week Before the publish date
Language (s): Thai
DAILY NEWSPAPER

Econ News 459739
Editorial: Econnews, 44/30-31 Ngamwongwan Rd., Lardyao, Chatuchak, Bangkok 10900
Tel: 66 29 5345026
Email: econnews@econnews.org **Web site:** http://www.econnews.org
Freq: Monthly; **Circ:** 25003 Not Audited
Profile: Target: Executive and over (A / B Class) in both public and private sectors. Cover events like the economy / society and politics.
Language (s): Thai
DAILY NEWSPAPER

Focus Pakati (Rai Sapda) 460295
Editorial: Focus Multimedia Group, 3, Soi 24, Niphatsongkhrao 1 Rd., Hadyai, Songkhla 90110
Tel: 66 74 3685223 20
Email: focuspaktai@yahoo.com **Web site:** http://www.focuspaktai.com
Freq: Weekly; **Circ:** 10003 Not Audited
Editor: Prasan Suksai
Profile: Covers of local news in south area.
Language (s): Thai
DAILY NEWSPAPER

Global Business 584924
Editorial: Global Business (Sri Benjachot Group), 1511/52, Phaholyothin Rd., Samsen Nai, Phayathai, Bangkok 10400 **Tel:** 66 26157003
Email: gb.newspaper@gmail.com **Web site:** http://www.globalbusiness.co.th
Freq: Weekly
Editor in Chief: Thitichai Atthawatchara
Profile: Covers business.
Language (s): Thai
DAILY NEWSPAPER

HotGolf 466544
Editorial: TTF International, 200/12-14 7th F., A.E. House, Ramkamhaeng 4, Ramkamhaeng, Suanluang, Bangkok 10250 **Tel:** 66 27172477 180
Email: hotgolfeditor@yahoo.com **Web site:** http://www.hotgolfclub.com
Freq: Semi-Monthly; **Circ:** 3001 Not Audited
Profile: Covers of golf industry.
Language (s): Thai
DAILY NEWSPAPER

Hua Hin Today 546217
Editorial: Hua Hin Today, 58 Naresdamri Rd., Hua Hin, Hua Hin 77110 **Tel:** 66 32 511535
Email: info@huahintoday.net **Web site:** http://www.huahintoday.net
Freq: Monthly; **Circ:** 7003 Not Audited
Editor: Julaporn Wannapruk
Profile: Providing information of Hua Hin.
Language (s): English
DAILY NEWSPAPER

Intertransport Logistics 578699
Editorial: ITL Trade Media, 230 Ladpraowanghin, Ladprao, Bangkok, Bangkok 10230
Tel: 66 251 42839
Email: itl@logisticsthailand.com **Web site:** http://www.logisticsthailand.com
Freq: Semi-Monthly
Editor: Arun Borirak
Profile: Covers latest news on logistics
Language (s): Thai
DAILY NEWSPAPER

Isaan Bizweek 607407
Editorial: Isaan Bizweek, 498, Moo 12, Baannonmuang, Sila, Muang, Khon Kaen 40000
Tel: 66 432 03683
Email: kunluk@yahoo.com
Freq: Semi-Monthly
Editor in Chief: Charoenrak Phetpradab
Profile: Covers of local news.
Language (s): Thai
DAILY NEWSPAPER

Jakkawan Muai 460008
Editorial: Central Express, 28/39 Soi Kehabangbua 4, Viphawadee 60 Rd., Taladbangken, Laksi, Bangkok 10210 **Tel:** 66 25 6148635
Email: centralexpress@hotmail.com
Freq: Weekly; **Circ:** 80003 Not Audited
Editor: Suwanna Srisongkram
Profile: Publishes twice a week.Focus: boxing
Language (s): Thai
DAILY NEWSPAPER

Job Express 381708
Editorial: Wattasarn Media, 105/7, Mooban Sasiwan, Moo 11, Soi Suanphak 32, Suanphak Rd., Talingchan, Talingchan, Bangkok 10170
Tel: 66 28842929
Email: webmaster@jobbyyou.com **Web site:** http://www.wm.co.th
Freq: Weekly
Profile: Covers information for college graduates.
Language (s): Thai
DAILY NEWSPAPER

Job Request 460007
Editorial: Sappasan, 71/17 Borommarachachonnanee Rd., Arun Amarin, Bangkok Noi, Bangkok 10700 **Tel:** 66 2435 2345 126
Web site: http://www.mrthaijob.com

Freq: Weekly; **Circ:** 80001 Not Audited
Profile: Covers the latest information on employment.
Language (s): Thai
DAILY NEWSPAPER

Joh Game 380463
Editorial: Siam Sport Syndicate, 66/26-29 Moo12, Soi Ramindra 40, Ramindra Rd., Nualjan, Buengkum, Bangkok 10310 **Tel:** 66 2508808586
Web site: http://www.siamsport.co.th
Freq: Daily; **Circ:** 100001 Not Audited
Profile: Covers of sport news.
Language (s): Thai
DAILY NEWSPAPER

Kanchon 460301
Editorial: Kanchon Newspaper, 34, Khuankhanun Rd., Tabtiang, Muang, Trang 92000
Tel: 66 89 7302889
Web site: http://www.trangtodaynews.com
Freq: Daily; **Circ:** 1203 Not Audited
Editor: Peerapol Janphak
Profile: Focus: local news
Language (s): Thai
DAILY NEWSPAPER

Kaohoon Thurakij Raiwan 460179
Editorial: BURAPA TASNA (1999) Co., Ltd, 48/5-6 2/F Preecha complex, Rajadapisek Rd., Samsennok, Huaykwang, Bangkok 10320
Tel: 66 2 6934555 108110
Email: kao_hoon@yahoo.com **Web site:** http://www.kaohoon.com
Freq: Daily; **Circ:** 70001 Not Audited
Publisher: Kaset Siwakua
Profile: Covers of stock news.
Language (s): Thai
DAILY NEWSPAPER

Khao Seree 539456
Editorial: Khao Seree, 324 Kantang Rd., Tabtiang, Muang, Trang 92000 **Tel:** 66 75213019
Email: kaosayre2535@hotmail.com
Freq: Weekly; **Circ:** 3003 Not Audited
Editor: Jessada Rakkhong
Profile: Covers business, politics, and local news.
Language (s): Thai
DAILY NEWSPAPER

Khaosod 459695
Owner: Matichon Group
Editorial: 12 Mooban Prachaniwes 1, Thedsaban Narumarn Rd, Lardyao, Chatuchak, Bangkok 10900
Tel: 66 29544999
Email: khaosod.eng@gmail.com **Web site:** http://www.khaosod.co.th
Freq: Daily; **Circ:** 500001 Not Audited
Editor: Thakoon Boonparn
Profile: Covers the latest in international and local news.
Language (s): Thai
DAILY NEWSPAPER

Komchadluek 459022
Editorial: The Nation, 1854 Bangna-Trad Road (KM 4.5), Bangkok 10260 **Tel:** 66 23383333 3325
Email: komchad@nationgroup.com **Web site:** http://www.komchadluek.com
Freq: Daily; **Circ:** 800001 Not Audited
Editor: Saranya Hai
Profile: Quality daily newspaper with strengths in the " different creative " by focusing on social responsibility. It is suitable for everyone in the family.
Language (s): Thai
DAILY NEWSPAPER

Krabi News 460292
Editorial: Krabi News, 17/6, Watchara Rd., Paknam, MuangKrabi Yai, Muang, Krabi 81000
Tel: 66 75620572
Email: krabinews17@yahoo.com
Freq: Semi-Monthly; **Circ:** 1001 Not Audited
Editor: Prasong Praditsap
Profile: Covers of local news
Language (s): Thai
DAILY NEWSPAPER

Krungthep Turakij 222236
Editorial: The Nation, 1854 Bangna-Trad Road (KM 4.5), Bangna, Bangkok 10260
Tel: 66 2338 3333 3386
Email: ktfor@nationgroup.com **Web site:** http://www.bangkokbiznews.com
Freq: Daily; **Circ:** 145503 Not Audited
Editor: Orawan Hoichan; **Editor in Chief:** Chalao Kanjana
Profile: Covers business.
Language (s): Thai
DAILY NEWSPAPER

Lannathai News 584292
Editorial: Great Sun & Stars Media (GSSM), 29/9-12, Thepharak Rd., Changphuek, Muang, Chiangmai 50300 **Tel:** 66 53 357977 14
Email: lannathainews@yahoo.com **Web site:** http://www.lannathai-news.com
Freq: Semi-Monthly
Editor: Nopniwat Krairoek
Profile: Covers local news.
Language (s): Thai
DAILY NEWSPAPER

Leader Time Newspaper 472884
Editorial: Leader Time, 1111/112 Baan Klangkrung (Ratchada-Ladprao), Ladyao, Jatujak, Bangkok 10900 **Tel:** 66 25139191 79
Email: ying99leadertime@gmail.com **Web site:** http://www.leadertimeonline.com
Freq: Semi-Monthly; **Circ:** 10003 Not Audited
Manager: Tiwawan Chaiterdkiat
Profile: Covers business.
Language (s): Thai
DAILY NEWSPAPER

Lok Wannee Raiwan 459777
Editorial: 71/30 Boromrajchonnee Rd, Arun-amarin, Bangkoknoi, Bangkok 10700 **Tel:** 66 2 422-8101 9
Email: editor@lokwannee.com **Web site:** http://www.dailyworldtoday.com
Freq: 2 Times/Week; **Circ:** 100000 Not Audited
Director: Tongkom Chincharoentham; **Editor:** Suntorn Kullawattanaworaphong
Profile: Covers of social issue, national news, sports, and business news.
Language (s): Thai
DAILY NEWSPAPER

Lok Wannee Wansuk 460413
Editorial: 71/30 Boromrajchonnee Road, Arun-amarin, Bangkoknoi, Bangkok 10700
Tel: 66 24228101
Email: editor@lokwannee.com **Web site:** http://www.dailyworldtoday.com
Freq: Weekly; **Circ:** 100001 Not Audited
Editor: Suntorn Kullawattanaworaphong
Profile: Covers news topics.
Language (s): Thai
DAILY NEWSPAPER

Matichon 378117
Editorial: Matichon Group, 12 Thedsaban Narumarn Rd., Ladyao, Jatujak, Bangkok 10900
Tel: 66 258 00021
Email: weekly@matichon.co.th **Web site:** http://www.matichon.co.th
Freq: Daily; **Circ:** 600001 Not Audited
Editor: Pairat Pongpanit
Profile: Covers of business, politics, economy, and international news.
Language (s): Thai
DAILY NEWSPAPER

Matitrang 460293
Editorial: Matitrang Newspaper, 35 Phattalung Rd., Muang, Trang 92000 **Tel:** 66 752 20931
Email: thong820@hotmail.com
Freq: Semi-Monthly; **Circ:** 1001 Not Audited
Profile: Covers of local news.
Language (s): Thai
DAILY NEWSPAPER

Maya Channel 381723
Editorial: Maya Channel, 90/106 Viphawadi 20, Viphawadi Rod, Bangkok 10900
Tel: 66 2691 5252 221
Freq: 2 Times/Week; **Circ:** 250003 Not Audited
Editor in Chief: Pakorn Thongboriboon
Profile: Covers celebrities, movies, and fashion.
Language (s): Thai
DAILY NEWSPAPER

Muay Siam Today 459778
Editorial: Siam Sport Syndicate, 66/26-29 Moo12, Soi Ramindra 40, Ramindra Rd., Nualchan, Buengkum, Bangkok 10230 **Tel:** 66 2 5088000
Email: webmaster@siamsport.co.th **Web site:** http://www.siamsport.co.th
Freq: Daily; **Circ:** 100003 Not Audited
Manager: Burachat Phatanaphong
Profile: Covers of boxing.
Language (s): Thai
DAILY NEWSPAPER

Naewna 378059
Editorial: Naewna Newspaper Co. Ltd., 96 Moo 3 Vibhavadee-Rangsit Road, Talard Bangken, Bangkok 10210 **Tel:** 66 29734250
Email: naewna@naewna.com **Web site:** http://www.naewna.com
Freq: Daily; **Circ:** 200001 Not Audited
Profile: covers of news
Language (s): Thai
DAILY NEWSPAPER

The Nation 159046
Editorial: 1854 Bangna-Trad Rd (KM 4.5), Bangna, Bangkok 10260 **Tel:** 66 2 3383333
Email: customer@nationgroup.com **Web site:** http://www.nationmultimedia.com
Freq: Daily; **Circ:** 68200 Not Audited
Editor: Achara Deboonme
Profile: Covers business, politics, international and local news.
Language (s): English
Ad Rate: Full Page Mono 254000.00
Ad Rate: Full Page Colour 304000.00
Currency: Thailand Baht
DAILY NEWSPAPER

Ngan Duan 460323
Editorial: Wattasarn Media, 105/7, Mooban Sasiwan, Moo 11, Soi Suanphak 32, Suanphak Rd, Talingchan, Talingchan, Bangkok 10170 **Tel:** 66 28842929
Email: webmaster@jobbyyou.com **Web site:** http://www.wm.co.th
Freq: Weekly
Profile: Covers employment and careers.
Language (s): Thai
DAILY NEWSPAPER

Ngan Tua Thai 459196
Editorial: Watta Classifieds, 71/30 Boromrajchonnee Road, Bangkoknoi, Bangkok 10700
Tel: 66 24228000 9
Email: ejobeasy@watta.co.th **Web site:** http://www.ejobeasy.com
Freq: Semi-Monthly; **Circ:** 80001 Not Audited
Profile: Covers of jobs, careers.
Language (s): Thai
DAILY NEWSPAPER

Northern Business Newspaper 475441
Editorial: Sveb Group, 36/2, Moo 4, Outer Ring Rd., San Pheesue, Muang, Chiangmai 50300
Tel: 66 5311 0677
Email: sveb_group@hotmail.com **Web site:** http://www.svebgroup.com
Freq: Monthly
Profile: Covers business in the northern area.
Language (s): Thai
DAILY NEWSPAPER

Palang Chon 460045
Editorial: Palang Chon, 110/1 Baan Pagrad Rd., Banpong, Rachaburi 70110 **Tel:** 66 818412992
Email: phalangchon@hotmail.com
Freq: Semi-Monthly; **Circ:** 5001 Not Audited
Editor: Surin Phiphakphakorn
Profile: Covers of local news
Language (s): Thai
DAILY NEWSPAPER

Patiroop 460203
Editorial: Patiroop, 28/1 Pokarong Rd., Tarab, Muang, Petchaburi 76000 **Tel:** 66 3240 01748
Email: reformnews@hotmail.com
Freq: Semi-Monthly; **Circ:** 5003 Not Audited
Manager: Anan Sitarom; **Editor:** Sirikul Sitarom
Profile: Publishes on the 1st and 16th of every month Covers of local news.
Language (s): Thai
DAILY NEWSPAPER

Pattaya Blatt 381721
Editorial: Pattaya Mail Publishing, 370/7-8 Pattaya Second Road, Chonburi, Pattaya 20260
Tel: 66 384 112401
Email: redaktion@pattayablatt.com **Web site:** http://www.pattayablatt.com
Freq: Weekly; **Circ:** 7001 Not Audited
Profile: Covers all the local news in Pattaya.
Language (s): German
DAILY NEWSPAPER

Pattaya Mail 378293
Editorial: Pattaya Mail Publishing, 370/7-8 Pattaya Second Road, Pattaya City, Chonburi 20150
Tel: 66 384112401
Email: ptymail@pattayamial.com **Web site:** http://www.pattayamail.com
Freq: Weekly; **Circ:** 10501 Not Audited
Profile: Covers local news.
Language (s): English
DAILY NEWSPAPER

Pattaya People Weekly 459492
Editorial: Dragon Enterprises, 20/15-16 M. 10 Soi Day-Night Hotel, South Pattaya Road, Pattaya City, Chonburi 20150 **Tel:** 66 38420707
Email: info@pattayapeople.com **Web site:** http://www.pattayapeople.com
Freq: Weekly; **Circ:** 5001 Not Audited
Profile: Covers of local news, international news., etc.
Language (s): Thai
DAILY NEWSPAPER

Pattaya Today 460400
Editorial: Siamese Mission Media, 42/91, M.9, Sukhumvit Rd., Nongprue, Banglamung, Chonburi 20150 **Tel:** 66 384 10077
Email: info@pattayatoday.net **Web site:** http://www.pattayatoday.net
Freq: Semi-Monthly; **Circ:** 8001 Not Audited
Editor: Lucksika Natham
Profile: Covers of real estate, business and local news.
Language (s): English
DAILY NEWSPAPER

Phalang Ras 460303
Editorial: Krasae Khao, 331/50, Makhamtia. Maung, Suratthani 84000 **Tel:** 66 772 82559
Email: krasaenewsofsouth@yahoo.com **Web site:** http://www.southnewsonline.co
Freq: Monthly; **Circ:** 2001 Not Audited
Profile: Focus: local news
Language (s): Thai
DAILY NEWSPAPER

Phitsanulok Today 537131
Editorial: Phitsanulok Today, 86/1 Moo 7, Watjan, Muang, Phitsanulok 65000 **Tel:** 66 55 216541
Email: plk_today@yahoo.com
Freq: Semi-Monthly; **Circ:** 2003 Not Audited
Editor: Yossakrai Kledjeen
Profile: Covers local news.
Language (s): Thai
DAILY NEWSPAPER

Phoo Chad Karn Rai Sapada 459708
Editorial: ASTV Manager, 102/1 Phra-Arthit Road, Chanasongkarm, Phranakhorn, Bangkok 10200
Tel: 66 26 294488
Web site: http://www.manager.co.th
Freq: Weekly; **Circ:** 180003 Not Audited
Profile: Covers news.
Language (s): Thai
DAILY NEWSPAPER

Phoo Chad Karn Rai Wan 459696
Editorial: ASTV Manager, 102/1 Phra-Arthit Road, Chanasongkarm, Phranakhorn, Bangkok 10200
Tel: 66 26 294488
Email: wm@manager.co.th **Web site:** http://www.gotomanager.com
Freq: Daily; **Circ:** 280003 Not Audited
Editor: Kriengsak Yiengsuphanon
Profile: Covers news.
Language (s): Thai
DAILY NEWSPAPER

Phuket Gazette 459201
Editorial: The Phuket Gazette, 79/94, Moo 4, Thepkasattree Rd., Koh Kaew, Muang, Phuket 83000
Tel: 66 762 73555
Email: info@phuketgazette.net **Web site:** http://www.phuketgazette.net
Freq: Weekly; **Circ:** 12001 Not Audited
Profile: Provides local news, in-depth analysis, lifestyle features and sports coverage for all with an interest in Phuket and the Andaman.
Language (s): English
DAILY NEWSPAPER

Post Today 378227
Editorial: The Post Publishing, 136 Na Ranong Road, Klong Toey, Bangkok 10110 **Tel:** 66 22403700
Web site: http://www.posttoday.com
Freq: Daily; **Circ:** 83001 Not Audited
Editor: Na Kan Loahawichai
Profile: Reports business news in a simple, comprehensive way for general readers and also covers politics, general, foreign and sports news and articles.
Language (s): Thai
DAILY NEWSPAPER

Prachachat Turakij 381715
Editorial: Matichon Group, 12 Mooban Prachaniwes 1, Thedsaban Narumarn Rd., Ladyao, Jatujak, Bangkok 10900 **Tel:** 66 25890020 1505
Email: pcconline@matichon.co.th **Web site:** http://www.prachachat.net
Freq: 2 Times/Week; **Circ:** 150001 Not Audited
Editor: Somprathana Khlaiwichian; **Editor:** Phattanaphan Wongphan
Profile: Covers of news.
Language (s): Thai
Ad Rate: Full Page Mono 240000.00
Ad Rate: Full Page Colour 312000.00
Currency: Thailand Baht
DAILY NEWSPAPER

Property Report Thailand 460291
Owner: Ensign Media
Editorial: Ensign Media Co. Ltd., 55 Bio House Bldg, 5th Fl, Bangkok 10110 **Tel:** 66 26625195
Email: editorial@property-report.com **Web site:** http://www.property-report.com
Freq: Monthly; **Circ:** 20002 Not Audited
Profile: Presents up-to-date information and coverage of industry trends and innovations. Each issue incorporates an in-depth special focus on one of the country's real estate hot spots, a key interview with an important industry figure and regular sections on construction, finance, legal issues, interiors and architecture. The remainder of the publication is devoted to pertinent reportage and in-depth analysis of property news.
Language (s): Thai
DAILY NEWSPAPER

Rak Trang 460294
Editorial: Rak Trang Group, 26/21 Soi 6, Wienkaphang Rd., Tabtieng, Muang, Trang 92000
Tel: 66 75 211480
Freq: Semi-Monthly; **Circ:** 1003 Not Audited
Editor: Methee Muangkaew
Profile: Coves local news.
Language (s): Thai
DAILY NEWSPAPER

Samak Duen 460006
Editorial: Sappasan, 71/17 Borommarachachonnanee Rd., Arun-Amarin, Bangkok-Noi, Bangkok 10700 **Tel:** 66 2435 2345 126
Web site: http://www.mrthaijob.com
Freq: 2 Times/Week; **Circ:** 140001 Not Audited
Profile: Shares information on government jobs.
Language (s): Thai
DAILY NEWSPAPER

Samila Times 460304
Editorial: Samila Times, 41 Khiongrian 2 Rd, Hatyai, Songkhla 90110 **Tel:** 66 74356804
Email: info@samilatimes.co.th **Web site:** http://www.samilatimes.co.th
Freq: Weekly; **Circ:** 5001 Not Audited
Editor: Sumrit Boonrat
Profile: Covers of local news.
Language (s): Thai
DAILY NEWSPAPER

Thailand

Sarn Pheun Sem 460215
Editorial: Semsikkha 29/15 Ramkhamhang 21, Ramkhamhang Road, Plubpla, Bangkok 10310
Tel: 66 231 473856
Email: semsikkhasam@yahoo.com **Web site:** http://www.semsikkha.org
Freq: Quarterly; **Circ:** 4001 Not Audited
Editor: Jenjira Rocha
Profile: Covers of lifestyle, religion, Buddhism.
Language (s): Thai
DAILY NEWSPAPER

Seangsawan 459078
Editorial: 49/1 Tachalab Road, Watmai, Muang, Chantaburi 22000 **Tel:** 66 39 311749
Email: sakda@chantaburi.com
Freq: Semi-Monthly; **Circ:** 3001 Not Audited
Editor in Chief: Sakda Yookasem
Profile: Covers information for people in Chantaburi and Trat Provinces.
Language (s): Thai
DAILY NEWSPAPER

Sentangnakkai 460020
Editorial: Sumret Dot Com, 1148/203-204 Pichai Condominium, Nakornchaisri Rd., Dusit, Bangkok 10300 **Tel:** 66 2 667401
Web site: http://www.nakkhai.com
Freq: Semi-Monthly; **Circ:** 75003 Not Audited
Manager: Panthep Rodpracha
Profile: Covers of business strategies.
Language (s): Thai
DAILY NEWSPAPER

Siam Banterng 459779
Owner: Inspire Entertainment Co., Ltd.
Editorial: 115/66 Moo12, Soi Ramindra 40, Klongkum, Buengkum, Bangkok 10230
Tel: 66 25088100
Web site: http://www.inspire.co.th
Freq: 2 Times/Week; **Circ:** 140001 Not Audited
Profile: Covers entertainment news.
Language (s): Thai
DAILY NEWSPAPER

Siam Dara 460411
Editorial: Siam Sport Syndicate, 66/26-29 Moo12, Soi Ramindra 40, Ramindra Rd., Nualjan, Buengkum, Bangkok 10230 **Tel:** 66 2508 8000
Email: webmaster@siamsport.co.th **Web site:** http://www.siamsport.co.th
Freq: Daily
Profile: Covers of celebrities, gossip star.
Language (s): Thai
DAILY NEWSPAPER

Siam Keela Raiwan 443717
Editorial: Siam Sport Syndicate, 66/26-29 Moo12, Soi Ramindra 40, Ramindra Rd., Nualjian, Buengkum, Bangkok 10310 **Tel:** 66 2508808586
Email: webmaster@siamsport.co.th **Web site:** http://www.siamsport.co.th
Freq: Daily; **Circ:** 200001 Not Audited
Profile: Covers of sports.
Language (s): Thai
DAILY NEWSPAPER

Siam Rath Raiwan 378309
Editorial: Siam Rath, 12 Building 6, Rajdamnoen Road, Bangkok 10200 **Tel:** 66 2662 1810 322
Email: siamrath@siamrath.co.th **Web site:** http://www.siamrath.co.th
Freq: Daily; **Circ:** 300003 Not Audited
Editor in Chief: Viroj Wattanathadakul
Profile: Covers news.
Language (s): Thai
DAILY NEWSPAPER

Siam Rath Sapda Wijan 459356
Editorial: Siam Rath, 12 Building 6, Rajdamnoen Road, Phranakorn, Bangkok 10200
Tel: 66 2662 1810 322
Email: siamweekly@hotmail.com **Web site:** http://www.siamrath.co.th
Freq: Weekly; **Circ:** 80003 Not Audited
Editor in Chief: Viroj Wattanathadakul
Profile: Weekly newspaper focusing on politics.
Language (s): Thai
DAILY NEWSPAPER

Siam Settakij 460212
Editorial: Siam Settakij, 12/3 Arun-amarin Rd., Bangkok Noi, Bangkok 10700 **Tel:** 66 24348080 19
Email: siam_settakij@hotmail.com
Freq: Monthly; **Circ:** 50003 Not Audited
Editor: Tongphoon Phensophee
Profile: Covers business news.
Language (s): Thai
DAILY NEWSPAPER

Siam Turakij 459738
Editorial: Siam Turakij Media, 6/88 Soi Ladphrao 25, Ladphrao Rd., Jankasem, Jatujak, Bangkok 10900
Tel: 66 29 381555
Web site: http://www.siamturakij.com
Freq: 2 Times/Week; **Circ:** 120003 Not Audited
Editor: Chaipom Janthanaroj; **Editor:** Jaturong Kobkaew
Profile: Covers business.
Language (s): Thai
DAILY NEWSPAPER

Siangtai Daily 460299
Editorial: Siangtai Raiwan, 1/25, Tepkasattree Rd., Tatsada, Muang, Phuket 83000 **Tel:** 66 76212751
Email: siangtai@e-mail.in.th **Web site:** http://www.siangtai.com
Freq: Daily; **Circ:** 35001 Not Audited
Editor: Chaowaphong Mekharakkul
Profile: Covers of local news.
Language (s): Thai
DAILY NEWSPAPER

Sing Sian Yit Pao 378222
Editorial: Sing Jong Eian, 267 New Road, Baan Bart, Pomprab, Bangkok 10100 **Tel:** 66 2 225-0070
Email: admin@singsian.net **Web site:** http://www.singsian.net
Freq: Daily; **Circ:** 70001 Not Audited
Profile: Covers topics for Chinese people living in Thailand.
Language (s): Chinese
DAILY NEWSPAPER

Sportman 459197
Editorial: Siam Sport Syndicate, 66/26-29 Moo12, Soi Ramindra 40, Ramindra Rd., Khlongkum, Buengkum, Bangkok 10230 **Tel:** 66 250 88000
Email: webmaster@siamsport.co.th **Web site:** http://www.sia, msport.co.th
Freq: Daily; **Circ:** 140001 Not Audited
Profile: A supplementary to Sport Pool in nature plus wider coverage in North American Sports.
Language (s): Thai
DAILY NEWSPAPER

Sportpool Rai Wan 459360
Editorial: Siam Sport Syndicate, 66/26-29 Moo12, Soi Ramindra 40, Ramindra Rd., Khlongkum, Buengkum, Bangkok 10310 **Tel:** 66 250 88000
Email: webmaster@siamsport.co.th **Web site:** http://www.siamsport.co.th
Freq: Daily; **Circ:** 300001 Not Audited
Profile: Covers of Sports (soccer)
Language (s): Thai
DAILY NEWSPAPER

Star Soccer Rai Wan 459361
Editorial: Siam Sport Syndicate, 66/26-29 Moo12, Soi Ramindra 40, Ramindra Rd., Khlongkum, Buengkum, Bangkok 10230 **Tel:** 66 250 88000
Email: webmaster@siamsport.co.th **Web site:** http://www.siamsport.co.th
Freq: Daily; **Circ:** 320001 Not Audited
Profile: Covers of soccer.
Language (s): Thai
DAILY NEWSPAPER

Sue Klang 460202
Editorial: Sueklang Advertising, 420/5 Chiengmai Land Village, Changkhlan Rd., Changkhlan, Muang, Chiangmai 50100 **Tel:** 66 532836345
Email: sueklang@hotmail.com
Freq: Weekly; **Circ:** 10001 Not Audited
Editor: Wariphan Thammawilaibutr
Profile: Covers of local news.
Language (s): Thai
DAILY NEWSPAPER

T -News inside 620462
Editorial: Multimedia Group, 50/33, Moo 5, Pracharat 1 Rd., Talad Kwan, Muang, Nontaburi 11000
Tel: 66 252 54242 103
Email: nantita@tnews.co.th **Web site:** http://www.tnews.co.th
Freq: Semi-Monthly
Profile: Covers of politics and business news.
Language (s): Thai
DAILY NEWSPAPER

Telecom Journal 459780
Editorial: Telecom Journal, 327/17-19 Soi Sri Amporn (Phaholyothin 32), Senanikom 1 Road, Lardyao, Chatuchak, Bangkok 10900
Tel: 66 2561 4993
Email: telecomjournal@yahoo.com **Web site:** http://www.telecomjournal.net
Freq: Weekly; **Circ:** 120003 Not Audited
Manager: Nucharee Bunchana
Profile: Focuses on telecommunication, IT and technology.
Language (s): Thai
DAILY NEWSPAPER

Thai Post 378219
Editorial: Thai Journal Group, 1850-1862 Kasemrath Road, Klongtoey, Bangkok 10110 **Tel:** 66 22402612
Email: reporter@thaipost.net **Web site:** http://www.thaipost.net
Freq: Daily; **Circ:** 200001 Not Audited
Editor in Chief: Chatchai Namtapee
Profile: Covers of politics, economics, sports, local and international business news.
Language (s): Thai
DAILY NEWSPAPER

Thai Rath 378052
Editorial: #1 Building, 10th St, 12th Fl, Vibhavadi, Rangsit Rd, Bangkok 10900 **Tel:** 66 2 2721030 1342
Email: thairathcare@thairath.co.th **Web site:** http://www.thairath.co.th
Freq: Daily; **Circ:** 1000001 Not Audited
Profile: Covers political, international, business, sports and local news.
Language (s): Thai
DAILY NEWSPAPER

Thainews 460204
Editorial: Banjob-Praphin Limjaroon, 56 Samlan Rd., Phrasingha, Muang, Chiangmai 50200
Tel: 66 532772524
Web site: http://www.thainews70.com
Freq: Daily; **Circ:** 50001 Not Audited
Profile: Covers of local news.
Language (s): Thai
DAILY NEWSPAPER

Thansettakij 381718
Editorial: Jutamas Building 7/F, 89/169-770 Vipavadee-Rangsit Road, Bangkok 10900
Tel: 66 2 973-5254
Email: editoronline@thannews.th.com **Web site:** http://www.thannews.th.com
Freq: 2 Times/Week; **Circ:** 120001 Not Audited
Editor: Suvipa Budsayabantoon
Profile: Covers the latest in business news.
Language (s): Thai
DAILY NEWSPAPER

Thunhoon 460180
Editorial: Traffic Corner Publishing, 21/59-60, Block C, 3/F, RCA, Soi Soonvijai, Phetchburi Rd., Bangkapi, Huaykhwang, Bangkok 10320 **Tel:** 66 22 031040 636
Email: tunhoon@yahoo.com **Web site:** http://www.thunhoon.com
Freq: Daily
Profile: Focus: stock
Language (s): Thai
DAILY NEWSPAPER

Tong Hua News 378310
Editorial: Tong Hua Communications Public Co., Ltd., 877-881 Chareon Krung Road, Talardnoi, Sompantawong, Bangkok 10100 **Tel:** 66 223601434
Email: tonghua_dailynews@tonghuagroup.com
Freq: Daily; **Circ:** 80003 Not Audited
Editor: Pavit Tokakuna
Profile: Chinese newspaper.
Language (s): Chinese
DAILY NEWSPAPER

Transport Journal 459357
Editorial: Sri Benjachot, 1/3 Moo 24, Soi Mooban Khetkhayaimai, Terddamri Rd., Bnagsue, Bangkok 10800 **Tel:** 66 25561624
Email: transport_j2004@yahoo.com **Web site:** http://www.transportnews.co.th
Freq: Weekly; **Circ:** 120003 Not Audited
Profile: Covers logistics, shipping and transportation.
Language (s): Thai
DAILY NEWSPAPER

Udomsarn Weekly 460205
Editorial: Catholic Social Communications of Thailand, 122/11 Soi Naksuwan, Nonsee Rd., Chongnonsee, Yannawa, Bangkok 10120
Tel: 66 26813900 180
Email: thcatcom@loxinfo.co.th **Web site:** http://www.udomsarn.com
Freq: Weekly
Profile: Covers of religion, society and culture.
Language (s): Thai
DAILY NEWSPAPER

Viang Chiangmai with Bangkok 460184
Editorial: Oriental Noise, 55/1, Soi 3, Rachawong Rd., Changmoi, Muang, Chiangmai 50300
Tel: 66 53 232383
Email: info@oriental-noise.com **Web site:** http://www.oriental-noise.com
Freq: Monthly; **Circ:** 5003 Not Audited
Publisher: Noritoshi Urano
Profile: Providing information about living in Chiangmai.
Language (s): Japanese
DAILY NEWSPAPER

Weekly News 460402
Editorial: Weekly News, 35/83 Mooban Yingruey Niwes, Prachachuen Road., Pakkred, Nontaburi 11120 **Tel:** 66 25734265
Email: weekly-news@hotmail.com
Freq: Weekly
Editor: Kasem Osathanukror
Profile: Focus on celebrities.
Language (s): Thai
DAILY NEWSPAPER

Yuadyan Newspaper (Automotive Newspaper) 459941
Editorial: Grand Prix International, 4/299, 2/F, Moo 5 Soi Lardplaklow 66, Lardplaklow Road, Autsawaree, Bangken, Bangkok 10220 **Tel:** 66 25 2217318
Email: yuadyan@grandprixgroup.com **Web site:** http://www.grandprixgroup.com
Freq: Semi-Monthly; **Circ:** 50003 Not Audited
Editor in Chief: Veerachot Duangruethai
Profile: Covers automotive industry news.
Language (s): Thai
DAILY NEWSPAPER

News Service/Syndicate

National News Bureau 467604
Editorial: National News Bureau, Government Public Relations Departmnet, 90/91 New Petchaburi Road, Bangkapi, Huay Kwang, BKK, Bangkok 10320
Tel: 66 2 369-2587
Email: thainews.nnt@gmail.com
Freq: Daily
Profile: Covers news and general interest throughout Thailand.
Language (s): Bahasa Indonesia
NEWS SERVICE/SYNDICATE

Togo

Time Difference: GMT
National Telephone Code: 228
Continent: Africa
Capital: Lomé

Newspapers

Le Canard Indépendant 225702
Owner: Le Canard Independant
Editorial: BP 8168, Lome **Tel:** 228 1 904 60 94
Email: lecanardin@yahoo.fr **Web site:** http://lecanard.fr
Freq: Weekly; **Circ:** 3000 Publisher's Statement
Editor in Chef: Augustin Koffi Amega
Profile: National weekly newspaper focusing on regional, national and international news, current affairs, politics, economics, society, entertainment and sports.
Language (s): French
Ad Rate: Full Page Mono 200000.00
Currency: Communauté Financière Africaine Francs BCEAO
DAILY NEWSPAPER

Tonga

Time Difference: GMT +13
National Telephone Code: 676
Continent: Oceania
Capital: Nuku'alofa (Tongatapu)

Community Newspaper

Ko e Kele'a 538736
Owner: 'Akilisi Pohiva
Editorial: Tonga, PO Box 1567, Kingdom Of Tonga
Tel: 676 25 480
Freq: Bi-Weekly
Editor: Tavake Fusimalohi
Language (s): English
COMMUNITY NEWSPAPER

Tonga Chronicle (Kalonikali Tonga) 538730
Owner: Government of Tonga
Editorial: PO Box 197, Old Vaiola (off Taufa'ahau Rd), Kingdom Of Tonga **Tel:** 676 23 302
Email: chroni@candw.to
Freq: Weekly
Profile: Published in English and Tongan covers current topics and news.
Language (s): English
COMMUNITY NEWSPAPER

Tunisia

Time Difference: GMT +1
National Telephone Code: 216
Continent: Africa
Capital: Tunis

Newspapers

Al Akhbar 430900
Owner: Dar Tunis Hebdo
Editorial: Rue Ali Bach Hamba, Tunis 1000
Tel: 216 71 344100
Email: alakhbar@planet.tn
Freq: Weekly; **Circ:** 70000 Publisher's Statement
General Manager: Mohamed Ben Youssef; **Editor in Chief:** Imed Jnane
Profile: Al Akhbar (The News) is a weekly Arabic newspaper covering local and international news, politics and arts. It launched in 1984 and is published on Thursdays.
Language (s): Arabic
DAILY NEWSPAPER

Akhbar Al-Joumhouria 430899
Owner: Media Plus
Editorial: 14, rue Ibn Al-Jazzar, Tunis 1002
Tel: 216 71 797055
Email: akhbar.joumhouria@gnet.tn **Web site:** http://jomhouria.com
Freq: Weekly; **Circ:** 80000 Publisher's Statement
News Editor: Chiraz Ben Mrad; **Managing Director:** Moncef Ben Mrad; **Editor in Chief:** Najib Khouildi; **Advertising Manager:** Rawdha Smida
Profile: Akhbar Al-Joumhouria (The Republic News) is a weekly newspaper covering society, politics, the arts and sport. It launched in 1990 and is published on Thursdays.
Language (s): Arabic
Ad Rate: Full Page Mono 500.00
Ad Rate: Full Page Colour 700.00
Currency: Tunisia Dinars
DAILY NEWSPAPER

Les Annonces de Tunisie 667673
Owner: TEC
Editorial: PO Box 2014, Megrine St Gobain, Route Z4, Ben Arous **Tel:** 216 71 432860
Email: nourikha@yahoo.fr
Freq: 2 Times/Week; **Circ:** 70000 Publisher's Statement
Editor in Chief: Khalid Al Nouri; **General Manager:** Nabil Azouz
Profile: Les Annonces de Tunisie is a bi-lingual (Arabic & French) newspaper covering news and current affairs, politics, sports, society and the arts. It launched in 1978 and is published twice a week on Tuesdays and Fridays.
Language (s): Arabic
Ad Rate: Full Page Mono 800.00
Ad Rate: Full Page Colour 1000.00
Currency: Tunisia Dinars
DAILY NEWSPAPER

Al Anwar 430901
Owner: Dar Anwar Press, Publishing & Distribution
Editorial: 25 Avenue Jean Jaures, Tunis 1000
Tel: 216 71 331000
Email: manbar@alanouar.com
Freq: Weekly; **Circ:** 90000 Publisher's Statement
Editor in Chief: Najmeddine Akkari; **Advertising Manager:** Ahmed Jabri
Profile: Al Anwar is a weekly newspaper covering local news, culture, social activities and sport. It launched in 1981 and is published on Saturdays.
Language (s): Arabic
Ad Rate: Full Page Mono 1067.50
Ad Rate: Full Page Colour 1225.00
Currency: Tunisia Dinars
DAILY NEWSPAPER

Assabah 324965
Owner: Dar Assabah
Editorial: PO Box 441, Boulevard Mohamed Bouazizi, El Menzah 1004 **Tel:** 216 71 238222
Email: rafik75.kram@yahoo.fr **Web site:** http://www.assabah.com.tn
Freq: Daily; **Circ:** 45000 Publisher's Statement
Editor in Chief: Ali Al Telili; **News Editor:** Rafik Benabdallah; **Advertising Manager:** Sihem Mokrani; **News Editor:** Mohssen Zoghlemi
Profile: Assabah (The Morning) is a newspaper covering national and international news, current affairs, politics, sport and entertainment. It launched in 1951 and is published daily, except Mondays.
Language (s): Arabic
Ad Rate: Full Page Mono 1540.00
Currency: Tunisia Dinars
DAILY NEWSPAPER

Assabah Al Ousboui 327494
Owner: Dar Assabah
Editorial: PO Box 441, Boulevard Mohamed Bouazizi, El Menzah 1004 **Tel:** 216 71 238222
Email: redaction@alousboui.com.tn
Freq: Weekly; **Circ:** 70000 Publisher's Statement
News Editor: Jamal Al Farchichi; **Editor in Chief:** Noureddine Ashour; **Advertising Manager:** Sihem Mokrani
Profile: Assabah Al Ousboui is a weekly newspaper covering national and international news, current affairs, politics, sports and entertainment. It launched in 1975 and is published on Mondays.
Language (s): Arabic
Ad Rate: Full Page Mono 785.40
Ad Rate: Full Page Colour 897.60
Currency: Tunisia Dinars
DAILY NEWSPAPER

Assarih 511151
Owner: Assarih
Editorial: PO Box 2058, Rue les Iles canaris, Ariana
Tel: 216 71 821715
Email: essarih1@gmail.com
Freq: Daily; **Circ:** 40000 Publisher's Statement
News Editor: Mohamed Abdelmoumen; **Advertising Manager:** Nadia Maghraoui
Profile: Assarih (The Virtuous) is a daily newspaper covering national and international news, business and sport. It was first published in 1995.
Language (s): Arabic
Ad Rate: Full Page Mono 1200.00
Ad Rate: Full Page Colour 1600.00
Currency: Tunisia Dinars
DAILY NEWSPAPER

Attounissia 824310
Owner: Dar Attounissia
Editorial: 7 Bis, rue Docteur Alfons Levarant, Belvedere, Tunis 1002 **Tel:** 216 71 890888
Email: attounissiajournal@yahoo.fr **Web site:** http://www.attounissia.com.tn
Freq: Daily; **Circ:** 70000 Publisher's Statement
General Manager: Nasreddine Ben Saida; **Editor in Chief:** Habib El Guizani; **National News Editor:** Mohamed Salah Elghanemi
Profile: Attounissia is a daily newspaper covering national and international news, business and sport. It was first published in 2011.
Language (s): Arabic
Ad Rate: Full Page Mono 1000.00
Ad Rate: Full Page Colour 1300.00
Currency: Tunisia Dinars
DAILY NEWSPAPER

El Bayane 667668
Owner: Union Tunisienne de l'Industrie du Commerce et de l'Artisanat
Editorial: 61, rue Abdel Razzak Al Charaibi, Tunis 1001 **Tel:** 216 71 339633
Email: albayane@gmail.com
Freq: Weekly; **Circ:** 90000 Publisher's Statement
Advertising Manager: Houda Ben-Najah; **News Editor:** Lotfi El Mekni
Profile: El Bayane is the weekly newspaper of the Union Tunisienne de l'Industrie du Commerce et de l'Artisanat and covers news, politics, business, arts and sport. It launched in 1977 and is published on Mondays.
Language (s): Arabic
Ad Rate: Full Page Mono 800.00
Ad Rate: Full Page Colour 1500.00
Currency: Tunisia Dinars
DAILY NEWSPAPER

Chams El-Janoub 668505
Owner: La Gazette Communication Group
Editorial: PO Box 609, Route de Teniour Km 3, Sfax 3018 **Tel:** 216 74 435500
Email: redaction@chamseljanoub.tn **Web site:** http://news.chamseljanoub.tn
Freq: Weekly; **Circ:** 8000 Publisher's Statement
Editor in Chief: Ali Baklouti
Profile: Chams El-Janoub is a regional newspaper distributed in the Sfax area in the south of Tunisia, and covers local news, current affairs, economics, sport, society and world news. The newspaper launched in 1980 and is published bi-monthly.
Language (s): Arabic
Ad Rate: Full Page Colour 600.00
Currency: Tunisia Dinars
DAILY NEWSPAPER

Al Chourouk 668468
Owner: Dar Anwar Press, Publishing & Distribution
Editorial: 25 Avenue Jean Jaures, Tunis 1000
Tel: 216 71 331000
Email: contact@alchourouk.com **Web site:** http://www.alchourouk.com
Freq: Daily; **Circ:** 110000 Publisher's Statement
News Editor: Sofiane El Aswad; **Advertising Manager:** Ahmed Jabri; **Co-Editor in Chief:** Fatma Karray
Profile: Al Chourouk (The Sunrise) is a daily, tabloid-sized newspaper covering national and international news, current affairs and politics. It was first published in 1982.
Language (s): Arabic
Ad Rate: Full Page Mono 1067.50
Ad Rate: Full Page Colour 1225.00
Currency: Tunisia Dinars
DAILY NEWSPAPER

Echaâb 667667
Owner: Union Générale Tunisienne du Travail (UGTT)
Editorial: 41, Avenue Ali Darghouth, Tunis 1001
Tel: 216 71 255020
Email: echaab_technique@yahoo.com **Web site:** http://www.echaab.info.tn
Freq: Weekly; **Circ:** 40000 Publisher's Statement
News Editor: Habib Chabi; **Advertising Manager:** Imad Farhat; **Editor in Chief:** Youssef Wetlati
Profile: Echaâb is the weekly newspaper of the Tunisian General Labour Union and covers local and international news, trade union affairs, culture and business. It launched in 1959 and is published on Fridays.
Language (s): Arabic
DAILY NEWSPAPER

Elhadath Journal 668507
Owner: Dar Jridi Press & Publishing
Editorial: 122, rue Radhia Haddad, Tunis 1000
Tel: 216 20 264426
Email: slahjeridi@gmail.com
Freq: Weekly; **Circ:** 45000 Publisher's Statement
Editor in Chief: Salah Jeridi; **News Editor:** Adel Talbi
Profile: Elhadath Journal is a weekly Arabic newspaper covering local news, current affairs and politics. It launched in 1993 and is published on Wednesdays.
Language (s): Arabic
DAILY NEWSPAPER

Es-Sahafa 324964
Owner: La SNIPE
Editorial: 17 Rue Ghari Baldi, Tunis 1000
Tel: 216 71 335025
Email: gwissemh@gmail.com **Web site:** http://www.essahafa.tn
Freq: Daily; **Circ:** 15000 Publisher's Statement
Picture Editor: Abdelfattah Belaid; **Advertising Manager:** Dhafer Miladi; **Editor in Chief:** Lotfi El Arbi Snoussi
Profile: Es-Sahafa (The Press) is a newspaper covering national and international news, current affairs, politics, sports and entertainment. It launched in 1989 and is published daily, except Mondays.
Language (s): Arabic
Ad Rate: Full Page Mono 1670.00
Currency: Tunisia Dinars
DAILY NEWSPAPER

Al Mijhar 857641
Owner: Societe Ramzi et Elissa
Editorial: 5th Floor, Al Saadi Building, Block CD 7, Place de 10 Decembre, Ariana **Tel:** 216 71 234909
Email: sendamechichi@gmail.com
Freq: Weekly; **Circ:** 50000
National News Editor: Hussam Bin Ahmed; **CEO & Editor in Chief:** Imad El Hadri
Profile: Al Mijhar (The Microscope) is a weekly tabloid-sized newspaper covering national and international news, business, sports and culture. The newspaper launched in January 2013 and is issued on Fridays.
Language (s): Arabic
Ad Rate: Full Page Mono 1200.00
Ad Rate: Full Page Colour 1450.00
Currency: Tunisia Dinars
DAILY NEWSPAPER

Al Moussawar 430903
Owner: Dar Al Moussawar for Publishing & Distribution
Editorial: 41, Immeuble Les Jardins de Bacha, Block 5, Avenue Khaireddine Bacha, Tunis 1073
Tel: 216 71 861190
Email: almoussawar_tunisie@yahoo.fr
Freq: Weekly; **Circ:** 55000 Publisher's Statement
Editor in Chief: Radia Abbou; **News Editor:** Walid Ferchichi; **Managing Director:** Omar Touil
Profile: Al Moussawar is a weekly Arabic newspaper covering news, business and sport. It launched in 1985 and is published on Mondays. The newspaper was formerly called El Ousbou Moussawar.
Language (s): Arabic
Ad Rate: Full Page Mono 800.00
Ad Rate: Full Page Colour 1300.00
Currency: Tunisia Dinars
DAILY NEWSPAPER

La Presse de Tunisie 306343
Owner: La SNIPE
Editorial: 17 Rue Ghari Baldi, Tunis 1000
Tel: 216 71 341066
Email: contact@lapresse.tn **Web site:** http://www.lapresse.tn
Freq: Daily; **Circ:** 50000 Publisher's Statement
Editor in Chief: Fouad Allani; **General Manager:** Belgassem Bentayaa; **Advertising Manager:** Dhafer Miladi
Profile: La Presse de Tunisie is a daily newspaper covering national and international news, economy, culture and sport. It was first published in 1936.
Language (s): French
Ad Rate: Full Page Mono 1670.00
Currency: Tunisia Dinars
DAILY NEWSPAPER

Le Quotidien 668467
Owner: Dar Anwar Press, Publishing & Distribution
Editorial: 25 Avenue Jean Jaures, Tunis 1000
Tel: 216 71 331000
Email: lequotidien222@yahoo.fr
Freq: Daily; **Circ:** 30000 Publisher's Statement
General Manager: Saida Al Ameri; **Co-Editor in Chief:** Choukri Baccouche; **News Editor:** Hassan Ghdiri; **Advertising Manager:** Ahmed Jabri
Profile: Le Quotidien is a newspaper covering national and international news, current affairs and politics. It launched in 2001 and is published daily, except Mondays.
Language (s): French
Ad Rate: Full Page Mono 1067.50
Ad Rate: Full Page Colour 1225.00
Currency: Tunisia Dinars
DAILY NEWSPAPER

Le Temps 306784
Owner: Dar Assabah
Editorial: PO Box 441, Boulevard Mohamed Al Bouazizi, El Menzah 1004 **Tel:** 216 71 238222
Email: redaction@letemps.com.tn **Web site:** http://www.letemps.com.tn
Freq: Daily; **Circ:** 35000 Publisher's Statement
Advertising Manager: Sihem Mokrani; **Editor in Chief:** Lotfi Wennich
Profile: Le Temps (The Time) is a newspaper covering national and international news, current affairs, politics, business, sport and entertainment. It launched in 1954 and is published daily, except Mondays.
Language (s): French
Ad Rate: Full Page Mono 1193.50
Ad Rate: Full Page Colour 1732.50
Currency: Tunisia Dinars
DAILY NEWSPAPER

Tunis Hebdo 327497
Owner: Dar Tunis Hebdo
Editorial: 11 Rue Ali Bach Hamba, Tunis 1000
Tel: 216 71 344100
Email: tunishebdo@tunishebdo.com.tn
Freq: Weekly; **Circ:** 35000 Publisher's Statement
Editor in Chief: Mohamed Ben Youssef; **Foreign News Editor:** Maher Chaabane; **News Editor:** Taher Selmi
Profile: Tunis Hebdo is a weekly newspaper covering national and international news, current affairs, politics, business, sport, culture and entertainment. It launched in 1973 and is published on Mondays.
Language (s): French
DAILY NEWSPAPER

News Service/Syndicate

Agence France-Presse - Tunis bureau 409560
Owner: Agence France-Presse
Editorial: 14, Rue 18 Janvier 1952, Tunis 1000
Tel: 216 71 249071
Email: afp.tunis@afp.com **Web site:** http://www.afp.com
Bureau Chief: Antoine Lambroschini
Profile: Tunis bureau of international French news agency.
Language (s): Arabic
NEWS SERVICE/SYNDICATE

Agence Tunis Afrique Presse 654825
Owner: Agence Tunis Afrique Presse
Editorial: 7, Avenue Slimane Ben Slimane, Manar II, Tunis 2092 **Tel:** 216 71 889000
Email: desk.national@email.ati.tn **Web site:** http://www.tap.info.tn
Editor in Chief: Lotfi Arfaoui; **General Manager:** Hamida Bour
Profile: Agence Tunis Afrique Presse is the national news agency of Tunisia and covers government news, matters of national importance, local news, politics, business, culture and sport.
Language (s): Arabic
NEWS SERVICE/SYNDICATE

Reuters - Tunis bureau 353730
Owner: Thomson Reuters
Editorial: PO Box 369, 3 rue Ibn Rachiq, Tunis 1002
Tel: 216 71 786655
Email: tarek.amara@reuters.com **Web site:** http://www.reuters.com
Profile: Tunis bureau of international news agency covering news, business and sport for a worldwide audience.
Language (s): Arabic
NEWS SERVICE/SYNDICATE

Turkey

Time Difference: GMT +2
National Telephone Code: 90
Continent: Europe
Capital: Ankara

Newspapers

?alom 447601
Editorial: Atiye Sk. Polar Apt. No:12/6 Tevikiye, Tevikiye, Istanbul **Tel:** 90 212 2319282
Email: sami@salom.com.tr **Web site:** http://www.salom.com.tr
Circ: 4000 Publisher's Statement
Editor: Ivo Molinas
Language (s): Turkish
DAILY NEWSPAPER

Ak?am 161050
Owner: Türkmedya
Editorial: Merkez Mahallesi 29 Ekim Caddesi, Binasi No: 11 34197 Bahcelievler, Istanbul
Tel: 90 212 449 30 00
Email: editor@aksam.com.tr **Web site:** http://www.aksam.com.tr
Freq: Daily; **Circ:** 103845 Publisher's Statement
Editor: Melis Apayd?n; **Editor:** Osman Can; **Editor:** Murat Kelkitlio?lu; **News Editor:** Özkan Tamirak
Profile: Newspaper focusing on national and international news and current affairs.
Language (s): Turkish
DAILY NEWSPAPER

Aktüel Gazete 871733
Editorial: Florya Senlikkoy Mh. Bakirkoy, Istanbul
Tel: 90 212 665 0656
Email: info@aktuelgazete.com **Web site:** http://www.aktuelgazete.com
Freq: Daily
Editor: Solmaz Akça
Language (s): Turkish
DAILY NEWSPAPER

Birgün 446647
Editorial: Kemeralt Cad. No:1-3 Kat 4, Karakoy, Istanbul **Tel:** 90 212 2440980
Email: info@birgun.net **Web site:** http://www.birgun.net
Freq: Daily; **Circ:** 22734 Publisher's Statement
Editor: Gülsen Candemir; **Editor:** Deniz Sar?
Profile: Daily newspaper with current news.
Language (s): Turkish
DAILY NEWSPAPER

Bugün 446697
Owner: Koza ?pek Bas?n ve Bas?m San. Tic. A.?.
Editorial: Meliha Avni Sozen Cad. No:17 B Blok Mecidiyekoy, ili, Istanbul **Tel:** 90 212 355 85 00
Web site: http://www.bugun.com.tr
Freq: Daily; **Circ:** 159629 Publisher's Statement
Editor-in-Chief: Erhan Ba?yurt

Profile: Daily newspaper in Turkey covering world political and business news from today and all major news.
Language (s): Turkish
DAILY NEWSPAPER

Cumhuriyet 161019
Owner: Cumhuriyet Grubu
Editorial: Prof. Nurettin Mazhar oktel Sok. No: 2 34381, ili, Istanbul **Tel:** 90 212 343 72 74
Email: editor@cumhuriyet.com.tr **Web site:** http://www.cumhuriyet.com.tr
Freq: Daily; **Circ:** 53845 Publisher's Statement
News Editor: O?uz Güven; **Editor:** Güray Öz
Profile: Newspaper containing national and international news, business, current affairs and sport.
Language (s): Turkish
DAILY NEWSPAPER

Cumhuriyet - Ankara 446729
Owner: Cumhuriyet Grubu
Editorial: Ahmet Rasim Sok. No: 14, cankaya, Ankara 6550 **Tel:** 90 312 442 30 50
Web site: http://www.cumhuriyet.com.tr
Freq: Weekly; **Circ:** 70450 Publisher's Statement
Profile: Regional edition and office of national newspaper.
Language (s): Turkish
DAILY NEWSPAPER

Daily Sabah 926147
Owner: Turkuvaz Gazete Dergi Bas?m A.?
Editorial: Barbaros Bulvar, 153, Balmumcu, Istanbul 34349 **Tel:** 90 212 354 3000
Email: editor@dailysabah.com **Web site:** http://www.dailysabah.com
Freq: Daily; **Circ:** 9317
Foreign News Editor: Yusuf Selman ?nanç; **News Editor:** Mehmet Solmaz
Profile: Founded in 2014, Daily Sabah provides latest headlines, special reports and interesting stories from Turkey and the world.
Language (s): English
DAILY NEWSPAPER

Dünya 446834
Owner: Dünya Grubu
Editorial: Basnevi 100.Yl Mahallesi, Baclar, Istanbul 34440 **Tel:** 90 212 440 24 24
Email: dunyaweb@dunya.com **Web site:** http://www.dunya.com
Freq: Daily; **Circ:** 54719 Publisher's Statement
News Editor: Ebru Sungur; **Editor:** Özgür Ta?p?nar
Profile: Daily newspaper covering national news, business and economics.
Language (s): Turkish
DAILY NEWSPAPER

Evrensel Gazetesi 448557
Owner: Bülten Bas?n Yay?n Reklamc?l?k Tic. Ltd. ?ti.
Editorial: cevre Tiyatrosu Sok, caykara Palas Apt. 1, Kocamustafapaa, Istanbul **Tel:** 90 212 5871799
Email: haber@evrensel.net **Web site:** http://www.evrensel.net
Freq: Daily; **Circ:** 7546
News Editor: Muzaffer Özkurt; **Editor:** Fatih Polat
Language (s): Turkish
DAILY NEWSPAPER

The Financial Times Turkey 874919
Editorial: Globus DÜNYA Basnevi 100.Yl Mahallesi, 34204 Baclar, Istanbul **Tel:** 90 212 4402424
Web site: http://www.ft.com
Freq: Daily
Profile: The Financial Times Turkey printed in Istanbul and distributed by Dunya publishing house.
Language (s): English
DAILY NEWSPAPER

Gözlem 446991
Editorial: Hürriyet Bulvar No: 8 / 806 Niyazi Ersoy Merkezi cankaya, Izmir **Tel:** 90 232 441 57 42
Email: haber@gozlemgazetesi.com **Web site:** http://www.gozlemgazetesi.com
Freq: Weekly; **Circ:** 32300 Not Audited
Language (s): Turkish
DAILY NEWSPAPER

Güne? 161047
Owner: Türkmedya Yay?n Grubu
Editorial: 29 Ekim Caddesi, Türkmedya Binas 11, Bahcelievler, Istanbul **Tel:** 90 212 449 30 00
Email: editor@turkmedya.com.tr **Web site:** http://www.gunes.com
Freq: Daily; **Circ:** 102927 Publisher's Statement
Editor: Ömer Özkaya; **Editor:** Nurettin Soydan
Profile: Newspaper featuring national and international news, economy, sport and features.
Language (s): Turkish
DAILY NEWSPAPER

Hürriyet 156639
Owner: Hürriyet Gazetecilik ve Matbaac?l?k A.?
Editorial: Hürriyet Dünyas, 100, Yl Mahallesi 2264. Sokak No:1, Baclar, Istanbul 34204
Tel: 90 212 6770000
Email: editor@hurriyet.com.tr **Web site:** http://www.hurriyet.com.tr
Freq: Daily; **Circ:** 339914 Publisher's Statement
Editor: Taha Akyol; **Editor:** Yalç?n Bayer; **Editor:** Ugur Cebeci; **Editor-in-Chief:** Sedat Ergin; **Editor:** Gökhan Kimsesizcan; **Editor:** Sava? Özbey; **Editor:** Cengiz Semercio?lu; **Editor:** Sahrap Soysal; **Editor:** Altan Tanrikulu
Profile: Newspaper focusing on national and international news, politics, business and sport.
Language (s): Turkish
DAILY NEWSPAPER

Hürriyet - Rome Bureau 508204
Owner: Hürriyet Gazetecilik ve Matbaac?l?k A.?
Editorial: Via dell'Umiltà, 83/C, Roma 187
Tel: 39 06 675911
Web site: http://www.hurriyet.com.tr
Circ: 600000 Publisher's Statement
Language (s): Italian
DAILY NEWSPAPER

Hürriyet Daily News 593952
Owner: Hürriyet Gazetecilik ve Matbaacilik A.?
Editorial: Hürriyet Dünyas, 100.Yl Mahallesi, Matbaaclar Caddesi, No : 78, Baclar, Istanbul 34204
Tel: 90 212 677 00 00
Email: hdnmail@hurriyet.com.tr **Web site:** http://www.hurriyetdailynews.com
Freq: Daily; **Circ:** 4975 Publisher's Statement
Editor-in-Chief: Murat Yetkin; **News Editor:** Barçin Yinanç
Profile: Daily newspaper in English covering domestic and world news, finance, lifestyle and sports.
Language (s): English
DAILY NEWSPAPER

Hürses 447089
Editorial: Yahya Kemal Mah. Talatpaa Cad. No:400/C, 34410 Gültepe, Istanbul **Tel:** 90 212 321 49 30
Email: editor@hursesgazetesi.com.tr **Web site:** http://www.hurses.com.tr
Freq: Daily; **Circ:** 1192 Publisher's Statement
Editor: Mehmet Emin Avc?
Language (s): Turkish
DAILY NEWSPAPER

Milat Gazetesi 789604
Editorial: ehit Erkan Alyanak Sk. No:2 Kat:4, Zeytinburnu, Istanbul **Tel:** 90 212 665 22 11 (
Email: ankaramilat@gmail.com **Web site:** http://www.milatgazetesi.com
Freq: Daily; **Circ:** 29936
Editor: Ahmet Zeki Gayberi
Language (s): Turkish
DAILY NEWSPAPER

Millet Gazetesi 949616
Owner: Koza ?pek Bas?n ve Bas?m San. Tic. A.?.
Editorial: Meliha Avni Sozen Cad. No:17 B Blok Mecidiyekoy, ili, Istanbul **Tel:** 90 212 355 85 00
Web site: http://www.millet.com.tr
Freq: Daily
Language (s): Turkish
DAILY NEWSPAPER

Milli Gazete 447678
Editorial: Muammer Aksoy Cad. Dere Sk. 70, Sefakoy-Kücükcekmece, Istanbul 34620
Tel: 90 212 697 10 00
Email: milli@milligazete.com.tr **Web site:** http://www.milligazete.com.tr
Freq: Daily; **Circ:** 22538 Publisher's Statement
Editor-in-Chief: Ercan Özcan
Profile: Provides political, economic news and developments in Turkey and the world's last-minute news, developments and information services.
Language (s): Turkish
DAILY NEWSPAPER

Milliyet 161022
Owner: Milliyet Gazetecilik ve Yay?nc?l?k A.?.
Editorial: zzet Paa Mah. Abide-i Hürriyet Cad. No:162, calayan-ili, Istanbul 34387
Tel: 90 212 337 99 99
Web site: http://www.milliyet.com.tr
Freq: Daily; **Circ:** 144598 Publisher's Statement
Editor: Sami Kohen
Profile: Newspaper focusing on national and international news, politics, business and sport.
Language (s): Turkish
DAILY NEWSPAPER

Önce Vatan 447436
Editorial: zzettin callar Cad. No: 3 D:8 Kat:1 - Bahcelievler, Istanbul **Tel:** 90 212 644 3207
Email: bilgi@oncevatan.com.tr **Web site:** http://www.oncevatan.com.tr
Freq: Daily; **Circ:** 6679 Publisher's Statement
Editor: Oguzhan Akosman
Language (s): Turkish
DAILY NEWSPAPER

Ortado?u 447422
Editorial: Fabrikalar Cd. No:1 K.2 Beyol, Sefakoy, Istanbul **Tel:** 90 212 425 36 50
Email: haber@ortadogugazetesi.net **Web site:** http://www.ortadogugazetesi.net
Freq: Daily; **Circ:** 5898 Publisher's Statement
Editor-in-Chief: Mehmet Müftüo?lu
Profile: Daily newspaper covering political news and issues.
Language (s): Turkish
DAILY NEWSPAPER

Özgür Gündem 447458
Editorial: Katip Mustafa celebi Mh.Abdullah Sk. No:3/8, Beyolu, Istanbul **Tel:** 90 212 251 86 54
Email: eposta@gundemimiz.com **Web site:** http://www.ozgur-gundem.com
Freq: Daily; **Circ:** 9925 Publisher's Statement
Language (s): Turkish
DAILY NEWSPAPER

Polis Bilimleri Dergisi 447480
Owner: Di?er
Editorial: Polis Akademisi 06580, Bakanlklar, Ankara
Tel: 90 312 2317840
Email: fberen@hotmail.com
Freq: Quarterly; **Circ:** 5000 Publisher's Statement
Language (s): Turkish
DAILY NEWSPAPER

Posta 161025
Owner: Do?an Gazetecilik A.?.
Editorial: Kutepe Mah. Mecidiyekoy Yolu Cad., Trump Towers Kule 2, Istanbul 34387
Tel: 90 212 5056111
Web site: http://www.posta.com.tr
Freq: Daily; **Circ:** 397299 Publisher's Statement
Editor-in-Chief: Mehmet Co?kundeniz; **Editor:** Canda? Tolga I??k
Profile: Newspaper focusing on national and international news, society, entertainment and sport.
Language (s): Turkish
DAILY NEWSPAPER

Radikal 161024
Owner: Hürriyet Gazetecilik ve Matbaac?l?k A.?
Editorial: Doan Medya Center 34204, Baclar, Istanbul **Tel:** 90 212 5056111
Email: iletisim@radikal.com.tr **Web site:** http://www.radikal.com.tr
Freq: Daily; **Circ:** 22024 Publisher's Statement
News Editor: Ömer Erbil; **Editor-in-Chief:** Eyup Can Sa?l?k; **Coumnist:** Murat Yetkin
Profile: Newspaper focusing on national and international news, economics, business and politics as well as culture and the arts.
Language (s): Turkish
DAILY NEWSPAPER

Sabah 156635
Owner: Turkuvaz Gazete Dergi Bas?m A.?.
Editorial: Barbaros Bulvar Cam Han No:125 K:5, Beikta, Istanbul **Tel:** 90 212 3543000
Email: editor@sabah.com.tr **Web site:** http://www.sabah.com.tr
Freq: Daily; **Circ:** 315525 Publisher's Statement
News Editor: Burak Artuner
Profile: Newspaper focusing on national and international news, politics, business and sport.
Language (s): Turkish
DAILY NEWSPAPER

Sol 447564
Owner: Güne? Bas?m Yay?m Organizasyon ve Ticaret Ltd. ?ti.
Editorial: Yeni Sahra Mahallesi, nonü Caddesi No: 9, Istanbul 34746 **Tel:** 90 216 315 14 00
Email: gazete@sol.org.tr **Web site:** http://gazete.sol.org.tr
Freq: Daily; **Circ:** 14550 Publisher's Statement
Editor: Hafize Kazc?
Language (s): Turkish
DAILY NEWSPAPER

Sözcü 448161
Owner: Estetik Yay?nc?l?k A.?
Editorial: Halkal Merkez Mah. Abay Cad. Atlas Sokak, Atlas Merkezi, A Blok, No: 6-8/4, Istanbul
Tel: 90 212 698 3535
Email: net@sozcu.com.tr **Web site:** http://www.sozcu.com.tr
Freq: Daily; **Circ:** 295990 Publisher's Statement
Editor: Mediha Olgun
Profile: Sözcü is a Turkish daily newspaper launched in 2007 and distributed nationwide.
Language (s): Turkish
DAILY NEWSPAPER

Star 161046
Owner: Star Medya Yay?nc?l?k A.?.
Editorial: Atatürk Mahallesi Bahariye, Cad. No:31 K.cekmece, Istanbul 34679 **Tel:** 90 212 473 20 00
Email: editor@stargazete.com **Web site:** http://www.star.com.tr
Freq: Daily; **Circ:** 102597 Publisher's Statement
Editor-in-Chief: Nuh Albayrak; **Editor:** Cengiz Ino?lu; **News Editor:** Mehmet Yücel
Profile: Newspaper focusing on national and international news, economy, current affairs and sport.
Language (s): Turkish
DAILY NEWSPAPER

Takvim Gazetesi 447622
Owner: Turkuvaz Gazete Dergi Bas?m A.?.
Editorial: Barbaros Bulvar, No:153, Cam Han, Kat:5 Beikta, Istanbul **Tel:** 90 212 354 30 00
Email: takvim@takvim.com.tr **Web site:** http://www.takvim.com.tr
Freq: Daily; **Circ:** 106953 Publisher's Statement
News Editor: Mevlüt Yüksel
Profile: Daily national newspaper with current political, economic and social news.
Language (s): Turkish
DAILY NEWSPAPER

Taraf 844647
Owner: Taraf Gazetecilik Sanayi ve Ticaret A.?
Editorial: Misbah Muhayye Damga ve Neet omer Sok. No:23-25, Kadkoy, Istanbul 34710
Tel: 210 216 348 99 22
Email: haber@taraf.com.tr **Web site:** http://www.taraf.com.tr
Freq: Daily; **Circ:** 69141
Profile: Taraf is a Turkish national newspaper in Turkey. It covers news, social and political affairs.
Language (s): Turkish
DAILY NEWSPAPER

Türkiye Gazetesi 156650
Owner: ?hlas Grubu
Editorial: Merkez Mahallesi 29 Ekim Caddesi, hlas Plaza No:11 A/41 34197, Istanbul
Tel: 90 212 641 8484
Email: info@tg.com.tr **Web site:** http://www.turkiyegazetesi.com.tr
Freq: Daily; **Circ:** 163374 Publisher's Statement
Profile: Newspaper focusing on national and international news, politics, business, culture and sport.
Language (s): Turkish
DAILY NEWSPAPER

Üsküdar 449136
Editorial: Ahmediye Meydan Katibim mrk. No:91/5, Üsküdar, Istanbul **Tel:** 90 216 3109848
Email: hergunhaber@gmail.com **Web site:** http://www.uskudargazetesi.com.tr
Circ: 20000 Publisher's Statement
Editor: O?uzhan Kaplan
Language (s): Turkish
DAILY NEWSPAPER

Vatan 449143
Owner: Vatan Gazetecilik A.?
Editorial: zzet Paa Mah. Abide-i Hürriyet Cad. No:162, calayan-ili, Istanbul 34387
Tel: 90 212 337 99 99
Email: bizeulasin@gazetevatan.com **Web site:** http://www.gazetevatan.com
Freq: Daily; **Circ:** 101871 Publisher's Statement
Editor: Burak Kara
Profile: National daily covering politics, economics, business, culture, social issues and entertainment.
Language (s): Turkish
DAILY NEWSPAPER

Yarin 449165
Editorial: Rumeli Cad. Matbaac Osmanbey Sok. No:67/4, ili, Istanbul
Email: bilgi@yarinhaber.net **Web site:** http://yarinhaber.net
Freq: Daily; **Circ:** 20000 Publisher's Statement
Language (s): Turkish
DAILY NEWSPAPER

Yeni ?afak 161045
Owner: Yeni ?afak Gazetecilik A.?.
Editorial: Yenidoan Mah. enay Sok. No:2 Kat:1, Bayrampaa, Istanbul **Tel:** 90 212 612 29 30
Email: sm@yenisafak.com.tr **Web site:** http://yenisafak.com.tr
Freq: Daily; **Circ:** 126630 Publisher's Statement
News Editor: Fatma Demircio?lu; **Editor-in-Chief:** Ibrahim Karagul; **Editor:** Idris Saruhan
Profile: Newspaper focusing on national and international news, economics, politics, culture, society and sport.
Language (s): Turkish
DAILY NEWSPAPER

Yeni Akit Gazetesi 795661
Editorial: ehit Mehmet Erol Sk. No:10/3 Mahmutbey, Bagclar, Istanbul **Tel:** 90 212 447 4200
Email: bilgi@yeniakit.com.tr **Web site:** http://www.yeniakit.com.tr
Freq: Daily; **Circ:** 55954
Language (s): Turkish
DAILY NEWSPAPER

Yeni As?r 161049
Owner: Sabah Grubu
Editorial: Gaziosmanpaa Bulvar No:5 35210, cankaya, Izmir **Tel:** 90 232 4415000
Email: yasir@yeniasir.com.tr **Web site:** http://www.yeniasir.com.tr
Freq: Daily; **Circ:** 37106 Publisher's Statement
Editor-in-Chief: ?ebnem Bursal?
Profile: Newspaper containing national and international news, business and current affairs.
Language (s): Turkish
DAILY NEWSPAPER

Yeni Asya 449182
Owner: Yeni Asya Gazetecilik, Matbaacilik ve Yayincilik AS
Editorial: Gülbahar Cad. Günay Sk. No:434212, Güneli, Istanbul **Tel:** 90 212 655 88 59
Email: iletisim@yeniasya.com.tr **Web site:** http://www.yeniasya.com.tr
Freq: Daily; **Circ:** 9300 Publisher's Statement
Editor in Chief: Kâzim Güleçyüz
Profile: Daily newspaper covering politics, economics, culture and sports.
Language (s): Turkish
DAILY NEWSPAPER

Yeni Ça? 449187
Editorial: A Yaynclk Gazetecilik ve Matbaaclk A. Bask Tesisleri cobanceme Mah. Kalender Sok., Yenibosna, Istanbul **Tel:** 90 212 4524040
Email: yenicag@yenicaggazetesi.com.tr **Web site:** http://www.yenicaggazetesi.com.tr
Freq: Daily; **Circ:** 56923 Not Audited
Editor: Ahmet Çelik
Profile: Daily newspaper providing political news, current news, entertainment and sports.
Language (s): Turkish
DAILY NEWSPAPER

Yeni Mesaj 449228
Editorial: enlikkoy Mahallesi, ehitozcan Canik Sokak, No: 4 / A Kat: 2, nonü Caddesi No: 96 Florya, Istanbul
Tel: 90 212 4251066
Email: editor@yenimesaj.com.tr **Web site:** http://www.yenimesaj.com.tr
Freq: Daily; **Circ:** 47282 Publisher's Statement
Editor: Mehmet Emin Koç
Profile: 'New Message' published in Turkey is a daily national newspaper.
Language (s): Turkish
DAILY NEWSPAPER

News Service/Syndicate

?hlas Haber Ajans? 957164
Owner: ?hlas Haber Ajans? A.?.
Editorial: Istanbul **Tel:** 90 212 454 33 33
Email: halklailiskiler@iha.com.tr **Web site:** http://www.iha.com.tr
Editor: ?ifa Kaymak
Language (s): Turkish
NEWS SERVICE/SYNDICATE

Anadolu Agency - Anadolu Ajans? 558816
Editorial: GMK Bulvar 128/C 06430 Maltepe, Ankara
Tel: 90 312 999 20 00
Email: kurumsaliletisim@aa.com.tr **Web site:** http://aa.com.tr/tr
News Editor: Addis Getachew; **Editor-in-Chief:** Metin Mutano?lu
Profile: Anadolu Agency is a press agency in Turkey and provides news in English, Turkish, Arabic, Bosnian, Kurdish, Russian and French.
NEWS SERVICE/SYNDICATE

BloombergHT 809548
Owner: C Görsel Yay?nlar A.?.
Editorial: Abdülhakhamit Cad., No:25 Beyolu/ Taksim, Istanbul 34437 **Tel:** 90 212 1316000
Email: editor@bloomberght.com **Web site:** http://www.bloomberght.com
Director: Cüneyt Ba?aran; **News Director:** Ahmet Öz; **Editor:** Tu?çe Özsoy; **Editor:** Süheyla Y?lmaz
Profile: BloombergHT is a 24-hour network providing business and financial news. Launched in 2010.
Language (s): Turkish
NEWS SERVICE/SYNDICATE

Turkmenistan

Time Difference: GMT +5
National Telephone Code: 993
Continent: Asia
Capital: Ashgabad

Newspapers

Neitralniy Turkmenistan 218486
Owner: Neytralniy Turkmenistan
Editorial: Garazhshyzlak shaily, Ashgabat
Tel: 993 12 38 61 18
Email: nt@online.tm **Web site:** http://www.turkmenistan.gov.tm
Freq: Daily; **Circ:** 39000 Publisher's Statement
Editor In Chief: Geren Taimova
Profile: Newspaper focusing on business, politics, economics, sport, culture and national and international news.
Language (s): Russian
DAILY NEWSPAPER

Turks and Caicos Islands

Time Difference: GMT -5
National Telephone Code: 1 649
Continent: The Americas
Capital: Cockburn Town (Grand Turk)

Community Newspaper

The Turks & Caicos Free Press 230283
Owner: Turks & Caicos Free Press Ltd
Editorial: The Marketplace, Leeward Highway, Providenciales **Tel:** 649 9415615
Email: news@tcifreepress.com **Web site:** http://www.tcifreepress.com
Freq: Weekly; **Circ:** 3500 Not Audited
Profile: The Turks & Caicos Free Press is a daily newspaper focusing on national news, business, politics and sports.
Language (s): English
Ad Rate: Full Page Mono 13.75
Currency: United States Dollars
COMMUNITY NEWSPAPER

Uganda

Time Difference: GMT +3
National Telephone Code: 256
Continent: Africa
Capital: Kampala

Newspapers

Bukedde 777405
Owner: Vision Group
Editorial: 19/21 First Street, Industrial Area, Kampala
Tel: 256 41 4337 000
Email: bukedde@newvision.co.ug **Web site:** http://bukedde.co.ug
Freq: Daily
Editor in Chief: Barbara Kaija
Profile: Newspaper covering regional and national news and current affairs including business, politics, entertainment and sports.
Language (s): English
DAILY NEWSPAPER

Daily Monitor 161252
Owner: Monitor Publications Ltd
Editorial: 29-35, 8th Street, Kampala
Tel: 256 41 7744100
Email: editorial@ug.nationmedia.com **Web site:** http://www.monitor.co.ug
Freq: Daily; **Circ:** 27000 Publisher's Statement
Bureau Chief: Michael Ssali
Profile: Newspaper covering national and international news and current affairs including business, politics, economics, sports, entertainment and culture.
Language (s): English
DAILY NEWSPAPER

The New Vision 156715
Owner: Vision Group
Editorial: 19/21 First Street, Industrial Area, Kampala
Tel: 256 414 337 000
Email: editorial@newvision.co.ug **Web site:** http://www.newvision.co.ug
Freq: Daily; **Circ:** 35186 Publisher's Statement
Editor in Chief: Barbara Kaija; **News Editor:** Hellen Mukiibi
Profile: Newspaper covering regional, national and international news and current affairs including sport, business, entertainment, health, multimedia and lifestyle.
Language (s): English
Ad Rate: Full Page Mono 3.00
Currency: United States Dollars
DAILY NEWSPAPER

The Observer 799023
Owner: Observer Media Ltd.
Editorial: 1, Tagore Crescent, Kamwokya, Kampala
Tel: 256 414 230433
Email: editor@observer.ug **Web site:** http://www.observer.ug
Freq: Daily
Editor: Richard Kavuma
Profile: Newspaper covering regional, national and international news and current affairs including business, economics, politics, education, lifestyle and sports.
Language (s): English
DAILY NEWSPAPER

Community Newspaper

ETOP 852717
Owner: Vision Group
Editorial: 19/21 First Street, Industrial Area, Kampala
Tel: 256 414 337 000
Email: editorial@newvision.co.ug **Web site:** http://www.etop.co.ug
Freq: Weekly
Editor in Chief: Barbara Kaija
Profile: Newspaper covering regional news and current affairs including relationship advice, sports, community news and gossip, business, pictorial and readers' letters and opinions. Published in Ateso weekly every Thursday, the main circulation area covers North Eastern Uganda, Soroti, Katakwa and Kumi.
COMMUNITY NEWSPAPER

Orumuri 852720
Owner: Vision Group
Editorial: 19/21 First Street, Industrial Area, Kampala
Tel: 256 414 337 000
Email: amakuru@newvision.co.ug **Web site:** http://www.orumuri.co.ug
Editor in Chief: Barbara Kaija
Profile: Newspaper covering regional news and current affairs including gossip, relationship education, politics, community news and gossip, wedding pictorial, business, herbal remedies, farming, weekly news round up and sports. Published in Runyakore/Rukiga weekly every Monday, the main circulation area is the western part of Uganda, from Masaka to Kabale, including Toro, Kasese, Bunyoro.
COMMUNITY NEWSPAPER

Rupiny 789885
Owner: Vision Group
Editorial: 19/21 First Street, Industrial Area, Kampala
Tel: 256 414 337 000
Email: editorial@newvision.co.ug **Web site:** http://rupiny.co.ug
Editor in Chief: Barbara Kaija
Profile: Newspaper covering regional news and current affairs including politics, relationship advice, sports, community news & gossip, business, leisure, crazy crazy country, pictorials and readers' letters and opinions. Published in Luo weekly every Wednesday, main circulation area is the northern part of Uganda including Gulu and Lira.
Language (s): English
COMMUNITY NEWSPAPER

Ukraine

Time Difference: GMT +2
National Telephone Code: 380
Continent: Europe
Capital: Kiev

Newspapers

Den 160100
Owner: The Ukrainian Press Group
Editorial: Bulvar Peremogi 121d, Kyiv 3115
Tel: 380 44 303-96-70
Email: chedit@day.kiev.ua **Web site:** http://day.kyiv.ua
Freq: Daily; **Circ:** 62500 Publisher's Statement
Profile: Newspaper in Ukrainian and Russian versions covering politics, current-affairs, economics and culture.
Language (s): English
Ad Rate: Full Page Mono 5000.00
Currency: United States Dollars
DAILY NEWSPAPER

Fakty i kommentarii 161224
Owner: Fakty i kommentarii
Editorial: ul. Vandy Vasilevskoi 27/29, Kiev 4116
Tel: 380 44 482 3201
Email: info@fakty.ua **Web site:** http://fakty.ua
Freq: Daily; **Circ:** 145000 Publisher's Statement
Editor In Chief: Aleksander Shvets
Profile: Newspaper covering news, politics, the economy, culture, foreign affairs and sport.
Language (s): Russian
Ad Rate: Full Page Colour 41000.00
Currency: Ukraine Hryvnia
DAILY NEWSPAPER

Kyiv Post 159089
Owner: Public Media
Editorial: 31A Pushkinska Street, Suite 600, 6th Floor, Kyiv 1004 **Tel:** 380 44 5913344
Email: news@kyivpost.com **Web site:** http://www.kyivpost.com
Circ: 25000 Publisher's Statement
Editor: Brian Bonner; **Advertising Manager:** Yulia Kovalenko; **Production Manager:** Tetyana Myturych; **Advertising Manager:** Lena Symonenko; **Project Manager:** Elena Viter
Profile: Newspaper containing national and international news, business and current affairs.
Language (s): English
Ad Rate: Full Page Colour 30300.00
Currency: Ukraine Hryvnia
DAILY NEWSPAPER

Segodnya 157132
Owner: Segodnya Multimedia
Editorial: Ul. Borshagovskaya 152-B, Kyiv 305656
Tel: 380 44 45 72 399
Email: info@segodnya.ua **Web site:** http://www.segodnya.ua
Freq: Daily; **Circ:** 150000 Publisher's Statement
Editor: Anastasiia Belousova; **News Editor:** Vladislava Darmostyuk; **Editor:** Polina Dorozhkina; **Editor-in-Chief:** Olga Guk; **News Editor:** Aleksandr Maruschak; **Editor:** Aleksandr Panchenko; **Editor:** Aleksey Ponomarenko; **Editor:** Konstantin Ryapolov
Profile: Newspaper covering national and international news, politics, sport and entertainment.
Language (s): Russian
DAILY NEWSPAPER

Sport Arena 539157
Owner: Donbass
Editorial: pr. Kievsky 48, 9 floor, Donetsk 83118
Tel: 380 62 38 56 289
Email: sport@donbass.dn.ua **Web site:** http://www.sport-arena.com.ua
Freq: 2 Times/Week; **Circ:** 15000 Not Audited
Editor-in-Chief: Eduard Kiselev
Profile: National newspaper on sports, sport events in Ukraine and abroad, interviews with sport celebrities and coaches.
Language (s): Russian
DAILY NEWSPAPER

Ukraina Moloda 161225
Owner: PP Ukraina Moloda
Editorial: pr. Peremogi 50, 5 floor, Kyiv 3047
Tel: 380 44 45 48 392
Email: post@umoloda.kiev.ua **Web site:** http://uamedia.visti.net/um
Freq: Daily; **Circ:** 130884 Publisher's Statement
Publisher: Mihailo Doroshenko; **Advertising Manager:** Natasha Yankovskaya
Profile: Informative -analytical newspaper covering news, politics and economic issues.
Language (s): Ukrainian
Ad Rate: Full Page Mono 18000.00
Currency: Ukraine Hryvnia
DAILY NEWSPAPER

Yuridicheskaya Practika 191449
Owner: Yuridicheskaya Practika Publishing
Editorial: 22 Zakrevskogo Str., 4 Floor, Kyiv 2660
Tel: 380 44 49 52 727
Email: info@yurpractika.com **Web site:** http://www.yurpractika.com
Freq: Weekly; **Circ:** 10000 Not Audited
Director: Anatoliy Shilenkov; **Advertising Manager:** Vadim Shpachuk; **Editor In Chief:** Yuriy Zabara
Profile: Newspaper focusing on law issues and legal practice includes advice on optimisation taxation, stock share issues, notary issues and family law.
Language (s): Russian
Ad Rate: Full Page Mono 1950.00
Ad Rate: Full Page Colour 2545.00
Currency: United States Dollars
DAILY NEWSPAPER

Zerkalo Nedeli. Ukraina 230013
Editorial: ul. Moskvoskaya 19/1, Kiev 1010
Tel: 380 44 280-04-85
Email: editor@zn.ua **Web site:** http://dt.ua
Circ: 57515 Publisher's Statement
Profile: Newspaper covering national and international news with features on business and finance, politics, lifestyle, entertainment and sport.
Language (s): Russian
DAILY NEWSPAPER

News Service/Syndicate

Interfax Ukraina 571890
Editorial: ul. Reitarskaya 8/5a, Kiev 1034
Tel: 380 44 270 74 65
Email: office@interfax.kiev.ua **Web site:** http://www.interfax.com.ua
Director General: Alexander Martynenko
Profile: News agency with coverage of news in three languages: Russian, Ukrainian and English.
Language (s): Ukrainian
NEWS SERVICE/SYNDICATE

Ukrinform 353219
Editorial: ul. Bogdana Khmelnytskogo 8/16, Kiev 1001 **Tel:** 380 44 279-81-52
Email: office@ukrinform.ua **Web site:** http://www.ukrinform.ua
Editor: Marina Tarnovska
Profile: Offers online free access to updated political, economic, financial, medicinal, cultural news in Russian, Ukrainian and English languages.
Language (s): Ukrainian
NEWS SERVICE/SYNDICATE

UNIAN 353719
Editorial: ul. Khreshatik 4, Kyiv 1001
Tel: 380 44 27 93 131
Email: info@unian.net **Web site:** http://www.unian.net
Editor-in-Chief: Mykhailo Gannytskyi
Profile: Provides political and economic news about most important events in Ukraine's capital and regions, official decisions of highest legislative and executive bodies, as well as unbiased comments of experts and politicians.
Language (s): Ukrainian
NEWS SERVICE/SYNDICATE

United Arab Emirates

Time Difference: GMT +4
National Telephone Code: 971
Continent: Asia
Capital: Abu Dhabi

Newspapers

Alroeya 584351
Owner: I-Media
Editorial: PO Box 502850, Mezzanine Floor, Shatha Tower, Dubai **Tel:** 971 4 439 2000
Email: press@alroeya.com **Web site:** http://www.alroeya.ae
Freq: Daily; **Circ:** 80000 Rate Card
News Editor: Firas Al Ali; **Editor In Chief:** Mohammed Al Tunisi
Profile: Alroeya is a daily newspaper covering news, business and sport. It launched in 2009 as business newspaper Alrroya Aleqtissadiya, before re-launching as Alroeya in December 2012.
Language (s): Arabic

Ad Rate: Full Page Colour 54060.00
Currency: United Arab Emirates Dirhams
DAILY NEWSPAPER

Al Bayan 157087
Owner: Dubai Media Incorporated
Editorial: PO Box 2710, Sheikh Zayed Road, Dubai **Tel:** 971 4 344 4400
Email: local@albayan.ae **Web site:** http://www.albayan.ae
Freq: Daily; **Circ:** 88800 Rate Card
Profile: Al Bayan is a daily, broadsheet-sized newspaper covering news, current affairs, politics, business and sport. The newspaper launched in 1980 and is owned by the Government of Dubai through Dubai Media Incorporated.
Language (s): Arabic
Ad Rate: Full Page Mono 41552.00
Ad Rate: Full Page Colour 47785.00
Currency: United Arab Emirates Dirhams
DAILY NEWSPAPER

Emarat Al Youm 360245
Owner: Dubai Media Incorporated
Editorial: PO Box 191919, Emarat Al Youm Building, Near Safa Park, Dubai **Tel:** 971 4 306 2222
Email: local@emaratalyoum.com **Web site:** http://www.emaratalyoum.com
Freq: Daily; **Circ:** 80000 Rate Card
Picture Editor: Osama Abughanim; **Editor In Chief:** Sami Al Reyami
Profile: Emarat Al Youm is a tabloid-sized newspaper covering local and international news, politics, business, entertainment, culture and sport. The daily newspaper was first published in 2005, and is owned by the Government of Dubai through Dubai Media Incorporated.
Language (s): Arabic
Ad Rate: Full Page Colour 28950.00
Currency: United Arab Emirates Dirhams
DAILY NEWSPAPER

Emirates Business 870179
Owner: Al Wathba For Media
Editorial: PO Box 54040, Building 35, Abu Dhabi **Tel:** 971 2 448 6000
Email: info@emirates-business.ae **Web site:** http://www.emirates-business.ae
Freq: Daily; **Circ:** 60000
Profile: Emirates Business is a daily, broadsheet newspaper covering business and finance. It was first published in July 2013, and was formerly called The Gulf Time until January 2016.
Language (s): English
Ad Rate: Full Page Colour 12000.00
Currency: United Arab Emirates Dirhams
DAILY NEWSPAPER

Gulf Madhyamam - UAE edition 355709
Owner: Gulf Madhyamam FZ LLC
Editorial: PO Box 4243, Office 232, Building 10, Dubai **Tel:** 971 4 390 2628
Email: dubai@gulfmadhyamam.net **Web site:** http://www.gulfmadhyamam.net
Freq: Daily; **Circ:** 63980 Rate Card
Editor-in-Chief: Hamzah Abbas; **Bureau Chief:** Anwarul Haque; **Chief Operating Officer:** Zakariya Mohammed
Profile: Gulf Madhyamam is an international Indian newspaper covering national and international news, current affairs, politics, business and sport. The newspaper is aimed at Malayalam speakers in the Gulf and publishes separate editions for the UAE, Saudi Arabia (Riyadh, Jeddah, Dammam & Abha), Qatar, Oman, Bahrain and Kuwait. The UAE edition was first published in 1999.
Language (s): Malayalam
DAILY NEWSPAPER

Gulf News 156714
Owner: Al Nisr Publishing LLC
Editorial: PO Box 6519, Gulf News Building, Dubai **Tel:** 971 4 344 7100
Email: editor@gulfnews.com **Web site:** http://www.gulfnews.com
Freq: Daily; **Circ:** 104351 BPA Worldwide
Editor In Chief: Abdul Hamid Ahmad; **Group Advertisement Manager:** Rajeev Khanna; **Advertising Manager:** Fariba Rezazadeh
Profile: Gulf News is a berliner-sized, daily newspaper covering local and international news, politics, business and sport. It includes tabloid!, an entertainment and lifestyle supplement from Sunday to Thursday, and the expanded tabloid! on Saturday on Saturdays. On Fridays, the newspaper includes lifestyle magazine supplement Friday and Weekend Review, which takes an in-depth look at the issues behind the news. The newspaper was first published as a tabloid in September 1978, and re-launched as a broadsheet in December 1985.
Language (s): English
Ad Rate: Full Page Colour 59600.00
Currency: United Arab Emirates Dirhams
DAILY NEWSPAPER

Al Ittihad 156819
Owner: Abu Dhabi Media
Editorial: PO Box 791, Abu Dhabi Media Building, Abu Dhabi **Tel:** 971 2 445 5555
Email: local@alittihad.ae **Web site:** http://www.alittihad.ae
Freq: Daily; **Circ:** 109640 Rate Card
Editor In Chief: Mohammed Al Hammadi; **Head of News:** Saeed Al Sawaf; **Picture Editor:** Sultan Bin Odaie
Profile: Al Ittihad (The Union) is a broadsheet-sized, daily Arabic newspaper covering local and international news, current affairs, politics, business and sport. It includes a daily lifestyle section, Dunia. The newspaper launched in 1969 and is owned by the Government of Abu Dhabi through its Abu Dhabi Media division.
Language (s): Arabic
Ad Rate: Full Page Colour 63918.00
Currency: United Arab Emirates Dirhams
DAILY NEWSPAPER

Al Khaleej 156861
Owner: Dar Al Khaleej for Press, Printing & Publishing
Editorial: PO Box 30, Al Khan Street, Sharjah **Tel:** 971 6 577 7777
Email: alkhaleej@alkhaleej.ae **Web site:** http://www.alkhaleej.ae
Freq: Daily; **Circ:** 147400 Rate Card
Advertising Manager: Ahmad Al Farhan; **Editor:** Sameh Al Laithi; **Head of News:** Jamal Dwairi; **Picture Editor:** Haidar Fouad; **News Editor:** Hajar Khamis; **Editor in Chief:** Khalid Omran
Profile: Al Khaleej (The Gulf) is a broadsheet-sized, daily Arabic newspaper covering local and international news, politics, business, economics, culture and sport. It was first published in 1970.
Language (s): Arabic
DAILY NEWSPAPER

Khaleej Times 156716
Owner: Galadari Printing & Publishing LLC
Editorial: PO Box 11243, Khaleej Times Offices, Dubai **Tel:** 971 4 338 3535
Email: news@khaleejtimes.com **Web site:** http://www.khaleejtimes.com
Freq: Daily; **Circ:** 96150 Publisher's Statement
Chief Photographer: Kiran Prasad
Profile: Khaleej Times is a broadsheet-sized, daily English newspaper covering local and international news, sport, business and finance. The newspaper was first published in 1978 and includes City Times, a daily tabloid supplement covering entertainment and celebrity news; wknd. magazine on Fridays; and a health supplement, Better Health, which is published twice a year in March and November.
Language (s): English
Ad Rate: Full Page Colour 55974.00
Currency: United Arab Emirates Dirhams
DAILY NEWSPAPER

Malayala Manorama - Gulf edition 457395
Owner: M M Publications Ltd
Editorial: PO Box 502638, Office 1505, Aurora Tower, Dubai **Tel:** 971 4 374 8920
Email: manoramagulf@gmail.com **Web site:** http://www.manoramaonline.com
Freq: Daily; **Circ:** 96000 Publisher's Statement
Bureau Chief: Jaimon George
Profile: Gulf edition of Indian newspaper Malayala Manorama. It covers international and local news, politics, sport, business, entertainment and technology. It was first published in 2006 and is aimed at Malayalam speakers in the Gulf.
Language (s): Malayalam
DAILY NEWSPAPER

Middle East Chandrika 457394
Owner: Kerala Muslim Printing and Publishing Co Ltd
Editorial: PO Box 50066, 1st Floor, Al Nakheel Center, Dubai **Tel:** 971 4 238 6888
Email: editor@mechandrika.ae **Web site:** http://www.chandrikadaily.com/category/gulf
Freq: Daily; **Circ:** 55000 Publisher's Statement
General Manager: Ibrahim Elettil; **Editor in Charge:** Abdul Jaleel Pattambi
Profile: Middle East Chandrika is the UAE edition of Indian newspaper Chandrika, and covers local and international news, sport, business, religion and politics. It was first published in 2005 and is aimed at Malayalam speakers in the UAE.
Language (s): Malayalam
Ad Rate: Full Page Mono 12000.00
Ad Rate: Full Page Colour 14000.00
Currency: United Arab Emirates Dirhams
DAILY NEWSPAPER

The National 526273
Owner: International Media Investments FZ LLC
Editorial: PO Box 769555, Building 6, Next to Park Rotana Hotel, Abu Dhabi **Tel:** 971 2 304 3600
Email: newsdesk@thenational.ae **Web site:** http://www.thenational.ae
Freq: Daily; **Circ:** 65000 Rate Card
Foreign News Editor: Jonathan Lessware; **News Editor:** Nic Ridley
Profile: The National is a berliner-sized newspaper covering local and international news, business and sport. The newspaper includes Arts & Lifestyle, an arts and lifestyle section from Sunday to Thursday; Weekend, a tabloid-sized lifestyle supplement on Fridays, and a monthly lifestyle magazine, Luxury. The newspaper launched in 2008 and was owned by the Government of Abu Dhabi through its Abu Dhabi Media division until 2017 when its ownership was transferred to International Media Investments (IMI), a subsidiary of Abu Dhabi Media Investment Corporation (ADMIC).
Language (s): English
Ad Rate: Full Page Colour 39900.00
Currency: United Arab Emirates Dirhams
DAILY NEWSPAPER

Al Watan 159069
Owner: Al Wathba For Media
Editorial: PO Box 54040, Street 21, Al Muroor, Abu Dhabi **Tel:** 971 2 448 6000
Email: info@al-watan.ae **Web site:** http://www.alwatannewspaper.ae
Freq: Daily; **Circ:** 109000 Publisher's Statement
Editor in Chief & General Manager: Abdul Rahman Al Shemiri
Profile: Al Watan is a daily newspaper covering news, business, politics and sport. It was first published in 1999 as Akhbar Al-Arab, later re-launching as Al Watan.
Language (s): Arabic
Ad Rate: Full Page Mono 38160.00
Ad Rate: Full Page Colour 43160.00
Currency: United Arab Emirates Dirhams
DAILY NEWSPAPER

XPRESS - Dubai edition 457212
Owner: Al Nisr Media FZ LLC
Editorial: PO Box 6519, Gulf News Building, Dubai **Tel:** 971 4 344 7100
Email: news@xpress4me.com **Web site:** http://gulfnews.com/xpress
Freq: Weekly; **Circ:** 43273 BPA Worldwide
Editor In Chief: Abdul Hamid Ahmad; **Group Advertisement Manager:** Rajeev Khanna; **Editor:** Bobby Naqvi
Profile: XPRESS is a free, tabloid-sized newspaper covering local news, features, sport, entertainment, human interest stories and leisure. The Dubai edition launched in March 2007 and is published on Thursdays. An Abu Dhabi edition was introduced in March 2013.
Language (s): English
Ad Rate: Full Page Colour 4000.00
Currency: United States Dollars
DAILY NEWSPAPER

News Service/Syndicate

Agence France-Presse - Dubai Bureau 370517
Owner: Agence France-Presse
Editorial: PO Box 502108, Villa 12, Boutique Offices, Dubai **Tel:** 971 4 366 4567
Email: afp.dubai@afp.com **Web site:** http://www.afp.com
Gulf Bureau Chief: Rene Slama
Profile: Dubai bureau of international news agency supplying news - text, graphics, video and pictures - to subscribers around the world.
Language (s): Arabic
NEWS SERVICE/SYNDICATE

Argus Media - Dubai bureau 681117
Owner: Argus Media
Editorial: PO Box 502821, Office 2607, Al Shatha Tower, Dubai **Tel:** 971 4 365 8667
Email: dubai@argusmedia.com **Web site:** http://www.argusmedia.com
Middle East Manager: Barbara Kalu
Profile: Dubai office of UK-based independent energy news agency.
Language (s): English
NEWS SERVICE/SYNDICATE

Associated Press - Dubai Bureau 370514
Owner: Associated Press
Editorial: PO Box 53872, Office 304, Building 4, Dubai **Tel:** 971 4 390 8120
Email: info@ap.org **Web site:** http://www.ap.org
Profile: Dubai bureau of international wire agency - covers the GCC and Iran from Dubai.
Language (s): English
NEWS SERVICE/SYNDICATE

Bloomberg - Dubai Bureau 370522
Owner: Bloomberg L.P.
Editorial: PO Box 506707, 10th Floor, Al Fattan Currency House, Dubai **Tel:** 971 4 364 1020
Email: mideastnews@bloomberg.net **Web site:** http://www.bloomberg.com
Bureau Chief: Claudia Maedler; **News Manager:** Shaji Mathew
Profile: Dubai bureau of financial news wire service.
Language (s): English
NEWS SERVICE/SYNDICATE

Deutsche Presse-Agentur - Dubai bureau 878255
Owner: Deutsche Presse-Agentur
Editorial: Al Safa Building, Sheikh Zayed Road, Dubai
Email: dpauae@yahoo.com **Web site:** http://www.dpa.com
Profile: Dubai bureau of German press agency - covers news, politics, sports, fashion, economy, conflicts, disasters, features and business in the Middle East.
Language (s): German
NEWS SERVICE/SYNDICATE

Dow Jones Newswires - Dubai bureau 370516
Owner: Dow Jones
Editorial: PO Box 502585, Office 314, Building 5, Dubai **Tel:** 971 4 446 1695
Email: djnews.dubai@dowjones.com **Web site:** http://www.dowjones.com
Middle East Bureau Chief: Bill Spindle
Profile: Financial newswire service - covers the UAE, Kuwait, Iran, Iraq, Oman, Qatar, Sudan and Saudi Arabia from Dubai.
Language (s): English
NEWS SERVICE/SYNDICATE

Emirates News Agency 370507
Owner: Emirates News Agency
Editorial: PO Box 3790, Ministry of Culture, Youth and Community Development Building, Abu Dhabi **Tel:** 971 2 404 4333
Email: edit@wam.ae **Web site:** http://www.wam.ae
General Director: Ibrahim Al Abed; **Editor in Chief:** Abdulkareem Al Jenaibi
Profile: Emirates News Agency (WAM) is the official news agency of the United Arab Emirates and covers government news and issues of national importance. It was founded in 1976.
Language (s): Arabic
NEWS SERVICE/SYNDICATE

Emirates News Agency - Dubai office 512601
Owner: Emirates News Agency
Editorial: PO Box 5010, Ministry of Culture Building, Dubai **Tel:** 971 4 261 5500
Email: dubai@wam.ae **Web site:** http://www.wam.ae
Editor: Halima Al Shamsi; **Editor:** Salma Al Shamsi; **Editor:** Munira Al Sumaiti; **Editor:** Aysha Al Suwaidy; **Office Manager:** Mubarak Khamees
Profile: Dubai office of the Emirates News Agency, which is the official news agency of the United Arab Emirates and covers government news and issues of national importance.
Language (s): Arabic
NEWS SERVICE/SYNDICATE

European Pressphoto Agency - UAE Bureau 492682
Owner: European Pressphoto Agency
Editorial: PO Box 454580, Dubai **Tel:** 971 4 363 9520
Email: haider@epa.eu **Web site:** http://www.epa.eu
Chief Photographer - Iraq & Gulf States: Ali Haider
Profile: European Pressphoto Agency is a picture agency representing eleven European news agencies (DPA, ANSA, EFE, Belga, APA, Athens News Agency, PAP, ANP, MTI, Keystone and LUSA). The UAE bureau covers news, politics, sports, fashion, economy, conflicts, disasters, features and business from the Gulf and Iraq.
Language (s): English
NEWS SERVICE/SYNDICATE

Platts - Dubai bureau 380846
Owner: McGraw-Hill Companies
Editorial: PO Box 506650, Office 501, Precinct Building 1, Dubai **Tel:** 971 4 372 7100
Email: tamsin.carlisle@platts.com **Web site:** http://www.platts.com
Profile: Platts is a worldwide energy information and price assessment agency. Coverage includes energy, oil and gas (upstream and downstream), OPEC affairs, analysis of energy trends and energy pricing - services include real time electronic news, daily newsletters and market reports.
Language (s): English
NEWS SERVICE/SYNDICATE

Reuters - Dubai Bureau 370518
Owner: Thomson Reuters
Editorial: PO Box 1426, 5th Floor, Thomson Reuters Building, Dubai **Tel:** 971 4 391 8301
Email: dubai.newsroom@thomsonreuters.com **Web site:** http://www.reuters.com
Photographer: Ahmed Jadallah; **Gulf Bureau Chief:** William Maclean
Profile: Dubai bureau of international news agency supplying news - text, graphics, video and pictures - to subscribers around the world.
Language (s): English
NEWS SERVICE/SYNDICATE

Reuters TV - Gulf Bureau 370503
Owner: Thomson Reuters
Editorial: PO Box 1426, Office 501, Thomson Reuters Building, Dubai **Tel:** 971 4 391 8300
Email: ahmed.seif@thomsonreuters.com **Web site:** http://www.reuters.com
Bureau Chief: William Maclean
Profile: Gulf bureau of Thomson Reuters TV providing television broadcasters and internet providers worldwide with international news video, including breaking news stories, human interest items, sport, business and entertainment news.
Language (s): English
NEWS SERVICE/SYNDICATE

Xinhua News Agency - Abu Dhabi Bureau 828730
Owner: Xinhua News Agency
Editorial: PO Box 44696, Chinese Embassy, Abu Dhabi **Tel:** 971 2 643 1397
Email: anjiang56@hotmail.com **Web site:** http://www.xinhuanet.com
Bureau Chief: An Jiang
Profile: Abu Dhabi bureau of the Xinhua News Agency, the official press agency of the People's Republic of China. Correspondence and press releases should be sent in Arabic or Chinese.
Language (s): Arabic
NEWS SERVICE/SYNDICATE

Xinhua News Agency - Dubai Bureau 856483
Owner: Xinhua News Agency
Editorial: PO Box 454385, Dubai **Tel:** 971 4 451 6739
Email: heitham2011@gmail.com **Web site:** http://www.xinhuanet.com
Profile: Dubai bureau of the Xinhua News Agency, the official press agency of the People's Republic of

China. Correspondence and press releases should be sent in Arabic or Chinese.
Language (s): Arabic
NEWS SERVICE/SYNDICATE

Community Newspaper

Al Gharbia Fee Ousbou 855251
Owner: Al Jewa Culture and Media
Editorial: PO Box 57887, Villa 213, Street 15, Abu Dhabi **Tel:** 971 2 552 1180
Email: info@algharbianews.ae **Web site:** http://algharbianews.ae
Freq: Weekly; **Circ:** 100000
General Manager: Afra Al Hamli
Profile: Al Gharbia Fee Ousbou is a tabloid-sized weekly newspaper covering news, business, sports, culture and society in the Western region of Abu Dhabi. The 32-page newspaper was launched in January 2013 and is issued on Sundays.
Language (s): Arabic
COMMUNITY NEWSPAPER

United States of America

Time Difference: GMT -5 (East Coast), GMT -8 (West Coast), GMT -9 (Alaska), GMT -10 (Hawaii)
National Telephone Code: 1
Continent: The Americas
Capital: Washington DC

Newspapers

Abbeville Meridional 14111
Owner: Louisiana State Newspapers
Editorial: 318 N Main St, Abbeville, Louisiana 70510-4608 **Tel:** 1 337 893-4223
Web site: http://vermiliontoday.com
Freq: Daily; **Circ:** 3847
Editor: Chris Rosa
Profile: Abbeville Meridional's editorial mission is to provide the most up-to-date news and information about the Abbeville, LA region. The publication is written for citizens in the Abbeville area as well as people all over the country who are interested with this part of the country. The Abbeville Meridional is a daily publication.
Language (s): English
Ad Rate: Full Page Mono 10.60
Currency: United States Dollars
DAILY NEWSPAPER

The Aberdeen American News 14650
Owner: Schurz Communications Inc.
Editorial: 124 S 2nd St, Aberdeen, South Dakota 57401-4010 **Tel:** 1 605 225-4100
Email: americannews@aberdeennews.com **Web site:** http://www.aberdeennews.com
Freq: Daily; **Circ:** 14958 Not Audited
Publisher: Cory Bollinger
Profile: The Aberdeen American News is a local daily newspaper serving 18 counties in South and North Dakota. It provides the local community with information on news, events, sports and weather.
Language (s): English
Ad Rate: Full Page Mono 23.25
Ad Rate: Full Page Colour 225.00
Currency: United States Dollars
DAILY NEWSPAPER

Abilene Reflector Chronicle 14030
Owner: Walls Newspapers
Editorial: 303 N Broadway St, Abilene, Kansas 67410-2616 **Tel:** 1 785 263-1000
Email: arc.editor@abilene-rc.com **Web site:** http://www.abilene-rc.com
Freq: Daily; **Circ:** 3387
Profile: Abilene Reflector Chronicle offers coverage of local news, sports, classifieds, deaths, community calendar, business, youth, a photo gallery and senior sections. The publication is geared toward residents of Abilene, KS and surrounding areas.
Language (s): English
Ad Rate: Full Page Mono 7.50
Ad Rate: Full Page Colour 57.87
Currency: United States Dollars
DAILY NEWSPAPER

Abilene Reporter-News 15415
Owner: Gannett Co., Inc.
Editorial: 101 Cypress St, Abilene, Texas 79601-5816 **Tel:** 1 325 673-4271
Email: publishme@reporternews.com **Web site:** http://www.reporternews.com
Freq: Daily; **Circ:** 15412 Not Audited
Profile: Abilene Reporter-News is a local daily newspaper written for residents of Abilene, TX. The newspaper provides information on news and events of interest to the local community. The lead time varies depending on the editorial material.
Language (s): English
Ad Rate: Full Page Mono 50.00
Ad Rate: Full Page Colour 316.85
Currency: United States Dollars
DAILY NEWSPAPER

Ada News 14507
Owner: Community Newspaper Holdings, Inc.
Editorial: 116 N Broadway Ave, Ada, Oklahoma 74820-5004 **Tel:** 1 580 332-4433
Email: adanewseditor@cableone.net **Web site:** http://www.theadanews.com
Freq: Daily; **Circ:** 7145
Profile: Ada News is a daily newspaper for the residents of Ada, OK, and the surrounding areas. It provides information on news and events of interest to the local community.
Language (s): English
Ad Rate: Full Page Mono 17.10
Ad Rate: Full Page Colour 17.10
Currency: United States Dollars
DAILY NEWSPAPER

Adirondack Daily Enterprise 14426
Owner: Ogden Newspapers
Editorial: 54 Broadway, Saranac Lake, New York 12983-1704 **Tel:** 1 518 891-2600
Email: adenews@adirondackdailyenterprise.com
Web site: http://www.adirondackdailyenterprise.com
Freq: Daily; **Circ:** 5300 Not Audited
Publisher: Catherine Moore; **News Editor:** Brittany Proulx
Profile: Adirondack Daily Enterprise is published for the residents of the Adirondack, NY region. Coverage includes local news, sports, community events and arts & entertainment.
Language (s): English
Ad Rate: Full Page Mono 20.41
Ad Rate: Full Page Colour 235.70
Currency: United States Dollars
DAILY NEWSPAPER

The Advertiser-Tribune 14493
Owner: Ogden Newspapers
Editorial: 320 Nelson St, Tiffin, Ohio 44883-8956 **Tel:** 1 419 448-3200
Email: newsroom@advertiser-tribune.com **Web site:** http://www.advertiser-tribune.com
Freq: Daily; **Circ:** 7219 Not Audited
Publisher: Chris Dixon; **Editor:** Nick Dutro; **News Editor:** MJ McVay; **Editor:** Rob Weaver
Profile: The Advertiser-Tribune is a local newspaper serving the Seneca County, OH area. It provides residents with information on local news, events, weather and sports. The lead time for editorial submissions is one week. Deadlines for the publication are one week before issue date.
Language (s): English
Ad Rate: Full Page Mono 21.15
Ad Rate: Full Page Colour 151.92
Currency: United States Dollars
DAILY NEWSPAPER

The Advocate 13807
Owner: Hearst Corporation
Editorial: 9A Riverbend Dr S, Stamford, Connecticut 06907-2524 **Tel:** 1 203 964-2200
Email: tips@ctnews.com **Web site:** http://www.stamfordadvocate.com
Freq: Daily; **Circ:** 8048 Not Audited
Profile: The Advocate is a regional daily newspaper that covers Fairfield County, CT. The editorial mission of the paper is to provide the best news and information with the highest journalistic integrity. The paper features local news, sports and business.
Language (s): English
Ad Rate: Full Page Mono 52.70
Ad Rate: Full Page Colour 55.08
Currency: United States Dollars
DAILY NEWSPAPER

The Advocate 14479
Owner: Gannett Co., Inc.
Editorial: 22 N 1st St, Newark, Ohio 43055 **Tel:** 1 740 345-4053
Email: advocate@newarkadvocate.com **Web site:** http://www.newarkadvocate.com
Freq: Daily; **Circ:** 11293 Not Audited
Profile: The Advocate is a daily local newspaper serving residents of the Newark, OH area. It covers local, national and international news as well as lifestyle, sports and entertainment information that pertains to the community.
Language (s): English
Ad Rate: Full Page Mono 35.50
Ad Rate: Full Page Colour 206.79
Currency: United States Dollars
DAILY NEWSPAPER

The Advocate 15348
Owner: Capital City Press
Editorial: 10705 Reiger Rd, Baton Rouge, Louisiana 70809-4520 **Tel:** 1 225 383-1111
Email: digitalmedia@theadvocate.com **Web site:** http://theadvocate.com
Freq: Daily; **Circ:** 126976 Not Audited
Editor: Peter Kovacs; **Publisher:** Dan Shea
Profile: The Advocate is a daily broadsheet newspaper distributed in the Baton Rouge, LA area. The newspaper covers local news, politics, government, education, entertainment, and sports, as well as travel, food and dining, religion, books, and community events. The publication also features national and international news coverage, but the content is taken almost exclusively from wire services. Deadlines vary, but final news deadlines fall at 11pm. The lead time is one day for breaking news and up to several months for features.
Language (s): English
Ad Rate: Full Page Mono 73.33
Ad Rate: Full Page Colour 950.00
Currency: United States Dollars
DAILY NEWSPAPER

The Advocate - Baton Rouge Bureau 16286
Editorial: 900 N 3rd St, Baton Rouge, Louisiana 70802-5236
Email: digitalmedia@theadvocate.com
Language (s): English
DAILY NEWSPAPER

The Advocate - Gonzales Bureau 16163
Editorial: 13057 Highway 44, Gonzales, Louisiana 70737-6863 **Tel:** 1 225 647-8447
Email: ascension@theadvocate.com
Language (s): English
DAILY NEWSPAPER

The Advocate - Lafayette Bureau 16159
Owner: Capital City Press
Editorial: 815 Johnston St, Lafayette, Louisiana 70501-7901 **Tel:** 1 337 234-0174
Bureau Chief: Richard Burgess
Language (s): English
DAILY NEWSPAPER

The Advocate - Port Allen Bureau 16162
Editorial: 911 7th St, Port Allen, Louisiana 70767-2113 **Tel:** 1 225 326-6627
Westside Bureau Chief: Terry Jones
Language (s): English
DAILY NEWSPAPER

The Advocate - Walker Bureau 16161
Editorial: 10291 Florida Blvd, Walker, Louisiana 70785 **Tel:** 1 225 664-9058
Language (s): English
DAILY NEWSPAPER

The Advocate-Messenger 14075
Owner: Schurz Communications Inc.
Editorial: 330 S 4th St, Danville, Kentucky 40422-2033 **Tel:** 1 859 236-2551
Web site: http://www.centralkynews.com/amnews
Freq: Mon thru Fri; **Circ:** 11995 Not Audited
Profile: The Advocate-Messenger is a local daily paper for residents in and around Danville, KY. The publication covers local news, sports and events.
Language (s): English
Ad Rate: Full Page Mono 18.10
Ad Rate: Full Page Colour 125.47
Currency: United States Dollars
DAILY NEWSPAPER

Aiken Standard 14640
Owner: Evening Post Publishing Co.
Editorial: 326 Rutland Dr, Aiken, South Carolina 29801-4010 **Tel:** 1 803 644-2401
Email: editorial@aikenstandard.com **Web site:** http://www.aikenstandard.com
Freq: Daily; **Circ:** 15759 Not Audited
Profile: Aiken Standard is a daily community newspaper published for the residents of Aiken, SC and its surrounding areas. The newspaper cover all aspects of local news, and offers national news relevant to the community.
Language (s): English
Ad Rate: Full Page Mono 32.82
Ad Rate: Full Page Colour 46.51
Currency: United States Dollars
DAILY NEWSPAPER

Akron Beacon Journal 15320
Owner: Black Press
Editorial: 44 E Exchange St, Akron, Ohio 44328-0001 **Tel:** 1 330 996-3000
Email: bjnews@thebeaconjournal.com **Web site:** http://www.ohio.com
Freq: Daily; **Circ:** 65783 Not Audited
Publisher: Mark Cohen
Profile: Akron Beacon Journal is a morning edition newspaper written for the general public in the Akron, OH area. The Business section is featured daily, covering local and national business stories, daily stock market rates, and real estate. Articles include features, breaking news, trends, analyses, profiles and investigative stories. The publication has won the Best in Business award by the Society of American Business Editors and Writers, along with four Pulitzer Prizes. The paper does not publish a Holiday Gift Guide.
Language (s): English
Ad Rate: Full Page Mono 89.28
Ad Rate: Full Page Colour 116.07
Currency: United States Dollars
DAILY NEWSPAPER

Alamogordo Daily News 14370
Owner: Gannett Co., Inc.
Editorial: 518 24th St, Alamogordo, New Mexico 88310-6104 **Tel:** 1 575 437-7120
Email: AlamogordoDailyNews@gannett.com **Web site:** http://www.alamogordonews.com
Freq: Fri; **Circ:** 5611
Profile: Alamogordo Daily News is published daily for the residents of Alamogordo, NM. The newspaper covers international, national and local news, sports, business, lifestyles and entertainment Deadlines are the day before issue at 5:30pm MT.
Language (s): English
Ad Rate: Full Page Mono 19.61
Ad Rate: Full Page Colour 129.56
Currency: United States Dollars
DAILY NEWSPAPER

Alaska Dispatch News 15354
Owner: Alaska Dispatch Publishing LLC
Editorial: 300 W 31st Ave, Anchorage, Alaska 99503-3878 **Tel:** 1 907 257-4301
Email: newstips@adn.com **Web site:** http://www.adn.com
Freq: Daily; **Circ:** 51266 Not Audited
News Editor: Mark Dent; **Publisher:** Alice Rogoff
Profile: Alaska Dispatch News provides local, national, and international news to readers in and around Anchorage, AK. It was first published as a weekly newspaper in 1946. It became a daily publication in 1948 and provided Alaska's first Sunday paper on June 13, 1965. Since then, the newspaper has expanded its services by becoming a member of the Associated Press and the Los Angeles Times/Washington Post News Service.
Language (s): English
Ad Rate: Full Page Mono 121.60
Ad Rate: Full Page Colour 399.20
Currency: United States Dollars
DAILY NEWSPAPER

Albany Democrat-Herald 14547
Owner: Lee Enterprises, Inc.
Editorial: 600 Lyon St S, Albany, Oregon 97321-2919 **Tel:** 1 541 926-2211
Email: news@dhonline.com **Web site:** http://www.democratherald.com
Freq: Daily; **Circ:** 12376
Profile: Albany Democrat-Herald is published daily for the residents of Albany, OR. The newspaper covers local news, business, sports and arts & entertainment. It also covers national and statewide stories that have a direct impact on the local area. The paper switched to morning delivery seven days a week in October 2010.
Language (s): English
Ad Rate: Full Page Mono 64.79
Ad Rate: Full Page Colour 211.50
Currency: United States Dollars
DAILY NEWSPAPER

The Albany Herald 13835
Owner: Southern Community Newspapers Inc.
Editorial: 126 N Washington St, Albany, Georgia 31701-2552 **Tel:** 1 229 888-9300
Email: news@albanyherald.com **Web site:** http://www.albanyherald.com
Freq: Daily; **Circ:** 12528 Not Audited
Publisher: Michael J. Gebhart
Profile: The Albany Herald is a daily newspaper written for the residents of Albany, GA. The newspaper covers local news, event calendars, sports, religion, business, arts & entertainment and lifestyles. Deadlines are on Wednesdays at 5pm ET.
Language (s): English
Ad Rate: Full Page Mono 51.81
Ad Rate: Full Page Colour 56.81
Currency: United States Dollars
DAILY NEWSPAPER

Albert Lea Tribune 14198
Owner: Boone Newspapers Inc.
Editorial: 808 W Front St, Albert Lea, Minnesota 56007-1947 **Tel:** 1 507 373-1411
Email: news@albertleatribune.com **Web site:** http://www.albertleatribune.com
Freq: Daily; **Circ:** 6006 Not Audited
Editor: Tim Engstrom; **Advertising Sales Manager:** Crystal Miller; **Publisher:** Scott Schmeltzer
Profile: Albert Lea Tribune is a community newspaper that is published six days a week for residents of southern Minnesota and northern Iowa. The publication is owned by Albert Lea Tribune Inc. According to the publisher, "one of our most important goals at The Albert Lea Tribune is to put our readers in touch with their neighbors. We offer much more than just what you see online. There are local parents' organizations trying to get their word to you about bake sales and car washes, clubs and community organizations with special programs, churches with special services, and businesses with prices and products to share."
Language (s): English
Ad Rate: Full Page Mono 17.85
Ad Rate: Full Page Colour 110.35
Currency: United States Dollars
DAILY NEWSPAPER

Albuquerque Journal 15321
Owner: Journal Publishing Co.
Editorial: 7777 Jefferson St NE, Albuquerque, New Mexico 87109-4343 **Tel:** 1 505 823-3800
Email: journal@abqjournal.com **Web site:** http://www.abqjournal.com
Freq: Daily; **Circ:** 91127 Not Audited
Washington Bureau Chief: Michael Coleman
Profile: Albuquerque Journal is New Mexico's most widely circulated daily newspaper. Coverage includes business, arts, science and technology, travel, sports, health and regional New Mexico news, as well as national news. Articles include feature and trend stories, company profiles, product announcements and reviews. The newspaper has special sections periodically throughout the year, including Mature Living, Summer Guide Journal, Indian Market Journal, Balloon Fiesta and High Country Holidays. It also has regional sections. Journal North and West Side Journal are daily sections, and the Mountain View Journal is a weekly section.
Language (s): English
Ad Rate: Full Page Mono 74.20
Ad Rate: Full Page Colour 79.55

Currency: United States Dollars
DAILY NEWSPAPER

Albuquerque Journal - Las Cruces Bureau 16147
Editorial: 345 N Water St, Las Cruces, New Mexico 88001-1220 **Tel:** 1 505 235-6908
Profile: Southern Bureau.
Language (s): English
DAILY NEWSPAPER

Albuquerque Journal - Santa Fe Bureau 15797
Editorial: 328 Galisteo St, Santa Fe, New Mexico 87501-2606 **Tel:** 1 505 988-8881
Email: jnorth@abqjournal.com
Bureau Chief: Dan Boyd
Language (s): English
DAILY NEWSPAPER

Alexander City Outlook 13679
Owner: Tallapoosa Publishers, Inc.
Editorial: 548 Cherokee Rd, Alexander City, Alabama 35010-2503 **Tel:** 1 256 234-4281
Email: editor@alexcityoutlook.com **Web site:** http://www.alexcityoutlook.com
Freq: Daily; **Circ:** 3445 Not Audited
Profile: Alexander City Outlook is a local newspaper that is published six days a week; Tuesday through Sunday. The publication is written for residents of Alexander City and Tallapoosa County, AL. The publication covers local news, sports, and community events.
Language (s): English
Ad Rate: Full Page Mono 13.90
Ad Rate: Full Page Colour 84.14
Currency: United States Dollars
DAILY NEWSPAPER

The Alliance Review 14432
Owner: GateHouse Media Inc.
Editorial: 40 S Linden Ave, Alliance, Ohio 44601-2447 **Tel:** 1 330 821-1200
Email: reviewedit@the-review.com **Web site:** http://www.the-review.com
Freq: Daily; **Circ:** 13200 Not Audited
Publisher: G. Charles Dix
Profile: This paper covers local news from Alliance, OH and surrounding counties.
Language (s): English
Ad Rate: Full Page Mono 16.95
Ad Rate: Full Page Colour 370.00
Currency: United States Dollars
DAILY NEWSPAPER

Alliance Times-Herald 14336
Owner: Alliance Publishing Company
Editorial: 114 E 4th St, Alliance, Nebraska 69301-3402 **Tel:** 1 308 762-3060
Email: athnews@alliancetimes.com **Web site:** http://www.alliancetimes.com
Freq: Daily; **Circ:** 3125 Not Audited
Profile: Alliance Times-Herald is published daily for the residents of Alliance, NE and surrounding communities. Coverage includes local news, sports, arts & entertainment, farm news, lifestyles and community events.
Language (s): English
Ad Rate: Full Page Mono 9.25
Ad Rate: Full Page Colour 30.75
Currency: United States Dollars
DAILY NEWSPAPER

The Alpena News 14158
Owner: Ogden Newspapers
Editorial: 130 Park Pl, Alpena, Michigan 49707-2828 **Tel:** 1 989 354-3111
Email: newsroom@thealpenanews.com **Web site:** http://www.thealpenanews.com
Freq: Mon thru Fri; **Circ:** 7661 Not Audited
Editor: Steve Murch; **Publisher:** Bill Speer
Profile: The Alpena News is written for the residents of Northeastern Michigan. Since 1899, the paper has played a significant role in reporting on the history and growth of the Northeastern Michigan region. It contains in-depth stories and telling photographs of both the tragedies and the triumphs of the area's people and industries. The majority of the content focuses on local and national news, local sports, lifestyle and entertainment. The Alpena News also contains classified and obituary sections. There are also special sections on certain days. Each Monday there is a special grocery section. On Thursdays there are special entertainment and real estate/business sections. A special entertainment section is run on Fridays as well. Finally, Saturday is the weekend edition filled with special outdoor, health and religion sections.
Language (s): English
Ad Rate: Full Page Mono 24.97
Currency: United States Dollars
DAILY NEWSPAPER

Altoona Mirror 14563
Owner: Ogden Newspapers
Editorial: 301 Cayuga Ave, Altoona, Pennsylvania 16602 **Tel:** 1 814 946-7411
Email: news@altoonamirror.com **Web site:** http://www.altoonamirror.com
Freq: Daily; **Circ:** 23159 Not Audited
Editor: John Cavrich; **Publisher:** Ed Kruger
Profile: Altoona Mirror is a daily newspaper published for the residents of Altoona, PA and surrounding areas. It provides local news and information.
Language (s): English
Ad Rate: Full Page Mono 55.49
Ad Rate: Full Page Colour 71.07
Currency: United States Dollars
DAILY NEWSPAPER

The Altus Times 14508
Owner: Heartland Publications
Editorial: 218 W Commerce St, Altus, Oklahoma 73521-3810 **Tel:** 1 580 482-1221
Web site: http://www.altustimes.com
Freq: Daily; **Circ:** 4400 Not Audited
Profile: The Altus Times is a daily, local newspaper serving residents of the Altus, OK area. It covers local and national news, lifestyle, features, entertainment and sports information.
Language (s): English
Ad Rate: Full Page Mono 9.70
Ad Rate: Full Page Colour 252.00
Currency: United States Dollars
DAILY NEWSPAPER

Alva Review-Courier 14509
Owner: Martin Broadcasting Corporation
Editorial: 620 Choctaw St, Alva, Oklahoma 73717-1626 **Tel:** 1 580 327-2200
Email: news@alvareviewcourier.net **Web site:** http://www.alvareviewcourier.com
Freq: Daily; **Circ:** 2300 Not Audited
Publisher: Lynn Martin; **Editor:** Marione Martin
Profile: Alva Review-Courier is a local daily newspaper serving residents in the Woods County, OK area. The paper is published everyday except Wednesday and Saturday. On Wednesday a free newspaper called the NewsGram is distributed in a three-county area. Advertising deadlines are at noon the day before publication.
Language (s): English
Ad Rate: Full Page Mono 5.20
Ad Rate: Full Page Colour 150.00
Currency: United States Dollars
DAILY NEWSPAPER

am New York 155097
Owner: Newsday Media Group
Editorial: 240 W 35th St Fl 9, New York, New York 10001-2506 **Tel:** 1 646 293-9499
Web site: http://www.amny.com
Freq: Mon thru Fri; **Circ:** 298759 Not Audited
Profile: Touted as "boiled down, high energy and to the point", am New York is a free commuter daily newspaper aimed at readers aged 18 to 35. The paper's regular features include an opinion page, a daily column and political cartoon. It also has weekend, entertainment and sports sections, classifieds and TV listings. It is designed to be read in 20 minutes, and gives those who normally don't read newspapers a quick update on New York City and their world.
Language (s): English
Ad Rate: Full Page Colour 209.47
Currency: United States Dollars
DAILY NEWSPAPER

Amarillo Globe-News 15431
Owner: GateHouse Media Inc.
Editorial: 900 S Harrison St, Amarillo, Texas 79101-3424 **Tel:** 1 806 376-4488
Email: citydesk@amarillo.com **Web site:** http://amarillo.com
Freq: Daily; **Circ:** 25418 Not Audited
Publisher: Lester Simpson
Profile: Amarillo Globe-News is a local daily newspaper published for the residents of Amarillo, TX and surrounding communities. The newspaper covers local, national, and international news, including politics, lifestyle, sports, entertainment, business and economics. The Amarillo Daily News and the Amarillo News & Globe-Times were both combined to create the Amarillo Globe-News.
Language (s): English
Ad Rate: Full Page Mono 56.49
Ad Rate: Full Page Colour 629.00
Currency: United States Dollars
DAILY NEWSPAPER

Amarillo Globe-News - Austin Bureau 16026
Editorial: Austin, Texas **Tel:** 1 210 481-3082
Freq: Daily
Profile: This bureau acts as the Austin bureau for all Morris Communications publications.
Language (s): English
DAILY NEWSPAPER

American Banker 12923
Owner: SourceMedia, Inc.
Editorial: 1 State St Fl 27, New York, New York 10004-1561 **Tel:** 1 212 803-8200
Web site: http://americanbanker.com
Freq: Mon thru Fri; **Circ:** 37100
Profile: Established in 1836 and geared towards banks, credit unions, government agencies, brokerage firms and insurance companies as a source for daily information, news and analysis about the financial services marketplace.
Language (s): English
Ad Rate: Full Page Mono 14945.00
Ad Rate: Full Page Colour 18840.00
Currency: United States Dollars
DAILY NEWSPAPER

American Banker - Arlington Bureau 959826
Editorial: 4401 Wilson Blvd Ste 910, Arlington, Virginia 22203-4197 **Tel:** 1 571 403-3850
DAILY NEWSPAPER

American Banker - Chicago Bureau 959828
Editorial: 550 W Van Buren St Ste 1110, Chicago, Illinois 60607-3805 **Tel:** 1 312 913-1334
DAILY NEWSPAPER

American Banker - Long Beach Bureau 959830
Editorial: 3416 E 2nd St Apt A, Long Beach, California 90803-5233 **Tel:** 1 562 434-5432
Language (s): English
DAILY NEWSPAPER

American Press 14101
Owner: Shearman Newspapers
Editorial: 4900 Highway 90 E, Lake Charles, Louisiana 70615-4037 **Tel:** 1 337 433-3000
Email: news@americanpress.com **Web site:** http://www.americanpress.com
Freq: Daily; **Circ:** 25686 Not Audited
Publisher: Thomas Shearman
Profile: American Press is a daily newspaper written for residents of the Lake Charles, LA area. The newspaper covers local news, weather, sports, and community events. Feature articles cover entertainment, lifestyle, business, finance, travel and leisure, and health.
Language (s): English
Ad Rate: Full Page Mono 35.00
Ad Rate: Full Page Colour 47.91
Currency: United States Dollars
DAILY NEWSPAPER

Anadarko Daily News 14510
Owner: Anadarko Publishing Company (The)
Editorial: 117 E Broadway St, Anadarko, Oklahoma 73005 **Tel:** 1 405 247-3331
Email: news@anadarko-news.com
Freq: Daily; **Circ:** 4207 Not Audited
Profile: Anadarko Daily News provides readers in the community with local, state and nationwide news coverage. Other features include sports, entertainment, classifieds, community events, politics, education, and health-related news. The advertising deadline is 10am CT.
Language (s): English
Ad Rate: Full Page Mono 7.50
Ad Rate: Full Page Colour 58.50
Currency: United States Dollars
DAILY NEWSPAPER

Andalusia Star News 13680
Owner: Boone Newspapers Inc.
Editorial: 207 Dunson St, Andalusia, Alabama 36420-3705 **Tel:** 1 334 222-2402
Email: editor@andalusiastarnews.com **Web site:** http://www.andalusiastarnews.com
Freq: Daily; **Circ:** 3400 Not Audited
Advertising Sales Manager: Ruck Ashworth
Profile: The Andalusia Star-News is published daily with the exception of Sunday, Monday and Christmas and New Year's Day by Andalusia Newspapers Inc. The newspaper focuses on local city and statewide news coverage, while sometimes even covering national news. Other features include sports, entertainment, lifestyle, health and classifieds.
Language (s): English
Ad Rate: Full Page Mono 9.80
Ad Rate: Full Page Colour 72.21
Currency: United States Dollars
DAILY NEWSPAPER

Anderson Independent-Mail 14641
Owner: Gannett Co., Inc.
Editorial: 1000 Williamston Rd, Anderson, South Carolina 29621-6508 **Tel:** 1 864 224-4321
Email: newsroom@independentmail.com **Web site:** http://www.independentmail.com
Freq: Daily; **Circ:** 19174 Not Audited
Profile: Anderson Independent-Mail reaches readers in the Anderson County, Oconee County, Pickens County, SC, and the Northeastern Georgia. Coverage includes local, national and international news, sports, lifestyle, business, editorials, weather, community events and obituaries. The paper does not publish a Holiday Gift Guide.
Language (s): English
Ad Rate: Full Page Mono 59.85
Currency: United States Dollars
DAILY NEWSPAPER

An-Nahar - New York Bureau 619599
Editorial: 405 E 42nd St, Rm L250A, New York, New York 10017-3507 **Tel:** 1 917 365-0942
Bureau Chief: Ali Barada
Profile: This is the New York bureau of An-Nehar in Beirut, Lebanon.
Language (s): Arabic
DAILY NEWSPAPER

Anniston Star 13663
Owner: Consolidated Publishing
Editorial: 4305 McClellan Blvd, Anniston, Alabama 36206-2812 **Tel:** 1 256 236-1551
Email: news@annistonstar.com **Web site:** http://www.annistonstar.com
Freq: Daily; **Circ:** 16043 Not Audited
Editor: Bob Davis
Profile: Anniston Star is a daily newspaper serving Anniston, AL and surrounding Calhoun County. The publication covers local and statewide news, business, entertainment, lifestyle and sports. The papers Monday edition is call jumpStart.
Language (s): English
Ad Rate: Full Page Mono 42.00
Ad Rate: Full Page Colour 475.00
Currency: United States Dollars
DAILY NEWSPAPER

Antelope Valley Press 14863
Owner: Antelope Valley Press, Inc.
Editorial: 37404 Sierra Hwy, Palmdale, California 93550-9343 **Tel:** 1 661 273-2700
Email: editor@avpress.com **Web site:** http://www.avpress.com
Freq: Daily; **Circ:** 19000 Not Audited
Advertising Sales Manager: Jay Curran
Profile: Antelope Valley Press is a local daily newspaper written for residents of North Los Angeles County and Southeastern Kern County, in Southern California. The paper covers local and national news, sports and religion.
Language (s): English
Ad Rate: Full Page Mono 68.84
Ad Rate: Full Page Colour 219.89
Currency: United States Dollars
DAILY NEWSPAPER

Antigo Daily Journal 14795
Owner: Berner Bros. Publishing Co., Inc.
Editorial: 612 Superior St, Antigo, Wisconsin 54409-2049 **Tel:** 1 715 623-4191
Web site: http://www.antigodailyjournal.com
Freq: Daily; **Circ:** 5074 Not Audited
Editor: Fred Berner; **News Editor:** Lisa Haefs;
Advertising Sales Manager: Denise Hale
Profile: Antigo Daily Journal is a the local newspaper for the Antigo, WI area. This daily newspaper covers local news and sports stories as well as important statewide and national stories that have an impact of their community.
Language (s): English
Ad Rate: Full Page Mono 6.78
Ad Rate: Full Page Colour 220.00
Currency: United States Dollars
DAILY NEWSPAPER

Appeal-Democrat 13737
Owner: Horizon Publications
Editorial: 1530 Ellis Lake Dr, Marysville, California 95901-4258 **Tel:** 1 530 741-2345
Email: adnewsroom@appealdemocrat.com **Web site:** http://www.appeal-democrat.com
Freq: Daily; **Circ:** 20428 Not Audited
News Editor: Andrew Cummins; **Editor:** Steve Miller;
Publisher: Glenn Stifflemire
Profile: Appeal-Democrat is a local daily newspaper covering news, weather, sports, events, arts & entertainment and education for the residents of Yuba City and Northern California.
Language (s): English
Ad Rate: Full Page Mono 27.00
Ad Rate: Full Page Colour 179.57
Currency: United States Dollars
DAILY NEWSPAPER

The Arcadian 78649
Editorial: 108 S Polk Ave, Arcadia, Florida 34266-3952 **Tel:** 1 863 494-7600
Email: arcadian.editor@gmail.com **Web site:** http://www.yoursun.net
Freq: Daily; **Circ:** 3000 Not Audited
Publisher: David Dunn-Rankin; **Advertising Sales Manager:** Joe Gallimore
Profile: The Arcadian Sun is a local daily newspaper written for the residents of Arcadia, FL.
Language (s): English
Ad Rate: Full Page Mono 11.00
Currency: United States Dollars
DAILY NEWSPAPER

Argus Leader 15413
Owner: Gannett Co. Inc.
Editorial: 200 S Minnesota Ave, Sioux Falls, South Dakota 57104-6314 **Tel:** 1 605 331-2200
Email: editor@argusleader.com **Web site:** http://www.argusleader.com
Freq: Daily; **Circ:** 35191 Not Audited
Publisher: William Albrecht
Profile: Argus Leader in Sioux Falls, SD aims to "provide reliable, fair and accurate news coverage in response to the changing interests and needs of our readers." The newspaper's readers are residents of Sioux Falls, SD and the surrounding area. They do not publish a holiday gift guide.
Language (s): English
Ad Rate: Full Page Mono 73.55
Ad Rate: Full Page Colour 544.40
Currency: United States Dollars
DAILY NEWSPAPER

Argus Observer 14558
Owner: Wick Communications Inc.
Editorial: 1160 SW 4th St, Ontario, Oregon 97914-4365 **Tel:** 1 541 889-5387
Email: editor@argusobserver.com **Web site:** http://www.argusobserver.com
Freq: Fri; **Circ:** 5582 Not Audited
Publisher: John Dillon
Profile: Argus Observer is a daily news publication written for local residents of Ontario, OR. The newspaper covers local news, events, sports, and politics. As of April 1998, the Acreage Magazine was implemented into the Argus Observer as the Farming section, printed every other Monday. Deadline for the Farming section is one week before issue date. There are four editorial editions for the Argus Observer: Travel, Car Care, and Home and Garden publish in the spring and winter; and a Farm Edition publishes in the summer.
Language (s): English
Ad Rate: Full Page Mono 13.00

Ad Rate: Full Page Colour 79.37
Currency: United States Dollars
DAILY NEWSPAPER

The Argus-Press 14188
Owner: Argus-Press Company (The)
Editorial: 201 E Exchange St, Owosso, Michigan 48867-3009 **Tel:** 1 989 725-5136
Email: news@argus-press.com **Web site:** http://www.argus-press.com
Freq: Daily; **Circ:** 10736 Not Audited
Publisher: Tom Campbell
Profile: The Argus-Press is a local newspaper that serves the Owosso, MI area and targets residents and businesses of Shiawassee County. It provides community residents with information on local news, events, weather and sports.
Language (s): English
Ad Rate: Full Page Mono 17.00
Ad Rate: Full Page Colour 59.21
Currency: United States Dollars
DAILY NEWSPAPER

Arizona Daily Star 13714
Owner: Lee Enterprises, Inc.
Editorial: 4850 S Park Ave, Tucson, Arizona 85714-1637 **Tel:** 1 520 573-4142
Email: metro@tucson.com **Web site:** http://www.tucson.com
Freq: Daily; **Circ:** 66930 Not Audited
Profile: Arizona Daily Star provides news and information for the residents of Tucson, Arizona. The paper features local, regional and state news, business and sports.
Language (s): English
Ad Rate: Full Page Mono 258.30
Ad Rate: Full Page Colour 335.79
Currency: United States Dollars
DAILY NEWSPAPER

Arizona Daily Sun 13711
Owner: Lee Enterprises, Inc.
Editorial: 1751 S Thompson St, Flagstaff, Arizona 86001-8716 **Tel:** 1 928 774-4545
Email: azdsnews@azdailysun.com **Web site:** http://www.azdailysun.com
Freq: Daily; **Circ:** 9136 Not Audited
Editor: Jake Bacon; **Publisher:** Don Rowley; **Editor:** Randy Wilson
Profile: Arizona Daily Sun is a daily newspaper serving Flagstaff and Northern Arizona. The newspaper provides residents with information on local news, weather, sports and events.
Language (s): English
Ad Rate: Full Page Mono 35.20
Ad Rate: Full Page Colour 358.50
Currency: United States Dollars
DAILY NEWSPAPER

The Arizona Republic 15296
Owner: Gannett Co., Inc.
Editorial: 200 E Van Buren St, Phoenix, Arizona 85004-2238 **Tel:** 1 602 444-8000
Email: newstips@arizonarepublic.com **Web site:** http://azcentral.com
Freq: Daily; **Circ:** 188467 Not Audited
Profile: The Arizona Republic is the state's largest newspaper. It offers readers a strong focus on local news, along with national and international news. There is also sports, business, features and lifestyle coverage. It debuted on May 19, 1890.
Language (s): English
Ad Rate: Full Page Mono 495.00
Ad Rate: Full Page Colour 668.00
Currency: United States Dollars
DAILY NEWSPAPER

The Arizona Republic - Mesa Bureau 16081
Editorial: 106 E Baseline Rd, Mesa, Arizona 85210-6204 **Tel:** 1 602 444-7931
Language (s): English
DAILY NEWSPAPER

Arkansas Democrat-Gazette 15323
Owner: Wehco Media Inc.
Editorial: 121 E Capitol Ave, Little Rock, Arkansas 72201-3819 **Tel:** 1 501 378-3400
Email: news@arkansasonline.com **Web site:** http://www.arkansasonline.com
Freq: Daily; **Circ:** 126980 Not Audited
Publisher: Walter Hussman
Profile: The Arkansas Democrat-Gazette is a daily regional, newspaper in Little Rock, Arkansas. The paper was first published as the Arkansas Gazette in 1819.
Language (s): English
Ad Rate: Full Page Mono 248.00
Ad Rate: Full Page Colour 788.20
Currency: United States Dollars
DAILY NEWSPAPER

Arkansas Democrat-Gazette - Conway Bureau 16258
Editorial: 1020 Main St, Conway, Arkansas 72032-5426 **Tel:** 1 501 327-5671
Bureau Chief: Debra Hale-Shelton
Language (s): English
DAILY NEWSPAPER

Arkansas Democrat-Gazette - Fort Smith Bureau 16259
Editorial: 101 N 10th St Ste G6, Fort Smith, Arkansas 72901-2716 **Tel:** 1 479 785-9966
Bureau Chief: Dave Hughes
Language (s): English
DAILY NEWSPAPER

Arkansas Democrat-Gazette - Jonesboro Bureau 16138
Owner: Wehco Media Inc.
Editorial: 201 W Washington Ave, Jonesboro, Arkansas 72401-2840 **Tel:** 1 870 932-3612
Email: news@arkansasonline.com
Bureau Chief: Kenneth Heard
Profile: This is the Jonesboro, AR bureau of the Arkansas Democrat-Gazette in Little Rock, AR.
Language (s): English
DAILY NEWSPAPER

Arkansas Democrat-Gazette - Little Rock Bureau 15601
Editorial: State Capitol Press Room, Little Rock, Arkansas 72201 **Tel:** 1 501 378-3438
Language (s): English
DAILY NEWSPAPER

Arkansas Democrat-Gazette - Springdale Bureau 16156
Editorial: 2560 N Lowell Rd, Springdale, Arkansas 72764-1818 **Tel:** 1 501 378-3400
Web site: http://www.arkansasonline.com
Language (s): English
DAILY NEWSPAPER

Arkansas Democrat-Gazette - Washington Bureau 15551
Editorial: 529 14th St NW Ste 1190, Washington, District Of Columbia 20045-2101 **Tel:** 1 202 662-7690
Language (s): English
DAILY NEWSPAPER

Artesia Daily Press 14371
Owner: Valley Newspapers Inc.
Editorial: 503 W Main St, Artesia, New Mexico 88210-2067 **Tel:** 1 575 746-3524
Email: news@artesianews.com **Web site:** http://www.artesianews.com
Freq: Daily; **Circ:** 3400
Advertising Sales Manager: Bev King
Profile: Artesia Daily Press is a local newspaper serving the area of Artesia, NM. It provides residents with information on local news, events, weather and sports. Deadines for editorial submissions are the previous noon MT during weekdays and Thursday for the Sunday edition. Do not send anything via e-mail.
Language (s): English
Ad Rate: Full Page Mono 6.85
Ad Rate: Full Page Colour 231.85
Currency: United States Dollars
DAILY NEWSPAPER

Asahi Shimbun International Satellite Edition 79986
Editorial: 620 8th Ave, New York, New York 10018-1618 **Tel:** 1 212 398-0257
Web site: http://www.asahi.com
Freq: Daily; **Circ:** 7500 Not Audited
Profile: Asahi Shimbun International Satellite Edition was established in 1986 in the United States and is widely read among Japanese Americans. It covers political and economic news, regional news, metro news, international news, sports news, science news and arts and culture. It also cites information that is useful both to newly transferred Japanese businessmen and their families and to readers already well established in the United States. The lead time is 12 hours. Deadlines for the publication are the day prior to the issue date at 11:30am and 10:30pm ET.
Language (s): Japanese
Ad Rate: Full Page Mono 24.37
Currency: United States Dollars
DAILY NEWSPAPER

Asbarez Armenian Daily News 79998
Owner: Armenian Media Network
Editorial: 1203 N Vermont Ave, Los Angeles, California 90029-1703 **Tel:** 1 323 284-9222
Email: editor@asbarez.com **Web site:** http://asbarez.com
Freq: Fri; **Circ:** 8000 Not Audited
Editor: Apo Borghigian
Profile: Asbarez Armenian Daily is a local newspaper serving the Armenian community of Fresno, CA and the surrounding area. It provides information on news and events of Armenian interest.
Language (s): Armenian
Ad Rate: Full Page Mono 3.50
Currency: United States Dollars
DAILY NEWSPAPER

Asbury Park Press 15388
Owner: Gannett Co., Inc.
Editorial: 3600 State Route 66, Neptune, New Jersey 07753-2605 **Tel:** 1 732 922-6000
Email: newstips@app.com **Web site:** http://www.app.com
Freq: Daily; **Circ:** 110859 Not Audited
Publisher: Tom Donovan
Profile: Asbury Park Press, a Gannett newspaper, reaches the New Jersey counties of Ocean, Monmouth, and Middlesex. According to the media kit, the publication considers itself the main newspaper reaching the edge of the New York DMA. Coverage includes world, national, regional, and local news, sports, weather, business, arts and entertainment, and health. The following sections run on Sunday: Turning Point, Well Being, On the Scene, Entertainment, Etc., Destinations, Business, Food, The Local Front, Impact, Real Estate & Home, Sports Weekend, and TV Week. The following sections run on Monday: Money Monday, Sports Weekend Wrap-up, Critters, Learning Curve, and Blitz (September - January). The Health and Whatever (teen) sections run on Tuesday. On Wednesday, the following sections appear: Food & Spirits, Community, TechWorld, Kid Stuff, and Brainstorm (12 times a year). The Home & Family and Day in the Life (monthly) sections run on Thursday. Jersey Alive, Wheels, and Real Estate run on Friday. On Saturday, readers can find Rally (school sports), Sports Weekend, Saturday People, Out and About, and Community Weekend. The Asbury Park Press shares some of its staff and stories with its sister newspapers, also published by Gannett, Inc.
Language (s): English
Ad Rate: Full Page Mono 225.86
Ad Rate: Full Page Colour 2060.27
Currency: United States Dollars
DAILY NEWSPAPER

Asbury Park Press - Trenton Bureau 15796
Editorial: Trenton, New Jersey **Tel:** 1 609 292-5171
Language (s): English
DAILY NEWSPAPER

Asheville Citizen-Times 15462
Owner: Gannett Co., Inc.
Editorial: 14 Ohenry Ave, Asheville, North Carolina 28801-2604 **Tel:** 1 828 252-5611
Email: news@citizen-times.com **Web site:** http://www.citizen-times.com
Freq: Daily; **Circ:** 28440 Not Audited
Profile: Asheville Citizen-Times is a daily broad sheet serving the greater Asheville, NC community. Sections include local news, business, arts & entertainment, features, city and county government, courts and law enforcement, education, politics, medicine and health. Regional news encompasses all of Western North Carolina outside the Buncombe-Madison area. Please mail all materials to the PO Box address. Advertising rates vary.
Language (s): English
Ad Rate: Full Page Mono 127.37
Ad Rate: Full Page Colour 366.75
Currency: United States Dollars
DAILY NEWSPAPER

Ashland Daily Press 14797
Owner: Macquarie Media Group
Editorial: 122 3rd St W, Ashland, Wisconsin 54806-1661 **Tel:** 1 715 682-2313
Email: pressnews@ashlanddailypress.net **Web site:** http://www.apg-wi.com/ashland_daily_press
Freq: Fri; **Circ:** 4489 Not Audited
Editor: Larry Servinsky
Profile: Ashland Daily Press is a daily newspaper published for the residents of Ashland, WI and surrounding areas. It provides information on local news and events. On Tuesdays, the paper is published online-only.
Language (s): English
Ad Rate: Full Page Mono 12.60
Ad Rate: Full Page Colour 14.05
Currency: United States Dollars
DAILY NEWSPAPER

Ashland Daily Tiding 14548
Owner: GateHouse Media Inc.
Editorial: 111 N Fir St, Medford, Oregon 97501-2772 **Tel:** 1 541 776-4411
Email: news@dailytidings.com **Web site:** http://www.dailytidings.com
Freq: Daily; **Circ:** 3800 Not Audited
Editor: Bert Etling; **Publisher:** James Grady Singletary
Profile: Ashland Daily Tidings is a local newspaper serving the Ashland, OR area. It provides information on news and events in the area. The newspaper focuses on Rogue Valley people and institutions. It offers a balanced selection on information, entertainment, opinion, and advertising. Please only send press releases with a local emphasis.
Language (s): English
Ad Rate: Full Page Mono 7.85
Ad Rate: Full Page Colour 11.43
Currency: United States Dollars
DAILY NEWSPAPER

Ashland Times-Gazette 14433
Owner: GateHouse Media Inc.
Editorial: 40 E 2nd St, Ashland, Ohio 44805-2304 **Tel:** 1 419 281-0581
Email: newsroom@times-gazette.com **Web site:** http://www.times-gazette.com
Freq: Daily; **Circ:** 11374 Not Audited
Profile: Ashland Times-Gazette is a local daily newspaper serving the Ashland County, OH area. It provides residents with information on local news, events, sports and weather. Deadlines for the publication are one week before issue date.
Language (s): English
Ad Rate: Full Page Mono 14.00
Currency: United States Dollars
DAILY NEWSPAPER

Aspen Daily News 13796
Owner: Dave Danforth
Editorial: 625 E Main St Ste 204, Aspen, Colorado 81611-1935 **Tel:** 1 970 925-2220
Web site: http://www.aspendailynews.com
Freq: Daily; **Circ:** 14500 Not Audited
Publisher: Dave Danforth
Profile: Aspen Daily News is a daily newspaper written for the residents of Aspen, Snowmass Village, Woody Creek, Basalt, El Jebel, Carbondale and Glenwood Springs, CO. It reports national and local news and community events.
Language (s): English
Ad Rate: Full Page Mono 10.50
Currency: United States Dollars
DAILY NEWSPAPER

Aspen Times 14924
Owner: Swift Newspapers
Editorial: 314 E Hyman Ave, Aspen, Colorado 81611-1918 **Tel:** 1 970 925-3414
Email: mail@aspentimes.com **Web site:** http://www.aspentimes.com
Freq: Mon thru Fri; **Circ:** 8141
Profile: Aspen Times is a daily newspaper written for the residents of Aspen, CO. It reports news and events in the local community.
Language (s): English
Ad Rate: Full Page Mono 29.27
Ad Rate: Full Page Colour 95.54
Currency: United States Dollars
DAILY NEWSPAPER

Athens Banner-Herald 13837
Owner: GateHouse Media Inc.
Editorial: 1 Press Pl, Athens, Georgia 30601-2605 **Tel:** 1 706 549-0123
Email: news@onlineathens.com **Web site:** http://www.onlineathens.com
Freq: Daily; **Circ:** 18575 Not Audited
Publisher: Scot Morrissey
Profile: Athens Banner-Herald is published daily for residents of Athens, GA and surrounding communities. The publication covers local news, weather, sports and community events.
Language (s): English
Ad Rate: Full Page Mono 35.27
Ad Rate: Full Page Colour 380.00
Currency: United States Dollars
DAILY NEWSPAPER

Athens Daily Review 14682
Owner: Athens Daily Review
Editorial: 201 S Prairieville St, Athens, Texas 75751-2541 **Tel:** 1 903 675-5626
Email: editor@athensreview.com **Web site:** http://www.athensreview.com
Freq: Fri; **Circ:** 5000 Not Audited
Editor: Jeff Riggs; **Publisher:** Lange Svehlak
Profile: Athens Daily Review is a daily newspaper published for the residents of Athens, TX area. The editorial content covers local sports, lifestyle and general news and to promote the goodwill of the community.
Language (s): English
Ad Rate: Full Page Mono 12.46
Ad Rate: Full Page Colour 89.23
Currency: United States Dollars
DAILY NEWSPAPER

The Athens Messenger 14435
Owner: American Consolidated Media
Editorial: 9300 Johnson Rd, Athens, Ohio 45701-9028 **Tel:** 1 740 592-6612
Email: info@athensmessenger.com **Web site:** http://www.athensmessenger.com
Freq: Daily; **Circ:** 12101 Not Audited
Editor: John Halley; **Publisher:** Monica Nieporte; **News Editor:** Steve Robb
Profile: Athens Messenger is written for the residents of Athens County, OH. It includes local news, classifieds and obituaries.
Language (s): English
Ad Rate: Full Page Mono 23.94
Ad Rate: Full Page Colour 145.73
Currency: United States Dollars
DAILY NEWSPAPER

Athol Daily News 14927
Owner: Athol Press Inc.
Editorial: 225 Exchange St, Athol, Massachusetts 01331-1843 **Tel:** 1 978 249-3535
Email: newsroom@atholdailynews.com **Web site:** http://www.atholdailynews.com
Freq: Daily; **Circ:** 5000 Not Audited
Publisher: Richard Chase; **Editor:** Deborah Porter
Profile: Athol Daily News serves the residents of Athol, MA.
Language (s): English
Ad Rate: Full Page Mono 7.60
Ad Rate: Full Page Colour 49.88
Currency: United States Dollars
DAILY NEWSPAPER

Atlanta Journal-Constitution 15317
Owner: Cox Media Group, Inc.
Editorial: 223 Perimeter Center Pkwy NE, Atlanta, Georgia 30346-1301 **Tel:** 1 404 526-7003
Email: newstips@ajc.com **Web site:** http://www.ajc.com
Freq: Daily; **Circ:** 122185 Not Audited
Editor: Kevin Riley
Profile: Atlanta Journal-Constitution (AJC) is the leading general interest daily paper in Atlanta. The Atlanta Constitution was founded in 1868 and the Atlanta Journal was founded in 1883. The two papers combined weekend sections in 1950, but did not fully combine until 2001. The paper covers world and local news as well as sports, entertainment, weather, business and travel. In August 2009, the paper joined a national sports content-sharing alliance with several other papers across the country. The paper also

offers multiple special sections, including a weekend arts section.
Language (s): English
Ad Rate: Full Page Mono 566.00
Ad Rate: Full Page Colour 600.29
Currency: United States Dollars
DAILY NEWSPAPER

Atlantic News-Telegraph 13865
Owner: Community Media Group
Editorial: 410 Walnut St, Atlantic, Iowa 50022-1378
Tel: 1 712 243-2624
Web site: http://www.atlanticnewstelegraph.com
Freq: Daily; **Circ:** 3241 Not Audited
Profile: Atlantic News-Telegraph is a daily newspaper for the residents of Atlantic, IA. It covers news and events in the local community.
Language (s): English
Ad Rate: Full Page Mono 13.10
Ad Rate: Full Page Colour 78.91
Currency: United States Dollars
DAILY NEWSPAPER

Auburn Journal 13770
Owner: Gold Country Media
Editorial: 1030 High St, Auburn, California 95603-4707 **Tel:** 1 530 885-5656
Email: ajournal@goldcountrymedia.com **Web site:** http://www.auburnjournal.com
Freq: Daily; **Circ:** 9670 Not Audited
Editor: Dennis Noone; **Editor:** Penne Usher; **Editor:** Gloria Young
Profile: Auburn Journal is a daily newspaper for the residents of Auburn, CA. It covers news and events in the local community.
Language (s): English
Ad Rate: Full Page Mono 21.25
Ad Rate: Full Page Colour 26.26
Currency: United States Dollars
DAILY NEWSPAPER

The Augusta Chronicle 15451
Owner: GateHouse Media Inc.
Editorial: 725 Broad St, Augusta, Georgia 30901-1336 **Tel:** 1 706 724-0851
Email: newsroom@augustachronicle.com **Web site:** http://chronicle.augusta.com
Freq: Daily; **Circ:** 43869 Not Audited
Profile: The Augusta Chronicle is the major daily newspaper for Augusta, Georgia. Founded in 1786, it is known to be one of the oldest US papers still in publication. It includes local and world news, sports, business, entertainment and classifieds sections. The newspaper has won acclaim for its coverage of the Masters Golf Tournament, and it has won many state and national awards, including the Georgia Press Association's top General Excellence Award in 1993.
Language (s): English
Ad Rate: Full Page Mono 54.41
Ad Rate: Full Page Colour 62.28
Currency: United States Dollars
DAILY NEWSPAPER

The Augusta Chronicle - Evans Bureau 16132
Editorial: 4272 Washington Rd Ste 3B, Evans, Georgia 30809-3073 **Tel:** 1 706 868-1222
Email: cnt@newstimesonline.com
Language (s): English
DAILY NEWSPAPER

Aurora Sentinel 238276
Owner: Aurora Media Group, LLC
Editorial: 12100 E Iliff Ave Ste 102, Aurora, Colorado 80014-1277 **Tel:** 1 303 750-7555
Email: news@aurorasentinel.com **Web site:** http://www.aurorasentinel.com
Freq: Mon thru Fri; **Circ:** 27635 Not Audited
Publisher: James Gold; **Editor:** Dave Perry
Profile: Aurora Sentinel Free Daily is issued Monday through Thursday and Aurora Sentinel Weekend on Friday. It is written for the residents of Aurora, CO.
Language (s): English
Ad Rate: Full Page Mono 28.00
Ad Rate: Full Page Colour 31.96
Currency: United States Dollars
DAILY NEWSPAPER

Austin American-Statesman 15369
Owner: Cox Media Group, Inc.
Editorial: 305 S Congress Ave, Austin, Texas 78704-1200 **Tel:** 1 512 445-3500
Email: newstips@statesman.com **Web site:** http://www.statesman.com
Freq: Daily; **Circ:** 95083 Not Audited
Publisher: Susie Ellwood; **Editor:** Debbie Hiott
Profile: Austin American-Statesman, "the paper of Central Texas," is a daily broadsheet covering regional, national and international news. The paper's daily sections include a Metro/state section, focusing on local and regional news, business, a Sports section, life/entertainment, as well as editorial articles and classified ads. In addition, the paper's weekly sections offer a more specific focus on a number of topics. Austin360 includes news and features on music, dance, dining and other topics related to arts and entertainment. The publication offers in-depth technology coverage in its Tech Monday section. Coverage includes consumer electronics, area technology firms, as well as computer and technology-related news. Other offerings include Weekly Business Review on Saturdays, a complete package of the entire week's stock market and mutual fund activity; Travel, featuring travel advice, and features related to travel and vacation destinations. Send holiday gift guide submissions to desk editors for specific coverage - there is no singular gift guide contact for the outlet overall.
Language (s): English
Ad Rate: Full Page Mono 78.00
Ad Rate: Full Page Colour 4380.57
Currency: United States Dollars
DAILY NEWSPAPER

Austin American-Statesman - Round Rock Bureau 83649
Editorial: 203 E Main St, Round Rock, Texas 78664-5207 **Tel:** 1 512 246-0040
Email: news@statesman.com
Language (s): English
DAILY NEWSPAPER

Austin Daily Herald 14199
Owner: Boone Newspapers Inc.
Editorial: 310 2nd St NE, Austin, Minnesota 55912-3436 **Tel:** 1 507 433-8851
Email: newsroom@austindailyherald.com **Web site:** http://www.austindailyherald.com
Freq: Daily; **Circ:** 3852 Not Audited
Advertising Sales Manager: Jana Gray
Profile: Austin Daily Herald is published daily for the residents of Austin, MN and surrounding areas. The newspaper provides information about local and state news, business, education, sports, lifestyles and entertainment.
Language (s): English
Ad Rate: Full Page Mono 18.50
Ad Rate: Full Page Colour 117.50
Currency: United States Dollars
DAILY NEWSPAPER

Baker City Herald 14550
Owner: Western Communications Inc.
Editorial: 1915 1st St, Baker City, Oregon 97814
Tel: 1 541 523-3673
Email: news@bakercityherald.com **Web site:** http://www.bakercityherald.com
Freq: Daily; **Circ:** 3396 Not Audited
Publisher: Kari Borgen; **Editor:** John Collins; **Editor:** Jayson Jacoby
Profile: Baker City Herald is published daily for the residents of Baker County, OR. The newspaper covers local and state news, business, sports, lifestyles and entertainment.
Language (s): English
Ad Rate: Full Page Mono 10.00
Ad Rate: Full Page Colour 65.63
Currency: United States Dollars
DAILY NEWSPAPER

Bakersfield Californian 15446
Owner: Moorhouse (Ginger)
Editorial: 1707 Eye St, Bakersfield, California 93301-5208 **Tel:** 1 661 395-7500
Email: local@bakersfield.com **Web site:** http://www.bakersfield.com
Freq: Daily; **Circ:** 35070 Not Audited
Profile: Bakersfield Californian is a daily newspaper written for the residents of Bakersfield, CA. The newspaper covers local news and events, sports, education and arts & entertainment.
Language (s): English
Ad Rate: Full Page Mono 45.79
Ad Rate: Full Page Colour 147.85
Currency: United States Dollars
DAILY NEWSPAPER

The Baltimore Sun 15285
Owner: tronc
Editorial: 501 N Calvert St, Baltimore, Maryland 21278-1000 **Tel:** 1 410 332-6000
Email: newstips@baltimoresun.com **Web site:** http://www.baltimoresun.com
Freq: Daily; **Circ:** 121351 Not Audited
Profile: The Baltimore Sun is a general interest daily newspaper written for the general public, business readers and consumers. It touts itself as "Maryland's leading provider of news for more than 150 years." Services used include Associated Press, Bloomberg News, The New York Times News Service, and Reuters. Coverage areas include news, business, consumer, health, and technology. The Business section, which is located inside the Maryland Section Tuesday through Friday, contains: Business Digest, a group of newsbriefs; Business Calendar, a listing of business events; and People on the Move, which lists personnel moves. On Sundays a Money & Life section runs as a stand-alone. The paper does not publish an editorial calendar. This is a morning newspaper. The outlet offers RRS (Real Simple Syndication). The paper is available for home delivery on Thursday and Sunday only. It is available at retail locations the rest of the week.
Language (s): English
Ad Rate: Full Page Mono 328.90
Ad Rate: Full Page Colour 685.03
Currency: United States Dollars
DAILY NEWSPAPER

Bangor Daily News 15399
Owner: Bangor Publishing Co.
Editorial: 1 Merchants Plz, Bangor, Maine 04401-8302 **Tel:** 1 207 990-8000
Email: bdnmail@bangordailynews.com **Web site:** http://www.bangordailynews.com
Freq: Daily; **Circ:** 42065
Publisher: Richard Warren
Profile: Bangor Daily News is a daily newspaper published for residents in all the Eastern and Northern region in Maine. The paper has four editions throughout the day and has three sections. The publication covers all local, national, and international news.
Language (s): English
Ad Rate: Full Page Mono 76.53
Ad Rate: Full Page Colour 250.60
Currency: United States Dollars
DAILY NEWSPAPER

Bangor Daily News - Augusta Bureau 621060
Editorial: Statehouse Station 50, Augusta, Maine 04333-0001
Language (s): English
DAILY NEWSPAPER

Bangor Daily News - Belfast Bureau 62419
Editorial: 93 Main St Ste 2, Belfast, Maine 04915-6595 **Tel:** 1 207 338-9546
Bureau Chief: Tom Groening
Language (s): English
DAILY NEWSPAPER

Bangor Daily News - Ellsworth Bureau 15756
Editorial: Ellsworth, Maine **Tel:** 1 207 667-9393
Language (s): English
DAILY NEWSPAPER

Bangor Daily News - Machias Bureau 671271
Owner: Bangor Publishing Co.
Editorial: 6 Myers Ln, Machias, Maine 04654-1095
Tel: 1 207 255-0618
Language (s): English
DAILY NEWSPAPER

Banner-Graphic 13986
Owner: Concord Publications, Inc.
Editorial: 100 N Jackson St, Greencastle, Indiana 46135-1240 **Tel:** 1 765 653-5151
Email: news@bannergraphic.com **Web site:** http://www.bannergraphic.com
Freq: Fri; **Circ:** 5800 Not Audited
Publisher: Randy List
Profile: Banner-Graphic is a local newspaper published daily except Sunday. It is targeted for the people of Putnam County, IN and the surrounding area. The paper includes articles about local news events, sports, weather and people.
Language (s): English
Ad Rate: Full Page Mono 14.25
Ad Rate: Full Page Colour 89.68
Currency: United States Dollars
DAILY NEWSPAPER

Baraboo News-Republic 14798
Owner: Capital Newspapers
Editorial: 714 Matts Ferry Rd, Baraboo, Wisconsin 53913-3152 **Tel:** 1 608 356-4808
Email: bnr-news@capitalnewspapers.com **Web site:** http://www.baraboonewsrepublic.com
Freq: Daily; **Circ:** 2903 Not Audited
Editor: Todd Krysiak
Profile: Baraboo News-Republic provides local news, sports and community events for residents of Baraboo and Sauk County, WI. Deadlines are at 10:30pm CT.
Language (s): English
Ad Rate: Full Page Mono 20.10
Ad Rate: Full Page Colour 97.83
Currency: United States Dollars
DAILY NEWSPAPER

Bartlesville Examiner-Enterprise 14512
Owner: GateHouse Media, LLC
Editorial: 4125 Nowata Rd, Bartlesville, Oklahoma 74006-5120 **Tel:** 1 918 335-8200
Web site: http://www.examiner-enterprise.com
Freq: Daily
Profile: Bartlesville Examiner-Enterprise is published daily for the residents of Bartlesville, OK. The newspaper covers local news, sports, entertainment, lifestyle, health and community events.
Language (s): English
Ad Rate: Full Page Mono 22.66
Ad Rate: Full Page Colour 30.09
Currency: United States Dollars
DAILY NEWSPAPER

Bastrop Daily Enterprise 14093
Owner: GateHouse Media Inc.
Editorial: 119 W Hickory Ave, Bastrop, Louisiana 71220-4549 **Tel:** 1 318 281-4421
Email: news@bastropenterprise.com **Web site:** http://www.bastropenterprise.com
Freq: Fri; **Circ:** 4697
Profile: Bastrop Daily Enterprise is a local daily newspaper published for the residents of the Morehouse Parish community. The publication covers local news, events and sports.
Language (s): English
Ad Rate: Full Page Mono 11.00
Ad Rate: Full Page Colour 72.56
Currency: United States Dollars
DAILY NEWSPAPER

Batavia Daily News 14392
Owner: Johnson Newspaper Corp.
Editorial: 2 Apollo Dr, Batavia, New York 14020-3002
Tel: 1 585 343-8000
Email: news@batavianews.com **Web site:** http://www.thedailynewsonline.com
Freq: Daily; **Circ:** 12499 Not Audited
Publisher: Michael Messerly
Profile: Batavia Daily News is published daily for the residents of Genesee, Wyoming and Orleans Counties, NY. The newspaper covers local news, events, weather, sports and other related topics.
Language (s): English
Ad Rate: Full Page Mono 22.94
Ad Rate: Full Page Colour 297.94
Currency: United States Dollars
DAILY NEWSPAPER

Batesville Daily Guard 13683
Owner: Batesville Guard-Record Co., Inc.
Editorial: 258 W Main St, Batesville, Arkansas 72501-6711 **Tel:** 1 870 793-2383
Email: news@guardonline.com **Web site:** http://www.guardonline.com
Freq: Mon thru Fri; **Circ:** 8928 Not Audited
Publisher: Pat Jones
Profile: Batesville Guard is a daily evening newspaper published for the residents of Batesville, AR and surrounding areas. It covers local news, features, sports, opinions, births and obituaries.
Language (s): English
Ad Rate: Full Page Mono 10.78
Ad Rate: Full Page Colour 41.34
Currency: United States Dollars
DAILY NEWSPAPER

Battle Creek Enquirer 14160
Owner: Gannett Co., Inc.
Editorial: 77 Michigan Ave E Ste 101, Battle Creek, Michigan 49017-7033 **Tel:** 1 269 964-7161
Web site: http://www.battlecreekenquirer.com
Freq: Daily; **Circ:** 12049 Not Audited
Profile: Battle Creek Enquirer is a daily newspaper published for the residents of Battle Creek, MI. The publication features news and information about local events, sports, business, crime, politics, and health.
Language (s): English
Ad Rate: Full Page Mono 53.28
Ad Rate: Full Page Colour 368.80
Currency: United States Dollars
DAILY NEWSPAPER

The Baxter Bulletin 13708
Owner: Gannett Co., Inc.
Editorial: 16 W 6th St, Mountain Home, Arkansas 72653-3508 **Tel:** 1 870 508-8000
Email: newsroom@baxterbulletin.com **Web site:** http://www.baxterbulletin.com
Freq: Daily; **Circ:** 8496 Not Audited
Profile: The Baxter Bulletin is published daily for the residents of Mountain Home and surrounding communities within Baxter County, AR. The newspaper covers local news, sports, schools, health, government and community events.
Language (s): English
Ad Rate: Full Page Mono 12.60
Ad Rate: Full Page Colour 15.60
Currency: United States Dollars
DAILY NEWSPAPER

Bay City Times 14161
Owner: MLive Media Group
Editorial: 311 5th St, Bay City, Michigan 48708-5806
Tel: 1 989 895-8551
Email: bcnews@mlive.com **Web site:** http://www.mlive.com/bctimes
Circ: 16548
Profile: Bay City Times is a daily newspaper published for the residents of Bay City, MI. The publication covers local news, business, sports, education, city and county government, police agencies, health, science, human services and community events. Deadlines are daily between 7:30am and 10am ET. Circulation figures for Thursday are 20,721, for Friday 21,235 and for Sunday 31,721.
Language (s): English
Ad Rate: Full Page Mono 38.27
Ad Rate: Full Page Colour 229.88
Currency: United States Dollars
DAILY NEWSPAPER

Baytown Sun 14684
Owner: Southern Newspapers, Inc.
Editorial: 1301 Memorial Dr, Baytown, Texas 77520-2401 **Tel:** 1 281 422-8302
Email: sunnews@baytownsun.com **Web site:** http://baytownsun.com
Freq: Fri; **Circ:** 7133 Not Audited
Editor & Publisher: Janie Halter Gray
Profile: Baytown Sun is a daily newspaper published for the residents of Baytown, TX. The newspaper covers local news, sports and lifestyle. The weekend edition of the paper is a combination of Saturday, Sunday and Monday.
Language (s): English
Ad Rate: Full Page Mono 14.94
Ad Rate: Full Page Colour 89.85
Currency: United States Dollars
DAILY NEWSPAPER

Beatrice Daily Sun 14337
Owner: Lee Enterprises, Inc.
Editorial: 110 S 6th St, Beatrice, Nebraska 68310-3912 **Tel:** 1 402 223-5233
Email: news@beatricedailysun.com **Web site:** http://www.beatricedailysun.com
Freq: Daily; **Circ:** 4524 Not Audited
Advertising Sales Manager: Janet Harms
Profile: Beatrice Daily Sun is a daily newspaper published everyday except Sunday for the residents of Gage County, NE. It reports the local news and events in the community. The lead time is the day prior to publication by 5pm CT. Deadline is one day prior to publication issue date.
Language (s): English
Ad Rate: Full Page Mono 16.46

Ad Rate: Full Page Colour 280.00
Currency: United States Dollars
DAILY NEWSPAPER

The Beaufort Gazette 14642
Owner: McClatchy Newspapers
Editorial: 10 Buck Island Rd, Bluffton, South Carolina 29910-5937 **Tel:** 1 843 524-3183
Email: gazette@beaufortgazette.com **Web site:** http://www.islandpacket.com/news/local/community/beaufort-news
Freq: Daily; **Circ:** 10439 Not Audited
Publisher: Sara Johnson Borton
Profile: The Beaufort Gazette is a daily newspaper for the residents of Beaufort, SC. The newspaper began printing in the early 1900s. It covers local news, sports, lifestyles and community events.
Language (s): English
Ad Rate: Full Page Mono 40.00
Ad Rate: Full Page Colour 234.48
Currency: United States Dollars
DAILY NEWSPAPER

Beaumont Enterprise 15416
Owner: Beaumont Enterprise-Hearst Newspapers
Editorial: 380 Main St, Beaumont, Texas 77701-2331 **Tel:** 1 409 833-3311
Email: localnews@beaumontenterprise.com **Web site:** http://www.beaumontenterprise.com
Freq: Daily; **Circ:** 21717 Not Audited
Editor: Tim Kelly
Profile: Beaumont Enterprise provides news coverage for residents of Beaumont and southeast Texas. The paper covers local and regional news, arts & entertainment, sports and business. Do not fax in press releases.
Language (s): English
Ad Rate: Full Page Mono 56.51
Ad Rate: Full Page Colour 183.36
Currency: United States Dollars
DAILY NEWSPAPER

Beauregard Daily News 14113
Owner: GateHouse Media Inc.
Editorial: 903 W 1st St, Deridder, Louisiana 70634-3701 **Tel:** 1 337 462-0616
Email: newsdeskbdn@gmail.com **Web site:** http://www.beauregarddailynews.net
Freq: Daily; **Circ:** 6700 Not Audited
Advertising Sales Manager: Cindy Sherman
Profile: Beauregard Daily News offers in-depth coverage of local news and sporting events for the residents of Deridder, LA.
Language (s): English
Ad Rate: Full Page Mono 13.70
Ad Rate: Full Page Colour 17.70
Currency: United States Dollars
DAILY NEWSPAPER

Beaver County Times 14564
Owner: Calkins Media
Editorial: 400 Fair Ave, Beaver, Pennsylvania 15009-1907 **Tel:** 1 724 775-3200
Email: timesnews@timesonline.com **Web site:** http://www.timesonline.com
Freq: Mon thru Fri; **Circ:** 25580 Not Audited
Profile: Beaver County Times' editorial mission is to provide local news coverage to the residents of Beaver County, PA. The publication is geared toward local residents. Deadlines for the publication are same day before issue date.
Language (s): English
Ad Rate: Full Page Mono 41.25
Ad Rate: Full Page Colour 54.66
Currency: United States Dollars
DAILY NEWSPAPER

Bedford Gazette 14565
Owner: Bedford Gazette
Editorial: 424 W Penn St, Bedford, Pennsylvania 15522-1230 **Tel:** 1 814 623-1151
Email: bedfordgazette@embarqmail.com **Web site:** http://www.bedfordgazette.com
Freq: Daily; **Circ:** 9837 Not Audited
Publisher: Joseph Beegle
Profile: Bedford Gazette is a daily newspaper for the residents of Bedford, PA. It covers news and events in the local community.
Language (s): English
Ad Rate: Full Page Mono 15.73
Ad Rate: Full Page Colour 53.00
Currency: United States Dollars
DAILY NEWSPAPER

Bellefontaine Examiner 14436
Owner: Hubbard Publishing Company
Editorial: 127 E Chillicothe Ave, Bellefontaine, Ohio 43311-1957 **Tel:** 1 937 592-3060
Email: news@examiner.org **Web site:** http://www.examiner.org
Freq: Daily; **Circ:** 9130 Not Audited
Editor: Miriam Baier; **Advertising Sales Manager:** Bob Chapman; **Editor:** Joel Mast
Profile: Bellefontaine Examiner is a daily newspaper for the residents of Bellefontaine, OH. For the past 110 years the Bellefontaine Examiner has been reporting the local news and events of Logan County.
Language (s): English
Ad Rate: Full Page Mono 11.75
Ad Rate: Full Page Colour 40.01
Currency: United States Dollars
DAILY NEWSPAPER

Belleville News-Democrat 13911
Owner: McClatchy Newspapers
Editorial: 120 S Illinois St, Belleville, Illinois 62220-2130 **Tel:** 1 618 234-1000
Email: Info@email.bnd.com **Web site:** http://www.bnd.com
Freq: Daily; **Circ:** 37626 Not Audited
Editor: Suzanne Boyle; **News Editor:** Mike Koziatek; **Publisher:** Jay Tebbe
Profile: Belleville News-Democrat is a daily newspaper serving residents in Southern Illinois. It focuses on local, breaking news and features about lifestyle, arts & entertainment and sports. On Fridays, the Pinckneyville (IL) Democrat is inserted in the paper to provide in-depth, local news about Pinckneyville and its residents.
Language (s): English
Ad Rate: Full Page Mono 53.77
Ad Rate: Full Page Colour 143.40
Currency: United States Dollars
DAILY NEWSPAPER

Belleville News-Democrat - Edwardsville Bureau 411835
Editorial: 142A N Main St, Ste 4, Edwardsville, Illinois 62025-1902 **Tel:** 1 618 692-9481
Language (s): English
DAILY NEWSPAPER

Bellingham Herald 14780
Owner: McClatchy Newspapers
Editorial: 1155 N State St, Bellingham, Washington 98225-5037 **Tel:** 1 360 676-2600
Email: newsroom@bellinghamherald.com **Web site:** http://www.bellinghamherald.com
Freq: Daily; **Circ:** 16320 Not Audited
Profile: Bellingham Herald is a daily newspaper for the residents of Bellingham, WA. It covers the news and events of the local community.
Language (s): English
Ad Rate: Full Page Mono 44.88
Ad Rate: Full Page Colour 145.85
Currency: United States Dollars
DAILY NEWSPAPER

Beloit Daily News 14800
Owner: Hagadone Corp.
Editorial: 149 State St, Beloit, Wisconsin 53511-6251 **Tel:** 1 608 365-8811
Email: news@beloitdailynews.com **Web site:** http://www.beloitdailynews.com
Freq: Daily; **Circ:** 11215
Editor: William Barth; **Publisher:** Kent Eymann
Profile: Beloit Daily News is a daily newspaper for Rock County, WI and Winnebago, IL. It covers news and events in the local community.
Language (s): English
Ad Rate: Full Page Mono 34.60
Currency: United States Dollars
DAILY NEWSPAPER

Belvidere Daily Republican 75709
Owner: Rock Valley Publishing LLC
Editorial: 130 S State St Ste 101, Belvidere, Illinois 61008-3697 **Tel:** 1 815 547-0084
Email: bdrnews@rvpublishing.com **Web site:** http://www.belvideredailyrepublican.net
Freq: Fri; **Circ:** 4317 Not Audited
Publisher: Pete Cruger; **Advertising Sales Manager:** Debra Werner
Profile: Belvidere Daily Republican is published for the residents of Boone County, IL. The newspaper covers news, business, sports, education and entertainment.
Language (s): English
Ad Rate: Full Page Mono 16.80
Ad Rate: Full Page Colour 19.90
Currency: United States Dollars
DAILY NEWSPAPER

The Bemidji Pioneer 14200
Owner: Forum Communications Co.
Editorial: 1320 Neilson Ave SE, Bemidji, Minnesota 56601-5406 **Tel:** 1 218 333-9200
Email: news@bemidjipioneer.com **Web site:** http://www.bemidjipioneer.com
Freq: Daily; **Circ:** 5655 Not Audited
Editor: Matt Cory; **Publisher:** Dennis Doeden
Profile: The mission of The Bemidji Pioneer is to be the source for news, sports, events and community coverage in North Central, MN. Readers of the paper are residents of North Central, MN. Topics covered include news, sports, government, education and others.
Language (s): English
Ad Rate: Full Page Mono 19.75
Ad Rate: Full Page Colour 64.60
Currency: United States Dollars
DAILY NEWSPAPER

Benicia Herald 14880
Owner: Gibson Group
Editorial: 820 1st St, Benicia, California 94510-3216
Email: beniciaherald@gmail.com **Web site:** http://beniciaheraldonline.com
Freq: Fri; **Circ:** 9000 Not Audited
Editor: Marc Ethier; **Publisher:** David Payne; **Advertising Sales Manager:** Pam Poppe
Profile: Benicia Herald is a local newspaper written for residents of Benicia, CA. The newspaper, published daily except for Monday and Saturday, covers local news, business, sports, social issues and community events.
Language (s): English
Ad Rate: Full Page Mono 12.60
Ad Rate: Full Page Colour 46.86
Currency: United States Dollars
DAILY NEWSPAPER

Bennington Banner 14771
Owner: New England Newspapers, Inc.
Editorial: 425 Main St, Bennington, Vermont 05201-2141 **Tel:** 1 802 447-7567
Email: news@benningtonbanner.com **Web site:** http://www.benningtonbanner.com
Freq: Daily; **Circ:** 5761 Not Audited
County News Editor: Mark Rondeau; **News Desk Editor:** Adam Samrov
Profile: Bennington Banner is a daily newspaper for the residents of Bennington, VT. It covers news and events of the local community as well as nationwide news.
Language (s): English
Ad Rate: Full Page Mono 22.60
Ad Rate: Full Page Colour 248.00
Currency: United States Dollars
DAILY NEWSPAPER

The Benton Evening News 13913
Owner: Paddock Publications
Editorial: 111 E Church St, Benton, Illinois 62812-2238 **Tel:** 1 618 438-5611
Email: newsroom@bentoneveningnews.com **Web site:** http://www.bentoneveningnews.com
Freq: Mon thru Fri; **Circ:** 3000 Not Audited
Profile: The Benton Evening News is a daily newspaper for the residents of Benton and Franklin County, IL. The publication covers news and events in the local and national community.
Language (s): English
Ad Rate: Full Page Mono 10.75
Ad Rate: Full Page Colour 35.04
Currency: United States Dollars
DAILY NEWSPAPER

The Berkshire Eagle 14131
Owner: New England Newspapers, Inc.
Editorial: 75 S Church St, Pittsfield, Massachusetts 01201-6157 **Tel:** 1 413 447-7311
Email: news@berkshireeagle.com **Web site:** http://www.berkshireeagle.com
Freq: Daily; **Circ:** 28608 Not Audited
Advertising Sales Manager: Warren Dews
Profile: The Berkshire Eagle is a daily, morning newspaper serving Berkshire County, MA and the surrounding area. It covers local and regional news, sports, health, lifestyle, business and obituaries.
Language (s): English
Ad Rate: Full Page Mono 38.35
Ad Rate: Full Page Colour 450.00
Currency: United States Dollars
DAILY NEWSPAPER

The Berlin Daily Sun 14897
Owner: Country News Club, Inc.
Editorial: 164 Main St, Berlin, New Hampshire 03570-2477 **Tel:** 1 603 752-5858
Email: bds@berlindailysun.com **Web site:** http://www.berlindailysun.com
Freq: Daily; **Circ:** 8925 Not Audited
Publisher: Mark Guerringue; **Editor:** Adam Hirshan
Profile: Berlin Daily Sun is a daily newspaper for the Northern New Hampshire Lakes Region. It covers news and events in the local communities.
Language (s): English
Ad Rate: Full Page Mono 6.50
Ad Rate: Full Page Colour 175.00
Currency: United States Dollars
DAILY NEWSPAPER

Big Spring Herald 14685
Owner: Horizon Publications Inc
Editorial: 710 Scurry St, Big Spring, Texas 79720-2723 **Tel:** 1 432 263-7331
Email: editor@bigspringherald.com **Web site:** http://www.bigspringherald.com
Freq: Daily; **Circ:** 4000 Not Audited
Profile: Big Spring Herald is a local newspaper written for the residents of Big Spring, TX. It covers local and national news, sports, politics, education and arts & entertainment. All releases should be addressed to the editor.
Language (s): English
Ad Rate: Full Page Mono 17.92
Ad Rate: Full Page Colour 20.10
Currency: United States Dollars
DAILY NEWSPAPER

Billings Gazette 15403
Owner: Lee Enterprises, Inc.
Editorial: 401 N 28th St, Billings, Montana 59101-1243 **Tel:** 1 406 657-1200
Email: citynews@billingsgazette.com **Web site:** http://www.billingsgazette.com
Freq: Daily; **Circ:** 36300 Not Audited
Editor: Darrell Ehrlick; **Publisher:** Michael Gulledge; **Advertising Sales Manager:** Dave Worstell
Profile: Billings Gazette is written daily for the residents of Billings, MT. The newspaper provides local news, community news, national news and world news.
Language (s): English
Ad Rate: Full Page Mono 76.50
Ad Rate: Full Page Colour 247.52
Currency: United States Dollars
DAILY NEWSPAPER

The Birmingham News 15324
Owner: Advance Publications, Inc.
Editorial: 1731 1st Ave N, Birmingham, Alabama 35203-2055 **Tel:** 1 205 325-4444
Email: bhamnews@al.com **Web site:** http://www.al.com/birmingham
Freq: 3 Times/Week; **Circ:** 60759 Not Audited
Profile: The Birmingham News features include the main News section, Metro-State news section, Sports, Money and LifeStyle sections. The LifeStyle section includes features covering a range of topics, including family life, fashion, fitness, food, consumer issues, fads and trends.
Language (s): English
Ad Rate: Full Page Mono 190.00
Ad Rate: Full Page Colour 643.74
Currency: United States Dollars
DAILY NEWSPAPER

The Bismarck Tribune 14328
Owner: Lee Enterprises, Inc.
Editorial: 707 E Front Ave, Bismarck, North Dakota 58504-5646 **Tel:** 1 701 223-2500
Email: news@bismarcktribune.com **Web site:** http://www.bismarcktribune.com
Freq: Daily; **Circ:** 22788 Not Audited
Profile: The Bismarck Tribune is published daily for the residents of Bismarck, ND and surrounding areas. The newspaper covers local and national news, sports, politics, arts & entertainment and education.
Language (s): English
Ad Rate: Full Page Mono 44.23
Ad Rate: Full Page Colour 133.20
Currency: United States Dollars
DAILY NEWSPAPER

Black Hills Pioneer 14659
Owner: Seaton Newspapers
Editorial: 315 Seaton Cir, Spearfish, South Dakota 57783-3212 **Tel:** 1 605 642-2761
Email: news@bhpioneer.com **Web site:** http://www.bhpioneer.com
Freq: Mon thru Fri; **Circ:** 3951 Not Audited
Publisher: Letitia Lister; **Advertising Sales Manager:** Dru Thomas
Profile: Black Hills Pioneer is a daily newspaper serving Spearfish, SD and the surrounding area. Newspaper coverage includes local news, sports, business, lifestyle and political items. Deadlines for the publication fall on the same day as the issue date.
Language (s): English
Ad Rate: Full Page Mono 11.95
Ad Rate: Full Page Colour 225.00
Currency: United States Dollars
DAILY NEWSPAPER

The Blade 15342
Owner: Block Communications Inc.
Editorial: 541 N Superior St, Toledo, Ohio 43660-1000 **Tel:** 1 419 724-6000
Email: citydesk@theblade.com **Web site:** http://www.toledoblade.com
Freq: Daily; **Circ:** 76642 Not Audited
News Editor: Tony Durham
Profile: The Blade, published since 1835, is a broadsheet, general interest, daily newspaper that covers regional, national and international news. It is Toledo's only morning newspaper and the primary newspaper of Northwest Ohio and Southeast Michigan. The paper prefers faxes be sent to the newsroom.
Language (s): English
Ad Rate: Full Page Mono 141.62
Ad Rate: Full Page Colour 160.45
Currency: United States Dollars
DAILY NEWSPAPER

The Blade - Columbus Bureau 15882
Owner: Block Communications Inc.
Editorial: 1 Capitol Sq Rm 107, Columbus, Ohio 43215-4275 **Tel:** 1 614 221-0496
Language (s): English
DAILY NEWSPAPER

Bluefield Daily Telegraph 14829
Owner: Community Newspaper Holdings, Inc.
Editorial: 928 Bluefield Ave, Bluefield, West Virginia 24701-2744 **Tel:** 1 304 327-2800
Email: news@bdtonline.com **Web site:** http://bdtonline.com
Freq: Daily; **Circ:** 12985 Not Audited
Editor: Charles Owens; **News Editor:** Andy Patton; **Editor:** Samantha Perry
Profile: Bluefield Daily Telegraph is a daily local newspaper that is written for those who live and/or are interested in the Bluefield, WV area. The newspaper covers local news, national news that has an impact on their readership, local sports, local politics, local arts & entertainment and local education issues. The publication welcomes submissions of community news, events or letters to the editor.
Language (s): English
Ad Rate: Full Page Mono 39.25
Ad Rate: Full Page Colour 125.57
Currency: United States Dollars
DAILY NEWSPAPER

Bluffton Today 62148
Owner: GateHouse Media Inc.
Editorial: 52 Persimmons St, Bluffton, South Carolina 29910-7682 **Tel:** 1 843 815-0800
Web site: http://www.blufftontoday.com
Freq: Daily; **Circ:** 17571 Not Audited
Editor: Lawrence Conneff
Profile: Bluffton Today is written for residents of Bluffton, SC. The outlet offers RSS (Really Simple Syndication).
Language (s): English
Ad Rate: Full Page Mono 23.04
Ad Rate: Full Page Colour 90.73
Currency: United States Dollars
DAILY NEWSPAPER

Blytheville Courier News 13685
Owner: Rust Communications
Editorial: 900 N Broadway St, Blytheville, Arkansas 72315-1714 **Tel:** 1 870 763-4461
Email: sspears@blythevillecourier.com **Web site:** http://www.blythevillecourier.com/
Freq: Fri; **Circ:** 3259 Not Audited
Profile: Blytheville Courier News is a daily local newspaper that is written for those who live and/or are interested in the Blytheville, AR area. The newspaper covers local news, national news that has an impact on their readership, sports, politics, arts & entertainment and education issues.
Language (s): English
Ad Rate: Full Page Mono 10.00
Ad Rate: Full Page Colour 36.21
Currency: United States Dollars
DAILY NEWSPAPER

Bogalusa Daily News 14094
Owner: Wick Communications Inc.
Editorial: 525 Avenue V, Bogalusa, Louisiana 70427-4413 **Tel:** 1 985 732-2565
Web site: http://www.bogalusadailynews.com/
Freq: Daily; **Circ:** 6500 Not Audited
Profile: Bogalusa Daily News is a local newspaper covering the community of Bogalusa, LA and its surrounding area. The newspaper is put out three times weekly; Wednesday, Friday, and Sunday, and covers all aspects of local news; including sports, weather, entertainment and community news.
Language (s): English
Ad Rate: Full Page Mono 8.75
Ad Rate: Full Page Colour 11.50
Currency: United States Dollars
DAILY NEWSPAPER

The Bolivar Commercial 14277
Owner: Walls Newspapers
Editorial: 821 N Chrisman Ave, Cleveland, Mississippi 38732-2110 **Tel:** 1 662 843-4241
Email: news@bolivarcommercial.com **Web site:** http://www.bolivarcommercial.com/
Freq: Daily; **Circ:** 6205 Not Audited
Advertising Sales Manager: David Laster; **Publisher & Editor:** Mark Williams
Profile: The Bolivar Commercial is a local daily newspaper geared toward the community of Cleveland, MS. The newspaper covers international, national and local news. Content consists of hard news, sports, lifestyle features, business news and What's Going On, a community-based news section.
Language (s): English
Ad Rate: Full Page Mono 10.50
Ad Rate: Full Page Colour 37.19
Currency: United States Dollars
DAILY NEWSPAPER

Bonner County Daily Bee 13907
Owner: Hagadone Corp.
Editorial: 310 Church St, Sandpoint, Idaho 83864-1345 **Tel:** 1 208 263-9534
Email: bcdailybee@bonnercountydailybee.com **Web site:** http://www.bonnercountydailybee.com
Freq: Daily; **Circ:** 5850 Not Audited
News Editor: Keith Kinnaird; **Editor:** Caroline Lobsinger
Profile: Bonner County Daily Bee is a local newspaper serving the residents of Bonner County, ID.
Language (s): English
Ad Rate: Full Page Mono 12.95
Ad Rate: Full Page Colour 54.82
Currency: United States Dollars
DAILY NEWSPAPER

Boone News-Republican 13866
Owner: Stephens Media
Editorial: 2136 Mamie Eisenhower Ave, Boone, Iowa 50036-4437 **Tel:** 1 515 432-6694
Email: news@newsrepublican.com **Web site:** http://www.newsrepublican.com
Freq: Daily; **Circ:** 2400 Not Audited
Publisher: Claudia Lovin
Profile: News-Republican is a newspaper covering local news, sports and community events for the residents of Boone, IA. The advertising deadline is at noon CT.
Language (s): English
Ad Rate: Full Page Mono 7.90
Ad Rate: Full Page Colour 185.00
Currency: United States Dollars
DAILY NEWSPAPER

Boonville Daily News 14221
Owner: GateHouse Media Inc.
Editorial: 412 High St, Boonville, Missouri 65233-1242 **Tel:** 1 660 882-5335
Web site: http://www.boonvilledailynews.com
Freq: Daily; **Circ:** 2574 Not Audited
Advertising Sales Manager: Mike Kellner
Profile: Boonville Daily News is a daily, local newspaper serving the residents of Boonville, MO and its surrounding communities. The newspaper covers all aspects of local, regional, national, and international news. Coverage of local news is extensive, including sports, entertainment, health, politics, and business news.
Language (s): English
Ad Rate: Full Page Mono 10.44
Ad Rate: Full Page Colour 36.67
Currency: United States Dollars
DAILY NEWSPAPER

Borger News-Herald 14686
Owner: Horizon Publications
Editorial: 207 N Main St, Borger, Texas 79007 **Tel:** 1 806 273-5611
Web site: http://www.borgernewsherald.com
Freq: Daily; **Circ:** 4255 Not Audited
Profile: Borger News-Herald is a local, daily newspaper that serves the residents of Borger, TX and its surrounding areas. The editorial content covers sports, technology, weather, business, and community news and events. The deadline is one day before the issue date. Advertising deadlines are one week prior to insertion.
Language (s): English
Ad Rate: Full Page Mono 11.38
Ad Rate: Full Page Colour 38.18
Currency: United States Dollars
DAILY NEWSPAPER

The Boston Globe 15309
Owner: Boston Globe Media Partners
Editorial: 53 State St, 1 Exchange Place, Boston, Massachusetts 02109-2820 **Tel:** 1 617 929-2000
Email: newstip@globe.com **Web site:** http://www.bostonglobe.com
Freq: Daily; **Circ:** 90
Editor: Brian McGrory
Profile: The Boston Globe focuses on news for the general public in the New England area as well as state, national and international news. Other coverage areas include business, healthcare, technology, features, lifestyle, arts and sports. There is also an emphasis on regional and suburban coverage. Lead times vary depending on the department. The staff won a 2003 Pulitzer prize for public service. The paper does not publish a Holiday Gift Guide.
Language (s): English
Ad Rate: Full Page Mono 577.00
Ad Rate: Full Page Colour 685.00
Currency: United States Dollars
DAILY NEWSPAPER

The Boston Globe - Boston City Hall Bureau 16157
Owner: Boston Globe Media Partners
Editorial: 1 City Hall Plz, Boston, Massachusetts 02108-2102 **Tel:** 1 617 367-4023
Email: newstip@globe.com
Bureau Chief: Andrew Ryan
Language (s): English
DAILY NEWSPAPER

The Boston Globe - Boston State House Bureau 16115
Owner: Boston Globe Media Partners
Editorial: Massachusetts State House #490, Boston, Massachusetts 2133 **Tel:** 1 617 367-4030
Bureau Chief: Frank Phillips
Language (s): English
DAILY NEWSPAPER

The Boston Globe - Washington Bureau 15529
Owner: Boston Globe Media Partners
Editorial: 1130 Connecticut Ave NW Ste 520, Washington, District Of Columbia 20036-3947 **Tel:** 1 202 857-5050
Language (s): English
DAILY NEWSPAPER

Boston Herald 15299
Owner: GateHouse Media Inc.
Editorial: 70 Fargo St Ste 600, Boston, Massachusetts 02210-2131 **Tel:** 1 617 426-3000
Email: newstips@bostonherald.com **Web site:** http://www.bostonherald.com
Freq: Daily; **Circ:** 81933 Not Audited
Publisher: Patrick Purcell
Profile: Boston Herald is a 70+ page general-interest tabloid with an emphasis on local area coverage. The morning paper aims to be the primary news and information source for Boston-area residents. Business coverage is company-oriented with the focus on more general news, not specific products. Significant breaking news that affects the high-tech industry and earnings reports is also covered. Consumer features run on Wednesday. Special sections include Business Extra (Monday), an expanded business section with all current local, national and international news, including personnel news; and Small Business (Tuesday) which focuses on small businesses and features advice columns and small business profiles. The Edge is the publication's Arts & Entertainment section.
Language (s): English
Ad Rate: Full Page Mono 71.84
Ad Rate: Full Page Colour 262.65
Currency: United States Dollars
DAILY NEWSPAPER

Bozeman Daily Chronicle 14278
Owner: Pioneer Newspapers
Editorial: 2820 W College St, Bozeman, Montana 59718-3925 **Tel:** 1 406 587-4491
Email: citydesk@dailychronicle.com **Web site:** http://www.bozemandailychronicle.com
Freq: Daily; **Circ:** 14668 Not Audited
Profile: Bozeman Daily Chronicle is a daily, local newspaper serving the residents of Bozeman, MT and its surrounding areas. It covers the outdoors, religion, health, travel, business and local news.
Language (s): English
Ad Rate: Full Page Mono 17.88
Ad Rate: Full Page Colour 53.09
Currency: United States Dollars
DAILY NEWSPAPER

Bradenton Herald 13813
Owner: McClatchy Newspapers
Editorial: 1111 3rd Ave W, Bradenton, Florida 34205-7834 **Tel:** 1 941 748-0411
Web site: http://www.bradenton.com
Freq: Daily; **Circ:** 21302 Not Audited
Profile: Bradenton Herald is a daily newspaper serving residents of Bradenton, Manatee and Sarasota, FL. It contains regional, national and international news. Coverage also extends to sports, business, education, entertainment, features, weather and community news. The paper is also printed for the residents of Lakewood Ranch, FL under the title Lakewood Ranch Herald.
Language (s): English
Ad Rate: Full Page Mono 59.99
Ad Rate: Full Page Colour 625.00
Currency: United States Dollars
DAILY NEWSPAPER

The Bradford Era 14567
Owner: Bradford Publishing Co.
Editorial: 43 Main St, Bradford, Pennsylvania 16701-2019 **Tel:** 1 814 362-6531
Email: news@bradfordera.com **Web site:** http://www.bradfordera.com
Freq: Fri; **Circ:** 11200 Not Audited
Advertising Sales Manager: Jill Henry; **Editor/Publisher:** John Satterwhite
Profile: The Bradford Era is a daily publication for residents of the Bradford, PA area. It reports news and events of the local area. Deadlines for the editorial submissions is one day prior to the issue date.
Language (s): English
Ad Rate: Full Page Mono 16.18
Ad Rate: Full Page Colour 375.00
Currency: United States Dollars
DAILY NEWSPAPER

The Brainerd Dispatch 14201
Owner: Forum Communications Co.
Editorial: 506 James St, Brainerd, Minnesota 56401-2942 **Tel:** 1 218 829-4705
Email: newstips@brainerddispatch.com **Web site:** http://www.brainerddispatch.com
Freq: Daily; **Circ:** 9613 Not Audited
Editor: Matt Erickson; **Editor:** Steve Kohls
Profile: Brainerd Daily Dispatch is regional newspaper serving Central Minnesota communities. It is issued six days per week, Sunday through Friday. The newspaper offers in depth coverage of international, national and local news. Content includes news, weather, politics, arts & entertainment, business, education, sports and community news, events and listings.
Language (s): English
Ad Rate: Full Page Mono 13.40
Ad Rate: Full Page Colour 49.73
Currency: United States Dollars
DAILY NEWSPAPER

Brattleboro Reformer 14772
Owner: New England Newspapers, Inc.
Editorial: 62 Black Mountain Rd, Brattleboro, Vermont 05301-9241 **Tel:** 1 802 254-2311
Email: news@reformer.com **Web site:** http://www.reformer.com
Freq: Mon thru Fri; **Circ:** 7550 Not Audited
Profile: Brattleboro Reformer is a daily, local newspaper serving the residents of Brattleboro, VT, and its surrounding areas. It provides in-depth local, regional, national and world news. Content also includes entertainment, business, sports, weather, education, health, religion and community events. Advertising deadlines are at 5pm ET. It shares offices with The Vermont Observer Brattleboro and the Town Crier.
Language (s): English
Ad Rate: Full Page Mono 25.30
Ad Rate: Full Page Colour 82.51
Currency: United States Dollars
DAILY NEWSPAPER

El Bravo - Brownsville Edition 520493
Owner: Comania Periodistica El Bravo
Editorial: 1114 Lincoln St Ste C, Brownsville, Texas 78521 **Tel:** 1 956 542-5800
Email: adpro@elbravo.com.mx **Web site:** http://www.elbravomatamoros.com
Freq: Daily; **Circ:** 5000 Not Audited
Publisher: Nancy Carretero
Profile: El Bravo is a Spanish-language newspaper for the residents of Brownsville, TX.
Language (s): Spanish
Ad Rate: Full Page Mono 52.13
Ad Rate: Full Page Colour 84.49
Currency: United States Dollars
DAILY NEWSPAPER

Brazil Times 13973
Owner: Rust Communications
Editorial: 100 N Meridian St, Brazil, Indiana 47834-2172 **Tel:** 1 812 446-2216
Email: wilson.braziltimes@gmail.com **Web site:** http://www.thebraziltimes.com
Freq: Fri; **Circ:** 5000 Not Audited
Publisher: Randy List; **Advertising Sales Manager:** Lynne Llewellyn
Profile: Brazil Times serves the residents of Clay County, IN. The paper covers local and regional news and occasionally reports on national news that directly affects the local area. Local coverage is extensive and covers sports, weather, business, education, crime, politics and community news and events.
Language (s): English
Ad Rate: Full Page Mono 12.21
Ad Rate: Full Page Colour 41.16
Currency: United States Dollars
DAILY NEWSPAPER

Breeze Courier 13963
Owner: Breeze Printing Company
Editorial: 212 S Main St, Taylorville, Illinois 62568-2219 **Tel:** 1 217 824-2233
Email: breezecourier@breezecourier.com **Web site:** http://www.breeze-courier.com
Freq: Mon thru Fri; **Circ:** 5541
Publisher & Editor: Marylee Lasswell
Profile: Breeze Courier is written for the residents of Taylorville, IL and their surrounding areas. It covers local news, weather, sports, business and announcements. It also includes an opinion column, classified ads and features stories. National news is covered when directly affecting the area. Deadlines are on the days prior to the issue date at 5pm CT.
Language (s): English
Ad Rate: Full Page Mono 8.50
Ad Rate: Full Page Colour 200.00
Currency: United States Dollars
DAILY NEWSPAPER

Brenham Banner-Press 14687
Owner: Hartman Newspapers, Inc.
Editorial: 2430 Stringer St, Brenham, Texas 77833-5724 **Tel:** 1 979 836-7956
Email: edit@brenhambanner.com **Web site:** http://www.brenhambanner.com
Freq: Daily; **Circ:** 6500 Not Audited
News Editor: Derek Hall; **Advertising Sales Manager:** Helen Nowicki
Profile: Brenham Banner-Press is written for the residents of Brenham, Burton, Bellville and College Station, TX. It covers local news, lifestyles, sports, education, arts & entertainment, politics, business, real estate and community events.
Language (s): English
Ad Rate: Full Page Mono 8.16
Ad Rate: Full Page Colour 270.00
Currency: United States Dollars
DAILY NEWSPAPER

Briefing 533520
Owner: A.H. Belo Corp.
Editorial: 508 Young St, Dallas, Texas 75202-4808 **Tel:** 1 214 977-8333
Email: briefing@dallasnews.com **Web site:** http://www.dallasnews.com/briefing
Freq: Fri; **Circ:** 250000
News Editor: Jamie Hancock
Profile: Briefing, launched on August 27, 2008, is aimed at time-crunched families who want a quick-read newspaper. It is distributed Wednesdays through Saturdays to households that don't currently subscribe to The Dallas Morning News, it's sister newspaper.
Language (s): English
Ad Rate: Full Page Mono 133.65
Ad Rate: Full Page Colour 149.52
Currency: United States Dollars
DAILY NEWSPAPER

Bristol Herald Courier 14751
Owner: BH Media Group
Editorial: 320 Bob Morrison Blvd, Bristol, Virginia 24201-3812 **Tel:** 1 276 669-2181
Web site: http://www.heraldcourier.com/
Freq: Daily; **Circ:** 21586 Not Audited
Profile: Bristol Herald Courier is a daily newspaper written for residents in the Mountain Empire Region (southwestern Virginia and northeastern Tennessee.) The newspaper covers both local and national news. Topics covered include news, sports, arts & entertainment, lifestyle, classifieds, business and community events. Deadlines are at 10pm ET the day before issue date.
Language (s): English
Ad Rate: Full Page Mono 56.95
Ad Rate: Full Page Colour 205.02
Currency: United States Dollars
DAILY NEWSPAPER

The Bristol Press 13797
Owner: Central Connecticut Communications
Editorial: 188 Main St, Bristol, Connecticut 06010-6308 **Tel:** 1 860 584-0501
Web site: http://www.bristolpress.com
Freq: Mon thru Fri; **Circ:** 4388 Not Audited
Advertising Sales Manager: Gary Curran
Profile: The Bristol Press is a local newspaper that covers Bristol, Plymouth, Plainville, Terryville, Thomaston and Burlington, CT. The paper provides readers with local news, business, education, lifestyle, sports, entertainment and classifieds. It combines with The Herald in New Britian, CT on Sundays.
Language (s): English
Ad Rate: Full Page Mono 29.48
Ad Rate: Full Page Colour 45.60
Currency: United States Dollars
DAILY NEWSPAPER

Brookhaven Daily Leader 14258
Owner: Brookhaven Newsmedia, LLC
Editorial: 128 N Railroad Ave, Brookhaven, Mississippi 39601-3043 **Tel:** 1 601 833-6961
Email: news@dailyleader.com **Web site:** http://www.dailyleader.com
Freq: Mon thru Fri; **Circ:** 5826 Not Audited
Profile: Brookhaven Daily Leader is a local newspaper distributed throughout Lincoln County, MS everyday except Saturday. The newspaper provides readers with local, regional and national news, as well as sports, business, entertainment and lifestyle coverage.
Language (s): English

Ad Rate: Full Page Mono 12.89
Ad Rate: Full Page Colour 49.19
Currency: United States Dollars
DAILY NEWSPAPER

Brookings Register 14651
Owner: News Media Corp.
Editorial: 312 5th St, Brookings, South Dakota 57006-1924 **Tel:** 1 605 692-6271
Email: registernews@brookingsregister.com **Web site:** http://www.brookingsregister.com
Freq: Daily; **Circ:** 3954 Not Audited
Editor: Doug Kott; **Publisher:** Will McMacken
Profile: Brookings Register is written for the residents of Brookings County, SD. The newspaper provides local community news and some national news to its readers. The focus is on the events occurring in the community and the people who live in the community. Some local features include sports, education, business, politics, entertainment, and classifieds.
Language (s): English
Ad Rate: Full Page Mono 16.00
Ad Rate: Full Page Colour 53.09
Currency: United States Dollars
DAILY NEWSPAPER

The Brooklyn Daily Eagle & Daily Bulletin 14939
Owner: Brooklyn Eagle Publications
Editorial: 16 Court St, Brooklyn, New York 11241-0102 **Tel:** 1 718 422-7400
Email: edit@brooklyneagle.net **Web site:** http://www.brooklyneagle.com
Freq: Daily; **Circ:** 10000 Not Audited
Publisher: Dozier Hasty; **Editor:** John Torenli
Profile: The Brooklyn Daily Eagle & Daily Bulletin is a daily newspaper serving readers in Brooklyn, NY with local and national news. Coverage also includes sports, business, education, politics, entertainment, lifestyle and classifieds.
Language (s): English
Ad Rate: Full Page Mono 21.00
Currency: United States Dollars
DAILY NEWSPAPER

The Brownsville Herald 14688
Owner: AIM Media Texas, LLC
Editorial: 1135 E Van Buren St, Brownsville, Texas 78520-7055 **Tel:** 1 956 542-4301
Web site: http://www.brownsvilleherald.com
Freq: Daily; **Circ:** 12935 Not Audited
Editor: Ryan Henry
Profile: The Brownsville Herald is published daily and distributed throughout Brownsville, TX and surrounding areas in Southern Texas. The newspaper provides readers with both local and national news coverage. It also features business, education, politics, lifestyle, entertainment, sports, classifieds and weather. It has a Spanish version called El Heraldo de Brownsville. The contacts are the same for both newspapers and should only be contacted once since both newspapers print the same content.
Language (s): English
Ad Rate: Full Page Mono 23.79
Ad Rate: Full Page Colour 85.64
Currency: United States Dollars
DAILY NEWSPAPER

Brownwood Bulletin 14689
Owner: American Consolidated Media
Editorial: 700 Carnegie St, Brownwood, Texas 76801-7040 **Tel:** 1 325 646-2541
Email: news@brownwoodbulletin.com **Web site:** http://www.brownwoodbulletin.com
Freq: Daily; **Circ:** 7120 Not Audited
Profile: Founded in 1900, Brownwood Bulletin is a daily newspaper which provides local and national news coverage to readers throughout Brown County, TX. It features sports, education, politics, lifestyle, entertainment, opinions, obituaries, weather, classifieds and letters to the editor.
Language (s): English
Ad Rate: Full Page Mono 14.78
Ad Rate: Full Page Colour 47.82
Currency: United States Dollars
DAILY NEWSPAPER

The Brunswick News 13838
Owner: Brunswick News Publishing Company
Editorial: 3011 Altama Ave, Brunswick, Georgia 31520-4059 **Tel:** 1 912 265-8320
Email: newsroom@thebrunswicknews.com **Web site:** http://www.thebrunswicknews.com
Freq: Daily; **Circ:** 17800
Publisher & Editor: C.H. Leavy
Profile: The Brunswick News is distributed throughout Brunswick and Golden Isles, GA. It provides local coverage of Brunswick, Jekyll Island, St. Simons Island and Brantley, Camden and McIntosh counties, GA. Local features include business, entertainment, sports and education. Deadlines are the day before publication at 1pm ET.
Language (s): English
Ad Rate: Full Page Mono 19.95
Ad Rate: Full Page Colour 319.95
Currency: United States Dollars
DAILY NEWSPAPER

The Bryan Times 14439
Owner: Bryan Publishing Company
Editorial: 127 S Walnut St, Bryan, Ohio 43506-1718 **Tel:** 1 419 636-1111
Email: news@bryantimes.com **Web site:** http://www.bryantimes.com
Freq: Daily; **Circ:** 7640 Not Audited
Publisher: Christopher Cullis
Profile: The Bryan Times provides local news to readers throughout Williams County, OH. The newspaper is published Monday through Saturday and focuses on local community news including business, lifestyle, entertainment, religion, farm, sports, school and service and classifieds.
Language (s): English
Ad Rate: Full Page Mono 11.80
Ad Rate: Full Page Colour 300.00
Currency: United States Dollars
DAILY NEWSPAPER

Bucks County Courier Times 14596
Owner: Calkins Media
Editorial: 8400 Bristol Pike, Levittown, Pennsylvania 19057-5117 **Tel:** 1 215 949-4000
Email: newstips@calkins.com **Web site:** http://www.buckscountycouriertimes.com
Freq: Mon thru Fri; **Circ:** 33769 Not Audited
Profile: Bucks County Courier Times is a daily newspaper published by Calkins Newspapers for the residents of Bucks County, PA and surrounding communities. The newspaper provides readers with local and national news coverage. Other features include business, entertainment, sports, education, lifestyle, real estate, community and classifieds. The lead time for submissions varies. Deadlines are one day prior to the issue date.
Language (s): English
Ad Rate: Full Page Mono 239.00
Ad Rate: Full Page Colour 695.00
Currency: United States Dollars
DAILY NEWSPAPER

Bucyrus Telegraph-Forum 14440
Owner: Gannett Co., Inc.
Editorial: 113 W Rensselaer St, Bucyrus, Ohio 44820-2215 **Tel:** 1 419 562-3333
Email: tfnews@nncogannett.com **Web site:** http://www.bucyrustelegraphforum.com
Freq: Daily; **Circ:** 105
Profile: Bucyrus Telegraph-Forum is a local daily newspaper serving Crawford County, OH. The newspaper focuses on local news and community events, also featuring national and international news. Local features include politics, business, lifestyle, education and sports.
Language (s): English
Ad Rate: Full Page Mono 15.50
Ad Rate: Full Page Colour 51.61
Currency: United States Dollars
DAILY NEWSPAPER

The Buffalo News 15325
Owner: BH Media Group
Editorial: 1 News Plz, Buffalo, New York 14203-2930 **Tel:** 1 716 849-3434
Email: citydesk@buffnews.com **Web site:** http://www.buffalonews.com
Freq: Daily; **Circ:** 121413 Not Audited
Editor: Mike Connelly; **Investigative News Editor:** Susan Schulman
Profile: The Buffalo News is a daily newspaper written for the general public in the greater Buffalo, NY area. The business section appears daily, covering local and national business stories, daily stock market rates and real estate. Articles include features, breaking news, trends, analysis, profiles and investigative stories. Consumer-related topics include: entertainment, lifestyles, TV topics, travel, viewpoints, health, money, a kid section, a computer page and a real estate section. Advertising rates are unavailable to media industry services and must be obtained by individual buyers through their sales department.
Language (s): English
Ad Rate: Full Page Mono 286.19
Ad Rate: Full Page Colour 8495.13
Currency: United States Dollars
DAILY NEWSPAPER

The Buffalo News - Albany Bureau 15813
Editorial: State Capitol LCA Pressroom 3rd Fl, Albany, New York 12224 **Tel:** 1 518 434-6365
Bureau Chief: Tom Precious
Language (s): English
DAILY NEWSPAPER

The Buffalo News - Washington Bureau 15553
Editorial: 1715 15th St NW Apt 24, Washington, District Of Columbia 20009-3876 **Tel:** 1 202 234-3188
Bureau Chief: Jerry Zremski
Language (s): English
DAILY NEWSPAPER

The Bulletin 13806
Owner: GateHouse Media Inc.
Editorial: 66 Franklin St, Norwich, Connecticut 06360-5806 **Tel:** 1 860 887-9211
Email: news@norwichbulletin.com **Web site:** http://www.norwichbulletin.com
Freq: Daily; **Circ:** 13287 Not Audited
Profile: The Bulletin is a daily newspaper written for residents in Eastern Connecticut. It covers local news, sports, lifestyle and technology.
Language (s): English
Ad Rate: Full Page Mono 35.35
Currency: United States Dollars
DAILY NEWSPAPER

The Bulletin 14551
Owner: Western Communications Inc.
Editorial: 1777 SW Chandler Ave, Bend, Oregon 97702-3200 **Tel:** 1 541 382-1811
Email: bulletin@bendbulletin.com **Web site:** http://www.bendbulletin.com
Freq: Daily; **Circ:** 26406 Not Audited
Profile: The Bulletin is published daily for the residents of Bend, OR, including Deschutes, Crook and Jefferson counties. The newspaper covers local and state news, business, sports, education, lifestyles and entertainment. Deadlines are one day prior to publications at 4pm PT.
Language (s): English
Ad Rate: Full Page Mono 45.60
Ad Rate: Full Page Colour 166.31
Currency: United States Dollars
DAILY NEWSPAPER

Burlington County Times 14367
Owner: Calkins Media
Editorial: 4284 Route 130, Willingboro, New Jersey 08046-2027 **Tel:** 1 609 871-8000
Email: mesposito@phillyburbs.com **Web site:** http://www.phillyburbs.com/news/local/burlington_county_times_news/
Freq: Mon thru Fri; **Circ:** 20147 Not Audited
Profile: Burlington County Times is a daily newspaper published for the residents of Burlington County, NJ. The newspaper focuses on local news and community events. Features include business, education, lifestyle, entertainment, sports, and politics. Deadlines are daily at noon ET.
Language (s): English
Ad Rate: Full Page Mono 239.00
Ad Rate: Full Page Colour 274.90
Currency: United States Dollars
DAILY NEWSPAPER

The Burlington Free Press 15420
Owner: Gannett Co., Inc.
Editorial: 100 Bank St Ste 700, Burlington, Vermont 05401-4946 **Tel:** 1 802 863-3441
Email: metro@burlingtonfreepress.com **Web site:** http://www.burlingtonfreepress.com
Freq: Daily; **Circ:** 32089 Not Audited
Profile: The Burlington Free Press is a daily newspaper serving the residents of Burlington, VT and surrounding communities. The publication covers local and national news, sports, business and community information.
Language (s): English
Ad Rate: Full Page Mono 81.10
Ad Rate: Full Page Colour 265.74
Currency: United States Dollars
DAILY NEWSPAPER

Butler County Times-Gazette 14041
Owner: GateHouse Media Inc.
Editorial: 114 N Vine St, El Dorado, Kansas 67042-2028 **Tel:** 1 316 321-1120
Web site: http://www.butlercountytimesgazette.com
Freq: 3 Times/Week; **Circ:** 1907 Not Audited
Profile: Butler County Times-Gazette is a daily newspaper covering Butler County, KS, the result of a 2013 merger between the El Dorado Times, Andover American and Augusta Gazette.
Language (s): English
Ad Rate: Full Page Mono 12.00
Ad Rate: Full Page Colour 15.00
Currency: United States Dollars
DAILY NEWSPAPER

Butler Eagle 14568
Owner: Eagle Printing Company
Editorial: 114 W Diamond St, Butler, Pennsylvania 16001-5747 **Tel:** 1 724 282-8000
Email: news@butlereagle.com **Web site:** http://www.butlereagle.com
Freq: Daily; **Circ:** 23859 Not Audited
Publisher: Vernon Wise
Profile: Butler Eagle is a daily newspaper published for the residents of Butler County, PA. The paper covers local news, business, education and sports. Deadlines are daily at 9:30am ET.
Language (s): English
Ad Rate: Full Page Mono 30.00
Ad Rate: Full Page Colour 97.87
Currency: United States Dollars
DAILY NEWSPAPER

Cadillac News 14163
Owner: Huckle (Chris)
Editorial: 130 N Mitchell St, Cadillac, Michigan 49601-1856 **Tel:** 1 231 775-6565
Email: news@cadillacnews.com **Web site:** http://www.cadillacnews.com
Freq: Daily; **Circ:** 9603 Not Audited
Publisher: T. Christopher Huckle; **Editor:** Matthew Seward
Profile: Cadillac News is written for the residents of Wexford, Missaukee, Osceola and Eastern Lake Counties, MI. It covers area news, events, sports, business and community information. Deadlines are daily at 8pm ET the day prior to the issue date.
Language (s): English
Ad Rate: Full Page Mono 17.40
Ad Rate: Full Page Colour 60.47
Currency: United States Dollars
DAILY NEWSPAPER

The Caledonian-Record 14776
Owner: Todd Smith
Editorial: 190 Federal St, Saint Johnsbury, Vermont 05819-5616 **Tel:** 1 802 748-8121
Email: news@caledonian-record.com **Web site:** http://caledonianrecord.com
Freq: Daily; **Circ:** 9849 Not Audited
Publisher: Mark Smith
Profile: The Caledonian-Record is a daily newspaper written for the residents of the Northeast Kingdom of Vermont and the North Country of New Hampshire. The publication covers local news, business, sports, entertainment, health, education, religion, food and fashion. They are only interested in releases directly germane to their five county area of distribution and coverage. Press releases should be submitted one week before an event is held. Deadlines fall two days prior to the issue date at 5pm ET. Please send all press releases to the PO Box.
Language (s): English
Ad Rate: Full Page Mono 8.25
Ad Rate: Full Page Colour 41.70
Currency: United States Dollars
DAILY NEWSPAPER

The Call 14639
Owner: R.I.S.N. Operations Inc.
Editorial: 75 Main St, Woonsocket, Rhode Island 02895-4312 **Tel:** 1 401 762-3000
Email: editor@woonsocketcall.com **Web site:** http://www.woonsocketcall.com
Freq: Daily; **Circ:** 6703 Not Audited
Profile: The Call is a daily newspaper written for the community of Woonsocket, RI. The paper includes local, state and some national and world news, politics, business, sports and entertainment.
Language (s): English
Ad Rate: Full Page Mono 26.53
Ad Rate: Full Page Colour 85.65
Currency: United States Dollars
DAILY NEWSPAPER

The Call-Leader 13982
Owner: Elwood Publishing Co.
Editorial: 317 S Anderson St, Elwood, Indiana 46036-2018 **Tel:** 1 765 552-3355
Email: elpub@elwoodpublishing.com **Web site:** http://www.elwoodpublishing.com
Freq: Daily; **Circ:** 2800 Not Audited
Editor: Sandy Burton; **Editor:** Ed Hamilton; **Publisher:** Robert Nash
Profile: The Call-Leader is written for the residents of Elwood, IN. It covers local news, sports, lifestyle, education, business and entertainment.
Language (s): English
Ad Rate: Full Page Mono 9.95
Ad Rate: Full Page Colour 159.95
Currency: United States Dollars
DAILY NEWSPAPER

Camden News 13686
Owner: Wehco Media Inc.
Editorial: 113 Madison Ave NE, Camden, Arkansas 71701-3514 **Tel:** 1 870 836-8192
Email: camdennews@camdenarknews.com **Web site:** http://www.camdenarknews.com
Freq: Daily; **Circ:** 4368 Not Audited
Editor: Kelly Blair; **Publisher:** Walter Hussman; **Advertising Sales Manager:** Sue Silliman
Profile: Camden News is a local daily newspaper serving Camden, AR. The newspaper covers local news, community events, weather and sports. It combines with the El Dorado (AR) News-Times and the Magnolia (AR) Banner-News on Sundays.
Language (s): English
Ad Rate: Full Page Mono 13.49
Ad Rate: Full Page Colour 45.93
Currency: United States Dollars
DAILY NEWSPAPER

The Cañon City Daily Record 13779
Owner: Lehman Communications Corp.
Editorial: 701 S 9th St, Canon City, Colorado 81212-4911 **Tel:** 1 719 275-7565
Web site: http://www.canoncitydailyrecord.com
Freq: Daily; **Circ:** 4882 Not Audited
Profile: Cañon City Daily Record publishes news for the residents of Fremont and Custard counties, CO. The newspaper covers local news, business, sports and arts & entertainment stories.
Language (s): English
Ad Rate: Full Page Mono 13.63
Currency: United States Dollars
DAILY NEWSPAPER

Cape Cod Times 14123
Owner: GateHouse Media Inc.
Editorial: 319 Main St, Hyannis, Massachusetts 02601-4037 **Tel:** 1 508 775-1200
Email: news@capecodonline.com **Web site:** http://www.capecodonline.com
Freq: Daily; **Circ:** 32527 Not Audited
Advertising Sales Manager: Lisa Maiden; **Publisher:** Peter Meyer; **Editor:** Paul Pronovost
Profile: Cape Cod Times is written for residents of Cape Cod, MA. The paper covers arts & entertainment, travel, technology, health and local news.
Language (s): English
Ad Rate: Full Page Mono 65.21
Ad Rate: Full Page Colour 206.22
Currency: United States Dollars
DAILY NEWSPAPER

Cape Cod Times - Orleans Bureau 62286
Editorial: 12 Main St, Orleans, Massachusetts 02653-2418 **Tel:** 1 508 255-0408
Language (s): English
DAILY NEWSPAPER

The Capital Gazette 14141
Owner: tronc
Editorial: 888 Bestgate Rd Ste 104, Annapolis, Maryland 21401-2950 **Tel:** 1 410 268-5000

Email: capstaff@capitalgazette.com **Web site:** http://www.capitalgazette.com
Freq: Daily; **Circ:** 29254 Not Audited
Editor: Rick Hutzell
Profile: The Capital is a daily newspaper serving the Annapolis, MD area. The publication dates back to the 18th century. The paper covers local news, sports, art & entertainment and business issues.
Language (s): English
Ad Rate: Full Page Mono 39.15
Ad Rate: Full Page Colour 129.99
Currency: United States Dollars
DAILY NEWSPAPER

Capital Journal 14655
Owner: Wick Communications Inc.
Editorial: 333 W Dakota Ave, Pierre, South Dakota 57501-4512 **Tel:** 1 605 224-7301
Email: news@capjournal.com **Web site:** http://www.capjournal.com
Freq: Mon thru Fri; **Circ:** 3903 Not Audited
Profile: Capital Journal is published daily for the residents of Pierre, SD and surrounding areas. The newspaper covers local news, sports, business and lifestyles. The paper is published 48 weeks out of the year.
Language (s): English
Ad Rate: Full Page Mono 9.63
Ad Rate: Full Page Colour 38.31
Currency: United States Dollars
DAILY NEWSPAPER

The Carmi Times 13917
Owner: GateHouse Media Inc.
Editorial: 323 E Main St, Carmi, Illinois 62821-1810 **Tel:** 1 618 382-4176
Email: carmitimes@clearwave.com **Web site:** http://www.carmitimes.com
Freq: Fri; **Circ:** 2735 Not Audited
Publisher: Kerry Kocher
Profile: The Carmi Times is a daily newspaper serving residents of Carmi, IL. The newspaper covers news, business, sports, entertainment and lifestyles.
Language (s): English
Ad Rate: Full Page Mono 12.99
Ad Rate: Full Page Colour 34.41
Currency: United States Dollars
DAILY NEWSPAPER

Carroll County Times 14148
Owner: tronc
Editorial: 115 Airport Dr Ste 170, Westminster, Maryland 21157-3056 **Tel:** 1 410 848-4400
Email: cctnews@carrollcountytimes.com **Web site:** http://www.carrollcountytimes.com
Freq: Daily; **Circ:** 20939 Not Audited
Profile: Carroll County Times is a daily newspaper serving the community of Carroll County, MD. The county has undergone a recent shift from an agricultural town to an affluent suburb of Baltimore and Washington, D.C. The paper focuses on local news and events but also covers some regional, national, and international news.
Language (s): English
Ad Rate: Full Page Mono 27.01
Ad Rate: Full Page Colour 635.00
Currency: United States Dollars
DAILY NEWSPAPER

The Carthage Press 14224
Owner: GateHouse Media Inc.
Editorial: 800 W Central Ave, Carthage, Missouri 64836-1023 **Tel:** 1 417 358-2422
Web site: http://www.carthagepress.com
Freq: Daily; **Circ:** 1000 Not Audited
Profile: Carthage Press is a daily newspaper distributed to the residents of Jasper County, MO. The paper focuses on local news and events but also includes some international news.
Language (s): English
Ad Rate: Full Page Mono 10.20
Ad Rate: Full Page Colour 68.70
Currency: United States Dollars
DAILY NEWSPAPER

Casa Grande Dispatch 13710
Owner: Kramer Publications
Editorial: 200 W 2Nd St, Casa Grande, Arizona 85122-4409 **Tel:** 1 520 836-7461
Email: ads@trivalleycentral.com **Web site:** http://www.trivalleycentral.com
Freq: Daily; **Circ:** 8568
Profile: Casa Grande Dispatch is a daily newspaper covering local news and events for residents of Casa Grande, AZ.
Language (s): English
Ad Rate: Full Page Mono 14.17
Ad Rate: Full Page Colour 52.27
Currency: United States Dollars
DAILY NEWSPAPER

Casper Star-Tribune 15423
Owner: Lee Enterprises, Inc.
Editorial: 170 Star Ln, Casper, Wyoming 82604-2883 **Tel:** 1 307 266-0520
Email: editors@trib.com **Web site:** http://www.trib.com
Freq: Daily; **Circ:** 23760 Not Audited
Profile: Casper Star-Tribune is a daily newspaper written for residents in Wyoming. The newspaper covers statewide news and events. The deadline is 7:30pm MT the day before publication.
Language (s): English
Ad Rate: Full Page Mono 41.96
Ad Rate: Full Page Colour 137.11
Currency: United States Dollars
DAILY NEWSPAPER

Cecil Whig 14875
Owner: Adams Publishing Group LLC
Editorial: 601 N Bridge St, Elkton, Maryland 21921-5307 **Tel:** 1 410 398-3311
Email: whigletters@chespub.com **Web site:** http://www.cecildaily.com
Freq: 3 Times/Week; **Circ:** 12756 Not Audited
Publisher: David Fike; **Advertising Sales Manager:** Renee Quietmeyer
Profile: Cecil Whig is a daily newspaper written for residents of Cecil County, MD. The publication covers local news, sports, features and community events.
Language (s): English
Ad Rate: Full Page Mono 22.95
Ad Rate: Full Page Colour 76.20
Currency: United States Dollars
DAILY NEWSPAPER

Cedar Valley Times 13894
Owner: Mid-America Publishing Corporation
Editorial: 108 E 5th St, Vinton, Iowa 52349-1759 **Tel:** 1 319 472-2311
Email: news@vintonnewspapers.com **Web site:** http://www.communitynewspapergroup.com/vinton_newspapers
Freq: Daily; **Circ:** 1200 Not Audited
Editor: Anelia Dimitrova; **Advertising Sales Manager:** Mona Garwood; **Publisher:** Deb Weigel
Profile: Cedar Valley Times is a daily community newspaper written for the residents of Vinton, IA and surrounding communities. The publication covers local news, events, sports and weather.
Language (s): English
Ad Rate: Full Page Mono 7.90
Ad Rate: Full Page Colour 35.90
Currency: United States Dollars
DAILY NEWSPAPER

Centre Daily Times 14618
Owner: McClatchy Newspapers
Editorial: 3400 E College Ave, State College, Pennsylvania 16801-7528 **Tel:** 1 814 238-5000
Email: communitynews@centredaily.com **Web site:** http://www.centredaily.com
Freq: Daily; **Circ:** 16921 Not Audited
Advertising Sales Manager: Diane Brown; **Editor:** Fran Jacobs
Profile: Centre Daily Times is a daily local newspaper written for residents of Centre County, PA. The newspaper covers local news, sports and events.
Language (s): English
Ad Rate: Full Page Mono 51.63
Ad Rate: Full Page Colour 221.00
Currency: United States Dollars
DAILY NEWSPAPER

The Chanute Tribune 14034
Owner: Family Media, Inc.
Editorial: 26 W Main St, Chanute, Kansas 66720-1701 **Tel:** 1 620 431-4100
Email: news@chanute.com **Web site:** http://www.chanute.com
Freq: Fri; **Circ:** 4100 Not Audited
Profile: Chanute Tribune is a daily newspaper published for the residents of Chanute, KS. The newspaper covers news, events and sports.
Language (s): English
Ad Rate: Full Page Mono 8.54
Ad Rate: Full Page Colour 28.59
Currency: United States Dollars
DAILY NEWSPAPER

Charles City Press 13870
Owner: Fortress Investment Group, LLC
Editorial: 801 Riverside Dr, Charles City, Iowa 50616-2248 **Tel:** 1 641 228-3211
Email: editor@charlescitypress.com **Web site:** http://www.charlescitypress.com
Freq: Daily; **Circ:** 3200 Not Audited
Advertising Sales Manager: Joel Gray; **Publisher:** Gene Hall
Profile: Charles City Press covers local news, sports and business in Charles City, IA.
Language (s): English
Ad Rate: Full Page Mono 13.42
Ad Rate: Full Page Colour 345.00
Currency: United States Dollars
DAILY NEWSPAPER

The Charleston Gazette-Mail 14830
Owner: Daily Gazette Co.
Editorial: 1001 Virginia St E, Charleston, West Virginia 25301-2816 **Tel:** 1 304 348-5100
Email: gazette@wvgazette.com **Web site:** http://www.wvgazettemail.com
Freq: Daily; **Circ:** 37384 Not Audited
Publisher: Elizabeth Chilton; **Advertising Sales Manager:** Jerry Rigs
Profile: On July 20, 2015, the Charleston Gazette combined with the Charleston Daily Mail to form the Charleston Gazette-Mail.The Gazette-Mail covers local news, sports, government, food and local industry news.
Language (s): English
Ad Rate: Full Page Mono 91.50
Ad Rate: Full Page Colour 96.85
Currency: United States Dollars
DAILY NEWSPAPER

The Charlotte Observer 15313
Owner: McClatchy Newspapers
Editorial: 550 S Caldwell St Fl 10, Charlotte, North Carolina 28202-2633 **Tel:** 1 704 358-5000
Email: localnews@charlotteobserver.com **Web site:** http://www.charlotteobserver.com
Freq: Daily; **Circ:** 106930 Not Audited

Profile: The Charlotte Observer is written for the general public in the greater Charlotte, NC area. The Business section is featured daily, covering local and national business stories, daily stock market rates, and real estate. Articles include features, breaking news, trends, analysis, profiles, and investigative stories. The paper asserts itself as being the only daily newspaper in America to win two Pulitzer Prizes for public service in the 1980s. It received a Pulitzer Prize in 1981 for reporting on brown-lung disease and the textile industry, and in 1988 for its coverage of Jim Bakker and the PTL.
Language (s): English
Ad Rate: Full Page Mono 361.00
Ad Rate: Full Page Colour 390.98
Currency: United States Dollars
DAILY NEWSPAPER

Charlotte Sun 13833
Owner: Sun Coast Media Group Inc.
Editorial: 23170 Harborview Rd, Port Charlotte, Florida 33980-2100 **Tel:** 1 941 206-1000
Email: feedback@sun-herald.com **Web site:** http://www.charlotte-sun.com
Freq: Daily; **Circ:** 28324 Not Audited
Publisher: David Dunn-Rankin; **Editor:** Phil Fernandez
Profile: Charlotte Sun is a daily newspaper serving the residents of Charlotte County, FL. It covers local and national news, business, sports, lifestyles and entertainment.
Language (s): English
Ad Rate: Full Page Mono 38.25
Ad Rate: Full Page Colour 49.25
Currency: United States Dollars
DAILY NEWSPAPER

Charlotte Sun 14941
Owner: Sun Coast Media Group Inc.
Editorial: 13487 Tamiami Trl, North Port, Florida 34287-1211 **Tel:** 1 941 429-3000
Web site: http://www.charlotte-sun.com/
Freq: Daily; **Circ:** 5500 Not Audited
Publisher: David Dunn-Rankin; **Advertising Sales Manager:** Glenn Nickerson
Profile: Charlotte Sun is a daily newspaper serving the local population of North Port, Fl. The newspaper includes coverage of local news events, business, lifestyle, real estate, and sports that impact the local readers. The publication is intended for readers in North Port, FL and surrounding communities.
Language (s): English
Ad Rate: Full Page Mono 12.95
Currency: United States Dollars
DAILY NEWSPAPER

Chattanooga Times Free Press 14661
Owner: Wehco Media Inc.
Editorial: 400 E 11th St, Chattanooga, Tennessee 37403-4203 **Tel:** 1 423 756-6900
Email: news@timesfreepress.com **Web site:** http://www.timesfreepress.com
Freq: Daily; **Circ:** 53130 Not Audited
Profile: Chattanooga Times Free Press is a local daily newspaper serving the city of Chattanooga, TN and the surrounding area. The publication covers local news, sports, business and community information.
Language (s): English
Ad Rate: Full Page Mono 63.91
Ad Rate: Full Page Colour 71.81
Currency: United States Dollars
DAILY NEWSPAPER

Chattanooga Times Free Press - Nashville Bureau 80633
Editorial: 28 Legislative Plaza, Nashville, Tennessee 37201 **Tel:** 1 615 255-0550
Language (s): English
DAILY NEWSPAPER

Cheboygan Tribune 14164
Owner: Fortress Investment Group, LLC
Editorial: 308 N Main St, Cheboygan, Michigan 49721-1545 **Tel:** 1 231 627-7144
Web site: http://www.cheboygannews.com
Freq: Daily; **Circ:** 4665 Not Audited
Editor: Richard Crofton; **Publisher:** Gary Lamberg
Profile: Cheboygan Tribune is a daily newspaper published for the residents of Cheboygan County, MI. The publication covers local news, sports, social issues, arts & entertainment, health, obituaries, community events and features.
Language (s): English
Ad Rate: Full Page Mono 11.50
Ad Rate: Full Page Colour 300.00
Currency: United States Dollars
DAILY NEWSPAPER

Cherokee Tribune 14968
Owner: Times Journal Inc.
Editorial: 521 E Main St, Canton, Georgia 30114-2805 **Tel:** 1 770 479-1441
Email: tribune@cherokeetribune.com **Web site:** http://tribuneledgernews.com
Freq: Fri; **Circ:** 4253 Not Audited
Publisher: Otis Brumby; **Advertising Sales Manager:** Kim Fowler
Profile: Cherokee Tribune is a local newspaper paper, published Wednesday through Sunday for the residents of Cherokee County, GA. It has four sections every day with four, full-color front pages. It provides readers with comprehensive local news and sports, as well as a new lifestyle section that focuses on food, religion, community events and neighbors. The Wednesday edition, called the Cherokee Tribune Plus, is sent to all nonsubscribers for free. Press releases can be sent by e-mail to the appropriate

editors. Only press releases containing information about Cherokee County are accepted. Advertising deadlines are at noon ET.
Language (s): English
Ad Rate: Full Page Mono 22.80
Ad Rate: Full Page Colour 450.00
Currency: United States Dollars
DAILY NEWSPAPER

Chesterton Tribune 13974
Owner: Chesterton Tribune, Inc.
Editorial: 193 S Calumet Rd, Chesterton, Indiana 46304-2433 **Tel:** 1 219 926-1131
Email: news@chestertontribune.com **Web site:** http://www.chestertontribune.com
Freq: Daily; **Circ:** 5000 Not Audited
Publisher: Warren Canright
Profile: Chesterton Tribune is published Monday through Friday for the residents of Chesterton, IN and surrounding areas. The newspaper covers local news, business, sports and community events. Deadlines for the editorial submissions are 5pm CT two days prior to the issue date.
Language (s): English
Ad Rate: Full Page Mono 7.00
Currency: United States Dollars
DAILY NEWSPAPER

Chicago Sun-Times 15361
Owner: ST Acquisition Holdings LLC
Editorial: 350 N Orleans St, Chicago, Illinois 60654-1975 **Tel:** 1 312 321-3000
Web site: http://chicago.suntimes.com
Freq: Daily; **Circ:** 129573 Not Audited
Editor: Bill Ruminski
Profile: Chicago Sun-Times is a daily newspaper offering news from international to local community news, sports, features, editorials, arts & entertainment, business and weather for the Chicago metro area.
Language (s): English
Ad Rate: Full Page Mono 277.67
Ad Rate: Full Page Colour 318.18
Currency: United States Dollars
DAILY NEWSPAPER

Chicago Sun-Times - Washington Bureau 15581
Editorial: 529 14th St NW Ste 1206, Washington, District Of Columbia 20045-2200 **Tel:** 1 202 662-8808
Bureau Chief: Lynn Sweet
Language (s): English
DAILY NEWSPAPER

Chicago Tribune 15284
Owner: tronc
Editorial: 435 N Michigan Ave, Chicago, Illinois 60611-4066 **Tel:** 1 312 222-3232
Email: tips@chicagotribune.com **Web site:** http://www.chicagotribune.com
Freq: Daily; **Circ:** 384962 Not Audited
Profile: Chicago Tribune covers local, regional, national and international news, as well as business, entertainment, lifestyle and sports. The paper was founded in 1847. Its editorial staff has won more than 24 Pulitzer Prizes. News is gathered at dozens of suburban, regional, national and foreign bureaus. In August 2009, Tribune Company formed a national sports content-sharing alliance between its properties, most notably between the Chicago Tribune and the Los Angeles Times. In October 2002, the paper launched its RedEye edition. This weekday tabloid is aimed at growing readership among young, urban professionals. In addition to reaching readers in print, the paper also operates related Web sites, including metromix.com, Chicago's complete entertainment guide; ChicagoSports.com, a comprehensive local sports site; and dogood.chicagotribune.com, a site linking Chicagoans with volunteer work.
Language (s): English
Ad Rate: Full Page Mono 667.00
Ad Rate: Full Page Colour 733.70
Currency: United States Dollars
DAILY NEWSPAPER

Chicago Tribune - Northlake Bureau 16089
Editorial: 505 Northwest Ave, Northlake, Illinois 60164-1662 **Tel:** 1 847 755-8911
Email: ctc-northwest@chicagotribune.com
Bureau Chief: Diana Wallace
Language (s): English
DAILY NEWSPAPER

Chicago Tribune - Springfield Bureau 15710
Editorial: 207 State House, Springfield, Illinois 62706 **Tel:** 1 217 782-4523
Language (s): English
DAILY NEWSPAPER

Chicago Tribune - Tinley Park Bureau 16167
Editorial: 18450 Crossing Dr, Tinley Park, Illinois 60487-9279 **Tel:** 1 708 342-5600
Email: ctc-southwest@chicagotribune.com
Bureau Chief: Patrick Regan
Language (s): English
DAILY NEWSPAPER

Chicago Tribune - Vernon Hills Bureau 16114
Editorial: 616 Atrium Dr Ste 200, Vernon Hills, Illinois 60061-1713 **Tel:** 1 847 918-2800

Email: ctc-northshore@chicagotribune.com
Language (s): English
DAILY NEWSPAPER

Chicago Tribune - Westchester Bureau 16068
Editorial: 3 Westbrook Corporate Ctr, Westchester, Illinois 60154-5703
Bureau Chief: Peter Hernon
Language (s): English
DAILY NEWSPAPER

Chico Enterprise-Record 13721
Owner: MediaNews Group
Editorial: 400 E Park Ave, Chico, California 95928-7127 **Tel:** 1 530 891-1234
Email: localnews@chicoer.com **Web site:** http://www.chicoer.com
Freq: Daily; **Circ:** 28695 Not Audited
Profile: Chico Enterprise-Record is a daily local newspaper serving residents in Butte County, CA and surrounding counties. The newspaper covers local and national news, lifestyle, sports, and arts and entertainment.
Language (s): English
Ad Rate: Full Page Mono 67.03
Ad Rate: Full Page Colour 600.00
Currency: United States Dollars
DAILY NEWSPAPER

Chillicothe Constitution-Tribune 14225
Owner: GateHouse Media Inc.
Editorial: 818 Washington St, Chillicothe, Missouri 64601-2232 **Tel:** 1 660 646-2411
Email: ctnews@chillicothenews.com **Web site:** http://www.chillicothenews.com
Freq: Daily; **Circ:** 3525 Not Audited
Editor: Laura Schuler
Profile: Chillicothe Constitution-Tribune is a local newspaper serving the residents of Livingston County, MO. The publication covers local news, sports and community events.
Language (s): English
Ad Rate: Full Page Mono 7.90
Ad Rate: Full Page Colour 160.00
Currency: United States Dollars
DAILY NEWSPAPER

Chillicothe Gazette 14443
Owner: Gannett Co., Inc.
Editorial: 50 W Main St, Chillicothe, Ohio 45601-3103 **Tel:** 1 740 773-2111
Email: gaznews@nncogannett.com **Web site:** http://www.chillicothegazette.com
Freq: Daily; **Circ:** 7714 Not Audited
Profile: Chillicothe Gazette is a daily local newspaper serving the residents in Pike, Chillicothe, and Ross Counties, OH. The publication covers local news and community events. The editorial mission is to supply their readers with current news.
Language (s): English
Ad Rate: Full Page Mono 4.55
Ad Rate: Full Page Colour 20.43
Currency: United States Dollars
DAILY NEWSPAPER

China Daily - Issy-Les-Moulineaux Bureau 830280
Editorial: 90 rue du Gouverneur General Eboue, Issy-Les-Moulineaux 92130 **Tel:** 33 1 82159686
Language (s): English
DAILY NEWSPAPER

China Daily (U.S. Edition) 584002
Owner: China Daily Distribution Corporation
Editorial: 1500 Broadway Ste 2800, New York, New York 10036-4097 **Tel:** 1 212 537-8888
Email: editor@chinadailyusa.com **Web site:** http://usa.chinadaily.com.cn
Freq: Mon thru Fri; **Circ:** 180000
National & International News Editor: William Hennelly
Profile: The U.S. Edition of China Daily is a tailor-made version of China Daily, China's national English-language newspaper, for North American readers. The paper launched in 2009 and is published Monday through Friday, providing a window into China with the Chinese perspective on major financial, political and social issues affecting China and the United States today. The U.S. Edition features reporting on Chinese business, politics, society, and culture from both sides of the Pacific.
Language (s): English
DAILY NEWSPAPER

China Press 79929
Editorial: 2121 W Mission Rd, Alhambra, California 91803-1420 **Tel:** 1 626 281-8500
Email: reporter@cpwc.com **Web site:** http://la.uschinapress.com
Freq: Daily; **Circ:** 30000 Not Audited
Advertising Sales Manager: Qing Lin; **Publisher & Editor:** Xiaodong Liu; **Editor:** Di Shen Wang
Profile: China Press is a newspaper serving the Chinese and Chinese American community.
Language (s): Chinese
Ad Rate: Full Page Mono 40.00
Currency: United States Dollars
DAILY NEWSPAPER

China Press 152839
Owner: Pacific Culture Enterprise
Editorial: 15 E 40th St, New York, New York 10016-0401 **Tel:** 1 212 683-8282
Email: news@chinapress.net **Web site:** http://www.uschinapress.com
Freq: Daily; **Circ:** 40000 Not Audited
Advertising Sales Manager: Sam Guo
Profile: China Press was founded on Jan. 5, 1990. The number one goal of the paper has always been to best serve the interests of Chinese Americans living in the United States.
Language (s): Chinese
Ad Rate: Full Page Mono 240.00
Currency: United States Dollars
DAILY NEWSPAPER

The Chippewa Herald 14801
Owner: Lee Enterprises, Inc.
Editorial: 321 Frenette Dr, Chippewa Falls, Wisconsin 54729-3372 **Tel:** 1 715 723-5515
Email: news@chippewa.com **Web site:** http://www.chippewa.com
Freq: Daily; **Circ:** 4049 Not Audited
Profile: The Chippewa Herald is a daily local newspaper serving residents of Chippewa County, WI. The publication covers local news and community events.
Language (s): English
Ad Rate: Full Page Mono 15.42
Ad Rate: Full Page Colour 225.00
Currency: United States Dollars
DAILY NEWSPAPER

The Chronicle 13810
Owner: Crosbie (Kevin)
Editorial: 1 Chronicle Rd, Willimantic, Connecticut 06226-1932 **Tel:** 1 860 423-8466
Email: news@thechronicle.com **Web site:** http://www.thechronicle.com
Freq: Daily; **Circ:** 8940 Not Audited
Advertising Sales Manager: Jean Beckley; **Editor:** Charles Ryan
Profile: The Chronicle is a daily newspaper published for residents of Willimantic, CT. It covers local events, sports and community news.
Language (s): English
Ad Rate: Full Page Mono 30.15
Ad Rate: Full Page Colour 350.00
Currency: United States Dollars
DAILY NEWSPAPER

The Chronicle 14782
Owner: Lafromboise Newspapers, Inc.
Editorial: 321 N Pearl St, Centralia, Washington 98531 **Tel:** 1 360 736-3311
Web site: http://www.chronline.com
Freq: Daily; **Circ:** 13912 Not Audited
Profile: The Chronicle is a daily local newspaper written for residents of Lewis County, WA. The newspaper covers local news, sports, lifestyle, police and courts, education and business.
Language (s): English
Ad Rate: Full Page Mono 16.25
Ad Rate: Full Page Colour 82.14
Currency: United States Dollars
DAILY NEWSPAPER

The Chronicle News 13795
Editorial: 200 Church St, Trinidad, Colorado 81082-2603 **Tel:** 1 719 846-3311
Web site: http://www.trinidadchroniclenews.com
Freq: Daily; **Circ:** 2200 Not Audited
Editor: Eric Monson; **Publisher:** Tom Shearman
Profile: The Chronicle News serves the residents of Trinidad, CO, The paper aims to provide up-to-date information and reports on local news, national news and community events.
Language (s): English
Ad Rate: Full Page Mono 11.13
Ad Rate: Full Page Colour 100.00
Currency: United States Dollars
DAILY NEWSPAPER

Chronicle Times 13871
Owner: Rust Communications
Editorial: 111 S 2nd St, Cherokee, Iowa 51012-1839 **Tel:** 1 712 225-5111
Email: editor@ctimes.biz **Web site:** http://www.chronicletimes.com
Freq: Fri; **Circ:** 6000 Not Audited
Publisher: Randy List
Profile: Chronicle Times, formerly Cherokee Daily Times, offers coverage of local news, sports and entertainment to the residents of Cherokee County, IA.
Language (s): English
Ad Rate: Full Page Mono 11.00
Ad Rate: Full Page Colour 35.09
Currency: United States Dollars
DAILY NEWSPAPER

The Chronicle-Telegram 14450
Owner: Lorain County Printing & Publishing
Editorial: 225 East Ave, Elyria, Ohio 44035-5634 **Tel:** 1 440 329-7000
Email: ctnews@chroniclet.com **Web site:** http://www.chroniclet.com
Freq: Daily; **Circ:** 23754 Not Audited
Publisher: A. Cooper Hudnutt; **News Editor:** Ben Nagy; **Advertising Sales Manager:** Jeff Pfeiffer; **Editor:** Andy Young
Profile: The Chronicle-Telegram brings local news to the tri-county area of Elyria, OH.
Language (s): English
Ad Rate: Full Page Mono 33.65
Ad Rate: Full Page Colour 300.00
Currency: United States Dollars
DAILY NEWSPAPER

Chronicle-Tribune 14001
Owner: Paxton Media Group
Editorial: 610 S Adams St, Marion, Indiana 46953-2041 **Tel:** 1 765 664-5111
Email: ctreport@indy.rr.com **Web site:** http://www.chronicle-tribune.com
Freq: Daily; **Circ:** 8201 Not Audited
Editor: David Penticuff
Profile: Chronicle Tribune is published daily for the residents of Grant County, IN. The newspaper provides information about local news, sports, entertainment and community events. Editorial deadlines are one day prior to issue date at noon ET.
Language (s): English
Ad Rate: Full Page Mono 18.00
Currency: United States Dollars
DAILY NEWSPAPER

The Cincinnati Enquirer 15377
Owner: Gannett Co., Inc.
Editorial: 312 Elm St, Cincinnati, Ohio 45202-2739 **Tel:** 1 513 721-2700
Email: localnews@enquirer.com **Web site:** http://www.cincinnati.com
Freq: Daily; **Circ:** 104354 Not Audited
Profile: The Cincinnati Enquirer is a broadsheet newspaper that covers local, national and world news. It is distributed to the eight counties in the greater Cincinnati area.
Language (s): English
Ad Rate: Full Page Mono 371.57
Ad Rate: Full Page Colour 433.23
Currency: United States Dollars
DAILY NEWSPAPER

The Cincinnati Enquirer - Columbus Bureau 15869
Editorial: 34 S 3rd St, Columbus, Ohio 43215-4201 **Tel:** 1 614 224-4640
Language (s): English
DAILY NEWSPAPER

The Cincinnati Enquirer - West Chester Bureau 16092
Owner: Gannett Co., Inc.
Editorial: 7700 Service Center Dr, West Chester, Ohio 45069-2442 **Tel:** 1 513 248-7111
Email: localnews@enquirer.com
Profile: This is the West Chester, OH bureau of The Cincinnati Enquirer.
Language (s): English
DAILY NEWSPAPER

The Circleville Herald 14444
Owner: American Consolidated Media
Editorial: 120 Watt St, Circleville, Ohio 43113-1747 **Tel:** 1 740 474-3131
Email: news@circlevilleherald.com **Web site:** http://www.circlevilletoday.com/
Freq: Daily; **Circ:** 7048 Not Audited
Profile: The Circleville Herald is a daily newspaper published for the residents of Circleville County, OH. The newspaper covers local news, sports, entertainment and business.
Language (s): English
Ad Rate: Full Page Mono 9.80
Currency: United States Dollars
DAILY NEWSPAPER

The Citizen 14391
Owner: Lee Publications, Inc.
Editorial: 25 Dill St, Auburn, New York 13021-3605 **Tel:** 1 315 253-5311
Email: citizennews@lee.net **Web site:** http://www.auburnpub.com
Freq: Daily; **Circ:** 6903
Publisher: Rob Forcey; **Advertising Sales Manager:** Tom Kirkwood
Profile: The Citizen is a daily newspaper serving the residents of Auburn, NY and the surrounding areas. It covers national, regional and local news, sports, weather, community events, public announcements and features.
Language (s): English
Ad Rate: Full Page Mono 23.33
Ad Rate: Full Page Colour 26.78
Currency: United States Dollars
DAILY NEWSPAPER

Citizen Tribune 14674
Owner: Lakeway Publishers, Inc.
Editorial: 1609 W 1st North St, Morristown, Tennessee 37814-3724 **Tel:** 1 423 581-5630
Email: ctmaned@lcs.net **Web site:** http://www.citizentribune.com
Freq: Daily; **Circ:** 18727 Not Audited
Publisher: Mike Fishman
Profile: Citizen Tribune is a local daily newspaper written for residents in the seven county area of Tennessee. The editorial mission is to deliver local and national news.
Language (s): English
Ad Rate: Full Page Mono 18.55
Ad Rate: Full Page Colour 450.00
Currency: United States Dollars
DAILY NEWSPAPER

The Citizens Voice 14630
Owner: Times-Shamrock Communications
Editorial: 75 N Washington St, Wilkes-Barre, Pennsylvania 18701 **Tel:** 1 570 821-2000
Email: citydesk@citizensvoice.com **Web site:** http://www.citizensvoice.com
Freq: Daily; **Circ:** 22873 Not Audited
Profile: The Citizens Voice is a local daily newspaper written for residents of Luzerne County, PA. The newspaper covers local news, sports, travel and events. The deadline for the newspaper falls at 7pm ET.
Language (s): English
Ad Rate: Full Page Mono 39.20
Ad Rate: Full Page Colour 335.20
Currency: United States Dollars
DAILY NEWSPAPER

Citrus County Chronicle 13831
Owner: Landmark Community Newspapers, Inc.
Editorial: 1624 N Meadowcrest Blvd, Crystal River, Florida 34429-8751 **Tel:** 1 352 563-6363
Email: newsdesk@chronicleonline.com **Web site:** http://www.chronicleonline.com
Freq: Daily; **Circ:** 21692 Not Audited
Editor: Michael Arnold; **Editor:** Matt Beck;
Publisher: Gerald Mulligan
Profile: Citrus County Chronicle is a daily newspaper serving the residents of Crystal River, FL.
Language (s): English
Ad Rate: Full Page Mono 38.73
Ad Rate: Full Page Colour 470.00
Currency: United States Dollars
DAILY NEWSPAPER

Clanton Advertiser 18538
Owner: Boone Newspapers Inc.
Editorial: 1109 7th St N, Clanton, Alabama 35045-2113 **Tel:** 1 205 755-5747
Email: newsroom@clantonadvertiser.com **Web site:** http://www.clantonadvertiser.com
Freq: Fri; **Circ:** 12100 Not Audited
Publisher: Tim Prince
Profile: Clanton Advertiser is a daily newspaper published for the residents of Clanton, AL. The newspaper covers local news and information. Please send all correspondence to the PO Box.
Language (s): English
Ad Rate: Full Page Mono 12.70
Currency: United States Dollars
DAILY NEWSPAPER

Claremore Daily Progress 14515
Owner: Community Newspaper Holdings, Inc.
Editorial: 315 W Will Rogers Blvd, Claremore, Oklahoma 74017-7021 **Tel:** 1 918 341-1101
Email: editor@claremoreprogress.com **Web site:** http://claremoreprogress.com
Freq: Daily; **Circ:** 6158 Not Audited
Editor & Publisher: John Dilmore; **Editor:** Tom Fink
Profile: Claremore Daily Progress is published daily for the residents of Claremore, OK and surrounding areas. The newspaper covers local and state news, sports, business, lifestyles and entertainment.
Language (s): English
Ad Rate: Full Page Mono 9.74
Ad Rate: Full Page Colour 1221.69
Currency: United States Dollars
DAILY NEWSPAPER

The Clarion-Ledger 14935
Owner: Gannett Co., Inc.
Editorial: 201 S Congress St, Jackson, Mississippi 39201-4202 **Tel:** 1 601 961-7000
Web site: http://www.clarionledger.com
Freq: Daily; **Circ:** 42584 Not Audited
Profile: The Clarion-Ledger is a daily newspaper covering news in Jackson, MS, and the surrounding areas with an emphasis on breaking events, local and state government, health, education, environment, business, finance, consumer issues and sports.
Language (s): English
Ad Rate: Full Page Mono 180.35
Ad Rate: Full Page Colour 547.45
Currency: United States Dollars
DAILY NEWSPAPER

Clay Center Dispatch 14035
Owner: Clay Center Publishing Co.
Editorial: 805 5th St, Clay Center, Kansas 67432-2502 **Tel:** 1 785 632-2127
Email: dispatch@claycenter.com **Web site:** http://www.ccenterdispatch.com
Freq: Mon thru Fri; **Circ:** 3900 Not Audited
Editor: Dave Berggren; **Editor:** Kay Ouellette;
Advertising Sales Manager: Hilary Thompson;
Editor: Ned Valentine; **Editor:** Ryan Wilson
Profile: Clay Center Dispatch is a daily local newspaper published for residents of Clay County, KS. The paper covers local news, weather and sports.
Language (s): English
Ad Rate: Full Page Mono 6.90
Ad Rate: Full Page Colour 80.00
Currency: United States Dollars
DAILY NEWSPAPER

Clayton News Daily 13845
Owner: Southern Community Newspapers Inc.
Editorial: 138 Church St, Jonesboro, Georgia 30236-3514 **Tel:** 1 770 478-5753
Email: news@news-daily.com **Web site:** http://www.news-daily.com
Freq: Daily; **Circ:** 6625 Not Audited
Profile: Clayton News Daily is a daily newspaper that covers local news, business, sports and community news in Clayton County, GA. It combines with the Daily Herald in McDonough, GA on Saturdays.
Language (s): English
Ad Rate: Full Page Mono 17.50
Ad Rate: Full Page Colour 320.00
Currency: United States Dollars
DAILY NEWSPAPER

Cleburne Times-Review 14691
Owner: Community Newspaper Holdings, Inc.
Editorial: 108 S Anglin St, Cleburne, Texas 76031-5602 **Tel:** 1 817 645-2441

Email: editor@trcle.com **Web site:** http://www.cleburnetimesreview.com
Freq: Mon thru Fri; **Circ:** 6443 Not Audited
News Editor: Monica Faram
Profile: Cleburne Times-Review is a local daily newspaper written for the residents of Cleburne and Johnson County, TX. Topics that do not directly pertain to the local residents are very rarely published. Deadlines are at noon CT, the day before issue date.
Language (s): English
Ad Rate: Full Page Mono 13.15
Ad Rate: Full Page Colour 380.00
Currency: United States Dollars
DAILY NEWSPAPER

Cleveland Daily Banner 14663
Owner: Cleveland Newspapers Inc.
Editorial: 1505 25th St NW, Cleveland, Tennessee 37311-3610 **Tel:** 1 423 472-5041
Email: news@clevelandbanner.com **Web site:** http://www.clevelandbanner.com
Freq: Daily; **Circ:** 11427 Not Audited
Profile: Cleveland Daily Banner is a local daily newspaper written for the residents of Cleveland, TN. The newspaper covers the local news of the Cleveland, TN area. The lead time is two to three days.
Language (s): English
Ad Rate: Full Page Mono 11.00
Ad Rate: Full Page Colour 300.00
Currency: United States Dollars
DAILY NEWSPAPER

Clinton Daily Democrat 14226
Owner: Democrat Publishing Co., Inc.
Editorial: 212 S Washington St, Clinton, Missouri 64735-2073 **Tel:** 1 660 885-2281
Email: ddem.news@embarqmail.com
Freq: Daily; **Circ:** 4000 Not Audited
Profile: Clinton Daily Democrat is a daily local newspaper written for the residents of Henry County, MO. Coverage includes local news and events, sports, business and social issues. The deadline is noon CT the day prior to issue date.
Language (s): English
Ad Rate: Full Page Mono 5.75
Ad Rate: Full Page Colour 70.00
Currency: United States Dollars
DAILY NEWSPAPER

Clinton Daily News 14516
Owner: Clinton Daily News Co.
Editorial: 522 Avant Ave, Clinton, Oklahoma 73601-3436 **Tel:** 1 580 323-5151
Email: cdnews@swbell.net **Web site:** http://www.clintondailynews.com
Freq: Daily; **Circ:** 5218 Not Audited
Advertising Sales Manager: Chris Crabtree; **Editor:** Gerald Green; **Publisher & Editor:** Rod Serfoss; **Editor:** Sean Stephens
Profile: Clinton Daily News is published daily for the residents of Clinton, OK and surrounding areas. The newspaper covers local and state news, sports, lifestyles and entertainment. Deadlines are at 1pm CT one day prior to issue date.
Language (s): English
Ad Rate: Full Page Mono 9.26
Ad Rate: Full Page Colour 100.00
Currency: United States Dollars
DAILY NEWSPAPER

Clinton Herald 13872
Owner: Community Newspaper Holdings, Inc.
Editorial: 221 6th Ave S, Clinton, Iowa 52732-4305 **Tel:** 1 563 242-7101
Email: news@clintonherald.com **Web site:** http://www.clintonherald.com
Freq: Mon thru Fri; **Circ:** 7790
Editor: Charlene Bielema
Profile: Clinton Herald is a daily newspaper written for the community of Clinton, IA. The newspaper covers local news, business, sports and arts & entertainment.
Language (s): English
Ad Rate: Full Page Mono 17.90
Currency: United States Dollars
DAILY NEWSPAPER

The Clinton-Graceville Northern Star 836276
Tel: 1 320 325-5152
Email: northernstar@mchsi.com
Profile: Provides news for the residents of Clinton and Graceville, MN.
Language (s): English
DAILY NEWSPAPER

Clovis News Journal 14373
Owner: Freedom Communications Inc.
Editorial: 521 Pile St, Clovis, New Mexico 88101-6637 **Tel:** 1 575 763-3431
Web site: http://cnjonline.com
Freq: Daily; **Circ:** 7050 Not Audited
News Editor: Robin Fornoff; **Editor:** David Stevens
Profile: Clovis News Journal is a local daily newspaper written for residents of Clovis, NM. The main topics covered are local news, sports and area features.
Language (s): English
Ad Rate: Full Page Mono 12.85
Ad Rate: Full Page Colour 1533.55
Currency: United States Dollars
DAILY NEWSPAPER

Coeur d'Alene Press 13900
Owner: Hagadone Corp.
Editorial: 201 N 2nd St, Coeur D Alene, Idaho 83814-2803 **Tel:** 1 208 664-8176
Email: news@cdapress.com **Web site:** http://www.cdapress.com
Freq: Daily; **Circ:** 24012 Not Audited
Profile: Coeur d'Alene Press is a daily newspaper published for the residents of Coeur d'Alene, ID. The publication features articles about local news, business, sports, and arts & entertainment.
Language (s): English
Ad Rate: Full Page Mono 32.67
Ad Rate: Full Page Colour 209.00
Currency: United States Dollars
DAILY NEWSPAPER

Coffeyville Journal 14036
Owner: Sumner Newspapers Inc.
Editorial: 302 W 8th St, Coffeyville, Kansas 67337-5829 **Tel:** 1 620 251-3300
Email: coffeyville1@gmail.com
Freq: Mon thru Fri; **Circ:** 3500 Not Audited
Publisher & Editor: Bethany Bunch; **Advertising Sales Manager:** Billy Noel
Profile: Coffeyville Journal provides community news for residents of Coffeyville, KS. The paper covers local and national news.
Language (s): English
Ad Rate: Full Page Mono 9.67
Ad Rate: Full Page Colour 62.20
Currency: United States Dollars
DAILY NEWSPAPER

Colby Free Press 14071
Owner: Haynes Publishing Company
Editorial: 155 W 5th St, Colby, Kansas 67701-2312 **Tel:** 1 785 462-3963
Email: colby.editor@nwkansas.com **Web site:** http://www.nwkansas.com/cfpwebpages/cfpmain.html
Freq: Daily; **Circ:** 2046 Not Audited
Publisher: Sharon Friedlander
Profile: Colby Free Press is a local daily newspaper written for the residents of Thomas County, KS which covers Colby, Brewster and Rexford, KS. The focus of the newspaper is on local news and events in Thomas County, KS. The Colby Free Press is published daily Monday through Friday.
Language (s): English
Ad Rate: Full Page Mono 7.95
Ad Rate: Full Page Colour 99.00
Currency: United States Dollars
DAILY NEWSPAPER

Columbia Basin Herald 14786
Owner: Hagadone Corp.
Editorial: 813 W 3rd Ave, Moses Lake, Washington 98837-2008 **Tel:** 1 509 765-4561
Email: editor@columbiabasinherald.com **Web site:** http://www.columbiabasinherald.com
Freq: Mon thru Fri; **Circ:** 8200 Not Audited
Publisher: Harlan Beagley
Profile: Columbia Basin Herald is a daily paper that provides the community with local news and information affecting the Columbia Basin area of Washington. Coverage includes sports, business, education and entertainment.
Language (s): English
Ad Rate: Full Page Mono 17.80
Ad Rate: Full Page Colour 60.60
Currency: United States Dollars
DAILY NEWSPAPER

Columbia Daily Tribune 14228
Owner: GateHouse Media Inc.
Editorial: 101 N 4th St, Columbia, Missouri 65201-4416 **Tel:** 1 573 815-1500 5
Web site: http://www.columbiatribune.com
Freq: Daily; **Circ:** 16429
Profile: Columbia Daily Tribune is published daily for the residents of Columbia, MO and the surrounding areas. The newspaper provides local and national news coverage, sports and features. Deadlines are at 11am CT one day prior to issue date.
Language (s): English
Ad Rate: Full Page Mono 15.00
Ad Rate: Full Page Colour 410.00
Currency: United States Dollars
DAILY NEWSPAPER

Columbia Missourian 14227
Owner: Missourian Publishing Association
Editorial: 221 S 8th St, Columbia, Missouri 65201-4868 **Tel:** 1 573 882-5700
Email: editor@columbiamissourian.com **Web site:** http://www.columbiamissourian.com
Freq: Fri; **Circ:** 5771 Not Audited
Editor: Phill Brooks; **Publisher:** Dean Mills; **Editor:** Scott Swafford; **Advertising Sales Manager:** Jack Swartz
Profile: Columbia Missourian is a daily newspaper published by the Missourian Publishing Association, which is affiliated with the University of Missouri. It provides state and local news, sports and campus news and events for readers in Columbia, MO and the surrounding area.
Language (s): English
Ad Rate: Full Page Mono 8.80
Ad Rate: Full Page Colour 9.90
Currency: United States Dollars
DAILY NEWSPAPER

The Columbian 15421
Owner: Columbian Publishing Co.
Editorial: 701 W 8th St, Vancouver, Washington 98660-3008 **Tel:** 1 360 694-3391
Email: metrodesk@columbian.com **Web site:** http://columbian.com
Freq: Daily; **Circ:** 45505 Not Audited
Editor: Lou Brancaccio; **Publisher:** Scott Campbell; **Editor:** Greg Jayne
Profile: The Columbian is a daily newspaper published for residents of Clark County, WA. Coverage includes local news, sports and general lifestyle stories.
Language (s): English
Ad Rate: Full Page Mono 63.50
Ad Rate: Full Page Colour 222.24
Currency: United States Dollars
DAILY NEWSPAPER

The Columbus Dispatch 15303
Owner: GateHouse Media Inc.
Editorial: 62 E Broad St, Columbus, Ohio 43215-3500 **Tel:** 1 614 461-5000
Email: storyideas@dispatch.com **Web site:** http://www.dispatch.com
Freq: Daily; **Circ:** 115063 Not Audited
National News Editor: Danny Goodwin; **Advertising Sales Manager:** Laura Hammett; **Editor:** Alan Miller
Profile: Columbus Dispatch is a daily newspaper serving Columbus, Ohio that covers regional as well as national and international news. Regular sections include features, business, international and national news and metropolitan Columbus news. Business coverage focuses on local business, personal finance, construction, manufacturing, banking and finance, insurance, retailers, automakers. Business coverage is featured daily and Sunday in the business pages.
Language (s): English
Ad Rate: Full Page Mono 319.31
Ad Rate: Full Page Colour 330.38
Currency: United States Dollars
DAILY NEWSPAPER

The Columbus Dispatch - Delaware Bureau 133750
Owner: GateHouse Media Inc.
Editorial: 2 W Winter St Ste 305, Delaware, Ohio 43015-1965 **Tel:** 1 740 363-0861
Email: storyideas@dispatch.com
Profile: This is the Delaware, OH bureau of The Columbus (OH) Dispatch.
Language (s): English
DAILY NEWSPAPER

The Columbus Dispatch - Lancaster Bureau 133751
Owner: GateHouse Media Inc.
Editorial: 117 W Main St Ste 105, Lancaster, Ohio 43130-3799 **Tel:** 1 740 653-3520
Email: storyideas@dispatch.com
Profile: This is the Lancaster, OH bureau of The Columbus (OH) Dispatch.
Language (s): English
DAILY NEWSPAPER

The Columbus Dispatch - Newark Bureau 133747
Owner: GateHouse Media Inc.
Editorial: 23 1/2 S Park Pl Ste 205, Newark, Ohio 43055-5500 **Tel:** 1 740 345-3688
Email: storyideas@dispatch.com **Web site:** http://www.dispatch.com
Profile: This is the Newark, OH bureau of The Columbus (OH) Dispatch.
Language (s): English
DAILY NEWSPAPER

The Columbus Dispatch - Washington Bureau 15501
Owner: GateHouse Media Inc.
Editorial: 400 N Capitol St NW Ste 750, Washington, District Of Columbia 20001-1536
Washington Bureau Chief: Jack Torry
Language (s): English
DAILY NEWSPAPER

Columbus Ledger-Enquirer 15394
Owner: McClatchy Newspapers
Editorial: 17 W 12th St, Columbus, Georgia 31901-5254 **Tel:** 1 706 324-5526
Email: newsroom@ledger-enquirer.com **Web site:** http://www.ledger-enquirer.com
Freq: Daily; **Circ:** 28283 Not Audited
Profile: Columbus Ledger-Enquirer is a daily newspaper serving Columbus, GA and surrounding communities. The paper covers local news, national news, sports, family, health, home, garden, business and entertainment.
Language (s): English
Ad Rate: Full Page Mono 69.25
Ad Rate: Full Page Colour 225.95
Currency: United States Dollars
DAILY NEWSPAPER

Columbus Telegram 14338
Owner: Lee Enterprises, Inc.
Editorial: 1254 27th Ave, Columbus, Nebraska 68601-5656 **Tel:** 1 402 564-2741
Web site: http://www.columbustelegram.com
Freq: Mon thru Fri; **Circ:** 7156 Not Audited
Editor: Tyler Ellyson
Profile: Columbus Telegram is dedicated to providing the latest news, sports and advertising to its readers. Since 1879, the paper has delivered news and shopping information to the homes and businesses of East-central Nebraska. Do not send them anything via e-mail.
Language (s): English
Ad Rate: Full Page Mono 14.23
Ad Rate: Full Page Colour 292.00
Currency: United States Dollars
DAILY NEWSPAPER

The Commercial Appeal 15337
Owner: Gannett Co., Inc.
Editorial: 495 Union Ave, Memphis, Tennessee 38103-3217 **Tel:** 1 901 529-2345
Web site: http://www.commercialappeal.com
Freq: Daily; **Circ:** 69866 Not Audited
Profile: The Commercial Appeal is published daily for the residents of Memphis, TN and surrounding areas. The newspaper covers local, national and international news, business, sports, arts & entertainment, technology and stock market listings. The Memphis Commercial (founded in 1889), The Appeal (founded in 1841) and The Avalanche (founded in 1867) consolidated into The Commercial Appeal in 1894.
Language (s): English
Ad Rate: Full Page Mono 284.85
Currency: United States Dollars
DAILY NEWSPAPER

Commercial Dispatch 14260
Owner: Imes Jr. (Birney)
Editorial: 516 Main St, Columbus, Mississippi 39701 **Tel:** 1 662 328-2424
Email: news@cdispatch.com **Web site:** http://www.cdispatch.com
Freq: Daily; **Circ:** 12184 Not Audited
Editor: Adam Minichino; **Advertising Sales Manager:** Beth Proffitt
Profile: Commercial Dispatch provides local news coverage for the Columbus, MS area. It is an afternoon paper which is published daily with the exception of Saturday.
Language (s): English
Ad Rate: Full Page Mono 12.90
Ad Rate: Full Page Colour 200.00
Currency: United States Dollars
DAILY NEWSPAPER

Commercial Recorder 778710
Owner: Ratcliff Publications, Inc.
Editorial: 3032 S Jones St, Fort Worth, Texas 76104-6747 **Tel:** 1 817 926-5351
Email: recorder@flash.net **Web site:** http://www.comlrec1.site.aplus.net
Freq: Mon thru Fri
Publisher: Genevieve Ratcliff
Profile: The Commercial Recorder is a daily newspaper providing current court and commercial information. It provides up-to-date court records, public notices, legal transactions, and business leads and business news each weekday.
Language (s): English
Ad Rate: Full Page Mono 8.20
Currency: United States Dollars
DAILY NEWSPAPER

The Commercial Review 14011
Owner: Graphic Printing Company Inc.
Editorial: 309 W Main St, Portland, Indiana 47371-1803 **Tel:** 1 260 726-8141
Email: news@thecr.com **Web site:** http://www.thecr.com
Freq: Daily; **Circ:** 5000
Advertising Sales Manager: Jeanne Lutz; **Publisher & Editor:** Jack Ronald
Profile: The Commercial Review is published for the residents of Portland, IN and surrounding areas. The newspaper covers local and state news, business, sports, education, lifestyles and entertainment.
Language (s): English
Ad Rate: Full Page Mono 9.25
Ad Rate: Full Page Colour 255.00
Currency: United States Dollars
DAILY NEWSPAPER

Commercial-News 13923
Owner: Community Newspaper Holdings, Inc.
Editorial: 17 W North St, Danville, Illinois 61832-5796 **Tel:** 1 217 446-1000
Email: info@dancomnews.com **Web site:** http://commercial-news.com
Freq: Daily; **Circ:** 10182
Editor: Larry Smith
Profile: Commercial-News is published daily for the residents of Danville, IL and surrounding areas. The newspaper covers local and regional news, business, sports, lifestyles and entertainment.
Language (s): English
Ad Rate: Full Page Mono 20.75
Ad Rate: Full Page Colour 46.75
Currency: United States Dollars
DAILY NEWSPAPER

Commonwealth Journal 14090
Owner: Community Newspaper Holdings, Inc.
Editorial: 110-112 E Mount Vernon St, Somerset, Kentucky 42501-1411 **Tel:** 1 606 678-8191
Email: news@somerset-kentucky.com **Web site:** http://www.somerset-kentucky.com
Freq: Mon thru Fri; **Circ:** 9700 Not Audited
Publisher: Jack McNeely; **News Editor:** Jeff Neal; **Editor:** Ken Shmidheiser
Profile: Commonwealth Journal is a daily newspaper published for the residents of Pulaski County, KY. It covers local news and information.
Language (s): English
Ad Rate: Full Page Mono 12.75
Ad Rate: Full Page Colour 1797.00
Currency: United States Dollars
DAILY NEWSPAPER

Concord Monitor 14351
Owner: Newspapers of New England
Editorial: 1 Monitor Dr, Concord, New Hampshire 03301-1834 **Tel:** 1 603 224-5301
Email: news@cmonitor.com **Web site:** http://www.concordmonitor.com
Freq: Daily; **Circ:** 19885 Not Audited
Editor: Steve Leone
Profile: Concord Monitor is a local daily newspaper serving Concord, NH and the surrounding areas. It covers local, state, New England, national and world news. The paper also covers politics, opinion, sports, business news, arts & entertainment and community news, including wedding, birth and engagement announcements.
Language (s): English
Ad Rate: Full Page Mono 16.75
Ad Rate: Full Page Colour 330.00
Currency: United States Dollars
DAILY NEWSPAPER

Concordia Blade-Empire 14038
Owner: Blade-Empire Publishing Co. Inc.
Editorial: 510 Washington St, Concordia, Kansas 66901-2117 **Tel:** 1 785 243-2424
Email: bladeempire@nckcn.com **Web site:** http://www.bladeempire.com
Freq: Daily; **Circ:** 3000 Not Audited
Editor: Sharon Coy; **Advertising Sales Manager:** Jessica LaDuke; **Publisher & Editor:** Brad Lowell
Profile: Concordia Blade-Empire is a daily publication that provides local news and sports coverage for the Concordia, KS area. Deadlines are at 2pm CT.
Language (s): English
Ad Rate: Full Page Mono 5.35
Ad Rate: Full Page Colour 70.00
Currency: United States Dollars
DAILY NEWSPAPER

Connecticut Post 14954
Owner: Hearst Corporation
Editorial: 410 State St, Bridgeport, Connecticut 06604-4501 **Tel:** 1 203 333-0161
Email: newsroom@ctpost.com **Web site:** http://www.ctpost.com
Freq: Daily; **Circ:** 29134 Not Audited
News Editor: Linda Levinson
Profile: Connecticut Post is a daily paper written for southwestern Connecticut. It covers local and national news, sports and entertainment.
Language (s): English
Ad Rate: Full Page Mono 95.35
Ad Rate: Full Page Colour 97.73
Currency: United States Dollars
DAILY NEWSPAPER

Connersville News-Examiner 13978
Owner: Paxton Media Group
Editorial: 406 N Central Ave, Connersville, Indiana 47331-1926 **Tel:** 1 765 825-0581 222
Email: newsexaminer@newsexaminer.com **Web site:** http://www.newsexaminer.com
Freq: Daily; **Circ:** 6500 Not Audited
Publisher: Rachael Raney; **Editor:** James Sprague
Profile: Connersville News-Examiner is a daily newspaper based in Connersville, IN. The publication covers local, state and national news.
Language (s): English
Ad Rate: Full Page Mono 17.96
Ad Rate: Full Page Colour 225.00
Currency: United States Dollars
DAILY NEWSPAPER

The Conway Daily Sun 14898
Owner: Country News Club, Inc.
Editorial: 64 Seavey St, North Conway, New Hampshire 03860-5355 **Tel:** 1 603 356-3456
Email: dailysun@conwaydailysun.com **Web site:** http://www.conwaydailysun.com
Freq: Daily; **Circ:** 14400 Not Audited
Publisher: Mark Guerringue; **Editor:** Adam Hirshan; **Advertising Sales Manager:** Rick Luksza
Profile: The Conway Daily Sun is a daily newspaper serving the community of Mount Washington Valley, NH. The publication covers news, with a special focus on the North Conway, NH region. Deadlines are one day prior to the issue date at noon ET.
Language (s): English
Ad Rate: Full Page Mono 7.00
Ad Rate: Full Page Colour 25.25
Currency: United States Dollars
DAILY NEWSPAPER

Cordele Dispatch 13840
Owner: Community Newspaper Holdings, Inc.
Editorial: 401 E 16th Ave Ste F, Cordele, Georgia 31015-1669 **Tel:** 1 229 273-2277
Web site: http://cordeledispatch.com
Freq: Fri; **Circ:** 5000 Not Audited
Publisher: Chris Lewis
Profile: Cordele Dispatch is a local newspaper written for residents of Cordele, GA. It covers local news, sports and events in the area.
Language (s): English
Ad Rate: Full Page Mono 16.50
Ad Rate: Full Page Colour 56.70
Currency: United States Dollars
DAILY NEWSPAPER

Corpus Christi Caller-Times 15417
Owner: Gannett Co., Inc.
Editorial: 820 N Lower Broadway St, Corpus Christi, Texas 78401-2025 **Tel:** 1 361 884-2011
Email: newstips@caller.com **Web site:** http://www.caller.com
Freq: Daily; **Circ:** 36173 Not Audited
Profile: Corpus Christi Caller-Times was founded in 1883. It is a daily publication. It was taken over by the Scripps-Howard group in 1997. It provides Corpus Christi, TX and its surrounding communities with local, regional, national and international news. It also covers sports, arts & entertainment, business and special reports.
Language (s): English
Ad Rate: Full Page Mono 188.67
Ad Rate: Full Page Colour 280.32
Currency: United States Dollars
DAILY NEWSPAPER

El Correo - New York Bureau 619698
Editorial: 405 E 42nd St, New York, New York 10017-3507 **Tel:** 1 212 935-1964
Email: mgallego@elcorreo.com
Profile: This is the New York bureau of El Correo in Spain.
Language (s): Spanish
DAILY NEWSPAPER

Corriere della Sera - New York Bureau 503827
Owner: RCS MediaGroup SpA
Editorial: 31 W 57th St Fl 4, New York, New York 10019-3496 **Tel:** 1 212 308-2000
Web site: http://www.corriere.it
Freq: Daily
Profile: Foreign bureau of the daily Corriere della Sera.
Language (s): English
DAILY NEWSPAPER

Corry Journal 14573
Owner: Sample News Group
Editorial: 28 W South St, Corry, Pennsylvania 16407-1810 **Tel:** 1 814 665-8291
Web site: http://www.thecorryjournal.com
Freq: Daily; **Circ:** 4100 Not Audited
Advertising Sales Manager: Dave Schwabenbauer; **Editor:** Stephen Sears
Profile: Corry Journal is published daily for the residents of Corry, PA and surrounding areas. The newspaper covers local and state news, business, sports, lifestyles and entertainment.
Language (s): English
Ad Rate: Full Page Mono 8.00
Ad Rate: Full Page Colour 9.50
Currency: United States Dollars
DAILY NEWSPAPER

Corsicana Daily Sun 14693
Owner: Community Newspapers Holdings, Inc.
Editorial: 405 E Collin St, Corsicana, Texas 75110-5325 **Tel:** 1 903 872-3931
Email: dailysun@corsicanadailysun.com **Web site:** http://corsicanadailysun.com
Freq: Fri; **Circ:** 3962 Not Audited
Publisher: Jake Mienk
Profile: Corsicana Daily Sun is the daily newspaper for Corsicana, TX. Sections include local news, world news, sports, lifestyle, business and arts & entertainment.
Language (s): English
Ad Rate: Full Page Mono 13.50
Ad Rate: Full Page Colour 300.00
Currency: United States Dollars
DAILY NEWSPAPER

Cortland Standard 14398
Owner: Cortland Standard Printing Company, Inc.
Editorial: 110 Main St, Cortland, New York 13045-6600 **Tel:** 1 607 756-5665
Email: news@cortlandstandard.net **Web site:** http://www.cortlandstandard.net
Freq: Daily; **Circ:** 10120 Not Audited
Advertising Sales Manager: Mike Anderson; **Publisher:** Kevin Howe
Profile: Cortland Standard is a local newspaper for residents of Cortland County, NY. The publication offers coverage of local news, weather and sports. Deadlines are at 12:30pm ET the day before issue date.
Language (s): English
Ad Rate: Full Page Mono 10.70
Ad Rate: Full Page Colour 270.00
Currency: United States Dollars
DAILY NEWSPAPER

Corvallis Gazette-Times 14553
Owner: Lee Enterprises, Inc.
Editorial: 1837 NW Circle Blvd, Corvallis, Oregon 97330-1310 **Tel:** 1 541 753-2641
Email: news@gazettetimes.com **Web site:** http://www.gazettetimes.com
Freq: Daily; **Circ:** 11075 Not Audited
Profile: Corvallis Gazette-Times is a daily newspaper for the residents of Mid-Willamette Valley in Oregon. The publication is a general newspaper that contains the sections news, sports, business, leisure, opinion, calendar, and classified ads. National and international news is provided by the Associated Press. Contact the publication for the advertising rates and editorial submission guidelines.
Language (s): English
Ad Rate: Full Page Mono 34.85
Ad Rate: Full Page Colour 375.00
Currency: United States Dollars
DAILY NEWSPAPER

Coshocton Tribune 14445
Owner: Gannett Co., Inc.
Editorial: 550 Main St, Coshocton, Ohio 43812
Tel: 1 740 622-1122
Email: coshocton@nncogannett.com **Web site:** http://www.coshoctontribune.com
Freq: Daily; **Circ:** 3688 Not Audited
Profile: Coshocton Tribune is a daily newspaper written for the residents of Coshocton, OH and the surrounding area. The publication covers local and regional news.
Language (s): English
Ad Rate: Full Page Mono 15.52
Ad Rate: Full Page Colour 175.00
Currency: United States Dollars
DAILY NEWSPAPER

Council Grove Republican 14039
Editorial: 208 W Main St, Council Grove, Kansas 66846 **Tel:** 1 620 767-5123
Email: cgnews@cgtelco.net
Freq: Daily; **Circ:** 2100 Not Audited
Advertising Sales Manager: Becky Evans; **Editor:** Craig McNeal
Profile: Council Grove Republican is a local newspaper serving the Morris County, KS community. It covers local news and area events.
Language (s): English
Ad Rate: Full Page Mono 5.55
Ad Rate: Full Page Colour 55.00
Currency: United States Dollars
DAILY NEWSPAPER

The Courier 13703
Owner: Paxton Media Group
Editorial: 201 E 2nd St, Russellville, Arkansas 72801-5102 **Tel:** 1 479 968-5252
Email: newsclerk@couriernews.com **Web site:** http://www.couriernews.com
Freq: Daily; **Circ:** 9358 Not Audited
News Editor: Adam Franks
Profile: The Courier is a daily newspaper published for the residents of Russellville, AR and surrounding communities. The publication covers local news, sports, lifestyles and community events.
Language (s): English
Ad Rate: Full Page Mono 15.15
Ad Rate: Full Page Colour 325.00
Currency: United States Dollars
DAILY NEWSPAPER

The Courier 13941
Owner: GateHouse Media Inc.
Editorial: 2201 Woodlawn Rd Ste 350, Lincoln, Illinois 62656-9645 **Tel:** 1 217 732-2101
Email: courier@lincolncourier.com **Web site:** http://www.lincolncourier.com
Freq: Daily; **Circ:** 5623 Not Audited
Profile: The Courier is published daily for the residents of Lincoln, IL and surrounding areas. The newspaper covers local news, sports, business, education and community events.
Language (s): English
Ad Rate: Full Page Mono 14.88
Ad Rate: Full Page Colour 256.00
Currency: United States Dollars
DAILY NEWSPAPER

The Courier 14452
Owner: Findlay Publishing Company (The)
Editorial: 701 W Sandusky St, Findlay, Ohio 45840-2325 **Tel:** 1 419 422-5151
Email: news@thecourier.com **Web site:** http://www.thecourier.com
Freq: Daily; **Circ:** 20878 Not Audited
Advertising Sales Manager: Kari Faulkner; **Publisher:** Karl Heminger; **Editor:** Peter Mattiace; **Editor:** Randy Roberts
Profile: The Courier is writen for residents of northwest Ohio. It covers local news, sports, editorial and community events. Deadlines are 11pm ET the day before publication.
Language (s): English
Ad Rate: Full Page Mono 16.45
Ad Rate: Full Page Colour 240.00
Currency: United States Dollars
DAILY NEWSPAPER

The Courier News 14357
Owner: Gannett Co., Inc.
Editorial: 92 E Main St Ste 202, Somerville, New Jersey 08876-2319 **Tel:** 1 908 243-6600
Email: cnmetro@mycentraljersey.com **Web site:** http://www.mycentraljersey.com
Freq: Daily; **Circ:** 14072 Not Audited
Advertising Sales Manager: Bernita Gilliam; **Editor:** Paul Grzella
Profile: The Courier News is a local newspaper serving the residents of Somerset, Hunterdon, Middlesex and Union counties, NJ. The newspaper covers local news, sports, arts & entertainment and business.
Language (s): English
Ad Rate: Full Page Mono 61.09
Ad Rate: Full Page Colour 600.00
Currency: United States Dollars
DAILY NEWSPAPER

The Courier of Montgomery County 14692
Owner: Hearst Newspapers
Editorial: 100 Avenue A, Conroe, Texas 77301-2946
Tel: 1 936 521-3300
Email: couriernews@hcnonline.com **Web site:** http://www.yourconroenews.com
Freq: Daily; **Circ:** 9562 Not Audited
Profile: The Courier of Montgomery County provides local news, community news, sports and events information for the residents of Conroe, TX.
Language (s): English
Ad Rate: Full Page Mono 18.00
Ad Rate: Full Page Colour 250.00
Currency: United States Dollars
DAILY NEWSPAPER

The Courier-Express 14576
Owner: McLean Publishing Co.
Editorial: 500 Jeffers St, Du Bois, Pennsylvania 15801-2430 **Tel:** 1 814 371-4200
Email: newsroom@thecourierexpress.com **Web site:** http://www.thecourierexpress.com
Freq: Daily; **Circ:** 14386
News Editor: Alisha Bish Sylvis; **Editor:** Tom Bukousky; **Editor:** Joy Norwood; **Advertising Sales Manager:** Linda Smith
Profile: The Courier-Express provides news and information to residents of DuBois, PA. It covers world, national and local news, features, lifestyles and entertainment.
Language (s): English
Ad Rate: Full Page Mono 22.18
Ad Rate: Full Page Colour 52.50
Currency: United States Dollars
DAILY NEWSPAPER

The Courier-Herald 13842
Owner: Courier Herald Publishing Company
Editorial: 115 S Jefferson St, Dublin, Georgia 31021-5146 **Tel:** 1 478 272-5522
Email: tchnewsroom61@gmail.com **Web site:** http://www.courier-herald.com
Freq: Mon thru Fri; **Circ:** 8768
Advertising Sales Manager: Pam Burney; **Publisher:** Griffin Lovett; **Editor:** DuBose Porter
Profile: The Courier-Herald is published daily for the residents of Dublin, GA and surrounding areas. The newspaper covers local and regional news, business, sports, lifestyle and entertainment.
Language (s): English
Ad Rate: Full Page Mono 14.25
Ad Rate: Full Page Colour 240.00
Currency: United States Dollars
DAILY NEWSPAPER

The Courier-Journal 15336
Owner: Gannett Co., Inc.
Editorial: 525 W Broadway, Louisville, Kentucky 40202-2206 **Tel:** 1 502 582-4691
Email: news@courier-journal.com **Web site:** http://www.courier-journal.com
Freq: Daily; **Circ:** 102895 Not Audited
Publisher: Wes Jackson
Profile: The Courier-Journal is a 70+ page, broadsheet newspaper aimed at the general public in the Louisville, KY area and southern Indiana. It covers local and regional news, business, sports, entertainment, and lifestyle. The Business section appears daily. A weekly, consumer-focused Health & Fitness section runs on Thursday.
Language (s): English
Ad Rate: Full Page Mono 327.66
Ad Rate: Full Page Colour 995.95
Currency: United States Dollars
DAILY NEWSPAPER

The Courier-Journal - Frankfort Bureau 15728
Editorial: 332 Capitol Ave, Frankfort, Kentucky 40601-2835 **Tel:** 1 502 875-5136
Bureau Chief: Tom Loftus
Language (s): English
DAILY NEWSPAPER

Courier-Post 15406
Owner: Gannett Co., Inc.
Editorial: 301 Cuthbert Blvd, Cherry Hill, New Jersey 08002-2905 **Tel:** 1 856 663-6000
Email: cpcommunities@courierpostonline.com **Web site:** http://www.courierpostonline.com
Freq: Daily; **Circ:** 39091 Not Audited
Profile: Courier-Post is a daily newspaper serving New Jersey. The publication covers local and regional news, business, lifestyle, arts & entertainment and sports. The newspaper's forerunner was founded in 1875 as a weekly newspaper. Gannett bought the publication in 1959. By the end of the 1970s, the paper became a daily, morning paper. In 1979, the first Sunday edition was published.
Language (s): English
Ad Rate: Full Page Mono 102.33
Ad Rate: Full Page Colour 538.26
Currency: United States Dollars
DAILY NEWSPAPER

Courier-Post - Trenton Bureau 16249
Editorial: Trenton, New Jersey **Tel:** 1 609 292-5171
Language (s): English
DAILY NEWSPAPER

The Courier-Times 14007
Owner: Paxton Media Group
Editorial: 201 S 14th St, New Castle, Indiana 47362-3328 **Tel:** 1 765 529-1111
Email: editor@thecouriertimes.com **Web site:** http://www.thecouriertimes.com
Freq: Daily; **Circ:** 9153 Not Audited
Profile: The Courier-Times is a daily newspaper serving residents of New Castle, IN and the surrounding area. The paper focuses on local news and sports.
Language (s): English

Ad Rate: Full Page Mono 17.00
Ad Rate: Full Page Colour 250.00
Currency: United States Dollars
DAILY NEWSPAPER

The Courier-Tribune 14288
Owner: Stephens Media Group
Editorial: 500 Sunset Ave, Asheboro, North Carolina 27203-5330 **Tel:** 1 336 625-2101
Web site: http://www.courier-tribune.com
Freq: Daily
Editor: Ray Criscoe; **Editor:** Dennis Garcia; **News Editor:** Annette Jordan
Profile: The Courier-Tribune offers coverage of events and issues in Randolph, Montgomery, Moore, and Chatham counties, as well as for the town of Denton in Davidson County in North Carolina. The newspaper is published daily and provides local information for the general public.
Language (s): English
Ad Rate: Full Page Mono 13.50
Ad Rate: Full Page Colour 118.50
Currency: United States Dollars
DAILY NEWSPAPER

Cowley CourierTraveler 14031
Owner: Seaton Newspapers
Editorial: 200 E 5th Ave, Arkansas City, Kansas 67005-2606 **Tel:** 1 620 442-4200
Email: advertising1@ctnewsonline.com **Web site:** http://ctnewsonline.com
Freq: Daily; **Circ:** 5000 Not Audited
Publisher: David Seaton
Profile: The Cowley CourierTraveler is a daily newspaper serving Arkansas City, KS. It provides residents with information on local news, events, weather, and sports. The lead time for is one day. Contact the managing editor with any further inquiries.
Language (s): English
Ad Rate: Full Page Mono 9.15
Ad Rate: Full Page Colour 165.00
Currency: United States Dollars
DAILY NEWSPAPER

Craig Daily Press 13780
Owner: WorldWest Limited Liability Co.
Editorial: 466 Yampa Ave, Craig, Colorado 81625-2610 **Tel:** 1 970 824-7031
Email: news@craigdailypress.com **Web site:** http://www.craigdailypress.com
Freq: Fri; **Circ:** 3550
Advertising Sales Manager: Sheli Steele
Profile: Craig Daily Press is published daily for residents of Moffat County, CO. As a community publication, its mission is to present the most unbiased information available to its readers.
Language (s): English
Ad Rate: Full Page Mono 10.00
Ad Rate: Full Page Colour 165.00
Currency: United States Dollars
DAILY NEWSPAPER

The Crescent-News 14446
Owner: GateHouse Media Inc.
Editorial: 624 W 2nd St, Defiance, Ohio 43512-2105 **Tel:** 1 419 784-5441
Email: crescent@crescent-news.com **Web site:** http://www.crescent-news.com
Freq: Daily; **Circ:** 14876 Not Audited
Editor: Darlene Prince; **Advertising Sales Manager:** Mark Ryan; **News Editor:** Al Smith
Profile: The Crescent-News is published daily for residents of Defiance, OH and surrounding areas. The publication is a general interest newspaper, including articles on local and national news, weather, sports, business, arts & entertainment and other information of interest to the Defiance community.
Language (s): English
Ad Rate: Full Page Mono 18.45
Ad Rate: Full Page Colour 335.00
Currency: United States Dollars
DAILY NEWSPAPER

Creston News Advertiser 13874
Owner: Shaw Media
Editorial: 503 W Adams St, Creston, Iowa 50801-3112 **Tel:** 1 641 782-2141
Email: news@crestonnews.com **Web site:** http://www.crestonnews.com
Freq: Daily; **Circ:** 5317 Not Audited
Publisher: Rich Paulsen
Profile: Creston News Advertiser is a daily newspaper written for residents of Union County, IA and surrounding communities. The publication is a general interest newspaper, covering local and national news, sports, business, arts and entertainment, and feature articles.
Language (s): English
Ad Rate: Full Page Mono 10.20
Ad Rate: Full Page Colour 85.00
Currency: United States Dollars
DAILY NEWSPAPER

Crookston Daily Times 14202
Owner: GateHouse Media Inc.
Editorial: 124 S Broadway, Crookston, Minnesota 56716-1955 **Tel:** 1 218 281-2730
Email: news@crookstontimes.com **Web site:** http://www.crookstontimes.com
Freq: Daily; **Circ:** 1025 Not Audited
Profile: Crookston Daily Times is published Monday through Friday for residents of Crookston, MN and surrounding areas. The publication is a general interest newspaper covering local news, sports, weather, business and arts & entertainment.
Language (s): English
Ad Rate: Full Page Mono 13.85
Currency: United States Dollars
DAILY NEWSPAPER

Crowley Post-Signal 14095
Owner: Louisiana State Newspapers
Editorial: 602 N Parkerson Ave, Crowley, Louisiana 70526-4354 **Tel:** 1 337 783-3450
Email: howie.dennis@crowleytoday.com **Web site:** http://www.acadiaparishtoday.com
Freq: Daily; **Circ:** 4350 Not Audited
News Editor: Howell Dennis; **Advertising Sales Manager:** Janet Doucet
Profile: Crowley Post-Signal is published daily for residents of Crowley and Arcadia Parish, LA. The publication is a general interest newspaper, providing local news, sports, business, entertainment and other information of interest to the Crowley community. The deadline for the publication is at noon CT.
Language (s): English
Ad Rate: Full Page Mono 10.18
Ad Rate: Full Page Colour 325.00
Currency: United States Dollars
DAILY NEWSPAPER

The Cullman Times 13665
Owner: Community Newspaper Holdings, Inc.
Editorial: 300 4th Ave SE, Cullman, Alabama 35055-3611 **Tel:** 1 256 734-2131
Email: sallee@cullmantimes.com **Web site:** http://www.cullmantimes.com
Freq: Daily; **Circ:** 11086 Not Audited
Publisher: Bill Morgan; **Editor:** David Palmer; **News Editor:** Amanda Shavers-Davis
Profile: The Cullman Times is published daily for residents of Cullman, AL and surrounding areas. It covers local news, weather, sports, business, arts & entertainment and other information of interest to local residents.
Language (s): English
Ad Rate: Full Page Mono 12.10
Ad Rate: Full Page Colour 220.00
Currency: United States Dollars
DAILY NEWSPAPER

Culpeper Star-Exponent 14754
Owner: BH Media Group
Editorial: 471 James Madison Hwy Ste 201, Culpeper, Virginia 22701-2364 **Tel:** 1 540 825-0771
Web site: http://www.dailyprogress.com/starexponent/
Freq: Daily; **Circ:** 4900 Not Audited
Publisher: Mitch Sneed
Profile: Culpeper Star-Exponent is published daily for residents of Culpeper, VA and surrounding areas. It is a general interest newspaper covering local news, sports, business, entertainment, education and other information of interest to the area.
Language (s): English
Ad Rate: Full Page Mono 18.30
Ad Rate: Full Page Colour 351.00
Currency: United States Dollars
DAILY NEWSPAPER

Cumberland Times-News 14143
Owner: Community Newspaper Holdings, Inc.
Editorial: 19 Baltimore St, Cumberland, Maryland 21502-3023 **Tel:** 1 301 722-4600
Email: ctn@times-news.com **Web site:** http://www.times-news.com
Freq: Daily; **Circ:** 20164 Not Audited
Editor: Jim Goldsworthy
Profile: Cumberland Times-News is published daily for the residents of Cumberland, Garrett, Allegany, Mineral and Hampshire, MD. It is a general interest newspaper that covers events, opportunities and community issues.
Language (s): English
Ad Rate: Full Page Mono 44.52
Ad Rate: Full Page Colour 299.00
Currency: United States Dollars
DAILY NEWSPAPER

Current-Argus 14372
Owner: Gannett Co., Inc.
Editorial: 620 S Main St, Carlsbad, New Mexico 88220-6243 **Tel:** 1 575 887-5501
Email: news@currentargus.com **Web site:** http://www.currentargus.com
Freq: Daily; **Circ:** 5943 Not Audited
Profile: Current-Argus is published daily for residents of Carlsbad, NM and surrounding areas. The publication is a general interest newspaper, including local, state, national and international news and features, comics and puzzles, syndicated columnists, classified and display advertising, weather, business and financial reports, obituaries, and local, state and national sports. The newspaper also includes editorials, letters and opinions, astrological forecasts, and other features as space permits. Deadlines are two weeks prior to the issue date.
Language (s): English
Ad Rate: Full Page Mono 17.15
Ad Rate: Full Page Colour 225.00
Currency: United States Dollars
DAILY NEWSPAPER

Daily & Sunday Review 14623
Owner: Scranton Times
Editorial: 116 Main St, Towanda, Pennsylvania 18848-1843 **Tel:** 1 570 265-2151
Email: reviewnews@thedailyreview.com **Web site:** http://www.thedailyreview.com
Freq: Daily; **Circ:** 8228 Not Audited
Editor: Kelly Andrus; **Publisher:** Greg Zyla
Profile: Daily & Sunday Review serves the residents of Towanda, PA and the surrounding areas. The newspaper provides local and national news, sports and entertainment. Send press releases by fax or mail to the city editor.
Language (s): English
Ad Rate: Full Page Mono 18.44
Ad Rate: Full Page Colour 75.00
Currency: United States Dollars
DAILY NEWSPAPER

The Daily Advance 14292
Owner: Cooke Communications, LLC
Editorial: 215 S Water St, Elizabeth City, North Carolina 27909-4844 **Tel:** 1 252 335-0841
Email: elizabethcity@dailyadvance.com **Web site:** http://www.dailyadvance.com
Freq: Daily; **Circ:** 9416 Not Audited
News Editor: Julian Eure; **Editor:** Michael Goodman; **Publisher:** Ann Hoffman
Profile: The Daily Advance is a local, daily newspaper for residents of Northeast Elizabeth City, NC. It covers community news and daily events.
Language (s): English
Ad Rate: Full Page Mono 19.93
Ad Rate: Full Page Colour 275.00
Currency: United States Dollars
DAILY NEWSPAPER

The Daily Advertiser 14100
Owner: Gannett Co., Inc.
Editorial: 1100 Bertrand Dr, Lafayette, Louisiana 70506-4110 **Tel:** 1 337 289-6300
Email: news@theadvertiser.com **Web site:** http://www.theadvertiser.com
Freq: Daily; **Circ:** 31314
Profile: The Daily Advertiser is a local newspaper written for residents in Acadiana, LA. The newspaper, published seven days a week, covers local news, sports, entertainment and community events.
Language (s): English
Ad Rate: Full Page Mono 45.50
Ad Rate: Full Page Colour 221.00
Currency: United States Dollars
DAILY NEWSPAPER

Daily American 14616
Owner: Schurz Communications Inc.
Editorial: 334 W Main St, Somerset, Pennsylvania 15501-1502 **Tel:** 1 814 444-5900
Email: news@dailyamerican.com **Web site:** http://www.dailyamerican.com
Freq: Daily; **Circ:** 11504 Not Audited
Publisher: Andrew Bruns; **News Editor:** Brian Schrock; **Editor:** Brian Whipkey
Profile: Daily American is a daily newspaper written for the residents of Somerset County, PA. The publication provides news, weather, sports and community events.
Language (s): English
Ad Rate: Full Page Mono 22.00
Ad Rate: Full Page Colour 380.00
Currency: United States Dollars
DAILY NEWSPAPER

Daily American Republic 14247
Owner: Rust Communications
Editorial: 208 Poplar St, Poplar Bluff, Missouri 63901-5808 **Tel:** 1 573 785-1414
Email: news@darnews.com **Web site:** http://www.darnews.com
Freq: Daily; **Circ:** 9537
Editor: Stan Berry; **Editor:** Paul Davis; **Editor:** Brian Rosener; **Publisher:** Don Schrieber
Profile: Daily American Republic is written for residents in and around Poplar Bluff, MO. The paper covers local news, sports and weather.
Language (s): English
Ad Rate: Full Page Mono 12.37
Ad Rate: Full Page Colour 400.00
Currency: United States Dollars
DAILY NEWSPAPER

The Daily Ardmoreite 14511
Owner: GateHouse Media Inc.
Editorial: 117 W Broadway St, Ardmore, Oklahoma 73401-6226 **Tel:** 1 580 223-2200
Email: yournews@ardmoreite.com **Web site:** http://www.ardmoreite.com
Freq: Daily; **Circ:** 8642 Not Audited
News Editor: Marsha Miller
Profile: The Daily Ardmoreite is published daily for the residents of Ardmoreite, OK and surrounding areas. The newspaper covers local and state news, business, sports, lifestyles and entertainment.
Language (s): English
Ad Rate: Full Page Mono 11.25
Ad Rate: Full Page Colour 130.00
Currency: United States Dollars
DAILY NEWSPAPER

The Daily Astorian 14549
Owner: East Oregonian Publishing Co.
Editorial: 949 Exchange St, Astoria, Oregon 97103-4605 **Tel:** 1 503 325-3211
Email: news@dailyastorian.com **Web site:** http://www.dailyastorian.com
Freq: Daily; **Circ:** 8082 Not Audited
Advertising Sales Manager: Betty Smith
Profile: The Daily Astorian is a daily newspaper for the residents of Astoria, OR. It covers news and events in the local community. Deadlines are one day prior to issue date.
Language (s): English
Ad Rate: Full Page Mono 17.05
Ad Rate: Full Page Colour 316.00
Currency: United States Dollars
DAILY NEWSPAPER

Daily Breeze 13757
Owner: Southern California News Group/Digital First Media
Editorial: 21250 Hawthorne Blvd Ste 170, Torrance, California 90503-5514 **Tel:** 1 310 540-5511
Email: entertainment@langnews.com **Web site:** http://www.dailybreeze.com
Freq: Daily; **Circ:** 79327 Not Audited
Profile: Daily Breeze is published for residents of Torrance, CA. This paper is a part of the Southern California News Group, a subsidiary of Digital First Media. The newspaper covers local news, sports and weather.
Language (s): English
Ad Rate: Full Page Mono 93.69
Ad Rate: Full Page Colour 101.22
Currency: United States Dollars
DAILY NEWSPAPER

Daily Challenge 14394
Owner: Challenge Group
Editorial: 1195 Atlantic Ave, Brooklyn, New York 11216-2709 **Tel:** 1 718 636-9500
Email: challengegroup@yahoo.com
Freq: Daily; **Circ:** 81000 Not Audited
Editor: Dawad Philip; **Publisher:** Tom Watkins
Profile: Daily Challenge is a daily newspaper serving the African-American community in the New York metropolitan area. The paper features local, national and international news from the Caribbean, Latin America and Africa and from wherever issues confronting Africans throughout the Diaspora are unfolding. Topics include entertainment, health, sports, books and a forum page.
Language (s): English
Ad Rate: Full Page Mono 67.98
Ad Rate: Full Page Colour 600.00
Currency: United States Dollars
DAILY NEWSPAPER

Daily Chief-Union 14495
Owner: Barnes Newspapers (Ray)
Editorial: 111 W Wyandot Ave, Upper Sandusky, Ohio 43351-1348 **Tel:** 1 419 294-2332
Email: dcueditor@dailychiefunion.com **Web site:** http://www.dailychiefunion.com
Freq: Daily; **Circ:** 3946 Not Audited
Advertising Sales Manager: David Barnes; **Publisher & Editor:** Jeff Barnes; **General News:** Alissa Paolella
Profile: Daily Chief-Union is written for the Upper Sandusky, OH community. The newspaper covers world news, local news, community news, sports news, obituaries, weather and job vacancies.
Language (s): English
Ad Rate: Full Page Mono 6.75
Ad Rate: Full Page Colour 75.00
Currency: United States Dollars
DAILY NEWSPAPER

Daily Chronicle 13924
Owner: Shaw Media
Editorial: 1586 Barber Greene Rd, Dekalb, Illinois 60115-7900 **Tel:** 1 815 756-4841
Email: news@daily-chronicle.com **Web site:** http://www.daily-chronicle.com
Freq: Mon thru Fri; **Circ:** 8419
Publisher: Don Bricker; **Editor:** Eric Olson; **Advertising Sales Manager:** Karen Pletsch
Profile: Daily Chronicle is published for the residents of Dekalb County, IL and surrounding areas. It covers local, national and international news, sports, weather, religion, legal and lifestyle.
Language (s): English
Ad Rate: Full Page Mono 29.15
Ad Rate: Full Page Colour 2669.10
Currency: United States Dollars
DAILY NEWSPAPER

The Daily Citizen 13704
Owner: Paxton Media Group
Editorial: 3000 E Race Ave, Searcy, Arkansas 72143-4808 **Tel:** 1 501 268-8621
Email: editor@thedailycitizen.com **Web site:** http://www.thedailycitizen.com
Freq: Daily; **Circ:** 6131 Not Audited
News Editor: Wendy Jones; **Publisher:** Mike Murphy
Profile: The Daily Citizen is a local newspaper serving Searcy, AR and the surrounding community. It provides readers with local news, sports, government and arts & entertainment coverage.
Language (s): English
Ad Rate: Full Page Mono 11.25
Ad Rate: Full Page Colour 125.00
Currency: United States Dollars
DAILY NEWSPAPER

The Daily Citizen 13841
Owner: Community Newspaper Holdings, Inc.
Editorial: 308 S Thornton Ave, Dalton, Georgia 30720-8268 **Tel:** 1 706 217-6397
Web site: http://daltondailycitizen.com
Freq: Daily; **Circ:** 11162 Not Audited
Publisher: William Bronson; **Editor:** Wes Chance; **Editor:** Jamie Jones; **Editor:** Victor Miller
Profile: The Daily Citizen is written for the Dalton, GA community. The newspaper covers local and state news, sports, business, lifestyles and entertainment.
Language (s): English
Ad Rate: Full Page Mono 19.50
Ad Rate: Full Page Colour 240.00
Currency: United States Dollars
DAILY NEWSPAPER

Daily Citizen 14799
Owner: Capital Newspapers
Editorial: 805 Park Ave, Beaver Dam, Wisconsin 53916-2205 **Tel:** 1 920 887-0321

Email: dc-news@capitalnewspapers.com **Web site:** http://www.wiscnews.com/bdc
Freq: Daily; **Circ:** 6865 Not Audited
Publisher & Editor: James Kelsh; **Advertising Sales Manager:** Scott Zeinemann
Profile: Daily Citizen is a local newspaper written for residents of Dodge County, WI. The newspaper covers local news, sports and events.
Language (s): English
Ad Rate: Full Page Mono 11.60
Ad Rate: Full Page Colour 72.04
Currency: United States Dollars
DAILY NEWSPAPER

Daily Comet 14109
Owner: GateHouse Media Inc.
Editorial: 104 Hickory St, Thibodaux, Louisiana 70301-2008 **Tel:** 1 985 448-7600
Web site: http://www.dailycomet.com
Freq: Mon thru Fri; **Circ:** 7695 Not Audited
Profile: Daily Comet serves the local community of Thibodaux, LA. The publication reports daily on local news, events and community programs, as well as regional and national highlights.
Language (s): English
Ad Rate: Full Page Mono 43.91
Currency: United States Dollars
DAILY NEWSPAPER

The Daily Commercial 13821
Owner: Harbor Point Media LLC
Editorial: 212 E Main St, Leesburg, Florida 34748-5227 **Tel:** 1 352 365-8200
Email: news@dailycommercial.com **Web site:** http://www.dailycommercial.com
Freq: Daily; **Circ:** 21093 Not Audited
Profile: The Daily Commercial is a local daily newspaper written for the residents of Lake and Sumter counties, FL. The newspaper covers local news, sports and community events.
Language (s): English
Ad Rate: Full Page Mono 28.91
Ad Rate: Full Page Colour 98.35
Currency: United States Dollars
DAILY NEWSPAPER

Daily Commercial Record 257354
Owner: Independent
Editorial: 706 Main St Bsmt 2, Dallas, Texas 75202-3620 **Tel:** 1 214 741-6366
Email: dcr@dailycommercialrecord.com **Web site:** http://www.dailycommercialrecord.com
Freq: Daily; **Circ:** 3200 Not Audited
Editor: Emily Cates; **Publisher:** Nuel Cates
Profile: The Daily Commercial Record is a daily newspaper providing current court and commercial information. It provides up-to-date court records, public notices, legal transactions, and business leads and business news each weekday.
Language (s): English
Ad Rate: Full Page Colour 306.00
Currency: United States Dollars
DAILY NEWSPAPER

Daily Corinthian 14261
Owner: Paxton Media Group
Editorial: 1607 S Harper Rd, Corinth, Mississippi 38834-6653 **Tel:** 1 662 287-6111
Email: news@dailycorinthian.com **Web site:** http://www.dailycorinthian.com
Freq: Fri; **Circ:** 6153 Not Audited
Advertising Sales Manager: Denise Mitchell; **Editor:** Lee Smith; **Publisher:** Reece Terry
Profile: Daily Corinthian provides local community news, weather and sports. The publication is written for residents of Corinth, MS.
Language (s): English
Ad Rate: Full Page Mono 16.95
Ad Rate: Full Page Colour 215.00
Currency: United States Dollars
DAILY NEWSPAPER

The Daily Courier 13713
Owner: Western Newspapers, Inc.
Editorial: 1958 Commerce Center Cir, Prescott, Arizona 86301-4454 **Tel:** 1 928 445-3333
Email: editorial@prescottaz.com **Web site:** http://www.dcourier.com
Freq: Daily; **Circ:** 14483 Not Audited
Publisher: Kelly Soldwedel; **Editor:** Les Stukenberg
Profile: The Daily Courier is a daily newspaper published by Western Newspapers Inc., for residents of Prescott, AZ. The newspaper covers local news, events and sports.
Language (s): English
Ad Rate: Full Page Mono 15.68
Ad Rate: Full Page Colour 690.00
Currency: United States Dollars
DAILY NEWSPAPER

The Daily Courier 14323
Owner: Paxton Media Group
Editorial: 601 Oak St, Forest City, North Carolina 28043-3471 **Tel:** 1 828 245-6431
Email: dc@thedigitalcourier.com **Web site:** http://www.thedigitalcourier.com
Freq: Daily; **Circ:** 6400 Not Audited
Editor: Matthew Clark
Profile: The Daily Courier provides the community with local news and information. The newspaper is written for residents of Forest City, NC and the surrounding area. Topics covered include local schools, government and the environment.
Language (s): English
Ad Rate: Full Page Mono 14.61
Currency: United States Dollars
DAILY NEWSPAPER

The Daily Courier 14572
Owner: West Penn Media Group, LLC
Editorial: 127 W Apple St, Connellsville, Pennsylvania 15425-3132 **Tel:** 1 724 628-2000
Email: newsroom@dailycourier.com **Web site:** http://www.dailycourier.com
Freq: Daily; **Circ:** 7544 Not Audited
Advertising Sales Manager: Karen Strickland
Profile: The Daily Courier is published daily for the residents of Connellsville, PA and surrounding areas. The newspaper cover local and regional news, business, sports, lifestyles and entertainment.
Language (s): English
Ad Rate: Full Page Mono 14.76
Ad Rate: Full Page Colour 64.76
Currency: United States Dollars
DAILY NEWSPAPER

Daily Courier-Observer 14909
Owner: St. Lawrence County Newspapers, Inc.
Editorial: 1 Harrowgate Commons, Massena, New York 13662-2201 **Tel:** 1 315 769-2451
Email: courier@ogd.com **Web site:** http://www.mpcourier.com
Freq: Fri; **Circ:** 7800 Not Audited
Advertising Sales Manager: Katie Nelson
Profile: Daily Courier-Observer is written for residents of Massena and Potsdam, NY. It covers international, national, state and local news, sports, editorials, social events and features of interest to local readers.
Language (s): English
Ad Rate: Full Page Mono 11.90
Ad Rate: Full Page Colour 70.00
Currency: United States Dollars
DAILY NEWSPAPER

The Daily Democrat 13767
Owner: MediaNews Group
Editorial: 711 Main St, Woodland, California 95695-3406 **Tel:** 1 530 662-5421
Email: news@dailydemocrat.com **Web site:** http://www.dailydemocrat.com
Freq: Daily; **Circ:** 8520 Not Audited
Publisher: Jim Gleim
Profile: The Daily Democrat is published for the residents of Woodland, CA and surrounding areas. The paper covers local and national news and finance with a democratic edge.
Language (s): English
Ad Rate: Full Page Mono 15.00
Ad Rate: Full Page Colour 2320.00
Currency: United States Dollars
DAILY NEWSPAPER

The Daily Dunklin Democrat 14236
Owner: Rust Communications
Editorial: 203 1st St, Kennett, Missouri 63857-2052 **Tel:** 1 573 888-4505
Web site: http://www.dddnews.com
Freq: Daily; **Circ:** 3068 Not Audited
Advertising Sales Manager: Terri Coleman; **Publisher:** Bud Hunt
Profile: The Daily Dunklin Democrat serves the residents of Kennett, MO and the surrounding area. The publication covers local and national news.
Language (s): English
Ad Rate: Full Page Mono 12.10
Ad Rate: Full Page Colour 280.00
Currency: United States Dollars
DAILY NEWSPAPER

Daily Freeman 14409
Owner: Digital First Media
Editorial: 79 Hurley Ave, Kingston, New York 12401-2832 **Tel:** 1 845 331-5000
Email: news@freemanonline.com **Web site:** http://www.dailyfreeman.com
Freq: Daily; **Circ:** 13675 Not Audited
Advertising Sales Manager: Barbara Norton; **Publisher:** Robert O'Leary
Profile: Daily Freeman is a daily newspaper published for the local community of Kingston, NY. The publication covers local news, events, people and sports in the area.
Language (s): English
Ad Rate: Full Page Mono 33.55
Ad Rate: Full Page Colour 312.00
Currency: United States Dollars
DAILY NEWSPAPER

Daily Freeman-Journal 13897
Owner: Marshalltown Newspaper Inc.
Editorial: 720 2nd St, Webster City, Iowa 50595-1463 **Tel:** 1 515 832-4350
Web site: http://www.freemanjournal.net
Freq: Daily; **Circ:** 2036 Not Audited
Advertising Sales Manager: Cory Bargfrede; **Publisher:** Terry Christensen
Profile: Daily Freeman-Journal is a daily newspaper which covers the news of Hamilton County, IA. The publication is written for residents of Hamilton County, IA and the surrounding areas.
Language (s): English
Ad Rate: Full Page Mono 10.30
Ad Rate: Full Page Colour 63.54
Currency: United States Dollars
DAILY NEWSPAPER

Daily Gate City 13882
Owner: Brehm Communications, Inc.
Editorial: 1016 Main St, Keokuk, Iowa 52632-4656 **Tel:** 1 319 524-8300
Email: dgceditor@dailygate.com **Web site:** http://www.dailygate.com
Freq: Daily; **Circ:** 5079 Not Audited
Editor: Brad Cameron
Profile: The Daily Gate City serves Keokuk, IA and surrounding communities. The publication provides local, regional and national news, business, sports, editorials and features of interest to readers in the area. Its delivery area extends from Farmington, IA in the north to Warsaw, IL in the south, Kahoka, MO to the west and Carthage, IL to the east.
Language (s): English
Ad Rate: Full Page Mono 15.90
Ad Rate: Full Page Colour 19.26
Currency: United States Dollars
DAILY NEWSPAPER

The Daily Gazette 15409
Owner: Daily Gazette Co.
Editorial: 2345 Maxon Rd Ext, Schenectady, New York 12308-1105 **Tel:** 1 518 395-3140
Email: news@dailygazette.net **Web site:** http://www.dailygazette.com
Freq: Daily; **Circ:** 50974 Not Audited
Publisher: John DeAugustine; **News Editor:** Bill Finelli; **Editor:** Jeff Haff; **Editor:** Judy Patrick
Profile: The Daily Gazette is published daily for residents of Schenectady, NY and surrounding communities. The newspaper covers local and national news, weather and sports. Feature articles cover business, arts & entertainment, lifestyle and community events.
Language (s): English
Ad Rate: Full Page Mono 49.20
Ad Rate: Full Page Colour 53.40
Currency: United States Dollars
DAILY NEWSPAPER

The Daily Globe 14175
Owner: Stevenson Newspapers
Editorial: 118 E McLeod Ave, Ironwood, Michigan 49938-2120 **Tel:** 1 906 932-2211
Email: news@yourdailyglobe.com **Web site:** http://www.yourdailyglobe.com
Freq: Daily; **Circ:** 5773 Not Audited
Profile: The Daily Globe is written for the citizens of Gogebic and Ononagon County, MI as well as Iron County, WI. The publication covers local news and sports. Deadlines are at noon CT two days prior to publication.
Language (s): English
Ad Rate: Full Page Mono 11.46
Ad Rate: Full Page Colour 60.00
Currency: United States Dollars
DAILY NEWSPAPER

Daily Globe 14220
Owner: Forum Communications Co.
Editorial: 300 11th St, Worthington, Minnesota 56187-2451 **Tel:** 1 507 376-9711
Email: dgnews@dglobe.com **Web site:** http://www.dglobe.com
Freq: Daily; **Circ:** 5108 Not Audited
Publisher: Joni Harms
Profile: Worthington Daily Globe is a local daily newspaper for residents of Nobles County, MN. The publication's editorial mission is to provide local news, sports, and events coverage for the area.
Language (s): English
Ad Rate: Full Page Mono 23.95
Ad Rate: Full Page Colour 510.00
Currency: United States Dollars
DAILY NEWSPAPER

Daily Guide 14256
Owner: GateHouse Media Inc.
Editorial: 108 Holly Dr, Saint Robert, Missouri 65584-4641 **Tel:** 1 573 336-3711
Web site: http://www.waynesvilledailyguide.com
Freq: Daily; **Circ:** 1550 Not Audited
Publisher: Tom Bookstaver; **Editor:** Mandy Matney
Profile: Daily Guide is a daily newspaper serving the residents of Crocker, Dixon, Laquey, Fort Leonard Wood, Richland, St. Robert and Waynesville, MO.
Language (s): English
Ad Rate: Full Page Mono 7.60
Ad Rate: Full Page Colour 50.00
Currency: United States Dollars
DAILY NEWSPAPER

Daily Hampshire Gazette 14130
Owner: Newspapers of New England
Editorial: 115 Conz St, Northampton, Massachusetts 01060-4426 **Tel:** 1 413 584-5000
Email: newsroom@gazettenet.com **Web site:** http://www.gazettenet.com
Freq: Mon thru Fri; **Circ:** 14475 Not Audited
Profile: Daily Hampshire Gazette is a daily broadsheet newspaper serving Northampton and Hampshire County, MA. The publication covers local news, entertainment, sports, and lifestyle. Local business coverage is contained primarily in the biweekly Business section in the Monday and Thursday editions. Other regular sections include Tuesday's Health, Wednesday's lifestyle and books page, Thursday's entertainment and home and garden sections, Friday's Hampshire Life Magazine and Real Estate EXTRA. The Saturday edition is the paper's expanded weekend edition, covering topics such as religion, senior issues, travel, society news, food, automotive, and television. The paper has no Sunday edition.
Language (s): English
Ad Rate: Full Page Mono 20.43
Ad Rate: Full Page Colour 465.00
Currency: United States Dollars
DAILY NEWSPAPER

Daily Herald 14310
Owner: Wick Communications Inc.
Editorial: 916 Roanoke Ave, Roanoke Rapids, North Carolina 27870-2720 **Tel:** 1 252 537-2505
Email: rrdailyherald@gmail.com **Web site:** http://www.rrdailyherald.com
Freq: Daily; **Circ:** 11153 Not Audited
Publisher: Titus Workman
Profile: Daily Herald is published weekly for the residents of Roanoke Rapids, NC and surrounding areas. It covers local news, sports, lifestyle, business, agriculture and entertainment.
Language (s): English
Ad Rate: Full Page Mono 17.45
Ad Rate: Full Page Colour 109.50
Currency: United States Dollars
DAILY NEWSPAPER

The Daily Herald 14624
Owner: Sample News Group
Editorial: 1067 Pennsylvania Ave, Tyrone, Pennsylvania 16686-1513 **Tel:** 1 814 684-4000
Email: news@thedailyherald.net
Freq: Daily; **Circ:** 1500 Not Audited
Advertising Sales Manager: Linda Daniels
Profile: The Daily Herald covers local news and community events for residents of Blair County, PA. Deadlines fall on the issue day at 9:30am ET.
Language (s): English
Ad Rate: Full Page Mono 7.10
Ad Rate: Full Page Colour 172.10
Currency: United States Dollars
DAILY NEWSPAPER

The Daily Herald 14664
Owner: Stephens Media
Editorial: 1115 S Main St, Columbia, Tennessee 38401 **Tel:** 1 931 388-6464
Email: newsroomc@c-dh.net **Web site:** http://www.columbiadailyherald.com
Freq: Daily
Editor: James Bennett; **Editor:** Susan Thurman
Profile: The Daily Herald is a local newspaper written for residents of Columbia, Maury County, and Southern Middle Tennessee. The newspaper covers local news, sports, government, business, schools, police and events.
Language (s): English
Ad Rate: Full Page Mono 13.45
Ad Rate: Full Page Colour 293.45
Currency: United States Dollars
DAILY NEWSPAPER

The Daily Herald 14784
Owner: Sound Publishing, Inc.
Editorial: 1800 41st St #S-300, Everett, Washington 98203-2355 **Tel:** 1 425 339-3000
Email: newstips@heraldnet.com **Web site:** http://www.heraldnet.com
Freq: Daily; **Circ:** 35201 Not Audited
News Editor: Mark Carlson
Profile: The Daily Herald is written for residents of Snohomish and Island counties in Washington. It features world, national, state and local news, sports, opinion and the economy. It also provides its readers with a lifestyle section each day of the week.
Language (s): English
Ad Rate: Full Page Mono 71.04
Ad Rate: Full Page Colour 1180.00
Currency: United States Dollars
DAILY NEWSPAPER

Daily Herald 14949
Owner: Ogden Newspapers, Inc.
Editorial: 1555 N Freedom Blvd, Provo, Utah 84604-2519 **Tel:** 1 801 373-5050
Web site: http://www.heraldextra.com
Freq: Daily; **Circ:** 23489 Not Audited
Profile: The Daily Herald is a daily newspaper that covers national, international and local news, sports, lifestyles, culture, and entertainment in Utah. Contact the publication for advertising and circulation information.
Language (s): English
Ad Rate: Full Page Mono 37.35
Ad Rate: Full Page Colour 225.00
Currency: United States Dollars
DAILY NEWSPAPER

Daily Herald - Cook County 16326
Owner: Paddock Publications
Editorial: 155 E Algonquin Rd, Arlington Heights, Illinois 60005-4617 **Tel:** 1 847 427-4300
Email: news@dailyherald.com **Web site:** http://www.dailyherald.com
Freq: Daily; **Circ:** 78878 Not Audited
News Editor: Michelle Holdway
Profile: Daily Herald - Cook County is a daily newspaper circulated primarily in the suburban area Northwest of Chicago. The paper features major local, regional, national and world news. Local stories come from around the city and surrounding suburbs. Business coverage includes national and world economic news, stock listings, and coverage of start-ups and local entrepreneurs. The newspaper also covers national and international news and features, arts & entertainment, travel, books, health and fitness, relationships, money, family and sports. The total circulation for the Daily Herald group of publications for the Cook, Dupage, McHenry and Lake markets is approximately 130,000.
Language (s): English
Ad Rate: Full Page Mono 133.95
Ad Rate: Full Page Colour 144.70
Currency: United States Dollars
DAILY NEWSPAPER

Daily Herald - DuPage County 363972
Owner: Paddock Publications
Editorial: 4300 Commerce Ct, Lisle, Illinois 60532-3709 **Tel:** 1 630 955-3500

Email: news@dailyherald.com **Web site:** http://www.dailyherald.com
Freq: Daily; **Circ:** 86865 Not Audited
Profile: The Daily Herald is a daily newspaper circulated primarily in the suburban areas of Chicago. The paper features major local, regional, national, and world news. Local stories come from around the city and surrounding suburbs. Business coverage includes national and world economic news, stock listings, and coverage of start-ups and local entrepreneurs. The newspaper also covers national and international news and features, arts and entertainment, travel, books, health and fitness, relationships, money, family, and sports. The total circulation for the Daily Herald group of publications for the Cook, Dupage, McHenry and Lake markets is approximately 130,000. See Daily Herald - Cook County for a list of special sections. Deadlines are two days before distribution.
Language (s): English
Ad Rate: Full Page Mono 133.95
Ad Rate: Full Page Colour 144.70
Currency: United States Dollars
DAILY NEWSPAPER

Daily Herald - Lake County 363488
Owner: Paddock Publications
Editorial: 1795 N Butterfield Rd Ste 100, Libertyville, Illinois 60048-1212 **Tel:** 1 847 680-5800
Email: news@dailyherald.com **Web site:** http://www.dailyherald.com
Freq: Daily; **Circ:** 86865 Not Audited
Bureau Chief & Lake County Editor: Pete Nenni
Profile: The Daily Herald is a daily newspaper circulated primarily in the suburban areas of Chicago. The paper features major local, regional, national, and world news. Local stories come from around the city and surrounding suburbs. Business coverage includes national and world economic news, stock listings, and coverage of start-ups and local entrepreneurs. The newspaper also covers national and international news and features, arts and entertainment, travel, books, health and fitness, relationships, money, family, and sports. The total circulation for the Daily Herald group of publications for the Cook, Dupage, McHenry and Lake markets is approximately 130,000. See Daily Herald, IL-D30 for a list of special sections. Deadlines are two days before distribution.
Language (s): English
Ad Rate: Full Page Mono 133.95
Ad Rate: Full Page Colour 144.70
Currency: United States Dollars
DAILY NEWSPAPER

Daily Herald - North Kane County 363895
Owner: Paddock Publications
Editorial: 385 Airport Rd Ste A, Elgin, Illinois 60123-9341 **Tel:** 1 847 608-2700
Email: news@dailyherald.com **Web site:** http://www.dailyherald.com
Freq: Daily; **Circ:** 86865 Not Audited
Profile: The Daily Herald is a series of daily newspapers circulated primarily in the suburban areas of Chicago. The papers feature major local, regional, national, and world news. Local stories come from around the city and surrounding suburbs. Business coverage includes national and world economic news, stock listings, and coverage of start-ups and local entrepreneurs. The newspapers also cover national and international news and features, arts and entertainment, travel, books, health and fitness, relationships, money, family, and sports. Deadlines are two days before distribution.
Language (s): English
Ad Rate: Full Page Mono 133.95
Ad Rate: Full Page Colour 144.70
Currency: United States Dollars
DAILY NEWSPAPER

The Daily Home 13676
Owner: Consolidated Publishing
Editorial: 4 Sylacauga Highway, Talladega, Alabama 35161 **Tel:** 1 256 362-1000
Email: news@dailyhome.com **Web site:** http://www.annistonstar.com/the_daily_home/
Freq: Daily; **Circ:** 9321 Not Audited
Editor: Anthony Cook; **Editor:** Laura Nation
Profile: The Daily Home is published for the residents of Talladega, Sylacauga and Pell City, AL. It covers local news and events.
Language (s): English
Ad Rate: Full Page Mono 9.75
Currency: United States Dollars
DAILY NEWSPAPER

The Daily Iberian 14105
Owner: Wick Communications Inc.
Editorial: 926 E Main St, New Iberia, Louisiana 70560-3866 **Tel:** 1 337 365-6773
Email: news@daily-iberian.com **Web site:** http://www.iberianet.com
Freq: Daily; **Circ:** 13193 Not Audited
Profile: The Daily Iberian is the official legal journal for the Iberia Parish.
Language (s): English
Ad Rate: Full Page Mono 16.76
Ad Rate: Full Page Colour 129.00
Currency: United States Dollars
DAILY NEWSPAPER

The Daily Independent 13774
Owner: GateHouse Media Inc.
Editorial: 224 E Ridgecrest Blvd, Ridgecrest, California 93555-3975 **Tel:** 1 760 375-4481
Web site: http://www.ridgecrestca.com
Freq: Daily; **Circ:** 7493 Not Audited
Publisher: John Watkins
Profile: The Daily Independent is published for the residents of Ridgecrest, CA and the surrounding areas. All mail must be sent to the P.O. box address.
Language (s): English
Ad Rate: Full Page Mono 12.27
Ad Rate: Full Page Colour 18.57
Currency: United States Dollars
DAILY NEWSPAPER

The Daily Independent 14072
Owner: Community Newspaper Holdings, Inc.
Editorial: 224 17th St, Ashland, Kentucky 41101-7606 **Tel:** 1 606 326-2600
Web site: http://dailyindependent.com
Freq: Daily; **Circ:** 12066 Not Audited
Publisher: Eddie Blakeley; **Editor:** Lee Ward
Profile: "The Ashland Independent is a daily newspaper in Ashland, Kentucky, USA covering local news, sports, business, jobs, and community events. <div> </div><div>The newspaper is published seven days a week.</div> <div> </div><div>The Independent (formerly known as The Daily Independent and The Sunday Independent) covers the city of Ashland and surrounding areas of Boyd County, Kentucky.</div>"
Language (s): English
Ad Rate: Full Page Mono 29.40
Ad Rate: Full Page Colour 380.00
Currency: United States Dollars
DAILY NEWSPAPER

The Daily Inter Lake 14284
Owner: Hagadone Corp.
Editorial: 727 E Idaho St, Kalispell, Montana 59901-3202 **Tel:** 1 406 755-7000
Email: edit@dailyinterlake.com **Web site:** http://www.dailyinterlake.com
Freq: Daily; **Circ:** 15112 Not Audited
Publisher: Rick Weaver
Profile: The Daily Inter Lake is a daily newspaper published for the residents of Kalispell, MT. It provides information on local news and events.
Language (s): English
Ad Rate: Full Page Mono 24.91
Ad Rate: Full Page Colour 161.27
Currency: United States Dollars
DAILY NEWSPAPER

Daily Iowegian 13869
Owner: Community Newspaper Holdings, Inc.
Editorial: 201 N 13th St, Centerville, Iowa 52544-1748 **Tel:** 1 641 856-6336
Email: newsroom@dailyiowegian.com **Web site:** http://dailyiowegian.com
Freq: Daily; **Circ:** 2500
Editor: Krystal Fowler; **Publisher:** Becky Maxwell
Profile: Daily Iowegian is a daily newspaper serving Appanoose County since 1864. The paper covers local news and community events for all or part of Appanoose, Wayne, Putnam, Sullivan counties including Centerville and surrounding communities.
Language (s): English
Ad Rate: Full Page Mono 8.00
Ad Rate: Full Page Colour 36.39
Currency: United States Dollars
DAILY NEWSPAPER

The Daily Item 14125
Owner: Hastings and Sons Publishing Co.
Editorial: 38 Exchange St, Lynn, Massachusetts 01901-1425 **Tel:** 1 781 593-7700
Email: contactus@itemlive.com **Web site:** http://www.itemlive.com
Freq: Daily; **Circ:** 13109 Not Audited
Publisher: Peter Gamage
Profile: The Daily Item is a family-owned, independent newspaper serving the Lynn, Lynnfield, Marblehead, Nahant, Peabody, Revere, Saugus and Swampscott, MA areas. The newspaper is published Monday through Saturday.
Language (s): English
Ad Rate: Full Page Mono 37.26
Ad Rate: Full Page Colour 122.10
Currency: United States Dollars
DAILY NEWSPAPER

The Daily Item 14620
Owner: Community Newspaper Holdings, Inc.
Editorial: 200 Market St, Sunbury, Pennsylvania 17801-3402 **Tel:** 1 570 286-5671
Email: news@dailyitem.com **Web site:** http://dailyitem.com
Freq: Daily; **Circ:** 19652 Not Audited
Profile: The Daily Item is a local newspaper for residents of Northumberland, Columbia, Snyder, Perry, Montour, Union and Juniata counties, PA. The newspaper covers local news, sports, entertainment, politics and community events.
Language (s): English
Ad Rate: Full Page Mono 53.91
Ad Rate: Full Page Colour 300.00
Currency: United States Dollars
DAILY NEWSPAPER

Daily Jefferson County Union 14804
Owner: Hoard & Sons Co. (W.D.)
Editorial: 28 Milwaukee Ave W, Fort Atkinson, Wisconsin 53538-2018 **Tel:** 1 920 563-5553
Email: dailyunion@dailyunion.com **Web site:** http://www.dailyunion.com
Freq: Mon thru Fri; **Circ:** 7139 Not Audited
Advertising Sales Manager: Robb Grindstaff; **Publisher:** Brian Knox; **Editor:** Ryan Whisner
Profile: Daily Jefferson County Union provides local and national news for residents of the Jefferson County, WI.
Language (s): English
Ad Rate: Full Page Mono 13.50
Ad Rate: Full Page Colour 76.47
Currency: United States Dollars
DAILY NEWSPAPER

The Daily Jeffersonian 14441
Owner: GateHouse Media Inc.
Editorial: 831 Wheeling Ave, Cambridge, Ohio 43725-2316 **Tel:** 1 740 439-3531
Email: newsroom@daily-jeff.com **Web site:** http://www.daily-jeff.com
Freq: Daily; **Circ:** 12625 Not Audited
Profile: The Daily Jeffersonian is published for the residents of Guernsey, Noble, Muskingum, Belmont and Tuscarawas counties in Southeastern Ohio. It covers local news, government, business, sports and lifestyle. The newspaper also features national stories if they have a direct impact on the readership.
Language (s): English
Ad Rate: Full Page Mono 16.00
Ad Rate: Full Page Colour 265.00
Currency: United States Dollars
DAILY NEWSPAPER

The Daily Journal 13937
Owner: Small Newspaper Group
Editorial: 8 Dearborn Sq, Kankakee, Illinois 60901-3909 **Tel:** 1 815 937-3300
Email: editors@daily-journal.com **Web site:** http://www.daily-journal.com
Freq: Mon thru Fri; **Circ:** 30000 Not Audited
Publisher: Robert Small
Profile: The Daily Journal is published daily for the residents of Kankakee, IL and surrounding areas. The newspaper covers local news, business, sports and entertainment.
Language (s): English
Ad Rate: Full Page Mono 30.71
Ad Rate: Full Page Colour 101.43
Currency: United States Dollars
DAILY NEWSPAPER

Daily Journal 13984
Owner: AIM Media Indiana
Editorial: 30 S Water St, Second Floor, Suite A, Franklin, Indiana 46131-2316 **Tel:** 1 317 736-7101
Email: newstips@dailyjournal.net **Web site:** http://www.dailyjournal.net
Freq: Mon thru Fri; **Circ:** 10744 Not Audited
Editor: Michele Holtkamp; **Publisher:** Chuck Wells
Profile: Daily Journal is a local newspaper written for residents of Johnson County, IN. The newspaper covers local news, sports and events.
Language (s): English
Ad Rate: Full Page Mono 19.80
Ad Rate: Full Page Colour 318.00
Currency: United States Dollars
DAILY NEWSPAPER

The Daily Journal 14206
Owner: Boone Newspapers Inc.
Editorial: 914 E Channing Ave, Fergus Falls, Minnesota 56537-3738 **Tel:** 1 218 736-7511
Email: newsroom@fergusfallsjournal.com **Web site:** http://www.fergusfallsjournal.com
Freq: Daily; **Circ:** 5168 Not Audited
Profile: The Daily Journal is written for residents in and around Fergus Falls, MN. The paper covers local news, sports, lifestyle and weather. The lead time varies.
Language (s): English
Ad Rate: Full Page Mono 17.80
Ad Rate: Full Page Colour 75.00
Currency: United States Dollars
DAILY NEWSPAPER

The Daily Journal 14230
Owner: Lee Enterprises, Inc.
Editorial: 1513 S Saint Joe Dr, Park Hills, Missouri 63601-2402 **Tel:** 1 573 431-2010
Email: editorial@dailyjournalonline.com **Web site:** http://www.dailyjournalonline.com
Freq: Daily; **Circ:** 4933 Not Audited
Profile: The Daily Journal is a local daily newspaper published for the residents of Parks Hill, MO. Covers local news, sports, entertainment, business and community events.
Language (s): English
Ad Rate: Full Page Mono 17.75
Ad Rate: Full Page Colour 230.00
Currency: United States Dollars
DAILY NEWSPAPER

The Daily Journal 14366
Owner: Gannett Co., Inc.
Editorial: 891 E Oak Rd, Vineland, New Jersey 08360-2311 **Tel:** 1 856 691-5000
Web site: http://www.thedailyjournal.com
Freq: Daily; **Circ:** 11337 Not Audited
Profile: The Daily Journal is published for the residents of Vineland, NJ and surrounding areas. The newspaper covers local and state news, sports, education, lifestyles and entertainment.
Language (s): English
Ad Rate: Full Page Mono 54.74
Ad Rate: Full Page Colour 468.00
Currency: United States Dollars
DAILY NEWSPAPER

Daily Journal 78522
Owner: SMDJ, LLC
Editorial: 1900 Alameda De Las Pulgas Ste 112, San Mateo, California 94403-1295 **Tel:** 1 650 344-5200
Email: news@smdailyjournal.com **Web site:** http://www.smdailyjournal.com
Freq: Daily; **Circ:** 15000 Not Audited
Publisher: Jerry Lee
Profile: Daily Journal is a local newspaper published six days a week for residents of San Mateo, CA, and surrounding communities. The newspaper covers local and national news, weather, sports and community events.
Language (s): English
Ad Rate: Full Page Mono 25.00
Ad Rate: Full Page Colour 299.00
Currency: United States Dollars
DAILY NEWSPAPER

Daily Leader 13955
Owner: GateHouse Media Inc.
Editorial: 318 N Main St, Pontiac, Illinois 61764-1930 **Tel:** 1 815 842-1153
Email: ldrnews@mchsi.com **Web site:** http://www.pontiacdailyleader.com
Freq: Mon; **Circ:** 4170 Not Audited
Advertising Sales Manager: Judy Sweitzer
Profile: Daily Leader is a local daily newspaper written for residents in and around Pontiac, IL and Livingston County, IL. The paper covers local news, sports, entertainment, business and weather.
Language (s): English
Ad Rate: Full Page Mono 11.87
Ad Rate: Full Page Colour 190.00
Currency: United States Dollars
DAILY NEWSPAPER

Daily Ledger 13915
Owner: GateHouse Media Inc.
Editorial: 53 W Elm St, Canton, Illinois 61520-2511 **Tel:** 1 309 647-5100
Email: editor@cantondailyledger.com **Web site:** http://www.cantondailyledger.com
Freq: Daily; **Circ:** 4932 Not Audited
Advertising Sales Manager: Jacquelin Caulkins; **Editor:** John Froehling
Profile: Daily Ledger is a local daily published newspaper written for the residents of Canton and Fulton County, IL. The publication covers local and national news, entertainment, health, sports and business issues.
Language (s): English
Ad Rate: Full Page Mono 12.30
Ad Rate: Full Page Colour 240.00
Currency: United States Dollars
DAILY NEWSPAPER

Daily Local News 14629
Owner: Digital First Media
Editorial: 250 N Bradford Ave, West Chester, Pennsylvania 19382-1912 **Tel:** 1 610 696-1775
Email: news@dailylocal.com **Web site:** http://www.dailylocal.com
Freq: Daily; **Circ:** 26772 Not Audited
Publisher: Ed Condra; **News Editor:** Mike Rellahan
Profile: Daily Local News in West Chester, PA covers local news, sports, events, business and politics affecting residents of Chester County, PA. It also covers national news if it has direct impact on the readership.
Language (s): English
Ad Rate: Full Page Mono 52.87
Ad Rate: Full Page Colour 865.00
Currency: United States Dollars
DAILY NEWSPAPER

The Daily Mail 14396
Owner: Johnson Newspaper Corp.
Editorial: 414 Main St, Catskill, New York 12414-1303 **Tel:** 1 518 943-2100
Email: editorial@thedailymail.net **Web site:** http://www.thedailymail.net
Freq: Fri; **Circ:** 2713 Not Audited
Editor: Raymond Pignone
Profile: The Daily Mail is a daily newspaper serving the residents of Green County, NY. The editorial content covers sports, technology, weather, business, and community news and events.
Language (s): English
Ad Rate: Full Page Mono 10.50
Currency: United States Dollars
DAILY NEWSPAPER

The Daily Messenger 14395
Owner: GateHouse Media Inc.
Editorial: 73 Buffalo St, Canandaigua, New York 14424-1001 **Tel:** 1 585 394-0770
Email: messengerpost@messengerpostmedia.com
Web site: http://www.mpnnow.com
Freq: Fri; **Circ:** 11255 Not Audited
Editor: Dave Wheeler
Profile: The Daily Messenger is a local daily newspaper for residents of Ontario County, NY. The paper is dedicated to linking its readers and advertisers to the greater Rochester and Western Finger Lakes, NY region by focusing on local and neighborhood news. The paper also provides national news coverage provided by news services.
Language (s): English
Ad Rate: Full Page Mono 17.80
Currency: United States Dollars
DAILY NEWSPAPER

The Daily Mining Gazette 14172
Owner: Ogden Newspapers
Editorial: 206 Shelden Ave, Houghton, Michigan 49931-2134 **Tel:** 1 906 482-1500
Email: clerk@mininggazette.com **Web site:** http://www.mininggazette.com
Freq: Mon thru Fri; **Circ:** 6142 Not Audited
Publisher: Michael Scott
Profile: The Daily Mining Gazette is published for residents of Houghton, MI and surrounding areas. The publication covers local news, business, sports, lifestyles and entertainment.
Language (s): English

Ad Rate: Full Page Mono 17.29
Ad Rate: Full Page Colour 2070.50
Currency: United States Dollars
DAILY NEWSPAPER

Daily Mountain Eagle 13671
Owner: Cleveland Newspapers Inc.
Editorial: 1301 Viking Dr, Jasper, Alabama 35501-4983 **Tel:** 1 205 221-2840
Email: jasper@mountaineagle.com **Web site:** http://www.mountaineagle.com
Freq: Daily; **Circ:** 7745 Not Audited
Editor: Ron Harris
Profile: Daily Mountain Eagle is written for the residents of Jasper, AL. It covers local news, high school sports and lifestyle.
Language (s): English
Ad Rate: Full Page Mono 18.06
Ad Rate: Full Page Colour 231.00
Currency: United States Dollars
DAILY NEWSPAPER

Daily News 13745
Owner: MediaNews Group
Editorial: 545 Diamond Ave, Red Bluff, California 96080-4302 **Tel:** 1 530 527-2151
Web site: http://www.redbluffdailynews.com
Freq: Mon thru Fri; **Circ:** 6727
Editor: Chip Thompson
Profile: The Daily News was founded in 1885. It is a daily newspaper serving the residents of Tehama County, CA.
Language (s): English
Ad Rate: Full Page Mono 16.98
Ad Rate: Full Page Colour 201.60
Currency: United States Dollars
DAILY NEWSPAPER

Daily News 14073
Owner: News Publishing Company
Editorial: 813 College St, Bowling Green, Kentucky 42101-2132 **Tel:** 1 270 781-1700
Email: editor@bgdailynews.com **Web site:** http://www.bgdailynews.com
Freq: Daily; **Circ:** 20279
Publisher: Pipes Gaines; **Editor:** Steve Gaines
Profile: Daily News is a local, weekly newspaper serving Bowling Green, KY and surrounding communities. The newspaper offers extensive local news, sports, weather, entertainment, community news and events and relevant national news. Deadlines for the publication are 3:30 p.m.CT day prior to, and 9:30 p.m. CT, date of issue.
Language (s): English
Ad Rate: Full Page Mono 22.42
Ad Rate: Full Page Colour 575.00
Currency: United States Dollars
DAILY NEWSPAPER

The Daily News 14128
Owner: Community Newspaper Holdings, Inc.
Editorial: 23 Liberty St, Newburyport, Massachusetts 01950-2750 **Tel:** 1 978 462-6666
Email: ndn@newburyportnews.com **Web site:** http://www.newburyportnews.com
Freq: Daily; **Circ:** 8456 Not Audited
Editor: Bryan Eaton; **Advertising Sales Manager:** Bill Trefethen
Profile: The Daily News provides local news and sports coverage and information about community events to the residents of Newburyport, MA.
Language (s): English
Ad Rate: Full Page Mono 22.50
Ad Rate: Full Page Colour 500.00
Currency: United States Dollars
DAILY NEWSPAPER

The Daily News 14169
Owner: Stafford Communications Group
Editorial: 109 N Lafayette St, Greenville, Michigan 48838-1853 **Tel:** 1 616 754-9301
Email: news@staffordgroup.com **Web site:** http://www.thedailynews.cc
Freq: Daily; **Circ:** 7754 Not Audited
Publisher: Rob Stafford
Profile: The Daily News is a local newspaper covering news, sports and entertainment for residents of Montcalm, Kent and Ionia County, MI. Deadlines are at 8am CT the day before issue date.
Language (s): English
Ad Rate: Full Page Mono 15.75
Ad Rate: Full Page Colour 18.75
Currency: United States Dollars
DAILY NEWSPAPER

The Daily News 14174
Owner: Ogden Newspapers
Editorial: 215 E Ludington St, Iron Mountain, Michigan 49801-2994 **Tel:** 1 906 774-2772
Email: news@ironmountaindailynews.com **Web site:** http://www.ironmountaindailynews.com
Freq: Mon thru Fri; **Circ:** 6958 Not Audited
News Editor: Jim Anderson
Profile: The Daily News is serves the communities of Iron Mountain and Kingsford on Michigan's upper peninsula. The publication covers local news, recreation, business and high school sports. Regional, national and international news is taken exclusively from news wires.
Language (s): English
Ad Rate: Full Page Mono 26.70
Ad Rate: Full Page Colour 370.00
Currency: United States Dollars
DAILY NEWSPAPER

The Daily News 14300
Owner: GateHouse Media Inc.
Editorial: 724 Bell Fork Rd, Jacksonville, North Carolina 28540-6311 **Tel:** 1 910 353-1171
Email: jdnhappenings@jdnews.com **Web site:** http://www.jdnews.com
Freq: Daily; **Circ:** 12982 Not Audited
Profile: The Daily News is the local newspaper for Jacksonville, NC and its surrounding community. It covers local business, news, lifestyle and sports stories. During the week, one page of the local news section is devoted to news about the military bases located in Eastern North Carolina. The page is called Liberty.
Language (s): English
Ad Rate: Full Page Mono 32.00
Ad Rate: Full Page Colour 387.00
Currency: United States Dollars
DAILY NEWSPAPER

The Daily News 14334
Owner: Wick Communications Inc.
Editorial: 601 Dakota Ave, Wahpeton, North Dakota 58075-4325 **Tel:** 1 701 642-8585
Email: editor@wahpetondailynews.com **Web site:** http://www.wahpetondailynews.com
Freq: Daily; **Circ:** 2584 Not Audited
Profile: The Daily News serves the Wahpeton, ND and Breckenridge, MN areas. The publication covers local news, sports and events.
Language (s): English
Ad Rate: Full Page Mono 10.50
Ad Rate: Full Page Colour 12.50
Currency: United States Dollars
DAILY NEWSPAPER

The Daily News 14584
Owner: Philadelphia Media Network Inc
Editorial: 325 Penn St, Huntingdon, Pennsylvania 16652-1455 **Tel:** 1 814 643-4040
Email: dnews@huntingdondailynews.com **Web site:** http://www.huntingdondailynews.com/
Freq: Daily; **Circ:** 9258 Not Audited
News Editor: Polly McMullin
Profile: The Daily News is written for residents of Huntington, PA and surrounding areas.
Language (s): English
Ad Rate: Full Page Mono 14.85
Ad Rate: Full Page Colour 240.00
Currency: United States Dollars
DAILY NEWSPAPER

The Daily News 14785
Owner: Lee Enterprises, Inc.
Editorial: 770 11th Ave, Longview, Washington 98632-2412 **Tel:** 1 360 577-2500
Email: frontdoor@tdn.com **Web site:** http://www.tdn.com
Freq: Daily; **Circ:** 19307 Not Audited
Publisher: Rick Parrish; **Advertising Sales Manager:** Steve Quaife; **Editor:** Roger Werth
Profile: The Daily News is written for the residents of the Longview, WA and the surrounding area. It covers local news, sports, outdoor recreation and arts & entertainment.
Language (s): English
Ad Rate: Full Page Mono 29.35
Ad Rate: Full Page Colour 33.40
Currency: United States Dollars
DAILY NEWSPAPER

The Daily News 349686
Editorial: 369 N 100 W Ste 1, Cedar City, Utah 84721-3590 **Tel:** 1 435 865-4520
Web site: http://www.thespectrum.com/cedar-city
Freq: Daily; **Circ:** 5692 Not Audited
Profile: The Daily News is a daily, local newspaper serving the residents of Cedar City and Iron County, UT. The newspaper covers local news, sports and other topics of interest to the readers.
Language (s): English
Ad Rate: Full Page Mono 12.80
Currency: United States Dollars
DAILY NEWSPAPER

The Daily News Journal 14675
Owner: Gannett Co., Inc.
Editorial: 224 N Walnut St, Murfreesboro, Tennessee 37130-3622 **Tel:** 1 615 893-5860
Email: news@dnj.com **Web site:** http://www.dnj.com
Freq: Daily; **Circ:** 10325 Not Audited
Profile: The Daily News Journal is a daily publication serving residents of Murfreesboro, TN and the surrounding counties. The paper focuses on local news, sports and politics with some national coverage.
Language (s): English
Ad Rate: Full Page Mono 21.06
Ad Rate: Full Page Colour 147.00
Currency: United States Dollars
DAILY NEWSPAPER

Daily News Publications - Palo Alto 500394
Owner: MediaNews Group
Editorial: 255 Constitution Dr, Menlo Park, California 94025-1108 **Tel:** 1 650 391-1000
Email: eventsandnews@dailynewsgroup.com **Web site:** http://www.mercurynews.com/peninsula
Freq: Daily; **Circ:** 21100 Not Audited
Language (s): English
DAILY NEWSPAPER

Daily News-Record 14757
Owner: Byrd Newspapers
Editorial: 231 S Liberty St, Harrisonburg, Virginia 22801-3621 **Tel:** 1 540 574-6200
Web site: http://www.dnronline.com
Freq: Daily; **Circ:** 25639 Not Audited
Editor & Publisher: Jeff Gauger
Profile: Daily News-Record covers local and world news for residents of Harrisonburg and the Shenandoah Valley, VA as well as counties in neighboring West Virginia. The publication also features business news, local politics, education, arts & entertainment and lifestyle.
Language (s): English
Ad Rate: Full Page Mono 26.00
Ad Rate: Full Page Colour 495.00
Currency: United States Dollars
DAILY NEWSPAPER

Daily News-Sun 13718
Owner: Independent Newsmedia Inc. USA
Editorial: 10102 W Santa Fe Dr, Sun City, Arizona 85351-3106 **Tel:** 1 623 977-8351
Email: wvnews@newszap.com **Web site:** http://www.yourwestvalley.com
Freq: Mon thru Fri; **Circ:** 7171 Not Audited
Advertising Sales Manager: Penny Bruns
Profile: Daily News-Sun is published for the residents of Sun City, Youngtown, El Mirage, Glendale, Peoria and Surprise, AZ and surrounding areas. It covers local news, sports and events.
Language (s): English
Ad Rate: Full Page Mono 16.00
Ad Rate: Full Page Colour 300.00
Currency: United States Dollars
DAILY NEWSPAPER

The Daily Nonpareil 13873
Owner: Southwest Iowa Newspaper Association
Editorial: 535 W Broadway Ste 300, Council Bluffs, Iowa 51503-0831 **Tel:** 1 712 328-1811
Email: web@nonpareilonline.com **Web site:** http://www.nonpareilonline.com
Freq: Fri; **Circ:** 12788
Publisher: Thomas Schmitt
Profile: The Daily Nonpareil is written for residents in and around Council Bluffs, IA. The paper covers local news, sports and weather.
Language (s): English
Ad Rate: Full Page Mono 25.00
Ad Rate: Full Page Colour 82.42
Currency: United States Dollars
DAILY NEWSPAPER

Daily Pilot 14893
Owner: tronc
Editorial: 10540 Talbert Ave Suite 300, Costa Mesa, California 92708 **Tel:** 1 714 966-4600
Email: dailypilot@latimes.com **Web site:** http://www.latimes.com/socal/daily-pilot
Freq: Fri; **Circ:** 17031 Not Audited
Editor: John Canalis
Profile: The Daily Pilot is a newspaper publishing Wednesday through Sunday, along with daily online updates, serving Costa Mesa, Newport Beach, Huntington Beach, Laguna Beach, Fountain Valley, Sunset Beach and Seal Beach. The paper is inserted into home delivered and newsstand versions in the Los Angeles Times, and is available for free at standalone racks locally. Merged with Coastline Pilot and Huntington Beach Independent in August 2016.
Language (s): English
Ad Rate: Full Page Mono 29.90
Ad Rate: Full Page Colour 325.00
Currency: United States Dollars
DAILY NEWSPAPER

Daily Post 399993
Owner: San Francisco Daily LLC
Editorial: 324 High St, Palo Alto, California 94301-1042 **Tel:** 1 650 328-7700
Email: news@padailypost.com **Web site:** http://www.padailypost.com
Freq: Mon thru Fri; **Circ:** 7500 Not Audited
Profile: Daily Post is a free newspaper that is published each weekday. Its focus is on the Marina, Cow Hollow, Fillmore, Noe Valley and Castro districts of San Francisco. Although neighborhood issues and local news dominate the paper, it also contains regional, national and international news stories. The paper is distributed in stores, coffee shops, restaurants and workplaces and circulates from Mountain View and Los Altos to the Golden Gate Bridge. Advertising deadlines are daily at 3pm PT.
Language (s): English
Ad Rate: Full Page Mono 15.00
Ad Rate: Full Page Colour 18.00
Currency: United States Dollars
DAILY NEWSPAPER

The Daily Post-Athenian 14660
Owner: Jones Media, Inc.
Editorial: 320 S Jackson St, Athens, Tennessee 37303-4715 **Tel:** 1 423 745-5664
Email: news@dailypostathenian.com **Web site:** http://www.dailypostathenian.com
Freq: Daily; **Circ:** 10413
Advertising Sales Manager: Rhonda Elkins; **Editor:** Douglas Headrick; **News Editor:** Autumn Hughes
Profile: The Daily Post-Athenian is a local newspaper written for residents of McMinn and Meigs counties in TN. The newspaper covers local news, sports, business and lifestyles.
Language (s): English
Ad Rate: Full Page Mono 15.50
Ad Rate: Full Page Colour 260.00
Currency: United States Dollars
DAILY NEWSPAPER

Daily Press 13762
Owner: GateHouse Media Inc.
Editorial: 13891 Park Ave, Victorville, California 92392-2435 **Tel:** 1 760 241-7744
Email: vvnews@vvdailypress.com **Web site:** http://www.vvdailypress.com
Freq: Daily; **Circ:** 25059 Not Audited
Editor: Steve Hunt
Profile: Daily Press is a newspaper serving Victorville, CA and the surrounding Victor Valley in San Bernardino County. The publication covers local news, sports, and entertainment.
Language (s): English
Ad Rate: Full Page Mono 38.12
Ad Rate: Full Page Colour 400.00
Currency: United States Dollars
DAILY NEWSPAPER

Daily Press 14167
Owner: Ogden Newspapers
Editorial: 600 Ludington St, Escanaba, Michigan 49829-3830 **Tel:** 1 906 786-2021
Email: news@dailypress.net **Web site:** http://www.dailypress.net
Freq: Mon thru Fri; **Circ:** 6652
Publisher: Dan McDonald; **Editor:** Brian Rowell; **Advertising Sales Manager:** Ann Troutman
Profile: Daily Press is published weekly for residents of Escanaba, MI. The newspaper covers local news and community events.
Language (s): English
Ad Rate: Full Page Mono 26.40
Ad Rate: Full Page Colour 205.00
Currency: United States Dollars
DAILY NEWSPAPER

The Daily Press 14617
Owner: Horizon Publications
Editorial: 245 Brusselles St, Saint Marys, Pennsylvania 15857-1501 **Tel:** 1 814 781-1596
Email: smnews@smdailypress.com **Web site:** http://www.smdailypress.com
Freq: Mon thru Fri; **Circ:** 5550 Not Audited
Publisher: Darlene Coder; **Advertising Sales Manager:** Betty Skrzypek
Profile: The Daily Press serves the residents of Saint Marys, PA. It provides local, regional and national news coverage.
Language (s): English
Ad Rate: Full Page Mono 9.05
Ad Rate: Full Page Colour 200.00
Currency: United States Dollars
DAILY NEWSPAPER

Daily Press 15435
Owner: tronc
Editorial: 703 Mariners Row, Newport News, Virginia 23606 **Tel:** 1 757 247-4600
Web site: http://www.dailypress.com
Freq: Daily; **Circ:** 41946 Not Audited
Profile: Daily Press is written for the residents of Newport, Hampton, York, Williamsburg, Gloucester, Matthews, Middlesex, Isle of Wight and Surrey, VA. The newspaper covers local, national and international news, along with sports, arts & entertainment and features.
Language (s): English
Ad Rate: Full Page Mono 81.64
Ad Rate: Full Page Colour 255.46
Currency: United States Dollars
DAILY NEWSPAPER

The Daily Progress 14752
Owner: BH Media Group
Editorial: 685 Rio Rd W, Charlottesville, Virginia 22901-1413 **Tel:** 1 434 978-7200
Web site: http://www.dailyprogress.com
Freq: Daily; **Circ:** 21085 Not Audited
Editor: Nick Mathews
Profile: The Daily Progress covers news for residents of Charlottesville, VA and Albemarle, Buckingham, Fluvanna, Greene, Louisa, Madison, Orange and Nelson Counties. Coverage includes local, national and international news, as well as business, local courts, arts & entertainment, politics and weather.
Language (s): English
Ad Rate: Full Page Mono 44.56
Ad Rate: Full Page Colour 1630.00
Currency: United States Dollars
DAILY NEWSPAPER

Daily Record 13940
Owner: Lewis Newspapers
Editorial: 1209 State St, Lawrenceville, Illinois 62439 **Tel:** 1 618 943-2331
Email: lawnews@lawdailyrecord.com **Web site:** http://www.lawdailyrecord.com
Freq: Mon thru Fri; **Circ:** 4012 Not Audited
Publisher: Kathleen Lewis; **Advertising Sales Manager:** Sandie Young
Profile: Daily Record is published for the residents of Lawrence County, IL. It provides information on local news and events.
Language (s): English
Ad Rate: Full Page Mono 7.50
Ad Rate: Full Page Colour 195.00
Currency: United States Dollars
DAILY NEWSPAPER

The Daily Record 14290
Owner: Record Publishing Co.
Editorial: 99 W Broad St, Dunn, North Carolina 28334-6031 **Tel:** 1 910 891-1234
Email: news@mydailyrecord.com **Web site:** http://www.mydailyrecord.com
Freq: Daily; **Circ:** 8517 Not Audited
Profile: The Daily Record is a daily newspaper serving Anderson Creek, Angier, Benson, Buies

Creek, Bunnlevel, Coats, Dunn, Erwin, Falcon, Godwin, Lillington, Linden and Newton Grove, North Carolina and the surrounding communities. It covers local and national news, business, government and lifestyle. Deadlines are daily at 9:30am ET.
Language (s): English
Ad Rate: Full Page Mono 13.40
Currency: United States Dollars
DAILY NEWSPAPER

The Daily Record 14502
Owner: GateHouse Media Inc.
Editorial: 212 E Liberty St, Wooster, Ohio 44691-4348 **Tel:** 1 330 264-1125
Email: news@the-daily-record.com **Web site:** http://www.the-daily-record.com
Freq: Daily; **Circ:** 19076 Not Audited
News Editor: Jeanine Kendle
Profile: The Daily Record is a daily, local newspaper serving the Wooster, OH area. Local, national and international news are covered, as well as local entertainment, sports, and lifestyle information.
Language (s): English
Ad Rate: Full Page Mono 29.52
Ad Rate: Full Page Colour 485.00
Currency: United States Dollars
DAILY NEWSPAPER

Daily Record 14783
Owner: Pioneer Newspapers
Editorial: 401 N Main St, Ellensburg, Washington 98926-3107 **Tel:** 1 509 925-1414
Web site: http://dailyrecordnews.com
Freq: Daily; **Circ:** 5700 Not Audited
Profile: Daily Record provides coverage of local news, sports, events and commentary to the residents of Kittitas County, WA.
Language (s): English
Ad Rate: Full Page Mono 13.15
Ad Rate: Full Page Colour 29.50
Currency: United States Dollars
DAILY NEWSPAPER

Daily Record 15461
Owner: Gannett Co., Inc.
Editorial: 6 Century Dr, Parsippany, New Jersey 07054-4608 **Tel:** 1 973 428-6200
Email: newsroom@dailyrecord.com **Web site:** http://www.dailyrecord.com
Freq: Daily; **Circ:** 14609 Not Audited
Profile: Daily Record is a local daily newspaper for Morris County, NJ. The paper covers local and national news, sports, government, entertainment, crime and business.
Language (s): English
Ad Rate: Full Page Mono 55.59
Currency: United States Dollars
DAILY NEWSPAPER

Daily Reflector 14295
Owner: Cooke Communications, LLC
Editorial: 1150 Sugg Pkwy, Greenville, North Carolina 27834-9077 **Tel:** 1 252 752-6166
Web site: http://www.reflector.com
Freq: Daily; **Circ:** 20465 Not Audited
Publisher: John Cooke, Jr.
Profile: Daily Reflector provides local news, sports and weather to the residents of Pitt County, NC.
Language (s): English
Ad Rate: Full Page Mono 12.55
Ad Rate: Full Page Colour 1985.80
Currency: United States Dollars
DAILY NEWSPAPER

Daily Reporter 13987
Owner: AIM Media Indiana
Editorial: 22 W New Rd, Greenfield, Indiana 46140-1090 **Tel:** 1 317 462-5528
Email: dr-editorial@greenfieldreporter.com **Web site:** http://www.greenfieldreporter.com
Freq: Fri; **Circ:** 7800 Not Audited
Editor: Noelle Steele; **Publisher:** Chuck Wells
Profile: Daily Reporter is a newspaper written for residents of Greenfield, IN and surrounding areas. The newspaper covers local news, arts & entertainment, sports and community events.
Language (s): English
Ad Rate: Full Page Mono 12.75
Ad Rate: Full Page Colour 18.75
Currency: United States Dollars
DAILY NEWSPAPER

The Daily Reporter 14165
Owner: Fortress Investment Group, LLC
Editorial: 15 W Pearl St, Coldwater, Michigan 49036-1912 **Tel:** 1 517 278-2318
Web site: http://www.thedailyreporter.com
Freq: Daily; **Circ:** 5562 Not Audited
Advertising Sales Manager: Lisa Vickers
Profile: The Daily Reporter is published for the residents of Coldwater, MI. It covers local news and sports.
Language (s): English
Ad Rate: Full Page Mono 14.69
Ad Rate: Full Page Colour 53.96
Currency: United States Dollars
DAILY NEWSPAPER

Daily Reporter-Herald 13790
Owner: MediaNews Group Inc.
Editorial: 201 E 5th St, Loveland, Colorado 80537-5605 **Tel:** 1 970 669-5050
Email: news@reporter-herald.com **Web site:** http://www.reporterherald.com
Freq: Daily; **Circ:** 17062 Not Audited
Profile: Daily Reporter-Herald is a daily newspaper written for the residents of Loveland, CO. The paper covers news and events on a local, state and national level.
Language (s): English
Ad Rate: Full Page Mono 26.01
Ad Rate: Full Page Colour 101.50
Currency: United States Dollars
DAILY NEWSPAPER

Daily Republic 13726
Owner: McNaughton Newspapers
Editorial: 1250 Texas St, Fairfield, California 94533-5748 **Tel:** 1 707 425-4646
Email: drnews@dailyrepublic.net **Web site:** http://www.dailyrepublic.com
Freq: Daily; **Circ:** 17710 Not Audited
Profile: Daily Republic is published for the residents of Fairfield, CA and surrounding areas. The newspaper covers local and state news, business, sports, lifestyles and arts & entertainment.
Language (s): English
Ad Rate: Full Page Mono 23.80
Ad Rate: Full Page Colour 96.95
Currency: United States Dollars
DAILY NEWSPAPER

The Daily Republic 14654
Owner: Forum Communications Co.
Editorial: 120 S Lawler St, Mitchell, South Dakota 57301-3443 **Tel:** 1 605 996-5514
Email: webmaster@mitchellrepublic.com **Web site:** http://www.mitchellrepublic.com
Freq: Daily; **Circ:** 12400 Not Audited
Advertising Sales Manager: Lorie Hansen; **Publisher:** Korrie Wenzel
Profile: The Daily Republic is published daily for the residents of Mitchell, SD and surrounding areas. The newspaper covers local news, business, sports, education and lifestyles.
Language (s): English
Ad Rate: Full Page Mono 21.30
Ad Rate: Full Page Colour 30.45
Currency: United States Dollars
DAILY NEWSPAPER

The Daily Review 14104
Owner: LSN Publishing Co. LLC
Editorial: 1014 Front St, Morgan City, Louisiana 70380-3226 **Tel:** 1 985 384-8370
Email: news@daily-review.com **Web site:** http://www.daily-review.com
Freq: Daily; **Circ:** 5621 Not Audited
Advertising Sales Manager: Charlie LeJeune; **Publisher & Editor:** Allan Von Werder
Profile: The Daily Review is published for the residents of Morgan City, LA. The newspaper covers local and world news and information.
Language (s): English
Ad Rate: Full Page Mono 8.40
Ad Rate: Full Page Colour 300.00
Currency: United States Dollars
DAILY NEWSPAPER

Daily Review Atlas 13946
Owner: GateHouse Media Inc.
Editorial: 400 S Main St, Monmouth, Illinois 61462-2164 **Tel:** 1 309 734-3176
Email: communitynews@reviewatlas.com **Web site:** http://www.reviewatlas.com
Freq: Fri; **Circ:** 2800 Not Audited
Profile: Daily Review Atlas is published daily for the residents of Monmouth, IL and surrounding areas. The newspaper offers local, national and international news.
Language (s): English
Ad Rate: Full Page Mono 11.25
Ad Rate: Full Page Colour 180.00
Currency: United States Dollars
DAILY NEWSPAPER

Daily Rocket-Miner 14853
Owner: Rock Springs Newspapers, Inc.
Editorial: 215 D St, Rock Springs, Wyoming 82901-6234 **Tel:** 1 307 362-3736
Email: editor@rocketminer.com **Web site:** http://www.rocketminer.com
Freq: Daily; **Circ:** 7379
Publisher: Holly Dabb; **Editor:** Michele DePue; **Advertising Sales Manager:** Rick Lee
Profile: Daily Rocket-Miner is a local news publication for Rock Springs, WY. The publication runs daily, with the exception of Sunday and Monday. The paper covers mainly local and national news.
Language (s): English
Ad Rate: Full Page Mono 12.56
Ad Rate: Full Page Colour 100.00
Currency: United States Dollars
DAILY NEWSPAPER

The Daily Sentinel 13785
Owner: Seaton Publishing
Editorial: 734 S 7th St, Grand Junction, Colorado 81501-7737 **Tel:** 1 970 242-5050
Email: letters@gjsentinel.com **Web site:** http://www.gjsentinel.com
Freq: Daily; **Circ:** 23708 Not Audited
Publisher: Jay Seaton
Profile: The Daily Sentinel is a local newspaper published for the residents of Grand Junction, CO. The newspaper covers national and local news, sports, business, education and events.
Language (s): English
Ad Rate: Full Page Mono 43.21
Ad Rate: Full Page Colour 750.00
Currency: United States Dollars
DAILY NEWSPAPER

Daily Sentinel 14718
Owner: Southern Newspapers, Inc.
Editorial: 4920 Colonial Dr, Nacogdoches, Texas 75965-3021 **Tel:** 1 936 564-8361
Web site: http://dailysentinel.com
Freq: Daily; **Circ:** 8724 Not Audited
Profile: Daily Sentinel provides readers with information about current news and events taking place in the area of Nacogdoches County, TX. Deadlines are at 4pm CT.
Language (s): English
Ad Rate: Full Page Mono 14.42
Ad Rate: Full Page Colour 315.00
Currency: United States Dollars
DAILY NEWSPAPER

The Daily Siftings Herald 13682
Owner: GateHouse Media Inc.
Editorial: 205 S 26th St, Arkadelphia, Arkansas 71923-5423 **Tel:** 1 870 246-5525
Email: siftingsherald@yahoo.com **Web site:** http://www.siftingsherald.com
Freq: Daily; **Circ:** 2800 Not Audited
Profile: Arkadelphia Daily Siftings Herald is a local newspaper serving the Arkadelphia, AR area. It provides residents with information on local news, sports, weather and events.
Language (s): English
Ad Rate: Full Page Mono 12.80
Ad Rate: Full Page Colour 262.80
Currency: United States Dollars
DAILY NEWSPAPER

Daily Sitka Sentinel 13661
Owner: Verstovia Corporation
Editorial: 112 Barracks St, Sitka, Alaska 99835-7532 **Tel:** 1 907 747-3219
Email: news@sitkasentinel.com **Web site:** http://www.sitkasentinel.com
Freq: Daily; **Circ:** 3010 Not Audited
Advertising Sales Manager: Susan McFadden
Profile: Daily Sitka Sentinel is written for residents of Sitka, AK. The publication covers local, international and national news.
Language (s): English
Ad Rate: Full Page Mono 13.85
Ad Rate: Full Page Colour 57.09
Currency: United States Dollars
DAILY NEWSPAPER

The Daily Standard 14442
Owner: Standard Printing Company (The)
Editorial: 123 E Market St, Celina, Ohio 45822-1798 **Tel:** 1 419 586-2371
Email: newsroom@dailystandard.com **Web site:** http://www.dailystandard.com
Freq: Daily; **Circ:** 10914 Not Audited
Publisher: Frank Snyder
Profile: The Daily Standard's editorial mission is to provide local coverage for the Grand Lake Saint Mary's area. It is written for residents in the in the county and community and also covers world and national news.
Language (s): English
Ad Rate: Full Page Mono 11.00
Ad Rate: Full Page Colour 230.00
Currency: United States Dollars
DAILY NEWSPAPER

The Daily Star 14097
Owner: Paxton Media Group
Editorial: 725 S Morrison Blvd, Hammond, Louisiana 70403-5401 **Tel:** 1 985 254-7827
Email: editor@hammondstar.com **Web site:** http://www.hammondstar.com
Freq: Daily; **Circ:** 9595
Publisher: Bailey Dabney; **Publisher:** Keenan Gingles
Profile: The Daily Star is published for the residents of Hammond, LA and surrounding areas. The newspaper covers local news, business, sports and arts & entertainment. It also features national and statewide stories if they have a direct impact on the community.
Language (s): English
Ad Rate: Full Page Mono 20.00
Ad Rate: Full Page Colour 365.00
Currency: United States Dollars
DAILY NEWSPAPER

The Daily Star 14420
Owner: Community Newspaper Holdings, Inc.
Editorial: 102 Chestnut St, Oneonta, New York 13820-2492 **Tel:** 1 607 432-1000
Email: news@thedailystar.com **Web site:** http://www.thedailystar.com
Freq: Daily; **Circ:** 10126 Not Audited
Editor: Sam Pollak
Profile: The Daily Star is a daily newspaper that offers coverage of local and national news, weather, sports, local arts & entertainment and opinion. The newspaper is written for residents of Oneonta, NY.
Language (s): English
Ad Rate: Full Page Mono 30.55
Ad Rate: Full Page Colour 350.00
Currency: United States Dollars
DAILY NEWSPAPER

The Daily Star-Journal 14255
Owner: The News-Press & Gazette Co.
Editorial: 135 E Market St, Warrensburg, Missouri 64093-1817 **Tel:** 1 660 747-8123
Web site: http://www.dailystarjournal.com
Freq: Daily; **Circ:** 4796 Not Audited
Editor: Jack Ventimiglia
Profile: The Daily Star-Journal is written for residents of Johnson County, MO. The publication covers local, international and national news, along with local sports, entertainment, agricultural news and milestones. Deadlines for the publication are two days before issue date.
Language (s): English
Ad Rate: Full Page Mono 10.50
Ad Rate: Full Page Colour 137.00
Currency: United States Dollars
DAILY NEWSPAPER

Daily Sun News 14865
Owner: Eagle Newspapers
Editorial: 600 S 6th St, Sunnyside, Washington 98944-2111 **Tel:** 1 509 837-4500
Email: dailysunnews@dailysunnews.com **Web site:** http://www.dailysunnews.com
Freq: Daily; **Circ:** 3800 Not Audited
Publisher: Tim Graff
Profile: Daily Sun News is published daily for residents of Sunnyside, WA and surrounding areas. It covers local news and events.
Language (s): English
Ad Rate: Full Page Mono 9.00
Ad Rate: Full Page Colour 180.00
Currency: United States Dollars
DAILY NEWSPAPER

The Daily Telegram 14156
Owner: GateHouse Media Inc.
Editorial: 133 N Winter St, Adrian, Michigan 49221-2042 **Tel:** 1 517 265-5111
Email: editor@lenconnect.com **Web site:** http://www.lenconnect.com
Freq: Daily; **Circ:** 12647 Not Audited
Editor: Marge Ferguson; **Editor:** Mark Lenz; **News Editor:** David Panian
Profile: The Daily Telegram is a daily, evening newspaper serving Adrian, MI. It covers news, sports, and entertainment. The lead time varies. Contact the publication for advertising rates and circulation figures.
Language (s): English
Ad Rate: Full Page Mono 26.25
Ad Rate: Full Page Colour 785.00
Currency: United States Dollars
DAILY NEWSPAPER

The Daily Times 14147
Owner: Gannett Co., Inc.
Editorial: 618 Beam St, Salisbury, Maryland 21801-7803 **Tel:** 1 410 749-7171
Email: newshub@delmarvanow.com **Web site:** http://www.delmarvanow.com
Freq: Daily; **Circ:** 14582 Not Audited
Profile: The Daily Times is a daily newspaper serving Salisbury, MD and the surrounding areas. It covers local and national news, sports and opinion.
Language (s): English
Ad Rate: Full Page Mono 30.32
Ad Rate: Full Page Colour 400.00
Currency: United States Dollars
DAILY NEWSPAPER

The Daily Times 14374
Owner: Gannett Co., Inc.
Editorial: 201 N Allen Ave, Farmington, New Mexico 87401-6212 **Tel:** 1 505 325-4545
Email: news@daily-times.com **Web site:** http://www.daily-times.com
Freq: Daily; **Circ:** 20140 Not Audited
Publisher: Sammy Lopez
Profile: The Daily News is a local daily newspaper written for the residents of Farmington, NM. The paper covers local news, sports and features.
Language (s): English
Ad Rate: Full Page Mono 23.10
Ad Rate: Full Page Colour 77.43
Currency: United States Dollars
DAILY NEWSPAPER

Daily Times 14537
Owner: Community Newspaper Holdings, Inc.
Editorial: 105 S Adair St, Pryor, Oklahoma 74361-3625 **Tel:** 1 918 825-3292
Email: prynews@swbell.net **Web site:** http://www.pryordailytimes.com
Freq: Daily; **Circ:** 3787 Not Audited
Publisher: Ken Jones
Profile: Daily Times is published daily for the residents of Pryor, OK and surrounding areas. The newspaper covers local news, business, sports, lifestyles and entertainment.
Language (s): English
Ad Rate: Full Page Mono 12.41
Ad Rate: Full Page Colour 16.41
Currency: United States Dollars
DAILY NEWSPAPER

The Daily Times 14673
Owner: Blount County Publishers LLC
Editorial: 307 E Harper Ave, Maryville, Tennessee 37804-5724 **Tel:** 1 865 981-1100
Email: editor@thedailytimes.com **Web site:** http://www.thedailytimes.com
Freq: Daily; **Circ:** 18425 Not Audited
News Editor: Richard Dodson; **Editor:** Bob Norris; **Editor:** Melanie Tucker; **Editor:** Steve Wildsmith
Profile: The Daily Times is a daily newspaper published for residents of Maryville, TN. The editorial content includes local news, sports, opinion, events, education, business, lifestyle and health. Advertising deadlines are at 2pm CT.
Language (s): English
Ad Rate: Full Page Mono 28.80
Ad Rate: Full Page Colour 450.00
Currency: United States Dollars
DAILY NEWSPAPER

Daily Times Chronicle 14139
Owner: Woburn Daily Times, Inc.
Editorial: 1 Arrow Dr, Woburn, Massachusetts 1801
Tel: 1 781 933-3700
Web site: http://www.woburnonline.com
Freq: Mon thru Fri; **Circ:** 10795 Not Audited
National News Editor: Mike Haggerty; **Publisher:** Peter Haggerty; **Advertising Sales Manager:** Thomas Kirk; **Editor:** Gordon Vincent
Profile: Daily Times Chronicle is a local newspaper written for the residents of Woburn, Reading, Burlington, Winchester and Wakefield, MA. It provides local and national news, community events, schools, businesses, politics, sports and features.
Language (s): English
Ad Rate: Full Page Mono 21.50
Ad Rate: Full Page Colour 150.00
Currency: United States Dollars
DAILY NEWSPAPER

Daily Times Leader 14274
Owner: Horizon Publications
Editorial: 227 Court St, West Point, Mississippi 39773-2926 **Tel:** 1 662 494-1422
Email: dtleditor@bellsouth.net **Web site:** http://www.dailytimesleader.com
Freq: Daily; **Circ:** 3410 Not Audited
Advertising Sales Manager: Donna Harris;
Publisher: Donald Norman
Profile: Daily Times Leader is written for residents of West Point, MS. Deadlines are daily at 10:30am CT.
Language (s): English
Ad Rate: Full Page Mono 8.70
Ad Rate: Full Page Colour 130.00
Currency: United States Dollars
DAILY NEWSPAPER

The Daily Tribune 14191
Owner: Journal Register Company
Editorial: 19176 Hall Rd Ste 200, Clinton Township, Michigan 48038-6914 **Tel:** 1 586 469-4510
Email: editor@dailytribune.com **Web site:** http://www.dailytribune.com
Freq: Fri; **Circ:** 6386 Not Audited
Publisher: Jim O'Rourke
Profile: The Daily Tribune is a daily newspaper serving Southern Oakland County, MI. It targets the communities of Hazel Park, Royal Oak, Troy, Clawson, Madison Heights, Berkley, Oak Park and Ferndale. Its sister paper is the Macomb Daily in Mount Clemens, MI. The Daily Tribune covers sports, news, city government, features, arts & entertainment, schools and police for the Southern Oakland County area.
Language (s): English
Ad Rate: Full Page Mono 14.15
Ad Rate: Full Page Colour 19.15
Currency: United States Dollars
DAILY NEWSPAPER

The Daily Tribune 14827
Owner: Gannett Co., Inc.
Editorial: 101 Riverview ExpressWay Ste 131, Wisconsin Rapids, Wisconsin 54495-4154
Tel: 1 715 423-7200
Email: wisconsincoe@gannett.com **Web site:** http://www.wisconsinrapidstribune.com
Freq: Daily; **Circ:** 6903 Not Audited
Advertising Sales Manager: Tara Marcoux
Profile: The Daily Tribune is a local newspaper serving the cities of Wisconsin Rapids and Nekoosa, WI, as well as the villages of Biron and Port Edwards, WI. It provides coverage of local news, events, politics, sports, lifestyle and more. It combines with the Marshfield News-Herald and the Stevens Point Journal on Sundays. Deadlines are one day prior to issue date.
Language (s): English
Ad Rate: Full Page Mono 32.00
Ad Rate: Full Page Colour 357.00
Currency: United States Dollars
DAILY NEWSPAPER

The Daily Tribune-News 13839
Owner: Walls Group
Editorial: 251 S Tennessee St, Cartersville, Georgia 30120-3605 **Tel:** 1 770 382-4545
Email: news@daily-tribune.com **Web site:** http://www.daily-tribune.com
Freq: Daily; **Circ:** 5335
Profile: The Daily Tribune-News is published for the residents of Cartersville, GA and surrounding areas. The newspaper covers local and regional news.
Language (s): English
Ad Rate: Full Page Mono 11.44
Ad Rate: Full Page Colour 200.00
Currency: United States Dollars
DAILY NEWSPAPER

Daily World 14106
Owner: Gannett Co., Inc.
Editorial: 2897 S Union St, Opelousas, Louisiana 70570-5738 **Tel:** 1 337 942-4971
Email: news@dailyworld.com **Web site:** http://www.dailyworld.com
Freq: Daily; **Circ:** 39
Profile: Daily World serves the residents of Opelousas, LA and surrounding areas. It covers news, sports, community events, editorials and entertainment.
Language (s): English
Ad Rate: Full Page Mono 30.11
Ad Rate: Full Page Colour 35.36
Currency: United States Dollars
DAILY NEWSPAPER

The Daily World 14778
Owner: Stephens Media Group
Editorial: 315 S Michigan St, Aberdeen, Washington 98520-6037 **Tel:** 1 360 532-4000
Email: press_releases@thedailyworld.com **Web site:** http://www.thedailyworld.com
Freq: 3 Times/Week
Profile: The Daily World is a local newspaper that serves the Grays Harbor and northern Pacific counties in Southwest Washington. It prides itself on being "the only daily newspaper on the coast of Washington state." The newspaper provides residents with important information on local news, politics, sports, lifestyles, recreation, entertainment, and more. The editorial deadline is one day prior to the issue date.
Language (s): English
Ad Rate: Full Page Mono 27.85
Ad Rate: Full Page Colour 490.00
Currency: United States Dollars
DAILY NEWSPAPER

The Dallas Morning News 15306
Owner: A.H. Belo Corp.
Editorial: 508 Young St, Dallas, Texas 75202-4808
Tel: 1 214 977-8222
Email: metro@dallasnews.com **Web site:** http://www.dallasnews.com
Freq: Daily; **Circ:** 258667 Not Audited
Profile: The Dallas Morning News is a daily newspaper covering regional, national and international news. Technology coverage runs daily in the business section. Business and technology-related editorial content consists mostly of news and trend articles analyzing the impact of technology on the economy and industry. Consumer-related topics include health and fitness, food, arts & entertainment, and book, movie and theater reviews. Deadlines for business news are daily at 5:30pm CT. The lead times for daily news is two hours. For features, the lead time is one to two weeks.
Language (s): English
Ad Rate: Full Page Mono 662.62
Ad Rate: Full Page Colour 747.50
Currency: United States Dollars
DAILY NEWSPAPER

The Dallas Morning News - Austin Bureau 15932
Editorial: 1005 Congress Ave Ste 930, Austin, Texas 78701-2415 **Tel:** 1 512 499-0581
Language (s): English
DAILY NEWSPAPER

The Dallas Morning News - Richardson Bureau 15937
Editorial: 1410 E Renner Rd Ste 260, Richardson, Texas 75082-2228 **Tel:** 1 469 330-5600
Profile: This is the Collin County Bureau.
Language (s): English
DAILY NEWSPAPER

The Dallas Morning News - Washington Bureau 15516
Editorial: 529 14th St NW Ste 930, Washington, District Of Columbia 20045-1901 **Tel:** 1 202 661-8410
Washington Bureau Chief: Todd Gillman
Language (s): English
DAILY NEWSPAPER

The Dalles Chronicle 14562
Owner: Eagle Newspapers
Editorial: 315 Federal St, The Dalles, Oregon 97058-2115 **Tel:** 1 541 296-2141
Email: tdchron@thedalleschronicle.com **Web site:** http://www.thedalleschronicle.com
Freq: Fri; **Circ:** 5067 Not Audited
News Editor: Mark Gibson; **News Editor:** RaeLynn Ricarte
Profile: The Dalles Chronicle is the largest newspaper in the Columbia River Gorge serving Wasco, Sherman, Hood River and Klickitat counties. This newspaper is the news source for metroplex technology leaders.
Language (s): English
Ad Rate: Full Page Mono 11.00
Ad Rate: Full Page Colour 300.00
Currency: United States Dollars
DAILY NEWSPAPER

Danville News 14574
Owner: Community Newspaper Holdings, Inc.
Editorial: 345 Mill St, Danville, Pennsylvania 17821-2063 **Tel:** 1 570 275-3235
Email: news@thedanvillenews.com **Web site:** http://www.thedanvillenews.com
Freq: Daily; **Circ:** 4200 Not Audited
Profile: Danville News is a daily newspaper written for the residents of Danville, Sunbury and Susquehanna Valley, PA. It covers local news, sports, events, business and classifieds.
Language (s): English
Ad Rate: Full Page Mono 8.42
Ad Rate: Full Page Colour 100.00
Currency: United States Dollars
DAILY NEWSPAPER

Danville Register and Bee 14755
Owner: BH Media Group
Editorial: 700 Monument St, Danville, Virginia 24541-1512 **Tel:** 1 434 793-2311
Email: news@registerbee.com **Web site:** http://www.godanriver.com
Freq: Daily; **Circ:** 13061 Not Audited
Publisher: Steve Kaylor

Profile: Danville Register and Bee is written for residents of Danville, VA. It covers local news, business, sports, arts & entertainment, national and statewide stories.
Language (s): English
Ad Rate: Full Page Mono 27.48
Ad Rate: Full Page Colour 404.25
Currency: United States Dollars
DAILY NEWSPAPER

The Davis Enterprise 13722
Owner: McNaughton Newspapers
Editorial: 315 G St, Davis, California 95616-4119
Tel: 1 530 756-0800
Email: newsroom@davisenterprise.net **Web site:** http://www.davisenterprise.com
Freq: Fri; **Circ:** 9468 Not Audited
Publisher: R. Burt McNaughton
Profile: The Davis Enterprise is a local daily newspaper written for residents of Davis, Woodland, El Macero, Winters and Dixon, CA. The newspaper covers local news, world news, sports and arts & entertainment.
Language (s): English
Ad Rate: Full Page Mono 18.00
Ad Rate: Full Page Colour 450.00
Currency: United States Dollars
DAILY NEWSPAPER

Dawn - New York Bureau 620263
Editorial: United Nations, Room S-344A, New York, New York 10017
Profile: This is the New York bureau of Dawn, based in Karachi, Pakistan.
Language (s): English
DAILY NEWSPAPER

The Day 13804
Owner: Day Publishing Co.
Editorial: 47 Eugene Oneill Dr, New London, Connecticut 06320-6306 **Tel:** 1 860 442-2200
Email: editor@theday.com **Web site:** http://www.theday.com
Freq: Daily; **Circ:** 23698 Not Audited
Advertising Sales Manager: Christine Brown;
Publisher: Gary Farrugia
Profile: The Day's editorial mission is to be the leading source of news and information for Eastern Connecticut. The publication is written for a general audience from teens to senior citizens.
Language (s): English
Ad Rate: Full Page Mono 36.22
Currency: United States Dollars
DAILY NEWSPAPER

Dayton Daily News 15329
Owner: Cox Media Group, Inc.
Editorial: 1611 S Main St, Dayton, Ohio 45409-2547
Tel: 1 937 225-2000
Email: newsdesk@cmgohio.com **Web site:** http://www.daytondailynews.com
Freq: Daily; **Circ:** 106657 Not Audited
Investigative News Editor: Brian Kollars;
Washington Bureau Chief: Jack Torry
Profile: Dayton Daily News is a daily newspaper serving the Dayton, OH area. Coverage includes local, regional, and national news, sports, entertainment and recreation. The Life sections covers entertainment and lifestyle topics, as well as health and food. Advertising rates are combined with Springfield News-Sun.
Language (s): English
Ad Rate: Full Page Mono 196.00
Ad Rate: Full Page Colour 253.56
Currency: United States Dollars
DAILY NEWSPAPER

Dayton Daily News - Columbus Bureau 15878
Editorial: 34 S 3rd St, Columbus, Ohio 43215-4201
Tel: 1 614 224-1608
Language (s): English
DAILY NEWSPAPER

The Daytona Beach News-Journal 15427
Owner: GateHouse Media Inc.
Editorial: 901 6th St, Daytona Beach, Florida 32117-3352 **Tel:** 1 386 252-1511
Email: metro@news-jrnl.com **Web site:** http://www.news-journalonline.com
Freq: Daily; **Circ:** 60803 Not Audited
Editor: Pat Rice
Profile: The Daytona Beach News-Journal covers local, state and national news, as well as business, sports, special reports and politics. There is also features and entertainment news, including lifestyles, movies, television and events. In 1986, The Morning Journal and The Evening News combined to create the current News-Journal. The paper was founded in 1928. Deadlines vary by department. The outlet offers RSS (Really Simple Syndication).
Language (s): English
Ad Rate: Full Page Mono 146.70
Ad Rate: Full Page Colour 441.70
Currency: United States Dollars
DAILY NEWSPAPER

The Decatur Daily 13666
Owner: Tennessee Valley Printing Co. Inc.
Editorial: 201 1st Ave SE, Decatur, Alabama 35601-2333 **Tel:** 1 256 353-4612
Email: news@decaturdaily.com **Web site:** http://www.decaturdaily.com
Freq: Daily; **Circ:** 16256
News Editor: Leah Daniels; **Publisher & Editor:** Clint Shelton

Profile: The Decatur Daily is a daily newspaper written for residents of Decatur, AL and surrounding areas. The publication covers local and state news, events, people, sports, business and arts & entertainment stories. On August 30, 2004 it became a morning newspaper.
Language (s): English
Ad Rate: Full Page Mono 34.27
Ad Rate: Full Page Colour 386.00
Currency: United States Dollars
DAILY NEWSPAPER

Decatur Daily Democrat 13980
Owner: Horizon Publications
Editorial: 141 S 2nd St, Decatur, Indiana 46733-1664
Tel: 1 260 724-2121
Email: comp@decaturdailydemocrat.com **Web site:** http://www.decaturdailydemocrat.com
Freq: Daily; **Circ:** 6000 Not Audited
Editor: J. Swygart
Profile: Decatur Daily Democrat is a local daily published newspaper. Its editorial mission is to cover news and events for the town of Decatur, IN and the surrounding communities.
Language (s): English
Ad Rate: Full Page Mono 12.35
Ad Rate: Full Page Colour 41.04
Currency: United States Dollars
DAILY NEWSPAPER

Del Norte Triplicate 14899
Owner: Western Communications Company
Editorial: 312 H St, Crescent City, California 95531-4018 **Tel:** 1 707 464-2141
Email: webmaster@triplicate.com **Web site:** http://www.triplicate.com
Freq: Fri; **Circ:** 4738 Not Audited
Editor: Matthew Durkee
Profile: Del Norte Triplicate is a local newspaper that is published Tuesday to Saturday. The editorial mission is to provide the residents of Del Norte County, CA with information on community news and events.
Language (s): English
Ad Rate: Full Page Mono 17.65
Ad Rate: Full Page Colour 62.71
Currency: United States Dollars
DAILY NEWSPAPER

Del Rio News-Herald 14695
Owner: Southern Newspapers, Inc.
Editorial: 2205 N Bedell Ave, Del Rio, Texas 78840-8007 **Tel:** 1 830 775-1551
Email: newsroom@delrionewsherald.com **Web site:** http://www.delrionewsherald.com
Freq: Daily; **Circ:** 4852 Not Audited
Profile: Del Rio News-Herald is a local daily newspaper written for residents of Del Rio, TX. The newspaper covers local news, sports and events.
Language (s): English
Ad Rate: Full Page Mono 14.10
Ad Rate: Full Page Colour 448.00
Currency: United States Dollars
DAILY NEWSPAPER

Delaware County Daily Times 14609
Owner: 21st Century Media
Editorial: 639 S. Chester Rd, Swarthmore, Pennsylvania 19081-2315 **Tel:** 1 610 622-8800
Email: newsroom@delcotimes.com **Web site:** http://www.delcotimes.com
Freq: Daily; **Circ:** 28837 Not Audited
Publisher: Ed Condra
Profile: Delaware County Daily Times serves residents of Delaware County, PA. The newspaper includes local community news and national news headlines. The national news is provided by the Associated Press. Local features cover entertainment, education, business, lifestyle, high school sports and classifieds. The paper does not publish a holiday gift guide.
Language (s): English
Ad Rate: Full Page Mono 72.40
Ad Rate: Full Page Colour 123.67
Currency: United States Dollars
DAILY NEWSPAPER

Delaware Gazette 14447
Owner: AIM Media Midwest
Editorial: 40 N Sandusky St Ste 202, Delaware, Ohio 43015-1973 **Tel:** 1 740 363-1161
Web site: http://www.delgazette.com
Freq: Daily; **Circ:** 6384 Not Audited
Profile: Delaware Gazette is a local daily newspaper serving the Delaware, OH area. It provides the local community with information on news, events, sports and weather. The lead time varies depending on the editorial material. Deadlines are at 9am ET before publication.
Language (s): English
Ad Rate: Full Page Mono 12.25
Ad Rate: Full Page Colour 180.00
Currency: United States Dollars
DAILY NEWSPAPER

Delaware State News 13811
Owner: Independent Newspapers Inc.
Editorial: 110 Galaxy Dr, Dover, Delaware 19901-9262 **Tel:** 1 302 674-3600
Email: newsroom@newszap.com **Web site:** http://delawarestatenews.net
Freq: Daily; **Circ:** 17250 Not Audited
Publisher: Ed Dulin; **Editor:** Andrew West
Profile: Delaware State News is a daily newspaper serving the residents of Dover, DE and surrounding

areas. It is a state-read publication that covers local, regional and national news and information.
Language (s): English
Ad Rate: Full Page Mono 34.11
Ad Rate: Full Page Colour 200.00
Currency: United States Dollars
DAILY NEWSPAPER

Delphos Daily Herald   14448
Owner: Delphos Herald Inc.
Editorial: 405 N Main St, Delphos, Ohio 45833-1577
Tel: 1 419 695-0015
Web site: http://www.delphosherald.com
Freq: Daily; **Circ:** 3682 Not Audited
Publisher: Murray Cohen; **Advertising Sales Manager:** Don Hemple; **Editor:** Nancy Spencer
Profile: Delphos Daily Herald is a local newspaper serving Delphos, OH and the surrounding area. It provides information on news and events.
Language (s): English
Ad Rate: Full Page Mono 10.00
Ad Rate: Full Page Colour 41.81
Currency: United States Dollars
DAILY NEWSPAPER

Delta Democrat Times   14262
Owner: Emmerich Newspapers Inc.
Editorial: 988 N Broadway St, Greenville, Mississippi 38701-2349 **Tel:** 1 662 335-1155
Web site: http://www.ddtonline.com
Freq: Mon thru Fri; **Circ:** 5707 Not Audited
Publisher & Editor: Jon Alverson
Profile: Delta Democrat Times is the local daily newspaper for the residents of Greenville, MS. The paper covers local news, sports, entertainment, business and events.
Language (s): English
Ad Rate: Full Page Mono 17.65
Ad Rate: Full Page Colour 300.00
Currency: United States Dollars
DAILY NEWSPAPER

Deming Headlight   14385
Owner: Gannett Co., Inc.
Editorial: 219 E Maple St, Deming, New Mexico 88030-4267 **Tel:** 1 575 546-2611
Web site: http://www.demingheadlight.com
Freq: Daily; **Circ:** 3668 Not Audited
Editor: Bill Armendariz
Profile: Deming Headlight is a local daily newspaper serving Deming, NM. It provides the local community with information on news, events, sports and weather.
Language (s): English
Ad Rate: Full Page Mono 11.85
Ad Rate: Full Page Colour 110.00
Currency: United States Dollars
DAILY NEWSPAPER

Democrat and Chronicle   15366
Owner: Gannett Co., Inc.
Editorial: 55 Exchange Blvd, Rochester, New York 14614-2001 **Tel:** 1 585 232-7100
Email: infodesk@democratandchronicle.com **Web site:** http://www.democratandchronicle.com
Freq: Daily; **Circ:** 82510 Not Audited
Profile: The Democrat and Chronicle began in 1833 as The Balance. Soon after, the name changed to the Daily Democrat. In 1870, the paper combined with the two-year-old Chronicle to become the Rochester Democrat and Chronicle. The newspaper aims to "be the highest valued source of news, information and advertising services in the Greater Rochester market." It was awarded Gannett's Outstanding Achievement Award for best overall performance in 1997. The paper features major local, regional, national and world news. Local stories come from around the city and surrounding suburbs. Business coverage includes national and world economic news, stock listings, and features on its "big three" local companies (Kodak, Xerox, B&L), as well as start-ups and entrepreneurs. Rochester Living, the lifestyle and feature section, was redesigned in 1996 and focuses on a different informational topic every day of the week: Sunday features arts, travel, and books; Monday features health; Tuesday features relationships; Wednesday features personal finance; Thursday features family; Friday features entertainment; and Saturday features home. Sports coverage includes news from around the region and nation.
Language (s): English
Ad Rate: Full Page Mono 480.75
Ad Rate: Full Page Colour 507.34
Currency: United States Dollars
DAILY NEWSPAPER

Demopolis Times   18493
Owner: Boone Newspapers Inc.
Editorial: 315 E Jefferson St, Demopolis, Alabama 36732-2255 **Tel:** 1 334 289-4017
Email: news@demopolistimes.com **Web site:** http://www.demopolistimes.com
Freq: Mon; **Circ:** 3300 Not Audited
Publisher & Editor: Justin Averette
Profile: Demopolis Times is a local newspaper serving Demopolis, AL and the surrounding area. It provides information on news and events of importance to the local community.
Language (s): English
Ad Rate: Full Page Mono 25.00
Currency: United States Dollars
DAILY NEWSPAPER

Denton Record-Chronicle   14696
Owner: A.H. Belo Corp.
Editorial: 314 E Hickory St, Denton, Texas 76201-4272 **Tel:** 1 940 387-3811

Email: drconline@dentonrc.com **Web site:** http://www.dentonrc.com
Freq: Daily; **Circ:** 13336 Not Audited
News Editor: Mark Finley; **Publisher:** Bill Patterson
Profile: Denton Record-Chronicle is a local daily newspaper published for the residents of Denton, TX. It provides information on news, events, sports, arts & entertainment and weather.
Language (s): English
Ad Rate: Full Page Mono 36.50
Ad Rate: Full Page Colour 220.00
Currency: United States Dollars
DAILY NEWSPAPER

The Denver Post   15357
Owner: Digital First Media
Editorial: 101 W Colfax Ave Ste 600, Denver, Colorado 80202-5315 **Tel:** 1 303 954-1010
Email: newsroom@denverpost.com **Web site:** http://www.denverpost.com
Freq: Daily; **Circ:** 196286 Not Audited
Profile: Denver Post is a general-interest broadsheet that reaches both a local and regional audience. The daily newspaper includes six sections, which are main news, local news, living, sports, business and classifieds.
Language (s): English
Ad Rate: Full Page Mono 862.64
Ad Rate: Full Page Colour 1055.07
Currency: United States Dollars
DAILY NEWSPAPER

Denver Post - Lakewood Bureau
155552
Editorial: 13949 W Colfax Ave Ste 195, Lakewood, Colorado 80401-3250 **Tel:** 1 303 278-3217
Web site: http://www.denverpost.com
Language (s): English
DAILY NEWSPAPER

Denver Post - Washington Bureau   63438
Editorial: 529 14th St NW Bldg, Washington, District Of Columbia 20045-1002 **Tel:** 1 202 662-8907
Language (s): English
DAILY NEWSPAPER

Denver Post - Westminster Bureau   331109
Editorial: 1333 W 120th Ave Ste 122, Westminster, Colorado 80234-2710 **Tel:** 1 720 929-0907
Language (s): English
DAILY NEWSPAPER

Des Moines Register   15330
Owner: Gannett Co., Inc.
Editorial: 400 Locust St Ste 500, Des Moines, Iowa 50309-2355 **Tel:** 1 515 284-8000
Email: metroiowa@dmreg.com **Web site:** http://www.desmoinesregister.com
Freq: Daily; **Circ:** 82371 Not Audited
Profile: Des Moines Register is the largest newspaper in Iowa. It was founded in 1849 as the Iowa Star and got its current name in 1915.
Language (s): English
Ad Rate: Full Page Mono 275.95
Ad Rate: Full Page Colour 3673.90
Currency: United States Dollars
DAILY NEWSPAPER

Deseret News   15419
Owner: Church of Jesus Christ of LDS (The)
Editorial: 55 N 300 W, Salt Lake City, Utah 84101-3502 **Tel:** 1 801 575-5600
Email: news@deseretnews.com **Web site:** http://www.deseretnews.com
Freq: Daily; **Circ:** 152210 Not Audited
Profile: Deseret News, established in 1850, is a daily broadsheet newspaper distributed in the Salt Lake City area. The publication covers local news, sports and entertainment, as well as regional, national and international news. The newspaper maintains joint advertising, printing, circulation and business functions with The Salt Lake Tribune, but the two papers operate independent editorial departments.
Language (s): English
Ad Rate: Full Page Mono 253.50
Ad Rate: Full Page Colour 695.18
Currency: United States Dollars
DAILY NEWSPAPER

Desert Dispatch   13720
Owner: GateHouse Media Inc.
Editorial: 130 Coolwater Ln, Barstow, California 92311-3222 **Tel:** 1 760 256-2257
Web site: http://www.desertdispatch.com
Freq: Daily; **Circ:** 3259
Editor: Steve Hunt; **Advertising Sales Manager:** Bea Lint
Profile: Desert Dispatch is a daily newspaper covering local news from Barstow, Daggett, Fort Irwin, Hinkley, Lenwood, Newberry Springs and Yermo, CA. The publication includes local news, sports and entertainment topics.
Language (s): English
Ad Rate: Full Page Mono 22.21
Ad Rate: Full Page Colour 330.00
Currency: United States Dollars
DAILY NEWSPAPER

The Desert Sun   14920
Owner: Gannett Co., Inc.
Editorial: 750 N Gene Autry Trl, Palm Springs, California 92262-5463 **Tel:** 1 760 322-8889
Email: localnews@thedesertsun.com **Web site:** http://www.desertsun.com

Freq: Daily; **Circ:** 38518 Not Audited
Publisher: Mark Winkler
Profile: The Desert Sun is a local daily newspaper that covers news and information in Coachella Valley, CA. Coverage includes local and national news, sports, business and lifestyle issues affecting the local community.
Language (s): English
Ad Rate: Full Page Mono 106.75
Ad Rate: Full Page Colour 337.06
Currency: United States Dollars
DAILY NEWSPAPER

DeSoto Times Tribune   14947
Owner: P.H. Publishing LLC
Editorial: 2445 Highway 51 S, Hernando, Mississippi 38632-1734 **Tel:** 1 662 429-6397
Email: editor@desototimestribune.com **Web site:** http://www.desototimes.com
Circ: 20000
Publisher: Cyndi Pittman; **News Editor:** Terri Smith
Profile: DeSoto Times Tribune is a local, daily newspaper serving DeSoto County, MS. It provides information on news and events of importance to the local community.
Language (s): English
Ad Rate: Full Page Mono 11.48
Currency: United States Dollars
DAILY NEWSPAPER

Detroit Free Press   15331
Owner: Gannett Co., Inc.
Editorial: 160 W Fort St, Detroit, Michigan 48226-3201 **Tel:** 1 313 222-6400 6
Web site: http://www.freep.com
Freq: Daily; **Circ:** 237369 Not Audited
Profile: Detroit Free Press is a general-interest daily newspaper written for the general public in Detroit. Founded in 1831 as the weekly Democratic Free Press and Michigan Intelligencer, the publication is one of the largest daily newspapers in the country. It has won eight Pulitzer Prizes. Coverage includes business, automotive, consumer, health and technology. Articles consist of news and trend stories, product announcements and reviews, case studies, company profiles, personality profiles and interviews. The publication has daily deadlines in the afternoon. It is best to contact staff editors and reporters before 3pm ET. The paper is distributed via home delivery on Thursdays, Fridays and Sundays. It is available daily on newsstands.
Language (s): English
Ad Rate: Full Page Mono 374.77
Ad Rate: Full Page Colour 430.99
Currency: United States Dollars
DAILY NEWSPAPER

Detroit Free Press - Lansing Bureau   15769
Editorial: 120 E Lenawee St, Lansing, Michigan 48919-1000 **Tel:** 1 517 372-8660
Language (s): English
DAILY NEWSPAPER

Detroit Free Press - Washington Bureau   395080
Editorial: 1100 New York Ave NW Ste 200E, Washington, District Of Columbia 20005-6116
Tel: 1 202 906-8203
Language (s): English
DAILY NEWSPAPER

The Detroit News   15300
Owner: Digital First Media
Editorial: 160 W Fort St, Detroit, Michigan 48226-3201 **Tel:** 1 313 222-2300
Email: newstips@detroitnews.com **Web site:** http://www.detroitnews.com
Freq: Mon thru Fri; **Circ:** 318531
Editor & Publisher: Jon Wolman
Profile: Detroit News is a general-interest daily newspaper written for the general public in Detroit and was founded in 1873 as The Evening News. The paper covers business, science, automotive, consumer, health and technology. The paper is distributed via home delivery on Thursdays, Fridays and Saturdays. It will be available daily on newsstands
Language (s): English
Ad Rate: Full Page Mono 299.43
Ad Rate: Full Page Colour 344.35
Currency: United States Dollars
DAILY NEWSPAPER

The Detroit News - Lansing Bureau   15774
Editorial: 124 W Allegan St Ste 1112, Boji Tower, Lansing, Michigan 48933-1748 **Tel:** 1 517 371-3660
Language (s): English
DAILY NEWSPAPER

The Detroit News - Washington Bureau   15504
Editorial: 529 14th St NW Ste 969, Washington, District Of Columbia 20045-1916 **Tel:** 1 202 662-8733
Washington Bureau Chief: David Shepardson
Language (s): English
DAILY NEWSPAPER

Devils Lake Journal   14329
Owner: Fortress Investment Group, LLC
Editorial: 516 4th St NE, Devils Lake, North Dakota 58301-2502 **Tel:** 1 701 662-2127
Email: news@devilslakejournal.com **Web site:** http://www.devilslakejournal.com
Freq: Daily; **Circ:** 3600 Not Audited

Editor: Louise Oleson
Profile: Devils Lake Journal is a local newspaper serving the Devils Lake, ND area. It provides information on local news, events, sports and weather.
Language (s): English
Ad Rate: Full Page Mono 12.10
Ad Rate: Full Page Colour 48.02
Currency: United States Dollars
DAILY NEWSPAPER

The Dexter Statesman   14229
Owner: Rust Communications
Editorial: 133 S Walnut St, Dexter, Missouri 63841-2141 **Tel:** 1 573 624-4545
Web site: http://www.dailystatesman.com
Freq: Daily; **Circ:** 2519 Not Audited
Advertising Sales Manager: Dea Glenn; **Publisher:** Bud Hunt; **Editor:** Noreen Hyslop
Profile: The Dexter Statesman is written for the citizens of Stoddard County, MO. The publication covers local, sports, national and international news.
Language (s): English
Ad Rate: Full Page Mono 12.00
Ad Rate: Full Page Colour 370.00
Currency: United States Dollars
DAILY NEWSPAPER

El Diario de El Paso   14963
Owner: Editora Paso del Norte
Editorial: 1801 Texas Ave, El Paso, Texas 79901-1811 **Tel:** 1 915 838-1600
Email: ayuda@redaccion.diario.com.mx **Web site:** http://www.diariousa.com
Freq: Daily; **Circ:** 20000 Not Audited
Profile: EL Diario de El Paso is a daily, Spanish-language newspaper serving the Hispanic community in El Paso, TX. It covers international and local news, sports, arts & entertainment, social events and real estate.
Language (s): Spanish
Ad Rate: Full Page Mono 224.00
Ad Rate: Full Page Colour 260.00
Currency: United States Dollars
DAILY NEWSPAPER

Diario Las Américas   14904
Owner: :as Americas Multimedia, LLC
Editorial: 888 Brickell Ave Fl 5, Miami, Florida 33131-2913 **Tel:** 1 305 633-3341
Email: diariolasamericas@gmail.com **Web site:** http://www.diariolasamericas.com
Freq: Fri; **Circ:** 32000 Not Audited
Editor: Laura Rivera
Profile: Diario Las Americas is a regional daily newspaper published for Spanish speaking residents of Miami. It covers international, national and local news, as well as arts & entertainment.
Language (s): English, Spanish
Ad Rate: Full Page Mono 36.20
Ad Rate: Full Page Colour 1200.00
Currency: United States Dollars
DAILY NEWSPAPER

El Diario Nueva York   14961
Owner: ImpreMedia LLC
Editorial: 1 Metrotech Ctr, Brooklyn, New York 11201-3948 **Tel:** 1 212 807-4600
Email: metro@eldiariony.com **Web site:** http://www.eldiariony.com
Freq: Daily; **Circ:** 36000
Advertising Sales Manager: Jorge Ayala; **Publisher:** Rossana Rosado
Profile: El Diario Nueva York is a daily newspaper written for Spanish communities of New York and surrounding areas. The editorial mission of the newspaper is to provide the Spanish communities of New York with cultural news and information.
Language (s): Spanish
Ad Rate: Full Page Mono 49.87
Ad Rate: Full Page Colour 168.39
Currency: United States Dollars
DAILY NEWSPAPER

The Dickinson Press   14330
Owner: Forum Communications Co.
Editorial: 1815 1st St W, Dickinson, North Dakota 58601-2463 **Tel:** 1 701 225-8111
Email: newsroom@thedickinsonpress.com **Web site:** http://www.thedickinsonpress.com
Freq: Daily; **Circ:** 6486 Not Audited
Publisher: Harvey Brock
Profile: Dickinson Press is a daily newspaper serving the Dickinson, ND community. It covers local and national news, lifestyle, business and government.
Language (s): English
Ad Rate: Full Page Mono 11.25
Ad Rate: Full Page Colour 70.00
Currency: United States Dollars
DAILY NEWSPAPER

The Dispatch   14304
Owner: GateHouse Media Inc.
Editorial: 30 E 1st Ave, Lexington, North Carolina 27292-3302 **Tel:** 1 336 249-3981
Email: news@the-dispatch.com **Web site:** http://www.the-dispatch.com
Freq: Fri; **Circ:** 7191 Not Audited
Publisher: Steve Skaggs; **Advertising Sales Manager:** Tammie Wright
Profile: The Dispatch is a daily local newspaper for Lexington, NC. The publication covers local news, business, lifestyle, sports and entertainment stories.
Language (s): English
Ad Rate: Full Page Mono 23.00
Ad Rate: Full Page Colour 300.00
Currency: United States Dollars
DAILY NEWSPAPER

Dispatch/Argus 586835
Owner: Small Newspaper Group
Editorial: 1720 5th Ave, Moline, Illinois 61265-7907
Tel: 1 309 764-4344
Email: press@qconline.com **Web site:** http://www.qconline.com
Editor: Jackie Chesser; **Publisher & Editor:** Gerald Taylor
Profile: Dispatch/Argus publishes both the Dispatch and the Rock Island Argus in Moline, IL.
Language (s): English
DAILY NEWSPAPER

Dodge City Daily Globe 14040
Owner: GateHouse Media Inc.
Editorial: 705 N 2nd Ave, Dodge City, Kansas 67801-4410 **Tel:** 1 620 225-4151
Email: dcnews@dodgeglobe.com **Web site:** http://www.dodgeglobe.com
Freq: Daily; **Circ:** 7000 Not Audited
Profile: Dodge City Daily Globe is a local newspaper for the Dodge City, KS area. The newspaper covers local news, business, sports and arts & entertainment stories. The newspaper also covers national and statewide stories if they have a direct impact on the newspaper's readership. All inquiries should be addressed to the managing editor. Deadlines for the publication are by noon CT the day before issue date.
Language (s): English
Ad Rate: Full Page Mono 9.87
Ad Rate: Full Page Colour 210.00
Currency: United States Dollars
DAILY NEWSPAPER

The Dominion Post 14840
Owner: The West Virginia Newspaper Publishing Company
Editorial: 1251 Earl L Core Rd, Morgantown, West Virginia 26505-5881 **Tel:** 1 304 292-6301
Email: newsroom@dominionpost.com **Web site:** http://www.dominionpost.com
Freq: Daily; **Circ:** 18691 Not Audited
Profile: The Dominion Post is a local daily newspaper published for the residents of Northern West Virginia. It covers local news and events. The lead time varies.
Language (s): English
Ad Rate: Full Page Mono 34.91
Ad Rate: Full Page Colour 575.00
Currency: United States Dollars
DAILY NEWSPAPER

The Dothan Eagle 13667
Owner: BH Media Group
Editorial: 227 N Oates St, Dothan, Alabama 36303-4555 **Tel:** 1 334 792-3141
Email: news@dothaneagle.com **Web site:** http://www.dothaneagle.com
Freq: Daily; **Circ:** 24134 Not Audited
Profile: The Dothan Eagle is a daily newspaper written for residents of Dothan, AL. The paper covers local and national news, sports and weather.
Language (s): English
Ad Rate: Full Page Mono 46.00
Ad Rate: Full Page Colour 375.00
Currency: United States Dollars
DAILY NEWSPAPER

Douglas County Sentinel 14864
Owner: Paxton Media Group
Editorial: 8501 Bowden St, Douglasville, Georgia 30134-1705 **Tel:** 1 770 942-6571
Email: douglascountysentinel@gmail.com **Web site:** http://www.douglascountysentinel.com
Freq: Fri; **Circ:** 3666 Not Audited
Publisher: Cathy New
Profile: Douglas County Sentinel's editorial mission is to bring to the citizens of Douglas news which directly affects and impacts their lives.
Language (s): English
Ad Rate: Full Page Mono 20.00
Ad Rate: Full Page Colour 150.00
Currency: United States Dollars
DAILY NEWSPAPER

Dowagiac Daily News 14166
Owner: Boone/Narragansett Publishing
Editorial: 205 Spaulding St, Dowagiac, Michigan 49047-1474 **Tel:** 1 269 782-2101
Web site: http://www.dowagiacnews.com
Freq: Daily; **Circ:** 1586 Not Audited
Editor: John Eby
Profile: Dowagiac Daily News is written for residents of Dowagiac, MI. The paper covers local news, sports, business and entertainment.
Language (s): English
Ad Rate: Full Page Mono 12.80
Currency: United States Dollars
DAILY NEWSPAPER

Draugas 573425
Owner: Lithuanian Catholic Press Society Inc.
Editorial: 4545 W 63rd St, Chicago, Illinois 60629-5532 **Tel:** 1 773 585-9500
Email: administracija@draugas.org **Web site:** http://www.draugas.org
Freq: Fri; **Circ:** 3000
Advertising Sales Manager: Danga Mackeviciene
Profile: Draugas is a daily newspaper publishing Tuesday through Saturday that delivers news, events and features to Lithuanian-speaking communities throughout the world. There is no publisher for the paper.
Language (s): Lithuanian
Ad Rate: Full Page Mono 7.00
Currency: United States Dollars
DAILY NEWSPAPER

Du Quoin Evening Call 13926
Owner: Paddock Publications
Editorial: 9 N Division St, Du Quoin, Illinois 62832-1405 **Tel:** 1 618 542-2133
Email: dqnews@frontier.com **Web site:** http://www.duquoin.com
Freq: Mon thru Fri; **Circ:** 3800 Not Audited
Profile: Du Quoin Evening Call provides local news to readers in Du Quoin, IL and the surrounding areas. All mail must be sent to the P.O. box address.
Language (s): English
Ad Rate: Full Page Mono 9.75
Ad Rate: Full Page Colour 100.00
Currency: United States Dollars
DAILY NEWSPAPER

Duluth News-Tribune 14203
Owner: Forum Communications Co.
Editorial: 424 W 1st St, Duluth, Minnesota 55802-1596 **Tel:** 1 218 723-5281
Email: news@duluthnewstribune.com **Web site:** http://www.duluthnewstribune.com
Freq: Daily; **Circ:** 23643 Not Audited
Profile: Duluth (MN) News-Tribune is daily newspaper serving the residents of Lake Superior and Duluth, MN that covers news, sports, entertainment and community events.
Language (s): English
Ad Rate: Full Page Mono 82.85
Ad Rate: Full Page Colour 400.00
Currency: United States Dollars
DAILY NEWSPAPER

The Duncan Banner 14518
Owner: Community Newspaper Holdings, Inc.
Editorial: 1001 W Elm Ave, Duncan, Oklahoma 73533-4746 **Tel:** 1 580 255-5354
Email: editor@duncanbanner.com **Web site:** http://www.duncanbanner.com
Freq: Daily; **Circ:** 8960 Not Audited
Advertising Sales Manager: Dana Boyles; **Editor & Publisher:** James Bright
Profile: The Duncan Banner is a daily newspaper that provides local and national news for residents in the Duncan, OK and surrounding areas.
Language (s): English
Ad Rate: Full Page Mono 14.45
Ad Rate: Full Page Colour 17.45
Currency: United States Dollars
DAILY NEWSPAPER

The Durango Herald 13781
Owner: Ballantine Communications, Inc.
Editorial: 1275 Main Ave, Durango, Colorado 81301-5137 **Tel:** 1 970 247-3504
Email: herald@durangoherald.com **Web site:** http://www.durangoherald.com
Freq: Daily; **Circ:** 6783 Not Audited
Publisher: Richard Ballantine; **News Editor:** Amy Maestas
Profile: The Durango Herald covers local and regional news for the residents of Durango, CO.
Language (s): English
Ad Rate: Full Page Mono 18.50
Ad Rate: Full Page Colour 450.00
Currency: United States Dollars
DAILY NEWSPAPER

Durant Daily Democrat 14519
Owner: Civitas Media
Editorial: 200 W Beech St, Durant, Oklahoma 74701-4316 **Tel:** 1 580 924-4388
Email: editor@durantdemocrat.com **Web site:** http://www.durantdemocrat.com
Freq: Daily; **Circ:** 5500 Not Audited
Profile: Durant Daily Democrat is the local, daily newspaper published for the Durant, OK area. The newspaper covers local news, sports and lifestyle topics. All inquiries should be addressed to the editor.
Language (s): English
Ad Rate: Full Page Mono 9.86
Ad Rate: Full Page Colour 225.00
Currency: United States Dollars
DAILY NEWSPAPER

Dyersburg State Gazette 14666
Owner: Rust Communications
Editorial: 294 Highway 51 Bypass, Dyersburg, Tennessee 38024 **Tel:** 1 731 285-4091
Web site: http://www.stategazette.com
Freq: Mon thru Fri; **Circ:** 7000 Not Audited
Publisher & Editor: Sheila Rouse
Profile: Dyersburg State Gazette has been serving Northwest Tennessee since 1865 and today stands as the largest information medium in the region. With coverage focused exclusively on local people and local events, in recent years the paper has expanded into regional prominence with an award-winning news staff and a skilled and creative advertising department. It is written for residents of Dyer County, TN and surrounding areas.
Language (s): English
Ad Rate: Full Page Mono 11.80
Ad Rate: Full Page Colour 14.13
Currency: United States Dollars
DAILY NEWSPAPER

Dziennik Zwi?zkowy 151201
Owner: Alliance Printers and Publishers Inc.
Editorial: 5711 N Milwaukee Ave, Chicago, Illinois 60646-6215 **Tel:** 1 773 763-3343
Email: dziennik@zwiazkowy.com **Web site:** http://www.dziennikzwiazkowy.com
Freq: Mon thru Fri; **Circ:** 25000 Not Audited
Editor: Wojtek Bialasiewicz; **Editor:** Peter Domaraezki; **Advertising Sales Manager:** Bogdan Mazur
Profile: Polish Daily News' editorial mission is to familiarize immigrants from Poland, Russia, Lithuania and the Ukraine with American culture, such as the laws and the politics in Washington, D.C. The newspaper, written in Polish, also works to maintain Polish traditions.
Language (s): Polish
Ad Rate: Full Page Mono 12.00
Ad Rate: Full Page Colour 150.00
Currency: United States Dollars
DAILY NEWSPAPER

The Eagle 14690
Owner: Evening Post Publishing Co.
Editorial: 1729 Briarcrest Dr, Bryan, Texas 77802-2712 **Tel:** 1 979 776-4444
Email: news@theeagle.com **Web site:** http://www.theeagle.com
Freq: Daily; **Circ:** 19132 Not Audited
Editor: Kelly Brown; **News Editor:** Elizabeth Webb
Profile: The Eagle provides readers with local, regional, and national news coverage. The newspaper is distributed throughout eight counties in the Brazos Valley, TX. The newspaper also covers business, education, politics, religion, sports, entertainment, lifestyle, and classifieds.
Language (s): English
Ad Rate: Full Page Mono 40.35
Ad Rate: Full Page Colour 510.00
Currency: United States Dollars
DAILY NEWSPAPER

Eagle Herald 14813
Owner: Bliss Communications, Inc.
Editorial: 1809 Dunlap Ave, Marinette, Wisconsin 54143-1706 **Tel:** 1 715 735-6611
Email: news@eagleherald.com **Web site:** http://www.ehextra.com
Freq: Daily; **Circ:** 9200 Not Audited
Profile: Eagle Herald is a daily newspaper published for the residents of Marinett, WI. It covers news and events in the local community.
Language (s): English
Ad Rate: Full Page Mono 28.08
Ad Rate: Full Page Colour 226.00
Currency: United States Dollars
DAILY NEWSPAPER

Eagle Times 14350
Owner: Eagle Publications, Inc.
Editorial: 401 River Rd, Claremont, New Hampshire 03743-5652 **Tel:** 1 603 543-3100
Email: news@eagletimes.com **Web site:** http://www.eagletimes.com/
Freq: Daily; **Circ:** 7793 Not Audited
Profile: Eagle Times is a daily newspaper that services Southwestern New Hampshire and Vermont.
Language (s): English
Ad Rate: Full Page Mono 17.00
Ad Rate: Full Page Colour 205.00
Currency: United States Dollars
DAILY NEWSPAPER

The Eagle-Tribune 14124
Owner: Community Newspaper Holdings Inc.
Editorial: 100 Turnpike St, North Andover, Massachusetts 01845-5033 **Tel:** 1 978 946-2000
Email: news@eagletribune.com **Web site:** http://www.eagletribune.com
Freq: Mon thru Fri; **Circ:** 28509
Publisher: Karen Andreas; **Advertising Sales Manager:** Mark Zappala
Profile: The Eagle-Tribune in North Andover, MA is published daily for residents of New Hampshire and Massachusetts and covers local, national and international news, arts, weather and sports.
Language (s): English
Ad Rate: Full Page Mono 40.65
Ad Rate: Full Page Colour 525.00
Currency: United States Dollars
DAILY NEWSPAPER

East Bay Times 15460
Owner: Digital First Media
Editorial: 175 Lennon Ln Ste 100, Walnut Creek, California 94598-2466 **Tel:** 1 925 935-2525
Email: ccnnewsrelease@bayareanewsgroup.com
Web site: http://www.eastbaytimes.com
Freq: Daily; **Circ:** 147510 Not Audited
Profile: Daily newspaper for residents in Northern California. It covers breaking news, features, profiles, trends, news analyses and investigative stories. The paper is a part of the Bay Area News Group subsidiary of MediaNews Group.
Language (s): English
Ad Rate: Full Page Mono 245.36
Ad Rate: Full Page Colour 541.49
Currency: United States Dollars
DAILY NEWSPAPER

East Oregonian 14559
Owner: East Oregonian Publishing Co.
Editorial: 211 SE Byers Ave, Pendleton, Oregon 97801-2346 **Tel:** 1 541 276-2211
Email: eonews@eastoregonian.com **Web site:** http://www.eastoregonian.com
Freq: Daily; **Circ:** 7890 Not Audited
Editor and Publisher: Kathryn Brown
Profile: East Oregonian is published daily for the residents of Pendleton, OR and surrounding areas. The newspaper covers local news, business, sports and community events.
Language (s): English
Ad Rate: Full Page Mono 18.83
Ad Rate: Full Page Colour 58.67
Currency: United States Dollars
DAILY NEWSPAPER

Les Echos - New York Bureau 503837
Owner: Groupe les Echos
Editorial: 1330 Avenue of the Americas Fl 14, New York, New York 10019-7682 **Tel:** 1 212 641-6500
Web site: http://www.lesechos.fr
Bureau Chief: Pierre de Gasquet
Profile: This is the New York bureau for Les Echos newspaper in Paris.
Language (s): French
DAILY NEWSPAPER

Edwardsville Intelligencer 13927
Owner: Hearst Newspapers
Editorial: 117 N 2nd St, Edwardsville, Illinois 62025-1938 **Tel:** 1 618 656-4700
Email: citydesk@edwpub.net **Web site:** http://www.theintelligencer.com
Freq: Daily; **Circ:** 4288 Not Audited
Advertising Sales Manager: Amy Schaake; **Publisher:** Denise Von Der Haar
Profile: Edwardsville Intelligencer is published daily for the residents of Edwardsville, IL and surrounding areas. The newspaper provides information about local news, business, sports and community events.
Language (s): English
Ad Rate: Full Page Mono 17.60
Currency: United States Dollars
DAILY NEWSPAPER

Effingham Daily News 13928
Owner: Community Newspaper Holdings, Inc.
Editorial: 201 N Banker St, Effingham, Illinois 62401-2304 **Tel:** 1 217 347-7151
Email: news@effinghamdailynews.com **Web site:** http://www.effinghamdailynews.com
Freq: Mon thru Fri; **Circ:** 9588
Profile: Effingham Daily News is is published daily for the residents of Effingham, IL an surrounding areas. The newspaper covers local news, sports, business, entertainment and lifestyles.
Language (s): English
Ad Rate: Full Page Mono 16.00
Ad Rate: Full Page Colour 55.81
Currency: United States Dollars
DAILY NEWSPAPER

El Dorado News-Times 13689
Owner: News-Times Publishing Co.
Editorial: 111 N Madison Ave, El Dorado, Arkansas 71730-6124 **Tel:** 1 870 862-6611
Email: editorial@eldoradonews.com **Web site:** http://www.eldoradonews.com
Freq: Daily; **Circ:** 7476 Not Audited
Publisher: Walter Hussman; **Advertising Sales Manager:** Nicole Patterson
Profile: El Dorado News-Times is a daily newspaper published for El Dorado, AR. The paper covers local news and events. It combines with the Camden (AR) News and the Magnolia (AR) Banner-News on Sundays.
Language (s): English
Ad Rate: Full Page Mono 18.85
Ad Rate: Full Page Colour 297.00
Currency: United States Dollars
DAILY NEWSPAPER

El Paso Times 15418
Owner: Gannett Co., Inc.
Editorial: 500 W Overland Ave Ste 150, El Paso, Texas 79901-1086 **Tel:** 1 915 546-6100
Email: borderland@elpasotimes.com **Web site:** http://www.elpasotimes.com
Freq: Daily; **Circ:** 29142 Not Audited
Editor: Robert Moore
Profile: El Paso Times is a local, daily newspaper published for the residents of El Paso, TX and Southern New Mexico. It covers news, sports, business, lifestyle and community events. Lead time for submissions vary with the content.
Language (s): English
Ad Rate: Full Page Mono 95.00
Ad Rate: Full Page Colour 1046.00
Currency: United States Dollars
DAILY NEWSPAPER

El Paso Times - Austin Bureau 15950
Editorial: 1005 Congress Ave, Austin, Texas 78701-2463
Language (s): English
DAILY NEWSPAPER

Elizabethton Star 14667
Owner: Elizabethton Newspapers Inc.
Editorial: 300 N Sycamore St, Elizabethton, Tennessee 37643-2742 **Tel:** 1 423 542-4151
Web site: http://www.starhq.com
Freq: Mon thru Fri; **Circ:** 7257 Not Audited
Advertising Sales Manager: Shirley Nave
Profile: Elizabethton Star is the daily newspaper for Carter County and Elizabethton County, TN. It is a general newspaper that covers local as well as regional news from Northeast Tennessee.
Language (s): English
Ad Rate: Full Page Mono 15.00
Ad Rate: Full Page Colour 245.00
Currency: United States Dollars
DAILY NEWSPAPER

Elk City Daily News 14520
Owner: Family Corporation
Editorial: 206 W Broadway Ave, Elk City, Oklahoma 73644-4742 **Tel:** 1 580 225-3000
Email: news@ecdailynews.com **Web site:** http://elkcitydailynews.com/
Freq: Daily; **Circ:** 5740 Not Audited

Editor: Cheryl Overstreet; **Publisher:** Larry Wade
Profile: Elk City Daily News is published for the residents of Elk City, OK and surrounding areas. The paper provides information on local news and community events. Deadlines are one day prior to issue date.
Language (s): English
Ad Rate: Full Page Mono 10.70
Ad Rate: Full Page Colour 920.10
Currency: United States Dollars
DAILY NEWSPAPER

The Elkhart Truth 13981
Owner: Paxton Media Group
Editorial: 421 S 2nd St, Elkhart, Indiana 46516-3238
Tel: 1 574 294-1661
Email: newsroom@elkharttruth.com **Web site:** http://www.elkharttruth.com
Freq: Daily; **Circ:** 15542 Not Audited
Profile: The Elkhart Truth is a daily newspaper for Elkhart, IN. The main goal of the paper is to be the dominant source of local news. The publication is written for residents of Elkhart County and the surrounding area. Topics covered include news about local schools, local government, and community organizations.
Language (s): English
Ad Rate: Full Page Mono 15.64
Currency: United States Dollars
DAILY NEWSPAPER

Elko Daily Free Press 14387
Owner: Lee Enterprises, Inc.
Editorial: 3720 E Idaho St, Elko, Nevada 89801-4611
Tel: 1 775 738-3118
Email: news@elkodaily.com **Web site:** http://elkodaily.com
Freq: Mon thru Fri; **Circ:** 6719
Profile: Elko Daily Free Press is a newspaper serving residents of Elko, NV and its surrounding area. It covers news, events, school news, sports, business, health and features of interest to local residents. Deadlines are two days prior to publication at noon PT.
Language (s): English
Ad Rate: Full Page Mono 15.30
Ad Rate: Full Page Colour 440.00
Currency: United States Dollars
DAILY NEWSPAPER

Ellwood City Ledger 14577
Owner: Calkins Media
Editorial: 501 Lawrence Ave, Ellwood City, Pennsylvania 16117-1927 **Tel:** 1 724 758-5573
Email: eclnews@ellwoodcityledger.com **Web site:** http://www.ellwoodcityledger.com
Freq: Mon thru Fri; **Circ:** 3341 Not Audited
Publisher: Alan Buncher; **Editor:** Larry Howsare
Profile: Ellwood City Ledger is published daily for the residents of Ellwood City, PA and surrounding areas. The newspaper offers local, state and national news, sports, business, lifestyles and entertainment.
Language (s): English
Ad Rate: Full Page Mono 15.23
Ad Rate: Full Page Colour 17.23
Currency: United States Dollars
DAILY NEWSPAPER

The Emporia Gazette 14042
Owner: White Corporation, Inc.
Editorial: 517 Merchant St, Emporia, Kansas 66801-7206 **Tel:** 1 620 342-4800
Email: news@emporia.com **Web site:** http://www.emporiagazette.com
Freq: Mon thru Fri; **Circ:** 5857
Profile: The Emporia Gazette's editorial mission is to provide readers with a complete daily package of local and regional news, plus the latest top stories from the state, nation and world. The publication is written for the communities of Lyon, Chase, Coffey, Greenwood, Morris and Osage counties in Kansas. It covers local and national news, sports, editorials, food, film reviews, youth columns, business news, agricultural news, Emporia State University news, and television listings.
Language (s): English
Ad Rate: Full Page Mono 10.56
Ad Rate: Full Page Colour 215.00
Currency: United States Dollars
DAILY NEWSPAPER

Englewood Sun 78650
Editorial: 120 W Dearborn St, Englewood, Florida 34223-3237 **Tel:** 1 941 681-3000
Web site: http://www.yoursun.com/csp/mediapool/sites/SunNews/Englewood/index.csp
Freq: Daily; **Circ:** 8400 Not Audited
Publisher: David Dunn-Rankin; **Advertising Sales Manager:** Glenn Nickerson
Profile: Englewood Sun is written for the residents of Englewood, FL.
Language (s): English
Ad Rate: Full Page Mono 13.70
Currency: United States Dollars
DAILY NEWSPAPER

Enid News and Eagle 14521
Owner: Community Newspaper Holdings, Inc.
Editorial: 227 W Broadway Ave, Enid, Oklahoma 73701-4017 **Tel:** 1 580 233-6600
Email: editor@enidnews.com **Web site:** http://enidnews.com
Freq: Daily; **Circ:** 12288 Not Audited
Publisher: Jeff Funk
Profile: Enid News and Eagle is a local weekly newspaper serving the residents of Enid, OK and the surrounding area. The newspaper covers local and national news, sports, arts & entertainment, editorial, business and community events. Deadlines are two days before issue dates.
Language (s): English
Ad Rate: Full Page Mono 25.75
Ad Rate: Full Page Colour 31.85
Currency: United States Dollars
DAILY NEWSPAPER

Ennis Daily News 14698
Owner: Fackelman Newspapers
Editorial: 213 N Dallas St, Ennis, Texas 75119-4096
Tel: 1 972 875-3801
Web site: http://www.ennisdailynews.com
Freq: Mon thru Fri; **Circ:** 3930 Not Audited
Profile: Ennis Daily News is a local newspaper serving the residents of Ennis, TX and the surrounding communities. The newspaper covers local news, sports, arts & entertainment, weather, business and community events.
Language (s): English
Ad Rate: Full Page Mono 9.00
Ad Rate: Full Page Colour 150.00
Currency: United States Dollars
DAILY NEWSPAPER

The Enquirer-Journal 14325
Owner: Paxton Media Group
Editorial: 500 W Jefferson St, Monroe, North Carolina 28112-4657 **Tel:** 1 704 289-1541
Email: news@theej.com **Web site:** http://www.enquirerjournal.com
Freq: 3 Times/Week; **Circ:** 6523 Not Audited
Profile: The Enquirer-Journal is a local daily newspaper serving the residents of Union County, NC. The newspaper covers local and national news, sports, arts, editorial, business and community events.
Language (s): English
Ad Rate: Full Page Mono 19.50
Ad Rate: Full Page Colour 290.00
Currency: United States Dollars
DAILY NEWSPAPER

The Enterprise 395332
Owner: GateHouse Media Inc.
Editorial: 1324 Belmont St, Brockton, Massachusetts 02301-4435 **Tel:** 1 508 586-6200
Email: newsroom@enterprisenews.com **Web site:** http://www.enterprisenews.com
Freq: Mon thru Fri; **Circ:** 18426
Profile: The Enterprise is a daily newspaper serving residents living South of Boston, including the community of Brockton, MA. It covers international, national and local news, sports, business, editorials, arts & entertainment and feature stories.
Language (s): English
Ad Rate: Full Page Mono 42.60
Currency: United States Dollars
DAILY NEWSPAPER

Enterprise Ledger 13668
Owner: BH Media Group
Editorial: 106 N Edwards St, Enterprise, Alabama 36330-2524 **Tel:** 1 334 347-9533
Email: news@eprisenow.com **Web site:** http://www.dothaneagle.com/enterprise_ledger/
Freq: Daily; **Circ:** 10372 Not Audited
Profile: Enterprise Ledger is a local newspaper serving the residents of Enterprise and Coffee County, AL. It covers local and national news, sports, entertainment, technology, food, weather, obituaries and business.
Language (s): English
Ad Rate: Full Page Mono 19.75
Ad Rate: Full Page Colour 230.00
Currency: United States Dollars
DAILY NEWSPAPER

Enterprise-Journal 14267
Owner: Emmerich Newspapers Inc.
Editorial: 112 Oliver Emmerich Dr, McComb, Mississippi 39648-6330 **Tel:** 1 601 684-2421
Email: news@enterprise-journal.com **Web site:** http://www.enterprise-journal.com
Freq: Daily; **Circ:** 8088 Not Audited
Advertising Sales Manager: Lauren Devereaux; **News Editor:** Karen Freeman; **Publisher & Editor:** Jack Ryan
Profile: Enterprise-Journal covers all news relevant to Southwest Mississippi. The editorial content of the newspaper includes local news, sports, lifestyle, outdoors and family.
Language (s): English
Ad Rate: Full Page Mono 18.81
Currency: United States Dollars
DAILY NEWSPAPER

Epoch Times 488945
Owner: Epoch Times International
Editorial: 229 W 28th St Fl 6, New York, New York 10001-5905 **Tel:** 1 212 239-2808
Email: nyc_news@epochtimes.com **Web site:** http://www.theepochtimes.com
Circ: 95000
Profile: Epoch Times is a Chinese-American daily newspaper in New York City.
Language (s): Chinese
Ad Rate: Full Page Mono 27.00
Ad Rate: Full Page Colour 44.30
Currency: United States Dollars
DAILY NEWSPAPER

Epoch Times - San Diego Bureau 962898
Owner: Epoch Times International
Editorial: 7925 Silverton Ave Ste 509, San Diego, California 92126-6350 **Tel:** 1 888 388-2518
Email: sandiego@epochtimes.com
Bureau Chief: Helen Zh
Language (s): Chinese
DAILY NEWSPAPER

Erie Times-News 14913
Owner: GateHouse Media Inc.
Editorial: 205 W 12th St, Erie, Pennsylvania 16534-0002
Email: newsdesk@timesnews.com **Web site:** http://www.goerie.com
Freq: Daily; **Circ:** 35648 Not Audited
Profile: Erie Times-News is published daily for the residents of Erie, PA, and the surrounding communities. The newspaper covers local and national news, sports, opinions, entertainment, business and community events. In October 2000, Morning News and Erie Daily Times merged into Erie Times-News.
Language (s): English
Ad Rate: Full Page Mono 76.22
Ad Rate: Full Page Colour 82.17
Currency: United States Dollars
DAILY NEWSPAPER

Estherville Daily News 13877
Owner: Ogden Newspapers
Editorial: 10 N 7th St, Estherville, Iowa 51334-2232
Tel: 1 712 362-2622
Web site: http://www.esthervilledailynews.com
Freq: Mon thru Fri; **Circ:** 2282 Not Audited
Publisher: Glen Caron; **Advertising Sales Manager:** Dar Isaackson
Profile: Estherville Daily News is a local daily newspaper serving the residents of Estherville, IA and the surrounding area. The newspaper covers local news, editorial, sports, arts & entertainment, business and community events.
Language (s): English
Ad Rate: Full Page Mono 5.30
Ad Rate: Full Page Colour 65.00
Currency: United States Dollars
DAILY NEWSPAPER

The Evansville Courier & Press 15428
Owner: Gannett Co., Inc.
Editorial: 300 E Walnut St, Evansville, Indiana 47713-1938 **Tel:** 1 812 424-7711
Email: news@courierpress.com **Web site:** http://www.courierpress.com
Freq: Daily; **Circ:** 36384 Not Audited
Editor: Tim Ethridge; **Publisher:** Jack Pate
Profile: The Evansville Courier & Press is a local daily newspaper serving the residents of Evansville, IN and the Indiana, Kentucky and Illinois tri-state area. The newspaper covers regional and local news, sports, arts & entertainment, business, health, law enforcement and politics. Press releases can be sent by mail or by e-mail.
Language (s): English
Ad Rate: Full Page Mono 49.70
Ad Rate: Full Page Colour 49.70
Currency: United States Dollars
DAILY NEWSPAPER

The Evening Leader 14491
Owner: Horizon Publications
Editorial: 102 E Spring St, Saint Marys, Ohio 45885-2310 **Tel:** 1 419 394-7414
Web site: http://www.theeveningleader.com
Freq: Daily; **Circ:** 5412 Not Audited
Publisher: Gayle Masonbrink
Profile: The Evening Leader is a local daily newspaper serving the residents of Auglaize County, OH. The newspaper covers local news, sports, police, entertainment, business and community events.
Language (s): English
Ad Rate: Full Page Mono 14.09
Ad Rate: Full Page Colour 259.09
Currency: United States Dollars
DAILY NEWSPAPER

The Evening News 14193
Owner: GateHouse Media Inc.
Editorial: 109 Arlington St, Sault Sainte Marie, Michigan 49783-1901 **Tel:** 1 906 632-2235
Email: edit@sooeveningnews.com **Web site:** http://www.sooeveningnews.com
Freq: Daily; **Circ:** 6996 Not Audited
Editor: Scott Brand; **Editor:** Kenn Filkins; **Publisher:** Howard Kaiser; **Editor:** Jack Storey; **Editor:** Brenda Weber
Profile: The Evening News is a local daily newspaper serving the residents of Chippewa County, Luce County and Macaneau County, MI. The newspaper mainly covers local and world news, sports, lifestyle, business, health and community events.
Language (s): English
Ad Rate: Full Page Mono 15.85
Ad Rate: Full Page Colour 195.50
Currency: United States Dollars
DAILY NEWSPAPER

The Evening Sun 14416
Owner: Snyder Communications Corporation
Editorial: 29 Lackawanna Ave, Norwich, New York 13815-1404 **Tel:** 1 607 334-3276
Email: news@evesun.com **Web site:** http://www.evesun.com
Freq: Daily; **Circ:** 4500 Not Audited
Advertising Sales Manager: Russ Foote; **Publisher:** Richard Snyder
Profile: The Evening Sun is a local daily newspaper serving the residents of Chenango County, NY. The newspaper mainly covers local news, sports, editorial, arts & entertainment, business and community events.
Language (s): English
Ad Rate: Full Page Mono 12.05
Ad Rate: Full Page Colour 225.00
Currency: United States Dollars
DAILY NEWSPAPER

The Evening Sun 14581
Owner: Gannett Co., Inc.
Editorial: 135 Baltimore St, Hanover, Pennsylvania 17331-3111 **Tel:** 1 717 637-3736
Email: news@eveningsun.com **Web site:** http://www.eveningsun.com
Freq: Daily; **Circ:** 18632 Not Audited
Profile: The Evening Sun is a local daily newspaper serving the residents of York County and Adams County, PA. The newspaper covers local and national news, sports, entertainment, style, editorial and community events.
Language (s): English
Ad Rate: Full Page Mono 45.58
Ad Rate: Full Page Colour 529.94
Currency: United States Dollars
DAILY NEWSPAPER

Evening Times 13707
Owner: Ricketson Newspapers Inc.
Editorial: 1010 State Highway 77, Marion, Arkansas 72364-9007 **Tel:** 1 870 735-1010
Email: news@theeveningtimes.com **Web site:** http://www.theeveningtimes.com
Freq: Daily; **Circ:** 7385 Not Audited
Publisher: Alex Coulter
Profile: Evening Times provides local news for Crittenden County and Eastern Arkansas.
Language (s): English
Ad Rate: Full Page Mono 13.92
Ad Rate: Full Page Colour 345.00
Currency: United States Dollars
DAILY NEWSPAPER

The Evening Tribune 14405
Owner: GateHouse Media Inc
Editorial: 32 Broadway Mall, Hornell, New York 14843-1920 **Tel:** 1 607 324-1425
Email: news@eveningtribune.com **Web site:** http://www.eveningtribune.com
Freq: Daily; **Circ:** 7562 Not Audited
Editor: John Anderson; **Publisher:** Tom Connors
Profile: The Evening Tribune is a local daily newspaper serving residents of Hornell, NY and the surrounding Canisteo Valley area. The newspaper covers local and world news, sports, entertainment, health and business. Deadlines fall one day prior to issue date.
Language (s): English
Ad Rate: Full Page Mono 9.65
Ad Rate: Full Page Colour 200.00
Currency: United States Dollars
DAILY NEWSPAPER

The Examiner 14233
Owner: GateHouse Media Inc.
Editorial: 410 S Liberty St, Independence, Missouri 64050-3805 **Tel:** 1 816 254-8600
Email: localnews@examiner.net **Web site:** http://www.examiner.net
Freq: Fri; **Circ:** 9373
Editor: Jeff Fox
Profile: The Examiner is published for the residents of Independence and Blue Springs, MO. The newspaper covers local and national news, sports, politics, arts & entertainment and education.
Language (s): English
Ad Rate: Full Page Mono 30.50
Ad Rate: Full Page Colour 283.00
Currency: United States Dollars
DAILY NEWSPAPER

Exponent Telegram 14831
Owner: NCWV Media
Editorial: 324 Hewes Ave, Clarksburg, West Virginia 26301-2744 **Tel:** 1 304 626-1400
Web site: http://www.theet.com
Freq: Daily; **Circ:** 14174 Not Audited
Advertising Sales Manager: Debbie Veltri
Profile: Exponent Telegram's editorial mission is to provide local news and sports to the community. It is written for residents of North Central West Virginia.
Language (s): English
Ad Rate: Full Page Mono 20.40
Ad Rate: Full Page Colour 300.00
Currency: United States Dollars
DAILY NEWSPAPER

The Express 14598
Owner: Ogden Newspapers
Editorial: 9 W Main St, Lock Haven, Pennsylvania 17745-1276 **Tel:** 1 570 748-6791
Email: news@lockhaven.com **Web site:** http://www.lockhaven.com
Freq: Daily; **Circ:** 7366
Editor: Lana Muthler; **Publisher:** Robert Rolley
Profile: The Express is the daily newspaper for Lock Haven, PA. It is a general interest newspaper that covers local, national, and international news and events.
Language (s): English
Ad Rate: Full Page Mono 14.50
Ad Rate: Full Page Colour 99.00
Currency: United States Dollars
DAILY NEWSPAPER

Express 152493

Owner: Washington Post Co.
Editorial: 1150 15th St NW Bldg LENNOX5, Washington, District Of Columbia 20071-0001
Tel: 1 202 334-6000
Email: inbox@readexpress.com **Web site:** http://www.washingtonpost.com/express
Freq: Mon thru Fri; **Circ:** 148928 Not Audited
Editor: Daniel Caccavaro
Profile: Express is a free commuter daily newspaper targeting readers and commuters in the Washington, D.C. metro area. It is provided complimentary in the Sunday edition. The editorial mix includes national, international and local news. Designed and owned by The Washington Post, the paper reaches readers whose busy schedules prevent them from reading newspapers frequently, mainly between the ages of 18 and 34. Much of the editorial content is pulled from wire services and the paper operates with a minimal staff.
Language (s): English
Ad Rate: Full Page Mono 106.00
Ad Rate: Full Page Colour 117.15
Currency: United States Dollars
DAILY NEWSPAPER

The Express-Star 14514

Owner: Community Newspaper Holdings, Inc.
Editorial: 411 W Chickasha Ave, Chickasha, Oklahoma 73018-2505 **Tel:** 1 405 224-2600
Email: james@chickashanews.com **Web site:** http://chickashanews.com
Freq: Daily; **Circ:** 4600 Not Audited
Editor & Publisher: James Bright; **Advertising Sales Manager:** Julie Durian
Profile: Express-Star is the local newspaper for the Chickasha, OK area. Feature stories focus on local, regional and national events. The paper is written to inform the community of any news, events or interesting human interest stories. Deadlines are daily at noon CT.
Language (s): English
Ad Rate: Full Page Mono 9.45
Ad Rate: Full Page Colour 12.45
Currency: United States Dollars
DAILY NEWSPAPER

The Express-Times 15456

Owner: NJ Advance Media
Editorial: 18 Centre Sq, Easton, Pennsylvania 18042-7746 **Tel:** 1 610 258-7171
Email: news@express-times.com **Web site:** http://www.lehighvalleylive.com
Freq: Daily; **Circ:** 21800
Profile: The Express-Times in Easton, PA is published daily for residents in Northampton County and parts of Lehigh County, PA. The paper covers both local and national news, sports, business, entertainment, lifestyle and events.
Language (s): English
Ad Rate: Full Page Mono 66.00
Ad Rate: Full Page Colour 375.00
Currency: United States Dollars
DAILY NEWSPAPER

The Facts 14745

Owner: Southern Newspapers, Inc.
Editorial: 720 S Main St, Clute, Texas 77531-5411
Tel: 1 979 265-7411
Email: news@thefacts.com **Web site:** http://www.thefacts.com
Freq: Daily; **Circ:** 16027 Not Audited
Advertising Sales Manager: Cindy Cornette
Profile: The Facts is written for Brazorian county community readers in and around Brazorian County.
Language (s): English
Ad Rate: Full Page Mono 14.50
Ad Rate: Full Page Colour 375.00
Currency: United States Dollars
DAILY NEWSPAPER

Fairbanks Daily News-Miner 14919

Owner: Snedden Foundation
Editorial: 200 N Cushman St, Fairbanks, Alaska 99701-2832 **Tel:** 1 907 456-6661
Email: digital@newsminer.com **Web site:** http://newsminer.com
Freq: Daily; **Circ:** 13767 Not Audited
Profile: Fairbanks Daily News-Miner is published daily for the residents of Fairbanks, AK and surrounding areas. The newspaper covers local and regional news, business, sports, lifestyles and entertainment.
Language (s): English
Ad Rate: Full Page Mono 25.88
Ad Rate: Full Page Colour 685.00
Currency: United States Dollars
DAILY NEWSPAPER

Fairfield Ledger 13878

Owner: Inland Industries Inc.
Editorial: 112 E Broadway Ave, Fairfield, Iowa 52556-3202 **Tel:** 1 641 472-4129
Email: fledger@lisco.com **Web site:** http://www.goldentrianglenewspapers.com
Freq: Mon thru Fri; **Circ:** 3000
Editor: Andy Hallman; **Advertising Sales Manager:** Gene Luedtke; **Publisher:** Jeff Wilson
Profile: Fairfield Ledger is a local daily newspaper serving the Fairfield, IA area. It provides residents of the local community with information on local news and events in and around the Fairfield and Jefferson county communities. Editorial submissions must be received by noon CT the day prior to publication.
Language (s): English
Ad Rate: Full Page Mono 10.88
Ad Rate: Full Page Colour 38.57
Currency: United States Dollars
DAILY NEWSPAPER

Fairmont Sentinel 14204

Owner: Ogden Newspapers
Editorial: 64 Downtown Plz, Fairmont, Minnesota 56031-1733 **Tel:** 1 507 235-3303
Email: news@fairmontsentinel.com **Web site:** http://www.fairmontsentinel.com
Freq: Mon thru Fri; **Circ:** 4626 Not Audited
Publisher: Gary Andersen; **Advertising Sales Manager:** Kathy Ratcliff; **Editor:** Lee Smith
Profile: Fairmont Sentinel is a local daily newspaper serving the Fairmont, MN area. It is written for residents of surrounding counties. The newspaper provides residents of the local community with information on local news and events in and around the Fairmont community. Contact the publication for the circulation information and advertisement rates.
Language (s): English
Ad Rate: Full Page Mono 19.55
Ad Rate: Full Page Colour 150.00
Currency: United States Dollars
DAILY NEWSPAPER

Faribault Daily News 14205

Owner: Huckle Media LLC
Editorial: 514 Central Ave N, Faribault, Minnesota 55021-4304 **Tel:** 1 507 333-3100
Email: editor@faribault.com **Web site:** http://www.southernminn.com/faribault_daily_news/
Freq: Daily; **Circ:** 14459 Not Audited
Profile: Faribault Daily News is written for the residents of Rice County, MN. It reports on local and national news and events of interest.
Language (s): English
Ad Rate: Full Page Mono 17.90
Ad Rate: Full Page Colour 370.00
Currency: United States Dollars
DAILY NEWSPAPER

The Fayetteville Observer 15432

Owner: GateHouse Media Inc.
Editorial: 458 Whitfield St, Fayetteville, North Carolina 28306-1614 **Tel:** 1 910 486-3500
Email: news@fayobserver.com **Web site:** http://www.fayobserver.com
Freq: Daily; **Circ:** 41371 Not Audited
Profile: The Fayetteville (NC) Observer provides coverage of local and regional news, the military, arts & entertainment, lifestyle news, sports and business. Lead times vary depending on the section and type of news involved.
Language (s): English
Ad Rate: Full Page Mono 51.50
Ad Rate: Full Page Colour 235.01
Currency: United States Dollars
DAILY NEWSPAPER

Finanz und Wirtschaft - New York Bureau 409741

Owner: Verlag Finanz und Wirtschaft AG
Editorial: 301 W 22nd St Apt 68, New York, New York 10011-2667 **Tel:** 1 212 529-1455
Email: newyork@fuw.ch **Web site:** http://www.fuw.ch
Freq: 2 Times/Week; **Circ:** 38354 Not Audited
Profile: Covers business, finance and economy.
Language (s): German
DAILY NEWSPAPER

Finger Lakes Times 14401

Owner: Community Media Group
Editorial: 218 Genesee St, Geneva, New York 14456-2323 **Tel:** 1 315 789-3333
Email: fltimes@fltimes.com **Web site:** http://www.fltimes.com
Freq: Daily; **Circ:** 14017 Not Audited
Publisher: Paul Barrett
Profile: Finger Lakes Times is published daily for the residents of Geneva, NY and surrounding areas. The newspaper covers local and state news, business, sports, lifestyles and entertainment.
Language (s): English
Ad Rate: Full Page Mono 20.50
Ad Rate: Full Page Colour 355.00
Currency: United States Dollars
DAILY NEWSPAPER

The Flint Journal 14928

Owner: MLive Media Group
Editorial: 540 S Saginaw St Ste 101, Flint, Michigan 48502-1813 **Tel:** 1 810 766-6100
Email: flnews@mlive.com **Web site:** http://www.mlive.com/flintjournal
Freq: Fri; **Circ:** 33501
Profile: The Flint Journal is written for the residents of Flint, MI. It covers local and world news, local events, sports, travel, food and music.
Language (s): English
Ad Rate: Full Page Mono 60.42
Ad Rate: Full Page Colour 69.48
Currency: United States Dollars
DAILY NEWSPAPER

Florence Morning News 14643

Owner: HB Media Group
Editorial: 310 S Dargan St, Florence, South Carolina 29506-2537 **Tel:** 1 843 317-6397
Web site: http://www.scnow.com
Freq: Daily; **Circ:** 28631 Not Audited
Publisher: M. Joseph Craig
Profile: Florence Morning News is a local newspaper serving the residents of Florence, SC. It includes news, weather, sports and lifestyles.
Language (s): English
Ad Rate: Full Page Mono 50.00
Ad Rate: Full Page Colour 54.50
Currency: United States Dollars
DAILY NEWSPAPER

The Florida Times-Union 15378

Owner: GateHouse Media Inc.
Editorial: 1 Riverside Ave, Jacksonville, Florida 32202-4917 **Tel:** 1 904 359-4111
Email: features@jacksonville.com **Web site:** http://www.jacksonville.com
Freq: Daily; **Circ:** 60399 Not Audited
Editor: Frank Denton; **Editor:** Carole Fader; **Publisher:** Mark Nusbaum
Profile: Founded in 1865, The Florida Times-Union is a general-interest, broadsheet newspaper with an emphasis on local area coverage, with some national and international wire coverage. It covers area news, politics, crime, professional and collegiate sports, and arts and culture, maintaining bureaus in several Florida and Georgia locations. The paper also produces skirt! magazine's Jacksonville edition and a host of weekly feature sections. It launched its Web arm in 1996, which became Jacksonville.com in 1997. The publication aims to be the primary news and information source for Northeast Florida residents.
Language (s): English
Ad Rate: Full Page Mono 236.00
Ad Rate: Full Page Colour 262.06
Currency: United States Dollars
DAILY NEWSPAPER

The Florida Times-Union - Brunswick Bureau 15671

Editorial: 3375 Community Rd, Brunswick, Georgia 31520-2867 **Tel:** 1 912 264-0405
Profile: Do NOT send faxes!
Language (s): English
DAILY NEWSPAPER

The Florida Times-Union - Tallahassee Bureau 15670

Editorial: Tallahassee, Florida
Language (s): English
DAILY NEWSPAPER

Florida Today 15426

Owner: Gannett Co., Inc.
Editorial: 1 Gannett Plaza, Melbourne, Florida 32940
Tel: 1 321 242-3500
Email: breakingnews@floridatoday.com **Web site:** http://www.floridatoday.com
Freq: Daily; **Circ:** 37780 Not Audited
Publisher: Jeff Kiel; **Editor:** John McCarthy
Profile: Florida Today serves Brevard County, FL and the area surrounding Cape Canaveral, FL. It also publishes five weekly and four monthly community newspapers, which cater to the distinct neighborhoods within Brevard County.
Language (s): English
Ad Rate: Full Page Mono 116.08
Ad Rate: Full Page Colour 131.83
Currency: United States Dollars
DAILY NEWSPAPER

Focus Daily News 63996

Owner: Focus Newspapers
Editorial: 1337 Marilyn Ave, Desoto, Texas 75115-6414 **Tel:** 1 972 223-9175
Email: editor@focusdailynews.com **Web site:** http://focusdailynews.com
Freq: Daily; **Circ:** 35786 Not Audited
Advertising Sales Manager: Carmela Hanson
Profile: Focus Daily News is written for the residents of DeSoto, Cedar Hill, Lancaster and Duncanville, TX. It covers local news, weather, sports, business and arts & entertainment.
Language (s): English
Ad Rate: Full Page Mono 46.00
Currency: United States Dollars
DAILY NEWSPAPER

Forrest City Times Herald 13691

Owner: Times-Herald Publishing Co., Inc.
Editorial: 222 N Izard St, Forrest City, Arkansas 72335-3324 **Tel:** 1 870 633-3130
Email: fctimes@thnews.com **Web site:** http://www.thnews.com
Freq: Daily; **Circ:** 5000 Not Audited
Profile: Forrest City Times Herald is a daily newspaper serving Forrest City, AR and the surrounding area. Sections include news, sports, arts & entertainment and opinions.
Language (s): English
Ad Rate: Full Page Mono 11.64
Ad Rate: Full Page Colour 250.00
Currency: United States Dollars
DAILY NEWSPAPER

Forsyth County News 15278

Editorial: 302 Veterans Memorial Blvd, Cumming, Georgia 30040-2644 **Tel:** 1 770 887-3126
Email: editor@forsythnews.com **Web site:** http://www.forsythnews.com
Freq: Fri; **Circ:** 12500 Not Audited
Advertising Sales Manager: Ryan Garmon; **Publisher:** Vince Johnson
Profile: The Forsyth County News is a local newspaper serving the residents of Forsyth County, GA. It includes information on local news, weather, sports, business, and entertainment. Reporters will often covering general news as needed, regardless of their usual beats.
Language (s): English
Ad Rate: Full Page Mono 16.45
Ad Rate: Full Page Colour 38.37
Currency: United States Dollars
DAILY NEWSPAPER

Fort Bend Herald & Texas Coaster 14727

Owner: Hartman Newspapers, Inc.
Editorial: 1902 4th St, Rosenberg, Texas 77471-5140
Tel: 1 281 342-4474
Email: newsroom@fbherald.com **Web site:** http://www.fbherald.com
Freq: Daily; **Circ:** 8200
Profile: Fort Bend Herald & Texas Coaster is a local, daily newspaper serving the Fort Bend, TX area. The paper's editorial mission is to print the news that affects people in the community. It covers local news and sports.
Language (s): English
Ad Rate: Full Page Mono 15.50
Ad Rate: Full Page Colour 275.00
Currency: United States Dollars
DAILY NEWSPAPER

Fort Collins Coloradoan 13782

Owner: Gannett Co., Inc.
Editorial: 1300 Riverside Ave, Fort Collins, Colorado 80524-4353 **Tel:** 1 970 493-6397
Email: news@coloradoan.com **Web site:** http://www.coloradoan.com
Freq: Daily; **Circ:** 19882 Not Audited
Profile: Fort Collins Coloradoan is a local newspaper serving the residents of Fort Collins, CO. It includes information on local news, weather, sports, business and entertainment.
Language (s): English
Ad Rate: Full Page Mono 59.40
Ad Rate: Full Page Colour 73.80
Currency: United States Dollars
DAILY NEWSPAPER

Fort Madison Daily Democrat 13880

Owner: Brehm Communications, Inc.
Editorial: 1226 Avenue H, Fort Madison, Iowa 52627-4544 **Tel:** 1 319 372-6421
Web site: http://www.dailydem.com
Freq: Daily; **Circ:** 5500
Editor: Robin Delaney
Profile: The Daily Democrat is published for the residents of Fort Madison, IA and surrounding areas. The newspaper covers local and state news, business, sports, lifestyles and entertainment.
Language (s): English
Ad Rate: Full Page Mono 14.40
Ad Rate: Full Page Colour 49.63
Currency: United States Dollars
DAILY NEWSPAPER

Fort Morgan Times 13783

Owner: MediaNews Group
Editorial: 329 Main St, Fort Morgan, Colorado 80701-2108 **Tel:** 1 970 867-5651
Email: editor@fmtimes.com **Web site:** http://www.fortmorgantimes.com
Freq: Daily; **Circ:** 2448 Not Audited
Editor: John La Porte
Profile: Fort Morgan Times is a local daily newspaper serving the residents of Fort Morgan, CO. The publication features local news, weather, sports, economy and business, and entertainment.
Language (s): English
Ad Rate: Full Page Mono 10.75
Currency: United States Dollars
DAILY NEWSPAPER

The Fort Scott Tribune 14043

Owner: Rust Communications
Editorial: 12 E Wall St, Fort Scott, Kansas 66701-1423 **Tel:** 1 620 644-5111
Email: editor@fstribune.com **Web site:** http://www.fstribune.com
Freq: Mon thru Fri; **Circ:** 3200 Not Audited
Profile: The Fort Scott Tribune is a local newspaper serving the residents of Fort Scott, KS. It includes information on local news, weather, sports, business and entertainment. The weekend edition, entitled the Sunday Herald-Tribune, is combined with the Nevada (MO) Daily Mail's weekend edition and is distributed to residents in both Vernon County, MO, and Bourbon County, KS.
Language (s): English
Ad Rate: Full Page Mono 6.25
Ad Rate: Full Page Colour 150.00
Currency: United States Dollars
DAILY NEWSPAPER

Fort Worth Star-Telegram 15332

Owner: McClatchy Newspapers
Editorial: 808 Throckmorton St, Fort Worth, Texas 76102-6315 **Tel:** 1 817 390-7827
Email: newsroom@star-telegram.com **Web site:** http://www.star-telegram.com
Freq: Daily; **Circ:** 97634 Not Audited
Profile: Fort Worth Star-Telegram, founded in 1906, is distributed in 23 North Texas counties in and around the Fort Worth, TX area. The Fort Worth Star-Telegram is a newspaper written for the general public. It offers regional and national news, and provides its readers with information on business, real estate, arts & entertainment, and sports. The business section offers breaking news, investigative reports, news and news analysis, features, columns and profiles. The Star-Telegram is a morning edition paper.
Language (s): English
Ad Rate: Full Page Mono 455.00
Ad Rate: Full Page Colour 492.10
Currency: United States Dollars
DAILY NEWSPAPER

The Forum 15410
Owner: Forum Communications Co.
Editorial: 101 5th St N, Fargo, North Dakota 58102-4826 **Tel:** 1 701 235-7311
Email: news@forumcomm.com **Web site:** http://www.inforum.com
Freq: Daily; **Circ:** 37267 Not Audited
News Editor: Dave Roepke; **Advertising Sales Manager:** Scott Schmeltzer
Profile: The Forum is a daily newspaper published for readers in the sister cities of Fargo, ND and Morehead, MN. The editorial content covers local and regional news, government, politics, business, technology, sports, entertainment and agriculture.
Language (s): English
Ad Rate: Full Page Mono 59.35
Currency: United States Dollars
DAILY NEWSPAPER

Forum - Bismarck Bureau 863334
Editorial: 600 E Boulevard Ave, Bismarck, North Dakota 58505-0601 **Tel:** 1 701 255-5607
Language (s): English
DAILY NEWSPAPER

Foster's Daily Democrat 14352
Owner: GateHouse Media Inc.
Editorial: 11 Main St, Dover, New Hampshire 03820-3811 **Tel:** 1 603 742-4455
Email: news@fosters.com **Web site:** http://www.fosters.com
Freq: Daily; **Circ:** 19023 Not Audited
Publisher: Therese Foster
Profile: Foster's Daily Democrat is a daily newspaper published for the residents of Southeastern New Hampshire. The newspaper provides information on local news, weather, sports, business and events.
Language (s): English
Ad Rate: Full Page Mono 20.95
Ad Rate: Full Page Colour 435.00
Currency: United States Dollars
DAILY NEWSPAPER

Fostoria Review Times 14453
Owner: Findlay Publishing Company (The)
Editorial: 113 E Center St, Fostoria, Ohio 44830-2905 **Tel:** 1 419 435-6641
Email: rtnews@reviewtimes.com **Web site:** http://www.reviewtimes.com
Freq: Daily; **Circ:** 3790 Not Audited
News Editor: Tom Pernecker; **News Editor:** Joel Sensenig
Profile: Fostoria Times Review is a local newspaper serving the residents of Fostoria, OH. It includes information on local and national news, weather, sports, business, and entertainment.
Language (s): English
Ad Rate: Full Page Mono 10.40
Ad Rate: Full Page Colour 175.00
Currency: United States Dollars
DAILY NEWSPAPER

Frankfurter Allgemeine - New York Bureau 503987
Owner: Frankfurter Allgemeine Zeitung GmbH
Editorial: 125 North 10th St, #S5B, Brooklyn, New York 11211-1169 **Tel:** 1 718 599-2750
Web site: http://www.faz.net
Profile: This is the New York bureau for Frankfurter Allgemeine Zeitung in Frankfurt, Germany.
Language (s): German
DAILY NEWSPAPER

Franklin Banner-Tribune 14096
Editorial: 115 Wilson St, Franklin, Louisiana 70538 **Tel:** 1 337 828-3706
Email: editor@banner-tribune.com **Web site:** http://www.banner-tribune.com
Freq: Daily; **Circ:** 3231 Not Audited
Publisher: Allan Von Werder; **Advertising Sales Manager:** Debbie Von Werder
Profile: Franklin Banner-Tribune is a newspaper for the residents of Franklin, Louisiana. The publication offers articles on local news, entertainment and events, sports, tourism, and weather.
Language (s): English
Ad Rate: Full Page Mono 6.84
Ad Rate: Full Page Colour 300.00
Currency: United States Dollars
DAILY NEWSPAPER

The Frederick News-Post 14145
Owner: Ogden Newspapers
Editorial: 351 Ballenger Center Dr, Frederick, Maryland 21703-7095 **Tel:** 1 301 662-1177
Web site: http://www.fredericknewspost.com
Freq: Fri; **Circ:** 27661 Not Audited
Advertising Sales Manager: Connie Hastings; **Publisher:** Geordie Wilson
Profile: The Frederick (MD) News-Post is a daily newspaper that covers local news, current events and sports.
Language (s): English
Ad Rate: Full Page Mono 25.50
Ad Rate: Full Page Colour 350.00
Currency: United States Dollars
DAILY NEWSPAPER

The Free Lance-Star 14756
Owner: BH Media Group
Editorial: 1340 Central Park Blvd Ste 100, Fredericksburg, Virginia 22401-4940 **Tel:** 1 540 374-5000
Email: newsroom@freelancestar.com **Web site:** http://www.fredericksburg.com
Freq: Daily; **Circ:** 34213 Not Audited
Editor: Richard Amrhine; **Editor:** Phil Jenkins
Profile: The Free Lance-Star is a daily newspaper serving the residents of Fredericksburg, VA and surrounding counties. It offers articles on local news, national news, events and business.
Language (s): English
Ad Rate: Full Page Mono 27.40
Ad Rate: Full Page Colour 96.15
Currency: United States Dollars
DAILY NEWSPAPER

The Free Press 14209
Owner: Community Newspaper Holdings, Inc.
Editorial: 418 S 2nd St, Mankato, Minnesota 56001-3727 **Tel:** 1 507 625-4451
Email: editor@mankatofreepress.com **Web site:** http://www.mankatofreepress.com
Freq: Daily; **Circ:** 16652 Not Audited
Publisher: John Elchert
Profile: The Free Press is published daily for residents of South Central Minnesota. The newspaper covers local news, weather, sports and community events. Feature articles cover business, education, arts & entertainment, lifestyle and other topics of interest to area residents. The lead time for editorial submissions is 3pm CT daily.
Language (s): English
Ad Rate: Full Page Mono 24.73
Ad Rate: Full Page Colour 338.00
Currency: United States Dollars
DAILY NEWSPAPER

The Freeman 14825
Owner: Conley Publishing Group
Editorial: 801 N Barstow St, Waukesha, Wisconsin 53186-4801 **Tel:** 1 262 542-2500
Email: news@conleynet.com **Web site:** http://www.gmtoday.com
Freq: Fri; **Circ:** 9308 Not Audited
Advertising Sales Manager: Jim Baumgart
Profile: The Freeman is a daily newspaper published for residents of Waukesha, WI and surrounding areas. It covers local news and events.
Language (s): English
Ad Rate: Full Page Mono 23.48
Ad Rate: Full Page Colour 184.92
Currency: United States Dollars
DAILY NEWSPAPER

Fremont Tribune 14339
Owner: Lee Enterprises, Inc.
Editorial: 135 N Main St, Fremont, Nebraska 68025-5673 **Tel:** 1 402 721-5000
Email: tribnews@ftrib.com **Web site:** http://fremonttribune.com
Freq: Daily; **Circ:** 6550 Not Audited
News Editor: Tammy McKeighan
Profile: Fremont Tribune is a local daily newspaper serving the residents of Fremont, NE and its surrounding communities. The publication offers local and national news, events, health, business and entertainment.
Language (s): English
Ad Rate: Full Page Mono 19.75
Ad Rate: Full Page Colour 380.00
Currency: United States Dollars
DAILY NEWSPAPER

The Fresno Bee 15355
Owner: McClatchy Newspapers
Editorial: 1626 E St, Fresno, California 93786-0001 **Tel:** 1 559 441-6111
Email: metro@fresnobee.com **Web site:** http://www.fresnobee.com
Freq: Daily; **Circ:** 66107 Not Audited
Profile: The Fresno Bee is published for the general public in the Fresno, CA area. Major news focuses are business, technology, state news, national news, local news, international news, lifestyle, sports and entertainment.
Language (s): English
Ad Rate: Full Page Mono 153.50
Ad Rate: Full Page Colour 252.00
Currency: United States Dollars
DAILY NEWSPAPER

The Fulton Sun 14231
Owner: Wehco Media Inc.
Editorial: 115 E 5th St, Fulton, Missouri 65251 **Tel:** 1 573 642-7272
Email: news@fultonsun.com **Web site:** http://www.fultonsun.com
Freq: Fri; **Circ:** 4500 Not Audited
Editor: Karen Atkins; **Advertising Sales Manager:** Rachel Reed; **Editor:** Kevin Smith
Profile: Fulton Sun is a newspaper serving the residents of Fulton, MO. The publication offers articles on local news and community events. Deadlines for the publication are 10am CT the day before issue date.
Language (s): English
Ad Rate: Full Page Mono 7.30
Ad Rate: Full Page Colour 10.30
Currency: United States Dollars
DAILY NEWSPAPER

The Gadsden Times 13670
Owner: GateHouse Media Inc.
Editorial: 401 Locust St, Gadsden, Alabama 35901-3737 **Tel:** 1 256 549-2000
Email: news@gadsdentimes.com **Web site:** http://www.gadsdentimes.com
Freq: Daily; **Circ:** 13473 Not Audited
Publisher: Glen Porter
Profile: The Gadsden Times is published daily for residents of Gadsden, AL and surrounding communities. The publication covers local, national and international news, weather, sports, religion and community events. Feature articles cover business, education, arts & entertainment, lifestyle and other information of interest to community residents.
Language (s): English
Ad Rate: Full Page Mono 39.50
Currency: United States Dollars
DAILY NEWSPAPER

Gainesville Daily Register 14699
Owner: Community Newspaper Holdings, Inc.
Editorial: 306 E California St, Gainesville, Texas 76240-4006 **Tel:** 1 940 665-5511
Web site: http://www.gainesvilleregister.com
Freq: Mon thru Fri; **Circ:** 5902 Not Audited
Profile: Gainesville Daily Register is a newspaper serving residents of Gainesville, TX. The publication covers local news and community events. Deadlines are one day prior to issue date at 10:30am MT.
Language (s): English
Ad Rate: Full Page Mono 9.90
Ad Rate: Full Page Colour 330.00
Currency: United States Dollars
DAILY NEWSPAPER

The Gainesville Sun 13817
Owner: GateHouse Media Inc.
Editorial: 2700 SW 13th St, Gainesville, Florida 32608-2015 **Tel:** 1 352 374-5000
Email: online@gvillesun.com **Web site:** http://www.gainesville.com
Freq: Daily; **Circ:** 26477 Not Audited
Publisher: James Doughton
Profile: The Gainesville Sun provides news and information to North Central Florida. As of November 2008, the publication has some combined operations with the Star-Banner in Ocala, FL.
Language (s): English
Ad Rate: Full Page Mono 120.30
Ad Rate: Full Page Colour 792.00
Currency: United States Dollars
DAILY NEWSPAPER

Galion Inquirer 14455
Owner: AIM Media Midwest
Editorial: 129 Harding Way E, Galion, Ohio 44833-1902 **Tel:** 1 419 468-1117
Email: editor@galioninquirer.com **Web site:** http://www.galioninquirer.com
Freq: Fri; **Circ:** 3860 Not Audited
Publisher: Vicki Taylor
Profile: Galion Inquirer is a local daily newspaper serving the residents of Galion, OH and surrounding areas. It covers local news and community events. Deadlines are the day before issue date.
Language (s): English
Ad Rate: Full Page Mono 9.15
Ad Rate: Full Page Colour 16.30
Currency: United States Dollars
DAILY NEWSPAPER

Gallipolis Daily Tribune 14456
Owner: AIM Media Midwest
Editorial: 825 3rd Ave, Gallipolis, Ohio 45631-1624 **Tel:** 1 740 446-2342
Web site: http://www.mydailytribune.com
Freq: Fri; **Circ:** 4466 Not Audited
Profile: Gallipolis Daily Tribune is a newspaper serving the residents of Gallipolis, OH. The publication covers local and national news, events, sports, business, and lifestyles. On Sundays, the paper joins with its sister newspaper, The Daily Sentinel in Pomeroy, OH to produce the Sunday Times-Sentinel. Advertising deadlines are two days prior to publication.
Language (s): English
Ad Rate: Full Page Mono 11.35
Ad Rate: Full Page Colour 180.00
Currency: United States Dollars
DAILY NEWSPAPER

The Galveston County Daily News 14700
Owner: Walls Investment Co.
Editorial: 8522 Teichman Rd, Galveston, Texas 77554-9119 **Tel:** 1 409 683-5200
Email: newsroom@galvnews.com **Web site:** http://www.galvnews.com/
Freq: Daily; **Circ:** 26838 Not Audited
News Editor: Dave Mathews; **Publisher:** Leonard Woolsey
Profile: The Galveston (TX) County Daily News provides news and information for the residents of Galveston County, TX.
Language (s): English
Ad Rate: Full Page Mono 29.00
Ad Rate: Full Page Colour 425.00
Currency: United States Dollars
DAILY NEWSPAPER

Garden City Telegram 14044
Owner: Harris Enterprises
Editorial: 310 N 7th St, Garden City, Kansas 67846-5521 **Tel:** 1 620 275-8500
Email: newsroom@gctelegram.com **Web site:** http://www.gctelegram.com
Freq: Daily; **Circ:** 7437 Not Audited
Editor & Publisher: Dena Sattler
Profile: Garden City Telegram provides news and information for the residents of southwest Kansas.
Language (s): English
Ad Rate: Full Page Mono 14.88
Ad Rate: Full Page Colour 295.00
Currency: United States Dollars
DAILY NEWSPAPER

The Garden Island 13863
Owner: Lee Enterprises, Inc.
Editorial: 3-3137 Kuhio Hwy, Lihue, Hawaii 96766-1141 **Tel:** 1 808 245-3681
Email: editor@thegardenisland.com **Web site:** http://thegardenisland.com
Freq: Daily; **Circ:** 10873 Not Audited
Profile: The Garden Island is published daily for the residents of Lihue, HI and surrounding areas. The newspaper covers local and national news, business, sports, lifestyles and entertainment.
Language (s): English
Ad Rate: Full Page Mono 24.00
Ad Rate: Full Page Colour 280.00
Currency: United States Dollars
DAILY NEWSPAPER

The Gardner News 14120
Owner: Gardner News, Inc. (The)
Editorial: 309 Central St, Gardner, Massachusetts 01440-3839 **Tel:** 1 978 632-8000
Email: editorial@thegardnernews.com **Web site:** http://www.thegardnernews.com
Freq: Daily; **Circ:** 4657 Not Audited
Publisher: Alberta Bell
Profile: The Gardner News is a local daily newspaper that provides news and information for the Gardner, MA area. Lead time for the Tuesday business special is the previous Friday.
Language (s): English
Ad Rate: Full Page Mono 8.25
Ad Rate: Full Page Colour 1332.00
Currency: United States Dollars
DAILY NEWSPAPER

Gaston Gazette 14293
Owner: GateHouse Media Inc.
Editorial: 1893 Remount Rd, Gastonia, North Carolina 28054-7413 **Tel:** 1 704 869-1700
Email: customerservice@gastongazette.com **Web site:** http://www.gastongazette.com
Freq: Daily; **Circ:** 20961 Not Audited
Publisher: Lucy Talley
Profile: Gaston Gazette is published daily for residents of Gaston, Lincoln, and Cleveland counties, NC and York County, SC. The newspaper covers local news, weather, sports and community events. Feature articles cover business, politics, education, arts & entertainment and lifestyle. The lead time and deadlines for the publication vary.
Language (s): English
Ad Rate: Full Page Mono 21.70
Ad Rate: Full Page Colour 500.00
Currency: United States Dollars
DAILY NEWSPAPER

The Gazette 15438
Owner: Gazette Company (The)
Editorial: 500 3rd Ave SE, Cedar Rapids, Iowa 52401-1608 **Tel:** 1 319 398-8313
Email: news@sourcemedia.net **Web site:** http://thegazette.com
Freq: Daily; **Circ:** 37786 Not Audited
Profile: The Gazette is a daily morning newspaper published in Cedar Rapids, IA. It provides Cedar Rapids and 16 counties in Eastern Iowa with local, regional, national and international news, sports, business, entertainment coverage and "information that is important to the readers."
Language (s): English
Ad Rate: Full Page Mono 78.17
Ad Rate: Full Page Colour 97.71
Currency: United States Dollars
DAILY NEWSPAPER

The Gazette 15439
Owner: Anschutz Corp.
Editorial: 30 E Pikes Peak Ave Ste 100, Colorado Springs, Colorado 80903-1580 **Tel:** 1 719 632-5511
Web site: http://www.gazette.com
Freq: Daily; **Circ:** 44072 Not Audited
Publisher: Dan Steever
Profile: The Gazette is a daily newspaper published for the residents of Colorado Springs, Colorado. It was founded in 1872 as The Out West. The newspaper's goal is to inform and connect all residents of the area to the world and to bolster the relationship between the military and non-military communities.
Language (s): English
Ad Rate: Full Page Mono 51.55
Ad Rate: Full Page Colour 61.22
Currency: United States Dollars
DAILY NEWSPAPER

The Gazette - Des Moines Bureau 16050
Editorial: 319 E 5th St, Des Moines, Iowa 50309-1927 **Tel:** 1 515 243-7220
Bureau Chief: Rod Boshart
Language (s): English
DAILY NEWSPAPER

The Gazette - Iowa City Bureau 16093
Editorial: 200 S Clinton St, Ste 201, Iowa City, Iowa 52240-4028 **Tel:** 1 319 339-3155
Email: iowacity@gazcomm.com
Language (s): English
DAILY NEWSPAPER

Gettysburg Times 14579
Owner: Times & News Publishing Co.
Editorial: 1570 Fairfield Rd, Gettysburg, Pennsylvania 17325-7252 **Tel:** 1 717 334-1131
Email: news@gettysburgtimes.com **Web site:** http://www.gettysburgtimes.com

Freq: Daily; Circ: 9001 Not Audited
Publisher: Harry Hartman
Profile: Gettysburg Times is a daily newspaper published Monday through Saturday for the residents of Adams County, PA. It provides news and information. Lead time and deadlines vary.
Language (s): English
Ad Rate: Full Page Mono 14.92
Ad Rate: Full Page Colour 18.72
Currency: United States Dollars
DAILY NEWSPAPER

Gillette News-Record 14849
Owner: Gillette News-Record
Editorial: 1201 W 2nd St, Gillette, Wyoming 82716-3301 Tel: 1 307 682-9306
Email: news@gillettenewsrecord.com Web site: http://www.gillettenewsrecord.com
Freq: Daily; Circ: 6900 Not Audited
Advertising Sales Manager: Cher Rhoades; Publisher & Editor: Ann Turner
Profile: Gillette News-Record is a daily newspaper for residents of Gillette and Campbell County, WY. Published daily except Saturday, the publication covers local news, sports, government, business, health, lifestyles and education information. Deadlines are daily at 9am MT.
Language (s): English
Ad Rate: Full Page Mono 14.30
Ad Rate: Full Page Colour 175.00
Currency: United States Dollars
DAILY NEWSPAPER

Glasgow Daily Times 14078
Owner: Community Newspaper Holdings, Inc.
Editorial: 100 Commerce Dr, Glasgow, Kentucky 42141-1192 Tel: 1 270 678-5171
Web site: http://glasgowdailytimes.com
Freq: Daily; Circ: 6455
Publisher: Bill Hanson
Profile: Glasgow Daily Times is a daily newspaper for the residents of Glasgow, KY and the surrounding area. Regular features include local news, sports, business and education. Deadlines are at noon CT on the day prior to publication.
Language (s): English
Ad Rate: Full Page Mono 13.44
Ad Rate: Full Page Colour 125.00
Currency: United States Dollars
DAILY NEWSPAPER

The Gleaner 14080
Owner: Gannett Co., Inc.
Editorial: 455 Klutey Park Plaza Dr, Henderson, Kentucky 42420-5213 Tel: 1 270 827-2000
Email: news@thegleaner.com Web site: http://www.thegleaner.com
Freq: Daily; Circ: 8047 Not Audited
Profile: The Gleaner is a local, daily newspaper serving residents of Henderson, KY. It covers local news and events, business, sports, obituaries and social issues.
Language (s): English
Ad Rate: Full Page Mono 16.26
Ad Rate: Full Page Colour 90.00
Currency: United States Dollars
DAILY NEWSPAPER

Glendale News-Press 13728
Owner: tronc
Editorial: 202 W 1st St, Los Angeles, California 90012-4299 Tel: 1 818 637-3200
Web site: http://www.latimes.com/socal/glendale-news-press/
Freq: Fri; Circ: 20000 Not Audited
Advertising Sales Manager: Hector Cabral
Profile: Glendale News-Press is published for the residents of Glendale, La Crescenta, La Canada Flintridge and Montrose, CA. The newspaper covers local news, sports, education, business, politics, crime and community events. It is distributed inside the Los Angeles Times and is available, free of charge, at select news racks throughout the area. It shares offices with the Burbank Leader. On Sundays, the paper combines with the Burbank Leader to put out a Sunday issue, the Sunday News-Press & Leader.
Language (s): English
Ad Rate: Full Page Mono 23.00
Ad Rate: Full Page Colour 250.00
Currency: United States Dollars
DAILY NEWSPAPER

Glenwood Springs Post Independent 14957
Owner: Swift Newspapers
Editorial: 824 Grand Ave, Glenwood Springs, Colorado 81601-3557 Tel: 1 970 945-8515
Email: news@postindependent.com Web site: http://www.postindependent.com
Freq: Daily; Circ: 9918 Not Audited
Publisher: Michael Bennett; Editor: Randy Essex
Profile: Glenwood Springs Post Independent is a daily newspaper written to provide news and information to the residents of Glenwood Springs, CO and surrounding communities. Sections include news, sports, arts & entertainment and letters to the editor.
Language (s): English
Ad Rate: Full Page Mono 35.78
Ad Rate: Full Page Colour 139.28
Currency: United States Dollars
DAILY NEWSPAPER

Globe Gazette 13885
Owner: Lee Enterprises, Inc.
Editorial: 300 N Washington Ave, Mason City, Iowa 50401-3222 Tel: 1 641 421-0500
Email: news@globegazette.com Web site: http://www.globegazette.com
Freq: Daily; Circ: 12689 Not Audited
News Editor: Bob Steenson; Editor: Tom Thoma
Profile: Globe Gazette is a published daily for the residents of Mason City, IA and surrounding areas. The newspaper covers local news, business and sports.
Language (s): English
Ad Rate: Full Page Mono 26.25
Currency: United States Dollars
DAILY NEWSPAPER

Gloucester Daily Times 14121
Owner: Community Newspaper Holdings, Inc.
Editorial: 36 Whittemore St, Gloucester, Massachusetts 01930-2553 Tel: 1 978 283-7000
Email: gdt@gloucestertimes.com Web site: http://www.gloucestertimes.com
Freq: Mon thru Fri; Circ: 6341 Not Audited
Profile: Gloucester Daily Times is a daily local newspaper serving the residents of Gloucester, MA and surrounding communities. It covers sports, business and local news. The publication's Web site offers a searchable database with purchase of the daily newspaper.
Language (s): English
Ad Rate: Full Page Mono 21.50
Currency: United States Dollars
DAILY NEWSPAPER

The Goldsboro News-Argus 14294
Owner: Buchheit News Management
Editorial: 310 N Berkeley Blvd, Goldsboro, North Carolina 27534-4326 Tel: 1 919 778-2211
Email: news@newsargus.com Web site: http://www.newsargus.com
Freq: Mon thru Fri; Circ: 14736 Not Audited
Editor: Renee Carey; Publisher: Hal Tanner
Profile: Goldsboro News-Argus is published daily for the residents of Wayne County, NC. The newspaper covers local news, sports and Seymour Johnson Air Force base news. Sections and departments regularly featured include business, church, classified, editorials, entertainment, lifestyle, sports and weather. Editorial deadlines are daily at 10:30am ET. The newspaper accepts non-disclosure agreements on a case-by-case basis.
Language (s): English
Ad Rate: Full Page Mono 24.60
Ad Rate: Full Page Colour 495.00
Currency: United States Dollars
DAILY NEWSPAPER

The Goshen News 13985
Owner: Community Newspaper Holdings, Inc.
Editorial: 114 S Main St, Goshen, Indiana 46526-3734 Tel: 1 574 533-2151
Email: news@goshennews.com Web site: http://goshennews.com
Freq: Fri; Circ: 9470
Profile: The Goshen News is published for the residents of Goshen, IN and surrounding areas. It provides information on local news, sports and weather.
Language (s): English
Ad Rate: Full Page Mono 24.00
Ad Rate: Full Page Colour 75.48
Currency: United States Dollars
DAILY NEWSPAPER

Grand Forks Herald 14973
Owner: Forum Communications Co.
Editorial: 375 2nd Ave N, Grand Forks, North Dakota 58203-3707 Tel: 1 701 780-1100
Email: news@gfherald.com Web site: http://www.grandforksherald.com
Freq: Daily; Circ: 26611 Not Audited
News Editor: Tu-Uyen Tran
Profile: Grand Forks Herald is a local daily newspaper written for residents of Grand Forks, ND. The newspaper covers local and statewide news, sports, and entertainment, as well as community events.
Language (s): English
Ad Rate: Full Page Mono 46.88
Ad Rate: Full Page Colour 524.00
Currency: United States Dollars
DAILY NEWSPAPER

Grand Haven Tribune 14168
Owner: Grand Haven Publishing Company
Editorial: 101 N 3rd St, Grand Haven, Michigan 49417-1209 Tel: 1 616 842-6400
Email: news@grandhaventribune.com Web site: http://www.grandhaventribune.com
Freq: Mon thru Fri; Circ: 8567 Not Audited
Editor: Marie Havenga; Publisher: Kevin Hook; News Editor: Becky Vargo
Profile: Grand Haven Tribune is published daily for the residents of Grand Haven, MI and surrounding areas. The newspaper covers local news, sports, arts & entertainment and community events.
Language (s): English
Ad Rate: Full Page Mono 18.68
Ad Rate: Full Page Colour 218.68
Currency: United States Dollars
DAILY NEWSPAPER

The Grand Island Independent 14340
Owner: Omaha World-Herald Co.
Editorial: 422 W 1st St, Grand Island, Nebraska 68801-5802 Tel: 1 308 646-0590
Email: newsdesk@theindependent.com Web site: http://www.theindependent.com
Freq: Daily; Circ: 18446 Not Audited
Publisher: Don Smith
Profile: Grand Island Independent is published daily for the residents of Grand Island, NE. The newspaper covers local news, sports, business news, arts & entertainment and community events.
Language (s): English
Ad Rate: Full Page Mono 25.73
Ad Rate: Full Page Colour 375.00
Currency: United States Dollars
DAILY NEWSPAPER

Grand Rapids Press 15385
Owner: MLive Media Group
Editorial: 169 Monroe Ave NW Ste 100, Grand Rapids, Michigan 49503-2632 Tel: 1 616 222-5400
Email: grnews@mlive.com Web site: http://www.mlive.com/grand-rapids
Freq: Daily; Circ: 60953
Editor: Julie Hoogland
Profile: Founded in 1892, Grand Rapids Press is a daily broadsheet covering West Michigan and outlying areas. It is an afternoon paper, therefore it is often best to contact members of the editorial staff in the late afternoon, rather than in the morning or at mid-day.
Language (s): English
Ad Rate: Full Page Colour 72.35
Currency: United States Dollars
DAILY NEWSPAPER

Grants Pass Daily Courier 14554
Owner: Courier Publishing Company
Editorial: 409 Se 7Th St, Grants Pass, Oregon 97526-3003 Tel: 1 541 474-3700
Email: news@thedailycourier.com Web site: http://www.thedailycourier.com
Freq: Mon thru Fri; Circ: 12263
Editor: Jeff Duewel; Publisher: Dennis Mack; News Editor: Patricia Snyder; Advertising Sales Manager: Debbie Thomas
Profile: Grants Pass Daily Courier is published daily for the residents of residents of Grants Pass, OR. The newspaper covers local and state news, sports, business and entertainment.
Language (s): English
Ad Rate: Full Page Mono 10.95
Ad Rate: Full Page Colour 325.00
Currency: United States Dollars
DAILY NEWSPAPER

Great Bend Tribune 14046
Owner: Morris Multimedia, Inc.
Editorial: 2012 Forest Ave, Great Bend, Kansas 67530-4014 Tel: 1 620 792-1211
Email: email@gbtribune.com Web site: http://www.gbtribune.com
Freq: Daily; Circ: 6195 Not Audited
Publisher: Mary Hoisington
Profile: Great Bend Tribune is published for the residents of Great Bend, KS and surrounding areas. It provides information on news, sports and community events.
Language (s): English
Ad Rate: Full Page Mono 12.06
Ad Rate: Full Page Colour 18.06
Currency: United States Dollars
DAILY NEWSPAPER

Great Falls Tribune 14280
Owner: Gannett Co., Inc.
Editorial: 205 River Dr S, Great Falls, Montana 59405-1854 Tel: 1 406 791-1444
Email: tribcity@greatfallstribune.com Web site: http://www.greatfallstribune.com
Freq: Daily; Circ: 22628 Not Audited
Publisher & Editor: Jim Strauss
Profile: Great Falls Tribune is written for the community and the surrounding area of Great Falls, MT. The publication covers local news, agriculture, outdoors, sports and community events.
Language (s): English
Ad Rate: Full Page Mono 48.20
Ad Rate: Full Page Colour 655.00
Currency: United States Dollars
DAILY NEWSPAPER

Green Bay Press-Gazette 14806
Owner: Gannett Co., Inc.
Editorial: 435 E Walnut St, Green Bay, Wisconsin 54301-5001 Tel: 1 920 435-4411
Email: metro@greenbaypressgazette.com Web site: http://www.greenbaypressgazette.com
Freq: Daily; Circ: 35868 Not Audited
Profile: Green Bay Press-Gazette is a local daily newspaper written for residents of Green Bay and Northeastern Wisconsin. The newspaper covers local, national and world news, sports, business, lifestyle, arts & entertainment and community events.
Language (s): English
Ad Rate: Full Page Mono 89.90
Ad Rate: Full Page Colour 96.77
Currency: United States Dollars
DAILY NEWSPAPER

Greene County Daily World 381857
Owner: Rust Communications
Editorial: 79 S Main St, Linton, Indiana 47441-1818 Tel: 1 812 847-4487
Email: greenecountynewsdesk@gmail.com Web site: http://www.gcdailyworld.com
Freq: Fri; Circ: 6300 Not Audited
Publisher: Randy List; Editor: Chris Pruett
Profile: Greene County Daily World is a weekday newspaper serving residents of Greene County, including Bloomfield and Linton, IN. It provides local, world and national news with sports, business, health and entertainment articles. The Daily World also contains public notices, community events, obituaries and classifieds. It was created in January 2006, when two local daily newspapers, the Linton Daily Citizen and the Evening World in Bloomfield, IN, were combined into a single publication. Deadlines are at 11am ET two days prior to issue date.
Language (s): English
Ad Rate: Full Page Mono 7.85
Ad Rate: Full Page Colour 90.00
Currency: United States Dollars
DAILY NEWSPAPER

Greene County Newspaper Group 86794
Owner: AIM Media Midwest
Editorial: 1836 W Park Sq, Xenia, Ohio 45385-2668 Tel: 1 937 372-4444
Web site: http://www.fairborndailyherald.com
Freq: Daily; Circ: 8224 Not Audited
Profile: The Greene County Newspaper Group is comprised of the Xenia Daily Gazette and Fairborn Daily Herald.
Language (s): English
DAILY NEWSPAPER

Greeneville Sun 14668
Owner: Jones Media, Inc.
Editorial: 121 W Summer St, Greeneville, Tennessee 37743-4923 Tel: 1 423 638-4181
Email: gsun@xtn.net Web site: http://www.greenevillesun.com
Freq: Daily; Circ: 13039 Not Audited
Editor: Kathy Knight
Profile: Greeneville Sun is a local daily newspaper written for residents of Greenville and Green County, TN. The publication's mission is to provide its readers with information about local news and events.
Language (s): English
Ad Rate: Full Page Mono 28.75
Ad Rate: Full Page Colour 93.57
Currency: United States Dollars
DAILY NEWSPAPER

Greensburg Daily News 13988
Owner: Community Newspaper Holdings, Inc.
Editorial: 135 S Franklin St, Greensburg, Indiana 47240-2023 Tel: 1 812 663-3111
Email: news@greensburgdailynews.com Web site: http://www.greensburgdailynews.com
Freq: Mon thru Fri; Circ: 5100 Not Audited
Publisher: Laura Welborn
Profile: Greensburg Daily News provides local and community news, including education, business and local sports coverage for the residents of Greensburg and Decatur County, IN.
Language (s): English
Ad Rate: Full Page Mono 17.20
Ad Rate: Full Page Colour 75.00
Currency: United States Dollars
DAILY NEWSPAPER

Greenville Daily Advocate 14457
Owner: AIM Media Midwest
Editorial: 428 S Broadway St, Greenville, Ohio 45331-1926 Tel: 1 937 548-3151
Email: pressrelease@dailyadvocate.com Web site: http://www.dailyadvocate.com
Freq: Fri; Circ: 7000 Not Audited
Editor: Christine Chalmers
Profile: Greenville Daily Advocate's editorial mission is to be committed to the community and to provide its readers with local news and information. The publication is written for Darke county residents.
Language (s): English
Ad Rate: Full Page Mono 16.50
Ad Rate: Full Page Colour 175.00
Currency: United States Dollars
DAILY NEWSPAPER

The Greenville News 15371
Owner: Gannett Co. Inc.
Editorial: 32 E Broad St, Greenville, South Carolina 29601-2602 Tel: 1 864 298-4100
Email: localnews@greenvillenews.com Web site: http://www.greenvilleonline.com
Freq: Daily; Circ: 41510 Not Audited
Profile: The Greenville News aims to provide Greenville, SC, and its surrounding communities, which include Pickens, Anderson and Spartanburg counties, with local, regional and national news. The paper became a part of Gannett when the company bought Multimedia in December 1995.
Language (s): English
Ad Rate: Full Page Mono 160.25
Ad Rate: Full Page Colour 176.25
Currency: United States Dollars
DAILY NEWSPAPER

The Greenville News - Columbia Bureau 15596
Editorial: 517 Amherst Ave, Columbia, South Carolina 29205-2601 Tel: 1 803 256-7367
Language (s): English
DAILY NEWSPAPER

Greenville Record-Argus 14580
Editorial: 205 Main St, Greenville, Pennsylvania 16125-2107 Tel: 1 724 588-5000
Email: news@recordargusnews.com Web site: http://www.recordargusnews.com/
Freq: Daily; Circ: 5400 Not Audited
Publisher: Steve Gargasz; Advertising Sales Manager: Jim Rust
Profile: Greenville Record-Argus is published daily for the residents of Greenville, PA and surrounding areas. The publication is a general interest newspaper covering local news, weather, sports,

education, business, arts & entertainment and other information of interest to the local community.
Language (s): English
Ad Rate: Full Page Mono 14.00
Currency: United States Dollars
DAILY NEWSPAPER

Greenwich Time 13799

Owner: Hearst Corporation
Editorial: 1445 E Putnam Ave, Old Greenwich, Connecticut 06870-1379 **Tel:** 1 203 625-4400
Email: gtcitydesk@scni.com **Web site:** http://www.greenwichtime.com
Freq: Daily; **Circ:** 5616 Not Audited
Profile: Greenwich Time covers news in Southern Connecticut. Its coverage includes local news, sports, business news and entertainment.
Language (s): English
Ad Rate: Full Page Mono 76.10
Ad Rate: Full Page Colour 525.00
Currency: United States Dollars
DAILY NEWSPAPER

Greenwood Commonwealth 14263

Owner: Emmerich Newspapers Inc.
Editorial: 329 Highway 82 W, Greenwood, Mississippi 38930-6538 **Tel:** 1 662 453-5312
Email: commonwealth@gwcommonwealth.com **Web site:** http://www.gwcommonwealth.com
Freq: Mon thru Fri; **Circ:** 5741 Not Audited
Advertising Sales Manager: Larry Alderman; **Publisher:** Tim Kalich; **News Editor:** David Monroe
Profile: Greenwood Commonwealth's editorial mission is to provide its readers with the finest in local news and information about the Greenwood, MS community.
Language (s): English
Ad Rate: Full Page Mono 14.90
Ad Rate: Full Page Colour 340.00
Currency: United States Dollars
DAILY NEWSPAPER

Griffin Daily News 13844

Owner: Paxton Media Group
Editorial: 323 E Solomon St, Griffin, Georgia 30223-3315 **Tel:** 1 770 227-3276
Web site: http://www.griffindailynews.com
Freq: Daily; **Circ:** 6936 Not Audited
Advertising Sales Manager: Joy Gaddy; **Editor:** John Sullivan
Profile: Griffin Daily News is published for the residents of Griffin, GA, and surrounding areas. The paper covers local and state news, business, sports and entertainment.
Language (s): English
Ad Rate: Full Page Mono 20.60
Ad Rate: Full Page Colour 370.00
Currency: United States Dollars
DAILY NEWSPAPER

The Grove Sun Daily 15048

Owner: GateHouse Media Inc.
Editorial: 16 W 3rd St, Grove, Oklahoma 74344-3223 **Tel:** 1 918 786-2228
Email: news@grovesun.com **Web site:** http://www.grandlakenews.com
Freq: Fri; **Circ:** 6000 Not Audited
Profile: The Grove Sun Daily is written for the residents of Grove, OK. It covers local news, events, sports and weather.
Language (s): English
Ad Rate: Full Page Mono 7.50
Ad Rate: Full Page Colour 100.00
Currency: United States Dollars
DAILY NEWSPAPER

Guymon Daily Herald 14523

Owner: Horizon Publications
Editorial: 515 N Ellison St, Guymon, Oklahoma 73942-4311 **Tel:** 1 580 338-3355
Email: guymondailyeditor@gmail.com **Web site:** http://www.guymondailyherald.com
Freq: Daily; **Circ:** 2332 Not Audited
Publisher: Allison Gipe
Profile: Guymon Daily Herald is written for residents of Guymon, OK and surrounding communities. It covers local news, weather, sports, arts & entertainment and business.
Language (s): English
Ad Rate: Full Page Mono 8.38
Ad Rate: Full Page Colour 75.00
Currency: United States Dollars
DAILY NEWSPAPER

Gwinnett Daily Post 14933

Owner: Southern Community Newspapers Inc.
Editorial: 725 Old Norcross Rd, Lawrenceville, Georgia 30046-4317 **Tel:** 1 770 963-9205
Email: news@gwinnettdailypost.com **Web site:** http://www.gwinnettdailypost.com
Freq: Daily; **Circ:** 60731 Not Audited
Profile: Gwinnett Daily Post is a daily local newspaper published for residents of Gwinnett County, GA and surrounding areas. The newspaper covers all local news, weather and sports. Mailings should be sent to the PO address.
Language (s): English
Ad Rate: Full Page Mono 83.67
Ad Rate: Full Page Colour 87.15
Currency: United States Dollars
DAILY NEWSPAPER

Hamodia 156460

Editorial: 207 Foster Ave, Brooklyn, New York 11230-2195 **Tel:** 1 718 853-9094
Web site: http://www.hamodia.com
Freq: Daily; **Circ:** 159931 Not Audited
Publisher & Editor: Ruth Lichtenstein; **Advertising Sales Manager:** Jonathan Moller
Profile: Hamodia is an independently owned, local, daily newspaper serving the Jewish community throughout the New York metro area. The newspaper covers a variety of local news and events, and also features public affairs, international news and cultural topics of interest. The lead times and deadlines for the publication vary. The outlet has requested to not have any email communication be published.
Language (s): English
Ad Rate: Full Page Mono 18.00
Ad Rate: Full Page Colour 625.00
Currency: United States Dollars
DAILY NEWSPAPER

Handelsblatt - New York Bureau 503949

Editorial: 33 Irving Pl Fl 10, New York, New York 10003-2332 **Tel:** 49 180 536-5365
Web site: http://www.handelsblatt.com
Freq: Daily
Profile: This is the New York bureau of Handelsblatt in Dusseldorf, Germany.
Language (s): English
DAILY NEWSPAPER

The Hanford Sentinel 13730

Owner: Lee Enterprises, Inc.
Editorial: 300 W 6th St, Hanford, California 93230-4518 **Tel:** 1 559 582-0471
Web site: http://www.hanfordsentinel.com
Freq: Mon thru Fri; **Circ:** 7448 Not Audited
Advertising Sales Manager: Annette Landi
Profile: The Hanford Sentinel is the local newspaper for the Hanford, CA area. The newspaper covers local news, business, sports, agriculture and news from their local state prisons and the U.S. Navy master jet base. The newspaper also covers national stories that have a direct impact on its readership.
Language (s): English
Ad Rate: Full Page Mono 32.50
Ad Rate: Full Page Colour 386.00
Currency: United States Dollars
DAILY NEWSPAPER

Hannibal Courier-Post 14232

Owner: GateHouse Media Inc.
Editorial: 200 N 3rd St, Hannibal, Missouri 63401-3504 **Tel:** 1 573 221-2800
Web site: http://www.hannibal.net
Freq: Fri; **Circ:** 4853 Not Audited
Profile: Hannibal Courier-Post is published for the residents of Hannibal, MO and surrounding areas. The newspaper covers local news, politics, sports, business and arts & entertainment. It also covers national stories that have an impact on the newspaper's readership.
Language (s): English
Ad Rate: Full Page Mono 15.10
Ad Rate: Full Page Colour 140.00
Currency: United States Dollars
DAILY NEWSPAPER

The Harlan Daily Enterprise 14079

Owner: Civitas Media
Editorial: 1548 S US Highway 421, Harlan, Kentucky 40831-2501 **Tel:** 1 606 573-4510
Web site: http://www.harlandaily.com
Freq: Mon thru Fri; **Circ:** 6581 Not Audited
Profile: The Harlan Daily Enterprise is a local, daily newspaper that provides local news coverage for residents of Harlan, KY. The paper covers local news, business, sports and arts & entertainment, as well as state and national news that has a direct impact on the newspaper's readership. Deadlines are at 1pm ET.
Language (s): English
Ad Rate: Full Page Mono 14.29
Ad Rate: Full Page Colour 275.00
Currency: United States Dollars
DAILY NEWSPAPER

Harrisburg Daily Newspapers 543282

Owner: Paddock Publications
Editorial: 35 S Vine St, Harrisburg, Illinois 62946-1725 **Tel:** 1 618 253-7146
Email: hbgnews@yourclearwave.com **Web site:** http://www.dailyregister.com
Freq: Daily; **Circ:** 7070 Not Audited
Publisher: Kevin Haezebroeck
Language (s): English
DAILY NEWSPAPER

Harrison Daily Times 13692

Owner: Neighbor Newspapers
Editorial: 111 W Rush Ave, Harrison, Arkansas 72601-4218 **Tel:** 1 870 741-2325
Email: news@harrisondaily.com **Web site:** http://www.harrisondaily.com
Freq: Daily; **Circ:** 10439 Not Audited
Advertising Sales Manager: Jason Overman
Profile: Harrison Daily Times is published Monday through Friday and on Sunday. The newspaper is distributed to five Arkansas counties and parts of Southern Missouri. It covers local and regional news, business, sports, consumer interest, finance, lifestyles and community events. Send information to PO Box address only.
Language (s): English
Ad Rate: Full Page Mono 13.15
Ad Rate: Full Page Colour 130.00
Currency: United States Dollars
DAILY NEWSPAPER

The Hartford City News Times 13989

Owner: Community Media Whitewater Valley Publishing
Editorial: 100 N Jefferson St, Hartford City, Indiana 47348-2201 **Tel:** 1 765 348-0110
Web site: http://www.hartfordcitynewstimes.com
Freq: Mon thru Fri; **Circ:** 1200 Not Audited
Publisher & Editor: Cynthia Payne; **Advertising Sales Manager:** Tami Roach
Profile: The News-Times, formerly known as Hartford City News Times, is written for residents of Hartford City, IN. The newspaper covers local news, business, sports and arts & entertainment. The newspaper also covers national and statewide stories if they have a direct impact on the newspaper's readership.
Language (s): English
Ad Rate: Full Page Mono 9.45
Ad Rate: Full Page Colour 20.00
Currency: United States Dollars
DAILY NEWSPAPER

The Hartford Courant 15333

Owner: tronc
Editorial: 285 Broad St, Hartford, Connecticut 06105-3785 **Tel:** 1 860 241-6200
Web site: http://www.courant.com
Freq: Daily; **Circ:** 103427 Not Audited
Editor: Andrew Julien
Profile: The Hartford Courant is a daily general-interest broadsheet newspaper published for the general public in the Hartford, CT area. Its mission is to provide news and information to a general readership.
Language (s): English
Ad Rate: Full Page Mono 330.00
Ad Rate: Full Page Colour 308.40
Currency: United States Dollars
DAILY NEWSPAPER

The Hartford Courant - Middletown Bureau 15653

Editorial: 373 E Main St, Middletown, Connecticut 06457-4556
Capitol Bureau Chief: Christopher Keating
Language (s): English
DAILY NEWSPAPER

The Hastings Tribune 14341

Owner: Seaton Newspapers
Editorial: 908 W 2Nd St, Hastings, Nebraska 68901-5063 **Tel:** 1 402 462-2131
Email: tribune@hastingstribune.com **Web site:** http://www.hastingstribune.com
Freq: Daily; **Circ:** 10811 Not Audited
Profile: The Hastings Tribune is a local, daily newspaper for the Hastings, NE area. The newspaper does not publish an edition on Sundays. It covers local news, business, sports and arts & entertainment. It also covers national and statewide stories if they have a direct impact on the newspaper's readership.
Language (s): English
Ad Rate: Full Page Mono 12.95
Ad Rate: Full Page Colour 55.13
Currency: United States Dollars
DAILY NEWSPAPER

Hattiesburg American 14265

Owner: Gannett Co., Inc.
Editorial: 825 N Main St, Hattiesburg, Mississippi 39401-3433 **Tel:** 1 601 582-4321
Email: news@hattiesburgamerican.com **Web site:** http://www.hattiesburgamerican.com
Freq: Daily; **Circ:** 8421 Not Audited
Profile: Hattiesburg American is the daily newspaper for the Hattiesburg, MS area. The newspaper covers local news, business, sports, and arts & entertainment stories. The newspaper also covers national and statewide stories if they have a direct impact on the newspaper's readership. All inquiries should be addressed to the executive editor.
Language (s): English
Ad Rate: Full Page Mono 28.25
Ad Rate: Full Page Colour 98.09
Currency: United States Dollars
DAILY NEWSPAPER

Havre Daily News 14282

Owner: Havre Daily News, Inc.
Editorial: 119 2nd St, Havre, Montana 59501-3507 **Tel:** 1 406 265-6795
Email: news@havredailynews.com **Web site:** http://www.havredailynews.com
Freq: Mon thru Fri; **Circ:** 4280 Not Audited
Profile: Havre Daily News is published for the residents of Havre, MT and surrounding areas. It focuses on local news, sports, agriculture, business, editorials and arts & entertainment. It also includes national stories if they have an impact on the newspaper's readership.
Language (s): English
Ad Rate: Full Page Mono 10.50
Ad Rate: Full Page Colour 4.00
Currency: United States Dollars
DAILY NEWSPAPER

Hawaii Hochi 83587

Owner: Shizuoka Shimbun
Editorial: 917 Kokea St, Honolulu, Hawaii 96817-4528 **Tel:** 1 808 845-2255
Email: oloi@hawaii.rr.com **Web site:** http://www.thehawaiihochi.com/
Freq: Daily; **Circ:** 3000 Not Audited
Advertising Sales Manager: Mamoru Tanji; **Publisher:** Paul Yempuku
Profile: Japanese & English language.
Language (s): English
Ad Rate: Full Page Mono 16.20
Currency: United States Dollars
DAILY NEWSPAPER

The Hawk Eye 13867

Owner: GateHouse Media Inc.
Editorial: 800 S Main St, Burlington, Iowa 52601-5870 **Tel:** 1 319 754-8461
Email: news@thehawkeye.com **Web site:** http://www.thehawkeye.com
Freq: Daily; **Circ:** 18777 Not Audited
Publisher & Editor: Steve Delaney; **Editor:** John Gaines; **Advertising Sales Manager:** Janet Stottmeister
Profile: The Hawk Eye is the daily local newspaper for the Des Moines, Lee, Henry, Jefferson, Washington, Louisa and Van Buren counties of Iowa. The newspaper covers local news, arts & entertainment, sports and business stories. Do NOT send any bulk emails to the outlet, as the server will always reject them. Per the news clerk, include the words, 'NOT SPAM' in the subject line, and the spam filter will let it go through.
Language (s): English
Ad Rate: Full Page Mono 21.28
Ad Rate: Full Page Colour 290.00
Currency: United States Dollars
DAILY NEWSPAPER

The Hays Daily News 14047

Owner: Harris Enterprises
Editorial: 507 Main St, Hays, Kansas 67601-4228 **Tel:** 1 785 628-1081
Email: newsroom@dailynews.net **Web site:** http://www.hdnews.net
Freq: Daily; **Circ:** 12514 Not Audited
Profile: The Hays Daily News is written for the residents of Hays, KS and surrounding areas. The newspaper covers local news, sports, weather, politics and community events.
Language (s): English
Ad Rate: Full Page Mono 16.07
Ad Rate: Full Page Colour 330.00
Currency: United States Dollars
DAILY NEWSPAPER

Henderson Daily Dispatch 14296

Owner: Paxton Media Group
Editorial: 304 S Chestnut St, Henderson, North Carolina 27536-4225 **Tel:** 1 252 436-2700
Email: news@hendersondispatch.com **Web site:** http://www.hendersondispatch.com
Freq: Daily; **Circ:** 6261 Not Audited
Profile: Henderson Daily Dispatch is the daily newspaper of Henderson and Vance counties, NC. It covers local and national news, lifestyle and sports. Deadlines are daily at 7pm ET.
Language (s): English
Ad Rate: Full Page Mono 19.02
Ad Rate: Full Page Colour 175.81
Currency: United States Dollars
DAILY NEWSPAPER

Henderson Daily News 14703

Owner: Hartman Newspapers, Inc.
Editorial: 1711 US Highway 79 S, Henderson, Texas 75654-4509 **Tel:** 1 903 657-2501
Web site: http://www.hendersondailynews.com
Freq: Daily; **Circ:** 6039 Not Audited
Editor & Publisher: Les Linebarger
Profile: Henderson Daily News covers community news for the residents of the Henderson, TX area. Deadlines are 11am CT one day prior to the issue date.
Language (s): English
Ad Rate: Full Page Mono 9.43
Ad Rate: Full Page Colour 11.52
Currency: United States Dollars
DAILY NEWSPAPER

Henry Daily Herald 14958

Owner: Southern Community Newspapers Inc.
Editorial: 38 Sloan St, McDonough, Georgia 30253-3102 **Tel:** 1 770 957-9161
Email: editor@henryherald.com **Web site:** http://www.henryherald.com
Freq: Daily; **Circ:** 18303
Profile: Henry Daily Herald is a newspaper written for residents of Henry County, GA. It covers local news, sports, government, education, business and events. It combines its coverage with the Clayton News Daily in Jonesboro, GA on Saturdays.
Language (s): English
Ad Rate: Full Page Mono 10.55
Currency: United States Dollars
DAILY NEWSPAPER

The Herald 13991

Owner: Jasper Herald Company
Editorial: 216 E 4th St, Jasper, Indiana 47546-3102 **Tel:** 1 812 482-2424
Email: news@dcherald.com **Web site:** http://duboiscountyherald.com
Freq: Mon thru Fri; **Circ:** 10100 Not Audited
Editor: Dawn Mazur
Profile: The Herald is published daily for resident of Jasper, IN and surrounding areas. The newspaper covers local and national news, sports, business and entertainment.
Language (s): English
Ad Rate: Full Page Mono 15.70
Currency: United States Dollars
DAILY NEWSPAPER

The Herald 14614
Owner: Community Newspaper Holdings, Inc.
Editorial: 52 S Dock St, Sharon, Pennsylvania 16146-1808 **Tel:** 1 724 981-6100
Email: newsroom@sharonherald.com **Web site:** http://www.sharonherald.com
Freq: Daily; **Circ:** 15250 Not Audited
Editor: Nancy Ash; **Editor:** Michael Roknick;
Publisher: Sharon Sorg
Profile: The Herald is the leading daily newspaper in the Mercer County, PA. area. It covers the Mercer County and the Shenango Valley as well as the adjacent towns in the New Wilmington/Volant area. The newspaper covers loca and national news, business, sports, religion, education, lifestyle and entertainment.
Language (s): English
Ad Rate: Full Page Mono 39.32
Ad Rate: Full Page Colour 54.44
Currency: United States Dollars
DAILY NEWSPAPER

The Herald 14647
Owner: McClatchy Newspapers
Editorial: 132 W Main St, Rock Hill, South Carolina 29730-4430 **Tel:** 1 803 329-4000
Email: assignmentdesk@heraldonline.com **Web site:** http://www.heraldonline.com
Freq: Daily; **Circ:** 22317 Not Audited
Editor: Paul Osmundson; **News Editor:** Chris Sherk
Profile: The Herald is a daily newspaper serving the counties of York, Chester and Lancaster, SC. The publication covers local news, community events, sports and lifestyles. Deadlines are the day prior to issue date.
Language (s): English
Ad Rate: Full Page Mono 43.82
Ad Rate: Full Page Colour 134.90
Currency: United States Dollars
DAILY NEWSPAPER

Herald & Review 15395
Owner: Lee Enterprises, Inc.
Editorial: 601 E William St, Decatur, Illinois 62523-1142 **Tel:** 1 217 429-5151
Email: hrnews@herald-review.com **Web site:** http://www.herald-review.com
Freq: Daily; **Circ:** 25026 Not Audited
Profile: Herald & Review is written for residents of Decatur, IL and the surrounding area. It covers, local news, weather, sports, politics, religion, business, entertainment, law, education, health, opinion and lifestyles in the Decatur, IL area.
Language (s): English
Ad Rate: Full Page Mono 50.80
Ad Rate: Full Page Colour 165.77
Currency: United States Dollars
DAILY NEWSPAPER

The Herald Bulletin 13967
Owner: Community Newspaper Holdings, Inc.
Editorial: 1133 Jackson St, Anderson, Indiana 46016-1433 **Tel:** 1 765 622-1212
Email: newsroom@heraldbulletin.com **Web site:** http://www.heraldbulletin.com
Freq: Daily; **Circ:** 16321 Not Audited
Statehouse Bureau Chief: Maureen Hayden
Profile: The Herald Bulletin is a daily newspaper written for Madison, Delaware, Hamilton and Henry counties, IN. The newspaper covers local and national news, sports, business, community news and obituaries. Deadlines are at 5pm ET.
Language (s): English
Ad Rate: Full Page Mono 31.00
Ad Rate: Full Page Colour 32.50
Currency: United States Dollars
DAILY NEWSPAPER

Herald Democrat 14946
Owner: GateHouse Media Inc.
Editorial: 603 S Sam Rayburn Fwy, Sherman, Texas 75090-7258 **Tel:** 1 903 893-8181
Email: news@heralddemocrat.com **Web site:** http://www.heralddemocrat.com
Freq: Daily
Editor: Jonathan Cannon
Profile: Herald Democrat is written for the residents of Sherman, TX. It covers local news, weather, sports, business and entertainment.
Language (s): English
Ad Rate: Full Page Mono 27.30
Ad Rate: Full Page Colour 28.30
Currency: United States Dollars
DAILY NEWSPAPER

Herald Journal 14004
Owner: Community Media Group
Editorial: 114 S Main St, Monticello, Indiana 47960-2328 **Tel:** 1 574 583-5121
Email: editor@thehj.com **Web site:** http://www.newsbug.info/monticello_herald_journal/
Freq: Daily; **Circ:** 4500 Not Audited
Editor: Daniel Thompson
Profile: Herald Journal is a local newspaper written for the residents of Monticello, IN. The newspaper is published daily Monday through Saturday. There is no Sunday edition. The publication covers local news, sports, education/schools and business in the Monticello, IN area. Deadlines are at noon CT.
Language (s): English
Ad Rate: Full Page Mono 14.50
Ad Rate: Full Page Colour 49.66
Currency: United States Dollars
DAILY NEWSPAPER

The Herald Journal 14749
Owner: Pioneer Newspapers
Editorial: 75 W 300 N, Logan, Utah 84321-3971
Tel: 1 435 752-2121
Email: hjnews@hjnews.com **Web site:** http://www.hjnews.com
Freq: Daily; **Circ:** 15533 Not Audited
News Editor: Chuck Nunn
Profile: The Herald Journal is written for the residents of the Logan, UT area. It covers local and city news, sports, arts & entertainment and other relevant topics of interest.
Language (s): English
Ad Rate: Full Page Mono 14.47
Ad Rate: Full Page Colour 280.00
Currency: United States Dollars
DAILY NEWSPAPER

The Herald News 14117
Owner: GateHouse Media Inc.
Editorial: 207 Pocasset St, Fall River, Massachusetts 2722 **Tel:** 1 508 676-8211
Email: news@heraldnews.com **Web site:** http://www.heraldnews.com
Freq: Daily; **Circ:** 12128 Not Audited
Profile: The Herald News is a daily newspaper serving Fall River, MA and the surrounding area. It covers news, sports, business and lifestyle.
Language (s): English
Ad Rate: Full Page Mono 35.00
Currency: United States Dollars
DAILY NEWSPAPER

Herald Republican 76419
Owner: KPC Media Group Inc.
Editorial: 45 S Public Sq, Angola, Indiana 46703-1926 **Tel:** 1 260 665-3117
Email: news@kpcmedia.com **Web site:** http://kpcnews.com/news/latest/heraldrepublican/
Freq: Daily; **Circ:** 4027
Publisher: Terry Housholder; **Editor:** Michael Marturello; **Editor:** Amy Oberlin
Profile: Herald Republican provides news and information for Steuben County, IN.
Language (s): English
Ad Rate: Full Page Mono 12.81
Ad Rate: Full Page Colour 46.80
Currency: United States Dollars
DAILY NEWSPAPER

Herald Times Reporter 14812
Owner: Gannett Co., Inc.
Editorial: 902 Franklin St, Manitowoc, Wisconsin 54220-4514 **Tel:** 1 920 684-4433
Email: htrnews@htrnews.com **Web site:** http://www.htrnews.com
Freq: Daily; **Circ:** 8389 Not Audited
Profile: Herald Times Reporter is a daily newspaper that serves the residents of Manitowoc, WI. It covers national, state and local news, business, community events, editorials, features, arts & entertainment and sports. It shares offices with the weekly Lakeshore Chronicle.
Language (s): English
Ad Rate: Full Page Mono 38.50
Ad Rate: Full Page Colour 50.81
Currency: United States Dollars
DAILY NEWSPAPER

The Herald-Argus 13995
Owner: Paxton Media Group
Editorial: 701 State St, La Porte, Indiana 46350-3328
Tel: 1 219 362-2161
Email: newsroom@heraldargus.com **Web site:** http://www.heraldargus.com
Freq: Daily; **Circ:** 5581 Not Audited
Publisher: Bill Hackney; **Editor:** Kim King
Profile: The Herald-Argus's editorial mission is to deliver news, weather, sports, and entertainment information to its readers. The publication is written for residents of LaPorte, IN.
Language (s): English
Ad Rate: Full Page Mono 15.46
Ad Rate: Full Page Colour 98.46
Currency: United States Dollars
DAILY NEWSPAPER

The Herald-Banner 14701
Owner: Community Newspaper Holdings, Inc.
Editorial: 2305 King St, Greenville, Texas 75401-3257 **Tel:** 1 903 455-4220
Web site: http://www.heraldbanner.com
Freq: Daily; **Circ:** 8283 Not Audited
Editor: Caleb Slinkard
Profile: The Herald-Banner is a local daily newspaper written for the residents of Greenville, TX. The newspaper covers local, national and international news, sports and features. The outlet offers RSS (Really Simple Syndication).
Language (s): English
Ad Rate: Full Page Mono 15.96
Ad Rate: Full Page Colour 270.00
Currency: United States Dollars
DAILY NEWSPAPER

Herald-Citizen 14665
Owner: Cookeville Newspapers Inc.
Editorial: 1300 Neal St, Cookeville, Tennessee 38501-4330 **Tel:** 1 931 526-9715
Email: editor@herald-citizen.com **Web site:** http://www.herald-citizen.com
Freq: Daily; **Circ:** 9352 Not Audited
Profile: Herald-Citizen is written for the residents of Cookeville and Putnam County, TN. The newspaper is published daily except for Saturday. It covers local news, sports, lifestyles, education, religion, business and entertainment. The paper does NOT accept press releases or submissions. Deadlines are 11am ET the day before issue date.
Language (s): English
Ad Rate: Full Page Mono 12.35
Ad Rate: Full Page Colour 106.00
Currency: United States Dollars
DAILY NEWSPAPER

The Herald-Dispatch 14835
Owner: Champion Industries Inc.
Editorial: 946 5th Ave, Huntington, West Virginia 25701 **Tel:** 1 304 526-4000
Email: news@herald-dispatch.com **Web site:** http://www.herald-dispatch.com
Freq: Daily; **Circ:** 25430 Not Audited
News Editor: Don Willis
Profile: The Herald-Dispatch is published for the residents of Huntington, WV, Southern Ohio, and Eastern Kentucky. The daily newspaper covers local news, sports, entertainment, police, education, health and religion.
Language (s): English
Ad Rate: Full Page Mono 82.73
Ad Rate: Full Page Colour 496.85
Currency: United States Dollars
DAILY NEWSPAPER

The Herald-Mail 16300
Owner: Schurz Communications Inc.
Editorial: 100 Summit Ave, Hagerstown, Maryland 21740-5509 **Tel:** 1 301 733-5131
Email: news@herald-mail.com **Web site:** http://www.heraldmailmedia.com
Freq: Daily; **Circ:** 23637 Not Audited
Publisher: Andy Bruns
Profile: The Herald-Mail is a local morning newspaper. It is published for the residents of the Washington County, MD tri-state area, which includes Washington and Frederick counties, MD; Fulton and Franklin counties, PA; Berkeley, Jefferson and Morgan counties, WV; and Frederick County, VA.
Language (s): English
Ad Rate: Full Page Mono 24.42
Ad Rate: Full Page Colour 34.42
Currency: United States Dollars
DAILY NEWSPAPER

The Herald-News 13936
Owner: Shaw Media
Editorial: 2175 Oneida St, Joliet, Illinois 60435-6560
Tel: 1 815 280-4100
Email: news@theherald-news.com **Web site:** http://www.theherald-news.com
Freq: Mon thru Fri; **Circ:** 33310 Not Audited
News Editor: Bob Okon; **Editor:** Kate Schott
Profile: The Herald-News is a daily newspaper written for the residents of Joliet, IL and the suburban communities of Chicago. The paper covers local news, business, sports and lifestyle.
Language (s): English
Ad Rate: Full Page Mono 33.00
Ad Rate: Full Page Colour 300.00
Currency: United States Dollars
DAILY NEWSPAPER

The Herald-Palladium 14197
Owner: Paxton Media Group
Editorial: 3450 Hollywood Rd, Saint Joseph, Michigan 49085-9155 **Tel:** 1 269 429-2400
Email: localnews@thehp.com **Web site:** http://www.heraldpalladium.com
Freq: Daily; **Circ:** 11659 Not Audited
Publisher: David Holgate
Profile: The Herald-Palladium is a daily newspaper focused on reporting the news in Southwest Michigan. The paper features local news, business, sports, world, health, stock market and entertainment news.
Language (s): English
Ad Rate: Full Page Mono 29.16
Ad Rate: Full Page Colour 475.00
Currency: United States Dollars
DAILY NEWSPAPER

Herald-Standard 14625
Owner: Calkins Media
Editorial: 8 E Church St #18, Uniontown, Pennsylvania 15401-3563 **Tel:** 1 724 439-7500
Email: hsnews@heraldstandard.com **Web site:** http://www.heraldstandard.com
Freq: Daily; **Circ:** 20636 Not Audited
Publisher: Bob Pinarski
Profile: Herald Standard is a local newspaper for the residents of Uniontown, PA. The editorial content covers local news, sports, community events and entertainment.
Language (s): English
Ad Rate: Full Page Mono 44.95
Ad Rate: Full Page Colour 264.71
Currency: United States Dollars
DAILY NEWSPAPER

Herald-Star 14492
Owner: Ogden Newspapers
Editorial: 401 Herald Sq, Steubenville, Ohio 43952-2090 **Tel:** 1 740 283-4711
Email: newsroom@heraldstaronline.com **Web site:** http://www.heraldstaronline.com
Freq: Daily; **Circ:** 11333
News Editor: Fred Rossano
Profile: Herald-Star is a daily, local newspaper serving the Steubenville, OH area. Local, national and international news are covered, as well as sports, entertainment and lifestyle information.
Language (s): English
Ad Rate: Full Page Mono 31.19
Ad Rate: Full Page Colour 484.56
Currency: United States Dollars
DAILY NEWSPAPER

The Herald-Sun 14291
Owner: McClatchy Newspapers
Editorial: 1530 N Gregson St, Durham, North Carolina 27701-1155 **Tel:** 1 919 419-6500
Email: news@heraldsun.com **Web site:** http://www.heraldsun.com
Freq: Daily; **Circ:** 21367 Not Audited
Publisher: Rick Bean
Profile: The Herald-Sun is a local, daily newspaper written primarily for residents of Durham, Orange, Granville, Person, and Chatham Counties in North Carolina. The newspaper covers, local, national, and international news, as well as sports, entertainment, business, religion, health, and technology. Contact the publication for lead time and deadlines.
Language (s): English
Ad Rate: Full Page Mono 72.45
Ad Rate: Full Page Colour 460.53
Currency: United States Dollars
DAILY NEWSPAPER

The Herald-Times 13971
Owner: Schurz Communications Inc.
Editorial: 1900 S Walnut St, Bloomington, Indiana 47401-7720 **Tel:** 1 812 332-4401
Email: webstaff@hoosiertimes.com **Web site:** http://www.heraldtimesonline.com
Freq: Daily; **Circ:** 20415 Not Audited
News Editor: Janice Rickert; **Editor:** Robert Zaltsberg
Profile: The Herald-Times is a daily newspaper written for residents of the Bloomington, IN area. It covers local news, sports and entertainment in. The publication combines with The Times-Mail and The Reporter-Times for the Sunday edition called the Hoosier Times.
Language (s): English
Ad Rate: Full Page Mono 33.70
Ad Rate: Full Page Colour 417.00
Currency: United States Dollars
DAILY NEWSPAPER

Hereford Brand 14746
Owner: Roberts Publishing Company
Editorial: 313 Lee Ave, Hereford, Texas 79045-5361
Tel: 1 806 364-2030
Email: editor@herefordbrand.com **Web site:** http://herefordbrand.com/web
Freq: Fri; **Circ:** 2500 Not Audited
Publisher & Editor: Grover Ford; **Advertising Sales Manager:** Ray Leverett
Profile: Hereford Brand is a daily newspaper published for the residents of Deaf Smith County and Hereford, TX. It provides local news coverage Tuesday through Saturday. No editions are published on Sunday or Monday.
Language (s): English
Ad Rate: Full Page Mono 7.00
Ad Rate: Full Page Colour 200.00
Currency: United States Dollars
DAILY NEWSPAPER

The Hibbing Daily Tribune 14207
Owner: American Consolidated Media
Editorial: 2142 1st Ave, Hibbing, Minnesota 55746-3759 **Tel:** 1 218 262-1011
Email: news@hibbingdailytribune.net **Web site:** http://www.hibbingmn.com
Freq: Fri; **Circ:** 4800 Not Audited
Editor: Kelly Grinsteinner; **Advertising Sales Manager:** Mark Roy
Profile: The Hibbing Daily Tribune is published for the residents of Hibbling, MN and surrounding areas. The newspaper covers local news, sports, government and weather. The paper's Monday edition only appears on the Web site.
Language (s): English
Ad Rate: Full Page Mono 17.15
Ad Rate: Full Page Colour 150.00
Currency: United States Dollars
DAILY NEWSPAPER

Hickory Daily Record 14298
Owner: World Media Enterprises, Inc.
Editorial: 1100 11th Avenue Blvd SE, Hickory, North Carolina 28602-4351 **Tel:** 1 828 322-4510
Email: news@hickoryrecord.com **Web site:** http://www.hickoryrecord.com
Freq: Daily; **Circ:** 16740 Not Audited
Editor: Scott Bryan
Profile: Hickory Daily Record is written for the residents of Hickory, NC. It covers news, business, sports, entertainment and community issues.
Language (s): English
Ad Rate: Full Page Mono 21.58
Ad Rate: Full Page Colour 182.25
Currency: United States Dollars
DAILY NEWSPAPER

High Plains Daily Leader 529055
Editorial: 218 S Kansas Ave, Liberal, Kansas 67901-3704 **Tel:** 1 620 626-0840
Email: news@hpleader.com **Web site:** http://www.hpleader.com
Freq: Mon thru Fri; **Circ:** 7000 Not Audited
Publisher: Earl Watt; **Advertising Sales Manager:** Rick Yearick
Profile: High Plains Daily Leader is a 14-page daily broadsheet newspaper serving the residents of Liberal, KA.
Language (s): English
Ad Rate: Full Page Mono 13.00
Ad Rate: Full Page Colour 123.60
Currency: United States Dollars
DAILY NEWSPAPER

High Point Enterprise 14299
Owner: Paxton Media Group
Editorial: 213 Woodbine St, High Point, North Carolina 27260-8339 **Tel:** 1 336 888-3500
Web site: http://www.hpenews.com
Freq: Daily; **Circ:** 16043 Not Audited
Publisher: Rick Bean; **Editor:** Megan Ward
Profile: High Point Enterprise is a daily newspaper serving High Point, NC and the surrounding communities. It covers local news, government, business, lifestyle and sports stories. It also covers national stories if they have an impact on the readership. The lead time for the publication varies.
Language (s): English
Ad Rate: Full Page Mono 31.24
Ad Rate: Full Page Colour 495.00
Currency: United States Dollars
DAILY NEWSPAPER

Highlands Today 257948
Owner: Media General Inc.
Editorial: 315 US Highway 27 N, Sebring, Florida 33870-2148 **Tel:** 1 863 386-5800
Email: highlandstoday@highlandstoday.com **Web site:** http://www.highlandstoday.com
Freq: Daily; **Circ:** 4373 Not Audited
Editor: Richard Hensley; **Publisher:** Tina McClelland Gottus
Profile: Highlands Today launched in August 1996, with a distinct focus on local news in Highlands, Hardee and DeSoto, FL. Advertising deadlines are at 5pm ET.
Language (s): English
Ad Rate: Full Page Mono 27.42
Ad Rate: Full Page Colour 93.55
Currency: United States Dollars
DAILY NEWSPAPER

Hillsdale Daily News 14170
Owner: GateHouse Media Inc.
Editorial: 2764 W Carleton Rd, Hillsdale, Michigan 49242-9191 **Tel:** 1 517 437-7351
Email: editor@thedailyreporter.com **Web site:** http://www.hillsdale.net
Freq: Daily; **Circ:** 7095 Not Audited
News Editor: Amanda VanAuker; **Advertising Sales Manager:** Lisa Vickers
Profile: Hillsdale Daily News is published for the residents of Hillsdale, MI. The newspaper covers local news, weather, sports and community events. Feature articles cover business developments, education, arts & entertainment and lifestyle. Deadlines are two days prior to issue date.
Language (s): English
Ad Rate: Full Page Mono 12.00
Ad Rate: Full Page Colour 126.00
Currency: United States Dollars
DAILY NEWSPAPER

Hobbs News-Sun 14376
Owner: Shearman Newspapers
Editorial: 201 N Thorp St, Hobbs, New Mexico 88240-6058 **Tel:** 1 575 393-2123
Email: editor@hobbsnews.com **Web site:** http://www.hobbsnews.com
Freq: Daily; **Circ:** 7564 Not Audited
Publisher & Editor: Daniel Russell
Profile: Hobbs News-Sun is a local newspaper serving residents of Lea County, NM. The publication covers news, local government, education, business, sports and community events. Send materials via email.
Language (s): English
Ad Rate: Full Page Mono 11.25
Ad Rate: Full Page Colour 325.00
Currency: United States Dollars
DAILY NEWSPAPER

Holdrege Daily Citizen 14342
Owner: Holdrege Daily Citizen, Inc.
Editorial: 418 Garfield St, Holdrege, Nebraska 68949-2219 **Tel:** 1 308 995-4441
Email: holdregecitizennews@gmail.com
Freq: Daily; **Circ:** 3174 Not Audited
Advertising Sales Manager: Barbara Penrod; **Editor:** Tunney Price
Profile: Holdrege Daily Citizen is a local newspaper serving the residents of Holdrege, NE. The publication covers local news and community events. Deadlines are daily at 1pm CT.
Language (s): English
Ad Rate: Full Page Mono 8.00
Ad Rate: Full Page Colour 330.00
Currency: United States Dollars
DAILY NEWSPAPER

The Holland Sentinel 14171
Owner: GateHouse Media Inc.
Editorial: 54 W 8th St, Holland, Michigan 49423-3104 **Tel:** 1 616 546-4200
Email: newsroom@hollandsentinel.com **Web site:** http://www.hollandsentinel.com
Freq: Daily; **Circ:** 11516 Not Audited
Publisher: Tricia Johnston
Profile: The Holland Sentinel is a daily local newspaper serving residents of Holland, MI. The publication covers news, entertainment, sports, business, religion and community events.
Language (s): English
Ad Rate: Full Page Mono 15.74
Ad Rate: Full Page Colour 106.50
Currency: United States Dollars
DAILY NEWSPAPER

Home News Tribune 14359
Owner: Gannett Co., Inc.
Editorial: 92 E Main St, Somerville, New Jersey 08876-2319 **Tel:** 1 732 246-5500
Email: hntmetro@mycentraljersey.com **Web site:** http://www.mycentraljersey.com
Freq: Daily; **Circ:** 21725 Not Audited
Editor: Paul Grzella
Profile: Home News Tribune is published daily for the residents of East Brunswick, NJ. The newspaper covers local news, business and community events.
Language (s): English
Ad Rate: Full Page Mono 225.86
Ad Rate: Full Page Colour 1481.56
Currency: United States Dollars
DAILY NEWSPAPER

Honolulu Star-Advertiser 13860
Owner: Black Press
Editorial: 500 Ala Moana Blvd Ste 210, 7 Waterfront Plaza, Honolulu, Hawaii 96813-4920 **Tel:** 1 808 529-4747
Web site: http://www.staradvertiser.com
Freq: Daily; **Circ:** 153399
Profile: Honolulu Star-Advertiser is a daily newspaper published for the residents of Honolulu and the Hawaiian Islands. It was first published in 1882 as the Honolulu Star Bulletin until June 2010 when the Star Bulletin bought out the Honolulu Advertiser, creating the Honolulu Star-Advertiser. The paper covers local, regional, state, national, and international news, as well as sports, business and entertainment news.
Language (s): English
Ad Rate: Full Page Mono 186.00
Ad Rate: Full Page Colour 239.00
Currency: United States Dollars
DAILY NEWSPAPER

Honolulu Star-Advertiser - Waikiki Bureau 828061
Editorial: Waikiki, Hawaii **Tel:** 1 808 284-5681
Bureau Chief: Allison Schaefers
Language (s): English
DAILY NEWSPAPER

Hope Star 13694
Owner: GateHouse Media Inc.
Editorial: 522 W 3rd St, Hope, Arkansas 71801-5001 **Tel:** 1 870 777-8841
Web site: http://www.hopestar.com
Freq: Daily; **Circ:** 3200 Not Audited
Advertising Sales Manager: Richard Haycox
Profile: Hope Star is a daily newspaper serving the residents of Hope, AR and surrounding areas. The paper covers local, national and international news.
Language (s): English
Ad Rate: Full Page Mono 15.65
Ad Rate: Full Page Colour 250.00
Currency: United States Dollars
DAILY NEWSPAPER

The Houma Courier 14098
Owner: GateHouse Media Inc.
Editorial: 3030 Barrow St, Houma, Louisiana 70360-7641 **Tel:** 1 985 850-1100
Email: news@houmatoday.com **Web site:** http://www.houmatoday.com
Freq: Daily; **Circ:** 11598
Profile: The Courier is published daily for the residents of Houma, LA and surrounding areas. The newspaper provides information on local and national news, business, sports and lifestyles. All advertising appeas in both The Courier and The Daily Comet.
Language (s): English
Ad Rate: Full Page Mono 43.91
Ad Rate: Full Page Colour 468.00
Currency: United States Dollars
DAILY NEWSPAPER

The Hour 13805
Owner: Hearst Corporation
Editorial: 1 Selleck St, Norwalk, Connecticut 06855-1120 **Tel:** 1 203 846-3281
Email: news@thehour.com **Web site:** http://www.thehour.com
Freq: Daily; **Circ:** 22954
Profile: The Hour is published daily for the residents of Norwalk, CT and surrounding areas. The newspaper covers local news, community events, historical features, people profiles, arts & entertainment and decorator trends.
Language (s): English
Ad Rate: Full Page Mono 52.54
Ad Rate: Full Page Colour 488.75
Currency: United States Dollars
DAILY NEWSPAPER

Houston Chronicle 15307
Owner: Hearst Newspapers
Editorial: 4747 Southwest Fwy, Houston, Texas 77027-6901 **Tel:** 1 713 362-7171
Email: citydesk@chron.com **Web site:** http://www.chron.com
Freq: Daily; **Circ:** 236092 Not Audited
News Editor: Charlie Crixell
Profile: Houston Chronicle is a daily, morning newspaper written for the general public in Texas. The state's largest daily newspaper, it is also the only daily in Houston. The newspaper offers full market coverage focusing on local business news and events, state and national economics, personal finance, government, business, personal computing and technology. Feature topics include the arts, health, beauty, entertainment, fashion, food, lifestyle issues, home, gardening and travel. Types of articles found in the paper include breaking news, trends, features, local company profiles and syndicated columns.
Language (s): English
Ad Rate: Full Page Mono 676.00
Ad Rate: Full Page Colour 871.00
Currency: United States Dollars
DAILY NEWSPAPER

Houston Chronicle - Austin Bureau 15942
Editorial: 1005 Congress Ave Ste 1060, Austin, Texas 78701-2469 **Tel:** 1 512 478-3495
Bureau Chief: Peggy Fikac
Profile: The San Antonio Express-News' and the Houston Chronicle's Austin burueas merged in 2006, and reporters cover news for both papers.
Language (s): English
DAILY NEWSPAPER

Houston Chronicle - Washington Bureau 15562
Owner: Hearst Newspapers
Editorial: 1331 H St NW Fl 11, Washington, District Of Columbia 20005-4706
Language (s): English
DAILY NEWSPAPER

Houston Home Journal 135361
Owner: Sun Multimedia, Inc.
Editorial: 1210 Washington St, Perry, Georgia 31069-2556 **Tel:** 1 478 987-1823
Web site: http://hhjonline.com
Freq: Daily; **Circ:** 14774 Not Audited
Publisher: Daniel Evans
Profile: Houston Home Journal is a daily newspaper serving Perry, GA and the surrounding area.
Language (s): English
Ad Rate: Full Page Mono 10.00
Ad Rate: Full Page Colour 100.00
Currency: United States Dollars
DAILY NEWSPAPER

Hoy Los Angeles 217754
Owner: tronc
Editorial: 202 W 1st St Fl 3, Los Angeles, California 90012-4299 **Tel:** 1 213 237-3001
Email: hola@vivelohoy.com **Web site:** http://www.hoylosangeles.com
Circ: 137221
Editor: Alejandro Maciel; **Circulation Manager:** George Martinez; **Publisher:** Roaldo Moran
Profile: Hoy is a free Spanish-language newspaper. The Los Angeles edition is split into four zoned editions, which include the areas of Los Angeles, Orange County, San Gabriel/Inland Empire and San Fernando Valley, CA. Each edition covers local, national and international news of interest to Hispanic populations in the local area. Sports, business news and entertainment news are also covered. Advertising deadlines are at 2pm PT two days prior to publication.
Language (s): Spanish/Bilingual
Ad Rate: Full Page Mono 54.33
Ad Rate: Full Page Colour 67.92
Currency: United States Dollars
DAILY NEWSPAPER

Hugo Daily News 14526
Owner: Hugo Publishing Company
Editorial: 128 E Jackson St, Hugo, Oklahoma 74743-4035 **Tel:** 1 580 326-3311
Email: editor@sbcglobal.net **Web site:** http://www.hugonews.com
Freq: Daily; **Circ:** 2900 Not Audited
Advertising Sales Manager: Linda Packard; **Publisher:** Stan Stamper
Profile: Hugo Daily News is a local, daily newspaper serving residents in Choctaw County and Northeastern Oklahoma. The publication covers local and community news, events and people. Deadlines are at noon CT.
Language (s): English
Ad Rate: Full Page Mono 6.00
Ad Rate: Full Page Colour 210.00
Currency: United States Dollars
DAILY NEWSPAPER

Huntington Herald-Press 13990
Owner: Paxton Media Group
Editorial: 7 N Jefferson St, Huntington, Indiana 46750-2839 **Tel:** 1 260 356-6700
Email: hpnews@h-ponline.com **Web site:** http://www.chronicle-tribune.com/hp_online
Freq: Daily; **Circ:** 7169 Not Audited
Editor: Rebecca Sandlin
Profile: Huntington Herald-Press is published daily for the residents of Huntington, IN and surrounding areas. It covers local news and community events.
Language (s): English
Ad Rate: Full Page Mono 18.00
Ad Rate: Full Page Colour 210.00
Currency: United States Dollars
DAILY NEWSPAPER

Huntsville Item 14704
Owner: Community Newspaper Holdings, Inc.
Editorial: 1409 10th St, Huntsville, Texas 77320-3805 **Tel:** 1 936 295-5407
Email: huntsvilleitem@gmail.com **Web site:** http://itemonline.com
Freq: Daily; **Circ:** 6940 Not Audited
Profile: Huntsville Item is a daily newspaper published for the residents of Huntsville, TX. It provides information on local news and events. Deadlines for the publication are the day before issue date.
Language (s): English
Ad Rate: Full Page Mono 19.50
Ad Rate: Full Page Colour 21.51
Currency: United States Dollars
DAILY NEWSPAPER

The Huntsville Times 15450
Owner: Advance Publications, Inc.
Editorial: 200 West Side Square Ste 100, Huntsville, Alabama 35801-5623 **Tel:** 1 256 532-4000
Email: hsvnews@al.com **Web site:** http://www.al.com/huntsville
Freq: 3 Times/Week; **Circ:** 38241 Not Audited
Profile: The Huntsville Times is a daily newspaper that covers weather, news, sports, entertainment, classified ads, politics, travel guides and Alabama commerce.
Language (s): English
Ad Rate: Full Page Mono 80.73
Ad Rate: Full Page Colour 264.21
Currency: United States Dollars
DAILY NEWSPAPER

Huron Daily Tribune 14159
Owner: Hearst Newspapers
Editorial: 211 N Heisterman St, Bad Axe, Michigan 48413-1239 **Tel:** 1 989 269-6461
Email: hdt_news@hearstnp.com **Web site:** http://www.michigansthumb.com
Freq: Fri; **Circ:** 6461 Not Audited
News Editor: Kate Hessling; **Editor:** Dave Shane
Profile: Huron Daily Tribune is written for residents of Huron, MI. It covers a wide range of topics including local sports, news and entertainment. Deadlines are at 8:30am CT daily.
Language (s): English
Ad Rate: Full Page Mono 19.30
Ad Rate: Full Page Colour 275.00
Currency: United States Dollars
DAILY NEWSPAPER

Huron Plainsman 14652
Owner: News Media Corp.
Editorial: 49 3rd St SE, Huron, South Dakota 57350-2015 **Tel:** 1 605 352-6401
Email: editor.plainsman@midconetwork.com **Web site:** http://www.plainsman.com
Freq: Daily; **Circ:** 5230 Not Audited
Publisher: Mark Davis
Profile: Huron Plainsman is a daily newspaper dedicated to bringing forth all of the pertinent local and national news. The publication is written for residents of Huron, SD and surrounding areas. Deadlines are at 3pm MT. The outlet offers RSS (Really Simple Syndication).
Language (s): English
Ad Rate: Full Page Mono 14.70
Ad Rate: Full Page Colour 19.23
Currency: United States Dollars
DAILY NEWSPAPER

The Hutchinson News 14049
Owner: Harris Enterprises
Editorial: 300 W 2nd Ave, Hutchinson, Kansas 67501-5211 **Tel:** 1 620 694-5700
Email: newsrelease@hutchnews.com **Web site:** http://www.hutchnews.com
Freq: Daily; **Circ:** 30653 Not Audited
Advertising Sales Manager: Dave Gilchrist; **News Editor:** Jason Probst
Profile: The Hutchinson News is a daily newspaper written for the residents of Wichita, Canton and Hutchinson, KS. The newspaper covers local and national news.
Language (s): English
Ad Rate: Full Page Mono 27.47
Ad Rate: Full Page Colour 94.55
Currency: United States Dollars
DAILY NEWSPAPER

IBD Weekly 15310
Owner: William O'Neil + Co. Inc.
Editorial: 12655 Beatrice St, Los Angeles, California 90066-7300 **Tel:** 1 310 448-6000
Email: ibdnews@investors.com **Web site:** http://www.investors.com
Freq: Weekly; **Circ:** 101224 Not Audited
News Editor: Ed Carson; **Publisher:** William O'Neil
Profile: Investor's Business Daily is a daily business newspaper aimed at senior executives, professionals and entrepreneurs, as well as individual and professional investors. The newspaper provides national business news, new management and investment ideas, and proprietary information used to make business and investment decisions, including stock data such as industry group rankings, relative strength, earnings per share ranking, volume percentage change and accumulation distribution. The paper is distributed weekly.
Language (s): English
Ad Rate: Full Page Mono 161.16
Ad Rate: Full Page Colour 238.05
Currency: United States Dollars
DAILY NEWSPAPER

IBD Weekly - Sunnyvale Bureau 15535
Editorial: 1270 Oakmead Pkwy Ste 208, Sunnyvale, California 94085-4041 **Tel:** 1 408 720-2129
Language (s): English
DAILY NEWSPAPER

IBD Weekly - Washington Bureau 15536
Editorial: 1001 Connecticut Ave NW Ste 415, Washington, District Of Columbia 20036-5587 **Tel:** 1 202 728-2150
Language (s): English
DAILY NEWSPAPER

Idaho Press-Tribune 13905
Owner: Pioneer Newspapers
Editorial: 1618 N Midland Blvd, Nampa, Idaho 83651-1751 **Tel:** 1 208 467-9251
Email: newsroom@idahopress.com **Web site:** http://www.idahopress.com
Freq: Daily; **Circ:** 21065 Not Audited
Publisher: Matt Davison; **Advertising Sales Manager:** Brian Doane
Profile: Idaho Press-Tribune is published daily for the residents of Nampa, ID. The newspaper covers local and national news, sports, business, politics, education, lifestyles and entertainment.
Language (s): English
Ad Rate: Full Page Mono 19.48
Ad Rate: Full Page Colour 20.55
Currency: United States Dollars
DAILY NEWSPAPER

Idaho State Journal 13906
Owner: Pioneer Newspapers
Editorial: 305 S Arthur Ave, Pocatello, Idaho 83204 **Tel:** 1 208 232-4161
Email: reporters@journalnet.com **Web site:** http://www.journalnet.com
Freq: Daily; **Circ:** 18149 Not Audited
Editor: Doug Lindley; **Publisher:** Andy Pennington
Profile: Idaho State Journal is a daily newspaper written for residents of Idaho. Topics covered include news, events, weather, sports, politics and business.
Language (s): English
Ad Rate: Full Page Mono 25.95
Ad Rate: Full Page Colour 390.00
Currency: United States Dollars
DAILY NEWSPAPER

The Idaho Statesman 15360
Owner: McClatchy Newspapers
Editorial: 1200 N Curtis Rd, Boise, Idaho 83706-1239 **Tel:** 1 208 377-6200
Email: newsroom@idahostatesman.com **Web site:** http://www.idahostatesman.com
Freq: Daily; **Circ:** 43903 Not Audited
Profile: The Idaho Statesman is written for residents in the Boise, ID, area. The paper covers local, regional, state, national and international news, as well as sports, business, arts & entertainment and special reports. It was founded as a weekly newspaper in 1864. The paper does not publish a holiday gift guide.
Language (s): English
Ad Rate: Full Page Mono 46.00
Ad Rate: Full Page Colour 46.00
Currency: United States Dollars
DAILY NEWSPAPER

Imperial Valley Press 13724
Owner: Schurz Communications Inc.
Editorial: 205 N 8th St, El Centro, California 92243-2301 **Tel:** 1 760 337-3400
Web site: http://www.ivpressonline.com
Freq: Daily; **Circ:** 11125 Not Audited
Profile: Imperial Valley Press is a daily newspaper published for the residents of Imperial County, CA and surrounding areas. Topics covered include local, national and world news, sports, weather, entertainment and health news.
Language (s): English
Ad Rate: Full Page Mono 26.35
Ad Rate: Full Page Colour 495.00
Currency: United States Dollars
DAILY NEWSPAPER

Independence Reporter 14050
Owner: Reporter Publishing Company, Inc.
Editorial: 320 N 6th St, Independence, Kansas 67301-3129 **Tel:** 1 620 331-3550
Freq: Fri; **Circ:** 7918 Not Audited
Advertising Sales Manager: Steve McBride; **Editor and Publisher:** Herbert Meyer; **Editor:** Brian Thomas
Profile: Independence Reporter is a bi-weekly newspaper published for Independence, KS. Coverage includes news, weather, sports, business and arts & entertainment.
Language (s): English
Ad Rate: Full Page Mono 6.93
Ad Rate: Full Page Colour 195.00
Currency: United States Dollars
DAILY NEWSPAPER

Independent 14375
Owner: Gallup Independent Co. (The)
Editorial: 500 N Ninth St, Gallup, New Mexico 87301-5379 **Tel:** 1 505 863-6811
Web site: http://www.gallupindependent.com
Freq: Daily; **Circ:** 12584 Not Audited
Publisher: Robert Zollinger
Profile: Independent is written for Navajo Indians and other residents of Gallup, NM. All press releases and other related correspondence must be mailed to the P.O. Box address. Deadlines for the publication are daily at 6:30am MT.
Language (s): English
Ad Rate: Full Page Mono 21.00
Currency: United States Dollars
DAILY NEWSPAPER

The Independent 14473
Owner: GateHouse Media Inc.
Editorial: 729 Lincoln Way E, Massillon, Ohio 44646-6829 **Tel:** 1 330 833-2631
Email: indenews@indeonline.com **Web site:** http://www.indeonline.com
Freq: Daily; **Circ:** 8854 Not Audited
Editor: Veronica VanDress
Profile: The Independent is published daily for the residents of Massillon, OH and surrounding areas. The paper focuses on local news, sports, business, education and city life.
Language (s): English
Ad Rate: Full Page Mono 19.75
Ad Rate: Full Page Colour 295.00
Currency: United States Dollars
DAILY NEWSPAPER

Independent Record 14283
Owner: Lee Enterprises, Inc.
Editorial: 317 N Cruse Ave, Helena, Montana 59601-5003 **Tel:** 1 406 447-4000
Email: irstaff@helenair.com **Web site:** http://www.helenair.com
Freq: Daily; **Circ:** 12541 Not Audited
News Editor: Leah Gilman
Profile: Independent Record is a daily newspaper published for the residents of Helena, MT and surrounding areas. It covers local, state and national news, weather, sports and community events.
Language (s): English
Ad Rate: Full Page Mono 20.62
Ad Rate: Full Page Colour 279.00
Currency: United States Dollars
DAILY NEWSPAPER

The Index-Journal 14644
Owner: Index Journal (The)
Editorial: 610 Phoenix St, Greenwood, South Carolina 29646-3253 **Tel:** 1 864 223-1411
Web site: http://www.indexjournal.com
Freq: Daily; **Circ:** 10730 Not Audited
Publisher: Judith Mundy Burns
Profile: The Index-Journal is a daily newspaper for Greenwood, SC and the surrounding community. It covers local and national news, lifestyle, business and sports.
Language (s): English
Ad Rate: Full Page Mono 23.10
Ad Rate: Full Page Colour 300.00
Currency: United States Dollars
DAILY NEWSPAPER

Indiana Gazette 14585
Owner: Community Newspaper Holdings, Inc.
Editorial: 899 Water St, Indiana, Pennsylvania 15701-1705 **Tel:** 1 724 465-5555
Email: news@indianagazette.net **Web site:** http://www.indianagazette.com
Freq: Daily; **Circ:** 12380
Publisher: Michael Donnelly
Profile: Indiana Gazette is a daily newspaper published for the residents of Indiana, PA and surrounding areas. The publication focuses on small-town journalism. It covers local news, sports, arts & entertainment and letters to the editor. Deadlines are daily at 10pm ET.
Language (s): English
Ad Rate: Full Page Mono 16.98
Ad Rate: Full Page Colour 159.95
Currency: United States Dollars
DAILY NEWSPAPER

The Indianapolis Star 15363
Owner: Gannett Co., Inc.
Editorial: 130 S Meridian St, Indianapolis, Indiana 46225-1046 **Tel:** 1 317 444-6000
Email: startips@indystar.com **Web site:** http://www.indystar.com
Freq: Daily; **Circ:** 166542 Not Audited
Profile: The Indianapolis Star is a 60+ page, four-color broadsheet read by the general public of Indiana. According to its publishers, the mission of Indianapolis Newspapers Inc. "is to be central Indiana's primary provider of news and information. To accomplish our mission, we will publish accurate, fair, and complete products of news, information, and opinion." The publication provides coverage of arts & entertainment, travel, real estate, health & fitness, automotive, city and state news, and sports. The paper runs business stories every day and publishes BusinessMonday, which contains in-depth, expanded business coverage with a local slant. The Indianapolis Star was founded in 1903. In 1995, the newspaper merged with its evening competitor, the Indianapolis News. The two were published separately until 1999, when the News was discontinued. The Holiday Gift Guide is an advertorial product and ONLY grants paid placement.
Language (s): English
Ad Rate: Full Page Mono 323.00
Ad Rate: Full Page Colour 359.43
Currency: United States Dollars
DAILY NEWSPAPER

Inland Valley Daily Bulletin 13741
Owner: Southern California News Group/Digital First Media
Editorial: 9616 Archibald Ave Ste 100, Rancho Cucamonga, California 91730-7940 **Tel:** 1 909 987-6397
Web site: http://www.dailybulletin.com
Freq: Daily; **Circ:** 60096 Not Audited
Profile: Inland Valley Daily Bulletin serves a 13-city region around Ontario, CA, stretching from Kellogg Hill in the west to Rialto in the east, Mount Baldy in the north to the southern towns of Chino and Chino Hills. This paper is a part of the Southern California News Group, a subsidiary of Digital First Media. It covers local, regional, state, national and international news, as well as business, sports, entertainment and special features.
Language (s): English
Ad Rate: Full Page Mono 126.00
Ad Rate: Full Page Colour 136.19
Currency: United States Dollars
DAILY NEWSPAPER

The Intelligencer 14575
Owner: Calkins Media
Editorial: 333 N Broad St, Doylestown, Pennsylvania 18901-3407 **Tel:** 1 215 345-3000
Email: intell_news@phillyburbs.com **Web site:** http://www.theintell.com
Freq: Mon thru Fri; **Circ:** 24447 Not Audited
Profile: The Intelligencer is a daily newspaper for the residents of Doylestown, PA and surrounding areas. The newspaper covers local news, sports, events, entertainment, business and politics.
Language (s): English
Ad Rate: Full Page Mono 33.73
Ad Rate: Full Page Colour 38.73
Currency: United States Dollars
DAILY NEWSPAPER

Intelligencer/News-Register 595500
Owner: Ogden Newspapers
Editorial: 1500 Main St, Wheeling, West Virginia 26003-2826 **Tel:** 1 304 233-0100
Web site: http://www.theintelligencer.net/
Circ: 12323
Publisher: Ogden Nutting
Language (s): English
DAILY NEWSPAPER

The Inter-Mountain 14833
Owner: Ogden Newspapers
Editorial: 520 Railroad Ave, Elkins, West Virginia 26241 **Tel:** 1 304 636-2121
Email: newsroom@theintermountain.com **Web site:** http://www.theintermountain.com
Freq: Daily; **Circ:** 6637 Not Audited
Editor: Edgar Kelley
Profile: The Inter-Mountain is a local daily newspaper written for residents of Randolph County, WV and the six surrounding counties. The newspaper covers local news and events in central West Virginia. The lead time for the newspaper is one week.
Language (s): English
Ad Rate: Full Page Mono 21.87
Ad Rate: Full Page Colour 71.70
Currency: United States Dollars
DAILY NEWSPAPER

Iola Register 14051
Owner: Iola Register Publishing, Inc.
Editorial: 302 S Washington Ave, Iola, Kansas 66749-3255 **Tel:** 1 620 365-2111
Email: editorial@iolaregister.com **Web site:** http://www.iolaregister.com
Freq: Daily; **Circ:** 3842 Not Audited
Advertising Sales Manager: Mark Hastings; **Editor:** Bob Johnson; **Publisher & Editor:** Susan Lynn
Profile: Iola Register is a local newspaper serving Allen County and the communities of Iola, Gas, Humboldt, Moran, LaHarpe and Colony, KS.
Language (s): English
Ad Rate: Full Page Mono 9.65
Ad Rate: Full Page Colour 82.50
Currency: United States Dollars
DAILY NEWSPAPER

Ionia Sentinel Standard 14173
Owner: GateHouse Media Inc.
Editorial: 114 N Depot St, Ionia, Michigan 48846-1688 **Tel:** 1 616 527-2100
Email: newsroom@sentinel-standard.com **Web site:** http://www.sentinel-standard.com
Freq: Daily; **Circ:** 3100 Not Audited
Profile: Ionia Sentinel Standard is written for residents of Ionia County, MI and surrounding areas. It cover local news and information.
Language (s): English
Ad Rate: Full Page Mono 14.75
Ad Rate: Full Page Colour 190.00
Currency: United States Dollars
DAILY NEWSPAPER

Iowa City Press-Citizen 13881
Owner: Gannett Co., Inc.
Editorial: 1725 N Dodge St, Iowa City, Iowa 52245-9589 **Tel:** 1 319 337-3181
Email: newsroom@press-citizen.com **Web site:** http://www.press-citizen.com
Freq: Mon thru Fri; **Circ:** 9836 Not Audited
Advertising Sales Manager: Shawn Reineke
Profile: Iowa City Press-Citizen is published daily for the residents of Iowa City, IA and surrounding areas. The newspaper covers local and state news, business, sports, lifestyles and entertainment.
Language (s): English
Ad Rate: Full Page Mono 41.64
Ad Rate: Full Page Colour 425.00
Currency: United States Dollars
DAILY NEWSPAPER

Irish Examiner - New York Bureau 620270
Editorial: 131 E 66th St, New York, New York 10065-6147 **Tel:** 1 212 734-8844
Profile: This is the New York bureau of the Irish Examiner.
Language (s): English
DAILY NEWSPAPER

Ironton Tribune 14460
Owner: Boone Newspapers Inc.
Editorial: 2903 S 5th St, Ironton, Ohio 45638-2866 **Tel:** 1 740 532-1441
Email: news@irontontribune.com **Web site:** http://www.irontontribune.com
Freq: Daily; **Circ:** 5486 Not Audited
Publisher & Editor: Mike Caldwell; **Advertising Sales Manager:** Shawn Randolph; **Editor:** Jessica St. James
Profile: Ironton Tribune's editorial mission is to provide news for the community of Ironton, OH. The publication contains sports, entertainment, news and events on a local scale. The paper is published every day except Saturday.
Language (s): English
Ad Rate: Full Page Mono 16.50
Ad Rate: Full Page Colour 175.00
Currency: United States Dollars
DAILY NEWSPAPER

The Island Packet 14858
Owner: McClatchy Newspapers
Editorial: 10 Buck Island Rd, Bluffton, South Carolina 29910-5937 **Tel:** 1 843 706-8100
Email: newsroom@islandpacket.com **Web site:** http://www.islandpacket.com
Freq: Daily; **Circ:** 19512 Not Audited
Publisher: Sara Johnson Borton
Profile: The Island Packet is a daily newspaper published for the residents of Southern Beaufort County, including Bluffton and Hilton Head Island, SC. It focuses on local news and events, business, real estate, editorial and feature articles. The paper is published the last Thursday of every month and items are due by the 15th of the month prior. Deadlines are on Mondays at 5pm ET.
Language (s): English
Ad Rate: Full Page Mono 40.00
Ad Rate: Full Page Colour 265.00
Currency: United States Dollars
DAILY NEWSPAPER

The Item 14648
Owner: Osteen Publishing Co.
Editorial: 20 N Magnolia St, Sumter, South Carolina 29150-4940 **Tel:** 1 803 774-1200
Email: news@theitem.com **Web site:** http://www.theitem.com
Freq: Fri; **Circ:** 18640 Not Audited
Publisher & Editor: Jack Osteen
Profile: The Item's editorial mission is to provide news, sports and events coverage for the Sumter, SC area.
Language (s): English
Ad Rate: Full Page Mono 17.50
Ad Rate: Full Page Colour 295.00
Currency: United States Dollars
DAILY NEWSPAPER

The Ithaca Journal 14407
Owner: Gannett Co., Inc.
Editorial: 123 W State St, Ithaca, New York 14850-5427 **Tel:** 1 607 272-2321
Email: ijnews@gannett.com **Web site:** http://www.ithacajournal.com/
Freq: Daily; **Circ:** 9050 Not Audited
Profile: The Ithaca Journal provides the communities of Ithaca and Tompkins County, NY with local news and information, sports, education, crime and weather. Deadlines are at noon ET.
Language (s): English
Ad Rate: Full Page Mono 42.85
Ad Rate: Full Page Colour 1750.00
Currency: United States Dollars
DAILY NEWSPAPER

The Jackson Citizen Patriot 14176
Owner: MLive Media Group
Editorial: 214 S Jackson St, Jackson, Michigan 49201 **Tel:** 1 517 787-2300
Email: janews@mlive.com **Web site:** http://www.mlive.com/jackson
Freq: Daily; **Circ:** 13688 Not Audited
Profile: The Jackson Citizen Patriot is a daily newspaper written for the residents of Jackson, MI. The publication covers local news, sports, weather and events. The Lansing, MI bureau contributes to all eight of the MLive-owned dailies, including: the Ann Arbor News, Bay City Times, Flint Journal, Grand Rapids Press, Jackson Citizen Patriot, Kalamazoo Gazette, Muskegon Chronicle and the Saginaw News.
Language (s): English
Ad Rate: Full Page Mono 40.40
Currency: United States Dollars
DAILY NEWSPAPER

Jackson County Floridan 13822
Owner: World Media Enterprises, Inc.
Editorial: 4403 Constitution Ln, Marianna, Florida 32448-4472 **Tel:** 1 850 526-3614
Email: editorial@jcfloridan.com **Web site:** http://www.jcfloridan.com
Freq: Fri; **Circ:** 4392 Not Audited
Publisher & Editor: Valeria Roberts
Profile: Jackson County Floridan is a community newspaper covering local and national news, weather and sports for the residents of Jackson County, FL.
Language (s): English
Ad Rate: Full Page Mono 23.00
Ad Rate: Full Page Colour 220.00
Currency: United States Dollars
DAILY NEWSPAPER

Jackson Hole Daily 390989
Owner: Jackson Hole Magazine
Editorial: 1225 Maple Way, Jackson, Wyoming 83001-8567 **Tel:** 1 307 733-2047
Email: daily@jhnewsandguide.com **Web site:** http://www.jhnewsandguide.com
Freq: Mon thru Fri; **Circ:** 8000 Not Audited
Editor: Thomas Dewell; **Editor:** Kevin Huelsmann; **Editor:** John Moses; **Publisher:** Michael Sellett

Profile: Jackson Hole Daily is a free newspaper distributed at outlets throughout Teton and Lincoln counties, WY and Teton Valley, ID. It offers news and information to local residents and visitors on topics such as local, state, regional, national, world, sports, business, entertainment and syndicated comics and features. Readership fluctuates dramatically during the summer and winter seasons due to increased circulation at restaurants and hospitality locations. Jackson Hole Daily shares its editorial staff and offices with its sister publication, the Jackson Hole News & Guide, a weekly paid-subscription newspaper. Do not send duplicate press materials to both publications. Deadlines are at 5pm MT two days prior to issue date.
Language (s): English
Ad Rate: Full Page Mono 10.20
Ad Rate: Full Page Colour 120.00
Currency: United States Dollars
DAILY NEWSPAPER

The Jackson Sun 15414
Owner: Gannett Co., Inc.
Editorial: 245 W Lafayette St, Jackson, Tennessee 38301-6126 **Tel:** 1 731 427-3333
Email: contactus@jacksonsun.com **Web site:** http://www.jacksonsun.com
Freq: Daily; **Circ:** 17829 Not Audited
Profile: The Jackson Sun is written for the surrounding communities of Jackson, TN. It covers local news of 13 counties.
Language (s): English
Ad Rate: Full Page Mono 61.75
Ad Rate: Full Page Colour 210.93
Currency: United States Dollars
DAILY NEWSPAPER

Jacksonville Daily Progress 14705
Owner: Community Newspaper Holdings, Inc.
Editorial: 525 E Commerce St, Jacksonville, Texas 75766-4909 **Tel:** 1 903 586-2236
Email: editor@jacksonvilleprogress.com **Web site:** http://www.jacksonvilleprogress.com
Freq: Daily; **Circ:** 3900 Not Audited
Editor: Amy Brocato Pearson; **Publisher:** Lange Svehlak
Profile: Jacksonville Daily Progress is a local daily newspaper written for residents of Jacksonville, TX and the surrounding areas. It is a general interest newspaper that covers local news, sports, finances, health, entertainment and events.
Language (s): English
Ad Rate: Full Page Mono 8.80
Ad Rate: Full Page Colour 225.00
Currency: United States Dollars
DAILY NEWSPAPER

Jacksonville Journal-Courier 13935
Owner: Civitas LLC
Editorial: 235 W State St, Jacksonville, Illinois 62650-2001 **Tel:** 1 217 245-6121
Email: news@myjournalcourier.com **Web site:** http://www.myjournalcourier.com
Freq: Daily; **Circ:** 8260 Not Audited
Editor: David Bauer; **Publisher:** Jim Shrader; **Advertising Sales Manager:** Karen Walker
Profile: Jacksonville Journal-Courier is published for the residents of Jacksonville, IL and surrounding areas. The newspaper cover local and regional news, business, sports, lifestyles and entertainment.
Language (s): English
Ad Rate: Full Page Mono 20.57
Ad Rate: Full Page Colour 69.82
Currency: United States Dollars
DAILY NEWSPAPER

The Jamestown Sun 14331
Owner: Forum Communications Co.
Editorial: 121 3rd St NW, Jamestown, North Dakota 58401-3127 **Tel:** 1 701 252-3120
Email: js@jamestownsun.com **Web site:** http://www.jamestownsun.com
Freq: Daily; **Circ:** 6234 Not Audited
Publisher: Rob Keller; **Advertising Sales Manager:** Gavin Kutz
Profile: The Jamestown Sun is a daily newspaper published Monday through Saturday that provides local news coverage for residents of the town. Deadlines are typically two days before an item's publication date.
Language (s): English
Ad Rate: Full Page Mono 13.60
Ad Rate: Full Page Colour 180.00
Currency: United States Dollars
DAILY NEWSPAPER

The Janesville Gazette 14807
Owner: Bliss Communications Inc.
Editorial: 1 S Parker Dr, Janesville, Wisconsin 53545 **Tel:** 1 608 754-3311
Email: newsroom@gazettextra.com **Web site:** http://www.gazettextra.com
Freq: Daily; **Circ:** 14953
Publisher: Skip Bliss; **Editor:** Ann Fiore; **Editor:** Sid Schwartz
Profile: The Janesville Gazette is a newspaper published daily for the residents of Rock and Walworth counties and the surrounding areas in southern Wisconsin. The newspaper covers local, national and international news, weather, sports and community events.
Language (s): English
Ad Rate: Full Page Mono 50.94
Ad Rate: Full Page Colour 611.00
Currency: United States Dollars
DAILY NEWSPAPER

Japanese Daily Sun 152972
Editorial: 20817 S Western Ave, Torrance, California 90501-1804 **Tel:** 1 310 222-8788
Email: jps753@aol.com
Freq: Mon thru Fri; **Circ:** 15000 Not Audited
Editor: Tomomi Kanemaru; **Advertising Sales Manager:** Satoshi Katana; **Editor:** Ty Makino
Profile: The Japanese Daily Sun is a daily tabloid paper containing various news, entertainment and sports stories.
Language (s): Japanese
Ad Rate: Full Page Mono 240.00
Ad Rate: Full Page Colour 1200.00
Currency: United States Dollars
DAILY NEWSPAPER

Jennings Daily News 14099
Owner: Fackelman Newspapers
Editorial: 238 Market St, Jennings, Louisiana 70546 **Tel:** 1 337 824-3011
Email: jdnnews@bellsouth.net **Web site:** http://www.jenningsdailynews.net
Freq: Daily; **Circ:** 5000 Not Audited
Editor: Rebecca Chaisson; **Publisher:** Dona Smith
Profile: Jennings Daily News covers local news and events of the Jeff Davis Parish for residents of Jennings, LA.
Language (s): English
Ad Rate: Full Page Mono 10.59
Ad Rate: Full Page Colour 15.30
Currency: United States Dollars
DAILY NEWSPAPER

The Jersey Journal 14358
Owner: NJ Advance Media
Editorial: 1 Harmon Plz Ste 1000, Secaucus, New Jersey 07094-2806 **Tel:** 1 201 653-1000
Web site: http://jjournal.com
Freq: Daily; **Circ:** 13093 Not Audited
Editor: Margaret Schmidt
Profile: The Jersey Journal is published daily for the residents of Jersey City, NJ and surrounding areas. The newspaper covers local and state news, business, sports, lifestyles and entertainment.
Language (s): English
Ad Rate: Full Page Mono 47.06
Ad Rate: Full Page Colour 135.00
Currency: United States Dollars
DAILY NEWSPAPER

Johnson City Press 14669
Owner: Sandusky Newspapers Inc.
Editorial: 204 W Main St, Johnson City, Tennessee 37604-6212 **Tel:** 1 423 929-3111
Email: newsroom@johnsoncitypress.com **Web site:** http://www.johnsoncitypress.com
Freq: Daily; **Circ:** 24358 Not Audited
News Editor: Sam Watson; **Publisher:** Justin Wilcox
Profile: Johnson City Press is a daily newspaper written for residents of Johnson City, TN and the surrounding area. The newspaper covers local news, sports, business, entertainment, lifestyles and events. Deadlines are everyday at midnight ET.
Language (s): English
Ad Rate: Full Page Mono 30.00
Ad Rate: Full Page Colour 419.00
Currency: United States Dollars
DAILY NEWSPAPER

The Joplin Globe 14235
Owner: Community Newspaper Holdings, Inc.
Editorial: 117 E 4th St, Joplin, Missouri 64801-2302 **Tel:** 1 417 623-3480
Email: news@joplinglobe.com **Web site:** http://www.joplinglobe.com
Freq: Daily; **Circ:** 19606 Not Audited
Publisher: Michael Beatty; **Editor:** Carol Stark
Profile: The Joplin Globe is a daily newspaper published in Joplin, MO. Founded in 1986, the paper provides in-depth news coverage and features for residents of Southwest Missouri, as well as over 90 surrounding communities in 14 counties.
Language (s): English
Ad Rate: Full Page Mono 31.95
Ad Rate: Full Page Colour 39.05
Currency: United States Dollars
DAILY NEWSPAPER

The Journal 14211
Owner: Ogden Newspapers
Editorial: 303 N Minnesota St, New Ulm, Minnesota 56073-1733 **Tel:** 1 507 359-2911
Email: news@nujournal.com **Web site:** http://www.nujournal.com
Freq: Daily; **Circ:** 5969 Not Audited
Editor: Kevin Sweeney; **News Editor:** Donna Weber
Profile: The Journal is a daily local newspaper covering news in southern Minnesota, including Brown and Sibley counties. The publication covers local, sports and community news.
Language (s): English
Ad Rate: Full Page Mono 27.11
Currency: United States Dollars
DAILY NEWSPAPER

The Journal 14839
Owner: Ogden Newspapers
Editorial: 207 W King St, Martinsburg, West Virginia 25401-3211 **Tel:** 1 304 263-8931
Email: news@journal-news.net **Web site:** http://www.journal-news.net
Freq: Daily; **Circ:** 11803 Not Audited
Publisher: Craig Bartoldson
Profile: The Journal is a local daily newspaper serving the residents of Berkley, Jefferson, and Morgan counties in West Virginia. It covers local, state and national news, sports, entertainment and community events.
Language (s): English
Ad Rate: Full Page Mono 24.90
Ad Rate: Full Page Colour 320.00
Currency: United States Dollars
DAILY NEWSPAPER

The Journal 358740
Owner: Eagle Media
Editorial: 210 W North 1st St, Seneca, South Carolina 29678-3250 **Tel:** 1 864 882-2375
Email: newsed@upstatetoday.com **Web site:** http://upstatetoday.com
Freq: Fri; **Circ:** 11456 Not Audited
Editor: Steven Bradley
Profile: The Journal is a daily local newspaper written for residents in and around Oconee County and Clemson County, SC including Seneca and Clemson, SC. It covers local news, events, politics, sports, weather, features and news from the local colleges and universities.
Language (s): English
Ad Rate: Full Page Mono 17.00
Currency: United States Dollars
DAILY NEWSPAPER

Journal & Courier 13996
Owner: Gannett Co., Inc.
Editorial: 823 Park East Blvd Ste C, Lafayette, Indiana 47905-0811 **Tel:** 1 765 423-5511
Email: editor@journalandcourier.com **Web site:** http://www.jconline.com
Freq: Daily; **Circ:** 16893 Not Audited
Profile: Journal & Courier is a daily newspaper published in Lafayette, IN. It is distributed in ten counties in west-central Indiana. The paper covers local and regional news, as well as business, lifestyle, sports, and entertainment. It is available in print form, online, and in Spanish once a month as Journal and Courier en Espanol.
Language (s): English
Ad Rate: Full Page Mono 57.87
Currency: United States Dollars
DAILY NEWSPAPER

The Journal Gazette 15362
Owner: Journal Gazette Company (The)
Editorial: 600 W Main St, Fort Wayne, Indiana 46802-1408 **Tel:** 1 260 461-8773
Email: jgnews@jg.net **Web site:** http://www.journalgazette.net
Freq: Daily; **Circ:** 49093 Not Audited
Publisher: Julie Inskeep
Profile: The Journal Gazette is a daily morning newspaper in Fort Wayne, IN that operates in conjunction with The News-Sentinel, the afternoon newspaper of the city. The papers have combined their business operations such as circulation, advertising, marketing and production, but the newsrooms work separately. The paper covers any news-related stories and particularly focuses on Northeast Indiana. Special sections also appear in the Fort Wayne News-Sentinel.
Language (s): English
Ad Rate: Full Page Mono 173.00
Ad Rate: Full Page Colour 188.45
Currency: United States Dollars
DAILY NEWSPAPER

The Journal Gazette - Indianapolis Bureau 15713
Editorial: 200 W Washington St Ste M8, Indianapolis, Indiana 46204-2755 **Tel:** 1 317 686-0901
Bureau Chief: Niki Kelly
Language (s): English
DAILY NEWSPAPER

Journal Gazette & Times-Courier 13945
Owner: Lee Enterprises, Inc.
Editorial: 700 Broadway Ave E Ste 9, Mattoon, Illinois 61938-4617 **Tel:** 1 217 235-5656
Email: editorial@jg-tc.com **Web site:** http://www.jg-tc.com
Freq: Daily; **Circ:** 11337 Not Audited
Profile: Journal Gazette/Times-Courier is published daily for residents of Mattoon, IL and Charleston, IL and surrounding areas. The publication is a general interest newspaper covering local news, weather, sports, education, business, arts & entertainment and other information of interest to the local community.
Language (s): English
DAILY NEWSPAPER

Journal Inquirer 13800
Owner: Ellis (Elizabeth)
Editorial: 306 Progress Dr, Manchester, Connecticut 06042-9011 **Tel:** 1 860 646-0500
Email: news@journalinquirer.com **Web site:** http://www.journalinquirer.com
Freq: Daily; **Circ:** 27338
Publisher: Elizabeth Ellis; **News Editor:** Ralph Williams
Profile: The Journal Inquirer was founded in 1968 and serves residents of north central Connecticut. The paper covers local news and events for 17 towns in the area of the state.
Language (s): English
Ad Rate: Full Page Mono 56.00
Ad Rate: Full Page Colour 400.00
Currency: United States Dollars
DAILY NEWSPAPER

The Journal News - Rockland Edition 87247
Owner: Gannett Co., Inc.
Editorial: 1 Crosfield Ave, West Nyack, New York 10994-2222 **Tel:** 1 845 578-2424
Email: letters@lohud.com **Web site:** http://www.lohud.com
Freq: Daily; **Circ:** 23545 Not Audited
Profile: The Journal News-Rockland Edition is published daily for residents of West Nyack, NY.
Language (s): English
Ad Rate: Full Page Mono 40.00
Ad Rate: Full Page Colour 58.00
Currency: United States Dollars
DAILY NEWSPAPER

Journal Review 13979
Owner: PTS, Inc.
Editorial: 119 N Green St, Crawfordsville, Indiana 47933-1708 **Tel:** 1 765 362-1200
Email: rop@jrpress.com **Web site:** http://www.journalreview.com
Freq: Daily; **Circ:** 7891 Not Audited
Publisher: Shawn Storie
Profile: Journal Review is a daily newspaper published in Crawfordsville, IN. The paper covers local news and events for local residents and the surrounding area, including parts of Hendrix, Boone, Montgomery and Putnam Counties, IN.
Language (s): English
Ad Rate: Full Page Mono 15.90
Ad Rate: Full Page Colour 250.00
Currency: United States Dollars
DAILY NEWSPAPER

Journal Star 14894
Owner: GateHouse Media Inc.
Editorial: 1 News Plz, Peoria, Illinois 61643-0001 **Tel:** 1 309 686-3000
Email: news@pjstar.com **Web site:** http://www.pjstar.com
Freq: Daily; **Circ:** 57658 Not Audited
Publisher: Ken Mauser
Profile: Journal Star is a daily newspaper written for the residents of Peoria, IL. The newspaper covers local news and events, business, sports and arts & entertainment. The newspaper also covers national and state news.
Language (s): English
Ad Rate: Full Page Mono 88.74
Ad Rate: Full Page Colour 291.70
Currency: United States Dollars
DAILY NEWSPAPER

The Journal Times 14818
Owner: Lee Enterprises, Inc.
Editorial: 212 4th St, Racine, Wisconsin 53403-1005 **Tel:** 1 262 634-3322
Web site: http://www.journaltimes.com
Freq: Daily; **Circ:** 18656 Not Audited
News Editor: Tom Farley; **Publisher:** Mark Lewis
Profile: The Journal Times is a daily newspaper serving Racine, WI. The newspaper covers local news sports, business, health, fitness, real estate and arts & entertainment. Press releases can be sent by e-mail. Deadlines for the editorial submissions is one week prior to the issue date.
Language (s): English
Ad Rate: Full Page Mono 46.75
Ad Rate: Full Page Colour 288.17
Currency: United States Dollars
DAILY NEWSPAPER

Journal Tribune 14152
Owner: Beacon Press Inc.
Editorial: 457 Alfred St, Biddeford, Maine 04005-9447 **Tel:** 1 207 282-1535
Email: jtcommunity@journaltribune.com **Web site:** http://www.journaltribune.com
Freq: Daily; **Circ:** 4558 Not Audited
Profile: Journal Tribune is the only daily newspaper in York County, ME. It serves readers in Wells and Old Orchard Beach, ME and its readership extends west to the New Hampshire border. The paper covers local news, sports and arts & entertainment.
Language (s): English
Ad Rate: Full Page Mono 16.25
Ad Rate: Full Page Colour 300.00
Currency: United States Dollars
DAILY NEWSPAPER

Journal-Advocate 13794
Owner: MediaNews Group
Editorial: 504 N 3rd St, Sterling, Colorado 80751-3203 **Tel:** 1 970 522-1990
Web site: http://www.journal-advocate.com
Freq: Daily; **Circ:** 2303
Profile: Journal-Advocate is a daily newspaper published for the residents of Sterling, CO and surrounding areas. It provides information on local and state news, government, politics and community events.
Language (s): English
Ad Rate: Full Page Mono 14.00
Ad Rate: Full Page Colour 16.00
Currency: United States Dollars
DAILY NEWSPAPER

Journal-News 14458
Owner: Cox Media Group, Inc.
Editorial: 228 Court St, Hamilton, Ohio 45011-2820 **Tel:** 1 513 863-8200
Email: butlercountynews@coxohio.com **Web site:** http://www.journal-news.com
Freq: Daily; **Circ:** 19956 Not Audited
Editor: Kevin Aldridge
Profile: Journal-News is a daily morning newspaper serving the residents of Butler County, OH since

1886. It contains news and advertising and serves as a forum for community issues. It has also been recognized as the best daily in Ohio in its circulation class by the Ohio Society of Professional Journalists.
Language (s): English
Ad Rate: Full Page Mono 21.50
Ad Rate: Full Page Colour 25.50
Currency: United States Dollars
DAILY NEWSPAPER

The Journal-Standard 13932
Owner: GateHouse Media Inc.
Editorial: 27 S State Ave, Freeport, Illinois 61032-4210 **Tel:** 1 815 232-1171
Email: frontdoor@journalstandard.com **Web site:** http://www.journalstandard.com
Freq: Fri; **Circ:** 7016 Not Audited
Profile: The Journal-Standard is published daily for the residents of Freeport, IL and surrounding areas. The newspaper covers local and national news, community events, sports and business news.
Language (s): English
Ad Rate: Full Page Mono 16.00
Ad Rate: Full Page Colour 2076.90
Currency: United States Dollars
DAILY NEWSPAPER

Junction City Daily Union 14052
Owner: Montgomery Communications, Inc.
Editorial: 222 W 6th St, Junction City, Kansas 66441-5500 **Tel:** 1 785 762-5000
Email: m.editor@thedailyunion.net **Web site:** http://www.yourdu.net
Freq: Fri; **Circ:** 4313 Not Audited
Editor & Publisher: Tim Hobbs
Profile: Junction City Daily Union is written for residents of Junction City, Fort Riley, Grandview Plaza, Milford, Chapman, Wakefield, Ogden, Herington, Woodbine, Dwight, White City, Parker Ville and Alta Vista, KS. It covers local news, business, politics, sports, people and community events.
Language (s): English
Ad Rate: Full Page Mono 8.60
Ad Rate: Full Page Colour 200.00
Currency: United States Dollars
DAILY NEWSPAPER

Juneau Empire 13659
Owner: GateHouse Media Inc.
Editorial: 3100 Channel Dr, Juneau, Alaska 99801-7837 **Tel:** 1 907 586-3740
Email: editor@juneauempire.com **Web site:** http://www.juneauempire.com
Freq: Daily; **Circ:** 4190
Publisher: Mark Bryan
Profile: Juneau Empire is published Monday through Friday afternoon and Sunday morning for readers in the Juneau, AK area. The newspaper covers local, national and international news, sports, business and arts.
Language (s): English
Ad Rate: Full Page Mono 25.85
Ad Rate: Full Page Colour 475.00
Currency: United States Dollars
DAILY NEWSPAPER

Kalamazoo Gazette 14177
Owner: MLive Media Group
Editorial: 300 S Kalamazoo Mall, Kalamazoo, Michigan 49007-4800 **Tel:** 1 269 345-3511
Email: kznews@mlive.com **Web site:** http://www.mlive.com/kzgazette
Freq: Daily; **Circ:** 27033 Not Audited
Profile: Kalamazoo (MI) Gazette covers local, national and international news. The lead time and deadlines for this publication vary. Contact the newspaper for details. It is published in the same office as the Kalamazoo Gazette Weeklies.
Language (s): English
Ad Rate: Full Page Mono 105.60
Ad Rate: Full Page Colour 168.75
Currency: United States Dollars
DAILY NEWSPAPER

Kane County Chronicle 14879
Owner: Shaw Media
Editorial: 333 N Randall Rd Ste 2, Saint Charles, Illinois 60174-1500 **Tel:** 1 630 232-9222
Email: editorial@kcchronicle.com **Web site:** http://www.kcchronicle.com
Freq: Fri; **Circ:** 10346 Not Audited
Editor: Kathy Gresey; **Publisher:** J. Thomas Shaw
Profile: Kane County Chronicle reports on local and national news for Kane County, IL.
Language (s): English
Ad Rate: Full Page Mono 20.95
Currency: United States Dollars
DAILY NEWSPAPER

The Kane Republican 14588
Owner: Horizon Publications
Editorial: 200 N Fraley St, Kane, Pennsylvania 16735-1177 **Tel:** 1 814 837-6000
Email: krnews1@zitomedia.net **Web site:** http://www.kanerepublican.com
Freq: Daily; **Circ:** 1973 Not Audited
Editor: Joseph Bell; **Publisher:** Darlene Coder
Profile: The Kane Republican is a daily local paper serving the residents of Mckean County, PA. The paper covers local news, government, education, athletics and community events. Deadlines fall on the day prior to the issue date at 2pm ET.
Language (s): English
Ad Rate: Full Page Mono 7.90
Ad Rate: Full Page Colour 9.20
Currency: United States Dollars
DAILY NEWSPAPER

The Kansas City Star 15292
Owner: McClatchy Newspapers
Editorial: 1729 Grand Blvd, Kansas City, Missouri 64108-1413 **Tel:** 1 816 234-4636
Web site: http://www.kansascity.com
Freq: Daily; **Circ:** 137084 Not Audited
News Editor: Charles Howland
Profile: The Kansas City Star is a 80+ page daily, broadsheet newspaper that was founded in 1880 covering local, regional, national and international news. Its mission is to be the "area's preeminent communications company because of a commitment to one ideal: Building our community through knowledge." The paper does not publish a Holiday Gift Guide.
Language (s): English
Ad Rate: Full Page Mono 538.00
Ad Rate: Full Page Colour 552.52
Currency: United States Dollars
DAILY NEWSPAPER

The Kansas City Star - Jefferson City Bureau 15783
Editorial: State Capitol Building #118A, Jefferson City, Missouri 65101 **Tel:** 1 573 634-3565
Language (s): English
DAILY NEWSPAPER

The Kansas City Star - Topeka Bureau 15781
Editorial: 300 SW 10th Ave Ste 132N, Topeka, Kansas 66612-1504
Language (s): English
DAILY NEWSPAPER

Kauppalehti - New York Bureau 504483
Owner: Kauppalehti Oy
Editorial: 225 Garfield Pl, Apt 2, Brooklyn, New York 11215-2264 **Tel:** 1 347 725-4172
Web site: http://www.kauppalehti.fi
Circ: 81337 Not Audited
Profile: This is the New York office for the Kauppalehti which is based in Finland.
Language (s): Finnish
DAILY NEWSPAPER

Kearney Hub 14343
Owner: Omaha World-Herald Co.
Editorial: 13 E 22nd St, Kearney, Nebraska 68847-5404 **Tel:** 1 308 237-2152
Email: news@kearneyhub.com **Web site:** http://www.kearneyhub.com
Freq: Daily; **Circ:** 11285 Not Audited
Editor: Lori Guthard; **Editor:** Brad Norton
Profile: Kearney Hub is a local daily newspaper published in Kearney, NE. The newspaper, founded in 1888, covers local and national news, sports, education, agriculture and business for the Southeastern Nebraska area. Fax or e-mail press releases to the assistant managing editor.
Language (s): English
Ad Rate: Full Page Mono 15.20
Ad Rate: Full Page Colour 56.26
Currency: United States Dollars
DAILY NEWSPAPER

The Keene Sentinel 14353
Owner: Keene Publishing Co.
Editorial: 60 West St, Keene, New Hampshire 03431-3373 **Tel:** 1 603 352-1234
Email: news@keenesentinel.com **Web site:** http://www.sentinelsource.com
Freq: Daily; **Circ:** 8928 Not Audited
Editor: Bill Bilodeau; **Publisher:** Thomas Ewing
Profile: The Keene Sentinel is a daily, local newspaper published for residents of the Keene, NH area. The editorial content of the newspaper covers local news, community events, sports, arts & entertainment, education and health.
Language (s): English
Ad Rate: Full Page Mono 13.60
Ad Rate: Full Page Colour 305.00
Currency: United States Dollars
DAILY NEWSPAPER

Kennebec Journal 14151
Owner: Maine Today Media Inc.
Editorial: 274 Western Ave, Augusta, Maine 04330-4976 **Tel:** 1 207 623-3811
Web site: http://www.centralmaine.com/
Freq: Daily; **Circ:** 8648 Not Audited
Advertising Sales Manager: Rick DeBruin
Profile: Kennebec Journal is a daily newspaper serving the residents of Augusta, ME and surrounding areas. The newspaper covers local and national news, sports, entertainment, business and community events.
Language (s): English
Ad Rate: Full Page Mono 58.37
Ad Rate: Full Page Colour 638.14
Currency: United States Dollars
DAILY NEWSPAPER

Kenosha News 14808
Owner: United Communications Corp.
Editorial: 5800 7th Ave, Kenosha, Wisconsin 53140-4131 **Tel:** 1 262 657-1000
Email: newsroom@kenoshanews.com **Web site:** http://www.kenoshanews.com
Freq: Daily; **Circ:** 19051 Not Audited
Profile: Kenosha News is a daily newspaper serving residents of Kenosha County, WI. The newspaper provides news, community events, entertainment and sports.
Language (s): English
Ad Rate: Full Page Mono 35.00
Ad Rate: Full Page Colour 38.55
Currency: United States Dollars
DAILY NEWSPAPER

Kent County Daily Times 404236
Owner: R.I.S.N. Operations Inc.
Editorial: 1353 Main St, West Warwick, Rhode Island 02893-3859 **Tel:** 1 401 821-7400
Web site: http://www.ricentral.com
Freq: Mon thru Fri; **Circ:** 1355 Not Audited
Publisher: Nanci Batson; **Editor:** Jeremiah Ryan
Profile: Kent County Daily Times is a daily newspaper serving Kent County, RI. It provides local, regional, national and international news. It also contains sports, entertainment, education, business and feature stories. Advertising deadlines are at 3pm ET three days prior to publication.
Language (s): English
Ad Rate: Full Page Mono 14.03
Ad Rate: Full Page Colour 480.00
Currency: United States Dollars
DAILY NEWSPAPER

Kenton Times 14461
Owner: Barnes Newspapers (Ray)
Editorial: 201 E Columbus St, Kenton, Ohio 43326-1583 **Tel:** 1 419 674-4066
Email: kteditor@kentontimes.com **Web site:** http://www.kentontimes.com
Freq: Daily; **Circ:** 7200 Not Audited
Publisher: Jeff Barnes; **Advertising Sales Manager:** Lesa Heacock; **Editor:** Tim Thomas
Profile: Kenton Times is the local newspaper for residents of Kenton, OH and the surrounding area. The newspaper covers the local news, sports, government, and events that are of interest to the community.
Language (s): English
Ad Rate: Full Page Mono 8.50
Ad Rate: Full Page Colour 255.00
Currency: United States Dollars
DAILY NEWSPAPER

The Kentucky Enquirer 15280
Owner: Gannett Co., Inc.
Editorial: 226 Grandview Dr, Fort Mitchell, Kentucky 41017-2702 **Tel:** 1 859 578-5555
Email: localnews@enquirer.com **Web site:** http://www.cincinnati.com/news/northern-kentucky
Freq: Daily; **Circ:** 21495 Not Audited
Profile: The Kentucky Enquirer is a supplement to the Cincinnati Enquirer and its coverage includes the three Northern counties of Kentucky.
Language (s): English
Ad Rate: Full Page Mono 58.00
Ad Rate: Full Page Colour 60.00
Currency: United States Dollars
DAILY NEWSPAPER

Kentucky New Era 14081
Owner: Kentucky New Era, Inc.
Editorial: 1618 E 9th St, Hopkinsville, Kentucky 42240-4430 **Tel:** 1 270 886-4444
Email: editor@kentuckynewera.com **Web site:** http://www.kentuckynewera.com
Freq: Mon thru Fri; **Circ:** 7361 Not Audited
Publisher: Taylor Hayes; **Editor:** Eli Pace
Profile: Kentucky New Era is a daily newspaper published for the residents of Christian, Todd, Caldwell and Trigg County, KY. The newspaper provides information on local and national news. Send all press releases to the managing editor.
Language (s): English
Ad Rate: Full Page Mono 11.00
Ad Rate: Full Page Colour 195.00
Currency: United States Dollars
DAILY NEWSPAPER

Kerrville Daily Times 14706
Owner: Southern Newspapers, Inc.
Editorial: 429 Jefferson St, Kerrville, Texas 78028-4412 **Tel:** 1 830 896-7000
Email: news@dailytimes.com **Web site:** http://dailytimes.com
Freq: Daily; **Circ:** 7852 Not Audited
Publisher & Editor: Mike Graxiola
Profile: Kerrville Daily Times is published daily for residents in Kerr County, TX. The newspaper covers local and national news, sports, business and lifestyle.
Language (s): English
Ad Rate: Full Page Mono 16.30
Ad Rate: Full Page Colour 320.00
Currency: United States Dollars
DAILY NEWSPAPER

Ketchikan Daily News 13660
Owner: Pioneer Printing Co., Inc.
Editorial: 501 Dock St, Ketchikan, Alaska 99901-6411 **Tel:** 1 907 225-3157
Email: news@ketchikandailynews.com **Web site:** http://www.ketchikandailynews.com
Freq: Daily; **Circ:** 3500
Publisher: Tena Williams
Profile: Ketchikan Daily News covers a mix of local, state, national and international news serving the residents of Ketchikan and other parts of Southeast Alaska. The newspaper is published every day except Sunday.
Language (s): English
Ad Rate: Full Page Mono 16.20
Ad Rate: Full Page Colour 320.00
Currency: United States Dollars
DAILY NEWSPAPER

The Key West Citizen 13818
Owner: Cooke Communications LLC
Editorial: 3420 Northside Dr, Key West, Florida 33040-4254 **Tel:** 1 305 292-7777
Email: editor@keysnews.com **Web site:** http://www.keysnews.com
Freq: Daily; **Circ:** 8468 Not Audited
Publisher: Paul Clarin; **Editor:** Kay Harris
Profile: The Key West Citizen is a local daily newspaper serving the residents of Key West, FL and surrounding areas. The publication covers local news events, weather, sports, business and arts & entertainment.
Language (s): English
Ad Rate: Full Page Mono 26.08
Currency: United States Dollars
DAILY NEWSPAPER

Killeen Daily Herald 14708
Owner: Maybom Enterprises
Editorial: 1809 Florence Rd, Killeen, Texas 76541-8977 **Tel:** 1 254 634-2125
Email: news@kdhnews.com **Web site:** http://www.kdhnews.com
Freq: Daily; **Circ:** 16534 Not Audited
Publisher: Sue Mayborn
Profile: Killeen Daily Herald is written for residents in Killeen, Fort Hood, Harker Heights and Copper's Cove, TX. It covers, local, national and state news, arts & entertainment, lifestyles, sports and courts. It shares offices with the Fort Hood Herald. Press releases should be e-mailed or faxed to the managing editor.
Language (s): English
Ad Rate: Full Page Mono 24.93
Ad Rate: Full Page Colour 85.13
Currency: United States Dollars
DAILY NEWSPAPER

Kingman Daily Miner 13712
Owner: Western Newspapers, Inc.
Editorial: 3015 N Stockton Hill Rd, Kingman, Arizona 86401-4162 **Tel:** 1 928 753-6397
Email: opinion@kdminer.com **Web site:** http://www.kingmandailyminer.com
Freq: Daily; **Circ:** 7595 Not Audited
Profile: Kingman Daily Miner is a newspaper written for the residents of Kingman, AZ. It provides local news, weather and sports.
Language (s): English
Ad Rate: Full Page Mono 17.07
Ad Rate: Full Page Colour 57.37
Currency: United States Dollars
DAILY NEWSPAPER

Kingsport Times-News 14671
Owner: Sandusky Newspapers Inc.
Editorial: 701 Lynn Garden Dr, Kingsport, Tennessee 37660-5607 **Tel:** 1 423 246-8121
Email: news@timesnews.net **Web site:** http://www.timesnews.net
Freq: Daily; **Circ:** 34230 Not Audited
Profile: Kingsport Times-News' editorial mission is to be the watchdog of the community, and to provide local news and information to its readers. The publication is written for Hawkins County and Southwest Virginia.
Language (s): English
Ad Rate: Full Page Mono 55.00
Ad Rate: Full Page Colour 294.90
Currency: United States Dollars
DAILY NEWSPAPER

The Kinston Free Press 14302
Owner: GateHouse Media Inc.
Editorial: 2103 N Queen St, Kinston, North Carolina 28501-1622 **Tel:** 1 252 527-3191
Web site: http://www.kinston.com
Freq: Daily; **Circ:** 6995 Not Audited
Profile: The Free Press covers local community news, sports and weather. The publication is written for the residents of Kinston, NC.
Language (s): English
Ad Rate: Full Page Mono 22.00
Ad Rate: Full Page Colour 230.00
Currency: United States Dollars
DAILY NEWSPAPER

Kirksville Daily Express 14237
Owner: GateHouse Media Inc.
Editorial: 110 E McPherson St, Kirksville, Missouri 63501-3506 **Tel:** 1 660 665-2808
Email: dailyexpresseditor@gmail.com **Web site:** http://www.kirksvilledailyexpress.com
Freq: Daily; **Circ:** 4270 Not Audited
Profile: Kirksville Daily Express is written for residents of Kirksville, MO. It covers local, national and international news, sports, food and health.
Language (s): English
Ad Rate: Full Page Mono 10.05
Currency: United States Dollars
DAILY NEWSPAPER

Kitsap Sun 14781
Owner: Gannett Co., Inc.
Editorial: 545 5th St, Bremerton, Washington 98337-1413 **Tel:** 1 360 377-3711
Email: sunnews@kitsapsun.com **Web site:** http://www.kitsapsun.com
Freq: Daily; **Circ:** 28262 Not Audited
Publisher: Brent Morris; **Editor:** David Nelson
Profile: Kitsap Sun in Bremerton, WA provides local news, events and sports coverage.
Language (s): English
Ad Rate: Full Page Mono 50.09
Ad Rate: Full Page Colour 352.32
Currency: United States Dollars
DAILY NEWSPAPER

Klamath Falls Herald and News 14555
Owner: Pioneer Newspapers
Editorial: 2701 Foothills Blvd, Klamath Falls, Oregon 97603-3785 **Tel:** 1 541 885-4410
Email: news@heraldandnews.com **Web site:** http://www.heraldandnews.com
Freq: Fri; **Circ:** 14947 Not Audited
Profile: Klamath Falls Herald and News is published daily for the residents of Klamath Falls, OR and surrounding areas. The newspaper covers local news, business, sports, entertainment and community events.
Language (s): English
Ad Rate: Full Page Mono 27.25
Ad Rate: Full Page Colour 48.93
Currency: United States Dollars
DAILY NEWSPAPER

Knoxville News Sentinel 15334
Owner: Gannett Co., Inc.
Editorial: 2332 News Sentinel Dr, Knoxville, Tennessee 37921-5766 **Tel:** 1 865 523-3131
Email: news@knoxnews.com **Web site:** http://www.knoxnews.com
Freq: Daily; **Circ:** 76525 Not Audited
Profile: The Knoxville News Sentinel is a daily newspaper for Knoxville and Eastern Tennessee residents. Coverage includes breaking news, business, arts & entertainment, lifestyle and sports.
Language (s): English
Ad Rate: Full Page Mono 109.73
Currency: United States Dollars
DAILY NEWSPAPER

Kodiak Daily Mirror 14862
Owner: MediaNews Group
Editorial: 1419 Selig St, Kodiak, Alaska 99615-6450 **Tel:** 1 907 486-3227
Email: info@kodiakdailymirror.com **Web site:** http://www.kodiakdailymirror.com
Freq: Daily; **Circ:** 3000 Not Audited
Publisher: Richard Harris
Profile: Kodiak Daily Mirror is a local paper serving residents of Kodiak, AK and surrounding villages. Coverage includes local news, sports and features.
Language (s): English
Ad Rate: Full Page Mono 12.75
Ad Rate: Full Page Colour 101.69
Currency: United States Dollars
DAILY NEWSPAPER

Kokomo Tribune 13994
Owner: Community Newspaper Holdings, Inc.
Editorial: 300 N Union St, Kokomo, Indiana 46901-4612 **Tel:** 1 765 459-3121
Email: ktnews@kokomotribune.com **Web site:** http://kokomotribune.com
Freq: Daily; **Circ:** 15595 Not Audited
Publisher: Robyn McCloskey
Profile: Kokomo Tribune is published daily for the residents of Howard County, IN. The newspaper covers local, national, and international news, as well as topics such as sports, business, agriculture, and education.
Language (s): English
Ad Rate: Full Page Mono 45.40
Ad Rate: Full Page Colour 145.92
Currency: United States Dollars
DAILY NEWSPAPER

The Korea Daily - Chicago 152992
Owner: JMNet USA
Editorial: 790 Busse Rd, Elk Grove Village, Illinois 60007-2118 **Tel:** 1 847 228-7200
Email: edited.chicago@koreadaily.com **Web site:** http://www.koreadaily.com
Freq: Mon thru Fri; **Circ:** 100000 Not Audited
Publisher: Hyun Kee Kwon; **Advertising Sales Manager:** Young Kwon
Profile: Korea Daily is a daily newspaper serving the Korean community of Chicago. Associated with Joongang Media Network.
Language (s): Korean
Ad Rate: Full Page Mono 31.53
Ad Rate: Full Page Colour 40.55
Currency: United States Dollars
DAILY NEWSPAPER

Korea Daily - Los Angeles 80004
Owner: JMNet USA
Editorial: 690 Wilshire Pl, Los Angeles, California 90005-3930 **Tel:** 1 213 368-2500
Web site: http://www.koreadaily.com
Freq: Daily; **Circ:** 72000 Not Audited
Publisher: Intek Park
Profile: Korea Daily is a daily newspaper providing news to the Korean community in Los Angeles. Associated with Joongang Media Network.
Language (s): English
Ad Rate: Full Page Mono 8.27
Currency: United States Dollars
DAILY NEWSPAPER

The Korea Daily - Los Angeles Bureau 663907
Owner: JMNet USA
Editorial: 690 Wilshire Pl, Los Angeles, California 90005-3930 **Tel:** 1 213 368-2500
Freq: Daily
Bureau Chief: Chang Yeon Hwa
Language (s): Korean
DAILY NEWSPAPER

The Korea Daily - New York 155457
Owner: JMNet USA
Editorial: 4327 36th St, Long Island City, New York 11101-1703 **Tel:** 1 718 361-7700
Email: nyopinion@koreadaily.com **Web site:** http://www.koreadaily.com
Freq: Daily; **Circ:** 58750 Not Audited
Advertising Sales Manager: Wansub Kong
Profile: Korea Daily news is a Korean language newspaper for residents in and around New York City. Associated with Joongang Media Network.
Language (s): Korean
Ad Rate: Full Page Mono 23.27
Ad Rate: Full Page Colour 4511.00
Currency: United States Dollars
DAILY NEWSPAPER

Korea Times Chicago Edition 152982
Owner: Korea Times
Editorial: 615 Milwaukee Ave Ste 12, Glenview, Illinois 60025-3878 **Tel:** 1 847 626-0388
Email: sub@chicagokoreatimes.com **Web site:** http://chi.koreatimes.com
Freq: Mon thru Fri; **Circ:** 50000 Not Audited
Advertising Sales Manager: Yun Huh; **Publisher & Editor:** Dustin Lee
Profile: Korea Times Chicago Edition is a daily, Korean-language paper serving the residents of Chicago. It provides local, national and international news.
Language (s): Korean
Ad Rate: Full Page Colour 50.00
Currency: United States Dollars
DAILY NEWSPAPER

Korea Times DC Edition 546587
Editorial: 7601 Little River Tpke, Annandale, Virginia 22003-2601 **Tel:** 1 703 941-8001
Email: edit@koreatimesdc.com **Web site:** http://koreatimes.com
Freq: Daily; **Circ:** 50000
Editor: Pae Park
Profile: Korea Times DC Edition in Annandale, VA is a daily newspaper serving the Korean population in Virginia and the District of Columbia.
Language (s): Vietnamese
Ad Rate: Full Page Mono 9.70
Ad Rate: Full Page Colour 77.66
Currency: United States Dollars
DAILY NEWSPAPER

Korea Times Los Angeles Edition 80005
Editorial: 4525 Wilshire Blvd, Los Angeles, California 90010 **Tel:** 1 323 692-2000
Web site: http://www.koreatimes.com
Freq: Daily; **Circ:** 70000 Not Audited
Publisher: Jae Min Chang; **International News Editor:** Kang Lee
Profile: Korea Times Los Angeles Edition (Hankook Ilbo) has been an integral part of the Korean American community since its founding in 1967. In partnership with Korean American communities nationwide, the Times seeks to provide hard news, which is presented from a culturally informed perspective. The paper is the most established Korean daily newspaper in the United States, in that it is the longest-running paper and the largest in terms of circulation. The paper features headline news from Korea and around the world, as well as coverage of breaking news in the United States.
Language (s): English
Ad Rate: Full Page Mono 22.00
Ad Rate: Full Page Colour 3528.00
Currency: United States Dollars
DAILY NEWSPAPER

Korea Times New York Edition 79982
Owner: Shin (Hak-Yeon)
Editorial: 4222 27th St, Long Island City, New York 11101-4107 **Tel:** 1 718 482-1122
Email: ktnyedit@gmail.com **Web site:** http://www.koreatimes.com
Freq: Mon thru Fri; **Circ:** 45000 Not Audited
Publisher: Jae Min Chang
Profile: Korea Times New York Edition covers local, regional, national and international news. It is geared toward a Korean audience. The ad rate provided is for the smallest size black-and-white ad available. The color rate is only offered for the front page, which is also for the smallest size available.
Language (s): Korean
Ad Rate: Full Page Mono 11.60
Ad Rate: Full Page Colour 28.98
Currency: United States Dollars
DAILY NEWSPAPER

Korea Times San Francisco Edition 80013
Owner: Korea Daily News, Inc.
Editorial: 8134 Capwell Dr, Oakland, California 94621-2110 **Tel:** 1 510 777-0909
Email: ktnews247@yahoo.com **Web site:** http://sf.koreatimes.com
Freq: Daily; **Circ:** 30000 Not Audited
Publisher: Michael Kang
Profile: Korean Times San Francisco is published daily for the Asian residents of San Francisco. The edition covers local news, arts & entertainment and sports and is written in Korean.
Language (s): English
Ad Rate: Full Page Mono 8.51
Ad Rate: Full Page Colour 25.94
Currency: United States Dollars
DAILY NEWSPAPER

Korea Times Seattle Edition 152984
Owner: Korea Times USA (The)
Editorial: 12532 Aurora Ave N, Seattle, Washington 98133-8036 **Tel:** 1 206 622-2229
Web site: http://www.koreatimes.com
Freq: Fri; **Circ:** 10000 Not Audited
Advertising Sales Manager: Hong Kim; **Editor and Publisher:** Yeo-chun Yun
Profile: The Korea Times is the oldest independent and most influential English daily in Korea, has served as Korea's bridge to the world since November 1, 1950.
Language (s): Korean
Ad Rate: Full Page Mono 40.00
Currency: United States Dollars
DAILY NEWSPAPER

L.A. Web Inc. Newspapers 349773
Owner: L.A. Web, Inc.
Editorial: 9639 Telstar Ave, El Monte, California 91731-3003 **Tel:** 1 626 453-8800
Web site: http://www.chinesedaily.com
Circ: 85000 Not Audited
Language (s): English
DAILY NEWSPAPER

La Crosse Tribune 14809
Owner: Lee Enterprises, Inc.
Editorial: 401 3rd St N, La Crosse, Wisconsin 54601 **Tel:** 1 608 782-9710
Email: news@lacrossetribune.com **Web site:** http://www.lacrossetribune.com
Freq: Daily; **Circ:** 28904
Publisher: Russell Cunningham; **Editor:** Scott Rada
Profile: La Crosse Tribune is a daily newspaper written for the residents of La Crosse, WI. It covers local news, sports, entertainment, events and health. The lead time varies according to topic.
Language (s): English
Ad Rate: Full Page Mono 35.96
Ad Rate: Full Page Colour 247.00
Currency: United States Dollars
DAILY NEWSPAPER

La Junta Tribune-Democrat 13787
Owner: GateHouse Media Inc.
Editorial: 422 Colorado Ave, La Junta, Colorado 81050-2336 **Tel:** 1 719 384-4475
Email: eevans@ljtdmail.com **Web site:** http://www.lajuntatribunedemocrat.com
Freq: Daily; **Circ:** 2500 Not Audited
Advertising Sales Manager: Jason Gallegos; **Editor & Publisher:** Candi Hill
Profile: La Junta Tribune-Democrat is a local newspaper written for the residents of La Junta, CO. It provides information on local news, weather and sports.
Language (s): English
Ad Rate: Full Page Mono 8.25
Ad Rate: Full Page Colour 60.00
Currency: United States Dollars
DAILY NEWSPAPER

Laconia Daily Sun 217090
Editorial: 65 Water St, Laconia, New Hampshire 03246-3378 **Tel:** 1 603 527-9299
Email: news@laconiadailysun.com **Web site:** http://www.laconiadailysun.com
Freq: Daily; **Circ:** 14000 Not Audited
Publisher: Mark Guerringue
Profile: Laconia Daily Sun is a local daily newspaper written for residents of Laconia, NH and the surrounding area. The publication covers local news and community events. Although there is no set deadline for press release submissions, it is suggested that they be sent one to two days prior to the issue date. After 80 years as an afternoon paper, it switched to morning circulation in November 2006.
Language (s): English
Ad Rate: Full Page Mono 6.00
Ad Rate: Full Page Colour 100.00
Currency: United States Dollars
DAILY NEWSPAPER

LaGrange Daily News 13846
Owner: Boone Newspapers Inc.
Editorial: 105 Ashton St, Lagrange, Georgia 30240-3111 **Tel:** 1 706 884-7311
Email: editor@lagrangenews.com **Web site:** http://www.lagrangenews.com
Freq: Daily; **Circ:** 10280 Not Audited
Publisher: Rick Thomason
Profile: LaGrange Daily News is published daily for the residents of Lagrange, GA and surrounding areas. The newspaper cover local and state news, business, sports, lifestyle and entertainment.
Language (s): English
Ad Rate: Full Page Mono 12.45
Ad Rate: Full Page Colour 75.63
Currency: United States Dollars
DAILY NEWSPAPER

Lake City Reporter 13819
Owner: Community Newspapers Inc.
Editorial: 180 E Duval St, Lake City, Florida 32055-4085 **Tel:** 1 386 752-1293
Email: news@lakecityreporter.com **Web site:** http://www.lakecityreporter.com
Freq: Daily; **Circ:** 6630
Editor: Robert Bridges; **Publisher:** Todd Wilson
Profile: Lake City Reporter's editorial mission is to provide the most accurate and fair comprehensive local news coverage to residents of Columbia and surrounding counties. The publication is written for residents of Columbia County, FL.
Language (s): English
Ad Rate: Full Page Mono 20.25
Ad Rate: Full Page Colour 225.00
Currency: United States Dollars
DAILY NEWSPAPER

Lake County Record-Bee 13733
Owner: MediaNews Group
Editorial: 2150 S Main St, Lakeport, California 95453-5620 **Tel:** 1 707 263-5636
Email: rbcommunitydesk@gmail.com **Web site:** http://www.record-bee.com
Freq: Fri; **Circ:** 4638 Not Audited
Profile: Lake County Record-Bee's editorial mission is to inform the public of Lake County, CA about local news and information.
Language (s): English
Ad Rate: Full Page Mono 13.00
Ad Rate: Full Page Colour 66.24
Currency: United States Dollars
DAILY NEWSPAPER

Lake Sun 14895
Owner: GateHouse Media Inc.
Editorial: 918 N Business Route 5, Camdenton, Missouri 65020-2648 **Tel:** 1 573 346-2132
Email: newsroom@lakesunonline.com **Web site:** http://www.lakenewsonline.com
Freq: Mon thru Fri; **Circ:** 6087
Profile: Lake Sun Leader is a daily newspaper written for the residents of Camdenton, MO. It covers local, national and international news, as well as local recreation, arts, sports and milestones, such as births, deaths and weddings.
Language (s): English
Ad Rate: Full Page Mono 8.80
Ad Rate: Full Page Colour 11.80
Currency: United States Dollars
DAILY NEWSPAPER

Lancaster Eagle-Gazette 14462
Owner: Gannett Co., Inc.
Editorial: 138 W Chestnut St, Lancaster, Ohio 43130-4308 **Tel:** 1 740 654-1321
Email: laneg@nncogannett.com **Web site:** http://www.lancastereaglegazette.com
Freq: Daily; **Circ:** 7687 Not Audited
Profile: Lancaster Eagle-Gazette covers local news and events for residents of Lancaster (Franklin County), OH. It is written for residents of Lancaster, OH and surrounding area.
Language (s): English
Ad Rate: Full Page Mono 29.40
Ad Rate: Full Page Colour 31.66
Currency: United States Dollars
DAILY NEWSPAPER

Lansing State Journal 14178
Owner: Gannett Co. Inc.
Editorial: 120 E Lenawee St, Lansing, Michigan 48919-1000 **Tel:** 1 517 377-1000
Email: metro@lsj.com **Web site:** http://www.lansingstatejournal.com
Freq: Daily; **Circ:** 33523 Not Audited
Advertising Sales Manager: Clark Schnepf
Profile: Lansing (MI) State Journal is a daily newspaper that covers local news, Michigan state government news, local business, entertainment, high school and Michigan State University athletics, and lifestyle topics.
Language (s): English
Ad Rate: Full Page Mono 103.00
Ad Rate: Full Page Colour 352.32
Currency: United States Dollars
DAILY NEWSPAPER

Laramie Daily Boomerang 14850
Owner: Wyoming Newspaper Group
Editorial: 320 E Grand Ave, Laramie, Wyoming 82070-3712 **Tel:** 1 307 742-2176
Email: news@laramieboomerang.com **Web site:** http://www.laramieboomerang.com
Freq: Daily; **Circ:** 5233 Not Audited
Profile: Laramie Daily Boomerang is a daily newspaper written for the residents of Laramie, WY and surrounding areas. The newspaper includes coverage of local news, weather, sports, business and lifestyle issues.
Language (s): English
Ad Rate: Full Page Mono 13.80
Ad Rate: Full Page Colour 580.00
Currency: United States Dollars
DAILY NEWSPAPER

Laredo Morning Times 14970
Owner: Hearst Newspapers
Editorial: 111 Esperanza Dr, Laredo, Texas 78041-2607 **Tel:** 1 956 728-2500
Email: times@lmtonline.com **Web site:** http://www.lmtonline.com
Freq: Daily; **Circ:** 13153 Not Audited
News Editor: Nick Georgiou; **Publisher:** William Green
Profile: Laredo Morning Times is a daily newspaper published in Laredo, TX. It covers local news, business, sports and entertainment. The paper also features a daily Spanish-language news section, Tiemp de Laredo. Deadlines are at 10pm daily.
Language (s): English
Ad Rate: Full Page Mono 51.35
Ad Rate: Full Page Colour 162.21
Currency: United States Dollars
DAILY NEWSPAPER

Las Cruces Sun-News 14377
Owner: Gannett Co., Inc.
Editorial: 256 W Las Cruces Ave, Las Cruces, New Mexico 88005-1804 **Tel:** 1 575 541-5400
Email: news@lcsun-news.com **Web site:** http://www.lcsun-news.com
Freq: Daily; **Circ:** 26745 Not Audited
Profile: Las Cruces Sun-News is the local daily newspaper for Las Cruces, NM and the surrounding communities. The editorial content covers local news, sports and business.
Language (s): English
Ad Rate: Full Page Mono 34.71
Ad Rate: Full Page Colour 238.82
Currency: United States Dollars
DAILY NEWSPAPER

Las Vegas Review-Journal 15301
Owner: News + Media Capital Group LLC
Editorial: 1111 W Bonanza Rd, Las Vegas, Nevada 89106-3545 **Tel:** 1 702 383-0211
Email: newstips@reviewjournal.com **Web site:** http://www.reviewjournal.com
Freq: Daily
Profile: Las Vegas Review-Journal is a daily newspaper written for the residents of Las Vegas. It covers local, regional and national news, business, entertainment, health, food, sports and lifestyle. The Las Vegas Sun is circulated daily within the Las Vegas Review-Journal as a six-to-10 page section. The Sun maintains its liberal editorial voice which is independent of the Review-Journal.
Language (s): English
Ad Rate: Full Page Mono 234.52
Ad Rate: Full Page Colour 262.51
Currency: United States Dollars
DAILY NEWSPAPER

Las Vegas Review-Journal - Carson City Bureau 15789
Editorial: Carson City, Nevada
Bureau Chief: Sean Whaley
Language (s): English
DAILY NEWSPAPER

Las Vegas Sun 14878
Owner: Greenspun Media Group
Editorial: 2275 Corporate Cir Ste 300, Henderson, Nevada 89074-7745 **Tel:** 1 702 385-3111
Web site: http://www.lasvegassun.com
Freq: Daily; **Circ:** 180000
Publisher & Editor: Brian Greenspun; **Advertising Sales Manager:** Stephanie Reviea
Profile: Las Vegas Sun is a daily newspaper covering local news, business, sports and travel for the Las Vegas community. It is published under a Joint Operating Agreement with the Las Vegas Review-Journal, but remains an independent and separate entity.
Language (s): English
Ad Rate: Full Page Mono 225.14
Ad Rate: Full Page Colour 1363.67
Currency: United States Dollars
DAILY NEWSPAPER

Las Vegas Sun - Carson City Bureau 231053
Editorial: 101 N Carson St, Carson City, Nevada 89701-3713 **Tel:** 1 775 687-5032
Bureau Chief: Cy Ryan
Language (s): English
DAILY NEWSPAPER

Latrobe Bulletin 14593
Owner: Sample News Group
Editorial: 1211 Ligonier St, Latrobe, Pennsylvania 15650-1921 **Tel:** 1 724 537-3351
Email: lb.news@verizon.net **Web site:** http://www.latrobebulletinnews.com/
Freq: Daily; **Circ:** 7988 Not Audited
News Editor: Marie McCandless; **Publisher:** Gary Siegel
Profile: Latrobe Bulletin is a newspaper written for residents of Latrobe, PA. The newspaper, published six days per week, covers local news and events in Latrobe, PA. The lead time varies. Contact the publication for advertising rates. The publication is not available on World Wide Web.
Language (s): English
Ad Rate: Full Page Mono 14.25
Ad Rate: Full Page Colour 150.00
Currency: United States Dollars
DAILY NEWSPAPER

Laurel Leader-Call 14266
Owner: Gin Creek Publishing
Editorial: 318 N Magnolia St, Laurel, Mississippi 39440-3932 **Tel:** 1 601 649-9388
Web site: http://leader-call.com
Freq: Sat; **Circ:** 6733 Not Audited
Profile: Laurel Leader-Call is a newspaper for the residents of Laurel County and Jones County, MS. It provides local and national news, business, lifestyle and sports.
Language (s): English
Ad Rate: Full Page Mono 12.50
Ad Rate: Full Page Colour 86.14
Currency: United States Dollars
DAILY NEWSPAPER

The Laurinburg Exchange 14940
Owner: Heartland Publications
Editorial: 211 W Cronly St, Laurinburg, North Carolina 28352-3637 **Tel:** 1 910 276-2311
Web site: http://www.laurinburgexchange.com
Freq: Daily; **Circ:** 8450 Not Audited
Profile: The Laurinburg Exchange is published daily for the residents of Laurinburg, NC and surrounding areas. The newspaper provides information on local news and community events. Deadlines are at 5pm ET one day prior to issue date.
Language (s): English
Ad Rate: Full Page Mono 9.85
Ad Rate: Full Page Colour 250.00
Currency: United States Dollars
DAILY NEWSPAPER

Lawrence Journal-World 14054
Owner: Ogden Newspapers
Editorial: 645 New Hampshire St, Lawrence, Kansas 66044-2243 **Tel:** 1 785 843-1000
Email: news@ljworld.com **Web site:** http://www2.ljworld.com/
Freq: Daily; **Circ:** 21245 Not Audited
Profile: Lawrence Journal-World is a daily newspaper published for the residents of Lawrence, KS and surrounding areas. The publication covers local, national and international news and sports.
Language (s): English
Ad Rate: Full Page Mono 27.95
Ad Rate: Full Page Colour 345.00
Currency: United States Dollars
DAILY NEWSPAPER

The Lawton Constitution 14528
Owner: Lawton Publishing Company, Inc.
Editorial: 102 SW 3rd St, Lawton, Oklahoma 73501-4031 **Tel:** 1 580 353-0620
Web site: http://www.swoknews.com
Freq: Daily; **Circ:** 18937 Not Audited
Editor: Steve Metzer; **News Editor:** De Ann Patterson
Profile: The Lawton Constitution is a daily newspaper distributed in the Lawton, OK area. The paper covers local news, recreation, high school sports and community events. National news is taken primarily from the wires. Deadlines are daily at 8pm CT.
Language (s): English
Ad Rate: Full Page Mono 19.45
Ad Rate: Full Page Colour 120.61
Currency: United States Dollars
DAILY NEWSPAPER

Le Mars Daily Sentinel 13883
Owner: Rust Communications
Editorial: 41 1st Ave NE, Le Mars, Iowa 51031-3535 **Tel:** 1 712 546-7031
Email: lemarssentinel@gmail.com **Web site:** http://www.lemarssentinel.com
Freq: Daily; **Circ:** 2684 Not Audited
Publisher: Randy List
Profile: Le Mars Daily Sentinel is published daily for the residents of Le Mars, IA and surrounding areas. It covers local and state news, business, sports and entertainment.
Language (s): English
Ad Rate: Full Page Mono 10.50
Ad Rate: Full Page Colour 100.00
Currency: United States Dollars
DAILY NEWSPAPER

The Leader 14397
Owner: Gatehouse Media, LLC
Editorial: 34 W Pulteney St, Corning, New York 14830-2211 **Tel:** 1 607 936-4651
Web site: http://www.the-leader.com
Freq: Daily; **Circ:** 13585 Not Audited
Profile: The Leader is a daily newspaper published for the residents Corning, Hornell and Bath, NY. It covers local news, sports and public opinions.
Language (s): English
Ad Rate: Full Page Mono 22.00
Ad Rate: Full Page Colour 142.66
Currency: United States Dollars
DAILY NEWSPAPER

Leader Times 14589
Owner: West Penn Media Group, LLC
Editorial: 11931 State Route 85 Ste E, Kittanning, Pennsylvania 16201-3741 **Tel:** 1 724 543-1303
Email: newsroom@leadertimes.com **Web site:** http://www.leadertimes.com
Freq: Mon thru Fri; **Circ:** 8104 Not Audited
Profile: Leader Times' editorial mission is to be the local source of news and information for Kittanning and Armstrong counties.
Language (s): English
Ad Rate: Full Page Mono 200.65
Ad Rate: Full Page Colour 1177.80
Currency: United States Dollars
DAILY NEWSPAPER

Leader-Herald 14403
Owner: Ogden Newspapers
Editorial: 8 E Fulton St, Gloversville, New York 12078-3283 **Tel:** 1 518 725-8616
Email: news@leaderherald.com **Web site:** http://www.leaderherald.com
Freq: Daily; **Circ:** 6937 Not Audited
Editor: Bill Trojan
Profile: Leader-Herald is a daily newspaper published for the residents of Gloversville, NY and surrounding areas. It provides information on local and national news, sports and community events. The lead time varies.
Language (s): English
Ad Rate: Full Page Mono 16.95
Ad Rate: Full Page Colour 215.00
Currency: United States Dollars
DAILY NEWSPAPER

Leader-Telegram 14802
Owner: Eau Claire Press Company
Editorial: 701 S Farwell St, Eau Claire, Wisconsin 54701-3831 **Tel:** 1 715 833-9200
Email: leadertelegram@ecpc.com **Web site:** http://www.leadertelegram.com
Freq: Daily; **Circ:** 18780 Not Audited
Editor: Andrew Dowd; **Publisher:** Pieter Graaskamp; **Editor:** Steve Kinderman
Profile: Leader-Telegram is a daily newspaper published for the residents of Eau Claire County, Chippewa Falls, and Menomonie, WI. The publication covers local news, sports, entertainment, government, business news, local schools, religion, food, health, travel, and community events.
Language (s): English
Ad Rate: Full Page Mono 33.10
Ad Rate: Full Page Colour 221.51
Currency: United States Dollars
DAILY NEWSPAPER

The Leaf-Chronicle 14662
Owner: Gannett Co., Inc.
Editorial: 200 Commerce St, Clarksville, Tennessee 37040-5101 **Tel:** 1 931 552-1808
Web site: http://www.theleafchronicle.com
Freq: Daily; **Circ:** 13207 Not Audited
Profile: The Leaf-Chronicle is a daily newspaper written for the residents of Clarksville, TN. The publication covers local news, sports, business news, local government, education and crime.
Language (s): English
Ad Rate: Full Page Mono 35.54
Ad Rate: Full Page Colour 250.00
Currency: United States Dollars
DAILY NEWSPAPER

The Leavenworth Times 14055
Owner: GateHouse Media Inc.
Editorial: 422 Seneca St, Leavenworth, Kansas 66048-1910 **Tel:** 1 913 682-0305
Email: news@leavenworthtimes.com **Web site:** http://www.leavenworthtimes.com
Freq: Daily; **Circ:** 6741 Not Audited
News Editor: Rimsie McConiga
Profile: The Leavenworth Times is a daily newspaper published for the residents of Leavenworth, KS. It covers local news and community events.
Language (s): English
Ad Rate: Full Page Mono 13.50
Ad Rate: Full Page Colour 75.88
Currency: United States Dollars
DAILY NEWSPAPER

Lebanon Daily News 14594
Owner: Gannett Co., Inc.
Editorial: 718 Poplar St, Lebanon, Pennsylvania 17042-6755 **Tel:** 1 717 272-5611
Email: citydesk@ldnews.com **Web site:** http://www.ldnews.com
Freq: Daily; **Circ:** 20606
Profile: Lebanon Daily News covers international, national, local, business, arts & entertainment and sports news. The publication is geared toward residents of Lebanon, PA and the surrounding area.
Language (s): English
Ad Rate: Full Page Mono 29.50
Ad Rate: Full Page Colour 425.00
Currency: United States Dollars
DAILY NEWSPAPER

Lebanon Daily Record 14238
Owner: Lebanon Publishing Company
Editorial: 100 E Commercial St, Lebanon, Missouri 65536 **Tel:** 1 417 532-9131
Email: editor@lebanondailyrecord.com **Web site:** http://www.lebanondailyrecord.com
Freq: Daily; **Circ:** 4496 Not Audited
Advertising Sales Manager: Rene Barker; **Editor:** Julie Turner-Crawford; **Publisher:** Dalton Wright
Profile: Lebanon Daily Record is published daily for the residents of Lebanon, MO. The newspaper covers local news, sports and community events. Deadlines are at 3pm CT.
Language (s): English
Ad Rate: Full Page Mono 8.55
Ad Rate: Full Page Colour 180.00
Currency: United States Dollars
DAILY NEWSPAPER

Lebanon Democrat 14672
Owner: Sandusky Newspapers Inc.
Editorial: 402 N Cumberland St, Lebanon, Tennessee 37087-2306 **Tel:** 1 615 444-3952
Email: newsclerk@lebanondemocrat.com **Web site:** http://www.lebanondemocrat.com
Freq: Daily; **Circ:** 6789 Not Audited
Publisher: Jesse Lindsey
Profile: Lebanon Democrat is a daily, local newspaper targeted at the Lebanon, TN area. The paper covers local news, sports, business and community events. Deadlines are noon CT on Mondays through Thursdays, and at 11am CT on Fridays.
Language (s): English
Ad Rate: Full Page Mono 12.25
Ad Rate: Full Page Colour 46.86
Currency: United States Dollars
DAILY NEWSPAPER

The Lebanon Reporter 13997
Owner: Community Newspaper Holdings, Inc.
Editorial: 117 E Washington St, Lebanon, Indiana 46052-2209 **Tel:** 1 765 482-4650
Email: news@reporter.net **Web site:** http://www.reporter.net
Freq: Daily; **Circ:** 5000 Not Audited
Advertising Sales Manager: Rick Whiteman
Profile: The Lebanon Reporter is published daily for the residents of Lebanon, IN and surrounding areas. The newspaper covers local and regional news, business, sports, lifestyles and entertainment.
Language (s): English
Ad Rate: Full Page Mono 10.50
Ad Rate: Full Page Colour 39.62
Currency: United States Dollars
DAILY NEWSPAPER

The Ledger 13820
Owner: GateHouse Media Inc.
Editorial: 300 W Lime St, Lakeland, Florida 33815-4649 **Tel:** 1 863 802-7000
Email: newstips@theledger.com **Web site:** http://www.theledger.com
Freq: Daily; **Circ:** 46406 Not Audited
Editor: Lenore Devore; **News Editor:** Chris George
Profile: The Ledger in Lakeland, FL covers local and regional news in Polk County, FL and surrounding areas.
Language (s): English
Ad Rate: Full Page Mono 116.80
Ad Rate: Full Page Colour 378.47
Currency: United States Dollars
DAILY NEWSPAPER

The Ledger - Winter Haven Bureau 80914
Editorial: 455 6th St NW, Winter Haven, Florida 33881 **Tel:** 1 863 401-6900
Language (s): English
DAILY NEWSPAPER

The Ledger-Independent 14084
Owner: Lee Enterprises, Inc.
Editorial: 120 Limestone St, Maysville, Kentucky 41056-1284 **Tel:** 1 606 564-9091
Web site: http://www.maysville-online.com
Freq: Mon thru Fri; **Circ:** 5439 Not Audited
Advertising Sales Manager: Patty Moore
Profile: The Ledger-Independent is a daily newspaper published for the residents of Maysville, KY and the surrounding area. It covers local news, sports and community events.
Language (s): English
Ad Rate: Full Page Mono 18.57
Ad Rate: Full Page Colour 114.99
Currency: United States Dollars
DAILY NEWSPAPER

Leesville Daily Leader 14110
Owner: GateHouse Media Inc.
Editorial: 206 E Texas St, Leesville, Louisiana 71446-4056 **Tel:** 1 337 239-3444
Email: news@leesvilledailyleader.com **Web site:** http://www.leesvilledailyleader.com
Freq: Daily; **Circ:** 2759 Not Audited
Advertising Sales Manager: Tracie Ganno; **News Editor:** Alix Kunkle
Profile: Leesville Daily Leader is a newspaper published for the residents of Leesville, LA. The publication covers local news, sports and community events.
Language (s): English
Ad Rate: Full Page Mono 13.46
Ad Rate: Full Page Colour 92.29
Currency: United States Dollars
DAILY NEWSPAPER

Lewiston Tribune 13903
Owner: tronc
Editorial: 505 Capital St, Lewiston, Idaho 83501-1843 **Tel:** 1 208 743-9411
Email: city@lmtribune.com **Web site:** http://www.lmtribune.com
Freq: Daily; **Circ:** 24515 Not Audited
Publisher & Editor: Nathan Alford
Profile: Lewiston Tribune is a daily newspaper published for the residents of Lewiston, ID. The publication covers local news, sports, business news and community events.
Language (s): English
Ad Rate: Full Page Mono 18.44
Ad Rate: Full Page Colour 114.58
Currency: United States Dollars
DAILY NEWSPAPER

Lexington Herald-Leader 15383
Owner: McClatchy Newspapers
Editorial: 100 Midland Ave, Lexington, Kentucky 40508-1943 **Tel:** 1 859 231-3100
Web site: http://www.kentucky.com
Freq: Daily; **Circ:** 61517 Not Audited
Editor: Peter Baniak; **Publisher:** Rufus Friday
Profile: Lexington Herald-Leader is a 58-page daily newspaper and a 135-page paper on Sunday. It is a voice for Central and Eastern Kentucky. There are 78 counties in the region, including Fayette, Bourbon, Clark, Jessamine, Madison, Scott and Woodford.
Language (s): English
Ad Rate: Full Page Mono 112.00
Ad Rate: Full Page Colour 338.97
Currency: United States Dollars
DAILY NEWSPAPER

Lexington Herald-Leader - Frankfort Bureau 16023
Editorial: 700 Capital Ave, Frankfort, Kentucky 40601-3410 **Tel:** 1 502 227-1198
Language (s): English
DAILY NEWSPAPER

Lexington Herald-Leader - Somerset Bureau 16024
Editorial: 513 Ogden St, Somerset, Kentucky 42501-1739 **Tel:** 1 606 678-4655
Bureau Chief: Bill Estep
Language (s): English
DAILY NEWSPAPER

The Lima News 14463
Owner: AIM Media Midwest
Editorial: 3515 Elida Rd, Lima, Ohio 45807-1538
Tel: 1 419 223-1010
Email: info@limanews.com **Web site:** http://limaohio.com/
Freq: Daily; **Circ:** 21644 Not Audited
Editor: Jim Krumel; **Editor:** Craig Orosz
Profile: The Lima News is a daily newspaper published for the residents of Lima, OH. It covers local news, sports, education, legal issues, arts & entertainment, local government and community events. Deadlines fall daily at 11:30pm ET prior to the issue date.
Language (s): English
Ad Rate: Full Page Mono 53.80
Ad Rate: Full Page Colour 358.84
Currency: United States Dollars
DAILY NEWSPAPER

Lincoln Journal Star 15440
Owner: Lee Enterprises, Inc.
Editorial: 926 P St, Lincoln, Nebraska 68508
Tel: 1 402 475-4200
Email: citydesk@journalstar.com **Web site:** http://www.journalstar.com
Freq: Daily; **Circ:** 47831 Not Audited
Editor: Dave Bundy; **Publisher:** Ava Thomas
Profile: Lincoln Journal Star is a daily newspaper written for residents in the Lincoln, NE area. The paper was formerly known as The Lincoln Journal and The Lincoln Star. The paper is a 50+ page newspaper, and its editorial mission is to "provide news, analysis and an open forum for the exchange of ideas and opinions." The paper covers local, regional, state, national and international news, as well as business, entertainment, sports and special reports. It was founded in 1873.
Language (s): English
Ad Rate: Full Page Mono 79.93
Ad Rate: Full Page Colour 87.31
Currency: United States Dollars
DAILY NEWSPAPER

Litchfield News-Herald 13942
Owner: Litchfield News-Herald, Inc.
Editorial: 112 E Ryder St, Litchfield, Illinois 62056-2031 **Tel:** 1 217 324-2121
Email: lfdnews@litchfieldil.com
Freq: Daily; **Circ:** 5880 Not Audited
Publisher: John Hanafin
Profile: Litchfield News-Herald is published daily for the residents of Litchfield, IL and surrounding areas. The newspaper covers local news, business, sports and entertainment.
Language (s): English
Ad Rate: Full Page Mono 3.80
Ad Rate: Full Page Colour 225.00
Currency: United States Dollars
DAILY NEWSPAPER

Livingston County Daily Press & Argus 70446
Owner: Gannett Co., Inc.
Editorial: 323 E Grand River Ave, Howell, Michigan 48843-2322 **Tel:** 1 517 548-2000
Web site: http://www.livingstondaily.com
Freq: Mon thru Fri; **Circ:** 9621 Not Audited
Profile: Livingston County Daily Press & Argus is published for the residents of Livingston County, MI and surrounding areas. It covers local news, sports and events.
Language (s): English
Ad Rate: Full Page Mono 33.48
Ad Rate: Full Page Colour 35.26
Currency: United States Dollars
DAILY NEWSPAPER

The Livingston Enterprise 14285
Owner: Yellowstone Newspapers
Editorial: 401 S Main St, Livingston, Montana 59047-3418 **Tel:** 1 406 222-2000
Email: news@livent.net **Web site:** http://www.livingstonenterprise.com
Freq: Daily; **Circ:** 3523 Not Audited
Advertising Sales Manager: Jim Durfey; **News Editor:** Dwight Harriman; **Publisher & Editor:** John Sullivan
Profile: The Livingston Enterprise is a daily afternoon newspaper that offers local, state, national and world news and events. The paper serves residents of towns located on the northern border of Yellowstone National Park, including: Livingston, Gardiner, Clyde Park, Wilsall, Cooke City, MT and surrounding areas. Deadlines are daily at 5pm MT.
Language (s): English
Ad Rate: Full Page Mono 7.60
Ad Rate: Full Page Colour 60.00
Currency: United States Dollars
DAILY NEWSPAPER

LNP 14590
Owner: Lancaster Newspapers, Inc.
Editorial: 8 W King St, Lancaster, Pennsylvania 17603-3824 **Tel:** 1 717 291-8811
Email: news@lnpnews.com **Web site:** http://www.lancasteronline.com
Freq: Daily; **Circ:** 52589
La Voz Editor: Enelly Betancourt; **News Editor:** Jon Ferguson; **News Editor:** Randy Montgomery
Profile: Intelligencer Journal/Lancaster New Era is a daily paper published for the residents of Lancaster County, PA and surrounding communities. The newspaper covers local, national and international news, weather, sports, and community events. Feature articles cover business developments, education, politics, arts & entertainment, and lifestyle. It previously was two separate publications, the Lancaster Intelligencer and the Lancaster New Era.
Language (s): English
Ad Rate: Full Page Mono 89.00
Ad Rate: Full Page Colour 95.30
Currency: United States Dollars
DAILY NEWSPAPER

Lockport Union-Sun & Journal 14411
Owner: Community Newspaper Holdings, Inc.
Editorial: 170 East Ave, Lockport, New York 14094-3835 **Tel:** 1 716 439-9222
Web site: http://www.lockportjournal.com
Freq: Daily; **Circ:** 5943
Profile: Lockport Union-Sun & Journal is written for the local residents of Lockport and Eastern Niagara County, NY. The publication covers local news, community events and issues.
Language (s): English
Ad Rate: Full Page Mono 23.00
Ad Rate: Full Page Colour 137.29
Currency: United States Dollars
DAILY NEWSPAPER

Lodi News-Sentinel 13734
Owner: Lodi News-Sentinel, Inc.
Editorial: 125 N Church St, Lodi, California 95240-2197 **Tel:** 1 209 369-2761
Email: news@lodinews.com **Web site:** http://www.lodinews.com
Freq: Mon thru Fri; **Circ:** 15771 Not Audited
Profile: Lodi News-Sentinel is a daily newspaper published for the residents of Lodi, CA and surrounding areas. It covers local and national news, sports, business and entertainment.
Language (s): English
Ad Rate: Full Page Mono 23.03
Ad Rate: Full Page Colour 496.94
Currency: United States Dollars
DAILY NEWSPAPER

Log Cabin Democrat 13687
Owner: GateHouse Media Inc.
Editorial: 1058 Front St, Conway, Arkansas 72032-4356 **Tel:** 1 501 327-6621
Email: editorial@thecabin.net **Web site:** http://www.thecabin.net
Freq: Daily; **Circ:** 10234 Not Audited
Profile: Log Cabin Democrat provides local and regional news coverage for much of Faulkner County, AR.
Language (s): English
Ad Rate: Full Page Mono 15.15
Ad Rate: Full Page Colour 290.15
Currency: United States Dollars
DAILY NEWSPAPER

The Logan Banner 14838
Owner: Civitas Media
Editorial: 437 Stratton St #447, Logan, West Virginia 25601-3913 **Tel:** 1 304 752-6950
Web site: http://www.loganbanner.com
Freq: Daily; **Circ:** 9166 Not Audited
Publisher: Ed Martin; **News Editor:** Debra Rolen
Profile: The Logan Banner is a daily newspaper published for the residents of Logan, WV and the surrounding counties of Lincoln, Boone and Mingo. It covers local news, business, lifestyles and sports.
Language (s): English
Ad Rate: Full Page Mono 13.45
Ad Rate: Full Page Colour 83.96
Currency: United States Dollars
DAILY NEWSPAPER

Logan Daily News 14465
Owner: American Consolidated Media
Editorial: 72 E Main St, Logan, Ohio 43138
Tel: 1 740 385-2107
Email: publisher@logandaily.com **Web site:** http://www.logandaily.com
Freq: Daily; **Circ:** 4161 Not Audited
Profile: Logan Daily News covers news and events in the Logan, OH community. Send all press releases to the main e-mail address.
Language (s): English
Ad Rate: Full Page Mono 14.95
Ad Rate: Full Page Colour 300.00
Currency: United States Dollars
DAILY NEWSPAPER

The Lompoc Record 13735
Owner: Lee Enterprises, Inc.
Editorial: 115 N H St, Lompoc, California 93436-6818 **Tel:** 1 805 736-2313
Web site: http://www.lompocrecord.com
Freq: Mon thru Fri; **Circ:** 3757
Editor: Marga Cooley; **Advertising Sales Manager:** George Fischer; **Publisher:** Cynthia Schur
Profile: The Lompoc Record publishes every day except Saturdays and provides local news coverage for residents of the Lompoc and Santa Ynez Valleys in California.
Language (s): English
Ad Rate: Full Page Mono 25.41
Ad Rate: Full Page Colour 153.88
Currency: United States Dollars
DAILY NEWSPAPER

Long Beach Press-Telegram 15335
Owner: Southern California News Group/Digital First Media
Editorial: 300 Oceangate, Long Beach, California 90802-6801 **Tel:** 1 562 435-1161
Email: ptnews@presstelegram.com **Web site:** http://www.presstelegram.com
Freq: Daily; **Circ:** 77334 Not Audited
Profile: Press-Telegram is a daily newspaper distributed in the Long Beach, CA area, South of Downtown Los Angeles. This paper is a part of the Southern California News Group, a subsidiary of Digital First Media. It covers local business, political and community news, as well as entertainment and recreation, lifestyle, travel and high school, collegiate and professional sports. Although the newspaper covers national business and political news, the newspaper's staff covers local news only; national news is taken almost exclusively from the Associated Press and other wire services. The advertising rates listed are for ads in the SCNG, as paper specific ads cannot be purchased.
Language (s): English
Ad Rate: Full Page Mono 204.00
Ad Rate: Full Page Colour 214.29
Currency: United States Dollars
DAILY NEWSPAPER

Longview News-Journal 14709
Owner: Texas Community Media LLC
Editorial: 320 E Methvin St, Longview, Texas 75601-7323 **Tel:** 1 903 757-3311
Email: clerks@news-journal.com **Web site:** http://www.news-journal.com
Freq: Daily; **Circ:** 20491 Not Audited
Editor: Richard Brack; **News Editor:** Sirena Mankins
Profile: Longview News-Journal is published daily for the residents of Longview, TX and surrounding areas. The newspaper covers local and regional news, business, sports, lifestyles and entertainment.
Language (s): English
Ad Rate: Full Page Mono 46.15
Ad Rate: Full Page Colour 275.73
Currency: United States Dollars
DAILY NEWSPAPER

Los Alamos Monitor 14384
Owner: Landmark Community Newspapers, Inc.
Editorial: 256 DP Rd, Los Alamos, New Mexico 87544-3233 **Tel:** 1 505 662-4185
Email: lanews@lamonitor.com **Web site:** http://www.lamonitor.com
Freq: Daily; **Circ:** 4751 Not Audited
Editor: John Severance
Profile: Los Alamos Monitor is a daily paper that provides coverage of local news, weather and sports for residents of the Los Alamos, NM community.
Language (s): English
Ad Rate: Full Page Mono 14.16
Ad Rate: Full Page Colour 16.06
Currency: United States Dollars
DAILY NEWSPAPER

Los Angeles Daily News 15375
Owner: Southern California News Group/Digital First Media
Editorial: 21860 Burbank Blvd Ste 200, Woodland Hills, California 91367-7439 **Tel:** 1 818 713-3000
Email: dnmetro@dailynews.com **Web site:** http://www.dailynews.com
Freq: Daily; **Circ:** 34658 Not Audited
Profile: The Los Angeles Daily News is a general interest broadsheet daily newspaper serving the residents of Los Angeles and San Fernando Valley, CA. This paper is a part of the Southern California News Group, a subsidiary of Digital First Media.
Language (s): English
Ad Rate: Full Page Mono 110.00
Ad Rate: Full Page Colour 155.35
Currency: United States Dollars
DAILY NEWSPAPER

Los Angeles Daily News - City Hall Bureau 15643
Editorial: 200 N Spring St Ste 345, Los Angeles, California 90012-1780 **Tel:** 1 213 978-0390
Language (s): English
DAILY NEWSPAPER

Los Angeles Times 15305
Owner: tronc
Editorial: 202 W 1st St, Los Angeles, California 90012-4299 **Tel:** 1 213 237-5000
Email: news@latimes.com **Web site:** http://www.latimes.com
Freq: Daily; **Circ:** 467309
South Asia Bureau Chief: Shashank Bengali; **Middle East Bureau Chief:** Laura King; **Editor:** Jack Leonard; **Editor:** Mary Ann Meek
Profile: Los Angeles Times is a general interest daily newspaper that covers regional, national and international news. The paper uses wire services and reports for certain content areas. In August 2009, Tribune Company formed a national sports content-sharing alliance between its properties, most notably between the Chicago Tribune and the Los Angeles Times. The staff honors news embargoes on a case-by-case basis. For FedEx mailing use: 130 S Broadway, Los Angeles, CA 90012. The outlet offers RSS (Really Simple Syndication).
Language (s): English
Ad Rate: Full Page Mono 223.13
Ad Rate: Full Page Colour 361.76
Currency: United States Dollars
DAILY NEWSPAPER

Los Angeles Times - Beijing Bureau 231098
Editorial: Jianguomenwai 71102, Beijing
Tel: 86 1065321982
Language (s): English
DAILY NEWSPAPER

Los Angeles Times - Beirut Bureau 698337
Editorial: Beirut
Email: daragahi@latimes.com
Beirut Bureau Chief: Patrick McDonnell
Language (s): English
DAILY NEWSPAPER

Los Angeles Times - Cairo Bureau 231102
Editorial: Cairo **Tel:** 20 27357424
Middle East Bureau Chief: Laura King
Language (s): English
DAILY NEWSPAPER

Los Angeles Times - Costa Mesa Bureau 16227
Editorial: 1375 Sunflower Ave, Costa Mesa, California 92626-1665 **Tel:** 1 714 966-7715
Language (s): English
DAILY NEWSPAPER

Los Angeles Times - Encinitas Bureau 15608
Editorial: 2224 Running Spring Pl, Encinitas, California 92024-3146
Language (s): English
DAILY NEWSPAPER

Los Angeles Times - Johannesburg Bureau 231153
Editorial: Johannesburg **Tel:** 27 118876055
Bureau Chief: Robyn Dixon
Language (s): English
DAILY NEWSPAPER

Los Angeles Times - New York Bureau 15524
Editorial: 220 E 42nd St, New York, New York 10017-5806 **Tel:** 1 212 448-2839
Language (s): English
DAILY NEWSPAPER

Los Angeles Times - Sacramento Bureau 15573
Editorial: 1215 K St Ste 1750, Sacramento, California 95814-3948 **Tel:** 1 916 321-4400
Language (s): English
DAILY NEWSPAPER

Lovington Daily Leader 14379
Owner: Wal-Roy Publishing, Inc.
Editorial: 14 W Avenue B, Lovington, New Mexico 88260-4404 **Tel:** 1 575 396-2844
Web site: http://www.lovingtonleaderonline.com/
Freq: Daily; **Circ:** 1965 Not Audited
Advertising Sales Manager: Joyce Clemens; **Publisher & Editor:** John Graham
Profile: Lovington Daily Leader's editorial mission is to provide local news to residents of Lovington, NM. Deadlines for the publication are one week before issue date.
Language (s): English
Ad Rate: Full Page Mono 8.00
Ad Rate: Full Page Colour 41.97
Currency: United States Dollars
DAILY NEWSPAPER

Lubbock Avalanche-Journal 14710
Owner: GateHouse Media Inc.
Editorial: 710 Avenue J, Lubbock, Texas 79401-1808
Tel: 1 806 762-8844
Email: ajnews@lubbockonline.com **Web site:** http://www.lubbockonline.com
Freq: Daily; **Circ:** 25825 Not Audited
Profile: Lubbock Avalanche-Journal is written for people in the Lubbock, TX area. It covers local and national news, as well as sports, entertainment, lifestyle, business and opinions. Deadlines for the publication are same day before issue date.
Language (s): English
Ad Rate: Full Page Mono 69.95
Ad Rate: Full Page Colour 75.78
Currency: United States Dollars
DAILY NEWSPAPER

Lubbock Avalanche-Journal - Austin Bureau 618033
Editorial: Austin, Texas
Profile: Serves as the Austin bureau for both Texas daily papers owned by Morris Communications: the Lubbock (TX) Avalanche-Journal and Amarillo (TX) Globe-News.
Language (s): English
DAILY NEWSPAPER

Ludington Daily News 14179
Owner: Shoreline Media, Inc.
Editorial: 202 N Rath Ave, Ludington, Michigan 49431-1663 **Tel:** 1 231 845-5181
Email: ldn@ludingtondailynews.com **Web site:** http://www.shorelinemedia.net/ludington_daily_news/
Freq: Daily; **Circ:** 6605 Not Audited

Publisher: Jeffrey Evans; **Editor:** Patti Klevorn; **Advertising Sales Manager:** John Walker
Profile: Ludington Daily News is a daily newspaper published for the residents of Ludington, MI and the surrounding counties of Mason, Manistee, Oceania and Lake. It covers local news and community events. Deadlines are daily at 10am CT.
Language (s): English
Ad Rate: Full Page Mono 14.00
Currency: United States Dollars
DAILY NEWSPAPER

The Lufkin Daily News 14711
Owner: Southern Newspapers, Inc.
Editorial: 300 Ellis Ave, Lufkin, Texas 75904-3817
Tel: 1 936 632-6631
Email: news@lufkindailynews.com **Web site:** http://lufkindailynews.com
Freq: Daily; **Circ:** 10400 Not Audited
Publisher: Janice Bell
Profile: The Lufkin Daily News is published for the residents of Lufkin, TX and surrounding areas. It provides information on local and national news, finance, sports, features, lifestyles, health and weather.
Language (s): English
Ad Rate: Full Page Mono 24.64
Ad Rate: Full Page Colour 152.67
Currency: United States Dollars
DAILY NEWSPAPER

The Macomb Daily 14184
Owner: Digital First Media
Editorial: 19176 Hall Rd Fl 2, Clinton Township, Michigan 48038-6914 **Tel:** 1 586 469-4510
Web site: http://www.macombdaily.com
Freq: Daily; **Circ:** 27581 Not Audited
Profile: The Macomb Daily in Clinton Township, MI is a daily newspaper serving residents of Macomb County, MI. The publication covers local news, sports, business, arts & entertainment and event information for the communities within its distribution area.
Language (s): English
Ad Rate: Full Page Mono 97.66
Ad Rate: Full Page Colour 318.02
Currency: United States Dollars
DAILY NEWSPAPER

Madera Tribune 13736
Owner: Madera Printing and Publishing
Editorial: 2591 Mitchell Ct Ste 107, Madera, California 93637-3807 **Tel:** 1 559 674-2424
Web site: http://www.maderatribune.com
Freq: 2 Times/Week; **Circ:** 4700 Not Audited
Publisher & Editor: Charles Doud; **News Editor:** John Rieping; **Advertising Sales Manager:** Corrie Valdez
Profile: Madera Tribune is a daily newspaper published Monday through Saturday for the residents of Madera, CA and surrounding areas. It covers local news, sports and community events.
Language (s): English
Ad Rate: Full Page Mono 14.00
Ad Rate: Full Page Colour 88.98
Currency: United States Dollars
DAILY NEWSPAPER

The Madison Courier 14000
Owner: Madison Courier, Inc.
Editorial: 310 Courier Sq, Madison, Indiana 47250-3799 **Tel:** 1 812 265-3641
Email: news@madisoncourier.com **Web site:** http://www.madisoncourier.com
Freq: Daily; **Circ:** 8700 Not Audited
Advertising Sales Manager: Mark McKee; **Editor:** Elliot Tompkin
Profile: The Madison Courier, established in 1837 and family owned since 1849, is published Monday through Saturday in Madison, IN. It serves Jefferson and Switzerland counties in Indiana and Trimble and Carroll counties in Kentucky. Deadlines for the publication are at 2pm CT.
Language (s): English
Ad Rate: Full Page Mono 12.35
Ad Rate: Full Page Colour 90.17
Currency: United States Dollars
DAILY NEWSPAPER

Madison Daily Leader 14653
Editorial: 214 S Egan Ave, Madison, South Dakota 57042-2911 **Tel:** 1 605 256-4555
Email: news@madisondailyleader.com **Web site:** http://www.dailyleaderextra.com
Freq: Daily; **Circ:** 3000 Not Audited
Advertising Sales Manager: Melissa Hegg; **Publisher:** Jon Hunter
Profile: Madison Daily Leader's editorial mission is to be the preferred source for news information and advertising. The publication is written for the county of Madison, SD. Deadlines for the publication are at 9am CT of the issue day.
Language (s): English
Ad Rate: Full Page Mono 10.40
Ad Rate: Full Page Colour 56.16
Currency: United States Dollars
DAILY NEWSPAPER

The Madison Press 14466
Owner: AIM Media Midwest
Editorial: 30 S Oak St, London, Ohio 43140-1066
Tel: 1 740 852-1616
Email: editor@madison-press.com **Web site:** http://www.madison-press.com
Freq: Fri; **Circ:** 6500 Not Audited
Profile: The Madison Press is a daily newspaper written for the residents of Madison County, OH and surrounding areas. It covers local news and community events.
Language (s): English
Ad Rate: Full Page Mono 8.85
Ad Rate: Full Page Colour 175.00
Currency: United States Dollars
DAILY NEWSPAPER

Magnolia Banner-News 13698
Owner: Wehco Media Inc.
Editorial: 130 S Washington, Magnolia, Arkansas 71753-3523 **Tel:** 1 870 234-5130
Email: news@bannernews.net **Web site:** http://www.bannernews.net
Freq: Daily; **Circ:** 4375 Not Audited
Advertising Sales Manager: Susan Gill; **Publisher:** Walter Hussman
Profile: Magnolia Banner-News is published daily for the residents of Magnolia, AR and surrounding areas. The newspaper covers local and state news, business, sports, lifestyles and entertainment. It combines with the Camden (AR) News and the El Dorado (AR) News-Times on Sundays.
Language (s): English
Ad Rate: Full Page Mono 11.93
Ad Rate: Full Page Colour 275.00
Currency: United States Dollars
DAILY NEWSPAPER

Mail Tribune 14557
Owner: GateHouse Media Inc.
Editorial: 111 N Fir St, Medford, Oregon 97501-2772
Tel: 1 541 776-4411
Email: news@mailtribune.com **Web site:** http://www.mailtribune.com
Freq: Daily; **Circ:** 20655 Not Audited
Editor: Bob Pennell; **Publisher:** James Grady Singletary
Profile: Mail Tribune is dedicated to the people's rights to know. The mission of the publication is to provide quality news and advertising information and services for readers and advertisers. It covers local news, sports, and opinion. The publication is written for adults ages 18 to 65 in the greater part of Oregon. Deadlines for the publication are daily at 5pm PT.
Language (s): English
Ad Rate: Full Page Mono 33024.00
Ad Rate: Full Page Colour 39.11
Currency: United States Dollars
DAILY NEWSPAPER

Malone Telegram 14412
Owner: Johnson Newspaper Corp.
Editorial: 469 E Main St Ste 4, Malone, New York 12953-2128 **Tel:** 1 518 483-4700
Email: news@mtelegram.com **Web site:** http://www.mtelegram.com
Freq: Mon thru Fri; **Circ:** 5346 Not Audited
Editor: Connie Jenkins
Profile: The Malone Telegram is written for residents of Franklin County, NY. It provides local news concerning the residents of Franklin County, NY. The lead time is the same day.
Language (s): English
Ad Rate: Full Page Mono 9.54
Ad Rate: Full Page Colour 60.87
Currency: United States Dollars
DAILY NEWSPAPER

Malvern Daily Record 13699
Owner: Horizon Publications
Editorial: 219 Locust St, Malvern, Arkansas 72104-3721 **Tel:** 1 501 337-7523
Email: editor@malvern-online.com **Web site:** http://www.malvern-online.com
Freq: Daily; **Circ:** 4200 Not Audited
Advertising Sales Manager: Michelle Cummins; **Publisher:** Richard Folds
Profile: Malvern Daily Record is published daily for the residents of Malvern, AR and surrounding areas. The newspaper covers local and state news, business, sports, lifestyles and entertainment.
Language (s): English
Ad Rate: Full Page Mono 11.45
Ad Rate: Full Page Colour 72.13
Currency: United States Dollars
DAILY NEWSPAPER

El Mañana 132610
Owner: Deanddar (Ramon Cantu)
Editorial: 6010 McPherson Rd, Laredo, Texas 78041-6206 **Tel:** 1 956 712-1122
Email: rio@elmanana.com.mx **Web site:** http://www.elmanana.com.mx
Freq: Daily; **Circ:** 25623 Not Audited
Publisher & Editor: Ramon Cantu Deandar; **Advertising Sales Manager:** Melissa Urteaga
Profile: El Mañana was founded in 1932. It is a Spanish language weekly publication serving the residents of Laredo, TX.
Language (s): Spanish/Bilingual
Ad Rate: Full Page Mono 6.45
Ad Rate: Full Page Colour 99.99
Currency: United States Dollars
DAILY NEWSPAPER

The Manhattan Mercury 14058
Owner: Seaton Newspapers
Editorial: 318 N 5th St, Manhattan, Kansas 66502-5910 **Tel:** 1 785 776-2200
Email: news@themercury.com **Web site:** http://www.themercury.com
Freq: Daily; **Circ:** 9424 Not Audited
Advertising Sales Manager: Steve Stallwitz
Profile: The Manhattan Mercury is published daily for residents of Manhattan, KS and its surrounding areas. The publication is a general interest newspaper, covering local news, sports, weather, business, education, arts and entertainment, and other information of interest to the local community. Deadlines for the publication vary.
Language (s): English
Ad Rate: Full Page Mono 13.83
Ad Rate: Full Page Colour 74.06
Currency: United States Dollars
DAILY NEWSPAPER

Manistee News-Advocate 14180
Owner: Pioneer Newspapers
Editorial: 75 Maple St, Manistee, Michigan 49660-1554 **Tel:** 1 231 723-3592
Email: advocate@pioneergroup.com **Web site:** http://www.manisteenews.com
Freq: Daily; **Circ:** 5000 Not Audited
Editor: Dave Barber; **Publisher:** Marilyn Barker
Profile: Manistee News-Advocate is a daily newspaper serving Manistee County, MI. It covers local news, sports and events.
Language (s): English
Ad Rate: Full Page Mono 11.75
Ad Rate: Full Page Colour 150.00
Currency: United States Dollars
DAILY NEWSPAPER

Manteca Bulletin 13771
Owner: Morris Multimedia, Inc.
Editorial: 531 E Yosemite Ave, Manteca, California 95336-5806 **Tel:** 1 209 249-3551
Email: news@mantecabulletin.com **Web site:** http://www.mantecabulletin.com
Freq: Daily; **Circ:** 6100 Not Audited
Profile: The Manteca Bulletin is published daily for residents of Manteca, CA and surrounding areas. The publication is a general interest newspaper, covering local news, sports, weather, business, education, arts and entertainment, and other information of interest to the local community.
Language (s): English
Ad Rate: Full Page Mono 14.33
Ad Rate: Full Page Colour 53.94
Currency: United States Dollars
DAILY NEWSPAPER

Marietta Daily Journal 14918
Owner: Times Journal Inc.
Editorial: 580 S Fairground St Se, Marietta, Georgia 30060-2751 **Tel:** 1 770 428-9411
Email: letters@mdjonline.com **Web site:** http://www.mdjonline.com
Freq: Daily; **Circ:** 14491 Not Audited
Publisher: Otis Brumby; **News Editor:** Leo Hohmann
Profile: Marietta Daily Journal is a daily newspaper that covers news, events, government and sports for the communities in Cobb County, including Marietta, GA.
Language (s): English
Ad Rate: Full Page Mono 26.45
Ad Rate: Full Page Colour 90.06
Currency: United States Dollars
DAILY NEWSPAPER

The Marietta Times 14469
Owner: Ogden Newspapers
Editorial: 700 Channel Ln, Marietta, Ohio 45750-2300 **Tel:** 1 740 373-2121
Email: news@mariettatimes.com **Web site:** http://www.mariettatimes.com
Freq: Daily; **Circ:** 7598 Not Audited
Publisher & Editor: Jennifer Houtman; **News Editor:** Kate York
Profile: The Marietta Times is a daily newspaper that is published for residents of Marietta, OH and surrounding areas. The publication is a general interest newspaper, covering local news, sports, business, education, arts & entertainment and other information of interest to the local community. Deadlines are at 3pm CT.
Language (s): English
Ad Rate: Full Page Mono 24.58
Ad Rate: Full Page Colour 175.60
Currency: United States Dollars
DAILY NEWSPAPER

Marin Independent Journal 13772
Owner: Digital First Media
Editorial: 4000 Civic Center Dr Ste 301, San Rafael, California 94903-4129 **Tel:** 1 415 883-8600
Email: localnews@marinij.com **Web site:** http://www.marinij.com
Freq: Daily; **Circ:** 27027
Profile: Marin Independent Journal is a daily newspaper serving the residents of Marin County, CA. It focuses on local news and events ONLY. Regional, state and international stories are covered by wire services. There is no travel section for this paper, so do not send any related stories or pitches.
Language (s): English
Ad Rate: Full Page Mono 155.00
Ad Rate: Full Page Colour 955.95
Currency: United States Dollars
DAILY NEWSPAPER

Marion Daily Republican 13944
Owner: Paddock Publications
Editorial: 502 W Jackson St, Marion, Illinois 62959-2355 **Tel:** 1 618 993-2626
Email: editor@dailyrepublicannews.com **Web site:** http://www.dailyrepublicannews.com
Freq: Mon thru Fri; **Circ:** 3069 Not Audited
Publisher: Kevin Haezebroeck; **Advertising Sales Manager:** Larry Henry
Profile: Marion Daily Republican is published daily for residents of Williamson County, IL and surrounding areas. The publication is a general interest newspaper covering local news, weather, sports, education, business and arts & entertainment.
Language (s): English
Ad Rate: Full Page Mono 11.65
Ad Rate: Full Page Colour 67.41
Currency: United States Dollars
DAILY NEWSPAPER

The Marion Star 14470
Owner: Gannett Co., Inc.
Editorial: 150 Court St, Marion, Ohio 43302-3026
Tel: 1 740 387-0400
Web site: http://www.marionstar.com
Freq: Daily; **Circ:** 5943 Not Audited
Profile: The Marion Star is a daily newspaper published for the residents of Marion, OH. It contains local, state, national and international news. Additional sections include sports, opinions, business, technology, travel and lifestyle. Press releases can be submitted through the paper's Web site.
Language (s): English
Ad Rate: Full Page Mono 26.80
Ad Rate: Full Page Colour 285.00
Currency: United States Dollars
DAILY NEWSPAPER

The Marshall Democrat-News 14240
Owner: Rust Communications
Editorial: 121 N Lafayette Ave, Marshall, Missouri 65340-1747 **Tel:** 1 660 886-2233
Email: sreed@marshallnews.com **Web site:** http://www.marshallnews.com
Freq: Daily; **Circ:** 3098 Not Audited
Advertising Sales Manager: Mike Davis
Profile: The Marshall Democrat-News is a daily newspaper published for the residents of Saline County, MO. It covers local and regional news, sports and community events.
Language (s): English
Ad Rate: Full Page Mono 8.66
Ad Rate: Full Page Colour 67.20
Currency: United States Dollars
DAILY NEWSPAPER

Marshall Independent 14210
Owner: Ogden Newspapers
Editorial: 508 W Main St, Marshall, Minnesota 56258
Tel: 1 507 537-1551
Email: news@marshallindependent.com **Web site:** http://www.marshallindependent.com
Freq: Mon thru Fri; **Circ:** 5422 Not Audited
Advertising Sales Manager: Tara Brandl; **Editor:** Karin Elton; **Editor:** Per Peterson
Profile: Marshall Independent is published daily for residents of Lyon County, MN and surrounding areas. The publication is a general interest newspaper, covering local news, weather, sports, education, business, arts & entertainment and other information of interest to the local community.
Language (s): English
Ad Rate: Full Page Mono 19.69
Currency: United States Dollars
DAILY NEWSPAPER

The Marshall News Messenger 14712
Owner: Texas Community Media LLC
Editorial: 309 E Austin St, Marshall, Texas 75670-3475 **Tel:** 1 903 935-7914
Email: newsmessenger@marshallnewsmessenger.com **Web site:** http://www.marshallnewsmessenger.com
Freq: Daily; **Circ:** 4517 Not Audited
Publisher & Editor: Phil Latham
Profile: Marshall News Messenger is published daily for residents of Marshall, TX and surrounding areas. It is a general interest newspaper, covering local news, weather, sports, business, education and other information of interest to local residents. Deadlines are two weeks prior to the issue date.
Language (s): English
Ad Rate: Full Page Mono 24.26
Ad Rate: Full Page Colour 39.32
Currency: United States Dollars
DAILY NEWSPAPER

Marshfield News-Herald 14814
Owner: Gannett Co., Inc.
Editorial: 111 W 3Rd St, Marshfield, Wisconsin 54449-2811 **Tel:** 1 715 384-3131
Email: areanews@marshfieldnewsherald.com **Web site:** http://www.marshfieldnewsherald.com
Freq: Daily; **Circ:** 6782 Not Audited
Advertising Sales Manager: Tara Marcoux
Profile: Marshfield News-Herald is published daily for residents of Marshfield, WI and surrounding areas. The publication is a general interest newspaper, covering local news, weather, sports, business, education, arts & entertainment and other information of interest to the local community. The paper combines with The Daily Tribune in Wisconsin Rapids and the Stevens Point Journal on Sundays. Lead times vary between one and three days.
Language (s): English
Ad Rate: Full Page Mono 32.00
Ad Rate: Full Page Colour 357.00
Currency: United States Dollars
DAILY NEWSPAPER

Martinsville Bulletin 14761
Owner: BH Media Group
Editorial: 204 Broad St, Martinsville, Virginia 24112-3704 **Tel:** 1 276 638-8801
Email: info@martinsvillebulletin.com **Web site:** http://www.martinsvillebulletin.com
Freq: Daily; **Circ:** 12508 Not Audited
Advertising Sales Manager: Tammy Jones
Profile: Martinsville Bulletin is published daily for residents of Martinsville, VA and surrounding areas. It

is a general interest newspaper covering local news, weather, sports, business, education and arts & entertainment. Deadlines are at noon ET.
Language (s): English
Ad Rate: Full Page Mono 17.72
Ad Rate: Full Page Colour 111.22
Currency: United States Dollars
DAILY NEWSPAPER

Marysville Journal Tribune 14472
Editorial: 207 N Main St, Marysville, Ohio 43040-1161 **Tel:** 1 937 644-9111
Web site: http://www.marysvillejt.com
Freq: Daily; **Circ:** 6495 Not Audited
Advertising Sales Manager: Marie Woodford
Profile: The Marysville Journal-Tribune is published daily for residents of Union County, OH, and surrounding areas. The publication is a general interest newspaper, covering local news, weather, sports, education, business, arts, entertainment and other information of interest to the local community. Deadlines for the publication are one week prior to the issue date.
Language (s): English
Ad Rate: Full Page Mono 12.25
Ad Rate: Full Page Colour 235.00
Currency: United States Dollars
DAILY NEWSPAPER

The Maryville Daily Forum 14241
Owner: GateHouse Media Inc.
Editorial: 111 E Jenkins St, Maryville, Missouri 64468-2318 **Tel:** 1 660 562-2424
Web site: http://www.maryvilledailyforum.com
Freq: Daily; **Circ:** 3200 Not Audited
News Editor: Tony Brown
Profile: The Maryville Daily Forum is published daily for residents of greater Maryville, MO and surrounding areas. The publication is a general interest newspaper, covering local news, weather, sports, education, business and arts & entertainment.
Language (s): English
Ad Rate: Full Page Mono 8.60
Ad Rate: Full Page Colour 48.58
Currency: United States Dollars
DAILY NEWSPAPER

Il Massaggero - New York Bureau 620282
Editorial: 350 5th Ave, Ste 5915, New York, New York 10118-0110 **Tel:** 1 212 601-2696
Profile: This is the New York bureau of Il Massaggero, based in Roma, Italy.
Language (s): Italian
DAILY NEWSPAPER

The Maui News 13861
Owner: Ogden Newspapers
Editorial: 100 Mahalani St, Wailuku, Hawaii 96793-2529 **Tel:** 1 808 244-3981
Web site: http://www.mauinews.com
Freq: Daily; **Circ:** 18134 Not Audited
Publisher: Joseph Bradley; **News Editor:** Lee Imada; **Advertising Sales Manager:** Dawne Miguel
Profile: The Maui News is published daily for residents of Wailuku, HI and surrounding areas. The publication is a general interest newspaper, covering local news, weather, sports, business, education, arts & entertainment and other information of importance to the local community.
Language (s): English
Ad Rate: Full Page Mono 35.60
Ad Rate: Full Page Colour 213.03
Currency: United States Dollars
DAILY NEWSPAPER

Mayfield Messenger 14083
Owner: Mayfield Messenger Corporation
Editorial: 201 N 8th St, Mayfield, Kentucky 42066-1825
Freq: Daily; **Circ:** 6200 Not Audited
Editor: Jim Abernathy; **Publisher:** Eric Hoffman
Profile: Mayfield Messenger is published daily for residents of Graves County, KY and surrounding areas. The publication is a general interest newspaper, covering local news, weather, sports, business, education, arts & entertainment and other information of interest to the local community. The outlet has requested their contact details not be listed.
Language (s): English
Ad Rate: Full Page Mono 8.30
Ad Rate: Full Page Colour 61.77
Currency: United States Dollars
DAILY NEWSPAPER

McAlester News-Capital 14529
Owner: Community Newspaper Holdings, Inc.
Editorial: 500 S 2nd St, McAlester, Oklahoma 74501-5812 **Tel:** 1 918 423-1700
Email: web@mcalesternews.com **Web site:** http://mcalesternews.com
Freq: Daily; **Circ:** 7500 Not Audited
Publisher: Amy Johns; **Advertising Sales Manager:** Scotty Maxwell
Profile: McAlester News-Capital is written for residents of McAlester, OK.
Language (s): English
Ad Rate: Full Page Mono 12.75
Ad Rate: Full Page Colour 316.75
Currency: United States Dollars
DAILY NEWSPAPER

McCook Daily Gazette 14344
Owner: Rust Communications
Editorial: West 1st and E St, McCook, Nebraska 69001 **Tel:** 1 308 345-4500
Email: editor@mccookgazette.com **Web site:** http://www.mccookgazette.com
Freq: Mon thru Fri; **Circ:** 5661 Not Audited
Editor: Bruce Crosby; **Publisher:** Shary Skiles
Profile: McCook Daily Gazette provides news to the communities of McCook and the Golden Plains of South Nebraska and Northwest Kansas.
Language (s): English
Ad Rate: Full Page Mono 10.20
Ad Rate: Full Page Colour 195.00
Currency: United States Dollars
DAILY NEWSPAPER

McCurtain Daily Gazette 14527
Owner: McCurtain County News, Inc. (The)
Editorial: 107 S Central Ave, Idabel, Oklahoma 74745-4847 **Tel:** 1 580 286-3321
Email: paper@mccurtain.com
Freq: Daily; **Circ:** 5850 Not Audited
Advertising Sales Manager: Shelly Davis; **Editor:** Bruce Willingham
Profile: McCurtain Daily Gazette is a local daily newspaper written for the residents of McCurtain County, OK.
Language (s): English
Ad Rate: Full Page Mono 7.35
Ad Rate: Full Page Colour 40.74
Currency: United States Dollars
DAILY NEWSPAPER

McDonough County Voice 13943
Owner: GateHouse Media Inc.
Editorial: 203 N Randolph St, Macomb, Illinois 61455-2273 **Tel:** 1 309 833-2114
Email: newsroom@mcdonoughvoice.com **Web site:** http://www.mcdonoughvoice.com
Freq: Fri; **Circ:** 6969 Not Audited
Publisher: Lynne Campbell
Profile: McDonough County Voice is a daily newspaper written for residents of Macomb, IL. It covers local, state and world news, sports and business.
Language (s): English
Ad Rate: Full Page Mono 14.00
Ad Rate: Full Page Colour 200.00
Currency: United States Dollars
DAILY NEWSPAPER

McDowell News 14324
Owner: World Media Enterprises, Inc.
Editorial: 136 N Logan St, Marion, North Carolina 28752-3754 **Tel:** 1 828 652-3313
Email: news@mcdowellnews.com **Web site:** http://www.mcdowellnews.com
Freq: Daily; **Circ:** 3526
Editor: Scott Hollifield
Profile: McDowell News is a daily newspaper published for the residents of McDowell County, including Macon, NC and Greenville, SC. It covers local news and entertainment. Deadlines are daily at 4pm ET.
Language (s): English
Ad Rate: Full Page Mono 9.02
Ad Rate: Full Page Colour 13.53
Currency: United States Dollars
DAILY NEWSPAPER

McPherson Sentinel 14059
Owner: GateHouse Media Inc.
Editorial: 116 S Main St, McPherson, Kansas 67460-4852 **Tel:** 1 620 241-2422
Email: news@mcphersonsentinel.com **Web site:** http://www.mcphersonsentinel.com
Freq: Fri; **Circ:** 4000
Publisher: Randy Mitchell
Profile: McPherson Sentinel provides news for the residents of McPherson County, KS. Deadlines are one day before issue date.
Language (s): English
Ad Rate: Full Page Mono 14.00
Currency: United States Dollars
DAILY NEWSPAPER

The Meadville Tribune 14600
Owner: Community Newspaper Holdings, Inc.
Editorial: 947 Federal Ct, Meadville, Pennsylvania 16335-3234 **Tel:** 1 814 724-6370
Email: tribune@meadvilletribune.com **Web site:** http://meadvilletribune.com
Freq: Daily; **Circ:** 10382 Not Audited
Publisher: James Galantis; **Advertising Sales Manager:** Heidi Gebhardt
Profile: The Meadville Tribune is a daily local newspaper published for Crawford County, PA residents. Regular features include local news, community announcements and sports. Deadlines are at 7pm ET.
Language (s): English
Ad Rate: Full Page Mono 25.40
Ad Rate: Full Page Colour 385.00
Currency: United States Dollars
DAILY NEWSPAPER

The Medina County Gazette 14474
Owner: Lorain County Printing & Publishing
Editorial: 885 W Liberty St, Medina, Ohio 44256-1312 **Tel:** 1 800 633-4623
Email: areanews@medina-gazette.com **Web site:** http://www.medina-gazette.com
Freq: Daily; **Circ:** 11538 Not Audited
Publisher: George Hudnutt; **News Editor:** Liz Sheaffer
Profile: The Medina County Gazette provides local news for Medina County, OH.
Language (s): English
Ad Rate: Full Page Mono 29.00
Currency: United States Dollars
DAILY NEWSPAPER

Merced Sun-Star 13738
Owner: McClatchy Newspapers
Editorial: 3033 G St, Merced, California 95340-2108 **Tel:** 1 209 722-1511
Web site: http://www.mercedsunstar.com
Freq: Mon thru Fri; **Circ:** 17854 Not Audited
Profile: Merced Sun-Star's editorial mission is to provide local news and community information for the people of Merced.
Language (s): English
Ad Rate: Full Page Mono 42.58
Ad Rate: Full Page Colour 140.24
Currency: United States Dollars
DAILY NEWSPAPER

The Mercury 14607
Owner: Digital First Media
Editorial: 24 N Hanover St, Pottstown, Pennsylvania 19464-5410 **Tel:** 1 610 323-3000
Email: mercury@pottsmerc.com **Web site:** http://www.pottsmerc.com
Freq: Daily; **Circ:** 24601
Publisher: Edward Condra; **Editor:** Tony Phyrillas
Profile: The Mercury is a published daily for readers in the greater Pottstown, PA area. The newspaper provides local news and community event information. News features include lifestyle, sports, business, classifieds and advertising. Some national news is provided by the Associated Press, but the newspaper primarily focuses on keeping its readers aware of news and events occurring in their community.
Language (s): English
Ad Rate: Full Page Mono 34.77
Ad Rate: Full Page Colour 48.68
Currency: United States Dollars
DAILY NEWSPAPER

The Mercury News 15343
Owner: Digital First Media
Editorial: 4 N 2nd St Ste 800, San Jose, California 95113-1308 **Tel:** 1 408 920-5000
Email: local@mercurynews.com **Web site:** http://www.mercurynews.com
Freq: Daily; **Circ:** 397754 Not Audited
Profile: Mercury News is a daily newspaper covering Silicon Valley, CA, including Santa Clara County, Southern Alameda County, Southern San Mateo County and Scotts Valley. The paper is read by a large number of high-tech professionals in the area. It serves its readership by presenting a variety of local business news, including many computer company stories and interviews. Coverage also includes news, business, consumer and technology. Consumer coverage includes lifestyles, health, food, fashion, arts & entertainment and travel. The outlet offers RSS (Really Simple Syndication). In 2016, the San Mateo Times merged with San Jose Mercury News to become Mercury News.
Language (s): English
Ad Rate: Full Page Mono 363.54
Ad Rate: Full Page Colour 436.25
Currency: United States Dollars
DAILY NEWSPAPER

Meridian Star 14268
Owner: Community Newspaper Holdings, Inc.
Editorial: 814 22nd Ave, Meridian, Mississippi 39301-5023 **Tel:** 1 601 693-1551
Email: editor@themeridianstar.com **Web site:** http://www.meridianstar.com
Freq: Daily; **Circ:** 16348 Not Audited
Editor: Ida Brown
Profile: Meridian Star provides local news and information to the residents of Meridian, MS.
Language (s): English
Ad Rate: Full Page Mono 29.45
Ad Rate: Full Page Colour 230.00
Currency: United States Dollars
DAILY NEWSPAPER

The Mesabi Daily News 14217
Owner: Macquarie Media Group
Editorial: 704 S 7th Ave, Virginia, Minnesota 55792-3086 **Tel:** 1 218 741-5544
Email: mdnedit@mesabidailynews.net **Web site:** http://www.virginiamn.com
Freq: Fri; **Circ:** 7800 Not Audited
Publisher & Editor: Bill Hanna; **Publisher:** Chris Knight
Profile: The Mesabi Daily News provides local news and information to the community of Virginia, MN.
Language (s): English
Ad Rate: Full Page Mono 11.41
Currency: United States Dollars
DAILY NEWSPAPER

The Messenger 13879
Owner: Ogden Newspapers
Editorial: 713 Central Ave, Fort Dodge, Iowa 50501-3813 **Tel:** 1 515 573-2141
Email: editor@messengernews.net **Web site:** http://www.messengernews.net
Freq: Daily; **Circ:** 11344 Not Audited
Publisher: Larry Bushman
Profile: The Messenger is a daily newspaper serving Fort Dodge, IA. The newspaper covers local and state news, business, agriculture, sports and entertainment.
Language (s): English
Ad Rate: Full Page Mono 23.35
Ad Rate: Full Page Colour 140.00
Currency: United States Dollars
DAILY NEWSPAPER

The Messenger 14082
Owner: Paxton Media Group
Editorial: 221 S Main St, Madisonville, Kentucky 42431-2567 **Tel:** 1 270 824-3300
Email: newsroom@the-messenger.com **Web site:** http://www.the-messenger.com
Freq: Fri; **Circ:** 7422 Not Audited
Publisher: Rick Welch
Profile: The Messenger is a local newspaper serving the residents of Madisonville, KY and the surrounding area. The publication covers local news, sports and community events. Deadlines are four working days in advance.
Language (s): English
Ad Rate: Full Page Mono 17.23
Ad Rate: Full Page Colour 290.00
Currency: United States Dollars
DAILY NEWSPAPER

Metro Boston 77714
Owner: Seabay Media Holdings LLC.
Editorial: 234 Congress St Fl 4, Boston, Massachusetts 02110-2470 **Tel:** 1 617 210-7905
Web site: http://www.metro.us/news/local-news/boston
Freq: Daily; **Circ:** 52218 Not Audited
Profile: Launched in May 2001, Metro Boston is a commuter daily newspaper serving commuters and residents of Boston. It reports national, regional and worldwide news, sports and arts and entertainment.
Language (s): English
Ad Rate: Full Page Colour 106.19
Currency: United States Dollars
DAILY NEWSPAPER

Metro New York 231921
Owner: Seabay Media Holdings LLC.
Editorial: 120 Broadway Fl 6, New York, New York 10271-1100 **Tel:** 1 212 457-7790
Web site: http://www.metro.us/news/local-news/new-york
Freq: Mon thru Fri; **Circ:** 176127 Not Audited
Profile: Metro New York is a commuter daily newspaper that is distributed for free each weekday. It is designed and packaged for young, urban, active and well-educated audiences and provides readers with the news that they need, condensed into a 15-minute read. Local, national and international news reports are combined with the latest entertainment listings and reviews.
Language (s): English
Ad Rate: Full Page Colour 178.80
Currency: United States Dollars
DAILY NEWSPAPER

Metro Philadelphia 62437
Owner: Seabay Media Holdings LLC.
Editorial: 30 S 15th St Fl 14, Philadelphia, Pennsylvania 19102-4806 **Tel:** 1 215 717-2600
Email: letters@metro.us **Web site:** http://www.metro.us/news/local-news/philadelphia
Freq: Daily; **Circ:** 75556 Not Audited
Profile: Philadelphia Metro is a free, commuter daily newspaper that is distributed to commuters and residents throughout the Philadelphia metropolitan area. It targets young professionals and is intended to be read during a 15-minute morning commute. The newspaper has concise articles that focus on local, national and international news, lifestyle, sports and arts & entertainment stories.
Language (s): English
Ad Rate: Full Page Colour 91.43
Currency: United States Dollars
DAILY NEWSPAPER

MetroWest Daily News 14119
Owner: GateHouse Media Inc.
Editorial: 33 New York Ave, Framingham, Massachusetts 01701-8857 **Tel:** 1 508 626-4412
Email: metrowest@wickedlocal.com **Web site:** http://www.metrowestdailynews.com
Freq: Daily; **Circ:** 14222 Not Audited
Profile: MetroWest Daily News is published for the residents of Boston and its Western suburbs. It covers regional, state, business, technology, sports, health, lifestyle and arts. The publication honors embargoes and accepts non-disclosure agreements. Advertisings deadlines are at 4pm ET.
Language (s): English
Ad Rate: Full Page Mono 41.25
Currency: United States Dollars
DAILY NEWSPAPER

The Mexico Ledger 14242
Owner: GateHouse Media Inc.
Editorial: 300 N Washington St, Mexico, Missouri 65265-2756 **Tel:** 1 573 581-1111
Email: news@mexicoledger.com **Web site:** http://www.mexicoledger.com
Freq: Mon thru Fri; **Circ:** 4049 Not Audited
Editor: Brenda Fike; **Advertising Sales Manager:** Martin Keller; **News Editor:** Janeen Sims
Profile: The Mexico Ledger is a daily newspaper that serves Mexico and Audrain counties, as well as portions of Boone, Callaway, Montgomery, Monroe and Ralls counties, MO. It provides all the news, events and happenings. Deadlines are at 9am CT.
Language (s): English
Ad Rate: Full Page Mono 13.00
Ad Rate: Full Page Colour 210.00
Currency: United States Dollars
DAILY NEWSPAPER

The Miami Herald 15315
Owner: McClatchy Newspapers
Editorial: 3511 NW 91st Ave, Doral, Florida 33172-1216 **Tel:** 1 305 350-2111

Email: dadenews@miamiherald.com **Web site:** http://www.miamiherald.com
Freq: Daily; **Circ:** 97974 Not Audited
Editor: Amy Driscoll
Profile: The Miami Herald, published daily, is a general interest broadsheet newspaper written for the general public in the greater Miami area. The publication aims to provide readers with breaking news and features and other general information. It includes partnerships with several community publications and features a number of neighborhood sub-domains on its Web site.
Language (s): English
Ad Rate: Full Page Mono 230.00
Ad Rate: Full Page Colour 310.62
Currency: United States Dollars
DAILY NEWSPAPER

The Miami Herald - Tallahassee Bureau 15675
Editorial: 336 E College Ave Ste 303, Tallahassee, Florida 32301-1560 **Tel:** 1 850 222-3095
Bureau Chief: Mary Ellen Klas
Language (s): English
DAILY NEWSPAPER

The Miami News-Record 14530
Owner: GateHouse Media Inc.
Editorial: 14 1st Ave NW, Miami, Oklahoma 74354-6224 **Tel:** 1 918 542-5533
Email: news@miaminewsrecord.com **Web site:** http://www.miamiok.com
Freq: Fri; **Circ:** 6000 Not Audited
Advertising Sales Manager: Mark Rogers
Profile: Miami News-Record is a daily publication, with the exception of Monday and offers news stories, events listings and general coverage. The publication is geared towards residents in and around Miami, OK.
Language (s): English
Ad Rate: Full Page Mono 12.75
Ad Rate: Full Page Colour 80.00
Currency: United States Dollars
DAILY NEWSPAPER

Middlesboro Daily News 14085
Owner: Heartland Publications
Editorial: 1275 N 25th St, Middlesboro, Kentucky 40965-1024 **Tel:** 1 606 248-1010
Web site: http://www.middlesborodailynews.com
Freq: Fri; **Circ:** 6143 Not Audited
Profile: The Daily News is a local newspaper serving the Kentucky area. The publication's editorial mission is to keep its readers aware of all news and events going on in the tri-state area.
Language (s): English
Ad Rate: Full Page Mono 15.02
Ad Rate: Full Page Colour 117.00
Currency: United States Dollars
DAILY NEWSPAPER

The Middletown Press 13802
Owner: Journal Register Company
Editorial: 386 Main Street Ext Fl 4, Middletown, Connecticut 06457-4406 **Tel:** 1 860 347-3331
Email: letters@middletownpress.com **Web site:** http://www.middletownpress.com
Freq: Mon thru Fri; **Circ:** 6114 Not Audited
Editor: John Berry
Profile: The Middletown Press is a local daily newspaper which provides readers in Middlesex County, CT with local, regional and national news. News features include sports, business, lifestyle, entertainment and classifieds. It combines with The Bristol (CT)Press and The Herald in New Britain, CT on Sundays.
Language (s): English
Ad Rate: Full Page Mono 21.41
Currency: United States Dollars
DAILY NEWSPAPER

Midland Daily News 14951
Owner: Hearst Newspapers
Editorial: 124 S McDonald St, Midland, Michigan 48640-5161 **Tel:** 1 989 835-7171
Email: info@mdn.net **Web site:** http://www.ourmidland.com
Freq: Daily; **Circ:** 10003 Not Audited
News Editor: Tony Lascari
Profile: Midland Daily News strives to be a thorough source of local area news and information for its Midland, MI readership.
Language (s): English
Ad Rate: Full Page Mono 31.00
Ad Rate: Full Page Colour 700.00
Currency: United States Dollars
DAILY NEWSPAPER

Midland Reporter-Telegram 14971
Owner: Hearst Newspapers
Editorial: 201 E Illinois Ave, Midland, Texas 79701-4852 **Tel:** 1 432 682-5311
Email: news@mrt.com **Web site:** http://www.mrt.com
Freq: Daily; **Circ:** 12299 Not Audited
Publisher: Mike Distelhorst; **News Editor:** Trevor Hawes
Profile: Midland Reporter-Telegram is a community newspaper that covers national and international events and news. It is published daily for residents of the Midland, TX area. Deadlines for the publication are 5pm MT.
Language (s): English
Ad Rate: Full Page Mono 23.50
Ad Rate: Full Page Colour 26.48
Currency: United States Dollars
DAILY NEWSPAPER

Miles City Star 14286
Owner: Yellowstone Newspapers
Editorial: 818 Main St, Miles City, Montana 59301-3221 **Tel:** 1 406 234-0450
Email: mceditor@midrivers.com **Web site:** http://www.milescitystar.com
Freq: Daily; **Circ:** 3300 Not Audited
Editor: Elaine Forman; **Editor:** Denise Hartse; **Advertising Sales Manager:** Alan Hauge; **Publisher:** Dan Killoy
Profile: Miles City Star is a daily newspaper serving the community of Miles City, MT. The publication provides readers with news stories, events listings, sports coverage and advertising.
Language (s): English
Ad Rate: Full Page Mono 7.96
Ad Rate: Full Page Colour 51.48
Currency: United States Dollars
DAILY NEWSPAPER

The Milford Daily News 14126
Owner: GateHouse Media Inc.
Editorial: 159 S Main St, Milford, Massachusetts 01757-3255 **Tel:** 1 508 634-7500
Email: milforddailynews@wickedlocal.com **Web site:** http://upton.wickedlocal.com
Freq: Daily; **Circ:** 4851 Not Audited
Profile: The Milford Daily News is a daily newspaper serving residents of Milford, MA. It covers local news, sports and arts. Advertising deadlines are at 4pm ET.
Language (s): English
Ad Rate: Full Page Mono 23.06
Ad Rate: Full Page Colour 425.00
Currency: United States Dollars
DAILY NEWSPAPER

Milwaukee Journal Sentinel 15338
Owner: Gannett Co., Inc.
Editorial: 333 W State St, Milwaukee, Wisconsin 53203-1305 **Tel:** 1 414 224-2000
Email: jsmetro@journalsentinel.com **Web site:** http://www.jsonline.com
Freq: Daily; **Circ:** 202508 Not Audited
Profile: Milwaukee Journal Sentinel is written for the residents of Milwaukee and surrounding areas. It covers local, state, national and international news, as well as business, entertainment, sports and lifestyle. The paper is the product of a 1995 merger between the Milwaukee Journal, founded in 1882, and the Milwaukee Sentinel, founded in 1837. The paper uses wire services, including the Associated Press, Reuters, Bloomberg News and Dow Jones News Service for much of its national and international news. In August 2009, the paper joined a national sports content-sharing alliance with several other papers across the country.
Language (s): English
Ad Rate: Full Page Mono 166.00
Ad Rate: Full Page Colour 197.54
Currency: United States Dollars
DAILY NEWSPAPER

Milwaukee Journal Sentinel - Madison Bureau 15979
Editorial: 10 E Doty St Ste 200, Madison, Wisconsin 53703-3354 **Tel:** 1 608 258-2262
Language (s): English
DAILY NEWSPAPER

Milwaukee Journal Sentinel - Washington Bureau 15566
Editorial: Washington, District Of Columbia
Language (s): English
DAILY NEWSPAPER

Minden Press-Herald 14102
Owner: Specht Newspapers Inc.
Editorial: 203 Gleason St, Minden, Louisiana 71055-3455 **Tel:** 1 318 377-1866
Email: bruce@press-herald.com **Web site:** http://www.press-herald.com
Freq: Daily; **Circ:** 5398 Not Audited
Publisher: Josh Beavers; **Editor:** Bruce Franklin
Profile: Minden Press-Herald is a daily newspaper serving the Minden, LA area. The publication features news and events listings as well as coverage of local sports and politics. Deadlines are at 11am CT the day before publication. Advertising in the Minden Press-Herald will also run in the Bossier Press-Tribune and the Bossier Banner Progress.
Language (s): English
Ad Rate: Full Page Mono 9.50
Ad Rate: Full Page Colour 250.00
Currency: United States Dollars
DAILY NEWSPAPER

Mineral Daily News-Tribune 14836
Owner: GateHouse Media Inc.
Editorial: 21 Shamrock Drive, Keyser, West Virginia 26726-3202 **Tel:** 1 304 788-3333
Email: newsroom@newstribune.info **Web site:** http://www.newstribune.info
Freq: Mon thru Fri; **Circ:** 6000 Not Audited
Publisher: David Boden
Profile: Mineral Daily News-Tribune is a daily newspaper written for the residents of Potomac Valley, WV. Do not contact the publication via fax.
Language (s): English
Ad Rate: Full Page Mono 8.06
Ad Rate: Full Page Colour 29.03
Currency: United States Dollars
DAILY NEWSPAPER

Mineral Wells Index 14716
Owner: Community Newspaper Holdings, Inc.
Editorial: 300 SE 1st St, Mineral Wells, Texas 76067-5331 **Tel:** 1 940 325-4465
Email: editor@mineralwellsindex.com **Web site:** http://mineralwellsindex.com
Freq: Daily; **Circ:** 3500 Not Audited
Editor: David May
Profile: Mineral Wells Index is a daily newspaper providing local news coverage for the Mineral Wells and Palo Pinto County, TX area.
Language (s): English
Ad Rate: Full Page Mono 12.50
Ad Rate: Full Page Colour 345.00
Currency: United States Dollars
DAILY NEWSPAPER

Ming Pao Free Daily 79984
Owner: Ming Pao Enterprise Corporation Ltd.
Editorial: 4331 33rd St, Long Island City, New York 11101-2316 **Tel:** 1 718 786-2888
Email: mpdailynews@yahoo.com **Web site:** http://www.mingpaony.com
Freq: Daily; **Circ:** 35000 Not Audited
Profile: Ming Pao Free Daily is a daily newspaper published for Chinese Americans. The publication covers news, business and entertainment in the United States.
Language (s): Chinese
Ad Rate: Full Page Mono 123.20
Ad Rate: Full Page Colour 1088.00
Currency: United States Dollars
DAILY NEWSPAPER

The Mining Journal 14181
Owner: Ogden Newspapers
Editorial: 249 W Washington St, Marquette, Michigan 49855-4321 **Tel:** 1 906 228-2500
Web site: http://www.miningjournal.net
Freq: Daily; **Circ:** 10268 Not Audited
Publisher: Jim Reevs
Profile: The Mining Journal is a daily newspaper published for the residents of Michigan's Upper Peninsula. The publication provides local and national news as well as sports, weather, obituaries and classifieds.
Language (s): English
Ad Rate: Full Page Mono 21.65
Ad Rate: Full Page Colour 240.00
Currency: United States Dollars
DAILY NEWSPAPER

Minot Daily News 14332
Owner: Ogden Newspapers
Editorial: 301 4th St SE, Minot, North Dakota 58701-4066 **Tel:** 1 701 857-1900
Email: news@minotdailynews.com **Web site:** http://www.minotdailynews.com
Freq: Daily; **Circ:** 13459 Not Audited
Profile: Minot Daily News is a daily newspaper for Minot, ND and the surrounding areas. The newspaper covers local news, sports, business, lifestyle and politics. The intended readership of the publication are local community residents with an interest in current local issues.
Language (s): English
Ad Rate: Full Page Mono 38.95
Ad Rate: Full Page Colour 470.00
Currency: United States Dollars
DAILY NEWSPAPER

Mississippi Press 14270
Owner: Advance Publications, Inc.
Editorial: 906 Convent Ave, Pascagoula, Mississippi 39567-4334 **Tel:** 1 228 762-1111
Email: msnews@themississippipress.com **Web site:** http://www.gulflive.com/mississippipress
Freq: Daily; **Circ:** 15050 Not Audited
Profile: Mississippi Press provides news and information to the residents of Gautier, MS.
Language (s): English
Ad Rate: Full Page Mono 13.00
Ad Rate: Full Page Colour 15.61
Currency: United States Dollars
DAILY NEWSPAPER

Missoulian 14287
Owner: Lee Enterprises, Inc.
Editorial: 500 S Higgins Ave, Missoula, Montana 59801-2736 **Tel:** 1 406 523-5200
Email: newsdesk@missoulian.com **Web site:** http://www.missoulian.com
Freq: Daily; **Circ:** 22197 Not Audited
Profile: Missoulian provides local news coverage for the Western Montana area. Missoulian keeps readers informed of the latest local and regional news, business, education, health, foods and the outdoors.
Language (s): English
Ad Rate: Full Page Mono 52.00
Ad Rate: Full Page Colour 375.00
Currency: United States Dollars
DAILY NEWSPAPER

Moberly Monitor-Index 14243
Owner: GateHouse Media Inc.
Editorial: 218 N Williams St, Moberly, Missouri 65270-1534 **Tel:** 1 660 263-4123
Web site: http://www.moberlymonitor.com
Freq: Mon thru Fri; **Circ:** 4029 Not Audited
Profile: Moberly Monitor-Index & Evening Democrat is written for residents in Moberly, MO. It covers local news, national news, business and sports. Deadlines are at noon CT.
Language (s): English
Ad Rate: Full Page Mono 14.20
Ad Rate: Full Page Colour 150.00
Currency: United States Dollars
DAILY NEWSPAPER

Mobile Press-Register 15437
Owner: Advance Publications, Inc.
Editorial: 18 South Royal St., Mobile, Alabama 36602 **Tel:** 1 251 219-5400
Email: local@al.com **Web site:** http://www.al.com/mobile
Freq: 3 Times/Week; **Circ:** 38440 Not Audited
Profile: Mobile Press-Register is Alabama's oldest newspaper, founded in 1813 and published continuously since then. It is a daily publication serving residents of Mobile and Baldwin counties, Alabama, with information on hard and local news, sports, business and finance, entertainment, events, lifestyle and weather. Deadlines are at noon ET two days prior to publication.
Language (s): English
Ad Rate: Full Page Mono 111.97
Ad Rate: Full Page Colour 124.49
Currency: United States Dollars
DAILY NEWSPAPER

The Modesto Bee 15433
Owner: McClatchy Newspapers
Editorial: 1325 H St, Modesto, California 95354-2427 **Tel:** 1 209 578-2000
Email: local@modbee.com **Web site:** http://www.modbee.com
Freq: Daily; **Circ:** 60106 Not Audited
Profile: The Modesto Bee, formerly known as Morning Herald News, was founded in 1849. The newspaper's editorial mission is to provide news, information and service that exceeds customers' expectations every day.
Language (s): English
Ad Rate: Full Page Mono 110.00
Ad Rate: Full Page Colour 2087.14
Currency: United States Dollars
DAILY NEWSPAPER

Mohave Valley Daily News 14923
Owner: Brehm Communications, Inc.
Editorial: 2435 Miracle Mile, Bullhead City, Arizona 86442-7311 **Tel:** 1 928 763-2505
Web site: http://www.mohavedailynews.com
Freq: Mon thru Fri; **Circ:** 8240 Not Audited
Editor: Bill McMillen; **Publisher:** Gary Milks
Profile: Mohave Valley Daily News is a local daily newspaper serving the Mohave Valley and Bullhead City, AZ. The publication provides information on news, events, sports and weather for the area.
Language (s): English
Ad Rate: Full Page Mono 25.10
Ad Rate: Full Page Colour 399.00
Currency: United States Dollars
DAILY NEWSPAPER

Monett Times 14244
Owner: Rust Communications
Editorial: 505 E Broadway St, Monett, Missouri 65708-2333 **Tel:** 1 417 235-3135
Email: editor@monett-times.com **Web site:** http://www.monett-times.com
Circ: 4100
Publisher: Jacob Brower; **Advertising Sales Manager:** Karen Waltrip
Profile: Monett Times is a daily newspaper that provides local news coverage for residents of Monett, MO. In addition to news, the publication also covers sports, business, and arts and entertainment. The paper is written for the general local community.
Language (s): English
Ad Rate: Full Page Mono 5.95
Ad Rate: Full Page Colour 120.00
Currency: United States Dollars
DAILY NEWSPAPER

The Monitor 14713
Owner: Aim Media
Editorial: 1400 E Nolana Ave, McAllen, Texas 78504-6111 **Tel:** 1 956 683-4000
Email: news@themonitor.com **Web site:** http://www.themonitor.com
Freq: Daily; **Circ:** 24590 Not Audited
Profile: The Monitor in McAllen, TX is a local daily newspaper that covers local news, sports, business and events.
Language (s): English
Ad Rate: Full Page Mono 50.22
Ad Rate: Full Page Colour 551.00
Currency: United States Dollars
DAILY NEWSPAPER

The Monroe News 14183
Owner: GateHouse Media Inc.
Editorial: 20 W 1st St, Monroe, Michigan 48161-2333 **Tel:** 1 734 242-1100
Web site: http://www.monroenews.com
Freq: Daily; **Circ:** 13521 Not Audited
National News Editor: Harry Orscheln; **Advertising Sales Manager:** David Zewicky
Profile: Monroe News is a daily newspaper that provides local news coverage for the Monroe County, MI area. The paper's editorial mission is to enhance the lives of its readers through information. All inquiries and press releases should be directed to the news editor by e-mail, or to the editorial department fax at 734-242-0937.
Language (s): English
Ad Rate: Full Page Mono 23.26
Ad Rate: Full Page Colour 26.76
Currency: United States Dollars
DAILY NEWSPAPER

The Monroe Times 14815
Owner: Morris Multimedia, Inc.
Editorial: 1065 4th Ave W, Monroe, Wisconsin 53566-1318 **Tel:** 1 608 328-4202
Web site: http://www.themonroetimes.com

Freq: Daily; **Circ:** 3431 Not Audited
Publisher: Skip Bliss; **Editor:** Mary Jane Grenzow; **News Editor:** Andrew Hellpap; **Advertising Sales Manager:** Laura Hughes
Profile: The Monroe Times is a local daily newspaper serving the residents of Green and Lafayette counties in Southern Wisconsin. The newspaper covers local and regional news, sports, entertainment, business and community events. Deadlines are at 9am CT the day before issue date.
Language (s): English
Ad Rate: Full Page Mono 34.00
Ad Rate: Full Page Colour 105.28
Currency: United States Dollars
DAILY NEWSPAPER

Montana Standard 14279
Owner: Lee Enterprises, Inc.
Editorial: 25 W Granite St, Butte, Montana 59701-9213 **Tel:** 1 406 496-5500
Email: editor@mtstandard.com **Web site:** http://www.mtstandard.com
Freq: Daily; **Circ:** 36300 Not Audited
Editor: Matt Christensen; **Advertising Sales Manager:** Jenean Kujawa
Profile: Montana Standard is a daily newspaper reporting local, national and international news to the residents of southern Montana.
Language (s): English
Ad Rate: Full Page Mono 33.00
Ad Rate: Full Page Colour 208.23
Currency: United States Dollars
DAILY NEWSPAPER

The Monterey County Herald 13739
Owner: MediaNews Group
Editorial: 2200 Garden Rd, Monterey, California 93940-5329 **Tel:** 1 831 372-3311
Email: editors@montereyherald.com **Web site:** http://www.montereyherald.com
Freq: Daily; **Circ:** 22524 Not Audited
Editor: Donald Miller; **Publisher:** Gary Omernick
Profile: The Monterey County Herald is a daily newspaper serving Salinas, Carmel and Monterey County, CA. It covers local news, entertainment, business and sports.
Language (s): English
Ad Rate: Full Page Mono 70.30
Ad Rate: Full Page Colour 754.00
Currency: United States Dollars
DAILY NEWSPAPER

Montgomery Advertiser 15463
Owner: Gannett Co., Inc.
Editorial: 425 Molton St, Montgomery, Alabama 36104-3523 **Tel:** 1 334 262-1611
Email: mgm-newsofrecord@gannett.com **Web site:** http://www.montgomeryadvertiser.com
Freq: Daily; **Circ:** 26521 Not Audited
Profile: Montgomery Advertiser's editorial mission is to be the number one source for news, information, and advertising needs for the Montgomery, AL metropolitan area. This publication provides a forum for diverse opinions, serves as a force for positive change, and acts as a watchdog for the public interest and the First Amendment.
Language (s): English
Ad Rate: Full Page Mono 27.00
Ad Rate: Full Page Colour 30.00
Currency: United States Dollars
DAILY NEWSPAPER

Montrose Daily Press 13791
Owner: Wick Communications Inc.
Editorial: 3684 N Townsend Ave, Montrose, Colorado 81401-5949 **Tel:** 1 970 249-3444
Email: editor@montrosepress.com **Web site:** http://www.montrosepress.com
Freq: Fri; **Circ:** 4542
Advertising Sales Manager: Dennis Anderson; **Publisher:** Vincent LaBoy
Profile: Montrose Daily Press is a local newspaper serving the residents of Montrose, CO. It includes information on local news, weather, sports, business and arts & entertainment.
Language (s): English
Ad Rate: Full Page Mono 13.00
Ad Rate: Full Page Colour 275.00
Currency: United States Dollars
DAILY NEWSPAPER

The Morning Call 15322
Owner: tronc
Editorial: 101 N 6th St, Allentown, Pennsylvania 18101-1403 **Tel:** 1 610 820-6500 3
Email: mcnews@mcall.com **Web site:** http://www.mcall.com
Freq: Daily; **Circ:** 65357 Not Audited
Profile: The Morning Call is a daily newspaper published in nine counties in Pennsylvania. It covers arts & entertainment, food, sports, travel, television, features, business and local, national and international news.
Language (s): English
Ad Rate: Full Page Mono 110.77
Ad Rate: Full Page Colour 1142.00
Currency: United States Dollars
DAILY NEWSPAPER

The Morning Call - Harrisburg Bureau 15895
Editorial: Main Capitol Bldg 524, Harrisburg, Pennsylvania 17120-0001 **Tel:** 1 717 783-7305
Language (s): English
DAILY NEWSPAPER

Morning Journal 14464
Owner: Ogden Newspapers
Editorial: 308 Maple St, Lisbon, Ohio 44432-1205
Tel: 1 330 424-9541
Web site: http://www.morningjournalnews.com
Freq: Daily; **Circ:** 8482 Not Audited
Publisher: Larry Dorschner; **Advertising Sales Manager:** Lori McIntosh; **Editor:** Dennis Spalvieri; **Editor:** Dorma Tolson
Profile: Morning Journal is a daily newspaper providing news for Lisbon, OH.
Language (s): English
Ad Rate: Full Page Mono 26.75
Currency: United States Dollars
DAILY NEWSPAPER

The Morning Journal 14467
Owner: Digital First Media
Editorial: 1657 Broadway, Lorain, Ohio 44052-3439
Tel: 1 440 245-6901
Email: news@morningjournal.com **Web site:** http://www.morningjournal.com
Freq: Daily; **Circ:** 23500 Not Audited
Profile: The Morning Journal is a daily newspaper serving the residents of Lorain, Erie, Huron and Cuyahoga County, OH. It includes information on local news, weather, sports, business and entertainment.
Language (s): English
Ad Rate: Full Page Mono 68.75
Ad Rate: Full Page Colour 251.70
Currency: United States Dollars
DAILY NEWSPAPER

The Morning News 13898
Owner: Horizon Publications
Editorial: 34 N Ash St, Blackfoot, Idaho 83221-2101
Tel: 1 208 785-1100
Email: mnews@am-news.com **Web site:** http://www.am-news.com
Freq: Daily; **Circ:** 4250 Not Audited
Advertising Sales Manager: Wayne Ingram; **Publisher:** Leonard Martin
Profile: The Morning News provides local news to the Blackfoot, ID community. The newspaper covers local news, business, sports and arts & entertainment stories.
Language (s): English
Ad Rate: Full Page Mono 14.50
Ad Rate: Full Page Colour 150.00
Currency: United States Dollars
DAILY NEWSPAPER

Morning Sentinel 14155
Owner: Maine Today Media Inc.
Editorial: 31 Front St, Waterville, Maine 04901-6626
Tel: 1 207 873-3341
Web site: http://www.centralmaine.com/
Freq: Daily; **Circ:** 11106 Not Audited
Advertising Sales Manager: Kirk Bird; **Advertising Sales Manager:** Rick DeBruin
Profile: Morning Sentinel is a local newspaper serving the residents of Waterville, ME. It includes information on local news, weather, sports, business and entertainment.
Language (s): English
Ad Rate: Full Page Mono 60.33
Ad Rate: Full Page Colour 657.28
Currency: United States Dollars
DAILY NEWSPAPER

The Morning Sun 14065
Owner: GateHouse Media Inc.
Editorial: 701 N Locust St, Pittsburg, Kansas 66762-4038 **Tel:** 1 620 231-2600
Web site: http://www.morningsun.net
Freq: Daily; **Circ:** 8145 Not Audited
Profile: The Morning Sun is a local newspaper serving the residents of Pittsburg, KS. It includes information on local news, weather, sports, business and arts & entertainment.
Language (s): English
Ad Rate: Full Page Mono 15.30
Ad Rate: Full Page Colour 185.00
Currency: United States Dollars
DAILY NEWSPAPER

Morning Sun 14185
Owner: Journal Register Company
Editorial: 711 W Pickard St, Mount Pleasant, Michigan 48858-1585 **Tel:** 1 989 779-6000
Email: news@michigannewspapers.com **Web site:** http://www.themorningsun.com
Freq: Daily; **Circ:** 10958 Not Audited
Advertising Sales Manager: Carol Turner
Profile: Morning Sun is a regional newspaper serving the residents of Gratiot County, Isabella County, and Southern Clare County, MI. It includes information on local news, weather, sports, business and arts & entertainment.
Language (s): English
Ad Rate: Full Page Mono 17.45
Currency: United States Dollars
DAILY NEWSPAPER

The Morning Times 14612
Owner: Sample News Group
Editorial: 201 N Lehigh Ave, Sayre, Pennsylvania 18840-2246 **Tel:** 1 570 888-9643
Email: whoweler@morning-times.com **Web site:** http://www.morning-times.com
Freq: Mon thru Fri; **Circ:** 6000 Not Audited
Publisher: Kelly Luvison
Profile: The Morning Times is published daily for residents of Sayre, Athens and South Waverly, PA and Waverly, NY. The newspaper covers local news, sports and community events.
Language (s): English
Ad Rate: Full Page Mono 12.54
Ad Rate: Full Page Colour 280.00
Currency: United States Dollars
DAILY NEWSPAPER

Morris Herald-News 13947
Owner: Shaw Media
Editorial: 1804 N Division St, Morris, Illinois 60450-1127 **Tel:** 1 815 942-3221
Email: news@morrisherald-news.com **Web site:** http://www.morrisherald-news.com
Freq: Daily; **Circ:** 6867 Not Audited
Publisher: Gerry Burke; **Editor:** Kate Schott; **Editor:** T.G. Smith
Profile: Morris Herald-News is a local newspaper serving the residents of Morris, IL. It includes information on local news, weather, sports, business and arts & entertainment.
Language (s): English
Ad Rate: Full Page Mono 16.10
Ad Rate: Full Page Colour 46.76
Currency: United States Dollars
DAILY NEWSPAPER

Moscow Pullman Daily News 13904
Owner: TPC Holdings
Editorial: 409 S Jackson St, Moscow, Idaho 83843-2251 **Tel:** 1 208 882-5561
Email: editor@dnews.com **Web site:** http://www.dnews.com
Freq: Daily; **Circ:** 7500 Not Audited
Publisher & Editor: Nathan Alford; **News Editor:** Devin Rokyta; **Advertising Sales Manager:** Craig Staszkow
Profile: Moscow Pullman Daily News is published for the residents of Moscow, Whitman County and Latah County, ID. The newspaper covers local news, weather, sports, arts & entertainment and business.
Language (s): English
Ad Rate: Full Page Mono 13.64
Ad Rate: Full Page Colour 42.58
Currency: United States Dollars
DAILY NEWSPAPER

The Moultrie Observer 13848
Owner: Community Newspaper Holdings, Inc.
Editorial: 25 N Main St, Moultrie, Georgia 31768-3861 **Tel:** 1 229 985-4545
Web site: http://www.moultrieobserver.com
Freq: Daily; **Circ:** 7485 Not Audited
Editor & Publisher: Dwain Walden
Profile: The Moultrie Observer is published daily for the residents of Moultrie, GA and surrounding areas. The newspaper covers local and regional news, sports, education, lifestyles and entertainment.
Language (s): English
Ad Rate: Full Page Mono 21.05
Ad Rate: Full Page Colour 294.00
Currency: United States Dollars
DAILY NEWSPAPER

Moundsville Daily Echo 14841
Owner: Self-Owned
Editorial: 715 Lafayette Ave, Moundsville, West Virginia 26041 **Tel:** 1 304 845-2660
Freq: Daily; **Circ:** 3805 Not Audited
Profile: The Moundsville Daily Echo is a local newspaper serving the residents of Moundsville, WV. It includes information on local news, weather, sports, business, and entertainment.
Language (s): English
Ad Rate: Full Page Mono 4.17
Currency: United States Dollars
DAILY NEWSPAPER

Mount Airy News 14326
Owner: Civitas Media
Editorial: 319 N Renfro St, Mount Airy, North Carolina 27030-3838 **Tel:** 1 336 786-4141
Email: mtanews@civitasmedia.com **Web site:** http://www.mtairynews.com
Freq: Daily; **Circ:** 11017 Not Audited
Profile: Mount Airy News is a local newspaper written for residents of Surry County, NC. The newspaper is published from Sunday through Saturday mornings and covers local news, sports, business and events. The deadline for submissions is generally three days prior to the issue date.
Language (s): English
Ad Rate: Full Page Mono 11.40
Ad Rate: Full Page Colour 90.00
Currency: United States Dollars
DAILY NEWSPAPER

Mount Carmel Register 13948
Owner: Brehm Communications, Inc.
Editorial: 115 E 4th St, Mount Carmel, Illinois 62863-2110 **Tel:** 1 618 262-5144
Email: news@mtcarmelregister.com **Web site:** http://www.mtcarmelregister.com
Freq: Daily; **Circ:** 3973 Not Audited
Editor: Andrea Howe; **Publisher:** Phil Summers
Profile: Mount Carmel Republican-Register is published daily for the residents of Wabash County, IL. The newspaper covers local news and community events.
Language (s): English
Ad Rate: Full Page Mono 12.15
Ad Rate: Full Page Colour 160.00
Currency: United States Dollars
DAILY NEWSPAPER

Mount Pleasant Daily Tribune 14717
Owner: Granite Publications
Editorial: 1705 Industrial Rd, Mount Pleasant, Texas 75455-2235 **Tel:** 1 903 572-1705
Email: news@dailytribune.net **Web site:** http://www.tribnow.com
Freq: Daily; **Circ:** 5000 Not Audited
Profile: Mount Pleasant Daily Tribune is published for the residents of Titus, Franklin, Camp and Morris counties, TX. It covers news, sports, education, healthcare, business, lifestyle and arts & entertainment.
Language (s): English
Ad Rate: Full Page Mono 15.00
Ad Rate: Full Page Colour 230.00
Currency: United States Dollars
DAILY NEWSPAPER

Mount Pleasant News 13886
Owner: Inland Media Inc.
Editorial: 215 W Monroe St, Mount Pleasant, Iowa 52641-2110 **Tel:** 1 319 385-3131
Email: pub@mpnews.net **Web site:** http://www.mpnews.net
Freq: Daily; **Circ:** 2450 Not Audited
Publisher & Editor: Bill Gray; **News Editor:** Brooks Taylor
Profile: Mount Pleasant News is a local newspaper serving the residents of Mount Pleasant, IA. It includes information on local news, weather, sports, business and entertainment.
Language (s): English
Ad Rate: Full Page Mono 10.84
Ad Rate: Full Page Colour 210.00
Currency: United States Dollars
DAILY NEWSPAPER

Mount Vernon News 14476
Owner: Progressive Communications
Editorial: 18 E Vine St, Mount Vernon, Ohio 43050-3200 **Tel:** 1 740 397-5333
Web site: http://www.mountvernonnews.com
Freq: Daily; **Circ:** 9099 Not Audited
Publisher: Kay Culbertson; **Advertising Sales Manager:** Corby Wise
Profile: Mount Vernon News is a local newspaper serving the residents of Mount Vernon, Fredericktown, Centerburg, Gambier, Danville, Sparta, Bladensburg and Utica, OH. It includes information on local news, weather, sports, business and entertainment.
Language (s): English
Ad Rate: Full Page Mono 15.00
Currency: United States Dollars
DAILY NEWSPAPER

Mountain Democrat 15041
Owner: McNaughton Newspapers
Editorial: 1360 Broadway, Placerville, California 95667-5902 **Tel:** 1 530 622-1255
Email: mtdemo@mtdemocrat.net **Web site:** http://www.mtdemocrat.com
Freq: Fri; **Circ:** 12544 Not Audited
Editor: Noel Stack
Profile: Mountain Democrat is a local newspaper serving the residents of El Dorado County, CA since 1854. Regular features include local news, weather, sports, business, and entertainment.
Language (s): English
Ad Rate: Full Page Mono 22.50
Ad Rate: Full Page Colour 73.87
Currency: United States Dollars
DAILY NEWSPAPER

Mountain Mail 13793
Owner: Arkansas Valley Publishing
Editorial: 125 E 2nd St, Salida, Colorado 81201-2114
Tel: 1 719 539-6691
Web site: http://www.themountainmail.com
Freq: Daily; **Circ:** 4000 Not Audited
Publisher & Editor: Merle Baranczyk
Profile: Mountain Mail is a daily local newspaper serving the residents of Salida, CO and surrounding areas. The publication features local news, weather, sports, business, and entertainment.
Language (s): English
Ad Rate: Full Page Mono 8.50
Ad Rate: Full Page Colour 70.00
Currency: United States Dollars
DAILY NEWSPAPER

The Mountain Press 14680
Owner: Paxton Media Group
Editorial: 119 River Bend Dr, Sevierville, Tennessee 37876-1943 **Tel:** 1 865 428-0746
Email: editor@themountainpress.com **Web site:** http://www.themountainpress.com
Freq: Daily; **Circ:** 8400 Not Audited
Editor: Jason Davis; **Publisher:** Jana Thomasson
Profile: The Mountain Press is a local newspaper serving the residents of Sevier County, TN. It includes information on local news, weather, sports, business and entertainment. Deadlines are the same day as the issue date.
Language (s): English
Ad Rate: Full Page Mono 21.11
Ad Rate: Full Page Colour 320.00
Currency: United States Dollars
DAILY NEWSPAPER

Murray Ledger & Times 14086
Owner: Murray Newspapers Inc.
Editorial: 1001 Whitnell Ave, Murray, Kentucky 42071-2975 **Tel:** 1 270 753-1916
Email: editor@murrayledger.com **Web site:** http://www.murrayledger.com
Freq: Mon thru Fri; **Circ:** 7159 Not Audited

Advertising Sales Manager: Chris Woodall
Profile: Murray Ledger & Times is a daily newspaper published for the residents of Murray, KY and the surrounding area. It covers local news, sports and business.
Language (s): English
Ad Rate: Full Page Mono 10.50
Ad Rate: Full Page Colour 125.00
Currency: United States Dollars
DAILY NEWSPAPER

Muscatine Journal 13887
Owner: Lee Enterprises, Inc.
Editorial: 301 E 3rd St, Muscatine, Iowa 52761-4116 **Tel:** 1 563 263-2331
Email: news@muscatinejournal.com **Web site:** http://www.muscatinejournal.com
Freq: Mon thru Fri; **Circ:** 5127
Publisher: Karla Pinner; **Advertising Sales Manager:** Jaime Weikert
Profile: Muscatine Journal is a local daily newspaper written for residents of Muscatine, IA. The publication's editorial mission is to attract as many readers as possible by providing the most up-to-date information about local news and events.
Language (s): English
Ad Rate: Full Page Mono 13.00
Currency: United States Dollars
DAILY NEWSPAPER

Muskegon Chronicle 14186
Owner: MLive Media Group
Editorial: 500 W Western Ave Ste 100, Muskegon, Michigan 49440-1000 **Tel:** 1 231 683-2329
Email: munews@mlive.com **Web site:** http://www.mlive.com/chronicle
Freq: Daily; **Circ:** 18644 Not Audited
Profile: Muskegon Chronicle is a local daily newspaper written for residents of Muskegon, MI and the surrounding area. The publication's editorial mission is to provide news and information to the community. Editorial deadlines are daily at 8:30am CT.
Language (s): English
Ad Rate: Full Page Mono 98.30
Ad Rate: Full Page Colour 775.00
Currency: United States Dollars
DAILY NEWSPAPER

Muskogee Daily Phoenix 14531
Owner: Community Newspaper Holdings, Inc.
Editorial: 214 Wall St, Muskogee, Oklahoma 74401-6644 **Tel:** 1 918 684-2828
Email: news@muskogeephoenix.com **Web site:** http://www.muskogeephoenix.com
Freq: Daily; **Circ:** 9079 Not Audited
Editor: Mike Kays
Profile: Muskogee Daily Phoenix's editorial mission is to bring the eight area counties local and national news, sports and features. The publication is written for the eight counties in northeast Oklahoma.
Language (s): English
Ad Rate: Full Page Mono 34.67
Ad Rate: Full Page Colour 349.00
Currency: United States Dollars
DAILY NEWSPAPER

The Napa Valley Register 13740
Owner: Lee Enterprises, Inc.
Editorial: 1615 2nd St, Napa, California 94559-2818 **Tel:** 1 707 226-3711
Web site: http://www.napavalleyregister.com
Freq: Daily; **Circ:** 11659
Publisher: Brenda Speth
Profile: The mission of Napa Valley Register is to provide news and information to the residents of Napa Valley, CA. The publication is written for residents of Napa Valley, CA and surrounding areas. The paper is delivered early in the morning to all subscribers and newsstands, seven days a week.
Language (s): English
Ad Rate: Full Page Mono 23.90
Ad Rate: Full Page Colour 27.40
Currency: United States Dollars
DAILY NEWSPAPER

Naples Daily News 13823
Owner: Gannett Co., Inc.
Editorial: 1100 Immokalee Rd, Naples, Florida 34110-4810 **Tel:** 1 239 262-3161
Email: news@naplesnews.com **Web site:** http://www.naplesnews.com
Freq: Daily; **Circ:** 44552 Not Audited
Editor: Manny Garcia; **Deadline News Editor:** Dave Osborn
Profile: Naples Daily News is a local newspaper published for the residents of Naples and Collier County, FL. The newspaper covers local and national news, business, arts & entertainment, events and sports.
Language (s): English
Ad Rate: Full Page Mono 83.70
Ad Rate: Full Page Colour 104.63
Currency: United States Dollars
DAILY NEWSPAPER

Natchez Democrat 14269
Owner: Boone Newspapers Inc.
Editorial: 503 N Canal St, Natchez, Mississippi 39120-2902 **Tel:** 1 601 442-9101
Email: newsroom@natchezdemocrat.com **Web site:** http://www.natchezdemocrat.com
Freq: Daily; **Circ:** 10500 Not Audited
Publisher: Kevin Cooper
Profile: Natchez Democrat's editorial mission is to provide news and information to the people of Natchez, MS and surrounding areas. The publication is written for the people of Natchez and Vidalia, MS and those that live on the Mississippi-Louisiana boarder. The publication covers all topics of interest to the local community.
Language (s): English
Ad Rate: Full Page Mono 22.50
Ad Rate: Full Page Colour 255.00
Currency: United States Dollars
DAILY NEWSPAPER

Natchitoches Times 14932
Owner: Natchitoches Times
Editorial: 904 South Dr, Natchitoches, Louisiana 71457 **Tel:** 1 318 352-3618
Email: news@natchitochestimes.com **Web site:** http://www.natchitochestimes.com
Freq: Daily; **Circ:** 4000 Not Audited
Editor: Carolyn Roy; **Publisher:** Lovan Thomas
Profile: Natchitoches Times' editorial mission is to provide news and information to its readers. The publication is written for the residents of Natchitoches, LA. The publication covers current news and events.
Language (s): English
Ad Rate: Full Page Mono 11.64
Currency: United States Dollars
DAILY NEWSPAPER

National Herald 79993
Editorial: 3710 30th St, Long Island City, New York 11101-2614 **Tel:** 1 718 784-5255
Email: info@thenationalherald.com **Web site:** http://www.thenationalherald.com
Freq: Daily; **Circ:** 80000 Not Audited
Publisher & Editor: Antonis Diamataris; **Athens News Editor:** Aris Papadopoulos
Profile: National Herald is published daily for Greek communities in New York and Massachusetts. The newspaper covers local, national and international news, business, culture and entertainment.
Language (s): English
Ad Rate: Full Page Mono 36.97
Ad Rate: Full Page Colour 40.30
Currency: United States Dollars
DAILY NEWSPAPER

Neosho Daily News 14245
Owner: GateHouse Media Inc.
Editorial: 1006 W Harmony St, Neosho, Missouri 64850-1631 **Tel:** 1 417 451-1520
Web site: http://www.neoshodailynews.com
Freq: Mon thru Fri; **Circ:** 3474 Not Audited
News Editor: Todd Higdon
Profile: Neosho Daily News is a local daily newspaper serving Neosho, MO and the surrounding area. It provides information on news and events of interest to the local community.
Language (s): English
Ad Rate: Full Page Mono 10.75
Ad Rate: Full Page Colour 50.00
Currency: United States Dollars
DAILY NEWSPAPER

Nevada Appeal 14386
Owner: Swift Newspapers
Editorial: 580 Mallory Way, Carson City, Nevada 89701-5360 **Tel:** 1 775 882-2111
Email: editor@nevadaappeal.com **Web site:** http://www.nevadaappeal.com
Freq: Fri; **Circ:** 16707 Not Audited
Publisher: Mark Raymond
Profile: Nevada Appeal is a local, daily newspaper serving Carson City, NV and the surrounding area. It covers news, events, sports and weather. Lead time varies.
Language (s): English
Ad Rate: Full Page Mono 35.80
Ad Rate: Full Page Colour 112.28
Currency: United States Dollars
DAILY NEWSPAPER

Nevada Daily Mail 14246
Owner: Rust Communications
Editorial: 131 S Cedar St, Nevada, Missouri 64772-3309 **Tel:** 1 417 667-3344
Email: editor@nevadadailymail.com **Web site:** http://www.nevadadailymail.com
Freq: Mon thru Fri; **Circ:** 2600 Not Audited
Advertising Sales Manager: Lorie Harter
Profile: Nevada Daily Mail is a local newspaper serving Bourbon County and Nevada, MO. It provides information, news, community events, sports, business and entertainment. The weekend edition, entitled the Sunday Herald-Tribune, is combined with the Fort Scott (KS) Tribune's weekend edition and is distributed to residents in both Vernon County, MO and Bourbon County, KS.
Language (s): English
Ad Rate: Full Page Mono 9.85
Ad Rate: Full Page Colour 150.00
Currency: United States Dollars
DAILY NEWSPAPER

New Braunfels Herald-Zeitung 14747
Owner: Southern Newspapers, Inc.
Editorial: 549 Landa St, New Braunfels, Texas 78130-6109 **Tel:** 1 830 625-9144
Email: news@herald-zeitung.com **Web site:** http://herald-zeitung.com
Freq: Fri; **Circ:** 8000 Not Audited
Advertising Sales Manager: Dave Burck
Profile: New Braunfels Herald-Zeitung is a local newspaper written for residents of Comal County, TX. The newspaper covers local news, sports and community events.
Language (s): English
Ad Rate: Full Page Mono 10.50
Ad Rate: Full Page Colour 250.00
Currency: United States Dollars
DAILY NEWSPAPER

New Britain Herald 13803
Owner: Central Connecticut Communications
Editorial: 1 Court St Fl 4, New Britain, Connecticut 06051-2262 **Tel:** 1 860 225-4601
Web site: http://www.newbritainherald.com
Freq: Daily; **Circ:** 4356 Not Audited
Advertising Sales Manager: Gary Curran
Profile: New Britain Herald covers local news, sports and information for residents of New Britain, CT. It combines with The Bristol (CT) Press on Sundays. It shares offices with Imprint Newspapers, a parent publisher of three community weeklies.
Language (s): English
Ad Rate: Full Page Mono 29.48
Currency: United States Dollars
DAILY NEWSPAPER

New Castle News 14603
Owner: Community Newspaper Holdings, Inc.
Editorial: 27 N Mercer St, New Castle, Pennsylvania 16101-3806 **Tel:** 1 724 654-6651
Email: nceditor@ncnewsonline.com **Web site:** http://www.ncnewsonline.com
Freq: Daily; **Circ:** 13272
Publisher: Lawrence Corvi
Profile: New Castle News is published daily for the residents of New Castle, PA and surrounding areas. The newspaper covers local and state news, business, sports, lifestyles and entertainment.
Language (s): English
Ad Rate: Full Page Mono 35.75
Ad Rate: Full Page Colour 295.00
Currency: United States Dollars
DAILY NEWSPAPER

The New Hampshire Union Leader 15405
Owner: Nackey S. Loeb School of Communications Inc.
Editorial: 100 William Loeb Dr, Manchester, New Hampshire 03109-5309 **Tel:** 1 603 668-4321
Email: news@unionleader.com **Web site:** http://www.unionleader.com
Freq: Daily; **Circ:** 50412
Publisher: Joseph McQuaid; **Advertising Sales Manager:** Robin Wilson
Profile: The New Hampshire Union Leader is published daily for residents of Manchester, NH and surrounding communities. The newspaper covers local, regional and national news as well as local recreation, entertainment, lifestyle and travel. The newspaper's Sunday edition is called the New Hampshire Sunday News.
Language (s): English
Ad Rate: Full Page Mono 51.15
Ad Rate: Full Page Colour 170.50
Currency: United States Dollars
DAILY NEWSPAPER

The New Hampshire Union Leader - Concord Bureau 15806
Editorial: State House Room 116, Concord, New Hampshire 03301-4951 **Tel:** 1 603 225-3500
Language (s): English
DAILY NEWSPAPER

New Haven Register 15358
Owner: Digital First Media
Editorial: 100 Gando Dr, New Haven, Connecticut 06513-1049 **Tel:** 1 203 789-5200
Web site: http://www.nhregister.com
Freq: Daily; **Circ:** 30572 Not Audited
Profile: New Haven Register is Connecticut's second largest daily newspaper. The publication provides readers throughout New Haven, CT and the surrounding areas with local, regional and national news.
Language (s): English
Ad Rate: Full Page Mono 142.14
Ad Rate: Full Page Colour 170.20
Currency: United States Dollars
DAILY NEWSPAPER

New Jersey Herald 14360
Owner: Quincy Newspapers, Inc.
Editorial: 2 Spring St, Newton, New Jersey 07860-2077 **Tel:** 1 973 383-1500
Email: newsroom@njherald.com **Web site:** http://www.njherald.com
Freq: Daily; **Circ:** 11814
Editor: Kathy Stevens
Profile: New Jersey Herald is published daily for the residents of Sussex County, NJ. The newspaper covers local and regional news, business, sports, lifestyles and entertainment.
Language (s): English
Ad Rate: Full Page Mono 24.76
Ad Rate: Full Page Colour 81.83
Currency: United States Dollars
DAILY NEWSPAPER

The New Orleans Advocate 842475
Owner: Capital City Press LLC
Editorial: 840 Saint Charles Ave, New Orleans, Louisiana 70130-3716 **Tel:** 1 504 636-7400
Email: newstips@theadvocate.com **Web site:** http://www.theadvocate.com/new_orleans
Freq: Daily
St. Tammany Bureau Chief: Sara Pagones
Profile: New Orleans Advocate is a Daily Newspaper providing Local, Community, Metro and City, Arts & Entertainment, Society, Sports and Business coverage for the residents of the New Orleans, LA metro area.
Language (s): English
DAILY NEWSPAPER

New York Daily News 15373
Owner: Daily News L.P.
Editorial: 4 New York Plz, New York, New York 10004-2413 **Tel:** 1 212 210-2100
Email: news@nydailynews.com **Web site:** http://www.nydailynews.com
Freq: Daily; **Circ:** 276122
Profile: Daily News is a general-interest daily newspaper serving the New York City and Long Island metropolitan area. Business coverage gives readers both a national and local perspective on news and carries the top stories from Wall Street, as well as the top performing stocks and mutual funds. Consumer topics include lifestyle issues, arts and entertainment, as well as health and medicine. Deadlines fall every afternoon at 5pm ET.
Language (s): English
Ad Rate: Full Page Mono 512.94
Ad Rate: Full Page Colour 589.88
Currency: United States Dollars
DAILY NEWSPAPER

New York Daily News - City Hall Bureau 16134
Editorial: Rm 9 City Hall, New York, New York 10007-1203 **Tel:** 1 212 210-2214
Language (s): English
DAILY NEWSPAPER

New York Daily News - Police Bureau 75174
Editorial: 1 Police Plz, New York, New York 10038-1403 **Tel:** 1 212 210-2234
Bureau Chief: Rocco Parascandola
Language (s): English
DAILY NEWSPAPER

New York Daily News - Statehouse Bureau 15820
Editorial: State Capitol LCA 3rd Floor, Albany, New York 12224 **Tel:** 1 518 463-4287
Bureau Chief: Kenneth Lovett
Language (s): English
DAILY NEWSPAPER

New York Post 15365
Owner: News America Publishing Inc.
Editorial: 1211 Avenue of the Americas, New York, New York 10036-8701 **Tel:** 1 212 930-8000 8
Email: tips@nypost.com **Web site:** http://www.nypost.com
Freq: Daily; **Circ:** 424721 Not Audited
Publisher: Jesse Angelo
Profile: New York Post is a tabloid-format newspaper aimed at the general public in the New York City area. The publication covers local and regional news, business, sports, entertainment, celebrities, fashion and travel.
Language (s): English
Ad Rate: Full Page Mono 1115.43
Ad Rate: Full Page Colour 844.50
Currency: United States Dollars
DAILY NEWSPAPER

New York Post - New York Bureau 15822
Editorial: 9 City Hall, New York, New York 10007-1200 **Tel:** 1 212 566-2367
Language (s): English
DAILY NEWSPAPER

New York Post - Washington Bureau 15588
Editorial: 529 14th St NW Ste 1114, Washington, District Of Columbia 20045-2101 **Tel:** 1 202 393-1787
Language (s): English
DAILY NEWSPAPER

The New York Times 15286
Owner: New York Times Company (The)
Editorial: 620 8th Ave, New York, New York 10018-1618 **Tel:** 1 212 556-1234
Email: news-tips@nytimes.com **Web site:** http://www.nytimes.com
Freq: Daily; **Circ:** 90
National News Editor: Jennifer Kingson; **Publisher:** Arthur Ochs Sulzberger
Profile: The New York Times offers the latest news from around the world. There are several different editions of the paper for Eastern and national regions. The paper gets much of its content and reporting from its many bureaus. The foreign desk is responsible for correspondents and stringers around the world. The paper offers DealBook pages Tuesdays through Fridays, with content corresponding with the DealBook blog. Daily deadlines are usually between 5pm and 6pm ET. The paper does not accept artwork. This outlet covers TCommerce (Television Commerce). The lead time for feature and news coverage is one day to one week. The lead time for advertising is 30 days.
Language (s): English
Ad Rate: Full Page Mono 621.00
Ad Rate: Full Page Colour 865.45
Currency: United States Dollars
DAILY NEWSPAPER

The New York Times - Albany Bureau 15828
Editorial: Albany, New York **Tel:** 1 518 436-0757
Bureau Chief: Susanne Craig
Language (s): English
DAILY NEWSPAPER

The New York Times - Atlanta Bureau 15825
Editorial: 8302 Dunwoody Pl Ste 300, Atlanta, Georgia 30350-3351 **Tel:** 1 770 643-0053
Language (s): English
DAILY NEWSPAPER

The New York Times - Baghdad Bureau 842765
Editorial: Address Restricted, Baghdad
Language (s): English
DAILY NEWSPAPER

The New York Times - Beijing Bureau 512308
Editorial: Jian Wai Diplomatic Compound 8-1-11, Beijing 100600 **Tel:** 86 106 532-3115
Bureau Chief: Edward Wong
Language (s): English
DAILY NEWSPAPER

The New York Times - Beirut Bureau 842769
Editorial: Address Restricted, Beirut **Tel:** 961 1 362-768
Language (s): English
DAILY NEWSPAPER

The New York Times - Berlin Bureau 154516
Editorial: Grolmanstrasse 52, Berlin 10623
Tel: 49 30 3127928
Language (s): English
DAILY NEWSPAPER

The New York Times - Cairo Bureau 842764
Editorial: Address Restricted, Cairo
Language (s): English
DAILY NEWSPAPER

The New York Times - Chicago Bureau 15514
Editorial: 111 E Wacker Dr Ste 2912, Chicago, Illinois 60601-4200 **Tel:** 1 312 552-7200
Email: chicago@nytimes.com
Bureau Chief: Monica Davey
Language (s): English
DAILY NEWSPAPER

The New York Times - City Hall Bureau 16158
Editorial: 1 City Hall Rm 9, New York, New York 10007-1212 **Tel:** 1 212 556-1947
Language (s): English
DAILY NEWSPAPER

The New York Times - Denver Bureau 15823
Editorial: Unavailable, Denver, Colorado
Tel: 1 303 629-7600
Email: denver@nytimes.com
Language (s): English
DAILY NEWSPAPER

The New York Times - Detroit Bureau 15515
Editorial: Birmingham, Michigan
Bureau Chief: Bill Vlasic
Language (s): English
DAILY NEWSPAPER

The New York Times - Hong Kong Bureau 551884
Editorial: 1706 K. Wah Centre, 191 Java Road, Hong Kong **Tel:** 852 2922 1188
Language (s): English
DAILY NEWSPAPER

The New York Times - Houston Bureau 15831
Editorial: 2510-A Van Buren St, Houston, Texas 77006 **Tel:** 1 713 752-2006
Bureau Chief: Manny Fernandez
Language (s): English
DAILY NEWSPAPER

The New York Times - Islamabad Bureau 815481
Editorial: Address Restricted, Islamabad
Bureau Chief: Declan Walsh
Language (s): English
DAILY NEWSPAPER

The New York Times - Istanbul Bureau 938470
Editorial: Address restricted, Istanbul
Language (s): English
DAILY NEWSPAPER

The New York Times - Jerusalem Bureau 231270
Tel: 972 2 625-3330
Bureau Chief: Jodi Rudoren
Language (s): English
DAILY NEWSPAPER

The New York Times - Johannesburg Bureau 953609
Editorial: Johannesburg
Language (s): English
DAILY NEWSPAPER

The New York Times - Kabul Bureau 842761
Editorial: Address Restricted, Kabul
Language (s): English
DAILY NEWSPAPER

The New York Times - London Bureau 71875
Editorial: 18 Museum Street, London, England WC1A 1JN **Tel:** 44 207 799-5050
Bureau Chief: Steven Erlanger
Language (s): English
DAILY NEWSPAPER

The New York Times - Los Angeles Bureau 15511
Editorial: 5900 Wilshire Blvd Ste 910, Los Angeles, California 90036-5027
Bureau Chief: Adam Nagourney
Language (s): English
DAILY NEWSPAPER

The New York Times - Madrid Bureau 842757
Editorial: Madrid
Language (s): English
DAILY NEWSPAPER

The New York Times - Mexico City Bureau 710743
Editorial: Mexico City, Distrito Federal
Tel: 52 55 5211-4160
Language (s): English
DAILY NEWSPAPER

The New York Times - Moscow Bureau 232254
Editorial: Canobar-Camoteyhar yn., 12/24, .56, Moscow 127051 **Tel:** 7 495 755-83-30
Language (s): English
DAILY NEWSPAPER

The New York Times - Nairobi Bureau 539303
Editorial: Nairobi
Email: nairobi@nytimes.com
Bureau Chief: Jeffrey Gettleman
Language (s): English
DAILY NEWSPAPER

The New York Times - New Delhi Bureau 231267
Editorial: 56 Jan Path, New Delhi 110001
Tel: 91 11 23321965
Bureau Chief, South Asia: Ellen Barry
Language (s): English
DAILY NEWSPAPER

The New York Times - Paris Bureau 71879
Editorial: Immeuble le Lavoisier, 4, place des Vosges, Courbevoie 92400 **Tel:** 33 1 41 43 93 00
Bureau Chief: Alissa Rubin
Profile: This is the headquarters of The International New York Times.
Language (s): English
DAILY NEWSPAPER

The New York Times - Rio De Janeiro Bureau 470621
Editorial: Rio De Janeiro **Tel:** 55 21 2513-4971
Circ: 1133763 Not Audited
Bureau Chief: Simon Romero
Language (s): English
DAILY NEWSPAPER

The New York Times - Rome Bureau 154524
Editorial: Rome **Tel:** 39 066833455
Language (s): English
DAILY NEWSPAPER

The New York Times - San Francisco Bureau 15512
Editorial: 221 Main St Ste 1250, San Francisco, California 94105-1961 **Tel:** 1 415 836-6700
Email: sfburo@nytimes.com
Profile: The bureau prefers all staff to be contacted by e-mail.
Language (s): English
DAILY NEWSPAPER

The New York Times - Seattle Bureau 15548
Editorial: Seattle, Washington **Tel:** 1 206 535-8474
Language (s): English
DAILY NEWSPAPER

The New York Times - Seoul Bureau 551885
Editorial: 18/F Korea Press Center, 25 Taepyongno-1-ga, Jung-gu, Seoul 100-101 **Tel:** 1 822 734-4686
Bureau Chief: Choe Sang-Hun
Language (s): English
DAILY NEWSPAPER

The New York Times - Shanghai Bureau 551883
Editorial: Address restricted, Shanghai
Tel: 86 21 62798585
Bureau Chief: David Barboza
Language (s): English
DAILY NEWSPAPER

The New York Times - Tehran Bureau 842758
Editorial: Address Restricted, Tehran
Bureau Chief: Thomas Erdbrink
Language (s): English
DAILY NEWSPAPER

The New York Times - Tokyo Bureau 130625
Editorial: Asahi Shimbun, 3-2, Tsukiji 5-chome, Tokyo 104-8011 **Tel:** 81 3 3545-0940
Language (s): English
DAILY NEWSPAPER

The New York Times - United Nations Bureau 16182
Editorial: Secretariat Bldg Rm S-317B, New York, New York 10017-0000 **Tel:** 1 212 935-8171
Language (s): English
DAILY NEWSPAPER

The New York Times - Warsaw Bureau 951132
Editorial: Warsaw **Tel:** 48 22 633-83-85
Bureau Chief, Central & Eastern Europe: Rick Lyman
Language (s): English
DAILY NEWSPAPER

The New York Times - Washington Bureau 15513
Editorial: 1627 I St NW Ste 700, Washington, District Of Columbia 20006-4007 **Tel:** 1 202 862-0300
Email: washington@nytimes.com
Bureau Chief & Political Editor: Carolyn Ryan; **Mid-Atlantic Bureau Chief:** Sheryl Gay Stolberg
Language (s): English
DAILY NEWSPAPER

The Newnan Times-Herald 14952
Owner: Thomasson Family
Editorial: 16 Jefferson St, Newnan, Georgia 30263-1913 **Tel:** 1 770 253-1576
Email: editor@newnan.com **Web site:** http://www.times-herald.com
Freq: Fri; **Circ:** 11860 Not Audited
News Editor: W. Winston Skinner
Profile: The Newnan Times-Herald is written for residents of Newnan, GA. It covers local news and events.
Language (s): English
Ad Rate: Full Page Mono 17.85
Ad Rate: Full Page Colour 100.00
Currency: United States Dollars
DAILY NEWSPAPER

Newport Daily Express 14773
Owner: Horizon Publications
Editorial: 178 Hill St, Newport, Vermont 05855-9430
Tel: 1 802 334-6568
Web site: http://newportvermontdailyexpress.com
Freq: Mon thru Fri; **Circ:** 4290 Not Audited
Profile: Newport Daily Express serves the residents of Newport, VT and its surrounding areas. The paper provides information on local news and events of interest to the community.
Language (s): English
Ad Rate: Full Page Mono 10.45
Ad Rate: Full Page Colour 11.99
Currency: United States Dollars
DAILY NEWSPAPER

The Newport Daily News 14635
Owner: Sherman Publishing Co.
Editorial: 101 Malbone Rd, Newport, Rhode Island 02840-1340 **Tel:** 1 401 849-3300
Email: newsroom@newportri.com **Web site:** http://www.newportri.com/newportdailynews/
Freq: Daily; **Circ:** 11678 Not Audited
Advertising Sales Manager: Lynn Abrams; **Publisher:** William Lucey; **News Editor:** Harvey Peters
Profile: The Newport Daily News is a local newspaper serving Newport, RI and the surrounding area. The newspaper provides information on news and events of interest to the local community. Advertising deadlines are at 4pm ET.
Language (s): English
Ad Rate: Full Page Mono 22.00
Ad Rate: Full Page Colour 325.00
Currency: United States Dollars
DAILY NEWSPAPER

The News & Advance 14759
Owner: BH Media Group
Editorial: 101 Wyndale Dr, Lynchburg, Virginia 24501-6710 **Tel:** 1 434 946-7195
Email: news@newsadvance.com **Web site:** http://www.newsadvance.com
Freq: Daily; **Circ:** 23972 Not Audited
Profile: News & Advance is a daily newspaper. Publication coverage includes local news, business, lifestyle and political information. The newspaper is intended for a readership of residents of Lynchburg, VA and surrounding areas.
Language (s): English
Ad Rate: Full Page Mono 56.10
Ad Rate: Full Page Colour 806.10
Currency: United States Dollars
DAILY NEWSPAPER

The News & Observer 15376
Owner: McClatchy Newspapers
Editorial: 215 S McDowell St, Raleigh, North Carolina 27601-1331 **Tel:** 1 919 829-4520
Email: metroeds@newsobserver.com **Web site:** http://www.newsobserver.com
Freq: Daily; **Circ:** 98158 Not Audited
Senior Editor, News: Dan Barkin
Profile: The News & Observer is a daily newspaper serving the Research Triangle of Raleigh, Durham, and Chapel Hill. The newspaper was started in the 1800s and was family-owned until 1997, when it was purchased by The McClatchy Company. The News & Observer runs seven days a week and includes national, regional, and local news, as well as sports, health, business, technology, and lifestyle information. Health and science, education, home, arts, auto, money, and business coverage run daily. In addition to the Research Triangle area, The News & Observer reaches Orange, Wake, Johnston, and Harnett counties. There is no editorial calendar available and deadlines are ongoing.
Language (s): English
Ad Rate: Full Page Mono 290.86
Currency: United States Dollars
DAILY NEWSPAPER

News & Record 15374
Owner: BH Media Group
Editorial: 200 E Market St, Greensboro, North Carolina 27401-2910 **Tel:** 1 336 373-7000
Web site: http://www.greensboro.com
Freq: Daily; **Circ:** 42095 Not Audited
Advertising Sales Manager: Keeley Duckworth; **Editor & Publisher:** Jeff Gauger
Profile: News & Record is a daily newspaper published for the residents of Greensboro, NC. It began as two smaller papers, The Daily Record and The Greensboro Daily News. The Daily Record was founded in 1890, The Greensboro Daily News in 1909. In 1982, the two papers merged and became a strictly morning paper and established its current name. It serves to inform Greensboro, Guilford, Randolph, Rockingham, Alamance, and Davidson, NC counties, the so-called Triad area, about current events, local and national news, culture, sports and world affairs. It is published in four different editions, which are all geared toward their respective area of distribution.
Language (s): English
Ad Rate: Full Page Mono 52.41
Ad Rate: Full Page Colour 992.41
Currency: United States Dollars
DAILY NEWSPAPER

News & Record - Reidsville Bureau 15858
Editorial: 1921 Vance St, Reidsville, North Carolina 27320-3254 **Tel:** 1 336 627-1781
Language (s): English
DAILY NEWSPAPER

News and Tribune 13992
Owner: News and Tribune
Editorial: 221 Spring St, Jeffersonville, Indiana 47130-3353 **Tel:** 1 812 283-6636
Email: newsroom@newsandtribune.com **Web site:** http://www.newsandtribune.com
Freq: Fri; **Circ:** 9725 Not Audited
Publisher: Bill Hanson; **Editor:** Shea Van Hoy
Profile: The News and Tribune is written for the residents of Clark and Floyd County, IN. It focuses on local news, with areas of emphasis education, government, police/courts, business, health and sports reporting.
Language (s): English
Ad Rate: Full Page Mono 18.50
Ad Rate: Full Page Colour 150.00
Currency: United States Dollars
DAILY NEWSPAPER

The News and Tribune - New Albany Bureau 14006
Editorial: 318 Pearl St Ste 100, New Albany, Indiana 47150-3450 **Tel:** 1 812 206-2155
Email: newsroom@newsandtribune.com **Web site:** http://www.newsandtribune.com
Circ: 8389 Not Audited
Profile: The News and Tribune is written for the residents of Clark and Floyd County, IN. It covers local news, sports, lifestyle and community events. The paper is published Tuesday through Sunday.
Language (s): English
Ad Rate: Full Page Mono 18.50
Ad Rate: Full Page Colour 150.00
Currency: United States Dollars
DAILY NEWSPAPER

News Chief 13830
Owner: GateHouse Media Inc.
Editorial: 455 6th St NW, Winter Haven, Florida 33881-4061 **Tel:** 1 863 401-6900
Email: news@newschief.com **Web site:** http://www.newschief.com
Freq: Daily; **Circ:** 2979 Not Audited
Advertising Sales Manager: Nanay Pittman
Profile: News Chief is a local daily newspaper serving the residents of Polk County, FL and its surrounding communities. The newspaper covers local and national news, business, entertainment and sports.
Language (s): English
Ad Rate: Full Page Mono 16.20
Ad Rate: Full Page Colour 150.00
Currency: United States Dollars
DAILY NEWSPAPER

The News Courier 13664
Owner: Community Newspaper Holdings, Inc.
Editorial: 410 W Green St, Athens, Alabama 35611-2518 **Tel:** 1 256 232-2720
Web site: http://www.enewscourier.com
Freq: Daily; **Circ:** 5970 Not Audited
Advertising Sales Manager: Shannon Elliot
Profile: The News Courier is a local daily newspaper serving the residents of Athens, AL and the surrounding communities. It covers local news and community events.
Language (s): English
Ad Rate: Full Page Mono 11.47
Ad Rate: Full Page Colour 39.50
Currency: United States Dollars
DAILY NEWSPAPER

The News Gazette 14029
Owner: Community Media Group
Editorial: 224 W Franklin St, Winchester, Indiana 47394-1808 **Tel:** 1 765 584-4501
Email: ngeditor@comcast.net **Web site:** http://www.winchesternewsgazette.com
Freq: Daily; **Circ:** 2500 Not Audited
Profile: The News Gazette is a daily newspaper published for residents of Winchester, IN. The paper covers local news, sports and business.
Language (s): English
Ad Rate: Full Page Mono 10.45
Ad Rate: Full Page Colour 135.00
Currency: United States Dollars
DAILY NEWSPAPER

The News Gram 21996
Editorial: 2543 Del Rio Blvd, Eagle Pass, Texas 78852-3627 **Tel:** 1 830 773-8610
Email: elgram@hilconet.com **Web site:** http://thenewsgramonline.dyndns.org:81
Freq: Fri; **Circ:** 3000 Not Audited
Publisher & Editor: Ruben Carrillo Mazuka
Profile: The News Gram is a daily, Spanish-English bilingual newspaper serving the residents of Eagle Pass, TX, which is a community near San Antonio. The publication covers local news and events. The deadline to submit press releases is 2pm CT.
Language (s): Spanish/Bilingual
Ad Rate: Full Page Mono 7.35
Ad Rate: Full Page Colour 150.00
Currency: United States Dollars
DAILY NEWSPAPER

The News Herald 13826
Owner: GateHouse Media Inc.
Editorial: 501 W 11th St, Panama City, Florida 32401-2330 **Tel:** 1 850 747-5000
Email: pcnhnews@pcnh.com **Web site:** http://www.newsherald.com
Freq: Mon thru Fri; **Circ:** 30829 Not Audited
Editor: Mike Cazalas; **Publisher:** Alan Davis
Profile: The News Herald is a daily newspaper that serves the Panama City, FL area. The newspaper covers local news, business, sports, lifestyle, business, government, military and community events.
Language (s): English
Ad Rate: Full Page Mono 60.69
Currency: United States Dollars
DAILY NEWSPAPER

The News Herald 14306
Owner: World Media Enterprises, Inc.
Editorial: 301 Collett St, Morganton, North Carolina 28655-3322 **Tel:** 1 828 437-2161
Email: news@morganton.com **Web site:** http://www.morganton.com
Freq: Daily; **Circ:** 10160 Not Audited
Advertising Sales Manager: Keeley Duckworth
Profile: The News Herald is a daily newspaper serving the Morganton, NC area. It includes local news, sports, lifestyle, business and arts & entertainment. The paper covers national news stories only if they have an impact on the readers.
Language (s): English
Ad Rate: Full Page Mono 13.58
Currency: United States Dollars
DAILY NEWSPAPER

News Journal 14468
Owner: Gannett Co., Inc.
Editorial: 70 W 4th St, Mansfield, Ohio 44903-1676 **Tel:** 1 419 522-3311
Email: yournews@mansfieldnewsjournal.com **Web site:** http://www.mansfieldnewsjournal.com
Freq: Daily; **Circ:** 16733 Not Audited
Profile: News Journal is a daily newspaper written for the residents of Mansfield, OH to provide local news coverage and community information.
Language (s): English
Ad Rate: Full Page Mono 38.70
Ad Rate: Full Page Colour 415.00
Currency: United States Dollars
DAILY NEWSPAPER

The News Journal 15453
Owner: Gannett Co., Inc.
Editorial: 950 W Basin Rd, New Castle, Delaware 19720-1008 **Tel:** 1 302 324-2500
Email: newsdesk@delawareonline.com **Web site:** http://www.delawareonline.com
Freq: Daily; **Circ:** 60620 Not Audited
Profile: The News Journal is the main newspaper for Wilmington, Delaware and the surrounding area. It is headquartered in unincorporated New Castle County, Delaware, near New Castle, and is owned by Gannett. The News Journal covers New Castle County most in-depth, but also offers considerable coverage of the Delaware General Assembly and the Delaware beaches. The paper also offers limited coverage of northeast Maryland and southeast Pennsylvania, mostly by means of short news briefs. The paper publishes national and international articles from wire services.The News Journal also maintains a Washington, D.C. bureau, mainly for covering Delaware's congressional delegation.
Language (s): English
Ad Rate: Full Page Mono 45.83
Ad Rate: Full Page Colour 51.79
Currency: United States Dollars
DAILY NEWSPAPER

The News Leader 14764
Owner: Gannett Co., Inc.
Editorial: 11 N Central Ave, Staunton, Virginia 24401-4212 **Tel:** 1 540 885-7281
Email: getpublished@newsleader.com **Web site:** http://www.newsleader.com
Freq: Daily; **Circ:** 12416 Not Audited
Publisher: Roger Watson
Profile: The News Leader is published daily for the residents of Staunton, VA and surrounding areas. The newspaper covers local, regional and national news, sports and community events.
Language (s): English
Ad Rate: Full Page Mono 39.95
Ad Rate: Full Page Colour 1070.00
Currency: United States Dollars
DAILY NEWSPAPER

The News Press 14541
Owner: Community Newspaper Holdings, Inc.
Editorial: 211 W 9th Ave, Stillwater, Oklahoma 74074-4406 **Tel:** 1 405 372-5000
Email: editor@stwnewspress.com **Web site:** http://www.stwnewspress.com
Freq: Daily; **Circ:** 6804 Not Audited
Publisher: Jeff Funk
Profile: The News Press is published daily for the residents of Stillwater, OK and surrounding areas. The newspaper covers local and national news, sports, entertainment, business, lifestyle and community events.
Language (s): English
Ad Rate: Full Page Mono 10.70
Ad Rate: Full Page Colour 225.00
Currency: United States Dollars
DAILY NEWSPAPER

The News Star 14103
Owner: Gannett Co., Inc.
Editorial: 411 N 4th St, Monroe, Louisiana 71201-6743 **Tel:** 1 318 322-5161
Email: news@thenewsstar.com **Web site:** http://www.thenewsstar.com
Freq: Daily; **Circ:** 26000 Not Audited
Profile: The News Star is a daily newspaper serving residents of northeastern Louisiana. Their mission is to provide accurate and comprehensive news, advertising and public service information to readers in a timely fashion every day of the year.
Language (s): English
Ad Rate: Full Page Mono 81.48
Ad Rate: Full Page Colour 595.00
Currency: United States Dollars
DAILY NEWSPAPER

The News Sun 13993
Owner: KPC Media Group Inc.
Editorial: 102 N Main St, Kendallville, Indiana 46755-1714 **Tel:** 1 260 347-0400
Web site: http://kpcnews.com/news/latest/newssun
Freq: Daily; **Circ:** 7934
Advertising Sales Manager: Lynette Donley; **Publisher:** Terry Housholder
Profile: The News Sun is written for the residents of Kendallville, IN. It covers news, sports, features, business, and more.
Language (s): English
Ad Rate: Full Page Mono 14.70
Ad Rate: Full Page Colour 30.14
Currency: United States Dollars
DAILY NEWSPAPER

News Tribune 13939
Owner: Daily News Tribune, Inc.
Editorial: 426 2nd St, La Salle, Illinois 61301-2334 **Tel:** 1 815 223-3200
Email: ntnews@newstrib.com **Web site:** http://www.newstrib.com
Freq: Mon thru Fri; **Circ:** 17626 Not Audited
Publisher: Joyce McCullough; **News Editor:** Craig Sterrett
Profile: News Tribune is published daily for the residents of La Salle, IL and the surrounding area. The newspaper covers local news, sports, lifestyles, business and community events.
Language (s): English
Ad Rate: Full Page Mono 24.00
Ad Rate: Full Page Colour 345.00
Currency: United States Dollars
DAILY NEWSPAPER

News Tribune 14234
Owner: Wehco Media Inc.
Editorial: 210 Monroe St, Jefferson City, Missouri 65101 **Tel:** 1 573 636-3131
Email: editor@newstribune.com **Web site:** http://www.newstribune.com
Freq: Daily; **Circ:** 15021
Advertising Sales Manager: Jane Haslag
Profile: News Tribune is a local daily newspaper serving the residents of Jefferson City, MO. It provides information on local news, events, sports and weather. Deadlines are at 11pm CT one day prior to issue date.
Language (s): English
Ad Rate: Full Page Mono 10.09
Ad Rate: Full Page Colour 180.00
Currency: United States Dollars
DAILY NEWSPAPER

The News Tribune 15370
Owner: McClatchy Newspapers
Editorial: 1950 S State St, Tacoma, Washington 98405-2817 **Tel:** 1 253 597-8742
Email: newstips@thenewstribune.com **Web site:** http://www.thenewstribune.com
Freq: Daily; **Circ:** 65264 Not Audited
Publisher: David Zeeck
Profile: The News Tribune is a daily newspaper reaching readers in Tacoma and Pierce County, WA. The paper covers sports with the following sections: Baseball, basketball, football, golf/tennis, hockey, college, UW Huskies and WSU Cougars. It covers business with market summaries and a Fortune 500 list. In addition, it covers government, crime and environmental issues. Arts & entertainment includes comics, puzzles, computers, food and restaurant coverage, family issues, travel and TV listings. Public opinion is represented in the following sections: Editorials, endorsements, letters and writers tips. The paper also covers technology issues in the greater South Puget Sound region. Deadlines are at noon PT three days before issue date.
Language (s): English
Ad Rate: Full Page Mono 162.80
Ad Rate: Full Page Colour 498.86
Currency: United States Dollars
DAILY NEWSPAPER

The News Tribune - Olympia Bureau 15977
Editorial: 1417 Columbia St SW, Olympia, Washington 98501-2342
Language (s): English
DAILY NEWSPAPER

The News Virginian 14767
Owner: BH Media Group
Editorial: 1300 W Main St, Waynesboro, Virginia 22980-2414 **Tel:** 1 540 949-8213
Email: enewstips@newsvirginian.com **Web site:** http://www.newsvirginian.com
Freq: Daily; **Circ:** 5733 Not Audited
Profile: The News Virginian is a daily newspaper covering Waynesboro, Staunton, Augusta County and Nelson County, VA and the surrounding areas. Topics include community events, business and sports.
Language (s): English
Ad Rate: Full Page Mono 23.85
Ad Rate: Full Page Colour 390.00
Currency: United States Dollars
DAILY NEWSPAPER

News-Banner 13972
Owner: News Banner Publications, Inc.
Editorial: 125 N Johnson St, Bluffton, Indiana 46714-1907 **Tel:** 1 260 824-0224
Email: newsroom@news-banner.com **Web site:** http://www.news-banner.com
Freq: Daily; **Circ:** 5059 Not Audited
Advertising Sales Manager: Jean Bordner; **Publisher:** Mark Miller
Profile: News-Banner is published Monday through Saturday for the residents of Bluffton, IN and surrounding areas. It cover local news and community events. Deadlines are at noon CT one day prior to issue date.
Language (s): English
Ad Rate: Full Page Mono 11.80
Ad Rate: Full Page Colour 240.00
Currency: United States Dollars
DAILY NEWSPAPER

Newsday 15312
Owner: Newsday Media Group
Editorial: 235 Pinelawn Rd, Melville, New York 11747-4226 **Tel:** 1 631 843-2700
Email: li@newsday.com **Web site:** http://www.newsday.com
Freq: Daily; **Circ:** 321296 Not Audited
Profile: Newsday is a daily tabloid covering local, national and international news, business, sports and features. Its mission is to provide breaking news and news analysis to the general public. The paper won a 1997 Pulitzer Prize for Spot News and a 2002 Best in Business Breaking News award from the Society of American Business Editors and Writers.
Language (s): English
Ad Rate: Full Page Mono 339.41
Ad Rate: Full Page Colour 377.58
Currency: United States Dollars
DAILY NEWSPAPER

Newsday - Albany Bureau 15816
Editorial: State Capitol LCA Pressroom, 3rd Floor, Albany, New York 12224 **Tel:** 1 518 465-2311
Bureau Chief: Yancey Roy
Language (s): English
DAILY NEWSPAPER

Newsday - Brooklyn Bureau 81195
Editorial: 225 Cadman Plz E Rm 695, Brooklyn, New York 11201-1832 **Tel:** 1 718 624-6880
Language (s): English
DAILY NEWSPAPER

Newsday - Mineola Bureau 408540
Editorial: 100 Supreme Court Dr, Mineola, New York 11501-4815
Language (s): English
DAILY NEWSPAPER

Newsday - Riverhead Bureau 15818
Editorial: 633 E Main St, Riverhead, New York 11901-7013 **Tel:** 1 631 727-7333
Language (s): English
DAILY NEWSPAPER

Newsday - Washington Bureau 15540
Editorial: 1090 Vermont Ave NW, Washington, District Of Columbia 20005-4905 **Tel:** 1 202 408-2715
Language (s): English
DAILY NEWSPAPER

The News-Dispatch 14003
Owner: Paxton Media Group
Editorial: 422 Franklin St Ste B, Michigan City, Indiana 46360-3386 **Tel:** 1 219 874-7211
Email: news@thenewsdispatch.com **Web site:** http://www.thenewsdispatch.com
Freq: Daily; **Circ:** 5965 Not Audited
Publisher: Bill Hackney; **Editor:** Amanda Haverstick
Profile: The News-Dispatch is published daily for the residents of Michigan City, IN and surrounding areas. The newspaper covers news, sports, business, events, entertainment, health and lifestyles.
Language (s): English
Ad Rate: Full Page Mono 15.10
Currency: United States Dollars
DAILY NEWSPAPER

The News-Enterprise 14076
Owner: Landmark Community Newspapers, Inc.
Editorial: 408 W Dixie Ave, Elizabethtown, Kentucky 42701-2455 **Tel:** 1 270 769-1200
Email: ne@thenewsenterprise.com **Web site:** http://www.thenewsenterprise.com
Freq: Daily; **Circ:** 12257 Not Audited
News Editor: Jeff D'Alessio; **Publisher:** Chris Ordway; **Editor:** Ben Sheroan
Profile: The News-Enterprise is written for the community of Elizabethtown, KY.
Language (s): English
Ad Rate: Full Page Mono 18.82
Ad Rate: Full Page Colour 348.82
Currency: United States Dollars
DAILY NEWSPAPER

The News-Gazette 13919
Owner: News-Gazette Inc.
Editorial: 15 E Main St, Champaign, Illinois 61820-3625 **Tel:** 1 217 351-5252
Email: news@news-gazette.com **Web site:** http://www.news-gazette.com
Freq: Daily; **Circ:** 35952
Editor: George Dobrik; **Publisher:** John Foreman
Profile: The News-Gazette is a newspaper serving the residents of Champaign, IL and its surrounding area. The publication covers local news, events, sports, arts & entertainment and business.
Language (s): English
Ad Rate: Full Page Mono 38.06
Ad Rate: Full Page Colour 41.96
Currency: United States Dollars
DAILY NEWSPAPER

The News-Herald 14501
Owner: Digital First Media
Editorial: 7085 Mentor Ave, Willoughby, Ohio 44094-7948 **Tel:** 1 440 951-0000
Email: editor@news-herald.com **Web site:** http://www.news-herald.com
Freq: Daily; **Circ:** 40238 Not Audited
Profile: The News-Herald provides local news, national news and sports coverage for the Northeast Ohio area.
Language (s): English
Ad Rate: Full Page Mono 48.05
Ad Rate: Full Page Colour 705.00
Currency: United States Dollars
DAILY NEWSPAPER

The News-Item 14613
Owner: Times-Shamrock Communications
Editorial: 707 N Rock St, Shamokin, Pennsylvania 17872-4930 **Tel:** 1 570 644-6397
Email: editorial@newsitem.com **Web site:** http://www.newsitem.com
Freq: Daily; **Circ:** 7650
Editor: Andy Heintzelman; **Publisher:** Henry Nyce
Profile: The News-Item provides local news and feature articles to residents in Northumberland County, PA.
Language (s): English
Ad Rate: Full Page Mono 15.65
Ad Rate: Full Page Colour 520.00

Currency: United States Dollars
DAILY NEWSPAPER

The News-Messenger 14454
Owner: Gannett Co., Inc.
Editorial: 1700 Cedar St, Fremont, Ohio 43420-1114 **Tel:** 1 419 332-5511
Email: newsdesk@thenews-messenger.com **Web site:** http://www.thenews-messenger.com
Freq: Daily; **Circ:** 5172
Editor: David Yonke
Profile: The News-Messenger is a daily newspaper serving the residents of Sandusky County and Fremont, OH. The publication covers local news, community events and sports.
Language (s): English
Ad Rate: Full Page Mono 29.20
Ad Rate: Full Page Colour 325.00
Currency: United States Dollars
DAILY NEWSPAPER

The News-Press 15429
Owner: Gannett Co., Inc.
Editorial: 2442 Dr Martin Luther King Blvd, Fort Myers, Florida 33901-3904 **Tel:** 1 239 335-0200
Email: mailbag@news-press.com **Web site:** http://www.news-press.com
Freq: Daily; **Circ:** 36275 Not Audited
Profile: The News-Press is a daily broadsheet newspaper located in Fort Myers, Florida serving primarily Lee County, as well as parts of Charlotte and Collier Counties. It was founded in 1884 by Stafford Cleveland. The newspaper joined the Gannett family in 1971. It publishes three different daily morning editions that are tailored to their respective distribution locations. These are Cape Coral, the area's largest city; Bonita Springs and South Lee County; and Fort Myers and surrounding Lee County. The newspaper covers local and regional, business, sports, lifestyles and entertainment news.
Language (s): English
Ad Rate: Full Page Mono 71.00
Ad Rate: Full Page Colour 99.40
Currency: United States Dollars
DAILY NEWSPAPER

The News-Review 14560
Owner: Swift Newspapers
Editorial: 345 NE Winchester St, Roseburg, Oregon 97470 **Tel:** 1 541 672-3321
Email: newsdesk@nrtoday.com **Web site:** http://www.nrtoday.com
Freq: Daily; **Circ:** 18287 Not Audited
Editor: Bruce Leonard; **Publisher:** Mark Raymond
Profile: The News-Review is a daily published for the residents of Roseburg, OR. It covers news and events in the local community.
Language (s): English
Ad Rate: Full Page Mono 30.90
Ad Rate: Full Page Colour 605.00
Currency: United States Dollars
DAILY NEWSPAPER

The News-Sentinel 15396
Owner: Ogden Newspapers
Editorial: 600 W Main St, Fort Wayne, Indiana 46802-1408 **Tel:** 1 260 461-8439
Email: metro@news-sentinel.com **Web site:** http://www.news-sentinel.com
Freq: Mon thru Fri; **Circ:** 49093
Publisher: Michael Christman; **Editor:** Kerry Hubartt
Profile: The News-Sentinel is a daily newspaper covering local news, features, business and sports for the residents of Fort Wayne, IN. The paper has special sections that print throughout the week: Business Monday covers the world of business and guides readers through workplace and industry news on Mondays; Food offers recipes and suggestions on cooking on Tuesdays; Home & Style offers gardening and home improvement advice on Saturdays; Prep Sports Monday provides in depth coverage of high school sport on Mondays; Ticket! is a weekend arts & entertainment guide for the area around Fort Wayne, IN that prints on Thursdays.
Language (s): English
Ad Rate: Full Page Mono 173.00
Ad Rate: Full Page Colour 188.45
Currency: United States Dollars
DAILY NEWSPAPER

The News-Times 13798
Owner: Hearst Corporation
Editorial: 333 Main St, Danbury, Connecticut 06810-5818 **Tel:** 1 203 744-5100
Email: news@newstimes.com **Web site:** http://www.newstimes.com
Freq: Daily; **Circ:** 15658 Not Audited
Advertising Sales Manager: Loraine Marshall
Profile: The News-Times is a daily newspaper written for the residents of Danbury, CT. It covers news, sports, entertainment, features and opinion. They prefer all press releases be sent to the main fax number, which reaches the newsroom directly.
Language (s): English
Ad Rate: Full Page Mono 46.57
Ad Rate: Full Page Colour 399.00
Currency: United States Dollars
DAILY NEWSPAPER

News-Topic 14303
Owner: Paxton Media Group
Editorial: 123 Pennton Ave NW, Lenoir, North Carolina 28645-4313 **Tel:** 1 828 758-7381
Web site: http://www.newstopicnews.com/
Freq: Daily; **Circ:** 7646 Not Audited
Editor: Guy Lucas
Profile: News-Topic is a daily newspaper published for the residents of Caldwell County, NC. The publication covers local news, sports, arts and entertainment, and community events. It is best to send releases at least one week in advance of the event, and it is preferable to send them in two weeks prior.
Language (s): English
Ad Rate: Full Page Mono 19.00
Ad Rate: Full Page Colour 196.44
Currency: United States Dollars
DAILY NEWSPAPER

Newton Citizen 153285
Owner: Southern Community Newspapers Inc.
Editorial: 969 S Main St NE, Conyers, Georgia 30012-4501 **Tel:** 1 770 483-7108
Email: news@newtoncitizen.com **Web site:** http://www.rockdalenewtoncitizen.com
Freq: Daily; **Circ:** 16170 Not Audited
Publisher: J.K. Murphy; **Editor:** Alice Queen
Profile: Newton Citizen is published daily for the residents of Covington, GA and surrounding areas. The newspaper provides information on local and regional news and community events.
Language (s): English
Ad Rate: Full Page Mono 18.04
Ad Rate: Full Page Colour 57.40
Currency: United States Dollars
DAILY NEWSPAPER

Newton Daily News 13888
Owner: Shaw Media
Editorial: 200 1st Ave E, Newton, Iowa 50208-3716 **Tel:** 1 641 792-3121
Email: newsroom@newtondailynews.com **Web site:** http://www.newtondailynews.com
Freq: Daily; **Circ:** 5800 Not Audited
Publisher: Dan Goetz; **Advertising Sales Manager:** Jeff Holschuh
Profile: Newton Daily News is published daily for the residents of Newton, IA and surrounding areas. It provides local news and information on community events.
Language (s): English
Ad Rate: Full Page Mono 10.20
Ad Rate: Full Page Colour 150.00
Currency: United States Dollars
DAILY NEWSPAPER

Newton Kansan 14060
Owner: GateHouse Media Inc.
Editorial: 121 W 6Th St, Newton, Kansas 67114-2117 **Tel:** 1 316 283-1500
Email: news@thekansan.com **Web site:** http://www.thekansan.com
Freq: Daily; **Circ:** 7513 Not Audited
Publisher: Randy Mitchell
Profile: Newton Kansan is a local daily newspaper written for residents of Newton, KS and the surrounding area. The newspaper covers local news, business, sports and arts & entertainment stories. The newspaper also covers national and statewide stories if they have a direct impact on the newspaper's readership.
Language (s): English
Ad Rate: Full Page Mono 16.08
Ad Rate: Full Page Colour 200.00
Currency: United States Dollars
DAILY NEWSPAPER

Nguoi Viet Daily News 80020
Owner: Nguoi Viet Inc.
Editorial: 14771 Moran St, Westminster, California 92683 **Tel:** 1 714 892-9414
Email: nv2@nguoi-viet.com **Web site:** http://www.nguoi-viet.com
Freq: Daily; **Circ:** 18000 Not Audited
Advertising Sales Manager: Vinh Hoang; **Editor:** Giao Pham; **Publisher:** Dat Phan
Profile: Nguoi Viet Daily News provides news and information to the Vietnamese community in the United States, particularly those living in California. The publication was the first Vietnamese language daily newspaper written outside of Vietnam. Advertising deadlines are at 2pm PT.
Language (s): English
Ad Rate: Full Page Mono 16.50
Ad Rate: Full Page Colour 1173.00
Currency: United States Dollars
DAILY NEWSPAPER

Niagara Gazette 14414
Owner: Community Newspaper Holdings, Inc.
Editorial: 473 3rd St, Niagara Falls, New York 14301-1500 **Tel:** 1 716 282-2311
Web site: http://www.niagara-gazette.com
Freq: Daily; **Circ:** 10420
Advertising Sales Manager: Jeff Calarco
Profile: Niagara Gazette is a daily, local newspaper for the area surrounding Niagara Falls, NY. The newspaper covers local news, business, sports, finance, health and arts & entertainment. It also covers national and statewide stories if they have a direct impact on the newspaper's readership. Deadlines are between 12:30pm and 1pm ET.
Language (s): English
Ad Rate: Full Page Mono 34.72
Currency: United States Dollars
DAILY NEWSPAPER

Niles Daily Star 14187
Owner: Leader Publications
Editorial: 217 N 4th St, Niles, Michigan 49120-2301 **Tel:** 1 269 683-2101
Email: news@leaderpub.com **Web site:** http://www.nilesstar.com
Freq: Daily; **Circ:** 1970 Not Audited
News Editor: Kimberly Wynn
Profile: Niles Daily Star is published daily for the residents of Niles, MI and surrounding areas. The newspaper covers local and regional news, business, sports and entertainment.
Language (s): English
Ad Rate: Full Page Mono 9.45
Currency: United States Dollars
DAILY NEWSPAPER

Norfolk Daily News 14346
Owner: Huse Publishing
Editorial: 525 W Norfolk Ave, Norfolk, Nebraska 68701-5236 **Tel:** 1 402 371-1020
Email: editor@norfolkdailynews.com **Web site:** http://www.norfolkdailynews.com
Freq: Daily; **Circ:** 14553 Not Audited
Publisher: Jerry Huse; **Editor:** Kent Warneke
Profile: Norfolk Daily News is a local newspaper for the Norfolk, NE area. The newspaper covers local, national and statewide news, business, sports and arts & entertainment. All inquiries should be addressed to the editor.
Language (s): English
Ad Rate: Full Page Mono 21.75
Ad Rate: Full Page Colour 476.00
Currency: United States Dollars
DAILY NEWSPAPER

The Norman Transcript 14532
Owner: Community Newspaper Holdings, Inc.
Editorial: 215 E Comanche St, Norman, Oklahoma 73069-6007 **Tel:** 1 405 321-1800
Email: editor@normantranscript.com **Web site:** http://www.normantranscript.com
Freq: Daily; **Circ:** 9500 Not Audited
Publisher: Mark Millsap
Profile: The Norman Transcript is a local daily newspaper that provides information on local news and topics of interest to residents of Norman, OK and surrounding communities. Coverage includes Oklahoma news, sports, business, real estate, editorials, outdoor news, arts & entertainment, lifestyles, religion, seniors, features, columnists, food, family, health, garden and more.
Language (s): English
Ad Rate: Full Page Mono 16.75
Ad Rate: Full Page Colour 295.00
Currency: United States Dollars
DAILY NEWSPAPER

The North Platte Telegraph 14347
Owner: Omaha World-Herald Co.
Editorial: 621 N Chestnut St, North Platte, Nebraska 69101-4131 **Tel:** 1 308 532-6000
Email: editor@nptelegraph.com **Web site:** http://www.nptelegraph.com
Freq: Daily; **Circ:** 10653 Not Audited
Advertising Sales Manager: Dee Klein
Profile: The North Platte Telegraph is the daily newspaper of North Platte, NE and the surrounding communities. It covers local news, sports, lifestyle, farming and legal stories. They also cover national stories if they have an impact on the readership.
Language (s): English
Ad Rate: Full Page Mono 16.55
Ad Rate: Full Page Colour 365.00
Currency: United States Dollars
DAILY NEWSPAPER

The Northeast Mississippi Daily Journal 14272
Owner: Journal Inc.
Editorial: 1242 S Green St, Tupelo, Mississippi 38804-6301 **Tel:** 1 662 842-2611
Email: info.news@journalinc.com **Web site:** http://djournal.com
Freq: Daily; **Circ:** 29642 Not Audited
Publisher: Clay Foster; **Editor:** Lloyd Gray
Profile: The Northeast Mississippi Daily Journal in Tupelo, MS provides local news, sports, business, entertainment and lifestyle coverage to residents of Northeast Mississippi.
Language (s): English
Ad Rate: Full Page Mono 35.19
Ad Rate: Full Page Colour 400.00
Currency: United States Dollars
DAILY NEWSPAPER

The Northern Virginia Daily 14765
Owner: Shenandoah Publishing House Inc.
Editorial: 152 N Holliday St, Strasburg, Virginia 22657-2143 **Tel:** 1 540 465-5137
Email: news@nvdaily.com **Web site:** http://www.nvdaily.com
Freq: Daily; **Circ:** 9153 Not Audited
Editor: Linda Ash; **Editor:** Rich Cooley
Profile: Northern Virginia Daily provides the latest in local news and information to local residents of Strasburg, VA. The newspaper covers local news, events, sports, business, arts & entertainment and lifestyles.
Language (s): English
Ad Rate: Full Page Mono 16.45
Ad Rate: Full Page Colour 370.00
Currency: United States Dollars
DAILY NEWSPAPER

Northern Wyoming Daily News 14855
Owner: McCraken Newspapers
Editorial: 201 N 8th St, Worland, Wyoming 82401 **Tel:** 1 307 347-3241
Web site: http://www.wyodaily.com
Freq: Fri; **Circ:** 4000 Not Audited
Advertising Sales Manager: Dustin Fuller; **Publisher & Editor:** Lee Lockhart; **Editor:** Karla Pomeroy
Profile: Northern Wyoming Daily News is written for residents of the Worland, WY area. It covers local news.
Language (s): English
Ad Rate: Full Page Mono 8.78
Ad Rate: Full Page Colour 120.00
Currency: United States Dollars
DAILY NEWSPAPER

Northwest Arkansas Democrat-Gazette 13690
Owner: Stephens Media Group
Editorial: 212 N East Ave, Fayetteville, Arkansas 72701-5225 **Tel:** 1 479 442-1700
Web site: http://www.nwaonline.com
Freq: Daily
Publisher & Editor: Rusty Turner
Profile: Northwest Arkansas Democrat Gazette is a daily newspaper serving Northwest Arkansas and surrounding areas. The publication covers news, sports, opinions, academics, business, health, agriculture and living. The outlet offers RSS (Really Simple Syndication).
Language (s): English
Ad Rate: Full Page Mono 248.10
Ad Rate: Full Page Colour 475.00
Currency: United States Dollars
DAILY NEWSPAPER

Northwest Florida Daily News 13816
Owner: GateHouse Media Inc.
Editorial: 2 Eglin Pkwy NE, Fort Walton Beach, Florida 32548-4915 **Tel:** 1 850 863-1111
Email: news@nwfdailynews.com **Web site:** http://www.nwfdailynews.com
Freq: Daily; **Circ:** 24496 Not Audited
Publisher: Diane Winnemuller
Profile: Northwest Florida Daily News is a local daily newspaper serving residents of Fort Walton, Navarre and Crestview, FL.
Language (s): English
Ad Rate: Full Page Mono 50.00
Ad Rate: Full Page Colour 159.83
Currency: United States Dollars
DAILY NEWSPAPER

Northwest Herald 14867
Owner: Shaw Media
Editorial: 7717 S Il Route 31, Crystal Lake, Illinois 60014-8132 **Tel:** 1 815 459-4040
Email: tips@nwherald.com **Web site:** http://www.nwherald.com
Freq: Daily; **Circ:** 27206 Not Audited
Publisher: John Rung
Profile: Northwest Herald is published daily for the residents of Crystal Lake, IL and surrounding areas. The newspaper covers local and state news, bussiness, sports and entertainment.
Language (s): English
Ad Rate: Full Page Mono 31.42
Ad Rate: Full Page Colour 142.15
Currency: United States Dollars
DAILY NEWSPAPER

Northwest Signal 14477
Owner: Bryan Publishing Company
Editorial: 595 E Riverview Ave, Napoleon, Ohio 43545-1865 **Tel:** 1 419 592-5055
Web site: http://www.northwestsignal.net
Freq: Daily; **Circ:** 4784 Not Audited
Publisher: Christopher Cullis; **News Editor:** Brian Koeller; **Editor:** Jen Lazenby
Profile: Northwest Signal is a local newspaper published Monday through Friday and serving the residents of the Northwest portion of Ohio. Each edition covers local, state, and national news, community event listings, entertainment updates and local weather and sports reports. Deadlines are at 9:30am on the day before issue date.
Language (s): English
Ad Rate: Full Page Mono 11.00
Ad Rate: Full Page Colour 210.00
Currency: United States Dollars
DAILY NEWSPAPER

Norwalk Reflector 14480
Owner: Sandusky Newspapers Inc.
Editorial: 61 E Monroe St, Norwalk, Ohio 44857-1532 **Tel:** 1 419 668-3771
Email: news@norwalkreflector.com **Web site:** http://www.norwalkreflector.com
Freq: Daily; **Circ:** 8053 Not Audited
Publisher: Andrew Prutsok; **News Editor:** Matthew Roche
Profile: Norwalk Reflector is a daily newspaper published for the residents of Norwalk, OH. It covers the latest news and information. Deadlines are two days prior to issue date.
Language (s): English
Ad Rate: Full Page Mono 13.00
Ad Rate: Full Page Colour 210.00
Currency: United States Dollars
DAILY NEWSPAPER

Nowy Dziennik 79994
Owner: Outwater Media Group
Editorial: 70 Outwater Ln, Garfield, New Jersey 07026-3847 **Tel:** 1 212 594-2266
Email: dziennik@me.com **Web site:** http://www.dziennik.com
Freq: Daily; **Circ:** 28000 Not Audited
News & Commentary Editor: Tomasz Deptula
Profile: Nowy Dziennik is a daily newspaper published in New Jersey. The publication's editorial mission is to provide its readers with the latest news and information. The publication is written for Polish-

speaking people, and those originating from Poland, of New York and surrounding areas.
Language (s): English
Ad Rate: Full Page Mono 10.00
Currency: United States Dollars
DAILY NEWSPAPER

El Nuevo Herald 14937
Owner: McClatchy Newspapers
Editorial: 3511 NW 91st Ave, Doral, Florida 33172-1216 **Tel:** 1 305 376-3535
Web site: http://www.elnuevoherald.com
Freq: Daily; **Circ:** 41760 Not Audited
Publisher: David Landsberg
Profile: El Nuevo Herald is the primary Spanish newspaper in South and Central Florida, since its launch in 1987. Coverage includes local and national news, sports and arts & entertainment.
Language (s): English, Spanish
Ad Rate: Full Page Mono 85.00
Ad Rate: Full Page Colour 442.69
Currency: United States Dollars
DAILY NEWSPAPER

El Nuevo Heraldo 14902
Owner: AIM Media Texas, LLC
Editorial: 1135 E Van Buren St, Brownsville, Texas 78520-7055 **Tel:** 1 956 542-4301
Web site: http://www.elnuevoheraldo.com
Freq: Daily; **Circ:** 7162 Not Audited
Profile: El Nuevo Heraldo is written for the residents of Brownsville, TX. It covers local news and events.
Language (s): Spanish
Ad Rate: Full Page Mono 8.95
Ad Rate: Full Page Colour 551.00
Currency: United States Dollars
DAILY NEWSPAPER

The Oak Ridger 14676
Owner: GateHouse Media Inc.
Editorial: 785 Oak Ridge Tpke, Oak Ridge, Tennessee 37830-7076 **Tel:** 1 865 482-1021
Email: oakridge@oakridger.com **Web site:** http://www.oakridger.com
Freq: Daily; **Circ:** 7700 Not Audited
Publisher: Darrell Richardson; **Editor:** Donna Smith
Profile: The Oak Ridger's editorial mission is to provide its readers with current local news and events. It is written for residents of Oak Ridge and Anderson Counties, TN. Deadlines are one day prior to the issue date. The outlet offers RSS (Really Simple Syndication).
Language (s): English
Ad Rate: Full Page Mono 14.60
Ad Rate: Full Page Colour 190.00
Currency: United States Dollars
DAILY NEWSPAPER

The Oakland Press 14190
Owner: Digital First Media
Editorial: 48 W Huron St, Pontiac, Michigan 48342-2101 **Tel:** 1 248 332-8181
Web site: http://www.theoaklandpress.com
Freq: Daily; **Circ:** 23080 Not Audited
Publisher: Jeannie Parent
Profile: The Oakland Press in Pontiac, MI is a daily newspaper for the residents of Oakland County, MI that covers the day's events, from the goings-on in local communities, schools, police departments and courts to the political events in the nation's capitol. It provides local, regional, state and national news, as well as sports, business, features, special reports and entertainment coverage. It strives to "deliver quality products and services that exceed our customers' expectations." Deadlines are three days prior to issue date.
Language (s): English
Ad Rate: Full Page Mono 80.00
Ad Rate: Full Page Colour 86.00
Currency: United States Dollars
DAILY NEWSPAPER

Observer 14399
Owner: Ogden Newspapers
Editorial: 8-10 E 2nd St, Dunkirk, New York 14048-1600 **Tel:** 1 716 366-3000
Email: editorial@observertoday.com **Web site:** http://www.observertoday.com
Freq: Daily; **Circ:** 6889 Not Audited
Publisher & Editor: John D'Agostino; **Advertising Sales Manager:** Meredith Patton
Profile: Observer is a daily community newspaper serving the residents of Northern Chautauqua County, NY. The newspaper covers local news, sports, entertainment, editorial, business and community events.
Language (s): English
Ad Rate: Full Page Mono 27.52
Ad Rate: Full Page Colour 372.52
Currency: United States Dollars
DAILY NEWSPAPER

The Observer 14556
Owner: Western Communications Inc.
Editorial: 1406 5th St, La Grande, Oregon 97850-2402 **Tel:** 1 541 963-3161
Web site: http://www.lagrandeobserver.com
Freq: Daily; **Circ:** 6029 Not Audited
Publisher: Kari Borgen; **Editor:** Andrew Cutler
Profile: La Grande Observer is a daily newspaper for the residents of La Grande, OR. It covers news and events in the local community. The lead time for La Grande Observer is three days. Deadline for the publication is three days before issue date.
Language (s): English
Ad Rate: Full Page Mono 12.70
Ad Rate: Full Page Colour 36.39
Currency: United States Dollars
DAILY NEWSPAPER

The Observer - New York Bureau 363911
Editorial: 2 Bank St Apt 1, New York, New York 10014-5248 **Tel:** 1 212 614-8576
Profile: This is the New York bureau for The Observer of London.
Language (s): English
DAILY NEWSPAPER

The Observer News Enterprise 14308
Owner: Horizon Publications
Editorial: 309 N College Ave, Newton, North Carolina 28658-3255 **Tel:** 1 828 464-0221
Email: onenews@observernewsonline.com **Web site:** http://www.observernewsonline.com
Freq: Mon thru Fri; **Circ:** 1299 Not Audited
Profile: The Observer News Enterprise is a newspaper that provides local news coverage for the Catawba County communities of Newton, Conover, Maiden, Claremont and Catawba, NC. The five-day newspaper comes out at noon ET each day with coverage of government activity, police and courts news, business developments, education and area sports. It also contains feature stories that highlight the people and places of Catawba County.
Language (s): English
Ad Rate: Full Page Mono 9.50
Ad Rate: Full Page Colour 75.00
Currency: United States Dollars
DAILY NEWSPAPER

Observer-Dispatch 14429
Owner: GateHouse Media Inc.
Editorial: 221 Oriskany St E, Utica, New York 13501-1201 **Tel:** 1 315 792-5000
Email: news@uticaod.com **Web site:** http://www.uticaod.com
Freq: Daily; **Circ:** 26637 Not Audited
News Editor: Fran Perritano
Profile: Observer-Dispatch is published daily for residents of Utica, NY and surrounding communities. The newspaper covers local and national news, as well as community events. Feature articles cover business, politics, education, arts & entertainment, lifestyle and other information of interest to those in the Mohawk Valley.
Language (s): English
Ad Rate: Full Page Mono 66.47
Ad Rate: Full Page Colour 69.47
Currency: United States Dollars
DAILY NEWSPAPER

Observer-Reporter 14627
Owner: Observer Publishing Comapny
Editorial: 122 S Main St, Washington, Pennsylvania 15301 **Tel:** 1 724 222-2200
Email: newsroom@observer-reporter.com **Web site:** http://www.observer-reporter.com
Freq: Daily; **Circ:** 29539 Not Audited
Editor: Brad Hundt; **Publisher:** Thomas Northrop; **Editor:** Linda Ritzer
Profile: Observer-Reporter is a local daily newspaper written for residents of Washington and Greene counties, PA. The newspaper covers local news, sports, business, religion and events.
Language (s): English
Ad Rate: Full Page Mono 42.50
Ad Rate: Full Page Colour 225.00
Currency: United States Dollars
DAILY NEWSPAPER

Ocala Star-Banner 15434
Owner: GateHouse Media Inc.
Editorial: 2121 SW 19th Avenue Rd, Ocala, Florida 34471-7752 **Tel:** 1 352 867-4010
Email: news@ocala.com **Web site:** http://www.ocala.com
Freq: Daily; **Circ:** 28651 Not Audited
Publisher: James Doughton; **State Capital Bureau Chief:** Lloyd Dunkelberger
Profile: Ocala (FL) Star-Banner is a daily morning newspaper providing news coverage to readers in Marion County, FL. The paper provides coverage of local and regional news, government, politics, business, entertainment, education, and real estate. As of November 2008, they have some combined operations with the Gainesville (FL) Sun.
Language (s): English
Ad Rate: Full Page Mono 93.61
Ad Rate: Full Page Colour 302.55
Currency: United States Dollars
DAILY NEWSPAPER

The Ocean County Signal 860316
Owner: Ocean Signal Media Group, LLC
Editorial: 195 Lehigh Ave Ste 1, Lakewood, New Jersey 08701-4555
Web site: http://www.oceancountysignal.com/
Freq: Daily
Profile: The Ocean County Signal is a daily newspaper covering Local News for the residents of Ocean County, NJ. Coverage includes Business and Community News, Events, Opinions, Politics, Schools, Sports and Towns in addition to other local topics. They do not accept pitching or press materials and have requested that their contact information not be listed.
Language (s): English
Ad Rate: Full Page Mono 1000.00
Ad Rate: Full Page Colour 1195.00
Currency: United States Dollars
DAILY NEWSPAPER

Odessa American 14719
Owner: AIM Media Texas, LLC
Editorial: 222 E 4th St, Odessa, Texas 79761-5122 **Tel:** 1 432 337-6262
Email: oanews@oaoa.com **Web site:** http://www.oaoa.com
Freq: Daily; **Circ:** 16633 Not Audited
Publisher: Patrick Canty
Profile: Odessa American is a daily newspaper written for residents of Odessa, TX. The newspaper covers local news, sports and entertainment in the Permian Basin area.
Language (s): English
Ad Rate: Full Page Mono 28.89
Ad Rate: Full Page Colour 395.00
Currency: United States Dollars
DAILY NEWSPAPER

Oelwein Daily Register 13889
Owner: Community Newspaper Group
Editorial: 25 1st St SE, Oelwein, Iowa 50662-2314 **Tel:** 1 319 283-2144
Email: news@oelweindailyregister.com **Web site:** http://www.oelweindailyregister.com
Freq: Daily; **Circ:** 2690 Not Audited
Publisher: Deb Weigel
Profile: Oelwein Daily Register is published daily for residents of Oelwein, IA and surrounding areas. The publication is a general interest newspaper, covering local news, weather, sports, education, business, arts & entertainment and other information of interest to the local community.
Language (s): English
Ad Rate: Full Page Mono 18.60
Ad Rate: Full Page Colour 250.00
Currency: United States Dollars
DAILY NEWSPAPER

Ogdensburg Journal 14417
Owner: St. Lawrence County Newspapers, Inc.
Editorial: 308 Isabella St, #312, Ogdensburg, New York 13669-1407 **Tel:** 1 315 393-1003
Email: journal@ogd.com **Web site:** http://www.ogd.com
Freq: Mon thru Fri; **Circ:** 5500 Not Audited
Profile: Ogdensburg Journal is a weekday newspaper serving residents of Ogdensburg, NY, and surrounding communities. It covers local and regional news, sports, arts & entertainment, events, editorials and features of interest to local readers.
Language (s): English
Ad Rate: Full Page Mono 9.75
Ad Rate: Full Page Colour 140.00
Currency: United States Dollars
DAILY NEWSPAPER

The Oklahoman 15304
Owner: Anschutz Corp.
Editorial: 100 W Main St Ste 100, Oklahoma City, Oklahoma 73102-9013 **Tel:** 1 405 475-3311
Email: news@newsok.com **Web site:** http://www.newsok.com
Freq: Daily; **Circ:** 96885 Not Audited
Editor: Nathan Poppe
Profile: The Oklahoman is a general-interest broadsheet newspaper serving readers in the Oklahoma City area. Business is covered in a daily business section, which also appears on Sunday. A large part of The Oklahoman's business coverage focuses on the oil industry. Types of articles included in the business section are short news items, company news, industry news, and trend stories.
Language (s): English
Ad Rate: Full Page Mono 384.95
Ad Rate: Full Page Colour 2677.83
Currency: United States Dollars
DAILY NEWSPAPER

The Oklahoman - Denver Bureau 156613
Editorial: Denver, Colorado **Tel:** 1 303 892-7151
Web site: http://www.newsok.com
Language (s): English
DAILY NEWSPAPER

Okmulgee Daily Times 14533
Owner: Sumner Newspapers Inc.
Editorial: 320 W 6th St, Okmulgee, Oklahoma 74447-5018 **Tel:** 1 918 756-3600
Email: okmulgeedailytimes@yahoo.com **Web site:** http://www.yourokmulgee.com
Freq: Daily; **Circ:** 4483 Not Audited
Editor: Herman Brown; **Advertising Sales Manager:** Robyn Brownfield
Profile: Okmulgee Daily Times is a daily newspaper written for the residents of Okmulgee, OK.
Language (s): English
Ad Rate: Full Page Mono 9.25
Ad Rate: Full Page Colour 150.00
Currency: United States Dollars
DAILY NEWSPAPER

Olney Daily Mail 13950
Owner: GateHouse Media Inc.
Editorial: 206 S Whittle Ave, Olney, Illinois 62450-2251 **Tel:** 1 618 393-2931
Email: news@olneydailymail.com **Web site:** http://www.olneydailymail.com
Freq: Daily; **Circ:** 4300 Not Audited
Editor: Mark Allen; **Advertising Sales Manager:** Miranda Holbrook; **Publisher:** Kerry Kocher
Profile: Olney Daily Mail is published daily for the residents of Olney, IL and surrounding areas. The newspaper covers local news, business, arts & entertainment, sports, health and government.
Language (s): English
Ad Rate: Full Page Mono 18.01
Ad Rate: Full Page Colour 225.00
Currency: United States Dollars
DAILY NEWSPAPER

The Olympian 14788
Owner: McClatchy Newspapers
Editorial: 111 Bethel St NE, Olympia, Washington 98506-4365 **Tel:** 1 360 754-5400
Email: news@theolympian.com **Web site:** http://www.theolympian.com
Freq: Daily; **Circ:** 19295 Not Audited
Profile: The Olympian is a local daily newspaper written for residents of Olympia, WA. The newspaper covers local news, sports, education, business, entertainment and politics.
Language (s): English
Ad Rate: Full Page Mono 67.00
Ad Rate: Full Page Colour 900.00
Currency: United States Dollars
DAILY NEWSPAPER

Omaha World-Herald 15294
Owner: BH Media Group
Editorial: 1314 Douglas St Ste 700, Omaha, Nebraska 68102-1811 **Tel:** 1 402 444-1000
Email: news@owh.com **Web site:** http://www.omaha.com
Freq: Daily; **Circ:** 104958 Not Audited
Profile: Omaha World-Herald is a daily, general interest broadsheet newspaper written for readers in the greater Omaha, NE, area. Coverage includes business, technology, working, entertainment, home, living, sports and local, regional and national news.
Language (s): English
Ad Rate: Full Page Mono 162.00
Ad Rate: Full Page Colour 591.60
Currency: United States Dollars
DAILY NEWSPAPER

Omaha World-Herald - Lincoln Bureau 15788
Editorial: 635 S 14th St Ste 320, Lincoln, Nebraska 68508-2701 **Tel:** 1 402 473-9580
Bureau Chief: Paul Hammel
Language (s): English
DAILY NEWSPAPER

Omaha World-Herald - Washington Bureau 15491
Editorial: 529 14th St NW Ste 1009, Washington, District Of Columbia 20045-2001 **Tel:** 1 202 997-9787
Bureau Chief: Joseph Morton
Language (s): English
DAILY NEWSPAPER

The Oneida Daily Dispatch 14419
Owner: Digital First Media
Editorial: 130 Broad St, Oneida, New York 13421-1684 **Tel:** 1 315 363-5100
Email: newsroom@oneidadispatch.com **Web site:** http://www.oneidadispatch.com
Freq: Mon thru Fri; **Circ:** 6715
Publisher: Robert O'Leary; **Editor:** Kurt Wanfried
Profile: The Oneida Daily Dispatch is written for Oneida and Madison County residents in New York.
Language (s): English
Ad Rate: Full Page Mono 16.29
Currency: United States Dollars
DAILY NEWSPAPER

Opelika-Auburn News 13673
Owner: BH Media Group
Editorial: 2901 Society Hill Rd, Opelika, Alabama 36804-4850 **Tel:** 1 334 749-6271
Email: editors@oanow.com **Web site:** http://www.oanow.com
Freq: Daily; **Circ:** 12748 Not Audited
Advertising Sales Manager: Sheila Haydel
Profile: Opelika-Auburn News is a daily newspaper published for the residents of Opelika, AL and surrounding areas. It provides local and national news and information.
Language (s): English
Ad Rate: Full Page Mono 31.93
Ad Rate: Full Page Colour 34.43
Currency: United States Dollars
DAILY NEWSPAPER

La Opinión 14960
Owner: ImpreMedia LLC
Editorial: 915 Wilshire Blvd Ste 850, Los Angeles, California 90017-3409 **Tel:** 1 213 622-8332
Email: laopinion@impremedia.com **Web site:** http://www.laopinion.com
Freq: Daily; **Circ:** 42120 Not Audited
News Editor: Carlos Avilés; **Editor:** Gabriel Lerner
Profile: La Opinión is a daily Spanish language newspaper for the Hispanic community of the Los Angeles area. It provides residents with information on local news, weather, sports and more. It maintains a commitment to diversity and immigration, as well as other issues specific to the Los Angeles Latino community. The paper is one of the most widely read and longest running Spanish-language newspapers in the country. It was first published in 1926. Previously focused on Mexico and Mexican and Mexican-American issues, the paper now serves a broader Hispanic readership with coverage of news and cultural topics from Central and South America, Cuba, Puerto Rico and The United States, in addition to international wire content. It is the recipient of a 2006 Jose Ortega y Gasset Award from El Pais newspaper in Spain. Contact the paper via Metro & News Editor.
Language (s): Spanish
Ad Rate: Full Page Mono 85.10
Ad Rate: Full Page Colour 1696.00

Currency: United States Dollars
DAILY NEWSPAPER

The Orange County Register 15339
Owner: Southern California News Group/Digital First Media
Editorial: 625 N Grand Ave, Santa Ana, California 92701-4347
Email: local@ocregister.com **Web site:** http://www.ocregister.com
Freq: Daily; **Circ:** 127597 Not Audited
Profile: The Orange County Register is published daily for the residents of Orange County, CA and surrounding areas. The newspaper covers local news and community events. Advertising rates reflect Monday, Tuesday and Wednesday. Rates for Thursday, Friday and Saturday are higher. This paper is a part of the Southern California News Group, a subsidiary of Digital First Media
Language (s): English
Ad Rate: Full Page Mono 361.85
Ad Rate: Full Page Colour 386.26
Currency: United States Dollars
DAILY NEWSPAPER

The Orange County Register - Laguna Woods Bureau 816300
Editorial: 24351 El Toro Rd, Laguna Woods, California 92637-4901 **Tel:** 1 949 837-5200
Language (s): English
DAILY NEWSPAPER

The Oregonian 15368
Owner: Oregonian Media Group
Editorial: 1500 SW 1st Ave Ste 400, Portland, Oregon 97201-5828 **Tel:** 1 503 221-8327 5
Email: newsroom@oregonian.com **Web site:** http://www.oregonlive.com
Freq: Daily; **Circ:** 142882 Not Audited
Profile: The Oregonian is a newspaper written for the general public in the Portland, OR area. It offers regional and national news and provides its readers with information on business, real estate, arts, entertainment, and sports. The business section offers breaking news, investigative reports, news and news analysis, features, columns and profiles on business in Oregon. The editorial staff only wants to receive information that pertains to Oregon businesses. The staff won a 2007 Pulitzer Prize for Breaking News.
Language (s): English
Ad Rate: Full Page Mono 263.70
Ad Rate: Full Page Colour 913.84
Currency: United States Dollars
DAILY NEWSPAPER

The Oregonian - Portland Bureau 15891
Editorial: 1675 SW Marlow Ave, Portland, Oregon 97225-5104 **Tel:** 1 503 294-5950
Email: west@oregonian.com
Language (s): English
DAILY NEWSPAPER

The Oregonian - Salem Bureau 16217
Editorial: 900 Court St NE Ste 43, Salem, Oregon 97301-4045 **Tel:** 1 503 221-8234
Email: politics@oregonian.com
Language (s): English
DAILY NEWSPAPER

L' Orient Le Jour - New York Bureau 620849
Editorial: United Nations, Room 450, New York, New York **Tel:** 1 212 963-5236
Profile: This is the New York bureau of L'Orient Le Jour, based in Beirut, Lebanon.
Language (s): Arabic
DAILY NEWSPAPER

Orlando Sentinel 15289
Owner: tronc
Editorial: 633 N Orange Ave, Orlando, Florida 32801-1300 **Tel:** 1 407 420-5000
Email: news@orlandosentinel.com **Web site:** http://www.orlandosentinel.com
Freq: Daily; **Circ:** 114225 Not Audited
News Editor: Steven Ford
Profile: Orlando Sentinel is a daily newspaper written for the general public in Orlando and East Central Florida, including the counties of Brevard, Flagler, Lake, Marion, Orange, Osceola, Seminole, Sumter and Volusia. Deadlines are two days prior to publication.
Language (s): English
Ad Rate: Full Page Mono 258.75
Currency: United States Dollars
DAILY NEWSPAPER

Orlando Sentinel - Tallahassee Bureau 15683
Editorial: 336 E College Ave Ste 105, Tallahassee, Florida 32301-1554 **Tel:** 1 850 222-5564
Language (s): English
DAILY NEWSPAPER

Orlando Sentinel - Tavares Bureau 15684
Editorial: 1898 E Burleigh Blvd, Tavares, Florida 32778-4366 **Tel:** 1 352 742-5920
Email: lake@orlandosentinel.com
Bureau Chief: Jerry Fallstrom
Language (s): English
DAILY NEWSPAPER

Oroville Mercury-Register 13742
Owner: MediaNews Group
Editorial: 2124 5th Ave, Oroville, California 95965-3400 **Tel:** 1 530 533-3131
Web site: http://www.orovillemr.com
Freq: Daily; **Circ:** 7000 Not Audited
Advertising Sales Manager: Sandra Lehman; **Editor:** David Little
Profile: Oroville Mercury-Register is a daily newspaper serving the residents of Oroville, CA and the Greater Mid-Valley area. It covers local news, sports, opinion, features and business.
Language (s): English
Ad Rate: Full Page Mono 67.03
Currency: United States Dollars
DAILY NEWSPAPER

Oshkosh Northwestern 14816
Owner: Gannett Co., Inc.
Editorial: 224 State St Floor 3, Oshkosh, Wisconsin 54901-4868 **Tel:** 1 920 235-7700
Email: oshkoshnews@thenorthwestern.com **Web site:** http://www.thenorthwestern.com
Freq: Daily; **Circ:** 15212
Profile: Oshkosh Northwestern is published daily for the residents of Oshkosh, WI and surrounding areas. The newspaper covers local and regional news, sports, entertainment, business and community events.
Language (s): English
Ad Rate: Full Page Mono 51.40
Ad Rate: Full Page Colour 312.36
Currency: United States Dollars
DAILY NEWSPAPER

Oskaloosa Herald 13890
Owner: Community Newspaper Holdings, Inc.
Editorial: 1901 A Ave W, Oskaloosa, Iowa 52577-1962 **Tel:** 1 641 672-2581
Email: oskynews@oskyherald.com **Web site:** http://www.oskaloosa.com
Freq: Daily; **Circ:** 3300
Editor: Duane Nollen; **Publisher:** Deb Van Engelenhoven
Profile: Oskaloosa Herald is published daily for the residents of Oskaloosa, IA and surrounding areas. The newspaper covers local news, sports, agriculture, government and lifestyle features.
Language (s): English
Ad Rate: Full Page Mono 8.17
Ad Rate: Full Page Colour 75.00
Currency: United States Dollars
DAILY NEWSPAPER

Ottawa Herald 14063
Owner: Harris Enterprises
Editorial: 214 S Hickory St, Ottawa, Kansas 66067-2309 **Tel:** 1 785 242-4700
Email: news@ottawaherald.com **Web site:** http://www.ottawaherald.com
Freq: Mon; **Circ:** 6100 Not Audited
Profile: Ottawa Herald is published daily for the residents of Franklin County, KS and surrounding areas. The newspaper covers news, sports, business and weather.
Language (s): English
Ad Rate: Full Page Mono 9.18
Ad Rate: Full Page Colour 135.00
Currency: United States Dollars
DAILY NEWSPAPER

Ottumwa Courier 13891
Owner: Community Newspaper Holdings, Inc.
Editorial: 213 E 2nd St, Ottumwa, Iowa 52501-2902 **Tel:** 1 641 684-4611
Email: news@ottumwacourier.com **Web site:** http://www.ottumwacourier.com/
Freq: Daily; **Circ:** 11772 Not Audited
Editor: Wanda Moeller
Profile: Ottumwa Courier is written for residents of Ottumwa, IA. It covers local news, sports, entertainment, health, state and national news.
Language (s): English
Ad Rate: Full Page Mono 20.25
Ad Rate: Full Page Colour 275.00
Currency: United States Dollars
DAILY NEWSPAPER

Owatonna People's Press 14212
Owner: Huckle Media LLC
Editorial: 135 W Pearl St, Owatonna, Minnesota 55060-2316 **Tel:** 1 507 451-2840
Email: news@owatonna.com **Web site:** http://www.southernminn.com/owatonna_peoples_press/
Freq: Daily; **Circ:** 11632 Not Audited
Profile: Owatonna People's Press is a local daily newspaper serving the residents of Owatonna, MN and the surrounding area. The newspaper mainly covers local news, sports, and community events. The paper accepts advertising at an open rate of $13.50 per column inch.
Language (s): English
Ad Rate: Full Page Mono 20.10
Ad Rate: Full Page Colour 370.00
Currency: United States Dollars
DAILY NEWSPAPER

Owensboro Messenger-Inquirer 14087
Owner: Paxton Media Group
Editorial: 1401 Frederica St, Owensboro, Kentucky 42301-4804 **Tel:** 1 270 926-0123
Email: news@messenger-inquirer.com **Web site:** http://www.messenger-inquirer.com
Freq: Daily; **Circ:** 20613 Not Audited
News and City Editor: Robert Bruck; **Publisher:** Bob Morris
Profile: Owensboro Messenger-Inquirer is a daily newspaper for residents of a seven-county area in Kentucky and Southern Indiana. The publication covers local news, events and sports. The editorial deadline is one day prior to the issue date.
Language (s): English
Ad Rate: Full Page Mono 34.47
Ad Rate: Full Page Colour 550.00
Currency: United States Dollars
DAILY NEWSPAPER

Oxford Eagle 14275
Owner: Oxford Eagle, Inc.
Editorial: 916 Jackson Ave E, Oxford, Mississippi 38655-3636 **Tel:** 1 662 234-4331
Email: news@oxfordeagle.com **Web site:** http://www.oxfordeagle.com
Freq: Daily; **Circ:** 6000 Not Audited
Editor: Stephanie Rebman; **News Editor:** Jon Scott
Profile: Oxford Eagle is a daily newspaper serving the residents of Lafayette County, MS. The newspaper provides news and sports coverage to the local community.
Language (s): English
Ad Rate: Full Page Mono 9.55
Ad Rate: Full Page Colour 264.55
Currency: United States Dollars
DAILY NEWSPAPER

The Paducah Sun 14088
Owner: Paxton Media Group
Editorial: 408 Kentucky Ave, Paducah, Kentucky 42003-1550 **Tel:** 1 270 575-8600
Email: news@paducahsun.com **Web site:** http://www.paducahsun.com
Freq: Daily; **Circ:** 20616 Not Audited
News Editor: Ron Clark; **Editor & Publisher:** Jim Paxton
Profile: The Paducah Sun is a daily newspaper serving Paducah, KY and the surrounding area. It covers news, business, sports, entertainment, outdoors and religion.
Language (s): English
Ad Rate: Full Page Mono 30.27
Currency: United States Dollars
DAILY NEWSPAPER

Palatka Daily News 13824
Owner: Community Newspapers Inc.
Editorial: 1825 Saint Johns Ave, Palatka, Florida 32177-4442 **Tel:** 1 386 312-5200
Email: palatkadailynews@yahoo.com **Web site:** http://www.palatkadailynews.com
Freq: Fri; **Circ:** 10300 Not Audited
Editor: Andy Hall; **Publisher:** Rusty Starr; **Editor:** Larry Sullivan
Profile: Palatka Daily News is a local newspaper serving the Palatka, FL community. The publication is published daily. It covers local news, sports and events.
Language (s): English
Ad Rate: Full Page Mono 23.22
Currency: United States Dollars
DAILY NEWSPAPER

Palestine Herald-Press 14721
Owner: Community Newspapers Holdings, Inc.
Editorial: 519 N Elm St, Palestine, Texas 75801-2927 **Tel:** 1 903 729-0281
Email: editor@palestineherald.com **Web site:** http://www.palestineherald.com
Freq: Fri; **Circ:** 7645 Not Audited
Publisher: Jake Mienk
Profile: Palestine Herald-Press is published daily for the residents of Palestine, TX and surrounding areas. The newspaper covers local news, sports and community events.
Language (s): English
Ad Rate: Full Page Mono 10.30
Ad Rate: Full Page Colour 100.00
Currency: United States Dollars
DAILY NEWSPAPER

Palladium-Item 14014
Owner: Gannett Co., Inc.
Editorial: 1175 N A St, Richmond, Indiana 47374-3226 **Tel:** 1 765 962-1575
Email: palitem@pal-item.com **Web site:** http://www.pal-item.com
Freq: Daily; **Circ:** 9271
Profile: Palladium-Item is a daily newspaper serving the greater Richmond, IN area. It covers local and national news, sports, politics and agricultural news.
Language (s): English
Ad Rate: Full Page Mono 41.28
Ad Rate: Full Page Colour 481.00
Currency: United States Dollars
DAILY NEWSPAPER

The Palladium-Times 14421
Owner: Sample News Group
Editorial: 140 W 1st St, Oswego, New York 13126-1514 **Tel:** 1 315 343-3800
Email: editor@palltimes.com **Web site:** http://www.oswegocountynewsnow.com/
Freq: Daily; **Circ:** 8507 Not Audited
Publisher: Jon Spaulding
Profile: The Palladium-Times is published daily for the residents of Oswego, NY and surrounding areas. The newspapers covers local and national news.
Language (s): English
Ad Rate: Full Page Mono 17.00
Ad Rate: Full Page Colour 375.00
Currency: United States Dollars
DAILY NEWSPAPER

Palm Beach Daily News 13825
Owner: Cox Media Group, Inc.
Editorial: 400 Royal Palm Way, Ste 100, Palm Beach, Florida 33480-4041 **Tel:** 1 561 820-3800
Email: copy@pbdailynews.com **Web site:** http://www.palmbeachdailynews.com
Freq: Daily; **Circ:** 7126 Not Audited
Editor: Elizabeth Clarke
Profile: Palm Beach Daily News is a sister publication to the Palm Beach Post. The newspaper covers local news, entertainment, politics and events of interest to residents of Palm Beach, FL. From mid-June through mid-September, this publication switches to a bi-weekly with print editions on Thursdays and Sundays.
Language (s): English
Ad Rate: Full Page Mono 59.28
Ad Rate: Full Page Colour 1573.00
Currency: United States Dollars
DAILY NEWSPAPER

The Palm Beach Post 15318
Owner: Cox Media Group, Inc.
Editorial: 2751 S Dixie Hwy, West Palm Beach, Florida 33405-1233 **Tel:** 1 561 820-4400
Email: pbmetro@pbpost.com **Web site:** http://www.palmbeachpost.com
Freq: Daily; **Circ:** 70394 Not Audited
Senior Editor, News: Carolyn DiPaolo
Profile: The Palm Beach Post is a metropolitan daily newspaper with bureaus throughout the state of Florida covering local, state, national and international news.
Language (s): English
Ad Rate: Full Page Mono 192.67
Ad Rate: Full Page Colour 238.41
Currency: United States Dollars
DAILY NEWSPAPER

The Palm Beach Post - Jupiter Bureau 15702
Editorial: 1838 Park Ln S, Jupiter, Florida 33458-8077 **Tel:** 1 561 820-3030
Language (s): English
DAILY NEWSPAPER

The Palm Beach Post - Washington Bureau 779218
Editorial: 400 N Capitol St NW Ste 750, Washington, District Of Columbia 20001-1536 **Tel:** 1 202 777-7090
Profile: This is the Washington D.C. bureau of The Palm Beach Post.
Language (s): English
DAILY NEWSPAPER

The Pampa News 14722
Owner: PTS, Inc.
Editorial: 403 W Atchison Ave, Pampa, Texas 79065-6303 **Tel:** 1 806 669-2525
Web site: http://www.thepampanews.com
Freq: Daily; **Circ:** 4578 Not Audited
Editor: Timothy Howsare; **Advertising Sales Manager:** Redonn Woods
Profile: The Pampa News is a community newspaper serving the Pampa, TX area. The publication covers local news, sports, an oil and gas report and community events.
Language (s): English
Ad Rate: Full Page Mono 12.80
Ad Rate: Full Page Colour 170.00
Currency: United States Dollars
DAILY NEWSPAPER

The Pantagraph 13914
Owner: Lee Enterprises, Inc.
Editorial: 301 W Washington St, Bloomington, Illinois 61701-3827 **Tel:** 1 309 829-9000
Email: newsroom@pantagraph.com **Web site:** http://www.pantagraph.com
Freq: Daily; **Circ:** 30900 Not Audited
Editor: Mark Pickering
Profile: The Pantagraph is a local daily newspaper published for residents in central Illinois. The newspaper covers local, national and international news, sports, business, and community events.
Language (s): English
Ad Rate: Full Page Mono 73.88
Ad Rate: Full Page Colour 112.63
Currency: United States Dollars
DAILY NEWSPAPER

Paper of Montgomery County 331052
Owner: Sagamore News Media
Editorial: 101 W Main St Ste 300, Crawfordsville, Indiana 47933-1742 **Tel:** 1 765 361-0100
Email: news@thepaper24-7.com **Web site:** http://www.thepaper24-7.com
Freq: Mon thru Fri; **Circ:** 1500 Not Audited
Publisher & Editor: Tim Timmons
Profile: The Paper of Montgomery County is written for the residents of Crawfordsville, IN.
Language (s): English
Ad Rate: Full Page Mono 8.00
Ad Rate: Full Page Colour 26.16
Currency: United States Dollars
DAILY NEWSPAPER

Paragould Daily Press 13701
Owner: Paxton Media Group
Editorial: 1401 W Hunt St, Paragould, Arkansas 72450 **Tel:** 1 870 239-8562
Email: newsinfo@paragoulddailypress.com **Web site:** http://www.paragoulddailypress.com

Freq: Daily; **Circ:** 5539 Not Audited
Editor: Steve Gillespie
Profile: Paragould Daily Press is a daily newspaper serving Paragould and Greene County, AR. The publication covers local news and sports. Features content is taken almost exclusively from wire services.
Language (s): English
Ad Rate: Full Page Mono 8.75
Ad Rate: Full Page Colour 160.00
Currency: United States Dollars
DAILY NEWSPAPER

Paris Beacon-News   13952
Owner: Edgar County Newspapers Inc.
Editorial: 218 N Main St, Paris, Illinois 61944-1738
Tel: 1 217 465-6424
Email: news@parisbeacon.com **Web site:** http://www.parisbeacon.com
Freq: Daily; **Circ:** 5400 Not Audited
Advertising Sales Manager: Stacy Rigdon
Profile: Paris Beacon-News is a daily newspaper serving the residents of Paris, IL. It covers local news, sports and community events.
Language (s): English
Ad Rate: Full Page Mono 10.00
Ad Rate: Full Page Colour 200.00
Currency: United States Dollars
DAILY NEWSPAPER

The Paris News   14881
Owner: Southern Newspapers, Inc.
Editorial: 5050 SE Loop 286, Paris, Texas 75460-6576 **Tel:** 1 903 785-8744
Email: editor@theparisnews.com **Web site:** http://theparisnews.com
Freq: Daily; **Circ:** 10000 Not Audited
Profile: The Paris News is a local newspaper written for residents of the Red River region in Texas. The newspaper covers local news, sports and events.
Language (s): English
Ad Rate: Full Page Mono 18.00
Ad Rate: Full Page Colour 295.00
Currency: United States Dollars
DAILY NEWSPAPER

Paris Post-Intelligencer   14677
Owner: Paris Publishing Co., Inc.
Editorial: 208 E Wood St, Paris, Tennessee 38242-4139 **Tel:** 1 731 642-1162
Email: parispi@parispi.net **Web site:** http://www.parispi.net
Freq: Daily; **Circ:** 8050 Not Audited
Advertising Sales Manager: Danny Peppers; **News Editor:** Ken Walker; **Publisher & Editor:** Michael Williams
Profile: Paris Post-Intelligencer provides local news to Henry County, TN.
Language (s): English
Ad Rate: Full Page Mono 9.85
Currency: United States Dollars
DAILY NEWSPAPER

Parkersburg News and Sentinel
14842
Owner: Ogden Newspapers
Editorial: 519 Juliana St, Parkersburg, West Virginia 26101-5135 **Tel:** 1 304 485-1891
Email: editorial@newsandsentinel.com **Web site:** http://www.newsandsentinel.com
Freq: Daily; **Circ:** 18095 Not Audited
Editor: Jesse Mancini; **Publisher:** Jim Spanner; **Advertising Sales Manager:** Matt Tranquill
Profile: Parkersburg News and Sentinel is a daily newspaper serving the area surrounding Parkersburg, West Virginia. The paper covers local news, business, sports, society and community events. Press releases should be sent to the managing editor regardless of content. Deadlines are one day prior to publication.
Language (s): English
Ad Rate: Full Page Mono 79.57
Ad Rate: Full Page Colour 487.30
Currency: United States Dollars
DAILY NEWSPAPER

Parsons Sun   14064
Owner: Family Media, Inc.
Editorial: 220 S 18th St, Parsons, Kansas 67357-4218 **Tel:** 1 620 421-2000
Email: news@parsonssun.com **Web site:** http://www.parsonssun.com
Freq: Fri; **Circ:** 6286 Not Audited
Profile: Parsons Sun is a daily newspaper serving residents of Southeast Kansas. It covers local news, sports and business.
Language (s): English
Ad Rate: Full Page Mono 10.50
Ad Rate: Full Page Colour 140.00
Currency: United States Dollars
DAILY NEWSPAPER

Pasadena Star-News   13743
Owner: Southern California News Group/Digital First Media
Editorial: 2 N Lake Ave Ste 150, Pasadena, California 91101-1896 **Tel:** 1 626 578-6300
Email: news.star-news@sgvn.com **Web site:** http://www.pasadenastarnews.com
Freq: Daily; **Circ:** 24880 Not Audited
Profile: Pasadena Star-News is a daily newspaper serving the residents of Pasadena, CA and surrounding communities. This paper is a part of the Southern California News Group, a subsidiary of Digital First Media. The paper's coverage includes news, sports, business and features. The paper is published 48 weeks out of the year.
Language (s): English

Ad Rate: Full Page Mono 651.00
Ad Rate: Full Page Colour 2121.50
Currency: United States Dollars
DAILY NEWSPAPER

The Patriot Ledger   14132
Owner: GateHouse Media Inc.
Editorial: 400 Crown Colony Dr, Quincy, Massachusetts 02169-0930 **Tel:** 1 617 786-7000
Email: newsroom@ledger.com **Web site:** http://www.patriotledger.com
Freq: Daily; **Circ:** 28670
Editor: Linda Shepherd
Profile: The Patriot Ledger in Quincy, MA is a daily regional newspaper covering news, sports and entertainment.
Language (s): English
Ad Rate: Full Page Mono 63.54
Ad Rate: Full Page Colour 220.05
Currency: United States Dollars
DAILY NEWSPAPER

The Patriot-News   15444
Owner: Advance Publications, Inc.
Editorial: 2020 Technology Pkwy Ste 300, Mechanicsburg, Pennsylvania 17050-9412
Tel: 1 717 255-8100
Email: newstips@pennlive.com **Web site:** http://www.pennlive.com
Freq: 3 Times/Week; **Circ:** 56983 Not Audited
Profile: The Patriot-News is a daily newspaper written for the residents of Harrisburg, PA and surrounding areas. The publication focuses on Pennsylvania-related news stories, but maintains a broad approach to reporting important national and international news. The special feature sections include recreation, weddings, sports and travel.
Language (s): English
Ad Rate: Full Page Mono 58.00
Ad Rate: Full Page Colour 94.45
Currency: United States Dollars
DAILY NEWSPAPER

The Patriot-News - Harrisburg Bureau   155438
Editorial: 501 N 3rd St Rm 524, Harrisburg, Pennsylvania 17120-0302
Language (s): English
DAILY NEWSPAPER

Pauls Valley Democrat   14534
Owner: Community Newspaper Holdings, Inc.
Editorial: 108 S Willow St, Pauls Valley, Oklahoma 73075-3834 **Tel:** 1 405 238-6464
Web site: http://www.paulsvalleydailydemocrat.com
Freq: Daily; **Circ:** 2474 Not Audited
Profile: Pauls Valley Democrat is a daily newspaper serving the residents of Pauls Valley, OK. The publication focuses on local news, sports and business.
Language (s): English
Ad Rate: Full Page Mono 7.25
Ad Rate: Full Page Colour 9.75
Currency: United States Dollars
DAILY NEWSPAPER

Pekin Daily Times   13954
Owner: GateHouse Media Inc.
Editorial: 20 S 4th St, Pekin, Illinois 61554-4203
Tel: 1 309 346-1111
Email: community@pekintimes.com **Web site:** http://www.pekintimes.com
Freq: Daily; **Circ:** 12537
Publisher: Gregg Ratliff
Profile: Pekin Daily Times is published daily for the residents of Pekin, IL and surrounding areas. The newspaper covers local news, sports, entertainment and community events.
Language (s): English
Ad Rate: Full Page Mono 21.00
Ad Rate: Full Page Colour 72.04
Currency: United States Dollars
DAILY NEWSPAPER

Peninsula Clarion   13662
Owner: GateHouse Media Inc.
Editorial: 150 Trading Bay Rd Ste 1, Kenai, Alaska 99611-7716 **Tel:** 1 907 283-7551
Email: news@peninsulaclarion.com **Web site:** http://www.peninsulaclarion.com
Freq: Daily; **Circ:** 4799 Not Audited
Editor: Will Morrow
Profile: Peninsula Clarion is a daily newspaper written for residents of Alaska's Kenai Peninsula. The publication covers news, sports, business, arts & entertainment, outdoor recreation and community events.
Language (s): English
Ad Rate: Full Page Mono 21.40
Ad Rate: Full Page Colour 300.00
Currency: United States Dollars
DAILY NEWSPAPER

Peninsula Daily News   14789
Owner: Black Press Ltd.
Editorial: 305 W 1st St, Port Angeles, Washington 98362-2205 **Tel:** 1 360 452-2345
Email: news@peninsuladailynews.com **Web site:** http://www.peninsuladailynews.com
Freq: Daily; **Circ:** 11748 Not Audited
News Editor: Michael Foster
Profile: Peninsula Daily News is a local newspaper serving residents of Washington's Olympic Peninsula. The publication covers local news, sports, business, education and community events.
Language (s): English
Ad Rate: Full Page Mono 28.12

Ad Rate: Full Page Colour 91.70
Currency: United States Dollars
DAILY NEWSPAPER

Pensacola News Journal   13827
Owner: Gannett Co., Inc.
Editorial: 2 N Palafox St, Pensacola, Florida 32502-5626 **Tel:** 1 850 435-8500
Email: news@pnj.com **Web site:** http://www.pnj.com
Freq: Daily; **Circ:** 27464 Not Audited
Profile: Pensacola News Journal is a daily regional newspaper for Northwest Florida and Southern Alabama. The publication offers investigative reports as well as information on health, education, arts & entertainment, news, food, recreation and sports.
Language (s): English
Ad Rate: Full Page Mono 153.34
Ad Rate: Full Page Colour 502.20
Currency: United States Dollars
DAILY NEWSPAPER

Perry Daily Journal   14535
Owner: Perry Publishing and Broadcasting
Editorial: 714 Delaware St, Perry, Oklahoma 73077-6425 **Tel:** 1 580 336-2222
Email: gloriapdjnews@yahoo.com **Web site:** http://www.pdjnews.com
Freq: Daily; **Circ:** 3250 Not Audited
Publisher: Phillip Reid
Profile: Perry Daily Journal is a local newspaper serving residents of Perry County, OK. The publication covers news, sports, arts & entertainment and community events.
Language (s): English
Ad Rate: Full Page Mono 10.42
Ad Rate: Full Page Colour 103.00
Currency: United States Dollars
DAILY NEWSPAPER

Peru Tribune   14009
Owner: Paxton Media Group
Editorial: 26 W 3rd St, Peru, Indiana 46970-2155
Tel: 1 765 473-6641
Web site: http://www.chronicle-tribune.com/peru_tribune
Freq: Daily; **Circ:** 7292 Not Audited
Profile: Peru Tribune is published for the residents of Peru and Miami County, IN. The newspaper covers local and state news, business, sports, lifestyles and entertainment.
Language (s): English
Ad Rate: Full Page Mono 18.00
Ad Rate: Full Page Colour 210.00
Currency: United States Dollars
DAILY NEWSPAPER

Petoskey News-Review   14189
Owner: Schurz Communications Inc.
Editorial: 319 State St, Petoskey, Michigan 49770-2746 **Tel:** 1 231 347-2544
Email: petoskeynews@petoskeynews.com **Web site:** http://www.petoskeynews.com
Freq: Daily; **Circ:** 9789 Not Audited
Publisher: Douglas Caldwell; **Advertising Sales Manager:** Christy Lyons
Profile: Petoskey News-Review is an evening weekday newspaper serving residents of Petoskey, Harbor Springs and Traverse City, MI. Coverage includes local and national news, sports and entertainment. It shares its offices and editorial staff with The Graphic, a free, weekly newspaper serving Petoskey, MI and surrounding communities. The lead time for submissions varies depending on content.
Language (s): English
Ad Rate: Full Page Mono 15.85
Ad Rate: Full Page Colour 55.88
Currency: United States Dollars
DAILY NEWSPAPER

Pharos-Tribune   13999
Owner: Community Newspaper Holdings, Inc.
Editorial: 517 E Broadway, Logansport, Indiana 46947-3154 **Tel:** 1 574 722-5000
Email: ptnews@pharostribune.com **Web site:** http://www.pharostribune.com
Freq: Daily; **Circ:** 9303 Not Audited
News Editor: Sarah Einselen; **Publisher:** Robyn McCloskey
Profile: Pharos-Tribune is a local daily newspaper serving residents of Logansport, Cass County and Central Indiana since 1844. The publication covers news, sports and community events taking place in and around Logansport. Regular features include local news, government, education and business. Deadlines are on the day of publication at 10:15am CT.
Language (s): English
Ad Rate: Full Page Mono 16.50
Ad Rate: Full Page Colour 57.87
Currency: United States Dollars
DAILY NEWSPAPER

Philadelphia Daily News   15455
Owner: Philadelphia Media Network
Editorial: 801 Market St Ste 300, Philadelphia, Pennsylvania 19107-3183 **Tel:** 1 215 854-5908
Web site: http://www.philly.com
Freq: Daily; **Circ:** 367160
Editor: Michael Days
Profile: Philadelphia Daily News, established in 1925, is a tabloid newspaper written specifically for Philadelphia residents. Emphasizing local news and events, its editorial content provides in-depth coverage of community, government, economic and business issues. Coverage extends to national and international news in the U.S. and World sections. Articles include features, breaking news, columns and accent features focusing on subjects such as careers and money. The paper does not publish a

Holiday Gift Guide. The black and white advertising rate is a combination rate for this paper and the Philadelphia Inquirer. Calendar listings are handled through a third party company, Event Source. When sending information via mail to the paper, clearly designate that it is for the newsroom.
Language (s): English
Ad Rate: Full Page Mono 1106.47
Ad Rate: Full Page Colour 2660.00
Currency: United States Dollars
DAILY NEWSPAPER

Philadelphia Daily News - Harrisburg Bureau   16176
Editorial: Press Office State Capital Bldg, Ste 524-E, Harrisburg, Pennsylvania 17108 **Tel:** 1 717 783-9666
Language (s): English
DAILY NEWSPAPER

The Philadelphia Inquirer   15287
Owner: Philadelphia Media Network
Editorial: 801 Market St Fl 3, Philadelphia, Pennsylvania 19107-3126 **Tel:** 1 215 854-2000 4502
Web site: http://www.philly.com/inquirer/
Freq: Daily; **Circ:** 227245 Not Audited
News Editor: Brian Leighton; **Editor:** Bill Marimow
Profile: Philadelphia Inquirer is a broadsheet newspaper written for residents in the Philadelphia area. It covers local, national and international news, as well as local zoned coverage of the suburbs and surrounding regions, business, technology, features, entertainment and sports. The paper won a 1997 Pulitzer Prize for Explanatory Journalism. Calendar listings are handled through a third party company, Event Source.
Language (s): English
Ad Rate: Full Page Mono 509.00
Ad Rate: Full Page Colour 802.98
Currency: United States Dollars
DAILY NEWSPAPER

Philadelphia Inquirer - Cherry Hill Bureau   15911
Editorial: 53 Haddonfield Rd Ste 300, Cherry Hill, New Jersey 08002-4802 **Tel:** 1 856 779-3840
Language (s): English
DAILY NEWSPAPER

Philadelphia Inquirer - Conshohocken Bureau   15918
Editorial: 800 River Rd Route 23, Conshohocken, Pennsylvania 19428-2632 **Tel:** 1 610 313-8000
Language (s): English
DAILY NEWSPAPER

Philadelphia Inquirer - Harrisburg Bureau   15916
Editorial: 524 State Capitol Building Fl E, Harrisburg, Pennsylvania 17120-0020
Language (s): English
DAILY NEWSPAPER

Philadelphia Inquirer - Trenton Bureau   15914
Editorial: 125 W State St, Trenton, New Jersey 08608-1101 **Tel:** 1 609 292-5775
Language (s): English
DAILY NEWSPAPER

Picayune Item   14276
Owner: Community Newspaper Holdings, Inc.
Editorial: 17 Richardson Ozona Rd, Picayune, Mississippi 39466-7865 **Tel:** 1 601 798-4766
Email: picayuneitem@bellsouth.net **Web site:** http://www.picayuneitem.com
Freq: Daily; **Circ:** 4343 Not Audited
Editor: Jeremy Pittari
Profile: Picayune Item is a daily newspaper serving the residents of Pearl River County, MS and surrounding areas. It covers local news, education, sports and community events.
Language (s): English
Ad Rate: Full Page Mono 11.33
Currency: United States Dollars
DAILY NEWSPAPER

The Pilot-News   14010
Owner: Horizon Publications
Editorial: 214 N Michigan St, Plymouth, Indiana 46563-2135 **Tel:** 1 574 936-3101
Email: news@thepilotnews.com **Web site:** http://www.thepilotnews.com
Freq: Daily; **Circ:** 7250 Not Audited
Publisher: Rick Kreps; **Advertising Sales Manager:** Cindy Stockton
Profile: The Pilot-News is published for residents of Marshall County, IN and surrounding areas. The newspapers covers local and state news, business, sports, lifestyles and entertainment.
Language (s): English
Ad Rate: Full Page Mono 10.20
Ad Rate: Full Page Colour 100.00
Currency: United States Dollars
DAILY NEWSPAPER

Pine Bluff Commercial   13702
Owner: Stephens Media
Editorial: 300 S Beech St, Pine Bluff, Arkansas 71601-4039 **Tel:** 1 870 534-3400
Email: pbcnews@pbcommercial.com **Web site:** http://www.pbcommercial.com
Freq: Fri
Editor: Sandra Hope

Profile: Pine Bluff Commercial is a daily newspaper written for residents in Southeast Arkansas. The paper covers local, regional and community news. The Monday edition of the paper is called PBC Today and is in tabloid format.
Language (s): English
Ad Rate: Full Page Mono 17.60
Ad Rate: Full Page Colour 250.00
Currency: United States Dollars
DAILY NEWSPAPER

Pioneer 14162
Owner: Pioneer Newspapers
Editorial: 115 N Michigan Ave, Big Rapids, Michigan 49307-1401 **Tel:** 1 231 796-4831
Email: pioinfo@pioneergroup.com **Web site:** http://www.bigrapidsnews.com
Freq: Daily; **Circ:** 5966 Not Audited
Publisher: John Norton; **Advertising Sales Manager:** Tim Zehr
Profile: Pioneer is a daily newspaper written for the residents of Big Rapids, greater Mecosta County, Osceola County and parts of Lake and Newaygo Counties, Michigan.
Language (s): English
Ad Rate: Full Page Mono 15.75
Ad Rate: Full Page Colour 165.00
Currency: United States Dollars
DAILY NEWSPAPER

Piqua Daily Call 14481
Owner: AIM Media Midwest
Editorial: 310 Spring St, Piqua, Ohio 45356-2334 **Tel:** 1 937 773-2721
Email: editorial@dailycall.com **Web site:** http://www.dailycall.com
Freq: Fri; **Circ:** 6567 Not Audited
Profile: Piqua Daily Call is published for the residents of Piqua, OH and surrounding areas. The newspaper covers local and state news, business, sports, lifestyles and entertainment. Deadlines are at 1pm the day prior to issue date.
Language (s): English
Ad Rate: Full Page Mono 15.25
Ad Rate: Full Page Colour 49.64
Currency: United States Dollars
DAILY NEWSPAPER

Pittsburgh Post-Gazette 15295
Owner: Block Communications Inc.
Editorial: 358 N Shore Dr Ste 300, Pittsburgh, Pennsylvania 15212-5870 **Tel:** 1 412 263-1100
Web site: http://www.post-gazette.com
Freq: Daily; **Circ:** 140987 Not Audited
Washington, D.C. Bureau Chief: Tracie Mauriello
Profile: Founded in 1786, the Pittsburgh Post-Gazette is a 70+ page broadsheet newspaper written for the general public in Pittsburgh and western Pennsylvania. The publication's mission statement is "to serve the community, our readers and advertisers as the region's indispensable source of news, advertising, and information." Business coverage in the publication includes local, regional and national news, features, investor information, personal finance tips, and technology information.
Language (s): English
Ad Rate: Full Page Mono 303.90
Ad Rate: Full Page Colour 4143.90
Currency: United States Dollars
DAILY NEWSPAPER

Pittsburgh Post-Gazette - Carnegie Bureau 151131
Editorial: 235 Hope St, Carnegie, Pennsylvania 15106-3655
Language (s): English
DAILY NEWSPAPER

Pittsburgh Post-Gazette - Cranberry Twp Bureau 232048
Editorial: 230 Executive Dr, Cranberry Twp, Pennsylvania 16066-6415 **Tel:** 1 724 772-4799
Language (s): English
DAILY NEWSPAPER

Pittsburgh Post-Gazette - Harrisburg Bureau 15920
Editorial: 524E Main Capitol Building, Harrisburg, Pennsylvania 17120-0022 **Tel:** 1 717 787-4254
Language (s): English
DAILY NEWSPAPER

The Plain Dealer 15302
Owner: Advance Publications, Inc.
Editorial: 1660 W 2nd St Ste 200, Cleveland, Ohio 44113-1446 **Tel:** 1 216 999-5000
Email: metrodesk@plaind.com **Web site:** http://www.cleveland.com/plaindealer
Freq: Daily; **Circ:** 200702 Not Audited
Profile: The Plain Dealer is a broadsheet daily newspaper distributed in Cuyahoga County, OH and covers local/metro, international, consumer, health, and business news. Monday's edition carries the Personal Finance section focusing on investments, savings, and spending money. The Tuesday Business section offers a look at business developments locally and around the world. In addition, on Tuesday, the Everywoman section deals with work, home, and the social concerns of women. Inside & Out, the paper's home and garden section, is published on Thursday. Friday Magazine features dining and local events in Northeast Ohio every Friday. In August 2009, the paper joined a national sports content-sharing alliance with several other papers across the country. The newspaper publishes seven times a week and provides home delivery three days a week, including Sunday.
Language (s): English
Ad Rate: Full Page Mono 520.00
Currency: United States Dollars
DAILY NEWSPAPER

The Plain Dealer - Columbus Bureau 15875
Editorial: 155 E Broad St, Columbus, Ohio 43215-3609 **Tel:** 1 614 228-8200
Bureau Chief: Robert Higgs
Language (s): English
DAILY NEWSPAPER

The Plain Dealer - Washington Bureau 15500
Editorial: 1625 K St NW, Washington, District Of Columbia 20006-1604
Washington Bureau Chief: Stephen Koff
Language (s): English
DAILY NEWSPAPER

Plainview Daily Herald 14972
Owner: Hearst Newspapers
Editorial: 820 Broadway St, Plainview, Texas 79072-7316 **Tel:** 1 806 296-1300
Web site: http://www.myplainview.com
Freq: Daily; **Circ:** 8000 Not Audited
News Editor: Homer Marquez; **Editor:** Doug McDonough
Profile: Plainview Daily Herald is a local daily newspaper written for the residents of Hale, Castro, Swisher, Briscoe, Lamb, and Floyd Counties in Texas. The newspaper primarily covers the local news, sports, features and lifestyles of Plainview, TX.
Language (s): English
Ad Rate: Full Page Mono 18.21
Ad Rate: Full Page Colour 300.00
Currency: United States Dollars
DAILY NEWSPAPER

Pocono Record 14619
Owner: GateHouse Media Inc.
Editorial: 511 Lenox St, Stroudsburg, Pennsylvania 18360-1516 **Tel:** 1 570 421-3000
Web site: http://www.poconorecord.com
Freq: Daily; **Circ:** 11617 Not Audited
Publisher: Joe Vanderhoof
Profile: Pocono Record's editorial mission is to provide the leading source of information in the Pocono Mountain area in Pennsylvania. The newspaper strives to provide an accurate, balanced, and fair news report. Pocono Record will exercise leadership, professionalism, and social responsibility for the betterment of the community. The local daily newspaper is written for residents in Monroe County and the Pocono Mountain area in Pennsylvania. Pocono Record covers local, national, and international news.
Language (s): English
Ad Rate: Full Page Mono 24.25
Ad Rate: Full Page Colour 324.25
Currency: United States Dollars
DAILY NEWSPAPER

Point Pleasant Register 14887
Owner: AIM Media Midwest
Editorial: 200 Main St, Point Pleasant, West Virginia 25550-1030 **Tel:** 1 304 675-1333
Email: news@mydailyregister.com **Web site:** http://www.mydailyregister.com
Freq: Fri; **Circ:** 3918 Not Audited
Profile: Point Pleasant Register is a local newspaper written for the residents of Point Pleasant, WV. The paper covers local news, sports, business and lifestyle.
Language (s): English
Ad Rate: Full Page Mono 11.35
Ad Rate: Full Page Colour 38.23
Currency: United States Dollars
DAILY NEWSPAPER

The Pomeroy Daily Sentinel 14482
Owner: AIM Media Midwest
Editorial: 200 Main St, Point Pleasant, West Virginia 25550-1030 **Tel:** 1 304 675-1333
Email: tdsnews@civitasmedia.com **Web site:** http://www.mydailysentinel.com
Freq: Fri; **Circ:** 3471 Not Audited
Profile: The Pomeroy Daily Sentinel is a daily newspaper serving the residents of Pomeroy and Middleport, OH. It contains world, national, state and local news, events, sports and editorial coverage. The paper is especially interested in receiving articles and photographs concerning new employees, promotions, club activities, civic organization programs, birthdays, anniversaries, weddings and engagements, honors and awards. On Sundays, the paper joins with its sister newspaper, the Gallipolis (OH) Daily Tribune to produce the Sunday Times-Sentinel.
Language (s): English
Ad Rate: Full Page Mono 10.05
Ad Rate: Full Page Colour 180.00
Currency: United States Dollars
DAILY NEWSPAPER

The Ponca City News 14536
Owner: Ponca City Publishing Company
Editorial: 300 N 3rd St, Ponca City, Oklahoma 74601-4336 **Tel:** 1 580 765-3311
Email: news@poncacitynews.com **Web site:** http://www.poncacitynews.com
Freq: Daily; **Circ:** 7436 Not Audited
Editor: Fred Hilton; **Advertising Sales Manager:** Patrick Jordan; **Editor & Publisher:** Tom Muchmore; **Editor:** Bob Patterson
Profile: The Ponca City News is a daily newspaper written for the residents of Ponca City, OK. The paper cover local news, education, sports, business and lifestyles.
Language (s): English
Ad Rate: Full Page Mono 12.00
Ad Rate: Full Page Colour 240.00
Currency: United States Dollars
DAILY NEWSPAPER

Port Arthur News 14726
Owner: Boone Newspapers
Editorial: 3501 Turtle Creek Dr, Port Arthur, Texas 77642-8053 **Tel:** 1 409 729-6397
Email: panews@panews.com **Web site:** http://www.panews.com
Freq: Daily; **Circ:** 8138 Not Audited
Advertising Sales Manager: Merle Hebert; **Publisher:** Rich Macke
Profile: The Port Arthur News is published daily for the residents of Jefferson County, TX. It delivers local news and information to residents of Jefferson County, TX. Topics covered also include national news, financial news, town hall news, arts and entertainment and health news.
Language (s): English
Ad Rate: Full Page Mono 35.00
Ad Rate: Full Page Colour 300.00
Currency: United States Dollars
DAILY NEWSPAPER

Port Clinton News Herald 14483
Owner: Gannett Co., Inc.
Editorial: 115 W 2Nd St, Port Clinton, Ohio 43452-1012 **Tel:** 1 419 734-3141
Email: newsherald@thenews-messenger.com **Web site:** http://www.portclintonnewsherald.com
Freq: Daily; **Circ:** 2190 Not Audited
Editor: David Yonke
Profile: Port Clinton News Herald is published for the residents in Ottawa County and Port Clinton, OH. It covers local and county news, features, business and community events. The paper dates back to 1865. After undergoing many name and ownership changes, the Port Clinton Herald and the Daily News merged in 1969 to become the News Herald.
Language (s): English
Ad Rate: Full Page Mono 19.20
Ad Rate: Full Page Colour 215.00
Currency: United States Dollars
DAILY NEWSPAPER

Portage Daily Register 14817
Owner: Capital Newspapers
Editorial: 1640 La Dawn Dr, Portage, Wisconsin 53901-8822 **Tel:** 1 608 745-3500
Email: pdr-news@capitalnewspapers.com **Web site:** http://www.wiscnews.com/portagedailyregister
Freq: Daily; **Circ:** 3350 Not Audited
Editor: Kerry Lechner
Profile: Portage Daily Register is published daily for the residents of Portage, Columbia and Market counties, WI. The newspaper provides local news and information.
Language (s): English
Ad Rate: Full Page Mono 20.10
Ad Rate: Full Page Colour 93.76
Currency: United States Dollars
DAILY NEWSPAPER

Portales News-Tribune 14380
Owner: Freedom Communications Inc.
Editorial: 101 E 1st St, Portales, New Mexico 88130 **Tel:** 1 575 356-4481
Email: pnt@yucca.net **Web site:** http://www.pntonline.com
Freq: Daily; **Circ:** 2200 Not Audited
Editor: David Stevens
Profile: Portales News-Tribune is published daily for the residents of Portales, NM. The newspaper focuses on news, sports, business and features about the community. Deadlines are daily at 10pm MT.
Language (s): English
Ad Rate: Full Page Mono 9.75
Ad Rate: Full Page Colour 247.20
Currency: United States Dollars
DAILY NEWSPAPER

Porterville Recorder 13744
Owner: Rhode Island Suburban Newspapers, Inc.
Editorial: 115 E Oak Ave, Porterville, California 93257-3807 **Tel:** 1 559 784-5000
Email: recorder@portervillerecorder.com **Web site:** http://www.recorderonline.com
Freq: Daily; **Circ:** 9118 Not Audited
Editor & Publisher: Rick Elkins
Profile: Porterville Recorder is written for residents of Southeastern Tulare County, CA.
Language (s): English
Ad Rate: Full Page Mono 34.00
Ad Rate: Full Page Colour 225.00
Currency: United States Dollars
DAILY NEWSPAPER

Portland Press Herald 15400
Owner: Maine Today Media Inc.
Editorial: 1 City Ctr Stop 5, Portland, Maine 04101-4009 **Tel:** 1 207 791-6650
Email: news@pressherald.com **Web site:** http://www.pressherald.com
Freq: Daily; **Circ:** 56722
Washington Bureau Chief: Kevin Miller
Profile: Portland Press Herald is a daily newspaper for residents of Portland that covers business, sports, entertainment, news, real estate and travel. The Sunday edition is named the Maine Sunday Telegram. Editorial lead times vary according to specific section.
Language (s): English
Ad Rate: Full Page Mono 84.00
Ad Rate: Full Page Colour 266.64
Currency: United States Dollars
DAILY NEWSPAPER

Portsmouth Daily Times 14484
Owner: AIM Media Midwest
Editorial: 1603 11th St., Portsmouth, Ohio 45662-3924 **Tel:** 1 740 353-3101
Email: pdtnews@aimmediamidwest.com **Web site:** http://www.portsmouth-dailytimes.com
Freq: Fri; **Circ:** 13733 Not Audited
Profile: Portsmouth Daily Times is a local newspaper serving the residents of Portsmouth, OH. The paper covers local news, sports, entertainment and lifestyle. Deadlines are at 10pm ET the day prior to the issue date.
Language (s): English
Ad Rate: Full Page Mono 18.75
Ad Rate: Full Page Colour 255.00
Currency: United States Dollars
DAILY NEWSPAPER

Portsmouth Herald 14356
Owner: GateHouse Media Inc.
Editorial: 111 NH Ave, Portsmouth, New Hampshire 03801-2864 **Tel:** 1 603 436-1800
Email: news@seacoastonline.com **Web site:** http://www.seacoastonline.com
Freq: Daily; **Circ:** 16601
Editor: Deb Cram; **Editor:** Christine French; **Publisher:** John Tabor
Profile: Portsmouth Herald is a local, daily newspaper providing news to residents of Portsmouth, NH. It is based in the same office as Seacost Newspapers, publisher of multiple community weeklies. Deadlines are at 5pm ET.
Language (s): English
Ad Rate: Full Page Mono 26.00
Ad Rate: Full Page Colour 465.00
Currency: United States Dollars
DAILY NEWSPAPER

The Post & Mail 13976
Owner: Horizon Publications
Editorial: 927 W Connexion Way, Columbia City, Indiana 46725-1031 **Tel:** 1 260 244-5153
Email: publisher@thepostandmail.com **Web site:** http://www.thepostandmail.com
Freq: Daily; **Circ:** 3583 Not Audited
Publisher: Rick Kreps
Profile: The Post & Mail provides local news, sports and events coverage for the Columbia City, IN area.
Language (s): English
Ad Rate: Full Page Mono 9.20
Ad Rate: Full Page Colour 100.00
Currency: United States Dollars
DAILY NEWSPAPER

The Post and Courier 15326
Owner: Evening Post Publishing Co.
Editorial: 134 Columbus St, Charleston, South Carolina 29403-4809 **Tel:** 1 843 577-7111
Web site: http://www.postandcourier.com
Freq: Daily; **Circ:** 69433 Not Audited
Profile: The Post and Courier was established in 1926 when The Daily Courier and The Evening Post combined. The newspaper kept separate staffs until the 1970s. In 1991, it was determined that the highest readership was for the morning edition so the evening edition stopped production. The news department is separated into four main areas: metro desk, copy desk, sports and features. The paper does not publish an editorial calendar.
Language (s): English
Ad Rate: Full Page Mono 167.87
Ad Rate: Full Page Colour 163.88
Currency: United States Dollars
DAILY NEWSPAPER

Post Falls Press 70659
Owner: Hagadone Corp.
Editorial: 201 N 2nd St, Coeur D Alene, Idaho 83814-2803 **Tel:** 1 208 664-8176
Web site: http://cdapress.com
Freq: Daily; **Circ:** 3729 Not Audited
Editor: Mark Nelke
Profile: Post Falls Press is written for the residents of Post Falls, ID. It combines with the Coeur d'Alene Press on Sunday.
Language (s): English
Ad Rate: Full Page Mono 32.67
Ad Rate: Full Page Colour 415.00
Currency: United States Dollars
DAILY NEWSPAPER

Post Register 13901
Owner: Post Company
Editorial: 333 Northgate Mile, Idaho Falls, Idaho 83401-2529 **Tel:** 1 208 522-1800
Email: news@postregister.com **Web site:** http://www.postregister.com
Freq: Fri; **Circ:** 25139 Not Audited
Publisher: Roger Plothow
Profile: Post Register is a daily local newspaper serving the Idaho Falls, ID area. Local, national and international news is covered, as well as lifestyle, entertainment and sports features.
Language (s): English
Ad Rate: Full Page Mono 24.85
Ad Rate: Full Page Colour 315.00
Currency: United States Dollars
DAILY NEWSPAPER

Post-Bulletin 14214

Owner: Small Newspaper Group
Editorial: 18 1st Ave SE, Rochester, Minnesota 55904-3722 **Tel:** 1 507 285-7600
Email: news@postbulletin.com **Web site:** http://www.postbulletin.com
Freq: Mon thru Fri; **Circ:** 32107 Not Audited
Publisher: Randy Chapman
Profile: Post-Bulletin in Rochester, MN is a daily newspaper that offers in-depth national and local news, including health, politics, entertainment, sports, technology, lifestyle, home, faith, food, and a section Teen Beat, specifically devoted to teenagers in the area.
Language (s): English
Ad Rate: Full Page Mono 55.10
Ad Rate: Full Page Colour 50.25
Currency: United States Dollars
DAILY NEWSPAPER

The Post-Crescent 14796

Owner: Gannett Co., Inc.
Editorial: 306 W Washington St, Appleton, Wisconsin 54911-5452 **Tel:** 1 920 993-1000
Email: pcnews@postcrescent.com **Web site:** http://www.postcrescent.com
Freq: Daily; **Circ:** 32048
Advertising Sales Manager: Nicole Mertes
Profile: The Post-Crescent is written for residents of Appleton, WI, and the surrounding counties. The newspaper covers news, sports, arts & entertainment, jobs and community information relevant to the area. Please send all correspondence to the PO Box.
Language (s): English
Ad Rate: Full Page Mono 89.90
Ad Rate: Full Page Colour 133.79
Currency: United States Dollars
DAILY NEWSPAPER

The Post-Crescent - Neenah Bureau 87424

Editorial: 307 S Commercial St, Neenah, Wisconsin 54956-5700 **Tel:** 1 920 729-6622
Bureau Chief: Rachel Rausch
Language (s): English
DAILY NEWSPAPER

The Post-Journal 14408

Owner: Ogden Newspapers
Editorial: 15 W 2nd St, Jamestown, New York 14701-5215 **Tel:** 1 716 487-1111
Email: editorial@post-journal.com **Web site:** http://www.post-journal.com
Freq: Daily; **Circ:** 12226 Not Audited
Publisher: Michael Bird; **Editor:** Chris Murphy; **Editor:** John Whittaker
Profile: The Post-Journal is written for residents of Chautauqua and Cattaraugus County, NY, and Warren County, PA. Deadlines are daily at 5pm ET.
Language (s): English
Ad Rate: Full Page Mono 50.44
Ad Rate: Full Page Colour 47.54
Currency: United States Dollars
DAILY NEWSPAPER

The Post-Standard 15449

Owner: Advance Publications
Editorial: 101 N Salina St, Syracuse, New York 13202-1030 **Tel:** 1 315 470-0011
Email: citynews@syracuse.com **Web site:** http://www.syracuse.com/poststandard
Freq: 3 Times/Week; **Circ:** 54685 Not Audited
Profile: The Post-Standard is a daily broadsheet newspaper distributed in the Syracuse, NY area. It covers central New York news, politics, education, sports and entertainment, as well as regional, national and international news. The paper was founded in 1829 as the Onondaga Standard.
Language (s): English
Ad Rate: Full Page Mono 439.06
Ad Rate: Full Page Colour 509.46
Currency: United States Dollars
DAILY NEWSPAPER

The Post-Standard - Arlington Bureau 16041

Editorial: 3900 Fairfax Dr, Arlington, Virginia 22203-1661 **Tel:** 1 571 970-3751
Language (s): English
DAILY NEWSPAPER

The Post-Star 14402

Owner: Lee Enterprises, Inc.
Editorial: 76 Lawrence St, Glens Falls, New York 12801-3741 **Tel:** 1 518 792-3131
Web site: http://www.poststar.com
Freq: Daily; **Circ:** 23525 Not Audited
Editor: Bob Condon
Profile: The Post-Star is a local daily newspaper written for residents of Saratoga County, Washington County and Warren County, NY.
Language (s): English
Ad Rate: Full Page Mono 28.38
Currency: United States Dollars
DAILY NEWSPAPER

Poteau Daily News & Sun 14872

Owner: Horizon Publications
Editorial: 804 N Broadway St, Poteau, Oklahoma 74953-3503 **Tel:** 1 918 647-3188
Email: editor@poteaudailynews.com **Web site:** http://www.poteaudailynews.com
Freq: Fri; **Circ:** 3900 Not Audited
Editor: Kim Ross; **Publisher:** Robert Shearon
Profile: Poteau Daily News & Sun is a local daily newspaper written for the residents of LeFlore County, OK. The newspaper covers news, business, sports, and arts & entertainment.
Language (s): English
Ad Rate: Full Page Mono 7.82
Ad Rate: Full Page Colour 9.57
Currency: United States Dollars
DAILY NEWSPAPER

Poughkeepsie Journal 14423

Owner: Gannett Co., Inc.
Editorial: 85 Civic Center Plz, Poughkeepsie, New York 12601-2498 **Tel:** 1 845 454-2000
Email: newsroom@poughkee.gannett.com **Web site:** http://www.poughkeepsiejournal.com
Freq: Daily; **Circ:** 22191 Not Audited
Profile: Poughkeepsie Journal is a daily newspaper serving the residents of the Poughkeepsie, NY area. Coverage includes local and city news, business, editorials, sports and lifestyle.
Language (s): English
Ad Rate: Full Page Mono 72.80
Ad Rate: Full Page Colour 753.00
Currency: United States Dollars
DAILY NEWSPAPER

Pratt Tribune 14066

Owner: Fortress Investment Group, LLC
Editorial: 320 S Main St, Pratt, Kansas 67124-2706 **Tel:** 1 620 672-5511
Web site: http://www.pratttribune.com
Freq: Mon thru Fri; **Circ:** 2000 Not Audited
Editor: Conrad Easterday; **Publisher:** Keith Lippoldt
Profile: Pratt Tribune is a daily newspaper that is written for residents of Pratt, KS. Articles include news, weather, travel and sports.
Language (s): English
Ad Rate: Full Page Mono 8.95
Ad Rate: Full Page Colour 100.00
Currency: United States Dollars
DAILY NEWSPAPER

Press & Sun-Bulletin 14393

Owner: Gannett Co., Inc.
Editorial: 33 Lewis Rd, Binghamton, New York 13905-1040 **Tel:** 1 607 798-1234
Email: bgm-newsroom@gannett.com **Web site:** http://www.pressconnects.com
Freq: Daily; **Circ:** 29809 Not Audited
Advertising Sales Manager: John Zych
Profile: Press & Sun-Bulletin was created in 1985 by the merger of the Evening Press and the morning Sun-Bulletin. It serves readers in Broome, Tioga, Chenango, Delaware and Otsego counties in New York, and Susquehanna and Bradford counties in Pennsylvania. Coverage includes local and regional news, national news affecting the paper's readers, sports, business, lifestyle and arts & entertainment. The lead time varies depending on the section and type of news involved.
Language (s): English
Ad Rate: Full Page Mono 107.52
Ad Rate: Full Page Colour 321.62
Currency: United States Dollars
DAILY NEWSPAPER

The Press Democrat 15464

Owner: Sonoma Media Investments LLC
Editorial: 427 Mendocino Ave, Santa Rosa, California 95401-6313 **Tel:** 1 707 526-8570
Web site: http://www.pressdemocrat.com
Freq: Daily; **Circ:** 46090 Not Audited
Profile: The Press Democrat is a local, daily newspaper based in Santa Rosa, CA, with additional bureaus in Petaluma and Ukiah, CA. The paper covers local, regional and national news of interest to residents of Northern California. Pitches are preferred via e-mail.
Language (s): English
Ad Rate: Full Page Mono 120.30
Ad Rate: Full Page Colour 132.20
Currency: United States Dollars
DAILY NEWSPAPER

The Press Democrat - Ukiah Bureau 16261

Editorial: 445 N State St, Ukiah, California 95482-4490 **Tel:** 1 707 462-6473
Language (s): English
DAILY NEWSPAPER

Press Journal 13834

Owner: Gannett Co., Inc.
Editorial: 1801 US Highway 1, Vero Beach, Florida 32960-5415 **Tel:** 1 772 562-2315
Email: yesdesk@tcpalm.com **Web site:** http://www.tcpalm.com
Freq: Daily; **Circ:** 29610
Profile: Press Journal in Vero Beach, FL is a daily newspaper published for residents of Indian River County, FL and surrounding communities. The newspaper covers local news, sports, events, business and lifestyle.
Language (s): English
Ad Rate: Full Page Mono 60.14
Ad Rate: Full Page Colour 662.00
Currency: United States Dollars
DAILY NEWSPAPER

The Press of Atlantic City 15407

Owner: BH Media
Editorial: 11 Devins Ln, Pleasantville, New Jersey 08232-4107 **Tel:** 1 609 272-7000
Email: newstips@pressofac.com **Web site:** http://www.pressofatlanticcity.com
Freq: Daily; **Circ:** 68542 Not Audited
Publisher: Mark Blum
Profile: The Press of Atlantic City is a daily newspaper distributed in Atlantic City, NJ and the surrounding counties. The newspaper covers local government, education, business and community news, as well as entertainment, sports and lifestyle. Business coverage focuses heavily on the area's legal gambling industry. The newspaper's staff covers local and state news only; national news is taken almost exclusively from wire services.
Language (s): English
Ad Rate: Full Page Mono 81.00
Ad Rate: Full Page Colour 265.51
Currency: United States Dollars
DAILY NEWSPAPER

The Press of Atlantic City - Cape May Court House Bureau 15808

Editorial: 1 S Main St, Cape May Court House, New Jersey 08210-2249 **Tel:** 1 609 463-6710
Bureau Chief: W.F. Keough
Language (s): English
DAILY NEWSPAPER

The Press of Atlantic City - Vineland Bureau 15811

Editorial: 22 W Landis Ave Ste F, Vineland, New Jersey 08360-8134 **Tel:** 1 856 794-5110
Email: wkeough@pressofac.com
Cape May/Vineland Bureau Chief: W.F. Keough
Profile: All mail should be sent to the main office.
Language (s): English
DAILY NEWSPAPER

Press-Enterprise 14566

Owner: Press-Enterprise, Inc.
Editorial: 3185 Lackawanna Ave, Bloomsburg, Pennsylvania 17815 **Tel:** 1 570 784-2121
Email: news@pressenterprise.net **Web site:** http://www.pressenterpriseonline.com
Freq: Daily; **Circ:** 21260 Not Audited
Editor: James Sachetti; **Advertising Sales Manager:** Sandra Sterner
Profile: Press-Enterprise is a daily newspaper serving Bloomsburg, PA and the surrounding communities. The newspaper provides residents with the latest information on news, weather and sports.
Language (s): English
Ad Rate: Full Page Mono 24.92
Ad Rate: Full Page Colour 34.12
Currency: United States Dollars
DAILY NEWSPAPER

The Press-Enterprise 15351

Owner: Southern California News Group/Digital First Media
Editorial: 1825 Chicago Ave Ste 100, Riverside, California 92507-2373 **Tel:** 1 951 684-1200
Email: news@pe.com **Web site:** http://www.pe.com
Freq: Daily; **Circ:** 108808 Not Audited
Profile: The Press-Enterprise, established in 1878, is a general interest newspaper serving the Riverside and San Bernardino counties in Southern California. This paper is a part of the Southern California News Group, a subsidiary of Digital First Media.
Language (s): English
Ad Rate: Full Page Mono 199.00
Ad Rate: Full Page Colour 216.46
Currency: United States Dollars
DAILY NEWSPAPER

Press-Republican 14422

Owner: Community Newspaper Holdings, Inc.
Editorial: 170 Margaret St, Plattsburgh, New York 12901-1899 **Tel:** 1 518 561-2300
Email: news@pressrepublican.com **Web site:** http://www.pressrepublican.com
Freq: Daily; **Circ:** 14804 Not Audited
Editor: Lois Clermont; **News Editor:** Suzanne Moore
Profile: Press-Republican's editorial mission is to be the leading print and online news source. The publication is written for Clinton, Franklin and Essex counties of Northeastern New York.
Language (s): English
Ad Rate: Full Page Mono 30.76
Ad Rate: Full Page Colour 38.56
Currency: United States Dollars
DAILY NEWSPAPER

Princeton Daily Clarion 14012

Owner: Brehm Communications, Inc.
Editorial: 100 N Gibson St, Princeton, Indiana 47670-1855 **Tel:** 1 812 385-2525
Email: news@pdclarion.com **Web site:** http://www.pdclarion.com
Freq: Daily; **Circ:** 6800 Not Audited
Editor: Andrea Howe
Profile: Princeton Daily Clarion is published daily for the residents of Gibson County, IN and surrounding areas. The newspaper covers local and state news, business, sports, lifestyles and entertainment.
Language (s): English
Ad Rate: Full Page Mono 14.35
Ad Rate: Full Page Colour 160.00
Currency: United States Dollars
DAILY NEWSPAPER

The Progress 14571

Owner: Progressive Publishing Co.
Editorial: 206 E Locust St, 2NDFL Fl, Clearfield, Pennsylvania 16830 **Tel:** 1 814 765-5581
Email: news@theprogressnews.com **Web site:** http://www.theprogressnews.com
Freq: Daily; **Circ:** 11680 Not Audited
Advertising Sales Manager: Jeannine Barger; **Editor:** Jill Golden; **Publisher:** Margaret Krebs
Profile: The Progress is written for the residents of Clearfield, PA and the surrounding area. It covers local news and community events. Deadlines are at 7am ET the day before publication date.
Language (s): English
Ad Rate: Full Page Mono 18.73
Ad Rate: Full Page Colour 22.21
Currency: United States Dollars
DAILY NEWSPAPER

The Progress-Index 14762

Owner: Scranton Times
Editorial: 15 Franklin St, Petersburg, Virginia 23803-4503 **Tel:** 1 804 732-3456
Email: newsroom@progress-index.com **Web site:** http://www.progress-index.com
Freq: Daily; **Circ:** 9150 Not Audited
Publisher: Cindy Morgan
Profile: The Progress-Index's editorial mission is to provide local news to the residents of Petersburg, VA and surrounding towns. The newspaper covers various local news and events, lifestyle, business, and other topics of general interest.
Language (s): English
Ad Rate: Full Page Mono 24.75
Ad Rate: Full Page Colour 380.00
Currency: United States Dollars
DAILY NEWSPAPER

The Providence Journal 15382

Owner: GateHouse Media Inc.
Editorial: 75 Fountain St, Providence, Rhode Island 02902-0050 **Tel:** 1 401 277-7000
Email: newstips@providencejournal.com **Web site:** http://www.providencejournal.com
Freq: Daily; **Circ:** 90342
Publisher: Janet Hasson
Profile: The Providence Journal is a general interest broadsheet newspaper written for the general public in the Providence, RI area. It is America's oldest major daily newspaper of general circulation in continuous publication. Its mission is "to publish an independent and profitable newspaper of unquestioned integrity devoted to the dissemination of local, state, national, and international news of interest and importance, and to do so in a manner noted for its excellence on a national scale while ever maintaining an outspoken voice for the welfare of Rhode Islanders."
Language (s): English
Ad Rate: Full Page Mono 300.30
Ad Rate: Full Page Colour 323.05
Currency: United States Dollars
DAILY NEWSPAPER

Public Opinion 14570

Owner: Gannett Co., Inc.
Editorial: 77 N 3rd St, Chambersburg, Pennsylvania 17201-1812 **Tel:** 1 717 264-6161
Email: newsdesk@publicopinionnews.com **Web site:** http://www.publicopiniononline.com
Freq: Daily; **Circ:** 16271 Not Audited
Editor: Becky Bennett; **Publisher:** Sara Glines
Profile: Public Opinion is published daily for the residents of Chambersburg, PA and surrounding areas. The newspaper covers local news, sports, entertainment and business news.
Language (s): English
Ad Rate: Full Page Mono 38.00
Ad Rate: Full Page Colour 47.50
Currency: United States Dollars
DAILY NEWSPAPER

The Pueblo Chieftain 15393

Owner: Star Journal Publishing Corporation
Editorial: 825 W 6th St, Pueblo, Colorado 81003-2313 **Tel:** 1 719 544-3520
Email: city@chieftain.com **Web site:** http://www.chieftain.com
Freq: Mon thru Fri; **Circ:** 36223
Publisher & Editor: Robert Rawlings; **News Editor:** Mike Spence
Profile: The Pueblo Chieftain is published daily for residents of Pueblo, CO and surrounding communities. The newspaper covers local news, weather, sports, and community events. Feature articles cover business developments, politics, education, arts & entertainment and lifestyle. Please use the main e-mail address for all press materials.
Language (s): English
Ad Rate: Full Page Mono 71.50
Ad Rate: Full Page Colour 216.82
Currency: United States Dollars
DAILY NEWSPAPER

Punxsutawney Spirit 14610

Owner: Horizon Publications
Editorial: 510 Pine St, Punxsutawney, Pennsylvania 15767-1404 **Tel:** 1 814 938-8740
Email: editor@punxsutawneyspirit.com **Web site:** http://www.punxsutawneyspirit.com
Freq: Mon thru Fri; **Circ:** 5105 Not Audited
Profile: Punxsutawney Spirit is a local daily newspaper written for residents in Punxsutawney, PA and provides local news and information.
Language (s): English
Ad Rate: Full Page Mono 12.00
Ad Rate: Full Page Colour 150.00
Currency: United States Dollars
DAILY NEWSPAPER

Quad-City Times 13875

Owner: Lee Enterprises, Inc.
Editorial: 500 E 3rd St, Davenport, Iowa 52801-1708 **Tel:** 1 563 383-2200
Email: newsroom@qctimes.com **Web site:** http://www.qctimes.com
Freq: Daily; **Circ:** 40247 Not Audited
Profile: Quad-City Times is a daily newspaper serving the residents of Davenport, IA and surrounding communities. Local and national news,

sports, entertainment and lifestyle information are included.
Language (s): English
Ad Rate: Full Page Mono 79.59
Ad Rate: Full Page Colour 275.88
Currency: United States Dollars
DAILY NEWSPAPER

Quad-City Times - Des Moines Bureau 86309
Editorial: 319 E. 5th St., Des Moines, Iowa 50309
Tel: 1 515 422-9061
Bureau Chief: Erin Murphy
Language (s): English
DAILY NEWSPAPER

Quincy Herald-Whig 13956
Owner: Quincy Newspapers, Inc.
Editorial: 130 S 5th St, Quincy, Illinois 62301-3916
Tel: 1 217 223-5100
Email: news@whig.com **Web site:** http://www.whig.com
Freq: Daily; **Circ:** 16278 Not Audited
Advertising Sales Manager: Tom Kelling
Profile: Quincy Herald-Whig is published daily for the residents of Quincy, IL and surrounding areas. The newspaper covers local news, sports, community events, health and lifestyles.
Language (s): English
Ad Rate: Full Page Mono 30.46
Ad Rate: Full Page Colour 107.68
Currency: United States Dollars
DAILY NEWSPAPER

Rafu Shimpo 80006
Editorial: 701 E 3rd St Ste 130, Los Angeles, California 90013-1789 **Tel:** 1 213 629-2231
Email: info@rafu.com **Web site:** http://www.rafu.com
Freq: Daily; **Circ:** 21000 Not Audited
Publisher: Michael Komai
Profile: Rafu Shimpo is a daily newspaper published for the Japanese American community in Los Angeles. The editorial content covers general interest articles, including local news, sports, personalities and events.
Language (s): English
Ad Rate: Full Page Mono 9.06
Currency: United States Dollars
DAILY NEWSPAPER

Rapid City Journal 14656
Owner: Lee Enterprises, Inc.
Editorial: 507 Main St, Rapid City, South Dakota 57701-2733 **Tel:** 1 605 394-8300
Email: news@rapidcityjournal.com **Web site:** http://www.rapidcityjournal.com
Freq: Daily; **Circ:** 23202 Not Audited
Publisher: Shannon Brinker
Profile: Rapid City Journal is published daily for residents of Rapid City, SD and surrounding areas. The publication is a general interest newspaper, covering local news, weather, sports, business, education, arts and entertainment, and other information of interest to the local community. Deadlines are daily at 9am MT. Emails sent to the main email address should not include attachments. Alternate email: rcy.news@lee.net.
Language (s): English
Ad Rate: Full Page Mono 87.20
Ad Rate: Full Page Colour 625.00
Currency: United States Dollars
DAILY NEWSPAPER

Ravalli Republic 14281
Owner: Lee Enterprises, Inc.
Editorial: 232 W Main St, Hamilton, Montana 59840-2552 **Tel:** 1 406 363-3300
Email: editor@ravallirepublic.com **Web site:** http://ravallirepublic.com
Freq: Daily; **Circ:** 6345 Not Audited
Profile: The Ravalli Republic is a daily newspaper serving the residents of Hamilton, MT. Articles are about local news, weather, sports and events. Deadlines are 24 hours prior to issue date.
Language (s): English
Ad Rate: Full Page Mono 13.78
Ad Rate: Full Page Colour 200.00
Currency: United States Dollars
DAILY NEWSPAPER

Rawlins Daily Times 14851
Owner: Rawlins Newspapers Inc.
Editorial: 522 W Buffalo St, Rawlins, Wyoming 82301-5623 **Tel:** 1 307 324-3411
Email: ekirk@rawlinstimes.com **Web site:** http://www.rawlinstimes.com
Freq: Fri; **Circ:** 3600 Not Audited
Publisher: Holly Dabb
Profile: Rawlins Daily Times covers local news, sports and community events for residents of Rawlins and Carbon County, WY. It has been serving south central Wyoming since 1889.
Language (s): English
Ad Rate: Full Page Mono 8.67
Ad Rate: Full Page Colour 154.35
Currency: United States Dollars
DAILY NEWSPAPER

The Reading Chronicle 761888
Owner: Woburn Daily Times, Inc.
Editorial: 531 Main St, Reading, Massachusetts 01867-3134 **Tel:** 1 781 944-2200
Email: reading@dailytimesinc.com **Web site:** http://homenewshere.com
Freq: Daily
Editor: Paul Feely; **Publisher:** Peter Haggerty
Profile: The Reading Chronicle covers community news for the residents of Reading, MA and Wakefield, MA. Coverage includes local news, editorials, lifestyles, sports, state and national news.
DAILY NEWSPAPER

Reading Eagle 14953
Owner: Reading Eagle Company
Editorial: 345 Penn St, Reading, Pennsylvania 19601-4029 **Tel:** 1 610 371-5000
Email: news@readingeagle.com **Web site:** http://www.readingeagle.com
Freq: Daily; **Circ:** 41217 Not Audited
Editor: Harry Deitz; **Publisher:** William Flippin; **News Editor:** Ron Southwick
Profile: Reading Eagle is written for residents of the Reading and Berks County, PA. It covers local, regional, state, national and international news, as well as sports, business, entertainment and special news features.
Language (s): English
Ad Rate: Full Page Mono 27.39
Ad Rate: Full Page Colour 75.29
Currency: United States Dollars
DAILY NEWSPAPER

The Record 14428
Owner: Digital First Media
Editorial: 501 Broadway, Troy, New York 12180-3324 **Tel:** 1 518 270-1200
Email: newsroom@troyrecord.com **Web site:** http://www.troyrecord.com
Freq: Daily; **Circ:** 8406 Not Audited
Publisher: Robert O'Leary; **News Editor:** Paul Tackett
Profile: The Record is a local daily newspaper for residents of Troy, NY and the surrounding area. It provides coverage of local news, sports, schools and community information, arts & entertainment, business and travel.
Language (s): English
Ad Rate: Full Page Mono 37.74
Ad Rate: Full Page Colour 320.00
Currency: United States Dollars
DAILY NEWSPAPER

The Record 15443
Owner: GateHouse Media Inc.
Editorial: 530 E Market St, Stockton, California 95202-3009 **Tel:** 1 209 943-6397
Email: newsroom@recordnet.com **Web site:** http://www.recordnet.com
Freq: Daily; **Circ:** 27266 Not Audited
Publisher: Roger Coover
Profile: The Record serves the Stockton, CA metro area. The publication offers local, state, national and world news as well as sports, business, entertainment and classifieds. It was established in 1896.
Language (s): English
Ad Rate: Full Page Mono 108.33
Ad Rate: Full Page Colour 328.83
Currency: United States Dollars
DAILY NEWSPAPER

The Record - San Andreas Bureau 16140
Editorial: San Andreas, California **Tel:** 1 209 607-1361
Language (s): English
DAILY NEWSPAPER

The Record & Herald News 609978
Owner: Gannett Co., Inc./North Jersey Media Group
Editorial: 1 Garret Mountain Plz, Woodland Park, New Jersey 07424-3320 **Tel:** 1 973 569-7000
Email: newsroom@northjersey.com **Web site:** http://www.northjersey.com
Freq: Daily; **Circ:** 150876
State House Bureau Chief: John McAlpin; **News Editor:** Scott Muller
Profile: The Record & Herald News are two daily newspapers, available only in a combined edition, and are not available separately.
Language (s): English
Ad Rate: Full Page Mono 287.24
Ad Rate: Full Page Colour 275.80
Currency: United States Dollars
DAILY NEWSPAPER

Record Searchlight 13746
Owner: Gannett Co., Inc.
Editorial: 1101 Twin View Blvd, Redding, California 96003-1531 **Tel:** 1 530 243-2424
Email: rrsedit@redding.com **Web site:** http://www.redding.com
Freq: Daily; **Circ:** 18250 Not Audited
Editor: Damon Arthur; **Editor:** Silas Lyons; **Publisher:** Steve Smith
Profile: Record Searchlight is written for residents of Redding, CA and surrounding areas. It offers a balance of news emphasizing local issues and pays attention to public spending, growth, development, government and literacy. In addition to helping victims of earthquakes and firestorms, it sponsors events and activities in the community. The outlet offers RSS (Really Simple Syndication).
Language (s): English
Ad Rate: Full Page Mono 53.50
Ad Rate: Full Page Colour 495.00
Currency: United States Dollars
DAILY NEWSPAPER

Record-Courier 14485
Owner: GateHouse Media Inc.
Editorial: 1050 W Main St, Kent, Ohio 44240-2006 **Tel:** 1 330 541-9400
Email: editor@recordpub.com **Web site:** http://www.recordpub.com
Freq: Daily; **Circ:** 17406 Not Audited
Editor: Roger DiPaolo; **News Editor:** Chad Murphy
Profile: Record-Courier provides news and information to the Canton County and Portage County, OH area. Deadlines are 8pm ET the day before the issue date.
Language (s): English
Ad Rate: Full Page Mono 18.12
Ad Rate: Full Page Colour 27.62
Currency: United States Dollars
DAILY NEWSPAPER

The Recorder 14122
Owner: Newspapers of New England
Editorial: 14 Hope St, Greenfield, Massachusetts 01301-3308 **Tel:** 1 413 772-0261
Email: news@recorder.com **Web site:** http://www.recorder.com
Freq: Daily; **Circ:** 11995 Not Audited
Profile: The Recorder is a daily newspaper published primarily for the residents of Greenfield, MA, as well as some parts of Franklin County, MA. Coverage includes local news, community events, arts & entertainment and sports. Deadlines are daily at 9pm ET.
Language (s): English
Ad Rate: Full Page Mono 15.98
Ad Rate: Full Page Colour 280.00
Currency: United States Dollars
DAILY NEWSPAPER

The Recorder 14390
Owner: William J. Kline & Sons, Inc.
Editorial: 1 Venner Rd, Amsterdam, New York 12010
Tel: 1 518 843-1100
Email: news@recordernews.com **Web site:** http://www.recordernews.com
Freq: Daily; **Circ:** 8116 Not Audited
Publisher: Kevin McClary
Profile: The Recorder provides national and local news for residents of Montgomery and Fulton counties, NY. It covers national and local news, sports, community happenings, opinions and arts.
Language (s): English
Ad Rate: Full Page Mono 14.95
Ad Rate: Full Page Colour 250.00
Currency: United States Dollars
DAILY NEWSPAPER

Record-Herald 14500
Owner: AIM Media Midwest
Editorial: 320 Washington Sq, Washington Court House, Ohio 43160-1751 **Tel:** 1 740 335-3611
Email: info@recordherald.com **Web site:** http://www.recordherald.com
Freq: Fri; **Circ:** 5533 Not Audited
Profile: Record-Herald is daily newspaper published for residents of Fayette County, OH and surrounding areas. The publication is a general interest newspaper, covering local news, weather, sports, business, education, arts & entertainment and other information of interest to the local community. It also publishes the South Central Ohio Shoppers Guide on Sundays.
Language (s): English
Ad Rate: Full Page Mono 12.25
Ad Rate: Full Page Colour 90.00
Currency: United States Dollars
DAILY NEWSPAPER

Record-Journal 13801
Owner: Record-Journal Publishing Company
Editorial: 11 Crown St, Meriden, Connecticut 06450-5713 **Tel:** 1 203 235-1661
Email: newsroom@record-journal.com **Web site:** http://www.myrecordjournal.com
Freq: Daily; **Circ:** 19541 Not Audited
Editor: Michael Misarski; **Publisher:** Eliot White
Profile: Record-Journal is a weekly newspaper serving the residents of Meriden and Wallingford, CT. The publication covers news, local events and sports.
Language (s): English
Ad Rate: Full Page Mono 50.50
Ad Rate: Full Page Colour 220.00
Currency: United States Dollars
DAILY NEWSPAPER

Redlands Daily Facts 13747
Owner: Southern California News Group/Digital First Media
Editorial: 700 Brookside Ave, Redlands, California 92373-5102 **Tel:** 1 909 793-3221
Email: editor@inlandnewspapers.com **Web site:** http://www.redlandsdailyfacts.com
Freq: Mon thru Fri; **Circ:** 6553
Profile: Redlands Daily Facts is a local daily newspaper written for residents of Redlands, CA and surrounding areas. This paper is a part of the Southern California News Group, a subsidiary of Digital First Media. The publication is a general interest newspaper that covers local news, weather, sports, education, business, arts and entertainment, and other information of interest to the local community.
Language (s): English
Ad Rate: Full Page Mono 15.00
Ad Rate: Full Page Colour 24.08
Currency: United States Dollars
DAILY NEWSPAPER

The Register Citizen 13808
Owner: Journal Register Company
Editorial: 190 Water St, Torrington, Connecticut 06790-5325 **Tel:** 1 860 489-3121
Email: editor@registercitizen.com **Web site:** http://www.registercitizen.com
Freq: Daily; **Circ:** 5211 Not Audited
Editor: John Berry
Profile: The Register Citizen is a daily newspaper that provides readers with local, regional and national news coverage. The newspaper focuses on local community news. Daily features include sports, business, entertainment, lifestyle and classifieds.
Language (s): English
Ad Rate: Full Page Mono 19.35
Currency: United States Dollars
DAILY NEWSPAPER

Register Star 14406
Owner: Johnson Newspaper Corp.
Editorial: 1 Hudson City Ctr Ste 202, Hudson, New York 12534-2355 **Tel:** 1 518 828-1616
Email: editorial@registerstar.com **Web site:** http://www.registerstar.com
Freq: Fri; **Circ:** 3381 Not Audited
Profile: Register Star is a local daily newspaper intended to serve the needs of the general public in Hudson, NY and the surrounding counties.
Language (s): English
Ad Rate: Full Page Mono 14.51
Ad Rate: Full Page Colour 300.00
Currency: United States Dollars
DAILY NEWSPAPER

The Register-Guard 15411
Owner: Guard Publishing Company
Editorial: 3500 Chad Dr, Eugene, Oregon 97408-7426 **Tel:** 1 541 485-1234
Email: rgnews@registerguard.com **Web site:** http://www.registerguard.com
Freq: Daily; **Circ:** 44697 Not Audited
News Editor: Chris Frisella; **Advertising Sales Manager:** Deborah Ramirez
Profile: The Register-Guard is published daily for residents of Eugene, OR and surrounding communities. It covers local news, weather, sports and community events. Feature articles cover business, lifestyle, arts & entertainment, education and other topics of interest to area residents.
Language (s): English
Ad Rate: Full Page Mono 39.40
Ad Rate: Full Page Colour 45.47
Currency: United States Dollars
DAILY NEWSPAPER

The Register-Guard - Salem Bureau 16191
Editorial: State Capitol Press Room, Salem, Oregon 97301-0001 **Tel:** 1 503 363-3451
Language (s): English
DAILY NEWSPAPER

The Register-Herald 14828
Owner: Community Newspaper Holdings, Inc.
Editorial: 801 N Kanawha St, Beckley, West Virginia 25801 **Tel:** 1 304 255-4400
Email: rhnews@register-herald.com **Web site:** http://www.register-herald.com
Freq: Daily; **Circ:** 18366 Not Audited
Editor: Mary Stillwell
Profile: The Register-Herald is for the residents of Southern West Virginia. It covers national news, local news, sports, events and politics.
Language (s): English
Ad Rate: Full Page Mono 39.68
Currency: United States Dollars
DAILY NEWSPAPER

The Register-Mail 13933
Owner: GateHouse Media Inc.
Editorial: 140 S Prairie St, Galesburg, Illinois 61401-4605 **Tel:** 1 309 343-7181
Email: news@register-mail.com **Web site:** http://www.galesburg.com
Freq: Daily; **Circ:** 9785
Editor: Tom Martin
Profile: The Register-Mail is a daily newspaper published for the residents of Galesburg, IL and surrounding areas.
Language (s): English
Ad Rate: Full Page Mono 20.59
Ad Rate: Full Page Colour 230.00
Currency: United States Dollars
DAILY NEWSPAPER

The Register-News 13949
Owner: Community Newspaper Holdings, Inc.
Editorial: 911 Broadway St, Mount Vernon, Illinois 62864-4008 **Tel:** 1 618 242-0113
Email: your.news@register-news.com **Web site:** http://www.register-news.com
Freq: Daily; **Circ:** 9155 Not Audited
Profile: The Register-News is published daily for the residents of Mount Vernon, IL abd surrounding areas. The newspaper covers local news, sports, business and entertainment.
Language (s): English
Ad Rate: Full Page Mono 13.86
Ad Rate: Full Page Colour 46.79
Currency: United States Dollars
DAILY NEWSPAPER

Reidsville Review & Eden News 597604
Owner: BH Media Group
Editorial: 1921 Vance St, Reidsville, North Carolina 27320-3254
Email: news@reidsvillereview.com **Web site:** http://www.newsadvance.com/rockingham_now
Freq: Daily; **Circ:** 6477
Publisher: Steve Kaylor
Language (s): English
DAILY NEWSPAPER

Reno Gazette-Journal 15404
Owner: Gannett Co. Inc.
Editorial: 955 Kuenzli St, Reno, Nevada 89502-1160 **Tel:** 1 775 788-6200
Email: news@rgj.com **Web site:** http://www.rgj.com
Freq: Daily; **Circ:** 37704 Not Audited
Publisher: John Maher
Profile: Reno Gazette-Journal is a local, daily newspaper providing Reno, NV residents with local and world-wide news coverage. The paper includes local and national news, sports, technology, business, outdoors and special reports.
Language (s): English
Ad Rate: Full Page Mono 271.34
Ad Rate: Full Page Colour 400.74
Currency: United States Dollars
DAILY NEWSPAPER

Rensselaer Republican 14013
Owner: Community Media Group
Editorial: 117 N Van Rensselaer St, Rensselaer, Indiana 47978-2651 **Tel:** 1 219 866-5111
Web site: http://www.newsbug.info/rensselaer_republican/
Freq: Daily; **Circ:** 2088 Not Audited
Editor & Publisher: Robert Blankenship
Profile: Rensselaer Republican is published daily for the residents of Rennsselaer, IN and surrounding areas. The newspaper covers local news, business, sports, lifestyles and entertainment.
Language (s): English
Ad Rate: Full Page Mono 13.00
Ad Rate: Full Page Colour 250.00
Currency: United States Dollars
DAILY NEWSPAPER

The Reporter 13776
Owner: MediaNews Group
Editorial: 916 Cotting Ln, Vacaville, California 95688-9338 **Tel:** 1 707 448-6401
Email: newsroom@thereporter.com **Web site:** http://www.thereporter.com
Freq: Daily; **Circ:** 17248 Not Audited
Publisher: Jim Gleim
Profile: The Reporter is a daily newspaper written for the residents of Northern Solano County, CA. The newspaper covers local news and events, public safety, education, county government, business in the area and courts.
Language (s): English
Ad Rate: Full Page Mono 35.85
Ad Rate: Full Page Colour 896.00
Currency: United States Dollars
DAILY NEWSPAPER

The Reporter 14592
Owner: Digital First Media
Editorial: 307 Derstine Ave, Lansdale, Pennsylvania 19446-3532 **Tel:** 1 215 855-8440
Email: citydesk@thereporteronline.com **Web site:** http://www.thereporteronline.com
Freq: Daily; **Circ:** 8480 Not Audited
Publisher: Edward Condra
Profile: The Reporter is a daily newspaper written for the residents of Lansdale, PA. It covers various local news for the Lansdale, PA region, including sports, arts and entertainment, business and lifestyle topics.
Language (s): English
Ad Rate: Full Page Mono 27.00
Ad Rate: Full Page Colour 620.00
Currency: United States Dollars
DAILY NEWSPAPER

The Reporter 14803
Owner: Gannett Co., Inc.
Editorial: N6637 Rolling Meadows Dr, Fond du Lac, Wisconsin 54937-9471 **Tel:** 1 920 922-4600
Email: news@fdlreporter.com **Web site:** http://www.fdlreporter.com
Freq: Mon thru Fri; **Circ:** 8639 Not Audited
Profile: The Reporter is a local, daily newspaper published by Gannett Newspapers for the residents of Fond Du Lac, WI and the surrounding area. It includes local, regional and national news.
Language (s): English
Ad Rate: Full Page Mono 51.40
Ad Rate: Full Page Colour 158.77
Currency: United States Dollars
DAILY NEWSPAPER

The Reporter-Times 14002
Owner: Schurz Communications Inc.
Editorial: 60 S Jefferson St, Martinsville, Indiana 46151-1968 **Tel:** 1 765 342-3311
Web site: http://www.reporter-times.com
Freq: Daily; **Circ:** 4849
Profile: The Reporter-Times is a local daily newspaper written for residents in Morgan County, IN. The publication's editorial mission is to strive for accuracy in local reporting. The publication combines with The Times-Mail and The Herald-Times for the Sunday edition called the Hoosier Times.
Language (s): English
Ad Rate: Full Page Mono 14.31
Ad Rate: Full Page Colour 230.00
Currency: United States Dollars
DAILY NEWSPAPER

The Repository 14922
Owner: GateHouse Media Inc.
Editorial: 500 Market Ave S, Canton, Ohio 44702-2112 **Tel:** 1 330 580-8300
Email: newsroom@cantonrep.com **Web site:** http://www.cantonrep.com
Freq: Daily; **Circ:** 41740
Profile: The Repository is a daily newspaper that supplies news coverage to residents of the Canton, OH area. The editorial content covers local and regional news, business, entertainment, sports and arts.
Language (s): English
Ad Rate: Full Page Mono 70.95
Ad Rate: Full Page Colour 231.64
Currency: United States Dollars
DAILY NEWSPAPER

The Republic 13977
Owner: AIM Media Texas, LLC
Editorial: 333 2nd St, Columbus, Indiana 47201-6709 **Tel:** 1 812 372-7811
Email: editorial@aimmediaindiana.com **Web site:** http://www.therepublic.com
Freq: Daily; **Circ:** 16013 Not Audited
Editor: Tom Jekel; **Publisher:** Chuck Wells
Profile: The Republic is a daily newspaper. The newspaper is written for residents of Brown, Jackson, Bartholomew, Decatur, and Jennings Counties in Indiana. The newspaper covers local news, sports, entertainment and events. The lead time varies.
Language (s): English
Ad Rate: Full Page Mono 27.52
Ad Rate: Full Page Colour 348.00
Currency: United States Dollars
DAILY NEWSPAPER

The Republican 15341
Owner: Newhouse Newspapers
Editorial: 1860 Main St, Springfield, Massachusetts 01103-1000 **Tel:** 1 413 788-1000
Email: news@repub.com **Web site:** http://www.masslive.com
Freq: Daily; **Circ:** 47550 Not Audited
Profile: The Republican was formerly the Springfield Union-News and is published daily for residents of Springfield, MA and surrounding communities in western Massachusetts. It covers local and national news, political news, arts & entertainment and sports.
Language (s): English
Ad Rate: Full Page Mono 92.00
Ad Rate: Full Page Colour 101.83
Currency: United States Dollars
DAILY NEWSPAPER

The Republican - Boston Bureau 69893
Editorial: Press Gallery at The State House, Room 455, Boston, Massachusetts 2133 **Tel:** 1 857 991-6812
Language (s): English
DAILY NEWSPAPER

Republican Herald 14608
Owner: Times-Shamrock Communications
Editorial: 111 Mahantongo St, Pottsville, Pennsylvania 17901-3071 **Tel:** 1 570 622-3456
Email: nuzdesk@republicanherald.com **Web site:** http://www.republicanherald.com
Freq: Daily; **Circ:** 20378 Not Audited
Publisher: Henry Nyce
Profile: Pottsville Republican & Herald is a local newspaper written for residents of Schuylkill County, PA. The newspaper covers local news and events.
Language (s): English
Ad Rate: Full Page Mono 40.00
Ad Rate: Full Page Colour 265.00
Currency: United States Dollars
DAILY NEWSPAPER

Republican-Times 14254
Owner: Rogers Printing Company, Inc. (W.B.)
Editorial: 122 E 8th St, Trenton, Missouri 64683-2183 **Tel:** 1 660 359-2212
Email: rtimes@lyn.net **Web site:** http://www.republican-times.com
Freq: Daily; **Circ:** 3197 Not Audited
Advertising Sales Manager: Angela Dugan; **Publisher:** Wendell Lenhart; **Editor:** Diane Lowrey
Profile: Republican-Times is a weekly community newspaper written for the residents of Trenton, MO. The paper covers local news and events.
Language (s): English
Ad Rate: Full Page Mono 6.30
Ad Rate: Full Page Colour 8.30
Currency: United States Dollars
DAILY NEWSPAPER

The Review 14449
Owner: Ogden Newspapers
Editorial: 210 E 4th St, East Liverpool, Ohio 43920-3144 **Tel:** 1 330 385-4545
Email: newsroom@reviewonline.com **Web site:** http://www.reviewonline.com
Freq: Daily; **Circ:** 5735 Not Audited
Editor: Jim Mackey; **Publisher:** Tammie McIntosh
Profile: The Review is a local daily newspaper serving the residents of the Ohio, West Virginia, and Pennsylvania tri-state area. The newspaper covers local news, sports, entertainment, business, weather, lottery and community events.
Language (s): English
Ad Rate: Full Page Mono 13.55
Ad Rate: Full Page Colour 225.00
Currency: United States Dollars
DAILY NEWSPAPER

Richmond County Daily Journal 14311
Owner: Heartland Publications
Editorial: 105 E Washington St, Rockingham, North Carolina 28379-3639 **Tel:** 1 910 997-3111
Web site: http://www.yourdailyjournal.com
Freq: Fri; **Circ:** 8439 Not Audited
Editor: Corey Friedman
Profile: Richmond County Daily Journal is published 5 days a week for the residents of Rockingham, NC and surrounding areas. The newspaper covers local and state news, business, education, sports and arts & entertainment. It offers a combined Saturday and Sunday edition called the Daily Journal Weekender.
Language (s): English
Ad Rate: Full Page Mono 14.50
Ad Rate: Full Page Colour 295.00
Currency: United States Dollars
DAILY NEWSPAPER

Richmond Register 14089
Owner: Community Newspaper Holdings, Inc.
Editorial: 380 Big Hill Ave, Richmond, Kentucky 40475 **Tel:** 1 859 623-1669
Email: editor@richmondregister.com **Web site:** http://www.richmondregister.com
Freq: Daily; **Circ:** 4060
Profile: The Richmond Register is written for residents of Madison County, KY. The publication delivers local and national news to the area. The Register reports on local events and human interest stories from the surrounding communities. The lead time is three days.
Language (s): English
Ad Rate: Full Page Mono 12.96
Ad Rate: Full Page Colour 255.00
Currency: United States Dollars
DAILY NEWSPAPER

Richmond Times-Dispatch 15347
Owner: BH Media Group
Editorial: 300 E Franklin St, Richmond, Virginia 23219-2214 **Tel:** 1 804 649-6000
Email: news@timesdispatch.com **Web site:** http://www.richmond.com
Freq: Daily; **Circ:** 90946 Not Audited
Editor: Paige Mudd; **Publisher:** Thomas Silvestri
Profile: Richmond Times-Dispatch is a 50+ page, four-color broadsheet newspaper written for the general public in the Richmond, VA area. The Business section is featured daily, covering local and national business stories, daily stock market rates, real estate, chemicals, manufacturing, retail, utilities, finance and healthcare. Articles include features, breaking news, trends, analysis, profiles and investigative stories.
Language (s): English
Ad Rate: Full Page Mono 184.00
Ad Rate: Full Page Colour 671.09
Currency: United States Dollars
DAILY NEWSPAPER

Ridgway Record 14611
Owner: Horizon Publications
Editorial: 325 Main St Ste A, Ridgway, Pennsylvania 15853-8019 **Tel:** 1 814 773-3161
Email: ridgwayrecord@shop-right.com **Web site:** http://www.ridgwayrecord.com
Freq: Mon thru Fri; **Circ:** 3150 Not Audited
Publisher: Darlene Coder
Profile: Ridgway Record is dedicated to providing the most local news possible to residents of Ridgeway, PA. It delivers local news and events weekly to the community.
Language (s): English
Ad Rate: Full Page Mono 8.15
Ad Rate: Full Page Colour 115.00
Currency: United States Dollars
DAILY NEWSPAPER

River Cities Daily Tribune 386856
Owner: Victory Publishing, LTD.
Editorial: 1007 Avenue K, Marble Falls, Texas 78654-5039 **Tel:** 1 830 693-7152
Email: info@thepicayune.com **Web site:** http://www.dailytrib.com
Freq: Fri; **Circ:** 4300 Not Audited
Profile: River Cities Daily Tribune is a local daily newspaper serving residents of Marble Falls, TX. It covers local news, community events, sports and features of interest to local readers. It shares its editorial staff with its sister weekly paper, the Picayune Tribune. Deadlines are at 4:30pm CT.
Language (s): English
Ad Rate: Full Page Mono 6.53
Ad Rate: Full Page Colour 43.29
Currency: United States Dollars
DAILY NEWSPAPER

Riverton Ranger 14852
Editorial: 421 E Main St, Riverton, Wyoming 82501-4438 **Tel:** 1 307 856-2244
Email: ranger@wyoming.com **Web site:** http://www.dailyranger.com
Freq: Fri; **Circ:** 7250
Editor: Wayne Nicholls; **Publisher & Editor:** Steven Peck
Profile: Riverton Ranger is a local daily newspaper for the residents of Freemont County, WY. The publication covers news and events in the local community. Deadlines are at noon, MT one day prior to issue date.
Language (s): English
Ad Rate: Full Page Mono 10.95
Ad Rate: Full Page Colour 150.00
Currency: United States Dollars
DAILY NEWSPAPER

The Roanoke Times 15389
Owner: BH Media Group
Editorial: 201 Campbell Ave SW, Roanoke, Virginia 24011-1105 **Tel:** 1 540 981-3100
Email: news@roanoke.com **Web site:** http://www.roanoke.com
Freq: Daily; **Circ:** 52800 Not Audited
Publisher: Terry Jamerson
Profile: The Roanoke Times is a daily newspaper serving Roanoke and 19 surrounding counties in Southwest Virginia. It provides readers with information on the latest local and national news, sports, weather, arts & entertainment, technology, health, business, automotive, political and other news. The paper also publishes the New River Valley Current, which serves readers in the Christiansburg-Blacksburg, VA area and surrounding New River Valley counties. Local tab publications are inserted into the regular newspaper for zoned news and advertising. The paper also publishes Blue Ridge Business Journal, Blue Ridge Sports Journal and Blue Ridge Employment Weekly.
Language (s): English
Ad Rate: Full Page Mono 52.70
Ad Rate: Full Page Colour 65.88
Currency: United States Dollars
DAILY NEWSPAPER

The Roanoke Times - Christiansburg Bureau 73879
Editorial: 1580 N Franklin St Ste 1, Christiansburg, Virginia 24073-1476 **Tel:** 1 540 381-1678
Email: newriver@roanoke.com
Bureau Chief: Todd Jackson
Language (s): English
DAILY NEWSPAPER

The Robesonian 14305
Owner: Civitas Media
Editorial: 2175 N Roberts Ave, Lumberton, North Carolina 28358-2867 **Tel:** 1 910 739-4322
Web site: http://www.robesonian.com
Freq: Fri; **Circ:** 12562 Not Audited
Editor: Donnie Douglas; **Advertising Sales Manager:** Robin Walker
Profile: The Robesonian is a daily newspaper serving the residents of Robeson County, NC. It covers news and events in the local community.
Language (s): English
Ad Rate: Full Page Mono 19.95
Ad Rate: Full Page Colour 72.06
Currency: United States Dollars
DAILY NEWSPAPER

Robinson Daily News 13957
Owner: Lewis Newspapers
Editorial: 302 S Cross St, Robinson, Illinois 62454-2137 **Tel:** 1 618 544-2101
Email: news@robdailynews.com **Web site:** http://www.robdailynews.com
Freq: Daily; **Circ:** 5262 Not Audited
Editor: Randy Harrison; **Publisher:** Kathleen Lewis; **Advertising Sales Manager:** Winnie Piper
Profile: Robinson Daily News is a local daily newspaper written for Crawford County, IL.
Language (s): English
Ad Rate: Full Page Mono 9.50
Ad Rate: Full Page Colour 195.00
Currency: United States Dollars
DAILY NEWSPAPER

Rochester Sentinel 14015
Owner: Sentinel Corporation (The)
Editorial: 118 E 8th St, Rochester, Indiana 46975-1508 **Tel:** 1 574 223-2111
Email: news@rochsent.com **Web site:** http://www.rochsent.com
Freq: Daily; **Circ:** 3900 Not Audited
Editor: Mike Kenny; **Publisher:** Sarah Overmyer Wilson; **Advertising Sales Manager:** Karen Vojtasek; **Editor:** W.S. Wilson
Profile: Rochester Sentinel is published daily for the residents of Rochester, IN and surrounding areas. The newspaper covers local and state news, business, sports, lifestyles and entertainment.
Language (s): English
Ad Rate: Full Page Mono 7.44
Ad Rate: Full Page Colour 110.00
Currency: United States Dollars
DAILY NEWSPAPER

Rockdale Citizen 13856
Owner: Southern Community Newspapers Inc.
Editorial: 969 S Main St NE, Conyers, Georgia 30012-4501
Email: news@rockdalecitizen.com **Web site:** http://www.rockdalecitizen.com
Freq: Daily; **Circ:** 5973
Editor: Jay Jones; **Publisher:** Alice Queen
Profile: Rockdale Citizen is a daily newspaper for the residents of Conyers, GA. The paper combines with the Newton Citizen on weekends.
Language (s): English
Ad Rate: Full Page Mono 29.62
Ad Rate: Full Page Colour 375.00
Currency: United States Dollars
DAILY NEWSPAPER

Rockford Register Star 15466
Owner: GateHouse Media Inc.
Editorial: 99 E State St, Rockford, Illinois 61104-1009 **Tel:** 1 815 987-1200
Email: local@rrstar.com **Web site:** http://www.rrstar.com
Freq: Daily; **Circ:** 71208 Not Audited
Publisher: Josh Trust
Profile: Rockford Register Star serves the Rockford, IL area by delivering news and local information to the city and surrounding communities. It is distributed to the Rock River Valley in Northwest Illinois. In addition to the city of Rockford, it serves suburban and regional readers in Loves Park, Machesney Park, Roscoe, Rockton and South Beloit, Winnebago County; Belvidere and other towns in Boone County; Byron, Oregon, and other communities in Ogle County, IL. They do not publish an editorial calendar.
Language (s): English
Ad Rate: Full Page Mono 128.03
Ad Rate: Full Page Colour 403.71

Currency: United States Dollars
DAILY NEWSPAPER

Rocky Ford Daily Gazette 13792
Owner: Rocky Ford Publishing Company
Editorial: 912 Elm Ave, Rocky Ford, Colorado 81067-1249 **Tel:** 1 719 254-3351
Email: news@rockyforddailygazette.com
Freq: Daily; **Circ:** 1948 Not Audited
Publisher & Editor: J.R. Thompson; **Advertising Sales Manager:** Laura Thompson
Profile: Rocky Ford Daily Gazette is a local newspaper serving the residents of Crowley and Otero County, CO. The newspaper covers local news, sports and community events.
Language (s): English
Ad Rate: Full Page Mono 6.10
Ad Rate: Full Page Colour 85.00
Currency: United States Dollars
DAILY NEWSPAPER

Rocky Mount Telegram 14312
Owner: Cooke Communications, LLC
Editorial: 1000 Hunter Hill Rd, Rocky Mount, North Carolina 27804-1727 **Tel:** 1 252 446-5161
Web site: http://www.rockymounttelegram.com
Freq: Daily; **Circ:** 14059 Not Audited
Editor: Jeff Herrin; **Publisher:** Mark Wilson
Profile: Rocky Mount Telegram is published daily for the residents of Rocky Mount, NC. It covers news and events in the local community.
Language (s): English
Ad Rate: Full Page Mono 22.36
Ad Rate: Full Page Colour 345.00
Currency: United States Dollars
DAILY NEWSPAPER

Rolla Daily News 14249
Owner: GateHouse Media Inc.
Editorial: 101 W 7Th St, Rolla, Missouri 65401-3243 **Tel:** 1 573 364-2468
Email: news@therolladailynews.com **Web site:** http://www.therolladailynews.com
Freq: Daily; **Circ:** 5021 Not Audited
Publisher: Tom Bookstaver; **Advertising Sales Manager:** Alissa Martin
Profile: Rolla Daily New is a daily newspaper for the residents of Rolla, MO. It covers news and events in the local community. Deadlines are the same day as the issue date.
Language (s): English
Ad Rate: Full Page Mono 12.05
Ad Rate: Full Page Colour 150.00
Currency: United States Dollars
DAILY NEWSPAPER

Rome News-Tribune 13849
Owner: News Publishing Company
Editorial: 305 E 6th Ave, Rome, Georgia 30161-6007 **Tel:** 1 706 298-5252
Email: romenewstribune@rn-t.com **Web site:** http://www.northwestgeorgianews.com/rome/
Freq: Daily; **Circ:** 14466 Not Audited
Editor: Michael Colombo; **Publisher:** Otis Raybon
Profile: Rome News-Tribune is a local daily newspaper serving the Rome, GA area. It's mission is to provide vital information to the communities it serves through growth, leadership and innovation.
Language (s): English
Ad Rate: Full Page Mono 23.86
Ad Rate: Full Page Colour 275.00
Currency: United States Dollars
DAILY NEWSPAPER

Rome Sentinel 14424
Owner: Rome Sentinel Company
Editorial: 333 W Dominick St, Rome, New York 13440-5701 **Tel:** 1 315 337-4000
Email: release@rny.com **Web site:** http://www.romesentinel.com
Freq: Daily; **Circ:** 9203 Not Audited
Publisher: Stephen Waters
Profile: Daily Sentinel is published for the residents of Rome, NY. It covers local news, community events, sports and arts & entertainment. Deadlines are daily at 11am ET.
Language (s): English
Ad Rate: Full Page Mono 15.19
Ad Rate: Full Page Colour 265.00
Currency: United States Dollars
DAILY NEWSPAPER

Roswell Daily Record 14381
Editorial: 2301 N Main St, Roswell, New Mexico 88201-6452 **Tel:** 1 575 622-7710
Email: news@rdrnews.com **Web site:** http://www.rdrnews.com
Freq: Daily; **Circ:** 11600 Not Audited
Publisher: Charles Fischer
Profile: Roswell Daily Record is a daily newspaper for the residents of Roswell, NM. It covers news and events in the local community.
Language (s): English
Ad Rate: Full Page Mono 15.20
Ad Rate: Full Page Colour 50.25
Currency: United States Dollars
DAILY NEWSPAPER

Ruston Daily Leader 14107
Owner: Fackelman Newspapers
Editorial: 212 W Park Ave, Ruston, Louisiana 71270-4314 **Tel:** 1 318 255-4353
Email: newsroom@rustonleader.com **Web site:** http://www.rustonleader.com
Freq: Daily; **Circ:** 5718 Not Audited
Editor: Buddy Davis; **Publisher:** Rick Hohlt
Profile: Ruston Daily Leader is published daily for the residents of Lincoln Parish, LA. The newspaper covers local news, sports, lifestyles, arts & entertainment and community events.
Language (s): English
Ad Rate: Full Page Mono 10.65
Ad Rate: Full Page Colour 175.00
Currency: United States Dollars
DAILY NEWSPAPER

Rutland Herald 14774
Owner: Maine Today Media Inc.
Editorial: 27 Wales St, Rutland, Vermont 05701-4027 **Tel:** 1 802 747-6121
Email: pressreleases@rutlandherald.com **Web site:** http://www.rutlandherald.com
Freq: Daily; **Circ:** 12569 Not Audited
Editor: Alan Keays; **Publisher:** R. John Mitchell; **Bureau Chief:** Louis Porter
Profile: Rutland Herald is a daily newspaper serving residents of Central and Southern Vermont. News coverage includes community events, breaking news, sports, opinion, home and garden, and business. Contact the newspaper for lead time and deadline information.
Language (s): English
Ad Rate: Full Page Mono 24.30
Ad Rate: Full Page Colour 152.27
Currency: United States Dollars
DAILY NEWSPAPER

The Sacramento Bee 15352
Owner: McClatchy Newspapers
Editorial: 2100 Q St, Sacramento, California 95816-6816 **Tel:** 1 916 321-1000
Email: metro@sacbee.com **Web site:** http://www.sacbee.com
Freq: Daily; **Circ:** 151316
Profile: The Sacramento Bee is a broadsheet newspaper with an emphasis on local coverage. It is written for the residents of the Sacramento, CA area. It covers local news and business, as well as local and regional entertainment, sports, lifestyle, politics, crime, and arts and culture. The paper's mission is to be the region's leading media company, providing a trusted and valued source of news and information to the communities they serve.
Language (s): English
Ad Rate: Full Page Mono 244.00
Ad Rate: Full Page Colour 315.00
Currency: United States Dollars
DAILY NEWSPAPER

The Sacramento Bee - Capitol Bureau 15604
Editorial: 925 L St Ste 600, Sacramento, California 95814-3763 **Tel:** 1 916 321-1199
Bureau Chief: Dan Smith
Language (s): English
DAILY NEWSPAPER

The Saginaw News 14192
Owner: MLive Media Group
Editorial: 100 S Michigan Ave Ste 3, Saginaw, Michigan 48602-2054 **Tel:** 1 989 752-7171
Email: sanews@mlive.com **Web site:** http://www.mlive.com/saginaw/#/0
Freq: Fri; **Circ:** 16602
Profile: The Saginaw News is a newspaper published for the residents of Saginaw County, MI. The publication covers local news, sports, law enforcement, courts, education, politics, government and community events. The Lansing, MI bureau contributes to all eight of the MLive Media Group publications, including: The Ann Arbor News, Bay City Times, Flint Journal, Grand Rapids Press, Jackson Citizen Patriot, Kalamazoo Gazette, Muskegon Chronicle and The Saginaw News. Press releases should be sent by fax and are due at least seven days prior to publication. Deadlines for the publication are not set, but items are generally needed by two days before issue date. Circulation for the Thursday edition is 25,789, for the Friday Edition it is 26,119 and for Sunday it is 37,223.
Language (s): English
Ad Rate: Full Page Mono 43.25
Ad Rate: Full Page Colour 182.00
Currency: United States Dollars
DAILY NEWSPAPER

Salem News 14133
Owner: Community Newspaper Holdings, Inc.
Editorial: 32 Dunham Rd, Beverly, Massachusetts 01915-1844 **Tel:** 1 978 922-1234
Email: sn@ecnnews.com **Web site:** http://www.salemnews.com
Freq: Mon thru Fri; **Circ:** 16855 Not Audited
Advertising Sales Manager: Bob MacDonald; **Editor:** David Olson
Profile: Salem News is written for the residents of Salem, MA. The publication covers local news, sports, police, courts, money, health, home, family and community events.
Language (s): English
Ad Rate: Full Page Mono 40.95
Ad Rate: Full Page Colour 470.00
Currency: United States Dollars
DAILY NEWSPAPER

Salem News 14486
Owner: Ogden Newspapers
Editorial: 161 N Lincoln Ave, Salem, Ohio 44460-2903 **Tel:** 1 330 332-4601
Email: salemnews@salemnews.net **Web site:** http://www.salemnews.net
Freq: Daily; **Circ:** 3998 Not Audited
Editor: John Celidonio; **Publisher:** Beth Volosin
Profile: Salem News delivers community news to the residents of Columbiana County, OH.
Language (s): English
Ad Rate: Full Page Mono 21.80
Currency: United States Dollars
DAILY NEWSPAPER

Salina Journal 14068
Owner: Harris Enterprises
Editorial: 333 S 4th St, Salina, Kansas 67401-3903 **Tel:** 1 785 823-6363
Email: news@salina.com **Web site:** http://www.salina.com
Freq: Daily; **Circ:** 28004 Not Audited
Publisher & Editor: M. Olaf Frandsen
Profile: Salina Journal is published daily for residents of Salina and northwestern Kansas. The newspaper covers local news, weather, sports and community events. Feature articles cover business, education, lifestyle and arts & entertainment.
Language (s): English
Ad Rate: Full Page Mono 21.95
Ad Rate: Full Page Colour 456.00
Currency: United States Dollars
DAILY NEWSPAPER

The Salinas Californian 13748
Owner: Gannett Co., Inc.
Editorial: 123 W Alisal St, Salinas, California 93901-2644 **Tel:** 1 831 424-2221
Email: newsroom@thecalifornian.com **Web site:** http://www.thecalifornian.com
Freq: Mon thru Fri; **Circ:** 7362 Not Audited
Advertising Sales Manager: Craig Hymovitz
Profile: The Salinas Californian is published daily for residents of Salinas Valley, CA. The newspaper covers local news, weather, sports, and community events. Feature articles cover business, education, arts and entertainment, lifestyle, and other information of interest to community residents.
Language (s): English
Ad Rate: Full Page Mono 59.19
Ad Rate: Full Page Colour 690.00
Currency: United States Dollars
DAILY NEWSPAPER

The Saline Courier 13684
Owner: Horizon Publications
Editorial: 321 N Market St, Benton, Arkansas 72015-3734 **Tel:** 1 501 315-8228
Web site: http://www.bentoncourier.com
Freq: Daily; **Circ:** 6563 Not Audited
Publisher: Terri Leifeste
Profile: The Saline Courier is a daily local newspaper serving Saline County, AR. It is published in the evening Monday through Friday and in the morning on Saturday and Sunday.
Language (s): English
Ad Rate: Full Page Mono 14.55
Ad Rate: Full Page Colour 46.90
Currency: United States Dollars
DAILY NEWSPAPER

Salisbury Post 14313
Owner: Evening Post Publishing Co.
Editorial: 131 W Innes St, Salisbury, North Carolina 28144-4338 **Tel:** 1 704 633-8950
Email: news@salisburypost.com **Web site:** http://www.salisburypost.com
Freq: Daily; **Circ:** 16046
Publisher: Greg Anderson; **Editor:** Elizabeth Cook; **News Editor:** Scott Jenkins
Profile: Salisbury Post is published daily for the residents of Rowan County, NC. The newspaper covers local news, sports, education and community events.
Language (s): English
Ad Rate: Full Page Mono 31.80
Ad Rate: Full Page Colour 399.00
Currency: United States Dollars
DAILY NEWSPAPER

The Salt Lake Tribune 14912
Owner: Huntsman (Paul)
Editorial: 90 S 400 W Ste 700, Salt Lake City, Utah 84101-1431 **Tel:** 1 801 257-8742
Email: newsroom@sltrib.com **Web site:** http://www.sltrib.com
Freq: Daily; **Circ:** 81306 Not Audited
Profile: The Salt Lake Tribune is the largest and most widely read daily newspaper in Utah. It was founded in 1872. The Tribune is published for a general consumer audience. Articles include features, breaking news, trends, analyses, profiles, and investigative stories. Topics covered also include entertainment, health, food and drink, sports, and reviews.
Language (s): English
Ad Rate: Full Page Mono 218.00
Ad Rate: Full Page Colour 327.45
Currency: United States Dollars
DAILY NEWSPAPER

The Salt Lake Tribune - Washington Bureau 133001
Editorial: 529 14th St NW Ste 1255, Washington, District Of Columbia 20045-2201 **Tel:** 1 202 662-8925
Language (s): English
DAILY NEWSPAPER

Sampson Independent 14327
Owner: Heartland Publications
Editorial: 303 W Elizabeth St, Clinton, North Carolina 28328-4426 **Tel:** 1 910 592-8137
Web site: http://www.clintonnc.com
Freq: Fri; **Circ:** 7000 Not Audited
Editor: Sherry Matthews
Profile: Sampson Independent is a daily newspaper published for the residents of Warsaw, Faison, Wallace, Sampson, Duplin, Harnett and Cumberland, NC. The newspaper covers local news, sports, business, lifestyles, education, agriculture, religion, arts & entertainment, courts, crime and community events.
Language (s): English
Ad Rate: Full Page Mono 15.10
Ad Rate: Full Page Colour 335.00
Currency: United States Dollars
DAILY NEWSPAPER

San Angelo Standard-Times 14728
Owner: Gannett Co., Inc.
Editorial: 34 W Harris Ave, San Angelo, Texas 76903-5838 **Tel:** 1 325 659-8200
Email: standard@gosanangelo.com **Web site:** http://www.gosanangelo.com
Freq: Daily; **Circ:** 18299 Not Audited
Publisher: Jeff DeLoach
Profile: San Angelo Standard-Times is a daily newspaper published for the residents of San Angelo, TX. The publication covers local news, sports, business, agriculture, city and county government, police, education, health and community events.
Language (s): English
Ad Rate: Full Page Mono 41.41
Ad Rate: Full Page Colour 420.00
Currency: United States Dollars
DAILY NEWSPAPER

San Antonio Express-News 15340
Owner: Hearst Newspapers
Editorial: 301 Avenue E, San Antonio, Texas 78205-2006 **Tel:** 1 210 250-3000
Email: citydesk@express-news.net **Web site:** http://www.mysanantonio.com
Freq: Daily; **Circ:** 98875 Not Audited
Editor: Richard Marini; **Publisher:** John McKeon
Profile: San Antonio Express-News is written for residents in the Southwest. The paper covers local, regional, national and international news, as well as business, technology, books, features, travel, home, garden and sports. It was founded in 1866. The Internet version of the paper is MySA.com.
Language (s): English
Ad Rate: Full Page Mono 364.11
Ad Rate: Full Page Colour 387.27
Currency: United States Dollars
DAILY NEWSPAPER

San Antonio Express-News - Austin Bureau 15944
Editorial: 1005 Congress Ave, Austin, Texas 78701-2463 **Tel:** 1 512 478-3495
Bureau Chief: Peggy Fikac
Profile: The San Antonio Express-News' and the Houston Chronicle's Austin bureaus merged in 2006, and reporters cover news for both papers.
Language (s): English
DAILY NEWSPAPER

The San Diego Union-Tribune 15356
Owner: tronc
Editorial: 600 B St #1201, San Diego, California 92101-4501 **Tel:** 1 619 299-3131
Web site: http://www.sandiegouniontribune.com
Freq: Daily; **Circ:** 180899 Not Audited
Publisher: Douglas Manchester
Profile: The San Diego Union-Tribune (previously U-T San Diego) is published daily for the residents of San Diego County, CA and surrounding areas. The newspaper offers comprehensive news and features of local happenings and the regional business economy. The outlet offers RSS (Really Simple Syndication). When sending mail, please note: 5260 Anna Ave, San Diego, CA 92110 is a corrected address UPS puts on packages. This address is only used for UPS packages, and is not the main or mailing address for the paper. The paper was previously titled The San Diego Union-Tribune.
Language (s): English
Ad Rate: Full Page Mono 583.00
Ad Rate: Full Page Colour 605.64
Currency: United States Dollars
DAILY NEWSPAPER

San Diego Union-Tribune - Sacramento Bureau 15621
Editorial: 925 L St Ste 1190, Sacramento, California 95814-3704 **Tel:** 1 916 445-2934
Language (s): English
DAILY NEWSPAPER

The San Diego Union-Tribune - San Marcos Bureau 16123
Editorial: 1152 Armorlite Dr, San Marcos, California 92069-1441 **Tel:** 1 760 592-4800
Language (s): English
DAILY NEWSPAPER

San Francisco Chronicle 15314
Owner: Hearst Newspapers
Editorial: 901 Mission St, San Francisco, California 94103-2905 **Tel:** 1 415 777-1111
Email: metro@sfchronicle.com **Web site:** http://www.sfchronicle.com
Freq: Daily; **Circ:** 167602 Not Audited
Publisher: Jeffrey Johnson
Profile: San Francisco Chronicle is the largest newspaper in northern California and the second largest in the Western United States. It is a regional, daily newspaper with circulation that stretches from

the Oregon border to Santa Barbara and includes the Silicon Valley.
Language (s): English
Ad Rate: Full Page Mono 280.92
Ad Rate: Full Page Colour 314.29
Currency: United States Dollars
DAILY NEWSPAPER

San Francisco Chronicle - Sacramento Bureau 15625
Editorial: 3 Television Cir, Sacramento, California 95814-0750
Language (s): English
DAILY NEWSPAPER

San Francisco Chronicle - Washington Bureau 15543
Editorial: 1850 K St NW Ste 1000, Washington, District Of Columbia 20006-2223
Bureau Chief: David McCumber
Language (s): English
DAILY NEWSPAPER

San Francisco Examiner 15344
Owner: San Francisco Newspaper Co.
Editorial: 835 Market St Ste 550, San Francisco, California 94103-1906 **Tel:** 1 415 359-2600
Email: newstips@sfexaminer.com **Web site:** http://www.sfexaminer.com
Freq: Mon thru Fri; **Circ:** 254171
Publisher: Glenn Zuehls
Profile: San Francisco Examiner is a free commuter newspaper targeting affluent urban readers in the San Francisco Metro area. With its heavy use of graphics and succinct articles, it delivers coverage of world and local events on the day they happen. The front page unveils breaking news; other sections include the Beyond the Bay, Arts & Culture and Sports. The paper is delivered to homes Thursdays and Sundays but is available by single-copy Monday through Friday and Sundays.
Language (s): English
Ad Rate: Full Page Mono 53.63
Currency: United States Dollars
DAILY NEWSPAPER

San Gabriel Valley Tribune 13765
Owner: Southern California News Group/Digital First Media
Editorial: 605 E Huntington Dr Ste 100, Monrovia, California 91016-6353 **Tel:** 1 626 657-0982
Email: news.tribune@sgvn.com **Web site:** http://www.sgvtribune.com
Freq: Daily; **Circ:** 56513 Not Audited
Profile: San Gabriel Valley Tribune is a daily newspaper serving the communities of West Covina, Monrovia, Temple City, Altadena, Arcadia, El Monte, CA and surrounding cities and towns. This paper is a part of the Southern California News Group, a subsidiary of Digital First Media. The paper's coverage includes news, sports, business, features, and real estate.
Language (s): English
Ad Rate: Full Page Mono 177.00
Ad Rate: Full Page Colour 185.71
Currency: United States Dollars
DAILY NEWSPAPER

San Marcos Daily Record 14729
Owner: Community Newspaper Holdings, Inc.
Editorial: 1910 S Interstate 35, San Marcos, Texas 78666-5901 **Tel:** 1 512 392-2458
Web site: http://www.sanmarcosrecord.com
Freq: Fri; **Circ:** 6464 Not Audited
News Editor: Anita Miller
Profile: San Marcos Daily Record is a daily newspaper published for the residents of San Marcos, TX. The publication covers local news, sports, and community events.
Language (s): English
Ad Rate: Full Page Mono 11.70
Ad Rate: Full Page Colour 350.00
Currency: United States Dollars
DAILY NEWSPAPER

Sandusky Register 14487
Owner: Sandusky Newspapers Inc.
Editorial: 314 W Market St, Sandusky, Ohio 44870-2410 **Tel:** 1 419 625-5500
Email: westerhold@sanduskyregister.com **Web site:** http://www.sanduskyregister.com
Freq: Daily; **Circ:** 18652 Not Audited
Profile: Sandusky Register is a daily newspaper published for the residents of Sandusky, OH. The publication covers local news, sports, and community events. They ONLY accept news items relating to north-central Ohio. They will NOT accept national press releases or product information.
Language (s): English
Ad Rate: Full Page Mono 23.06
Ad Rate: Full Page Colour 317.20
Currency: United States Dollars
DAILY NEWSPAPER

The Sanford Herald 14314
Owner: Paxton Media Group
Editorial: 208 Saint Clair Ct, Sanford, North Carolina 27330-3916 **Tel:** 1 919 708-9000
Email: news@sanfordherald.com **Web site:** http://www.sanfordherald.com
Freq: Daily; **Circ:** 8162 Not Audited
Profile: The Sanford Herald is published daily for the residents of Sanford, NC and surrounding areas. The newspaper provides information about local news, business, sports, lifestyle and entertainment. The paper will publish national news stories only if it has a direct impact on the local area.
Language (s): English
Ad Rate: Full Page Mono 13.65
Currency: United States Dollars
DAILY NEWSPAPER

Santa Barbara News-Press 13751
Owner: Ampersand Publishing Company
Editorial: 715 Anacapa St, Santa Barbara, California 93101 **Tel:** 1 805 564-5200
Web site: http://www.newspress.com
Freq: Daily; **Circ:** 26200 Not Audited
Editor: Scott Steepleton
Profile: Santa Barbara News-Press is a daily newspaper serving the Santa Barbara, CA area. The publication covers local news, business, entertainment, lifestyle and sports.
Language (s): English
Ad Rate: Full Page Mono 63.86
Ad Rate: Full Page Colour 440.00
Currency: United States Dollars
DAILY NEWSPAPER

Santa Cruz Sentinel 13752
Owner: MediaNews Group
Editorial: 1800 Green Hills Rd Ste 210, Scotts Valley, California 95066-4985 **Tel:** 1 831 423-4242
Web site: http://www.santacruzsentinel.com
Freq: Daily; **Circ:** 23465 Not Audited
News Editor: Donald Fukui; **Editor:** Donald Miller
Profile: Santa Cruz Sentinel is a daily newspaper written for the residents of Santa Cruz, CA. The newspaper covers local news, sports, education, arts & entertainment, business and events. It only covers Santa Cruz County in California. Do NOT send pitches without a strong Santa Cruz tie.
Language (s): English
Ad Rate: Full Page Mono 40.56
Ad Rate: Full Page Colour 133.37
Currency: United States Dollars
DAILY NEWSPAPER

The Santa Fe New Mexican 14382
Owner: Robin Martin
Editorial: 202 E Marcy St, Santa Fe, New Mexico 87501-2021 **Tel:** 1 505 983-3303
Email: citydesk@sfnewmexican.com **Web site:** http://www.santafenewmexican.com
Freq: Daily; **Circ:** 19228 Not Audited
Profile: The Santa Fe New Mexican is a daily newspaper published for the residents of Santa Fe, NM. The publication covers local news, sports, business news, travel, health, science, food, the outdoors, arts & entertainment and community events. The outlet offers RSS (Really Simple Syndication).
Language (s): English
Ad Rate: Full Page Mono 29.75
Ad Rate: Full Page Colour 34.75
Currency: United States Dollars
DAILY NEWSPAPER

Santa Maria Times 13753
Owner: Lee Enterprises, Inc.
Editorial: 3200 Skyway Dr, Santa Maria, California 93455-1824 **Tel:** 1 805 925-2691
Web site: http://www.santamariatimes.com
Freq: Daily; **Circ:** 10749 Not Audited
Editor: Marga Cooley; **Publisher:** Cynthia Schur
Profile: Santa Maria Times is published daily for the residents of Santa Maria, CA. The publication covers local news, sports and community events. The newspaper shares a staff with Times-Press-Recorder and Adobe Press.
Language (s): English
Ad Rate: Full Page Mono 25.70
Currency: United States Dollars
DAILY NEWSPAPER

Santa Monica Daily Press 78010
Editorial: 1640 5th St Ste 218, Santa Monica, California 90401-3325 **Tel:** 1 310 458-7737
Web site: http://www.smdp.com
Freq: Daily; **Circ:** 10450 Not Audited
Publisher: Ross Furukawa; **Advertising Sales Manager:** Rob Schwenker
Profile: Santa Monica Daily Press is a local daily tabloid-size newspaper serving Santa Monica, CA and the surrounding area. It provides residents with information on news and events of interest to the community.
Language (s): English
Ad Rate: Full Page Mono 20.00
Ad Rate: Full Page Colour 95.00
Currency: United States Dollars
DAILY NEWSPAPER

Sapulpa Daily Herald 14538
Owner: Sumner Newspapers Inc.
Editorial: 16 S Park St, Sapulpa, Oklahoma 74066-4220 **Tel:** 1 918 224-5185
Email: editor@sapulpaheraldonline.com
Freq: Fri; **Circ:** 4501 Not Audited
Editor: Eric Bruce; **Advertising Sales Manager:** Cindy Leslie; **Publisher:** Darren Sumner
Profile: Sapulpa Daily Herald is a daily newspaper written for the residents of Sapulpaa, OK. The paper covers national and local news, sports and arts & entertainment.
Language (s): English
Ad Rate: Full Page Mono 19.00
Ad Rate: Full Page Colour 62.10
Currency: United States Dollars
DAILY NEWSPAPER

Sarasota Herald-Tribune 15465
Owner: GateHouse Media
Editorial: 1777 Main St, Sarasota, Florida 34236-5845 **Tel:** 1 941 953-7755
Email: advocate@heraldtribune.com **Web site:** http://www.heraldtribune.com
Freq: Daily; **Circ:** 50606
Publisher: Patrick Dorsey
Profile: Sarasota Herald-Tribune is a daily general-interest newspaper serving Sarasota, Manatee and Charlotte counties on Florida's Gulf Coast. The paper has been published continuously since 1925. Articles include features, breaking news, trends, analyses, profiles and investigative stories.
Language (s): English
Ad Rate: Full Page Mono 77.95
Ad Rate: Full Page Colour 85.08
Currency: United States Dollars
DAILY NEWSPAPER

Sarasota Herald-Tribune - Bradenton Bureau 87543
Editorial: 2025 Lakewood Ranch Blvd Ste 202, Bradenton, Florida 34211-4948 **Tel:** 1 941 745-7808
Language (s): English
DAILY NEWSPAPER

Sarasota Herald-Tribune - Venice Bureau 16263
Editorial: 300 Tamiami Trl S, Venice, Florida 34285-2422 **Tel:** 1 941 486-3030
Language (s): English
DAILY NEWSPAPER

The Saratogian 14427
Owner: Digital First Media
Editorial: 20 Lake Ave, Saratoga Springs, New York 12866-2314 **Tel:** 1 518 584-4242
Email: news@saratogian.com **Web site:** http://www.saratogian.com
Freq: Daily; **Circ:** 6475 Not Audited
Publisher: Robert O'Leary; **News Editor:** Paul Tackett
Profile: The Saratogian is a daily local newspaper serving the residents of Saratoga Springs and Saratoga County, NY. The publication covers local news, national news, lifestyle, sports, and features a weekly entertainment calendar. Press releases can be faxed to the appropriate staff member according to topic.
Language (s): English
Ad Rate: Full Page Mono 35.22
Ad Rate: Full Page Colour 536.00
Currency: United States Dollars
DAILY NEWSPAPER

Sauk Valley Newspapers 382356
Owner: Sauk Valley Newspapers
Editorial: 3200 E Lincolnway, Sterling, Illinois 61081-1773 **Tel:** 1 815 625-3600
Email: news@svnmail.com **Web site:** http://www.saukvalley.com
Freq: Mon thru Fri; **Circ:** 16521
Advertising Sales Manager: Jennifer Baratta; **Publisher:** Trevis Mayfield
Profile: Sauk Valley Newspapers publishes newspapers covering Dixon, Sterling and Rock Falls, IL.
Language (s): English
DAILY NEWSPAPER

Savannah Morning News 13850
Owner: GateHouse Media, Inc.
Editorial: 1375 Chatham Pkwy, Savannah, Georgia 31405-0301 **Tel:** 1 912 236-9511
Web site: http://www.savannahnow.com
Freq: Daily; **Circ:** 30698 Not Audited
Publisher: Michael Traynor
Profile: Savannah Morning News is a regional daily morning newspaper published for the residents of Savannah, GA and the surrounding communities. It has a very strict anti-spam policy in place. Please contact the paper for specific information about e-mailing reporters on staff.
Language (s): English
Ad Rate: Full Page Mono 95.00
Ad Rate: Full Page Colour 620.23
Currency: United States Dollars
DAILY NEWSPAPER

Scottsboro Daily Sentinel 13674
Owner: Southern Newspapers, Inc.
Editorial: 701 Veterans Dr, Scottsboro, Alabama 35768-2132 **Tel:** 1 256 259-1020
Email: dsnews@thedailysentinel.com **Web site:** http://www.thedailysentinel.com
Freq: Daily; **Circ:** 4200 Not Audited
Publisher: Brad Shurett
Profile: Scottsboro Daily Sentinel is a local newspaper published daily except for Saturday and Monday. The newspaper covers local news, sports, education, and government for all of Jackson County, AL.
Language (s): English
Ad Rate: Full Page Mono 9.20
Ad Rate: Full Page Colour 204.20
Currency: United States Dollars
DAILY NEWSPAPER

Scripps/Tribune - Capitol Bureau 924434
Owner: E.W. Scripps Co.
Editorial: Tallahassee, Florida
Web site: http://www.politicalfixflorida.com
Profile: Bureau is a joint effort between The Tampa Tribune and Naples Daily News to provide coverage of Florida state government and politics news.
Language (s): English
DAILY NEWSPAPER

The Seattle Times 15390
Owner: Seattle Times Co.
Editorial: 1000 Denny Way, Seattle, Washington 98109-5340 **Tel:** 1 206 464-2111
Email: newstips@seattletimes.com **Web site:** http://seattletimes.com
Freq: Daily; **Circ:** 195778 Not Audited
Editor: Kathy Best; **Publisher:** Frank Blethen
Profile: The Seattle Times is a daily newspaper serving the Seattle, Washington area. It is the largest daily newspaper in the state of Washington and covers local, national and international news, as well as business, technology, real estate, travel, food, features, entertainment and sports. The Sunday issue is combined with the Seattle Post-Intelligencer. It was founded in 1896.
Language (s): English
Ad Rate: Full Page Mono 425.50
Ad Rate: Full Page Colour 4790.50
Currency: United States Dollars
DAILY NEWSPAPER

Security Council Report - New York Bureau 620045
Editorial: 1 Dag Hammarskjold Plz Fl 21, New York, New York 10017-2201 **Tel:** 1 212 759-5186
Email: contact@securitycouncilreport.org
Profile: This is the New York Bureau of the Security Council Report association.
Language (s): English
DAILY NEWSPAPER

The Sedalia Democrat 14250
Owner: Freedom Communications Inc.
Editorial: 700 S Massachusetts Ave, Sedalia, Missouri 65301-4548 **Tel:** 1 660 826-1000
Email: news@sedaliademocrat.com **Web site:** http://www.sedaliademocrat.com
Freq: Mon thru Fri; **Circ:** 7602
Publisher: Denny Koenders
Profile: The Sedalia Democrat is a daily newspaper serving the Sedalia, MO area. The paper covers local news, entertainment and recreation, lifestyle, and high school sports. Regional and national news, as well as collegiate and professional sports coverage, is taken solely from the wires.
Language (s): English
Ad Rate: Full Page Mono 17.44
Ad Rate: Full Page Colour 232.88
Currency: United States Dollars
DAILY NEWSPAPER

Seguin Daily News 437522
Owner: Guadalupe Media, LTD.
Editorial: 609 E Court St, Seguin, Texas 78155-5713 **Tel:** 1 830 379-2234
Email: news@kwed1580.com **Web site:** http://www.seguintoday.com
Freq: Mon thru Fri; **Circ:** 3500 Not Audited
Profile: Seguin Daily News is written for the residents of Seguin, TX. News topics include community, farm, religion, health, military, home & garden and a local citizen profile.
Language (s): English
Ad Rate: Full Page Mono 2.34
Currency: United States Dollars
DAILY NEWSPAPER

Seguin Gazette 14748
Owner: Southern Newspapers, Inc.
Editorial: 1012 Schriewer, Seguin, Texas 78155-7473 **Tel:** 1 830 379-5404
Email: editor@seguingazette.com **Web site:** http://www.seguingazette.com
Freq: Fri; **Circ:** 3991 Not Audited
News Editor: Jessica Sanders
Profile: Seguin Gazette-Enterprise is published Tuesday through Friday and Sunday in the morning. The editorial mission is to provide news and sports information to the county. The paper primarily covers local news for the residents of Seguin and Guadalupe County, TX. Send press releases to the news editor by e-mail.
Language (s): English
Ad Rate: Full Page Mono 12.00
Ad Rate: Full Page Colour 285.00
Currency: United States Dollars
DAILY NEWSPAPER

The Selma Times-Journal 13675
Owner: Boone Newspapers Inc.
Editorial: 1018 Water Ave, Selma, Alabama 36701-4617 **Tel:** 1 334 875-2110
Email: news@selmatimesjournal.com **Web site:** http://www.selmatimesjournal.com
Freq: Daily; **Circ:** 10043 Not Audited
News Editor: Rick Couch; **Publisher:** Dennis Palmer
Profile: The Selma Times-Journal is written for residents in Selma and The Black Belt, AL. It covers a mixture of national and local news and sports.
Language (s): English
Ad Rate: Full Page Mono 23.45
Ad Rate: Full Page Colour 176.45
Currency: United States Dollars
DAILY NEWSPAPER

Seminole Producer 14539
Editorial: 121 N Main St, Seminole, Oklahoma 74868-4627 **Tel:** 1 405 382-1100
Email: news@seminoleproducer.com **Web site:** http://www.seminoleproducer.com

Freq: Daily; Circ: 5400 Not Audited
Publisher & Editor: Stu Phillips
Profile: Seminole Producer is published daily for the residents of Seminole County, OK. The newspaper covers local news, sports and community events. Deadlines are one day prior to issue date at 10am CT.
Language (s): English
Ad Rate: Full Page Mono 6.30
Ad Rate: Full Page Colour 70.00
Currency: United States Dollars
DAILY NEWSPAPER

The Sentinel 14569
Owner: Lee Enterprises, Inc.
Editorial: 457 E North St, Carlisle, Pennsylvania 17013-2655 Tel: 1 717 243-2611
Email: frontdoor@cumberlink.com Web site: http://www.cumberlink.com
Freq: Daily; Circ: 15156
Profile: The Sentinel is a daily newspaper serving residents in Cumberland County, PA. The publication covers local, national, state and international news, sports, entertainment and community announcements. Press releases should be faxed to the appropriate editor. Deadlines for the publication are before 8am ET the day of publication.
Language (s): English
Ad Rate: Full Page Mono 29.50
Ad Rate: Full Page Colour 34.95
Currency: United States Dollars
DAILY NEWSPAPER

The Sentinel 14597
Owner: Ogden Newspapers
Editorial: 352 6th St, Lewistown, Pennsylvania 17044-1213 Tel: 1 717 248-6741
Email: sentinel@lewistownsentinel.com Web site: http://www.lewistownsentinel.com
Freq: Daily; Circ: 9008 Not Audited
Advertising Sales Manager: Matthew Bolich; Publisher: Ruth Eddy
Profile: The Sentinel is published six days a week Monday through Saturday. It covers a wide variety of topics including national and local news, seniors, outdoors, government, entertainment, sports, health, business, schools, religion and agriculture. Press releases can be sent by fax to the appropriate editor. The newspaper coves six central Pennsylvania counties.
Language (s): English
Ad Rate: Full Page Mono 18.88
Ad Rate: Full Page Colour 280.00
Currency: United States Dollars
DAILY NEWSPAPER

Sentinel & Enterprise 14118
Owner: MediaNews Group
Editorial: 808 Main St, Fitchburg, Massachusetts 01420-3153 Tel: 1 978 343-6911
Email: news@sentinelandenterprise.com Web site: http://www.sentinelandenterprise.com
Freq: Daily; Circ: 15514 Not Audited
Publisher: Mark O'Neil
Profile: Sentinel & Enterprise is a daily local newspaper serving residents of Central Massachusetts. The newspaper covers local news, national news, business, obituaries and sports. Lead time varies.
Language (s): English
Ad Rate: Full Page Mono 28.00
Ad Rate: Full Page Colour 200.00
Currency: United States Dollars
DAILY NEWSPAPER

The Sentinel-Record 13695
Owner: Wehco Media Inc.
Editorial: 300 Spring St, Hot Springs National Park, Arkansas 71901-4148 Tel: 1 501 623-7711
Web site: http://www.hotsr.com
Freq: Daily; Circ: 13893 Not Audited
Publisher: Walter Hussman
Profile: The Sentinel-Record is a daily newspaper serving residents of Hot Springs National Park, AR and adjoining towns. The publication covers local news, business, lifestyles, arts & entertainment and sports.
Language (s): English
Ad Rate: Full Page Mono 30.75
Ad Rate: Full Page Colour 98.99
Currency: United States Dollars
DAILY NEWSPAPER

Sentinel-Tribune 14438
Owner: The Sentinel Co.
Editorial: 300 E Poe Rd, Bowling Green, Ohio 43402-1329 Tel: 1 419 352-4611
Email: letters@sentinel-tribune.com Web site: http://www.sent-trib.com
Freq: Daily; Circ: 10550 Not Audited
Publisher: Thomas Haswell; Editor: Jan Larson McLaughlin
Profile: Sentinel-Tribune is a daily newspaper serving residents of Wood County, OH. It covers local and national news, arts & entertainment, education, farming, lifestyles, real estate, religion and sports. Advertising deadlines are at 5pm ET.
Language (s): English
Ad Rate: Full Page Mono 14.10
Ad Rate: Full Page Colour 250.00
Currency: United States Dollars
DAILY NEWSPAPER

The Shawano Leader 14820
Owner: BlueLine Media Holdings
Editorial: 1464 E Green Bay St, Shawano, Wisconsin 54166-2258 Tel: 1 715 526-2121
Email: news@wolfrivermedia.com Web site: http://www.shawanoleader.com
Freq: Daily; Circ: 4400 Not Audited
Publisher: Greg Mellis
Profile: Shawano Leader is a local daily newspaper serving the residents of Shawano County, WI. The newspaper mainly covers local and world news, sports, financial and community events. Deadlines for the publication are at 10am CT the day before issue date.
Language (s): English
Ad Rate: Full Page Mono 16.78
Ad Rate: Full Page Colour 135.00
Currency: United States Dollars
DAILY NEWSPAPER

The Shawnee News-Star 14540
Owner: GateHouse Media Inc.
Editorial: 215 N Bell Ave, Shawnee, Oklahoma 74801-6913 Tel: 1 405 273-4200
Email: newsroom@news-star.com Web site: http://www.news-star.com
Freq: Daily; Circ: 7175 Not Audited
Editor: Kim Morava
Profile: The Shawnee News-Star is a local newspaper serving the residents of Shawnee, OK. It includes information on local news, weather, sports, business and arts & entertainment.
Language (s): English
Ad Rate: Full Page Mono 10.00
Currency: United States Dollars
DAILY NEWSPAPER

The Sheboygan Press 14821
Owner: Gannett Co., Inc.
Editorial: 632 Center Ave, Sheboygan, Wisconsin 53081-4621 Tel: 1 920 457-7711
Email: news@sheboyganpress.com Web site: http://www.sheboyganpress.com
Freq: Daily; Circ: 12284
Profile: The Sheboygan Press is a local daily newspaper written for residents of Sheboygan, WI. The newspaper covers local news, sports, and events as well as national news that effects the residents of Sheboygan, WI.
Language (s): English
Ad Rate: Full Page Mono 51.40
Ad Rate: Full Page Colour 300.00
Currency: United States Dollars
DAILY NEWSPAPER

Shelby Globe 14488
Owner: Shelby Daily Globe, Inc.
Editorial: 37 W Main St, Shelby, Ohio 44875
Tel: 1 419 342-4276
Web site: http://www.sdgnewsgroup.com
Freq: Daily; Circ: 4200 Not Audited
Publisher: Scott Gove; Editor: Jodi Myers; Editor: Chuck Ridenour
Profile: The Shelby Daily Globe is a local newspaper serving the residents of Shelby, OH. It includes information on local news, weather, sports, business, and entertainment. The lead time and deadline are the same day as issue date. Contact the publication for advertising rates.
Language (s): English
Ad Rate: Full Page Mono 11.35
Currency: United States Dollars
DAILY NEWSPAPER

The Shelby Star 14315
Owner: GateHouse Media Inc.
Editorial: 315 E Graham St, Shelby, North Carolina 28150-5452 Tel: 1 704 484-7000
Email: shelbystar@shelbystar.com Web site: http://www.shelbystar.com
Freq: Daily; Circ: 11982 Not Audited
Profile: The Shelby Star is a local newspaper serving the residents of Shelby, NC. It includes information on local news, weather, sports, business and entertainment.
Language (s): English
Ad Rate: Full Page Mono 22.75
Ad Rate: Full Page Colour 77.35
Currency: United States Dollars
DAILY NEWSPAPER

Shelbyville Daily Union 13959
Owner: Community Newspaper Holdings, Inc.
Editorial: 100 W Main St, Shelbyville, Illinois 62565-1652 Tel: 1 217 774-2161
Email: news@shelbyvilledailyunion.com Web site: http://www.shelbyvilledailyunion.com
Freq: Weekly; Circ: 3200 Not Audited
Profile: Shelbyville Daily Union is a local daily newspaper serving Shelbyville, Windsor, Findlay, Moweaqua and Stewardson, IL. The newspaper covers community news, politics, sports and entertainment. Advertising deadlines are at noon CT the day before issue date.
Language (s): English
Ad Rate: Full Page Mono 6.65
Ad Rate: Full Page Colour 75.00
Currency: United States Dollars
DAILY NEWSPAPER

Shelbyville News 14018
Owner: Paxton Media Group
Editorial: 123 E Washington St, Shelbyville, Indiana 46176-1463 Tel: 1 317 398-6631
Email: shelbynews@shelbynews.com Web site: http://www.shelbynews.com
Freq: Daily; Circ: 8655 Not Audited
Publisher: Rachael Raney
Profile: The Shelbyville Times is a local newspaper serving the residents of Shelbyville, IN. It includes information on local news, weather, sports, business, and entertainment. This publication serves the local community of Shelbyville, IN. The staff prefers to be contacted via e-mail.
Language (s): English
Ad Rate: Full Page Mono 17.00
Ad Rate: Full Page Colour 230.00
Currency: United States Dollars
DAILY NEWSPAPER

Shelbyville Times-Gazette 14678
Owner: Rust Communications
Editorial: 323 E Depot St, Shelbyville, Tennessee 37160-4027 Tel: 1 931 684-1200
Email: tgnews@t-g.com Web site: http://www.t-g.com
Freq: Fri; Circ: 7385 Not Audited
Advertising Sales Manager: Sandra Smith
Profile: Shelbyville Times-Gazette is a local newspaper serving the residents of Shelbyville, TN.
Language (s): English
Ad Rate: Full Page Mono 9.14
Ad Rate: Full Page Colour 250.00
Currency: United States Dollars
DAILY NEWSPAPER

Sheridan Press 14854
Owner: Sheridan Newspapers, Inc.
Editorial: 144 E Grinnell St, Sheridan, Wyoming 82801-3933 Tel: 1 307 672-2431
Web site: http://www.thesheridanpress.com
Freq: Daily; Circ: 6750 Not Audited
Advertising Sales Manager: Beth Smith; Publisher: Steven Woody
Profile: Sheridan Press is a local newspaper serving the residents of Sheridan, WY. It includes information on local news, weather, sports, business and entertainment.
Language (s): English
Ad Rate: Full Page Mono 14.00
Ad Rate: Full Page Colour 89.81
Currency: United States Dollars
DAILY NEWSPAPER

Shoshone News-Press 13902
Owner: Hagadone Corp.
Editorial: 620 E Mullan Ave, Osburn, Idaho 83849
Tel: 1 208 752-1120
Web site: http://www.shoshonenewspress.com
Freq: Daily; Circ: 4006 Not Audited
Profile: Shoshone News-Press is a local newspaper serving the residents of Shoshone County, ID. The paper includes information on local news, weather, sports, business and entertainment.
Language (s): English
Ad Rate: Full Page Mono 13.83
Ad Rate: Full Page Colour 200.00
Currency: United States Dollars
DAILY NEWSPAPER

The Sidney Daily News 14489
Owner: AIM Media Midwest
Editorial: 1451 N Vandemark Rd, Sidney, Ohio 45365-3547 Tel: 1 937 498-8088
Email: sdnnews@civitasmedia.com Web site: http://www.sidneydailynews.com
Freq: Fri; Circ: 13141 Not Audited
Advertising Sales Manager: Becky Smith; Editor: Melanie Speicher
Profile: The Sidney Daily News is a daily, local paper serving the residents of the Sidney, OH area. It covers local news, sports, entertainment and lifestyle information as well as comprehensive event listings.
Language (s): English
Ad Rate: Full Page Mono 18.90
Ad Rate: Full Page Colour 27.90
Currency: United States Dollars
DAILY NEWSPAPER

Sierra Sun 18653
Owner: Swift Newspapers
Editorial: 12315 Deerfield Dr, Truckee, California 96161-0452 Tel: 1 530 587-6061
Email: editor@sierrasun.com Web site: http://www.sierrasun.com
Freq: 2 Times/Week; Circ: 5871 Not Audited
Profile: Sierra Sun is a community newspaper serving residents of Truckee, Tahoe City, Sqaw Valley and Kings Beach, CA. It covers regional and local news, sports, editorials and lifestyle stories. Tahoe World, an arts, entertainment and recreation guide to the North Shore area, is inserted into the paper on Wednesdays.
Language (s): English
Ad Rate: Full Page Mono 13.00
Ad Rate: Full Page Colour 16.00
Currency: United States Dollars
DAILY NEWSPAPER

Sierra Vista Herald/Bisbee Daily Review 457812
Owner: Wick Communications Inc.
Editorial: 102 Fab Ave, Sierra Vista, Arizona 85635-1741 Tel: 1 520 458-9440
Email: publisher@svherald.com Web site: http://www.svherald.com
Circ: 10876 Not Audited
Advertising Sales Manager: Becky Bjork
Language (s): English
DAILY NEWSPAPER

The Signal 14861
Owner: Morris Multimedia, Inc.
Editorial: 24000 Creekside Rd, Santa Clarita, California 91355-1726 Tel: 1 661 259-1234
Email: citydesk@signalscv.com Web site: http://www.signalscv.com/
Freq: Daily; Circ: 9329 Not Audited
Profile: The Signal is a local daily newspaper written for residents of northern Los Angeles County, including the communities of Santa Clarita, Agua Dolce, Canyon Country, Castaic, Newhall, Saugus, Stevenson Ranch, Valencia and Val Verde, CA. It covers local news, schools, business, sports, editorials, community events and arts & entertainment.
Language (s): English
Ad Rate: Full Page Mono 39.90
Ad Rate: Full Page Colour 127.46
Currency: United States Dollars
DAILY NEWSPAPER

Silver City Daily Press & Independent 14383
Owner: Independent Publishing Co./Christina Ely Owner
Editorial: 300 W Market St, Silver City, New Mexico 88061-4956 Tel: 1 575 388-1576
Email: dthompson@silvercitydailypress.net Web site: http://www.scdailypress.com
Freq: Daily; Circ: 9072 Not Audited
Publisher: Tina Ely; Editor: Dean Thompson
Profile: Silver City Daily Press & Independent serves the residents of Silver City, NM. It covers local news, weather, sports, business and entertainment.
Language (s): English
Ad Rate: Full Page Mono 16.25
Ad Rate: Full Page Colour 17.25
Currency: United States Dollars
DAILY NEWSPAPER

Silver City Sun-News 430456
Owner: Gannett Co., Inc.
Editorial: 208 W Broadway St, Silver City, New Mexico 88061-5353 Tel: 1 575 538-5893
Web site: http://www.scsun-news.com
Freq: Daily; Circ: 2200 Not Audited
Profile: Silver City Sun-News is a daily newspaper serving the residents of Silver City, NM. It covers news, sports, features, business and opinion articles. It shares some of its editorial content with the Las Cruces (NM) Sun-News.
Language (s): English
Ad Rate: Full Page Mono 9.50
Ad Rate: Full Page Colour 50.00
Currency: United States Dollars
DAILY NEWSPAPER

Sing Tao Daily 79987
Owner: Sing Tao Newspapers Ltd.
Editorial: 188 Lafayette St, New York, New York 10013 Tel: 1 212 431-9030
Email: editor@nysingtao.com Web site: http://www.nysingtao.com
Freq: Daily; Circ: 55000 Not Audited
Editor: Lotus Chau; Editor: Alice Lee; Publisher: Robin Mui
Profile: Sing Tao Daily is a daily newspaper published for the members of the Chinese speaking community. The newspaper covers local, regional, national and international news as well as entertainment, business and finance and lifestyle issues.
Language (s): Chinese
Ad Rate: Full Page Mono 6.00
Ad Rate: Full Page Colour 8.40
Currency: United States Dollars
DAILY NEWSPAPER

Sing Tao Daily 80014
Owner: Sing Tao Newspapers (S.F.) Ltd.
Editorial: 5000 Shoreline Ct Ste 300, South San Francisco, California 94080-1956 Tel: 1 650 808-8800
Email: editor@singtaousa.com Web site: https://www.singtaousa.com/sf
Freq: Daily; Circ: 10000 Not Audited
Publisher: Tim Lau
Profile: Sing Tao Daily is a newspaper covering local, national and international news relevant to Chinese Americans in the San Francisco Bay area. Advertising deadlines are at noon PT.
Language (s): Chinese
Ad Rate: Full Page Mono 7.50
Ad Rate: Full Page Colour 11.00
Currency: United States Dollars
DAILY NEWSPAPER

Sing Tao Daily - Boston Bureau 151966
Editorial: 130 Lincoln St, Boston, Massachusetts 02111-2506 Tel: 1 617 426-9642
Email: singtaoboston@yahoo.com
Freq: Daily
Bureau Chief: Klysler Yen
Language (s): Chinese
DAILY NEWSPAPER

Sing Tao Daily - Chicago Bureau 151963
Editorial: 2109 S China Pl, B, Chicago, Illinois 60616-1536 Tel: 1 312 842-3191
Email: chicago@nysingtao.com
Bureau Chief: Michelle Teo
Language (s): English
DAILY NEWSPAPER

Sing Tao Daily - Los Angeles Bureau 800441
Editorial: 17059 Green Dr, City of Industry, California 91745-1812 Tel: 1 626 956-8210
Email: editor@singtaola.com
DAILY NEWSPAPER

Sing Tao Daily - San Francisco Bureau 359504
Owner: Sing Tao Newspapers Ltd.
Editorial: 625 Kearny St, San Francisco, California 94108-1849 **Tel:** 1 415 989-7111
Language (s): English
DAILY NEWSPAPER

The Sioux City Journal 13892
Owner: Lee Enterprises, Inc.
Editorial: 515 Pavonia St, Sioux City, Iowa 51101-2245 **Tel:** 1 712 293-4250
Email: frontdoor@siouxcityjournal.com **Web site:** http://www.siouxcityjournal.com
Freq: Daily; **Circ:** 27951 Not Audited
Editor: Bruce Miller; **Publisher:** Ron Peterson
Profile: The Sioux City Journal is a daily local newspaper serving the residents of Sioux City, IA and the surrounding area. The newspaper covers news, sports, government, politics and entertainment.
Language (s): English
Ad Rate: Full Page Mono 56.15
Ad Rate: Full Page Colour 219.11
Currency: United States Dollars
DAILY NEWSPAPER

Siskiyou Daily News 13768
Owner: GateHouse Media Inc.
Editorial: 309 S Broadway St, Yreka, California 96097-2905 **Tel:** 1 530 842-5777
Email: news@siskiyoudaily.com **Web site:** http://www.siskiyoudaily.com
Freq: Daily; **Circ:** 6061 Not Audited
Publisher: Sean McDonald
Profile: Siskiyou Daily News is a local daily newspaper serving Siskiyou County, CA and the surrounding area. It provides information on news and events of interest to the local community.
Language (s): English
Ad Rate: Full Page Mono 15.95
Ad Rate: Full Page Colour 285.00
Currency: United States Dollars
DAILY NEWSPAPER

Skagit Valley Herald 14787
Owner: Skagit Valley Publishing Co.
Editorial: 1215 Anderson Rd, Mount Vernon, Washington 98274-7615 **Tel:** 1 360 424-3251
Email: news@skagitpublishing.com **Web site:** http://www.goskagit.com
Freq: Daily; **Circ:** 17231 Not Audited
Publisher: Heather Hernandez; **Editor:** Colette Weeks
Profile: Skagit Valley Herald is a local daily newspaper serving Mount Vernon, WA and the surrounding area. It provides information on news and events of interest to the local community, as well as sports, entertainment and community issues.
Language (s): English
Ad Rate: Full Page Mono 23.45
Currency: United States Dollars
DAILY NEWSPAPER

Snyder Daily News 14730
Owner: McQueen (Roy)
Editorial: 3600 College Ave, Snyder, Texas 79549-4637 **Tel:** 1 325 573-5486
Email: news@snyderdailynews.com **Web site:** http://www.snyderdailynews.com
Freq: Daily; **Circ:** 5000 Not Audited
Editor: Shirley Gorman; **News Editor:** Jeff West
Profile: Snyder Daily News is written for residents of Snyder, TX and the surrounding area. It covers local news, sports and community events.
Language (s): English
Ad Rate: Full Page Mono 9.25
Currency: United States Dollars
DAILY NEWSPAPER

El Sol Latino Newspaper 819765
Owner: Grupo Bogota, Inc.
Editorial: 198 W Chew Ave, Philadelphia, Pennsylvania 19120-2465 **Tel:** 1 215 424-1200
Email: editorial@elsoln1.com **Web site:** http://www.elsoln1.com
Freq: Weekly; **Circ:** 45000
Publisher: Ricardo Hurtado
Profile: El Sol Latino Newspaper is a Spanish paper featuring local news in the Philadelphia market.
Language (s): English
DAILY NEWSPAPER

South Bend Tribune 14019
Owner: Schurz Communications Inc.
Editorial: 225 W Colfax Ave, South Bend, Indiana 46626-1000 **Tel:** 1 574 235-6161
Email: sbtnews@sbtinfo.com **Web site:** http://www.southbendtribune.com
Freq: Daily; **Circ:** 44951 Not Audited
Profile: South Bend Tribune provides local and regional news coverage. The paper covers business news, sports and arts & entertainment.
Language (s): English
Ad Rate: Full Page Mono 64.02
Ad Rate: Full Page Colour 72.75
Currency: United States Dollars
DAILY NEWSPAPER

South Florida Sun Sentinel 15288
Owner: tronc
Editorial: 500 E Broward Blvd Ste 900, Fort Lauderdale, Florida 33394-3019 **Tel:** 1 954 356-4000
Web site: http://www.sun-sentinel.com
Freq: Daily; **Circ:** 106053 Not Audited
News Editor: Dana Banker; **Editor:** Howard Saltz
Profile: South Florida Sun Sentinel is a daily, broadsheet newspaper written for the general public in Southern Florida, particularly in Palm Beach, Broward and Dade counties. The Business Section offers features, breaking news, and cover stories on various business issues. The Monday edition offers the Weekly Business section, a tabloid-sized pull-out featuring articles on business, personal finance and the economic pulse of various regional areas. Articles include software reviews and South Florida Web sites in the Technology section; Business Leads, TeachSmart, People on the Move, and columns in the Your Business section; trade growth and networking in the International Business section; Savings Game, IRA investing and columns in the Personal Finance section; industry trends; and cover stories. Society Scene is published Wednesdays in the paper and covers charity happenings. Other topics included in Sun Sentinel are art, books, food, music and travel.
Language (s): English
Ad Rate: Full Page Mono 196.00
Ad Rate: Full Page Colour 225.40
Currency: United States Dollars
DAILY NEWSPAPER

South Florida Sun Sentinel - Deerfield Beach Bureau 15662
Editorial: 333 SW 12th Ave, Deerfield Beach, Florida 33442-3107 **Tel:** 1 561 243-6600
Profile: The bureau is physically located in Delray Beach, Palm Beach County. All mail correspondence for the office must be sent to the address in Deerfield Beach, FL. Due to safety precautions, mail will not be accepted at the Delray office.
Language (s): English
DAILY NEWSPAPER

South Florida Sun Sentinel - Tamarac Bureau 15663
Editorial: 6501 Nob Hill Rd, Tamarac, Florida 33321-6422 **Tel:** 1 954 572-2050
Language (s): English
DAILY NEWSPAPER

South Jersey Times 14369
Owner: NJ Advance Media
Editorial: 161 Bridgeton Pike #E, Mullica Hill, New Jersey 08062-2669 **Tel:** 1 856 845-3300
Web site: http://www.nj.com/southjerseytimes/
Freq: Daily; **Circ:** 37339
Profile: South Jersey Times is a daily newspaper published by South Jersey Newspapers. The newspaper provides readers in Salem County, Gloucester County, and Cumberland, NJ with local and national news. Other features include lifestyle, entertainment, sports, business and classifieds.
Language (s): English
Ad Rate: Full Page Mono 85.00
Ad Rate: Full Page Colour 89.09
Currency: United States Dollars
DAILY NEWSPAPER

Southbridge Evening News 14134
Owner: Stonebridge Press
Editorial: 25 Elm St, Southbridge, Massachusetts 01550-2605 **Tel:** 1 508 764-4325
Web site: http://www.southbridgeeveningnews.com
Freq: Mon thru Fri; **Circ:** 4098 Not Audited
Advertising Sales Manager: Jean Ashton; **Publisher:** Frank Chilinski; **Editor:** Adam Minor
Profile: The Southbridge Evening News is a local daily newspaper written for residents of Southbridge, MA and the surrounding towns. The newspaper covers local news, sports, arts and entertainment, business, and national stories if they have a direct impact on the readership.
Language (s): English
Ad Rate: Full Page Mono 15.00
Currency: United States Dollars
DAILY NEWSPAPER

Southeast Missourian 14223
Owner: Rust Communications
Editorial: 301 Broadway St, Cape Girardeau, Missouri 63701-7330 **Tel:** 1 573 335-6611
Email: news@semissourian.com **Web site:** http://www.semissourian.com
Freq: Mon thru Fri; **Circ:** 11216 Not Audited
Editor: Bob Miller; **Publisher:** Jon Rust
Profile: Southeast Missourian is a local daily newspaper devoted to keeping the residents of Southeastern Missouri informed about the news of their community. The articles in the newspaper focus on local news, arts, sports and business, as well as national stories that have an impact on the readership.
Language (s): English
Ad Rate: Full Page Mono 19.28
Ad Rate: Full Page Colour 330.00
Currency: United States Dollars
DAILY NEWSPAPER

Southern Chinese Daily News - Houston Edition 152789
Owner: Southern Chinese Daily News
Editorial: 11122 Bellaire Blvd, Houston, Texas 77072-2608 **Tel:** 1 281 498-4310
Email: wealee@aol.com **Web site:** http://www.scdaily.com
Freq: Daily; **Circ:** 25000 Not Audited
Editor: Jun Gai; **Publisher:** Wea Lee; **Advertising Sales Manager:** Hilda Poon
Profile: Southern Chinese Daily News-Houston Edition is a daily newspaper that serves the Chinese community of Houston.
Language (s): Chinese
Ad Rate: Full Page Mono 34.00
Currency: United States Dollars
DAILY NEWSPAPER

The Southern Illinoisan 13916
Owner: Lee Enterprises, Inc.
Editorial: 710 N Illinois Ave, Carbondale, Illinois 62901-1283 **Tel:** 1 618 529-5454
Email: news@thesouthern.com **Web site:** http://www.thesouthern.com
Freq: Daily; **Circ:** 23099 Not Audited
Editor: Autumn Phillips; **Editor:** Les Winkeler
Profile: The Southern Illinoisan is published daily for the residents of Carbondale, IL and surrounding areas. The newspaper covers local news, business, sports and community events.
Language (s): English
Ad Rate: Full Page Mono 45.40
Ad Rate: Full Page Colour 79.91
Currency: United States Dollars
DAILY NEWSPAPER

Southwest Daily News 14112
Owner: Fortress Investment Group, LLC
Editorial: 716 E Napoleon St, Sulphur, Louisiana 70663-3402 **Tel:** 1 337 527-7075
Email: sdneditorial@yahoo.com **Web site:** http://www.sulphurdailynews.com
Freq: Fri; **Circ:** 3077 Not Audited
Advertising Sales Manager: Jill Humphrey; **Editor:** Marilyn Monroe
Profile: Southwest Daily News is a daily newspaper, locally written for residents of Southwestern Louisiana. The newspaper covers local news, business, sports and arts & entertainment stories. The newspaper also covers national and statewide stories if they have a direct impact on the newspaper's readership. All inquiries should be addressed to the editor. Deadlines are at noon CT the day before publication.
Language (s): English
Ad Rate: Full Page Mono 14.39
Currency: United States Dollars
DAILY NEWSPAPER

The Southwest Times 14763
Owner: Southwest Publishers, Inc.
Editorial: 34 5th St NE, Pulaski, Virginia 24301
Tel: 1 540 980-5220
Web site: http://www.southwesttimes.com
Freq: Fri; **Circ:** 5200 Not Audited
Publisher: Kay Kline; **Editor:** Melinda Williams
Profile: The Southwest Times' editorial mission is to deliver local news and community information to its readers in Pulaski County, Western Wythe County, Radford and Western Montgomery, VA.
Language (s): English
Ad Rate: Full Page Mono 12.00
Ad Rate: Full Page Colour 250.00
Currency: United States Dollars
DAILY NEWSPAPER

The Sparks Tribune 14882
Owner: Battle Born Media
Editorial: 155 Glendale Ave Ste 10, Sparks, Nevada 89431-5751 **Tel:** 1 775 358-8062
Web site: http://sparkstrib.com
Freq: Daily; **Circ:** 6374 Not Audited
Profile: The Sparks Tribune is a local daily newspaper. Its editorial mission is to present the best news to the residents of Sparks, NV. It covers national and local news.
Language (s): English
Ad Rate: Full Page Mono 17.00
Ad Rate: Full Page Colour 60.32
Currency: United States Dollars
DAILY NEWSPAPER

Spartanburg Herald-Journal 15452
Owner: GateHouse Media Inc.
Editorial: 189 W Main St, Spartanburg, South Carolina 29306-2334 **Tel:** 1 864 582-4511
Email: online@shj.com **Web site:** http://www.goupstate.com
Freq: Daily; **Circ:** 27138 Not Audited
Profile: Spartanburg (SC) Herald-Journal serves readers in the state's upstate region and covers local and regional news, business, sports, arts & entertainment and community news. The outlet offers RSS (Really Simple Syndication).
Language (s): English
Ad Rate: Full Page Mono 63.19
Ad Rate: Full Page Colour 1200.00
Currency: United States Dollars
DAILY NEWSPAPER

The Spectrum 14750
Owner: Gannett Co., Inc.
Editorial: 275 E Saint George Blvd, Saint George, Utah 84770-2986 **Tel:** 1 435 674-6200
Web site: http://www.thespectrum.com
Freq: Daily; **Circ:** 18456 Not Audited
Publisher: Donnie Welch
Profile: The Spectrum is a daily local newspaper serving the residents of St. George, UT. The newspaper covers local and national news, sports and other topics of interest to the readers.
Language (s): English
Ad Rate: Full Page Mono 18.60
Ad Rate: Full Page Colour 515.00
Currency: United States Dollars
DAILY NEWSPAPER

Spencer Daily Reporter 13893
Owner: Rust Communications
Editorial: 310 E Milwaukee St, Spencer, Iowa 51301-4569 **Tel:** 1 712 262-6610
Email: news@spencerdailyreporter.com **Web site:** http://www.spencerdailyreporter.com
Freq: Daily; **Circ:** 3900 Not Audited
Publisher: Paula Buenger; **Editor:** Randy Cauthron
Profile: Spencer Daily Reporter is written for the community of Spencer, IA. The publication provides local news, sports, agriculture, and community events coverage.
Language (s): English
Ad Rate: Full Page Mono 8.40
Ad Rate: Full Page Colour 215.00
Currency: United States Dollars
DAILY NEWSPAPER

Spencer Evening World 14020
Owner: Spencer Evening World, Inc.
Editorial: 114 E Franklin St, Spencer, Indiana 47460-1818 **Tel:** 1 812 829-2255
Email: editor@spencereveningworld.com **Web site:** http://www.spencereveningworld.com
Freq: Daily; **Circ:** 3800 Not Audited
Advertising Sales Manager: Judy Deckard; **Publisher:** John Gillaspy
Profile: Spencer Evening World is a local daily newspaper serving residents of Owen County, IN. It covers local news, lifestyle and community events. Advertising deadlines are at 5pm the day before publication. News deadlines are at 10am ET the day of issue.
Language (s): English
Ad Rate: Full Page Mono 5.50
Ad Rate: Full Page Colour 85.00
Currency: United States Dollars
DAILY NEWSPAPER

The Spokesman-Review 15447
Owner: Cowles Publishing Company
Editorial: 999 W Riverside Ave, Spokane, Washington 99201-1006 **Tel:** 1 509 459-5000
Email: news@spokesman.com **Web site:** http://www.spokesman.com
Freq: Daily; **Circ:** 70534 Not Audited
Publisher: William Cowles
Profile: The Spokesman-Review is a daily newspaper written for the general public of the Spokane, WA area. The business section includes articles on technology, employment, growth and development, agriculture, economy, logging, media and mining. Articles include trends, breaking news, analyses, profiles and investigative stories. Additional articles include travel, genealogy, books, theater and music. The paper has won the Best in Business Award by the Society of American Business Editors and Writers.
Language (s): English
Ad Rate: Full Page Mono 104.53
Ad Rate: Full Page Colour 997.75
Currency: United States Dollars
DAILY NEWSPAPER

The Spokesman-Review - Coeur D Alene Bureau 16097
Editorial: 608 Northwest Blvd, Coeur D Alene, Idaho 83814-2174 **Tel:** 1 208 765-7100
Email: idaho@spokesman.com
Language (s): English
DAILY NEWSPAPER

The Spokesman-Review Boise Bureau 151967
Editorial: 2601 W Hillway Dr, Boise, Idaho 83702-0937 **Tel:** 1 208 336-2854
Email: news@spokesman.com **Web site:** http://spokesman.com/blogs/boise
Profile: This helps keep an eye on the happenings in the state capital, from government and politics to court cases and southern Idaho oddities.
Language (s): English
DAILY NEWSPAPER

The Springfield News-Leader 14252
Owner: Gannett Co., Inc.
Editorial: 651 N Boonville Ave, Springfield, Missouri 65806-1005 **Tel:** 1 417 836-1100
Email: webeditor@news-leader.com **Web site:** http://www.news-leader.com
Freq: Daily; **Circ:** 30201 Not Audited
Profile: The Springfield (MO) News-Leader is a daily, general interest publication written for residents of Southwest Missouri. The publication covers news, business, sports and arts & entertainment.
Language (s): English
Ad Rate: Full Page Mono 100.33
Ad Rate: Full Page Colour 120.84
Currency: United States Dollars
DAILY NEWSPAPER

Springfield News-Sun 14490
Owner: Cox Media Group, Inc.
Editorial: 202 N Limestone St, Springfield, Ohio 45503-4202 **Tel:** 1 937 328-0300
Email: newssun@coxinc.com **Web site:** http://www.springfieldnewssun.com
Freq: Daily; **Circ:** 16232 Not Audited
Editor: Ben McLaughlin
Profile: Springfield News Sun is published daily for residents of Springfield, OH. The newspaper covers local and national news, sports and arts & entertainment. Deadlines are on Mondays at noon ET.
Language (s): English
Ad Rate: Full Page Mono 36.25
Ad Rate: Full Page Colour 103.19
Currency: United States Dollars
DAILY NEWSPAPER

St. Albans Messenger 14775
Owner: Vermont Media Publishing Co.
Editorial: 281 N Main St, Saint Albans, Vermont 05478-2503 **Tel:** 1 802 524-9771

Email: news@samessenger.com **Web site:** http://www.samessenger.com
Freq: Daily; **Circ:** 5000 Not Audited
Advertising Sales Manager: Jeremy Read
Profile: St. Albans Messenger provides Franklin County, VT residents with local news, sports and coverage of community events.
Language (s): English
Ad Rate: Full Page Mono 14.25
Ad Rate: Full Page Colour 48.75
Currency: United States Dollars
DAILY NEWSPAPER

The St. Augustine Record 13829

Owner: GateHouse Media Inc.
Editorial: 1 News Pl, Saint Augustine, Florida 32086-6520 **Tel:** 1 904 829-6562
Email: editor@staugustine.com **Web site:** http://www.staugustine.com
Freq: Daily; **Circ:** 17607 Not Audited
Profile: The St. Augustine Record is published daily for the residents of St. Augustine, FL and surrounding areas. The newspaper covers local and state news, business, sports, lifestyles and entertainment.
Language (s): English
Ad Rate: Full Page Mono 23.00
Currency: United States Dollars
DAILY NEWSPAPER

St. Cloud Times 14215

Owner: Gannett Co., Inc.
Editorial: 3000 7th St N, Saint Cloud, Minnesota 56303-3108 **Tel:** 1 320 255-8700
Email: newsroom@stcloudtimes.com **Web site:** http://www.sctimes.com
Freq: Daily; **Circ:** 19809 Not Audited
Profile: St. Cloud Times is written for the residents of Saint Cloud, MN. It includes local, business, sports and recreational news.
Language (s): English
Ad Rate: Full Page Mono 59.04
Ad Rate: Full Page Colour 220.27
Currency: United States Dollars
DAILY NEWSPAPER

St. Joseph News-Press 14253

Owner: NPG Newspapers
Editorial: 825 Edmond St, Saint Joseph, Missouri 64501-2737 **Tel:** 1 816 271-8500
Web site: http://www.newspressnow.com
Freq: Daily; **Circ:** 23596 Not Audited
Publisher: David Bradley
Profile: St. Joseph News-Press is a daily newspaper covering over twenty counties in Northwest Missouri. The publication covers local news, events, lifestyle, business, and political issues affecting the area. The newspaper is written for a readership of local community residents.
Language (s): English
Ad Rate: Full Page Mono 54.57
Ad Rate: Full Page Colour 176.03
Currency: United States Dollars
DAILY NEWSPAPER

St. Louis Post-Dispatch 15293

Owner: Lee Enterprises, Inc.
Editorial: 900 N Tucker Blvd, Saint Louis, Missouri 63101-1069 **Tel:** 1 314 340-8000
Email: metro@post-dispatch.com **Web site:** http://www.stltoday.com
Freq: Daily; **Circ:** 124712 Not Audited
Profile: Founded by Joseph Pulitzer in 1878, the St. Louis Post-Dispatch is a daily four-color broadsheet newspaper that covers regional, national, and international news. The platform of the publication, according to Pulitzer, is that it "will always fight for progress and reform, never tolerate injustice or corruption, always fight demagogues of all parties, never belong to any party, always oppose privileged classes and public plunderers, never lack sympathy with the poor, always remain devoted to the public welfare, never be satisfied with merely printing news, always be drastically independent, never be afraid to attack wrong, whether by predatory plutocracy or predatory poverty." Other topics covered in the publication include music, travel, theater, arts, food, and books. The publication's staff does not accept unsolicited e-mail attachments due to virus dangers. All calendar and event items should be submitted through http://events.stltoday.com/listings.
Language (s): English
Ad Rate: Full Page Mono 245.71
Ad Rate: Full Page Colour 331.72
Currency: United States Dollars
DAILY NEWSPAPER

St. Louis Post-Dispatch - Clayton Bureau 16117

Editorial: 200 S Bemiston Ave, Clayton, Missouri 63105-1915 **Tel:** 1 314 863-2812
Language (s): English
DAILY NEWSPAPER

St. Louis Post-Dispatch - Jefferson City Bureau 15787

Editorial: Jefferson City, Missouri **Tel:** 1 573 556-6181
Language (s): English
DAILY NEWSPAPER

St. Louis Post-Dispatch - Saint Charles Bureau 16016

Editorial: 190 Spring Dr, Saint Charles, Missouri 63303-3255 **Tel:** 1 636 255-7201
Email: stcharles@post-dispatch.com
Language (s): English
DAILY NEWSPAPER

St. Louis Post-Dispatch - Washington Bureau 15490

Editorial: 1025 Connecticut Ave NW, Washington, District Of Columbia 20036-5405 **Tel:** 1 202 298-6880
Language (s): English
DAILY NEWSPAPER

The St. Lucie News Tribune 16355

Owner: Gannett Co., Inc.
Editorial: 1939 S. Federal Highway, Stuart, Florida 34994 **Tel:** 1 772 461-2050
Email: feedback@tcpalm.com **Web site:** http://www.tcpalm.com
Freq: Daily; **Circ:** 51124 Not Audited
Profile: The St. Lucie News Tribune shares staff and editorial content with the Stuart (FL) News. The newspaper covers local news and community events. Other sister publications include the Jupiter (FL) Courier, Vero Beach (FL) Press Journal, and Sebastian (FL) Sun.
Language (s): English
Ad Rate: Full Page Mono 176.90
Ad Rate: Full Page Colour 260.00
Currency: United States Dollars
DAILY NEWSPAPER

St. Paul Pioneer Press 15345

Owner: Digital First Media
Editorial: 10 River Park Plz Ste 700, Saint Paul, Minnesota 55107-1223 **Tel:** 1 651 222-1111
Email: news@pioneerpress.com **Web site:** http://www.twincities.com
Freq: Daily; **Circ:** 194195 Not Audited
Publisher: Guy Gilmore; **Dakota Editor:** David Knutson
Profile: Founded in 1849, The St. Paul Pioneer Press is a daily, 60+ page, four-color broadsheet newspaper published for a general audience in Minnesota and Wisconsin. It aims to be the "leading provider of news and information for an audience that spans the Twin Cities, parts of Minnesota, and a large part of Wisconsin." It covers national and regional news, editorials, sports, business and technology. Consumer issues covered include fashion, food, health, travel, arts and entertainment, music, movies and theater. Outside of the St. Paul area, the paper is known as the Minnesota Pioneer Press.
Language (s): English
Ad Rate: Full Page Mono 242.00
Ad Rate: Full Page Colour 4200.00
Currency: United States Dollars
DAILY NEWSPAPER

Standard Democrat 14251

Owner: Rust Communications
Editorial: 205 S New Madrid St, Sikeston, Missouri 63801-2953 **Tel:** 1 573 471-1137
Email: news@standard-democrat.com **Web site:** http://www.standard-democrat.com
Freq: Mon thru Fri; **Circ:** 4793
Publisher: Michael Jensen; **Advertising Sales Manager:** DeAnna Nelson
Profile: Standard Democrat is a daily newspaper of Sikeston, MO and the surrounding areas. The newspaper covers local and national news, sports, business, lifestyle, and local events. It is intended for a readership of community subscribers.
Language (s): English
Ad Rate: Full Page Mono 11.53
Ad Rate: Full Page Colour 350.00
Currency: United States Dollars
DAILY NEWSPAPER

Standard-Examiner 14955

Owner: Ogden Publishing Corp.
Editorial: 332 Standard Way, Ogden, Utah 84404-1371 **Tel:** 1 801 625-4200
Email: cityed@standard.net **Web site:** http://www.standard.net
Freq: Daily; **Circ:** 64332 Not Audited
Publisher: Charles Horton
Profile: Standard-Examiner covers local, regional and national news for the Ogden, Layton, Kaysville, Davis and Cache, UT area. Deadlines are at 8pm MT before issue date. It was first published as The Standard in 1888.
Language (s): English
Ad Rate: Full Page Mono 46.93
Ad Rate: Full Page Colour 51.40
Currency: United States Dollars
DAILY NEWSPAPER

Standard-Journal 14601

Owner: Sample News Group
Editorial: 21 N Arch St, Milton, Pennsylvania 17847-1211 **Tel:** 1 570 742-9671
Email: newsroom@standard-journal.com **Web site:** http://www.standard-journal.com
Freq: Daily; **Circ:** 3245 Not Audited
Editor: Chris Brady; **Publisher:** Amy Moyer
Profile: Standard-Journal is a local daily newspaper published for the residents of Lewisburg, PA. The publication covers local news, sports and community events.
Language (s): English
Ad Rate: Full Page Mono 15.00
Ad Rate: Full Page Colour 300.00
Currency: United States Dollars
DAILY NEWSPAPER

Standard-Speaker 14582

Owner: Times-Shamrock Communications
Editorial: 21 N Wyoming St, Hazleton, Pennsylvania 18201-6068 **Tel:** 1 570 455-3636
Email: editorial@standardspeaker.com **Web site:** http://www.standardspeaker.com
Freq: Daily; **Circ:** 20008 Not Audited
Profile: Standard-Speaker is a daily newspaper written for residents of Hazelton, PA and surrounding areas. The publication covers local news, sports and community events. Send press materials to the main email.
Language (s): English
Ad Rate: Full Page Mono 22.58
Ad Rate: Full Page Colour 265.00
Currency: United States Dollars
DAILY NEWSPAPER

The Standard-Times 14127

Owner: GateHouse Media Inc.
Editorial: 25 Elm St, New Bedford, Massachusetts 02740-6228 **Tel:** 1 508 997-7411
Email: newsroom@s-t.com **Web site:** http://www.southcoasttoday.com
Freq: Daily; **Circ:** 17307 Not Audited
Advertising Sales Manager: Modesta Levesque
Profile: The Standard-Times is a daily newspaper located in New Bedford, MA. The features include sports, religion, social issues, education, career, healthcare and lifestyle. The lead time is two weeks. Contact the publication for advertising rates.
Language (s): English
Ad Rate: Full Page Mono 47.50
Ad Rate: Full Page Colour 187.03
Currency: United States Dollars
DAILY NEWSPAPER

Star 13968

Owner: KPC Media Group Inc.
Editorial: 118 W 9th St, Auburn, Indiana 46706-2225 **Tel:** 1 260 925-2611
Email: info@kpcmedia.com **Web site:** http://www.kpcnews.com/news/latest/eveningstar
Freq: Daily; **Circ:** 6255
Publisher: Terry Housholder; **Editor:** David Kurtz
Profile: The Evening Star provides news and information for the Auburn, IN area. Deadlines are the day before issue date.
Language (s): English
Ad Rate: Full Page Mono 3.40
Ad Rate: Full Page Colour 55.30
Currency: United States Dollars
DAILY NEWSPAPER

Star Beacon 14434

Owner: Community Newspaper Holdings, Inc.
Editorial: 4626 Park Ave, Ashtabula, Ohio 44004-6933 **Tel:** 1 440 998-2323
Web site: http://www.starbeacon.com
Freq: Daily; **Circ:** 11424 Not Audited
Editor: Matt Hutton
Profile: Star Beacon provides news to the residents of Ashtabula, OH. Deadlines are at noon ET.
Language (s): English
Ad Rate: Full Page Mono 25.08
Ad Rate: Full Page Colour 305.00
Currency: United States Dollars
DAILY NEWSPAPER

Star Courier 13938

Owner: GateHouse Media Inc.
Editorial: 105 E Central Blvd, Kewanee, Illinois 61443-2245 **Tel:** 1 309 852-2181
Email: editor@starcourier.com **Web site:** http://www.starcourier.com
Freq: Fri; **Circ:** 6200 Not Audited
Editor: Mike Landis; **Advertising Sales Manager:** Diane Mikenas
Profile: Star Courier is published daily for the residents of Kewanee, IL and surrounding areas. The newspaper covers local news, business, sports, education and community events.
Language (s): English
Ad Rate: Full Page Mono 10.45
Currency: United States Dollars
DAILY NEWSPAPER

The Star Press 14005

Owner: Gannett Co., Inc.
Editorial: 345 S High St, Muncie, Indiana 47305-2326 **Tel:** 1 765 747-5700
Email: news@muncie.gannett.com **Web site:** http://www.thestarpress.com
Freq: Daily; **Circ:** 15003 Not Audited
Profile: The Star Press is a regional newspaper of East Central Indiana. The paper covers national, as well as local news stories. Coverage also includes, sports, business and cultural items. The main goal of the paper is to provide the most accurate and up-to-date news and information for their readers.
Language (s): English
Ad Rate: Full Page Mono 38.49
Ad Rate: Full Page Colour 146.49
Currency: United States Dollars
DAILY NEWSPAPER

Star Tribune 15291

Owner: Star Tribune Media Co.
Editorial: 650 3rd Ave S Ste 1300, Minneapolis, Minnesota 55402-1947 **Tel:** 1 612 673-4000
Email: releases@startribune.com **Web site:** http://www.startribune.com
Freq: Daily; **Circ:** 285129 Not Audited
Publisher: Michael Klingensmith; **Investigative News Editor:** Jeffrey Meitrodt
Profile: Star Tribune is a broadsheet written for the general public in the Twin Cities. There are separate Minneapolis and St. Paul editions. Although they focus on news in their respective regions, both editions offer the same international, national, state, metro and consumer news. In August 2009, the paper joined a national sports content-sharing alliance with several other papers across the country.
Language (s): English
Ad Rate: Full Page Mono 199.00
Ad Rate: Full Page Colour 325.00
Currency: United States Dollars
DAILY NEWSPAPER

Star Tribune - Saint Paul Bureau 577638

Editorial: 75 Rev Dr Martin Luther King Jr Blvd, Saint Paul, Minnesota 55155-1605 **Tel:** 1 651 222-1636
Language (s): English
DAILY NEWSPAPER

Star Tribune - Washington Bureau 15488

Editorial: 1090 Vermont Ave NW, Washington, District Of Columbia 20005-4905
Language (s): English
DAILY NEWSPAPER

Star Tribune - Woodbury Bureau 793235

Editorial: 8360 City Centre Dr Ste 130, Woodbury, Minnesota 55125-3381 **Tel:** 1 651 925-5040
Profile: The Star Tribune bureau located in Woodbury, MN is also known as the Eastern Suburbs bureau.
DAILY NEWSPAPER

The Star-Democrat 14144

Owner: ACM / Chesapeake Publishing and Printing
Editorial: 29088 Airpark Dr, Easton, Maryland 21601-7000 **Tel:** 1 410 822-1500
Email: stardem@chespub.com **Web site:** http://www.stardem.com
Freq: Daily; **Circ:** 16398 Not Audited
Publisher: David Fike; **Advertising Sales Manager:** Betsy Griffin
Profile: The Star-Democrat is published daily for the residents of Talbot, MD. The newspaper covers local news and community events.
Language (s): English
Ad Rate: Full Page Mono 24.90
Ad Rate: Full Page Colour 255.00
Currency: United States Dollars
DAILY NEWSPAPER

Star-Gazette 14400

Owner: Gannett Co., Inc.
Editorial: 310 E Church St, Elmira, New York 14901-2704 **Tel:** 1 607 734-5151
Email: sgnews@gannett.com **Web site:** http://www.stargazette.com
Freq: Daily; **Circ:** 13289 Not Audited
Advertising Sales Manager: John Zych
Profile: Star-Gazette is a daily local newspaper serving residents of Elmira, NY and surrounding communities. The newspaper covers local and national news, weather, sports and community events. Feature articles cover business developments, local and national politics, education, arts & entertainment and lifestyle.
Language (s): English
Ad Rate: Full Page Mono 62.50
Ad Rate: Full Page Colour 665.00
Currency: United States Dollars
DAILY NEWSPAPER

Star-Herald 14348

Owner: Omaha World-Herald Co.
Editorial: 1405 Broadway, Scottsbluff, Nebraska 69361-3151 **Tel:** 1 308 632-9000
Email: news@starherald.com **Web site:** http://www.starherald.com
Freq: Fri; **Circ:** 12311 Not Audited
Publisher: Greg Awtry
Profile: Star-Herald is the daily newspaper of Scottsbluff, NE and the surrounding region. It covers local and national news, lifestyle and sports. Lead time varies.
Language (s): English
Ad Rate: Full Page Mono 20.78
Ad Rate: Full Page Colour 78.03
Currency: United States Dollars
DAILY NEWSPAPER

Starkville Daily News 14271

Owner: Horizon Publications
Editorial: 304 E Lampkin St, Starkville, Mississippi 39759-2910 **Tel:** 1 662 323-1642
Email: editor@starkvilledailynews.com **Web site:** http://www.starkvilledailynews.com
Freq: Daily; **Circ:** 7875 Not Audited
Publisher: Donald Norman
Profile: Starkville Daily News is the successor to the Starkville News (established in 1901) and the East Mississippi Times (established in 1867), which were consolidated in 1926. It has been published daily since October 31, 1960. The publication is written for residents of Starkville, MS. The lead time for Starkville Daily News is same day. Deadlines for the publication end two days prior to the issue date.
Language (s): English
Ad Rate: Full Page Mono 10.25
Ad Rate: Full Page Colour 325.00
Currency: United States Dollars
DAILY NEWSPAPER

Starkville Dispatch 597537

Owner: Commercial Dispatch Publishing Company
Editorial: 101 S Lafayette St Ste 16, Starkville, Mississippi 39759-2914 **Tel:** 1 661 323-2424
Web site: https://www.cdispatch.com/news/index.asp?id=25
Freq: Daily; **Circ:** 2500
Advertising Sales Manager: Beth Proffitt
Profile: The Starkville Dispatch is printed for the residents of Starkville, MS. It shares much of its

content with the Commercial Dispatch in Columbus, MS.
Language (s): English
Ad Rate: Full Page Mono 12.90
Currency: United States Dollars
DAILY NEWSPAPER

The Star-Ledger 15364
Owner: NJ Advance Media
Editorial: 1 Gateway Ctr Ste 1100, Newark, New Jersey 07102-5323 **Tel:** 1 973 392-4141
Web site: http://www.nj.com/starledger
Freq: Daily; **Circ:** 156489 Not Audited
Publisher: Richard Vezza
Profile: The Star-Ledger is a 95+ page, four-color broadsheet written for the general public in the New Jersey area. The newspaper aims to serve the greater New Jersey region. The business section is featured daily, covering local and national business stories, daily stock market rates, and real estate. The largest business sections appear in the Tuesday and Sunday editions. Articles include features, breaking news, trends, analyses, profiles, and investigative stories.
Language (s): English
Ad Rate: Full Page Mono 506.34
Ad Rate: Full Page Colour 551.02
Currency: United States Dollars
DAILY NEWSPAPER

The Star-Ledger - Trenton Bureau 16045
Editorial: 50 W State St, Trenton, New Jersey 08608-1220 **Tel:** 1 609 989-0012
Email: trenton@njadvancemedia.com
Language (s): English
DAILY NEWSPAPER

The Star-Ledger - Wall Township Bureau 75317
Editorial: 1305 Campus Pkwy Ste 200, Wall Township, New Jersey 07753-6813 **Tel:** 1 732 919-0381
Language (s): English
DAILY NEWSPAPER

StarNews 14320
Owner: GateHouse Media Inc.
Editorial: 1003 S 17th St, Wilmington, North Carolina 28401-8023 **Tel:** 1 910 343-2000
Email: breakingnews@starnewsonline.com **Web site:** http://www.starnewsonline.com
Freq: Daily; **Circ:** 35339 Not Audited
Publisher: Robert Gruber
Profile: StarNews is a daily newspaper aimed at providing local, national and global news coverage to the Wilmington, NC area. The paper's sections include local news, sports, entertainment, business, leisure and marketplace.
Language (s): English
Ad Rate: Full Page Mono 152.38
Ad Rate: Full Page Colour 226.41
Currency: United States Dollars
DAILY NEWSPAPER

The State 15328
Owner: McClatchy Newspapers
Editorial: 1401 Shop Rd, Columbia, South Carolina 29201-4843 **Tel:** 1 803 771-6161
Email: state@thestate.com **Web site:** http://www.thestate.com
Freq: Daily; **Circ:** 51154 Not Audited
Profile: The State is a daily four-color newspaper serving residents of Columbia, SC. The newspaper focuses on coverage of state and local matters instead of national stories. According to the publishers, "our readers have a greater opportunity to affect what happens at the state and local level than at the national level." The newspaper includes the following sections: Business, Classifieds, Columnists, Features, Opinion, Local News, Sports, Weather and Obituaries. The paper contains a strong local focus on politics and the government. As explained by the publishers, the aim of the newspaper is "to place the news in context, and to help readers have a deeper understanding of the issues." The publication is a 2002 winner of the Best in Business award, given by the Society of American Business Editors and Writers.
Language (s): English
Ad Rate: Full Page Mono 169.11
Ad Rate: Full Page Colour 185.77
Currency: United States Dollars
DAILY NEWSPAPER

The State Journal 14077
Owner: Boone Newspapers
Editorial: 1216 Wilkinson Blvd, Frankfort, Kentucky 40601-1243 **Tel:** 1 502 227-4556
Web site: http://www.state-journal.com
Freq: Daily; **Circ:** 8633 Not Audited
News Editor: Shannon Brock
Profile: The State Journal is written for residents of Frankfort, KY. It covers local news, sports, business, education and events.
Language (s): English
Ad Rate: Full Page Mono 11.50
Ad Rate: Full Page Colour 190.00
Currency: United States Dollars
DAILY NEWSPAPER

The State Journal-Register 13960
Owner: GateHouse Media Inc.
Editorial: 1 Copley Plz, Springfield, Illinois 62701-1927 **Tel:** 1 217 788-1513
Email: sjr@sj-r.com **Web site:** http://www.sj-r.com
Freq: Daily; **Circ:** 37171 Not Audited
Publisher: Clarissa Williams
Profile: The State Journal-Register is a daily newspaper for residents of Springfield, IL and the central part of the state. The publication covers local and national news, sports, business and arts & entertainment.
Language (s): English
Ad Rate: Full Page Mono 223.50
Ad Rate: Full Page Colour 327.21
Currency: United States Dollars
DAILY NEWSPAPER

Staten Island Advance 15424
Owner: Advance Publications, Inc.
Editorial: 950 W Fingerboard Rd, Staten Island, New York 10305-1453 **Tel:** 1 718 981-1234
Email: tips@siadvance.com **Web site:** http://www.silive.com
Freq: Daily; **Circ:** 30632 Not Audited
Publisher: Caroline Diamond Harrison; **Editor:** Brian Laline; **News Editor:** Richard Ryan
Profile: Staten Island Advance is a daily regional newspaper for residents of Staten Island, NY. The paper features business, sports, living, entertainment and national, regional and local news. The paper's travel section found in the Sunday paper is provided by The Star-Ledger, a sister publication. The mission of the publication is to provide the most accurate and comprehensive news for the readers with the highest of journalistic integrity.
Language (s): English
Ad Rate: Full Page Mono 65.89
Ad Rate: Full Page Colour 211.05
Currency: United States Dollars
DAILY NEWSPAPER

Staten Island Advance - New York Bureau 62341
Editorial: 9 City Hall, New York, New York 10007-1200 **Tel:** 1 718 304-7307
Language (s): English
DAILY NEWSPAPER

Statesboro Herald 13858
Owner: Morris Multimedia, Inc.
Editorial: 1 Proctor St, Statesboro, Georgia 30458-1387 **Tel:** 1 912 764-9031
Web site: http://www.statesboroherald.com/
Freq: Fri; **Circ:** 8544 Not Audited
Profile: Statesboro Herald is written for the residents of Bulloch County, GA. The outlet offers RSS (Really Simple Syndication).
Language (s): English
Ad Rate: Full Page Mono 13.04
Ad Rate: Full Page Colour 195.00
Currency: United States Dollars
DAILY NEWSPAPER

Statesman Journal 14561
Owner: Gannett Co. Inc.
Editorial: 280 Church St NE, Salem, Oregon 97301-3734 **Tel:** 1 503 399-6611
Email: newsroom@statesmanjournal.com **Web site:** http://www.statesmanjournal.com
Freq: Daily; **Circ:** 30066
Capital Bureau Chief: Carol Currie
Profile: The Statesman Journal is a daily newspaper published for the residents of Salem, OR and surrounding areas. The newspaper covers local and state news, business, sports, lifestyles and entertainment.
Language (s): English
Ad Rate: Full Page Mono 92.09
Ad Rate: Full Page Colour 124.48
Currency: United States Dollars
DAILY NEWSPAPER

Statesville Record & Landmark 14316
Owner: World Media Enterprises, Inc.
Editorial: 222 E Broad St, Statesville, North Carolina 28677-5325 **Tel:** 1 704 873-1451
Email: news@statesville.com **Web site:** http://www.statesville.com
Freq: Daily; **Circ:** 13269 Not Audited
Publisher: Tim Dearman; **Editor:** Dave Ibach
Profile: Statesville Record & Landmark is written for residents of Statesville, NC.
Language (s): English
Ad Rate: Full Page Mono 12.07
Currency: United States Dollars
DAILY NEWSPAPER

Steamboat Pilot & Today 14869
Owner: WorldWide Ltd. Liability Co.
Editorial: 1901 Curve Plaza, Steamboat Springs, Colorado 80487 **Tel:** 1 970 879-1502
Web site: http://www.steamboattoday.com/
Freq: Daily; **Circ:** 4543 Not Audited
Publisher: Suzanne Schlicht
Profile: Steamboat Pilot & Today is a local newspaper for residents of Steamboat Springs, CO. The paper covers local news, business, sports and arts & entertainment. It also covers national and statewide stories if they have a direct impact on the newspaper's readership.
Language (s): English
Ad Rate: Full Page Mono 12.52
Currency: United States Dollars
DAILY NEWSPAPER

Stephenville Empire-Tribune 14731
Owner: GateHouse Media Inc.
Editorial: 590 E South Loop, Stephenville, Texas 76401-5310 **Tel:** 1 254 965-3124
Email: news@empiretribune.com **Web site:** http://www.yourstephenvilletx.com
Freq: Daily; **Circ:** 4384 Not Audited
Profile: Stephenville Empire-Tribune's editorial mission is to be the premiere source of local information to the residents of Erath County, TX. Deadlines are at 2pm CT the day before publication. Deadlines for Sunday's edition are at noon CT the Friday before.
Language (s): English
Ad Rate: Full Page Mono 14.65
Ad Rate: Full Page Colour 125.00
Currency: United States Dollars
DAILY NEWSPAPER

Stevens Point Journal 14822
Owner: Gannett Co., Inc.
Editorial: 1200 3rd St, Stevens Point, Wisconsin 54481-2855 **Tel:** 1 715 344-6100
Email: news@stevenspointjournal.com **Web site:** http://www.stevenspointjournal.com
Freq: Daily; **Circ:** 6240 Not Audited
Profile: Combines with The Daily Tribune in Wisconsin Rapids and the Marshfield News-Herald on Sundays.
Language (s): English
Ad Rate: Full Page Mono 31.10
Ad Rate: Full Page Colour 357.00
Currency: United States Dollars
DAILY NEWSPAPER

Stuart News 16330
Owner: Gannett Co., Inc.
Editorial: 1939 SE Federal Hwy, Stuart, Florida 34994-3915 **Tel:** 1 772 287-1550
Email: yesdesk@tcpalm.com **Web site:** http://www.tcpalm.com
Freq: Daily; **Circ:** 51124 Not Audited
Publisher: Bob Brunjes; **Advertising Sales Manager:** Chris Stonecipher
Profile: Stuart News is published daily for residents of Stuart, FL and surrounding communities. The publication covers local news, features and community events. The newspaper has several sister publications including The Port St. Lucie (FL) News, Fort Pierce (FL) Tribune, Vero Beach (FL) Press Journal, and the Sebastian (FL) Sun. Press releases should be directed to the appropriate editor.
Language (s): English
Ad Rate: Full Page Mono 98.25
Currency: United States Dollars
DAILY NEWSPAPER

Sturgis Journal 14194
Owner: Liberty
Editorial: 209 John St, Sturgis, Michigan 49091-1459 **Tel:** 1 269 651-5407
Email: newsroom@sturgisjournal.com **Web site:** http://www.sturgisjournal.com
Freq: Daily; **Circ:** 7000 Not Audited
Advertising Sales Manager: Brenda Kane; **Editor:** Candice Phelps; **Publisher:** Dan Tollefson
Profile: Sturgis Journal is published daily for the residents of Sturgis, MI and surrounding areas. The newspaper covers local and regional news, business, sports, lifestyles and entertainment.
Language (s): English
Ad Rate: Full Page Mono 12.50
Ad Rate: Full Page Colour 235.00
Currency: United States Dollars
DAILY NEWSPAPER

Stuttgart Daily Leader 13706
Owner: GateHouse Media Inc.
Editorial: 111 W 6th St, Stuttgart, Arkansas 72160-4243 **Tel:** 1 870 673-8533
Email: editor@stuttgartdailyleader.com **Web site:** http://www.stuttgartdailyleader.com
Freq: Daily; **Circ:** 2552 Not Audited
Profile: Stuttgart Daily Leader is written for residents of Stuttgart, AR. It covers local news, sports and entertainment.
Language (s): English
Ad Rate: Full Page Mono 12.50
Ad Rate: Full Page Colour 200.00
Currency: United States Dollars
DAILY NEWSPAPER

Suffolk News-Herald 14766
Owner: Boone Newspapers Inc.
Editorial: 130 S Saratoga St, Suffolk, Virginia 23434-5323 **Tel:** 1 757 539-3437
Web site: http://www.suffolknewsherald.com
Freq: Daily; **Circ:** 3930 Not Audited
Publisher: John Carr
Profile: Suffolk News-Herald provides news and information for the Suffolk, VA area.
Language (s): English
Ad Rate: Full Page Mono 21.74
Ad Rate: Full Page Colour 350.00
Currency: United States Dollars
DAILY NEWSPAPER

Sullivan Daily Times 14021
Owner: Kelk Publishing
Editorial: 115 W Jackson St, Sullivan, Indiana 47882-1505 **Tel:** 1 812 268-6356
Email: editor.sdt@gmail.com **Web site:** http://www.sullivan-times.com
Freq: Daily; **Circ:** 4300
Editor: Pete Wilson
Profile: Sullivan Daily Times provides news and information for Sullivan, IN. Deadlines are at noon CT on the issue date.
Language (s): English
Ad Rate: Full Page Mono 7.25
Ad Rate: Full Page Colour 240.00
Currency: United States Dollars
DAILY NEWSPAPER

Sulphur Springs News-Telegram 14732
Owner: Southern Newspapers, Inc.
Editorial: 401 Church St, Sulphur Springs, Texas 75482-2681 **Tel:** 1 903 885-8663
Email: news@ssnewstelegram.com **Web site:** http://www.myssnews.com
Freq: Daily; **Circ:** 5500 Not Audited
News Editor: Faith Huffman
Profile: Sulphur Springs News-Telegram is a local daily newspaper written for residents of Sulphur Springs, TX. The newspaper primarily covers local news. Deadlines are at noon CT the day prior to publication.
Language (s): English
Ad Rate: Full Page Mono 11.48
Ad Rate: Full Page Colour 358.00
Currency: United States Dollars
DAILY NEWSPAPER

Summit Daily News 14929
Owner: Swift Newspapers
Editorial: 331 W Main St, Frisco, Colorado 80443 **Tel:** 1 970 668-3998
Email: news@summitdaily.com **Web site:** http://www.summitdaily.com
Freq: Daily; **Circ:** 9218 Not Audited
Publisher: Matt Sandberg
Profile: Summit Daily News provides news and information for the Frisco, CO area.
Language (s): English
Ad Rate: Full Page Mono 10.75
Currency: United States Dollars
DAILY NEWSPAPER

The Sun 13697
Owner: Paxton Media Group
Editorial: 518 Carson St, Jonesboro, Arkansas 72401-3128 **Tel:** 1 870 935-5525
Email: newsroom@jonesborosun.com **Web site:** http://www.jonesborosun.com
Freq: Daily; **Circ:** 19830 Not Audited
Publisher: David Mosesso; **Editor:** Chris Wessel
Profile: The Sun is published daily for the residents of Jonesboro, AR and surrounding areas. The newspaper covers local and state news, sports, lifestyles and entertainment.
Language (s): English
Ad Rate: Full Page Mono 27.25
Ad Rate: Full Page Colour 3440.25
Currency: United States Dollars
DAILY NEWSPAPER

The Sun 15425
Owner: Southern California News Group/Digital First Media
Editorial: 290 N D St Ste 102, San Bernardino, California 92401-1734 **Tel:** 1 909 889-9666
Web site: http://www.sbsun.com
Freq: Daily; **Circ:** 52281 Not Audited
Profile: The Sun is a daily newspaper that serves San Bernadino, CA. This paper is a part of the Southern California News Group, a subsidiary of Digital First Media. The publication features local, regional, state, national and international news, as well as sports, business and entertainment.
Language (s): English
Ad Rate: Full Page Mono 651.00
Ad Rate: Full Page Colour 2121.48
Currency: United States Dollars
DAILY NEWSPAPER

The Sun 15430
Owner: MediaNews Group
Editorial: 491 Dutton St, Lowell, Massachusetts 01854-4289 **Tel:** 1 978 458-7100
Web site: http://www.lowellsun.com
Freq: Daily; **Circ:** 24275 Not Audited
Editor: James Campanini
Profile: The Sun is a daily newspaper covering news for all of Northern Middlesex County and parts of Northern Essex County, MA and Southern New Hampshire. Coverage includes local news, politics, sports, lifestyle and entertainment.
Language (s): English
Ad Rate: Full Page Mono 54.30
Ad Rate: Full Page Colour 756.30
Currency: United States Dollars
DAILY NEWSPAPER

The Sun Chronicle 14114
Owner: United Communications Corp.
Editorial: 34 S Main St, Attleboro, Massachusetts 02703-2920 **Tel:** 1 508 222-7000
Email: news@thesunchronicle.com **Web site:** http://www.thesunchronicle.com
Freq: Daily; **Circ:** 12486 Not Audited
Publisher: Oreste D'Arconte; **Editor:** Mike Kirby
Profile: The Sun Chronicle is a daily newspaper for the Attleboro, MA area. It provides news, special reports, features, opinions, sports and announcements.
Language (s): English
Ad Rate: Full Page Mono 16.33
Ad Rate: Full Page Colour 395.00
Currency: United States Dollars
DAILY NEWSPAPER

Sun Herald 15402
Owner: McClatchy Newspapers
Editorial: 205 Debuys Rd, Gulfport, Mississippi 39507-2838 **Tel:** 1 228 896-2100
Web site: http://www.sunherald.com
Freq: Daily; **Circ:** 28966 Not Audited
Advertising Sales Manager: James Dick; **International & National News Editor:** Paul Hampton

Profile: Sun Herald is a daily newspaper for the residents of Biloxi, MS. The publication covers news, people and events nationally, as well as local news along the Mississippi Coast.
Language (s): English
Ad Rate: Full Page Mono 57.12
Ad Rate: Full Page Colour 191.36
Currency: United States Dollars
DAILY NEWSPAPER

Sun Journal 14154
Owner: Lewiston Sun Journal Inc.
Editorial: 104 Park St, Lewiston, Maine 04240-7202 **Tel:** 1 207 784-5411
Email: editor@sunjournal.com **Web site:** http://www.sunjournal.com
Freq: Daily; **Circ:** 44218 Not Audited
Profile: Sun Journal in Lewiston, ME is a daily newspaper covering local news and events.
Language (s): English
Ad Rate: Full Page Mono 43.80
Ad Rate: Full Page Colour 46.58
Currency: United States Dollars
DAILY NEWSPAPER

Sun Journal 14307
Owner: GateHouse Media Inc.
Editorial: 3200 Wellons Blvd, New Bern, North Carolina 28562-5234 **Tel:** 1 252 638-8101
Web site: http://www.newbernsj.com
Freq: Daily; **Circ:** 11310 Not Audited
Profile: Sun Journal is a daily newspaper for New Bern, NC and the surrounding communities. The newspaper covers local news, arts and entertainment, sports, business, and lifestyle stories. Contact the publication for circulation information and advertisements rates.
Language (s): English
Ad Rate: Full Page Mono 24.00
Ad Rate: Full Page Colour 435.00
Currency: United States Dollars
DAILY NEWSPAPER

The Sun News 14645
Owner: McClatchy Newspapers
Editorial: 914 Frontage Rd E, Myrtle Beach, South Carolina 29577-6700 **Tel:** 1 843 626-8555
Email: sneditors@thesunnews.com **Web site:** http://www.myrtlebeachonline.com/
Freq: Daily; **Circ:** 38304 Not Audited
Profile: The Sun News is a daily newspaper published for the residents of Myrtle Beach, SC and surrounding areas. It provides information on local news and community events.
Language (s): English
Ad Rate: Full Page Mono 59.05
Ad Rate: Full Page Colour 202.39
Currency: United States Dollars
DAILY NEWSPAPER

Sun-Telegraph 14950
Owner: Stevenson Newspapers
Editorial: 817 12th Ave, Sidney, Nebraska 69162-1625 **Tel:** 1 308 254-2818
Web site: http://www.suntelegraph.com
Freq: Daily; **Circ:** 2350 Not Audited
Publisher: Rob Langrell
Profile: Sun-Telegraph provides news and information for the Sidney, NE area.
Language (s): English
Ad Rate: Full Page Mono 9.50
Ad Rate: Full Page Colour 75.00
Currency: United States Dollars
DAILY NEWSPAPER

Super Express USA 879411
Owner: Media Express USA
Editorial: 111 John St. Floor 28, New York, New York 10038 **Tel:** 1 212 227-5800
Email: reklama@seusa.info **Web site:** http://www.se.pl
Freq: Mon thru Fri; **Circ:** 20000
Profile: Super Express USA is a daily newspaper published in Polish, and the largest newspaper serving the Polish-American audience in the United States, with editions for New York and Chicago. The U.S. edition is a division of the Super Express tabloid in Poland. News from Poland is featured, along with features on Polish-American everyday life.
Language (s): Polish
DAILY NEWSPAPER

Svet 394647
Owner: Svet Russian Media Group
Editorial: 350 E Dundee Rd, Ste 206, Wheeling, Illinois 60090-3104 **Tel:** 1 847 243-0838
Email: svet@svet.com **Web site:** http://www.svet.com
Freq: Mon thru Fri; **Circ:** 7500 Not Audited
Publisher: Emily Etman; **Advertising Sales Manager:** Kate Migdalovich
Profile: Svet is a free, daily newspaper published in the Russian language and serving the Russian community throughout the Chicago metro area. Since 1992, the paper has provided local and international news and features of interest to the Russian-American population. The Saturday edition, called Saturday Plus Weekly is devoted to photo stories, featuring the rich and famous here and abroad, with helpful hints on where to go and what to do in and around Chicago. The paper is available for pick-up at newsstands throughout Chicago.
Language (s): Russian
Ad Rate: Full Page Mono 10.67
Currency: United States Dollars
DAILY NEWSPAPER

Sweetwater Reporter 14733
Owner: Horizon Publications
Editorial: 112 W 3rd St, Sweetwater, Texas 79556 **Tel:** 1 325 236-6677
Email: editor@sweetwaterreporter.com **Web site:** http://www.sweetwaterreporter.com
Freq: Daily; **Circ:** 3724
Editor: Tatiana Rodriguez
Profile: Sweetwater Reporter provides news and information for Nolan County, TX and surrounding communities. Published daily except Saturdays, the lead time and deadline for the weekdays are 10am CT on the issue date. For the Sunday edition, editorial submissions must be in by 10am CT Saturday.
Language (s): English
Ad Rate: Full Page Mono 10.75
Ad Rate: Full Page Colour 250.00
Currency: United States Dollars
DAILY NEWSPAPER

Tahlequah Daily Press 14546
Owner: Community Newspaper Holdings, Inc.
Editorial: 106 W 2nd St, Tahlequah, Oklahoma 74464-4724 **Tel:** 1 918 456-8833
Email: news@tahlequahdailypress.com **Web site:** http://www.tahlequahdailypress.com
Freq: Daily; **Circ:** 6881 Not Audited
Profile: Tahlequah Daily Press is a newspaper serving the community of Tahlequah, OK. The publication covers local news, sports and community events. Deadlines are at 11am CT the day before publication.
Language (s): English
Ad Rate: Full Page Mono 8.50
Ad Rate: Full Page Colour 85.00
Currency: United States Dollars
DAILY NEWSPAPER

Tallahassee Democrat 15359
Owner: Gannett Co. Inc.
Editorial: 277 N Magnolia Dr, Tallahassee, Florida 32301-2664 **Tel:** 1 850 599-2100
Email: letters@tallahassee.com **Web site:** http://www.tallahassee.com
Freq: Daily; **Circ:** 29181 Not Audited
Publisher: Skip Foster
Profile: Tallahassee Democrat is a daily newspaper published for the residents of Tallahassee and Leon County, FL. The paper covers local news, business, city and state government, entertainment, high school and college sports, lifestyle, and entertainment.
Language (s): English
Ad Rate: Full Page Mono 103.25
Ad Rate: Full Page Colour 339.98
Currency: United States Dollars
DAILY NEWSPAPER

Tampa Bay Times 15290
Owner: Poynter Institute for Media Studies
Editorial: 490 1st Ave S Fl 4, Saint Petersburg, Florida 33701-4204 **Tel:** 1 727 893-8111
Email: local@tampabay.com **Web site:** http://www.tampabay.com
Freq: Daily; **Circ:** 166995 Not Audited
News Editor: Dawn Cate; **Advertising Sales Manager:** Kelly Spamer
Profile: Tampa Bay Times (formerly St. Petersburg Times) is a general-interest broadsheet newspaper written for readers in the greater St. Petersburg, Tampa, and Clearwater, FL. The mission of the newspaper is to provide news and information to the general public.
Language (s): English
Ad Rate: Full Page Mono 770.00
Ad Rate: Full Page Colour 2431.86
Currency: United States Dollars
DAILY NEWSPAPER

Tampa Bay Times - Hernando Bureau 15685
Editorial: 13045 Cortez Blvd, Brooksville, Florida 34613-4838 **Tel:** 1 352 754-6100
Email: hernando@tampabay.com **Web site:** http://www.tampabay.com/news/hernando
Bureau Chief: Mike Konrad
Language (s): English
DAILY NEWSPAPER

Tampa Bay Times - Pasco County Bureau 15690
Editorial: 11321 US Highway 19, Port Richey, Florida 34668-1416 **Tel:** 1 727 869-6235
Email: pasco@tampabay.com **Web site:** http://www.tampabay.com/news/pasco
Language (s): English
DAILY NEWSPAPER

Tampa Bay Times - Pinellas County Bureau 15686
Editorial: 1130 Cleveland St, Clearwater, Florida 33755-4841 **Tel:** 1 727 445-4111
Language (s): English
DAILY NEWSPAPER

Tampa Bay Times - Riverview Bureau 231319
Editorial: 11268 Winthrop Main St Ste 101, Riverview, Florida 33578-4266 **Tel:** 1 813 661-2425
Email: local@sptimes.com
Language (s): English
DAILY NEWSPAPER

Tampa Bay Times - Tallahassee Bureau 15692
Editorial: 336 E College Ave Ste 303, Tallahassee, Florida 32301-1560 **Tel:** 1 850 224-7263
Bureau Chief: Steve Bousquet
Language (s): English
DAILY NEWSPAPER

Tampa Bay Times - Tampa Bureau 15693
Editorial: 1000 N Ashley Dr, Tampa, Florida 33602-3716 **Tel:** 1 813 226-3300
Email: tampa@tampabay.com
Language (s): English
Ad Rate: Full Page Mono 5.00
Currency: United States Dollars
DAILY NEWSPAPER

Tampa Bay Times - Washington Bureau 15487
Editorial: 1100 Connecticut Ave NW Ste 440, Washington, District Of Columbia 20036-4152
Tel: 1 202 463-0571
Bureau Chief: Alex Leary
Language (s): English
DAILY NEWSPAPER

Taunton Daily Gazette 14135
Owner: GateHouse Media Inc.
Editorial: 5 Cohannet St, Taunton, Massachusetts 02780-3903 **Tel:** 1 508 880-9000
Email: newsroom@tauntongazette.com **Web site:** http://www.tauntongazette.com
Freq: Daily; **Circ:** 5642 Not Audited
Profile: Taunton Daily Gazette is a local daily newspaper for the residents of Taunton, MA and the surrounding area. The publication covers local and national news, community events and sports.
Language (s): English
Ad Rate: Full Page Mono 22.95
Ad Rate: Full Page Colour 250.00
Currency: United States Dollars
DAILY NEWSPAPER

Taylor Daily Press 14734
Owner: Blackland Publications
Editorial: 211 W 3rd St, Taylor, Texas 76574-3518 **Tel:** 1 512 352-8535
Email: news@taylordailypress.net **Web site:** http://www.taylordailypress.net
Freq: Mon thru Fri; **Circ:** 5300 Not Audited
Profile: Taylor Daily Press is a newspaper serving the residents of Taylor, TX. The publication covers local news, entertainment, sports and community events.
Language (s): English
Ad Rate: Full Page Mono 8.75
Ad Rate: Full Page Colour 200.00
Currency: United States Dollars
DAILY NEWSPAPER

tbt* 390939
Owner: Poynter Institute for Media Studies
Editorial: 490 1st Ave S Fl 4, Saint Petersburg, Florida 33701-4204 **Tel:** 1 727 893-8111
Email: tbteditors@tampabay.com **Web site:** http://www.tampabay.com/tbt
Freq: Mon thru Fri; **Circ:** 78047 Not Audited
Advertising Sales Manager: Dawn Philips
Profile: tbt*, launched as a weekly newspaper in September 2004, also known as the Tampa Bay Times, is a free, commuter and alternative daily newspaper that is distributed each weekday. It contains concise versions of the day's local and national news, along with sports, entertainment and consumer features. It provides restaurant reviews, movie listings and information about places to go and things to do in the area. The Friday edition features a special entertainment pullout section. Advertising deadlines are at noon ET.
Language (s): English
Ad Rate: Full Page Mono 44.00
Ad Rate: Full Page Colour 66.26
Currency: United States Dollars
DAILY NEWSPAPER

Telegram & Gazette 15384
Owner: GateHouse Media Inc.
Editorial: 100 Front St Fl 5, Worcester, Massachusetts 01608-1425 **Tel:** 1 508 793-9100
Email: newstips@telegram.com **Web site:** http://www.telegram.com
Freq: Daily; **Circ:** 69406
Profile: Established in 1866, the Telegram & Gazette is a daily broadsheet providing local, national, and international news coverage to the Worcester, MA area. The Telegram & Gazette is a morning paper. The publication's coverage includes technology, real estate, business news, food, travel, music, the arts, and lifestyle topics.
Language (s): English
Ad Rate: Full Page Mono 128.28
Ad Rate: Full Page Colour 95.87
Currency: United States Dollars
DAILY NEWSPAPER

The Telegraph 13847
Owner: McClatchy Newspapers
Editorial: 487 Cherry St, Macon, Georgia 31201-7972 **Tel:** 1 478 744-4200
Email: breaking@macon.com **Web site:** http://www.macon.com
Freq: Daily; **Circ:** 36960 Not Audited
Advertising Sales Manager: Lisa Berrian
Profile: The Telegraph is a daily newspaper that covers local and regional news. It includes sports, lifestyle, arts & entertainment and business. The paper also produces editions specifically for Houston and Peach Counties, GA.
Language (s): English
Ad Rate: Full Page Mono 81.30
Ad Rate: Full Page Colour 274.50
Currency: United States Dollars
DAILY NEWSPAPER

The Telegraph 13909
Owner: Civitas Media, LLC
Editorial: 111 E Broadway, Alton, Illinois 62002-6218 **Tel:** 1 618 463-2500
Email: telegraph@thetelegraph.com **Web site:** http://www.thetelegraph.com
Freq: Daily; **Circ:** 24032 Not Audited
Edwardsville Bureau Chief: Sanford Schmidt; **Publisher:** Jim Shrader
Profile: The Telegraph is a local daily newspaper for residents of Madison, Jersey, Calhoun, Macoupin and Greene counties, IL.
Language (s): English
Ad Rate: Full Page Mono 45.33
Ad Rate: Full Page Colour 149.36
Currency: United States Dollars
DAILY NEWSPAPER

The Telegraph 14355
Owner: Ogden Newspapers, Inc.
Editorial: 110 Main St Ste 1, Nashua, New Hampshire 03060-2723 **Tel:** 1 603 594-1266
Email: news@nashuatelegraph.com **Web site:** http://www.nashuatelegraph.com
Freq: Daily; **Circ:** 14473 Not Audited
Profile: The Telegraph is a daily newspaper for residents of Nashua, NH and Southern New Hampshire. The paper covers local news, weather, sports, community events, business, education, arts & entertainment, lifestyle and other information of interest to community residents.
Language (s): English
Ad Rate: Full Page Mono 35.10
Ad Rate: Full Page Colour 120.85
Currency: United States Dollars
DAILY NEWSPAPER

The Telegraph - Warner Robins Bureau 153035
Editorial: 16 Green St Ste B, Warner Robins, Georgia 31093-2606 **Tel:** 1 478 923-5650
Profile: The Telegraph, formerly The Macon Telegraph, maintains its own office and shares its editorial staff with the main office in Macon, GA. The bureau covers Houston County news, information and events.
Language (s): English
DAILY NEWSPAPER

Telegraph Herald 13876
Owner: Woodward Communications, Inc.
Editorial: 801 Bluff St, Dubuque, Iowa 52001-4661 **Tel:** 1 563 588-5611
Email: thonline@wcinet.com **Web site:** http://www.telegraphherald.com
Freq: Daily; **Circ:** 24586 Not Audited
News Editor: Monty Gilles
Profile: Telegraph Herald is a general interest daily newspaper covering topics such as news, employment, education, tourism, recreation, holidays, events, special interests, sports, business, health and family. The weekend edition prints on Saturday.
Language (s): English
Ad Rate: Full Page Mono 1.83
Currency: United States Dollars
DAILY NEWSPAPER

Telluride Daily Planet 14930
Editorial: 307 E Colorado, Telluride, Colorado 81435 **Tel:** 1 970 728-9788
Email: editor@telluridedailyplanet.com **Web site:** http://www.telluridenews.com
Freq: Daily; **Circ:** 3350
Advertising Sales Manager: Maureen Pellison
Profile: Telluride Daily Planet is a daily local paper serving residents in the Telluride, CO area.
Language (s): English
Ad Rate: Full Page Mono 11.00
Ad Rate: Full Page Colour 14.00
Currency: United States Dollars
DAILY NEWSPAPER

Temple Daily Telegram 14916
Owner: Mayborn Enterprises
Editorial: 10 S 3rd St, Temple, Texas 76501-7619 **Tel:** 1 254 778-4444
Email: tdt@tdtnews.com **Web site:** http://www.tdtnews.com/
Freq: Daily; **Circ:** 16525 Not Audited
Advertising Sales Manager: Gary Garner; **Editor & Publisher:** Sue Mayborn
Profile: Temple Daily Telegram is a newspaper serving the residents of Temple, Texas. The publication covers local news, community events, business, and sports. The hours are 8 a.m. to 5 p.m. Monday-Friday, 8 a.m. to noon Saturday
Language (s): English
Ad Rate: Full Page Mono 24.50
Ad Rate: Full Page Colour 536.00
Currency: United States Dollars
DAILY NEWSPAPER

The Tennessean 15436
Owner: Gannett Co., Inc.
Editorial: 1100 Broadway, Nashville, Tennessee 37203-3116 **Tel:** 1 615 259-8000
Email: local@tennessean.com **Web site:** http://www.tennessean.com
Freq: Daily; **Circ:** 83645 Not Audited

Profile: The Tennessean is a daily newspaper in Nashville, Tennessee, and covers local and regional news, as well as entertainment, lifestyle, sports and business. The circulation area covers 39 counties in middle Tennessee and eight counties in Southern Kentucky.
Language (s): English
Ad Rate: Full Page Mono 188.00
Ad Rate: Full Page Colour 197.92
Currency: United States Dollars
DAILY NEWSPAPER

Terrell Tribune 14735
Owner: Hartman Newspapers, Inc.
Editorial: 150 9th St, Terrell, Texas 75160-3061 **Tel:** 1 972 563-6476
Email: editor@terrelltribune.com **Web site:** http://www.terrelltribune.com
Freq: Daily; **Circ:** 6200 Not Audited
Profile: Terrell Tribune is published daily for the residents of Terrell, TX and surrounding areas. The newspaper covers local and state news, business, sports, lifestyles and entertainment. Editorial deadlines are daily at noon CT.
Language (s): English
Ad Rate: Full Page Mono 10.00
Ad Rate: Full Page Colour 330.00
Currency: United States Dollars
DAILY NEWSPAPER

Texarkana Gazette 14736
Owner: Wehco Media Inc.
Editorial: 101 E Broad St, Texarkana, Arkansas 71854-5901 **Tel:** 1 870 330-7550
Email: clerk@texarkanagazette.com **Web site:** http://www.texarkanagazette.com
Freq: Daily; **Circ:** 17807 Not Audited
News Editor: Andrea Miller; **Editor:** Les Minor
Profile: Texarkana Gazette is the daily newspaper for the community of Texarkana, TX. The publication covers local news, sports, entertainment and community events. Deadlines are at 9am CT.
Language (s): English
Ad Rate: Full Page Mono 26.84
Ad Rate: Full Page Colour 33.27
Currency: United States Dollars
DAILY NEWSPAPER

Thomasville Times-Enterprise 13851
Owner: Community Newspaper Holdings, Inc.
Editorial: 106 South St, Thomasville, Georgia 31792-6061 **Tel:** 1 229 226-2400
Web site: http://www.timesenterprise.com
Freq: Daily; **Circ:** 7927 Not Audited
Profile: Thomasville Times-Enterprise's editorial mission is to provide news and information to the Thomasville, GA community.
Language (s): English
Ad Rate: Full Page Mono 22.05
Ad Rate: Full Page Colour 340.00
Currency: United States Dollars
DAILY NEWSPAPER

Three Rivers Commercial-News 14195
Owner: Three Rivers Commercial, Inc.
Editorial: 124 N Main St, Three Rivers, Michigan 49093-1522 **Tel:** 1 269 279-7488
Email: news@threeriversnews.com **Web site:** http://www.threeriversnews.com
Freq: Daily; **Circ:** 2940 Not Audited
Advertising Sales Manager: Marnie Apa; **Publisher:** Dirk Milliman
Profile: Three Rivers Commercial-News provides local news and sports coverage for the Three Rivers, MI area.
Language (s): English
Ad Rate: Full Page Mono 11.07
Ad Rate: Full Page Colour 275.00
Currency: United States Dollars
DAILY NEWSPAPER

Tifton Gazette 13852
Owner: Community Newspaper Holdings, Inc.
Editorial: 211 Tift Ave N, Tifton, Georgia 31794-4463 **Tel:** 1 229 382-4321
Web site: http://www.tiftongazette.com
Freq: Daily; **Circ:** 9500 Not Audited
Profile: Tifton Gazette provides local news and sports coverage for the Tifton, GA area.
Language (s): English
Ad Rate: Full Page Mono 21.70
Ad Rate: Full Page Colour 294.00
Currency: United States Dollars
DAILY NEWSPAPER

The Times 13843
Owner: Morris Multimedia Inc.
Editorial: 345 Green St NW, Gainesville, Georgia 30501-3370 **Tel:** 1 770 532-1234
Email: news@gainesvilletimes.com **Web site:** http://www.gainesvilletimes.com
Freq: Daily; **Circ:** 22000 Not Audited
Publisher: Charlotte Atkins
Profile: The Times was founded in 1947. It provides daily news, including features, entertainment, business and sports for the residents of Gainesville, GA.
Language (s): English
Ad Rate: Full Page Mono 23.12
Ad Rate: Full Page Colour 402.00
Currency: United States Dollars
DAILY NEWSPAPER

The Times 13951
Owner: Small Newspaper Group
Editorial: 110 W Jefferson St, Ottawa, Illinois 61350-5010 **Tel:** 1 815 433-2000
Email: newsroom@mywebtimes.com **Web site:** http://www.mywebtimes.com
Freq: Mon thru Fri; **Circ:** 15850 Not Audited
Advertising Sales Manager: Mike Bertok; **Editor:** Mike Murphy; **Publisher:** John Newby
Profile: The Times, formerly known as the Daily Times, is a newspaper serving the Ottawa community, and the surrounding areas of Lasselle County, IL. They do not want to receive ANYTHING via fax.
Language (s): English
Ad Rate: Full Page Mono 18.90
Ad Rate: Full Page Colour 230.00
Currency: United States Dollars
DAILY NEWSPAPER

The Times 13983
Owner: Paxton Media Group
Editorial: 211 N Jackson St, Frankfort, Indiana 46041-1936 **Tel:** 1 765 659-4622
Email: news@ftimes.com **Web site:** http://www.chronicle-tribune.com/ftimes/
Freq: Daily; **Circ:** 6000 Not Audited
Publisher: Sharon Bardonner
Profile: The Times is a local, weekly newspaper for the residents of Frankfort, IN. The paper includes news, weather, travel, sports and community events.
Language (s): English
Ad Rate: Full Page Mono 18.00
Ad Rate: Full Page Colour 210.00
Currency: United States Dollars
DAILY NEWSPAPER

The Times 14364
Owner: NJ Advance Media
Editorial: 413 River View Plz, Trenton, New Jersey 08611-3420 **Tel:** 1 609 989-5454
Email: news@njtimes.com **Web site:** http://www.nj.com/times
Freq: Daily; **Circ:** 31971 Not Audited
Editor: Kelly King
Profile: The Times is published daily and distributed throughout Mercer County, NJ. The newspaper provides readers with local and national news. Readers will also find other features, such as sports, business, education, entertainment, lifestyle, community and classifieds.
Language (s): English
Ad Rate: Full Page Mono 62.42
Ad Rate: Full Page Colour 270.57
Currency: United States Dollars
DAILY NEWSPAPER

The Times 14636
Owner: R.I.S.N. Operations Inc.
Editorial: 23 Exchange St, Pawtucket, Rhode Island 02860-2026 **Tel:** 1 401 722-4000
Email: editor@pawtuckettimes.com **Web site:** http://www.pawtuckettimes.com
Freq: Daily; **Circ:** 5068 Not Audited
Profile: The Times is a local daily newspaper for the residents of Pawtucket, Central Falls, Lincoln, East Providence and Cumberland, RI and Seekonk and Attleboro, MA. The publication covers local news and community events.
Language (s): English
Ad Rate: Full Page Mono 21.71
Ad Rate: Full Page Colour 23.44
Currency: United States Dollars
DAILY NEWSPAPER

The Times 15277
Owner: Lee Enterprises, Inc.
Editorial: 601 45th Ave, Munster, Indiana 46321-2875 **Tel:** 1 219 933-3200
Email: newstips@nwitimes.com **Web site:** http://www.nwitimes.com
Freq: Daily; **Circ:** 71184 Not Audited
Editor: Bob Heisse; **Publisher:** Christopher White
Profile: The Times is a daily newspaper that serves Munster, IN; Lake County, IN; the Southern part of Cook County, IL; the west end of Porter County, IN; and the Northwest portion of LaPorte County, IN. The publication covers local, state, national and international news, as well as sports, business and arts & entertainment.
Language (s): English
Ad Rate: Full Page Mono 90.75
Ad Rate: Full Page Colour 108.90
Currency: United States Dollars
DAILY NEWSPAPER

The Times 15398
Owner: Gannett Co., Inc.
Editorial: 222 Lake St, Shreveport, Louisiana 71101-3738 **Tel:** 1 318 459-3200
Email: shreveporttimes@gannett.com **Web site:** http://www.shreveporttimes.com
Freq: Daily; **Circ:** 36111 Not Audited
Profile: The Times, founded in 1872, is a daily, morning broadsheet newspaper distributed in Northwestern Louisiana. It covers local, regional and national news, as well as local sports, religion, politics, entertainment and lifestyle stories. Contact the appropriate section editor with press releases and general questions. The lead time varies, but can be as short as one day. Advertising is due by 5pm CT.
Language (s): English
Ad Rate: Full Page Mono 145.00
Ad Rate: Full Page Colour 368.77
Currency: United States Dollars
DAILY NEWSPAPER

The Times 19195
Owner: The Paper of Montgomery County
Editorial: 920 Logan St Ste 101, Noblesville, Indiana 46060-2225 **Tel:** 1 317 770-7777
Email: news@thetimes24-7.com **Web site:** http://thetimes24-7.com
Freq: Daily; **Circ:** 7074 Not Audited
Editor: Betsy Reason; **Publisher:** Tim Timmons
Profile: Noblesville Daily Times is a local newspaper published for the residents of Arcadia, Atlanta, Carmel, Cicero, Fishers, Noblesville, Sheridan and Westfield in Hamilton County, Indiana. It covers community events, local news, education, government, weather and sports. Deadlines are on Thursdays at noon ET. The paper does not publish on Tuesdays or Sundays.
Language (s): English
Ad Rate: Full Page Mono 11.50
Ad Rate: Full Page Colour 14.71
Currency: United States Dollars
DAILY NEWSPAPER

The Times - Crown Point Bureau 76059
Editorial: 2080 N Main St, Crown Point, Indiana 46307-2002 **Tel:** 1 219 662-5300
Email: newstips@nwi.com
Language (s): English
DAILY NEWSPAPER

The Times - Indianapolis Bureau 829848
Editorial: 150 W Market St Ste 135, Indianapolis, Indiana 46204-2841 **Tel:** 1 317 637-9078
Bureau Chief: Dan Carden
Language (s): English
DAILY NEWSPAPER

The Times - Portage Bureau 152135
Editorial: 3410 Delta Dr, Portage, Indiana 46368-5120 **Tel:** 1 219 762-4334
Language (s): English
DAILY NEWSPAPER

The Times - Valparaiso Bureau 76062
Editorial: 1111 Glendale Blvd, Valparaiso, Indiana 46383-3724 **Tel:** 1 219 462-5151
Profile: The Valparaiso bureau staff put out the paper's zoned edition, The Vidette Times.
Language (s): English
DAILY NEWSPAPER

The Times & Democrat 14646
Owner: Lee Enterprises, Inc.
Editorial: 1010 Broughton St, Orangeburg, South Carolina 29115-5962 **Tel:** 1 803 533-5500
Email: news@timesanddemocrat.com **Web site:** http://www.thetandd.com
Freq: Daily; **Circ:** 13259
Editor: Lee Harter; **Publisher:** Cathy Hughes
Profile: The Times & Democrat is a daily newspaper written for the residents of Central South Carolina. It covers local news, sports, features and events. Deadlines are the day prior to publication between 6pm and 8pm ET.
Language (s): English
Ad Rate: Full Page Mono 18.23
Ad Rate: Full Page Colour 571.00
Currency: United States Dollars
DAILY NEWSPAPER

The Times Argus 14770
Owner: Maine Today Media Inc.
Editorial: 540 N Main St, Barre, Vermont 05641-2504 **Tel:** 1 802 479-0191 3
Email: news@timesargus.com **Web site:** http://www.timesargus.com
Freq: Daily; **Circ:** 7216 Not Audited
Publisher: R. John Mitchell; **Editor:** Steven Pappas
Profile: The Times Argus written for the residents of Barre, VT. It covers local news, sports and state government.
Language (s): English
Ad Rate: Full Page Mono 13.98
Ad Rate: Full Page Colour 40.83
Currency: United States Dollars
DAILY NEWSPAPER

Times Herald 14418
Owner: Bradford Publishing Co.
Editorial: 639 W Norton Dr, Olean, New York 14760-1402 **Tel:** 1 716 372-3121
Email: news@oleantimesherald.com **Web site:** http://www.oleantimesherald.com
Freq: Daily; **Circ:** 10083 Not Audited
Publisher: Jim Bonn; **Advertising Sales Manager:** Debbie Perry
Profile: Times Herald is a daily newspaper based in Olean, NY. It covers community news, sports, births and deaths, business, weather and other news for St. Bonaventure University and Cattaraugus, Allegany, McKean, Potter and Cameron Counties.
Language (s): English
Ad Rate: Full Page Mono 22.27
Currency: United States Dollars
DAILY NEWSPAPER

Times Herald 14604
Owner: Journal Register Company
Editorial: 410 Markley St, Norristown, Pennsylvania 19401-4617 **Tel:** 1 610 272-2500
Email: editors@timesherald.com **Web site:** http://www.timesherald.com
Freq: Daily; **Circ:** 10138 Not Audited
Publisher: Edward Condra
Profile: Times Herald is published daily for the residents of Norristown, PA and surrounding areas. The newspaper provides information about local, national and global news, business, sports, entertainment and features.
Language (s): English
Ad Rate: Full Page Mono 41.55
Ad Rate: Full Page Colour 690.00
Currency: United States Dollars
DAILY NEWSPAPER

The Times Herald 14969
Owner: Gannett Co., Inc.
Editorial: 911 Military St, Port Huron, Michigan 48060-5414 **Tel:** 1 810 985-7171
Email: timesherald@gannett.com **Web site:** http://www.thetimesherald.com
Freq: Daily; **Circ:** 15016
Editor: Michael Eckert
Profile: Times Herald is published daily for the residents of Port Huron, MI and surrounding areas. The newspaper covers local and state news, business, sports, lifestyles and entertainment.
Language (s): English
Ad Rate: Full Page Mono 40.55
Currency: United States Dollars
DAILY NEWSPAPER

Times Herald-Record 15457
Owner: GateHouse Media Inc.
Editorial: 40 Mulberry St, Middletown, New York 10940-6302 **Tel:** 1 845 343-2181
Email: news@th-record.com **Web site:** http://www.recordonline.com
Freq: Daily; **Circ:** 45859 Not Audited
Publisher: Joe Vanderhoof
Profile: Times Herald-Record is a daily newspaper serving residents of the Hudson Valley and the Catskills, NY. The newspaper covers local, national and international news, as well as business, sports, arts & entertainment, editorials and community events.
Language (s): English
Ad Rate: Full Page Mono 105.20
Ad Rate: Full Page Colour 344.45
Currency: United States Dollars
DAILY NEWSPAPER

Times Herald-Record - Kingston Bureau 16201
Editorial: 34 John St, Kingston, New York 12401-3822 **Tel:** 1 845 340-4910
Language (s): English
DAILY NEWSPAPER

The Times Leader 14471
Owner: Ogden Newspapers
Editorial: 200 S 4th St, Martins Ferry, Ohio 43935-1312 **Tel:** 1 740 633-1131
Email: timesleader@timesleaderonline.com **Web site:** http://www.timesleaderonline.com
Freq: Daily; **Circ:** 10389 Not Audited
Publisher: Lori Figurski
Profile: The Times Leader is a daily, local newspaper for the Martins Ferry, OH area. It covers local news, sports, business, government and lifestyle stories. The paper also covers national stories if they are of interest to the readership.
Language (s): English
Ad Rate: Full Page Mono 22.92
Ad Rate: Full Page Colour 255.00
Currency: United States Dollars
DAILY NEWSPAPER

The Times Leader 14634
Owner: Civitas Media
Editorial: 15 N Main St, Wilkes-Barre, Pennsylvania 18711-0250 **Tel:** 1 570 829-7100
Email: news@timesleader.com **Web site:** http://www.timesleader.com
Freq: Daily; **Circ:** 33632 Not Audited
News Editor: Dan Burnett; **Publisher:** Doug Olsson; **Advertising Sales Manager:** Anthony Spina
Profile: The Times Leader in Wilkes-Barre, PA serves Northeastern PA and covers local and national news, sports, arts & entertainment, business and lifestyle topics.
Language (s): English
Ad Rate: Full Page Mono 63.03
Ad Rate: Full Page Colour 495.00
Currency: United States Dollars
DAILY NEWSPAPER

The Times News 14595
Owner: Pencor Services
Editorial: 594 Blakeslee Boulevard Dr W, Lehighton, Pennsylvania 18235-9818 **Tel:** 1 610 377-2051
Email: tneditor@tnonline.com **Web site:** http://www.tnonline.com
Freq: Daily; **Circ:** 11623
Publisher: Fred Masenheimer; **Editor:** Emmett McCall
Profile: The Times News is a daily newspaper serving the counties of Carbon, Schuylkill, Lehigh, Monroe and Northampton, PA. The publication not only covers local news in each county, but state-wide news as well. Sections include news, sports, calendars, announcements and classified ads.
Language (s): English
Ad Rate: Full Page Mono 10.95
Ad Rate: Full Page Colour 19.24
Currency: United States Dollars
DAILY NEWSPAPER

Times Observer 14626
Owner: Ogden Newspapers
Editorial: 205 Pennsylvania Ave W, Warren, Pennsylvania 16365-2412 **Tel:** 1 814 723-8200
Email: editorial@timesobserver.com **Web site:** http://www.timesobserver.com
Freq: Daily; **Circ:** 8798 Not Audited
Publisher: Bob Patchen
Profile: Times Observer's editorial mission is to provide local, national, and international news and information. This publication serves residents of Warren County, PA. Deadline for Warren Times Observer is the day before issue date.
Language (s): English
Ad Rate: Full Page Mono 21.62
Ad Rate: Full Page Colour 30.18
Currency: United States Dollars
DAILY NEWSPAPER

The Times Record 14153
Owner: Sample News Group
Editorial: 3 Business Pkwy, Brunswick, Maine 04011-7390 **Tel:** 1 207 729-3311
Email: news@timesrecord.com **Web site:** http://www.timesrecord.com
Freq: Daily; **Circ:** 7722 Not Audited
Profile: The Times Record serves the mid-Coastal Maine area. It focuses on local news and sports.
Language (s): English
Ad Rate: Full Page Mono 16.50
Ad Rate: Full Page Colour 300.00
Currency: United States Dollars
DAILY NEWSPAPER

Times Record 15392
Owner: Stephens Media
Editorial: 3600 Wheeler Ave, Fort Smith, Arkansas 72901-6621 **Tel:** 1 479 785-7700
Email: press@swtimes.com **Web site:** http://www.swtimes.com
Freq: Daily
Profile: Times Record is a daily newspaper for the residents of Fort Smith, AR.
Language (s): English
Ad Rate: Full Page Mono 40.98
Ad Rate: Full Page Colour 137.70
Currency: United States Dollars
DAILY NEWSPAPER

Times Record News 14744
Owner: Gannett Co., Inc.
Editorial: 1301 Lamar St, Wichita Falls, Texas 76301-7032 **Tel:** 1 940 767-8341
Web site: http://www.timesrecordnews.com
Freq: Daily; **Circ:** 18574 Not Audited
Publisher: Dwayne Bivona; **Editor:** Deanna Watson
Profile: Times Record News is a daily newspaper written for the residents of Wichita Falls, TX. The newspaper covers current news and events. The deadline for the publication is 5pm CT, the day before issue date.
Language (s): English
Ad Rate: Full Page Mono 38.91
Ad Rate: Full Page Colour 184.20
Currency: United States Dollars
DAILY NEWSPAPER

Times Recorder 14505
Owner: Gannett Co., Inc.
Editorial: 3871 Gorsky Dr Ste G1, Zanesville, Ohio 43701-3449 **Tel:** 1 740 452-4561
Email: tmews@zanesvilletimesrecorder.com **Web site:** http://www.zanesvilletimesrecorder.com
Freq: Daily; **Circ:** 11186 Not Audited
Profile: Times Recorder is a daily newspaper providing News and Current Affairs information for the residents of Muskingum County and Zanesville, OH.
Language (s): English
Ad Rate: Full Page Mono 35.50
Ad Rate: Full Page Colour 335.00
Currency: United States Dollars
DAILY NEWSPAPER

Times Telegram 14404
Owner: GateHouse Media, Inc.
Editorial: 111 Green St, Herkimer, New York 13350-1914 **Tel:** 1 315 866-2220
Email: news@timestelegram.com **Web site:** http://www.timestelegram.com
Freq: Daily; **Circ:** 6657 Not Audited
Profile: The Times Telegram is a daily, local newspaper written for the local residents of Herkimer and Little Falls, NY. The newspaper covers local news and events in Herkimer County, NY, and is the result of an August 2015 merger between the Herkimer Telegram and Little Falls Times.
Language (s): English
Ad Rate: Full Page Mono 10.66
Ad Rate: Full Page Colour 310.00
Currency: United States Dollars
DAILY NEWSPAPER

Times Union 15372
Owner: Hearst Newspapers
Editorial: 645 Albany Shaker Rd, Albany, New York 12211-1158 **Tel:** 1 518 454-5694
Email: tucitydesk@timesunion.com **Web site:** http://www.timesunion.com
Freq: Daily; **Circ:** 45275 Not Audited
Publisher: George Hearst; **Editor:** Rex Smith
Profile: Times Union is a daily newspaper serving the capital region of New York, which includes Albany, Schenectady, Troy, Rensselaer and Saratoga ONLY. It provides readers with the latest news, weather, entertainment and sports information. The paper dates back to 1856. After a merger with a competitor, the Evening Union, the Times Union was forged in 1891. In 1937, Hearst took over the newspaper and ended 72 years of afternoon publication by moving the Times Union into the morning field. The paper will no longer accept event listings submitted by phone, fax, email or traditional mail. Print calendars will only include those events submitted online. To submit, go to http://events.timesunion.com/ and follow the directions. There is a help page at the site should you need assistance.
Language (s): English
Ad Rate: Full Page Mono 636.88
Ad Rate: Full Page Colour 986.88
Currency: United States Dollars
DAILY NEWSPAPER

Times Union - Albany Bureau 75245
Editorial: Albany, New York **Tel:** 1 518 454-5420
Bureau Chief & State Government Editor: Casey Seiler
Language (s): English
DAILY NEWSPAPER

Times West Virginian 14834
Owner: MediaNews Group
Editorial: 300 Quincy St, Fairmont, West Virginia 26554-3136 **Tel:** 1 304 367-2500
Email: timeswv@timeswv.com **Web site:** http://www.timeswv.com
Freq: Daily; **Circ:** 8343 Not Audited
News Editor: Cliff Nichols; **Advertising Sales Manager:** Craig Richards
Profile: Times West Virginian is published daily for the residents of Marion County, WV. The newspaper covers local and state news, business, sports, lifestyles and entertainment.
Language (s): English
Ad Rate: Full Page Mono 20.05
Ad Rate: Full Page Colour 24.05
Currency: United States Dollars
DAILY NEWSPAPER

Times-Call 13789
Owner: Digital First Media
Editorial: 350 Terry St, Longmont, Colorado 80501-5440 **Tel:** 1 303 776-2244
Email: news@times-call.com **Web site:** http://www.timescall.com
Freq: Daily; **Circ:** 19256 Not Audited
Profile: Daily Times-Call's editorial mission is to provide the most comprehensive news coverage about public and private news issues. The publication is written for the general public in Boulder, Weld and Larimer counties, CO.
Language (s): English
Ad Rate: Full Page Mono 21.78
Ad Rate: Full Page Colour 536.00
Currency: United States Dollars
DAILY NEWSPAPER

TimesDaily 13669
Owner: Tennessee Valley Printing Co. Inc.
Editorial: 219 W Tennessee St, Florence, Alabama 35630-5440 **Tel:** 1 256 766-3434
Email: vent@timesdaily.com **Web site:** http://www.timesdaily.com
Freq: Daily; **Circ:** 21349 Not Audited
Publisher: Darrell Sandlin
Profile: TimesDaily is a newspaper written for the residents of Northwest Alabama. It covers local news, sports, entertainment and events.
Language (s): English
Ad Rate: Full Page Mono 59.15
Ad Rate: Full Page Colour 190.42
Currency: United States Dollars
DAILY NEWSPAPER

Times-Gazette 14459
Owner: AIM Media Midwest
Editorial: 209 S High St, Hillsboro, Ohio 45133-1444 **Tel:** 1 937 393-3456
Email: info@timesgazette.com **Web site:** http://www.timesgazette.com
Freq: Fri; **Circ:** 4667 Not Audited
Editor & Publisher: Gary Abernathy; **Advertising Sales Manager:** Mickey Parrott
Profile: Times-Gazette is written for the residents of Highland County, OH. It covers local news and sports. Deadlines are at 4:30pm ET the day before publication.
Language (s): English
Ad Rate: Full Page Mono 10.30
Ad Rate: Full Page Colour 195.00
Currency: United States Dollars
DAILY NEWSPAPER

Times-Georgian 13859
Owner: Paxton Media Group
Editorial: 901 Hays Mill Rd, Carrollton, Georgia 30117-9576 **Tel:** 1 770 834-6631
Web site: http://www.times-georgian.com
Freq: Daily; **Circ:** 8019 Not Audited
Editor: Bruce Browning; **Editor:** Amy Lavender
Profile: Times-Georgian's editorial mission is to report current news and information to the public. It is written for the residents of Carroll County and Haralson County, GA and covers current news and events that affect the community. Deadlines are one day before issue date.
Language (s): English
Ad Rate: Full Page Mono 20.00
Ad Rate: Full Page Colour 150.00
Currency: United States Dollars
DAILY NEWSPAPER

The Times-Herald 13761
Owner: Digital First Media
Editorial: 440 Curtola Pkwy, Vallejo, California 94590-6923 **Tel:** 1 707 644-1141
Web site: http://www.timesheraldonline.com
Freq: Daily; **Circ:** 15782 Not Audited
Publisher: Jim Gleim
Profile: The Times-Herald is the local daily newspaper written for the residents of Vallejo, Benicia and American County, CA and the surrounding communities. The newspaper covers international, national and local news, sports, events and arts & entertainment.
Language (s): English
Ad Rate: Full Page Mono 26.50
Ad Rate: Full Page Colour 625.00
Currency: United States Dollars
DAILY NEWSPAPER

The Times-Herald 13868
Owner: Herald Publishing Company
Editorial: 508 N Court St, Carroll, Iowa 51401-2747 **Tel:** 1 712 792-3573
Email: newspaper@carrollspaper.com **Web site:** http://www.carrollspaper.com
Freq: Daily; **Circ:** 6525 Not Audited
Editor: Larry Devine; **Advertising Sales Manager:** Marcia Jensen
Profile: The Times-Herald is a local, daily newspaper serving Carroll, IA and surrounding communities.
Language (s): English
Ad Rate: Full Page Mono 6.10
Currency: United States Dollars
DAILY NEWSPAPER

Times-Journal 13681
Owner: Southern Newspapers, Inc.
Editorial: 811 Greenhill Blvd NW, Fort Payne, Alabama 35967-3675 **Tel:** 1 256 845-2550
Email: news@times-journal.com **Web site:** http://www.times-journal.com
Freq: Daily; **Circ:** 5897 Not Audited
Advertising Sales Manager: Gloria Jackson
Profile: Times-Journal is a local daily newspaper serving Fort Payne, AL. The paper covers local news, weather, sports and opinion.
Language (s): English
Ad Rate: Full Page Mono 9.40
Ad Rate: Full Page Colour 40.44
Currency: United States Dollars
DAILY NEWSPAPER

The Times-Mail 13969
Owner: Schurz Communications Inc.
Editorial: 813 16th St, Bedford, Indiana 47421-3822 **Tel:** 1 812 275-3355
Email: lragle@schurz.com **Web site:** http://www.tmnews.com
Freq: Mon thru Fri; **Circ:** 9000
Profile: The Times-Mail's editorial mission is to provide news and information to the public with a heavy emphasis on local events, personalities and trends that affect the residents of south central Indiana. The publication combines with The Times-Mail and The Reporter-Times for the Sunday edition called the Hoosier Times.
Language (s): English
Ad Rate: Full Page Mono 17.83
Ad Rate: Full Page Colour 310.00
Currency: United States Dollars
DAILY NEWSPAPER

The Times-News 13908
Owner: Lee Enterprises, Inc.
Editorial: 132 Fairfield St W, Twin Falls, Idaho 83301-5492 **Tel:** 1 208 733-0931 3
Email: frontdoor@magicvalley.com **Web site:** http://www.magicvalley.com
Freq: Daily; **Circ:** 15275 Not Audited
Profile: The Times-News is a daily newspaper serving the community of Twin Falls, ID and surrounding southern Idaho communities, including Jerome and Burley, ID and Gooding County, ID. The newspaper includes national and local news, business, sports and lifestyle sections.
Language (s): English
Ad Rate: Full Page Mono 26.84
Ad Rate: Full Page Colour 420.00
Currency: United States Dollars
DAILY NEWSPAPER

Times-News 14289
Owner: GateHouse Media Inc.
Editorial: 707 S Main St, Burlington, North Carolina 27215-5844 **Tel:** 1 336 227-0131
Web site: http://www.thetimesnews.com
Freq: Daily; **Circ:** 18141 Not Audited
Publisher: Paul Mauney
Profile: Times-News is published daily for residents of Burlington, NC and surrounding communities. The newspaper covers local, national, and international news, weather, sports and community events. Feature articles cover business developments, politics, education, arts & entertainment, lifestyle and other topics of interest to the local community.
Language (s): English
Ad Rate: Full Page Mono 24.37
Ad Rate: Full Page Colour 460.00
Currency: United States Dollars
DAILY NEWSPAPER

Times-News 14297
Owner: GateHouse Media Inc.
Editorial: 106 Henderson Crossing Plz, Hendersonville, North Carolina 28792-2879 **Tel:** 1 828 692-0505
Email: lifestyle@blueridgenow.com **Web site:** http://www.blueridgenow.com
Freq: Daily; **Circ:** 10641 Not Audited
Publisher: Larry Riley
Profile: Times-News is a daily newspaper serving the Hendersonville, NC region. The publication covers local news, sports and community events.
Language (s): English
Ad Rate: Full Page Mono 25.73
Ad Rate: Full Page Colour 450.00
Currency: United States Dollars
DAILY NEWSPAPER

The Times-Picayune 15311
Owner: Newhouse Newspapers
Editorial: 365 Canal St Ste 3100, New Orleans, Louisiana 70130-6509 **Tel:** 1 504 826-3000
Web site: http://www.nola.com
Freq: 3 Times/Week; **Circ:** 103085 Not Audited
Profile: The Times-Picayune is a 70+ page, four-color broadsheet newspaper, published for the New Orleans general consumer audience. The business section, entitled Money, is featured daily, covering local and national business stories, daily stock market rates, and real estate. Articles include features, breaking news, trends, analyses, profiles, reviews, and investigative stories. Topics covered include entertainment, travel, health, food and drink, technology, and sports. As of October 1, 2012, The Times-Picayune is no longer publishing seven days a week, but produces expanded editions on Wednesday, Friday and Sunday, and much of the editorial staff's focus has shifted to their digital platform, NOLA.com.
Language (s): English
Ad Rate: Full Page Mono 186.20
Ad Rate: Full Page Colour 217.49
Currency: United States Dollars
DAILY NEWSPAPER

The Times-Picayune - Baton Rouge Bureau 128365
Editorial: 301 Main St Ste 101, Baton Rouge, Louisiana 70801-1200 **Tel:** 1 225 342-7315
Language (s): English
DAILY NEWSPAPER

The Times-Picayune - Covington Bureau 230999
Editorial: 1001 N Highway 190, Covington, Louisiana 70433-8962 **Tel:** 1 985 898-4825
Language (s): English
DAILY NEWSPAPER

The Times-Picayune - Gretna Bureau 15732
Editorial: 2520 Belle Chasse Hwy, Gretna, Louisiana 70053-6767 **Tel:** 1 504 826-3781
Language (s): English
DAILY NEWSPAPER

The Times-Picayune - Metairie Bureau 15734
Editorial: 4013 N I 10 Service Rd W, Metairie, Louisiana 70002-6718 **Tel:** 1 504 883-7050
Language (s): English
DAILY NEWSPAPER

The Times-Picayune - Slidell Bureau 15735
Editorial: 2070 Gause Blvd E, Slidell, Louisiana 70461-5431 **Tel:** 1 985 645-2850
Language (s): English
DAILY NEWSPAPER

The Times-Reporter 14478
Owner: GateHouse Media Inc.
Editorial: 629 Wabash Ave Nw, New Philadelphia, Ohio 44663-4145 **Tel:** 1 330 364-5577
Email: news@timesreporter.com **Web site:** http://www.timesreporter.com
Freq: Daily; **Circ:** 16300 Not Audited
News Editor: Joe Wright
Profile: The Times Reporter is a daily newspaper written for residents of the Dover and New Philadelphia, OH area. The editorial mission is to provide news and information to the public. The deadlines are 5pm ET the day before issue date.
Language (s): English
Ad Rate: Full Page Mono 25.95
Ad Rate: Full Page Colour 360.00
Currency: United States Dollars
DAILY NEWSPAPER

Times-Republic 13964
Owner: Community Media Group
Editorial: 1492 E Walnut St, Watseka, Illinois 60970-1806 **Tel:** 1 815 432-5227
Email: reporter@intranix.com **Web site:** http://www.newsbug.info/iroquois_countys_times-republic/
Freq: Daily; **Circ:** 2890 Not Audited
Publisher: Don Hurd; **Advertising Sales Manager:** Roberta Kempten
Profile: The Times-Republic is written for the communities in Iroquois County, IL.
Language (s): English
Ad Rate: Full Page Mono 9.35
Currency: United States Dollars
DAILY NEWSPAPER

Times-Republican 13884
Owner: Marshalltown Newspaper Inc.
Editorial: 135 W Main St, Marshalltown, Iowa 50158-5800 **Tel:** 1 641 753-6611
Email: news@timesrepublican.com **Web site:** http://www.timesrepublican.com
Freq: Daily; **Circ:** 6737

Publisher: Mike Schlesinger
Profile: Times-Republican is a daily newspaper serving Central Iowa. Articles include news, weather, travel, sports and local events.
Language (s): English
Ad Rate: Full Page Mono 24.52
Ad Rate: Full Page Colour 209.52
Currency: United States Dollars
DAILY NEWSPAPER

Times-Standard 13725

Owner: Digital First Media
Editorial: 930 6th St, Eureka, California 95501-1112 **Tel:** 1 707 441-0500
Email: editor@times-standard.com **Web site:** http://www.times-standard.com
Freq: Daily; **Circ:** 18284 Not Audited
Profile: Times-Standard is published daily for the residents of Eureka, CA and surrounding areas. The newspaper covers local and state news, business, sports, lifestyles and entertainment. The paper no longer prints Monday editions, but is available online.
Language (s): English
Ad Rate: Full Page Mono 33.00
Ad Rate: Full Page Colour 625.00
Currency: United States Dollars
DAILY NEWSPAPER

The Times-Tribune 14074

Owner: Community Newspaper Holdings, Inc.
Editorial: 201 N Kentucky Ave, Corbin, Kentucky 40701-1529 **Tel:** 1 606 528-2464
Email: newsroom@thetimestribune.com **Web site:** http://www.thetimestribune.com
Freq: Mon thru Fri; **Circ:** 9464 Not Audited
Profile: The Times-Tribune is a daily newspaper published for the residents of Southeastern Kentucky. The paper covers local news, sports, business and lifestyle.
Language (s): English
Ad Rate: Full Page Mono 12.15
Ad Rate: Full Page Colour 250.00
Currency: United States Dollars
DAILY NEWSPAPER

The Times-Tribune 15445

Owner: Times-Shamrock Communications
Editorial: 149 Penn Ave, Scranton, Pennsylvania 18503-2055 **Tel:** 1 570 348-9100
Email: yesdesk@timesshamrock.com **Web site:** http://www.thetimes-tribune.com
Freq: Daily; **Circ:** 37807 Not Audited
Publisher: George Lynett
Profile: The Times-Tribune is published daily for the residents of Scranton, PA and surrounding areas. The newspaper provides information about local and national news, business, sports, lifestyles and entertainment.
Language (s): English
Ad Rate: Full Page Mono 62.03
Ad Rate: Full Page Colour 189.15
Currency: United States Dollars
DAILY NEWSPAPER

Times-Union 14027

Owner: Chandler Williams
Tel: 1 574 267-3111
Email: news@timesuniononline.com **Web site:** http://www.timesuniononline.com
Freq: Daily; **Circ:** 7586 Not Audited
Publisher: Lane Hartle; **Advertising Sales Manager:** William Hays; **Editor:** Siera Sparkman
Profile: Times-Union covers local news, sports and community events for residents of Kosciusko County, IN.
Language (s): English
Ad Rate: Full Page Mono 13.15
Ad Rate: Full Page Colour 180.00
Currency: United States Dollars
DAILY NEWSPAPER

Tipton County Tribune 14023

Owner: Elwood Publishing Co.
Editorial: 116 S Main St Ste A, Tipton, Indiana 46072-1864 **Tel:** 1 765 675-2115
Email: tiptontri@netscape.net **Web site:** http://www.elwoodpublishing.com
Freq: Daily; **Circ:** 3000 Not Audited
Publisher: Robert Nash
Profile: Tipton County Tribune is published daily for the residents of Tipton, IN and surrounding areas. The newspaper covers local and state news, business, sports, lifestyles and entertainment.
Language (s): English
Ad Rate: Full Page Mono 9.95
Ad Rate: Full Page Colour 150.00
Currency: United States Dollars
DAILY NEWSPAPER

Titusville Herald 14622

Owner: Titusville Herald, Inc.
Editorial: 209 W Spring St, Titusville, Pennsylvania 16354-1687 **Tel:** 1 814 827-3634
Email: news@titusvilleherald.com **Web site:** http://www.titusvilleherald.com
Freq: Daily; **Circ:** 4000 Not Audited
Profile: Titusville Herald provides news for residents of Titusville, PA. It covers local news and events that effect the community. Deadlines are two days before issue date.
Language (s): English
Ad Rate: Full Page Mono 9.60
Ad Rate: Full Page Colour 255.00
Currency: United States Dollars
DAILY NEWSPAPER

Today's News-Herald 14906

Owner: River City Newspapers, L.L.C.
Editorial: 2225 Acoma Blvd W, Lake Havasu City, Arizona 86403-2907 **Tel:** 1 928 453-4237
Email: news@havasunews.com **Web site:** http://www.havasunews.com
Freq: Daily; **Circ:** 10000 Not Audited
Editor: Pam Ashley; **Publisher:** Michael Quinn
Profile: Today's News-Herald is a weekly newspaper serving residents of Lake Havasu City, AZ and surrounding communities. The newspaper covers local and national news, community events, weather and sports.
Language (s): English
Ad Rate: Full Page Mono 20.36
Ad Rate: Full Page Colour 69.86
Currency: United States Dollars
DAILY NEWSPAPER

Topeka Capital-Journal 15397

Owner: GateHouse Media Inc.
Editorial: 616 SE Jefferson St, Topeka, Kansas 66607-1137 **Tel:** 1 785 295-1111
Email: news@cjonline.com **Web site:** http://www.cjonline.com
Freq: Daily; **Circ:** 26468 Not Audited
Editor: Tomari Quinn
Profile: Topeka Capital-Journal is published daily for residents of Topeka, KS and surrounding communities. The newspaper covers state government, as well as regional news in 23 Northeast Kansas counties.
Language (s): English
Ad Rate: Full Page Mono 81.89
Ad Rate: Full Page Colour 1250.00
Currency: United States Dollars
DAILY NEWSPAPER

Town Crier 80346

Editorial: 218 Genesee St, Geneva, New York 14456-2323 **Tel:** 1 315 789-5186
Email: info@thetowncrier.com
Freq: Daily; **Circ:** 3800 Not Audited
Publisher & Editor: Jeri Marcuccilli
Profile: Town Crier services the Finger Lakes region of New York with news, events and more.
Language (s): English
Ad Rate: Full Page Mono 80.00
Currency: United States Dollars
DAILY NEWSPAPER

The Town Talk 14092

Owner: Gannett Co., Inc.
Editorial: 1201 3rd St, Alexandria, Louisiana 71301-8246 **Tel:** 1 318 487-6397
Email: metro@thetowntalk.com **Web site:** http://www.thetowntalk.com
Freq: Daily; **Circ:** 16029 Not Audited
Profile: The Town Talk is a daily newspaper serving Alexandria, LA and the surrounding area. It covers news, sports, features, business, technology and entertainment.
Language (s): English
Ad Rate: Full Page Mono 39.80
Ad Rate: Full Page Colour 210.18
Currency: United States Dollars
DAILY NEWSPAPER

Traverse City Record-Eagle 14196

Owner: Community Newspaper Holdings, Inc.
Editorial: 120 W Front St, Traverse City, Michigan 49684-2202 **Tel:** 1 231 946-2000
Web site: http://www.record-eagle.com
Freq: Daily; **Circ:** 14071 Not Audited
Publisher: Paul Heidbreder
Profile: Traverse City Record-Eagle is a daily morning newspaper that circulates in 13 counties in lower Northwest Michigan. Newspaper coverage includes local news, sports, weather, lifestyle and business. The intended readership of the newspaper is local community residents.
Language (s): English
Ad Rate: Full Page Mono 31.83
Ad Rate: Full Page Colour 37.08
Currency: United States Dollars
DAILY NEWSPAPER

The Trentonian 14365

Owner: Journal Register Company
Editorial: 600 Perry St, Trenton, New Jersey 08618-3934 **Tel:** 1 609 989-7800
Email: editor@trentonian.com **Web site:** http://www.trentonian.com
Freq: Daily; **Circ:** 23145 Not Audited
Publisher: Edward Condra
Profile: The Trentonian is a daily newspaper published for the residents of Trenton, NJ and the Mercer, Burlington and Bucks areas. The newspaper covers local news, business, sports and lifestyle information.
Language (s): English
Ad Rate: Full Page Mono 167.43
Currency: United States Dollars
DAILY NEWSPAPER

The Tribune 13749

Owner: McClatchy Newspapers
Editorial: 3825 S Higuera St, San Luis Obispo, California 93401-7438 **Tel:** 1 805 781-7800
Email: newsroom@thetribunenews.com **Web site:** http://www.sanluisobispo.com
Freq: Daily; **Circ:** 29353 Not Audited
Profile: The Tribune is a daily newspaper serving the San Luis Obispo, CA area. The publication covers local news, business, events and sports.
Language (s): English
Ad Rate: Full Page Mono 32.20
Ad Rate: Full Page Colour 470.00
Currency: United States Dollars
DAILY NEWSPAPER

The Tribune 13786

Owner: Swift Newspapers
Editorial: 501 8th Ave, Greeley, Colorado 80631-3913 **Tel:** 1 970 352-0211
Web site: http://www.greeleytribune.com
Freq: Daily; **Circ:** 29792 Not Audited
Editor: Randy Bangert; **Publisher:** Bart Smith
Profile: The Tribune is a daily local newspaper for residents of Greeley and Weld County, CO. Its mission is to provide its readers with community news, events and information.
Language (s): English
Ad Rate: Full Page Mono 28.23
Ad Rate: Full Page Colour 30.23
Currency: United States Dollars
DAILY NEWSPAPER

The Tribune 13864

Owner: Stephens Media
Editorial: 317 5th St, Ames, Iowa 50010-6101 **Tel:** 1 515 232-2160
Email: news@amestrib.com **Web site:** http://www.amestrib.com
Freq: Fri; **Circ:** 10000 Not Audited
Editor: Michael Crumb
Profile: The Tribune is published daily for the residents of Ames, IA and surrounding areas. The newspaper covers local and state news, business, sports, lifestyles and entertainment.
Language (s): English
Ad Rate: Full Page Mono 17.20
Ad Rate: Full Page Colour 154.80
Currency: United States Dollars
DAILY NEWSPAPER

The Tribune 14017

Owner: AIM Media Indiana Network
Editorial: 100 Saint Louis Ave, Seymour, Indiana 47274-2304 **Tel:** 1 812 522-4871
Email: readersubmit@tribtown.com **Web site:** http://www.tribtown.com
Freq: Daily; **Circ:** 8400 Not Audited
Advertising Sales Manager: Melissa Bane; **Publisher:** Chuck Wells; **Editor:** Aubrey Woods
Profile: The Seymour Daily Tribune is a local newspaper serving the residents of Seymour, IN. It includes information on local news, weather, sports, business, and entertainment.
Language (s): English
Ad Rate: Full Page Mono 13.44
Ad Rate: Full Page Colour 250.00
Currency: United States Dollars
DAILY NEWSPAPER

Tribune Chronicle 14499

Owner: Ogden Newspapers
Editorial: 240 Franklin St SE, Warren, Ohio 44483-5711 **Tel:** 1 330 841-1600
Web site: http://www.tribtoday.com
Freq: Mon thru Fri; **Circ:** 21844 Not Audited
Publisher: Charles Jarvis; **Editor:** Brenda Linert
Profile: Tribune Chronicle strives to give its vast readership comprehensive coverage of all the local area news and information that impacts the lives of those in and around Warren, OH.
Language (s): English
Ad Rate: Full Page Mono 65.45
Ad Rate: Full Page Colour 785.00
Currency: United States Dollars
DAILY NEWSPAPER

Tribune Star 14022

Owner: Community Newspaper Holdings, Inc.
Editorial: 222 S 7th St, Terre Haute, Indiana 47807-3601 **Tel:** 1 812 231-4200
Email: community@tribstar.com **Web site:** http://www.tribstar.com
Freq: Daily; **Circ:** 16978 Not Audited
Editor: Max Jones; **Advertising Sales Manager:** Erin Powell
Profile: Tribune Star is a daily newspaper covering local, regional, and national news, weather, and sports. The newspaper serves Vigo, Clay, Sullivan, Greene, Parke, and Vermillion IN, and Edgar, Clark, and Crawford, IL.
Language (s): English
Ad Rate: Full Page Mono 40.27
Ad Rate: Full Page Colour 45.50
Currency: United States Dollars
DAILY NEWSPAPER

The Tribune-Democrat 14587

Owner: Community Newspaper Holdings, Inc.
Editorial: 425 Locust St, Johnstown, Pennsylvania 15901-1817 **Tel:** 1 814 532-5199
Email: tribdem@tribdem.com **Web site:** http://www.tribdem.com
Freq: Daily; **Circ:** 27525 Not Audited
Editor: Renee Carthew; **Editor:** Chip Minemyer; **Publisher:** Robin Quillon
Profile: The Tribune-Democrat is a daily newspaper serving the residents of Johnstown and west central Pennsylvania. It features news, business, sports and editorials.
Language (s): English
Ad Rate: Full Page Mono 48.25
Ad Rate: Full Page Colour 655.00
Currency: United States Dollars
DAILY NEWSPAPER

Tribune-Herald 14917

Owner: Stephens Media Group
Editorial: 355 Kinoole St, Hilo, Hawaii 96720-2945 **Tel:** 1 808 935-6621
Web site: http://www.hawaiitribune-herald.com
Freq: Daily
Publisher & Editor: David Bock; **Advertising Sales Manager:** Alice Sledge
Profile: Tribune-Herald is a daily newspaper that delivers news and events to the Big Island, HI area.
Language (s): English
Ad Rate: Full Page Mono 30.50
Ad Rate: Full Page Colour 550.00
Currency: United States Dollars
DAILY NEWSPAPER

Tribune-Review 15459

Owner: Tribune-Review Publishing Co.
Editorial: 622 Cabin Hill Dr, Greensburg, Pennsylvania 15601-1657 **Tel:** 1 724 836-6675
Email: release@tribweb.com **Web site:** http://triblive.com/local/westmoreland
Freq: Daily; **Circ:** 89807 Not Audited
Editor: Susan McFarland
Profile: Tribune-Review is a daily newspaper that covers news from Greensburg, PA and the counties of Westmoreland, Fayette and Indiana. It contains business, entertainment, style and regional, national and international news. The newspaper has several regional editions, including the Pittsburgh Tribune-Review.
Language (s): English
Ad Rate: Full Page Mono 70.00
Ad Rate: Full Page Colour 570.00
Currency: United States Dollars
DAILY NEWSPAPER

Tri-City Herald 14793

Owner: McClatchy Newspapers
Editorial: 333 W Canal Dr, Kennewick, Washington 99336-3811 **Tel:** 1 509 582-1500
Email: news@tricityherald.com **Web site:** http://www.tri-cityherald.com
Freq: Daily; **Circ:** 25617 Not Audited
Publisher: Gregg McConnell
Profile: Tri-City Herald is the local daily newspaper for the residents of Kennewick, WA. Coverage includes local news, sports, arts & entertainment, food, nutrition, lifestyle and weather.
Language (s): English
Ad Rate: Full Page Mono 60.64
Ad Rate: Full Page Colour 215.96
Currency: United States Dollars
DAILY NEWSPAPER

Troy Daily News 14494

Owner: AIM Media Midwest
Editorial: 224 S Market St, Troy, Ohio 45373-3327 **Tel:** 1 937 335-5634
Email: editorial@tdnpublishing.com **Web site:** http://www.tdn-net.com
Freq: Fri; **Circ:** 10568 Not Audited
Profile: Troy Daily News (TDN) is a daily newspaper serving residents of Troy, OH and surrounding communities. It covers local, national and international news, weather, and sports. Feature articles cover business, politics, health, education, arts & entertainment, lifestyle, and other topics of interest to members of the local community.
Language (s): English
Ad Rate: Full Page Mono 18.85
Ad Rate: Full Page Colour 27.85
Currency: United States Dollars
DAILY NEWSPAPER

Troy Messenger 13677

Owner: Boone Newspapers Inc.
Editorial: 918 S Brundidge St, Troy, Alabama 36081-3222 **Tel:** 1 334 566-4270
Web site: http://www.troymessenger.com
Freq: Daily; **Circ:** 2814 Not Audited
Profile: Troy Messenger is a daily newspaper written for residents of Troy and Pike County, AL.
Language (s): English
Ad Rate: Full Page Mono 12.50
Ad Rate: Full Page Colour 200.00
Currency: United States Dollars
DAILY NEWSPAPER

Tryon Daily Bulletin 14318

Editorial: 16 N Trade St, Tryon, North Carolina 28782-6656 **Tel:** 1 828 859-9151
Email: news@tryondailybulletin.com **Web site:** http://www.tryondailybulletin.com
Freq: Daily; **Circ:** 4374 Not Audited
Profile: Tryon Daily Bulletin is a daily newspaper serving residents of Tryon, NC and surrounding communities. The newspaper covers local, national and international news, weather, sports, business, education, health, politics and arts & entertainment.
Language (s): English
Ad Rate: Full Page Mono 12.56
Currency: United States Dollars
DAILY NEWSPAPER

Tulare Advance-Register 13758

Owner: Gannett Co., Inc.
Editorial: 330 N West St, Tulare, California 93274 **Tel:** 1 559 735-3200
Email: online@visaliatimesdelta.com **Web site:** http://www.visaliatimesdelta.com/section/tulare/
Freq: Mon thru Fri; **Circ:** 5874
Profile: Tulare Advance-Register is written for residents in Tulare and the surrounding Tulare County, CA. It covers local news and events only, and takes regional and national coverage entirely from wire services. Tulare Advance-Register shares much of its content and staff with sister publication Visalia Times-Delta in neighboring Visalia, CA.
Language (s): English
Ad Rate: Full Page Mono 54.09

Currency: United States Dollars
DAILY NEWSPAPER

Tulsa World 15379

Owner: BH Media Group
Editorial: 315 S Boulder Ave, Tulsa, Oklahoma 74103-3401 **Tel:** 1 918 581-8400
Email: news@tulsaworld.com **Web site:** http://www.tulsaworld.com
Freq: Daily; **Circ:** 61817 Not Audited
Profile: Tulsa World is written for the greater metropolitan Tulsa, OK, region. Coverage includes local, regional and national news, business, entertainment, sports and features. The paper does not publish an editorial calendar.
Language (s): English
Ad Rate: Full Page Mono 102.00
Ad Rate: Full Page Colour 98.94
Currency: United States Dollars
DAILY NEWSPAPER

Tulsa World - Oklahoma City Bureau 15887

Editorial: State Capitol Bldg, Rm 430, Oklahoma City, Oklahoma 73105 **Tel:** 1 405 528-2465
Bureau Chief: Barbara Hoberock
Language (s): English
DAILY NEWSPAPER

Turkish Journal - New York Bureau 620047

Editorial: 4330 48th St.., #D15, New York, New York 11104 **Tel:** 1 917 365-6087
Email: seleuk@turkjournal.com **Web site:** http://www.turkishjournal.com
Profile: This is the New York Bureau for Turkish Journal which is based in Istanbul, Turkey.
Language (s): Turkish
DAILY NEWSPAPER

The Tuscaloosa News 13678

Owner: GateHouse Media Inc.
Editorial: 315 28th Ave, Tuscaloosa, Alabama 35401-1022 **Tel:** 1 205 345-0505
Email: news@tuscaloosanews.com **Web site:** http://www.tuscaloosanews.com
Freq: Daily; **Circ:** 25678 Not Audited
Publisher: Jim Rainey
Profile: The Tuscaloosa News's editorial mission is to provide local and national news for the residents of the Tuscaloosa, AL area.
Language (s): English
Ad Rate: Full Page Mono 49.25
Currency: United States Dollars
DAILY NEWSPAPER

Tyler Morning Telegraph 14738

Owner: T.B. Butler Publishing Co., Inc.
Editorial: 410 W Erwin St, Tyler, Texas 75702-7133 **Tel:** 1 903 597-8111
Email: opinion@tylerpaper.com **Web site:** http://www.tylerpaper.com
Freq: Daily; **Circ:** 17631 Not Audited
Publisher: C. Nelson Clyde; **Editor:** Allison Pollan
Profile: Tyler Morning Telegraph is published daily for the residents of Tyler, TX and surrounding areas. The newspaper covers local and state news, business, sports, lifestyles and entertainment.
Language (s): English
Ad Rate: Full Page Mono 28.33
Ad Rate: Full Page Colour 400.00
Currency: United States Dollars
DAILY NEWSPAPER

Ukiah Daily Journal 13760

Owner: MediaNews Group
Editorial: 590 S School St, Ukiah, California 95482-5438 **Tel:** 1 707 468-3500
Email: udj@ukiahdj.com **Web site:** http://www.ukiahdailyjournal.com
Freq: Daily; **Circ:** 5006 Not Audited
Publisher: Kevin McConnell; **Editor:** K.C. Meadows
Profile: The Ukiah Daily Journal's mission is to provide its readers with the latest in local news and information. The publication is written for the residents of Ukiah, CA and its surrounding area.
Language (s): English
Ad Rate: Full Page Mono 16.00
Ad Rate: Full Page Colour 2323.43
Currency: United States Dollars
DAILY NEWSPAPER

The Union 13729

Owner: Swift Newspapers
Editorial: 464 Sutton Way, Grass Valley, California 95945-4102 **Tel:** 1 530 273-9561
Email: letters@theunion.com **Web site:** http://www.theunion.com
Freq: Mon thru Fri; **Circ:** 16571 Not Audited
Profile: The Union is a daily newspaper covering western Nevada County, CA, including Nevada City and Grass Valley. The publication covers local news, sports, community news, local events and entertainment.
Language (s): English
Ad Rate: Full Page Mono 26.46
Ad Rate: Full Page Colour 295.00
Currency: United States Dollars
DAILY NEWSPAPER

Union City Daily Messenger 14679

Editorial: 613 E Jackson St, Union City, Tennessee 38261-5239 **Tel:** 1 731 885-0744
Email: ucdm@ucmessenger.com **Web site:** http://www.nwtntoday.com
Freq: Daily; **Circ:** 8000 Not Audited
Editor & Publisher: David Critchlow; **Advertising Sales Manager:** Lynette Wagster
Profile: Union City Daily Messenger is a local newspaper written for the residents of Union City, TN. It covers local news and events.
Language (s): English
Ad Rate: Full Page Mono 8.50
Ad Rate: Full Page Colour 55.38
Currency: United States Dollars
DAILY NEWSPAPER

Union Daily Times 14649

Owner: Civitas Media
Editorial: 100 Times Blvd, Union, South Carolina 29379-7705 **Tel:** 1 864 427-1234
Web site: http://www.uniondailytimes.com
Freq: Fri; **Circ:** 4000 Not Audited
Editor: Charles Warner
Profile: Union Daily Times is written for the residents of Union, SC and surrounding areas. The newspaper covers local and state news, business, sports, education, lifestyles and entertainment.
Language (s): English
Ad Rate: Full Page Mono 12.50
Ad Rate: Full Page Colour 15.65
Currency: United States Dollars
DAILY NEWSPAPER

The Union Democrat 13754

Owner: Western Communications Inc.
Editorial: 84 S Washington St, Sonora, California 95370-4711 **Tel:** 1 209 532-7151
Email: editor@uniondemocrat.com **Web site:** http://www.uniondemocrat.com
Freq: Mon thru Fri; **Circ:** 8753 Not Audited
Editor: Lyn Riddle
Profile: The Union Democrat's editorial mission is to serve the community by providing the latest in local news and information. The publication is written for residents of Mother Lode, Yosemite, and the Sierra Nevada.
Language (s): English
Ad Rate: Full Page Mono 21.00
Ad Rate: Full Page Colour 455.00
Currency: United States Dollars
DAILY NEWSPAPER

Union-Recorder 13857

Owner: Community Newspaper Holdings, Inc.
Editorial: 165 Garrett Way NW, Milledgeville, Georgia 31061-2371 **Tel:** 1 478 452-0567
Email: newsroom@unionrecorder.com **Web site:** http://www.unionrecorder.com
Freq: Daily; **Circ:** 7500 Not Audited
Publisher: Keith Barlow
Profile: Union-Recorder provides its readers with the latest in local news and information in the Milledgeville, GA area. Please contact them only with information of local interest.
Language (s): English
Ad Rate: Full Page Mono 14.40
Ad Rate: Full Page Colour 270.00
Currency: United States Dollars
DAILY NEWSPAPER

Urbana Daily Citizen 14496

Owner: AIM Media Midwest
Editorial: 220 E Court St, Urbana, Ohio 43078-1805 **Tel:** 1 937 652-1331
Email: editor@urbanacitizen.com **Web site:** http://www.urbanacitizen.com
Freq: Mon thru Fri; **Circ:** 5616 Not Audited
Publisher: Lane Moon
Profile: Urbana Daily Citizen is a local newspaper written for residents of Champaign County, OH. The newspaper covers local news, sports and events.
Language (s): English
Ad Rate: Full Page Mono 12.15
Ad Rate: Full Page Colour 300.00
Currency: United States Dollars
DAILY NEWSPAPER

USA Today 15308

Owner: Gannett Co., Inc.
Editorial: 7950 Jones Branch Dr, Mc Lean, Virginia 22107-0002 **Tel:** 1 703 854-3400
Email: newstips@usatoday.com **Web site:** http://www.usatoday.com
Freq: Mon thru Fri; **Circ:** 2203610 Not Audited
National News Editor: Mike James
Profile: USA Today is a national, general interest newspaper covering consumer-driven and general interest topics. There are many trend stories and profiles, as well as news from around the world. Coverage also includes business, technology, entertainment, travel, movie and book reviews, television, food, fashion, health and sports. The paper is broken down into the sections News, Money, Sports, Life, Travel, Tech and Weather. It also makes heavy use of color and graphics. Lead times vary for departments and reporters. The ad rates in their media kit are based on modular sizes. Editors and reporters honor non-disclosure agreements on a case-by-case basis. They also publish an e-Edition copy of the print publication and a Saturday-Sunday e-edition called USA Today EXTRA. It was founded in 1982.
Language (s): English
Ad Rate: Full Page Mono 996.83
Ad Rate: Full Page Colour 1579.37
Currency: United States Dollars
DAILY NEWSPAPER

USA Today - Los Angeles Bureau 15527

Editorial: 6060 Center Dr Ste 900, Los Angeles, California 90045-8854 **Tel:** 1 310 444-2100
Language (s): English
DAILY NEWSPAPER

USA Today - New York Bureau 15528

Editorial: 535 Madison Ave Fl 20, New York, New York 10022-4214
Email: newstips@usatoday.com
Language (s): English
DAILY NEWSPAPER

USA Today - San Francisco Bureau 71034

Editorial: San Francisco, California
Profile: The San Francisco bureau of USA Today does not want a main line or mailing address listed, as many reporters and staff work from home. Staff prefers to be contacted via email and do not want unsolicited physical materials being sent.
Language (s): English
DAILY NEWSPAPER

USA Today - Washington Bureau 76772

Editorial: 1575 I St NW Ste 350, Washington, District Of Columbia 20005-1114 **Tel:** 1 703 854-8900
Washington Bureau Chief: Susan Page
Language (s): English
DAILY NEWSPAPER

Vail Daily 14908

Owner: Swift Newspapers
Editorial: 40780 US Highway 6 and 24, Avon, Colorado **Tel:** 1 970 949-0555
Email: newsroom@vaildaily.com **Web site:** http://www.vaildaily.com
Freq: Daily; **Circ:** 10385
Publisher & Editor: Don Rogers
Profile: Vail Daily is a local daily newspaper written for the local residents and tourists of Vail, CO. The publication covers local news, community events, sports, arts & entertainment, editorials and advertisements. Use the street address when mailing items through UPS and Fedex, and use the PO box when mailing items through USPS.
Language (s): English
Ad Rate: Full Page Mono 97.59
Currency: United States Dollars
DAILY NEWSPAPER

The Valdosta Daily Times 13853

Owner: Community Newspaper Holdings, Inc.
Editorial: 201 N Troup St, Valdosta, Georgia 31601-5774 **Tel:** 1 229 244-1880
Email: valdostadailytimes.editorial@gaflnews.com
Web site: http://www.valdostadailytimes.com
Freq: Daily; **Circ:** 13595 Not Audited
Publisher: Sandy Sanders
Profile: The Valdosta Daily Times's editorial mission is to provide news about Valdosta, GA and its surrounding counties in South Florida and North Georgia.
Language (s): English
Ad Rate: Full Page Mono 27.30
Ad Rate: Full Page Colour 500.00
Currency: United States Dollars
DAILY NEWSPAPER

Valley City Times-Record 14333

Owner: Horizon Publications
Editorial: 146 3rd St NE, Valley City, North Dakota 58072-3047 **Tel:** 1 701 845-0463
Web site: http://www.times-online.com
Freq: Daily; **Circ:** 2355 Not Audited
Editor: Paul Riemerman
Profile: Valley City Times-Record is the daily newspaper for Valley City, ND and the surrounding communities. It covers local news, sports and lifestyle topics in the region.
Language (s): English
Ad Rate: Full Page Mono 9.95
Ad Rate: Full Page Colour 180.00
Currency: United States Dollars
DAILY NEWSPAPER

The Valley Courier 13777

Owner: Alamosa Newspapers, Inc.
Editorial: 2205 State Ave, Alamosa, Colorado 81101-3559 **Tel:** 1 719 589-2553
Email: news@alamosanews.com **Web site:** http://www.alamosanews.com
Freq: Daily; **Circ:** 5265 Not Audited
Publisher: Keith Cerny; **Editor:** Lloyd Engen
Profile: The Valley Courier serves the businesses and residents of Alamosa, CO with local and regional news.
Language (s): English
Ad Rate: Full Page Mono 14.30
Ad Rate: Full Page Colour 80.00
Currency: United States Dollars
DAILY NEWSPAPER

The Valley Dispatch 76174

Owner: MediaNews Group
Editorial: 491 Dutton St, Lowell, Massachusetts 01854-4221 **Tel:** 1 978 458-7100
Web site: http://www.thevalleydispatch.com
Freq: Daily; **Circ:** 14500 Not Audited
Editor: David McArdle
Profile: The Valley Dispatch is a newspaper for residents of Lowel, MA. Deadlines are at noon ET.
Language (s): English
Ad Rate: Full Page Mono 12.00
Ad Rate: Full Page Colour 51.71
Currency: United States Dollars
DAILY NEWSPAPER

Valley Morning Star 14702

Owner: AIM Media Texas, LLC
Editorial: 1310 S Commerce St, Harlingen, Texas 78550-7711 **Tel:** 1 956 430-6200
Web site: http://www.valleymorningstar.com
Freq: Daily; **Circ:** 18439 Not Audited
Publisher: Tyler Patton; **Editor:** Lisa Seiser
Profile: Valley Morning Star is published daily for residents of Harlingen, TX and surrounding communities. The newspaper covers local news, weather, sports, features, business, politics, arts & entertainment, lifestyle and community events.
Language (s): English
Ad Rate: Full Page Mono 46.25
Ad Rate: Full Page Colour 551.00
Currency: United States Dollars
DAILY NEWSPAPER

Valley News 14777

Owner: Newspapers of New England
Editorial: 24 Interchange Dr, West Lebanon, New Hampshire 03784-2003 **Tel:** 1 603 298-8711
Email: newseditor@vnews.com **Web site:** http://www.vnews.com
Freq: Daily; **Circ:** 16522 Not Audited
News Editor: Martin Frank; **News Editor:** John Gregg; **Editor:** Ernie Kohlsaat; **Publisher:** Dan McClory
Profile: Valley News is a local, daily newspaper serving residents of Grafton County, NH and White River Junction, VT. The paper covers local news, business, community events and sports.
Language (s): English
Ad Rate: Full Page Mono 25.52
Ad Rate: Full Page Colour 85.25
Currency: United States Dollars
DAILY NEWSPAPER

Valley News Dispatch 14621

Owner: Tribune-Review Publishing Co.
Editorial: 210 E 4th Ave, Tarentum, Pennsylvania 15084-1708 **Tel:** 1 724 226-4666
Email: vndcity@tribweb.com **Web site:** http://triblive.com/news/valleynewsdispatch
Freq: Daily; **Circ:** 28135 Not Audited
Profile: Valley News Dispatch is a local daily newspaper written for the Tarentum, PA community. The publication focuses on local, regional, and national news coverage.
Language (s): English
Ad Rate: Full Page Mono 49.28
Currency: United States Dollars
DAILY NEWSPAPER

The Valley Times-News 13672

Editorial: 220 N 12th St, Lanett, Alabama 36863-6422 **Tel:** 1 334 644-8100
Email: news@valleytimes-news.com **Web site:** http://www.valleytimes-news.com
Freq: Daily; **Circ:** 8000 Not Audited
Editor: Scott Sickler; **Publisher & Editor:** Cy Wood
Profile: The Valley Times-News is written for the residents of Lanett, AL.
Language (s): English
Ad Rate: Full Page Mono 9.50
Ad Rate: Full Page Colour 300.00
Currency: United States Dollars
DAILY NEWSPAPER

Van Wert Times-Bulletin 14497

Owner: Ohio Community Media LLC.
Editorial: 700 Fox Rd, Van Wert, Ohio 45891-2485 **Tel:** 1 419 238-2285
Email: info@timesbulletin.com **Web site:** http://www.timesbulletin.com
Freq: Fri; **Circ:** 7000 Not Audited
Publisher: Kirk Dougal; **Editor:** Ed Gebert; **Editor:** Sherry Missler
Profile: Van Wert Times-Bulletin is written for the community residents in and around Van Wert, OH. It covers community news, events, schools, sports, businesses, agriculture and editorials.
Language (s): English
Ad Rate: Full Page Mono 12.50
Ad Rate: Full Page Colour 135.00
Currency: United States Dollars
DAILY NEWSPAPER

Venango Newspapers 704359

Owner: Venango Newspapers Inc.
Editorial: 1510 W 1st St, Oil City, Pennsylvania 16301-3211 **Tel:** 1 814 676-7444
Email: newsroom.thederrick@gmail.com **Web site:** http://www.thederrick.com
Publisher: Ned Cowart
Profile: Venango Newspapers includes The Derrick and The News-Herald, which cover local news for the residents of Venango County, Pennsylvania.
Language (s): English
DAILY NEWSPAPER

Ventura County Star 407134

Owner: Gannett Co., Inc.
Editorial: 550 Camarillo Center Dr, Camarillo, California 93010-7700 **Tel:** 1 805 437-0000
Email: news@vcstar.com **Web site:** http://www.vcstar.com
Freq: Daily; **Circ:** 49735
Profile: Ventura County Star is a local daily newspaper serving the residents of Ventura County,

CA. The publication features local news, weather, sports, business, and entertainment.
Language (s): English
Ad Rate: Full Page Mono 128.00
Ad Rate: Full Page Colour 425.13
Currency: United States Dollars
DAILY NEWSPAPER

Vernon Daily Record 14739
Owner: North Central Texas Publishing Company
Editorial: 3214 Wilbarger St, Vernon, Texas 76384
Tel: 1 940 552-5454
Email: vdr@vernonrecord.com **Web site:** http://www.vernonrecord.com
Freq: Daily; **Circ:** 4546 Not Audited
Publisher: Larry Crabtree; **Advertising Sales Manager:** Jimmy Surber; **News Editor:** Daniel Walker
Profile: Vernon Daily Record's editorial mission is to provide daily news coverage to its readers. Deadlines are by 10am CT the day before.
Language (s): English
Ad Rate: Full Page Mono 7.90
Ad Rate: Full Page Colour 150.00
Currency: United States Dollars
DAILY NEWSPAPER

Vicksburg Post 14273
Owner: Vicksburg Printing and Publishing Co.
Editorial: 1601F N Frontage Rd, Vicksburg, Mississippi 39180-5149 **Tel:** 1 601 636-4545
Email: newsreleases@vicksburgpost.com **Web site:** http://www.vicksburgpost.com
Freq: Daily; **Circ:** 12254 Not Audited
Editor: Jan Griffey; **Publisher:** Jeff Schumacher
Profile: Vicksburg Post is a daily newspaper which covers local news, business, sports and arts & entertainment for the residents of Vicksburg, MS. The newspaper, established in 1883, was awarded the Pulitzer Prize.
Language (s): English
Ad Rate: Full Page Mono 17.78
Ad Rate: Full Page Colour 210.00
Currency: United States Dollars
DAILY NEWSPAPER

Victoria Advocate 14740
Owner: Victoria Advocate Publishing Co.
Editorial: 311 E Constitution St, Victoria, Texas 77901-8140 **Tel:** 1 361 575-1451
Email: newsroom@vicad.com **Web site:** http://www.victoriaadvocate.com
Freq: Daily; **Circ:** 19796 Not Audited
Editor: Chris Cobler
Profile: Victoria Advocate is a daily newspaper written for residents of Victoria, TX. It covers business, sports, arts & entertainment, features and news stories.
Language (s): English
Ad Rate: Full Page Mono 61.40
Ad Rate: Full Page Colour 855.00
Currency: United States Dollars
DAILY NEWSPAPER

Vien-Dong Daily News 577812
Owner: Vietnamese America Media Corporation
Editorial: 14891 Moran St, Westminster, California 92683-5535 **Tel:** 1 714 379-2851
Email: viendong@aol.com **Web site:** http://www.viendongdaily.com
Freq: Daily; **Circ:** 25000
Publisher & Editor: Nhuan Nguyen-Tong
Profile: Vien-Dong Daily News is a daily newspaper for Vietnamese speaking residents in and around Los Angeles and Orange County, CA. It also publishes a weekly edition on Saturdays culling regionally specific news from each week for residents of San Diego, CA. The paper launched in 1993.
Language (s): Vietnamese
Ad Rate: Full Page Mono 9.00
Ad Rate: Full Page Colour 655.50
Currency: United States Dollars
DAILY NEWSPAPER

Viet Bao Daily News 25559
Editorial: 14841 Moran St, Westminster, California 92683 **Tel:** 1 714 894-2500
Email: info@vietbao.com **Web site:** http://www.vietbao.com
Freq: Daily; **Circ:** 20000 Not Audited
Editor: Phan Tan Hai; **Publisher:** Hoabinh Le-Munzer; **Editor:** Kha Nguyen
Profile: Viet Bao Daily News serves the Vietnamese community in Southern California. The editorial mission is to keep the Vietnamese communities informed of local news and events, business, lifestyle, politics, education and entertainment.
Language (s): English, Vietnamese
Ad Rate: Full Page Mono 4.07
Ad Rate: Full Page Colour 1700.00
Currency: United States Dollars
DAILY NEWSPAPER

Vietnam - The Daily News 23295
Owner: Pacific Press Corporation
Editorial: 2350 S 10th St, San Jose, California 95112-4109 **Tel:** 1 408 292-3422
Email: vnnb@vietnamdaily.com **Web site:** http://www.vietnamdaily.com
Freq: Fri; **Circ:** 13000 Not Audited
Publisher & Editor: Gwen Nguyen
Profile: Vietnam - The Daily News is a daily paper focusing on the Vietnamese community of California.
Language (s): English, Vietnamese
Ad Rate: Full Page Mono 4.61
Ad Rate: Full Page Colour 23.54
Currency: United States Dollars
DAILY NEWSPAPER

The Villages Daily Sun 14945
Owner: Villages Media Group
Editorial: 1100 Main St, The Villages, Florida 32159-7719 **Tel:** 1 352 753-1119
Email: dailysun@thevillagesmedia.com **Web site:** http://www.thevillagesdailysun.com
Freq: Daily; **Circ:** 39581 Not Audited
Publisher: Phillip Markward; **Advertising Sales Manager:** Dan Sprung
Profile: The Villages Daily Sun is published daily for the residents of the Villages, a retirement community in The Villages, FL. It covers local news, sports, features and community events. Advertising deadlines are at 3pm ET.
Language (s): English
Ad Rate: Full Page Mono 21.50
Ad Rate: Full Page Colour 190.00
Currency: United States Dollars
DAILY NEWSPAPER

Vincennes Sun-Commercial 14025
Owner: Paxton Media Group
Editorial: 702 Main St, Vincennes, Indiana 47591-2910 **Tel:** 1 812 886-9955
Email: vscnews@suncommercial.com **Web site:** http://www.suncommercial.com
Freq: Fri; **Circ:** 8841
Advertising Sales Manager: Kim Gordon; **News Editor:** Jenny Peter
Profile: Vincennes Sun-Commercial's editorial mission is to be the best source of local news and information including accuracy and fairness. Vincennes Sun-Commercial is written for residents of Knox County, IN.
Language (s): English
Ad Rate: Full Page Mono 17.23
Ad Rate: Full Page Colour 285.00
Currency: United States Dollars
DAILY NEWSPAPER

The Vindicator 14504
Owner: Vindicator Printing Company
Editorial: 107 Vindicator Sq, Youngstown, Ohio 44503-1136 **Tel:** 1 330 747-1471
Email: news@vindy.com **Web site:** http://www.vindy.com
Freq: Daily; **Circ:** 39776 Not Audited
Editor: Todd Franko; **Publisher:** Betty Jagnow; **Ohio Statehouse Bureau Chief:** Marc Kovac
Profile: The Vindicator is a daily newspaper providing news coverage for readers in the greater Youngstown, OH area. The newspaper focuses on events and people in the community. Other features include area sports coverage, business news, local entertainment, lifestyle and classified ads. The newspaper is published daily except on Saturday.
Language (s): English
Ad Rate: Full Page Mono 73.86
Ad Rate: Full Page Colour 243.13
Currency: United States Dollars
DAILY NEWSPAPER

Vinita Daily Journal 14542
Owner: Wetherford News
Editorial: 138 S Wilson St, #140, Vinita, Oklahoma 74301-3730 **Tel:** 1 918 256-6422
Email: vdjnews@cableone.net **Web site:** http://www.vdjonline.com
Freq: Daily; **Circ:** 4331 Not Audited
Editor: David Burgess; **Editor:** Brenda Haskell; **Advertising Sales Manager:** Janet Link; **Publisher:** John Link
Profile: Vinita Daily Journal is a daily newspaper serving the residents of Vinita, OK and the surrounding areas. The newspaper covers local news, business, sports and arts & entertainment stories. It also covers national and statewide stories if they have a direct impact on the newspaper's readership. All inquiries should be addressed to the editor. Deadlines are at 2pm CT the day before issue date.
Language (s): English
Ad Rate: Full Page Mono 12.12
Ad Rate: Full Page Colour 90.00
Currency: United States Dollars
DAILY NEWSPAPER

Virginian Review 14753
Owner: Covington Virginian, Inc.
Editorial: 128 N Maple Ave, Covington, Virginia 24426-1545 **Tel:** 1 540 962-2121
Email: virginianreview@aol.com **Web site:** http://www.thevirginianreview.com
Freq: Daily; **Circ:** 6379 Not Audited
Editor & Publisher: Horton Beirne
Profile: Virginian Review is a local newspaper serving the residents of Covington, Clifton Forge, Allegheny County, and Bath County, VA. The publication features local news, sports, weather, real estate, tourism, education, health services and other pertinent information for the area.
Language (s): English
Ad Rate: Full Page Mono 9.25
Ad Rate: Full Page Colour 220.00
Currency: United States Dollars
DAILY NEWSPAPER

The Virginian-Pilot 15386
Owner: Landmark Media Enterprises, LLC
Editorial: 150 W Brambleton Ave, Norfolk, Virginia 23510-2018 **Tel:** 1 757 446-2000
Email: tips@pilotonline.com **Web site:** http://www.pilotonline.com
Freq: Daily; **Circ:** 108162 Not Audited
Profile: The Virginian-Pilot is a daily newspaper serving the Hampton Roads community of Virginia which includes 12 cities and counties. It covers food, business, technology, real estate, entertainment and travel. Do NOT send press releases for product promotions or product reviews. The Virginian-Pilot is ONLY interested in news concerning Virginia and, moreover, the Hampton Roads communities. Press releases should be sent to the appropriate journalists and editors.
Language (s): English
Ad Rate: Full Page Mono 232.00
Ad Rate: Full Page Colour 708.58
Currency: United States Dollars
DAILY NEWSPAPER

The Virginian-Pilot - Chesapeake Bureau 15956
Editorial: 921 Battlefield Blvd N, Chesapeake, Virginia 23320-4803 **Tel:** 1 757 222-5200
Email: clipper@pilotonline.com
Language (s): English
DAILY NEWSPAPER

The Virginian-Pilot - Suffolk Bureau 15959
Editorial: 157 N Main St Ste B, Suffolk, Virginia 23434-4565 **Tel:** 1 757 222-5550
Email: thesun@pilotonline.com
Language (s): English
DAILY NEWSPAPER

The Virginian-Pilot - Virginia Beach Bureau 15960
Editorial: 4549 Commerce St Ste 101, Virginia Beach, Virginia 23462-3370 **Tel:** 1 757 222-5100
Editor: Matthew Bowers
Language (s): English
DAILY NEWSPAPER

Visalia Times-Delta 13763
Owner: Gannett Co., Inc.
Editorial: 330 N West St, Visalia, California 93291-6010 **Tel:** 1 559 735-3200
Email: news@visaliatimesdelta.com **Web site:** http://www.visaliatimesdelta.com
Freq: Daily; **Circ:** 15557 Not Audited
Editor: Mike Hazelwood
Profile: Visalia Times-Delta is a daily newspaper covering local news and sports in Visalia and the surrounding Tulare County, CA. The paper covers local news and events only, and takes regional and national coverage entirely from wire services.
Language (s): English
Ad Rate: Full Page Mono 60.31
Ad Rate: Full Page Colour 900.00
Currency: United States Dollars
DAILY NEWSPAPER

Wabash Plain Dealer 14026
Owner: Paxton Media Group
Editorial: 123 W Canal St, Wabash, Indiana 46992-3042 **Tel:** 1 260 563-2131
Email: news@wabashplaindealer.com **Web site:** http://www.chronicle-tribune.com/wabashplaindealer
Freq: Daily; **Circ:** 6108 Not Audited
Profile: Wabash Plain Dealer is published daily for the residents of Wabash County, IN and surrounding areas. The newspaper provides information on news and community events.
Language (s): English
Ad Rate: Full Page Mono 18.00
Ad Rate: Full Page Colour 225.00
Currency: United States Dollars
DAILY NEWSPAPER

Waco Tribune-Herald 14741
Owner: Berkshire Hathaway Media
Editorial: 900 Franklin Ave, Waco, Texas 76701-1906
Tel: 1 254 757-5757
Email: news@wacotrib.com **Web site:** http://www.wacotrib.com
Freq: Daily; **Circ:** 24180 Not Audited
Publisher: Jim Wilson
Profile: Waco Tribune-Herald is a daily newspaper for the residents of the Waco County, TX. It covers national and local news and events. Deadlines are the same day as the issue date. The outlet offers RSS (Really Simple Syndication).
Language (s): English
Ad Rate: Full Page Mono 55.51
Ad Rate: Full Page Colour 487.00
Currency: United States Dollars
DAILY NEWSPAPER

Wakefield Daily Item 14136
Owner: Wakefield Item Co.
Editorial: 26 Albion St, Wakefield, Massachusetts 01880-2803 **Tel:** 1 781 245-0080
Email: news@wakefielditem.com **Web site:** http://www.wakefielditem.com
Freq: Mon thru Fri; **Circ:** 4556 Not Audited
Publisher: Glenn Dolbeare; **Editor:** Peter Rossi
Profile: Wakefield Daily Item is published daily for residents of Wakefield, MA and surrounding communities. The newspaper covers local news, weather, sports and community events. Feature artivles cover business, arts and entertainment and lifestyle.
Language (s): English
Ad Rate: Full Page Mono 20.00
Ad Rate: Full Page Colour 225.00
Currency: United States Dollars
DAILY NEWSPAPER

The Wall Street Journal 15283
Owner: News Corporation Ltd.
Editorial: 1211 Avenue of the Americas Fl 4, New York, New York 10036-0003 **Tel:** 1 212 416-2000
Email: nywireroom@wsj.com **Web site:** http://www.wsj.com
Freq: Daily
South America Bureau Chief: Juan Forero; **News Editor:** Chris Gay; **World News Editor:** James Graff; **News Editor:** Lisa Kalis; **Global News Editor:** Susan Lillo; **News Editor:** Tom Loftus; **News Editor:** Cristina Lourosa-Ricardo; **New York Bureau Chief:** Bob Rose; **News Editor:** Richard Taliaferro; **News Editor:** Robert Walzer; **National News Desk Editor:** Bart Ziegler
Profile: The Wall Street Journal is considered the most widely-read periodical in the nation's business and investment community. Information in the paper is also distributed to many Dow Jones outlets, including news service and specialized financial and commodity reports. The paper produces tabloid-style supplements that appear several times each year called The Wall Street Journal Reports. Report topics include small business, world business, telecommunications, technology, executive pay and personal finance. Several sections appear throughout the week, including the Personal Journal, which covers health, automotive, technology and personal finance, a Greater New York metro section, which provides general consumer news content for their New York City readership and WSJ Weekend, which features lifestyle related news, cultural coverage and reviews. National supplement The Sunday Journal provides business content from the paper to business sections of many external daily newspapers. The lead time for feature and news coverage is one day to one week. The lead time for The Wall Street Journal Reports is three to five months, although stories are often developed during the two or three months immediately preceding the issue. The lead time for Marketplace and Enterprise is two months. Deadlines are at 5:30pm ET for in-depth business and Marketplace stories and 3pm ET for shorter stories. The paper does not publish a Holiday Gift Guide.
Language (s): English
Ad Rate: Full Page Mono 2200.00
Ad Rate: Full Page Colour 2870.74
Currency: United States Dollars
DAILY NEWSPAPER

The Wall Street Journal - Amsterdam Bureau 964889
Editorial: Jozef Israelkade 48H, Amsterdam 1072 SB
Tel: 31 20 623-5616
Email: djnews.amsterdam@dowjones.com
Bureau Chief: Robin van Daalen
Language (s): English
DAILY NEWSPAPER

The Wall Street Journal - Atlanta Bureau 15476
Editorial: 1201 W Peachtree St NW Ste 2550, Atlanta, Georgia 30309-3489
Email: atspot@wsj.com
Bureau Chief & Southeast U.S. Editor: Betsy McKay
Language (s): English
DAILY NEWSPAPER

The Wall Street Journal - Bangkok Bureau 153308
Editorial: 540 Mercury Tower, 5th Floor Rm #502-503 Ploenchit Rd, Bangkok 10330 **Tel:** 66 2 238-2661
Language (s): English
DAILY NEWSPAPER

The Wall Street Journal - Beijing Bureau 153279
Editorial: 3F, Raffles City Beijing Office Tower, No. 1, Dongzhimen South Street Dongcheng District, Beijing 100007 **Tel:** 86 10 8400-7700
Bureau Chief: Charles Hutzler
Language (s): English
DAILY NEWSPAPER

The Wall Street Journal - Berlin Bureau 15506
Editorial: Pressehaus Zimmer 6195, Schiffbauerdamm 40, Berlin 10117 **Tel:** 49 30 288-8410
Language (s): English
DAILY NEWSPAPER

The Wall Street Journal - Beverly Hills Bureau 15472
Editorial: 407 N Maple Dr Ste 104, Beverly Hills, California 90210-3818
Bureau Chief: Ethan Smith
Language (s): English
DAILY NEWSPAPER

The Wall Street Journal - Boston Bureau 15478
Editorial: 53 State St Ste 1201, Boston, Massachusetts 02109-3000 **Tel:** 1 617 654-6700
Language (s): English
DAILY NEWSPAPER

The Wall Street Journal - Brussels Bureau 15526
Editorial: Avenue de Cortenbergh 60/4F, Brussels B-1000 **Tel:** 32 2 741-1211
Brussels Editor & Bureau Chief: Stephen Fidler
Profile: Contact staff via fax.
Language (s): English
DAILY NEWSPAPER

The Wall Street Journal - Buenos Aires Bureau 964657
Editorial: Ing. Butty 240 Piso 5, Buenos Aires 1001
Tel: 54 11 4590-2428
Language (s): English
DAILY NEWSPAPER

The Wall Street Journal - Chicago Bureau 15477
Editorial: 1 S Wacker Dr Ste 1700, Chicago, Illinois 60606-4653 **Tel:** 1 312 750-4000
Bureau Chief: Jason Dean
Language (s): English
DAILY NEWSPAPER

The Wall Street Journal - Dallas Bureau 15481
Editorial: 2515 McKinney Ave Ste 850, Dallas, Texas 75201-7617 **Tel:** 1 214 951-7100
Email: lonestar.bureau@wsj.com
Language (s): English
DAILY NEWSPAPER

The Wall Street Journal - Detroit Bureau 15479
Editorial: 2000 Town Ctr Ste 750, Southfield, Michigan 48075-1127 **Tel:** 1 248 204-5500
Bureau Chief: John Stoll
Language (s): English
DAILY NEWSPAPER

The Wall Street Journal - Dubai Bureau 564336
Editorial: Building 5, Office 314, Dubai
Tel: 971 4 331-4260
Email: djnews.dubai@dowjones.com
Bureau Chief: Peter Wonacott
Language (s): English
DAILY NEWSPAPER

The Wall Street Journal - Frankfurt Bureau 133836
Editorial: Wilhelm-Leuschner-Strasse 78, Baseler Arkaden, Frankfurt 60329 **Tel:** 49 69 2972-5550
Email: djnews.frankfurt@dowjones.com
Language (s): English
DAILY NEWSPAPER

The Wall Street Journal - Hong Kong Bureau 15508
Editorial: Suite 2404 & 25/F Central Plaza, 18 Harbour Rd, Hong Kong **Tel:** 852 2573-7121
Email: wsj.ltrs@wsj.com **Web site:** http://www.wsj-asia.com
Bureau Chief: Ken Brown
Language (s): English
DAILY NEWSPAPER

The Wall Street Journal - Houston Bureau 15482
Editorial: 1200 Smith St Ste 615, Houston, Texas 77002-4311 **Tel:** 1 713 227-5440
Email: lonestar.bureau@wsj.com
Language (s): English
DAILY NEWSPAPER

The Wall Street Journal - Jakarta Bureau 153289
Editorial: Deutsche Bank Building 1402, Jalan Imam Bonjol 80, Jakarta 10310 **Tel:** 62 21 3983-1277
Bureau Chief: Patrick McDowell
Language (s): English
DAILY NEWSPAPER

The Wall Street Journal - Johannesburg Bureau 651822
Editorial: 12th Floor, Sandton City Office Tower, 158 5th St., Sandhurst ext. 3, Johannesburg 2196
Tel: 27 11 783-7848
Africa Bureau Chief: Joe Parkinson
Language (s): English
DAILY NEWSPAPER

The Wall Street Journal - Kuala Lumpur Bureau 153292
Editorial: Sdn Bhd Suite 34-02, Level 34, Menara Dion 27, Jalan Sultan Ismail, Kuala Lumpur 50250
Tel: 60 3 2026-1233
Email: djn.kl@dowjones.com
Bureau Chief: Patrick McDowell
Language (s): English
DAILY NEWSPAPER

The Wall Street Journal - London Bureau 15509
Editorial: 1 London Bridge St, London, England SE1 9GF **Tel:** 44 20 7842-9200
Web site: http://europe.wsj.com/home-page
Middle East and Africa, News Editor: Craig Nelson
Language (s): English
DAILY NEWSPAPER

The Wall Street Journal - Madrid Bureau 231453
Editorial: Calle de Espronceda 32, Fl 1, Madrid 28003 **Tel:** 34 91 395-8122
Email: djmadrid@dowjones.com
Bureau Chief: Richard Boudreaux
Language (s): English
DAILY NEWSPAPER

The Wall Street Journal - Manila Bureau 564708
Editorial: 1209-1210 12Fl Tower 1 Exchange Plaza, Ayala Triangle, Ayala Avenue, Manila **Tel:** 63 2 848-5051
Bureau Chief: Cris Larano
Language (s): English
DAILY NEWSPAPER

The Wall Street Journal - Mexico City Bureau 16065
Editorial: Tennyson 96, Col. Chapultepec Polanco, Mexico City, Distrito Federal 11560 **Tel:** 52 55 5281-0902
Email: mexico@dowjones.com
Language (s): English
DAILY NEWSPAPER

Wall Street Journal - Milano Bureau 907743
Editorial: Via Marco Burigozzo 5, Milano 20122
Tel: 39 02 5821-1901
Email: djitaly@dowjones.com
Bureau Chief: Deborah Ball
Language (s): English
DAILY NEWSPAPER

The Wall Street Journal - Moscow Bureau 15534
Editorial: Petrovka str. 5, 5th floor, Moscow 107031
Tel: 7 495 232-9198
Language (s): English
DAILY NEWSPAPER

The Wall Street Journal - Mumbai Bureau 535836
Editorial: Unit 93, 9th Floor 2 North Ave, Maker Maxity Bandra Kurla Complex, Bandra (East), Mumbai 400-051 **Tel:** 91 22 6145-6100
Language (s): English
DAILY NEWSPAPER

The Wall Street Journal - New Delhi Bureau 492368
Editorial: 4th Floor, Birla Tower, 25 Barakhamba Road, New Delhi 1100 001 **Tel:** 91 11 2307-4032
Web site: http://india.wsj.com
Bureau Chief: Gordon Fairclough
Language (s): English
DAILY NEWSPAPER

Wall Street Journal - Oslo Bureau 928705
Editorial: Holbergs Gate 1, Oslo 166
DAILY NEWSPAPER

Wall Street Journal - Ottawa Bureau 963758
Editorial: 1 Rideau St Suite 700, Ottawa, Ontario K1N 8S7 **Tel:** 1 613 237-0668
Language (s): English
DAILY NEWSPAPER

The Wall Street Journal - Paris Bureau 15532
Editorial: 6 Bd Haussmann, Paris 75009
Tel: 33 1 4017-1819
News Editor: Matthew Curtin; **Bureau Chief:** Grainne McCarthy
Language (s): English
DAILY NEWSPAPER

The Wall Street Journal - Pittsburgh Bureau 15480
Editorial: 1 Ppg Pl Ste 3030, Pittsburgh, Pennsylvania 15222-9812 **Tel:** 1 412 553-6900
Bureau Chief: Clare Ansberry
Language (s): English
DAILY NEWSPAPER

The Wall Street Journal - Rio De Janeiro Bureau 543437
Editorial: Praia de Botafogo, 501, Torre Pao de Acucar, 1 andar, Sala 156, Rio De Janeiro 22250-040
Tel: 55 21 2586-6000
Language (s): English
DAILY NEWSPAPER

The Wall Street Journal - Rome Bureau 543434
Editorial: Via Santa Maria, Via 12, Rome 187
Tel: 39 06 678-2543
Email: djitaly@dowjones.com
Bureau Chief: Deborah Ball
Language (s): English
DAILY NEWSPAPER

The Wall Street Journal - San Francisco Bureau 15473
Editorial: 201 California St Fl 10, San Francisco, California 94111-5002 **Tel:** 1 415 986-6886
Editor: Cassandra Sweet
Language (s): English
DAILY NEWSPAPER

The Wall Street Journal - Sao Paulo Bureau 543441
Editorial: Av Paulista 854 13th floor, Sao Paulo CEP 01310-913 **Tel:** 55 11 3826-2648
Email: brazil@dowjones.com
Language (s): English
DAILY NEWSPAPER

The Wall Street Journal - Seoul Bureau 153291
Editorial: 14th Floor Young Poong Building, Cheonggyecheon-ro 41 Jongro-gu, Seoul
Bureau Chief: Alastair Gale
Language (s): English
DAILY NEWSPAPER

The Wall Street Journal - Shanghai Bureau 153287
Editorial: Suites 1504-1508, Two ICC, Shanghai International, Commerce Center No. 288 South Shaanxi Road, Shanghai 200031 **Tel:** 86 21 6120-1200
Bureau Chief: Shen Hong
Language (s): English
DAILY NEWSPAPER

The Wall Street Journal - Singapore Bureau 153297
Editorial: 10 Anson Road #32-08, International Plaza, Singapore 79903 **Tel:** 65 6415-4240
Email: djn.singapore.bureau@dowjones.com
Language (s): English
DAILY NEWSPAPER

Wall Street Journal - Stockholm Bureau 823697
Editorial: Kungsgatan 12-14, 7th Floor, Stockholm 11135 **Tel:** 46 8 5451-3090
Email: djnews.stockholm@dowjones.com
Freq: Daily
Language (s): English
DAILY NEWSPAPER

Wall Street Journal - Sydney Bureau 600216
Editorial: Level 2, 2 Holt Street, Surry Hills NSW 2010
Tel: 61 2 8272-4680
Email: djnews.sydney@dowjones.com
Bureau Chief: David Winning
Language (s): English
DAILY NEWSPAPER

The Wall Street Journal - Tokyo Bureau 15510
Editorial: Otemachi First Square East Tower 19F, 1-5-1 Otemachi Chiyoda-ku, Tokyo 100-0004
Tel: 81 3 6269-2770
Email: japanrealtime@wsj.com
Language (s): English
DAILY NEWSPAPER

The Wall Street Journal - Toronto Bureau 739314
Editorial: 145 King St W Suite 730, Toronto, Ontario M5H 1J8 **Tel:** 1 416 306-2100
Language (s): English
DAILY NEWSPAPER

The Wall Street Journal - Washington Bureau 15474
Editorial: 1025 Connecticut Ave NW Ste 800, Washington, District Of Columbia 20036-5419
Tel: 1 202 862-9200
Language (s): English
DAILY NEWSPAPER

The Wall Street Journal - Zurich Bureau 605262
Editorial: 59 Loewenstrasse, Zurich CH-8001
Tel: 41 43 443-8059
Email: zurichdjnews@dowjones.com
Bureau Chief: Andrew Morse
Language (s): English
DAILY NEWSPAPER

Walla Walla Union-Bulletin 14790
Owner: Seattle Times Co.
Editorial: 112 S 1st Ave, Walla Walla, Washington 99362-3011 **Tel:** 1 509 525-3301
Web site: http://www.union-bulletin.com
Freq: Daily; **Circ:** 12730 Not Audited
Profile: Walla Walla Union-Bulletin provides news for the local community. It is written for readers of all ages in Walla Walla, WA. Deadlines are five days before issue date.
Language (s): English
Ad Rate: Full Page Mono 23.20
Ad Rate: Full Page Colour 486.00
Currency: United States Dollars
DAILY NEWSPAPER

Wapakoneta Daily News 14498
Owner: Horizon Publications
Editorial: 520 Industrial Dr, Wapakoneta, Ohio 45895-9200 **Tel:** 1 419 738-2128
Web site: http://www.wapakdailynews.com
Freq: Mon thru Fri; **Circ:** 5300 Not Audited
Profile: Wapakoneta Daily News strives to provide news and information to the residents of Wapakoneta, OH. Please send all mail correspondence to the PO Box address.
Language (s): English
Ad Rate: Full Page Mono 13.34
Ad Rate: Full Page Colour 294.00
Currency: United States Dollars
DAILY NEWSPAPER

Washington Daily News 14319
Owner: Washington Newsmedia, LLC
Editorial: 217 N Market St, Washington, North Carolina 27889-4949 **Tel:** 1 252 946-2144
Email: news@thewashingtondailynews.com **Web site:** http://www.wdnweb.com
Freq: Fri; **Circ:** 9459 Not Audited
News Editor: Vail Rumley; **Advertising Sales Manager:** Amy Whitaker
Profile: Washington Daily News's editorial mission is to report local news to the community of Washington, NC. The paper is focused towards all age groups and all topics concerning the general public. The lead time for Washington Daily News is same day.
Language (s): English
Ad Rate: Full Page Mono 20.00
Ad Rate: Full Page Colour 169.00
Currency: United States Dollars
DAILY NEWSPAPER

Washington Evening Journal 13895
Owner: Inland Media Comapny, Inc.
Editorial: 111 N Marion Ave, Washington, Iowa 52353 **Tel:** 1 319 653-2191
Web site: http://www.washjrnl.com
Freq: Daily; **Circ:** 3850 Not Audited
Publisher & Editor: Mathew Bryant; **News Editor:** David Holte
Profile: Washington Evening Journal is a local daily newspaper written for the residents of Washington County, IA. The publication focuses on local news of Washington County, but national news is also included if it applies to the community.
Language (s): English
Ad Rate: Full Page Mono 10.88
Ad Rate: Full Page Colour 34.61
Currency: United States Dollars
DAILY NEWSPAPER

The Washington Post 15297
Owner: Washington Post Co.
Editorial: 1301 K St NW, One Franklin Square, Washington, District Of Columbia 20005-3317
Tel: 1 202 334-6000
Email: tellus@washpost.com **Web site:** http://www.washingtonpost.com
Freq: Daily; **Circ:** 356768 Not Audited
Moscow Bureau Chief: Michael Birnbaum; **White House Bureau Chief:** Juliet Eilperin; **Bureau Chief:** Anthony Faiola; **Africa Bureau Chief:** Sudarsan Raghavan; **Publisher:** Frederick Ryan; **Kabul Bureau Chief:** Kevin Sieff
Profile: The Washington Post focuses on news from the nation's capital, including national business, political issues, commerce, federal regulations and finance. There is also coverage of sports, entertainment, features, local and world news. It has a content share agreement for technology stories from The Verge. Lead times vary.
Language (s): English
Ad Rate: Full Page Mono 393.76
Ad Rate: Full Page Colour 452.55
Currency: United States Dollars
DAILY NEWSPAPER

The Washington Post - Alexandria Bureau 16088
Editorial: 526 King St Ste 203, Alexandria, Virginia 22314-3181 **Tel:** 1 703 518-3000
Language (s): English
DAILY NEWSPAPER

The Washington Post - Annapolis Bureau 16146
Editorial: 3 Church Cir, Annapolis, Maryland 21401-1932
Email: aaextra@washpost.com
Language (s): English
DAILY NEWSPAPER

The Washington Post - Beijing Bureau 231409
Editorial: 45329, Jianwai Diplomatic Compound, Beijing 100600 **Tel:** 86 1065323464
Email: foreign@washpost.com
Language (s): English
DAILY NEWSPAPER

The Washington Post - Cairo Bureau 844008
Owner: Washington Post Co.
Editorial: Restricted Address, Cairo
Language (s): English
DAILY NEWSPAPER

The Washington Post - Fairfax Bureau 16203
Editorial: 4020 University Dr, Fairfax, Virginia 22030-6802 **Tel:** 1 703 383-5100
Email: fxliving@washpost.com
Language (s): English
DAILY NEWSPAPER

The Washington Post - Islamabad Bureau 832566
Owner: Washington Post Co.
Editorial: Address Restricted, Islamabad
Language (s): English
DAILY NEWSPAPER

The Washington Post - Largo Bureau 16211
Editorial: 9500 Arena Dr, Largo, Maryland 20774-3701 **Tel:** 1 301 618-1720
Email: pgextra@washpost.com
Language (s): English
DAILY NEWSPAPER

The Washington Post - Leesburg Bureau 16122
Editorial: 305 Harrison St SE, Leesburg, Virginia 20175-3729 **Tel:** 1 703 771-4102
Email: lextra@washpost.com
Language (s): English
DAILY NEWSPAPER

The Washington Post - London Bureau 87822
Tel: 44 20 74338094
Bureau Chief: Griff Witte
Language (s): English
DAILY NEWSPAPER

The Washington Post - Manassas Bureau 16215
Editorial: 9420 Battle St, Manassas, Virginia 20110-5432 **Tel:** 1 703 392-1303
Language (s): English
DAILY NEWSPAPER

The Washington Post - Moscow Bureau 83786
Editorial: 7/4 Kutuzovsky Prospekt #2, Moscow 121248 **Tel:** 7 0957776661
Email: moscow@washpost.ru
Moscow Bureau Chief: Michael Birnbaum
Language (s): English
DAILY NEWSPAPER

The Washington Post - New Delhi Bureau 850063
Editorial: Restricted, New Delhi
Language (s): English
DAILY NEWSPAPER

The Washington Post - Richmond Bureau 15661
Editorial: 1001 E Main St Ste 203, Richmond, Virginia 23219-3536 **Tel:** 1 804 649-7575
Language (s): English
DAILY NEWSPAPER

The Washington Post - Rockville Bureau 16214
Editorial: 51 Monroe St, Rockville, Maryland 20850-2419 **Tel:** 1 301 294-2600
Email: mocoextra@washpost.com
Profile: This bureau publishes the Montgomery Extra print edition of the Washington Post.
Language (s): English
DAILY NEWSPAPER

The Washington Post - Tokyo Bureau 16020
Editorial: Avex Bldg, 3-1-30 Minami-Aoyama Minato-ku, Tokyo 107 **Tel:** 81 354116031
Language (s): English
DAILY NEWSPAPER

The Washington Times 15454
Owner: The Washington Times LLC
Editorial: 3600 New York Ave NE, Washington, District Of Columbia 20002-1947 **Tel:** 1 202 636-3000
Web site: http://www.washingtontimes.com
Freq: Mon thru Fri; **Circ:** 59185 Not Audited
National News Editor: Victor Morton
Profile: The Washington Times is a general interest daily newspaper that offers coverage of the greater Washington, D.C. area. Its mission is to provide readers with breaking news and news analysis. It offers a complete listing of the day's important scheduled events, a daily congressional briefing and an international briefing about happenings in the diplomatic community. Send all press materials directly to the Managing Editor, that address is configured to be a general inbox for the newsroom.
Language (s): English
DAILY NEWSPAPER

Washington Times-Herald 14028
Owner: Community Newspaper Holdings, Inc.
Editorial: 102 E Van Trees St, Washington, Indiana 47501-2943 **Tel:** 1 812 254-0480
Email: newsroom@washtimesherald.com **Web site:** http://www.washtimesherald.com
Freq: Daily; **Circ:** 6849
Editor: Melody Brunson
Profile: Washington Times-Herald is published daily for residents of Washington, IN and the surrounding area. The newspaper covers local and state news, business, sports, lifestyles and entertainment.
Language (s): English
Ad Rate: Full Page Mono 10.90
Currency: United States Dollars
DAILY NEWSPAPER

Waterbury Republican-American 13809
Owner: American-Republican Inc.
Editorial: 389 Meadow St, Waterbury, Connecticut 06702-1808 **Tel:** 1 203 574-3636
Email: releases@rep-am.com **Web site:** http://www.rep-am.com
Freq: Daily; **Circ:** 36477 Not Audited
Advertising Sales Manager: Fred Hull; **Publisher & Editor:** William J. Pape
Profile: Waterbury Republican-American was founded in 1844. Its editorial mission is to provide local, national and international news to the residents of Waterbury, CT.
Language (s): English
Ad Rate: Full Page Mono 30.84
Ad Rate: Full Page Colour 36.40
Currency: United States Dollars
DAILY NEWSPAPER

Waterbury Republican-American - Southbury Bureau 76910
Editorial: 207 Playhouse Cor, Southbury, Connecticut 06488-2265 **Tel:** 1 203 264-5554
Email: communitynews@rep-am.com
Language (s): English
DAILY NEWSPAPER

Waterbury Republican-American - Torrington Bureau 76908
Editorial: 122 Franklin St, Torrington, Connecticut 06790-5508 **Tel:** 1 860 489-4615
Language (s): English
DAILY NEWSPAPER

The Waterloo-Cedar Falls Courier 13896
Owner: Lee Enterprises, Inc.
Editorial: 100 E 4th St, Waterloo, Iowa 50703-4714 **Tel:** 1 319 291-1400
Email: newsroom@wcfcourier.com **Web site:** http://www.wcfcourier.com
Freq: Mon thru Fri; **Circ:** 38732
Publisher: David Braton; **News Editor:** Pat Kinney; **Editor:** Nancy Raffensperger Newhoff
Profile: Waterloo-Cedar Falls Courier is a daily, local newspaper for the Waterloo/Cedar Falls, IA area. The newspaper covers local news, business, sports and arts & entertainment stories. It also covers national and statewide stories if they have a direct impact on the newspaper's readership.
Language (s): English
Ad Rate: Full Page Mono 43.13
Ad Rate: Full Page Colour 475.00
Currency: United States Dollars
DAILY NEWSPAPER

Watertown Daily Times 14430
Owner: Johnson Newspaper Corp.
Editorial: 260 Washington St, Watertown, New York 13601-3301 **Tel:** 1 315 782-1000
Email: news@wdt.net **Web site:** http://www.watertowndailytimes.com
Freq: Daily; **Circ:** 18319 Not Audited
Publisher & Editor: John Johnson; **Editor:** Mary Kaskan
Profile: Watertown Daily Times is a daily newspaper written for residents of Northern New York. The newspaper covers local, state, and national news, events and sports.
Language (s): English
Ad Rate: Full Page Mono 12.72
Ad Rate: Full Page Colour 185.00
Currency: United States Dollars
DAILY NEWSPAPER

Watertown Daily Times 14824
Owner: Times Publishing Company
Editorial: 113 W Main St, 115115, Watertown, Wisconsin 53094-7623 **Tel:** 1 920 261-5161
Email: news1@wdtimes.com **Web site:** http://www.wdtimes.com
Freq: Daily; **Circ:** 6850 Not Audited
Editor: James Clifford; **Advertising Sales Manager:** Judy Kluetzman
Profile: Watertown Daily Times is a local newspaper written for residents in Watertown, WI. The newspaper covers local, national and international news, sports and community events.
Language (s): English
Ad Rate: Full Page Mono 15.65
Ad Rate: Full Page Colour 185.00
Currency: United States Dollars
DAILY NEWSPAPER

Watertown Public Opinion 14657
Owner: Schurz Communications Inc.
Editorial: 120 3rd Ave NW, Watertown, South Dakota 57201-2311 **Tel:** 1 605 886-6901
Email: news@thepublicopinion.com **Web site:** http://www.thepublicopinion.com
Freq: Daily; **Circ:** 11228
Editor: Roger Merriam; **Editor:** Terry O'Keefe; **Advertising Sales Manager:** Tim Oviatt; **Publisher:** Mark Roby
Profile: Watertown Public Opinion is a daily newspaper written for residents of Watertown, SD and surrounding areas. The newspaper covers local and regional news, sports, education, lifestyles and entertainment.
Language (s): English
Ad Rate: Full Page Mono 25.00
Ad Rate: Full Page Colour 190.00
Currency: United States Dollars
DAILY NEWSPAPER

Wausau Daily Herald 14826
Owner: Gannett Co., Inc.
Editorial: 800 Scott St, Wausau, Wisconsin 54403-4951 **Tel:** 1 715 842-2101
Email: announcements@wdhprint.com **Web site:** http://www.wausaudailyherald.com
Freq: Daily; **Circ:** 12506 Not Audited
Profile: Wausau Daily Herald is a local daily newspaper written for residents of Marathon County and Lincoln County, WI. Deadlines are at 8am CT.
Language (s): English
Ad Rate: Full Page Mono 51.40
Ad Rate: Full Page Colour 719.30
Currency: United States Dollars
DAILY NEWSPAPER

Waxahachie Daily Light 14742
Owner: Waxahachie Newspapers Inc.
Editorial: 200 W Marvin Ave, Waxahachie, Texas 75165-3040 **Tel:** 1 972 937-3310
Web site: http://www.waxahachietx.com
Freq: Mon thru Fri; **Circ:** 5027 Not Audited
Profile: Waxahachie Daily Light, founded in 1867, has been providing news for Waxahachie, TX and the surrounding communities for more than 133 years. Its focus is providing readers with local news - the events and people of note in Ellis County, TX. Deadlines are at 10am CT.
Language (s): English
Ad Rate: Full Page Mono 9.70
Ad Rate: Full Page Colour 175.00
Currency: United States Dollars
DAILY NEWSPAPER

Waycross Journal-Herald 13855
Owner: Waycross Journal-Herald Inc.
Editorial: 400 Isabella St, Waycross, Georgia 31501-3637 **Tel:** 1 912 283-2244
Email: newsroom@wjhnews.com **Web site:** http://www.wjhnews.com
Freq: Daily; **Circ:** 10100 Not Audited
Editor: Scott Cooper; **Editor:** Jack Williams; **Publisher:** Roger Williams
Profile: Waycross Journal-Herald is the official legal organ of Ware County, GA. The daily paper that has been serving Waycross County, GA and the surrounding area since 1875.
Language (s): English
Ad Rate: Full Page Mono 15.00
Ad Rate: Full Page Colour 200.00
Currency: United States Dollars
DAILY NEWSPAPER

Wayne County News 15282
Editorial: 310 Central Ave, Wayne, West Virginia 25570-9602 **Tel:** 1 304 272-3433
Web site: http://www.waynecountynews.com
Freq: Daily; **Circ:** 5100 Not Audited
Advertising Sales Manager: Ruth Adkins; **Publisher & Editor:** Thomas George
Profile: Wayne County News is written for residents of Wayne County, WV and the surrounding area. The publication aims to bring local news to the community.
Language (s): English
Ad Rate: Full Page Mono 11.75
Currency: United States Dollars
DAILY NEWSPAPER

The Wayne Independent 14583
Owner: Fortress Investment Group, LLC
Editorial: 220 8th St, Honesdale, Pennsylvania 18431-1854 **Tel:** 1 570 253-3055
Web site: http://www.wayneindependent.com
Freq: Daily; **Circ:** 4297 Not Audited
Publisher: Michelle Fleece
Profile: The Wayne Independent is written for the residents of Wayne County, PA. Deadlines are two days before publication date at 5pm ET.
Language (s): English
Ad Rate: Full Page Mono 15.25
Ad Rate: Full Page Colour 19.02
Currency: United States Dollars
DAILY NEWSPAPER

Waynesboro Record Herald 14628
Owner: Gatehouse Media, LLC
Editorial: 30 Walnut St, Waynesboro, Pennsylvania 17268-1644 **Tel:** 1 717 762-2151
Email: news@therecordherald.com **Web site:** http://www.therecordherald.com
Freq: Mon thru Fri; **Circ:** 9928 Not Audited
Editor: Shawn Hardy; **Publisher:** Pat Patterson
Profile: Waynesboro Record Herald is written for the residents of Waynesboro, PA and the surrounding area. It brings local news, sporting events and general community events to the residents of the area. Deadlines are at 10:30am ET the day of publication.
Language (s): English
Ad Rate: Full Page Mono 14.90
Ad Rate: Full Page Colour 56.21
Currency: United States Dollars
DAILY NEWSPAPER

Weatherford Daily News 14543
Editorial: 118 S Broadway St, Weatherford, Oklahoma 73096 **Tel:** 1 580 772-3301
Email: wdn@wdnonline.com **Web site:** http://www.wdnonline.com
Freq: Daily; **Circ:** 4893 Not Audited
Publisher: Phillip Reid
Profile: Weatherford Daily News is the daily newspaper for Weatherford, OK. The newspaper focuses on local news and events for the area's residents. Sections include news, sports, public records, community calendar, school calendar and classified ads.
Language (s): English
Ad Rate: Full Page Mono 13.74
Ad Rate: Full Page Colour 85.00
Currency: United States Dollars
DAILY NEWSPAPER

Weatherford Democrat 14743
Owner: Community Newspaper Holdings, Inc.
Editorial: 512 Palo Pinto St, Weatherford, Texas 76086-4197 **Tel:** 1 817 594-7447
Email: editor@weatherforddemocrat.com **Web site:** http://www.weatherforddemocrat.com
Freq: Daily; **Circ:** 6500 Not Audited
Editor: Sally Sexton
Profile: Weatherford Democrat's editorial mission is to provide the local news and information to Weatherford and Parker County residents. The deadline for the publication is the day before issue date by 10am CT.
Language (s): English
Ad Rate: Full Page Mono 12.50
Ad Rate: Full Page Colour 250.00
Currency: United States Dollars
DAILY NEWSPAPER

Weirton Daily Times 14844
Owner: Ogden Newspapers
Editorial: 401 Herald Sq, Steubenville, Ohio 43952-2059 **Tel:** 1 304 748-0606
Email: newsroom@heraldstaronline.com **Web site:** http://www.weirtondailytimes.com
Freq: Daily; **Circ:** 3664 Not Audited
Profile: Weirton Daily Times is a daily newspaper that provides local, national and international news for the residents of Weirton, WV.
Language (s): English
Ad Rate: Full Page Mono 48.44
Ad Rate: Full Page Colour 312.61
Currency: United States Dollars
DAILY NEWSPAPER

Wellington Daily News 14069
Owner: Fortress Investment Group, LLC
Editorial: 113 W Harvey Ave, Wellington, Kansas 67152-3840 **Tel:** 1 620 326-3326
Web site: http://www.wellingtondailynews.com
Freq: Daily; **Circ:** 2900 Not Audited
Publisher: Randy Mitchell
Profile: Wellington Daily News is published daily for the residents of Wellington, KS and surrounding areas. The newspaper covers local and state news, business, sports, lifestyles and arts & entertainment.
Language (s): English
Ad Rate: Full Page Mono 9.00
Ad Rate: Full Page Colour 11.00
Currency: United States Dollars
DAILY NEWSPAPER

Wellsville Daily Reporter 14431
Owner: Fortress Investment Group, LLC
Editorial: 159 N Main St, Wellsville, New York 14895-1149 **Tel:** 1 585 593-5300
Web site: http://www.wellsvilledaily.com
Freq: Daily; **Circ:** 4500 Not Audited
Publisher: Oak Duke; **Advertising Sales Manager:** Jody Wood
Profile: Wellsville Daily Reporter is written to bring local news to Alleghany County, NY.
Language (s): English
Ad Rate: Full Page Mono 8.50
Ad Rate: Full Page Colour 100.00
Currency: United States Dollars
DAILY NEWSPAPER

Wenatchee World 14791
Owner: World Publishing Co.
Editorial: 14 N Mission St, Wenatchee, Washington 98801-2250 **Tel:** 1 509 663-5161
Email: circulation@wenatcheeworld.com **Web site:** http://www.wenatcheeworld.com
Freq: Daily; **Circ:** 19356 Not Audited
Publisher & Editor: Rufus Woods
Profile: Wenatchee World is a daily newspaper that covers regional news for Wenatchee, WA. The newspaper features topics such as local business, recreation, arts and entertainment, sports, business, agriculture, community, classifieds, government, transportation, family, faith and health.
Language (s): English
Ad Rate: Full Page Mono 32.10
Ad Rate: Full Page Colour 103.46
Currency: United States Dollars
DAILY NEWSPAPER

West Bend Daily Times & Hartford Times Press 826566
Editorial: 100 S 6th Ave, West Bend, Wisconsin 53095-3309 **Tel:** 1 262 338-0622
Web site: http://www.gmtoday.com
DAILY NEWSPAPER

West Central Tribune 14218
Owner: Forum Communications Co.
Editorial: 2208 Trott Ave Sw, Willmar, Minnesota 56201-2723 **Tel:** 1 320 235-1150
Email: news@wctrib.com **Web site:** http://www.wctrib.com
Freq: Daily; **Circ:** 11477 Not Audited
Publisher: Steve Ammermann; **Editor:** Kelly Boldan; **News Editor:** Susan Lunneborg

Profile: West Central Tribune is a daily newspaper written for the residents of Willmar, MN. It covers local news, business, community news, entertainment and sports.
Language (s): English
Ad Rate: Full Page Mono 21.57
Ad Rate: Full Page Colour 463.00
Currency: United States Dollars
DAILY NEWSPAPER

West County Times 13773

Owner: MediaNews Group
Editorial: 1050 Marina Way S, Richmond, California 94804-3741 **Tel:** 1 510 262-2732
Email: ccnnewsrelease@bayareanewsgroup.com
Web site: http://www.contracostatimes.com/west-county-times
Freq: Daily; **Circ:** 33000 Not Audited
Profile: West County Times in Richmond, CA is a daily newspaper that covers news, sports, arts & entertainment and more.
Language (s): English
Ad Rate: Full Page Mono 57.00
Currency: United States Dollars
DAILY NEWSPAPER

West Hawaii Today 13862

Owner: Stephens Media Group
Editorial: 75-5580 Kuakini Hwy, Kailua Kona, Hawaii 96740-1647 **Tel:** 1 808 329-9311
Email: wht@aloha.net **Web site:** http://www.westhawaiitoday.com
Freq: Daily
Publisher & Editor: David Bock
Profile: West Hawaii Today is written for Kailua-Kona, HI and the surrounding areas.
Language (s): English
Ad Rate: Full Page Mono 23.00
Ad Rate: Full Page Colour 405.00
Currency: United States Dollars
DAILY NEWSPAPER

West Plains Daily Quill 14257

Owner: Quill Press Company, Inc.
Editorial: 205 Washington Ave, West Plains, Missouri 65775-3439 **Tel:** 1 417 256-9191
Email: news@wpdailyquill.net **Web site:** http://www.westplainsdailyquill.net
Freq: Mon thru Fri; **Circ:** 6922 Not Audited
Publisher: Jim Perry
Profile: West Plains Daily Quill is published weekly for residents of Howell County, MO. The newspaper covers local news and community events.
Language (s): English
Ad Rate: Full Page Mono 12.10
Ad Rate: Full Page Colour 250.00
Currency: United States Dollars
DAILY NEWSPAPER

West Virginia Daily News 14837

Owner: Moffitt Newspapers
Editorial: 200 S Court St, Lewisburg, West Virginia 24901-1310 **Tel:** 1 304 645-1206
Email: wvdailynews@suddenlinkmail.com **Web site:** http://wvdailynews.net/
Freq: Mon thru Fri; **Circ:** 4200 Not Audited
Advertising Sales Manager: Barbara Cordall; **Publisher:** Judy Steele
Profile: West Virginia Daily News's editorial mission is to keep the area informed about what's going on in the local community. The publication is written for Lewisburg, WV and the immediate surrounding area.
Language (s): English
Ad Rate: Full Page Mono 6.85
Ad Rate: Full Page Colour 120.00
Currency: United States Dollars
DAILY NEWSPAPER

The Westerly Sun 14638

Owner: Record-Journal Publishing Company
Editorial: 99 Mechanic St, Pawcatuck, Connecticut 06379-2132 **Tel:** 1 401 348-1000
Email: editorial@thewesterlysun.com **Web site:** http://www.thewesterlysun.com
Freq: Daily; **Circ:** 8665 Not Audited
Profile: The Westerly Sun is a local, daily newspaper serving the Westerly, RI and Stonington, CT areas. The paper covers local news, sports and entertainment. It is the main source of local news and advertising in Southern Rhode Island and Southeastern Connecticut.
Language (s): English
Ad Rate: Full Page Mono 18.11
Ad Rate: Full Page Colour 300.00
Currency: United States Dollars
DAILY NEWSPAPER

The Westfield News 14138

Owner: Allbritton Communications Co.
Editorial: 62 - 64 School St, Westfield, Massachusetts 01085-2890 **Tel:** 1 413 562-4181
Email: pressreleases@thewestfieldnews.com **Web site:** http://thewestfieldnews.com
Freq: Daily; **Circ:** 5300 Not Audited
Profile: Westfield News is a local daily newspaper distributed nightly Monday through Friday. The Saturday edition is a morning paper. It delivers local news and event information to the Westfield, MA community. Deadline is approximately a week before issue date.
Language (s): English
Ad Rate: Full Page Mono 12.80
Ad Rate: Full Page Colour 375.00
Currency: United States Dollars
DAILY NEWSPAPER

Whittier Daily News 13766

Owner: Southern California News Group/Digital First Media
Editorial: 7612 Greenleaf Ave, Whittier, California 90602-1625 **Tel:** 1 562 698-0955
Email: news.wdn@sgvn.com **Web site:** http://www.whittierdailynews.com
Freq: Daily; **Circ:** 13757
Profile: Whittier Daily News is a daily newspaper written for the residents of Whittier, CA. This paper is a part of the Southern California News Group, a subsidiary of Digital First Media. It covers local news, sports, business, features and arts & entertainment in Whittier and Southeast Los Angeles.
Language (s): English
Ad Rate: Full Page Mono 651.00
Ad Rate: Full Page Colour 2121.50
Currency: United States Dollars
DAILY NEWSPAPER

The Wichita Eagle 15316

Owner: McClatchy Newspapers
Editorial: 330 N Mead, Wichita, Kansas 67202
Tel: 1 316 268-6000
Email: wenews@wichitaeagle.com **Web site:** http://www.kansas.com
Freq: Daily; **Circ:** 46709 Not Audited
Editor: Sherry Chisenhall
Profile: The Wichita Eagle is a daily newspaper covering Wichita, KS and the surrounding area. The paper covers local and national news, sports, business and the arts. The best way to contact the paper is by fax. The editorial deadline varies depending on the section. The lead times vary depending on the story. The editorial department accepts non-disclosure agreements on a case-by-case basis.
Language (s): English
Ad Rate: Full Page Mono 52.54
Ad Rate: Full Page Colour 70.54
Currency: United States Dollars
DAILY NEWSPAPER

Williamson Daily News 14847

Owner: Heartland Publications
Editorial: 100 E 3rd Ave, Williamson, West Virginia 25661-3620 **Tel:** 1 304 235-4242
Web site: http://www.williamsondailynews.com
Freq: Daily; **Circ:** 10578 Not Audited
Editor: Kyle Lovern; **Publisher:** Ed Martin
Profile: Williamson Daily News is a daily newspaper written for the residents of Mingo and Logan County, WV as well as Pike and Martin County, KY. The newspaper covers local news, events, sports and entertainment. Deadlines for the publication are 6pm ET the day prior to issue date.
Language (s): English
Ad Rate: Full Page Mono 9.85
Ad Rate: Full Page Colour 300.00
Currency: United States Dollars
DAILY NEWSPAPER

Williamsport Sun-Gazette 14631

Owner: Ogden Newspapers
Editorial: 252 W 4th St, Williamsport, Pennsylvania 17701 **Tel:** 1 570 326-1551
Email: news@sungazette.com **Web site:** http://www.sungazette.com
Freq: Daily; **Circ:** 23575 Not Audited
Editor: Laura Janssen; **Publisher:** Bernie Oravec; **Editor:** Dave Troisi
Profile: Williamsport Sun-Gazette is published daily for residents of Williamsport, PA and surrounding communities. The newspaper covers local and national news, weather, sports and community events. Feature articles cover business developments, politics, education, arts & entertainment and lifestyle. Deadlines are the day prior to the issue date at 5pm ET.
Language (s): English
Ad Rate: Full Page Mono 40.00
Ad Rate: Full Page Colour 305.00
Currency: United States Dollars
DAILY NEWSPAPER

Williston Herald 14335

Owner: Wick Communications Inc.
Editorial: 14 4th St W, Williston, North Dakota 58801-5308 **Tel:** 1 701 572-2165
Email: news@willistonherald.com **Web site:** http://www.willistonherald.com
Freq: Daily; **Circ:** 4134 Not Audited
Publisher: Mitzi Moe
Profile: Williston Daily Herald is a daily newspaper written for residents of Williston, ND and the surrounding areas. The paper covers local news and events. There is no Saturday edition. The paper is affiliated with the Plains Reporter.
Language (s): English
Ad Rate: Full Page Mono 12.60
Ad Rate: Full Page Colour 103.00
Currency: United States Dollars
DAILY NEWSPAPER

Wilmington News-Journal 14914

Owner: AIM Media Midwest
Editorial: 761 S Nelson Ave, Wilmington, Ohio 45177-2517 **Tel:** 1 937 382-2574
Email: info@wnewsj.com **Web site:** http://www.wnewsj.com
Freq: Fri; **Circ:** 7292 Not Audited
Editor & Publisher: Thomas Barr
Profile: Wilmington News-Journal is written for residents of Clinton County, OH. Deadlines are at 4pm ET. The Monday shopper edition of the paper is called the Star Republican. The paper was established in 1837.
Language (s): English
Ad Rate: Full Page Mono 15.50
Ad Rate: Full Page Colour 22.31
Currency: United States Dollars
DAILY NEWSPAPER

The Wilson Times 14321

Owner: The Wilson Times Company
Editorial: 2001 Downing St SW, Wilson, North Carolina 27893-4611 **Tel:** 1 252 243-5151
Email: editor@wilsontimes.com **Web site:** http://www.wilsontimes.com
Freq: Mon thru Fri; **Circ:** 12320
Publisher: Morgan Dickerman
Profile: Wilson Daily Times is a local daily newspaper serving residents of Wilson, NC and surrounding communities. The newspaper covers local, state, and national news, weather, sports and community events. Feature articles cover business developments, education, politics, arts & entertainment and lifestyle. The editorial lead time for the publication varies. Deadlines for the publication are one day prior to the issue date.
Language (s): English
Ad Rate: Full Page Mono 13.23
Ad Rate: Full Page Colour 350.00
Currency: United States Dollars
DAILY NEWSPAPER

The Winchester Star 14768

Owner: Byrd Newspapers
Editorial: 2 N Kent St, Winchester, Virginia 22601-5038 **Tel:** 1 540 667-3200
Email: news@winchesterstar.com **Web site:** http://www.winchesterstar.com
Freq: Daily; **Circ:** 18199 Not Audited
Profile: Winchester Star is written for residents of Frederick County, VA.
Language (s): English
Ad Rate: Full Page Mono 21.10
Ad Rate: Full Page Colour 24.27
Currency: United States Dollars
DAILY NEWSPAPER

Winchester Sun 14091

Owner: Schurz Communications Inc.
Editorial: 20 Wall St, Winchester, Kentucky 40391-1900 **Tel:** 1 859 744-3123
Email: news@winchestersun.com **Web site:** http://www.centralkynews.com/winchestersun
Freq: Daily; **Circ:** 7300 Not Audited
Profile: Winchester Sun is written for the community of Winchester, KY. The publication covers local news, sports and community events.
Language (s): English
Ad Rate: Full Page Mono 11.25
Currency: United States Dollars
DAILY NEWSPAPER

Winona Daily News 14219

Owner: Lee Enterprises, Inc.
Editorial: 902 E 2nd St Ste 110, Winona, Minnesota 55987-6512 **Tel:** 1 507 453-3500
Email: news@winonadailynews.com **Web site:** http://www.winonadailynews.com
Freq: Daily; **Circ:** 7637 Not Audited
Editor: Jerome Christenson; **Publisher:** Russell Cunningham; **Editor:** Darrell Ehrlick
Profile: Winona Daily News is written for surrounding communities of Winona, MN.
Language (s): English
Ad Rate: Full Page Mono 22.92
Ad Rate: Full Page Colour 300.00
Currency: United States Dollars
DAILY NEWSPAPER

Winston-Salem Journal 15367

Owner: BH Media Group
Editorial: 418 N Marshall St, Winston Salem, North Carolina 27101-2815 **Tel:** 1 336 727-7211
Email: news@wsjournal.com **Web site:** http://www.journalnow.com
Freq: Daily; **Circ:** 42651 Not Audited
Profile: Winston-Salem Journal is a daily newspaper with a primary coverage area of Forsyth County, and nine other counties in Northwest North Carolina including Alleghany, Ashe, Davidson, Davie, Stokes, Surry, Watauga, Wilkes and Yadkin. The paper features local, state and national news, business, arts & entertainment, sports and classifieds. The paper uses a percentage rate for color advertisements.
Language (s): English
Ad Rate: Full Page Mono 109.00
Ad Rate: Full Page Colour 136.25
Currency: United States Dollars
DAILY NEWSPAPER

Wisconsin State Journal 14811

Owner: Lee Enterprises
Editorial: 1901 Fish Hatchery Rd, Madison, Wisconsin 53713-1248 **Tel:** 1 608 252-6100
Web site: http://host.madison.com/wsj/
Freq: Daily; **Circ:** 71222 Not Audited
Editor: John Smalley
Profile: Wisconsin State Journal covers national, regional and local news as well as sports and politics.
Language (s): English
Ad Rate: Full Page Mono 112.43
Ad Rate: Full Page Colour 119.86
Currency: United States Dollars
DAILY NEWSPAPER

Wisconsin State Journal - Madison Bureau 62897

Editorial: State Capital Press Room, Madison, Wisconsin 53701
Web site: http://www.madison.com
Profile: The reporters in this bureau work out of the state capital press room.
Language (s): English
DAILY NEWSPAPER

Woodward News 14544

Owner: Community Newspaper Holdings, Inc.
Editorial: 904 Oklahoma Ave, Woodward, Oklahoma 73801-4660 **Tel:** 1 580 256-2200
Email: editor@woodwardnews.net **Web site:** http://www.woodwardnews.net
Freq: Daily; **Circ:** 5000 Not Audited
Publisher: Sheila Gay; **Editor:** Johnny McMahan
Profile: Woodward News is written for residents of Woodward County, OK. Deadlines are 5pm CT, the prior day before issue date.
Language (s): English
Ad Rate: Full Page Mono 10.12
Ad Rate: Full Page Colour 170.00
Currency: United States Dollars
DAILY NEWSPAPER

The World 14552

Owner: Lee Enterprises, Inc.
Editorial: 350 Commercial Ave, Coos Bay, Oregon 97420-2269 **Tel:** 1 541 269-1222
Email: theworldnews@theworldlink.com **Web site:** http://www.theworldlink.com
Freq: Mon thru Fri; **Circ:** 7808 Not Audited
News Editor: Ron Jackimowicz
Profile: The World is published daily for the residents of Coos Bay, OR and surrounding areas. The newspaper covers news, national news, sports, outdoors, home and garden, business, coast life and entertainment. It is published daily except on Sunday, Labor Day, or Christmas.
Language (s): English
Ad Rate: Full Page Mono 30.20
Ad Rate: Full Page Colour 97.27
Currency: United States Dollars
DAILY NEWSPAPER

World Journal: Los Angeles Edition 800828

Editorial: 1588 Corporate Center Dr, Monterey Park, California 91754-7624 **Tel:** 1 323 268-4982
Email: citydesk-la@worldjournal.com **Web site:** http://www.worldjournal.com/category/losangeles
Profile: World Journal: Los Angeles Edition is a daily community newspaper.
Language (s): English
DAILY NEWSPAPER

World Journal: New York Edition 152827

Owner: World Journal Inc.
Editorial: 14107 20th Ave, Whitestone, New York 11357-3062 **Tel:** 1 718 746-8889
Email: citydesk@worldjournal.com **Web site:** http://www.worldjournal.com
Freq: Daily; **Circ:** 75000 Not Audited
Profile: World Journal: New York Edition is a Chinese-language newspaper published daily for residents in North America. The paper covers political and social developments in China, Hong Kong, Taiwan, and Southeast Asia, as well as business, sports, arts & entertainment and sports news.
Language (s): Chinese
Ad Rate: Full Page Colour 26.50
Currency: United States Dollars
DAILY NEWSPAPER

World Journal: San Francisco Edition 80007

Owner: World Journal Inc.
Editorial: 231 Adrian Rd, Millbrae, California 94030-3102 **Tel:** 1 650 692-9936
Web site: http://www.worldjournal.com/sf
Freq: Daily; **Circ:** 250000 Not Audited
Editor: Yu-Ru Chen; **Publisher:** Pili Wang
Profile: World Journal: San Francisco Edition is a local daily newspaper written for the Chinese and Chinese-American community of San Francisco and surrounding areas.
Language (s): Chinese
Ad Rate: Full Page Mono 6.70
Ad Rate: Full Page Colour 10.00
Currency: United States Dollars
DAILY NEWSPAPER

Wyoming Tribune-Eagle 14848

Owner: Cheyenne Newspapers, Inc.
Editorial: 702 W Lincolnway, Cheyenne, Wyoming 82001-4397 **Tel:** 1 307 634-3361
Email: news@wyomingnews.com **Web site:** http://www.wyomingnews.com
Freq: Daily; **Circ:** 14061 Not Audited
Profile: Wyoming Tribune-Eagle is a daily newspaper that is written for surrounding communities of Cheyenne, WY. The newspaper covers local news, events, business, entertainment, and sports stories.
Language (s): English
Ad Rate: Full Page Mono 22.50
Ad Rate: Full Page Colour 80.06
Currency: United States Dollars
DAILY NEWSPAPER

Yakima Herald-Republic 14792

Owner: Seattle Times Co.
Editorial: 114 N 4th St, Yakima, Washington 98901-2707 **Tel:** 1 509 248-1251
Email: news@yakima-herald.com **Web site:** http://www.yakimaherald.com
Freq: Daily; **Circ:** 25695 Not Audited
Editor: Bob Crider
Profile: Yakima Herald-Republic is a local daily newspaper written for the residents of Yakima, WA.

The newspaper covers the local news, business, entertainment and sports, as well as national and limited international stories.
Language (s): English
Ad Rate: Full Page Mono 40.87
Ad Rate: Full Page Colour 683.00
Currency: United States Dollars
DAILY NEWSPAPER

Yankton Daily Press & Dakotan
14658
Owner: Yankton Media Inc.
Editorial: 319 Walnut St, Yankton, South Dakota 57078-4309 **Tel:** 1 605 665-7811
Email: news@yankton.net **Web site:** http://www.yankton.net
Freq: Mon thru Fri; **Circ:** 8303 Not Audited
Publisher & Editor: Gary Wood
Profile: Yankton Daily Press & Dakotan is published daily for the residents of Yankton, SD and surrounding areas. The newspaper covers local and regional news, business, sports, education and entertainment.
Language (s): English
Ad Rate: Full Page Mono 18.36
Ad Rate: Full Page Colour 60.03
Currency: United States Dollars
DAILY NEWSPAPER

York Daily Record
14632
Owner: Gannett Co., Inc.
Editorial: 1891 Loucks Rd, York, Pennsylvania 17408-9708 **Tel:** 1 717 771-2000
Email: news@ydr.com **Web site:** http://www.ydr.com
Freq: Daily; **Circ:** 51337
Editor: James McClure
Profile: York Daily Record is written for the residents of York County, PA. It covers national and local news, sports, business and events. The Sunday edition of the paper is called York Sunday News.
Language (s): English
Ad Rate: Full Page Mono 61.00
Ad Rate: Full Page Colour 901.50
Currency: United States Dollars
DAILY NEWSPAPER

The York Dispatch
14633
Owner: Gannett Co. Inc.
Editorial: 1891 Loucks Rd, York, Pennsylvania 17408-9708 **Tel:** 1 717 854-1575
Email: news@yorkdispatch.com **Web site:** http://www.yorkdispatch.com
Freq: Daily; **Circ:** 37688 Not Audited
Editor: Allison Cooper; **Publisher:** David Martens
Profile: The York Dispatch is a daily, evening newspaper serving the York, PA area. The paper covers local news, business, entertainment, sports and lifestyle. On Sundays, it combines with the York Daily Record. The lead time is two weeks and the absolute deadline is one week before issue date.
Language (s): English
Ad Rate: Full Page Mono 61.00
Ad Rate: Full Page Colour 146.19
Currency: United States Dollars
DAILY NEWSPAPER

York News-Times
14349
Owner: Omaha World-Herald Co.
Editorial: 327 N Platte Ave, York, Nebraska 68467-3547 **Tel:** 1 402 362-4478
Email: news@yorknewstimes.com **Web site:** http://www.yorknewstimes.com
Freq: Daily; **Circ:** 4328 Not Audited
Profile: York News-Times is a local daily newspaper written for residents of York, NE. The publication's editorial mission is to report the local news of York, NE.
Language (s): English
Ad Rate: Full Page Mono 12.50
Ad Rate: Full Page Colour 119.00
Currency: United States Dollars
DAILY NEWSPAPER

The Yuma Sun
13715
Owner: Rhode Island Suburban Newspapers, Inc.
Editorial: 2055 S Arizona Ave, Yuma, Arizona 85364-6549 **Tel:** 1 928 783-3333
Email: newsroom@yumasun.com **Web site:** http://www.yumasun.com
Freq: Daily; **Circ:** 15932 Not Audited
Editor: Roxanne Molenar
Profile: The Yuma Sun is a daily newspaper serving the Yuma, AZ area. The publication covers local news, sports, lifestyle and entertainment for the residents of Yuma.
Language (s): English
Ad Rate: Full Page Mono 30.01
Ad Rate: Full Page Colour 797.00
Currency: United States Dollars
DAILY NEWSPAPER

News Service/Syndicate

Accuracy in Media
30819
Owner: Accuracy in Media Inc.
Editorial: 4350 E West Hwy Ste 555, Bethesda, Maryland 20814-4582 **Tel:** 1 202 364-4401
Email: info@aim.org **Web site:** http://www.aim.org
Profile: Accuracy in Media is a non-profit, grassroots citizens watchdog of the news media that critiques botched and bungled news stories and sets the record straight on important issues that have received slanted coverage. Column focus is on examples of media bias, distortion and erroneous coverage.
Language (s): English
NEWS SERVICE/SYNDICATE

AccuWeather
30888
Owner: AccuWeather Inc.
Editorial: 385 Science Park Rd, State College, Pennsylvania 16803-2215 **Tel:** 1 814 237-0309
Email: salesmail@accuweather.com **Web site:** http://www.accuweather.com
Profile: AccuWeather provides a portfolio of products and services via the Internet, in print and behind the scenes for millions of people worldwide. It services 300,000 paying customers in media, business, government and institutions, and millions more through AccuWeather.com. It also provides content to more than 10,000 Internet sites, including CNN Interactive, ABC's owned and operated stations, The Washington Post, USA Today and The New York Times.
Language (s): English
NEWS SERVICE/SYNDICATE

African American Newswire
88079
Tel: 1 413 221-7931
Email: jfondon@unityfirst.com **Web site:** http://www.unityfirst.com
Profile: African American Newswire is a news service that reaches communities of color, including community-based organizations, business and professional groups, social associations and spiritual outlets across the country.
Language (s): English
NEWS SERVICE/SYNDICATE

AlterNet
31088
Owner: Independent Media Institute
Editorial: 1881 Harmon St, Berkeley, California 94703-2415
Email: info@alternet.org **Web site:** http://www.alternet.org
Profile: AlterNet is a non-profit organization devoted to promoting and strengthening the independent press. About 45 stories a week are syndicated on the virtual newswire. Categories include: news and features; media culture review; essays, columns and opinions; shorts; arts & entertainment and books and authors. Coverage often includes new media and technology, political commentary, the environment, sex, personal essays and noteworthy literary writing. More than 200 media outlets subscribe.
Language (s): English
NEWS SERVICE/SYNDICATE

American Baptist News Service
588707
Editorial: 588 N Gulph Rd, King of Prussia, Pennsylvania 19406-2831 **Tel:** 1 610 768-2322
Email: webmaster@abc-usa.org **Web site:** http://www.abc-usa.org
Profile: The American Baptist News Service provides information on events and developments in the American Baptist Churches USA.
Language (s): English
NEWS SERVICE/SYNDICATE

American Chemical Society News Service
31061
Editorial: 1155 16th St NW, Washington, District Of Columbia 20036-4839 **Tel:** 1 800 333-9511
Email: newsroom@acs.org **Web site:** http://www.chemistry.org
Profile: American Chemical Society News Service provides expert commentary on a variety of topics related to the chemical sciences. Also distributes news briefs and features on many of the research findings presented at its national meetings and in its numerous scientific journals.
Language (s): English
NEWS SERVICE/SYNDICATE

American Federation of Teachers
30774
Owner: American Federation of Teachers
Editorial: 555 New Jersey Ave NW, Washington, District Of Columbia 20001-2029 **Tel:** 1 202 879-4400
Email: online@aft.org **Web site:** http://www.aft.org
Profile: Monthly review and opinion column focusing on current issues affecting education, children and labor/management relations. Monthly radio spots are also done on the same subject matter.
Language (s): English
NEWS SERVICE/SYNDICATE

American Lawyer Media
281714
Owner: ALM Media Properties, LLC
Editorial: 120 Broadway Fl 5, New York, New York 10271-1100 **Tel:** 1 212 457-9408
Email: editorial@alm.com **Web site:** http://www.alm.com
Profile: American Lawyer Media is the nation's leading source of news and information for the legal industry. The news service owns and publishes 33 award-winning national and regional legal trade newspapers and magazines, including The American Lawyer and The National Law Journal. Other services for legal professionals include book, custom and newsletter publishing, court verdict and settlement reporting, production of legal trade shows and conferences, educational seminars and distribution of content related to the legal industry.
Language (s): English
NEWS SERVICE/SYNDICATE

American-International News Syndicate
73631
Editorial: 695 Olive Rd, Santa Barbara, California 93108-1442 **Tel:** 1 805 969-5848

Profile: The syndicate's main features, Ask The Expert and The Discriminating Traveler, cover restaurants, food, new books, art and luxury travel news. The features explore hotels, spas, wines and cruises and syndicated to 25 newspapers across the country.
Language (s): English
NEWS SERVICE/SYNDICATE

Amok
30949
Editorial: 287 Margaret Way, Ripon, California 95366-9317 **Tel:** 1 415 730-5610
Web site: http://www.amok.com
Profile: The author looks at news and issues affecting America's ethnic minorities, with special emphasis on Asian-Americans. He also includes coverage of sports, politics, movies, entertainment, public policy, Washington events, California, high-tech, computers and the Internet.
Language (s): English
NEWS SERVICE/SYNDICATE

Ampersand Communications
31013
Editorial: 2311 S Bayshore Dr, Miami, Florida 33133-4728 **Tel:** 1 305 285-2200
Email: amprsnd@aol.com **Web site:** http://www.ampersandcom.com
Profile: Ampersand Communications is a diversified news features syndication firm that specializes in coverage of food, travel, books, healthcare and other topics. The firm provides editorial copy to online publications as well as newspapers, magazines and trade journals.
Language (s): English
NEWS SERVICE/SYNDICATE

Anadolu Agency - New York Bureau
619604
Editorial: 801 2nd Ave Rm 502, New York, New York 10017-8602 **Tel:** 1 646 596-8484
Email: newyork@aa.com.tr **Web site:** http://www.aa.com.tr/en/
Bureau Chief: Huseyin Kosger
Profile: This is the New York Bureau of Anadolu Agency in Turkey; the agency's other bureau is in Washington, D.C. Both agencies cover developments in the U.S. that are relevant to Turkey.
Language (s): Turkish
NEWS SERVICE/SYNDICATE

Andrews McMeel Syndication
30750
Owner: Andrews McMeel Universal
Editorial: 1130 Walnut St, Kansas City, Missouri 64106-2109 **Tel:** 1 816 581-7300
Web site: http://syndication.andrewsmcmeel.com
Editor: Lee Salem
Profile: Andrews McMeel Syndication offers a lineup of features, from insightful and provocative commentary to useful and delightful lifestyle, consumer and entertainment information, advice and opinion on a wide range of topics including: parenting, advice, food and recipes, fashion, healthcare, computers, home remodeling, business, personal finance, entertainment and travel, plus comic strips, comic panels and editorial cartoons.
Language (s): English
NEWS SERVICE/SYNDICATE

AP Money & Markets
504495
Owner: Associated Press, Inc.
Editorial: 1 World Financial Ctr Lbby 5, New York, New York 10281-1011 **Tel:** 1 212 621-1500
Email: stocks@ap.org **Web site:** http://markets.ap.org/moneyMarkets.htm
Editor: Joyce Rosenberg
Profile: Money & Markets is an off-shoot of the Associated Press and provides analytical, forward-looking financial data in the form of graphs, data and reports. The service offers modular, customized business and financial sections and is distributed in newspapers nationwide. It is designed to offer the quick-paced changes of the financial world in both print and online content formats. The service also offers Money & Markets Extra, which is geared towards newspapers' weekend editions.
Language (s): English
NEWS SERVICE/SYNDICATE

Army News Service
231607
Email: arnews.dma@mail.mil **Web site:** https://www.army.mil/arnews
Editor: Gary Sheftick
Profile: Army News Service keeps the United States Army's obligation of informing the American people and the Army of the latest Army news, including news on policies and combat updates.
Language (s): English
NEWS SERVICE/SYNDICATE

Army Times News Service
238913
Editorial: 1919 Gallows Rd Fl 4, Vienna, Virginia 22182-3964 **Tel:** 1 703 750-7400
Email: armylet@armytimes.com **Web site:** http://www.armytimes.com
News Editor: Karen Small
Profile: Army Times News Service offers exclusive, original, in-depth news and analysis about an Army career, pay and benefits and issues impacting professional advancement. It also has community information and active lifestyle features of interest to Army personnel and their families. There are over 18 supplements during the year, including valuable military resource guides, a special annual historical

issue, military healthcare specials and important second career and educational supplements.
Language (s): English
NEWS SERVICE/SYNDICATE

Ask Jerry
242244
Tel: 1 202 244-2222
Email: askjerry@earthlink.net
Profile: Eclectic, entertaining consumer advice column featured in daily newspapers throughout the United States. Ask Jerry solutions appear in the Features, Business and Sunday magazine sections, where millions of readers learn to find the unobtainable and solve the impossible.
Language (s): English
NEWS SERVICE/SYNDICATE

Assist News Service
232274
Editorial: 23591 El Toro Rd, Lake Forest, California 92630-4774 **Tel:** 1 949 472-0974
Email: danjuma1@aol.com **Web site:** http://assistnews.net
Profile: Assist News Service offers news on religious happenings around the world, focusing on international news from a Christian perspective.
Language (s): English
NEWS SERVICE/SYNDICATE

Associated Designs
476034
Editorial: 1100 Jacobs Dr, Eugene, Oregon 97402-1983 **Tel:** 1 541 461-2082
Email: info@associateddesigns.com **Web site:** http://www.associateddesigns.com
Editor: Rick McAlexander
Profile: Associated Designs home plans are created by talented designers with more than 50 years of combined home design experience. Weekly columns feature plans that are published in newspapers around the country. Since the company was founded, more than 60,000 home plans have been sold.
Language (s): English
NEWS SERVICE/SYNDICATE

Associated Press
31014
Owner: Associated Press, Inc.
Editorial: 200 Liberty St, New York, New York 10281-1003 **Tel:** 1 212 621-1500
Email: info@ap.org **Web site:** https://apnews.com
Profile: Founded in 1848, Associated Press is an international news organization offering news, photos, graphics, audio and video for 1,700 newspapers and 5,000 radio and television outlets in the United States as well as newspaper, radio and television subscribers internationally. There are bureaus worldwide representing over one hundred countries. It features a massive digital photo network, a continuously updated online news service, a television news service and one of the largest radio networks in the United States. Daybook items for New York City should go to the alternate email.
Language (s): English
NEWS SERVICE/SYNDICATE

Associated Press - Albany Bureau
31261
Owner: Associated Press, Inc.
Editorial: 645 Albany Shaker Rd, Albany, New York 12211-1158 **Tel:** 1 518 458-7821
Email: apalbany@ap.org
Language (s): English
NEWS SERVICE/SYNDICATE

Associated Press - Albuquerque Bureau
31134
Owner: Associated Press, Inc.
Editorial: 5130 San Francisco Rd NE Ste A, Albuquerque, New Mexico 87109-4618
Tel: 1 505 822-9022
Email: apalbuquerque@ap.org
Language (s): English
NEWS SERVICE/SYNDICATE

Associated Press - Allentown Bureau
334442
Owner: Associated Press Inc.
Editorial: Allentown, Pennsylvania **Tel:** 1 610 207-9297
Email: phillyap@ap.org
Language (s): English
NEWS SERVICE/SYNDICATE

Associated Press - Amman Bureau
732079
Owner: Associated Press, Inc.
Editorial: Amman **Tel:** 962 6 461-4660
Email: apamman@ap.org
Bureau Chief: Karin Laub
Language (s): English
NEWS SERVICE/SYNDICATE

Associated Press - Amsterdam Bureau
217842
Owner: Associated Press, Inc.
Editorial: Hoogte Kadijk 143/F20, Amsterdam 1018
Tel: 31 20 623-5057
Chief Correspondent: Mike Corder
Language (s): English
NEWS SERVICE/SYNDICATE

Associated Press - Anchorage Bureau
31235
Owner: Associated Press, Inc.
Editorial: 750 W 2nd Ave Ste 102, Anchorage, Alaska 99501-2167 **Tel:** 1 907 272-7549

United States of America

Email: apanchorage@ap.org
News Editor: Mark Thiessen
Language (s): English
NEWS SERVICE/SYNDICATE

Associated Press - Ankara Bureau
377894
Owner: Associated Press, Inc.
Editorial: Ankara **Tel:** 90 312 428-2709
Email: apankara@ap.org
Language (s): English
NEWS SERVICE/SYNDICATE

Associated Press - Annapolis Bureau
31293
Owner: Associated Press, Inc.
Editorial: 100 State Cir, Annapolis, Maryland 21401-1924 **Tel:** 1 410 269-0196
Email: balpr@ap.org
Language (s): English
NEWS SERVICE/SYNDICATE

Associated Press - Asuncion Bureau
964230
Owner: Associated Press, Inc.
Editorial: Asuncion **Tel:** 595 21 606-334
Language (s): English
NEWS SERVICE/SYNDICATE

Associated Press - Athens Bureau
377388
Owner: Associated Press, Inc.
Editorial: 34 Filellinon St, Athens 10558
Tel: 30 21 0331-0802
Email: apathens@ap.org
Bureau Chief: Elena Becatoros
Language (s): English
NEWS SERVICE/SYNDICATE

Associated Press - Atlanta Bureau
31106
Owner: Associated Press, Inc.
Editorial: 101 Marietta St NW Ste 2450, Atlanta, Georgia 30303-2772 **Tel:** 1 404 522-8971
Email: apatlanta@ap.org
Profile: South Daybook department items for regional South coverage can be sent to the South Daybook Department e-mail.
Language (s): English
NEWS SERVICE/SYNDICATE

Associated Press - Augusta Bureau
31255
Owner: Associated Press, Inc.
Editorial: Capitol St & State St, Augusta, Maine 4333
Tel: 1 207 622-3018
Email: apmaine@ap.org
Language (s): English
NEWS SERVICE/SYNDICATE

Associated Press - Austin Bureau
31308
Owner: Associated Press, Inc.
Editorial: 1005 Congress Ave Ste 1060, Austin, Texas 78701-2469 **Tel:** 1 512 472-4004
Email: austaff@ap.org
Language (s): English
NEWS SERVICE/SYNDICATE

Associated Press - Baghdad Bureau
851588
Owner: Associated Press, Inc.
Editorial: Address restricted, Baghdad
Tel: 44 207 482-7726
Bureau Chief: Vivian Salama
Language (s): English
NEWS SERVICE/SYNDICATE

Associated Press - Baltimore Bureau
31122
Owner: Associated Press, Inc.
Editorial: 218 N Charles St Ste 330, Baltimore, Maryland 21201-4018 **Tel:** 1 410 837-8315
Email: balpr@ap.org
News Editor: Amanda Kell
Language (s): English
NEWS SERVICE/SYNDICATE

Associated Press - Bangkok Bureau
217846
Owner: Associated Press, Inc.
Editorial: 15/F Ramaland Bldg., 952 Rama IV Road, Bangarak, Bangkok 10500 **Tel:** 66 (0) 2632-6911
Email: apbangkok@ap.org
Language (s): English
NEWS SERVICE/SYNDICATE

Associated Press - Baton Rouge Bureau
31292
Owner: Associated Press, Inc.
Editorial: Capitol Lake Dr., Baton Rouge, Louisiana 70804 **Tel:** 1 225 343-1325
Email: nrle@ap.org
Language (s): English
NEWS SERVICE/SYNDICATE

Associated Press - Beijing Bureau
71772
Owner: Associated Press, Inc.
Editorial: LG Twin Towers Suite E-2201, B-12 Jianguo Ave., Beijing 100022 **Tel:** 86 10 6568-0330
Email: apbeijing@ap.org
Language (s): English
NEWS SERVICE/SYNDICATE

Associated Press - Beirut Bureau
409139
Owner: Associated Press, Inc.
Editorial: Oueini & Shaker Bldg, Riad El Solh Square Fl 4, Beirut 2023 6516 **Tel:** 961 1 985-190
Email: apbeirut@ap.org
Bureau Chief: Zeina Karam
Language (s): English
NEWS SERVICE/SYNDICATE

Associated Press - Belgrade Bureau
391087
Owner: Associated Press, Inc.
Editorial: Palmoticeva 9, Belgrade 11000
Tel: 381 11 3234-166
Language (s): English
NEWS SERVICE/SYNDICATE

Associated Press - Berlin Bureau
217847
Owner: Associated Press, Inc.
Editorial: Reinhardtstrasse 52, Berlin 10117
Tel: 49 30 437-3670
Email: apberlin@ap.org
Language (s): English
NEWS SERVICE/SYNDICATE

Associated Press - Billings Bureau
70013
Owner: Associated Press, Inc.
Editorial: 401 N 28th St, C/O Billings Gazette, Billings, Montana 59101-1243 **Tel:** 1 406 896-1528
Email: apmontana@ap.org
Language (s): English
NEWS SERVICE/SYNDICATE

Associated Press - Birmingham Bureau
31125
Owner: Associated Press, Inc.
Editorial: 2201 4th Ave N, Birmingham, Alabama 35203-3863 **Tel:** 1 205 251-4221
Email: apalabama@ap.org
Language (s): English
NEWS SERVICE/SYNDICATE

Associated Press - Bismarck Bureau
31273
Owner: Associated Press, Inc.
Editorial: 707 E Front Ave, Bismarck, North Dakota 58504-5646 **Tel:** 1 701 223-8450
Email: apbismarck@ap.org
Language (s): English
NEWS SERVICE/SYNDICATE

Associated Press - Bogota Bureau
217848
Owner: Associated Press, Inc.
Editorial: Bogota **Tel:** 57 1 602-1414
Bureau Chief: Joshua Goodman
Language (s): English
NEWS SERVICE/SYNDICATE

Associated Press - Boise Bureau
31252
Owner: Associated Press, Inc.
Editorial: 101 S Capitol Blvd Ste 304, Boise, Idaho 83702-7738 **Tel:** 1 208 343-1894
Email: apboise@ap.org
Language (s): English
NEWS SERVICE/SYNDICATE

Associated Press - Boston Bureau
31107
Owner: Associated Press, Inc.
Editorial: 184 High St Fl 3, Boston, Massachusetts 02110-3029 **Tel:** 1 617 357-8100
Email: apboston@ap.org
Language (s): English
NEWS SERVICE/SYNDICATE

Associated Press - Brussels Bureau
390818
Owner: Associated Press, Inc.
Editorial: 1 Bd. Charlemagne, Box 49, Int'l Press Center, Brussels 1041 **Tel:** 32 2 285-0112
Email: apbrussels@ap.org
Language (s): English
NEWS SERVICE/SYNDICATE

Associated Press - Bucharest Bureau
821136
Owner: Associated Press, Inc.
Editorial: Bucharest **Tel:** 40 21 310-2488
Chief Correspondent: Alison Mutler
Language (s): English
NEWS SERVICE/SYNDICATE

Associated Press - Budapest Bureau
851591
Owner: Associated Press, Inc.
Editorial: Bajcsy-Zsilinszky ut 12, Room 602-603, Budapest 1051 **Tel:** 36 1 267-0625
Language (s): English
NEWS SERVICE/SYNDICATE

Associated Press - Buenos Aires Bureau
154701
Owner: Associated Press, Inc.
Editorial: Leandro N Alem 712 Piso 4 (1101), Buenos Aires C1006ABG **Tel:** 54 11 4311-0081
Language (s): English
NEWS SERVICE/SYNDICATE

Associated Press - Buffalo Bureau
31301
Owner: Associated Press, Inc.
Editorial: 1 News Plz, C/O Buffalo News, Buffalo, New York 14203-2930 **Tel:** 1 716 852-1051
Email: apbuffalo@ap.org **Web site:** http://www.ap.org/state/east/new-york
Language (s): English
NEWS SERVICE/SYNDICATE

Associated Press - Cairo Bureau
430961
Owner: Associated Press, Inc.
Editorial: 1117 Corniche el-Nil St, Cairo 11221
Tel: 20 2 2578-4091
Email: apcairo@ap.org
Language (s): English
NEWS SERVICE/SYNDICATE

Associated Press - Canberra Bureau
964213
Owner: Associated Press, Inc.
Editorial: Canberra **Tel:** 61 2 8235-2999
Email: apsydney@ap.org
Language (s): English
NEWS SERVICE/SYNDICATE

Associated Press - Caracas Bureau
217850
Owner: Associated Press, Inc.
Editorial: Edificio el Universal Avinida Urdaneta, Esquina Animas Piso 9 Oficina D, Caracas 1010
Tel: 58 212 564-1834
Language (s): English
NEWS SERVICE/SYNDICATE

Associated Press - Charleston Bureau
31142
Owner: Associated Press, Inc.
Editorial: 500 Virginia St E Ste 1150, Charleston, West Virginia 25301-2167 **Tel:** 1 304 346-0897
Email: chwpr@ap.org
News Editor: Steve McMillan
Language (s): English
NEWS SERVICE/SYNDICATE

Associated Press - Charlotte Bureau
31143
Owner: Associated Press, Inc.
Editorial: 1100 S Tryon St Ste 310, Charlotte, North Carolina 28203-4297 **Tel:** 1 704 334-4624
Email: apraleigh@ap.org
Language (s): English
NEWS SERVICE/SYNDICATE

Associated Press - Cheyenne Bureau
31274
Owner: Associated Press, Inc.
Editorial: 320 W 25th St Ste 310, Cheyenne, Wyoming 82001-3005 **Tel:** 1 307 632-9351
Email: apcheyenne@ap.org
Language (s): English
NEWS SERVICE/SYNDICATE

Associated Press - Chicago Bureau
31108
Owner: Associated Press, Inc.
Editorial: 440 S La Salle St Ste 1000, Chicago, Illinois 60605-1028 **Tel:** 1 312 781-0500
Email: chifax@ap.org
Bureau Chief: George Garties
Profile: This is a central bureau for Illinois coverage. Daybook items should go to the main e-mail address.
Language (s): English
NEWS SERVICE/SYNDICATE

Associated Press - Cincinnati Bureau
31136
Owner: Associated Press, Inc.
Editorial: 312 Elm St Ste 2300, C/O the Cincinnati Enquirer, Cincinnati, Ohio 45202-2727
Tel: 1 513 241-2386
Email: apcolumbus@ap.org
Language (s): English
NEWS SERVICE/SYNDICATE

Associated Press - Cleveland Bureau
31124
Owner: Associated Press, Inc.
Editorial: 700 W Saint Clair Ave Ste 318, Cleveland, Ohio 44113-1226 **Tel:** 1 216 771-2172
Email: apcolumbus@ap.org

Bureau Chief: Eva Parziale
Language (s): English
NEWS SERVICE/SYNDICATE

Associated Press - Colombo Bureau
551873
Owner: Associated Press, Inc.
Editorial: Colombo **Tel:** 94 11 230-4940
NEWS SERVICE/SYNDICATE

Associated Press - Columbia Bureau
31198
Owner: Associated Press, Inc.
Editorial: 4312 Williamsburg Dr, Columbia, South Carolina 29203-5440 **Tel:** 1 803 799-5510
Email: apcolumbia@ap.org
Language (s): English
NEWS SERVICE/SYNDICATE

Associated Press - Columbus Bureau
31109
Owner: Associated Press, Inc.
Editorial: 1103 Schrock Rd Ste 300, Columbus, Ohio 43229-1179 **Tel:** 1 614 885-2727
Email: apcolumbus@ap.org
Language (s): English
NEWS SERVICE/SYNDICATE

Associated Press - Concord Bureau
31260
Owner: Associated Press, Inc.
Editorial: 2 Capital Plz Ste 400, Concord, New Hampshire 03301-4911 **Tel:** 1 603 224-3327
Email: apconcord@ap.org
Language (s): English
NEWS SERVICE/SYNDICATE

Associated Press - Copenhagen Bureau
884838
Owner: Associated Press, Inc.
Editorial: Radhuspladsen 37, Kobenhavn V, Copenhagen 1550 **Tel:** 45 3311 1504
Email: copenhagen@ap.org
NEWS SERVICE/SYNDICATE

Associated Press - Dakar Bureau
390777
Owner: Associated Press, Inc.
Editorial: 7 Avenue Carde, Immeuble Carde, 4EME, Dakar 14221 **Tel:** 221 33 849-2620
Email: apdakar@ap.org
Bureau Chief: Krista Larson
Language (s): English
NEWS SERVICE/SYNDICATE

Associated Press - Dallas Bureau
31110
Owner: Associated Press, Inc.
Editorial: 4851 Lyndon B Johnson Fwy Ste 300, Dallas, Texas 75244-6047 **Tel:** 1 972 991-2100
Email: aptexas@ap.org
Language (s): English
NEWS SERVICE/SYNDICATE

Associated Press - Denver Bureau
31111
Owner: Associated Press, Inc.
Editorial: 1120 N Lincoln St Ste 901, Denver, Colorado 80203-2138 **Tel:** 1 303 825-0123
Email: apdenver@ap.org
Bureau Chief: Jim Clarke
Language (s): English
NEWS SERVICE/SYNDICATE

Associated Press - Des Moines Bureau
31129
Owner: Associated Press, Inc.
Editorial: 505 5th Ave Ste 1000, Des Moines, Iowa 50309-2315 **Tel:** 1 515 243-3281
Email: apdesmoines@ap.org
News Editor: Scott McFetridge
Language (s): English
NEWS SERVICE/SYNDICATE

Associated Press - Detroit Bureau
31112
Owner: Associated Press, Inc.
Editorial: 300 River Place Dr Ste 2400, Detroit, Michigan 48207-5064 **Tel:** 1 313 259-0650
Email: apmichigan@ap.org
Language (s): English
NEWS SERVICE/SYNDICATE

Associated Press - Dhaka Bureau
964215
Owner: Associated Press, Inc.
Editorial: 69/1 New Circular Road, Cosmos Center, Dhaka **Tel:** 880 2 933-1411
Language (s): English
NEWS SERVICE/SYNDICATE

Associated Press - Dover Bureau
31247
Owner: Associated Press, Inc.
Editorial: William Penn St, Dover, Delaware
Tel: 1 302 674-3037
Email: balpr@ap.org
Language (s): English
NEWS SERVICE/SYNDICATE

Associated Press - Dubai Bureau 431043
Owner: Associated Press, Inc.
Editorial: Dubai Media City, Building 4 Office 304, Dubai Tel: 971 4 390-8120
Email: apdubai@ap.org
Language (s): English
NEWS SERVICE/SYNDICATE

Associated Press - Dublin Bureau 391072
Owner: Associated Press, Inc.
Editorial: 146 Chapelgate, Saint Alphonsus Road, Dublin Dublin 9 Tel: 353 1 882-8281
Language (s): English
NEWS SERVICE/SYNDICATE

Associated Press - Fargo Bureau 31342
Owner: Associated Press, Inc.
Editorial: 101 5th St N, Fargo, North Dakota 58102-4826 Tel: 1 701 235-1908
Email: apbismarck@ap.org
Language (s): English
NEWS SERVICE/SYNDICATE

Associated Press - Fort Worth Bureau 31144
Owner: Associated Press, Inc.
Editorial: TCU Moudy Building South, Convergence Center, Fort Worth, Texas Tel: 1 817 348-0367
Email: aptexas@ap.org
Language (s): English
NEWS SERVICE/SYNDICATE

Associated Press - Frankfort Bureau 31290
Owner: Associated Press, Inc.
Editorial: 700 Capital Ave Rm 243, Frankfort, Kentucky 40601-3415 Tel: 1 502 227-2410
Email: aplouisville@ap.org
Language (s): English
NEWS SERVICE/SYNDICATE

Associated Press - Frankfurt Am Main Bureau 71746
Owner: Associated Press, Inc.
Editorial: Wilhelm-Leuschner-Str. 41, Frankfurt Am Main 60329 Tel: 46 69 2722-1730
Language (s): English
NEWS SERVICE/SYNDICATE

Associated Press - Geneva Bureau 231913
Owner: Associated Press, Inc.
Editorial: Palais des Nations, Room C12 CH-1211, Geneva Tel: 41 22 919-4222
Email: apgeneva@ap.org
Language (s): English
NEWS SERVICE/SYNDICATE

Associated Press - Guatemala Bureau 884528
Owner: Associated Press, Inc.
Editorial: Guatemala Tel: 502 2332-0618
Language (s): English
NEWS SERVICE/SYNDICATE

Associated Press - Hanoi Bureau 217853
Owner: Associated Press, Inc.
Editorial: Hanoi Tel: 84 4 825-0732
Language (s): English
NEWS SERVICE/SYNDICATE

Associated Press - Harrisburg Bureau 31264
Owner: Associated Press, Inc.
Editorial: Main Capitol, Rm 526, E Floor, Harrisburg, Pennsylvania 17120-0001 Tel: 1 717 238-9413
Email: phillyap@ap.org
Language (s): English
NEWS SERVICE/SYNDICATE

Associated Press - Hartford Bureau 31206
Owner: Associated Press, Inc.
Editorial: 10 Columbus Blvd Ste 23, Hartford, Connecticut 06106-1976 Tel: 1 860 246-6876
Email: aphartford@ap.org
Language (s): English
NEWS SERVICE/SYNDICATE

Associated Press - Havana Bureau 561554
Owner: Associated Press, Inc.
Editorial: Edificio Lonja del Comercio, Lamparilla 2, Piso 6, Local B, Havana Tel: 53 7 866-0370
Bureau Chief: Michael Weissenstein
Language (s): English
NEWS SERVICE/SYNDICATE

Associated Press - Helena Bureau 31259
Owner: Associated Press, Inc.
Editorial: 321 Fuller Ave #2, Helena, Montana 59601-5005 Tel: 1 406 442-7440

Email: apmontana@ap.org
Language (s): English
NEWS SERVICE/SYNDICATE

Associated Press - Helsinki Bureau 390912
Owner: Associated Press, Inc.
Editorial: Erottajankatu 9B, 7th Floor, Helsinki 130 Tel: 358 9 680-2394
Email: aphelsinki@ap.org
Language (s): English
NEWS SERVICE/SYNDICATE

Associated Press - Hong Kong Bureau 217854
Editorial: 18 Harbour Road, Wan Chai, Suite 4808, 48F, Central Plaza, Hong Kong 10020-1605 Tel: 852 2802-4324
Language (s): English
NEWS SERVICE/SYNDICATE

Associated Press - Honolulu Bureau 31251
Owner: Associated Press, Inc.
Editorial: 500 Ala Moana Blvd Ste 7-590, Honolulu, Hawaii 96813-4925 Tel: 1 808 536-5510
Email: aphonolulu@ap.org
Language (s): English
NEWS SERVICE/SYNDICATE

Associated Press - Houston Bureau 31113
Owner: Associated Press, Inc.
Editorial: 16945 Northchase Dr Ste 2110, Houston, Texas 77060-2151 Tel: 1 281 872-8900
Email: aptexas@ap.org
News Editor, South Central Region: Maud Beelman
Language (s): English
NEWS SERVICE/SYNDICATE

Associated Press - Indianapolis Bureau 31121
Owner: Associated Press, Inc.
Editorial: 251 N Illinois St Ste 1600, Indianapolis, Indiana 46204-1943 Tel: 1 317 639-5501
Email: indy@ap.org
Language (s): English
NEWS SERVICE/SYNDICATE

Associated Press - Iowa City Bureau 31287
Owner: Associated Press, Inc.
Editorial: 103 E College St Ste 208, Iowa City, Iowa 52240-4008 Tel: 1 319 337-5615
Email: apdesmoines@ap.org
Language (s): English
NEWS SERVICE/SYNDICATE

Associated Press - Islamabad Bureau 231455
Owner: Associated Press, Inc.
Editorial: Address restricted, Islamabad Tel: 92 51 282-8397
Language (s): English
NEWS SERVICE/SYNDICATE

Associated Press - Istanbul Bureau 429803
Owner: Associated Press, Inc.
Editorial: Reasürans Han 2, No. 61/4 Kat 4 Macka, Istanbul 34367 Tel: 90 212 231-1616
Email: apturkey@ap.org
Language (s): English
NEWS SERVICE/SYNDICATE

Associated Press - Jackson Bureau 31217
Owner: Associated Press, Inc.
Editorial: 125 S Congress St Ste 1330, Jackson, Mississippi 39201-3310 Tel: 1 601 948-5897
Email: jkme@ap.org
Language (s): English
NEWS SERVICE/SYNDICATE

Associated Press - Jakarta Bureau 377892
Owner: Associated Press, Inc.
Editorial: Deutsche Bank Building, Fl 14, Ste 1403-1404, Jakarta 10310 Tel: 62 21 3983-1269
Bureau Chief: Margie Mason
Language (s): English
NEWS SERVICE/SYNDICATE

Associated Press - Jefferson City Bureau 31258
Owner: Associated Press, Inc.
Editorial: 201 W Capitol Ave Rm 118B, Jefferson City, Missouri 65101-1556 Tel: 1 573 636-9415
Email: apkansascity@ap.org
Language (s): English
NEWS SERVICE/SYNDICATE

Associated Press - Jerusalem Bureau 154539
Owner: Associated Press, Inc.
Editorial: 206 Jaffa Rd, JCS Building, Fl 2, Jerusalem 91342 Tel: 44 20 7427-4300
Email: apjerusalem@ap.org

Bureau Chief: Josef Federman
Language (s): English
NEWS SERVICE/SYNDICATE

Associated Press - Johannesburg Bureau 363164
Owner: Associated Press, Inc.
Editorial: Menton Centre, 5th Floor, 1 Park Road Richmond, Johannesburg 2092 Tel: 27 11 628-7700
Email: africadesk@ap.org
Africa News Editor: Andrew Selsky
Language (s): English
NEWS SERVICE/SYNDICATE

Associated Press - Juneau Bureau 31236
Owner: Associated Press, Inc.
Editorial: 319 Seward St Ste 12, Juneau, Alaska 99801-1173 Tel: 1 907 586-1515
Email: apjuneau@ap.org
Language (s): English
NEWS SERVICE/SYNDICATE

Associated Press - Kabul Bureau 543083
Owner: Associated Press, Inc.
Editorial: House 1, Street 15, Wazir Akbar Khan, Kabul Tel: 93 20 230-0335
Email: apkabul@ap.org
Bureau Chief: Lynne O'Donnell
Language (s): English
NEWS SERVICE/SYNDICATE

Associated Press - Kansas City Bureau 31114
Owner: Associated Press, Inc.
Editorial: 215 W Pershing Rd Ste 221, Kansas City, Missouri 64108-4316 Tel: 1 816 421-4844
Email: apkansascity@ap.org
Bureau Chief: Kia Breaux
Language (s): English
NEWS SERVICE/SYNDICATE

Associated Press - Kathmandu Bureau 851587
Owner: Associated Press, Inc.
Editorial: Address restricted, Kathmandu Tel: 977 1 4224-705
Chief Correspondent: Binaj Gurubacharya
Language (s): English
NEWS SERVICE/SYNDICATE

Associated Press - Kuala Lumpur Bureau 429319
Owner: Associated Press, Inc.
Editorial: Suite 21A-8-2 Level 8, Faber Imperial Court, Kuala Lumpur 50250 Tel: 60 3 2181-8134
Email: apklnews@ap.org
Language (s): English
NEWS SERVICE/SYNDICATE

Associated Press - La Paz Bureau 964216
Owner: Associated Press, Inc.
Editorial: La Paz
Language (s): English
NEWS SERVICE/SYNDICATE

Associated Press - Lagos Bureau 851599
Owner: Associated Press, Inc.
Editorial: 16 Adeyemi Lawson Road, Ikoyi, Lagos Tel: 234 803 403-0364
Language (s): English
NEWS SERVICE/SYNDICATE

Associated Press - Lansing Bureau 31295
Owner: Associated Press, Inc.
Editorial: 215 S Washington Sq Ste 170, Lansing, Michigan 48933-1889 Tel: 1 517 482-8011
Email: apmichigan@ap.org
Language (s): English
NEWS SERVICE/SYNDICATE

Associated Press - Las Vegas Bureau 31219
Owner: Associated Press, Inc.
Editorial: 300 S 4th St Ste 810, Las Vegas, Nevada 89101-6009 Tel: 1 702 382-7440
Email: aplasvegas@ap.org
Language (s): English
NEWS SERVICE/SYNDICATE

Associated Press - Lincoln Bureau 31296
Owner: Associated Press, Inc.
Editorial: 926 P St, Lincoln, Nebraska 68508-3615 Tel: 1 402 476-2525
Email: omahane@ap.org
Language (s): English
NEWS SERVICE/SYNDICATE

Associated Press - Lisbon Bureau 658170
Owner: Associated Press, Inc.
Editorial: Atrium Saldanha 8-J, Pr. Duque de Saldanha 1, Lisbon 1050-094 Tel: 351 308 805-522
Language (s): English
NEWS SERVICE/SYNDICATE

Associated Press - Little Rock Bureau 31128
Owner: Associated Press, Inc.
Editorial: 10810 Executive Center Dr Ste 308, Little Rock, Arkansas 72211-4388 Tel: 1 501 225-3668
Email: pebbles@ap.org
News Editor: Kelly Kissel
Language (s): English
NEWS SERVICE/SYNDICATE

Associated Press - London Bureau 31350
Owner: Associated Press, Inc.
Editorial: The Interchange, 32 Oval Road, London, England NW1 7DZ Tel: 44 20 7482-7400
Email: aplondon@ap.org
News Editor: Danica Kirka
Language (s): English
NEWS SERVICE/SYNDICATE

Associated Press - Los Angeles Bureau 31115
Owner: Associated Press, Inc.
Editorial: 221 S Figueroa St Ste 300, Los Angeles, California 90012-2552 Tel: 1 213 626-1200
Email: losangeles@ap.org
Profile: This is a central bureau for California coverage. Daybook items should go to the main e-mail address.
Language (s): English
NEWS SERVICE/SYNDICATE

Associated Press - Louisville Bureau 31130
Owner: Associated Press, Inc.
Editorial: 525 W Broadway, Louisville, Kentucky 40202-2206 Tel: 1 502 583-7718
Email: aplouisville@ap.org
News Editor: Scott Stroud; Bureau Chief: Adam Yeomans
Language (s): English
NEWS SERVICE/SYNDICATE

Associated Press - Madison Bureau 31314
Owner: Associated Press, Inc.
Editorial: 119 Martin Luther King Jr Blvd, Madison, Wisconsin 53703-3355 Tel: 1 608 255-3679
Email: apmlw@ap.org
Language (s): English
NEWS SERVICE/SYNDICATE

Associated Press - Madrid Bureau 232023
Owner: Associated Press, Inc.
Editorial: Esproceda 32, 5th Floor, Madrid 28003 Tel: 34 913 95-81-01
Bureau Chief: Alan Clendenning
Language (s): English
NEWS SERVICE/SYNDICATE

Associated Press - Manila Bureau 217857
Owner: Associated Press, Inc.
Editorial: Manila Tel: 63 2 525-9217
Chief Correspondent: Jim Gomez
Language (s): English
NEWS SERVICE/SYNDICATE

Associated Press - Mc Lean Bureau 31311
Owner: Associated Press, Inc.
Editorial: 7950 Jones Branch Dr, C/O Usa Today, Mc Lean, Virginia 22107-0002 Tel: 1 703 761-0187
Email: aprichmond@ap.org
Language (s): English
NEWS SERVICE/SYNDICATE

Associated Press - Memphis Bureau 839488
Owner: Associated Press, Inc.
Editorial: 495 Union Ave, C/O Commerical Appeal, Memphis, Tennessee 38103-3217 Tel: 1 901 525-1972
Email: apnashville@ap.org
Profile: The Memphis Bureau of the Associated Press covers local, regional and national news.
NEWS SERVICE/SYNDICATE

Associated Press - Mexico City Bureau 71775
Owner: Associated Press, Inc.
Editorial: Reforma 350, Piso 9, Mexico City, Distrito Federal 6600 Tel: 52 55 5080-3473
Email: apmexico@ap.org
Language (s): Spanish
NEWS SERVICE/SYNDICATE

Associated Press - Miami Bureau 31116
Owner: Associated Press, Inc.
Editorial: 9100 NW 36th St Ste 111, Doral, Florida 33178-2432 Tel: 1 305 594-5825
Email: miami@ap.org
Bureau Chief: Jim Baltzelle
Language (s): English
NEWS SERVICE/SYNDICATE

United States of America

Associated Press - Milan Bureau 578676
Owner: Associated Press, Inc.
Editorial: Via Daniele Manin, 37, Milan 20121
Tel: 39 02 2906-0700
Email: aprome@ap.org
Chief Correspondent: Colleen Barry
Language (s): English
NEWS SERVICE/SYNDICATE

Associated Press - Milwaukee Bureau 31140
Owner: Associated Press, Inc.
Editorial: 111 E Wisconsin Ave Ste 1925, Milwaukee, Wisconsin 53202-4825 Tel: 1 414 225-3580
Email: apmlw@ap.org
Language (s): English
NEWS SERVICE/SYNDICATE

Associated Press - Minneapolis Bureau 31123
Owner: Associated Press, Inc.
Editorial: Minneapolis, Minnesota Tel: 1 612 332-2727
Email: apminneapolis@ap.org
News Editor: Doug Glass
Profile: This is a central bureau for Minnesota coverage. Daybook items should go to the main e-mail address.
Language (s): English
NEWS SERVICE/SYNDICATE

Associated Press - Montevideo Bureau 964231
Owner: Associated Press, Inc.
Editorial: Montevideo Tel: 598 2 902-0309
Email: uruguay@ap.org
Language (s): English
NEWS SERVICE/SYNDICATE

Associated Press - Montgomery Bureau 31126
Owner: Associated Press, Inc.
Editorial: 201 Monroe St Ste 1940, Montgomery, Alabama 36104-3721 Tel: 1 334 262-5947
Email: apalabama@ap.org
Language (s): English
NEWS SERVICE/SYNDICATE

Associated Press - Montpelier Bureau 31266
Owner: Associated Press, Inc.
Editorial: 535 Stone Cutters Way Ste 101A, Montpelier, Vermont 05602-3796 Tel: 1 802 229-0577
Email: apvermont@ap.org
Language (s): English
NEWS SERVICE/SYNDICATE

Associated Press - Moscow Bureau 815030
Owner: Associated Press, Inc.
Editorial: Kutuzovsky Prospekt 7/4, Corpus 5, Office 33, Moscow 121248 Tel: 7 495 974-1654
Email: mosed@ap.org
News Editor: Lynn Berry
Language (s): English
NEWS SERVICE/SYNDICATE

Associated Press - Nairobi Bureau 217858
Owner: Associated Press, Inc.
Editorial: Nairobi Tel: 254 20 285-9000
Language (s): English
NEWS SERVICE/SYNDICATE

Associated Press - Nashville Bureau 31139
Owner: Associated Press, Inc.
Editorial: 1207 18th Ave S Ste 261A, Nashville, Tennessee 37212-2822 Tel: 1 615 373-9988
Email: apnashville@ap.org
Language (s): English
NEWS SERVICE/SYNDICATE

Associated Press - New Delhi Bureau 217852
Owner: Associated Press, Inc.
Editorial: Statesman Building Fl 1 B-102103, Barakahamba Road, New Delhi 110001
Tel: 94 11 230-4940
Language (s): English
NEWS SERVICE/SYNDICATE

Associated Press - New Orleans Bureau 31131
Owner: Associated Press, Inc.
Editorial: 1515 Poydras Ste 2100, New Orleans, Louisiana 70112-3800 Tel: 1 504 523-3931
Email: nrle@ap.org
Language (s): English
NEWS SERVICE/SYNDICATE

Associated Press - Newark Bureau 31231
Owner: Associated Press, Inc.
Editorial: 50 Park Pl Ste 800, Newark, New Jersey 07102-4305 Tel: 1 973 642-0151
Email: aptrenton@ap.org
Language (s): English
NEWS SERVICE/SYNDICATE

Associated Press - Nicosia Bureau 731975
Owner: Associated Press
Editorial: Nicosia Tel: 357 2249-2599
Email: apnicosia@ap.org
Language (s): English
NEWS SERVICE/SYNDICATE

Associated Press - Oklahoma City Bureau 31137
Owner: Associated Press, Inc.
Editorial: 100 W Main St Ste 100, Oklahoma City, Oklahoma 73102-9013 Tel: 1 405 525-2121
Email: apoklahoma@ap.org
Language (s): English
NEWS SERVICE/SYNDICATE

Associated Press - Olympia Bureau 31270
Owner: Associated Press, Inc.
Editorial: 1417 Columbia St SW Fl 1, Olympia, Washington 98501-2342 Tel: 1 360 753-7222
Email: apseattle@ap.org
Language (s): English
NEWS SERVICE/SYNDICATE

Associated Press - Omaha Bureau 31132
Owner: Associated Press, Inc.
Editorial: 909 N 96th St Ste 104, Omaha, Nebraska 68114-2508 Tel: 1 402 391-0031
Email: omahane@ap.org
Language (s): English
NEWS SERVICE/SYNDICATE

Associated Press - Orlando Bureau 31172
Owner: Associated Press, Inc.
Editorial: 501 N Magnolia Ave Ste 100, Orlando, Florida 32801-1364 Tel: 1 407 425-4547
Email: miami@ap.org
Language (s): English
NEWS SERVICE/SYNDICATE

Associated Press - Panama Bureau 888972
Owner: Associated Press, Inc.
Editorial: Panama
Language (s): English
NEWS SERVICE/SYNDICATE

Associated Press - Paris Bureau 71745
Owner: Associated Press, Inc.
Editorial: 162 rue du Faubourg Saint Honore, Paris 75008 Tel: 33 1 4359-8676
Bureau Chief: Angela Charlton
Language (s): English
NEWS SERVICE/SYNDICATE

Associated Press - Philadelphia Bureau 31117
Owner: Associated Press, Inc.
Editorial: 1835 Market St Ste 1700, Philadelphia, Pennsylvania 19103-2945 Tel: 1 215 561-1133
Email: phillyap@ap.org Web site: http://www.ap.org/state/east/pennsylvania
Bureau Chief: Sally Hale; News Editor: Larry Rosenthal
Language (s): English
NEWS SERVICE/SYNDICATE

Associated Press - Phnom Penh Bureau 964226
Owner: Associated Press, Inc.
Editorial: Phnom Penh Tel: 84 4 825-0732
Language (s): English
NEWS SERVICE/SYNDICATE

Associated Press - Phoenix Bureau 31127
Owner: Associated Press, Inc.
Editorial: 1850 N Central Ave Ste 640, Phoenix, Arizona 85004-4573 Tel: 1 602 258-8934
Email: aparizona@ap.org
Language (s): English
NEWS SERVICE/SYNDICATE

Associated Press - Pierre Bureau 31343
Owner: Associated Press, Inc.
Editorial: 124 S Euclid Ave Ste 104, Pierre, South Dakota 57501-3168 Tel: 1 605 224-7811
Email: apsiouxfalls@ap.org
Language (s): English
NEWS SERVICE/SYNDICATE

Associated Press - Pittsburgh Bureau 31169
Owner: Associated Press, Inc.
Editorial: 11 Stanwix St Ste 1020, Pittsburgh, Pennsylvania 15222-1312 Tel: 1 412 281-3747
Email: appittsburgh@ap.org Web site: http://www.ap.org/state/east/pennsylvania
Language (s): English
NEWS SERVICE/SYNDICATE

Associated Press - Pleasantville Bureau 31299
Owner: Associated Press, Inc.
Editorial: 1000 W Washington Ave, C/O the Press of Atlantic City, Pleasantville, New Jersey 08232-3861
Tel: 1 609 645-2063
Email: aptrenton@ap.org
Language (s): English
NEWS SERVICE/SYNDICATE

Associated Press - Portland Bureau 31146
Owner: Associated Press, Inc.
Editorial: 121 SW Salmon St Ste 1450, Portland, Oregon 97204-2924 Tel: 1 503 228-2169
Email: apportland@ap.org
Language (s): English
NEWS SERVICE/SYNDICATE

Associated Press - Portland Bureau 31207
Owner: Associated Press, Inc.
Editorial: 75 Market St Ste 402, Portland, Maine 04101-5031 Tel: 1 207 772-4157
Email: apmaine@ap.org
Language (s): English
NEWS SERVICE/SYNDICATE

Associated Press - Prague Bureau 845785
Owner: Associated Press, Inc.
Editorial: Prague Tel: 4202 21 085-266
Language (s): English
NEWS SERVICE/SYNDICATE

Associated Press - Providence Bureau 31138
Owner: Associated Press, Inc.
Editorial: 10 Dorrance St Ste 601, Providence, Rhode Island 02903-2018 Tel: 1 401 274-2270
Email: approvidence@ap.org
Language (s): English
NEWS SERVICE/SYNDICATE

Associated Press - Pyongyang Bureau 886164
Owner: Associated Press, Inc.
Editorial: Address restricted, Pyongyang
Email: pyongyang@ap.org
Bureau Chief: Eric Talmadge
Language (s): English
NEWS SERVICE/SYNDICATE

Associated Press - Quito Bureau 964227
Owner: Associated Press, Inc.
Editorial: Quito Tel: 593 2 222-7701
Email: apquito@ap.org
Language (s): English
NEWS SERVICE/SYNDICATE

Associated Press - Raleigh Bureau 31135
Owner: Associated Press, Inc.
Editorial: 4800 Six Forks Rd Ste 210, Raleigh, North Carolina 27609-5245 Tel: 1 919 510-8937
Email: apraleigh@ap.org
Language (s): English
NEWS SERVICE/SYNDICATE

Associated Press - Reno Bureau 31298
Owner: Associated Press, Inc.
Editorial: 1 E Liberty St Ste 507, Reno, Nevada 89501-2117 Tel: 1 775 322-3639
Email: aplasvegas@ap.org
Language (s): English
NEWS SERVICE/SYNDICATE

Associated Press - Richmond Bureau 31233
Owner: Associated Press, Inc.
Editorial: 600 E Main St Ste 1250, Richmond, Virginia 23219-2440 Tel: 1 804 643-6646
Email: aprichmond@ap.org
Language (s): English
NEWS SERVICE/SYNDICATE

Associated Press - Rio De Janeiro Bureau 562212
Owner: Associated Press, Inc.
Editorial: Praia de Botafogo, 228 - Sala 1105, Botafogo, Rio De Janeiro 22250-906 Tel: 55 21 3288-5000
Email: apbrazil@ap.org
Language (s): English
NEWS SERVICE/SYNDICATE

Associated Press - Rome Bureau 71867
Owner: Associated Press Inc.
Editorial: Piazza Grazioli 5, Rome 186
Tel: 39 06 6974-7260
Email: aprome@ap.org
Language (s): English
NEWS SERVICE/SYNDICATE

Associated Press - Sacramento Bureau 31168
Owner: Associated Press, Inc.
Editorial: 1215 K St Ste 960, Sacramento, California 95814-3946 Tel: 1 916 448-9555
Email: sacramento@ap.org
Language (s): English
NEWS SERVICE/SYNDICATE

Associated Press - Saint Louis Bureau 31216
Owner: Associated Press, Inc.
Editorial: 900 N Tucker Blvd Ste 400, Saint Louis, Missouri 63101-1098 Tel: 1 314 241-2496
Email: apkansascity@ap.org
Chief Correspondent: Jim Salter
Language (s): English
NEWS SERVICE/SYNDICATE

Associated Press - Saint Petersburg Bureau 31149
Owner: Associated Press, Inc.
Editorial: 490 1st Ave S Ste 2009, Saint Petersburg, Florida 33701-4204 Tel: 1 727 823-4721
Email: apmiami@ap.org
Language (s): English
NEWS SERVICE/SYNDICATE

Associated Press - Salem Bureau 31306
Owner: Associated Press, Inc.
Editorial: 900 Court St NE Ste 43, Salem, Oregon 97301-4045 Tel: 1 503 363-0010
Email: apportland@ap.org
Language (s): English
NEWS SERVICE/SYNDICATE

Associated Press - Salt Lake City Bureau 31148
Owner: Associated Press, Inc.
Editorial: 90 S 400 W Ste 670, Salt Lake City, Utah 84101-1374 Tel: 1 801 322-3405
Email: apsaltlake@ap.org
News Editor, Nevada & Utah: Tom Tait
Language (s): English
NEWS SERVICE/SYNDICATE

Associated Press - San Diego Bureau 31171
Owner: Associated Press, Inc.
Editorial: 964 5th Ave Ste 407, San Diego, California 92101-6102 Tel: 1 619 231-9365
Email: sandiego@ap.org
Language (s): English
NEWS SERVICE/SYNDICATE

Associated Press - San Francisco Bureau 31120
Owner: Associated Press, Inc.
Editorial: 300 Montgomery St Ste 700, San Francisco, California 94104-1917 Tel: 1 415 495-1708
Email: sanfrancisco@ap.org
Language (s): English
NEWS SERVICE/SYNDICATE

Associated Press - San Juan Bureau 231383
Owner: Associated Press, Inc.
Editorial: San Juan Tel: 52 55 5080-3400
Email: apsanjuan@ap.org
Language (s): English
NEWS SERVICE/SYNDICATE

Associated Press - San Salvador Bureau 964228
Owner: Associated Press, Inc.
Editorial: San Salvador Tel: 503 2265-2222
Email: apelsalvador@ap.org
Language (s): English
NEWS SERVICE/SYNDICATE

Associated Press - Sao Paulo Bureau 390849
Owner: Associated Press, Inc.
Editorial: Av. Paulista, 854, 13 Andar, Conj. 131, Sao Paulo 01310-913 Tel: 55 21 3512-8600
Email: apbrazil@ap.org
Bureau Chief: Bradley Brooks
Language (s): English
NEWS SERVICE/SYNDICATE

Associated Press - Seattle Bureau 31118
Owner: Associated Press, Inc.
Editorial: 1000 Denny Way Ste 501, Seattle, Washington 98109-5323 Tel: 1 206 682-1812
Email: apseattle@ap.org
News Editor: Chris Grygiel
Language (s): English
NEWS SERVICE/SYNDICATE

Associated Press - Seoul Bureau 418443
Owner: Associated Press, Inc.
Editorial: 85-1 Fusong, Jongro-ku, Ste 603, Seoul 1110-140 Tel: 82 2 721-0551
Email: apseoul@ap.org
Language (s): English
NEWS SERVICE/SYNDICATE

Associated Press - Shanghai Bureau 773041
Owner: Associated Press, Inc.
Editorial: Shanghai **Tel:** 86 21 6218-0707
Email: apbeijing@ap.org
Language (s): English
NEWS SERVICE/SYNDICATE

Associated Press - Spokane Bureau 31267
Owner: Associated Press, Inc.
Editorial: 818 W Riverside Ave Ste 500, Spokane, Washington 99201-0909 **Tel:** 1 509 624-1258
Email: apseattle@ap.org
Language (s): English
NEWS SERVICE/SYNDICATE

Associated Press - Springfield Bureau 31215
Owner: Associated Press, Inc.
Editorial: 301 S 2nd St, Springfield, Illinois 62706-1720 **Tel:** 1 217 789-2700
Email: chifax@ap.org
Language (s): English
NEWS SERVICE/SYNDICATE

Associated Press - Stockholm Bureau 217306
Owner: Associated Press, Inc.
Editorial: Klarabersgatan 37, Stockholm 111 21
Tel: 46 8 545-130-80
Bureau Chief: Karl Ritter
Language (s): English
NEWS SERVICE/SYNDICATE

Associated Press - Sydney Bureau 72217
Owner: Associated Press, Inc.
Editorial: 309 Kent Street, Suite 1 Level 6, Sydney 2000 **Tel:** 61 2 8235-2999
Email: apsydney@ap.org
Bureau Chief: Kristen Gelineau
Language (s): English
NEWS SERVICE/SYNDICATE

Associated Press - Tallahassee Bureau 31250
Owner: Associated Press, Inc.
Editorial: 336 E College Ave Ste 301, Tallahassee, Florida 32301-1560 **Tel:** 1 850 224-1211
Email: apmiami@ap.org
Language (s): English
NEWS SERVICE/SYNDICATE

Associated Press - Tirana Bureau 964212
Owner: Associated Press, Inc.
Editorial: Tirana **Tel:** 995 35 982-461
Email: tirana@ap.org
Language (s): English
NEWS SERVICE/SYNDICATE

Associated Press - Tokyo Bureau 71764
Owner: Associated Press, Inc.
Editorial: Shidome Media Tower 7th Fl, 1-7-1 Higashi-Shimbashi Minato-ku, Tokyo 105-7207
Tel: 81 3 6215-8931
Language (s): English
NEWS SERVICE/SYNDICATE

Associated Press - Toledo Bureau 31262
Owner: Associated Press, Inc.
Editorial: 541 N Superior St, C/O the Blade, Toledo, Ohio 43660-1000 **Tel:** 1 419 255-7113
Email: apcolumbus@ap.org
Language (s): English
NEWS SERVICE/SYNDICATE

Associated Press - Topeka Bureau 31254
Owner: Associated Press, Inc.
Editorial: 300 SW 10th Ave Ste 134N, Topeka, Kansas 66612-1512 **Tel:** 1 785 234-5654
Email: apkansascity@ap.org
Language (s): English
NEWS SERVICE/SYNDICATE

Associated Press - Toronto Bureau 71744
Owner: Associated Press, Inc.
Editorial: 36 King St E Fl 5 #550, Toronto, Ontario M5C 1E5 **Tel:** 1 416 368-1388
Bureau Chief: Rob Gillies
Language (s): English
NEWS SERVICE/SYNDICATE

Associated Press - Traverse City Bureau 31257
Owner: Associated Press, Inc.
Editorial: 120 W Front St, Traverse City, Michigan 49684-2202 **Tel:** 1 231 929-4180
Email: apmichigan@ap.org
Language (s): English
NEWS SERVICE/SYNDICATE

Associated Press - Trenton Bureau 31133
Owner: Associated Press, Inc.
Editorial: 50 W State St Ste 1114, Trenton, New Jersey 08608-1220 **Tel:** 1 609 392-3622
Email: aptrenton@ap.org
Language (s): English
NEWS SERVICE/SYNDICATE

Associated Press - Tulsa Bureau 31263
Owner: Associated Press, Inc.
Editorial: 315 S Boulder Ave, Tulsa, Oklahoma 74103-3401 **Tel:** 1 918 584-4346
Email: apoklahoma@ap.org
Language (s): English
NEWS SERVICE/SYNDICATE

Associated Press - Tustin Bureau 31325
Owner: Associated Press, Inc.
Editorial: 17291 Irvine Blvd Ste 263, Tustin, California 92780-2930 **Tel:** 1 714 573-7888
Email: orangecountyca@ap.org
Language (s): English
NEWS SERVICE/SYNDICATE

Associated Press - United Nations Bureau 505254
Owner: Associated Press, Inc.
Editorial: 405 E 42nd St Rm S-320, New York, New York 10017-3507 **Tel:** 1 212 621-7921
NEWS SERVICE/SYNDICATE

Associated Press - Vienna Bureau 217862
Owner: Associated Press, Inc.
Editorial: Laimgrubengasse 10,1960, Vienna 1199
Tel: 43 1 3684-1560
Email: apvienna@ap.org
Bureau Chief: George Jahn
Language (s): English
NEWS SERVICE/SYNDICATE

Associated Press - Warsaw Bureau 560547
Owner: Associated Press, Inc.
Editorial: Al. Przyjaciol 9/9, Warsaw 00-433
Tel: 48 22 628-72-31
Language (s): English
NEWS SERVICE/SYNDICATE

Associated Press - Washington Bureau 31119
Editorial: 1100 13th St NW Ste 500, Washington, District Of Columbia 20005-4051 **Tel:** 1 202 641-9000
Email: apwashington@ap.org
Bureau Chief: Sally Buzbee; **News Editor:** Eugene Kim
Profile: Daybook items for the D.C. area should be sent to the main email address.
Language (s): English
NEWS SERVICE/SYNDICATE

Associated Press - Wellington Bureau 732069
Owner: Associated Press, Inc.
Editorial: Press Gallery Parliament Buildings, Wellington 6160 **Tel:** 64 4 471-2990
Language (s): English
NEWS SERVICE/SYNDICATE

Associated Press - Wichita Bureau 31150
Owner: Associated Press, Inc.
Editorial: 825 E Douglas Ave, Wichita, Kansas 67202-3512 **Tel:** 1 316 263-4601
Email: apkansascity@ap.org
Language (s): English
NEWS SERVICE/SYNDICATE

Associated Press - Yangon Bureau 870417
Owner: Associated Press, Inc.
Tel: 95 1 524-666
Email: yangon@ap.org
NEWS SERVICE/SYNDICATE

Associated Press en Espanol 517880
Owner: Associated Press, Inc.
Editorial: 200 Liberty St, New York, New York 10281-1003 **Tel:** 1 212 621-1500
Email: info@ap.org **Web site:** http://hosted.ap.org/dynamic/fronts/NOTICIAS_FINANCIERAS?SITE=AP&SECTION=HOME
Profile: Associated Press en Espanol is a news service that provides a mix of articles translated to Spanish, as well as original Spanish language content.
Language (s): Spanish/Bilingual
NEWS SERVICE/SYNDICATE

Auto Reviews Plus 30874
Owner: Moorhead, Ron
Editorial: 75 N Main St, Willits, California 95490-3107
Tel: 1 707 367-4608
Email: glenmoorent@yahoo.com **Web site:** http://www.autoreviewsplus.com
Profile: Information provided by this group includes auto road tests, auto industry news, auto Q & A, travel features, lifestyle features outdoor adventures and recreational vehicle adventures. A column called Vibrant Senior Life on lifestyles for seniors, is scheduled to begin October, 2014.
Language (s): English
NEWS SERVICE/SYNDICATE

Automotive News Syndicate 31021
Owner: Crain Communications
Editorial: 1155 Gratiot Ave, Detroit, Michigan 48207-2732 **Tel:** 1 313 446-6000
Email: autonews@crain.com **Web site:** http://www.automotivenews.com
Editor: Jason Stein
Profile: Automotive News Syndicate is a news and feature service that provides automotive industry news from Crain publications to other media, primarily general circulation newspapers and magazines worldwide.
Language (s): English
NEWS SERVICE/SYNDICATE

Baptist News Global 31089
Owner: Baptist News Global
Email: info@baptistnews.com **Web site:** http://baptistnews.com
News Editor: Bob Allen
Profile: Baptist News Global offers news, features and commentary every business day for a global audience of Baptists and other Christians.
Language (s): English
NEWS SERVICE/SYNDICATE

Baptist Press 31090
Editorial: 901 Commerce St, Nashville, Tennessee 37203-3620 **Tel:** 1 615 782-8617
Email: bpress@sbc.net **Web site:** http://www.bpnews.net
Editor: Art Toalston
Profile: Founded in 1946, this is a news service of the Southern Baptist Convention. Stories go out to 40 state Baptist newspapers with a combined readership of 1.16 million. There are also offices in Richmond, VA; Atlanta; and Washington.
Language (s): English
NEWS SERVICE/SYNDICATE

Bay City News Service 31048
Editorial: 1 Kaiser Plz Ste 470, Oakland, California 94612-3675 **Tel:** 1 510 251-8100
Email: newsroom@baycitynews.com **Web site:** http://www.baycitynews.com
Profile: Bay City News Service is a regional, general interest news wire service which operates 24 hours a day gathering information from in and around the greater San Francisco Bay area. Established in 1979, it provides a real-time news report delivered directly to media organizations, Web sites, public relations firms, government agencies and more than 100 newsrooms via a satellite, dedicated phone line and Internet network.
Language (s): English
NEWS SERVICE/SYNDICATE

BestWire 238640
Editorial: 1 Ambest Rd, Oldwick, New Jersey 08858-7000 **Tel:** 1 908 439-2200
Email: editor_bw@ambest.com **Web site:** http://www.ambest.com
News Editor: Mark Dobrow; **Editor:** Caroline Saucer
Profile: BestWire offers insurance industry news on earnings, litigation, state rate actions, mergers and acquisitions, industry trends, legislative actions and upcoming industry conferences and events. The service accepts press releases from insurers, state insurance departments, insurance trade groups and consulting and equity analysis companies.
Language (s): English
NEWS SERVICE/SYNDICATE

Biopharm Insight 492894
Owner: Pearson PLC
Editorial: 41 Farnsworth St Fl 1, Boston, Massachusetts 02210-1236 **Tel:** 1 781 762-9450
Email: info@biopharminsight.com **Web site:** http://www.biopharminsight.com
Editor: Querida Anderson
Profile: Biopharm Insight, a Financial Times Group publication, launched in September 2007. It publishes real-time news and data concerning the most price sensitive issues in the global pharmaceutical market. Built for financial professionals, the wire covers product approvals, litigation, licensing deals and mergers and acquisitions. Its clients are financial professionals who subscribe to the news service, and the articles found online can also be sent to clients' email and BlackBerry. Online content is available through a paid subscription and through mergermarket.com. Print weekly prints in the Financial Times.
Language (s): English
NEWS SERVICE/SYNDICATE

Biopharm Insight - London Bureau 696232
Owner: Pearson PLC
Editorial: 80 Strand, London, England WC2R 0RL
Tel: 44 020 70596100
Web site: http://www.biopharminsight.com
Language (s): English
NEWS SERVICE/SYNDICATE

Biopharm Insight - Shanghai Bureau 809952
Editorial: 11A New Shanghai International Tower, 360 Pudong Road S, Shanghai 200120
Tel: 86 21 6886 3061
NEWS SERVICE/SYNDICATE

Biopharm Insight - Tokyo Bureau 809678
Editorial: Nishi Shimbashi 1-5-8, Kawate Building, 9th Floor, Tokyo
NEWS SERVICE/SYNDICATE

Black Press Service, Inc. 31015
Editorial: 375 5th Ave Fl 3, New York, New York 10016-3323 **Tel:** 1 212 686-6850
Email: news@blackradionetwork.com **Web site:** http://nnpa.org/
Editor: Roy Thompson
Profile: Specializes in news and features with a minority perspective. Syndicated to about 170 minority-oriented print and broadcast news outlets.
Language (s): English
NEWS SERVICE/SYNDICATE

Bloomberg News 31053
Owner: Bloomberg L.P.
Editorial: 731 Lexington Ave, New York, New York 10022-1331 **Tel:** 1 212 617-2300
Email: release@bloomberg.net **Web site:** http://www.bloomberg.com
News Editor: Nathaniel Baker; **Editor:** Lisa Beyer; **Editor:** Clive Crook; **Editor:** Mary Duenwald; **News Editor:** Andrew Dunn; **Editor:** Paula Dwyer; **Editor:** James Greiff; **Editor:** Tobin Harshaw; **Editor:** Timothy Lavin; **Editor:** Brendan Walsh; **Editor:** Frank Wilkinson; **Breaking News Editor:** Erin Zlomek
Profile: Bloomberg News is an international wire service, including print, television, radio and Internet, that provides news, data and analysis to business and media professionals around the world. Bloomberg publishes over 6,000 stories on an average day, syndicating to over 450 newspapers worldwide with a combined circulation of 80 million people. The service is part of Bloomberg Financial Markets and covers business, financial and economic issues, as well as technology, international, national, political, entertainment and sports news. In 2010, it launched a government platform, Bloomberg Government and breaking news platform, Bloomberg First Word. In 2011, it launched its first opinion section, Bloomberg View. In 2015, Bloomberg Gadfly was formed, which is described as a fast business commentary team.
Language (s): English
NEWS SERVICE/SYNDICATE

Bloomberg News - Amman Bureau 738522
Owner: Bloomberg News
Editorial: Regus Business Center Room 206, Al Husari Street, Shmeisani, Amman 11194
Tel: 962 6500 7405
Profile: Bloomberg News is an international wire service, including print, television, radio and Internet, that provides news, data and analysis to business and media professionals around the world. Bloomberg publishes over 6,000 stories on an average day, syndicating to over 450 newspapers worldwide with a combined circulation of 80 million people. The service is part of Bloomberg Financial Markets and covers business, financial and economic issues, as well as technology, international, national, political, entertainment and sports news. In 2010, it launched a government platform, Bloomberg Government and breaking news platform, Bloomberg First Word. In 2011, it launched its first opinion section, Bloomberg View. In 2015, Bloomberg Gadfly was formed, which is described as a fast business commentary team.
NEWS SERVICE/SYNDICATE

Bloomberg News - Amsterdam Bureau 31211
Editorial: Stadhouderskade 14B, Amsterdam 1054
Tel: 31 20 589-8500
Bureau Chief: Fred Pals
Language (s): English
NEWS SERVICE/SYNDICATE

Bloomberg News - Ankara Bureau 433033
Editorial: Piyabe Sokak, Portakal Bldg Cicegi, Apt 18, C Block #7, Ankara 6540 **Tel:** 90 312 4388990
News Editor and Correspondent: Elizabeth Konstantinova
Language (s): English
NEWS SERVICE/SYNDICATE

Bloomberg News - Athens Bureau 306260
Editorial: Vasilisis Sofias 60, Athens 11528
Tel: 30 2107419090
Email: athensnews@bloomberg.net
Language (s): English
NEWS SERVICE/SYNDICATE

Bloomberg News - Atlanta Bureau 31224
Editorial: 235 Peachtree St NE Ste 2210, Atlanta, Georgia 30303-1406 **Tel:** 1 404 507-1300
Bureau Chief: Anita Sharpe
Language (s): English
NEWS SERVICE/SYNDICATE

United States of America

Bloomberg News - Bangkok Bureau 217892
Editorial: 87 Wireless Road, Bangkok 10330
Tel: 66 26540255
Email: thainews@bloomberg.net
Bureau Chief: Tony Jordan
Language (s): English
NEWS SERVICE/SYNDICATE

Bloomberg News - Beijing Bureau 217894
Editorial: 1 Jian Guo Men Wai Avenue, Unit 15, Beijing 100004 **Tel:** 86 106 66497500
Email: chinanews@bloomberg.net
Editor: John Liu; **Editor:** Feifei Shen
Language (s): English
NEWS SERVICE/SYNDICATE

Bloomberg News - Berlin Bureau 87054
Editorial: Pariser Platz 4A, Berlin 10117
Tel: 49 30 700106200
Bureau Chief: Angela Cullen
Language (s): English
NEWS SERVICE/SYNDICATE

Bloomberg News - Bogota Bureau 230994
Editorial: Carrera 7 Numero 71-21, Torre B, Oficina 502, Bogota 801 **Tel:** 57 13137640
Bureau Chief: Matthew Bristow
Language (s): English
NEWS SERVICE/SYNDICATE

Bloomberg News - Boston Bureau 31200
Editorial: 100 Summer St Ste 2810, Boston, Massachusetts 02110-2108 **Tel:** 1 617 210-4600
Email: release@bloomberg.net
Bureau Chief: Tom Moroney
Language (s): English
NEWS SERVICE/SYNDICATE

Bloomberg News - Brasilia Bureau 231578
Editorial: SCN-Q2 Bloco A 5th Fl Off 13-14, Corporate Financial Center Brasilia St, Brasilia 70712-900 **Tel:** 55 61 3329-6057
Language (s): English
NEWS SERVICE/SYNDICATE

Bloomberg News - Brussels Bureau 235276
Editorial: Internation Press Center, Boulevard Charlemagne 1 Box 28, Brussels 1041
Tel: 32 2 2854300
Email: belgium@bloomberg.net
Bureau Chief: Kevin Costelloe
Language (s): English
NEWS SERVICE/SYNDICATE

Bloomberg News - Budapest Bureau 232230
Editorial: Regus House Budapest, Kalman Imre Utca 1 1054, Budapest **Tel:** 36 1 4751180
Email: budapest@bloomberg.net
Editor: Andras Gergely; **Bureau Chief:** Zoltan Simon
Language (s): English
NEWS SERVICE/SYNDICATE

Bloomberg News - Buenos Aires Bureau 154705
Editorial: Corrientes 485 Piso 9, Buenos Aires C1043AAE **Tel:** 54 11 5280-7700
Email: release@bloomberg.net
Bureau Chief: Daniel Cancel
Language (s): English
NEWS SERVICE/SYNDICATE

Bloomberg News - Cairo Bureau 727633
Owner: Bloomberg L.P.
Editorial: 22nd Floor, North Tower, Nile City Towers, Corniche El Nil, Cairo 116 24 **Tel:** 20 22 739 6400
Email: egyptnews@bloomberg.net
Bureau Chief: Tarek El-Tablawy
Profile: Bloomberg News is an international wire service, including print, television, radio and Internet, that provides news, data and analysis to business and media professionals around the world. Bloomberg publishes over 6,000 stories on an average day, syndicating to over 450 newspapers worldwide with a combined circulation of 80 million people. The service is part of Bloomberg Financial Markets and covers business, financial and economic issues, as well as technology, international, national, political, entertainment and sports news. In 2010, it launched a government platform, Bloomberg Government and breaking news platform, Bloomberg First Word. In 2011, it launched its first opinion section, Bloomberg View. In 2015, Bloomberg Gadfly was formed, which is described as a fast business commentary team.
Language (s): English
NEWS SERVICE/SYNDICATE

Bloomberg News - Caracas Bureau 231013
Editorial: Avda. Francisco de Miranda con Avenida El Parque, Torre Edicampo, Piso 5 Oficina 51-52, Caracas **Tel:** 58 212 277-3700
Bureau Chief: Nathan Crooks
Language (s): English
NEWS SERVICE/SYNDICATE

Bloomberg News - Chicago Bureau 31199
Editorial: 111 S Wacker Dr Ste 4950, Chicago, Illinois 60606-4418 **Tel:** 1 312 443-5900
Language (s): English
NEWS SERVICE/SYNDICATE

Bloomberg News - Chiyoda-Ku, Tokyo Bureau 31205
Editorial: Marunouchi Bldg, Fl 22, 2-4-1 Marunouchi, Chiyoda-Ku, Tokyo 100-6321 **Tel:** 81 3 32018950
Email: tokyonews@bloomberg.net
News Editor: Kyung Cho; **Editor:** Dave McCombs; **Bureau Chief:** Chian Wei Teo
Language (s): English
NEWS SERVICE/SYNDICATE

Bloomberg News - Colombo Bureau 377811
Editorial: World Trade Center, Level 26, East Tower, Colombo **Tel:** 94 11 2351-333
Language (s): English
NEWS SERVICE/SYNDICATE

Bloomberg News - Copenhagen Bureau 230993
Editorial: Dronningens Tvaergarde 30, Copenhagen 1302 **Tel:** 45 33322121
Email: copenhagen@bloomberg.net
Bureau Chief: Christian Wienberg
Language (s): English
NEWS SERVICE/SYNDICATE

Bloomberg News - Dallas Bureau 31197
Editorial: 2001 Ross Ave Ste 350, Dallas, Texas 75201-2911 **Tel:** 1 214 954-9430
Email: release@bloomberg.net
Bureau Chief: Susan Warren
Language (s): English
NEWS SERVICE/SYNDICATE

Bloomberg News - Detroit Bureau 31210
Editorial: 2000 Town Ctr Ste 220, Southfield, Michigan 48075-1121 **Tel:** 1 248 455-2300
Bureau Chief: Jeff Green
Language (s): English
NEWS SERVICE/SYNDICATE

Bloomberg News - Dubai Bureau 230996
Editorial: The Gate, 84 West, Dubai
Tel: 971 4 364 1020
Language (s): English
NEWS SERVICE/SYNDICATE

Bloomberg News - Dublin Bureau 230997
Editorial: Harcourt Road, Regus House, Dublin
Tel: 011 353 1523-9520
Email: dublinnews@bloomberg.net
Bureau Chief: Dara Doyle
Language (s): English
NEWS SERVICE/SYNDICATE

Bloomberg News - Edinburgh Bureau 235170
Editorial: 93-95 Hanover Street, Edinburgh, Scotland EH2 1DJ **Tel:** 44 131 301-5035
Editor: Tim Farrand
Language (s): English
NEWS SERVICE/SYNDICATE

Bloomberg News - Frankfurt Am Main Bureau 31212
Editorial: Neue Mainzer Strasse 75, Frankfurt Am Main 60311 **Tel:** 49 69 92041200
Email: germany@bloomberg.net
Editor: Jana Randow
Language (s): English
NEWS SERVICE/SYNDICATE

Bloomberg News - Geneva Bureau 513443
Editorial: 40 Rue du Marche, Geneva 1204
Tel: 41 22 3179200
Email: switzerland@bloomberg.net
Editor: Thomas Mulier
Language (s): English
NEWS SERVICE/SYNDICATE

Bloomberg News - Hanoi Bureau 671357
Owner: Bloomberg News
Editorial: 14 Tran Binh Trong, Hanoi
Tel: 84 4 3936 6727
Bureau Chief: Oanh Ha
Profile: Bloomberg News is an international wire service, including print, television, radio and Internet, that provides news, data and analysis to business and media professionals around the world. Bloomberg publishes over 6,000 stories on an average day, syndicating to over 450 newspapers worldwide with a combined circulation of 80 million people. The service is part of Bloomberg Financial Markets and covers business, financial and economic issues, as well as technology, international, national, political, entertainment and sports news. In 2010, it launched a government platform, Bloomberg Government and breaking news platform, Bloomberg First Word. In 2011, it launched its first opinion section, Bloomberg View. In 2015, Bloomberg Gadfly was formed, which is described as a fast business commentary team.
Language (s): English
NEWS SERVICE/SYNDICATE

Bloomberg News - Helsinki Bureau 235172
Editorial: Mannerheimintie 12, Regus Business Center Luna House Rm 504, Helsinki 100
Tel: 358 9 2512-3732
Email: helsinkinews@bloomberg.net
Bureau Chief: Kati Pohjanpalo
Language (s): English
NEWS SERVICE/SYNDICATE

Bloomberg News - Hong Kong Bureau 87471
Editorial: 2 Queens Road Central, 27th Floor Cheung Kong Centre, Hong Kong **Tel:** 86 852 2977-6600
Email: hknews@bloomberg.net
Editor: Young-Sam Cho; **Editor:** Paul Panckhurst
Language (s): English
NEWS SERVICE/SYNDICATE

Bloomberg News - Houston Bureau 77382
Editorial: 811 Main St Ste 4650, Houston, Texas 77002-6227 **Tel:** 1 713 547-8400
Bureau Chief: Richard Stubbe
Language (s): English
NEWS SERVICE/SYNDICATE

Bloomberg News - Istanbul Bureau 561449
Owner: Bloomberg News
Editorial: Kanyon Office Block, Buyukdere Cd.; Kat 4, Istanbul **Tel:** 90 212 317 3950
Email: turkeynews@bloomberg.net
Profile: Bloomberg News is an international wire service, including print, television, radio and Internet, that provides news, data and analysis to business and media professionals around the world. Bloomberg publishes over 6,000 stories on an average day, syndicating to over 450 newspapers worldwide with a combined circulation of 80 million people. The service is part of Bloomberg Financial Markets and covers business, financial and economic issues, as well as technology, international, national, political, entertainment and sports news. In 2010, it launched a government platform, Bloomberg Government and breaking news platform, Bloomberg First Word. In 2011, it launched its first opinion section, Bloomberg View. In 2015, Bloomberg Gadfly was formed, which is described as a fast business commentary team.
Language (s): English
NEWS SERVICE/SYNDICATE

Bloomberg News - Jakarta Bureau 232227
Editorial: Wisma Antara Suite 1604A, JLN Medan Merdeka Selatan 17, Jakarta 10110 **Tel:** 62 21 3435-3020
Bureau Chief: Neil Chatterjee
Language (s): English
NEWS SERVICE/SYNDICATE

Bloomberg News - Jerusalem Bureau 515115
Editorial: 23 Hillel St, 10th Flr, Jerusalem 61336
Tel: 972 26401110
Bureau Chief: Gwen Ackerman; **Editor:** Amy Teibel
Language (s): English
NEWS SERVICE/SYNDICATE

Bloomberg News - Johannesburg Bureau 310108
Tel: 27 112861900
Email: johannesburg@bloomberg.net
Africa Correspondent: Mike Cohen
Language (s): English
NEWS SERVICE/SYNDICATE

Bloomberg News - Kuala Lumpur Bureau 230998
Editorial: Menara 3 Petronas Twin Towers, Level 24, Persiaran KLCC, Kuala Lumpur 50088
Tel: 60 323027800
Bureau Chief: Shamim Adam
Language (s): English
NEWS SERVICE/SYNDICATE

Bloomberg News - Lagos Bureau 920049
Editorial: Africa Head Office, 35 Oladipo Bateye Street, Lagos **Tel:** 234 1 775-5486
Bureau Chief: Chris Kay
Language (s): English
NEWS SERVICE/SYNDICATE

Bloomberg News - Lima Bureau 458194
Editorial: Avenida Republica de Panama 3545, Piso 11 Oficina 1101, Lima 27 **Tel:** 51 16146806
Language (s): English
NEWS SERVICE/SYNDICATE

Bloomberg News - Lisbon Bureau 411105
Editorial: Regis Business Centre, 110, Avenida de Liberdad, Lisbon 1269-046 **Tel:** 351 213404545
Email: libsonnews@bloomberg.net
Bureau Chief: Joao Lima
Language (s): English
NEWS SERVICE/SYNDICATE

Bloomberg News - London Bureau 31204
Editorial: 39-45 Finsbury Square, London, England EC2A 1PQ **Tel:** 44 20 73307500
Email: newsalert@bloomberg.net
News Editor: Heather Burke; **Editor:** Will Kennedy; **Editor:** Patricia Lui; **Breaking News Editor:** Douglas Lytle; **Editor:** Jon Menon; **Bureau Chief:** Emma Ross-Thomas; **Editor:** John Viljoen
Language (s): English
NEWS SERVICE/SYNDICATE

Bloomberg News - Los Angeles Bureau 31326
Editorial: 1999 Avenue of the Stars Ste 3100, Los Angeles, California 90067-6018 **Tel:** 1 310 201-3400
Bureau Chief: Anthony Palazzo; **Editor:** Anne Reifenberg
Language (s): English
NEWS SERVICE/SYNDICATE

Bloomberg News - Madrid Bureau 231010
Editorial: Paseo de la Castellana 9, Madrid 28046
Tel: 34 91 700-9650
Email: madridnews@bloomberg.net
Bureau Chief: Charles Penty
Language (s): English
NEWS SERVICE/SYNDICATE

Bloomberg News - Manila Bureau 431749
Editorial: 1101-1103 Tower One and Exchange Plaza, Ayala Triangle, Ayala Ave, Makati City 1226
Tel: 63 28497100
Language (s): English
NEWS SERVICE/SYNDICATE

Bloomberg News - Melbourne Bureau 231002
Editorial: 101 Collins Street, Level 20, Melbourne 3000 **Tel:** 61 3 9228-8701
Language (s): English
NEWS SERVICE/SYNDICATE

Bloomberg News - Mexico City Bureau 235300
Editorial: Paseo de la Reforma 265, Piso 12, Mexico City, Distrito Federal 6500 **Tel:** 52 55 5242-9200
Bureau Chief: Jose Enrique Arrioja; **Deputy Bureau Chief:** Carlos Rodriguez
Language (s): English
NEWS SERVICE/SYNDICATE

Bloomberg News - Miami Bureau 826260
Editorial: 1111 Brickell Ave Fl 11, Miami, Florida 33131-3122 **Tel:** 1 305 579-4330
Email: miaminews@bloomberg.net
Bureau Chief: Bill Faries
Language (s): English
NEWS SERVICE/SYNDICATE

Bloomberg News - Milan Bureau 231000
Editorial: Piazza Fontana 1, Milan 20122
Tel: 39 0280644274
Bureau Chief: Dan Liefgreen
Language (s): English
NEWS SERVICE/SYNDICATE

Bloomberg News - Montreal Bureau 231279
Editorial: 1 Place Ville Marie Suite 2001, Montreal, Quebec H3B 2C4 **Tel:** 1 514 669-4400
Email: release@bloomberg.net **Web site:** http://www.bloomberg.com/news/canada
Bureau Chief: Frederic Tomesco
Language (s): English
NEWS SERVICE/SYNDICATE

Bloomberg News - Moscow Bureau 231001
Editorial: Romanov Dvor II, Romanov Pereulok 4, Moscow 125009 **Tel:** 7 0957717717
Email: moscowbn@bloomberg.net
Bureau Chief: Torrey Clark
Language (s): English
NEWS SERVICE/SYNDICATE

Bloomberg News - Mumbai Bureau
231458
Editorial: 51-A Maker Chambers 4, Nariman Point, Mumbai 400 021 **Tel:** 91 22 6120-3604
Email: indianews@bloomberg.net
Bureau Chief: Stephen Foxwell; **News Editor:** Hari Govind; **Editor:** Pratish Narayanan; **Deputy Bureau Chief & Government Reporter:** Natalie Obiko Pearson
Language (s): English
NEWS SERVICE/SYNDICATE

Bloomberg News - Munich Bureau
515232
Owner: Bloomberg News
Editorial: Maximilian Strasse 8, Munich 80539
Tel: 49 89 244478800
Email: germany@bloomberg.net
Bureau Chief: Oliver Suess
Profile: Bloomberg News is an international wire service, including print, television, radio and Internet, that provides news, data and analysis to business and media professionals around the world. Bloomberg publishes over 6,000 stories on an average day, syndicating to over 450 newspapers worldwide with a combined circulation of 80 million people. The service is part of Bloomberg Financial Markets and covers business, financial and economic issues, as well as technology, international, national, political, entertainment and sports news. In 2010, it launched a government platform, Bloomberg Government and breaking news platform, Bloomberg First Word. In 2011, it launched its first opinion section, Bloomberg View. In 2015, Bloomberg Gadfly was formed, which is described as a fast business commentary team.
Language (s): English
NEWS SERVICE/SYNDICATE

Bloomberg News - Nairobi Bureau
745144
Owner: Bloomberg News
Editorial: 3rd Floor, International House, Mama Ngina St., Nairobi **Tel:** 25 42 031-3440
Email: pmrichardson@bloomberg.net
Profile: Bloomberg News is an international wire service, including print, television, radio and Internet, that provides news, data and analysis to business and media professionals around the world. Bloomberg publishes over 6,000 stories on an average day, syndicating to over 450 newspapers worldwide with a combined circulation of 80 million people. The service is part of Bloomberg Financial Markets and covers business, financial and economic issues, as well as technology, international, national, political, entertainment and sports news. In 2010, it launched a government platform, Bloomberg Government and breaking news platform, Bloomberg First Word. In 2011, it launched its first opinion section, Bloomberg View. In 2015, Bloomberg Gadfly was formed, which is described as a fast business commentary team.
Language (s): English
NEWS SERVICE/SYNDICATE

Bloomberg News - New Delhi Bureau
151664
Editorial: PTI Building, 4 Parliament Street, New Delhi 110001 **Tel:** 91 1141792020
Email: indianews@bloomberg.net
Bureau Chief: Sam Nagarajan
Language (s): English
NEWS SERVICE/SYNDICATE

Bloomberg News - Oslo Bureau
310070
Editorial: C.J. Hambros Plass 2C, Fl 2, Oslo 164
Tel: 47 22 008208
Language (s): English
NEWS SERVICE/SYNDICATE

Bloomberg News - Ottawa Bureau
83302
Editorial: 46 Elgin St Suite 110, Ottawa, Ontario K1P 5K6 **Tel:** 1 613 667-4800
Bureau Chief: Theophilos Argitis
Language (s): French/Bilingual
NEWS SERVICE/SYNDICATE

Bloomberg News - Paris Bureau
31213
Editorial: 7 Rue Scribe, Paris 75009
Tel: 33 153655000
Email: parisnews@bloomberg.net
Bureau Chief: Geraldine Amiel; **Editor:** Frank Connelly
Language (s): English
NEWS SERVICE/SYNDICATE

Bloomberg News - Perth Bureau
584629
Owner: Bloomberg News
Editorial: Regus Forrest Centre Level 29, 221 St Georges Terrace, Perth 6000 **Tel:** 61 8 9480 3750
Profile: Bloomberg News is an international wire service, including print, television, radio and Internet, that provides news, data and analysis to business and media professionals around the world. Bloomberg publishes over 6,000 stories on an average day, syndicating to over 450 newspapers worldwide with a combined circulation of 80 million people. The service is part of Bloomberg Financial Markets and covers business, financial and economic issues, as well as technology, international, national, political, entertainment and sports news. In 2010, it launched a government platform, Bloomberg Government and breaking news platform, Bloomberg First Word. In 2011, it launched its first opinion section, Bloomberg View. In 2015, Bloomberg Gadfly was formed, which is described as a fast business commentary team.
Language (s): English
NEWS SERVICE/SYNDICATE

Bloomberg News - Portland Bureau
217242
Editorial: 121 SW Salmon St, Portland, Oregon 97204-2908 **Tel:** 1 503 471-1358
Language (s): English
NEWS SERVICE/SYNDICATE

Bloomberg News - Prague Bureau
310071
Editorial: NA Prikope 19-21, Mislbek Building, Prague 11719 **Tel:** 420 2 2442-2100
Language (s): English
NEWS SERVICE/SYNDICATE

Bloomberg News - Rio De Janeiro Bureau
231004
Editorial: Avenue Rio Branco 1, #1802, Rio De Janeiro RJ 2009003 **Tel:** 55 21 3956-2500
Bureau Chief: Peter Millard
Language (s): English
NEWS SERVICE/SYNDICATE

Bloomberg News - Riyadh Bureau
590947
Owner: Bloomberg News
Editorial: Regus Kingdom Centre, Fl 28, Riyadh
Tel: 966 1 211 8033
Profile: Bloomberg News is an international wire service, including print, television, radio and Internet, that provides news, data and analysis to business and media professionals around the world. Bloomberg publishes over 6,000 stories on an average day, syndicating to over 450 newspapers worldwide with a combined circulation of 80 million people. The service is part of Bloomberg Financial Markets and covers business, financial and economic issues, as well as technology, international, national, political, entertainment and sports news. In 2010, it launched a government platform, Bloomberg Government and breaking news platform, Bloomberg First Word. In 2011, it launched its first opinion section, Bloomberg View. In 2015, Bloomberg Gadfly was formed, which is described as a fast business commentary team.
Language (s): English
NEWS SERVICE/SYNDICATE

Bloomberg News - Rome Bureau
231008
Editorial: Piazza del Popolo 18, 4th Floor, Rome 187
Tel: 39 06 4520-6333
Email: italynews@bloomberg.net
Bureau Chief: Alessandra Migliaccio
Language (s): English
NEWS SERVICE/SYNDICATE

Bloomberg News - Sacramento Bureau
80718
Editorial: 770 L St Ste 950, Sacramento, California 95814-3361 **Tel:** 1 415 912-2960
Language (s): English
NEWS SERVICE/SYNDICATE

Bloomberg News - San Francisco Bureau
31315
Editorial: 3 Pier Ste 101, San Francisco, California 94111-2036 **Tel:** 1 415 617-7100
Editor: Dan Reichl; **News Editor:** Vivek Shankar;
Bureau Chief: Jeff Taylor
Language (s): English
NEWS SERVICE/SYNDICATE

Bloomberg News - Santiago Bureau
217896
Editorial: Mira Flores 222 Edificio de las Americas, Piso 13 Rm 1302, Santiago 10022-1240
Tel: 56 2 487-4000
Language (s): English
NEWS SERVICE/SYNDICATE

Bloomberg News - Sao Paulo Bureau
231009
Editorial: Avenida Nacões Unidas, 12551 - 21o Andar, World Trade Center, Sao Paulo 04578-903
Tel: 55 11 2395-9000
Email: bnbrazil@bloomberg.net
Bureau Chief: Jessica Brice
Language (s): English
NEWS SERVICE/SYNDICATE

Bloomberg News - Seattle Bureau
31244
Editorial: 1420 5th Ave, Seattle, Washington 98101-4087 **Tel:** 1 206 262-4140
Bureau Chief: Peter Robison
Language (s): English
NEWS SERVICE/SYNDICATE

Bloomberg News - Seoul Bureau
238251
Editorial: 139 Sjong-Ro Chongro-Ju Dong-A, Ilbo Media Center Building 15-F, Seoul 110-110
Tel: 82 2 3702-1600
Language (s): English
NEWS SERVICE/SYNDICATE

Bloomberg News - Shanghai Bureau
493452
Owner: Bloomberg News
Editorial: Unit 3404/3405 Bank of China Tower, 200 Ying Cheng Rd, Shanghai 200120
Tel: 86 21 6104 3000
Bureau Chief: Matthew Brooker
Profile: Bloomberg News is an international wire service, including print, television, radio and Internet, that provides news, data and analysis to business and media professionals around the world. Bloomberg publishes over 6,000 stories on an average day, syndicating to over 450 newspapers worldwide with a combined circulation of 80 million people. The service is part of Bloomberg Financial Markets and covers business, financial and economic issues, as well as technology, international, national, political, entertainment and sports news. In 2010, it launched a government platform, Bloomberg Government and breaking news platform, Bloomberg First Word. In 2011, it launched its first opinion section, Bloomberg View. In 2015, Bloomberg Gadfly was formed, which is described as a fast business commentary team.
Language (s): English
NEWS SERVICE/SYNDICATE

Bloomberg News - Singapore Bureau
232205
Editorial: 12th Floor Capital Square, 23 Church St, Singapore 49481 **Tel:** 65 6212-1200
Email: spnews@bloomberg.net
Bureau Chief: Linus Chua; **Editor:** Alexander Kwiatkowski; **Editor:** James Poole
Language (s): English
NEWS SERVICE/SYNDICATE

Bloomberg News - Stockholm Bureau
231011
Editorial: Sturegatan 4 Plan 2, Stockholm 11483
Tel: 46 8 610-0700
Email: stockholmnew@bloomberg.net
Editor: Charles Daly
Language (s): English
NEWS SERVICE/SYNDICATE

Bloomberg News - Sydney Bureau
231012
Editorial: 1 McQuarie Place, Level 36, Sydney 2000
Tel: 61 2 9777-8601
Email: sydnews@bloomberg.net
Editor: Garfield Reynolds
Language (s): English
NEWS SERVICE/SYNDICATE

Bloomberg News - Taipei Bureau
232206
Editorial: 10-C Hung Tai Century Building, 156 Ming Cheng Rd East Section 3, Taipei **Tel:** 886 2 7719-1500
Bureau Chief: Janet Ong
Language (s): English
NEWS SERVICE/SYNDICATE

Bloomberg News - Tel-Aviv Bureau
154541
Editorial: Sderot Rothschild 41, Tel-Aviv 65784
Tel: 11 97 23542-7106
Language (s): English
NEWS SERVICE/SYNDICATE

Bloomberg News - Toronto Bureau
31203
Editorial: 161 Bay St Suite 4300, Toronto, Ontario M5J 2S1 **Tel:** 1 416 203-5700
Web site: http://www.bloomberg.com/news/canada
Bureau Chief: Jacqueline Thorpe
Profile: Toronto bureau of Bloomberg News.
Language (s): English
NEWS SERVICE/SYNDICATE

Bloomberg News - Trenton Bureau
377177
Editorial: 125 W State St, Trenton, New Jersey 08608-1101 **Tel:** 1 609 278-3170
Bureau Chief: Stacie Sherman
Language (s): English
NEWS SERVICE/SYNDICATE

Bloomberg News - Vancouver Bureau
217070
Editorial: 666 Burrard St, Vancouver, British Columbia V6C 2X8 **Tel:** 1 604 331-1310
Email: release@bloomberg.net
Language (s): English
NEWS SERVICE/SYNDICATE

Bloomberg News - Vienna Bureau
711958
Owner: Bloomber News
Editorial: Palais Corso, Kaerntenr Ring 9-13, Vienna Win 1010 **Tel:** 43 1513 2660 50
Profile: Bloomberg News is an international wire service, including print, television, radio and Internet, that provides news, data and analysis to business and media professionals around the world. Bloomberg publishes over 6,000 stories on an average day, syndicating to over 450 newspapers worldwide with a combined circulation of 80 million people. The service is part of Bloomberg Financial Markets and covers business, financial and economic issues, as well as technology, international, national, political, entertainment and sports news. In 2010, it launched a government platform, Bloomberg Government and breaking news platform, Bloomberg First Word. In 2011, it launched its first opinion section, Bloomberg View. In 2015, Bloomberg Gadfly was formed, which is described as a fast business commentary team.
Language (s): English
NEWS SERVICE/SYNDICATE

Bloomberg News - Warsaw Bureau
231014
Editorial: Emil Plater 53, 23 Fl Warsaw Financial Centre, Warsaw 00-113 **Tel:** 48 22 4334444
Email: release@bloomberg.net
Language (s): English
NEWS SERVICE/SYNDICATE

Bloomberg News - Washington Bureau
31195
Editorial: 1101 K St NW #500, Washington, District Of Columbia 20005-4210 **Tel:** 1 202 624-1860
Breaking News Editor: Nicholas Johnston; **Editor:** Joi Preciphs; **Editor:** Bennett Roth
Language (s): English
NEWS SERVICE/SYNDICATE

Bloomberg News - Wellington Bureau
231015
Editorial: 171 Featherton Street, Level 13 HP Tower, Wellington **Tel:** 64 44982201
Bureau Chief: Chris Bourke
Language (s): English
NEWS SERVICE/SYNDICATE

Bloomberg News - Wilmington Bureau
31238
Editorial: 1201 N Market St Fl 12, Wilmington, Delaware 19801-1147 **Tel:** 1 302 661-7600
Bureau Chief: Jef Feeley
Language (s): English
NEWS SERVICE/SYNDICATE

Bloomberg News - Zurich Bureau
235171
Editorial: Seidengasse 20, CH-8001, Zurich
Tel: 41 44 2244130
Email: switzerland@bloomberg.net
Language (s): English
NEWS SERVICE/SYNDICATE

Cagle World
238733
Editorial: 906 Chelham Way, Santa Barbara, California 93108-1049 **Tel:** 1 805 969-2829
Web site: http://www.cagle.com
Profile: Cagle Cartoons features political cartoons and syndicated political columns. All of them are available for purchase to be used in any publication.
Language (s): English
NEWS SERVICE/SYNDICATE

Capital News Service
31092
Owner: Phillip Merrill College of Journalism, University of Marylan
Editorial: 7765 Alumni Dr, Philip Merrill College of Journalism, College Park, Maryland 20742
Tel: 1 301 405-2399
Email: azcapmedia@cs.com **Web site:** http://cnsmaryland.org/home
Profile: Capital News Service serves as a source of Maryland state and federal government news for 14 daily newspapers and wire services, more than 60 weekly and monthly newspapers and newsletters, a news-radio station, a statewide public television network and several online services. The news service is operated by the Philip Merrill College of Journalism at the University of Maryland, College Park. It is only in operation during the months school is in session, from August to May. Students' stories have appeared in The Washington Post, The Baltimore Sun and The Washington Times.
Language (s): English
NEWS SERVICE/SYNDICATE

Capital News Service - Annapolis Bureau
217766
Editorial: 48 Maryland Ave Ste 301, Annapolis, Maryland 21401-8005 **Tel:** 1 410 626-1008
Web site: https://cnsmaryland.org/home
Bureau Chief: Karen Denny
Language (s): English
NEWS SERVICE/SYNDICATE

Capitol Media Services
76080
Editorial: 1820 W Washington St Rm, Phoenix, Arizona 85007-3208 **Tel:** 1 602 390-1850
Email: capmedia@hotmail.com
Editor: Howard Fischer
Profile: Content centers on political, legal and business issues and syndicates to daily and weekly newspapers throughout the state as well as radio stations.
Language (s): English
NEWS SERVICE/SYNDICATE

Catholic News Service 31045
Editorial: 3211 4th St NE, Washington, District Of Columbia 20017-1104 **Tel:** 1 202 541-3250
Email: cns@catholicnews.com **Web site:** http://www.catholicnews.com
Profile: The mission of Catholic News Service is to spread the Gospel and report the news that affects Catholics in their everyday lives. It is the oldest and largest news wire service specializing in reporting on religion, and is the primary source of national and world news that appears in the United States Catholic press. It is also a leading source of news for Catholic print and broadcast media throughout the world. It was created in 1920 by the bishops of the United States but is editorially independent.
Language (s): English
NEWS SERVICE/SYNDICATE

Center for Investigative Reporting 601931
Editorial: 1400 65th St Ste 200, Emeryville, California 94608-1020 **Tel:** 1 510 809-3160
Email: info@cironline.org **Web site:** http://www.revealnews.org
Editor: Bob Salladay
Profile: Founded in 1977, the Center for Investigative Reporting is the nation's oldest nonprofit investigative news organization, producing multimedia reporting that has impact and is relevant to people's lives.
Language (s): English
NEWS SERVICE/SYNDICATE

The Center for Investigative Reporting - San Francisco Bureau 863180
Editorial: 126 Post St, San Francisco, California 94108-4713 **Tel:** 1 415 821-8520
Web site: https://www.revealnews.org
Profile: The Center for Investigative Reporting San Francisco office, formerly The Bay Citizen, launched in May 2010 as a non-profit, publicly supported news organization offering original coverage of Bay Area civic and community news. It focuses on government and public policy, education, the arts and cultural affairs, the environment, food, wine and neighborhood news. The organization also provides content for The New York Times' Bay Area edition.
Language (s): English
NEWS SERVICE/SYNDICATE

Chad, Norman 408109
Editorial: 12747 Pacific Ave Apt 1, Los Angeles, California 90066-4245
Email: asktheslouch@aol.com
Profile: He writes a weekly sports-based syndicated column called Couch Slouch. Each column closes with the feature Ask the Slouch; if a reader's question is selected, the reader wins $1.25 in cash. "Pay the man, Shirley," is frequently cited as a response to readers who have fulfilled the comedy quotient for their particular question. His column has become infamous for many references to his ex-wives and his strong dislike of what he terms "showboating in poker."
Language (s): English
NEWS SERVICE/SYNDICATE

Chinese News Service 506312
Editorial: 15 E 40th St Rm 1101, New York, New York 10016-0411 **Tel:** 1 212 481-2510
Email: gaojian@chinanews.com.cn **Web site:** http://www.chinanews.com.cn
Profile: China News Service is a government-owned news service distributing China-related news to outlets around the world. It covers national and international news, business, politics, life, culture and sports, and is one of the two largest news service agencies in China.
Language (s): Chinese
NEWS SERVICE/SYNDICATE

The Christian Science Monitor News Service 154327
Editorial: 210 Massachusetts Ave, Boston, Massachusetts 02115-3012 **Tel:** 1 617 450-2300
Email: syndication@csmonitor.com **Web site:** http://www.csmonitor.com
Profile: This syndicate covers international and United States news and features.The syndicate has been the recipient of seven Pulitzer Prizes and more than a dozen Overseas Press Club awards.
Language (s): English
NEWS SERVICE/SYNDICATE

City News Service, Inc. 30871
Editorial: 11400 W Olympic Blvd Ste 780, Los Angeles, California 90064-1553 **Tel:** 1 310 481-0404
Email: citynews@pacbell.net **Web site:** http://www.socalnews.com
Editor: Lori Streifler
Profile: City News Service, Inc. is America's largest regional news service. It provides Southern California news 24 hours a day to print and broadcast media outlets. Specifically, it covers news in Los Angeles, Orange, Riverside and San Diego counties, including goverment, crime, court and entertainment stories.
Language (s): English
NEWS SERVICE/SYNDICATE

The Classified Guys 231500
Editorial: 12 Bates Pl, Danbury, Connecticut 06810-6803 **Tel:** 1 888 242-3644
Email: comments@classifiedguys.com **Web site:** http://www.classifiedguys.com
Profile: The Classified Guys produces products and services that help newspapers generate more revenue from their classified sections. Their product line includes being the largest supplier of garage sale kits and car selling kits in North America.
Language (s): English
NEWS SERVICE/SYNDICATE

Cleveland Clinic News Service 430028
Editorial: 9500 Euclid Ave #JJN4-01, Cleveland, Ohio 44195-0001 **Tel:** 1 216 444-0141
Email: healthhub@ccf.org **Web site:** https://newsroom.clevelandclinic.org
Profile: Cleveland Clinic News Service provides reliable information from one of the nation's top academic medical centers. Provides daily stories with two sound bites and b-roll. Also releases Patient Feature Stories and provides video upon request to media outlets.
Language (s): English
NEWS SERVICE/SYNDICATE

Commercial Real Estate Direct 31011
Owner: FM Financial Publishing, LLC
Editorial: 350 S Main St Ste 312, Doylestown, Pennsylvania 18901-4829 **Tel:** 1 267 247-0112
Web site: http://www.crenews.com
Profile: Founded in 1999, Commercial Real Estate Direct tries to bring high-end news and information to professionals in the commercial real estate industry. Since it is a complex industry, people must understand who is raising equity, from whom and for what. They also have to know who is providing debt and at what cost.
Language (s): English
NEWS SERVICE/SYNDICATE

Community Features 30981
Editorial: 1733 Dawsonville Hwy, Gainesville, Georgia 30501-1531 **Tel:** 1 770 287-3798
Email: commfeat@charter.net **Web site:** http://www.communityfeatures.com
Editor: Bill Johnson
Profile: Contains religious features for religion pages that are designed to encourage people to worship regularly. Also sells church pages and bible verse pages for newspapers.
Language (s): English
NEWS SERVICE/SYNDICATE

Content That Works 72193
Editorial: 134 Columbus St, Charleston, South Carolina 29403-4809 **Tel:** 1 773 728-8326
Email: editorial@contentthatworks.com **Web site:** http://www.contentthatworks.com
Profile: Content That Works creates original content that helps its local media partners build audiences, drive revenue and strengthen brands. More than 1000 local media organizations use CTW content in print or online, including CTW's fully designed print publications, individual stories or online feeds. Primary topics covered by the outlet include real estate, jobs/careers, automotive, home decorating/home improvement, bridal, parenting, health & wellness, 50-plus, food, couponing, eco-wise, holiday entertaining, holiday decorating, holiday gift guides and holiday PixelGrams.
Language (s): English
NEWS SERVICE/SYNDICATE

Continental News Service 31070
Editorial: 501 W Broadway, Plaza A PMB#265, San Diego, California 92101-3536 **Tel:** 1 858 492-8696
Email: continentalnewsservice@yahoo.com **Web site:** http://continentalnewsservice.com
Profile: Travel destination stories and food features/recipes are offered along with investigative reports and coverage of unreported news. CF/CNS is a national and international news service and newspaper-feature agency that continues to publish the periodic, general-interest newsmagazine, Continental Newstime and the on-line children's newspaper, Kids' Newstime. While CF/CNS continues to publish a San Diego News Edition periodically, as well, and a Northern California community newspaper regularly, they started publishing intermittent special complimentary Washington D.C., Chicago, Atlanta, Honolulu, Boston and Seattle News Editions, as well.
Language (s): English
NEWS SERVICE/SYNDICATE

Creators Syndicate 30746
Editorial: 737 3rd St, Hermosa Beach, California 90254-4714 **Tel:** 1 310 337-7003
Email: info@creators.com **Web site:** http://www.creators.com
Profile: Creators Syndicate distributes a variety of features, including advice, lifestyle and opinion columns, as well as comics and editorial cartoons. Send press releases by fax or e-mail. Press releases will be forwarded to the appropriate contact. The service was founded in 1987.
Language (s): English
NEWS SERVICE/SYNDICATE

Critics Inc. 30865
Editorial: 6724 Perimeter Loop Rd, Dublin, Ohio 43017-3202 **Tel:** 1 614 408-3865
Email: comments@critics.com **Web site:** http://www.criticsinc.com
Profile: Critics Inc. serves as a source of new film and video criticism for nationwide media outlets. For each movie, the staff presents a wrap-up review as well as ratings from 15 prominent critics. Ultimately, the editors paint a picture of the national critical consensus. They also offer a dueling critics portion, including two quotes, one from the critic who gave the highest rating and one from the critic giving the lowest rating.
Language (s): English
NEWS SERVICE/SYNDICATE

Cronkite News 515130
Owner: Arizona State University
Editorial: 555 N Central Ave Ste 302, Phoenix, Arizona 85004-1248 **Tel:** 1 602 496-5020
Email: cronkitenews@asu.edu **Web site:** http://cronkitenews.azpbs.org
Profile: Cronkite News features stories, photos and video packages about Arizona issues. The news service is a part of Arizona State University and serves as a professional experience for the students of the Walter Cronkite School of Journalism and Mass Communication.
Language (s): English
NEWS SERVICE/SYNDICATE

Cronkite News Service - Washington Bureau 828457
Owner: Arizona State University
Editorial: 1834 Connecticut Ave NW, Washington, District Of Columbia 20009-5732 **Tel:** 1 202 684-2400
Email: cronkitedc@asu.edu
Bureau Chief: Steve Crane
Language (s): English
NEWS SERVICE/SYNDICATE

Curt Schleier Reviews 30777
Owner: Curt Schleier
Editorial: 646 Jones Rd, Rivervale, New Jersey 07675-6034 **Tel:** 1 201 391-7135
Email: writa1@me.com
Profile: Curt Schleier Reviews focuses on author and celebrity interviews, book industry news, book reviews, DVD and CD-ROM reviews and television reviews.
Language (s): English
NEWS SERVICE/SYNDICATE

Dave Goodwin & Associates 30741
Tel: 1 305 865-0158
Web site: http://davegoodwin.weebly.com/
Editor: Dave Goodwin
Profile: Dave Goodwin & Associates target the consumer with Q&A, commentary, and compiled information on insurance and travel.
Language (s): English
NEWS SERVICE/SYNDICATE

Dave Says 242209
Owner: Dave Ramsey
Editorial: 1749 Mallory Ln, Brentwood, Tennessee 37027-2931 **Tel:** 1 615 371-8881
Email: davesays@daveramsey.com **Web site:** http://www.daveramsey.com/davesays/
Editor: David Taylor
Profile: Dave Says column is a compilation of transcripts from calls taken on The Dave Ramsey Show radio program, which focuses on life and how it happens to revolve around money. Ramsey's common sense advice helps people change their lives by getting out of debt and building wealth.
Language (s): English
NEWS SERVICE/SYNDICATE

Davidson, Jim 30965
Owner: Davidson, Jim
Editorial: 2 Bentley Dr, Conway, Arkansas 72034-9602 **Tel:** 1 800 242-2618
Web site: http://www.jimdavidsoncolumn.com
Profile: This is a self-syndicated weekly column offering practical and down to earth ideas and concepts for everyday life. He stresses traditional values, hard work and high moral standards. It is syndicated to around 250 newspapers.
Language (s): English
NEWS SERVICE/SYNDICATE

The Diet Detective 154653
Editorial: 17 E 17th St Fl 4, New York, New York 10003-1943 **Tel:** 1 212 367-7575
Web site: http://www.dietdetective.com
Profile: Charles Stuart Platkin's Diet Detective is the largest syndicated nutrition and fitness column in the United States. It appears in more than 100 daily newspapers including Rochester (NY) Democrat & Chronicle, Omaha (NE) World-Herald, The State, Honolulu (HI) Advertiser and more. The author works with an in-house team of registered dietitians and fitness professionals, as well as additional expert sources from around the country to investigate timely topics in nutrition, food, weight control and fitness.
Language (s): English
NEWS SERVICE/SYNDICATE

Dow Jones Corporate Filings Alert 382292
Owner: News Corporation Ltd.
Editorial: 1025 Connecticut Ave NW Ste 1100, Washington, District Of Columbia 20036-5405
Tel: 1 202 862-7100
Web site: http://www.djnewswires.com
Profile: Dow Jones Corporate Filings Alert is a news service delivering coverage on news uncovered in SEC filings and bankruptcy courts.
Language (s): English
NEWS SERVICE/SYNDICATE

Dow Jones Newswires 31023
Owner: News Corporation Ltd.
Editorial: 1211 Avenue of the Americas, New York, New York 10036-8701 **Tel:** 1 212 416-2000
Web site: https://www.dowjones.com
Breaking News Editor: Lauren Pollock
Profile: Dow Jones Newswires provides news for financial professionals in the equities, fixed-income, foreign exchange, energy and stock markets. Dow Jones Newswires provides real-time business news and information to approximately 438,000 financial professionals around the world. The division also offers news for financial firms' Web sites and Dow Jones Newsletters' sector-specific content. Dow Jones & Company also publishes The Wall Street Journal and its international and online editions, Barron's and the Far Eastern Economic Review, Dow Jones Indexes and the Ottaway group of community newspapers.
Language (s): English
NEWS SERVICE/SYNDICATE

Dow Jones Newswires - Athens Bureau 231694
Editorial: Filellinon 34, 105 58, Athens 10558
Tel: 30 21 0331-2881
Email: djnews.athens@dowjones.com
Language (s): English
NEWS SERVICE/SYNDICATE

Dow Jones Newswires - Bangkok Bureau 154745
Editorial: 540 Mercury Tower 5th Fl Room #502-503, Ploenchit Rd Lumpini, Pathumwan, Bangkok 10330
Tel: 66 2 690-4200
Email: djnews.bangkok@dowjones.com
Language (s): English
NEWS SERVICE/SYNDICATE

Dow Jones Newswires - Beijing Bureau 154747
Editorial: 3F, Raffles City Beijing Office Tower, No.1, Dongzhimen South Street - Dongcheng District, Beijing 100007 **Tel:** 86 10 6588-5848
Language (s): English
NEWS SERVICE/SYNDICATE

Dow Jones Newswires - Berlin Bureau 231696
Editorial: Pressehaus Zimmer 6195, Schiffbauerdamm 40, Berlin 10117 **Tel:** 49 30 288-8410
Language (s): English
NEWS SERVICE/SYNDICATE

Dow Jones Newswires - Bogota Bureau 231697
Editorial: Carrera 14 No 94-44, Torre B, Piso 8, Bogota
Email: colombia@dowjones.com
Language (s): English
NEWS SERVICE/SYNDICATE

Dow Jones Newswires - Brasilia Bureau 231700
Editorial: SRTVS Q. 701 Ed, Centro Empresarial Brasilia, Bloco B-Sala 507, Brasilia 70340-907
Tel: 55 61 3335-0832
Language (s): English
NEWS SERVICE/SYNDICATE

Dow Jones Newswires - Brussels Bureau 231678
Editorial: Avenue de Cortenbergh 60/4F, Brussels B-1000 **Tel:** 32 2 741-1211
Brussels Editor & Bureau Chief: Stephen Fidler; **Deputy Bureau Chief:** Laurence Norman
Language (s): English
NEWS SERVICE/SYNDICATE

Dow Jones Newswires - Buenos Aires Bureau 154704
Editorial: Ing. Butty 240 Piso 5, Buenos Aires 1001
Tel: 54 11 4590-2428
Language (s): English
NEWS SERVICE/SYNDICATE

Dow Jones Newswires - Canberra Bureau 231740
Editorial: Suite 117, Press Gallery, Parliament House, Canberra 2600 **Tel:** 61 2 6208-0901
Language (s): English
NEWS SERVICE/SYNDICATE

Dow Jones Newswires - Caracas Bureau 231704
Editorial: Edificio El Universal, Avenida Urdaneta Esquina Animas Piso 2 Oficina D, Caracas 1010
Tel: 58 25642911
Language (s): English
NEWS SERVICE/SYNDICATE

Dow Jones Newswires - Chicago Bureau 31277
Editorial: 1 S Wacker Dr Ste 1700, Chicago, Illinois 60606-4653 **Tel:** 1 312 750-4000
Deputy Bureau Chief: Doug Cameron; **Bureau Chief:** Jason Dean
Language (s): English
NEWS SERVICE/SYNDICATE

Dow Jones Newswires - Detroit Bureau 31333
Editorial: 2000 Town Ctr Ste 750, Southfield, Michigan 48075-1127 **Tel:** 1 248 204-5500
Bureau Chief: John Stoll
Language (s): English
NEWS SERVICE/SYNDICATE

Dow Jones Newswires - Dubai Bureau 231707
Editorial: Building 5, Office 314, Dubai
Tel: 971 4 331-4260
Email: djnews.dubai@dowjones.com
Profile: This bureau operates as the Arabic-language Zawya Dow Jones News Service. Produced jointly by Dow Jones Newswires and ABQ Zawya, it is the English and Arabic-language news service covering the Middle East's financial markets. It provides news, commentary and analysis, covering public, private and state-owned enterprises, as well as those companies looking to join the region's stock markets. It also covers regional stock markets and mergers and acquisitions activity; government privatizations and budgetary moves; economic trends and infrastructure tenders.
Language (s): English
NEWS SERVICE/SYNDICATE

Dow Jones Newswires - Frankfurt Bureau 231058
Editorial: Wilhelm-Leuschner-Strasse 78, Baseler Arkaden, Frankfurt 60329 **Tel:** 49 69 2972-5500
Email: djnews.frankfurt@dowjones.com
Language (s): English
NEWS SERVICE/SYNDICATE

Dow Jones Newswires - Hanoi Bureau 231060
Editorial: #701 Phu Quy Building, 209 Giang Vo St. - Dong Da District, Hanoi **Tel:** 84 4 3512-3041
Language (s): English
NEWS SERVICE/SYNDICATE

Dow Jones Newswires - Hong Kong Bureau 231061
Editorial: Suite 2404 & 25/F Central Plaza, 18 Harbour Road, Wanchai **Tel:** 852 2802-7002
Email: djnews.honkong@dowjones.com
Bureau Chief: Ken Brown
Language (s): English
NEWS SERVICE/SYNDICATE

Dow Jones Newswires - Houston Bureau 72937
Editorial: 600 Travis St Ste 1965, Houston, Texas 77002-2911 **Tel:** 1 713 227-5440
Deputy Bureau Chief & Energy Editor: Lynn Cook
Language (s): English
NEWS SERVICE/SYNDICATE

Dow Jones Newswires - Jakarta Bureau 231716
Editorial: Jalan Asia Afrika, No. 8 Gelora Bung Karno, Jakarta 10270 **Tel:** 62 21 3983-1277
Bureau Chief: Patrick McDowell
Language (s): English
NEWS SERVICE/SYNDICATE

Dow Jones Newswires - Johannesburg Bureau 779121
Editorial: 12th Floor, Sandton City Office Tower, 158 5th St., Sandhurst ext. 3, Johannesburg 2196
Tel: 27 11 783-7848
Africa Bureau Chief: Peter Wonacott
Language (s): English
NEWS SERVICE/SYNDICATE

Dow Jones Newswires - Kuala Lumpur Bureau 577908
Editorial: Sdn Bhd Suite 34-02, Level 34, Menara Dion 27, Jalan Sultan Ismail, Kuala Lumpur 50250
Tel: 60 3 2026-1233
Email: djnews.kl@dowjones.com
Language (s): English
NEWS SERVICE/SYNDICATE

Dow Jones Newswires - Lima Bureau 231721
Editorial: Los Rosales 460 3rd Floor, San Isidro, Lima
Tel: 51 1 221-7050
Email: peru@dowjones.com
Language (s): English
NEWS SERVICE/SYNDICATE

Dow Jones Newswires - London Bureau 31353
Editorial: 1 London Bridge St, London, England SE1 9GF **Tel:** 44 20 7842-9200
Email: generaldesklondon@dowjones.com
Language (s): English
NEWS SERVICE/SYNDICATE

Dow Jones Newswires - Madrid Bureau 72227
Editorial: Calle de Espronceda 32, Fl 1, Madrid 28003 **Tel:** 34 91 395-8122
Email: djmadrid@dowjones.com
Bureau Chief: Richard Boudreaux
Language (s): English
NEWS SERVICE/SYNDICATE

Dow Jones Newswires - Manila Bureau 231725
Editorial: 1209-1210 12Fl Tower 1 Exchange Plaza, Ayala Triangle, Ayala Avenue, Manila **Tel:** 63 2 848-5051
Bureau Chief: Cris Larano
Language (s): English
NEWS SERVICE/SYNDICATE

Dow Jones Newswires - Mexico City Bureau 231731
Editorial: Tennyson 96, Col. Chapultepec Polanco, Mexico City, Distrito Federal 11560 **Tel:** 52 55 5281-0902
Email: mexico@dowjones.com
Language (s): English
NEWS SERVICE/SYNDICATE

Dow Jones Newswires - Milano Bureau 231732
Editorial: Via Marco Burigozzo 5, Milano 20122
Tel: 39 02 5821-1901
Email: djitaly@dowjones.com
Bureau Chief: Deborah Ball
Language (s): English
NEWS SERVICE/SYNDICATE

Dow Jones Newswires - Moscow Bureau 231733
Editorial: Petrovka str. 7, 7th floor, Moscow 107031
Tel: 7 495 232-9198
Language (s): English
NEWS SERVICE/SYNDICATE

Dow Jones Newswires - Mumbai Bureau 570348
Editorial: Unit 93, 9th Floor 2 North Ave, Maker Maxity Bandra Kurla Complex, Bandra (East), Mumbai 400-051 **Tel:** 91 22 6145-6100
Language (s): English
NEWS SERVICE/SYNDICATE

Dow Jones Newswires - New Delhi Bureau 537612
Editorial: 4th Floor, Birla Tower, 25 Barakhamba Road, New Delhi 1100 001 **Tel:** 91 11 2307-4032
Bureau Chief: Gordon Fairclough; **News Editor for Commodities:** Biman Mukherji
Language (s): English
NEWS SERVICE/SYNDICATE

Dow Jones Newswires - Ottawa Bureau 83300
Editorial: 1 Rideau St Suite 700, Ottawa, Ontario K1N 8S7 **Tel:** 1 613 237-0668
Language (s): English
NEWS SERVICE/SYNDICATE

Dow Jones Newswires - Paris Bureau 31354
Editorial: 6 Bd Haussmann, Paris 75009
Tel: 33 1 4017-1740
Email: paris@priority.emea.dowjones.com
News Editor: Matthew Curtin; **Bureau Chief:** Grainne McCarthy
Language (s): English
NEWS SERVICE/SYNDICATE

Dow Jones Newswires - Rio De Janeiro Bureau 231744
Editorial: Praia de Botafogo, 501, Torre Pao de Acucar, 1 andar, Sala 156, Rio De Janeiro 22250-040
Tel: 55 21 2586-6000
Language (s): English
NEWS SERVICE/SYNDICATE

Dow Jones Newswires - Rome Bureau 231745
Editorial: Via Santa Maria, Via 12, Rome 187
Tel: 39 06 678-2543
Email: djitaly@dowjones.com
Language (s): English
NEWS SERVICE/SYNDICATE

Dow Jones Newswires - San Francisco Bureau 238600
Editorial: 201 California St Fl 10, San Francisco, California 94111-5002 **Tel:** 1 415 986-6886
Editor: Cassandra Sweet
Language (s): English
NEWS SERVICE/SYNDICATE

Dow Jones Newswires - Sao Paulo Bureau 231747
Editorial: Av Paulista 854 13th floor, Sao Paulo CEP 01310-913 **Tel:** 55 11 3145-1479
Email: brazil@dowjones.com
Language (s): English
NEWS SERVICE/SYNDICATE

Dow Jones Newswires - Seoul Bureau 231065
Editorial: 14th Floor Young Poong Building, Cheonggyecheon-ro 41 Jongro-gu, Seoul
Bureau Chief: Alastair Gale
Language (s): English
NEWS SERVICE/SYNDICATE

Dow Jones Newswires - Shanghai Bureau 154746
Editorial: Suites 1504-1508, Two ICC, Shanghai International, Commerce Center No. 288 South Shaanxi Road, Shanghai 200031 **Tel:** 86 21 6120-1200
Bureau Chief: Shen Hong
Language (s): English
NEWS SERVICE/SYNDICATE

Dow Jones Newswires - Singapore Bureau 231066
Editorial: 10 Anson Road #32-08, International Plaza, Singapore 79903 **Tel:** 65 6415-4140
Email: djn.singapore.bureau@dowjones.com
News Editor, Realtime Desk: Colin Ng
Language (s): English
NEWS SERVICE/SYNDICATE

Dow Jones Newswires - Stockholm Bureau 231067
Editorial: Kungsgatan 12-14, 7th Floor, Stockholm 11135 **Tel:** 46 8 5451-3090
Email: djnews.stockholm@dowjones.com
Language (s): English
NEWS SERVICE/SYNDICATE

Dow Jones Newswires - Sydney Bureau 231749
Editorial: Press Gallery Parliament House Suite 117, Surry Hills NSW 2010 **Tel:** 61 2 8272-4600
Email: djnews.sydney@dowjones.com
Language (s): English
NEWS SERVICE/SYNDICATE

Dow Jones Newswires - Tokyo Bureau 156571
Editorial: Otemachi First Square East Tower 19F, 1-5-1 Otemachi Chiyoda-ku, Tokyo 100-0004
Tel: 81 3 6269-2770
Email: tokyo.djnews@dowjones.com
Language (s): English
NEWS SERVICE/SYNDICATE

Dow Jones Newswires - Toronto Bureau 31351
Editorial: 145 King St W Suite 730, Toronto, Ontario M5H 1J8 **Tel:** 1 416 306-2100
Email: djcanada@dowjones.com
Language (s): English
NEWS SERVICE/SYNDICATE

Dow Jones Newswires - Washington Bureau 31201
Editorial: 1025 Connecticut Ave NW Ste 800, Washington, District Of Columbia 20036-5419
Tel: 1 202 862-9200
Deputy Bureau Chief: Mark Anderson
Language (s): English
NEWS SERVICE/SYNDICATE

Dow Jones Newswires - Wellington Bureau 231755
Editorial: Level 5, EMC2, 5-7 Wilestone Street, Wellington 6011 **Tel:** 64 4 471-5990
Language (s): English
NEWS SERVICE/SYNDICATE

Dow Jones Newswires - Zurich Bureau 231757
Editorial: 59 Loewenstrasse, Zurich CH-8032
Tel: 41 43 443-8059
Email: zurichdjnews@dowjones.com
Bureau Chief: Andrew Morse
Language (s): English
NEWS SERVICE/SYNDICATE

DTN News Service 217756
Owner: Schneider Electric
Editorial: 9110 W Dodge Rd Ste 300, Omaha, Nebraska 68114-3316 **Tel:** 1 800 485-4000
Email: agnews@dtn.com **Web site:** http://www.dtnpf.com
News Editor: Anthony Greder
Profile: Founded in 1984, DTN News Service delivers 24-hour information about agriculture, refined fuels, commodities, futures trading, public safety, aviation, turf, recreation, construction and transportation. It is the leading business-to-business provider of real-time market, news and weather information services to agriculture, energy trading markets and other weather-sensitive industries. They deliver on-demand market information, commodity cash prices, industry news and in-depth analysis, and location-specific weather to over 120,000 subscribers for agriculture, refined fuels and trading markets.
Language (s): English
NEWS SERVICE/SYNDICATE

Earth Talk 493041
Owner: Earth Action Network, Inc.
Web site: http://www.earthtalk.org
Profile: Earth Talk provides a weekly question and answer column focused on environmental issues. It is distributed to more than 1,100 publications nationwide.
Language (s): English
NEWS SERVICE/SYNDICATE

Elfman, Doug 436748
Owner: Elfman, Doug
Editorial: 3674 Wild Springs St, Las Vegas, Nevada 89129-5051 **Tel:** 1 702 336-2625
Email: elfmonster@gmail.com **Web site:** http://www.dougelfman.com
Profile: Syndication packages include the weekly column, briefs, Top 10 lists and high-resolution photos. The editorial objective is to reach both video gamers, parents, adult gamers and general-interest newspaper readers. Weekly adult readership is in the millions in print and online. The Game Dork column appears in more than 20 daily newspapers including the Las Vegas Review-Journal, The Kansas City Star; the Times-Picayune in New Orleans; and The Commercial Appeal in Memphis, TN.
Language (s): English
NEWS SERVICE/SYNDICATE

Engelbert Wine & Food Service 30811
Editorial: 3204 Sawmill Rd, Newtown Square, Pennsylvania 19073-1901 **Tel:** 1 610 353-4870
Email: herbeng@earthlink.net
Profile: Provides print, radio and TV commentary on selecting wines to compliment foods, understanding wine labels, wine and health, cooking with wine and interviews with wine makers and wine personalities.
Language (s): English
NEWS SERVICE/SYNDICATE

Entertainment Report 30913
Editorial: 322 Mall Blvd Ste 237, Monroeville, Pennsylvania 15146-2241 **Tel:** 1 412 371-1399
Email: tvj.entertainment.report@gmail.com **Web site:** http://theentertainmentreport.org
Editor: Doris Alma; **Editor:** Jane Otis; **Editor:** Alan Petrucelli; **Editor:** Bill Self
Profile: Entertainment Report provides entertainment and travel news with features on music, films, books, science, health, food, lifestyles, children and home decoration. It covers new product reviews in radio, television and print mediums. The music, book and DVD news and review column is part of the Dow Jones Newswires. 156 papers carry their content. Their website is currently being updated.
Language (s): English
NEWS SERVICE/SYNDICATE

Environment News Service 31101
Owner: Naturalist Com Inc.
Editorial: 1150 Darlene Ln Apt 344, Eugene, Oregon 97401-1102 **Tel:** 1 206 605-3757
Email: news@ens-news.com **Web site:** http://www.ens-newswire.com
Profile: Environment News Service is a daily international wire service. Its mission is to provide late-breaking environmental news in a fair and balanced manner. Contributors around the world cover issues and events that affect the environment. They do not want to be contacted via mail.
Language (s): English
NEWS SERVICE/SYNDICATE

Episcopal News Service 155403
Editorial: 815 2nd Ave, New York, New York 10017-4503 **Tel:** 1 212 716-6000
Email: news@episcopalchurch.org **Web site:** http://episcopaldigitalnetwork.com/ens/
Editor: Matthew Davies; **Editor:** Mary Frances Schjonberg; **Editor:** Lynette Wilson
Profile: Episcopal News Service provides news about the Episcopal Church in the United States and the Anglican Communion worldwide.
Language (s): English
NEWS SERVICE/SYNDICATE

Executive Intelligence Review News Services 30844
Editorial: 729 15th St NW, Washington, District Of Columbia 20005-2105 **Tel:** 1 703 297-8434
Email: eirns@larouchepub.com **Web site:** http://www.larouchepub.com
Profile: Serves as a source of economic and political news for media outlets and clients worldwide. Columns about international affairs and environmentalism also are included. Bureaus of the service are located in European and South American cities. A major emphasis is placed on economic and political intelligence for policy makers internationally.
Language (s): English
NEWS SERVICE/SYNDICATE

Eyes on Mississippi 30838
Tel: 1 601 366-4089
Web site: http://www.jacksonfreepress.com/news/2015/apr/15/eyes-bill-minor/
Profile: Political commentary drawing on 60 years of covering Mississippi politics, government and social change. Self-syndicated to 15 newspapers.
Language (s): English
NEWS SERVICE/SYNDICATE

FairWarning 670333
Editorial: 55 S Grand Ave, Pasadena, California 91105-1602 **Tel:** 1 818 453-8785
Web site: http://www.fairwarning.org
Editor: Myron Levin
Profile: FairWarning is a non-profit news organization that aims to provide in-depth, investigative reporting on issues such as health, saftey and corporate conduct. It launched in March 2010.
Language (s): English
NEWS SERVICE/SYNDICATE

Family Features Editorial Syndicate, Inc. 30873
Editorial: 5825 Dearborn St, Mission, Kansas 66202-2745 **Tel:** 1 913 722-0055
Email: editor@familyfeatures.com **Web site:** http://www.familyfeatures.com
Profile: An industry leader in food and lifestyle content, Family Features helps brands reach and engage consumers through a network of over 8,000 editors at nearly 4,000 print and online outlets. Family Features' clients include the nation's top food, beverage and lifestyle products manufacturers, commodity boards and associations, and their advertising and public relations agencies. Celebrating its 40th anniversary in 2014, Family Features connects, brands consumers and media.
Language (s): English
NEWS SERVICE/SYNDICATE

Featurewell 80756
Editorial: 238 W 4th St, New York, New York 10014-2610 **Tel:** 1 212 924-2283
Email: contactus@featurewell.com **Web site:** http://www.featurewell.com
Profile: Featurewell syndicates both original and non-original content covering culture, business, technology, sports, sex, science, food, health, entertainment, travel and politics to both print and online outlets. It serves as a global marketplace offering articles and photos from some of the world's finest journalists.
Language (s): English
NEWS SERVICE/SYNDICATE

Federal Information & News Dispatch, Inc. 31079
Editorial: 103 John F Kennedy Pkwy, Short Hills, New Jersey 07078-2708 **Tel:** 1 512 374-4500
Email: agenda@find-inc.com **Web site:** http://www.hoovers.com/
Bureau Chief: C. Patrick Thorne
Profile: Federal Information & News Dispatch, Inc., serves as a source of government and business news for major news services, online services and other media and business outlets. Their clients include Lexis-Nexis, Dow Jones Factiva, the Denver Post, NewsEdge, the National Journal and Federal News Service, among others.
Language (s): English
NEWS SERVICE/SYNDICATE

Federal News Service 30935
Owner: Federal News Service, Inc.
Editorial: 77 K St NE Fl 8, Washington, District Of Columbia 20002-4681 **Tel:** 1 202 650-6500
Email: info@fednews.com **Web site:** http://www.fednews.com
Profile: Founded in 1985, Federal News Service offers real-time verbatim transcripts of Congressional hearings, government briefings, speeches, press conferences and other newsmaker events to news bureaus and other governmental and nongovernmental organizations through its Washington Transcription subscription service. The transcripts are sent out within 24 hours. FNS also offers on-demand transcription, translation and media monitoring services. There are also offices in Moscow and Jerusalem that do regional transcription work.
Language (s): English
NEWS SERVICE/SYNDICATE

Feeley Enterprises 31034
Editorial: 3141 Washington Ave, Wilmette, Illinois 60091-2082 **Tel:** 1 847 251-7191
Editor: Jim Limper; **News Editor:** Barry Stockton
Profile: Feeley Enterprises provides news and features daily to more than 1100 print publications with a rated 86.3 million readership and more than 900 electronic media outlets. Primary focus includes leisure, entertainment, travel, sports and product reviews. Business news briefs, product and trade show coverage also are available.
Language (s): English
NEWS SERVICE/SYNDICATE

Fleet Hometown News Center 797570
Owner: Armed Forces
Editorial: 9420 3rd Ave Ste 100, Norfolk, Virginia 23511-2131 **Tel:** 1 301 222-6691
Email: fleethometownnews@navy.mil **Web site:** http://jhns.dma.mil/
News Release Processing Coordinator: Deborah Grant
Profile: Designed to increase national awareness of the activities of United States sailors, marines and coast guardsmen through written stories and documented images about them to hometown markets. Includes positive news stories to friends and family of US serviceman in their hometown.
Language (s): English
NEWS SERVICE/SYNDICATE

FNA News 281734
Tel: 1 801 355-3336
Email: mg2@utah.edu **Web site:** http://www.fnanews.com
Editor: Cindy Richie
Profile: FNA News was formed in March 1980, in Salt Lake City, and has been responsible for bringing many stories to the front page of attention in the Salt Lake City metro area, as well as the nation and beyond. See fnanews.com to see what the news agency does.
Language (s): English
NEWS SERVICE/SYNDICATE

Gannett Washington 31047
Owner: Gannett Co., Inc.
Editorial: 1575 I St NW Ste 350, Washington, District Of Columbia 20005-1114 **Tel:** 1 703 854-6000
Email: pr@gannett.com **Web site:** http://www.gannett.com
Profile: Formerly Gannett News Service and Gannett ContentOne, this is the headquarters of Gannett's Washington staff, who report for various Gannett papers nationwide.
Language (s): English
NEWS SERVICE/SYNDICATE

Gary R. Gruber, Ph.D. 949412
Email: garyg@drgarygruber.com **Web site:** http://www.drgarygruber.com/
Profile: Dr. Gruber is a columnist and author who writes columns on critical thinking and test-taking skills as well as puzzles and brain teasers. He has sold more than 7 million books focused on standardized test preparation as well as books of puzzles and brain teasers.
Language (s): English
NEWS SERVICE/SYNDICATE

GateHouse News Service - Springfield Bureau 31185
Editorial: One Copley Plaza, Springfield, Illinois 62701 **Tel:** 1 217 788-1518
Email: sjr@sj-r.com **Web site:** http://www.sj-r.com
Profile: Gatehouse News Service provides stories on Illinois politics, government and healthcare for the GateHouse newspapers in Illinois, including the Rockford (IL) Register-Star, Peoria (IL) Journal-Star and Star Courier in Kewanee, IL.
Language (s): English
NEWS SERVICE/SYNDICATE

Getty Images 30841
Owner: Getty Images Inc.
Editorial: 75 Varick St, New York, New York 10013-1917 **Tel:** 1 646 613-4000
Email: pressreleases@gettyimages.com **Web site:** http://www.gettyimages.com
Profile: Getty Images provides photos from major news, arts & entertainment, sports, political events any other newsworthy event. There are also travel shots and celebrities. It is syndicated to hundreds of countries and is also available to more than 1,800 newspapers.
Language (s): English
NEWS SERVICE/SYNDICATE

Getty Images - London Bureau 853718
Editorial: 101 Bayham St., London, England NW1 0AG **Tel:** 44 20 7579-5759
Web site: http://www.gettyimages.co.uk
Language (s): English
NEWS SERVICE/SYNDICATE

Globe Photos 690799
Owner: Whelan (Mary Beth)
Editorial: 24 Edmore Ln S, West Islip, New York 11795-4016 **Tel:** 1 631 661-3131
Email: info@globephotos.com **Web site:** http://www.globephotos.com
Profile: Globe Photos is a news service that provides specialized coverage of the entertainment industry to a variety of markets, including multimedia, television, film, advertising, corporate, editorial and publishing industries. It maintains a comprehensive stock photography archive.
Language (s): English
NEWS SERVICE/SYNDICATE

The Gold Sheet 30827
Editorial: 4717 Van Nuys Blvd Fl 3, Sherman Oaks, California 91403-2153 **Tel:** 1 800 798-4653
Email: goldshee@goldsheet.com **Web site:** http://www.goldsheet.com
Editor: Gary Olshan
Profile: The Gold Sheet is a sports information newsletter covering football and basketball. It offers insight and analysis on teams across the nation. For football coverage, there is comprehensive pointspread coverage, college and pro power ratings, statistical reviews and detailed reports on injuries and lineup changes. There are also reports on college games with in-depth analysis of each game.
Language (s): English
NEWS SERVICE/SYNDICATE

Goldsborough, Reid 30984
Editorial: 756 Suffolk Rd, Rydal, Pennsylvania 19046-3426
Email: reidgoldsborough@gmail.com **Web site:** http://www.reidgold.com
Profile: This is a nationally-syndicated bi-weekly column focusing on personal computers and related technology, including software, hardware and the Internet. The focus is on issues and trends. Do not send press releases about personnel changes or company acquisitions.
Language (s): English
NEWS SERVICE/SYNDICATE

Golf Publishing Syndicate 30898
Editorial: 2743 Saxon St, Allentown, Pennsylvania 18103-2825 **Tel:** 1 610 437-4982
Email: info@galvgolf.com **Web site:** http://www.galvgolf.com
Editor: Karl Gilbert
Profile: Golf Publishing Syndicate offers features on golf equipment, golf etiquette, learning how to play better golf and professional golf analysis.
Language (s): English
NEWS SERVICE/SYNDICATE

Gongwer News Service 151672
Editorial: 17 S High St Ste 630, Columbus, Ohio 43215-3413 **Tel:** 1 614 221-1992
Email: gongwer@gongwer-oh.com **Web site:** http://www.gongwer-oh.com
Editor: Kent Cahlander
Profile: Gongwer News Service provides comprehensive, accurate, timely and balanced daily news reports on the activities of state government, with a particular emphasis on legislative activities. The news service provides subscribers with a complete package of information about Ohio's state government, including real time email alerts and bill tracking.
Language (s): English
NEWS SERVICE/SYNDICATE

Gongwer News Service - Lansing Bureau 151676
Editorial: 124 W Allegan St Ste 1200, Lansing, Michigan 48933-1768 **Tel:** 1 517 482-3500
Email: gongwer@gongwer.com **Web site:** http://www.gongwer.com
Editor: Zachary Gorchow
Profile: The Lansing bureau of Gongwer News Service provides The Michigan Report, a comprehensive, accurate, timely report on the activities of state government, with a particular emphasis on legislative activities.
Language (s): English
NEWS SERVICE/SYNDICATE

Gracenote 958185
Owner: Nielsen Company (The)
Editorial: 2000 Powell St, Emeryville, California 94608-1804 **Tel:** 1 510 428-7200
Email: support@gracenote.com **Web site:** http://www.gracenote.com
Profile: Gracenote is a digital and print content distributor, focusing on Arts & Entertainment and TV Listings content.
Language (s): English
NEWS SERVICE/SYNDICATE

Grochowski, John 407975
Tel: 1 312 321-2351
Email: casinoanswerman@casinoanswerman.com
Web site: http://casinoanswerman.blogspot.com/
Profile: John Grochowski self-syndicates a weekly casino column that runs in several Midwest newspapers and beyond including Atlantic City Weekly and the Denver Post's "The Deal" publication. Some clients include Casino Player, Strictly Slots, and Southern Gaming and Destinations. His column is sometimes labeled as The Casino Answer Man.
Language (s): English
NEWS SERVICE/SYNDICATE

Guidry News Service 153240
Owner: Guidry (Lynda)
Editorial: 4001 Fannin St Apt 4432, Houston, Texas 77004-4077 **Tel:** 1 409 763-6397
Email: news@guidrynews.com **Web site:** http://www.guidrynews.com
Profile: Guidry News Service publishes Gulf Coast E-news, a newsletter delivered by e-mail five days a week; the Online News Station, a news magazine covering events impacting the Gulf Coast region of Texas and Louisiana; and The Guidry News Gazette, published weekly on its Web site. It primarily focuses on coverage in five counties in the Texas Gulf Coast. Topics covered include Government & Politics, Education, Arts & Entertainment, Ports, Obituaries, Opinion & Editorial, Business & Industry, Faith & Values, Gardening, Economics, Weather, and Events.
Language (s): English
NEWS SERVICE/SYNDICATE

Hannah News Service 583992
Editorial: 21 W Broad St Ste 1000, Columbus, Ohio 43215-4100 **Tel:** 1 614 228-3113
Email: pressreleases@hannah.com **Web site:** http://hannah.com
Editor: Paul Teasley
Profile: Hannah News Service covers state government and the state house, including legislative, healthcare and education news.
Language (s): English
NEWS SERVICE/SYNDICATE

Hearst News Service 31025
Editorial: 700 12th St NW Ste 100, Washington, District Of Columbia 20005-3945 **Tel:** 1 212 649-2000
Bureau Chief: David McCumber
Profile: Hearst News Service combines daily stories from each Hearst newspaper, along with contributions from its own Washington staff, and transmits them to the group's daily newspapers and subscribers to the New York Times News Service. The Washington staff regularly covers the White House, Congress, the economy and national security for its readers in Houston, San Antonio, San Francisco, Albany (N.Y.) and Connecticut.
Language (s): English
NEWS SERVICE/SYNDICATE

The Hechinger Report 797575
Editorial: 475 Riverside Dr, New York, New York 10115-0002 **Tel:** 1 585 502-8499
Email: dobo@hechingerreport.org **Web site:** http://hechingerreport.org
Editor: Liz Willen
Profile: The Hechinger Report is a non-profit news organization that is focused on producing in-depth education journalism. Working with in-house and freelance reporters, The Report covers education issues, including investigative reporting, detailed analysis, and occasionally featuring opinion from some of the leading thinkers in education. These stories appear nationwide in newspapers and on websites, as well as on the Hechinger Report's website. The Hechinger Report is an independently funded unit of Teachers College at Columbia University. This outlet offers RSS (Really Simple Syndication).
Language (s): English
NEWS SERVICE/SYNDICATE

High Country News Service 238871
Editorial: 119 Grand Ave, Paonia, Colorado 81428-9905 **Tel:** 1 970 527-4898
Email: editor@hcn.org **Web site:** http://www.hcn.org
Profile: High Country News Service reports on the West's natural resources, public lands and changing communities. It covers 11 Western states, from the Great Plains to the northwest, and from the northern Rockies to the desert southwest. It offers environmental news, analysis and commentary on water, logging, wildlife, grazing, public lands, economic growth and other issues changing the face of the West.
Language (s): English
NEWS SERVICE/SYNDICATE

Hollister Kids 281745
Editorial: 3 E Wynnewood Rd, Wynnewood, Pennsylvania 19096-1917 **Tel:** 1 484 829-0021
Web site: http://www.hollisterkids.com
Profile: Hollister Kids offers educational supplements for newspapers in education programs. It features try to reach, teach and entertain young readers and their families with a new topic every week.
Language (s): English
NEWS SERVICE/SYNDICATE

Hollywood News Calendar 30802
Editorial: 13636 Ventura Blvd Ste 303, Sherman Oaks, California 91423-3700 **Tel:** 1 818 990-5945
Email: editor@newscalendar.com **Web site:** http://www.newscalendar.com
Profile: Hollywood News Calendar offers information for covering the entertainment industry, including which celebrities are available for interviews, what celebrities are going to which parties, where the premieres are being held or when a celebrity is appearing in court. It is sent out Monday through Friday to subscribers.
Language (s): English
NEWS SERVICE/SYNDICATE

Homeland Security News Wire 496624
Editorial: 220 Old Country Rd Ste 200, Mineola, New York 11501-4208 **Tel:** 1 202 518-0029
Email: editor@newswirepubs.com **Web site:** http://www.homelandsecuritynewswire.com
Profile: Homeland Security News Wire is designed for executives, investors and senior decision makers involved in the homeland security market. It provides daily reports on trends, technologies and emerging market directions, and is international in its coverage and readership. Issues covered include biodefense and food supply safety, biometrics and identity authentication, border security, business continuity and disaster recovery, critical infrastructure and IT security, detection, emergency response and management, homeland security budget, intelligence, surveillance, training and simulation technologies and transportation security.
Language (s): English
NEWS SERVICE/SYNDICATE

Hot Topics Publications Inc. 30942
Owner: Carroll (Ned) & Carroll (Debby)
Tel: 1 800 352-5444
Email: nie@hottopicshotserials.com **Web site:** http://www.hottopicshotserials.com
Editor: Ned Carroll
Profile: Hot Topics Publications provides materials for educational environments. The products include 16-page tabloid supplements with full color covers and teacher's guides. Experienced teachers help write lesson plans so that editors and reporters can get an intuitive product.
Language (s): English
NEWS SERVICE/SYNDICATE

Hughes, Mike 561305
Editorial: 1149 Woodside Dr, Haslett, Michigan 48840-9780 **Tel:** 1 517 339-5051
Email: hughestvmike@aol.com **Web site:** http://mikehughes.tv
Profile: This self-syndicated column covers television. It provides readers with reviews and previews of upcoming television programs.
Language (s): English
NEWS SERVICE/SYNDICATE

Icon Sportswire 724708
Owner: XML Team Solutions
Editorial: 531A N Hollywood Way #221, Burbank, California 91505-3406 **Tel:** 1 855 333-4266
Email: info@iconsportswire.com **Web site:** http://iconsportswire.com/

Profile: Icon Sports Media is a digital photography wire service.
Language (s): English
NEWS SERVICE/SYNDICATE

IDG News Service 133069
Owner: International Data Group
Editorial: 1 Exeter Plaza, 15th Floor, Boston, Massachusetts 2116 **Tel:** 1 617 534-1200
Email: newsbox@idg.com **Web site:** http://www.idg.com
Profile: IDG News Service is a technology media, research and event company. The parent company, International Data Group, publishes more than 300 magazines and newspapers. It is updated six days a week, 24 hours a day, and has correspondents worldwide, covering their respective markets. The mission of the service is to provide major breaking news stories to its affiliates, including the majority of news stories that run in IDG publications and Web sites around the world.
Language (s): English
NEWS SERVICE/SYNDICATE

IDG News Service - Bangalore Bureau 588167
Owner: International Data Group
Editorial: 302 Koramangala Comforts, No. 1, 9th Main, 6th Cross, S.T. Bed, Bangalore 560 034
Tel: 91 802-553-3341
Email: idgnews@idg.com
Language (s): English
NEWS SERVICE/SYNDICATE

IDG News Service - New York Bureau 588166
Owner: International Data Group
Editorial: 224 W 4th St Ste 200, New York, New York 10014-3188 **Tel:** 1 212 400-0524
Email: idgnews@idg.com
Language (s): English
NEWS SERVICE/SYNDICATE

IDG News Service - San Francisco Bureau 153201
Owner: International Data Group
Editorial: 501 2nd St Ste 600, San Francisco, California 94107-4133
Email: idgnews@idg.com **Web site:** http://www.idg.com
Profile: IDG News Service is a technology media, research and event company. The parent company, International Data Group, publishes more than 300 magazines and newspapers. It is updated six days a week, 24 hours a day, and has correspondents worldwide, covering their respective markets. The mission of the service is to provide major breaking news stories to its affiliates, including the majority of news stories that run in IDG publications and Web sites around the world.
Language (s): English
NEWS SERVICE/SYNDICATE

IDG News Service - Suresnes Bureau 153232
Owner: International Data Group
Editorial: 40 bd Henri Sellier, Suresnes F-92150
Tel: 33 141970197
Email: idgnews@idg.com **Web site:** http://www.idgnews.net
Bureau Chief: Peter Sayer
Language (s): English
NEWS SERVICE/SYNDICATE

IDG News Service - Sydney Bureau 857140
Owner: International Data Group
Tel: 61 2 9902-2719
Email: idgnews@idg.com
NEWS SERVICE/SYNDICATE

Independence Institute 281748
Editorial: 727 E 16th Ave, Denver, Colorado 80203-2048 **Tel:** 1 303 279-6536
Email: info@i2i.org **Web site:** http://www.i2i.org
Profile: This syndicate is in a variety of publications and provides citizens of Colorado and the nation with specific recommendations to help resolve important issues. Issues include improving the educational system, healthcare costs, economic freedom and controlling violent crime. It offers issue papers and editorials. They are interested in pieces focused on Colorado or Colorado localities. The service is associated with a public policy think tank with many writers.
Language (s): English
NEWS SERVICE/SYNDICATE

inewsource 694952
Owner: San Diego State University
Editorial: 5500 Campanile Dr Psfa 361C, San Diego, California 92182-0001 **Tel:** 1 619 594-5100
Email: contact@inewsource.org **Web site:** http://inewsource.org
Profile: inewsource is an independent non-profit news service at San Diego State University, providing investigative journalism to the citizens of San Diego and Imperial County, CA, and is partnered with KPBS, the PBS-NPR affiliate in San Diego.
Language (s): English
NEWS SERVICE/SYNDICATE

Inman News 30745
Editorial: 4225 Hollis St, Emeryville, California 94608-3507 **Tel:** 1 510 658-9252
Email: press@inman.com **Web site:** http://www.inman.com
Profile: Founded in 1983, Inman News is a real estate news service and syndicate based in the San Francisco Bay area. It is a daily news feed and reports on residential and commercial real estate, including market trends, emerging technologies and news for homebuyers and sellers. Editorial content is licensed to over 250 newspapers and 50,000 Web sites.
Language (s): English
NEWS SERVICE/SYNDICATE

International Fashion Syndicate 235329
Editorial: 35 Park Ave, New York, New York 10016-3838 **Tel:** 1 646 742-9307
Email: marylouluther@gmail.com
Profile: International Fashion Syndicate syndicates Clotheslines, a weekly question-and-answer fashion advice feature that includes tips on the latest trends and designers.
Language (s): English
NEWS SERVICE/SYNDICATE

International News Features Network 31060
Editorial: 415 E 52nd St, New York, New York 10022-6424 **Tel:** 1 212 753-2939
Email: generalstrategics@msn.com
Editor: Edward Mahoney
Profile: International News Features Network offers print and broadcast media clients packaged features covering a variety of general interest topics, such as travel, book reviews, food, personal finance, entertainment, medical/health and the arts.
Language (s): English
NEWS SERVICE/SYNDICATE

International News Group 133148
Editorial: 2535 NW 2nd Ter, Gresham, Oregon 97030-5278 **Tel:** 1 866 335-4710
Email: pitch@internationalnewsgroup.com **Web site:** http://www.internationalnewsgroup.com
Profile: International News Group is a privately held subscriber supported wire service established in 1972. It primarily provides features for print and broadcast. The service mainly looks at feature stories rather than hard news. Currently their Web site is only available to paid subscribing news outlets. International News Group is updated four times a day, seven days a week, and has offices in Oregon, California, Dallas, Hilton Head Island, London England, and Karmi'el Israel.
Language (s): English
NEWS SERVICE/SYNDICATE

Jacobi, Dana 88262
Owner: Jacobi, Dana
Editorial: 460 E 79th St, New York, New York 10075-1443 **Tel:** 1 212 744-0939
Email: djacobi@aol.com **Web site:** http://www.danajacobi.com
Profile: The column targets mainstream readers interested in good food and healthful eating. Please only send press releases that are strictly related to food.
Language (s): English
NEWS SERVICE/SYNDICATE

Jandon Features 30764
Editorial: 2319 S 105th Ave, Omaha, Nebraska 68124-1821 **Tel:** 1 402 502-4367
Web site: http://midwestgardening.com
Profile: Jandon Features provides weekly columns and seasonal features that focus on gardening and landscaping in the Midwest. It also includes product reviews. It is syndicated to daily and weekly newspapers in cities from Ohio to Nebraska, including Chicago, Milwaukee, Omaha, NE, Sioux City, IA, and Peoria, IL.
Language (s): English
NEWS SERVICE/SYNDICATE

Jiji Press America 31086
Owner: JIJI Press LTD.
Editorial: 70 E 55th St Fl 4, New York, New York 10022-3222 **Tel:** 1 646 231-6300
Email: edit@jijiusa.com **Web site:** http://www.jiji.com
Bureau Chief: Itsuro Umemoto
Profile: JiJi Press America is a Japanese wire service serving newspapers in Japan on varied topics with emphasis on financial and business news.
Language (s): English
NEWS SERVICE/SYNDICATE

JiJi Press America - Chicago Bureau 31359
Editorial: 300 W Adams St Ste 322, Chicago, Illinois 60606-5107 **Tel:** 1 312 750-1415
Web site: http://www.jiji.com
Profile: This is the Chicago bureau of JiJi Press America.
Language (s): English
NEWS SERVICE/SYNDICATE

JiJi Press America - Silicon Valley Bureau 31360
Editorial: 700 Promontory Point Ln Apt 1208, Foster City, California 94404-4018 **Tel:** 1 650 784-6877
Email: jijila@jijiusa.com
Bureau Chief: Yoshihisa Tamura
Profile: This is the Silicon Valley bureau.
Language (s): English
NEWS SERVICE/SYNDICATE

Jiji Press America - Washington Bureau 532662
Editorial: 529 14th St NW, Ste 550, Washington, District Of Columbia 20045-1500 **Tel:** 1 202 783-4330
Email: jijipressdc@nationalpress.com
Bureau Chief: Yoshiki Kishida
Profile: This is the Washington bureau of JiJi Press America.
Language (s): Japanese
NEWS SERVICE/SYNDICATE

JTA 30823
Owner: Jewish Telegraphic Agency
Editorial: 24 W 30th St Fl 4, New York, New York 10001-4443 **Tel:** 1 212 643-1890
Email: newsdesk@jta.org **Web site:** http://www.jta.org
Profile: The Jewish Telegraphic Agency is a news service covering domestic and international news of interest to Jewish people. It hopes to provide accurate reports and informative analysis of the issues and news developments, including coverage of political, economic and social developments affecting Jews around the world.
Language (s): English
NEWS SERVICE/SYNDICATE

JTA - Washington Bureau 88299
Editorial: 1025 Vermont Ave NW, Ste 504, Washington, District Of Columbia 20005-3578
Tel: 1 202 737-0935
Email: newsdesk@jta.org **Web site:** http://www.jta.org
Bureau Chief: Ron Kampeas
Profile: JTA is a global news service serving the Jewish community.
Language (s): English
NEWS SERVICE/SYNDICATE

Kaiser Health News 556001
Owner: Kaiser Family Foundation (Henry J.)
Editorial: 1330 G St NW, Washington, District Of Columbia 20005-3004 **Tel:** 1 202 347-5270
Email: khnnews@kff.org **Web site:** http://khn.org/
Editor: Stephanie Stapleton
Profile: Kaiser Health News launched in early 2009. It is an independent news service that focuses on the nation's healthcare system and related political and policy issues. The news service provides in-depth stories on developments, initiatives and debates in the healthcare system. In addition to reporting, the news service features columns, video, graphics and multimedia elements. News content is also provided online.
Language (s): English
NEWS SERVICE/SYNDICATE

Keister-Williams Newspaper Services, Inc. 30822
Editorial: 1807 Emmet St N Ste 6B, Charlottesville, Virginia 22901-3616 **Tel:** 1 434 293-4709
Email: kw@kwnews.com **Web site:** http://www.kwnews.com
Editor: Carol Lindsay
Profile: Keister-Williams Newspaper Services, Inc., offers a weekly feature with daily Bible readings for the newspapers it serves. The features are non-denominational messages to encourage church attendance.
Language (s): English
NEWS SERVICE/SYNDICATE

Kid Scoop 281765
Owner: Whiting (Vicki)
Tel: 1 707 996-6077
Email: info@kidscoop.com **Web site:** http://www.kidscoop.com
Profile: Kid Scoop provides award-winning internationally syndicated print and online content full of educational puzzles, games and fun for young readers aged 5 to 13. Every week there are two or more Newspapers in Education lessons that direct readers to other parts of the newspaper. There is also a weekly writing prompt that encourages children to get something published. It is designed to make reading the newspaper fun and engaging.
Language (s): English
NEWS SERVICE/SYNDICATE

King Features Syndicate 30749
Owner: Hearst Corporation (The)
Editorial: 300 W 57th St Unit A, New York, New York 10019-3741 **Tel:** 1 212 969-7550
Email: kfswriters@hearst.com **Web site:** http://www.kingfeatures.com
Profile: King Features Syndicate is a member of Hearst Entertainment and Syndication Group, which combines Hearst Corporation's cable network partnerships, television programming activities and newspaper syndication and merchandise licensing operations. It is a premier distributor of comics, columns, editorial cartoons, puzzles and games, distributing in print and online some 150 features to nearly 5,000 newspapers around the globe. Its columns cover business, personal finance, commentary, entertainment, lifestyle, advice, health, fitness and sports.
Language (s): English
NEWS SERVICE/SYNDICATE

King Features Weekly Service 434360
Owner: Hearst Corporation (The)
Editorial: 28 Virginia Dr, Orlando, Florida 32803-1858
Tel: 1 407 894-7300
Email: jclarke@hearstsc.com **Web site:** http://kingfeatures.com
Profile: King Features Weekly Service is a features syndicator to weekly, monthly and college newspapers, with more than 1,300 subscribers nationwide. It offers weekly packages with more than 75 comics, puzzles, columns and features. Features include color comics, a weekly Sudoku puzzle, cartoons, a birding graphic, a bible trivia quiz, a cooking/celebrities feature and a police log review.
Language (s): English
NEWS SERVICE/SYNDICATE

Knight, Bill 869353
Email: bill.knight@hotmail.com **Web site:** http://billknightcolumn.blogspot.com
Profile: Knight is a self-syndicated opinion columnist for some Illinois-based GateHouse Media newspapers, including the Daily Register in Canton, IL and the Pekin (IL) Daily Times. He writes two columns a week on various subjects, of both national and Illinois state significance, and is also a commentator for Tri-States Public Radio, WIUM-FM 91.3, which also features his columns on their web site.
Language (s): English
NEWS SERVICE/SYNDICATE

Kuwait News Agency - United Nations Bureau 503981
Editorial: 405 E 72nd St Ste 315, Un Secretariat, New York, New York 10021-4407 **Tel:** 1 929 264-8000
Web site: http://www.kuna.net.kw
Profile: This is the United Nations bureau of the Kuwait News Agency.
Language (s): Arabic
NEWS SERVICE/SYNDICATE

Kuwait News Agency - Washington Bureau 615601
Editorial: 529 14th St NW Ste 906, Washington, District Of Columbia 20045-1901 **Tel:** 1 202 347-5554
Web site: http://www.kuna.net.kw
Profile: The Washington Bureau of the Kuwait News Wire Service reports and distributes news relevant to Kuwait to media organizations.
Language (s): Arabic
NEWS SERVICE/SYNDICATE

Kyodo News English Language 31058
Editorial: 780 3rd Ave Rm 1101, New York, New York 10017-2158 **Tel:** 1 212 508-5460
Email: kni@kyodonews.com **Web site:** http://www.kyodonews.com
Bureau Chief: Hajime Ozaki; **Deputy Bureau Chief:** Keiko Tatsuta
Profile: Founded in 1945, Kyodo is based in Japan and has bureaus all over the world. It is a Japanese news agency independent of government, political and commercial interests. It provides a Japanese-language news service that is distributed to virtually all newspapers and broadcast networks in Japan, as well as English and Chinese language services that reach news agencies, newspapers, and radio and television broadcasters in various parts of the world.
Language (s): English
NEWS SERVICE/SYNDICATE

Kyodo News English Language - Los Angeles Bureau 31329
Editorial: 250 E 1st St Ste 302, Los Angeles, California 90012-3819 **Tel:** 1 213 680-9448
Email: kyodolosangeles@gmail.com
Bureau Chief: Masahiro Watanabe
Profile: This is the Los Angeles bureau for Kyodo News.
Language (s): English
NEWS SERVICE/SYNDICATE

Kyodo News English Language - New York Bureau 506296
Editorial: 747 3rd Ave Fl 1801, New York, New York 10017-2879 **Tel:** 1 212 508-5460
Profile: This is the United Nations bureau for the news service.
Language (s): English
NEWS SERVICE/SYNDICATE

Kyodo News English Language - Washington Bureau 953703
Editorial: 529 14th St NW Ste 400, Washington, District Of Columbia 20045-1401 **Tel:** 1 202 347-5767
Deputy Bureau Chief: Takuya Arai; **Bureau Chief:** Hideomi Kinoshita
Profile: This is the Washington bureau for Kyodo News.
Language (s): English
NEWS SERVICE/SYNDICATE

LaPolitics News Service 858546
Owner: Maginnis (John)
Tel: 1 225 395-1316
Email: jja@lapolitics.com **Web site:** http://www.lapolitics.com
Profile: Covers Louisiana Politics and Government for several outlets in Louisiana. Founded by the late John McGinnis.
Language (s): English
NEWS SERVICE/SYNDICATE

Lasky, Jane 31003
Editorial: 1009 Coronado Ter, Los Angeles, California 90026-3007 **Tel:** 1 213 819-5054
Email: janelasky@gmail.com **Web site:** http://www.axs.com/thelatestonaxs

Profile: This self-syndicated column appears in both national and international daily newspapers. It focuses on travel trends, hotel news, airline updates, luxury travel and cultural etiquette. Most readers are business travelers, future business travelers and armchair travelers. It also provides travel insights through anecdotes and insider's tips.
Language (s): English
NEWS SERVICE/SYNDICATE

Lempert, Phil 232213
Editorial: 3015 Main St Ste 320, Santa Monica, California 90405-6402 **Tel:** 1 310 392-0448
Email: phil@supermarketguru.com **Web site:** http://www.supermarketguru.com
Profile: This syndicated column covers trends and products in the food industry, including new foods, diet tips, healthy eating and recipes. There is analysis and the author identifies and explains trends to both industry and consumers in a thought provoking manner.
Language (s): English
NEWS SERVICE/SYNDICATE

Linximages 950078
Editorial: 2770 Broxton Mill Ct, Snellville, Georgia 30039-4437 **Tel:** 1 678 612-5883
Web site: http://www.linximages.com
Profile: Linximages provides photos from major news, arts & entertainment, sports, political events any other newsworthy event in the Atlanta, Georgia area.
Language (s): English
NEWS SERVICE/SYNDICATE

Lisa Miller Film Preview 696250
Editorial: 824 Marsh Ave, Reno, Nevada 89509-1945
Profile: Lisa Miller Film Preview offers the lastest movie entertainment news and provides in-depth reviews of new movie releases.
Language (s): English
NEWS SERVICE/SYNDICATE

Listening Inc. 30813
Editorial: 103 E. Third St, Hobart, Indiana 46342
Tel: 1 219 947-5478
Email: listeninginc@comcast.net **Web site:** http://www.listeninginc.com
Bureau Chief: Richard Bennett
Profile: Listening Inc. distributes a variety of weekly columns by a husband and wife writing team. The columns offer advice and lifestyle information about remarriage, step-family living, attention deficit disorder and the challenges of mid-life.
Language (s): English
NEWS SERVICE/SYNDICATE

Literary Features Syndicate 30991
Editorial: 88 Briarcliff Rd, Larchmont, New York 10538-1758 **Tel:** 1 914 834-7480
Web site: https://literaryfeaturessyndicate.com/
Editor: Barbara Basbanes
Profile: Literary Features Syndicate offers profiles of authors, a children's book review package, seasonal choices and the author's thoughts on certain works. There are also links to her various appearances and guest spots, as well as quotes about her works. She also writes about all matters concerning books collecting, book culture and the future of the medium.
Language (s): English
NEWS SERVICE/SYNDICATE

Long News Service 472324
Editorial: 2103B Pompton Dr, Austin, Texas 78757-8216 **Tel:** 1 512 478-5663
Editor: Bill Kidd
Profile: Long News Service provides articles and information relating to state government, politics and business developments to several daily newspapers in Texas. It also syndicates to some national publications dealing primarily with education, healthcare, law enforcement, insurance and workers compensation matters.
Language (s): English
NEWS SERVICE/SYNDICATE

Lubavitch News Service 679090
Editorial: 770 Eastern Pkwy, Brooklyn, New York 11213-3409 **Tel:** 1 718 774-4000
Email: info@lubavitch.com **Web site:** http://lubavitch.com
Profile: Lubavitch News Service is the official news network of the Chabad Lubavitch movement. It provides news and information about Jewish life worldwide. The news service was founded in 1958.
Language (s): English
NEWS SERVICE/SYNDICATE

Lutheran News Service 328180
Editorial: 8765 W Higgins Rd, Chicago, Illinois 60631-4101 **Tel:** 1 773 380-2700
Email: news@elca.org **Web site:** http://www.elca.org/news
Profile: Lutheran News Service is a news service of the Evangelical Lutheran Church in America. Reports on the church's ministries and provides stories about its people and their faith to journalists, religion writers and columnists, as well as other members of the media.
Language (s): English
NEWS SERVICE/SYNDICATE

Lynch-Hudson, Regina 30944
Editorial: 1865 River Falls Dr, Roswell, Georgia 30076-5114 **Tel:** 1 770 998-9911
Email: info@thewritepublicist.com **Web site:** http://www.thewritepublicist.com
Profile: Lynch-Hudson writes and makes national placements for a consortium of columns including "Doing Biz In," which covers destinations for the business traveler and has appeared in Atlanta Tribune: The Magazine for 15 years, and "Blissbehavin' In," which covers top destinations for adventure travelers.
Language (s): English
NEWS SERVICE/SYNDICATE

Maghreb Arabe Press - United Nations Bureau 506280
Editorial: 405 E 42nd St Rm S-486, New York, New York 10017-3507 **Tel:** 1 212 963-4068
Profile: This is the United Nations bureau of Maghreb Arabe Press in Morocco.
Language (s): Arabic
NEWS SERVICE/SYNDICATE

MAI Photo/News Agency, Inc. 30957
Editorial: 6601 Ashmere Ln, Centreville, Virginia 20120-3753 **Tel:** 1 703 968-0030
Email: staff@maiphoto.com **Web site:** http://maiphoto.com
Profile: Provides news and photos covering national security, the military and politics. Encompasses the State Department, United States Congress, the Department of Defense and the White House.
Language (s): English
NEWS SERVICE/SYNDICATE

Market News International 31040
Owner: Hale Global
Editorial: 40 Fulton St Fl 5, New York, New York 10038-5092 **Tel:** 1 212 669-6400
Email: editorial@marketnews.com **Web site:** http://mninews.marketnews.com
Profile: Market News International is a news service that offers a broad selection of market news reports on major economies, monetary policy, currencies, bonds and derivatives. These stories deliver the same exclusive and incisive coverage successful traders and fund managers count on for their edge in the fast-moving global markets. The focus is on political and economic news briefs and features for professionals in the fixed income and foreign exchange markets.
Language (s): English
NEWS SERVICE/SYNDICATE

Market News International - Chicago Bureau 859740
Editorial: 223 W Jackson Blvd Ste 1250, Chicago, Illinois 60606-6950 **Tel:** 1 708 784-1849
Language (s): English
NEWS SERVICE/SYNDICATE

Market News International - Paris Bureau 860324
Editorial: 38, Rue des Blancs Manteaux, Paris 75004
Tel: 1 331 42715540
Bureau Chief: Stephen Sandelius
Language (s): English
NEWS SERVICE/SYNDICATE

Market News International - Singapore Bureau 860410
Editorial: 9 Raffles Place, #56-01, Republic Plaza, Singapore 48319 **Tel:** 1 656 632-3411
Email: editorial@mni-news.com
Language (s): English
NEWS SERVICE/SYNDICATE

Market News International - Tokyo Bureau 860406
Editorial: 2-7-1 Yurakucho, Chiyoda-ku, 12/F, Yurakucho ITOCiA, Tokyo 100-0006
Tel: 81 90 21750040
Bureau Chief: Max Sato
Language (s): English
NEWS SERVICE/SYNDICATE

Market News International - Washington Bureau 31196
Editorial: 529 14th St NW Ste 1100, Washington, District Of Columbia 20045-2101 **Tel:** 1 202 371-2121
Email: dcoffice@marketnews.com
Deputy Bureau Chief, Economic Data Operations: Kevin Kastner; **Deputy Bureau Chief, News:** Yali N'Diaye
Language (s): English
NEWS SERVICE/SYNDICATE

Mavrix Photo 897490
Owner: Mavrix Photo Inc.
Editorial: 11271 Ventura Blvd #403, Studio City, California 91604-3136 **Tel:** 1 305 542-9275
Email: sales@mavrixphoto.com **Web site:** http://www.mavrixphoto.com
Profile: Mavrix Photo is a global celebrity news photo agency, located both in Miami Beach and Los Angeles.
Language (s): English
NEWS SERVICE/SYNDICATE

Maximo TV 946727
Owner: Ricomix Productions
Editorial: 1811 Ivar Ave Apt 4, Los Angeles, California 90028-5060 **Tel:** 1 818 389-1306
Email: press@maximotv.com **Web site:** http://www.maximotv.com
Profile: Entertainment news video wire service of celebrity red carpet events for editorial use.
Language (s): English
NEWS SERVICE/SYNDICATE

McClatchy Newspapers 30909
Owner: McClatchy Newspapers
Editorial: 1025 Connecticut Ave NW Ste 1100, Washington, District Of Columbia 20036-5405
Tel: 1 202 383-6000
Email: web@mcclatchydc.com **Web site:** http://www.mcclatchydc.com
Profile: Serves as the Washington bureau for all 30 McClatchy daily newspapers. It also oversees the operations of 8 international bureaus. The news service covers Politics, Economy, International and National News, and Special Investigative Reports. They do NOT cover Arts & Entertainment, Sports, Food, Home & Gardening, Lifestyle, Fashion or Beauty topics.
Language (s): English
NEWS SERVICE/SYNDICATE

McManus Syndicate 30747
Editorial: 9311 Harrington Dr, Potomac, Maryland 20854-4510 **Tel:** 1 301 469-5870
Web site: http://www.marriagesavers.org
Editor: Harriet McManus
Profile: McManus Syndicate covers religious and ethical issues with a focus on improving and stabilizing marriages. It also hopes to prepare people for lifelong marriages, strengthen existing marriages and restore troubled marriages. There are also reports on major events with a moral component and suggests ways to raise ethical standards.
Language (s): English
NEWS SERVICE/SYNDICATE

Meadowlands Media Group 354963
Editorial: 20 Nevins St, Rutherford, New Jersey 07070-2819 **Tel:** 1 201 978-8524
Editor: Catherine Salfino
Profile: Meadowlands Media Group syndicates fantasy sports columns for football and baseball and provides editorial content for publishers, including the Wall St. Journal and Yahoo.
Language (s): English
NEWS SERVICE/SYNDICATE

Medill News Service 80899
Owner: Medill News Service
Editorial: 1325 G St NW Ste 730, Washington, District Of Columbia 20005-3127 **Tel:** 1 202 661-0127
Email: medilldc@gmail.com **Web site:** http://www.medilldc.net
Editor: Josh Meyer; **Bureau Chief:** Ellen Shearer
Profile: Medill News Service is comprised of graduate journalism students at Northwestern University. The program begins on a smaller scale in Evanston, while the Washington, D.C. operation is the more advanced level. Students in Washington, D.C. report on federal politics and government, "focusing on how public policy affects people's lives," and specializes in investigative reporting with multimedia coverage. Topics are varied, and include business, technology, environment, religion/ethics, finance, economy, health, science, immigration, national security, politics and sports. It serves 18 newspapers, five Web sites, nine television stations and eight radio stations.
Language (s): English
NEWS SERVICE/SYNDICATE

Medill News Service - Chicago Bureau 395479
Owner: Medill News Service
Editorial: 105 W Adams St, Ste 200, Chicago, Illinois 60603-6202 **Tel:** 1 312 503-4100
Web site: http://news.medill.northwestern.edu/chicago
Profile: The focus of the Chicago-based Medill News Service is on business, economy, science, medicine and urban affairs in the Chicagoland area, and specifically partners with Chicago media outlets such as the Daily Herald, and The Times of Munster.
Language (s): English
NEWS SERVICE/SYNDICATE

Merrell Enterprises 30847
Editorial: 2610 Garfield St NW, Washington, District Of Columbia 20008-4104 **Tel:** 1 202 265-1925
Email: jesse@jessehmerrell.com **Web site:** http://www.merrell-enterprises.com
Profile: Focus is on political commentary on current events and news from a moral and religious perspective.
Language (s): English
NEWS SERVICE/SYNDICATE

Metro Feature Syndicate 31024
Owner: Metro Publishing Group
Editorial: 626 McCarthy Dr, New Milford, New Jersey 07646-1029 **Tel:** 1 201 385-2000
Email: metropub@aol.com
Profile: Metro Feature Syndicate is a news service that targets weekly newspapers in the metropolitan New York and New Jersey areas. The service provides various columns to weekly newspapers in these areas. The news service contains articles on skiing, travel, book reviews and theatre. Bob and Sandy Nesoff also write a monthly travel column for New York City Resident Magazine and a weekly column for Courier Publications (Queens, Brooklyn, Long Island) and Cruising Squared. They are also travel columnists for L'Chaim Magazine published by North Jersey Media.
Language (s): English
NEWS SERVICE/SYNDICATE

MIC Insurance Services 30901
Editorial: 170 Kinnelon Rd Rm 11, Kinnelon, New Jersey 07405-2324 **Tel:** 1 973 492-2828
Web site: http://www.micinsurance.com
Editor: Betsy Chandler
Profile: MIC Insurance Services appears in several newspapers in New Jersey each Sunday. It provides news about long term care, individual and group health, and medicine and medigap insurances. Sometimes there is analysis of different coverages. Overall, it tries to help readers understand the world of health insurance.
Language (s): English
NEWS SERVICE/SYNDICATE

Midnight Trader 377231
Owner: MidnightTrader Inc.
Editorial: 4923 Bethesda Ave Ste A, Bethesda, Maryland 20814-5203 **Tel:** 1 888 559-0073 2
Email: editor@mtnewswires.com **Web site:** http://www.midnighttrader.com
Profile: Midnight Trader provides public company news, data and market analysis focused on the after-hours markets. It offers real-time extended-hours coverage of stocks moving after-hours and likely to move in the following regular session. The goal of the news service is to provide opportunities for readers to be better prepared for the extended-hours trading session by staying ahead of Wall Street with live pre-market stock trading news from 6:45am to 10am EST, and late breaking after-hours coverage from 3:30pm to 8pm ET. The service is subscription-based.
Language (s): English
NEWS SERVICE/SYNDICATE

Midwest Features Syndicate 153850
Tel: 1 608 274-8925
Email: info@roadstraveled.com **Web site:** http://www.roadstraveled.com
Profile: Midwest Features Syndicate produces a weekly travel and food column whose content emphasizes the Midwest US. Also produces other travel and Midwest features for various publications. Stock photography on file.
Language (s): English
NEWS SERVICE/SYNDICATE

Military Update 30923
Tel: 1 703 830-6863
Email: milupdate@aol.com **Web site:** https://militaryadvantage.military.com/category/military-update/
Profile: The weekly news column reaches two million readers and covers breaking news affecting the lives of service members and their families, including analysis of issues affecting pay, benefits and lifestyles of active duty members, retirees and reservists. It is intended for daily newspapers near military bases.
Language (s): English
NEWS SERVICE/SYNDICATE

Moisés Naím 850087
Editorial: 1779 Massachusetts Ave NW, Washington, District Of Columbia 20036-2109 **Tel:** 1 202 317-1015
Email: vcano@moisesnaim.com **Web site:** http://www.moisesnaim.com
Profile: Moisés Naím is a syndicated columnist covering both national and international politics for outlets in the United States, Spain, Italy and Latin America. His column appears in The New York Times, The Financial Times, The Washington Post, Newsweek, Time, Foreign Policy and Foreign Affairs. All contact should be directed to his publicist.
Language (s): English
NEWS SERVICE/SYNDICATE

More Content Now 945778
Owner: GateHouse Media, LLC
Tel: 1 630 348-3350
Web site: http://morecontentnow.com/
Editor: Lisa Glowinski
Profile: More Content Now is a syndicate service offering print and online publishers prepaginated special sections, weekly lifestyle and sports pages, editorial cartoons, entertainment features, lifestyle and opinion columnists and more. MCN is also behind much of GateHouse Media sites' syndicated content.
Language (s): English
NEWS SERVICE/SYNDICATE

Morem, Sue 238882
Tel: 1 610 710-1907
Email: info@suemorem.com **Web site:** http://www.suemorem.com
Profile: This nationally syndicated column helps people get the jobs of their dreams, present themselves with enthusiasm in every social situation, dazzle company presidents and clients alike with their people skills, out-shine the competition and epitomize the look of career success.
Language (s): English
NEWS SERVICE/SYNDICATE

Motor Matters 30792
Tel: 1 302 998-1650
Email: info@motormatters.biz **Web site:** http://www.motormatters.biz

Profile: Autowriters Associates Inc., provides automotive content to print and online media and various automotive-related businesses.
Language (s): English
NEWS SERVICE/SYNDICATE

Motor News Media Corporation 31078
Owner: Motor News Media Corp.
Editorial: 3710 SE Capitol Cir Ste F, Grimes, Iowa 50111-5046 **Tel:** 1 515 986-1155
Email: motornewsmedia@live.com **Web site:** http://www.motornewsmedia.com
Profile: This is a customer-focused news service that provides automotive news, features and photos to educate and entertain readers.
Language (s): English
NEWS SERVICE/SYNDICATE

My Suburban Life Media 475462
Owner: Shaw Media
Editorial: 1101 31st St Ste 100, Downers Grove, Illinois 60515-5581 **Tel:** 1 630 368-1100
Email: national@gatehousemedia.com **Web site:** http://www.mysuburbanlife.com/downersgrove
Profile: Suburban Life Media is a leading provider of community information and advertising in the western suburbs of Chicago across print, online and mobile channels. Suburban Life Media is a division of Shaw Media.
Language (s): English
NEWS SERVICE/SYNDICATE

National News Bureau 613993
Editorial: 3343 W School House Ln, Philadelphia, Pennsylvania 19129-5517 **Tel:** 1 215 849-9016
Email: nnbfeature@aol.com **Web site:** http://www.nationalnewsbureau.com
Editor: Debra Cruz
Profile: Established in 1979 and features syndicate servicing in excess of 300 publications in the United States. Covers Travel, "What's hot", "How to" columns, Beauty, Fashion, Theater, Music, Video, Movies, Books, Food & Wine, and all leisure and entertainment-oriented fields.
Language (s): English
NEWS SERVICE/SYNDICATE

New America Media 31028
Owner: Pacific News Service
Editorial: 209 9th St Ste 200, San Francisco, California 94103-6800 **Tel:** 1 415 503-4170
Web site: http://www.newamericamedia.org
Editor: Anthony Advincula; **Editor:** Andrew Lam
Profile: New America Media syndicates daily stories through the Associated Press wire to subscribing mainstream and community newspapers across the country. It serves as a conduit for youth, ethnic and other voices that aren't heard as much in mainstream media. It offers feature-length commentary, news analysis and investigative reporting about topics such as immigration, civil liberties threats and hybrid identities, health, education, environment, etc.
Language (s): English
NEWS SERVICE/SYNDICATE

New Car News Syndicate 153755
Editorial: 41 Quercus Cir, Little Rock, Arkansas 72223-5159 **Tel:** 1 501 425-9737
Email: carnews@aol.com
Profile: New Car News Syndicate provides news and information on automotive trends. Geared toward auto shoppers, the publication features car and truck testing, brand reviews and product reviews.
Language (s): English
NEWS SERVICE/SYNDICATE

New York German Press 504159
Editorial: 11 Broadway Ste 851, New York, New York 10004-1306 **Tel:** 1 212 269-3438
Email: jkorte@newyorkgermanpress.com **Web site:** http://www.nygp.info/
Editor: Jens Korte
Profile: New York German Press is the main independent press agency covering the United States financial markets for German language media. The agency covers developments in the United States securities market as well as the broader aspects of the United States economy.
NEWS SERVICE/SYNDICATE

The New York Times News Service/Syndicate 30743
Owner: New York Times Company (The)
Editorial: 620 8th Ave, New York, New York 10018-1618 **Tel:** 1 212 556-1927
Email: nytns@nytimes.com **Web site:** http://www.nytsyn.com
Profile: The New York Times News Service/Syndicate offers a variety of nationally syndicated columnists and content from The New York Times and other newspapers and wire services to its subscribers. There are columns, special features and book excerpts from many different countries and points of view. It Serves more than 2,000 clients on five continents and transmits material in English and Spanish. It works closely with The New York Times News Service and transmits material in English and Spanish.
Language (s): English
NEWS SERVICE/SYNDICATE

News Service of Florida 779143
Editorial: 336 E College Ave, Tallahassee, Florida 32301-1551 **Tel:** 1 850 656-6400
Email: news@newsserviceflorida.com **Web site:** http://www.newsserviceflorida.com
Profile: The News Service of Florida is an independent wire service providing journalists, lobbyists, government officials and other civic leaders with comprehensive information about the activities of Florida state government.
Language (s): English
NEWS SERVICE/SYNDICATE

News-Features Syndicate 152786
Editorial: New York, New York **Tel:** 1 212 229-1111
Email: newsfeatsyndicate@gmail.com
Editor: Caroline Howe
Profile: News-Features Syndicate offers its varied media clients in-depth stories on a variety of subjects, including book reviews, celebrity profiles, human interest, style, fashion, trends, technology, media and consumerism. Veteran journalists and experienced freelancers around the globe are members of the team servicing publications across the country.
Language (s): English
NEWS SERVICE/SYNDICATE

Newswatch Feature Service 75483
Editorial: 11166 Fairfax Blvd Ste 403, Fairfax, Virginia 22030-5017 **Tel:** 1 703 662-8180
Email: info@newswatchtv.com **Web site:** http://newswatchtv.com/
Profile: Newswatch Feature Service is an independent news feature service providing editorial content, including articles, photo features, pictorials, column pieces and special sections, to national trade, technical, professional and consumer magazines. It specializes in covering technology, public safety, entertainment and travel.
Language (s): English
NEWS SERVICE/SYNDICATE

Nielsen Entertainment News Wire - Los Angeles Bureau 31368
Editorial: 5055 Wilshire Blvd Fl 7, Los Angeles, California 90036-6100 **Tel:** 1 323 525-2335
Bureau Chief: Angela Dawson
Language (s): English
NEWS SERVICE/SYNDICATE

NNPA News Service 231990
Editorial: 1816 12th St NW Fl 2, Washington, District Of Columbia 20009-4422 **Tel:** 1 202 588-8764
Web site: http://www.nnpa.org
Profile: Founded during World War II, the NNPA News Service is a national black news service that distributes investigative reports, news and feature articles, as well as political and social commentary to its member papers.
Language (s): English
NEWS SERVICE/SYNDICATE

Northwest Auto News Service 429772
Editorial: 4213 Glen Terra Dr SE, Olympia, Washington 98503-7165 **Tel:** 1 360 438-3825
Email: lhall@nwautonews.com
Profile: Northwest Auto News Service is a newspaper syndicate that focuses on the automotive industry. Topics covered include new-car test drives and feature articles ranging from car care to technology. It syndicates to several newspapers and Web sites, including The Oregonian in Portland, OR; The News Tribune in Tacoma, WA; the Peninsula Gateway in Gig Harbor, WA; The Sequim (WA) Gazette; The Forks (WA) Forum; the Port Townsend (WA) News; the Mountain Mail in Salida, CO; The Chaffee County Times in Buena Vista, CO; and the Herald Democrat in Leadville, CO as well as MSN Autos and NBCNews.com.
Language (s): English
NEWS SERVICE/SYNDICATE

Notimex - Miami Bureau 858683
Editorial: 3191 Coral Way Ste 501, Coral Gables, Florida 33145-3227 **Tel:** 1 305 445-0716
Language (s): Spanish
NEWS SERVICE/SYNDICATE

NYCity News Service 842580
Owner: CUNY Graduate School of Journalism
Editorial: 219 W 40th St, New York, New York 10018-1507 **Tel:** 1 646 758-7700
Web site: http://nycitynewsservice.com
Profile: NYCity News Service is a Web-based news service operated by the CUNY Graduate School of Journalism in New York City, with content primarily provided by attending students, overseen by faculty. The focus of coverage is local New York City news. Content is distributed to media outlets internationally.
Language (s): English
NEWS SERVICE/SYNDICATE

On Computers 622825
Editorial: 1630 Chicago Ave Apt 1513, Evanston, Illinois 60201-4595 **Tel:** 1 847 570-9881
Web site: http://www.oncomp.com
Profile: On Computers is a weekly syndicated newspaper column that features the latest in computer and technology news. Coverage includes computer hardware and software, new technology in phones and cameras, video games, Web sites and Web services, technology trends, books, user studies and surveys and GPS. The column appears in the Arkansas Democrat Gazette in Little Rock, AR, and the Worcester (MA) Telegram & Gazette.
Language (s): English
NEWS SERVICE/SYNDICATE

Outdoor News Service 30995
Tel: 1 909 887-3444
Email: odwriter@verizon.net **Web site:** http://www.outdoornewsservice.com
Editor: Jim Matthews
Profile: Outdoor News Service offers news about Southern California fishing reports, waterfowl coverage, outdoor packages and columns that are distributed to daily newspapers and Internet sites throughout the region for use on outdoor pages. It is syndicated to about 11 daily papers.
Language (s): English
NEWS SERVICE/SYNDICATE

Pacific Perspectives 417433
Owner: Plate, Tom
Editorial: 11372 Bunche Hall, Los Angeles, California 90095-1487 **Tel:** 1 310 825-9110
Email: platecolumn@gmail.com **Web site:** http://pacificperspectives.blogspot.com/
Profile: Discusses news from the Asia Pacific region, as well as all aspects of the media in Asia, including its role in regional and national economies, societies and political debate. Columns are syndicated to several national and international publications including The South China Morning Post, Mainichi Shimbun, the China Times, the Korea Times, the Khaleej Times, the Seattle Times, the San Diego Business Journal and the Straits Times.
Language (s): English
NEWS SERVICE/SYNDICATE

Passage Media 242457
Editorial: 24541 S Wildwood Trl, Crete, Illinois 60417-3735
Email: workwise@comcast.net
Profile: Dr. Mildred L. Culp's WorkWise commentary, first syndicated in 1994, covers national emerging trends in job hunting/employment and recruiting and is distributed via Passage Media. These columns and special assignment articles have found their way into many daily newspapers and their niche publications, including more than 50 major dailies, both in print and on 142 news and 115 commercial websites. Dr. Culp has freelanced widely. Publications span USA Today's Hispanic Living, The Hartford Courant, New York's Daily News, Los Angeles Times, Chicago Sun-Times, The Seattle Times, and UTAH CEO magazine.
Language (s): English
NEWS SERVICE/SYNDICATE

Plain Label Press 72019
Tel: 1 636 207-9880
Email: lower79124@mypacks.net **Web site:** http://creativeon-line.com/syndicate
Profile: Plain Label Press is a specialty syndicate serving both print and online publications. It offers a family of humorous features that try and stray from the mainstream.
Language (s): English
NEWS SERVICE/SYNDICATE

Platts Global Alert 156060
Owner: McGraw-Hill Companies
Editorial: 2 Penn Plz Fl 25, New York, New York 10121-0101 **Tel:** 1 212 904-3070
Email: releases@platts.com **Web site:** http://www.platts.com
Profile: Platts Global Alert is an energy news and information provider. It aims to help global energy markets enhance their performance through such offerings as independent industry news and price benchmarks. There are 15 offices worldwide that cover the oil, natural gas, electricity, nuclear power, coal, petrochemical and metals markets.
Language (s): English
NEWS SERVICE/SYNDICATE

Platts Global Alert - Houston Bureau 156062
Owner: McGraw-Hill Companies
Editorial: 1111 Bagby St, Heritage Plaza, Houston, Texas 77002-2551 **Tel:** 1 713 658-9261
Language (s): English
NEWS SERVICE/SYNDICATE

Platts Global Alert - London Bureau 864010
Owner: McGraw-Hill Companies
Editorial: 20 Canada Square, 12th Floor, Canary Wharf, London, England E14 5LH
Tel: 44 20 71767000
Language (s): English
NEWS SERVICE/SYNDICATE

Platts Global Alert - Moscow Bureau 778483
Owner: McGraw-Hill Companies
Editorial: Business Center Mokhovaya, 4/7 Vozdvizhenka Street, Moscow 125009
Tel: 7 495 783-4141
Profile: Platts Global Alert is an energy news and information provider. It aims to help global energy markets enhance their performance through such offerings as independent industry news and price benchmarks. There are 15 offices worldwide that cover the oil, natural gas, electricity, nuclear power, coal, petrochemical and metals markets.
Language (s): English
NEWS SERVICE/SYNDICATE

Platts Global Alert - Tokyo Bureau 851108
Owner: McGraw-Hill Companies
Editorial: Marunouchi Kitaguchi Building, 28th Floor, 1-6-5 Marunouchi Chiyoda-ku, Tokyo 100-0005
Tel: 81 3 4550-8842
Language (s): Spanish
NEWS SERVICE/SYNDICATE

Platts Global Alert - Washington Bureau 156063
Owner: McGraw-Hill Companies
Editorial: 1200 G St Nw Ste 1000, Washington, District Of Columbia 20005-3845 **Tel:** 1 202 383-2000
Editor: Jasmin Melvin
Language (s): English
NEWS SERVICE/SYNDICATE

Polaris Images 431228
Editorial: 259 W 30th St Fl 14, New York, New York 10001-2863 **Tel:** 1 212 967-5656
Email: editors@polarisimages.com **Web site:** http://www.polarisimages.com
Profile: Polaris Images represents photographers and distributes photos and media content to editorial and corporate clients in more than 30 countries.
Language (s): English
NEWS SERVICE/SYNDICATE

Presbyterian News Service 155421
Editorial: 100 Witherspoon St, Louisville, Kentucky 40202-1396 **Tel:** 1 800 728-7228
Email: info@pcusa.org **Web site:** http://www.pcusa.org/pcnews
Editor: Gregg Brekke
Profile: This is the official news agency of the Presbyterian Church. They gather and disseminate news and information about the denomination and its work to church members, church officials, religious and secular media, and the public. Their editorial freedom allows them to fairly report on all aspects of the church, both good and bad.
Language (s): English
NEWS SERVICE/SYNDICATE

Press Trust of India/PTI - New York Bureau 503935
Editorial: S 450 United Nations, New York, New York 10017
Email: techsupport@pti.in **Web site:** http://ptinews.com
Profile: Press Trust of India (PTI) is India's premier news agency
NEWS SERVICE/SYNDICATE

Press Trust of India/PTI - Washington Bureau 504583
Editorial: 5705 Brewer House Cir Apt 302, Rockville, Maryland 20852-5425 **Tel:** 1 917 817-0859
Email: techsupport@pti.in **Web site:** http://www.ptinews.com
Chief Correspondent: Lalit Jha
Profile: The Press Trust of India is the largest news agency in India.
NEWS SERVICE/SYNDICATE

Pulliam Weston, Liz 491580
Editorial: 3940 Laurel Canyon Blvd, Studio City, California 91604-3709
Web site: http://www.asklizweston.com
Profile: Liz Pulliam Weston writes a nationally syndicated question and answer column appears in newspapers throughout the country, including the Los Angeles Times, the Palm Beach (FL) Post, the Portland (OR) Oregonian, Stars & Stripes and others.
Language (s): English
NEWS SERVICE/SYNDICATE

Purcell, Tom 30954
Owner: Purcell, Tom
Tel: 1 571 216-6265
Email: tom@tompurcell.com **Web site:** http://www.tompurcell.com
Profile: Purcell is a self-syndicated humor columnist who touches on the controversies of public policy as well as complications of everyday existence. He offers stories about issues and events, and delivers suggested truths and common sense through satire. The column runs 680 words per week and appears in over a dozen newspapers.
Language (s): English
NEWS SERVICE/SYNDICATE

Q Syndicate 281827
Owner: Q Syndicate, LLC
Editorial: 20222 Farmington Rd, Livonia, Michigan 48152-1412 **Tel:** 1 734 290-7200 22
Email: qsyndicate@pridesource.com **Web site:** http://www.qsyndicate.com
Editor: Chris Azzopardi
Profile: Q Syndicate offers content and community to the gay and lesbian press. Features include travel, entertainment, sports, editorial cartoons, puzzles, movies and more.
Language (s): English
NEWS SERVICE/SYNDICATE

Racing Information Service 30958
Editorial: 6141 Sunset Ln, Indianapolis, Indiana 46228-1455 **Tel:** 1 317 251-4371
Email: brickyard@indy.net **Web site:** http://www.ris-news.com
Bureau Chief: Tom Beeler

Profile: Racing Information Service is the oldest and largest interactive newswire dedicated to motor sports. It covers every form of auto racing and motorcycles worldwide, including NASCAR, Formula One, GP2, Champ Car, IRL, SCCA, Professional Sports Car Racing, AMA, World of Outlaws, USAC, BTCC, FIA GT, IKF and karting. It also provides racing book, software and movie reviews. It serves around 150 newspapers, several magazines and electronic outlets.
Language (s): English
NEWS SERVICE/SYNDICATE

Raia, James 281828
Editorial: 122 43rd St, Sacramento, California 95819-2102 **Tel:** 1 916 508-5122
Email: james@byjamesraia.com **Web site:** http://sacramentonewsservice.com
Profile: This is a site offering columns about car reviews. Columns are picked up by various media outlets.
Language (s): English
NEWS SERVICE/SYNDICATE

Rautzhan, Kendal 30956
Editorial: 118 S 5th St, Lewisburg, Pennsylvania 17837-1810 **Tel:** 1 570 898-2929
Email: kendal@sunlink.net
Profile: Books to Borrow...Books to Buy is a syndicated weekly column providing parenting and educational tips to get books and kids connected. The primary emphasis stresses the importance of adults reading to children every day and also providing reflective thought on the role of a parent to a child. The column is followed by children's book reviews. Syndicated to more than 45 newspapers across the country. The companion website, Greatest Books for Kids, features numerous additional chidren's book reviews.
Language (s): English
NEWS SERVICE/SYNDICATE

Real Estate Matters Syndicate 30924
Editorial: 361 Park Ave Ste 200, Glencoe, Illinois 60022-1585 **Tel:** 1 847 242-0550
Email: questions@thinkglink.com **Web site:** http://www.thinkglink.com
Profile: This self-syndicated column provides homeowners with the information they need to proceed with confidence when buying, selling, renovating or refinancing their home. It focuses on a wide range of timely national topics, including discrimination, mortgage financing, buyer brokerage, disclosure and property taxes. It appears in more than 30 newspapers.
Language (s): English
NEWS SERVICE/SYNDICATE

Red Line Report 30907
Editorial: 11 Patch Ln, Lake Placid, New York 12946-3034 **Tel:** 1 518 523-4289
Email: kyle@redlinereport.com **Web site:** http://redlinereport.com
Profile: Weekly humorous hockey column that looks at the National Hockey League, Major Junior and International Leagues.
Language (s): English
NEWS SERVICE/SYNDICATE

Reel to Real Celebrity Profiles 30947
Editorial: 8643 N Fielding Rd, Milwaukee, Wisconsin 53217-2427 **Tel:** 1 414 352-7998
Web site: http://www.reeltoreal.com
Editor: David Fantle
Profile: This is a self-syndicated weekly column featuring two-on-one, face-to-face interviews with show business personalities and celebrities. They mainly do in-depth features about those in the entertainment industry. The column runs in dozens of publications throughout the country.
Language (s): English
NEWS SERVICE/SYNDICATE

Religion News Service 30853
Owner: Religion News Association
Editorial: 529 14th St NW Ste 1009, Washington, District Of Columbia 20045-2001 **Tel:** 1 202 463-8777
Email: info@religionnews.com **Web site:** http://www.religionnews.com
Profile: Religion News Service offers news about religion, ethics, spirituality and moral issues. There is a network of correspondents around the world providing news and information on all faiths and religious movements. They hope to provide intelligent, objective coverage of all religions, including Judaism, Christianity, Islam, Asian religions and private spirituality.
Language (s): English
NEWS SERVICE/SYNDICATE

Reuters 31029
Owner: Thomson Reuters
Editorial: 3 Times Sq, New York, New York 10036-6564 **Tel:** 1 646 223-4000
Email: nyc.equities.newsroom@news.reuters.com
Web site: http://www.reuters.com
Profile: Founded in 1851, Reuters offers 24-hour coverage of global happenings for professionals around the world. With 196 editorial bureaus in 130 countries and 2,400 editorial staff members, it covers international news, regional news, politics, social issues, health, business, sports and media. The news service also provides text, graphics, pictures, in-depth news analysis, features and profiles. They also offer a complimentary newsletter, Reuters Washington Extra, that includes the outlet's most popular stories of the day with an introductory from the Washington bureau chief.
Language (s): English
NEWS SERVICE/SYNDICATE

Reuters - Amman Bureau 727641
Editorial: Mahmoud Al Abidi Street, 1st Floor, Building 1, Amman 11118 **Tel:** 926 6 462-3776
Web site: http://www.thomsonreuters.com
Language (s): English
NEWS SERVICE/SYNDICATE

Reuters - Amsterdam Bureau 394893
Editorial: Antonio Vivaldistraat 50, Amsterdam 1083 HK **Tel:** 31 20 504-5045
Email: amsterdam.newsroom@thomsonreuters.com
Bureau Chief: Anthony Deutsch
Language (s): English
NEWS SERVICE/SYNDICATE

Reuters - Athens Bureau 231217
Editorial: 8 Othonos Street, 5th Floor, Athens
Tel: 30 210 331-1800
Email: athens.newsroom@news.reuters.com
Language (s): English
NEWS SERVICE/SYNDICATE

Reuters - Baghdad Bureau 696417
Editorial: Restricted Address, Baghdad
Tel: 964 7901917033
NEWS SERVICE/SYNDICATE

Reuters - Bangalore Bureau 785521
Editorial: Divyasree Technopolis, 36/2 & 124 Yamalur, Varthur Hobli, Bangalore 560037
Tel: 91 80 6749-1130
Email: bangalore.newsroom@thomsonreuters.com
NEWS SERVICE/SYNDICATE

Reuters - Bangkok Bureau 231219
Editorial: 34-35th Floor U Chu Liang Building, 968 Rama IV Road, Silom, Bangrak, Bangkok 10500
Tel: 66 2 648-9600
Email: bangkok.newsroom@thomsonreuters.com
Language (s): English
NEWS SERVICE/SYNDICATE

Reuters - Beijing Bureau 231220
Editorial: Chemsunny World Trade Center, Central Tower 2F, No 28 Fuxingmennei St, Xicheng District, Beijing 100031
Email: beijing.newsroom@thomsonreuters.com
Language (s): English
NEWS SERVICE/SYNDICATE

Reuters - Beirut Bureau 431848
Editorial: Hibat Al Maarad Bldg, Fl 3, Riad El Solh Sq, Beirut 2011 4810 **Tel:** 961 1 983-839
Email: lebanon.news@thomsonreuters.com
Bureau Chief: Dominic Evans
Language (s): English
NEWS SERVICE/SYNDICATE

Reuters - Belgrade Bureau 562310
Editorial: Vladimira Popovica 6, Genex International Building, Apt B 37, 30, Belgrade 11070
Tel: 381 11 304-4900
Email: belgrade.newsroom@thomsonreuters.com
Language (s): English
NEWS SERVICE/SYNDICATE

Reuters - Berlin Bureau 231221
Editorial: Schiffbauerdamm 22, Berlin 102 10117
Tel: 49 30 28885230
Email: berlin.newsroom@thomsonreuters.com
Bureau Chief: Noah Barkin
Language (s): English
NEWS SERVICE/SYNDICATE

Reuters - Bogota Bureau 327624
Editorial: Calle 94-A, No 13-34 Piso 4, Bogota
Tel: 57 16344090
Email: bogota.newsroom@thomsonreuters.com
Bureau Chief: Helen Murphy
Language (s): English
NEWS SERVICE/SYNDICATE

Reuters - Boston Bureau 31180
Editorial: 22 Thomson Pl, Boston, Massachusetts 02210-1212 **Tel:** 1 617 856-4401
Email: boston.newsroom@thomsonreuters.com
Language (s): English
NEWS SERVICE/SYNDICATE

Reuters - Brasilia Bureau 573896
Editorial: Srtvs -QD 701 - Conj DBIA, Sala 723 Centro Empresarial, Brasilia 70340-907
Tel: 55 61 3426-7000
Language (s): English
NEWS SERVICE/SYNDICATE

Reuters - Bratislava Bureau 613359
Editorial: Plynarenska 1, Bratislava 82109
Tel: 421 253418402
Language (s): English
NEWS SERVICE/SYNDICATE

Reuters - Brussels Bureau 231222
Editorial: Avenue Marnix 17, Brussels 1000
Tel: 32 2 287-6611
Email: belgium.newsroom@thomsonreuters.com
Bureau Chief: Alastair MacDonald
Language (s): English
NEWS SERVICE/SYNDICATE

Reuters - Bucharest Bureau 684783
Editorial: Premium Point Bucharest, 78-80 Buzesti Street, 9th floor, Bucharest 11017 **Tel:** 40 21 305-5285
Email: bucharest.newsroom@thomsonreuters.com
Web site: http://www.reuters.ro
Language (s): English
NEWS SERVICE/SYNDICATE

Reuters - Buenos Aires Bureau 154703
Editorial: Av E Madero 942 - 24 Piso, Buenos Aires C1106ACW **Tel:** 54 114 510-2500
Email: buenosaires.newsroom@thomsonreuters.com
Language (s): English
NEWS SERVICE/SYNDICATE

Reuters - Cairo Bureau 727637
Editorial: 153 Mohamed Farid Street, 21st Floor, Banque Misr Tower, Cairo 11511 **Tel:** 20 2 5577150
Email: cairo.newsroom@thomsonreuters.com
Bureau Chief: Michael Georgy
Language (s): English
NEWS SERVICE/SYNDICATE

Reuters - Calgary Bureau 31365
Editorial: 407 2 St SW Suite 312, Calgary, Alberta T2P 2Y3 **Tel:** 1 403 531-1624
Web site: http://ca.reuters.com/
Profile: Thomson Reuters is the world's leading source of intelligent information for businesses and professionals.
Language (s): English
NEWS SERVICE/SYNDICATE

Reuters - Caracas Bureau 231256
Editorial: Ave Eugenio Mendoza Angel Lamas, Edftorre La Castellane Piso #4, Caracas D.F.1060
Tel: 58 115 5547334
Email: caracas.newsroom@thomsonreuters.com
Web site: http://lta.reuters.com
Bureau Chief: Andrew Cawthorne
Language (s): English
NEWS SERVICE/SYNDICATE

Reuters - Chicago Bureau 31151
Editorial: 311 S Wacker Dr Ste 1200, Chicago, Illinois 60606-6623 **Tel:** 1 312 408-8500
Bureau Chief: David Greising
Language (s): English
NEWS SERVICE/SYNDICATE

Reuters - Colombo Bureau 431846
Editorial: Level 8 - East Tower, World Trade Center, Echelon Sq, Colombo **Tel:** 94 11 232-5540
Email: colombo.newsroom@thomsonreuters.com
Language (s): English
NEWS SERVICE/SYNDICATE

Reuters - Copenhagen Bureau 431858
Editorial: Meldahlsgade 5 4th Floor, DK-1613, Copenhagen **Tel:** 45 33969696 50
Email: copenhagen.newsroom@thomsonreuters.com
Language (s): Danish
NEWS SERVICE/SYNDICATE

Reuters - Dakar Bureau 734460
Editorial: Rue des Ecrivains, angle Rue G, Dakar
Email: dakar.newsroom@thomsonreuters.com
NEWS SERVICE/SYNDICATE

Reuters - Dallas Bureau 906105
Editorial: 1601 Elm St, Dallas, Texas 75201-4701
Language (s): English
NEWS SERVICE/SYNDICATE

Reuters - Detroit Bureau 31154
Editorial: 1155 Brewery Park Blvd Ste 250, Detroit, Michigan 48207-2640 **Tel:** 1 313 202-6920
Email: detroitnewsroom@reuters.com
Language (s): English
NEWS SERVICE/SYNDICATE

Reuters - Dubai Bureau 231223
Editorial: Reuters Building, Sheikh Zayed Road, Dubai **Tel:** 971 4391-8301
Email: dubai.newsroom@thomsonreuters.com
Editor: Sami Aboudi
Language (s): English
NEWS SERVICE/SYNDICATE

Reuters - Dublin Bureau 601182
Editorial: 12-13 Exchange Place, IFSC, Dublin 5001500 **Tel:** 3 531 500-1500
Email: dublin.newsroom@thomsonreuters.com
Chief Correspondent: Padriac Halpin
Language (s): English
NEWS SERVICE/SYNDICATE

Reuters - Frankfurt Bureau 231225
Editorial: Friedrich-Ebert Anlage 49, Frankfurt 60308
Tel: 49 69 7565-1245
Email: frankfurt.newsroom@reuters.com
Language (s): English
NEWS SERVICE/SYNDICATE

Reuters - Geneva Bureau 377487
Editorial: 153 Route De Thonon, Geneva 1245
Tel: 41 58 306-2828
Email: geneva.newsroom@thomsonreuters.com
Chief Correspondent: Tom Miles
Language (s): English
NEWS SERVICE/SYNDICATE

Reuters - Hanoi Bureau 231228
Editorial: 8 Tran Hung Dao, 4th Floor, Hanoi
Tel: 84 43 825 9623
Email: hanoi.newsroom@thomsonreuters.com
Language (s): English
NEWS SERVICE/SYNDICATE

Reuters - Havana Bureau 231229
Editorial: Calle 21st #104 Apt 3, Vedado, Havana
Tel: 53 78333145
Web site: http://www.reuters.com/places/cuba
Language (s): English
NEWS SERVICE/SYNDICATE

Reuters - Helsinki Bureau 431859
Editorial: Urho Kekkosen katu 5, 00100, Helsinki FI-00100 **Tel:** 46 358 9 680501
Email: helsinki.newsroom@thomsonreuters.com
Language (s): Finnish
NEWS SERVICE/SYNDICATE

Reuters - Hong Kong Bureau 231230
Editorial: Cityplaza Three 14 Tai Koo Wan Road, Quarry Bay, Hong Kong **Tel:** 852 2 843-6363
Email: hongkong.newsroom@reuters.com **Web site:** http://www.reuters.com/places/china
Bureau Chief: Charlie Zhu
Language (s): English
NEWS SERVICE/SYNDICATE

Reuters - Houston Bureau 31158
Editorial: 500 Dallas St Ste 3010, Houston, Texas 77002-4804 **Tel:** 1 713 210-8500
Language (s): English
NEWS SERVICE/SYNDICATE

Reuters - Islamabad Bureau 363423
Editorial: Islamabad **Tel:** 92 51 281-0017
Web site: http://www.reuters.com/places/pakistan
Language (s): English
NEWS SERVICE/SYNDICATE

Reuters - Istanbul Bureau 584306
Editorial: Is Kuleleri Kule 2 Kat 1-2, Istanbul 806204 LEVENT **Tel:** 90 212 350-7000
Email: istanbul.newsroom@thomsonreuters.com
Bureau Chief: Nicholas Tattersall
Language (s): English
NEWS SERVICE/SYNDICATE

Reuters - Jakarta Bureau 231235
Editorial: Kantor Berita Reuter, Jakarta 10001
Tel: 62 213846364
Chief Correspondent: Randy Fabi
Language (s): English
NEWS SERVICE/SYNDICATE

Reuters - Jerusalem Bureau 154546
Editorial: Jerusalem Technology Center, Tower Bld, 12th Flr, Jerusalem 96951 **Tel:** 972 26322202
Email: jerusalem.newsroom@thomsonreuters.com
Web site: http://www.reuters.com/places/israel
Bureau Chief: Luke Baker; **Bureau Chief:** Crispian Balmer
Language (s): English
NEWS SERVICE/SYNDICATE

Reuters - Johannesburg Bureau 231237
Editorial: The Chelsea Building, 4th Floor, 138 West Street, Johannesburg **Tel:** 27 11 775-3000
Web site: http://af.reuters.com
Language (s): English
NEWS SERVICE/SYNDICATE

Reuters - Kabul Bureau 696418
Editorial: Restricted Address, Kabul
Tel: 93 799335284
NEWS SERVICE/SYNDICATE

Reuters - Kiev Bureau 857776
Editorial: Room 112 - 115, Ulitsa Bogdana Khmelnitskovo 8-16, Kiev 252006 **Tel:** 380 44 244-91-50
Language (s): English
NEWS SERVICE/SYNDICATE

Reuters - Kuala Lumpur Bureau
726185
Owner: Thomson Reuters
Editorial: Reuters Malaysia Sdn Bhd, Level 32, Petronas Tower 2, Kuala Lumpur 5088 **Tel:** 60 3 23-338000
Email: malaysia.newsroom@thomsonreuters.com
Language (s): English
NEWS SERVICE/SYNDICATE

Reuters - Lagos Bureau
538174
Editorial: KPMG Towers, Bishop Aboyade Cole Street, Lagos **Tel:** 234 1 270-4080
Email: nigeria.newsroom@thomsonreuters.com
Bureau Chief: Tim Cocks
NEWS SERVICE/SYNDICATE

Reuters - Lima Bureau
431844
Editorial: Av. Victor Andres Belaunde 332, Oficina 302, Oficinas 901-902, Lima **Tel:** 51 08 007-7116
Email: lima.newsroom@thomsonreuters.com
Language (s): English
NEWS SERVICE/SYNDICATE

Reuters - Lisbon Bureau
235297
Editorial: Avenida da Liberdade, 190-2 A, 1250-147, Lisbon **Tel:** 351 213509200
Email: lisbon.newsroom@thomsonreuters.com **Web site:** http://reuters.com/places/portugal
Deputy Bureau Chief: Sergio Goncalves
Language (s): English
NEWS SERVICE/SYNDICATE

Reuters - London Bureau
77000
Editorial: The Reuters Building, 30 South Colonnade, London, England E14 5EP **Tel:** 44 20 7250-1122
Bureau Chief: Guy Faulconbridge; **News Editor:** Peter Graff; **News Editor:** Louise Ireland; **News Editor:** Janet McBride; **Deputy Bureau Chief:** Andrew Osborn
Language (s): English
NEWS SERVICE/SYNDICATE

Reuters - Los Angeles Bureau
31152
Editorial: 633 W 5th St, Los Angeles, California 90071-2005 **Tel:** 1 213 380-2014
Language (s): English
NEWS SERVICE/SYNDICATE

Reuters - Madrid Bureau
231238
Editorial: Piso de la Casellana 37-41, Madrid 28046
Tel: 34 91 585-2100
Email: madrid.newsroom@thomsonreuters.com **Web site:** http://www.reuters.es
Language (s): English
NEWS SERVICE/SYNDICATE

Reuters - Manila Bureau
394680
Editorial: 6 floor three world square, Upper McKinley Rd, Manila **Tel:** 63 916328418900
Email: manila.newsroom@thomsonreuters.com
Language (s): English
NEWS SERVICE/SYNDICATE

Reuters - Mexico City Bureau
71791
Editorial: Manuel Avila Camacho Blvd., #36, Torre Esmeralda II, Piso 19, Mexico City, Distrito Federal 11000 **Tel:** 52 55 5282-7000
Email: mexicocity.newsroom@thomsonreuters.com
Web site: http://mx.reuters.com
Bureau Chief: Simon Gardner
Language (s): Spanish
NEWS SERVICE/SYNDICATE

Reuters - Miami Bureau
31155
Editorial: 5201 Blue Lagoon Dr, Miami, Florida 33126-2064 **Tel:** 1 305 810-2688
Email: miami.newsroom@thomsonreuters.com
Language (s): English
NEWS SERVICE/SYNDICATE

Reuters - Milan Bureau
599739
Editorial: Via Santa Margherita 1/A, Milan 20121
Tel: 39 02 661-291
Email: milan.newsroom@thomsonreuters.com
Language (s): English
NEWS SERVICE/SYNDICATE

Reuters - Moscow Bureau
231247
Editorial: 5 Petrovka Street, Berlin Haus Business Centre, Moscow 103031 **Tel:** 7 495 961-0100
Email: moscow.newsroom@reuters.com **Web site:** http://ru.reuters.com
Editor: Dmitry Antonov; **Editor:** Anton Zverev
Language (s): English
NEWS SERVICE/SYNDICATE

Reuters - Mumbai Bureau
431849
Editorial: Nicholas Piramal Tower, 4th Floor, Peninsula Corporate Park, Ganpatrao Kadam Marg, Mumbai 400 013 **Tel:** 91 22 6180-7001
Language (s): English
NEWS SERVICE/SYNDICATE

Reuters - Nairobi Bureau
492868
Editorial: Loita St, Finance House, 12th Floor, Nairobi
Tel: 254 20 222-4717
Email: nairobi.newsroom@thomsonreuters.com
Bureau Chief: Edmund Blair; **Africa Correspondent:** Abdiqani Hassan
Profile: This is the central East Africa bureau and serves as the forwarding office for contacts in the area, including those in Mogadishu, Somalia, Burundi and Uganda.
Language (s): English
NEWS SERVICE/SYNDICATE

Reuters - New Delhi Bureau
231243
Editorial: 10th Floor, East Birla Towers, 25 Barakhamba Road, New Delhi 110001
Tel: 91 11 4178-1000
Bureau Chief: Tony Tharakan
Language (s): English
NEWS SERVICE/SYNDICATE

Reuters - Oslo Bureau
238271
Editorial: Karl Johans Gate 37B, 162, Oslo
Tel: 47 22936900
Email: oslo.newsroom@thomsonreuters.com **Web site:** http://www.reuters.com/places/norway
Bureau Chief: Balazs Koranyi
Language (s): English
NEWS SERVICE/SYNDICATE

Reuters - Ottawa Bureau
31320
Editorial: 165 Sparks St Suite 400, Ottawa, Ontario K1P 5B9 **Tel:** 1 613 235-6745
Email: ottawa.newsroom@thomsonreuters.com **Web site:** http://ca.reuters.com
Language (s): English
NEWS SERVICE/SYNDICATE

Reuters - Paris Bureau
238255
Editorial: 6/8 bd Haussmann, 75457 Paris Cedex 09, Paris **Tel:** 33 1 4949-5452
Email: paris.newsroom@thomsonreuters.com
Editor: Mark John; **Editor:** Yann Le Guernigou
Language (s): English
NEWS SERVICE/SYNDICATE

Reuters - Quito Bureau
387538
Editorial: Avenida Republica, 500 Y La Pradera Edificio Pucara of 402, Quito **Tel:** 593 2 252-3560
Email: quito.newsroom@thomsonreuters.com
Language (s): English
NEWS SERVICE/SYNDICATE

Reuters - Rio De Janeiro Bureau
793069
Editorial: Av. Presidente Wilson, 231, Sala 1201, Rio De Janeiro **Tel:** 55 21 2223-7100
Language (s): English
NEWS SERVICE/SYNDICATE

Reuters - Rome Bureau
411441
Editorial: Corso D'Italia 39, Rome 198
Tel: 39 348 760-4350
Email: rome.newsroom@thomsonreuters.com
Bureau Chief: James Mackenzie
Language (s): English
NEWS SERVICE/SYNDICATE

Reuters - Sacramento Bureau
841483
Editorial: 1750 Creekside Oaks Dr Ste 100, Sacramento, California 95833-3647 **Tel:** 1 916 576-6200
Language (s): English
NEWS SERVICE/SYNDICATE

Reuters - San Francisco Bureau
31230
Editorial: 50 California St Ste 200, San Francisco, California 94111-4605 **Tel:** 1 415 344-6000
Language (s): English
NEWS SERVICE/SYNDICATE

Reuters - Santiago Bureau
350288
Editorial: Edificio Centenario, Piso 10, Miraflores 383, Santiago **Tel:** 5411 5554 7306
Language (s): English
NEWS SERVICE/SYNDICATE

Reuters - Sao Paulo Bureau
394852
Editorial: Av. Cardoso de Melo, 1855, 13, Andar, Vila Olimpia, Sao Paulo **Tel:** 55 11 56447500
Language (s): English
NEWS SERVICE/SYNDICATE

Reuters - Sarajevo Bureau
727797
Editorial: Fra Andjela Zvizdovica 1, Sarajevo 71000
Tel: 387 3366 3864
Email: sarajevo.newsroom@thomsonreuters.com
Web site: http://www.thomsonreuters.com
Bureau Chief: Daria Sito-Sucic
Language (s): English
NEWS SERVICE/SYNDICATE

Reuters - Seattle Bureau
31221
Editorial: 600 University St, Seattle, Washington 98101-1176
Language (s): English
NEWS SERVICE/SYNDICATE

Reuters - Seoul Bureau
431847
Editorial: 14F Gwanghwamun Building, 149 Sejong-daero, Jongno-gu, Seoul 3186 **Tel:** 82 2 37045500
Email: seoul.newsroom@thomsonreuters.com
Deputy Bureau Chief: Choonsik Yoo
Language (s): Korean
NEWS SERVICE/SYNDICATE

Reuters - Shanghai Bureau
382928
Editorial: 3004 AZIA Centre, 1233 Lujiazui Huan Rd, Shanghai 200120 **Tel:** 86 21 6104-1688
Email: shanghai.newsroom@thomsonreuters.com
Web site: http://reuters.com/places/china
Bureau Chief: Jason Subler; **Chief Correspondent:** Pete Sweeney
Language (s): English
NEWS SERVICE/SYNDICATE

Reuters - Singapore Bureau
231249
Editorial: 18 Science Park Drive, Singapore 118229
Tel: 65 6 775-5088
Email: singapore.newsroom@thomsonreuters.com
Bureau Chief: Rachel Armstrong
Language (s): English
NEWS SERVICE/SYNDICATE

Reuters - Sofia Bureau
727800
Editorial: 16 Ivan Vazov Street, Suite 1000, Sofia
Tel: 3592 9399 700
Web site: http://www.thomsonreuters.com
Language (s): English
NEWS SERVICE/SYNDICATE

Reuters - Stockholm Bureau
231253
Editorial: Kungsgatan 15, Stockholm 11143
Tel: 46 8 700-1000
Email: stockholm.newsroom@thomsonreuters.com
Bureau Chief: Alistair Scrutton
Language (s): English
NEWS SERVICE/SYNDICATE

Reuters - Sydney Bureau
231218
Editorial: 60 Margaret Street, Sydney NSW 2000
Tel: 61 2 9373-1500
Email: sydney.newsroom@thomsonreuters.com
Bureau Chief: Mark Bendeich; **Bureau Chief:** Lincoln Feast; **Chief Correspondent:** Michael Perry; **Deputy Bureau Chief & Chief Companies Correspondent:** Jane Wardell
Language (s): English
NEWS SERVICE/SYNDICATE

Reuters - Taipei Bureau
411111
Editorial: 10 Fl 196 Chien Kuo North Road, Section 2, Taipei **Tel:** 886 225080815
Deputy Bureau Chief: Faith Hung
Language (s): English
NEWS SERVICE/SYNDICATE

Reuters - Tirana Bureau
727804
Editorial: 1 Nikolla Tupe Street, 2nd Floor, Tirana Unavailable **Tel:** 355 4 222-9824
Web site: http://www.thomsonreuters.com
NEWS SERVICE/SYNDICATE

Reuters - Tokyo Bureau
231254
Editorial: 30F Akasaka Biz Tower, 5-3-1 Akasaka, Minato-ku, Tokyo 107-6330 **Tel:** 81 334324141
Email: tokyo.newsroom@thomsonreuters.com **Web site:** http://www.reuters.com/places/japan
News Editor, Japanese Service: Kazuhiko Tamaki
Language (s): English
NEWS SERVICE/SYNDICATE

Reuters - Toronto Bureau
31223
Editorial: 333 Bay St Suite 400, Toronto, Ontario M5H 2R2- **Tel:** 1 416 687 7500
Email: toronto.newsroom@thomsonreuters.com **Web site:** http://ca.reuters.com
Language (s): English
NEWS SERVICE/SYNDICATE

Reuters - Tunis Bureau
728175
Editorial: Tunis **Tel:** 216 7 178-7711
Web site: http://www.reuters.com
Language (s): English
NEWS SERVICE/SYNDICATE

Reuters - United Nations Bureau
31337
Editorial: United Nations #C-316, New York, New York 10017 **Tel:** 1 212 355-6053
Email: un.newsroom@thomsonreuters.com
Profile: This bureau is based at the United Nations.
Language (s): English
NEWS SERVICE/SYNDICATE

Reuters - Vienna Bureau
232187
Editorial: Boersegasse 11, A-1010, Vienna x
Tel: 43 1 5311 20
Email: vienna.newsroom@reuters.com
Chief Correspondent: Michael Shields
Language (s): English
NEWS SERVICE/SYNDICATE

Reuters - Warsaw Bureau
728407
Editorial: Atrium Business Centre Wola, Aleja Jana Pawla 2, Warsaw 00-854
Email: warsaw.newsroom@thomsonreuters.com
Language (s): English
NEWS SERVICE/SYNDICATE

Reuters - Washington Bureau
31153
Editorial: 1333 H St NW, Washington, District Of Columbia 20005-4707 **Tel:** 1 202 898-8300
Email: washington.newsroom@thomsonreuters.com
Web site: http://downtowndc.org/go/reuters
Breaking News Desk Editor: Peter Cooney
Language (s): English
NEWS SERVICE/SYNDICATE

Reuters - Wellington Bureau
347774
Owner: Thomson Reuters
Editorial: PO Box 11-744, Wellington 6140
Tel: 64 4 471 4234
Email: wellington.newsroom@thomsonreuters.com
Web site: http://www.reuters.com
Language (s): English
NEWS SERVICE/SYNDICATE

Reuters - Zurich Bureau
411507
Editorial: Hufgasse 10, Zurich 8022 **Tel:** 41 44 631-7311
Email: zurich.newsroom@reuters.com
Chief Correspondent: Katharina Bart; **Bureau Chief:** Emma Thomasson
Language (s): English
NEWS SERVICE/SYNDICATE

Reuters America
726267
Owner: Thomson Reuters
Editorial: 3 Times Sq, New York, New York 10036-6564 **Tel:** 1 646 223-4000
Web site: http://www.thomsonreuters.com
Profile: Reuters America serves as a domestic news and information service. If provides state-by-state general and political news. Other topics covered include professional and college sports, business news and financial data as well as entertainment, lifestyle and feature stories. Its launch was announced in mid-December 2010.
Language (s): English
NEWS SERVICE/SYNDICATE

Reuters Health Information
31081
Owner: Thomson Reuters
Editorial: 3 Times Sq, New York, New York 10036-6564
Email: healtheditor@thomsonreuters.com **Web site:** http://www.reutershealth.com
Profile: Reuters Health provides medical and healthcare news. They try to offer unbiased, authoritative, timely and dependable news. They use an international staff from bureaus around the world to produce stories for their three news wires: Reuters Health eLine, Reuters Medical News and Reuters Health Industry Briefing. Pitches should be sent via the main e-mail. They ask that PR professionals not pitch them via phone.
Language (s): English
NEWS SERVICE/SYNDICATE

Reuters Life!
518787
Editorial: 3 Times Sq, New York, New York 10036-6564 **Tel:** 1 646 223-4000
Web site: http://www.reuters.com/news/lifestyle
Profile: Reuters Life! is a wire of lifestyle stories that covers news and trends in the fields of entertainment, celebrities, leisure, lifestyles, health, the environment and odd news. It carries approximately 60 stories a day, about 20 of which are exclusive to Reuters Life! clients.
Language (s): English
NEWS SERVICE/SYNDICATE

Rex by Shutterstock
690292
Editorial: 350 5th Ave Fl 21, New York, New York 10118-2100 **Tel:** 1 646 419-4452
Email: support@shutterstock.com **Web site:** http://www.rexusa.com
Profile: This is the Los Angeles bureau of Rex Features. It serves as a photo press agency and also offers feature articles on various topics including travel, human interest, animals, science and technology, general interest and offbeat news.
Language (s): English
NEWS SERVICE/SYNDICATE

Rinker, Harry
134054
Owner: Harry L. Rinker LLC
Editorial: 5955 Mill Point Ct SE, Kentwood, Michigan 49512-9364 **Tel:** 1 484 695-5628
Email: harrylrinker@aol.com **Web site:** http://www.harryrinker.com
Profile: This is a self-syndicated text and Q&A column focusing on collectibles made after 1920 and offers appraisal and consulting advice in the antiques and collectibles field. It attempts to offer the widest range of antiques and collectibles informational services possible. The column appears in more than 10 publications nationwide.
Language (s): English
NEWS SERVICE/SYNDICATE

Risk & Compliance Journal
853327
Owner: News Corporation Ltd.
Editorial: 1211 Avenue of the Americas, New York, New York 10036-8701
Email: riskjournal@wsj.com **Web site:** http://online.wsj.com/public/page/risk-compliance-journal.html
Editor: Ben DiPietro
Profile: Risk & Compliance Journal is a News and Information Service that provides news coverage of a wide span of governance, risk and compliance issues, including analysis of laws and regulations, the risks of global market and trademark expansion, and

practical guidance on how companies and corporate boards can uphold their corporate reputations.
Language (s): English
NEWS SERVICE/SYNDICATE

Robertson Treatment 76079
Owner: Robertson, Gil
Editorial: 324 S Beverly Dr #136, Beverly Hills, California 90212-4801 **Tel:** 1 323 878-2399
Web site: http://www.robertsontreatment.com
Editor: Gil Robertson
Profile: Robertson Treatment takes an in-depth look at the entertainment community and travel and concentrates on breakthrough African American artists, as well as issues affecting people of color in the entertainment world. The column is syndicated throughout the country to over 30 African American news weeklies and has a readership around 3 million.
Language (s): English
NEWS SERVICE/SYNDICATE

Roth Content Services 852210
Tel: 1 414 455-2091
Email: info@rothcontent.com **Web site:** http://rothcontent.com
Editor: Jay Roth
Profile: Roth Content Services provides publications with small to medium circulations with up-to-date reviews focusing on business and technology products, services, books as well as specialty content on a contracted basis.
Language (s): English
NEWS SERVICE/SYNDICATE

Saddle Ridge Communications 30837
Tel: 1 304 686-2630
Profile: Weekly columns, which are syndicated to 20 newspapers, cover anecdotes, information and occasional commentaries on conservation issues, ecology and the environment, natural wildlife history and back-to-nature travel destinations.
Language (s): English
NEWS SERVICE/SYNDICATE

Saenger Syndicate 31080
Editorial: 2121 Star Ln, Alpine, California 91901-2868
Tel: 1 619 445-4105
Email: editor@reviewexpress.com **Web site:** http://www.classicmovieguide.com
Editor: Diana Saenger
Profile: Founded in 1990, Saenger Syndicate offers reviews of film, books and DVDs and celebrity interviews appear in print and online media of weekly and monthly publications. They cover all markets, from children to adults.
Language (s): English
NEWS SERVICE/SYNDICATE

Sallan, Bruce 689160
Owner: Sallan, Bruce
Editorial: 1317 Santa Barbara St, Santa Barbara, California 93101-2016 **Tel:** 1 818 648-0748
Email: bruce@brucesallan.com **Web site:** http://www.brucesallan.com
Profile: Bruce Sallan is a self-syndicated columnist who focuses on fatherhood and single-parent issues ranging from teen parenting to dating.
Language (s): English
NEWS SERVICE/SYNDICATE

Saudi Press Agency 503950
Editorial: 601 New Hampshire Ave NW, Washington, District Of Columbia 20037-2405 **Tel:** 1 800 453-3177
Email: news@saudipressagency.com **Web site:** http://www.spa.gov.sa/home.php?lang=en
Bureau Chief: Naila Al-Sowayel
Profile: This is the Washington bureau for the Saudi Press Agency and is the main bureau for the service's coverage of the United States.
Language (s): Arabic
NEWS SERVICE/SYNDICATE

Saudi Press Agency - New York Bureau 503951
Editorial: 405 E 42nd St, United Nations Rm S-301, New York, New York 10017 **Tel:** 1 212 308-2412
Profile: This is the United Nations bureau of the Saudi Press Agency.
Language (s): English
NEWS SERVICE/SYNDICATE

Savvy Senior 112695
Tel: 1 405 360-4228
Email: editor@savvysenior.org **Web site:** http://www.savvysenior.org
Editor: Jim Miller
Profile: Savvy Senior is a nationally syndicated newspaper column that offers valuable resources to seniors and the families who support them. It also provides tips and information through a resource book, a weekly radio show and regular television features on PBS, CNN Headline Newsand the NBC Today show. The column started in 2002 and now has more than 400 daily newspapers and other clients.
Language (s): English
NEWS SERVICE/SYNDICATE

Sel, Selacia 30986
Editorial: 171 Pier Ave, Santa Monica, California 90405-5311 **Tel:** 1 424 231-5122
Email: selacia@selacia.com **Web site:** http://www.selacia.com
Profile: This is a self-syndicated feature column focusing on alternative health, personal growth, lifestyle issues, technology, spirituality, social issues and female empowerment. Her features appear in numerous publications, including Mount Shasta Magazine, Let's Live, Cosmic Link, Whole Life Times and Whole Life News. She also reviews books and Web sites on spirituality and personal growth.
Language (s): English
NEWS SERVICE/SYNDICATE

Senior Wire News Service 31051
Editorial: 2377 Elm St, Denver, Colorado 80207-3206
Tel: 1 303 355-3882
Email: clearmountain@tde.com **Web site:** http://www.seniorwire.net
Profile: Started in 1990, Senior Wire News Service offers content aimed specifically at mature publications and readers. It provides senior and boomer-oriented news, including features, health, psychology, sports, beauty, humor, travel and grandparenting. Topics include legislation, health, finances, travel, aging, commentary and advice. Stories appear in publications across the United States, Canada and Mumbai, India. Primary topics should include: legislation, health, finances, travel and aging gracefully commentary and advice.
Language (s): English
NEWS SERVICE/SYNDICATE

South Florida News Service 560440
Owner: Florida International University
Editorial: 3000 NE 151st St, North Miami, Florida 33181-3605
Web site: http://sfnsonline.com
Profile: Launched in January 2009, South Florida News Service provides local South Florida news, written by journalism students at Florida International University. Content is provided to the Sun Sentinel, The Miami Herald, The Palm Beach Post and The Scripps Treasure Coast newspapers in Stuart.
Language (s): English
NEWS SERVICE/SYNDICATE

Southern California Focus 30815
Editorial: 1720 Oak St, Santa Monica, California 90405-4804 **Tel:** 1 310 452-3918
Email: tdelias@aol.com **Web site:** http://www.californiafocus.net/
Editor: Thomas Elias
Profile: Southern California Focus offers commentary on public affairs and any issue that affects California: political, business, economical, ecological, science, books, education, transportation, etc. Syndicated bi-weekly to 94 newspapers.
Language (s): English
NEWS SERVICE/SYNDICATE

Southern Ohio News Media 535977
Editorial: 9935 Fite Ave, Hamersville, Ohio 45130-8792 **Tel:** 1 513 317-8430
Email: southernohionews@aol.com
Editor: Matt Ernst
Profile: Launched in 2008, Southern Ohio News Media covers Southern Ohio, Northern Kentucky and Southeastern Indiana.
Language (s): English
NEWS SERVICE/SYNDICATE

Splash Newswire 614780
Owner: Corbis Corporation
Editorial: 333 Washington Blvd Ste 508, Marina del Rey, California 90292-5152 **Tel:** 1 310 821-2666
Email: newsdesk@splashnews.com **Web site:** http://www.splashnews.com
Profile: Offers photos of celebrity sightings with commentary. Its main offices are based in London.
Language (s): English
NEWS SERVICE/SYNDICATE

Starcott Media Services 30787
Editorial: 6906 Royalgreen Dr, Cincinnati, Ohio 45244-4004 **Tel:** 1 513 231-6034
Email: contact@dulley.com **Web site:** http://www.dulley.com
Profile: Started in 1982, and syndicated to over 400 newspapers and magazines, this Q&A column covers a broad range of money-saving topics, including air conditioning units, furnaces, fireplaces, energy-efficient light bulbs, solar window heaters, water conservation, geodesic dome homes, refrigerators and landscaping. There is detailed information about a variety of topics but presented in a way that average readers can understand.
Language (s): English
NEWS SERVICE/SYNDICATE

Stark's News Service 30938
Owner: J-C Communications Co. Inc.
Editorial: 318 W Adams St Ste 1406, Chicago, Illinois 60606-5173 **Tel:** 1 312 236-5122
Email: sns@starks-news.com **Web site:** http://www.starks-news.com
Profile: Stark's News Service is a source of late-breaking news, statistics and up-to-the-minute market outlooks about cars, trucks, farm and construction machinery. The features focus on the business of production, sales and inventory and are published twice a month in the newsletter.
Language (s): English
NEWS SERVICE/SYNDICATE

State House News Service 155361
Editorial: 24 Beacon St Ste 458, Boston, Massachusetts 02133-1099 **Tel:** 1 617 722-2439
Email: news@statehousenews.com **Web site:** http://www.statehousenews.com
Editor: Michael Norton
Profile: State House News Service offers daily coverage of the legislative happenings on Beacon Hill. It offers news without a political slant or bias. Stories appear in newspapers and online publications throughout Massachusetts, as well as in Washington, D.C., due to their focus on government and policy.
Language (s): English
NEWS SERVICE/SYNDICATE

State Net 281832
Editorial: 2101 K St, Sacramento, California 95816-4920 **Tel:** 1 916 444-0840
Email: info@statenet.com **Web site:** http://www.statenet.com
Editor: Rich Ehisen
Profile: State Net offers data, legislative intelligence and in-depth reporting for people who care about the actions of government. It monitors every bill in the 50 states, District of Columbia, Congress and every state agency regulation.
Language (s): English
NEWS SERVICE/SYNDICATE

Steyn, Mark 594040
Email: mailbox@steynonline.com **Web site:** http://www.steynonline.com
Profile: This column covers politics, arts and culture and can be read each week throughout much of the English-speaking world. In the United States, his column appears in newspapers from The Washington Times to The Evening Bulletin in Philadelphia, The Orange County Register in California to Black & White in Birmingham, Alabama. It also appears in The Jerusalem Post, The Australian, Investigate and Hawke's Bay Today in New Zealand; and more occasionally in The Wall Street Journal and (translated into Italian) Il Foglio.
Language (s): English
NEWS SERVICE/SYNDICATE

Stoneberg, Diana 30971
Editorial: 2730 W Highway 89A Ste 11-281, Sedona, Arizona 86336 **Tel:** 1 928 202-4777
Email: info@gadgetgrrl.com **Web site:** http://www.gadgetgrrl.com
Profile: The service presents technology in a fun and entertaining way, including the latest technologies, games, electronics, appliances, toys, music, MP3, consumer electronics, wireless devices and the Internet. The author looks at all the latest and biggest technology gadgets. Her columns run both online, including TheStreet.com and housekeeping channel.com, as well as in print with a circulation of about 3 million readers. Gadget Grrl is appears on TV News and Talk Shows featuring the latest consumer electronics services and apps. She also hosts a daily podcast.
Language (s): English
NEWS SERVICE/SYNDICATE

The Straight Dope 281833
Owner: Atalaya Capital Management
Editorial: 11 E Illinois St, Chicago, Illinois 60611-5652
Tel: 1 312 828-0350
Web site: http://www.straightdope.com
Profile: The Straight Dope is a nationally distributed column and newsletter that answers questions about scientific phenomena and complicated or interesting questions. It appears mostly in alternative weekly newspapers.
Language (s): English
NEWS SERVICE/SYNDICATE

Strange But True 30975
Editorial: 1237 Rae Rd, Lyndhurst, Ohio 44124-1409
Tel: 1 440 460-0330
Email: strangetrue@cs.com **Web site:** http://strangefacts.com
Profile: Strange But True is a self-syndicated lifestyle or magazine column featuring strange but true stories. It has been syndicated to more than 75 papers on six continents. Each column features questions submitted by readers that are answered by the writers. Its focus is to provide readers answers to everything you wondered about (and some things you never wanted to know).
Language (s): English
NEWS SERVICE/SYNDICATE

Sun-Times Media Wire 387591
Editorial: 350 N Orleans St, Chicago, Illinois 60654-1975 **Tel:** 1 312 321-2147
Email: wire@suntimes.com
Editor: Jeff Mayes
Profile: Sun-Times Media Wire is a service launched by the Chicago Sun-Times. It delivers news and notices from organizations to print and electronic media serving the area. It serves as a hub for consideration of releases, meeting notices, event announcements and other important information. It specializes in breaking news in and around Chicago 24 hours per day.
Language (s): English
NEWS SERVICE/SYNDICATE

Talk Media News 31099
Editorial: 300 New Jersey Ave NW Ste 900, Washington, District Of Columbia 20001-2271
Tel: 1 202 337-5322
Email: info@talkmedianews.com **Web site:** http://www.talkmedianews.com
Bureau Chief: Ellen Ratner
Profile: Talk Media News Service is a news booking and host service dedicated to serving the talk radio community. It provides local talk radio stations, producers, hosts and their listeners with up-to-date information and behind the scenes scoops from the nation's capitol.
Language (s): English
NEWS SERVICE/SYNDICATE

The Talk Media News - New York Bureau 831842
Editorial: 405 E 42nd St, 4th Floor, S-0422-A, New York, New York 10017-3507 **Tel:** 1 212 918-1995
Profile: This is the United Nations bureau for Talk Media News.
Language (s): English
NEWS SERVICE/SYNDICATE

Targeted News Service 432351
Editorial: 7723 Harwood Pl, Springfield, Virginia 22152-2014 **Tel:** 1 703 304-1897
Email: editor@targetednews.com **Web site:** http://www.targetednews.com
Editor: Myron Struck
Profile: Targeted News Service is an editorial services company providing focused news products. It offers a wide range of news and support services to newspapers. The news service assists in gathering a wide range of raw government and congressional documents documents and makes that information available directly to newspapers and other end-users in a targeted manner.
Language (s): English
NEWS SERVICE/SYNDICATE

Tech With Kids 234986
Editorial: 903 Falls Bridge Ln, Great Falls, Virginia 22066-1347 **Tel:** 1 703 444-9005
Email: jinny@techwithkids.com **Web site:** http://www.techwithkids.com
Profile: Tech With Kids is a weekly online magazine that reviews of children's software and apps, video games, Web sites and tech toys. It issues BEST PICK Awards for the outstanding products in each category. The column appears in USAToday and Gannett newspapers.
Language (s): English
NEWS SERVICE/SYNDICATE

This is True 30941
Owner: This is True Inc.
Tel: 1 970 626-6030
Web site: http://www.thisistrue.com
Profile: This is True provides humorous commentary on the news and reports on bizarre-but-true news items from legitimate printed news sources from around the world.
Language (s): English
NEWS SERVICE/SYNDICATE

Trade News Service 30886
Editorial: 3701 State Route 21, Canandaigua, New York 14424-9020 **Tel:** 1 585 396-0027
Email: tns@fats-and-oils.com **Web site:** http://www.fats-and-oils.com
Editor: Dennis Maxfield
Profile: Weekly information service for producers, traders and consumers of edible and inedible fats and oils. Included are price histories, import/export data and numerous news and statistical reports for the trade.
Language (s): English
NEWS SERVICE/SYNDICATE

Tribune Content Agency 31030
Owner: tronc
Editorial: 435 N Michigan Ave Ste 1400, Chicago, Illinois 60611-7551 **Tel:** 1 312 222-4131
Email: story@tribpub.com **Web site:** http://www.tribunecontentagency.com
Profile: Tribune Content Agency is a leading media content company that provides syndicated information and entertainment products to print, electronic and on-air media worldwide. It is a subsidiary of Tribune Publishing. Editorial content is provided by syndicated columnists and writers.
Language (s): English
NEWS SERVICE/SYNDICATE

Tribune Content Agency - Specialty Products 445911
Owner: tronc
Editorial: 435 N Michigan Ave Ste 1400, Chicago, Illinois 60611-7551 **Tel:** 1 800 637-4082
Web site: http://www.tmsspecialtyproducts.com
Profile: Tribune Content Agency - Specialty Products writes, designs and edits print content for newspaper classified and editorial special sections. It offers single stories, as well as complete advertorial sections. Niche content is created to target specific demographics, readers and advertisers. Employment and careers, entertainment and lifestyles packages are published weekly, and dozens of topic-specific special sections are available annually, quarterly or by request.
Language (s): English
NEWS SERVICE/SYNDICATE

Tribune News Service 30752
Owner: tronc
Editorial: 435 N Michigan Ave Ste 500, Tribune Content Agency, Chicago, Illinois 60611-6222
Tel: 1 312 222-4131
Email: tcaeditors@tribune.com **Web site:** http://www.mctdirect.com
Profile: Tribune News Service provides news and feature stories, photos, print and Web news, feature graphics, illustrations, caricatures and paginated news products to news organizations around the world. The service relies on America's top newspapers for its content and does not accept

outside articles for distribution. Content includes health, science, weather information, business, lifestyle topics and more. With contributions from more than 70 newspapers plus its own staff in the United States and Europe, its services appear in more than 1,000 newspapers worldwide and is represented on leading online services.
Language (s): English
NEWS SERVICE/SYNDICATE

Tribune Washington News Bureau 558441
Owner: tronc
Editorial: 1090 Vermont Ave NW, Washington, District Of Columbia 20005-4905 **Tel:** 1 202 824-8200
Deputy Bureau Chief: Bob Drogin; **Bureau Chief:** David Lauter
Profile: Serves as the Washington bureau for all Tribune Company newspapers.
Language (s): English
NEWS SERVICE/SYNDICATE

Trivia Guy 155198
Editorial: 282 Spring Dr, Spartanburg, South Carolina 29302-3248 **Tel:** 1 864 621-7129
Email: trivguy@bellsouth.net **Web site:** http://www.triviaguy.com
Profile: The column started in 1999. Wilson Casey, a Guiness World Record holder also known as the Trivia Guy, provides topical multiple choice trivia questions and answers. His column runs seven times a week, 365 days a year. He writes a biblical trivia column once a week; the other six days, the column features trivia of a general nature. It is syndicated in over 500 newspapers.
Language (s): English
NEWS SERVICE/SYNDICATE

United Methodist News Service 30964
Editorial: 810 12th Ave S, Nashville, Tennessee 37203-4704 **Tel:** 1 615 742-5470
Email: newsdesk@umcom.org **Web site:** http://www.umc.org/news-and-media/united-methodist-news
News Editor: Vicki Brown
Profile: Founded in 1940, United Methodist News Service gathers news about the United Methodist Church for dissemination to the religious and secular media. It seeks to assure that the United Methodist Church is reflected in the media as fairly and accurately as possible. The publication targets United Methodist parishioners.
Language (s): English
NEWS SERVICE/SYNDICATE

United Nations News Service 155401
Editorial: Office of the Spokesman/Sec General, United Nations S-378, New York, New York 10017
Tel: 1 212 963-7162
Email: inquiries2@un.org **Web site:** http://www.un.org/news
Profile: United Nations News Service provides current information on the office of the Secretary General and United Nations missions around the globe. Updates are available in English, French, Spanish, Chinese and Russian. They do NOT want to be contacted.
Language (s): Chinese
NEWS SERVICE/SYNDICATE

United Nations Secretariat 621183
Editorial: 1st Avenue, New York, New York 10017
Tel: 1 609 529-6129
Email: nosh.nalavala@climatemedia.org **Web site:** http://climatemedia.org/
Bureau Chief: Naosherwan Nalavala
Profile: United Nations Secretariat is a media organization that covers issues affecting the developing world including disease, hunger, climate change, poverty and humanitarian efforts. This news service is based at the United Nations in New York.
Language (s): English
NEWS SERVICE/SYNDICATE

United Press International 31032
Owner: News World Communications, Inc.
Editorial: 1133 19th St NW, Washington, District Of Columbia 20036-3604 **Tel:** 1 202 898-8000
Email: nationaldesk@upi.com **Web site:** http://www.upi.com
Profile: United Press International, since 1907, has been a leading provider of critical information to media outlets, businesses, governments and researchers worldwide. Covering a wide range of topics, UPI's journalists provide in-depth reports and analysis of global issues affecting business and policy decisions, short news bulletins, and a headline service. Products include original content in English, Spanish and Arabic text and photos. Headquarters are in Washington, with offices in Hong Kong; London; Santiago, Chile; Seoul, South Korea; and Tokyo.
Language (s): English
NEWS SERVICE/SYNDICATE

United Press International - Hong Kong Bureau 358959
Editorial: Wui Tat Centre 18/F, 55 Connaught Road West, Hong Kong **Tel:** 86 85228582774
Web site: http://www.upiasiaonline.com
Language (s): English
NEWS SERVICE/SYNDICATE

United Press International - Valencia Bureau 31161
Editorial: 25348 Via Pacifica, Valencia, California 91355-2634 **Tel:** 1 661 670-8023
Profile: This is the West Coast bureau of United Press International. All releases should be in the form of email and sent to the News Editor.
Language (s): English
NEWS SERVICE/SYNDICATE

USA Today Sports Images 604813
Owner: Gannett Co., Inc.
Editorial: 535 Madison Ave Fl 20, New York, New York 10022-4214 **Tel:** 1 646 601-7202
Email: info@usatodaysportsimages.com **Web site:** http://www.usatodaysportsimages.com
Profile: USA Today Sports Images is a global leader in premium digital media content creation and distribution to media companies worldwide. It offers some of the industry's premium sports content to exceed the demand of the digital media world's ever changing needs. Its content is distributed on deadline for editorial usage and accessed via their Web site or direct wire feed to our creative professional clients.
Language (s): English
NEWS SERVICE/SYNDICATE

Veterinary Information Network News Service 670331
Owner: Veterinary Information Network, Inc.
Editorial: 777 W Covell Blvd, Davis, California 95616-5916 **Tel:** 1 530 756-4881
Email: news@vin.com **Web site:** http://news.vin.com
Editor: Jennifer Fetterman
Profile: News wire focusing on veterinary news.
Language (s): English
NEWS SERVICE/SYNDICATE

The Washington Post News Service/Syndicate 31033
Owner: Washington Post Co.
Editorial: 1301 K St NW, One Franklin Square, Washington, District Of Columbia 20005-3317
Tel: 1 202 334-6375
Email: wp.syndicate@washpost.com **Web site:** https://www.washingtonpost.com/syndication
Profile: The Washington Post News Service/Syndicate provides features with an emphasis on national and international political and social commentary with both liberal and conservative viewpoints. General features cover personal finance, book reviews, real estate and movie reviews.
Language (s): English
NEWS SERVICE/SYNDICATE

Western News Service 30977
Editorial: 866 Oneonta Dr, Los Angeles, California 90065-4125 **Tel:** 1 323 256-3625
Email: jim.thompson@wnsnews.com
Profile: Western News Service offers information about national and international news, travel features and technology. It is used by more than 35 newspapers and 350 radio stations.
Language (s): English
NEWS SERVICE/SYNDICATE

Whitegate Features Syndicate 30751
Editorial: 71 Faunce Dr, Providence, Rhode Island 02906-4805 **Tel:** 1 401 274-2149
Web site: http://www.whitegatefeatures.com
Profile: Founded in 1988, Whitegate Features Syndicate offers feature columns on a variety of topics, including food, wine, gardening, beauty, entertainment, fashion, dining, home decorating, lifestyle issues, health and travel. It also provides reviews of books, software and music CDs. Articles are syndicated to more than 200 newspapers around the world. Whitegate Features Syndicate does accept press releases and news items delivered via mail.
Language (s): English
NEWS SERVICE/SYNDICATE

Williams, Armstrong 324838
Editorial: 201 Massachusetts Ave NE Ste C1, Washington, District Of Columbia 20002-4988
Tel: 1 202 546-5400
Email: arightside@aol.com **Web site:** http://www.armstrongwilliams.com/
Profile: This self-syndicated column provides intelligent and value-oriented commentary on American culture and politics with a reputation for taking tough political issues and making them personal for its readers. It is from a conservative and Christian perspective.
Language (s): English
NEWS SERVICE/SYNDICATE

Winning Investing 281775
Editorial: 199 Quail Run Rd, Aptos, California 95003-3433 **Tel:** 1 831 685-1932
Email: hdomash@winninginvesting.com **Web site:** http://www.winninginvesting.com
Profile: Winning Investing describes how professionals employ fundamental analysis strategies to pinpoint the best stocks and mutual funds.
Language (s): English
NEWS SERVICE/SYNDICATE

WireImage 358802
Editorial: 75 Varick St, New York, New York 10013-1917 **Tel:** 1 646 613-4000
Email: nydesk@wireimage.com **Web site:** http://www.wireimage.com
Editor: Pancho Bernasconi
Profile: WireImage is a photography news service reaching professional publishing, broadcast and online media. They also provide photo and press release distribution through other newswires, including the Associated Press, Reuters Pictures, Business Wire, Gannett News Service and The New York Times News Service. Photos can be delivered to either a broad or targeted list of media outlets.
Language (s): English
NEWS SERVICE/SYNDICATE

WireImage - Los Angeles Bureau 678805
Editorial: 6300 Wilshire Blvd, 16th Floor, Los Angeles, California 90048-5204 **Tel:** 1 323 202-4101
Email: ladesk@wireimage.com **Web site:** http://www.wireimage.com
Profile: Wire Image is a top ranking digital photo agency and wire service for entertainment photography.
Language (s): English
NEWS SERVICE/SYNDICATE

World News Syndicate, Ltd. 30761
Owner: Lane (Nancy)
Editorial: 519 Alameda St, Altadena, California 91001-2904 **Tel:** 1 323 469-2333
Web site: http://wnsltd.com/
Profile: World News Syndicate provides information and reviews of new music, books, CDs, DVDs as well as political, automotive, religious and health and beauty topics. Also, features news and gossip from Hollywood and the film world. Monthly columns are sent to roughly 164 smaller newspapers across the country and Canada including minority publications. Will be launching a travel and entertainment supplement and website in December, 2014.
Language (s): English
NEWS SERVICE/SYNDICATE

WorldWatch Affairs Syndicate 30773
Editorial: 14421 Charter Rd, Jamaica, New York 11435-6386 **Tel:** 1 718 591-7246
Email: jjmcolumn@att.net **Web site:** http://www.worldtribune.com/
Editor: John Metzler
Profile: WorldWatch Affairs Syndicate is a weekly roundup of key diplomatic, defense and developmental issues filed from the United Nations and abroad. Self-syndicated to 16 newspapers and premium Web sites.
Language (s): English
NEWS SERVICE/SYNDICATE

World-Wire 232091
Editorial: 620 NE Vineyard Ln Unit 303, Seattle, Washington 98110-2431 **Tel:** 1 541 992-5901
Email: editor@world-wire.com **Web site:** http://www.world-wire.com
Profile: World-Wire provides press releases from environmentally relevant organizations and corporations that keeps readers up to date on this fast-changing field.
Language (s): English
NEWS SERVICE/SYNDICATE

Zimmerman, Sandy 579240
Tel: 1 702 731-6491
Email: sandyzimm2003@yahoo.com **Web site:** http://www.discovertheultimate.com
Profile: Zimmerman writes the Best in Las Vegas and Best in the World columns, covering Shows, Entertainment, Dining, Travel, Cars, Beauty, Fashion, Spas, Famous Chefs, Openings, Interviews and Reviews. She is syndicated with over 1,000 newspapers and magazines around the world.
Language (s): English
NEWS SERVICE/SYNDICATE

Zuma Press 334335
Editorial: 408 N El Camino Real, San Clemente, California 92672-4717 **Tel:** 1 949 481-3747
Email: licensing@zumapress.com **Web site:** http://www.zumapress.com
Profile: Zuma Press in San Clemente, CA offers local and international news, sports, entertainment, in-depth investigative stories, features and travel stories produced by photojournalists.
Language (s): English
NEWS SERVICE/SYNDICATE

Community Newspaper

1870 Magazine 359821
Owner: 614 Media Group
Editorial: 458 E Main St, Columbus, Ohio 43215-5344 **Tel:** 1 614 488-4400 17
Email: editor@1870now.com **Web site:** https://1870now.com
Freq: Wed; **Circ:** 16000 Not Audited
Publisher: Wayne Lewis
Profile: 1870 Magazine is a monthly newspaper serving the areas in and around Ohio State University's campus in Columbus, OH. The paper is independently-owned and not affiliated with the university. It covers campus news, events, sports music, movies, television shows, technology and gadgets and features relevant to the student population. The production schedule usually halts for portions of December and June. Send pitches by e-mail.
Language (s): English
Ad Rate: Full Page Mono 10.00
Currency: United States Dollars
COMMUNITY NEWSPAPER

280 Living 777051
Owner: Starnes Publshing
Editorial: 1833 27th Ave S, Homewood, Alabama 35209-1962 **Tel:** 1 205 313-1780
Email: editor@280living.com **Web site:** http://280living.com
Freq: Weekly; **Circ:** 13500
Publisher: Dan Starnes
Profile: 280 Living is a monthly newspaper providing Local and Community News coverage to the residents living in the 280 Corridor along Highway 280, encompassing the communities of Birmingham, Cahaba Heights, Inverness, Mountain Brook, Chelsea and Oak Park, AL
Language (s): English
COMMUNITY NEWSPAPER

5 Towns Jewish Times 927167
Tel: 1 516 569-0502
Email: editor@5tjt.com **Web site:** http://5tjt.com
Freq: Weekly
Editor & Publisher: Larry Gordon
Profile: 5 Towns Jewish Times is a weekly newspaper serving the Orthodox Jewish community in Nassau County, NY, which includes Inwood, Lawrence, Cedarhurst, Woodmere and Hewlett.
Language (s): English
Ad Rate: Full Page Mono 13.10
Ad Rate: Full Page Colour 16.27
Currency: United States Dollars
COMMUNITY NEWSPAPER

ACE Weekly 69925
Owner: Realitytruck LLC
Editorial: 118 Constitution St, Lexington, Kentucky 40507-2111 **Tel:** 1 859 225-4889
Email: publisher@aceweekly.com **Web site:** http://www.aceweekly.com
Freq: Thu; **Circ:** 10000 Not Audited
Publisher & Editor: Rob Kirkland
Profile: ACE Weekly is a free newspaper that features arts, commentary, entertainment and current events in the Lexington, KY area. The mailing address is only used for billing and accounting; send press releases to the street address. The fax number is used only by the advertising department.
Language (s): English
Ad Rate: Full Page Mono 27.79
Currency: United States Dollars
COMMUNITY NEWSPAPER

AcheiUSA 726098
Owner: Jose Nunes
Editorial: 816 SE 9th St Ste E, Deerfield Beach, Florida 33441-5640 **Tel:** 1 954 570-7568
Email: contato@acheiusa.com **Web site:** http://www.acheiusa.com
Freq: Weekly; **Circ:** 12000
Publisher: Jorge Nunes; **Advertising Sales Manager:** Esterliz Nunez
Profile: Launched on November 2000, the newspaper covers news of interest to the Brazilian Community in Florida (in Portuguese).
Language (s): Portuguese
Ad Rate: Full Page Mono 41.90
Currency: United States Dollars
COMMUNITY NEWSPAPER

The AD Times 758131
Owner: Allentown Catholic Communications, Inc.
Tel: 1 610 871-5200 264
Email: adtimes@allentowndiocese.org **Web site:** http://www.allentowndiocese.org/ad_times.html
Freq: Bi-Weekly; **Circ:** 60000
Publisher: John Barres; **Editor:** Jill Caravan
Profile: A.D. Times is newspaper written for the Diocese of Allentown, PA serving the counties of Berks, Carbon, Lehigh, Northampton and Schuylkill. Advertising Deadline is the Monday the week before publication, News copy must be recieved by Thursday of the week before publication.
Language (s): English
Ad Rate: Full Page Mono 20.00
Currency: United States Dollars
COMMUNITY NEWSPAPER

Addison County Independent 21084
Owner: Angelo Lynn
Editorial: 58 Maple St, Middlebury, Vermont 05753-1276 **Tel:** 1 802 388-4944
Email: news@addisonindependent.com **Web site:** http://www.addisonindependent.com
Freq: Mon; **Circ:** 7800 Not Audited
Publisher & Editor: Angelo Lynn
Profile: Addison County Independent is a twice weekly newspaper for the 23 towns within Vermont's Addison County. The newspaper covers local events and news and is published on Monday and Thursday. The total circulation for the Thursday and Monday editions is 7,500 and 5,600 respectively.
Language (s): English
Ad Rate: Full Page Mono 10.75
Ad Rate: Full Page Colour 1234.00
Currency: United States Dollars
COMMUNITY NEWSPAPER

Addison Eagle 24144
Owner: Newmarket Press
Editorial: 16 Creek Rd Ste 5A, Middlebury, Vermont 05753-1376 **Tel:** 1 802 388-6397
Email: newmarketpress@denpubs.com **Web site:** http://www.denpubs.com
Freq: Sat; **Circ:** 12266 Not Audited
Publisher: Edward Coats
Profile: Addison Eagle is a weekly newspaper serving residents of Addison County, VT including the

communities of Bristol, Huntington, Ferrisburg, Hinesburg, Monkton, New Haven, Starkboro, Middlebury, Orwell, Bridport and Shoreham, VT. It covers local news, sports, schools, businesses, arts & entertainment and features of interest. National and state news stories are also covered if they have a direct impact on the paper's audience. Advertising deadlines are at 4pm ET.
Language (s): English
Ad Rate: Full Page Mono 19.00
Currency: United States Dollars
COMMUNITY NEWSPAPER

Addison Post
22443
Editorial: 42 Main St, Addison, New York 14801-1210 **Tel:** 1 607 359-2238
Email: addisonpost@gmail.com **Web site:** http://www.addisonpost.net
Freq: Sat; **Circ:** 6400 Not Audited
Publisher & Editor: Oakley Hayes
Profile: Addison Post is written for residents in Addision, NY. It covers local news and events.
Language (s): English
Ad Rate: Full Page Mono 5.90
Currency: United States Dollars
COMMUNITY NEWSPAPER

Adelante Valle
520312
Owner: Schurz Communications Inc.
Editorial: 205 N 8th St, El Centro, California 92243-2301 **Tel:** 1 760 337-3400
Email: webmaster@ivpressonline.com **Web site:** http://www.adelantevalle.com
Freq: Thu; **Circ:** 8000 Not Audited
Editor: Arturo Bojorquez
Profile: Adelante Valle is a weekly Spanish-language newspaper written for residents of El Centro, CA and the surrounding areas. It covers local, regional and national news of interest for the Hispanic community of the Valley, as well as international briefs, news from Mexico, arts, culture, entertainment and sports.
Language (s): Spanish
Ad Rate: Full Page Mono 14.10
Ad Rate: Full Page Colour 332.06
Currency: United States Dollars
COMMUNITY NEWSPAPER

The Adirondack Express
698786
Owner: Port Jackson Media
Editorial: 2942 St. Rt. 28, Old Forge, New York 13420 **Tel:** 1 315 369-2237
Email: adkexpress@gmail.com **Web site:** http://www.adirondackexpress.com
Freq: Tue; **Circ:** 39000
Publisher: Kevin McClary; **Editor:** M. Lisa Monroe
Profile: The Adirondack Express is a community newspaper serving residents of Old Forge, NY and the surrounding areas.
Language (s): English
Ad Rate: Full Page Mono 6.35
Currency: United States Dollars
COMMUNITY NEWSPAPER

The Advance
18843
Editorial: 205 E 1st St, Vidalia, Georgia 30474-4717 **Tel:** 1 912 537-3131
Email: theadvancenews@gmail.com **Web site:** http://www.theadvancenews.com
Freq: Wed; **Circ:** 7000 Not Audited
Circulation Manager: Gail Cauley; **Advertising Sales Manager:** Daniel Ford; **Publisher & Editor:** William Ledford
Profile: The Advance is a local newspaper for residents of the Vidalia, GA area. It provides feature articles on local and national news, community happenings, events, and classifieds. Deadlines fall on Mondays at noon ET before issue date.
Language (s): English
Ad Rate: Full Page Mono 6.75
Currency: United States Dollars
COMMUNITY NEWSPAPER

Advance Ohio
24671
Owner: Advance Publications
Editorial: 1801 Superior Ave E Ste 100, Cleveland, Ohio 44114-2135 **Tel:** 1 216 999-3900
Email: marketing@advance-ohio.com **Web site:** https://www.advance-ohio.com/
Freq: Weekly; **Circ:** 124614 Not Audited
Profile: Advance Ohio produces the weekly Sun Newspapers, and are sister company of The Plain Dealer and Cleveland.com.
Language (s): English
COMMUNITY NEWSPAPER

The Advertiser
24443
Owner: Hearst Newspapers
Editorial: 29 Sheer Rd, Averill Park, New York 12018-4722 **Tel:** 1 518 674-2841
Email: articles@theadvertiser.us **Web site:** http://www.crwnewspapers.net
Freq: Weekly; **Circ:** 34000 Not Audited
Profile: The Advertiser is a weekly newspaper written for residents of Rensselaer County, NY. There are two editions of the newspaper, one for South Rensselaer County and one for North Rensselaer County. It covers local news, sports, government and lifestyles. The majority of the editorial copy is written by freelancers. Send all press materials to the main e-mail address.
Language (s): English
Ad Rate: Full Page Mono 27.49
Ad Rate: Full Page Colour 1921.00
Currency: United States Dollars
COMMUNITY NEWSPAPER

Advertiser Democrat
19490
Owner: The Oxford Group
Editorial: 1 Pikes Hl, Norway, Maine 04268-4350 **Tel:** 1 207 743-7011
Email: newsteam@advertiserdemocrat.com **Web site:** http://www.advertiserdemocrat.com
Freq: Thu; **Circ:** 6500 Not Audited
Circulation Manager: Patricia Crowder; **Publisher:** Edward Snook
Profile: Advertiser Democrat is a local, weekly newspaper for residents of Western Maine. The publication covers local news, community events and general interest stories relevant to the local community.
Language (s): English
Ad Rate: Full Page Mono 8.95
Currency: United States Dollars
COMMUNITY NEWSPAPER

The Advertiser Gleam
18504
Editorial: 2218 Taylor St, Guntersville, Alabama 35976-1126 **Tel:** 1 256 582-3232
Email: news@advertisergleam.com **Web site:** http://www.advertisergleam.com
Freq: Sat; **Circ:** 10000 Not Audited
Circulation Manager: Taunya Buchanan
Profile: The Advertiser Gleam is a local newspaper for Marshall County, AL. It is published twice a week.
Language (s): English
Ad Rate: Full Page Mono 9.00
Currency: United States Dollars
COMMUNITY NEWSPAPER

The Advertiser News of Spring Hill
238998
Owner: Stephens Media
Editorial: 1115 S. Main St, Spring Hill, Tennessee 38401 **Tel:** 1 615 302-0647
Email: advertiser@c-dh.net **Web site:** http://www.columbiadailyherald.com/advertisernews
Freq: Wed; **Circ:** 14400 Not Audited
Publisher & Editor: Jeff Bryant
Profile: The Advertiser News of Spring Hill is a community newspaper written for the residents of Spring Hill, TN and the surrounding areas.
Language (s): English
Ad Rate: Full Page Mono 10.02
Currency: United States Dollars
COMMUNITY NEWSPAPER

The Advertizer Herald Publishing Co.
24809
Editorial: 369 McGee St, Bamberg, South Carolina 29003-1338 **Tel:** 1 803 245-5204
Email: ahpublisher@bellsouth.net **Web site:** http://www.advertizerherald.com
Circ: 5550 Not Audited
Advertising Sales Manager: Vicki Cleveland; **Publisher & Editor:** Joyce Searson
Language (s): English
COMMUNITY NEWSPAPER

The Advocate
23146
Owner: Newspapers of New England
Editorial: 124 American Legion Dr, North Adams, Massachusetts 1247 **Tel:** 1 413 664-6900
Email: news@advocateweekly.com **Web site:** http://www.advocateweekly.com
Freq: Thu; **Circ:** 15000 Not Audited
Publisher: Robert Chapman; **Advertising Sales Manager:** Mary Rochelo
Profile: The Advocate is a weekly newspaper serving the residents of Berkshire County, MA, and Southern Vermont. It contains local news, arts & entertainment, community events and features. Advertising deadlines are at 4pm ET.
Language (s): English
Ad Rate: Full Page Mono 11.85
Ad Rate: Full Page Colour 50.00
Currency: United States Dollars
COMMUNITY NEWSPAPER

The Advocate and Democrat
29074
Owner: Jones Media, Inc.
Editorial: 609 E North St, Sweetwater, Tennessee 37874-3137 **Tel:** 1 423 337-7101
Web site: http://www.advocateanddemocrat.com
Freq: Sun; **Circ:** 14500 Not Audited
Editor: Tommy Millsaps; **Circulation Manager:** David Smith
Profile: The Advocate and Democrat provides local news and sports coverage for the Monroe County, TN area.
Language (s): English
Ad Rate: Full Page Mono 13.50
Currency: United States Dollars
COMMUNITY NEWSPAPER

African-American News & Issues
151392
Editorial: 6130 Wheatley St, Houston, Texas 77091-3947 **Tel:** 1 713 692-1892
Email: news@aframnews.com **Web site:** http://www.aframnews.com
Freq: Mon; **Circ:** 200000 Not Audited
Advertising Sales Manager: Fred Smith
Profile: African-American News & Issues is a weekly African American newspaper serving Austin, San Antonio, Dallas, Galveston, Harris, Tarrant, Bexar, Jefferson, Travis, Fort Bend, Bell, Smith, McLennan, El Paso, Gregg, Bowie, Brazoria, Denton, Lubbock, Coryell, Harrison, Collin and Brazos, TX.
Language (s): English
Ad Rate: Full Page Mono 69.00

Currency: United States Dollars
COMMUNITY NEWSPAPER

African-American Observer
86879
Editorial: 213 W 35th St Rm 807, New York, New York 10001-1976 **Tel:** 1 212 586-4141
Freq: Tue; **Circ:** 55000 Not Audited
Profile: The African-American Observer is a weekly newspaper written for the African-American, Caribbean and African communities in New York, NY. The advertising deadline is 5pm ET on Thursdays. Editorial submissions are due at 1pm ET on Fridays.
Language (s): English
Ad Rate: Full Page Mono 59.00
Ad Rate: Full Page Colour 64.90
Currency: United States Dollars
COMMUNITY NEWSPAPER

Agua Dulce/Acton Country Journal
521097
Owner: Lillian Smith Enterprises
Editorial: 35327 Glenwall St, Agua Dulce, California 91390-4555 **Tel:** 1 661 269-0884
Email: countryjournal91@earthlink.net
Freq: Sat; **Circ:** 6000 Not Audited
Publisher & Editor: Lillian Smith
Profile: Agua Dulce/Acton Country Journal is a weekly newspaper written for the residents of Agua Dulce, CA and the surrounding areas.
Language (s): English
Ad Rate: Full Page Mono 1.72
Currency: United States Dollars
COMMUNITY NEWSPAPER

Ahora
825210
Owner: Puerto Rican Congress of New Jersey, Inc.
Editorial: 571 Saint Pauls Ave, Cliffside Park, New Jersey 07010-1712 **Tel:** 1 201 478-3997
Email: redaccion@ahoranews.net **Web site:** http://www.ahoranews.net
Freq: Weekly
Profile: Ahora is a Spanish-language community newspaper providing International and Local News coverage to the Residents of Bergen County, NJ and New York, NY. The newspaper also covers Arts & Entertainment, Health, Sports, Business, People and Travels.
Language (s): Spanish
COMMUNITY NEWSPAPER

Ahora Now Newspaper
75921
Editorial: 601 E San Ysidro Blvd Ste 180, San Ysidro, California 92173-3132 **Tel:** 1 619 428-2277
Email: ahoranow2008@hotmail.com
Freq: Thu; **Circ:** 10000 Not Audited
Publisher & Editor: Bertha Gonzalez
Profile: Ahora Now is a weekly Spanish language newspaper serving residents in San Diego. It covers local news, arts & entertainment, health and general topics of interest to the Hispanic community.
Language (s): Spanish
Ad Rate: Full Page Mono 18.00
Currency: United States Dollars
COMMUNITY NEWSPAPER

Ahora si!
310250
Owner: Cox Media Group Inc.
Editorial: 305 S Congress Ave, Austin, Texas 78704-1200 **Tel:** 1 512 445-3637
Email: events@ahorasi.com **Web site:** http://www.ahorasi.com
Freq: Thu; **Circ:** 25000 Not Audited
Editor: Josefina Villicana Casati
Profile: Ahora si! is a Spanish newspaper written for the Spanish-speaking community and residents in central Texas.
Language (s): Spanish
Ad Rate: Full Page Mono 21.30
Currency: United States Dollars
COMMUNITY NEWSPAPER

Ahwatukee Foothills News
21429
Owner: 10/13 Communications
Editorial: 1620 W Fountainhead Pkwy Ste 219, Tempe, Arizona 85282-1848 **Tel:** 1 480 898-7900
Email: afnnews@aztrib.com **Web site:** http://www.ahwatukee.com
Freq: 3 Times/Week; **Circ:** 28000 Not Audited
Profile: Ahwatukee Foothills News twice weekly community newspaper geared toward the residents of the Ahwatukee Foothills in Arizona. Coverage includes community politics, crime, education, sports, travel, arts & entertainment and special interest stories.
Language (s): English
Ad Rate: Full Page Mono 19.00
Currency: United States Dollars
COMMUNITY NEWSPAPER

Al Dia
153768
Owner: A.H. Belo Corp.
Editorial: 508 Young St Fl 2, Dallas, Texas 75202-4808 **Tel:** 1 469 -977-3740
Web site: http://www.aldiadallas.com/
Freq: Sat; **Circ:** 99676
Local News Editor: Julian Resendiz
Profile: Al Dia is a Spanish language newspaper serving the residents of Dallas.
Language (s): English
Ad Rate: Full Page Mono 65.00
Ad Rate: Full Page Colour 500.00
Currency: United States Dollars
COMMUNITY NEWSPAPER

Al Dia en América
520122
Owner: Donis (Jose Neil)
Editorial: 2210 Goldsmith Ln, Louisville, Kentucky 40218-1038 **Tel:** 1 502 451-8489
Email: news@aldiaenamerica.com **Web site:** http://www.aldiaenamerica.com
Freq: Bi-Weekly; **Circ:** 65000 Not Audited
Profile: Al Dia en America is a bi-weekly newspaper written for Latin Americans in Louisville, KY, and the surrounding areas. Contact them via e-mail.
Language (s): Spanish
Ad Rate: Full Page Mono 5.50
Currency: United States Dollars
COMMUNITY NEWSPAPER

Al Día News
22715
Owner: Al Dia Newspaper Inc.
Editorial: 1835 Market St Ste 450, Philadelphia, Pennsylvania 19103-2939 **Tel:** 1 215 569-4666
Email: editor@aldianews.com **Web site:** http://aldianews.com
Freq: Sun; **Circ:** 62000 Not Audited
Advertising Sales Manager: Mergie Castro; **Publisher & Editor:** Hernan Guaracao
Profile: Al Dia is weekly published Spanish-language newspaper that features news for the Hispanic/Latino community of Philadelphia, it promotes American journalism on Hispanic/Latino issues.
Language (s): English, Spanish
Ad Rate: Full Page Mono 56.00
Ad Rate: Full Page Colour 3820.00
Currency: United States Dollars
COMMUNITY NEWSPAPER

Alameda Sun
491561
Owner: Steller Media Group
Editorial: 3215 Encinal Ave Ste J, Alameda, California 94501-4882 **Tel:** 1 510 263-1470
Email: editor@alamedasun.com **Web site:** http://www.alamedasun.com
Freq: Thu; **Circ:** 23000 Not Audited
Profile: Alameda Sun is a community newspaper written for the residents of Alameda, CA. It covers local news, sports, events, features, business, politics and education.
Language (s): English
Ad Rate: Full Page Mono 22.00
Currency: United States Dollars
COMMUNITY NEWSPAPER

Alaska Post
22354
Owner: U.S. Army Garrison Fort Wainwright
Tel: 1 907 353-6701
Email: usarmy.wainwright.imcom-pacific.list.pao@mail.mil **Web site:** https://www.dvidshub.net/publication/561/alaska-post
Freq: Fri; **Circ:** 10000 Not Audited
Profile: Alaska Post is a military newspaper for the Fort Wainwright Air Force Base, AK. The publication is written for military personnel, retired military and their family members. The deadline for the newspaper is Tuesdays at noon PT.
Language (s): English
Ad Rate: Full Page Mono 9.90
Ad Rate: Full Page Colour 1200.00
Currency: United States Dollars
COMMUNITY NEWSPAPER

Alaska Star
18473
Owner: GateHouse Media Inc.
Editorial: 11401 Old Glenn Hwy Ste 105, Eagle River, Alaska 99577-7747 **Tel:** 1 907 694-2727
Email: editor@alaskastar.com **Web site:** http://www.alaskastar.com
Freq: Thu; **Circ:** 8500 Not Audited
Profile: Alaska Star is a weekly newspaper distributed throughout Anchorage, Eagle River, and the Mat-Su Valley, AK. According to the publisher, "one fifth of our readers in Anchorage and a fourth of our readers in Eagle River do not read a daily newspaper, but rely on The Star as their sole source of information for local news. The Star is known for its fair and accurate coverage of local news - with an emphasis on the community, not the same news you'll find on the wire services. We take a moderate to conservative editorial position and a positive approach to news coverage."
Language (s): English
Ad Rate: Full Page Mono 18.80
Currency: United States Dollars
COMMUNITY NEWSPAPER

Alexandria Times
375949
Owner: Alex Times LLC
Editorial: 110 S Pitt St Ste 200, Alexandria, Virginia 22314-3126 **Tel:** 1 703 739-0001
Web site: http://www.alextimes.com
Freq: Thu; **Circ:** 19311 Not Audited
Circulation Manager: Pat Booth; **Publisher:** Denise Dunbar
Profile: Alexandria Times is a free, weekly newspaper serving residents of Alexandria, VA. It strives to be an alternative voice of news and information, which focuses on local government, politics, business, sports, culture, arts, lifestyle, entertainment and social issues of particular interest to the local community.
Language (s): English
Ad Rate: Full Page Mono 24.87
Currency: United States Dollars
COMMUNITY NEWSPAPER

Algemeiner Journal
22031
Owner: Gershon Jacobson Foundation
Editorial: 508 Montgomery St, Brooklyn, New York 11225-3023 **Tel:** 1 212 376-4988
Email: editor@algemeiner.com **Web site:** http://www.algemeiner.com

Freq: Fri; **Circ:** 25000 Not Audited
Publisher: Simon Jacobson
Profile: The Algemeiner provides readers with news and commentary from Israel, the Middle East and other Jewish communities around the world.
Language (s): English
Ad Rate: Full Page Mono 15.71
Currency: United States Dollars
COMMUNITY NEWSPAPER

Alianza Metropolitan News 23266
Owner: Alianza Media Group
Editorial: 1090 Lincoln Ave Ste 8, San Jose, California 95125-3156
Email: info@alianzamediagroup.com **Web site:** http://www.alianzanews.com
Freq: Bi-Weekly; **Circ:** 40000 Not Audited
Publisher: Rossana Drumond; **Editor:** Gerardo Fernández
Profile: Alianza Metropolitan News is a weekly newspaper published for the Hispanic community in San Francisco and San Jose, CA. The editorial content covers business-related information, classifieds, entertainment news, events, food, Hispanic issues, travel, local issues, politics, sports, and information for women and youth.
Language (s): Spanish/Bilingual
Ad Rate: Full Page Mono 24.50
Currency: United States Dollars
COMMUNITY NEWSPAPER

Allied News 20563
Owner: Community Newspaper Holdings Inc.
Editorial: 201 Erie St Ste A, Grove City, Pennsylvania 16127-1659 **Tel:** 1 724 458-5010
Email: alliednewspaper@gmail.com **Web site:** http://alliednews.com
Freq: Sat; **Circ:** 15000 Not Audited
Editor: Kim Curry; **Publisher:** Sharon Sorg; **Circulation Manager:** Devon Stout
Profile: Allied News is written for residents in the Grove City, PA area. It focuses on news that affects county residents, including business and educational news, sports, entertainment and life-event news.
Language (s): English
Ad Rate: Full Page Mono 16.91
Ad Rate: Full Page Colour 1854.00
Currency: United States Dollars
COMMUNITY NEWSPAPER

The Almanac 22735
Owner: Embarcadero Publishing Co.
Editorial: 3525 Alameda De Las Pulgas, Menlo Park, California 94025-6544 **Tel:** 1 650 854-2626
Email: editor@almanacnews.com **Web site:** http://www.almanacnews.com
Freq: Wed; **Circ:** 18000 Not Audited
News Editor: Renee Batti; **Editor:** Richard Hine
Profile: The Almanac is published weekly for the San Francisco peninsula communities of Menlo Park, Atherton, Portola Valley, Woodside, Ladera, Los Trancos Woods, Sharon Heights, Stanford Hills and southern San Mateo County, CA. The newspaper covers local news, sports, lifestyle, business, arts & entertainment and community events. The news deadline falls on Thursday, the week prior to publication.
Language (s): English
Ad Rate: Full Page Mono 21.00
Ad Rate: Full Page Colour 400.00
Currency: United States Dollars
COMMUNITY NEWSPAPER

The Almanac 22890
Owner: Observer Publishing Company
Editorial: 2600 Boyce Plaza Rd Ste 142, Pittsburgh, Pennsylvania 15241-3949 **Tel:** 1 724 941-7725
Email: aanews@thealmanac.net **Web site:** http://www.thealmanac.net
Freq: Wed; **Circ:** 50000 Not Audited
Profile: The Almanac is published weekly for the residents of Washington County, PA. The newspaper covers local news, sports, education, crime and community events. News deadlines are on Fridays at 5pm ET.
Language (s): English
Ad Rate: Full Page Mono 33.06
Currency: United States Dollars
COMMUNITY NEWSPAPER

Alpine Avalanche 22690
Owner: Granite Publications
Editorial: 118 N 5th St, Alpine, Texas 79830-4602 **Tel:** 1 432 837-3334
Email: publisher@alpineavalanche.com **Web site:** http://www.alpineavalanche.com
Freq: Weekly; **Circ:** 5000 Not Audited
Profile: The Alpine Avalanche has served Alpine, TX and the entire Big Bend, TX region since 1891. The Avalanche focuses on local news and local sports. The Avalanche is published each Thursday morning. It is a member of the Granite Publications family of newspapers.
Language (s): English
Ad Rate: Full Page Mono 7.75
Ad Rate: Full Page Colour 9.42
Currency: United States Dollars
COMMUNITY NEWSPAPER

Altamont Enterprise & Albany County Post 20244
Owner: Gardner (James E.)
Editorial: 123 Maple Ave, Altamont, New York 12009-7719 **Tel:** 1 518 861-4026
Email: info@altamontenterprise.com **Web site:** http://www.altamontenterprise.com
Freq: Thu; **Circ:** 5000 Not Audited
Circulation Manager: Ellen Schreibstein
Profile: Altamont Enterprise & Albany County Post, better known as the Altamont Enterprise, is a local news weekly for Albany County, NY. Topics covered include local news, planning, zoning, schools, and features in the following towns: Guilderland, New Scotland, Berne, Know, Westerlo, and Rensselerville.
Language (s): English
Ad Rate: Full Page Mono 12.10
Ad Rate: Full Page Colour 1084.00
Currency: United States Dollars
COMMUNITY NEWSPAPER

Altavista Journal 21042
Owner: Womack Newspapers Inc.
Editorial: 701 5th St, Altavista, Virginia 24517-1719 **Tel:** 1 434 369-6688
Email: aljournal@altavistajournal.com **Web site:** http://www.altavistajournal.com
Freq: Wed; **Circ:** 6400 Not Audited
Publisher: Chad Harrison
Profile: Altavista Journal is published weekly for the residents of Altavista, VA. The newspaper provides information about local news, people and community events.
Language (s): English
Ad Rate: Full Page Mono 10.25
Currency: United States Dollars
COMMUNITY NEWSPAPER

Altoona Herald-Mitchellville Index 18864
Owner: Des Moines Register & Tribune Inc.
Editorial: 400 Locust St Ste 500, Des Moines, Iowa 50309-2355 **Tel:** 1 515 699-7000
Web site: http://www.desmoinesregister.com/communities/altoona/
Freq: Wed; **Circ:** 5300 Not Audited
Editor: Adam Wilson
Profile: Altoona Herald-Mitchellville Index is a weekly, local newspaper based in Des Moines, IA that serves the communities of Altoona and Mitchellville, IA. Deadlines are on Fridays at 3pm CT.
Language (s): English
Ad Rate: Full Page Mono 10.50
Currency: United States Dollars
COMMUNITY NEWSPAPER

Al-Watan 87222
Editorial: 800 S Brookhurst St Ste 3G, Anaheim, California 92804-4301 **Tel:** 1 714 726-6026
Email: editor@watan.com **Web site:** http://www.watan.com
Freq: Fri; **Circ:** 35000 Not Audited
Publisher & Editor: Inam Gundy
Language (s): Arabic
Ad Rate: Full Page Mono 35.00
Currency: United States Dollars
COMMUNITY NEWSPAPER

The Amelia Bulletin Monitor 21667
Owner: ABM Enterprises, Inc.
Editorial: 16311 Goodes Bridge Rd, Amelia Court House, Virginia 23002 **Tel:** 1 804 561-3655
Email: contactus@ameliamonitor.com **Web site:** http://www.ameliamonitor.com
Freq: Thu; **Circ:** 10500 Not Audited
Editor: Wayne Russell; **Publisher:** Ann Salster; **Advertising Sales Manager:** Beverly Thompson
Profile: The Amelia Bulletin Monitor is a weekly newspaper which covers local news and events occurring in the Amelia County area. The newspaper has been serving the citizens of Amelia County and surrounding areas since 1973 with news, commentary and advertising.
Language (s): English
Ad Rate: Full Page Mono 8.25
Currency: United States Dollars
COMMUNITY NEWSPAPER

America Oggi 23155
Owner: Gruppo Editoriale Oggi, Inc.
Editorial: 475 Walnut St, Norwood, New Jersey 07648-1318 **Tel:** 1 201 358-6692
Email: americoggi@aol.com **Web site:** http://www.americaoggi.info
Freq: Daily; **Circ:** 40000 Not Audited
International News Editor: Antonio Cirino; **Circulation Manager:** Domenico Delli Carpini; **Publisher & Editor:** Andrea Mantineo; **Advertising Sales Manager:** Maria Suriano
Profile: America Oggi is a daily newspaper published for Italian communities in the tri-state area around New York City. The publication covers state and national news, entertainment, features and sports. It does not cover local news.
Language (s): Italian
Ad Rate: Full Page Mono 25.00
Currency: United States Dollars
COMMUNITY NEWSPAPER

American Canyon Eagle 483134
Owner: Lee Enterprises/Napa Valley Publishing
Editorial: 1615 Soscol Ave, Napa, California 94559-1901 **Tel:** 1 707 256-2269
Email: editor@americancanyoneagle.com **Web site:** http://napavalleyregister.com/eagle
Freq: Weekly
Editor: Noel Brinkerhoff; **Publisher:** Brenda Speth
Profile: American Canyon Eagle is a weekly newspaper serving residents of American Canyon, CA.
Language (s): English
COMMUNITY NEWSPAPER

American Free Press 76040
Editorial: 645 Pennsylvania Ave SE Ste 100, Washington, District Of Columbia 20003-4379 **Tel:** 1 202 544-5977
Email: editor@americanfreepress.net **Web site:** http://www.americanfreepress.net
Freq: Mon; **Circ:** 39000 Not Audited
Advertising Sales Manager: Sharon Elsworth
Profile: American Free Press is a weekly community newspaper written for residents of Washington, D.C. It covers local and national news. Contact the newspaper via online form.
Language (s): English
Ad Rate: Full Page Mono 17.84
Currency: United States Dollars
COMMUNITY NEWSPAPER

The American Israelite 24437
Owner: Deutsch (Netanel)
Editorial: 18 W 9th St Ste 2, Cincinnati, Ohio 45202-2037 **Tel:** 1 513 621-3145
Web site: http://www.americanisraelite.com
Freq: Thu; **Circ:** 6000 Not Audited
Editor & Publisher: Netanel Deutsch
Profile: The American Israelite is written for Jewish residents in Cincinnati. It focuses on local news and community events.
Language (s): English
Ad Rate: Full Page Mono 26.00
Currency: United States Dollars
COMMUNITY NEWSPAPER

The American Jewish World 63326
Owner: Mordecai Specktor
Editorial: 4820 Minnetonka Blvd Ste 104, Minneapolis, Minnesota 55416-2278 **Tel:** 1 952 920-6205
Email: news@ajwnews.com **Web site:** http://www.ajwnews.com
Freq: Bi-Weekly; **Circ:** 5000 Not Audited
Circulation Manager: Lori Bieds; **Editor and Publisher:** Mordecai Specktor
Profile: American Jewish World is a weekly community newspaper written for Jewish residents of St. Paul, Minneapolis, Duluth and Rochester, MN.
Language (s): English
Ad Rate: Full Page Mono 12.00
Currency: United States Dollars
COMMUNITY NEWSPAPER

Americus Times-Recorder 13836
Owner: Community Newspaper Holdings, Inc.
Editorial: 101 GA-27, Americus, Georgia 31709-3500 **Tel:** 1 229 924-2751
Email: news@americustimesrecorder.com **Web site:** http://americustimesrecorder.com
Circ: 5800
Profile: Americus Times-Recorder is a daily local newspaper in South Georgia. It covers local news, sports, classifieds, business, politics, entertainment and obituaries.
Language (s): English
Ad Rate: Full Page Mono 21.55
Ad Rate: Full Page Colour 514.80
Currency: United States Dollars
COMMUNITY NEWSPAPER

Amerika Woche 772164
Owner: ONA Publishing Corp.
Tel: 1 516 771-3181
Email: info@amerikawoche.com **Web site:** http://www.amerikawoche.com
Freq: Bi-Weekly; **Circ:** 27000
Publisher & Editor: Peter Lobl; **Advertising Sales Manager:** Alyson McLean
Profile: Amerika Woche is the oldest and largest German-American newspaper. It was established in 1859. It is a bi-weekly newspaper for the residents of Gladwyne, PA.
Ad Rate: Full Page Mono 2895.00
Ad Rate: Full Page Colour 3290.00
Currency: United States Dollars
COMMUNITY NEWSPAPER

Amery Free Press 21144
Owner: Sentinel Publications LLC
Editorial: 215 Keller Ave S, Amery, Wisconsin 54001-1275 **Tel:** 1 715 268-8101
Email: editor@theameryfreepress.com **Web site:** http://www.theameryfreepress.com/
Freq: Tue; **Circ:** 5000 Not Audited
Circulation Manager: Diane Stangl; **Editor & Publisher:** Tom Stangl
Profile: Community newspaper written for the residents of Amery, WI. The paper covers local news, sports, arts and entertainment, lifestyle, business and community issues and events.
Language (s): English
Ad Rate: Full Page Mono 7.25
Currency: United States Dollars
COMMUNITY NEWSPAPER

Amherst Bulletin 22076
Owner: Newspapers of New England
Editorial: 115 Conz St, Northampton, Massachusetts 01060-4444 **Tel:** 1 413 584-5000
Email: amherst@gazettenet.com **Web site:** http://www.amherstbulletin.com/
Freq: Fri; **Circ:** 14000 Not Audited
Editor: Larry Parnass; **Advertising Manager:** Jonathan Stafford
Profile: Amherst Bulletin is a weekly newspaper which brings readers in the Amherst, MA area local and national news. Other features include editorials, letters to the editor, classifieds, real estate, employment opportunities and community events. Do not send ANY information via fax. Deadlines are Monday morning.
Language (s): English
Ad Rate: Full Page Mono 16.61
Currency: United States Dollars
COMMUNITY NEWSPAPER

The Amherst Citizen 23120
Editorial: 16 Pine Acres Rd, Amherst, New Hampshire 3031 **Tel:** 1 603 672-9444
Email: news@amherstcitizen.com **Web site:** http://www.amherstcitizen.com
Freq: Bi-Weekly; **Circ:** 6200 Not Audited
Editor: Cliff Ann Wales
Profile: The Amherst Citizen is published for the residents of Amherst, NH and surrounding areas. The newspaper is released bi-weekly on the second and fourth Tuesdays from September to June and monthly on the last Tuesdays of July and August.
Language (s): English
Ad Rate: Full Page Mono 12.95
Currency: United States Dollars
COMMUNITY NEWSPAPER

The Anchor 21509
Owner: Diocese of Fall River
Editorial: 887 Highland Ave, Fall River, Massachusetts 02720-3820 **Tel:** 1 508 675-7151
Email: theanchor@anchornews.org **Web site:** http://www.anchornews.org
Freq: Fri; **Circ:** 28000 Not Audited
Editor: Dave Jolivet; **Advertising Sales Manager:** Wayne Powers
Profile: The Anchor is a weekly community newspaper serving the Catholic residents of Fall River, MA and surrounding areas.
Language (s): English
Ad Rate: Full Page Mono 17.50
Currency: United States Dollars
COMMUNITY NEWSPAPER

The Anchorage Press 80387
Owner: Wick Communications Inc.
Editorial: 540 E 5th Ave, Anchorage, Alaska 99501-2636 **Tel:** 1 907 561-7737
Email: contact@anchoragepress.com **Web site:** http://www.anchoragepress.com
Freq: Thu; **Circ:** 20000 Not Audited
Editor: Victoria Barber; **Advertising Sales Manager:** Bridget Mackey
Profile: The Anchorage Press is a weekly newspaper written for residents of Anchorage, AK.
Language (s): English
Ad Rate: Full Page Mono 22.00
Currency: United States Dollars
COMMUNITY NEWSPAPER

The Anderson News 19352
Owner: Landmark Community Newspapers Inc.
Editorial: 504 W Broadway St Ste D, Lawrenceburg, Kentucky 40342-1541 **Tel:** 1 502 839-6906
Email: news@theandersonnews.com **Web site:** http://www.theandersonnews.com
Freq: Wed; **Circ:** 5700 Not Audited
Publisher & Editor: Ben Carlson
Profile: The Anderson News is published weekly for the residents of Anderson County, KY. Coverage includes local news, sports, community events and arts & entertainment. Press releases should be submitted at least one week prior to publication. Deadlines are on Mondays at noon ET.
Language (s): English
Ad Rate: Full Page Mono 10.33
Currency: United States Dollars
COMMUNITY NEWSPAPER

Andover Townsman 217290
Owner: Community Newspaper Holdings, Inc.
Editorial: 33 Chestnut St, Andover, Massachusetts 01810-3623 **Tel:** 1 978 475-7000
Email: townsman@andovertownsman.com **Web site:** http://www.andovertownsman.com
Freq: Thu; **Circ:** 8750 Not Audited
Editor: Sonya Vartabedian
Profile: The Andover Townsman is a weekly newspaper established in 1887 and is published every Thursday. It covers local news and happenings in and around Andover, MA. Other features include: education, editorials, arts and entertainment, local high school sports, and obituaries. The deadline is Monday at 5:00 p.m. ET before publication date. Contact the publication for advertising information.
Language (s): English
Ad Rate: Full Page Mono 22.45
Currency: United States Dollars
COMMUNITY NEWSPAPER

Ankeny Register & Press-Citizen 18867
Owner: Gannett Co. Inc.
Editorial: 400 Locust St Ste 500, Des Moines, Iowa 50309-2355 **Tel:** 1 515 284-8000
Email: community@dmreg.com **Web site:** http://www.desmoinesregister.com/communities/ankeny
Freq: Tue; **Circ:** 22000 Not Audited
Profile: Ankeny Register & Press-Citizen is a free, weekly newspaper serving the residents of Ankeny, IA. Coverage includes local news, sports, community events and arts & entertainment. The news and advertising deadlines fall on Thursdays at noon CT.
Language (s): English
Ad Rate: Full Page Mono 11.20
Currency: United States Dollars
COMMUNITY NEWSPAPER

United States of America

The Ann Arbor News 594823
Owner: MLive Media Group
Editorial: 111 N Ashley St Ste 100, Ann Arbor, Michigan 48104-1307 **Tel:** 1 734 222-0071
Email: news@annarbor.com **Web site:** http://www.mlive.com/annarbor
Freq: 2 Times/Week; **Circ:** 25396
Editor: Paula Gardner
Profile: Ann Arbor News was established in July 2009 for residents and visitors of Ann Arbor, Mich., and features news and information from the area. Editorial content focuses on government, education, crime, business, health care, the environment and more. Part of MLive Media Group.
Language (s): English
COMMUNITY NEWSPAPER

Anna Maria Island Sun 70939
Editorial: 9801 Gulf Dr Ste 6, Anna Maria, Florida 34216 **Tel:** 1 941 778-3986
Email: news@amisun.com **Web site:** http://www.amisun.com
Freq: Wed; **Circ:** 15000 Not Audited
Circulation Manager: Bob Alexander; **Advertising Sales Manager:** Changelle Lewin
Profile: Anna Maria Island Sun is published weekly for the residents of Anna Maria, FL. Coverage includes local news, business news, sports and community events. The news deadline falls on Wednesdays.
Language (s): English
Ad Rate: Full Page Mono 10.90
Currency: United States Dollars
COMMUNITY NEWSPAPER

Apache Junction Gold Canyon News 24419
Owner: Foothills Publishing
Editorial: 1075 S Idaho Rd Ste 102, Apache Junction, Arizona 85119-6497 **Tel:** 1 480 982-6397
Email: ajnews@ajnews.com **Web site:** http://www.ajnews.com
Freq: Mon; **Circ:** 24500 Not Audited
Profile: Apache Junction News is published weekly for the residents of Apache Junction, AZ. Coverage includes local news, sports, arts & entertainment and community events. Deadlines are on Thursdays at 5pm MT.
Language (s): English
Ad Rate: Full Page Mono 20.60
Currency: United States Dollars
COMMUNITY NEWSPAPER

APG News 27143
Owner: Homestead Publishing
Editorial: US Army Garrison APG, Attn: APG News-Bldg 2201, Aberdeen Proving Ground, Maryland 21005-5001 **Tel:** 1 410 278-1150
Web site: https://www.apg.army.mil/APGNews
Freq: Thu; **Circ:** 8900 Not Audited
Editor: Pat Beauchamp; **Editor:** Amanda Rominiecki
Profile: APG News is published weekly for the members of the military and civilians living and working at Aberdeen Proving Ground, MD. Articles cover topics such as general military issues, community events, local news, members of the community and local sports. A community calendar of events is also included. Press releases are accepted, however they must be directly related to the military.
Language (s): English
Ad Rate: Full Page Mono 9.07
Currency: United States Dollars
COMMUNITY NEWSPAPER

Apna Roots 527710
Editorial: 12414 82 Ave Unit 104, Surrey, British Columbia V3W 3E9 **Tel:** 1 604 599-5021
Email: staff@apnaroots.com **Web site:** http://www.apnaroots.com
Freq: Bi-Weekly; **Circ:** 100000
Profile: This biweekly paper features local news geared toward the Indo-Canadian and South Asian community.
Ad Rate: Full Page Mono 34.67
Ad Rate: Full Page Colour 49.27
Currency: Canada Dollars
COMMUNITY NEWSPAPER

Appalachian News-Express 397092
Owner: Lancaster (Charles)
Editorial: 129 Caroline Ave, Pikeville, Kentucky 41501-1101 **Tel:** 1 606 437-4054
Email: editor@news-expressky.com **Web site:** http://www.news-expressky.com
Freq: Fri; **Circ:** 9000
Editor: Russ Cassady; **Circulation Manager:** Lisa Moore; **Publisher:** Jeff Vanderbeck
Profile: Appalachian News-Express in Pikeville, KY is a local newspaper serving residents of eastern Kentucky. It covers news, sports, editorials, businesses, events and features of interest to residents of eastern Kentucky.
Language (s): English
Ad Rate: Full Page Mono 9.95
Currency: United States Dollars
COMMUNITY NEWSPAPER

The Arab American News 78573
Editorial: 5706 Chase Rd, Dearborn, Michigan 48126-2102 **Tel:** 1 313 582-4888
Email: info@arabamericannews.com **Web site:** http://www.arabamericannews.com
Freq: Sat; **Circ:** 35000 Not Audited

Profile: Bilingual Arab and English newspaper offering an Arab perspective on American, Arab and international news.
Language (s): Arabic
Ad Rate: Full Page Mono 24.38
Currency: United States Dollars
COMMUNITY NEWSPAPER

Arab Tribune 18481
Editorial: 619 S Brindlee Mountain Pkwy, Arab, Alabama 35016-1502 **Tel:** 1 256 586-3188
Email: tribnews@otelco.net **Web site:** http://www.thearabtribune.com
Freq: Sat; **Circ:** 6500 Not Audited
Advertising Sales Manager: Janet Calhoun; **Publisher:** Ed Reed; **Editor:** Charles Whisenant
Profile: Arab Tribune is a twice weekly community newspapers serving the residents of Arab, AL.
Language (s): English
Ad Rate: Full Page Mono 9.15
Currency: United States Dollars
COMMUNITY NEWSPAPER

Arab Voice 87242
Owner: Arab Voice Inc.
Editorial: 85-99 Hazel St, Paterson, New Jersey 07503-2462 **Tel:** 1 973 523-7815
Web site: http://www.arabvoice.com
Freq: Sat; **Circ:** 35000 Not Audited
Advertising Sales Manager: Nadil Rabah; **Publisher & Editor:** Walid Rabah
Profile: Arab Voice in Paterson, NJ, is a weekly newspaper that serves Arab-Americans in five states.
Language (s): English
Ad Rate: Full Page Mono 9.00
Currency: United States Dollars
COMMUNITY NEWSPAPER

The Arab World 87238
Owner: Alam (Ahmad)
Editorial: 512 S Brookhurst St Ste 4, Anaheim, California 92804-2448 **Tel:** 1 714 758-3507
Email: lanamanale@aol.com **Web site:** http://www.arabworldnewspaper.com
Freq: Fri; **Circ:** 45000 Not Audited
Editor: Riad Saeid
Profile: The Arab World in Anaheim, CA is a weekly newspaper written for Arabic-speaking residents and covers local news and events.
Language (s): Arabic
Ad Rate: Full Page Mono 10.00
Currency: United States Dollars
COMMUNITY NEWSPAPER

Arcade Herald 20245
Owner: Neighbor to Neighbor News, Inc.
Editorial: 223 Main St, Arcade, New York 14009-1209 **Tel:** 1 716 496-5013
Email: heraldnews@roadrunner.com **Web site:** http://www.arcadeherald.com
Freq: Thu; **Circ:** 5000 Not Audited
Advertising Sales Manager: Cyndi Gradl; **Publisher:** Grant Hamilton
Profile: Arcade Herald is a weekly newspaper written for residents of Arcade, NY and the surrounding area. The newspaper covers information on local news and community events. Editorial deadlines are on Mondays at 5pm ET.
Language (s): English
Ad Rate: Full Page Mono 13.95
Currency: United States Dollars
COMMUNITY NEWSPAPER

Arctic Warrior 789210
Editorial: 10480 22nd St, Elmendorf AFB, Alaska 99506-2501 **Tel:** 1 907 552-8918
Email: arctic.warrior@gmail.com **Web site:** http://www.arcticwarrior.net
Freq: Weekly
Profile: Weekly paper printed in the interest of families within Joint Base Elmendorf-Richardson (JBER) community near Anchorage, Alaska.
Language (s): English
Ad Rate: Full Page Mono 17.00
Currency: United States Dollars
COMMUNITY NEWSPAPER

The Argonaut 18663
Owner: Southland Publishing, Inc.
Editorial: 5301 Beethoven St Ste 183, Los Angeles, California 90066-7066 **Tel:** 1 310 822-1629
Web site: http://www.argonautnews.com
Freq: Thu; **Circ:** 30000 Not Audited
Publisher: David Comden; **Editor:** Joe Piasecki
Profile: The Argonaut is published weekly for residents of Marina del Rey, Playa del Rey, Westchester, Venice and Santa Monica, CA. The newspaper covers local news, weather, sports and community events. Feature articles cover business, education, arts & entertainment and lifestyle.
Language (s): English
Ad Rate: Full Page Mono 26.25
Currency: United States Dollars
COMMUNITY NEWSPAPER

Arizona Hispana 822978
Editorial: 2334 S 4th Ave, Tucson, Arizona 85713-3515 **Tel:** 1 520 770-9261
Email: contacto@arizonahispana.com **Web site:** http://www.arizonahispana.com
Freq: Bi-Weekly
Publisher & Editor: Francisco Rojas
Profile: Arizona Hispana is a bi-weekly newspaper providing Local and Community News coverage for the Hispanic community in Tucson, AZ.
Language (s): English
COMMUNITY NEWSPAPER

Arizona Informant 18598
Editorial: 1301 E Washington St Ste 101, Phoenix, Arizona 85034-1173 **Tel:** 1 602 257-9300
Web site: http://azinformant.com
Freq: Wed; **Circ:** 15000 Not Audited
Profile: Arizona Informant is a weekly African American newspaper for Arizona residents. Deadlines are on Fridays.
Language (s): English
Ad Rate: Full Page Mono 45.83
Currency: United States Dollars
COMMUNITY NEWSPAPER

Arizona Jewish Post 22488
Owner: Jewish Federation of Southern Arizona
Editorial: 3822 E River Rd Ste 300, Tucson, Arizona 85718-6635 **Tel:** 1 520 319-1112
Email: localnews@azjewishpost.com **Web site:** http://www.azjewishpost.com
Freq: Bi-Weekly; **Circ:** 5600 Not Audited
Profile: Arizona Jewish Post is a biweekly newspaper for the Jewish community of Arizona. It provides the community with information on local, national and international news of Jewish importance. Lead times vary depending on the editorial material. Contact the editor with any further inquiries.
Language (s): English
Ad Rate: Full Page Mono 23.00
Currency: United States Dollars
COMMUNITY NEWSPAPER

Arkansas Catholic 21922
Owner: Diocese of Little Rock
Editorial: 2500 N Tyler St, Little Rock, Arkansas 72207-3743 **Tel:** 1 501 664-0125
Web site: http://www.arkansas-catholic.org
Freq: Sat; **Circ:** 7400 Not Audited
Editor: Malea Hargett; **Circulation Manager:** Rose Harrigan; **Publisher:** Anthony Taylor
Profile: Arkansas Catholic is the official newspaper of the Diocese of Little Rock. The publication is written for Catholics in Little Rock, AR, containing news about religious events in the diocese. The paper also contains national and international news about Catholic communities elsewhere in the world. Any PR materials must directly pertain to the Diocese of Little Rock or to Catholic communities. There also is a Spanish edition of the paper, Arkansas Catholic en Espanol.
Language (s): English
Ad Rate: Full Page Mono 17.00
Currency: United States Dollars
COMMUNITY NEWSPAPER

Arkansas Times 1809
Owner: Arkansas Writers Project, Inc.
Editorial: 201 E Markham St Ste 200, Little Rock, Arkansas 72201-1696 **Tel:** 1 501 375-2985
Web site: http://www.arktimes.com
Freq: Weekly; **Circ:** 32724 Not Audited
Publisher: Alan Leveritt; **Editor:** Lindsey Millar
Profile: Profiles the business, political and social culture in Arkansas. Devoted to recreation and entertainment guides to Arkansas, and its customs, politics, people and lifestyles.
Language (s): English
Ad Rate: Full Page Mono 2615.00
Ad Rate: Full Page Colour 3035.00
Currency: United States Dollars
COMMUNITY NEWSPAPER

Arkansas Weekly 135418
Owner: W. R. D. Entertainment, Inc.
Editorial: 920 Harrison St Ste C, Batesville, Arkansas 72501-6949 **Tel:** 1 870 793-4196
Email: arwkly@swbell.net **Web site:** http://www.arkansasweekly.com
Freq: Wed; **Circ:** 21500 Not Audited
Advertising Sales Manager: Matt Johnson
Profile: Arkansas Weekly is a direct-mailed community newspaper written for the residents of Independence County, Newport and Cave City, AR, featuring community news, events and opinion.
Language (s): English
Ad Rate: Full Page Mono 8.95
Currency: United States Dollars
COMMUNITY NEWSPAPER

Arlington Catholic Herald 21910
Owner: Catholic Diocese of Arlington
Editorial: 200 N Glebe Rd Ste 600, Arlington, Virginia 22203-3763 **Tel:** 1 703 841-2590
Email: editorial@catholicherald.com **Web site:** http://www.catholicherald.com
Freq: Thu; **Circ:** 63000 Not Audited
Advertising Sales Manager: Carlos Salinas
Profile: Arlington Catholic Herald is written for Catholics in Arlington, VA.
Language (s): English
Ad Rate: Full Page Mono 31.50
Currency: United States Dollars
COMMUNITY NEWSPAPER

Armenian Observer 23317
Owner: Keshian (Osheen)
Editorial: 6646 Hollywood Blvd Ste 210, Hollywood, California 90028-6231 **Tel:** 1 323 467-6767
Email: okesh@aol.com **Web site:** http://www.thearmenianobserver.com
Freq: Wed; **Circ:** 5000 Not Audited
Publisher & Editor: Osheen Keshishian
Profile: Armenian Observer is a weekly newspaper written for the Armenian American residents of Hollywood, CA.
Language (s): English
Ad Rate: Full Page Mono 6.00
Ad Rate: Full Page Colour 200.00

Currency: United States Dollars
COMMUNITY NEWSPAPER

Army Flier 397553
Owner: Fort Rucker Army Aviation Center
Editorial: Fort Rucker Public Affairs Office, Building 131, Fort Rucker, Alabama 36362 **Tel:** 1 334 255-1239
Web site: http://www.dothaneagle.com/army_flier
Freq: Thu; **Circ:** 10000 Not Audited
Editor: Jim Hughes
Profile: Army Flier is a free, weekly newspaper serving the military personnel and residents of the U.S. Army's Aviation Training and Command Center in Fort Rucker, AL. It has an emphasis on local news, family activities, command news, Department of Defense news and social events. All editorial content is supplied by military personnel, while advertising is handled by the Dothan (AL) Eagle . Deadlines are at 5pm ET.
Language (s): English
Ad Rate: Full Page Mono 11.50
Currency: United States Dollars
COMMUNITY NEWSPAPER

Aroostook Republican & News 27299
Owner: Northeast Publishing Co.
Editorial: 92 Bennett Dr, Caribou, Maine 04736-1952 **Tel:** 1 207 496-3251
Email: republican@nepublish.com **Web site:** http://www.republican-me.com
Freq: Wed; **Circ:** 5000 Not Audited
Profile: Aroostook Republican & News is a local weekly newspaper serving the Caribou, ME area. It provides residents with information on local news and events. Deadlines for the publication are the Monday afternoon before issue date.
Language (s): English
Ad Rate: Full Page Mono 12.50
Currency: United States Dollars
COMMUNITY NEWSPAPER

Around Town 22630
Owner: Around Town Publications Inc.
Editorial: 1280 S Powerline Rd Ste 28, Pompano Beach, Florida 33069-4342 **Tel:** 1 954 971-8008
Email: editor@aroundtownnews.com **Web site:** http://www.aroundtownnews.com
Freq: Bi-Weekly; **Circ:** 22000 Not Audited
Publisher & Editor: Patrick Mascola
Profile: Around Town is a bi-weekly publication for residents of South Florida. The newspaper covers hospitality and social events.
Language (s): English
Ad Rate: Full Page Mono 23.50
Currency: United States Dollars
COMMUNITY NEWSPAPER

Arvin Tiller & Lamont Reporter Newspapers 153315
Owner: Reed, (Frank and Donald)
Editorial: 5409 Aldrin Ct, Bakersfield, California 93313-2104 **Tel:** 1 661 845-3704
Email: lamontreporter@earthlink.net
Freq: Wed; **Circ:** 8100 Not Audited
Editor: Michael Wafford
Profile: Arvin Tiller & Lamont Reporter Newspapers provides news to the community of Shafter, CA.
Language (s): English
COMMUNITY NEWSPAPER

Ashland City Times 24341
Owner: Gannett Co., Inc.
Editorial: 202 N Main St Ste A, Ashland City, Tennessee 37015-1318 **Tel:** 1 615 946-7549
Email: actimes@mtcngroup.com **Web site:** http://www.tennessean.com/counties/cheatham
Freq: Wed; **Circ:** 5900 Not Audited
Profile: Ashland City Times is a weekly newspaper serving residents of Cheatham County, TN. Its editorial mission is to keep the community informed of local events and news. Deadlines for the publication are Mondays at 11am ET before issue date.
Language (s): English
Ad Rate: Full Page Mono 8.77
Currency: United States Dollars
COMMUNITY NEWSPAPER

Asian American Press 128802
Editorial: 7124 90th Ave N, Brooklyn Park, Minnesota 55445-3227 **Tel:** 1 651 755-6864
Email: aanews@aapress.com **Web site:** http://aapress.com
Freq: Fri; **Circ:** 15000
Publisher & Editor: Nghi Huynh
Profile: Asian American Press is a weekly newspaper serving the Asian community of Minneapolis and St. Paul, MN.
Language (s): English
Ad Rate: Full Page Mono 32.00
Currency: United States Dollars
COMMUNITY NEWSPAPER

Asian American Times 150731
Owner: Fu (Tim)
Editorial: 2011 S Henkel, Mesa, Arizona 85202-6500 **Tel:** 1 480 839-5139
Email: news@asianamericantimes.us **Web site:** http://www.asianamericantimes.us
Freq: Weekly; **Circ:** 8000 Not Audited
News Editor: Pu Chen; **News Editor:** Quinney Fu; **News Editor:** Michelle Kim; **News Editor:** John Tang

Profile: Asian American Times is weekly community newspaper serving Asian American residents of Mesa, AZ.
Language (s): Chinese
Ad Rate: Full Page Mono 50.00
Currency: United States Dollars
COMMUNITY NEWSPAPER

The Asian Reporter 78576
Owner: Asian Reporter Publications, Inc.
Editorial: 922 N Killingsworth St, Portland, Oregon 97217-2261 **Tel:** 1 503 283-4440
Email: news@asianreporter.com **Web site:** http://www.asianreporter.com
Freq: Mon; **Circ:** 25000 Not Audited
Publisher: Jamie Lim; **Editor:** Jeff Wenger
Profile: The Asian Reporter is written for Asian-Americans living in Oregon. It covers international, national and local news and events with an Asian focus.
Language (s): English
Ad Rate: Full Page Mono 23.00
Ad Rate: Full Page Colour 1788.00
Currency: United States Dollars
COMMUNITY NEWSPAPER

Asian Times 258016
Owner: Le (Nhi)
Tel: 1 617 542-2244
Email: asiantimesboston@gmail.com
Freq: Fri; **Circ:** 30000
Publisher & Circulation Manager: Nan Le
Profile: Asian Times is written for the residents of Boston.
Language (s): English
Ad Rate: Full Page Mono 20.00
Currency: United States Dollars
COMMUNITY NEWSPAPER

Aspen Times Weekly 21545
Owner: Swift Newspapers
Editorial: 314 E Hyman Ave, Aspen, Colorado 81611-1918 **Tel:** 1 970 925-3414
Email: mail@aspentimes.com **Web site:** http://www.aspentimes.com
Freq: Sun; **Circ:** 7000 Not Audited
Profile: Aspen Times Weekly is a weekly newspaper for tourists and residents of the Aspen, CO area. It covers various events, activities and places to visit that are not covered in the Aspen Times. Deadlines for the publication are two to three days before issue date.
Language (s): English
Ad Rate: Full Page Mono 7.00
Ad Rate: Full Page Colour 240.00
Currency: United States Dollars
COMMUNITY NEWSPAPER

Atascadero News 18601
Owner: North County Newspapers
Editorial: 4401 El Camino Real Ste G, Atascadero, California 93422-2708 **Tel:** 1 805 466-2585
Email: news@atascaderonews.com **Web site:** http://www.atascaderonews.com
Freq: Fri; **Circ:** 5500 Not Audited
Profile: Atascadero News is written for the residents of Atascadero, CA and surrounding areas. It covers local news, sports, business and arts and entertainment issues that impact local residents.
Language (s): English
Ad Rate: Full Page Mono 8.80
Currency: United States Dollars
COMMUNITY NEWSPAPER

Athens News 21320
Owner: Adams Publishing Group LLC
Editorial: 14 N Court St, Athens, Ohio 45701-2429 **Tel:** 1 740 594-8219
Email: news@athensnews.com **Web site:** http://www.athensnews.com
Freq: Mon; **Circ:** 17500 Not Audited
Editor: Terry Smith
Profile: Athens News is a twice-weekly newspaper serving residents of Athens, OH. It covers news and events occurring in Athens, OH and at Ohio University. It is Athens County's only locally owned newspaper.
Language (s): English
Ad Rate: Full Page Mono 9.65
Currency: United States Dollars
COMMUNITY NEWSPAPER

Atlanta Chinese News 152787
Owner: Atlanta Chinese News Inc.
Tel: 1 770 455-0880
Email: info@atlantachinesenews.com **Web site:** http://www.atlantachinesenews.com
Freq: Fri; **Circ:** 10000 Not Audited
Publisher & Editor: Amy Sheu
Profile: Atlanta Chinese News is a local newspaper written for the Chinese community of Atlanta.
Language (s): Chinese
Ad Rate: Full Page Mono 7.32
Currency: United States Dollars
COMMUNITY NEWSPAPER

Atlanta Daily World 21956
Owner: Interactive One, LLC
Editorial: 875 Old Roswell Rd Ste C100, Roswell, Georgia 30076-1660 **Tel:** 1 770 587-0501
Web site: https://atlantadailyworld.com
Freq: Thu; **Circ:** 27000 Not Audited
Profile: Atlanta Daily World is a weekly newspaper for the African American residents of Atlanta.
Language (s): English
Ad Rate: Full Page Mono 47.00
Currency: United States Dollars
COMMUNITY NEWSPAPER

The Atlanta Inquirer 18848
Owner: Smith Sr. (John)
Editorial: 947 Martin Luther King Jr Dr NW, Atlanta, Georgia 30314-2947 **Tel:** 1 404 523-6086
Email: news@atlinq.com **Web site:** http://www.atlinq.com
Freq: Thu; **Circ:** 40000 Not Audited
Profile: The Atlanta Inquirer is a local newspaper written for the African-American community in Atlanta.
Language (s): English
Ad Rate: Full Page Mono 32.34
Ad Rate: Full Page Colour 3713.34
Currency: United States Dollars
COMMUNITY NEWSPAPER

Atlanta Jewish Times 18857
Owner: Zadok Publishing, LLC
Editorial: 270 Carpenter Dr Ste 320, Atlanta, Georgia 30328-4933 **Tel:** 1 404 883-2130
Web site: http://www.atlantajewishtimes.com
Freq: Fri; **Circ:** 15000
Profile: Atlanta Jewish Times is a local newspaper written for the Jewish community of Atlanta, GA. The paper covers a calendar of events, arts and entertainment and lifestyle features.
Language (s): English
Ad Rate: Full Page Mono 27.95
Currency: United States Dollars
COMMUNITY NEWSPAPER

The Atlanta Voice 18849
Owner: Janis Ware
Editorial: 633 Pryor St SW, Atlanta, Georgia 30312-2738 **Tel:** 1 404 524-6426
Email: info@theatlantavoice.com **Web site:** http://www.theatlantavoice.com
Freq: Fri; **Circ:** 54955 Not Audited
Publisher: Janis Ware; **Editor:** Stan Washington
Profile: Atlanta Voice, established in 1966, is a weekly newspaper designed to serve and salute the African American community throughout metro Atlanta. It covers local and national news, sports and entertainment.
Language (s): English
Ad Rate: Full Page Mono 68.43
Ad Rate: Full Page Colour 72.11
Currency: United States Dollars
COMMUNITY NEWSPAPER

Atwater Signal 383187
Editorial: 3033 G St, Merced, California 95340-2108
Tel: 1 209 722-1511
Web site: http://www.mercedsunstar.com/news/local/community/atwater
Freq: Sat; **Circ:** 10000
Profile: The Atwater Signal is a free weekly newspaper published for the residents of Atwater, CA. It is published from the offices of the Merced Sun-Star.
Language (s): English
Ad Rate: Full Page Mono 10.25
Currency: United States Dollars
COMMUNITY NEWSPAPER

The AUC Digest 389680
Editorial: 117 Vine St SW, Atlanta, Georgia 30314-4205 **Tel:** 1 404 523-6136
Email: aucdigestmail@aol.com
Freq: Mon; **Circ:** 25000 Not Audited
Publisher & Editor: Lo Jelks
Profile: The AUC Digest is a local newspaper that is distributed throughout the Atlanta University Center to students and faculty of Clark Atlanta University, Morehouse College, Morehouse School of Medicine, Morris Brown College, Spelman College and ITC, the Interdominational Theological Center.
Language (s): English
COMMUNITY NEWSPAPER

The Auglaize Merchandiser 26557
Owner: Horizon Publications
Editorial: 520 Industrial Dr, Wapakoneta, Ohio 45895-9200 **Tel:** 1 419 738-2128
Web site: http://www.wapakdailynews.com
Freq: Tue; **Circ:** 11200 Not Audited
Editor: William Laney
Profile: The Auglaize Merchandiser is a weekly newspaper written for the residents of Wapakoneta, OH. The paper covers news, social issues, business, sports and events in the local community.
Language (s): English
Ad Rate: Full Page Mono 6.15
Currency: United States Dollars
COMMUNITY NEWSPAPER

Austin Chronicle 21611
Owner: Austin Chronicle Corp.
Editorial: 4000 N Interstate 35, Austin, Texas 78751-4801 **Tel:** 1 512 454-5766
Email: newseditors@austinchronicle.com **Web site:** http://www.austinchronicle.com
Freq: Thu; **Circ:** 72505 Not Audited
Publisher: Nick Barbaro; **Editor:** Louis Black; **Circulation Manager:** Dan Hardick; **News Editor:** Michael King
Profile: Austin Chronicle is written for residents of Austin, TX. It covers political and environmental concerns, the local cultural scene and in-depth information on arts & entertainment, which includes venues, restaurants, recreational activities and outdoor excursions. Do NOT send pitches for alcohol & spirits, beer and wine to the food editor; direct those pitches to the appropriate writer.
Language (s): English
Ad Rate: Full Page Mono 5.00
Currency: United States Dollars
COMMUNITY NEWSPAPER

The Avenue News 87027
Owner: Adams Publishing Group
Editorial: 4 N Center Pl, Dundalk, Maryland 21222-4300 **Tel:** 1 410 687-7775
Email: editor@avenuenews.com **Web site:** http://www.avenuenews.com
Freq: Thu; **Circ:** 47000 Not Audited
Editor: Dan Baldwin; **Publisher:** David Fike; **Circulation Manager:** Bill Sims
Profile: The Avenue News is a weekly newspaper written for the local residents of Baltimore, MD. The newspaper covers local news, sports, business, special events, lifestyles and general information. Deadlines for editorial submissions are on Tuesdays at noon ET prior to the issue date.
Language (s): English
Ad Rate: Full Page Mono 25.00
Currency: United States Dollars
COMMUNITY NEWSPAPER

Avery Post 86579
Owner: Burleson (Bertie)
Editorial: 435 Pineola St, Newland, North Carolina 28657-7603 **Tel:** 1 828 733-1407
Email: averypost@yahoo.com
Freq: Wed; **Circ:** 5000 Not Audited
Publisher & Editor: Bertie Burleson; **Advertising Sales Manager:** Denise Johnson
Profile: The Avery Post is an independently-owned weekly newspaper providing local and community news coverage to residents of Avery County, NC.
Language (s): English
Ad Rate: Full Page Mono 4.65
Currency: United States Dollars
COMMUNITY NEWSPAPER

El Aviso 23326
Owner: El Aviso De Ocasion Inc.
Editorial: 6728 Seville Ave, Huntington Park, California 90255-4804 **Tel:** 1 323 586-9199
Email: elaviso@aol.com **Web site:** http://www.elaviso.com
Freq: Mon; **Circ:** 275000 Not Audited
Advertising Sales Manager: Juan Hernandez; **Publisher:** Jose Zepeda
Profile: El Aviso is a weekly Spanish language magazine for the Hispanic community of Los Angeles. It acts primarily as a television guide, but it also provides useful advice on personal health and relationships, as well as sports coverage. Deadlines are on Thursdays at noon PT.
Language (s): Spanish
Ad Rate: Full Page Mono 48.08
Currency: United States Dollars
COMMUNITY NEWSPAPER

Avoyelles Journal 28105
Editorial: 105 N Main St, Marksville, Louisiana 71351
Tel: 1 318 253-5413
Email: newsonline@avoyelles.com **Web site:** http://www.avoyellestoday.com
Freq: Sun; **Circ:** 16500 Not Audited
Publisher & Editor: Randy DeCuir; **Advertising Sales Manager:** Kathie Lipe
Profile: The Avoyelles Journal is a news source for Marksville, LA and the surrounding towns.
Language (s): English
Ad Rate: Full Page Mono 10.90
Currency: United States Dollars
COMMUNITY NEWSPAPER

Azteca News 21798
Owner: Romano (Rossana)
Editorial: 1823 E 17th St Ste 312, Santa Ana, California 92705-8630 **Tel:** 1 714 972-9912
Email: aztecanews@aol.com **Web site:** http://www.aztecanews.com
Freq: Wed; **Circ:** 42000 Not Audited
Editor: Fernando Velo
Profile: Azteca News in Santa Ana, CA is a weekly newspaper that covers local news and community events for the Spanish-speaking community.
Language (s): Spanish
Ad Rate: Full Page Mono 21.50
Currency: United States Dollars
COMMUNITY NEWSPAPER

Bajo El Sol 30226
Owner: Rhode Island Suburban Newspapers Inc
Editorial: 2055 S Arizona Ave, Yuma, Arizona 85364-6549 **Tel:** 1 928 783-3333
Email: newsroom@yumasun.com **Web site:** http://www.yumasun.com/bajo_el_sol
Freq: Fri; **Circ:** 15000 Not Audited
Editor: John Vaughn
Profile: Bajo El Sol is a local newspaper for the Hispanic community of Yuma, AZ. The newspaper covers national, local and community news.
Language (s): Spanish
Ad Rate: Full Page Mono 21.69
Ad Rate: Full Page Colour 3192.40
Currency: United States Dollars
COMMUNITY NEWSPAPER

The Baker County Press 18758
Owner: Baker County Press Inc.
Editorial: 104 S 5th St, Macclenny, Florida 32063-2304 **Tel:** 1 904 259-2400
Email: editor@bakercountypress.com **Web site:** http://www.bakercountypress.com
Freq: Thu; **Circ:** 5800 Not Audited
Publisher & Editor: James McGauley
Profile: The Baker County Press in Macclenny, FL is published weekly for the residents of Baker County, FL. Coverage includes local news, sports, community events and arts & entertainment. Deadlines are on Mondays at 4pm ET.
Language (s): English
Ad Rate: Full Page Mono 6.70
Currency: United States Dollars
COMMUNITY NEWSPAPER

The Bakersfield Voice 399929
Owner: Mercado Nuevo
Tel: 1 661 716-8640
Web site: http://www.bakersfieldvoice.com
Freq: Sun; **Circ:** 146000 Not Audited
Editor: Sandra Molen
Profile: The Bakersfield Voice is a free, weekly newspaper that is home-delivered to residents of Bakersfield, CA. It provides information on local news, community events, schools, churches, sports, businesses, real estate, land development, reader-submitted letters, recipes, features stories and photos for and about the area. Most of the information and pictures in the paper are submitted by readers, community organizations, churches and schools. Its policy is to publish all correspondence received, at least on its Web site, given that it pertains to the local area, respects the publication's terms and is submitted via the Web site. Its Web site is updated daily. The Voice is operated by Mercado Neuvo, an independent subsidiary of The Bakersfield Californian. Advertising deadlines are at 5pm PT.
Language (s): English
Ad Rate: Full Page Mono 20.63
Currency: United States Dollars
COMMUNITY NEWSPAPER

Ballard News-Tribune 21140
Owner: Robinson Newspapers
Editorial: 14006 1St Ave S Ste B, Burien, Washington 98168-3402 **Tel:** 1 206 708-1378
Email: bnteditor@robinsonnews.com **Web site:** http://www.ballardnewstribune.com
Freq: Fri; **Circ:** 7334 Not Audited
Editor: Ken Robinson
Profile: Ballard News-Tribune is written for residents of Ballard, WA. It covers local news and events.
Language (s): English
Ad Rate: Full Page Mono 30.00
Ad Rate: Full Page Colour 1500.00
Currency: United States Dollars
COMMUNITY NEWSPAPER

The Baltimore Afro American 28276
Editorial: 2519 N Charles St, Baltimore, Maryland 21218 **Tel:** 1 410 554-8200
Email: editor@afro.com **Web site:** http://www.afro.com
Freq: Sat; **Circ:** 5285 Not Audited
Publisher: John Oliver
Profile: The Baltimore Afro American is a weekly newspaper written for the African-American community in Baltimore. Its editorial mission is to inform readers about positive news and happenings in their communities. News deadlines are on Mondays at noon ET. Advertising deadlines are at 3pm ET.
Language (s): English
Ad Rate: Full Page Mono 46.56
Currency: United States Dollars
COMMUNITY NEWSPAPER

Bangla Patrika 155143
Editorial: 3806 31st St Fl 2, Long Island City, New York 11101-2719 **Tel:** 1 718 753-0086
Email: banglapatrikausa@gmail.com **Web site:** http://www.banglapatrikausa.com/
Freq: Mon; **Circ:** 15000 Not Audited
Publisher & Editor: Abu Taher
Profile: Bangla Patrika is a weekly newspaper written for the residents of Jackson Heights, NY.
Language (s): English
Ad Rate: Full Page Mono 15.00
Currency: United States Dollars
COMMUNITY NEWSPAPER

The Banner 18791
Owner: E.W. Scripps Co.
Editorial: 1100 Immokalee Rd, Naples, Florida 34110-4810 **Tel:** 1 239 263-4842
Email: news@naplesnews.com **Web site:** http://www.naplesnews.com/community/the-banner
Freq: Sat; **Circ:** 30000 Not Audited
Editor: Elysa Delcorto
Profile: The Banner is a bi-weekly local newspaper, geared toward the residents of Bonita, FL. The newspaper covers all aspects of local news, including sports, weather, entertainment and community news.
Language (s): English
Ad Rate: Full Page Mono 10.00
Ad Rate: Full Page Colour 925.00
Currency: United States Dollars
COMMUNITY NEWSPAPER

The Banner 22148
Owner: Saylor Broadcasting
Editorial: 345 Main St, Crab Orchard, Kentucky 40419-8617 **Tel:** 1 606 355-2370
Email: bannernewspaper@aol.com **Web site:** http://www.thebanner.us
Freq: Semi-Monthly; **Circ:** 16000 Not Audited
Profile: The Banner is a local newspaper written for residents of Mount Vernon, KY.
Language (s): English
Ad Rate: Full Page Mono 5.00
Ad Rate: Full Page Colour 9.00
Currency: United States Dollars
COMMUNITY NEWSPAPER

The Banner 282009
Owner: Eric Cox & Stacy Cox
Editorial: 24 N Washington St, Knightstown, Indiana 46148-1275 **Tel:** 1 765 345-2292
Web site: http://www.thebanneronline.com
Freq: Wed; **Circ:** 5000 Not Audited
Publisher and Editor: Eric Cox
Profile: Knightstown Banner provides news, sports and events coverage for the community of Knightstown, IN, and the surrounding areas.
Language (s): English
Ad Rate: Full Page Mono 6.00
Currency: United States Dollars
COMMUNITY NEWSPAPER

Banner Journal 21149
Owner: News Publishing Co.
Editorial: 409 E Main St, Black River Falls, Wisconsin 54615-1460 **Tel:** 1 715 284-4304
Email: news@bannerjournal.com
Freq: Wed; **Circ:** 5000 Not Audited
Editor: Jo Dee Brooke; **Publisher:** Dan Witte
Profile: Banner Journal is published weekly for the residents of Black River Falls, WI. The newspaper covers local news and community events.
Language (s): English
Ad Rate: Full Page Mono 9.00
Currency: United States Dollars
COMMUNITY NEWSPAPER

The Banner Press Newspaper 21526
Owner: Regional Newspapers Inc.
Editorial: 1217 Bowie St, Columbus, Texas 78934-2343 **Tel:** 1 979 732-6243
Email: bannercolumbus@sbcglobal.net **Web site:** http://www.bannerpresspaper.com
Freq: Thu; **Circ:** 5000 Not Audited
Publisher & Editor: Chad Ferguson; **Advertising Sales Manager:** Nora Rollins
Profile: The Banner Press Newspaper is a local weekly newspaper written for the residents of Austin, Colorado and Fayette counties, TX.
Language (s): English
Ad Rate: Full Page Mono 9.59
Currency: United States Dollars
COMMUNITY NEWSPAPER

The Baptist Courier 543276
Editorial: 100 Manly St, Greenville, South Carolina 29601-3025 **Tel:** 1 864 232-8736
Email: news@baptistcourier.com **Web site:** http://www.baptistcourier.com
Freq: Bi-Weekly; **Circ:** 69000 Not Audited
Advertising Sales Manager: Debbie Grooms;
Editor: Don Kirkland
Profile: The Baptist Courier is a bi-weekly newspaper serving Southern Baptist churches and individuals in South Carolina.
Language (s): English
Ad Rate: Full Page Mono 75.00
Currency: United States Dollars
COMMUNITY NEWSPAPER

Baptist Messenger 22713
Owner: Baptist General Convention of Oklahoma
Editorial: 3800 N May Ave, Oklahoma City, Oklahoma 73112-6639 **Tel:** 1 405 942-3800
Email: baptistmessenger@okbaptist.net **Web site:** http://baptistmessenger.com
Freq: Thu; **Circ:** 59665 Not Audited
Circulation Manager: Jana Gabrielse
Profile: The Baptist Messenger is a local newspaper written for churches in Oklahoma. Editorial mission is to do the work of Jesus Christ by assisting churches in accomplishing their Biblical mission and providing channels for cooperative ministry in Oklahoma and the world.
Language (s): English
Ad Rate: Full Page Mono 63.00
Currency: United States Dollars
COMMUNITY NEWSPAPER

Baptist Standard 23037
Editorial: 5151 Headquarters Dr, Plano, Texas 75024-5962 **Tel:** 1 214 630-4571
Web site: http://www.baptiststandard.com
Freq: Bi-Weekly; **Circ:** 40000 Not Audited
Publisher & Editor: Marv Knox; **Advertising Sales Manager:** Julie Sorrels
Profile: Baptist Standard in Plano, TX is a weekly newspaper written for Southern Baptists in Texas. Regular features include Around the State, On the Move, a religious cartoon, and Bible study. Deadlines for the publication fall one week before issue date.
Language (s): English
Ad Rate: Full Page Mono 65.00
Currency: United States Dollars
COMMUNITY NEWSPAPER

Baptist Trumpet 22038
Owner: Baptist Missionary of Arkansas (The)
Editorial: 10712 Interstate 30, Little Rock, Arkansas 72209-5835 **Tel:** 1 501 565-4601
Web site: http://www.baptisttrumpet.com
Freq: Wed; **Circ:** 10000 Not Audited
Editor: Diane Spriggs
Profile: Baptist Trumpet in Little Rock, AR is the official publication of the Baptist Missionary Association of Arkansas.
Language (s): English
Ad Rate: Full Page Mono 15.00
Currency: United States Dollars
COMMUNITY NEWSPAPER

Barberton Herald 20316
Owner: Vespoint Publishing Co.
Editorial: 70 4th St NW, Barberton, Ohio 44203-2572 **Tel:** 1 330 753-1068
Email: news@barbertonherald.com **Web site:** http://www.barbertonherald.com
Freq: Thu; **Circ:** 6500 Not Audited
Advertising Sales Manager: Jim Colombo;
Publisher: Cheryl Vespoint
Profile: Barberton Herald, established in 1923, is published weekly for the residents of Southwest Summit County, OH. Coverage includes local news, sports and community events. The news deadlines are Mondays at noon ET.
Language (s): English
Ad Rate: Full Page Mono 17.50
Currency: United States Dollars
COMMUNITY NEWSPAPER

The Barbour Democrat 21269
Owner: Cutright (J.Eric)
Editorial: 113 Church St, Philippi, West Virginia 26416 **Tel:** 1 304 457-2222
Email: thebarbourdemocratic@yahoo.com **Web site:** http://www.barbourdemocratwv.com
Freq: Wed; **Circ:** 5300 Not Audited
Editor: Lars Byrne; **Publisher:** Eric Cutright
Profile: The Barbour Democrat is a weekly newspaper written for residents of Philippi, WV and the surrounding area. The newspaper covers local news and community events.
Language (s): English
Ad Rate: Full Page Mono 5.25
Currency: United States Dollars
COMMUNITY NEWSPAPER

Barbourville Mountain Advocate 19319
Owner: Mountain Advocate Media
Editorial: 214 Knox St, Barbourville, Kentucky 40906-1428 **Tel:** 1 606 546-9225
Web site: http://www.mountainadvocate.com
Freq: Thu; **Circ:** 5500
Circulation Manager: Mollie Hale; **Publisher:** Jay Nolan
Profile: Barbourville Mountain Advocate is a weekly community newspaper serving the residents of Barbourville, KY.
Language (s): English
Ad Rate: Full Page Mono 12.15
Ad Rate: Full Page Colour 42.26
Currency: United States Dollars
COMMUNITY NEWSPAPER

The Barksdale Warrior 258069
Owner: Gannett Co. Inc.
Editorial: 222 Lake St, Shreveport, Louisiana 71101-3738 **Tel:** 1 318 456-3241
Email: warrior@gannett.com **Web site:** http://www.shreveporttimes.com/apps/pbcs.dll/section?category=barksdsdalewarrior
Freq: Fri; **Circ:** 10000 Not Audited
Editor: Benjamin Raughton; **Publisher:** Judi Terzotis
Profile: The Barksdale Warrior is a weekly newspaper serving the Barksdale Air Force Base, LA 2nd Bomb Wing. It provides local news, military news, events and stories of interest to military personnel, civilian residents and employees of the Air Force base. All editorial content is provided by the 2nd Bomb Wing Public Affairs office. Advertising is handled by The Times in Shreveport, LA. Editorial submissions should be e-mailed or mailed to the Public Affairs office by 4:30pm CT. Advertising should be sent to The Times by 4:30pm CT.
Language (s): English
Ad Rate: Full Page Mono 15.00
Currency: United States Dollars
COMMUNITY NEWSPAPER

Barnesville Herald-Gazette 21352
Owner: Geiger (Walter)
Editorial: 509 Greenwood St, Barnesville, Georgia 30204-1502 **Tel:** 1 770 358-0754
Email: news@barnesville.com **Web site:** http://www.barnesville.com
Freq: Tue; **Circ:** 5000 Not Audited
Publisher, Editor, Advertising Sales & Circulation Manager: Walter Geiger
Profile: Barnesville Herald-Gazette is a local newspaper written for the residents of Barnesville, GA. The newspaper covers local news and events. Deadlines are Fridays at noon ET.
Language (s): English
Ad Rate: Full Page Mono 6.85
Currency: United States Dollars
COMMUNITY NEWSPAPER

The Barnstable Patriot 19449
Owner: Gatehouse Media Group
Editorial: 4 Ocean St, Hyannis, Massachusetts 02601-4006 **Tel:** 1 508 771-1427
Email: news@barnstablepatriot.com **Web site:** http://www.barnstablepatriot.com
Freq: Fri; **Circ:** 5000 Not Audited
Profile: Barnstable Patriot is a weekly newspaper covering general news, business, sports and editorials. Local coverage includes the town of Barnstable, MA and surrounding areas.
Language (s): English
Ad Rate: Full Page Mono 14.50
Currency: United States Dollars
COMMUNITY NEWSPAPER

The Barrow County News 24169
Owner: Schwartz-Morris Media
Editorial: 189 W Athens St, Winder, Georgia 30680-2295 **Tel:** 1 770 867-7557
Email: news@barrowcountynews.com **Web site:** http://www.barrowcountynews.com
Freq: Sun; **Circ:** 8000 Not Audited
Publisher: Debbie Burgamy; **Circulation Manager:** JoAnn Craven
Profile: The Barrow County News is a local newspaper for the communities of Barrow and Jackson counties, GA. Deadlines for the publication are Mondays and Thursdays prior to publication.
Language (s): English
Ad Rate: Full Page Mono 9.20
Currency: United States Dollars
COMMUNITY NEWSPAPER

Barry County Advertiser 21683
Editorial: 904 West St, Cassville, Missouri 65625-1356 **Tel:** 1 417 847-4475
Email: events@4bca.com **Web site:** http://www.4bcaonline.com
Freq: Wed; **Circ:** 12500 Not Audited
Profile: Barry County Advertiser is published weekly for residents in Barry County, MO. The newspaper covers local news and community events. Deadlines are on Tuesdays at noon CT.
Language (s): English
Ad Rate: Full Page Mono 4.65
Currency: United States Dollars
COMMUNITY NEWSPAPER

The Base 68113 23000
Owner: Omaha World-Herald Co.
Editorial: 109 Washington Sq, Ste 221, Offutt AFB, Nebraska 68113 **Tel:** 1 402 294-3663
Email: airpulse@offutt.af.mil **Web site:** http://www.offutt.af.mil
Freq: Fri; **Circ:** 13200 Not Audited
Publisher: Shon Barenklau
Profile: The Base 68113 provides news and information for and about the Offutt Air Base in Nebraska. The publication is written for active duty members of the Air Force at the Offutt Air Base. The publication does not accept press releases or editorial submissions.
Language (s): English
Ad Rate: Full Page Mono 24.70
Ad Rate: Full Page Colour 29.70
Currency: United States Dollars
COMMUNITY NEWSPAPER

Bastrop Advertiser 22983
Owner: Cox Media Group, Inc.
Editorial: 908 Water St, Bastrop, Texas 78602-3834 **Tel:** 1 512 321-2557
Email: news@bastropadvertiser.com **Web site:** http://www.statesman.com/news/local/bastrop-advertiser/
Freq: Sat; **Circ:** 5760 Not Audited
Publisher: Mark Gwin
Profile: Bastrop Advertiser is published twice weekly for the residents of Bastrop and Bastrop County, TX. The publication features local news, community events and advertisements. The news deadline falls on Monday at 3pm CT for the Thursday edition. The deadline for the Saturday editon is Thursday at 3pm CT.
Language (s): English
Ad Rate: Full Page Mono 14.35
Currency: United States Dollars
COMMUNITY NEWSPAPER

The Bath County News-Outlook 19370
Editorial: 18 Water St, Owingsville, Kentucky 40360 **Tel:** 1 859 289-6425
Email: melissa@kynewsgroup.com
Freq: Wed; **Circ:** 11000 Not Audited
Publisher & Editor: Melissa Mitchell
Profile: The Bath County News-Outlook is a weekly newspaper published for the residents of Bath County, KY. The publication features local news, sports, and community events. The news deadline falls on Tuesday at noon ET.
Language (s): English
Ad Rate: Full Page Mono 4.50
Ad Rate: Full Page Colour 587.80
Currency: United States Dollars
COMMUNITY NEWSPAPER

Baxley News-Banner 22421
Owner: Gardner Newspapers Inc
Editorial: 241 E Parker St, Baxley, Georgia 31513-0009 **Tel:** 1 912 367-2468
Email: mail@baxleynewsbanner.com **Web site:** http://www.baxleynewsbanner.com
Freq: Weekly; **Circ:** 5000 Not Audited
Publisher & Editor: Jamie Gardner; **Advertising Sales Manager:** Matt Gardner
Profile: Baxley News-Banner is a local paper written for the residents of Baxley, GA. The paper covers local news and events. Deadlines are on Fridays at 4pm ET.
Language (s): English
Ad Rate: Full Page Mono 6.45
Currency: United States Dollars
COMMUNITY NEWSPAPER

The Bay Area Observer 858321
Owner: Bay Area Observer
Editorial: PO Box 82, La Porte, Texas 77572-0082 **Tel:** 1 281 907-3140
Email: editor@bayareaobserver.com **Web site:** http://www.bayareaobserver.com
Freq: Thu
Publisher & Editor: Rebecca Collins
Profile: The Bay Area Observer is a weekly newspaper providing Local and Community News coverage for the residents of Seabrook, La Porte, Kemah, TX, as well as the Galveston Bay Area, TX.
Language (s): English
COMMUNITY NEWSPAPER

The Bay Beacon 30176
Owner: Beacon Newspapers
Editorial: 1181 John Sims Pkwy E, Niceville, Florida 32578-2752 **Tel:** 1 850 678-1080
Email: info@baybeacon.com **Web site:** http://baybeacon.com
Freq: Wed; **Circ:** 15500 Not Audited
Advertising Sales Manager: Sara Kent; **Publisher & Editor:** Stephen Kent
Profile: The Bay Beacon is a weekly newspaper published for the residents of Niceville, Valparaiso, Blue Water Bay and Freeport, FL.
Language (s): English
Ad Rate: Full Page Mono 14.95
Currency: United States Dollars
COMMUNITY NEWSPAPER

The Bay City Tribune 80325
Owner: Southern Newspapers, Inc.
Editorial: 2901 Carey Smith Blvd, Bay City, Texas 77414-3768 **Tel:** 1 979 245-5555
Email: news@baycitytribune.com **Web site:** http://baycitytribune.com
Freq: Sun; **Circ:** 5200 Not Audited
Advertising Sales Manager: Susie Phillips;
Circulation Manager: Porfirio Rodriguez
Profile: The Bay City Tribune is a community newspaper serving the residents of Bay City, TX.
Language (s): English
Ad Rate: Full Page Mono 6.10
Currency: United States Dollars
COMMUNITY NEWSPAPER

The Bay State Banner 19463
Owner: Banner Publications
Editorial: 1100 Washington St Ste 303, Dorchester Center, Massachusetts 02124-5520 **Tel:** 1 617 261-4600
Email: news@bannerpub.com **Web site:** http://www.baystatebanner.com
Freq: Thu; **Circ:** 30000 Not Audited
Publisher & Editor: Melvin Miller
Profile: The Bay State Banner covers news stories for the African-American community of Greater Boston.
Language (s): English
Ad Rate: Full Page Mono 24.00
Ad Rate: Full Page Colour 1925.76
Currency: United States Dollars
COMMUNITY NEWSPAPER

Bay Times 28325
Owner: Chesapeake Publishing and Printing
Editorial: 1101 Butterworth Ct Ste 201, Stevensville, Maryland 21666-2662 **Tel:** 1 410 643-7770
Web site: http://www.myeasternshoremd.com/qa/bay_times/
Freq: Wed; **Circ:** 6100 Not Audited
Publisher: David Fike; **Editor:** Angela Price
Profile: Bay Times' editorial mission is to provide local news and information regarding community events for residents of Kent Island and Grasonville, MD.
Language (s): English
Ad Rate: Full Page Mono 11.25
Currency: United States Dollars
COMMUNITY NEWSPAPER

Bay Weekly 22168
Owner: New Bay Enterprises, Inc.
Editorial: 1160 Spa Rd Ste 1A, Annapolis, Maryland 21403-1097 **Tel:** 1 410 626-9888
Email: editor@bayweekly.com **Web site:** http://bayweekly.com
Freq: Thu; **Circ:** 19000 Not Audited
Publisher & Editor: Sandra Martin
Profile: Bay Weekly is written for the residents of Severna Park, greater Annapolis, southern Anne Arundel County and Calvert County, MD. The news deadlines fall on Fridays at noon ET.
Language (s): English
Ad Rate: Full Page Mono 30.00
Currency: United States Dollars
COMMUNITY NEWSPAPER

The Bayonet 18847
Owner: Landmark Military Newspapers
Editorial: 6460 Way Ave Ste 102, Fort Benning, Georgia 31905-3771 **Tel:** 1 706 545-4622
Email: lori.egan@us.army.mil **Web site:** http://www.ledger-enquirer.com/bayonet
Freq: Fri; **Circ:** 22000 Not Audited
Publisher & Editor: Lori Egan; **Circulation Manager:** Rick Wade
Profile: The Bayonet is a weekly newspaper published for Fort Benning Base, GA. The publication covers local news and community events. Deadlines are on Fridays at noon, ET.
Language (s): English
Ad Rate: Full Page Mono 22.00
Currency: United States Dollars
COMMUNITY NEWSPAPER

Bayonne Community News 21695
Owner: Hudson Reporter Newspapers
Editorial: 447 Broadway, Bayonne, New Jersey 07002-3623 **Tel:** 1 201 437-2460
Email: bcneditorial@hudsonreporter.com **Web site:** http://hudsonreporter.com
Freq: Weekly; **Circ:** 28000 Not Audited

Advertising Sales Manager: Tish Kraszyk; **Circulation Manager:** Roberto Lopez; **Editor:** Kate Rounds
Profile: Bayonne (NJ) Community News is a weekly newspaper that covers local news and events in a region that includes Country Village, Society Hill, Franklin Park and Port Liberte in Jersey City, NJ.
Language (s): English
Ad Rate: Full Page Mono 19.25
Currency: United States Dollars
COMMUNITY NEWSPAPER

The Bayou Journal 868394
Owner: Bayou Co. LLC
Editorial: 3415 Highway 70 S, Pierre Part, Louisiana 70339-4524 **Tel:** 1 985 252-0501
Email: bayoujournal@teche.net **Web site:** http://www.bayoujournal.com
Freq: Weekly
Advertising Sales Manager: Sue Hebert; **Editor & Publisher:** Tracy Hebert
Profile: The Bayou Journal is a weekly community newspaper serving the Assumption Parish communities of Pierre Part and Belle River, LA, and also surrounding communities in Ascension and Saint Mary Parishes. The publications includes community news, events and sports.
Language (s): English
COMMUNITY NEWSPAPER

Bayside Gazette 154160
Owner: Flag Publications
Editorial: 11 S Main St Ste 1A, Berlin, Maryland 21811-1426 **Tel:** 1 410 641-0039
Email: Info@baysidegazette.com **Web site:** http://www.baysideoc.com
Freq: Thu; **Circ:** 10000 Not Audited
Advertising Sales Manager: Mary Cooper; **Editor:** Stewart Dobson
Profile: Bayside Gazette is a weekly community newspaper written for the residents of Berlin, MD and the surrounding areas.
Language (s): English
Ad Rate: Full Page Mono 15.00
Currency: United States Dollars
COMMUNITY NEWSPAPER

BDN weekend 525351
Owner: Fortress Investment Group, LLC
Editorial: 412 High St, Boonville, Missouri 65233-1242 **Tel:** 1 660 882-5335
Email: news@boonvilledailynews.com **Web site:** http://www.boonvilledailynews.com
Freq: Wed; **Circ:** 10000 Not Audited
Circulation Manager: Edward Lang
Profile: BDN Weekend is a free weekly newspaper that is available on newsstands and is also delivered to subscribers of Boonville Daily News as an insert in the paper. It previews and lists local weekend happenings.
Language (s): English
Ad Rate: Full Page Mono 12.30
Currency: United States Dollars
COMMUNITY NEWSPAPER

Beach Breeze 350387
Owner: Woodham (Gary)
Editorial: 740 Baldwin Ave, Defuniak Springs, Florida 32435-2598 **Tel:** 1 850 231-0918
Email: beachbreezenews@gmail.com **Web site:** http://www.defuniakherald.com
Freq: Thu; **Circ:** 5500 Not Audited
Editor: Bruce Collier; **Publisher:** Gary Woodham
Profile: Beach Breeze is a community newspaper in Santa Rosa Beach, FL, covering the south side of Walton County, FL. The publication features stories on schools, sports, state capitol news and entertainment. Advertising deadlines are Tuesdays at 5pm ET.
Language (s): English
Ad Rate: Full Page Mono 4.50
Currency: United States Dollars
COMMUNITY NEWSPAPER

The Beach Reporter 21467
Owner: MediaNews Group
Editorial: 2615 Pacific Coast Hwy Ste 329, Hermosa Beach, California 90254-2229 **Tel:** 1 310 372-0388
Web site: http://www.tbrnews.com
Freq: Thu; **Circ:** 44000 Not Audited
Publisher: Simon Grieve
Profile: The Beach Reporter in Hermosa Beach, CA covers local news, business, sports, health, entertainment and community events for residents of Manhattan Beach, Hermosa Beach, Redondo Beach and El Segundo, CA.
Language (s): English
Ad Rate: Full Page Mono 9.90
Ad Rate: Full Page Colour 276.00
Currency: United States Dollars
COMMUNITY NEWSPAPER

Beachcomber 281735
Owner: Beeler & Associates
Editorial: 5199 E Pacific Coast Hwy Ste 608, Long Beach, California 90804-3364 **Tel:** 1 562 597-8000
Email: editor@beachcomber.news **Web site:** https://beachcomber.news
Freq: Bi-Weekly; **Circ:** 39000 Not Audited
Publisher: Jay Beeler
Profile: Beachcomber in Long Beach, CA is a community newspaper that covers local news and events.
Language (s): English
Ad Rate: Full Page Mono 36.00
Currency: United States Dollars
COMMUNITY NEWSPAPER

Beachcomber News 24154
Owner: MLAR Inc.
Editorial: 1000 W Washington Ave, Pleasantville, New Jersey 08232-3861 **Tel:** 1 609 601-5194
Email: beachcombernews@aol.com **Web site:** http://brigantine.shorenewstoday.com
Freq: Fri; **Circ:** 5000 Not Audited
Advertising Sales Manager: James Miller
Profile: Beachcomber News is a weekly newspaper published for the residents of Brigantine, NJ. The publication covers local news and community events. Deadlines are on Monday at 5pm ET.
Language (s): English
Ad Rate: Full Page Mono 16.00
Currency: United States Dollars
COMMUNITY NEWSPAPER

The Beacon 20360
Owner: Schaffner (John)
Editorial: 205 SE Catawba Rd Ste G, Port Clinton, Ohio 43452-2669 **Tel:** 1 419 732-2154
Email: editor@thebeacon.net **Web site:** http://www.thebeacon.net
Freq: Thu; **Circ:** 14239 Not Audited
Editor: Jasmine Cupp; **Circulation Manager:** Bruce Dinse; **Publisher & Editor:** John Schaffner
Profile: The Beacon in Port Clinton, OH is a weekly newspaper serving Ottawa County, OH. It covers news related to arts & entertainment, sports, business and health. Deadlines for news releases, classifieds and advertisements are at 4pm on Mondays.
Language (s): English
Ad Rate: Full Page Mono 13.75
Currency: United States Dollars
COMMUNITY NEWSPAPER

Beacon 22885
Owner: Highland Community News
Editorial: 895 Baucom Ave SE Bldg 323, March ARB, California 92518-2293 **Tel:** 1 951 655-4137
Email: 452amw.paworkflow@us.af.mil **Web site:** http://www.aerotechnews.com/marcharb
Freq: Fri; **Circ:** 6000 Not Audited
Editor: Megan Just
Profile: Beacon is a military newspaper written for the military personnel of March Air Reserve Base, CA.
Language (s): English
Ad Rate: Full Page Mono 7.95
Currency: United States Dollars
COMMUNITY NEWSPAPER

The Beacon 74345
Owner: West Publishing and Advertising, Inc.
Editorial: N2759 State Road 67, Williams Bay, Wisconsin 53191-3704 **Tel:** 1 262 245-1877
Email: beaconnews@charter.net **Web site:** http://www.readthebeacon.com
Freq: Bi-Weekly; **Circ:** 20000 Not Audited
Publisher & Editor: Dennis West; **Advertising Sales Manager:** Mark West
Profile: The Beacon is published weekly for the residents of Williams Bay, WI and surrounding areas. The newspaper covers local news, features and community events.
Language (s): English
Ad Rate: Full Page Mono 13.00
Currency: United States Dollars
COMMUNITY NEWSPAPER

The Beacon 755873
Owner: Diocese of Paterson
Editorial: 775 Valley Rd, Clifton, New Jersey 07013-2205 **Tel:** 1 973 279-8845
Email: catholicbeacon@patersondiocese.org **Web site:** http://www.patersondiocese.org
Freq: Weekly; **Circ:** 30000
Circulation Manager: Joyce Deceglie; **News Editor:** Michael Wojcik
Profile: The Beacon is written for the Diocese of Paterson, NJ.
Language (s): English
Ad Rate: Full Page Mono 25.50
Currency: United States Dollars
COMMUNITY NEWSPAPER

Bedford Bulletin 21044
Owner: Landmark Community Newspapers, Inc.
Editorial: 402 E Main St, Bedford, Virginia 24523-2017 **Tel:** 1 540 586-8612
Email: news@bedfordbulletin.com **Web site:** http://www.bedfordbulletin.com
Freq: Wed; **Circ:** 7200 Not Audited
Publisher: Jay Bondurant; **Editor:** Tom Wilmoth
Profile: Bedford Bulletin is a newspaper for the residents of Bedford, VA. It reports news and events in the community. Deadlines are on Fridays at 5pm.
Language (s): English
Ad Rate: Full Page Mono 12.00
Currency: United States Dollars
COMMUNITY NEWSPAPER

Bedford Now 72495
Owner: Monroe Publishing Company
Editorial: 20 W 1st St, Monroe, Michigan 48161-2333 **Tel:** 1 734 242-1100
Email: info@bedfordnow.com **Web site:** http://www.bedfordnow.com
Freq: Sat; **Circ:** 12000 Not Audited
Publisher: Lonnie Cappler-Moyer
Profile: Bedford Now brings news to the residents of Monroe county, MI.
Language (s): English
Ad Rate: Full Page Mono 12.50
Currency: United States Dollars
COMMUNITY NEWSPAPER

Bedford Press 22595
Editorial: 3363 Hemmingway Ln, Lambertville, Michigan 48144-9653 **Tel:** 1 734 8566680
Email: bedfordpress@aol.com
Freq: Bi-Weekly; **Circ:** 14000 Not Audited
Editor/Publisher: Karen Daggett
Profile: The Bedford Press is a local weekly newspaper serving the residents of Southern Monroe County, MI. It provides local news and information for Southern Monroe County, MI. Currently, the paper does not have a Website.
Language (s): English
Ad Rate: Full Page Mono 8.75
Currency: United States Dollars
COMMUNITY NEWSPAPER

Beeville Bee-Picayune 21690
Owner: Beeville Publishing Company
Editorial: 111 N Washington St, Beeville, Texas 78102-4508 **Tel:** 1 361 358-2550
Email: news@mysoutex.com **Web site:** http://www.mysoutex.com
Freq: Sat; **Circ:** 5200 Not Audited
Editor: Jason Collins
Profile: Beeville Bee-Picayune is a twice weekly newspaper for the residents of Beeville, Texas. The newspaper covers news and events about the local community. Contact the editor or general manager with article ideas, story submissions, and/or general questions and comments about the Beeville Bee-Picayune. The deadline for the Wednesday edition is Monday at noon CT, and the deadline for the Friday edition of the Beeville Bee-Picayune is Wednesday at noon CT. Contact the advertising department at the Beeville Bee-Picayune to discuss advertising frequency discounts.
Language (s): English
Ad Rate: Full Page Mono 9.30
Currency: United States Dollars
COMMUNITY NEWSPAPER

Beirut Times 23138
Owner: Beirut Times Publishing Co.
Editorial: 1214 E Colorado Blvd Ste 208, Pasadena, California 91106-1899 **Tel:** 1 626 844-7777
Email: 44beirut@gmail.com **Web site:** http://www.beiruttimes.com
Freq: Thu; **Circ:** 35000 Not Audited
Publisher & Editor: Michelle Absi; **Advertising Sales Manager:** Linda Smith
Profile: Beirut Times is a weekly newspaper for Lebanese and Arab Americans. It provides a forum by which their voices can be heard with an internationally expanding circulation. It serves as an alternative to the American news media. Local, national and international news is reported on. Foreign correspondents, posted in vital news centers in the Arab world and Europe, transmit on the scene coverage with specific details not available through the general media. It is written entirely in Arabic, although advertising appears in both English and Arabic.
Language (s): Arabic
Ad Rate: Full Page Mono 35.00
Ad Rate: Full Page Colour 37.00
Currency: United States Dollars
COMMUNITY NEWSPAPER

Belleville Telescope 19228
Owner: Arnold (Fred)
Editorial: 1314 19th St, Belleville, Kansas 66935-2216 **Tel:** 1 785 527-2244
Email: btelescope@sbcglobal.net **Web site:** http://thebellevilletelescope.com/
Freq: Thu; **Circ:** 5600 Not Audited
Publisher & Editor: Fred Arnold
Profile: Belleville Telescope is a weekly newspaper written for the residents of Belleville, KS. It reports the local news and events in the community. Deadlines are on Mondays at noon CT.
Language (s): English
Ad Rate: Full Page Mono 8.50
Currency: United States Dollars
COMMUNITY NEWSPAPER

Bellevue Reporter 242168
Owner: Black Press
Editorial: 2700 Richards Rd Ste 201, Bellevue, Washington 98005-4200 **Tel:** 1 425 453-4270
Email: editor@bellevuereporter.com **Web site:** http://www.bellevuereporter.com
Freq: Fri; **Circ:** 43000
Advertising Manager: Jim Gatens; **Publisher:** William Shaw
Profile: Bellevue Reporter is a local, weekly newspaper serving residents of Bellevue, WA. The paper includes local news, entertainment, business, sports and community events.
Language (s): English
Ad Rate: Full Page Mono 34.15
Currency: United States Dollars
COMMUNITY NEWSPAPER

Beloit Chronicle 155942
Editorial: 1872 Porter Ave, Beloit, Wisconsin 53511-3659 **Tel:** 1 608 363-9110
Email: fraggle142@sbcglobal.net **Web site:** http://www.beloitchronicle.com
Freq: Fri; **Circ:** 8000 Not Audited
Publisher & Editor: Eugene Relerford
Profile: Beloit Chronicle is written for the African American residents in and around Beloit, WI. It provides information on local news, community events, schools, businesses and features of interest to local readers.
Language (s): English
Ad Rate: Full Page Mono 8.00
Currency: United States Dollars
COMMUNITY NEWSPAPER

Belvoir Eagle 21050
Owner: BH Media Group
Editorial: 9820 Flagler Rd, Fort Belvoir, Virginia 22060-5610 **Tel:** 1 703 805-2019
Email: editor@belvoireagleonline.com **Web site:** http://www.belvoireagle.com
Freq: Thu; **Circ:** 20000 Not Audited
Advertising Manager: Tom Spargur; **Editor:** Margaret Steele
Profile: Belvoir Eagle is a weekly newspaper written for active duty military personnel in Fort Belvoir, VA. It covers news and events.
Language (s): English
Ad Rate: Full Page Mono 15.00
Currency: United States Dollars
COMMUNITY NEWSPAPER

Benton County Enterprise 19832
Owner: Benton County Enterprise Company Inc.
Editorial: 107 W Main St, Warsaw, Missouri 65355 **Tel:** 1 660 438-6312
Email: bentoncountyenterprise@yahoo.com **Web site:** http://www.bentoncountyenterprise.com
Freq: Thu; **Circ:** 5700 Not Audited
Publisher & Editor: James Mahlon White
Profile: Benton County Enterprise in Warsaw, MO is published weekly for the residents of Benton County, MO. The newspaper covers local news, business, community events, sports and industry news.
Language (s): English
Ad Rate: Full Page Mono 5.00
Currency: United States Dollars
COMMUNITY NEWSPAPER

The Berlin Citizen 22552
Owner: Record-Journal Publishing Company
Editorial: 500 S Broad St Ste 2, Meriden, Connecticut 06450-6643 **Tel:** 1 203 235-1661
Email: newsroom@record-journal.com **Web site:** http://www.theberlincitizen.com
Freq: Thu; **Circ:** 10000 Not Audited
News Editor: Nick Carroll; **Publisher:** Eliot White
Profile: The Berlin Citizen is a weekly newspaper for residents and businesses in Berlin, East Berlin and Kensington, CT. The publication covers news and events. Deadlines are Thursdays at 5pm ET.
Language (s): English
Ad Rate: Full Page Mono 16.45
Currency: United States Dollars
COMMUNITY NEWSPAPER

Bernardsville News 29754
Owner: PowerOne Media
Editorial: 17 Morristown Rd, 19, Bernardsville, New Jersey 07924-2312 **Tel:** 1 908 766-3900
Web site: http://newjerseyhills.com
Freq: Thu; **Circ:** 7900 Not Audited
Editor: Charles Zavalick
Profile: Bernardsville News is a weekly newspaper that covers the five counties surrounding Bernardsville, NJ. They cover all local news and the occasional national news feature that has an impact on their readership. They also cover local business, politics, sports, and arts & entertainment. All releases should be addressed to the editor. Deadlines for the publication are Tuesday evening before issue date.
Language (s): English
Ad Rate: Full Page Mono 22.00
Currency: United States Dollars
COMMUNITY NEWSPAPER

Bernice Banner-News 22127
Owner: Boyett (Jessie)
Editorial: 227 Boyette Rd, Bernice, Louisiana 71222-5327 **Tel:** 1 318 285-7424
Email: bernicebanner@oeccwildblue.com
Freq: Weekly; **Circ:** 12000 Not Audited
Editor & Publisher: Jessie Boyett
Profile: Bernice (LA) Banner-News is a weekly publication written for residents of the Bernice, Junction City, Spearsville and Lillie, LA. The newspaper focuses on local and national news, politics, sports, education and arts & entertainment. Deadlines are Mondays at noon CT.
Language (s): English
Ad Rate: Full Page Mono 5.00
Currency: United States Dollars
COMMUNITY NEWSPAPER

Bettendorf News 18872
Owner: Lee Enterprises Inc.
Editorial: 500 E 3rd St, Davenport, Iowa 52801-1708 **Tel:** 1 563 383-2396
Email: bettnews@qctimes.com **Web site:** http://qctimes.com/news/local/bettendorf/
Freq: Thu; **Circ:** 10000 Not Audited
Profile: Bettendorf News is written for those who live and/or are interested in Bettendorf, LeClaire, Pleasant Valley and Riverdale, IA. The newspaper covers local news, national news that has an impact on their readership, local sports, local politics, local arts & entertainment and local education issues. Deadlines are on Mondays.
Language (s): English
Ad Rate: Full Page Mono 18.75
Currency: United States Dollars
COMMUNITY NEWSPAPER

Beverly Hills Courier 18602
Owner: Beverly Hills Courier, LLC
Editorial: 499 N Canon Dr Ste 100, Beverly Hills, California 90210-6192 **Tel:** 1 310 278-1322
Email: editorial@bhcourier.com **Web site:** http://www.bhcourier.com
Freq: Weekly; **Circ:** 40000 Not Audited
Advertising Sales Manager: Evelyn Portugal
Profile: Beverly Hills Courier is a local newspaper published for the residents of Beverly Hills, California

area and distributed in Beverly Hills, Bel Air, Holmby Hills, Westwood, Brentwood, and the Desert. The newspaper covers local and national news, sports, politics, arts & entertainment and education issues.
Language (s): English
Ad Rate: Full Page Mono 65.30
Ad Rate: Full Page Colour 75.38
Currency: United States Dollars
COMMUNITY NEWSPAPER

Beverly Hills Weekly 63818
Editorial: 140 S Beverly Dr Ste 201, Beverly Hills, California 90212-3050 **Tel:** 1 310 887-0788
Email: editor@bhweekly.com **Web site:** http://www.bhweekly.com
Freq: Thu; **Circ:** 15000 Not Audited
Publisher: Josh Gross
Profile: Beverly Hills Weekly is the weekly local newspaper written for those who live and/or are interested in Beverly Hills, CA. The newspaper covers local news, sports, politics, arts & entertainment and education issues. It also covers national news that has an impact on their readership. All releases should be addressed to the editor. Deadlines for the publication are three days before publication before issue date.
Language (s): English
Ad Rate: Full Page Mono 13.13
Currency: United States Dollars
COMMUNITY NEWSPAPER

Beverly Press/Park Labrea News 27858
Owner: Villalpando (Michael)
Editorial: 5150 Wilshire Blvd Ste 330, Los Angeles, California 90036-4480 **Tel:** 1 323 933-5518
Email: editor@beverlypress.com **Web site:** http://www.beverlypress.com
Freq: Weekly; **Circ:** 13000 Not Audited
Profile: Beverly Press/Park Labrea News is a weekly, local newspaper written for residents of Los Angeles and Beverly Hills, CA. It publishes the same content under two different banners, Park Labrea News or Beverly Press, depending on its area of distribution.
Language (s): English
Ad Rate: Full Page Mono 16.00
Ad Rate: Full Page Colour 20.38
Currency: United States Dollars
COMMUNITY NEWSPAPER

The Beverly Review 19153
Owner: TR Communications, Inc.
Editorial: 10546 S Western Ave, Chicago, Illinois 60643-2528 **Tel:** 1 773 238-3366
Email: general@beverlyreview.net **Web site:** http://www.beverlyreview.net
Freq: Wed; **Circ:** 6300 Not Audited
Editor: Kyle Garmes; **Advertising Sales Manager:** Bob Olszewski; **Publisher:** Toby Olszewski; **Circulation Manager:** Katherine Robbins
Profile: The Beverly Review offers weekly news and events featuring local personalities in the greater Chicago area. The newspaper provides news affecting the community with a local perspective. Deadlines are four days before issue date.
Language (s): English
Ad Rate: Full Page Mono 10.85
Ad Rate: Full Page Colour 42.30
Currency: United States Dollars
COMMUNITY NEWSPAPER

Biblical Recorder 22949
Owner: Biblical Recorder, Inc.
Editorial: 205 Convention Dr, Cary, North Carolina 27511-4257 **Tel:** 1 919 847-2127
Email: editor@brnow.org **Web site:** http://www.brnow.org
Freq: Sat; **Circ:** 20000 Not Audited
Profile: Biblical Recorder is a weekly newspaper in Raleigh, NC, serving North Carolina's Baptist community, with news articles, feature stories, editorials, and an events calendar.
Language (s): English
Ad Rate: Full Page Mono 52.00
Ad Rate: Full Page Colour 1750.00
Currency: United States Dollars
COMMUNITY NEWSPAPER

The Big Sandy News 19356
Owner: WCM Investments
Tel: 1 606 788-9962
Email: info@bigsandynews.com **Web site:** http://www.bigsandynews.com
Freq: Wed; **Circ:** 8000 Not Audited
Advertising Sales Manager: Becky Crum; **Publisher:** Chris McGhee
Profile: The Big Sandy News is a local newspaper written for those who live and/or are interested in Lawerence, Martin, Johnston and Magoffin counties in Eastern Kentucky's Big Sandy Valley. It covers local news, sports, politics, arts & entertainment and education, as well as national news that has an impact on their readership.
Language (s): English
Ad Rate: Full Page Mono 8.25
Currency: United States Dollars
COMMUNITY NEWSPAPER

The Bilingual News 407516
Editorial: 5th Ave., Bay Shore, New York 11706
Tel: 1 800 256-8161
Email: bilingualnews@gmail.com **Web site:** http://www.thebilingualnews.com
Freq: Mon; **Circ:** 115000 Not Audited
Publisher & Editor: Jason Garzon; **Advertising Sales Manager:** Jose Mejia
Profile: The Bilingual News is a free, weekly newspaper published in English and Spanish that serves the residents of Long Island, Nassau, West Suffolk, East Suffolk, Queens, Brooklyn, the Bronx and Manhattan, NY. It covers general interest news, education, technology, business, science, advice, culture, sports, entertainment and health. Send press releases via e-mail, not fax. Deadlines are at noon ET.
Language (s): Spanish/Bilingual
Ad Rate: Full Page Mono 8.64
Currency: United States Dollars
COMMUNITY NEWSPAPER

The Biloxi D'Iberville Press 19915
Owner: Bay Newspapers Inc.
Editorial: 819 Jackson St, Biloxi, Mississippi 39530-4235 **Tel:** 1 228 435-0720
Email: publisher@biloxi-diberville-press.com **Web site:** http://www.biloxi-diberville-press.com
Freq: Thu; **Circ:** 6000 Not Audited
Editor: Vicki Fox; **Publisher & Advertising Manager:** Cindy Picard
Profile: The Biloxi D'Iberville Press is a local newspaper that is written for those who live and/or are interested in Biloxi, MS. The newspaper covers local news, sports, politics, arts & entertainment, education issues and national news that has an impact on their readership. Deadlines are on the Monday prior to the issue date.
Language (s): English
Ad Rate: Full Page Mono 11.00
Currency: United States Dollars
COMMUNITY NEWSPAPER

The Birmingham Times 18483
Owner: Birmingham Times Publishing Co.
Editorial: 115 3rd Ave W, Birmingham, Alabama 35204-4114 **Tel:** 1 205 251-5158
Web site: http://www.birminghamtimes.com
Freq: Thu; **Circ:** 16500 Not Audited
Circulation Manager: Philip Eldridge
Profile: The Birmingham Times is a weekly newspaper that covers the news and events of the local African American community of Birmingham, AL. The publication covers local news, sports, entertainment and religious issues.
Language (s): English
Ad Rate: Full Page Mono 15.20
Currency: United States Dollars
COMMUNITY NEWSPAPER

Birmingham Weekly 22960
Owner: Magnolia Media LLC
Editorial: 130 41st St S Ste 103, Birmingham, Alabama 35222-1966 **Tel:** 1 205 991-4440
Email: bhamweekly@gmail.com **Web site:** http://www.bhamweekly.com
Freq: Thu; **Circ:** 20000 Not Audited
Publisher & Editor: Stephen Humphreys; **Advertising Sales Manager:** Mike Walker
Profile: Birmingham Weekly is written for residents of Birmingham, AL.
Language (s): English
Ad Rate: Full Page Mono 26.75
Currency: United States Dollars
COMMUNITY NEWSPAPER

Bitterroot Star 21478
Owner: Bitterroot Star, Inc.
Editorial: 215 Main St, Stevensville, Montana 59870-2112 **Tel:** 1 406 777-3928
Email: editor@bitterrootstar.com **Web site:** http://www.bitterrootstar.com
Freq: Weekly; **Circ:** 7050 Not Audited
Profile: Bitterroot Star is a weekly community newspaper serving residents of Corvallis, Darby, Florence, Hamilton, Stevensville and Victor, MT with local news, sports, opinion and events.
Language (s): English
Ad Rate: Full Page Mono 10.20
Currency: United States Dollars
COMMUNITY NEWSPAPER

Bi-Weekly Post 132423
Tel: 1 317 894-8777
Email: biweeklypost@aol.com **Web site:** http://www.bi-weeklypost.com
Freq: Bi-Weekly; **Circ:** 50000
Advertising Sales Manager: Maggie Thomas; **Editor and Publisher:** Tom Wills
Profile: Fomerly known as Indiana WEEKENDER, this publication started in 1989 in Shelbyville, IN. It was a four-page paper known as the Shelby Weekly and covered Shelby, Rush, and Decatur counties. In 1990, the paper became the Shelby Tri-County Weekly, increased to eight pages, and added Bartholomew and Hancock counties. During the course of the last 12 years the paper has grown and increased its circulation into eight counties. The paper features a TV Section, Dining Out, Job Services, Nightlife, Entertainment, Sports, Bingo, Auto Market, and Real Estate sections. Deadlines are on Wednesdays at noon ET.
Language (s): English
Ad Rate: Full Page Mono 15.00
Currency: United States Dollars
COMMUNITY NEWSPAPER

The Black Chronicle 20441
Owner: Perry Publishing And Broadcasting
Editorial: 1528 NE 23rd St, Oklahoma City, Oklahoma 73111-3260 **Tel:** 1 405 424-4695
Email: alindsey@blackchronicle.com **Web site:** http://www.blackchronicle.com
Freq: Thu; **Circ:** 31000 Not Audited
Advertising Sales Manager: Tiffany Cooper; **Publisher:** Russell Perry
Profile: The Black Chronicle is a weekly newspaper that is written for the African-American community in Oklahoma City, OK. The newspaper aims to bring its readers information on local and national news, sports and events. Deadlines are on Tuesdays at 1pm CT.
Language (s): English
Ad Rate: Full Page Mono 16.44
Currency: United States Dollars
COMMUNITY NEWSPAPER

Black News 22545
Owner: Diversity City Media
Editorial: 1310 Harden St, Columbia, South Carolina 29204 **Tel:** 1 803 799-5252
Email: scbnews@aol.com **Web site:** http://www.scblacknews.com
Freq: Thu; **Circ:** 75000 Not Audited
Publisher & Editor: Isaac Washington
Profile: Black News is a local paper written for the African American community of Columbia, SC. The paper covers state and local news, sports, arts & entertainment, lifestyle and health. Deadlines are on Fridays.
Language (s): English
Ad Rate: Full Page Mono 36.91
Currency: United States Dollars
COMMUNITY NEWSPAPER

The Black Sheep 591867
Owner: Black Card Media LLC
Editorial: 350 N Orleans St Ste 9000N, Chicago, Illinois 60654-1701 **Tel:** 1 217 390-1747
Email: brendan@theblacksheeponline.com **Web site:** http://theblacksheeponline.com
Freq: Wed; **Circ:** 7000
Editor: Brendan Bonham; **Publisher:** Atish Doshi
Profile: The Black Sheep is a newspaper distributed on college campuses, featuring humor and satire aimed at college students. Previously produced as The Booze News and Rough Draft.
Language (s): English
Ad Rate: Full Page Mono 12.50
Currency: United States Dollars
COMMUNITY NEWSPAPER

Black Star News 23244
Editorial: 2429 Southern Blvd Apt 2, Bronx, New York 10458-6508 **Tel:** 1 646 261-7566
Email: editor@blackstarnews.com **Web site:** http://www.blackstarnews.com
Freq: Thu; **Circ:** 50000 Not Audited
Advertising Sales Manager: Dianne Cooper
Profile: Black Star News is a weekly newspaper written for the African American population of New York.
Language (s): English
Ad Rate: Full Page Mono 56.00
Currency: United States Dollars
COMMUNITY NEWSPAPER

The Black Voice News 18646
Owner: Ohio Community Media LLC
Editorial: 4144 10th St, Riverside, California 92501-3110 **Tel:** 1 951 682-6070
Email: info@blackvoicenews.com **Web site:** http://www.blackvoicenews.com
Freq: Thu; **Circ:** 10000 Not Audited
Editor: Lee Ragin
Profile: The Black Voice News is a weekly newspaper concentrating on news, events, and issues effecting the African American community. In addition to news and weather, the publication covers topics such as health, travel, and money.
Language (s): English
Ad Rate: Full Page Mono 35.06
Currency: United States Dollars
COMMUNITY NEWSPAPER

Blackstone Courier-Record 21045
Editorial: 111 W Maple St, Blackstone, Virginia 23824-1707 **Tel:** 1 434 292-3019
Email: news@courier-record.com **Web site:** http://www.courier-record.com
Freq: Thu; **Circ:** 6535 Not Audited
Publisher: James Coleburn; **Editor:** William Coleburn
Profile: Blackstone Courier-Record is a weekly newspaper written for the residents of Blackstone, VA. The newspaper aims to bring its readers information on local news, politics, education and community events. Deadlines are one week before issue date.
Language (s): English
Ad Rate: Full Page Mono 6.75
Currency: United States Dollars
COMMUNITY NEWSPAPER

Blackstone Valley Tribune 23165
Owner: Stonebridge Press
Editorial: 25 Elm St, Southbridge, Massachusetts 01550-2605 **Tel:** 1 508 909-4130
Web site: http://www.blackstonevalleytribune.com
Freq: Fri; **Circ:** 10000 Not Audited
Publisher: Frank Chilinski; **Editor:** Adam Minor
Profile: Blackstone Valley Tribune is a free weekly newspaper that covers local news and events. The newspaper is written for residents of Oxbridge, Northbridge, and Uxbridge, MA.
Language (s): English
Ad Rate: Full Page Mono 10.00
Currency: United States Dollars
COMMUNITY NEWSPAPER

The Blount Countian 18520
Owner: Southern Democrat Inc. (The)
Editorial: 217 3rd St S, Oneonta, Alabama 35121-2189 **Tel:** 1 205 625-3231
Email: countian@otelco.net **Web site:** http://www.blountcountian.com
Freq: Wed; **Circ:** 5100 Not Audited
Advertising Sales Manager: Kim Hipp; **Publisher:** Molly Howard; **Editor:** Rob Rice; **Circulation Manager:** Jenna Wood
Profile: The Blount Countian is a weekly newspaper in Oneonta, AL that serves the residents of Blount County, Alabama. The goal of the newspaper is to provide the community with information on local news, events, recreation, sports, and more.
Language (s): English
Ad Rate: Full Page Mono 8.00
Currency: United States Dollars
COMMUNITY NEWSPAPER

Blue Mountain Town & Country Gazette 594193
Owner: Innovative Designs & Publishing, Inc.
Editorial: 4685 Lehigh Dr, Walnutport, Pennsylvania 18088-9574 **Tel:** 1 610 767-9600
Email: AskUs@TownandCountryGazette.com **Web site:** http://www.townandcountrygazette.com
Freq: Bi-Weekly; **Circ:** 11000
Editor: Joe Korba; **Publisher:** Paul Prass
Profile: Blue Mountain Town & Country Gazette is written for the residents of Walnutport, PA.
Language (s): English
Ad Rate: Full Page Mono 5.00
Ad Rate: Full Page Colour 7.00
Currency: United States Dollars
COMMUNITY NEWSPAPER

Blythewood Country Chronicle 591172
Owner: Camden Media Co.
Tel: 1 803 432-6157
Email: tpage@countrychronicle.com **Web site:** http://countrychronicle.com/
Freq: Thu; **Circ:** 12300
Publisher: Mike Mischner
Profile: The Country Chronicle is a weekly, community newspaper distributed in Blythewood (SC), Ridgeway (SC) and Winnsboro (SC).
Language (s): English
Ad Rate: Full Page Mono 13.15
Currency: United States Dollars
COMMUNITY NEWSPAPER

Boardman News 20322
Editorial: 8302 Southern Blvd Ste 2A, Boardman, Ohio 44512-6353 **Tel:** 1 330 758-6397
Email: bnews@zoominternet.net **Web site:** http://www.boardmannews.net
Freq: Thu; **Circ:** 9000 Not Audited
Publisher & Editor: John Darnell
Profile: The Boardman News was founded at Boardman Centre in Nov., 1947 by Jack A Darnell and has been a continually published since that time. The newpaper is the longest consecutively published community newspaper in Mahoning County. The newspaper is now operated by John A Darnell Jr., Jack's son, and his wife, Gwen. The Boardman is published once a week, every Thursday. Deadline for the news and advertising is noon, the Tuesday before publication.
Language (s): English
Ad Rate: Full Page Mono 6.50
Currency: United States Dollars
COMMUNITY NEWSPAPER

Boca Beacon 21390
Editorial: 431 Park Ave, Boca Grande, Florida 33921-0313 **Tel:** 1 941 964-2995
Email: info@bocabeacon.com **Web site:** http://www.bocabeacon.com
Freq: Fri; **Circ:** 6000 Not Audited
Publisher: Dusty Hopkins; **Advertising Sales Manager:** Dizey Lindquist; **Editor:** Marcy Shortuse
Profile: Boca Beacon is a local newspaper serving the residents of Boca Grande, FL and its surrounding communities. The newspaper offers local news, weather and sports. Deadlines are on Wednesdays. Please use PO Box when mailing releases.
Language (s): English
Ad Rate: Full Page Mono 8.49
Ad Rate: Full Page Colour 950.00
Currency: United States Dollars
COMMUNITY NEWSPAPER

Boca Raton Tribune 703745
Editorial: 141 NW 20th St Ste B5, Boca Raton, Florida 33431-7961 **Tel:** 1 561 807-6300
Email: news@bocaratontribune.com **Web site:** http://bocaratontribune.com
Freq: Weekly; **Circ:** 21800
Profile: Boca Raton (FL) Tribune was founded in January 15, 2010 and provides news for the communities of Boca Raton, Highland Beach, and Delray Beach, FL. It is published every Thursday. Do NOT call the publication. Send all press releases via email.
Language (s): English
Ad Rate: Full Page Mono 16.75
Ad Rate: Full Page Colour 43.85
Currency: United States Dollars
COMMUNITY NEWSPAPER

Boerne Star 20785
Owner: Hill Country Newspapers, Inc.
Editorial: 941 N School St, Boerne, Texas 78006-5922 **Tel:** 1 830 249-2441
Email: news@boernestar.com **Web site:** http://www.boernestar.com
Freq: Weekly; **Circ:** 8200 Not Audited
Publisher: Brian Cartwright; **Advertising Sales Manager:** Frank Shubert
Profile: Boerne Star is published weekly for the residents of Kendall County, TX. The newspaper

covers local news, weather, sports and entertainment.
Language (s): English
Ad Rate: Full Page Mono 20.00
Currency: United States Dollars
COMMUNITY NEWSPAPER

Boise Weekly 22527
Owner: Bar Bar Inc.
Editorial: 523 W Broad St, Boise, Idaho 83702-7642 **Tel:** 1 208 344-2055
Email: info@boiseweekly.com **Web site:** http://www.boiseweekly.com
Freq: Wed; **Circ:** 35000 Not Audited
Circulation Manager: Meg Andersen; **Publisher:** Sally Freeman; **News Editor:** George Prentice
Profile: Boise Weekly is a community newspaper serving Boise, ID, and its surrounding communities. The newspaper is an alternative, independent publication covering hard local news as well as other feature stories pertinent to the area.
Language (s): English
Ad Rate: Full Page Mono 51.80
Currency: United States Dollars
COMMUNITY NEWSPAPER

Bolivar Bulletin Times 20716
Owner: Delphis Herald
Editorial: 200 E Market St, Bolivar, Tennessee 38008-2362 **Tel:** 1 731 658-3691
Email: btnews1@yahoo.com **Web site:** http://www.bulletintimesnews.com
Freq: Weekly; **Circ:** 5200 Not Audited
Profile: Bolivar Bulletin-Times is a weekly newspaper published for the residents of Hardeman County, TN. The publication features local and county news, business information, sports, and community events.
Language (s): English
Ad Rate: Full Page Mono 8.30
Currency: United States Dollars
COMMUNITY NEWSPAPER

Bolivar Herald-Free Press 28100
Owner: Neighbor Newspapers
Editorial: 335 S Springfield Ave, Bolivar, Missouri 65613-2040 **Tel:** 1 417 326-7636
Email: news@bolivarmonews.com **Web site:** http://www.bolivarmonews.com
Freq: Fri; **Circ:** 6800 Not Audited
Circulation Manager: Jim Kennedy
Profile: Bolivar Herald-Free Press, is a twice-weekly, local newspaper. It is geared toward the residents of Polk County. MO and its surrounding areas. The newspaper covers all aspect of national and local news. Content includes sports news, business news, education news, entertainment news, and community news.
Language (s): English
Ad Rate: Full Page Mono 7.81
Currency: United States Dollars
COMMUNITY NEWSPAPER

Booneville Banner-Independent 19860
Owner: Paxton Media Group
Editorial: 208 N Main St, Booneville, Mississippi 38829-3317 **Tel:** 1 662 728-6214
Email: boonevillebanner@bellsouth.net **Web site:** http://www.dailycorinthian.com/pages/banner_independent
Freq: Thu; **Circ:** 5000 Not Audited
Editor: Brant Sappington; **Publisher:** Reece Terry
Profile: The Booneville Banner-Independent is a local, weekly newspaper serving the residents of Booneville, MS. The newspaper covers all aspects of local news, including weather, sports, business and community news. Features stories are also offered often. The newspaper occasionally reports national news that directly affects the residents of the Booneville community. Deadlines are on Mondays at noon CT.
Language (s): English
Ad Rate: Full Page Mono 9.00
Currency: United States Dollars
COMMUNITY NEWSPAPER

The Booster 28004
Editorial: 2435 Miracle Mile, Bullhead City, Arizona 86442-7311 **Tel:** 1 928 763-2505
Web site: http://www.mohavedailynews.com
Freq: Sun; **Circ:** 12663 Not Audited
Circulation Manager: Dave Horchak; **Editor:** Bill McMillen
Profile: The Booster is a twice-weekly newspaper reporting local news and events of Bullhead City and the Mohave Valley, AZ.
Language (s): English
Ad Rate: Full Page Mono 15.11
Ad Rate: Full Page Colour 120.00
Currency: United States Dollars
COMMUNITY NEWSPAPER

Boothbay Register 24441
Owner: Maine-OK Enterprises
Editorial: 97 Townsend Ave, Boothbay Harbor, Maine 04538-1843 **Tel:** 1 207 633-4620
Email: editcopy@boothbayregister.com **Web site:** http://www.boothbayregister.com/
Freq: Thu; **Circ:** 5356 Not Audited
Editor: Kevin Burnham; **Advertising Sales Manager:** Kathy Frizzell
Profile: Boothbay Register is a weekly newspaper serving the Boothbay, Boothbay Harbor, Southport, and Edgecomb, ME communities. The newspaper covers sports, weather, business, education, and community news and events.
Language (s): English
Ad Rate: Full Page Mono 9.48
Currency: United States Dollars
COMMUNITY NEWSPAPER

Bossier Press-Tribune 25161
Owner: Specht Newspapers Inc.
Editorial: 6346 Venecia Dr, Bossier City, Louisiana 71111-7454 **Tel:** 1 318 747-7900
Email: newsroom@bossierpress.com **Web site:** http://www.bossierpress.com
Freq: 3 Times/Week; **Circ:** 20000
Advertising Sales Manager: Randy Brown
Profile: Bossier Press-Tribune is a local newspaper serving the residents of Bossier City, LA and is distributed Monday through Friday. The newspaper offers extensive coverage of local and regional news, including weather, sports, business and community news. National and world headlines are also often covered.
Language (s): English
Ad Rate: Full Page Mono 18.00
Ad Rate: Full Page Colour 62.00
Currency: United States Dollars
COMMUNITY NEWSPAPER

Boston Chinese News 257563
Editorial: 1105 Massachusetts Ave Apt 3E, Cambridge, Massachusetts 02138-5221
Tel: 1 617 354-4154
Email: info@bostonchinesenews.com **Web site:** http://www.bostonchinesenews.com
Freq: Fri; **Circ:** 10000 Not Audited
Editor: Emerald Wu
Profile: Boston Chinese News is a weekly newspaper for Chinese-Americans in the Boston region. The newspaper offers local news and event listings, as well as news from China. Deadlines are Tuesdays prior to the issue date.
Language (s): Chinese
Ad Rate: Full Page Mono 7.14
Currency: United States Dollars
COMMUNITY NEWSPAPER

Boston City Paper 257566
Owner: Feeney (Paul)
Editorial: 143 Dorchester St, Boston, Massachusetts 02127-2647 **Tel:** 1 617 265-4205
Email: boscitpap@aol.com **Web site:** http://www.bostoncitypaper.org/index.html
Freq: Sat; **Circ:** 8000 Not Audited
Editor & Publisher: Paul Feeney
Profile: Boston City Paper, founded in 1967, covers local news and events in the communities of Dorchester, South Boston, West Roxbury, Roslindale, Jamaica Plain, Hyde Park, Mattapan and Boston's South End. Press Releases and Public Relation stories need to be sent in a word document as an attachment for them to be published.
Language (s): English
Ad Rate: Full Page Mono 14.58
Currency: United States Dollars
COMMUNITY NEWSPAPER

Bothell-Kenmore Reporter 593509
Owner: Sound Publishing, Inc.
Editorial: 11630 Slater Ave NE Ste 8/9, Kirkland, Washington 98034-4100 **Tel:** 1 425 483-3732
Email: editor@bothell-reporter.com **Web site:** http://www.bothell-reporter.com
Freq: Bi-Weekly; **Circ:** 20518
Profile: Bothell/Kenmore Reporter in Kirkland, WA is a publisher of community newspapers. This community newspaper is owned by Sound Publishing, Inc., which produces a variety of weekly newspapers in Washington state; these papers share content, and news releases, as well as calendar listings can be posted online for review by the paper's editorial staff.
Language (s): English
Ad Rate: Full Page Mono 23.45
Ad Rate: Full Page Colour 30.32
Currency: United States Dollars
COMMUNITY NEWSPAPER

Boulder Weekly 21954
Owner: Sallo (Stewart)
Editorial: 690 S Lashley Ln, Boulder, Colorado 80305-5920 **Tel:** 1 303 494-5511
Email: editorial@boulderweekly.com **Web site:** http://www.boulderweekly.com
Freq: Thu; **Circ:** 25000 Not Audited
Editor: Joel Dyer; **Publisher:** Stewart Sallo;
Circulation Manager: Cal Winn
Profile: Boulder (CO) Weekly is a weekly newspaper that covers local and national news relevant to the Boulder County area.
Language (s): English
Ad Rate: Full Page Mono 22.50
Currency: United States Dollars
COMMUNITY NEWSPAPER

The Boulevard Sentinel 522561
Owner: AJLA OGNA Inc
Tel: 1 323 255-1053
Email: boulevardsentinel@gmail.com **Web site:** http://www.boulevardsentinel.com
Freq: Monthly; **Circ:** 12000 Not Audited
Publisher & Editor: Tom Topping
Profile: The Boulevard Sentinel is a community newspaper written for the residents of Los Angeles. The paper was launched in 1997.
Language (s): English
Ad Rate: Full Page Mono 9.00
Currency: United States Dollars
COMMUNITY NEWSPAPER

Bowie County Citizens Tribune 25402
Owner: Westward Communications, LLC
Editorial: 133 E North Front St., New Boston, Texas 75570-2924 **Tel:** 1 903 628-5801
Email: kmitchell@bowiecountynow.com **Web site:** http://www.bowiecountynow.com
Freq: 2 Times/Week; **Circ:** 12500 Not Audited
Profile: Bowie County Citizens Tribune is a weekly community newspaper serving the Bowie County, TX area, including news, sports, lifestyle, opinion and community event listings.
Language (s): English
Ad Rate: Full Page Mono 9.05
Currency: United States Dollars
COMMUNITY NEWSPAPER

Box Elder News Journal 21026
Owner: Claybaugh (Casey)
Editorial: 55 S 100 W, Brigham City, Utah 84302-2540 **Tel:** 1 435 723-3471
Email: editor@benewsjournal.com **Web site:** http://www.benewsjournal.com
Freq: Weekly; **Circ:** 5800 Not Audited
Publisher: Casey Claybaugh
Profile: Box Elder News Journal is a weekly, local paper serving the Box Elder and Brigham, UT communities. The paper focuses on the people and places of Box Elder County, UT. It strictly covers local and community news. Content includes religion and church reports from every denomination, sports news, hunting, and fishing news. Contact the publication for advertising details. Deadlines for the paper are Friday at 5pm MT for publication the following Wednesday.
Language (s): English
Ad Rate: Full Page Mono 10.50
Ad Rate: Full Page Colour 12.09
Currency: United States Dollars
COMMUNITY NEWSPAPER

Bradford Journal 26585
Owner: Nichols (Grand) & Nichols (Debra)
Editorial: 69 Garlock Holw, Bradford, Pennsylvania 16701-3420 **Tel:** 1 814 465-3468
Email: bradfordjournal@gmail.com **Web site:** http://www.bradfordjournal.com
Freq: Thu; **Circ:** 5500 Not Audited
Editor: Debra Nichols; **Publisher:** Grant Nichols
Profile: Bradford Journal is written for the residents of Bradford, PA and its surrounding area. It covers local news, regional and national news, sports, weather, business, education, politics and community news and events. Press releases may be sent via e-mail to the editor.
Language (s): English
Ad Rate: Full Page Mono 8.32
Currency: United States Dollars
COMMUNITY NEWSPAPER

Branson Tri-Lakes News 14896
Owner: Lancaster Management Inc.
Editorial: 200 Industrial Park Dr, Hollister, Missouri 65672-5327 **Tel:** 1 417 334-3161
Web site: http://bransontrilakesnews.com
Freq: Sat; **Circ:** 9851
Circulation Manager: Robert Erickson; **Advertising Sales Manager:** Shane Walton
Profile: Branson Tri-Lakes News serves residents of Branson, MO and the surrounding area. It offers extensive coverage of local and regional news and provides syndicated national news. Content also includes sports, weather, entertainment, business and community events. Deadlines are at 10am CT two days before issue date.
Language (s): English
Ad Rate: Full Page Mono 11.50
Ad Rate: Full Page Colour 100.00
Currency: United States Dollars
COMMUNITY NEWSPAPER

Braxton Citizens' News 21280
Owner: Given (Edward Ray)
Editorial: 501 Main St, Sutton, West Virginia 26601-1320 **Tel:** 1 304 765-5193
Email: editor@bcn-news.com **Web site:** http://www.bcn-news.com
Freq: Tue; **Circ:** 6500 Not Audited
Advertising Sales Manager: Allison Given; **Editor:** Edward Ray Given
Profile: Braxton Citizens' News is a local, weekly newspaper serving the residents of Braxton, WV and its surrounding areas. The newspapers offers extensive local and regional news and covers national news when directly affecting the Braxton community. Content includes sports, weather, business, entertainment, and community news and events. The lead time for Braxton Citizens' News is one week. Deadlines for the publication are Thursday before issue date at 4pm ET.
Language (s): English
Ad Rate: Full Page Mono 7.25
Currency: United States Dollars
COMMUNITY NEWSPAPER

Brazilian Times 23210
Editorial: 311 Broadway Ste 108, Somerville, Massachusetts 02145-1933 **Tel:** 1 877 625-0079
Email: news@braziliantimes.com **Web site:** http://www.braziliantimes.com
Freq: Fri; **Circ:** 16000 Not Audited
Editor & Publisher: Edirson Paiva
Profile: Brazilian Times is a weekly newspaper targeted toward the Brazilian community of New England. The newspaper aims to bring together the public and the private sectors to support, strengthen and benefit from the integration of Brazil and the world. This includes providing timely information on Brazil and access to Brazilian resources, as well as promoting Brazilian perspectives on issues of global interest. Deadlines are on Thursdays at noon ET.
Language (s): English, Portuguese
Ad Rate: Full Page Mono 9.04
Ad Rate: Full Page Colour 9.34
Currency: United States Dollars
COMMUNITY NEWSPAPER

Brazilian Voice 231130
Editorial: 412 Chestnut St, Newark, New Jersey 07105-2433 **Tel:** 1 973 491-6200
Email: info@brazilianvoice.com **Web site:** http://www.brazilianvoice.com
Freq: Sat; **Circ:** 55000 Not Audited
Advertising Sales Manager: Fabianne Lima;
Publisher & Editor: Roberto Lima
Profile: Brazilian Voice is a newspaper serving the Brazilian-American community.
Language (s): Portuguese
Ad Rate: Full Page Mono 50.00
Currency: United States Dollars
COMMUNITY NEWSPAPER

Brazoria County News 24451
Editorial: 113 E Bernard St, West Columbia, Texas 77486-3213 **Tel:** 1 979 345-3127
Email: bcneditor@embarqmail.com **Web site:** http://www.brazoriacountynews.com
Freq: Thu; **Circ:** 11000 Not Audited
Profile: Brazoria County News is a weekly newspaper written for residents of Brazoria County, TX. The newspaper covers local news, government, sports and lifestyle.
Language (s): English
Ad Rate: Full Page Mono 7.00
Ad Rate: Full Page Colour 1080.00
Currency: United States Dollars
COMMUNITY NEWSPAPER

The Breese Journal 19059
Owner: Breese Journal and Publishing
Editorial: 8060 Old US Highway 50, Breese, Illinois 62230-3924 **Tel:** 1 618 526-7211
Email: info@thebreesejournal.com **Web site:** http://www.thebreesejournal.com
Freq: Thu; **Circ:** 6629 Not Audited
Editor: Vicky Albers; **Editor:** Jeremy Chawgo;
Publisher: Steve Mahlandt; **Advertising Sales Manager:** Mandy Ribbing
Profile: The Breese Journal is a local newspaper serving Clinton County, IL. The paper covers local news, sports, weather, business, education, arts & entertainment and crime.
Language (s): English
Ad Rate: Full Page Mono 7.43
Currency: United States Dollars
COMMUNITY NEWSPAPER

Brentwood News 21955
Owner: MediaNews Group
Editorial: 1700 Cavallo Rd, Antioch, California 94509-1930 **Tel:** 1 925 634-2125
Email: bnews@bayareanewsgroup.com **Web site:** http://www.contracostatimes.com/brentwood
Freq: Fri; **Circ:** 41000 Not Audited
Circulation Manager: Jerry Magee; **Editor:** Judy Prieve; **Advertising Sales Manager:** Robbie Simmonds
Profile: Brentwood News is a weekly insert newspaper included in the East County Times serving residents of Brentwood, CA. It operates out of the office of the East County Times in Antioch, CA.
Language (s): English
Ad Rate: Full Page Mono 18.00
Currency: United States Dollars
COMMUNITY NEWSPAPER

Bridgeport News 21584
Owner: Feldman (Joseph)
Editorial: 3506 S Halsted St, Chicago, Illinois 60609-1605 **Tel:** 1 773 927-0025
Email: jrbridgeportnews@aol.com **Web site:** http://www.bridgeportnews.net
Freq: Weekly; **Circ:** 25300 Not Audited
Publisher: Joseph Feldman; **Editor:** Janice Racinowski
Profile: Bridgeport News in Chicago, IL is published weekly and focuses on local news and community events, including high school sports, local entertainment, business, breaking news and classifieds.
Language (s): English
Ad Rate: Full Page Mono 33.00
Currency: United States Dollars
COMMUNITY NEWSPAPER

The Bridgton News 19479
Owner: Bridgton News Corp.
Editorial: 118 Main St, Bridgton, Maine 04009-1127 **Tel:** 1 207 647-2851
Email: bnews@roadrunner.com **Web site:** http://www.bridgton.com
Freq: Thu; **Circ:** 6500 Not Audited
Circulation Manager: Elaine Rioux; **Editor:** Wayne Rivet
Profile: The Bridgton News is written for the residents of Bridgton, ME and surrounding areas. It covers news, events and issues. Mail should be sent to the paper's PO Box. Deadlines are on Mondays at 5pm ET.
Language (s): English
Ad Rate: Full Page Mono 6.25
Currency: United States Dollars
COMMUNITY NEWSPAPER

The Brigantine Times 847432
Editorial: 902 W Brigantine Ave, Brigantine, New Jersey 08203-2341 **Tel:** 1 609 266-2486
Email: etinbrig@comcast.net **Web site:** http://www.brigantinetimes.com
Freq: Fri
Editor: Emmett Turner
Profile: The Brigantine Times is a weekly newspaper providing Local and Community News coverage for the residents of Brigantine, NJ.
Language (s): English
COMMUNITY NEWSPAPER

Brighton Park/McKinley Park Life 19069
Editorial: 2949 W Pope John Paul II Dr, Chicago, Illinois 60632-2554 **Tel:** 1 773 523-3663
Email: brightonparklife@aol.com **Web site:** http://www.brightonparklife.com
Freq: Thu; **Circ:** 16500 Not Audited
Advertising Sales Manager: Donna Rooney; **Publisher & Editor:** Albert Silinski
Profile: Brighton Park-Mckinley Life's editorial mission is to provide Chicago residnets with local news and information. The publication is written for Chicago, IL residents.
Language (s): English
Ad Rate: Full Page Mono 10.00
Currency: United States Dollars
COMMUNITY NEWSPAPER

The Bristol Observer 946957
Owner: Maitland Publishing, LLC.
Editorial: 213 Spring St, Southington, Connecticut 06489-1542 **Tel:** 1 860 628-9645
Web site: http://bristolobserver.com
Freq: Fri
Editor: Michael Chaiken
Profile: The Bristol Observer is a weekly newspaper devoted to the Bristol, CT community and the surrounding area. The newspaper covers local news, business, sports and arts & entertainment stories. The newspaper also covers national and statewide stories if they have a direct impact on the newspaper's readership. All inquiries should be addressed to the editor.
Language (s): English
COMMUNITY NEWSPAPER

Bristol Phoenix 23098
Owner: East Bay Newspapers
Editorial: 1 Bradford St, Bristol, Rhode Island 02809-1906 **Tel:** 1 401 253-6000
Email: bristol@eastbaynewspapers.com **Web site:** http://www.eastbayri.com/bristol
Freq: Weekly; **Circ:** 3584 Not Audited
Publisher: Matthew Hayes; **Editor:** Scott Pickering
Profile: Bristol Phoenix is a weekly newspaper published for the residents of Bristol, RI. The editorial content includes community news and events, high school sports, weather, editorials and a community guide.
Language (s): English
Ad Rate: Full Page Mono 18.50
Ad Rate: Full Page Colour 24.98
Currency: United States Dollars
COMMUNITY NEWSPAPER

British Weekly 23202
Editorial: 171 Pier Ave, Santa Monica, California 90405-5311 **Tel:** 1 310 452-2621
Email: editor@british-weekly.com **Web site:** http://www.british-weekly.com
Freq: Sat; **Circ:** 30000 Not Audited
Advertising Sales Manager: Steve George
Profile: British Weekly in Santa Monica, CA is the only newspaper in the USA serving the British expat market. It is published every Saturday and offers readers a 20-page digest of news, entertainment and sport from the United Kingdom, plus news from Southern California's British expat community.
Language (s): English
Ad Rate: Full Page Mono 14.78
Currency: United States Dollars
COMMUNITY NEWSPAPER

The Brodhead Free Press 590598
Editorial: 925 W Exchange St, Brodhead, Wisconsin 53520-1470 **Tel:** 1 608 897-4797
Email: brodheadfreepress@frontier.com
Freq: Wed; **Circ:** 8300
Advertising Sales Manager: Debbie Fitzgerald; **Publisher & Editor:** Gary Rosendahl
Profile: The Brodhead Free Press is a weekly community newspaper written for the residents of Brodhead, WI and the surrounding communities.
Language (s): English
Ad Rate: Full Page Mono 9.00
Currency: United States Dollars
COMMUNITY NEWSPAPER

The Bronx Free Press 851106
Editorial: 2030 Broadway Ste 807, New York, New York 10023-5060
Web site: http://bronxfreepress.com
Freq: Weekly
Editor: Debralee Santos
Profile: The Bronx Free Press is a weekly bilingual newspaper serving the Latin American community in The Bronx, NY, focusing on local news. The paper includes articles in English and Spanish.
Language (s): English
COMMUNITY NEWSPAPER

Broomfield Enterprise 21704
Owner: MediaNews Group
Editorial: 2500 55th St Ste 210, Boulder, Colorado 80301-5740 **Tel:** 1 303 448-9898
Web site: http://www.broomfieldenterprise.com
Freq: Fri; **Circ:** 20000 Not Audited
Advertising Sales Manager: Christine Labozan; **Publisher:** Albert Manzi
Profile: Broomfield Enterprise is distributed throughout Boulder County, CO on Wednesday afternoons and Saturday mornings. The newspaper is owned by Boulder Publishing and provides local news to readers in the community. Local features include high school sports, business, education, government and politics, and lifestyle. The best time to reach the editorial department is in the early afternoon MT. Deadlines for the publication are Tuesdays for the Wednesdays issue and Thursdays for the Saturdays issue.
Language (s): English
Ad Rate: Full Page Mono 15.34
Currency: United States Dollars
COMMUNITY NEWSPAPER

Broward Palm Beach New Times 22749
Owner: Voice Media Group
Editorial: 2450 Hollywood Blvd Ste 301A, Hollywood, Florida 33020-6642 **Tel:** 1 954 342-7700
Email: feedback@browardpalmbeach.com **Web site:** http://www.browardpalmbeach.com
Freq: Thu; **Circ:** 5400 Not Audited
Editor: Chuck Strouse
Profile: New Times is a weekly newspaper written for the residents of Broward and Palm Beach counties in Florida. It covers local news, arts & entertainment, restaurants, culture and community events.
Language (s): English
Ad Rate: Full Page Mono 50.43
Currency: United States Dollars
COMMUNITY NEWSPAPER

The Brown County Press 21656
Owner: Sun Group Newspapers
Editorial: 219 S High St, Mount Orab, Ohio 45154-9039 **Tel:** 1 937 444-3441
Email: bcpress@frontier.com **Web site:** http://www.browncountypress.com
Freq: Sun; **Circ:** 18000 Not Audited
Editor: Wayne Gates
Profile: Brown County Press is a local, weekly newspaper serving the residents of Brown County, OH. The publication focuses on local news and community events. Deadlines are Thursdays at 4pm ET.
Language (s): English
Ad Rate: Full Page Mono 9.05
Currency: United States Dollars
COMMUNITY NEWSPAPER

The Brunswick Beacon 20006
Owner: Landmark Community Newspapers, Inc.
Editorial: 208 Smith Ave, Shallotte, North Carolina 28470-4458 **Tel:** 1 910 754-6890
Web site: http://www.brunswickbeacon.com
Freq: Thu; **Circ:** 17000 Not Audited
Profile: The Brunswick Beacon is a weekly newspaper which provides readers throughout Brunswick County, NC with local community news. The newspaper covers local issues such as: politics, education, entertainment, business, lifestyle, classifieds, and weather. Their mission is to keep the community connected by focusing on local events and people. Deadlines are on Mondays at noon ET.
Language (s): English
Ad Rate: Full Page Mono 15.59
Currency: United States Dollars
COMMUNITY NEWSPAPER

Bryan County Now 448926
Owner: GateHouse Media Inc.
Editorial: 10610 Ford Ave, Richmond Hill, Georgia 31324-5976 **Tel:** 1 912 756-5566
Web site: http://savannahnow.com/bryancountynow
Freq: Thu; **Circ:** 10000 Not Audited
Publisher: Michael Traynor
Profile: Bryan County Now is a local, weekly newspaper serving residents of Richmond Hill and Bryan County, GA. The paper includes local news, business, politics, arts & entertainment, sports and community information. The paper shares a few of the same staff members at the Savannah (GA) Morning News. Advertising rates are based on a minimum one-week run.
Language (s): English
Ad Rate: Full Page Mono 12.48
Ad Rate: Full Page Colour 180.00
Currency: United States Dollars
COMMUNITY NEWSPAPER

Buckeye Lake Beacon 23041
Owner: Impact Publications
Editorial: 4675 Walnut Rd, Buckeye Lake, Ohio 43008-7770 **Tel:** 1 740 928-5541
Email: news@buckeyelakebeacon.net **Web site:** http://www.buckeyelakebeacon.net
Freq: Sat; **Circ:** 14700 Not Audited
Publisher & Editor: Charles Prince
Profile: Buckeye Lake Beacon is a local weekly newspaper that is distributed to readers throughout Perry, Fairfield, and Licking County, OH. The paper provides readers with local news and community events. Some local features include politics, business, education, lifestyle, sports and classifieds. Deadlines are Fridays at 4pm ET.
Language (s): English
Ad Rate: Full Page Mono 8.30
Currency: United States Dollars
COMMUNITY NEWSPAPER

Bucks County Herald 349776
Owner: Bucks County Herald Corp.
Editorial: 5761 Lower York Road, Lahaska, Pennsylvania 18938 **Tel:** 1 215 794-1096
Email: herald@buckscountyherald.com **Web site:** http://www.buckscountyherald.com
Freq: Thu; **Circ:** 25000 Not Audited
Editor: Bridget Wingert; **Publisher:** Joseph Wingert
Profile: Bucks County Herald in Lahaska, PA is a community newspaper that covers local news, events, school districts, sports and features. Editorial deadlines are on Tuesdays at 12 noon ET. Advertising deadlines are on Mondays at 5 p.m. ET.
Language (s): English
Ad Rate: Full Page Mono 22.00
Currency: United States Dollars
COMMUNITY NEWSPAPER

The Budget 20366
Owner: Sugarcreek Budget Publishers, Inc.
Editorial: 134 N Factory St, Sugarcreek, Ohio 44681 **Tel:** 1 330 852-4634
Email: localnews@thebudgetnewspaper.com **Web site:** http://thebudgetnewspaper.com
Freq: Wed; **Circ:** 19200 Not Audited
Editor: Fannie Erb-Miller; **Circulation Manager:** Loretta Harding; **Advertising Sales Manager:** Milo Miller
Profile: The Budget is written for members of Amish and Mennonite communities. Deadlines are on Fridays at 5pm ET.
Language (s): English
Ad Rate: Full Page Mono 12.15
Currency: United States Dollars
COMMUNITY NEWSPAPER

The Buffalo Criterion 20308
Owner: Evelyn Merri
Editorial: 623 William St, Buffalo, New York 14206-1648 **Tel:** 1 716 853-2973
Email: criterion@apollo3.com **Web site:** http://www.buffalocriterion.com
Freq: Weekly; **Circ:** 10000 Not Audited
Publisher: Evelyn Merriweather; **Editor:** Frances Merriweather
Profile: The Buffalo Criterion is a weekly newspaper written for residents of the inner city community in Buffalo, NY. The editorial mission is to try to keep the community appraised of important events and news that would be vital to the survival of the community. The newspaper includes news and editorials on local and national events, education, fitness, health, arts, and other information of interest to the community. It is written for the African American community in Buffalo, NY and surrounding areas. Deadlines are Mondays by 5pm prior to the issue dates.
Language (s): English
Ad Rate: Full Page Mono 13.50
Ad Rate: Full Page Colour 1479.50
Currency: United States Dollars
COMMUNITY NEWSPAPER

Buffalo Rocket 25091
Owner: Rocket Communications, Inc.
Editorial: 1249 Hertel Ave, Buffalo, New York 14216-2728 **Tel:** 1 716 873-2594
Email: editor.buffalorocket@gmail.com **Web site:** http://www.buffalorocket.com
Freq: Thu; **Circ:** 10000 Not Audited
Publisher: David Gallagher
Profile: Buffalo Rocket is a local, weekly newspaper serving residents of North Buffalo, West Side and Riverside, NY. The paper includes local news, business, sports, arts & entertainment and community information.
Language (s): English
Ad Rate: Full Page Mono 10.00
Currency: United States Dollars
COMMUNITY NEWSPAPER

Bukharian Times 217221
Editorial: 10616 70th Ave Fl 5, Forest Hills, New York 11375-4253 **Tel:** 1 718 261-1595
Email: bukhariantimes@aol.com **Web site:** http://www.bukhariantimes.org
Freq: Fri; **Circ:** 10000 Not Audited
Language (s): English
Ad Rate: Full Page Mono 50.00
Currency: United States Dollars
COMMUNITY NEWSPAPER

The Bulletin 140182
Owner: J & S Communications Inc.
Tel: 1 979 849-5407
Email: john.bulletin@gmail.com **Web site:** http://mybulletinnewspaper.com
Freq: Tue; **Circ:** 8000 Not Audited
Publisher & Editor: John Toth
Profile: The Bulletin is a weekly newspaper serving the residents of Brazoria County, TX.
Language (s): English
Ad Rate: Full Page Mono 10.00
Currency: United States Dollars
COMMUNITY NEWSPAPER

Bullseye 22344
Owner: Aerotech News and Review Inc.
Editorial: 3355 Spring Mountain Rd Ste 44, Las Vegas, Nevada 89102-8637 **Tel:** 1 702 876-4589
Email: bullseye@aerotechnews.com **Web site:** http://www.nellisafbnews.com
Freq: Fri; **Circ:** 12000 Not Audited
Advertising Sales Manager: Barry Anderson; **Editor:** Stuart Ibberson; **Publisher:** Paul Kinison
Profile: Bullseye is a weekly newspaper for active members of the United States Air Force stationed at Nellis Air Force Base in Nevada. Deadlines are on Thursdays prior to issue date.
Language (s): English
Ad Rate: Full Page Mono 15.70
Currency: United States Dollars
COMMUNITY NEWSPAPER

Burbank Leader 28352
Owner: tronc
Editorial: 202 W 1st St Fl 2, Los Angeles, California 90012-4299 **Tel:** 1 818 637-3200
Email: burbankleader@latimes.com **Web site:** http://www.latimes.com/socal/burbank-leader
Freq: Sat; **Circ:** 10223 Not Audited
Profile: Burbank Leader is a bi-weekly newspaper published by the Tribune Company for the residents of Burbank. It covers local news, business, sports, arts and entertainment. The paper is inserted within the Los Angeles Times and it is also available for free at area news racks. Deadlines fall on Fridays at 5pm PT for the Wednesday issue and on Thursdays at 5pm PT for the Saturday issue. On Sundays, the paper combines with the Glendale News-Press to put out a Sunday issue, the Sunday News-Press & Leader.
Language (s): English
Ad Rate: Full Page Mono 22.95
Currency: United States Dollars
COMMUNITY NEWSPAPER

The Burbank Times 21715
Editorial: 3917 W Riverside Dr Fl 2, Burbank, California 91505-4327 **Tel:** 1 818 841-6397
Email: burbanktimes@gmail.com
Freq: Fri; **Circ:** 25000 Not Audited
Publisher & Editor: Bruce Tiger
Profile: The Burbank Times is published weekly for the residents of Burbank, Glendale and North Hollywood, CA. The newspaper covers local news, business, sports, entertainment and community events.
Language (s): English
Ad Rate: Full Page Mono 24.50
Currency: United States Dollars
COMMUNITY NEWSPAPER

Bureau County Republican 22112
Owner: Shaw Media
Editorial: 800 Ace Rd, Princeton, Illinois 61356-9201 **Tel:** 1 815 875-4461
Email: news@bcrnews.com **Web site:** http://www.bcrnews.com
Freq: Sat; **Circ:** 7340 Not Audited
Circulation Manager: Abbie Clark; **Publisher:** Sam Fisher; **Editor:** Kevin Hieronymus; **Editor:** Terri Simon
Profile: The Bureau County Republican is a newspaper in Princeton, Illinois covering local news and events. Founded in 1847, the paper publishes three times a week, on Tuesday, Thursday, and Saturday.
Language (s): English
Ad Rate: Full Page Mono 12.35
Currency: United States Dollars
COMMUNITY NEWSPAPER

Burleson-Crowley Connection 492431
Owner: Community Newspaper Holdings Inc.
Editorial: 108 S Anglin St, Cleburne, Texas 76031-5602 **Tel:** 1 817 645-2441
Email: editor@trcle.com **Web site:** http://burlesoncrowley.com
Freq: Tue; **Circ:** 20000 Not Audited
News Editor: Monica Faram; **Circulation Manager:** Toscha Vaughan
Profile: Burleson-Crowley Connection is a community newspaper written for the residents of Cleburne, Burleson and Crowley, TX. It covers local news and sports.
Language (s): English
Ad Rate: Full Page Mono 10.50
Currency: United States Dollars
COMMUNITY NEWSPAPER

The Burton View 949407
Owner: JAMS Media
Editorial: 220 N Main St, Davison, Michigan 48423-1432 **Tel:** 1 810 653-3511
Email: buveditor@mihomepaper.com **Web site:** http://burtonview.mihomepaper.com/
Freq: Weekly; **Circ:** 11910
Profile: The Burton View is a weekly community newspaper serving residents of Burton, MI with community news, sports and lifestyle.
Language (s): English
COMMUNITY NEWSPAPER

The Butner-Creedmoor News 19974
Owner: Granville Publishing Company, Inc.
Editorial: 418 N Main St, Creedmoor, North Carolina 27522-8809 **Tel:** 1 919 528-2393
Email: bcnews@mindspring.com **Web site:** http://www.butnercreedmoornews.org
Freq: Thu; **Circ:** 5400 Not Audited
Publisher & Editor: Elizabeth Coleman; **Circulation Manager:** Gail Locklear
Profile: The Butner-Creedmoor News is a weekly newspaper published for the residents of Butner and Creedmoor, NC. The publication covers the communities of Butner, Creedmoor and Stem, as well as Southern Granville, Northern Wake and Northern Durham counties. The newspaper features local news, politics, sports and community events. Deadlines are on Tuesdays at 3pm ET.
Language (s): English

Ad Rate: Full Page Mono 11.00
Ad Rate: Full Page Colour 948.15
Currency: United States Dollars
COMMUNITY NEWSPAPER

Cairo Messenger 18798
Editorial: 31 1st Ave NE, Cairo, Georgia 39828-2102 **Tel:** 1 229 377-2032
Email: news@cairomessenger.com **Web site:** http://www.cairomessenger.com
Freq: Wed; **Circ:** 13195 Not Audited
Advertising Sales Manager: Mesha Wind; **Editor and Publisher:** Randolph Wind
Profile: Cairo Messenger covers local news in and around Cairo, GA. Deadlines for editorial submissions are on Mondays at noon ET.
Language (s): English
Ad Rate: Full Page Mono 6.60
Ad Rate: Full Page Colour 893.80
Currency: United States Dollars
COMMUNITY NEWSPAPER

The Calhoun Liberty Journal 18738
Editorial: 11493 NW Summers Rd, Bristol, Florida 32321-3364 **Tel:** 1 850 643-3333
Email: thejournal@fairpoint.net **Web site:** http://www.cljnews.com
Freq: Wed; **Circ:** 5550 Not Audited
Publisher: Johnny Eubanks; **Editor:** Teresa Eubanks
Profile: The Calhoun Liberty Journal is a local newspaper serving the counties of Calhoun and Liberty, FL. It provides the local communities with information on news, events, weather and sports.
Language (s): English
Ad Rate: Full Page Mono 6.00
Currency: United States Dollars
COMMUNITY NEWSPAPER

Calhoun Times 24385
Owner: News Publishing Company
Editorial: 215 W Line St, Calhoun, Georgia 30701-1815 **Tel:** 1 706 629-2231
Web site: http://www.calhountimes.com
Freq: Sat; **Circ:** 8500 Not Audited
Advertising Sales Manager: Billy Steele
Profile: Calhoun Times is a local biweekly newspaper serving the Gordon County, GA area. It provides the local community with information on local news, events, sports and weather.
Language (s): English
Ad Rate: Full Page Mono 10.76
Currency: United States Dollars
COMMUNITY NEWSPAPER

California Advocate 18617
Owner: Kimber (Mark and Les)
Editorial: 1555 E St, Fresno, California 93706-2005 **Tel:** 1 559 268-0941
Email: newsroom@caladvocate.com **Web site:** http://www.caladvocate.com
Freq: Fri; **Circ:** 33013 Not Audited
Editor & Publisher: Mark Kimber
Profile: California Advocate is a newspaper serving the Fresno, CA area. It provides the African-American community with information on important issues and events. Deadlines are on Mondays before the issue date.
Language (s): English
Ad Rate: Full Page Mono 39.50
Currency: United States Dollars
COMMUNITY NEWSPAPER

California Crusader News 24124
Editorial: 12519 Crenshaw Blvd, Hawthorne, California 90250 **Tel:** 1 424 269-1359
Email: calcrus@pacbell.net **Web site:** http://www.calcrusnews.com
Freq: Thu; **Circ:** 25000 Not Audited
Advertising Sales Manager: Kim Lopez
Profile: California Crusader News in Hawthorne, CA covers local news, sports, entertainment, health, food, religion and events for residents of Inglewood, CA, Los Angeles and surrounding communities.
Language (s): English
Ad Rate: Full Page Mono 30.00
Currency: United States Dollars
COMMUNITY NEWSPAPER

California Sun Times 281575
Editorial: 3010 Wilshire Blvd, Ste 553, Los Angeles, California 90010 **Tel:** 1 213 614-0534 115
Email: calsuntimes2@yahoo.com
Freq: Fri
Circulation Manager: Stan Miles; **Publisher:** Dave Shumann
Profile: California Sun Times is published weekly for the residents of Los Angeles and surrounding areas. The newspaper provides information about local news and community events.
Language (s): English
Ad Rate: Full Page Mono 15.00
Currency: United States Dollars
COMMUNITY NEWSPAPER

The Call 19837
Owner: Stewart (Donna)
Editorial: 1715 E 18th St, Kansas City, Missouri 64108-1611 **Tel:** 1 816 842-3804
Email: kccallnews@hotmail.com **Web site:** http://www.kccall.com
Freq: Fri; **Circ:** 15000 Not Audited
Editor & Publisher: Donna Stewart; **Advertising Sales Manager:** Barbara Way
Profile: The Call is one of the six largest African American weeklies in the country and serves the communities surrounding Kansas City, MO. The newspaper covers local news, social issues, religion, education and community events.
Language (s): English
Ad Rate: Full Page Mono 15.00
Currency: United States Dollars
COMMUNITY NEWSPAPER

Call and Post 26507
Owner: King Media Enterprises Inc.
Editorial: 11800 Shaker Blvd, Cleveland, Ohio 44120-1919 **Tel:** 1 216 588-6700
Email: info@call-post.com **Web site:** http://www.callandpost.com
Freq: Wed; **Circ:** 45600 Not Audited
Publisher: Don King; **Circulation Manager:** Carl Matthews
Profile: Call and Post is dedicated to providing news to the African-American communities in Cincinnati and Cleveland. It covers local news, business, arts & entertainment and sports.
Language (s): English
Ad Rate: Full Page Mono 65.49
Currency: United States Dollars
COMMUNITY NEWSPAPER

The Calvert Recorder 28320
Owner: Gazette Newspapers Inc.
Tel: 1 301 855-1029
Web site: http://www.somdnews.com/recorder
Freq: Fri; **Circ:** 12000 Not Audited
Advertising Sales Manager: Christy Bailey; **Editor:** Rob Perry
Profile: The Calvert Recorder is a local newspaper covering all of Calvert County, MD. Coverage includes local news, events, sports, arts & entertainment, travel, food and lifestyle topics.
Language (s): English
Ad Rate: Full Page Mono 12.85
Currency: United States Dollars
COMMUNITY NEWSPAPER

Camas-Washougal Post Record 21095
Owner: Columbian Publishing Co.
Editorial: 425 NE 4th Ave, Camas, Washington 98607-2129 **Tel:** 1 360 834-2141
Web site: http://www.camaspostrecord.com
Freq: Weekly; **Circ:** 10000 Not Audited
Editor: Heather Acheson; **Publisher:** Mike Gallagher
Profile: Camas-Washougal Post Record is a local weekly newspaper serving Camas and Washougal, WA. It provides residents with information on news, events, sports and weather.
Language (s): English
Ad Rate: Full Page Mono 10.60
Ad Rate: Full Page Colour 1206.30
Currency: United States Dollars
COMMUNITY NEWSPAPER

The Camden Chronicle 24322
Owner: Magic Valley Publishing, Inc.
Editorial: 144 W Main St, Camden, Tennessee 38320 **Tel:** 1 731 584-7200
Web site: http://www.thecamdenchronicle.com
Freq: Thu; **Circ:** 5163 Not Audited
Advertising Sales Manager: Bethany Hargis; **Publisher:** Dennis Richardson; **Editor:** Lisa Richardson
Profile: The Camden Chronicle is a local weekly newspaper serving the Benton County, TN area. It provides the local community with information on news, events, sports and weather. Deadlines for the paper are Mondays at noon ET.
Language (s): English
Ad Rate: Full Page Mono 8.00
Currency: United States Dollars
COMMUNITY NEWSPAPER

Camden Herald 23110
Owner: Village NetMedia
Editorial: 5 Bayview Lndg, Camden, Maine 04843-2249 **Tel:** 1 207 236-8511
Email: cherald@courierpub.com **Web site:** http://www.camdenherald.com
Freq: Sat; **Circ:** 5400 Not Audited
Editor: Daniel Dunkle
Profile: The Camden Herald is a regional newspaper serving Knox County, Maine with news, sports, weather, events and photos. Circulation figures unavailable.
Language (s): English
Ad Rate: Full Page Mono 12.48
Ad Rate: Full Page Colour 1771.00
Currency: United States Dollars
COMMUNITY NEWSPAPER

Cam-News 24123
Editorial: 1305 Raymond Ave Ste A, Long Beach, California 90804-2282 **Tel:** 1 562 987-4532
Email: cam-news@hotmail.com **Web site:** http://www.camnews.org
Freq: Bi-Weekly; **Circ:** 10000 Not Audited
Publisher & Editor: Borann Duong
Profile: CAM-News is a bi-weekly Cambodian language newspaper in San Francisco.
Language (s): Cambodian, English
Ad Rate: Full Page Mono 27.00
Currency: United States Dollars
COMMUNITY NEWSPAPER

La Campana 154584
Owner: Cisneros (Ramon)
Editorial: 250 Chatfield Way, Franklin, Tennessee 37067-6238 **Tel:** 1 615 764-0240
Email: lacampana@comcast.net **Web site:** http://www.lacampana.us
Freq: Mon; **Circ:** 8500 Not Audited
Editor & Publisher: Ramon Cisneros
Profile: La Campana is a weekly community newspaper serving Spanish-speaking residents of Franklin, TN.
Language (s): Spanish
Ad Rate: Full Page Mono 26.00
Currency: United States Dollars
COMMUNITY NEWSPAPER

Campus News 913445
Owner: Johnson (Darren)
Editorial: 39 County Route 70, Greenwich, New York 12834-6300 **Tel:** 1 518 507-6359
Email: editor@campus-news.org **Web site:** http://campus-news.org
Freq: Bi-Weekly; **Circ:** 10000
Editor & Publisher: Darren Johnson
Profile: Founded in February 2010, Campus News is a community newspaper serving college students at New York, New England and New Jersey two-year colleges. The paper prints monthly/bi-weekly during the school year and is distributed to 27 campus in the region. Writers are all college students and faculty, with occasional pieces from Scripps interns and student freelancers.
Language (s): English
Ad Rate: Full Page Mono 18.71
Ad Rate: Full Page Colour 21.29
Currency: United States Dollars
COMMUNITY NEWSPAPER

Canarsie Courier 20248
Owner: Canarsie Courier Publications, Inc.
Editorial: 1142 E 92nd St, Brooklyn, New York 11236-3624 **Tel:** 1 718 257-0600
Email: editor@canarsiecourier.com **Web site:** http://www.canarsiecourier.com
Freq: Weekly; **Circ:** 8500 Not Audited
Advertising Sales Manager: Catherine Rosa
Profile: Canarsie Courier is a community newspaper serving Brooklyn, NY. It provides residents with information on local news and events.
Language (s): English
Ad Rate: Full Page Mono 5.11
Currency: United States Dollars
COMMUNITY NEWSPAPER

Canby Herald 22963
Owner: Pamplin Media Group
Editorial: 241 N Grant St, Canby, Oregon 97013-3629 **Tel:** 1 503 266-6831
Email: cherald@canbyherald.com **Web site:** http://www.pamplinmedia.com/canby-herald-news
Freq: Sat; **Circ:** 5500 Not Audited
Editor: John Baker; **Publisher:** Georgia Newton
Profile: Canby Herald provides news, sports and events coverage for residents of Canby, OR. Deadlines are two days before issue date.
Language (s): English
Ad Rate: Full Page Mono 11.00
Currency: United States Dollars
COMMUNITY NEWSPAPER

Cannon Connections 387606
Owner: Clovis Media
Editorial: 521 Pile St, Clovis, New Mexico 88101-6637 **Tel:** 1 575 763-3431
Web site: http://cannonconnections.com
Freq: Fri; **Circ:** 6000 Not Audited
Editor: David Stevens
Profile: Cannon Connections is a free, weekly newspaper serving military personnel and civilian employees and residents of Cannon Air Force Base in Clovis, NM. It provides readers with local news and information pertinent to the local community and the military both here and abroad. Although it is owned by the Clovis News Journal, which handles printing and advertising, all editorial content is supplied by military staff members. Editorial submissions are due to the base's Public Affairs office on Fridays at noon CT one week before issue date. Advertising is due to the offices of the Clovis News Journal on Friday one week prior to publication.
Language (s): English
Ad Rate: Full Page Mono 7.00
Currency: United States Dollars
COMMUNITY NEWSPAPER

Canyon News 281917
Owner: Kelly Media
Editorial: 9465 Wilshire Blvd Ste 300, Beverly Hills, California 90212-2612 **Tel:** 1 310 277-6017
Email: staff@canyon-news.com **Web site:** http://www.canyon-news.com
Freq: Sun; **Circ:** 40000 Not Audited
Editor: Rachel Knuese
Profile: Canyon News in Beverly Hills, CA is a weekly newspaper covering all of the Canyon, including Bel Air, Beachwood Canyon, Benedict Canyon, Brentwood, Laurel Canyon, Los Feliz, Malibu, Melrose, Pacific Palisades, Santa Monica, Sherman Oaks, Studio City, Topanga Canyon, Westwood, Woodland Hills and all of the Hollywood Hills, CA. Publication requests that users register on website; it does not take calls from publicists.
Language (s): English
Ad Rate: Full Page Mono 7.24
Currency: United States Dollars
COMMUNITY NEWSPAPER

The Cap Times 14810
Owner: Capital Newspapers
Editorial: 1901 Fish Hatchery Rd, Madison, Wisconsin 53713-1248 **Tel:** 1 608 252-6400
Email: citydesk@madison.com **Web site:** http://host.madison.com/ct/
Freq: Weekly; **Circ:** 73519
News Editor: Jason Joyce
Profile: The Cap Times is a weekly magazine style print publication featuring news, commentary and other content on Madison. The paper was previously known as a daily, The Capital Times.
Language (s): English
COMMUNITY NEWSPAPER

The Cape Cod Chronicle 19462
Owner: Hyora Publications
Editorial: 60 Munson Meeting Way Ste C, Chatham, Massachusetts 02633-1992 **Tel:** 1 508 945-2220
Email: editor@capecodchronicle.com **Web site:** http://www.capecodchronicle.com
Freq: Thu; **Circ:** 9900 Not Audited
Advertising Sales Manager: Debra Decosta; **Publisher:** Henry Hyora; **Editor:** Timothy J. Wood
Profile: The Cape Cod Chronicle is written for the residents of Cape Cod, MA. It covers news, sports, entertainment and lifestyle topics.
Language (s): English
Ad Rate: Full Page Mono 15.10
Currency: United States Dollars
COMMUNITY NEWSPAPER

Cape Gazette 22169
Owner: Cape Gazette Ltd.
Editorial: 17585 Nassau Commons Blvd, Lewes, Delaware 19958-6286 **Tel:** 1 302 645-7700
Email: newsroom@capegazette.com **Web site:** http://www.capegazette.com
Freq: Fri; **Circ:** 13000 Not Audited
Publisher: Dennis Forney; **Community News Editor:** Laura Ritter
Profile: Cape Gazette is a local weekly newspaper serving Delaware's Cape region. It provides residents with information on local news, events, sports and weather. Deadlines are on Wednesdays at noon ET.
Language (s): English
Ad Rate: Full Page Mono 12.35
Currency: United States Dollars
COMMUNITY NEWSPAPER

The Cape May Star and Wave 23023
Owner: Sample Media, Inc.
Editorial: 600 Park Blvd Ste 28, West Cape May, New Jersey 08204-1267 **Tel:** 1 609 884-3466
Email: cmstarwave@comcast.net **Web site:** http://www.starandwave.com
Freq: Wed; **Circ:** 6700 Not Audited
Editor: Jack Fichter; **Publisher:** David Nahan; **Advertising Sales Manager:** Jay Young
Profile: The Cape May Star and Wave is a local weekly newspaper serving the Cape May, NJ area. It provides information on local news and events.
Language (s): English
Ad Rate: Full Page Mono 8.30
Currency: United States Dollars
COMMUNITY NEWSPAPER

Capital City Weekly 21641
Owner: GateHouse Media Inc.
Editorial: 134 N Franklin St, Juneau, Alaska 99801-1223 **Tel:** 1 907 789-4144
Email: editor@capweek.com **Web site:** http://www.capitalcityweekly.com
Freq: Wed; **Circ:** 15550 Not Audited
Profile: Capital City Weekly is a local weekly newspaper serving residents of Juneau, AK. It provides residents of Southeastern Alaska with information on news, events, sports and weather.
Language (s): English
Ad Rate: Full Page Mono 17.82
Currency: United States Dollars
COMMUNITY NEWSPAPER

Carbondale News 20551
Owner: GateHouse Media Inc.
Editorial: 41 N Church St, Carbondale, Pennsylvania 18407-1904 **Tel:** 1 570 282-3300
Web site: http://www.thecarbondalenews.com
Freq: Wed; **Circ:** 6500
Publisher: Michelle Fleece; **Advertising Manager:** Guy Matthews; **Editor:** Ryan O'Malley
Profile: Carbondale News is written for the residents of Carbondale, PA.
Language (s): English
Ad Rate: Full Page Mono 4.60
Currency: United States Dollars
COMMUNITY NEWSPAPER

Carbondale Times 75288
Owner: Paddock Publications
Editorial: 701 W Main St, Carbondale, Illinois 62901-2643 **Tel:** 1 618 457-4084
Email: ctimes@midwest.net **Web site:** http://carbondaletimes.com
Freq: Wed; **Circ:** 8500 Not Audited
Advertising Sales Manager: Debbie Thomas; **Publisher:** Jason Thomas
Profile: Carbondale Times is a weekly community newspaper serving Carbondale, IL, including local news, sports and events.
Language (s): English
Ad Rate: Full Page Mono 11.50
Currency: United States Dollars
COMMUNITY NEWSPAPER

Caribbean National Weekly 585297
Owner: Ferguson (Hugh)
Tel: 1 954 739-6618
Email: editor@cnweeklynews.com **Web site:** http://www.cnweeklynews.com
Freq: Thu; **Circ:** 30000
Profile: Written for the Caribbean-American community in Florida. It is distributed throughout

Miami-Dade, Broward and Palm counties as well as Tampa, Orlando, Melbourne and Jacksonville, FL. It covers news from the nations of the Caribbean and other information of relevance to Caribbean-Americans. The publication launched in December 2004. Advertising deadlines are Tuesdays at 10AM ET.
Language (s): English
Ad Rate: Full Page Mono 20.00
Currency: United States Dollars
COMMUNITY NEWSPAPER

The Carmel Pine Cone 22556
Owner: Miller (Paul)
Editorial: 734 Lighthouse Ave, Pacific Grove, California 93950-2522 **Tel:** 1 831 624-0162
Email: mail@carmelpinecone.com **Web site:** http://www.carmelpinecone.com
Freq: Fri; **Circ:** 20000 Not Audited
Advertising Sales Manager: Jackie Edwards; **Publisher & Editor:** Paul Miller
Profile: The Carmel Pine Cone is a weekly newspaper covering the town of Carmel-by-the-Sea, CA. The paper provides local news and events for residents of the town.
Language (s): English
Ad Rate: Full Page Mono 17.20
Currency: United States Dollars
COMMUNITY NEWSPAPER

Carolina Beach Island Gazette 19970
Owner: McKee (Roger)
Editorial: 1003 Bennet Ln Ste F, Carolina Beach, North Carolina 28428-5770 **Tel:** 1 910 458-8156
Email: islandgazette@aol.com **Web site:** http://www.islandgazette.net
Freq: Wed; **Circ:** 8000 Not Audited
Publisher: Roger McKee
Profile: Carolina Beach Island Gazette is published weekly for the residents of Carolina Beach, NC and surrounding areas. The newspaper covers local news, sports and community events. Editorial deadlines are on Mondays at 5pm ET.
Language (s): English
Ad Rate: Full Page Mono 12.00
Currency: United States Dollars
COMMUNITY NEWSPAPER

The Carolina Forest Chronicle 527812
Editorial: 2510 Main St, Conway, South Carolina 29526-3365 **Tel:** 1 843 248-6671
Email: info@myhorrynews.com **Web site:** http://www.myhorrynews.com
Freq: Thu; **Circ:** 13500 Not Audited
Publisher: Steve Robertson
Profile: The Carolina Forest Chronicle is written for the residents of Forestbrook, SC and surrounding areas. The publication was incepted in November 2007. The newspaper covers local news and community events.
Language (s): English
Ad Rate: Full Page Mono 14.00
Currency: United States Dollars
COMMUNITY NEWSPAPER

Carolina Panorama 22530
Owner: MDB Media
Editorial: 2346 Two Notch Rd, Columbia, South Carolina 29204-2279 **Tel:** 1 803 256-4015
Email: cpanorama@aol.com **Web site:** http://www.carolinapanorama.com
Freq: Thu; **Circ:** 16000 Not Audited
Editor: Nat Abraham
Profile: Carolina Panorama is a weekly newspaper that provides local news coverage for residents of Columbia, South Carolina.
Language (s): English
Ad Rate: Full Page Mono 15.00
Currency: United States Dollars
COMMUNITY NEWSPAPER

Carolina Peacemaker 20031
Editorial: 400 Summit Ave, Greensboro, North Carolina 27405-7748 **Tel:** 1 336 274-6210
Email: editor@carolinapeacemaker.com **Web site:** http://peacemakeronline.com/
Freq: Thu; **Circ:** 9100 Not Audited
Editor: Afrique Kilimanjaro
Profile: Carolina Peacemaker is a local newspaper written for the African American residents of Greensboro, NC. Deadlines are on Mondays at 5pm ET.
Language (s): English
Ad Rate: Full Page Mono 30.00
Currency: United States Dollars
COMMUNITY NEWSPAPER

The Carolina Times 19975
Owner: United Publishers Incorporated
Editorial: 923 Old Fayetteville St, Durham, North Carolina 27701-3914 **Tel:** 1 919 682-2913
Email: thecarolinatimes@cs.com
Freq: Thu; **Circ:** 6009 Not Audited
Publisher, Editor, Advertising Sales & Circulation Manager: Kenneth Edmonds
Profile: The Carolina Times is written or residents in Durham, NC. It covers city and county government, local education and regional and state issues affecting African Americans. Please e-mail or mail all press releases and other related materials. Do NOT fax this paper.
Language (s): English
Ad Rate: Full Page Mono 24.50
Currency: United States Dollars
COMMUNITY NEWSPAPER

The Caroline Progress 28913
Owner: Lakeway Publishers, Inc.
Editorial: 204 N Main St, Bowling Green, Virginia 22427-9416 **Tel:** 1 804 633-5005
Email: cpeditor@lcs.net **Web site:** http://www.carolineprogress.com
Freq: Thu; **Circ:** 9000 Not Audited
Editor: Toni Stinson; **Publisher:** Mosby Wigginton; **Advertising Sales Manager:** Rusty Wornom
Profile: The Caroline Progress is a weekly newspaper that provides local news coverage for the residents of Caroline County. The deadline for the Caroline Progress is the Monday prior to the issue date at noon ET.
Language (s): English
Ad Rate: Full Page Mono 11.43
Currency: United States Dollars
COMMUNITY NEWSPAPER

The Carolinian 20036
Editorial: 519 S Blount St, Raleigh, North Carolina 27601-1827 **Tel:** 1 919 834-5558
Email: thecarolinian@bellsouth.net **Web site:** http://www.raleighcarolinian.com
Freq: Mon; **Circ:** 14202 Not Audited
Circulation Manager: Andrew Alston; **Editor:** Kevin Jervay; **Editor:** Cash Michaels
Profile: The Carolinian is written for African American residents in Raliegh, NC. It covers local news, business, sports and arts & entertainment stories. It also covers national and statewide stories if they have a direct impact on the readership.
Language (s): English
Ad Rate: Full Page Mono 24.00
Currency: United States Dollars
COMMUNITY NEWSPAPER

Carriage Towne News 73119
Owner: Community Newspaper Holdings, Inc.
Editorial: 14 Church St, Kingston, New Hampshire 03848-3062 **Tel:** 1 603 642-4499
Email: info@carriagetownenews.com **Web site:** http://www.carriagetownenews.com
Freq: Thu; **Circ:** 30614 Not Audited
Publisher: Karen Andreas; **Publisher & Editor:** Elisha Blaisdell
Profile: Carriage Towne News is a local newspaper covering news in Atkinson, Brentwood, Danville, East Hampstead, East Kingston, Epping, Exeter, Fremont, Hampstead, Kensington, Kingston, Newton, Newton Junction, Plaistow, Raymond, Sandown, South Hampton and Stratham, NH.
Language (s): English
Ad Rate: Full Page Mono 20.25
Currency: United States Dollars
COMMUNITY NEWSPAPER

The Carroll News 22604
Owner: Civitas Media
Editorial: 707 N Main St, Hillsville, Virginia 24343-1455 **Tel:** 1 276 728-7311
Web site: http://thecarrollnews.com
Freq: Wed; **Circ:** 13500 Not Audited
Advertising Sales Manager: Sherry Stanley
Profile: The Carroll News is a local newspaper written for the residents of Hillsville, VA. The paper provides local news and events.
Language (s): English
Ad Rate: Full Page Mono 10.95
Currency: United States Dollars
COMMUNITY NEWSPAPER

Carson City Gazette 19501
Owner: Stafford Communications Group
Editorial: 109 N Lafayette St, Greenville, Michigan 48838-1853 **Tel:** 1 616 754-9303
Web site: http://www.thedailynews.cc
Freq: Mon; **Circ:** 8646 Not Audited
Publisher: Rob Stafford
Profile: Carson City Gazette is written for the residents of Carson City, MI. It covers local news, sports, entertainment and events.
Language (s): English
Ad Rate: Full Page Mono 6.95
Currency: United States Dollars
COMMUNITY NEWSPAPER

The Carteret County News-Times 19992
Owner: Carteret Publishing Company
Editorial: 4206 Bridges St, Morehead City, North Carolina 28557-2942 **Tel:** 1 252 726-7081
Web site: http://www.carolinacoastonline.com
Freq: Fri; **Circ:** 10500 Not Audited
Circulation Manager: Joyce Ferrell; **Advertising Sales Manager:** Kim Moseley; **Publisher:** Lockwood Phillips
Profile: The Carteret County News-Times is a local newspaper written for the residents of Morehead City, NC. The circulation rate is 9,515 on on Wednesday and Friday and 10,924 on Sunday.
Language (s): English
Ad Rate: Full Page Mono 13.10
Currency: United States Dollars
COMMUNITY NEWSPAPER

Carthage Carthaginian 19863
Owner: Prather (Waid)
Editorial: 122 W Franklin St, Carthage, Mississippi 39051-3754 **Tel:** 1 601 267-4501
Web site: http://www.thecarthaginian.com
Freq: Thu; **Circ:** 5700 Not Audited
Advertising Sales Manager: Mandy Farrow
Profile: Carthage Carthaginian is a weekly newspaper covering news and events of interest to residents of Leake County, MS. Deadlines are on Tuesdays at noon CT.
Language (s): English
Ad Rate: Full Page Mono 7.35
Currency: United States Dollars
COMMUNITY NEWSPAPER

Carthage Courier 20719
Owner: Lake (Hershel)
Editorial: 509 Main St N, Carthage, Tennessee 37030-1270 **Tel:** 1 615 735-1110
Email: news@carthagecourier.com **Web site:** http://www.carthagecourier.com
Freq: Thu; **Circ:** 5350 Not Audited
Circulation Manager: Susanne Tisdale
Profile: Carthage Courier is a weekly newspaper covering news and events of interest to the residents of Smith County, TN. Deadlines for submission are Mondays at 4pm ET.
Language (s): English
Ad Rate: Full Page Mono 5.50
Currency: United States Dollars
COMMUNITY NEWSPAPER

Cascadia Weekly 405474
Owner: Cascadia Newspaper Co. LLC
Editorial: 1155 N State St Ste 600, Bellingham, Washington 98225-5392 **Tel:** 1 360 647-8200
Email: info@cascadiaweekly.com **Web site:** http://www.cascadiaweekly.com
Freq: Wed; **Circ:** 20000 Not Audited
Publisher & Editor: Tim Johnson
Profile: Cascadia Weekly is published weekly for the residents of Bellingham, WA and surrounding areas. The newspaper covers local news, arts and entertainment. Deadlines are at noon PT prior to issue date.
Language (s): English
Ad Rate: Full Page Mono 11.47
Currency: United States Dollars
COMMUNITY NEWSPAPER

The Casey County News 19354
Owner: Landmark Community Newspapers, Inc.
Editorial: 720 Campbellsville St, Liberty, Kentucky 42539-3106 **Tel:** 1 606 787-7171
Web site: http://www.caseynews.net
Freq: Wed; **Circ:** 5543 Not Audited
Profile: The Casey County News is a weekly newspaper for residents of Casey County, KY. Submission deadlines are Mondays at 4pm ET.
Language (s): English
Ad Rate: Full Page Mono 9.11
Currency: United States Dollars
COMMUNITY NEWSPAPER

The Cash-Book Journal 19781
Editorial: 210 W Main St, Jackson, Missouri 63755-1822 **Tel:** 1 573 243-3515
Email: cashbook@mvp.net **Web site:** http://www.thecash-book.com
Freq: Wed; **Circ:** 6000
Circulation Manager: Elaine Hale; **Publisher:** Gina Raffety; **Advertising Sales Manager:** Jim Salzman
Profile: The Cash-Book Journal is a weekly community newspaper issued on Wednesday. It has been covering local news and sports for Cape Girardeau County, MO since 1870.
Language (s): English
Ad Rate: Full Page Mono 10.50
Currency: United States Dollars
COMMUNITY NEWSPAPER

Casper Journal 21304
Owner: Lee Enterprises, Inc.
Editorial: 170 Star Ln, Casper, Wyoming 82604-2883 **Tel:** 1 307 266-0520
Web site: http://trib.com/casperjournal
Freq: Wed; **Circ:** 26000 Not Audited
Publisher & Editor: Dale Bohren
Profile: Casper Journal is a weekly newspaper written for the residents of Casper, WY. The newspaper covers local news, entertainment, sports, politics and community events. The deadlines for the publication are on Wednesdays at 5pm MT.
Language (s): English
Ad Rate: Full Page Mono 23.00
Ad Rate: Full Page Colour 38.00
Currency: United States Dollars
COMMUNITY NEWSPAPER

Cass County Democrat-Missourian 22742
Owner: McClatchy Newspapers
Editorial: 301 S Lexington St, Harrisonville, Missouri 64701-2446 **Tel:** 1 816 234-4449
Web site: http://www.demo-mo.com
Freq: Fri; **Circ:** 5900 Not Audited
Advertising Manager: Kristi Feiss
Profile: Cass County Democrat-Missourian is a local weekly newspaper serving Harrisonville, MO and the surrounding area. It provides the local community with information on news, events, sports and weather. Deadlines are on Tuesdays at 5pm CT.
Language (s): English
Ad Rate: Full Page Mono 22.00
Currency: United States Dollars
COMMUNITY NEWSPAPER

Castro Valley Forum 22855
Owner: Zehnder (Fred)
Editorial: 3742 Castro Valley Blvd, Castro Valley, California 94546-4406 **Tel:** 1 510 537-1792
Freq: Wed; **Circ:** 22500 Not Audited
Advertising Sales Manager: Mary Florence
Profile: Castro Valley Forum is a community newspaper for residents of Castro Valley, CA.
Language (s): English
Ad Rate: Full Page Mono 16.50
Currency: United States Dollars
COMMUNITY NEWSPAPER

The Catalina Islander 22958
Owner: Community Media Corporation
Editorial: 635 Crescent Avenue, Suite A, Avalon, California 90704 **Tel:** 1 310 510-0500
Email: editor@catalinaislander.com **Web site:** http://www.thecatalinaislander.com/
Freq: Fri; **Circ:** 5000 Not Audited
Publisher: Vincent Bodiford; **Editor:** Dennis Kaiser
Profile: Catalina Islander is a weekly newspaper covering Catalina Island and Avalon. It covers local news, community events, sports, public announcements and features of interest to residents and tourists to the area. Calendar items are due on Mondays at noon PT. News submissions are due on Mondays at 5pm PT. Advertising deadlines are on Tuesdays at 2pm PT. This paper does not want to be contacted for any reason.
Language (s): English
Ad Rate: Full Page Mono 10.00
Currency: United States Dollars
COMMUNITY NEWSPAPER

Catholic Accent 21891
Owner: Roman Catholic Diocese of Greensburg
Editorial: 725 E Pittsburgh St, Greensburg, Pennsylvania 15601-2660 **Tel:** 1 724 834-4010
Email: news@dioceseofgreensburg.org **Web site:** http://www.dioceseofgreensburg.org
Freq: Bi-Weekly; **Circ:** 46370 Not Audited
Circulation Manager: Nancy Balfe; **Publisher:** Lawrence Brandt; **Editor:** Jerry Zufelt
Profile: Catholic Accent is a bi-weekly newsletter that provides news, event calendars and scripture for members of the Diocese of Greensburg, PA. The articles also provide interviews with priests who answer questions relating to faith.
Language (s): English
Ad Rate: Full Page Mono 16.50
Currency: United States Dollars
COMMUNITY NEWSPAPER

Catholic Advance 21920
Owner: Diocese of Wichita
Editorial: 424 N Broadway St, Wichita, Kansas 67202-2310 **Tel:** 1 316 269-3965
Email: advancenews@cdowk.org **Web site:** http://www.catholicdioceseofwichita.org/advance
Freq: Bi-Weekly; **Circ:** 37800 Not Audited
Circulation Manager: Kristina Glicksman; **Advertising Sales Manager:** Molly Martin; **Editor:** Christopher Riggs
Profile: The Catholic Advance in Wichita, KS targets residents in the Diocese of Wichita and covers news and commentary of interest to Catholics.
Language (s): English
Ad Rate: Full Page Mono 12.25
Currency: United States Dollars
COMMUNITY NEWSPAPER

Catholic Anchor 749854
Owner: Archdiocese of Anchorage
Editorial: 225 Cordova St, Anchorage, Alaska 99501-2409 **Tel:** 1 907 297-7730
Email: catholicanchor@gci.net **Web site:** http://www.catholicanchor.org/wordpress
Freq: Monthly; **Circ:** 11000
Editor: Joel Davidson; **Publisher:** Roger Schweitz
Profile: Catholic Anchor is a monthly newspaper for the Archdiocese of Anchorage, AK.
Language (s): English
Ad Rate: Full Page Mono 17.00
Currency: United States Dollars
COMMUNITY NEWSPAPER

The Catholic Chronicle 22770
Owner: Catholic Diocese of Toledo
Editorial: 1933 Spielbusch Ave, Toledo, Ohio 43604-5360 **Tel:** 1 419 244-6711
Email: ccnews@toledodiocese.org **Web site:** http://www.catholicchronicle.org
Freq: Monthly; **Circ:** 31000 Not Audited
Publisher: Leonard Blair; **Circulation Manager:** Rose Anne Conrad; **Editor:** Angela Kessler
Profile: The Catholic Chronicle in in Toledo, OH is a monthly newspaper published by the Catholic diocese that covers local, national and international Catholic news. Press releases should be sent by fax to the attention of the editor.
Language (s): English
Ad Rate: Full Page Mono 43.00
Ad Rate: Full Page Colour 1495.00
Currency: United States Dollars
COMMUNITY NEWSPAPER

The Catholic Free Press 21886
Owner: Roman Catholic Bishop of Worcester
Editorial: 51 Elm St, Worcester, Massachusetts 01609-2514 **Tel:** 1 508 757-6387
Email: editor@catholicfreepress.org **Web site:** http://www.catholicfreepress.org
Freq: Fri; **Circ:** 11000 Not Audited
Advertising Sales Manager: Robert Ballantine; **Circulation Manager:** Judy Curini; **Publisher:** Robert McManus
Profile: The Catholic Free Press is a weekly publication written for the catholics in the Diocese of Worcester, MA.
Language (s): English
Ad Rate: Full Page Mono 16.30
Currency: United States Dollars
COMMUNITY NEWSPAPER

Catholic Herald 21921
Owner: Diocese of Sacramento
Editorial: 2110 Broadway, Sacramento, California 95818-2518 **Tel:** 1 916 733-0173
Web site: http://www.catholicheraldsacramento.org
Freq: Bi-Weekly; **Circ:** 42000 Not Audited
Editor: Julie Sly
Profile: Catholic Herald is a biweekly newspaper published in Sacramento, California. The paper aims to reach members of the diocese and provide them with local, national, and international news of the Catholic church. The publication comes bi-weekly with the exception of coming out monthly in July, August and December.
Language (s): English
Ad Rate: Full Page Mono 35.00
Currency: United States Dollars
COMMUNITY NEWSPAPER

The Catholic Herald 759445
Owner: Diocese of Madison
Editorial: 702 S High Point Rd, Madison, Wisconsin 53719-3522 **Tel:** 1 608 821-3070
Email: info@madisoncatholicherald.org **Web site:** http://www.madisoncatholicherald.org
Freq: Thu; **Circ:** 26000
Publisher: Robert Morlino; **Editor:** Mary Uhler
Profile: The Catholic Herald is a weekly newspaper written for the Diocese of Madison, WI.
Language (s): English
Ad Rate: Full Page Mono 20.85
Currency: United States Dollars
COMMUNITY NEWSPAPER

Catholic Herald 821567
Owner: Milwaukee Catholic Press Apostolate
Editorial: 3501 S Lake Dr, Saint Francis, Wisconsin 53235-0900 **Tel:** 1 414 769-3500
Email: catholicherald@archmil.org **Web site:** http://www.chnonline.org
Freq: Weekly; **Circ:** 46898
Publisher: Jerome Listecki; **Advertising Sales Manager:** Mary Wojes
Profile: The Catholic Herald is the official newspaper for the Archdiocese of Milwaukee. It provides weekly Community News content for the members of the Catholic faith community in Milwaukee, WI and southeastern Wisconsin.
Language (s): English
Ad Rate: Full Page Mono 42.46
Ad Rate: Full Page Colour 51.86
Currency: United States Dollars
COMMUNITY NEWSPAPER

The Catholic Key 22268
Owner: Catholic Diocese of Kansas City
Editorial: 300 E 36th St, Kansas City, Missouri 64111-1410 **Tel:** 1 816 756-1850
Email: catholickey@diocesekcsj.org **Web site:** http://www.catholickey.org
Freq: Fri; **Circ:** 22000 Not Audited
Editor: Jack Smith
Profile: The Catholic Key is a weekly newspaper published by the Diocese of Kansas City-St. Joseph. The publication covers local and world Catholic news for members of the diocese. Display advertising deadlines are on Thursdays. Classified advertising deadlines are on Mondays at 3pm CT.
Language (s): English
Ad Rate: Full Page Mono 19.55
Ad Rate: Full Page Colour 960.00
Currency: United States Dollars
COMMUNITY NEWSPAPER

The Catholic Light 758424
Owner: Roman Catholic Diocese of Scranton
Editorial: 300 Wyoming Ave Ste 10, Scranton, Pennsylvania 18503-1242 **Tel:** 1 570 207-2229
Web site: http://www.dioceseofscranton.org/media/catholic-light
Freq: Semi-Monthly; **Circ:** 45000
Publisher: Joseph Bambera; **Circulation Manager:** Pamela Haefele; **Advertising Sales Manager:** Eileen Manley
Profile: The Catholic Light is a monthly newspaper for the Diocese of Scranton, PA.
Language (s): English
Ad Rate: Full Page Mono 20.00
Currency: United States Dollars
COMMUNITY NEWSPAPER

The Catholic Messenger 21973
Owner: Diocese of Davenport
Editorial: 780 W Central Park Ave, Davenport, Iowa 52804-1901 **Tel:** 1 563 323-9959
Email: messenger@davenportdiocese.org **Web site:** http://www.catholicmessenger.org
Freq: Thu; **Circ:** 18508 Not Audited
Publisher: Martin Amos; **Editor:** Barbara Arland-Fye; **Circulation Manager:** Nancy Hamerlinck; **Advertising Manager:** Phil Hart
Profile: The Catholic Messenger is a weekly newspaper published in Davenport, IA. The paper covers local, national and international news regarding the Catholic church.
Language (s): English
Ad Rate: Full Page Mono 10.00
Currency: United States Dollars
COMMUNITY NEWSPAPER

Catholic Mirror 21972
Owner: Diocese of Des Moines, IA
Editorial: 601 Grand Ave, Des Moines, Iowa 50309-2501 **Tel:** 1 515 243-7653
Email: mirror@dmdiocese.org **Web site:** http://www.dmdiocese.org
Freq: Monthly; **Circ:** 35000 Not Audited
Editor: Anne Marie Cox
Profile: Catholic Mirror in Des Moines, IA serves the members of the local diocese and focuses on local news, events and political issues that affect the Catholic community. It also provides advice to its readers on how to include religion in everyday life.
Language (s): English
Ad Rate: Full Page Mono 13.50
Currency: United States Dollars
COMMUNITY NEWSPAPER

Catholic Miscellany 21908
Owner: Diocese of Charleston
Editorial: 119 Broad St, Charleston, South Carolina 29401-2435 **Tel:** 1 843 261-0522
Email: editor@catholic-doc.org **Web site:** http://www.themiscellany.org
Freq: Bi-Weekly; **Circ:** 29100 Not Audited
Publisher: Robert Guglielmone; **Editor:** Deidre Mayes
Profile: Catholic Miscellany is published weekly except for the second and last weeks of June, July, August and the last week in December.
Language (s): English
Ad Rate: Full Page Mono 10.00
Currency: United States Dollars
COMMUNITY NEWSPAPER

Catholic Missourian 21888
Owner: Catholic Diocese of Jefferson City
Editorial: 2207 W Main St, Jefferson City, Missouri 65110 **Tel:** 1 573 635-9127
Email: cathmo@diojeffcity.org **Web site:** http://www.diojeffcity.org
Freq: Fri; **Circ:** 22000 Not Audited
Publisher: John Gaydos; **Advertising Sales Manager:** Kelly Martin; **Editor:** Jay Nies
Profile: Catholic Missourian is a weekly newspaper written for the Catholic community of Jefferson City, MO and surrounding areas.
Language (s): English
Ad Rate: Full Page Mono 10.00
Currency: United States Dollars
COMMUNITY NEWSPAPER

The Catholic Moment 21913
Owner: Roman Catholic Diocese of Lafayette
Editorial: 610 Lingle Ave, Lafayette, Indiana 47901-1740 **Tel:** 1 765 742-2050
Email: moment@dol-in.org **Web site:** http://www.thecatholicmoment.org
Freq: Sun; **Circ:** 28000 Not Audited
Publisher: Timothy Doherty
Profile: The Catholic Moment in Lafayette, IN is published weekly and focuses on local news, events and political issues that affect the Roman Catholic community of North Central Indiana.
Language (s): English
Ad Rate: Full Page Mono 13.00
Currency: United States Dollars
COMMUNITY NEWSPAPER

Catholic New York 21929
Owner: Ecclesiastical Communications Corp.
Editorial: 1011 1st Ave Ste 1721, New York, New York 10022-4112 **Tel:** 1 212 688-2399
Email: cny@cny.org **Web site:** http://www.cny.org
Freq: Bi-Weekly; **Circ:** 132327 Not Audited
News Editor: Christie Chicoine; **Publisher:** Timothy Dolan; **Circulation Manager:** Mary Gregory; **Advertising Sales Manager:** Matt Schiller
Profile: Catholic New York is a bi-weekly newspaper published by the Archdiocese of New York. It covers news and events of the Archdiocese for members of the church, focusing on positive and practical information. It also provides human interest stories about priests, lay people, and international religious works, such as disaster relief efforts. It began publication in August 1981.
Language (s): English
Ad Rate: Full Page Mono 60.60
Currency: United States Dollars
COMMUNITY NEWSPAPER

The Catholic Post 751167
Owner: Diocese of Peoria
Editorial: 419 NE Madison Ave, Peoria, Illinois 61603-3719 **Tel:** 1 800 340-5630
Email: cathpost@mcleodusa.net **Web site:** http://www.thecatholicpost.com/post
Freq: Bi-Weekly; **Circ:** 14000
Publisher: Richard Jenky; **Advertising Sales Manager:** Sonia Nelson
Profile: The Catholic Post is a bi-weekly newspaper for the Diocese of Peoria.
Language (s): English
Ad Rate: Full Page Mono 15.50
Currency: United States Dollars
COMMUNITY NEWSPAPER

The Catholic Register 758418
Owner: Diocese of Altoona-Johnstown
Editorial: 925 S Logan Blvd, Hollidaysburg, Pennsylvania 16648-3035 **Tel:** 1 814 695-7563
Web site: http://www.dioceseaj.org/catholic-register
Freq: Bi-Weekly; **Circ:** 34000
Publisher: Mark Bartchak; **Circulation Manager:** Frances Logrando; **Editor:** Timothy Stein
Profile: The Catholic Register is a bi-weekly newspaper for the Diocese of Altoona-Johnstown, PA covering news, events and issues.
Language (s): English
Ad Rate: Full Page Mono 15.00
Currency: United States Dollars
COMMUNITY NEWSPAPER

Catholic Review 21884
Owner: Cathedral Foundation
Editorial: 880 Park Ave, Baltimore, Maryland 21201-4822 **Tel:** 1 443 524-3150
Email: mail@catholicreview.org **Web site:** http://www.catholicreview.org
Freq: Bi-Weekly; **Circ:** 47000 Not Audited
Publisher: William Lori
Profile: Catholic Review in Baltimore, MD is a weekly newspaper of record for the Archdiocese of Baltimore, covering most of the state. It provides news about events and issues of interest to people who are involved in parishes, schools and other Catholic activities.
Language (s): English
Ad Rate: Full Page Mono 45.00
Currency: United States Dollars
COMMUNITY NEWSPAPER

Catholic San Francisco 23811
Owner: Archdiocese of San Francisco
Editorial: 1 Peter Yorke Way, San Francisco, California 94109-6602 **Tel:** 1 415 614-5632
Email: info@sfarchdiocese.org **Web site:** http://www.catholic-sf.org
Freq: Fri; **Circ:** 77000 Not Audited
Editor: Rick DelVecchio
Profile: Catholic San Francisco is a weekly newspaper for the Catholic community of San Francisco, CA and the surrounding area. It provides information on developments within the Archdiocese of San Francisco as well as other topics of interest to the Catholic community.
Language (s): English
Ad Rate: Full Page Mono 48.00
Ad Rate: Full Page Colour 3800.00
Currency: United States Dollars
COMMUNITY NEWSPAPER

The Catholic Spirit 22388
Owner: Diocese of Metuchen (The)
Editorial: 146 Metlars Ln, Piscataway, New Jersey 08854-4303 **Tel:** 1 732 562-2424
Email: news@catholicspirit.com **Web site:** http://www.catholicspirit.com
Freq: Bi-Weekly; **Circ:** 20000 Not Audited
Publisher: Paul Bootkoski; **Advertising Sales Manager:** Nanette Kubian
Profile: The Catholic Spirit is a weekly publication for the Catholic communities within the Diocese of Metuchen, New Jersey, which encompasses Middlesex, Somerset, Hunterdon and Warren counties.
Language (s): English
Ad Rate: Full Page Mono 24.00
Currency: United States Dollars
COMMUNITY NEWSPAPER

The Catholic Spirit 759435
Editorial: 1300 Byron St, Wheeling, West Virginia 26003-3315 **Tel:** 1 304 233-0880
Web site: http://www.thecatholicspiritwv.org
Freq: Bi-Weekly; **Circ:** 35000
Publisher: Michael Bransfield; **Editor:** Colleen Rowan
Profile: The Catholic Spirit is a bi-weekly newspaper that is written for the Diocese of Wheeling/Charleston.
Language (s): English
Ad Rate: Full Page Mono 13.38
Currency: United States Dollars
COMMUNITY NEWSPAPER

Catholic Star Herald 21914
Owner: Catholic Diocese of Camden, NJ
Editorial: 15 N 7th St, Pastoral Center, Camden, New Jersey 08102-1104 **Tel:** 1 856 756-7900
Web site: http://www.catholicstarherald.org
Freq: Fri; **Circ:** 65000 Not Audited
Publisher: Joseph Galante; **Advertising Sales Manager:** Paul Worthington
Profile: Catholic Star Herald provides news and information to the members of the Catholic community in the Diocese of Camden, NJ.
Language (s): English
Ad Rate: Full Page Mono 40.00
Currency: United States Dollars
COMMUNITY NEWSPAPER

The Catholic Sun 21852
Owner: Roman Catholic Diocese of Phoenix
Editorial: 400 E Monroe St, Phoenix, Arizona 85004-2336 **Tel:** 1 602 354-2139
Email: info@catholicsun.org **Web site:** http://www.catholicsun.org
Freq: Bi-Weekly; **Circ:** 117105 Not Audited
Advertising Sales Manager: Jennifer Ellis; **Circulation Manager:** Mary Navarro; **Publisher:** Thomas Olmsted
Profile: The Catholic Sun is a local community newspaper for the Catholic members of the Diocese of Phoenix and the surrounding Catholic communities.
Language (s): English, Spanish/Bilingual
Ad Rate: Full Page Mono 42.00
Currency: United States Dollars
COMMUNITY NEWSPAPER

Catholic Sun 257062
Owner: Diocese of Syracuse
Editorial: 424 Montgomery St, Syracuse, New York 13202-2920 **Tel:** 1 315 422-8153
Email: catholicsun@yahoo.com **Web site:** http://thecatholicsun.com/
Freq: Thu; **Circ:** 21327 Not Audited
Editor: Connie Berry; **Publisher:** Robert Cunningham; **Advertising Sales Manager:** Mark Klenz
Profile: Catholic Sun is the weekly newspaper of the Diocese of Syracuse, NY.
Language (s): English
Ad Rate: Full Page Mono 24.00
Currency: United States Dollars
COMMUNITY NEWSPAPER

Catholic Times 21905
Owner: Diocese of Columbus
Editorial: 197 E Gay St, Columbus, Ohio 43215-3229 **Tel:** 1 614 224-5195
Email: commailbox@colsdioc.org **Web site:** http://www.ctonline.org
Freq: Sun; **Circ:** 15000
Publisher: Frederick Campbell; **Editor:** David Garick
Profile: Catholic Times is the official newspaper of the Catholic Diocese of Columbus, which includes 23 counties across Central and Southern Ohio. It is written for Catholics of Columbus, OH.
Language (s): English
Ad Rate: Full Page Mono 18.55
Currency: United States Dollars
COMMUNITY NEWSPAPER

Catholic Times 21906
Owner: Diocese of Springfield in Illinois
Editorial: 1615 W Washington St, Springfield, Illinois 62702-4757 **Tel:** 1 217 698-8500
Email: catholictimes@dio.org **Web site:** http://www.dio.org
Freq: Bi-Weekly; **Circ:** 45000 Not Audited
Editor & Publisher: Scott Mulford; **Advertising Sales Manager:** Paula Ruot
Profile: Catholic Times is a local newspaper for the Catholic community in Springfield, IL.
Language (s): English
Ad Rate: Full Page Mono 16.25
Currency: United States Dollars
COMMUNITY NEWSPAPER

The Catholic Times 21912
Owner: Diocese of LaCrosse
Editorial: 3710 East Ave S, La Crosse, Wisconsin 54601-7215 **Tel:** 1 608 788-1524
Email: catholictimes@dioceseoflacrosse.com **Web site:** http://www.thecatholictimes.com
Freq: Bi-Weekly; **Circ:** 31500 Not Audited
Editor: Stanton Gould
Profile: The Catholic Times in La Crosse, WI is a bi-weekly newspaper that features news, events and other issues of importance to members of the local Catholic community.
Language (s): English
Ad Rate: Full Page Mono 32.00
Currency: United States Dollars
COMMUNITY NEWSPAPER

Catholic Voice 22224
Editorial: 6060 NW Radial Hwy, Omaha, Nebraska 68104-3426 **Tel:** 1 402 558-6611
Email: tcvomaha@archomaha.org **Web site:** http://www.catholicvoiceomaha.com
Freq: Semi-Monthly; **Circ:** 49000 Not Audited
Publisher: George Lucas; **News Editor:** Joe Ruff; **Circulation Manager:** Karen Suchy
Profile: Catholic Voice in Omaha, NE is the publication of the Archdiocese of Omaha, NE. The newspaper focuses on local news, events, and political issues that affect the Catholic community. The paper also provides advice to its readers on how to include religion in everyday life. All inquiries should be addressed to the editor.
Language (s): English
Ad Rate: Full Page Mono 31.00
Currency: United States Dollars
COMMUNITY NEWSPAPER

The Catholic Witness 758416
Owner: Diocese of Harrisburg
Editorial: 4800 Union Deposit Rd, Harrisburg, Pennsylvania 17111-3710 **Tel:** 1 717 657-4804 201
Email: witness@hbgdiocese.org **Web site:** http://www.hbgdiocese.org
Freq: Bi-Weekly; **Circ:** 80000
Publisher: Joseph McFadden; **Editor:** Jen Reed
Profile: The Catholic Witness is a bi-weekly newspaper published for the Diocese of Harrisburg, PA. The paper does not accept outside advertising.
Language (s): English
COMMUNITY NEWSPAPER

Cedar Springs Post 21738
Owner: Allen (Lois)
Editorial: 36 E Maple St., Cedar Springs, Michigan 49319-5135 **Tel:** 1 616 696-3655
Email: newsreleases@cedarspringspost.com **Web site:** http://cedarspringspost.com
Freq: Thu; **Circ:** 5000 Not Audited
Publisher: Lois Allen; **Editor:** Judy Reed
Profile: Cedar Springs Post (MI) is a weekly newspaper that provides in-depth local and regional news, weather, arts & entertainment, business, political news and sports.
Language (s): English
Ad Rate: Full Page Mono 7.95
Currency: United States Dollars
COMMUNITY NEWSPAPER

Cedar Street Times 824975
Owner: Jameson (Marge Ann)
Editorial: 306 Grand Ave, Pacific Grove, California 93950-3422 **Tel:** 1 831 324-4742
Email: editor@cedarstreettimes.com **Web site:** http://cedarstreettimes.com
Freq: Weekly
Editor & Publisher: Marge Ann Jameson

Profile: Cedar Street Times is a weekly community newspaper serving residents of Pacific Grove, CA with local news, sports, opinion, and features. Deadlines are Wednesdays at noon PT.
Language (s): English
Ad Rate: Full Page Mono 18.00
Ad Rate: Full Page Colour 22.50
Currency: United States Dollars
COMMUNITY NEWSPAPER

Celebration Independent 537213
Owner: Club Publications
Tel: 1 407 566-1700
Web site: http://celebrationindependent.com
Freq: Bi-Weekly; **Circ:** 25000 Not Audited
Profile: Celebration Independent will re-launch in November 2013. It will be a bi-weekly newspaper written for residents of Celebration, FL and the surrounding communities.
Language (s): English
Ad Rate: Full Page Mono 12.00
Currency: United States Dollars
COMMUNITY NEWSPAPER

El Central Hispanic News 22714
Owner: Sanchez Communications
Editorial: 4124 W Vernor Hwy, Detroit, Michigan 48209-2145 **Tel:** 1 313 841-0100
Email: elcentral1@aol.com
Freq: Thu; **Circ:** 14000 Not Audited
Publisher & Editor: Dolores Sanchez
Profile: El Central Hispanic News provides news and information to Michigan's Hispanic population. The publication covers local, national and international news.
Language (s): Spanish/Bilingual
Ad Rate: Full Page Mono 16.00
Ad Rate: Full Page Colour 1705.00
Currency: United States Dollars
COMMUNITY NEWSPAPER

Central Illinois Business 257362
Owner: News Gazette Media Grp
Editorial: 15 E Main St, Champaign, Illinois 61820-3625 **Tel:** 1 217 351-5276
Web site: http://www.centralillinoisbusiness.com
Freq: Daily; **Circ:** 40000 Not Audited
Editor: Jodi Heckel
Profile: Central Illinois Business is a weekly section within the Champaign News-Gazette, a local newspaper in Champaign, IL. The publication covers business within Clinton and the surrounding Champaign County area.
Language (s): English
Ad Rate: Full Page Colour 750.00
Currency: United States Dollars
COMMUNITY NEWSPAPER

Central Kentucky News-Journal 19327
Owner: Landmark Community Newspapers, Inc.
Editorial: 200 Albion Way, Campbellsville, Kentucky 42718-1565 **Tel:** 1 270 465-8111
Web site: http://www.cknj.com
Freq: Mon; **Circ:** 7400 Not Audited
Publisher & Editor: Jeff Moreland
Profile: Central Kentucky News-Journal is a weekly newspaper covering local news, sports, events, arts and entertainment for the Taylor County, KY area. Deadlines for the Monday edition fall on the previous Friday at 10am CT. Deadlines for the Thursday edition fall on the Tuesday prior to the issue date at 10am CT.
Language (s): English
Ad Rate: Full Page Mono 11.46
Currency: United States Dollars
COMMUNITY NEWSPAPER

The Central Virginian 21058
Owner: Lakeway Publishers, Inc.
Editorial: 89 Rescue Ln, Louisa, Virginia 23093-4105
Tel: 1 540 967-0368
Web site: http://www.thecentralvirginian.com
Freq: Thu; **Circ:** 10000 Not Audited
Publisher: Steve Weddle
Profile: The Central Virginian is a weekly local newspaper serving the counties of Louisa and Fluvanna, VA. The publication covers local news, events, sports and arts & entertainment. It also includes the regional section named the Goochland Courier.
Language (s): English
Ad Rate: Full Page Mono 12.85
Currency: United States Dollars
COMMUNITY NEWSPAPER

Central Wisconsin Sunday 324433
Editorial: 800 Scott St, Wausau, Wisconsin 54403
Tel: 1 715 842-2101
Web site: http://www.wausaudailyherald.com
Freq: Sun; **Circ:** 21000 Not Audited
Advertising Sales Manager: Tara Marcoux
Profile: Central Wisconsin Sunday is published on Sundays by the four local Gannett dailies: The Daily Tribune in Wisconsin Rapids, WI, Marshfield (WI) News-Herald, Stevens Point (WI) Journal and Wausau (WI) Daily Herald. It is included in the Sunday edition of these four papers, but readers can also purchase a seperate subscription. The contact information is for The Wausau Daily Herald.
Language (s): English
Ad Rate: Full Page Mono 29.60
Currency: United States Dollars
COMMUNITY NEWSPAPER

Centro Tampa 363283
Owner: Tampa Media Group, LLC
Editorial: 202 S Parker St Ste 202, Tampa, Florida 33606-2308
Email: advertising@centrotampa.com **Web site:** http://www.centrotampa.com
Freq: Fri; **Circ:** 48860 Not Audited
Publisher: Brian Burns
Profile: Centro Tampa is a Spanish-language community newspaper serving the Latino population of Tampa Bay, FL. The paper covers news, events and features stories in conjunction with Media General's other Spanish-language products, centrotampa.com, its Web site and Centro Capsulas, which provides radio and television broadcasting. Deadlines are on Tuesdays at 5pm ET.
Language (s): Spanish
Ad Rate: Full Page Mono 18.00
Currency: United States Dollars
COMMUNITY NEWSPAPER

Ceres Courier 18608
Owner: Morris Multimedia Inc.
Editorial: 138 S Center St, Turlock, California 95380-4508 **Tel:** 1 209 537-5032
Web site: http://www.cerescourier.com
Freq: Wed; **Circ:** 18500 Not Audited
Editor: Jeff Benziger; **Publisher:** Hank Vander Veen
Profile: Ceres Courier is a community newspaper located in Ceres, CA. It is published weekly and covers local news, events, sports, and government issues.
Language (s): English
Ad Rate: Full Page Mono 12.95
Currency: United States Dollars
COMMUNITY NEWSPAPER

Challenger Community News 20307
Owner: Banks
Editorial: 1337 Jefferson Ave, Buffalo, New York 14208-1808 **Tel:** 1 716 881-1051
Email: thechallengernews@gmail.com **Web site:** http://www.thechallengernews.com
Freq: Wed; **Circ:** 11000 Not Audited
Publisher & Editor: Al-Nisa Banks
Profile: Challenger Community News is a weekly newspaper published for the African American communities of Buffalo, NY. The publication covers local news and community events. News deadlines are on Fridays at 5pm ET.
Language (s): English
Ad Rate: Full Page Mono 16.00
Currency: United States Dollars
COMMUNITY NEWSPAPER

Challenger Newspapers 25110
Owner: Greenwood Newspapers, Inc.
Tel: 1 317 888-3376
Email: news@indychallenger.com **Web site:** http://www.challengernewspapers.com
Freq: Wed; **Circ:** 15677 Not Audited
Publisher & Editor: Doug Chambers
Language (s): English
COMMUNITY NEWSPAPER

The Champion 22532
Owner: ACE III Communications, Inc.
Editorial: 114 New St Ste E, Decatur, Georgia 30030-5356 **Tel:** 1 404 373-7779
Web site: http://thechampionnewspaper.com/
Freq: Thu; **Circ:** 25000 Not Audited
Profile: The Champion is published weekly for the residents of DeKalb County, GA. The newspaper covers local news, business, lifestyle, sports and community events. Press releases should be sent directly to the editor.
Language (s): English
Ad Rate: Full Page Mono 10.00
Ad Rate: Full Page Colour 1550.00
Currency: United States Dollars
COMMUNITY NEWSPAPER

Chanhassen Villager 86377
Owner: Red Wing Publishing Co.
Editorial: 123 W 2nd St, Chaska, Minnesota 55318-1907 **Tel:** 1 952 448-2650
Email: editor@chaskaherald.com **Web site:** http://www.swnewsmedia.com/chanhassen_villager
Freq: Thu; **Circ:** 6200 Not Audited
Circulation Manager: Ruby Winings
Profile: Chanhassen Villager is published weekly for the residents of Chanhassen, MN and surrounding areas. The newspaper covers local news, sports and community events. Deadlines are on Mondays at 10am CT.
Language (s): English
Ad Rate: Full Page Mono 11.45
Currency: United States Dollars
COMMUNITY NEWSPAPER

Charleston Chronicle 20646
Owner: French (Jim)
Editorial: 1111 King St, Charleston, South Carolina 29403-3761 **Tel:** 1 843 723-2785
Email: news@charlestonchronicle.net **Web site:** http://www.thecharlestonchronicle.net
Freq: Wed; **Circ:** 6000 Not Audited
Publisher & Editor: Jim French; **Advertising Sales Manager:** Tolbert Smalls
Profile: Charleston Chronicle is a weekly newspaper serving the Charleston, SC African-American community. The publication covers local news, community events and social issues related to the community.
Language (s): English
Ad Rate: Full Page Mono 15.10
Currency: United States Dollars
COMMUNITY NEWSPAPER

Charleston City Paper 23121
Owner: Jones Street Publishers, LLC
Editorial: 1049 Morrison Dr, Charleston, South Carolina 29403-3875 **Tel:** 1 843 577-5304
Email: editor@charlestoncitypaper.com **Web site:** http://www.charlestoncitypaper.com
Freq: Wed; **Circ:** 40000 Not Audited
Publisher: Noel Mermer
Profile: Charleston (SC) City Paper is a community newspaper that covers local news, opinion articles, music and restaurant reviews.
Language (s): English
Ad Rate: Full Page Mono 21.14
Currency: United States Dollars
COMMUNITY NEWSPAPER

Charleston Enterprise-Courier 19762
Owner: Bennett (Carlin)
Editorial: 101 E Main St, East Prairie, Missouri 63845-1136 **Tel:** 1 573 683-3351
Email: news@enterprisecourier.com **Web site:** http://www.enterprisecourier.com
Freq: Tue; **Circ:** 5000 Not Audited
Publisher: Carlin Bennett; **Editor:** Maiory Wagner
Profile: Charleston Enterprise-Courier is a local newspaper published in combination with the East Prairie Eagle, for the residents of Charleston and East Prairie, MO. The publication covers local news, events, sports and community information.
Language (s): English
Ad Rate: Full Page Mono 4.00
Currency: United States Dollars
COMMUNITY NEWSPAPER

The Charlotte Post 20028
Owner: Charlotte Post Publishing Co.
Editorial: 1531 Camden Rd, Charlotte, North Carolina 28203-4753 **Tel:** 1 704 376-0496
Web site: http://www.thecharlottepost.com
Freq: Thu; **Circ:** 12000 Not Audited
Publisher: Gerald Johnson; **Advertising Sales Manager:** Jeri Thompson
Profile: The Charlotte Post covers local news, events, sports, health, travel, business, life and religious topics for the African American community in Charlotte, NC. Send press releases to the editor in chief.
Language (s): English
Ad Rate: Full Page Mono 35.00
Currency: United States Dollars
COMMUNITY NEWSPAPER

Chaska Herald 22123
Owner: Red Wing Publishing Co.
Editorial: 123 W 2nd St, Chaska, Minnesota 55318-1907 **Tel:** 1 952 448-2650
Email: editor@chaskaherald.com **Web site:** http://www.swnewsmedia.com/chaska_herald
Freq: Thu; **Circ:** 6900 Not Audited
Editor: Mark Olson; **Circulation Manager:** Ruby Winings
Profile: Chaska Herald is published weekly for the residents of Chaska, MN. The newspaper covers local news, sports and community events.
Language (s): English
Ad Rate: Full Page Mono 11.45
Currency: United States Dollars
COMMUNITY NEWSPAPER

Chatsworth Times 18799
Editorial: 224 N 3rd Ave, Chatsworth, Georgia 30705-2536 **Tel:** 1 706 695-4646
Email: manager@chatsworthtimes.com **Web site:** http://www.chatsworthtimes.com/
Freq: Wed; **Circ:** 5600 Not Audited
Circulation Manager: Trannon Goble; **Advertising Sales Manager:** Pat Oxford
Profile: Chatsworth (GA) Times serves the residents of Murray County, GA. The publication covers local news, community events and sports.
Language (s): English
Ad Rate: Full Page Mono 6.95
Currency: United States Dollars
COMMUNITY NEWSPAPER

Chattanooga Pulse 231672
Owner: Brewer Media Group
Editorial: 1305 Carter St, Chattanooga, Tennessee 37402-4412 **Tel:** 1 423 648-7857
Email: info@chattanoogapulse.com **Web site:** http://www.chattanoogapulse.com
Freq: Wed; **Circ:** 36400 Not Audited
Advertising Sales Manager: Mike Baskin; **Editor:** Gary Poole
Profile: Chattanooga Pulse is a local newspaper serving the residents of Chattanooga, TN. The alternative paper provides articles on news, columns, art, music, dining guides and a calendar of events for the area.
Language (s): English
Ad Rate: Full Page Mono 12.60
Currency: United States Dollars
COMMUNITY NEWSPAPER

Cherokee Ledger-News 22795
Owner: Lakeside Publishing, Inc.
Editorial: 103 E Main St, Woodstock, Georgia 30188-5008 **Tel:** 1 770 928-0706
Web site: http://tribuneledgernews.com
Freq: Wed; **Circ:** 40000 Not Audited
Profile: Cherokee Ledger-News is a community newspaper published for residents of Cherokee County, GA. It covers news, local events and entertainment.
Language (s): English
Ad Rate: Full Page Mono 19.95
Currency: United States Dollars
COMMUNITY NEWSPAPER

Cherokee Post 331216
Owner: Crawford (David)
Editorial: 100 E Main St, Centre, Alabama 35960-1517 **Tel:** 1 256 927-4476
Email: info@postpaper.com **Web site:** http://www.postpaper.com
Freq: Mon; **Circ:** 17000 Not Audited
Publisher: David Crawford; **Advertising Sales Manager:** Tanya Smith; **Editor:** Scott Wright
Profile: Cherokee Post is published weekly for the residents of Centre, AL and surrounding areas. The newspaper covers local news and community events.
Language (s): English
Ad Rate: Full Page Mono 5.00
Currency: United States Dollars
COMMUNITY NEWSPAPER

Cherokee Scout 19994
Owner: Community Newspapers Inc.
Editorial: 89 Sycamore St, Murphy, North Carolina 28906-2954 **Tel:** 1 828 837-5122
Email: news@cherokeescout.com **Web site:** http://www.cherokeescout.com
Freq: Wed; **Circ:** 8500 Not Audited
Publisher: David Brown; **Advertising Sales Manager:** Donna Cook; **Editor:** Matthew Osborne
Profile: Cherokee Scout is a local weekly newspaper written for residents of Cherokee County, NC. The publication covers local news, events, politics, opinions and sports. Deadlines are 5pm ET on the Fridays.
Language (s): English
Ad Rate: Full Page Mono 14.25
Currency: United States Dollars
COMMUNITY NEWSPAPER

Cherokee Tribune Plus 22966
Owner: Times Journal Inc.
Editorial: 521 E Main St, Canton, Georgia 30114-2805 **Tel:** 1 770 479-1441
Web site: http://www.cherokeetribune.com
Freq: Wed; **Circ:** 16577 Not Audited
Publisher: Otis Brumby; **Advertising Sales Manager:** Kim Fowler
Profile: Cherokee Tribune Plus is a free, weekly newspaper distributed for free to nonsubscribers of the daily newspaper, the Cherokee Tribune, in Cherokee County, GA. The paper shares its editorial staff and content with the daily. Press releases can be sent by fax to the appropriate editors. Only press releases containing information about Cherokee County are accepted. Advertising deadlines are at noon ET.
Language (s): English
Ad Rate: Full Page Mono 22.80
Ad Rate: Full Page Colour 200.00
Currency: United States Dollars
COMMUNITY NEWSPAPER

Cheshire Herald 18727
Owner: True Publishing Co. (The)
Editorial: 1079 S Main St, Cheshire, Connecticut 06410-3414 **Tel:** 1 203 272-5316
Email: news@cheshireherald.com **Web site:** http://www.cheshireherald.com
Freq: Thu; **Circ:** 7200 Not Audited
Publisher: Joseph Jakubisyn; **Advertising Manager:** Mary Malavenda
Profile: Cheshire Herald is written for the residents of Cheshire, CT. Deadlines are Mondays at 5pm ET.
Language (s): English
Ad Rate: Full Page Mono 12.00
Currency: United States Dollars
COMMUNITY NEWSPAPER

Chester County Independent 20728
Owner: American Hometown Publishing
Editorial: 218 S Church Ave, Henderson, Tennessee 38340-2638 **Tel:** 1 731 989-4624
Email: news@chestercountyindependent.com **Web site:** http://www.chestercountyindependent.com
Freq: Thu; **Circ:** 5100 Not Audited
Advertising Sales Manager: Marvin Croom; **Publisher:** Tim Stratton
Profile: Chester County Independent is a weekly local paper serving residents in Henderson and Chester County, TN. It covers local news, community events, sports, education, entertainment and editorials. The editor is the main PR contact. Press releases may be sent by e-mail or fax.
Language (s): English
Ad Rate: Full Page Mono 6.50
Currency: United States Dollars
COMMUNITY NEWSPAPER

Chester County Press 22456
Owner: Ad Pro, Inc.
Editorial: 144 S Jennersville Rd, West Grove, Pennsylvania 19390-9430 **Tel:** 1 610 869-5553
Email: info@chestercounty.com **Web site:** http://www.chestercounty.com
Freq: Wed; **Circ:** 14900 Not Audited
Editor: Steve Hoffman; **Publisher:** Randall Lieberman
Profile: Chester County Press is a weekly newspaper serving the residents of Southern Chester County, including the communities of Oxford, West Grove, Avondale, New London, Kemblesville, Landenberg and Kennett Square, PA. It provides local news,

events, lifestyle stories and sports. Advertising deadlines are at noon ET.
Language (s): English
Ad Rate: Full Page Mono 14.70
Currency: United States Dollars
COMMUNITY NEWSPAPER

Chesterfield Observer 449035
Owner: The Observer, Inc.
Editorial: 4600 Market Square Ln, Midlothian, Virginia 23112-4875 **Tel:** 1 804 545-7500
Web site: http://www.chesterfieldobserver.com
Freq: Wed; **Circ:** 70789 Not Audited
Editor: Scott Bass; **News Editor:** Michael Buettner
Profile: Chesterfield Observer is a local, weekly newspaper serving residents of Chesterfield and Midlothian, VA and surrounding areas. The paper includes local and national news, business, politics, sports and entertainment.
Language (s): English
Ad Rate: Full Page Mono 95.00
Currency: United States Dollars
COMMUNITY NEWSPAPER

Chesterland News 22968
Owner: Chesterland News, LLC.
Editorial: 8389 Mayfield Rd Ste B-5, Chesterland, Ohio 44026-2553 **Tel:** 1 440 729-7667
Email: news@chesterlandnews.com **Web site:** http://www.chesterlandnews.com
Freq: Wed; **Circ:** 6500 Not Audited
Publisher: Jeffrey Karlovec; **Editor:** John Karlovec
Profile: Chesterland News is published weekly for the residents of Chesterland, OH and surrounding areas. The newspaper covers local news and community events.
Language (s): English
Ad Rate: Full Page Mono 8.86
Currency: United States Dollars
COMMUNITY NEWSPAPER

Chestnut Hill Local 20584
Owner: Chestnut Hill Community Association
Editorial: 8434 Germantown Ave, Philadelphia, Pennsylvania 19118-3302 **Tel:** 1 215 248-8800
Web site: http://www.chestnuthilllocal.com
Freq: Thu; **Circ:** 7000 Not Audited
Editor: Pete Mazzaccaro
Profile: Chestnut Hill Local is an independent weekly newspaper that serves the neighborhood of Chestnut Hill and surrounding communities in the Northwest Philadelphia region. It covers local politics, business and quality of life. It also publishes stories about local personalities, the arts and cultural happenings in the region. The sports section offers in-depth coverage of independent school athletics. Press releases should be faxed to the editor.
Language (s): English
Ad Rate: Full Page Mono 17.65
Currency: United States Dollars
COMMUNITY NEWSPAPER

The Cheyenne Edition 600874
Owner: Walter Publishing Co.
Editorial: 30 E Pikes Peak Ave, Colorado Springs, Colorado 80942-1000 **Tel:** 1 719 476-4872
Email: hannah@gazettecommunitynews.com **Web site:** http://www.gazettecommunitynews.com/
Freq: Weekly; **Circ:** 8000
Advertising Sales Manager: Jenny Hillstrom
Profile: The Cheyenne Edition is published every Friday and is delivered free to households in the Cheyenne Mountain School District 12.
Language (s): English
Ad Rate: Full Page Mono 13.75
Currency: United States Dollars
COMMUNITY NEWSPAPER

The Chicago Crusader 21334
Owner: Chicago Crusader Newspaper
Editorial: 6429 S King Dr, Chicago, Illinois 60637-3116 **Tel:** 1 773 752-2500
Email: news@chicagocrusader.com **Web site:** http://www.chicagocrusader.com
Freq: Thu; **Circ:** 90071 Not Audited
Publisher & Editor: Dorothy Leavell; **Editor:** Raymond Ward
Profile: The Chicago Crusader is a local newspaper published every Saturday for African Americans in Chicago. The newspaper covers topics on employment, equal rights, social justice, sports and entertainment. The paper prefers not to be contacted on Wednesday.
Language (s): English
Ad Rate: Full Page Mono 136.24
Currency: United States Dollars
COMMUNITY NEWSPAPER

The Chicago Defender 13921
Owner: Real Times Media, Inc.
Editorial: 4445 S King Dr, Chicago, Illinois 60653-3310 **Tel:** 1 312 225-2400
Email: editorial@chicagodefender.com **Web site:** http://www.chicagodefender.com
Freq: Wed; **Circ:** 30000 Not Audited
Circulation Manager: Bertha Cromwell
Profile: The Chicago Defender is a weekly newspaper, website and multi-platform news organization providing relevant content to Chicago's influential African-American community. Topics covered include news, business, politics, arts & culture, technology, commentary, African and African-American issues, neighborhood news, religion, entertainment, lifestyle, society news and sports.
Language (s): English
Ad Rate: Full Page Mono 131.22
Currency: United States Dollars
COMMUNITY NEWSPAPER

Chicago Deportivo 81498
Editorial: 3748 Cleveland Ave, Brookfield, Illinois 60513-1510 **Tel:** 1 708 387-7724
Web site: http://www.chicagodeportivo.net
Freq: Fri; **Circ:** 10000
Profile: Offers news and sports to Chicago's Hispanic communities.
Language (s): Spanish/Bilingual
Ad Rate: Full Page Mono 8.50
Currency: United States Dollars
COMMUNITY NEWSPAPER

Chicago Jewish News 22160
Editorial: 5301 Dempster St Ste 100, Skokie, Illinois 60077-1800 **Tel:** 1 847 966-0606
Web site: http://www.chicagojewishnews.com
Freq: Fri; **Circ:** 40000 Not Audited
Publisher & Editor: Joseph Aaron
Profile: Chicago Jewish News reports news, events and features that are relevant to the Jewish communities in and around Chicago.
Language (s): English
Ad Rate: Full Page Mono 37.50
Ad Rate: Full Page Colour 2840.00
Currency: United States Dollars
COMMUNITY NEWSPAPER

Chicago Jewish Star 22102
Owner: Star Media Group Inc.
Tel: 1 847 674-7827
Email: chicagojewishstar@comcast.net
Freq: Bi-Weekly; **Circ:** 19000 Not Audited
Editor/Publisher: Doug Wertheimer
Profile: Chicago Jewish Star is a bi-weekly newspaper. The publication reports on local, national, and international news of Jewish interest for the Jewish community in and around Chicago. The newspaper is published every two weeks. The editor is the most appropriate PR and editorial contact.
Language (s): English
Ad Rate: Full Page Mono 27.00
Currency: United States Dollars
COMMUNITY NEWSPAPER

Chicago Reader 19071
Owner: ST Acquisition Holdings LLC
Editorial: 350 N Orleans St, Chicago, Illinois 60654-1975 **Tel:** 1 312 222-6920
Email: mail@chicagoreader.com **Web site:** http://www.chicagoreader.com
Freq: Wed; **Circ:** 90040 Not Audited
Editor: Jake Malooley
Profile: Chicago Reader serves residents and commuters of Chicago. It focuses on specialized features over news and covers urban issues and politics, arts & culture and literary work. It also publishes a separate guide to arts & entertainment happenings in Chicago and the surrounding area. Press releases that are faxed to the editorial office will be forwarded to the appropriate staff member. Advertising and editorial deadlines are the Fridays prior to publication.
Language (s): English
Ad Rate: Full Page Mono 30.00
Currency: United States Dollars
COMMUNITY NEWSPAPER

Chicago Shimpo 78634
Owner: Urayama (Yoshiko)
Editorial: 4670 N Manor Ave, Chicago, Illinois 60625-3718 **Tel:** 1 773 478-6170
Email: shimpo@mc.net
Freq: Fri; **Circ:** 5000 Not Audited
Publisher & Editor: Yoshiko Urayama
Profile: Chicago Shimpo was founded in 1945 and is the only Japanese language newspaper published in the Midwest. Chicago Shimpo's editorial mission is to facilitate communication among diverse Japanese American communities. The paper covers local community news and international news from Japan, the United States and around the world. Most of the publication is written in Japanese, but includes two pages of English text. The intended audience is Japanese Americans and Japanese men and women living in or visiting the United States.
Language (s): Japanese
Ad Rate: Full Page Mono 80.00
Currency: United States Dollars
COMMUNITY NEWSPAPER

Chico News & Review 21330
Owner: Chico Community Publishing, Inc.
Editorial: 353 E 2nd St, Chico, California 95928-5469 **Tel:** 1 530 894-2300
Email: chiconewstips@newsreview.com **Web site:** http://www.newsreview.com/chico
Freq: Thu; **Circ:** 41600 Not Audited
Editor: Melissa Daugherty; **Advertising Sales Manager:** Jamie DeGarmo; **Publisher:** Jeff von Kaenel
Profile: Chico News & Review is a local newspaper published for residents of Chico and surrounding Butte County, CA. It covers local and national news, calendar & events information, sustainability, arts & entertainment, the environment, politics, diversity and women's issues.
Language (s): English
Ad Rate: Full Page Mono 32.00
Currency: United States Dollars
COMMUNITY NEWSPAPER

The Chicopee Register 30200
Owner: Turley Publications, Inc.
Editorial: 24 Water St, Palmer, Massachusetts 01069-1885 **Tel:** 1 413 682-0007
Web site: http://chicopeeregister.turley.com
Freq: Thu; **Circ:** 13000 Not Audited
Advertising Sales Manager: Wendy Bellcamp; **Circulation Manager:** Charlann Griswold; **Publisher:** Patrick Turley
Profile: The Chicopee Register is a weekly local paper serving the readers of Chicopee, MA. It covers all aspects of local news from politics to sports. The newspaper was founded in 1998. Advertising and editorial deadlines are Tuesdays at noon ET.
Language (s): English
Ad Rate: Full Page Mono 11.50
Currency: United States Dollars
COMMUNITY NEWSPAPER

The Chief 22902
Owner: NY Civil Service Employees Publishing Co., Inc.
Editorial: 277 Broadway Ste 1506, New York, New York 10007-2008 **Tel:** 1 212 962-2690
Email: thechiefsubs@rcn.com **Web site:** http://www.thechief-leader.com
Freq: Fri; **Circ:** 26228 Not Audited
Publisher: Edward Prial; **Editor:** Richard Steier
Profile: The Chief is a weekly newspaper for civil service employees in New York, NY. The newspaper focuses on job opportunities, the civil service examination, and other relevant issues for employees of governmental organizations. Deadlines for the publication are on the Monday before issue date. This paper will not accept unsolicited information sent via e-mail. Send press releases by fax.
Language (s): English
Ad Rate: Full Page Mono 35.00
Currency: United States Dollars
COMMUNITY NEWSPAPER

Chinese American Post 778770
Editorial: 2555 S Santa Fe Dr Unit 240, Denver, Colorado 80223-4458 **Tel:** 1 303 934-1773
Email: chineseamericanpost@gmail.com **Web site:** http://www.chineseamericanpost.net/
Freq: Thu; **Circ:** 6500
Publisher: Wanning Feng; **Editor:** Harrison Gu
Profile: Chinese American Post is a weekly newspaper for the Chinese community of Denver, CO.
Language (s): Chinese
Ad Rate: Full Page Mono 1.92
Currency: United States Dollars
COMMUNITY NEWSPAPER

Chinese News 509841
Editorial: 4463 University Ave, San Diego, California 92105-1731 **Tel:** 1 619 280-3388
Email: chinesenews@cox.net
Freq: Fri; **Circ:** 12000 Not Audited
Publisher & Editor: Stanley Ting; **Advertising Sales Manager:** Anne Young
Profile: Chinese News is a weekly newspaper focused to the Chinese residents in the San Diego area.
Language (s): Chinese
Ad Rate: Full Page Mono 5.10
Currency: United States Dollars
COMMUNITY NEWSPAPER

Chinook Observer 21115
Owner: East Oregonian Publishing Co.
Editorial: 205 Bolstad Ave E #2, Long Beach, Washington 98631-9200 **Tel:** 1 360 642-8181
Email: pressrelease@chinookobserver.com **Web site:** http://www.chinookobserver.com
Freq: Wed; **Circ:** 6800 Not Audited
Publisher & Editor: Matt Winters
Profile: Chinook Observer is a weekly community newspaper serving the residents of Long Beach Peninsula, WA. The newspaper was founded in 1900 by shipwrecked sailors. Chinook Observer covers local, national, and international news, in addition to sports, features and an opinions page. The newspaper is published each Wednesday.
Language (s): English
Ad Rate: Full Page Mono 15.10
Currency: United States Dollars
COMMUNITY NEWSPAPER

The Choctaw Sun/Advocate 331437
Owner: Campbell (Dee Ann)
Editorial: 13440 Choctaw Ave, Gilbertown, Alabama 36908-9502 **Tel:** 1 251 843-6397
Email: choctawsun@millry.net **Web site:** http://www.choctawsun.com
Freq: Wed; **Circ:** 5100 Not Audited
Editor: Dee Ann Campbell; **Advertising Sales Manager:** Virginia Loftus
Profile: The Choctaw Sun/Advocate brings weekly news to the people of Choctaw County, AL and the surrounding areas. Deadlines are Monday mornings.
Language (s): English
Ad Rate: Full Page Mono 9.00
Currency: United States Dollars
COMMUNITY NEWSPAPER

The Christian Index 22036
Owner: Georgia Baptist Convention
Editorial: 6405 Sugarloaf Pkwy, Duluth, Georgia 30097-4092 **Tel:** 1 770 936-5590
Email: editor@christianindex.org **Web site:** http://www.christianindex.org
Freq: Bi-Weekly; **Circ:** 35000 Not Audited
Circulation Manager: Lonette Godwin; **Editor:** J. Harris; **Advertising Sales Manager:** Donna Ward
Profile: Christian Index was founded in 1822 and is the oldest religious newspaper in the nation. The publication is written for Baptists living in Georgia. It covers news and issues facing the Baptist religion.
An online-only subscription is available for $6 per year.
Language (s): English
Ad Rate: Full Page Mono 30.00
Currency: United States Dollars
COMMUNITY NEWSPAPER

The Christian Science Monitor 15298
Owner: First Church of Christ, Scientist
Editorial: 210 Massachusetts Ave, Boston, Massachusetts 02115-3012 **Tel:** 1 617 450-2000
Web site: http://www.csmonitor.com
Freq: Weekly; **Circ:** 48509
Editor: Clayton Collins; **International News Editor:** Amelia Newcomb; **Publisher:** Jonathan Wells
Profile: Founded in 1908, The Christian Science Monitor is recognized as one of the leading U.S. newspapers specializing in international reporting. With a reputation for balanced coverage of complex issues and in-depth analysis of events, the award-winning paper offers both news and features from its 16 bureaus in the U.S. and abroad and from freelance reporters across the globe. Please send press materials via e-mail.
Language (s): English
Ad Rate: Full Page Mono 1800.00
Ad Rate: Full Page Colour 2000.00
Currency: United States Dollars
COMMUNITY NEWSPAPER

The Chronicle 21080
Editorial: 133 Water, Barton, Vermont 05822-8814
Tel: 1 802 525-3531
Email: news@bartonchronicle.com **Web site:** http://www.bartonchronicle.com
Freq: Wed; **Circ:** 7900 Not Audited
Publisher: Chris Braithwaite; **Advertising Sales Manager:** LeAnn Cady; **News Editor:** Tena Starr; **Circulation Manager:** Georgia Young
Profile: The Chronicle is published weekly for the residents of Orleans County, VT. The newspaper covers local news, business, sports, local government and community events. The paper does not cover national news unless it relates to the local area.
Language (s): English
Ad Rate: Full Page Mono 11.25
Ad Rate: Full Page Colour 489.00
Currency: United States Dollars
COMMUNITY NEWSPAPER

The Chronicle 21455
Owner: Lone Oak Publishing Co., Inc.
Editorial: 15 Ridge St, Glens Falls, New York 12801-3608 **Tel:** 1 518 792-1126
Email: chronicle@loneoak.com **Web site:** http://www.readthechronicle.com
Freq: Thu; **Circ:** 30000 Not Audited
Advertising Sales Manager: Valeria Erceg; **Editor:** Mark Frost; **News Editor:** Gordon Woodworth
Profile: The Chronicle is an arts weekly in the greater Glens Falls/Lake George region, covering Warren, Washington and northern Saratoga Counties.
Language (s): English
Ad Rate: Full Page Mono 21.00
Currency: United States Dollars
COMMUNITY NEWSPAPER

The Chronicle 21553
Owner: Country Media, Inc.
Editorial: 1805 Columbia Blvd, Saint Helens, Oregon 97051-6220 **Tel:** 1 503 397-0116
Web site: http://www.thechronicleonline.com
Freq: Wed; **Circ:** 6200 Not Audited
Publisher: Don Patterson; **Editor:** Shari Phiel
Profile: The Chronicle is published for the residents of Columbia County, OR. The newspaper covers local news and community events.
Language (s): English
Ad Rate: Full Page Mono 7.50
Currency: United States Dollars
COMMUNITY NEWSPAPER

The Chronicle 657915
Owner: Great Lakes Media, Inc.
Editorial: 61 Indiana Ave Ste A, Valparaiso, Indiana 46383-5500 **Tel:** 1 219 462-1488
Email: editorial@thechroniclenwi.com **Web site:** http://www.thechroniclenwi.com
Freq: Wed; **Circ:** 30000
Editor: Kathy Mitchell
Profile: The Chronicle is a community newspaper written for the residents of Valparaiso, IN.
Language (s): English
Ad Rate: Full Page Mono 18.00
Currency: United States Dollars
COMMUNITY NEWSPAPER

The Chronicle 735543
Tel: 1 410 658-5740
Email: opcnews@zoominternet.net **Web site:** http://www.heraldandchronicle.com/the-chronicle.html
Freq: Tue; **Circ:** 8200
Advertising Sales Manager: Gerry Salsbury; **Editor:** Jim Wolf
Profile: The Chronicle is a weekly newspaper written for the residents of Southern Lancaster County, PA. It covers local, community news.
Language (s): English
Ad Rate: Full Page Mono 6.75
Ad Rate: Full Page Colour 125.00
Currency: United States Dollars
COMMUNITY NEWSPAPER

The Chronicle of Grand Lake
923627

Tel: 1 918 782-4408
Email: grandchr@grand-chronicle.com **Web site:** http://www.grand-chronicle.com
Freq: Weekly
Publisher: Brian Ruth
Profile: Provides news in the Grand Lake region, Oklahoma.
Language (s): English
COMMUNITY NEWSPAPER

The Chronicle of Mount Juliet
21877

Owner: Robinson (Bill)
Editorial: 11509 Lebanon Rd, Mount Juliet, Tennessee 37122-5500 **Tel:** 1 615 754-6111
Email: thechronicle@thechronicleofmtjuliet.com **Web site:** http://www.thechronicleofmtjuliet.com
Freq: Wed; **Circ:** 12000 Not Audited
Profile: The Chronicle of Mount Juliet is a community newspaper serving residents of Mount Juliet, TN. The paper covers wedding and birth announcements, community news, events and local business news.
Language (s): English
Ad Rate: Full Page Mono 10.99
Ad Rate: Full Page Colour 13.70
Currency: United States Dollars
COMMUNITY NEWSPAPER

The Chronicle Shopper
22425

Owner: Chronicle Printing Co. Inc.
Editorial: 1 Chronicle Rd, Willimantic, Connecticut 06226-1932 **Tel:** 1 860 423-8466
Email: news@thechronicle.com **Web site:** http://www.thechronicle.com
Freq: Thu; **Circ:** 27470 Not Audited
Advertising Sales Manager: Jean Beckley; **Editor:** Charles Ryan
Profile: The Chronicle Shopper is a free, weekly newspaper published by The Chronicle. It is sent to non-subscribers of The Chronicle and provides local news, community events and feature stories of interest to residents in northeastern Connecticut. Advertising must be purchased as a combination buy with the daily paper.
Language (s): English
Ad Rate: Full Page Mono 28.75
Currency: United States Dollars
COMMUNITY NEWSPAPER

Cibola Beacon
22159

Owner: Orion El Faro, LLC dba Cibola Beacon
Editorial: 325 W Santa Fe Ave, Grants, New Mexico 87020-2531 **Tel:** 1 505 287-4411
Email: editor@cibolabeacon.com **Web site:** http://www.cibolabeacon.com
Freq: Fri; **Circ:** 8600 Not Audited
Advertising Sales Manager: Sylvia Anzures Gonzales; **Publisher & Editor:** Don Jaramillo; **Circulation Manager:** Aaryn Tribbey
Profile: Cibola Beacon is a local twice-weekly published newspaper written for residents of Cibola County, NM. The editorial deadlines are Mondays at noon MT for the Tuesday issue and Thursdays at noon MT for the Friday issue.
Language (s): Spanish/Bilingual
Ad Rate: Full Page Mono 10.00
Currency: United States Dollars
COMMUNITY NEWSPAPER

Citizen News
22173

Editorial: 79 State Route 39, New Fairfield, Connecticut 06812-4120 **Tel:** 1 203 746-4669
Email: citizennews@aol.com **Web site:** http://www.fairfieldcitizenonline.com
Freq: Wed; **Circ:** 7890 Not Audited
Publisher & Editor: Ellen Burnett
Profile: Citizen News provides current news to the residents in suburban and upper Fairfield County, CT. Deadlines for the publication are at noon ET.
Language (s): English
Ad Rate: Full Page Mono 7.50
Currency: United States Dollars
COMMUNITY NEWSPAPER

Citizens' Advocate
21391

Owner: Murph (Jean) & Meara (Dan) Inc.
Editorial: 446 W Bethel Rd, Coppell, Texas 75019-4416 **Tel:** 1 972 462-8192
Email: citizensadvocate2000@yahoo.com **Web site:** http://www.coppellcitizensadvocate.com
Freq: Fri; **Circ:** 5000 Not Audited
Publisher & Editor: Jean Murph
Profile: Citizens' Advocate is a community newspaper targeted at the residents of Coppell and Valley Ranch, TX.
Language (s): English
Ad Rate: Full Page Mono 12.00
Currency: United States Dollars
COMMUNITY NEWSPAPER

Citizen's News
24454

Owner: Maitland Publishing, LLC.
Editorial: 71 Weid Dr, Naugatuck, Connecticut 06770-4764 **Tel:** 1 203 729-2228
Email: editor@mycitizensnews.com **Web site:** http://www.mycitizensnews.com
Freq: Thu; **Circ:** 15000 Not Audited
Editor: Elio Gugliotti; **Advertising Sales Manager:** Paul Roth
Language (s): English
Ad Rate: Full Page Mono 7.70
Currency: United States Dollars
COMMUNITY NEWSPAPER

The Citizen-Times
19378

Owner: Pitchford (Robert)
Editorial: 611 E Main St, Scottsville, Kentucky 42164-1628 **Tel:** 1 270 237-3441
Email: ctimes@nctc.com **Web site:** http://www.thecitizen-times.com
Freq: Thu; **Circ:** 5400 Not Audited
Editor: Matt Pedigo; **Publisher:** Robert Pitchford; **Advertising Sales Manager:** Jennetta Stinson
Profile: The Citizen-Times is published weekly for the residents of Scottsville, KY and surrounding areas. The newspaper covers local news and community events.
Language (s): English
Ad Rate: Full Page Mono 7.70
Currency: United States Dollars
COMMUNITY NEWSPAPER

City Beat
22231

Owner: Lightborne Publishing Inc.
Editorial: 811 Race St, Cincinnati, Ohio 45202-2041 **Tel:** 1 513 665-4700
Email: letters@citybeat.com **Web site:** http://www.citybeat.com
Freq: Wed; **Circ:** 50000 Not Audited
Circulation Manager: Steve Ferguson
Profile: City Beat in Cincinnati, OH aims to provide an alternative source of information for progressive, open-minded readers, and to explore, explain and discuss issues involving the community in a way that encourages readers to participate as better citizens. The newspaper is written for the people of Greater Cincinnati and Northern Kentucky. The newspaper covers local news, social issues and arts & entertainment, including: film, live and recorded music, theater and dance, art and literature.
Language (s): English
Ad Rate: Full Page Mono 56.72
Currency: United States Dollars
COMMUNITY NEWSPAPER

City Newspaper
21322

Owner: WMT Publications Inc.
Editorial: 250 Goodman St N, Rochester, New York 14607-1100 **Tel:** 1 585 244-3329
Email: themail@rochester-citynews.com **Web site:** http://www.rochestercitynewspaper.com
Freq: Wed; **Circ:** 39000 Not Audited
News Editor: Christine Fien; **Advertising Sales Manager:** Betsy Matthews; **Circulation Manager:** Kate Stathis
Profile: City Newspaper is written for Rochester, NY residents. The editorial mission is to provide coverage of arts and alternative lifestyles.
Language (s): English
Ad Rate: Full Page Colour 1937.00
Currency: United States Dollars
COMMUNITY NEWSPAPER

City Pages
19748

Owner: Star Tribune Media Co.
Editorial: 800 N 1st St Ste 300, Minneapolis, Minnesota 55401-5050 **Tel:** 1 612 375-1015
Email: news@citypages.com **Web site:** http://www.citypages.com
Freq: Wed; **Circ:** 50000 Not Audited
Profile: City Pages is a weekly newspaper published for the residents of Minneapolis, MN. The newspaper covers news, sports and entertainment.
Language (s): English
Ad Rate: Full Page Mono 61.54
Ad Rate: Full Page Colour 74.59
Currency: United States Dollars
COMMUNITY NEWSPAPER

City Pages
21869

Owner: Stezenski (Tammy)
Editorial: 300 N 3rd St, Wausau, Wisconsin 54403-5458 **Tel:** 1 715 845-5171
Email: advertising@thecitypages.com **Web site:** http://www.thecitypages.com
Freq: Thu; **Circ:** 16720 Not Audited
Publisher & Editor: Tammy Stezenski
Profile: City Pages' editorial mission is to provide news to residents of Central Wisconsin. The paper based in Wausau, WI only wants to receive news of local, regional or state interest. National press information is generally ignored. Deadlines are Mondays at 5pm CT.
Language (s): English
Ad Rate: Full Page Mono 25.00
Currency: United States Dollars
COMMUNITY NEWSPAPER

City Paper
19467

Owner: tronc
Editorial: 501 N Calvert St, Baltimore, Maryland 21278-1000 **Tel:** 1 410 523-2300
Email: letters@citypaper.com **Web site:** http://www.citypaper.com
Freq: Wed; **Circ:** 48843 Not Audited
Profile: City Paper is a weekly newspaper written for the residents of Baltimore, MD. The editorial mission of the newspaper is to serve as a resource of arts & entertainment. The newspaper provides coverage of local news, politics, communities, culture and arts & entertainment.
Language (s): English
Ad Rate: Full Page Mono 18.25
Currency: United States Dollars
COMMUNITY NEWSPAPER

City Pulse
76946

Owner: To The Max LLC
Editorial: 1905 E Michigan Ave, Lansing, Michigan 48912-2828 **Tel:** 1 517 371-5600
Web site: http://lansingcitypulse.com
Freq: Wed; **Circ:** 20000 Not Audited
News Editor: Andy Balaskovitz; **News Editor:** Sam Inglot; **Publisher & Editor:** Berl Schwartz
Profile: City Pulse is a weekly newspaper written for the residents of Lansing, MI. The editorial content includes news, entertainment, events, arts and other topics of general interest.
Language (s): English
Ad Rate: Full Page Mono 37.00
Currency: United States Dollars
COMMUNITY NEWSPAPER

The City Sentinel
231020

Owner: Frost Entertainment LLC
Tel: 1 405 605-6062
Email: news@city-sentinel.com **Web site:** http://www.city-sentinel.com
Freq: Thu; **Circ:** 8000 Not Audited
Advertising Manager: Pam Paul
Profile: The City Sentinel is a weekly, legal newspaper serving downtown, central and northwest Oklahoma City. Focusing on community and neighborhood news, the paper is now serving as the source for news from the heart of Oklahoma City.
Language (s): English
Ad Rate: Full Page Mono 11.95
Currency: United States Dollars
COMMUNITY NEWSPAPER

City Suburban News
22301

Owner: Klein (Robert M.)
Tel: 1 610 667-6623
Email: citysuburbannews@mac.com
Freq: Wed; **Circ:** 8500 Not Audited
Publisher: Robert Klein; **Editor:** Leslie Swan
Profile: City Suburban News is a weekly newspaper published for residents of Mainline and Western Philadelphia, including the communities of Bala Cynwyd, Merion, Narberth, Penn Valley, Ardmore, Wynnewood, Havertown, Bryn Mawr, Haverford, Overbrook Park, Overbrook, Balwynne Park and Wynnefield Heights, PA. It covers local news and events, profiles of local people and businesses, education news and features of interest.
Language (s): English
Ad Rate: Full Page Mono 13.00
Currency: United States Dollars
COMMUNITY NEWSPAPER

Cityview
22622

Owner: Big Green Umbrella
Editorial: 5619 NW St. Suite 600, Johnston, Iowa 50131 **Tel:** 1 515 953-4822
Email: editor@dmcityview.com **Web site:** http://www.dmcityview.com
Freq: Thu; **Circ:** 30000 Not Audited
Circulation Manager: Brent Antisdel; **Publisher & Editor:** Shane Goodman; **Advertising Sales Manager:** Ashley Sohl
Profile: Cityview in Johnston, IA aims to provide an alternative news source for residents of Des Moines and central Iowa, and covers local events, music, arts & entertainment, food and trends.
Language (s): English
Ad Rate: Full Page Mono 77.00
Ad Rate: Full Page Colour 2223.00
Currency: United States Dollars
COMMUNITY NEWSPAPER

Claiborne Progress
22144

Owner: Community Newspaper Holdings, Inc.
Editorial: 1705 Main St, Tazewell, Tennessee 37879-3413 **Tel:** 1 423 626-3222
Web site: http://www.claiborneprogress.net
Freq: Wed; **Circ:** 7000 Not Audited
Editor: Marisa Anders
Profile: Tazewell Claiborne Progress provides local news for the residents of Claiborne, TN.
Language (s): English
Ad Rate: Full Page Mono 7.05
Currency: United States Dollars
COMMUNITY NEWSPAPER

The Clare County Review
19512

Owner: Wilcox Enterprise
Editorial: 105 W 4th St, Clare, Michigan 48617-1458 **Tel:** 1 989 386-4414
Email: info@clarecountyreview.com **Web site:** http://www.clarecountyreview.com
Freq: Fri; **Circ:** 10000 Not Audited
Editor & Publisher: Mike Wilcox
Profile: The Clare County Review is a weekly community newspaper. Its editorial mission is to provide residents of Clare County, MI with local news, sports and entertainment. Deadlines are on Wednesdays at 5pm ET.
Language (s): English
Ad Rate: Full Page Mono 15.00
Currency: United States Dollars
COMMUNITY NEWSPAPER

Claremont Courier
24474

Editorial: 1420 N Claremont Blvd, Ste 205B, Claremont, California 91711-3528 **Tel:** 1 909 621-4761
Email: editor@claremont-courier.com **Web site:** http://www.claremont-courier.com
Freq: 2 Times/Week; **Circ:** 6253 Not Audited
Circulation Manager: Dee Proffitt; **Advertising Sales Manager:** Mary Rose; **Publisher & Editor:** Peter Weinberger
Profile: Claremont Courier is a bi-weekly newspaper carrying news relevant to the Claremont, CA community. It covers local news and events, social issues, education, business and community news. Deadlines for submissions are Mondays at 3pm PT for the Wednesday issue and Thursdays at 3pm PT for the Saturday issue.
Language (s): English
Ad Rate: Full Page Mono 11.00
Currency: United States Dollars
COMMUNITY NEWSPAPER

The Clarion
830068

Editorial: 2819 Veterans Dr, Scottsboro, Alabama 35769-4225 **Tel:** 1 256 259-2455
Email: info@theclarion.org **Web site:** http://www.theclarion.org
Freq: Wed; **Circ:** 15000
Profile: The Clarion is a weekly community newspaper in Scottsboro, AL.
Ad Rate: Full Page Mono 8.20
Currency: United States Dollars
COMMUNITY NEWSPAPER

Clarion Dispatch
21640

Owner: GateHouse Media Inc.
Editorial: 150 Trading Bay Rd Ste 1, Kenai, Alaska 99611-7716 **Tel:** 1 907 283-7551
Email: news@peninsulaclarion.com **Web site:** http://peninsulaclarion.com/dispatch
Freq: Wed; **Circ:** 10000 Not Audited
Profile: Clarion Dispatch is a weekly community newspaper servicing the residents of Kenai, AK.
Language (s): English
Ad Rate: Full Page Mono 11.47
Currency: United States Dollars
COMMUNITY NEWSPAPER

Clarion Herald
21571

Owner: Clarion Herald Publishing Company
Editorial: 1000 Howard Ave Ste 400, New Orleans, Louisiana 70113-1926 **Tel:** 1 504 596-3035
Email: clarionherald@clarionherald.org **Web site:** http://www.clarionherald.org
Freq: Sat; **Circ:** 56000 Not Audited
Publisher: Gregory Aymand
Profile: Clarion Herald is the official Catholic newspaper of the Archdiocese of New Orleans. The paper's editorial mission is to enable readers to grow and develop into mature, well-informed Catholics and to deepen their commitment to the Lord, their Catholic faith and their church.
Language (s): English
Ad Rate: Full Page Mono 36.00
Currency: United States Dollars
COMMUNITY NEWSPAPER

Clarion News
20552

Owner: Boyles (Patrick)
Editorial: 860 S 5th Ave Ste 4, Clarion, Pennsylvania 16214-8614 **Tel:** 1 814 226-7000
Web site: http://www.theclarionnews.com
Freq: Thu; **Circ:** 6924 Not Audited
Publisher: Ned Cowart; **Advertising Manager:** Mary Logue; **Editor:** Rodney Sherman
Profile: Clarion News is a bi-weekly newspaper written for residents of Clarion County, Armstrong County and Jefferson County, PA. The newspaper covers local news, weather and sports.
Language (s): English
Ad Rate: Full Page Mono 14.42
Currency: United States Dollars
COMMUNITY NEWSPAPER

El Clasificado
81475

Owner: de la Torre (Martha)
Editorial: 11205 Imperial Hwy, Norwalk, California 90650-2229 **Tel:** 1 323 278-5310
Email: elclasificado@elclasificado.com **Web site:** http://www.elclasificado.com
Freq: Tue; **Circ:** 510012 Not Audited
Editor: Hilda Hernandez
Profile: El Clasificado offers goods and services to the Latino community of greater Los Angeles. Classified sections include automotive sales, automotive services, rentals, employment opportunites, free community events, general services, home services, miscellaneous services, professional services, real estate and business opportunities.
Language (s): English
Ad Rate: Full Page Mono 110.91
Currency: United States Dollars
COMMUNITY NEWSPAPER

The Clayton News-Star
22541

Editorial: 109 S Ellington St, Clayton, North Carolina 27520-2305 **Tel:** 1 919 553-7234
Email: claytonnews@newsobserver.com **Web site:** http://www.claytonnewsstar.com
Freq: Wed; **Circ:** 5400 Not Audited
Editor: Johnny Whitfield
Profile: The Clayton News-Star is for residents of Clayton, NC. It covers local news, weather and sports. Deadlines are on noon ET Fridays.
Language (s): English
Ad Rate: Full Page Mono 11.30
Currency: United States Dollars
COMMUNITY NEWSPAPER

Clayton Pioneer
331141

Editorial: 6200 Center St, Clayton, California 94517-1446 **Tel:** 1 925 672-0500
Web site: http://www.claytonpioneer.com
Freq: Bi-Weekly; **Circ:** 9000 Not Audited
Publisher & Editor: Tamara Steiner
Profile: Clayton Pioneer is published bi-weekly for the residents of Clayton, CA and surrounding areas. The newspaper provides information about local news and community events, and does not want to be contacted by PR professionals.
Language (s): English
Ad Rate: Full Page Mono 16.50
Currency: United States Dollars
COMMUNITY NEWSPAPER

The Clayton Tribune 22310
Owner: Community Newspapers Inc.
Editorial: 120 N Main St, Clayton, Georgia 30525-4266 **Tel:** 1 706 782-3312
Email: thetribune@theclaytontribune.com **Web site:** http://www.theclaytontribune.com
Freq: Thu; **Circ:** 6200 Not Audited
Editor: Klark Byrd
Profile: The Clayton Tribune is a local weekly newspaper written for the residents of Clayton, GA.
Language (s): English
Ad Rate: Full Page Mono 15.00
Currency: United States Dollars
COMMUNITY NEWSPAPER

The Cleveland Jewish News 22099
Owner: Cleveland Jewish Publication Co.
Editorial: 23880 Commerce Park Ste 1, Beachwood, Ohio 44122-5830 **Tel:** 1 216 454-8300
Email: editorial@cjn.org **Web site:** http://www.clevelandjewishnews.com
Freq: Fri; **Circ:** 8000 Not Audited
Circulation Manager: Abby Royer
Profile: The Cleveland Jewish News is written for northeast Ohio's Jewish Community with local, national and international news, features and commentary.
Language (s): English
Ad Rate: Full Page Mono 31.97
Currency: United States Dollars
COMMUNITY NEWSPAPER

Cleveland Scene 128782
Owner: Euclid Media Group
Editorial: 737 Bolivar Rd Ste 4100, Cleveland, Ohio 44115-1259 **Tel:** 1 216 241-7550
Email: scene@clevescene.com **Web site:** http://www.clevescene.com
Freq: Wed; **Circ:** 45000 Not Audited
Editor: Vince Grzegorek; **Publisher:** Chris Keating
Profile: Cleveland Scene is written for residents of Cleveland. It features magazine-style news and features, award-winning music coverage with film and theater sections, restaurant reviews and listings, and a comprehensive regional calendar of events. The publication targets young urban professionals hungry for smart, uncompromising civic journalism. The paper merged with the Cleveland Free Times on July 30, 2008.
Language (s): English
Ad Rate: Full Page Mono 28.66
Currency: United States Dollars
COMMUNITY NEWSPAPER

Clifton Insider Passaic County Edition 387391
Owner: Clifton Insider LLC
Tel: 1 973 865-7691
Email: editor@insidernewsnj.com **Web site:** http://insidernewsnj.com
Freq: Bi-Weekly; **Circ:** 15000 Not Audited
Publisher, Editor & Advertising Sales Manager: Nicholas Veliky
Profile: Clifton Insider is a community newspaper circulated every other week to residents of Clifton, NJ and the surrounding area. It reports on community news, financial, technology and business news, local politics and consumer news. Feature articles include the topics of entertainment, food, health, social events and calendar listings. It is best to contact the paper mid-week by e-mail.
Language (s): English
Ad Rate: Full Page Mono 15.00
Currency: United States Dollars
COMMUNITY NEWSPAPER

Clifton Journal 81585
Owner: Gannett Co., Inc./North Jersey Media Group
Editorial: 777 Passaic Ave, Clifton, New Jersey 07012-1804
Email: newsroom@northjersey.com **Web site:** http://www.northjersey.com/local
Freq: Fri; **Circ:** 30000 Not Audited
Advertising Sales Manager: Peter Bocchieri; **Editor:** Albina Sportelli
Profile: Clifton Journal is a community newspaper serving Clifton, NJ and the surrounding areas.
Language (s): English
Ad Rate: Full Page Mono 17.50
Currency: United States Dollars
COMMUNITY NEWSPAPER

CNI Newspapers 24738
Owner: Journal Communications
Editorial: 1741 Dolphin Dr Ste A, Waukesha, Wisconsin 53186-1493 **Tel:** 1 414 224-2100
Email: news@cninow.com **Web site:** http://www.mycommunitynow.com
Circ: 36864 Not Audited
Editor: Darryl Enriquez; **Editor:** Jim Riccioli
Language (s): English
COMMUNITY NEWSPAPER

Coachella Valley Weekly 822566
Editorial: Coachella, California **Tel:** 1 760 501-6228
Email: info@coachellavalleyweekly.com **Web site:** http://coachellavalleyweekly.com
Freq: Weekly; **Circ:** 20000
Publisher & Editor: Tracy Dietlin
Profile: The Coachella Valley Weekly is a weekly community newspaper covering news, business, entertainment, fashion and sports for Coachella Valley residents.
Language (s): English
COMMUNITY NEWSPAPER

Coal Valley News 28470
Owner: Heartland Publications
Editorial: 350 Main St, Madison, West Virginia 25130-1293 **Tel:** 1 304 369-1165
Web site: http://www.coalvalleynews.com
Freq: Wed; **Circ:** 5400 Not Audited
Editor: Fred Pace
Profile: Coal Valley News is written for the residents of Boone County, WV. Deadlines are 5pm ET on Fridays.
Language (s): English
Ad Rate: Full Page Mono 6.00
Currency: United States Dollars
COMMUNITY NEWSPAPER

Coalinga Recorder 532553
Owner: Madera Printing and Publishing
Editorial: 192 E Elm Ave Ste 103, Coalinga, California 93210-2835 **Tel:** 1 559 935-3434
Freq: Wed; **Circ:** 5000 Not Audited
Publisher: Charles Doud; **Advertising Sales Manager:** Katrina Soliz
Profile: Coalinga Recorder is a weekly community newspaper serving local news, arts & entertainment and sports to the residents of Coalinga, CA.
Language (s): English
Ad Rate: Full Page Mono 7.00
Currency: United States Dollars
COMMUNITY NEWSPAPER

The Coast Star 23015
Owner: Star News Group, Inc.
Editorial: 13 Broad St, Manasquan, New Jersey 08736-2906 **Tel:** 1 732 223-0076
Email: info@thecoaststar.com **Web site:** http://www.starnewsgroup.com
Freq: Weekly; **Circ:** 12287 Not Audited
Publisher: James Manser; **Editor:** Doug Paviluk
Profile: The Coast Star is a local newspaper written for residents of Southern Monmouth County, NJ and the communities of Avon, Brielle, Belmar, Manasquan, Sea Girt, South Belmar, Spring Lake, Spring Lake Heights and Wall, NJ.
Language (s): English
Ad Rate: Full Page Mono 9.01
Ad Rate: Full Page Colour 10.48
Currency: United States Dollars
COMMUNITY NEWSPAPER

The Coastal Bend Herald News 21007
Owner: Riley (Kerry A.)
Tel: 1 361 729-1828
Email: coastalbendherald1@yahoo.com **Web site:** http://www.theheraldonline.com
Freq: Thu; **Circ:** 5000 Not Audited
Advertising Sales Manager: Michelle Perdue; **Circulation Manager:** Jerry Reynolds; **Publisher & Editor:** Kerry Riley
Profile: The Coastal Bend Herald News is a regional newspaper published weekly for residents of San Patricio and Aransas Counties, TX.
Language (s): English
Ad Rate: Full Page Mono 12.75
Currency: United States Dollars
COMMUNITY NEWSPAPER

The Coastal Courier 18816
Owner: Morris Multimedia, Inc.
Editorial: 125 S Main St, Hinesville, Georgia 31313-3217 **Tel:** 1 912 876-0156
Email: editor@coastalcourier.com **Web site:** http://www.coastalcourier.com
Freq: 3 Times/Week; **Circ:** 5000 Not Audited
Profile: Coastal Courier is a local weekly newspaper written for residence of Liberty County, GA. The main topic of the newspaper is the local news in the Liberty County, GA area. The lead time for Coastal Courier is 24 hours.
Language (s): English
Ad Rate: Full Page Mono 10.75
Currency: United States Dollars
COMMUNITY NEWSPAPER

The Coastal Journal 21518
Owner: Maine Today Media Inc.
Editorial: 832 Washington St, Bath, Maine 04530-2662 **Tel:** 1 207 443-6241
Web site: http://www.coastaljournal.com
Freq: Thu; **Circ:** 20000 Not Audited
Profile: Coastal Journal is published weekly for the residents of Freeport and Rockland, ME. The newspaper covers local news, sports and community events.
Language (s): English
Ad Rate: Full Page Mono 16.00
Currency: United States Dollars
COMMUNITY NEWSPAPER

Coastal Observer 21506
Owner: Southwestern Publishing Company, Inc.
Editorial: 97 Commerce Dr, Pawley's Island, South Carolina 29585 **Tel:** 1 843 237-8438
Web site: http://www.coastalobserver.com
Freq: Thu; **Circ:** 5300 Not Audited
Editor: Charles Swenson; **Publisher:** M.P. Swenson
Profile: Coastal Observer is a local weekly newspaper written for residents in the Waccamaw Neck River area, SC. Deadlines are at 5pm ET on Mondays.
Language (s): English
Ad Rate: Full Page Mono 8.15
Currency: United States Dollars
COMMUNITY NEWSPAPER

Coastal View 22209
Owner: RMG Ventures, LLC
Editorial: 4856 Carpinteria Ave, Carpinteria, California 93013-1935 **Tel:** 1 805 684-4428
Email: news@coastalview.com **Web site:** http://www.coastalview.com
Freq: Thu; **Circ:** 6502 Not Audited
Publisher: Gary Dobbins
Profile: Coastal View News is a local weekly newspaper written for the community of Carpinteria, CA. The main topic the newspaper covers is the local news of Carpinteria, CA.
Language (s): English
Ad Rate: Full Page Mono 16.50
Ad Rate: Full Page Colour 50.00
Currency: United States Dollars
COMMUNITY NEWSPAPER

The Coaster 21699
Editorial: 1011 Main St, Asbury Park, New Jersey 07712-5963 **Tel:** 1 732 775-6379
Web site: http://thecoaster.net/wordpress
Freq: Thu; **Circ:** 5000 Not Audited
Publisher & Editor: Ellen Carroll
Profile: The Coaster is published weekly for the residents of Asbury Park, NJ and surrounding areas. The newspaper covers local news and community events.
Language (s): English
Ad Rate: Full Page Mono 7.00
Currency: United States Dollars
COMMUNITY NEWSPAPER

The Coastland Times 19988
Owner: Times Printing Co.
Editorial: 501 Budleigh Street, Manteo, North Carolina 27954 **Tel:** 1 252 473-2105
Email: news@thecoastlandtimes.net
Freq: Sun; **Circ:** 7500
Publisher & Editor: Susan Simpson; **Advertising Sales Manager:** Teresa Simpson
Profile: The Coastland Times is the official newspaper of the Walter Raleigh Coastland. It is published three times per week for residents of Dare County, NC. The publication is a general interest newspaper, covering local news, weather, sports, business, education, arts and entertainment, and other information of interest to the local community.
Language (s): English
Ad Rate: Full Page Mono 8.16
Currency: United States Dollars
COMMUNITY NEWSPAPER

Cody Enterprise 21284
Owner: Sage Publishing
Editorial: 3101 Big Horn Ave, Cody, Wyoming 82414-9250 **Tel:** 1 307 587-2231
Email: office@codyenterprise.com **Web site:** http://www.codyenterprise.com
Freq: Mon; **Circ:** 7100 Not Audited
Profile: Cody Enterprise is a local newspaper written for residents of Cody, WY. The newspaper covers local news. Deadlines are on Mondays and Wednesdays at 10am MT.
Language (s): English
Ad Rate: Full Page Mono 13.00
Currency: United States Dollars
COMMUNITY NEWSPAPER

El Colombiano 407511
Owner: Latinwork Publishing Co.
Editorial: 3408 W 84th St Ste 206, Hialeah, Florida 33018-4942 **Tel:** 1 954 430-1090
Email: editor@elcolombiano.net **Web site:** http://www.elcolombiano.net
Freq: Fri; **Circ:** 35000 Not Audited
Publisher & Editor: Alfredo Mantilla
Profile: El Colombiano is a free, weekly newspaper serving the Hispanic population and Colombian Americans in Miami-Dade, Broward and Palm Beach counties, FL. It relays current events occurring in Colombia, everything from news to entertainment. It also provides analysis of international news.
Language (s): Spanish/Bilingual
Ad Rate: Full Page Mono 20.00
Currency: United States Dollars
COMMUNITY NEWSPAPER

Colorado Chinese News 152792
Owner: Colorado Chinese News Inc.
Editorial: 1548 W Alameda Ave Ste A, Denver, Colorado 80223-1973 **Tel:** 1 303 722-8268
Email: editor@cocnews.com **Web site:** http://www.cocnews.com
Freq: Fri; **Circ:** 6500 Not Audited
Publisher: Frank Chao; **Advertising Sales Manager:** Wendy Chao
Profile: The Colorado Chinese News is written for the residents of Denver, CO.
Language (s): Chinese
Ad Rate: Full Page Mono 28.00
Currency: United States Dollars
COMMUNITY NEWSPAPER

Colorado Hometown Weekly 28450
Editorial: 5450 Western Ave, Boulder, Colorado 80301-2709 **Tel:** 1 303 776-2244
Email: news@coloradohometownweekly.com **Web site:** http://www.coloradohometownweekly.com
Freq: Wed; **Circ:** 18400 Not Audited
Profile: Colorado Hometown Weekly is a local weekly newspaper serving the residents of Louisville, Erie, Lafayette and Superior, CO. The newspaper covers local news, sports, schools, opinion, and community events.
Language (s): English
Ad Rate: Full Page Mono 14.50
Ad Rate: Full Page Colour 249.00
Currency: United States Dollars
COMMUNITY NEWSPAPER

Colorado Springs Independent 21960
Owner: Colorado Publishing House
Editorial: 235 S Nevada Ave, Colorado Springs, Colorado 80903-1906 **Tel:** 1 719 577-4545
Email: news@csindy.com **Web site:** http://www.csindy.com
Freq: Wed; **Circ:** 35500 Not Audited
Profile: Colorado Springs (CO) Independent is a weekly alternative newspaper featuring arts & entertainment, dining, music, film, opinion, events and news.
Language (s): English
Ad Rate: Full Page Mono 52.00
Ad Rate: Full Page Colour 59.39
Currency: United States Dollars
COMMUNITY NEWSPAPER

The Columbia County News-Times 22562
Owner: GateHouse Media Inc.
Editorial: 4272 Washington Rd Ste 3B, Evans, Georgia 30809-3073 **Tel:** 1 706 863-6165
Email: cnt@newstimesonline.com **Web site:** http://newstimes.augusta.com
Freq: Sun; **Circ:** 48000 Not Audited
Publisher: Steve Crawford; **Advertising Sales Manager:** Suzanne Liverett
Profile: The Columbia County News-Times provides local and national news coverage for the Columbia County, GA area.
Language (s): English
Ad Rate: Full Page Mono 21.50
Currency: United States Dollars
COMMUNITY NEWSPAPER

The Columbia Star 20621
Owner: Star Reporter Corp. (The)
Editorial: 723 Queen St, Columbia, South Carolina 29205-1723 **Tel:** 1 803 771-0219
Web site: http://www.thecolumbiastar.com
Freq: Fri; **Circ:** 15000 Not Audited
Publisher: Mimi Maddock
Profile: The Columbia Star is written for the residents of Columbia, SC. It covers local news, society, education and legal sections. Deadlines for publication are Fridays at 5pm ET.
Language (s): English
Ad Rate: Full Page Mono 15.00
Currency: United States Dollars
COMMUNITY NEWSPAPER

The Columbian Progress 19867
Owner: Emmerich Newspapers Inc.
Editorial: 318 Second St, Columbia, Mississippi 39429-2954 **Tel:** 1 601 736-2611
Email: news@columbianprogress.com **Web site:** http://www.columbiams.info
Freq: Sat; **Circ:** 5000 Not Audited
Publisher: Adam Prestridge
Profile: The Columbian-Progress provides local news coverage for Columbia, MS.
Language (s): English
Ad Rate: Full Page Mono 11.00
Currency: United States Dollars
COMMUNITY NEWSPAPER

Columbus Alive 21610
Owner: GateHouse Media Inc.
Editorial: 34 S 3rd St, Columbus, Ohio 43215-4201
Tel: 1 614 221-2449
Web site: http://www.columbusalive.com
Freq: Weekly; **Circ:** 55000 Not Audited
Editor: Justin McIntosh
Profile: Columbus Alive is written for residents of Columbus, OH. It covers news, arts and culture as well as commentary on national issues that are of concern to the readership.
Language (s): English
Ad Rate: Full Page Mono 19.96
Currency: United States Dollars
COMMUNITY NEWSPAPER

The Columbus Federal Voice 22709
Owner: Defense Logistics Agency
Editorial: 3990 E Broad St, Columbus, Ohio 43213
Tel: 1 614 692-2328
Email: publicaffairs.dscc@dla.mil **Web site:** http://www.federalvoice.defensesupplycentercolumbus.dla.mil/voice
Freq: Bi-Weekly; **Circ:** 8000 Not Audited
Editor: Dan Bender
Language (s): English
Ad Rate: Full Page Mono 32.00
Currency: United States Dollars
COMMUNITY NEWSPAPER

The Columbus Post 22374
Owner: Freedom Media Group of Ohio Inc.
Editorial: 770 E Main St, Columbus, Ohio 43205-1715 **Tel:** 1 614 224-6723
Email: publisher@columbuspost.com **Web site:** http://www.columbuspost.com
Freq: Weekly; **Circ:** 5000 Not Audited
Publisher & Editor: Alan W. Sorter
Profile: Columbus Post is written for African American residents of Columbus, OH. It covers local and national news.
Language (s): English
Ad Rate: Full Page Mono 33.60
Ad Rate: Full Page Colour 41.40

Currency: United States Dollars
COMMUNITY NEWSPAPER

The Columbus Times 18802
Owner: Columbus Times
Editorial: 2230 Buena Vista Rd, Columbus, Georgia 31906-3111 **Tel:** 1 706 324-2404
Web site: http://www.columbustimes.com
Freq: Wed; **Circ:** 10000 Not Audited
Editor: Ophelia Mitchell
Profile: The Columbus Times is a weekly publication covering regional, national and international news of minority and race issues for the residents of Columbus, GA and Ft. Benning and Phoenix City, AL. Deadlines are on Mondays at 5pm ET.
Language (s): English
Ad Rate: Full Page Mono 21.25
Currency: United States Dollars
COMMUNITY NEWSPAPER

El Colusa News 520450
Editorial: 2550 NW 72nd Ave Ste 308, Miami, Florida 33122-1348 **Tel:** 1 786 845-6868
Email: info@elcolusa.com **Web site:** http://www.elcolusa.com
Freq: Thu; **Circ:** 27000 Not Audited
Editor: Johanna Amorocho
Profile: El Colusa News is a free weekly community newspaper distributed in the Miami area.
Language (s): Spanish
Ad Rate: Full Page Mono 10.15
Currency: United States Dollars
COMMUNITY NEWSPAPER

El Comercio de Colorado 819762
Owner: Image Impressions
Editorial: 6805 Broadway, Denver, Colorado 80221-2878 **Tel:** 1 303 308-9486
Email: elcomercio@imageimpressions.com **Web site:** http://www.elcomerciocolorado.com
Freq: Thu; **Circ:** 30000
Editor: Eva Tejada
Profile: El Comercio de Colorado is a weekly Spanish-language newspaper providing Local and Community News coverage to the Arvada, Aurora, Boulder, Brighton, Commerce City, Dacono, Denver, Federal Heights, Fort Lupton, Golden, Greeley, Lafayette, Lakewood, Littleton, Longmont, Loveland, Northglenn, Parker, Thornton, Westminster and Wheat Ridge.
Language (s): Spanish
COMMUNITY NEWSPAPER

The Commons 579373
Owner: Vermont Independent Media
Editorial: 139 Main St Rm 604, Brattleboro, Vermont 05301-2871 **Tel:** 1 802 246-6397
Email: news@commonsnews.org **Web site:** http://www.commonsnews.org
Freq: Weekly; **Circ:** 6500
Advertising Sales Manager: Nancy Gauthier
Profile: The Commons is printed for the residents of Windham County, VT.
Language (s): English
Ad Rate: Full Page Mono 10.25
Ad Rate: Full Page Colour 12.50
Currency: United States Dollars
COMMUNITY NEWSPAPER

Community 154794
Owner: Jewish Community Federation
Editorial: 3600 Dutchmans Ln, Louisville, Kentucky 40205-3302 **Tel:** 1 502 459-0660
Email: jcl@jewishlouisville.org **Web site:** http://www.jewishlouisville.org
Freq: Bi-Weekly; **Circ:** 5800 Not Audited
Profile: Community is the official publication of the Jewish Community of Louisville.
Language (s): English
Ad Rate: Full Page Mono 12.00
Currency: United States Dollars
COMMUNITY NEWSPAPER

Community Advertiser 22460
Editorial: 20 Peter Path, Farmingdale, Maine 04344-2930 **Tel:** 1 207 582-8486
Email: ads@comadvertiser.com
Freq: Mon; **Circ:** 13000 Not Audited
Publisher & Editor: Keith Peters
Profile: The Community Advertiser is a weekly publication, mailed free of charge to every address in several central Maine communities. The publication provides local news coverage. The lead time for Community Advertiser is three days.
Language (s): English
Ad Rate: Full Page Mono 7.50
Ad Rate: Full Page Colour 400.00
Currency: United States Dollars
COMMUNITY NEWSPAPER

Community Advocate 23197
Owner: Community Advocate, Inc.
Editorial: 32 South St, Westborough, Massachusetts 01581-1619 **Tel:** 1 508 366-5500
Email: news@communityadvocate.com **Web site:** http://www.communityadvocate.com
Freq: Weekly; **Circ:** 19000 Not Audited
Publisher, Editor & Owner: David Bagdon; **Editor:** Kathy Behan
Profile: Community Advocate is a weekly community newspaper serving Westborough, MA.
Language (s): English
Ad Rate: Full Page Mono 12.95
Currency: United States Dollars
COMMUNITY NEWSPAPER

Community Common 22864
Owner: AIM Media Midwest
Editorial: 637 6th St, Portsmouth, Ohio 45662-3924 **Tel:** 1 740 353-1151
Web site: http://www.communitycommon.com
Freq: Sun; **Circ:** 36700 Not Audited
Editor & Publisher: Hope Comer; **Circulation Manager:** Ed Literal
Profile: Community Common provides local news coverage for the Ohio and Kentucky areas. Coverage includes local news and events, business, politics and social issues.
Language (s): English
Ad Rate: Full Page Mono 15.50
Ad Rate: Full Page Colour 1768.50
Currency: United States Dollars
COMMUNITY NEWSPAPER

Community Courier 682725
Editorial: 92 E Main St Ste 202, Somerville, New Jersey 08876-2319 **Tel:** 1 908 243-6630
Web site: http://www.mycentraljersey.com/news/courier-news
Freq: Thu; **Circ:** 49000
Advertising Sales Manager: Bernita Gilliam; **Editor:** Paul Grzella
Profile: Community Courier is written for the residents of Somerville County, NJ.
Language (s): English
Ad Rate: Full Page Mono 16.00
Currency: United States Dollars
COMMUNITY NEWSPAPER

Community Journal 21769
Editorial: 2042 N Country Rd, Wading River, New York 11792-1639 **Tel:** 1 631 929-4927
Freq: Thu; **Circ:** 7000 Not Audited
Publisher & Editor: Bernadette Smith Budd
Profile: Community Journal is a community newspaper targeted at the residents of Wading River, NY.
Language (s): English
Ad Rate: Full Page Mono 17.00
Currency: United States Dollars
COMMUNITY NEWSPAPER

Community Ledger 139840
Owner: S & R Publications, LLC
Editorial: 945 Laurie Ln, Gallatin, Tennessee 37066-3850 **Tel:** 1 615 391-4826
Email: theledger@bellsouth.net
Freq: Wed; **Circ:** 22000 Not Audited
Profile: Community Ledger is a local community newspaper for the residents of Hermitage, TN and the surrounding communities.
Language (s): English
Ad Rate: Full Page Mono 12.00
Currency: United States Dollars
COMMUNITY NEWSPAPER

The Community Merchant 359345
Owner: AIM Media Midwest
Editorial: 1451 N Vandemark Rd, Sidney, Ohio 45365-3547 **Tel:** 1 937 498-8088
Email: sdnews@civitasmedia.com **Web site:** http://www.sidneydailynews.com
Freq: Mon; **Circ:** 12000 Not Audited
News Editor: Melanie Speicher
Profile: The Community Merchant is a free, weekly newspaper published by the Sidney Daily News. It is mailed directly to households in and around Sidney and Wapakoneta, OH, including portions of Shelby, Auglaize, Champaign and Logan counties. In addition to offering expanded market opportunities for advertisers, the paper also provides news and entertainment features of interest to local readers. Each issue includes human-interest articles, a review of local news highlights and previews of stories slated to appear in upcoming issues of the Sidney Daily News. Deadlines are Thursdays at 5pm ET prior to distribution.
Language (s): English
Ad Rate: Full Page Mono 8.00
Currency: United States Dollars
COMMUNITY NEWSPAPER

Community News 21578
Owner: Journal Register Company
Editorial: 20 Lake Ave, Saratoga Springs, New York 12866-2314 **Tel:** 1 518 290-3896
Email: cnews@saratogian.com **Web site:** http://www.cnweekly.com
Freq: Fri; **Circ:** 28501 Not Audited
Profile: Community News in Saratoga Springs, NY is written for residents of Southern Saratoga County, NY.
Language (s): English
Ad Rate: Full Page Mono 12.75
Currency: United States Dollars
COMMUNITY NEWSPAPER

Community News - South 397883
Owner: Gannett Co., Inc./North Jersey Media Group
Editorial: 1 Garret Mountain Plz, Woodland Park, New Jersey 07424-3320
Email: communitynews@northjersey.com **Web site:** http://www.northjersey.com
Freq: Wed; **Circ:** 78404 Not Audited
Profile: Community News - South is a weekly newspaper written for the residents of Garfield and Wallington, Hasbrouck, Heights, Lodi, Maywood, Rochelle Park and Wood Ridge, NJ
Language (s): English
COMMUNITY NEWSPAPER

Community Times 21783
Owner: Landmark Community Newspapers, Inc.
Editorial: 201 Railroad Ave, Westminster, Maryland 21157-4823 **Tel:** 1 410 875-5449
Email: ctimes@lcniofmd.com **Web site:** http://www.carrollcountytimes.com/communities
Freq: Wed; **Circ:** 13000 Not Audited
Profile: Community Times is published weekly for the residents of Westminster, MD and surrounding areas. The newspaper covers local news, government, education, business and community events.
Language (s): English
Ad Rate: Full Page Mono 13.25
Ad Rate: Full Page Colour 2047.00
Currency: United States Dollars
COMMUNITY NEWSPAPER

The Community Times 22091
Owner: DBS Communications
Tel: 1 843 667-1818
Web site: http://www.scvillagevoices.com
Freq: Thu; **Circ:** 36000 Not Audited
Publisher: Diana Smith
Profile: The Community Times is a local newspaper written for the African American community of Florence, SC. The paper covers local news.
Language (s): English
Ad Rate: Full Page Mono 16.00
Ad Rate: Full Page Colour 1648.00
Currency: United States Dollars
COMMUNITY NEWSPAPER

The Community Voice 22133
Owner: Shah (Yatin)
Editorial: 100 Professional Center Dr Ste 110, Rohnert Park, California 94928-2137 **Tel:** 1 707 584-2222
Email: news@thecommunityvoice.com **Web site:** http://www.thecommunityvoice.com
Freq: Weekly; **Circ:** 8000 Not Audited
Circulation Manager: Bill Poole
Profile: The Community Voice provides local news coverage for the Rohnert Park, Cotati and Penngrove, CA communities.
Language (s): English
Ad Rate: Full Page Mono 24.00
Currency: United States Dollars
COMMUNITY NEWSPAPER

The Community Voice 155360
Owner: TCV Publishing, Inc.
Editorial: 2918 E Douglas Ave, Wichita, Kansas 67214-4709 **Tel:** 1 316 681-1155
Email: press@tcvpub.com **Web site:** http://www.voiceitwichita.com
Freq: Thu; **Circ:** 10000 Not Audited
Publisher & Editor: Bonita Gooch
Profile: The Community Voice is a local newspaper written for African American residents in Wichita, KS.
Language (s): English
Ad Rate: Full Page Mono 20.00
Currency: United States Dollars
COMMUNITY NEWSPAPER

The Commuter Times 22881
Owner: Conner (Fred)
Tel: 1 415 509-7056
Email: rhalstead@marinij.com
Freq: Thu; **Circ:** 7500 Not Audited
Publisher & Editor: Fred Conner
Profile: The Commuter Times is a local newspaper written for residents of Marin and San Francisco County, CA. It covers community news and stories regarding transportation issues.
Language (s): English
Ad Rate: Full Page Mono 17.41
Currency: United States Dollars
COMMUNITY NEWSPAPER

The Compton Bulletin/Carson Bulletin/Wilmington Beacon/ The Californian 24442
Owner: American Print Media
Editorial: 800 E Compton Blvd, Compton, California 90221 **Tel:** 1 310 635-6776
Web site: http://www.thecomptonbulletin.com
Freq: Wed; **Circ:** 75000 Not Audited
Profile: The Compton Bulletin/Carson Bulletin/ Wilmington Beacon/The Californian is a weekly newspaper that provides local news coverage for residents in the Compton, Carson and Wilmington, CA area. It covers news relating to politics, business, social issues and community events. Advertising deadlines are at 3pm PT.
Language (s): English
Ad Rate: Full Page Mono 35.00
Ad Rate: Full Page Colour 250.00
Currency: United States Dollars
COMMUNITY NEWSPAPER

Comunidade News 608370
Editorial: 155 Main St Ste 212, Danbury, Connecticut 06810-7844 **Tel:** 1 203 748-0123
Email: info@comunidadenews.com **Web site:** http://www.comunidadenews.com
Freq: Tue; **Circ:** 80000
Profile: Offers news and events to the Brazilian and Portuguese language communities of Connecticut, New Jersey and New York.
Language (s): Portuguese
Ad Rate: Full Page Mono 10.20
Currency: United States Dollars
COMMUNITY NEWSPAPER

Condo News 22623
Editorial: 2827 Exchange Ct Ste C, West Palm Beach, Florida 33409-4000 **Tel:** 1 561 471-0329
Email: info@condonewsonline.com **Web site:** http://www.condonewsonline.com
Freq: Bi-Weekly; **Circ:** 13000 Not Audited
Editor: Betty Thomas; **Publisher:** C.E. Tzoumas
Profile: Condo News is distributed to condominium complex clubhouses in Palm Beach County, FL. It provides local news coverage. Regular features include Food Fun & Entertainment, Out & About, and Fit after Fifty. It is a socially oriented newspaper featuring news supplied by correspondents from the various communities. The lead time for editorial submissions falls on Friday prior to publication date.
Language (s): English
Ad Rate: Full Page Mono 13.25
Currency: United States Dollars
COMMUNITY NEWSPAPER

La Conexion 23352
Tel: 1 919 832-1225
Email: press@laconexionusa.com **Web site:** http://www.laconexionusa.com
Freq: Tue; **Circ:** 21000 Not Audited
Editor: Paola Jaramillo
Profile: La Conexion is a local newspaper written for the Hispanic community of Raleigh, NC. The paper covers local and national news, arts & entertainment, sports, business, horoscopes and classifieds.
Language (s): Spanish
Ad Rate: Full Page Mono 12.40
Currency: United States Dollars
COMMUNITY NEWSPAPER

Conexion 235394
Owner: Hearst Newspapers
Editorial: 301 Ave E & 3rd St, San Antonio, Texas 78205 **Tel:** 1 210 250-2535
Web site: http://www.conexionsa.com
Freq: Wed; **Circ:** 80859 Not Audited
Profile: Conexion in San Antonio, TX is a weekly bicultural publication that targets Hispanic and bicultural households in south Texas. It is published by the San Antonio Express-News. Advertising and news submissions must be received by 5pm CT.
Language (s): Spanish/Bilingual
Ad Rate: Full Page Mono 34.36
Currency: United States Dollars
COMMUNITY NEWSPAPER

Connect Savannah 790905
Editorial: 1800 E Victory Dr Ste 7, Savannah, Georgia 31404-4195 **Tel:** 1 912 238-2040
Web site: http://www.connectsavannah.com
Advertising Sales Manager: Chris Griffin
Profile: Connect Savannah is a weekly community newspaper serving the residents of Savannah, GA. It covers a range of topics including News, Entertainment, Music, Film and Culture.
COMMUNITY NEWSPAPER

El Conquistador 483781
Owner: Huyke (Victor)
Editorial: 4531 W Forest Home Ave, Milwaukee, Wisconsin 53219-4837 **Tel:** 1 414 383-1000
Email: conquistador@bizwi.rr.com **Web site:** http://spanishelconquistador.com/
Freq: Fri; **Circ:** 20000 Not Audited
Publisher & Editor: Victor Huyke
Profile: El Conquistador is a weekly Hispanic newspaper writting for the residents of Milwaukee, WI. It covers local news, health, home politics, sports culture and arts & entertainment.
Language (s): Spanish/Bilingual
Ad Rate: Full Page Mono 12.00
Currency: United States Dollars
COMMUNITY NEWSPAPER

The Contact 791253
Owner: Ajit Weekly
Editorial: 2-7015 Tranmere Dr 2, Mississauga, Ontario L5S 1T7 **Tel:** 1 905 671-4761
Email: info@ajitweekly.com **Web site:** http://www.ajitweekly.com/epaper/the-contact-english.html
Freq: Weekly
Profile: The Contact is a weekly newspaper providing Community News and International News coverage to the Punjabi and Indian community in Mississauga, ON.
Language (s): English
COMMUNITY NEWSPAPER

Continental 23175
Editorial: 200 49th St, Union City, New Jersey 07087-7727 **Tel:** 1 201 864-9505
Email: continews@aol.com
Freq: Fri; **Circ:** 35000 Not Audited
Profile: Continental is a weekly Spanish newspaper serving the Hispanic community of Union City, NJ. The newspaper covers local news, arts & entertainment, health and general interest topics.
Language (s): Spanish
Ad Rate: Full Page Mono 35.00
Currency: United States Dollars
COMMUNITY NEWSPAPER

Co-op City Times 21655
Owner: Riverbay Corporation
Editorial: 2049 Bartow Ave Rm 21, Bronx, New York 10475-4613 **Tel:** 1 718 320-3375
Web site: https://issuu.com/cctimes
Freq: Sat; **Circ:** 18000 Not Audited
Publisher & Editor: Rozaan Boone; **Advertising Sales Manager:** Jennifer Flynn
Profile: Co-op City Times is a weekly newspaper written for the residents of Co-op City, NY.
Language (s): English
Ad Rate: Full Page Mono 5.45

Currency: United States Dollars
COMMUNITY NEWSPAPER

Coopersville Observer 377302
Owner: Coopersville Observer, Inc.
Editorial: 298 Creekside Dr, Coopersville, Michigan 49404-9489 **Tel:** 1 616 997-5049
Email: info@coopersvilleobserver.com **Web site:** http://www.coopersvilleobserver.com
Freq: Bi-Weekly; **Circ:** 6600 Not Audited
Profile: Coopersville Observer is a free, bi-weekly publication serving the communities of Coopersville, Conklin, Marne, Lamont and Ravenna, MI. It contains news, events and information about its community members and what is important to them.
Language (s): English
Ad Rate: Full Page Mono 10.93
Currency: United States Dollars
COMMUNITY NEWSPAPER

Copiah County Courier 19874
Editorial: 103 S Ragsdale Ave, Hazlehurst, Mississippi 39083-3037 **Tel:** 1 601 894-3141
Email: office@copiahcountycourier.com **Web site:** http://www.copiahcountycourier.com
Freq: Wed; **Circ:** 5425 Not Audited
Publisher: Joe Coates
Profile: Copiah County Courier is a local newspaper serving the residents of Copiah County, MS. The paper covers local news and sports.
Language (s): English
Ad Rate: Full Page Mono 7.80
Currency: United States Dollars
COMMUNITY NEWSPAPER

Copper Country News 21842
Owner: New Media Corp.
Editorial: 298 N Pine St, Globe, Arizona 85501-2516 **Tel:** 1 928 425-0355
Email: news@coppercountrynews.com **Web site:** http://www.coppercountrynews.com
Freq: Wed; **Circ:** 20000 Not Audited
Publisher & Editor: Marc Marin; **Circulation Manager:** Cassie Tafoya
Profile: The Copper Country News is a weekly community newspaper serving Globe, AZ.
Language (s): English
Ad Rate: Full Page Mono 14.50
Currency: United States Dollars
COMMUNITY NEWSPAPER

The Corvallis Advocate 858838
Owner: Corvallis Advocate
Tel: 1 541 766-3675
Email: editor@corvallisadvocate.com **Web site:** http://www.corvallisadvocate.com
Freq: Thu
Editor: Johnny Beaver; **Publisher:** Steve Schultz
Profile: The Corvallis Advocate is an Alternative Weekly newspaper providing Local News, Arts & Entertainment, Literature for the residents of Corvallis, OR.
Language (s): English
COMMUNITY NEWSPAPER

Country Gazette 22850
Owner: GateHouse Media Inc.
Editorial: 197 S Main St, Milford, Massachusetts 1757 **Tel:** 1 508 634-7500
Email: gazette@wickedlocal.com **Web site:** http://bellingham.wickedlocal.com
Freq: Fri; **Circ:** 31030 Not Audited
Editor: Heather McCarron; **Circulation Manager:** Linda Vahey-Stole
Profile: Country Gazette is a free, weekly newspaper serving residents of Millford, Bellingham, Franklin, Foxboro, Wrentham, Medway, Millis and Norfolk, MA and surrounding areas. It covers local news and events. Advertising deadlines are on Tuesdays at 3pm ET.
Language (s): English
Ad Rate: Full Page Mono 41.25
Ad Rate: Full Page Colour 100.00
Currency: United States Dollars
COMMUNITY NEWSPAPER

The Country Today 21249
Owner: Eau Claire Press Company
Editorial: 701 S Farwell St, Eau Claire, Wisconsin 54701-3831 **Tel:** 1 715 833-9270
Email: thecountrytoday@ecpc.com **Web site:** http://www.thecountrytoday.com
Freq: Wed; **Circ:** 22602 Not Audited
Publisher: Pieter Graaskamp; **Editor:** Jim Massey
Profile: The Country Today is an agricultural newspaper focusing on farming industry news and trends. It also covers general agricultural business and the rural lifestyle.
Language (s): English
Ad Rate: Full Page Mono 19.71
Currency: United States Dollars
COMMUNITY NEWSPAPER

County Journal 19149
Editorial: 1101 E Pine St, Percy, Illinois 62272-1333 **Tel:** 1 618 497-8272
Email: cjournal@egyptian.net
Freq: Thu; **Circ:** 7500 Not Audited
Advertising Sales Manager: John Falkenhein
Profile: County Journal is published weekly for the residents of Percy, IL and surrounding areas. The newspaper covers local news, sports and community events.
Language (s): English
Ad Rate: Full Page Mono 9.00
Currency: United States Dollars
COMMUNITY NEWSPAPER

The County News 400091
Editorial: 211 S Center St Ste 307, Statesville, North Carolina 28677-5873 **Tel:** 1 704 873-1054
Email: production@countynews4you.com
Freq: Wed; **Circ:** 12000
Publisher & Editor: Fran Farrer
Profile: The County News is a newspaper published on Wednesdays. It caters to the African American population in Iredell County, NC. It provides county news, government, sports and features of interest to readers in the area.
Language (s): English
Ad Rate: Full Page Mono 20.00
Ad Rate: Full Page Colour 75.00
Currency: United States Dollars
COMMUNITY NEWSPAPER

The County Shopper 573173
Owner: Mitchell (Wayne & Catherine)
Editorial: 420 2Nd St, Belmont, Mississippi 38827-7700 **Tel:** 1 662 454-7196
Email: jmlb@bellsouth.net
Freq: Wed; **Circ:** 7025
Publisher: M. Wayne Mitchell
Profile: The County Shopper is a local weekly newspaper serving Belmont, Dennis, Golden and Tishomingo, MS.
Language (s): English
Ad Rate: Full Page Mono 7.75
Currency: United States Dollars
COMMUNITY NEWSPAPER

County Times 444150
Owner: Southern Maryland Publishing
Editorial: 43251 Rescue Lane, Hollywood, Maryland 20636 **Tel:** 1 301 373-4125
Email: news@countytimes.net **Web site:** http://countytimes.somd.com
Freq: Thu; **Circ:** 12000 Not Audited
Advertising Manager: Kit Carson; **Editor:** Angie Kalnasy; **Publisher:** Thomas McKay
Profile: County Times in Hollywood, MD is a locally owned and operated newspaper that serves the St. Mary's County, MD area. Published weekly, the paper reports the news as it happens while focusing strongly on the local community.
Language (s): English
Ad Rate: Full Page Mono 7.26
Currency: United States Dollars
COMMUNITY NEWSPAPER

The Courier 20753
Owner: Hurd
Editorial: 375 Main St, Savannah, Tennessee 38372-2056 **Tel:** 1 731 925-6397
Email: info@courieranywhere.com **Web site:** http://www.courieranywhere.com
Freq: Thu; **Circ:** 9249 Not Audited
Advertising Sales Manager: Candy Chine; **Publisher:** Joe Hurd
Profile: The Courier is a weekly community newspaper written for the residents of Savannah, TN.
Language (s): English
Ad Rate: Full Page Mono 5.50
Currency: United States Dollars
COMMUNITY NEWSPAPER

The Courier 884825
Owner: Osteen Publishing Co.
Editorial: 901 N McKenzie St, Foley, Alabama 36535-3546 **Tel:** 1 251 249-0163
Email: courier@gulfcoastnewspapers.com **Web site:** http://www.gulfcoastnewstoday.com/the-courier/
Freq: Weekly
Editor: Crystal Cole
Profile: The Courier is a weekly community newspaper serving residents of Fairhope, Daphne, Spanish Fort, Malbis, Montrose, Barnwell and Point Clear, AL with local news, events, and sports coverage.
Language (s): English
COMMUNITY NEWSPAPER

Courier Journal 18499
Owner: Colbert Courier, Inc.
Editorial: 1828 Darby Dr, Florence, Alabama 35630-2623 **Tel:** 1 256 764-4268
Email: editor@courierjournal.net **Web site:** http://www.courierjournal.net
Freq: Wed; **Circ:** 71567 Not Audited
Publisher & Editor: Thomas Magazzu
Profile: Courier Journal is a weekly advertising newspaper serving the consumers of Northwestern Alabama. The publication only runs advertising, and does not regularly publish articles. The lead time is one week and deadlines are one week prior to publication.
Language (s): English
Ad Rate: Full Page Mono 19.50
Ad Rate: Full Page Colour 1245.00
Currency: United States Dollars
COMMUNITY NEWSPAPER

The Courier MAX! 358867
Owner: Community Newspaper Holdings, Inc.
Editorial: 213 E 2nd St, Ottumwa, Iowa 52501-2902 **Tel:** 1 641 684-4611
Email: news@ottumwacourier.com **Web site:** http://www.ottumwacourier.com
Freq: Sat; **Circ:** 22500 Not Audited
Profile: The Courier MAX! is a free weekly newspaper created and distributed by the Ottumwa (IA) Courier. The MAX, which stands for Maximum Audience eXposure, provides news and advertising to residents and businesses in the Ottumwa, IA area. It attempts to reach non-subscribers of the daily newspaper. Advertising rates are based on the Courier's rates plus an additional charge for the greater readership. Advertising within the MAX! must also run in the Courier.
Language (s): English
Ad Rate: Full Page Mono 20.25
Currency: United States Dollars
COMMUNITY NEWSPAPER

Courier News Weekly 22611
Owner: Buxmont Media LLC
Editorial: 70 Souderton Hatfield Pike Ste 250, Souderton, Pennsylvania 18964-1939 **Tel:** 1 267 663-6300
Web site: http://www.buxmontmedia.com
Freq: Wed; **Circ:** 48666 Not Audited
Publisher & Editor: Susan Lapp
Profile: Courier News Weekly is a community newspaper serving the residents of Indian Valley, Perkiomen Valley and Harleysville, PA. The publication covers local news and community events.
Language (s): English
Ad Rate: Full Page Mono 43.88
Currency: United States Dollars
COMMUNITY NEWSPAPER

Courier Tribune 22778
Owner: NPG Newspapers
Editorial: 104 N Main St, Liberty, Missouri 64068-1640 **Tel:** 1 816 781-4941
Email: news@mycouriertribune.com **Web site:** http://www.mycouriertribune.com
Freq: Weekly; **Circ:** 7000 Not Audited
Profile: The Courier Tribune is a weekly newspaper serving residents of Kearney, Smithville and Liberty, MO. It covers local news, sports, business and community events. Deadlines are on Mondays at noon CT. The paper was previously three distinct titles: Liberty Tribune, Smithville Herald and Kearney Courier.
Language (s): English
Ad Rate: Full Page Mono 15.25
Ad Rate: Full Page Colour 150.00
Currency: United States Dollars
COMMUNITY NEWSPAPER

The Courier-Gazette 153532
Owner: Village NetMedia
Editorial: 91 Camden St Ste 403, Rockland, Maine 04841-2421 **Tel:** 1 207 594-4401
Email: news@villagesoup.com **Web site:** http://knox.villagesoup.com
Freq: Sat; **Circ:** 9500 Not Audited
Editor: Daniel Dunkle
Profile: The Courier-Gazette is a local newspaper serving the residents of Knox County, ME. It covers local news, sports, arts & entertainment, business and community events. It was previously split between two community weeklies, the Courier-Gazette and the Camden Herald. It still keeps offices in both Rockland and Camden, ME.
Language (s): English
Ad Rate: Full Page Mono 14.41
Currency: United States Dollars
COMMUNITY NEWSPAPER

The Courier-News 21725
Owner: Republic Newspapers, Inc.
Editorial: 233 N Hicks St, Clinton, Tennessee 37716-2919 **Tel:** 1 865 457-2515
Email: editor@hometownclinton.com **Web site:** http://www.hometownclinton.com
Freq: Sun; **Circ:** 5300 Not Audited
Publisher: Allen Handley; **Editor:** Ken Leinart
Profile: The Courier-News is a local publication providing news to the community of Clinton, TN.
Language (s): English
Ad Rate: Full Page Mono 9.50
Currency: United States Dollars
COMMUNITY NEWSPAPER

Courier-Standard-Enterprise 22877
Owner: Port Jackson Media LLC
Editorial: 1 Venner Rd, Amsterdam, New York 12010-5617 **Tel:** 1 518 843-1100
Email: news@recordernews.com **Web site:** http://www.courierstandardenterprise.com
Freq: Thu; **Circ:** 5500 Not Audited
Circulation Manager: Richard Kretser; **Publisher:** Kevin McClary; **Editor:** Joshua Thomas
Profile: Courier-Standard-Enterprise is written for residents of Western Montgomery County, NY. Its editorial mission is to provide community-focused news for the villages of Fort Plain, Saint Johnsville and Canajoharie, NY. It is published from the offices of The Reporter and shares its editorial staff with the paper. Deadlines are at 5pm ET.
Language (s): English
Ad Rate: Full Page Mono 10.40
Currency: United States Dollars
COMMUNITY NEWSPAPER

The Courier-Times 20005
Owner: Brinn Clayton
Editorial: 109 Clayton Ave, Roxboro, North Carolina 27573-4611 **Tel:** 1 336 599-0162
Email: ctimes@roxboro-courier.com **Web site:** http://www.roxboro-courier.com
Freq: Sat; **Circ:** 7400 Not Audited
Publisher: Brinn Clayton
Profile: The Courier-Times is published twice weekly for the residents of Roxboro, NC and surrounding areas. The newspaper provides information on local news and community events. Deadlines are on Tuesdays and Fridays at 3pm ET prior to issue date.
Language (s): English
Ad Rate: Full Page Mono 12.36
Currency: United States Dollars
COMMUNITY NEWSPAPER

Cove Herald 155985
Editorial: 102 Cove Terrace, Copperas Cove, Texas 76522 **Tel:** 1 254 501-7470
Email: covenews@kdhnews.com **Web site:** http://kdhnews.com/copperas_cove_herald
Freq: Thu; **Circ:** 8000 Not Audited
Profile: Cove Herald is published weekly for the residents of Copperas Cove, TX and surrounding areas. The newspaper covers local news, sports and community events.
Language (s): English
Ad Rate: Full Page Mono 6.50
Currency: United States Dollars
COMMUNITY NEWSPAPER

The Covington News 29173
Owner: Morris Multimedia, Inc.
Editorial: 1166 Usher St NW, Covington, Georgia 30014-2451 **Tel:** 1 770 787-6397
Email: news@covnews.com **Web site:** http://www.covnews.com
Freq: Fri; **Circ:** 5200 Not Audited
Circulation Manager: Amanda Ellington; **News Editor:** Michelle Kim; **Editor:** Jenny Long; **Publisher:** Charles Morriss
Profile: The Covington News is a local newspaper serving the residents of Newton, Rockdale and Walton counties, GA. Editorial coverage includes local news, police, courts, government, features, lifestyle and sports. Deadlines fall at noon ET on Mondays, Wednesdays and Fridays.
Language (s): English
Ad Rate: Full Page Mono 9.29
Currency: United States Dollars
COMMUNITY NEWSPAPER

Cranberry Eagle 29437
Owner: Eagle Printing Company
Editorial: 20701 Route 19, Cranberry Twp, Pennsylvania 16066-6009 **Tel:** 1 724 776-4270
Email: cranberryads@gmail.com **Web site:** http://www.thecranberryeagle.com
Freq: Sun; **Circ:** 22585 Not Audited
Publisher: John Wise
Profile: The Cranberry Eagle provides local news, weather, and sports information to the residents of Cranberry Township, PA.
Language (s): English
Ad Rate: Full Page Mono 12.50
Currency: United States Dollars
COMMUNITY NEWSPAPER

Creative Loafing Atlanta 24164
Owner: Eason (Ben)
Editorial: 115 Martin Luther King Jr Dr SW Ste 301, Atlanta, Georgia 30303-3536 **Tel:** 1 404 688-5623
Web site: http://www.clatl.com
Freq: Wed; **Circ:** 65014 Not Audited
Publisher: Sharry Smith; **News Editor:** Thomas Wheatley
Profile: Creative Loafing is written for socially conscious and aware readers who want to experience what Atlanta has to offer in its growing arts & entertainment scene.
Language (s): English
Ad Rate: Full Page Mono 148.24
Currency: United States Dollars
COMMUNITY NEWSPAPER

Creative Loafing Charlotte 73583
Owner: Womack Newspapers Inc.
Editorial: 1000 NC Music Factory Blvd Apt C2, Charlotte, North Carolina 28206-6010 **Tel:** 1 704 522-8334
Web site: http://www.clclt.com
Freq: Thu; **Circ:** 44000 Not Audited
Advertising Sales Manager: Amy Mularski; **Publisher:** Charles Womack
Profile: Creative Loafing is a weekly newspaper covering arts & entertainment and public issues generally geared toward readers ages 22 to 45 in the metro Charlotte, NC area. Features include classifieds, entertainment and dining as well as social and political views. Deadlines fall on Wednesdays.
Language (s): English
Ad Rate: Full Page Mono 11.88
Currency: United States Dollars
COMMUNITY NEWSPAPER

Creative Loafing Tampa 21831
Owner: Atalaya Capital Management
Editorial: 1911 N 13th St Ste W200, Tampa, Florida 33605-3652 **Tel:** 1 813 739-4800
Web site: http://www.cltampa.com
Freq: Wed; **Circ:** 37644 Not Audited
News and Politics Editor: Kate Bradshaw
Profile: Creative Loafing is a weekly newspaper covering arts & entertainment and public issues in Tampa, FL. Features include classifieds, entertainment and dining as well as social and political views. The newspaper shares some stories with the Sarasota edition.
Language (s): English
Ad Rate: Full Page Mono 26.25
Ad Rate: Full Page Colour 150.00
Currency: United States Dollars
COMMUNITY NEWSPAPER

Crescenta Valley Weekly 615640
Owner: Goldsworthy (Robin)
Editorial: 3800 La Crescenta Ave, La Crescenta, California 91214-3924 **Tel:** 1 818 248-2740
Email: wizard@cvweekly.com **Web site:** http://www.crescentavalleyweekly.com
Freq: Thu; **Circ:** 8300
Publisher & Editor: Robin Goldsworthy; **Advertising Sales Manager:** Kim Mekelburg

Profile: Crescenta Valley Weekly offers local news, features, sports and entertainment to the communities of La Crescenta and Montrose and parts of Glendale, La Canada and Tujunga in California. The paper was established in September 2009.
Language (s): English
Ad Rate: Full Page Mono 22.50
Ad Rate: Full Page Colour 24.75
Currency: United States Dollars
COMMUNITY NEWSPAPER

Cresco Times-Plain Dealer 18886
Owner: Evans Publishing LLC.
Editorial: 214 N Elm St, Cresco, Iowa 52136-1522 **Tel:** 1 563 547-3601
Email: info@crescotimes.com **Web site:** http://www.crescotimes.com
Freq: Wed; **Circ:** 12300 Not Audited
Publisher: Daniel Evans; **Advertising Sales Manager:** Lacey Mader
Profile: Cresco Times-Plain Dealer is the official newspaper of Howard County, IA and the city of Cresco. Published weekly, it is both a source of information about the people and events of Howard and surrounding counties and an historical record of the times. Each newspaper published since the 1860s is on file at the Times Plain Dealer offices and is a constant source of information for historians, genealogists, students and people interested in researching their family history.
Language (s): English
Ad Rate: Full Page Mono 9.18
Currency: United States Dollars
COMMUNITY NEWSPAPER

The Crested Butte News 18675
Owner: Crested Butte News Inc.
Editorial: 301 Bellevue Ave, Unit 6A, Crested Butte, Colorado 81224 **Tel:** 1 970 349-0500
Email: editorial@crestedbuttenews.com **Web site:** http://www.crestedbuttenews.com
Freq: Thu; **Circ:** 5500 Not Audited
Editor: Mark Reaman
Profile: Crested Butte News serves the community of Crested Butte (CO) with news and relevant information.
Language (s): English
Ad Rate: Full Page Mono 10.30
Currency: United States Dollars
COMMUNITY NEWSPAPER

Crete News 25263
Editorial: 1201 Linden Ave, Crete, Nebraska 68333-2252 **Tel:** 1 402 826-2147
Email: newsdesk@cretenews.net **Web site:** http://www.cretenews.net
Freq: Weekly; **Circ:** 8000 Not Audited
Advertising Sales Manager: Pat Hier
Language (s): English
COMMUNITY NEWSPAPER

Crewe-Burkeville Journal 21046
Owner: Gunter (Rick)
Editorial: 107 W Carolina Ave, Crewe, Virginia 23930-1803 **Tel:** 1 434 645-7534
Email: cbjournal@meckcom.net **Web site:** http://www.thecrewburkevillejournal.com
Freq: Thu; **Circ:** 6000 Not Audited
Publisher & Editor: Rick Gunter
Profile: Crewe-Burkeville Journal is a local newspaper providing the community of Crewe, VA with news.
Language (s): English
Ad Rate: Full Page Mono 7.00
Currency: United States Dollars
COMMUNITY NEWSPAPER

The Criterion 21916
Owner: Roman Catholic Archdiocese of Indianapolis
Editorial: 1400 N Meridian St, Indianapolis, Indiana 46202-2305 **Tel:** 1 317 236-1570
Email: criterion@archindy.org **Web site:** http://www.CriterionOnline.com
Freq: Fri; **Circ:** 68000 Not Audited
Editor: Mike Krokos; **Advertising Sales Manager:** Ron Massey; **Publisher:** Joseph Tobin
Profile: The Criterion is the official weekly newspaper for the Roman Catholic Archdiocese of Indianapolis. The newspaper's focus is on religion.
Language (s): English
Ad Rate: Full Page Mono 8.76
Currency: United States Dollars
COMMUNITY NEWSPAPER

Cronicas 434156
Owner: Grupo Pro Y
Tel: 1 707 363-3021
Email: cronicas@cronicasnewspaper.com **Web site:** http://www.cronicasnewspaper.com
Freq: Bi-Weekly; **Circ:** 10000 Not Audited
Profile: Cronicas is a weekly, tabloid-style Spanish language newspaper serving Hispanic, bilingual and Spanish-speaking residents of Marin, Sonoma, Solano and Napa counties, CA. The paper includes local and national news, education, immigration, business, sports, editorials, columns and a community calendar.
Language (s): Spanish
COMMUNITY NEWSPAPER

The Cross Roads 754063
Owner: Diocese of Lexington
Editorial: 1310 W Main St, Lexington, Kentucky 40508-2048 **Tel:** 1 859 253-1993
Web site: http://www.crossroads.cdlex.org/index.cfm
Freq: Weekly
Publisher & Editor: Thomas Shaughnessy
Profile: The Cross Roads is a weekly newspaper for the Diocese of Lexington, KY.
Language (s): English
COMMUNITY NEWSPAPER

CTNow 884985
Owner: Tribune Broadcasting
Editorial: 285 Broad St, Hartford, Connecticut 06105-3785 **Tel:** 1 860 548-9300
Email: info@ct.com **Web site:** http://www.ctnow.com
Freq: Weekly; **Circ:** 150000
Profile: CTNow is a weekly publication focusing on Music and Arts and Entertainment in the state of Connecticut. It is distributed on newsstands in addition to being included in the Thursday edition of the Hartford Courant.
Language (s): English
COMMUNITY NEWSPAPER

The Cullman Tribune 18492
Owner: Blalock Publishing, L.L.C.
Editorial: 300 4th Ave SE, Cullman, Alabama 35055-3611 **Tel:** 1 256 734-2131
Web site: http://cullmantimes.com
Freq: Thu; **Circ:** 15000 Not Audited
Publisher & Editor: Delton Blalock; **Circulation Manager:** Ron Kepler
Profile: The Cullman Tribune is a local weekly newspaper serving the residents of Cullman, AL. Coverage includes local news and events, business, politics and social issues. Deadline for submission of press releases is Monday at noon CT.
Language (s): English
Ad Rate: Full Page Mono 12.00
Ad Rate: Full Page Colour 874.00
Currency: United States Dollars
COMMUNITY NEWSPAPER

The Culvert Chronicles 554555
Editorial: 13545 227Th St, Laurelton, New York 11413-2447 **Tel:** 1 718 276-0405
Email: culvertchronicles@nyc.rr.com **Web site:** http://theculvertchronicles.com
Freq: Thu; **Circ:** 60000
Publisher & Editor: Edward Culvert
Profile: The Culvert Chronicles is a weekly community newspaper serving the African-American community of Laurelton, NY.
Language (s): English
Ad Rate: Full Page Mono 25.00
Currency: United States Dollars
COMMUNITY NEWSPAPER

Cumberland County Reminder 22875
Owner: Cohansey Cove Publishing, Inc.
Editorial: 2 W Vine St, Millville, New Jersey 08332-3823 **Tel:** 1 856 825-8811
Email: editor@remindernewspaper.net **Web site:** http://www.reminderusa.net
Freq: Wed; **Circ:** 24352 Not Audited
Editor: Dan Podehl
Profile: Cumberland County Reminder is a weekly newspaper for residents of Millville, NJ and surrounding areas. The paper provides community news, education information, entertainment, sports and more. Deadlines are Fridays before the issue date.
Language (s): English
Ad Rate: Full Page Mono 14.36
Currency: United States Dollars
COMMUNITY NEWSPAPER

Curry Coastal Pilot 20492
Owner: Western Communications Inc.
Editorial: 507 Chetco Ave, Brookings, Oregon 97415-8159 **Tel:** 1 541 469-3123
Email: mail@currypilot.com **Web site:** http://www.currypilot.com
Freq: Sat; **Circ:** 7000 Not Audited
Editor: Scott Graves
Profile: Curry Coastal Pilot is a community newspaper serving Curry County on the Southern Oregon Coast from Brookings, Oregon. The newspaper focuses on providing local news and community event information to its readers. Some local features include sports, business, weather, port information, surf and tide forecasts, obituaries and classifieds. Some regional and national news is provided. The newspaper also keeps fishermen and boaters aware of local weather conditions in the newspaper and on their web site.
Language (s): English
Ad Rate: Full Page Mono 14.90
Currency: United States Dollars
COMMUNITY NEWSPAPER

C-Ville Weekly 21979
Owner: C-Ville Holdings, LLC.
Editorial: 308 E Main St, Charlottesville, Virginia 22902-5234 **Tel:** 1 434 817-2749
Email: editor@c-ville.com **Web site:** http://www.c-ville.com
Freq: Wed; **Circ:** 25000 Not Audited
Publisher: Frank Dubec
Profile: C-Ville Weekly is the weekly news and arts paper of Charlottesville, VA. It is the largest locally owned paper in Charlottesville. The paper is published every Tuesday. It is distributed to residents of Charlottesville and Albemarle County. The publication covers music, film, and photography. Special issues cover notable artists from the area such as Dave Matthews Band and Dispatch.
Language (s): English
Ad Rate: Full Page Mono 19.84
Currency: United States Dollars
COMMUNITY NEWSPAPER

Dahlonega Nugget 24331
Owner: Community Newspapers Inc.
Editorial: 1074 Morrison Moore Pkwy W, Dahlonega, Georgia 30533-1425 **Tel:** 1 706 864-3613
Web site: http://www.thedahloneganugget.com
Freq: Wed; **Circ:** 6400 Not Audited
Publisher & Editor: Wayne Knuckles; **Advertising Sales Manager:** Rebecca Ladewige
Profile: Dahlonega Nugget is written for the town of Dahlonega, GA. It covers weekly events and stories from around the town.
Language (s): English
Ad Rate: Full Page Mono 7.70
Currency: United States Dollars
COMMUNITY NEWSPAPER

Dallas Chinese Daily 232007
Owner: Lee (Wei)
Editorial: 12809 Audelia Rd, Dallas, Texas 75243-2275 **Tel:** 1 972 907-1919
Email: chinese9071919@yahoo.com **Web site:** http://www.agdct.com
Freq: Fri; **Circ:** 10000 Not Audited
Editor: William Chang; **Publisher:** Wei Lee
Profile: Dallas (TX) Chinese Daily is a community newspaper that covers news and events relevant to the Chinese community. The paper is Tuesday through Sunday weekly.
Language (s): Chinese
Ad Rate: Full Page Mono 20.00
Currency: United States Dollars
COMMUNITY NEWSPAPER

Dallas New Era 18803
Editorial: 121 W Spring St, Dallas, Georgia 30132-4138 **Tel:** 1 770 445-3379
Email: newerapr@bellsouth.net **Web site:** http://www.thedallasnewera.com
Freq: Thu; **Circ:** 7000 Not Audited
Advertising Sales Manager: Jolee Kitchen; **Circulation Manager:** Darlene Parker
Profile: The Dallas New Era is a community newspaper serving the residents of Paulding County, Georgia. It covers local news, sports, and community events.
Language (s): English
Ad Rate: Full Page Mono 3.50
Currency: United States Dollars
COMMUNITY NEWSPAPER

Dallas Observer 21316
Owner: Voice Media Group
Editorial: 2501 Oak Lawn Ave Ste 700, Dallas, Texas 75219-4058 **Tel:** 1 214 757-9000
Email: retail@dallasobserver.com **Web site:** http://www.dallasobserver.com
Freq: Thu; **Circ:** 50000 Not Audited
Profile: Dallas Observer is a community newspaper written for the residents of Dallas. It includes investigative stories about government, politics, business, sports, music and the arts.
Language (s): English
Ad Rate: Full Page Mono 36.00
Currency: United States Dollars
COMMUNITY NEWSPAPER

Dallas Post Tribune 20985
Owner: Lee (Dr. T.R.)
Editorial: 2726 S Beckley Ave, Dallas, Texas 75224-2938 **Tel:** 1 214 946-7678
Email: posttrib@airmail.net **Web site:** http://www.dallasposttrib.com
Freq: Thu; **Circ:** 10000 Not Audited
Circulation Manager: Elester Coleman
Profile: Dallas Post Tribune is weekly newspaper that promotes equality in the Dallas area. Deadlines are on Mondays at noon CT.
Language (s): English
Ad Rate: Full Page Mono 35.00
Currency: United States Dollars
COMMUNITY NEWSPAPER

The Dallas Weekly 20986
Editorial: 3101 Martin Luther King Jr Blvd, Dallas, Texas 75215-2415 **Tel:** 1 214 428-8958
Email: editorial@dallasweekly.com **Web site:** http://www.dallasweekly.com
Freq: Thu; **Circ:** 17500 Not Audited
Publisher: Jim Washington
Profile: The Dallas Weekly covers local news and events of interest to the African American community in Dallas.
Language (s): English
Ad Rate: Full Page Mono 41.00
Ad Rate: Full Page Colour 3186.00
Currency: United States Dollars
COMMUNITY NEWSPAPER

Daniel Island News 317894
Editorial: 225 Seven Farms Dr., Daniel Island, Charleston, South Carolina 29492 **Tel:** 1 843 856-1999
Web site: http://www.thedanielislandnews.com
Freq: Thu; **Circ:** 8000 Not Audited
Circulation Manager: Jan Marvin; **Advertising Sales Manager:** Ronda Shilling
Profile: Daniel Island News is a local paper written for the residents of Daniel Island, SC.
Language (s): English
Ad Rate: Full Page Mono 10.50
Currency: United States Dollars
COMMUNITY NEWSPAPER

Dan's Papers 24929
Owner: Manhattan Media LLC
Editorial: 158 Country Road 39, Southampton, New York 11968 **Tel:** 1 631 537-0500
Email: editor@danspapers.com **Web site:** http://www.danshamptons.com
Freq: Weekly; **Circ:** 26800
Publisher: Steve McKenna
Profile: Dan's Papers' editorial mission is to provide entertainment and take stances on current events. The publications are written for people interested in elegant lifestyles in Long Island, NY.
Language (s): English
Ad Rate: Full Page Mono 2630.00
Ad Rate: Full Page Colour 3230.00
Currency: United States Dollars
COMMUNITY NEWSPAPER

Darien Times 23029
Owner: Hersam Acorn Newspapers
Editorial: 10 Corbin Dr Fl 3, Darien, Connecticut 06820-5403 **Tel:** 1 203 656-4230
Email: editor@darientimes.com **Web site:** http://www.darientimes.com
Freq: Thu; **Circ:** 6751 Not Audited
Editor: Steven Buono; **Publisher:** Donald Hersam; **Editor:** Susan Shultz
Profile: Darien Times is published weekly for the residents of Darien, CT. The newspaper covers local news, sports, travel and community events. Deadlines for the publication are on Tuesdays at noon ET. The newspaper is free for residents of Darien.
Language (s): English
Ad Rate: Full Page Mono 13.00
Currency: United States Dollars
COMMUNITY NEWSPAPER

Darlington News & Press 20622
Editorial: 117 S Main St, Darlington, South Carolina 29532-3207 **Tel:** 1 843 393-3811
Email: editor@newsandpress.net **Web site:** http://www.newsandpressonline.com
Freq: Wed; **Circ:** 6200 Not Audited
Profile: Darlington News & Press is a local newspaper written for residents of Darlington, SC. The paper covers local news and events.
Language (s): English
Ad Rate: Full Page Mono 10.95
Currency: United States Dollars
COMMUNITY NEWSPAPER

Das Yidishe Licht 234970
Owner: Rochman (Jacob)
Editorial: 150 Wilson St, Brooklyn, New York 11211-7707 **Tel:** 1 718 387-3166
Freq: Fri; **Circ:** 5000 Not Audited
Editor & Publisher: Jacob Rochman
Profile: Das Yidische Licht is a newspaper serving the Jewish community in Brooklyn, NY.
Language (s): Yiddish
Ad Rate: Full Page Mono 10.00
Currency: United States Dollars
COMMUNITY NEWSPAPER

Davie County Enterprise-Record 27942
Owner: Davie Publishing Co.
Editorial: 171 S Main St, Mocksville, North Carolina 27028-2424 **Tel:** 1 336 751-2129
Email: ernews@davie-enterprise.com **Web site:** http://www.ourdavie.com
Freq: Thu; **Circ:** 9200 Not Audited
Profile: Davie County Enterprise-Record is a local newspaper written for the residents of Mocksville, NC.
Language (s): English
Ad Rate: Full Page Mono 10.50
Currency: United States Dollars
COMMUNITY NEWSPAPER

Davis County Clipper 24462
Owner: Clipper Publishing Co., Inc.
Editorial: 1370 S 500 W, Woods Cross, Utah 84010-8141 **Tel:** 1 801 295-2251
Email: news@davisclipper.com **Web site:** http://www.davisclipper.com
Freq: Thu; **Circ:** 11350 Not Audited
Publisher: R. Gail Stahle
Profile: Davis County Clipper provides residents of Davis County, UT with local news.
Language (s): English
Ad Rate: Full Page Mono 14.00
Currency: United States Dollars
COMMUNITY NEWSPAPER

The Davison Index 19508
Owner: JAMS Media
Editorial: 220 N Main St, Davison, Michigan 48423-1432 **Tel:** 1 810 653-3511
Email: daveditor@mihomepaper.com **Web site:** http://www.thedavisonindex.com
Freq: Thu; **Circ:** 14139 Not Audited
Publisher: Rick Burrough
Profile: The Davison Index is published weekly for the residents of Davison and Richfield, MI. The newspaper provides information on local news and community events.
Language (s): English
Ad Rate: Full Page Mono 12.82
Currency: United States Dollars
COMMUNITY NEWSPAPER

Dayton City Paper 22903
Owner: Dayton City Media, LLC
Editorial: 126 N Main St Ste 240, Dayton, Ohio 45402-1766 **Tel:** 1 937 222-8855
Email: pr@daytoncitypaper.com **Web site:** http://www.daytoncitypaper.com
Freq: Tue; **Circ:** 18000 Not Audited
Publisher: Paul Noah

Profile: Dayton City Paper is a local newspaper serving the Miami Valley, including Dayton, OH and its suburbs.
Language (s): English
Ad Rate: Full Page Mono 22.83
Currency: United States Dollars
COMMUNITY NEWSPAPER

Dayton Leader 895387
Tel: 1 515 571-1666
Email: daytonleader@gmail.com **Web site:** http://daytonleader.wix.com/daytonleader
Freq: Weekly
Editor: Kendra Breitsprecher
Profile: Provides news in news and happenings in Dayton, IA and the surrounding area.
Language (s): English
COMMUNITY NEWSPAPER

Dayton Weekly News 257187
Owner: Black (Don)
Editorial: 118 Salem Ave, Dayton, Ohio 45406-5803 **Tel:** 1 937 223-8060
Email: daytonweek@aol.com
Freq: Thu; **Circ:** 25000 Not Audited
Publisher, Editor & Advertising Sales Manager: Don Black; **Circulation Manager:** Ellis Hutchinson
Profile: Dayton Weekly News is written for the African American residents in Dayton, OH. It covers news and trends.
Language (s): English
Ad Rate: Full Page Mono 22.00
Currency: United States Dollars
COMMUNITY NEWSPAPER

Daytona Times 18783
Owner: Central Florida Communications Group, LLC
Tel: 1 877 352-4455
Email: news@flcourier.com **Web site:** http://www.daytonatimes.com
Freq: Thu; **Circ:** 15000 Not Audited
Publisher: Charles Cherry; **Circulation Manager:** Eugene Leach; **Editor:** Jenise Morgan
Profile: Daytona Times is written for the African-American community in Daytona Beach, FL and the surrounding area. It contains local and national news, investigative reports, editorials, entertainment and sports stories.
Language (s): English
Ad Rate: Full Page Mono 25.00
Currency: United States Dollars
COMMUNITY NEWSPAPER

Dearborn Times Herald 21618
Owner: Bewick Publications
Editorial: 13730 Michigan Ave, Dearborn, Michigan 48126-3520 **Tel:** 1 313 584-4000
Email: timesheraldads@yahoo.com **Web site:** http://downriversundaytimes.com
Freq: Sun; **Circ:** 27000 Not Audited
Publisher: Michael Bewick; **Editor:** Scott Bewick; **Advertising Sales Manager:** Gloria Fox; **Editor:** Zeinab Najm; **Circulation Manager:** John Walton
Profile: Dearborn (MI) Times Herald is published twice per week and covers local news, weather, sports, business, features and community events. Deadlines fall on Friday.
Language (s): English
Ad Rate: Full Page Mono 23.50
Ad Rate: Full Page Colour 2135.00
Currency: United States Dollars
COMMUNITY NEWSPAPER

Decatur Tribune 19142
Owner: Osborne Publications, Inc.
Editorial: 132 S Water St Ste 424, Decatur, Illinois 62523-2306 **Tel:** 1 217 422-9702
Email: decaturtribune@aol.com **Web site:** http://www.decaturtribune.com
Freq: Wed; **Circ:** 25000 Not Audited
Editor & Publisher: Paul Osborne
Profile: The publication is written to serve their customers with the news of Decatur, IL and surrounding areas. The lead time for Decatur Tribune is one week. Deadlines for the publication are one week before issue date.
Language (s): English
Ad Rate: Full Page Mono 7.00
Currency: United States Dollars
COMMUNITY NEWSPAPER

Defender Newspaper 20868
Owner: Defender Media Group
Editorial: 12401 S. Post Oak Rd., Ste.223, Houston, Texas 77045 **Tel:** 1 713 663-6996
Email: news@defendermediagroup.com **Web site:** http://defendernetwork.com
Freq: Thu; **Circ:** 23000 Not Audited
Publisher: Sonceria Messiah Jiles; **Advertising Sales Manager:** Selma Tyler
Profile: Defender Newspaper is written for African American residents in the Houston area. The publication covers national and global news, sports, business, food, health and arts & entertainment news. Deadlines are on Mondays at 5pm CT.
Language (s): English
Ad Rate: Full Page Mono 36.00
Ad Rate: Full Page Colour 4432.00
Currency: United States Dollars
COMMUNITY NEWSPAPER

DeFuniak Herald 350385
Owner: Woodham (Gary)
Editorial: 740 Baldwin Ave, Defuniak Springs, Florida 32435-2598 **Tel:** 1 850 892-3232
Email: dfsherald@gmail.com **Web site:** http://www.defuniakherald.com
Freq: Thu; **Circ:** 5500 Not Audited
Editor: Bruce Collier; **Publisher:** Gary Woodham
Profile: DeFuniak Herald is a community newspaper written for the residents of DeFuniak Springs, FL. The DeFuniak Herald does not cover Panama City, FL. The paper covers features, schools, sports, legal notices, letters to the editor, state capitol news and arts & entertainment.
Language (s): English
Ad Rate: Full Page Mono 4.50
Currency: United States Dollars
COMMUNITY NEWSPAPER

Delaware Wave 21585
Owner: Gannett Co., Inc.
Editorial: 618 Beacon St, Salisbury, Maryland 21801 **Tel:** 1 410 749-7171
Email: wave@dmg.gannett.com **Web site:** http://www.delmarvanow.com
Freq: Tue; **Circ:** 22500 Not Audited
Profile: Delaware Wave is a local weekly newspaper serving the Bethany Beach, DE area. It provides the local community with information on news, events, sports and weather.
Language (s): English
Ad Rate: Full Page Mono 16.38
Currency: United States Dollars
COMMUNITY NEWSPAPER

Delta County Independent 18677
Owner: Leader Publishing Co. Inc.
Editorial: 401 Meeker St, Delta, Colorado 81416-1918 **Tel:** 1 970 874-4421
Email: editor@deltacountyindependent.com **Web site:** http://www.deltacountyindependent.com
Freq: Wed; **Circ:** 6300 Not Audited
Advertising Sales Manager: Roxanne McCormick; **Editor:** Pat Sunderland
Profile: Delta County Independent is a local weekly newspaper serving Delta County, CO. It provides information on news and events of importance to residents of the county.
Language (s): English
Ad Rate: Full Page Mono 10.00
Currency: United States Dollars
COMMUNITY NEWSPAPER

Delta Star 20556
Owner: Star Printing
Editorial: 811 Main St, Delta, Pennsylvania 17314-8945 **Tel:** 1 717 456-5692
Email: thestar@thestarprinting.com
Freq: Weekly; **Circ:** 5000 Not Audited
Editor & Publisher: Ron Sommer
Profile: Delta Star is a local weekly newspaper serving Delta, PA and the surrounding area. It provides the local community with information on news and events in the area. Deadlines are one week before issue date. Contact the editor with any further inquiries.
Language (s): English
Ad Rate: Full Page Mono 4.10
Currency: United States Dollars
COMMUNITY NEWSPAPER

Democrat Publishing Company 25418
Editorial: 212 S Washington St, Clinton, Missouri 64735-2073 **Tel:** 1 660 885-2281
Circ: 14400 Not Audited
Advertising Sales Manager: Sarah Anderson
Profile: Send press releases by fax.
Language (s): English
COMMUNITY NEWSPAPER

The Democrat-Reporter 18511
Owner: Sutton (Goodloe)
Editorial: 108 E Coats Ave, Linden, Alabama 36748-1526 **Tel:** 1 334 295-5224
Email: dreporter2@yahoo.com **Web site:** http://drp.stparchive.com
Freq: Thu; **Circ:** 8000 Not Audited
Advertising Sales Manager: Billie Jo Eatmon; **Publisher & Editor:** Goodloe Sutton
Profile: Democrat-Reporter in Linden, AL is a local weekly newspaper serving the Marengo County, AL area. It provides the local community with information on news, events, sports, and weather. The lead time for Democrat-Reporter varies depending on the editorial material.
Language (s): English
Ad Rate: Full Page Mono 10.00
Currency: United States Dollars
COMMUNITY NEWSPAPER

Denver Catholic Register 22044
Editorial: 1300 S Steele St, Denver, Colorado 80210 **Tel:** 1 303 715-3215
Email: editor@archden.org **Web site:** http://www.archden.org
Freq: Wed; **Circ:** 81507 Not Audited
Advertising Sales Manager: Chad Andrzejewski; **Publisher:** Charles Chaput; **Editor:** Roxanne King
Profile: Denver Catholic Register is a weekly publication published by the Archdiocese of Denver. It provides local and regional news about Catholic parishes, as well as local Denver news. Denver Catholic Register also reports on news in the archdiocese of Denver and news and updates from the Vatican. Deadlines are at 3pm CT. Special sections submissions must be received 10 days prior to publication date.
Language (s): English
Ad Rate: Full Page Mono 38.90
Currency: United States Dollars
COMMUNITY NEWSPAPER

Denver Weekly News 18680
Editorial: 2937 Welton St, Denver, Colorado 80205-3021 **Tel:** 1 303 292-5158
Email: dwnews2@yahoo.com **Web site:** http://www.denverweeklynews.net
Freq: Thu; **Circ:** 10000 Not Audited
Publisher & Editor: Lenora Alexander; **Editor:** Lynn Durant; **Advertising Sales Manager:** Alexandria Harris
Profile: Denver Weekly News is a newspaper for the African American community of Denver, CO. It provides information on news and events of importance to the city's African American community. The lead time for Denver Weekly News is two weeks. Deadlines for the publication are two weeks before issue date on Monday at 5pm CT. Contact the editor with any further inquiries.
Language (s): English
Ad Rate: Full Page Mono 30.00
Currency: United States Dollars
COMMUNITY NEWSPAPER

Der Blatt 217213
Owner: Wider (Sam)
Editorial: 76 Rutledge St, Brooklyn, New York 11249-7814 **Tel:** 1 718 625-3400
Email: news@derblatt.com
Freq: Thu; **Circ:** 10000 Not Audited
Publisher & Editor: Sam Wider
Language (s): Yiddish
Ad Rate: Full Page Mono 12.00
Currency: United States Dollars
COMMUNITY NEWSPAPER

Der Yid 23299
Editorial: 84 Broadway, Brooklyn, New York 11211-8665 **Tel:** 1 718 797-3900
Email: adv@deryid.org
Freq: Thu; **Circ:** 51000 Not Audited
Publisher & Editor: Aron Friedman; **Advertising Sales Manager:** Herman Friedman
Profile: Der Yid weekly newspaper carrying world news widely read within the "black hat" community. It uses a Yiddish dialect more common to Satmar Chasidim.
Language (s): English, Hebrew, Yiddish
Ad Rate: Full Page Mono 14.00
Currency: United States Dollars
COMMUNITY NEWSPAPER

Desert Mobile Home News 21593
Owner: Brehm Communications, Inc.
Editorial: 41995 Boardwalk Ste L2, Palm Desert, California 92211-9065 **Tel:** 1 760 568-6633
Email: news@desertmobilehomenews.com
Freq: Thu; **Circ:** 6000 Not Audited
Editor: Jose De La Cruz
Profile: Desert Mobile Home is a community paper that covers general and local news. The publication is written for mobile home seniors in Coachella Valley, CA.
Language (s): English
COMMUNITY NEWSPAPER

Desert Star Weekly 818239
Owner: Praxis Communications, Inc.
Editorial: 66538 8th St, Desert Hot Springs, California 92240-3217 **Tel:** 1 760 671-6604
Email: editor@desertstarweekly.com **Web site:** http://desertstarweekly.com
Freq: Weekly; **Circ:** 10000
Publisher: Richard Perry
Profile: Desert Star Weekly is a community newspaper serving the Coachella Valley and High Desert region of Southern California.
Language (s): English
COMMUNITY NEWSPAPER

Desert Valley Times 24447
Owner: Gannett Co., Inc.
Editorial: 355 W Mesquite Blvd Ste C10, Mesquite, Nevada 89027-8117 **Tel:** 1 702 346-7495
Email: news@dvtnv.com **Web site:** http://www.thespectrum.com/mesquite
Freq: Fri; **Circ:** 7800 Not Audited
Publisher: Donnie Welch
Profile: Desert Valley News is a local weekly newspaper serving the Mesquite, NV area. It provides information on news and events of interest to the local community.
Language (s): English
Ad Rate: Full Page Mono 7.90
Currency: United States Dollars
COMMUNITY NEWSPAPER

Desi Talk New York 25554
Owner: Parikh Worldwide Media LLC
Editorial: 115 W 30th Street, Suite 1206, New York, New York 10001-4043 **Tel:** 1 212 675-7515
Email: editor@newsindiatimes.com **Web site:** http://www.desitalk.com
Freq: Weekly; **Circ:** 14000 Not Audited
Editor: Sunil Adam; **Publisher:** Sudhir Parikh
Profile: Desi Talk New York is a weekly newspaper serving the New York-New Jersey-Connecticut region with Indian-American news coverage. Owner: Parikh Worldwide Media LLC
Language (s): English
Ad Rate: Full Page Mono 40.00
Currency: United States Dollars
COMMUNITY NEWSPAPER

The Destin Log 86250
Owner: GateHouse Media Inc.
Editorial: 3508 Emerald Coast Parkway, Destin, Florida 32541-2909 **Tel:** 1 850 837-2828
Email: news@thedestinlog.com **Web site:** http://www.thedestinlog.com
Freq: Sat; **Circ:** 7618 Not Audited
Publisher: Diane Winnemuller
Profile: The Destin Log is written for residents in Destin and South Walton County, FL. It covers news and events.
Language (s): English
Ad Rate: Full Page Mono 17.43
Ad Rate: Full Page Colour 43.57
Currency: United States Dollars
COMMUNITY NEWSPAPER

The Detroit Jewish News 22253
Owner: Renaissance Media
Editorial: 29200 Northwestern Hwy Ste 110, Southfield, Michigan 48034-1055 **Tel:** 1 248 354-6060
Web site: http://www.thejewishnews.com
Freq: Thu; **Circ:** 23000 Not Audited
Advertising Sales Manager: Keith Farber; **Publisher:** Arthur Horwitz
Profile: The Detroit Jewish News is a weekly newspaper serving the Jewish residents of Detroit. It covers local, national and global news with an emphasis on events in Israel. It also features articles on all aspects of Jewish life, from the arts to care for the elderly.
Language (s): English
Ad Rate: Full Page Mono 37.50
Currency: United States Dollars
COMMUNITY NEWSPAPER

Detroit Metro Times 21324
Owner: Times Shamrock Group
Editorial: 1200 Woodward Hts, Ferndale, Michigan 48220-1427 **Tel:** 1 313 961-4060
Email: letters@metrotimes.com **Web site:** http://www.metrotimes.com
Freq: Wed; **Circ:** 65000 Not Audited
Circulation Manager: Justin Hatch; **Publisher:** Chris Keating
Profile: Detroit Metro Times is a local, weekly newspaper serving the tri-county area surrounding Detroit, MI. It provides information on news, events, and arts and entertainment of interest to the local community. In May 2014, the publication merged with fellow alternative newsweekly Real Detroit Weekly.
Language (s): English
Ad Rate: Full Page Mono 54.12
Currency: United States Dollars
COMMUNITY NEWSPAPER

El Dia 21810
Editorial: 6331 26th St, Berwyn, Illinois 60402-2631 **Tel:** 1 708 652-6397
Email: eldia@eldianewschicago.com **Web site:** http://www.eldianewschicago.com
Freq: Fri; **Circ:** 60000 Not Audited
Editor: Ana Maria Montes de Oca; **Advertising Sales Manager:** Christopher Montes de Oca; **Publisher:** Jorge Montes de Oca
Profile: El Dia's editorial mission is to provide the Spanish community with information on community activities and current events. The publication is written for the Old Spanish community of Cicero, IL. Deadlines are on Wednesdays at 5pm CT.
Language (s): Spanish
Ad Rate: Full Page Mono 31.00
Currency: United States Dollars
COMMUNITY NEWSPAPER

The Dialog 18735
Owner: Catholic Press Inc.
Editorial: 1925 Delaware Ave, Wilmington, Delaware 19806-2301 **Tel:** 1 302 573-3109
Email: news@thedialog.org **Web site:** http://thedialog.org/
Freq: Fri; **Circ:** 26000 Not Audited
Editor: Mike Lang; **Publisher:** W. Francis Malooly; **Editor:** Joseph Ryan; **Advertising Sales Manager:** Sue Uniatowski
Profile: The Dialog is a weekly Catholic newspaper serving the Catholic community of Delaware and the Eastern Maryland.
Language (s): English
Ad Rate: Full Page Mono 42.70
Ad Rate: Full Page Colour 100.00
Currency: United States Dollars
COMMUNITY NEWSPAPER

Dickson Herald 20765
Owner: Gannett Co., Inc.
Editorial: 104 Church St, Dickson, Tennessee 37055-1826 **Tel:** 1 615 446-2811
Email: feedback@tennessean.com **Web site:** http://www.dicksonherald.com
Freq: Fri; **Circ:** 7500 Not Audited
Editor: Chris Gadd
Profile: Dickson Herald is published twice a week for the residents of Dickson County, TN. The newspaper covers local news, events, sports and community events. Deadlines are at 3pm CT two days prior to issue date.
Language (s): English
Ad Rate: Full Page Mono 18.90
Currency: United States Dollars
COMMUNITY NEWSPAPER

Dig Magazine 359629
Owner: University Media Group
Editorial: 5261 Highland Rd #167, Ste 167, Baton Rouge, Louisiana 70808-6547 **Tel:** 1 225 248-1229
Email: editor@digbatonrouge.com **Web site:** https://digbr.com
Freq: Wed; **Circ:** 20000 Not Audited
Profile: Dig Magazine is a free, weekly newspaper serving the areas immediately surrounding Louisiana

## United States of America

State University's campus in Baton Rouge, LA. The paper is independently-owned and in no way affiliated with the university. It covers campus news, events, sports and features relevant to the student population. The production schedule follows that of the university and usually halts for portions of December, January and May.
Language (s): English
Ad Rate: Full Page Mono 11.91
Currency: United States Dollars
COMMUNITY NEWSPAPER

The Dillon Herald   20623
Owner: Herald Publishing Co., Inc.
Editorial: 505 Highway 301 N, Dillon, South Carolina 29536-2957 Tel: 1 843 774-3311
Email: dillonherald@yahoo.com Web site: http://www.thedillonherald.com
Freq: 2 Times/Week; Circ: 7488 Not Audited
Advertising Sales Manager: Johnnie Daniels;
Editor: Betsy Finklea
Profile: The Dillon Herald is written for residents of Dillon County, SC. It covers local news and events.
Language (s): English
Ad Rate: Full Page Mono 8.19
Ad Rate: Full Page Colour 10.37
Currency: United States Dollars
COMMUNITY NEWSPAPER

The Dispatch   21107
Owner: RIM Publications
Editorial: 133 Mashell Avenue North, Eatonville, Washington 98328 Tel: 1 360 832-4411
Email: editor@dispatchnews.com Web site: http://www.dispatchnews.com
Freq: Wed; Circ: 8950 Not Audited
Language (s): English
Ad Rate: Full Page Mono 11.00
Currency: United States Dollars
COMMUNITY NEWSPAPER

Dispatch-Post USA   153540
Owner: Missouri Minority Press Service, Inc.
Editorial: 8401 New Jersey Ave., Kansas City, Kansas 66112 Tel: 1 913 481-4727
Email: dispatchpostusanewspaper@gmail.com
Freq: Thu; Circ: 30000 Not Audited
Editor & Publisher: David Jordon
Profile: Dispatch-Post USA provides weekly news updates to the African-American communities of Missouri. Local community news is covered, as well as some national news.
Language (s): English
Ad Rate: Full Page Mono 15.86
Currency: United States Dollars
COMMUNITY NEWSPAPER

Dixon Tribune   80980
Owner: Gibson Radio & Publishing Co.
Editorial: 145 E A St, Dixon, California 95620-3531 Tel: 1 707 678-5594
Email: editor@dixontribune.com
Freq: Fri; Circ: 6000 Not Audited
Editor: Jared Kohls; Publisher: David Payne
Profile: The Dixon Tribune is a local newspaper catering to Dixon, California and surrounding areas.
Language (s): English
Ad Rate: Full Page Mono 8.00
Currency: United States Dollars
COMMUNITY NEWSPAPER

Dixon's Independent Voice   258033
Owner: Scholl (Dave)
Editorial: 350 W A St, Dixon, California 95620-2918 Tel: 1 707 678-8917
Email: staff@independentvoice.com Web site: http://www.independentvoice.com
Freq: Fri; Circ: 5000 Not Audited
Publisher & Editor: Dave Scholl
Profile: Dixon's Independent Voice is the local newspaper for Dixon, CA. It provides local news, events and weather and some national news. It also features articles on business, health and sports news.
Language (s): English
Ad Rate: Full Page Mono 6.95
Currency: United States Dollars
COMMUNITY NEWSPAPER

The Dodge County News   21718
Owner: Middle Georgia Publishing Inc.
Editorial: 226 Main St, Eastman, Georgia 31023-6240 Tel: 1 478 374-6397
Email: dcn@dodgecountynews.com Web site: http://www.dodgecountynews.com
Freq: Wed; Circ: 5000 Not Audited
Editor/Publisher: Chuck Eckles
Profile: The Dodge County News prints the news of Eastman and Dodge County. Deadlines are Mondays at 5pm ET.
Language (s): English
Ad Rate: Full Page Mono 7.05
Currency: United States Dollars
COMMUNITY NEWSPAPER

The Dodgeville Chronicle   21171
Owner: Reilly (T. Michael) & Reilly (J. Patrick)
Editorial: 106 W Merrimac St, Dodgeville, Wisconsin 53533-1440 Tel: 1 608 935-2331
Email: news@thedodgevillechronicle.com Web site: https://www.thedodgevillechronicle.com
Freq: Thu; Circ: 5600 Not Audited
Profile: The Dodgeville Chronicle is a community newspaper serving the residents of Dodgeville, WI.
Language (s): English
Ad Rate: Full Page Mono 8.25
Currency: United States Dollars
COMMUNITY NEWSPAPER

The Dolphin   21516
Owner: 21st Century Media
Editorial: Naval Submarine Base PAO Box 44, Groton, Connecticut 06349-5044 Tel: 1 860 694-3514
Email: dolphin@ctcentral.com Web site: http://www.dolphin-news.com
Freq: Thu; Circ: 8500 Not Audited
Publisher: John Slater; Editor: Sheryl Walsh
Profile: The Dolphin is a weekly newspaper published by the Journal Register Company, a private firm in no way connected with the US Navy, under exclusive agreement with Naval Submarine Base New London. The newspaper covers Navy activities in Connecticut. It is written for people interested in the US Navy.
Language (s): English
Ad Rate: Full Page Mono 14.00
Currency: United States Dollars
COMMUNITY NEWSPAPER

Door County Advocate   21232
Owner: Gannett Co. Inc.
Editorial: 235 N 3rd Ave, Sturgeon Bay, Wisconsin 54235-2417 Tel: 1 920 743-3321
Email: advocate@doorcountyadvocate.com Web site: http://www.greenbaypressgazette.com/door-co/
Freq: Sat; Circ: 10500 Not Audited
Editor: Warren Bluhm; Advertising Sales Manager: Leah Clover
Profile: Door County Advocate is a twice-weekly newspaper serving residents of Door County, WI. Each edition covers county news, sports, births, deaths and public announcements, opinion articles, classified advertising and television listings. The weekday edition also contains local business news and a section called Community. Community provides columns submitted by neighborhood freelance writers, along with stories about the local YMCA, Door County Library, schools and senior centers. The weekend edition of the paper carries a section titled Family, which celebrates local peoples' accomplishments in school, service clubs and elsewhere in addition to wedding and anniversary announcements. The Family section relies heavily on reader-submitted photographs and information.
Language (s): English
Ad Rate: Full Page Mono 14.00
Currency: United States Dollars
COMMUNITY NEWSPAPER

Dorchester Star   28323
Owner: Chesapeake Publishing and Printing
Editorial: 511 Poplar St, Cambridge, Maryland 21613-1833 Tel: 1 410 228-0222
Web site: http://www.dorchesterstar.com
Freq: Fri; Circ: 11000 Not Audited
Editor: Gale Dean; Publisher: David Fike; Editor: Dustin Holt; Advertising Sales Manager: Paul Myers
Profile: Dorchester Star's editorial mission is to provide local news and event information for residents of Dorchester County, MD.
Language (s): English
Ad Rate: Full Page Mono 11.25
Currency: United States Dollars
COMMUNITY NEWSPAPER

Dos Mundos   22266
Editorial: 902A Southwest Blvd, Kansas City, Missouri 64108-2341 Tel: 1 816 221-4747
Email: newsstaff@dosmundos.com Web site: http://www.dosmundos.com
Freq: Thu; Circ: 20000 Not Audited
Advertising Sales Manager: Diana Raymer; Editor: Clara Reyes; Publisher: Manuel Reyes
Profile: Dos Mundos delivers news to the Hispanic community of Kansas City, MO.
Language (s): Spanish/Bilingual
Ad Rate: Full Page Mono 14.00
Ad Rate: Full Page Colour 2184.00
Currency: United States Dollars
COMMUNITY NEWSPAPER

Dothan Progress   27419
Owner: BH Media Group
Editorial: 227 N Oates St, Dothan, Alabama 36303-4555 Tel: 1 334 792-3141
Freq: Thu; Circ: 25000 Not Audited
Advertising Sales Manager: Jerry Morgan
Profile: Dothan Progress is written for the residents of Dothan, Headland and Ashford, AL. It covers local news, education, entertainment and food.
Language (s): English
Ad Rate: Full Page Mono 11.50
Currency: United States Dollars
COMMUNITY NEWSPAPER

Douglas County Post-Gazette   22284
Owner: Overmann (Penny)
Editorial: 2929 N 204th St Ste 117, Elkhorn, Nebraska 68022-1201 Tel: 1 402 289-2329
Email: editor@dcpostgazette.com Web site: http://www.dcpostgazette.com
Freq: Tue; Circ: 16000 Not Audited
Publisher: Penny Overmann; Editor: Mary Lou Rodgers
Profile: Douglas County Post-Gazette is a local weekly newspaper. Its editorial mission is to be the best local news source for the communities of Elkhorn, Waterloo, Bennington, and Valley, NE. Deadlines are on Fridays at 9am CT.
Language (s): English
Ad Rate: Full Page Mono 17.50
Currency: United States Dollars
COMMUNITY NEWSPAPER

The Downey Patriot   86615
Owner: Dekay-Girens (Jennifer)
Editorial: 8301 Florence Ave Ste 100, Downey, California 90240-3946 Tel: 1 562 904-3668
Email: news@thedowneypatriot.com Web site: http://www.thedowneypatriot.com
Freq: Thu; Circ: 25000 Not Audited
Publisher: Jennifer Dekay-Givens
Profile: The Downey Patriot is a community newspaper serving Downey, CA and the surrounding areas. It includes local news, sports, business, health news, opinion and community events.
Language (s): English
Ad Rate: Full Page Mono 19.00
Currency: United States Dollars
COMMUNITY NEWSPAPER

Downtown News   21466
Owner: Southland Publishing
Editorial: 1264 W 1st St, Los Angeles, California 90026-5831 Tel: 1 213 481-1448
Email: realpeople@downtownnews.com Web site: http://www.ladowntownnews.com
Freq: Mon; Circ: 37615 Not Audited
Profile: Downtown News is a weekly newspaper for the people who work in downtown Los Angeles. Its editorial mission is to provide news about business, politics, arts and culture.
Language (s): English
Ad Rate: Full Page Mono 44.00
Ad Rate: Full Page Colour 7428.00
Currency: United States Dollars
COMMUNITY NEWSPAPER

Dripping Springs Century-News   28389
Tel: 1 512 858-4163
Email: dscenturynews@gmail.com Web site: http://www.drippingspringsnews.com
Freq: Wed; Circ: 1500 Not Audited
Profile: Century-News is a community newspaper serving the Dripping Springs, TX area. The publication covers local news, sports and events within the community. Deadlines are noon CT on Wednesdays for Saturdays issue and noon CT on Fridays for Wednesdays issue.
Language (s): English
Ad Rate: Full Page Mono 8.00
Currency: United States Dollars
COMMUNITY NEWSPAPER

The Dundalk Eagle   19471
Owner: Kimbel Publication Inc.
Editorial: 4 N Center Pl, Dundalk, Maryland 21222-4300 Tel: 1 410 288-6060
Email: info@dundalkeagle.net Web site: http://www.dundalkeagle.com
Freq: Thu; Circ: 16000 Not Audited
Publisher: Deborah Cornely; Editor: Steve Matrazzo; Advertising Manager: Jason O'Neill
Profile: The Dundalk (MD) Eagle is a weekly newspaper that covers local news and events.
Language (s): English
Ad Rate: Full Page Mono 19.60
Currency: United States Dollars
COMMUNITY NEWSPAPER

The Dunwoody Crier   18856
Owner: Crier Newspapers, LLC
Editorial: 5064 Nandina Ln Ste C, Dunwoody, Georgia 30338-4115 Tel: 1 770 451-4147
Email: thecrier@mindspring.com Web site: http://www.thecrier.net
Freq: Wed; Circ: 23000 Not Audited
Editor & Publisher: Dick Williams
Profile: The Dunwoody Crier is a local newspaper written for residents of Dunwoody, GA. The newspaper covers local news, sports, weather, business and arts & entertainment.
Language (s): English
Ad Rate: Full Page Mono 31.76
Ad Rate: Full Page Colour 31.76
Currency: United States Dollars
COMMUNITY NEWSPAPER

Duowei News   507016
Owner: Chinese Media Net Inc. (CMN)
Editorial: 6 E 46th St Rm 302, New York, New York 10017-2432 Tel: 1 212 219-3892
Email: newsdesk@dwnews.com Web site: http://www.dwnews.com
Freq: Fri; Circ: 20000 Not Audited
Publisher: Bettina Yang
Profile: Duowei News is a Chinese-language weekly covering national and international news. It also covers local news, life in North America, arts & entertainment and real estate.
Language (s): Chinese
Ad Rate: Full Page Mono 30.00
Currency: United States Dollars
COMMUNITY NEWSPAPER

Durango Telegraph   617091
Editorial: 1309 E 3rd Ave Unit 25, Durango, Colorado 81301-5257 Tel: 1 970 259-0133
Email: telegraph@durangotelegraph.com Web site: http://www.durangotelegraph.com
Freq: Thu; Circ: 5500
Advertising Sales Manager: Lainie Maxson
Profile: Durango Herald is a local community newspaper written for the residents of Durango, CO and the surrounding communities.
Language (s): English
Ad Rate: Full Page Mono 7.61
Currency: United States Dollars
COMMUNITY NEWSPAPER

The Eagle   134081
Owner: Associated Newspapers
Tel: 1 734 467-1900
Email: editor@journalgroup.com Web site: http://www.associatednewspapers.net
Freq: Weekly; Circ: 15000 Not Audited
Profile: The Eagle is a community newspaper for residents of Western Wayne County, MI.
Language (s): English
Ad Rate: Full Page Mono 11.70
Currency: United States Dollars
COMMUNITY NEWSPAPER

The Early Bird   20312
Owner: Ball Publishing Company
Editorial: 5312 Sebring Warner Rd, Greenville, Ohio 45331-8787 Tel: 1 937 548-3330
Email: publisher@earlybirdpaper.com Web site: https://www.earlybirdpaper.com
Freq: Sun; Circ: 27558 Not Audited
Profile: The Early Bird is a weekly newspaper established in 1968, written for the residents of County Target, OH. It covers news and events in the local community. Deadlines are Thursdays at noon CT.
Language (s): English
Ad Rate: Full Page Mono 65.00
Currency: United States Dollars
COMMUNITY NEWSPAPER

Early County News   18795
Owner: Early County News Inc.
Editorial: 529 College St, Blakely, Georgia 39823-2235 Tel: 1 229 723-4376
Email: ecnews@windstream.net Web site: http://www.earlycountynews.com
Freq: Wed; Circ: 11400
Editor and Publisher: William Fleming
Profile: The Early County News is a weekly community newspaper serving residents of Early County, GA. Deadlines for the publication fall on Fridays at 5pm ET.
Language (s): English
Ad Rate: Full Page Mono 6.23
Currency: United States Dollars
COMMUNITY NEWSPAPER

East Allen Courier   324701
Owner: Corp Courier Printing Co
Editorial: 13720 Main St, Grabill, Indiana 46741-2011 Tel: 1 260 627-2728
Email: eacourier@mediacombb.net Web site: http://www.courierprinting.biz/east-allen-courier
Freq: Tue; Circ: 7500 Not Audited
Profile: The East Allen Courier is a weekly newspaper that was founded in 1935, when it was known as the Woodburn Booster. It served the residents of Grabill, IN, Leo, IN, Cedarville, IN, Woodburn, IN, and Spencerville, IN. It focuses on news in the communities of Allen County, IN, and is published every Tuesday.
Language (s): English
Ad Rate: Full Page Mono 5.00
Currency: United States Dollars
COMMUNITY NEWSPAPER

East Bay Express   21331
Owner: Telegraph Media
Editorial: 318 Harrison St Ste 302, Oakland, California 94607-4134 Tel: 1 510 879-3700
Email: editor@eastbayexpress.com Web site: http://www.eastbayexpress.com
Freq: Wed; Circ: 50000 Not Audited
Publisher: Jody Colley; Advertising Sales Manager: Ben Grambergu
Profile: East Bay Express in Oakland, CA is a weekly newspaper for the residents of the East Bay, CA area, covering local news and events.
Language (s): English
Ad Rate: Full Page Mono 20.30
Currency: United States Dollars
COMMUNITY NEWSPAPER

The East County Californian   62146
Owner: San Diego Neighborhood Newsapapers Inc.
Editorial: 119 N Magnolia Ave, El Cajon, California 92020-3903 Tel: 1 619 441-0400
Web site: http://www.eccalifornian.com
Freq: Thu; Circ: 32500 Not Audited
Editor: Albert Fulcher
Profile: The East County Californian serves the cities of El Cajon, Santee, La Mesa, Lemon Grove, and the communities of Spring Valley, Lakeside, Blossom Valley, Flinn Springs, Rancho San Diego, Casa de Oro, Dehesa, Dulzura, and Crest all, CA. Coverage includes local news, sports, business, arts and entertainment, food, and business.
Language (s): English
Ad Rate: Full Page Mono 91.80
Currency: United States Dollars
COMMUNITY NEWSPAPER

East County Gazette   291571
Editorial: 1130 Broadway, El Cajon, California 92021-4805 Tel: 1 619 444-5774
Email: gazettenews@sbcglobal.net Web site: http://www.eastcountygazette.com
Freq: Thu; Circ: 20000 Not Audited
Publisher & Editor: Debbie Norman; Advertising Sales Manager: Brionna Thomas
Profile: East County Gazette is a weekly newspaper written for the residents of East County, CA.
Language (s): English
Ad Rate: Full Page Mono 10.50
Currency: United States Dollars
COMMUNITY NEWSPAPER

The East County Herald 510053
Owner: The San Diego County Herald, LLC
Tel: 1 619 445-0374
Web site: http://www.eastcountyherald.com
Freq: Weekly; **Circ:** 10000 Not Audited
Publisher: Dee Dean; **Editor:** Steve Hamann
Profile: The East County Herald is a free weekly community newspaper covering local news and events.
Language (s): English
Ad Rate: Full Page Mono 8.50
Currency: United States Dollars
COMMUNITY NEWSPAPER

The East County Times 22342
Editorial: 513 Eastern Blvd, Baltimore, Maryland 21221-6702 **Tel:** 1 410 780-3303
Email: ecteditorial@comcast.net **Web site:** http://www.eastcountytimesonline.com
Freq: Thu; **Circ:** 45000 Not Audited
Advertising Sales Manager: Linda Mrok; **Publisher:** George Wilbanks
Profile: The East County Times is a weekly newspaper that was founded in 1970. The paper's editorial mission is to uplift the community and neighborhood in which we live to encourage people to make their homes here and work here. The publication is written for all ages and was formerly known as Essex Times. This is a 48-page tabloid newspaper.
Language (s): English
Ad Rate: Full Page Mono 12.60
Currency: United States Dollars
COMMUNITY NEWSPAPER

East Hampton Star 20261
Owner: East Hampton Star Inc.
Editorial: 153 Main St, East Hampton, New York 11937-2716 **Tel:** 1 631 324-0002
Email: editor@easthamptonstar.com **Web site:** http://www.easthamptonstar.com
Freq: Thu; **Circ:** 15200 Not Audited
Circulation Manager: Jane Callan; **Editor:** David Rattray; **Publisher:** Helen Rattray; **Advertising Sales Manager:** Min Spear-Hefner
Profile: East Hampton Star is a local weekly newspaper for the residents of East Hampton, NY. It covers news and events in the local community.
Language (s): English
Ad Rate: Full Page Mono 28.00
Currency: United States Dollars
COMMUNITY NEWSPAPER

East Side Daily News 22101
Editorial: 11400 Woodland Ave, Cleveland, Ohio 44104-2636 **Tel:** 1 216 721-1674
Email: esdn1@yahoo.com **Web site:** http://www.eastsidedailynews.com
Freq: Weekly; **Circ:** 20000 Not Audited
Publisher & Editor: Ulysses Glen
Profile: East Side Daily News is written for the African American residents of Cleveland, OH. It covers news and events in the African American community.
Language (s): English
Ad Rate: Full Page Mono 25.00
Currency: United States Dollars
COMMUNITY NEWSPAPER

East St. Louis Monitor 19143
Editorial: 1501 State St, East St. Louis, Illinois 62205-2011 **Tel:** 1 618 271-0468
Email: media@estlmonitor.com
Freq: Thu; **Circ:** 8650 Not Audited
Editor: Lonnie Davidson; **Publisher and Editor:** Anne Jordan; **Advertising Sales Manager:** George Laktzian
Profile: East St. Louis Monitor is a local newspaper serving residents of East St. Louis, IL. The publication covers local news and community events. Deadlines are on Mondays at 5pm ET.
Language (s): English
Ad Rate: Full Page Mono 17.60
Currency: United States Dollars
COMMUNITY NEWSPAPER

East Tennessee Times 20770
Owner: East Tennessee Times Inc.
Editorial: 2533 Sand Pike Blvd Ste 3, Pigeon Forge, Tennessee 37863-6230 **Tel:** 1 865 680-1891
Email: news@easttntimes.com **Web site:** http://www.easttntimes.com
Freq: Wed; **Circ:** 9542 Not Audited
Advertising Sales Manager: Rebecca Dodgen; **Editor & Publisher:** Gwen Ford
Profile: East Tennessee Times provides local news and community events to the residents of Sevier and Jefferson County, Tennessee.
Language (s): English
Ad Rate: Full Page Mono 7.00
Currency: United States Dollars
COMMUNITY NEWSPAPER

East Texas Review 217529
Editorial: 517 S Mobberly Ave, Longview, Texas 75602-1827 **Tel:** 1 903 236-0406
Email: graphics@easttexasreview.com
Freq: Thu; **Circ:** 10000 Not Audited
Editor: Joycelyne Fadojutimi; **Publisher:** Robert Fadojutimi
Profile: East Texas Review is a weekly community newspaper serving Longview, TX.
Language (s): English
Ad Rate: Full Page Mono 42.50
Currency: United States Dollars
COMMUNITY NEWSPAPER

East Valley Tribune 16353
Owner: 10/13 Communications
Editorial: 1620 W Fountainhead Pkwy Ste 219, Tempe, Arizona 85282-1848 **Tel:** 1 480 898-6500
Email: newstips@evtrib.com **Web site:** http://www.eastvalleytribune.com
Freq: Fri; **Circ:** 52303
Profile: East Valley Tribune is a newspaper covering local, national and international news. It serves suburban Phoenix, specifically the communities of Ahwatukee, Apache Junction, Chandler, Gilbert, Mesa, Queen Creek and Tempe, AZ. The paper also offers a section specifically about Scottsdale. It is printed Wednesday, Friday and Saturday but is available online 7 days a week.
Language (s): English
Ad Rate: Full Page Mono 59.59
Ad Rate: Full Page Colour 624.18
Currency: United States Dollars
COMMUNITY NEWSPAPER

The Eastern Gazette 19481
Owner: Gazette, Inc
Editorial: 97 Church St, Dexter, Maine 04930-1332
Tel: 1 207 924-7402
Email: gazette@easterngazette.com **Web site:** http://www.easterngazette.com
Freq: Fri; **Circ:** 17250 Not Audited
Publisher & Editor: Robert Shank
Profile: The Eastern Gazette is published weekly for the residents of Dexter, ME and surrounding areas. The newspaper covers local news and community events.
Language (s): English
Ad Rate: Full Page Mono 12.50
Ad Rate: Full Page Colour 75.00
Currency: United States Dollars
COMMUNITY NEWSPAPER

Eastern Shore Post 554740
Editorial: 25248 Lankford Hwy, Onley, Virginia 23418
Tel: 1 757 789-7678
Web site: http://www.easternshorepost.com
Freq: Weekly; **Circ:** 13000
Advertising Manager: Troy Justis; **Editor:** Cheryl Nowak
Profile: Eastern Shore Post is weekly community newspaper serving residents of Onley, VA, with a focus on local news, sports, and events.
Language (s): English
COMMUNITY NEWSPAPER

Eastern Wake News 137305
Owner: McClatchy Newspapers
Editorial: 110 N Arendell Ave, Zebulon, North Carolina 27597-2602 **Tel:** 1 919 269-6101
Email: jwhitfield@newsobserver.com **Web site:** http://www.easternwakenews.com
Freq: Sun; **Circ:** 21600 Not Audited
Profile: Eastern Wake News is a weekly newspaper covering Knightdale, Wendell, Zebulon and neighboring communities like Middlesex, Pilot, Archer Lodge, Lizard Lick, Hopkins, Shotwell, Pearces, Eagle Rock and Bunn, NC. It is a source for in-depth coverage of issues that affect the area: news, photos, honor rolls and schools; exclusive reports and photos from recreation teams; town government coverage; and more stories and photos of the Carolina Mudcats and high school sports than any other source.
Language (s): English
Ad Rate: Full Page Mono 27.45
Currency: United States Dollars
COMMUNITY NEWSPAPER

Eastland/Callahan County Newspapers 24704
Owner: Eastland/Callahan County Newspapers
Editorial: 215 S Seaman St, Eastland, Texas 76448-2745 **Tel:** 1 254 629-1707
Web site: http://www.eastlandcountytoday.com/
Circ: 5006 Not Audited
Publisher & Editor: H.V. O'Brien
Language (s): English
COMMUNITY NEWSPAPER

Easy Reader 22565
Owner: 2100 Trust LLC
Editorial: 2200 Pacific Coast Hwy Ste 101, Hermosa Beach, California 90254-2716 **Tel:** 1 310 372-4611
Email: easyreader@easyreadernews.com **Web site:** http://www.easyreadernews.com
Freq: Thu; **Circ:** 57000 Not Audited
Editor & Publisher: Kevin Cody
Profile: Easy Reader is published weekly for the residents of Manhattan Beach, El Segundo, Redondo Beach and Hermosa Beach, CA. The newspaper covers local news, sports, entertainment and community events.
Language (s): English
Ad Rate: Full Page Mono 28.00
Currency: United States Dollars
COMMUNITY NEWSPAPER

Ebony News Today 135468
Owner: Cain (Ben)
Editorial: 1783 Mission Bay Cir, P-304, Rockledge, Florida 32955-6685 **Tel:** 1 321 220-4216
Web site: http://www.ebonynewstoday.com
Freq: Thu; **Circ:** 35000 Not Audited
Publisher & Editor: Ben Cain
Profile: Ebony News Today is written for the African American population of Brevard, Orange and Osceola Counties in Florida. It provides relevant news and information.
Language (s): English
Ad Rate: Full Page Mono 15.00
Currency: United States Dollars
COMMUNITY NEWSPAPER

The Echo 29680
Owner: Helotes Echo, LLC
Editorial: 7205 Bandera Rd, Leon Valley, Texas 78238-1226 **Tel:** 1 210 695-3613
Email: helotesecho@gmail.com **Web site:** http://helotesecho.com
Freq: Wed; **Circ:** 16000 Not Audited
Advertising Sales Manager: Veronica Gonzales
Profile: The Echo is a weekly newspaper written for residents in Boerne, TX. Articles include news, weather and local events. The paper is published by Texas Heritage Newspaper Group.
Language (s): English
Ad Rate: Full Page Mono 10.05
Currency: United States Dollars
COMMUNITY NEWSPAPER

Echo Press 22137
Owner: Forum Communications
Editorial: 225 7th Ave E, Alexandria, Minnesota 56308-1831 **Tel:** 1 320 763-3133
Email: echo@echopress.com **Web site:** http://www.echopress.com
Freq: Fri; **Circ:** 9500 Not Audited
News & Opinion Editor: Al Edenloff
Profile: Echo Press is a twice weekly newspaper for the residents of Douglas County, MN. It covers news and events in the local community. Deadlines are on Mondays and Wednesdays at 10am ET. The outlet offers RRS (Real Simple Syndication).
Language (s): English
Ad Rate: Full Page Mono 15.50
Currency: United States Dollars
COMMUNITY NEWSPAPER

El Eco de Virginia-Weekly 520498
Editorial: 204 Brackenridge Ave, Norfolk, Virginia 23505-4322 **Tel:** 1 757 625-1341
Email: elecodeva@yahoo.com **Web site:** http://www.ecohispanic.com
Freq: Wed; **Circ:** 30000 Not Audited
Publisher & Editor: Augusto Ratti-Angulo;
Advertising Sales Manager: Gabriel Ratti-Angulo;
Circulation Manager: Sebastian Simon Ratti-Angulo
Profile: El Eco de Virginia-Weekly is a Spanish-language newspaper written for Hispanic residents of Norfolk, VA and the surrounding area.
Language (s): Spanish
Ad Rate: Full Page Mono 27.62
Currency: United States Dollars
COMMUNITY NEWSPAPER

Ecuador News 152259
Owner: Arboleda (Edgar)
Editorial: 6403 Roosevelt Ave Fl 2, Woodside, New York 11377-3643 **Tel:** 1 718 205-7014
Email: ecuanews@inch.com **Web site:** http://www.ecuadornews.com.ec
Freq: Wed; **Circ:** 45000 Not Audited
Publisher & Editor: Edgar Arboleda; **Advertising Sales Manager:** Julio Garino
Profile: Ecuador News in Woodside, NY is a weekly newspaper written for Ecuadorian and Hispanic communities in New York, New Jersey and other U.S. cities.
Language (s): Spanish
Ad Rate: Full Page Mono 21.54
Currency: United States Dollars
COMMUNITY NEWSPAPER

The Edmonds Beacon 23340
Owner: Beacon Publishing, Inc.
Editorial: 806 5th St, Mukilteo, Washington 98275-1628 **Tel:** 1 425 347-1711
Web site: http://edmondsbeacon.villagesoup.com
Freq: Thu; **Circ:** 9700 Not Audited
Publisher: Paul Archipley; **Editor:** Pat Ratliff
Profile: Edmonds Beacon is a weekly newspaper providing Local News coverage to the residents of Edmonds, WA, including Woodway and Lynnwood neighborhoods.
Language (s): English
Ad Rate: Full Page Mono 22.00
Currency: United States Dollars
COMMUNITY NEWSPAPER

EdPrint, Inc. 24790
Owner: EdPrint, Inc.
Editorial: 13400 NE 175th St Ste C, Woodinville, Washington 98072-7037 **Tel:** 1 425 483-0606
Email: editor@woodinville.com **Web site:** http://www.nwnews.com
Circ: 30200 Not Audited
Editor: Lisa Allen; **Publisher:** Julie Bosely; **Editor:** Karen Diefendorf
Profile: Ed Print is a community newspaper publisher in Woodinville, WA.
Language (s): English
COMMUNITY NEWSPAPER

Edward A. Sherman Publishing Co. 24694
Editorial: 101 Malbone Rd, Newport, Rhode Island 2840 **Tel:** 1 401 849-3300
Circ: 15000 Not Audited
Editor: Richard Alexander; **Editor:** Janine Weisman
Profile: Edward A. Sherman Publishing Co. is a weekly community newspaper publisher serving the residents of Newport, RI.
Language (s): English
COMMUNITY NEWSPAPER

Effingham Now 429765
Owner: GateHouse Media Inc.
Editorial: 5946 S Columbia Ave, Rincon, Georgia 31326-9027 **Tel:** 1 912 826-1290
Web site: http://savannahnow.com/effinghamnow
Freq: Wed; **Circ:** 12500 Not Audited
Editor: Deann Komanecky; **Publisher:** Michael Traynor
Profile: Effingham Now is a newspaper distributed weekly to subscribers of the Savannah (GA) Morning News and residents of Effingham County, GA. Please do not send any mail to the street address.
Language (s): English
Ad Rate: Full Page Mono 9.66
Currency: United States Dollars
COMMUNITY NEWSPAPER

Eintracht 22494
Owner: Eintracht, Inc.
Editorial: 9456 Lawler Ave, Skokie, Illinois 60077-1271 **Tel:** 1 847 679-0599
Email: eintrachtinc@aceweb.com
Freq: Weekly; **Circ:** 5000 Not Audited
News Editor: Annerose Goerge; **Publisher:** Ilse Juengling; **Editor:** Klaus Juengling
Profile: Eintracht is a weekly newspaper published in Skokie, IL. Three quarters of the news is written in German, and the rest is in English. The paper provides news coverage for German-speaking residents of Chicago and the surrounding area.
Language (s): English, German
Ad Rate: Full Page Mono 9.00
Currency: United States Dollars
COMMUNITY NEWSPAPER

El Campo Leader-News 20828
Owner: Wharton County Newspapers
Editorial: 203 E Jackson St, El Campo, Texas 77437-4413 **Tel:** 1 979 543-3363
Email: news@leader-news.com **Web site:** http://www.leader-news.com
Freq: Sat; **Circ:** 5700 Not Audited
News Editor: Shannon Crabtree; **Advertising Sales Manager:** Keri Mahalitic; **Editor:** Quala Matocha; **Publisher:** Jay Strasner
Profile: El Campo Leader-News covers local news and events of interest for residents of Wharton County, TX. Deadlines are 10am CT on Tuesdays for the Wednesday edition and 10am CT on Fridays for the Saturday edition.
Language (s): English
Ad Rate: Full Page Mono 7.85
Ad Rate: Full Page Colour 983.70
Currency: United States Dollars
COMMUNITY NEWSPAPER

El Dorado Springs Sun 19769
Owner: Sun Newspapers
Editorial: 125 N Main St, El Dorado Springs, Missouri 64744-1141 **Tel:** 1 417 876-3841
Email: sunnews@socket.net **Web site:** http://www.eldoradospringsmo.com
Freq: Thu; **Circ:** 7000 Not Audited
Advertising Sales Manager: Wanda Baldwin; **Editor:** Kenneth Long; **Publisher:** Kimball Long; **News Editor:** Mary TRUE
Profile: El Dorado Springs Sun is a weekly newspaper for residents of El Dorado Springs, MO. The paper covers local news and events.
Language (s): English
Ad Rate: Full Page Mono 8.00
Currency: United States Dollars
COMMUNITY NEWSPAPER

El Segundo Herald Newspapers 70111
Owner: Herald Publications
Editorial: 312 E Imperial Ave, El Segundo, California 90245-2441 **Tel:** 1 310 322-1830
Email: pr@heraldpublications.com **Web site:** http://www.heraldpublications.com
Freq: 2 Times/Week; **Circ:** 60000 Not Audited
Editor: Heidi Maerker; **Publisher:** Richard Van Vranken
Language (s): English
COMMUNITY NEWSPAPER

Eldridge North Scott Press 19026
Editorial: 214 N 2nd St, Eldridge, Iowa 52748-1208
Tel: 1 563 285-8111
Web site: http://www.northscottpress.com
Freq: Wed; **Circ:** 5500 Not Audited
Editor: Scott Campbell; **Advertising Sales Manager:** Jeff Martens; **Publisher:** William Tubbs; **Circulation Manager:** Becky Wentworth
Profile: Eldridge (IA) North Scott Press is a weekly newspaper published for residents of Scott County, IA. The paper provides local news.
Language (s): English
Ad Rate: Full Page Mono 12.00
Currency: United States Dollars
COMMUNITY NEWSPAPER

Elk Grove Citizen 27275
Owner: Herburger Publications, Inc.
Editorial: 8970 Elk Grove Blvd, Elk Grove, California 95624-1971 **Tel:** 1 916 685-3945
Email: egnews@herburger.net **Web site:** http://www.egcitizen.com
Freq: Fri; **Circ:** 10350 Not Audited
Publisher: David Herburger; **Editor:** Cameron MacDonald
Profile: Elk Grove Citizen is written for residents of Elk Grove, CA. It covers local news and events.
Language (s): English
Ad Rate: Full Page Mono 9.50
Currency: United States Dollars
COMMUNITY NEWSPAPER

The Elk Valley Times 20726
Owner: Lakeway Publishers, Inc.
Editorial: 418 Elk Ave N, Fayetteville, Tennessee 37334-2512 **Tel:** 1 931 433-6151
Email: evtpub@lcs.net **Web site:** http://www.elkvalleytimes.com
Freq: Wed; **Circ:** 9093 Not Audited
Editor & Publisher: Lucy Carter; **Advertising Sales Manager:** Amber Gentry; **News Editor:** Sandy Williams
Profile: The Elk Valley Times is published weekly for the residents of Elk Valley, TN and surrounding areas. The newspaper covers local news and community events.
Language (s): English
Ad Rate: Full Page Mono 13.90
Ad Rate: Full Page Colour 306.74
Currency: United States Dollars
COMMUNITY NEWSPAPER

Elkin Tribune 19976
Owner: Civitas Media
Editorial: 214 E Main St, Elkin, North Carolina 28621-3431 **Tel:** 1 336 835-1513
Web site: http://www.elkintribune.com
Freq: Fri; **Circ:** 5195 Not Audited
Editor: Wendy Byerly Wood
Profile: Elkin Tribune is for residents of Elkin, NC. It covers local, national and international news, weather and sports. Feature articles cover business, politics, health, education, lifestyle and arts & entertainment.
Language (s): English
Ad Rate: Full Page Mono 10.00
Currency: United States Dollars
COMMUNITY NEWSPAPER

The Ellsworth American 19483
Owner: Ellsworth American, Inc.
Editorial: 30 Water St, Ellsworth, Maine 04605-2033 **Tel:** 1 207 667-2576
Email: news@ellsworthamerican.com **Web site:** http://www.ellsworthamerican.com
Freq: Thu; **Circ:** 10800 Not Audited
Publisher: Alan Baker; **Advertising Sales Manager:** Julie Clark
Profile: Ellsworth American is a weekly newspaper written for residents of Hancock County, ME. Deadlines for the publication are Mondays at 5pm ET.
Language (s): English
Ad Rate: Full Page Mono 21.25
Currency: United States Dollars
COMMUNITY NEWSPAPER

Embarcadero Publishing - Palo Alto 620352
Owner: Embarcadero Publishing Co.
Editorial: 450 Cambridge Ave, Palo Alto, California 94306-1507 **Tel:** 1 650 326-8210
Email: editor@paweekly.com **Web site:** http://paloaltoonline.com
Circ: 59000
Editor: Jocelyn Dong; **Editor and Publisher:** Richard Hine; **Publisher:** William Johnson
Profile: Embarcadero Publishing in Palo Alto, CA publishes The Almanac, Mountain View Voice and Palto Alto Weekly.
Language (s): English
COMMUNITY NEWSPAPER

Emmetsburg Democrat & Reporter 24509
Owner: Ogden Newspapers
Editorial: 1122 Broadway St Ste B, Emmetsburg, Iowa 50536-1767 **Tel:** 1 712 852-2323
Web site: http://www.emmetsburgnews.com
Circ: 5200 Not Audited
Circulation Manager: Linda Hill; **Publisher:** Dan McCain
Profile: The Emmetsburg Reporter/Democrat covers the area news of Emmetsburg, Iowa. Circulation figure unavailable.
Language (s): English
COMMUNITY NEWSPAPER

Empire Publishing Corporation 25347
Editorial: 1525 Central Ave, Far Rockaway, New York 11691-4019 **Tel:** 1 516 594-4000
Email: lijeworld@aol.com
Freq: 2 Times/Week; **Circ:** 90000 Not Audited
Language (s): English
Ad Rate: Full Page Mono 10.00
Currency: United States Dollars
COMMUNITY NEWSPAPER

Engle Publishing Company 25283
Editorial: 1425 W Main St, Mount Joy, Pennsylvania 17552 **Tel:** 1 717 653-1833
Email: news@engleonline.com **Web site:** http://www.engleonline.com
Circ: 398678 Not Audited
Publisher: Charles Engle; **Editor:** Francine Fulton; **Advertising Sales Manager:** John Hemperley
Language (s): English
COMMUNITY NEWSPAPER

Englewood Independent 86948
Owner: AIM Media Midwest
Editorial: 69 N Dixie Dr, Vandalia, Ohio 45377-2060 **Tel:** 1 937 890-6030 204
Web site: http://www.englewoodindependent.com
Freq: Wed; **Circ:** 6000 Not Audited
Editor: Ron Nunnari
Profile: Englewood Independent is a local, weekly newspaper serving the residents of Englewood, Clayton, Trotwood, Union and Phillisburg, OH. The publication covers local news, sports, politics, entertainment and community events. Deadlines are Mondays at noon ET.
Language (s): English
Ad Rate: Full Page Mono 6.70
Currency: United States Dollars
COMMUNITY NEWSPAPER

The Englewood Review 86224
Owner: Newton (Tom)
Editorial: 370 W Dearborn St Ste B, Englewood, Florida 34223-3167 **Tel:** 1 941 474-4351
Email: pr@englewoodreview.com **Web site:** http://www.englewoodreview.com
Freq: Bi-Weekly; **Circ:** 7000 Not Audited
Publisher, Editor & Advertising Sales Manager: Tom Newton
Profile: The Englewood Review is a local newspaper serving the residents of Englewood, FL. The publication covers local news, arts & entertainment and community events. Deadlines are on Fridays prior to issue date at noon ET.
Language (s): English
Ad Rate: Full Page Mono 20.80
Ad Rate: Full Page Colour 840.00
Currency: United States Dollars
COMMUNITY NEWSPAPER

Enquirer-Democrat 19063
Owner: Macoupin County Enquirer Inc. (The)
Editorial: 125 E Main St, Carlinville, Illinois 62626-1726 **Tel:** 1 217 854-2534
Email: editorial@enquirerdemocrat.com **Web site:** http://www.enquirerdemocrat.com
Freq: Thu; **Circ:** 5500 Not Audited
Publisher & Editor: Jay Endress; **Advertising Sales Manager:** Roger Michalek
Profile: Enquirer-Democrat is a local newspaper serving the community of Macoupin County, IL. The newspaper covers local news, sports, entertainment, business and community events. Deadlines are Tuesdays at noon CT.
Language (s): English
Ad Rate: Full Page Mono 6.30
Currency: United States Dollars
COMMUNITY NEWSPAPER

Enquirer-Herald 20645
Owner: McClatchy Newspapers
Editorial: 23 E Liberty St, York, South Carolina 29745-1546 **Tel:** 1 803 684-9903
Email: news@enquirerherald.com **Web site:** http://www.heraldonline.com/news/local/community/enquirer-herald/
Freq: Thu; **Circ:** 7143 Not Audited
Editor: Jennifer Becknell
Profile: Enquirer-Herald is a local weekly newspaper that reports the local news of York, Clover and Western York County, SC. It offers community news, events, schools, sports, lifestyle stories and editorials.
Language (s): English
Ad Rate: Full Page Mono 8.19
Currency: United States Dollars
COMMUNITY NEWSPAPER

The Enterprise 21070
Owner: Miona Publications
Editorial: 129 N Main St, Stuart, Virginia 24171-8802 **Tel:** 1 276 694-3101
Email: mail@theenterprise.net **Web site:** http://www.theenterprise.net
Freq: Wed; **Circ:** 5900 Not Audited
Publisher: Gail Harding; **Editor:** Nancy Lindsey; **Advertising Sales Manager:** Lindsay Roberson
Profile: The Enterprise is published every Wednesday for the residents of Stuart, VA.
Language (s): English
Ad Rate: Full Page Mono 4.00
Currency: United States Dollars
COMMUNITY NEWSPAPER

The Enterprise 87088
Owner: Gazette Newspapers Inc.
Editorial: 23125 Camden Way, California, Maryland 20619-2404 **Tel:** 1 301 862-2111
Web site: http://www.somdnews.com/enterprise
Freq: Fri; **Circ:** 16000 Not Audited
Advertising Manager: Al Bailey; **Editor:** Rick Boyd; **Circulation Manager:** Phyllis Dietz; **Community News Editor:** Jesse Yeatman
Profile: The Enterprise is a local weekly newspaper written for the residents of Lexington Park, MD and surrounding areas. The publication covers local news, sports, area schools and community events.
Language (s): English
Ad Rate: Full Page Mono 14.79
Currency: United States Dollars
COMMUNITY NEWSPAPER

Enterprise and Pioneer Newspapers 25381
Owner: Hometown Publishing, LLC
Editorial: 3341 Los Padres Drive, Frazier Park, California 93225 **Tel:** 1 661 245-3794
Web site: http://www.mountainenterprise.com
Circ: 7000 Not Audited
Publisher: Gary Meyer
Language (s): English
COMMUNITY NEWSPAPER

Enterprise Publishing - Seward 756638
Owner: Enterprise Publishing Co.
Editorial: 129 S 6Th St, Seward, Nebraska 68434-2003 **Tel:** 1 402 643-3676
Freq: Weekly
Editor: Jill Martin
Profile: The Enterprise Publishing Co. publishes two newspapers in Seward, Nebraska: The Seward County (NE) Independent and The Sentinel in Friend, NE.
Language (s): English
COMMUNITY NEWSPAPER

Enterprise Publishing Company, Inc. 24620
Owner: Enterprise Publishing Co.
Editorial: 138 N 16th St, Blair, Nebraska 68008-1633 **Tel:** 1 402 426-2121
Email: news@enterprisepub.com **Web site:** http://www.enterprisepub.com
Circ: 9505 Not Audited
Editor: Doug Barber; **Circulation Manager:** Rich Hain; **Advertising Sales Manager:** Lynette Hansen; **Publisher:** Mark Rhoades; **Editor:** Melissa Rice
Language (s): English
COMMUNITY NEWSPAPER

The Ephrata Review 20560
Owner: Lancaster Newspapers Inc.
Editorial: 1 E Main St, Ephrata, Pennsylvania 17522-2713 **Tel:** 1 717 733-6397
Web site: http://ephratareview.com
Freq: Wed; **Circ:** 9000 Not Audited
Circulation Manager: John Betz; **Editor & Publisher:** Andy Fasnacht; **Advertising Sales Manager:** Beverly Kent
Profile: Ephrata Review is a local weekly newspaper written for residents in the Ephrata, PA area. The newspaper covers local news, community events, sports, entertainment, and business. The lead time is two days. The deadline is one week before issue date.
Language (s): English
Ad Rate: Full Page Mono 20.01
Currency: United States Dollars
COMMUNITY NEWSPAPER

The Epoch Times 331140
Editorial: 50 Cragwood Rd Suite 305, South Plainfield, New Jersey 7080 **Tel:** 1 732 548-0380
Email: nj@epochtimes.com **Web site:** http://epochtimes.com
Freq: Fri; **Circ:** 20000 Not Audited
Circulation Manager: Jerry Lin; **Publisher & Editor:** Helen Xu; **Advertising Sales Manager:** Doris Yip
Profile: Epoch Times is a Chinese-American weekly newspaper. They distribute an English as well as a Chinese version.
Language (s): English
Ad Rate: Full Page Mono 15.00
Currency: United States Dollars
COMMUNITY NEWSPAPER

Epoch Times-Chicago Edition 334687
Owner: Tu (Andrew)
Editorial: 3249 S Halsted St, Epoch Times, Chicago, Chicago, Illinois 60608-6605 **Tel:** 1 312 808-9410
Email: midwest@epochtimes.com **Web site:** http://www.theepochtimes.com
Freq: Fri; **Circ:** 12000 Not Audited
Advertising Sales Manager: Stacey Tang; **Publisher:** Andrew Tu; **Editor:** Catherine Wen
Profile: Epoch Times-Chicago Edition is a free newspaper for American and Chinese-American residents and businesses in Chicago. Their mission is to enrich local communities with news and perspectives on current events which are often overlooked by mainstream media, especially by outlets inside China. It strives to present an alternative and uncensored view to the propaganda generated by the People's Republic of China.
Language (s): English
Ad Rate: Full Page Mono 25.70
Currency: United States Dollars
COMMUNITY NEWSPAPER

Erie Reader 877840
Editorial: 1001 State St Ste 901, Erie, Pennsylvania 16501-1829 **Tel:** 1 814 314-9364
Email: contact@eriereader.com **Web site:** http://www.eriereader.com
Freq: Weekly; **Circ:** 10000
Profile: Independent publication serving the residents of Erie, Pennsylvania. Covers everything from news, politics and events, to culture, food, drink and sports.
Language (s): English
COMMUNITY NEWSPAPER

The Erwin Record 22330
Owner: Sandusky Newspapers Inc.
Editorial: 218 Gay St, Erwin, Tennessee 37650-1230 **Tel:** 1 423 743-4112
Email: news@erwinrecord.net **Web site:** http://www.erwinrecord.net
Freq: Weekly; **Circ:** 5000 Not Audited
News Editor: Keeli Parkey; **Publisher:** Keith Whitson
Profile: Erwin Record is a local weekly newspaper serving the residents of Unicoi County, TN. The newspaper covers local and world news, local sports, entertainment, business news, and community events.
Language (s): English
Ad Rate: Full Page Mono 6.50
Currency: United States Dollars
COMMUNITY NEWSPAPER

ESP Publications 24661
Editorial: 1 W Main St Ste 200, Smithtown, New York 11787-2620 **Tel:** 1 631 265-3500
Email: messenger127e@aol.com
Circ: 32500 Not Audited
Publisher & Editor: Phillip Sciarillo
Profile: ESP Publications is a weekly community newspaper publisher serving the residents of Brookhaven, Ronkonkoma, Smithtown, Patchogue and Medford, NY.
Language (s): English
COMMUNITY NEWSPAPER

El Especial 23273
Editorial: 175 Fontainebleau Blvd Ste 2J2, Miami, Florida 33172-4511 **Tel:** 1 305 225-3742
Web site: http://elespecial.com
Freq: Fri; **Circ:** 25000 Not Audited
Publisher: Antonio Ibarria; **Editor:** José Sibaja
Profile: El Especial is a weekly Spanish newspaper. The publication provides the Hispanic community in Miami with local news, business, politics, education, sports and arts & entertainment.
Language (s): Spanish
Ad Rate: Full Page Colour 55.95
Currency: United States Dollars
COMMUNITY NEWSPAPER

El Especialito 21812
Owner: Ibarria Media Group
Editorial: 3711 Hudson Ave, Union City, New Jersey 07087-6015 **Tel:** 1 201 348-1959
Email: news@elespecial.com **Web site:** http://www.elespecialitomk.com
Freq: Tue; **Circ:** 295000 Not Audited
Publisher: Antonio Ibarria
Profile: El Especial provides news, information and entertainment to Latin Americans in New York, New Jersey, and Miami. This paper does not offer black and white advertising.
Language (s): Spanish
Ad Rate: Full Page Colour 23.50
Currency: United States Dollars
COMMUNITY NEWSPAPER

El Especialito 389632
Editorial: 3510 Bergenline Ave, Union City, New Jersey 07087-4775 **Tel:** 1 201 348-1959
Web site: http://www.elespecial.com
Circ: 253463
Language (s): Spanish/Bilingual
COMMUNITY NEWSPAPER

Essex Reporter & Colchester Sun Newspapers 153665
Owner: Lynn Publication
Editorial: 42 Severance Green #108, Colchester, Vermont 5446 **Tel:** 1 802 878-5282
Circ: 19000 Not Audited
Advertising Sales Manager: Wendy Ewing; **Editor:** Jason Starr
Language (s): English
COMMUNITY NEWSPAPER

Estes Park News 318474
Owner: Hazelton (Gary) and Hazelton (Kris)
Editorial: 1191 Woodstock Dr, Estes Park, Colorado 80517-5412 **Tel:** 1 970 586-5800
Email: info@estesparknews.com **Web site:** http://www.estesparknews.com
Freq: Fri; **Circ:** 8000
Profile: Estes Park News provides local news, sports and events coverage for the community of Estes Park, CO and the surrounding areas.
Language (s): English
Ad Rate: Full Page Mono 20.00
Currency: United States Dollars
COMMUNITY NEWSPAPER

La Estrella de Tucson 389686
Owner: Lee Enterprises, Inc.
Editorial: 4850 S Park Ave, Tucson, Arizona 85714-1637 **Tel:** 1 520 573-4419
Email: metro@azstarnet.com **Web site:** http://www.laestrelladetucson.com
Freq: Fri; **Circ:** 40000 Not Audited
Advertising Sales Manager: Vanessa Mendivil; **Editor:** Ernesto Portillo
Profile: La Estrella de Tucson is a weekly newspaper aimed at Spanish-speaking and bilingual Hispanics in southern Arizona. It is published by the Arizona Daily Star and operates from its offices.
Language (s): Spanish
Ad Rate: Full Page Mono 24.20
Currency: United States Dollars
COMMUNITY NEWSPAPER

Eufaula Tribune 18494
Owner: BH Media Group
Editorial: 514 E Barbour St, Eufaula, Alabama 36027-1704 **Tel:** 1 334 687-3506
Email: editorial@eufaulatribune.com **Web site:** http://www.eufaulatribune.com
Freq: Sun; **Circ:** 6350 Not Audited
Circulation Manager: Cindy Pastre; **Advertising Sales Manager:** Dennis Shelley
Profile: Eufaula Tribune is a community newspaper serving the residents of Eufaula and Barbour County, AL. It covers local news, community events, schools, sports, religion, local businesses and features of interest to readers. News submissions for Wednesday's paper must be received on Mondays at 10am CT.
Language (s): English
Ad Rate: Full Page Mono 7.50
Currency: United States Dollars
COMMUNITY NEWSPAPER

Eugene Weekly 22248

Owner: Johnson (Art & Anita)
Editorial: 1251 Lincoln St, Eugene, Oregon 97401-3418 **Tel:** 1 541 484-0519
Email: office@eugeneweekly.com **Web site:** http://www.eugeneweekly.com
Freq: Thu; **Circ:** 39850 Not Audited
Circulation Manager: Paula Hoemann; **Editor:** Ted Taylor
Profile: Eugene Weekly is a local newspaper serving the residents of Eugene, OR and the surrounding area. The newspaper covers local news, opinions, environmental issues, arts & entertainment and community events. It also contains personal and classified ads. Deadlines are Fridays before issue date.
Language (s): English
Ad Rate: Full Page Mono 25.55
Ad Rate: Full Page Colour 1565.00
Currency: United States Dollars
COMMUNITY NEWSPAPER

Eureka Springs Independent

888744

Editorial: 178A W Van Buren, Eureka Springs, Arkansas 72632-3655 **Tel:** 1 479 253-6101
Email: newsdesk@eurekaspringsindependent.com
Web site: http://www.eurekaspringsindependent.com
Freq: Weekly
Editor: Mary Pat Boian
Profile: Eureka Springs Independent is a weekly community newspaper covering local news, events, opinion, sports and features for Eureka Springs, AR and Carroll County, AR residents.
Language (s): English
COMMUNITY NEWSPAPER

The Evangelist 24132

Owner: Albany Catholic Press Association, Inc.
Editorial: 40 N Main Ave, Albany, New York 12203-1481 **Tel:** 1 518 453-6688
Web site: http://www.evangelist.org
Freq: Thu; **Circ:** 50253 Not Audited
Editor: Kate Blain; **Advertising Sales Manager:** John Salvione; **Publisher:** Edward Scharfenberger
Profile: The Evangelist's editorial mission is to provide Catholic news to 14 counties surrounding Albany, NY. The publication is written for members of the Roman Catholic Diocese of Albany, NY. It contains Catholic news, local parish features, daily scripture readings, people in the news and a community calendar.
Language (s): English
Ad Rate: Full Page Mono 23.50
Currency: United States Dollars
COMMUNITY NEWSPAPER

Evanston RoundTable 408205

Owner: Evanston RoundTable LLC
Editorial: 1124 Florence Ave Ste 3, Evanston, Illinois 60202-5829 **Tel:** 1 847 864-7741
Email: info@evanstonroundtable.com **Web site:** http://www.evanstonroundtable.com
Freq: Bi-Weekly; **Circ:** 18000 Not Audited
Publisher and Editor: Mary Helt Gavin
Profile: Evanston RoundTable is a bi-weekly newspaper serving residents of Evanston, IL. It covers local news, traffic, arts & entertainment, business, lifestyle, opinions, schools and sports.
Language (s): English
Ad Rate: Full Page Mono 25.00
Currency: United States Dollars
COMMUNITY NEWSPAPER

Evansville Review 21173

Editorial: 8409 N US Highway 14, Evansville, Wisconsin 53536 **Tel:** 1 608 882-5220
Email: gildner@litewire.net
Freq: Wed; **Circ:** 5400 Not Audited
Language (s): English
Ad Rate: Full Page Mono 6.00
Currency: United States Dollars
COMMUNITY NEWSPAPER

Evening Post Publishing Company 669009

Owner: Evening Post Publishing Co.
Editorial: 104 E Doty Ave, Summerville, South Carolina 29483-6300 **Tel:** 1 843 572-0511
Web site: http://www.journalscene.com
Circ: 22000
Editor: Frank Johnson; **Publisher:** Steve Wagenlander
Language (s): English
COMMUNITY NEWSPAPER

Evening Star 151782

Owner: Copperas Cove Newspapers, Inc.
Editorial: 302 Millers Xing, Harker Heights, Texas 76548-5659 **Tel:** 1 254 699-3998
Email: editor@hheveningstar.com **Web site:** http://hheveningstar.com
Freq: Fri; **Circ:** 5000 Not Audited
Publisher & Editor: Cedric Iglehart; **Advertising Sales Manager:** Cory Wheeler
Profile: Evening Star is a weekly community newspaper serving the residents of Harker Heights, TX.
Language (s): English
Ad Rate: Full Page Mono 7.50
Currency: United States Dollars
COMMUNITY NEWSPAPER

Everett Leader Herald News Gazette 19446

Owner: Curnane
Editorial: 28 Church St, Everett, Massachusetts 02149-2719 **Tel:** 1 617 387-4570
Email: everettleader@comcast.net
Freq: Thu; **Circ:** 15000 Not Audited
Publisher & Editor: Joseph Curnane
Profile: Everett Leader Herald News Gazette is a community newspaper targeted at the residents of Everett, MA.
Language (s): English
Ad Rate: Full Page Mono 12.00
Currency: United States Dollars
COMMUNITY NEWSPAPER

Evergreen Newspapers, Inc.

24856

Owner: Landmark Community Newspapers, Inc.
Editorial: 27902 Meadow Dr Unit 200, Evergreen, Colorado 80439-2106 **Tel:** 1 303 674-5534
Email: news@evergreenco.com **Web site:** http://www.canyoncourier.com
Circ: 10050 Not Audited
Editor: Doug Bell; **Editor:** Ian Neligh; **Publisher:** Tim Zeman
Profile: Evergreen Newspapers, Inc. produces the Clear Creek Courant in Idaho Springs, ID, the High Timber Times in Conifer, CO, the Columbine (CO) Courier and the Canyon Courier in Evergreen, CO, where the main offices are located. The editorial staff is shared and moves between the offices as needed.
Language (s): English
COMMUNITY NEWSPAPER

EWA Publications 25003

Editorial: 2446 E 65th St, Brooklyn, New York 11234-6718 **Tel:** 1 718 763-7034
Email: editman1000@yahoo.com
Circ: 523000 Not Audited
Advertising Sales Manager: Susan Berger;
Publisher: Kenneth Brown; **Editor:** Kevin Browne
Language (s): English
COMMUNITY NEWSPAPER

The Examiner 411953

Owner: Reaud (Wayne)
Editorial: 795 Willow St, Beaumont, Texas 77701-1829 **Tel:** 1 409 832-1400
Email: mail@theexaminer.com **Web site:** http://www.theexaminer.com
Freq: Thu; **Circ:** 30000 Not Audited
Publisher, Editor & Advertising Sales Manager: Don Dodd
Profile: The Examiner is a weekly newspaper serving the residents of Beaumont, TX. It contains local news, community events, sports, schools, businesses and features of interest to local readers.
Language (s): English
Ad Rate: Full Page Mono 23.50
Currency: United States Dollars
COMMUNITY NEWSPAPER

Examiner Media 782973

Owner: Examiner Media
Tel: 1 914 864-0878
Web site: http://www.theexaminernews.com
Freq: Weekly
Publisher: Adam Stone
Profile: Examiner Media is publishes the weekly newspapers the Examiner, the Putnam Examiner, the Northern Westchester Examiner and the White Plains Examiner.
Language (s): English
COMMUNITY NEWSPAPER

El Exito 155307

Owner: Latin American Press
Editorial: 1904 Silver Birch Ln, Las Vegas, Nevada 89104-4252 **Tel:** 1 702 431-1904
Web site: http://www.elexitolasvegas.com
Freq: Fri; **Circ:** 10000 Not Audited
Circulation Manager: Luz Delgado; **Publisher & Editor:** Maggy Ruiz
Profile: El Exito is a free weekly newspaper published in Spanish and English, providing News coverage for the Hispanic community in Las Vegas, NV. It is published on Fridays and is available in print and online.
Language (s): Spanish
Ad Rate: Full Page Mono 18.00
Currency: United States Dollars
COMMUNITY NEWSPAPER

The Exponent 22546

Owner: Schepeler Corporation
Editorial: 160 S Main St, Brooklyn, Michigan 49230
Tel: 1 517 592-2122
Email: news@theexponent.com **Web site:** http://www.theexponent.com
Freq: Tue; **Circ:** 6000 Not Audited
Advertising Sales Manager: Dorothy Booth;
Publisher: Matt Schepeler; **Editor:** Jeff Steers
Profile: The Exponent serves the residents of the Irish Hills, which consists of Brooklyn, Addison and Olmstead counties, MI.
Language (s): English
Ad Rate: Full Page Mono 7.00
Ad Rate: Full Page Colour 10.66
Currency: United States Dollars
COMMUNITY NEWSPAPER

The Expositor 20756

Owner: Smith Newspapers
Editorial: 34 W Bockman Way, Sparta, Tennessee 38583-2015 **Tel:** 1 931 836-3284

Web site: http://spartalive.com
Freq: 2 Times/Week; **Circ:** 5000 Not Audited
Publisher: Jim Shanks; **Editor:** Kim Swindell Wood
Profile: The Expositor is a bi-weekly newspaper written for the residents of Sparta, TN and the surrounding area. The newspaper aims to bring its readers information on local news and events. Send press materials to the editor.
Language (s): English
Ad Rate: Full Page Mono 8.50
Ad Rate: Full Page Colour 150.00
Currency: United States Dollars
COMMUNITY NEWSPAPER

El Extra 23158

Editorial: 1214 Gardenview Dr, Dallas, Texas 75217-4311 **Tel:** 1 214 309-0990
Email: pressrelease@elextranewspaper.com **Web site:** http://www.elextranewspaper.com
Freq: Thu; **Circ:** 20370 Not Audited
Circulation Manager: Joanna Luna; **Publisher & Editor:** Emmy Silva
Profile: El Extra is published weekly for the Hispanic community of the Dallas metropolitan area. The newspaper provides local, national and international news, business, politics and community events. Deadlines are on Tuesdays at 1pm CT.
Language (s): Spanish
Ad Rate: Full Page Mono 23.00
Ad Rate: Full Page Colour 126.38
Currency: United States Dollars
COMMUNITY NEWSPAPER

El Extra 82617

Owner: AIM Media Texas, LLC
Editorial: 1400 E Nolana Ave, McAllen, Texas 78504-6111 **Tel:** 1 956 683-4162
Freq: Fri; **Circ:** 43000 Not Audited
Editor: G. Zulema Baez-Ahumada; **Publisher:** Frank Escobedo; **Editor:** Santos Garcia
Profile: El Extra is a weekly Spanish-language newspaper covering local news and events.
Language (s): Spanish
Ad Rate: Full Page Mono 9.28
Currency: United States Dollars
COMMUNITY NEWSPAPER

Facts 21141

Editorial: 1112 34th Ave, Seattle, Washington 98122-5139 **Tel:** 1 206 324-0552
Web site: http://nwfacts.com
Freq: Wed; **Circ:** 100000 Not Audited
Profile: Facts provides community news to residents of Tacoma and Seattle, WA.
Language (s): English
Ad Rate: Full Page Mono 22.50
Currency: United States Dollars
COMMUNITY NEWSPAPER

Fairchild Flyer 22836

Owner: Journal News Publishing Co.
Editorial: 1 E Bong St Bldg 2285, Fairchild AFB, Washington 99011-9433 **Tel:** 1 509 247-5705
Email: e-connection@fairchild.af.mil **Web site:** http://www.fairchild.af.mil/news/fairchildflyer.asp
Freq: Fri; **Circ:** 7600 Not Audited
Editor: Joseph Buzanowski
Profile: The Fairchild Flyer is written for the Fairchild, Washington airforce base. It provides residents of the base community with information on local news and events in and around the Fairchild Air Force Base. Deadlines are on Fridays.
Language (s): English
Ad Rate: Full Page Mono 7.50
Currency: United States Dollars
COMMUNITY NEWSPAPER

The Fairfax County Times 28063

Owner: Post Community Media, LLC
Editorial: 1920 Association Dr Ste 500, Reston, Virginia 20191-1562 **Tel:** 1 703 437-5400
Web site: http://www.fairfaxtimes.com
Freq: Wed; **Circ:** 102225 Not Audited
Advertising Sales Manager: Marta Wallace
Profile: The Fairfax County Times is a weekly newspaper serving Fairfax County, VA. It is dedicated to providing local news coverage with an emphasis on people, events, sports, businesses, government, real estate and entertainment. Deadlines are at 3pm ET. It was previously published through multiple regional editions, but as of September 2008 has been under a single edition.
Language (s): English
Ad Rate: Full Page Mono 52.00
Ad Rate: Full Page Colour 140.00
Currency: United States Dollars
COMMUNITY NEWSPAPER

Fairfield Towne Crier 217738

Owner: McMillen (Esther)
Editorial: 1594 Stonewall Dr, Newark, Ohio 43055-1725 **Tel:** 1 740 344-7555
Email: freedomptg@roadrunner.com **Web site:** http://www.fairfieldtownecrier.com
Freq: Bi-Weekly; **Circ:** 35000 Not Audited
Editor: Edward Heaton; **Publisher:** Esther McMillen-Heaton
Profile: Fairfield Towne Crier in Newark, OH s a community newspaper covering local news and events. The paper has two editions, the Fairfield Towne Crier and the Eastern Towne Crier, that are published every other week.
Language (s): English
Ad Rate: Full Page Mono 13.00
Currency: United States Dollars
COMMUNITY NEWSPAPER

Fairmont Photo Press 19629

Owner: BuddBay Media LLC
Editorial: 112 E 1st St, Fairmont, Minnesota 56031-2807 **Tel:** 1 507 238-9456
Email: frontdesk@fairmontphotopress.com **Web site:** http://www.fairmontphotopress.com
Freq: Wed; **Circ:** 12140 Not Audited
Advertising Sales Manager: Randy Chirpich; **Editor:** Sherman Kumba
Profile: Fairmont Photo Press is a local weekly newspaper written for the Fairmont, MN, community.
Language (s): English
Ad Rate: Full Page Mono 11.85
Currency: United States Dollars
COMMUNITY NEWSPAPER

Faith West Tennessee 759458

Owner: Diocese of Memphis
Editorial: 5825 Shelby Oaks Dr, Memphis, Tennessee 38134-7316 **Tel:** 1 901 373-1200
Email: fwt.editor@cc.cdom.org **Web site:** http://www.cdom.org
Freq: Weekly; **Circ:** 10000
Publisher: J. Terry Steib
Profile: West Tennessee Catholic is a weekly paper written for the Diocese of Memphis, TN.
Language (s): English
Ad Rate: Full Page Mono 0.36
Currency: United States Dollars
COMMUNITY NEWSPAPER

Falls Church News-Press 21774

Owner: Benton Communications
Editorial: 200 Little Falls St Ste 508, Falls Church, Virginia 22046-4302 **Tel:** 1 703 532-3267
Email: fcnp@fcnp.com **Web site:** http://www.fcnp.com
Freq: Thu; **Circ:** 10000 Not Audited
Circulation Manager: Julio Ictrobo
Profile: Falls Church News-Press is a weekly community newspaper servicing the residents of Falls Church, VA.
Language (s): English
Ad Rate: Full Page Mono 38.50
Currency: United States Dollars
COMMUNITY NEWSPAPER

Fannin Sentinel 828463

Owner: Owen (Elaine) & Owen (James)
Editorial: 29 State St., Blue Ridge, Georgia
Tel: 1 706 258-3406
Email: fanninsentinel.lisag@gmail.com **Web site:** http://fanninsentinel.com
Freq: Weekly
Editor & Publisher: Elaine Owen
Profile: Fannin Sentinel is a community newspaper serving Fannin County, GA, including local news and community events.
Language (s): English
COMMUNITY NEWSPAPER

Farmer's Weekly Review 19097

Owner: Will County Publications, Inc.
Editorial: 100 Manhattan Rd, Joliet, Illinois 60433-2757 **Tel:** 1 815 727-4811
Email: farmersweekly@sbcglobal.net **Web site:** http://www.farmers-weekly-review.com
Freq: Weekly; **Circ:** 13000 Not Audited
Editor & Publisher: Michael Cleary; **Advertising Sales Manager:** Debbie Werner
Profile: Farmer's Weekly Review is written to inform residents of Will County, IL and the surrounding area of local farming news.
Language (s): English
Ad Rate: Full Page Mono 11.25
Currency: United States Dollars
COMMUNITY NEWSPAPER

The Farmville Herald 21048

Owner: Farmville Newsmedia, LLC
Editorial: 114 North St, Farmville, Virginia 23901-1312 **Tel:** 1 434 392-4151
Web site: http://www.farmvilleherald.com
Freq: Fri; **Circ:** 9000 Not Audited
Advertising Sales Manager: Jacqueline Newman
Profile: The Farmville Herald covers local news and events of interest to the community in Farmville, VA and Prince Edward County, VA .
Language (s): English
Ad Rate: Full Page Mono 9.75
Currency: United States Dollars
COMMUNITY NEWSPAPER

Farragut Press 20766

Owner: Republic Newspapers, Inc.
Editorial: 11863 Kingston Pike, Knoxville, Tennessee 37934-3833 **Tel:** 1 865 675-6397
Email: editor@farragutpress.com **Web site:** http://www.farragutpress.com
Freq: Thu; **Circ:** 15000 Not Audited
Publisher & Editor: Dan Barile
Profile: Farragut Press is a local paper providing news to the community of Farragut, TN.
Language (s): English
Ad Rate: Full Page Mono 12.65
Currency: United States Dollars
COMMUNITY NEWSPAPER

The Fayette County Record 20886

Owner: Keilers (Regina Barton)
Editorial: 127 S Washington St, La Grange, Texas 78945-2628 **Tel:** 1 979 968-3155
Web site: http://www.fayettecountyrecord.com
Freq: Fri; **Circ:** 5201 Not Audited
Publisher: Regina Barton Keilers; **Circulation Manager:** Theresia Karstedt; **Editor:** Jeff Wick; **Advertising Sales Manager:** Becky Wiese

Profile: Fayette County Record is a weekly newspaper serving the residents of Fayette and La Grange Counties. It is published every Tuesday and Friday.
Language (s): English
Ad Rate: Full Page Mono 10.10
Currency: United States Dollars
COMMUNITY NEWSPAPER

Fayetteville Free Weekly 324337
Owner: Stephens Media
Editorial: 212 N East Ave, Fayetteville, Arkansas 72701-5225 **Tel:** 1 479 521-4550
Web site: http://www.freeweekly.com
Freq: Thu; **Circ:** 12000 Not Audited
Profile: Fayetteville Free Weekly is a community newspaper written for the residents of Fayetteville, AR.
Language (s): English
Ad Rate: Full Page Mono 9.00
Currency: United States Dollars
COMMUNITY NEWSPAPER

Federal Way Mirror 22808
Owner: Sound Publishing Inc.
Editorial: 31919 1st Ave S Ste 101, Federal Way, Washington 98003-5258 **Tel:** 1 253 925-5565
Email: editor@fedwaymirror.com **Web site:** http://www.federalwaymirror.com
Freq: Sat; **Circ:** 30400 Not Audited
Editor: Carrie Rodriguez
Profile: Federal Way Mirror is a local newspaper that covers local legislation, news and events for residents of Federal Way, WA. Deadlines are Mondays and Wednesdays before issue date. All editorial correspondence should be sent to the street address. All advertising correspondence should be sent to Federal Way Mirror, c/o Sound Publishing, 7869 NE Day Rd., Bainbridge Island, WA 98110. This community newspaper is owned by Sound Publishing, Inc., which produces a variety of weekly newspapers in Washington state; these papers share content, and news releases, as well as calendar listings can be posted online for review by the paper's editorial staff.
Language (s): English
Ad Rate: Full Page Mono 27.50
Currency: United States Dollars
COMMUNITY NEWSPAPER

Fentress Courier 20731
Editorial: 114 White Oak St, Jamestown, Tennessee 38556-4204 **Tel:** 1 931 879-4040
Email: fencourier@twlakes.net **Web site:** http://www.fentresscouriernews.com
Freq: Weekly; **Circ:** 5400 Not Audited
Editor & Publisher: Bill Bowden
Profile: Fentress Courier is a local newspaper written for the residents of Jamestown, TN. The paper covers local news and events.
Language (s): English
Ad Rate: Full Page Mono 5.00
Currency: United States Dollars
COMMUNITY NEWSPAPER

FilAm Star 844945
Owner: Fortune News Media, Inc.
Editorial: 1028 Mission St, San Francisco, California 94103-2813 **Tel:** 1 415 593-5955
Email: admin@filamstar.com **Web site:** http://www.filamstar.net
Profile: FilAm Star is a bi-weekly publication that keeps San Franciscans up-to-date with news and features in the Bay Area and the Philippines. The paper can be found in Asian/American stores, supermarkets and restaurants. The paper's reach extends from Sacramento to all of Silicon Valley. The online edition is updated regularly. It was first published in 2007.
COMMUNITY NEWSPAPER

The Filipino Express 23132
Owner: Filipino Express, Inc.
Editorial: 2711 John F Kennedy Blvd, Jersey City, New Jersey 07306-5712 **Tel:** 1 201 434-1114
Email: filexpress@aol.com **Web site:** http://www.filipinoexpress.com
Freq: Fri; **Circ:** 25000 Not Audited
Publisher & Editor: Lito Gajilan
Profile: The Filipino Express is a weekly publication for the Filipino-American community. The paper brings residents news, opinions, entertainment, real estate/business, sports and classifieds.
Language (s): English
Ad Rate: Full Page Mono 100.00
Currency: United States Dollars
COMMUNITY NEWSPAPER

Filipino Press 509843
Editorial: 600 E 8th St Ste 3, National City, California 91950-2400 **Tel:** 1 619 477-1720
Email: filpress@aol.com **Web site:** http://www.filipinopress.com
Freq: Sat; **Circ:** 25000 Not Audited
Publisher, Editor & Advertising Sales Manager: Susan Delos Santos
Profile: Filipino Press is a weekly newspaper that is written for the Filipino residents in the San Diego area.
Language (s): English
Ad Rate: Full Page Mono 12.69
Currency: United States Dollars
COMMUNITY NEWSPAPER

The Filipino Reporter 23185
Owner: Filipino Reporter Enterprises, Inc.
Editorial: 350 5th Ave, 59th Floor, New York, New York 10118-0600 **Tel:** 1 212 967-5784
Email: filipinoreporter@aol.com **Web site:** http://www.filipinoreporter.us
Freq: Fri; **Circ:** 25000
Publisher & Editor: Bert Pelayo; **Circulation Manager:** Patrick Pelayo; **News Editor:** Edmund Silvestre
Profile: The Filipino Reporter is a weekly newspaper written for Filipino Americans in the tri-state area of New York, New Jersey and Connecticut. The newspaper covers news, entertainment, sports and immigration.
Language (s): English
Ad Rate: Full Page Mono 15.00
Currency: United States Dollars
COMMUNITY NEWSPAPER

Fillmore County Journal 21538
Editorial: 136 Saint Anthony St N, Preston, Minnesota 55965 **Tel:** 1 507 765-2151
Email: news@fillmorecountyjournal.com **Web site:** http://www.fillmorecountyjournal.com
Freq: Mon; **Circ:** 12000 Not Audited
Editor & Publisher: Jason Sethre
Profile: The Fillmore County Journal is a free local newspaper written to share stories and news with the local community.
Language (s): English
Ad Rate: Full Page Mono 14.64
Currency: United States Dollars
COMMUNITY NEWSPAPER

The Fincastle Herald 26716
Owner: Main Street Newspapers, Inc.
Editorial: 9 S Roanoke St, Fincastle, Virginia 24090-3103 **Tel:** 1 540 473-2741
Email: fincastle@ourvalley.org **Web site:** http://www.ourvalley.org
Freq: Wed
Editor: Ed McCoy; **Advertising Sales Manager:** Debbie Starr
Profile: The Fincastle Herald is a local newspaper serving Botetourt County, VA. It includes news, weather, sports and classifieds. Deadlines for the publication are Mondays at 5pm before issue date.
Language (s): English
COMMUNITY NEWSPAPER

Finger Lakes Community Newspapers 24652
Editorial: 109 N Cayuga St, Ithaca, New York 14850-4341 **Tel:** 1 607 277-7000
Email: editor@flcn.org
Circ: 7495 Not Audited
Publisher: Jim Bilinski; **Advertising Sales Manager:** Tom Olson; **Circulation Manager:** Danielle Simoens
Language (s): English
COMMUNITY NEWSPAPER

Fitchburg Star 24253
Editorial: 133 Enterprise Dr, Verona, Wisconsin 53593-9122 **Tel:** 1 608 845-9559
Email: fitchburgstar@wcinet.com **Web site:** http://www.unifiednewsgroup.com/fitchburg_star
Freq: Bi-Weekly; **Circ:** 7250 Not Audited
Editor: Kurt Gutkencht; **Advertising Sales Manager:** Lisa Kersten; **Circulation Manager:** Diane Odegard
Profile: Fitchburg Star is a community newspaper written for the residents of Fitchburg, WI. The paper covers local news, events, weather, sports, business and arts & entertainment.
Language (s): English
Ad Rate: Full Page Mono 9.10
Currency: United States Dollars
COMMUNITY NEWSPAPER

The Flagship 22951
Owner: Flagship
Editorial: 258 Granby St, Norfolk, Virginia 23510-1812 **Tel:** 1 757 222-3990
Email: news@flagshipnews.com **Web site:** http://www.norfolknavyflagship.com
Freq: Thu; **Circ:** 40000 Not Audited
Publisher: Laura Baxter
Profile: The Flagship is a weekly newspaper that serves members of the U.S. Navy and their families in the Norfolk, VA area it includes the latest news and events of the Navy and other branches of the military.
Language (s): English
Ad Rate: Full Page Mono 19.09
Currency: United States Dollars
COMMUNITY NEWSPAPER

Flagstaff Live 725254
Editorial: 1751 S Thompson St, Flagstaff, Arizona 86001-8716 **Tel:** 1 928 779-1877
Web site: http://www.flaglive.com
Freq: Thu; **Circ:** 7500
Publisher: Don Rowley; **Editor:** Andrew Wisniewski
Profile: Flagstaff Live is a weekly community newspaper for the residents of Flagstaff, AZ and the surrounding communities.
Language (s): English
Ad Rate: Full Page Mono 5.41
Ad Rate: Full Page Colour 6.49
Currency: United States Dollars
COMMUNITY NEWSPAPER

Flashes 22593
Editorial: 115 Grand St, Eaton Rapids, Michigan 48827 **Tel:** 1 517 663-2361
Email: flashesnews@sbcglobal.net
Freq: Tue; **Circ:** 7927 Not Audited
Publisher: Rod McLaughlin
Profile: Flashes Shoppers Guide & News provides local news coverage for the Eaton Rapids, MI area. Press releases and editorial submissions should relate to the Eaton Rapids, MI area.
Language (s): English
Ad Rate: Full Page Mono 8.15
Currency: United States Dollars
COMMUNITY NEWSPAPER

Flathead Beacon 484225
Owner: Povich (Maury)
Editorial: 217 Main St, Kalispell, Montana 59901-4453 **Tel:** 1 406 257-9220
Email: news@flatheadbeacon.com **Web site:** http://www.flatheadbeacon.com
Freq: Wed; **Circ:** 25000 Not Audited
Circulation Manager: Rob Ford
Profile: Flathead Beacon is a weekly community newspaper for the residents of Flathead Valley, MT and the surrounding areas. The paper does not offer black and white ads.
Language (s): English
Ad Rate: Full Page Mono 18.33
Ad Rate: Full Page Colour 25.00
Currency: United States Dollars
COMMUNITY NEWSPAPER

Florida Chinese News 152859
Owner: Florida Chinese News Inc.
Editorial: 3325 Griffin Rd Ste 193, Fort Lauderdale, Florida 33312-5500 **Tel:** 1 954 966-5264
Email: info@floridachinese.com **Web site:** http://www.floridachinesenews.com
Freq: Thu; **Circ:** 9000 Not Audited
Publisher & Editor: Raymond Ching
Profile: Florida Chinese News is a local newspaper written for the Chinese community of Fort Lauderdale, FL.
Language (s): English
Ad Rate: Full Page Mono 20.00
Currency: United States Dollars
COMMUNITY NEWSPAPER

Florida Courier 397550
Owner: Central Florida Communications Group Inc.
Tel: 1 813 620-1300
Email: news@flcourier.com **Web site:** http://www.flcourier.com
Freq: Fri; **Circ:** 88438 Not Audited
Publisher: Charles Cherry; **Editor:** Jenise Morgan
Profile: Florida Courier is written for African American residents in Tampa, FL. It contains state and local news, editorials, investigative reports and entertainment stories. Press releases must be sent via e-mail to be considered for publication.
Language (s): English
Ad Rate: Full Page Mono 85.00
Currency: United States Dollars
COMMUNITY NEWSPAPER

Florida Sentinel-Bulletin 18766
Editorial: 2207 E 21st Ave, Tampa, Florida 33605-2043 **Tel:** 1 813 248-1921
Email: editor@flsentinel.com **Web site:** http://flsentinel.com
Freq: Fri; **Circ:** 21600
Circulation Manager: Harold Adams; **Publisher:** Sybil Kay Andrews-Wells; **Editor:** Gwendolyn Hayes
Profile: Florida Sentinel Bulletin is a local newspaper serving the African American community in the Tampa, FL area. The editorial mission is to keep the community informed of news and events relevant to African Americans. The newspaper covers both local and national news. Florida Sentinel Bulletin is published twice a week on Tuesday and Friday.
Language (s): English
Ad Rate: Full Page Mono 14.00
Currency: United States Dollars
COMMUNITY NEWSPAPER

The Florida Star 18787
Tel: 1 904 766-8834
Email: info@thefloridastar.com **Web site:** http://www.thefloridastar.com
Freq: Fri; **Circ:** 10500 Not Audited
Advertising Sales Manager: Hannah Kirkwood
Profile: The Florida Star is a local newspaper serving the African-American community in Jacksonville, FL.
Language (s): English
Ad Rate: Full Page Mono 16.50
Currency: United States Dollars
COMMUNITY NEWSPAPER

Florida Sun 155896
Editorial: 2700 Catalina Dr, Orlando, Florida 32805-5808 **Tel:** 1 407 219-9285
Email: sunreview@aol.com **Web site:** http://www.floridasunreview.com
Freq: Thu; **Circ:** 10000 Not Audited
Circulation Manager: Sandi Lewis; **Publisher & Editor:** James Madison; **Advertising Sales Manager:** Thomas Owens
Profile: Florida Sun is published weekly for the residents of Orlando, FL and surrounding areas. The newspaper covers Local News, Entertainment and Community Events.
Language (s): English
Ad Rate: Full Page Mono 17.50
Currency: United States Dollars
COMMUNITY NEWSPAPER

Florida Weekly - Bonita Springs 947720
Owner: Florida Media Group LLC
Editorial: 9051 Tamiami Trl N Ste 202, Naples, Florida 34108-2520 **Tel:** 1 239 325-1960
Email: news@floridaweekly.com **Web site:** http://bonitasprings.floridaweekly.com/
Freq: Weekly
Publisher: Shelley Hobbs
Profile: Florida Weekly is published for the residents of Bonita Springs, FL. It covers news, entertainment, dining, business and real estate.
Language (s): English
COMMUNITY NEWSPAPER

Florida Weekly - Charlotte County 593407
Owner: Florida Media Group LLC
Editorial: 1205 Elizabeth St Ste G, Punta Gorda, Florida 33950-6054 **Tel:** 1 239 333-2135
Email: news@floridaweekly.com **Web site:** http://charlotte.floridaweekly.com
Freq: Weekly; **Circ:** 12800
Publisher: Michael Hearn
Profile: Charlotte County Florida Weekly is a community newspaper written for residents of Punta Gorda and Southwest Florida. It covers local governments, politics, arts, nightlife, social scene, events, features and investigative reports.
Language (s): English
Ad Rate: Full Page Mono 15.68
Currency: United States Dollars
COMMUNITY NEWSPAPER

Florida Weekly - Fort Myers 469646
Owner: Florida Media Group LLC
Editorial: 4300 Ford St Ste 105, Fort Myers, Florida 33916-9318 **Tel:** 1 239 333-2135
Email: news@floridaweekly.com **Web site:** http://fortmyers.floridaweekly.com
Freq: Thu; **Circ:** 63000 Not Audited
Publisher: Angela Schivinski
Profile: Florida Weekly is published for the residents of Fort Myers, FL and West Palm Peach, FL. It covers news, entertainment, dining, business and real estate.
Language (s): English
Ad Rate: Full Page Mono 30.00
Currency: United States Dollars
COMMUNITY NEWSPAPER

Florida Weekly - Naples 545986
Owner: Florida Media Group LLC
Editorial: 9051 Tamiami Trl N Ste 202, Naples, Florida 34108-2520 **Tel:** 1 239 325-1960
Email: news@floridaweekly.com **Web site:** http://naples.floridaweekly.com
Freq: Thu; **Circ:** 18000
Publisher: Shelley Hobbs
Profile: Naples Florida Weekly, launched October 2, 2008, is a weekly newspaper written for residents of Naples and Collier County, FL. It covers news, arts & entertainment, dining, regional business and real estate.
Language (s): English
Ad Rate: Full Page Mono 15.44
Currency: United States Dollars
COMMUNITY NEWSPAPER

Florida Weekly - Palm Beach 947717
Owner: Florida Media Group LLC
Editorial: 11380 Prosperity Farms Rd Ste 103, Palm Beach Gardens, Florida 33410-3450 **Tel:** 1 561 904-6470
Email: news@floridaweekly.com **Web site:** http://palmbeach.floridaweekly.com
Freq: Weekly
Publisher: Michelle Noga
Profile: Florida Weekly is published for the residents of Palm Beach, FL and West Palm Peach, FL. It covers news, entertainment, dining, business and real estate.
Language (s): English
COMMUNITY NEWSPAPER

The Floyd County Times 19389
Owner: Civitas Media
Editorial: 263 S Central Ave, Prestonsburg, Kentucky 41653-1958 **Tel:** 1 606 886-8506
Email: news@floydcountytimes.com **Web site:** http://www.floydcountytimes.com
Freq: Fri; **Circ:** 5200 Not Audited
Advertising Sales Manager: Barb Marshall
Profile: The Floyd County Times is a local newspaper serving the residents of Floyd County, KY. It includes news, weather, sports and classifieds.
Language (s): English
Ad Rate: Full Page Mono 9.00
Ad Rate: Full Page Colour 900.00
Currency: United States Dollars
COMMUNITY NEWSPAPER

The FM Extra 893740
Owner: New Century Press
Editorial: 810 4th Ave S Ste 120, Moorhead, Minnesota 56560-2800 **Tel:** 1 218 284-1288
Email: extra@ncppub.com **Web site:** http://thefmextra.com
Freq: Weekly; **Circ:** 9037
Editor: Tammy Finney
Profile: The Extra is a popular weekly newspaper covers Fargo, ND and Moorhead, MN into eastern North Dakota, Grand Forks, and the Minnesota lakes country.
Language (s): English
Ad Rate: Full Page Mono 6.50
Ad Rate: Full Page Colour 500.00
Currency: United States Dollars
COMMUNITY NEWSPAPER

Focus 257859
Owner: Roberti
Editorial: 2 Leslie Dr, Brodheadsville, Pennsylvania 18322-9724 **Tel:** 1 570 992-9300
Email: thefocus@ptd.net **Web site:** http://www.focuscommunitynewspaper.com
Freq: Fri; **Circ:** 25000 Not Audited
Publisher & Editor: Pauline Roberti
Profile: Focus is a publication for residents in Monroe County, PA. It covers local news, dining, entertainment, health and fitness, home improvement, real estate and automotive. It is distributed to more than 40 towns.
Language (s): English
Ad Rate: Full Page Mono 9.00
Currency: United States Dollars
COMMUNITY NEWSPAPER

Folio Weekly 21952
Editorial: 45 W Bay St, Jacksonville, Florida 32202-3600 **Tel:** 1 904 260-9770
Email: themail@folioweekly.com **Web site:** http://www.folioweekly.com
Freq: Tue; **Circ:** 51000 Not Audited
Profile: Folio Weekly is published for the residents of Northeastern Florida. The publication provides news, arts and entertainment and other feature articles.
Language (s): English
Ad Rate: Full Page Mono 35.00
Currency: United States Dollars
COMMUNITY NEWSPAPER

Fontana Herald News 21626
Owner: Century Group (The)
Editorial: 16981 Foothill Blvd, Ste N, Fontana, California 92335-3573 **Tel:** 1 909 822-2231
Web site: http://www.fontanaheraldnews.com
Freq: Fri; **Circ:** 11500 Not Audited
Editor: Russell Ingold
Profile: Fontana Herald News is a local newspaper serving the residents of Fontana, CA. It includes information on local news, weather, sports, business, and entertainment. Deadlines for the publication are two days before issue date.
Language (s): English
Ad Rate: Full Page Mono 19.65
Currency: United States Dollars
COMMUNITY NEWSPAPER

The Foothills Focus 584271
Owner: The Foothills Focus, LLC.
Editorial: 46641 N Black Canyon Hwy, New River, Arizona 85087-6941 **Tel:** 1 623 465-5808
Email: foothillsfocus@qwestoffice.net **Web site:** http://www.thefoothillsfocus.com
Freq: Wed; **Circ:** 30000
Editor: Elizabeth Medora
Profile: The Foothills Focus offers local news, sports and events to residents of the northeast and northwest Valley communities in Arizona, including Anthem, Cave Creek, Carefree, Desert Hills, Diamond Creek Estates, Dove Valley Estates, Dove Valley Ranch, Mountain Gate, New River, North Phoenix, North Scottsdale, Tramonto, Tatum Ranch and Tatum Highlands.
Language (s): English
Ad Rate: Full Page Mono 43.70
Currency: United States Dollars
COMMUNITY NEWSPAPER

The Foothills Sun-Gazette 70075
Editorial: 120 N E St, Exeter, California 93221-1729 **Tel:** 1 559 592-3171
Email: news@thesungazette.com **Web site:** http://www.thesungazette.com
Freq: Wed; **Circ:** 21225 Not Audited
Advertising Sales Manager: Syble Davis; **Publisher & Editor:** Reggie Ellis
Profile: The Foothills Sun-Gazette is a weekly newspaper serving the foothill communities of Exeter, CA. The publication provides information on community news, events, sports, business and education. Deadlines are on Tuesdays at noon ET.
Language (s): English
Ad Rate: Full Page Mono 12.93
Currency: United States Dollars
COMMUNITY NEWSPAPER

The Foothills Trader 257358
Tel: 1 860 489-3121
Web site: http://www.foothillstrader.com
Freq: Weekly; **Circ:** 60000 Not Audited
Profile: Serves Northwest Connecticut and the Farmington Valley. Provides information on deals in merchandise for sale, autos and real estate.
Language (s): English
COMMUNITY NEWSPAPER

The Forecaster 22178
Owner: Lewiston Daily Sun Inc.
Editorial: 5 Fundy Rd, Falmouth, Maine 04105-1774 **Tel:** 1 207 781-3661
Email: editor@theforecaster.net **Web site:** http://www.theforecaster.net
Freq: Weekly; **Circ:** 69500 Not Audited
Editor: Mo Mehlsak; **Publisher:** Karen Rajotte
Profile: The Forecaster provides local coverage to the Greater Portland, ME area. It publishes the Forecaster North, Forecaster South, Forecaster Portland City and Forecaster Mid-Coast Editions on a weekly basis.
Language (s): English
COMMUNITY NEWSPAPER

Forest Blade Publishing Company 25213
Owner: Smith Newspapers
Editorial: 416 W Moring St, Swainsboro, Georgia 30401-3177 **Tel:** 1 478 237-9971
Email: news@emanuelcountylive.com **Web site:** http://emanuelcountylive.com
Circ: 15985 Not Audited
Publisher: Gail Williamson
Language (s): English
COMMUNITY NEWSPAPER

Forks Forum 21110
Owner: Sound Publishing
Editorial: 490 S Forks Ave, Forks, Washington 98331-9155 **Tel:** 1 360 374-3311
Email: editor@forksforum.com **Web site:** http://www.forksforum.com
Freq: Thu; **Circ:** 5000 Not Audited
Editor: Christi Baron
Profile: Forks Forum is a local newspaper serving the residents of Forks, WA. It includes information on local news, weather, sports, business and entertainment. This community newspaper is owned by Sound Publishing, Inc., which produces a variety of weekly newspapers in Washington state; these papers share content, and news releases, as well as calendar listings can be posted online for review by the paper's editorial staff.
Language (s): English
Ad Rate: Full Page Mono 10.25
Currency: United States Dollars
COMMUNITY NEWSPAPER

Fort Bend Star 76613
Editorial: 3944 Bluebonnet Dr, Stafford, Texas 77477-3952 **Tel:** 1 281 690-4200
Email: editor@fortbendstar.com **Web site:** http://www.fortbendstar.com
Freq: Wed; **Circ:** 62094 Not Audited
Advertising Sales Manager: Michael Frederickson
Profile: Fort Bend Star is published weekly for the residents of Fort Bend County, TX. The newspaper covers local news, sports, business news, education, arts & entertainment and community events.
Language (s): English
Ad Rate: Full Page Mono 23.50
Ad Rate: Full Page Colour 3960.50
Currency: United States Dollars
COMMUNITY NEWSPAPER

The Fort Bliss Bugle 472730
Owner: Laven Publishing Co.
Tel: 1 915 568-4088
Email: fortblissbugle@gmail.com **Web site:** http://fortblissbugle.com/
Freq: Thu; **Circ:** 15000 Not Audited
Publisher: Susan Laven
Profile: The Fort Bliss Bugle is a free, weekly newspaper providing news and information on the Fort Bliss military base in Fort Bliss, TX. Advertising for the paper is handled by Laven Publishing in El Paso, TX.
Language (s): English
Ad Rate: Full Page Mono 22.44
Currency: United States Dollars
COMMUNITY NEWSPAPER

Fort Campbell Courier 257197
Editorial: 2574 23rd St, Fort Campbell, Kentucky 42223-5307 **Tel:** 1 270 798-6090
Email: campbell.courier.editor@gmail.com **Web site:** http://www.fortcampbellcourier.com
Freq: Thu; **Circ:** 24000 Not Audited
Publisher: Bob Jenkins
Profile: Fort Campbell Courier is a local newspaper that serves members of the Army in Fort Campbell, KY.
Language (s): English
Ad Rate: Full Page Mono 12.00
Currency: United States Dollars
COMMUNITY NEWSPAPER

Fort Drum Mountaineer 22073
Editorial: 10012 S Riva Ridge Loop, Fort Drum, New York 13602-5492 **Tel:** 1 315 772-5469
Email: drum.pao@conus.army.mil **Web site:** http://www.drum.army.mil
Freq: Thu; **Circ:** 10000 Not Audited
Circulation Manager: Laurie Danesha
Profile: The Fort Drum Mountaineer is a local newspaper serving the military and their families in Fort Drum, NY. Contact via the form.
Language (s): English
Ad Rate: Full Page Mono 24.55
Ad Rate: Full Page Colour 79.13
Currency: United States Dollars
COMMUNITY NEWSPAPER

Fort Gordon Globe 473071
Owner: U.S. Army Garrison
Editorial: 307 Chamberlain Ave Bldg 33720, Room 382, Fort Gordon, Georgia 30905-5730
Tel: 1 706 791-7069
Web site: http://www.fortgordonglobe.com
Freq: Fri; **Circ:** 18000 Not Audited
Editor: Wilson Rivera
Profile: Fort Gordon Globe is a free weekly civilian enterprise newspaper published for all personnel at Fort Gordon, GA.
Language (s): English
Ad Rate: Full Page Mono 10.75
Currency: United States Dollars
COMMUNITY NEWSPAPER

Fort Hood Herald 232058
Owner: Mayborn Enterprises
Editorial: 1809 Florence Rd, Killeen, Texas 76541-8977 **Tel:** 1 254 634-2125
Email: news@kdhnews.com **Web site:** http://kdhnews.com
Freq: Daily; **Circ:** 40000 Not Audited
Circulation Manager: Cottril Dickerson; **Advertising Sales Manager:** Tamika Galmore; **Editor:** Vanessa Lynch
Profile: Fort Hood Herald is a weekly newspaper serving the military personnel of Fort Hood and residents of Kileen, TX. In addition to newsstand availability, the paper is also inserted into the Killeen (TX) Daily Herald, with which it shares offices.
Language (s): English
Ad Rate: Full Page Mono 8.73
Currency: United States Dollars
COMMUNITY NEWSPAPER

Fort Hood Sentinel 20968
Owner: Mayborn Enterprises
Editorial: Fort Hood U.S. Army Base, 1001 Rim W105 Corps Public Affairs Office, Fort Hood, Texas 76544 **Tel:** 1 254 287-2436
Email: usarmy.hood.iii-corps.mbx.pao@mail.mil **Web site:** http://www.forthoodsentinel.com
Freq: Thu; **Circ:** 26500 Not Audited
Editor: Todd Pruden
Profile: Fort Hood Sentinel is a free, weekly newspaper serving military personnel and civilian employees and residents of the U.S. Army Base in Fort Hood, TX.
Language (s): English
Ad Rate: Full Page Mono 12.00
Currency: United States Dollars
COMMUNITY NEWSPAPER

The Fort Huachuca Scout 18599
Owner: Aerotech News and Review Inc.
Editorial: 3015 Carnahan St, Public Affairs Office - Building 21115, Fort Huachuca, Arizona 85613-5040 **Tel:** 1 520 533-1987
Email: kenneth.a.robinson@us.army.mil **Web site:** http://www.aerotechnews.com/forthuachuca/
Freq: Thu; **Circ:** 8700 Not Audited
Editor: Amy Sunseri
Profile: The Fort Huachuca Scout is a local weekly newspaper published and written by and for the U.S. Army community of Fort Huachuca, AZ. The paper covers local news, event listings and a variety of general interest articles. Since it is a military publication, some e-mail may be rejected due to security measures.
Language (s): English
Ad Rate: Full Page Mono 7.75
Currency: United States Dollars
COMMUNITY NEWSPAPER

Fort Jackson Leader 245019
Owner: Morris Multimedia, Inc.
Tel: 1 803 751-7045
Email: fjleader@gmail.com **Web site:** http://www.fortjacksonleader.com
Freq: Thu; **Circ:** 15000 Not Audited
Publisher: Mike Mischner
Profile: Fort Jackson Leader is a military newspaper in Camden, SC. The paper covers community news, events and sports.
Language (s): English
Ad Rate: Full Page Mono 14.70
Currency: United States Dollars
COMMUNITY NEWSPAPER

Fort Leavenworth Lamp 257713
Owner: GateHouse Media Inc.
Editorial: 290 Grant Ave, Fort Leavenworth, Kansas 66027-1254 **Tel:** 1 913 684-5267
Email: editor@ftleavenworthlamp.com **Web site:** http://www.ftleavenworthlamp.com
Freq: Thu; **Circ:** 8000 Not Audited
Publisher: Sandy Hattock; **Editor:** Robert Kerr
Profile: Fort Leavenworth Lamp is a weekly newspaper written for residents of Fort Leavenwoth, KS, including military personnel and their family members. The newspaper covers local news, community events, perspectives, entertainment, and health. Editorial deadlines are on Fridays prior to the issue date. Contact the Liberty Group Publishing office (913)-758-1334 for advertising information.
Language (s): English
Ad Rate: Full Page Mono 9.70
Currency: United States Dollars
COMMUNITY NEWSPAPER

Fort Lee Traveller 22438
Owner: Military Newspapers of Virginia
Editorial: 114 Charlotte Ave Ste A, Colonial Heights, Virginia 23834-3007 **Tel:** 1 804 526-8656
Email: armyfortlee.pao@mail.mil **Web site:** http://www.fortleetraveller.com
Freq: Thu; **Circ:** 11000 Not Audited
Publisher: Laura Baxter
Profile: Fort Lee Traveller is written for soldiers, civilians, family members and retirees of the U.S. Army. It covers news and feature articles about the Fort Lee, VA community.
Language (s): English
Ad Rate: Full Page Mono 12.24
Currency: United States Dollars
COMMUNITY NEWSPAPER

Fort Mill Times 20625
Owner: McClatchy Newspapers
Editorial: 422 Highway 21, Fort Mill, South Carolina 29715-1739
Email: news@fortmilltimes.com **Web site:** http://www.heraldonline.com/news/local/community/fort-mill-times/
Freq: Wed; **Circ:** 24000 Not Audited
Editor: Michael Harrison
Profile: Fort Mill Times is a local newspaper for Fort Mill, Tega Cay and Indian Land, SC. The publication features local and national news, weather, sports, business and entertainment. The newspaper also includes news about local schools, government, community and church activities. Deadlines are on Fridays at noon ET.
Language (s): English
Ad Rate: Full Page Mono 25.00
Ad Rate: Full Page Colour 1257.00
Currency: United States Dollars
COMMUNITY NEWSPAPER

Fort Polk Guardian 69981
Owner: News Leader, Inc.
Editorial: 7033 Magnolia Dr., Leesville, Louisiana 71459-5329 **Tel:** 1 337 531-4033
Email: kimberly.reischling@us.army.mil **Web site:** http://www.fortpolkguardian.com
Freq: Fri; **Circ:** 13000 Not Audited
Editor: Jean Dubiel
Profile: Fort Polk Guardian is a local newspaper serving military personnel and their families in Fort Polk, LA. Press releases should go to the Editor in Chief directly.
Language (s): English
Ad Rate: Full Page Mono 23.87
Currency: United States Dollars
COMMUNITY NEWSPAPER

Fort Worth Weekly 22823
Editorial: 3311 Hamilton Ave, Fort Worth, Texas 76107-1877 **Tel:** 1 817 321-9700
Email: feedback@fwweekly.com **Web site:** http://www.fwweekly.com
Freq: Wed; **Circ:** 37954 Not Audited
Publisher: Lee Newquist
Profile: Fort Worth Weekly serves the residents of Fort Worth, TX. It provides coverage of news, sports, entertainment and other lifestyle stories.
Language (s): English
Ad Rate: Full Page Mono 32.09
Currency: United States Dollars
COMMUNITY NEWSPAPER

Forum Publishing Group, Inc. 24781
Owner: Sun Sentinel
Editorial: 1701 Green Rd, Pompano Beach, Florida 33064-1074 **Tel:** 1 954 698-6397
Web site: http://www.sun-sentinel.com/forum-publishing
Circ: 599098 Not Audited
Editor: Kari Barnett; **Editor:** Alan Goch
Profile: Forum Publishing Group is a community newspaper chain publishing 32 newspapers in Florida regions.
Language (s): English
COMMUNITY NEWSPAPER

Forum South 20285
Owner: BJP Publications
Editorial: 15519 Lahn St, Howard Beach, New York 11414-2858 **Tel:** 1 718 845-3221
Email: forumwest@gmail.com **Web site:** http://theforumnewsgroup.com
Freq: Thu; **Circ:** 60000 Not Audited
Publisher: Patricia Adams
Profile: Forum South is a free weekly newspaper serving Queens County, NY. It offers local news, world events, lifestyle topics, food, health, sports and education. Deadlines are on Mondays.
Language (s): English
Ad Rate: Full Page Mono 40.00
Currency: United States Dollars
COMMUNITY NEWSPAPER

The Forward Newspapers 21915
Owner: Forward Association (The)
Editorial: 125 Maiden Ln, New York, New York 10038-4912 **Tel:** 1 212 889-8200
Email: website@forward.com **Web site:** http://www.forward.com
Freq: Fri; **Circ:** 29428 Not Audited
Profile: The Forward began publishing in 1897 as a daily Yiddish newspaper, but now publishes weekly on Fridays, with a Yiddish version that publishes bi-weekly. The paper still publishes in Yiddish and began an English version in 1990. The newspaper covers news, politics and culture in the Jewish world. Please ONLY send press materials with a Jewish angle. Publications were previously known as The Jewish Daily Forward.
Language (s): English
COMMUNITY NEWSPAPER

Foster City Islander 21598
Editorial: 1185 Chess Dr Ste B, Foster City, California 94404-1109 **Tel:** 1 650 574-5952
Freq: Wed; **Circ:** 6000 Not Audited
Publisher & Editor: Marge Felser
Profile: The Foster City Islander is a local newspaper serving the residents of Foster City, CA. It includes information on local news, weather, sports, business, and entertainment.
Language (s): English
Ad Rate: Full Page Mono 15.00
Currency: United States Dollars
COMMUNITY NEWSPAPER

United States of America

Foto News
21376

Owner: Journal Community Publishing Group
Editorial: 807 E 1st St, Merrill, Wisconsin 54452-2412
Tel: 1 715 536-7121
Email: tschreiber@mmclocal.com **Web site:** http://www.merrillfotonews.com
Freq: Wed; **Circ:** 16400 Not Audited
Editor: Collin Lueck
Profile: Foto News is a weekly community newspaper written for residents in Merrill, WI and surrounding areas.
Language (s): English
Ad Rate: Full Page Mono 25.40
Currency: United States Dollars
COMMUNITY NEWSPAPER

The Franklin County Times
18529

Owner: Franklin County Newspapers Inc.
Editorial: 14131 Highway 43, Russellville, Alabama 35653-2847 **Tel:** 1 256 332-1881
Web site: http://www.franklincountytimes.com
Freq: Sat; **Circ:** 13000 Not Audited
Advertising Sales Manager: Peggy Hyde; **Publisher & Editor:** Jonathan Willis
Profile: Franklin County Times is a newspaper serving the residents of Franklin County, Alabama. The publication offers articles on local and national news, sports, and events. The lead time for Franklin County Times is two days.
Language (s): English
Ad Rate: Full Page Mono 12.07
Currency: United States Dollars
COMMUNITY NEWSPAPER

Franklin Favorite
19340

Owner: Paxton Media Group
Editorial: 103 N High St, Franklin, Kentucky 42134-1801 **Tel:** 1 270 586-4481
Web site: http://www.franklinfavorite.com
Freq: Thu; **Circ:** 5500
Circulation Manager: Brian Davis; **Advertising Sales Manager:** Betty Gentry; **Editor:** Brian Hancock
Profile: Franklin Favorite is a weekly newspaper for the residents of Franklin, Kentucky, and south-central Kentucky. The publication offers articles on local news, events, sports and editorials.
Language (s): English
Ad Rate: Full Page Mono 8.90
Currency: United States Dollars
COMMUNITY NEWSPAPER

The Franklin News-Post
21064

Owner: BH Media Group
Editorial: 310 S Main St, Rocky Mount, Virginia 24151-1711 **Tel:** 1 540 483-5113
Email: info@franklinnews-post.com **Web site:** http://www.thefranklinnewspost.com
Freq: Fri; **Circ:** 8000 Not Audited
Profile: The Franklin News-Post is written for the residents of Franklin County, VA and surrounding communities. It covers local news and events.
Language (s): English
Ad Rate: Full Page Mono 8.70
Currency: United States Dollars
COMMUNITY NEWSPAPER

Franklin Press
22639

Owner: Community Newspapers Inc.
Editorial: 40 Depot St, Franklin, North Carolina 28734-2704 **Tel:** 1 828 524-2010
Email: news@thefranklinpress.com **Web site:** http://www.thefranklinpress.com
Freq: Fri; **Circ:** 7093 Not Audited
Publisher: Rachel Hoskins; **News Editor:** Michael Lewis; **Editor:** Jessica Waters
Profile: Franklin Press is a local newspaper written for the residents of Franklin, NC. The newspaper covers community news and events, sports, arts & entertainment and weather.
Language (s): English
Ad Rate: Full Page Mono 15.45
Ad Rate: Full Page Colour 200.00
Currency: United States Dollars
COMMUNITY NEWSPAPER

The Franklin Square Bulletin
23083

Owner: Nassau Border Papers, Inc.
Editorial: 139 Tulip Ave, Floral Park, New York 11001
Tel: 1 516 775-7700
Freq: Thu; **Circ:** 8700 Not Audited
Editor and Publisher: Carla Cohen
Profile: Franklin Square Bulletin is a weekly newspaper written for the residents of Franklin Square, New York. The publication offers articles on local news and events.
Language (s): English
Ad Rate: Full Page Mono 12.38
Currency: United States Dollars
COMMUNITY NEWSPAPER

The Franklin Sun
23199

Owner: Hanna Publishing Co., Inc.
Editorial: 514 Prairie St, Winnsboro, Louisiana 71295-2737 **Tel:** 1 318 435-4521
Web site: http://www.franklinsun.com
Freq: Wed; **Circ:** 6200 Not Audited
Publisher: Mary Sue Hanna; **Advertising Sales Manager:** Monica Huff; **Editor:** Matt Reynolds
Profile: Franklin Sun is a newspaper serving the residents of Franklin Parish, Louisiana. The publication offers articles on local news and government, events, and sports. The lead time for Franklin Sun is three to four days before publication. Deadlines for the publication are noon CT on the Monday before publication.
Language (s): English

Ad Rate: Full Page Mono 6.50
Ad Rate: Full Page Colour 1214.00
Currency: United States Dollars
COMMUNITY NEWSPAPER

The Franklin Times
19986

Owner: Franklin County Newspapers, Inc.
Editorial: 109 S Bickett Blvd, Louisburg, North Carolina 27549 **Tel:** 1 919 496-6503
Email: news@thefranklintimes.com **Web site:** http://www.thefranklintimes.com
Freq: Sat; **Circ:** 7700 Not Audited
Publisher: Gary Cunard; **Editor:** Asher Johnson
Profile: The Franklin Times is published weekly for residents of Louisburg, NC and surrounding areas. The newspaper provides information on local news, government, weather and community events. Deadlines are on Mondays and Thursdays at noon ET.
Language (s): English
Ad Rate: Full Page Mono 11.75
Currency: United States Dollars
COMMUNITY NEWSPAPER

Franklin Township Informer
150749

Owner: Franklin Township Civic League Inc.
Editorial: 8822 Southeastern Ave, Indianapolis, Indiana 46239-1341 **Tel:** 1 317 862-1774
Web site: http://www.ftcivicleague.org
Freq: Wed; **Circ:** 5000 Not Audited
Publisher & Editor: Kasie Foster
Profile: The Franklin Township Informer in Indianapolis, IN is a weekly community newspaper that covers local news and events.
Language (s): English
Ad Rate: Full Page Mono 6.00
Currency: United States Dollars
COMMUNITY NEWSPAPER

Fredericksburg Standard-Radio Post
20842

Owner: Fredericksburg Publishing Co. Inc.
Editorial: 712 W Main St, Fredericksburg, Texas 78624-3134 **Tel:** 1 830 997-2155
Email: fbgnews@fredericksburgstandard.com **Web site:** http://www.fredericksburgstandard.com
Freq: Wed; **Circ:** 8400 Not Audited
Publisher & Editor: Ken Cooke; **Circulation Manager:** Sherrie Geistweidt; **Advertising Sales Manager:** Kim Jung
Profile: Fredericksburg Standard-Radio Post is a local weekly newspaper serving the residents of Fredericksburg, TX. The publication offers articles on local news and events, sports, and weather. The lead time is one day.
Language (s): English
Ad Rate: Full Page Mono 11.65
Ad Rate: Full Page Colour 943.00
Currency: United States Dollars
COMMUNITY NEWSPAPER

Free Press
22166

Owner: Cooke Communications LLC
Editorial: 91731 Overseas Hwy, Tavernier, Florida 33070-2649 **Tel:** 1 305 853-7277
Email: freepress@keysnews.com **Web site:** http://www.keysnews.com
Freq: Wed; **Circ:** 18000 Not Audited
Editor: Dan Campbell; **Publisher:** Paul Clarin
Profile: Free Press is a weekly local newspaper covering local news and community events. There are two editions of the paper. One is sent to Key Largo and Homestead, FL, and the other is sent to Islamorada and Tavernier, FL. The two issues are identical in content and have the same staff. Circulation figures are the combination of the two different editions.
Language (s): English
Ad Rate: Full Page Mono 14.73
Currency: United States Dollars
COMMUNITY NEWSPAPER

The Free Press
22179

Owner: The Free Press Inc.
Editorial: 8 N Main St Ste 101, Rockland, Maine 04841-3154 **Tel:** 1 207 596-0055
Email: freepress@freepressonline.com **Web site:** http://www.freepressonline.com
Freq: Thu; **Circ:** 12000 Not Audited
Circulation Manager: Robin Anderson; **Advertising Sales Manager:** Steve Davis
Profile: The Free Press is a weekly newspaper serving midcoast Maine. It covers community news, shopping, dining and entertainment.
Language (s): English
Ad Rate: Full Page Mono 11.00
Currency: United States Dollars
COMMUNITY NEWSPAPER

The Free Press Standard
20326

Owner: Maynard Buck Jr.
Editorial: 43 E Main St, Carrollton, Ohio 44615-1221
Tel: 1 330 627-5591
Email: fps44615@yahoo.com **Web site:** http://www.freepressstandard.com
Freq: Thu; **Circ:** 7500 Not Audited
Publisher: Maynard Buck; **Editor:** Carol McIntire
Profile: The Free Press Standard is published weekly for the residents of Carrollton, OH and surrounding areas. The newspaper covers local news and community events.
Language (s): English
Ad Rate: Full Page Mono 10.97
Currency: United States Dollars
COMMUNITY NEWSPAPER

Free Times
22756

Owner: Evening Post Publishing Co.
Editorial: 1534 Main St, Columbia, South Carolina 29201-2808 **Tel:** 1 803 765-0707
Email: editor@free-times.com **Web site:** http://www.free-times.com
Freq: Wed; **Circ:** 35000 Not Audited
News Editor: Eva Moore
Profile: Free Times is published weekly for residents of Columbia, SC and surrounding communities. The publication offers articles on local and national news, events and entertainment, including music, movies and theater.
Language (s): English
Ad Rate: Full Page Mono 22.20
Ad Rate: Full Page Colour 1340.00
Currency: United States Dollars
COMMUNITY NEWSPAPER

Freestone County Times
441239

Owner: Freestone County Times, Inc.
Editorial: 401 E Commerce St, Fairfield, Texas 75840-1603 **Tel:** 1 903 389-6397
Email: news@freestonecountytimes.com **Web site:** http://www.freestonecountytimes.com
Freq: Weekly
Editor: Karen Leidy; **Publisher:** Scott Marsters
Profile: The Freestone County Times is a weekly newspaper providing Local News coverage to the communities in Freestone County, TX.
Language (s): English
COMMUNITY NEWSPAPER

Friday Flyer
22865

Owner: Golding Publications
Editorial: 31558 Railroad Canyon Rd, Canyon Lake, California 92587-9427 **Tel:** 1 951 244-1966
Email: news@goldingpublications.com **Web site:** http://www.thefridayflyer.com
Freq: Fri; **Circ:** 6000 Not Audited
Publisher: Chuck Golding
Profile: Friday Flyer is a weekly newspaper for Canyon Lake, CA residents and mailed to all property owners, including those living outside the community. Deadlines are at noon PT on Mondays.
Language (s): English
Ad Rate: Full Page Mono 4.50
Currency: United States Dollars
COMMUNITY NEWSPAPER

Front Range Guardian
494101

Owner: Gannett Co., Inc.
Editorial: 205 River Dr S, Great Falls, Montana 59405-1854 **Tel:** 1 406 791-1444
Web site: http://www.greatfallstribune.com
Freq: Fri; **Circ:** 12000 Not Audited
Publisher: Jim Strauss
Profile: Front Range Guardian is a military publication written for the military personnel of the Malmstrom Air Force Base.
Language (s): English
Ad Rate: Full Page Mono 14.05
Currency: United States Dollars
COMMUNITY NEWSPAPER

The Frontline
661379

Editorial: 112 Vilseck Rd Suite 109, Fort Stewart, Georgia 31314 **Tel:** 1 912 767-5669
Email: usarmy.stewart.3-id.list.
pao-frontline-news-desk@mail.mil **Web site:** http://www.stewart.army.mil
Freq: Thu; **Circ:** 25000
Profile: The Frontline is written for the army community of Fort Stewart, GA.
Language (s): English
Ad Rate: Full Page Mono 13.00
Currency: United States Dollars
COMMUNITY NEWSPAPER

Fullerton Observer
22303

Tel: 1 714 525-6402
Email: observernews@earthlink.net **Web site:** http://www.fullertonobserver.com
Freq: Bi-Weekly; **Circ:** 10000 Not Audited
Editor: Sharon Kennedy
Profile: The Fullerton Observer Community Newspaper, founded in 1978, is staffed by local citizen for community of Fullerton, CA. Its purpose is to cover local news and features, informing local residents about the institutions and other societal forces which most impact their lives. It is published twice per month except in July, August and January. Only send materials that are directly relevant to local events and news.
Language (s): English
Ad Rate: Full Page Mono 12.00
Currency: United States Dollars
COMMUNITY NEWSPAPER

Fulton County News
20571

Editorial: 417 East Market St, McConnellsburg, Pennsylvania 17233 **Tel:** 1 717 485-3811
Email: fultoncountynews@comcast.net **Web site:** http://www.fultoncountynews.com
Freq: Thu; **Circ:** 6400 Not Audited
Advertising Manager: Charles Dean; **Circulation Manager:** Trudy Gelvin; **Publisher & Editor:** Jamie Greathead
Profile: Fulton County News is a newspaper serving the residents of Fulton County, PA. Deadlines are Tuesdays at noon ET.
Language (s): English
Ad Rate: Full Page Mono 7.20
Currency: United States Dollars
COMMUNITY NEWSPAPER

La Gaceta
86363

Owner: La Gaceta Publishing Inc.
Editorial: 3210 E 7th Ave, Tampa, Florida 33605-4302 **Tel:** 1 813 248-3921
Email: lagaceta@tampabay.rr.com **Web site:** http://www.lagacetanewspaper.com
Freq: Fri; **Circ:** 18110 Not Audited
Publisher & Editor: Patrick Manteiga; **Circulation Manager:** Gene Siudut
Profile: La Gaceta is written for the Spanish, Italian and English residents in Tampa, FL. It covers local news and events.
Language (s): Italian
Ad Rate: Full Page Mono 12.00
Currency: United States Dollars
COMMUNITY NEWSPAPER

Gadsden County Times
18764

Owner: Landmark Community Newspapers Inc.
Editorial: 15 S Madison St, Quincy, Florida 32351-3137 **Tel:** 1 850 627-7649
Email: editor@gadcotimes.com **Web site:** http://www.gadcotimes.com
Freq: Thu; **Circ:** 6000 Not Audited
Advertising Sales Manager: Tricia Collins; **Circulation Manager:** Wayne Conner; **Editor:** Alice Dupont
Profile: Gadsden County Times in Quincy, FL is a local newspaper written for the residents of Gadsden County, FL. The paper covers local news and community events. Deadlines are on Mondays at 5pm ET.
Language (s): English
Ad Rate: Full Page Mono 14.71
Ad Rate: Full Page Colour 854.34
Currency: United States Dollars
COMMUNITY NEWSPAPER

The Gaffney Ledger
20626

Owner: Sossamon (Cody)
Editorial: 1604 W Floyd Baker Blvd, Gaffney, South Carolina 29341-1206 **Tel:** 1 864 489-1131
Email: editor@gaffneyledger.com **Web site:** http://www.gaffneyledger.com
Freq: Fri; **Circ:** 8500 Not Audited
Editor: Klonie Jordan; **Publisher:** Cody Sossamon
Profile: The Gaffney Ledger is a local newspaper serving the residents of Gaffney, SC. The publication features local news, events, sports, lifestyle and education. Deadlines are at 5pm ET.
Language (s): English
Ad Rate: Full Page Mono 10.50
Currency: United States Dollars
COMMUNITY NEWSPAPER

Gainesville Guardian
355368

Owner: Halifax Media
Editorial: 2700 SW 13th St, Gainesville, Florida 32608-2015 **Tel:** 1 352 337-0376
Email: news@gainesville.com **Web site:** http://blogs.gainesville.com/section/guardian
Freq: Thu; **Circ:** 10000 Not Audited
Publisher: James Doughton; **Advertising Sales Manager:** Lisa Wiggs
Profile: Gainesville Guardian is a community newspaper written for the African American community of Gainsville, FL. The paper covers local news, events, businesses, schools, sports and feature stories.
Language (s): English
Ad Rate: Full Page Mono 14.35
Currency: United States Dollars
COMMUNITY NEWSPAPER

Gainesville Voice
444459

Owner: New York Times Company (The)
Editorial: 2700 SW 13th St, Gainesville, Florida 32608-2015 **Tel:** 1 352 374-5000
Web site: http://blogs.gainesvillevoice.com
Freq: Thu; **Circ:** 15000 Not Audited
Publisher: James Doughton; **Advertising Sales Manager:** Lisa Wiggs
Profile: Gainesville Voice is a local newspaper written for the residents of Gainesville, FL. Deadlines are on Thursdays at 4pm ET.
Language (s): English
Ad Rate: Full Page Mono 14.44
Ad Rate: Full Page Colour 125.00
Currency: United States Dollars
COMMUNITY NEWSPAPER

The Galena Gazette
21859

Owner: Newton (P. Carter)
Editorial: 716 S Bench St, Galena, Illinois 61036-2502 **Tel:** 1 815 777-0019
Web site: http://www.galenagazette.com
Freq: Wed; **Circ:** 5390 Not Audited
Advertising Sales Manager: Jay Dickerson; **Circulation Manager:** Julie Eggleston; **Publisher:** P. Carter Newton
Profile: The Galena Gazette is a local weekly newspaper written for residents of Galena, Il. The publication features articles covering local and national news, events, sports and business.
Language (s): English
Ad Rate: Full Page Mono 14.00
Currency: United States Dollars
COMMUNITY NEWSPAPER

The Gallatin News Examiner
22909

Owner: Gannett Co., Inc.
Editorial: 1100 Broadway, Nashville, Tennessee 37203-3116 **Tel:** 1 615 259-8000
Email: gnenews@mtcngroup.com **Web site:** http://www.tennessean.com/counties/sumner
Freq: 3 Times/Week; **Circ:** 5284 Not Audited

Editor: Mealand Ragland-Hudgins; **Advertising Sales Manager:** Robyn Williams
Profile: The News Examiner is a local newspaper that is published three times a week for residents of Gallatin, TN and surrounding areas. The publication covers local news, community events, sports and business.
Language (s): English
Ad Rate: Full Page Mono 13.65
Currency: United States Dollars
COMMUNITY NEWSPAPER

The Gallatin Newspaper 411991
Owner: MainStreet Media, LLC
Editorial: 450 W Main St Ste 101, Gallatin, Tennessee 37066-3193 **Tel:** 1 615 452-4940
Web site: http://www.thegallatinnews.com
Freq: Thu; **Circ:** 5500 Not Audited
Publisher: David Gould; **Circulation Manager:** Patrick Gould; **Editor:** Sherry Mitchell; **Advertising Manager:** Randy Moore
Profile: The Gallatin Newspaper is a local newspaper serving the residents of Gallatin, TN. It covers local news, people and events.
Language (s): English
Ad Rate: Full Page Mono 10.75
Currency: United States Dollars
COMMUNITY NEWSPAPER

Gallup Town Talk 442101
Owner: Veazey (Doug)
Editorial: 1503 Linda Dr, Gallup, New Mexico 87301-5617 **Tel:** 1 505 879-0515
Email: gallupstowntalk@yahoo.com **Web site:** http://www.gallupstowntalk.com
Freq: Wed; **Circ:** 5500 Not Audited
Publisher & Editor: Doug Veazey
Profile: Gallup Town Talk is a community newspaper written for the residents of Gallup, NM. When sending faxes, please address them to the attention of the Town Talk or editor.
Language (s): English
Ad Rate: Full Page Mono 13.51
Currency: United States Dollars
COMMUNITY NEWSPAPER

The Galt Herald 22869
Owner: Herburger Publications, Inc.
Editorial: 604 N Lincoln Way, Galt, California 95632-8601 **Tel:** 1 209 745-1551
Email: editor_galtherald@herburger.net **Web site:** http://www.galtheraldonline.com
Freq: Wed; **Circ:** 11700 Not Audited
Editor: Bonnie Rodriguez
Profile: The Galt Herald provides news and information for the residents of Galt, CA and Southern Sacramento County. Deadlines are Mondays before the issue date.
Language (s): English
Ad Rate: Full Page Mono 9.50
Currency: United States Dollars
COMMUNITY NEWSPAPER

Gambit Weekly 21325
Owner: Gambit Communications, Inc.
Editorial: 3923 Bienville St, New Orleans, Louisiana 70119-5102 **Tel:** 1 504 486-5900
Email: response@gambitweekly.com **Web site:** http://www.bestofneworleans.com
Freq: Tue; **Circ:** 37914 Not Audited
Editor: Kevin Allman; **Publisher:** Margo DuBos
Profile: Gambit Weekly is a weekly newspaper covering the New Orleans arts & entertainment scene, as well as politics and culture. The publication provides an alternative view of New Orleans' diverse communities.
Language (s): English
Ad Rate: Full Page Mono 169.00
Ad Rate: Full Page Colour 3262.00
Currency: United States Dollars
COMMUNITY NEWSPAPER

La Ganga Especial 383306
Owner: MediaNews Group
Editorial: 23 E Beach St Ste 205, Watsonville, California 95076-4638 **Tel:** 1 831 724-6564
Web site: http://www.lagangaonline.com
Freq: Weekly; **Circ:** 25000 Not Audited
Publisher & Editor: Mauricio Urzua
Profile: La Ganga, part of the Bay Area News Group, publishes a variety of lifestyle stories for 70 cities along the Central Coast of California.
Language (s): Spanish
Ad Rate: Full Page Mono 45.00
Currency: United States Dollars
COMMUNITY NEWSPAPER

Gardena Valley News 18618
Owner: Verdugo (Edward)
Editorial: 15005 S Vermont Ave, Gardena, California 90247-3004 **Tel:** 1 310 329-6351
Email: info@gardenavalleynews.org **Web site:** http://www.gardenavalleynews.org
Freq: Thu; **Circ:** 10000 Not Audited
Editor: Gary Kohatsu
Profile: Gardena Valley News is a local newspaper that provides news and information for the Gardena, CA area. Regular features include local news, arts & entertainment, community events and sports.
Language (s): English
Ad Rate: Full Page Mono 9.00
Currency: United States Dollars
COMMUNITY NEWSPAPER

The Gardner News 25042
Owner: Gardner News LLC
Editorial: 136 E Main St, Gardner, Kansas 66030-1310 **Tel:** 1 913 856-7615
Email: submissions@gardnernews.com **Web site:** http://www.gardnernews.com
Freq: Weekly; **Circ:** 10000 Not Audited
Advertising Sales Manager: Dave Highfill; **Publisher:** Mark Humble; **Editor:** Danedri Thompson
Profile: Gardner News is a community newspaper serving Gardner, KS, including local news, sports and community events.
Language (s): English
Ad Rate: Full Page Mono 14.00
Currency: United States Dollars
COMMUNITY NEWSPAPER

Garner-Cleveland Record 794082
Owner: McClatchy Newspapers
Editorial: 110 N Arendell Ave, Zebulon, North Carolina 27597-2602 **Tel:** 1 919 836-5703
Email: garnercleveland@newsobserver.com **Web site:** http://garnercleveland.com
Freq: Sun
Editor: Scott Bolejack
Profile: Garner-Cleveland Record is a twice-weekly newspaper providing local news coverage for the residents of Garner and surrounding Johnston County, NC.
Language (s): English
COMMUNITY NEWSPAPER

Garrett County Weekender 23051
Owner: Community Newspaper Holdings, Inc.
Editorial: 19 Baltimore St, Cumberland, Maryland 21502 **Tel:** 1 301 722-4600
Email: gcweekender@times-news.com **Web site:** http://www.times-news.com
Freq: Fri; **Circ:** 16000 Not Audited
Profile: Garrett County Weekender is a local weekly newspaper that provides news and information to the communities of Garrett County, MD. Deadlines are on Tuesdays at noon ET.
Language (s): English
Ad Rate: Full Page Mono 9.31
Ad Rate: Full Page Colour 1132.02
Currency: United States Dollars
COMMUNITY NEWSPAPER

The Gary Crusader 19222
Owner: Chicago Crusader Newspaper
Editorial: 1549 Broadway, Gary, Indiana 46407-2240 **Tel:** 1 219 885-4357
Email: garycrusadernews@aol.com **Web site:** http://www.garycrusader.com
Freq: Thu; **Circ:** 56519 Not Audited
Editor & Publisher: Dorothy Leavell
Profile: The Gary Crusader is a weekly newspaper written for African Americans in Northwest Indiana. The newspaper covers employment, equal rights, social justice, sports and entertainment. The publication is a sister publication of the Chicago Crusader, which covers the same topics in the Chicago area.
Language (s): English
COMMUNITY NEWSPAPER

Gasparilla Gazette 21627
Owner: Boca Beacon
Editorial: 431 Park Ave, Boca Grande, Florida 33921 **Tel:** 1 941 964-2995
Email: info@bocabeacon.com
Freq: Tue; **Circ:** 5000 Not Audited
Circulation Manager: Lynn Erb; **Publisher:** Dusty Hopkins; **Advertising Sales Manager:** Dizey Lindquist; **Editor:** Marcy Shortuse
Profile: Gasparilla Gazette is a local, weekly newspaper written for residents of Boca Grande, FL. The publication covers local news, events, lifestyle issues and people in the area. Deadlines are on Fridays at 5pm ET. Please use PO Box when mailing releases.
Language (s): English
Ad Rate: Full Page Mono 7.14
Ad Rate: Full Page Colour 723.00
Currency: United States Dollars
COMMUNITY NEWSPAPER

Gateway Newspapers 24686
Owner: Trib Total Media
Editorial: 460 Rodi Rd, Penn Hills, Pennsylvania 15235-4547 **Tel:** 1 412 856-7400
Web site: http://triblive.com
Circ: 41332 Not Audited
Editor: Nafari Vanaski
Language (s): English
COMMUNITY NEWSPAPER

Gaylord Herald Times 19515
Owner: Schurz Communications Inc.
Editorial: 2058 S Otsego Ave, Gaylord, Michigan 49735-9422 **Tel:** 1 989 732-1111
Email: editor@gaylordheraldtimes.com **Web site:** http://www.petoskeynews.com/gaylord/
Freq: 2 Times/Week; **Circ:** 6572 Not Audited
Publisher: Douglas Caldwell; **Advertising Sales Manager:** Christy Lyons; **Editor:** Jeremy Speer
Profile: Gaylord (MI) Herald Times is a local newspaper for residents of Otsego County, MI and the surrounding area. The paper provides information on local news, events, sports and people. Lead times are determined by space availability and department.
Language (s): English
Ad Rate: Full Page Mono 9.25
Currency: United States Dollars
COMMUNITY NEWSPAPER

Gazeta Brazilian News 726304
Owner: Vuelma (Zigomar)
Editorial: 4390 N Federal Hwy Ste 207, Fort Lauderdale, Florida 33308-5200 **Tel:** 1 954 938-9292
Email: news@gazetanews.com **Web site:** http://www.gazetanews.com
Freq: Weekly; **Circ:** 16000
Advertising Sales Manager: Rose Nunes; **Publisher:** Zigomar Vuelma
Profile: Launched in 1994, offers entertainment, sports, politics, society and general interest news for the Brazilian community in Florida.
Language (s): Portuguese
Ad Rate: Full Page Mono 5.92
Ad Rate: Full Page Colour 11.11
Currency: United States Dollars
COMMUNITY NEWSPAPER

The Gazette 18728
Owner: Acorn Media Services, LLC
Editorial: 1406 Main St, East Hartford, Connecticut 06108-1684 **Tel:** 1 860 289-6468
Email: editor@ehgazette.com **Web site:** http://www.ehgazette.com
Freq: Thu; **Circ:** 15000 Not Audited
Editor & Publisher: Bill Doak; **Advertising Sales Manager:** Nancy Phaneuf
Profile: The Gazette is a weekly newspaper, covering local sports, government, news, and entertainment for residents of East Hartford, CT.
Language (s): English
Ad Rate: Full Page Mono 19.18
Currency: United States Dollars
COMMUNITY NEWSPAPER

The Gazette 21052
Owner: Landmark Community Newspapers, Inc.
Editorial: 108 W Stuart Dr, Galax, Virginia 24333-2114 **Tel:** 1 276 236-5178
Email: news@galaxgazette.com **Web site:** http://www.galaxgazette.com
Freq: Fri; **Circ:** 8400 Not Audited
Circulation Manager: Vicki Ayers; **Publisher:** Chuck Burress; **Editor:** Brian Funk; **Advertising Sales Manager:** Randy Kegley
Profile: The Gazette, published three times a week, serves the towns of Galax, Grayson and Carroll, VA. The newspaper covers local news, sports and community events.
Language (s): English
Ad Rate: Full Page Mono 14.97
Currency: United States Dollars
COMMUNITY NEWSPAPER

The Gazette 22120
Owner: GateHouse Media Inc.
Editorial: 40 Middleberry St, Middletown, New York 1940 **Tel:** 1 845 341-1100
Email: pjgazette@gmail.com **Web site:** http://www.recordonline.com
Freq: Fri; **Circ:** 6200 Not Audited
Editor: Eric Stutz; **Publisher:** Joseph Vanderhoof
Profile: The Gazette is a weekly community-based publication that serves residents in and around Port Jervis, NY, Pike County, PA and Sussex, NJ. Deadlines are on Fridays.
Language (s): English
Ad Rate: Full Page Mono 3.39
Currency: United States Dollars
COMMUNITY NEWSPAPER

Gazette 22414
Editorial: 1335 W Harrison St, Chicago, Illinois 60607-3318 **Tel:** 1 312 243-4288
Email: pjgazette@gazettechicago.com **Web site:** http://www.gazettechicago.com
Freq: Monthly; **Circ:** 17000 Not Audited
Advertising Sales Manager: Carmen Valentino; **Publisher & Editor:** Mark Valentino
Profile: Gazette is a community newspaper serving Near West/Tri-Taylor, University Village/UIC South Campus, West Loop, South Loop, West Haven, Bridgeport/Armour Square, Bronzeville, Chinatown, West Town, and Heart of Chicago communities of Chicago, IL. The paper is published the first Friday of each month.
Language (s): English
Ad Rate: Full Page Mono 50.00
Currency: United States Dollars
COMMUNITY NEWSPAPER

The Gazette 23342
Owner: Rock Valley Publishing LLC
Editorial: 111 W 4th St, Pecatonica, Illinois 61063 **Tel:** 1 815 239-1028
Email: news@rvpublishing.com **Web site:** http://www.rvpublishing.com
Freq: Thu; **Circ:** 8630 Not Audited
Publisher: Pete Cruger; **Advertising Sales Manager:** Rhonda Marshall; **Editor:** Doug Schroder
Profile: The Gazette provides local news, sports and events to residents of Pecatonica, Winnebago, Durand, Davis and Dakota, IL.
Language (s): English
Ad Rate: Full Page Mono 14.00
Currency: United States Dollars
COMMUNITY NEWSPAPER

Gazette Newspaper 22870
Editorial: 7770 Brecksville Rd, Brecksville, Ohio 44141-1000 **Tel:** 1 440 526-7977
Email: production1@gazette-news.com **Web site:** http://www.gazette-news.com
Freq: Bi-Weekly; **Circ:** 12000 Not Audited
Editor: Joyce McFadden
Profile: The Gazette Newspaper is a bi-weekly publication that covers Brecksville, Broadview Heights, Independence, Parma and Seven Hills in Ohio.
Language (s): English
Ad Rate: Full Page Mono 15.00
Currency: United States Dollars
COMMUNITY NEWSPAPER

Gazette van Detroit 791822
Editorial: 18740 E. 13 Mile Rd., Roseville, Michigan 48066-1378
Email: editor@gazettevandetroit.com **Web site:** http://www.gazettevandetroit.com
Freq: Bi-Weekly
Editor: Carine Christiaens Acks
Profile: Gazette van Detroit is a community newspaper.
Language (s): English
COMMUNITY NEWSPAPER

The Gazette-Virginian 21067
Owner: Halifax Gazette Publishing Co.
Editorial: 3201 Halifax Rd #3209, South Boston, Virginia 24592-4907 **Tel:** 1 434 572-3945
Email: gazette@gazettevirginian.com **Web site:** http://www.gazettevirginian.com
Freq: Fri; **Circ:** 9500 Not Audited
Editor: Paula Bryant; **Advertising Sales Manager:** Donna Guthrie
Profile: The Gazette-Virginian is a community newspaper serving South Boston, VA.
Language (s): English
Ad Rate: Full Page Mono 9.55
Currency: United States Dollars
COMMUNITY NEWSPAPER

Geauga County Maple Leaf 22384
Owner: Legal News
Editorial: 100 Center St Ste 250, Chardon, Ohio 44024-1177 **Tel:** 1 440 285-2013
Email: info@geaugamapleleaf.com **Web site:** http://www.geaugacountymapleleaf.com
Freq: Weekly; **Circ:** 5000 Not Audited
Advertising Sales Manager: Diane Evans; **Publisher:** Jeff Karlovec; **Editor:** John Karlovec; **News Editor:** Cassandra Shofar
Profile: Geauga County Maple Leaf is a local weekly newspaper serving the residents of Geauga County, OH. The paper covers local news, sports and events.
Language (s): English
Ad Rate: Full Page Mono 11.00
Currency: United States Dollars
COMMUNITY NEWSPAPER

Gente Bonita 217351
Editorial: 2840 29th Ave NE, Naples, Florida 34120-7414 **Tel:** 1 239 438-7506
Email: gentebonita@msn.com
Freq: Bi-Weekly; **Circ:** 5000 Not Audited
Editor: Maria Alvarez; **Publisher:** Jose Herrera
Profile: Gente Bonita is a Spanish-language newspaper for residents of Naples, FL.
Language (s): Spanish
Ad Rate: Full Page Mono 100.00
Currency: United States Dollars
COMMUNITY NEWSPAPER

George County Times 19886
Owner: Sellers (O.G.)
Editorial: 5133 Main St, Lucedale, Mississippi 39452-6523 **Tel:** 1 601 947-2967
Email: gctimes@bellsouth.net **Web site:** http://www.gctimesonline.com
Freq: Thu; **Circ:** 6000 Not Audited
Advertising Sales Manager: Jan Hilbun; **Publisher & Editor:** O.G. Sellers
Profile: George County Times is a weekly newspaper published for the residents of George County, MS and the surrounding area. It provides local news and information. Deadlines are on Tuesdays at noon CT.
Language (s): English
Ad Rate: Full Page Mono 6.75
Currency: United States Dollars
COMMUNITY NEWSPAPER

The Georgetown News-Graphic 19341
Owner: Lancaster Newspapers Inc.
Editorial: 1481 Cherry Blossom Way, Georgetown, Kentucky 40324-8953 **Tel:** 1 502 863-1111
Email: news@news-graphic.com **Web site:** http://www.news-graphic.com
Freq: Sat; **Circ:** 5500
Editor: Jerry Boggs; **Circulation Manager:** Cheri Kuhns; **Advertising Manager:** Vivien Loos; **Publisher:** Mike Scogin
Profile: Georgetown News-Graphic is a local morning newspaper that provides news and information for the residents of Georgetown, KY. Regular features include local and national news, arts & entertainment and sports. Advertising deadlines are at 2pm ET.
Language (s): English
Ad Rate: Full Page Mono 9.00
Currency: United States Dollars
COMMUNITY NEWSPAPER

Georgetown Times 27753
Owner: Evening Post Publishing Co.
Editorial: 615 Front St, Georgetown, South Carolina 29440-3623 **Tel:** 1 843 546-4148
Email: news@southstrandnews.com **Web site:** http://www.southstrandnews.com/georgetown-times
Freq: Fri; **Circ:** 8446 Not Audited
Circulation Manager: Eugena Poterala
Profile: Georgetown Times is a local newspaper serving the residents of Georgetown County, SC. It covers local news, sports, business, education, crime, the courts, arts & entertainment, health & fitness, food and community events. Advertising deadlines are at 2pm ET.
Language (s): English
Ad Rate: Full Page Mono 8.85

Ad Rate: Full Page Colour 90.00
Currency: United States Dollars
COMMUNITY NEWSPAPER

The Georgia Bulletin 21919

Editorial: 2401 Lake Park Dr SE, Smyrna, Georgia 30080-8862 **Tel:** 1 404 920-7430
Email: editor@georgiabulletin.org **Web site:** http://www.georgiabulletin.org
Freq: Thu; **Circ:** 80000 Not Audited
Advertising Sales Manager: Tom Aisthorpe; **Publisher:** Wilton Gregory; **Editor:** Gretchen Keiser; **Circulation Manager:** Tina Levitt
Profile: The Georgia Bulletin is the official newspaper of the Archdiocese of Atlanta and covers local Catholic news and feature stories. Deadlines are on the Thursday before the issue date.
Language (s): English
Ad Rate: Full Page Mono 14.00
Currency: United States Dollars
COMMUNITY NEWSPAPER

Germantown News 20727

Owner: Crittendon Publishing
Editorial: 7545 North St, Germantown, Tennessee 38138-3822 **Tel:** 1 901 754-0337
Email: news@germantownnews.com **Web site:** http://www.germantownnews.com
Freq: Wed; **Circ:** 7500 Not Audited
Profile: Germantown News provides news and information for the Germantown, TN. The publication covers local news, sports, community events and business. Deadlines are on Fridays at 5pm CT.
Language (s): English
Ad Rate: Full Page Mono 13.94
Currency: United States Dollars
COMMUNITY NEWSPAPER

Giddings Times & News 20845

Owner: Preuss (Buddy)
Editorial: 170 N Knox Ave, Giddings, Texas 78942-3439 **Tel:** 1 979 542-2222
Email: gtimes@verizon.net
Freq: Thu; **Circ:** 6200 Not Audited
Publisher: Buddy Preuss
Profile: Giddings Times & News' editorial mission is to inform the public about current news and events. The publication is written for residents of Giddings, TX and surrounding areas. The publication covers current news topics of importance to the people of Giddings, TX.
Language (s): English
Ad Rate: Full Page Mono 13.00
Currency: United States Dollars
COMMUNITY NEWSPAPER

Gilbert Publishing 24873

Editorial: 15624 Betroit Ave, Gilbert, Minnesota 55741-5007 **Tel:** 1 218 741-4445
Email: esgh@dz.net
Publisher & Editor: James Krause
Language (s): English
COMMUNITY NEWSPAPER

The Gilbert Times 338446

Owner: Civitas Media
Editorial: 38 W 2nd Ave, Williamson, West Virginia 25661-3500 **Tel:** 1 304 235-4242
Web site: http://www.gilberttimes.net
Freq: Wed; **Circ:** 15000 Not Audited
Editor and Publisher: Joshua Byers; **Circulation Manager:** Mike Murray
Profile: The Gilbert Times is a weekly paper distributed throughout Gilbert, WV and surrounding areas. It features stories on community news and events, education, sports and local businesses.
Language (s): English
Ad Rate: Full Page Mono 13.00
Currency: United States Dollars
COMMUNITY NEWSPAPER

Gladstone Dispatch 863272

Owner: NPG Newspapers
Editorial: 104 N. Main St., Liberty, Missouri 64068-1640 **Tel:** 1 816 781-4941
Email: gladstonenews@npgco.com **Web site:** http://gladstonedispatch.com
Freq: Weekly
Profile: Gladstone Dispatch is a weekly community newspaper serving residents of Gladstone, MO with community news, sports, education, opinion and events.
Language (s): English
COMMUNITY NEWSPAPER

Gladwin County Record & Beaverton Clarion 19516

Owner: Macquarie Media Group
Editorial: 700 E Cedar Ave, Gladwin, Michigan 48624-2218 **Tel:** 1 989 426-9411
Email: customerservice@thegladwincountyrecord.com **Web site:** http://www.gladwinmi.com
Freq: Wed; **Circ:** 7200 Not Audited
Publisher: Mike Drey
Profile: The Gladwin County Record & Clarion's editorial mission is to provide local news and community information to its readers. The publication is written for residents of Gladwin County, MI.
Language (s): English
Ad Rate: Full Page Mono 11.10
Currency: United States Dollars
COMMUNITY NEWSPAPER

Glastonbury Citizen, Inc. 25021

Editorial: 87 Nutmeg Ln, Glastonbury, Connecticut 06033-2314 **Tel:** 1 860 633-4691
Email: bulletin@glcitizen.com
Circ: 35085 Not Audited
Circulation Manager: Janki Buch; **Publisher & Editor:** James Hallas; **Advertising Sales Manager:** Carole Saucier; **Editor:** Mike Thompson
Language (s): English
COMMUNITY NEWSPAPER

Glen Rose Newspaper 778758

Editorial: 615 Ne Big Bend Trl, Glen Rose, Texas 76043-4866 **Tel:** 1 254 897-4536
Email: editor@glenrosenewspaper.com **Web site:** http://www.glenrosenewspaper.com
Publisher and Editor: Steve Monroe
Profile: Glen Rose Newspaper is a weekly newspaper providing Local News coverage to residents in Somervell County and Glen Rose, TX.
COMMUNITY NEWSPAPER

The Globe 19023

Editorial: 1825 Jackson St, Sioux City, Iowa 51105-1055 **Tel:** 1 712 255-2550
Web site: http://www.catholicglobe.org
Freq: Thu; **Circ:** 26000 Not Audited
Editor: Joanne Fox; **Advertising Sales Manager:** Trina Joines; **Publisher:** Walker Nickless
Profile: Sioux City Globe is the official newspaper of the Diocese of Sioux City, IA. It covers local news and events for the area Catholic community. The lead time varies between 10 days and two weeks.
Language (s): English
Ad Rate: Full Page Mono 12.70
Currency: United States Dollars
COMMUNITY NEWSPAPER

The Globe 387350

Owner: Landmark Military Newspapers
Editorial: 149 Rea St. Suite 100, Jacksonville, North Carolina 28540-5203 **Tel:** 1 910 451-7403
Email: staff@lejeuneglobe.com **Web site:** http://www.camplejeuneglobe.com
Freq: Thu; **Circ:** 30000 Not Audited
Advertising Sales Manager: Bobby Stone
Profile: The Globe is a free, weekly newspaper serving military personnel and civilian employees and residents of the Camp Lejeune Marine Corps Base, NC. Although the paper is printed and distributed by Landmark Military Newspapers of North Carolina, all editorial content is provided by military personnel. Deadlines are Wednesdays at 11am ET.
Language (s): English
Ad Rate: Full Page Mono 21.52
Ad Rate: Full Page Colour 300.00
Currency: United States Dollars
COMMUNITY NEWSPAPER

Gloucester-Mathews Gazette-Journal 21053

Owner: Tidewater Newspapers Inc.
Editorial: 6625 Main St, Gloucester, Virginia 23061-5194 **Tel:** 1 804 693-3101
Email: info@gazettejournal.net **Web site:** http://www.gazettejournal.net
Freq: Thu; **Circ:** 11331 Not Audited
Community News Editor: Charlie Koenig; **Publisher:** Elsa Verbyla
Profile: Gloucester-Mathews Gazette-Journal is a local newspaper written for the residents of Gloucester, VA. The paper covers local news and events. Deadlines are on Tuesdays at noon ET.
Language (s): English
Ad Rate: Full Page Mono 9.50
Ad Rate: Full Page Colour 1396.00
Currency: United States Dollars
COMMUNITY NEWSPAPER

Gold Coast Gazette 22074

Editorial: 57 Glen St, Glen Cove, New York 11542-2755 **Tel:** 1 516 671-2360
Email: mail@goldcoastgazette.net **Web site:** http://www.goldcoastgazette.net
Freq: Thu; **Circ:** 7000 Not Audited
Publisher & Editor: Kevin Horton
Profile: Gold Coast Gazette is a local weekly newspaper written for the residents and schools of Glen Cove and Sea Cliff, NY. Articles cover local news, events and people. Deadlines for the publication are on Tuesdays before the issue date. A free online e-edition of the paper is also available. Advertising rate sheet available upon request.
Language (s): English
Ad Rate: Full Page Mono 4.25
Ad Rate: Full Page Colour 1125.00
Currency: United States Dollars
COMMUNITY NEWSPAPER

The Gold Standard 19392

Owner: United States Army
Editorial: Building 1110, Wing B; 6th Street, Fort Knox, Kentucky 40121-5199 **Tel:** 1 502 624-1095
Web site: http://www.fkgoldstandard.com
Freq: Thu; **Circ:** 17200 Not Audited
Editor: Lynsie Dickerson
Profile: The Gold Standard in Fort Knox, KY covers local news and events for military personnel and retirees.
Language (s): English
COMMUNITY NEWSPAPER

Goochland Gazette 27237

Owner: BH Media Group
Tel: 1 804 746-1235
Email: news@goochlandgazette.com **Web site:** http://www.goochlandgazette.com
Freq: Thu; **Circ:** 10226 Not Audited
Publisher: Joy Monopoli
Profile: Goochland Gazette is a local newspaper serving residents of Goochland County, VA. The paper covers local news, community activities, sports, opinion and features.
Language (s): English
Ad Rate: Full Page Mono 11.20
Ad Rate: Full Page Colour 8.00
Currency: United States Dollars
COMMUNITY NEWSPAPER

Good Times 22435

Owner: Mainstreet Media Group
Editorial: 1101 Pacific Ave Ste 320, Santa Cruz, California 95060-7510 **Tel:** 1 831 458-1100
Email: info@goodtimes.sc **Web site:** http://goodtimes.sc
Freq: Thu; **Circ:** 40000 Not Audited
News Editor: Jacob Pierce; **Circulation Manager:** Pamela Pollard; **Publisher:** Debra Whizin
Profile: Good Times Weekly of Santa Cruz County is written for residents in Santa Cruz, CA. It is Santa Cruz County's guide to entertainment and events, presents news of ongoing local interest and reflects the voice, character and spirit of the unique community. It is available free of charge but limited to one copy per reader. Deadlines are Fridays before publication.
Language (s): English
COMMUNITY NEWSPAPER

Gosport 257395

Owner: U.S. Navy
Editorial: 150 Hase Rd, Pensacola, Florida 32508-1051 **Tel:** 1 850 452-4466
Web site: http://www.gosportpensacola.com
Freq: Fri; **Circ:** 25000 Not Audited
Editor: Scott Hallford
Profile: Gosport is written for the civilian community and military community surrounding the Pensacola Naval Air Station. It provides base news and information. They do not do book reviews, but if it's a government source of military news, they would welcome it.
Language (s): English
Ad Rate: Full Page Mono 15.04
Currency: United States Dollars
COMMUNITY NEWSPAPER

Government Center Gazette & Van Nuys News Press 714267

Tel: 1 818 707-2507
Email: editor@vannuysnewspress.com **Web site:** http://www.vannuysnewspress.com
Freq: Mon; **Circ:** 12000
Editor: Joanne Lewis
Profile: Government Center Gazette & Van Nuys News Press is a local community newspaper for the residents of Van Nuys, CA and the surrounding communities.
Language (s): English
Ad Rate: Full Page Mono 7.35
Currency: United States Dollars
COMMUNITY NEWSPAPER

Gowanda News 23009

Owner: Community Newspapers of Western New York
Editorial: 49 W Main St, Gowanda, New York 14070-1305 **Tel:** 1 716 532-2288
Freq: Sun; **Circ:** 11462 Not Audited
Publisher: Bernard Bradpiece; **Editor:** Mary Pankow; **Circulation Manager:** Teri Scott
Profile: Gowanda News is a weekly newspaper serving the residents of Gowanda, NY and its surrounding areas. The paper serves as a news provider and as a consumer's magazine.
Language (s): English
Ad Rate: Full Page Mono 8.23
Currency: United States Dollars
COMMUNITY NEWSPAPER

Grand Haven West Michigan News Review 19582

Owner: Rau (David)
Editorial: 101 N 3rd St, Grand Haven, Michigan 49417-1209 **Tel:** 1 616 842-6400
Email: news@grandhaventribune.com **Web site:** http://www.grandhaventribune.com
Freq: Sat; **Circ:** 8400 Not Audited
Publisher: Kevin Hook; **Advertising Sales Manager:** Lauri Wagner
Profile: Grand Haven West Michigan News Review is a weekly community newspaper serving Grand Haven, MI.
Language (s): English
Ad Rate: Full Page Mono 3.30
Currency: United States Dollars
COMMUNITY NEWSPAPER

Grand Rapids Herald-Review 19640

Owner: Macquarie Media Group
Editorial: 301 NW 1st Ave, Grand Rapids, Minnesota 55744-2704 **Tel:** 1 218 326-6623
Email: news@grandrapidsheraldreview.net **Web site:** http://www.grandrapidsmn.com
Freq: Sun; **Circ:** 19000 Not Audited
Editor: Britta Arendt; **Publisher:** Mark Roy
Profile: Grand Rapids Herald-Review is a local publication that provides information to the local community of Grand Rapids, MN.
Language (s): English
Ad Rate: Full Page Mono 13.50
Currency: United States Dollars
COMMUNITY NEWSPAPER

The Grand Rapids Times 28930

Editorial: 2016 Eastern Ave SE, Grand Rapids, Michigan 49507-3235 **Tel:** 1 616 245-8737
Email: staff@grtimes.com **Web site:** http://www.grtimes.com
Freq: Fri; **Circ:** 6000 Not Audited
Advertising Sales Manager: Sally Calloway
Profile: The Grand Rapids Times is a regional newspaper written for residents of Grand Rapids and Kalamazoo, MI. The paper reports on local news, events, politics, sports and weather. Deadlines are Wednesdays at noon ET.
Language (s): English
Ad Rate: Full Page Mono 17.50
Currency: United States Dollars
COMMUNITY NEWSPAPER

Grant County Press 21268

Owner: Fouch (William)
Editorial: 47 S Main St, Petersburg, West Virginia 26847-1766 **Tel:** 1 304 257-1844
Email: news@grantcountypress.com **Web site:** http://www.grantcountypress.com
Freq: Tue; **Circ:** 5005 Not Audited
Advertising Sales Manager: Jodi Fouch; **Publisher & Editor:** William Fouch; **Circulation Manager:** Mary Simmons
Profile: Grant County Press is published weekly for the residents of Petersburg, WV and surrounding areas. The newspaper covers local news and community events.
Language (s): English
Ad Rate: Full Page Mono 7.50
Currency: United States Dollars
COMMUNITY NEWSPAPER

Grapevine Newspaper 695281

Editorial: 907 N Main Rd Ste 205, Vineland, New Jersey 08360-8200 **Tel:** 1 856 457-7815
Email: letters@grapevinenewspaper.com **Web site:** http://www.grapevinenewspaper.com
Freq: Wed; **Circ:** 8000
Publisher & Editor: Mike Epifanio; **Advertising Sales Manager:** Sherry Munyan
Profile: Grapevine Newspaper was founded in early 2008. It is a weekly community newspaper published every Wednesday, serving the residents of Vineland, NJ and Cumberland County, NJ.
Language (s): English
Ad Rate: Full Page Mono 31.00
Ad Rate: Full Page Colour 106.00
Currency: United States Dollars
COMMUNITY NEWSPAPER

The Graphic 86273

Owner: Schurz Communications Inc.
Editorial: 319 State St, Petoskey, Michigan 49770-2746 **Tel:** 1 231 347-2544
Email: petoskeynews@petoskeynews.com **Web site:** http://www.thegraphicweekly.com
Freq: Thu; **Circ:** 14000 Not Audited
Publisher: Douglas Caldwell; **Circulation Manager:** Mark Fedus; **Advertising Sales Manager:** Christy Lyons; **Editor:** Sheri McWhirter-O'Donnell
Profile: The Graphic is a free, weekly newspaper serving residents of Petoskey, MI and the surrounding communities of Mackinac Island, Atwood, Gaylord and Carlevoix, MI. The paper covers news and information, shopping, new food, drinks and activities, events, arts and weird and unusual jobs. It shares its offices and editorial staff with the Petoskey News-Review.
Language (s): English
Ad Rate: Full Page Mono 15.85
Currency: United States Dollars
COMMUNITY NEWSPAPER

Gratiot County Herald 22283

Owner: MacDonald Publications
Editorial: 123 N Main St, Ithaca, Michigan 48847-1131 **Tel:** 1 989 875-4151
Email: gcherald@gcherald.com **Web site:** http://www.gcherald.com
Freq: Thu; **Circ:** 5000 Not Audited
Publisher: Thomas MacDonald
Profile: Gratiot County Herald's editorial mission is to deliver news and community information to the residents of Gratiot County, MI.
Language (s): English
Ad Rate: Full Page Mono 9.55
Currency: United States Dollars
COMMUNITY NEWSPAPER

Grayson County News-Gazette 21550

Owner: Heartland Publications
Editorial: 40 Public Sq, Leitchfield, Kentucky 42754-1105 **Tel:** 1 270 259-9622
Web site: http://www.gcnewsgazette.com
Freq: Sat; **Circ:** 9000
Profile: Grayson County News-Gazette is a bi-weekly newspaper serving the residents of Leitchfield, KY and surrounding areas. The publication covers local and national news, entertainment, events, business and health. Deadlines are on Fridays at 10am CT for the Monday edition and Tuesdays at 10am CT for the Thursday edition.
Language (s): English
Ad Rate: Full Page Mono 8.15
Currency: United States Dollars
COMMUNITY NEWSPAPER

Grayson Journal 24378

Owner: Community Newspaper Holdings, Inc.
Editorial: 211 S Carol Malone Blvd Ste B, Grayson, Kentucky 41143-1355 **Tel:** 1 606 474-5101
Web site: http://www.journal-times.com
Freq: Wed; **Circ:** 6000 Not Audited
Advertising Sales Manager: Dan Duncan

Profile: Grayson Journal-Enquirer provides coverage of local news and community events to residents of Carter County, KY.
Language (s): English
Ad Rate: Full Page Mono 6.35
Ad Rate: Full Page Colour 898.85
Currency: United States Dollars
COMMUNITY NEWSPAPER

Great Lakes Bulletin
257011
Owner: NorthWest News Group
Editorial: 2601A Paul Jones Street, Grayslake, Illinois 60088 **Tel:** 1 847 688-4808
Email: editor.bulletin@yahoo.com **Web site:** http://cnic.navy.mil/greatlakes
Freq: Fri; **Circ:** 14000 Not Audited
Editor: Paul Engstrom; **Publisher:** John Rung
Profile: Great Lakes Bulletin is a weekly newspaper aimed at naval personnel and residents of the Naval Training Center in Great Lakes, IL. Features include local news, military information, recreation, health, wellness and weather. Deadlines are on Mondays at 4pm CT.
Language (s): English
Ad Rate: Full Page Mono 12.00
Currency: United States Dollars
COMMUNITY NEWSPAPER

Greater Diversity News
22519
Owner: Greater Diversity News
Editorial: 272 N Front St Ste 300A, Wilmington, North Carolina 28401-4059 **Tel:** 1 910 762-1337
Web site: http://www.greaterdiversity.com
Freq: Weekly; **Circ:** 5000 Not Audited
Profile: Greater Discovery News is written for minorities and women. The publication is expanding the equal opportunity umbrella in economics, employment and business.
Language (s): English
Ad Rate: Full Page Mono 30.00
Currency: United States Dollars
COMMUNITY NEWSPAPER

Greater Meadowbrook News
739128
Owner: Greater Meadowbrook News
Editorial: 2320 Oakland Blvd Ste 207, Fort Worth, Texas 76103-3239 **Tel:** 1 817 413-0019
Email: meadowbrooknews@sbcglobal.net **Web site:** http://www.greatermeadowbrooknews.com
Freq: Bi-Weekly; **Circ:** 21000
Profile: Greater Meadowbrook News offers local news and information for residents and businesses of East Forth Worth, West Arlington and Richland Hills, TX.
Language (s): English
Ad Rate: Full Page Mono 25.00
Ad Rate: Full Page Colour 25.00
Currency: United States Dollars
COMMUNITY NEWSPAPER

Greek News
153920
Owner: Greek News Inc.
Editorial: 3507 23rd Ave, Astoria, New York 11105-2204 **Tel:** 1 718 545-4888
Email: info@greeknewsonline.com **Web site:** http://www.greeknewsonline.com
Freq: Mon; **Circ:** 16000 Not Audited
Publisher & Editor: Apostolos Zoupaniotis
Profile: Greek News is a weekly newspaper and provides news and events listings, along with cultural programs information to members of the Greek-American community. Contact the publication for advertisement rates.
Language (s): English
Ad Rate: Full Page Mono 7.88
Currency: United States Dollars
COMMUNITY NEWSPAPER

The Green Mountain Outlook
22612
Owner: New Market Press, Inc.
Editorial: 16 Creek Rd Ste 5A, Middlebury, Vermont 05753-1376 **Tel:** 1 802 388-6397
Email: newmarketpress@denpubs.com **Web site:** http://www.denpubs.com
Freq: Wed; **Circ:** 7863 Not Audited
Publisher: Edward Coats
Profile: The Green Mountain Outlook is a free, weekly newspaper serving residents of Rutland and Windsor counties from Brandon to Ludlo and including Chester, the greater Rutland region and the Castleton-Fair-Haven-Poultney area in Vermont. It covers local news, sports, schools, businesses, arts, entertainment and features of interest to local readers. National and state news stories are also covered if they have a direct impact on the paper's audience. Advertising deadlines are at 4pm ET.
Language (s): English
Ad Rate: Full Page Mono 18.75
Currency: United States Dollars
COMMUNITY NEWSPAPER

Green Valley News and Sun Publishing
25370
Owner: Wick Communications Inc.
Editorial: 18705 S I 19 Frontage Rd Ste 125, Green Valley, Arizona 85614-5014 **Tel:** 1 520 625-5511
Email: editorial@gvnews.com **Web site:** http://www.gvnews.com
Circ: 19000 Not Audited
Publisher: Rebecca Bradner; **Editor:** Dan Shearer;
Advertising Sales Manager: Kelly Walter;
Circulation Manager: Donna West
Profile: Santa Cruz Valley Sun is a weekly newspaper serving residents of Sahuarita, Green Valley, Amado, Tubac, Patagonia and Sonoita in Arizona. It is

distributed free. It covers local news, sports and events.
Language (s): English
COMMUNITY NEWSPAPER

Greenbelt News Review
19472
Owner: Greenbelt Co-operative Publishing Assn.
Editorial: 15 Crescent Rd Ste 100, Greenbelt, Maryland 20770-0807 **Tel:** 1 301 474-4131
Email: editor@greenbeltnewsreview.com **Web site:** http://www.greenbeltnewsreview.com
Freq: Thu; **Circ:** 11000 Not Audited
News Editor: Elaine Skolnik; **Editor:** Mary Lou Williamson
Profile: Greenbelt News Review ONLY covers news and events concerning residents of Greenbelt, MD. The paper does not accept or use regional events and news and cannot use anything that is not in its coverage area.
Language (s): English
Ad Rate: Full Page Mono 14.40
Currency: United States Dollars
COMMUNITY NEWSPAPER

Greenpoint Gazette
492722
Owner: Mann (Jeff)
Editorial: 597 Manhattan Ave, Brooklyn, New York 11222-3981 **Tel:** 1 718 389-6067
Web site: http://www.greenpointnews.com
Freq: Fri; **Circ:** 6000 Not Audited
Publisher & Editor: Jeff Mann
Profile: Greenpoint Gazette is a community newspaper covering the news and events of the Greenpoint, NY area. The paper has been publishing since the early 1970s.
Language (s): English
Ad Rate: Full Page Mono 8.69
Currency: United States Dollars
COMMUNITY NEWSPAPER

The Greenville Advocate
19091
Editorial: 305 S 2nd St, Greenville, Illinois 62246-1726 **Tel:** 1 618 664-3144
Email: advocateil@sbcglobal.net **Web site:** http://www.thegreenvilleadvocate.com
Freq: Thu; **Circ:** 5100 Not Audited
Editor: Nancy Nowlin
Profile: The Greenville Advocate's editorial mission is to serve the community and report news that is in the best interest of the community. The publication is written for residents of Bond County, IL. Deadlines for the publication are three days prior to issue date.
Language (s): English
Ad Rate: Full Page Mono 7.40
Currency: United States Dollars
COMMUNITY NEWSPAPER

Greenwich Citizen
133624
Owner: Hearst Corporation
Editorial: 1455 E Putnam Ave Ste 102, Old Greenwich, Connecticut 06870-1360 **Tel:** 1 203 625-4400
Email: gcitizen@bcnnew.com **Web site:** http://www.greenwichcitizen.com
Freq: Fri; **Circ:** 12516 Not Audited
Profile: Greenwich Citizen is a weekly newspaper published for the residents of Greenwich, CT. The newspaper is comprised of three main sections: News, which includes local/regional news, sports, living, police reports and obituaries; classifieds, which includes CT Job Hunter and CT Auto Pix; and features, which includes a weather section.
Language (s): English
Ad Rate: Full Page Mono 20.00
Currency: United States Dollars
COMMUNITY NEWSPAPER

Greenwich Post
22427
Owner: Hersam Acorn Newspapers
Editorial: 10 Corbin Dr Fl 3, Darien, Connecticut 06820-5403 **Tel:** 1 203 861-9191
Email: editor@greenwich-post.com **Web site:** http://www.greenwich-post.com
Freq: Thu; **Circ:** 16000 Not Audited
Publisher: Thomas Nash
Profile: Greenwich Post is published weekly for the residents of Greenwich, CT and surrounding areas. The newspaper covers local news and community events. Deadlines are Tuesdays at noon ET.
Language (s): English
Ad Rate: Full Page Mono 12.60
Currency: United States Dollars
COMMUNITY NEWSPAPER

The Greer Citizen
20627
Owner: Buchheit News Management Co.
Editorial: 317 Trade St, Greer, South Carolina 29651-3431 **Tel:** 1 864 877-2076
Email: ads@greercitizen.com **Web site:** http://www.greercitizen.com
Freq: Wed; **Circ:** 11000 Not Audited
Publisher: Steve Blackwell; **Editor:** Billy Cannada
Profile: The Greer Citizen is a weekly newspaper serving residents of Greer, SC. It provides local news, sports, government issues and other pertinent information. The deadlines are on Tuesdays at noon ET.
Language (s): English
Ad Rate: Full Page Mono 9.50
Currency: United States Dollars
COMMUNITY NEWSPAPER

Grenada Star
14264
Owner: Daily Sentinel Star, Inc
Editorial: 50 Corporate Row, Grenada, Mississippi 38901-2823 **Tel:** 1 662 226-4321
Email: editor@grenadastar.com **Web site:** http://www.grenadastar.com

Freq: Fri; **Circ:** 6000
Circulation Manager: Stephanie Dees; **Editor:** Lue Harbin; **Publisher:** Joe Lee; **Advertising Sales Manager:** Anita Turner
Profile: Grenada is written for the residents of Greneda, MS.
Language (s): English
Ad Rate: Full Page Mono 12.40
Ad Rate: Full Page Colour 225.00
Currency: United States Dollars
COMMUNITY NEWSPAPER

The Gresham Outlook
81552
Owner: Community Newspapers Inc.
Editorial: 1190 NE Division St, Gresham, Oregon 97030-5727 **Tel:** 1 503 665-2181
Web site: http://www.pamplinmedia.com/gresham-outlook-news/
Freq: 2 Times/Week; **Circ:** 10000 Not Audited
Circulation Manager: Kim Stephens; **Advertising Sales Manager:** Cheryl Swart
Profile: Gresham Outlook is a community newspaper serving the residents of Multnomah County, including the communities of Gresham, Troutdale, Fairview and Wood Village, OR. It covers local news, schools, businesses, sports, people, government and features.
Language (s): English
Ad Rate: Full Page Mono 13.59
Ad Rate: Full Page Colour 95.00
Currency: United States Dollars
COMMUNITY NEWSPAPER

Gretna Guide & News
22285
Owner: Overmann (Mike)
Editorial: 620 N Highway 6, Gretna, Nebraska 68028-8090 **Tel:** 1 402 332-3232
Email: editor@gretnaguide.com **Web site:** http://www.dcpostgazette.com/gretnaguide/
Freq: Wed; **Circ:** 5000 Not Audited
Editor: Mike Fischer; **Publisher:** Mike Overmann
Profile: Gretna Guide & News' editorial mission is to provide its readers with local news and information. The publication is written for the residents of the Gretna, NE community.
Language (s): English
Ad Rate: Full Page Mono 13.50
Currency: United States Dollars
COMMUNITY NEWSPAPER

Gringo Gazette
154940
Editorial: 303 Magnolia Dr, Laguna Beach, California 92651-1720 **Tel:** 1 562 714-6735
Web site: http://www.gringogazette.com
Freq: Bi-Weekly; **Circ:** 16000 Not Audited
Publisher & Editor: Carrie Duncan
Profile: Gringo Gazette is an English language paper for Southern Baja California, Mexico. The Mexico office phone number is 01152-624-14-30865. All correspondence may be sent to the California office.
Language (s): English
Ad Rate: Full Page Mono 20.00
Currency: United States Dollars
COMMUNITY NEWSPAPER

Grosse Pointe News
25131
Owner: Point News Group
Editorial: 21316 Mack Ave, Grosse Pointe Woods, Michigan 48236-1047 **Tel:** 1 313 882-6900
Email: editor@grossepointenews.com **Web site:** http://www.grossepointenews.com
Freq: Thu; **Circ:** 12500 Not Audited
Publisher: Robert Liggett; **Editor:** Joe Warner
Profile: Grosse Pointe News is a community newspaper written for residents of Grosse Pointe and Harper Woods, MI.
Language (s): English
Ad Rate: Full Page Mono 25.00
Currency: United States Dollars
COMMUNITY NEWSPAPER

Guidon
29794
Owner: Gannett
Editorial: 320 Illinois Ave, Fort Leonard Wood, Missouri 65473 **Tel:** 1 573 563-5014
Email: guidoneditor@myguidon.com **Web site:** http://www.myguidon.com
Freq: Thu; **Circ:** 10000 Not Audited
Advertising Sales Manager: Mike Brame
Profile: Guidon is a military publication for members of the U.S. Army and headquartered in the Public Affairs Office at Fort Leanard Wood, where all editorial content is edited and approved.
Language (s): English
Ad Rate: Full Page Mono 10.40
Currency: United States Dollars
COMMUNITY NEWSPAPER

Guilford Gazette
821574
Owner: Adventure Enterprises of Maryland LLC
Tel: 1 410 777-8467
Email: news@guilfordgazette.com **Web site:** http://www.guilfordgazette.com
Freq: Weekly
Publisher, Editor & Advertising Sales Manager: Ricardo Whitaker
Profile: The Guilford Gazette is a local newspaper in the Columbia, Maryland area that specializes in news and information of interest to residents, schools, and businesses in and around Guilford (east of Columbia).
Language (s): English
Ad Rate: Full Page Mono 4.69
Currency: United States Dollars
COMMUNITY NEWSPAPER

Gujarat Times
155563
Owner: Parikh Worldwide Media, LLC
Editorial: 37 W 20TH St Ste 1009, New York, New York 10011-3714 **Tel:** 1 212 206-7361
Email: info@gujarattimesusa.com **Web site:** http://www.gujarattimesusa.com
Freq: Fri; **Circ:** 15000 Not Audited
Advertising Sales Manager: Shairu Desai;
Publisher: Sudhir Parikh
Profile: Gujarat Times is written for Gujarati-speaking members of the Indian community in the United States. Provides news and events coverage.
Language (s): English
Ad Rate: Full Page Mono 20.00
Currency: United States Dollars
COMMUNITY NEWSPAPER

Gulf Breeze News
231957
Owner: Newell (Lisa) & Papajohn (Vici)
Editorial: 913 Gulf Breeze Pkwy Ste 35, Gulf Breeze, Florida 32561-4729 **Tel:** 1 850 932-8986
Email: news@gulfbreezenews.com **Web site:** http://www.gulfbreezenews.com
Freq: Thu; **Circ:** 7800 Not Audited
Advertising Manager: Janna DeMotts; **Editor:** Mathew Pellegrino
Profile: Gulf Breeze News is a weekly community newspaper serving residents of Gulf Breeze, FL.
Language (s): English
Ad Rate: Full Page Mono 34.72
Currency: United States Dollars
COMMUNITY NEWSPAPER

Gulf Pine Catholic
22033
Owner: Catholic Diocese of Biloxi
Editorial: 1790 Popps Ferry Rd, Biloxi, Mississippi 39532-2118 **Tel:** 1 228 702-2126
Email: gulfpinecatholic@biloxidiocese.org **Web site:** http://www.gulfpinecatholic.com
Freq: Bi-Weekly; **Circ:** 16800 Not Audited
Editor: Terry Dickson; **Publisher:** Roger Morin;
Advertising Sales Manager: Debbie Mowrey
Profile: Gulf Pine Catholic's mission is to spread the gospel through contemporary means of communication. The publication serves the Catholic Family in the Diocese of Biloxi. Deadlines for the publication are every Friday.
Language (s): English
Ad Rate: Full Page Mono 10.00
Currency: United States Dollars
COMMUNITY NEWSPAPER

The Gulfport Gabber
24168
Editorial: 1419 49th St S, Gulfport, Florida 33707-4301 **Tel:** 1 727 321-6965
Email: news@thegabber.com **Web site:** http://www.thegabber.com
Freq: Thu; **Circ:** 14000 Not Audited
Profile: The Gulfport Gabber is a local weekly newspaper written for residents of Gulfport, FL and the surrounding communities. The publication's mission is to provide readers with information about local news, community events, and in-depth classifieds.
Language (s): English
Ad Rate: Full Page Mono 23.00
Currency: United States Dollars
COMMUNITY NEWSPAPER

Haïti Progrès
23151
Tel: 1 917 548-5568
Email: editor@haiti-progres.com **Web site:** http://www.haitiprogres.com
Freq: Weekly; **Circ:** 21000 Not Audited
Advertising Sales Manager: Dianne Cooper
Profile: Haïti Progrès is a weekly newspaper written for the Haitian and Haitian American community.
Language (s): Creole, English, French, Spanish
Ad Rate: Full Page Mono 40.49
Currency: United States Dollars
COMMUNITY NEWSPAPER

The Haitian Times
24466
Editorial: 495 Flatbush Ave Fl 2, Brooklyn, New York 11225-3706 **Tel:** 1 646 770-2687
Email: thehaitiantimes@gmail.com **Web site:** http://haitiantimes.com/
Freq: Wed; **Circ:** 15000 Not Audited
Publisher & Editor: Garry Pierre-Pierre
Profile: The Haitian Times is written for Haitian Americans living in New York City and the surrounding areas. The articles focus on news about Haiti and New York. The publication covers sports, arts & entertainment, business, and features on prominent Haitians throughout the United States. The editorial deadlines are Fridays prior to the issue date.
Language (s): English
Ad Rate: Full Page Mono 13.00
Ad Rate: Full Page Colour 2435.94
Currency: United States Dollars
COMMUNITY NEWSPAPER

Half Moon Bay Review
18620
Owner: Wick Communications Inc.
Editorial: 714 Kelly St, Half Moon Bay, California 94019-1919 **Tel:** 1 650 726-4424
Web site: http://www.hmbreview.com
Freq: Wed; **Circ:** 6300 Not Audited
Circulation Manager: Barb Anderson; **Editor:** Clay Lambert; **Publisher:** Bill Murray; **Advertising Manager:** Linda Pettengill
Profile: Half Moon Bay Review has been serving the San Mateo County, CA since 1898. The newspaper covers local news, politics, sports and national stories that have an affect on its readership.
Language (s): English
Ad Rate: Full Page Mono 17.25

Currency: United States Dollars
COMMUNITY NEWSPAPER

Halston Media 879202
Owner: Halston Media, LLC
Editorial: 360 Underhill Ave, the Grace Building, Yorktown Heights, New York 10598-4558
Web site: http://www.halstonmedia.com
Freq: Weekly
Publisher: Brett Freeman; **Circulation Manager:** Lauren Freeman
Profile: Halston Media is a community newspaper publisher in Yorktown Heights, NY, producing the Mahopac (NY) News, The Somers (NY) Record and Yorktown (NY) News.
Language (s): English
COMMUNITY NEWSPAPER

The Hamden Journal 29495
Owner: Hamden Journal LLC
Tel: 1 203 688-6307
Web site: http://www.hamdenjournal.com
Freq: Bi-Weekly; **Circ:** 7500 Not Audited
Profile: The Hamden Journal is written for the residents of Hamden, CT. It covers local news, business, sports and arts & entertainment. It also covers national and statewide stories if they have a direct impact on the newspaper's readership. The paper publishes the first and third Fridays of each month.
Language (s): English
Ad Rate: Full Page Mono 6.03
Ad Rate: Full Page Colour 6.41
Currency: United States Dollars
COMMUNITY NEWSPAPER

Hamilton County Express 22878
Owner: Port Jackson Media
Editorial: c/o Amsterdam Recorder, 1 Verner Road, Amsterdam, New York 12010 **Tel:** 1 800 453-6397
Email: news@recordernews.com **Web site:** http://www.hamiltoncountyexpress.com
Freq: Weekly; **Circ:** 5000 Not Audited
Publisher: Kevin McClary
Profile: Hamilton County Express provides local news and information for Hamilton County, NY.
Language (s): English
Ad Rate: Full Page Mono 9.30
Currency: United States Dollars
COMMUNITY NEWSPAPER

Hammonton Gazette 217329
Owner: Donio (Gabriel)
Editorial: 233 Bellevue Ave, Hammonton, New Jersey 08037-1751 **Tel:** 1 609 704-1939
Email: editor@hammontongazette.com **Web site:** http://www.hammontongazette.com
Freq: Wed; **Circ:** 8000 Not Audited
Publisher: Gabriel Donio; **Editor:** Gina Rullo
Profile: Hammonton Gazette is a local publication providing news to the community of Hammonton, NJ with news.
Language (s): English
Ad Rate: Full Page Mono 8.50
Currency: United States Dollars
COMMUNITY NEWSPAPER

Hampshire Review 21273
Editorial: 25 S Grafton St, Romney, West Virginia 26757-1802 **Tel:** 1 304 822-3871
Email: news@hampshirereview.com **Web site:** http://www.hampshirereview.com
Freq: Wed; **Circ:** 7150 Not Audited
Advertising Sales Manager: Lana Bean; **Publisher:** Charles See; **Editor:** Sallie See
Profile: Hampshire Review is a local weekly paper written for the Romney, WV community. Its editorial mission is to provide information on news developing locally in Romney and Hamphire County, West Virginia.
Language (s): English
Ad Rate: Full Page Mono 3.42
Ad Rate: Full Page Colour 1006.00
Currency: United States Dollars
COMMUNITY NEWSPAPER

The Hanahan, Goose Creek & North Charleston News 28852
Editorial: 1231 Yeamans Hall Rd, Hanahan, South Carolina 29410-2745 **Tel:** 1 843 744-8000
Email: hanahancom@aol.com
Freq: Wed; **Circ:** 14000 Not Audited
Publisher & Editor: Kirk Luther
Profile: The Hanahan, Goose Creek & North Charleston News is a community newspaper for the residents of North Charleston, SC.
Language (s): English
Ad Rate: Full Page Mono 10.00
Currency: United States Dollars
COMMUNITY NEWSPAPER

The Hansconian 22402
Owner: Gatehouse Media
Editorial: 9 Eglin St, Hanscom AFB, Massachusetts 01731-2143 **Tel:** 1 781 225-1685
Email: hanscom.hansconian@us.af.mil **Web site:** http://www.hanscom.af.mil
Freq: Fri; **Circ:** 6000 Not Audited
Editor: Mark Wyatt
Profile: The Hansconian's editorial mission is to be a communication tool for the United States Air Force community stationed at Hanscom Air Force Base.
Language (s): English
Ad Rate: Full Page Mono 16.05
Currency: United States Dollars
COMMUNITY NEWSPAPER

Harbor Country News 21384
Owner: Paxton Media Group
Editorial: 122 N Whittaker St, New Buffalo, Michigan 49117-1169 **Tel:** 1 269 469-1410
Email: news@harborcountry-news.com **Web site:** http://www.harborcountry-news.com
Freq: Thu; **Circ:** 13500 Not Audited
Advertising Sales Manager: Isis Cains; **Publisher:** Bill Hackney; **Editor:** David Johnson
Profile: Harbor Country News is the local newspaper for the regions of New Buffalo, Three Oaks and Bridgeman, MI. It covers local news, business, sports and arts & entertainment, as well as national and statewide stories if they have a direct impact on the readership. Deadlines are on Fridays at 5pm ET.
Language (s): English
Ad Rate: Full Page Mono 10.50
Currency: United States Dollars
COMMUNITY NEWSPAPER

Hardin County News 21661
Owner: Beaumont Enterprise-Hearst Newspapers
Editorial: 522 N Main St, Lumberton, Texas 77657-7351 **Tel:** 1 409 755-4912
Email: localnews@beaumontenterprise.com **Web site:** http://www.beaumontenterprise.com/hardincountynews/
Freq: Wed; **Circ:** 21000 Not Audited
Advertising Sales Manager: Joy Wooley
Profile: Hardin County News is a weekly local newspaper for Hardin County, TX. The newspaper covers local news, business, sports, religion, education and arts & entertainment stories. The newspaper also covers national and statewide stories if they have a direct impact on the newspaper's readership. All inquiries should be addressed to the editor. Deadlines are Fridays at 5pm CT for the Wednesday issue.
Language (s): English
Ad Rate: Full Page Mono 10.00
Currency: United States Dollars
COMMUNITY NEWSPAPER

Harlan Newspapers 24511
Owner: Tribune Newspapers Inc
Editorial: 1114 7th St, Harlan, Iowa 51537
Tel: 1 712 755-3111
Email: news2@harlanonline.com **Web site:** http://www.harlanonline.com
Circ: 10216 Not Audited
Editor: Bob Bjoin; **Advertising Sales Manager:** Mike Kolbe; **Editor:** Mike Oeffner; **Editor:** Kim Wegener
Language (s): English
COMMUNITY NEWSPAPER

Harlem Community Newspapers 966216
Owner: Harlem Community Newspapers, Inc.
Tel: 1 212 996-6006
Email: harlemnewsinc@aol.com **Web site:** http://harlemcommunitynews.com
Freq: Thu; **Circ:** 50000
Publisher & Editor: Pat Stevenson
Profile: Harlem Community Newspapers is a publisher of community newspapers for the residents of the Harlem, Brooklyn, The Bronx, and Queens neighborhoods in New York City. Focuses on positive news and uplifting stories from the community. Cover releases include Harlem Community News, Queens Community News, Brooklyn Community News and Bronx Community News.
Language (s): English
Ad Rate: Full Page Mono 52.25
Ad Rate: Full Page Colour 58.34
Currency: United States Dollars
COMMUNITY NEWSPAPER

Harrison News-Herald 20323
Owner: Schloss Media Inc.
Editorial: 144 S Main St, Cadiz, Ohio 43907-1133
Tel: 1 740 942-2118
Email: newsroom@harrisonnewsherald.com **Web site:** http://www.harrisonnewsherald.com
Freq: Sat; **Circ:** 6000 Not Audited
Profile: Harrison News-Herald is published weekly for the Harrison County and Cadiz, OH area. The newspaper covers local news, sports, business and arts & entertainment. It also covers national stories if they have a local impact.
Language (s): English
Ad Rate: Full Page Mono 9.95
Currency: United States Dollars
COMMUNITY NEWSPAPER

Hartsville Messenger 20628
Owner: BH Media Group
Editorial: 212 Swift Creek Rd, Hartsville, South Carolina 29550-4383 **Tel:** 1 843 332-6545
Web site: http://www.scnow.com/messenger
Freq: Fri; **Circ:** 5200 Not Audited
Profile: This outlet has requested its main email not be listed. Hartsville Messenger is the local newspaper for the Hartsville, SC region. The newspaper covers local news, sports, business, and arts & entertainment stories. They will also cover national stories that have an impact on the Hartsville Messenger's readership.
Language (s): English
Ad Rate: Full Page Mono 9.00
Ad Rate: Full Page Colour 851.34
Currency: United States Dollars
COMMUNITY NEWSPAPER

Hartwell Sun 24395
Owner: Community Newspapers Inc.
Editorial: 8 Benson St, Hartwell, Georgia 30643-1990
Tel: 1 706 376-8025
Web site: http://www.thehartwellsun.com
Freq: Thu; **Circ:** 6900 Not Audited
Editor: Mark Hynds; **Publisher:** Robert Rider
Profile: Hartwell Sun is a local newspaper published for the residents of Hartwell, GA. The newspaper covers local news, sports, business and arts & entertainment.
Language (s): English
Ad Rate: Full Page Mono 11.45
Ad Rate: Full Page Colour 1063.40
Currency: United States Dollars
COMMUNITY NEWSPAPER

Hastings Star Gazette 19645
Owner: Forum Communications Co.
Editorial: 745 Spiral Blvd, Hastings, Minnesota 55033-3651 **Tel:** 1 651 437-6153
Email: news@hastingsstargazette.com **Web site:** http://www.hastingsstargazette.com
Freq: Thu; **Circ:** 5100 Not Audited
Advertising Manager: Jean Brown
Profile: Hastings Star Gazette is written for the residents of Hastings, MN. It covers local news, business, sports and arts & entertainment. It also covers national and statewide stories if they have a direct impact on the newspaper's readership.
Language (s): English
Ad Rate: Full Page Mono 13.45
Currency: United States Dollars
COMMUNITY NEWSPAPER

Hattiesburg Impact 963948
Editorial: 219 S 40th Ave Ste E, Hattiesburg, Mississippi 39402-1623 **Tel:** 1 601 264-8181
Web site: http://impact360.ms
Freq: 2 Times/Week; **Circ:** 65009
Profile: Focuses on Community News in Hattiesburg, MS.
Language (s): English
Ad Rate: Full Page Mono 21.00
Currency: United States Dollars
COMMUNITY NEWSPAPER

The Haverhill Gazette 22906
Owner: Community Newspaper Holdings, Inc.
Editorial: 100 Turnpike St, North Andover, Massachusetts 01845-5033 **Tel:** 1 978 946-2000
Email: hgnews@hgazette.com **Web site:** http://www.hgazette.com
Freq: Thu; **Circ:** 6517 Not Audited
Editor: Bill Cantwell; **Advertising Sales Manager:** Ed Wholley
Profile: The Haverhill Gazette is a newspaper serving the residents of Haverhill, MA. The publication covers local news, sports and community events. Deadlines for the publication are Tuesdays at 10am ET.
Language (s): English
Ad Rate: Full Page Mono 12.75
Currency: United States Dollars
COMMUNITY NEWSPAPER

Hawaii Army Weekly 22970
Owner: Gannett Co., Inc.
Editorial: Public Affairs Office, USAG-HI, 314 Sasaoka St, Schofield Barracks, Hawaii 96857
Tel: 1 808 656-3155
Email: editor@hawaiiarmyweekly.com **Web site:** http://www.hawaiiarmyweekly.com
Freq: Fri; **Circ:** 15300 Not Audited
News Editor: Sarah Pacheco; **Circulation Manager:** Steve Tomino
Profile: Hawaii Army Weekly provides news and information for and about the United States Army Base in Achifield Barracks, HI. The weekly newspaper is published for soldiers, their family members and civilians. Deadlines are on Fridays prior to issue date.
Language (s): English
Ad Rate: Full Page Mono 13.21
Currency: United States Dollars
COMMUNITY NEWSPAPER

Hawaii Marine 22975
Owner: RFD Publications, Inc.
Editorial: MCB Hawaii Public Affairs Office, Bldg 216 Box 63002, Kaneohe Bay, Hawaii 96863
Tel: 1 808 257-8836
Email: hawaiimarineeditor@gmail.com **Web site:** http://www.mcbh.usmc.mil/news/news.htm
Freq: Fri; **Circ:** 7850 Not Audited
Profile: Hawaii Marine provides new and information to military personnel and their families, sailors, retirees and reservists on Marine Base Hawaii. The deadlines for the paper are Fridays prior to issue date.
Language (s): English
Ad Rate: Full Page Mono 11.05
Currency: United States Dollars
COMMUNITY NEWSPAPER

Hawthorne Press 20199
Editorial: 463 Lafayette Ave, Hawthorne, New Jersey 07506-2521 **Tel:** 1 973 427-3330
Email: hawthornepress@optonline.net
Freq: Thu; **Circ:** 9500 Not Audited
Editor & Publisher: Linda Missonellie
Profile: Hawthorne Press is the weekly local newspaper for the Hawthorne, NJ area. The newspaper covers local news, business, sports, and arts & entertainment stories. The newspaper also covers national and statewide stories if they have a direct impact on the newspaper's readership. All inquiries should be addressed to the editor.
Language (s): English
Ad Rate: Full Page Mono 7.80
Currency: United States Dollars
COMMUNITY NEWSPAPER

The Hazard Herald 19347
Owner: Heartland Publications
Editorial: 439 High St, Hazard, Kentucky 41701-1701
Tel: 1 606 436-5771
Web site: http://www.hazard-herald.com
Freq: Wed; **Circ:** 6420 Not Audited
Advertising Sales Manager: Barb Anderson; **Circulation Manager:** Jenny Jones; **Editor:** Cris Ritchie
Profile: The Hazard Herald is written for residents of Perry County, KY and covers news and events. Deadlines are on Fridays at 4pm ET.
Language (s): English
Ad Rate: Full Page Mono 9.25
Currency: United States Dollars
COMMUNITY NEWSPAPER

Headlight Newspapers 25015
Owner: Fisher's Publishing Co.
Editorial: 908 W Broadway St, Morrilton, Arkansas 72110-3329 **Tel:** 1 501 354-2451
Email: pjch@suddenlinkmail.com **Web site:** http://www.headlightnews.com
Freq: Wed; **Circ:** 6800 Not Audited
Publisher: David Fisher; **Advertising Sales Manager:** Sharon Judkins; **Editor:** Larry Miller
Language (s): English
Ad Rate: Full Page Mono 13.00
Currency: United States Dollars
COMMUNITY NEWSPAPER

Headlight-Herald 20534
Owner: Country Media Inc.
Editorial: 1908 2nd St, Tillamook, Oregon 97141-2206 **Tel:** 1 503 842-7535
Web site: http://www.tillamookheadlightherald.com
Freq: Wed; **Circ:** 8700 Not Audited
Profile: Headlight-Herald is a local weekly newspaper written for Tillamook County, OR. The publication features local news, sports, opinion and community events. Deadlines are on Mondays before the issue date at noon PT.
Language (s): English
Ad Rate: Full Page Mono 12.27
Currency: United States Dollars
COMMUNITY NEWSPAPER

Hellenic Times 23258
Editorial: 823 11th Ave Fl 5, New York, New York 10019-3557 **Tel:** 1 212 986-6881
Email: hellenictimes@aol.com
Freq: Fri; **Circ:** 15000 Not Audited
Profile: Hellenic Times serves Greek Americans and those interested in the Greek American community. The newspaper contains news and features that are relevant and of interest to the Greek American community.
Language (s): English
Ad Rate: Full Page Mono 9.00
Currency: United States Dollars
COMMUNITY NEWSPAPER

Hendersonville Lightning 853846
Editorial: 1111 Asheville Hwy, Hendersonville, North Carolina 28791-3633 **Tel:** 1 828 698-0407
Email: news@hendersonvillelightning.com **Web site:** http://www.hendersonvillelightning.com
Freq: Weekly
Editor & Publisher: Bill Moss
Profile: Hendersonville Lightning is a weekly community newspaper serving Henderson County, NC and the surrounding areas, including Hendersonville, Mills River, Fletcher, Flat Rock, Laurel Park, Edneyville, Etowah and Green River. The paper includes local news, politics, business, sports, entertainment, events and editorials.
Language (s): English
COMMUNITY NEWSPAPER

The Hendersonville Standard 716085
Owner: Main Street Media LLC
Editorial: 450 W Main St Ste 101, Gallatin, Tennessee 37066-3193 **Tel:** 1 615 452-4940
Email: news@hendersonvillestandard.com **Web site:** http://www.hendersonvillestandard.com
Freq: Tue; **Circ:** 5000
Publisher: David Gould; **Circulation Manager:** Patrick Gould; **Advertising Sales Manager:** Ginger McClendon; **Editor:** Sherry Mitchell
Profile: The Hendersonville Standard in Gallatin, TN, is a local community newspaper for residents of Hendersonville, TN and surrounding communities.
Language (s): English
Ad Rate: Full Page Mono 8.75
Currency: United States Dollars
COMMUNITY NEWSPAPER

The Hendersonville Star News 22908
Owner: Gannett Co., Inc.
Editorial: 1100 Broadway, Gallatin, Tennessee 37203
Tel: 1 615 259-8000
Email: hsnnews@mtcngroup.com **Web site:** http://www.tennessean.com/counties/sumner
Freq: Fri; **Circ:** 18500 Not Audited
Editor: Mealand Ragland-Hudgins
Profile: The Star News is a free publication written for residents of Sumner County, TN. It covers local news, sports, and events. Deadlines for the publication are Monday for the Wednesday issue and Wednesday for the Friday issue.
Language (s): English
Ad Rate: Full Page Mono 17.00
Currency: United States Dollars
COMMUNITY NEWSPAPER

Henrico Citizen 242560
Owner: T3 Media, LLC
Editorial: 6924 Lakeside Ave Ste 307, Henrico, Virginia 23228-5240 **Tel:** 1 804 262-1700
Email: citizen@henricocitizen.com **Web site:** http://www.henricocitizen.com
Freq: Bi-Weekly; **Circ:** 17500 Not Audited
Publisher & Editor: Tom Lappas
Profile: Henrico Citizen is a bi-weekly newspaper written for the residents of Richmond, VA.
Language (s): English
Ad Rate: Full Page Mono 40.00
Currency: United States Dollars
COMMUNITY NEWSPAPER

Henry County Local 19367
Owner: Landmark Community Newspapers Inc.
Editorial: 18 S Penn Ave, Eminence, Kentucky 40019-1036 **Tel:** 1 502 845-2858
Email: news@hclocal.com **Web site:** http://www.hclocal.com
Freq: Wed; **Circ:** 9500 Not Audited
Circulation Manager: Tawnja Morris; **Editor:** Jonna Priester
Profile: Henry County Local is written for residents of Henry County, KY. Its editorial mission is to be the dominant information provider in Henry County, KY. It covers community news, entertainment, sports, health, school and agriculture. Deadlines are on Fridays at 3pm CT.
Language (s): English
Ad Rate: Full Page Mono 8.55
Currency: United States Dollars
COMMUNITY NEWSPAPER

Henry County Times 86495
Owner: Jackson (Mickie)
Editorial: 48 Racetrack Rd, McDonough, Georgia 30253-6829 **Tel:** 1 770 957-6314
Web site: http://www.henrycountytimes.com
Freq: Wed; **Circ:** 8000 Not Audited
Publisher & Editor: Mickie Jackson
Profile: Henry County Times is a local newspaper serving McDonough, GA and the surrounding area. The newspaper covers local news and community events.
Language (s): English
Ad Rate: Full Page Mono 10.00
Currency: United States Dollars
COMMUNITY NEWSPAPER

The Herald 18854
Editorial: 1803 Barnard St, Savannah, Georgia 31401-8022 **Tel:** 1 912 232-4505
Email: news@savannahherald.net **Web site:** http://www.savannahherald.net
Freq: Wed; **Circ:** 12000 Not Audited
Publisher & Editor: Floyd Adams
Profile: The Herald is written for the African American community in Savannah, GA. The paper features social events, editorial columns and a church section. Deadlines are on Mondays at noon ET.
Language (s): English
Ad Rate: Full Page Mono 12.00
Ad Rate: Full Page Colour 1107.00
Currency: United States Dollars
COMMUNITY NEWSPAPER

The Herald 20007
Owner: McClatchy Newspapers
Editorial: 228 E Market St, Smithfield, North Carolina 27577-3918 **Tel:** 1 919 934-2176
Web site: http://smithfieldherald.com
Freq: Sun; **Circ:** 42418 Not Audited
Profile: The Herald is a published weekly for the residents of Smithfield, NC and surrounding areas. The newspaper covers local news, sports, business and arts & entertainment.
Language (s): English
Ad Rate: Full Page Mono 33.67
Ad Rate: Full Page Colour 36.96
Currency: United States Dollars
COMMUNITY NEWSPAPER

The Herald 21124
Owner: McClatchy Newspapers
Editorial: 510 E Main, Puyallup, Washington 98372-5698 **Tel:** 1 253 841-2481
Web site: http://www.puyallupherald.com
Freq: Wed; **Circ:** 25000 Not Audited
Circulation Manager: Mary Morgan
Profile: The Herald, formerly known as the Pierce County Herald, is a weekly newspaper serving the residents of Puyallup, South Hill, Sumner, Bonney Lake and Edgewood, WA. Deadlines are on Mondays at noon PT.
Language (s): English
Ad Rate: Full Page Mono 9.50
Currency: United States Dollars
COMMUNITY NEWSPAPER

Herald Community Newspapers 24644
Editorial: 2 Endo Blvd, Garden City, New York 11530-6707 **Tel:** 1 516 569-4000
Email: srichner@liherald.com **Web site:** http://liherald.com/
Circ: 89534 Not Audited
Editor: Jeff Bessen; **Editor:** Scott Brinton; **Editor:** Alex Costello; **Editor:** Andrew Hackmack
Profile: Richner Communications Inc. in Garden City, NY publishes 15 community newspapers in the Nassau County, NY.
Language (s): English
COMMUNITY NEWSPAPER

The Herald News 21726
Owner: Rhea County Publishing Co.
Editorial: 3687 Rhea County Hwy, Dayton, Tennessee 37321-5819 **Tel:** 1 423 775-6111
Email: news@rheaheraldnews.com **Web site:** http://www.rheaheraldnews.com
Freq: Sun; **Circ:** 13700 Not Audited
Publisher: Sarah Jane Locke
Profile: The Herald News is a local newspaper published for the residents in Rhea County, TN. The newspaper covers local news, events, sports, business and weather.
Language (s): English
Ad Rate: Full Page Mono 12.00
Currency: United States Dollars
COMMUNITY NEWSPAPER

The Herald of Randolph 21086
Owner: Drysdale (M. Dickey)
Editorial: 30 Pleasant St, Randolph, Vermont 5060 **Tel:** 1 802 728-3232
Email: editor@ourherald.com **Web site:** http://www.rherald.com
Freq: Weekly; **Circ:** 5700 Not Audited
Editor: Sandy Cooch; **Publisher & Editor:** M. Dickey Drysdale
Profile: The Herald of Randolph (VT) is a weekly community newspaper.
Language (s): English
Ad Rate: Full Page Mono 10.92
Currency: United States Dollars
COMMUNITY NEWSPAPER

The Herald-Chronicle 20763
Owner: Lakeway Publishers, Inc.
Editorial: 906 Dinah Shore Blvd, Winchester, Tennessee 37398-1102 **Tel:** 1 931 967-2272
Email: whcnews@lcs.net **Web site:** http://www.heraldchronicle.com
Freq: Fri; **Circ:** 9400 Not Audited
Circulation Manager: Cathy Beasley; **Publisher & Editor:** Davis Sons
Profile: The Herald-Chronicle is a local newspaper written for residents of Franklin County, TN. The newspaper covers local news and sports. Deadlines are 2pm CT Fridays or Wednesdays before issue date.
Language (s): English
Ad Rate: Full Page Mono 12.73
Currency: United States Dollars
COMMUNITY NEWSPAPER

The Herald-Leader 18810
Editorial: 202 E Central Ave #204, Fitzgerald, Georgia 31750-2503 **Tel:** 1 229 423-9331
Email: butlerherald@gmail.com **Web site:** http://www.herald-leader.net
Freq: Wed; **Circ:** 5200 Not Audited
Advertising Sales Manager: Becky Anderson; **Publisher & Editor:** Tim Anderson
Profile: The Herald-Leader is a local newspaper written for the residents of Fitzgerald, GA. Deadlines are on Fridays at noon ET.
Language (s): English
Ad Rate: Full Page Mono 6.00
Currency: United States Dollars
COMMUNITY NEWSPAPER

Herald-Leader 27846
Owner: Wehco Media Inc.
Editorial: 101 N Mount Olive St, Siloam Springs, Arkansas 72761-3156 **Tel:** 1 479 524-5144
Email: hleditor@nwaonline.com **Web site:** http://www.nwaonline.com
Freq: Weekly; **Circ:** 5000 Not Audited
Advertising Sales Manager: Steve Peters
Profile: The Herald-Leader is a bi-weekly community newspaper that serves residents of Siloam Springs, AR. The Sunday edition, published under the name of Siloam Sunday, contains the same locally-focused editorial content of the weekday edition, but it is distributed as an insert to the daily newspaper, the Arkansas Democrat-Gazette. Lead times are on Tuesdays one week before distribution. Advertising deadlines are on Mondays bedore issue date.
Language (s): English
Ad Rate: Full Page Mono 9.06
Currency: United States Dollars
COMMUNITY NEWSPAPER

Herald-News 19344
Owner: Breckinridge Herald News
Editorial: 120 Old Highway 60, Hardinsburg, Kentucky 40143 **Tel:** 1 270 756-2109
Email: editorialthn@bbtel.com
Freq: Weekly; **Circ:** 5000 Not Audited
Circulation Manager & Advertising Sales Manager: Nadean Collins; **Advertising Sales Manager:** Angelia Wheatley
Profile: Herald-News is published weekly for the residents of Breckinridge County, KY. The newspaper covers local news and community events. Deadlines are on Mondays at 5pm CT.
Language (s): English
Ad Rate: Full Page Mono 6.25
Currency: United States Dollars
COMMUNITY NEWSPAPER

El Heraldo de Colorado 405656
Editorial: 6450 E Colfax Ave, Denver, Colorado 80220-1604 **Tel:** 1 720 436-5104
Email: elheraldodeco@hotmail.com **Web site:** http://elheradodecolorado.jimdo.com
Freq: Bi-Weekly; **Circ:** 5000 Not Audited
Publisher & Editor: Concepcion Wallrer
Profile: El Heraldo de Colorado is a free, bi-weekly, bilingual newspaper serving the Hispanic community in and around Denver. It covers local and international news, events, sports, entertainment and features of interest to Hispanic readers.
Language (s): Spanish/Bilingual
Ad Rate: Full Page Mono 13.91
Currency: United States Dollars
COMMUNITY NEWSPAPER

Heraldo Hispano 235125
Owner: Argueta (Oscar)
Editorial: 705 E Monroe St, Mount Pleasant, Iowa 52641-1928 **Tel:** 1 319 385-3431
Email: coca43@hotmail.com
Freq: Bi-Weekly; **Circ:** 6500 Not Audited
Publisher & Editor: Oscar Argueta
Profile: Heraldo Hispano is a weekly Spanish-language newspaper written for the residents of Mount Pleasant, IA.
Language (s): Spanish/Bilingual
Ad Rate: Full Page Mono 10.25
Currency: United States Dollars
COMMUNITY NEWSPAPER

El Heraldo News 81510
Editorial: 4532 Columbia Ave, Dallas, Texas 75226-1016 **Tel:** 1 214 827-9700
Email: editorial@elheraldonews.com **Web site:** http://www.elheraldonews.com
Freq: Fri; **Circ:** 25000 Not Audited
Profile: El Heraldo News is a Spanish-language newspaper serving the Dallas metro area. It contains local, national and international news, sports and entertainment stories of interest to the local Hispanic population.
Language (s): Spanish
Ad Rate: Full Page Mono 25.00
Currency: United States Dollars
COMMUNITY NEWSPAPER

Herald-Progress 21043
Owner: Lakeway Publishers, Inc.
Editorial: 11159 Air Park Rd Ste 1, Ashland, Virginia 23005-3500 **Tel:** 1 804 798-9031
Email: hpnews@herald-progress.com **Web site:** http://www.herald-progress.com
Freq: Thu; **Circ:** 7000 Not Audited
Editor: Dan Sherrier
Profile: Herald-Progress is a local publication providing the community of Ashland, VA with news.
Language (s): English
Ad Rate: Full Page Mono 10.95
Currency: United States Dollars
COMMUNITY NEWSPAPER

Heritage Florida Jewish News 18784
Owner: Gaeser (Jeffrey)
Editorial: 207 Obrien Rd Ste 101, Fern Park, Florida 32730-2838 **Tel:** 1 407 834-8787
Email: info@heritagefl.com **Web site:** http://heritagefl.com
Freq: Fri; **Circ:** 5000 Not Audited
Publisher, Editor, Advertising Sales & Circulation Manager: Jeffrey Gaeser
Profile: Heritage Florida Jewish News is a local newspaper serving Central Florida's Jewish community. The publication covers local news, community events and religious news.
Language (s): English
Ad Rate: Full Page Mono 13.25
Currency: United States Dollars
COMMUNITY NEWSPAPER

Hesperia Star 151358
Owner: Freedom Communications Inc.
Editorial: 15550 Main St Ste C11, Hesperia, California 92345-3492 **Tel:** 1 760 956-7827
Email: editor@hesperiastar.com **Web site:** http://www.hesperiastar.com
Freq: Tue; **Circ:** 20000 Not Audited
Advertising Sales Manager: Shelia Mockett
Profile: Hesperia Star is a publication providing local news to the community of Hesperia, CA.
Language (s): English
Ad Rate: Full Page Mono 17.25
Currency: United States Dollars
COMMUNITY NEWSPAPER

Hickman County Times 20721
Editorial: 104 N Central Ave, Centerville, Tennessee 37033-1406 **Tel:** 1 931 729-4283
Email: hc.times@att.net **Web site:** http://www.hickmancountytimes.net
Freq: Mon; **Circ:** 5800 Not Audited
Publisher: Jim Crawford; **Advertising Sales Manager:** Theresa Cunningham; **Editor:** Bradley Martin
Profile: Hickman County Times is a local weekly newspaper serving residents of Hickman County, TN and the surrounding area. The publication covers local news, business, sports and community events. Editorial deadlines are Thursdays at noon ET.
Language (s): English
Ad Rate: Full Page Mono 7.65
Currency: United States Dollars
COMMUNITY NEWSPAPER

Hickory Focus 21673
Owner: Panther (Tammy)
Editorial: 264 1st Ave NW, Hickory, North Carolina 28601-6103 **Tel:** 1 828 322-1036
Email: focusnews@centurylink.net **Web site:** http://www.focusnewspaper.com
Freq: Thu; **Circ:** 37500 Not Audited
Publisher: Tammy Panther
Profile: Hickory (NC) Focus is a free, weekly newspaper serving eight counties and providing reviews, feature stories and a directory.
Language (s): English
Ad Rate: Full Page Mono 8.63
Ad Rate: Full Page Colour 650.00
Currency: United States Dollars
COMMUNITY NEWSPAPER

Hi-Desert Star 27290
Owner: Brehm Communications, Inc.
Editorial: 56445 29 Palms Hwy, Yucca Valley, California 92284-2861 **Tel:** 1 760 365-3315
Email: news@hidesertstar.com **Web site:** http://www.hidesertstar.com
Freq: Sat; **Circ:** 7800 Not Audited
Circulation Manager: Steve Austin; **Publisher:** Cindy Melland; **Editor:** Stacy Moore
Profile: Hi-Desert Star is a local newspaper serving Morongo Basin, CA. It covers news, business developments, local schools, sports, entertainment and community events.
Language (s): English
Ad Rate: Full Page Mono 18.45
Currency: United States Dollars
COMMUNITY NEWSPAPER

High Country Press 515199
Editorial: 130 N Depot St, Boone, North Carolina 28607-3603 **Tel:** 1 828 264-2262
Email: news@highcountrypress.com **Web site:** http://www.highcountrypress.com
Freq: Thu; **Circ:** 10000 Not Audited
Publisher & Editor: Kenneth Ketchie; **News Editor:** Jesse Wood
Profile: High Country Press serves the residents of Watauga and Avery, NC. The weekly newspaper covers local news, sports, business and community events.
Language (s): English
Ad Rate: Full Page Mono 6.00
Currency: United States Dollars
COMMUNITY NEWSPAPER

High Desert Advocate 22058
Owner: Coyote Publishing Co.
Editorial: 2028 Elko Ave, West Wendover, Nevada 89883 **Tel:** 1 775 664-3415
Email: advocate@cut.net **Web site:** http://www.coyote-tv.com
Freq: Thu; **Circ:** 7500 Not Audited
Profile: High Desert Advocate is a local, weekly newspaper serving the residents of Alcove, Eureka, Wendover and Wells, NV. The paper covers local news and community events. Editorial deadlines are on Tuesdays prior to the issue date.
Language (s): English
Ad Rate: Full Page Mono 10.00
Currency: United States Dollars
COMMUNITY NEWSPAPER

High Desert Warrior 156438
Editorial: Inner Loop Rd, Bldg 983, Fort Irwin, California 92310 **Tel:** 1 760 380-4511
Web site: http://www.aerotechnews.com/ntcfortirwin
Freq: Thu; **Circ:** 6500 Not Audited
Profile: The High Desert Warrior is a free weekly newspaper distributed to members of the U. S. Army and Fort Irwin, CA community. Deadlines are at noon PT on Thursdays before publication days.
Language (s): English
Ad Rate: Full Page Mono 7.65
Currency: United States Dollars
COMMUNITY NEWSPAPER

Highland Community News 22408
Owner: Century Group (The)
Editorial: 27000 Base Line St, Highland, California 92346-3163 **Tel:** 1 909 862-1771
Email: news@highlandnews.net **Web site:** http://www.highlandnews.net
Freq: Fri; **Circ:** 15000 Not Audited
Editor: Charles Roberts
Profile: Highland Community News is a local weekly newspaper serving the Highland, CA area. The publication focuses on local, community-related news and events.
Language (s): English
Ad Rate: Full Page Mono 17.70
Currency: United States Dollars
COMMUNITY NEWSPAPER

Highland News Leader 19094
Owner: McClatchy Newspapers
Editorial: 1 Woodcrest Professional Park, Highland, Illinois 62249-1254 **Tel:** 1 618 654-2366
Email: hnlnews@bnd.com **Web site:** http://www.bnd.com/highland-news-leader
Freq: Thu; **Circ:** 6000 Not Audited
Advertising Sales Manager: Gay Bentlage; **Publisher:** Todd Eschman; **County News Editor:** Mark Hodapp; **Editor:** Curt Libbra
Profile: Highland News Leader is a local newspaper serving the Highland, IL area. It covers news, sports, local business, local government and community events.
Language (s): English
Ad Rate: Full Page Mono 17.25
Ad Rate: Full Page Colour 1283.60
Currency: United States Dollars
COMMUNITY NEWSPAPER

The Highlander 22692
Owner: Bar 30 Media, LLC
Editorial: 304 Highlander Cir, Marble Falls, Texas 78654-6322 **Tel:** 1 830 693-4367
Email: newscopy@highlandernews.com **Web site:** http://www.highlandernews.com

Freq: 2 Times/Week; **Circ:** 6060 Not Audited
Profile: The Highlander is a bi-weekly newspaper written for residents of Marble Falls, TX. The publication covers local news, events, entertainment and sports.
Language (s): English
Ad Rate: Full Page Mono 9.00
Currency: United States Dollars
COMMUNITY NEWSPAPER

Highlands Highlander 22640
Owner: Community Newspapers Inc.
Editorial: 134 N 5th St, Highlands, North Carolina 28741 **Tel:** 1 828 526-4114
Email: news@highlandsnews.com **Web site:** http://www.highlandsnews.com
Freq: Thu; **Circ:** 2321 Not Audited
Editor: Carolyn Morrisroe; **Publisher:** Brad Spaulding; **Circulation Manager:** Della Stanfield
Profile: Highlands Highlander is a local newspaper serving Highlands, NC. The publication covers local news and community events. It is published on Thursdays from December to April and Tuesdays and Fridays from May to November. Deadlines are Mondays.
Language (s): English
Ad Rate: Full Page Mono 12.35
Ad Rate: Full Page Colour 200.00
Currency: United States Dollars
COMMUNITY NEWSPAPER

Hi-Lites 21581
Editorial: 217 N Franklin St, Watkins Glen, New York 14891-1201 **Tel:** 1 607 535-9866
Email: ads@hilites.net **Web site:** http://www.hilites.net
Freq: Sun; **Circ:** 8500 Not Audited
Publisher & Editor: Bridget Goodman
Profile: Hi-Lites is a community newspaper written for the residents of Schuyler County, NY. The advertising deadline is Thursday at noon ET.
Language (s): English
Ad Rate: Full Page Mono 8.00
Currency: United States Dollars
COMMUNITY NEWSPAPER

Hill Country Community Journal 778767
Editorial: 303 Earl Garrett St, Kerrville, Texas 78028-4529 **Tel:** 1 830 257-2828
Email: journal@ktc.com **Web site:** http://www.hccommunityjournal.com
Freq: Weekly
Publisher and Editor: Tammy Prout
Profile: Hill Country Community Journal is a weekly newspaper providing Local News coverage to the residents of Kerrville, TX.
Language (s): English
COMMUNITY NEWSPAPER

Hillsboro Free Press 310363
Editorial: 116 S Main St, Hillsboro, Kansas 67063-1526 **Tel:** 1 620 947-5702
Web site: http://www.hillsborofreepress.com
Freq: Weekly; **Circ:** 7141
Advertising Sales Manager: Natalie Hoffman; **Circulation Manager:** Kevin Hower; **Editor:** Don Ratzlaff; **Publisher:** Joey Young
Profile: Hillsboro Free Press is a weekly newspaper providing local and community news coverage to the residents of Hillsboro and Marion County, KS.
Language (s): English
Ad Rate: Full Page Mono 10.50
Currency: United States Dollars
COMMUNITY NEWSPAPER

Hilltop Times 21433
Owner: Ogden Publishing Corp.
Editorial: 332 Standard Way, Ogden, Utah 84404-1371 **Tel:** 1 801 625-4200
Web site: http://www.hilltoptimes.com
Freq: Weekly; **Circ:** 12000 Not Audited
Editor: Mark Shenefelt
Profile: Hilltop Times is geared toward servicemen and families of Hill Air Force Base, UT. The publication covers base news, sports, and event listings. Deadlines are on Thursdays prior to the issue date at 3pm MT.
Language (s): English
Ad Rate: Full Page Mono 18.00
Ad Rate: Full Page Colour 21.97
Currency: United States Dollars
COMMUNITY NEWSPAPER

The Hinsdalean 476264
Owner: Lannom (Pamela) and Slonoff (Jim)
Editorial: 7 W 1st St, Hinsdale, Illinois 60521-4103 **Tel:** 1 630 323-4422
Email: news@thehinsdalean.com **Web site:** http://www.thehinsdalean.com
Freq: Thu; **Circ:** 6000 Not Audited
Editor: Pamela Lannom; **Advertising Sales Manager:** Lisa Skrapka; **Publisher:** Jim Slonoff
Profile: The Hinsdalean is a local community newspaper providing local news for the residents of Hinsdale, IL.
Language (s): English
Ad Rate: Full Page Mono 11.38
Ad Rate: Full Page Colour 125.00
Currency: United States Dollars
COMMUNITY NEWSPAPER

The Hippo 239012
Owner: Reese (Jody)
Editorial: 49 Hollis St, Manchester, New Hampshire 03101-1239 **Tel:** 1 603 625-1855
Email: news@hippopress.com **Web site:** http://www.hippopress.com
Freq: Thu; **Circ:** 42561 Not Audited
Advertising Sales Manager: Charlene Cesarini; **Circulation Manager:** Doug Ladd; **Publisher:** Jody Reese
Profile: The Hippo is published weekly for the residents of Manchester, NH and surrounding areas. The newspaper covers local news, sports and entertainment.
Language (s): English
Ad Rate: Full Page Mono 45.00
Currency: United States Dollars
COMMUNITY NEWSPAPER

El Hispanic News 21854
Owner: Brilliant Media LLC
Editorial: 1206 Jantzen Beach Ctr, Portland, Oregon 97217-7836 **Tel:** 1 503 228-3139
Email: info@elhispanicnews.com **Web site:** http://www.elhispanicnews.com
Freq: Thu; **Circ:** 20000 Not Audited
Publisher: Melanie Davis; **Advertising Sales Manager:** Larry Lewis
Profile: El Hispanic News is a weekly publication written for the Hispanic community of Portland, OR. The publication focuses on Pacific Northwest news, national news, international news, sports, people and business. Deadlines are the day before issue date. The publication does not publish an editorial calendar.
Language (s): Spanish/Bilingual
Ad Rate: Full Page Mono 22.00
Ad Rate: Full Page Colour 2593.00
Currency: United States Dollars
COMMUNITY NEWSPAPER

El Hispano 21803
Owner: Larenas (Patrick)
Editorial: 1903 21st St, Sacramento, California 95811-6813 **Tel:** 1 916 442-0267
Email: blarenas2@yahoo.com
Freq: Weekly; **Circ:** 15000 Not Audited
Publisher & Editor: Patrick Larenas
Profile: El Hispano's editorial mission is to inform and transform the image of the Latino community in Sacramento, CA. The publication covers issues such as sports, local news and entertainment. The newspaper is published primarily in Spanish but does have an English section as well.
Language (s): Spanish/Bilingual
Ad Rate: Full Page Mono 15.29
Currency: United States Dollars
COMMUNITY NEWSPAPER

El Hispano 21826
Owner: Lopez Publications, Inc.
Editorial: 50 N State Rd, Springfield, Pennsylvania 19064-1332 **Tel:** 1 484 472-6059
Web site: http://www.el-hispano.com
Freq: Weekly; **Circ:** 16500 Not Audited
Editor: Sara Lopez; **Circulation Manager:** Josue Rodriguez; **News Editor:** James Smith
Profile: El Hispano's editorial mission is to inform the Hispanic communities of Southeastern Pennsylvania and Northeastern New Jersey about local and national news and events. Editorial deadlines are on Mondays.
Language (s): Spanish/Bilingual
Ad Rate: Full Page Mono 30.00
Currency: United States Dollars
COMMUNITY NEWSPAPER

El Hispano 152343
Owner: EMES Publications, Inc.
Editorial: 1200 Del Mar Pkwy, Aurora, Colorado 80010-3318 **Tel:** 1 303 340-0303
Email: elhispano@comcast.net **Web site:** http://www.elhispanonewspaper.com
Freq: Thu; **Circ:** 20000 Not Audited
Advertising Sales Manager: Rodrigo Chavez; **Publisher & Editor:** Roberto Martinez
Profile: El Hispano is a Spanish-language newspaper providing news and information to the residents of Aurora, Colorado.
Language (s): Spanish
Ad Rate: Full Page Mono 45.05
Currency: United States Dollars
COMMUNITY NEWSPAPER

El Hispano News 21799
Owner: Colmenero (Lupita)
Editorial: 2102 Empire Central, Dallas, Texas 75235-4302 **Tel:** 1 214 357-2186
Email: editor@elhispanonews.com **Web site:** http://www.elhispanonews.com
Freq: Thu; **Circ:** 20081 Not Audited
Publisher: Lupita Colmenero
Profile: El Hispano News is a local newspaper written for the Hispanic community in Dallas, TX. The paper covers healthcare, education, immigration, politics, business, sports and arts & entertainment.
Language (s): Spanish/Bilingual
Ad Rate: Full Page Mono 26.00
Currency: United States Dollars
COMMUNITY NEWSPAPER

Hispanos Unidos 23220
Owner: AH/HU Associates, Inc.
Editorial: 411 W 9th Ave, Escondido, California 92025-5034 **Tel:** 1 760 740-9561
Email: info@hispanosnews.com **Web site:** http://www.hispanosnews.com
Freq: Fri; **Circ:** 26000 Not Audited
Editor: Jaime Castaneda; **Publisher:** Ana Hannegan
Profile: Hispanos Unidos is published weekly for the residents of San Diego and Riverside, CA. The newspaper focuses on showing a better picture of the Hispanic issues and community. Coverage includes local, national and international news, sports, business and social issues.
Language (s): Spanish
Ad Rate: Full Page Mono 24.00
Ad Rate: Full Page Colour 375.00
Currency: United States Dollars
COMMUNITY NEWSPAPER

Hmong Times 77672
Tel: 1 651 224-9395
Email: hmongtimes@gmail.com **Web site:** http://www.hmongtimes.com
Freq: Bi-Weekly; **Circ:** 15000 Not Audited
Publisher & Editor: Dick Wetzler; **Advertising Sales Manager:** Steve Wetzler
Profile: Hmong Times is published bi-monthly for the Hmong community of Minnesota.
Language (s): English
Ad Rate: Full Page Mono 18.00
Currency: United States Dollars
COMMUNITY NEWSPAPER

Hockessin Community News 25408
Owner: GateHouse Media Inc.
Editorial: 24 W Main St, Middletown, Delaware 19709-1039 **Tel:** 1 302 378-9531
Email: editor@communitypub.com **Web site:** http://www.hockessincommunitynews.com/
Freq: Weekly
News Editor: Ben Mace
Profile: Hockessin Community News offers local news and information to residents in and around Hockessin, Pike Creek and Brandywine (New Castle County), Delaware.
Language (s): English
COMMUNITY NEWSPAPER

Hola Arkansas 328247
Owner: Hola Arkansas Hispanic Media & Publishing Co. LLC
Tel: 1 501 771-5007
Email: publisher@hola-arkansas.com **Web site:** http://www.hola-arkansas.com
Freq: Weekly; **Circ:** 15000 Not Audited
Publisher & Editor: Maura Lozano-Yancy
Profile: Hola Arkansas is a bilingual newspaper written for Hispanic residents in Little Rock, AR.
Language (s): Spanish/Bilingual
Ad Rate: Full Page Mono 15.00
Currency: United States Dollars
COMMUNITY NEWSPAPER

Hola Noticias 521084
Owner: Norsan Media
Editorial: 9831-7 Beach Blvd, Jacksonville, Florida 32246-4703 **Tel:** 1 904 683-2198
Email: hola@norsanmedia.com **Web site:** http://www.holanoticias.com
Freq: Wed; **Circ:** 10000 Not Audited
Editor in Chief & Publisher: Mayra Arteaga; **Advertising Sales Manager:** Jorge López
Profile: Hola Noticias is a weekly Spanish-language newspaper written for the Hispanic residents of Jacksonville, FL and the surrounding areas.
Language (s): Spanish
Ad Rate: Full Page Mono 17.72
Currency: United States Dollars
COMMUNITY NEWSPAPER

Holyoke Sun 88233
Owner: Turley Publications, Inc.
Editorial: 24 Water St, Palmer, Massachusetts 01069-1885 **Tel:** 1 413 612-2310
Web site: http://www.holyokesunonline.com
Freq: Fri; **Circ:** 6000 Not Audited
Advertising Sales Manager: Beth Baker; **Publisher:** Patrick Turley; **Editor:** Kristin Will
Profile: Holyoke Sun is a community newspaper written for the residents of Chicopee, MA.
Language (s): English
Ad Rate: Full Page Mono 11.75
Currency: United States Dollars
COMMUNITY NEWSPAPER

Hometown Journal 20365
Editorial: 32 State St, Ste 204, Struthers, Ohio 44471-1952 **Tel:** 1 330 755-2155
Email: news@hometownjournal.biz **Web site:** http://www.hometownjournal.biz
Freq: Thu; **Circ:** 6000 Not Audited
Editor & Publisher: Nancy Johngrass
Profile: Hometown Journal is published weekly for the residents of Struthers, OH and surrounding areas. The newspaper covers local news and community events. Deadlines are on Mondays at 4pm ET.
Language (s): English
Ad Rate: Full Page Mono 8.00
Currency: United States Dollars
COMMUNITY NEWSPAPER

Hometown News 25462
Owner: Heart of Texas Media
Editorial: 2816 N 19th St Apt C, Waco, Texas 76708-2872 **Tel:** 1 254 754-3511
Email: editor@heartoftexasmedia.com **Web site:** http://www.thecitizencourier.com
Freq: Weekly
Editor and Publisher: Steve Ray
Profile: Hometown News is a weekly community newspaper serving residents of McLennan County, TX with local news, sports, business, lifestyle and opinion. Prior to purchase by Heart of Texas Media, the paper was known as the Citizen Courier.
Language (s): English
Ad Rate: Full Page Mono 10.00
Currency: United States Dollars
COMMUNITY NEWSPAPER

Hondo Anvil Herald 26672
Editorial: 1601 Avenue K, Hondo, Texas 78861-1838 **Tel:** 1 830 426-3346
Email: anvil@hondo.net **Web site:** http://www.hondoanvilherald.com
Freq: Thu; **Circ:** 5400 Not Audited
Publisher & Editor: Jeff Berger; **Advertising Sales Manager:** Lois Davis; **Circulation Manager:** Cathy Walton
Profile: Hondo Anvil Herald is written for residents of Medina County, TX.
Language (s): English
Ad Rate: Full Page Mono 7.00
Currency: United States Dollars
COMMUNITY NEWSPAPER

Hood County News 20853
Owner: Tidwell (Jerry)
Editorial: 1501 S Morgan St, Granbury, Texas 76048-2791 **Tel:** 1 817 573-7066
Email: editor@hcnews.com **Web site:** http://www.hcnews.com
Freq: Sat; **Circ:** 12200 Not Audited
Advertising Sales Manager: Rick Craig; **Editor:** Roger Enlow; **Circulation Manager:** Derek Tidwell; **Publisher:** Jerry Tidwell
Profile: Hood County News is written for the residents of Granbury, TX. It covers local events that are newsworthy, interesting or otherwise important to the Granbury community.
Language (s): English
Ad Rate: Full Page Mono 11.00
Ad Rate: Full Page Colour 706.14
Currency: United States Dollars
COMMUNITY NEWSPAPER

Hood River News 20509
Owner: Eagle Newspapers
Editorial: 419 State St, Hood River, Oregon 97031-2075 **Tel:** 1 541 386-1234
Email: hrnews@hoodrivernews.com **Web site:** http://www.gorgenews.com
Freq: Sat; **Circ:** 5800 Not Audited
Local News Editor: Kirby Neumann-Rea
Profile: The Hood River News is a twice-weekly community newspaper serving Hood River County, Oregon. The publication, which is distributed on Wednesday and Saturday, covers local news, entertainment, information, and sports which pertain to the residents of Hood River County.
Language (s): English
Ad Rate: Full Page Mono 12.35
Ad Rate: Full Page Colour 1302.50
Currency: United States Dollars
COMMUNITY NEWSPAPER

Ho'okele 22969
Owner: Oahu Publishing
Editorial: 850 Ticonderoga St Ste 110, Navy Region Hawaii Public Affairs Office, Pearl Harbor, Hawaii 96860-5101 **Tel:** 1 808 473-2888
Email: editor@hookelenews.com **Web site:** http://www.hookelenews.com
Freq: Fri; **Circ:** 16800
Profile: Ho'okele is a free weekly newspaper, published every Friday, written for the naval personnel at Navy Region Hawaii and published by the Honolulu Star-Advertiser. It contains stories, news, events and articles pertaining to Navy Region Hawaii. Deadlines for the publication are Friday the week before issue date.
Language (s): English
Ad Rate: Full Page Mono 13.21
Currency: United States Dollars
COMMUNITY NEWSPAPER

The Hoosier Topics 324670
Editorial: 1 N Main St, Cloverdale, Indiana 46120-8538 **Tel:** 1 765 795-4438
Email: htopics@ccrtc.com **Web site:** http://www.thehoosiertopics.com
Freq: Tue; **Circ:** 20183 Not Audited
Advertising Manager: Jenny Snyder
Profile: The Hoosier Topics is a free, weekly newspaper written for and about Cloverdale, Greencastle, Quincy, Poland, Eminence, Reelsville, Putnamville, Coatesville, Stilesville, Fillmore, Roachdale, Bainbridge and Spencer, IN. It covers local news, community events, businesses, sports, schools and editorials. Deadlines are at noon ET.
Language (s): English
Ad Rate: Full Page Mono 6.75
Currency: United States Dollars
COMMUNITY NEWSPAPER

Hopkinton Independent 232115
Editorial: 6 Fenton St, Hopkinton, Massachusetts 01748-1812 **Tel:** 1 508 435-5188
Email: hopkintonindependent@comcast.net **Web site:** http://www.hopkintonindependent.com
Freq: Bi-Weekly; **Circ:** 6800 Not Audited
Publisher & Editor: Sarah Lothrop Duckett
Profile: Hopkinton Independent is a bi-weekly newspaper that provides local news to the community of Hopkinton, MA.
Language (s): English
Ad Rate: Full Page Mono 48.00
Currency: United States Dollars
COMMUNITY NEWSPAPER

The Horry Independent 20647
Owner: Robertson (Steve)
Editorial: 2510 Main St, Conway, South Carolina 29526-3365 **Tel:** 1 843 248-6671

Email: info@myhorrynews.com **Web site:** http://www.myhorrynews.com
Freq: Thu; **Circ:** 6000 Not Audited
Publisher: Steve Robertson; **Editor:** Kathy Ropp
Profile: The Horry Independent is a local newspaper written for residents of Conway, SC. The paper covers local news, weather and sports.
Language (s): English
Ad Rate: Full Page Mono 10.00
Currency: United States Dollars
COMMUNITY NEWSPAPER

Hot Springs Village Voice 74017
Owner: Stephens Media Group
Editorial: 3576 N Highway 7, Hot Springs Village, Arkansas 71909-9608 **Tel:** 1 501 623-6397
Email: news@hsvvoice.com **Web site:** http://www.hsvvoice.com
Freq: Wed
Advertising Manager: Jennifer Allen
Profile: Hot Springs Village Voice is a weekly community newspaper written for the residents of Hot Springs Village, AR.
Language (s): English
Ad Rate: Full Page Mono 10.85
Currency: United States Dollars
COMMUNITY NEWSPAPER

Houghton Lake Resorter 19523
Editorial: 4049 W Houghton Lake Dr, Houghton Lake, Michigan 48629-9208 **Tel:** 1 989 366-5341
Email: news@houghtonlakeresorter.com **Web site:** http://www.houghtonlakeresorter.com
Freq: Thu; **Circ:** 6031 Not Audited
Advertising Sales Manager: Patricia Tribelhorn
Profile: Houghton Lake Resorter is written for residents of Houghton Lake and Roscommon County, MI.
Language (s): English
Ad Rate: Full Page Mono 8.75
Ad Rate: Full Page Colour 1147.20
Currency: United States Dollars
COMMUNITY NEWSPAPER

Houlton Pioneer Times 27300
Owner: Northeast Publishing Co.
Editorial: 23 Court St, Houlton, Maine 04730-1745 **Tel:** 1 207 532-2281
Email: pioneertimes@nepublish.com **Web site:** http://www.pioneertimes-me.com
Freq: Wed; **Circ:** 5000 Not Audited
Advertising Sales Manager: Dave Bates; **Publisher:** Richard Warren
Profile: Houlton Pioneer Times is written for the people of Houlton, ME and the surrounding areas.
Language (s): English
Ad Rate: Full Page Mono 16.05
Currency: United States Dollars
COMMUNITY NEWSPAPER

The Hour Publishing Company 135789
Owner: Hearst Corporation
Editorial: 1 Selleck St, Norwalk, Connecticut 06855-1120 **Tel:** 1 203 846-3281
Email: news@thehour.com
Circ: 28000 Not Audited
Editor: Chase Wright
Language (s): English
COMMUNITY NEWSPAPER

Houston County Courier 22597
Owner: Polk County Publishing
Editorial: 102 S 7Th St, Crockett, Texas 75835-2146 **Tel:** 1 936 544-2238
Email: news@houstoncountycourier.com **Web site:** http://www.easttexasnews.com/courier.htm
Freq: Sun; **Circ:** 5500 Not Audited
Advertising Sales Manager: Sherry Driskell
Profile: Houston County Courier is published twice weekly for the residents of Crockett, TX and surrounding areas. The newspaper covers local news and community events. Deadlines are on Tuesdays and Fridays at 10am CT.
Language (s): English
Ad Rate: Full Page Mono 8.85
Ad Rate: Full Page Colour 1157.40
Currency: United States Dollars
COMMUNITY NEWSPAPER

Houston Press 22931
Owner: Voice Media Group
Editorial: 2603 La Branch St, Houston, Texas 77004-1136 **Tel:** 1 713 280-2400
Email: letters@houstonpress.com **Web site:** http://www.houstonpress.com
Freq: Thu; **Circ:** 61000 Not Audited
Editor: Margaret Downing; **Publisher:** Stuart Folb
Profile: Houston Press is the metropolitan weekly that has become one of Houston's most respected and most read newspapers. The Press is dedicated to hard-hitting journalism, smart criticism, lively features and good old-fashioned muckraking.
Language (s): English
Ad Rate: Full Page Mono 28.69
Currency: United States Dollars
COMMUNITY NEWSPAPER

Houston Style 22084
Owner: Minority Print Media, LLC
Editorial: 2646 S Loop W Ste 270, Houston, Texas 77054-5608 **Tel:** 1 713 748-6300
Email: editorial@stylemagazine.com **Web site:** http://www.stylemagazine.com
Freq: Thu; **Circ:** 50000 Not Audited
Advertising Sales Manager: Lewis Miller; **Publisher and Editor:** Francis Page
Profile: Houston Style is a magazine published twice a month. The editorial content covers a wide range of topics stemming from entertainment to travel and tourism and is targeted toward the urban community. The deadline for the magazine falls on Monday.
Language (s): English
Ad Rate: Full Page Mono 44.50
Ad Rate: Full Page Colour 50.65
Currency: United States Dollars
COMMUNITY NEWSPAPER

Houston Sun 705627
Editorial: 1520 Isabella St, Houston, Texas 77004-4042 **Tel:** 1 713 524-0786
Web site: http://www.houstonsun.com/
Freq: Weekly
Publisher and Editor: Dorris Ellis
Profile: Houston Sun is a weekly newspaper providing local and community news coverage to the African-American community residing in Houston, TX.
Language (s): English
COMMUNITY NEWSPAPER

Hoy 23276
Owner: tronc
Editorial: 435 N Michigan Ave Fl 22, Chicago, Illinois 60611-7552 **Tel:** 1 312 527-8400
Email: hola@vivelohoy.com **Web site:** http://www.vivelohoy.com
Freq: Mon thru Fri; **Circ:** 99776 Not Audited
Profile: Hoy is a free, weekly Spanish-language newspaper published by the Tribune Company. It publishes three geographic editions, Chicago, New York and Los Angeles. Each edition covers local, national and international news of interest to Hispanic populations in the local area. Sports, business news and entertainment news are also covered. Each daily edition also contains special sections: Mondays include Sports and Education; Tuesdays feature a Trips section; Wednesdays offer a Health section; Thursdays feature Style and Fashion, Real Estate and Home sections; and on Fridays, an Auto section is included. Vida Hoy is the weekend supplement covering restaurants, events, music, TV, movies and other entertainment news and features. The Wall Street Journal provides an eight-page financial section on Thursdays. Additionally, Hoy dedicates region-specific pages each day to news from Central America, South America, Mexico, Puerto Rico and the Caribbean.
Language (s): Spanish/Bilingual
Ad Rate: Full Page Mono 55.73
Ad Rate: Full Page Colour 112.65
Currency: United States Dollars
COMMUNITY NEWSPAPER

Hoy San Diego 900351
Owner: San Diego Union-Tribune, LLC
Editorial: 1669 Brandywine Ave, Chula Vista, California 91911-6073 **Tel:** 1 619 293-1039
Email: editorial@mienlace.com **Web site:** http://www.vidalatinasd.com
Freq: Fri; **Circ:** 128694
Editor: Lilia O'Hara
Profile: Hoy San Diego, formerly titled Enlace, is a weekly newspaper providing Local and Community News to the Hispanic and Spanish-speaking communities in San Diego, CA and Tijuana, Baja California, Mexico published by the San Diego Union-Tribune.
Language (s): English
Ad Rate: Full Page Mono 51.70
Currency: United States Dollars
COMMUNITY NEWSPAPER

Hudson Star-Observer 24337
Owner: Forum Communications Co.
Editorial: 226 Locust St, Hudson, Wisconsin 54016-1569 **Tel:** 1 715 386-9333
Email: hso@rivertowns.net **Web site:** http://www.hudsonstarobserver.com
Freq: Thu; **Circ:** 6035 Not Audited
Editor: Douglas Stohlberg
Profile: Hudson Star-Observer is a local weekly newspaper written for the residents of Hudson, WI. The newspaper covers local news, business, education, arts & entertainment, sports and community events. Deadlines are on Fridays at 5pm CT prior to issue date.
Language (s): English
Ad Rate: Full Page Mono 12.98
Currency: United States Dollars
COMMUNITY NEWSPAPER

The Hudson Valley Press 21569
Owner: Stewart (Chuck)
Editorial: 343 Broadway, Newburgh, New York 12550-5301 **Tel:** 1 845 562-1313
Email: news@hvpress.net **Web site:** http://www.hvpress.net
Freq: Wed; **Circ:** 31800 Not Audited
Publisher & Editor: Chuck Stewart
Profile: The Hudson Valley Press in Newburgh, NY is a local publication which is written for the Latino and African American communities in Ulster, Putnam, Dutchess and Sullivan counties. The newspaper is published on a weekly basis and covers local news, sports, entertainment and cultural stories. The editorial deadline for the publication is Monday at 5pm ET.
Language (s): English
Ad Rate: Full Page Mono 29.00
Currency: United States Dollars
COMMUNITY NEWSPAPER

The Huntington County Tab 22910
Owner: Huntington TAB Inc.
Editorial: 1670 Etna Ave, Huntington, Indiana 46750-4132 **Tel:** 1 260 356-1107
Email: tabnewsroom@comcast.net **Web site:** http://www.huntingtoncountytab.com
Freq: Mon; **Circ:** 16142 Not Audited
Editor: Cindy Klepper
Profile: Huntington County Tab's editorial mission is to serve the people of Huntington County and offer them the foremost in enlightening news information. This local publication is written for Huntington residents. Articles include news, travel, weather and community events. Deadlines for the publication are one week before issue date.
Language (s): English
Ad Rate: Full Page Mono 8.20
Currency: United States Dollars
COMMUNITY NEWSPAPER

Hutchinson Leader 19652
Owner: Red Wing Publishing
Editorial: 170 Shady Ridge Rd NW Ste 100, Hutchinson, Minnesota 55350-1454 **Tel:** 1 320 587-5000
Email: news@hutchinsonleader.com **Web site:** http://www.hutchinsonleader.com
Freq: Sun; **Circ:** 5000 Not Audited
Circulation Manager: Alan Fuchs; **Publisher:** Brent Schacherer; **Advertising Sales Manager:** Kevin TRUE
Profile: Hutchinson Leader is published weekly for residents of Hutchinson, MN. The newspaper covers local news, business, sports and community events.
Language (s): English
Ad Rate: Full Page Mono 13.39
Ad Rate: Full Page Colour 1006.41
Currency: United States Dollars
COMMUNITY NEWSPAPER

Hutto News 154429
Owner: Granite Publications
Editorial: 101 East St, Hutto, Texas 78634-4510 **Tel:** 1 512 578-5229
Email: newsdesk@thehuttonews.com **Web site:** http://www.thehuttonews.com
Freq: Wed; **Circ:** 6600 Not Audited
Editor: Christine Bolanos
Profile: Hutto News is a weekly newspaper for the residents of Hutto, TX. It covers local news, sports, business, events, education and entertainment.
Language (s): English
Ad Rate: Full Page Mono 7.00
Ad Rate: Full Page Colour 23.43
Currency: United States Dollars
COMMUNITY NEWSPAPER

Idaho Catholic Register 19028
Owner: Roman Catholic Diocese of Boise
Editorial: 1501 S Federal Way, Boise, Idaho 83705-2588 **Tel:** 1 208 342-1311
Email: information@rcdb.org **Web site:** http://www.catholicidaho.org
Freq: Bi-Weekly; **Circ:** 12000 Not Audited
Advertising Sales Manager: Ann Bixby; **Editor:** Michael Brown; **Publisher:** Michael P. Driscoll; **Circulation Manager:** Loretta Gossi
Profile: Idaho Catholic Register in Boise, ID covers Catholicism, religious and social issues. It hopes to inform, unify, inspire and educate the Catholic population. Deadlines for the publication are two weeks before the issue date.
Language (s): English
Ad Rate: Full Page Mono 12.65
Currency: United States Dollars
COMMUNITY NEWSPAPER

Idaho Mountain Express 21350
Owner: Express Publishing, Inc.
Editorial: 591 N 1st Ave, Ketchum, Idaho 83340 **Tel:** 1 208 726-8060
Email: news@mtexpress.com **Web site:** http://www.mtexpress.com
Freq: 2 Times/Week; **Circ:** 13500 Not Audited
Editor: Greg Foley; **Publisher:** Pam Morris; **Circulation Manager:** Ben Varner
Profile: Idaho Mountain Express appears twice weekly for people around the Sun Valley, ID resort area. The paper covers local news, sports and arts. It contains a calendar of regional events. Deadlines for the publication are one week before issue date.
Language (s): English
Ad Rate: Full Page Mono 17.30
Currency: United States Dollars
COMMUNITY NEWSPAPER

Identidad Latina 154583
Editorial: 593 Farmington Ave, Hartford, Connecticut 06105-3038 **Tel:** 1 860 231-9891
Email: news@identidadlatina.com **Web site:** http://www.identidadlatina.com
Freq: Bi-Weekly; **Circ:** 15000
Editor: Jorge Alatrista; **Advertising Sales Manager:** Adelia Cruz; **Publisher:** Ruth Espinoza
Profile: Identidad Latina is a community newspaper serving the Hispanic community of Hartford, CT.
Language (s): English
Ad Rate: Full Page Mono 18.70
Currency: United States Dollars
COMMUNITY NEWSPAPER

Illinois Times 19152
Owner: Central Illinois Communications Inc.
Editorial: 1320 S State St, Springfield, Illinois 62704-3654 **Tel:** 1 217 753-2226
Email: editor@illinoistimes.com **Web site:** http://www.illinoistimes.com
Freq: Thu; **Circ:** 28000 Not Audited
Editor: Fletcher Farrar; **Circulation Manager:** Brenda Matheis; **Publisher:** Sharon Whalen
Profile: Illinois Times is published weekly for residents of Springfield, IL and surrounding communities. It is an alternative to the mainstream media for arts and local news. It covers local news, community events, arts & entertainment and nightlife. Please send editorial submissions and press materials to the main e-mail address.
Language (s): English
Ad Rate: Full Page Mono 6.25
Currency: United States Dollars
COMMUNITY NEWSPAPER

Illyria 23179
Owner: Ekrem Newspaper, L.L.C.
Editorial: 481 8th Ave Ste 536, New York, New York 10001-1809 **Tel:** 1 212 868-2224
Email: info@illyriapress.com **Web site:** http://www.illyriapress.com
Freq: Fri; **Circ:** 10000 Not Audited
Editor: Ruben Avxhiu; **Publisher:** Vebi Bharami
Profile: Illyria is an Albanian American newspaper in New York. It covers events in Albania, Kosovo, the Albanian territories of Macedonia, Montenegro and the diaspora. The paper is written for Albanian Americans and those interested in the politics and history of Albania and the former Yugoslavia.
Language (s): English
Ad Rate: Full Page Mono 5.93
Currency: United States Dollars
COMMUNITY NEWSPAPER

Impacto Latin News 21794
Editorial: 225 W 35th St Ste 305, New York, New York 10001-1904 **Tel:** 1 212 807-0400
Email: media@impactony.com **Web site:** http://www.impactony.com
Freq: Wed; **Circ:** 57000 Not Audited
Publisher: Gail Smith-Carillo
Profile: Impacto Latin News is a local weekly newspaper serving the Latin communities of New York. It covers community, national, international news, sports coverage and movie reviews. Deadlines are on Fridays at noon ET.
Language (s): Spanish
Ad Rate: Full Page Mono 66.65
Currency: United States Dollars
COMMUNITY NEWSPAPER

Impacto USA 217288
Owner: Los Angeles Newspaper Group
Editorial: 21250 Hawthorne Blvd Ste 170, Torrance, California 90503-5514 **Tel:** 1 562 499-1415
Web site: http://www.impactousa.com
Freq: Sat; **Circ:** 193220
Editor: Jose Fuentes
Profile: Impacto USA is a community newspaper written for the residents of Torrance, CA and the surrounding areas.
Language (s): English
Ad Rate: Full Page Mono 147.50
Currency: United States Dollars
COMMUNITY NEWSPAPER

The Independent 21465
Owner: Seppala (Joan)
Editorial: 2250 1st St, Livermore, California 94550-3143 **Tel:** 1 925 447-8700
Email: editmail@compuserve.com **Web site:** http://www.independentnews.com
Freq: Thu; **Circ:** 33000 Not Audited
Editor: Janet Armantrout; **Circulation Manager:** Doug Jorgensen; **Advertising Sales Manager:** Tina Rose; **Publisher:** Joan Kinney Seppala
Profile: The Independent provides local news coverage to residents of Livermore, Pleasanton and Sunol, CA. Deadlines are at 5pm PT on the Friday prior to the issue date.
Language (s): English
Ad Rate: Full Page Mono 26.10
Currency: United States Dollars
COMMUNITY NEWSPAPER

The Independent 21947
Owner: East Hampton Independent News Company Inc.
Editorial: 74 Montauk Hwy Unit 16, East Hampton, New York 11937-3268 **Tel:** 1 631 324-2500
Email: news@indyeastend.com **Web site:** http://www.indyeastend.com
Freq: Wed; **Circ:** 19769 Not Audited
Publisher: Jim Mackin; **News Editor:** Kitty Merrill; **Circulation Manager:** Ben Sneed
Profile: The Independent is a weekly newspaper serving the communities of East Hampton, South Hampton, Riverhead, Southold and Shelter Island, NY. It covers community news, events, sports, business and features of interest to local readers. Deadlines are at noon ET.
Language (s): English
Ad Rate: Full Page Mono 55.44
Currency: United States Dollars
COMMUNITY NEWSPAPER

The Independent 791698
Owner: Independent Publishing Company
Editorial: 40 N 300 E Ste 103, Saint George, Utah 84770-2900 **Tel:** 1 435 656-1555
Email: editor@infowest.com **Web site:** http://www.suindependent.com
Freq: Monthly; **Circ:** 20500
Editor: Greta Hyland; **Publisher:** Josh Warburton
Profile: The Independent is a monthly newspaper providing Arts & Entertainment News and Listings to the residents of Saint George, UT and the greater Southern Utah area. Copies are published the first Friday of each month.
Language (s): English
Ad Rate: Full Page Colour 16.81
Currency: United States Dollars
COMMUNITY NEWSPAPER

Independent Appeal 21333
Owner: McNairy County Publishing, LLC
Editorial: 111 N 2nd St, Selmer, Tennessee 38375
Tel: 1 731 645-5346
Email: submissions@independentappeal.com **Web site:** http://www.independentappeal.com
Freq: Wed; **Circ:** 7289 Not Audited
Editor: John Philleo; **Publisher:** Janet Rail
Profile: The Independent Appeal is a weekly newspaper written for residents of McNairy County, TN and the surrounding area. The newspaper covers the community news and events.
Language (s): English
Ad Rate: Full Page Mono 4.50
Currency: United States Dollars
COMMUNITY NEWSPAPER

Independent Herald 21271
Owner: Civitas Media
Editorial: 683 Appalachian Highway, Pineville, West Virginia 24874 **Tel:** 1 304 732-6060
Web site: http://www.independentherald.com
Freq: Wed; **Circ:** 6000 Not Audited
Editor: John Conley
Profile: Pineville Independent Herald is a local weekly newspaper in Pineville, WV. The publication's editorial mission is to inform the residents of Pineville, WV about local news and current events in Wyoming County, WV. The newspaper is published weekly on Wednesdays. Deadlines are on Fridays before issue date at 5pm ET.
Language (s): English
Ad Rate: Full Page Mono 4.50
Currency: United States Dollars
COMMUNITY NEWSPAPER

The Independent Journal 19808
Owner: The Independent-Journal Corp
Editorial: 119 E High St, Potosi, Missouri 63664-1906
Tel: 1 573 438-5141
Email: ijnews@centurytel.net **Web site:** http://www.theijnews.com
Freq: Thu; **Circ:** 5300 Not Audited
Advertising Sales Manager: Kris Richards
Profile: The Independent Journal is a community newspaper written for the residents of Potosi, MO.
Language (s): English
Ad Rate: Full Page Mono 6.00
Currency: United States Dollars
COMMUNITY NEWSPAPER

Independent Messenger 80824
Owner: Womack Newspapers Inc.
Editorial: 111 Baker St, Emporia, Virginia 23847-1703 **Tel:** 1 434 634-4153
Email: news@imnewspaper.com **Web site:** http://www.emporiaindependentmessenger.com
Freq: Sun; **Circ:** 9600 Not Audited
Advertising Sales Manager: Becky Hinkle; **Publisher & Editor:** Don Koralewski
Profile: The Independent Messenger is written for the residents of Emporia, VA.
Language (s): English
Ad Rate: Full Page Mono 9.65
Currency: United States Dollars
COMMUNITY NEWSPAPER

Independent News 18774
Owner: Outzen (Rick)
Editorial: 226 Palafox Pl, Pensacola, Florida 32502-5846 **Tel:** 1 850 438-8115
Email: info@inweekly.net **Web site:** http://www.inweekly.net
Freq: Thu; **Circ:** 25000 Not Audited
Publisher & Editor: Rick Outzen
Profile: Independent News is a local newspaper written for the residents of Pensacola, FL.
Language (s): English
Ad Rate: Full Page Mono 25.54
Ad Rate: Full Page Colour 50.00
Currency: United States Dollars
COMMUNITY NEWSPAPER

The Independent News 19144
Owner: News-Gazette Inc.
Editorial: 137 N. Walnut St., Danville, Illinois 61832
Tel: 1 217 443-8484
Email: indnews@news-gazette.com **Web site:** http://www.the-independent-news.com
Freq: Wed; **Circ:** 16000 Not Audited
Circulation Manager: Melinda Carpenter; **Editor:** Vicki Delhaye; **Publisher:** John Foreman; **Advertising Sales Manager:** Jan Lynn Long
Profile: The Independent News is a weekly, community newspaper serving residents of Georgetown and surrounding areas in Vermilion County, IL. It contains local news, events and feature stories.
Language (s): English
Ad Rate: Full Page Mono 10.25
Currency: United States Dollars
COMMUNITY NEWSPAPER

The Independent News 22873
Owner: Two Rivers Publishing Co. Inc
Editorial: 25 Saint Anthony Ln, Florissant, Missouri 63031-6720 **Tel:** 1 314 831-4645
Email: independentnws@aol.com **Web site:** http://www.flovalleynews.com
Freq: Thu; **Circ:** 27000 Not Audited
News Editor: Carol Arnett; **Publisher & Editor:** Bob Lindsey; **Circulation Manager:** Phil Tankersley
Profile: The Independent News is a weekly publication covering news and events for the cities of Florissant and Hazelwood, MO. Topics include local sports, community news, events, city politics and features.
Language (s): English
Ad Rate: Full Page Mono 12.50
Currency: United States Dollars
COMMUNITY NEWSPAPER

Independent Tribune 14301
Owner: World Media Enterprises, Inc.
Editorial: 363 Church St N Ste 140, Concord, North Carolina 28025-4590 **Tel:** 1 704 782-3155
Email: alert@independenttribune.com **Web site:** http://www.independenttribune.com
Freq: Fri; **Circ:** 16910
Circulation Manager: Bud Welch
Profile: Independent Tribune is a weekly newspaper written for the communities of Concord and Kannapolis, NC. It covers local news, sports and lifestyle stories.
Language (s): English
Ad Rate: Full Page Mono 16.17
Ad Rate: Full Page Colour 23.88
Currency: United States Dollars
COMMUNITY NEWSPAPER

The Independent Weekly 21321
Owner: City of Roses Newspaper Co.
Editorial: 201 W Main St Ste 101, Durham, North Carolina 27701-3228 **Tel:** 1 919 286-1972
Email: editors@indyweek.com **Web site:** http://www.indyweek.com
Freq: Wed; **Circ:** 45000 Not Audited
Circulation Manager: Brenna Berry-Stewart; **Advertising Sales Manager:** Ruth Gierisch
Profile: Independent Weekly is written for residents of Durham, NC. It covers local news, social issues, arts & entertainment, music and lifestyle.
Language (s): English
Ad Rate: Full Page Mono 31.00
Ad Rate: Full Page Colour 1900.21
Currency: United States Dollars
COMMUNITY NEWSPAPER

India Abroad 22571
Owner: India Abroad Publishing Inc.
Editorial: 42 Broadway Ste 1836, New York, New York 10004-3855 **Tel:** 1 212 929-1727
Email: editorial@indiaabroad.com **Web site:** http://www.indiaabroad.com
Freq: Fri; **Circ:** 38000 Not Audited
Community News Editor: George Joseph; **Advertising Sales Manager:** Jitender Sharma
Profile: India Abroad in New York is published weekly for members of the Indian American Center for Political Awareness. The newspaper covers all social and political issues affecting the Indian community in America. The publication's editorial mission is to increase awareness in the Indian American community and encourage participation in American democracy. Deadlines for the publication are on Tuesdays.
Language (s): English
Ad Rate: Full Page Mono 46.00
Currency: United States Dollars
COMMUNITY NEWSPAPER

India Bulletin 918883
Tel: 1 847 674-7941
Email: pressrelease@indiabulletinusa.com
Freq: Bi-Weekly; **Circ:** 27000
Profile: This bi-weekly publication is aimed at the Indian community in the Midwest. Covers the latest news and events.
Language (s): English
COMMUNITY NEWSPAPER

India Globe 504137
Editorial: 27025 McPherson Square Station, Washington, District Of Columbia 20038
Tel: 1 202 271-1100
Email: indiaglobe@hotmail.com
Freq: Weekly; **Circ:** 10000 Not Audited
Editor & Publisher: Raghubir Goyal
Profile: India Globe is a weekly community newspaper distributed to the Indian residents of Washington, D.C. and the surrounding areas.
Language (s): English
Ad Rate: Full Page Mono 300.00
Currency: United States Dollars
COMMUNITY NEWSPAPER

India Journal 79705
Owner: Premier Media Inc.
Editorial: 13353 Alondra Blvd Ste 115, Santa Fe Springs, California 90670-5588 **Tel:** 1 562 802-9720
Email: info@indiajournal.com **Web site:** http://www.indiajournal.com
Freq: Fri; **Circ:** 20500 Not Audited
Publisher: Navneet Chugh; **Advertising Sales Manager:** Kamaljit Kaur; **Editor:** Nimmi Raghunathan
Profile: India Journal is a weekly newspaper that serves southern California's South Asian community. It features local news, sports and entertainment. Editorial deadlines are on Mondays. Advertising deadlines are on Fridays.
Language (s): English
Ad Rate: Full Page Mono 4.75
Currency: United States Dollars
COMMUNITY NEWSPAPER

INDIA New England 62669
Owner: Mishra Group, Inc. (The)
Editorial: 1344 Maine St., Waltham, Massachusetts 2451 **Tel:** 1 781 373-3220
Email: editorial@mishragroup.com **Web site:** http://www.indianewengland.com
Freq: Bi-Weekly; **Circ:** 12000 Not Audited
Editor: Martin Desmarais
Profile: India New England is written for the Indo-American community throughout New England. It covers business, entrepreneurship, cultural and community news and events.
Language (s): English
Ad Rate: Full Page Mono 22.65
Currency: United States Dollars
COMMUNITY NEWSPAPER

India This Week/Express India 681827
Editorial: 7908 Kennewick Ave Apt 101, Takoma Park, Maryland 20912-7413 **Tel:** 1 301 445-0200
Email: indiathisweekeditorial@gmail.com **Web site:** http://www.indiathisweek.us
Circ: 22000
Publisher & Editor: Rajan George; **Advertising Sales Manager:** Geofrey Gilbert
Language (s): English
COMMUNITY NEWSPAPER

India Tribune 22493
Editorial: 3302 W Peterson Ave, Chicago, Illinois 60659-3510 **Tel:** 1 773 588-5077
Email: prashant@indiatribune.com **Web site:** http://www.indiatribune.com
Freq: Sat; **Circ:** 40000 Not Audited
Publisher: Eric Shah; **Publisher:** Prashant Shah
Profile: India Tribune, an English weekly newspaper, was launched in 1977 in Chicago to serve the Asian Indian settlers in the USA. It is published in three editions: Chicago, New York and Atlanta. The publication is written for the Indian community in the United States. The lead time for India Tribune is one week.
Language (s): English
Ad Rate: Full Page Mono 25.71
Currency: United States Dollars
COMMUNITY NEWSPAPER

India West 22489
Owner: India West Publications
Editorial: 933 MacArthur Blvd, San Leandro, California 94577-3062 **Tel:** 1 510 383-1140
Email: news@indiawest.com **Web site:** http://www.indiawest.com
Freq: Fri; **Circ:** 150000 Not Audited
Editor: Bina Murarka; **Publisher:** Ramesh Murarka
Profile: India West is a weekly newspaper published for the Indian American community in San Leandro, CA and the surrounding area. The paper covers news, local events, business, sports, religion, lifestyle and entertainment. Some articles are also reprinted from Indianlifeandstyle.com, an online-only magazine targeting the Indian American community.
Language (s): English
Ad Rate: Full Page Mono 30.00
Ad Rate: Full Page Colour 2100.00
Currency: United States Dollars
COMMUNITY NEWSPAPER

Indiana Newspaper Group 25181
Owner: MC Communications, Inc.
Editorial: 407 E Main St, Gas City, Indiana 46933-1532 **Tel:** 1 765 674-0070
Circ: 14000 Not Audited
Publisher: Greg LeNeave; **Advertising Sales Manager:** Bill Shelton; **Editor:** Rachel Terry
Language (s): English
COMMUNITY NEWSPAPER

The Indianapolis Recorder 19217
Owner: George P. Stewart Publishing Co.
Editorial: 2901 N Tacoma Ave, Indianapolis, Indiana 46218-2737 **Tel:** 1 317 924-5143
Email: newsroom@indyrecorder.com **Web site:** http://www.indianapolisrecorder.com
Freq: Fri; **Circ:** 13300 Not Audited
Profile: The Indianapolis Recorder's editorial mission is to empower and enlighten the African American community of Indianapolis. Deadline for the publication is one week before issue date.
Language (s): English
Ad Rate: Full Page Mono 16.34
Currency: United States Dollars
COMMUNITY NEWSPAPER

Indo American News 769533
Owner: IndoAmerican News Inc.
Editorial: 7457 Harwin Dr Ste 262, Houston, Texas 77036-2025 **Tel:** 1 713 789-6397
Email: indoamericannews@yahoo.com **Web site:** http://www.indoamerican-news.com
Freq: Weekly; **Circ:** 6000
Community News Editor: Vanshika Vipin
Profile: Indo American News serves the South Asian population of Greater Houston. Offers news on Houston and South Asia. Coverage includes business, features, art, culture, entertainment, health, food, sports, travel, education and more.
Language (s): English
Ad Rate: Full Page Mono 15.00
Currency: United States Dollars
COMMUNITY NEWSPAPER

La Informacion Newspapers 25551
Owner: Martinez (Lina)
Editorial: 6065 Hillcroft St Ste 400B, Houston, Texas 77081-1013 **Tel:** 1 713 272-0100
Web site: http://www.lainformacion.us
Circ: 200000 Not Audited
Editor: Emilio Martinez-Paula
Language (s): English, Spanish
COMMUNITY NEWSPAPER

El Informador del Valle 23287
Owner: Felix (Hector)
Editorial: 82015 US Highway 111, Indio, California 92201-5686 **Tel:** 1 760 342-7558
Email: elinformads@yahoo.com **Web site:** http://www.elinformadordelvalle.com
Freq: Thu; **Circ:** 40000 Not Audited
Publisher & Editor: Hector Felix
Profile: El Informador del Valle is a Spanish-language newspaper for Indio, CA. It provides the Hispanic community with information on local news, arts & entertainment and more.
Language (s): Spanish
Ad Rate: Full Page Mono 15.00
Currency: United States Dollars
COMMUNITY NEWSPAPER

Inglewood Today 349681
Owner: Brown (Willie)
Editorial: 9111 S La Cienega Blvd Ste 100, Inglewood, California 90301-4411 **Tel:** 1 310 670-9600
Email: willie@inglewoodtoday.com **Web site:** http://www.inglewoodtoday.com
Freq: Thu; **Circ:** 25000 Not Audited
Circulation Manager: Daryl McLamore
Profile: Inglewood Today is a free, weekly community paper that serves the residents, businesses and local government of Inglewood, CA. The tabloid paper covers community news, events, politics, school districts, businesses and locally-related editorials. Some national news issues and happenings are also covered, if they are relevant to local readers. The paper encourages article contributions from area residents. The lead time is Mondays at noon PT.
Language (s): English
Ad Rate: Full Page Mono 49.50
Currency: United States Dollars
COMMUNITY NEWSPAPER

Inland Empire Community News 24850
Editorial: 1809 Commercenter W, San Bernardino, California 92408-3303 **Tel:** 1 909 381-9898
Email: iecn1@mac.com **Web site:** http://www.iecn.com
Circ: 20000 Not Audited
Circulation Manager: Keith Armstrong
Profile: Inland Empire Community News covers San Bernardino, CA, offering readers news, sports, features and more.
Language (s): English
COMMUNITY NEWSPAPER

Inland Valley News 23298
Owner: Inland Valley News, Inc.
Editorial: 2009 Porter Field Way Ste C, Upland, California 91786-1106 **Tel:** 1 909 985-0072
Email: info@inlandvalleynews.com **Web site:** http://www.inlandvalleynews.com
Freq: Weekly; **Circ:** 18000 Not Audited
Profile: Inland Valley News is written for the African American community living in the Inland Valley area of Southern California.
Language (s): English
Ad Rate: Full Page Mono 24.90
Currency: United States Dollars
COMMUNITY NEWSPAPER

The Inlander 22678
Editorial: 1227 W Summit Pkwy, Spokane, Washington 99201-7003 **Tel:** 1 509 325-0634
Email: editor@inlander.com **Web site:** http://www.inlander.com
Freq: Thu; **Circ:** 47000 Not Audited
Editor: Jacob Fries; **Advertising Sales Manager:** Kristi Gotzian; **Publisher & Editor:** Ted McGregor
Profile: The Inlander in Spokane, WA is published weekly and covers local news, weather, sports, arts, features and community events.
Language (s): English
Ad Rate: Full Page Mono 49.00
Currency: United States Dollars
COMMUNITY NEWSPAPER

Inner City 22533
Owner: Penfield Communication
Editorial: 50 Fitch St, New Haven, Connecticut 06515-1366 **Tel:** 1 203 387-0354
Freq: Wed; **Circ:** 20000 Not Audited
Advertising Sales Manager: Keith Jackson; **Publisher & Editor:** John Thomas
Profile: Inner City's editorial mission is to cover local news, sports, government, arts & entertainment for residents of greater Bridgeport and New Haven, CT.
Language (s): English
Ad Rate: Full Page Mono 55.00
Currency: United States Dollars
COMMUNITY NEWSPAPER

The Inquirer & Mirror 19453
Owner: GateHouse Media Inc.
Editorial: 1 Old South Rd, Nantucket, Massachusetts 02554-2836 **Tel:** 1 508 228-0001
Email: newsroom@inkym.com **Web site:** http://www.ack.net
Freq: Thu; **Circ:** 8000 Not Audited
Advertising Sales Manager: Lora Kebbati; **Publisher & Editor:** Marianne Stanton
Profile: The Inquirer & Mirror is written for the residents of Nantucket, MA. It covers local news, events and weather.
Language (s): English
Ad Rate: Full Page Mono 26.23
Currency: United States Dollars
COMMUNITY NEWSPAPER

Inquiring News
24497
Owner: Hales (Reggie)
Editorial: 51 Gilbert Ave, Bloomfield, Connecticut 06002-3824 **Tel:** 1 860 983-7587
Email: inqnews@aol.com **Web site:** http://www.inqnews.com
Freq: Wed; **Circ:** 55000 Not Audited
Publisher & Editor: Reggie Hales
Profile: Inquiring News is a local, community newspaper serving residents of Hartford, New Haven, Bridgeport, Springfield and Waterbury, CT. The paper includes local news, business, sports, arts & entertainment and community events.
Language (s): English
Ad Rate: Full Page Mono 35.82
Currency: United States Dollars
COMMUNITY NEWSPAPER

The Inquisitor
258050
Owner: Danny Lawler Enterprises, LLC
Editorial: 7781 Highway 1, Shreveport, Louisiana 71107-8148 **Tel:** 1 318 929-5152
Email: news@nwcable.net **Web site:** http://www.theinquisitor.com
Freq: Fri; **Circ:** 36000 Not Audited
Publisher & Editor: Danny Lawler; **Advertising Sales Manager:** Wendy Lawler; **Circulation Manager:** Elizabeth Morace
Profile: The Inquisitor in Shreveport, LA is a weekly newspaper that covers local news, events, business, politics and lifestyle for residents of Caddo and Bossier parishes.
Language (s): English
Ad Rate: Full Page Mono 10.00
Currency: United States Dollars
COMMUNITY NEWSPAPER

Inside NoVa - North Stafford
27400
Owner: Northern Virginia Media Services
Editorial: 1372 Old Bridge Rd Ste 101, Woodbridge, Virginia 22192-2755 **Tel:** 1 703 318-1836
Email: info@insidenova.com **Web site:** https://www.insidenova.com
Freq: Fri; **Circ:** 20000 Not Audited
Advertising Manager: Tom Spargur
Profile: Inside NoVa - North Stafford (formerly Stafford County Sun) is written for residents of Stafford County, VA. It covers local news and information, community events and stories of interest to area readers.
Language (s): English
Ad Rate: Full Page Mono 12.00
Ad Rate: Full Page Colour 205.00
Currency: United States Dollars
COMMUNITY NEWSPAPER

Inside NoVa - Prince William
883293
Owner: Northern Virginia Media Services
Editorial: 1372 Old Bridge Rd Ste 101, Woodbridge, Virginia 22192-2755 **Tel:** 1 703 318-1386
Email: info@insidenova.com **Web site:** http://www.insidenova.com
Freq: Weekly
Advertising Sales Manager: Connie Fields; **Editor:** Kari Pugh
Profile: Inside NoVa - Prince William Edition (formerly Prince William Today) is a weekly newspaper for residents of Prince William County, Manassas and Manassas Park, VA. It covers local news, sports and events. Launched in January 2013.
Language (s): English
COMMUNITY NEWSPAPER

Inside Publications
583920
Owner: Inside Publications
Editorial: 6221 N Clark St, Chicago, Illinois 60660-1207 **Tel:** 1 773 465-9700
Email: insidepublicationschicago@gmail.com **Web site:** http://www.insideonline.com
Circ: 50000
Publisher & Editor: Ronald Roenigk
Profile: Inside Publications is a local newspaper providing the community of Chicago, IL with news.
Language (s): English
Ad Rate: Full Page Mono 25.00
Currency: United States Dollars
COMMUNITY NEWSPAPER

Insight News
21983
Owner: Insight News, Inc.
Editorial: 1815 Bryant Ave N, Minneapolis, Minnesota 55411-3212 **Tel:** 1 612 588-1313
Email: info@insightnews.com **Web site:** http://www.insightnews.com
Freq: Weekly; **Circ:** 35000 Not Audited
Publisher: Batala-Ra McFarlane; **Circulation Manager:** Jamal Mohamed
Profile: Insight News is written for African American residents of Minneapolis. It covers information, instruction and inspiration in a user-friendly, culturally relevant way. It provides preferred access to African American consumers for businesses, agencies and organizations.
Language (s): English
Ad Rate: Full Page Mono 69.84
Currency: United States Dollars
COMMUNITY NEWSPAPER

Inter-County Leader
21176
Editorial: 303 Wisconsin Ave N, Frederic, Wisconsin 54837-9048 **Tel:** 1 715 327-4236
Email: editor@leadernewsroom.com **Web site:** http://www.leadernewsroom.com
Freq: Wed; **Circ:** 6000 Not Audited
Editor: Gary King

Profile: Inter-County Leader is a local newspaper written for the residents of Frederic, WI. The paper offers articles on local and national news, arts & entertainment, events and sports. Deadlines are Tuesdays at 10am CT.
Language (s): English
Ad Rate: Full Page Mono 2.30
Currency: United States Dollars
COMMUNITY NEWSPAPER

Intermountain Catholic
21909
Owner: Catholic Diocese of Salt Lake City
Editorial: 27 C St, Salt Lake City, Utah 84103-2302 **Tel:** 1 801 328-8641
Email: icnews@icatholic.org **Web site:** http://www.icatholic.org
Freq: Fri; **Circ:** 15000 Not Audited
Circulation Manager: Arthur Heredia; **Editor:** Marie Mischel; **Advertising Sales Manager:** Cris Paulsen; **Publisher:** John Wester
Profile: Intermountain Catholic is a weekly newspaper that provides news and information for the Diocese of Salt Lake City.
Language (s): English
Ad Rate: Full Page Mono 20.00
Currency: United States Dollars
COMMUNITY NEWSPAPER

Intermountain Jewish News
71254
Owner: Goldberg (Miriam)
Editorial: 1177 Grant St Ste 200, Denver, Colorado 80203-2362 **Tel:** 1 303 861-2234
Email: email@ijn.com **Web site:** http://www.ijn.com
Freq: Fri; **Circ:** 50000 Not Audited
Advertising Sales Manager: Lori Aron; **Circulation Manager:** Carol Coen; **Publisher & Editor:** Miriam Harris Goldberg
Profile: Intermountain Jewish News's editorial mission is to provide news and information of interest to the Jewish population of Colorado, New Mexico, Wyoming, Utah and Montana.
Language (s): English
Ad Rate: Full Page Mono 68.63
Currency: United States Dollars
COMMUNITY NEWSPAPER

Intertown Record
22190
Owner: Bog Mountain Publishing LLC.
Editorial: 1526 Rt 114, Unit D, North Sutton, New Hampshire 03260-9999 **Tel:** 1 603 927-4028
Email: info@intertownrecord.com **Web site:** http://www.intertownrecord.com
Freq: Tue; **Circ:** 5000 Not Audited
Advertising Sales Manager: Diane Rosewood
Profile: Intertown Record is published weekly for the residents of North Sutton, NH and surrounding areas. The newspaper covers local news and community events. Deadlines are on Thursdays prior to issue date.
Language (s): English
Ad Rate: Full Page Mono 7.50
Currency: United States Dollars
COMMUNITY NEWSPAPER

The Inyo Register
22866
Owner: Horizon Publications
Editorial: 1180 N Main St Ste 108, Bishop, California 93514-2472 **Tel:** 1 760 873-3535
Email: editor@inyoregister.com **Web site:** http://www.inyoregister.com
Freq: Sat; **Circ:** 6000 Not Audited
Circulation Manager: Aime Banta; **Editor:** Darcy Ellis; **Advertising Sales Manager:** Terry Langdon; **Publisher:** Carol Ross
Profile: The Inyo Register is written for the community of Owens County, CA.
Language (s): English
Ad Rate: Full Page Mono 12.85
Currency: United States Dollars
COMMUNITY NEWSPAPER

Iowa Bystander & El Communicador Newspapers
217162
Owner: IPJ Media, LLC
Editorial: Des Moines, Iowa **Tel:** 1 515 288-7677
Web site: http://iowabystander.com
Circ: 10500 Not Audited
Publisher: Jerald Bratley; **Editor:** Jonathan Narcisse
Language (s): English
COMMUNITY NEWSPAPER

Iowa County Newspapers
24513
Owner: Gannett Co., Inc.
Editorial: 100 W Main St, Marengo, Iowa 52301-4705 **Tel:** 1 319 642-5506
Circ: 13307 Not Audited
Publisher: Dan DeBettignies; **Editor:** J.O. Parker; **Advertising Sales Manager:** John Rotter
Language (s): English
COMMUNITY NEWSPAPER

Iowa Information, Inc.
24514
Editorial: 227 9th St, Sheldon, Iowa 51201-1419
Circ: 7900 Not Audited
Editor: Jeff Grant; **Advertising Sales Manager:** Denise Rust; **Publisher:** Peter Wagner; **Circulation Manager:** Lori Wiersma
Language (s): English
COMMUNITY NEWSPAPER

Iranians Newspaper
24187
Owner: Washington Iranians Media, Inc.
Editorial: 43861 Arborvitae Dr, Ashburn, Virginia 20147 **Tel:** 1 703 724-9680

Email: iranians@iraniansnewspaper.com **Web site:** http://www.iraniansnewspaper.com
Freq: Weekly; **Circ:** 120000 Not Audited
Advertising Sales Manager: Ali Khaligh; **Editor:** Taghi Mokhtar
Profile: Iranians Newspaper is published weekly in Persian. The newspaper serves the Iranian community of the United States. It provides information on developments within the Iranian community and other topics of importance to Iranians.
Language (s): English
Ad Rate: Full Page Mono 12.50
Currency: United States Dollars
COMMUNITY NEWSPAPER

Irish Echo
21958
Editorial: 165 Madison Ave Rm 302, New York, New York 10016-5431 **Tel:** 1 212 482-4818
Email: letters@irishecho.com **Web site:** http://www.irishecho.com
Freq: Wed; **Circ:** 62000 Not Audited
Circulation Manager: Madeline O'Boyle; **Publisher:** Mairtin O'Muilleoir
Profile: Irish Echo, founded in 1928, is the largest circulation Irish American newspaper in the United States. It covers arts & leisure, business and sports. The deadlines are 4pm ET every Friday.
Language (s): English
Ad Rate: Full Page Mono 32.70
Currency: United States Dollars
COMMUNITY NEWSPAPER

IrishCentral
317662
Editorial: 875 Avenue of the Americas Ste 201, New York, New York 10001-3507 **Tel:** 1 212 871-0111 200
Email: editors@irishcentral.com **Web site:** http://www.irishcentral.com
Circ: 20000 Not Audited
Publisher: Connell Gallagher; **Editor:** Kate Hickey; **Advertising Sales Manager:** Peter Walsh
Profile: Covers news and interests of Irish descendants in North America. Tells stories of Irish culture, roots, history, genealogy, and serves as a leading source for news and politics for Irish Americans and Ireland.
Language (s): English
COMMUNITY NEWSPAPER

Iron County Reporter
19525
Editorial: 801 W Adams St, Iron River, Michigan 49935-1218 **Tel:** 1 906 265-9927
Email: news@ironcountyreporter.com **Web site:** http://www.ironcountyreporter.com
Freq: Wed; **Circ:** 6000 Not Audited
Circulation Manager: Nan Burske; **Publisher:** Margaret Christensen
Profile: Iron County Reporter is a newspaper for the community of Iron County, MI and northern WI. The publication covers local news, community events and sports. Deadlines are on Fridays prior to issue dates at 4pm CT.
Language (s): English
Ad Rate: Full Page Mono 6.75
Currency: United States Dollars
COMMUNITY NEWSPAPER

Iron Mountain Advertiser
22397
Owner: Ogden Newspapers
Editorial: 421 S Stephenson Ave, Iron Mountain, Michigan 49801-3454 **Tel:** 1 906 774-3708
Email: advertiser@ironmountainadvertiser.com
Freq: Tue; **Circ:** 20600 Not Audited
Editor: Joe Edelbeck
Language (s): English
Ad Rate: Full Page Mono 17.00
Currency: United States Dollars
COMMUNITY NEWSPAPER

Isanti County News
22829
Owner: ECM Publishers, Inc.
Editorial: 234 Main St S, Cambridge, Minnesota 55008-1643 **Tel:** 1 763 691-6000
Email: editor.countynews@ecm-inc.com **Web site:** http://www.isanticountynews.com
Freq: Wed; **Circ:** 12472 Not Audited
Publisher: Julian Andersen; **Editor:** Rachel Kytonen; **Circulation Manager:** Cathy Nelson
Profile: Isanti County News is a weekly newspaper serving Isanti, Cambridge and Braham counties, MN. It provides the local community with information on news, events, sports and weather.
Language (s): English
Ad Rate: Full Page Mono 10.10
Currency: United States Dollars
COMMUNITY NEWSPAPER

Island Park News
156336
Tel: 1 208 558-0267
Email: ipnews@mac.com **Web site:** http://www.islandparknewsonline.com
Freq: Fri; **Circ:** 5000
Editor: Elizabeth Laden; **Advertising Sales Manager:** John Losch
Profile: Island Park News is published weekly for the residents of Island Park, ID and surrounding areas. The newspaper covers local and community news.
Language (s): English
Ad Rate: Full Page Mono 5.50
Currency: United States Dollars
COMMUNITY NEWSPAPER

Island Sand Paper
355170
Editorial: 1661 Estero Blvd Ste 4A, Fort Myers Beach, Florida 33931-2846 **Tel:** 1 239 463-4461
Email: sandpaperfmb@gmail.com **Web site:** http://www.islandsandpaper.com

Freq: Fri; **Circ:** 10000 Not Audited
Circulation Manager: Don Block; **Publisher:** Bob Layfield; **Editor:** Missy Layfield
Profile: The Island Sand Paper is a weekly newspaper serving residents and businesses in Ft. Myers Beach, Florida. "By Islanders, For Islanders" is their motto and readers are assured of seeing the inside scoop on what's happening on and around the island. The paper covers local news, events, politics, features, editorials, businesses and profiles of community members. Advertising deadlines are Wednesdays at 5 pm ET.
Language (s): English
Ad Rate: Full Page Mono 10.13
Currency: United States Dollars
COMMUNITY NEWSPAPER

Island Sun
24166
Editorial: 1640 Periwinkle Way Ste 2, Sanibel, Florida 33957-4401 **Tel:** 1 239 395-1213
Email: press@islandsunnews.com **Web site:** http://www.islandsunnews.com
Freq: Fri; **Circ:** 11000 Not Audited
Profile: Island Sun is a weekly newspaper written for the communities of Lee County, FL.
Language (s): English
Ad Rate: Full Page Mono 8.65
Ad Rate: Full Page Colour 545.00
Currency: United States Dollars
COMMUNITY NEWSPAPER

Islander
21495
Editorial: 21 Sunset View Rd, South Hero, Vermont 05486-4503 **Tel:** 1 802 372-5600
Email: islander@vermontislander.com **Web site:** http://www.lakechamplainislander.com
Freq: Tue; **Circ:** 7000 Not Audited
Publisher & Editor: George Fowler; **Advertising Sales Manager:** Courtney Schaetz
Profile: Islander provides news for residents of Grand Isle County, VT, Clinton County, NY, Milton, VT and Swanton, VT. Its coverage includes local news and politics, articles about education and business and stories about local entertainment.
Language (s): English
Ad Rate: Full Page Mono 6.00
Currency: United States Dollars
COMMUNITY NEWSPAPER

The Islander
22056
Editorial: 5604 Marina Dr Ste B, Holmes Beach, Florida 34217-1556 **Tel:** 1 941 778-7978
Email: news@islander.org **Web site:** http://www.islander.org
Freq: Wed; **Circ:** 17000 Not Audited
Publisher & Editor: Bonner Joy
Profile: The Islander is a weekly newspaper bringing local news to the residents of Holmes Beach, FL. It covers topics related to business, health, sports and events.
Language (s): English
Ad Rate: Full Page Mono 12.00
Currency: United States Dollars
COMMUNITY NEWSPAPER

Issaquah Press, Inc.
310374
Owner: Seattle Times Company
Editorial: 45 Front St S, Issaquah, Washington 98027-3820 **Tel:** 1 425 392-6434
Email: news@isspress.com
Freq: Weekly; **Circ:** 48400 Not Audited
Editor: Tim Pfarr
Language (s): English
COMMUNITY NEWSPAPER

Issaquah/Sammamish Reporter
593505
Owner: Black Press
Editorial: 2700 Richards Rd Ste 201, Bellevue, Washington 98005-4200 **Tel:** 1 425 391-0363
Email: news@issaquahreporter.com **Web site:** http://www.issaquahreporter.com
Circ: 32000
Publisher: William Shaw
Language (s): English
COMMUNITY NEWSPAPER

Isthmus
21314
Owner: Isthmus Publishing Co., Inc.
Editorial: 100 State St Ste 301, Madison, Wisconsin 53703-3430 **Tel:** 1 608 251-5627
Email: isthmus@isthmus.com **Web site:** http://www.isthmus.com
Freq: Thu; **Circ:** 60000 Not Audited
Advertising Manager: Chad Hopper
Profile: Isthmus is written for residents in Madison, WI. It covers local news and events. Deadlines fall on Mondays at 5pm CT.
Language (s): English
Ad Rate: Full Page Mono 63.97
Ad Rate: Full Page Colour 2350.00
Currency: United States Dollars
COMMUNITY NEWSPAPER

Italian Tribune
22497
Editorial: 7 N Willow St, Ste 8C, Montclair, New Jersey 7042 **Tel:** 1 973 860-0101
Email: mail@italiantribune.com **Web site:** http://www.italiantribune.com
Freq: Thu; **Circ:** 97000 Not Audited
Editor: Joseph Cannavo; **Publisher:** A.J. Buddy Fortunato
Profile: Italian Tribune is a community newspaper serving Italian Americans in the Northeast. The paper focuses on current events and happenings of interest in the Italian American community.
Language (s): English

Ad Rate: Full Page Mono 16.52
Currency: United States Dollars
COMMUNITY NEWSPAPER

The Italian Voice 23193

Tel: 1 973 942-2814
Freq: Thu; **Circ:** 6000 Not Audited
Profile: The Italian Voice is a community newspaper written for the residents of Paterson and Totowa, NJ and the surrounding areas. Features community, business, industrial and residential news.
Language (s): English, Italian
Ad Rate: Full Page Mono 7.72
Currency: United States Dollars
COMMUNITY NEWSPAPER

L' Italo Americano 23240

Owner: L'Italo American Foundation
Editorial: 10631 Vinedale St, Sun Valley, California 91352-2825 **Tel:** 1 626 359-7715
Email: info.italoamericano@gmail.com **Web site:** http://www.italoamericano.com
Freq: Thu; **Circ:** 30000 Not Audited
Publisher: Robert Barbera
Profile: L'Italo Americano provides news coverage and features for Italian-Americans in Sun Valley, CA and surrounding areas. The weekly publication covers news and events within the Italian-American community.
Language (s): Italian
Ad Rate: Full Page Mono 10.00
Ad Rate: Full Page Colour 1100.00
Currency: United States Dollars
COMMUNITY NEWSPAPER

Ithaca Times 22454

Owner: Newski Inc.
Editorial: 109 N Cayuga St, Ithaca, New York 14850-4341 **Tel:** 1 607 277-7000
Email: front@ithacatimes.com **Web site:** http://www.ithacatimes.com
Freq: Wed; **Circ:** 20382 Not Audited
Publisher: Jim Bilinski
Profile: Ithaca Times is a local weekly newspaper written for residents of Tompkins County, NY and surrounding areas. The newspaper covers local and national news, community events, sports and arts & entertainment. Deadlines for the publication are Fridays the week before issue date.
Language (s): English
Ad Rate: Full Page Mono 29.00
Currency: United States Dollars
COMMUNITY NEWSPAPER

j. - The Jewish News Weekly of Northern California 21849

Owner: San Francisco Jewish Community Publications Inc.
Editorial: 225 Bush St Ste 480, San Francisco, California 94104-4252 **Tel:** 1 415 263-7200
Email: info@jweekly.com **Web site:** http://www.jweekly.com
Freq: Fri; **Circ:** 18000 Not Audited
Editor: Sue Fishkoff; **Publisher:** Steven Gellman
Profile: J. - The Jewish News Weekly of Northern California is a community newspaper targeted at the Jewish community of San Francisco. The publication is interested only in press materials that have a Jewish angle.
Language (s): English
Ad Rate: Full Page Mono 168.25
Currency: United States Dollars
COMMUNITY NEWSPAPER

Jackson Advocate 19916

Owner: Tisdale, (Alice)
Editorial: 100 W Hamilton St, Jackson, Mississippi 39202-3237 **Tel:** 1 601 948-4122
Email: thejacksonadvocate@gmail.com **Web site:** http://www.jacksonadvocateonline.com
Freq: Thu; **Circ:** 8000 Not Audited
Profile: Jackson Advocate is a weekly newspaper written for African American residents of Jackson, MS. The newspaper covers African American community news and history. Deadlines are noon CT on Tuesdays.
Language (s): English
Ad Rate: Full Page Mono 43.70
Currency: United States Dollars
COMMUNITY NEWSPAPER

The Jackson County Times-Journal 22862

Owner: APG Media of Ohio, LLC
Editorial: 73 E Huron St Ste B, Jackson, Ohio 45640-1939 **Tel:** 1 740 286-2187
Email: info@timesjournal.com **Web site:** http://www.timesjournal.com
Freq: Sun; **Circ:** 5700 Not Audited
Circulation Manager: Paul Brown; **Community News Editor:** Jackie Denuit; **Publisher:** Norman Gilliland; **Editor:** Jennifer Hughes
Profile: The Jackson County Times-Journal is a general interest, weekly newspaper covering local news, sports and community stories as well as national, state and regional stories that impact Jackson, OH.
Language (s): English
Ad Rate: Full Page Mono 10.95
Currency: United States Dollars
COMMUNITY NEWSPAPER

The Jackson Herald 24317

Owner: MainStreet Newspapers Inc.
Editorial: 33 Lee St, Jefferson, Georgia 30549-1345 **Tel:** 1 706 367-5233
Email: news@mainstreetnews.com **Web site:** http://www.jacksonheraldtoday.com
Freq: Wed; **Circ:** 8400 Not Audited
Editor: Mike Buffington
Profile: The Jackson Herald is a local weekly newspaper serving Jefferson, GA. The paper covers local news, sports and opinion. Deadlines are on Mondays at noon ET.
Language (s): English
Ad Rate: Full Page Mono 7.75
Currency: United States Dollars
COMMUNITY NEWSPAPER

Jackson Hole News & Guide 21290

Owner: Teton Media Works
Editorial: 1225 Maple Way, Jackson, Wyoming 83001-8567 **Tel:** 1 307 732-7063
Email: editor@jhnewsandguide.com **Web site:** http://www.jhnewsandguide.com
Freq: Wed; **Circ:** 11000 Not Audited
Editor: John Moses; **Publisher:** Kevin Olson
Profile: Jackson Hole News & Guide is a local weekly newspaper written for the residents of Jackson and Teton County, WY. It features local news, community events, arts & entertainment, sports, society, health and business. The paper shares its editorial staff and offices with its sister publication, the Jackson Hole Daily. Please do not send duplicate press materials to both publications. E-mail submissions or send them to the PO Box address. Deadlines are on Fridays at 5pm MT.
Language (s): English
Ad Rate: Full Page Mono 19.45
Ad Rate: Full Page Colour 80.00
Currency: United States Dollars
COMMUNITY NEWSPAPER

Jacksonville Free Press 22512

Owner: Jacksonville Free Press
Editorial: 1122 Edgewood Ave W, Jacksonville, Florida 32208-3419 **Tel:** 1 904 634-1993
Email: jfreepress@aol.com **Web site:** http://www.jacksonvillefreepress.com
Freq: Thu; **Circ:** 45256 Not Audited
Editor: Charles Griggs; **Publisher:** Rita Perry; **Editor:** Sylvia Perry
Profile: Jacksonville Free Press is a weekly newspaper published by Jacksonville Free Press. The editorial content covers positive African-American news as well as other races. Contact the newspaper for deadline and lead time information.
Language (s): English
Ad Rate: Full Page Mono 30.50
Ad Rate: Full Page Colour 34.30
Currency: United States Dollars
COMMUNITY NEWSPAPER

J-Ad Graphics 24776

Owner: J-Ad Graphics
Editorial: 1351 N M 43 Hwy, Hastings, Michigan 49058-8499 **Tel:** 1 269 945-9554
Email: ads@j-adgraphics.com **Web site:** http://www.j-adgraphics.com/
Freq: Weekly; **Circ:** 132742 Not Audited
News Editor: Jeanne Boss; **News Editor:** John Hendler; **Advertising Sales Manager:** Scott Ommen; **Circulation Manager:** Dennis Rasey
Profile: J-Ad Graphics is a community newspaper publisher and printing service offering several weekly community newspapers to Central Michigan communities, including The Hastings Banner, The (Hastings) Reminder, The Sun & News, Maple Valley News, Lakewood News, Lowell Ledger and the Advisor & Chronicle.
Language (s): English
COMMUNITY NEWSPAPER

Jamestown Press 22191

Editorial: 45 Narragansett Ave, Jamestown, Rhode Island 02835-1150 **Tel:** 1 401 423-3200
Email: news@jamestownpress.com **Web site:** http://www.jamestownpress.com
Freq: Thu; **Circ:** 6100 Not Audited
Advertising Sales Manager: Katie Lucas; **Publisher:** Jeffrey McDonough; **Editor:** Tim Riel
Profile: Jamestown Press is a weekly newspaper written for residents of Jamestown, RI. The newspaper covers local news, sports and community events. Deadlines are on Mondays at 3pm ET.
Language (s): English
Ad Rate: Full Page Mono 9.54
Currency: United States Dollars
COMMUNITY NEWSPAPER

Jasper County Sun Times 28531

Owner: GateHouse Media Inc.
Editorial: 138 S Railroad Ave, Ridgeland, South Carolina 29936-9128 **Tel:** 1 843 726-6161
Email: news@jaspercountysun.com **Web site:** http://www.jaspersuntimes.com
Freq: Wed; **Circ:** 7000 Not Audited
Editor: Anthony Garzilli; **Publisher:** Ann Kennedy
Profile: Jasper County Sun Times is a community newspaper published every Wednesday in Richland, South Carolina. The paper covers news and events of interest to residents of Jasper County, SC.
Language (s): English
Ad Rate: Full Page Mono 9.27
Ad Rate: Full Page Colour 723.00
Currency: United States Dollars
COMMUNITY NEWSPAPER

Jefferson County Neighbors 22362

Owner: Spirit Publishing, Co.
Editorial: 510 Pine St, Punxsutawney, Pennsylvania 15767-1404 **Tel:** 1 814 938-8740
Web site: http://www.punxsutawneyspirit.com
Freq: Sat; **Circ:** 7665 Not Audited
Editor: Zak Lantz; **Circulation Manager:** Cathy Smith; **Publisher:** Tracy Smith
Profile: Jefferson County Neighbors is a weekly community newspaper published for residents of Punxsutawney, PA. The paper covers local news and events for the five county area with a focus on the Brookvale area in the northern part of the county. Deadlines are on Thursdays.
Language (s): English
Ad Rate: Full Page Mono 18.00
Currency: United States Dollars
COMMUNITY NEWSPAPER

The Jefferson Post 86498

Owner: Civitas Media
Editorial: 203 W Second St, West Jefferson, North Carolina 28694 **Tel:** 1 336 846-7164
Web site: http://www.jeffersonpost.com
Freq: Fri; **Circ:** 5000 Not Audited
Profile: The Jefferson Post is a community newspaper written for the residents of West Jefferson, NC. The paper covers local news and events, sports and weather. Deadlines are on Fridays at noon ET for the Tuesday edition and Tuesdays at noon ET for the Friday edition.
Language (s): English
Ad Rate: Full Page Mono 50.00
Ad Rate: Full Page Colour 926.10
Currency: United States Dollars
COMMUNITY NEWSPAPER

The Jeffersonian 28350

Owner: JAMS Media
Editorial: 65 S Elk St, Sandusky, Michigan 48471-1337 **Tel:** 1 810 648-4000
Email: jeffersonian@mihomepaper.com **Web site:** http://www.mihomepaper.com/
Freq: Sun; **Circ:** 5187
Editor: Carol Seifferlein; **Publisher:** Jane Vanderpool
Profile: The Jeffersonian is a free weekly newspaper serving residents in Sanilac County, MI.
Language (s): English
Ad Rate: Full Page Mono 13.40
Currency: United States Dollars
COMMUNITY NEWSPAPER

Jersey & Courier Times 685085

Editorial: 285 W Side Ave Suite 250, Jersey City, New Jersey 07305-1130 **Tel:** 1 201 333-6885
Circ: 94800
Publisher & Editor: James Adams
Language (s): English
COMMUNITY NEWSPAPER

Jersey County Journal 152104

Owner: Campbell Publications
Editorial: 832 S State St, Jerseyville, Illinois 62052-2343 **Tel:** 1 618 498-1234
Email: jcjnews@campbellpublications.net **Web site:** http://www.jerseycountyjournal.com
Freq: Weekly; **Circ:** 10700 Not Audited
Publisher & Editor: Julie Boren
Profile: Jersey County Journal is a weekly community newspaper written for the residents of Jerseyville, IL.
Language (s): English
Ad Rate: Full Page Mono 10.06
Currency: United States Dollars
COMMUNITY NEWSPAPER

Jet Observer 22440

Editorial: 1750 Tomcat Blvd, Virginia Beach, Virginia 23460 **Tel:** 1 757 433-3360
Email: jet@militarynews.com **Web site:** http://www.oceanajetobserver.com
Freq: Thu; **Circ:** 8000 Not Audited
Editor: Cathy Heimer
Profile: Jet Observer is a military newspaper published weekly in Virginia Beach, Virginia. The paper covers news and events of interest to base personnel as well as civilians living in the area.
Language (s): English
Ad Rate: Full Page Mono 23.22
Currency: United States Dollars
COMMUNITY NEWSPAPER

The Jewish Advocate 86626

Owner: The Jewish Advocate, Inc.
Editorial: 15 School St, Boston, Massachusetts 02108-4307 **Tel:** 1 617 367-9100
Web site: http://www.thejewishadvocate.com
Freq: Fri; **Circ:** 30000 Not Audited
Editor: Daniel Kimmel; **Publisher:** Yitzchok Aharon Korff; **Community News Editor:** Alexandra Lapkin
Profile: The Jewish Advocate is published weekly for members of the Jewish community in Boston. The publication aims to provide detailed information on all local, national and international issues relevant to the Jewish religion, culture and community.
Language (s): English
Ad Rate: Full Page Mono 37.05
Currency: United States Dollars
COMMUNITY NEWSPAPER

The Jewish Chronicle 21895

Owner: Pittsburgh Jewish Periodical and Education Foundation
Editorial: 5915 Beacon St, Pittsburgh, Pennsylvania 15217-2005 **Tel:** 1 412 687-1000
Email: newsdesk@thejewishchronicle.net **Web site:** http://www.thejewishchronicle.net
Freq: Thu; **Circ:** 8000 Not Audited
Community News Editor: Angela Leibowicz
Profile: The Jewish Chronicle is published weekly for the Jewish population in and around Pittsburgh. The paper covers news about the Jewish community in the area, as well as national and international news of concern.
Language (s): English
Ad Rate: Full Page Mono 21.50
Currency: United States Dollars
COMMUNITY NEWSPAPER

Jewish Community Voice 154699

Editorial: 1301 Springdale Rd #250, Cherry Hill, New Jersey 08003-2763 **Tel:** 1 856 751-9500 217
Email: jvoice@jfedsnj.org **Web site:** http://www.jewishvoicesnj.org
Freq: Bi-Weekly; **Circ:** 12500 Not Audited
Publisher: Sally Grossman; **Editor:** David Portnoe
Profile: Jewish Community Voice is a community newspaper written for the Jewish community in and around Cherry Hill, NJ.
Language (s): English
Ad Rate: Full Page Mono 30.25
Currency: United States Dollars
COMMUNITY NEWSPAPER

Jewish Exponent 21892

Owner: Jewish Publishing Group
Editorial: 2100 Arch St Fl 4, Philadelphia, Pennsylvania 19103-1300 **Tel:** 1 215 832-0700
Web site: http://www.jewishexponent.com
Freq: Weekly; **Circ:** 35369 Not Audited
Circulation Manager: Nicole McNally
Profile: Jewish Exponent in Philadelphia, PA is a weekly newspaper for the Jewish community that covers local, national and international news; offers an opinion section about all the important issues of the day; features about people and institutions in the community; weekly pages for kids, teens and college students; and arts, books, business, science, health, travel, food and dining.
Language (s): English
Ad Rate: Full Page Mono 38.59
Currency: United States Dollars
COMMUNITY NEWSPAPER

The Jewish Herald 22998

Owner: American Jewish Publishing Corporation
Editorial: 1689 46th St, Brooklyn, New York 11204 **Tel:** 1 718 972-4000
Freq: Thu; **Circ:** 340000 Not Audited
Profile: The Jewish Herald is written for the Jewish community nationwide. It focuses on informing the Jewish community about world and local news, features, commentary, events, lifestyle, religion and other topics of general interest.
Language (s): English
Ad Rate: Full Page Mono 75.00
Ad Rate: Full Page Colour 600.00
Currency: United States Dollars
COMMUNITY NEWSPAPER

Jewish Herald-Voice 21992

Owner: Jeanne Samuels - Herald Publishing
Editorial: 3403 Audley St, Houston, Texas 77098-1923 **Tel:** 1 713 630-0391
Email: articles@jhvonline.com **Web site:** http://jhvonline.com/index96.htm
Freq: Thu; **Circ:** 5000 Not Audited
Circulation Manager: Lawrence Levy; **Editor and Publisher:** Jeanne Samuels
Profile: Jewish Herald-Voice is a weekly newspaper published in Houston, Texas. The paper serves the greater Houston-area Jewish community & globally, and offers news of interest to the Jewish community. The paper has been in continuous publication since 1908. It also publishes five annual magazines.
Language (s): English
Ad Rate: Full Page Mono 40.00
Currency: United States Dollars
COMMUNITY NEWSPAPER

The Jewish Journal 22539

Owner: TRIBE Media Corp.
Editorial: 3250 Wilshire Blvd Ste 1250, Los Angeles, California 90010-1601 **Tel:** 1 213 368-1661
Email: editor@jewishjournal.com **Web site:** http://www.jewishjournal.com
Freq: Fri; **Circ:** 49975 Not Audited
Editor in Chief & Publisher: Robert Eshman
Profile: The Jewish Journal of greater Los Angeles is a non-profit community weekly newspaper serving the city's Jewish community. Coverage includes news, business, events, arts and entertainment, and other information relevant to the Jewish community. It was founded in 1985.
Language (s): English
Ad Rate: Full Page Mono 47.50
Ad Rate: Full Page Colour 3375.00
Currency: United States Dollars
COMMUNITY NEWSPAPER

Jewish Journal - Boston North 22197

Owner: North Shore Jewish Press, LTD
Editorial: 27 Congress St Ste 501, Salem, Massachusetts 01970-5577 **Tel:** 1 978 745-4111
Email: pr@jewishjournal.org **Web site:** http://www.jewishjournal.org
Freq: Bi-Weekly; **Circ:** 13000 Not Audited
Circulation Manager: Chester Baker; **Advertising Sales Manager:** Lois Kaplan; **Publisher:** Barbora Schneider
Profile: Jewish Journal - Boston North is written for Jewish residents in Northeastern Massachusetts. It covers international, national and local news, arts & entertainment and health.
Language (s): English
Ad Rate: Full Page Mono 24.53
Currency: United States Dollars
COMMUNITY NEWSPAPER

Jewish Ledger 154791
Editorial: 2535 Brighton Henrietta Town Line Rd, Rochester, New York 14623-2711 **Tel:** 1 585 427-2434
Email: editor@jewishledger.com
Freq: Thu; **Circ:** 6500
Publisher & Editor: Barbara Morgenstern
Profile: Jewish Ledger is a weekly newspaper written for the Jewish community of Rochester, NY and surrounding areas.
Language (s): English
Ad Rate: Full Page Mono 30.00
Currency: United States Dollars
COMMUNITY NEWSPAPER

Jewish News 154783
Owner: United Jewish Federation of Tidewater
Editorial: 5000 Corporate Woods Dr Ste 200, Virginia Beach, Virginia 23462-4429 **Tel:** 1 757 965-6100
Email: news@ujft.org **Web site:** http://www.jewishnewsva.org
Freq: Bi-Weekly; **Circ:** 5000 Not Audited
Circulation Manager: Marilyn Cerase; **Editor:** Terri Denison
Profile: Jewish News is written for Jewish communities in Chesapeake, Norfolk, Portsmouth, Suffolk, Virginia Beach in Southeastern, VA.
Language (s): English
Ad Rate: Full Page Mono 15.65
Ad Rate: Full Page Colour 19.57
Currency: United States Dollars
COMMUNITY NEWSPAPER

Jewish News of Greater Phoenix 18597
Owner: Phoenix Jewish News Inc.
Editorial: 1430 E Missouri Ave Ste B225, Phoenix, Arizona 85014-2489 **Tel:** 1 602 870-9470
Email: publisher@jewishaz.com **Web site:** http://www.jewishaz.com
Freq: Fri; **Circ:** 7500 Not Audited
Circulation Manager: Stephanie Shink; **Publisher:** Jamie Stern
Profile: Jewish News of Greater Phoenix is written for the Jewish community in the Phoenix, AZ area.
Language (s): English
Ad Rate: Full Page Mono 48.00
Currency: United States Dollars
COMMUNITY NEWSPAPER

The Jewish Post of New York 22838
Owner: Link Marketing & Promotions, Inc.
Editorial: 31 E 32nd St Ste 300, New York, New York 10016-5509 **Tel:** 1 212 563-9219
Email: jewishpost@yahoo.com **Web site:** http://www.jewishpost.com
Freq: Fri; **Circ:** 55000 Not Audited
Publisher: Henry Levy; **Editor:** Scott Levy
Profile: The Jewish Post of New York is published for members of the New York Jewish community. The editorial content includes local Jewish news, international news, community events, travel, business and the arts.
Language (s): English
Ad Rate: Full Page Mono 42.00
Currency: United States Dollars
COMMUNITY NEWSPAPER

The Jewish Press 24133
Owner: Jewish Press, Inc.
Editorial: 4915 16th Ave, Brooklyn, New York 11204-1115 **Tel:** 1 718 330-1100
Email: ads@jewishpress.com **Web site:** http://www.jewishpress.com
Freq: Weekly; **Circ:** 96000 Not Audited
Editor: Chumi Friedman; **Circulation Manager:** Joe Hochber; **Advertising Manager:** Heshy Korenblit; **Publisher:** Naomi Mauer
Profile: The Jewish Press is a weekly newspaper published in Brooklyn, NY. The paper covers local, national and international news of interest to the Jewish community in New York and abroad. The publication's coverage includes politics, opinions, special features, Torah lessons and Jewish lifestyle articles. The newspaper is distributed nationally and internationally.
Language (s): English
Ad Rate: Full Page Mono 91.00
Currency: United States Dollars
COMMUNITY NEWSPAPER

Jewish Press 154687
Owner: The Jewish Press Group of Tampa Bay
Editorial: 1101 Belcher Rd S, Ste H, Largo, Florida 33771 **Tel:** 1 727 535-4400
Email: jewishpress@aol.com **Web site:** http://www.jewishpresstampabay.com
Circ: 11700 Not Audited
Publisher: Jim Dawkins
Language (s): English
COMMUNITY NEWSPAPER

The Jewish Star 151508
Owner: The Jewish Star LLC
Editorial: 2 Endo Blvd, Garden City, New York 11530-6707 **Tel:** 1 516 632-5205
Email: newsroom@thejewishstar.com **Web site:** http://www.thejewishstar.com
Freq: Fri; **Circ:** 13000 Not Audited
Publisher: Ed Weintrob
Profile: The Jewish Star is a weekly newspaper serving the Orthodox Jewish communities of the South Shore in New York.
Language (s): English
Ad Rate: Full Page Mono 30.37
Currency: United States Dollars
COMMUNITY NEWSPAPER

The Jewish Voice 81065
Owner: Jewish Alliance of Greater Rhode Island
Editorial: 401 Elmgrove Ave, Providence, Rhode Island 02906-3451 **Tel:** 1 401 421-4111
Email: editor@jewishallianceri.org **Web site:** http://jvhri.org
Freq: Bi-Weekly; **Circ:** 10000 Not Audited
Editor: Fran Ostendorf; **Advertising Sales Manager:** Tricia Stearly
Profile: The Jewish Voice covers news and opinions of interest to Jewish residents in Rhode Island and Southeastern Massachusetts. Deadlines for submissions are on Mondays at 4pm ET.
Language (s): English
Ad Rate: Full Page Mono 20.00
Currency: United States Dollars
COMMUNITY NEWSPAPER

The Jewish Week, Inc. 25193
Owner: Jewish Week, Inc. (The)
Editorial: 1501 Broadway Ste 505, New York, New York 10036-5501 **Tel:** 1 212 921-7822
Web site: http://www.thejewishweek.com
Freq: Weekly; **Circ:** 98100 Not Audited
Publisher & Editor: Gary Rosenblatt
Profile: The Jewish Week, Inc., an independent community newspaper, is recognized widely as the largest and most respected Jewish newspaper in America. It has five regional editions including Manhattan, Long Island, Queens, Westchester/The Bronx, and Brooklyn/Staten Island. In covering the Jewish world, from Midtown to the Mideast, The Jewish Week reports on news, trends, features, and analysis from Israel as well as from throughout the New York metropolitan area. Deadlines are one week prior to the issue date.
Language (s): English
COMMUNITY NEWSPAPER

The Jewish World 24192
Owner: Jewish World Inc. (The)
Editorial: 1635 Eastern Pkwy, Schenectady, New York 12309-6011 **Tel:** 1 518 344-7018
Email: news@jewishworldnews.org **Web site:** http://www.jewishworldnews.org
Freq: Thu; **Circ:** 5000 Not Audited
Editor: Laurie Clevenson; **Circulation Manager:** Shelly Liebmann; **Advertising Sales Manager:** Frank McGivern
Profile: The Jewish World is a weekly publication serving the Jewish community in Northeastern New York, Vermont and Western Massachusetts region. The publication focuses on local, Jewish related news. Press releases must deal with the publication's specialization.
Language (s): English
Ad Rate: Full Page Mono 13.50
Currency: United States Dollars
COMMUNITY NEWSPAPER

JH Weekly 217515
Editorial: 567 W Broadway Ave, Jackson, Wyoming 83001-8641 **Tel:** 1 307 732-0299
Email: editor@planetjh.com **Web site:** http://planetjh.com
Freq: Wed; **Circ:** 12000 Not Audited
Publisher & Editor: Mary Grossman
Profile: JH Weekly is a Local News and Entertainment weekly newspaper.
Language (s): English
Ad Rate: Full Page Mono 11.24
Currency: United States Dollars
COMMUNITY NEWSPAPER

JHL Ledger Publications 87178
Owner: JHL Ledger Publications
Editorial: 36 Woodland St, Hartford, Connecticut 06105-2325 **Tel:** 1 860 231-2424
Email: editorial@jewishledger.com **Web site:** http://www.jewishledger.com
Circ: 37000 Not Audited
Advertising Sales Manager: Debra Cohen; **Editor:** Stacey Dresner; **Editor:** Judie Jacobson; **Circulation Manager:** Hillary Pasternak
Language (s): English
COMMUNITY NEWSPAPER

Jobe Publishing - Horse Cave 24576
Owner: Jobe Publishing Inc.
Editorial: 570 S Dixie St, Horse Cave, Kentucky 42749 **Tel:** 1 270 786-2679
Email: print@scrtc.com **Web site:** http://www.jpinews.com
Circ: 22750 Not Audited
Editor: Candace Geralds; **Publisher:** Jeff Jobe; **Editor:** Jerry Matera; **Advertising Sales Manager:** Tresia Sexton
Language (s): English
COMMUNITY NEWSPAPER

Jobe Publishing - Morgantown 19364
Owner: Jobe Publishing Inc.
Editorial: 120 E Ohio St, Morgantown, Kentucky 42261 **Tel:** 1 270 487-8666
Web site: http://www.jpinews.com
Circ: 10900 Not Audited
Publisher: Diane Dyer
Profile: Cave Country Newspapers-Morgantown is a community newspaper publisher serving the residents of Morgantown, KY.
Language (s): English
COMMUNITY NEWSPAPER

Johnlor Publishing, Inc. 25518
Editorial: 20 Medford Ave, Route 112, Patchogue, New York 11772-1220 **Tel:** 1 631 475-1000
Circ: 18350 Not Audited
Editor: Liz Finnegan; **Editor:** Linda Leuzzi; **Publisher:** John Tuthill; **Advertising Sales Manager:** Rory Upton
Profile: Johnlor Publishing, Inc. in Patchogue, NY publishes the community newspapers Islip Bulletin, Suffolk County News and Long Island Advance. The Islip Bulletin and Suffolk County share editorial staff, while the Long Island Advance has a separate editor and reporter.
Language (s): English
COMMUNITY NEWSPAPER

The Johnson City News & Neighbor 24439
Owner: The Shopping News, LLC
Editorial: 1114 Sunset Dr Ste 1, Johnson City, Tennessee 37604-2969 **Tel:** 1 423 979-1300
Email: news@jcnewsandneighbor.com **Web site:** http://www.newsandneighboronline.com
Freq: Weekly; **Circ:** 30797 Not Audited
Circulation Manager: Roy Jenkins; **Editor:** Scott Robertson
Profile: The Johnson City News & Neighbor is a community newspaper for residents of Johnson City, TN.
Language (s): English
Ad Rate: Full Page Mono 17.95
Currency: United States Dollars
COMMUNITY NEWSPAPER

Johnson County Graphic 18547
Owner: The Johnson County Graphic Inc.
Editorial: 203 E Cherry St, Clarksville, Arkansas 72830-3101 **Tel:** 1 479 754-2005
Email: news@thegraphic.org **Web site:** http://www.thegraphic.org
Freq: Wed; **Circ:** 7800 Not Audited
Publisher: Ron Wylie
Profile: Johnson County Graphic is written for the residents of Johnson County, AR. It covers local news, sports and community events. Deadlines are on Fridays at 3pm CT.
Language (s): English
Ad Rate: Full Page Mono 12.00
Currency: United States Dollars
COMMUNITY NEWSPAPER

La Jornada Latina 24189
Owner: Gate West Coast Ventures, LLC
Editorial: 4412 Carver Woods Dr Ste 200, Blue Ash, Ohio 45242-5539 **Tel:** 1 513 891-1000
Email: editor@tsjnews.com **Web site:** http://www.tsjnews.com
Freq: Weekly; **Circ:** 15000 Not Audited
Publisher: Brian Wiles
Profile: La Jornada Latina is distributed to local businesses and areas heavy in Hispanic population in the Greater Cincinnati, Northern Kentucky and Dayton regions. It includes local community and organizational news, local editorial content, special events, sports and entertainment.
Language (s): Spanish/Bilingual
Ad Rate: Full Page Mono 30.38
Currency: United States Dollars
COMMUNITY NEWSPAPER

O Jornal 22206
Owner: GateHouse Media Inc.
Editorial: 10 Purchase St, Fall River, Massachusetts 2720 **Tel:** 1 508 678-3844
Email: editorial@ojornal.com **Web site:** http://www.ojornal.com
Freq: Fri; **Circ:** 14500 Not Audited
Editor: Lurdes DaSilva; **Publisher:** Ric Oliveira
Profile: O Jornal is a weekly newspaper that covers Portuguese culture in English and Portuguese. The paper is a bilingual community newspaper distributed in Massachusetts and Rhode Island.
Language (s): Portuguese
Ad Rate: Full Page Mono 16.50
Currency: United States Dollars
COMMUNITY NEWSPAPER

The Journal 22070
Owner: Comprint Military Publications
Editorial: 8901 Rockville Pike, Bethesda, Maryland 20889-0001 **Tel:** 1 301 295-5727
Web site: http://www.dcmilitary.com/journal/
Freq: Weekly; **Circ:** 11500 Not Audited
Publisher: John Rives
Profile: The Journal is a weekly communtiy newspaper located in Bethesda, MD. It's main focus is on military personnal and lifestyle.
Language (s): English
Ad Rate: Full Page Mono 19.93
Currency: United States Dollars
COMMUNITY NEWSPAPER

The Journal 30184
Owner: Minnesota Premier Publications
Editorial: 1115 Hennepin Ave, Minneapolis, Minnesota 55403-1705 **Tel:** 1 612 825-9205
Email: editor@mnpubs.com **Web site:** http://www.journalmpls.com
Freq: Bi-Weekly; **Circ:** 30000 Not Audited
Circulation Manager: Marlo Johnson; **Advertising Sales Manager:** Melissa Ungerman
Profile: The Journal, also known as the Skyway News, is a local weekly newspaper serving Minneapolis and Saint Paul, MN. Its editorial mission is to provide the connection between the two cities. It provides information on news, events and arts of interest to the local community.
Language (s): English
Ad Rate: Full Page Mono 48.59
Ad Rate: Full Page Colour 2022.00
Currency: United States Dollars
COMMUNITY NEWSPAPER

Journal & Topics Newspapers 24529
Owner: Wessell Family
Editorial: 622 Graceland Ave, Des Plaines, Illinois 60016-4519 **Tel:** 1 847 299-5511
Email: journalnews@journal-topics.info **Web site:** http://www.journal-topics.com
Circ: 70166 Not Audited
Editor: Todd Wessell
Profile: The Journal & Topics Journal covers news on Chicago's Great Northwest Suburbs. Chicago DMA
Language (s): English
COMMUNITY NEWSPAPER

Journal Newspapers 25369
Editorial: 211 Main St, White Haven, Pennsylvania 18661-1406 **Tel:** 1 570 443-9131
Email: hellojournal@gmail.com **Web site:** http://poconownewspapers.com
Circ: 23000 Not Audited
Publisher: Clara Holder; **Advertising Sales Manager:** Seth Isenberg
Language (s): English
COMMUNITY NEWSPAPER

The Journal Newspapers 76411
Owner: Barron Communications
Editorial: 306 E Newmark Ave, Monterey Park, California 91755-2908 **Tel:** 1 626 572-7450
Email: news@sgvjournal.com **Web site:** http://www.sgvjournal.com
Circ: 10000 Not Audited
Language (s): English
COMMUNITY NEWSPAPER

Journal Press, Inc. 25333
Owner: Jessica Herrink
Editorial: 10250 Kings Hwy, King George, Virginia 22485-3429 **Tel:** 1 540 775-2024
Email: news@journalpress.com **Web site:** http://www.journalpress.com
Circ: 16000 Not Audited
Editor: Jessica Herrink; **Publisher:** Ruth Herrink
Language (s): English
COMMUNITY NEWSPAPER

Journal Publications 24868
Editorial: 431 S Main St, Hillsboro, Illinois 62049 **Tel:** 1 217 532-3933
Email: thejournal-news@consolidated.net **Web site:** http://www.thejournal-news.net
Circ: 8108 Not Audited
Advertising Sales Manager: Joyce Connor
Language (s): English
COMMUNITY NEWSPAPER

Journal Register Company-Kennett Square 354977
Owner: Journal Register Company
Editorial: 250 N Bradford Ave, West Chester, Pennsylvania 19382-1912 **Tel:** 1 610 444-6590
Email: kennettpaper@gmail.com **Web site:** http://www.southernchestercountyweeklies.com/
Circ: 9500 Not Audited
Editor: Chris Barber; **Editor:** Fran Kaye
Profile: Journal Register Company-Kennett Square publishes the Avon Grove Sun and The Kennet Paper weekly newspapers, providing Local News coverage to Kennett Square, Chadds Ford, Avon Grove and Oxford, PA communities.
Language (s): English
COMMUNITY NEWSPAPER

Joyce Media, Inc. 25289
Editorial: 3413 Soledad Canyon Rd, Acton, California 93510 **Tel:** 1 661 269-1169
Email: help@joycemediainc.com **Web site:** http://www.joycemediainc.com
Circ: 19940 Not Audited
Editor: Gayle Joyce; **Publisher:** John Joyce
Language (s): English
COMMUNITY NEWSPAPER

Juniata News 151436
Editorial: Philadelphia, Pennsylvania **Tel:** 1 215 739-8197
Email: juniatapress@comcast.net
Freq: Tue; **Circ:** 9000 Not Audited
Publisher: Gerard Lineman; **Editor:** Thomas Lineman
Profile: The Juniata News is a community newspaper written for the residents of Philadelphia.
Language (s): English
Ad Rate: Full Page Mono 7.00
Currency: United States Dollars
COMMUNITY NEWSPAPER

Juniata Sentinel 20578
Owner: Advance Publications of Perry and Juniata Counties
Editorial: 1806 William Penn Hw, Mifflintown, Pennsylvania 17059 **Tel:** 1 717 436-8206
Freq: Wed; **Circ:** 5800 Not Audited
Publisher: Curtis Dreibelbis
Profile: Juniata Sentinel in Mifflintown, PA is a weekly newspaper that covers local news and events for residents of Juniata County, PA.
Language (s): English

Ad Rate: Full Page Mono 7.25
Currency: United States Dollars
COMMUNITY NEWSPAPER

The Jupiter Courier 18752
Owner: Gannett Co., Inc.
Editorial: 1939 S Federal Hwy, Stuart, Florida 34994-3915 **Tel:** 1 561 745-3311
Web site: http://www.tcpalm.com
Freq: Sun; **Circ:** 25000
Advertising Sales Manager: Chris Stonecipher
Profile: The Jupiter Courier in Stuart, FL is a local newspaper for the residents of Jupiter, Tequesta, and Juno Beach, FL areas. The publication reports only on local news and community events. It offers a TMC edition on Wednesday. Press releases should be mailed or faxed to the office. The staff understands that public relations companies send out more than one copy of the same item, however they do not wish to receive the same press release eight times.
Language (s): English
Ad Rate: Full Page Mono 21.89
Currency: United States Dollars
COMMUNITY NEWSPAPER

Kaechele Publications 24752
Owner: Kaechele, (Cheryl)
Editorial: 231 Trowbridge St Ste 17, Allegan, Michigan 49010-1330 **Tel:** 1 269 673-5534
Email: editor@allegannews.com **Web site:** http://www.allegannews.com
Circ: 5384 Not Audited
Publisher: Cheryl Kaechele; **Editor:** Ryan Lewis; **Editor:** Scott Sullivan
Language (s): English
COMMUNITY NEWSPAPER

Kanawha-Putnam Ad Mailer 81600
Owner: Valley Publications
Editorial: 6050 State Route 34, Winfield, West Virginia 25213 **Tel:** 1 304 755-0270
Web site: http://www.kpadmailer.com
Freq: Sun; **Circ:** 113000 Not Audited
Publisher: Jim Spanner
Profile: Kanawha-Putnam Ad Mailer is written for residents of the Kanawha and Putnam counties in West Virginia. Deadlines are on Wednesdays.
Language (s): English
Ad Rate: Full Page Mono 27.50
Currency: United States Dollars
COMMUNITY NEWSPAPER

Kansas City Globe 19838
Owner: Jordon Communications Company
Editorial: 615 E 29th St, Kansas City, Missouri 64109-1110 **Tel:** 1 816 531-5253
Email: kcglobe@swbell.net **Web site:** http://www.thekcglobe.com
Freq: Thu; **Circ:** 10500 Not Audited
Publisher & Editor: Marion Jordon; **Circulation Manager:** Marion Jordon Jr.
Profile: Kansas City Globe is published weekly for the African American community in Kansas City, MO. The newspaper covers local news, sports, features, business and community events. Deadlines are on Mondays at noon CT.
Language (s): English
Ad Rate: Full Page Mono 22.84
Currency: United States Dollars
COMMUNITY NEWSPAPER

Kansas City Hispanic News 24135
Owner: Arce Communications
Editorial: 2918 Southwest Blvd, Kansas City, Missouri 64108-3615 **Tel:** 1 816 472-5246
Email: kchnews@swbell.net **Web site:** http://www.kchispanicnews.com
Freq: Thu; **Circ:** 14000 Not Audited
Publisher: Joe Arce; **News Editor:** Ramona Arce; **Advertising Sales Manager:** Lisa Arce-Sidenstick; **Editor:** Jose Faus
Profile: Kansas City Hispanic News is a local newspaper serving residents in the metropolitan Kansas City, MO area. The newspaper is published in English and Spanish, and reports on local and national news, features, business and finance. The newspaper's main audience is Hispanic men and women. The editorial deadline is the Friday before publication.
Language (s): Spanish/Bilingual
Ad Rate: Full Page Mono 14.00
Ad Rate: Full Page Colour 1700.00
Currency: United States Dollars
COMMUNITY NEWSPAPER

Kansas City Jewish Chronicle 28072
Owner: MetroMedia Publishers, Inc.
Editorial: 4210 Shawnee Mission Pkwy Ste 314A, Fairway, Kansas 66205-2546 **Tel:** 1 913 951-8425
Email: chronicle@metromediapublishers.com **Web site:** http://www.kcjc.com
Freq: Weekly; **Circ:** 7500 Not Audited
Editor: Barbara Bayer; **Community News Editor:** Marcia Montgomery; **Publisher:** David Small
Profile: Kansas City Jewish Chronicle's editorial mission is to provide news and event information that concerns the local Jewish community in Kansas City, MO.
Language (s): English
Ad Rate: Full Page Mono 25.30
Currency: United States Dollars
COMMUNITY NEWSPAPER

Kanzhongguo 791595
Owner: SC Times Media Inc
Editorial: 886 College St, Toronto, Ontario M6H 1A3
Tel: 1 416 543-2018
Email: editor@kanzhongguo.com **Web site:** https://www.secretchina.com/
Freq: Weekly; **Circ:** 6000
Publisher & Editor: Frank Zhuo
Profile: Kanzhongguo is a weekly newspaper providing Community and International News Coverage for the Chinese communities in serving Mississauga, North York, GTA, Brampton, Scarborough, Hamilton, London, ON.
Language (s): Chinese
COMMUNITY NEWSPAPER

The Katy News 961765
Owner: Wilson (Pat)
Editorial: Katy, Texas **Tel:** 1 281 396-3333
Email: ads@thekatynews.com **Web site:** http://thekatynews.com
Freq: Weekly; **Circ:** 32000
Editor, Publisher & Owner: Pat Wilson
Profile: Founded in 1989, The Katy News is a weekly, locally owned community newspaper offering content on community events, local school news, church events and generally upbeat topics.
Language (s): English
Ad Rate: Full Page Colour 11.88
Currency: United States Dollars
COMMUNITY NEWSPAPER

Katy Times 20878
Owner: Hartman Newspapers, LLC
Editorial: 5319 E 5th St, Katy, Texas 77493-2520
Tel: 1 281 391-3141
Web site: http://www.katytimes.com
Freq: Weekly; **Circ:** 6000 Not Audited
Profile: Katy Times is a weekly paper that serves the residents of Katy, TX. The newspaper reports on local news, sports, features, and police news. The editor is the main PR contact. Press releases can be faxed or e-mailed.
Language (s): English
Ad Rate: Full Page Mono 12.50
Currency: United States Dollars
COMMUNITY NEWSPAPER

Katy Trail Weekly 925766
Owner: Trail Publishing Group, Inc.
Tel: 1 214 278-7245
Email: info@katytrailweekly.com **Web site:** http://www.katytrailweekly.com
Freq: Weekly
Managing Director: Nancy Black; **Publisher:** Rex Cumming
Profile: Katy Trail Weekly is a community newspaper serving various Dallas neighborhoods, including: Downtown, Uptown, Cedar Springs/Oak Lawn, the Design District, Medical District and Park Cities. Content includes local news, sports, entertainment, events and opinion.
Language (s): English
COMMUNITY NEWSPAPER

Keene Sentinel Weeklies 324362
Editorial: 60 West St, Keene, New Hampshire 03431-3373 **Tel:** 1 603 352-1234
Email: news@keenesentinel.com **Web site:** http://www.sentinelsource.com
Freq: Weekly; **Circ:** 9000 Not Audited
Advertising Sales Manager: Michael Breshears; **Publisher:** Thomas Ewing
Language (s): English
Ad Rate: Full Page Mono 13.60
Currency: United States Dollars
COMMUNITY NEWSPAPER

Kendall County Record Inc. 25119
Editorial: 222 S Bridge St, Yorkville, Illinois 60560-1502 **Tel:** 1 630 553-7034
Email: news@kendallcountyrecord.com **Web site:** http://www.kendallcountynow.com/
Circ: 22227 Not Audited
Editor: John Etheredge; **Publisher:** Jeff Farren; **Editor:** Kathy Farren
Language (s): English
COMMUNITY NEWSPAPER

Kent County News 19470
Owner: Adams Publishing Group
Editorial: 223 High St, Chestertown, Maryland 21620-1517 **Tel:** 1 410 778-2011
Email: editor@thekentcountynews.com **Web site:** http://www.myeasternshoremd.com/news/kent_county
Freq: Thu; **Circ:** 7500 Not Audited
Editor: Dan Divilio; **Publisher:** David Fike
Profile: Kent County News is a local weekly newspaper whose editorial mission is to deliver local news and event information to its readers. The publication is written for residents of Kent County, MD.
Language (s): English
Ad Rate: Full Page Mono 13.00
Currency: United States Dollars
COMMUNITY NEWSPAPER

Kentucky Publishing Inc. 24823
Owner: Leneave (Greg & Teresa)
Editorial: 1540 McCracken Blvd, Paducah, Kentucky 42001-9192 **Tel:** 1 270 442-7389
Web site: http://www.ky-news.com
Circ: 26600 Not Audited
Publisher: Greg LeNeave; **Advertising Sales Manager:** Larrah Workman
Language (s): English
COMMUNITY NEWSPAPER

The Kentucky Standard 19320
Owner: Landmark Community Newspapers Inc.
Editorial: 110 W Stephen Foster Ave, Bardstown, Kentucky 40004-1416 **Tel:** 1 502 348-9003
Email: news@kystandard.com **Web site:** http://www.kystandard.com
Freq: Fri; **Circ:** 8643 Not Audited
Editor: Forrest Berkshire; **Circulation Manager:** Brandi Cheatham; **Publisher:** Jamie Sizemore
Profile: The Kentucky Standard is a weekly newspaper providing Local Coverage to residents of Bardstown, KY and surrounding areas in Nelson County. Deadlines are one day prior to issue date.
Language (s): English
Ad Rate: Full Page Mono 58.30
Currency: United States Dollars
COMMUNITY NEWSPAPER

Kenwood Press 23066
Owner: Kenwood Press, Inc.
Editorial: 8910 Sonoma Highway, Kenwood, California 95452 **Tel:** 1 707 833-5155
Email: info@kenwoodpress.com **Web site:** http://www.kenwoodpress.com
Freq: Bi-Weekly; **Circ:** 8000 Not Audited
Profile: Kenwood Press is a local newspaper serving residents of Kenwood, Glen Ellen and Oakmont, CA. The publication provides coverage of local news and community events.
Language (s): English
Ad Rate: Full Page Mono 4.91
Currency: United States Dollars
COMMUNITY NEWSPAPER

Kern Valley Sun 18621
Owner: Smith (Marsha S.)
Editorial: 6416 Lake Isabella Blvd, Lake Isabella, California 93240-9475 **Tel:** 1 760 379-3667
Email: editor@kvsun.com **Web site:** http://www.kernvalleysun.com
Freq: Wed; **Circ:** 5100 Not Audited
Circulation Manager: Steve Rinehart; **Publisher & Editor:** Marsha Smith
Profile: Kern Valley Sun is a local newspaper for residents of Kern County, CA. The newspaper reports on local news, community events and sports.
Language (s): English
Ad Rate: Full Page Mono 13.60
Currency: United States Dollars
COMMUNITY NEWSPAPER

Kernersville News 19982
Owner: Carter Publishing Company
Editorial: 300 E Mountain St, Kernersville, North Carolina 27284-2943 **Tel:** 1 336 993-2161
Email: editor@kernersvillenews.com **Web site:** http://www.kernersvillenews.com
Freq: Sat; **Circ:** 18300 Not Audited
News Editor: Wendy Davis; **Circulation Manager:** Connie Owensby; **Publisher, Managing Editor & Advertising Sales Manager:** John Owensby
Profile: Kernersville News is a local newspaper written for the residents of Kernersville, NC. The paper covers schools, local government, health, arts & entertainment, lifestyle, recreation, crafts, sports, real estate and community events. Deadlines are one day prior to the issue day at noon ET.
Language (s): English
Ad Rate: Full Page Mono 19.50
Currency: United States Dollars
COMMUNITY NEWSPAPER

KerWest, Inc. 24859
Editorial: 14693 W Whitesbridge Ave, Kerman, California 93630-1131 **Tel:** 1 559 846-6689
Email: kerwest@msn.com **Web site:** http://www.kerwestnewspapers.com
Circ: 12200 Not Audited
Publisher & Editor: Mark Kilen; **Advertising Sales Manager:** Merlyn Wilcox
Language (s): English
COMMUNITY NEWSPAPER

Kewaunee County Star-News 27982
Editorial: 203 Ellis St, Kewaunee, Wisconsin 54216-1051 **Tel:** 1 920 388-3175
Email: editorial@gokewauneecounty.com **Web site:** http://www.greenbaypressgazette.com/news/kewaunee-county-star-news
Freq: Sat; **Circ:** 10000 Not Audited
Editor: Warren Bluhm
Profile: Kewaunee County Star-News, launched September 18, 2010, is a local weekly newspaper serving residents of Kewaunee County, WI. The paper covers general news, business, sports, education and arts & entertainment.
Language (s): English
Ad Rate: Full Page Mono 13.00
Currency: United States Dollars
COMMUNITY NEWSPAPER

Key West Keynoter 152192
Editorial: 3015 Overseas Hwy, Marathon, Florida 33050-2236 **Tel:** 1 305 743-5551
Email: keynoter@keysnet.com **Web site:** http://keysinfonet.com
Freq: Sat; **Circ:** 35000 Not Audited
Editor: Larry Kahn; **Publisher:** Richard Tamborrino; **Circulation Manager:** Carter Townshend
Profile: Key West Keynoter is a local newspaper written for the residents of Key West, FL.
Language (s): English
Ad Rate: Full Page Mono 27.85
Currency: United States Dollars
COMMUNITY NEWSPAPER

Keynoter Newspapers 433433
Owner: Keynoter Publishing Company Inc.
Editorial: 3015 Overseas Hwy, Marathon, Florida 33050-2236 **Tel:** 1 305 743-5551
Email: keynoter@keynoter.com **Web site:** http://www.keysnet.com
Circ: 43000 Not Audited
Editor: Larry Kahn
Profile: Keynoter Newspapers is a community newspaper publisher serving residents of Marathon, FL.
Language (s): English
COMMUNITY NEWSPAPER

Kings Mountain Herald 27710
Owner: Gemini Newspapers
Editorial: 700 E King St, Kings Mountain, North Carolina 28086-3116 **Tel:** 1 704 739-7496
Web site: http://kmherald.com
Freq: Wed; **Circ:** 5300 Not Audited
Advertising Sales Manager: Rick Hord
Profile: Kings Mountain Herald is a local newspaper written for the residents of Kings Mountain, NC.
Language (s): English
Ad Rate: Full Page Mono 9.60
Currency: United States Dollars
COMMUNITY NEWSPAPER

Kingsett Publications 620119
Owner: Kingsett LLC
Editorial: 1103 S Milford Rd, Highland, Michigan 48357-4856 **Tel:** 1 248 360-6397
Email: editor@scnmail.com **Web site:** http://spinalcolumnonline.com
Circ: 79000
Advertising Sales Manager: Cindie Audia; **Publisher & Circulation Manager:** James Stevenson
Language (s): English
COMMUNITY NEWSPAPER

The Kingsville Record and Bishop News 20883
Owner: King Ranch Inc.
Editorial: 1831 W. Santa Gertrudis St., Kingsville, Texas 78363 **Tel:** 1 361 592-4304
Web site: http://www.kingsvillerecord.com
Freq: Sun; **Circ:** 5500 Not Audited
Publisher and Editor: Christopher Maher; **Circulation Manager:** Irma Reyes
Profile: The Kingsville (TX) Record and Bishop News' editorial mission is to provide local news to the community of Kingsville, TX.
Language (s): English
Ad Rate: Full Page Mono 8.00
Currency: United States Dollars
COMMUNITY NEWSPAPER

Kirkland Reporter 27336
Owner: Black Press
Editorial: 11630 Slater Ave NE Ste 8/9, Kirkland, Washington 98034-4100 **Tel:** 1 425 822-9166
Email: editor@kirklandreporter.com **Web site:** http://www.kirklandreporter.com
Freq: Wed; **Circ:** 26350 Not Audited
Circulation Manager: Dennis Osborn
Profile: Kirkland Reporter is a weekly newspaper for residents of Kirkland, WA. It began publishing in 1978 and was acquired by Pacific Publishing in 1991. It was sold in April 2007 to Black Press Ltd.
Language (s): English
Ad Rate: Full Page Mono 27.50
Ad Rate: Full Page Colour 395.00
Currency: United States Dollars
COMMUNITY NEWSPAPER

The Kirtland Air Force Base Nucleus 387605
Owner: RR Community Publishing, LLC
Editorial: 1594 Sara Rd SE, Ste D, Kirtland, New Mexico 87124 **Tel:** 1 505 892-8080
Email: nuceditor@rrobserver.com **Web site:** http://www.kafbnucleus.com
Freq: Thu; **Circ:** 10000 Not Audited
Publisher: Rockford Hayes
Profile: The Kirtland Air Force Base Nucleus is a free, weekly newspaper serving the military personnel, civilian employees and residents of Kirtland Air Force Base, NM. It provides readers with local news and information pertinent to the local community and military members in the United States and abroad. Although printing and advertising are managed externally, all editorial content is supplied by military staff members. Editorial submissions are due to the base's Public Affairs office on Fridays at 9am CT and advertising is due on Fridays at 5pm CT.
Language (s): English
Ad Rate: Full Page Mono 17.50
Currency: United States Dollars
COMMUNITY NEWSPAPER

Kitsap Sun Weekly Newspapers 502398
Owner: Journal Media Group
Editorial: 545 5th St, Bremerton, Washington 98337
Tel: 1 360 377-3711
Circ: 48043 Not Audited

Local News Editor: Kimberly Rubenstein; **Publisher:** Rob White
Language (s): English
COMMUNITY NEWSPAPER

Kitsap Weekly 400030
Owner: Sound Publishing, Inc./Kitsap News Group
Editorial: 19351 8th Ave NE Ste 106, Poulsbo, Washington 98370-8710 **Tel:** 1 360 779-8276
Web site: http://www.kitsapdailynews.com
Circ: 39895 Not Audited
Language (s): English
COMMUNITY NEWSPAPER

Knob Rock Rattler 426517
Editorial: Bridgeway Plaza, Shell Knob, Missouri 65747 **Tel:** 1 417 858-3910
Email: therattler@centurytel.net
Freq: Wed; **Circ:** 7300 Not Audited
Publisher & Editor: Jeannie Jones
Profile: Knob Rock Rattler is a weekly newspaper covering local events in Shell Knob, MO. Deadlines are on Fridays at noon CT.
Language (s): English
Ad Rate: Full Page Mono 21.60
Currency: United States Dollars
COMMUNITY NEWSPAPER

The Knox County Neighbors 429379
Owner: GateHouse Media Inc.
Editorial: 140 S Prairie St, Galesburg, Illinois 61401-4605 **Tel:** 1 309 344-3800
Web site: http://www.galesburg.com/the_paper
Freq: Wed; **Circ:** 23000 Not Audited
Circulation Manager: Jan Blair; **News Editor:** Tom Martin; **Advertising Sales Manager:** Donna Moore
Profile: Knox County Neighbors is a weekly newspaper serving residents of Knox County, IL and the community of Alpha, IL. It covers local news, community events, sports, business, features, editorials, education, entertainment, health and women's issues. In each edition, the paper will feature a local profile of a community leader, a community volunteer, a senior citizen, a community military veteran or personnel, a teacher or student and a coach or athlete. Advertising and editorial deadlines are on Fridays at 5pm CT.
Language (s): English
Ad Rate: Full Page Mono 8.90
Currency: United States Dollars
COMMUNITY NEWSPAPER

Knoxville County FOCUS 257141
Owner: Hunley (Steve)
Editorial: 4109 Central Avenue Pike, Knoxville, Tennessee 37912-4306 **Tel:** 1 865 686-9970
Email: staff@knoxfocus.com **Web site:** http://www.knoxfocus.com
Freq: Weekly; **Circ:** 20000 Not Audited
Publisher: Steve Hunley; **Circulation Manager:** Rose King
Profile: Knoxville/Knox County FOCUS provides residents of Knoxville, TN and surrounding communities with information about local news, government, sports, education, and entertainment. The paper is published every Wednesday.
Language (s): English
Ad Rate: Full Page Mono 12.50
Ad Rate: Full Page Colour 1140.00
Currency: United States Dollars
COMMUNITY NEWSPAPER

Kokomo Perspective 151382
Owner: Wilson Media Group
Editorial: 209 N Main St, Kokomo, Indiana 46901-4623 **Tel:** 1 765 452-0055
Email: editor@kokomoperspective.com **Web site:** http://www.kokomoperspective.com
Freq: Wed; **Circ:** 31000
Advertising Sales Manager: Bill Eldridge; **Publisher:** Don Wilson
Profile: Kokomo Perspective is published weekly for the residents of Kokomo, IN and surrounding areas. The newspaper covers local news, opinions and community events.
Language (s): English
Ad Rate: Full Page Mono 16.95
Currency: United States Dollars
COMMUNITY NEWSPAPER

Korean Bergen News 154837
Owner: KBN Publishing Group Inc.
Editorial: 210 Sylvan Ave Ste 23, Englewood Cliffs, New Jersey 07632-2503 **Tel:** 1 201 894-9061
Email: koreanbergennews@gmail.com **Web site:** http://www.koreanbergennews.com
Freq: Fri; **Circ:** 8000 Not Audited
Publisher: Thomas Bae
Profile: Korean Bergen News is a local newspaper written for Korean residents of Bergen County, NJ.
Language (s): Korean
Ad Rate: Full Page Mono 60.00
Currency: United States Dollars
COMMUNITY NEWSPAPER

Korean Journal 232008
Owner: Korean Journal Media Group
Editorial: 2828 Forest Ln Ste 1159, Dallas, Texas 75234-7533 **Tel:** 1 972 406-2800
Email: kjdtx21@yahoo.com **Web site:** http://www.dallaskj.com
Freq: Fri; **Circ:** 8000 Not Audited
Publisher: Jung Ho Kim; **Editor:** Bong Suh
Language (s): Korean
Ad Rate: Full Page Mono 77.00
Currency: United States Dollars
COMMUNITY NEWSPAPER

Korean Phila Times 879230
Owner: KoreanPhila Times Inc.
Editorial: 103 Township Line Rd, Rockledge, Pennsylvania 19046-5127 **Tel:** 1 215 740-2218
Web site: http://juganphila.com
Freq: Weekly; **Circ:** 15000
Editor: Justin Lee
Profile: Korean Phila Times is a weekly community newspaper serving the Korean-American community in the Philadelphia area, including Montgomery County, Delaware County, Bucks County, Southern New Jersey and Delaware.
Language (s): Korean
Ad Rate: Full Page Mono 6.95
Ad Rate: Full Page Colour 11.30
Currency: United States Dollars
COMMUNITY NEWSPAPER

Koreaworld 538330
Owner: The Koreaworld, Inc.
Editorial: 9610 Long Point Rd Ste 340, Houston, Texas 77055-4259 **Tel:** 1 713 827-0063
Email: withkoreaworld@gmail.com
Freq: Fri; **Circ:** 12000 Not Audited
Profile: Koreaworld is a weekly, Korean-language newspaper serving the Korean-American communities of Houston, Austin, Killeen, and San Antonio. The paper features Korean politics, economics, entertainment and other news.
Language (s): Korean
Ad Rate: Full Page Mono 2.60
Currency: United States Dollars
COMMUNITY NEWSPAPER

Kwik Konnection Printing & Publishing, Inc. 25422
Editorial: 213 W Main St, Staunton, Illinois 62088-1454 **Tel:** 1 618 635-3172
Email: editor@kwikkonnection.com **Web site:** http://www.kwikkonnection.com
Circ: 9000 Not Audited
Editor: William Napper
Language (s): English
COMMUNITY NEWSPAPER

The Kyocharo News 23286
Editorial: 1260 B St, Hayward, California 94541-2955 **Tel:** 1 510 728-1236
Email: sundaytopic@yahoo.com **Web site:** http://www.asianmediaguide.com
Freq: Sat; **Circ:** 17000 Not Audited
Publisher & Editor: Dae Kim
Profile: The Kyocharo News is published in Korean to provide news and information concerning the Korean American population. The publication provides local Korean American community news, national and international headlines, news from Korea and a section dealing with women's issues and interests. Deadlines are noon PT on Fridays.
Language (s): English, Korean
Ad Rate: Full Page Mono 3.81
Currency: United States Dollars
COMMUNITY NEWSPAPER

L & M Publications 24886
Owner: L & M Publications Inc.
Editorial: 1840 Merrick Ave, Merrick, New York 11566 **Tel:** 1 516 378-5320
Email: lmpub@optonline.net **Web site:** http://www.merricklife.com
Circ: 10476 Not Audited
Circulation Manager: Joan Oliva; **Publisher:** Linda Toscano
Profile: L & M Publications is a community newspaper publisher servicing the residents of New York, Northern NJ and Long Island, NY.
Language (s): English
COMMUNITY NEWSPAPER

La Canada Flintridge Outlook Weeklies 524237
Editorial: 800 Foothill Blvd, La Canada Flintridge, California 91011-3336 **Tel:** 1 818 790-7500
Email: outlooknews@outlooknewspapers.com **Web site:** http://www.lacanadaoutlook.com
Circ: 22500 Not Audited
Publisher & Editor: Charlie Plowman
Language (s): English
COMMUNITY NEWSPAPER

La Canada Valley Sun 155053
Owner: tronc
Editorial: 202 W 1st St, Los Angeles, California 90012-4299 **Tel:** 1 818 495-4440
Email: lcnews@valleysun.net **Web site:** http://www.lacanadaonline.com
Freq: Thu; **Circ:** 10000 Not Audited
Editor: Carol Cormaci
Profile: La Canada Valley Sun is a weekly, community newspaper serving areas in and surrounding La Canada, CA. Coverage includes local news, events, sports, religion, entertainment, schools and editorials. Please use the news release form on their website or e-mail all press releases to the appropriate editor or reporter. Valley Sun newspapers will NOT accept materials that are faxed or mailed. Deadlines for calendar submissions are on Mondays at 11 a.m. PT.
Language (s): English
Ad Rate: Full Page Mono 24.50
Currency: United States Dollars
COMMUNITY NEWSPAPER

La Estrella En Casa 23338
Owner: McClatchy Newspapers
Editorial: 400 W 7th St, Fort Worth, Texas 76102-4701
Web site: http://www.diariolaestrella.com
Freq: Fri; **Circ:** 118936 Not Audited
Publisher & Editor: Juan Antonio Ramos
Profile: La Estrella En Casa is a weekly, Spanish-language newspaper serving the Hispanic community throughout Dallas and Fort Worth, TX.
Language (s): Spanish
Ad Rate: Full Page Mono 40.00
Ad Rate: Full Page Colour 658.00
Currency: United States Dollars
COMMUNITY NEWSPAPER

La Feria News 155991
Owner: Wright (Donald and Mary E.)
Editorial: 102 S Main St, La Feria, Texas 78559-5005 **Tel:** 1 956 797-9920
Email: news@laferianews.net **Web site:** http://www.laferianews.net
Freq: Wed; **Circ:** 5000 Not Audited
Advertising Sales Manager: Bill Keltner; **Publisher:** Donald R. Wright; **Editor:** Mary Beth Wright
Profile: La Feria (TX) News is a community newspaper covering news and events for the local Hispanic community.
Language (s): English
Ad Rate: Full Page Mono 8.00
Currency: United States Dollars
COMMUNITY NEWSPAPER

La Follette Press Publications 24888
Owner: Landmark Community Newspapers, Inc.
Editorial: 225 N 1st St, La Follette, Tennessee 37766 **Tel:** 1 423 562-8468
Email: stories@lafollettepress.com **Web site:** http://www.lafollettepress.com
Circ: 11000 Not Audited
Circulation Manager: Michell Daugherty; **Advertising Sales Manager:** Ann Rutherford
Language (s): English
COMMUNITY NEWSPAPER

La Jolla Light 23035
Owner: Mainstreet Media Group
Editorial: 565 Pearl St Ste 300, La Jolla, California 92037-5051 **Tel:** 1 858 459-4201
Email: talkback@lajollalight.com **Web site:** http://www.lajollalight.com
Freq: Thu; **Circ:** 20047 Not Audited
Editor: Susan DeMaggio; **Publisher:** Phyllis Pfeiffer
Profile: La Jolla Light is dedicated to delivering local news, business, sports, entertainment and religious news to the community of La Jolla, CA.
Language (s): English
Ad Rate: Full Page Mono 32.95
Currency: United States Dollars
COMMUNITY NEWSPAPER

La Mirada Lamplighter 887983
Tel: 1 562 407-3873
Email: lmlamplighter@gmail.com **Web site:** http://www.lmlamplighter.com
Freq: Sat; **Circ:** 74000
Publisher: Brian Hews
Profile: La Mirada Lamplighter is a weekly newspaper providing Community and Local News coverage for the residents of La Mirada, CA in Southeast Los Angeles.
Language (s): English
COMMUNITY NEWSPAPER

LA Watts Times 22370
Owner: Bakewell Media
Editorial: 3800 Crenshaw Blvd, Los Angeles, California 90008-1813 **Tel:** 1 323 299-3800
Email: brandon@lasentinel.net **Web site:** http://www.lawattstimes.com
Freq: Thu; **Circ:** 40000 Not Audited
Publisher: Danny Bakewell; **Advertising Sales Manager:** Bernard Lloyd; **Advertising Sales Manager:** Clifford Russell
Profile: L.A. Watts Times is a local weekly newspaper written for the African American community in Los Angeles County, CA. The paper publishes information on education, business, health, legal, financial, entertainment, career and employment opportunities as well as many current and historical topics.
Language (s): English
Ad Rate: Full Page Mono 58.24
Ad Rate: Full Page Colour 4560.00
Currency: United States Dollars
COMMUNITY NEWSPAPER

LA Weekly 22689
Owner: Voice Media Group
Editorial: 3861 Sepulveda Blvd, Culver City, California 90230-4605 **Tel:** 1 310 574-7100
Web site: http://www.laweekly.com
Freq: Thu; **Circ:** 89683 Not Audited
Editor: Mara Shalhoup
Profile: LA Weekly is published every Thursday for the young, affluent residents of Los Angeles. The publication covers news, entertainment, art, culture and lifestyle. Sections include Calendar, Picks, Scoring the Clubs, News, Film, Music, Theater, Art, Books, Radio, Politics, Dining and Cyber. Submit releases to the appropriate section editor. The editorial deadline falls on Monday at noon PT.
Language (s): English
Ad Rate: Full Page Mono 84.00
Currency: United States Dollars
COMMUNITY NEWSPAPER

Ladue News 21932
Owner: Lee Enterprises Inc.
Editorial: 8811 Ladue Rd Ste D, Saint Louis, Missouri 63124-2084 **Tel:** 1 314 863-3737
Email: pressreleases@laduenews.com **Web site:** http://www.laduenews.com
Freq: Fri; **Circ:** 38122 Not Audited
Circulation Manager: Megan Langford
Profile: Ladue News is written for residents in the St. Louis, MO area and covers news and events.
Language (s): English
Ad Rate: Full Page Mono 2.05
Currency: United States Dollars
COMMUNITY NEWSPAPER

Ladysmith News 21188
Owner: Bell Press
Editorial: 120 W 3rd St S, Ladysmith, Wisconsin 54848-1764 **Tel:** 1 715 532-5591
Web site: http://www.ladysmithnews.com
Freq: Thu; **Circ:** 5550 Not Audited
Publisher: James Bell; **Advertising Sales Manager:** Scott Bingham; **Editor:** Oliver Fink
Profile: Ladysmith News aims to provide residents of Ladysmith and Rusk County, WI with local stories, community news and weather.
Language (s): English
Ad Rate: Full Page Mono 7.95
Ad Rate: Full Page Colour 1160.63
Currency: United States Dollars
COMMUNITY NEWSPAPER

The Lafourche Gazette 22839
Owner: Legendre (Earl P.)
Editorial: 12958 E Main St, Larose, Louisiana 70373-1450 **Tel:** 1 985 693-7229
Email: news@tlgnewspaper.com **Web site:** http://www.thelafourchegazette.com
Freq: Sun; **Circ:** 15300 Not Audited
Editor: Vicki Chaisson; **Publisher:** Adrian Legendre
Profile: The Lafourche Gazette's editorial mission is to be a free news source for the local communities of Lafourche and Larose, LA.
Language (s): English
Ad Rate: Full Page Mono 14.92
Currency: United States Dollars
COMMUNITY NEWSPAPER

Laguna Beach Independent 238888
Owner: Firebrand Media LLC.
Editorial: 250 Broadway St, Laguna Beach, California 92651-1807 **Tel:** 1 949 715-4100
Email: editor@lbindy.com **Web site:** http://www.lagunabeachindy.com/
Freq: Fri; **Circ:** 15000 Not Audited
Profile: Laguna Beach Independent is a weekly newspaper serving the residents of Laguna Beach, CA.
Language (s): English
Ad Rate: Full Page Mono 9.53
Ad Rate: Full Page Colour 880.00
Currency: United States Dollars
COMMUNITY NEWSPAPER

Laguna Woods Globe 88353
Owner: Southern California News Group/Digital First Media
Editorial: 24351 El Toro Rd, Laguna Woods, California 92637-4901 **Tel:** 1 949 837-5200
Web site: http://www.ocregister.com/sections/city-pages/lagunawoods
Freq: Thu; **Circ:** 7264 Not Audited
Profile: Laguna Woods Globe is written for residents of Laguna Woods Village, a retirement community located in Orange County, CA. It covers local news and community events. Editorial deadlines are on Mondays at noon PT.
Language (s): English
Ad Rate: Full Page Mono 44.52
Currency: United States Dollars
COMMUNITY NEWSPAPER

Lake Country Publications 24733
Owner: Journal Community Publishing Group
Editorial: 810 Cardinal Ln Ste 200, Hartland, Wisconsin 53029-2390 **Tel:** 1 262 367-3272
Email: lakenews@jcpgroup.com **Web site:** http://www.livinglakecountry.com
Freq: Weekly; **Circ:** 10427 Not Audited
Language (s): English
COMMUNITY NEWSPAPER

Lake Eufaula Publishing 25308
Owner: Sumner Newspapers Inc.
Editorial: 109 S Main St, Eufaula, Oklahoma 74432 **Tel:** 1 918 689-2191
Circ: 15900 Not Audited
Editor: Jack Fallor; **Publisher & Editor:** Donna Pierce
Language (s): English
Ad Rate: Full Page Mono 8.00
Currency: United States Dollars
COMMUNITY NEWSPAPER

Lake Geneva Regional News 29561
Owner: United Communications Corp.
Editorial: 315 Broad St, Lake Geneva, Wisconsin 53147-1811 **Tel:** 1 262 248-4444
Web site: http://www.lakegenevanews.net
Freq: Thu; **Circ:** 5000 Not Audited
Circulation Manager: Sue Hinske
Profile: Lake Geneva Regional News is a weekly newspaper serving the residents of Lake Geneva, WI.

The publication features coverage of local news, community events and recreational activities.
Language (s): English
Ad Rate: Full Page Mono 11.50
Currency: United States Dollars
COMMUNITY NEWSPAPER

Lake Norman Citizen 594608
Owner: Hager (Irvin)
Editorial: 307 Gilead Rd, Huntersville, North Carolina 28078-6896 **Tel:** 1 704 948-3348
Email: news@lakenormancitizen.com **Web site:** http://www.lakenormancitizen.com
Freq: Wed; **Circ:** 30000
Publisher: Kim Clark; **Circulation Manager:** Steve Podielsky; **Editor:** Andy Warfield
Profile: Lake Norman Citizen is a weekly community newspaper written for the residents of Huntersville, Cornelius and Davidson, NC. The paper began publishing in June 2009.
Language (s): English
Ad Rate: Full Page Mono 26.00
Ad Rate: Full Page Colour 100.00
Currency: United States Dollars
COMMUNITY NEWSPAPER

Lake Norman Publications 88117
Owner: Newsman LLC
Editorial: 209 Delburg St, Davidson, North Carolina 28036-6913 **Tel:** 1 704 766-2100
Email: news@huntersvilleherald.com **Web site:** http://www.lakenormanpublications.com
Circ: 37000 Not Audited
Profile: Lake Norman Publications in Davidson, NC publishes community newspapers for residents of Union and Mecklenburg County, NC.
Language (s): English
COMMUNITY NEWSPAPER

Lake Oconee Breeze 394914
Owner: Community Newspaper Holdings, Inc.
Editorial: 165 Garrett Way NW, Milledgeville, Georgia 31061-2318 **Tel:** 1 478 453-1450
Email: breeze@unionrecorder.com **Web site:** http://www.lakeoconeebreeze.net
Freq: Thu; **Circ:** 9000 Not Audited
Publisher: Keith Barlow; **Editor:** Natalie Davis; **Circulation Manager:** Michael Evans
Profile: Lake Oconee Breeze is a community newspaper covering local news for the residents of Milledgeville, GA.
Language (s): English
Ad Rate: Full Page Mono 7.90
Ad Rate: Full Page Colour 100.00
Currency: United States Dollars
COMMUNITY NEWSPAPER

Lake Stevens Journal 22016
Owner: Lake Stevens Journal Inc.
Editorial: 1816 S Lake Stevens Rd Ste 2, Lake Stevens, Washington 98258-7960 **Tel:** 1 425 334-9252
Email: lakestevensjournalpublisher@gmail.com
Freq: Wed; **Circ:** 16000 Not Audited
Editor and Publisher: Desiree Cahoon; **Advertising Manager:** Marcy Little
Profile: Lake Stevens Journal is written for residents of Lake Stevens and Granite Falls, WA. Deadlines are on Thursdays at 5pm PT.
Language (s): English
Ad Rate: Full Page Mono 23.00
Currency: United States Dollars
COMMUNITY NEWSPAPER

The Lake Today 939040
Owner: Wehco Media Inc.
Editorial: 101 Crossings W Ste 203, Lake Ozark, Missouri 65049-8707 **Tel:** 1 573 365-2827
Web site: http://www.thelaketoday.com
Freq: Weekly; **Circ:** 13000
Editor: Samantha Edmondson; **Publisher:** Walter Hussman; **Advertising Manager:** Jennifer Vanderpool
Profile: The Lake Today is a full-color weekly community newspaper covering local news, sports, entertainment, human interest, education, outdoors and recreation for Lake Ozark, MO residents.
Language (s): English
Ad Rate: Full Page Colour 10.50
Currency: United States Dollars
COMMUNITY NEWSPAPER

Lake Worth Herald Press, Inc. 24500
Editorial: 130 S H St, Lake Worth, Florida 33460-4431 **Tel:** 1 561 585-9387
Email: lwherald@bellsouth.net **Web site:** http://www.lwherald.com
Circ: 38000 Not Audited
Publisher & Editor: Mark Easton
Language (s): English
COMMUNITY NEWSPAPER

Lake Wylie Pilot 22732
Owner: McClatchy Newspapers
Editorial: 264 Latitude Ln Ste 102 E-F, Clover, South Carolina 29710-8129 **Tel:** 1 803 831-8166
Email: news@lakewyliepilot.com **Web site:** http://www.lakewyliepilot.com
Freq: Tue; **Circ:** 11000 Not Audited
Editor: Catherine Muccigrosso; **Advertising Sales Manager:** Wendi Samples
Profile: Lake Wylie Pilot provides local news to Lake Wylie, SC and the surrounding counties. Deadlines are on Wednesdays prior to the next issue date.
Language (s): English
Ad Rate: Full Page Mono 15.60
Currency: United States Dollars
COMMUNITY NEWSPAPER

The Lakeland Times 21199
Owner: Walker (Gregg)
Editorial: 510 Chippewa St, Minocqua, Wisconsin 54548-9395 **Tel:** 1 715 356-5236
Email: editor@lakelandtimes.com **Web site:** http://www.lakelandtimes.com
Freq: Fri; **Circ:** 10000 Not Audited
Publisher: Gregg Walker
Profile: The Lakeland Times is written for Oneida and Vilas counties, WI.
Language (s): English
Ad Rate: Full Page Mono 6.95
Ad Rate: Full Page Colour 558.80
Currency: United States Dollars
COMMUNITY NEWSPAPER

The Lakelander 777584
Editorial: 1221A N Brazos St, Whitney, Texas 76692-2018 **Tel:** 1 254 694-4344
Email: lakelander@valornet.com
Freq: Weekly
Editor: Deanna Eubank; **Publisher:** Ron Eubank
Profile: The Lakelander is a weekly community newspaper.
COMMUNITY NEWSPAPER

The Laker 522503
Owner: Panoramic Publishing Group, LLC
Editorial: 83 Center St, Wolfeboro, New Hampshire 03894-4368 **Tel:** 1 603 569-5257
Email: lkr@thelaker.com **Web site:** http://www.thelaker.com
Freq: Mon; **Circ:** 20000 Not Audited
Publisher & Editor: Brad Lipe
Profile: The Laker is a weekly community newspaper serving the Lakes Region in New Hampshire.
Language (s): English
Ad Rate: Full Page Mono 3.14
Ad Rate: Full Page Colour 4.09
Currency: United States Dollars
COMMUNITY NEWSPAPER

Lakes Area Review 24179
Owner: Hawk Publishing Inc.
Editorial: 106 Norwood St SW, New London, Minnesota 56273 **Tel:** 1 320 354-2945
Email: lakesareareview@tds.net
Freq: Sat; **Circ:** 6263 Not Audited
Editor: Dori Moudry
Profile: Lakes Area Review is a weekly newspaper serving the residents of Kandiyohi County, including New London and Spicer, MN. It mostly covers local news and community events.
Language (s): English
Ad Rate: Full Page Mono 11.00
Currency: United States Dollars
COMMUNITY NEWSPAPER

Lakeshore Chronicle 21248
Owner: Gannett Co., Inc.
Editorial: 902 Franklin St, Manitowoc, Wisconsin 54220-4514 **Tel:** 1 920 684-4433
Email: htrnews@htrnews.com **Web site:** http://www.htrnews.com
Freq: Sun; **Circ:** 31500 Not Audited
Circulation Manager: Bruce Tischer
Profile: Lakeshore Chronicle is published twice weekly for residents of Manitowoc County, WI. The publication covers local news, weather, sports and community events. Feature articles cover business, education, arts & entertainment, lifestyle and other topics of importance to community residents. It shares offices and Web site with the daily Herald Times Reporter.
Language (s): English
Ad Rate: Full Page Mono 23.52
Currency: United States Dollars
COMMUNITY NEWSPAPER

Lakeshore Newspapers 25273
Owner: Conley Publishing Group
Editorial: W61N306 Washington Ave Ste L1, Cedarburg, Wisconsin 53012-2451 **Tel:** 1 262 375-5100
Email: webmaster@conleynet.com **Web site:** http://www.gmtoday.com
Circ: 36952 Not Audited
Language (s): English
COMMUNITY NEWSPAPER

Lakeshore Weekly News 74137
Owner: Southwest News Media
Editorial: 1001 Twelve Oaks Center Dr Ste 1017, Wayzata, Minnesota 55391-4310 **Tel:** 1 952 473-0890
Web site: http://www.swnewsmedia.com/lakeshore_weekly
Freq: Tue; **Circ:** 16000 Not Audited
Profile: Lakeshore Weekly News provides information on news and events to the residents of Wayzata, MN.
Language (s): English
Ad Rate: Full Page Mono 31.00
Currency: United States Dollars
COMMUNITY NEWSPAPER

The Lakeville Journal 24219
Owner: Lakeville Journal Co. (The)
Editorial: 33 Bissell St, Lakeville, Connecticut 6039 **Tel:** 1 860 435-9873
Email: editor@lakevillejournal.com **Web site:** http://www.tricornernews.com
Freq: Thu; **Circ:** 5000 Not Audited
Publisher: Janet Manko
Profile: Lakeville Journal is a weekly newspaper for residents of Lakeville, CT and surrounding areas. The newspaper covers local news and community events. Deadlines are on Tuesdays prior to issue date.
Language (s): English
Ad Rate: Full Page Mono 13.00
Currency: United States Dollars
COMMUNITY NEWSPAPER

Lakeway Publishers, Inc. 25169
Owner: Lakeway Publishers, Inc.
Editorial: 20 Business Park Dr, Troy, Missouri 63379 **Tel:** 1 636 528-9550
Email: lcjeditor@lcs.net **Web site:** http://www.lakewaypublishers.com
Circ: 16000 Not Audited
Advertising Sales Manager: Sandy Turner; **Publisher:** Pat Whiteside
Language (s): English
COMMUNITY NEWSPAPER

Lamorinda Sun 18623
Owner: MediaNews Group
Editorial: 175 Lennon Ln Ste 100, Walnut Creek, California 94598-2466 **Tel:** 1 925 943-8241
Email: ccsun@bayareanewsgroup.com
Freq: Fri; **Circ:** 15000 Not Audited
Editor: Sam Richards
Profile: Lamorinda Sun is a local weekly newspaper serving Lafayette, CA. The paper covers local news, weather, sports, business and arts & entertainment. The paper is a part of the Bay Area News Group subsidiary of MediaNews Group.
Language (s): English
Ad Rate: Full Page Mono 28.00
Currency: United States Dollars
COMMUNITY NEWSPAPER

The Lancaster News 426624
Owner: Landmark Community Newspapers Inc.
Editorial: 701 N White St, Lancaster, South Carolina 29720-2174 **Tel:** 1 800 844-9344 223
Email: news@thelancasternews.com **Web site:** http://www.thelancasternews.com
Circ: 20543 Not Audited
Publisher: Susan Rowell; **Editor:** Barbara Rutledge; **Advertising Sales Manager:** Leigh Sullivan
Language (s): English
COMMUNITY NEWSPAPER

The Landmark 19465
Owner: Holden Landmark Corporation
Editorial: 1161 Main St, Holden, Massachusetts 01520-1222 **Tel:** 1 508 829-5981
Email: editor@thelandmark.com **Web site:** http://www.thelandmark.com
Freq: Thu; **Circ:** 9006 Not Audited
Editor: Michael Ballway; **Advertising Sales Manager:** Barbara Brown
Profile: The Landmark is a community newspaper serving the five-town Wachusett, MA region. It reports on a wide spectrum of news about the people of Holden, Paxton, Princeton, Rutland and Sterling, MA. Deadlines are on Mondays at noon ET.
Language (s): English
Ad Rate: Full Page Mono 22.56
Currency: United States Dollars
COMMUNITY NEWSPAPER

Lansing Community Newspapers 24597
Owner: Gannett Co., Inc.
Editorial: 300 S Washington Sq #300, Lansing, Michigan 48933-2115 **Tel:** 1 517 377-1000
Web site: http://www.lsj.com
Freq: Weekly; **Circ:** 149114 Not Audited
Editor: Barbara Modrack
Language (s): English
COMMUNITY NEWSPAPER

Lapeer Area View 153183
Owner: JAMS Media
Editorial: 1521 Imlay City Rd, Lapeer, Michigan 48446-3175 **Tel:** 1 810 245-9343
Email: editor@mihomepaper.com **Web site:** http://www.mihomepaper.com
Freq: Thu; **Circ:** 35000 Not Audited
Profile: Lapeer Area View is a community newspaper for the residents of Lapeer, MI. It covers local news, weather and sports.
Language (s): English
Ad Rate: Full Page Mono 12.19
Currency: United States Dollars
COMMUNITY NEWSPAPER

Larned Tiller & Toiler Newspapers 393940
Owner: Star Communications Corp.
Editorial: 115 W 5th St, Larned, Kansas 67550 **Tel:** 1 620 285-3111
Email: tiller@star.kscoxmail.com
Circ: 16750 Not Audited
Publisher: John Settle
Language (s): English
COMMUNITY NEWSPAPER

Larson Newspapers 25099
Owner: Larson Newspapers, LLC
Editorial: 298 Van Deren Rd, Sedona, Arizona 86336-4826 **Tel:** 1 928 282-7795
Email: editor@larsonnewspapers.com **Web site:** http://www.redrocknews.com
Circ: 15800 Not Audited
Publisher: Robert Larson; **Circulation Manager:** Eric Mageary
Language (s): English
COMMUNITY NEWSPAPER

Las Americas Newspaper 258018
Owner: Alvarez (Fernando)
Editorial: 3809 Bell Manor Ct, Falls Church, Virginia 22041-1665 **Tel:** 1 703 256-4200
Email: lasamericasnewspaper@yahoo.com **Web site:** http://www.lasamericasnews.com
Freq: Fri; **Circ:** 25000 Not Audited
Publisher: Fernando Alvarez; **Advertising Sales Manager:** Cecilia Sanlillan; **Editor:** Abraham Ustariz
Profile: Las Americas Newspaper is a weekly Spanish-language newspaper covering local, national and Latino news and serving readers in Virginia, Maryland and Washington, D.C. Deadlines fall on Mondays at 5pm ET.
Language (s): Spanish
Ad Rate: Full Page Mono 20.00
Currency: United States Dollars
COMMUNITY NEWSPAPER

Las Cruces Bulletin 20225
Owner: OPC News
Editorial: 840 N Telshor Blvd Ste E, Las Cruces, New Mexico 88011-8205 **Tel:** 1 575 524-8065
Email: editor@lascrucesbulletin.com **Web site:** http://www.lascrucesbulletin.com
Freq: Fri; **Circ:** 20000 Not Audited
Publisher: Richard Coltharp; **Advertising Sales Manager:** Claire Frohs
Profile: Las Cruces Bulletin's editorial mission is to provide local news first to the residents of the Mesilla Valley, NM. Each issue features exclusive local content, including news, photography, features, sports, business, arts and entertainment, editorials, letters to the editor, local calendars, television listings and classified advertising.
Language (s): English
Ad Rate: Full Page Mono 20.00
Ad Rate: Full Page Colour 1303.40
Currency: United States Dollars
COMMUNITY NEWSPAPER

Las Vegas Chinese Daily News 349734
Editorial: 4215 Spring Mountain Rd Ste B206A, Las Vegas, Nevada 89102-8747 **Tel:** 1 702 312-3998
Web site: http://www.lvcdn.com
Freq: Fri; **Circ:** 20000 Not Audited
Advertising Sales Manager: Minyan Liu; **Editor:** Annie Yen
Profile: Las Vegas Chinese Daily News provides international and local news, business, real estate, entertainment and lifestyle news to the Las Vegas Chinese community. The paper is written in Mandarin Chinese to appeal to readers from China, Hong Kong, Singapore and Taiwan. The paper teams up with leading news source providers in China and Taiwan. Their mission is to provide objective reporting on the most updated news and events to the growing Asian population. It is distributed to local Chinese retail stores, doctor's offices, supermarkets, libraries and restaurants at no cost to its readers.
Language (s): Chinese
Ad Rate: Full Page Mono 11.54
Currency: United States Dollars
COMMUNITY NEWSPAPER

Las Vegas Chinese News Network 873207
Owner: Las Vegas Chinese News Network Corp.
Editorial: 3552 Wynn Rd, Las Vegas, Nevada 89103-1710 **Tel:** 1 702 685-6600
Email: ad@lvcnn.com **Web site:** http://www.lvcnn.com
Freq: Fri
Profile: Las Vegas Chinese News Network is a newspaper that provides Local and Community News coverage for Chinese-speaking residents in the Las Vegas, NV area.
Language (s): English
COMMUNITY NEWSPAPER

Las Vegas Israelite 154696
Owner: Jewish Newspaper of Las Vegas Inc.
Tel: 1 702 876-1255
Email: lasvegasisraelite@cox.net
Freq: Bi-Weekly; **Circ:** 43000 Not Audited
Publisher, Editor, Advertising Sales & Circulation Manager: Michael Tell
Profile: Las Vegas Israelite's editorial mission is to be positive about Israel, and to serve the Jewish business community and retirees. The publication provides local, national, and international news.
Language (s): English
Ad Rate: Full Page Mono 20.00
Currency: United States Dollars
COMMUNITY NEWSPAPER

Las Vegas Optic 14378
Owner: Landmark Community Newspapers, Inc.
Editorial: 614 Lincoln St, Las Vegas, New Mexico 87701-3935 **Tel:** 1 505 425-6796
Email: optic@lasvegasoptic.com **Web site:** http://www.lasvegasoptic.com
Freq: Fri; **Circ:** 5200
Circulation Manager: Crissy Johnson; **Publisher & Editor:** Martin Salazar
Profile: Las Vegas Optic is a weekly newspaper written for residents of Las Vegas, NM and the surrounding area.
Language (s): English
Ad Rate: Full Page Mono 12.21
Ad Rate: Full Page Colour 70.00

Currency: United States Dollars
COMMUNITY NEWSPAPER

Las Vegas Tribune 152725
Owner: Larraz (Rolando)
Editorial: 820 E Charleston Blvd, Las Vegas, Nevada 89104-1512 **Tel:** 1 702 426-6022
Email: newsdesk@lasvegastribune.com **Web site:** http://www.lasvegastribune.com
Freq: Wed; **Circ:** 41500 Not Audited
Editor in Chief & Publisher: Rolando Larraz; **Circulation Manager:** John Thomas
Profile: Las Vegas Tribune is a weekly newspaper serving residents of Las Vegas. It contains community news and politics, editorials, sports and an entertainment section. Some national news is reported if it is of interest to local readers.
Language (s): English
Ad Rate: Full Page Mono 15.00
Currency: United States Dollars
COMMUNITY NEWSPAPER

Lassen County Times 28690
Owner: Feather Publishing Co.
Editorial: 100 Grand Ave, Susanville, California 96130-4451 **Tel:** 1 530 257-5321
Email: lctimes@lassennews.com **Web site:** http://www.lassennews.com
Freq: Tue; **Circ:** 9550 Not Audited
Advertising Sales Manager: Jill Atkinson; **Publisher:** Michael Taborski
Profile: Lassen County Times is written for the residents of Susanville and Honey Valley Lake, CA. The publication covers local news and community events. Editorial deadlines are on Fridays at noon PT.
Language (s): English
Ad Rate: Full Page Mono 8.75
Currency: United States Dollars
COMMUNITY NEWSPAPER

Latin Opinion 719087
Editorial: 211 Eastern Ave, Suite 300, Baltimore, Maryland 21231 **Tel:** 1 410 522-0297
Email: alba@latinopinionbaltimore.com **Web site:** http://www.latinopinionbaltimore.com
Freq: Bi-Weekly; **Circ:** 10000
Profile: Latin Opinion is a bi-weekly newspaper serving the Latin community in Baltimore.
Language (s): Spanish
Ad Rate: Full Page Mono 15.65
Currency: United States Dollars
COMMUNITY NEWSPAPER

El Latino 74120
Owner: Arkansas Times
Editorial: 201 E Markham St, Ste 200, Little Rock, Arkansas 72201 **Tel:** 1 501 374-0853
Email: el-latino@arktimes.com **Web site:** http://ellatinoarkansas.com
Freq: Thu; **Circ:** 6000 Not Audited
Advertising Sales Manager: Luis Garcia; **Circulation Manager:** Anitra Hickman; **Editor:** Michel Leidermann; **Publisher:** Alan Leveritt
Profile: El Latino is a weekly Spanish publication for Little Rock and Benton, AR. The paper covers Spanish community news, entertainment, sports and weather.
Language (s): Spanish/Bilingual
Ad Rate: Full Page Mono 45.00
Ad Rate: Full Page Colour 1675.00
Currency: United States Dollars
COMMUNITY NEWSPAPER

El Latino 135709
Owner: Ramos (Jose)
Editorial: 3318 Cambridge St, Des Moines, Iowa 50313-4655 **Tel:** 1 515 266-3399
Email: info@latinonewspaper.com **Web site:** http://www.latinonewspaper.com
Freq: Thu; **Circ:** 5000 Not Audited
Publisher & Editor: Jose Ramos
Profile: El Latino is a weekly Spanish newspaper in Des Moines, IA that serves adults, ages 25 and older, in Iowa. The paper covers news and sports throughout Central America, South America and the United States. The paper can be found at restaurants, hotels and Hispanic business throughout Iowa.
Language (s): Spanish
Ad Rate: Full Page Mono 5.00
Currency: United States Dollars
COMMUNITY NEWSPAPER

Latino 242150
Owner: Leon (Wilfredo)
Editorial: 303 N Main St, Mauldin, South Carolina 29662-2303 **Tel:** 1 864 627-1945
Email: editor@latinonewspaper.net **Web site:** http://www.latino4u.net
Freq: Fri; **Circ:** 35000 Not Audited
Editor & Publisher: Wilfredo Leon
Profile: Latino in Mauldin, SC is a Spanish newspaper written for the residents of Greenville, SC and surrounding areas. Its editorial mission is to enhance society by creating, collecting and distributing high quality news, information and entertainment.
Language (s): Spanish
Ad Rate: Full Page Mono 10.40
Currency: United States Dollars
COMMUNITY NEWSPAPER

Latino Communications Network 396798
Owner: Latino Communications Network
Editorial: 2909 Bryant Ave S Ste 301, Minneapolis, Minnesota 55408-4966 **Tel:** 1 612 729-5900
Email: sales@lcnmedia.com **Web site:** http://www.lcnmedia.com
Circ: 45000 Not Audited
Profile: Latino Communications Network is a publisher dedicated to reaching Minnesota's Latino community.
Language (s): English
COMMUNITY NEWSPAPER

El Latino de Hoy 324183
Tel: 1 503 493-1106
Email: contact@ellatinodehoy.com **Web site:** http://www.ellatinodehoy.com
Freq: Wed; **Circ:** 25000 Not Audited
Editor & Publisher: Rodrigo Aguilar
Profile: El Latino de Hoy is a weekly Spanish-language newspaper written for residents of Portland, OR.
Language (s): Spanish
Ad Rate: Full Page Mono 18.00
Currency: United States Dollars
COMMUNITY NEWSPAPER

Latino News 520228
Editorial: 2522 Valleydale Rd Ste 301, Hoover, Alabama 35244-2703 **Tel:** 1 205 533-7808
Email: alabama@latino-news.com **Web site:** http://www.latino-news.com
Freq: Fri; **Circ:** 10000 Not Audited
Publisher & Editor: Jairo Vargas
Profile: Latino News is a weekly Spanish-language newspaper covering local, national and Latino news.
Language (s): Spanish
Ad Rate: Full Page Mono 30.00
Currency: United States Dollars
COMMUNITY NEWSPAPER

Latino Press 71749
Owner: Latino Press, Inc.
Editorial: 6301 Michigan Ave, Detroit, Michigan 48210-2954 **Tel:** 1 313 361-3000
Email: editorial@latinodetroit.com **Web site:** http://www.latinodetroit.com
Freq: Thu; **Circ:** 20000 Not Audited
Publisher & Editor: Elias Gutierrez
Profile: Latino Press is published weekly for the Hipanic community in Detroit, MI and surrounding areas. The newspaper covers local news, national news, Mexico news, community events, sports, immigration and education.
Language (s): Spanish
Ad Rate: Full Page Mono 57.00
Currency: United States Dollars
COMMUNITY NEWSPAPER

El Latino San Diego 23219
Owner: Latina Associates Inc.
Editorial: 555 H St, Chula Vista, California 91910-4330 **Tel:** 1 619 426-1491
Email: editor@ellatino.net **Web site:** http://www.ellatinoonline.com
Freq: Fri; **Circ:** 57351 Not Audited
Publisher & Editor: Fanny Miller
Profile: El Latino San Diego is a weekly publication for the Hispanic communities located in Southern California. The publication covers local news and events.
Language (s): English, Spanish
Ad Rate: Full Page Mono 53.50
Currency: United States Dollars
COMMUNITY NEWSPAPER

El Latino Semanal 23225
Owner: El Latino, Inc.
Editorial: 4404 Georgia Ave, West Palm Beach, Florida 33405-2524 **Tel:** 1 561 835-4913
Email: ellatino@msn.com **Web site:** http://www.ellatinodigital.com
Freq: Fri; **Circ:** 39000 Not Audited
Editor: Miguel Lavin; **Editor:** Olga Vazquez
Profile: El Latino Semanal is a local newspaper written for the Hispanic community of West Palm Beach, FL. Topics covered include immigration, health, sports and arts & entertainment.
Language (s): Spanish
Ad Rate: Full Page Mono 16.00
Currency: United States Dollars
COMMUNITY NEWSPAPER

Lauderdale County Enterprise 24701
Editorial: 145 E Jackson Ave, Ripley, Tennessee 38063-1556 **Tel:** 1 731 635-1771
Email: enterprisenewspaper@hotmail.com
Freq: Weekly; **Circ:** 5969 Not Audited
Profile: Lauderdale County Enterprise is written for the general public in Tennessee.
Language (s): English
Ad Rate: Full Page Colour 666.00
Currency: United States Dollars
COMMUNITY NEWSPAPER

Laughlin Nevada Times 22730
Owner: Brehm Communications, Inc.
Editorial: 2435 Miracle Mile, Bullhead City, Arizona 86442-7311 **Tel:** 1 928 763-2505
Email: gmco53@clippintheriver.com **Web site:** http://www.mohavedailynews.com/laughlin_times/
Freq: Wed; **Circ:** 8000 Not Audited
Editor: Bill McMillen; **Publisher:** Gary Milks; **Circulation Manager:** Don Orth
Profile: Laughlin Nevada Times is published weekly for the residents of Laughlin, NV. It covers local news, sports, arts & and entertainment, health, real estate and community events. Deadlines are on Thursdays.
Language (s): English
Ad Rate: Full Page Mono 19.56
Ad Rate: Full Page Colour 120.00
Currency: United States Dollars
COMMUNITY NEWSPAPER

Laurel Group Newspapers 24796
Owner: Tribune-Review Publishing Co.
Editorial: 228 Pittsburgh St, Scottdale, Pennsylvania 15683-1735 **Tel:** 1 724 887-7400
Web site: http://www.laurelgrouponline.com
Circ: 18626 Not Audited
Editor: Deborah Brehun; **Editor:** Mary Kaufman; **Editor:** Kristie Linden; **Editor:** Paul Paterra; **Editor:** William Zirkle
Language (s): English
COMMUNITY NEWSPAPER

Laurens County Advertiser 20632
Owner: Brown (Marc & James)
Editorial: 226 W Laurens St, Laurens, South Carolina 29360-2960 **Tel:** 1 864 984-2586
Email: news@lcadvertiser.com **Web site:** http://www.laurenscountyadvertiser.net
Freq: Wed; **Circ:** 8000 Not Audited
Circulation Manager: Tara Brown
Profile: Laurens County Advertiser is a local newspaper written for Laurens County, SC and surrounding areas. The publication features local news, community events and advertising in the Wednesday edition. The Saturday issue does not feature editorials. Deadlines are 5pm ET for editorials.
Language (s): English
Ad Rate: Full Page Mono 10.25
Currency: United States Dollars
COMMUNITY NEWSPAPER

Lawndale News 22643
Owner: Lawndale Press, Inc.
Editorial: 5533 W 25th St, Cicero, Illinois 60804-3319 **Tel:** 1 708 656-6400
Email: subscribe@lawndalenews.com **Web site:** http://www.lawndalenews.com
Freq: Weekly; **Circ:** 192200 Not Audited
Editor: Ashmar Mandou; **Publisher:** Lynda Nardini
Profile: Lawndale News is written for the Hispanic residents of Chicago. It covers local news and events. Deadlines are on Thursdays at 5pm CT.
Language (s): English, Spanish
Ad Rate: Full Page Mono 55.00
Ad Rate: Full Page Colour 3810.00
Currency: United States Dollars
COMMUNITY NEWSPAPER

Lawrence County Advocate 20767
Owner: Kennedy (Sam)
Editorial: 121 N Military Ave, Lawrenceburg, Tennessee 38464-3323 **Tel:** 1 931 762-1726
Email: lawcoadv@bellsouth.net **Web site:** http://www.lawrencecountyadvocate.net
Freq: Sun; **Circ:** 16400 Not Audited
Circulation Manager: Dorothy Belew; **Advertising Sales Manager:** Janice Butler; **Publisher/Editor:** Sam Kennedy; **Editor:** Sandy Mashburn
Profile: Lawrence County Advocate is a local newspaper written for residents of Lawrence County, Tennessee. The publication regularly features local news and sometimes features national news.
Language (s): English
Ad Rate: Full Page Mono 5.60
Ad Rate: Full Page Colour 691.80
Currency: United States Dollars
COMMUNITY NEWSPAPER

Lawrenceburg Democrat Union 20735
Owner: Crawford (Jim, Jr.)
Editorial: 238 Hughes St, Lawrenceburg, Tennessee 38464-3364 **Tel:** 1 931 762-2222
Email: duadv@bellsouth.net
Freq: 2 Times/Week; **Circ:** 6869 Not Audited
Publisher & Editor: Jim Crawford
Profile: Lawrenceburg Democrat Union is a local newspaper serving the Lawrenceburg, TN area. It provides information on news, events, politics and other information of importance to the local community. The lead time is one week.
Language (s): English
Ad Rate: Full Page Mono 6.95
Currency: United States Dollars
COMMUNITY NEWSPAPER

Le Roy Pennysaver & News 768253
Editorial: 1 Church St, Le Roy, New York 14482-1017 **Tel:** 1 585 768-2201
Email: office@leroyny.com **Web site:** http://www.leroypennysavernews.com
Freq: Weekly; **Circ:** 7700
Profile: The Le Roy Pennysaver & News is a free community newspaper written for the residents of Le Roy, NY and the surrounding area. Includes calendar & events, local news, sports and features.
Language (s): English
Ad Rate: Full Page Mono 9.91
Currency: United States Dollars
COMMUNITY NEWSPAPER

The Leader 21123
Editorial: 226 Adams St, Port Townsend, Washington 98368-5706 **Tel:** 1 360 385-2900
Email: news@ptleader.com **Web site:** http://www.ptleader.com
Freq: Wed; **Circ:** 8000 Not Audited
Advertising Sales Manager: Catherine Brewer; **Circulation Manager:** Susan Jackson
Profile: The Leader is written for residents of Jefferson County, WA. It covers news and events. Deadlines are on Fridays at 3pm PT.
Language (s): English
Ad Rate: Full Page Mono 14.85
Currency: United States Dollars
COMMUNITY NEWSPAPER

The Leader 22332
Owner: American Hometown Publishing
Editorial: 2001 Highway 51 S, Covington, Tennessee 38019-3631 **Tel:** 1 901 476-7116
Email: news@covingtonleader.com **Web site:** http://www.covingtonleader.com
Freq: Thu; **Circ:** 6070 Not Audited
Publisher: Brian Blackley; **Circulation Manager:** Kathy Griffin
Profile: The Leader is a weekly newspaper serving the residents of Tipton County, TN. The paper covers local, state and national news, arts & entertainment, sports, lifestyle and editorial articles.
Language (s): English
Ad Rate: Full Page Mono 10.51
Currency: United States Dollars
COMMUNITY NEWSPAPER

The Leader 152593
Editorial: 404 Graham Rd, Jacksonville, Arkansas 72076-3813 **Tel:** 1 501 982-9421
Web site: http://www.arkansasleader.com
Freq: Sat; **Circ:** 28866 Not Audited
Publisher & Editor: Garrick Feldman
Profile: The Leader is a local newspaper written for the residents of Pulaski, Lonoke and White counties with an emphasis on Jacksonville, Sherwood, Cabot, Ward, Lonoke, Austin and Beebe, Arkansas.
Language (s): English
Ad Rate: Full Page Mono 17.50
Currency: United States Dollars
COMMUNITY NEWSPAPER

The Leader 777708
Owner: Burge Publishing Corporation
Editorial: 3500 A East T.C. Jester Blvd, Houston, Texas 77292 **Tel:** 1 713 686-8494
Web site: http://www.theleadernews.com
Freq: Weekly
COMMUNITY NEWSPAPER

Leader Group 25028
Owner: Community Newspapers Inc.
Editorial: 1114 Beach Blvd, Jacksonville Beach, Florida 32250-3404 **Tel:** 1 904 249-9033
Web site: http://www.beachesleader.com
Circ: 34600 Not Audited
Circulation Manager: Steve Fouraker; **Publisher:** Tom Wood
Profile: Leader Group in Jacksonville Beach, FL publishes the Ponte Vedra Leader and Beaches Leader community newspapers.
Language (s): English
COMMUNITY NEWSPAPER

Leader Publications 25417
Owner: West Side Publishing Co.
Editorial: 3075 Smith Rd Ste 204, Fairlawn, Ohio 44333-4454 **Tel:** 1 330 665-9595
Email: editor@akron.com **Web site:** http://www.akron.com
Circ: 64997
Editor: Kathryn Core; **Circulation Manager:** Stephanie Goehler
Profile: Leader Publications is a community newspaper publisher serving Akron, OH and surrounding areas.
Language (s): English
COMMUNITY NEWSPAPER

Leader Publications 25434
Owner: Leader Publications
Editorial: 503 N 2nd St, Festus, Missouri 63028-1829 **Tel:** 1 636 931-7560
Email: nvrweekly@aol.com **Web site:** http://www.myleaderpaper.com
Freq: Weekly; **Circ:** 58190 Not Audited
Editor: Peggy Bess; **Publisher & Circulation Manager:** Pam LaPlant; **Advertising Sales Manager:** Glenda O'Tool Potts; **Editor:** Kim Robertson; **News Editor:** Peggy Scott
Profile: Leader Publications provides a local newspaper to the community of Festus, MO.
Language (s): English
Ad Rate: Full Page Mono 59.00
Currency: United States Dollars
COMMUNITY NEWSPAPER

Leader Publishing Company 24564
Editorial: 117 E Walnut St, Salem, Indiana 47167-2044 **Tel:** 1 812 883-3281
Web site: http://www.salemleader.com
Circ: 12300 Not Audited
Editor: Stephanie Ferriell; **Publisher:** Nancy Grossman; **Advertising Sales Manager:** Debbi Hayes
Language (s): English
COMMUNITY NEWSPAPER

Leader-Times, Inc. 25172
Owner: Corbin (Horace)
Editorial: 251 North Ave W, Westfield, New Jersey 07090-1499 **Tel:** 1 908 232-4407
Email: press@goleader.com **Web site:** http://www.goleader.com
Freq: Thu; **Circ:** 7600 Not Audited
Circulation Manager: Robert Connelly; **Publisher and Editor:** Horace Corbin
Profile: Leader-times Inc is a local newspaper in Westfield, NJ.
Language (s): English

Ad Rate: Full Page Mono 12.00
Currency: United States Dollars
COMMUNITY NEWSPAPER

Lebanon Enterprise 19353
Owner: Landmark Community Newspapers Inc.
Editorial: 119 S Proctor Knott Ave, Lebanon, Kentucky 40033-1217 **Tel:** 1 270 692-6026
Web site: http://www.lebanonenterprise.com
Freq: Wed; **Circ:** 6000 Not Audited
Circulation Manager: Barbara Battcher; **Advertising Sales Manager:** Mary Anne Blair; **Publisher:** Stevie Lowery
Profile: Lebanon Enterprise is a weekly newspaper written for the residents of Lebanon, KY. The publication covers local news, sports and community events.
Language (s): English
Ad Rate: Full Page Mono 9.80
Ad Rate: Full Page Colour 1151.55
Currency: United States Dollars
COMMUNITY NEWSPAPER

Lebanon News 21056
Editorial: 20 Clinch Mountain Ave, Lebanon, Virginia 24266 **Tel:** 1 276 889-2112
Email: lebnews@verizon.net **Web site:** http://www.thelebanonnews.com
Freq: Wed; **Circ:** 5600 Not Audited
Publisher & Editor: Jerry Lark; **Advertising Sales Manager:** Louise Yates
Profile: Lebanon News is a weekly newspaper published for the residents of Lebanon, VA. The publication covers local news sports and community events. Deadlines are on Mondays at 2pm ET.
Language (s): English
Ad Rate: Full Page Mono 7.10
Currency: United States Dollars
COMMUNITY NEWSPAPER

Lee Newspapers 25258
Owner: Lee Enterprises, Inc.
Editorial: 2045 Grant St, Selma, California 93662-3508 **Tel:** 1 559 896-1976
Circ: 8024 Not Audited
Circulation Manager: Deborah Collette
Profile: Moreover.
Language (s): English
COMMUNITY NEWSPAPER

Leelanau Enterprise & Tribune 19528
Editorial: 7200 E Duck Lake Rd, Lake Leelanau, Michigan 49653-9779 **Tel:** 1 231 256-9827
Email: info@leelanaunews.com **Web site:** http://www.leelanaunews.com/drupal
Freq: Thu; **Circ:** 8600 Not Audited
Circulation Manager: Rochelle Briggerman; **Publisher & Editor:** Alan Campbell; **Advertising Sales Manager:** Debra Campbell; **News Editor:** Amy Hubbell; **News Editor:** Mike Spencer
Profile: Leelanau Enterprise & Tribune is a weekly newspaper published for the residents of Leelanau, MI. The publication covers local news and community events. The news deadline falls on Monday morning.
Language (s): English
Ad Rate: Full Page Mono 10.45
Currency: United States Dollars
COMMUNITY NEWSPAPER

Lee's Summit Journal & Blue Springs Journal 524284
Owner: McClatchy Newspapers
Editorial: 415 SE Douglas St, Lee's Summit, Missouri 64063 **Tel:** 1 816 524-2345
Web site: http://www.lsjournal.com
Circ: 30400 Not Audited
Language (s): English
COMMUNITY NEWSPAPER

The Legislative Gazette 76068
Editorial: Empire State Plaza, Concourse Level - Rm106, Albany, New York 12224 **Tel:** 1 518 473-9739
Web site: http://www.legislativegazette.com
Freq: Tue; **Circ:** 13000 Not Audited
Publisher: Alan Chartock; **Editor:** James Gormley; **Circulation Manager:** Beth Rider
Profile: Covers New York state government. Offers news and special reports.
Language (s): English
Ad Rate: Full Page Mono 32.89
Currency: United States Dollars
COMMUNITY NEWSPAPER

Lehigh Acres Citizen 22664
Owner: Breeze Newspapers
Editorial: 14051 Jetport Loop, Fort Myers, Florida 33913-7705 **Tel:** 1 239 368-3944
Email: citizen936@hotmail.com **Web site:** http://www.lehighacrescitizen.com
Freq: Wed; **Circ:** 12000 Not Audited
Publisher: Scott Blonde; **Editor:** Mel Toadvine
Profile: Lehigh Acres Citizen is written for the residents of Lehigh Acres, Alva, Buckingham and East Lee County, FL. It covers community news, sports and events. Deadlines are on Mondays at 5pm ET.
Language (s): English
Ad Rate: Full Page Mono 11.62
Currency: United States Dollars
COMMUNITY NEWSPAPER

Leisure World Seal Beach Golden Rain News 21638
Owner: Golden Rain Foundation
Editorial: 13533 Seal Beach Blvd, Seal Beach, California 90740 **Tel:** 1 562 430-0534
Freq: Thu; **Circ:** 9000 Not Audited
Editor: Cathie Merz
Profile: Seal Beach Leisure World Golden Rain News is published weekly for senior citizens. The newspaper provides senior citizens with news, lifestyle issues and information about social activities within the Leisure World community in Seal Beach, CA.
Language (s): English
Ad Rate: Full Page Mono 15.45
Currency: United States Dollars
COMMUNITY NEWSPAPER

La Lengua 519649
Owner: E.B.S., Inc.
Editorial: 118 W. Shepherd, Lufkin, Texas 75901
Tel: 1 936 632-8444
Email: ebs@suddenlinkmail.com
Freq: Wed; **Circ:** 10000 Not Audited
Editor: Ino Reyes; **Publisher:** Roy Reyes
Profile: La Lengua is a free, Spanish-language weekly community newspaper serving Lufkin, Nacogdoches and other communities in East Texas. It covers local news, education, government, events and human interest features with a Hispanic angle.
Language (s): Spanish
Ad Rate: Full Page Mono 7.00
Currency: United States Dollars
COMMUNITY NEWSPAPER

LEO Weekly 24424
Owner: Yarmuth (Aaron)
Editorial: 301 E Main St Ste 201, Louisville, Kentucky 40202-1247 **Tel:** 1 502 895-9770
Email: leo@leoweekly.com **Web site:** http://www.leoweekly.com
Freq: Wed; **Circ:** 30000 Not Audited
Editor & Publisher: Aaron Yarmuth
Profile: LEO Weekly is published weekly for residents of Louisville, KY and surrounding communities. The newspaper reports on a variety of lifestyle topics of interest to area residents, including local news, the arts, government, sports and the environment.
Language (s): English
Ad Rate: Full Page Mono 32.02
Currency: United States Dollars
COMMUNITY NEWSPAPER

Leominster Champion 397142
Owner: Holden Landmark Corp.
Editorial: 285 Central St Ste 202, Leominster, Massachusetts 01453-6144 **Tel:** 1 978 534-6006
Email: editor@leominsterchamp.com **Web site:** http://www.leominsterchamp.com
Freq: Fri; **Circ:** 9000 Not Audited
Editor: Cheryl Cuddahy; **Editor:** David Dore
Profile: The Leominster Champion is a free, weekly newspaper serving residents of Leominster, MA. It focuses exclusively on local news with a particular emphasis on people, schools, business, culture and youth sports. News submissions are due on Tuesdays by noon ET. Advertising deadlines are on Mondays at noon ET.
Language (s): English
Ad Rate: Full Page Mono 7.70
Ad Rate: Full Page Colour 70.00
Currency: United States Dollars
COMMUNITY NEWSPAPER

Levelland News Press 20998
Owner: Hockley County Publishing Co., Inc.
Editorial: 711 Austin St, Levelland, Texas 79336-4523 **Tel:** 1 806 894-3121
Email: levellandnews@valornet.com **Web site:** http://www.levellandnews.net
Freq: 2 Times/Week; **Circ:** 5000 Not Audited
Advertising Sales Manager: Michelle Davis; **Editor:** John Rigg
Profile: Levelland News Press is published twice a week for the residents of Hockley County, TX. The newspaper covers local news, sports, lifestyles and community events. Deadlines are on Fridays for the Sunday edition and on Tuesdays for the Wednesday edition.
Language (s): English
Ad Rate: Full Page Mono 7.75
Currency: United States Dollars
COMMUNITY NEWSPAPER

Lexington County Chronicle 22052
Owner: Lexington Publishing Co. Inc.
Editorial: 131 Swartz Rd, Lexington, South Carolina 29072-3623 **Tel:** 1 803 359-7633
Email: lexingtonchronicle@gmail.com **Web site:** http://www.lexingtonchronicle.com
Freq: Thu; **Circ:** 6000 Not Audited
Advertising Manager: MacLeod Bellune; **Editor:** Mark Bellune
Profile: Lexington County Chronicle & Dispatch-News is a newspaper started at the request of Lexington County residents to fill a local news void created by out-of-state ownership of other newspapers in the area. It is locally owned and operated. The paper's editor requests that only information involving Lexington County, SC, be sent.
Language (s): English
Ad Rate: Full Page Mono 13.00
Currency: United States Dollars
COMMUNITY NEWSPAPER

Lexington Progress 20736
Owner: Lexington Progress, Inc.
Editorial: 508 S Broad St, Lexington, Tennessee 38351-2211 **Tel:** 1 731 968-6397
Email: news@lexingtonprogress.com **Web site:** http://www.lexingtonprogress.com
Freq: Wed; **Circ:** 7500 Not Audited
Publisher: Tom Franklin; **Editor:** Mike Reed; **Advertising Sales Manager:** Susan Small
Profile: Lexington Progress is a local paper written for the residents of Lexington, TN.
Language (s): English
Ad Rate: Full Page Mono 5.50
Currency: United States Dollars
COMMUNITY NEWSPAPER

Liberty Gazette 21694
Owner: Smith (Cynthia)
Editorial: 314 Main St, Liberty, Texas 77575
Tel: 1 936 336-6416
Email: mail@libertygazette.com **Web site:** http://www.libertygazette.com
Freq: Tue; **Circ:** 9100 Not Audited
Publisher: Cynthia Smith
Profile: Liberty Gazette is a local weekly newspaper written for the residents of Liberty, TX. The publication covers local news, sports, and community events.
Language (s): English
Ad Rate: Full Page Mono 5.79
Currency: United States Dollars
COMMUNITY NEWSPAPER

Liberty Herald & UC Review 24874
Owner: Whitewater Publications
Editorial: 10 N Market St, Liberty, Indiana 47353-1122 **Tel:** 1 765 458-5114
Email: info@whitewaterpub.com **Web site:** http://www.whitewaterpub.com/?page=liberty
Circ: 6700 Not Audited
Editor: John Estridge; **Advertising Sales Manager:** Chris Louden; **Publisher:** Gary Wolf
Profile: Local Weekly paper owned by Whitewater Publications covering Community News in the Liberty, IN area.
Language (s): English
COMMUNITY NEWSPAPER

The Liberty Hill Independent 22605
Owner: Free State Media Group
Tel: 1 512 778-5577
Email: news@lhindependent.com **Web site:** http://lhindependent.com
Freq: Thu
Profile: The Independent is a weekly newspaper for residents of Liberty Hill, TX.
Language (s): English
COMMUNITY NEWSPAPER

The Liberty Lake Splash 70030
Owner: Peridot Publishing LLC
Editorial: 2310 N Molter Rd Ste 305, Liberty Lake, Washington 99019-8630 **Tel:** 1 509 242-7752
Email: editor@libertylakesplash.com **Web site:** http://www.libertylakesplash.com
Freq: Thu; **Circ:** 6000 Not Audited
Publisher & Editor: Josh Johnson
Profile: Liberty Lake Splash is a weekly newspaper written for the residents of Liberty Lake, WA. The publication covers local news, sports and community events. Deadlines are on Fridays prior to issue date.
Language (s): English
Ad Rate: Full Page Mono 21.00
Currency: United States Dollars
COMMUNITY NEWSPAPER

Libre 23174
Owner: Libre, L.L.C.
Editorial: 2700 SW 8th St, Miami, Florida 33135-4619
Tel: 1 305 643-4200
Web site: http://www.libreonline.com
Freq: Tue; **Circ:** 15000 Not Audited
Publisher & Editor: Demetrio Perez
Profile: Libre is a weekly billingual newspaper written for the residents of Miami. The publication covers local community news, as well as national and international topics of interest.
Language (s): Spanish
Ad Rate: Full Page Mono 30.00
Currency: United States Dollars
COMMUNITY NEWSPAPER

Life Newspapers 25508
Owner: McNaughton Newspapers
Editorial: 981 Governor Dr, Ste 101, El Dorado Hills, California 95762 **Tel:** 1 530 622-1255
Email: editor@villagelife.com
Circ: 32100 Not Audited
Editor: Noel Stack
Language (s): English
COMMUNITY NEWSPAPER

Lighthouse 152973
Owner: Komiyama (Yoichi)
Editorial: 2958 Columbia St, Torrance, California 90503-3806 **Tel:** 1 310 782-1260
Email: lighthouse@us-lighthouse.com **Web site:** http://www.us-lighthouse.com
Freq: Bi-Weekly; **Circ:** 95000 Not Audited
Publisher: Yoichi Komiyama
Profile: Lighthouse in Torrance, CA is community newspaper serving the Japanese community in and around Torrance, CA.
Language (s): Japanese
Ad Rate: Full Page Mono 34.78
Currency: United States Dollars
COMMUNITY NEWSPAPER

Lillie Suburban Newspapers 24604
Owner: Lillie Suburban Newspapers
Editorial: 2515 7th Ave E, Saint Paul, Minnesota 55109-3004 **Tel:** 1 651 777-8800
Email: news@lillienews.com **Web site:** http://lillienews.com
Circ: 124405 Not Audited
Advertising Sales Manager: Tony Fragnito; **Circulation Manager:** Laura Young
Profile: Lillie Suburban Newspapers is a community newspaper publisher in North Saint Paul, MN. The publications are only interested in news that pertains to Minnesota.
Language (s): English
COMMUNITY NEWSPAPER

Lincoln County News 19480
Owner: Lincoln County Publishing Company
Editorial: 116 Mills Rd, Newcastle, Maine 4553
Tel: 1 207 563-3171
Email: info@lcnme.com **Web site:** http://lcnme.com/
Freq: Thu; **Circ:** 9000 Not Audited
Advertising Sales Manager: Joyce Gill; **Publisher:** Christopher Roberts
Profile: Lincoln County News is a weekly newspaper published for the residents of Lincoln County, ME. The publication covers local news, sports, and community events. The news deadline falls on Tuesday.
Language (s): English
Ad Rate: Full Page Mono 8.00
Currency: United States Dollars
COMMUNITY NEWSPAPER

The Lincoln Journal, Inc. 24741
Owner: Lincoln Journal, Inc.
Editorial: 328 Walnut St, Hamlin, West Virginia 25523
Tel: 1 304 824-5101
Email: lincolnjournal@zoominternet.net
Circ: 17557
Publisher & Editor: Thomas Robinson
Language (s): English
COMMUNITY NEWSPAPER

Lincoln News 19486
Editorial: 78 W Broadway, Lincoln, Maine 04457-1312 **Tel:** 1 207 794-6532
Email: lincnews@midmaine.com **Web site:** http://www.lincnews.com
Freq: Thu; **Circ:** 6800 Not Audited
Publisher & Editor: Kevin Tenggren; **Advertising Sales Manager:** David Whalen
Profile: Lincoln News provides in-depth local, area and state news for the greater Lincoln, ME area.
Language (s): English
Ad Rate: Full Page Mono 7.00
Currency: United States Dollars
COMMUNITY NEWSPAPER

Lincoln News Messenger 18624
Owner: Gold Country Media
Editorial: 553 F St, Lincoln, California 95648-1849
Tel: 1 916 645-7733
Email: messenger@goldcountrymedia.com **Web site:** http://www.lincolnnewsmessenger.com
Freq: Thu; **Circ:** 6500 Not Audited
Circulation Manager: Dawn Baron; **Editor:** Carol Feineman; **Publisher:** Beth O'Brien
Profile: Lincoln News Messenger is a weekly newspaper written for residents in and around Lincoln, CA. The paper covers local news, sports and weather as well as national reports. Deadlines are one day prior to issue date.
Language (s): English
Ad Rate: Full Page Mono 10.80
Currency: United States Dollars
COMMUNITY NEWSPAPER

Lincoln Times-News 19985
Editorial: 119 W Water St, Lincolnton, North Carolina 28092-2623 **Tel:** 1 704 735-3031
Email: news@ltnews.com **Web site:** http://www.lincolntimesnews.com
Freq: Fri; **Circ:** 8000 Not Audited
Circulation Manager: Robin Ledford; **Advertising Sales Manager:** Lisa Matthews
Profile: Lincoln Times-News is published weekly for the residents of Lincolnton, NC and surrounding areas. The newspaper covers local news and community events.
Language (s): English
Ad Rate: Full Page Mono 10.00
Currency: United States Dollars
COMMUNITY NEWSPAPER

Lincoln Trail Publishing Co. 25127
Owner: CornerStone Media
Editorial: 216 S Central Ave, Casey, Illinois 62420-1726 **Tel:** 1 217 932-5211
Web site: http://www.lincolntrailpublishing.com
Circ: 9150 Not Audited
Editor: JJ Aten; **Publisher:** Charlotte Land; **Editor:** Nancy Lawson; **Editor & Publisher:** Chris Russell
Language (s): English
COMMUNITY NEWSPAPER

Lititz Record-Express 20568
Owner: Lancaster Newspapers, Inc.
Editorial: 1 E Main St, Ephrata, Pennsylvania 17522-2713 **Tel:** 1 717 626-2191
Web site: http://www.lititzrecord.com
Freq: Thu; **Circ:** 8100 Not Audited

Circulation Manager: John Betz; **Editor:** Andy Fasnacht; **Advertising Manager:** Beverly Kent
Profile: Lititz Record-Express is a local weekly newspaper in Lititz, PA. The publication covers local and state events, news, weather, and sports as well as some national news. The newspaper is written for residents of Lititz, PA and neighboring towns.
Language (s): English
Ad Rate: Full Page Mono 16.35
Currency: United States Dollars
COMMUNITY NEWSPAPER

Litmore Publishing Corp. 24642
Editorial: 81 E Barclay St, Hicksville, New York 11801 **Tel:** 1 516 931-0012
Email: editor@gcnews.com **Web site:** http://www.gcnews.com
Circ: 37933 Not Audited
Editor: Ann Cadigan; **Advertising Sales Manager:** Ed Norris
Profile: Litmore Publishing Corp. is a weekly community newspaper publisher serving the residents of Bethpage, Hicksville, Williston, Syosset and Hyde Park, NY.
Language (s): English
COMMUNITY NEWSPAPER

Little Saigon News 151359
Editorial: 13861 Seaboard Cir, Garden Grove, California 92843-3908 **Tel:** 1 714 265-0800
Email: saigonnho@gmail.com **Web site:** http://www.littlesaigonnow.com
Freq: Fri; **Circ:** 10000 Not Audited
Publisher & Editor: Brigitte Hynh; **Advertising Sales Manager:** Joseph Le
Profile: Little Saigon News is a publication providing the Vietnamese community of Garden Grove, CA with news.
Language (s): English
Ad Rate: Full Page Mono 10.00
Currency: United States Dollars
COMMUNITY NEWSPAPER

Littleton Courier 28666
Owner: Salmon Press LLC
Editorial: 16 Mill St, Littleton, New Hampshire 03561-4000 **Tel:** 1 603 444-3927
Email: couriernews@salmonpress.com **Web site:** http://www.courier-littletonnh.com
Freq: Wed; **Circ:** 6000 Not Audited
Publisher: Frank Chilinski
Profile: Littleton Courier covers local news, businesses, sports and events of interest to residents of Grafton County, including the towns of Littleton, Bethlehem, Franconia, Lincoln, Lisbon, North Woodstock, Sugar Hill, Whitefield, Bath, Bretton Woods, Dalton, Easton, Jefferson, Landaff, Lyman, Monroe, North Haverhill, Twin Mountain and Woodsville, NH, and Lower Waterford and Wells River, VT.
Language (s): English
Ad Rate: Full Page Mono 10.00
Currency: United States Dollars
COMMUNITY NEWSPAPER

Livewire Printing Co. 24941
Editorial: 310 2nd St, Jackson, Minnesota 56143-1640 **Tel:** 1 507 847-3771
Email: info@livewireprinting.com **Web site:** http://livewireprinting.com
Circ: 12311
Publisher & Editor: Justin Lessman; **Advertising Sales Manager:** Dallas Luhmann
Language (s): English
COMMUNITY NEWSPAPER

The Living Magazines 364183
Owner: Community Publications, Inc.
Editorial: 179 Fairfield Ave, Bellevue, Kentucky 41073-3410 **Tel:** 1 859 291-1412
Email: pr@livingmagazines.com **Web site:** http://www.livingmagazines.com
Circ: 30000 Not Audited
Editor: Vicki Black; **Editor:** Mark Collier; **Editor:** Grace DeGregorio; **Editor:** Amy Elliot; **Editor:** Moira Grainger; **Publisher:** Jim Lied
Profile: Community Publications Inc. publishes free, monthly news magazines called Fort Mitchell Living, Fort Thomas Living, Hyde Park Living, Indian Hill Living, Sycamore Living and Wyoming Living. Please only send one press release via fax, direct mail or to the main e-mail address. The lead times are by the 10th of the month two months prior to publication. Advertising deadlines are by the 15th of the month two months prior to issue date.
Language (s): English
COMMUNITY NEWSPAPER

Livingston Chronicle 349860
Owner: McClatchy Newspapers
Editorial: 3033 G St, Merced, California 95340
Tel: 1 209 722-1511
Web site: http://mercedsunstar.com
Freq: Wed; **Circ:** 10500 Not Audited
Profile: Livingston Chronicle is a free, weekly newspaper distributed to residents in Livingston, CA and the surrounding area. It is published by the Merced (CA) Sun Star and distributed to its subscribers. The paper only carries local news, events, features and editorials; all national and wire stories are featured within the daily edition of the Merced Sun Star.
Language (s): English
Ad Rate: Full Page Mono 11.00
Currency: United States Dollars
COMMUNITY NEWSPAPER

Livingston County News 21567
Owner: Johnson Newspaper Corp.
Editorial: 122 Main St, Geneseo, New York 14454-1230 **Tel:** 1 585 243-0296
Email: news@livingstonnews.com **Web site:** http://thelcn.com
Freq: Thu; **Circ:** 6500 Not Audited
Publisher: Thomas Turnbull
Profile: Livingston County News is a local weekly newspaper written for residents of Livingston County, NY. The publication provides coverage of local news and community events. The editorial deadline is Friday at 5pm ET.
Language (s): English
Ad Rate: Full Page Mono 8.51
Currency: United States Dollars
COMMUNITY NEWSPAPER

Livingston Enterprise 20738
Owner: Mitchell Media, Inc.
Editorial: 203 S Church St, Livingston, Tennessee 38570-1942 **Tel:** 1 931 823-1274
Email: stories@livingstonenterprise.net **Web site:** http://www.livingstonenterprise.net
Freq: Tue; **Circ:** 5429 Not Audited
Publisher & Editor: Andy Mitchell
Profile: Livingston Enterprise is a local paper written for the residents of Livingston, TN.
Language (s): English
Ad Rate: Full Page Mono 5.15
Currency: United States Dollars
COMMUNITY NEWSPAPER

The Local News 23141
Editorial: 5901 Warner Ave, #429, Huntington Beach, California 92649-4659 **Tel:** 1 714 914-9797
Email: hbnews1@aol.com **Web site:** http://www.MyHBGold.com
Freq: Bi-Weekly; **Circ:** 20000 Not Audited
Editor and Publisher: David Garofalo
Profile: The Local News is written for people stationed in and around Hamilton Air Force Base in Novato, CA. It covers local and national news stories and events as well as special interests, new product development and humor.
Language (s): English
Ad Rate: Full Page Mono 11.54
Currency: United States Dollars
COMMUNITY NEWSPAPER

Lockhart Post-Register 20895
Owner: Garrett (Dana)
Editorial: 111 S Church St, Lockhart, Texas 78644-2641 **Tel:** 1 512 398-4886
Email: news@post-register.com **Web site:** http://www.post-register.com
Freq: Thu; **Circ:** 12000 Not Audited
Editor: Kathi Bliss; **Publisher:** Dana Garrett; **Advertising Manager:** Patty Rodriguez
Profile: The Lockhart Post-Register provides residents of Lockhart, Texas with local community news, politics, and sports updates weekly.
Language (s): English
Ad Rate: Full Page Mono 12.50
Currency: United States Dollars
COMMUNITY NEWSPAPER

Logan County Courier 922795
Editorial: Crescent, Oklahoma **Tel:** 1 405 969-2215
Email: news@lccourier.com
Freq: Weekly
Publisher & Editor: Mark Radford
Profile: Weekly paper published on Thursdays that covers Crescent and western Logan County, Oklahoma.
Language (s): English
COMMUNITY NEWSPAPER

Long Beach/Carson/Compton Times Newspaper 342808
Tel: 1 562 715-5641
Email: lbtimes@aol.com **Web site:** http://www.longbeachtimes.org/
Freq: Wed; **Circ:** 33000 Not Audited
Publisher & Editor: Richard Love; **Advertising Sales Manager:** Robin Thorne
Profile: Long Beach/Carson/Compton Times Newspaper is a a weekly, bilingual newspaper serving residents in Long Beach, Carson and Compton, CA. It covers local, regional and national news, editorials, education, business, economic development and family stories. It also profiles prominent African American business leaders and provides Hispanic and Cambodian current events. Deadlines are at noon PT.
Language (s): Spanish/Bilingual
Ad Rate: Full Page Mono 28.00
Currency: United States Dollars
COMMUNITY NEWSPAPER

Long Island Catholic 21930
Owner: RVC Diocese
Editorial: 200 W Centennial Ave, Roosevelt, New York 11575-1937 **Tel:** 1 516 594-1000
Email: editor@licatholic.org **Web site:** http://www.licatholic.org
Freq: Wed; **Circ:** 35000 Not Audited
Profile: Long Island Catholic is a local weekly newspaper written for Catholic residents of Nassau and Suffolk counties, NY. The newspaper covers Catholic news, information, and events, both locally and around the world. Deadlines fall on Fridays prior to the issue date.
Language (s): English
Ad Rate: Full Page Mono 63.00
Currency: United States Dollars
COMMUNITY NEWSPAPER

Long Island Press 136795
Owner: Schneps Communications
Editorial: 575 Underhill Blvd Ste 210, Syosset, New York 11791-3432 **Tel:** 1 516 284-3300
Web site: http://www.longislandpress.com
Freq: Thu; **Circ:** 73903 Not Audited
News Editor: Timothy Bolger; **Circulation Manager:** Tom Butcher
Profile: Long Island Press, formerly the New Island Ear, covers music and entertainment in the Long Island, NY area. Established in 1978, it is distributed free through record stores, bars, restaurants and movie theaters. The publication focuses particularly on popular music, but also offers limited coverage of other forms of entertainment media, such as films and Web sites. It contains concert and events listings, music and film reviews, classified ads for local musicians and profiles of entertainment personalities. Editorial deadlines are on the second Friday of each month.
Language (s): English
Ad Rate: Full Page Mono 31.20
Currency: United States Dollars
COMMUNITY NEWSPAPER

Long Islander Newspapers 24766
Owner: Spend Navigator LLC
Editorial: 14 Wall St, Huntington, New York 11743
Tel: 1 631 427-7000
Email: info@longislandergroup.com **Web site:** http://www.longislandernews.com
Circ: 33462 Not Audited
Profile: Long Islander Newspapers in Huntintgton, NY is a weekly community newspaper publisher serving the residents of Northport, Troy, Long Island and Dix Hills, NY as well as the surrounding areas.
Language (s): English
COMMUNITY NEWSPAPER

Longboat Key News 781225
Editorial: 5370 Gulf Of Mexico Dr Ste 210, Longboat Key, Florida 34228-2047 **Tel:** 1 941 387-2200
Email: editorial@lbknews.com **Web site:** http://www.lbknews.com/
Freq: Weekly
Publisher & Editor: Steve Reid
Profile: Longboat Key News is weekly newspaper providing Community News, focusing on the residents of Longboat Key and the neighboring areas of St. Armands Key, Bird Key and Lido Key. The newspaper covers Longboat Key town government, Real Estate, Local Business and cultural activities.
Language (s): English
COMMUNITY NEWSPAPER

The Longboat Observer 21347
Owner: Observer Media Group Inc. (The)
Editorial: 5570 Gulf of Mexico Dr, Longboat Key, Florida 34228-1904 **Tel:** 1 941 383-5509
Email: longboatnews@yourobserver.com **Web site:** http://www.yourobserver.com/news/longboat-key/Front-Page
Freq: Thu; **Circ:** 17000 Not Audited
Advertising Sales Manager: Jill Raleigh
Profile: Longboat Observer provides local news and community information to Longboat, St. Armands, Lido and Bird Keys, FL.
Language (s): English
Ad Rate: Full Page Mono 28.65
Ad Rate: Full Page Colour 100.00
Currency: United States Dollars
COMMUNITY NEWSPAPER

Longmont Weekly 689939
Owner: Prairie Mountain Publishing)
Editorial: 350 Terry St, Longmont, Colorado 80501-5440 **Tel:** 1 303 776-2244
Web site: http://www.longmontweekly.com
Freq: Wed; **Circ:** 16205
Profile: Longmont Weekly is a local community newspaper for the residents of Longmont, CO and the surrounding communities. It is based in the same office as the Times-Call. It merged with the Longmont Ledger in 2010.
Language (s): English
Ad Rate: Full Page Mono 11.62
Currency: United States Dollars
COMMUNITY NEWSPAPER

Los Altos Town Crier 22291
Owner: Nyberg (Paul)
Editorial: 138 Main St, Los Altos, California 94022-2905 **Tel:** 1 650 948-9000
Web site: http://www.losaltosonline.com
Freq: Wed; **Circ:** 16500 Not Audited
Editor: Bruce Barton; **Editor:** Pete Borello; **Advertising Sales Manager:** Kathy Lera; **Publisher:** Paul Nyberg
Profile: Los Altos Town Crier is a weekly paper written for residents of Los Altos, CA. The paper covers local news, sports and weather.
Language (s): English
Ad Rate: Full Page Mono 26.02
Currency: United States Dollars
COMMUNITY NEWSPAPER

Los Angeles Sentinel 18662
Owner: Bakewell Media
Editorial: 3800 Crenshaw Blvd, Los Angeles, California 90008-1813 **Tel:** 1 323 299-3800
Web site: https://lasentinel.net/
Freq: Thu; **Circ:** 30000 Not Audited
Publisher: Danny Bakewell; **Circulation Manager:** Angela Howard; **Advertising Sales Manager:** Bernard Lloyd
Profile: Los Angeles Sentinel is a local, weekly newspaper providing community, business and political news to the African American community in Southern Los Angeles, Orange and San Diego counties, CA. It is Southern California's oldest continually published black newspaper. The paper also contains an insert of Healthy Choices, which focuses on the elimination of certain health problems that affect racial and ethnic minorities.
Language (s): English
Ad Rate: Full Page Mono 35.00
Currency: United States Dollars
COMMUNITY NEWSPAPER

Los Cerritos Community News 151222
Owner: Hews (Brian)
Editorial: 13047 Artesia Blvd Ste C102, Cerritos, California 90703-1389 **Tel:** 1 562 407-3873
Web site: http://loscerritosnews.net
Freq: Fri; **Circ:** 45000 Not Audited
Editor: Jerry Bernstein; **Publisher:** Brian Hews
Profile: Los Cerritos Community News is a weekly newspaper written for the residents of Cerritos, CA.
Language (s): English
Ad Rate: Full Page Mono 21.00
Currency: United States Dollars
COMMUNITY NEWSPAPER

Loudoun Times-Mirror 75362
Owner: Times Community Newspapers
Editorial: 9 E Market St, Leesburg, Virginia 20176-3013 **Tel:** 1 703 777-1111
Web site: http://www.loudountimes.com
Freq: Wed; **Circ:** 57351 Not Audited
Publisher: Peter Arundel; **Editor:** Dale Peskin; **Circulation Manager:** Ron Sauer
Profile: Loudoun Times-Mirror is a local weekly newspaper written for residents in and around Loudoun County, VA. It covers local news and events, sports, business and features. Deadlines are at 9am ET.
Language (s): English
Ad Rate: Full Page Mono 41.18
Currency: United States Dollars
COMMUNITY NEWSPAPER

Louisa Publishing 24860
Editorial: 301 James L Hodges Ave S, Wapello, Iowa 52653-1242 **Tel:** 1 319 523-4631
Email: lpc@louisacomm.net
Circ: 9950 Not Audited
Editor: Rusty Ebert; **Editor:** Evelyn Garmoe; **Publisher & Editor:** Michael Hodges; **Editor:** Connie Street
Profile: Louisa Publishing is a community newspaper publisher in Wapello, IA and publishes the Van Buren County Register, New London Journal, Clarion Plainsman, Morning Sun News-Herald, Wapello Republican and Des Moines County News.
Language (s): English
COMMUNITY NEWSPAPER

Louisiana State Newspapers 25717
Owner: Louisiana State Newspapers
Editorial: 241 Martin Luther St, Columbia, Louisiana 71418 **Tel:** 1 318 649-6411
Email: caldwellwatchman@bellsouth.net
Circ: 9400 Not Audited
Editor: Becky Stapleton
Profile: The Post Office Box address should be used for USPS deliveries only. The street address should be used for deliveries by other couriers.
Language (s): English
COMMUNITY NEWSPAPER

The Louisiana Weekly 19437
Owner: Hall (Renette)
Editorial: 2215 Pelopidas St, New Orleans, Louisiana 70122-4957 **Tel:** 1 504 282-3705
Email: info@louisianaweekly.com **Web site:** http://www.louisianaweekly.com
Freq: Mon; **Circ:** 6500 Not Audited
Profile: The Louisiana Weekly is written for Louisiana's African-American residents. It covers economic, social and scientific information from business, culture, natural and social sciences.
Language (s): English
Ad Rate: Full Page Mono 21.35
Ad Rate: Full Page Colour 2895.00
Currency: United States Dollars
COMMUNITY NEWSPAPER

Lovely County Citizen 328248
Owner: Rust Communications
Editorial: 3022 E Van Buren Ste H, Eureka Springs, Arkansas 72632-9800 **Tel:** 1 479 253-0070
Email: citizen.editor.eureka@gmail.com **Web site:** http://www.lovelycitizen.com
Freq: Thu; **Circ:** 6500 Not Audited
Editor: David Blankenship
Profile: Lovely County Citizen is a weekly paper written for residents of Eureka Springs, AR and surrounding towns.
Language (s): English
Ad Rate: Full Page Mono 3.75
Currency: United States Dollars
COMMUNITY NEWSPAPER

Luso-Americano 22498
Editorial: 66 Union St, Newark, New Jersey 07105-1417 **Tel:** 1 973 344-3200
Email: news@lusoamericano.com **Web site:** http://www.lusoamericano.com
Freq: Fri; **Circ:** 28400 Not Audited
Publisher: Antonio Matinho; **News Editor:** Luis Pires
Profile: Luso-Americano's editorial mission is to serve as a means of social communication among Portuguese communities nationally and

internationally. Deadlines are Tuesdays at 10:30am ET for the Wednesday editions, and Thursdays by noon ET for the Friday editions.
Language (s): English, Portuguese
Ad Rate: Full Page Mono 10.00
Currency: United States Dollars
COMMUNITY NEWSPAPER

The Luverne Journal 18513
Owner: Boone Newspapers Inc.
Editorial: 94 S Glenwood Ave, Luverne, Alabama 36049-2149 **Tel:** 1 334 335-3541
Email: editor@luvernejournal.com **Web site:** http://www.greenvilleadvocate.com
Freq: Wed; **Circ:** 9350 Not Audited
Circulation Manager: Tammy Faulk; **Editor:** Fred Guarino; **Publisher:** Tracy Salter
Profile: The Luverne Journal is a local weekly newspaper published every Wednesday in Luverne, AL. The publication's editorial mission is to report local news to the residents of Luverne, AL.
Language (s): English
Ad Rate: Full Page Mono 6.75
Currency: United States Dollars
COMMUNITY NEWSPAPER

Lynden Tribune 28761
Owner: Lewis Publishing Co., Inc.
Editorial: 113 6th St, Lynden, Washington 98264-1901 **Tel:** 1 360 354-4444
Email: reporter@lyndentribune.com **Web site:** http://www.lyndentribune.com
Freq: Wed; **Circ:** 6000 Not Audited
Circulation Manager: Karina DeLange; **Advertising Sales Manager:** Mary Jo Lewis; **Publisher:** Michael Lewis
Profile: Lynden Tribune is written for local farmers in Whatcom County, WA. It covers local news and agricultural issues.
Language (s): English
Ad Rate: Full Page Mono 20.50
Ad Rate: Full Page Colour 300.00
Currency: United States Dollars
COMMUNITY NEWSPAPER

The Macon County News & Shopping Guide 342649
Owner: Gooder (Betsey)
Editorial: 26 W Main St, Franklin, North Carolina 28734-3006 **Tel:** 1 828 369-6767
Email: maconcountynews@gmail.com **Web site:** http://www.maconnews.com
Freq: Thu; **Circ:** 12500 Not Audited
Publisher: Betsey Gooder; **Editor:** Teresa Tabor
Profile: The Macon County News & Shopping Guide is a lcoal newspaper serving the residents of Franklin, NC. The paper covers community news and events.
Language (s): English
Ad Rate: Full Page Mono 6.83
Currency: United States Dollars
COMMUNITY NEWSPAPER

Madison County Record 18563
Owner: Kreth (Ellen)
Editorial: 201 Church St, Huntsville, Arkansas 72740 **Tel:** 1 479 738-2141
Email: editor@mcrecordonline.com **Web site:** http://www.mcrecordonline.com
Freq: Thu; **Circ:** 5100 Not Audited
Publisher: Ellen Kreth
Profile: Madison County Record is a weekly newspaper in Huntsville, AR that covers local news and events.
Language (s): English
Ad Rate: Full Page Mono 7.00
Currency: United States Dollars
COMMUNITY NEWSPAPER

The Madison Record 18514
Owner: Boone Newspapers Inc.
Editorial: 14 Main St Ste C, Madison, Alabama 35758-2084 **Tel:** 1 256 772-6677
Email: news@themadisonrecord.com **Web site:** http://www.themadisonrecord.com
Freq: Sat; **Circ:** 10000 Not Audited
Profile: The Madison Record is a community newspaper serving Madison, AL with local news, sports, commentary, lifestyle, business, education news and community events.
Language (s): English
Ad Rate: Full Page Mono 11.50
Currency: United States Dollars
COMMUNITY NEWSPAPER

The Madison Times 24217
Editorial: 313 W Beltline Hwy Ste 120, Madison, Wisconsin 53713-2680 **Tel:** 1 608 270-9470
Web site: http://themadisontimes.themadent.com
Freq: Thu; **Circ:** 8000 Not Audited
Publisher: Ray Allen; **Editor:** David Dahmer
Profile: The Madison Times is written for the African American community of Madison, WI.
Language (s): English
Ad Rate: Full Page Mono 26.00
Currency: United States Dollars
COMMUNITY NEWSPAPER

The Madisonian/Morgan County Citizen 22629
Owner: Mainstreet Communications
Editorial: 259 N Second St, Madison, Georgia 30650-1317 **Tel:** 1 706 342-7440
Email: morgancountycitizen@gmail.com **Web site:** http://www.morgancountycitizen.com
Freq: Weekly; **Circ:** 5000 Not Audited
Publisher, Editor & Advertising Sales Manager: Patrick Yost
Profile: The Madisonian/Morgan County Citizen is a local newspaper serving the residents of Morgan County, GA. The paper covers local news, weather, sports, business and arts & entertainment. Deadlines are on Mondays.
Language (s): English
Ad Rate: Full Page Mono 6.75
Currency: United States Dollars
COMMUNITY NEWSPAPER

Mahogany Revue 22806
Editorial: 903 NE Osceola Ave, Ocala, Florida 34470-5208 **Tel:** 1 352 368-2002
Email: psa@mahoganyrevue.com **Web site:** http://www.mahoganyrevue.com
Freq: Bi-Weekly; **Circ:** 33000 Not Audited
Profile: Mahogany Revue is published bi-weekly for African Americans and Latin Americans in Ocala, FL. The newspaper provides information on local news and community events. Deadlines are on Thursdays prior to issue date.
Language (s): English
Ad Rate: Full Page Mono 14.55
Currency: United States Dollars
COMMUNITY NEWSPAPER

Main Street Journal 491542
Owner: Ash (Jim)
Editorial: 186 Main St, Marlborough, Massachusetts 01752-3813 **Tel:** 1 508 460-1166
Email: news@msjnews.com **Web site:** http://msjnews.com/
Freq: Sat; **Circ:** 5075 Not Audited
Publisher & Editor: Jim Ash
Profile: Main Street Journal is a weekly newspaper covering local news and events for residents of Marlborough, MA.
Language (s): English
Ad Rate: Full Page Mono 7.83
Currency: United States Dollars
COMMUNITY NEWSPAPER

The Maine Edge 801197
Owner: Edge Media Group
Editorial: 157 Park St Ste 25, Bangor, Maine 04401-5063 **Tel:** 1 207 942-2901
Email: yournews@themaineedge.com **Web site:** http://www.themaineedge.com
Freq: Weekly; **Circ:** 18000
Publisher: Michael Fern
Profile: The Maine Edge is a free weekly newspaper that provides Lifestyle and Cultural Arts coverage to the residents of Bangor, ME, as well as Penobscot and Hancock counties.
Language (s): English
Ad Rate: Full Page Mono 32.67
Currency: United States Dollars
COMMUNITY NEWSPAPER

Malibu Surfside News 18629
Owner: 22nd Century Media
Editorial: 28990 Pacific Coast Hwy #C116, Malibu, California 90265-3952 **Tel:** 1 310 457-2112
Email: news@malibusurfsidenews.com **Web site:** http://www.malibusurfsidenews.com
Freq: Thu; **Circ:** 13500 Not Audited
Advertising Sales Manager: Andrew Nicks
Profile: Malibu Surfside News provides local news to the residents of Malibu, CA. Deadlines for the publication are on Tuesdays at noon PT.
Language (s): English
Ad Rate: Full Page Mono 15.00
Currency: United States Dollars
COMMUNITY NEWSPAPER

Malibu Times 18630
Editorial: 3864 Las Flores Canyon Rd, Malibu, California 90265-5239 **Tel:** 1 310 456-5507
Email: webeditor@malibutimes.com **Web site:** http://www.malibutimes.com
Freq: Thu; **Circ:** 12000 Not Audited
Profile: Malibu Times provides the residents of Malibu, CA with local news, weather and community events. Deadlines are on Tuesdays at 5pm PT.
Language (s): English
Ad Rate: Full Page Mono 32.00
Currency: United States Dollars
COMMUNITY NEWSPAPER

Mammoth Times 21637
Owner: Horizon Publications
Editorial: 501 Old Mammoth Rd Ste 9, Mammoth Lakes, California 93546 **Tel:** 1 760 934-3929
Email: editor@mammothtimes.com **Web site:** http://www.mammothtimes.com
Freq: Weekly; **Circ:** 5000 Not Audited
Profile: Mammoth Times in Mammoth Lakes, CA is a weekly newspaper that covers local news, weather, travel, sports and community events.
Language (s): English
Ad Rate: Full Page Mono 6.85
Currency: United States Dollars
COMMUNITY NEWSPAPER

The Manchester Enterprise 19359
Editorial: 103 3rd St, Manchester, Kentucky 40962-1119 **Tel:** 1 606 598-2319
Web site: http://www.themanchesterenterprise.com
Freq: Thu; **Circ:** 7500 Not Audited
Advertising Sales Manager: Jessica Bowling; **Publisher:** Glen Gray; **Editor:** Jim Wilson
Profile: The Manchester Enterprise is published weekly for residents of Clay and Laurel Counties, KY. The publication is a general interest newspaper covering local news, sports, weather, business, education, arts & entertainment and other information of interest to the local community.
Language (s): English
Ad Rate: Full Page Mono 6.50
Currency: United States Dollars
COMMUNITY NEWSPAPER

Manchester Journal 21083
Owner: New England Newspapers, Inc.
Editorial: 51 Memorial Ave, Manchester Center, Vermont 05255-5100 **Tel:** 1 802 362-2222
Email: news@manchesterjournal.com **Web site:** http://www.manchesterjournal.com
Freq: Fri; **Circ:** 10750 Not Audited
Advertising Sales Manager: Susan Plaisance
Profile: Manchester Journal is published weekly for the residents of Manchester Center, VT and surrounding areas. The newspaper covers local news, weather, sports, business, education and entertainment.
Language (s): English
Ad Rate: Full Page Mono 13.06
Currency: United States Dollars
COMMUNITY NEWSPAPER

Manchester Signal 20346
Editorial: 414 E 7Th St, Manchester, Ohio 45144-1402 **Tel:** 1 937 549-2800
Email: thesignal1@frontier.com
Freq: Thu; **Circ:** 5137 Not Audited
Editor: William Woolard
Profile: Manchester Signal is a community newspaper for residents of Manchester, OH and surrounding areas. The publication is a general interest newspaper, covering local news, sports, weather, business, education, arts and entertainment.
Language (s): English
Ad Rate: Full Page Mono 9.25
Currency: United States Dollars
COMMUNITY NEWSPAPER

Manchester Times 20742
Owner: Lakeway Publishers Inc.
Editorial: 300 N Spring St, Manchester, Tennessee 37355-1567 **Tel:** 1 931 728-7577
Email: mteditor@lcs.net **Web site:** http://www.manchestertimes.com
Freq: Wed; **Circ:** 6700 Not Audited
Advertising Manager: Teresa Bare; **Publisher:** Jack Owens; **Editor:** Josh Peterson
Profile: Manchester Times is a local newspaper written for the residents of Manchester, TN. The publication is a general interest newspaper, covering local news, sports, weather, business, education, and arts & entertainment.
Language (s): English
Ad Rate: Full Page Mono 12.48
Currency: United States Dollars
COMMUNITY NEWSPAPER

Manila Mail 389681
Owner: Media First Corp.
Editorial: 12 Avalon Dr, Daly City, California 94015-4551 **Tel:** 1 650 992-5474
Email: info@emanilamail.com **Web site:** http://www.emanilamail.com/home.html
Freq: Wed; **Circ:** 25500 Not Audited
Publisher: Ruben Bunag; **Editor:** Benji Solis
Profile: Manila Mail in Daly City, CA is a weekly newspaper serving Filipino American residents in the San Francisco metro area. Published in English, the publication provides readers with local and international news and feature stories that are pertinent to Filipino readers and their culture.
Language (s): English
Ad Rate: Full Page Mono 15.00
Currency: United States Dollars
COMMUNITY NEWSPAPER

Mansfield News-Mirror 20900
Owner: McClatchy Newspapers
Editorial: 119 N Main St, Mansfield, Texas 76063-1723 **Tel:** 1 817 473-4451
Web site: http://www.mansfieldnewsmirror.com
Freq: Wed; **Circ:** 27000 Not Audited
Profile: Mansfield News-Mirror is published twice per week for residents of Tarrant, Johnson, Ellis, and Dallas counties, TX. The publication is a general interest newspaper, covering local news, sports, business, government, education, social, and other information of interest to the local community. The Mansfield News-Mirror is the most complete source of information about Mansfield government and community activities.
Language (s): English
Ad Rate: Full Page Mono 15.50
Currency: United States Dollars
COMMUNITY NEWSPAPER

Marco Eagle 18788
Owner: Gannett Co., Inc.
Editorial: 579 E Elkcam Cir, Marco Island, Florida 34145-2876 **Tel:** 1 239 213-5300
Email: mail@marcoeagle.com **Web site:** http://www.naplesnews.com/community/macro-eagle
Freq: Fri; **Circ:** 10000
Editor: Bill Green; **Advertising Sales Manager:** Mary Quinton
Profile: Marco Eagle is a community newspaper, serving the residents of Marco Island, FL and its surrounding areas. It covers all aspects of local news, weather, sports, entertainment and community news. It is published by the Naples (FL) Daily News.
Language (s): English
Ad Rate: Full Page Mono 15.00
Currency: United States Dollars
COMMUNITY NEWSPAPER

Marco Island Sun Times 258023
Owner: Gannett
Editorial: 847 N Collier Blvd, Marco Island, Florida 34145-2258 **Tel:** 1 239 394-4050
Email: mail@misuntimes.com **Web site:** http://www.marcoislandflorida.com
Freq: Thu; **Circ:** 13500 Not Audited
Editor: Joe Taylor
Profile: Marco Island Sun Times is a community newspaper written for residents of Marco Island, FL. The paper covers local news, events and sports.
Language (s): English
Ad Rate: Full Page Mono 15.50
Currency: United States Dollars
COMMUNITY NEWSPAPER

Marinscope Community Newspapers 24491
Owner: Mallya, (Vijay)
Editorial: 1301 Grant Ave, Novato, California 94945-3143 **Tel:** 1 415 892-1516
Email: scope@marinscope.com **Web site:** http://www.marinscope.com
Circ: 44942 Not Audited
Publisher: Greg Andersen; **Editor:** Soren Hemmila; **Circulation Manager:** Linda Mallin; **Editor:** Derek Wilson; **Editor:** Joe Wolfcale
Language (s): English
COMMUNITY NEWSPAPER

Mariposa Gazette 27421
Editorial: 5024 Hwy 140, Mariposa, California 95338-0038 **Tel:** 1 209 966-2500
Email: editor@mariposagazette.com **Web site:** http://www.mariposagazette.com
Freq: Thu; **Circ:** 5300 Not Audited
Publisher: R.D. Tucker
Profile: Mariposa Gazette is a local newspaper written for the residents of Mariposa, CA. The paper covers local news, weather, sports, business, education and arts & entertainment.
Language (s): English
Ad Rate: Full Page Mono 15.00
Currency: United States Dollars
COMMUNITY NEWSPAPER

Marksville Weekly News 23204
Owner: Avoyelles Publishing Company
Editorial: 105 N Main St, Marksville, Louisiana 71351-2405 **Tel:** 1 318 253-5413
Email: news@avoyelles.com **Web site:** http://avoyellestoday.com
Freq: Thu; **Circ:** 5000 Not Audited
Publisher: Randy DeCuir; **Editor:** Susan DeCuir; **Advertising Sales Manager:** Amy Ducote; **News Editor:** Garland Foreman; **Circulation Manager:** Rachel Gaspard
Profile: The Marksville Weekly News was founded in 1843, and is the oldest weekly newspaper in the state of Louisiana. The newspaper is published for residents of Avoyelles Parish, LA and the surrounding communities. The publication is a general interest newspaper containing information on local news and events.
Language (s): English
Ad Rate: Full Page Mono 7.06
Currency: United States Dollars
COMMUNITY NEWSPAPER

Marlboro Herald-Advocate 20615
Owner: Marlboro Publishing Co., Inc.
Editorial: 100 Fayetteville Ave, Bennettsville, South Carolina 29512-4022 **Tel:** 1 843 479-3815
Email: ads@heraldadvocate.com **Web site:** http://www.heraldadvocate.com
Freq: Thu; **Circ:** 6800 Not Audited
Advertising Sales Manager: Linda Wilson
Profile: Marlboro Herald-Advocate is published twice per week for residents of Marlboro County, SC and surrounding areas. The publication is a general interest newspaper, covering local news, weather, sports, social, and other information of interest to the local community. The deadline for the Monday edition is Friday at noon ET. The deadline for the Thursday edition is Wednesday at noon ET.
Language (s): English
Ad Rate: Full Page Mono 7.05
Currency: United States Dollars
COMMUNITY NEWSPAPER

Marshall County Tribune 382183
Owner: Rust Communications
Editorial: 111 W Commerce St, Lewisburg, Tennessee 37091-3343 **Tel:** 1 931 359-1188
Web site: http://www.marshalltribune.com
Freq: 2 Times/Week; **Circ:** 5545 Not Audited
Profile: Marshall County Tribune is a community newspaper written for the residents of Lewisburg, TN. The paper provides community news and events, local sports, editorial pieces, columns, lifestyle articles and education news.
Language (s): English
Ad Rate: Full Page Mono 10.15
Currency: United States Dollars
COMMUNITY NEWSPAPER

Martha's Vineyard Times 19451
Owner: Martha's Vineyard Times Corporation Inc.
Editorial: 30 Beach Rd, Vineyard Haven, Massachusetts 02568-5582 **Tel:** 1 508 693-6100
Email: mvt@mvtimes.com **Web site:** http://www.mvtimes.com
Freq: Thu; **Circ:** 14000 Not Audited
Advertising Sales Manager: Carrie Waltersdorf
Profile: Martha's Vineyard Times is written for residents of Vineyard Haven, MA and surrounding areas. It covers local news and weather, tourist

information, arts & entertainment, real estate listings, and tidal and beach updates.
Language (s): English
Ad Rate: Full Page Mono 28.00
Ad Rate: Full Page Colour 1700.00
Currency: United States Dollars
COMMUNITY NEWSPAPER

Martin County Currents 884160
Tel: 1 772 245-6564
Email: editor@martincountycurrents.com **Web site:** http://hobesoundcurrents.com
Circ: 20000
Publisher & Editor: Barbara Clowdus
Profile: A newspaper by locals, for locals, about locals of Martin County, Florida. Serves as an independent voice intended to celebrate life in the area and among neighbors and to promote their businesses.
COMMUNITY NEWSPAPER

The Martin County Enterprise & Weekly Herald 27718
Owner: Cooke Communications, LLC
Editorial: 106 W Main St, Williamston, North Carolina 27892-2471 **Tel:** 1 252 792-1181
Email: enterprise@ncweeklies.com
Freq: Thu; **Circ:** 4334 Not Audited
Editor: Angela Harne; **Publisher:** Kyle Stevens; **Advertising Sales Manager:** Lou Ann VanLandingham
Profile: The Martin County Enterprise & Herald in Williamston, NC is a semi-weekly community newspaper created by the merger of the Williamston Enterprise and the Robersonville Weekly Herald.
Language (s): English
Ad Rate: Full Page Mono 8.50
Currency: United States Dollars
COMMUNITY NEWSPAPER

Martinez News-Gazette 80982
Owner: Gibson Publications
Editorial: 615 Estudillo St, Martinez, California 94553-1119 **Tel:** 1 925 228-6400
Email: editor@martinezgazette.com **Web site:** http://www.martinezgazette.com
Freq: Sun; **Circ:** 14000 Not Audited
Circulation Manager: Jenny Croghan; **Editor:** Yael Li-Ron; **Publisher:** David Payne
Profile: Martinez News-Gazette is a local newspaper written for the residents of Martinez, CA.
Language (s): English
Ad Rate: Full Page Mono 7.81
Currency: United States Dollars
COMMUNITY NEWSPAPER

Maryland Coast Dispatch 22093
Owner: Green (James Steven)
Editorial: 10012 Old Ocean City Blvd, Berlin, Maryland 21811-1145 **Tel:** 1 410 641-4561
Email: editor@mdcoastdispatch.com **Web site:** http://www.mdcoastdispatch.com
Freq: Fri; **Circ:** 25000 Not Audited
Publisher, Managing Editor, Advertising Sales & Circulation Manager: Steven Green; **Editor:** Shawn Soper
Profile: The Maryland Coast Dispatch in Berlin, MD covers local news, sports, editorials, classifieds and obituaries for Ocean City, Md. and northern Worcester County .
Language (s): English
Ad Rate: Full Page Mono 10.18
Currency: United States Dollars
COMMUNITY NEWSPAPER

Maryland Independent 75074
Owner: Gazette Newspapers Inc.
Editorial: 7 Industrial Park Dr, Waldorf, Maryland 20602-2753 **Tel:** 1 301 645-9480
Web site: http://www.somdnews.com/independent
Freq: Fri; **Circ:** 24500 Not Audited
Profile: Maryland Independent is published twice per week for residents of Charles County, MD and surrounding areas. The publication is a general interest newspaper covering local news, weather, sports, community events and other information of interest to area residents and newcomers. Deadlines are Wednesdays and Fridays at 5pm ET.
Language (s): English
Ad Rate: Full Page Mono 24.13
Ad Rate: Full Page Colour 2653.68
Currency: United States Dollars
COMMUNITY NEWSPAPER

Marysville Advocate 19273
Editorial: 107 S 9th St, Marysville, Kansas 66508-1825 **Tel:** 1 785 562-2317
Web site: http://www.marysvilleonline.net
Freq: Thu; **Circ:** 5135 Not Audited
News Editor: Sally Gray; **Editor & Publisher:** Sarah Kessinger; **Advertising Manager:** Ashley Kracht; **Circulation Manager:** Jan Smith
Profile: Marysville Advocate is published weekly for residents of Marysville, KS and surrounding areas. The publication is a general interest newspaper, covering local news, weather, sports, business, education, arts & entertainment and other information of interest to the local community. Deadlines are on Wednesdays prior to publication at noon CT.
Language (s): English
Ad Rate: Full Page Mono 7.00
Currency: United States Dollars
COMMUNITY NEWSPAPER

Maui Time Weekly 152915
Owner: MauiTime
Editorial: 16 S Market St Ste 2K, Wailuku, Hawaii 96793-2201 **Tel:** 1 808 244-0777
Email: editor@mauitime.com **Web site:** http://mauitime.com
Freq: Thu; **Circ:** 18000 Not Audited
Publisher: Thomas Russo
Profile: Maui Time Weekly covers a variety of issues and topics including local Maui and Hawaii news, arts and entertainment features, weekly restaurant reviews, live music and club info, and listings on over 100 events happening on Maui every day.
Language (s): English
Ad Rate: Full Page Mono 121.00
Currency: United States Dollars
COMMUNITY NEWSPAPER

Maywood Our Town 20203
Owner: JimCam Publishing Inc.
Editorial: 19 W Pleasant Ave, Maywood, New Jersey 07607-1320 **Tel:** 1 201 843-5700
Email: rtownmaywoodrp@aol.com **Web site:** http://www.ourtownnewsonline.com
Freq: Thu; **Circ:** 8500 Not Audited
Profile: Maywood Our Town is a local weekly newspaper serving the residents of Maywood, Saddle Brook, and Rochelle Park, NJ. The newspaper provides information on news and events of interest to the local communities.
Language (s): English
Ad Rate: Full Page Mono 10.50
Currency: United States Dollars
COMMUNITY NEWSPAPER

The McDonough Democrat 19060
Owner: McDonough Democrat
Editorial: 358 E Main St, Bushnell, Illinois 61422-1338 **Tel:** 1 309 772-2129
Email: info@themcdonoughdemocrat.com **Web site:** http://www.themcdonoughdemocrat.com
Freq: Mon; **Circ:** 6000 Not Audited
Circulation Manager: Bruce Lorton; **Advertising Sales Manager:** Adam Morrow; **Publisher & Editor:** David Norton
Profile: The McDonough Democrat is published weekly for the residents of Bushnell, IL and surrounding areas. The newspaper covers local news and community events. Deadlines are on Thursdays at 10am CT.
Language (s): English
Ad Rate: Full Page Mono 8.00
Currency: United States Dollars
COMMUNITY NEWSPAPER

The Mechanicsville Local 26878
Owner: BH Media Group
Editorial: 6400 Mechanicsville Tpke, Mechanicsville, Virginia 23111-4579 **Tel:** 1 804 746-1235
Email: news@mechlocal.com **Web site:** http://www.mechlocal.com
Freq: Wed; **Circ:** 29864 Not Audited
News Editor: Meredith Rigsby
Profile: The Mechanicsville Local is a weekly newspaper serving residents of Mechanicsville, VA. It covers local news, community events, sports, editorials and features of interest to area readers. Deadlines are at 5pm ET.
Language (s): English
Ad Rate: Full Page Mono 30.00
Ad Rate: Full Page Colour 8.00
Currency: United States Dollars
COMMUNITY NEWSPAPER

The Mecklenburg Sun 21074
Owner: McLaughlin (Tom)
Editorial: 602 Virginia Ave, Clarksville, Virginia 23927-9121 **Tel:** 1 434 374-8152
Email: news@themecklenburgsun.com **Web site:** http://www.sovanow.com
Freq: Wed; **Circ:** 15500 Not Audited
Advertising Sales Manager: Sylvia McLaughlin; **Editor & Publisher:** Tom McLaughlin
Profile: Mecklenburg Sun is a local newspaper providing the community of Clarksville, VA with news.
Language (s): English
Ad Rate: Full Page Mono 8.13
Currency: United States Dollars
COMMUNITY NEWSPAPER

Medford's News & Review 22300
Owner: Hayden (Nathaniel)
Tel: 1 541 778-8164
Email: sneakpreview@medford.net **Web site:** http://www.sneakpre.com
Freq: Monthly; **Circ:** 40000 Not Audited
Advertising Sales Manager: Kasey Hayden; **Publisher, Editor, & Circulation Manager:** Nathaniel Hayden
Profile: Medford's News & Review is a monthly paper released the first Friday of the month offering local news and events to residents in and around Medford, OR.
Language (s): English
Ad Rate: Full Page Mono 19.85
Currency: United States Dollars
COMMUNITY NEWSPAPER

Memphis Silver Star News 22375
Editorial: 3015 Park Ave, Memphis, Tennessee 38114-2723 **Tel:** 1 901 452-8828
Email: silverstarnews@bellsouth.net
Freq: Wed; **Circ:** 28000 Not Audited
Publisher & Editor: Jimmy Delnoah Williams
Profile: Memphis Silver Star News provides news to the African-American community in Memphis, TN. Deadlines are on Fridays.
Language (s): English
Ad Rate: Full Page Mono 18.70
Currency: United States Dollars
COMMUNITY NEWSPAPER

Mennonite World Review 21899
Owner: Mennonite World Review Inc.
Editorial: 129 W 6th St, Newton, Kansas 67114-2117 **Tel:** 1 316 283-3670
Web site: http://www.mennoworld.org
Freq: Bi-Weekly; **Circ:** 7200 Not Audited
Editor and Publisher: Paul Schrag
Profile: Mennonite World Review is a national newspaper that focuses on news and information concerning the North American Mennonite population. The paper includes Mennonite news and activities, ideas for congregations and families, opinions on church issues and current events, editorials, book reviews and Sunday school lesson comments. Editorial deadlines fall on Tuesdays prior to issue dates at noon CT.
Language (s): English
Ad Rate: Full Page Mono 25.00
Currency: United States Dollars
COMMUNITY NEWSPAPER

El Mensajero 81509
Owner: Godoy (Dr. Ramon)
Editorial: 2430 SW 8th Ave, Amarillo, Texas 79106-6612 **Tel:** 1 806 371-7084
Email: lmensajero@aol.com
Freq: Wed; **Circ:** 5000 Not Audited
Advertising Sales Manager: Amada Godoy; **Editor & Publisher:** Ramon Godoy
Profile: El Mensajero in Amarillo, TX is a weekly newspaper that covers local news and events affecting the Hispanic community.
Language (s): Spanish/Bilingual
Ad Rate: Full Page Mono 48.00
Currency: United States Dollars
COMMUNITY NEWSPAPER

Mercersburg Journal 20573
Editorial: 11 S Main St, Mercersburg, Pennsylvania 17236-1515 **Tel:** 1 717 328-3223
Email: news@mercersburgjournal.com
Freq: Wed; **Circ:** 8200 Not Audited
Profile: Mercersburg Journal is a weekly newspaper published for the residents of Mercersburg, PA. The newspaper covers local news, sports, entertainment, business, events and industry news.
Language (s): English
Ad Rate: Full Page Mono 8.82
Currency: United States Dollars
COMMUNITY NEWSPAPER

Mesquite Local News 596153
Owner: Battle Born Media
Editorial: 114 N Sandhill Blvd Ste C, Mesquite, Nevada 89027-4703 **Tel:** 1 702 346-6397
Email: admin@mesquitelocalnews.com **Web site:** http://www.mesquitelocalnews.com
Freq: Thu; **Circ:** 6500
Profile: Mesquite Local News is a community newspaper written for residents of Mesquite, NV.
Language (s): English
Ad Rate: Full Page Mono 6.00
Currency: United States Dollars
COMMUNITY NEWSPAPER

The Message 751708
Owner: Diocese of Evansville
Editorial: 4200 N Kentucky Ave, Evansville, Indiana 47711-2752 **Tel:** 1 812 424-5536
Email: message@evdio.org **Web site:** http://themessageonline.org
Freq: Fri; **Circ:** 5000
Editor: Tim Lilley; **Publisher:** Charles Thompson
Profile: The Message is a weekly newspaper for the Diocese of Evansville, IN.
Language (s): English
Ad Rate: Full Page Mono 8.00
Currency: United States Dollars
COMMUNITY NEWSPAPER

The Messenger 22389
Editorial: 630 Broad St, Gadsden, Alabama 35901 **Tel:** 1 256 547-1049
Web site: http://www.gadsdenmessenger.com
Freq: Wed; **Circ:** 7500 Not Audited
Advertising Sales Manager: Gail Keeling; **Circulation Manager:** Michelle McCloud; **Publisher:** Art Segers
Profile: The Messenger is written for the residents of Gadsden, AL.
Language (s): English
Ad Rate: Full Page Mono 8.00
Currency: United States Dollars
COMMUNITY NEWSPAPER

The Messenger 22955
Owner: Granite Quill Publishers
Editorial: 246 W Main St, Hillsboro, New Hampshire 03244-5251 **Tel:** 1 603 464-3388
Email: granitequill@mcttelecom.com **Web site:** http://www.granitequill.com/publications/the-messenger
Freq: Fri; **Circ:** 17000 Not Audited
Editor: Joyce Bosse; **Publisher:** Leigh Bosse
Profile: The Messenger is written for residents of Hillsboro, NH. It covers local news and community events. Deadlines are on Mondays at 5pm ET.
Language (s): English
Ad Rate: Full Page Mono 9.00
Currency: United States Dollars
COMMUNITY NEWSPAPER

Messenger Index 19034
Owner: Pioneer Newspapers
Editorial: 120 N Washington Ave, Emmett, Idaho 83617-2973 **Tel:** 1 208 365-6066
Email: newsroom@messenger-index.com **Web site:** http://www.messenger-index.com
Freq: Wed; **Circ:** 7000 Not Audited
Profile: Messenger Index in Emmett, ID is published weekly for the residents of Gem County, ID. The newspaper covers local news and community events.
Language (s): English
Ad Rate: Full Page Mono 6.25
Currency: United States Dollars
COMMUNITY NEWSPAPER

The Metro Courier 18851
Owner: Gordon (Barbara)
Editorial: 314 Walton Way, Augusta, Georgia 30901-2436 **Tel:** 1 706 724-6556
Email: metrocourier@comcast.net **Web site:** http://www.themetrocourieraugusta.com
Freq: Thu; **Circ:** 29100 Not Audited
Publisher and Editor: Barbara Gordon
Profile: The Metro Courier's editorial mission is to address the issues and concerns of the African-American community in Augusta. The publication is written for the African American communities of Augusta, GA.
Language (s): English
Ad Rate: Full Page Mono 16.50
Currency: United States Dollars
COMMUNITY NEWSPAPER

Metro Group Inc. 426584
Owner: Strategic Publications LLC
Editorial: 495 Arrow Dr., Cheektowaga, New York 14227-2707 **Tel:** 1 716 668-5223
Email: edit@metrowny.com **Web site:** http://www.metrowny.com
Circ: 282051 Not Audited
Advertising Sales Manager: Fred Cohen; **Publisher:** Gerard Grabowski; **Editor:** Matt Ondesko
Language (s): English
COMMUNITY NEWSPAPER

Metro North Media Inc. 25194
Owner: Wolf (Andrew)
Editorial: 5752 Fieldston Rd, Bronx, New York 10471-2508 **Tel:** 1 718 543-5200
Email: bxny@aol.com
Circ: 53500 Not Audited
Advertising Sales Manager: Robert Nilva; **Publisher and Editor:** Andrew Wolf
Profile: Metro North Media Inc. in the Bronx, NY publishes the Riverdale Review and the Bronx Press-Review.
Language (s): English
COMMUNITY NEWSPAPER

Metro San Diego Communications Inc. 63023
Owner: REP Publishing, Inc
Editorial: 1250 6th Ave Fl 12, San Diego, California 92101-4300
Web site: http://www.sandiegometro.com
Circ: 16000 Not Audited
Publisher: Rebeca Page
Profile: SD Metro is a local newspaper covering Downtown San Diego.
Language (s): English
COMMUNITY NEWSPAPER

Metro Silicon Valley 25094
Owner: Metro Publishing Group
Editorial: 380 S 1st St, San Jose, California 95113-2803 **Tel:** 1 408 298-8000
Email: letters@metronews.com **Web site:** http://www.metrosiliconvalley.com
Freq: Wed; **Circ:** 60000
News Editor: Josh Koehn
Profile: Metro is a weekly newspaper published by Metro Publishing Group, for the residents of Silicon Valley, CA. The newspaper covers local news, business, entertainment and music.
Language (s): English
Ad Rate: Full Page Mono 50.83
Currency: United States Dollars
COMMUNITY NEWSPAPER

Metropolis Newspapers 25122
Owner: Paxton Media Group
Editorial: 111 E 5th St, Metropolis, Illinois 62960-2108 **Tel:** 1 618 524-2141
Email: news@metropolisplanet.com **Web site:** http://www.metropolisplanet.com
Circ: 15950 Not Audited
Editor: Linda Kennedy
Language (s): English
COMMUNITY NEWSPAPER

Metropolitan News Company 409038
Owner: Grace Communications, Inc.
Editorial: 210 S Spring St, Los Angeles, California 90012 **Tel:** 1 213 346-0033
Email: news@metnews.com **Web site:** http://www.mnc.net
Circ: 43230 Not Audited
Publisher: Roger Grace
Language (s): English
COMMUNITY NEWSPAPER

MetroWest Publishing 24803
Owner: Landmark Community Newspapers, Inc.
Editorial: 139 N Main St, Brighton, Colorado 80601
Tel: 1 303 659-2522 200
Email: news@metrowestnewspapers.com **Web site:** http://www.metrowestfyi.com
Circ: 26625 Not Audited
Publisher: Allen Messick
Language (s): English
COMMUNITY NEWSPAPER

El Mexicano 390796
Owner: Zapari (Fernando)
Editorial: 2301 Fairfield Ave Ste 102, Fort Wayne, Indiana 46807-1247 **Tel:** 1 260 456-6843
Email: elmexica@earthlink.net **Web site:** http://www.elmexicanonews.com
Freq: Monthly; **Circ:** 10000 Not Audited
Advertising Sales Manager: Ron Latham; **Publisher & Editor:** Fernando Zapari
Profile: El Mexicano is a free, monthly, Spanish-language newspaper in Fort Wayne, IN. It is distributed the first Friday of each month at newsstands, restaurants and businesses with a large Hispanic clientèle throughout Fort Wayne, South Bend, Ligonier and the surrounding area, including communities in southern Michigan. It covers regional and international news, events, sports and entertainment of interest to a Hispanic audience.
Language (s): Spanish
Ad Rate: Full Page Mono 12.00
Currency: United States Dollars
COMMUNITY NEWSPAPER

Miami County Republic 21777
Owner: NPG Newspapers
Editorial: 121 S Pearl St, Paola, Kansas 66071-1754
Tel: 1 913 294-2311
Email: republic@republic-online.com **Web site:** http://www.republic-online.com
Freq: Wed; **Circ:** 5400 Not Audited
Advertising Sales Manager: Teresa Morrow
Profile: Miami County Republic is a local weekly newspaper serving the residents of Miami County, KS. Its focus is intensely local, covering city council, school boards, sports teams and local people and family news. On Fridays, subscribers also receive the Miami County Weekend Republic, which contains stories written by a combined staff of the Osawatomie Graphic, Miami County Republic and the Louisburg Herald. Deadlines are on Mondays at 10am CT. Deadlines for the weekend edition are on Wednesdays at 10am CT.
Language (s): English
Ad Rate: Full Page Mono 6.30
Currency: United States Dollars
COMMUNITY NEWSPAPER

Miami New Times 21613
Owner: Voice Media Group
Editorial: 2750 NW 3rd Ave Ste 24, Miami, Florida 33127-4143 **Tel:** 1 305 576-8000
Email: editorial@miaminewtimes.com **Web site:** http://www.miaminewtimes.com
Freq: Wed; **Circ:** 49565 Not Audited
Editor: Chuck Strouse
Profile: Miami New Times is a weekly newspaper written for residents and tourists in the Miami area. The newspaper covers local news and events, business, politics, social issues, travel and other news of interests to the local community.
Language (s): English
Ad Rate: Full Page Mono 24.20
Currency: United States Dollars
COMMUNITY NEWSPAPER

The Miami Times 18790
Editorial: 900 NW 54th St, Miami, Florida 33127-1818 **Tel:** 1 305 694-6210
Email: editorial@miamitimesonline.com **Web site:** http://www.miamitimesonline.com
Freq: Wed; **Circ:** 17178 Not Audited
Circulation Manager: Karen Franklin; **Publisher:** Rachel Reeves
Profile: The Miami (FL) Times is written for Miami's African American community. It provides news, cultural and lifestyle information.
Language (s): English
Ad Rate: Full Page Mono 47.75
Currency: United States Dollars
COMMUNITY NEWSPAPER

Miami Valley Newspapers 133625
Owner: Miller Publishing Co.
Editorial: 230 S 2nd St, Miamisburg, Ohio 45342-2925 **Tel:** 1 947 866-3331
Email: news@miamivalleynewspapers.com **Web site:** http://www.miamivalleynewspapers.com
Circ: 14900 Not Audited
Advertising Sales Manager: D.J. Miller; **Publisher:** Don Miller; **Editor:** Steve Sandlin
Language (s): English
COMMUNITY NEWSPAPER

Miami-Dade Calle Ocho 521443
Owner: Rosell (Marta)
Editorial: 321 NW 63rd Ct, Miami, Florida 33126-4542 **Tel:** 1 786 521-9130
Email: pressnet@comcast.net **Web site:** http://calleochonews.com/
Freq: Bi-Weekly; **Circ:** 40000 Not Audited
Editor: JC Bacallo; **Publisher:** Louis Thomas
Profile: Miami-Dade Calle Ocho is a Spanish-language biweekly newspaper serving the Hispanic residents of Miami and the surrounding area.
Language (s): Spanish
Ad Rate: Full Page Mono 10.00
Ad Rate: Full Page Colour 17.00

Currency: United States Dollars
COMMUNITY NEWSPAPER

Miami's Community Newspapers 24501
Owner: Your Hometown Newspapers Inc.
Editorial: 6796 SW 62nd Ave, South Miami, Florida 33143-3306 **Tel:** 1 305 669-7355
Email: michael@communitynewspapers.com **Web site:** http://www.communitynewspapers.com
Circ: 127000 Not Audited
Editor: David Berkowitz; **Advertising Sales Manager:** Georgia Tait
Profile: Miami's Community Newspapers in South Miami, FL serves communities in the North Miami Beach, North Miami and North Bay Village areas of Broward and Dade Counties, FL. It distributes free newspapers featuring community news, events, business, health, entertainment and sports stories.
Language (s): English
COMMUNITY NEWSPAPER

The Michigan Catholic 22020
Owner: Archdiocese of Detroit
Editorial: 305 Michigan Ave, Detroit, Michigan 48226-2631 **Tel:** 1 313 224-8000
Email: themichigancatholic@aod.org **Web site:** http://www.aodonline.org
Freq: Bi-Weekly; **Circ:** 18410 Not Audited
Advertising Sales Manager: Vince Kenson;
Circulation Manager: Carlen Neely; **Publisher:** Allen Vigneron
Profile: The Michigan Catholic in Detroit, MI is a weekly newspaper written that covers local, national and international issues relevant to the Catholic community.
Language (s): English
Ad Rate: Full Page Mono 17.00
Currency: United States Dollars
COMMUNITY NEWSPAPER

Michigan Chronicle 19580
Owner: Real Times, Inc.
Editorial: 479 Ledyard St, Detroit, Michigan 48201-2641 **Tel:** 1 313 963-5522
Web site: http://www.michronicleonline.com
Freq: Wed; **Circ:** 45000 Not Audited
Publisher: Hiram Jackson; **Advertising Sales Manager:** Joyce Johnson; **Editor:** Keith Owens
Profile: Michigan Chronicle is a weekly newspaper that is written for the African-American community in Detroit. The paper covers local and national news, sports, arts & entertainment and travel.
Language (s): English
Ad Rate: Full Page Mono 60.95
Ad Rate: Full Page Colour 9.92
Currency: United States Dollars
COMMUNITY NEWSPAPER

Michigan Publishers Auxiliary 810909
Tel: 1 517 937-5546
Email: alanwade-mpa@sbcglobal.net **Web site:** http://www.mpaux.com
Editor & Publisher: George Wade
Profile: Michigan Publisher's Auxiliary is a community newspaper publisher based in Lansing, MI, producing papers aimed at Michigan minorities, primarily the African-American, but also the Latin American and Arab American communities. They produce two newspapers in house, and also assist other minority-aimed newspapers in Michigan with advertising efforts.
COMMUNITY NEWSPAPER

Micromedia Publications 429907
Owner: Micromedia Publications, Inc.
Editorial: 15 Union Ave, Lakehurst, New Jersey 8733
Tel: 1 732 657-7344
Web site: http://www.micromediapubs.com
Circ: 105000 Not Audited
Advertising Sales Manager: Sean Curry;
Circulation Manager: Laura Hoban; **News Editor:** Eric San Juan; **Publisher:** Stewart Swan
Language (s): English
COMMUNITY NEWSPAPER

Mid Valley Publishing - Reedley 24771
Editorial: 1130 G St, Reedley, California 93654
Tel: 1 559 638-2244
Web site: http://www.reedleyexponent.com
Circ: 13100 Not Audited
Publisher: Fred Hall; **Editor:** Doug Hoagland;
Advertising Sales Manager: Janie Lucio; **Editor:** George Villagrana
Profile: Mid Valley Publishing - Reedley is a weekly community newspaper publisher serving the residents of Reedley, Orange Cove and Parlier, CA.
Language (s): English
COMMUNITY NEWSPAPER

The Middleboro Gazette 23168
Owner: GateHouse Media Inc.
Editorial: 148 W Grove St, Middleboro, Massachusetts 02346-1457 **Tel:** 1 508 947-1760
Web site: http://www.southcoasttoday.com/Gazette
Freq: Thu; **Circ:** 5485 Not Audited
Profile: The Middleboro Gazette is a weekly community newspaper serving residents of Middleboro, MA. The newspaper covers local news and community events.
Language (s): English
Ad Rate: Full Page Mono 18.53
Currency: United States Dollars
COMMUNITY NEWSPAPER

The Middletown Transcript 24371
Owner: GateHouse Media Inc.
Editorial: 24 W Main St, Middletown, Delaware 19709 **Tel:** 1 302 378-9531
Web site: http://www.middletowntranscript.com
Freq: Thu; **Circ:** 6000 Not Audited
Profile: The Middletown Transcript is a newspaper for the residents of Middletown, DE and the surrounding area. The publication strives to provide pertinent local area news and information. Deadlines are Mondays at 10am ET.
Language (s): English
Ad Rate: Full Page Mono 9.10
Currency: United States Dollars
COMMUNITY NEWSPAPER

Midsouth Newspapers 25155
Editorial: Highway 195 East, Haleyville, Alabama 35565-0430 **Tel:** 1 205 486-9461
Email: nwanews@centurytel.net **Web site:** http://www.mytrpaper.com
Circ: 21000 Not Audited
Publisher: Horace Moore
Language (s): English
COMMUNITY NEWSPAPER

The Mid-South Tribune 22411
Owner: A J M Enterprises Inc.
Editorial: 1801 Edward Ave, Memphis, Tennessee 38107-3015
Email: blackinfohwy@prodigy.net **Web site:** http://blackinformationhighway.wordpress.com
Freq: Fri; **Circ:** 24402 Not Audited
Profile: The Mid-South Tribune is a weekly newspaper written for the African American and Hispanic population in Memphis, TN. The newspaper covers news, business, sports and entertainment. Due to the enormous amount of e-mail the newspaper receives, the staff requests that all business, economic, or Internet news be e-mailed, and they request a phone and fax not be listed.
Language (s): English
Ad Rate: Full Page Mono 25.00
Currency: United States Dollars
COMMUNITY NEWSPAPER

Mid-Valley News 24434
Owner: Private Owner
Editorial: 11401 Valley Blvd, Masterson Building Suite 200B, El Monte, California 91731-3242
Tel: 1 626 443-1753
Email: editor@midvalleynews.com **Web site:** http://midvalleynews.com
Freq: Wed; **Circ:** 30000 Not Audited
Editor: Joanne Disney; **Publisher:** Clarke Moseley
Profile: Mid-Valley News is a weekly newspaper serving the San Gabriel Valley, CA area. It provides information on local news, sports and lifestyles.
Language (s): English
Ad Rate: Full Page Mono 13.00
Currency: United States Dollars
COMMUNITY NEWSPAPER

Mid-Valley Publications 24486
Owner: Derby (John)
Editorial: 2221 K St, Merced, California 95340-3868
Tel: 1 209 358-5311
Email: info@midvalleypub.com **Web site:** http://www.midvalleypublications.com
Circ: 29200
Publisher & Editor: John Derby
Profile: Mid-Valley Publications in Winton, CA, publishes the following weekly newspapers: El Tiempo in Winton, CA; Merced (CA) County Times; Hilmar (CA) Times; Waterford (CA) News; and Atwater-Winton (CA) Times.
Language (s): English
COMMUNITY NEWSPAPER

The Mid-Valley Town Crier 24468
Owner: AIM Media Texas, LLC
Editorial: 401 S Iowa Ave, Weslaco, Texas 78596-6255 **Tel:** 1 956 969-2543
Web site: http://www.themonitor.com/mvtc/
Freq: Sun; **Circ:** 22500
Publisher: John Greider
Profile: The Mid-Valley Town Crier is written for the residents of Weslaco, TX. It covers local news and events.
Language (s): English
Ad Rate: Full Page Mono 11.79
Ad Rate: Full Page Colour 1587.99
Currency: United States Dollars
COMMUNITY NEWSPAPER

The MidWeek 21426
Owner: Shaw Media
Editorial: 1586 Barber Greene Rd, Dekalb, Illinois 60115-7900 **Tel:** 1 815 756-4841
Email: readit@midweeknews.com **Web site:** http://www.midweeknews.com
Freq: Wed; **Circ:** 31000 Not Audited
Publisher: Don Bricker; **Circulation Manager:** Kara Hansen
Profile: The Midweek in Dekalb, IL is a weekly community newspaper that covers local news and events.
Language (s): English
Ad Rate: Full Page Mono 35.12
Currency: United States Dollars
COMMUNITY NEWSPAPER

MidWeek 217222
Owner: MidWeek Printing Inc.
Editorial: 500 Ala Moana Blvd Ste 7-500, Honolulu, Hawaii 96813-4930 **Tel:** 1 808 529-4700
Web site: http://www.midweek.com

Circ: 300000 Not Audited
Circulation Manager: Sharene Chun; **Publisher:** Ron Nagasawa
Profile: Midweek is a newspaper in Kaneohe, HI, covering local events and entertainment. The tabloid reports on everything from business news, to entertainment, travel, politics, dining, fashion and more for the Hawaiian islands. It is published each Wednesday.
Language (s): English
COMMUNITY NEWSPAPER

Midwest Buy Line 257955
Owner: Keute (Todd)
Editorial: 522 Beltrami Ave NW Ste 100, Bemidji, Minnesota 56601-3002 **Tel:** 1 218 759-1139
Freq: Sat; **Circ:** 14500 Not Audited
Publisher & Editor: Todd Keute
Profile: Midwest Buy Line is a weekly newspaper serving residents in a 50-mile radius of Bemidji, MN. It covers local news and events in the area. Deadlines are on Wednesdays.
Language (s): English
Ad Rate: Full Page Mono 11.00
Currency: United States Dollars
COMMUNITY NEWSPAPER

The Mid-York Weekly 20267
Owner: Gatehouse Media
Editorial: 14 Utica St, Hamilton, New York 13346-1135 **Tel:** 1 315 824-2150
Email: midyork@yahoo.com **Web site:** http://www.themidyorkweekly.com
Freq: Thu; **Circ:** 10000 Not Audited
Profile: The Mid-York Weekly is written for residents of Hamilton, NY.
Language (s): English
Ad Rate: Full Page Mono 8.25
Currency: United States Dollars
COMMUNITY NEWSPAPER

Milan Mirror-Exchange 20745
Owner: Parkins (Victor)
Editorial: 1104 S Main St, Milan, Tennessee 38358-2726 **Tel:** 1 731 686-1632
Email: melissa@milanmirrorexchange.com **Web site:** http://www.milanmirrorexchange.com
Freq: Tue; **Circ:** 5600 Not Audited
Advertising Manager: Scarlet Elliott; **Editor & Publisher:** Victor Parkins; **Circulation Manager:** Melissa West
Profile: Milan Mirror-Exchange is a community-based publication that specializes in covering pertinent local area news and information in Milan, TN.
Language (s): English
Ad Rate: Full Page Mono 8.75
Currency: United States Dollars
COMMUNITY NEWSPAPER

Mile High Newspapers 24807
Owner: Colorado Community Media
Editorial: 110 N Rubey Dr Unit 120, Golden, Colorado 80403-3200 **Tel:** 1 303 279-5541
Email: calendar@coloradocommunitymedia.com
Web site: http://coloradocommunitymedia.com
Circ: 56775 Not Audited
Circulation Manager: Robin Sant
Language (s): English
COMMUNITY NEWSPAPER

The Military Press 22886
Owner: Military Press Group
Editorial: 430 N Cedar St Ste C, Escondido, California 92025-4650 **Tel:** 1 858 537-2280
Email: editor@militarypress.com **Web site:** http://www.militarypress.com
Freq: Bi-Weekly; **Circ:** 100000 Not Audited
Publisher: Richard Matz
Profile: The Military Press is a newspaper written for military personnel in San Diego. The paper covers military news, sports and entertainment.
Language (s): English
Ad Rate: Full Page Mono 41.66
Ad Rate: Full Page Colour 297.29
Currency: United States Dollars
COMMUNITY NEWSPAPER

Mill Creek View Newspaper 258053
Owner: Fillbrook & Associates
Editorial: 16212 Bothell Everett Hwy Ste F-313, Mill Creek, Washington 98012-1603 **Tel:** 1 425 357-0549
Email: info@millcreekview.com **Web site:** http://www.millcreekview.com
Freq: Bi-Weekly; **Circ:** 14500 Not Audited
Publisher: Fred Fillbrook
Profile: Mill Creek View Newspaper is a bi-weekly newspaper for the residents of Mill Creek, WA. The newspaper provides coverage on topics such as local news, sports, arts & entertainment and community events.
Language (s): English
Ad Rate: Full Page Mono 15.00
Currency: United States Dollars
COMMUNITY NEWSPAPER

Millbrook Independent 152735
Editorial: 3455 Main St, Millbrook, Alabama 36054-3216 **Tel:** 1 334 285-1299
Email: news@millbrookindependent.com **Web site:** http://www.millbrookindepedent.com
Freq: Thu; **Circ:** 8042 Not Audited
Publisher: Bob Martin; **Editor:** Art Parker
Language (s): English
Ad Rate: Full Page Mono 7.00

Currency: United States Dollars
COMMUNITY NEWSPAPER

Milton Independent 22205
Editorial: 77 River St, Milton, Vermont 05468-3644
Tel: 1 802 893-2028
Email: news@miltonindependent.com **Web site:** http://www.miltonindependent.com
Freq: Thu; **Circ:** 5500 Not Audited
Editor: Courtney Landin; **Advertising Sales Manager:** Kevin Letiecq; **Publisher:** Emerson Lynn
Profile: Milton Independent is a local newspaper that specializes in covering area news and information. Deadlines are on Fridays at 5pm ET.
Language (s): English
Ad Rate: Full Page Mono 10.00
Currency: United States Dollars
COMMUNITY NEWSPAPER

The Milwaukee Community Journal 21629
Editorial: 3612 N Dr Martin Luther King Dr, Milwaukee, Wisconsin 53212 **Tel:** 1 414 265-5300
Email: editorial@communityjournal.net **Web site:** http://www.communityjournal.net
Freq: Fri; **Circ:** 61350 Not Audited
Editor: Tom Mitchell; **Publisher:** Patricia Pattillo
Profile: The Milwaukee Community Journal is a publication that specializes in covering news and information on a local and national level. It strives to serve its readership with the necessary information to keep them informed of pertinent events and happenings.
Language (s): English
Ad Rate: Full Page Mono 34.00
Currency: United States Dollars
COMMUNITY NEWSPAPER

Milwaukee Courier 24734
Editorial: 6310 N Port Washington Rd, Milwaukee, Wisconsin 53217-4300 **Tel:** 1 414 449-4860
Email: milwaukeecourier@aol.com **Web site:** http://www.milwaukeecourieronline.com
Circ: 80000 Not Audited
Editor: Romel Brown; **Publisher:** Jerrel Jones
Language (s): English
COMMUNITY NEWSPAPER

The Milwaukee Times Weekly 21705
Owner: Conyers (Lynda Jackson)
Editorial: 1936 N Dr Martin Luther King Dr, Milwaukee, Wisconsin 53212-3642 **Tel:** 1 414 263-5088
Email: miltimes@gmail.com **Web site:** http://www.milwaukeetimes.com
Freq: Thu; **Circ:** 20000 Not Audited
Editor: Jacquelyn Heath; **Publisher:** Lynda Jackson Conyers
Profile: The Milwaukee Times Weekly is a weekly newspaper serving the African American community in Milwaukee and its surrounding areas. It covers national and local news, sports, lifestyle, opinions and community events.
Language (s): English
Ad Rate: Full Page Mono 15.00
Currency: United States Dollars
COMMUNITY NEWSPAPER

Minco-Union City Times 957986
Editorial: 553 N Mustang Rd, Mustang, Oklahoma 73064-7002 **Tel:** 1 405 376-6688
Email: mustangtimesnews@sbcglobal.net **Web site:** http://www.mustangpaper.com/4291/1586/minco-union-city-times
Freq: Weekly
Profile: Minco-Union City Times is written for residents of Minco, OK.
Language (s): English
COMMUNITY NEWSPAPER

Miniondas 23316
Owner: Velasquez Publishing Inc.
Editorial: 17291 Irvine Blvd. Suite 255, Tustin, California 92780 **Tel:** 1 714 668-1010
Email: editorial@miniondas.com **Web site:** http://www.miniondas.com
Freq: Thu; **Circ:** 60000 Not Audited
Editor: Jesus Morales; **Publisher:** Sergio Velasquez
Profile: Miniondas provides local news coverage for the Spanish speaking community in Orange County, CA.
Language (s): Spanish
Ad Rate: Full Page Mono 20.70
Currency: United States Dollars
COMMUNITY NEWSPAPER

Minnesota Spokesman-Recorder 26251
Owner: Williams-Dillard (Tracey)
Editorial: 3744 4th Ave S, Minneapolis, Minnesota 55409-1327 **Tel:** 1 612 827-4021
Web site: http://www.spokesman-recorder.com
Freq: Weekly; **Circ:** 10000 Not Audited
Advertising Sales Manager: Raymond Boyd; **Publisher:** Tracey Williams-Dillard
Profile: Minnesota Spokesman-Recorder provides local news for the African American community in Minneapolis. Deadlines are on Fridays at noon CT.
Language (s): English
Ad Rate: Full Page Mono 45.92
Currency: United States Dollars
COMMUNITY NEWSPAPER

Minority Communicator News Group 238798
Owner: Minority Community News Group
Editorial: 90 W Campus View Blvd, Columbus, Ohio 43235-1447 **Tel:** 1 614 781-1160
Email: tcneditor@aol.com **Web site:** http://www.communicatornews.homestead.com
Freq: Weekly; **Circ:** 153000 Not Audited
Publisher: Jack Harris
Profile: Minority Communicator News publishes regional editions of The Communicator, which covers community news with a focus on relevance to Central Ohio's African American population. Editions for Columbus, Cleveland, Cincinnati and Dayton are available.
Language (s): English
Ad Rate: Full Page Mono 27.00
Ad Rate: Full Page Colour 33.00
Currency: United States Dollars
COMMUNITY NEWSPAPER

Minority Reporter 687915
Editorial: 282 Hollenbeck St, Rochester, New York 14621-3235 **Tel:** 1 585 301-4199
Email: info@minorityreporter.net **Web site:** http://www.minorityreporter.net
Freq: Fri; **Circ:** 6000
Editor & Publisher: Dave McCleary
Profile: Minority Reporter is a local community newspaper for the African-American Residents of Rochester, NY and the surrounding communities.
Language (s): English
Ad Rate: Full Page Mono 20.00
Currency: United States Dollars
COMMUNITY NEWSPAPER

Minuteman/County Times Publications - Westport, CT 134071
Owner: Journal Register Company
Editorial: 100 Gando Dr, New Haven, Connecticut 06513-1049 **Tel:** 1 203 752-2711
Web site: http://minutemannewscenter.com
Circ: 38000 Not Audited
Editor: Tom Henry; **Editor:** Donna Saracco
Profile: Minuteman/County Times Publications in Westport, CT publishes the Westport (CT) Minuteman and the Fairfield (CT) Minuteman community newspapers.
Language (s): English
COMMUNITY NEWSPAPER

The Mirror 21890
Owner: Diocese of Springfield-Cape Girardeau
Editorial: 601 S Jefferson Ave, Springfield, Missouri 65806-3107 **Tel:** 1 417 866-0841
Web site: http://www.dioscg.org/
Freq: Bi-Weekly; **Circ:** 16000 Not Audited
Editor: Leslie Eidson; **Publisher:** James Vann Johnston
Profile: The Mirror is the newspaper of the Catholic Diocese of Springfield-Cape Girardeau, MO. It written for southern Missouri Catholics. The Mirror strives to provide current diocesan content to southern Missouri Catholics, as well as create a sense of Catholic community.
Language (s): English
Ad Rate: Full Page Mono 13.50
Currency: United States Dollars
COMMUNITY NEWSPAPER

Mirror Media Group 74613
Owner: Mirror Media Group, INC
Editorial: 3435 Ocean Park Blvd Ste 210, Santa Monica, California 90405-3315 **Tel:** 1 310 577-6507
Freq: Thu; **Circ:** 25000 Not Audited
Profile: Santa Monica Mirror is written for residents in and around Santa Monica, CA, including the towns of Pacific Palisades, Brentwood, Marina del Ray, Venice, West Los Angeles, Malibu, Playa del Rey and Mar Vista. It reflects the concerns of the community, thematically focusing on housing issues, agenda items and topics before the city council, local notables and school successes. Deadlines are on Fridays at noon.
Language (s): English
Ad Rate: Full Page Mono 28.00
Currency: United States Dollars
COMMUNITY NEWSPAPER

The Mirror Newspapers 523529
Editorial: 113 W Wayne St, Maumee, Ohio 43537
Tel: 1 419 893-8135
Email: info@themirrornewspaper.com **Web site:** http://www.themirrornewspaper.com
Circ: 19695 Not Audited
Publisher & Editor: Michael McCarthy
Language (s): English
COMMUNITY NEWSPAPER

Missile Ranger 472726
Editorial: Building 1782, White Sands, New Mexico 88002 **Tel:** 1 575 678-2716
Email: usarmy.wsmr.atec.list.ranger@mail.mil **Web site:** http://www.missileranger.com
Freq: Thu; **Circ:** 6000 Not Audited
Editor: Miriam Rodriguez
Profile: Missile Ranger is a free weekly newspaper serving the White Sands Missile Range community. The paper is printed by the Las Cruces (NM) Sun-News, and all advertising is handled through their office.
Language (s): English
Ad Rate: Full Page Mono 9.00
Currency: United States Dollars
COMMUNITY NEWSPAPER

The Mission News Group 25474
Owner: Mission News Group
Editorial: 23472 Vista Del Verde, Coto de Caza, California 92679-3930 **Tel:** 1 949 589-9990
Email: newseditorials@yahoo.com **Web site:** http://missionviejonewsgroup.com
Circ: 62877 Not Audited
Publisher & Editor: Jerry White
Profile: The Mission News Group is a community newspaper publisher that services the residents of Los Angeles, Long Beach, and Santa Ana, CA.
Language (s): English
COMMUNITY NEWSPAPER

Mission Progress-Times 20912
Owner: Brunson (James)
Editorial: 1217 N Conway Ave, Mission, Texas 78572-4112 **Tel:** 1 956 585-4893
Email: news@progresstimes.net **Web site:** http://www.progresstimes.net
Freq: Fri; **Circ:** 10000 Not Audited
Publisher: James Brunson; **Community News Editor:** Mendi Brunson; **Editor:** Julie Silva
Profile: The Mission Progress-Times provides local news coverage for the Mission, TX area.
Language (s): Spanish/Bilingual
Ad Rate: Full Page Mono 12.50
Ad Rate: Full Page Colour 1259.00
Currency: United States Dollars
COMMUNITY NEWSPAPER

The Mississippi Link 78577
Owner: Mississippi Link Inc.
Editorial: 2659 Livingston Rd, Jackson, Mississippi 39213-6926 **Tel:** 1 601 896-0084
Email: editor@mississippilink.com **Web site:** http://themississippilink.com
Freq: Weekly; **Circ:** 16332
Publisher: Jackie Hampton
Profile: The Mississippi Link is a local, weekly newspaper providing news for and about the Jackson, MS area. It covers local news, sports, editorials, city notices, arts & entertainment and classified advertising.
Language (s): English
Ad Rate: Full Page Mono 18.00
Ad Rate: Full Page Colour 21.17
Currency: United States Dollars
COMMUNITY NEWSPAPER

Missoula Independent 22953
Owner: Lee Enterprises
Editorial: 317 S Orange St, Missoula, Montana 59801-1810 **Tel:** 1 406 543-6609
Email: editor@missoulanews.com **Web site:** http://missoulanews.bigskypress.com
Freq: Thu; **Circ:** 20000 Not Audited
Advertising Manager: Carolyn Bartlett
Profile: Missoula Independent is written for residents of Missoula, MT. Its editorial mission is to provide news and information about current politics and culture of Western Montana. Deadlines are on Mondays by 5pm MT.
Language (s): English
Ad Rate: Full Page Mono 29.48
Currency: United States Dollars
COMMUNITY NEWSPAPER

Missouri Dakota Publishing Inc. 24985
Owner: Bridge City Publishing, Inc.
Editorial: 110 S Exene St, Gettysburg, South Dakota 57442 **Tel:** 1 605 765-2464
Email: pcnews@pottercountynews.com
Circ: 5000
Editor: Nancy Anderson; **Publisher:** Larry Atkinson; **Editor:** Molly McRoberts
Language (s): English
COMMUNITY NEWSPAPER

Mitchell Newspapers, Inc. 24863
Owner: Trib Publications, Inc.
Editorial: 13 S Scott St, Camilla, Georgia 31730-1705 **Tel:** 1 229 336-5265
Email: camillaenterprise@camillaga.net
Circ: 10100 Not Audited
Editor & Publisher: Carl Stokes
Language (s): English
COMMUNITY NEWSPAPER

Moab Sun News 817358
Owner: Mirrington (Andrew)
Editorial: 30 S 100 E, Moab, Utah 84532-2638
Tel: 1 435 259-6261
Email: editor@moabsunnews.com **Web site:** http://moabsunnews.com
Freq: Weekly
Editor: Rudy Herndon; **Publisher:** Andrew Mirrington
Profile: Moab Sun News is a free weekly community newspaper serving residents of Moab, UT. The paper began publishing in April 2012.
Language (s): English
COMMUNITY NEWSPAPER

Moapa Valley Progress 76592
Owner: JZR Communications Co. LLC
Editorial: 145 S Moapa Valley Blvd, Suite #4, Overton, Nevada 89040 **Tel:** 1 702 397-6246
Email: progress@mvdsl.com **Web site:** http://www.mvprogress.com
Freq: Wed; **Circ:** 5600 Not Audited
Profile: Moapa Valley Progress is a weekly community newspaper written for the residents of Clark County, NV.
Language (s): English
Ad Rate: Full Page Mono 5.60
Currency: United States Dollars
COMMUNITY NEWSPAPER

Mobile Beacon And Alabama Citizen 18516
Owner: Mobile Beacon Inc.
Editorial: 2311 Costarides St, Mobile, Alabama 36617-2442 **Tel:** 1 251 479-0629
Email: mobilebeaconinc@bellsouth.net
Freq: Wed; **Circ:** 7000 Not Audited
Publisher & Editor: Cleretta Blackmon
Profile: Mobile Beacon and Alabama Citizen is a local weekly newspaper serving Mobile, AL and the surrounding areas. The publication covers local news, sports, business and arts & entertainment issues that impact local residents. All editorial submissions should be sent at least one week in advance. Deadlines for the publication are the Monday before issue date.
Language (s): English
Ad Rate: Full Page Mono 20.95
Ad Rate: Full Page Colour 24029.70
Currency: United States Dollars
COMMUNITY NEWSPAPER

El Mojave 231518
Owner: Local Media Group
Editorial: 13891 Park Ave, Victorville, California 92392-2435 **Tel:** 1 760 241-7744
Web site: http://www.elmojave.com
Freq: Sat; **Circ:** 10000 Not Audited
Profile: El Mojave is a community newspaper written for the residents of Victorville, CA and the surrounding areas.
Language (s): Spanish
Ad Rate: Full Page Mono 9.25
Currency: United States Dollars
COMMUNITY NEWSPAPER

Monadnock Ledger-Transcript 20187
Owner: Newspapers of New England
Editorial: 20 Grove St, Peterborough, New Hampshire 03458-1470 **Tel:** 1 603 924-7172
Email: news@ledgertranscript.com **Web site:** http://www.ledgertranscript.com
Freq: 2 Times/Week; **Circ:** 8701 Not Audited
Editor: Ben Conant; **Circulation Manager:** Emily Manns; **Publisher:** Heather McKernan
Profile: Monadnock Ledger-Transcript is published twice-weekly for the residents of Peterborough, NH and surrounding areas. The newspaper covers local news and community events. Deadlines are on Tuesdays at noon ET.
Language (s): English
Ad Rate: Full Page Mono 9.75
Ad Rate: Full Page Colour 75.00
Currency: United States Dollars
COMMUNITY NEWSPAPER

Monadnock Shopper News 22276
Owner: Publishers, Inc.
Editorial: 445 West St, Keene, New Hampshire 03431-2448 **Tel:** 1 603 352-5250
Email: shopper@shoppernews.com **Web site:** http://www.shoppernews.com
Freq: Wed; **Circ:** 42750 Not Audited
Editor: Michelle Green; **Circulation Manager:** Linda Joyce; **Publisher:** Mitchell Shakour
Profile: Monadnock Shopper News is published weekly for the residents of Keene, NH. The newspaper provides local news, business, sports, entertainment, real estate and a shopping guide.
Language (s): English
Ad Rate: Full Page Mono 18.28
Currency: United States Dollars
COMMUNITY NEWSPAPER

The Monitor 22387
Owner: Diocese of Trenton
Editorial: 701 Lawrenceville Rd, Trenton, New Jersey 8648 **Tel:** 1 609 406-7404
Email: monitor@dioceseoftrenton.org **Web site:** http://www.dioceseoftrenton.org
Freq: Thu; **Circ:** 20000 Not Audited
News Editor: Mary Stadnyk; **Advertising Sales Manager:** Frank Weber
Profile: The Monitor is the weekly newspaper written for Catholics in the Trenton, NJ area. Its editorial mission is to keep members up-to-date on the news and events of the Diocese of Trenton. It covers news, activities, anniversaries and events of local parishes and the Diocese.
Language (s): English
Ad Rate: Full Page Mono 32.00
Ad Rate: Full Page Colour 1560.00
Currency: United States Dollars
COMMUNITY NEWSPAPER

The Monitor 133634
Owner: Hermes Publications
Editorial: 20121 Cox Rd, Sutherland, Virginia 23885-9457 **Tel:** 1 804 733-8636
Email: dmmonitor@earthlink.net **Web site:** http://www.dmwiddie-montior.com
Freq: Wed; **Circ:** 10080 Not Audited
Publisher & Editor: Evan Jones; **Advertising Sales Manager:** Helene McDaniels
Profile: The Monitor is a local weekly newspaper serving residents of the Petersburg, VA area. The publication covers local news and community events. Deadlines are 5pm ET the Friday before issue date.
Language (s): English
Ad Rate: Full Page Mono 7.00
Currency: United States Dollars
COMMUNITY NEWSPAPER

Monitor/Lake Area Leader 492885
Owner: MediaOne LLC
Editorial: 1316 S 3rd St, Mabank, Texas 75147-7680 **Tel:** 1 903 887-4511
Email: publisher@themonitor.net **Web site:** http://www.themonitor.net
Circ: 31000 Not Audited
Publisher: John Buzzetta
Profile: Monitor/Lake Area Leader in Mabank, TX publishes The Monitor and The Lake Area Leader, both community newspapers that cover local news and events.
COMMUNITY NEWSPAPER

The Monmouth Journal 238701
Owner: Monmouth Journal, LLC (The)
Editorial: 212 Maple Ave, Red Bank, New Jersey 07701-1758 **Tel:** 1 732 747-7007
Email: news@themonmouthjournal.com **Web site:** http://www.themonmouthjournal.com
Freq: Fri; **Circ:** 10000 Not Audited
Profile: The Monmouth Journal is published weekly for the residents of Red Bank, NJ and surrounding areas. The newspaper covers local news and community events.
Language (s): English
Ad Rate: Full Page Mono 7.00
Currency: United States Dollars
COMMUNITY NEWSPAPER

Monroe County Independent 397162
Owner: Independent Media Group, Ltd.
Editorial: 120 N Main St, Columbia, Illinois 62236-1761 **Tel:** 1 618 281-8000
Email: independent@htc.net **Web site:** http://www.monroecountynews.net
Freq: Bi-Weekly; **Circ:** 5000 Not Audited
Profile: Monroe County Independent in Columbia, IL, is a bi-monthly newspaper serving the residents of Monroe County, IL. It covers local news, events and other stories of interest to area readers. It is mailed to subscribers' homes on the first and third Fridays of each month.
Language (s): English
Ad Rate: Full Page Mono 10.25
Currency: United States Dollars
COMMUNITY NEWSPAPER

Monroe County Publishers, Inc. 24736
Owner: MCP Inc.
Editorial: 1302 River Rd, Sparta, Wisconsin 54656-2498 **Tel:** 1 608 269-3186
Email: news@monroecountyherald.com **Web site:** http://www.spartanewspapers.com
Freq: Mon; **Circ:** 9850
Advertising Sales Manager: Dan Elliott; **Editor:** William Gleiss; **Editor:** Patrick Mulvaney
Profile: Monroe County Publishers, Inc. provides the community of Sparta, WI with news.
Language (s): English
Ad Rate: Full Page Mono 9.00
Currency: United States Dollars
COMMUNITY NEWSPAPER

Monroe Dispatch 19435
Owner: Monroe Dispatch Corporation
Editorial: 830 Martin Luther King Jr Dr, Monroe, Louisiana 71203-5521 **Tel:** 1 318 325-2858
Email: monroedispatch@yahoo.com
Freq: Thu; **Circ:** 12250 Not Audited
Publisher: Frank DeTiege
Profile: Monroe Dispatch is a weekly newspaper published for the African American communities of Monroe, LA. The newspaper covers local news, lifestyles, interests and concerns. Editorial deadlines are on Mondays at 6pm CT. Contact Frank DeTeige, Jr. to submit press releases.
Language (s): English
Ad Rate: Full Page Mono 11.50
Currency: United States Dollars
COMMUNITY NEWSPAPER

Monroe Free Press 22515
Editorial: 216 Collier St, Monroe, Louisiana 71201-7202 **Tel:** 1 318 388-1310
Email: support@monroefreepress.com **Web site:** http://www.monroefreepress.com
Freq: Thu; **Circ:** 14000 Not Audited
Advertising Sales Manager: Sylvia Campbell; **Publisher & Editor:** Roosevelt Wright
Profile: Monroe Free Press is a local newspaper written for the African American community of Monroe, LA. The paper serves as an advocate for minorities, working people and women's issues. The paper also provides local news and sports coverage. Deadlines are Mondays at 5pm CT.
Language (s): English
Ad Rate: Full Page Mono 17.00
Currency: United States Dollars
COMMUNITY NEWSPAPER

The Monroe Journal 18517
Owner: Bolton Newspapers Inc.
Editorial: 49 Hines St, Monroeville, Alabama 36460-1833 **Tel:** 1 251 575-3282
Email: news@monroejournal.com **Web site:** http://www.monroejournal.com
Freq: Thu; **Circ:** 7773 Not Audited
Advertising Sales Manager: Michael Lambeth
Profile: The editorial mission of Monore Journal is to keep readers informed of local news and events. It is written for residents of the Monroeville, GA area.
Language (s): English
Ad Rate: Full Page Mono 9.72
Currency: United States Dollars
COMMUNITY NEWSPAPER

Monroe Journal 19854
Owner: Journal Publishing Company
Editorial: 115 Main St S, Amory, Mississippi 38821-3407 **Tel:** 1 662 256-5647
Email: news1@monroe360.com **Web site:** http://www.monroe360.com
Freq: Wed; **Circ:** 7000 Not Audited
Advertising Sales Manager: Jeannie Murphree; **Editor:** Ray Van Dusen
Profile: Monroe Journal is a local weekly newspaper written for the residents of Amory and Aberdeen, MS.
Language (s): English
Ad Rate: Full Page Mono 5.90
Ad Rate: Full Page Colour 200.00
Currency: United States Dollars
COMMUNITY NEWSPAPER

The Montclair Times 23018
Owner: Gannett Co., Inc./North Jersey Media Group
Editorial: 632 Pompton Ave, Cedar Grove, New Jersey 07009-1736 **Tel:** 1 973 569-7100
Email: contactus@montclairtimes.com **Web site:** http://www.northjersey.com/towns/montclair
Freq: Thu; **Circ:** 8020 Not Audited
Publisher: Kathleen Hivish; **Editor:** Mark Porter
Profile: The Montclair Times is a local newspaper serving the residents of Montclair, NJ and the surrounding communities. Sections include local news, sports, arts & entertainment, editorial, education, opinion, community news and events.
Language (s): English
Ad Rate: Full Page Mono 16.90
Currency: United States Dollars
COMMUNITY NEWSPAPER

Montecito Journal 22603
Editorial: 1206 Coast Village Cir Ste D, Montecito, California 93108-2710 **Tel:** 1 805 565-1860
Email: news@montecitojournal.net **Web site:** http://www.montecitojournal.net
Freq: Wed; **Circ:** 12000 Not Audited
Advertising Sales Manager: Sue Brooks; **Publisher & Editor:** Tim Buckley
Profile: Montecito Journal is written for the residents of Montecito, CA. It covers local fashion, design, travel, real estate, restaurants and business.
Language (s): English
Ad Rate: Full Page Mono 28.75
Currency: United States Dollars
COMMUNITY NEWSPAPER

Monterey County Weekly 21594
Owner: Milestone Communications
Editorial: 668 Williams Ave, Seaside, California 93955-5736 **Tel:** 1 831 394-5656
Email: mail@mcweekly.com **Web site:** http://www.montereycountyweekly.com
Freq: Thu; **Circ:** 40000 Not Audited
Publisher: Erik Cushman; **Advertising Sales Manager:** Carrie Kuhl
Profile: Monterey County Weekly is published weekly for the residents of Seaside, CA and surrounding areas. The newspaper covers local news, sports and community events.
Language (s): English
Ad Rate: Full Page Mono 26.84
Ad Rate: Full Page Colour 2164.00
Currency: United States Dollars
COMMUNITY NEWSPAPER

Montgomery County News 777718
Editorial: 14375 Liberty St, Montgomery, Texas 77356-4668 **Tel:** 1 936 499-6395
Email: news@montgomerycountynews.net **Web site:** http://montgomerycountynews.net
Freq: Weekly; **Circ:** 6200
Publisher: Monte West
Profile: The Montgomery County news is a community newspaper for residents of Montgomery County, TX.
COMMUNITY NEWSPAPER

The Montgomery County Sentinel 19477
Owner: Montgomery Sentinel Publishing, Inc.
Editorial: 22 W Jefferson St Ste 309, Rockville, Maryland 20850-4259 **Tel:** 1 301 838-0788
Web site: http://www.thesentinel.com
Freq: Thu; **Circ:** 10000 Not Audited
Advertising Sales Manager: Lonnie Johnson; **Publisher:** Lynn Kapiloff; **Editor:** Brian Karem
Profile: The Montgomery County Sentinel is published weekly for the residents of Rockville, MD and surrounding areas. The newspaper covers local news and community events.
Language (s): English
Ad Rate: Full Page Mono 18.00
Currency: United States Dollars
COMMUNITY NEWSPAPER

Montgomery Herald 20015
Owner: Womack Newspapers Inc.
Editorial: 139 Bruton St, Troy, North Carolina 27371-2815 **Tel:** 1 910 576-6051
Email: sendnews@montgomeryherald.com **Web site:** http://www.montgomeryherald.com
Freq: Wed; **Circ:** 5200 Not Audited
Editor: Tammy Dunn
Profile: Montgomery Herald is a weekly newspaper serving the residents in Montgomery County, NC. It covers local news and events.
Language (s): English
Ad Rate: Full Page Mono 9.45
Currency: United States Dollars
COMMUNITY NEWSPAPER

The Montgomery Independent 18518
Owner: Ram Publications Inc.
Editorial: 141 Market Pl, Montgomery, Alabama 36117-4900 **Tel:** 1 334 265-7323
Email: art@montgomeryindependent.com **Web site:** http://www.al.com
Freq: Thu; **Circ:** 5264 Not Audited
Editor: Bob Martin
Profile: Montgomery Independent is a local weekly newspaper that serves Montgomery, AL and surrounding areas. The newspaper covers local news, business, arts & entertainment and sports issues that impact local residents.
Language (s): English
Ad Rate: Full Page Mono 9.50
Currency: United States Dollars
COMMUNITY NEWSPAPER

Montgomery Newspapers 24684
Owner: Journal Register Company
Editorial: 307 Derstine Ave, Lansdale, Pennsylvania 19446-3532 **Tel:** 1 215 542-0200
Email: editorial@montgomerynews.com **Web site:** http://www.montgomerynews.com
Circ: 36742 Not Audited
News Editor: Thomas Celona; **Publisher:** Elizabeth Wilson
Profile: Montgomery Newspapers covers local news and events in Montgomery County and Bucks County, Pa. Serves as the host website for the Ambler Gazette, Colonial News, Glenside News & Globe News & Times Chronicle, Montgomery Life, North Penn Life, Perkasie News-Herald, Public Spirit & Willow Grove Guide, Roxborough Review, Souderton Independent, Springfield Sun and Spring-Ford Reporter & Valley Item.
Language (s): English
COMMUNITY NEWSPAPER

Montgomery Publishing, LLC 491136
Editorial: 1633 W Main St, Salem, Virginia 24153-3115 **Tel:** 1 540 389-9355
Web site: http://www.ourvalley.org
Circ: 11700 Not Audited
Editor: Meg Hibbert; **Editor:** Ed McCoy
COMMUNITY NEWSPAPER

Moorefield Examiner & The Weekender Newspapers 25207
Owner: Heishman (Phoebe)
Editorial: 132 S Main St, Moorefield, West Virginia 26836-1102 **Tel:** 1 304 530-6397
Email: examiner@hardynet.com **Web site:** http://www.moorefieldexaminer.com
Circ: 9076 Not Audited
Advertising Sales Manager: Lisa Duan; **Publisher & Editor:** Phoebe Heishman
Language (s): English
COMMUNITY NEWSPAPER

The Mooresville Tribune 25453
Owner: World Media Enterprises, Inc.
Editorial: 147 E Center Ave, Mooresville, North Carolina 28115-2513 **Tel:** 1 704 664-5554
Email: news@mooresvilletribune.com **Web site:** http://www.mooresvilletribune.com
Freq: Fri; **Circ:** 10767 Not Audited
Publisher: Tim Dearman; **Editor:** Dale Gowing; **Editor:** Karen Kistler
Profile: The Mooresville Tribune is a community newspaper serving residents of Mooresville, NC, including local news, sports, commentary, entertainment and community events.
Language (s): English
Ad Rate: Full Page Mono 9.22
Currency: United States Dollars
COMMUNITY NEWSPAPER

The Mooresville/Decatur Times 22267
Owner: Schurz Communications Inc.
Editorial: 23 E Main St, Mooresville, Indiana 46158-1403 **Tel:** 1 317 831-0280
Email: webstaff@hoosiertimes.com **Web site:** http://www.reporter-times.com/mdt
Freq: Sat; **Circ:** 5000 Not Audited
Circulation Manager: Tim Smith
Profile: The Mooresville/Decatur Times is a local newspaper serving the residents of Mooresville, IN. It includes information on local news, weather, sports, business, and entertainment.
Language (s): English
Ad Rate: Full Page Mono 14.31
Currency: United States Dollars
COMMUNITY NEWSPAPER

The Morehead News 28513
Owner: Community Newspaper Holdings, Inc.
Editorial: 722 W 1st St, Morehead, Kentucky 40351-1404 **Tel:** 1 606 784-4116
Email: newsroom@themoreheadnews.com **Web site:** http://www.themoreheadnews.com
Freq: Fri; **Circ:** 5458 Not Audited
Advertising Sales Manager: Dan Duncan
Profile: The Morehead News is a local newspaper serving the residents of Morehead, KY. It includes information on local news, weather, sports, business and arts & entertainment.
Language (s): English
Ad Rate: Full Page Mono 7.85
Currency: United States Dollars
COMMUNITY NEWSPAPER

Morgan County News 27292
Editorial: 202 N Maiden Street, Wartburg, Tennessee 37887 **Tel:** 1 423 346-6225
Web site: http://www.morgancountynews.net
Freq: Wed; **Circ:** 5613 Not Audited
Profile: Morgan County News is a local newspaper written for the residents of Morgan County and Wartburg, TN, and the surrounding area. The paper covers local news, business, sports and arts & entertainment stories.
Language (s): English
Ad Rate: Full Page Mono 7.05
Currency: United States Dollars
COMMUNITY NEWSPAPER

The Morgan Messenger 21252
Owner: Morgan Messenger, Inc. (The)
Editorial: 16 N Mercer St, Berkeley Springs, West Virginia 25411-1587 **Tel:** 1 304 258-1800
Email: news@morganmessenger.com **Web site:** http://www.morganmessenger.com
Freq: Wed; **Circ:** 5700 Not Audited
Editor: Kate Shunney
Profile: The Morgan Messenger is a local newspaper serving the residents of Berkeley Springs, WV. It includes information on local news, weather, sports, business and entertainment. The lead time is four days.
Language (s): English
Ad Rate: Full Page Mono 9.70
Currency: United States Dollars
COMMUNITY NEWSPAPER

Morning Star Publications 25400
Owner: Richardson (Bryant)
Editorial: 951 Norman Eskridge Hwy, Seaford, Delaware 19973-1719 **Tel:** 1 302 629-9788
Email: editor@mspublications.com
Circ: 7600 Not Audited
Circulation Manager: Karen Cherrix; **Publisher:** Bryant Richardson; **Editor:** Daniel Richardson
Profile: Mornings Star Publications is a community newspaper publisher serving the residents of Salisbury, MD.
Language (s): English
COMMUNITY NEWSPAPER

Morris Multimedia, Inc. 24808
Editorial: 122 S 3rd Ave, Oakdale, California 95361 **Tel:** 1 209 847-3021
Email: ads@oakdaleleader.com
Circ: 22700 Not Audited
Language (s): English
COMMUNITY NEWSPAPER

Morrison County Record 21420
Owner: ECM Publishers, Inc.
Editorial: 216 1st St SE, Little Falls, Minnesota 56345-3004 **Tel:** 1 320 632-2345
Email: mcr@mcrecord.com **Web site:** http://www.mcrecord.com
Freq: Sun; **Circ:** 19000 Not Audited
Publisher: Julian Andersen; **Circulation Manager:** Karen Grittner; **News Editor:** Terry Lehrke; **Advertising Sales Manager:** Carmen Meyer
Profile: Morrison County Record is a local newspaper serving the residents of Morrison County, MN. It covers local news, weather, sports, business and arts & entertainment. Deadlines fall on the Wednesday before publication.
Language (s): English
Ad Rate: Full Page Mono 9.10
Currency: United States Dollars
COMMUNITY NEWSPAPER

Morrisons Cove Herald 20569
Owner: Bassler (Allan) and Bassler (Karen)
Editorial: 113 N Market St, Martinsburg, Pennsylvania 16662 **Tel:** 1 814 793-2144
Email: news@mcheraldonline.com
Freq: Thu; **Circ:** 7150 Not Audited
Publisher & Editor: Allan Bassler; **Advertising Manager:** Cynthia DiAndrea
Profile: Morrisons Cove Herald is a local newspaper serving the residents of Martinsburg, PA.
Language (s): English
Ad Rate: Full Page Mono 12.00
Currency: United States Dollars
COMMUNITY NEWSPAPER

The Moscow Villager 21537
Owner: GateHouse Media Inc.
Editorial: 220 8th St, Honesdale, Pennsylvania 18431-1854 **Tel:** 1 570 844-1999
Email: news@moscowvillager.com **Web site:** http://www.moscowvillager.com
Freq: Wed; **Circ:** 5000 Not Audited
Editor: Ryan O'Malley
Profile: Community news source covering news, sports, business, weather, and other topics for the residents of Moscow, Pennsylvania and surrounding areas.
Language (s): English
Ad Rate: Full Page Mono 9.47
Currency: United States Dollars
COMMUNITY NEWSPAPER

Moulton Advertiser 18519
Owner: Moulton Advertiser Inc.
Editorial: 659 Main St, Moulton, Alabama 35650-1512 **Tel:** 1 256 974-1114
Email: editor@moultonadvertiser.com **Web site:** http://www.moultonadvertiser.com
Freq: Thu; **Circ:** 13500 Not Audited

Publisher: Clint Shelton
Profile: Moulton Advertiser is a local newspaper serving the residents of Moulton, AL. It includes information on local news, weather, sports, business and entertainment. Deadlines are on Mondays.
Language (s): English
Ad Rate: Full Page Mono 10.85
Currency: United States Dollars
COMMUNITY NEWSPAPER

Moultrie News 26638
Owner: Evening Post Publishing Co.
Editorial: 134 Columbus St, Charleston, South Carolina 29403-4809 **Tel:** 1 843 849-1778
Email: editor@moultrienews.com **Web site:** http://www.moultrienews.com
Freq: Wed; **Circ:** 28225 Not Audited
Editor: Sully Witte
Profile: Moultrie News is the weekly local newspaper written for the residents of Mount Pleasant, SC and the surrounding area. The newspaper aims to bring the general news, events and information of the community to its residents.
Language (s): English
Ad Rate: Full Page Mono 15.00
Currency: United States Dollars
COMMUNITY NEWSPAPER

Mount Desert Islander 79122
Owner: Baker, Alan
Editorial: 310 Main St, Bar Harbor, Maine 04609-1638 **Tel:** 1 207 288-0556
Email: news@mdislander.com **Web site:** http://www.mdislander.com
Freq: Weekly; **Circ:** 5000 Not Audited
Publisher: Alan Baker; **Editor:** Earl Brechlin; **Advertising Sales Manager:** Julie Clark
Profile: Mount Desert Islander is a community newspaper written for residents of Bar Harbor, ME.
Language (s): English
Ad Rate: Full Page Mono 9.60
Currency: United States Dollars
COMMUNITY NEWSPAPER

Mount Olive Tribune 19993
Editorial: 214 N Center St, Mount Olive, North Carolina 28365-1702 **Tel:** 1 919 658-9456 7012
Email: editor@mountolivetribune.com **Web site:** http://www.mountolivetribune.com
Freq: Wed; **Circ:** 5000 Not Audited
Editor: John Cate; **Advertising Sales Manager:** Denise Lassiter; **Publisher & Circulation Manager:** Barry Merrill
Profile: Mount Olive Tribune is a local newspaper written for the residents of Mount Olive, NC. The paper covers local news, weather, sports, business and arts & entertainment.
Language (s): English
Ad Rate: Full Page Mono 13.50
Currency: United States Dollars
COMMUNITY NEWSPAPER

Mount Sterling Advocate 19365
Owner: Hasco Newspapers Inc.
Editorial: 219 Midland Trl, Mount Sterling, Kentucky 40353-9070 **Tel:** 1 859 498-2222
Email: news@msadvocate.com **Web site:** http://www.msadvocate.com
Freq: Thu; **Circ:** 7000 Not Audited
Publisher: Matt Hall; **Advertising Sales Manager:** Sharon Manning
Profile: Mount Sterling Advocate is a local newspaper in Mount Sterling, KY providing local news, sports and local entertainment coverage.
Language (s): English
Ad Rate: Full Page Mono 5.86
Currency: United States Dollars
COMMUNITY NEWSPAPER

Mount Vernon Voice 152857
Editorial: 7946 Fort Hunt Rd, Alexandria, Virginia 22308-1249 **Tel:** 1 703 360-0080
Email: mountvernonvoice@aol.com **Web site:** http://www.mountvernonvoice.com
Freq: Wed; **Circ:** 12000 Not Audited
Profile: Mount Vernon Voice is a local newspaper providing local news to the community of Alexandria, VA.
Language (s): English
Ad Rate: Full Page Mono 19.00
Currency: United States Dollars
COMMUNITY NEWSPAPER

Mountain Citizen 19394
Owner: New Wave Communications
Editorial: 20 W Main St, Inez, Kentucky 41224-6003 **Tel:** 1 606 298-7570
Email: mountaincitizen@bellsouth.net
Freq: Wed; **Circ:** 6000 Not Audited
Editor: Gary Ball; **Circulation Manager:** Becky Smith; **Advertising Sales Manager:** Diane Smith; **Publisher:** Roger Smith
Profile: Mountain Citizen is a local newspaper serving the residents of Inez, KY. It includes information on local news, weather, sports, business, and entertainment.
Language (s): English
Ad Rate: Full Page Mono 6.17
Currency: United States Dollars
COMMUNITY NEWSPAPER

Mountain City Publishing Company 76659
Editorial: 112 N Watauga Ln, Lookout Mountain, Tennessee 37350-1356 **Tel:** 1 423 822-6397
Email: mtncpub@bellsouth.net **Web site:** http://www.mountainmirror.com
Circ: 9500 Not Audited
Publisher: William Parker; **Editor:** Ferris Robinson
Language (s): English
COMMUNITY NEWSPAPER

The Mountain Echo 19780
Owner: Pribble (Sue) & Pribble (Randy)
Editorial: 110 N Main St, Ironton, Missouri 63650-1108 **Tel:** 1 573 546-3917
Web site: http://www.myironcountynews.com
Freq: Wed; **Circ:** 6584 Not Audited
Advertising Sales Manager: Dory Hackett; **Editor & Publisher:** Randy Pribble; **Circulation Manager:** Sue Pribble
Profile: The Mountain Echo is a local newspaper serving the residents of Ironton, MO. It includes information on local news, weather, sports, business and entertainment.
Language (s): English
Ad Rate: Full Page Mono 7.75
Currency: United States Dollars
COMMUNITY NEWSPAPER

Mountain Home News Publishing 25377
Owner: Rust Communications
Editorial: 195 S 3rd E, Mountain Home, Idaho 83647 **Tel:** 1 208 587-3331
Web site: http://www.mountainhomenews.com
Freq: Weekly; **Circ:** 16300
Community News Editor: Melanie Brown; **Advertising Sales Manager:** Miranda Hannah
Profile: Mountain Home News Publishing is a community newspaper publisher servicing the residents of Boise, ID.
Language (s): English
Ad Rate: Full Page Mono 10.55
Currency: United States Dollars
COMMUNITY NEWSPAPER

Mountain Jackpot 22393
Owner: Wind Ridge Press Inc.
Tel: 1 719 687-0803
Email: mountainjackpot@gmail.com **Web site:** http://www.mountainjackpot.com
Freq: Tue; **Circ:** 7000 Not Audited
Editor: Rick Langenberg; **Publisher:** Robert Leininger
Profile: The Mountain Jackpot is a free local weekly newspaper serving the residents of Teller County, CO. The publication includes information on local news, weather, sports, business and entertainment. Deadlines are Fridays at 5pm MT.
Language (s): English
Ad Rate: Full Page Mono 12.50
Currency: United States Dollars
COMMUNITY NEWSPAPER

The Mountain Sun 778434
Owner: Southern Newspapers, Inc.
Editorial: 429 Jefferson St, Kerrville, Texas 78028-4412 **Tel:** 1 830 896-7000
Email: news@dailytimes.com **Web site:** http://dailytimes.com
Freq: Weekly
Publisher & Editor: Mike Graxiola
Profile: The Mountain Sun is Kerrville Daily Times free weekly community newspaper. The newspaper covers local and national news, sports, business and lifestyle.
COMMUNITY NEWSPAPER

The Mountain Times 21493
Owner: Outer Limits Publishing, LLC
Editorial: 5465 Route 4, Killington, Vermont 5751 **Tel:** 1 802 422-2399
Email: editor@mountaintimes.info **Web site:** http://www.mountaintimes.info
Freq: Thu; **Circ:** 10500 Not Audited
Profile: Mountain Times is a regional weekly newspaper serving the residents of Central Vermont. The publication features local news, weather, sports, business and entertainment. Deadlines are on Fridays prior to issue date. The paper cannot accept attachments. Please include information in the body of the e-mail.
Language (s): English
Ad Rate: Full Page Mono 10.70
Currency: United States Dollars
COMMUNITY NEWSPAPER

Mountain Times & Watauga Democrat 696977
Owner: Jones Media, Inc.
Editorial: 474 Industrial Park Dr, Boone, North Carolina 28607-3937 **Tel:** 1 828 264-6397
Email: newspaper@mountaintimes.com **Web site:** http://www.mountaintimes.com
Circ: 28503
Publisher: Gene Fowler; **Advertising Sales Manager:** Charlie Price
Profile: The Boone Mountain Times is a newspaper in Boone, North Carolina. The newspaper is published once a week on Thursday. The Mountain Times began publication in 1978. It is part of Mountain Times Publications.
Language (s): English
COMMUNITY NEWSPAPER

The Mountain Valley News 21711
Owner: Hometown Publications
Editorial: 367 Main St E, Rainsville, Alabama 35986-4545 **Tel:** 1 256 638-6397
Email: mtnvalley@farmerstel.com **Web site:** http://mountainvalleynewspaper.com
Freq: Thu; **Circ:** 5000 Not Audited
Circulation Manager: Patsy Overby
Profile: Mountain Valley News is a community newspaper serving Dekalb and Jackson counties, AL, with local news, sports and community events.
Language (s): English
Ad Rate: Full Page Mono 10.00
Currency: United States Dollars
COMMUNITY NEWSPAPER

The Mountain View Telegraph 309881
Owner: Albuquerque Publishing Co.
Editorial: 717 W Abrahames Rd, Moriarty, New Mexico 87035-8197 **Tel:** 1 505 823-7101
Email: editor@mvtelegraph.com **Web site:** http://www.mvtelegraph.com
Freq: Thu; **Circ:** 7000 Not Audited
Editor: Rory McClannahan
Profile: The Mountain View Telegraph is a community newspaper serving the residents of Moriarty, NM. It covers local news, sports and events.
Language (s): English
Ad Rate: Full Page Mono 18.77
Currency: United States Dollars
COMMUNITY NEWSPAPER

Mountain Xpress 81209
Owner: Green Line Media, Inc.
Editorial: 2 Wall St, Asheville, North Carolina 28801-2721 **Tel:** 1 828 251-1333
Email: news@mountainx.com **Web site:** http://www.mountainx.com
Freq: Wed; **Circ:** 25448 Not Audited
Editor & Publisher: Jeff Fobes; **Circulation Manager:** Jeff Tallman
Profile: Mountain Xpress is a local newspaper written for the residents of Asheville, NC. The paper covers local news, weather, sports, business and arts & entertainment.
Language (s): English
Ad Rate: Full Page Mono 20.00
Ad Rate: Full Page Colour 145.00
Currency: United States Dollars
COMMUNITY NEWSPAPER

The Mountaineer 20020
Owner: Mountaineer Publishing Company
Editorial: 220 N Main St, Waynesville, North Carolina 28786-3812 **Tel:** 1 828 452-0661
Email: info@themountaineer.com **Web site:** http://www.themountaineer.com
Freq: Fri; **Circ:** 7900 Not Audited
Editor: Vicki Hyatt; **Publisher:** Jonathan Key
Profile: The Mountaineer is a local newspaper for the residents of Haywood County, NC. Its editorial mission is to be Haywood County's leader for news coverage. The publication covers local news, sports, lifestyles, education, entertainment, business and community events.
Language (s): English
Ad Rate: Full Page Mono 17.85
Ad Rate: Full Page Colour 180.00
Currency: United States Dollars
COMMUNITY NEWSPAPER

Mountaineer 22815
Editorial: 31 E Platte Ave Ste 300, Colorado Springs, Colorado 80903-1246 **Tel:** 1 719 526-4144
Email: fcmountaineer@hotmail.com **Web site:** http://www.csmng.com/mountaineer
Freq: Fri; **Circ:** 20000 Not Audited
Editor: Devin Fisher; **Advertising Sales Manager:** Aimee Grable
Profile: Mountaineer is a weekly newspaper published in the interest of the 7th Infantry Division and the Fort Carson, CO community. Editorial coverage includes local news, sports, arts, events, health and nutrition.
Language (s): English
Ad Rate: Full Page Mono 18.82
Ad Rate: Full Page Colour 1330.00
Currency: United States Dollars
COMMUNITY NEWSPAPER

Mukilteo Beacon 22015
Owner: Beacon Publishing Inc.
Editorial: 806 5th St, Mukilteo, Washington 98275-1628 **Tel:** 1 425 347-5634
Email: editor@mukilteobeacon.com **Web site:** http://www.mukilteobeacon.com
Freq: Wed; **Circ:** 65250 Not Audited
Advertising Sales Manager: Caitlin Archipley; **Publisher:** Paul Archipley; **Editor:** Sara Bruestle; **Circulation Manager:** Carolyn Hart-Mylie
Profile: Mukilteo Beacon is published weekly for the residents of Mukilteo, WA and surrounding areas. The newspaper covers local news, government and sports.
Language (s): English
Ad Rate: Full Page Mono 24.00
Currency: United States Dollars
COMMUNITY NEWSPAPER

El Mundo 23173
Editorial: 760 N Eastern Ave Ste 110, Las Vegas, Nevada 89101-2888 **Tel:** 1 702 649-8553
Email: editorial@elmundo.net **Web site:** http://www.elmundo.net
Freq: Fri; **Circ:** 29597 Not Audited
Circulation Manager: Nick Escobedo; **Editor:** Valdemar Gonzalez; **Advertising Sales Manager:** Flor Hernandez
Profile: El Mundo is a weekly, Spanish-language community newspaper. Deadlines for press releases are Tuesdays by 2pm PT.
Language (s): Spanish
Ad Rate: Full Page Mono 16.50
Ad Rate: Full Page Colour 1488.00
Currency: United States Dollars
COMMUNITY NEWSPAPER

El Mundo 23218
Owner: El Mundo Communications Co.
Editorial: 11410 Ne 124Th St #441, Kirkland, Washington 98034-4305 **Tel:** 1 800 797-4544
Email: info@elmundous.com **Web site:** http://www.elmundous.com
Freq: Thu; **Circ:** 20000 Not Audited
Publisher: Martha Montoya
Profile: El Mundo is written for the Hispanic community in Wenatchee, WA. It covers news and current events occurring in Mexico.
Language (s): Spanish
Ad Rate: Full Page Mono 14.00
Currency: United States Dollars
COMMUNITY NEWSPAPER

El Mundo 23261
Owner: Banner Publications, Inc.
Editorial: 408 S Huntington Ave, Boston, Massachusetts 02130-4814 **Tel:** 1 617 522-5060
Email: editor@elmundoboston.com **Web site:** http://www.elmundoboston.com
Freq: Thu; **Circ:** 30000 Not Audited
Profile: El Mundo is a weekly newspaper that provides local and national news to Hispanic communities around Boston. The newspaper also provides weekly features in business, politics, education, health and sports. Deadlines are on Mondays at 2pm ET.
Language (s): Spanish/Bilingual
Ad Rate: Full Page Mono 25.00
Ad Rate: Full Page Colour 2350.00
Currency: United States Dollars
COMMUNITY NEWSPAPER

El Mundo 137040
Owner: Angulo (Roberto)
Editorial: 2112 E Cesar Chavez St, Austin, Texas 78702-4514 **Tel:** 1 512 476-8636
Email: info@elmundonewspaper.com **Web site:** http://www.elmundonewspaper.com
Freq: Thu; **Circ:** 45725 Not Audited
Circulation Manager: Monica Angulo; **Editor:** Roberto Angulo; **Advertising Sales Manager:** Sahabel Porto
Profile: El Mundo in Austin, TX is a weekly Spanish newspaper that covers local news and events in a region that includes Round Rock, Georgetown, Cedar Park, Lockhart, Bastrop, Buda, and Kyle. Deadlines are on Mondays prior to publication.
Language (s): Spanish
Ad Rate: Full Page Mono 25.00
Currency: United States Dollars
COMMUNITY NEWSPAPER

Mundo Hispanico 23222
Owner: Atlanta Journal-Constitution (The)
Editorial: 6455 Best Friend Rd, Norcross, Georgia 30071-2914 **Tel:** 1 404 881-0441
Email: editorial@mundohispanico.com **Web site:** http://www.mundohispanico.com
Freq: Thu; **Circ:** 63901 Not Audited
Circulation Manager: Jimmy Vega
Profile: Mundo Hispanico is a local newspaper written for the Hispanic population of Atlanta. The newspaper covers local news, sports and arts & entertainment. Deadlines are on Mondays prior to issue date.
Language (s): English, Spanish
Ad Rate: Full Page Mono 40.13
Currency: United States Dollars
COMMUNITY NEWSPAPER

The Murfreesboro Post 514889
Owner: Fryar (Ron)
Editorial: 2955 S Rutherford Blvd Ste I, Murfreesboro, Tennessee 37130-0719
Tel: 1 615 869-0800
Email: online@murfreesboropost.com **Web site:** http://www.murfreesboropost.com
Freq: Weekly; **Circ:** 25000 Not Audited
Circulation Manager: Sally Clark; **Publisher:** Ron Fryar; **Advertising Sales Manager:** Travis Swann
Profile: The Murfreesboro Post is a community-based weekly newspaper serving the households and businesses of the Mufreesboro market. Daily breaking news is offered on the Web site.
Language (s): English
Ad Rate: Full Page Mono 23.00
Currency: United States Dollars
COMMUNITY NEWSPAPER

Muslim Journal 22528
Owner: Muslim Journal Enterprises, Inc.
Editorial: 231 E. 51st St., Chicago, Illinois 60615 **Tel:** 1 773 952-8177
Email: muslimjrnl@comcast.net **Web site:** http://muslimjournal.net
Freq: Fri; **Circ:** 10000 Not Audited
Publisher & Editor: Ayesha Mustafaa
Profile: Muslim Journal is written for the Muslim communities in the United States, Australia and the Middle East. It covers political and social issues of interest to the Muslim community. Deadlines are on Tuesdays at 5pm CT.
Language (s): English
Ad Rate: Full Page Mono 15.00
Currency: United States Dollars
COMMUNITY NEWSPAPER

The Muslim Observer 440086
Owner: Muslim Media Network
Editorial: 29004 W 8 Mile Rd, Farmington Hills, Michigan 48336-5910 **Tel:** 1 248 426-7777

Email: submissions@muslimobserver.com **Web site:** http://www.muslimobserver.com
Freq: Thu; **Circ:** 10000 Not Audited
Publisher: A.S. Nakadar
Profile: The Muslim Observer is a weekly newspaper tabloid covering international, national and community news for Muslims. Based in Wisconsin, it distributed across the United States including South Florida and the Detroit, Houston, Chicago and San Francisco metro areas.
Language (s): English
Ad Rate: Full Page Mono 5.71
Currency: United States Dollars
COMMUNITY NEWSPAPER

Mustang Times 704019
Editorial: 553 N Mustang Rd, Mustang, Oklahoma 73064-7002 **Tel:** 1 405 376-6688
Email: mustangtimesnews@sbcglobal.net **Web site:** http://www.mustangpaper.com/4289/1586/mustang-times
Freq: Weekly
Profile: Mustang Times is written for residents of Mustang, OK.
Language (s): English
COMMUNITY NEWSPAPER

My Backyard 217550
Editorial: 34 Rosewood Ave, South Attleboro, Massachusetts 02703-5913 **Tel:** 1 508 212-4454
Email: mybackyard@comcast.net **Web site:** http://www.mybackyardnews.com
Freq: Semi-Monthly; **Circ:** 13000 Not Audited
Editor: James Hanley; **Advertising Sales Manager:** Sherri Oldfield
Profile: My Backyard is a weekly newspaper written for residents of Rhode Island and Southeastern Massachusetts, including East Providence, Pawtucket, Lincoln, Central Falls and Cumberland, RI and Attleboro, MA. The paper is publised the 1st and 3rd Friday each month.
Language (s): English
Ad Rate: Full Page Mono 10.00
Currency: United States Dollars
COMMUNITY NEWSPAPER

Myrtle Beach Herald 62790
Owner: Waccamaw Publishers, Inc.
Editorial: 4761 Highway 501 Ste 3, Myrtle Beach, South Carolina 29579-9457 **Tel:** 1 843 626-3131
Email: hipub@sccoast.net **Web site:** http://www.myrtlebeachherald.com
Freq: Fri; **Circ:** 5900 Not Audited
Publisher & Editor: Stephen Robertson
Profile: Myrtle Beach Herald is a local weekly newspaper written for the residents of Myrtle Beach, SC. The publication covers the latest news and events taking place in and around Myrtle Beach, SC.
Language (s): English
Ad Rate: Full Page Mono 9.00
Currency: United States Dollars
COMMUNITY NEWSPAPER

Mystic River Press 22181
Owner: Sun Publishing Company
Editorial: 99 Mechanic St, Stonington, Connecticut 6379 **Tel:** 1 860 536-9577
Email: news@themysticriverpress.com **Web site:** http://www.thewesterlysun.com/news/mysticriverpress/
Freq: Thu; **Circ:** 10815 Not Audited
Profile: Mystic River Press is a local, weekly newspaper serving residents of of Mystic, Groton, and Stonington, CT. Its editorial mission is to provide readers with the latest news and information. Deadlines are on Mondays.
Language (s): English
Ad Rate: Full Page Mono 12.50
Currency: United States Dollars
COMMUNITY NEWSPAPER

La Nacion Hispana 137110
Owner: Hispanic Marketing, Inc.
Editorial: 1601 Cedar Lane Rd Ste 14, Greenville, South Carolina 29617-2347 **Tel:** 1 864 246-4110
Email: manager@lanacionhispana.com **Web site:** http://www.lanacionhispana.com
Freq: Wed; **Circ:** 10000 Not Audited
Publisher & Editor: Carlos Puello Mejia
Profile: La Nacion Hispana is written for Hispanic residents of Greenville, SC. It covers community, national and international news, sports, weather and lifestyles. Deadlines are Fridays.
Language (s): Spanish
Ad Rate: Full Page Mono 10.44
Currency: United States Dollars
COMMUNITY NEWSPAPER

El Nacional de Oklahoma 21796
Editorial: 304 SW 25th St, Oklahoma City, Oklahoma 73109-5922 **Tel:** 1 405 632-4531
Email: noticias@elnacionalmedia.net **Web site:** http://www.noticiasoklahoma.com
Freq: Thu; **Circ:** 65000 Not Audited
Editor & Publisher: Rosa King
Profile: El Nacional de Oklahoma is a Spanish language newspaper written for Hispanics in and around Oklahoma City, OK.
Language (s): Spanish
Ad Rate: Full Page Mono 15.50
Currency: United States Dollars
COMMUNITY NEWSPAPER

Nadig Newspapers 24525
Owner: Nadig Newspapers
Editorial: 4937 N Milwaukee Ave, Chicago, Illinois 60630-2114 **Tel:** 1 773 286-6100
Email: news@nadignewspapers.com **Web site:** http://www.nadignewspapers.com
Circ: 24000 Not Audited
Editor: Randy Erickson
Profile: Nadig newspapers serves the Far Northwest Side of Chicago and the surrounding suburbs providing local and community news.
Language (s): English
Ad Rate: Full Page Mono 43.00
Currency: United States Dollars
COMMUNITY NEWSPAPER

Nashoba Publications Inc. 24579
Owner: Fitchburg Publishing Co.
Editorial: 78 Barnum Rd, Ayer, Massachusetts 01434-3508 **Tel:** 1 978 772-0777
Email: editor@nashobapub.com **Web site:** http://www.nashobapublishing.com
Circ: 25009 Not Audited
Managing Editor & News Director: Kate Walsh King
Profile: Please send all postal correspondence to the PO address.
Language (s): English
COMMUNITY NEWSPAPER

The Nashville News 19107
Owner: Riccon, Inc.
Editorial: 211 W Saint Louis St, Nashville, Illinois 62263-1161 **Tel:** 1 618 327-3411
Email: news@nashnews.net **Web site:** http://www.nash-news.com
Freq: Wed; **Circ:** 5000 Not Audited
Profile: The Nashville News provides news for residents in Nashville, IL and surrounding areas. The newspaper covers local news, business, sports, and arts & entertainment stories. It also covers national and statewide stories if they have a direct impact on the newspaper's readership. All editorial inquiries should be addressed to the editor.
Language (s): English
Ad Rate: Full Page Mono 6.35
Currency: United States Dollars
COMMUNITY NEWSPAPER

Nashville Scene 21621
Owner: Southcomm, Inc.
Editorial: 210 12th Ave S Ste 100, Nashville, Tennessee 37203-4046 **Tel:** 1 615 244-7989
Email: editor@nashvillescene.com **Web site:** http://www.nashvillescene.com
Freq: Thu; **Circ:** 44817 Not Audited
News Editor: Steve Cavendish; **Publisher:** Mike Smith
Profile: Nashville Scene is a weekly newspaper published for the residents of Nashville, TN and surrounding areas. The publication covers local news and community events.
Language (s): English
Ad Rate: Full Page Mono 46.47
Ad Rate: Full Page Colour 2882.00
Currency: United States Dollars
COMMUNITY NEWSPAPER

Nassau Border Papers, Inc. 24639
Owner: Cushing Media Group
Editorial: 139 Tulip Ave, Floral Park, New York 11001-2783 **Tel:** 1 516 775-2700
Email: nassaubdr@optonline.net
Circ: 28700 Not Audited
Editor and Publisher: Scott Cushing; **Advertising Manager:** Anna McCarthy
Profile: Nassau Border Papers in Floral Park, NY publishes the Franklin Square Bulletin, the Gateway and the Floral Park Bulletin community newspapers.
Language (s): English
COMMUNITY NEWSPAPER

Nassau County Record 22464
Owner: Community Newspapers Inc.
Editorial: 617317 Brandies Ave, Callahan, Florida 32011-3704 **Tel:** 1 904 879-2727
Email: editor@nassaucountyrecord.com **Web site:** http://www.nassaucountyrecord.com
Freq: Weekly; **Circ:** 5000 Not Audited
Publisher: Foy Maloy; **Editor:** Amanda Ream
Profile: Nassau County Record is a weekly newspaper written for residents of Nassau County, FL. The publication covers news and events. Deadlines for the publication are Fridays at 4pm ET before issue date.
Language (s): English
Ad Rate: Full Page Mono 8.92
Currency: United States Dollars
COMMUNITY NEWSPAPER

Native Sun News 584991
Editorial: 1026 Jackson Blvd, Rapid City, South Dakota 57702-4334 **Tel:** 1 605 721-1266
Email: editor@nsweekly.com **Web site:** http://www.nsweekly.com
Freq: Wed; **Circ:** 7000
Advertising Sales Manager: Kirk Dickerson; **Editor:** Brandon Ecoffey
Profile: Native Sun News offers community and tribal news to residents in and around Rapid City, SD and communities in northern Nebraska in addition to the nine Native American Reservations in South Dakota as well as tribal colleges and highschools throughout the United States.
Language (s): English
Ad Rate: Full Page Mono 18.00
Currency: United States Dollars
COMMUNITY NEWSPAPER

Navajo County Publishers 281861
Owner: Navajo County Publishers
Editorial: 200 E Hopi Dr, Holbrook, Arizona 86025-2628 **Tel:** 1 928 524-6203
Email: tribunenews@cableone.net **Web site:** http://www.azjournal.com
Freq: Fri; **Circ:** 8801 Not Audited
Publisher: Matthew Barger; **Editor:** Francie Payne
Profile: Navajo County Publishers produces Silver Creek Herald in Snowflake, AZ and the Holbrook (AZ) Tribune-News.
Language (s): English
Ad Rate: Full Page Mono 9.85
Currency: United States Dollars
COMMUNITY NEWSPAPER

Navajo Times 21427
Owner: Navajo Times Publishing Co., Inc.
Editorial: Highway 264 Route 12, Window Rock, Arizona 86515 **Tel:** 1 928 871-1130
Email: editor@navajotimes.com **Web site:** http://www.navajotimes.com
Freq: Thu; **Circ:** 24000 Not Audited
Publisher: Tom Arviso; **Editor:** Candace Begody; **Circulation Manager:** Rhonda Joe; **Advertising Sales Manager:** Vernon Yazzie
Profile: Navajo Times is a local newspaper published weekly for the Native American population of Window Rock, AZ and surrounding areas. It covers local news, government and community events.
Language (s): English
Ad Rate: Full Page Mono 14.00
Currency: United States Dollars
COMMUNITY NEWSPAPER

Navajo-Hopi Observer 22072
Owner: Western Newspapers, Inc.
Editorial: 2717 N 4th St Ste 110, Flagstaff, Arizona 86004-1813 **Tel:** 1 928 226-9696
Email: nhoeditorial@nhonews.com **Web site:** http://www.nhonews.com
Freq: Wed; **Circ:** 15000 Not Audited
Advertising Sales Manager: Robb Smart
Profile: Navajo-Hopi Observer is published weekly for the Native American Indians of Flagstaff, AZ. The publication informs the Navajo and Hopi, who live on reservations, about local news, government and community events. Deadlines are on Thursdays at 4pm MT.
Language (s): English
Ad Rate: Full Page Mono 15.54
Currency: United States Dollars
COMMUNITY NEWSPAPER

Navarre Press 310140
Editorial: 7502 Harvest Village Ct, Navarre, Florida 32566-7319 **Tel:** 1 850 939-8040
Email: news@navarrepress.com **Web site:** http://www.navarrepress.com
Freq: Thu; **Circ:** 7500 Not Audited
Advertising Manager: Gail Acosta; **Publisher:** Sandi Kemp; **Circulation Manager:** Brandy Wiser
Profile: Navarre Press is a local newspaper written for the residents of Navarre, FL.
Language (s): English
Ad Rate: Full Page Mono 15.00
Currency: United States Dollars
COMMUNITY NEWSPAPER

The Navigator & Journal-Register Newspapers 24900
Owner: S&R Media, LLC
Editorial: 19 W Main St, Albion, Illinois 62806-1006 **Tel:** 1 618 445-2355
Email: navigator@nwcable.net
Freq: Weekly; **Circ:** 17200 Not Audited
Circulation Manager: Carolyn Hallam; **Advertising Sales Manager:** Steve Hartsock; **Publisher:** Patrick Seil
Profile: The Navigator & Journal-Register is written for residents that live in and around Albion, IL. The publication covers news and events.
Language (s): English
COMMUNITY NEWSPAPER

Nearby News 358752
Owner: Times Media Group
Editorial: 3200 N Hayden Rd Ste 210, Scottsdale, Arizona 85251-6654 **Tel:** 1 480 654-4460
Email: info@nearbynews.com **Web site:** http://www.nearbynews.com
Circ: 30000 Not Audited
Profile: Nearby News in Scottsdale, AZ provides local news and information to nine communities in the East Valley, in North Scottsdale and in North Chandler.
Language (s): English
COMMUNITY NEWSPAPER

Neighbor News 25479
Owner: Gannett Co., Inc./North Jersey Media Group
Editorial: 1 Garret Mountain Plz, Woodland Park, New Jersey 07424-3320
Email: newsroom@northjersey.com **Web site:** http://www.northjersey.com
Circ: 88413 Not Audited
Profile: Neighbor News is a community newspaper serving residents of North New Jersey.
Language (s): English
COMMUNITY NEWSPAPER

Neighbor Newspapers 62580
Owner: Neighbor Newspapers
Editorial: 225 N Clay St, Marshfield, Missouri 65706-1652 **Tel:** 1 417 859-2013
Email: news@marshfieldmail.com **Web site:** http://www.marshfieldmail.com
Circ: 21900 Not Audited
Publisher: Dave Berry
Language (s): English
COMMUNITY NEWSPAPER

Neighbor Newspapers 242297
Owner: Neighbor Newspapers
Editorial: 116 N 2nd Ave, Ozark, Missouri 65721-8453 **Tel:** 1 417 581-3541
Email: news@ccheadliner.com
Circ: 7200 Not Audited
Publisher: Dave Berry; **Editor:** Emilia Wigton
Language (s): English
COMMUNITY NEWSPAPER

Neighbor Newspapers 518015
Owner: LI Media Group LLC
Editorial: 565 Broadhollow Rd, Farmingdale, New York 11735-4831 **Tel:** 1 631 226-2636
Email: editors@southbaynews.com **Web site:** http://www.theneighbornewspapers.com
Circ: 667919 Not Audited
Publisher: Jeff Lambert; **Editor:** Jamie Lynn Ryan
Profile: Also known as South Bay's Neighbor, writes community newspapers for the state of New York.
Language (s): English
COMMUNITY NEWSPAPER

Neighbor Newspapers - Cobb 25146
Editorial: 580 S Fairground St Se, Marietta, Georgia 30060-2751 **Tel:** 1 770 428-9411
Email: mdjnews@mdjonline.com **Web site:** http://www.neighbornewspapers.com
Circ: 99950 Not Audited
Publisher: Otis Brumby
Language (s): English
COMMUNITY NEWSPAPER

Neighbor Newspapers - DeKalb 25147
Owner: Marietta Journal
Editorial: 10930 Crabapple Rd Ste 9, Roswell, Georgia 30075-5812 **Tel:** 1 770 454-9388
Email: dekalb@neighbornewspapers.com **Web site:** http://www.neighbornewspapers.com
Circ: 49200 Not Audited
Publisher: Otis Brumby; **Editor:** LaTria Garnigan; **Advertising Sales Manager:** Denise Weaver
Profile: Neighbor Newspapers - DeKalb in Roswell, GA publishes the North DeKalb Neighbor, the DeKalb Neighbor and Dunwoody Neighbor community newspapers.
Language (s): English
COMMUNITY NEWSPAPER

Neighbor Newspapers - North Fulton 25388
Owner: Neighbor Newspapers
Editorial: 10930 Crabapple Rd, Roswell, Georgia 30075-5813 **Tel:** 1 770 993-7400
Email: nfulton@neighbornewspapers.com **Web site:** http://www.neighbornewspapers.com
Freq: Weekly; **Circ:** 47980 Not Audited
Publisher: Otis Brumby
Profile: Neighbor Newspapers, based in Marietta, GA, produces weekly newspapers serving metro Atlanta's suburban communities.
Language (s): English
COMMUNITY NEWSPAPER

Neighbor Newspapers - Northside Atlanta 25148
Owner: Neighbor Newspapers, Inc.
Editorial: 5290 Roswell Rd Ste M, Sandy Springs, Georgia 30342-1978 **Tel:** 1 404 256-3100
Email: nside@neighbornewspapers.com **Web site:** http://www.neighbornewspapers.com
Circ: 35086
Publisher: Otis Brumby; **News Editor:** Everett Catts; **Advertising Sales Manager:** Stephanie DeJarnette; **Circulation Manager:** Dave Gossett; **Editor:** Greg Oshust
Profile: Neighbor Newspapers - Northside Atlanta is a community newspaper publisher servicing the residents of Atlanta, as well as Sandy Springs and Marietta, GA.
Language (s): English
COMMUNITY NEWSPAPER

Neighbor Newspapers - South Metro 25323
Owner: Neighbor Newspapers
Editorial: 5442 Frontage Rd, Ste 130, Forest Park, Georgia 30297 **Tel:** 1 404 363-8484
Email: smetro@neighbornewspapers.com **Web site:** http://www.neighbornewspapers.com
Freq: Weekly; **Circ:** 97775 Not Audited
Editor: Bill Baldowski; **Publisher:** Otis Brumby; **Advertising Sales Manager:** Gregg Ewing
Language (s): English
COMMUNITY NEWSPAPER

The Neighbor Newspapers - West Metro 671346
Owner: Neighbor Newspapers
Editorial: 4471 Jimmy Lee Smith Pkwy, Ste 200 and 201C, Hiram, Georgia 30141-2725 **Tel:** 1 770 445-9401
Web site: http://www.neighbornewspapers.com
Circ: 46125
Publisher: Otis Brumby; **Editor:** Monica Burge; **Advertising Sales Manager:** Charlene Kay; **Editor:** Tom Spigolon

Profile: The Neighbor Newspapers - West Metro in Hiram, GA publishes the Paulding Neighbor, the Douglas Neighbor and the Bartow Neighbor.
Language (s): English
COMMUNITY NEWSPAPER

Neighbor to Neighbor News, Inc. 24933
Editorial: 710 Main St, East Aurora, New York 14052-2406 **Tel:** 1 716 652-0320
Email: eanews@eastaurorany.com **Web site:** http://www.eastaurorany.com
Circ: 5600
Publisher: Grant Hamilton; **Advertising Sales Manager:** Sharon Holtz; **Circulation Manager:** Christina Peterman
Profile: Neighbor to Neighbor News, Inc. is a community newspaper publisher servicing the residents of Buffalo and Niagara Falls, NY.
Language (s): English
COMMUNITY NEWSPAPER

The Neighborhood Leader 607308
Owner: Jaramogi Communications
Editorial: 2227 N Broad St, Philadelphia, Pennsylvania 19132-4502 **Tel:** 1 267 970-5632
Email: neighborhoodlead@aol.com
Freq: Bi-Weekly; **Circ:** 20000
Publisher & Editor: Heshimu Jaramogi
Profile: Neighborhood Leader is a local community newspaper for the residents of Philadelphia and the surrounding communities.
Language (s): English
Ad Rate: Full Page Mono 14.84
Currency: United States Dollars
COMMUNITY NEWSPAPER

The Neighborhood News/ Garfield Heights Tribune 22100
Owner: Psenicka (Ellen)
Editorial: 8613 Garfield Blvd, Garfield Heights, Ohio 44125-1317 **Tel:** 1 216 441-2141
Email: nnews1923@aol.com **Web site:** http://www.theneighborhoodnews.com
Freq: Weekly; **Circ:** 15000 Not Audited
Advertising Sales Manager: Michael Psenicka
Profile: Neighborhood News/Garfield Heights Tribune is a local weekly newspaper in Garfield Heights, OH. The publication's editorial mission is to provide news and information to the community. The publication is written for the communities in Garfield Heights and Southeast Ohio. The paper covers all news and events that affect the community.
Language (s): English
Ad Rate: Full Page Mono 10.00
Currency: United States Dollars
COMMUNITY NEWSPAPER

Neighborhood Publications Inc. 24810
Owner: Union Leader Corp.
Editorial: 100 William Loeb Dr, Manchester, New Hampshire 03109-5309 **Tel:** 1 603 314-0447
Email: editor@yourneighborhoodnews.com **Web site:** http://www.newhampshire.com/section/newhampshire14
Circ: 64050 Not Audited
Editor: Christine Heiser; **Advertising Manager:** Charlotte Ingalls; **Editor:** Jerry Liptak
Language (s): English
COMMUNITY NEWSPAPER

The Neshoba Democrat 19895
Owner: Neshoba Democrat Publishing Co. Inc
Editorial: 439 E Beacon St, Philadelphia, Mississippi 39350-2950 **Tel:** 1 601 656-4000
Email: news@neshobademocrat.com **Web site:** http://www.neshobademocrat.com
Freq: Wed; **Circ:** 8200 Not Audited
Advertising Sales Manager: Mandy Meazell; **Publisher & Editor:** Jim Prince; **Circulation Manager:** Aida Ward
Profile: The Neshoba Democrat is a local weekly newspaper serving Neshoba County, MS. It provides local, national and international news to the residents of Neshoba County, MS. Deadlines are Mondays at noon CT.
Language (s): English
Ad Rate: Full Page Mono 10.50
Currency: United States Dollars
COMMUNITY NEWSPAPER

Nevada Journal & Tri-County Times Newspapers 153173
Owner: Stephens Media
Editorial: 922 Lincoln Hwy, Nevada, Iowa 50201-1722 **Tel:** 1 515 382-2161
Circ: 6105 Not Audited
Editor & Publisher: Marlys Barker; **Advertising Sales Manager:** Jerry Simmermaker
Language (s): English
COMMUNITY NEWSPAPER

The New Era 20533
Owner: Scott Miriam Inc.
Editorial: 1313 Main St, Sweet Home, Oregon 97386-1611 **Tel:** 1 541 367-2135
Email: news@sweethomenews.com **Web site:** http://www.sweethomenews.com
Freq: Wed; **Circ:** 7800 Not Audited
Advertising Sales Manager: Miriam Swanson; **Publisher & Editor:** Scott Swanson
Language (s): English
Ad Rate: Full Page Mono 9.90
Currency: United States Dollars
COMMUNITY NEWSPAPER

New Jersey Hills Media Group - Chester 25535
Owner: Parker Publications
Editorial: 530 Main St, Chester, New Jersey 07930-2669 **Tel:** 1 908 879-4100
Web site: http://newjerseyhills.com
Circ: 16600 Not Audited
Editor: Mike Condon
Language (s): English
COMMUNITY NEWSPAPER

New Jersey Hills Media Group - Clinton 515602
Owner: Parker Publications
Editorial: 14 E Main St, Clinton, New Jersey 08809-1394 **Tel:** 1 908 647-1187
Web site: http://newjerseyhills.com
Circ: 23131 Not Audited
COMMUNITY NEWSPAPER

New Jersey Jewish Media Group 25409
Owner: Jewish Media Group
Editorial: 1086 Teaneck Rd, Teaneck, New Jersey 07666-4854 **Tel:** 1 201 837-8818
Email: pr@jewishmediagroup.com **Web site:** http://www.jstandard.com
Circ: 58500 Not Audited
Community News Editor: Beth Chananie; **Publisher:** James Janoff; **Advertising Sales Manager:** Natalie Jay; **Editor:** Joanne Palmer
Language (s): English
COMMUNITY NEWSPAPER

New Jersey Jewish Newspapers 25546
Owner: Jewish Times (The)
Editorial: 901 State Route 10, Whippany, New Jersey 07981-1105 **Tel:** 1 973 739-8110
Email: editorial@njjewishnews.com **Web site:** http://www.njjewishnews.com
Circ: 51968 Not Audited
Community News Editor: Lori Brauner; **Bureau Chief:** Debra Rubin
Profile: New Jersey Jewish News in Whippany, NJ, covers news and events pertinent to Jewish communities in Greater Middlesex County, Greater Monmouth County, and Princeton Mercer Bucks, NJ counties. Published by the Jewish Federation of Greater MetroWest NJ, the North Jersey Jewish News has five editions.
Language (s): English
COMMUNITY NEWSPAPER

New Journal & Guide 21077
Editorial: 5127 E Virginia Beach Blvd, Norfolk, Virginia 23502-3412 **Tel:** 1 757 543-6531
Email: njguide@gmail.com **Web site:** http://www.thenewjournalandguide.com
Freq: Thu; **Circ:** 15000 Not Audited
Publisher & Editor: Brenda Andrews
Profile: New Journal and Guide is a weekly newspaper written for the African-American community of Norfolk, Virginia Beach, Chesapeake, Suffolk, Portsmouth, Hampton, and Newport News, VA. The newspaper aims to bring its readers information on local, national and international news and events.
Language (s): English
Ad Rate: Full Page Mono 15.60
Currency: United States Dollars
COMMUNITY NEWSPAPER

New Milford Spectrum 258034
Owner: Hearst Corporation
Editorial: 45B Main St, New Milford, Connecticut 06776-2807 **Tel:** 1 860 355-7324
Email: ed@ctnews.com **Web site:** http://www.newmilfordspectrum.com
Freq: Fri; **Circ:** 20614 Not Audited
Editor: Norm Cummings
Profile: New Milford Spectrum is a weekly newspaper for the town of New Milford, CT. The paper provides local information on current events, movies, entertainment, recreation and specialty columns.
Language (s): English
Ad Rate: Full Page Mono 17.51
Currency: United States Dollars
COMMUNITY NEWSPAPER

The New Monitor 22398
Owner: Megaphone Media
Tel: 1 248 439-1863
Email: detroitmonitor@gmail.com
Freq: Thu; **Circ:** 35000 Not Audited
Publisher & Editor: Horst Mann; **Advertising Sales Manager:** Roger Smith
Profile: The New Monitor is a weekly newspaper serving residents of Detroit. It covers local news, community events and family-oriented feature stories.
Language (s): English
Ad Rate: Full Page Mono 16.50
Currency: United States Dollars
COMMUNITY NEWSPAPER

New Orleans Data News Weekly 19436
Owner: Data Enterprises Inc.
Editorial: 3501 Napoleon Ave, New Orleans, Louisiana 70125-4843 **Tel:** 1 504 821-7421
Email: datanewsad@bellsouth.net **Web site:** http://www.ladatanews.com
Freq: Sat; **Circ:** 25000 Not Audited
Editor: Edwin Buggage; **Publisher:** Terry Jones
Profile: New Orleans Data News Weekly is a local weekly newspaper serving African-American residents in the New Orleans, LA area. The publication provides information on news and events of interest to the local community. The lead time for New Orleans Data News Weekly is one week.
Language (s): English
Ad Rate: Full Page Mono 74.12
Currency: United States Dollars
COMMUNITY NEWSPAPER

New Pittsburgh Courier 20587
Owner: Real Times, Inc.
Editorial: 315 E Carson St, Pittsburgh, Pennsylvania 15219-1202 **Tel:** 1 412 481-8302
Email: newsroom@newpittsburghcourier.com **Web site:** http://www.newpittsburghcourier.com
Freq: Wed; **Circ:** 10000 Not Audited
Publisher: Rod Doss; **Advertising Sales Manager:** Eric Gaines; **Circulation Manager:** Jeff Marion
Profile: New Pittsburgh Courier is a weekly newspaper written for the African American community in Western Pennsylvania. It covers local news and community events of interest to African Americans.
Language (s): English
Ad Rate: Full Page Mono 26.52
Currency: United States Dollars
COMMUNITY NEWSPAPER

The New Republic 20574
Owner: Gindlesperger (Linda A.)
Editorial: 145 Center St, Meyersdale, Pennsylvania 15552-1320 **Tel:** 1 814 634-8321
Email: news@tnrnewspaper.com **Web site:** http://www.tnrnewspaper.com
Freq: Weekly; **Circ:** 5000 Not Audited
Editor: Kerri Belardi; **Advertising Sales Manager:** George Menser
Language (s): English
Ad Rate: Full Page Mono 14.00
Currency: United States Dollars
COMMUNITY NEWSPAPER

The New Standard 155087
Owner: The Standard Publications
Editorial: 620 Alum Creek Dr Fl 3, Columbus, Ohio 43205-1653 **Tel:** 1 614 371-2595
Email: info@thenewstandard.com **Web site:** http://www.thenewstandardonline.com
Freq: Bi-Weekly; **Circ:** 10000 Not Audited
Publisher & Editor: Doug Smith
Profile: The New Standard is a bi-weekly newspaper written for the Jewish community of Columbus, OH.
Language (s): English
Ad Rate: Full Page Mono 145.00
Currency: United States Dollars
COMMUNITY NEWSPAPER

New Times 21328
Owner: New Times Media Group
Editorial: 1010 Marsh St, San Luis Obispo, California 93401-3630 **Tel:** 1 805 546-8208
Email: letters@newtimesslo.com **Web site:** http://www.newtimesslo.com
Freq: Thu; **Circ:** 35235 Not Audited
Circulation Manager: Jim Parsons; **Publisher:** Bob Rucker
Profile: New Times is published weekly for the residents of San Luis Obispo County, CA and surrounding areas. The newspaper covers local news, community events and lifestyle. Deadlines are on Fridays prior to issue date.
Language (s): English
Ad Rate: Full Page Mono 12.28
Ad Rate: Full Page Colour 13.87
Currency: United States Dollars
COMMUNITY NEWSPAPER

The New Town Press 22420
Owner: Viereck (Karen)
Editorial: 421 Stone Meeting House Rd, Woolwich Township, New Jersey 08085-3609 **Tel:** 1 856 467-3113
Email: newtownpress@comcast.net **Web site:** http://www.newtownpress.com
Freq: Monthly; **Circ:** 15364 Not Audited
Editor & Publisher: Karen Viereck
Profile: The New Town Press is a local monthly newspaper serving the Woolwich Township, NJ area. It provides information on local news and events of interest to the community. Deadlines for the publication are three weeks before issue date. Please contact the editor in chief with any further inquiries.
Language (s): English
Ad Rate: Full Page Mono 12.00
Currency: United States Dollars
COMMUNITY NEWSPAPER

New Ulm Shopper Post Review 21403
Editorial: 514 3rd North St, New Ulm, Minnesota 56073-1705 **Tel:** 1 507 359-2091
Email: nushopper@nujournal.com **Web site:** http://nujournal.com
Freq: Tue; **Circ:** 16500 Not Audited
Advertising Sales Manager: Becky Tykwinski
Profile: New Ulm Shopper Post Review is written for residents of New Ulm, MN and surrounding areas. It provides information on news and events of interest to the local community.
Language (s): English
Ad Rate: Full Page Mono 5.45
Currency: United States Dollars
COMMUNITY NEWSPAPER

New World Publications 70512
Owner: Catholic Archdiocese of Chicago
Editorial: 835 N Rush St, Chicago, Illinois 60611-2030 **Tel:** 1 312 534-7777
Email: editorial@catholicnewworld.com **Web site:** http://www.catholicnewworld.com
Circ: 108000 Not Audited
Editor: Joyce Duriga; **Publisher:** Francis George
Profile: New World Publications' mission is to be the key source of information about the Catholic church in Chicago. It provides news, analysis and commentary about the church at the world, national and local levels and about issues of concern to the Catholic community. It acts as an instrument of evangelization by providing current information and guidance in matters of faith, morals and spiritual life.
Language (s): English
COMMUNITY NEWSPAPER

New York Amsterdam News 20302
Owner: Am News Corp.
Editorial: 2340 Frederick Douglass Blvd, New York, New York 10027-3619 **Tel:** 1 212 932-7400
Email: info@amsterdamnews.com **Web site:** http://www.amsterdamnews.com
Freq: Thu; **Circ:** 12587 Not Audited
Editor: Nayaba Arinde
Profile: New York Amsterdam News covers the African-American community in and around New York City. Includes news and events from the community, social issues and business. Also contains an insert of Healthy Choices, which focuses on the elimination of certain health problems that affect racial and ethnic minorities.
Language (s): English
Ad Rate: Full Page Mono 65.60
Ad Rate: Full Page Colour 76.37
Currency: United States Dollars
COMMUNITY NEWSPAPER

New York Awam 155642
Owner: New York Awam Inc.
Editorial: 373 Broadway Rm D20, New York, New York 10013-3976 **Tel:** 1 212 219-1331
Email: nypawam@aol.com **Web site:** http://newyorkawam.org
Freq: Fri; **Circ:** 50000 Not Audited
Publisher & Editor: Hameed Minhas
Profile: New York AWAM is a weekly, Urdu-language newspaper based in New York.
Language (s): English
Ad Rate: Full Page Mono 60.00
Currency: United States Dollars
COMMUNITY NEWSPAPER

New York Beacon 20306
Owner: Smith Haj Group
Editorial: 237 W 37th St Rm 201, New York, New York 10018-6958 **Tel:** 1 212 213-8585
Email: newyorkbeacon@yahoo.com **Web site:** http://www.newyorkbeacon.net
Freq: Thu; **Circ:** 71000 Not Audited
Profile: New York Beacon is a weekly general newspaper serving the Bronx, Brooklyn, Manhattan, Queens, Staten Island, Westchester and Long Island, NY as well as New Jersey and Connecticut. The newspaper covers sports, personalities, entertainment, health, local and world news and events.
Language (s): English
Ad Rate: Full Page Mono 65.70
Currency: United States Dollars
COMMUNITY NEWSPAPER

The New York Carib News 21773
Owner: Carib News Corporation
Editorial: 1745 Broadway Fl 17, New York, New York 10019-4642 **Tel:** 1 212 944-1991
Email: caribdesk@gmail.com **Web site:** http://www.nycaribnews.com
Freq: Wed; **Circ:** 67000 Not Audited
Editor: Michael Roberts; **Publisher:** Karl Rodney; **Advertising Sales Manager:** June Williams
Profile: Launched in 1983, The New York Carib News, a 50-page tabloid-sized newspaper, is published weekly for the Caribbean-American community of New York City. The publication covers local news, sports, fashion, travel, community events and lifestyle information from and about the Caribbean. Deadlines are on Fridays at 6pm ET.
Language (s): English
Ad Rate: Full Page Mono 45.00
Ad Rate: Full Page Colour 5670.00
Currency: United States Dollars
COMMUNITY NEWSPAPER

The Newberg Graphic 20519
Owner: Eagle Newspapers
Editorial: 500 E Hancock St, Newberg, Oregon 97132-2898 **Tel:** 1 503 538-2181
Email: nbgnews@newberggraphic.com **Web site:** http://www.pamplinmedia.com/newberg-graphic-news
Freq: Sat; **Circ:** 5500 Not Audited
Publisher: Allen Herriges
Profile: The Newberg Graphic is a bi-weekly newspaper written for residents of Newberg, OR and the surrounding communities. Deadlines are on Mondays and Thursdays at 10am PT.
Language (s): English
Ad Rate: Full Page Mono 10.75
Currency: United States Dollars
COMMUNITY NEWSPAPER

The Newberry Observer 20635
Owner: Civitas Media
Editorial: 1716 Main St, Newberry, South Carolina 29108-3548 **Tel:** 1 803 276-0625
Email: news@newberryobserver.com **Web site:** http://www.newberryobserver.com
Freq: 3 Times/Week; **Circ:** 6150 Not Audited
Circulation Manager: Leesa Chavis
Profile: The Newberry (SC) Observer is published weekly for the residents of Newberry, SC and surrounding areas. The newspaper covers local news, sports, local government and community events. Deadlines are on Mondays at 11am ET.
Language (s): English
Ad Rate: Full Page Mono 11.00
Currency: United States Dollars
COMMUNITY NEWSPAPER

Newcity 21614
Owner: New City Communications, Inc.
Editorial: 47 W Polk St Ste 100-223, Chicago, Illinois 60605-2000 **Tel:** 1 312 243-8786
Email: editorial@newcity.com **Web site:** http://www.newcity.com
Freq: Thu; **Circ:** 40000 Not Audited
Profile: New City is published weekly for young adults in Chicago and surrounding communities. The newspaper mainly covers arts & entertainment, but also focuses on topics of interest to young adult audiences, including politics, subcultures, work, money, travel, health & fitness, love, sex, fashion and shopping. They prefer pitches be sent to topic specific editors.
Language (s): English
Ad Rate: Full Page Mono 55.00
Currency: United States Dollars
COMMUNITY NEWSPAPER

Newport Beach Independent 619365
Owner: Firebrand Media LLC
Editorial: 250 Broadway St, Laguna Beach, California 92651-1807 **Tel:** 1 949 715-4100
Web site: http://www.newportbeachindy.com
Circ: 25500
Editor: Christopher Trela
Profile: Founded in June 2009, this newspaper aims to fill the vacuum created by relentless cuts made to local news coverage. Provides news, commentary and information about Newport Beach, CA and Costa Mesa, CA.
Language (s): English
Ad Rate: Full Page Colour 11.07
Currency: United States Dollars
COMMUNITY NEWSPAPER

The Newport Plain Talk 15040
Owner: Jones Media, Inc.
Editorial: 145 E Broadway, Newport, Tennessee 37821-2324 **Tel:** 1 423 623-6171
Email: comments@newportplaintalk.com **Web site:** http://www.newportplaintalk.com
Freq: 3 Times/Week; **Circ:** 6677
Circulation Manager: Pat Helms; **News Editor:** Duay O'Neil
Profile: The Newport Plain Talk is a local newspaper serving Newport, TN. It provides news and events of interest to the local community.
Language (s): English
Ad Rate: Full Page Mono 18.08
Ad Rate: Full Page Colour 19.35
Currency: United States Dollars
COMMUNITY NEWSPAPER

Newport This Week 484129
Editorial: 86 Broadway, Newport, Rhode Island 02840-2750 **Tel:** 1 401 847-7766
Email: news@newportthisweek.net **Web site:** http://www.newportthisweek.com
Freq: Thu; **Circ:** 13800 Not Audited
Publisher & Editor: Lynne Tungett
Profile: Newport This Week, is a weekly newspaper written for the residents of Newport, RI. The editorial content includes community news and events, sports, weather, editorials and a community guide. The editorial lead time is on Mondays at 5pm ET. Advertising deadlines are at noon ET.
Language (s): English
Ad Rate: Full Page Mono 14.00
Currency: United States Dollars
COMMUNITY NEWSPAPER

News & Observer Weeklies - Chapel Hill 587902
Owner: McClatchy Newspapers
Editorial: 505 W Franklin St, Chapel Hill, North Carolina 27516-2315 **Tel:** 1 919 932-2000
Email: chnclerk@newsobserver.com **Web site:** http://chapelhillnews.com
Circ: 92300 Not Audited
Circulation Manager: Sean O'Rourke; **Editor:** Mark Schultz
COMMUNITY NEWSPAPER

News & Reporter 20618
Owner: Landmark Community Newspapers, Inc.
Editorial: 104 York St, Chester, South Carolina 29706-1427 **Tel:** 1 803 385-3177
Email: newsdepartment@onlinechester.com **Web site:** http://www.onlinechester.com
Freq: Fri; **Circ:** 8500 Not Audited
Advertising Sales Manager: Fran Dodds; **Editor:** Travis Jenkins
Profile: News & Reporter is a local newspaper written for the residents of Chester, SC. The paper covers local news, events, sports, business and lifestyles. Deadlines are at noon ET the day prior to issue date.
Language (s): English
Ad Rate: Full Page Mono 8.62
Currency: United States Dollars
COMMUNITY NEWSPAPER

The News and Farmer and Wadley Herald / The Jefferson Reporter 22457
Owner: GateHouse Media Inc.
Editorial: 615 Mulberry St, Louisville, Georgia 30434-1645 **Tel:** 1 478 625-7722
Email: news@thenewsandfarmer.com **Web site:** http://www.thenewsandfarmer.com
Freq: Thu; **Circ:** 5100 Not Audited
Publisher & Editor: Parish L. Howard; **Advertising Sales Manager:** David Irwin
Profile: The News and Farmer and Wadley Herald / The Jefferson Reporter is a local newspaper written for the residents of Louisville, GA. The paper covers local news and events. Deadlines are Mondays at noon ET.
Language (s): English
Ad Rate: Full Page Mono 8.00
Currency: United States Dollars
COMMUNITY NEWSPAPER

News Barometer 22898
Editorial: 30344 Overseas Hwy, Big Pine Key, Florida 33043-3352 **Tel:** 1 305 872-0106
Email: bigpinenews@aol.com **Web site:** http://www.newsbarometer.com
Freq: Fri; **Circ:** 10000 Not Audited
Advertising Sales Manager: Holly Estes; **Publisher & Editor:** Steve Estes
Profile: News Barometer is a local weekly newspaper serving the residents of Big Pine, FL. The publication covers local news and community events. Deadlines are Tuesdays at noon ET.
Language (s): English
Ad Rate: Full Page Mono 7.00
Ad Rate: Full Page Colour 616.00
Currency: United States Dollars
COMMUNITY NEWSPAPER

News Chronicle Company, Inc. 24690
Owner: Sample News Group
Editorial: 22 E King St, Shippensburg, Pennsylvania 17257-1308 **Tel:** 1 717 532-4101
Email: nceditor@gmail.com **Web site:** http://shipnc.com
Circ: 6800 Not Audited
Publisher: Joe Beegle; **Circulation Manager:** Judy Marlin
Profile: News Chronicle Company, Inc. is a community newspaper publisher servicing the residents of Harrisburg and Carlisle, PA.
Language (s): English
COMMUNITY NEWSPAPER

The News Democrat 25427
Owner: Ohio Community Media LLC.
Editorial: 111 E State St, Georgetown, Ohio 45121-1412 **Tel:** 1 937 378-6161
Email: info@newsdemocrat.com **Web site:** http://www.newsdemocrat.com
Freq: Weekly; **Circ:** 26385 Not Audited
Advertising Sales Manager: Billy Maxfield; **Publisher & Editor:** Steven Triplett
Profile: The News-Democrat, located in Georgetown, OH, publishes local weekly newspapers serving in and around Brown County, OH.
Language (s): English
COMMUNITY NEWSPAPER

News Extra 22706
Owner: BH Media Group
Editorial: 310 S Dargan St, Florence, South Carolina 29506-2537 **Tel:** 1 843 317-6397
Web site: http://www.scnow.com
Freq: Wed; **Circ:** 12500 Not Audited
Editor: Don Kausler; **Publisher:** Stephen Wade
Profile: This outlet has requested its main email not be listed. News Extra is a supplemental publication of Morning News, circulated to residents of Florence, SC. The newspaper covers news, community events, sports and arts & entertainment.
Language (s): English
Ad Rate: Full Page Mono 6.00
Currency: United States Dollars
COMMUNITY NEWSPAPER

News For You 22361
Owner: New Readers Press
Editorial: 104 Marcellus St, Syracuse, New York 13204-2952 **Tel:** 1 315 422-9121
Email: nrp@proliteracy.org **Web site:** http://www.newsforyouonline.com
Freq: Wed; **Circ:** 67387 Not Audited
Profile: News for You is a weekly newspaper circulated nationally to schools. It is written at the reading level of four to six. Each issue includes the top news of the week, world news, national news, people in the news and special features such as A Look at Work, Health News and The Law. The publication does not accept press releases or advertisements.
Language (s): English
COMMUNITY NEWSPAPER

The News Guard 20514
Owner: Country Media Inc.
Editorial: 1818 NE 21st St., Lincoln City, Oregon 97367 **Tel:** 1 541 994-2178
Email: info@thenewsguard.com **Web site:** http://www.thenewsguard.com
Freq: Wed; **Circ:** 5500 Not Audited
Profile: The News Guard is a newspaper serving the residents of Lincoln City, OR. The publication covers local news and community events.
Language (s): English
Ad Rate: Full Page Mono 13.60
Currency: United States Dollars
COMMUNITY NEWSPAPER

The News Journal 21363
Owner: Swartz Media
Editorial: 312 Railroad Ave, Florence, South Carolina 29506-2583 **Tel:** 1 843 667-9656
Web site: http://www.florencenewsjournal.com
Freq: Wed; **Circ:** 20500 Not Audited
Editor: Brenda Harrison; **Publisher:** Don Swartz
Profile: The News Journal is a local newspaper written for the residents of Florence, SC.
Language (s): English
Ad Rate: Full Page Mono 15.75
Currency: United States Dollars
COMMUNITY NEWSPAPER

News Journal 25503
Editorial: 215 N Main St, Corbin, Kentucky 40701-1451 **Tel:** 1 606 528-9767
Web site: http://www.thenewsjournal.net
Freq: Wed; **Circ:** 8500 Not Audited
Circulation Manager: Jennifer Benfield; **Publisher & Editor:** Don Estep; **Advertising Sales Manager:** Melissa Hudson; **Community News Editor:** Trent Knuckles; **News Editor:** Mark White
Profile: News Journal is a weekly community newspaper written for the residents of Corbin, KY.
Language (s): English
Ad Rate: Full Page Mono 11.67
Currency: United States Dollars
COMMUNITY NEWSPAPER

News Korea Weekly 518798
Owner: News Korea Texas Inc.
Editorial: 2000 Royal Ln, Ste 200, Dallas, Texas 75229 **Tel:** 1 972 247-9111
Web site: http://www.wnewskorea.com
Freq: Fri; **Circ:** 10500 Not Audited
Publisher: Timothy Choe; **Editor:** Yun Choi
Profile: News Korea Weekly is a free community newspaper providing regional and local news to the Korean American populations of many cities in Texas. The paper is distributed in the Dallas/Ft. Worth area as well as Austin, Houston, San Antonio and Killeen, TX.
Language (s): Korean
Ad Rate: Full Page Mono 4.30
Ad Rate: Full Page Colour 6.45
Currency: United States Dollars
COMMUNITY NEWSPAPER

News Leader 18746
Owner: Community Newspapers Inc.
Editorial: 511 Ash St, Fernandina Beach, Florida 32034-3930 **Tel:** 1 904 261-3696
Email: pegdavis@fbnewsleader.com **Web site:** http://www.fbnewsleader.com
Freq: Fri; **Circ:** 12200 Not Audited
Editor: Peg Davis; **Publisher:** Foy Maloy
Profile: News Leader is a newspaper serving the residents of Fernandina Beach, FL. The publication covers local news, community events and sports.
Language (s): English
Ad Rate: Full Page Mono 24.73
Currency: United States Dollars
COMMUNITY NEWSPAPER

News Leader Newspapers 156305
Owner: Lakeway Publishers of Florida
Editorial: 637 8th St, Clermont, Florida 34711-2159 **Tel:** 1 352 242-9818
Email: thenewsleader@cfl.rr.com **Web site:** http://clermontnewsleader.com
Circ: 84000 Not Audited
Profile: News Leader Newspapers in Clermont, FL publishes the Clermont News Leader, the four Corners News Leader and the Sumter Shopper.
Language (s): English
COMMUNITY NEWSPAPER

The News Observer 18796
Owner: Community Newspapers Inc.
Editorial: 5748 Appalachian Hwy, Blue Ridge, Georgia 30513-4240 **Tel:** 1 706 632-2019
Email: news@thenewsobserver.com **Web site:** http://www.thenewsobserver.com
Freq: Fri; **Circ:** 9100 Not Audited
Publisher: Glenn Harbison
Profile: The News Observer is a bi-weekly newspaper written for the residents of Fannin County, GA and surrounding communities.
Language (s): English
Ad Rate: Full Page Mono 13.65
Currency: United States Dollars
COMMUNITY NEWSPAPER

News Publishing Company - Ringgold 25707
Editorial: 7513 Nashville St, Ringgold, Georgia 30736 **Tel:** 1 706 935-2621
Email: catoosacountynews@catoosanews.com **Web site:** http://www.catoosanews.com
Circ: 8745 Not Audited
Editor: Misty Martin-Chastain; **Editor & Publisher:** Don Stilwell
Language (s): English
COMMUNITY NEWSPAPER

The News Reporter 24142
Owner: News Reporter Company Inc.
Editorial: 127 W Columbus St, Whiteville, North Carolina 28472-4023 **Tel:** 1 910 642-4104
Web site: http://www.whiteville.com
Freq: Mon; **Circ:** 10483 Not Audited
Editor: Dan Biser; **News Editor:** Clara Cartrette; **Advertising Sales Manager:** Max Greer; **Publisher:** James High; **Editor:** Les High
Profile: News Reporter is a weekly newspaper serving the residents of Whiteville, NC.
Language (s): English
Ad Rate: Full Page Mono 12.12
Currency: United States Dollars
COMMUNITY NEWSPAPER

News Review 21557
Editorial: 109 N Sanders St, Ridgecrest, California 93555-3848 **Tel:** 1 760 371-4301
Email: info@news-ridgecrest.com **Web site:** http://www.news-ridgecrest.com
Freq: Wed; **Circ:** 8200
Editor: Patti Cosner; **Publisher:** Patricia Farris
Language (s): English
Ad Rate: Full Page Mono 8.00
Currency: United States Dollars
COMMUNITY NEWSPAPER

The News Times 24143
Owner: News Reporter Company Inc.
Editorial: 114 E 1st Ave, Chadbourn, North Carolina 28431-1802 **Tel:** 1 910 654-3762
Email: newstimes@whiteville.com
Freq: Wed; **Circ:** 9000 Not Audited
Publisher: James High; **Editor:** Bob Morgan
Profile: News Times is a community newspaper written for residents of Chadbourn, NC. It covers local news. They do not want to receive any press information.
Language (s): English
Ad Rate: Full Page Mono 7.00
Currency: United States Dollars
COMMUNITY NEWSPAPER

News-Bulletin Times 25330
Editorial: 501 Madrid St, Castroville, Texas 78009-4570 **Tel:** 1 830 538-2556
Email: cornerstonenews@sbcglobal.net **Web site:** http://www.cornerstonenewspapers.com/news-bulletin.html
Circ: 5200 Not Audited
Publisher: Natalie Spencer
Language (s): English
COMMUNITY NEWSPAPER

News-Democrat & Leader 21818
Owner: Heartland Publications
Editorial: 120 SW Park Sq, Russellville, Kentucky 42276-1436 **Tel:** 1 270 726-8394
Web site: http://www.newsdemocratleader.com
Freq: Fri; **Circ:** 5600 Not Audited
Editor: OJ Stapleton
Profile: News-Democrat & Leader is a newspaper serving the residents of Russellville, KY. The newspaper covers local news and community events.
Language (s): English
Ad Rate: Full Page Mono 6.80
Currency: United States Dollars
COMMUNITY NEWSPAPER

News-Enterprise 24465
Owner: CommunityMedia Corporation
Editorial: 11110 Los Alamitos Blvd Ste 101, Los Alamitos, California 90720-3602 **Tel:** 1 562 431-1397
Email: office@newsenterprise.net **Web site:** http://newsenterprise.net/
Freq: Wed; **Circ:** 30000 Not Audited
Editor: Ted Apodaca; **Publisher:** Vincent Bodiford; **Advertising Sales Manager:** John Griffin
Profile: News-Enterprise is a newspaper serving the residents of Los Alamitos, Rossmoor, Cypress, La Palma, Seal Beach, Hawaiian Gardens and El Dorado Estates, CA. The publication covers local news and community events. Deadlines for the publication are Fridays at 5pm PT.
Language (s): English
Ad Rate: Full Page Mono 16.00
Currency: United States Dollars
COMMUNITY NEWSPAPER

The News-Gazette 21057
Owner: News-Gazette Inc.
Editorial: 20 W Nelson St, Lexington, Virginia 24450-2034 **Tel:** 1 540 463-3113
Web site: http://www.thenews-gazette.com
Freq: Wed; **Circ:** 8150 Not Audited
Publisher: Matt Paxton; **Advertising Sales Manager:** Shannon Tinsley; **Editor:** Darryl Woodson
Profile: The News-Gazette is published weekly for the residents of Lexington, VA and surrounding areas. The newspaper covers local news, sports, education and community events. Deadlines are on Fridays at 4pm ET.
Language (s): English
Ad Rate: Full Page Mono 12.15
Currency: United States Dollars
COMMUNITY NEWSPAPER

News-Herald 21727
Editorial: 201 Simpson Rd, Lenoir City, Tennessee 37771-6567 **Tel:** 1 865 986-6581
Email: news@news-herald.net **Web site:** http://www.news-herald.net
Freq: Mon; **Circ:** 7800 Not Audited
Publisher: Kevin Burcham; **Advertising Sales Manager:** Cindy White; **Editor:** Greg Wilkerson

Profile: News-Herald is a local newspaper written for the residents of Lenoir City, TN.
Language (s): English
Ad Rate: Full Page Mono 8.50
Currency: United States Dollars
COMMUNITY NEWSPAPER

NewsHopper 472869
Owner: NewsHopper
Editorial: 100 Viola Ave. N, Ironton, Minnesota 56401-5549 **Tel:** 1 218 772-0300
Email: hopper@crosbyironton.net **Web site:** http://www.newshopper.net
Freq: Sat; **Circ:** 25000 Not Audited
Profile: NewsHopper is a local newspaper written for the residents of Aitkin, MN.
Language (s): English
Ad Rate: Full Page Mono 12.50
Currency: United States Dollars
COMMUNITY NEWSPAPER

Newsleaders 439855
Owner: Von Meyer Publishing, Inc.
Editorial: 32 1st Ave NW, Saint Joseph, Minnesota 56374-4524 **Tel:** 1 320 363-7741
Email: news@thenewsleaders.com **Web site:** http://www.thenewsleaders.com
Freq: Weekly; **Circ:** 12000
Publisher & Editor: Janelle Von Pinnon
Profile: Newsleaders is a local newspaper in Saint Joseph, MN.
Language (s): English
Ad Rate: Full Page Mono 31.00
Currency: United States Dollars
COMMUNITY NEWSPAPER

The News-Progress 22426
Owner: Womack Newspapers Inc.
Editorial: 850 E 2nd St, Chase City, Virginia 23924 **Tel:** 1 434 372-5156
Email: news@thenewsprogress.com **Web site:** http://www.thenewsprogress.com
Freq: Wed; **Circ:** 5700 Not Audited
Publisher: Leigh Shields; **Editor:** Dallas Weston
Profile: The News-Progress is a weekly newspaper serving residents of Chase City, VA.
Language (s): English
Ad Rate: Full Page Mono 5.50
Currency: United States Dollars
COMMUNITY NEWSPAPER

News-Record 139777
Owner: Gannett Co. Inc.
Editorial: 306 W Washington St, Appleton, Wisconsin 54911-5452 **Tel:** 1 920 993-1000
Email: information@newsrecord.net **Web site:** http://www.postcrescent.com/
Freq: Wed; **Circ:** 23900 Not Audited
Publisher: Pamela Henson; **Advertising Manager:** Sandy Prinsen; **Editor:** Rachel Rausch
Profile: News-Record is a local newspaper written for the residents of Neenah, WI. The paper covers news, sports and arts & entertainment. This outlet offers RSS (Really Simple Syndication.)
Language (s): English
Ad Rate: Full Page Mono 15.35
Currency: United States Dollars
COMMUNITY NEWSPAPER

The News-Record & Sentinel 71093
Owner: Gannett Co., Inc.
Editorial: 58 Back St., Marshall, North Carolina 28753-9115 **Tel:** 1 828 649-1075
Email: info@newsrecordandsentinel.com **Web site:** http://www.newsrecordandsentinel.com
Freq: Wed; **Circ:** 6700 Not Audited
Profile: The News-Record & Sentinel is written for residents of Hot Springs, Marshall, Mars Hill and Weaverville, NC.
Language (s): English
Ad Rate: Full Page Mono 7.00
Currency: United States Dollars
COMMUNITY NEWSPAPER

News-Register 20516
Owner: News-Register Publishing Co.
Editorial: 611 NE 3rd St, McMinnville, Oregon 97128-4518 **Tel:** 1 503 472-5114
Email: news@newsregister.com **Web site:** http://www.newsregister.com
Freq: Sat; **Circ:** 10921 Not Audited
Editor & Publisher: Jeb Bladine; **Advertising Sales Manager:** Christy Nielsen; **Editor:** Racheal Winter
Profile: News-Register is published weekly for the residents of McMinnville, OR and surrounding areas. The newspaper covers local news, sports and community events.
Language (s): English
Ad Rate: Full Page Mono 10.00
Currency: United States Dollars
COMMUNITY NEWSPAPER

The News-Sun 18765
Owner: Sun Coast Media Group LLC
Editorial: 2227 US Highway 27 S, Sebring, Florida 33870-4936 **Tel:** 1 863 385-6155
Email: editor@newssun.com **Web site:** http://www.newssun.com
Freq: Fri; **Circ:** 17000 Not Audited
Editor: Scott Dressel
Profile: The News-Sun in Sebring, FL is a weekly newspaper serving residents of Highlands County, FL. Coverage includes local news, features, lifestyle, sports and business.
Language (s): English
Ad Rate: Full Page Mono 16.39
Currency: United States Dollars
COMMUNITY NEWSPAPER

Newstime 592467
Owner: Lakeway Publishers, Inc.
Editorial: 11102 Veterans Memorial Pkwy, Lake Saint Louis, Missouri 63367-1113 **Tel:** 1 636 625-3081
Web site: http://www.newstime-mo.com
Freq: Sat; **Circ:** 17000
Publisher: Carol Clark; **Editor:** Tim Hager
Profile: Newstime is a local community newspaper written for the residents of Lake Saint Louis, MO and the surrounding communities.
Language (s): English
Ad Rate: Full Page Mono 10.50
Ad Rate: Full Page Colour 60.50
Currency: United States Dollars
COMMUNITY NEWSPAPER

News-Times 21336
Owner: News Media Corp.
Editorial: 831 NE Avery St, Newport, Oregon 97365-3033 **Tel:** 1 541 265-8571
Web site: http://www.newportnewstimes.com
Freq: Fri; **Circ:** 10300 Not Audited
Editor: Steve Card; **Advertising Sales Manager:** Barb Moore
Profile: News-Times is published weekly for residents of Lincoln County, OR and surrounding areas. It covers local news, sports, business, entertainment and events.
Language (s): English
Ad Rate: Full Page Mono 19.76
Currency: United States Dollars
COMMUNITY NEWSPAPER

Niagara Frontier Publications 24762
Owner: Mazenauer (Skip)
Editorial: 1859 Whitehaven Rd, Grand Island, New York 14072-1803 **Tel:** 1 716 773-7676
Web site: http://www.wnypapers.com
Circ: 31350 Not Audited
Editor: Larry Austin; **Publisher:** Skip Mazenauer; **Circulation Manager:** Lisa Sorri
Profile: Niagara Frontier Publications in Grand Island, NY is a publisher of community newspapers.
Language (s): English
COMMUNITY NEWSPAPER

Nichi Bei Weekly 651862
Owner: Nichi Bei Foundation
Editorial: 1832 Buchanan St Ste 207, San Francisco, California 94115-3252 **Tel:** 1 415 673-1009
Email: news@nichibeiweekly.org **Web site:** http://www.nichibei.org
Freq: Thu; **Circ:** 8000
Profile: Nichi Bei Weekly offers local news, sports and events primarily to Japanese communities within California, with some limited national distribution.
Language (s): English
Ad Rate: Full Page Mono 23.07
Currency: United States Dollars
COMMUNITY NEWSPAPER

The Nicholas Chronicle 21275
Owner: Yeager (Charlotte)
Editorial: 718 Broad St, Summersville, West Virginia 26651-1648 **Tel:** 1 304 872-2251
Email: news@nicholaschronicle.com **Web site:** https://www.nicholaschronicle.com
Freq: Thu; **Circ:** 8700 Not Audited
Advertising Sales Manager: Steve Beal; **News Editor:** Ray Corbin; **Editor:** Matthew Yeager
Profile: The Nicholas Chronicle provides news and information for residents of Nicholas County, WV and the surrounding communities. Deadlines are Fridays at 5pm ET before the issue date.
Language (s): English
Ad Rate: Full Page Mono 5.30
Currency: United States Dollars
COMMUNITY NEWSPAPER

NikkeiWest 73707
Editorial: 123 E San Carlos St Ste 521, San Jose, California 95112-3680 **Tel:** 1 408 998-0920
Email: editor@nikkeiwest.com **Web site:** http://www.nikkeiwest.com
Freq: Bi-Weekly; **Circ:** 12000 Not Audited
Publisher & Editor: Jeffrey Kimoto
Profile: NikkeiWest is for Japanese Americans residing in northern California. The editorial content includes local and national news, events, sports, history and other topics of general interest.
Language (s): English
Ad Rate: Full Page Mono 6.50
Ad Rate: Full Page Colour 1700.00
Currency: United States Dollars
COMMUNITY NEWSPAPER

NJ Advance Media Publishing - Flemington 24625
Owner: NJ Advance Media
Editorial: 8 Minneakoning Rd, Flemington, New Jersey 08822-5725 **Tel:** 1 908 782-4747
Web site: http://www.nj.com/hunterdon
Circ: 151548
Editor: Michael Kelly; **Circulation Manager:** Mary Krovatin; **News Editor:** Beth Wade
Profile: NJ Advance Media Publishing is a weekly community newspaper publisher serving the residents of New Jersey.
Language (s): English
COMMUNITY NEWSPAPER

NJToday.net 69860
Owner: CMD Media
Tel: 1 908 352-3100
Email: news@njtoday.net **Web site:** http://www.njtoday.net
Freq: Weekly; **Circ:** 35000 Not Audited
Circulation Manager: Steve Campbell; **Editor:** Paul Hadsall; **Publisher:** Lisa McCormick
Profile: NJToday.net is a weekly newspaper serving Union and Middlesex County, NJ, and distributed throughout the area. The paper covers news and events of interest to local residents.
Language (s): English
Ad Rate: Full Page Mono 40.00
Currency: United States Dollars
COMMUNITY NEWSPAPER

Nogales International & Weekly Bulletin 87105
Owner: Wick Communications Inc.
Editorial: 268 W View Point Dr, Nogales, Arizona 85621-4114 **Tel:** 1 520 375-5760
Web site: http://www.nogalesinternational.com/the_bulletin
Circ: 6300 Not Audited
Advertising Sales Manager: Maria Castillo; **Circulation Manager:** Ricardo Villareal
Profile: Nogales International and Weekly Bulletin are sister newspapers covering Santa Cruz County, AZ. Nogales International is the flagship paper, publishing on Tuesdays and Fridays, while the Weekly Bulletin publishes Wednesdays.
Language (s): English
COMMUNITY NEWSPAPER

Nokoa - The Observer 22129
Owner: Evans (Akwasi)
Editorial: 5200 King Charles Dr, Austin, Texas 78724-5318 **Tel:** 1 512 499-8713
Email: nokoatheobserver@gmail.com **Web site:** http://www.nokoanewspaper.com/
Freq: Thu; **Circ:** 5000 Not Audited
Publisher & Editor: Akwasi Evans
Profile: Nokoa - The Observer is a weekly newspaper serving the residents of Austin, TX. The publication covers local news and events.
Language (s): English
Ad Rate: Full Page Mono 35.00
Currency: United States Dollars
COMMUNITY NEWSPAPER

The Nome Nugget 18476
Owner: McGuire (Nancy)
Editorial: 304 Front St, Nome, Alaska 99762 **Tel:** 1 907 443-5235
Email: nugget@nomenugget.com **Web site:** http://www.nomenugget.net
Freq: Thu; **Circ:** 6000 Not Audited
Profile: Nome Nugget is the weekly, local newspaper for the Nome, AK area. The newspaper covers local news, business, sports and arts & entertainment stories. The newspaper also covers national and statewide stories if they have a direct impact on the newspaper's readership.
Language (s): English
Ad Rate: Full Page Mono 24.00
Currency: United States Dollars
COMMUNITY NEWSPAPER

Nordstjernan 22500
Owner: Swedish News Inc.
Tel: 1 212 490-3900
Email: info@nordstjernan.com **Web site:** http://www.nordstjernan.com
Freq: Semi-Monthly; **Circ:** 18000 Not Audited
Editor & Publisher: Ulf Martensson
Profile: Nordstjernan is a semi-monthly newspaper focusing on news from Sweden and the United States dealing with business, financial, commercial, political, sports and current events. The paper is 80 percent in English and 20 percent in Swedish.
Language (s): English
Ad Rate: Full Page Mono 29.75
Ad Rate: Full Page Colour 6400.00
Currency: United States Dollars
COMMUNITY NEWSPAPER

Normal Newspapers 25087
Owner: Pyne, (Edward)
Editorial: 1702 W College Ave Ste G, Normal, Illinois 61761-2793 **Tel:** 1 309 454-5476
Email: thenormalite@gmail.com
Circ: 5900 Not Audited
Editor: Patty Fye; **Publisher:** Edward Pyne
Language (s): English
COMMUNITY NEWSPAPER

North America Weekly Times 791575
Owner: Times, North America
Editorial: 800-200 Consumers Rd 800, North York, Ontario M2J 4R4 **Tel:** 1 416 850-1100
Email: info@naweeklytimes.com **Web site:** http://www.naweeklytimes.com
Freq: Weekly; **Circ:** 12000
Publisher & Editor: Gary Gao
Profile: The North America Weekly Times is a weekly newspaper providing International and Community News to the Chinese community in North York, ON. The newspaper also provides insight of community cultural events taking place in the area.
Language (s): Chinese
Ad Rate: Full Page Mono 7.00
Currency: Canada Dollars
COMMUNITY NEWSPAPER

North American Post 22647
Editorial: 519 6th Ave S Ste 200, Seattle, Washington 98104-2878 **Tel:** 1 206 623-0100
Email: info@napost.com **Web site:** http://www.napost.com
Freq: Wed; **Circ:** 6000 Not Audited
Publisher: Tomio Moriguchi; **Editor:** Shiho Sasaki
Profile: North American Post is written for Japanese Americans in Seattle. It is published in Japanese and English.
Language (s): English, Japanese
Ad Rate: Full Page Mono 15.25
Currency: United States Dollars
COMMUNITY NEWSPAPER

North Attleborough Free Press 21512
Owner: GateHouse Media Inc.
Editorial: 31 N Washington St, North Attleboro, Massachusetts 02760-1650 **Tel:** 1 508 699-6755
Email: news@nafreepress.com **Web site:** http://www.nafreepress.com
Freq: Wed; **Circ:** 17000 Not Audited
Advertising Manager: Cheryl Robinson
Profile: North Attleborough Free Press is written for residents in North Attleborough, MA. It covers local news and events. Deadlines for the paper are on Fridays prior to the issue date at noon ET.
Language (s): English
Ad Rate: Full Page Mono 10.00
Currency: United States Dollars
COMMUNITY NEWSPAPER

North Augusta Today 831526
Owner: GateHouse Media Inc.
Editorial: 725 Broad St, Augusta, Georgia 30901-1336 **Tel:** 1 706 724-0851
Web site: http://natoday.augusta.com
Freq: Weekly; **Circ:** 17000
Profile: North Augusta Today is a free weekly community newspaper under the Augusta (GA) Chronicle banner, and includes local news, sports, education and community events for the North Augusta, GA community.
Language (s): English
COMMUNITY NEWSPAPER

North Bay Bohemian 21712
Owner: Metro Publishing Group
Editorial: 847 5th St, Santa Rosa, California 95404-4526 **Tel:** 1 707 527-1200
Web site: http://www.bohemian.com
Freq: Weekly; **Circ:** 25000 Not Audited
Editor: Stett Holbrook; **Publisher:** Rosemary Olson
Profile: North Bay Bohemian in Santa Rosa, CA is a weekly newspaper that covers local news, business, entertainment and sports in Sonoma, Napa and Marin counties.
Language (s): English
Ad Rate: Full Page Mono 32.76
Currency: United States Dollars
COMMUNITY NEWSPAPER

North Country This Week 22446
Owner: Shumway (William)
Editorial: 19 Depot St, Potsdam, New York 13676-1191 **Tel:** 1 315 265-1000
Email: news@northcountrynow.com **Web site:** http://www.northcountrynow.com
Freq: Wed; **Circ:** 19159 Not Audited
Advertising Sales Manager: John Basham; **News Editor:** Craig Freilich; **Publisher:** William Shumway
Profile: North Country This Week is the weekly, local newspaper for St. Lawrence County, NY. The newspaper covers local news, business, sports and arts & entertainment stories. The newspaper also covers national and statewide stories if they have a direct impact on the newspaper's readership.
Language (s): English
Ad Rate: Full Page Mono 12.45
Currency: United States Dollars
COMMUNITY NEWSPAPER

North Fort Myers Neighbor 376367
Owner: Breeze Newspapers
Editorial: 2510 Del Prado Blvd S, Cape Coral, Florida 33904-5750 **Tel:** 1 239 656-5248
Email: nfmneighbor@breezenewspapers.com **Web site:** http://www.breezenewspapers.com
Freq: Wed; **Circ:** 24000 Not Audited
Publisher: Scott Blonde; **Advertising Sales Manager:** Malcolm Johnson; **Editor:** Chris Strine
Profile: North Fort Myers Neighbor is a weekly newspaper written for residents of North Fort Myers, FL. It covers community events, school news and sports, business profiles, real estate, human interest stories and government issues that affect local residents. Editorial and advertising deadlines are on Fridays at 5pm ET.
Language (s): English
Ad Rate: Full Page Mono 11.62
Currency: United States Dollars
COMMUNITY NEWSPAPER

North Georgia News 24206
Editorial: 266 Cleveland St, Blairsville, Georgia 30512-8537 **Tel:** 1 706 745-6343
Email: ngnews@windstream.net **Web site:** http://www.nganews.com
Freq: Wed; **Circ:** 10800 Not Audited
Editor: Charles Duncan; **Advertising Sales Manager:** Justin Owenvy; **Publisher:** Kenneth West
Profile: North Georgia News is a local newspaper written for the residents of Blairsville, GA. The paper covers local news, business, sports and arts & entertainment.
Language (s): English

Ad Rate: Full Page Mono 9.50
Currency: United States Dollars
COMMUNITY NEWSPAPER

North Haven Citizen 358849
Owner: Record-Journal Publishing Company
Editorial: 11 Crown St, Meriden, Connecticut 6450 **Tel:** 1 203 235-1661
Email: news@thenorthhavencitizen.com **Web site:** http://www.thenorthhavencitizen.com
Freq: Fri; **Circ:** 11500 Not Audited
News Editor: Nick Carroll; **Publisher:** Eliot White
Profile: North Haven Citizen is written for the residents of North Haven, CT. It seeks to provide the readers with community news and information through stories on local news, sports, community groups, businesses, politics and schools. It encourages the submissions of photos, stories, events, schedules, press releases and birth and wedding announcements.
Language (s): English
Ad Rate: Full Page Mono 11.35
Currency: United States Dollars
COMMUNITY NEWSPAPER

North Jackson Progress 18530
Owner: Glass (Larry O.)
Editorial: 1202 Kentucky Ave., Stevenson, Alabama 35772-5411 **Tel:** 1 256 437-2395
Email: njprogresslog@aol.com **Web site:** http://www.northjacksonprogress.com
Freq: Mon; **Circ:** 5200 Not Audited
Publisher & Editor: Larry Glass; **Circulation Manager:** Machelle McCrary
Profile: The North Jackson Progress is a weekly newspaper serving the area of Stevenson, AL and the surrounding communities that make up North Jackson. The newspaper covers local news, sports, business, and arts and entertainment issues that impact local residents. The publication is intended for a local readership.
Language (s): English
Ad Rate: Full Page Mono 7.90
Currency: United States Dollars
COMMUNITY NEWSPAPER

North Jersey Media Group - Cresskill 63132
Owner: Gannett Co., Inc./North Jersey Media Group
Editorial: 210 Knickerbocker Rd Ste 1200, Cresskill, New Jersey 07626-1801 **Tel:** 1 201 894-6700
Web site: http://www.northjersey.com
Circ: 105496 Not Audited
Editor: Chris Lang
Language (s): English
COMMUNITY NEWSPAPER

North Kitsap Herald 22470
Owner: Sound Publishing, Inc./Kitsap News Group
Editorial: 19351 8th Ave NE Ste 106, Poulsbo, Washington 98370-8710 **Tel:** 1 360 779-4464
Email: editor@northkitsapherald.com **Web site:** http://www.kitsapdailynews.com
Freq: Fri; **Circ:** 12800 Not Audited
Publisher: Donna Etchey; **Editor:** Richard Walker
Profile: North Kitsap Herald is a community newspaper serving the Poulsbo, Kingston, Suquamish, Hansville, Indianola and Little Boston, WA area. The paper offers local news, features, editorial and sports. Send all editorial correspondence to the PO Box address. Send advertising correspondence to North Kitsap Herald, c/o Sound Publishing, 7689 NE Day Rd., Bainbridge Island, WA 98110. Ads will also run in the paper's sister publications, including Bainbridge Island Review, Bremerton Patriot and Port Orchard Independent.
Language (s): English
Ad Rate: Full Page Mono 18.70
Currency: United States Dollars
COMMUNITY NEWSPAPER

North Lawndale Community News 231172
Owner: Strategic Human Services
Editorial: 325 S California Ave, Chicago, Illinois 60612-3669 **Tel:** 1 773 940-1953
Email: nlcn1@yahoo.com **Web site:** http://www.nlcn.org
Freq: Weekly; **Circ:** 15000
Publisher & Editor: Isaac Lewis; **Advertising Sales Manager:** Andre Stokes
Profile: North Lawndale Community News is published weekly for African-American residents of Chicago.
Language (s): English
Ad Rate: Full Page Mono 30.00
Currency: United States Dollars
COMMUNITY NEWSPAPER

North Myrtle Beach Times 29420
Owner: Polly Lowman
Editorial: 203 Highway 17 N, North Myrtle Beach, South Carolina 29582-2937 **Tel:** 1 843 249-3525
Email: nmbtimes@sc.rr.com **Web site:** http://www.nmbtimes.com
Freq: Thu; **Circ:** 12400 Not Audited
Editor: Polly Lowman
Profile: North Myrtle Beach Times is a local newspaper written for the residents of North Myrtle Beach, SC.
Language (s): English
Ad Rate: Full Page Mono 8.00
Currency: United States Dollars
COMMUNITY NEWSPAPER

North Raleigh News & Midtown Raleigh News 823919
Owner: McClatchy Newspapers
Editorial: 215 S McDowell St, Raleigh, North Carolina 27601-1331
Email: nrnews@newsobserver.com **Web site:** http://www.newsobserver.com/news/local/community/north-raleigh-news/
Freq: Weekly
Language (s): English
COMMUNITY NEWSPAPER

North River News 21564
Owner: North River Publishing
Editorial: 604 6th St W, Palmetto, Florida 34221-5136 **Tel:** 1 941 722-1088
Email: nr.news@verizon.net **Web site:** http://www.northrivernewsonline.com
Freq: Thu; **Circ:** 9000 Not Audited
Editor: Barbara Nielsen
Profile: North River News is a local newspaper written for the residents of Palmetto, FL. The newspaper covers local news and events.
Language (s): English
Ad Rate: Full Page Mono 9.65
Currency: United States Dollars
COMMUNITY NEWSPAPER

North Shore Today 432294
Editorial: 17 W John St Unit 1, Hicksville, New York 11801-1045 **Tel:** 1 516 496-4300
Email: events@northshoretoday.com **Web site:** http://www.northshoretoday.com
Freq: Weekly; **Circ:** 150000
Editor: Rachel Schlau
Profile: North Shore Today is a weekly community newspaper featuring fashion and community events, and news, and dining reviews.
Language (s): English
COMMUNITY NEWSPAPER

The North Shore Weekend 838036
Owner: JWC Media
Editorial: 445 Sheridan Rd Ste 100, Highwood, Illinois 60040-1317 **Tel:** 1 847 926-0911
Web site: http://www.northshoreweekend.com
Freq: Weekly
Profile: North Shore Weekend is a weekly newspaper covering the North Shore region in the Chicagoland area.
Language (s): English
COMMUNITY NEWSPAPER

The Northcountry News 258042
Owner: Flagg (Bryan) & Flagg (Suzanne)
Tel: 1 603 764-5807
Email: ncnewsnh@gmail.com **Web site:** http://www.northcountrynewsnh.com
Freq: Bi-Weekly; **Circ:** 9000 Not Audited
Publisher: Bryan Flagg; **Editor:** Suzanne Flagg
Profile: The Northcountry News is a newspaper for the residents of Warren, NH. It contains local happenings, editorials, news, political views, educational issues, the outdoors, cooking, history and sports. The paper was launched in April 1989.
Language (s): English
Ad Rate: Full Page Mono 6.00
Ad Rate: Full Page Colour 7.00
Currency: United States Dollars
COMMUNITY NEWSPAPER

Northeast and North Forest Newspapers 155315
Owner: Grafikpress Corp.
Editorial: 5327 Aldine Mail Rd, Houston, Texas 77039-4919 **Tel:** 1 281 449-9945
Email: nenewsroom@aol.com **Web site:** http://www.nenewsroom.com
Circ: 45000 Not Audited
Publisher: Gilbert Hoffman
Profile: Northeast and North Forest Newspapers cover the local area ONLY. They do not want to be contacted via e-mail.
Language (s): English
COMMUNITY NEWSPAPER

The Northeast Georgian 24330
Owner: Community Newspapers Inc.
Editorial: 2440 Old Athens Hwy, Cornelia, Georgia 30531-5364 **Tel:** 1 706 778-4215
Email: news@thenortheastgeorgian.com **Web site:** http://www.thenortheastgeorgian.com
Freq: Fri; **Circ:** 8850 Not Audited
Editor: Rob Moore; **Publisher:** Alan NeSmith
Profile: The Northeast Georgian is a local newspaper that is published twice a week for residents of Habersham County, GA. The publication's editorial mission is to publish a distinguished and profitable newspaper that is community oriented. The editorial deadlines are 8am ET on Friday for the Tuesday edition and 8am ET on Wednesday for the Friday edition.
Language (s): English
Ad Rate: Full Page Mono 17.85
Ad Rate: Full Page Colour 1450.00
Currency: United States Dollars
COMMUNITY NEWSPAPER

The Northeast News 338014
Owner: Linc Inc.
Editorial: 7707 Saint Andrews Rd, Irmo, South Carolina 29063-2835 **Tel:** 1 803 865-5563
Email: info@thenortheastnews.com **Web site:** http://www.thenortheastnews.com
Freq: Thu; **Circ:** 10000 Not Audited
Editor: Keith Boudreaux; **Advertising Sales Manager:** Jacqueline Kleynenberg; **Publisher:** Kirk Luther
Profile: The Northeast News is written for the residents of Columbia, SC. It covers community news and events, sports, features and editorials with a local focus.
Language (s): English
Ad Rate: Full Page Mono 9.80
Currency: United States Dollars
COMMUNITY NEWSPAPER

Northeast News 861918
Editorial: 5715 St. John Ave., Kansas City, Missouri 64123 **Tel:** 1 816 241-0765
Email: northeastnews@socket.net **Web site:** http://northeastnews.net
Freq: Weekly; **Circ:** 12450
Publisher: Michael Bushnell; **Editor:** Leslie Collins; **Advertising Manager:** Joe Keefhaver
Profile: Northeast News is a weekly community newspaper covering the northeast Kansas City area, including local news, sports, features and community events.
Language (s): English
Ad Rate: Full Page Mono 9.00
Currency: United States Dollars
COMMUNITY NEWSPAPER

Northeaster 238987
Owner: Pro Media Inc.
Editorial: 2844 Johnson St NE, Minneapolis, Minnesota 55418-3056 **Tel:** 1 612 788-9003
Email: contact@mynortheaster.com **Web site:** http://www.mynortheaster.com/
Circ: 63500 Not Audited
Editor and Publisher: Margo Ashmore
Profile: Northeaster in Minneapolis, MN is a community newspaper.
Language (s): English
COMMUNITY NEWSPAPER

Northend Agent's, LLC 22183
Editorial: 680 Blue Hills Ave, Hartford, Connecticut 06112-1210 **Tel:** 1 860 827-1010
Email: northendagents@aol.com **Web site:** http://www.northendagents.com
Freq: Wed; **Circ:** 40000 Not Audited
Editor: John Allen
Profile: Northend Agent's, LLC is a weekly newspaper which provides its readers with the latest in news and information. It cover local news, community news, and lifestyle issues in the Hartford, CT area.
Language (s): English
Ad Rate: Full Page Mono 15.30
Ad Rate: Full Page Colour 1600.00
Currency: United States Dollars
COMMUNITY NEWSPAPER

The Northern Cross 391060
Owner: Diocese of Duluth
Editorial: 2830 E 4th St, Duluth, Minnesota 55812-1501 **Tel:** 1 218 724-9111
Web site: http://www.dioceseduluth.org
Freq: Monthly; **Circ:** 30000 Not Audited
Advertising Sales Manager: Pauline Davies; **Editor:** Kyle Eller; **Publisher:** Paul Sirba
Profile: The Northern Cross is a monthly newspaper for the Diocese of Duluth, MN. It is mailed on the first Friday of the month. It strives to keep Catholics in the Arrowhead area of Minnesota well informed about their faith.
Language (s): English
Ad Rate: Full Page Mono 45.00
Ad Rate: Full Page Colour 145.00
Currency: United States Dollars
COMMUNITY NEWSPAPER

Northern Express 257015
Editorial: 109 S Union St Ste 303, Traverse City, Michigan 49684-2575 **Tel:** 1 231 947-8787
Email: info@northernexpress.com **Web site:** http://www.northernexpress.com
Freq: Mon; **Circ:** 33000 Not Audited
Publisher & Editor: Luke Haase; **Advertising Sales Manager:** Kathy Johnson
Profile: Northern Express is written for residents of Traverse City, MI. Its mission is to provide readers with the latest in local nightlife, news, opinions, events and happenings.
Language (s): English
Ad Rate: Full Page Mono 19.80
Currency: United States Dollars
COMMUNITY NEWSPAPER

The Northern Light 24243
Owner: Point Roberts Press, Inc.
Editorial: 225 Marine Dr Ste 200, Blaine, Washington 98230-4052 **Tel:** 1 360 332-1777
Email: editor@thenorthernlight.com **Web site:** http://www.thenorthernlight.com
Freq: Weekly; **Circ:** 10300 Not Audited
Publisher & Editor: Patrick Grubb
Profile: The Northern Light is a community newspaper serving the towns of Blaine and Birch Bay, WA, and the surrounding areas. It includes local news, features, sports and community events.
Language (s): English
Ad Rate: Full Page Mono 23.00
Currency: United States Dollars
COMMUNITY NEWSPAPER

Northern Neck News 28912
Owner: Lakeway Publishers, Inc.
Editorial: 132 Court Circle, Warsaw, Virginia 22572 **Tel:** 1 804 333-6397
Email: nnneditor@lcs.net **Web site:** http://www.northernnecknews.com
Freq: Wed; **Circ:** 9000 Not Audited
Editor: Lee Francis; **Publisher:** Mosby Wigginton
Profile: Northern Neck News provides the latest local news and information for the residents of Northern Neck, VA. Deadlines for the publication are Fridays at noon before issue date.
Language (s): English
Ad Rate: Full Page Mono 10.90
Currency: United States Dollars
COMMUNITY NEWSPAPER

Northern Sentry 383225
Owner: BHG Inc.
Editorial: 315 Main St S Ste 202, Minot, North Dakota 58701-3956 **Tel:** 1 701 839-0946
Email: news@bhgnews.com **Web site:** http://www.northernsentry.com
Freq: Fri; **Circ:** 6000 Not Audited
Editor: Tonya Stuart
Profile: Northern Sentry provides news, events and information to military personnel, civilian employees and residents of the Minot Air Force Base. Deadlines are on Fridays at noon CT.
Language (s): English
Ad Rate: Full Page Mono 8.85
Currency: United States Dollars
COMMUNITY NEWSPAPER

Northland Neighbors 551760
Owner: McClatchy Newspapers
Editorial: 17 W 12th St, Columbus, Georgia 31901-5254 **Tel:** 1 706 324-5526
Email: neighbors@ledger-enquirer.com
Freq: Wed; **Circ:** 51000
Editor: Marcia McAllister
Profile: Northland Neighbors is a weekly paper that is inserted in the Columbus (GA) Ledger-Enquirer and is also distributed on racks throughout North Columbus and South Harris County, GA. Coverage is highly localized and features stories about youth, sports, recreation, family, home, dining and entertainment.
Language (s): English
Ad Rate: Full Page Mono 17.00
Currency: United States Dollars
COMMUNITY NEWSPAPER

The Northport Gazette 86563
Owner: Millport Gazette Inc. (The)
Editorial: 401 20th Ave Ste 5, Northport, Alabama 35476-5045 **Tel:** 1 205 759-3091
Email: northportgazette@northportgazette.com **Web site:** http://www.northportgazette.com
Freq: Wed; **Circ:** 8000 Not Audited
Editor & Publisher: Paula Bryant; **Advertising Manager:** Lateekia Gunter
Profile: The Northport Gazette is a local community newspaper for the residents of Northport, AL and the surrounding communities.
Language (s): English
Ad Rate: Full Page Mono 7.50
Currency: United States Dollars
COMMUNITY NEWSPAPER

Northside Sun 19879
Owner: Emmerich Newspapers Inc.
Editorial: 246 Briarwood Dr #101, Jackson, Mississippi 39206-3027 **Tel:** 1 601 957-1122
Email: sun@northsidesun.com **Web site:** http://www.northsidesun.com
Freq: Thu; **Circ:** 11000 Not Audited
Publisher: Wyatt Emmerich; **Circulation Manager:** Dani Poe; **Editor:** Jimmye Sweat
Profile: Northside Sun's mission is to provide its readers with the local news and information. The publication is written for residents of northern Mississippi.
Language (s): English
Ad Rate: Full Page Mono 18.30
Currency: United States Dollars
COMMUNITY NEWSPAPER

Northwest Guardian 22233
Owner: McClatchy Newspapers
Editorial: Fort Lewis Military Base, Building 2026B, Fort Lewis, Washington 98433 **Tel:** 1 253 967-0171
Email: nwgeditor@thenewstribune.com **Web site:** http://www.nwguardian.com
Freq: Fri; **Circ:** 20700 Not Audited
Publisher: Charles Jacoby; **Editor:** David Kuhns
Profile: Northwest Guardian is a community newspaper that serves active military personnel, civilians and employees of the army base in Fort Lewis, WA. Although the paper is printed and distributed by The News Tribune in Tacoma, WA all editorial content is created by military staff. Contact The News Tribune for advertising inquiries by phone at (253)597-8742, or by mail at: PO Box 11000; Tacoma, WA 98411.
Language (s): English
Ad Rate: Full Page Mono 35.85
Currency: United States Dollars
COMMUNITY NEWSPAPER

Northwest Indiana Catholic Newspaper 750373
Owner: Northwest Indiana Catholic Publications
Editorial: 9292 Broadway, Merrillville, Indiana 46410-7047 **Tel:** 1 219 769-9292
Email: nwic@dcgary.org **Web site:** http://www.nwicatholic.com
Freq: Weekly; **Circ:** 15000
Circulation Manager: Carol Macinga
Profile: Northwest Indiana Catholic Newspaper is a community newspaper for the Diocese of Gary, IN.
Language (s): English
Ad Rate: Full Page Mono 10.14

Currency: United States Dollars
COMMUNITY NEWSPAPER

Northwest Observer 128731
Owner: PS Communications Inc.
Editorial: 1616 Nc Highway 68 N, Oak Ridge, North Carolina 27310-9667 **Tel:** 1 336 644-7035
Email: info@nwobserver.com **Web site:** http://www.nwobserver.com
Freq: Fri; **Circ:** 13000 Not Audited
Publisher: Patti Stokes
Profile: Northwest Observer is a weekly newspaper serving the Oak Ridge, NC area.
Language (s): English
Ad Rate: Full Page Mono 58.82
Currency: United States Dollars
COMMUNITY NEWSPAPER

Northwest Prime Time 258054
Owner: Roedell (Michelle) & Mitchell (Chris)
Tel: 1 206 824-8600
Email: editor@nwprimetime.com **Web site:** http://www.northwestprimetime.com
Freq: Semi-Monthly; **Circ:** 50000 Not Audited
Profile: Northwest Prime Time is a monthly newspaper for senior residents in Seattle, WA. The newspaper covers topics such as health, finance, arts & entertainment and travel.
Language (s): English
Ad Rate: Full Page Mono 42.58
Ad Rate: Full Page Colour 2550.00
Currency: United States Dollars
COMMUNITY NEWSPAPER

Norwood News 22567
Owner: Mosholu Preservation Corp.
Editorial: 3400 Reservoir Oval E, Bronx, New York 10467-3102 **Tel:** 1 718 324-4998
Email: norwoodnews@norwoodnews.org **Web site:** http://www.norwoodnews.org
Freq: Bi-Weekly; **Circ:** 15000 Not Audited
Profile: Norwood News is a local newspaper serving Bronx, NY, including Norwood, Bedford Park, and Fordham Bedford since 1988. The publication offers information about local news and community events.
Language (s): English
Ad Rate: Full Page Mono 12.78
Currency: United States Dollars
COMMUNITY NEWSPAPER

The Norwood Record 560345
Owner: Bulletin Newspapers, Inc. (The)
Editorial: 695 Truman Hwy Ste B103, Hyde Park, Massachusetts 02136-3552 **Tel:** 1 781 769-1725
Email: news@norwoodrecord.com **Web site:** http://www.norwoodrecord.com
Freq: Weekly; **Circ:** 6500
Profile: The Norwood Record is a free community weekly distributed to local business throughout Norwood, MA. It offers community news, sports and events.
Language (s): English
Ad Rate: Full Page Mono 32.55
Ad Rate: Full Page Colour 38.64
Currency: United States Dollars
COMMUNITY NEWSPAPER

The Notes 22271
Owner: LaBrie (Mark) & LaBrie (Andrew)
Editorial: 33 Yarmouth Crossing Dr, Yarmouth, Maine 04096-6740 **Tel:** 1 207 846-4112
Email: news@thenotes.org **Web site:** http://www.thenotes.org
Freq: Tue; **Circ:** 10000 Not Audited
Publisher & Editor: Andrew LaBrie; **Advertising Sales Manager:** Mark LaBrie
Profile: The Notes is a community newspaper serving Yarmouth, ME with local news and community events.
Language (s): English
Ad Rate: Full Page Mono 9.60
Currency: United States Dollars
COMMUNITY NEWSPAPER

Noticia 23228
Owner: L.I. Media Communications Inc.
Editorial: 53 E Merrick Rd Ste 353, Freeport, New York 11520-4056 **Tel:** 1 516 223-5678
Email: editorial@noticiali.com **Web site:** http://www.noticiali.com
Freq: Wed; **Circ:** 48500 Not Audited
Advertising Sales Manager: Silvana Diaz
Profile: Noticia is a Spanish newspaper serving Long Island, NY and the five boroughs.The publication provides information on local news, community events and entertainment.
Language (s): Spanish
Ad Rate: Full Page Mono 13.00
Currency: United States Dollars
COMMUNITY NEWSPAPER

La Noticia 75742
Editorial: 5936 Monroe Rd, Charlotte, North Carolina 28212 **Tel:** 1 704 568-6966
Email: editor@lanoticia.com **Web site:** http://www.lanoticia.com
Freq: Wed; **Circ:** 72900 Not Audited
Editor: Diego Barahona; **Advertising Sales Manager:** Alvaro Gurdian; **Publisher:** Hilda Gurdian
Profile: La Noticia is written for Hispanic residents in Asheville and Charlotte, NC. It covers local, national and international news, sports, real estate, entertainment, politics, education and business.
Language (s): Spanish
Ad Rate: Full Page Mono 37.82
Ad Rate: Full Page Colour 45.28
Currency: United States Dollars
COMMUNITY NEWSPAPER

Noticias 359847
Owner: Vazquez (Alejandro)
Editorial: 505 W Hemlock St, Abbotsford, Wisconsin 54405-9730 **Tel:** 1 715 613-2168
Email: noticias@noticiaswi.com **Web site:** http://www.noticiaswi.com
Freq: Bi-Weekly; **Circ:** 7000 Not Audited
Publisher & Editor: Alejandro Vazquez
Profile: Noticias is a free, Spanish-language newspaper circulating twice-a-month throughout Vernon, Monrow, Jackson, Wood, Clark, Lincoln, Eau Claire, La Cross, Winnebajo, Fond du Lac and Marathon counties, WI. It provides stories of interest to the Hispanic population and topics include local and international news, events and sports.
Language (s): Spanish
Ad Rate: Full Page Mono 9.39
Currency: United States Dollars
COMMUNITY NEWSPAPER

Las Noticias De Fort Bend 21813
Owner: Morales (Joe)
Editorial: 924 3rd St Ste 4, Rosenberg, Texas 77471-2660 **Tel:** 1 281 342-1622
Email: noticiasdefb@aol.com
Freq: Wed; **Circ:** 7500 Not Audited
Publisher & Editor: Joe Morales
Profile: Las Noticias de Fort Bend is a weekly Spanish publication that covers local news and events in Fort Bend, TX. Deadlines are on Fridays at 5pm CT.
Language (s): Spanish/Bilingual
Ad Rate: Full Page Mono 12.00
Currency: United States Dollars
COMMUNITY NEWSPAPER

Noticias Libres 442122
Owner: Wehco Media Inc.
Editorial: 400 E 11th St, Chattanooga, Tennessee 37403 **Tel:** 1 423 756-6900
Web site: http://www.noticiaslibres.com
Freq: Thu; **Circ:** 12000 Not Audited
Editor: Luis Carrasco
Profile: Noticias Libres is a local, weekly newspaper serving Hispanic and Spanish-speaking residents of Tennesee and North Georgia. The paper includes local news and information pertaining to the local Hispanic community. The paper shares an office with the Chattanooga (TN) Times Free Press.
Language (s): Spanish
Ad Rate: Full Page Mono 7.50
Ad Rate: Full Page Colour 50.00
Currency: United States Dollars
COMMUNITY NEWSPAPER

El Noticiero 22625
Tel: 1 954 766-4492
Email: elnoti2@aol.com
Freq: Bi-Weekly; **Circ:** 18000 Not Audited
Editor: Rodrigo Martinez; **Publisher:** Eduardo Quiroga
Profile: El Noticiero is a local newspaper published for Hispanic residents of Fort Lauderdale, FL. The newspaper covers local and national news, community events and social issues affecting the local and national Hispanic community.
Language (s): Spanish/Bilingual
Ad Rate: Full Page Mono 48.00
Currency: United States Dollars
COMMUNITY NEWSPAPER

Noticiero Colombiano Hispano 154755
Editorial: 437 Linden Ave, Elizabeth, New Jersey 7202 **Tel:** 1 908 351-9390
Email: noticolomb@aol.com **Web site:** http://www.noticierohispano.com
Freq: Weekly; **Circ:** 62000 Not Audited
Publisher & Editor: Nelson Franco; **Advertising Sales Manager:** Gloria Vargas
Profile: Noticiero Colombiano Hispano is written for Colombian residents in Elizabeth, NJ. It covers news, arts & entertainment and Hispanic culture. Monthly supplements include special articles on automobiles, tourism, real estate and health.
Language (s): Spanish
Ad Rate: Full Page Mono 30.00
Currency: United States Dollars
COMMUNITY NEWSPAPER

Noticiero Semanal 152346
Owner: Porterville Recorder
Editorial: 115 E Oak Ave, Porterville, California 93257-3807 **Tel:** 1 559 784-5000
Email: recorder@portervillerecorder.com **Web site:** http://www.noticierosemanal.com
Freq: Thu; **Circ:** 30000 Not Audited
Editor & Publisher: Rick Elkins; **Circulation Manager:** Alex Larson
Profile: Noticiero Semanal in Porterville, CA is a Spanish-language newspaper that covers local news and community events.
Language (s): Spanish/Bilingual
Ad Rate: Full Page Mono 46.00
Currency: United States Dollars
COMMUNITY NEWSPAPER

Novedades News 23217
Owner: Puerto (Sergio)
Editorial: 121 S Zang Blvd, Dallas, Texas 75208-4530 **Tel:** 1 214 943-2932
Email: editorial@novedadesnews.com **Web site:** http://www.novedadesnews.com
Freq: Wed; **Circ:** 37800 Not Audited
Profile: Novedades News' editorial mission is to provide news and information to the Hispanic community of Dallas. Deadlines are on Fridays.
Language (s): Spanish
Ad Rate: Full Page Mono 22.00
Ad Rate: Full Page Colour 740.00
Currency: United States Dollars
COMMUNITY NEWSPAPER

Nuestra Comunidad 232170
Owner: Gannett Co. Inc.
Editorial: 891 E Oak Rd, Vineland, New Jersey 08360-2311 **Tel:** 1 856 563-5206
Freq: Fri; **Circ:** 13000 Not Audited
Advertising Manager: Robin Adams; **Editor:** Pablo Mansilla
Profile: Nuestra Comunidad is a weekly community newspaper for the residents of Vineland, NJ. It covers sports, arts & entertainment, politics, health, environment, technology and youth.
Language (s): Spanish
Ad Rate: Full Page Mono 6.56
Currency: United States Dollars
COMMUNITY NEWSPAPER

Nueva America 23307
Owner: Hispanic Millenium Media, Corp.
Editorial: 990 Suffolk Ave, Brentwood, New York 11717-4502 **Tel:** 1 631 231-6222
Email: nuameric@aol.com **Web site:** http://www.nuevamericany.com
Freq: Thu; **Circ:** 75000
Editor: Claudia Canales; **Publisher:** Ivan Guerrero
Profile: Nueva America is published weekly for the Latino population of Long Island, NY and surrounding areas. The publication contains community and national news of interest to the readers. A local events calendar is also included. The publication does not have a Web site. The lead time and deadlines vary.
Language (s): English, Spanish
Ad Rate: Full Page Mono 8.00
Currency: United States Dollars
COMMUNITY NEWSPAPER

Nuevas Raices 583279
Tel: 1 540 560-5335
Email: info@nuevasraices.com **Web site:** http://www.nuevasraices.com
Freq: Weekly; **Circ:** 14000
Editor: Fernando Gamboa
Language (s): Spanish
Ad Rate: Full Page Mono 4.18
Currency: United States Dollars
COMMUNITY NEWSPAPER

El Nuevo Patria 23284
Owner: Patria Media Foundation Inc.
Editorial: 1393 SW 1st St Ste 400, Miami, Florida 33135-2321 **Tel:** 1 305 698-8787
Email: patrianews@aol.com **Web site:** http://elnuevopatria.com
Freq: Fri; **Circ:** 30000 Not Audited
Publisher: Eladio Jose Armesto; **Advertising Sales Manager:** Patricia Armesto
Profile: El Nuevo Patria is a local, Hispanic newspaper serving the Cuban community of South Florida. It includes information on local news, weather, sports, business and entertainment.
Language (s): Spanish
Ad Rate: Full Page Mono 19.25
Ad Rate: Full Page Colour 325.00
Currency: United States Dollars
COMMUNITY NEWSPAPER

Nuevo Siglo 23223
Editorial: 7137 N Armenia Ave Ste B, Tampa, Florida 33604-5263 **Tel:** 1 813 493-7079
Email: nuevosiglonews@gmail.com **Web site:** http://www.nuevosiglotampa.com
Freq: Thu; **Circ:** 27000 Not Audited
Advertising Sales Manager: Karol Escalante
Profile: Nuevo Siglo in Tampa, FL is a local publication dedicated to the Hispanic community of Hillsborough County, FL.
Language (s): Spanish
Ad Rate: Full Page Mono 12.00
Currency: United States Dollars
COMMUNITY NEWSPAPER

Nuevo Siglo 154627
Owner: Bandia (Ezequiel)
Editorial: 2644 W 47th St, Chicago, Illinois 60632-1350 **Tel:** 1 773 890-1656
Email: ns@nuevosiglonews.com **Web site:** http://www.nuevosiglo.com
Freq: Weekly; **Circ:** 30000 Not Audited
Publisher & Editor: Ezequiel Banda; **Advertising Sales Manager:** Leon Martinez
Profile: Nuevo Siglo is a weekly newspaper written for Spanish-speaking residents of Chicago.
Language (s): Spanish
Ad Rate: Full Page Mono 52.00
Currency: United States Dollars
COMMUNITY NEWSPAPER

The Nugget 22755
Editorial: 442 E Main Ave, Sisters, Oregon 97759
Tel: 1 541 549-9941
Web site: http://www.nuggetnews.com
Freq: Wed; **Circ:** 7600 Not Audited
Advertising Sales Manager: Lisa Buckley; **Editor:** Jim Cornelius; **Publisher:** Kiki Dolson; **Circulation Manager:** Teresa Mahnken
Profile: The Nugget was founded as an independently owned, weekly newspaper in the mountain town of Sisters, OR in 1978. It provides comprehensive coverage of city government, school, forest service and other local news. Weekly features include editorials and letters to the editor, business briefs and features, columns, the sheriff's report, music and arts and stories on local events and people in the Sisters community. Its readership spans Western Deschutes County from the Santiam Pass toward Bend and Redmond and includes Camp Sherman and Black Butte Ranch, Sisters, Crossroads, Tollgate, Indian Ford and development in the Plainview and Cloverdale, OR areas.
Language (s): English
Ad Rate: Full Page Mono 11.50
Currency: United States Dollars
COMMUNITY NEWSPAPER

Number Nine Media Inc 25096
Owner: Number Nine Media Inc.
Editorial: 1837 Camino Del Llano, Belen, New Mexico 87002-2619 **Tel:** 1 505 864-4472
Email: vcnb@news-bulletin.com **Web site:** http://www.news-bulletin.com
Circ: 45000 Not Audited
Editor: Clara Garcia; **Publisher:** Rocky Hayes; **Circulation Manager:** Alex Raab
Language (s): English
COMMUNITY NEWSPAPER

Nutfield Publishing 334171
Owner: Nutfield Publishing
Editorial: 2 Litchfield Rd, Londonderry, New Hampshire 03053-2625 **Tel:** 1 603 537-2760
Email: ads@nutpub.net **Web site:** http://www.nutpub.net
Freq: Weekly; **Circ:** 28407 Not Audited
Editor: Leslie O'Donnell
Profile: Nutfield Publishing, of Londonderry, NH, produces newspapers that serve the communities of Londonderry, Derry, East Derry, Chester, Sandown, Hampstead and East Hampstead.
Language (s): English
Ad Rate: Full Page Mono 32.10
Currency: United States Dollars
COMMUNITY NEWSPAPER

Nutley Sun 24872
Owner: Gannett Co., Inc./North Jersey Media Group
Editorial: 632 Pompton Ave, Cedar Grove, New Jersey 07009-1736 **Tel:** 1 973 569-7087
Email: newsroom@northjersey.com **Web site:** http://www.northjersey.com
Circ: 10131 Not Audited
Editor: Mollie Gray; **Publisher:** Kathleen Hivish; **Editor:** Owen Proctor
Profile: Nutley Sun's mission is to provide its readers with the latest in local news and information. The publication is written for residents of the Nutley, NJ area. Deadlines are one week prior to issue date.
Language (s): English
COMMUNITY NEWSPAPER

NUVO 21459
Owner: NUVO Inc.
Editorial: 3951 N Meridian St Ste 200, Indianapolis, Indiana 46208-4078 **Tel:** 1 317 254-2400
Email: editors@nuvo.net **Web site:** http://www.nuvo.net
Freq: Wed; **Circ:** 34000 Not Audited
Publisher & Editor: Kevin McKinney; **News Editor:** Amber Stearns
Profile: NUVO is written for the residents of Indianapolis and surrounding areas. The newspaper is published every Wednesday and covers politics, culture, cuisine, arts & entertainment, music reviews and a community calendar of events. The best day to reach the paper is on Fridays between 9 a.m. and 5 p.m. The outlet offers RSS (Really Simple Syndication).
Language (s): English
Ad Rate: Full Page Mono 48.52
Ad Rate: Full Page Colour 2875.00
Currency: United States Dollars
COMMUNITY NEWSPAPER

NY Cool Japan 971240
Owner: New York Seikatsu Press, Inc.
Editorial: West 47th St. Suite 307, New York, New York 10036 **Tel:** 1 212 213-6069
Email: post@nyseikatsu.com **Web site:** http://www.nyseikatsu.com/?cat=68
Freq: Weekly; **Circ:** 20000
Editor: Kaoru Komi
Profile: NY Cool Japan is a Weekly Japanese Lifestyle publication launched in January 2004 in New York.
Language (s): Japanese
COMMUNITY NEWSPAPER

NY Japion 155517
Editorial: 411 Lafayette St Fl 3, New York, New York 10003-7032 **Tel:** 1 212 431-9970
Email: reader@nyjapion.com **Web site:** http://www.ejapion.com
Freq: Weekly; **Circ:** 23000 Not Audited
Publisher & Editor: Hitonshi Onishi
Profile: NY Japion is a free community newspaper serving New York City's Japanese-American community.
Language (s): Japanese
Ad Rate: Full Page Mono 60.00
Currency: United States Dollars
COMMUNITY NEWSPAPER

Oakwood Register 22077
Owner: Winkler Co. (The)
Editorial: 435 Patterson Rd, Dayton, Ohio 45419-4309 **Tel:** 1 937 294-2662

Email: editor@oakwoodregister.com **Web site:** http://www.oakwoodregister.com
Freq: Tue; **Circ:** 6500 Not Audited
Circulation Manager: Vicki Auditor; **Advertising Sales Manager:** Dee Dee Nagel; **Publisher:** Dolores Wagner; **Editor:** Lance Winkler
Profile: Oakwood Register is a local newspaper for residents of Oakwood, OH. The paper covers local news, events, people, sports, arts & entertainment and education.
Language (s): English
Ad Rate: Full Page Mono 14.00
Ad Rate: Full Page Colour 738.00
Currency: United States Dollars
COMMUNITY NEWSPAPER

The Obion County Weekly 429266
Owner: Critchlow (David) & Critchlow (Scott)
Editorial: 613 E Jackson St, Union City, Tennessee 38261-5239 **Tel:** 1 731 885-0744
Email: dgc@ucmessenger.com **Web site:** http://nwtntoday.com
Freq: Wed; **Circ:** 5400 Not Audited
Editor & Publisher: David Critchlow; **Advertising Manager:** Todd Tilghman; **Circulation Manager:** John Trevathan
Profile: The Obion County Weekly is a free newspaper serving residents of Obion County, TN. It covers news, events and features stories in addition to an extensive advertising section. Published by the Union City Daily Messenger, it shares its offices and editorial staff with the daily. To advertise in the paper, advertising must also run in the daily. Deadlines are at 10am ET.
Language (s): English
Ad Rate: Full Page Mono 3.00
Currency: United States Dollars
COMMUNITY NEWSPAPER

El Observador 21797
Editorial: 1042 W Hedding St Ste 250, San Jose, California 95126-1206 **Tel:** 1 408 938-1700
Web site: http://www.el-observador.com
Freq: Fri; **Circ:** 84000 Not Audited
Profile: El Observador is a weekly bilingual publication that covers sports, entertainment, local, national and international news for Santa Clara, San Mateo and Encino, CA. It covers both Hispanic and American community issues. Deadlines are on Fridays prior to issue date.
Language (s): Spanish
Ad Rate: Full Page Mono 30.00
Currency: United States Dollars
COMMUNITY NEWSPAPER

L' Observateur 19415
Owner: LaPlace News Media, LLC
Editorial: 116 Newspaper Dr, La Place, Louisiana 70068-4509 **Tel:** 1 985 652-9545
Web site: http://www.lobservateur.com
Freq: 2 Times/Week; **Circ:** 5000 Not Audited
Publisher & Editor: Stephen Hemelt; **Advertising Sales Manager:** J. Kennon
Profile: L'Observateur is a local paper written for the residents of La Place, LA. The paper covers local events, sports and politics. The paper releases a free edition of the paper on Thursdays.
Language (s): English
Ad Rate: Full Page Mono 10.50
Currency: United States Dollars
COMMUNITY NEWSPAPER

Observation Post 28620
Owner: Hi-Desert Publishing
Editorial: Public Affairs Office, MCAGCC Building 1417, Twentynine Palms, California 92278
Tel: 1 760 830-6213
Email: smbplmswebpao@usmc.mil **Web site:** http://www.29palms.marines.mil/news/opconnection.aspx
Freq: Fri; **Circ:** 8600 Not Audited
Profile: Observation Post is a military publication for the Marine Corps members of Twentynine Palms, CA.
Language (s): English
Ad Rate: Full Page Mono 12.25
Currency: United States Dollars
COMMUNITY NEWSPAPER

The Observer 18745
Owner: Deerfield Publishing
Editorial: 201 N Federal Hwy Ste 103, Deerfield Beach, Florida 33441-3621
Email: observernews@comcast.net **Web site:** http://www.observernewspaperonline.com
Freq: Thu; **Circ:** 30000 Not Audited
Publisher: David Eller
Profile: The Observer is published weekly for the residents of Broward County, FL. The newspaper provides information about local news, sports, education and community events.
Language (s): English
Ad Rate: Full Page Mono 9.50
Currency: United States Dollars
COMMUNITY NEWSPAPER

The Observer 20201
Owner: Tortoreti (Mary)
Editorial: 39 Seeley Ave, Kearny, New Jersey 07032-1806 **Tel:** 1 201 991-1600
Email: editorial@theobserver.com **Web site:** http://www.theobserver.com
Freq: Wed; **Circ:** 32500
Editor: Karen Zautyk
Profile: The Observer is published weekly for the residents of Kearny, NJ and surrounding areas. The newspaper covers local news, sports and community events.
Language (s): English
Ad Rate: Full Page Mono 18.00
Currency: United States Dollars
COMMUNITY NEWSPAPER

The Observer 20232
Owner: Rio Rancho Observer, LLC
Editorial: 1594 Sara Rd SE, Rio Rancho, New Mexico 87124-1862 **Tel:** 1 505 892-8080
Email: editor@rrobserver.com **Web site:** http://www.rrobserver.com
Freq: Sun; **Circ:** 23500 Not Audited
Publisher: Rockford Hayes
Profile: The Observer is a community newspaper that serves Rio Rancho, NM and the surrounding communities on the west side of Albuquerque, NM. It includes news, sports and information about the people who make up the community. The news deadlines for the Wednesday edition are Mondays at noon and for Fridays the deadlines are Wednesdays at noon MT.
Language (s): English
Ad Rate: Full Page Mono 18.00
Currency: United States Dollars
COMMUNITY NEWSPAPER

Observer 389565
Owner: Diocese of Rockford
Editorial: 555 Colman Center Dr, Rockford, Illinois 61108-2747 **Tel:** 1 815 399-4300
Email: observer@rockforddiocese.org **Web site:** http://observer.rockforddiocese.org
Freq: Fri; **Circ:** 25500 Not Audited
Circulation Manager: Jill Bonk; **News Editor:** Amanda Hudson; **Publisher:** David Malloy; **Advertising Sales Manager:** Kevin McCarthy; **Editor:** Penny Wiegert
Profile: Observer is a weekly newspaper for the Diocese of Rockford, IL. It offers columns from the bishop, profiles of leaders and a weekly calendar of events.
Language (s): English
Ad Rate: Full Page Mono 16.15
Currency: United States Dollars
COMMUNITY NEWSPAPER

Observer & Eccentric Newspapers - Detroit 24591
Owner: Gannett Co., Inc.
Editorial: 615 W Lafayette Blvd, Detroit, Michigan 48226-3124 **Tel:** 1 586 826-7494
Web site: http://www.hometownlife.com
Circ: 158439 Not Audited
Profile: Observer & Eccentric Newspapers offer local news, sports and events to residents of suburban Detroit. It has other offices in Sterling Heights, MI and Plymouth, MI, where main reception is maintained. All news faxes go to the Detroit newsroom.
Language (s): English
COMMUNITY NEWSPAPER

Observer & Eccentric Newspapers - Sterling Heights 598267
Owner: Gannett Co. Inc
Editorial: 6200 Metropolitan Pkwy, Sterling Heights, Michigan 48312-1022 **Tel:** 1 586 826-7494
Web site: http://www.hometownlife.com
Editor: Sandy Armbruster
Profile: Observer & Eccentric Newspapers offer local news, sports and events to residents of suburban Detroit. It has other offices in Detroit, MI and Plymouth, MI, where main reception is maintained. All news faxes go to the Detroit newsroom.
Language (s): English
COMMUNITY NEWSPAPER

The Observer Group Newspapers of Southern California 24745
Editorial: 1219 20th St, Bakersfield, California 93301
Tel: 1 661 324-9466
Email: observernews@gmail.com
Circ: 97315 Not Audited
Publisher & Editor: Ellen Coley
Language (s): English
COMMUNITY NEWSPAPER

Observer Newspapers 860827
Owner: Observer Media Group Inc. (The)
Editorial: 1970 Main St, Sarasota, Florida 34236-5921 **Tel:** 1 941 366-3468
Web site: http://www.yourobserver.com
Freq: Weekly
News Editor: Pam Eubanks; **Advertising Sales Manager:** Jill Raleigh; **Publisher:** Matt Walsh
Language (s): English
COMMUNITY NEWSPAPER

OC Weekly 22337
Owner: McIntosh Co. Inc. (Duncan)
Editorial: 18475 Bandilier Cir, Fountain Valley, California 92708-7000 **Tel:** 1 714 550-5900
Web site: http://www.ocweekly.com
Freq: Thu; **Circ:** 45088 Not Audited
Editor: Gustavo Arellano
Profile: OC Weekly is published for the residents of Orange County, CA and surrounding areas. The newspaper covers local and national news, music, arts, politics and sports.
Language (s): English
Ad Rate: Full Page Mono 20.84
Ad Rate: Full Page Colour 27.59
Currency: United States Dollars
COMMUNITY NEWSPAPER

Ocean City Sentinel 23022
Owner: Sample Media, Inc.
Editorial: 112 E 8th St, Ocean City, New Jersey 08226-3736 **Tel:** 1 609 399-5411
Email: oceancitysentinel@comcast.net **Web site:** http://www.oceancitysentinel.com
Freq: Thu; **Circ:** 10000 Not Audited
Community News Editor: Kristen Keller; **Publisher & Editor:** David Nahan; **Advertising Sales Manager:** Marshall Smith; **Circulation Manager:** Mary Jane Weissenberg
Profile: Ocean City Sentinel serves residents of Ocean City, NJ. The paper focuses on local news, sports and community events.
Language (s): English
Ad Rate: Full Page Mono 14.57
Currency: United States Dollars
COMMUNITY NEWSPAPER

Ocean City Today 355201
Owner: Flag Publications
Editorial: 8200 Coastal Hwy, Ocean City, Maryland 21842-2834 **Tel:** 1 410 723-6397
Email: editor@oceancitytoday.net **Web site:** http://www.oceancitytoday.net
Freq: Fri; **Circ:** 18000 Not Audited
Advertising Sales Manager: Elaine Brady; **Publisher & Editor:** Stewart Dobson
Profile: Ocean City (MD) Today is a weekly newspaper serving the Maryland coast.
Language (s): English
Ad Rate: Full Page Mono 11.50
Ad Rate: Full Page Colour 75.00
Currency: United States Dollars
COMMUNITY NEWSPAPER

The Ocean Star 23016
Owner: Star News Group, Inc.
Editorial: 421 River Ave, Point Pleasant Beach, New Jersey 08742-2569 **Tel:** 1 732 899-7606
Email: info@theoceanstar.com **Web site:** http://www.starnewsgroup.com
Freq: Fri; **Circ:** 6192 Not Audited
Publisher: James Manser; **Editor:** Doug Paviluk
Profile: The Ocean Star is published weekly for the residents of Point Pleasant Beach, NJ and surrounding areas. The newspaper provides information about local news and community events.
Language (s): English
Ad Rate: Full Page Mono 5.61
Currency: United States Dollars
COMMUNITY NEWSPAPER

Oceana's Herald-Journal 19521
Owner: Shoreline Media, Inc.
Editorial: 123 S State St, Hart, Michigan 49420-1124 **Tel:** 1 231 873-5602
Email: editor@oceanaheraldjournal.com **Web site:** http://www.oceanaheraldjournal.com
Freq: Weekly; **Circ:** 6428 Not Audited
Editor: Mary Sanford; **Publisher:** James Young
Profile: Oceana's Herald-Journal is a local weekly newspaper written for residents of Oceana County, MI. The newspaper primarily covers the local news, however, some national news is covered when it pertains to the local residents.
Language (s): English
Ad Rate: Full Page Mono 10.65
Currency: United States Dollars
COMMUNITY NEWSPAPER

The Oconee Leader 861901
Owner: Peecher Communcations LLC
Tel: 1 706 208-2221
Email: news.oconeeleader@gmail.com **Web site:** http://www.theoconeeleader.com/
Freq: Weekly; **Circ:** 12500
Publisher & Editor: Robert Peecher
Profile: The Oconee Leader is a weekly community newspaper covering local news and events in Oconee County, GA.
Language (s): English
Ad Rate: Full Page Mono 1000.00
Ad Rate: Full Page Colour 1125.00
Currency: United States Dollars
COMMUNITY NEWSPAPER

Oconomowoc Enterprise 21208
Owner: Conley Publishing Group
Editorial: 801 N Barstow St, Waukesha, Wisconsin 53186-4801 **Tel:** 1 262 567-5511
Email: enterprise@conleynet.com **Web site:** http://www.gmtoday.com
Freq: Thu; **Circ:** 5000 Not Audited
Advertising Sales Manager: Jim Baumgart; **Publisher:** Jim Conley; **Circulation Manager:** Barb Parker
Profile: Oconomowoc Enterprise is written for residents of Northwestern Waukesha County in Wisconsin.
Language (s): English
Ad Rate: Full Page Mono 8.24
Currency: United States Dollars
COMMUNITY NEWSPAPER

Oconto County Reporter 21209
Owner: Gannett Co. Inc.
Editorial: 648 Brazeau Ave, Oconto, Wisconsin 54153-1946 **Tel:** 1 920 834-4242
Email: editorial@gocontocounty.com **Web site:** http://www.ocontocountyreporter.com
Freq: Weekly; **Circ:** 5000 Not Audited
Profile: Oconto (WI) County Reporter is a weekly newspaper that provides in-depth local and regional news, including sports, weather, business, politics, entertainment and community news.
Language (s): English
Ad Rate: Full Page Mono 6.25
Currency: United States Dollars
COMMUNITY NEWSPAPER

Ogemaw County Herald 19563
Owner: Sunrise Printing & Publishing, Inc.
Editorial: 215 W Houghton Ave, West Branch, Michigan 48661-1219 **Tel:** 1 989 345-0044
Email: editor@ogemawherald.com **Web site:** http://www.ogemawherald.com
Freq: Thu; **Circ:** 6150 Not Audited
Publisher: Elizabeth Gorske
Profile: The editorial mission of Ogemaw County Herald is to keep readers informed of local news and events. Ogemaw County Herald is written for the population of Ogemaw, MI. The lead time for Ogemaw County Herald is three days.
Language (s): English
Ad Rate: Full Page Mono 7.70
Currency: United States Dollars
COMMUNITY NEWSPAPER

The Ogle County Life 23345
Editorial: 311 Washington St, Oregon, Illinois 61061-1621 **Tel:** 1 815 732-2156
Email: news@oglecountylife.com **Web site:** http://www.oglecountylife.com
Freq: Mon; **Circ:** 12700
Editor: Tina Ketter
Profile: The Ogle County Life is a community newspaper written for residents of Oregon, IL.
Language (s): English
Ad Rate: Full Page Mono 18.70
Currency: United States Dollars
COMMUNITY NEWSPAPER

Oklahoma City Friday 20443
Owner: Nichols Hills Publishing Co.
Editorial: 10801 Quail Plaza Dr, Oklahoma City, Oklahoma 73120-3118 **Tel:** 1 405 755-3311
Web site: http://www.okcfriday.com
Freq: Fri; **Circ:** 8460 Not Audited
Profile: Oklahoma City Friday's editorial mission is to report Oklahoma happenings. The publication is written for the most affluent market in Oklahoma. Deadlines for the publication are one week before issue date.
Language (s): English
Ad Rate: Full Page Mono 26.00
Currency: United States Dollars
COMMUNITY NEWSPAPER

The Oklahoma City Herald 922791
Editorial: 7416 Broadway Ext Ste G, Oklahoma City, Oklahoma 73116-9066 **Tel:** 1 405 842-7827
Email: news@okcherald.org **Web site:** http://okcherald.org
Freq: Weekly
Community News Editor: Alvah Boyd; **Editor:** John Reed
Profile: The Oklahoma City Herald was established to provide a positive communication medium for and about Oklahoma's minority communities. The weekly publication covers community, state, national and international news of interest to the African American population in particular, but appeals to persons of all races.
Language (s): English
Ad Rate: Full Page Mono 900.00
Currency: United States Dollars
COMMUNITY NEWSPAPER

The Oklahoma Eagle 20468
Editorial: 624 E Archer St, Tulsa, Oklahoma 74120-1000 **Tel:** 1 918 582-7124
Email: news@theoklahomaeagle.net **Web site:** http://www.theoklahomaeagle.net
Freq: Thu; **Circ:** 15000 Not Audited
Circulation Manager: Jeane Winston
Profile: The Oklahoma Eagle is written for the African-American community of Tulsa, OK.
Language (s): English
Ad Rate: Full Page Mono 16.00
Currency: United States Dollars
COMMUNITY NEWSPAPER

Oklahoma Gazette 21319
Owner: Gazette Media Inc.
Editorial: 3701 N Shartel Ave, Oklahoma City, Oklahoma 73118-7102 **Tel:** 1 405 528-6000
Web site: http://www.okgazette.com
Freq: Wed; **Circ:** 51332 Not Audited
Circulation Manager: Chad Bleakley
Profile: Oklahoma Gazette is a free weekly newspaper for the residents of central Oklahoma. The newspaper's mission is to analyze elements that affect the quality of life in central Oklahoma; to stimulate thought and participation with information and opinion on entertainment opportunities and social needs; to expose conditions and actions that detract from our quality of life; and to recognize those individuals and actions that deserve commendation within the community. The lead time varies per issue.
Language (s): English
Ad Rate: Full Page Mono 75.24
Ad Rate: Full Page Colour 2232.00
Currency: United States Dollars
COMMUNITY NEWSPAPER

The Olathe News 786685
Owner: The McClatchy Company
Editorial: 1729 Grand Blvd, Kansas City, Missouri 64108-1413 **Tel:** 1 816 234-4636
Web site: http://www.theolathenews.com
Freq: Bi-Weekly; **Circ:** 25000
Profile: The Olathe News is a bi-weekly community news edition of the Kansas City Star written for the

residents of Johnson County, KS. Covers local news, sports, opinion and entertainment.
COMMUNITY NEWSPAPER

The Oldham Era 19350
Owner: Landmark Community Newspapers, Inc.
Editorial: 202 S 1st St, La Grange, Kentucky 40031-2208 **Tel:** 1 502 222-7183
Email: editor@oldhamera.com **Web site:** http://www.oldhamera.com
Freq: Thu; **Circ:** 5500 Not Audited
Profile: The Oldham Era is a local community newspaper written for the residents of Oldham County, KY. It covers local government news, sports and other local information of interest. Announcements for weddings, engagements, anniversaries, births, first birthdays and obituaries are published free of charge as a community service. Deadline for submissions is Thurday, 3 p.m. EST.
Language (s): English
Ad Rate: Full Page Mono 11.17
Ad Rate: Full Page Colour 40.99
Currency: United States Dollars
COMMUNITY NEWSPAPER

Olympia Review 27567
Owner: BT Publications
Editorial: 102 S. Main St, Minier, Illinois 61759
Tel: 1 309 392-2414
Email: olympiareview@frontier.com
Freq: Tue; **Circ:** 5100 Not Audited
Publisher & Editor: Lois Rickard
Profile: Olympia Review is a local community newspaper written for the residents of Minier, IL.
Language (s): English
Ad Rate: Full Page Mono 9.50
Currency: United States Dollars
COMMUNITY NEWSPAPER

Omaha Star 20142
Owner: Washington (Marguerita)
Editorial: 2216 N 24th St, Omaha, Nebraska 68110-2213 **Tel:** 1 402 346-4041
Web site: http://www.theomahastarinc.com
Freq: Fri; **Circ:** 30000 Not Audited
Advertising Sales Manager: Phyllis Hicks
Profile: Omaha Star is written for the African-American community in Omaha, NE, and the surrounding areas. Deadlines for the publication are Tuesdays by noon before issue date. Published bi-weekly.
Language (s): English
Ad Rate: Full Page Mono 18.00
Currency: United States Dollars
COMMUNITY NEWSPAPER

The Omak-Okanogan County Chronicle 24178
Owner: Eagle Newspapers
Editorial: 618 Okoma Dr, Omak, Washington 98841
Tel: 1 509 826-1110
Email: news@omakchronicle.com **Web site:** http://www.omakchronicle.com
Freq: Sun; **Circ:** 7092 Not Audited
Publisher & Editor: Roger Harnack
Profile: Omak-Okanogan County Chronicle is published weekly for the residents of Okanogan County, WA. It covers local news and community events. Deadlines are on Fridays at noon PT.
Language (s): English
Ad Rate: Full Page Mono 15.50
Currency: United States Dollars
COMMUNITY NEWSPAPER

On Common Ground News 472860
Editorial: 1240 Sigman Rd NW Ste 107, Conyers, Georgia 30012-3934 **Tel:** 1 678 526-1910
Email: editor@ocgnews.com **Web site:** http://www.ocgnews.com
Freq: Weekly; **Circ:** 30000 Not Audited
Advertising Sales Manager: Richard Hill
Profile: On Common Ground News is a bi-weekly newspaper written for the residents of DeKalb County, GA. The newspaper covers local news, education, business, arts & entertainment, health and real estate. It is issued on the 1st and 15th of each month.
Language (s): English
Ad Rate: Full Page Mono 53.00
Currency: United States Dollars
COMMUNITY NEWSPAPER

One Nation News 86988
Owner: Black Heart Publishing Inc.
Editorial: 1614 Harmon Pl Ste 203, Minneapolis, Minnesota 55403-1964 **Tel:** 1 763 205-6751
Email: info@onenationnews.com **Web site:** http://www.onenationnews.com
Freq: Wed; **Circ:** 10000 Not Audited
Publisher: Joe Bryson; **Editor:** Kay Hansen
Profile: One Nation News is a weekly newspaper serving the African-American residents in the Twin Cities in Minnesota. It is published every Wednesday.
Language (s): English
Ad Rate: Full Page Mono 59.00
Currency: United States Dollars
COMMUNITY NEWSPAPER

One Voice 21923
Owner: Diocese of Birmingham
Tel: 1 205 838-8305
Email: onevoice@bhmdiocese.org
Freq: Fri; **Circ:** 19000 Not Audited
Publisher: Robert Baker; **Circulation Manager:** Ann Lanzi
Profile: One Voice is a weekly newspaper whose editorial mission is to provide information pertaining to the church. The publication is written for the Catholic community. The publication does not accept press releases.
Language (s): English
Ad Rate: Full Page Mono 10.00
Currency: United States Dollars
COMMUNITY NEWSPAPER

Oneida Independent Herald 20769
Owner: Liberty Press Inc.
Editorial: 19391 Alberta St, Oneida, Tennessee 37841-3359 **Tel:** 1 423 569-6343
Web site: http://www.ihoneida.com
Freq: Thu; **Circ:** 5000 Not Audited
Editor: Ben Garrett
Profile: Oneida Independent Herald is written for residents in Scott County, TN.
Language (s): English
Ad Rate: Full Page Mono 4.99
Currency: United States Dollars
COMMUNITY NEWSPAPER

La Opinión de la Bahía 22728
Owner: ImpreMedia LLC
Editorial: 225 W Ohio St Fl 3, Chicago, Illinois 60654-7898 **Tel:** 1 855 340-0180
Web site: http://www.laopiniondebahia.com
Freq: Sun; **Circ:** 103800 Not Audited
Profile: La Opinión de la Bahía is written for the Latino and Spanish-speaking community of the San Francisco Bay area. The paper covers local news, international news, local entertainment and sports.
Language (s): English, Spanish
Ad Rate: Full Page Mono 85.00
Ad Rate: Full Page Colour 400.00
Currency: United States Dollars
COMMUNITY NEWSPAPER

The Opp News 18521
Owner: Pujol Printing & Publishing, LLC
Editorial: 200 W Covington Ave, Opp, Alabama 36467-2046 **Tel:** 1 334 493-3595
Web site: http://www.oppnewsonline.com
Freq: Thu; **Circ:** 5500 Not Audited
Publisher: Maurice Pujol; **Editor:** Jay Thomas
Profile: Opp News is a weekly newspaper published for residents of Opp, AL. The publication covers local news. Deadlines are one week before the issue date.
Language (s): English
Ad Rate: Full Page Mono 9.50
Currency: United States Dollars
COMMUNITY NEWSPAPER

Orange County Neighborhood Newspapers Inc. 24880
Owner: CommunityMedia Corporation
Editorial: 9559 Valley View St, Cypress, California 90630 **Tel:** 1 714 220-0292
Circ: 73500 Not Audited
Language (s): English
COMMUNITY NEWSPAPER

Orange County Publishing Co., Inc. 24563
Owner: Orange County Publishing
Editorial: 131 N West Court St, Paoli, Indiana 47454
Tel: 1 812 723-2572
Email: ocpinc@ocpnews.com
Freq: Weekly; **Circ:** 18009 Not Audited
Publisher: Art Hampton; **Advertising Sales Manager:** Peggy Manship
Language (s): English
Ad Rate: Full Page Mono 716.00
Currency: United States Dollars
COMMUNITY NEWSPAPER

The Orange County Register Community Newspapers 25292
Owner: Southern California News Group/Digital First Media
Editorial: 2190 S Towne Centre Pl, Anaheim, California 92806-6128 **Tel:** 1 714 796-7000
Email: local@ocregister.com **Web site:** http://www.ocregister.com
Language (s): English
COMMUNITY NEWSPAPER

Orange County Review 86836
Owner: BH Media Group
Editorial: 146 Byrd St, Orange, Virginia 22960-1631
Tel: 1 540 672-1266
Email: news@orangenews.com **Web site:** http://www.orangenews.com
Freq: Thu; **Circ:** 7000 Not Audited
Circulation Manager: Carmen Stroll
Profile: Orange Review is a weekly newspaper written for the residents of Orange County, VA. The publication covers community news and events. The lead time for editorial submissions is one week before issue date. Contact the publication for advertising rates.
Language (s): English
Ad Rate: Full Page Mono 17.99
Currency: United States Dollars
COMMUNITY NEWSPAPER

Oregon Coast Today 837739
Owner: East Oregonian Publishing Co.
Editorial: 820 SE Highway 101 Ste A, Lincoln City, Oregon 97367-2773 **Tel:** 1 541 921-0413
Email: news@oregoncoasttoday.com **Web site:** http://www.oregoncoasttoday.com
Freq: Weekly; **Circ:** 17500
Editor: Patrick Alexander
Profile: Oregon Coast Today is a free weekly newspaper providing Local and Community News coverage for the residents of Newport, Lincoln City, Yachats, Tillamook, Pacific City and Depoe Bay, OR.
Language (s): English
COMMUNITY NEWSPAPER

The Oregon Sentinel 472401
Editorial: Oregon Military Dept, Public Affairs, AGPA Rm 204, Salem, Oregon 997309 **Tel:** 1 503 584-3917
Web site: https://www.oregon.gov/OMD/AGPA/pages/publications.aspx
Freq: Semi-Monthly; **Circ:** 15000 Not Audited
Editor: Jeff Thompson
Profile: The Oregon Sentinel is a free semi-monthly publication providing news and features about the Oregon National Guard. It changed its name from Azuwur in 2003. The paper does not accept advertising.
Language (s): English
COMMUNITY NEWSPAPER

The Orlando Advocate 22257
Owner: Trexel Communications and Publishing Group Inc.
Editorial: 30 Coburn Ave, Orlando, Florida 32805-2138 **Tel:** 1 407 648-1162
Email: newsdesk@orlandoadvocate.com **Web site:** http://orlandoadvocate.com
Freq: Fri; **Circ:** 9900 Not Audited
Circulation Manager: Robert Brown; **Publisher:** Kevin Seraaj
Profile: The Advocate is a local, weekly newspaper serving residents of Central Florida. The paper covers local news, education, politics and community events. Advertising deadlines are on Mondays at noon ET.
Language (s): English
Ad Rate: Full Page Mono 10.65
Currency: United States Dollars
COMMUNITY NEWSPAPER

The Orlando Times 18773
Owner: Calvin Collins, Jr.
Editorial: 4403 Vineland Rd Ste B5, Orlando, Florida 32811-7362 **Tel:** 1 407 841-3052
Email: keepupwiththetimes@gmail.com **Web site:** http://www.orlando-times.com
Freq: Thu; **Circ:** 10000 Not Audited
Publisher: Calvin Collins; **Editor:** Kevin Collins;
Circulation Manager: Margaret Davis
Profile: The Orlando Times is geared toward the African American residents of Orlando, FL and surrounding areas in central Florida. Topics covered in the newspaper include education, religion, local news and information of interest to the black community residing in Orlando, FL.
Language (s): English
Ad Rate: Full Page Mono 18.50
Currency: United States Dollars
COMMUNITY NEWSPAPER

Orlando Weekly 21664
Owner: Euclid Media
Editorial: 16 W Pine St, Orlando, Florida 32801-2612
Tel: 1 407 377-0400
Email: letters@orlandoweekly.com **Web site:** http://www.orlandoweekly.com
Freq: Weekly; **Circ:** 45000 Not Audited
Publisher: Graham Jarrett
Profile: Orlando (FL) Weekly covers local news, politics, music, arts & entertainment, dining, social issues and community events.
Language (s): English
Ad Rate: Full Page Mono 63.00
Currency: United States Dollars
COMMUNITY NEWSPAPER

Osage Valley Newspapers 25287
Owner: Standard Herald, Inc.
Editorial: 205 S Main St, Windsor, Missouri 65360-1869 **Tel:** 1 660 647-2121
Circ: 6800
Editor: Colby Gordon; **Advertising Sales Manager:** Jess Kellock; **Editor:** Frank Mercer
Language (s): English
COMMUNITY NEWSPAPER

Osceola News-Gazette 29443
Owner: Sun Publications of Florida
Editorial: 108 Church St, Kissimmee, Florida 34741-5055 **Tel:** 1 407 846-7600
Email: display@osceolanewsgazette.com **Web site:** http://www.osceolanewsgazette.com
Freq: Sat; **Circ:** 44410 Not Audited
Circulation Manager: Kathy Beckham; **Publisher:** Matt Plocha
Profile: Osceola News-Gazette in Kissimmee, FL covers local news, sports, arts and entertainment, opinion and community events. Deadlines are three days prior to issue date
Language (s): English
Ad Rate: Full Page Mono 20.35
Ad Rate: Full Page Colour 1491.00
Currency: United States Dollars
COMMUNITY NEWSPAPER

El Osceola Star 154489
Editorial: 922 Brack St, Kissimmee, Florida 34744-4510 **Tel:** 1 407 933-0174
Email: starnews@aol.com **Web site:** http://www.elosceolastar.com
Freq: Fri; **Circ:** 15000 Not Audited
Advertising Sales Manager: Yolanda Lopez
Profile: El Osceola Star is a local newspaper written for the Hispanic residents of Kissimmee, FL. Advertising deadlines are Mondays at 5PM ET.
Language (s): Spanish/Bilingual
Ad Rate: Full Page Mono 14.00
Currency: United States Dollars
COMMUNITY NEWSPAPER

Osprey Observer Inc. 217057
Owner: Osprey Observer Inc.
Editorial: 900 Lithia Pinecrest Rd, Brandon, Florida 33511-6121 **Tel:** 1 813 657-2418
Email: editor@ospreyobserver.com **Web site:** http://www.ospreyobserver.com
Circ: 86000 Not Audited
Publisher & Editor: Marie Gilmore; **Advertising Sales Manager:** Patricia Tracy
Profile: Osprey Observer Inc. in Brandon, FL is a community newspaper publisher that serves the residents of Tampa, St. Petersburg and Clearwater, FL.
Language (s): English
COMMUNITY NEWSPAPER

Ossian Journal-News 24915
Owner: News-Banner Publications
Editorial: 1002 Dehner Dr, Ossian, Indiana 46777-9787 **Tel:** 1 260 622-4108
Email: ossianj@adamswells.com **Web site:** http://www.news-banner.com
Circ: 9802 Not Audited
Advertising Sales Manager: Jean Bordner; **Publisher & Editor:** Mark Miller
Language (s): English
COMMUNITY NEWSPAPER

Osteen Publishing Company - Ponte Vedra 564643
Owner: Osteen Publishing Company
Editorial: 1102 A1A North, Unit 108, Ponte Vedra Beach, Florida 32082 **Tel:** 1 904 285-8831
Email: pvrecorder@opcfla.com **Web site:** http://www.pontevedrarecorder.com
Circ: 35000
Publisher: Susan Griffin
COMMUNITY NEWSPAPER

Osteen Publishing Group 135850
Owner: Osteen Publishing Group
Editorial: 3513 U.S. Hwy. 17, Fleming Island, Florida 32003 **Tel:** 1 904 264-3200
Web site: http://www.claytodayonline.com
Circ: 12000 Not Audited
Publisher: Jon Cantrell; **Circulation Manager:** Rob Conwell; **Advertising Sales Manager:** Peggy Oddy
Language (s): English
COMMUNITY NEWSPAPER

The Oswego County Weeklies 24646
Owner: Backus (Mark)
Editorial: 80 N Jefferson St, Mexico, New York 13114-3001 **Tel:** 1 315 963-7813
Email: ocweeklies@cnymail.com
Circ: 34567 Not Audited
Publisher: Mark Backus
Profile: The Oswego County Weeklies is a community newspaper publisher n Mexico, NY.
Language (s): English
COMMUNITY NEWSPAPER

The Other Paper 21623
Editorial: 1340 Williston Rd, South Burlington, Vermont 05403-6469 **Tel:** 1 802 864-6670
Email: news@otherpapersbvt.com **Web site:** http://www.otherpapersbvt.com
Freq: Thu; **Circ:** 9750 Not Audited
Publisher & Editor: Judy Kearns
Profile: The Other Paper is a local newspaper published for residents of South Burlington, VT. It covers local news and community events.
Language (s): English
Ad Rate: Full Page Mono 12.41
Ad Rate: Full Page Colour 675.00
Currency: United States Dollars
COMMUNITY NEWSPAPER

The Ouachita Citizen 22390
Owner: SJR Publishing Co. Inc.
Editorial: 1400 N 7th St, West Monroe, Louisiana 71291-4340 **Tel:** 1 318 322-3161
Email: news@ouachitacitizen.com **Web site:** http://www.hannapub.com/ouachitacitizen
Freq: Thu; **Circ:** 5200 Not Audited
Advertising Sales Manager: Rick Day; **Publisher:** Sam Hanna; **Editor:** Zach Parker
Profile: The Ouachita Citizen is a local, weekly newspaper serving the residents of West Monroe, LA. The newspaper covers local news, sports and community events. Deadlines are on Mondays.
Language (s): English
Ad Rate: Full Page Mono 5.50
Currency: United States Dollars
COMMUNITY NEWSPAPER

Our Place Newspapers 25537
Editorial: 1515 Veterans Hwy Ste 340, Islandia, New York 11749-4802 **Tel:** 1 631 224-9500
Email: ourplace20@optonline.net **Web site:** http://www.ourplacenews.com
Circ: 64000 Not Audited
Language (s): English
COMMUNITY NEWSPAPER

Our Time Press 155357
Owner: DGB Media Publishers
Editorial: 679 Lafayette Ave, Brooklyn, New York 11216-1009 **Tel:** 1 718 599-6828
Email: editors@ourtimepress.com **Web site:** http://www.ourtimepress.com

Freq: Thu; **Circ:** 20000 Not Audited
Profile: Our Time Press is an African-American owned and operated free tabloid-sized paper published in Brooklyn, New York.
Language (s): English
Ad Rate: Full Page Mono 75.00
Currency: United States Dollars
COMMUNITY NEWSPAPER

Our Town 24299
Owner: Straus News
Editorial: 36 Ridge St, Pearl River, New York 10965-2407 **Tel:** 1 845 735-1342
Email: news@ourtownnews.com **Web site:** http://www.ourtownnews.com
Freq: Wed; **Circ:** 14400 Not Audited
Publisher & Editor: Arthur Aldrich
Profile: Our Town is a weekly newspaper serving the residents of Rockland and Northern Bergen, NY.
Language (s): English
Ad Rate: Full Page Mono 14.35
Currency: United States Dollars
COMMUNITY NEWSPAPER

Outer Banks Sentinel 73118
Owner: Womack Newspapers Inc.
Editorial: 2910 S Croatan Hwy, Nags Head, North Carolina 27959-9026 **Tel:** 1 252 480-2234
Email: editor@obsentinel.com **Web site:** http://www.obsentinel.com
Freq: Wed; **Circ:** 8450 Not Audited
News Editor: Neel Keller; **Publisher:** Charles Womack
Profile: Outer Banks Sentinel is published weekly for the residents of Outer Banks, NC and the surrounding areas. The newspaper covers news, politics, business, finance, entertainment, health and sports.
Language (s): English
Ad Rate: Full Page Mono 8.00
Currency: United States Dollars
COMMUNITY NEWSPAPER

Outlook 409674
Owner: Horizon Publications
Editorial: 309 N College Ave, Newton, North Carolina 28658-3255 **Tel:** 1 828 464-0221
Email: onenews2@observernewsonline.com **Web site:** http://www.observernewsonline.com
Freq: Thu; **Circ:** 10000 Not Audited
Advertising Sales Manager: James Jennings; **Publisher:** Seth Mabry
Profile: Outlook is a free, weekly publication that emphasizes positive news about Catawba County, NC. From feature stories to arts & entertainment and the social scene, it is filled with local names and people. Published by The Observer News Enterprise, Outlook is included in every Thursday edition of the daily newspaper and is also available at area newsstands and businesses.
Language (s): English
Ad Rate: Full Page Mono 7.50
Currency: United States Dollars
COMMUNITY NEWSPAPER

Over the Mountain Journal 21874
Owner: Wald (Maury)
Editorial: 2016 Columbiana Rd, Birmingham, Alabama 35216-2147 **Tel:** 1 205 823-9646
Email: editorial@otmj.com **Web site:** http://www.otmj.com
Freq: Bi-Weekly; **Circ:** 40000 Not Audited
Editor: Keysha Drexel; **Advertising Sales Manager:** Julie Edwards
Profile: Over the Mountain Journal in Birmingham, AL is a bi-weekly newspaper that covers local news, community events and lifestyle topics of interest to the surrounding communities. Deadlines are three weeks prior to the issue date.
Language (s): English
Ad Rate: Full Page Mono 50.00
Ad Rate: Full Page Colour 2500.00
Currency: United States Dollars
COMMUNITY NEWSPAPER

Overton County News 20739
Owner: Oliver (Carson)
Editorial: 415 W Main St, Livingston, Tennessee 38570-1831 **Tel:** 1 931 823-6485
Email: info@overtoncountynews.com **Web site:** http://www.overtoncountynews.com
Freq: Tue; **Circ:** 5550 Not Audited
Publisher & Circulation Manager: Carson Oliver; **Advertising Sales Manager:** Darren Oliver; **Editor:** Dewain Peek
Profile: Overton County News is published weekly for the residents of Overton County, TN and surrounding areas. The newspaper covers local news, sports, society and community events. Deadlines are on Mondays at 5pm CT.
Language (s): English
Ad Rate: Full Page Mono 6.45
Currency: United States Dollars
COMMUNITY NEWSPAPER

Owego Pennysaver 28452
Owner: Times Shamrock Group
Editorial: 181-183 Front St Ste 2, Owego, New York 13827-1592 **Tel:** 1 607 687-2434
Email: opennysaver@stny.rr.com **Web site:** http://www.owegopennysaver.com
Freq: Sun; **Circ:** 20023 Not Audited
Circulation Manager: Ken Chaffee; **Editor:** Wendy Post; **Advertising Manager:** Vicki Wooden; **Publisher:** Greg Zyla
Profile: Owego Pennysaver is a local weekly newspaper serving the residents of Tioga County, NY and the Northeastern portion of Bradford County, PA. The newspaper is comprised mainly of advertising, but it also contains some local news and features of interest to the local community. Deadlines are on Wednesday mornings.
Language (s): English
Ad Rate: Full Page Mono 14.12
Currency: United States Dollars
COMMUNITY NEWSPAPER

Owyhee Avalanche 19037
Editorial: 20 E Idaho Ave, Homedale, Idaho 83628-3228 **Tel:** 1 208 337-4681
Email: owyheeavalanche@cableone.net **Web site:** http://www.owyheeavalanche.com/
Freq: Wed; **Circ:** 8000 Not Audited
Editor and Publisher: Joe Aman; **Advertising Sales Manager:** Rob Aman
Profile: Owyhee Avalanche is published weekly for the residents of Owyhee County, ID. The newspaper covers local news, sports and community events. Deadlines are on Mondays at noon ET.
Language (s): English
Ad Rate: Full Page Mono 6.00
Currency: United States Dollars
COMMUNITY NEWSPAPER

Oxford Public Ledger 19998
Editorial: 200 W Spring St, Oxford, North Carolina 27565-3247 **Tel:** 1 919 693-2646
Email: opl@earthlink.net
Freq: Mon; **Circ:** 6500 Not Audited
Profile: Oxford Public Ledger aims to provide local news and information to residents of Oxford County, NC. The deadlines are Tuesday at noon ET for the Thursday publication and Friday at 5pm ET for the Monday publication.
Language (s): English
Ad Rate: Full Page Mono 9.50
Currency: United States Dollars
COMMUNITY NEWSPAPER

Oyster Bay Guardian 20278
Owner: Oyster Bay Guardian Corp.
Editorial: 2 Endo Blvd, Garden City, New York 11530-6707 **Tel:** 1 516 509-4000 327
Web site: http://www.oysterbayguardian.com/
Freq: Fri; **Circ:** 6000 Not Audited
Editor: Laura Lane
Profile: Oyster Bay Guardian is a local weekly newspaper serving the residents of Oyster Bay, NY and the surrounding communities. It covers local news, sports and community events. Deadlines are one week before issue date.
Language (s): English
Ad Rate: Full Page Mono 8.96
Currency: United States Dollars
COMMUNITY NEWSPAPER

Ozark Spectator 18575
Owner: Bevil (Bob)
Editorial: 207 W Main St, Ozark, Arkansas 72949-3231 **Tel:** 1 479 667-2136
Email: spectator@centurytel.net **Web site:** http://www.ozarkspectator.net
Freq: Wed; **Circ:** 5800 Not Audited
Publisher: Bob Bevil; **Editor:** Jo Eveld; **Advertising Sales Manager:** Tracey Kendrick
Profile: Ozark (AR) Spectator is a local weekly newspaper serving Franklin, Johnson, Crawford, Logan, Madison and Sebastian counties, AR. It provides information on news and events of interest to the local communities.
Language (s): English
Ad Rate: Full Page Mono 5.50
Currency: United States Dollars
COMMUNITY NEWSPAPER

Pacific Publishing Company 24728
Owner: Pacific Publishing Co. Inc.
Editorial: 636 S Alaska St, Seattle, Washington 98108-1727 **Tel:** 1 206 461-1300
Web site: http://www.pacificpublishingcompany.com
Circ: 40000 Not Audited
Publisher: Robert Munford
Profile: Pacific Publishing Co. in Seattle, WA publishes City Living Seattle, Madison Park Times and Queen Anne News & Magnolia News.
Language (s): English
COMMUNITY NEWSPAPER

Pacific Sun 18664
Owner: Metro Publishing Group
Editorial: 835 4th St Ste B, San Rafael, California 94901-3260 **Tel:** 1 415 485-6700
Email: letters@pacificsun.com **Web site:** http://www.pacificsun.com
Freq: Fri; **Circ:** 22000 Not Audited
Publisher: Bob Heinen; **Editor:** Molly Oleson
Profile: Pacific Sun is a local weekly newspaper serving the residents of Marin County, CA, and Sonoma County, CA. It is an independent, alternative paper and content focuses on local news, entertainment, lifestyle and politics. The lead time for the paper varies per article.
Language (s): English
Ad Rate: Full Page Mono 29.90
Currency: United States Dollars
COMMUNITY NEWSPAPER

Packet Publications - Princeton 545890
Owner: Packet Media LLC
Editorial: 300 Witherspoon St, Princeton, New Jersey 08542-3401 **Tel:** 1 609 924-3244
Email: feedback@centraljersey.com **Web site:** http://www.centraljersey.com
Circ: 12680 Not Audited
Editor: Ruth Peterson Luse
Profile: Packet Publications in Princeton, NJ, publishes 11 community weekly papers, 7 TMC weekly publications, 1 lifestyle glossy magazine, and centraljersey.com. The Princeton Packet is the most widely read of their newspapers.
Language (s): English
COMMUNITY NEWSPAPER

Page News & Courier 21059
Owner: Byrd Newspapers
Editorial: 17 S Broad St, Luray, Virginia 22835-1904 **Tel:** 1 540 743-5123
Email: community@pagenewspaper.com **Web site:** http://www.shenvalleynow.com/index.php/newspapers/C1
Freq: Thu; **Circ:** 7212 Not Audited
Editor: Randy Arrington; **Publisher:** Thomas Byrd; **Advertising Sales Manager:** Jackie Elliott; **Community News Editor:** Deloris Judy
Profile: Page News & Courier is written for the residents of Page County, VA. It covers local news, sports, business, education and entertainment.
Language (s): English
Ad Rate: Full Page Mono 11.75
Currency: United States Dollars
COMMUNITY NEWSPAPER

Pahrump Valley Times 21485
Owner: News + Media Capital Group LLC
Editorial: 2160 E Calvada Blvd Ste A, Pahrump, Nevada 89048-5892 **Tel:** 1 775 727-5102
Email: pvtads@pvtimes.com **Web site:** https://pvtimes.com
Freq: Fri; **Circ:** 8000 Not Audited
Profile: Pahrump Valley Times is written for the residents of Nye County, NV. It covers local and community news, local sports, entertainment, editorials, business and events.
Language (s): English
Ad Rate: Full Page Mono 10.98
Currency: United States Dollars
COMMUNITY NEWSPAPER

Paintsville Herald 19371
Owner: Johnson County Newspapers Inc.
Editorial: 978 Broadway St, Paintsville, Kentucky 41240-1346 **Tel:** 1 606 789-5315
Email: news@paintsvilleherald.com **Web site:** http://www.paintsvilleherald.com
Freq: Fri; **Circ:** 5200 Not Audited
Advertising Sales Manager: Rita Brock; **Publisher & Editor:** Paula Halm
Profile: Paintsville Herald is a local newspaper serving the residents of Johnson County, KY. The newspaper mainly covers local news, sports, lifestyle, editorial and community events.
Language (s): English
Ad Rate: Full Page Mono 7.00
Currency: United States Dollars
COMMUNITY NEWSPAPER

Pakistan Link 79549
Owner: Mansuri (Arif)
Tel: 1 714 400-3400
Email: editor@pakistanlink.com **Web site:** http://www.pakistanlink.com
Freq: Fri; **Circ:** 25000 Not Audited
Editor: Akhtar Faruqui
Profile: Pakistan Link provides the Pakistani community in and around Anaheim, CA, with relevant information.
Language (s): English
Ad Rate: Full Page Mono 8.00
Currency: United States Dollars
COMMUNITY NEWSPAPER

Pakistan Post 155630
Editorial: 7826 Parsons Blvd, Fresh Meadows, New York 11366-1930 **Tel:** 1 718 739-2976
Email: postnewyork@aol.com **Web site:** http://www.pakistanpost.net
Freq: Wed; **Circ:** 81000 Not Audited
Profile: Pakistan Post is a community newspaper targeted at the Pakistani community of Jamaica, NY.
Language (s): English
Ad Rate: Full Page Mono 35.00
Currency: United States Dollars
COMMUNITY NEWSPAPER

Pakistan Publications 231997
Owner: Pakistan Publications, Inc. (The)
Editorial: 6666 Harwin Dr Ste 365, Houston, Texas 77036-2263 **Tel:** 1 713 914-0786
Email: pakistanchronicle@gmail.com **Web site:** http://pc.thepakistanpublications.com
Freq: Weekly; **Circ:** 90000 Not Audited
Publisher: Nasreen Khan; **Editor and Publisher:** Tariq Khan; **Advertising Sales Manager:** Jamil Siddiqui
Profile: Pakistan Publications publishes three weekly newspapers targeting South Asians and Muslims in the United States: The Pakistan Journal, which publishes in Urdu; The Pakistan Chronicle, which publishes in English, and the South Asian Chronicle, which also publishes in English.
Language (s): English
Ad Rate: Full Page Mono 20.00
Currency: United States Dollars
COMMUNITY NEWSPAPER

Palisadian Post 18637
Owner: Smolinisky (Alan)
Editorial: 881 Alma Real Dr Ste 213, Pacific Palisades, California 90272-3737 **Tel:** 1 310 454-1321
Email: info@palipost.com **Web site:** http://www.palipost.com
Freq: Thu; **Circ:** 15000 Not Audited
Publisher: Alan Smolinisky
Profile: Palisadian Post is a local newspaper written for the residents of Pacific Palisades, CA. The paper covers local news and community events.
Language (s): English
Ad Rate: Full Page Mono 28.05
Currency: United States Dollars
COMMUNITY NEWSPAPER

Palo Verde Valley & Quartzsite Times 18603
Owner: Yuma Sun, Inc.
Editorial: 153 S Broadway, Blythe, California 92225-2501 **Tel:** 1 760 922-3181
Email: webmaster@pvvt.com **Web site:** http://www.pvvt.com
Freq: 2 Times/Week; **Circ:** 5000
Profile: Covers Blythe News, Quartzsite News, Sports, Opinion, Features, Business, Events, Obituaries, Public Notices, and Multimedia.
Language (s): English
COMMUNITY NEWSPAPER

Palos Verdes Peninsula News 18639
Owner: MediaNews Group
Editorial: 609 Deep Valley Dr Ste 229, Rolling Hills Estates, California 90274-3629 **Tel:** 1 310 372-0388
Email: letters@pvnews.com **Web site:** http://www.pvnews.com
Freq: Thu; **Circ:** 18400 Not Audited
Profile: Palos Verdes Peninsula News is a twice-weekly newspaper serving the Palos Verdes Peninsula, including Palos Verdes Estates, Rolling Hills Estates, Rolling Hills and Rancho Palos Verdes, CA. It covers local news, business, sports, health, entertainment and community events. An edition of the paper is circulated for free to non-subscribers in the area on the third Saturday of each month.
Language (s): English
Ad Rate: Full Page Mono 22.54
Ad Rate: Full Page Colour 117.00
Currency: United States Dollars
COMMUNITY NEWSPAPER

Panola Watchman 22125
Owner: Texas Community Media
Editorial: 109 W Panola St, Carthage, Texas 75633-2631 **Tel:** 1 903 693-7888
Email: news@panolawatchman.com **Web site:** http://www.panolawatchman.com
Freq: 2 Times/Week; **Circ:** 5000 Not Audited
Editor: Becky Barlish; **Publisher:** Jerry Pye; **Advertising Sales Manager:** Dana Vega
Profile: Panola Watchman is a local newspaper serving the town of Carthage and Panola County, TX. The publication covers local news and community events.
Language (s): English
Ad Rate: Full Page Mono 9.35
Currency: United States Dollars
COMMUNITY NEWSPAPER

The Panolian 19857
Owner: Panolian, Inc. (The)
Editorial: 363 Highway 51 N, Batesville, Mississippi 38606-2311 **Tel:** 1 662 563-4591
Email: newsroom@panolian.com **Web site:** http://www.panolian.com
Freq: Fri; **Circ:** 6000 Not Audited
Advertising Sales Manager: Margaret Buntin; **Publisher:** John Howell; **News Editor:** Rita Howell
Profile: The Panolian is a local newspaper serving Batesville, MS. The publication covers local news and community events.
Language (s): English
Ad Rate: Full Page Mono 8.00
Currency: United States Dollars
COMMUNITY NEWSPAPER

Panorama 23332
Editorial: 7080 Hollywood Blvd, Ste 504, Los Angeles, California 90028 **Tel:** 1 323 463-7224
Email: pmgnews@sbcglobal.net **Web site:** http://www.kmnb.com
Freq: Wed; **Circ:** 60000
Publisher: Eugene Levin; **Editor:** Irene Parker; **Circulation Manager:** Boris Shpuut
Profile: Panorama is a Russian language newspaper serving the Russian community of Los Angeles.
Language (s): English
Ad Rate: Full Page Mono 11.97
Currency: United States Dollars
COMMUNITY NEWSPAPER

The Paper 23350
Owner: Boma (Mark) & Boma (Mary)
Editorial: 204 E Chippewa St, Dwight, Illinois 60420-1408 **Tel:** 1 815 584-1901
Email: thepaper1901@sbcglobal.net **Web site:** http://thepaper1901.com
Freq: Wed; **Circ:** 10000 Not Audited
Profile: The Paper is a community newspaper serving the following communities: Dwight, Gardner, Mazon, Odell, Reddick, Campus, Essex, Cullom, Kempton, Buckingham, Union Hill, Ransom, Blackstone, Cabery, Sauneminn Emington, Kinsman, Verona, Braceville, Herscher and South Wilmington, IL. It contains stories on community news, events, schools, government, sports, business and features.
Language (s): English
Ad Rate: Full Page Mono 12.00
Currency: United States Dollars
COMMUNITY NEWSPAPER

The Paper 359278
Owner: Aylward (Terry) and Lewis (Paul)
Editorial: 3 N Adair St Ste A, Pryor, Oklahoma 74361-2479 **Tel:** 1 918 825-2860
Email: thepaper@mayescounty.com **Web site:** http://www.mayescounty.com
Freq: Mon; **Circ:** 5000 Not Audited
Profile: The Paper is a weekly newspaper serving the residents of Mayes County, including communities in and around Pryor, OK. Stories include local news, events, sports, opinions, features and columns. The Paper is available via home delivery or for purchase at area newstands. The lead time is at least one week before distribution. Deadlines are on Thursdays a week prior to publication.
Language (s): English
Ad Rate: Full Page Mono 6.00
Currency: United States Dollars
COMMUNITY NEWSPAPER

The Paper 613863
Editorial: 3643 Grand Ave Ste A, San Marcos, California 92078-2336 **Tel:** 1 760 747-7119
Email: thepaper@cox.net **Web site:** http://www.thecommunitypaper.com
Freq: Thu; **Circ:** 20000
Publisher & Editor: Lyle Davis
Profile: The Paper is a local community newspaper for the residents ot San Marcos, CA and the surrounding communities.
Language (s): English
Ad Rate: Full Page Mono 22.00
Currency: United States Dollars
COMMUNITY NEWSPAPER

The Paper of Wabash County 21562
Tel: 1 260 563-8326
Email: news@thepaperofwabash.com **Web site:** http://www.thepaperofwabash.com
Freq: Tue; **Circ:** 16225 Not Audited
Publisher: Wayne Rees; **Editor:** Brent Swan
Profile: The Paper Of Wabash County is a community newspaper serving the residents of Wabash County, IN.
Language (s): English
Ad Rate: Full Page Mono 6.85
Currency: United States Dollars
COMMUNITY NEWSPAPER

The Papers Incorporated 24912
Owner: Baumgartner (Ronald)
Editorial: 206 S Main St, Milford, Indiana 46542-3004 **Tel:** 1 574 658-4111
Web site: http://www.the-papers.com
Circ: 58203 Not Audited
Publisher: Ron Baumgartner; **Publications Manager:** Kip Schumm
Profile: The Papers, Inc. is a printing and publishing company based in Milford, IN.
Language (s): English
COMMUNITY NEWSPAPER

Paradise Post 18640
Owner: MediaNews Group
Editorial: 5399 Clark Rd, Paradise, California 95969-6325 **Tel:** 1 530 877-4413
Email: newsroom@paradisepost.com **Web site:** http://www.paradisepost.com
Freq: Sat; **Circ:** 5303 Not Audited
Profile: Paradise Post serves the residents of Paradise, CA and surrounding areas. It covers local news, events, sports and business.
Language (s): English
Ad Rate: Full Page Mono 17.00
Currency: United States Dollars
COMMUNITY NEWSPAPER

Paraglide 789229
Editorial: Fort Bragg PAO, Reilly Road Stop A, Fort Bragg, North Carolina 28310-5000 **Tel:** 1 910 432-5007
Email: paraglidebragg@gmail.com **Web site:** http://paraglideonline.net
Freq: Weekly
Editor: Sandy Aubrey
Profile: The Paraglide is a weekly community newspaper serving Fort Bragg, NC, with local news, sports and features of interest to the military community.
Language (s): English
COMMUNITY NEWSPAPER

Park Cities News 20816
Owner: Waters (Marjorie)
Editorial: 4136 Greenbrier Dr, Dallas, Texas 75225-6635 **Tel:** 1 214 369-7570
Email: pcn@parkcitiesnews.com **Web site:** http://www.parkcitiesnews.com
Freq: Thu; **Circ:** 8000 Not Audited
Publisher & Editor: Marjorie Waters
Profile: Park Cities News is published weekly for the Highland Park, University Park and North Dallas, TX area. The newspaper covers local news and community events.
Language (s): English
Ad Rate: Full Page Mono 36.00
Currency: United States Dollars
COMMUNITY NEWSPAPER

Park Rapids Enterprise 19692
Owner: Forum Communications Co.
Editorial: 203 Henrietta Ave N, Park Rapids, Minnesota 56470-2617 **Tel:** 1 218 732-3364
Web site: http://www.parkrapidsenterprise.com
Freq: Sat; **Circ:** 6000 Not Audited
Editor: Vance Carlson; **Editor:** Kevin Cederstrom; **Circulation Manager:** Kathy Dennis; **Advertising Sales Manager:** Candy Parks
Profile: Park Rapids Enterprise is written for the residents of Park Rapids, MN and the surrounding area. The newspaper covers local news, sports and community events. Deadlines are on Mondays and Thursdays.
Language (s): English
Ad Rate: Full Page Mono 14.90
Currency: United States Dollars
COMMUNITY NEWSPAPER

The Park Record 21039
Owner: MediaNews Group
Editorial: 1670 Bonanza Dr Ste 202, Park City, Utah 84060-7239 **Tel:** 1 435 649-9014
Email: editor@parkrecord.com **Web site:** http://www.parkrecord.com
Freq: 2 Times/Week; **Circ:** 7500 Not Audited
Circulation Manager: Lacy Brundy; **Editor:** Nan Chalat-Noaker; **News Editor:** Jay Hamburger
Profile: Park Record is published bi-weekly for the residents of Park City, UT and surrounding areas. The newspaper covers local news, business, education, community events and entertainment. Deadlines are on Mondays and Wednesdays at 5pm MT.
Language (s): English
Ad Rate: Full Page Mono 16.00
Ad Rate: Full Page Colour 20.17
Currency: United States Dollars
COMMUNITY NEWSPAPER

Pasadena Weekly 21591
Owner: Southland Publishing
Editorial: 50 S De Lacey Ave Ste 200, Pasadena, California 91105-3806 **Tel:** 1 626 584-1500
Web site: http://www.pasadenaweekly.com
Freq: Thu; **Circ:** 30000 Not Audited
Publisher: Jon Guynn; **Circulation Manager:** Don Margolin; **Editor:** Kevin Uhrich
Profile: Pasadena (CA) Weekly covers local news, sports, business, politics and community events.
Language (s): English
Ad Rate: Full Page Mono 26.02
Ad Rate: Full Page Colour 1694.00
Currency: United States Dollars
COMMUNITY NEWSPAPER

The Pasadena/San Gabriel Valley Journal 22401
Editorial: 1541 N Lake Ave, Pasadena, California 91104-2374 **Tel:** 1 626 798-3972
Email: journal@pasadenajournal.com **Web site:** http://www.pasadenajournal.com
Freq: Thu; **Circ:** 12000 Not Audited
Publisher & Editor: Ruthie Hopkins
Profile: The Pasadena/San Gabriel Valley Journal is a weekly publication serving the African American community within the towns of Pasadena, Altadena, and San Gabriel Valley, CA. The publication covers local news, national news, arts & entertainment and community events. Deadlines are on Fridays at noon PT.
Language (s): English
Ad Rate: Full Page Mono 30.00
Currency: United States Dollars
COMMUNITY NEWSPAPER

Pascack Press 851653
Owner: Press Group, INC
Editorial: 192 3rd Ave Ste 14, Westwood, New Jersey 07675-2100 **Tel:** 1 201 664-2105
Email: pascackpress@thepressgroup.net
Freq: Weekly
Editor: Tom Clancey
Profile: Pascack Press is a weekly newspaper providing Local and Community News coverage for the residents of the Emerson, Hillsdale, Montvale, Park Ridge, River Vale, Township of Washington, Westwood and Woodcliff Lake, NJ region.
Language (s): English
COMMUNITY NEWSPAPER

Pascack Valley Community Life 21698
Owner: Gannett Co., Inc.
Editorial: 372 Kinderkamack Rd, Westwood, New Jersey 07675-1653 **Tel:** 1 201 664-2501
Email: pvcommunitylife@northjersey.com **Web site:** http://www.pvcommunitylife.com
Freq: Thu; **Circ:** 23298 Not Audited
Profile: Pascack Valley Community Life is a member of North Jersey Community Newspapers-Bergen Division. It is a weekly, community newspaper serving residents of Pascack Valley, NJ (Montvale, Park Ridge, Woodcliff Lake, Hillsdale, Westwood, River Vale, Washington Township and Emerson). It covers local news, events, schools, sports, business and features stories.
Language (s): English
Ad Rate: Full Page Mono 13.60
Currency: United States Dollars
COMMUNITY NEWSPAPER

Paso Robles Newspapers Inc. 133617
Owner: News Media Corp.
Editorial: 502 First St, Ste C, Paso Robles, California 93446-3742 **Tel:** 1 805 237-6060
Web site: http://www.pasoroblespress.com
Circ: 14400 Not Audited
Publisher: Jason Cross; **Editor:** Brian Williams
Language (s): English
COMMUNITY NEWSPAPER

Pataskala Post 24463
Editorial: 190 E Broad St, Pataskala, Ohio 43062-7104 **Tel:** 1 740 964-6226
Email: pataskalapost@earthlink.net **Web site:** http://home.earthlink.net/~pataskalapost
Freq: Thu; **Circ:** 11152 Not Audited
Publisher & Editor: Randy Almendinger; **Circulation Manager:** Brian McGuire
Profile: Pataskala Post covers local news, the city council, the school board, high school sports and community events.
Language (s): English
Ad Rate: Full Page Mono 6.45
Currency: United States Dollars
COMMUNITY NEWSPAPER

The Patriot 22835
Owner: Community Press, Inc.
Editorial: 102 E Hill Blvd #223, Charleston AFB, South Carolina 29404-5019 **Tel:** 1 843 412-5861
Email: info@charlestonmilitary.com **Web site:** http://www.charlestonmilitary.com
Freq: Fri; **Circ:** 7500 Not Audited
Profile: The Airlift Dispatch is a military newspaper for the Charleston Air Force Base, SC. The publication is written for military personnel, retired military and their family members.
Language (s): English
Ad Rate: Full Page Mono 9.00
Currency: United States Dollars
COMMUNITY NEWSPAPER

Patterson Irrigator 21948
Owner: Tank Town Media LLC
Editorial: 26 N 3rd St, Patterson, California 95363-2507 **Tel:** 1 209 892-6187
Email: news@pattersonirrigator.com **Web site:** http://www.pattersonirrigator.com
Freq: Thu; **Circ:** 8600 Not Audited
Editor: Maddy Houk; **Advertising Sales Manager:** Marybeth Marin
Profile: Patterson Irrigator is a local newspaper written for residents of Patterson, CA. The newspaper covers local news and events in the Patterson, CA area. Deadlines are on Fridays at noon for the Tuesday edition and on Tuesdays at noon for the Thursday edition.
Language (s): English
Ad Rate: Full Page Mono 8.50
Currency: United States Dollars
COMMUNITY NEWSPAPER

Pawnee Republican 20150
Owner: Puhalla (Ronald)
Editorial: 600 G St, Pawnee City, Nebraska 68420 **Tel:** 1 402 852-2575
Email: news@pawneenews.com **Web site:** http://www.pawneenews.com
Freq: Thu; **Circ:** 13000
Editor: Ray Kappel; **Advertising Sales Manager:** Elaine Karel
Profile: Pawnee Republican is the official newspaper of Pawnee County, NE. Its coverage area includes Pawnee County and the surrounding communities, including the school districts of Pawnee City, Lewston Consolidated and Humboldt Table Rock Steinauer.
Language (s): English
Ad Rate: Full Page Mono 7.50
Currency: United States Dollars
COMMUNITY NEWSPAPER

The Paxton Herald 21961
Owner: Antoun (Annette)
Editorial: 101 Lincoln St, Harrisburg, Pennsylvania 17112-2543 **Tel:** 1 717 545-9540
Email: thepaxtonherald@verizon.net **Web site:** http://www.thepaxtonherald.com
Freq: Wed; **Circ:** 22000 Not Audited
Publisher & Editor: Annette Antoun; **Circulation Manager:** Jon Antoun; **Advertising Sales Manager:** Jim Riordan
Profile: The Paxton Herald is a weekly newspaper serving Lancaster, Northern York, Perry and Cumberland counties, PA. The publication is in a "long tabloid format" and covers local news and community events.
Language (s): English
Ad Rate: Full Page Mono 6.95
Currency: United States Dollars
COMMUNITY NEWSPAPER

Paxton Media Group - High Point 25464
Owner: Paxton Media Group
Editorial: 210 Church Ave, High Point, North Carolina 27262-4806 **Tel:** 1 336 472-9500
Circ: 23600 Not Audited
Publisher: Rick Bean; **Editor:** Kathy Stuart
Language (s): English
COMMUNITY NEWSPAPER

Peach Publications 25494
Owner: Peach Publishing Co. Inc.
Editorial: 109 Anderson Ave, Fort Valley, Georgia 31030-4141 **Tel:** 1 478 825-2432
Web site: http://theleadertribune.net
Circ: 12100 Not Audited
News Editor: Victor Kulkosky; **Publisher:** Judy Robinson
Language (s): English
COMMUNITY NEWSPAPER

Pearisburg Virginian-Leader 21061
Owner: Virginian Leader Corp.
Editorial: 511 Mountain Lake Ave, Pearisburg, Virginia 24134 **Tel:** 1 540 921-3434
Email: office@virginianleader.com **Web site:** http://virginianleader.com
Freq: Wed; **Circ:** 5542 Not Audited
Editor: Roger Mullins; **Publisher:** Kenneth Rakes
Profile: The Pearisburg Virginian - Leader is a newspaper in Pearisburg, Virginia covering local news, sports, business, jobs, and community events.
Language (s): English
Ad Rate: Full Page Mono 6.10
Currency: United States Dollars
COMMUNITY NEWSPAPER

The Pender-Topsail Post & Voice 19968
Owner: Post Publishers, Inc.
Editorial: 108 W. Wilmington St, Burgaw, North Carolina 28425 **Tel:** 1 910 259-9111
Email: posteditor@post-voice.com **Web site:** http://post-voice.com
Freq: Thu; **Circ:** 5000 Not Audited
Circulation Manager: Michelle Charles; **Publisher & Editor:** Andy Pettigrew
Profile: The Pender-Topsail Post & Voice is a local publication serving residents of Pender County and Hampstead, NC. The newspaper covers local news and community events.
Language (s): English
Ad Rate: Full Page Mono 7.00
Ad Rate: Full Page Colour 567.00
Currency: United States Dollars
COMMUNITY NEWSPAPER

Peninsula Gateway 21112
Owner: McClatchy Newspapers
Editorial: 1950 S State St, Tacoma, Washington 98405-2817 **Tel:** 1 253 358-4141
Email: gatewayeditor@gateline.com **Web site:** http://www.gateline.com
Freq: Wed; **Circ:** 20000 Not Audited
Editor: Tyler Hemstreet
Profile: Peninsula Gateway is published weekly for the residents of Gig Harbor, WA. The publication covers local news, sports, business, lifestyle and community events. Deadlines are on Fridays at 5pm PT.
Language (s): English
Ad Rate: Full Page Mono 20.90
Currency: United States Dollars
COMMUNITY NEWSPAPER

Peninsula Warrior 476240
Owner: Military Newspapers of Virginia
Editorial: 150 W Brambleton Ave, Norfolk, Virginia 23510-2018 **Tel:** 1 757 878-4920
Email: pw@militarynews.com **Web site:** http://www.peninsulawarrior.com
Freq: Fri; **Circ:** 14000 Not Audited
Publisher: Laura Baxter
Profile: Peninsula Warrior is written for the Langley Air Force Base and Armed Forces communities in Hampton Roads, VA, producing two editions, for Air Force and Army.
Language (s): English
Ad Rate: Full Page Mono 17.77
Currency: United States Dollars
COMMUNITY NEWSPAPER

Penn-Franklin News Publishing Co. 25298
Editorial: 4021 Old William Penn Hwy, Murrysville, Pennsylvania 15668 **Tel:** 1 724 327-3471
Email: news@penn-franklin.com **Web site:** http://www.penn-franklin.com
Circ: 6000 Not Audited
Publisher & Editor: Georgia Cooper Boring; **Circulation Manager:** David Kenneth Boring; **Advertising Sales Manager:** Charlene Word
Profile: The Penn-Franklin News Publishing Co. publishes the Penn-Franklin News, the Penn-Trafford News and the Delmont-Salem News. They only accept local news tips. They do NOT accept e-mail attachments.
Language (s): English
COMMUNITY NEWSPAPER

Pennyrile Plus 22341
Editorial: 221 S Main St, Madisonville, Kentucky 42431-2557 **Tel:** 1 270 824-3300
Email: newsroom@the-messenger.com **Web site:** http://www.the-messenger.com/pennyrile_plus
Freq: Wed; **Circ:** 8000 Not Audited
Publisher: Rick Welch
Profile: Pennyrile Plus is a weekly lifestyle guide for residents of Madisonville, KY. The publication covers the local entertainment scene. Deadlines are on Fridays.
Language (s): English
Ad Rate: Full Page Mono 17.23
Currency: United States Dollars
COMMUNITY NEWSPAPER

Pennysaver Weekly News 389631
Owner: Hope (Linda) and Hope (Gail)
Editorial: 10546 N Florida Ave, Tampa, Florida 33612-6711 **Tel:** 1 813 935-3115
Email: pennysavernews@aol.com **Web site:** http://www.pennysaverweeklynews.com
Freq: Thu; **Circ:** 5000 Not Audited
Profile: The Pennysaver Weekly News is a weekly newspaper serving residents of Hillsborough County, including the communities of Tampa, Temple Terrace and Plant City, FL. It contains news, lifestyle and

entertainment stories and an extensive advertising section. It is distributed for a fee at newstands or through paid home subscriptions. Deadlines are on Tuesdays at noon ET before issue date.
Language (s): English
Ad Rate: Full Page Mono 5.00
Currency: United States Dollars
COMMUNITY NEWSPAPER

Penobscot Bay Press 25045
Editorial: 69 Main St, Stonington, Maine 4681
Tel: 1 207 367-2200
Email: news@pbp.me **Web site:** http://www.penobscotbaypress.com
Circ: 5880
Circulation Manager: Beverley Andrews; **Editor:** R. Nathaniel Barrows
Profile: Penobscot Bay Press is a community newspaper publisher servicing the residents of Bangor, ME.
Language (s): English
COMMUNITY NEWSPAPER

The Pensacola Voice 18775
Owner: Pensacola Voice Inc. (The)
Editorial: 213 E Yonge St, Pensacola, Florida 32503-3766 **Tel:** 1 850 434-6963
Email: info@pensacolavoice.com **Web site:** http://www.pensacolavoice.com
Freq: Thu; **Circ:** 35684 Not Audited
Publisher & Editor: Jacqueline Miles; **Circulation Manager:** Glover Powell
Profile: Pensacola Voice is a newspaper serving the African American community of Pensacola, FL. The publication covers news, sports, entertainment, health and religion. It also provides news of importance for and relating to African Americans. Deadlines are Tuesdays at noon ET.
Language (s): English
Ad Rate: Full Page Mono 19.65
Ad Rate: Full Page Colour 22.82
Currency: United States Dollars
COMMUNITY NEWSPAPER

Pentagram 21949
Owner: Comprint Military Publications
Editorial: 204 Lee Ave Bldg 59, Fort Myer, Virginia 22211-1114 **Tel:** 1 703 696-5401
Web site: http://www.dcmilitary.com/pentagram/
Freq: Weekly; **Circ:** 24000 Not Audited
Publisher: John Rives
Profile: Pentagram is written to provide news and event information to the Fort Meyers, VA military community. Deadlines are on Fridays.
Language (s): English
Ad Rate: Full Page Mono 39.62
Currency: United States Dollars
COMMUNITY NEWSPAPER

People Newspapers 25248
Owner: City Newspapers, LP
Editorial: 750 N Saint Paul St Ste 2100, Dallas, Texas 75201-3214 **Tel:** 1 214 739-2244
Email: editor@peoplenewspapers.com **Web site:** http://www.peoplenewspapers.com
Freq: Weekly; **Circ:** 23500 Not Audited
Editor: Todd Jorgenson; **Publisher:** Patricia Martin
Profile: People Newspapers is a weekly newspaper publisher in Northern Dallas. The papers cover news, sports, entertainment, arts, politics and features in the North Dallas area. The target audience is affluent readers in the community.
Language (s): English
COMMUNITY NEWSPAPER

The People's Defender 21332
Owner: Civitas Media
Editorial: 229 N Cross St, West Union, Ohio 45693-1266 **Tel:** 1 937 544-2391
Email: wuninfo@peoplesdefender.com **Web site:** http://www.peoplesdefender.com
Freq: Wed; **Circ:** 8700 Not Audited
Advertising Sales Manager: Terry Rigdon; **Editor:** Steven Triplett
Profile: The People's Defender is a local newspaper serving the residents of Adams County, OH. The publication covers local news and community events.
Language (s): English
Ad Rate: Full Page Mono 8.75
Currency: United States Dollars
COMMUNITY NEWSPAPER

The People's Tribune 22346
Owner: People's Tribune Inc. (The)
Editorial: 17 N Main Cross St, Bowling Green, Missouri 63334-1643 **Tel:** 1 573 324-6111
Email: peoplestribune@sbcglobal.net **Web site:** http://www.thepeoplestribune.com
Freq: Tue; **Circ:** 9000 Not Audited
Circulation Manager: Nancy Case; **Editor:** April Fronick; **Publisher:** Jerry Hickerson
Profile: The People's Tribune is published weekly for the residents of Bowling Green, MS and surrounding areas. The newspaper covers local news, sports, education and community events.
Language (s): English
Ad Rate: Full Page Mono 7.50
Currency: United States Dollars
COMMUNITY NEWSPAPER

El Periodico U.S.A. 23280
Owner: Spanish Point, Inc.
Editorial: 801 E Fir Ave, McAllen, Texas 78501-9320
Tel: 1 956 631-5628
Email: usa1@sc2000.net **Web site:** http://www.elperiodicousa.com
Freq: Wed; **Circ:** 68573 Not Audited
Publisher: Kathy Letelier
Profile: El Periodico U.S.A. provides national news and information for and about the Hispanic population across the country. Deadlines are on Fridays at noon CT.
Language (s): Spanish
Ad Rate: Full Page Mono 25.00
Currency: United States Dollars
COMMUNITY NEWSPAPER

Periódico Visión 824533
Editorial: Calle Ramon E. Betances 178 Sur, Mayaguez 680 **Tel:** 1 787 834-6829
Email: periodicovision@gmail.com **Web site:** http://puertoricoserver.net/pvision
Freq: Weekly; **Circ:** 53907
Editor: Maria Cotto
Profile: Periódico Visión is a community newspaper serving the Mayaguez area in Puerto Rico, including local news, features and events.
Language (s): Spanish
Ad Rate: Full Page Mono 26.00
Currency: United States Dollars
COMMUNITY NEWSPAPER

Perris Progress and City News 18642
Owner: GG Publications Inc.
Editorial: 1307C W 6th St Ste 139, Corona, California 92882-3140 **Tel:** 1 951 737-9784
Email: lmsentinel@aol.com **Web site:** http://www.theperrisprogress.com
Freq: Wed; **Circ:** 8500 Not Audited
Publisher & Editor: Gary Lendennie
Profile: Perris Progress is a local weekly newspaper based in Corona, CA. It covers local news, sports, weather, business, and arts & entertainment issues that impact readers. The publication is written for residents of Perris Valley, CA and surrounding areas.
Language (s): English
Ad Rate: Full Page Mono 110.00
Currency: United States Dollars
COMMUNITY NEWSPAPER

The Perry County News 19210
Owner: Landmark Community Newspapers, Inc.
Editorial: 537 Main St, Tell City, Indiana 47586-2210
Tel: 1 812 547-3424
Web site: http://www.perrycountynews.com
Freq: Mon; **Circ:** 6600 Not Audited
Advertising Sales Manager: Cindy Dauby; **Editor:** Vince Luecke
Profile: The Perry County News is published weekly for the residents of Tell City, IN and surrounding areas. The publication covers local news, sports, business and community events.
Language (s): English
Ad Rate: Full Page Mono 10.75
Currency: United States Dollars
COMMUNITY NEWSPAPER

Perry Newspapers 24897
Editorial: 123 S Jefferson St, Perry, Florida 32347
Tel: 1 850 584-5513
Email: newsdesk@perrynewspapers.com **Web site:** http://www.perrynewspapers.com
Circ: 10200 Not Audited
Publisher: Donald Lincoln
Profile: Perry Newspapers is a weekly community newspaper publisher serving the residents of Perry, FL.
Language (s): English
COMMUNITY NEWSPAPER

Peshtigo Times 21215
Owner: Gardon (Charles)
Editorial: 841 Maple St, Peshtigo, Wisconsin 54157-1341 **Tel:** 1 715 582-4541
Email: news@peshtigotimes.com **Web site:** http://www.peshtigotimes.com
Freq: Wed; **Circ:** 10450 Not Audited
Publisher & Editor: Mary Ann Gardon
Profile: The Peshtigo Times is a local newspaper serving the residents of Wisconsin's Marinette and Oconto counties in Wisconsin and Menominee County, MI. It covers local news, sports, education and community events. Deadlines are at 10am CT.
Language (s): English
Ad Rate: Full Page Mono 7.20
Currency: United States Dollars
COMMUNITY NEWSPAPER

Petaluma Argus-Courier 21868
Owner: Sonoma Media Investments LLC
Editorial: 719 Southpoint Blvd Ste C, Petaluma, California 94954-8004 **Tel:** 1 707 762-4541
Web site: http://www.petaluma360.com
Freq: Weekly
Editor: Matt Brown
Profile: Petaluma Argus-Courier is published weekly for the residents of Petaluma, CA and surrounding areas. The newspaper covers local news, government, education, business, sports and community events. Deadlines are on Mondays at 5pm PT.
Language (s): English
COMMUNITY NEWSPAPER

The Philadelphia Sunday Sun 21825
Owner: Philadelphia Sun Group (The)
Editorial: 6661 Germantown Ave, Philadelphia, Pennsylvania 19119-2251 **Tel:** 1 215 848-7864
Email: infosundaysun@yahoo.com **Web site:** http://www.philasun.com
Freq: Sun; **Circ:** 20000 Not Audited
Circulation Manager: Mike Baker; **Editor and Publisher:** J. Whyatt Mondesire
Profile: The Philadelphia (PA) Sunday Sun is published weekly for the residents of Philadelphia and surrounding areas. The newspaper provides information on local news and community events. Deadlines are on Wednesdays at noon ET.
Language (s): English
Ad Rate: Full Page Mono 47.20
Currency: United States Dollars
COMMUNITY NEWSPAPER

The Philadelphia Tribune 20608
Owner: The Philadelphia Tribune, Co.
Editorial: 520 S 16th St, Philadelphia, Pennsylvania 19146-1565 **Tel:** 1 215 893-4050
Email: newsroom@phillytrib.com **Web site:** http://www.phillytrib.com
Freq: Fri; **Circ:** 23090 Not Audited
News Editor: Johann Calhoun
Profile: The Philadelphia Tribune is written for the African American residents of Philadelphia, Delaware County and parts of Montgomery County, PA. It covers local news, sports, arts & entertainment, crime, health, business news, religion, politics and community events. The Sunday circulation is 10,380, Tuesday is 14,177 and Friday is 7,792.
Language (s): English
Ad Rate: Full Page Mono 117.15
Currency: United States Dollars
COMMUNITY NEWSPAPER

Philippine News 151883
Editorial: 1818 Gilbreth Rd, St 220, Burlingame, California 94010-1225 **Tel:** 1 650 552-9775
Email: feedback@gmanews.tv **Web site:** http://www.philippinenews.com
Freq: Fri; **Circ:** 64000
Advertising Sales Manager: Margarita Argenge; **Editor:** Cherie Querol Moreno
Profile: Philippine News is published weekly for the Filipino American community of Southern San Francisco. The newspaper provides information on local news, business, culture, arts & entertainment and community events.
Language (s): English
Ad Rate: Full Page Mono 35.00
Currency: United States Dollars
COMMUNITY NEWSPAPER

Philly Weekly 21617
Owner: Broad Street Media LLC
Editorial: 2 Executive Campus Ste 400, Cherry Hill, New Jersey 08002-4102 **Tel:** 1 215 563-7400
Email: mail@phillyweekly.com **Web site:** http://www.philadelphiaweekly.com
Freq: Wed; **Circ:** 55000 Not Audited
Profile: Philadelphia Weekly is published for the residents of Philadelphia, Southern New Jersey and Northern Delaware. Founded in 1971, this alternative newspaper focuses on the entertainment scene in Philadelphia as well as local and national news, government and politics.
Language (s): English
Ad Rate: Full Page Mono 46.00
Ad Rate: Full Page Colour 3474.00
Currency: United States Dollars
COMMUNITY NEWSPAPER

Phoenix New Times 18595
Owner: Voice Media Group
Editorial: 1201 E Jefferson St, Phoenix, Arizona 85034-2300 **Tel:** 1 602 271-0040
Email: feedback@newtimes.com **Web site:** http://www.phoenixnewtimes.com
Freq: Thu; **Circ:** 68861 Not Audited
Publisher: Kurtis Barton
Profile: Phoenix New Times is a weekly newspaper published for the residents of Phoenix, Arizona. The paper focuses on news, culture, music, film, dining, and local events. The lead time and deadlines for this publication vary. Contact the publication for updated advertising rates.
Language (s): English
Ad Rate: Full Page Mono 44.99
Currency: United States Dollars
COMMUNITY NEWSPAPER

Photo Star 20375
Owner: Bunner, (Judith E.)
Editorial: 307 State St., Willshire, Ohio 45898
Tel: 1 419 495-2696
Email: photostarnews@frontier.com
Freq: Wed; **Circ:** 11200 Not Audited
Editor: Judith Bunner
Profile: Photo Star is a local newspaper serving residents of the Willshire, OH area. The publication covers local news and community events.
Language (s): English
Ad Rate: Full Page Mono 8.50
Ad Rate: Full Page Colour 725.00
Currency: United States Dollars
COMMUNITY NEWSPAPER

The Picatinny Voice 22920
Owner: Picatinny Arsenal
Editorial: Public Affairs Office, 93 Ramsey Ave, Picatinny Arsenal, New Jersey 07806-5000
Tel: 1 973 724-6366
Email: usarmy.picatinny.netcom.list.acc-nj-procnet@mail.mil **Web site:** http://www.pica.army.mil/evoice/PDF/VOICE.pdf
Freq: Bi-Weekly; **Circ:** 5000 Not Audited
Editor: Ed Lopez
Profile: The Picatinny Voice is a military publication in Picatinny Arsenal written for members of the U.S. Army. They do not publish press releases or use outside contact by regulation.
Language (s): English
Ad Rate: Full Page Mono 11.00
Currency: United States Dollars
COMMUNITY NEWSPAPER

The Picayune 28955
Owner: Victory Publishing, LTD.
Editorial: 1007 Avenue K, Marble Falls, Texas 78654-5039 **Tel:** 1 830 693-7152
Email: info@thepicayune.com **Web site:** http://www.thepicayunetv.com/
Freq: Wed; **Circ:** 24409 Not Audited
Profile: The Picayune is a local newspaper serving residents of Picayune and areas around Marble Falls, TX. It covers local news, community events, sports and features of interest to local readers. It shares its editorial staff with its sister daily paper, the River Cities Daily Tribune in Marble Falls, TX. Deadlines are on Mondays at noon CT.
Language (s): English
Ad Rate: Full Page Mono 12.49
Currency: United States Dollars
COMMUNITY NEWSPAPER

Picayune-Times 758815
Owner: GateHouse Media Inc.
Editorial: 522 W 3rd St, Hope, Arkansas 71801-5001
Tel: 1 870 887-2002
Web site: http://www.picayune-times.com
Profile: Picayune-Times is a weekly newspaper serving Nevada County, AR. It provides information on news and events of interest to the local community. It is written for both past and present residents of Nevada County, AR. Deadlines are 5pm CT on Fridays.
Language (s): English
COMMUNITY NEWSPAPER

Pickens County News & LINK 542343
Owner: Gannett Co. Inc.
Editorial: 305 S Main St, Greenville, South Carolina 29601-2605 **Tel:** 1 864 298-4100
Email: localnews@greenvillenews.com **Web site:** http://greenvilleonline.com
Circ: 75000 Not Audited
Profile: Pickens County News & LINK is a community newspaper publisher in Greenville, SC.
Language (s): English
COMMUNITY NEWSPAPER

Pickens County Progress 18817
Editorial: 94 N Main St, Jasper, Georgia 30143-1510
Tel: 1 706 253-2457
Email: progress@ellijay.com **Web site:** http://www.pickensprogress.com
Freq: Thu; **Circ:** 7500 Not Audited
Circulation Manager: Sheri Crowe; **Editor:** Dan Pool; **Publisher:** John Pool; **Advertising Sales Manager:** Martha Pool
Profile: The Pickens County Progress is a local newspaper serving residents of Pickens County, GA. The publication covers local news, sports, and community events. The lead time for Pickens County Progress is one week. Deadlines for the publication fall one week before issue date.
Language (s): English
Ad Rate: Full Page Mono 16.50
Currency: United States Dollars
COMMUNITY NEWSPAPER

Picket Fence Media 737688
Owner: Picket Fence Media
Editorial: 34932 Calle Del Sol Ste B, Capistrano Beach, California 92624-1664 **Tel:** 1 949 388-7700
Circ: 41500
Profile: Picket Fence Media is a local newspaper providing news to the community of Capistrano Beach, CA.
Language (s): English
COMMUNITY NEWSPAPER

PICT Partnership 25337
Owner: Douthit Communications Inc.
Editorial: 158 Lear Rd, Avon Lake, Ohio 44012-1908
Tel: 1 440 933-5100
Email: news@westlifenews.com **Web site:** http://westlife.northcoastnow.com/
Freq: Weekly; **Circ:** 19500 Not Audited
Publisher: Harold Douthit
Language (s): English
Ad Rate: Full Page Mono 14.50
Currency: United States Dollars
COMMUNITY NEWSPAPER

Pierce County Community Newspaper Group 377251
Owner: Weymer (John)
Editorial: 2588 Pacific Highway, Fife, Washington 98424 **Tel:** 1 253 759-5773
Email: news@tacomaweekly.com **Web site:** http://www.tacomaweekly.com
Circ: 54000 Not Audited
Circulation Manager: Dave Davison; **Editor:** Matt Nagle; **Advertising Sales Manager:** Rose Thiele; **Publisher:** John Weymer
Profile: Pierce County Community Newspaper Group is a weekly newspaper publisher in Fife, WA.
Language (s): English
COMMUNITY NEWSPAPER

Pike County Dispatch 20579
Owner: Doty-Lloyd (Sue)
Editorial: 105 W Catherine St, Milford, Pennsylvania 18337-1417 **Tel:** 1 570 296-6641
Email: ads@pikedispatch.com **Web site:** http://www.pikedispatch.com
Freq: Thu; **Circ:** 6500 Not Audited
Publisher: Sue Doty-Lloyd; **Editor:** Christopher Jones; **Circulation Manager:** Amanda Markwalter; **Advertising Sales Manager:** Carol Markwalter
Profile: Pike County Dispatch is written for residents of Pike County, PA and the surrounding areas.
Language (s): English
Ad Rate: Full Page Mono 16.95
Currency: United States Dollars
COMMUNITY NEWSPAPER

Pikes Peak Newspapers 25353
Owner: ASP Westward LP
Editorial: 1200 E US Highway 24, Woodland Park, Colorado 80863-9213 **Tel:** 1 719 687-3006
Web site: http://coloradocommunitynewspapers.com
Circ: 18000 Not Audited
Advertising Sales Manager: Barb Stolte
Language (s): English
COMMUNITY NEWSPAPER

The Pilot 19461
Owner: Roman Catholic Archdiocese of Boston
Editorial: 66 Brooks Dr, Braintree, Massachusetts 02184-3839 **Tel:** 1 617 779-3782
Email: editorial@pilotcatholicnews.com **Web site:** http://www.pilotcatholicnews.com
Freq: Fri; **Circ:** 24000 Not Audited
Circulation Manager: Ernesto Cuevas; **Editor:** Antonio Enrique; **Publisher:** Seán O'Malley; **Advertising Sales Manager:** Larry Ricardo
Profile: The Pilot is a weekly newspaper written for members of the Roman Catholic Archdiocese of Boston. The paper covers local news and issues pertaining to the Roman Catholic Church.
Language (s): English
Ad Rate: Full Page Mono 25.00
Ad Rate: Full Page Colour 1980.00
Currency: United States Dollars
COMMUNITY NEWSPAPER

The Pilot 20008
Owner: The Pilot LLC
Editorial: 145 W Pennsylvania Ave, Southern Pines, North Carolina 28387-5428 **Tel:** 1 910 692-7271
Web site: http://www.thepilot.com
Freq: Fri; **Circ:** 13500 Not Audited
Editor: Steve Bouser; **Editor:** John Nagy; **Publisher:** David Woronoff
Profile: The Pilot is a local newspaper written for residents of Pinehurst, Southern Pines and the rest of the Sandhills in NC. The newspaper, published three days a week, covers local news and events. The lead time varies. Deadlines for The Pilot are noon ET on Thursdays for the Monday issue, Mondays for the Wednesday issue or Wednesdays for the Friday issue.
Language (s): English
Ad Rate: Full Page Mono 15.00
Currency: United States Dollars
COMMUNITY NEWSPAPER

Pine Cone Press-Citizen 21760
Owner: DeLost (Dave)
Editorial: 166 Hardy Ln, Longville, Minnesota 56655 **Tel:** 1 218 363-2002
Email: presscit@arvig.net **Web site:** http://www.pineconepresscitizen.com
Freq: Tue; **Circ:** 7814 Not Audited
Profile: Pine Cone Press-Citizen is a local newspaper written for residents of Cass County, MN. The newspaper covers local news, sports and events.
Language (s): English
Ad Rate: Full Page Mono 9.20
Currency: United States Dollars
COMMUNITY NEWSPAPER

Pine Creek Journal 427151
Owner: Trib Total Media, Inc.
Editorial: 535 Keystone Dr, Warrendale, Pennsylvania 15086-7538 **Tel:** 1 724 779-8742
Web site: http://www.yournorthhills.com/pinecreekjournal
Freq: Thu; **Circ:** 26000 Not Audited
Advertising Sales Manager: Jill Paschl
Profile: Pine Creek Journal is a local weekly newspaper serving residents of Seneca Valley and Pine Creek, PA. It covers local news, business, sports and arts & entertainment stories. It also provides national and statewide stories if they have a direct impact on the newspaper's readership. All inquiries should be addressed to the editor.
Language (s): English
Ad Rate: Full Page Mono 14.97
Currency: United States Dollars
COMMUNITY NEWSPAPER

Pine Island Eagle 24218
Owner: Breeze Newspapers
Editorial: 10700 Stringfellow Rd Ste 60, Bokeelia, Florida 33922-3232 **Tel:** 1 239 283-2022
Email: pineisland@breezenewspapers.com **Web site:** http://www.pineisland-eagle.com
Freq: Wed; **Circ:** 8500 Not Audited
Publisher: Scott Blonde
Profile: Pine Island Eagle is a local newspaper written for the residents of Bokeelia, FL. The newspaper covers local news. Deadlines are on Fridays at noon ET.
Language (s): English
Ad Rate: Full Page Mono 12.78
Currency: United States Dollars
COMMUNITY NEWSPAPER

Pioneer Group 24841
Editorial: 115 N Michigan Ave, Big Rapids, Michigan 49307-1401 **Tel:** 1 231 796-4831
Email: info@pioneergroup.com **Web site:** http://www.pioneergroup.net
Circ: 33645 Not Audited
Circulation Manager: Candy Allan; **Editor:** Bob Allen; **Publisher:** John Norton; **Advertising Sales Manager:** Tim Zehr
Language (s): English
COMMUNITY NEWSPAPER

Pioneer Press 24547
Owner: tronc
Editorial: 435 N Michigan Ave, Chicago, Illinois 60611-4066
Email: suburbs@tribpub.com **Web site:** http://www.chicagotribune.com/suburbs
Freq: Weekly; **Circ:** 121562 Not Audited
News Editor: Charles Berman; **News Editor:** Rich Bird; **News Editor:** Jennifer Fisher; **News Editor:** Ben Meyerson; **Editor:** John Puterbaugh
Profile: Placing an ad in just one paper is not an option, the advertising rate provided is based on an estimated group rate. Single ads can be placed in the Glencoe News for the rate listed.
Language (s): English
COMMUNITY NEWSPAPER

The Pioneer-News 19380
Owner: Landmark Community Newspapers, Inc.
Editorial: 455 N Buckman St, Shepherdsville, Kentucky 40165-5902 **Tel:** 1 502 543-2288
Email: editor@pioneernews.net **Web site:** http://www.pioneernews.net
Freq: Mon; **Circ:** 6800 Not Audited
Editor & Publisher: Thomas Barr
Profile: The Pioneer-News is published twice a week for residents of Bullitt County, KY. The newspaper covers local news, business, education, sports and community events.
Language (s): English
Ad Rate: Full Page Mono 21.39
Currency: United States Dollars
COMMUNITY NEWSPAPER

The Piscataquis Observer 27301
Owner: Northeast Publishing Co.
Editorial: 12 E Main St, Dover Foxcroft, Maine 04426-1414 **Tel:** 1 207 564-8355
Email: observer@nepublish.com **Web site:** http://www.observer-me.com
Freq: Wed; **Circ:** 5225 Not Audited
Advertising Sales Manager: Keri Foster
Profile: The Piscataquis Observer is a weekly community newspaper written for the residents of Piscataquis County in ME.
Language (s): English
Ad Rate: Full Page Mono 13.70
Currency: United States Dollars
COMMUNITY NEWSPAPER

The Pitch 21721
Owner: SouthComm Inc.
Editorial: 1627 Main St, 7th Flr, Kansas City, Missouri 64108-1368 **Tel:** 1 816 561-6061
Email: tips@pitch.com **Web site:** http://www.pitch.com
Freq: Weekly; **Circ:** 40000 Not Audited
Editor: Scott Wilson
Profile: The Pitch in Kansas City, MO is a weekly newspaper providing in-depth local news, lifestyle and arts & entertainment coverage.
Language (s): English
Ad Rate: Full Page Mono 45.00
Currency: United States Dollars
COMMUNITY NEWSPAPER

Pittsburgh Catholic 21894
Editorial: 135 1st Ave, Ste 200, Pittsburgh, Pennsylvania 15222 **Tel:** 1 412 471-1252
Email: info@pittsburghcatholic.org **Web site:** http://www.pittsburghcatholic.org
Freq: Fri; **Circ:** 111750 Not Audited
Editor: William Cone; **Circulation Manager:** Peggy Zezza
Profile: Pittsburgh Catholic serves as an instrument of education by presenting readers with accurate news and information about the church on a local, national and universal level. Its main goal is to provide a forum for expression of views, in a manner consistent with the teachings of the church and the principle of respect for others. The weekly newspaper is written for Catholics in the six county Diocese of Pittsburgh. Deadlines are at noon ET on Fridays, one week before issue date.
Language (s): English
Ad Rate: Full Page Mono 58.00
Ad Rate: Full Page Colour 3780.60
Currency: United States Dollars
COMMUNITY NEWSPAPER

Pittsburgh City Paper 21781
Owner: Eagle Media
Editorial: 650 Smithfield St Ste 2200, Pittsburgh, Pennsylvania 15222-3925 **Tel:** 1 412 316-3342
Web site: http://www.pghcitypaper.com
Freq: Wed; **Circ:** 61118 Not Audited
News Editor: Charlie Deitch; **Publisher:** Michael Frischling; **Editor:** Chris Potter
Profile: Pittsburgh City Paper is a local weekly newspaper serving residents of the Pittsburgh area. It features local news, sports, arts & entertainment and event listings.
Language (s): English
Ad Rate: Full Page Mono 54.10
Currency: United States Dollars
COMMUNITY NEWSPAPER

Pittsburgh Union 20589
Editorial: 1719 Liberty Ave, Pittsburgh, Pennsylvania 15222 **Tel:** 1 412 281-8533
Freq: Bi-Weekly; **Circ:** 11000 Not Audited
Editor: Anna D'Alo; **Publisher:** Larry Frediani
Profile: Pittsburgh Union is written for The Italian Sons and Daughters of America, a fraternal organization located mainly in Pennsylvania, New York, Ohio, West Virginia, Illinois, Indiana and Florida. The newspaper covers news and events regarding The Italian Sons and Daughters of America. There is no e-mail nor Web site for Pittsburgh Union. Advertising is not accepted.
Language (s): English
COMMUNITY NEWSPAPER

Placer Herald 18647
Owner: Gold Country Media
Editorial: 5055 Pacific St, Rocklin, California 95677-2707 **Tel:** 1 916 624-9713
Email: jeffr@goldcountrymedia.com **Web site:** http://www.placerherald.com
Freq: Thu; **Circ:** 14350 Not Audited
Editor: Scott Anderson; **Advertising Sales Manager:** Beth O'Brien
Profile: Placer Herald is a local weekly newspaper written for the residents of Rocklin, CA. Deadlines are at 5pm PT on Fridays.
Language (s): English
Ad Rate: Full Page Mono 24.00
Currency: United States Dollars
COMMUNITY NEWSPAPER

Plaindealer Publishing 24976
Owner: Lee Enterprises, Inc.
Editorial: 707 S 13th St, Tekamah, Nebraska 68061 **Tel:** 1 402 374-2226
Email: support@midwestmessenger.com **Web site:** http://www.midwestmessenger.com
Circ: 128767 Not Audited
Language (s): English
COMMUNITY NEWSPAPER

The Plains Reporter 20076
Owner: Wick Communications Inc.
Editorial: 14 4th St W, Williston, North Dakota 58801-5308 **Tel:** 1 701 572-2165
Email: news@willistonherald.com **Web site:** http://www.willistonherald.com
Freq: Wed; **Circ:** 15100 Not Audited
Profile: The Plains Reporter is a local weekly newspaper written for the residents of Williston, ND and the surrounding area.
Language (s): English
Ad Rate: Full Page Mono 9.10
Currency: United States Dollars
COMMUNITY NEWSPAPER

Plainville Citizen 88068
Owner: Record-Journal Publishing Company
Editorial: 500 S Broad St, Meriden, Connecticut 06450-6643 **Tel:** 1 860 410-1857
Email: news@plainvillecitizen.com **Web site:** http://www.plainvillecitizen.com
Freq: Thu; **Circ:** 9200 Not Audited
News Editor: Nick Carroll; **Advertising Sales Manager:** Christine Nadeau
Profile: Plainville Citizen is a community newspaper targeted at the residents of Plainville, CT.
Language (s): English
Ad Rate: Full Page Mono 15.85
Currency: United States Dollars
COMMUNITY NEWSPAPER

El Planeta 363372
Owner: Planeta Media LLC/MasTV
Editorial: 285 Broadway, Chelsea, Massachusetts 02150-2807 **Tel:** 1 617 379-0216
Email: editor@elplaneta.com **Web site:** http://www.elplaneta.com
Freq: Fri; **Circ:** 50000 Not Audited
Editor: Rafael Ulloa
Profile: El Planeta in Chelsea, MA is a weekly Spanish-language newspaper serving the Latino population in the Boston metro area and throughout New England. The paper covers regional, national and international news, politics, sports and arts & entertainment. Copies are distributed via subscriptions, picked-up at retailers and newsstands or they are handed out. Advertising deadlines are on Fridays at 5pm ET.
Language (s): Spanish/Bilingual
Ad Rate: Full Page Mono 22.00
Ad Rate: Full Page Colour 150.00
Currency: United States Dollars
COMMUNITY NEWSPAPER

Platte County Citizen 19842
Owner: Stubbs Publishing Company
Editorial: 1110 Branch St, Platte City, Missouri 64079-9714 **Tel:** 1 816 858-5154
Email: newsdesk1@plattecountycitizen.com **Web site:** http://www.plattecountycitizen.com
Freq: Wed; **Circ:** 11850 Not Audited
Profile: Platte County Citizen is a local weekly newspaper written for the residents of Platte County, MO. The paper offers comprehensive and complete coverage of the Platte County Commission, Sheriff's Department and municipal governments in Platte City, Weston, Camden Point, Dearborn and Edgerton, MO. The newspaper also features local coverage of Platte County R-3, West Platte R-2 and North Platte R-1 School Districts, including reports from Board of Education meetings and other school-related events and activities. The paper also covers local high school sports, including results and features on all Pirate, Bluejay and Panthers teams. The newspaper strives to provide its readers with not only timely news stories, but also features about the people and places that make the northern Platte County area unique and special.
Language (s): English
Ad Rate: Full Page Mono 10.00
Currency: United States Dollars
COMMUNITY NEWSPAPER

Platte County Newspapers 25243
Owner: News Media Corp.
Editorial: 1007 8th St, Wheatland, Wyoming 82201 **Tel:** 1 307 322-2627
Email: pceditor@pcrecordtimes.com **Web site:** http://www.pcrecordtimes.com
Circ: 6930 Not Audited
Circulation Manager: Teri Cordingly; **Editor:** Amber Ningen
Language (s): English
COMMUNITY NEWSPAPER

Pleasant Hill Times 21942
Owner: Powell (F. Kirk)
Editorial: 126 S 1st St, Pleasant Hill, Missouri 64080-1604 **Tel:** 1 816 540-3500
Email: phtimes@comcast.net **Web site:** http://www.phtimes.net
Freq: Wed; **Circ:** 10200 Not Audited
Advertising Sales Manager: Cheryl Miller
Profile: Pleasant Hill (MO) Times is a weekly newspaper that covers local news, government, business, schools and sports. Deadlines are Fridays at 5pm CT.
Language (s): English
Ad Rate: Full Page Mono 6.75
Currency: United States Dollars
COMMUNITY NEWSPAPER

Pleasanton Express 20930
Owner: Wilersons (Judith)
Editorial: 114 W Goodwin St, Pleasanton, Texas 78064 **Tel:** 1 830 281-2341
Email: news@pleasantonexpress.com **Web site:** http://www.pleasantonexpress.com
Freq: Wed; **Circ:** 8400 Not Audited
Advertising Sales Manager: Megan Benishek; **Editor:** Sue Brown
Profile: Pleasanton Express is a local weekly newspaper written for the residents of Atascosa County, TX. The newspaper covers the local news, sports, and lifestyles in Atascosa County, TX. Deadlines for the publication are on Monday by noon CT.
Language (s): English
Ad Rate: Full Page Mono 15.55
Currency: United States Dollars
COMMUNITY NEWSPAPER

Pocahontas Record-Democrat, Buena Vista County Journal & Laurens Sun Newspapers 242120
Editorial: 218 N Main St, Pocahontas, Iowa 50574-1624 **Tel:** 1 712 335-3553
Email: publisher@pokyrd.com
Circ: 7195 Not Audited
Advertising Sales Manager: Marcia Hamp; **Publisher & Editor:** Chris Vrba
Language (s): English
COMMUNITY NEWSPAPER

Pocahontas Star Herald 18578
Owner: JV Rockwell Publishing
Editorial: 109 N Van Bibber St, Pocahontas, Arkansas 72455-3319 **Tel:** 1 870 892-4451
Email: starherald@jvrhomes.com **Web site:** http://starheraldnews.com
Freq: Thu; **Circ:** 5000 Not Audited
Editor: Anita Murphy; **Publisher:** Thelma Rockwell
Profile: Pocahontas Star Herald is a local weekly newspaper written for residents of Pocahontas, AR. The newspaper covers the local news and events in Randolf County, AR. There is no Web site for Pocahontas Star Herald.
Language (s): English
Ad Rate: Full Page Mono 6.00
Currency: United States Dollars
COMMUNITY NEWSPAPER

Poinciana Pioneer 945891
Owner: Association of Poinciana Villages
Editorial: 401 Walnut St, Kissimmee, Florida 34759-4329 **Tel:** 1 321 402-0401
Email: pioneer@apvinc.net **Web site:** http://www.poincianapioneer.com
Freq: Bi-Weekly
Profile: Poinciana Pioneer is a twice-monthly publication providing Community News coverage to the residents of Poinciana, Florida.
Language (s): English
COMMUNITY NEWSPAPER

Polish Times 879407
Owner: S.M.I. Publishing, Inc.
Editorial: Sterling Heights, Michigan **Tel:** 1 313 721-3369
Email: polishtimes@comcast.net **Web site:** http://mypolishtimes.com
Freq: Weekly
Profile: Polish Times is a bilingual weekly newspaper covering news, culture, sports and entertainment news relevant to Polish-American audiences in the

Detroit metropolitan area, including both local news, and news from Europe and Poland.
Language (s): English
COMMUNITY NEWSPAPER

Polk County Publishing 24711
Owner: Polk County Publishing Co.
Editorial: 100 E Calhoun St, Livingston, Texas 77351 **Tel:** 1 936 327-4357
Email: enterprise@easttexasnews.com **Web site:** http://www.easttexasnews.com
Circ: 31048 Not Audited
Publisher: Alvin Holley; **Advertising Sales Manager:** Linda Holley; **Editor:** Greg Peak; **Editor:** Kim Popham; **Editor:** Jim Powers; **Editor:** Darlene Pyle
Language (s): English
COMMUNITY NEWSPAPER

Pomerado Newspapers 24858
Owner: Union Tribune Community Press
Editorial: 14023 Midland Rd, Poway, California 92064-3959 **Tel:** 1 858 218-7200
Email: news@pomeradonews.com **Web site:** http://www.pomeradonews.com
Circ: 32000 Not Audited
Editor: Steve Dreyer; **Publisher:** Douglas Manchester
Language (s): English
COMMUNITY NEWSPAPER

The Pompano Pelican 22228
Editorial: 1500 E Atlantic Blvd Ste A, Pompano Beach, Florida 33060-6769 **Tel:** 1 954 783-8700
Web site: http://www.pompanopelican.com
Freq: Fri; **Circ:** 15000 Not Audited
Editor and Publisher: Anne Hanby Siren
Profile: The Pompano Pelican's editorial mission is to produce the news that people need to know and want to know. It is focused on the local community and is written for residents of Pompano Beach, FL. Deadlines are noon ET, Wednesdays before issue date.
Language (s): English
Ad Rate: Full Page Mono 12.00
Currency: United States Dollars
COMMUNITY NEWSPAPER

Ponchatoula Times 19432
Editorial: 170 N 7th St, Ponchatoula, Louisiana 70454-3305 **Tel:** 1 985 386-2877
Email: editor@ponchatoula.com **Web site:** http://www.ponchatoula.com/ptimes
Freq: Thu; **Circ:** 7500 Not Audited
Publisher & Editor: Bryan McMahon
Profile: Ponchatoula Times is written for residents of Tangipahoa Parish, LA. It covers local news, sports and events.
Language (s): English
Ad Rate: Full Page Mono 6.49
Currency: United States Dollars
COMMUNITY NEWSPAPER

Pontotoc Progress 19896
Owner: Journal Publishing Co.
Editorial: 13 E Jefferson St, Pontotoc, Mississippi 38863-2807 **Tel:** 1 662 489-3511
Email: pontprog@journalinc.com **Web site:** http://www.pontotoc360.com
Freq: Wed; **Circ:** 7100 Not Audited
Editor: David Helms; **Advertising Manager:** Angie Quarles
Profile: Pontotoc Progress is published weekly for the residents of Pontotoc, MS and surrounding areas. The newspaper provides information on local news and community events.
Language (s): English
Ad Rate: Full Page Mono 7.60
Currency: United States Dollars
COMMUNITY NEWSPAPER

El Popular 23278
Owner: El Popular, Inc.
Editorial: 404 Truxtun Ave, Bakersfield, California 93301-5316 **Tel:** 1 661 398-1000
Email: news@elpopularnews.com **Web site:** http://www.elpopularnews.com
Freq: Fri; **Circ:** 24000 Not Audited
Profile: El Popular is a local weekly newspaper serving western Kern County, CA. It covers local community news, upcoming events, local sports, health, food and arts & entertainment. It also contains the section Our Culture.
Language (s): Spanish
Ad Rate: Full Page Mono 17.50
Currency: United States Dollars
COMMUNITY NEWSPAPER

Port Orchard Independent 24373
Owner: Sound Publishing, Inc./Kitsap News Group
Editorial: 2465 Bethel Rd SE Ste 102, Port Orchard, Washington 98366-2407 **Tel:** 1 360 876-4414
Web site: http://www.kitsapdailynews.com
Freq: Fri; **Circ:** 18300 Not Audited
Circulation Manager: Noreen Hamren; **Editor:** Jeff Rhodes
Profile: Port Orchard Independent is a weekly newspaper written for the residents of Port Orchard, WA and surrounding areas. The paper covers local news, business, sports and community events. Deadlines are at noon PT prior to issue date. Send all editorial correspondence to the PO Box address. Send advertising correspondence to Port Orchard Independent, c/o Sound Publishing, 7689 NE Day Rd., Bainbridge Island, WA 98110. Ads will also run in the paper's sister publications, including Bainbridge Island Review, Bremerton Patriot and North Kitsap Herald.
Language (s): English
Ad Rate: Full Page Mono 22.40
Currency: United States Dollars
COMMUNITY NEWSPAPER

Port Publications, Inc. 779830
Owner: Port Publications, Inc.
Editorial: 125 E Main St, Port Washington, Wisconsin 53074-1915 **Tel:** 1 262 284-3494
Email: news@ozaukeepress.com **Web site:** http://www.ozaukeepress.com/
Circ: 19300
Advertising Sales Manager: Holly Ostermann; **Publisher & Editor:** William Schanen
Language (s): English
COMMUNITY NEWSPAPER

Portage County Gazette 245117
Editorial: 1024 Main St, Stevens Point, Wisconsin 54481-2859 **Tel:** 1 715 343-8045
Email: news@pcgazette.com **Web site:** http://www.pcgazette.com
Freq: Fri; **Circ:** 5361 Not Audited
Editor: Nathanael Enwald; **Advertising Manager:** Joey Hetzel; **Publisher:** Peter Leahy
Profile: Portage County Gazette is published weekly for the residents of Stevens Point and Portage County, WI. The publication provides information on local news and community events.
Language (s): English
Ad Rate: Full Page Mono 9.75
Currency: United States Dollars
COMMUNITY NEWSPAPER

The Portland Mercury 152525
Owner: Index Publishing LLC
Editorial: 115 SW Ash St Ste 600, Portland, Oregon 97204-3549 **Tel:** 1 503 294-0840
Email: news@portlandmercury.com **Web site:** http://www.portlandmercury.com
Freq: Thu; **Circ:** 45000 Not Audited
Publisher: Rob Crocker; **Editor:** William Humphrey; **Advertising Sales Manager:** Rob Thompson
Profile: Portland Mercury is a free weekly arts, entertainment, and culture newspaper. It is targeted at 20-somethings in Portland, OR and its surrounding areas. The paper offers extensive entertainment listings, music reviews, political news and local news. It is also filled with humorous parodies of the news.
Language (s): English
Ad Rate: Full Page Mono 41.78
Currency: United States Dollars
COMMUNITY NEWSPAPER

Portland Observer 20523
Owner: Northwest Print Inc.
Editorial: 4747 NE M L King Blvd, Portland, Oregon 97211-3398 **Tel:** 1 503 288-0033
Email: news@portlandobserver.com **Web site:** http://www.portlandobserver.com
Freq: Wed; **Circ:** 39534 Not Audited
Advertising Sales Manager: Leonard Latin; **Editor:** Mike Leighton
Profile: Portland Observer is a weekly newspaper written for residents of Portland, OR. Deadlines are 5pm PT, Friday before issue date. Contact the publication for advertisement rates.
Language (s): English
Ad Rate: Full Page Mono 70.00
Currency: United States Dollars
COMMUNITY NEWSPAPER

The Portland Phoenix 24457
Owner: Portland News Club LLC
Editorial: 65 W Commercial St Ste 207, Portland, Maine 04101-4788 **Tel:** 1 207 773-8900
Email: submit@phx.com **Web site:** http://portlandphoenix.me
Freq: Fri; **Circ:** 44500 Not Audited
News Editor: David Carkhuff; **Publisher:** Stephen Mindich
Profile: The Portland (ME) Phoenix is written for residents of Maine and New Hampshire. It covers local news, events and entertainment. Deadlines are on Tuesdays at 5pm ET.
Language (s): English
Ad Rate: Full Page Mono 13.33
Currency: United States Dollars
COMMUNITY NEWSPAPER

Portuguese Times 257065
Owner: Lima (Linda)
Editorial: 1501 Acushnet Ave, New Bedford, Massachusetts 02746-2223 **Tel:** 1 508 997-3118
Email: ptimes@aol.com **Web site:** http://www.portuguesetimes.com
Freq: Wed; **Circ:** 16000 Not Audited
Advertising Sales Manager: Gus Pessoa; **Editor and Publisher:** Frank Resendes
Profile: Portuguese Times in New Bedford, MA covers news relevant to Portuguese community in the local region and nationally.
Language (s): Portuguese
Ad Rate: Full Page Mono 10.00
Currency: United States Dollars
COMMUNITY NEWSPAPER

Post Eagle 20193
Owner: Post Publishing Co.
Editorial: 107 Mount Prospect Ave, Clifton, New Jersey 07013-1919 **Tel:** 1 973 473-5414
Email: posteagle@aol.com **Web site:** http://www.posteaglenewspaper.com
Freq: Wed; **Circ:** 10000 Not Audited
Publisher & Editor: Christine Grabowski-Witmyer
Profile: Post Eagle is published weekly for the residents of Clifton, NJ and surrounding areas. The newspaper covers local news, sports and community events.
Language (s): English
Ad Rate: Full Page Mono 11.00
Currency: United States Dollars
COMMUNITY NEWSPAPER

The Post Newspapers 769166
Owner: Post Newspapers (The)
Editorial: 5164 Normandy Park Dr Ste 100, Medina, Ohio 44256-5903 **Tel:** 1 330 721-7678
Email: news@thepostnewspapers.com **Web site:** http://www.thepostnewspapers.com
Freq: Weekly; **Circ:** 108600
Advertising Manager: Tara Leffel; **Publisher:** Bruce Trogdon; **Circulation Manager:** Ronnie Zack
Profile: The Post Newspapers offer local news and information in nine different community newspapers in the Medina, Ohio area.
Language (s): English
Ad Rate: Full Page Mono 2998.00
Ad Rate: Full Page Colour 3597.60
Currency: United States Dollars
COMMUNITY NEWSPAPER

Post Newspapers, Inc. 25481
Owner: MediaNews Group
Editorial: 59 Marylinn Dr, Milpitas, California 95035-4311 **Tel:** 1 408 262-2454
Circ: 70900 Not Audited
Editor: Rob Devincenzi
Profile: Post Newspapers Inc. in Milpitas, CA publishes the Berryessa Sun, Fremont Bulletin, Milpitas Post and Newark Connection.
Language (s): English
COMMUNITY NEWSPAPER

Post-Gazette 21497
Owner: Donnaruma (Pamela)
Editorial: 5 Prince St, Boston, Massachusetts 02113-2443 **Tel:** 1 617 227-8929
Email: postgazette@aol.com **Web site:** http://www.bostonpostgazette.com
Freq: Fri; **Circ:** 25900 Not Audited
Publisher and Editor: Pamela Donnaruma
Profile: Post-Gazette in Boston is a community newspaper that covers local news and events pertinent to the Italian-American community in New England. Deadlines are Wednesdays at noon ET.
Language (s): English
Ad Rate: Full Page Mono 20.00
Currency: United States Dollars
COMMUNITY NEWSPAPER

The Post-Searchlight 18794
Owner: Bainbridge Media, LLC
Editorial: 301 N Crawford St, Bainbridge, Georgia 39817-3612 **Tel:** 1 229 246-2827
Email: news@thepostsearchlight.com **Web site:** http://www.thepostsearchlight.com
Freq: 2 Times/Week; **Circ:** 43602 Not Audited
Advertising Sales Manager: Nichole Buchanan; **Publisher:** Jeff Findley
Profile: The Post-Searchlight's editorial mission is to present news and information of interest to residents of Bainbridge and Decatur County, GA. Deadlines are 9am ET, Monday before Wednesday's issue date and 9am ET, Thursday before Saturday's issue date.
Language (s): English
Ad Rate: Full Page Mono 8.60
Currency: United States Dollars
COMMUNITY NEWSPAPER

Powdersville Post & Easley Progress 524505
Owner: Heartland Publications
Editorial: 205 Russell St, Easley, South Carolina 29640-3056 **Tel:** 1 864 855-0355
Email: news@theeasleyprogress.com
Circ: 17000 Not Audited
Profile: A community newspaper covering local news and events in Easley, South Carolina.
COMMUNITY NEWSPAPER

Powell Valley News 21062
Editorial: 41798 E Morgan Ave, Pennington Gap, Virginia 24277-3216 **Tel:** 1 276 546-1210
Email: dlock.pvn@sunsetcom.com
Freq: Sat; **Circ:** 6428 Not Audited
Editor: Rick Watson
Language (s): English
Ad Rate: Full Page Mono 10.00
Currency: United States Dollars
COMMUNITY NEWSPAPER

The Prairie Advocate 21765
Owner: Sauk Valley Publishing
Editorial: 104 N Broad St, Lanark, Illinois 61046-1004 **Tel:** 1 815 493-2560
Email: news@prairieadvocate.com **Web site:** http://www.prairieadvocate.com
Freq: Wed; **Circ:** 15800 Not Audited
Editor: Jeff Rogers; **Advertising Manager:** Andrew Williamson
Profile: The Prairie Advocate is a weekly local newspaper written for the residents of Carroll County, IL. The publication is a general interest newspaper covering local news and community events. Deadlines are noon CT Fridays before issue date.
Language (s): English
Ad Rate: Full Page Mono 18.00
Currency: United States Dollars
COMMUNITY NEWSPAPER

Precinct Reporter Group 24851
Owner: Townsend (Brian)
Editorial: 670 N Arrowhead Ave Ste B, San Bernardino, California 92401-1102 **Tel:** 1 909 889-0597
Email: news@precinctreporter.com **Web site:** http://online.precinctreporter.com/
Circ: 80000
Publisher & Editor: Brian Townsend
Language (s): English
COMMUNITY NEWSPAPER

La Prensa 23184
Owner: ImpreMedia LLC
Editorial: 685 S Ronald Reagan Blvd, Longwood, Florida 32750-6435 **Tel:** 1 407 767-0070
Email: info@laprensa.com **Web site:** http://www.laprensafl.com
Freq: Thu; **Circ:** 35000 Not Audited
Advertising Sales Manager: Elio Aguilar; **Publisher:** Dora Casanova de Toro
Profile: La Prensa Newspaper's editorial mission is to provide a voice for the Spanish residents Longwood, FL. The publication includes topics of fashion, beauty, community news, national and local news, health news and immigration topics. The lead time for La Prensa Newspaper is one week.
Language (s): Spanish
Ad Rate: Full Page Mono 35.36
Currency: United States Dollars
COMMUNITY NEWSPAPER

La Prensa 154498
Editorial: 1704 E 5th St Ste 103, Austin, Texas 78702-4482 **Tel:** 1 512 478-3090
Email: laprensanews@aol.com **Web site:** http://www.laprensaofaustin.com
Freq: Thu; **Circ:** 20000 Not Audited
Publisher & Editor: Catherine Vasquez-Revilla
Profile: La Prensa is a local newspaper written for the residents of Austin, TX.
Language (s): Spanish
Ad Rate: Full Page Mono 18.25
Currency: United States Dollars
COMMUNITY NEWSPAPER

La Prensa de Chicago 903517
Editorial: 4518 W Fullerton Ave, Chicago, Illinois 60639-1934 **Tel:** 1 773 521-7286
Email: laprensachicago@hotmail.com **Web site:** http://www.laprensaus.com
Freq: Fri
Editor: Diego Giraldo; **Publisher:** Martha González
Profile: La Prensa de Chicago is a weekly newspaper providing Local and Community News for the Hispanic and Spanish-speaking community in Chicago, IL.
Language (s): Spanish
COMMUNITY NEWSPAPER

La Prensa de Colorado 902713
Owner: La Prensa de Colorado
Editorial: 7280 Irving St Ste A-106, Westminster, Colorado 80030-4933 **Tel:** 1 303 287-4105
Email: news@laprensadecolorado.com **Web site:** http://www.laprensadecolorado.com
Freq: Fri; **Circ:** 10000
News Editor: Germán Gónzalez
Profile: La Prensa de Colorado is a weekly Spanish-language newspaper providing Local and Community News coverage for the residents of Westminster, CO.
Language (s): English
COMMUNITY NEWSPAPER

La Prensa de Houston 882961
Editorial: 7100 Regency Square Blvd Ste 217, Houston, Texas 77036-3187 **Tel:** 1 713 334-4959
Email: editorial@prensadehouston.com **Web site:** http://www.prensadehouston.com
Freq: Weekly; **Circ:** 96500
Profile: La Prensa de Houston is a weekly publication in Spanish committed to providing international, national and local advertisers with the best medium to reach Spanish-speaking consumers in the Houston metropolitan and suburban areas with more than 3,700 points of distribution. Each issue features a balanced content of news, reports, business information and entertainment for the entire family.
Language (s): Spanish
COMMUNITY NEWSPAPER

La Prensa De San Antonio 23235
Owner: Duran Duran Industries
Editorial: 230 N Medina St, San Antonio, Texas 78207-3022 **Tel:** 1 210 242-7900
Web site: http://www.laprensasa.com
Freq: Sun; **Circ:** 60581 Not Audited
Profile: La Prensa De San Antonio is a bilingual newspaper written for the Hispanic community of San Antonio. The newspaper aims to encourage the community by reporting on positive news stories, as well as cultural issues and entertainment news and information.
Language (s): English, Spanish
Ad Rate: Full Page Mono 18.00
Currency: United States Dollars
COMMUNITY NEWSPAPER

La Prensa Del Noroeste de Arkansas 75794
Owner: Stephens Media Group
Editorial: 212 N East Ave, Fayetteville, Arkansas 72701-5225 **Tel:** 1 479 872-5035
Web site: http://www.laprensanwa.com
Freq: Thu; **Circ:** 8200 Not Audited
Advertising Sales Manager: Biasnhey Grimaldo

Profile: La Prensa Del Noroeste de Arkansas is a weekly Spanish-language publication distributed throughout Arkansas. It focuses on bringing the Spanish community information on entertainment, sports, community news and weather.
Language (s): Spanish/Bilingual
Ad Rate: Full Page Mono 10.00
Currency: United States Dollars
COMMUNITY NEWSPAPER

La Prensa en Iowa 823509
Owner: Lopez (Lorena)
Editorial: 109 S Main St, Denison, Iowa 51442-1958 **Tel:** 1 712 790-1563
Email: info@laprensaiowa.com **Web site:** http://www.laprensaiowa.com
Freq: Bi-Weekly
Advertising Sales Manager: Carlos Aguello; **Editor & Publisher:** Lorena Lopez
Profile: La Prensa en Iowa is a bi-weekly community newspaper serving the Hispanic population of Western Iowa, including Storm Lake, Denison, Carroll, Perry, Des Moines, and Ames. The paper includes local, national, and international news, as well as sports, health, and immigration news.
Language (s): Spanish
Ad Rate: Full Page Mono 6.81
Ad Rate: Full Page Colour 8.27
Currency: United States Dollars
COMMUNITY NEWSPAPER

Prensa Hispana 75770
Owner: Hispanic Press
Editorial: 809 E Washington St Ste 209, Phoenix, Arizona 85034-1018 **Tel:** 1 602 256-2443
Email: ml@prensahispana.org **Web site:** http://www.prensahispanaaz.com
Freq: Wed; **Circ:** 64925 Not Audited
Advertising Sales Manager: Laty Garcia; **Publisher & Editor:** Manny Garcia
Profile: Prensa Hispana is a regional newspaper for the Hispanic community of Arizona. It covers international, national and local news, sports, art and events.
Language (s): English
Ad Rate: Full Page Mono 48.07
Ad Rate: Full Page Colour 4830.00
Currency: United States Dollars
COMMUNITY NEWSPAPER

La Prensa Hispana 407527
Owner: HIM, Inc.
Editorial: 45102 Smurr St, Indio, California 92201-4404 **Tel:** 1 760 342-2565
Email: laprehis@aol.com **Web site:** http://www.laprensahispananewspaper.com
Freq: 2 Times/Week; **Circ:** 46500 Not Audited
Profile: La Prensa Hispana is a bilingual newspaper written for residents in Indio, CA.
Language (s): Spanish/Bilingual
Ad Rate: Full Page Mono 35.00
Currency: United States Dollars
COMMUNITY NEWSPAPER

La Prensa Hispana-L.A. 23265
Owner: OSA Communications
Editorial: 815 S Central Ave, Ste 12B, Glendale, California 91204 **Tel:** 1 818 500-8103
Email: laprensahispana@aol.com **Web site:** http://laprensahispanala.com
Freq: Weekly; **Circ:** 50000 Not Audited
Profile: La Prensa Hispana-L.A. covers the concerns of the Hispanic community in California.
Language (s): Spanish
Ad Rate: Full Page Mono 18.50
Currency: United States Dollars
COMMUNITY NEWSPAPER

La Prensa Latina 258021
Owner: Mendelson and Associates
Editorial: 995 S Yates Rd Ste 3, Memphis, Tennessee 38119-0882 **Tel:** 1 901 751-2100
Email: sidney@laprensalatina.com **Web site:** http://www.laprensalatina.com
Freq: Sun; **Circ:** 37000 Not Audited
Editor: Vivian Fernandez; **Publisher:** Sidney Mendelson
Profile: La Prensa Latina in Memphis, TN is a local newspaper written for Hispanic residents and covers community news, sports, social events, education, arts & entertainment and features.
Language (s): Spanish/Bilingual
Ad Rate: Full Page Mono 14.49
Currency: United States Dollars
COMMUNITY NEWSPAPER

La Prensa Ohio/Michigan 22505
Owner: Aztlan Communications, Inc.
Tel: 1 419 870-6565
Email: latinoprensa@yahoo.com **Web site:** http://www.laprensa1.com
Freq: Weekly; **Circ:** 13000 Not Audited
Circulation Manager: Olga Castilleja; **Advertising Manager:** Adrianne Chasteen
Profile: La Prensa is a weekly, bilingual newspaper serving the Latino and Hispanic communities in Northern Ohio, including Toledo and Cleveland, and Southern Michigan, including Detroit. It provides readers with community news about education, people, politics and events. It also offers in-depth cultural articles on literature, art, poetry, dance, travel and Tejano music. It is distributed to Latino dining and entertainment establishments, retail and specialty stores, hotels, museums, libraries, universities and other educational facilities. The paper is also available by paid subscription. Advertising deadlines are at 11am ET.
Language (s): Spanish/Bilingual
Ad Rate: Full Page Mono 15.00
Ad Rate: Full Page Colour 15.79
Currency: United States Dollars
COMMUNITY NEWSPAPER

La Prensa San Diego 21805
Owner: Castanares (Art)
Editorial: 1712 Logan Ave, San Diego, California 92113-1007 **Tel:** 1 619 425-7400
Email: laprensasd@gmail.com **Web site:** http://www.laprensa-sandiego.org
Freq: Fri; **Circ:** 35000 Not Audited
Profile: La Prensa San Diego is a weekly newspaper that aims to be the voice of the Mexican-American and Latino communities. Deadline for the publication is on Tuesday at 5pm PT prior to Friday publication.
Language (s): Spanish
Ad Rate: Full Page Mono 28.00
Currency: United States Dollars
COMMUNITY NEWSPAPER

The Presbyterian Outlook 22041
Owner: Presbyterian Outlook Foundation Inc.
Editorial: 1 N 5th St Ste 500, Richmond, Virginia 23219-2231 **Tel:** 1 804 359-8442
Email: info@pres-outlook.org **Web site:** http://www.pres-outlook.org
Freq: Mon; **Circ:** 7300 Not Audited
Editor & Publisher: Jill Duffield
Profile: The Presbyterian Outlook is a weekly newspaper serving the Presbyterian community of Richmond, VA. It covers news and opinion information that is useful for educating the decision makers of the church. All press releases must be of a Presbyterian nature with proper contact information. Deadlines are on Fridays.
Language (s): English
Ad Rate: Full Page Mono 64.00
Currency: United States Dollars
COMMUNITY NEWSPAPER

Prescott Newspapers 25007
Owner: Prescott Newspapers, Inc.
Editorial: 8307 E State Route 69 Ste B, Prescott Valley, Arizona 86314-8482 **Tel:** 1 928 445-3333
Email: editorial@prescottaz.com **Web site:** http://www.dcourier.com
Circ: 27330 Not Audited
Publisher: Kelly Soldwedel; **Editor:** Tim Wiederaenders
Profile: Prescott Newspapers in Prescott Valley, AZ publishes the Chino Valley Review and the Prescott Valley Tribune.
Language (s): English
COMMUNITY NEWSPAPER

Presque Isle Newspapers 24935
Editorial: 104 S 3rd St, Rogers City, Michigan 49779 **Tel:** 1 989 734-2105
Email: editor@piadvance.com **Web site:** http://www.piadvance.com
Circ: 5850 Not Audited
Advertising Sales Manager: Cella Bade; **Publisher:** Richard Lamb
Language (s): English
COMMUNITY NEWSPAPER

The Press - Lehigh Valley Press 25174
Owner: Times News, Inc - A Pencor Company
Editorial: 1633 N 26th St, Allentown, Pennsylvania 18104-1805 **Tel:** 1 610 740-0944
Web site: http://www.tnonline.com
Circ: 25507 Not Audited
Editor: Johanna Billings; **Circulation Manager:** Kathy Carpenter; **Editor:** Debra Galbraith; **Publisher:** Scott Masenheimer; **Editor:** Debra Palmieri; **Editor:** George Taylor
Profile: East Penn Publishing is a weekly community newspaper publisher serving the residents of Parkland, Whitehall, Coplay, Northampton, Salisbury and Catasauqua, PA as well as the surrounding areas. The advertising rate provided is based on a placement in all eight papers.
Language (s): English
COMMUNITY NEWSPAPER

The Press & Banner 20612
Owner: Banner Corporation
Editorial: 107 W Pickens St, Abbeville, South Carolina 29620-2415 **Tel:** 1 864 366-5461
Email: pb@bannercorp.net **Web site:** http://pressandbanner.tripod.com/
Freq: Wed; **Circ:** 7500 Not Audited
Publisher & Editor: John West
Profile: The Press & Banner is a local newspaper written for residents of Abbeville, SC. The paper covers local and general interest news and community events. Deadlines are on Fridays at 5pm ET.
Language (s): English
Ad Rate: Full Page Mono 9.50
Currency: United States Dollars
COMMUNITY NEWSPAPER

The Press & Standard 20642
Owner: Smith Newspapers
Editorial: 1025 Bells Hwy, Walterboro, South Carolina 29488-2507 **Tel:** 1 843 549-2586
Email: editor@lowcountry.com **Web site:** http://www.colletontoday.com
Freq: Fri; **Circ:** 5000 Not Audited
Circulation Manager: Tammy Hiott; **Publisher:** Barry Moore
Profile: The Press & Standard is a biweekly newspaper that covers local news and events for the Walterboro, SC area. Articles include news, weather, travel and sports. Deadlines are on Wednesdays and Fridays at noon ET.
Language (s): English
Ad Rate: Full Page Mono 7.50
Currency: United States Dollars
COMMUNITY NEWSPAPER

The Press and Journal 20576
Owner: Sukle (Joseph)
Editorial: 20 S Union St, Middletown, Pennsylvania 17057-1445 **Tel:** 1 717 944-4628
Email: info@pressandjournal.com **Web site:** http://www.pressandjournal.com
Freq: Wed; **Circ:** 9319 Not Audited
Advertising Sales Manager: David Brown; **Editor:** Jim Lewis; **Publisher:** Joseph Sukle
Profile: The Press and Journal is a weekly newspaper covering local news for residents of Dauphin, Lancaster and Lebanon County, PA.
Language (s): English
Ad Rate: Full Page Mono 15.44
Currency: United States Dollars
COMMUNITY NEWSPAPER

The Press Dispatch 19201
Owner: Pike Publishing
Editorial: 820 E Poplar St, Petersburg, Indiana 47567-1258 **Tel:** 1 812 354-8500
Email: contact@pressdispatch.net **Web site:** http://www.pressdispatch.net
Freq: Wed; **Circ:** 5650 Not Audited
Editor: Andrew Heuring; **Publisher:** Frank Heuring; **Advertising Sales Manager:** John Heuring
Profile: The Press Dispatch is a weekly newspaper serving residents of Petersburg, IN.
Language (s): English
Ad Rate: Full Page Mono 5.50
Currency: United States Dollars
COMMUNITY NEWSPAPER

The Press Newspapers 24879
Owner: DCI
Editorial: 1550 Woodville Rd, Millbury, Ohio 43447-9619 **Tel:** 1 419 836-2221
Email: news@presspublications.com **Web site:** http://www.presspublications.com
Freq: Weekly; **Circ:** 33977 Not Audited
News Editor: Kelly Kaczala; **News Editor:** Larry Limpf; **Advertising Manager:** Abbey Schell; **Circulation Manager:** Jordan Szozda
Language (s): English
Ad Rate: Full Page Mono 33.32
Currency: United States Dollars
COMMUNITY NEWSPAPER

Press Publications 24607
Editorial: 4779 Bloom Ave, White Bear Lake, Minnesota 55110-2764 **Tel:** 1 651 407-1200
Email: news@presspubs.com **Web site:** http://www.presspubs.com
Circ: 55547
Publisher: Carter Johnson; **Circulation Manager:** Wade Martin
Language (s): English
Ad Rate: Full Page Mono 22.00
Currency: United States Dollars
COMMUNITY NEWSPAPER

Press Publishing Company 24683
Owner: Press Publishing Co.
Editorial: 3245 Garrett Rd, Drexel Hill, Pennsylvania 19026-2338 **Tel:** 1 610 259-4141
Email: mail@presspublishing.org
Freq: Weekly; **Circ:** 14500 Not Audited
Publisher & Editor: P.A. Girard
Language (s): English
COMMUNITY NEWSPAPER

Press-Banner 28518
Owner: Tank Town Media LLC
Editorial: 5215 Scotts Valley Dr Ste F, Scotts Valley, California 95066-3522 **Tel:** 1 831 438-2500
Email: pbeditor@pressbanner.com **Web site:** http://www.pressbanner.com
Freq: Fri; **Circ:** 20000 Not Audited
Profile: Press Banner is a weekly local newspaper serving residents of Lorenzo Valley and Scotts Valley, CA. The newspaper covers local news, sports and community events.
Language (s): English
Ad Rate: Full Page Mono 13.00
Currency: United States Dollars
COMMUNITY NEWSPAPER

The Press-Sentinel 18818
Owner: Community Newspapers Inc.
Editorial: 8252 W Walnut St, Jesup, Georgia 31545 **Tel:** 1 912 427-3757
Email: thepress@bellsouth.net **Web site:** http://www.thepress-sentinel.com
Freq: 2 Times/Week; **Circ:** 7200 Not Audited
Editor: Drew Davis; **Circulation Manager:** Bob Whitley
Profile: The Press-Sentinel is a local newspaper written for the residents of Jesup, GA. The paper covers local news, sports and events. The newspaper prefers to be contacted by e-mail. Deadlines are on Fridays at noon for the Sunday edition and on Tuesdays at 2pm for the Wednesday edition.
Language (s): English
Ad Rate: Full Page Mono 64.38
Currency: United States Dollars
COMMUNITY NEWSPAPER

Press-Tribune Publishing 231568
Owner: Gold Country Media
Editorial: 188 Cirby Way, Roseville, California 95678-6481 **Tel:** 1 916 786-8746
Web site: http://www.thepresstribune.com
Freq: Sat; **Circ:** 31000 Not Audited
Language (s): English
COMMUNITY NEWSPAPER

The Preston County Journal 21260
Owner: NCWV Media
Editorial: 208 W Main St, Kingwood, West Virginia 26537-1419 **Tel:** 1 304 329-0090
Email: news@prestonnj.com **Web site:** http://www.theet.com/prestoncountyjournal
Freq: Sat; **Circ:** 5700 Not Audited
Editor: John Dahlia; **Advertising Sales Manager:** Carol Peters
Profile: Preston County Journal is written for residents of Preston County, WV.
Language (s): English
Ad Rate: Full Page Mono 5.00
Currency: United States Dollars
COMMUNITY NEWSPAPER

The Pride of the Prairie 844155
Owner: Pride Publications
Editorial: 2018 2nd St, Bowdle, South Dakota 57428 **Tel:** 1 608 281-0421
Email: bowdlepride@gmail.com **Web site:** http://www.pridepublications.net/pride.html
Freq: Weekly
Profile: The Pride of the Prairie is a weekly newspaper providing Local News and Community News for the residents of Bowdle, SD.
Language (s): English
COMMUNITY NEWSPAPER

Priest River Times 19045
Owner: Hagadone Corp.
Editorial: 5809 Highway 2 Ste C, Priest River, Idaho 83856 **Tel:** 1 208 448-2431
Email: prtimes@priestrivertimes.com **Web site:** http://www.priestrivertimes.com
Freq: Wed; **Circ:** 9200 Not Audited
Circulation Manager: Shannon Foote
Profile: Priest River Times is written for residents of Priest River, ID and the surrounding communities. Deadlines are on Mondays before noon PT.
Language (s): English
Ad Rate: Full Page Mono 12.00
Currency: United States Dollars
COMMUNITY NEWSPAPER

Prime Publishers Inc. 25083
Owner: Prime Publishers Inc.
Editorial: 55 Heritage Rd, Southbury, Connecticut 06488-3888 **Tel:** 1 203 262-6631
Email: newsdesk@ctvoices.com **Web site:** http://www.primepublishers.com/voicesnews/
Circ: 64205 Not Audited
Publisher: Rudy Mazurosky; **Circulation Manager:** Walter Mazurosky; **Editor:** Pattie Wesley
Language (s): English
COMMUNITY NEWSPAPER

Prime Time Military Newspapers 25410
Owner: Hearst Corporation (The)
Editorial: 2203 S Hackberry, San Antonio, Texas 78210-4119 **Tel:** 1 210 534-8848
Email: fshnewsleader@gmail.com
Circ: 136789 Not Audited
Editor: Steve Elliott
Profile: Prime Time Military Newspapers provides local news coverage for military and civilian personnel at Ft. Sam Houston and Kelly, Lackland, Brooks Air Force Bases in the San Antonio, TX area.
Language (s): English
COMMUNITY NEWSPAPER

Prime Time Newspapers 25212
Owner: Prime Time Newspapers Inc.
Editorial: 301 Avenue E, San Antonio, Texas 78205-2006 **Tel:** 1 210 250-3000
Email: news@mysanantonio.com **Web site:** http://www.mysanantonio.com
Circ: 201610 Not Audited
Language (s): English
COMMUNITY NEWSPAPER

The Prince George's Post 21583
Editorial: 15207 Marlboro Pike, Upper Marlboro, Maryland 20772-3111 **Tel:** 1 301 627-0900
Web site: http://www.pgpost.com
Freq: Thu; **Circ:** 10000 Not Audited
Advertising Sales Manager: Brenda Boice; **Editor & Publisher:** Legusta Floyd; **Editor:** Michael Fragia
Profile: The Prince George's Post is written for the African-American community of Prince George County, MD.
Language (s): English
Ad Rate: Full Page Mono 21.00
Currency: United States Dollars
COMMUNITY NEWSPAPER

Prince George's Sentinel 19474
Owner: Berlyn Inc.
Editorial: 9458 Lanham Severn Rd, Seabrook, Maryland 20706-2600 **Tel:** 1 301 306-9500
Email: editor-pg@thesentinel.com **Web site:** http://www.thesentinel.com
Freq: Thu; **Circ:** 46000 Not Audited

Circulation Manager: Oonnie Johnson; **Publisher:** Lynn Kapiloff
Profile: Prince George's Sentinel is written for residents of Prince George County, MD. The publication provides news on community events, sports, business and local entertainment.
Language (s): English
Ad Rate: Full Page Mono 34.92
Currency: United States Dollars
COMMUNITY NEWSPAPER

Princeton Times
21272
Owner: Community Newspaper Holdings, Inc.
Editorial: 109 Thorn St, Princeton, West Virginia 24740-3571 **Tel:** 1 304 425-8191
Email: news@ptonline.net **Web site:** http://www.ptonline.net
Freq: Fri; **Circ:** 5200 Not Audited
Advertising Sales Manager: Natalie Fanning; **Editor:** Tammie Toler
Profile: Princeton Times is a local weekly newspaper for residents of Princeton and Mercer County, WV. The publication provides coverage of community news, sports, consumer interests and finance.
Language (s): English
Ad Rate: Full Page Mono 11.50
Currency: United States Dollars
COMMUNITY NEWSPAPER

Printer's Inc.
25225
Owner: Printer's Inc.
Editorial: 209 S Main Ave, Wagner, South Dakota 57380 **Tel:** 1 605 384-5616
Email: announcer@hcinet.net **Web site:** http://www.announceronline.com
Circ: 8670 Not Audited
Publisher & Editor: Monica Wepking
Language (s): English
COMMUNITY NEWSPAPER

El Progreso Hispano
154585
Editorial: 756 Tyvola Rd Ste 102, Charlotte, North Carolina 28217-3535 **Tel:** 1 704 529-6624
Email: ephpres@progresohispanonews.com **Web site:** http://progresohispanonews.com
Freq: Bi-Weekly; **Circ:** 27000 Not Audited
Publisher & Editor: Jose Herrera
Profile: El Progresso Hispano is a bi-weekly Spanish-language newspaper written for residents in Charlotte, NC.
Language (s): Spanish
Ad Rate: Full Page Mono 250.00
Currency: United States Dollars
COMMUNITY NEWSPAPER

The Progress News
22956
Editorial: 410 Main St, Emlenton, Pennsylvania 16373 **Tel:** 1 724 867-1112
Email: news@myprogressnews.com **Web site:** http://www.theprogressnews.com
Freq: Tue; **Circ:** 14000 Not Audited
Publisher & Editor: David Staab
Profile: The Progress News provides local news and information for the residents of Venengo, Clarion, Butler and Armstrong County, PA.
Language (s): English
Ad Rate: Full Page Mono 10.00
Currency: United States Dollars
COMMUNITY NEWSPAPER

Providence En Espanol
217489
Owner: Cuenca (Victor)
Editorial: 280 Broadway, Providence, Rhode Island 02903-3007 **Tel:** 1 401 834-5552
Email: news@providenceenespanol.com **Web site:** http://www.providenceenespanol.com
Freq: Fri; **Circ:** 25000 Not Audited
Publisher & Editor: Victor Cuenca
Profile: Providence (RI) en Espanol was founded in 1999 as the only weekly newspaper serving Rhode Island's Latino population. It is published every Friday.
Language (s): Spanish
Ad Rate: Full Page Mono 35.00
Currency: United States Dollars
COMMUNITY NEWSPAPER

Provincetown Banner
22299
Owner: GateHouse Media Inc.
Editorial: 167 Commercial St, Provincetown, Massachusetts 02657-2144 **Tel:** 1 508 487-7400
Email: editor@provincetownbanner.com **Web site:** http://truro.wickedlocal.com
Freq: Thu; **Circ:** 7000 Not Audited
Profile: Provincetown Banner is a weekly newspaper that covers general news, arts & entertainment, weather and sports in the city of Provincetown, MA. Deadlines are on Mondays at 1pm ET.
Language (s): English
Ad Rate: Full Page Mono 22.00
Currency: United States Dollars
COMMUNITY NEWSPAPER

El Pueblo Latino
153750
Owner: MassPublishing Co. LLC
Editorial: 1860 Main St, Springfield, Massachusetts 01103-1000 **Tel:** 1 413 788-1213
Email: elpueblolatino@repub.com **Web site:** http://www.masslive.com/elpueblolatino/
Freq: Thu; **Circ:** 11500 Not Audited
Publisher: Anita Rivera; **Editor:** Lucilla Santana
Profile: El Pueblo Latino is a free, weekly newspaper serving Latinos and Spanish-speaking residents and businesses in Western Massachusetts. It covers Latino community leaders, news, events, businesses and features. It is available for pick-up at local

retailers, libraries, schools and restaurants. Deadlines are on Tuesdays at 5pm ET.
Language (s): Spanish
Ad Rate: Full Page Mono 13.00
Currency: United States Dollars
COMMUNITY NEWSPAPER

Pueblo Publishers, Inc.
24845
Editorial: 7122 N 59th Ave, Glendale, Arizona 85301-2436 **Tel:** 1 623 842-6000
Circ: 20000 Not Audited
Editor: Carolyn Dryer; **Publications Manager:** Mike Kenny; **Publisher:** William Toops; **Advertising Sales Manager:** Connie Williams
Profile: Pueblo Publishers, Inc. is a weekly community newspaper publisher serving the residents of Glendale and Peoria, AZ.
Language (s): English
COMMUNITY NEWSPAPER

Pueblo West View
281875
Editorial: 825 W 6th St, Pueblo, Colorado 81003-2313 **Tel:** 1 719 547-9606
Email: comments@pueblowestview.com **Web site:** http://www.pueblowestview.com/home/
Freq: Thu; **Circ:** 12000 Not Audited
Editor: Christine Casillas; **Advertising Sales Manager:** Bob Hudson; **Publisher:** Robert Rawlings
Profile: Pueblo West View is a community newspaper targeted at the residents of Pueblo, CO.
Language (s): English
Ad Rate: Full Page Mono 12.45
Currency: United States Dollars
COMMUNITY NEWSPAPER

El Puente
155303
Owner: El Puente, LLC
Editorial: 1906 W Clinton St, Goshen, Indiana 46526-1618 **Tel:** 1 574 533-9082
Email: mail@webelpuente.com **Web site:** http://www.webelpuente.com
Freq: Bi-Weekly; **Circ:** 9000 Not Audited
Advertising Sales Manager: Yizzar Prieto
Profile: El Puente, which translates to "The Bridge," is a bilingual newspaper serving the Spanish population in and around South Bend, Goshen and Elkhart, IN, and Three Rivers, Niles and Sturgis, MI. The publication attempts to connect the Anglo and Hispanic communities within its coverage area. It contains local, national and international news, in addition to legal and cultural information of interest to Hispanics.
Language (s): Spanish/Bilingual
Ad Rate: Full Page Mono 14.08
Currency: United States Dollars
COMMUNITY NEWSPAPER

The Pulaski Citizen
27783
Owner: Pulaski Publishing, Inc.
Editorial: 955 W College St, Pulaski, Tennessee 38478-3600 **Tel:** 1 931 363-4548
Web site: http://www.pulaskicitizen.com
Freq: Tue; **Circ:** 6982 Not Audited
Publisher: Steve Lake
Profile: The Pulaski Citizen is a local newspaper written for the residents of Pulaski, TN. The paper covers local news and information. Deadlines are on Mondays at noon CT.
Language (s): English
Ad Rate: Full Page Mono 9.95
Currency: United States Dollars
COMMUNITY NEWSPAPER

Pulaski County Press
25114
Owner: Pulaski County Press, Inc.
Editorial: 114 W Main St, Winamac, Indiana 46996-1208 **Tel:** 1 574 946-6628
Email: news@pulaskijournal.com **Web site:** http://www.pulaskijournal.com
Circ: 12400 Not Audited
Profile: Pulaski County Press produces The Pulaski County Journal and The Independent, serving the Pulaski County, IN area.
Language (s): English
Ad Rate: Full Page Mono 8.75
Currency: United States Dollars
COMMUNITY NEWSPAPER

Pulse-Journal Newspapers
25365
Owner: Cox Media Group, Inc.
Editorial: 7320 Yankee Rd, Liberty Township, Ohio 45044-9168 **Tel:** 1 513 829-7900
Email: butlercountynews@coxohio.com **Web site:** http://www.pulsejournal.com
Circ: 68733 Not Audited
Editor: Kevin Aldridge; **Editor:** Jennifer Collins
Language (s): English
COMMUNITY NEWSPAPER

The Purcell Register
20448
Owner: McClain County Publishing
Editorial: 225 W Main St, Purcell, Oklahoma 73080-4221 **Tel:** 1 405 527-2126
Email: purcellregister@gmail.com **Web site:** http://www.purcellregister.com
Freq: Weekly; **Circ:** 5000 Not Audited
Profile: The Purcell Register's editorial mission is to be a conservative force, as well as a local news source, for Oklahoma. The publication is written for residents of McClain County in Central Oklahoma. Deadlines for the publication are on Tuesdays at 11am CT.
Language (s): English
Ad Rate: Full Page Mono 10.00
Currency: United States Dollars
COMMUNITY NEWSPAPER

Purcellville Gazette
686595
Owner: Pregartner-Weber (Kim)
Editorial: 130 N 21st St, Purcellville, Virginia 20132-5609 **Tel:** 1 540 431-8507
Email: editor@purcellvillegazette.com **Web site:** http://www.purcellvillegazette.com
Freq: Fri; **Circ:** 16500
Profile: Purcellville Gazette is a local newspaper serving residents of Purcellville, VA and the surrounding areas.
Language (s): English
Ad Rate: Full Page Mono 9.62
Currency: United States Dollars
COMMUNITY NEWSPAPER

Puro Futbol
402959
Owner: Zepeda (Oscar)
Editorial: 4248 Lake Park Ave, Gurnee, Illinois 60031-3035 **Tel:** 1 847 858-7493
Email: info@purofutbolonline.com **Web site:** http://www.purofutbolonline.com
Freq: Wed; **Circ:** 15000 Not Audited
Profile: Puro Futbol is Spanish-language weekly newspaper written for the amateur, youth and professional soccer teams in Northern Illinois. The paper includes player statistics, league information and team biographies.
Language (s): Spanish/Bilingual
Ad Rate: Full Page Mono 11.23
Currency: United States Dollars
COMMUNITY NEWSPAPER

Putnam County Press
24645
Owner: Hall (Don)
Editorial: 928 S Lake Blvd, Mahopac, New York 10541-3242 **Tel:** 1 845 628-8400
Email: putnampress@aol.com
Freq: Weekly; **Circ:** 12400 Not Audited
Publisher & Editor: Don Hall
Profile: Putnam County Press is a local weekly newspaper written for residents of Putnam County, NY. Deadlines are Fridays at noon ET.
Language (s): English
COMMUNITY NEWSPAPER

Putnam County Sentinel
20357
Owner: Delphos Herald Inc.
Editorial: 224 E Main St, Ottawa, Ohio 45875-1944 **Tel:** 1 419 523-5709
Email: news@putnamsentinel.com **Web site:** http://www.putnamsentinel.com
Freq: Wed; **Circ:** 6000 Not Audited
Advertising Sales Manager: Kristen Pickens; **Editor:** Charles Warniment
Profile: Putnam County Sentinel is a local weekly newspaper written for residents of Putnam County, OH. The publication's editorial mission is to provide local news coverage and information to its readers.
Language (s): English
Ad Rate: Full Page Mono 12.85
Currency: United States Dollars
COMMUNITY NEWSPAPER

Putnam Town Crier & Northeast Ledger
22174
Editorial: 158 Main St Ste 9, Putnam, Connecticut 06260-1965 **Tel:** 1 860 933-3744
Email: ptcrier@gmail.com **Web site:** http://www.putnamtowncrier.com
Freq: Thu; **Circ:** 12000 Not Audited
Publisher & Editor: Linda Lemmon
Profile: Putnam Town Crier & Northeast Ledger is a community newspaper that targets the area of Putnam, CT.
Language (s): English
Ad Rate: Full Page Mono 9.00
Currency: United States Dollars
COMMUNITY NEWSPAPER

QST Publications
25376
Owner: Quattenbaum (Caroline) & Quattenbaum (Russell)
Editorial: 628 Glover Ave, Enterprise, Alabama 36330-2014 **Tel:** 1 334 393-2969
Email: news@southeastsun.com **Web site:** www.southeastsun.com
Circ: 22000 Not Audited
Circulation Manager: Janet Corneil; **Publisher:** Russell Quattlebaum
Language (s): English
COMMUNITY NEWSPAPER

Quantico Sentry
29101
Owner: BH Media Group
Editorial: 3250 Catlin Ave, Quantico, Virginia 22134-5109 **Tel:** 1 703 784-2741
Email: sentry.quantico@usmc.mil **Web site:** http://www.quantico.usmc.mil
Freq: Thu; **Circ:** 11000 Not Audited
Publisher: John Rives; **Editor:** David White
Profile: Quantico Sentry is published for the Marine Corp and residents of Quantico, VA. It covers local news and information.
Language (s): English
Ad Rate: Full Page Mono 16.10
Currency: United States Dollars
COMMUNITY NEWSPAPER

Que Pasa - Greensboro/ Winston-Salem
81505
Owner: Latino Communications
Editorial: 3025 Waughtown St Ste G, Winston Salem, North Carolina 27107-1679 **Tel:** 1 336 784-9004
Email: editor@quepasamedia.com **Web site:** http://greensboro.quepasanoticias.com
Freq: Thu; **Circ:** 55744 Not Audited

Publisher: Jose Isasi
Profile: Que Pasa is a community newspaper which provides Hispanic readers with local and national news. The publication has two editions; one is distributed throughout the Greensboro, NC area and the other is distributed throughout the Raleigh-Durham, NC area. All contents are the same except for editorials. Other features include sports, entertainment, business, education and classifieds. The deadline for press releases is the Friday prior to issue date.
Language (s): Spanish
Ad Rate: Full Page Mono 28.00
Currency: United States Dollars
COMMUNITY NEWSPAPER

Que Pasa - Raleigh
239039
Owner: Winston-Salem Media
Editorial: 4600 New Bern Ave Ste 101, Raleigh, North Carolina 27610-1881 **Tel:** 1 919 645-1680
Email: editor@quepasamedia.com **Web site:** http://raleigh.quepasanoticias.com
Freq: Wed; **Circ:** 25000 Not Audited
Advertising Sales Manager: Roberto Aisenberg; **Publisher:** Jose Isasi; **Local News Editor:** Eloy Tupayachi
Profile: Que Pasa is a weekly Spanish language newspaper written for the residents of Raleigh, NC.
Language (s): Spanish
Ad Rate: Full Page Mono 12.60
Currency: United States Dollars
COMMUNITY NEWSPAPER

Que Pasa Mi Gente
239037
Owner: Latino Communications
Editorial: 7508 E Independence Blvd Ste 109, Charlotte, North Carolina 28227-9409 **Tel:** 1 704 319-5044
Email: editor@quepasamedia.com **Web site:** http://www.quepasa-migente.com
Freq: Tue
Publisher: Julio Suarez; **News Editor:** Eloy Tupayachi
Profile: Previously two separate publications, Mi Gente and Que Pasa Charlotte. Offers local news and information to Spanish-speaking residents of Mecklenburg, Gaston, Union, Cabarrus, Iredell, Lincoln, Rowan, Catawba and Burke Counties in North Carolina and York and Lancaster Counties in South Carolina.
Language (s): Spanish
Ad Rate: Full Page Mono 34.89
Ad Rate: Full Page Colour 34.89
Currency: United States Dollars
COMMUNITY NEWSPAPER

Queen Central News
21454
Owner: Van Winkle (James)
Editorial: 39 Main St, Camden, New York 13316-1301 **Tel:** 1 315 245-1849
Email: theqcn@gmail.com **Web site:** http://www.queencentralnews.com
Freq: Mon; **Circ:** 8500 Not Audited
Editor & Publisher: James Van Winkle; **Advertising Sales Manager:** Darla Woodcock
Profile: Queen Central News' editorial mission is to provide local news and information to the residents of Camden, Redfield, Ashfield and North Bay, NY.
Language (s): English
Ad Rate: Full Page Mono 5.25
Currency: United States Dollars
COMMUNITY NEWSPAPER

Queens Chronicle
25374
Owner: Mark I Publications, Inc.
Editorial: 6233 Woodhaven Blvd, Rego Park, New York 11374-3731 **Tel:** 1 718 205-8000
Email: mailbox@qchron.com **Web site:** http://www.qchron.com
Freq: Weekly; **Circ:** 160000 Not Audited
Advertising Sales Manager: Dave Abramowitz; **Publisher:** Mark Weidler
Profile: Queens Chronicles publishes eight different editions of the Queens Chronicle newspapers with a combined circulation of 160,000. The papers cover local and national news, weather, sports, and community events. Feature articles cover business developments, local politics, education, arts and entertainment, lifestyle, and other topics of interest to local residents. Do not send any materials unless they have a Queens connection.
Language (s): English
COMMUNITY NEWSPAPER

Queens Gazette Publishing
25195
Owner: Service Publications Inc.
Editorial: 4216 34th Ave, Astoria, New York 11101-1110 **Tel:** 1 718 361-6161
Email: qgazette@aol.com **Web site:** http://www.qgazette.com
Circ: 90000 Not Audited
Editor: Jason Antos; **Publisher & Editor:** Tony Barsamian; **Advertising Sales Manager:** Mark Lipmann
Profile: Queens Gazette Publishing in Astoria, NY publishes Western Queens Gazette, Queens Gazette and Eastern Queens Gazette.
Language (s): English
COMMUNITY NEWSPAPER

Queens Ledger Newspaper Group
24658
Owner: Queens Ledger Greenpoint Star, Inc.
Editorial: 6960 Grand Ave, Maspeth, New York 11378 **Tel:** 1 718 639-7000
Email: news@queensledger.com **Web site:** http://www.queensledger.com
Circ: 99453

Circulation Manager: Jesse Almonte; **Advertising Sales Manager:** Tammy Sanchez; **Publisher and Editor:** Walter Sanchez
Profile: Queens Ledger Newspaper Group is a weekly community newspaper publisher serving the resident of Queens and Brooklyn, NY.
Language (s): English
COMMUNITY NEWSPAPER

Queens Times 22978
Owner: C.T. Publishing, Corp.
Editorial: 4808 111th St, Corona, New York 11368-2920 **Tel:** 1 718 592-2196
Email: editor@queenstimes.com **Web site:** http://www.queenstimes.com
Freq: Thu; **Circ:** 90000 Not Audited
Publisher & Editor: James Lisa
Profile: Queens Times's editorial mission is to be an informative and positive news source. The publication is written for residents of Queens, NY. Founded in 1995, the Queens Times is a 16-page tabloid publication.
Language (s): English
Ad Rate: Full Page Mono 20.90
Currency: United States Dollars
COMMUNITY NEWSPAPER

Queens Tribune Newspapers 24761
Owner: Tribco, LLC
Editorial: 15050 14th Rd, Whitestone, New York 11357-2609 **Tel:** 1 718 357-7400
Email: news@queenstribune.com **Web site:** http://www.queenstribune.com
Circ: 171000 Not Audited
Publisher: Michael Schenkler
Language (s): English
COMMUNITY NEWSPAPER

The Quincy Sun 19455
Editorial: 1372 Hancock St, Quincy, Massachusetts 02169-5107 **Tel:** 1 617 471-3100
Email: thequincysun@verizon.net **Web site:** http://www.thequincysun.com
Freq: Wed; **Circ:** 7000
Publisher & Editor: Robert Bosworth
Profile: The Quincy Sun is published weekly for the residents of Quincy, MA and surrounding areas. The newspaper provides information about local news and community events.
Language (s): English
Ad Rate: Full Page Mono 12.00
Currency: United States Dollars
COMMUNITY NEWSPAPER

The Raleigh Telegram 691933
Owner: The Raleigh Telegram
Editorial: 64 TW Alexander Drive, Durham, North Carolina 27709 **Tel:** 1 919 760-3110
Email: raleightelegram@yahoo.com **Web site:** http://www.raleightelegram.com
Freq: Weekly
Profile: The Raleigh Telegram is a weekly newspaper providing Local and Community News coverage to the residents of the Raleigh-Durham and Chapel Hill, NC area.
Language (s): English
COMMUNITY NEWSPAPER

Ramona Sentinel 22484
Owner: Mainstreet Media Group
Editorial: 425 10Th St Ste A, Ramona, California 92065-3936 **Tel:** 1 760 789-1350
Email: news@ramonasentinel.com **Web site:** http://www.ramonasentinel.com
Freq: Thu; **Circ:** 14000 Not Audited
Advertising Sales Manager: Nancy Lund; **Publisher:** Jeff Mitchell; **Editor:** Maureen Robertson
Profile: Ramona Sentinel is a local, weekly newspaper serving residents of Ramona, CA. It focuses on local sports and community news.
Language (s): English
Ad Rate: Full Page Mono 16.66
Currency: United States Dollars
COMMUNITY NEWSPAPER

Rancho Cordova Independent 21590
Owner: Messenger Publishing Group
Editorial: 7144 Fair Oaks Blvd, Carmichael, California 95608-6434 **Tel:** 1 916 773-1111
Email: publisher@ranchocordovaindependent.com
Web site: http://www.rcgrapevine.com
Freq: Fri; **Circ:** 11000 Not Audited
Circulation Manager: Gabriel Scholl; **Publisher & Editor:** Paul Scholl
Profile: Grapevine Independent covers news and sports in Rancho Cordova and Eastern Sacramento County, CA.
Language (s): English
Ad Rate: Full Page Mono 12.75
Currency: United States Dollars
COMMUNITY NEWSPAPER

Randall Publishing Corporation 528589
Editorial: 8803 Sudley Rd Ste 201, Manassas, Virginia 20110-4718 **Tel:** 1 703 369-5253
Email: editor@obsvr.com **Web site:** http://bullrunnow.com
Circ: 70000 Not Audited
Publisher & Editor: Randi Reid; **Advertising Sales Manager:** Ellen Wilson
Profile: Randall Publishing Corp. in Manassas, VA is a community newspaper publisher.
Language (s): English
COMMUNITY NEWSPAPER

The Randolph Leader 18527
Owner: Randoph Publishers Inc.
Editorial: 524 Main St, Roanoke, Alabama 36274-1440 **Tel:** 1 334 863-2819
Web site: http://www.therandolphleader.com
Freq: Weekly; **Circ:** 7000 Not Audited
Advertising Sales Manager: Peggy Seabolt; **News Editor:** Vanessa Sorrell Burnside; **Editor & Publisher:** John W. Stevenson; **Circulation Manager:** Rodney Wright
Profile: The Randolph Leader is written for residents of Randolph County, AL. The publication covers local news and events ONLY. They are not interested in press information relevant to the Atlanta area. Deadlines are on Mondays at 5pm CT.
Language (s): English
Ad Rate: Full Page Mono 8.12
Currency: United States Dollars
COMMUNITY NEWSPAPER

Rantoul Press 25125
Owner: News-Gazette Inc.
Editorial: 1332 Harmon Dr, Rantoul, Illinois 61866-3310 **Tel:** 1 217 892-9613
Email: news@rantoulpress.com **Web site:** http://www.rantoulpress.com
Freq: Wed; **Circ:** 9550 Not Audited
Circulation Manager: Melinda Carpenter
Language (s): English
Ad Rate: Full Page Mono 18.00
Currency: United States Dollars
COMMUNITY NEWSPAPER

Rappahannock Record 21055
Owner: Rappahannock Record
Editorial: 27 North Main St, Kilmarnock, Virginia 22482 **Tel:** 1 804 435-1701
Email: editor@rrecord.com **Web site:** http://www.rrecord.com
Freq: Thu; **Circ:** 9000 Not Audited
Advertising Sales Manager: Sara Amiss; **Publisher:** Frederick Gaskins; **Editor:** Robert Mason
Profile: Rappahannock Record is published weekly for residents of Lancaster County, VA and surrounding areas. The publication is a general interest newspaper, covering local news, weather, sports, business, education, arts and entertainment and other information of interest to the local community. Deadlines are on Tuesdays at 2pm ET.
Language (s): English
Ad Rate: Full Page Mono 9.00
Currency: United States Dollars
COMMUNITY NEWSPAPER

Rappahannock Times 21063
Editorial: 622 Charlotte St, Tappahannock, Virginia 22560 **Tel:** 1 804 443-2200
Email: rapptimes@gmail.com **Web site:** http://www.rappnews.com
Freq: Thu; **Circ:** 5500 Not Audited
Publisher & Editor: Chris Rose
Profile: Rappahannock Times is written for residents of Tappahannock, VA and surrounding areas. It covers local news, weather, sports, business, education, arts & entertainment and other information of interest to the local community. Deadlines are on Tuesdays at noon ET.
Language (s): English
Ad Rate: Full Page Mono 6.20
Currency: United States Dollars
COMMUNITY NEWSPAPER

Rare Reminder & The Chronicle 685818
Owner: Rare Reminder, Inc. (The)
Editorial: 222 Dividend Rd, Rocky Hill, Connecticut 06067-3740 **Tel:** 1 860 563-9386
Email: greg@rarereminder.com **Web site:** http://rarereminder.com
Circ: 43332
Advertising Sales Manager: Greg Barton; **Editor:** Kate Kelleher
Profile: Rare Reminder & The Chronicle in Rocky Hill, CT is a community newspaper publisher.
Language (s): English
Ad Rate: Full Page Mono 21.87
Currency: United States Dollars
COMMUNITY NEWSPAPER

La Raza 21808
Owner: ImpreMedia LLC
Editorial: 225 W Ohio St Fl 3, Chicago, Illinois 60654-7898 **Tel:** 1 312 870-7000
Email: agenda@laraza.com **Web site:** http://www.laraza.com
Freq: Weekly; **Circ:** 153660 Not Audited
Profile: La Raza's editorial mission is to be the organ of accountability for the Hispanic community in Chicago. Coverage in the weekly newspaper includes local, city and national news, as well as business and finance, arts & entertainment and health news.
Language (s): Spanish/Bilingual
Ad Rate: Full Page Mono 97.50
Ad Rate: Full Page Colour 108.86
Currency: United States Dollars
COMMUNITY NEWSPAPER

La Raza del Noroeste 436002
Owner: Washington Post Co.
Editorial: 1213 California St, Everett, Washington 98201-3445 **Tel:** 1 425 673-6633
Email: editor@nuestronoroeste.com **Web site:** http://www.larazanw.com
Freq: Fri; **Circ:** 24000 Not Audited
Editor & Publisher: Alvaro Guillen
Profile: La Raza de Noroeste is a local, weekly Spanish language newspaper serving Hispanic residents of Everett and Puget Sound, WA. The paper includes strong Mexican content and Mexican news by region. It also focuses on arts & entertainment and Hispanic-related news in the community, such as education and schools, police issues and immigration. The paper also features profiles of successful Hispanics, Mexican sports like soccer and content with newcomer relevance, such as how to behave in public places and how to access the government and other public services.
Language (s): Spanish/Bilingual
Ad Rate: Full Page Mono 25.95
Currency: United States Dollars
COMMUNITY NEWSPAPER

RC News 25340
Owner: RCN Corporation
Editorial: 207 E Government St, Brandon, Mississippi 39042-3151 **Tel:** 1 601 825-8333
Email: rankincn@aol.com
Circ: 23400 Not Audited
Editor & Publisher: Marcus Bowers
Language (s): English
COMMUNITY NEWSPAPER

Reader & Perico 624396
Owner: Heaston (John)
Editorial: 2314 M St, Omaha, Nebraska 68107-2828 **Tel:** 1 402 341-7323
Email: news@thereader.com **Web site:** http://www.thereader.com
Profile: Reader & Perico in Omaha, NE publishes the following community newspapers: El Perico and The Reader.
COMMUNITY NEWSPAPER

Real Change 22579
Editorial: 219 1st Ave Suite 220, Seattle, Washington 98104 **Tel:** 1 206 441-3247
Email: webmaster@realchangenews.org **Web site:** http://www.realchangenews.org
Freq: Wed; **Circ:** 12000 Not Audited
Publisher: Timothy Harris; **Editor:** Nicole Myles
Profile: Real Change is published twice a month for and by the homeless community of Seattle and surrounding areas. The newspaper publishes the views of poor and homeless people and their advocates. Its editorial mission is to organize, educate, and build alliances to find community-based solutions to homelessness and poverty in Seattle and nationwide. Each issue contains 32 pages of quality journalism, poetry, opinion, art and photography, much of it produced by the poor and homeless themselves. It also shares book and film reviews, interviews and other feature stories with members of the International Network of Streetpapers.
Language (s): English
Ad Rate: Full Page Mono 90.00
Currency: United States Dollars
COMMUNITY NEWSPAPER

The Real McCoy 473057
Owner: Fort McCoy Garrison
Editorial: 100 E. Headquarters Road, Sparta, Wisconsin 54656 **Tel:** 1 608 388-2769
Email: usarmy.mccoy.imcom-central.list.pao-admin@mail.mil **Web site:** http://www.mccoy.army.mil
Freq: Bi-Weekly; **Circ:** 5000 Not Audited
Editor: Lou-Ann Mittelstaedt
Profile: The Real McCoy is a free newspaper providing news and information on the Fort McCoy army base in Fort McCoy, WI.
Language (s): English
Ad Rate: Full Page Mono 6.75
Currency: United States Dollars
COMMUNITY NEWSPAPER

Reboli Newspapers 24835
Tel: 1 973 227-4433
Circ: 38313 Not Audited
Advertising Sales Manager: Joan Bonadeo; **Editor:** Kelly Kilborn; **Editor:** Sherilyn Learner; **Editor:** Bob Meling; **Editor:** Samuel Miller; **Editor:** Tami Jean Morgan; **Publisher:** John Reboli; **Editor:** Michele Santoro; **Editor:** Dennis Wilson; **Editor:** John Wiss
Language (s): English
COMMUNITY NEWSPAPER

The Record 19262
Editorial: 14690 Parallel Rd, Basehor, Kansas 66007-3007 **Tel:** 1 913 724-3444
Email: news@recordnews.com **Web site:** http://www.recordnews.com
Freq: Thu; **Circ:** 6000 Not Audited
Editor: Jon Males
Profile: The Record is published weekly for residents of Kansas City, KS and surrounding areas. The newspaper covers local news, weather, sports, education, business and arts & entertainment.
Language (s): English
Ad Rate: Full Page Mono 7.50
Currency: United States Dollars
COMMUNITY NEWSPAPER

The Record 21563
Owner: Landmark Community Newspapers Inc.
Editorial: 209C White Oak Rd, Leitchfield, Kentucky 42754-5816 **Tel:** 1 270 259-6061
Email: news@graysonrecord.com **Web site:** http://www.graysonrecord.com
Freq: Thu; **Circ:** 5000 Not Audited
News Editor: DeAnna Lasley; **Publisher:** Chris Ordway
Profile: The Record in Leitchfield, KY is a weekly newspaper that covers local news and events affecting Grayson County.
Language (s): English
Ad Rate: Full Page Mono 6.00
Currency: United States Dollars
COMMUNITY NEWSPAPER

Record 21901
Editorial: 1200 S Shelby St, Louisville, Kentucky 40203-2627 **Tel:** 1 502 636-0296
Email: record@archlou.org **Web site:** http://therecordnewspaper.org
Freq: Thu; **Circ:** 64000 Not Audited
Profile: The Record is a weekly publication run by the Archdiose of Louisville.
Language (s): English
Ad Rate: Full Page Mono 20.00
Currency: United States Dollars
COMMUNITY NEWSPAPER

Record & Banner 25501
Editorial: 3203 Highway 367 N, Bald Knob, Arkansas 72010 **Tel:** 1 501 724-0398
Email: wcrecord@centurytel.net
Circ: 5500 Not Audited
Publisher and Editor: Barth Grayson
Language (s): English
COMMUNITY NEWSPAPER

The Record Newspapers 25311
Editorial: 333 W Round Bunch Rd, Bridge City, Texas 77611-2445 **Tel:** 1 409 735-5305
Email: therecordnews@sbcglobal.net **Web site:** http://therecordlive.com
Circ: 34000 Not Audited
Publisher: Roy Dunn; **Advertising Sales Manager:** Liz Weaver
Profile: The Record Newspapers of Bridge City, TX, publishes weeklies with news and events of local interest to residents of Orange County, TX.
Language (s): English
COMMUNITY NEWSPAPER

Record Publishing Company 24669
Owner: GateHouse Media Inc.
Editorial: 1050 W Main St, Kent, Ohio 44240-2006 **Tel:** 1 330 541-9400
Web site: http://www.recordpub.com
Circ: 107805 Not Audited
Editor: Jamie Gerard; **Circulation Manager:** Margaret Gotschall; **Editor:** Phil Keren; **Editor:** Eric Marotta; **Editor:** Andrew Schunk
Profile: Record Publishing Company in Kent, OH is a community newspaper publisher.
Language (s): English
COMMUNITY NEWSPAPER

The Record-Courier 20238
Owner: Swift Communications
Editorial: 1503 US Highway 395 N Ste G, Gardnerville, Nevada 89410-5227 **Tel:** 1 775 782-5121
Email: editor@recordcourier.com **Web site:** http://www.recordcourier.com
Freq: Fri; **Circ:** 6000 Not Audited
Publisher: Pat Bridges; **Editor:** Kurt Hildebrand
Profile: The Record-Courier has been serving Douglas County, NV since 1880.
Language (s): English
Ad Rate: Full Page Mono 20.00
Currency: United States Dollars
COMMUNITY NEWSPAPER

The Recorder 21060
Owner: Snowy Mountain Publishing Inc.
Editorial: 43 Water St, Monterey, Virginia 24465 **Tel:** 1 540 468-2147
Email: recorder@htcnet.org **Web site:** http://www.therecorderonline.com
Freq: Thu; **Circ:** 5000 Not Audited
Circulation Manager: Brandi Bussard; **Advertising Sales Manager:** Jessica Rogers
Profile: The Recorder in Monterey, VA is a weekly newspaper that covers local news and community events.
Language (s): English
Ad Rate: Full Page Mono 8.75
Currency: United States Dollars
COMMUNITY NEWSPAPER

Recorder Community Newspapers - Bernardsville 25533
Owner: New Jersey Hills Media Group
Editorial: 23 Morristown Rd., Bernardsville, New Jersey 7924 **Tel:** 1 973 377-2000
Web site: http://www.newjerseyhills.com
Circ: 16410 Not Audited
Editor: Garry Herzog; **Editor:** Jim Lent
Language (s): English
COMMUNITY NEWSPAPER

Recorder Community Newspapers - Caldwell 363952
Owner: Recorder Community Newspapers
Editorial: 10 Brookside Ave, Caldwell, New Jersey 07006-5600 **Tel:** 1 973 226-8900
Web site: http://www.newjerseyhills.com
Circ: 19000 Not Audited
Language (s): English
COMMUNITY NEWSPAPER

The Record-Herald and Indianola Tribune 18919

Owner: Des Moines Register & Tribune Inc.
Editorial: 112 N Howard St, Indianola, Iowa 50125-2510 **Tel:** 1 515 961-2511
Email: customerservice@registermedia.com **Web site:** http://www.indianolarecordherald.com
Freq: Wed; **Circ:** 6500 Not Audited
Publisher: Amy Duncan; **Advertising Sales Manager:** Cindy Nelson
Profile: The Record-Herald & Indianola (IA)Tribune is published weekly for residents of Indianola, IA and surrounding areas. The publication is a general-interest newspaper, covering local news, weather, sports, business, education, arts & entertainment and other information of interest to the local community. Deadlines for the publication are one day prior to the issue date.
Language (s): English
Ad Rate: Full Page Mono 9.50
Currency: United States Dollars
COMMUNITY NEWSPAPER

Record-Observer 29288

Owner: APG Media of Chesapeake
Editorial: 114 Broadway, Centreville, Maryland 21617-1006 **Tel:** 1 410 758-1400
Email: newsroom@recordobserver.com **Web site:** http://myeasternshoremd.com
Freq: Fri; **Circ:** 5000 Not Audited
Publisher: David Fike; **Circulation Manager:** Pat Mayer; **Editor:** Angie Price
Profile: Record-Observer is a local weekly newspaper for residents of Queen Anne's County, MD. The editorial deadline is Monday at 5pm ET.
Language (s): English
Ad Rate: Full Page Mono 10.00
Currency: United States Dollars
COMMUNITY NEWSPAPER

Red Latina 412400

Owner: Velazquez, Cecilia
Editorial: 625 N Euclid Ave Ste 602B, Saint Louis, Missouri 63108-1676 **Tel:** 1 314 772-3515
Email: redlatinastl@hotmail.com **Web site:** http://www.redlatinastl.com
Freq: Bi-Weekly; **Circ:** 22000 Not Audited
Publisher & Editor: Cecilia Velazquez; **Circulation Manager:** Shadia Wade; **Advertising Manager:** Katrina Wiggind
Profile: Red Latina is written for the Hispanic community of Saint Louis, MO. The paper is published the 1st and 15th of each month.
Language (s): Spanish
Ad Rate: Full Page Mono 11.43
Currency: United States Dollars
COMMUNITY NEWSPAPER

Red Oak Express 18973

Owner: Landmark Community Newspapers Inc.
Editorial: 20012 Commerce Dr, Red Oak, Iowa 51566 **Tel:** 1 712 623-2566
Email: news@redoakexpress.com **Web site:** http://www.redoakexpress.com
Freq: Tue; **Circ:** 11480 Not Audited
Advertising Sales Manager: Barb Gray; **Publisher & Editor:** Gregory Orear; **Circulation Manager:** Angie Quick; **Community News Editor:** Marge Warder
Profile: Red Oak Express is published weekly for residents of Red Oak, IA and surrounding areas. The publication covers local news, weather, sports, education, business, arts & entertainment and other information of interest to the local community. Deadlines for the publication are Thursdays at 5pm CT.
Language (s): English
Ad Rate: Full Page Mono 11.73
Currency: United States Dollars
COMMUNITY NEWSPAPER

Red Wing Republican Eagle 14213

Owner: Forum Communications Co.
Editorial: 2760 N Service Dr, Red Wing, Minnesota 55066-1985 **Tel:** 1 651 388-8235
Email: news@republican-eagle.com **Web site:** http://www.republican-eagle.com
Freq: 2 Times/Week; **Circ:** 5600
Advertising Sales Manager: Steve Gall; **Editor:** Anne Jacobson; **Publisher:** Steve Messick
Profile: Red Wing Republican Eagle is written for residents of Red Wing, MN and surrounding areas. It covers local news, weather, sports, education, business, arts & entertainment and other information of interest to the local community. Deadlines are noon CT.
Language (s): English
Ad Rate: Full Page Mono 14.41
Currency: United States Dollars
COMMUNITY NEWSPAPER

RedEye 128175

Owner: tronc
Editorial: 435 N Michigan Ave, Chicago, Illinois 60611-4066 **Tel:** 1 312 222-4970
Email: redeye@redeyechicago.com **Web site:** http://www.chicagotribune.com/redeye
Freq: Mon thru Fri; **Circ:** 165348 Not Audited
News Editor: Lisa Donovan
Profile: RedEye is a free, commuter weekly newspaper that is owned by the Chicago Tribune. It offers a unique approach to news and entertainment and targets urban commuters in metro Chicago. The paper, designed for a 20-minute read, features everything from top news stories and sports to celebrity gossip. The publication is also coupled with Metromix.com, the Tribune's online entertainment guide.
Language (s): English

Ad Rate: Full Page Mono 118.12
Ad Rate: Full Page Colour 118.12
Currency: United States Dollars
COMMUNITY NEWSPAPER

Redmond Reporter 78981

Owner: Black Press
Editorial: 8105 166th Ave NE Ste 102, Redmond, Washington 98052-3999 **Tel:** 1 425 867-0353
Email: editor@redmond-reporter.com **Web site:** http://www.redmond-reporter.com/
Freq: Fri; **Circ:** 25000
Advertising Sales Manager: Jim Gatens; **Editor:** Andy Nystrom
Profile: Redmond Reporter is a local, weekly newspaper serving residents of Redmond, WA. The paper includes local news, sports, business, arts & entertainment and community events.
Language (s): English
Ad Rate: Full Page Mono 27.50
Currency: United States Dollars
COMMUNITY NEWSPAPER

The Reflector 21093

Owner: Case Publishing Inc.
Editorial: 208 SE 1st St., Battle Ground, Washington 98604 **Tel:** 1 360 687-5151
Email: news@thereflector.com **Web site:** http://www.thereflector.com
Freq: Wed; **Circ:** 28000 Not Audited
Publisher: Christine Fossett; **Editor:** Ken Vance
Profile: The Reflector in Battle Ground, WA is published weekly for the residents of Clark County, WA and surrounding areas. The newspaper provides information on local news and community events. All mail must be sent to the PO Box.
Language (s): English
Ad Rate: Full Page Mono 15.10
Currency: United States Dollars
COMMUNITY NEWSPAPER

Reflejos 83624

Owner: Paddock Publications
Editorial: 155 E Algonquin Rd, Arlington Heights, Illinois 60005-4617 **Tel:** 1 847 427-4300
Email: copy@reflejos.com **Web site:** http://www.reflejos.com
Freq: Sun; **Circ:** 100000 Not Audited
Editor: Marco Ortiz; **Publisher:** Doug Ray
Profile: Reflejos is a free, weekly, bilingual newspaper serving the suburban Chicago Latino community. Its focus is motivational, educational and inspirational news in the Cook, DuPage, Kane, Lake and McHenry counties. Deadlines are at 5pm CT.
Language (s): Spanish/Bilingual
Ad Rate: Full Page Mono 34.88
Currency: United States Dollars
COMMUNITY NEWSPAPER

The Register 22035

Owner: Diocese of Salina
Editorial: 103 N 9th St, Salina, Kansas 67401-2503 **Tel:** 1 785 827-8746
Web site: http://www.salinadiocese.org
Freq: Bi-Weekly; **Circ:** 18000 Not Audited
Publisher: Edward Weisenburger; **Editor:** Doug Weller
Profile: The Register provides the Diocese of Salina, KS, with a source for religious news and information. The free publication is sent to all registered Catholics; donations are requested. The lead time varies. Deadlines are on Sundays.
Language (s): English
Ad Rate: Full Page Mono 7.50
Currency: United States Dollars
COMMUNITY NEWSPAPER

Register Publications, Inc. 24561

Owner: Delphos Herald Inc.
Editorial: 126 W High St, Lawrenceburg, Indiana 47025-1908 **Tel:** 1 812 537-0063
Email: newsroom@registerpublications.com **Web site:** http://www.registerpublications.com
Freq: Weekly; **Circ:** 14538 Not Audited
Publisher: Tom Brooker; **Editor:** Jim Buchberger
Language (s): English
COMMUNITY NEWSPAPER

The Register-Herald 20337

Owner: AIM Media Midwest
Editorial: 200 Eaton Lewisburg Rd, Eaton, Ohio 45320-1190 **Tel:** 1 937 456-5553
Web site: http://www.registerherald.com
Freq: Sat; **Circ:** 7200 Not Audited
Editor: Eddie Mowen
Profile: The Register-Herald is published weekly for the residents of Eaton, OH and surrounding areas. The newspaper provides information on local news and community events.
Language (s): English
Ad Rate: Full Page Mono 9.50
Currency: United States Dollars
COMMUNITY NEWSPAPER

Register-Pajaronian 13764

Owner: News Media Corp.
Editorial: 100 Westridge Dr, Watsonville, California 95076-6602 **Tel:** 1 831 761-7300
Email: newsroom@register-pajaronian.com **Web site:** http://www.register-pajaronian.com
Freq: Sat; **Circ:** 5000
Publisher: John Bartlett; **Advertising Sales Manager:** Allison Stenberg; **Circulation Manager:** Rosa Vizcara
Profile: Register-Pajaronian covers news in and around Watsonville and Santa Cruz County, CA. It covers local and community news, business,

features, dining, education, arts & entertainment, health, fitness, home improvement, real estate, shopping and travel.
Language (s): English
Ad Rate: Full Page Mono 16.16
Currency: United States Dollars
COMMUNITY NEWSPAPER

Reminder Press, Inc. 25227

Editorial: 130 Old Town Rd, Vernon, Connecticut 06066-2322 **Tel:** 1 860 875-3366
Web site: http://www.courant.com/reminder-news/
Freq: Weekly; **Circ:** 242019 Not Audited
Publisher: Ken Hovland
Language (s): English
Ad Rate: Full Page Colour 977.40
Currency: United States Dollars
COMMUNITY NEWSPAPER

Reminder Publications Inc. 73127

Owner: Reminder Publications Inc.
Editorial: 280 N Main St, East Longmeadow, Massachusetts 01028-1868 **Tel:** 1 413 525-6661
Email: news@reminderpublications.com **Web site:** http://www.thereminder.com
Freq: Fri; **Circ:** 45300 Not Audited
Profile: Reminder Publications Inc. is a local newspaper in East Longmeadow, MA.
Language (s): English
Ad Rate: Full Page Mono 42.25
Currency: United States Dollars
COMMUNITY NEWSPAPER

Reno News & Review 22525

Owner: Chico Community Publishing, Inc.
Editorial: 405 Marsh Ave Fl 3, Reno, Nevada 89509-1516 **Tel:** 1 775 324-4440
Email: renoletters@newsreview.com **Web site:** http://www.newsreview.com/reno/home
Freq: Thu; **Circ:** 21726 Not Audited
Editor: Kelley Lang; **News Editor:** Dennis Myers; **Publisher:** Jeff von Kaenel
Profile: Reno News & Review is published weekly for the residents of Reno, NV and surrounding areas. The newspaper offers community news, arts & entertainment and event listings. Do not send press releases via fax.
Language (s): English
Ad Rate: Full Page Mono 65.09
Currency: United States Dollars
COMMUNITY NEWSPAPER

The Reporter 20379

Editorial: 1088 S Main St, Akron, Ohio 44301-1206 **Tel:** 1 330 535-7061
Email: reporter14@juno.com
Freq: Fri; **Circ:** 18000 Not Audited
Publisher & Editor: William Ellis; **Advertising Sales Manager:** Carl Gordon
Profile: The Reporter is a weekly community newspaper written for residents of Akron, OH. Its main focus is on local news with an emphasis on the African American Community.
Language (s): English
Ad Rate: Full Page Mono 29.50
Currency: United States Dollars
COMMUNITY NEWSPAPER

The Reporter 20867

Owner: Galle (Roger)
Tel: 1 254 582-3431
Email: ads@hillsbororeporter.com **Web site:** http://www.hillsbororeporter.com
Freq: 2 Times/Week; **Circ:** 5000 Not Audited
Editor and Publisher: Roger Galle
Profile: The Hillsboro Reporter is a community newspaper serving Hillsboro, TX and the surrounding areas and covers local news, events and sports.
Language (s): English
Ad Rate: Full Page Mono 8.15
Currency: United States Dollars
COMMUNITY NEWSPAPER

The Reporter 22620

Owner: McClatchy Newspapers
Editorial: 91655 Overseas Hwy, Tavernier, Florida 33070-2558 **Tel:** 1 305 852-3216
Web site: http://www.keysnet.com
Freq: Fri; **Circ:** 13000 Not Audited
Editor: David Goodhue; **Circulation Manager:** Carter Townshend
Profile: The Reporter is a local newspaper written for the residents of Tavernier, FL. The newspaper covers local and national news, weather, sports and community events.
Language (s): English
Ad Rate: Full Page Mono 10.28
Currency: United States Dollars
COMMUNITY NEWSPAPER

The Reporter 446406

Owner: Sound Publishing, Inc.
Editorial: 27116 167th Pl SE Ste 114, Covington, Washington 98042-7341 **Tel:** 1 425 432-1209
Email: letters@maplevalleyreporter.com **Web site:** http://www.maplevalleyreporter.com/
Freq: Sat; **Circ:** 24000 Not Audited
Publisher: Bill Marcum
Profile: The Reporter is a community newspaper covering Covington, Maple Valley and Black Diamond, WA. This community newspaper is owned by Sound Publishing, Inc., which produces a variety of weekly newspapers in Washington state; these papers share content, and news releases, as well as calendar listings can be posted online for review by the paper's editorial staff.
Language (s): English

Ad Rate: Full Page Mono 23.00
Currency: United States Dollars
COMMUNITY NEWSPAPER

The Reporter Group 154733

Owner: Jewish Federation of Broome County
Editorial: 500 Clubhouse Rd, Vestal, New York 13850-4700 **Tel:** 1 607 724-2360
Email: treporter@aol.com **Web site:** http://www.thereportergroup.org
Freq: Bi-Weekly; **Circ:** 17027 ABC-Audit Bureau of Circulations
Advertising Sales Manager: Bonnie Rozen
Profile: The Reporter Group is a community newspaper publisher serving the Jewish communities of New York, Pennsylvania and Connecticut.
Language (s): English
COMMUNITY NEWSPAPER

Reporter Newspapers 446287

Owner: Springs Publishing, LLC
Editorial: 6065 Roswell Rd Ste 225, Springs Publishing Llc, Sandy Springs, Georgia 30328-4012 **Tel:** 1 404 917-2200
Email: editor@reporternewspapers.net **Web site:** http://www.reporternewspapers.net
Circ: 66000 Not Audited
Publisher: Steve Levene
Profile: Reporter Newspapers in Sandy Springs, GA is a community newspaper publisher serving the residents of Atlanta.
COMMUNITY NEWSPAPER

Reporter Newspapers 951319

Owner: Sound Publishing Inc.
Editorial: 19426 68th Ave S Ste A, Kent, Washington 98032-1193 **Tel:** 1 425 255-3484
Profile: Reporter Newspapers produces the Kent Reporter, Auburn Reporter, Renton Reporter and Tukwila Reporter. This community newspaper is owned by Sound Publishing, Inc., which produces a variety of weekly newspapers in Washington state; these papers share content, and news releases, as well as calendar listings can be posted online for review by the paper's editorial staff.
COMMUNITY NEWSPAPER

Reporter Today 790291

Owner: Reporter Today
Tel: 1 508 252-6575
Email: news@rehobothreporter.com **Web site:** http://www.reportertoday.com
Publisher: Barbara Georgia; **Editor:** Dick Georgia; **Advertising Sales Manager:** Mary Nascimento
Profile: Reporter Today publishes the East Providence Reporter, Rehoboth Reporter and Seekonk Reporter.
COMMUNITY NEWSPAPER

The Republican 19475

Owner: NCWV Media
Editorial: 108 S 2nd St, Oakland, Maryland 21550-1520 **Tel:** 1 301 334-3963
Email: newsroom@therepublicannews.com **Web site:** http://www.therepublicannews.com
Freq: Thu; **Circ:** 7310 Not Audited
Advertising Sales Manager: Lisa Rook; **Editor:** Donald Sincell
Profile: Republican News' editorial mission is to cover local news and events of Garrett County. The publication is written for residents of Garrett County, MD. The lead time for Republican News is two days.
Language (s): English
Ad Rate: Full Page Mono 5.20
Currency: United States Dollars
COMMUNITY NEWSPAPER

The Republican Journal 23114

Owner: Village NetMedia
Editorial: 71 High St, Belfast, Maine 04915-6246 **Tel:** 1 207 338-3333
Email: news@villagesoup.com **Web site:** http://waldo.villagesoup.com
Freq: Thu; **Circ:** 6000 Not Audited
Editor: Dan West
Profile: The Republican Journal is a local weekly newspaper written for the citizens of Belfast, ME. It delivers local news, events, and interests. Deadline varies by content but is between one and three days before issue date.
Language (s): English
Ad Rate: Full Page Mono 12.45
Currency: United States Dollars
COMMUNITY NEWSPAPER

The Republic-Monitor 22105

Owner: PTS Inc.
Editorial: 10 W Sainte Marie St, Perryville, Missouri 63775-1347 **Tel:** 1 573 547-4567
Email: webeditor@perryvillenews.com **Web site:** http://www.perryvillenews.com
Freq: Thu; **Circ:** 5511 Not Audited
Publisher: Beth Chism; **Advertising Sales Manager:** Sandy Schnurbusch
Profile: The Republic-Monitor is a community newspaper featuring news, sports, classifieds and events about Perryville and Perry County, MO. Deadlines for the Tuesday edition are Fridays at 5pm CT. Deadlines for the Thursday edition are Tuesdays at 5pm CT.
Language (s): English
Ad Rate: Full Page Mono 8.95
Currency: United States Dollars
COMMUNITY NEWSPAPER

The Resident 21630
Owner: Ann (Alexis)
Editorial: 252 S Broad St, Pawcatuck, Connecticut 06379-7924 **Tel:** 1 860 608-0467
Email: editor@theresident.com **Web site:** http://theresidentgoodnews.com
Freq: Bi-Weekly; **Circ:** 30000 Not Audited
Publisher & Editor: Alexis Ann; **Circulation Manager:** Joel Kelly
Profile: The Resident in Pawcatuck, CT is a bi-weekly newspaper written that covers local news and events, including the regional casino industry.
Language (s): English
Ad Rate: Full Page Mono 31.00
Currency: United States Dollars
COMMUNITY NEWSPAPER

Retrospect 21677
Owner: Ainsworth Media Inc.
Editorial: 732 Haddon Ave, Collingswood, New Jersey 8108 **Tel:** 1 856 854-1400
Email: editor@theretrospect.com **Web site:** http://www.theretrospect.com
Freq: Fri; **Circ:** 5600
Publisher: Brett Ainsworth
Language (s): English
Ad Rate: Full Page Mono 12.65
Currency: United States Dollars
COMMUNITY NEWSPAPER

The Revere Independent Newspaper Group 24854
Owner: Independent Newspaper Group
Editorial: 385 Broadway Ste 105, Revere, Massachusetts 02151-3049 **Tel:** 1 781 485-0588
Circ: 50100 Not Audited
Advertising Sales Manager: Deborah Digregoriou; **Editor:** John Lynds; **Publisher:** Stephen Quigley
Profile: The Revere Independent Newspaper Group is a weekly community newspaper publisher serving the residents of Revere, Charlestown, East Boston, Chelsea, Winthrop, Lynn and Everett, MA.
Language (s): English
COMMUNITY NEWSPAPER

Review Independent 27334
Owner: Yakima Valley Publishing Co.
Editorial: 416 S 3rd St, Yakima, Washington 98901-2834 **Tel:** 1 509 457-4886
Email: news@yvpub.com
Freq: Weekly; **Circ:** 7800 Not Audited
Publisher: Bruce Smith; **Editor:** Jack Smith
Profile: Review Independent is a weekly newspaper written for the residents of the Lower Valley in Yakima, WA.
Language (s): English
Ad Rate: Full Page Mono 10.00
Currency: United States Dollars
COMMUNITY NEWSPAPER

Review/Beacon Publishing 25411
Owner: Kozak Publishing
Tel: 1 415 831-0461
Email: editor@sfrichmondreview.com **Web site:** http://www.sunsetbeacon.com
Circ: 50500 Not Audited
Publisher & Editor: Paul Kozakiewicz
Profile: Review/Beacon Publishing in San Francisco is a community newspaper publisher.
Language (s): English
COMMUNITY NEWSPAPER

Review-Roxborough 22239
Owner: Digital First Media
Editorial: 307 Derstine Ave, Lansdale, Pennsylvania 19446-3532 **Tel:** 1 215 542-0200
Web site: http://www.montgomerynews.com/roxborough_review
Freq: Wed; **Circ:** 15000 Not Audited
Profile: Review-Roxborough is a weekly newspaper serving the Roxborough, Manayunk, Andorra, Wissahickon and East Falls sections of the Philadelphia area. Editorial deadlines are on Fridays at noon ET. Advertising deadlines are on Mondays at 4pm ET. Deadlines are a day earlier when holidays fall on a Friday or Monday.
Language (s): English
Ad Rate: Full Page Mono 26.76
Currency: United States Dollars
COMMUNITY NEWSPAPER

RH Weekly 689950
Owner: Prairie Mountain Publishing)
Editorial: 201 E 5Th St, Loveland, Colorado 80537-5605 **Tel:** 1 970 669-5050
Freq: Wed; **Circ:** 15000
Editor: Jeff Stahla
Profile: RH Weekly is a local community newspaper for the residents of Loveland, CO and the surrounding communities.
Language (s): English
Ad Rate: Full Page Mono 8.93
Currency: United States Dollars
COMMUNITY NEWSPAPER

Rhode Island Catholic 21907
Owner: Diocese of Providence
Editorial: 1 Cathedral Sq, Providence, Rhode Island 02903-3601 **Tel:** 1 401 272-1010
Email: editor@thericatholic.com **Web site:** http://thericatholic.com
Freq: Thu; **Circ:** 30000 Not Audited
Circulation Manager: Danuta Lesnikowski
Profile: Rhode Island Catholic in Providence, RI is a weekly newspaper that covers news and events of interest to the Catholic community.
Language (s): English
Ad Rate: Full Page Mono 19.00
Currency: United States Dollars
COMMUNITY NEWSPAPER

Rice Lake Chronotype 21223
Owner: Chronotype Publishing Co.
Editorial: 28 S Main St, Rice Lake, Wisconsin 54868-2269 **Tel:** 1 715 234-2121
Email: newsroom@chronotype.com **Web site:** http://www.apg-wi.com/rice_lake_chronotype/
Freq: Wed; **Circ:** 7779 Not Audited
Advertising Sales Manager: Bob Dorrance; **Publisher:** Warren Dorrance; **Circulation Manager:** Jim Stavran
Profile: Rice Lake Chronotype is published weekly for the residents of Rice Lake, WI and surrounding areas. The newspaper delivers information on local news, sports and community events. Deadlines are at 10am CT.
Language (s): English
Ad Rate: Full Page Mono 11.25
Currency: United States Dollars
COMMUNITY NEWSPAPER

Richards Publishing Company, Inc. 24601
Editorial: 2nd and Main St, Gonvick, Minnesota 56644 **Tel:** 1 218 487-5225
Email: richards@gvtel.com **Web site:** http://www.tricocanary.com
Circ: 5300 Not Audited
Editor: Corrine Richards; **Publisher:** Richard Richards
Language (s): English
COMMUNITY NEWSPAPER

Richfield Reaper 21606
Owner: Brehm Communications, Inc.
Editorial: 65 W Center St, Richfield, Utah 84701-2546 **Tel:** 1 435 896-5476
Email: reapered@richfieldreaper.com **Web site:** http://www.richfieldreaper.com
Freq: Wed; **Circ:** 6300 Not Audited
Editor: Sandy Phillips
Profile: Richfield Reaper is a weekly local newspaper delivering local news and event information to the community of Richfield, UT and Southern Utah. Its editorial mission is to provide quality community journalism. Deadlines fall on the Fridays before issue date.
Language (s): English
Ad Rate: Full Page Mono 12.50
Currency: United States Dollars
COMMUNITY NEWSPAPER

Richlands News-Press 24281
Owner: BH Media Group
Editorial: 1945 2nd St, Richlands, Virginia 24641-2303 **Tel:** 1 276 963-1081
Web site: http://www.richlands-news-press.com
Freq: Wed; **Circ:** 8300 Not Audited
Editor: Mark Sage
Profile: Richlands News-Press is published weekly for the residents of Richlands, VA and surrounding communities. The newspaper provides information on local news and community events.
Language (s): English
Ad Rate: Full Page Mono 15.00
Currency: United States Dollars
COMMUNITY NEWSPAPER

Richmond Free Press 22523
Owner: Paradigm Communications, Inc.
Editorial: 422 E Franklin St, Richmond, Virginia 23219-2226 **Tel:** 1 804 644-0496
Email: news@richmondfreepress.com **Web site:** http://www.richmondfreepress.com
Freq: Thu; **Circ:** 36905 Not Audited
Editor and Publisher: Jean Boone
Profile: Richmond Free Press is written for the residents of Richmond, VA. It covers local news and events.
Language (s): English
Ad Rate: Full Page Mono 32.60
Currency: United States Dollars
COMMUNITY NEWSPAPER

Rio Grande Sun 20223
Owner: Sun Publishing, Inc.
Editorial: 123 N Railroad Ave, Espanola, New Mexico 87532-2627 **Tel:** 1 505 753-2126
Email: rgsun@cybermesa.com **Web site:** http://www.riograndesun.com
Freq: Thu; **Circ:** 11126 Not Audited
Editor: Jennifer Garcia; **Advertising Sales Manager:** Maria Garcia; **Publisher:** Robert Trapp
Profile: Rio Grande Sun is a local weekly newspaper for the residents of Rio Arriba and Northern Santa Fe County, NM. The publication covers local news, events, sports, arts & entertainment and education. The editorial deadlines are Mondays at 5pm MT.
Language (s): English
Ad Rate: Full Page Mono 9.50
Currency: United States Dollars
COMMUNITY NEWSPAPER

Ripley Publishing Company, Inc. 24566
Editorial: 115 S Washington St, Versailles, Indiana 47042-8016 **Tel:** 1 812 689-6364
Email: publication@ripleynews.com **Web site:** http://www.ripleynews.com
Circ: 9600 Not Audited
Publisher: Linda Chandler; **Editor:** Mary Mattingly
Language (s): English
COMMUNITY NEWSPAPER

Rising Publications 24657
Owner: Rising Media Group LLC
Editorial: 25 Warburton Ave, Yonkers, New York 10701-7079 **Tel:** 1 914 965-4000
Email: risingmediagroup@gmail.com **Web site:** http://www.risingmediagroup.com
Freq: Weekly; **Circ:** 54496 Not Audited
Profile: Rising Publications in Yonkers, NY publishes the following community newspapers: North Castle Rising; Pelham Rising; Rye Rising: Yonkers Rising; Sound View Rising; Harrison Rising; Eastchester Rising; Westchester Rising; and Mt. Vernon Rising.
Language (s): English
COMMUNITY NEWSPAPER

River Cities' Reader 22326
Owner: McGreevy (Todd)
Editorial: 532 W 3rd St, Davenport, Iowa 52801-1117 **Tel:** 1 563 324-0049
Email: info@rcreader.com **Web site:** http://www.rcreader.com
Freq: Bi-Weekly; **Circ:** 22000 Not Audited
Circulation Manager: Rick Martin; **Editor:** Kathleen McCarthy; **Publisher:** Todd McGreevy
Profile: River Cities' Reader is a weekly newspaper for the residents of Davenport, IA. The editorial mission is to report the local news of Davenport as well as provide comprehensive and critical arts, music, and culture coverage.
Language (s): English
Ad Rate: Full Page Mono 20.09
Currency: United States Dollars
COMMUNITY NEWSPAPER

River Publishing 25011
Editorial: 308 W Cedar St, Brinkley, Arkansas 72021-2710 **Tel:** 1 870 734-1056
Circ: 10100 Not Audited
Publisher: Katie Jacques; **Editor:** Trisha Rogers
Language (s): English
COMMUNITY NEWSPAPER

The River Reporter 21457
Owner: Stuart Communications
Editorial: 93 Erie Ave, Narrowsburg, New York 12764-6423 **Tel:** 1 845 252-7414
Email: editor@riverreporter.com **Web site:** http://www.riverreporter.com
Freq: Thu; **Circ:** 5000 Not Audited
Editor: Fritz Mayer; **Publisher:** Laurie Stuart
Profile: The River Reporter is a community newspaper published for the residents of Narrowsburg, NY that covers local news and events.
Language (s): English
Ad Rate: Full Page Mono 8.70
Ad Rate: Full Page Colour 14.19
Currency: United States Dollars
COMMUNITY NEWSPAPER

River Valley Newspapers 25339
Owner: River Valley Newspaper Group
Editorial: 401 N. Third St., La Crosse, Wisconsin 54601-3281 **Tel:** 1 608 782-9710
Email: information@lee.net **Web site:** http://www.rivervalleynewspapers.com
Circ: 6988 Not Audited
Editor: Randy Erickson
Language (s): English
COMMUNITY NEWSPAPER

River Valley Times 22917
Owner: Herburger Publications, Inc.
Tel: 1 800 700-2166
Email: rvt@herburger.net
Freq: Wed; **Circ:** 5600 Not Audited
Publisher: David Herburger
Profile: The River Valley Times provides news and relevant information to the residents of Wilton, CA.
Language (s): English
Ad Rate: Full Page Mono 7.80
Currency: United States Dollars
COMMUNITY NEWSPAPER

The River Weekly News 86054
Owner: Lorken Publications
Editorial: 1609 Hendry St Ste 15, Fort Myers, Florida 33901-2913 **Tel:** 1 239 415-7732
Email: press@riverweekly.com **Web site:** http://www.islandsunnews.com
Freq: Thu; **Circ:** 8000 Not Audited
Editor: Isabel Rasi
Profile: The River Weekly News is a community newspaper written for residents of Fort Myers, FL.
Language (s): English
Ad Rate: Full Page Mono 6.44
Currency: United States Dollars
COMMUNITY NEWSPAPER

The Riverdale Press 20247
Owner: Richner Communications
Editorial: 5676 Riverdale Ave Ste 311, Bronx, New York 10471-2100 **Tel:** 1 718 543-6065
Email: newsroom@riverdalepress.com **Web site:** http://www.riverdalepress.com
Freq: Thu; **Circ:** 10000 Not Audited
Publisher: Richard Stein
Profile: The Riverdale Press is a weekly newspaper for residents of the Northwest Bronx, NY area. The editorial mission is to provide the community with accurate and up-to-date local news and information. Deadlines for the publication are on Mondays before issue date.
Language (s): English
COMMUNITY NEWSPAPER

Riverfront Times 21323
Owner: Euclid Media Group
Editorial: 6358 Delmar Blvd Ste 200, Saint Louis, Missouri 63130-4718 **Tel:** 1 314 754-5966
Email: feedback@riverfronttimes.com **Web site:** http://www.riverfronttimes.com
Freq: Thu; **Circ:** 33000 Not Audited
Profile: Riverfront Times is a weekly newspaper published for the residents of St. Louis and surrounding areas. It covers local news, culture, arts & entertainment and weather.
Language (s): English
Ad Rate: Full Page Mono 40.83
Ad Rate: Full Page Colour 54.31
Currency: United States Dollars
COMMUNITY NEWSPAPER

Riverland News 24209
Owner: Landmark Community Newspapers, Inc.
Editorial: 20441 E Pennsylvania Ave, Dunnellon, Florida 34432-6035 **Tel:** 1 352 489-2731
Email: editor@riverlandnews.com **Web site:** http://www.riverlandnews.com
Freq: Thu; **Circ:** 9000 Not Audited
Editor: Pat Faherity; **Publisher:** Gerald Mulligan
Profile: Riverland News is a weekly newspaper for the residents of Dunnellon, FL. It covers news and events, sports, business and other topics. The lead time falls on Mondays prior to the issue date. Deadlines are one week before issue date.
Language (s): English
Ad Rate: Full Page Mono 16.48
Currency: United States Dollars
COMMUNITY NEWSPAPER

The Riverside County Record 21481
Owner: N.C. Publications, Inc.
Editorial: 8175 Limonite Ave Ste A8, Riverside, California 92509-6121 **Tel:** 1 951 685-6191
Email: recorddhb@aol.com **Web site:** http://www.countyrecordnews.com
Freq: Thu; **Circ:** 5000 Not Audited
Profile: The Riverside County Record is a weekly newspaper for the residents of Riverside, CA. It covers news and events in the local community.
Language (s): English
Ad Rate: Full Page Mono 6.50
Currency: United States Dollars
COMMUNITY NEWSPAPER

Riverside Review 20249
Owner: Mack (Richard)
Editorial: 215 Military Rd, Buffalo, New York 14207-2631 **Tel:** 1 716 877-8400
Email: rich@buffaloreview.com
Freq: Wed; **Circ:** 12000 Not Audited
Publisher & Editor: Richard Mack
Profile: Riverside Review is a weekly newspaper for the residents of northwest Buffalo, NY. It covers news and events in the local community.
Language (s): English
Ad Rate: Full Page Mono 9.50
Currency: United States Dollars
COMMUNITY NEWSPAPER

Rivertowns Enterprise 22570
Owner: W.H. White Publications
Editorial: 95 Main St, Dobbs Ferry, New York 10522-1673 **Tel:** 1 914 478-2787
Web site: http://www.rivertownsenterprise.net/Rivertowns_Enterprise/Home.html
Freq: Fri; **Circ:** 6100 Not Audited
Editor: Timothy Lamorte; **Advertising Sales Manager:** Marilyn Petrosa; **Publisher:** Deborah White
Profile: Rivertowns Enterprise is a weekly newspaper for the residents of Hastings-on-Hudson, Dobbs Ferry, Ardsley and Irvington, NY.
Language (s): English
Ad Rate: Full Page Mono 11.50
Currency: United States Dollars
COMMUNITY NEWSPAPER

Roane Newspapers 24770
Editorial: 204 Franklin St, Kingston, Tennessee 37763 **Tel:** 1 865 376-3481
Email: newsroom@roanecounty.com **Web site:** http://www.roanecounty.com
Circ: 15987 Not Audited
Circulation Manager: Sara Baylis; **Advertising Sales Manager:** Kevin Kile; **Editor:** Terri Likens
Language (s): English
COMMUNITY NEWSPAPER

The Roanoke Star-Sentinel 512303
Owner: Whisper One Media Inc.
Tel: 1 540 400-0990
Email: info@newsroanoke.com **Web site:** http://www.newsroanoke.com
Freq: Fri; **Circ:** 77000 Not Audited
News Editor: Gene Marrano; **Publisher & Editor:** Stuart Revercomb
Profile: The Roanoke Star-Sentinel is a weekly newspaper written for the residents of Roanoke, VA. It covers local news, sports and community events.
Language (s): English
Ad Rate: Full Page Mono 15.00
Currency: United States Dollars
COMMUNITY NEWSPAPER

Roanoke Tribune 21078
Editorial: 2318 Melrose Ave NW, Roanoke, Virginia 24017-3906 **Tel:** 1 540 343-0326
Email: trib@rt.roacoxmail.com **Web site:** http://theroanoketribune.org
Freq: Thu; **Circ:** 6000 Not Audited
Publisher: Claudia Whitworth
Profile: Roanoke Tribune is written for the African American community of Roanoke, VA. It covers news and events in the local community. Deadlines are on Mondays at 5pm ET.
Language (s): English
Ad Rate: Full Page Mono 7.20
Currency: United States Dollars
COMMUNITY NEWSPAPER

Robertson County Times 20757
Owner: Gannett Co., Inc.
Editorial: 505 W Court Sq, Springfield, Tennessee 37172-2413 **Tel:** 1 615 384-3567
Email: rctnews@mtcngroup.com **Web site:** http://www.rctimes.com
Freq: Wed; **Circ:** 8400 Not Audited
Editor: Eric Miller
Profile: Robertson County Times is a weekly newspaper for the residents of Robertson County, TN. It covers news and events in the local community. Deadlines for the publication are 5pm ET, Monday before issue date.
Language (s): English
Ad Rate: Full Page Mono 14.00
Currency: United States Dollars
COMMUNITY NEWSPAPER

Robins Rev-Up 133858
Editorial: 620 North St., Bldg 905, Warner Robins, Georgia 31098-2255 **Tel:** 1 478 468-2137
Web site: http://www.robins.af.mil/library/rev.asp
Freq: Fri; **Circ:** 15000 Not Audited
Editor: Lanorris Askew; **Publisher:** Rick Brewer
Profile: Robins Rev-Up is a weekly paper written for current and former members of the U.S. military services. Deadlines are Mondays at 4pm ET.
Language (s): English
Ad Rate: Full Page Mono 13.00
Currency: United States Dollars
COMMUNITY NEWSPAPER

Robinson Newspapers 156297
Owner: Robinson Newspapers
Editorial: 14006 1st Ave S, Suite B, Burien, Washington 98168 **Tel:** 1 206 708-1378
Web site: http://www.robinsonnews.com
Freq: Weekly; **Circ:** 49000 Not Audited
Circulation Manager: Dave Kellog; **Editor:** Eric Mathison; **Advertising Manager:** Dona Ozier; **Publisher:** Jerry Robinson
Language (s): English
COMMUNITY NEWSPAPER

Robson Publishing 75697
Editorial: 9532 E Riggs Rd, Sun Lakes, Arizona 85248-7463 **Tel:** 1 480 895-4216
Email: advertising@robson.com **Web site:** http://www.robsonpublishing.com
Circ: 29500 Not Audited
Publisher: Linda Gosnel; **Editor:** Linda Robson
Profile: Robson Publishing is a publication that provides the community of Sun Lakes, AZ with community newspapers.
Language (s): English
COMMUNITY NEWSPAPER

The Rochester Times 24175
Editorial: 1 Old Dover Rd Ste, Rochester, New Hampshire 03867-3438 **Tel:** 1 603 332-2300
Email: thetimes@fosters.com **Web site:** http://www.fosters.com
Freq: Thu; **Circ:** 15000 Not Audited
Profile: The Rochester Times is a weekly newspaper published for the residents of Rock County, NE. The publication features local news and community events. The news deadline falls on Tuesday at noon CT.
Language (s): English
Ad Rate: Full Page Mono 10.80
Currency: United States Dollars
COMMUNITY NEWSPAPER

The Rock River Times 22652
Owner: Rock River Times Inc. (The)
Editorial: 128 N Church St, Rockford, Illinois 61101-1002 **Tel:** 1 815 964-9767
Email: contact@rockrivertimes.com **Web site:** http://www.rockrivertimes.com
Freq: Wed; **Circ:** 22000 Not Audited
Advertising Manager: Judy Marshall; **Publisher & Editor:** Frank Schier
Profile: The Rock River Times is a weekly newspaper written for residents of Illinois and Madison, WI. The publication focuses on local news and events, but it also covers state, national and international news. News deadlines are on Thursdays at 4pm CT. The best days to contact reporters and editors are Tuesdays, Wednesdays and Thursdays between 10am and 5pm CT. The publication prefers to receive press materials via mail, fax and e-mail, in that order.
Language (s): English
Ad Rate: Full Page Mono 9.08
Ad Rate: Full Page Colour 10.72
Currency: United States Dollars
COMMUNITY NEWSPAPER

Rock Valley Publishing, LLC. 473464
Editorial: 11512 N 2nd St, Machesney Park, Illinois 61115-1101 **Tel:** 1 815 654-4850
Email: info@rvpublishing.com **Web site:** http://www.rvpublishing.com
Freq: Weekly; **Circ:** 12463 Not Audited
Editor: Melanie Bradley; **Publisher:** Pete Cruger; **Circulation Manager:** Lindy Sweet
Profile: Rock Valley Publishing prints and publishes both weekly and monthly community newspapers, distributed in Northern Illinois, Southern Wisconsin, and the Chicagoland area.
Language (s): English
COMMUNITY NEWSPAPER

The Rockaway Times 919458
Owner: Boyle (Kevin) & Adams (Patricia)
Editorial: 11404 Beach Channel Dr, Rockaway Park, New York 11694-2211 **Tel:** 1 718 634-3030
Email: news@rockawaytimes.com **Web site:** http://rockawaytimes.com
Freq: Weekly; **Circ:** 10000
Editor & Publisher: Kevin Boyle
Profile: Launched June 26, 2014, The Rockaway Times is a free, weekly community newspaper covering news, events, arts and entertainment in the Rockaways, a Queens neighborhood in New York.
Language (s): English
COMMUNITY NEWSPAPER

The Rockford Squire 19548
Owner: Altena (Beth)
Editorial: 331 Northland Dr NE, Rockford, Michigan 49341-1025 **Tel:** 1 616 866-4465
Web site: http://www.rockfordsquire.com
Freq: Thu; **Circ:** 11500 Not Audited
Editor & Publisher: Beth Altena
Profile: The Rockford Squire is a weekly newspaper for the residents of Rockford, MI. It covers news and events in the local community.
Language (s): English
Ad Rate: Full Page Mono 10.00
Currency: United States Dollars
COMMUNITY NEWSPAPER

Rockland County Times 22743
Owner: Citizen Publishing Co.
Editorial: 119 Main St, Nanuet, New York 10954-2882 **Tel:** 1 845 627-1414
Email: editor@rocklandcountytimes.com **Web site:** http://www.rocklandcountytimes.com
Freq: Thu; **Circ:** 12000 Not Audited
Circulation Manager: Marge Formato; **Publisher:** Ken Herndon; **Publisher:** Kenneth Herndon; **Advertising Sales Manager:** Terri Warner
Profile: Rockland County Times is a local weekly newspaper for the residents of Rockland County, NY. The publication covers information on news and events occurring in the local community.
Language (s): English
Ad Rate: Full Page Mono 11.18
Currency: United States Dollars
COMMUNITY NEWSPAPER

Rockland Review 22744
Owner: Angel Media & Publishing Co.
Editorial: 26 Snake Hill Rd, West Nyack, New York 10994-1625 **Tel:** 1 845 727-4114
Email: rocklandreview@optonline.net **Web site:** http://www.rocklandreviewnews.com
Freq: Weekly; **Circ:** 25000 Not Audited
Publisher: Joseph Miele; **Editor:** Meryl Raffman
Profile: Rockland Review is a community newspaper written for the residents of West Nyack, NY.
Language (s): English
Ad Rate: Full Page Mono 16.00
Currency: United States Dollars
COMMUNITY NEWSPAPER

Rockport Pilot 20941
Owner: Hartman Newspapers Inc.
Editorial: 1002 E Wharf St, Rockport, Texas 78382-2662 **Tel:** 1 361 729-9900
Email: editorial@rockportpilot.com **Web site:** http://www.rockportpilot.com
Freq: Sat; **Circ:** 5300 Not Audited
Advertising Sales Manager: Kim Gove; **Publisher & Editor:** Mike Probst; **Circulation Manager:** Marie Simon
Profile: Rockport Pilot is a twice weekly newspaper for the residents of Rockport, TX. It covers news and events in the local community.
Language (s): English
Ad Rate: Full Page Mono 9.50
Currency: United States Dollars
COMMUNITY NEWSPAPER

Rogersville Review 21728
Owner: Jones Media
Editorial: 316 E Main St, Rogersville, Tennessee 37857-3468 **Tel:** 1 423 272-7422
Email: review@xtn.net **Web site:** http://www.therogersvillereview.com
Freq: Sat; **Circ:** 7000 Not Audited
Advertising Manager: Sharon Roberts; **Circulation Manager:** Pat Smith
Profile: Rogersville Review is a local newspaper written for the residents of Rogersville, TN. The paper covers local news and events.
Language (s): English
Ad Rate: Full Page Mono 12.00
Currency: United States Dollars
COMMUNITY NEWSPAPER

rolling out UrbanStyle Weekly 238966
Owner: Steed Media Group
Editorial: 770 English Ave NW, Atlanta, Georgia 30318-8400 **Tel:** 1 404 635-1313
Email: editorial@rollingout.com **Web site:** http://www.rollingout.com
Freq: Weekly; **Circ:** 1201817 Not Audited
Advertising Sales Manager: Randy Fling; **Publisher:** Munson Steed
Profile: rolling out UrbanStyle Weekly is a newspaper that offers African Americans mainstream reviews of celebrities, entertainment, movies, politics and society. The newspaper is involved in the transformation of urban America by shaping and perpetuating the continuity of African American culture. The paper provides African Americans with instructions on how to live and with paradigms of what they can aspire to be. The paper is distributed in all major cities throughout the United States.
Language (s): English
COMMUNITY NEWSPAPER

Rolling Thunder Express 22096
Owner: Angel-Currier (Sylvia)
Editorial: 134A Main St, Newport, Maine 04953-3105 **Tel:** 1 207 368-2028
Email: info@rollingthunderexpress.com **Web site:** http://www.rollingthunderexpress.com
Freq: Mon; **Circ:** 16200 Not Audited
Editor and Publisher: Sylvia Angel-Currier; **Circulation Manager:** Dave Dube
Profile: Rolling Thunder Express is a local weekly newspaper serving the residents of Newport, Corinna, East Newport, Detroit, Dixmont, Exeter, Cambridge, Parkman, Hartland, St. Albans, Garland, Stetson, Burnham, Ripley, Abbot, Willimantic, Pittsfield, Dexter, Palmyra, Etna, Plymouth, Guilford, Sangerville, Blanchard, Harmony, Carmel, Clinton, Dover-Foxcroft, Levant, Unity, Canaan, Monson, East Corinth, Troy, Athens and Greenville, ME. The newspaper mainly covers local news, sports, entertainment, education and community events.
Language (s): English
Ad Rate: Full Page Mono 7.69
Currency: United States Dollars
COMMUNITY NEWSPAPER

Rossmoor News 18654
Owner: Golden Rain Foundation
Editorial: 1006 Stanley Dollar Dr, Walnut Creek, California 94595-2913 **Tel:** 1 925 988-7800
Email: news@rossmoor.com **Web site:** http://www.rossmoornews.com
Freq: Wed; **Circ:** 6700 Not Audited
Profile: Rossmoor News is the weekly newspaper written for residents of Rossmoor, CA, a senior adult community. The newspaper covers news and events in the community.
Language (s): English
Ad Rate: Full Page Mono 14.00
Currency: United States Dollars
COMMUNITY NEWSPAPER

Round Rock Leader/ Pflugerville Pflag 722050
Owner: Cox Media Group, Inc.
Editorial: 1111 N Interstate 35 Ste 230, Round Rock, Texas 78664-4244 **Tel:** 1 512 255-5827
Freq: Weekly; **Circ:** 14700
Language (s): English
COMMUNITY NEWSPAPER

Royalton Recorder 257486
Editorial: 13737 State Rd, North Royalton, Ohio 44133-3907 **Tel:** 1 440 237-2235
Email: rrnews@aol.com **Web site:** http://www.nroyaltonchamber.com
Freq: Semi-Monthly; **Circ:** 16000 Not Audited
Profile: Royalton Recorder is a community newspaper written for the residents of North Royalton, OH. It covers news and events in the local community. Deadlines for the publication are one week before the issue date.
Language (s): English
Ad Rate: Full Page Mono 55.00
Currency: United States Dollars
COMMUNITY NEWSPAPER

Rumbo 231377
Owner: Suda Inc. dba Rumbo
Editorial: 60 Island St Ste 211, Lawrence, Massachusetts 01840-1835 **Tel:** 1 978 794-5360
Email: rumbo@rumbonews.com **Web site:** http://www.rumbonews.com
Freq: Weekly; **Circ:** 5000 Not Audited
Profile: Rumbo is a local community newspaper written for Hispanic residents of Lawrence, MA and surrounding areas. It covers local news, entertainment, education, business, religion and sports.
Language (s): Spanish/Bilingual
Ad Rate: Full Page Mono 8.00
Currency: United States Dollars
COMMUNITY NEWSPAPER

Rumores 87279
Owner: Torres (Abel)
Editorial: 429 S Bristol St, Santa Ana, California 92703-4500 **Tel:** 1 714 547-8283
Email: editorial@rumoresnews.com
Freq: Wed; **Circ:** 30000 Not Audited
Publisher & Editor: Abel Torres
Profile: Rumores in Santa Ana, CA targets the Spanish-speaking community and covers local news, arts & entertainment, health and general interest topics.
Language (s): Spanish
Ad Rate: Full Page Mono 10.00
Currency: United States Dollars
COMMUNITY NEWSPAPER

Rural Virginian 22367
Owner: Media General Inc.
Editorial: 685 Rio Road West, Charlottesville, Virginia 22901 **Tel:** 1 434 978-7216
Email: rv@dailyprogress.com **Web site:** http://www.ruralvirginian.com
Freq: Wed; **Circ:** 14000 Not Audited
Editor: Terry Karnes
Profile: Rural Virginian is a weekly newspaper for the residents of Charlottesville, VA. It covers community news and events.
Language (s): English
Ad Rate: Full Page Mono 15.50
Currency: United States Dollars
COMMUNITY NEWSPAPER

Rural-Urban Record 20329
Owner: Boise (Lee)
Editorial: 24487 Squire Rd, Columbia Station, Ohio 44028-9672 **Tel:** 1 440 236-8982
Email: news@rural-urbanrecord.com **Web site:** http://www.rural-urbanrecord.com
Freq: Mon; **Circ:** 22274 Not Audited
Advertising Sales Manager: Stephanie Hunt
Profile: Rural-Urban Record is written for the residents of Columbia Station, OH and surrounding areas. It covers news and events in the local community. Deadlines are on Wednesdays at 5pm ET.
Language (s): English
Ad Rate: Full Page Mono 16.00
Currency: United States Dollars
COMMUNITY NEWSPAPER

Russell County Newspapers Inc. 24923
Owner: Times Journal Inc.
Editorial: 120 Wilson St, Russell Springs, Kentucky 42642-4315 **Tel:** 1 270 866-3191
Email: news@russellcountynewspapers.com **Web site:** http://www.russellcountynewspapers.com
Circ: 14500 Not Audited
Editor: Derek Aaron; **Publisher:** Patsy Judd; **Advertising Sales Manager:** Stephanie Smith
Language (s): English
COMMUNITY NEWSPAPER

Russian Bazaar 155514
Editorial: 8518 17th Ave, Brooklyn, New York 11214-2810 **Tel:** 1 718 266-4444
Email: rusbazaar@yahoo.com **Web site:** http://www.russian-bazaar.com
Freq: Thu; **Circ:** 19000
Advertising Sales Manager: Margarita Shapiro; **Publisher & Editor:** Natasha Shapiro
Profile: Russian bazaar is a weekly community newspaper for the Russian community of Brooklyn, NY.
Language (s): Russian
Ad Rate: Full Page Mono 7.20
Currency: United States Dollars
COMMUNITY NEWSPAPER

Russkaya Reklama 22566
Owner: Courier-Life
Editorial: 2699 Coney Island Ave, Brooklyn, New York 11235-5004 **Tel:** 1 718 769-3000
Email: reklama2000@yahoo.com **Web site:** http://www.rusrek.com
Freq: Fri; **Circ:** 40000 Not Audited
Publisher: Paul Smukler; **Editor:** Michael Tripolsky
Profile: Russkaya Reklama is a Russian-language paper distributed in Brooklyn, NY.
Language (s): Russian
Ad Rate: Full Page Mono 10.37
Ad Rate: Full Page Colour 62.22
Currency: United States Dollars
COMMUNITY NEWSPAPER

The Rye Record 491534
Owner: Jovanovich, Robin
Editorial: 14 Elm Pl, Rye, New York 10580-2951 **Tel:** 1 914 925-0540
Email: ryerecordweb@aol.com **Web site:** http://www.ryerecord.com
Freq: Bi-Weekly; **Circ:** 10000 Not Audited
Advertising Sales Manager: Carla Eggers; **Publisher:** Robin Jovanovich
Profile: The Rye Record provides local news and events to the Rye, NY community.
Language (s): English
Ad Rate: Full Page Mono 25.00
Currency: United States Dollars
COMMUNITY NEWSPAPER

SabaH 155202
Owner: Dzidzovic (Sukrija)
Editorial: 5205 Gravois Ave, Saint Louis, Missouri 63116-2309 **Tel:** 1 314 351-0201
Email: sabahbos@hotmail.com **Web site:** http://www.sabahusa.com
Freq: Mon; **Circ:** 50000 Not Audited
Publisher & Editor: Sukrija Dzidzovic
Profile: SabaH, which means sunrise, is a Bosnian-language newspaper in Saint Louis, MO that provides political news from the Balkans. It also covers events of interest to Bosnian-Americans in the U.S., especially in St. Louis, Chicago, New York, Detroit, Grand Rapids, MI, and other cities with large Bosnian populations. It is distributed throughout the U.S. and Canada.
Language (s): Bosnian
Ad Rate: Full Page Mono 150.00
Currency: United States Dollars
COMMUNITY NEWSPAPER

Sabine Index/Around the Bend
603248

Owner: Thomas (Lovan B.)
Editorial: 875 San Antonio Ave, Many, Louisiana 71449-3140 **Tel:** 1 318 256-3495
Email: news@sabineindex.net **Web site:** http://www.thesabineindex.com
Advertising Sales Manager: Steve Colwell
Profile: The Sabine Index and Around the Bend are published for the communities of Sabine Parrish, LA.
Language (s): English
COMMUNITY NEWSPAPER

Sac-Osage Publishing
24954

Tel: 1 417 646-2211
Email: sacosagenews@centurytel.net
Circ: 7950 Not Audited
Advertising Sales Manager: Donna White
Language (s): English
COMMUNITY NEWSPAPER

Sacramento News & Review
21599

Owner: Chico Community Publishing, Inc.
Editorial: 1124 Del Paso Blvd, Sacramento, California 95815-3607 **Tel:** 1 916 498-1234
Email: sactonewstips@newsreview.com **Web site:** http://www.newsreview.com/sacramento/home
Freq: Thu; **Circ:** 77793 Not Audited
Advertising Sales Manager: Richard Brown;
Circulation Manager: Greg Erwin
Profile: Sacramento News & Review is written for residents of the Sacramento, CA area. The publication provides news, community arts & entertainment, a calendar of events and several special features, including the annual Women's Issues in October.
Language (s): English
Ad Rate: Full Page Mono 8.40
Currency: United States Dollars
COMMUNITY NEWSPAPER

Sacramento Observer
18648

Owner: Observer Newspapers
Editorial: 2330 Alhambra Blvd, Sacramento, California 95817-1121 **Tel:** 1 916 452-4781
Web site: http://www.sacobserver.com
Freq: Thu; **Circ:** 49090 Not Audited
Editor: Larry Lee; **Publisher & Editor:** William Lee;
Advertising Sales Manager: Joe Stinson
Profile: Sacramento Observer delivers local, national and international news aimed toward the African-American population of Sacramento, CA. The weekly newspaper provides information on sports, business, religion, health issues, government, education and the economy. Within the SOUL section, readers can find articles about entertainment, shopping, poetry, literature and stories about local and national influential African-Americans. The paper also publishes a calendar of events, a real estate guide and several columns. Send all press releases directly to the editors.
Language (s): English
Ad Rate: Full Page Mono 90.00
Ad Rate: Full Page Colour 6370.00
Currency: United States Dollars
COMMUNITY NEWSPAPER

Sada E Pakistan
155518

Tel: 1 718 360-1934
Email: sadaepakis@aol.com **Web site:** http://www.sada-e-pakistan.net
Freq: Wed; **Circ:** 30000
Publisher: Ahsan Chughtai; **Editor:** Mohsin Zaheer
Profile: Sada E Pakistan is a weekly newspaper written for the Pakistani and Pakistani American community.
Language (s): English
Ad Rate: Full Page Mono 5.95
Currency: United States Dollars
COMMUNITY NEWSPAPER

Saigon Times
153126

Editorial: 9234 Valley Blvd, Rosemead, California 91770-1922 **Tel:** 1 626 288-2696
Email: sgtimes@aol.com **Web site:** http://www.saigontimesusa.com
Freq: Fri; **Circ:** 20000 Not Audited
Editor: Hap Thai; **Publisher:** Cam Tran
Profile: Saigon Times is a weekly newspaper written for the Vietnamese-speaking residents of Rosemead, CA.
Language (s): Vietnamese
Ad Rate: Full Page Mono 11.23
Currency: United States Dollars
COMMUNITY NEWSPAPER

Salem Times Commoner Newspapers
25266

Tel: 1 618 548-3330
Email: stceditor@salemtc.net
Circ: 20300 Not Audited
Publisher & Editor: Dennis Rosenberger
Language (s): English
COMMUNITY NEWSPAPER

Salem Weekly
586451

Editorial: 1342 Capitol St NE, Salem, Oregon 97301-7849 **Tel:** 1 503 569-1841
Email: editors@willamettemedia.com **Web site:** http://www.willamettelive.com
Freq: Bi-Weekly
Publisher: A.P. Walther

Profile: Salem Weekly is an alternative, free weekly newspaper offering local news, thought and culture to the greater Salem, OR area.
Language (s): English
COMMUNITY NEWSPAPER

Salisbury Independent
949764

Owner: Independent Newsmedia Inc.
Tel: 1 410 543-4500
Email: salisburyindependent@newszap.com **Web site:** http://www.salisburyindependent.net
Freq: Weekly
Publisher: Darel La Prade
Profile: Salisbury Independent is a weekly newspaper providing Local and Community News for the residents of Salisbury and Wicomico County, Maryland.
Language (s): English
COMMUNITY NEWSPAPER

Salmon Press - Lancaster
578524

Owner: Salmon Press LLC
Tel: 1 603 788-4939
Web site: http://www.newhampshirelakesandmountains.com
Circ: 9200
Publisher: Frank Chilinski
COMMUNITY NEWSPAPER

Salmon Press - Meredith
338336

Owner: Salmon Press LLC
Editorial: 5 Water St, Meredith, New Hampshire 03253-6233 **Tel:** 1 603 279-4516
Web site: http://www.newhampshirelakesandmountains.com
Circ: 14965 Not Audited
Editor: Brendan Berube; **Publisher:** Frank Chilinski;
Editor: Erin Plummer
Language (s): English
COMMUNITY NEWSPAPER

Salmon Press - Wolfeboro
334450

Owner: Salmon Press LLC
Editorial: Clark Plaza, 35 Center St, Wolfeboro, New Hampshire 3896 **Tel:** 1 603 569-3126
Web site: http://www.newhampshirelakesandmountains.com
Circ: 10500 Not Audited
Editor: Thomas Beeler; **Publisher:** Frank Chilinski;
Editor: Joshua Spalding; **Circulation Manager:** Nancy Turner
Language (s): English
COMMUNITY NEWSPAPER

Salt Lake City Weekly
21616

Owner: Copperfield Publishing, Inc.
Editorial: 248 S Main St, Salt Lake City, Utah 84101-2001 **Tel:** 1 801 575-7003
Email: tips@cityweekly.net **Web site:** http://www.cityweekly.net
Freq: Thu; **Circ:** 47717 Not Audited
Publisher: John Saltas; **Editor:** Jerre Wroble
Profile: Salt Lake City Weekly is published for the residents of Salt Lake City, UT and surrounding areas. The newspaper covers local news and entertainment.
Language (s): English
Ad Rate: Full Page Mono 67.20
Currency: United States Dollars
COMMUNITY NEWSPAPER

Salt River Journal
22113

Editorial: 200 N 3Rd St, Hannibal, Missouri 63401-3504 **Tel:** 1 573 221-2800
Email: webmaster@courierpost.com **Web site:** http://www.hannibal.net
Freq: Wed; **Circ:** 10100 Not Audited
Profile: Salt River Journal is a weekly newspaper published for the residents of Hannibal, MO and surrounding communities. The publication covers hunting and fishing news and information.
Language (s): English
Ad Rate: Full Page Mono 7.36
Currency: United States Dollars
COMMUNITY NEWSPAPER

El Salvador Dia a Dia
152350

Editorial: 3325 Wilshire Blvd Ste 739, Los Angeles, California 90010-1769 **Tel:** 1 213 674-8549
Email: diaadianews@yahoo.com **Web site:** http://www.diaadianews.com
Freq: Fri; **Circ:** 40000 Not Audited
Publisher & Editor: Carlos Martinez-Herrera
Profile: El Salvador Dia a Dia is a community newspaper written for the Spanish-speaking residents of Los Angeles.
Language (s): Spanish
Ad Rate: Full Page Mono 25.00
Currency: United States Dollars
COMMUNITY NEWSPAPER

Sampan
22061

Owner: Asian American Civic Association
Editorial: 87 Tyler St Fl 5, Boston, Massachusetts 02111-1833 **Tel:** 1 617 426-9492
Email: editor@sampan.org **Web site:** http://www.sampan.org
Freq: Bi-Weekly; **Circ:** 7000 Not Audited
Advertising Sales Manager: Amy Chen; **Editor:** Ling-Mei Wong
Profile: Sampan is the only Chinese-English bilingual newspaper in the New England area. It is published on the first and third Friday of each month primarily for the Asian-American community in the greater New England area. The newspaper offers information on

news and events in the area. Deadlines are on Fridays before the publication day.
Language (s): Chinese, English
Ad Rate: Full Page Mono 12.00
Currency: United States Dollars
COMMUNITY NEWSPAPER

The Sampson Weekly
825164

Editorial: 404 Sunset Ave, Clinton, North Carolina 28328-3942 **Tel:** 1 910 590-2102
Email: info@thesampsonweekly.com **Web site:** http://www.thesampsonweekly.com
Freq: Weekly
Editor: Melvin Henderson; **Advertising Sales Manager:** Bill Roberson
Profile: The Sampson Weekly is a weekly newspaper that provides Local and Community News coverage to the residents of Clinton, NC and Sampson County.
Language (s): English
COMMUNITY NEWSPAPER

Sam's Good News
74094

Owner: Sammy G. Media Corp.
Editorial: 162 N Main St, Stony Brook Plaza, Rutland, Vermont 05701-3024 **Tel:** 1 802 773-4040
Email: samsgoodnews@aol.com **Web site:** http://www.samsgoodnews.com
Freq: Wed; **Circ:** 11000 Not Audited
Editor: Rosemary Finley; **Publisher:** Samuel Gorruso
Profile: Sam's Good News' editorial mission is to provide good, positive news and information to the people in Vermont communities. The newspaper has 500 distribution points, including some in New York state. Topics include local news, real estate, business, horoscopes and sports in addition to other relevant topics. Deadline for submission of press releases falls on Friday prior to the issue date.
Language (s): English
Ad Rate: Full Page Mono 12.00
Ad Rate: Full Page Colour 1344.00
Currency: United States Dollars
COMMUNITY NEWSPAPER

San Antonio Current
21315

Owner: Times Shamrock Group
Editorial: 915 Dallas St, San Antonio, Texas 78215-1433 **Tel:** 1 210 227-0044
Email: sacalendar@sacurrent.com **Web site:** http://www.sacurrent.com
Freq: Wed; **Circ:** 46613 Not Audited
Profile: San Antonio (TX) Current is a local alternative weekly newspaper focusing on investigative reports, alternative news, entertainment and lifestyle.
Language (s): English
Ad Rate: Full Page Mono 51.03
Ad Rate: Full Page Colour 2250.00
Currency: United States Dollars
COMMUNITY NEWSPAPER

San Antonio Observer
155375

Owner: Observer Newspaper Group
Editorial: 3427 Belgium Ln, San Antonio, Texas 78219-2501 **Tel:** 1 210 212-6397
Web site: http://www.saobserver.com
Freq: Wed; **Circ:** 60000 Not Audited
Profile: San Antonio Observer is a community newspaper written for the residents of San Antonio, TX.
Language (s): English
Ad Rate: Full Page Mono 50.00
Currency: United States Dollars
COMMUNITY NEWSPAPER

The San Bernardino American News
18665

Owner: Don Roberto Group Inc.
Editorial: 14443 Park Ave, C-2, Victorville, California 92392-2927 **Tel:** 1 909 889-7677
Email: samerisam1@earthlink.net **Web site:** http://www.sbnews.us
Freq: Thu; **Circ:** 10000 Not Audited
Advertising Sales Manager: John Banks; **Editor & Publisher:** Mary Harris
Profile: The San Bernardino American News is written for the residents of San Bernardino, CA. The newspaper covers minority issues and local news.
Language (s): English
Ad Rate: Full Page Mono 49.00
Currency: United States Dollars
COMMUNITY NEWSPAPER

San Bernardino Sun City Newspapers
359873

Owner: MediaNews Group
Editorial: 290 N D St Ste 102, San Bernardino, California 92401-1734 **Tel:** 1 909 889-9666
Email: citydesk@inlandnewspapers.com **Web site:** http://www.sbsun.com
Circ: 137250 Not Audited
Profile: Produced by the San Bernardino (CA) Sun, City Newspapers consist of five weekly newspapers that target specific communities throughout the area. Each newspaper is inserted within the Friday edition of the San Bernardino (CA) Sun and also mailed to selected non-subscribers on Saturdays. The papers cover the lifestyles and events of the communities and residents in the area. They rely heavily on readers' submissions of photos and stories concerning neighborhood news, volunteerism, community events, hobbies and youth sports.
Language (s): English
Ad Rate: Full Page Mono 651.00
Currency: United States Dollars
COMMUNITY NEWSPAPER

San Diego CityBeat
155129

Owner: Southland Publishing
Editorial: 3047 University Ave Ste 202, San Diego, California 92104-3039 **Tel:** 1 619 281-7526
Web site: http://www.sdcitybeat.com
Freq: Wed; **Circ:** 44000 Not Audited
Publisher: Kevin Hellman
Profile: San Diego CityBeat is an alternative weekly newspaper distributed throughout San Diego County.
Language (s): English
Ad Rate: Full Page Mono 30.40
Ad Rate: Full Page Colour 38.22
Currency: United States Dollars
COMMUNITY NEWSPAPER

San Diego Community News Network
837529

Owner: San Diego Community News Network
Editorial: 123 Camino De La Reina Ste 202E, San Diego, California 92108-3006 **Tel:** 1 619 283-9747
Email: editor@sdcnn.com **Web site:** http://sdcnn.com
Freq: Fri; **Circ:** 107000
Editor: Doug Curlee; **Advertising Sales Manager:** Mike Rosensteel
Profile: San Diego Community News Network produces three monthly community newspapers covering the San Diego metropolitan area: Mission Times Courier, La Mesa Courier and Mission Valley News, as well as the combined Web site, Scoop San Diego.
Language (s): English
COMMUNITY NEWSPAPER

San Diego Downtown News
830853

Owner: San Diego Community News Network
Editorial: 3737 5th Ave Ste 201, San Diego, California 92103-4217 **Tel:** 1 619 519-7775
Email: info@sdcnn.com **Web site:** http://www.sandiegodowntownnews.com
Circ: 18000
Publisher: David Mannis
Profile: San Diego Downtown News is a monthly community newspaper serving downtown San Diego, including the Columbia, Core/Civic, Cortez Hill, East Village, Gaslamp/Horton Plaza, Little Italy and Marina neighborhoods. The paper includes local news, business, entertainment, opinion, and event calendars.
Language (s): English
COMMUNITY NEWSPAPER

San Diego Monitor News
23314

Editorial: 3570 Olive St, Lemon Grove, California 91945-1737 **Tel:** 1 619 668-1007
Email: sdmonitor@outlook.com
Freq: Sat; **Circ:** 15000 Not Audited
Publisher & Editor: Willie Morrow
Profile: San Diego Monitor News is published twice a month for residents of San Diego. The publication covers local news, sports and community events. Deadlines for the publication are Tuesdays.
Language (s): English
Ad Rate: Full Page Mono 15.50
Currency: United States Dollars
COMMUNITY NEWSPAPER

San Diego Reader
21329

Editorial: 2323 Broadway, San Diego, California 92102-1955 **Tel:** 1 619 235-3000
Email: info@sandiegoreader.com **Web site:** http://www.sandiegoreader.com
Freq: Thu; **Circ:** 97878 Not Audited
Publisher & Editor: Jim Holman; **News Editor:** Matt Potter
Profile: San Diego Reader is a weekly newspaper written for the residents of San Diego. The newspaper cover local news, arts and entertainment, politics and events.
Language (s): English
Ad Rate: Full Page Mono 89.45
Ad Rate: Full Page Colour 5254.00
Currency: United States Dollars
COMMUNITY NEWSPAPER

San Diego Uptown News
624488

Owner: San Diego Community News Network
Editorial: 3737 5th Ave Ste 201, San Diego, California 92103-4217 **Tel:** 1 619 519-7775
Web site: http://sduptownnews.com
Freq: Bi-Weekly; **Circ:** 22000
Publisher: David Mannis
Profile: San Diego Uptown News is a free, bi-weekly newspaper serving the communities of Mission Hills, Bankers Hill, Hillcrest, University Heights, North Park, South Park, Normal Heights, Kensington and surrounding areas.
Language (s): English
Ad Rate: Full Page Mono 20.41
Currency: United States Dollars
COMMUNITY NEWSPAPER

The San Diego Voice & Viewpoint
18649

Owner: Warren (John)
Editorial: 3619 College Ave, San Diego, California 92115-7041 **Tel:** 1 619 266-2233
Email: news@sdvoice.info **Web site:** http://sdvoice.info/index1.htm
Freq: Thu; **Circ:** 30000 Not Audited
Publisher & Editor: John Warren
Profile: The San Diego Voice & Viewpoint is written for the residents of San Diego. Deadlines for the paper are Mondays prior to issue date.
Language (s): English
Ad Rate: Full Page Mono 26.00

United States of America

Currency: United States Dollars
COMMUNITY NEWSPAPER

San Diego Yu-Yu
23254

Owner: International Times Corp.
Editorial: 4655 Ruffner St Ste 290, San Diego, California 92111-2270 **Tel:** 1 858 576-9016
Email: info@sandiegoyuyu.com **Web site:** http://www.sandiegoyuyu.com
Freq: Bi-Weekly; Circ: 8000 Not Audited
Publisher: Noriko Sato
Profile: San Diego Yu-Yu is a Japanese-language newspaper serving Japanese communities in San Diego, Los Angeles, San Jose and Orange County, CA.
Language (s): English, Japanese
Ad Rate: Full Page Mono 19.81
Currency: United States Dollars
COMMUNITY NEWSPAPER

The San Fernando Sun
25782

Owner: San Fernando Valley Sun Newspapers, Inc.
Editorial: 601 S Brand Blvd Ste 202, San Fernando, California 91340-4950 **Tel:** 1 818 365-3111
Web site: http://www.sanfernandosun.com
Freq: Thu; Circ: 10000 Not Audited
Advertising Sales Manager: Yesenia Galvan
Profile: The San Fernando Sun is a local newspaper published every Thursday by San Fernando Valley Sun Newspaper. It is published for the residents of the San Fernando, CA area. The newspaper covers local news, sports, social and community events and business.
Language (s): English
Ad Rate: Full Page Mono 19.00
Currency: United States Dollars
COMMUNITY NEWSPAPER

San Francisco Catolico
23226

Owner: Roman Catholic Archdiocese of San Francisco
Editorial: 1 Peter Yorke Way, San Francisco, California 94109-6602 **Tel:** 1 415 614-5633
Web site: http://www.catholic-sf.org
Freq: Bi-Weekly; Circ: 8000 Not Audited
Editor: Lorena Rojas
Profile: El Heraldo Catolico's editorial mission is to help Hispanics throughout the Diocese of San Francisco, Oakland and Sacramento, CA maintain their faith and adapt in a new country. Coverage includes local, regional, national and international news. Deadlines for the publication fall on the 15th of the month prior to the month it is issued.
Language (s): Spanish
Ad Rate: Full Page Mono 20.50
Currency: United States Dollars
COMMUNITY NEWSPAPER

San Gabriel Valley Newspaper Group
24487

Owner: MediaNews Group
Editorial: 1210 N Azusa Canyon Rd, West Covina, California 91790 **Tel:** 1 626 962-8811
Email: news.tribune@sgvn.com **Web site:** http://www.sgvtribune.com
Freq: Weekly; Circ: 139000 Not Audited
Profile: San Gabriel Valley Newspaper Group covers local stories and features for the communities of San Gabriel Valley, CA.
Language (s): English
Ad Rate: Full Page Mono 100.25
Currency: United States Dollars
COMMUNITY NEWSPAPER

San Juan Record
21031

Owner: Boyle (Bill)
Editorial: 49 South Main Street, Monticello, Utah 84535 **Tel:** 1 435 587-2277
Email: sjrnews@frontiernet.net **Web site:** http://www.sjrnews.com
Freq: Weekly; Circ: 5500 Not Audited
Publisher & Editor: Bill Boyle
Profile: San Juan Record is a weekly newspaper published for the residents of San Juan County, UT. The publication covers local news, sports and community events. Deadlines are on Fridays at noon MT.
Language (s): English
Ad Rate: Full Page Mono 5.00
Currency: United States Dollars
COMMUNITY NEWSPAPER

San Juan Sun
22852

Owner: MediaNews Group
Editorial: 201 N Allen Ave, Farmington, New Mexico 87401-6212 **Tel:** 1 505 325-4545
Freq: Wed; Circ: 15000 Not Audited
Profile: San Juan Sun is written for the residents of San Juan County, NM. The publication features advertisements, as well as some news briefs. Deadlines are on Mondays at 3:30pm MT.
Language (s): English
Ad Rate: Full Page Mono 6.70
Ad Rate: Full Page Colour 2927.96
Currency: United States Dollars
COMMUNITY NEWSPAPER

San Marino Tribune
18650

Editorial: 1441 San Marino Ave, San Marino, California 91108-2027 **Tel:** 1 626 792-6397
Web site: http://www.sanmarinotribune.com
Freq: Thu; Circ: 15000 Not Audited
Circulation Manager: Kate Boyce; Editor: Mitch Lehman
Profile: San Marino Tribune is a weekly, local paper serving the residents of the San Marino, CA. It covers local news and sports, lifestyles, events,

entertainment calendars, home and garden tips and dining reviews. Deadlines are on Wednesdays at noon PT.
Language (s): English
Ad Rate: Full Page Mono 20.00
Currency: United States Dollars
COMMUNITY NEWSPAPER

The Sand Mountain Reporter
18480

Owner: Southern Newspapers, Inc.
Editorial: 1603 Progress Dr, Albertville, Alabama 35950-8547 **Tel:** 1 256 840-3000
Email: news@sandmountainreporter.com **Web site:** http://www.sandmountainreporter.com
Freq: Weekly; Circ: 10628 Not Audited
Circulation Manager: Mike Warren
Profile: The Sand Mountain Reporter is published three times a week for the residents of Albertville, AL. The newspaper covers local news, sports and community events. Deadlines fall on the day prior to publication at at 10am CT.
Language (s): English
Ad Rate: Full Page Mono 10.90
Currency: United States Dollars
COMMUNITY NEWSPAPER

The Sandspur
411494

Owner: GateHouse Media Inc.
Editorial: 458 Whitfield St, Fayetteville, North Carolina 28306-1614 **Tel:** 1 910 323-4848
Web site: http://www.sandspuronline.com
Freq: Wed; Circ: 68000 Not Audited
Editor: Kim Hasty
Profile: The Sandspur is published weekly for the residents of Fayetteville, NC. The newspaper covers community news, business, people profiles, education, religion and outdoor recreation.
Language (s): English
Ad Rate: Full Page Mono 16.45
Currency: United States Dollars
COMMUNITY NEWSPAPER

The Sanford Herald
71136

Owner: Radiate Media
Editorial: 217 E 1st St, Sanford, Florida 32771-1376 **Tel:** 1 407 322-2611
Web site: http://www.mysanfordherald.com
Freq: Sun; Circ: 5000 Not Audited
Editor: Rachel Delinski; Circulation Manager: Tony Smith
Profile: The Sanford Herald, formerly The Seminole Herald since 1999, is published twice weekly and covers local news and sports for Sanford, northern Seminole County and Heathrow, FL. Deadlines are on Mondays at noon ET for the Wednesday edition, and Thursdays at noon ET for the Saturday edition.
Language (s): English
Ad Rate: Full Page Mono 6.99
Currency: United States Dollars
COMMUNITY NEWSPAPER

Sanford News
21515

Owner: George J. Foster Co. Inc.
Editorial: 835 Main St, Sanford, Maine 04073-3522 **Tel:** 1 207 324-5986
Email: news@sanfordnews.com **Web site:** http://www.fosters.com
Freq: Thu; Circ: 6800 Not Audited
Publisher: Patrice Foster; Advertising Sales Manager: Chris Olio; Circulation Manager: Jim Russell; Editor: Shawn Sullivan
Profile: Sanford News is published weekly for the residents of Sanford, ME and surrounding areas. The newspaper covers local news, sports and community events. Deadlines are on Tuesdays at 3pm ET. The Web site can be opened by going to Foster's Daily Democrat website, www.fosters.com, and clicking on the Sanford News tab.
Language (s): English
Ad Rate: Full Page Mono 10.25
Currency: United States Dollars
COMMUNITY NEWSPAPER

Sanibel Captiva Islander
29305

Owner: Breeze Newspapers
Editorial: 2340 Periwinkle Way, Sanibel, Florida 33957-3220 **Tel:** 1 239 472-1587
Web site: http://www.captivasanibel.com
Freq: Weekly; Circ: 6575 Not Audited
Publisher: Scott Blonde
Profile: Sanibel Captiva Islander is a community newspaper for residents in and around Sanibel Island, FL. It is published by Breeze Newspapers. Also includes the Island Reporter.
Language (s): English
Ad Rate: Full Page Colour 10.00
Currency: United States Dollars
COMMUNITY NEWSPAPER

Sanilac County News
28351

Owner: JAMS Media
Editorial: 65 S Elk St, Sandusky, Michigan 48471-1337 **Tel:** 1 810 648-4000
Email: info@mihomepaper.com **Web site:** http://www.mihomepaper.com
Freq: Wed; Circ: 6363
Editor: Eric Levine; Publisher: Jane Vanderpoel
Profile: Sanilac County News is a weekly newspaper serving the residents of Sanilac County, MI. The publication covers local news and community events. Deadlines are at 5pm ET on Mondays.
Language (s): English
Ad Rate: Full Page Mono 14.25
Currency: United States Dollars
COMMUNITY NEWSPAPER

Santa Barbara Independent
21327

Editorial: 122 W Figueroa St, Santa Barbara, California 93101-3106 **Tel:** 1 805 965-5205
Email: news@independent.com **Web site:** http://www.independent.com
Freq: Thu; Circ: 40000 Not Audited
Profile: The Santa Barbara (CA) Independent is a weekly newspaper published for the residents of Santa Barbara County, CA. The publication covers local news, arts, entertainment, business news, politics, and sports. Contact the publication for advertisement rates. The news deadline falls on Monday at noon PT.
Language (s): English
Ad Rate: Full Page Mono 30.32
Currency: United States Dollars
COMMUNITY NEWSPAPER

The Santa Clara Weekly
21469

Owner: Barber (Miles)
Editorial: 3000 Scott Blvd Ste 105, Santa Clara, California 95054-3321 **Tel:** 1 408 243-2000
Email: scweekly@ix.netcom.com **Web site:** http://www.santaclaraweekly.com
Freq: Wed; Circ: 40000 Not Audited
Publisher: Miles Barber, Editor: Angie Tolliver
Profile: The Santa Clara Weekly is published for the residents of Santa Clara, CA and surrounding areas. The newspaper covers local news, sports and community events. It is distributed via newstands and local businesses. The paper also publishes a color edition once a month that is distributed directly to the homes of area residents. The color edition has a circulation of 31,000 and is issued on the second to last Wednesday of each month. The news deadline for both editions is Fridays the week prior to publication.
Language (s): English
Ad Rate: Full Page Mono 37.33
Currency: United States Dollars
COMMUNITY NEWSPAPER

Santa Fe Reporter
20233

Owner: City of Roses Newspaper Co.
Editorial: 132 E Marcy St, Santa Fe, New Mexico 87501-2054 **Tel:** 1 505 988-5541
Email: editor@sfreporter.com **Web site:** http://www.sfreporter.com
Freq: Wed; Circ: 17000 Not Audited
Circulation Manager: Andy Bramble; Publisher: Jeff Norris
Profile: Santa Fe Reporter is a weekly newspaper published for the residents of Santa Fe, NM. The publication covers local news, arts, culture and community events.
Language (s): English
Ad Rate: Full Page Mono 41.45
Currency: United States Dollars
COMMUNITY NEWSPAPER

The Santa Maria Sun
63133

Owner: Santa Maria Sun LLC
Editorial: 2540 Skyway Dr, Santa Maria, California 93455-1514 **Tel:** 1 805 347-1968
Email: mail@santamariasun.com **Web site:** http://www.santamariasun.com
Freq: Thu; Circ: 19000 Not Audited
Circulation Manager: Cindy Rucker
Profile: The Santa Maria Sun is a local weekly newspaper published for the residents of Santa Maria, CA. The publication covers local news, arts & entertainment, business, crime, sports, religion, cultural and social issues, local politics, education, agriculture, health and environmental issues. Deadlines are on Tuesdays.
Language (s): English
Ad Rate: Full Page Mono 17.96
Ad Rate: Full Page Colour 1228.00
Currency: United States Dollars
COMMUNITY NEWSPAPER

Santa Paula Times
21828

Owner: Johnson (Deborah)
Editorial: 120 Davis St, Santa Paula, California 93060-2730 **Tel:** 1 805 525-1890
Email: santapaulatimes@gmail.com **Web site:** http://www.santapaulatimes.com
Freq: Fri; Circ: 9000 Not Audited
Advertising Sales Manager: Debbie Johnson; Publisher & Editor: Don Johnson; Circulation Manager: Diana Ramos
Profile: Santa Paula Times serves the residents of Santa Paula, CA. It covers local news, sports, the police, city council, area schools and community events. News deadlines for the Wednesday issue fall on Mondays at noon PT; for the Friday edition deadlines are Thursdays at noon PT.
Language (s): English
Ad Rate: Full Page Mono 8.25
Currency: United States Dollars
COMMUNITY NEWSPAPER

Santa Rosa Press Gazette & Free Press
24896

Owner: GateHouse Media Inc.
Editorial: 6629 Elva St, Milton, Florida 32570-4735 **Tel:** 1 850 623-2120
Email: news@srpressgazette.com **Web site:** http://www.srpressgazette.com
Circ: 22800 Not Audited
Advertising Sales Manager: Debbie Coon; Publisher: Diane Winnemuller
Language (s): English
COMMUNITY NEWSPAPER

SanTan Sun News
73261

Tel: 1 480 348-0343
Email: news@santansun.com **Web site:** http://www.santansun.com
Freq: Bi-Weekly; Circ: 38000 Not Audited
Publisher: Laurie Fagen
Profile: SanTan Sun News is a bi-weekly newspaper serving the communities of Ocotillo, Southern Chandler and Gilbert, AZ. Articles cover local news, education, youth, recreation, arts & entertainment and religion. The paper is not published in January and July.
Language (s): English
Ad Rate: Full Page Mono 15.00
Currency: United States Dollars
COMMUNITY NEWSPAPER

Saratoga Today
396811

Owner: Saratoga Publishing LLC
Editorial: 5 Case St, Saratoga Springs, New York 12866-3501 **Tel:** 1 518 581-2480
Web site: http://www.saratogatodaynewspaper.com
Freq: Fri; Circ: 10000 Not Audited
Editor & Publisher: Chad Beatty; Circulation Manager: Kim Beatty
Profile: Saratoga Today is a free community newspaper published weekly for residents of Saratoga Springs and communities such as Ballston Spa, Malta, Milton, Wilton, Schuylerville and Greenfield, NY. It provides local news, sports and community events happening in the area. It is distributed at news racks, convenience stores and retailers in the distribution area.
Language (s): English
Ad Rate: Full Page Mono 21.45
Currency: United States Dollars
COMMUNITY NEWSPAPER

Saturday Morning Press
155811

Editorial: 466 Yampa Ave, Craig, Colorado 81625-2610 **Tel:** 1 970 824-7031
Email: editor@craigdailypress.com **Web site:** http://www.craigdailypress.com
Freq: Sat; Circ: 9600
Profile: Saturday Morning Press is a weekly community newspaper written for the residents of Craig, CO.
Language (s): English
Ad Rate: Full Page Mono 10.70
Currency: United States Dollars
COMMUNITY NEWSPAPER

Savanna Newspapers
24908

Editorial: 308 N Main St, Mount Carroll, Illinois 61053-1024 **Tel:** 1 815 244-2965
Email: mirrordem@grics.net
Circ: 12900 Not Audited
Advertising Sales Manager: Pam Villalobos; Editor and Publisher: Robert Watson
Language (s): English
COMMUNITY NEWSPAPER

Sawyer County Record
21181

Owner: Adams Publishing Group
Editorial: 15617 US Highway 63, Hayward, Wisconsin 54843-4244 **Tel:** 1 715 634-4881
Email: news@sawyercountyrecord.net **Web site:** http://www.apg-wi.com/sawyer_county_record
Freq: Wed; Circ: 7000 Not Audited
Profile: Sawyer County Record is a weekly local newspaper serving residents of Sawyer County, WI. The publication covers local news, business and sports. Deadlines are on Mondays at 5pm CT.
Language (s): English
Ad Rate: Full Page Mono 9.75
Currency: United States Dollars
COMMUNITY NEWSPAPER

The Scarsdale Inquirer
22569

Owner: S.I. Communications, Inc.
Editorial: 14 Harwood Ct, Ste 510, Scarsdale, New York 10583-4183 **Tel:** 1 914 725-2500
Web site: http://www.scarsdalenews.com/Scarsdale_Inquirer/Home.html
Freq: Fri; Circ: 7000 Not Audited
Editor: Todd Sliss; Publisher: Deborah White; Advertising Sales Manager: Barbara Yeaker
Profile: The Scarsdale Inquirer is a community newspaper serving residents of the Scarsdale, NY area. The newspaper covers local news and contains a calendar listing community events. Editorial deadlines are Mondays prior to publication.
Language (s): English
Ad Rate: Full Page Mono 19.25
Currency: United States Dollars
COMMUNITY NEWSPAPER

Schneps Publications Inc.
24930

Editorial: 38-15 Bell Blvd, Bayside, New York 11361 **Tel:** 1 718 224-5863
Circ: 95000 Not Audited
Publisher & Editor: Victoria Schneps
Language (s): English, Spanish
COMMUNITY NEWSPAPER

The Scoop Today
155338

Owner: Rock Valley Publishing LLC
Editorial: 213 S Center St, Lena, Illinois 61048-8711 **Tel:** 1 815 369-4112
Email: scoopshopper@rvpublishing.com **Web site:** http://www.belvideredailyrepublican.net/
Freq: Wed; Circ: 8600
Editor: Todd Nielsen
Profile: The Scoop Today covers Stockton and Lena, IL and the surrounding communities.
Language (s): English
Ad Rate: Full Page Mono 6.95

Currency: United States Dollars
COMMUNITY NEWSPAPER

Scoop U.S.A. 22520
Owner: Driver (Sunny)
Editorial: 942 N Watts St, Philadelphia, Pennsylvania 19123-1000 **Tel:** 1 215 232-5974
Email: phillyscoop@aol.com **Web site:** http://www.scoopusanewspaper.com
Freq: Fri; **Circ:** 35000 Not Audited
Editor: R. Sonny Driver
Profile: Scoop U.S.A. is a weekly community newspaper providing community news and public service announcements to residents in Philadelphia.
Language (s): English
Ad Rate: Full Page Mono 22.00
Ad Rate: Full Page Colour 2712.00
Currency: United States Dollars
COMMUNITY NEWSPAPER

The Scott County Times 19872
Owner: Emmerich Newspapers Inc.
Editorial: 311 Smith Ave, Forest, Mississippi 39074-4159 **Tel:** 1 601 469-2561
Email: news@sctonline.net **Web site:** http://www.sctonline.net
Freq: Wed; **Circ:** 6000 Not Audited
News Editor: Chris Baker; **Publisher & Editor:** Tim Beeland; **Circulation Manager:** Brian Stevens
Profile: The Scott County Times is a local newspaper published every Wednesday. It is published for the residents of Scott County, MS area. The newspaper covers local news, sports, entertainment, business, and events.
Language (s): English
Ad Rate: Full Page Mono 11.00
Ad Rate: Full Page Colour 1053.00
Currency: United States Dollars
COMMUNITY NEWSPAPER

Scott County Virginia Star 21504
Owner: Scott County Herald-Virginia, Inc.
Editorial: 255 W Jackson St, Gate City, Virginia 24251-4129 **Tel:** 1 276 386-6300
Email: info@virginiastar.org **Web site:** http://www.virginiastar.net
Freq: Wed; **Circ:** 6500 Not Audited
Publisher & News Editor: Lisa Watson McCarty
Profile: Scott County Virginia Star is a weekly local newspaper serving residents of Scott County, VA. The newspaper provides local news and community events. Deadlines are on Mondays at 5pm ET.
Language (s): English
Ad Rate: Full Page Mono 8.50
Currency: United States Dollars
COMMUNITY NEWSPAPER

The Scout & Eastern Colorado News Newspapers 155321
Owner: I-70 Publishing Company Inc.
Editorial: 1522 Main St, Strasburg, Colorado 80136-7507 **Tel:** 1 303 622-9796
Email: dclaussen@i-70scout.com **Web site:** http://www.i-70scout.com
Freq: Fri; **Circ:** 8000 Not Audited
Publisher & Editor: Doug Claussen; **Advertising Manager:** Jason Kero; **Circulation Manager:** LuAnne Stegner
Language (s): English
Ad Rate: Full Page Mono 13.62
Currency: United States Dollars
COMMUNITY NEWSPAPER

The Scuppernong Reminder 857526
Owner: Washington News Media
Editorial: 217 N Market St, Washington, North Carolina 27889-4949
Email: scuppernong@thewashingtondailynews.com
Freq: Weekly
Editor: Jurgen Boerema; **Publisher:** Ashley VanSant
Profile: The Scuppernong Reminder is a Washington Newsmedia LLC publication covering Tyrrell County and eastern Washington County in Washington, NC.
Language (s): English
COMMUNITY NEWSPAPER

Sea Coast Echo 19858
Owner: BSL Newspapers Inc.
Editorial: 124 Court St, Bay Saint Louis, Mississippi 39520-4516 **Tel:** 1 228 467-5474
Web site: http://www.seacoastecho.com
Freq: Sat; **Circ:** 8100 Not Audited
News Editor: Geoff Belcher; **Publisher & Editor:** James Ponder; **Advertising Sales Manager:** Maurice Singleton
Profile: Sea Coast Echo is a local newspaper written for residents of Bay Saint Louis, MS. Published twice weekly, the newspaper covers the local news, sports and business in the Bay Saint Louis, MS area. Deadlines are three days prior to issue date.
Language (s): English
Ad Rate: Full Page Mono 23.00
Currency: United States Dollars
COMMUNITY NEWSPAPER

Seacoast Newspapers 24622
Owner: GateHouse Media Inc.
Editorial: 111 NH Ave, Portsmouth, New Hampshire 03801-2864 **Tel:** 1 603 436-1800
Web site: http://www.seacoastonline.com
Circ: 56397
Editor: Jennifer Feals; **Advertising Sales Manager:** Katrina Green; **Editor:** Aaron Sanborn; **Publisher:** John Tabor
Profile: Seacoast Newspapers offers several community, weekly newspapers to residents in and around Portsmouth, NH. It is based in the same office as the Portsmouth (NH) Herald.
Language (s): English
COMMUNITY NEWSPAPER

Seattle Weekly 22761
Owner: Sound Publishing
Editorial: 307 3rd Ave S Fl 2, Seattle, Washington 98104-2684 **Tel:** 1 206 623-0500
Email: info@seattleweekly.com **Web site:** http://www.seattleweekly.com
Freq: Wed; **Circ:** 54909 Not Audited
Circulation Manager: Jay Kraus
Profile: Seattle Weekly is a newspaper published every Friday for the residents of Seattle. The newspaper covers national and local news, entertainment, events, education, politics, and business. Seattle Weekly publishes an extensive calendar listing. Contact the publication for advertising information.
Language (s): English
Ad Rate: Full Page Mono 47.00
Currency: United States Dollars
COMMUNITY NEWSPAPER

La Semana Del Sur 217650
Owner: Guillermo Rojas
Editorial: 100 W 5th St Ste 701, Tulsa, Oklahoma 74103-4290 **Tel:** 1 918 744-9502
Web site: http://www.lasemanadelsur.com
Freq: Wed; **Circ:** 15000 Not Audited
Publisher & Editor: Guillermo Rojas
Language (s): Spanish/Bilingual
Ad Rate: Full Page Mono 9.00
Currency: United States Dollars
COMMUNITY NEWSPAPER

Semana News 342756
Owner: NEWSPAN Media Corp.
Editorial: 6601 Tarnef Dr Ste 200, Houston, Texas 77074-3634 **Tel:** 1 713 774-4652
Email: editorial@semananews.com **Web site:** http://www.semananews.com
Freq: Weekly; **Circ:** 130252 Not Audited
Profile: Focuses on the Hispanic community in the Houston area. Reports on local and national headlines, including lifestyle pertinent to Spanish speaking families. Highlights on everything from sports to people active in community life.
Language (s): Spanish
Ad Rate: Full Page Mono 5132.40
Ad Rate: Full Page Colour 6143.28
Currency: United States Dollars
COMMUNITY NEWSPAPER

El Semanario 87227
Owner: Weekly Issue/El Semanario Inc.
Editorial: 8400 E Crescent Pkwy Ste 600, Greenwood Village, Colorado 80111-2842
Tel: 1 303 672-0800
Email: semanario@aol.com **Web site:** http://www.elsemanario.us/
Freq: Thu; **Circ:** 25000 Not Audited
Editor: Toni Fresquez
Profile: El Semanario is a weekly newspaper written for the Hispanic residents of Denver interested in local news. The publication covers news, sports, business and entertainment.
Language (s): Spanish/Bilingual
Ad Rate: Full Page Mono 22.00
Currency: United States Dollars
COMMUNITY NEWSPAPER

Semanario Argentino 858328
Editorial: 20900 ME 30 Ave #200, Aventura, Florida 33160 **Tel:** 1 786 277-5148
Email: posedente@hotmail.com **Web site:** http://www.seminarioargentino.com
Freq: Tue; **Circ:** 43000
Editor: María Amelia Castro; **Publisher:** Oscar Posedente
Profile: Seminario Argentino is a weekly that provides news and information to the Argentine and Hispanic community of South Florida.
Language (s): Spanish
COMMUNITY NEWSPAPER

The Sentinel 21458
Owner: E.W. Smith Publishing Co., Inc.
Editorial: 36 Merline Ave, New Windsor, New York 12553-6520 **Tel:** 1 845 562-1218
Web site: https://ocpostsentinel.wordpress.com/contact-us/
Freq: Fri; **Circ:** 7000 Not Audited
Editor: Mark Gerlach; **Advertising Sales Manager:** Joanne McCormick; **Publisher:** Everett Smith
Profile: The Sentinel is a weekly local newspaper serving residents in Granville, NY and the surrounding area. The newspaper covers local news and community events. The Sentinel shares a website with its sister paper, Orange County Post in Washingtonville, NY, though the physical offices are separate.
Language (s): English
Ad Rate: Full Page Mono 9.95
Currency: United States Dollars
COMMUNITY NEWSPAPER

El Sentinel del Sur del la Florida 87984
Owner: tronc
Editorial: 6501 Nob Hill Rd, Tamarac, Florida 33321-6422 **Tel:** 1 954 356-4000
Email: agenda@elsentinel.com **Web site:** http://www.sun-sentinel.com/elsentinel
Freq: Sat; **Circ:** 138911 Not Audited
Advertising Sales Manager: Ariel Gonzalez; **Editor:** Deborah Ramirez
Profile: El Sentinel del Sur del la Florida is a free, weekly Spanish-language newspaper serving Hispanic residents in Broward and Palm Beach counties, including the city of Fort Lauderdale, FL. It covers local, national and international news pertinent to the Hispanic community. Other features include sports, lifestyle, food, events and a classifieds section. It is published from the offices of the South Florida Sun-Sentinel. Deadlines are on Tuesdays at 5pm ET.
Language (s): Spanish
Ad Rate: Full Page Mono 32.00
Ad Rate: Full Page Colour 1200.00
Currency: United States Dollars
COMMUNITY NEWSPAPER

El Sentinel Orlando 75936
Owner: tronc
Editorial: 633 N Orange Ave, Orlando, Florida 32801-1300 **Tel:** 1 407 420-5000
Web site: http://www.orlandosentinel.com/elsentinel
Freq: Sat; **Circ:** 99150 Not Audited
Editor: Rafael Palacio
Profile: El Sentinel Orlando is a free, weekly Spanish-language newspaper serving Hispanic residents in Orange, Seminole, Osceola, Lake and West Volusia, FL counties, which includes the cities of Orlando, Daytona Beach and Melbourne, FL. It covers local, national and international news pertinent to the Hispanic community. Other features include sports, lifestyle, food, events and a classifieds section. The paper is home delivered to local Hispanics and is also available for pick-up at area businesses. It is published from the offices of the Orlando Sentinel. Advertising rates are a combination run with the Orlando Sentinel. Deadlines are on Thursdays at noon ET before publication.
Language (s): Spanish
Ad Rate: Full Page Mono 31.00
Currency: United States Dollars
COMMUNITY NEWSPAPER

Sentinel Weekly News 151413
Owner: GG Publications, Inc.
Editorial: 1307B W 6th St Ste 119C, Corona, California 92882-3170 **Tel:** 1 951 737-9784
Email: sentinelweekly@aol.com
Freq: Wed; **Circ:** 11000 Not Audited
Advertising Sales Manager: Jerry Chrysong; **Editor:** Ellisa May Lendennie; **Publisher:** Gary Lendennie
Profile: Sentinel Weekly News is written for the residents of Corona, CA. It covers local news.
Language (s): English
Ad Rate: Full Page Mono 125.00
Currency: United States Dollars
COMMUNITY NEWSPAPER

The Sentinel-Echo 19355
Owner: Community Newspaper Holdings, Inc.
Editorial: 123 W 5th St, London, Kentucky 40741-1837 **Tel:** 1 606 878-7400
Web site: http://www.sentinel-echo.com
Freq: Fri; **Circ:** 10000 Not Audited
Editor: Carrie Dillard
Profile: Sentinel-Echo is a local newspaper serving residents of the town London and Laurel county, KY. The newspaper is published three times a week on Monday, Wednesday, and Friday. Sentinel-Echo covers local and community news for the area. Press releases should be e-mailed to the managing editor.
Language (s): English
Ad Rate: Full Page Mono 7.90
Currency: United States Dollars
COMMUNITY NEWSPAPER

The Sentinel-News 76999
Owner: Landmark Community Newspapers, Inc.
Editorial: 703 Taylorsville Rd, Shelbyville, Kentucky 40065 **Tel:** 1 502 633-2526
Web site: http://www.sentinelnews.com
Freq: Fri; **Circ:** 8000 Not Audited
Advertising Sales Manager: Dan Barry; **Editor:** Todd Martin
Profile: The Sentinel-News is a local newspaper serving the residents of Shelby County, KY. Deadlines are Mondays and Wednesdays at noon ET.
Language (s): English
Ad Rate: Full Page Mono 15.15
Currency: United States Dollars
COMMUNITY NEWSPAPER

The Sentry 21345
Owner: Amendment One Inc.
Editorial: 2500 SE 5th Ct, Pompano Beach, Florida 33062-6108 **Tel:** 1 954 532-2000
Email: news@flsentry.com **Web site:** http://www.flsentry.com
Freq: Thu; **Circ:** 5000 Not Audited
Editor: M. Ross Shulmister
Profile: The Sentry is a local weekly newspaper written for residents of Broward County, FL.
Language (s): English
Ad Rate: Full Page Mono 17.95
Ad Rate: Full Page Colour 2561.00
Currency: United States Dollars
COMMUNITY NEWSPAPER

The Sequim Gazette 21143
Owner: Olympic View Publishing
Editorial: 147 W Washington St, Sequim, Washington 98382-3372 **Tel:** 1 360 683-3311
Web site: http://www.sequimgazette.com
Freq: Wed; **Circ:** 8100 Not Audited
Editor: Michael Dashiell
Profile: The Sequim Gazette is a local newspaper that covers news affecting Sequim area residents. News coverage includes sports, education, government, environment, healthcare and business. The Deadline is one week prior to issue date. Do not send press releases - the paper only covers local news.
Language (s): English
Ad Rate: Full Page Mono 13.20
Ad Rate: Full Page Colour 1576.00
Currency: United States Dollars
COMMUNITY NEWSPAPER

Sequoyah County Times 20452
Owner: Cookson Hills Publishers, Inc.
Editorial: 111 N Oak St, Sallisaw, Oklahoma 74955-4637 **Tel:** 1 918 775-4433
Email: news@seqcotimes.com **Web site:** http://www.sequoyahcountytimes.com
Freq: Sun; **Circ:** 6600 Not Audited
Publisher: Jim Mayo; **News Editor:** Regina Smith
Profile: Sequoyah County Times is a local newspaper serving the residents of Sequoyah County, OK. The newspaper covers local and community news. Deadlines for the paper are Wednesdays by 10am CT.
Language (s): English
Ad Rate: Full Page Mono 6.40
Currency: United States Dollars
COMMUNITY NEWSPAPER

Sereechai Newspaper 689185
Editorial: 1253 Vine St Ste 16A, Los Angeles, California 90038-1682 **Tel:** 1 323 465-7550
Email: sereechai@sbcglobal.net **Web site:** http://www.sereechai.com
Freq: Weekly; **Circ:** 15000
Publisher: Teck Bna-Snenguraipam; **Editor:** Somchet Phayakarit
Profile: Sereechai is a Thai newspaper written for the residents of the greater Los Angeles area. Includes community and international news, arts and entertainment, lifestyle and society, law and editorial sections.
Language (s): Thai
Ad Rate: Full Page Mono 7.00
Currency: United States Dollars
COMMUNITY NEWSPAPER

Sesh Communications Newspapers 25515
Owner: Sesh Communications Newspapers
Editorial: 3440 Burnet Ave Ste 130, Cincinnati, Ohio 45229-2857 **Tel:** 1 513 961-3331
Email: sesh@seshnow.com **Web site:** http://seshnow.com
Circ: 28800 Not Audited
Publisher: Jan-Michele Lemon Kearney
Language (s): English
COMMUNITY NEWSPAPER

Seven Days 23105
Owner: Da Capo Publishing
Editorial: 255 S Champlain St, Burlington, Vermont 05401-4881 **Tel:** 1 802 865-1020
Web site: http://www.sevendaysvt.com
Freq: Wed; **Circ:** 35976 Not Audited
Circulation Manager: Steve Hadeka; **News Editor:** Matthew Roy
Profile: Seven Days is a weekly arts newspaper serving residents in the greater Burlington, Middlebury, Montpelier, Stow, The Mad River Valley, Rutland, St. Albans and Plattsburgh, VT areas. The newspaper covers music, film and art and contains a calendar listing local events. Deadlines for the publication are on Thursdays by 5pm ET.
Language (s): English
Ad Rate: Full Page Mono 26.44
Currency: United States Dollars
COMMUNITY NEWSPAPER

SF Weekly 21622
Owner: San Francisco Newspaper Co.
Editorial: 835 Market St Ste 550, San Francisco, California 94103-1906 **Tel:** 1 415 536-8100
Web site: http://www.sfweekly.com
Freq: Wed; **Circ:** 68883 Not Audited
Publisher: Glenn Zuehls
Profile: SF Weekly is an award-winning news and arts weekly for the San Francisco area. It provides residents with information on local news, arts & entertainment, cultural affairs and much more.
Language (s): English
COMMUNITY NEWSPAPER

Shakopee Valley News 86381
Owner: Red Wing Publishing Co.
Editorial: 12925 Eagle Creek Pkwy, Savage, Minnesota 55378-1271 **Tel:** 1 952 445-3333
Email: editor@shakopeenews.com **Web site:** http://www.swnewsmedia.com/shakopee_valley_news
Freq: Thu; **Circ:** 5650 Not Audited
Circulation Manager: Ruby Winings
Profile: The Shakopee Valley News is a community newspaper covering Shakopee, MN.
Language (s): English
Ad Rate: Full Page Mono 9.18
Currency: United States Dollars
COMMUNITY NEWSPAPER

Shaw Media - Downers Grove, IL 24531
Owner: Shaw Media
Editorial: 1101 31st St, Suite 260, Downers Grove, Illinois 60515-5515 **Tel:** 1 630 368-1100
Web site: http://www.mysuburbanlife.com
Freq: Weekly; **Circ:** 43689 Not Audited
Advertising Sales Manager: Bill Korbel; **News Editor:** Anna Schier; **News Editor:** Alex Soulier

Profile: Shaw Media - Downers Grove, IL is a weekly community newspaper publisher serving the residents of Berwyn, Brookfield, La Grange, Lemont and Riverside, IL. The circulation provided for each weekly newspaper published is a combination total.
Language (s): English
Ad Rate: Full Page Colour 2594.00
Currency: United States Dollars
COMMUNITY NEWSPAPER

Shaw Media - St. Charles, IL 25378
Owner: Shaw Media
Editorial: 333 N Randall Rd Ste 2, Saint Charles, Illinois 60174-1500 **Tel:** 1 630 232-9222
Web site: http://www.mysuburbanlife.com
Circ: 29775 Not Audited
Publisher: J. Thomas Shaw
Language (s): English
COMMUNITY NEWSPAPER

The Shawnee Dispatch 130585
Owner: Ogden Newspapers
Editorial: 6301 Pflumm Rd Ste 102, Shawnee, Kansas 66216-2497 **Tel:** 1 913 962-3000
Web site: http://www.shawneedispatch.com
Freq: Wed; **Circ:** 6800 Not Audited
Profile: The Shawnee Dispatch is a local newspaper written for the residents of Shawnee, KS.
Language (s): English
Ad Rate: Full Page Mono 17.60
Currency: United States Dollars
COMMUNITY NEWSPAPER

Shawngunk Journal 961010
Tel: 1 845 647-9190
Email: info@gunkjournal.com **Web site:** http://www.shawangunkjournal.com
Freq: Weekly
Profile: The Shawangunk Journal is a weekly newspaper that covers news and information relevant to the people of Wawarsing, Crawford, Mamakating, Rochester and Shawangunk in New York.
Language (s): English
COMMUNITY NEWSPAPER

Shelby County Reporter 86769
Owner: Shelby County Newspapers, Inc.
Editorial: 115 N Main St, Columbiana, Alabama 35051-5359 **Tel:** 1 205 669-3131
Web site: http://www.shelbycountyreporter.com
Freq: Wed; **Circ:** 33900 Not Audited
Profile: Shelby County Reporter is a weekly newspaper serving the residents of Shelby County, AL. The publication covers local news and community events. Deadlines are on Mondays at 10am ET.
Language (s): English
Ad Rate: Full Page Mono 21.10
Currency: United States Dollars
COMMUNITY NEWSPAPER

Shelton-Mason County Journal Inc. 21127
Owner: Shelton-Mason County Journal Inc.
Editorial: 227 W Cota St, Shelton, Washington 98584-2263 **Tel:** 1 360 426-4412
Email: news@masoncounty.com **Web site:** http://masoncounty.com
Freq: Thu; **Circ:** 17022 Not Audited
Circulation Manager: Margo Brand
Profile: Shelton-Mason County Journal is a local newspaper serving the residents of Shelton, WA. It includes information on local news, weather, sports, business and entertainment.
Language (s): English
COMMUNITY NEWSPAPER

Shepherd Express 21313
Owner: Alternative Publications Employees Cooperative
Editorial: 207 E Buffalo St Ste 410, Milwaukee, Wisconsin 53202-5712 **Tel:** 1 414 276-2222
Email: editor@shepex.com **Web site:** http://www.expressmilwaukee.com
Freq: Thu; **Circ:** 59849 Not Audited
Publisher & Editor: Louis Fortis
Profile: Shepherd Express is written for the residents of Milwaukee. It provides coverage of local music, arts and culture. It also includes listing of local events in the area.
Language (s): English
Ad Rate: Full Page Mono 16.95
Currency: United States Dollars
COMMUNITY NEWSPAPER

Sherburne County Citizen 24305
Owner: Meyer Publications
Editorial: 14054 Bank St, Becker, Minnesota 55308-8865 **Tel:** 1 763 261-5880
Email: citizennewspaper@midconetwork.com **Web site:** http://www.citizennewspaper.com
Freq: Sat; **Circ:** 11200 Not Audited
Publisher & Editor: Gary Meyer
Profile: Sherburne County Citizen is a local newspaper serving the residents of Sherburne County, MN. It includes information on local news, weather, sports, business and entertainment.
Language (s): English
Ad Rate: Full Page Mono 10.05
Currency: United States Dollars
COMMUNITY NEWSPAPER

Sher-E-Panjab 155605
Owner: Singh (Baldev)
Editorial: 2477 Poppy St, East Meadow, New York 11554-5211 **Tel:** 1 516 783-1001
Email: mail@sher-e-panjab.com **Web site:** http://www.sher-e-panjab.com
Freq: Fri; **Circ:** 14500 Not Audited
Circulation Manager: Aman Grewal; **Publisher & Editor:** Baldev Grewal; **Advertising Sales Manager:** Deepi Grewal; **News Editor:** Aman Hammi
Profile: Sher-E-Panjab is a weekly Panjabi (Indian language) newspaper published for the residents of New York, NY.
Language (s): Punjabi
Ad Rate: Full Page Mono 12.00
Currency: United States Dollars
COMMUNITY NEWSPAPER

Sherman Publications, Inc. 25049
Owner: Sherman Publications Inc.
Editorial: 666 S Lapeer Rd, Oxford, Michigan 48371-5034 **Tel:** 1 248 628-4801
Email: shermanpub@aol.com **Web site:** http://www.oxfordleader.com
Circ: 37600 Not Audited
Editor: C.J. Carnacchio; **Editor:** Phil Custadio; **Editor:** David Fleet; **Advertising Sales Manager:** Eric Lewis; **Circulation Manager:** Luan Offer; **Publisher:** Jim Sherman; **Editor:** Dan Shriner
Profile: Sherman Publications, Inc. publishes The Citizen, The Clarkston News, The Lake Orion Review, The Oxford Leader, providing local coverage for the Oxford, Lake Orion, Clarkston, Ortonville/Brandon and Goodrich, MI communities.
Language (s): English
COMMUNITY NEWSPAPER

Shippensburg Sentinel 238893
Owner: Lee Enterprises, Inc.
Editorial: 81 W King St, Shippensburg, Pennsylvania 17257-1224 **Tel:** 1 717 530-2444
Web site: http://www.cumberlink.com
Freq: Sat; **Circ:** 13500
Profile: Shippensburg Sentinel is published twice weekly for residents of Shippensburg, PA.
Language (s): English
Ad Rate: Full Page Mono 7.09
Currency: United States Dollars
COMMUNITY NEWSPAPER

Shop Right 151443
Owner: Horizon Publications
Editorial: 325 Main St Ste A, Ridgway, Pennsylvania 15853-8019 **Tel:** 1 814 776-2121
Email: ridgwayrecord@shop-right.com **Web site:** http://www.ridgewayrecord.com
Freq: Mon; **Circ:** 27111
Editor: Joe Bell; **Advertising Sales Manager:** Christi Gardner; **Circulation Manager:** Brandon Leiphner; **Publisher:** Joe Piccirrillo
Profile: Shop Right in Ridgway, PA is a weekly newspaper that covers community news and events.
Language (s): English
Ad Rate: Full Page Mono 11.60
Currency: United States Dollars
COMMUNITY NEWSPAPER

The Shoppers Guide 22360
Owner: Gazette Newspapers
Editorial: 6 E Main St, Everett, Pennsylvania 15537-1256 **Tel:** 1 814 623-1151
Email: shopperguide@embarqmail.com **Web site:** http://www.bedfordgazette.com
Freq: Sat; **Circ:** 26027 Not Audited
Publisher & Editor: Holly Claycomb; **Advertising Sales Manager:** Paul Price
Profile: The Shoppers Guide is a weekly community newspaper serving residents of the Everett, PA area. It covers local news, sports and entertainment.
Language (s): English
Ad Rate: Full Page Mono 10.25
Currency: United States Dollars
COMMUNITY NEWSPAPER

The Shopping News of Lancaster County 21970
Owner: Hocking Printing Co. Inc.
Editorial: 615 E Main St, Ephrata, Pennsylvania 17522-2537 **Tel:** 1 717 738-1151
Email: snews@ptd.net **Web site:** http://www.snews.com
Freq: Wed; **Circ:** 37925 Not Audited
Publisher & Editor: John Hocking
Profile: The Shopping News of Lancaster County in Ephrata, PA is a weekly newspaper that covers local news and events.
Language (s): English
Ad Rate: Full Page Mono 13.25
Currency: United States Dollars
COMMUNITY NEWSPAPER

Shore Publishing - Madison 154872
Owner: Shore Publishing LLC
Editorial: 724 Boston Post Rd Ste 202, Madison, Connecticut 06443-3039 **Tel:** 1 203 245-1877
Email: news@shorepublishing.com **Web site:** http://www.shorepublishing.com
Circ: 70102 Not Audited
Publisher: Robyn Collins; **Circulation Manager:** Lisa Strickland
Profile: Shore Publishing - Madison (CT) offers superior local news coverage delivered to every home and business every week. The publications feature informative articles about issues that are important to local residents and affect their daily lives, including weekly resident profiles and regular reports on town projects, boards, and committees. News coverage is complemented by columns from state senators, local authors, and naturalists, letters to the editor, opinion pieces and submissions from readers.
Language (s): English
COMMUNITY NEWSPAPER

Shoreline Publishing 25496
Owner: Shapiro (Edward)
Editorial: 629 Fifth Ave Ste 213, Pelham, New York 10803-3708 **Tel:** 1 914 738-7869
Email: shorelineproduction@gmail.com **Web site:** http://www.shorelinepub.com
Circ: 47303 Not Audited
Publisher: Edward Shapiro
Profile: Shoreline Publishing provides a local newspaper for Pelham, NY.
Language (s): English
COMMUNITY NEWSPAPER

Shoreline Times 86820
Owner: Shore Line Newspaper Group
Editorial: 100 Gando Dr, New Haven, Connecticut 06513-1049 **Tel:** 1 203 789-5200
Web site: http://www.shorelinetimes.com
Freq: Weekly; **Circ:** 30902 Not Audited
Editor: Susan Braden
Profile: The Shoreline Times is a weekly community newspaper focusing on news along the shoreline of New Haven, CT.
Language (s): English
Ad Rate: Full Page Mono 31.85
Currency: United States Dollars
COMMUNITY NEWSPAPER

Shreveport Sun 19426
Editorial: 2224 Jewella Ave, Shreveport, Louisiana 71109-2410 **Tel:** 1 318 631-6222
Email: sunweekly@aol.com **Web site:** http://www.sunweeklynews.com
Freq: Thu; **Circ:** 7000 Not Audited
Editor: Sonya Collins Landry; **Advertising Sales Manager:** Larry Rogers
Profile: The Shreveport Sun is a local newspaper serving the African American residents of Shreveport, LA. It includes information on local news, weather, sports, business and entertainment.
Language (s): English
Ad Rate: Full Page Mono 9.80
Currency: United States Dollars
COMMUNITY NEWSPAPER

Shun Pao News 791583
Editorial: 5695 Talaton Trail, Mississauga, Ontario L5R 3N6 **Tel:** 1 905 273-5291
Email: infospnews@gmail.com
Freq: Weekly; **Circ:** 10000
Publisher & Editor: Tony Kamg
Profile: Shun Pao News is a weekly newspaper providing Community News coverage and Cultural Event reports for the Chinese community in Mississauga, ON.
Language (s): Chinese
Ad Rate: Full Page Mono 39.50
Currency: Canada Dollars
COMMUNITY NEWSPAPER

Siam Media Weekly Thai Newspaper 23296
Owner: Siam Media, Inc.
Editorial: 9266 Valley Blvd, Rosemead, California 91770-1922 **Tel:** 1 626 307-9119
Email: siammedia@gmail.com **Web site:** http://www.siammedia.org
Freq: Fri; **Circ:** 10000 Not Audited
Advertising Sales Manager: Aporn Sripipat
Profile: Siam Media Weekly Thai Newspaper provides news and information for and about the Thai and Southeast Asian community living in the United States. Deadlines are on Fridays at 6pm PT.
Language (s): English
Ad Rate: Full Page Mono 2.07
Currency: United States Dollars
COMMUNITY NEWSPAPER

Sicangu Sun Times 21633
Editorial: BIA Hwy I, Rosebud, South Dakota 57570 **Tel:** 1 605 747-2280
Email: suntimes@goldenwest.net **Web site:** http://www.sicangusuntimes.com
Freq: Semi-Monthly; **Circ:** 15000 Not Audited
Advertising Sales Manager: Nancy Brooks; **Publisher & Editor:** Paul Gregg-Bear
Profile: Sicangu Sun Times is a local newspaper serving the Native American residents of Rosebud, SD. It includes information on local news, weather, sports, business and entertainment.
Language (s): English
Ad Rate: Full Page Mono 9.00
Currency: United States Dollars
COMMUNITY NEWSPAPER

Sie7e Dias 231074
Editorial: 2555 Porter Lake Dr Ste 107, Sarasota, Florida 34240-7865 **Tel:** 1 941 341-0000
Email: info@7dias.us **Web site:** http://www.7dias.us
Freq: Sat; **Circ:** 23000 Not Audited
Publisher & Editor: Luis Baron
Profile: Sie7E Dias is a local newspaper written for the Hispanic community of Sarasota, Pinellas, FL.
Language (s): Spanish
Ad Rate: Full Page Mono 17.00
Currency: United States Dollars
COMMUNITY NEWSPAPER

Siete Días 217149
Editorial: 12005 NE 12th St Ste 26, Bellevue, Washington 98005-2420 **Tel:** 1 425 646-8846
Web site: http://www.elsietedias.com
Freq: Wed; **Circ:** 7000 Not Audited
Publisher & Editor: Raul Perez-Calleja
Profile: Siete Dias is a free, weekly newspaper serving Spanish-speaking residents in King, Pierce and Snohomish counties, WA. Coverage includes stories on local and international news, events, sports and entertainment that are of interest to the local Latino community. Siete Dias is available for pick-up at Latin stores and Hispanic businesses and organizations throughout the coverage area. Deadlines are at noon PT.
Language (s): Spanish
Ad Rate: Full Page Mono 13.33
Currency: United States Dollars
COMMUNITY NEWSPAPER

The Signal Tribune 87916
Owner: Strichart (Neena)
Editorial: 939 E 27th St, Signal Hill, California 90755-2703 **Tel:** 1 562 427-8678
Email: newspaper@signaltribune.com **Web site:** http://www.signaltribune.com
Freq: Thu; **Circ:** 25000 Not Audited
Publisher & Editor: Neena Strichart
Profile: The Signal Tribune covers news and events for the community of Signal Hill, CA.
Language (s): English
Ad Rate: Full Page Mono 18.00
Currency: United States Dollars
COMMUNITY NEWSPAPER

Silicon Valley Community Newspapers 25715
Owner: MediaNews Group
Editorial: 1095 The Alameda, San Jose, California 95126-3142 **Tel:** 1 408 200-1000
Web site: http://www.mercurynews.com/san-jose-neighborhoods
Circ: 148779 Not Audited
Language (s): English
COMMUNITY NEWSPAPER

Silicon Valley Community Newspapers - Los Gatos 291444
Owner: MediaNews Group
Editorial: 1095 The Alameda, San Jose, California 95126-3142 **Tel:** 1 408 200-1000
Web site: http://www.mercurynews.com/my-town
Circ: 29750 Not Audited
Editor: Dick Sparrer
Language (s): English
COMMUNITY NEWSPAPER

Silsbee Bee 20957
Owner: Reneau Publishing Co.
Editorial: 404 Highway 96 S, Silsbee, Texas 77656-4810 **Tel:** 1 409 385-5278
Web site: http://www.silsbeebee.com
Freq: Wed; **Circ:** 5000 Not Audited
Editor: Daniel Elizondo; **Circulation Manager:** Debbie Gordon
Profile: Silsbee Bee is a local newspaper serving the residents of Silsbee, TX. It includes information on local news, weather, sports, business and entertainment. Deadlines are at 5pm Fridays before issue date.
Language (s): English
Ad Rate: Full Page Mono 6.75
Currency: United States Dollars
COMMUNITY NEWSPAPER

Simpson Publishing Co., Inc. 25031
Owner: Emmerich Newspapers Inc.
Editorial: 206 Main Ave N, Magee, Mississippi 39111-3536 **Tel:** 1 601 849-3434
Email: pbrown@mageecourier.ms **Web site:** http://www.mageecourier-countynews.com
Circ: 6450 Not Audited
Advertising Sales Manager: Nancy Brown; **Publisher and Editor:** Pat Brown
Profile: Simpson Publishing Co., Inc. provides local news to the community of Magee, MS.
Language (s): English
Ad Rate: Full Page Mono 11.12
Currency: United States Dollars
COMMUNITY NEWSPAPER

The Siuslaw News 20505
Owner: News Media Corp.
Editorial: 148 Maple St, Florence, Oregon 97439 **Tel:** 1 541 997-3441
Email: pressreleases@thesiuslawnews.com **Web site:** http://www.thesiuslawnews.com
Freq: Sat; **Circ:** 6571 Not Audited
Publisher: John Bartlett; **Advertising Sales Manager:** Susan Gutierrez
Profile: The Siuslaw News is a local newspaper serving Lane County, OR. It provides information on local news and events of interest to the local community. Deadlines for the Wednesday edition are on Mondays at 3pm PT. Deadlines for the Saturday edition are on Thursdays at 3pm PT.
Language (s): English
Ad Rate: Full Page Mono 15.71
Currency: United States Dollars
COMMUNITY NEWSPAPER

Skagit Valley Community Newspapers - Mount Vernon 577800
Owner: Skagit Valley Publishing Co.
Editorial: 1215 Anderson Rd, Mount Vernon, Washington 98274-7615 **Tel:** 1 360 424-3251

Email: weeklyeditor@skagitpublishing.com **Web site:** http://www.goskagit.com
Circ: 17839
Editor: Kathy Boyd
Profile: Skagit Valley Newspapers - Mount Vernon offers local and community news to residents in and around Mount Vernon. It shares offices with the Skagit Valley Herald.
Language (s): English
COMMUNITY NEWSPAPER

The Skanner 20542
Owner: The Skanner Newspaper Group
Editorial: 415 N Killingsworth St, Portland, Oregon 97217-2440 **Tel:** 1 503 285-5555
Email: news@theskanner.com **Web site:** http://www.theskanner.com
Freq: Thu; **Circ:** 30000 Not Audited
Advertising Sales Manager: Ted Banks; **News Editor:** Christen McCurdy; **News Editor:** Brian Stinson
Profile: The Skanner is written for African American residents of Portland, OR. It covers local news and events.
Language (s): English
Ad Rate: Full Page Mono 69.50
Currency: United States Dollars
COMMUNITY NEWSPAPER

The Skanner 21602
Editorial: 415 N Killingsworth St, Portland, Oregon 97217-2440 **Tel:** 1 503 285-5555
Email: seattle@theskanner.com **Web site:** http://www.theskanner.com
Freq: Thu; **Circ:** 20000 Not Audited
Publisher: Bernie Foster; **Advertising Sales Manager:** Jerry Foster
Language (s): English
Ad Rate: Full Page Mono 69.50
Currency: United States Dollars
COMMUNITY NEWSPAPER

Skywrighter 22774
Owner: Cox Media Group
Editorial: 5135 Pearson Rd, Area A, Wright Patterson AFB, Ohio 45433-5346 **Tel:** 1 937 522-3251
Email: 88abw.skywrighter@us.as.mil **Web site:** http://www.skywrighter.com
Freq: Fri; **Circ:** 16000 Not Audited
Circulation Manager: Gary Henderson; **Editor:** Jim Tyler
Profile: Skywrighter is a local weekly newspaper serving Wright-Patterson Air Force Base and the surrounding area. It provides the community with information on news and events related to the base and the local community.
Language (s): English
Ad Rate: Full Page Mono 16.00
Currency: United States Dollars
COMMUNITY NEWSPAPER

The Slidell Independent 809153
Owner: Chiri (Kevin)
Tel: 1 985 607-8852
Email: sliindenews@gmail.com **Web site:** http://www.slidell-independent.com
Freq: Weekly; **Circ:** 15000
Publisher & Editor: Kevin Chiri
Profile: The Slidell Independent is a community newspaper serving the residents of Slidell, LA, including community news, lifestyle, business and sports. This outlet offers RSS (Really Simple Syndication).
Language (s): English
Ad Rate: Full Page Mono 12.00
Currency: United States Dollars
COMMUNITY NEWSPAPER

The Smithfield Times 21066
Owner: Times Publishing Company
Editorial: 228 Main St, Smithfield, Virginia 23430-1325 **Tel:** 1 757 357-3288
Email: news@smithfieldtimes.com **Web site:** http://www.smithfieldtimes.com
Freq: Wed; **Circ:** 6200 Not Audited
Circulation Manager: Natalie Bangley; **Editor/ Publisher:** John Edwards; **Advertising Sales Manager:** Wendy Kantsios; **News Editor:** Diana McFarland
Profile: The Smithfield Times is a local, weekly newspaper serving the Smithfield, VA area. It provides information on news and events of interest to the local community.
Language (s): English
Ad Rate: Full Page Mono 9.76
Currency: United States Dollars
COMMUNITY NEWSPAPER

The Smithtown News, Inc. 24651
Owner: North Shore News Group
Editorial: 1 Brooksite Dr, Smithtown, New York 11787-3454 **Tel:** 1 631 265-2100
Email: info@smithtownnews.com **Web site:** http://www.northshorenewsgroup.com
Circ: 37740 Not Audited
Editor: David Ambro
Language (s): English
COMMUNITY NEWSPAPER

Smoky Mountain News 342425
Owner: McLeod (Scott)
Editorial: 144 Montgomery St, Waynesville, North Carolina 28786-3720 **Tel:** 1 828 452-4251
Email: news@smokymountainnews.com **Web site:** http://www.smokymountainnews.com
Freq: Wed; **Circ:** 16318 Not Audited
Publisher & Editor: Scott McLeod; **Circulation Manager:** Amanda Singletary; **Editor:** Jessi Stone
Profile: Smoky Mountain News is a weekly newspaper covering Haywood, Jackson, Macon and Swain counties in NC. It features hard news, editorials on local issues and an extensive arts, entertainment, books and outdoors section. The paper caters to both residents and tourists. Deadlines for editorial content and advertising are Thursdays at 3 p.m. ET for the following week's publication.
Language (s): English
Ad Rate: Full Page Mono 712.00
Currency: United States Dollars
COMMUNITY NEWSPAPER

The Smyth County News & Messenger 28856
Owner: BH Media Group
Editorial: 119 S Sheffey St, Marion, Virginia 24354-2523 **Tel:** 1 276 783-5121
Web site: http://www.swvatoday.com/news/smyth_county
Freq: Sat; **Circ:** 6000 Not Audited
Publisher: Jim Maxwell; **Editor:** Jerry Orr; **Editor:** Stephanie Porter-Nichols
Profile: The Smyth County News & Messenger is a local newspaper serving Smyth County, VA. The publication provides information on news and events of interest to the local community. Deadlines are Wednesday and Friday at 4pm ET, one week prior to issue date.
Language (s): English
Ad Rate: Full Page Mono 11.30
Currency: United States Dollars
COMMUNITY NEWSPAPER

Sneak Preview - Ashland 584262
Owner: Hayden (Curt) & Colvin (Penny)
Editorial: 2305 Ashland St, Ste C, Ashland, Oregon 97520-3777 **Tel:** 1 541 482-0368
Email: sneakpre@mind.net **Web site:** http://www.sneakpre.com
Circ: 44000
Profile: Sneak Preview - Ashland is a monthly community newspaper publisher serving the residents of Ashland, OR.
Language (s): English
COMMUNITY NEWSPAPER

Snyder County Times 20575
Editorial: 405 E Main St, Middleburg, Pennsylvania 17842-1215 **Tel:** 1 570 837-6065
Email: scuc@ptd.net **Web site:** http://www.thesnydercountytimes.com
Freq: Fri; **Circ:** 16108 Not Audited
Publisher: Susan Weaver
Profile: Snyder County Times is a weekly newspaper written for the residents of Snyder County, PA. The newspaper aims to bring its readers information on local news, politics, education, sports and community events.
Language (s): English
Ad Rate: Full Page Mono 8.00
Currency: United States Dollars
COMMUNITY NEWSPAPER

Socialist Worker 342516
Owner: Maass (Alan)
Tel: 1 773 583-5069
Email: contact@internationalsocialist.org **Web site:** http://www.socialistworker.org
Freq: Fri; **Circ:** 5500 Not Audited
Publisher & Editor: Alan Maass
Profile: Socialist Worker is published weekly by the International Socialist Organization. The ISO has branches and members in about 40 cities across the U.S. and is headquartered in Chicago. The Socialist Worker features updates, news and events for all branches and members. The paper does not solicit advertising.
Language (s): English
Ad Rate: Full Page Mono 12.00
Currency: United States Dollars
COMMUNITY NEWSPAPER

El Sol 23148
Owner: Gannett Co., Inc.
Editorial: 123 W Alisal St, Salinas, California 93901-2644 **Tel:** 1 831 424-2221
Email: mivozenelsol@thecalifornian.com **Web site:** http://www.elsoldesalinas.com
Freq: Sat; **Circ:** 20000 Not Audited
Advertising Sales Manager: Craig Hymovitz
Profile: El Sol is a weekly, Spanish-language newspaper serving the Hispanic community in Monterey, Santa Cruz and San Benito counties, CA. It is published by the staff of the Salinas (CA) Californian daily newspaper. Deadlines for Saturday's edition are on Thursdays at noon PT. Send press releases to the editor directly.
Language (s): Spanish
Ad Rate: Full Page Mono 38.69
Currency: United States Dollars
COMMUNITY NEWSPAPER

El Sol de Cleveland 358677
Owner: RB Publishing & Media Services
Editorial: 3157 W 105th St, Cleveland, Ohio 44111-2727 **Tel:** 1 216 535-9388
Email: elsoldecleveland@att.net **Web site:** http://www.elsoldecleveland.com
Freq: Bi-Weekly; **Circ:** 25000 Not Audited
Advertising Sales Manager: Randy Michael
Profile: El Sol de Cleveland is a semi-monthly newspaper serving the Latino community in and around Cleveland. It is available for pick-up at local retailers, restaurants, community centers and newsstands.
Language (s): Spanish/Bilingual
Ad Rate: Full Page Mono 9.00
Currency: United States Dollars
COMMUNITY NEWSPAPER

El Sol de la Florida 823386
Owner: El Sol Group, Inc.
Editorial: 2717 Michigan Ave, Kissimmee, Florida 34744-1551 **Tel:** 1 407 572-8855
Email: admin@elsoldelaflorida.com **Web site:** http://www.elsoldelaflorida.com
Freq: Weekly; **Circ:** 65000
Publisher & Editor: Marcos Tejeda
Profile: El Sol de la Florida is a weekly newspaper providing local and community news coverage for the Hispanic community in Miami-Dade, Broward and Palm Beach as well Orlando, Kissimmee, Tampa and Fort Myers, FL.
Language (s): Spanish
Ad Rate: Full Page Mono 21.95
Currency: United States Dollars
COMMUNITY NEWSPAPER

El Sol de New York 217262
Tel: 1 845 429-7764
Email: elsol1@aol.com **Web site:** http://www.elsoldeny.com
Freq: Bi-Weekly; **Circ:** 25000 Not Audited
Publisher & Editor: Ramon Soto
Profile: Sol de New York is a Spanish language newspaper serving the Spanish-speaking residents of New York with relevant news and information.
Language (s): Spanish
Ad Rate: Full Page Mono 18.78
Currency: United States Dollars
COMMUNITY NEWSPAPER

El Sol de Yakima 156170
Owner: Seattle Times Co.
Editorial: 114 N 4th St, Yakima, Washington 98901-2707 **Tel:** 1 509 249-6181
Email: adsmailbox@yakimaherald.com **Web site:** http://elsoldeyakima.com
Freq: Thu; **Circ:** 13250 Not Audited
Language (s): Spanish
Ad Rate: Full Page Mono 14.71
Currency: United States Dollars
COMMUNITY NEWSPAPER

El Sol Del Valle Imperial 152894
Editorial: 280 Campillo St Ste D, Calexico, California 92231-3200 **Tel:** 1 760 353-8711
Email: meza1120@yahoo.com
Freq: Fri; **Circ:** 12000 Not Audited
Publisher & Editor: Felix Meza
Profile: El Sol Del Valle Imperial is a spanish newspaper written for the residents of El Centro, CA. Call ahead before sending them a fax.
Language (s): Spanish
Ad Rate: Full Page Mono 24.00
Currency: United States Dollars
COMMUNITY NEWSPAPER

El Sol News 155402
Owner: Arteaga (Servio)
Editorial: 1 Bank St Ste 304, Stamford, Connecticut 06901-3006 **Tel:** 1 203 323-8400
Email: info@elsolnews.com **Web site:** http://www.elsolnews.com
Freq: Fri; **Circ:** 50000 Not Audited
Editor: Raul Arteaga
Profile: El Sol News is a weekly newspaper written for the Hispanic community of Stamford, CT.
Language (s): Spanish
Ad Rate: Full Page Mono 14.00
Currency: United States Dollars
COMMUNITY NEWSPAPER

Somerset Herald 24195
Owner: Gannett Co., Inc.
Editorial: 11779 Somerset Ave Ste 13, Princess Anne, Maryland 21853-1271 **Tel:** 1 410 651-1600
Email: somersetherald@gannett.com **Web site:** http://www.delmarvanow.com
Freq: Wed; **Circ:** 7800 Not Audited
Editor: Ben Penserga
Profile: Somerset Herald provides local news and information for the residents of greater Princess Anne and Crisfield, MD.
Language (s): English
Ad Rate: Full Page Mono 10.42
Currency: United States Dollars
COMMUNITY NEWSPAPER

The Somerville Times 238653
Editorial: 699 Broadway, Somerville, Massachusetts 02144-2223 **Tel:** 1 617 666-4010
Email: news@thesomervilletimes.com **Web site:** http://www.thesomervilletimes.com
Freq: Wed; **Circ:** 6000 Not Audited
Editor: Jim Clark; **Publisher:** Donald Norton
Profile: The Somerville News is a community newspaper written for residents of Somerville, MA. The paper will print only local news dealing with Somerville. They will not print anything else.
Language (s): English
Ad Rate: Full Page Mono 10.00
Currency: United States Dollars
COMMUNITY NEWSPAPER

Somos Frontera 448943
Owner: MediaNews Group
Editorial: 500 W Overland, El Paso, Texas 79901
Tel: 1 915 546-6100
Web site: http://www.somosfrontera.com
Freq: Sat; **Circ:** 50000 Not Audited
Editor: Juan Antonio Rodriguez
Profile: Somos Frontera is a local, weekly Spanish-language newspaper serving Hispanic and Spanish-speaking residents of El Paso, TX. The paper includes local news, business, sports, arts & entertainment and other information. It is published out of the same office as the El Paso (TX) Times and shares some of its staff.
Language (s): Spanish
Ad Rate: Full Page Mono 24.15
Currency: United States Dollars
COMMUNITY NEWSPAPER

Sonoma Index-Tribune 22132
Owner: Sonoma Media Investments LLC
Editorial: 117 W Napa St, Sonoma, California 95476-6647 **Tel:** 1 707 938-2111
Email: info@sonomanews.com **Web site:** http://www.sonomanews.com
Freq: 2 Times/Week; **Circ:** 8500 Not Audited
Publisher: John Burns
Profile: Sonoma Index Tribune is a local newspaper serving Sonoma, CA.
Language (s): English
Ad Rate: Full Page Mono 32.00
Currency: United States Dollars
COMMUNITY NEWSPAPER

Sonoma Valley Sun Newspapers 238547
Editorial: 158 W Napa St, Sonoma, California 95476-6625 **Tel:** 1 707 933-0101
Email: news@sonomasun.com **Web site:** http://sonomasun.com/
Circ: 22700 Not Audited
Advertising Sales Manager: Kelly Magner; **Editor:** Jody Purdom
Language (s): English
COMMUNITY NEWSPAPER

Sonoran News 22760
Owner: Conestoga Merchants Inc.
Editorial: 6812 E Cave Creek Rd Ste 1, Cave Creek, Arizona 85331-8627 **Tel:** 1 480 488-2021
Email: news@sonorannews.com **Web site:** http://www.sonorannews.com
Freq: Bi-Weekly; **Circ:** 44000 Not Audited
Advertising Sales Manager: Charles Blankenship
Profile: Sonoran News is published weekly and distributed free of charge to more than 38,000 homes and businesses throughout the Cave Creek, Carefree, Desert Hills, New River, Tatum Ranch, Rio Verde, N. Phoenix and N. Scottsdale areas including Anthem, Desert Mountain, Terravita, Legend Trail, Winfield, Tramonto, Troon, Boulders and Pinnacle Peak. Deadlines are 5pm Thursday for advertising and 5pm Friday for editorial material.
Language (s): English
Ad Rate: Full Page Mono 32.00
Currency: United States Dollars
COMMUNITY NEWSPAPER

The Sooner Catholic 757890
Editorial: 7501 NW Expressway, Oklahoma City, Oklahoma 73132-1551
Email: tips@archokc.org **Web site:** http://www.archokc.org/sooner-catholic
Freq: Bi-Weekly; **Circ:** 37000
Publisher: Paul Coakley; **Editor:** Ray Dyer
Profile: The Sooner Catholic is a newspaper written for the members of the Archdiocese of Oklahoma City. The paper is bi-weekly with the exceptions of once in July and twice in December. The paper does not accept outside advertising. They have requested that all contact info not be listed.
Language (s): English
COMMUNITY NEWSPAPER

Soundoff! 27378
Editorial: 4409 Llewellyn Ave, Fort Meade, Maryland 20755 **Tel:** 1 301 677-6806
Email: joyce.p.brayboy.civ@mail.mil **Web site:** http://www.ftmeade.army.mil
Freq: Thu; **Circ:** 11946 Not Audited
Editor: Joyce Brayboy
Profile: Soundoff! provides local news, sports and entertainment information to the military personnel of Fort Meade, MD and people in the surrounding county.
Language (s): English
Ad Rate: Full Page Mono 46.86
Currency: United States Dollars
COMMUNITY NEWSPAPER

The Sounds 21882
Editorial: 4541 W Peterson Ave, Chicago, Illinois 60646-5819 **Tel:** 1 773 216-2094
Email: soundsnewspaper@comcast.net **Web site:** http://www.soundsnewspaper.com
Freq: Sat; **Circ:** 7000 Not Audited
Advertising Sales Manager: Judy Fasold
Profile: The Sounds is a weekly community newspaper serving the residents of Chicago.
Language (s): English
Ad Rate: Full Page Mono 10.00
Currency: United States Dollars
COMMUNITY NEWSPAPER

The Source Newspapers 24595
Owner: Journal Register Company
Editorial: 19176 Hall Rd Ste 200, Clinton Township, Michigan 48038-6914 **Tel:** 1 586 716-8100
Web site: http://www.sourcenewspapers.com
Circ: 125536
Advertising Sales Manager: Debbie Loggins; **Editor:** Jody McVeigh; **Publisher:** Jim O'Rourke

Profile: Advisor & Source Newspapers is a newspaper covering local news in Macomb County, Michigan.
Language (s): English
COMMUNITY NEWSPAPER

South Arkansas Sunday News 389568

Owner: Wehco Media Inc.
Editorial: 111 N Madison Ave, El Dorado, Arkansas 71730-6124 **Tel:** 1 870 862-6611
Email: editorial@eldoradonews.com **Web site:** http://www.eldoradonews.com
Freq: Daily; **Circ:** 7476 Not Audited
Publisher: Walter Hussman; **Circulation Manager:** Danny Leftridge; **Advertising Sales Manager:** Nicole Patterson
Profile: South Arkansas Sunday News is a weekly newspaper covering El Dorado, AR and surrounding communities.
Language (s): English
Ad Rate: Full Page Mono 23.75
Currency: United States Dollars
COMMUNITY NEWSPAPER

South Beach Bulletin 22021

Owner: Stephens Media Group
Tel: 1 360 268-0736
Email: southbeachbulletin@comcast.net **Web site:** http://southbeachbulletin.com/
Freq: Thu; **Circ:** 5400 Not Audited
Profile: South Beach Bulletin is a free local weekly newspaper serving Westport, WA and the surrounding area. It provides information on news and events of interest to the greater South Beach area. It is written for community members as well as tourists. The advertising deadline for the publication is 4pm PT on Mondays.
Language (s): English
Ad Rate: Full Page Mono 6.00
Currency: United States Dollars
COMMUNITY NEWSPAPER

South Belt-Ellington Leader 778174

Editorial: 11555 Beamer Rd, Houston, Texas 77089-2357 **Tel:** 1 281 481-5656
Email: mynews@southbeltleader.com **Web site:** http://www.southbeltleader.com
Freq: Weekly
Publisher & Editor: Marie Flickinger
Profile: The South Belt-Ellington Leader is a weekly community newspaper.
COMMUNITY NEWSPAPER

South Bergenite 20209

Owner: Gannett Co., Inc./North Jersey Media Group
Editorial: 1 Garret Mountain Plz, Woodland Park, New Jersey 07424-3320 **Tel:** 1 201 933-1166
Email: southbergenite@northjersey.com **Web site:** http://www.northjersey.com/towns/south-bergen
Freq: Thu; **Circ:** 26327 Not Audited
Editor: Jamie Winters
Profile: South Bergenite is a weekly newspaper for residents of Rutherford, East Rutherford, Lyndhurst, Carlstadt, North Arlington and Meadowlands, NJ. The newspaper covers local news, business, sports and arts & entertainment. The newspaper also covers national and statewide stories if they have a direct impact on the newspaper's readership.
Language (s): English
Ad Rate: Full Page Mono 20.59
Currency: United States Dollars
COMMUNITY NEWSPAPER

South Boston Online 257101

Editorial: 700 E Broadway, South Boston, Massachusetts 2127 **Tel:** 1 617 269-5550
Email: mail@southbostononline.com **Web site:** http://www.southbostononline.com
Freq: Thu; **Circ:** 13000 Not Audited
Profile: South Boston Online is written for the residents in South Boston. It covers news, events, people and politics. Deadlines are on Tuesdays.
Language (s): English
Ad Rate: Full Page Mono 12.50
Currency: United States Dollars
COMMUNITY NEWSPAPER

South Cheatham Advocate 324203

Owner: Graham (Dale)
Editorial: 1065 Crane Ct, Kingston Springs, Tennessee 37082-5208 **Tel:** 1 615 952-5554
Email: scadvocate@aol.com **Web site:** http://www.scadvocate.com
Freq: Sat; **Circ:** 5000 Not Audited
Profile: South Cheatham Advocate's deadline is Tuesday at 4pm CT.
Language (s): English
Ad Rate: Full Page Mono 7.75
Currency: United States Dollars
COMMUNITY NEWSPAPER

South County Newspapers, LLC. 24476

Owner: News Media Corp.
Editorial: 522 Broadway St, Ste A, King City, California 93930 **Tel:** 1 831 385-4880
Email: editor@southcountynewspapers.com
Circ: 5500 Not Audited
Advertising Sales Manager: Sheryl Bailey; **Publisher:** Jason Cross
Profile: South County Newspapers, LLC. is a weekly community newspaper publisher serving the residents of King City, Gonzales, Greenfield and Soledad, CA.
Language (s): English
COMMUNITY NEWSPAPER

South County Publications 24518

Editorial: 110 N 5th St, Auburn, Illinois 62615-1449 **Tel:** 1 217 438-6155
Email: southco@royell.org **Web site:** http://www.southcountypublications.net
Circ: 10275 Not Audited
Circulation Manager: Patrice Huber; **Advertising Sales Manager:** Connie Michelich; **Publisher & Editor:** Joe Michelich; **Editor:** Byron Painter; **Editor:** Joe Pritchett
Language (s): English
COMMUNITY NEWSPAPER

South Dade News Leader 21697

Owner: Calkins-Media
Editorial: 205 N Flagler Ave, Homestead, Florida 33030-6130 **Tel:** 1 305 245-2311
Web site: http://www.southdadenewsleader.com
Freq: Thu; **Circ:** 12000 Not Audited
Publisher: Dale Machesic; **Editor:** Frank Maradiaga
Profile: South Dade News Leader is a local newspaper serving South Dade, FL and the surrounding area. The publication provides information on news and events of interest to the local community. The lead time for the publication varies depending on the material.
Language (s): English
Ad Rate: Full Page Mono 18.90
Currency: United States Dollars
COMMUNITY NEWSPAPER

The South End News & Bay Windows Publications 25416

Editorial: 28 Damrell St Ste 204, Boston, Massachusetts 02127-3077 **Tel:** 1 617 464-7280
Email: news.baywindows@gmail.com **Web site:** http://www.baywindows.com
Circ: 39000 Not Audited
Language (s): English
COMMUNITY NEWSPAPER

South Florida Sun Times 87915

Editorial: 305 NW 10th Ter, Hallandale Beach, Florida 33009-3103 **Tel:** 1 954 458-0635
Email: sfsuntimes@aol.com **Web site:** http://www.southfloridasun.net
Freq: Thu; **Circ:** 60000 Not Audited
Editor: Larry Bluestein; **Publisher:** Craig Farquhar
Profile: South Florida Sun Times is a local newspaper written for the residents of Hallandale, FL.
Language (s): English
Ad Rate: Full Page Mono 23.00
Currency: United States Dollars
COMMUNITY NEWSPAPER

South Florida Times 29282

Owner: Beatty (Robert)
Editorial: 3020 NE 32nd Ave Ste 200, Fort Lauderdale, Florida 33308-7233 **Tel:** 1 954 356-9360
Email: news@sfltimes.com **Web site:** http://www.sfltimes.com
Freq: Fri; **Circ:** 26000 Not Audited
Publisher: Robert Beatty
Profile: South Florida Times is distributed every Friday throughout Broward County, FL. The newspaper focuses on local news and events that are important to the African American community. Features include business, politics, lifestyle, entertainment and sports. Deadlines are on Wednesdays at noon ET.
Language (s): English
Ad Rate: Full Page Mono 34.95
Ad Rate: Full Page Colour 3876.00
Currency: United States Dollars
COMMUNITY NEWSPAPER

South Haven Tribune 22748

Owner: Paxton Media Group
Editorial: 308 Kalamazoo St, South Haven, Michigan 49090-1308 **Tel:** 1 269 637-1104
Email: southhaventribune@yahoo.com
Freq: Sun; **Circ:** 14000 Not Audited
Editor: Becky Burkert; **Publisher:** David Holgate
Profile: South Haven Tribune is a community newspaper serving South Haven, MI and the surrounding area. The publication provides information on news and events of interest to the local community. Deadlines are Wednesdays at 5pm CT.
Language (s): English
Ad Rate: Full Page Mono 11.36
Currency: United States Dollars
COMMUNITY NEWSPAPER

The South Hill Enterprise 21069

Owner: GateHouse Media Inc.
Editorial: 914 W Danville St, South Hill, Virginia 23970 **Tel:** 1 434 447-3178
Email: editor@southhillenterprise.com **Web site:** http://www.southhillenterprise.com
Freq: Sun; **Circ:** 6300 Not Audited
News Editor: Keith Corum; **Publisher:** David Crawley; **Advertising Sales Manager:** Baretta Taylor
Profile: South Hill Enterprise News is a weekly local paper serving the residents of Mecklenburg and Brunswick Counties, VA. It reports on local news, weather and sports. The editor is the main PR contact. Press releases can be faxed or e-mailed. Contact the publication for advertising information.
Language (s): English
Ad Rate: Full Page Mono 8.20
Currency: United States Dollars
COMMUNITY NEWSPAPER

South Lake Press 18742

Owner: Halifax Media Group
Editorial: 732 W Montrose St, Clermont, Florida 34711-2122 **Tel:** 1 352 394-2183
Email: slpress@dailycommercial.com **Web site:** http://www.southlakepress.com
Freq: Wed; **Circ:** 40000 Not Audited
Circulation Manager: Paul Nikolai
Profile: South Lake Press is a local newspaper serving Clermont, Minneola, Groveland, Mascotte and Montverde in Lake County, FL. The publication provides information on news, sports, arts & entertainment and events of interest to the local community.
Language (s): English
Ad Rate: Full Page Mono 11.25
Currency: United States Dollars
COMMUNITY NEWSPAPER

South Marion Citizen 24211

Editorial: 8810 Sw Highway 200 Unit 104, Ocala, Florida 34481-7824 **Tel:** 1 352 854-3986
Web site: http://www.smcitizen.com
Freq: Fri; **Circ:** 15000 Not Audited
Editor: Jim Clark; **Publisher:** Gerry Mulligan
Profile: South Marion Citizen is a local newspaper written for the residents of Ocala, FL.
Language (s): English
Ad Rate: Full Page Mono 14.87
Currency: United States Dollars
COMMUNITY NEWSPAPER

The South Pittsburgh Reporter 20588

Owner: Smith (William)
Tel: 1 412 481-0266
Email: news@sopghreporter.com **Web site:** http://sopghreporter.com
Freq: Tue; **Circ:** 10000 Not Audited
Publisher & Editor: William Smith
Profile: The South Pittsburgh Reporter is a local newspaper for the residents of Pittsburgh.
Language (s): English
Ad Rate: Full Page Mono 9.00
Currency: United States Dollars
COMMUNITY NEWSPAPER

South Potomac Pilot 472875

Owner: Comprint Military Publications
Editorial: 6509 Sampson Rd, Dahlgren, Virginia 22448-5176 **Tel:** 1 540 653-8153
Web site: http://www.dcmilitary.com/section/news07
Freq: Weekly; **Circ:** 8000 Not Audited
Editor: Jeron Hayes; **Publisher:** John Rives
Profile: South Potomac Pilot is a weekly newspaper serving the Dahlgren, VA Air Force Base. Deadlines are on Fridays at 3pm ET.
Language (s): English
Ad Rate: Full Page Mono 13.91
Currency: United States Dollars
COMMUNITY NEWSPAPER

The South Reporter 19875

Editorial: 157 S Center St, Holly Springs, Mississippi 38635-3040 **Tel:** 1 662 252-4261
Email: southreporter@dixie-net.com **Web site:** http://www.southreporter.com
Freq: Thu; **Circ:** 5200 Not Audited
Publisher & Editor: Barry Burleson; **Advertising Sales Manager:** Barbara Taylor
Profile: The South Reporter is written for residents of Holly Springs, MS. The local publication covers a number of events, including local news, sports, business and entertainment. Deadlines are on Mondays at 5pm CT.
Language (s): English
Ad Rate: Full Page Mono 5.90
Currency: United States Dollars
COMMUNITY NEWSPAPER

South Shore Press 231649

Owner: South Shore Press Inc.
Editorial: 2 Coraci Blvd Ste 7, Shirley, New York 11967-4833 **Tel:** 1 631 878-7800
Email: sspress2000@aol.com **Web site:** http://southshorepress.net
Freq: Wed; **Circ:** 45000 Not Audited
Editor: Jeannie Kubik
Profile: South Shore Press in Shirley, NY, is a weekly newspaper that covers local news and events.
Language (s): English
Ad Rate: Full Page Mono 220.00
Currency: United States Dollars
COMMUNITY NEWSPAPER

South Shore Tribune 24813

Owner: Frank G Naudus
Editorial: 4 California Pl N, Island Park, New York 11558-2215 **Tel:** 1 516 431-5628
Email: info@litribune.com **Web site:** http://www.litribune.com
Freq: Weekly; **Circ:** 32366 Not Audited
Profile: South Shore Tribune is a local newspaper published every Thursday. It is published for the residents of the South Shore of Long Island, NY. The newspaper covers local news, sports, entertainment, and lifestyle issues.
Language (s): English
COMMUNITY NEWSPAPER

South Washington County Bulletin 24224

Owner: Forum Communications Co.
Editorial: 7584 80th St S, Cottage Grove, Minnesota 55016-3100 **Tel:** 1 651 319-4280
Email: editor@swcbulletin.com **Web site:** http://www.swcbulletin.com
Freq: Wed; **Circ:** 6000 Not Audited
Editor: Scott Wente
Profile: South Washington County Bulletin is written for residents of Southern Washington County, MN. It covers a broad array of topics including local news, sports, business and entertainment. Deadlines are on Wednesdays at noon CT.
Language (s): English
Ad Rate: Full Page Mono 14.63
Currency: United States Dollars
COMMUNITY NEWSPAPER

South Whidbey Record 22473

Owner: Sound Publishing, Inc.
Editorial: 5575 S Harbor Ave Ste 207A, Freeland, Washington 98239 **Tel:** 1 360 221-5300
Email: editor@southwhidbeyrecord.com **Web site:** http://www.southwhidbeyrecord.com
Freq: Sat; **Circ:** 5375 Not Audited
Editor: Justin Burnett; **Circulation Manager:** Diane Smothers
Profile: The South Whidbey Record serves the south end of Whidbey Island, covering the commnunities of Clinton, Langley, Freeland and Greenbank. It covers local news, sports and entertainment. Deadlines are on Mondays and Wednesdays before issue the date.
Language (s): English
Ad Rate: Full Page Mono 16.15
Currency: United States Dollars
COMMUNITY NEWSPAPER

South Whidbey Record/ Whidbey News-Times 623884

Owner: Sound Publishing, Inc.
Editorial: 107 S Main St Ste E101, Coupeville, Washington 98239-3569 **Tel:** 1 360 221-5300
Circulation Manager: Diane Smothers
Profile: The Whidbey News-Times/Whidbey Examiner provide Local and Community News coverage for Whidbey Island, WA. The Whidbey News-Times covers North and Central Whidbey Island, from Greenbank to Deception Pass. The Whidbey Examiner is a weekly newspaper serving the community of Coupewille, WA. This community newspaper is owned by Sound Publishing, Inc., which produces a variety of weekly newspapers in Washington state; these papers share content, and news releases, as well as calendar listings can be posted online for review by the paper's editorial staff.
Language (s): English
COMMUNITY NEWSPAPER

The Southampton Press - Eastern Edition 23094

Owner: Southampton Press Publishing Co.
Editorial: 135 Windmill Ln, Southampton, New York 11968-4840 **Tel:** 1 631 283-4100
Email: mailbag@pressnewsgroup.com **Web site:** http://www.southamptonpress.com
Freq: Thu; **Circ:** 9599 Not Audited
Advertising Sales Manager: Paul Conroy; **Publisher:** Joseph Louchheim; **Editor:** Joseph Shaw
Language (s): English
Ad Rate: Full Page Mono 8.69
Currency: United States Dollars
COMMUNITY NEWSPAPER

The Southampton Press - Western Edition 23093

Owner: Southampton Town Newspapers
Editorial: 12 Mitchell Rd, Westhampton Beach, New York 11978-2609 **Tel:** 1 631 288-1100
Email: mailbag@pressnewsgroup.com **Web site:** http://www.27east.com
Freq: Thu; **Circ:** 7500 Not Audited
Advertising Sales Manager: Paul Conroy; **Editor:** Frank Costanza; **Publisher:** Joseph Louchheim
Profile: The Southampton Press - Western Edition is the newspaper of record for the town of Southampton, NY. Established in 1897, the paper includes two zoned editions. The Western edition focuses on local news and events for Hampton Bays, East Quogue, Quogue, Westhampton, Speonk, Eastport, and parts of Flanders and Riverhead, NY.
Language (s): English
Ad Rate: Full Page Mono 64.00
Currency: United States Dollars
COMMUNITY NEWSPAPER

The Southeast Christian Outlook 785527

Editorial: 920 Blankenbaker Pkwy, Louisville, Kentucky 40243-1845 **Tel:** 1 502 253-8950
Web site: http://www.southeastoutlook.org
Freq: Weekly; **Circ:** 70000
Editor: Brent Adams; **Advertising Sales Manager:** Larry Stewart
Profile: The Southeast Christian Outlook is a weekly publication serving the members of the Southeast Christian Church in Louisville, Kentucky. It features a Devotions section, as well as articles concerning the Christian religion in the context of Global, American, Kentucky, and Louisville life.
Language (s): English
COMMUNITY NEWSPAPER

Southern Cross 21918
Owner: Roman Catholic Diocese of Savannah
Editorial: 601 E Liberty St, Savannah, Georgia 31401-5118 **Tel:** 1 912 201-4100
Email: southerncross@diosav.org **Web site:** http://www.southerncross.diosav.org
Freq: Thu; **Circ:** 26000 Not Audited
Circulation Manager and Advertising Sales Manager: Sarah Dixon; **Publisher:** Gregory Hartmayer; **Editor:** Michael Johnson
Profile: Southern Cross in Savannah, GA is published weekly and covers news of interest to Catholics. Deadlines are on Fridays prior to issue date.
Language (s): English
COMMUNITY NEWSPAPER

Southern Dutchess News 24765
Editorial: 84 E Main St, Wappingers Falls, New York 12590 **Tel:** 1 845 297-3723
Email: newsplace@aol.com **Web site:** http://sdutchessnews.com
Freq: Weekly; **Circ:** 15000 Not Audited
Editor: Kate Goldsmith; **Editor:** Melina Makris; **Publisher:** Al Osten
Language (s): English
COMMUNITY NEWSPAPER

Southern Lakes Newspapers LLC. - Burlington 24732
Editorial: 700 N Pine St, Burlington, Wisconsin 53105-1261 **Tel:** 1 262 763-3511
Email: delavaneditor@southernlakesnewspapers.com **Web site:** http://www.southernlakesnewspapers.com
Circ: 14800 Not Audited
Publisher: Jack Cruger
Language (s): English
COMMUNITY NEWSPAPER

Southern Lakes Newspapers LLC. - Elkhorn 80984
Owner: Southern Lakes Newspapers LLC
Editorial: 11 W Walworth St, Elkhorn, Wisconsin 53121-1736 **Tel:** 1 262 723-2921
Email: elkinde@elkhornindependent.com **Web site:** http://www.mywalworthcounty.com
Freq: Thu
Publisher: Jack Cruger; **Advertising Sales Manager:** Pete Hansen
Language (s): English
COMMUNITY NEWSPAPER

Southern Rhode Island Newspapers 828404
Editorial: 187 Main St., Wakefield, Rhode Island 2879 **Tel:** 1 401 789-9744
Web site: http://www.ricentral.com
Publisher: Nanci Batson; **Editor:** Gabbi Falletta; **Circulation Manager:** Phil Rowell; **Editor:** Jeremiah Ryan
Profile: Southern Rhode Island is a community newspaper publisher, affiliated with the Kent County Daily Times, and publishes five papers: The Narragansett Times, The Standard-Times, The East Greenwich Pendulum, The Chariho Times, and The Coventry Courier.
COMMUNITY NEWSPAPER

Southern Sentinel 19903
Owner: Journal Publishing Co.
Editorial: 1701 City Ave N, Ripley, Mississippi 38663-1124 **Tel:** 1 662 837-8111
Email: news@tippah360.com **Web site:** http://www.southern-sentinel.com
Freq: Sat; **Circ:** 6800 Not Audited
Circulation Manager: Jessica Davis; **Publisher:** Tim Watson
Profile: Southern Sentinel is a community newspaper written for the residents of Ripley, MS. The paper covers local news, events, education, businesses, sports and features.
Language (s): English
Ad Rate: Full Page Mono 12.70
Currency: United States Dollars
COMMUNITY NEWSPAPER

Southern Standard 22430
Owner: Morris Multimedia Inc.
Editorial: 105 College St, Mc Minnville, Tennessee 37110-2537 **Tel:** 1 931 473-2191
Web site: http://www.southernstandard.com
Freq: Fri; **Circ:** 9000 Not Audited
Editor: James Clark; **Publisher:** Patricia Zechman
Profile: Southern Standard is the local newspaper for Warren County, TN. The newspaper covers local news, business, sports, and arts & entertainment stories. The newspaper also covers national and statewide stories if they have a direct impact on the newspaper's readership. All inquiries should be addressed to the editor.
Language (s): English
Ad Rate: Full Page Mono 8.25
Currency: United States Dollars
COMMUNITY NEWSPAPER

The Southern Star 18522
Owner: Adams (Joe)
Editorial: 373 Ed Lisenby Dr, Ozark, Alabama 36360-1473 **Tel:** 1 334 774-2715
Email: southernstar@centurytel.net
Freq: Wed; **Circ:** 5000 Not Audited
Publisher and Editor: Joseph Adams; **Advertising Sales Manager:** Charlie Dawkins
Profile: Southern Star is the local newspaper for the Ozark, AL area. The newspaper covers local news, business, sports, and arts & entertainment stories. The newspaper also covers national and statewide stories if they have a direct impact on the newspaper's readership. All inquiries should be addressed to the editor. The lead time for the publication is one week.
Language (s): English
Ad Rate: Full Page Mono 6.30
Currency: United States Dollars
COMMUNITY NEWSPAPER

The Southington Citizen 239013
Owner: Record-Journal Publishing Company
Editorial: 11 Crown St, Meriden, Connecticut 06450-5713 **Tel:** 1 860 620-5960
Email: news@thesouthingtoncitizen.com **Web site:** http://www.southingtoncitizen.com
Freq: Fri; **Circ:** 22000
Advertising Manager: Kimberly Boath; **News Editor:** Nick Carroll; **Publisher:** Eliot White
Profile: The Southington Citizen is published weekly for the residents of Southington, CT and surrounding areas. The newspaper covers local news and community events.
Language (s): English
Ad Rate: Full Page Mono 12.20
Currency: United States Dollars
COMMUNITY NEWSPAPER

Southington Observer 18729
Owner: Maitland Publishing, LLC.
Editorial: 213 Spring St, Southington, Connecticut 06489-1542 **Tel:** 1 860 621-6751
Web site: http://southingtonobserver.com
Freq: Fri; **Circ:** 5600 Not Audited
Publisher: William Pape
Profile: Southington Observer is a weekly newspaper devoted to the Southington, CT community and the surrounding area. The newspaper covers local news, business, sports and arts & entertainment stories. The newspaper also covers national and statewide stories if they have a direct impact on the newspaper's readership. All inquiries should be addressed to the editor. Deadlines for the publication are on Tuesdays at noon ET.
Language (s): English
Ad Rate: Full Page Mono 9.00
Currency: United States Dollars
COMMUNITY NEWSPAPER

Southside Times 19158
Owner: Times-Leader Publications LLC
Editorial: 7670 US 31 S, Indianapolis, Indiana 46227-8547 **Tel:** 1 317 300-8782
Email: news@ss-times.com **Web site:** http://www.ss-times.com
Freq: Thu; **Circ:** 21500 Not Audited
Editor: Nicole Davis; **Circulation Manager:** Curtis Dodd; **Publisher:** Rick Myers
Profile: Southside Times is written for the residents of the south side of Indianapolis and Greenwood in Johnson County, IN. It is a weekly local newspaper that covers local news, sports, business and entertainment stories. Deadlines are at 10am ET.
Language (s): English
Ad Rate: Full Page Mono 15.30
Currency: United States Dollars
COMMUNITY NEWSPAPER

The Southsider Voice 578602
Owner: Sum (Denise)
Editorial: 6025 Madison Ave Ste B, Indianapolis, Indiana 46227-4722 **Tel:** 1 317 781-0023
Email: news@southsidervoice.com **Web site:** http://www.southsidervoice.com
Freq: Weekly; **Circ:** 25000
Editor: Denise Summers
Profile: The Southsider Voice, launched in February 2009, is a community weekly newspaper that serves residents of Indianapolis's south side. It offers local news, sports and arts & entertainment.
Language (s): English
Ad Rate: Full Page Mono 4.16
Ad Rate: Full Page Colour 4.85
Currency: United States Dollars
COMMUNITY NEWSPAPER

Southwest Community News Group 24526
Owner: Southwest Community News Group
Editorial: 7676 W 63rd St, Summit, Illinois 60501-1812 **Tel:** 1 708 496-0265
Email: vonpub@aol.com **Web site:** http://www.swnewsherald.com
Circ: 61500 Not Audited
Circulation Manager: Dave Andersen; **Editor:** Joseph Boyle; **Publisher:** Mark Hornung; **Advertising Sales Manager:** Jose Reyes
Profile: Southwest Community News Group in Summit, IL is a community newspaper publisher.
Language (s): English
COMMUNITY NEWSPAPER

Southwest Globe Times 584244
Owner: Southwest CDC
Editorial: 6328 Paschall Ave, Philadelphia, Pennsylvania 19142-2315 **Tel:** 1 215 727-7777
Email: globe.times@yahoo.com **Web site:** http://www.swglobetimes.com
Freq: Bi-Weekly; **Circ:** 7000
Publisher: Ted Behr
Profile: Southwest Globe Times is a community paper published bi-weekly for residents of Philadelphia's southwest neighborhoods.
Language (s): English
Ad Rate: Full Page Mono 19.00
Currency: United States Dollars
COMMUNITY NEWSPAPER

Southwest Kansas Register 257750
Owner: Diocese of Dodge City
Editorial: 910 Central Ave, Dodge City, Kansas 67801-4905 **Tel:** 1 620 227-1519
Email: skregister@dcdiocese.org **Web site:** http://dcdiocese.org/register
Freq: Bi-Weekly; **Circ:** 6500 Not Audited
Publisher: John Brungardt; **Editor:** Dave Myers
Profile: Southwest Kansas Register is published bi-weekly for Catholics in Southwestern Kansas. The newspaper covers news and topics of interest pertaining to the Diocese of Dodge City, KS.
Language (s): English
Ad Rate: Full Page Mono 15.00
Currency: United States Dollars
COMMUNITY NEWSPAPER

Southwest Messenger Press 24541
Owner: Lysen (Lucinda)
Editorial: 3840 147th St, Midlothian, Illinois 60445-3452 **Tel:** 1 708 388-2425
Email: info@southwestmessengerpress.com **Web site:** http://southwestmessengerpress.com
Circ: 73829 Not Audited
Advertising Sales Manager: Carol Beymer; **Editor:** Lori Taylor
Profile: Southwest Messenger Press in Midlothian, IL is a community newspaper publisher.
Language (s): English
COMMUNITY NEWSPAPER

Southwest News Media 86464
Owner: Big Fish Works
Editorial: 12925 Eagle Creek Pkwy, Savage, Minnesota 55378-1271 **Tel:** 1 952 445-3333
Email: sales@swnewsmedia.com **Web site:** http://www.swnewsmedia.com
Circ: 14700 Not Audited
Publisher: Laurie Hartmann; **Circulation Manager:** Ruby Winings
Profile: Southwest News Media is a weekly community newspaper publisher serving the residents of Prior Lake and Savage, MN.
Language (s): English
COMMUNITY NEWSPAPER

Southwest Sun 19917
Owner: Emmerich Newspapers Inc.
Editorial: 112 Oliver Emmerich Dr, McComb, Mississippi 39648-6330 **Tel:** 1 601 684-2421
Email: news@enterprise-journal.com **Web site:** http://www.enterprise-journal.com
Freq: Wed; **Circ:** 7200 Not Audited
Advertising Sales Manager: Vicky Deere; **Editor & Publisher:** Jack Ryan
Profile: Southwest Sun is a weekly newspaper written for the residents of McComb, MS. It covers local, statewide and national news, business, sports and arts & entertainment.
Language (s): English
Ad Rate: Full Page Mono 2.50
Currency: United States Dollars
COMMUNITY NEWSPAPER

Space Observer 22816
Owner: Colorado Springs Military Newspaper Group
Editorial: 31 E Platte Ave Ste 300, Colorado Springs, Colorado 80903-1246 **Tel:** 1 719 556-4351
Email: info@csmng.com **Web site:** http://csmng.com
Freq: Thu; **Circ:** 7000 Not Audited
Profile: Space Observer is a weekly newspaper written for the residents and military members of Peterson Air Forc Base, CO.
Language (s): English
Ad Rate: Full Page Mono 15.02
Currency: United States Dollars
COMMUNITY NEWSPAPER

Spanish Journal 154506
Owner: Welch (Rhonda)
Editorial: 611 W National Ave Ste 316, Milwaukee, Wisconsin 53204-1714 **Tel:** 1 414 643-5683
Email: spanishjournalads@yahoo.com **Web site:** http://www.spanishjournal.com
Freq: Thu; **Circ:** 20000 Not Audited
Editor: Robert Miranda; **Publisher:** Rhonda Welch
Profile: Spanish Journal is a Spanish-language publication written for the Hispanic-American residents of Milwaukee.
Language (s): Spanish/Bilingual
Ad Rate: Full Page Mono 1.30
Currency: United States Dollars
COMMUNITY NEWSPAPER

Spare Change News 23310
Editorial: 1151 Massachusetts Ave, Cambridge, Massachusetts 02138-5201 **Tel:** 1 617 497-1595
Email: editor@sparechangenews.net **Web site:** http://www.sparechangenews.net
Freq: Bi-Weekly; **Circ:** 8000 Not Audited
Editor: Osagyefo Sekou; **Advertising Sales Manager:** Samuel Weems
Profile: Spare Change News is published as a means to help end homelessness. It covers news and events of interest to persons in Cambridge, Boston and Somerville, MA.
Language (s): English
Ad Rate: Full Page Mono 10.00
Currency: United States Dollars
COMMUNITY NEWSPAPER

Speakin' Out News 22366
Owner: Smothers (William)
Editorial: 201 Oakwood Ave NE, Huntsville, Alabama 35811-1901 **Tel:** 1 256 551-1020
Email: wsmoth3193@aol.com **Web site:** http://www.speakinoutweeklynews.com
Freq: Wed; **Circ:** 26500 Not Audited
Advertising Sales Manager: Knegleshia Smothers; **Publisher & Editor:** William Smothers
Profile: Speakin' Out News is an African-American publication written for residents of Huntsville, AL. It covers local news, business, sports, health, religion and arts & entertainment. Deadlines are on Mondays at noon CT.
Language (s): English
Ad Rate: Full Page Mono 34.00
Ad Rate: Full Page Colour 2996.00
Currency: United States Dollars
COMMUNITY NEWSPAPER

Spectator 22675
Owner: GateHouse Media Inc.
Editorial: 32 Broadway Mall, Hornell, New York 14843-1920 **Tel:** 1 607 324-1425
Email: news@eveningtribune.com **Web site:** http://www.eveningtribune.com
Freq: Sun; **Circ:** 14500 Not Audited
Editor: John Anderson; **Publisher:** Tom Connors
Profile: Spectator is written for the residents of Hornell, NY. It covers local news, business, sports and arts & entertainment stories. It also covers national and statewide stories if they have a direct impact on the newspaper's readership. All inquiries should be addressed to the editor.
Language (s): English
Ad Rate: Full Page Mono 9.65
Currency: United States Dollars
COMMUNITY NEWSPAPER

The Spectator & Fall River Spirit 542829
Owner: GateHouse Media Inc.
Editorial: 25 Elm St, New Bedford, Massachusetts 02740-6228 **Tel:** 1 508 979-4440
Web site: http://www.southcoasttoday.com
Circ: 16000 Not Audited
Editor: George Austin; **Advertising Sales Manager:** Jerry Reis; **Publisher & Editor:** Richard Snizek
Language (s): English
COMMUNITY NEWSPAPER

The Spencer County Journal-Democrat 19202
Owner: Landmark Community Newspapers, Inc.
Editorial: 541 Main St, Rockport, Indiana 47635-1429 **Tel:** 1 812 649-9196
Email: news@spencercountyjournal.com **Web site:** http://spencercountyjournal.com
Freq: Thu; **Circ:** 5700 Not Audited
Editor: Vince Luecke; **Advertising Manager:** Steve Weedman
Profile: Spencer County Journal-Democrat is a local weekly newspaper in Rockport, IN. The publication is written for residents of Spencer County, IN and surrounding areas. The paper covers local news and community events. Deadlines are on Tuesdays at 10am CT.
Language (s): English
Ad Rate: Full Page Mono 9.15
Currency: United States Dollars
COMMUNITY NEWSPAPER

Spencer Newspapers, Inc. 24742
Editorial: 210 E Main St, Spencer, West Virginia 25276-1602 **Tel:** 1 304 927-2360
Circ: 5417 Not Audited
Editor: Jim Cooper; **Advertising Sales Manager:** Annie Hedges; **Publisher:** David J. Hedges
Language (s): English
COMMUNITY NEWSPAPER

Spokane Valley News Herald 21129
Owner: Free Press Publishing Inc.
Editorial: 1212 N Argonne Road, Spokane, Washington 99212 **Tel:** 1 509 924-2440
Email: vnh@onemain.com
Freq: Fri; **Circ:** 5000 Not Audited
Publisher: Harlan Shellabarger
Profile: Spokane Valley News Herald is written for Spokane, WA community residents and also covers county news. Deadlines for the publication are on Tuesday by 5pm PT.
Language (s): English
Ad Rate: Full Page Mono 11.00
Currency: United States Dollars
COMMUNITY NEWSPAPER

Spotlight Newspapers 24932
Owner: Eagle Media Partners LP
Editorial: 341 Delaware Avenue, Delmar, New York 12054 **Tel:** 1 518 439-4949
Email: news@spotlightnews.com **Web site:** http://www.spotlightnews.com
Freq: Weekly; **Circ:** 58395 Not Audited
Publisher: John McIntyre
Language (s): English
COMMUNITY NEWSPAPER

Spring Creek Sun 21566
Owner: Starrett City, Inc.
Editorial: 1540 Van Siclen Ave, Brooklyn, New York 11239-2412 **Tel:** 1 718 642-2718
Web site: http://springcreeksunonline.com
Freq: Bi-Weekly; **Circ:** 8500 Not Audited

Profile: Spring Creek Sun is a local newspaper written for residents of Brooklyn, NY. The newspaper primarily covers local news in the Brooklyn area.
Language (s): English
Ad Rate: Full Page Mono 8.16
Currency: United States Dollars
COMMUNITY NEWSPAPER

The Springfield Paper 788120
Owner: Penda Publishing
Editorial: 1026 N Plum St, Springfield, Ohio 45504-2108 **Tel:** 1 937 327-9017
Email: editor@pendapublishing.com **Web site:** http://www.thespringfieldpaper.com
Freq: Wed; **Circ:** 50000
Publisher & Editor: David Reeves
Profile: The Springfield Paper is a weekly newspaper providing Local News, Community News, Sports and Lifestyle coverage to the residents of Springfield, OH and Clark County. The newspaper also focuses on religious news pertaining to the area.
Language (s): English
COMMUNITY NEWSPAPER

Springhill Press 28339
Owner: Thomas (Thomas)
Editorial: 403 Butler St, Springhill, Louisiana 71075-2735 **Tel:** 1 318 539-3511
Email: nattimes@wnonline.net
Freq: Thu; **Circ:** 30000 Not Audited
Profile: Springhill (LA) Press is a weekly newspaper that covers local news, events, sports, politics and social issues. Deadlines are on Fridays.
Language (s): English
Ad Rate: Full Page Mono 6.25
Ad Rate: Full Page Colour 717.00
Currency: United States Dollars
COMMUNITY NEWSPAPER

The St. Bernard News 217815
Owner: Roberson Advertising
Editorial: 3010 Lausat St, Metairie, Louisiana 70001-5924 **Tel:** 1 504 832-1481
Email: editor@thestbernardnews.com **Web site:** http://thestbernardnews.com/
Freq: Wed; **Circ:** 18000 Not Audited
Advertising Sales Manager: Joe Latino; **Publisher:** Michael Roberson
Profile: The St. Bernard News is published weekly for the residents of Metairie, LA and the surrounding St. Bernard Parish area. The newspaper covers local news and community events.
Language (s): English
Ad Rate: Full Page Mono 12.95
Currency: United States Dollars
COMMUNITY NEWSPAPER

St. Charles Herald-Guide 19433
Owner: Louisiana Publishing Corp, LLC
Editorial: 14236 Highway 90, Boutte, Louisiana 70039-3516 **Tel:** 1 985 758-2795
Web site: http://www.heraldguide.com
Freq: Thu; **Circ:** 6000 Not Audited
Editor: Jonathan Menard; **Circulation Manager:** Ricky Naquin
Profile: St. Charles Herald- Guide is a local newspaper providing community members with current events, news, articles, features, classifieds, and advertising. The publication is written for community members of Botte, LA. Deadlines for the publication are one week before the issue date.
Language (s): English
Ad Rate: Full Page Mono 8.73
Currency: United States Dollars
COMMUNITY NEWSPAPER

St. Clair Times 63397
Owner: Consolidated Publishing
Editorial: 1911 Martin St S Ste 7, Pell City, Alabama 35128-2372 **Tel:** 1 205 884-3400
Web site: http://www.dailyhome.com/stclair/dh-stclair.htm
Freq: Thu; **Circ:** 33700 Not Audited
Circulation Manager: John Knoll
Profile: St. Clair Times in Pell City, AL is a weekly newspaper that covers local news and events.
Language (s): English
Ad Rate: Full Page Mono 8.75
Currency: United States Dollars
COMMUNITY NEWSPAPER

St. Cloud Visitor 21885
Owner: Diocese of St. Cloud
Editorial: 305 7th Ave N Ste 206, Saint Cloud, Minnesota 56303-3633 **Tel:** 1 320 251-3022
Email: news@stcloudvisitor.org **Web site:** http://stcloudvisitor.org/
Freq: Bi-Weekly; **Circ:** 44500 Not Audited
Publisher: Donald Kettler; **Advertising Sales Manager:** Rose Kruger-Fuchs; **Circulation Manager:** Paula Lemke; **Editor:** Joe Towalski
Profile: St. Cloud Visitor provides news to the Catholic residents of central Minnesota. Coverage includes religious issues and events.
Language (s): English
Ad Rate: Full Page Mono 25.00
Ad Rate: Full Page Colour 1181.00
Currency: United States Dollars
COMMUNITY NEWSPAPER

The St. Johns Review 22292
Owner: Patton (Gayla)
Editorial: 6635 N Baltimore Ave #261, Portland, Oregon 97203-5454 **Tel:** 1 503 283-5086
Email: reviewnewspaper@gmail.com **Web site:** http://www.stjohnsreview.com
Freq: Bi-Weekly; **Circ:** 5500 Not Audited
Editor & Publisher: Gayla Patton
Profile: The St. Johns Review is Portland's oldest community newspaper and has been the St. Johns community newspaper since 1904. It is a source of history for the St. Johns and North Portland area. If verification is needed regarding an event in years past, they look it up in the St. Johns Review newspaper. It is published on a bi-weekly basis, continuing the history for future residents.
Language (s): English
Ad Rate: Full Page Mono 13.50
Currency: United States Dollars
COMMUNITY NEWSPAPER

St. Lawrence County Newspapers 25143
Owner: St. Lawrence County Newspapers, Inc.
Editorial: 308 Isabella St, Ogdensburg, New York 13669-1409 **Tel:** 1 315 393-1000
Circ: 25629 Not Audited
Advertising Sales Manager: Barbara Ward
Language (s): English
COMMUNITY NEWSPAPER

St. Louis American 19844
Editorial: 2315 Pine St, Saint Louis, Missouri 63103-2218 **Tel:** 1 314 533-8000
Web site: http://www.stlamerican.com
Freq: Thu; **Circ:** 66875 Not Audited
Advertising Sales Manager: Kevin Jones; **Publisher:** Donald Suggs
Profile: St. Louis American is a weekly newspaper geared toward African-Americans. Topics covered include news, religion, entertainment, sports and profiles of successful local African-Americans in business, healthcare or public service. The paper was founded in 1928.
Language (s): English
Ad Rate: Full Page Mono 60.50
Currency: United States Dollars
COMMUNITY NEWSPAPER

St. Louis Chinese American News 281580
Editorial: 8041 Olive Blvd, Saint Louis, Missouri 63130-2022 **Tel:** 1 314 432-3858
Email: editor@scanews.com **Web site:** http://www.scanews.com
Freq: Thu; **Circ:** 6000 Not Audited
Publisher: Sandy Psai; **Editor:** Tracy Wang; **Advertising Sales Manager:** May Wu
Profile: St. Louis Chinese American News is a weekly bilingual newspaper serving the greater St. Louis area since 1990. The paper is free at newstands but subscriptions are also available. The paper is 28 to 32 pages and in color. The St. Louis Chinese American News Yellow Pages are put out by the paper annually. St. Louis Community Information Network said "SCANews.com is an invaluable resource for the Chinese American community in St. Louis."
Language (s): Chinese
Ad Rate: Full Page Mono 7.00
Currency: United States Dollars
COMMUNITY NEWSPAPER

The St. Louis Evening Whirl 19847
Owner: Thomas Publishing Co. Inc.
Editorial: 4244 McPherson Ave, Saint Louis, Missouri 63108-2908 **Tel:** 1 678 778-2616
Email: contact@thewhirlonline.com **Web site:** http://www.thewhirlonline.com
Freq: Mon; **Circ:** 52500 Not Audited
Publisher: Barry Thomas
Profile: The St. Louis Evening Whirl is written for residents of Saint Louis, Jefferson and Saint Charles counties, MO, as well as Saint Clair, Madison and Bond counties, IL, and focuses heavily on crime in the area.
Language (s): English
Ad Rate: Full Page Mono 31.75
Currency: United States Dollars
COMMUNITY NEWSPAPER

St. Louis Jewish Light 21931
Owner: St. Louis Jewish Light
Editorial: 6 Millstone Campus Dr Ste 3010, Saint Louis, Missouri 63146-6603 **Tel:** 1 314 743-3660
Email: news@thejewishlight.com **Web site:** http://www.stljewishlight.com
Freq: Wed; **Circ:** 12000 Not Audited
Editor: Ellen Futterman; **Publisher:** Larry Levin; **Advertising Sales Manager:** Julie Schack
Profile: St. Louis Jewish Light is published for Jewish residents of St. Louis. The paper covers local news, community events and announcements.
Language (s): English
Ad Rate: Full Page Mono 45.00
Currency: United States Dollars
COMMUNITY NEWSPAPER

St. Louis Metro Sentinel Journal 864583
Owner: Metro Publishing Group, Inc.
Editorial: 2002 Saint Louis Ave, Saint Louis, Missouri 63106-2415 **Tel:** 1 314 531-2101
Email: metrosentinel@sbcglobal.net **Web site:** http://www.metrosentinel.net/
Freq: Weekly
Editor & Publisher: Michael Williams
Profile: St. Louis Metro Sentinel Journal is a weekly community newspaper serving the St. Louis African-American community with relevant news and editorials.
Language (s): English
COMMUNITY NEWSPAPER

St. Louis Review 21889
Editorial: 20 Archbishop May Dr, Saint Louis, Missouri 63119 **Tel:** 1 314 792-7500
Web site: http://www.stlouisreview.com
Freq: Fri; **Circ:** 86000 Not Audited
Publisher: Robert Hermann; **Circulation Manager:** Theresa Orozco
Profile: St. Louis Review is a newspaper published by the Archdiocese of St. Louis and should be only sent appropriate material. The publication is not generally open to receiving PR materials, as they are a niche publication strictly covering the Catholic Church in St. Louis.
Language (s): English
Ad Rate: Full Page Mono 25.75
Currency: United States Dollars
COMMUNITY NEWSPAPER

St. Martinville Teche News 29471
Owner: Louisiana State Newspapers
Editorial: 214 N Main St, Saint Martinville, Louisiana 70582-4028 **Tel:** 1 337 394-6232
Web site: http://www.techetoday.com
Freq: Wed; **Circ:** 5400 Not Audited
Advertising Sales Manager: Kristy Bourque; **Publisher & Editor:** Ken Grissom
Profile: The Teche News was founded in 1886 by Albert Bienvenu and George Eastin. It was then known as the Weekly Messenger, and the printer was Albert's 12-year-old brother, Laizaire E. Bienvenu. Laizaire took over in 1912, and was succeeded by his son, Marcel "Blackie" Bienvenu, in 1935, and Blackie's son, Henri Clay Bienvenu, took over the reins in 1982. Henri still serves as editor-publisher emeritus, helping to preserve the continuity of three generations. The newspaper's name was changed to Teche News in 1948. Published on Wednesdays, it serves the entire parish of St. Martin, providing in-depth local news and sports coverage, public notices and affordable advertising reaching St. Martin consumers.No general email provided.
Language (s): English
Ad Rate: Full Page Mono 7.00
Currency: United States Dollars
COMMUNITY NEWSPAPER

St. Paul Publishing Co. 25358
Editorial: 1643 Robert St S, #60B, West St. Paul, Minnesota 55118-3903 **Tel:** 1 651 457-1177
Email: sppc@stpaulpublishing.com **Web site:** http://www.stpaulpublishing.com
Circ: 37250
Advertising Sales Manager: John Ahlstrom; **Publisher & Editor:** Tim Spitzack
Profile: St. Paul Publishing Co. is a local newspaper providing news to the community of St. Paul, MN.
Language (s): English
Ad Rate: Full Page Mono 70.92
Currency: United States Dollars
COMMUNITY NEWSPAPER

St. Tammany Farmer 19402
Owner: Courtney (Karen)
Editorial: 321 N New Hampshire St, Covington, Louisiana 70433-2805 **Tel:** 1 985 892-2323
Email: news@sttammanyfarmer.net **Web site:** http://www.theadvocate.com/new_orleans/news/communities/st_tammany
Freq: Thu; **Circ:** 5000 Not Audited
Publisher: Karen Goodwyn Courtney; **Advertising Sales Manager:** Brenda Willis
Profile: St. Tammany Farmer is written for residents of Covington, LA. It covers local news, sports and community events. Deadlines for the publication are at noon CT on Tuesdays before issue date.
Language (s): English
Ad Rate: Full Page Mono 6.00
Currency: United States Dollars
COMMUNITY NEWSPAPER

Staats-Zeitung Newspapers 533683
Tel: 1 941 926-1426
Circ: 34000 Not Audited
Advertising Sales Manager: Margita Baldeweg; **Publisher & Editor:** Jes Rau
Language (s): English
COMMUNITY NEWSPAPER

The Standard 608364
Owner: Warrick Publishing
Editorial: 204 W Locust St, Boonville, Indiana 47601-1522 **Tel:** 1 812 897-2330
Email: gwneal@aol.com **Web site:** http://warricknews.com
Freq: Thu
Profile: Boonville Standard is a newspaper in Boonville, Indiana, USA covering local news, sports, business, jobs, and community events. The Boonville Standard began publication in 1873.
Language (s): English
COMMUNITY NEWSPAPER

The Standard Banner 20733
Owner: Jefferson County Standard Publishing Co., Inc.
Editorial: 122 W Old Andrew Johnson Hwy, Jefferson City, Tennessee 37760-1945 **Tel:** 1 865 475-2081
Email: news@standardbanner.com **Web site:** http://www.standardbanner.com
Freq: Thu; **Circ:** 63420 Not Audited
Advertising Sales Manager: Shane Cook
Profile: Standard-Banner is a local community newspaper for the residents of Jefferson City, TN and the surrounding communities.
Language (s): English
Ad Rate: Full Page Mono 7.90
Currency: United States Dollars
COMMUNITY NEWSPAPER

Standard Journal 232103
Owner: Pioneer Newspapers
Editorial: 23 S 1st E, Rexburg, Idaho 83440-1901 **Tel:** 1 208 356-5441
Email: circulation@uvsj.com **Web site:** http://www.uvsj.com
Freq: Sat; **Circ:** 5000
Publisher: Scott Anderson
Profile: Standard Journal is a local newspaper written for the residents of Rexburg, ID. The publication features local news, sports and events.
Language (s): English
Ad Rate: Full Page Mono 17.70
Ad Rate: Full Page Colour 43.95
Currency: United States Dollars
COMMUNITY NEWSPAPER

The Stanly News and Press 19964
Owner: Stanly County Newspapers, Inc.
Editorial: 237 W North St, Albemarle, North Carolina 28001-3923 **Tel:** 1 704 982-2121
Web site: http://www.thesnaponline.com
Freq: Sun; **Circ:** 9664
Advertising Manager: Tracey Almond; **Publisher:** Sandy Selvy; **News Editor:** Ritchie Starnes
Profile: Stanly News and Press is for residents of Stanly County, NC. It covers local news and events.
Language (s): English
Ad Rate: Full Page Mono 11.55
Currency: United States Dollars
COMMUNITY NEWSPAPER

Stanwood/Camano News 21130
Owner: Pinkham (Dave) & Pinkham (Pam)
Editorial: 9005 271st St NW, Stanwood, Washington 98292 **Tel:** 1 360 629-2155
Email: newsroom@scnews.com **Web site:** http://www.scnews.com
Freq: Tue; **Circ:** 18675 Not Audited
Profile: Stanwood/Camano News is written for the residents of Snohomish and Island Counties, WA. The newspaper covers local news and community events, as well as general news stories of interest to its readership.
Language (s): English
Ad Rate: Full Page Mono 17.80
Currency: United States Dollars
COMMUNITY NEWSPAPER

The Star 19604
Owner: Northstar Media
Editorial: 930 Cleveland St S, Cambridge, Minnesota 55008-1785 **Tel:** 1 763 689-1181
Email: editor@countystar.com **Web site:** http://www.isantichisagocountystar.com
Freq: Sat; **Circ:** 16000 Not Audited
Advertising Sales Manager: Eric Champion; **Publisher:** Keith Hansen; **Editor:** Linda Noyce
Profile: Star is a local community newspaper published for the residents of Cambridge, MN. and the surrounding communities.
Language (s): English
Ad Rate: Full Page Mono 10.50
Currency: United States Dollars
COMMUNITY NEWSPAPER

The Star 21682
Owner: Tri County Publishing, Inc.
Editorial: 105 S Main St, El Dorado Springs, Missouri 64744-1123 **Tel:** 1 417 876-2500
Email: thestar@socket.net
Freq: Weekly; **Circ:** 8000 Not Audited
Publisher: Pat Brownlee
Profile: The Star is published weekly for the residents of in El Dorado Springs, MO and surrounding areas. The newspaper covers local news, sports and community events.
Language (s): English
Ad Rate: Full Page Mono 5.50
Currency: United States Dollars
COMMUNITY NEWSPAPER

The Star News 21195
Owner: Central Wisconsin Publications, Inc.
Editorial: 116 Wisconsin Ave, Medford, Wisconsin 54451-1749 **Tel:** 1 715 748-2626
Email: starnews@centralwinews.com **Web site:** http://www.centralwinews.com/star-news
Freq: Thu; **Circ:** 6200 Not Audited
Publisher: Carol O'Leary; **Advertising Sales Manager:** Kelly Schmidt; **Editor:** Brian Wilson
Profile: The Star News covers local news, sports and events of interest to residents of Taylor County, WI. Deadlines are on Tuesdays at 5pm CT.
Language (s): English
Ad Rate: Full Page Mono 9.25
Currency: United States Dollars
COMMUNITY NEWSPAPER

Star News 28676
Owner: ECM Publishers, Inc.
Editorial: 506 Freeport Ave NW Ste A, Elk River, Minnesota 55330-4755 **Tel:** 1 763 441-3500
Email: print.elkriver@ecm-inc.com **Web site:** http://erstarnews.com
Freq: Sat; **Circ:** 20600 Not Audited
Publisher: Julian Andersen; **Editor:** Jim Boyle; **Editor:** Bruce Strand
Profile: Star News is a community newspaper published in Elk River, MN. The paper covers local news and events for residents of the town and the surrounding area. Deadlines are Fridays at 10am CT prior to issue date.
Language (s): English

Ad Rate: Full Page Mono 17.00
Currency: United States Dollars
COMMUNITY NEWSPAPER

Star Publishing Group 25063
Owner: Graham Newspapers, Inc.
Editorial: 319 N Burleson Blvd, Burleson, Texas 76028-3907 **Tel:** 1 817 295-0486
Web site: http://www.thestargroup.com
Circ: 15950 Not Audited
Editor: Mike Eskridge; **Editor:** Brian Porter
Profile: Star Publishing Group is a community newspaper publisher servicing the residents of Dallas, as well as Fort Worth and Arlington, TX.
Language (s): English
COMMUNITY NEWSPAPER

The Star-Herald 27298
Owner: Northeast Publishing Co.
Editorial: 40 North St Ste B, Presque Isle, Maine 04769-2269 **Tel:** 1 207 768-5431
Email: starherald@nepublish.com **Web site:** http://www.starherald-me.com
Freq: Wed; **Circ:** 5725 Not Audited
Advertising Sales Manager: Scott Galipeau;
Publisher: Richard Warren
Profile: The Star-Herald is a weekly newspaper covering local news in the city of Presque Isle, ME, and the surrounding towns of Fort Fairfield, Washburn, Ashland, Mars Hill, Mapleton, Castle Hill, Chapman, Blaine, Bridgewater, Easton and Westfield.
Language (s): English
Ad Rate: Full Page Mono 16.50
Currency: United States Dollars
COMMUNITY NEWSPAPER

Star-Mercury Publications 24504
Owner: Grimes Publications
Editorial: 3051 Roosevelt Hwy, Manchester, Georgia 31816 **Tel:** 1 706 846-3188
Circ: 11600 Not Audited
Editor: Jim Grimes; **Publisher & Editor:** John Kuykendall; **Circulation Manager:** Elisha Passmore;
Editor: Rob Richardson
Language (s): English
COMMUNITY NEWSPAPER

The Star-News 22959
Owner: San Diego Neighborhood Newspapers, Inc.
Editorial: 296 3rd Ave, Chula Vista, California 91910-2701 **Tel:** 1 619 427-3000
Email: staff@thestarnews.com **Web site:** http://www.thestarnews.com
Freq: Fri; **Circ:** 33750 Not Audited
Editor: Carlos Davalos; **Publisher:** John Moreno
Profile: Star News is a weekly newspaper providing Local News coverage to the residents of Chula Vista, National City, Bonita, East Lake and Otay Ranch, CA. Coverage includes local news and events, business, sports and social issues.
Language (s): English
Ad Rate: Full Page Mono 20.25
Currency: United States Dollars
COMMUNITY NEWSPAPER

El Starous News 778546
Owner: Observer Newspaper Group
Editorial: 3427 Belgium Ln, San Antonio, Texas 78219-2501 **Tel:** 1 210 212-6397
Email: taylor2039@aol.com
Freq: Weekly
Editor: Waseem Ali
Profile: El Starous News provides Local News coverage to the African-American Community in San Antonio, TX.
Language (s): English
COMMUNITY NEWSPAPER

The Star-Republican 20320
Owner: AIM Media Midwest
Editorial: 761 S Nelson Ave, Wilmington, Ohio 45177-2517 **Tel:** 1 937 382-2574
Email: wnjinfo@civitasmedia.com **Web site:** http://www.wnewsj.com
Freq: Mon; **Circ:** 16000 Not Audited
Editor: Laura Abernathy; **Circulation Manager:** Dawn Gunkel
Profile: The Star-Republican is a local newspaper serving Clinton County, OH, including Blanchester and Wilmington, OH and covering local news, sports, commentary and entertainment.
Language (s): English
Ad Rate: Full Page Mono 17.00
Currency: United States Dollars
COMMUNITY NEWSPAPER

Star-Tribune 28650
Owner: Womack Newspapers Inc.
Editorial: 28 S Main St, Chatham, Virginia 24531-5436 **Tel:** 1 434 432-2791
Email: news@chathamstartribune.com **Web site:** http://www.chathamstartribune.com
Freq: Wed; **Circ:** 9100 Not Audited
Advertising Sales Manager: Alisa Davis; **Publisher:** Chad Harrison; **Editor:** Susan Light
Profile: Star-Tribune is a weekly paper serving the residents of Pittsylvania County, VA.
Language (s): English
Ad Rate: Full Page Mono 10.30
Currency: United States Dollars
COMMUNITY NEWSPAPER

State Gazette 75069
Owner: Rust Communications
Editorial: 294 US Highway 51 Byp N, Dyersburg, Tennessee 38024-3659 **Tel:** 1 731 287-1555
Email: editor@stategazette.com **Web site:** http://www.stategazette.com
Freq: Fri; **Circ:** 6663 Not Audited
Advertising Sales Manager: Charles Dawson;
Editor: Mike Smith
Profile: State Gazette is a weekly newspaper for the residents of Dyersburg, TN. The paper reports on local news and events in the community.
Language (s): English
Ad Rate: Full Page Mono 11.25
Currency: United States Dollars
COMMUNITY NEWSPAPER

The State Port Pilot 20009
Owner: State Port Pilot, Inc. (The)
Editorial: 114 E Moore St, Southport, North Carolina 28461-3926 **Tel:** 1 910 457-4568
Email: pilot@stateportpilot.com **Web site:** http://www.stateportpilot.com
Freq: Wed; **Circ:** 8800 Not Audited
Editor: Ed Harper; **Circulation Manager:** Jan Keyes;
Advertising Sales Manager: Carol Magnani
Profile: The State Port Pilot is a weekly newspaper serving Southeastern Brunswick County, NC. It covers local news and special events, business, social issues, and weather.
Language (s): English
Ad Rate: Full Page Mono 10.00
Currency: United States Dollars
COMMUNITY NEWSPAPER

Statesman-Examiner 21101
Owner: Horizon Publications
Editorial: 220 S Main St, Colville, Washington 99114-2408 **Tel:** 1 509 684-4567
Web site: http://www.statesmanexaminer.com
Freq: Wed; **Circ:** 6000 Not Audited
Advertising Sales Manager: Dennis Branstetter;
Circulation Manager: Denise Lee
Profile: Statesman-Examiner's editorial mission is to provide the residents of Eastern Washington with current local news and information on a weekly basis. Deadlines for the publication are Friday at 5pm PT.
Language (s): English
Ad Rate: Full Page Mono 12.90
Currency: United States Dollars
COMMUNITY NEWSPAPER

Stephens Media - Cabot 25010
Owner: Stephens Media
Editorial: 903 S Pine St, Cabot, Arkansas 72023
Tel: 1 501 843-3534
Web site: http://www.pulaskinews.net
Circ: 14065 Not Audited
Advertising Manager: Kathy Lenzen; **Editor:** Jeremy Peppas; **Editor:** Greg Rayburn
Language (s): English
COMMUNITY NEWSPAPER

Stephens Media Group-Van Alstyne 359695
Owner: Stephens Media
Editorial: 209 N Dallas St, Van Alstyne, Texas 75495
Tel: 1 903 482-5253
Circ: 17500 Not Audited
Editor: Jeremy Corley; **Advertising Sales Manager:** Peggy Schoggin
Language (s): English
COMMUNITY NEWSPAPER

The Steuben Courier-Advocate 22673
Owner: GateHouse Media Inc.
Editorial: 10 W Steuben St, Bath, New York 14810-1512 **Tel:** 1 607 776-2121
Email: news@steubencourier.com **Web site:** http://www.steubencourier.com
Freq: Sun; **Circ:** 10800 Not Audited
Profile: Steuben Courier-Advocate is written for the residents of Steuben County, NY.
Language (s): English
Ad Rate: Full Page Mono 7.20
Currency: United States Dollars
COMMUNITY NEWSPAPER

Steubenville Register 257456
Owner: Roman Catholic Diocese of Steubenville
Editorial: 422 Washington St, Steubenville, Ohio 43952-2159 **Tel:** 1 740 282-3631
Email: register@diosteub.org **Web site:** http://www.diosteub.org
Freq: Bi-Weekly; **Circ:** 15000 Not Audited
Editor: Pat DeFrancis; **Publisher:** Jeffrey Monforton;
Advertising Sales Manager: Janice Ward
Profile: Steubenville Register's editorial mission is to inform about the Catholic church locally and internationally. The publication is written for the Catholic residents in 13 counties in Ohio.
Language (s): English
Ad Rate: Full Page Mono 7.25
Currency: United States Dollars
COMMUNITY NEWSPAPER

Stevens County Times 622691
Owner: Forum Communications, Co.
Editorial: 607 Pacific Ave, Morris, Minnesota 56267-1942 **Tel:** 1 320 589-2525
Email: news@stevenscountytimes.com **Web site:** http://www.stevenscountytimes.com
Publisher: Sue Dieter; **Editor:** Kim Ukura
Profile: The Stevens County Times provides regional community news for Stevens County in Minnesota. Combining the Morris Sun Tribune and Hancock Record, Stevens County Times covers Community News, High School and Local Sports, Local Events and Affairs.
Language (s): English
COMMUNITY NEWSPAPER

The Stewart-Houston Times 24342
Owner: Gannett Co., Inc.
Editorial: 310 Spring St, Dover, Tennessee 37058-3233 **Tel:** 1 931 232-5421
Web site: http://www.theleafchronicle.com/news/stewart-houston-times/
Freq: Tue; **Circ:** 5600 Not Audited
Editor: Mark Hicks
Profile: Stewart-Houston Times is written for the residents of Stewart and Houston counties, TN.
Language (s): English
Ad Rate: Full Page Mono 8.35
Currency: United States Dollars
COMMUNITY NEWSPAPER

Stillwater Gazette 740759
Owner: ECM Publishers, Inc.
Editorial: 1931 Curve Crest Blvd W, Stillwater, Minnesota 55082-6063 **Tel:** 1 651 439-3130
Web site: http://www.stillwatergazette.com
Freq: 3 Times/Week; **Circ:** 22819
Publisher: Mark Berriman
Profile: The Stillwater Gazette is a group of local newspapers that provides Local News coverage of the St. Croix Valley region. They do not accept any press info that is not related to Minnesota.
Language (s): English
COMMUNITY NEWSPAPER

Stillwater Valley Advertiser 20331
Owner: Arens Publications
Editorial: 395 S High St, Covington, Ohio 45318-1121 **Tel:** 1 937 473-2028
Web site: http://www.arenspub.com
Freq: Wed; **Circ:** 10378 Not Audited
Editor: Jean Devlin; **Publisher:** Gary Godfrey;
Advertising Sales Manager: Don Selanders
Profile: Stillwater Valley Advertiser is written for residents of Covington, OH.
Language (s): English
Ad Rate: Full Page Mono 11.62
Currency: United States Dollars
COMMUNITY NEWSPAPER

Stilwell Democrat-Journal 20461
Owner: Community Newspaper Holdings, Inc.
Editorial: 118 N 2nd St, Stilwell, Oklahoma 74960-3028 **Tel:** 1 918 696-2228
Email: stilwelldj@windstream.net
Freq: Weekly; **Circ:** 5000 Not Audited
Advertising Sales Manager: Kristal Diver;
Publisher: Gary Jackson; **Editor:** Keith Neale
Profile: Stilwell Democrat-Journal is a local newspaper written for the residents of Stilwell, OK. It provides the local community with information on news, events, sports and weather. Deadlines are Mondays at 4pm CT.
Language (s): English
Ad Rate: Full Page Mono 7.15
Ad Rate: Full Page Colour 623.25
Currency: United States Dollars
COMMUNITY NEWSPAPER

The Stokes News & The Weekly Independent 83257
Owner: Civitas Media, LLC
Editorial: 1072 N Main St, Walnut Cove, North Carolina 27052-9312 **Tel:** 1 336 591-8191
Web site: http://www.thestokesnews.com
Freq: Thu; **Circ:** 6920 Not Audited
Editor: Shannon Fenner
Language (s): English
COMMUNITY NEWSPAPER

Stonebridge Press Newspapers 24855
Owner: Stonebridge Press
Editorial: 25 Elm St, Southbridge, Massachusetts 01550-2605 **Tel:** 1 508 764-4325
Web site: http://www.theheartofmassachusetts.com/
Circ: 49320 Not Audited
Advertising Sales Manager: Jean Ashton;
Publisher: Frank Chilinski; **Editor:** Adam Minor
Profile: Stonebridge Press Newspapers is a weekly community newspaper publisher serving the residents of Spencer, Webster, Auburn, Sturbridge, Charlton and Southbridge, MA.
Language (s): English
COMMUNITY NEWSPAPER

Stowe Reporter Group 445779
Owner: Stowe Reporter LLC
Editorial: 49 School St, Stowe, Vermont 05672-4447
Tel: 1 802 253-2101
Email: news@stowereporter.com **Web site:** http://www.stowetoday.com
Freq: Weekly; **Circ:** 9300 Not Audited
Advertising Sales Manager: Greg Popa
Profile: The Stowe Reporter Group is comprised of the Stowe Reporter, Waterbury Record, and News & Citizen.
Language (s): English
COMMUNITY NEWSPAPER

The Stranger 22194
Owner: Index Publishing LLC
Editorial: 1535 11th Ave Fl 3, Seattle, Washington 98122-3933 **Tel:** 1 206 323-7101
Email: editor@thestranger.com **Web site:** http://www.thestranger.com
Freq: Thu; **Circ:** 58587 Not Audited
Editor: Christopher Frizzelle; **Publisher:** Tim Keck;
Circulation Manager: Kevin Shurtluff
Profile: Stranger is a tabloid weekly publication written for the residents of Seattle. The newspaper covers news on recent events.
Language (s): English
Ad Rate: Full Page Mono 25.60
Currency: United States Dollars
COMMUNITY NEWSPAPER

Straus News 24653
Owner: Straus (Jeanne)
Editorial: 20 West Ave, Chester, New York 10918-1032 **Tel:** 1 845 469-9000
Email: nyoffice@strausnews.com **Web site:** http://www.strausnews.com
Circ: 35943 Not Audited
Publisher: Jeanne Straus
Profile: Straus News is a community newspaper publisher headquartered in Chester, NY.
Language (s): English
COMMUNITY NEWSPAPER

Straus News 25290
Editorial: 1A Main St Ste 9, Sparta, New Jersey 07871-1909 **Tel:** 1 973 300-0890
Email: njoffice@strausnews.com **Web site:** http://www.strausnews.com
Circ: 50723 Not Audited
Publisher: Jeanne Straus
Language (s): English
COMMUNITY NEWSPAPER

Straus News Manhattan 25191
Owner: Straus News
Editorial: 33 7th Ave, New York, New York 10011-6602 **Tel:** 1 212 868-0190
Email: nyoffice@strausnews.com **Web site:** http://nypress.com
Freq: Weekly; **Circ:** 205200 Not Audited
Circulation Manager: Jessica Reyes
Language (s): English
COMMUNITY NEWSPAPER

Street Sense 155785
Editorial: 1317 G St NW, Washington, District Of Columbia 20005-3102 **Tel:** 1 202 347-2006
Email: info@streetsense.org **Web site:** http://www.streetsense.org
Freq: Bi-Weekly; **Circ:** 12000 Not Audited
Profile: Street Sense is published bi-weekly on Wednesday for the residents of Washington, D.C. The newspaper is written and published by homeless men and women as part of a mission to help them earn income. It explores issues related to poverty, homelessness and other social problems.
Language (s): English
Ad Rate: Full Page Mono 25.00
Currency: United States Dollars
COMMUNITY NEWSPAPER

StreetWise 22578
Owner: Streetwise, Inc.
Editorial: 4454 N Broadway St Suite 350, Chicago, Illinois 60640-5660 **Tel:** 1 773 334-6600
Email: pressreleases@streetwise.org **Web site:** http://www.streetwise.org
Freq: Wed; **Circ:** 13000 Not Audited
Editor: Suzanne Hanney; **Publisher:** Jim LoBianco
Profile: StreetWise was founded to meet a vitally important area of need among the homeless of Chicago. Through its operation of a street newspaper, the organization seeks to empower men and women who are homeless, or at risk of becoming so, as they work toward gainful employment. The newspaper provides news and information for the Chicago area.
Language (s): English
Ad Rate: Full Page Mono 9.56
Currency: United States Dollars
COMMUNITY NEWSPAPER

Stumpf Publishing 24606
Editorial: 924 Whitewater Ave, Saint Charles, Minnesota 55972-1131 **Tel:** 1 507 932-3663
Circ: 6200 Not Audited
Editor: Laura Berndt
Language (s): English
COMMUNITY NEWSPAPER

Style Weekly 21988
Owner: Landmark Media Enterprises, LLC
Editorial: 24 E 3rd St, Richmond, Virginia 23224-4246 **Tel:** 1 804 358-0825
Email: info@styleweekly.com **Web site:** http://www.styleweekly.com
Freq: Wed; **Circ:** 35100 Not Audited
Publisher: Lori Collier Waran
Profile: Style Weekly is a weekly newspaper that provides news and information with a slant toward recreation for the Richmond, VA area. The papers covers local news, sports, entertainment and events.
Language (s): English
Ad Rate: Full Page Mono 27.62
Currency: United States Dollars
COMMUNITY NEWSPAPER

Suburban Flint Newspaper Group 25079
Owner: Newhouse Newspapers
Editorial: 200 E 1st St, Flint, Michigan 48502
Tel: 1 810 766-6100
Email: fj@flintjournal.com **Web site:** http://www.flintjournal.com

Circ: 93645 Not Audited
Language (s): English
COMMUNITY NEWSPAPER

Suburban Gazette 20572
Owner: Schramm (Virginia DiNardo)
Editorial: 421 Locust St, McKees Rocks, Pennsylvania 15136-3509 **Tel:** 1 412 331-2645
Email: gazette1892@verizon.net **Web site:** http://www.gazette1892.com
Freq: Wed; **Circ:** 8300 Not Audited
Publisher: Virginia Schramm
Profile: Suburban Gazette is community newspaper written for residents of McKees Rocks, PA. The publication provides coverage of local news and events.
Language (s): English
Ad Rate: Full Page Mono 15.00
Currency: United States Dollars
COMMUNITY NEWSPAPER

Suburban Journals - Madison County 25325
Owner: Lee Enterprises, Inc.
Editorial: 2 Eastport Executive Drive, Collinsville, Illinois 62234 **Tel:** 1 618 344-0264
Email: metroeastnews@yourjournal.com **Web site:** http://www.stltoday.com/suburban-journals/illinois
Circ: 55105 Not Audited
Language (s): English
COMMUNITY NEWSPAPER

Suburban Journals - St. Charles County 24839
Owner: Lee Enterprises, Inc.
Editorial: 14522 S Outer 40 Rd, Town and Country, Missouri 63017-5737 **Tel:** 1 314 821-1110
Email: goodnews@yourjournal.com **Web site:** http://www.stltoday.com/suburban-journals
Circ: 79988 Not Audited
Advertising Sales Manager: Andrea Griffith
Language (s): English
COMMUNITY NEWSPAPER

Suburban News 24975
Owner: Midlands Newspapers, Inc.
Editorial: 604 Fort Crook Rd N, Bellevue, Nebraska 68005-4557 **Tel:** 1 402 773-7300
Web site: http://www.omaha.com
Circ: 8450
Publisher: Shon Barenklau; **Advertising Manager:** Lowell Miller; **Circulation Manager:** Melissa Vanek
Language (s): English
COMMUNITY NEWSPAPER

Suburban Newspapers, Inc. 24705
Owner: Underwood (Robert)
Editorial: 7820 Wyatt Dr, Fort Worth, Texas 76108-2533 **Tel:** 1 817 246-2473
Email: suburbannews@sbcglobal.net
Freq: Thu; **Circ:** 30000 Not Audited
Editor: Lori Ball; **Publisher:** Bo Underwood
Profile: Suburban Newspapers, Inc. is a local newspaper in Fort Worth, TX.
Language (s): English
Ad Rate: Full Page Mono 13.50
Currency: United States Dollars
COMMUNITY NEWSPAPER

Suburban Trends 140015
Owner: Gannett Co., Inc./North Jersey Media Group
Editorial: 632 Pompton Ave, Cedar Grove, New Jersey 07009-1736 **Tel:** 1 973 283-5600
Email: suburbantrends@northjersey.com **Web site:** http://www.northjersey.com
Circ: 60757 Not Audited
Editor: Jai Agnish; **Editor:** Matt Fagan; **Editor:** Donna Rolando
Profile: Suburban Trends is a regional newspaper that covers regional news, local news, breaking news, local events in Bloomingdale, Butler, Kinnelon, Lincoln Park, Pequannock, Pompton Lakes, Ringwood, Riverdale, Wanaque and West Milford in New Jersey.
Language (s): English
COMMUNITY NEWSPAPER

Suburban Washington Newspapers 63807
Owner: Northern Virginia Media
Editorial: 131 E Broad St Ste 202, Falls Church, Virginia 22046-4520 **Tel:** 1 703 738-2520
Web site: http://www.insidenova.com
Freq: Weekly; **Circ:** 67949 Not Audited
Editor: Scott McCaffrey
Language (s): English
COMMUNITY NEWSPAPER

Sullivan County Democrat 20250
Owner: Catskill-Delaware Publications Inc.
Editorial: 5 Lower Main St, Callicoon, New York 12723-5000 **Tel:** 1 845 887-5200
Email: info@scdemocratonline.com **Web site:** http://www.sc-democrat.com
Freq: 2 Times/Week; **Circ:** 7000 Not Audited
Circulation Manager: Sandy Schrader; **Publisher:** Fred Stabbert
Profile: Sullivan County Democrat is a local newspaper that provides news and information for the communities of Sullivan County, NY. Regular features include local news, community events and sports.
Language (s): English
Ad Rate: Full Page Mono 14.05
Currency: United States Dollars
COMMUNITY NEWSPAPER

Sullivan Independent News 21401
Owner: Manion, (Kathleen)
Editorial: 411 Scottsdale Dr, Sullivan, Missouri 63080-1307 **Tel:** 1 573 468-6511
Email: nuz4u@fidnet.com **Web site:** http://www.mysullivannews.com
Freq: Wed; **Circ:** 6000 Not Audited
Publisher: Kathleen Abell-Manion; **Editor:** Jim Bartle; **Advertising Sales Manager:** Mark Hilse
Profile: Sullivan Independent News provides news and information for the Sullivan, MO area. Deadlines are at noon CT on Saturdays before the issue date.
Language (s): English
Ad Rate: Full Page Mono 6.00
Currency: United States Dollars
COMMUNITY NEWSPAPER

The Sullivan Review 20557
Owner: Shoemaker (John)
Editorial: 211 Water St., Dushore, Pennsylvania 18614 **Tel:** 1 570 928-8403
Email: news@thesullivanreview.com **Web site:** http://www.thesullivanreview.com
Freq: Wed; **Circ:** 7000 Not Audited
Publisher: John Shoemaker; **Editor:** T.W. Shoemaker
Profile: Sullivan Review provides news and information for the Dushore, PA area. Published on Thursday, the lead time is 12:00 p.m. CT Monday before the issue date.
Language (s): English
Ad Rate: Full Page Mono 7.00
Currency: United States Dollars
COMMUNITY NEWSPAPER

The Summerville News 18838
Owner: Espy Publishing Company Inc.
Editorial: 20 Wildlife Lake Rd, Summerville, Georgia 30747-5300 **Tel:** 1 706 857-2494
Email: admin@thesummervillenews.com **Web site:** http://www.thesummervillenews.com
Freq: Thu; **Circ:** 7200 Not Audited
Publisher & Editor: Winston Espy
Profile: The Summerville News is a local newspaper written for the residents Summerville, GA. The paper covers local news, sports and business. Deadlines are Tuesdays at 5pm ET.
Language (s): English
Ad Rate: Full Page Mono 3.50
Currency: United States Dollars
COMMUNITY NEWSPAPER

The Sumter County Record-Journal 21343
Editorial: 210 S Washington, Livingston, Alabama 35470 **Tel:** 1 205 652-6100
Email: scrjmedia@yahoo.com **Web site:** http://www.recordjournal.net
Freq: Thu; **Circ:** 5125 Not Audited
Community News Editor: Kasey DeCastra; **Publisher & Editor:** Tommy McGraw; **Advertising Sales Manager:** Herman Ward
Profile: The Sumter County Record-Journal is written for the residents of Sumter County, AL. It covers news and information.
Language (s): English
Ad Rate: Full Page Mono 6.75
Currency: United States Dollars
COMMUNITY NEWSPAPER

The Sun 20565
Owner: The Sun Ink, Corp.
Editorial: 40 W Main St Ste 102, Hummelstown, Pennsylvania 17036-1528 **Tel:** 1 717 566-3251
Email: news@thesunontheweb.com **Web site:** http://www.thesunontheweb.com
Freq: Thu; **Circ:** 7642 Not Audited
Editor: David Buffington; **Publisher:** Deb Buffington; **Circulation Manager:** Lois Musser; **Advertising Manager:** Amber Topper
Profile: The Sun is a local weekly newspaper for the residents of Hummelstown, PA. The paper covers local news, sports, business and events.
Language (s): English
Ad Rate: Full Page Mono 10.00
Currency: United States Dollars
COMMUNITY NEWSPAPER

Sun Advocate 24267
Owner: Brehm Communications, Inc.
Editorial: 845 E Main St, Price, Utah 84501-2708 **Tel:** 1 435 637-0732
Email: editor@sunad.com **Web site:** http://www.sunad.com
Freq: Thu; **Circ:** 5300 Not Audited
Circulation Manager: Darla Lee; **Editor:** C.J. McManus
Profile: Sun Advocate provides news and information for Carbon County, UT.
Language (s): English
Ad Rate: Full Page Mono 8.20
Currency: United States Dollars
COMMUNITY NEWSPAPER

Sun Coast Media Newspapers 25024
Owner: Sun Coast Media Group Inc.
Editorial: 190 S Florida Ave, Bartow, Florida 33830-4701 **Tel:** 1 863 533-4183
Email: news@polkcountydemocrat.com **Web site:** http://www.polkcountydemocrat.com
Circ: 16651 Not Audited
Publisher: Jim Gouvellis; **Editor:** Jeff Roslow
Language (s): English
COMMUNITY NEWSPAPER

Sun Current Newspapers 24760
Owner: ECM Publishers, Inc.
Editorial: 10917 Valley View Rd, Eden Prairie, Minnesota 55344-3730 **Tel:** 1 952 829-0797
Email: keith.anderson@ecm-inc.com **Web site:** http://current.mnsun.com
Circ: 54253 Not Audited
Profile: The Sun Current Central group encompasses coverage from the Minnesota cities of Bloomington, Richfield, Edina and Eden Prairie.
Language (s): English
COMMUNITY NEWSPAPER

The Sun Newspapers 22155
Owner: Community Media Corporation
Editorial: 216 Main St, Seal Beach, California 90740-6318 **Tel:** 1 562 430-7555
Email: receptionist@sunnews.org **Web site:** http://www.sunnews.org
Freq: Thu; **Circ:** 32000 Not Audited
Publisher: Lindsay Evans; **Editor:** Donna Leedy
Profile: The Sun Newspapers is a local paper serving the residents and tourists of the communities of Seal Beach, Huntington Harbour, Rossmoor/Los Alamitos and Sunset Beach, CA. It contains local news, entertainment, events, sports and lifestyle features. It also provides comprehensive event listings and information on travel services.
Language (s): English
Ad Rate: Full Page Mono 20.80
Currency: United States Dollars
COMMUNITY NEWSPAPER

The Sun Patriot Newspapers 62343
Owner: ECM Publishers, Inc.
Editorial: 8 S Elm St, Waconia, Minnesota 55387-1412 **Tel:** 1 952 442-4414
Web site: http://sunpatriot.com
Circ: 14191
Publisher: Julian Andersen
Profile: The Sun Patriot Newspapers is a community newspaper publisher servicing the residents Waconia, Minneapolis and St. Paul, MN.
Language (s): English
COMMUNITY NEWSPAPER

Sun Post News 73190
Owner: Southern California News Group/Digital First Media
Editorial: 625 N Grand Ave, Santa Ana, California 92701-4347 **Tel:** 1 949 492-5127
Email: sunpostnews@ocregister.com **Web site:** http://www.ocregister.com/sections/city-pages/sanclemente/
Freq: Fri; **Circ:** 10667 Not Audited
Profile: Sun Post News is a newspaper serving residents of San Clemente, CA, that is published three times per week. This paper is a part of the Southern California News Group, a subsidiary of Digital First Media.
Language (s): English
Ad Rate: Full Page Mono 16.14
Ad Rate: Full Page Colour 197.00
Currency: United States Dollars
COMMUNITY NEWSPAPER

Sun Press & News Publications 24605
Owner: Press & News Publications
Editorial: 33 2nd St NE, Osseo, Minnesota 55369-1252 **Tel:** 1 763 425-3323
Email: sunpressnews@ecm-inc.com **Web site:** http://www.pressnews.com
Circ: 36320 Not Audited
Profile: Sun Press & News Publications is a local newspaper for the community of Osseo, MN.
Language (s): English
COMMUNITY NEWSPAPER

Sun Publishing Company 364686
Owner: Record-Journal Publishing Company
Editorial: 99 Mechanic St, Pawcatuck, Connecticut 06379-2132 **Tel:** 1 401 348-1000
Email: advertising@thewesterlysun.com **Web site:** http://www.thewesterlysun.com
Circ: 31729 Not Audited
Publisher: Elliot White
Language (s): English
COMMUNITY NEWSPAPER

Sun Thisweek Newspapers 397743
Owner: ECM Publishers, Inc.
Editorial: 15322 Galaxie Ave Ste 219, Apple Valley, Minnesota 55124-3150 **Tel:** 1 952 846-2011
Web site: http://www.sunthisweek.com
Circ: 66346 Not Audited
Editor: Laura Adelmann; **Publisher:** Julian Andersen; **Editor:** John Gessner; **Advertising Manager:** Mike Jetchick; **Editor:** Andrew Miller
Profile: Sun ThisWeek Newspapers, of Apple Valley, MN, provide news, information, entertainment, sports and events to residents of the following communities: Burnsville, Apple Valley, Farmington, Rosemont, Lakeville, and Dakota County.
Language (s): English
COMMUNITY NEWSPAPER

Sun Times 19555
Owner: Nester (Robert)
Editorial: 9573 Dexter Pinckney Rd, Pinckney, Michigan 48169-9667 **Tel:** 1 734 648-0837
Email: info@thesuntimesnews.com **Web site:** http://www.thesuntimesnews.com
Freq: Tue; **Circ:** 23727 Not Audited
Publisher: Robert Nester; **Editor:** Wendy Wood
Profile: Sun Times is a weekly publication that provides news and information to the residents of Chelsea, Dexter, Pinckney, Stockbridge, Waterloo, Unadilla, Lyndon, Sylvan, White Oak, Bunker Hill and surrounding areas. Content includes hyperlocal community news, events, editorials and sports.
Language (s): English
Ad Rate: Full Page Mono 10.00
Currency: United States Dollars
COMMUNITY NEWSPAPER

Sunbury News 20367
Owner: AIM Media Midwest
Editorial: 40 N Sandusky St Ste 202, Delaware, Ohio 43015-1973 **Tel:** 1 740 363-1161
Email: snnews@sunburynews.com **Web site:** http://www.sunburynews.com
Freq: Thu; **Circ:** 10000 Not Audited
Profile: Sunbury News is a local weekly newspaper written for residents of the Big Walnut school district in Delaware, OH. The newspaper covers local news, sports and events. Deadlines are on Mondays at noon ET.
Language (s): English
Ad Rate: Full Page Mono 5.20
Currency: United States Dollars
COMMUNITY NEWSPAPER

Suncoast News - New Port Richey 25029
Owner: Media General Inc.
Editorial: 8069 Regency Park Boulevard, Port Richey, Florida 34668 **Tel:** 1 727 815-1000
Web site: http://www.suncoastnews.com
Freq: 2 Times/Week; **Circ:** 147245 Not Audited
Editor: Robert Hibbs; **Community News Editor:** Carl Orth
Profile: Suncoast News is published twice a week for the residents of west Pasco County, FL. The newspaper covers local news, sports, entertainment and community events. Deadlines for the publication vary.
Language (s): English
COMMUNITY NEWSPAPER

The Suncook Valley Sun 22277
Owner: Morse (Arthur)
Editorial: 21 Broadway St, Pittsfield, New Hampshire 03263-3831 **Tel:** 1 603 435-6291
Email: svsun@aol.com **Web site:** http://www.suncookvalleysun.com
Freq: Wed; **Circ:** 9000 Not Audited
Publisher: Arthur Morse
Profile: The Suncook Valley Sun provides news for residents of Pittsfield, NH. Deadlines are on Thursdays at 4:30pm ET.
Language (s): English
Ad Rate: Full Page Mono 11.25
Currency: United States Dollars
COMMUNITY NEWSPAPER

Sunday Dispatch 20590
Owner: Civitas Media
Editorial: 109 New St, Pittston, Pennsylvania 18640-2147 **Tel:** 1 570 655-1418
Email: sd@psdispatch.com **Web site:** http://psdispatch.com
Freq: Sun; **Circ:** 14000
Profile: Sunday Dispatch is a local, weekly newspaper written for residents of Pittston, PA. The publication provides coverage of local news, sports, arts & entertainment and events. Deadlines are at 5pm ET.
Language (s): English
Ad Rate: Full Page Mono 11.27
Currency: United States Dollars
COMMUNITY NEWSPAPER

The Sunday Independent 21385
Owner: Flores (Michael)
Editorial: 1907 W M 21, Owosso, Michigan 48867-9317 **Tel:** 1 989 723-1118
Email: indysales@owossoindependent.com **Web site:** http://www.owossoindependent.com
Freq: 2 Times/Week; **Circ:** 42774 Not Audited
Publisher: Michael Flores; **Advertising Sales Manager:** Kim Lazar; **Circulation Manager:** Chris Rushka
Profile: The Sunday Independent is a community newspaper providing news and information for the Owosso, MI area.
Language (s): English
Ad Rate: Full Page Mono 27.85
Ad Rate: Full Page Colour 28.69
Currency: United States Dollars
COMMUNITY NEWSPAPER

Sunday News 22348
Owner: Lancaster Newspapers, Inc.
Editorial: 8 W King St, Lancaster, Pennsylvania 17603-3824 **Tel:** 1 717 291-8811
Email: sunnews@lnpnews.com **Web site:** http://www.lancasteronline.com/pages/paper/sundaynews
Freq: Sun; **Circ:** 101702 Not Audited
Profile: Sunday News is a weekly newspaper published for the residents of Lancaster, PA and surrounding areas. It provides local and state news and information on community events.
Language (s): English
Ad Rate: Full Page Mono 58.00

Currency: United States Dollars
COMMUNITY NEWSPAPER

Sun-Reporter Publishing Company 24490

Owner: Sun Reporter Publishing
Editorial: 1791 Bancroft Ave, San Francisco, California 94124 **Tel:** 1 415 671-1000
Email: sunmedia97@aol.com **Web site:** http://www.sunreporter.com
Circ: 170452 Not Audited
Editor: Gail Berkley
Profile: Sun-Reporter Publishing Company provides newspapers in the San Francisco Bay area which focus on news that truly affects the lives and families throughout the black community.
Language (s): English
COMMUNITY NEWSPAPER

Superior Telegram 14823

Owner: Superior Telegram and Forum Communications Co.
Editorial: 1226 Ogden Ave, Superior, Wisconsin 54880-1584 **Tel:** 1 715 395-5000
Email: editorial@superiortelegram.com **Web site:** http://www.superiortelegram.com
Freq: Fri; **Circ:** 6500 Not Audited
Publisher: JoAnn Buelteman; **News Editor:** Shelley Nelson; **Advertising Sales Manager:** Ryan Olmstead
Profile: Superior Telegram serves the residents of Douglas County, WI and Northwest Wisconsin. It covers local news, lifestyles, sports and opinions.
Language (s): English
Ad Rate: Full Page Mono 16.96
Ad Rate: Full Page Colour 54.33
Currency: United States Dollars
COMMUNITY NEWSPAPER

Susquehanna County Transcript 20595

Owner: County Transcript, Inc.
Editorial: 36 Exchange St, Susquehanna, Pennsylvania 18847-2610 **Tel:** 1 570 853-3134
Email: susqtran@epix.net **Web site:** http://www.susquehannatranscript.com
Freq: Wed; **Circ:** 6000 Not Audited
Publisher & Editor: Charles Ficarro; **Advertising Sales Manager:** Lauren Ficarro
Profile: Susquehanna County Transcript provides news and information for Susquehanna County, PA.
Language (s): English
Ad Rate: Full Page Mono 10.90
Currency: United States Dollars
COMMUNITY NEWSPAPER

Suwannee Democrat/Mayo Free Press 590834

Owner: Community Newspaper Holdings, Inc.
Editorial: 521 Demorest St SE, Live Oak, Florida 32064-3320 **Tel:** 1 386 362-1734
Email: nf.editorial@gaflnews.com **Web site:** http://www.suwanneedemocrat.com
Circ: 7098
Publisher: Myra Regan; **Advertising Sales Manager:** Monja Robinson
Language (s): English
COMMUNITY NEWSPAPER

Swarner Communications 24887

Owner: Swarner, (Ken & Ron)
Editorial: 8312 Custer Rd SW, Lakewood, Washington 98499-2526 **Tel:** 1 253 584-1212
Email: feedback@weeklyvolcano.com **Web site:** http://www.northwestmilitary.com
Circ: 69250 Not Audited
Language (s): English
COMMUNITY NEWSPAPER

Sylva Herald & Ruralite 20012

Owner: Sylva Herald Publishing Co., Inc. (The)
Editorial: 539 W Main St, Sylva, North Carolina 28779-5551 **Tel:** 1 828 586-2611
Email: news@thesylvaherald.com **Web site:** http://www.thesylvaherald.com
Freq: Thu; **Circ:** 5402 Not Audited
Advertising Sales Manager: Margo Gray; **Publisher:** Steven Gray; **Editor:** Lynn Hotaling
Profile: Sylva Herald & Ruralite is a local weekly newspaper written for the residents of Sylva and Jackson County, NC. The newspaper covers local news, community events, and sports of Sylva and Jackson County, NC. The lead time is three days. Advertising is accepted by this publication, please call for a quote.
Language (s): English
Ad Rate: Full Page Mono 5.85
Ad Rate: Full Page Colour 190.00
Currency: United States Dollars
COMMUNITY NEWSPAPER

The Sylvania Telephone 18839

Owner: GateHouse Media Inc.
Editorial: 208 N Main St, Sylvania, Georgia 30467-1831 **Tel:** 1 912 564-2045
Email: enoch.autry@sylvaniatelephone.com **Web site:** http://www.sylvaniatelephone.com
Freq: Thu; **Circ:** 9500 Not Audited
Publisher & Editor: Enoch Autry
Profile: The Sylvania Telephone is a local newspaper written for the residents of Sylvania, GA and covers community news.
Language (s): English
Ad Rate: Full Page Mono 8.15
Currency: United States Dollars
COMMUNITY NEWSPAPER

Syracuse New Times 20305

Owner: Brod (William)
Editorial: 1415 W Genesee St, Syracuse, New York 13204-2119 **Tel:** 1 315 422-7011
Email: editorial@syracusenewtimes.com **Web site:** http://www.syracusenewtimes.com
Freq: Wed; **Circ:** 40000 Not Audited
Publisher: William Brod
Profile: Syracuse (NY) New Times provides local news, sports and arts & entertainment coverage.
Language (s): English
Ad Rate: Full Page Mono 50.33
Currency: United States Dollars
COMMUNITY NEWSPAPER

The Tablet 23001

Owner: Tablet Publishing Company
Editorial: 1712 10th Ave, Brooklyn, New York 11215-6215 **Tel:** 1 718 965-7333
Email: ewilkinson@desalesmedia.org **Web site:** http://www.thetablet.org
Freq: Sat; **Circ:** 73954
Advertising Sales Manager: Kimberly Benn; **Publisher:** Nicholas DiMarzio; **Editor:** Ed Wilkinson
Profile: The Tablet is written for the Catholic residents in Brooklyn, NY. It covers news about the Catholic religion.
Language (s): English
Ad Rate: Full Page Mono 35.67
Ad Rate: Full Page Colour 2950.00
Currency: United States Dollars
COMMUNITY NEWSPAPER

Tahoe Daily Tribune 13755

Owner: Swift Newspapers
Editorial: 3079 Harrison Ave, South Lake Tahoe, California 96150-7931 **Tel:** 1 530 541-3880
Web site: http://www.tahoedailytribune.com
Freq: Fri; **Circ:** 9000
Profile: Tahoe Daily Tribune is a newspaper serving South Lake Tahoe, CA. The publication covers national and local news, and community events.
Language (s): English
Ad Rate: Full Page Mono 19.45
Ad Rate: Full Page Colour 140.00
Currency: United States Dollars
COMMUNITY NEWSPAPER

Tahoe World 18652

Owner: Swift Newspapers
Editorial: 3079 Harrison Ave, South Lake Tahoe, California 96150-7976 **Tel:** 1 530 541-3880
Email: editor@sierrasun.com **Web site:** http://www.tahoedailytribune.com
Freq: Wed; **Circ:** 14000 Not Audited
Profile: Tahoe World is a free, weekly source for arts, entertainment, dining and recreation in the North Shore, including Truckee, Tahoe City, Squaw Valley and Kings Beach, CA. It provides residents and tourists with stories that celebrate the Tahoe lifestyle, including a calendar of events, live music and movie reviews, local columnists, outdoor activities and feature articles. It is inserted within the Sierra Sun daily newspaper in Truckee, CA, and the North Lake Tahoe Bonanza paper in Incline Village, NV. It is also available at newsstands throughout the area. All mail must be sent to the PO Box. Advertising deadlines are at noon PT.
Language (s): English
Ad Rate: Full Page Mono 16.00
Currency: United States Dollars
COMMUNITY NEWSPAPER

Tailwind 21838

Owner: Daily Republic
Editorial: 400 Brennan Cir, Travis AFB, California 94535-5001 **Tel:** 1 707 424-0131
Email: tailwind@travis.af.mil **Web site:** http://tailwind.dailyrepublic.net
Freq: Fri; **Circ:** 10040 Not Audited
Editor: Amber Carter
Profile: Tailwind is the official news publication of Travis Air Force Base in Travis, CA. The newspaper is written for members of the base and covers local news, base news, events, information and sports. It is put out by The Daily Republic, though the Air Force is still responsible for all content. The editorial deadline is Fridays at 4:30pm PT.
Language (s): English
Ad Rate: Full Page Mono 13.00
Currency: United States Dollars
COMMUNITY NEWSPAPER

Tallahassee Capital Outlook 18780

Owner: Holmes, Jr. (Rev. Dr. R.B.)
Editorial: 1363 E Tennessee St, Tallahassee, Florida 32308-5107 **Tel:** 1 850 877-0105
Email: info@capitaloutlook.com **Web site:** http://capitaloutlook.com/
Freq: Thu; **Circ:** 12000 Not Audited
Editor: Tiffany Harris; **Publisher:** R.B. Holmes; **Editor:** Angeline Taylor
Profile: Tallahassee Capital Outlook is a newspaper serving African American residents of Tallahassee, FL. The publication covers Local and National News, Sports, and Community Events.
Language (s): English
Ad Rate: Full Page Mono 33.00
Currency: United States Dollars
COMMUNITY NEWSPAPER

Tama/Grundy Publishing Inc. 25041

Owner: Marshalltown Newspaper Inc.
Editorial: 220 W 3rd St, Tama, Iowa 52339
Tel: 1 641 484-2841
Email: editor@tamatoledonews.com **Web site:** http://www.tamatoledonews.com
Circ: 6400 Not Audited
Publisher: Mike Schlesinger; **Editor:** John Speer; **Advertising Sales Manager:** Nancy Sund
Language (s): English
COMMUNITY NEWSPAPER

The Taos News 20228

Owner: Watkin (Robin)
Editorial: 226 Albright St, Taos, New Mexico 87571-6312 **Tel:** 1 575 758-2241
Email: editor@taosnews.com **Web site:** http://www.taosnews.com
Freq: Thu; **Circ:** 11020 Not Audited
Publisher: Chris Baker; **Circulation Manager:** Saul Rodriquez; **Editor:** Rick Romancito; **Advertising Sales Manager:** Chris Wood
Profile: Taos News is a local, weekly newspaper serving the community of Taos, NM. The publication covers local news, community events, lifestyle, education, business and other topics of general interest. Deadlines are on Fridays at noon MT.
Language (s): Spanish/Bilingual
Ad Rate: Full Page Mono 16.40
Currency: United States Dollars
COMMUNITY NEWSPAPER

Tate Record 19906

Owner: Lee (John, III)
Editorial: 219 E Main St, Senatobia, Mississippi 38668-2123 **Tel:** 1 662 562-4414
Web site: http://www.taterecord.com
Freq: Tue; **Circ:** 5200 Not Audited
Publisher & Editor: Joseph Lee; **Advertising Sales Manager:** Shirley Trimm
Profile: The Tate Record is a community newspaper written for the residents of Senatobia, MS. The paper covers community news, lifestyle and business.
Language (s): English
Ad Rate: Full Page Mono 8.90
Currency: United States Dollars
COMMUNITY NEWSPAPER

Taylorsville Times 20014

Owner: Sharpe (Walter)
Editorial: 24 E Main Ave, Taylorsville, North Carolina 28681-2541 **Tel:** 1 828 632-2532
Email: taylorsvilletimes@taylorsvilletimes.com **Web site:** http://www.taylorsvilletimes.com
Freq: Wed; **Circ:** 7200 Not Audited
Advertising Sales Manager: Steve Garland; **Editor:** Walter Sharpe
Profile: Taylorsville Times is a newspaper serving the residents of Taylorsville, NC. The publication covers local news and community events. Deadlines are Mondays at 5pm ET.
Language (s): English
Ad Rate: Full Page Mono 6.40
Currency: United States Dollars
COMMUNITY NEWSPAPER

Tazewell County Free Press 21977

Editorial: 1249 Front St, Richlands, Virginia 24641
Tel: 1 276 963-0127
Email: freepres@netscope.net
Freq: Wed; **Circ:** 13500 Not Audited
Editor & Publisher: Lynna Mitchell
Profile: Tazewell County Free Press is a newspaper serving the residents of Tazewell County, VA. The publication covers local news and community events. Deadlines are on Mondays at 5pm ET.
Language (s): English
Ad Rate: Full Page Mono 8.00
Currency: United States Dollars
COMMUNITY NEWSPAPER

El Tecolote 154540

Editorial: 2958 24th St, San Francisco, California 94110-4132 **Tel:** 1 415 648-1045
Email: editor@eltecolote.org **Web site:** http://www.eltecolote.org
Freq: Bi-Weekly; **Circ:** 10000 Not Audited
Advertising Manager: Mabel Jimenez; **Editor:** Alexis Terrazas
Profile: El Tecolote is a bilingual, bi-monthly newspaper for the Latino population of the San Francisco Bay area. 10,000 copies are distributed freely throughout sites in the Mission District and East Bay. Its primary goal, according to the newspaper's mission statement, is "to provide a vehicle of information and organization to the Chicano/Latino communities of the Bay Area, articulating its social, cultural, political and economic needs through our ongoing and timely coverage of issues." It has also established itself as an effective training ground for aspiring Latino journalists. The paper was founded in 1970 by Juan Gonzales as part of a project in his La Raza studies class at San Francisco State University. It is the longest running Spanish/English bilingual newspaper in California and remains a centerpiece to Mission District arts, culture and community. It is mostly staffed by volunteers and is a member of the San Francisco Neighborhood Newspaper Association and founding member New America Media.
Language (s): Spanish/Bilingual
Ad Rate: Full Page Mono 16.25
Currency: United States Dollars
COMMUNITY NEWSPAPER

The Telegram 20372

Owner: Jackson County Broadcasting Inc.
Editorial: 920 Veterans Dr Unit D, Jackson, Ohio 45640-2175 **Tel:** 1 740 286-3604
Web site: http://thetelegramnews.com
Freq: Sat; **Circ:** 5000 Not Audited
Advertising Sales Manager: Jeanne Gillum; **Circulation Manager:** Rayanna Puckett; **Community News Editor:** Pam Wilson
Profile: The Telegram is written for the residents of Jackson and Vinton Counties, OH. The editorial content includes community news, events, sports and politics.
Language (s): English
Ad Rate: Full Page Mono 8.25
Currency: United States Dollars
COMMUNITY NEWSPAPER

Telegram Newspaper 19581

Owner: Gina C. Wilson
Editorial: 10748 W Jefferson Ave, River Rouge, Michigan 48218-1232 **Tel:** 1 313 928-2955
Email: telegram@telegramnews.net **Web site:** http://www.telegramnews.net
Freq: Thu; **Circ:** 12000 Not Audited
Publisher & Editor: Gina Steward
Profile: Telegram Newspaper is published weekly for the residents of Ecorse, MI and surrounding areas. The newspaper covers local news, sports and community events.
Language (s): English
Ad Rate: Full Page Mono 21.00
Currency: United States Dollars
COMMUNITY NEWSPAPER

Telegraph Newspapers 231576

Owner: Gold Country Media
Editorial: 921 Sutter St Ste 100, Folsom, California 95630-2441 **Tel:** 1 916 985-2581
Web site: http://www.goldcountrymedia.com
Circ: 23600 Not Audited
Circulation Manager: Kelly Liebold
Language (s): English
COMMUNITY NEWSPAPER

Telluride Watch 324317

Owner: S. Cagin
Editorial: 307 E Colorado Ave, Telluride, Colorado 81435 **Tel:** 1 970 728-4496
Email: publisher@telluridenews.com **Web site:** http://www.telluridenews.com/the_watch
Freq: Thu; **Circ:** 11500
Profile: Telluride Watch is published twice a week for the residents of Telluride, CO. All materials must be sent to the PO Box address.
Language (s): English
Ad Rate: Full Page Mono 15.00
Currency: United States Dollars
COMMUNITY NEWSPAPER

Tempe-Chandler Wrangler News 73217

Editorial: 2145 E Warner Rd Ste 102, Tempe, Arizona 85284-3497 **Tel:** 1 480 966-0845
Email: editor@wranglernews.com **Web site:** http://www.wranglernews.com
Freq: Bi-Weekly; **Circ:** 20000 Not Audited
Editor & Publisher: Don Kirkland
Profile: The Tempe-Chandler Wrangler News is a bi-weekly community newspaper serving the residents of Tempe, AZ.
Language (s): English
Ad Rate: Full Page Mono 10.00
Currency: United States Dollars
COMMUNITY NEWSPAPER

Tempo News 469302

Editorial: 2826 Leonard Reid Ave, Sarasota, Florida 34234-6231 **Tel:** 1 941 359-1065
Email: temponews@comcast.net **Web site:** http://www.temponewsflorida.com
Freq: Thu; **Circ:** 40000 Not Audited
Editor: Inez Hunter; **Publisher:** Johnny Hunter; **Advertising Sales Manager:** Danny Preston
Profile: Tempo News is published weekly for the African-American communities of Manatee and Sarasota, FL. The newspaper provides information about local news, cultural issues and community events.
Language (s): English
Ad Rate: Full Page Mono 15.00
Currency: United States Dollars
COMMUNITY NEWSPAPER

Tennessee Register 21902

Owner: Diocese of Nashville
Editorial: 2400 21st Ave S, Nashville, Tennessee 37212-5302 **Tel:** 1 615 783-0750
Email: tnregister@dioceseofnashville.com **Web site:** http://www.dioceseofnashville.com/tnregister.pdf
Freq: Bi-Weekly; **Circ:** 19000 Not Audited
Publisher: David Choby; **Advertising Sales Manager:** Byron Warner
Profile: Tennessee Register is a bi-weekly newspaper serving the Catholic community in Nashville, TN.
Language (s): English
Ad Rate: Full Page Mono 15.42
Currency: United States Dollars
COMMUNITY NEWSPAPER

The Tennessee Tribune 7451

Owner: Perry & Perry & Associates
Editorial: 1501 Jefferson St, Nashville, Tennessee 37208-3016 **Tel:** 1 615 321-3268
Email: tennesseetribunenews@aol.com **Web site:** http://tntribune.com
Freq: Weekly; **Circ:** 45000 Not Audited
Publisher & Editor: Rosetta Miller Perry
Profile: Focused on issues of interest to members of the black community. Included are regular departments on health, entertainment, business,

education, society, and history. Reviews on books, fashion, and travel are also covered.
Language (s): English
Ad Rate: Full Page Mono 3078.00
Ad Rate: Full Page Colour 2673.00
Currency: United States Dollars
COMMUNITY NEWSPAPER

Tester 21950
Owner: Comprint Military Publications
Editorial: 22268 Cedar Point Rd Bldg 409, Patuxent River, Maryland 20670-1154 **Tel:** 1 301 757-6748
Email: webmaster@gazette.net **Web site:** http://www.dcmilitary.com/tester/
Freq: Weekly; **Circ:** 15000 Not Audited
Publisher: John Rives
Profile: Tester provides news and information for the Patuxent Naval Air Test Center. The weekly newspaper is read by the Patuxent Naval Air Test Center personnel.
Language (s): English
Ad Rate: Full Page Mono 19.16
Ad Rate: Full Page Colour 2572.64
Currency: United States Dollars
COMMUNITY NEWSPAPER

Texas News Topics 794638
Tel: 1 214 431-9241
Email: info@tntpaper.com **Web site:** http://tntpaper.com
Freq: Fri; **Circ:** 35000
Editor & Publisher: Bettye Williams
Profile: Texas News Topics is a Community Newspaper in Cedar Hill, Texas serving the residents of the Dallas / Fort Worth Metroplex community. Topics covered include News, Sports, Entertainment, and Weather.
Language (s): English
COMMUNITY NEWSPAPER

Thang Long 256541
Owner: Nguyen (Cuong)
Editorial: 18 Faulkner St Apt 1, Dorchester, Massachusetts 02122-1339 **Tel:** 1 617 436-4036
Email: nvietnam04@yahoo.com **Web site:** http://www.conong.com
Freq: Tue; **Circ:** 22000 Not Audited
Editor: Charles Nguyen; **Publisher:** Cuong Nguyen
Profile: Thang Long is a Vietnamese-language publication written for the Vietnamese community in Boston and the surrounding area. The newspaper focuses on local, national and international news. It also covers entertainment and business issues.
Language (s): Vietnamese
Ad Rate: Full Page Mono 8.33
Currency: United States Dollars
COMMUNITY NEWSPAPER

Thangatheepam 791141
Editorial: 8130 Sheppard Ave E Suite 201, Scarborough, Ontario M1B 3W3 **Tel:** 1 416 266-8383
Email: thangatheepam@yahoo.com **Web site:** http://thangatheepam.com
Freq: Weekly; **Circ:** 10000
Publisher & Editor: Kandiah Sivaneswaran
Profile: Thangatheepam is a bilingual Tamil and English weekly newspaper providing Community News coverage to the Tamil-speaking community in Scarborough, ON.
Language (s): English
Ad Rate: Full Page Mono 4.90
Currency: Canada Dollars
COMMUNITY NEWSPAPER

The Island News 962208
Editorial: 308 Charles St, Beaufort, South Carolina 29902-5532 **Tel:** 1 843 3218281
Email: theislandnews@gmail.com **Web site:** http://www.yourislandnews.com
Freq: Weekly
Profile: The Island News is a hyper-local weekly newspaper that covers news and information for the people of Beaufort, South Carolina.
Language (s): English
COMMUNITY NEWSPAPER

The Sheet 961006
Editorial: 3343 Main St, Mammoth Lakes, California 93546 **Tel:** 1 760 924-0048
Email: lunch@thesheetnews.com **Web site:** http://thesheetnews.com
Freq: Weekly
Profile: Covers news and information for Lone Pine, Coleville and the surrounding areas of California.
Language (s): English
COMMUNITY NEWSPAPER

Thief River Falls Times, Inc. 24947
Owner: MCM Media, LLC
Editorial: 324 Main Ave N, Thief River Falls, Minnesota 56701-1906 **Tel:** 1 218 681-4450
Email: trftimes@trftimes.com **Web site:** http://www.trftimes.com
Freq: Weekly; **Circ:** 28250 Not Audited
Advertising Sales Manager: DeDe Coltom; **Editor:** Dave Hill; **Publisher:** Randal Hultgren
Profile: Thief River Falls Times, Inc. provides local news and sports for the residents of Thief River Falls, MN.
Language (s): English
COMMUNITY NEWSPAPER

Thikana 830177
Owner: Prometheus International, Inc.
Editorial: 4502 11th St, Long Island City, New York 11101-5206 **Tel:** 1 718 472-0700
Email: wthikana@aol.com **Web site:** http://www.thikana.net
Freq: Weekly; **Circ:** 30000
Advertising Sales Manager: Monjur Hossain; **Editor:** Muhammad Rahman
Profile: Thikana is a weekly community newspaper serving the Bengali American population in New York City and is published in Bengali, the official language of Bangladesh. It contains local, national and international news of importance to readers.
Language (s): Bengali
COMMUNITY NEWSPAPER

This Week 21873
Owner: Lee Enterprises Inc.
Editorial: 600 Lyon St S, Albany, Oregon 97321-2919 **Tel:** 1 541 926-2211
Freq: Wed; **Circ:** 17500 Not Audited
Profile: This Week is a weekly newspaper written for the residents of Albany, OR and targeting non-subscribers of Mid-Valley Newspapers.
Language (s): English
Ad Rate: Full Page Mono 5.50
Currency: United States Dollars
COMMUNITY NEWSPAPER

This Week From Indian Country Today 21470
Owner: Four Directions Media
Editorial: ICTMN, Attn: Business Affairs, Verona, New York 13478 **Tel:** 1 315 829-8355
Email: editor@ictmn.com **Web site:** http://www.indiancountrytodaymedianetwork.com
Freq: Weekly
Editor: Theresa Braine; **Advertising Sales Manager:** Heather Donovan; **Editor:** Ken Polisse; **Circulation Manager:** Sabrina Sharkey
Profile: This Week From Indian Country Today magazine features stories and perspectives from Native American journalists that include news, entertainment, business, politics and education.
Language (s): English
COMMUNITY NEWSPAPER

ThisWeek Community Newspapers 24798
Owner: GateHouse Media Inc.
Editorial: 7801 N Central Dr, Lewis Center, Ohio 43035-9407 **Tel:** 1 740 888-6100
Email: editorial@thisweeknews.com **Web site:** http://www.thisweeknews.com
Freq: Weekly; **Circ:** 323534 Not Audited
News Editor: Julanne Hohbach; **Community News Editor:** Tim Krumlauf; **Community News Editor:** Dennis Laycock; **Community News Editor:** Lisa Proctor; **Community News Editor:** Neil Thompson
Profile: ThisWeek Community Newspapers publishes more than 20 local papers in the Columbus, OH region. All are distributed for free to subscribers of the Columbus Dispatch.
Language (s): English
COMMUNITY NEWSPAPER

Thoi Báo Houston 546500
Owner: Nguyen (Dave)
Editorial: 11360 Bellaire Blvd Ste 870, Houston, Texas 77072-2567 **Tel:** 1 281 568-4600
Email: mail@thoibao.com **Web site:** http://www.thoibao.com
Freq: Fri; **Circ:** 6500
Publisher: Dave Nguyen; **Editor:** Thinh Nguyen
Profile: Thoi Báo Houston is a free weekly Vietnamese-language newspaper serving the Asian communities of the greater Houston area.
Language (s): Vietnamese
Ad Rate: Full Page Mono 9.09
Currency: United States Dollars
COMMUNITY NEWSPAPER

Thousand Islands Sun 20243
Owner: Thousand Islands Printing Co. Inc.
Tel: 1 315 482-2581
Email: tisun@gisco.net
Freq: Wed; **Circ:** 7000 Not Audited
Advertising Sales Manager: Angela Jury; **Editor:** David Schwartzentruber; **Publisher:** Craig Snow
Profile: Thousand Islands Sun is a local weekly newspaper written for the residents of Alexandria Bay, NY. It covers local news.
Language (s): English
Ad Rate: Full Page Mono 4.80
Currency: United States Dollars
COMMUNITY NEWSPAPER

Thousandsticks Newspapers 24922
Editorial: 22009 Main St, Hyden, Kentucky 41749
Tel: 1 606 672-3399
Circ: 7300 Not Audited
Publisher & Editor: Reba Baker
Language (s): English
COMMUNITY NEWSPAPER

Thunderbolt 22887
Editorial: 8208 Hangar Loop Dr, Ste 14, Tampa, Florida 33621-5545 **Tel:** 1 813 828-4586
Web site: http://www.macdillthunderbolt.com
Freq: Bi-Weekly; **Circ:** 8800 Not Audited
Publisher: Denise Palmer; **Editor:** Nick Stubbs
Profile: Thunderbolt is the official newspaper of MacDill Air Force Base in Tampa, Florida. The publication features the latest news on the base, the people, and the activities, and includes a mix of local and Air Force news, features, sports, and community happenings.
Language (s): English
Ad Rate: Full Page Mono 19.70
Currency: United States Dollars
COMMUNITY NEWSPAPER

The Thunderbolt 156447
Editorial: 14185 W Falcon, Luke Air Force Base, Phoenix, Arizona 85309 **Tel:** 1 623 856-6055
Email: luke.thunderbolt@us.af.mil **Web site:** http://www.aerotechnews.com/lukeafb/
Freq: Fri; **Circ:** 15000 Not Audited
Editor: Deborah Leuthold
Profile: Thunderbolt is the official newspaper of Luke Air Force Base, AZ. The weekly publication features the latest news on the base, the people, the events, and includes a mix of local and Air Force news, features, sports, and community happenings. Thunderbolt is published by Pueblo Publishers, Inc., a private firm in no way connected with the US Air Force, under exclusive written contract with the 56th Support Group, Luke Air Force Base, AZ. This commercial enterprise Air Force newspaper is an authorized publication for members of the US military services. Contents of the "Thunderbolt" are not necessarily the official views of, or endorsed by, the US government, the Department of Defense, or the Department of the Air Force.
Language (s): English
Ad Rate: Full Page Mono 15.70
Ad Rate: Full Page Colour 984.00
Currency: United States Dollars
COMMUNITY NEWSPAPER

Tidewater Hispanic News 824981
Tel: 1 757 474-1233
Email: twhispanic@msn.com **Web site:** http://twhispanicnews.com
Freq: Bi-Weekly; **Circ:** 9000
Editor: Regina Gomez; **Advertising Sales Manager:** Gigy Torres
Profile: Tidewater Hispanic News is a bi-weekly community newspaper serving the Hispanic community of Virginia, including Virginia Beach, Norfolk, Chesapeake, Portsmouth, Suffolk, Smithfield, Newport News, Hampton, Yorktown, Williamsburg, New Kent County, York County, James City County, Chesterfield County, Henrico County, Richmond City, Elizabeth City and Manteo.
Language (s): Spanish/Bilingual
Ad Rate: Full Page Mono 10.48
Currency: United States Dollars
COMMUNITY NEWSPAPER

The Tidewater News 80826
Owner: Tidewater Publications
Editorial: 1000 Armory Dr, Franklin, Virginia 23851-1852 **Tel:** 1 757 562-3187
Email: tnnews@tidewaternews.com **Web site:** http://www.tidewaternews.com
Freq: Fri; **Circ:** 8800 Not Audited
Advertising Sales Manager: Betty Ramsey; **Circulation Manager:** Michelle Stainback
Profile: The Tidewater News is a local newspaper written for the residents of Franklin, VA. The paper covers local news.
Language (s): English
Ad Rate: Full Page Mono 11.80
Currency: United States Dollars
COMMUNITY NEWSPAPER

Tidewater Review 28901
Owner: tronc
Editorial: 425 12th Street, West Point, Virginia 23181 **Tel:** 1 804 843-2282
Email: mail@tidewaterreview.com **Web site:** http://www.tidewaterreview.com
Freq: Wed; **Circ:** 5000 Not Audited
Advertising Sales Manager: Jennifer Haynes
Profile: The Tidewater Review is a weekly newspaper that provides local news coverage for the West Point, VA area. The lead time for Tidewater Review is two days. Deadlines for publication are Monday at 2:00 ET for Wednesday issue date. Advertising rates are not available at this time.
Language (s): English
Ad Rate: Full Page Mono 7.39
Currency: United States Dollars
COMMUNITY NEWSPAPER

El Tiempo 24418
Owner: Vegas Review Journal (Las)
Editorial: 1111 W Bonanza Rd, Las Vegas, Nevada 89106 **Tel:** 1 702 387-2972
Web site: http://www.eltiempolv.com
Freq: Fri; **Circ:** 50000 Not Audited
Profile: El Tiempo is an independent product of the Las Vegas Review-Journal. It is written for Latinos. Send press releases to the editor directly.
Language (s): Spanish/Bilingual
Ad Rate: Full Page Mono 45.00
Currency: United States Dollars
COMMUNITY NEWSPAPER

El Tiempo Hispano 719850
Editorial: 123 Rosemary Ct, Bear, Delaware 19701-6015 **Tel:** 1 302 588-9584
Email: editor@eltiempohispano.com **Web site:** http://www.eltiempohispano.com
Freq: Bi-Weekly; **Circ:** 8000
Profile: El Tiempo Hispano is a community newspaper in Bear, DE geared toward Hispanic bilingual readers. It offers community news and information on local events.
Language (s): Spanish/Bilingual
Ad Rate: Full Page Mono 14.00
Currency: United States Dollars
COMMUNITY NEWSPAPER

El Tiempo Latino 21853
Owner: Washington Post Co.
Editorial: 1440 G St NW, Washington, District Of Columbia 20005-2001 **Tel:** 1 202 334-9100
Web site: http://www.eltiempolatino.com
Freq: Fri; **Circ:** 49967 Not Audited
Circulation Manager: Luis Torrico
Profile: El Tiempo Latino in Washington, DC is a weekly Spanish newspaper that covers local, national and international news for the Hispanic community in the metropolitan region, including Arlington, VA.
Language (s): Spanish
Ad Rate: Full Page Mono 43.50
Currency: United States Dollars
COMMUNITY NEWSPAPER

Tierra Times 21784
Owner: Serra Services
Tel: 1 858 292-1037
Email: dspehn1@san.rr.com
Freq: Thu; **Circ:** 10000 Not Audited
Advertising Sales Manager: Richard Spehn
Profile: Tierra Times is a monthly community newspaper written for residents of San Diego, CA.
Language (s): English
Ad Rate: Full Page Mono 17.90
Currency: United States Dollars
COMMUNITY NEWSPAPER

Tilden Newspapers 25037
Editorial: 202 E 2nd St, Tilden, Nebraska 68781
Tel: 1 402 368-5315
Email: tildencitizen@cableone.net
Circ: 15750 Not Audited
Advertising Sales Manager: Lynn Carter; **Editor:** Donna Smith; **Publisher:** Verlyn Thomas
Language (s): English
COMMUNITY NEWSPAPER

Tiloben Publishing Co. 24786
Editorial: 2600 S Jackson St, Seattle, Washington 98144 **Tel:** 1 888 909-3070
Web site: http://www.seattlemedium.com
Circ: 64500 Not Audited
Editor: Chris Bennet
Language (s): English
COMMUNITY NEWSPAPER

The Times 28134
Owner: GateHouse Media Inc.
Editorial: 129 Commerce St, Apalachicola, Florida 32320-1717 **Tel:** 1 850 653-8868
Web site: http://www.apalachtimes.com
Freq: Thu; **Circ:** 5500 Not Audited
Editor: David Adlerstein; **Editor:** Tim Croft; **Publisher:** Alan Davis
Profile: The Times is written for residents of Apalachicola and Carrabelle, FL. It covers local news, politics, sports and business.
Language (s): English
Ad Rate: Full Page Mono 7.90
Currency: United States Dollars
COMMUNITY NEWSPAPER

Times Beacon Record Newspapers 25047
Owner: Donnief (Leah)
Editorial: 185 Main St, Setauket, New York 11733-2803 **Tel:** 1 631 751-7744
Web site: http://tbrnewsmedia.com
Circ: 53888 Not Audited
Publisher & Editor: Leah Dunaief; **Editor:** Elena Glowatz; **Editor:** Patricia Kalish
Profile: Publishes The Port Times Record, The Times of Northport, The Times of Huntington, The Times of Middle Country, The Village Times Herald, The Village Beacon Record, and The Times of Smithtown.
Language (s): English
COMMUNITY NEWSPAPER

Times Community Newspapers 24959
Editorial: 300 Stony Brook Ct, Newburgh, New York 12550 **Tel:** 1 845 561-0170
Web site: http://www.timescommunitypapers.com
Circ: 8500 Not Audited
Language (s): English
COMMUNITY NEWSPAPER

Times Community Newspapers - Warrenton 408672
Owner: Virginia News Group
Editorial: 39 Culpeper St, Warrenton, Virginia 20186-3319 **Tel:** 1 540 347-4222
Web site: http://fauquier.com
Circ: 55114 Not Audited
Advertising Sales Manager: Kathy Godfrey
Profile: Times Community Newspapers- Warrenton (VA) serve residents of Culpeper County, Fauquier County and Prince William County, VA.
Language (s): English
COMMUNITY NEWSPAPER

The Times Group - New London 154882
Owner: Day Publishing Co.
Editorial: 47 Eugene Oneill Dr, New London, Connecticut 06320-6306 **Tel:** 1 860 442-2200
Email: tips@theday.com **Web site:** http://www.theday.com
Circ: 79063 Not Audited

Publisher: Gary Farrugia; **Advertising Sales Manager:** Bence Strickland
Language (s): English
COMMUNITY NEWSPAPER

Times Indicator 19514
Owner: TI Publications
Editorial: 44 W Main St, Fremont, Michigan 49412-1136 **Tel:** 1 231 924-4400
Email: news@ncats.net **Web site:** http://www.timesindicator.com
Freq: Wed; **Circ:** 7500 Not Audited
Circulation Manager: Jenna Flanery; **Publisher & Editor:** Richard Wheater
Profile: Times Indicator's editorial mission is to inform the public about local news and events that take place in and around Fremont, MI. The publication is written for the residents of Fremont, MI and covers local news and events.
Language (s): English
Ad Rate: Full Page Mono 8.00
Currency: United States Dollars
COMMUNITY NEWSPAPER

Times Leader 19374
Editorial: 607 W Washington St, Princeton, Kentucky 42445-1941 **Tel:** 1 270 365-5588
Email: newsroom@timesleader.net **Web site:** http://www.timesleader.net
Freq: Sat; **Circ:** 5700 Not Audited
Advertising Sales Manager: Kathy Boyd; **Publisher:** Chip Hutcheson
Profile: Times Leader is a local newspaper serving Princeton and Caldwell counties, KY. It covers local news, sports and features. Deadlines are on Mondays for the Wednesday issue and Thursdays for the Saturday issue.
Language (s): English
Ad Rate: Full Page Mono 6.00
Currency: United States Dollars
COMMUNITY NEWSPAPER

Times Media Inc. 25492
Owner: Bellou (William)
Editorial: 1900 Camden Ave, San Jose, California 95124 **Tel:** 1 408 494-7000
Email: times@timesmediainc.com **Web site:** http://www.timesmediainc.com
Circ: 55000 Not Audited
Publisher: William Bellou; **Advertising Sales Manager:** Brigitte Jones
Profile: Times Media Inc. is the local newspaper providing the community of San Jose, CA with news.
Language (s): English
COMMUNITY NEWSPAPER

Times Newsweekly 20303
Owner: Ridgewood Times Printing and Publishing Company, Inc.
Editorial: 6071 Woodbine St, Ridgewood, New York 11385-3242 **Tel:** 1 718 821-7500
Email: editorial@queenscourier.com **Web site:** http://www.timesnewsweekly.com
Freq: Thu; **Circ:** 30000 Not Audited
Advertising Sales Manager: Jose Vargas
Profile: Times Newsweekly is written for the residents of Queens, NY. It covers local news and events.
Language (s): English
Ad Rate: Full Page Mono 10.50
Currency: United States Dollars
COMMUNITY NEWSPAPER

The Times of Acadiana 21309
Owner: Gannett Co., Inc.
Editorial: 1100 Bertrand Dr, Lafayette, Louisiana 70506-4110 **Tel:** 1 337 289-6300
Email: calendar@theadvertiser.com **Web site:** http://www.theadvertiser.com/topic/91888a22-d739-4f28-bc33-1829bcfeeb0e/times-of-acadiana
Freq: Thu; **Circ:** 29500 Not Audited
Circulation Manager: Chalisa Davis
Profile: The Times of Acadiana is a free, alternative news magazine covering entertainment, recreation, politics, culture, food and business in Lafayette, LA, and the surrounding Acadiana region of southern Louisiana. Columns review movies, music, the arts, food and wine, books and sporting events.
Language (s): English
Ad Rate: Full Page Mono 21.05
Currency: United States Dollars
COMMUNITY NEWSPAPER

The Times of Wayne County 22449
Owner: Times of Wayne County, Inc.
Tel: 1 315 986-4300
Email: news@waynetimes.com **Web site:** http://www.waynetimes.com
Freq: Mon; **Circ:** 12700 Not Audited
Publisher & Editor: Ron Holdraker
Profile: The Times of Wayne County is published weekly for the residents of Wayne County, NY. The newspaper covers local news and community events. Deadlines for the publication are on Fridays at 5pm ET.
Language (s): English
Ad Rate: Full Page Mono 20.00
Currency: United States Dollars
COMMUNITY NEWSPAPER

Times Publishing Group 137244
Owner: Patrice Edwards
Editorial: 9601 Soquel Dr, Aptos, California 95003-4163 **Tel:** 1 831 688-7549
Email: info@cyber-times.com **Web site:** http://www.tpgonlinedaily.com
Circ: 36000 Not Audited
Publisher: Patrice Edwards; **Editor:** Noel Smith
Language (s): English
COMMUNITY NEWSPAPER

The Times Weekly 21762
Owner: C & C Publications
Editorial: 254 E Cass St, Joliet, Illinois 60432-2813 **Tel:** 1 815 723-0325
Email: info@thetimesweekly.com **Web site:** http://www.thetimesweekly.com
Freq: Thu; **Circ:** 28000 Not Audited
Advertising Sales Manager: Tamika Archibald; **Publisher & Editor:** Jayme Cain; **Circulation Manager:** Jason Vertin
Profile: The Times Weekly provides news and information on topics that affect African Americans in the Joliet, IL community.
Language (s): English
Ad Rate: Full Page Mono 46.12
Currency: United States Dollars
COMMUNITY NEWSPAPER

Times/Ledger Newspapers 24825
Owner: News Corporation Ltd.
Editorial: 4102 Bell Blvd Ste 2, Bayside, New York 11361-2794 **Tel:** 1 718 229-0300
Email: timesledgernews@cnglocal.com **Web site:** http://www.timesledger.com
Circ: 46975 Not Audited
Editor: Roz Liston; **Circulation Manager:** Roberto Palacios; **Publisher:** Brian Rice; **News Editor:** Kevin Zimmerman
Language (s): English
COMMUNITY NEWSPAPER

Times-Beacon Newspapers 24777
Owner: Gannett Co., Inc.
Editorial: 3600 State Route 66, Neptune, New Jersey 07753-2605 **Tel:** 1 732 922-6000
Web site: http://www.timesbeacon.com
Circ: 15887 Not Audited
Publisher: Thomas Donovan
Language (s): English
COMMUNITY NEWSPAPER

Times-Courier 18809
Owner: Bunch III, (George N.)
Editorial: 47 River St, Ellijay, Georgia 30540-3174 **Tel:** 1 706 635-4313
Email: news@timescourier.com **Web site:** http://www.timescourier.com
Freq: Wed; **Circ:** 6450 Not Audited
News Editor: Mark Millican
Profile: Times-Courier offers weekly news and events featuring local personalities in the Gilmer county area. The newspaper provides news affecting the Ellijay, GA area with a local perspective.
Language (s): English
Ad Rate: Full Page Mono 7.75
Currency: United States Dollars
COMMUNITY NEWSPAPER

Times-Journal 19969
Owner: Trib Publications
Editorial: 22 N Main St, Burnsville, North Carolina 28714-2925 **Tel:** 1 828 682-2120
Web site: http://www.yanceytimesjournal.com
Freq: Wed; **Circ:** 7000 Not Audited
Circulation Manager: Audria Briggs; **Editor:** David Grindstaff
Profile: The Times-Journal is a weekly published for the residents of Burnsville, NC.
Language (s): English
Ad Rate: Full Page Mono 8.60
Currency: United States Dollars
COMMUNITY NEWSPAPER

Times-Journal 21782
Editorial: 108 Division St, Cobleskill, New York 12043-4699 **Tel:** 1 518 234-2515
Email: tjournalnews@yahoo.com **Web site:** http://www.timesjournalonline.com
Freq: Wed; **Circ:** 7100 Not Audited
Editor: Patsy Nicosia; **Publisher:** Jim Poole; **Advertising Sales Manager:** Kathleen Rivenburg
Language (s): English
Ad Rate: Full Page Mono 7.57
Currency: United States Dollars
COMMUNITY NEWSPAPER

Times-Review Media Group 24961
Owner: Times-Review Newspapers
Editorial: 7785 Main Rd, Mattituck, New York 11952-1518 **Tel:** 1 631 298-3200
Email: editor@timesreview.com **Web site:** http://timesreview.com
Circ: 17900 Not Audited
Advertising Sales Manager: Cheryl Behr; **Publisher:** Andrew Olsen; **Advertising Sales Manager:** Joseph Tumminello
Language (s): English
COMMUNITY NEWSPAPER

The Times-Sentinel Newspapers 62466
Owner: Times Sentinel Newspaper Group LLC
Editorial: 125 N Main St, Goddard, Kansas 67052-8871 **Tel:** 1 316 540-0500
Email: classifieds@tsnews.com **Web site:** http://www.tsnews.com
Circ: 22300
Profile: Times-Sentinel Newspapers provides local news coverage for communities in Cheney, Clearwater, Garden Plain and Goddard, KS.
Language (s): English
COMMUNITY NEWSPAPER

Times-Shamrock Group 25297
Owner: Times-Shamrock Media Group
Editorial: 149 Penn Ave, Scranton, Pennsylvania 18503-2055 **Tel:** 1 570 348-9100
Web site: http://timesshamrock.com
Circ: 19650 Not Audited
Editor: Robert Baker; **Advertising Manager:** Vicki Wooden
Language (s): English
COMMUNITY NEWSPAPER

The Times-Villager 80693
Owner: Kaukauna Times Publishing Inc.
Editorial: 1900 Crooks Ave, Kaukauna, Wisconsin 54130 **Tel:** 1 920 759-2000
Email: editor@timesvillager.com **Web site:** http://www.timesvillager.com
Freq: Sat; **Circ:** 5400 Not Audited
Editor: Brian Roebke; **Advertising Sales Manager:** Diane Verhagen
Profile: The Times-Villager is a weekly newspaper that was founded in 1880, serving the residents of Kaukauna, WI, Kimberly, WI and Little Chute, WI. It is published every Wednesday and Saturday.
Language (s): English
Ad Rate: Full Page Mono 10.00
Currency: United States Dollars
COMMUNITY NEWSPAPER

Times-Virginian 21692
Owner: Womack Newspapers Inc.
Editorial: 589 Court St, Appomattox, Virginia 24522 **Tel:** 1 434 352-8215
Email: editor@timesvirginian.com **Web site:** http://www.timesvirginian.com
Freq: Wed; **Circ:** 8800 Not Audited
Advertising Sales Manager: Steve Atkinson; **Editor:** Marvin Hamlett; **Publisher:** Chad Harrison
Profile: Times-Virginian is written for the residents of Appomattox, VA.
Language (s): English
Ad Rate: Full Page Mono 8.90
Currency: United States Dollars
COMMUNITY NEWSPAPER

Tinker Take Off 920656
Owner: Journal Record Publishing Company
Editorial: 3000 S Douglas Blvd, 72nd Air Base Wing Headquarters - Bldg 460, Rm 125, Oklahoma City, Oklahoma 73150-1003 **Tel:** 1 405 739-5780
Email: tinker.takeoff@us.af.mil **Web site:** http://journalrecord.com/tinkertakeoff
Freq: Weekly
Editor: April McDonald
Profile: Tinker Take Off is a weekly community newspaper serving Tinker Air Force Base in Oklahoma City, OK.
Language (s): English
COMMUNITY NEWSPAPER

Tinnen Publishing 25186
Editorial: 102 E Maple St, Plattsburg, Missouri 64477-1246 **Tel:** 1 816 539-2111
Email: leader@clintoncountyleader.com **Web site:** http://www.clintoncountyleader.com
Circ: 21362 Not Audited
Advertising Sales Manager: Ray Freeman; **Publisher:** Steve Tinnen
Profile: Tinnen Publishing is a weekly community newspaper publisher serving the residents of Kansas City, MO.
Language (s): English
COMMUNITY NEWSPAPER

Tinytown Gazette 76612
Owner: Kasperowitz (Tanna)
Editorial: 172 S Main St, Cohasset, Massachusetts 02025-2009 **Tel:** 1 781 383-6704
Email: tinytown@comcast.net **Web site:** http://www.tinytowngazette.com
Freq: Bi-Weekly; **Circ:** 10000 Not Audited
Profile: Tinytown Gazette is a community newspaper blog written for the residents of Cohasset and area towns in MA.
Language (s): English
Ad Rate: Full Page Mono 10.00
Currency: United States Dollars
COMMUNITY NEWSPAPER

Tioga Publishing 25299
Owner: Community Media Group
Editorial: 25 East Ave, Wellsboro, Pennsylvania 16901-1618 **Tel:** 1 814 274-8044
Web site: http://www.tiogapublishing.com/
Circ: 10000
Language (s): English
COMMUNITY NEWSPAPER

Tioga Publishing - Wellsboro 542066
Owner: Community Media Group
Editorial: 25 East Ave, Wellsboro, Pennsylvania 16901-1618 **Tel:** 1 570 724-2287
Web site: http://www.tiogapublishing.com
Circ: 6700 Not Audited
Advertising Sales Manager: Nicole Hilfiger; **Editor:** Natalie Kennedy
Language (s): English
COMMUNITY NEWSPAPER

Tionesta Forest Press 20597
Owner: Sample, Mike
Editorial: 150 Elm St, Tionesta, Pennsylvania 16353 **Tel:** 1 814 755-4900
Email: news@myforestpress.com
Freq: Weekly; **Circ:** 5000 Not Audited
Editor: Kathy Culver; **Advertising Sales Manager:** Laura Davis
Profile: Tionesta Forest Press' editorial mission is to provide news and information to the residents of Tionesta, PA. The publication covers local news and events that affect the community. Deadlines are on Mondays at 4pm ET.
Language (s): English
Ad Rate: Full Page Mono 5.00
Currency: United States Dollars
COMMUNITY NEWSPAPER

Tishomingo County News 19878
Owner: Biggs (John)
Editorial: 120 W Front St, Iuka, Mississippi 38852-2325 **Tel:** 1 662 423-2211
Email: tcnews@bellsouth.net
Freq: Thu; **Circ:** 6000 Not Audited
Publisher: John Biggs; **Circulation Manager:** Nancy Hughes; **Editor:** Charlotte McVay; **Advertising Sales Manager:** Susan Thompson
Profile: Tishomingo County News is published weekly for the residents of Tishomingo County, MS. The newspaper covers local news and community events. Deadlines are on Tuesdays at noon CT.
Language (s): English
Ad Rate: Full Page Mono 5.00
Currency: United States Dollars
COMMUNITY NEWSPAPER

T-News Weekly 338387
Owner: Halifax Media
Editorial: 315 28th Ave, Tuscaloosa, Alabama 35401-1022 **Tel:** 1 205 345-0505
Email: news@tuscaloosanews.com **Web site:** http://www.tuscaloosanews.com
Freq: Wed; **Circ:** 21934 Not Audited
Circulation Manager: NaTa'sha Black; **Publisher:** Jim Rainey
Profile: T-News Weekly is a free publication mailed to non-subscribers of the Tuscaloosa News and distributed to area newsstands. The paper features stories of local interest, neighborhood announcements, growth projects, school activities, entertainment and events. It also contains the week's major news headlines and a classified section.
Language (s): English
Ad Rate: Full Page Mono 7.50
Currency: United States Dollars
COMMUNITY NEWSPAPER

The Toccoa Record 24333
Owner: Community Newspapers Inc.
Editorial: 67 W Doyle St, Toccoa, Georgia 30577-1787 **Tel:** 1 706 886-9476
Email: toccoarecord@windstream.net **Web site:** http://www.thetoccoarecord.com
Freq: Thu; **Circ:** 7200 Not Audited
Publisher & Editor: Tom Law
Profile: The Toccoa Record is a local newspaper written for the residents of Toccoa, GA. The paper covers local news and events.
Language (s): English
Ad Rate: Full Page Mono 12.55
Currency: United States Dollars
COMMUNITY NEWSPAPER

Today's Catholic 21846
Owner: Diocese of Fort Wayne – South Bend
Editorial: 915 S Clinton St, Fort Wayne, Indiana 46802-2601 **Tel:** 1 260 456-2824
Email: editor@diocesefwsb.org **Web site:** http://www.todayscatholicnews.org
Freq: Sun; **Circ:** 52000 Not Audited
Publisher: Kevin Rhoades
Profile: Today's Catholic is a local catholic newspaper for residents of Fort Wayne, IN and the surrounding counties. It provides local and national news of interest to the Catholic community, and comes out once a week on Sundays.
Language (s): English
Ad Rate: Full Page Mono 15.00
Currency: United States Dollars
COMMUNITY NEWSPAPER

Today's Catholic Newspaper 759300
Owner: Archdiocese of San Antonio
Editorial: 2718 W Woodlawn Ave, San Antonio, Texas 78228-5124 **Tel:** 1 210 734-1692
Email: tcpaper@arch.org **Web site:** http://www.satodayscatholic.com
Freq: Bi-Weekly; **Circ:** 30000
Publisher: Gustavo Garcia-Siller
Profile: Today's Catholic Newspaper is written for the Archdiocese of San Antonio.
Language (s): English
Ad Rate: Full Page Mono 14.44
Currency: United States Dollars
COMMUNITY NEWSPAPER

The Toledo Journal 20383
Editorial: 3021 Douglas, Toledo, Ohio 43606-5001 **Tel:** 1 419 472-4521
Email: toljour@aol.com **Web site:** http://www.thetoledojournal.com
Freq: Wed; **Circ:** 63000 Not Audited
Editor: Myron Stewart; **Publisher:** Sandra Stewart
Profile: The Toledo Journal's editorial mission is to provide news and information to the African American community in Toledo, Sylvania, Oregon and

Springfield Township, OH. It covers national and local news and events that affect its readers.
Language (s): English
Ad Rate: Full Page Mono 23.40
Ad Rate: Full Page Colour 502.00
Currency: United States Dollars
COMMUNITY NEWSPAPER

Tolosa Press 527729
Owner: Central Coast News Group, LLC
Editorial: 615 Clarion Ct Ste 2, San Luis Obispo, California 93401-8197 **Tel:** 1 805 543-6397
Email: dana@tolosapress.com **Web site:** http://www.tolosapressnews.com
Circ: 24000 Not Audited
Editor: Neil Farrell; **Advertising Sales Manager:** Dana McGraw; **Editor:** Theresa Wilson
Profile: Tolosa Press is a local newspaper providing the community of San Luis Obispo, CA with news.
Language (s): English
COMMUNITY NEWSPAPER

The Tolucan Times and Canyon Crier 18628
Owner: Ticor
Editorial: 10701 Riverside Dr, Toluca Lake, California 91602-2384 **Tel:** 1 818 762-2171
Email: editorial@tolucantimes.com **Web site:** http://www.tolucantimes.com
Freq: Wed; **Circ:** 40000 Not Audited
Publisher & Editor: Mardi Rustam
Profile: The Tolucan Times and Canyon Crier is a local weekly newspaper serving residents of Glendale, Burbank, North Hollywood, NoHo Arts District, Universal City, Toluca Lake, Valley Village, Studio City, Sherman Oaks and Encino, CA. Advertising deadlines are at noon PT.
Language (s): English
Ad Rate: Full Page Mono 30.00
Currency: United States Dollars
COMMUNITY NEWSPAPER

Tomah Journal Newspapers 25178
Owner: Lee Enterprises, Inc.
Editorial: 903 Superior Ave Ste 1, Tomah, Wisconsin 54660-2060 **Tel:** 1 608 372-4123
Email: tomahnews@lee.net **Web site:** http://www.tomahjournal.com
Circ: 10600 Not Audited
Editor: Steve Rundio
Profile: Tomah Journal Newspapers is a weekly community newspaper publisher serving the residents of Tomah, WI.
Language (s): English
COMMUNITY NEWSPAPER

The Tomahawk 22329
Owner: Sandusky Newspapers Inc.
Editorial: 116 S Church St, Mountain City, Tennessee 37683-1502 **Tel:** 1 423 727-6121
Email: letters2editor@thetomahawk.com **Web site:** http://www.thetomahawk.com
Freq: Wed; **Circ:** 5700
Advertising Manager: Ann Badal; **Editor:** Angie Gambill; **Publisher:** Bill Thomas
Profile: The Tomahawk is a weekly newspaper written for the residents of Mountain City, TN.
Language (s): English
Ad Rate: Full Page Mono 9.40
Currency: United States Dollars
COMMUNITY NEWSPAPER

Tomahawk Leader 21234
Owner: Tomahawk Leader
Editorial: 315 W Wisconsin Ave, Tomahawk, Wisconsin 54487-1133 **Tel:** 1 715 453-2151
Email: news@tomahawkleader.com **Web site:** http://www.tomahawkleader.com
Freq: Tue; **Circ:** 8800 Not Audited
Profile: Tomahawk Leader provides news and information to the public. The publication is written for residents of Tomahawk and Lincoln County, WI. The publication covers news and events that affect the community.
Language (s): English
Ad Rate: Full Page Mono 11.45
Currency: United States Dollars
COMMUNITY NEWSPAPER

Tooele Transcript-Bulletin 21785
Owner: Transcript Bulletin Publishing
Editorial: 58 N Main St, Tooele, Utah 84074-2139 **Tel:** 1 435 882-0050
Email: tbp@tooeletranscript.com **Web site:** http://www.tooeletranscript.com
Freq: 2 Times/Week; **Circ:** 8200 Not Audited
Editor: David Bern; **Publisher:** Scott Dunn; **Community News Editor:** Darren Vaughan
Profile: Tooele Transcript Bulletin's editorial mission is to inform the public of news and events that affect the residents of Tooele, UT.
Language (s): English
Ad Rate: Full Page Mono 7.94
Ad Rate: Full Page Colour 9.53
Currency: United States Dollars
COMMUNITY NEWSPAPER

Topsail Advertiser 825312
Owner: GateHouse Media Inc.
Editorial: 206A S Topsail Dr, Surf City, North Carolina 28445-6744 **Tel:** 1 910 328-3033
Web site: http://www.topsailadvertiser.com
Freq: Weekly
Profile: Topsail Advertiser is a weekly community newspaper serving Pender, Onslow, and New Hanover counties, NC. The paper includes local news and community events.
Language (s): English
COMMUNITY NEWSPAPER

The Tower/Soudan Timberjay 21759
Editorial: 414 Main St, Tower, Minnesota 55790 **Tel:** 1 218 753-2950
Email: editor@timberjay.com **Web site:** http://www.timberjay.com
Freq: Sat; **Circ:** 7600 Not Audited
Publisher: Marshall Helmberger; **Editor:** Jodi Summit
Profile: The Tower/Soudan Timberjay is a weekly newspaper that provides local news coverage for the communities of Tower and Soudan, MN.
Language (s): English
Ad Rate: Full Page Mono 8.10
Currency: United States Dollars
COMMUNITY NEWSPAPER

Town & Village 23089
Owner: Hagedorn Communications
Editorial: 20 W 22nd St, New York, New York 10010-5804 **Tel:** 1 212 777-6611 111
Email: editor@townvillage.net **Web site:** https://town-village.com
Freq: Thu; **Circ:** 8000 Not Audited
Publisher: Chris Hagedorn; **Editor:** Sabina Mollot
Profile: Formerly New York Town & Village, Town & Village is a weekly newspaper serving the residents of New York, NY. It provides information on news and events of interest to the local communities.
Language (s): English
Ad Rate: Full Page Mono 21.50
Currency: United States Dollars
COMMUNITY NEWSPAPER

Town and Country 20583
Owner: LJR Publishing, LLC
Editorial: 2508 Kutztown Rd, Pennsburg, Pennsylvania 18073-1914 **Tel:** 1 215 679-5060
Email: townandcountry@upvnews.com **Web site:** http://www.upvnews.com
Freq: Thu; **Circ:** 6000 Not Audited
Publisher & Editor: Larry Roeder; **Advertising Manager:** Wayne Suhl
Profile: Town and Country is a community newspaper covering local news and events for the residents of Red Hill, PA.
Language (s): English
Ad Rate: Full Page Mono 7.75
Currency: United States Dollars
COMMUNITY NEWSPAPER

The Town Common 359525
Owner: Maravalli (Marc)
Editorial: 77 Wethersfield St, Rowley, Massachusetts 01969-1713 **Tel:** 1 978 948-8696
Email: editor@thetowncommon.com **Web site:** http://www.thetowncommon.com
Freq: Wed; **Circ:** 18000 Not Audited
Editor & Publisher: Marc Maravalli
Profile: The Town Common serves the residents within the Triton Regional School district and the towns of Rowley, Newbury, Salisbury, Byfield and Plum Island, MA. Coverage includes local news, events and school and community happenings.
Language (s): English
Ad Rate: Full Page Mono 23.80
Currency: United States Dollars
COMMUNITY NEWSPAPER

The Town Courier 851623
Editorial: 309 Main St., Gaithersburg, Maryland **Tel:** 1 301 330-0132
Email: news@towncourier.com **Web site:** http://www.towncourier.com
Freq: Bi-Weekly; **Circ:** 14500
Editor & Publisher: Diane Dorney
Profile: The Town Courier is a bi-weekly community newspaper serving Gaithersburg, MD and the surrounding areas, including local news, business, education, sports, opinion and features. The paper publishes a Gaithersburg, MD edition on the 1st and 3rd Fridays of each month, and an Urbana, MD edition on the 4th Friday of each month.
Language (s): English
Ad Rate: Full Page Mono 10.28
Ad Rate: Full Page Colour 14.05
Currency: United States Dollars
COMMUNITY NEWSPAPER

Town Crier 22667
Owner: Flannery Publications
Editorial: 203 NE 1st St, Winlock, Washington 98596 **Tel:** 1 360 785-3151
Email: towncrier@flannerypubs.com **Web site:** http://www.hometowndebate.com/section/town-crier-news
Freq: Wed; **Circ:** 12000 Not Audited
Editor: Kim Collucci; **Publisher:** Patrick Myers
Profile: The Town Crier is a local weekly newspaper written for the residents of Lewis County, WA. The publication covers local news, sports, and community events. Editorial deadlines are on Fridays at noon PT.
Language (s): English
Ad Rate: Full Page Mono 8.90
Currency: United States Dollars
COMMUNITY NEWSPAPER

The Town Crier 23171
Owner: Graphic Word Publications
Editorial: 48 Mechanic St, Upton, Massachusetts 01568-1578 **Tel:** 1 508 529-7791
Email: thetowncrier@charter.net **Web site:** http://www.towncrier.us
Freq: Bi-Weekly; **Circ:** 5700 Not Audited
Editor: Jane Bigda; **Publisher:** Alfred Holman
Profile: The Town Crier is a local newspaper written for the communities of Milford, Mendon and Upton, MA.
Language (s): English
Ad Rate: Full Page Mono 14.42
Currency: United States Dollars
COMMUNITY NEWSPAPER

Town Crier Community Newspapers 25476
Owner: Ogden Newspapers
Editorial: 200 Franklin St Se, Warren, Ohio 44483-5711 **Tel:** 1 330 629-6200
Web site: http://www.towncrieronline.com
Freq: Weekly; **Circ:** 20000 Not Audited
Editor: Amy Wilson
Profile: Town Crier's editorial mission is to provide news and information that affects the community. The publication is written for the residents of Boardman, OH and surrounding areas.
Language (s): English
COMMUNITY NEWSPAPER

Town Crier Newspapers 25392
Owner: Woburn Daily Times, Inc.
Editorial: 1 Arrow Dr, Woburn, Massachusetts 01801-2039 **Tel:** 1 978 658-2346 100
Web site: http://www.homenewshere.com
Freq: Thu; **Circ:** 6900 Not Audited
Circulation Manager: Mary Early; **Publisher:** Peter Haggerty; **News Editor:** Jayne Miller; **Advertising Sales Manager:** Marcy Ragucci
Language (s): English
COMMUNITY NEWSPAPER

Town Journal 24632
Owner: Gannett Co., Inc./North Jersey Media Group
Editorial: 41 Oak St, Ridgewood, New Jersey 07450-3805 **Tel:** 1 201 612-5400
Email: townjournal@northjersey.com **Web site:** http://www.northjersey.com
Circ: 71125 Not Audited
Profile: Town Journal is a weekly, community newspaper serving residents of Allendale, Ho-Ho-Kus, Saddle River, Upper Saddle River, NJ. It covers local news, events, schools, sports, business and features stories.
Language (s): English
COMMUNITY NEWSPAPER

The Town Line 24147
Owner: Town Line, Inc. (The)
Editorial: 16 Jones Brook Xing, South China, Maine 04358-5246 **Tel:** 1 207 445-2234
Email: townline@fairpoint.net **Web site:** http://www.townline.org
Freq: Thu; **Circ:** 15000 Not Audited
Advertising Sales Manager: Diane Bickford; **Circulation Manager:** Claire Breton; **Editor:** Roland Hallee
Profile: The Town Line is a weekly newspaper serving the towns of Albion, China, Palermo, Vassalboro, Windsor and Winslow, ME. The editorial deadline is Mondays at 4pm ET.
Language (s): English
Ad Rate: Full Page Mono 12.50
Currency: United States Dollars
COMMUNITY NEWSPAPER

Town Reminder 23144
Owner: Turley Publications, Inc.
Editorial: 138 College St Ste 2, South Hadley, Massachusetts 01075-1500 **Tel:** 1 413 536-5333
Email: townreminder@turley.com **Web site:** http://townreminder.turley.com
Freq: Fri; **Circ:** 11800
Editor: Aimee Henderson; **Publisher:** Patrick Turley
Profile: Town Reminder is published weekly for the residents of South Hadley, MA. The newspaper covers local news, sports and community events.
Language (s): English
Ad Rate: Full Page Mono 11.50
Ad Rate: Full Page Colour 1360.00
Currency: United States Dollars
COMMUNITY NEWSPAPER

Town Talk Newspapers 25356
Owner: Journal Register Company
Editorial: 1914 Parker Ave, Holmes, Pennsylvania 19043-1414 **Tel:** 1 610 583-4432
Web site: http://www.delconewsnetwork.com
Circ: 48650 Not Audited
Publisher: Richard Crowe; **Editor:** Christina Parker
Language (s): English
COMMUNITY NEWSPAPER

Town Times 22182
Owner: Record-Journal Publishing Company
Editorial: 488 Main St, Middlefield, Connecticut 06455-1210 **Tel:** 1 860 349-8000
Email: news@towntimes.com **Web site:** http://www.towntimes.com
Freq: Fri; **Circ:** 10000 Not Audited
Advertising Sales Manager: Joy Boone; **Publisher:** Eliot White; **Editor:** Stephanie Wilcox
Profile: Town Times is a weekly newspaper serving Durham, Middlefield and Rockfall, CT.
Language (s): English
Ad Rate: Full Page Mono 15.30
Currency: United States Dollars
COMMUNITY NEWSPAPER

Town Topics 20207
Editorial: 305 Witherspoon St, Princeton, New Jersey 08542-3454 **Tel:** 1 609 924-2200
Email: editor@towntopics.com **Web site:** http://www.towntopics.com
Freq: Wed; **Circ:** 15500 Not Audited
Publisher/Editor: Lynn Smith
Profile: Town Topics is a weekly newspaper that concentrates on events and people in Princeton Borough and Township, NJ. Deadlines are on Fridays.
Language (s): English
Ad Rate: Full Page Mono 14.95
Ad Rate: Full Page Colour 1173.60
Currency: United States Dollars
COMMUNITY NEWSPAPER

The Town-Crier Newspaper 135531
Owner: Newspaper Publishiers, Inc.
Editorial: 12794 Forest Hill Blvd Ste 31, Wellington, Florida 33414-4758 **Tel:** 1 561 793-7606
Email: news@gotowncrier.com **Web site:** http://www.gotowncrier.com
Circ: 35500 Not Audited
Publisher: Barry Manning
Profile: Town-Crier Newspaper is a local newspaper for the community of Wellington, FL.
Language (s): English
COMMUNITY NEWSPAPER

Towns County Herald 24207
Editorial: 482 N Main St, Hiawassee, Georgia 30546-2258 **Tel:** 1 706 896-4454
Email: tcherald@windstream.net **Web site:** http://www.townscountyherald.net
Freq: Wed; **Circ:** 5300 Not Audited
Editor: Charles Duncan; **Publisher:** Kenneth West
Profile: Towns County Herald is a weekly newspaper covering local news for residents of Towns County, GA.
Language (s): English
Ad Rate: Full Page Mono 7.75
Currency: United States Dollars
COMMUNITY NEWSPAPER

The Township Times 22819
Editorial: 1668 Midland Rd, Saginaw, Michigan 48638-4338 **Tel:** 1 989 799-3200
Email: office@twptimes.com **Web site:** http://www.twptimes.com
Freq: Wed; **Circ:** 5000 Not Audited
Publisher: Ed Belles; **Advertising Sales Manager:** Tari Newvine
Profile: The Township Times is written for residents of Saginaw, MI.
Language (s): English
Ad Rate: Full Page Mono 8.50
Currency: United States Dollars
COMMUNITY NEWSPAPER

TP Printing Company 24729
Owner: TP Printing Company
Editorial: 103 W Spruce St, Abbotsford, Wisconsin 54405 **Tel:** 1 715 223-2342
Email: tp@tpprinting.com **Web site:** http://www.centralwinews.com
Circ: 5300 Not Audited
Circulation Manager: Jane Kroeplin; **Publisher:** Carol O'Leary; **Advertising Sales Manager:** Kelly Schmidt; **Editor:** Peter Weinschenk
Language (s): English
COMMUNITY NEWSPAPER

Tracy Press 13775
Owner: Tank Town Media LLC
Editorial: 131 W 10th St, Tracy, California 95376-3903 **Tel:** 1 209 835-3030
Email: tpnews@tracypress.com **Web site:** http://www.goldenstatenewspapers.com/tracy_press/
Freq: Fri; **Circ:** 19904 Not Audited
Editor: Michael Langley; **Circulation Manager:** Nancy Matthews; **Community News Editor:** Melanie Smith
Profile: Tracy Press strives to provide its readers with comprehensive coverage of local news and information, while keeping a keen eye toward national events and happenings.
Language (s): English
Ad Rate: Full Page Mono 26.00
Ad Rate: Full Page Colour 33.85
Currency: United States Dollars
COMMUNITY NEWSPAPER

The Transylvania Times 19967
Owner: Trapp (Stella)
Editorial: 37 N Broad St, Brevard, North Carolina 28712-3725 **Tel:** 1 828 883-8156
Email: news@transylvaniatimes.com **Web site:** http://www.transylvaniatimes.com
Freq: Mon; **Circ:** 6500 Not Audited
Circulation Manager: Barbara Conley; **Advertising Sales Manager:** John Connelly; **Editor:** John Lanier; **News Editor:** Derrick McKissock; **Publisher:** Stella Trapp
Profile: Transylvania Times is a publication that specifically deals with pertinent local area news and information. The audience for the publication is the community in and around Transylvania, NC. Deadlines for the publication are Tuesday and Friday at 3pm ET.
Language (s): English
Ad Rate: Full Page Mono 8.50
Currency: United States Dollars
COMMUNITY NEWSPAPER

Trempealeau County Times
726093
Owner: News Publishing Company, Inc.
Editorial: 36435 Main St, Whitehall, Wisconsin 54773-9108 **Tel:** 1 715 538-4765
Web site: http://www.arrow-times.com
Freq: Weekly; **Circ:** 5000
Editor: Scott Thomson
Profile: Trempealeau County Times is a weekly community newspaper serving Trempealeau County, WI. It covers communities including Arcadia, Whitehall, Independence, Galesville and Ettrick, WI.
Language (s): English
COMMUNITY NEWSPAPER

Tri City Ledger
18497
Owner: Thomas (Joe)
Editorial: 20766 Highway 31 South, Flomaton, Alabama 36441-1916 **Tel:** 1 251 296-3491
Email: newsroom@tricityledger.com
Freq: Thu; **Circ:** 5300 Not Audited
Circulation Manager: Michelle Hendrichs; **Publisher & Editor:** Joe Thomas
Profile: The Tri City Ledger is a weekly newspaper serving residents of Flomaton, AL and surrounding communities. The newspaper covers local news, community events, weather, and sports. Feature articles cover business, politics, education, health, lifestyle, arts & entertainment, and other topics of interest to the local community. Deadlines for the paper are Monday evening or early Tuesday morning prior to the issue date. It is not available online.
Language (s): English
Ad Rate: Full Page Mono 5.25
Currency: United States Dollars
COMMUNITY NEWSPAPER

Tri City Times
19570
Owner: Heim
Editorial: 594 N Almont Ave, Imlay City, Michigan 48444-1072 **Tel:** 1 810 724-2615
Email: tct@pageone-inc.com **Web site:** http://www.tricitytimes-online.com
Freq: Wed; **Circ:** 6322 Not Audited
Publisher: Delores Heim; **Editor:** Catherine Minolli Oudin
Profile: The Tri City Times is written for the residents of Imlay City, MI.
Language (s): English
Ad Rate: Full Page Mono 7.45
Currency: United States Dollars
COMMUNITY NEWSPAPER

Triad City Beat
915309
Owner: Beat Media, Inc.
Editorial: 1451 S Elm Eugene St, Greensboro, North Carolina 27406-2200 **Tel:** 1 336 256-9320
Web site: http://triad-city-beat.com
Freq: Weekly
Publisher: Allen Broach
Profile: Launched in March 2014, Triad City Beat is a hyperlocal alternative newsweekly, covering community news and culture in Greensboro, High Point and Winston-Salem, NC.
Language (s): English
Ad Rate: Full Page Mono 10.26
Ad Rate: Full Page Colour 12.31
Currency: United States Dollars
COMMUNITY NEWSPAPER

Triangle News Leader
475385
Owner: Independent Publications Inc.
Editorial: 4645 N Highway 19A, Mount Dora, Florida 32757-2039 **Tel:** 1 352 589-8811
Web site: http://www.trianglenewsleader.com
Freq: Wed; **Circ:** 31100 Not Audited
Editor: Linda Briody
Profile: Triangle News Leader is a community newspaper written for the residents of Mount Dora, FL. It covers local news, health, education, events and entertainment.
Language (s): English
Ad Rate: Full Page Mono 75.00
Ad Rate: Full Page Colour 11.33
Currency: United States Dollars
COMMUNITY NEWSPAPER

The Triangle Tribune
22805
Owner: Charlotte Post Publishing Co.
Editorial: 115 Market St Ste 360H, Durham, North Carolina 27701-3241 **Tel:** 1 919 688-9408 22
Email: editor@triangletribune.com **Web site:** http://www.triangletribune.com
Freq: Sun; **Circ:** 10000 Not Audited
Publisher: Gerald Johnson; **Advertising Sales Manager:** Jeri Thompson
Profile: The Triangle Tribune is published for African-American residents of Raleigh and Durham, NC. The newspaper covers local news, weather, sports and community events of interest to members of the African American community in the "Triangle."
Language (s): English
Ad Rate: Full Page Mono 24.00
Currency: United States Dollars
COMMUNITY NEWSPAPER

La Tribuna de New Jersey
23306
Editorial: 300 36th St, Union City, New Jersey 07087-4724 **Tel:** 1 201 617-1360
Freq: Bi-Weekly; **Circ:** 53000 Not Audited
Publisher & Editor: Ruth Molenaar
Profile: La Tribuna de New Jersey is a bi-monthly newspaper written for Hispanic residents and others interested in the Hispanic culture in Union City, NJ. The newspaper focuses on general news and Hispanic affairs.
Language (s): Spanish
Ad Rate: Full Page Mono 19.80
Currency: United States Dollars
COMMUNITY NEWSPAPER

La Tribuna Hispana - USA
23279
Editorial: 48 Main St Fl 2, Hempstead, New York 11550-4052 **Tel:** 1 516 486-6457
Email: editorial@latribunahispana.com **Web site:** http://www.tribunahispanausa.com/
Freq: Wed; **Circ:** 49000 Not Audited
Publisher & Editor: Luis Aguilar; **Advertising Sales Manager:** Emilio Alfaror Ruiz
Profile: La Tribuna Hispana - USA is published weekly for New York's Spanish-speaking residents. The newspaper covers news, arts & entertainment, religion, family, politics and community events. Deadlines fall on Tuesdays at noon ET.
Language (s): English, Spanish
Ad Rate: Full Page Mono 25.50
Currency: United States Dollars
COMMUNITY NEWSPAPER

Tribuna Newspaper
974685
Editorial: 281 Main St, Danbury, Connecticut 06810-6607 **Tel:** 1 203 730-0457
Email: editor@tribunact.com **Web site:** http://www.tribunact.com
Freq: Bi-Weekly
Publisher: Celia Bacelar; **Advertising Sales Manager:** Angela Barbosa; **Editor:** Emanuela Leaf
Profile: Tribuna Is a free bi-weekly trilingual publication In English, Portuguese and Spanish covering Connecticut Since 1999.
Language (s): English
COMMUNITY NEWSPAPER

Tribune
21106
Owner: Horizon Publications
Editorial: 104 N Main St, Deer Park, Washington 99006-5086 **Tel:** 1 509 276-5043
Web site: http://www.dptribune.com/
Freq: Wed; **Circ:** 12447 Not Audited
Editor: Thomas Costigan
Profile: The Tribune is a weekly newspaper providing Local News coverage for the residents for Deer Park, WA.
Language (s): English
Ad Rate: Full Page Mono 8.50
Currency: United States Dollars
COMMUNITY NEWSPAPER

Tribune
22506
Editorial: 173 Coquina Ave, Ormond Beach, Florida 32174-3303 **Tel:** 1 434 979-0373
Email: tribune54@gmail.com
Freq: Thu; **Circ:** 12000 Not Audited
Publisher & Editor: Agnes White
Profile: Tribune is published weekly for members of the African American community in Charlottesville, VA. The newspaper covers local news, community events and social issues. Deadlines for the publication are on Tuesdays.
Language (s): English
Ad Rate: Full Page Mono 16.94
Currency: United States Dollars
COMMUNITY NEWSPAPER

The Tribune & Georgian
18855
Owner: Community Newspapers Inc.
Editorial: 206 Osborne St, Saint Marys, Georgia 31558-8400 **Tel:** 1 912 882-4927
Email: editor1@tds.net **Web site:** http://www.tribune-georgian.com
Freq: Fri; **Circ:** 8200 Not Audited
Circulation Manager: Barbara Boyd; **Community News Editor:** Emily Heglund; **Editor & Publisher:** Jill Helton; **Advertising Manager:** Brad Spaulding
Profile: The Tribune & Georgian is a local newspaper serving Camden County, GA. It provides the local community with information on news, events, sports and weather
Language (s): English
Ad Rate: Full Page Mono 14.44
Currency: United States Dollars
COMMUNITY NEWSPAPER

The Tribune Newspapers
445468
Owner: Hartburg Publications
Editorial: 18525 W Lake Houston Pkwy, Ste 102, Humble, Texas 77346 **Tel:** 1 281 540-8742
Web site: http://www.ourtribune.com
Freq: Wed; **Circ:** 55000 Not Audited
Publisher & Editor: Cynthia Calvert
Profile: The Tribune Newspapers is a weekly newspaper serving the Humble, TX community. Deadlines are Thursdays at 5pm, CT.
Language (s): English
Ad Rate: Full Page Mono 26.50
Currency: United States Dollars
COMMUNITY NEWSPAPER

Tribune Papers
359711
Owner: Tribune Papers Inc. (The)
Editorial: 1 Boston Way, Asheville, North Carolina 28803-2653 **Tel:** 1 828 277-1760
Web site: http://www.thetribunepapers.com/
Circ: 25000
Publisher: David Morgan; **Editor:** Clint Parker
Profile: Tribune Papers in Asheville, NC publishes the Asheville Tribune and Weaverville Tribune community newspapers.
Language (s): English
COMMUNITY NEWSPAPER

Tribune Publishing Company
24580
Editorial: 700 E Broadway, Boston, Massachusetts 02127-1504 **Tel:** 1 617 269-5550
Email: mail@southbostononline.com **Web site:** http://www.southbostononline.com
Circ: 30400 Not Audited
Profile: South Boston Online is a free weekly news publication for South Boston and its surrounding neighborhoods.
Language (s): English
COMMUNITY NEWSPAPER

The Tribune-Courier
19322
Owner: Paxton Media Group
Editorial: 86B Commerce Blvd, Benton, Kentucky 42025-1110 **Tel:** 1 270 527-3162
Email: emcgill@tribunecourier.com **Web site:** http://www.tribunecourier.com
Freq: Tue; **Circ:** 5200 Not Audited
Circulation Manager: Hilda Norwood; **Editor:** Jody Norwood; **Advertising Sales Manager:** Selena Ward
Profile: The Tribune-Courier is a local weekly newspaper written for residents of Marshall County, KY. The newspaper covers local news, sports and events.
Language (s): English
Ad Rate: Full Page Mono 7.70
Currency: United States Dollars
COMMUNITY NEWSPAPER

Tribune-Times
24309
Owner: Greenville News/Gannett
Editorial: 305 S Main St, Greenville, South Carolina 29601-2605 **Tel:** 1 864 298-4100
Email: tletters@tribunetimes.com **Web site:** http://www.tribunetimes.com
Freq: Wed; **Circ:** 43525 Not Audited
Profile: Tribune-Times is a weekly publication written for residents of Greenville, SC. It mainly focuses on local news and sports.
Language (s): English
Ad Rate: Full Page Mono 19.65
Currency: United States Dollars
COMMUNITY NEWSPAPER

Tri-City Voice
355562
Owner: What's Happening Inc.
Editorial: 39737 Paseo Padre Pkwy, Fremont, California 94538-2996 **Tel:** 1 510 494-1999
Email: tricityvoice@aol.com **Web site:** http://www.tricityvoice.com
Freq: Weekly; **Circ:** 25500 Not Audited
Profile: Tri-City Voice in Fremont, CA is a weekly community newspaper covering the cities of Fremont, Newark, Union City, Hayward, Sunol, and Milpitas, CA. Through a blend of local coverage of sports, culture and art & entertainment, the newspaper has become an essential resource for understanding, exploring, and celebrating the area's heritage. Tri-City Voice speaks with a distinctive voice to a large multicultural audience. It is distributed to over 2,500 locations including community centers, government offices, libraries, all major businesses, high-end apartments, hotels, restaurants, medical centers, recreational facilities, schools, and high traffic retail locations, in addition to our subscribers. Deadlines are on Thursdays at 5 pm PT.
Language (s): English
Ad Rate: Full Page Mono 18.82
Ad Rate: Full Page Colour 400.00
Currency: United States Dollars
COMMUNITY NEWSPAPER

triCityNews
541871
Editorial: 601 Bangs Ave, Ste 609, Asbury Park, New Jersey 07712-6925 **Tel:** 1 732 897-9779
Email: news@trinews.com **Web site:** http://www.trinews.com
Freq: Thu; **Circ:** 8500 Not Audited
Publisher: Dan Jacobson
Profile: triCityNews is an alternative newspaper focusing on the arts, culture and politics in Eastern Monmouth County, NJ. The free weekly paper aims to uncover interesting artists, businesses and characters of all stripes in suburban New Jersey.
Language (s): English
Ad Rate: Full Page Mono 4.71
Ad Rate: Full Page Colour 3.00
Currency: United States Dollars
COMMUNITY NEWSPAPER

Tri-County Citizen
22818
Owner: JAMS Media
Editorial: 110 S Chapman St, Chesaning, Michigan 48616-1221 **Tel:** 1 989 845-7403
Email: tccnews@mihomepaper.com **Web site:** http://www.tricountycitizen.com
Freq: Sun; **Circ:** 18000 Not Audited
Editor: Keith Salisbury
Profile: Tri-County Citizen is a publication providing residents of Chesaning, MI with coverage of local area news and information.
Language (s): English
Ad Rate: Full Page Mono 9.45
Currency: United States Dollars
COMMUNITY NEWSPAPER

Tri-County Herald
920642
Owner: News Leader Co. Inc.
Editorial: 620 W Carl Hubbell Blvd, Meeker, Oklahoma 74855 **Tel:** 1 405 279-2363
Email: news@tricountyherald.com **Web site:** http://www.okemahnewsleader.com/77278/1578/online-editiontricounty-herald
Freq: Weekly
Editor & Publisher: Lynn Thompson
Profile: Tri-County Herald is a weekly community newspaper serving Meeker, Harrah, McLoud and Newalla, OK with community news, events and sports coverage.
Language (s): English
COMMUNITY NEWSPAPER

Tri-County Newspapers
24609
Editorial: 217 S Alvaredo Ave, Belle, Missouri 65013 **Tel:** 1 573 859-3328
Email: tcnpub3@gmail.com
Circ: 5300 Not Audited
Publisher: Kurt Lewis; **Editor:** Ron Lewis
Profile: Covers local news in Belle, MO. Also operates under the name the Belle Banner.
Language (s): English
COMMUNITY NEWSPAPER

Tri-County Publishing, Inc.
25060
Owner: Tri County Publishing, Inc.
Editorial: 3 Banner Row, Mc Kenzie, Tennessee 38201 **Tel:** 1 731 352-3323
Email: banner@mckenziebanner.com **Web site:** http://mckenziebanner.com
Circ: 10000 Not Audited
Advertising Sales Manager: Jennifer Sims; **Editor:** Joel Washburn; **Publisher:** Ramona Washburn
Profile: Tri-County Publishing, Inc. is a community newspaper publisher that services the residents of Jackson, TN.
Language (s): English
COMMUNITY NEWSPAPER

Tri-County Sentry
137097
Owner: Hunt Communications, LLC
Editorial: 1200 N Ventura Rd Ste G, Oxnard, California 93030-3827 **Tel:** 1 805 983-0015
Email: sentry1234@aol.com **Web site:** http://www.tricountysentry.com
Freq: Fri; **Circ:** 10000 Not Audited
Advertising Sales Manager: Debby Hunt; **Publisher & Editor:** Peggy Hunt
Profile: Tri-County Sentry is a local newspaper written for the African American community of Oxnard, CA.
Language (s): English
Ad Rate: Full Page Mono 21.50
Currency: United States Dollars
COMMUNITY NEWSPAPER

Tri-County Sunday
794025
Owner: McLean Publishing Co.
Editorial: 500 Jeffers St, Du Bois, Pennsylvania 15801 **Tel:** 1 814 371-4200
Web site: http://www.thecourierexpress.com
Freq: Sun; **Circ:** 16500
Editor: Joy Norwood
Profile: The Tri-County Sunday is the Sunday delivered version of the Courier-Express. The Tri-County Sunday covers the topics and areas as the Courier-Express, and is published at the same offices.
Language (s): English
COMMUNITY NEWSPAPER

Tri-County Times
22256
Owner: Rockman Communications
Editorial: 256 N Fenway Dr, Fenton, Michigan 48430-2699 **Tel:** 1 810 629-8282
Email: news@tctimes.com **Web site:** http://www.tctimes.com
Freq: 2 Times/Week; **Circ:** 22898 Not Audited
Publisher: Craig Rockman; **Editor:** Sharon Stone; **Editor:** Dave Troppens
Profile: Tri-County Times is a community-based publication that looks to give its followers comprehensive coverage of local area news and events. The lead time is two days. Deadline is two days before the publication date.
Language (s): English
Ad Rate: Full Page Mono 28.56
Currency: United States Dollars
COMMUNITY NEWSPAPER

Tri-State Defender
20744
Owner: Best Media Properties
Editorial: 203 Beale St Ste 200, Memphis, Tennessee 38103-3727 **Tel:** 1 901 523-1818
Email: editorial@tri-statedefender.com **Web site:** http://www.tri-statedefender.com
Freq: Thu; **Circ:** 36000 Not Audited
Circulation Manager: Kelly Evans
Profile: Tri-State Defender is a local weekly newspaper written for residents in and around Memphis, TN. The publication strives to provide its readership with comprehensive coverage of local area news and information. Deadlines are Mondays at 5pm ET.
Language (s): English
Ad Rate: Full Page Mono 32.07
Currency: United States Dollars
COMMUNITY NEWSPAPER

Troy-Somerset Gazette
28757
Owner: Gazette Newspapers Inc.
Editorial: 6966 Crooks Rd Ste 22, Troy, Michigan 48098-1798 **Tel:** 1 248 524-4868
Email: news@gazettemediagroup.com **Web site:** http://www.troy-somersetgazette.com
Freq: Mon; **Circ:** 25000 Not Audited
Advertising Sales Manager: Pam Brown; **Publisher:** Claire Weber
Profile: Troy-Somerset Gazette in Troy, MI is a community newspaper that covers local news and events. Deadlines for the publication are Mondays at 5pm ET.
Language (s): English

Ad Rate: Full Page Mono 15.60
Currency: United States Dollars
COMMUNITY NEWSPAPER

The Trussville Tribune 788192
Owner: ADLAB Communications
Editorial: 5850 Valley Rd Ste 90, Trussville, Alabama 35235-8683 **Tel:** 1 205 533-8664
Email: news@trussvilletribune.com **Web site:** http://www.trussvilletribune.com
Freq: Weekly
Publisher: Scott Buttram
Profile: The Trussville Tribune is a weekly newspaper providing Local and Community News coverage to the residents of Trussville, AL.
Language (s): English
COMMUNITY NEWSPAPER

Tu Decides/You Decide 489198
Owner: Campos (Gracie), Campos (Ismael), Torres (Albert) dba Tu Decides Media
Editorial: 8220 W Gage Blvd, Kennewick, Washington 99336-8113 **Tel:** 1 509 591-0495
Email: info@tudecidesmedia.com **Web site:** http://www.tudecidesmedia.com
Freq: Fri; **Circ:** 20000 Not Audited
Circulation Manager: Ismael Campos
Profile: Tu Decides/You Decide is a weekly bilingual newspaper for the residents of Kennewick, WA and the surrounding areas. It covers local news, events, arts & entertainment and religion.
Language (s): Spanish/Bilingual
Ad Rate: Full Page Mono 17.68
Currency: United States Dollars
COMMUNITY NEWSPAPER

Tucson Local Media 152125
Owner: 10/13 Communications
Editorial: 7225 N Mona Lisa Rd Ste 125, Tucson, Arizona 85741-2581 **Tel:** 1 520 797-4384
Email: editor@explorernews.com **Web site:** http://tucsonlocalmedia.com
Freq: Wed; **Circ:** 98625 Not Audited
Circulation Manager: Laura Horvath
Profile: Tucson Local Media is a community newspaper publisher producing the Explorer, Foothills News, Marana News, Desert Times, Tucson Weekly and Inside Tucson Business.
Language (s): English
COMMUNITY NEWSPAPER

Tullahoma Newspapers 25061
Owner: Lakeway Publishers, Inc.
Editorial: 505 Lake Way Pl, Tullahoma, Tennessee 37388 **Tel:** 1 931 455-4545
Email: tnased@lcs.net **Web site:** http://www.tullahomanews.com
Circ: 17900 Not Audited
Publisher & Editor: Jeff Fishman
Language (s): English
COMMUNITY NEWSPAPER

Tulsa Beacon 920666
Owner: Biggs (Charles) & Biggs (Susan)
Editorial: 6784 S 67th East Ave, Tulsa, Oklahoma 74133-1723 **Tel:** 1 918 523-4425
Web site: http://tulsabeacon.com
Freq: Weekly
Profile: Tulsa Beacon is a weekly community newspaper serving residents of Tulsa, OK with community news, opinion, sports and entertainment.
Language (s): English
COMMUNITY NEWSPAPER

Turley Publications, Inc. 25167
Owner: Turley Publications, Inc.
Editorial: 24 Water St, Palmer, Massachusetts 01069-1885 **Tel:** 1 413 283-8393
Web site: http://www.turley.com
Circ: 38404 Not Audited
Editor: Charles Bennett; **Circulation Manager:** Charlann Griswold; **Editor:** Emily Thurlow; **Publisher:** Patrick Turley; **Editor:** Tyler Witkop
Language (s): English
COMMUNITY NEWSPAPER

TurleyCT Community Publications 75516
Owner: TurleyCT Community Publications
Editorial: 540 Hopmeadow St, Simsbury, Connecticut 06070-2496 **Tel:** 1 860 651-4700
Web site: http://www.turleyct.com
Circ: 142700 Not Audited
Editor: Mark Jahne; **Editor:** Nancy Thompson; **Publisher:** Keith Turley; **Editor:** Lynn Woike
Profile: TurleyCT Community Publications features community newspaper mailed to households in West Hartford, Avon, Burlington, Canton, Farmington, Rocky Hill, Newington, Wethersfield, and Glastonbury, and Simsbury, CT. The publications cover local news with a focus on events, town meetings, schools, sports and business.
Language (s): English
COMMUNITY NEWSPAPER

Turlock Journal 13759
Owner: Morris Newspaper Corp.
Editorial: 138 S Center St, Turlock, California 95380-4508 **Tel:** 1 209 634-9141
Email: news@turlockjournal.com **Web site:** http://www.turlockjournal.com
Freq: Sat; **Circ:** 6000
Publisher: Hank Vander Veen
Profile: Turlock Journal's mission is to provide its readers with the latest in local news and information. The publication is written for residents of Turlock, CA and its surrounding area. Deadlines are one day prior to issue dates.
Language (s): English
Ad Rate: Full Page Mono 14.20
Currency: United States Dollars
COMMUNITY NEWSPAPER

Turner Publishing 242211
Owner: Turner Publishing Inc.
Editorial: 5 Fern St, Turner, Maine 4282
Tel: 1 207 225-2076
Email: articles@turnerpublishing.net **Web site:** http://www.turnerpublishing.net
Circ: 161406 Not Audited
Editor & Publisher: Jodi Cornelio
Language (s): English
COMMUNITY NEWSPAPER

Turnstile Media Group 88011
Owner: Turnstile Media Group
Editorial: 1500 Park Center Dr, Orlando, Florida 32835-5705 **Tel:** 1 407 515-2605
Web site: http://www.wpmobserver.com
Freq: Weekly; **Circ:** 5000 Not Audited
Publisher: Tracy Craft
Profile: Turnstile Media Group newspapers are published for the residents of Winter Park and Maitland, FL.
Language (s): English
Ad Rate: Full Page Mono 14.00
Currency: United States Dollars
COMMUNITY NEWSPAPER

Turtle Creek News 128875
Editorial: 1812 N Haskell Ave Ste 200, Dallas, Texas 75204-3762 **Tel:** 1 214 887-0737
Freq: Fri; **Circ:** 25000 Not Audited
Publisher: Lance Brennan; **Editor:** Chris Libby
Profile: Turtle Creek News is a local newspaper written for the residents of Dallas. Do not send press releases to the paper by fax.
Language (s): English
Ad Rate: Full Page Mono 30.00
Currency: United States Dollars
COMMUNITY NEWSPAPER

Tuscola County Advertiser 19500
Owner: Edwards Publications
Editorial: 344 N State St, Caro, Michigan 48723-1538
Tel: 1 989 673-3181
Email: ads@tcadvertiser.com **Web site:** http://www.tuscolatoday.com
Freq: Sat; **Circ:** 7500 Not Audited
Circulation Manager: Lori Gandy; **Publisher:** Tim Murphy; **Advertising Sales Manager:** Jean Norton
Profile: Tuscola County Advertiser is written for the residents of Caro and eastern Saginaw Valley, MI and its surrounding areas.
Language (s): English
Ad Rate: Full Page Mono 10.82
Currency: United States Dollars
COMMUNITY NEWSPAPER

Tuscumbia Newspapers 25005
Editorial: 106 W 5th St, Tuscumbia, Alabama 35674-2412 **Tel:** 1 256 383-8471
Email: colbertcountyreporter@earthlink.net
Circ: 5700 Not Audited
Publisher and Editor: Jim Crawford
Language (s): English
COMMUNITY NEWSPAPER

Twin City Times 156407
Owner: Steele (Laurie)
Editorial: 33 Dunn St, Auburn, Maine 04210-6822
Tel: 1 207 795-5017
Email: editor@twincitytimes.com **Web site:** http://www.twincitytimes.com
Freq: Thu; **Circ:** 34697 Not Audited
Publisher: Laurie Steele
Profile: The Twin City Times is a community newspaper written for the residents of Auburn, ME and the surrounding areas.
Language (s): English
Ad Rate: Full Page Mono 19.00
Currency: United States Dollars
COMMUNITY NEWSPAPER

Twin Valley Publications 25054
Editorial: 10 S Main St, West Alexandria, Ohio 45381-1216 **Tel:** 1 937 839-4733
Email: twinvpub@infinet.com **Web site:** http://twinvalleypublications.com
Circ: 8000 Not Audited
Advertising Sales Manager: Cindy Shortes; **Publisher & Editor:** Sam Shortes
Language (s): English
COMMUNITY NEWSPAPER

The Two River Times 21649
Editorial: 75 W Front St, Red Bank, New Jersey 07701-1659 **Tel:** 1 732 219-5788
Email: editor@tworivertimes.com **Web site:** http://trtnj.com
Freq: Thu; **Circ:** 10000 Not Audited
Publisher: Ellen McCarthy
Profile: Two River Times provides local residents of Red Bank, NJ with local news and information.
Language (s): English
Ad Rate: Full Page Mono 11.90
Currency: United States Dollars
COMMUNITY NEWSPAPER

The U.P. Catholic 382454
Owner: Catholic Diocese of Marquette
Editorial: 1004 Harbor Hills Dr, Marquette, Michigan 49855-8851 **Tel:** 1 906 227-9131
Email: jfee@dioceseofmarquette.org **Web site:** http://www.dioceseofmarquette.org
Freq: Bi-Weekly; **Circ:** 20000 Not Audited
Editor: John Fee; **Advertising Sales Manager:** Stephen Gretzinger; **Circulation Manager:** Sheila Wickenheiser
Profile: The U.P. Catholic is a bi-weekly newspaper published on the first and third Fridays of each month by the Catholic Diocese of Marquette, MI. Its mission is to unite all Catholic households in the Upper Peninsula with the Diocesan Church through a newspaper that brings residents news and information that broaden their perspectives, leading to greater closeness to Christ as they live with faith in their daily lives.
Language (s): English
Ad Rate: Full Page Mono 13.98
Currency: United States Dollars
COMMUNITY NEWSPAPER

U.S. 1 Newspaper 22269
Editorial: 12 Roszel Rd, Princeton, New Jersey 08540-6234 **Tel:** 1 609 452-7000
Email: info@princetoninfo.com **Web site:** http://www.princetoninfo.com
Freq: Wed; **Circ:** 19000 Not Audited
Publisher & Editor: Richard Rein
Profile: U.S. 1 Newspaper is a business focused publication written for professionals in the greater Princeton, NJ area.
Language (s): English
Ad Rate: Full Page Mono 14.10
Currency: United States Dollars
COMMUNITY NEWSPAPER

Uintah Basin Standard 21034
Owner: Unitah Basin Media
Editorial: 268 S Main St, Roosevelt, Utah 84066-3109 **Tel:** 1 435 722-5131
Email: editor@ubstandard.com **Web site:** http://www.ubmedia.biz/touch5/
Freq: Weekly; **Circ:** 5500 Not Audited
Publisher: Kevin Ashby
Profile: Uintah Basin Standard is written for the residents of Roosevelt, UT. Deadlines are on Thursdays at 5pm MT.
Language (s): English
Ad Rate: Full Page Mono 8.50
Currency: United States Dollars
COMMUNITY NEWSPAPER

The Ukrainian Weekly & Svoboda 25548
Owner: Ukrainian National Association, Inc.
Editorial: 2200 State Rt 10, Parsippany, New Jersey 07054-5304 **Tel:** 1 973 292-9800
Circ: 16000
Advertising Sales Manager: Walter Honcharyk
Profile: The Ukrainian Weekly is community newspaper published every Fridays covering Ukrainian news, culture, and events.
Language (s): English
COMMUNITY NEWSPAPER

Ulster Publishing Co. - Kingston 73254
Owner: Ulster Publishing
Editorial: 322 Wall St, Kingston, New York 12401-3820 **Tel:** 1 845 334-8200
Web site: http://www.ulsterpublishing.com
Circ: 17400 Not Audited
Editor: Dan Barton; **Editor:** Will Dendis; **Editor:** Brian Hollander; **Publisher:** Geddy Sveikauskas
Language (s): English
COMMUNITY NEWSPAPER

Ultima Nota 824786
Editorial: 4768 Broadway, New York, New York 10034-4916 **Tel:** 1 917 567-8565
Web site: http://www.ultimanota.com
Freq: Weekly
Editor & Publisher: Félix Jerez
Profile: Ultima Nota is a weekly newspaper providing Local and Community News coverage to the Hispanic community in New Jersey, New York and Connecticut.
Language (s): Spanish
COMMUNITY NEWSPAPER

Unidos en el Sur de California 903808
Owner: 2100 Trust LLC
Editorial: 523 N Grand Ave, Santa Ana, California 92701-4345 **Tel:** 1 951 368-9330
Email: laprensaeditors@pe.com **Web site:** http://www.unidossc.com
Freq: Weekly; **Circ:** 57852
Profile: Unidos en el Sur de California is a weekly Spanish language community newspaper serving the Latino population in Southern California with news (Noticias), sports (Deportes) and NEXT, a bilingual entertainment guide. Four zoned editions are offered, serving Orange County, Inland Southern California, Coachella Valley and Los Angeles.
Language (s): Spanish
COMMUNITY NEWSPAPER

Union Banner 19064
Owner: Centralia Press Ltd.
Editorial: 671 10th St, Carlyle, Illinois 62231-1443
Tel: 1 618 594-3131
Email: mhodapp@unionbanner.net
Freq: Wed; **Circ:** 6200 Not Audited
Editor: Mark Hodapp; **Publisher:** John Perrine
Profile: Union Banner's editorial mission is to inform people of the news in the Carlyle and Clinton counties of Illinois and its surrounding area. The publication includes local news, local politics, arts & entertainment and sports. Deadlines for the publicatoin are one week before issue date.
Language (s): English
Ad Rate: Full Page Mono 5.18
Currency: United States Dollars
COMMUNITY NEWSPAPER

The Union Star 152950
Owner: Womack Newspapers Inc.
Editorial: 241 Main St, Brookneal, Virginia 24528
Tel: 1 434 376-2795
Email: news@theunionstar.com **Web site:** http://www.theunionstar.com
Freq: Weekly; **Circ:** 5600 Not Audited
Publisher: Chad Harrison; **Advertising Sales Manager:** Amanda Letterman
Profile: The Union Star serves residents of Brookneal, VA with community news coverage.
Language (s): English
COMMUNITY NEWSPAPER

Upper Dauphin Sentinel 20580
Owner: Kocher (Ben)
Editorial: 510 Union St, Millersburg, Pennsylvania 17061-1470 **Tel:** 1 717 692-4737
Email: news@sentinelnow.com **Web site:** http://www.sentinelnow.com
Freq: Tue; **Circ:** 7700 Not Audited
Editor: Duane Good; **Publisher:** Ben Kocher
Profile: Upper Dauphin Sentinel is a local newspaper serving residents in and around Dauphin County, PA. The newspaper covers local news, community events and sports. Deadlines are on Thursdays at 4pm ET.
Language (s): English
Ad Rate: Full Page Mono 10.60
Currency: United States Dollars
COMMUNITY NEWSPAPER

Upstate Newspapers, Inc. 25074
Owner: Keowee Publications, Inc.
Editorial: 100 E Main St, Westminster, South Carolina 29693-1715 **Tel:** 1 864 647-5404
Email: westnews@bellsouth.net
Circ: 6300 Not Audited
Editor: Ashton Hester; **Editor:** Rolann Lee;
Publisher: Robert Tribble
Language (s): English
COMMUNITY NEWSPAPER

Urdu Times USA 811155
Owner: Urdu Media Network, Inc.
Editorial: 16920 Hillside Ave, Jamaica, New York 11432-4435 **Tel:** 1 718 297-8700
Email: urdutimesny@aol.com **Web site:** http://www.urdutimesusa.com
Freq: Weekly; **Circ:** 17000
Profile: The Urdu Times USA is a weekly newspaper providing Community News coverage for the Indian, Pakastani and Urdu-speaking community in the United States.
Language (s): Urdu
Ad Rate: Full Page Mono 20.00
Currency: United States Dollars
COMMUNITY NEWSPAPER

Urdu Times USA - California 811222
Owner: Urdu Media Network, Inc.
Editorial: 3632 Redondo Beach Blvd Apt D, Torrance, California 90504-1328 **Tel:** 1 310 704-3939
Web site: http://www.urdutimesusa.com
Freq: Weekly; **Circ:** 7000
Profile: The Urdu Times USA is a weekly newspaper providing Community News coverage for the Indian, Pakastani and Urdu-speaking community in the Torrance, CA area.
Language (s): Urdu
Ad Rate: Full Page Mono 20.00
Currency: United States Dollars
COMMUNITY NEWSPAPER

Urdu Times USA - Chicago 811175
Owner: Urdu Media Network, Inc.
Editorial: 7450 Skokie Blvd, Skokie, Illinois 60077-3374 **Tel:** 1 773 274-3100
Email: urdutimes@hotmail.com **Web site:** http://www.urdutimesusa.com/chicago
Freq: Weekly; **Circ:** 10000
Bureau Chief: Tariq Khawaja
Profile: The Urdu Times USA is a weekly newspaper providing Community News coverage for the Indian, Pakastani and Urdu-speaking community in the Chicago, IL area.
Language (s): Urdu
Ad Rate: Full Page Mono 20.00
Currency: United States Dollars
COMMUNITY NEWSPAPER

Urdu Times USA - Florida 811238
Owner: Urdu Media Network, Inc.
Tel: 1 954 873-3681
Web site: http://www.urdutimesusa.com
Freq: Weekly; **Circ:** 5000
Bureau Chief: Masood Akhtar
Profile: The Urdu Times USA is a weekly newspaper providing Community News coverage for the Indian, Pakastani and Urdu-speaking community in the Fort Lauderdale, FL area.
Language (s): Urdu
Ad Rate: Full Page Mono 20.00

Currency: United States Dollars
COMMUNITY NEWSPAPER

Urdu Times USA - Texas 811245
Owner: Urdu Media Network, Inc.
Editorial: 13100 W Bellfort Ave, Houston, Texas 77099-4828
Web site: http://www.urdutimesusa.com
Freq: Weekly
Bureau Chief: Ahmed Mahmood
Profile: The Urdu Times USA is a weekly newspaper providing Community News coverage for the Indian, Pakastani and Urdu-speaking community in the Houston, TX area.
Language (s): Urdu
Ad Rate: Full Page Mono 20.00
Currency: United States Dollars
COMMUNITY NEWSPAPER

Urdu Times USA - Washington DC 811182
Owner: Urdu Media Network, Inc.
Editorial: 8254 Richmond Hwy, Alexandria, Virginia 22309-8220 **Tel:** 1 202 812-1252
Web site: http://www.urdutimesusa.com
Freq: Weekly; **Circ:** 7000
Bureau Chief: Ahmad Shakil Mian
Profile: The Urdu Times USA is a weekly newspaper providing Community News coverage for the Indian, Pakastani and Urdu-speaking community in the Washington, DC area.
Language (s): Urdu
Ad Rate: Full Page Mono 20.00
Currency: United States Dollars
COMMUNITY NEWSPAPER

UT Community Press 535371
Owner: UT Community Press
Editorial: 3702 Via De La Valle Ste 202W, Del Mar, California 92014-4255 **Tel:** 1 858 756-1403
Email: editor@delmartimes.net **Web site:** http://www.delmartimes.net
Circ: 44596 Not Audited
Circulation Manager: Dara Elstein; **Publisher:** Phyllis Pfeiffer
Profile: UT Community Press publishes weekly newspapers for surrounding area suburbs of San Diego. Four papers are located in the Del Mar, CA office, one, Encinatas Advocate in Encinatas, California, and one, La Jolla Light, is a standalone in La Jolla, CA. The papers cover local news, sports and events.
Language (s): English
COMMUNITY NEWSPAPER

Uvalde Leader-News 20971
Owner: Garnett (Chris)
Editorial: 110 N East St, Uvalde, Texas 78801-5312
Tel: 1 830 278-3335
Web site: http://www.uvaldeleadernews.com
Freq: Sun; **Circ:** 5233 Not Audited
Advertising Sales Manager: Steve Balke; **Publisher & Editor:** Craig Garnett; **Circulation Manager:** Pete Luna
Profile: Uvalde Leader-News is written for the citizens of Uvalde, TX and the surrounding areas.
Language (s): English
Ad Rate: Full Page Mono 10.00
Currency: United States Dollars
COMMUNITY NEWSPAPER

V Novom Svete 155663
Editorial: 55 Broad St Fl 20, New York, New York 10004-2501 **Tel:** 1 212 482-0303
Email: editor@vnsnews.com **Web site:** http://www.vnovomsvete.
Freq: Thu; **Circ:** 47500 Not Audited
Editor: Olga Kochetkova; **Advertising Sales Manager:** Anastasia Stetsum
Profile: V Novom Svete in New York is a weekly newspaper serving the Russian and Russian American Community.
Language (s): English
Ad Rate: Full Page Mono 100.00
Currency: United States Dollars
COMMUNITY NEWSPAPER

Vacation News 22793
Editorial: 3797 Highway 54, Osage Beach, Missouri 65065-2138 **Tel:** 1 573 348-4577
Web site: http://www.lakenewsonline.com
Freq: Bi-Weekly; **Circ:** 11500 Not Audited
Advertising Sales Manager: Mary Montgomery; **Editor:** Charis Patris
Profile: Vacations News is a bi-weekly community newspaper written for residents of Osage Beach, MO.
Language (s): English
Ad Rate: Full Page Mono 6.52
Currency: United States Dollars
COMMUNITY NEWSPAPER

Valley Advocate 22918
Owner: Newspapers of New England
Editorial: 115 Conz St, Northampton, Massachusetts 01060-4444 **Tel:** 1 413 529-2840
Email: editor@valleyadvocate.com **Web site:** http://www.valleyadvocate.com
Freq: Thu; **Circ:** 40000 Not Audited
Profile: Valley Advocate is written for residents of Hampden, Hampshire, Franklin and Berkshire counties in Massachusetts. It covers news, lifestyle, arts & entertainment and community events. Its editorial mission is to provide an alternative to the mainstream press with articles written for an audience of primarily young, educated college graduates.
Language (s): English
Ad Rate: Full Page Mono 40.74
Currency: United States Dollars
COMMUNITY NEWSPAPER

Valley Breeze Newspapers 25724
Owner: Breeze Publications
Editorial: 6 Blackstone Valley Pl Ste 204, Lincoln, Rhode Island 02865-1112 **Tel:** 1 401 334-9555
Email: news@valleybreeze.com **Web site:** http://www.valleybreeze.com
Circ: 35500
News Editor: Nancy O'Halloran; **Publisher:** Tom Ward
Language (s): English
COMMUNITY NEWSPAPER

The Valley Chronicle 74407
Owner: Century Group (The)
Editorial: 227 E Florida Ave, Hemet, California 92543-4205 **Tel:** 1 951 652-6529
Email: info@thevalleychronicle.com **Web site:** http://www.thevalleychronicle.com
Freq: Thu; **Circ:** 40000 Not Audited
Publisher: Eric Buskirk; **Advertising Sales Manager:** Kimberly Nichols
Profile: The Valley Chronicle is published twice a month for the residents of Hemet, San Jacinto, Valle Vista and Winchester, CA. The editorial content includes local news, business, sports, arts and events.
Language (s): English
Ad Rate: Full Page Mono 27.00
Ad Rate: Full Page Colour 2775.00
Currency: United States Dollars
COMMUNITY NEWSPAPER

Valley Community Newspapers, Inc. 25312
Editorial: 2709 Riverside Blvd, Sacramento, California 95818 **Tel:** 1 916 429-9901
Email: editor@valcomnews.com **Web site:** http://www.valcomnews.com
Circ: 60000 Not Audited
Publisher and Editor: George Macko; **Advertising Sales Manager:** Linda Pohl
Profile: Valley Community Newspapers, Inc. is a community newspaper publisher serving the Sacramento, CA area.
Language (s): English
COMMUNITY NEWSPAPER

The Valley Dispatch 21502
Owner: MediaNews Group
Editorial: 491 Dutton St, Lowell, Massachusetts 01854-4289 **Tel:** 1 978 458-7100
Web site: http://www.thevalleydispatch.com/
Freq: Weekly; **Circ:** 37841 Not Audited
Profile: The Valley Dispatch is a free weekly publication for the residents of Nashua, NH area.
Language (s): English
Ad Rate: Full Page Mono 18.00
Ad Rate: Full Page Colour 4500.00
Currency: United States Dollars
COMMUNITY NEWSPAPER

Valley Free Press 458198
Editorial: 1586 Barber Greene Rd, Dekalb, Illinois 60115-7900 **Tel:** 1 815 756-4841
Email: news@valleylifepress.com **Web site:** http://www.vfpnews.com
Freq: Tue; **Circ:** 13200 Not Audited
Publisher: Don Bricker; **Advertising Sales Manager:** Rob Dancey
Profile: Valley Free Press is published weekly for the residents of Sandwich, IL and surrounding areas. The newspaper covers local news, sports and community events.
Language (s): English
Ad Rate: Full Page Mono 7.00
Currency: United States Dollars
COMMUNITY NEWSPAPER

Valley Journal 876616
Owner: Goddard (Summer) & Goddard (Boone)
Editorial: 331 Main St SW, Ronan, Montana 59864-2708 **Tel:** 1 406 676-8989
Email: vjeditor@valleyjournal.net **Web site:** http://www.valleyjournal.net
Freq: Weekly; **Circ:** 7875
Advertising Manager: Boone Goddard; **Publisher:** Summer Goddard; **Editor:** Linda Sappington
Profile: Valley Journal is a weekly community newspaper serving residents of Lake County, MT, including Mission, Jocko, and Flathead Valley, MT.
Language (s): English
Ad Rate: Full Page Colour 13.04
Currency: United States Dollars
COMMUNITY NEWSPAPER

The Valley Mirror 20549
Owner: Woodland Publishing Co.
Editorial: 3315 Main St, Munhall, Pennsylvania 15120-3200 **Tel:** 1 412 462-0626
Email: valleymirror@comcast.net **Web site:** http://www.ca.rca-pa.com
Freq: Thu; **Circ:** 5000 Not Audited
Publisher & Editor: Marilyn Schiavoni
Profile: The Valley Mirror is the only weekly newspaper serving the Steel Valley communities of Homestead, West Homestead, West Mifflin, and Whitaker; and the Woodland Hills communities of Braddock, Braddock Hills, Chalfant, East Pittsburgh, Forest Hills, North Braddock, Rankin, Swissvale, and Turtle Creek.
Language (s): English
Ad Rate: Full Page Mono 7.00
Currency: United States Dollars
COMMUNITY NEWSPAPER

The Valley News 24127
Owner: Sample News Group
Editorial: 67 S 2nd St, Fulton, New York 13069-1725
Tel: 1 315 598-6397
Email: editor@fultonvalleynews.com **Web site:** http://www.oswegocountynewsnow.com
Freq: 2 Times/Week; **Circ:** 5000 Not Audited
Editor: Colin Hogan
Profile: The Valley News in Fulton, NY is written for residents in Oswego County, NY and is also circulated outside of the county and state. Deadlines for the Wednesday edition are on Fridays by 5pm ET. Deadlines for the Saturday edition are on Wednesdays by 5pm ET.
Language (s): English
Ad Rate: Full Page Mono 8.83
Currency: United States Dollars
COMMUNITY NEWSPAPER

Valley News Group 24894
Editorial: 23009 Ventura Blvd #303, Woodland Hills, California 91364-1107 **Tel:** 1 818 313-9545
Email: valleynewsgroup@gmail.com **Web site:** http://www.valleynewsgroup.com
Freq: Fri; **Circ:** 35000 Not Audited
Publisher & Editor: Kathleen Sterling
Profile: Valley News Group is written for the residents of Woodland Hills, CA. It covers local news and events.
Language (s): English
Ad Rate: Full Page Mono 25.00
Currency: United States Dollars
COMMUNITY NEWSPAPER

Valley Newspapers 25450
Owner: Valley Newspapers Holdings, LP
Editorial: 1811 N 23rd St, McAllen, Texas 78501-6121 **Tel:** 1 956 682-2423
Email: otc@valleytowncrier.com **Web site:** http://www.yourvalleyvoice.com
Freq: Weekly; **Circ:** 123710 Not Audited
Publisher: Linda Medrano; **Editor:** Pedro Perez
Language (s): English
Ad Rate: Full Page Colour 2265.00
Currency: United States Dollars
COMMUNITY NEWSPAPER

Valley Publishing Co. 24726
Editorial: 613 7th St, Prosser, Washington 99350
Tel: 1 509 786-1711
Web site: http://www.valleypublishing.us
Circ: 5800 Not Audited
Advertising Sales Manager: Dianne Buxton; **Publisher:** Danielle Fournier; **Editor:** Mike Marino
Language (s): English
COMMUNITY NEWSPAPER

Valley Publishing Newspapers 154556
Owner: Valley Publishing
Editorial: 2987 Lake Monticello Rd, Palmyra, Virginia 22963-4820 **Tel:** 1 434 591-1000
Web site: http://www.fluvannareview.com
Circ: 14000 Not Audited
Publisher & Editor: Carlos Santos
Language (s): English
COMMUNITY NEWSPAPER

Valley Ranger 257396
Owner: Moffitt Newspapers
Editorial: 200 S Court St, Lewisburg, West Virginia 24901-1310 **Tel:** 1 304 645-1206
Email: wvdailynews@suddenlinkmail.com **Web site:** http://www.wvdailynewsandvalleyranger.com
Freq: Sun; **Circ:** 23932 Not Audited
Editor: Sharon Boone; **Advertising Manager:** Susan Linton; **Publisher:** Judy Steele; **Circulation Manager:** Gary Walkup
Profile: The Valley Ranger (Tmc)'s editorial mission is to provide its readers with news and information. The publication is written for local residents of the Greenbrier Valley, WV area.
Language (s): English
Ad Rate: Full Page Mono 11.00
Currency: United States Dollars
COMMUNITY NEWSPAPER

The Valley Voice 21308
Owner: White (Cheryl)
Editorial: 656 Exchange St Ste 2, Middlebury, Vermont 05753-1522 **Tel:** 1 802 388-6366
Email: info@vvoice.org **Web site:** http://vvoice.org
Freq: Tue; **Circ:** 8800 Not Audited
Publisher: Cheryl White
Profile: The weekly Valley Voice newspaper of Middlebury, VT serves residents of the Champlain Valley.
Language (s): English
Ad Rate: Full Page Mono 8.00
Currency: United States Dollars
COMMUNITY NEWSPAPER

Valley Wide Newspapers 24817
Owner: Pryke (Raymond)
Editorial: 16925 Main St Ste A, Hesperia, California 92345-6038 **Tel:** 1 760 244-0021
Email: valleywide@valleywidenews.com **Web site:** http://www.valleywidenewspaper.com
Circ: 25900 Not Audited
Editor & Publisher: Raymond Pryke
Profile: Valley Wide Newspapers is a weekly newspaper publisher serving the residents of Apple Valley, Hesperia, Adelanto and Victorville, CA.
Language (s): English
COMMUNITY NEWSPAPER

Valley/Pymatuning Area News 593504
Editorial: 46 W Jefferson St, Jefferson, Ohio 44047-1028 **Tel:** 1 440 576-9115
Circulation Manager: Cheryl Copehand; **Publisher:** Bob Halsted
Language (s): English
COMMUNITY NEWSPAPER

Van Buren Publishing 25239
Owner: Stephens Media
Editorial: 100 N 11th St, Van Buren, Arkansas 72956
Tel: 1 479 474-5215
Web site: http://www.pressargus.com
Circ: 17731 Not Audited
Editor: Kenneth Fry; **Publisher:** Gene Kincy
Language (s): English
COMMUNITY NEWSPAPER

Van Zandt Newspapers, L.L.C. 24994
Owner: Van Zandt Newspapers, LLC
Editorial: 109 N 5th St, Wills Point, Texas 75169-2058 **Tel:** 1 903 873-2525
Email: vznews@aol.com **Web site:** http://www.vanzandtnews.com/
Circ: 17100 Not Audited
Publisher: John Buzzetta
Language (s): English
COMMUNITY NEWSPAPER

Vandalia Drummer 559123
Owner: AIM Media Midwest
Editorial: 694 W National Rd, Vandalia, Ohio 45377-1032 **Tel:** 1 937 236-4990
Web site: http://www.vandaliadrummernews.com/
Circ: 13000 Not Audited
Profile: The information sourse of record for Vandalia and Butler Township since 1979.
COMMUNITY NEWSPAPER

La Vanguardia Hoy 823510
Tel: 1 513 835-2481
Web site: http://lavanguardiahoy.com
Freq: Bi-Weekly; **Circ:** 10000
Publisher: Mauricio Bach; **Editor:** Claudia Prada
Profile: La Vanguardia Hoy is a Spanish language, bi-weekly community newspaper.
Language (s): Spanish
COMMUNITY NEWSPAPER

El Venezolano 152340
Owner: Grupo Editorial El Venezolano
Editorial: 3625 NW 82nd Ave Ste 406, Doral, Florida 33166-7602 **Tel:** 1 305 717-3209
Email: editor@elvenezolanonews.com **Web site:** http://www.elvenezolanonews.com
Freq: Thu; **Circ:** 20000 Not Audited
Editor: José Hernández
Profile: El Venezolano is a local newspaper written for the Hispanic, specifically Venezuelan, community of Doral, FL.
Language (s): Spanish
Ad Rate: Full Page Mono 140.00
Currency: United States Dollars
COMMUNITY NEWSPAPER

Venezuela al Dia 217379
Editorial: 8245 NW 36th St Ste 3, Doral, Florida 33166-6636 **Tel:** 1 786 201-8523
Web site: http://www.venezuelaaldia.com
Freq: Weekly; **Circ:** 10000 Not Audited
Editor: Armando Chirinos
Profile: Venezuela al Dia is a newspaper serving the Venezuelan community abroad in Miami and the surrounding area. It includes international and national news, sports, editorial and entertainment stories of interest to Venezuelan readers.
Language (s): Spanish
Ad Rate: Full Page Mono 30.00
Currency: United States Dollars
COMMUNITY NEWSPAPER

Venice Gondolier Sun 78651
Owner: Sun Coast Media Group Inc.
Editorial: 200 E Venice Ave, Venice, Florida 34285-1941 **Tel:** 1 941 207-1000
Web site: http://www.venicegondolier.com
Freq: Sat; **Circ:** 31000 Not Audited
Publisher: Lang Capasso; **Editor:** Bob Mudge
Profile: Venice Gondolier Sun is a local newspaper that is published for the residents of Sarasota County in Florida. The publication covers local news, events, business, entertainment and sports.
Language (s): English
Ad Rate: Full Page Mono 19.30
Currency: United States Dollars
COMMUNITY NEWSPAPER

Ventura Breeze 502432
Editorial: 1575 Spinnaker Dr #105B-393, Ventura, California 93001-4381 **Tel:** 1 805 653-0791
Email: editor@venturabreeze.com **Web site:** http://www.venturabreeze.com
Freq: Bi-Weekly; **Circ:** 11000 Not Audited
Publisher & Editor: Sheldon Brown
Profile: Ventura Breeze is a local community newspaper written for the residents of Ventura, CA.

The paper covers local news, governments, schools, business, arts & entertainment, local events and weather. Send all press materials to the main e-mail address.
Language (s): English
Ad Rate: Full Page Mono 20.00
Currency: United States Dollars
COMMUNITY NEWSPAPER

Ventura County Reporter 21671
Owner: Southland Publishing
Editorial: 700 E Main St, Ventura, California 93001-2906 **Tel:** 1 805 648-2244
Email: editor@vcreporter.com **Web site:** http://www.vcreporter.com
Freq: Weekly; **Circ:** 33000 Not Audited
Publisher: David Comden; **Editor:** Michael Sullivan
Profile: Ventura (CA) County Reporter is an alternative weekly publication that provides in-depth features, investigative reporting and arts & entertainment coverage.
Language (s): English
Ad Rate: Full Page Mono 28.33
Currency: United States Dollars
COMMUNITY NEWSPAPER

Verde Valley Newspapers Inc. 25139
Owner: Western Newspapers, Inc.
Editorial: 116 S Main St, Cottonwood, Arizona 86326-3909 **Tel:** 1 928 634-2241
Web site: http://verdenews.com/
Circ: 21522 Not Audited
Editor: Dan Engler; **Publisher:** Pam Miller
Language (s): English
COMMUNITY NEWSPAPER

Vermont Journal 445191
Owner: KMA Inc.
Editorial: 8 High St, Ludlow, Vermont 05149-1008
Tel: 1 802 228-3600
Email: editor@vermontjournal.com **Web site:** http://www.vermontjournal.com
Freq: Wed; **Circ:** 28862 Not Audited
Editor: Donna Allen; **Publisher:** Bob Miller
Profile: Vermont Journal is a local, weekly newspaper serving residents of Ludlow, VT. The paper includes an editorial page and local news, as well as some national and international news relevant to the local community. Advertising deadlines are on Fridays at noon.
Language (s): English
Ad Rate: Full Page Mono 12.00
Ad Rate: Full Page Colour 60.00
Currency: United States Dollars
COMMUNITY NEWSPAPER

The Vermont News Guide 21494
Owner: Hersam Acorn Newspapers
Editorial: 4483 Main St, Manchester, Vermont 5255
Tel: 1 802 362-3535
Email: jmurren@hersamacorn.com **Web site:** http://www.vermontnews-guide.com
Freq: Wed; **Circ:** 16000 Not Audited
Editor: Liz Schafer
Profile: The Vermont News Guide is a weekly publication which announces surrounding area up and coming events in the Manchester Center, VT region. Deadlines for the publication are on Thursdays.
Language (s): English
Ad Rate: Full Page Mono 10.65
Currency: United States Dollars
COMMUNITY NEWSPAPER

The Vermont Standard 21089
Owner: Vermont Standard Inc.
Editorial: 43 Lincoln Corners Way, Woodstock, Vermont 05091-4022 **Tel:** 1 802 457-1313
Email: info@thevermontstandard.com **Web site:** http://www.thevermontstandard.com
Freq: Thu; **Circ:** 13600 Not Audited
Publisher: Phillip Camp
Profile: The Vermont Standard is a community newspaper for the residents of Woodstock, VT.
Language (s): English
Ad Rate: Full Page Mono 8.25
Currency: United States Dollars
COMMUNITY NEWSPAPER

Vernal Express 21037
Owner: Uintah Basin Media
Editorial: 60 E 100 N, Vernal, Utah 84078-2122
Tel: 1 435 789-3511
Web site: http://www.ubmedia.biz/vernal
Freq: Weekly; **Circ:** 5630 Not Audited
Publisher: Kevin Ashby
Profile: The Vernal Express is a publication written for the community of Vernal, UT.
Language (s): English
Ad Rate: Full Page Mono 8.50
Currency: United States Dollars
COMMUNITY NEWSPAPER

Vernon County Broadcaster 29560
Owner: Lee Enterprises, Inc.
Editorial: 124 W Court St, Viroqua, Wisconsin 54665-1505 **Tel:** 1 608 637-3137
Email: vcb.news@lee.net **Web site:** http://www.vernonbroadcaster.com
Freq: Thu; **Circ:** 6000 Not Audited
News Editor: Angie Cina
Profile: Vernon County Broadcaster is a weekly newspaper that serves residents of Vernon County, WI. It informs readers about public issues, news and local events and entertains them with feature stories.
Language (s): English
Ad Rate: Full Page Mono 8.00
Currency: United States Dollars
COMMUNITY NEWSPAPER

Vernon Publishing - Eldon 24951
Owner: Vernon Publishing, Inc.
Editorial: 415 S Maple St, Eldon, Missouri 65026-1856 **Tel:** 1 573 392-5658
Web site: http://www.vernonpublishing.com
Circ: 5850 Not Audited
Editor: Tim Flora; **Publisher:** Trevor Vernon
Language (s): English
COMMUNITY NEWSPAPER

Vero Beach Hometown News 151183
Owner: Hometown News, L.C.
Editorial: 1020 Old Dixie Hwy, Vero Beach, Florida 32960-4359 **Tel:** 1 772 465-5656
Email: info@hometownnewsol.com **Web site:** http://www.myhometownnews.net
Freq: Fri; **Circ:** 18900 Not Audited
Circulation Manager: Dolan Hoggatt; **Advertising Sales Manager:** Michele Muccigrosso; **Publisher:** Vernon Smith
Profile: Vero Beach Hometown News is a local publication providing news to the community of Vero Beach, FL.
Language (s): English
Ad Rate: Full Page Mono 19.25
Currency: United States Dollars
COMMUNITY NEWSPAPER

The Vici Vision 920669
Owner: McCormick (Jennifer)
Editorial: 107 1/2 E Broadway, Vici, Oklahoma
Tel: 1 580 995-3425
Email: vicichamber@vicihorizon.com **Web site:** http://vicivision.wordpress.com
Freq: Weekly
Editor & Publisher: Jennifer McCormick
Profile: The Vici Vision is a weekly community newspaper serving residents of Vici, OK with community news and events coverage.
Language (s): English
COMMUNITY NEWSPAPER

Vida 22720
Editorial: 130 Palm Dr, Oxnard, California 93030-4979 **Tel:** 1 805 483-1008
Email: vidanews@aol.com **Web site:** http://www.vidanewspaper.com
Freq: Thu; **Circ:** 45000 Not Audited
Editor: Carlos Olea; **Editor:** Loury Smith; **Editor:** Jose Valencia
Profile: Vida is written for Hispanic and Latino residents throughout Southern California. It features local and national news, in addition to sports, business, lifestyles and arts & entertainment coverage. The deadlines are on Fridays.
Language (s): Spanish/Bilingual
Ad Rate: Full Page Mono 49.50
Ad Rate: Full Page Colour 53.47
Currency: United States Dollars
COMMUNITY NEWSPAPER

Vida en el Valle 21792
Owner: McClatchy Newspapers
Editorial: 1626 E St, Fresno, California 93786-0001
Tel: 1 559 441-6780
Email: noticias@vidaenelvalle.com **Web site:** http://www.vidaenelvalle.com
Freq: Wed; **Circ:** 157285 Not Audited
Editor: Juan Esparza; **Advertising Sales Manager:** Bill Gutierrez
Profile: Vida en el Valle is a weekly newspaper which provides news of importance to the Latino community of the central San Joaquin Valley, CA. The newspaper covers topics such as education, politics, business, sports and arts & entertainment. The paper promotes cultural contributions of Latinos in the Valley.
Language (s): Spanish/Bilingual
Ad Rate: Full Page Mono 136.40
Ad Rate: Full Page Colour 1241.00
Currency: United States Dollars
COMMUNITY NEWSPAPER

La Vida News/The Black Voice 22721
Owner: La Vida News
Editorial: 5601 Bridge St, Ste 300, Fort Worth, Texas 76112-2355 **Tel:** 1 817 543-2095
Email: newsdesk@lavidanewstheblackvoice.com
Web site: http://lavidanewstheblackvoice.com
Freq: Thu; **Circ:** 10700 Not Audited
Publisher & Editor: Ted Pruitt; **Advertising Sales Manager:** Sanford Sims
Profile: La Vida News/The Black Voice is a weekly community newspaper serving the African-American community in Fort Worth, TX and the surrounding areas. The paper was founded in 1957.
Language (s): English
Ad Rate: Full Page Mono 47.00
Currency: United States Dollars
COMMUNITY NEWSPAPER

Vida Nueva/Tidings 622156
Owner: Catholic Archdiocese of Los Angeles
Editorial: 3424 Wilshire Blvd, Los Angeles, California 90010-2263 **Tel:** 1 213 637-7360
Editor: Victor Aleman; **Publisher:** José H. Gómez;
Circulation Manager: Chris Krause
Language (s): English
COMMUNITY NEWSPAPER

Viet Nam Moi 546369
Editorial: 8060 Boone Rd, Houston, Texas 77072-4925 **Tel:** 1 281 933-9283
Freq: Sat; **Circ:** 10000
Publisher & Editor: Hoa Van Vu
Profile: Viet Nam Moi is a weekly newspaper written for the Vietnamese community. Advertising rates available upon request.
Language (s): Vietnamese
COMMUNITY NEWSPAPER

Viet Tide 79335
Owner: Tuan Bao Viet Tide Corp.
Editorial: 9315 Bolsa Ave #620, Westminster, California 92683-5902 **Tel:** 1 714 262-7028
Email: baoviettide@yahoo.com
Freq: Fri; **Circ:** 20000 Not Audited
Profile: Viet Tide is a community newspaper providing Community News coverage for the Vietnamese community in Westminster, CA.
Language (s): Vietnamese
Ad Rate: Full Page Mono 10.50
Currency: United States Dollars
COMMUNITY NEWSPAPER

The Vietnam Post & Thuongmoi Viet Nam 546434
Owner: Yang (Kimberly)
Editorial: 10515 Harwin Dr Ste 120, Houston, Texas 77036-1533 **Tel:** 1 713 777-4848
Email: ad@thevietnampost.com **Web site:** http://www.thevietnampost.com
Circ: 74000
Editor: Angelo Hoang; **Publisher:** Missy Nguyan;
Advertising Sales Manager: John Yung
Profile: The Vietnam Post & Thuongmoi Viet Nam are free Vietnamese-language newspapers serving the Asian communities of the greater Houston area. They are also distributed on international flights to Asia.
Language (s): Vietnamese
COMMUNITY NEWSPAPER

View Newspapers 25256
Owner: News + Media Capital Group LLC
Editorial: 1111 W Bonanza Rd, Las Vegas, Nevada 89106-3545 **Tel:** 1 702 383-0211
Web site: http://www.reviewjournal.com/view
Circ: 511000 Not Audited
Editor: Ginger Meurer
Language (s): English
COMMUNITY NEWSPAPER

Village & Southwest Newspapers 338282
Owner: Responsive Newspapers, L.P.
Editorial: 5160 Spruce St, Bellaire, Texas 77401
Tel: 1 713 668-9293
Email: mynews@village-southwest-news.com **Web site:** http://village-southwest-news.com
Circ: 40000 Not Audited
Editor & Publisher: Kathleen Ballanfant; **Advertising Sales Manager:** Buzz Crainer
Language (s): English
COMMUNITY NEWSPAPER

Village News 151438
Editorial: 4607 W Hundred Rd, Chester, Virginia 23831-1743 **Tel:** 1 804 751-0421
Email: info@villagepublishing.com **Web site:** http://www.villagenewsonline.com
Freq: Wed; **Circ:** 12000 Not Audited
Advertising Sales Manager: Elliot Fausz; **Publisher:** Linda Fausz; **Editor:** Mark Fausz
Profile: Village News is a local publication providing news to the community of Chester, VA.
Language (s): English
Ad Rate: Full Page Mono 13.73
Ad Rate: Full Page Colour 20.40
Currency: United States Dollars
COMMUNITY NEWSPAPER

Village View Publications, Inc. 25530
Owner: Dixon (Annette)
Editorial: 1160 S Michigan Ave Apt 1306, Chicago, Illinois 60605-3701 **Tel:** 1 708 425-1910
Email: vvnew@sbcglobal.net **Web site:** http://vvnew.com
Freq: Bi-Weekly; **Circ:** 25000
Circulation Manager: Steve Bilski; **Publisher & Editor:** Annette Dixon
Profile: Village View Publications is the Publisher of four free bi-weekly community newspapers covering the South and far-South suburban Chicagoland: B-MAC - Blue Island/Midlothian/Alsip/Crestwood; Suburban-Oak Lawn/Burbank/Justice/Hickory Hills/ Evergreen Park; South Suburban - Chicago Ridge/ Worth/Palos Hills/Palos Park/Palos Heights; Far South -Oak Forest/Orland Park/Tinley Park. Covers local news, community events, local business, schools, sports, arts & entertainment, travel, food and restaurant reviews.
Language (s): English
Ad Rate: Full Page Mono 25.00
Currency: United States Dollars
COMMUNITY NEWSPAPER

The Village Voice 20275
Owner: Black Walnut Holdings
Editorial: 80 Maiden Ln Rm 2105, New York, New York 10038-4893 **Tel:** 1 212 475-3300
Email: tips@villagevoice.com **Web site:** http://www.villagevoice.com
Freq: Wed; **Circ:** 75212 Not Audited
Profile: The Village Voice was founded in 1955. Called "the father of alternative weeklies," the Village Voice "introduced free-form, high-spirited, and passionate journalism." The weekly covers New York politics, national politics, and the arts. This publication is known as the "writer's paper." Deadlines are on Monday evenings. The editorial department accepts non-disclosure agreements on a case by case basis.
Language (s): English
Ad Rate: Full Page Mono 14.57
Ad Rate: Full Page Colour 2531.00
Currency: United States Dollars
COMMUNITY NEWSPAPER

The Villager 20993
Owner: Black Registry Publishing Company
Editorial: 4132 E 12th St, Austin, Texas 78721-1905
Tel: 1 512 476-0082
Email: vil3202@aol.com **Web site:** http://www.theaustinvillager.com
Freq: Weekly; **Circ:** 6000 Not Audited
Editor & Publisher: T.L. Wyatt
Profile: The Villager is a weekly community newspaper serving the Austin, TX African-American community. Topics covered include local news, politics, state government, lifestyle, events, sports and schools. All editorial contact is filtered through the publisher.
Language (s): English
Ad Rate: Full Page Mono 20.00
Ad Rate: Full Page Colour 25.95
Currency: United States Dollars
COMMUNITY NEWSPAPER

Villager 27662
Editorial: 757 Snelling Ave S, Saint Paul, Minnesota 55116-2250 **Tel:** 1 651 699-1462
Email: news@myvillager.com **Web site:** http://www.myvillager.com
Freq: Bi-Weekly; **Circ:** 59927 Not Audited
Publisher: Michael Mischke
Profile: Villager is a local newspaper serving Saint Paul, MN. The publication features general interest news, local news and community events.
Language (s): English
Ad Rate: Full Page Mono 50.00
Currency: United States Dollars
COMMUNITY NEWSPAPER

The Villager Newspaper Group 24893
Editorial: 8933 E Union Ave Ste 230, Greenwood Village, Colorado 80111-1357 **Tel:** 1 303 773-8313
Email: news@villagerpublishing.com **Web site:** http://www.villagerpublishing.com
Freq: Weekly; **Circ:** 21700 Not Audited
Publisher & Editor: Gerri Sweeney; **Advertising Sales Manager:** Sharon Sweeney
Profile: The Villager Newspaper Group is a weekly community newspaper publisher serving the residents of Greenwood Village, CO.
Language (s): English
COMMUNITY NEWSPAPER

Villager Newspapers 377446
Owner: Stonebridge Press
Tel: 1 860 928-1818
Web site: http://www.villagernewspapers.com
Circ: 20000 Not Audited
Advertising Sales Manager: Jean Ashton;
Publisher: Frank Chilinski; **Editor:** Adam Minor
Language (s): English
COMMUNITY NEWSPAPER

Vineyard Gazette 19445
Editorial: 34 S Summer St, Edgartown, Massachusetts 02539-8104 **Tel:** 1 508 627-4311
Email: news@mvgazette.com **Web site:** http://www.mvgazette.com
Freq: Fri; **Circ:** 12500 Not Audited
Circulation Manager: Kathy Agin; **Publisher:** Jane Seagrave; **Editor:** Julia Wells
Profile: Vineyard Gazette is written for the residents of Martha's Vineyard, MA. Deadlines are on Mondays and Wednesdays prior to issue date.
Language (s): English
Ad Rate: Full Page Mono 23.50
Currency: United States Dollars
COMMUNITY NEWSPAPER

The Virginia Gazette 28902
Owner: tronc
Editorial: 216 Ironbound Rd, Williamsburg, Virginia 23188-2618 **Tel:** 1 757 220-1736
Email: letters@vagazette.com **Web site:** http://www.vagazette.com
Freq: Sat; **Circ:** 19500 Not Audited
Editor: Rusty Carter; **Advertising Sales Manager:** Olivia Hartman
Profile: The Virginia Gazette is published twice a week for the residents of Williamsburg, VA. It covers local news, sports, opinion, events, education, opinion and legal notices.
Language (s): English
Ad Rate: Full Page Mono 18.53
Ad Rate: Full Page Colour 2083.00
Currency: United States Dollars
COMMUNITY NEWSPAPER

The Virginia Mountaineer 21054
Owner: Mountaineer Publishing Company
Editorial: 1133 Plaza Dr Ste 2400, Grundy, Virginia 24614-6780 **Tel:** 1 276 935-2123

Email: virginiamountaineer@gmail.com **Web site:** http://www.virginiamountaineer.com
Freq: Thu; **Circ:** 8200 Not Audited
Publisher & Editor: Lodge Compton; **News Editor:** Scotty Wampler
Profile: The Virginia Moutaineer is a local newspaper written for the residents of Grundy, VA. The paper covers news, sports and features.
Language (s): English
Ad Rate: Full Page Mono 7.98
Currency: United States Dollars
COMMUNITY NEWSPAPER

La Vision de Georgia 152756
Owner: Chacon (Victoria)
Editorial: 1394 Indian Trail Lilburn Rd Ste 202, Norcross, Georgia 30093-2678 **Tel:** 1 770 963-7521
Email: comentarios@lavisionnewspaper.com **Web site:** http://www.lavisionnewspaper.com
Freq: Fri; **Circ:** 40000 Not Audited
Publisher: Victoria Chacon; **Advertising Sales Manager:** Oromi Leon
Profile: La Vision de Georgia in Norcross, GA is s a free weekly newspaper for the Hispanic community in the metropolitan Atlanta area. It covers community, national and Latin American news.
Language (s): Spanish/Bilingual
Ad Rate: Full Page Mono 16.67
Ad Rate: Full Page Colour 95.00
Currency: United States Dollars
COMMUNITY NEWSPAPER

Vision Hispana 844952
Editorial: 1151 Harbor Bay Pkwy, Alameda, California 94502-6540 **Tel:** 1 510 865-6274
Email: contact@visionhispanausa.com **Web site:** http://www.visionhispanausa.com/
Publisher & Editor: Elena Miramar
Profile: Vision Hispana is a a community newspaper informing the citizens of Alameda, CA on local news, events, education, health & safety and travel in regards to the Hispanic community. The paper was founded in 2003.
COMMUNITY NEWSPAPER

Vocero Hispano 22195
Owner: Vocero Hispano, Inc.
Editorial: 335 Chandler St Ste 8, Worcester, Massachusetts 01602-3441 **Tel:** 1 508 792-1942
Email: voceronews@aol.com **Web site:** http://www.vocerohispano.com
Freq: Fri; **Circ:** 20000 Not Audited
Editor & Publisher: Sergio Rivera
Profile: Vocero Hispano, published weekly, focuses on news within the Hispanic communities across Massachusetts. The paper covers local news, business, sports and arts & entertainment stories.
Language (s): Spanish
Ad Rate: Full Page Mono 18.00
Currency: United States Dollars
COMMUNITY NEWSPAPER

El Vocero Hispano 217380
Owner: Abreu (Andres)
Editorial: 2818 Vineland Ave SE, Grand Rapids, Michigan 49508-1453 **Tel:** 1 616 246-6023
Email: elvocero@elvoceromi.com **Web site:** http://www.elvocerous.com
Freq: Fri; **Circ:** 20000 Not Audited
Publisher & Editor: Andres Abreu
Profile: El Vocero Hispano in Grand Rapids, MI is written for the Hispanic communities in Michigan. The newspaper covers community news, cultural events and services and national news of interest to Hispanic communities.
Language (s): Spanish/Bilingual
Ad Rate: Full Page Mono 13.00
Ad Rate: Full Page Colour 1200.00
Currency: United States Dollars
COMMUNITY NEWSPAPER

Voice Media 832041
Owner: Voice Media
Editorial: 1511 Ritchie Hwy Ste 304, Arnold, Maryland 21012-2471
Web site: http://www.voicemediagroup.com/
Editor: Hayley Gable Bowerman
Profile: Voice Media is a community newspaper publisher serving Anne Arundel County in Maryland, and produces three monthly papers: the Pasadena (MD) Voice, the Severna Park (MD) Voice, and the Arundel Voice. The editorial staff is shared, though there are separate PO boxes for each publication.
Language (s): English
COMMUNITY NEWSPAPER

The Voice Newspapers 25179
Owner: Journal Register Company
Editorial: 19176 Hall Rd Ste 200, New Baltimore, Michigan 48038 **Tel:** 1 586 716-8100
Email: editor@voicenews.com **Web site:** http://www.voicenews.com
Circ: 74336 Not Audited
Advertising Sales Manager: Dawn Emke; **Editor:** Jeff Payne
Profile: The Voice Newspapers in New Baltimore, MI is a publisher of community newspapers.
Language (s): English
COMMUNITY NEWSPAPER

The Voice Newspapers 408528
Owner: Megamedia Enterprises Inc.
Editorial: 5236 W North Ave, Chicago, Illinois 60639-4467 **Tel:** 1 773 889-0880
Email: tvoicenews@gmail.com **Web site:** http://thevoicenewspapers.blogspot.com
Circ: 30000 Not Audited
Editor: Brad Cummings; **Advertising Sales Manager:** Donell Jones; **Publisher:** Isaac Jones
Profile: The Voice Newspapers in Chicago publishes The Garfield-Lawndale Voice and The Austin Voice, both weekly neighborhood newspapers.
Language (s): English
COMMUNITY NEWSPAPER

Voice of the Valley 22017
Editorial: 26909 206th Ave SE, Maple Valley, Washington 98042 **Tel:** 1 425 432-9696
Email: news@voiceofthevalley.com **Web site:** http://www.voiceofthevalley.com
Freq: Tue; **Circ:** 17300 Not Audited
Publisher & Editor: Donna Hayes
Profile: Voice of the Valley covers news for the local residents of Maple Valley, WA. The lead time for Voice of the Valley is two to three weeks, depending on the story.
Language (s): English
Ad Rate: Full Page Mono 17.50
Ad Rate: Full Page Colour 1080.00
Currency: United States Dollars
COMMUNITY NEWSPAPER

The Voice-Tribune 19358
Owner: Blue Equity
Editorial: 735 E Main St, Louisville, Kentucky 40202-1005 **Tel:** 1 502 897-8900
Email: kcoursey@lifestylemediapublishing.com **Web site:** http://www.voice-tribune.com
Freq: Thu; **Circ:** 13301 Not Audited
Profile: The Voice-Tribune provides community news for Jefferson County and Eastern Louisville, KY.
Language (s): English
Ad Rate: Full Page Mono 2000.00
Ad Rate: Full Page Colour 2000.00
Currency: United States Dollars
COMMUNITY NEWSPAPER

Voyager Media 377320
Owner: Voyager Media Inc.
Editorial: 23856 W Andrew Rd, Plainfield, Illinois 60585-8770 **Tel:** 1 815 436-2431
Web site: http://www.buglenewspapers.com
Circ: 64200 Not Audited
Editor: Nick Reiher
Profile: Voyager Media in Plainfield, IL is a publisher of community newspapers.
Language (s): English
COMMUNITY NEWSPAPER

La Voz 74836
Owner: Cruz (Andres)
Editorial: 560 E Third St, Lexington, Kentucky 40508-1738 **Tel:** 1 859 621-2106
Email: info@lavozky.com **Web site:** http://www.lavozky.com
Freq: Bi-Weekly; **Circ:** 10000 Not Audited
Publisher & Editor: Andres Cruz
Profile: La Voz is a Spanish-language newspaper written for residents of Lexington, KY.
Language (s): Spanish/Bilingual
Ad Rate: Full Page Mono 12.00
Currency: United States Dollars
COMMUNITY NEWSPAPER

La Voz 152895
Owner: The Voice Publishing Corp.
Editorial: 1020 Kipling Rd, Elizabeth, New Jersey 07208-1039 **Tel:** 1 908 352-6654
Email: lavoznj@aol.com **Web site:** http://www.lavoznj.com
Freq: Bi-Weekly; **Circ:** 38000 Not Audited
Publisher: Daniel Garcia; **Editor:** Virginia Iturralde
Profile: La Voz in Elizabeth, NJ is a bi-weekly Spanish-language newspaper written for Spanish-speaking residents in the region.
Language (s): Spanish
Ad Rate: Full Page Mono 12.40
Currency: United States Dollars
COMMUNITY NEWSPAPER

La Voz Arizona 75643
Owner: Gannett Co., Inc.
Editorial: 200 E Van Buren St, Phoenix, Arizona 85004-2238 **Tel:** 1 602 444-3800
Web site: http://www.lavozarizona.com
Freq: Weekly; **Circ:** 57958 Not Audited
Editor: Elvia Diaz
Profile: La Voz Arizona is a free Spanish-language newspaper serving Hispanic residents in Phoenix, Mesa, Tempe and West Valley, AZ. It covers local news, sports and community events. It shares offices with the Arizona Republic.
Language (s): Spanish
Ad Rate: Full Page Mono 27.00
Currency: United States Dollars
COMMUNITY NEWSPAPER

La Voz De Dalton 505373
Owner: Palacios Communications
Editorial: 737 Riverbend Rd, Dalton, Georgia 30721-4789 **Tel:** 1 706 272-0113
Email: lavozdalton@gmail.com **Web site:** http://www.lavoz.us
Freq: Thu; **Circ:** 15000 Not Audited
Publisher & Editor: Francisco Palacios
Profile: La Voz is a bilingual English and Spanish newspaper covering News for the Hispanic community residing in the Dalton, GA area.
Language (s): Spanish/Bilingual
Ad Rate: Full Page Mono 17.00
Ad Rate: Full Page Colour 150.00
Currency: United States Dollars
COMMUNITY NEWSPAPER

La Voz De La Calle 23275
Owner: The Voice Publishing Corp.
Editorial: 4696 E 10th Ct, Hialeah, Florida 33013-2108 **Tel:** 1 305 687-5555
Email: informes@lavozdelacalle.com.pe **Web site:** http://www.lavozdelacalle.com.pe
Freq: Fri; **Circ:** 25000 Not Audited
Circulation Manager: Paul Debeda; **Editor:** Rosa Martinez; **Advertising Sales Manager:** Vicente Rodriguez; **News Editor:** Raul Tapanez Estrella
Profile: La Voz De La Calle is a weekly newspaper published for the Spanish-speaking Latin American community in Hialeah, FL. The newspaper is printed in Spanish and provides local, state and national news to its readers. Deadlines are on Wednesdays at noon ET.
Language (s): Spanish
Ad Rate: Full Page Mono 30.00
Ad Rate: Full Page Colour 30.00
Currency: United States Dollars
COMMUNITY NEWSPAPER

La Voz Hispana 23160
Editorial: 159 E 116th St, New York, New York 10029-1399 **Tel:** 1 212 348-8270
Email: discomund@aol.com **Web site:** http://www.lavozhispanany.com
Freq: Thu; **Circ:** 68082 Not Audited
Publisher: Nick Lugo
Profile: La Voz Hispana is a weekly newspaper which is printed in Spanish. The newspaper is distributed throughout New York City every Thursday. La Voz Hispana provides the Hispanic communities with local and national news. Other features include education, business, politics, entertainment, sports, and classifieds.
Language (s): English, Spanish
Ad Rate: Full Page Mono 32.00
Currency: United States Dollars
COMMUNITY NEWSPAPER

La Voz Hispana 154384
Owner: Lancaster Newspapers, Inc.
Editorial: 8 W King St, Lancaster, Pennsylvania 17603-3824 **Tel:** 1 717 481-8488
Email: lavoz@lavozlancaster.com **Web site:** http://lavozlancaster.com/
Freq: Bi-Weekly; **Circ:** 5100 Not Audited
Editor: Enelly Betancourt
Profile: La Voz Hispana is a bi-weekly Spanish-language publication written for Hispanic residents in Pennsylvania.
Language (s): Spanish
Ad Rate: Full Page Mono 14.10
Currency: United States Dollars
COMMUNITY NEWSPAPER

La Voz Hispana 154613
Owner: Rodriguez (Norma) and King (Abelardo)
Editorial: 51 Elm St Ste 307, New Haven, Connecticut 06510-2049 **Tel:** 1 203 865-2272
Email: info@lavozhispanact.com **Web site:** http://www.lavozhispanact.com
Freq: Weekly; **Circ:** 35000 Not Audited
Advertising Sales Manager: Norma Rodriguez
Profile: La Voz Hispana is a community newspaper serving the Hispanic community in and around New Haven, CT.
Language (s): Spanish
Ad Rate: Full Page Mono 11.65
Currency: United States Dollars
COMMUNITY NEWSPAPER

La Voz Hispana 334128
Owner: La Voz Hispana
Editorial: 3552 Sullivant Ave, Columbus, Ohio 43204-1106 **Tel:** 1 614 274-5505
Email: lavozh@yahoo.com **Web site:** http://www.lavozhispana.com
Freq: Fri; **Circ:** 20000 Not Audited
Editor: Cynthia Aguilar; **Publisher:** Alejandro Flores; **Advertising Sales Manager:** Rachel Perez
Profile: La Voz Hispana is a local newspaper providing news to the community of Columbus, OH.
Language (s): Spanish
Ad Rate: Full Page Mono 45.00
Currency: United States Dollars
COMMUNITY NEWSPAPER

La Voz Hispanic 152124
Editorial: 1901 N 4th Ave, Pasco, Washington 99301-3728 **Tel:** 1 509 545-3055
Email: lavoz@bmi.net
Freq: Thu; **Circ:** 16000 Not Audited
Publisher: David Cortinas
Profile: La Voz Hispanic is a weekly Spanish-language community newspaper.
Language (s): Spanish
Ad Rate: Full Page Mono 14.60
Currency: United States Dollars
COMMUNITY NEWSPAPER

La Voz Independiente 151123
Editorial: 200 Burrell Ave, Brevard, North Carolina 28712-6328 **Tel:** 1 828 687-1132
Web site: http://www.lavozindependiente.com
Freq: Wed; **Circ:** 9000 Not Audited
Publisher & Editor: Robert McCarson
Language (s): Spanish
Ad Rate: Full Page Mono 8.19
Currency: United States Dollars
COMMUNITY NEWSPAPER

La Voz Nueva 21801
Owner: La Voz Publishing Company, Inc
Editorial: 1027 21st St, Denver, Colorado 80205-2503 **Tel:** 1 303 936-8556
Email: news@lavozcolorado.com **Web site:** http://www.lavozcolorado.com
Freq: Wed; **Circ:** 30000 Not Audited
Circulation Manager: Jim Koucherik; **Publisher, Editor & Advertising Sales Manager:** Pauline Rivera
Profile: La Voz Nueva is a weekly newspaper distributed throughout Denver. The newspaper is bilingual but is geared toward the Latino community. It provides regional news.
Language (s): Spanish/Bilingual
Ad Rate: Full Page Mono 21.00
Currency: United States Dollars
COMMUNITY NEWSPAPER

The Wake Weekly 20018
Owner: Allen Publishing LLC
Editorial: 229 E Owen Ave, Wake Forest, North Carolina 27587-2717 **Tel:** 1 919 556-3182
Email: news@wakeweekly.com **Web site:** http://www.wakeweekly.com
Freq: Thu; **Circ:** 10000 Not Audited
Publisher: Todd Allen; **Circulation Manager:** Shelia Cattaruzza
Profile: The Wake Weekly is a community newspaper for the residents of Wake Forest, NC. The paper covers local news, business, sports and arts & entertainment in zip codes 27587, 27571, 27614, 27616, 27525, 27596, 27549.
Language (s): English
Ad Rate: Full Page Mono 11.00
Currency: United States Dollars
COMMUNITY NEWSPAPER

Wakulla News 22141
Owner: Landmark Community Newspapers, Inc.
Editorial: 3119 Crawfordville Hwy, Crawfordville, Florida 32327 **Tel:** 1 850 926-7102
Freq: Thu; **Circ:** 5500 Not Audited
Publisher: Gerry Mulligan; **Editor:** William Snowden
Profile: Wakulla News is a local newspaper for Wakulla County, FL. The newspaper covers local news, business, sports and arts & entertainment stories. Deadlines are on Tuesdays at noon ET.
Language (s): English
Ad Rate: Full Page Mono 8.27
Currency: United States Dollars
COMMUNITY NEWSPAPER

Walnut Creek Journal 28175
Editorial: 175 Lennon Ln, Walnut Creek, California 94598-2485 **Tel:** 1 925 943-8241
Email: wcjournal@bayareanewsgroup.com **Web site:** http://www.contracostatimes.com/walnut-creek-alamo
Freq: Thu; **Circ:** 17651
Editor: Sam Richards
Profile: Covering Walnut Creek, California. A weekly newspaper from the Bay Area News Group.
Language (s): English
Ad Rate: Full Page Mono 15.65
Currency: United States Dollars
COMMUNITY NEWSPAPER

Walpole Times 19457
Owner: GateHouse Media Inc.
Editorial: 7 West St, Walpole, Massachusetts 02081-2856 **Tel:** 1 781 433-8282
Email: walpole@wickedlocal.com **Web site:** http://walpole.wickedlocal.com
Freq: Thu; **Circ:** 6100 Not Audited
Publisher: Chuck Goodrich
Profile: Walpole Times is a weekly newspaper serving the residents of Walpole, MA. It is published every Thursday.
Language (s): English
Ad Rate: Full Page Mono 9.00
Currency: United States Dollars
COMMUNITY NEWSPAPER

The Walton and Loganville Tribune Newspapers 389814
Owner: Southern Newspapers, Inc.
Editorial: 124 N Broad St, Monroe, Georgia 30655-1842 **Tel:** 1 770 267-8371
Email: news@waltontribune.com **Web site:** http://waltontribune.com
Circ: 17300 Not Audited
Circulation Manager: Billie Burch
Language (s): English
COMMUNITY NEWSPAPER

The Walton Reporter 20290
Owner: Decker Advertising
Editorial: 132 Delaware St, Walton, New York 13856-1486 **Tel:** 1 607 865-4131
Email: news@waltonreporter.com **Web site:** http://www.waltonreporter.com
Freq: Wed; **Circ:** 5150 Not Audited
Advertising Sales Manager: Bernice Bates; **Publisher:** Randy Shepherd
Profile: The Walton Reporter is a weekly newspaper which provides complete coverage of county, town and village news within Delaware County, NY and adjacent municipalities. Deadlines are on Tuesdays at noon ET.
Language (s): English
Ad Rate: Full Page Mono 10.35
Currency: United States Dollars
COMMUNITY NEWSPAPER

The Walton Sun 22583
Owner: GateHouse Media Inc.
Editorial: 5597 US Highway 98 W Ste 203, Santa Rosa Beach, Florida 32459-3283 **Tel:** 1 850 267-4555
Email: news@waltonsun.com **Web site:** http://www.waltonsun.com
Freq: Sat; **Circ:** 12000 Not Audited

Publisher: Diane Winnemuller
Profile: The Walton Sun is written for residents and visitors of Walton County, FL.
Language (s): English
Ad Rate: Full Page Mono 10.36
Currency: United States Dollars
COMMUNITY NEWSPAPER

The Wanderer 22576
Owner: Wanderer Printing Co.
Editorial: 201 Ohio St, Saint Paul, Minnesota 55107-2003 **Tel:** 1 651 224-5733
Email: editorial@thewandererpress.com **Web site:** http://www.thewandererpress.com
Freq: Thu; **Circ:** 17000 Not Audited
Advertising Sales Manager: Monica Hamilton; **Editor:** Alphonse Matt
Profile: The Wanderer is a weekly newspaper written for residents in Saint Paul, MN and surrounding areas.
Language (s): English
Ad Rate: Full Page Mono 14.00
Currency: United States Dollars
COMMUNITY NEWSPAPER

Warren County Report 533512
Editorial: 122 W 14th St, Front Royal, Virginia 22630-3608 **Tel:** 1 540 636-1014
Web site: http://www.nj.com/warrenreporter
Freq: Bi-Weekly; **Circ:** 9000 Not Audited
Circulation Manager: Leslie Bennett; **Advertising Sales Manager:** Leanne Bryant; **Publisher & Editor:** Dan McDermott
Profile: Warren County Report is a free, bi-weekly community newspaper serving local government news, arts & entertainment, education, business and sports features to residents of Warren County, VA. The paper also features national and international stories with a local angle and runs syndicated cartoons, puzzles and games.
Language (s): English
Ad Rate: Full Page Mono 7.50
Currency: United States Dollars
COMMUNITY NEWSPAPER

The Warren Record 20019
Owner: Womack Newspapers Inc.
Editorial: 112 N Main St, Warrenton, North Carolina 27589-1922 **Tel:** 1 252 257-3341
Email: news@warrenrecord.com **Web site:** http://www.warrenrecord.com
Freq: Wed; **Circ:** 5000 Not Audited
Advertising Sales Manager: Nettie Ayscue; **Circulation Manager:** Janie Miller
Profile: The Warren Record is a weekly local paper for residents in Warren County, NC. The publication is part of the Womack Publishing Company family of newspapers. The editor is the best PR contact. Press releases should be e-mailed.
Language (s): English
Ad Rate: Full Page Mono 7.30
Currency: United States Dollars
COMMUNITY NEWSPAPER

Warren Sentinel 21788
Owner: Wyoming Newspapers Inc.
Editorial: 5305 Randall Ave., Bldg. 250, Rm 201, Warren AFB, Wyoming 82005 **Tel:** 1 307 773-3381
Web site: http://www.warren.af.mil
Freq: Fri; **Circ:** 5200 Not Audited
Editor: Michael Tryon; **Publisher:** Jim Wood
Profile: Warren Sentinel is a free, weekly newspaper providing news and information about the 90th Space Wing to military personnel, civilian employees and residents of F. E. Warren (WY) Air Force Base. All editorial content is provided by the public affairs office at the base, but the paper is owned, printed and distributed by Wyoming Newspapers Inc. Deadlines are Thursdays at 4:30pm CT before the issue date. Advertising deadlines are on Tuesdays at 11am CT the week of publication.
Language (s): English
COMMUNITY NEWSPAPER

The Washington Afro American 18730
Editorial: 1917 Benning Rd NE, Washington, District Of Columbia 20002-4723 **Tel:** 1 202 332-0080
Email: editor@afro.com **Web site:** http://www.afro.com
Freq: Sat; **Circ:** 5737 Not Audited
Editor: Edgar Brookins; **Advertising Sales Manager:** Lenora Howze; **Publisher:** John Oliver
Profile: The Washington Afro American is published weekly for the African American community in Washington D.C. and Virginia. The newspaper covers local news, diversity issues and community events.
Language (s): English
Ad Rate: Full Page Mono 49.15
Currency: United States Dollars
COMMUNITY NEWSPAPER

Washington Chinese News 137242
Owner: Lee & Lee Washington, Inc.
Editorial: 5848 Hubbard Dr, Rockville, Maryland 20852-4820 **Tel:** 1 301 984-8988
Email: news@wchns.com **Web site:** http://www.wchns.com
Freq: Sat; **Circ:** 15000 Not Audited
Publisher: Ray Hwang; **Editor:** Yen Lin; **Editor:** Ching Shu
Profile: Washington Chinese News is a community newspaper written for Chinese Americans in Rockville, MD.
Language (s): Chinese
Ad Rate: Full Page Mono 5.75
Currency: United States Dollars
COMMUNITY NEWSPAPER

Washington City Paper 21326
Owner: SouthComm, Inc.
Editorial: 734 15th St NW Ste 400, Washington, District Of Columbia 20005-1013 **Tel:** 1 202 332-2100
Email: mail@washingtoncitypaper.com **Web site:** http://www.washingtoncitypaper.com
Freq: Fri; **Circ:** 63829 Not Audited
Editor: Steve Cavendish
Profile: Washington City Paper is written for those living in or around Washington, D.C. The newspaper's editorial mission is to provide information regarding city life and arts & entertainment for single people, ages 20 to 50.
Language (s): English
Ad Rate: Full Page Mono 25.44
Currency: United States Dollars
COMMUNITY NEWSPAPER

Washington County News 18489
Owner: Gray and Gray Inc.
Editorial: 81 Grenade Ave, Chatom, Alabama 36518 **Tel:** 1 251 847-2599
Email: news@washcountynews.com **Web site:** http://www.washcountynews.com
Freq: Fri; **Circ:** 11500 Not Audited
Editor: Jason Boothe; **Publisher:** Willie Gray
Profile: Washington County News is a local, weekly newspaper written for the residents of Chatom, AL.
Language (s): English
Ad Rate: Full Page Mono 9.00
Currency: United States Dollars
COMMUNITY NEWSPAPER

Washington County News 21041
Owner: BH Media Group
Editorial: 102 Wall St SW, Abingdon, Virginia 24210-3204 **Tel:** 1 276 628-7101
Web site: http://www.swvatoday.com/news/washington_county
Freq: Wed; **Circ:** 6000 Not Audited
Editor: Mark Sage
Profile: Washington County News is written for local residents of Abingdon, VA. The publication covers local and national news, as it applies to the community.
Language (s): English
Ad Rate: Full Page Mono 11.42
Currency: United States Dollars
COMMUNITY NEWSPAPER

Washington Hispanic 22717
Owner: Washington Hispanic, Inc.
Editorial: 8455 Colesville Rd Ste 700, Silver Spring, Maryland 20910-3318 **Tel:** 1 202 667-8881
Email: info@washingtonhispanic.com **Web site:** http://www.washingtonhispanic.com
Freq: Fri; **Circ:** 45000 Not Audited
Editor: Nelly Carrion
Profile: Washington Hispanic is an independent weekly Spanish-language newspaper which serves the Washington metropolitan area. The publication's goal is to inform the area's Hispanic community as well as other community groups about local, national, and international news and events. The lead time for Washington Hispanic is three days.
Language (s): Spanish
Ad Rate: Full Page Mono 40.00
Currency: United States Dollars
COMMUNITY NEWSPAPER

The Washington Informer 18732
Owner: Lion Heart Digital
Editorial: 3117 Martin Luther King Jr Ave SE, Washington, District Of Columbia 20032-1537 **Tel:** 1 202 561-4100
Email: news@washingtoninformer.com **Web site:** http://www.washingtoninformer.com
Freq: Thu; **Circ:** 7500 Not Audited
Advertising Sales Manager: Ron Burke; **Publisher:** Denise Rolark-Barnes
Profile: The Washington Informer is a weekly newspaper covering news, issues and features relating to the African American community of Washington, D.C. Deadlines are on Mondays at 5pm ET. The editorial staff asks that all press materials be directed to the main e-mail address.
Language (s): English
Ad Rate: Full Page Mono 37.98
Ad Rate: Full Page Colour 2311.00
Currency: United States Dollars
COMMUNITY NEWSPAPER

Washington Jewish Week 21848
Owner: Washington Jewish Week, LLC
Editorial: 11900 Parklawn Dr Ste 300, Rockville, Maryland 20852-2768 **Tel:** 1 301 230-2222
Web site: http://www.washingtonjewishweek.com
Freq: Thu; **Circ:** 20000 Not Audited
Publisher: Craig Burke
Profile: Washington Jewish Week is a weekly newspaper that covers social issues affecting the Jewish communities of Washington, D.C., Maryland and northern Virginia.
Language (s): English
Ad Rate: Full Page Mono 23.60
Currency: United States Dollars
COMMUNITY NEWSPAPER

Washington Sun 22509
Editorial: 830 Kennedy St NW Ste B2, Washington, District Of Columbia 20011-2948 **Tel:** 1 202 882-1021
Email: thewashingtonsun@aol.com **Web site:** http://thewashingtonsun.com
Freq: Thu; **Circ:** 55000 Not Audited
Profile: Washington Sun is published weekly for members of the African American community throughout the United States. The newspaper covers local, national and international news, social issues and other topics of interest to African Americans.
Language (s): English
Ad Rate: Full Page Mono 16.80
Currency: United States Dollars
COMMUNITY NEWSPAPER

The Washington Times - National Weekly Edition 22161
Owner: Washington Times, LLC
Editorial: 3600 New York Ave NE, Washington, District Of Columbia 20002-1947 **Tel:** 1 202 636-3000
Web site: http://www.washingtontimes.com
Freq: Sun; **Circ:** 42997 Not Audited
Profile: The Washington Times - National Weekly edition was founded in 1994. Send all press materials directly to the Managing Editor, that address is configured to be a general inbox for the newsroom.
Language (s): English
Ad Rate: Full Page Mono 1800.00
Currency: United States Dollars
COMMUNITY NEWSPAPER

Watertown Town Times 23053
Owner: Prime Publishers Inc.
Editorial: 469 Main St, Watertown, Connecticut 06795-2628 **Tel:** 1 860 274-8851
Email: newsdept@towntimesnews.com **Web site:** http://www.towntimesnews.com
Freq: Thu; **Circ:** 17000 Not Audited
Editor: James Dreher; **Publisher:** Rudy Mazurosky; **Circulation Manager:** Walter Mazurosky; **Editor:** James Taylor
Profile: Watertown Town Times is written for the residents of Watertown, CT and the surrounding area. It covers local and national news. Deadlines are on Fridays.
Language (s): English
Ad Rate: Full Page Mono 15.96
Currency: United States Dollars
COMMUNITY NEWSPAPER

Waushara Argus 21240
Owner: Wautoma Newspaper Inc
Editorial: 7781 W State Road 21 & 73, Wautoma, Wisconsin 54982 **Tel:** 1 920 787-3334
Email: argus@wausharaargus.com **Web site:** http://www.wausharaargus.com
Freq: Wed; **Circ:** 6200 Not Audited
News Editor: Katie Schaefer
Profile: Serving Waushara County since 1859, the Waushara Argus is the county seat's weekly, broadsheet newspaper. It provides readers with an in-depth look into local issues, interesting people, county board news and high school sports. It is dedicated to producing a quality newspaper that promotes Waushara County as a great place to live and vacation. Advertising deadlines are at 5pm CT.
Language (s): English
Ad Rate: Full Page Mono 7.90
Currency: United States Dollars
COMMUNITY NEWSPAPER

The Wave and Los Angeles Independent Newspaper Group 24488
Owner: Equal Access Media Inc.
Editorial: 3731 Wilshire Blvd Ste 840, Los Angeles, California 90010-2851 **Tel:** 1 323 556-5720
Email: newsroom@wavepublication.com **Web site:** http://www.laindependent.com
Freq: Weekly; **Circ:** 298435 Not Audited
Publisher: Pluria Marshall; **Circulation Manager:** Feras Shamuon
Language (s): English
COMMUNITY NEWSPAPER

Wave of Long Island 20304
Owner: Wave Publishing Co.
Editorial: 8808 Rockaway Beach Blvd, Rockaway Beach, New York 11693-1608 **Tel:** 1 718 634-4000
Email: editor@rockawave.com **Web site:** http://www.rockawave.com
Freq: Fri; **Circ:** 9000 Not Audited
Publisher: Susan Locke
Profile: Wave of Long Island is a local newspaper that serves the residents of Rockaway Beach, NY. It covers local news, weather and sports.
Language (s): English
Ad Rate: Full Page Mono 20.00
Ad Rate: Full Page Colour 760.00
Currency: United States Dollars
COMMUNITY NEWSPAPER

Wave Publishing Company 24719
Editorial: 165 S 100 W, Heber City, Utah 84032-2001 **Tel:** 1 435 654-1471
Email: editor@wasatchwave.com **Web site:** http://www.wasatchwave.com
Freq: 2 Times/Week; **Circ:** 11200 Not Audited
Advertising Sales Manager: Kari McFee; **County News Editor:** Cheryl Ovard; **Editor & Publisher:** Laurie Wynn
Profile: The Wave Publishing Company produces two weekly community newspapers serving residents of Wasatch County, UT: The Wasatch Wave (Wed) and Summit County News (Fri).
Language (s): English
COMMUNITY NEWSPAPER

Waverly Newspapers 24515
Owner: Community Media Group
Editorial: 311 W Bremer Ave, Waverly, Iowa 50677 **Tel:** 1 319 352-3334
Email: news@waverlynewspapers.com **Web site:** http://www.waverlynewspapers.com
Circ: 12800 Not Audited
Editor: Anelia Dimitrova; **Advertising Sales Manager:** Michael Izer
Language (s): English
COMMUNITY NEWSPAPER

Wayne County News 20762
Owner: American Hometown Publishing
Editorial: 119 E Hollis St, Waynesboro, Tennessee 38485-2154 **Tel:** 1 931 722-5429
Email: advertising@waynecountynews.net **Web site:** http://waynecountynews.net
Freq: Wed; **Circ:** 5200 Not Audited
Publisher & Editor: Dan Cole; **Circulation Manager:** Linda Hayes; **Advertising Sales Manager:** Misty Richardson
Profile: Wayne County News is a local publication providing the community of Waynesboro, TN with news.
Language (s): English
Ad Rate: Full Page Mono 5.15
Currency: United States Dollars
COMMUNITY NEWSPAPER

Wayne County Outlook 19362
Owner: Community Newspaper Holdings Inc.
Editorial: 109 E Columbia Ave, Monticello, Kentucky 42633 **Tel:** 1 606 348-3338
Web site: http://www.wcoutlook.com
Freq: Wed; **Circ:** 5800 Not Audited
Circulation Manager: Jerrena Chaplin; **Publisher:** Melinda Jones; **Editor:** Melodie Phelps
Profile: Wayne County Outlook is written for the residents of Wayne County, KY and the surrounding area. The publication aims to bring local news, sports and events to the community. Deadlines for publication are noon ET on Mondays.
Language (s): English
Ad Rate: Full Page Mono 6.00
Currency: United States Dollars
COMMUNITY NEWSPAPER

Wayne County Press 19082
Editorial: 213 E Main St, Fairfield, Illinois 62837-2028 **Tel:** 1 618 842-2662
Email: news@waycopress.com **Web site:** http://www.waycopress.com/
Freq: Mon; **Circ:** 6850 Not Audited
Circulation Manager: Sherry Auvil; **Publisher & Editor:** Tom Mathews; **Advertising Sales Manager:** Carol Tannahill
Profile: Wayne County Press is written for the residents of Wayne County, IL. The publication offers local news, sports and information on the schools and events. The deadline for publication is 10am CT.
Language (s): English
Ad Rate: Full Page Mono 11.48
Currency: United States Dollars
COMMUNITY NEWSPAPER

Wayne Today 140018
Owner: Gannett Co., Inc./North Jersey Media Group
Editorial: 1 Garret Mountain Plz, Woodland Park, New Jersey 07424-3320 **Tel:** 1 973 659-7100
Email: today@northjersey.com **Web site:** http://www.northjersey.com
Circ: 30873 Not Audited
Profile: Wayne Today is a community newspaper covering news and community events for the residents of Passaic, NJ.
Language (s): English
COMMUNITY NEWSPAPER

Waynedale News 324706
Editorial: 2505 Lower Huntington Rd, Fort Wayne, Indiana 46809-2634 **Tel:** 1 219 747-4535
Email: news@waynedalenews.com **Web site:** http://www.waynedalenews.com
Freq: Bi-Weekly; **Circ:** 11000 Not Audited
Profile: The Waynedale News is a free, bi-weekly newspaper written for the residents of southwest Fort Wayne, IN, including the communities of Waynedale, Wildwood, Foster Park, Time Corners, Coventry, Zanesville and surrounding areas. It covers local news, businesses, schools, government, sports, editorials and features of interest to area readers.
Language (s): English
Ad Rate: Full Page Mono 13.00
Currency: United States Dollars
COMMUNITY NEWSPAPER

Wayuga Community Newspapers, Inc. 24650
Editorial: 6784 W Main St, Red Creek, New York 13143 **Tel:** 1 315 754-6229
Email: star@wayuga.com **Web site:** http://www.wayuga.com
Circ: 5500 Not Audited
Editor: Louise Broach; **Publisher:** Angelo Palermo
Language (s): English
COMMUNITY NEWSPAPER

WCL Advertising & Publishing 133416
Editorial: Restricted address, Stuyvesant, New York 12173-3108 **Tel:** 1 518 799-5811
Circ: 32000 Not Audited
Editor: Joan Lundquest; **Publisher:** William Lundquest
Profile: WCL Advertising & Publishing is a Community Publisher that releases Hudson River Sampler - Northern Dutchess County and Hudson River Sampler - Columbia County. The publication has requested that its contact information not be listed.
Language (s): English
COMMUNITY NEWSPAPER

Weatherford Star-Telegram
530684

Owner: McClatchy Newspapers
Editorial: 112 S Main St, Weatherford, Texas 76086-4320 **Tel:** 1 817 594-9902
Web site: http://www.star-telegram.com/news/local/community/weatherford-star-telegram
Freq: Wed; **Circ:** 34000
Advertising Sales Manager: Gary Cruse
Profile: Weatherford Star-Telegram is published weekly for the residents of Weatherford, TX and surrounding areas. The newspaper cover local news, sports, lifestyles, religion and community events.
Language (s): English
Ad Rate: Full Page Mono 24.07
Currency: United States Dollars
COMMUNITY NEWSPAPER

Webster County Publishing Company, Inc.
25199

Owner: Webster County Publishing Co. Inc.
Editorial: 221 S Commercial St, Seymour, Missouri 65746-8743 **Tel:** 1 417 935-2257
Email: citizen190@gmail.com **Web site:** http://www.webstercountycitizen.com
Circ: 5116 Not Audited
Advertising Sales Manager: Beverly Hannum; **Publisher & Editor:** Dan Wehmer
Language (s): English
COMMUNITY NEWSPAPER

Webster-Kirkwood Times, Inc.
24955

Owner: Bitikofer (Dwight)
Editorial: 122 W Lockwood Ave Fl 2, Saint Louis, Missouri 63119-2916 **Tel:** 1 314 968-2699
Email: newsroom@timesnewspapers.com **Web site:** http://www.timesnewspapers.com
Circ: 72400 Not Audited
Circulation Manager: Kim Besterfeldt; **Publisher:** Dwight Bitikofer; **Advertising Sales Manager:** Mary Chambers
Language (s): English
COMMUNITY NEWSPAPER

Wedgwood Shopping News
445908

Editorial: 6001 Granbury Rd, Fort Worth, Texas 76133-2719 **Tel:** 1 817 292-2260
Email: wsn@mesh.net
Freq: Bi-Weekly; **Circ:** 25000 Not Audited
Publisher: Carla Duke
Profile: Wedgwood Shopping News is a local newspaper serving the residents of Fort Worth, TX. The paper includes local news, a shopping guide, profiles on advertisers and community information.
Language (s): English
Ad Rate: Full Page Mono 10.60
Currency: United States Dollars
COMMUNITY NEWSPAPER

Wednesday Journal Publishing Co.
25032

Owner: Wednesday Journal Inc.
Editorial: 141 S Oak Park Ave, Oak Park, Illinois 60302-2972 **Tel:** 1 708 524-8300
Web site: http://www.oakpark.com
Circ: 59350 Not Audited
Advertising Manager: Dawn Ferencak; **Publisher:** Dan Haley
Profile: Wednesday Journal Publishing Co. in Oak Park, IL publishes the Riverside Landmark, Austin Weekly News, Wednesday Journal and Forest Park Review.
Language (s): English
COMMUNITY NEWSPAPER

The Weekender
62276

Owner: Sentinel-Standard Inc.
Editorial: 114 N Depot St, Ionia, Michigan 48846 **Tel:** 1 616 527-2100
Web site: http://www.sentinel-standard.com
Freq: Sun; **Circ:** 23500 Not Audited
Editor: Lori Kilchermann
Profile: The Weekender is a local daily newspaper written for citizens of Ionia County, MI. The publication provides coverage of local news and events, as well as national and international news that pertains to the community.
Language (s): English
Ad Rate: Full Page Mono 14.75
Currency: United States Dollars
COMMUNITY NEWSPAPER

The Weekly
22262

Owner: Paper of Montgomery Co. (The)
Editorial: 101 W Main St, Ste 300, Crawfordsville, Indiana 47933 **Tel:** 1 765 361-0100
Email: news@thepaper24-7.com **Web site:** http://www.thepaper24-7.com
Freq: Tue; **Circ:** 12500 Not Audited
Advertising Sales Manager: Jill Pursell; **Publisher & Editor:** Tim Timmons
Profile: The Weekly provides local and national news to Montgomery, Fountain, Park and Putman counties, IN. It shares its editorial staff and offices with The Paper of Montgomery County.
Language (s): English
Ad Rate: Full Page Mono 16.00
Currency: United States Dollars
COMMUNITY NEWSPAPER

Weekly & Beacon
594477

Owner: Northeast Publishing
Editorial: 491 Main St, Bangor, Maine 04401-6296 **Tel:** 1 207 990-8139
Email: beacon@bangordailynews.com **Web site:** http://www.maineville.com
Advertising Sales Manager: Beth Grant; **Editor:** Ardeana Hamlin; **Publisher:** Richard Warren
Language (s): English
COMMUNITY NEWSPAPER

Weekly Alibi
22162

Owner: NuCity Publications
Editorial: 413 Central Ave NW, Albuquerque, New Mexico 87102-3219 **Tel:** 1 505 346-0660
Email: editorial@alibi.com **Web site:** http://www.alibi.com
Freq: Thu; **Circ:** 45000 Not Audited
Advertising Sales Manager: John Hankinson
Profile: Weekly Alibi in Albuquerque, NM is a weekly newspaper that covers local news and events.
Language (s): English
Ad Rate: Full Page Mono 80.96
Currency: United States Dollars
COMMUNITY NEWSPAPER

The Weekly Challenger
18779

Owner: Weekly Challenger Inc.
Editorial: 2500 Dr Martin Luther King Jr St S Ste F, Saint Petersburg, Florida 33705-3554 **Tel:** 1 727 896-2922
Email: contactus@theweeklychallenger.com **Web site:** http://www.theweeklychallenger.com
Freq: Thu; **Circ:** 25000 Not Audited
Advertising Sales Manager: Irene Johnson
Profile: The Weekly Challenger in Saint Petersburg, FL is published weekly for African American residents of north central Florida, Tampa and Saint Petersburg, FL. The newspaper covers local news, weather, sports and community events. Feature articles cover African American history, business, politics, education, arts & entertainment and lifestyle. The publication is a member of the National Newspaper Publishers Association Inc.
Language (s): English
Ad Rate: Full Page Mono 28.00
Ad Rate: Full Page Colour 325.00
Currency: United States Dollars
COMMUNITY NEWSPAPER

The Weekly News
884200

Owner: Armijo Newspapers & Public Relations
Editorial: 14144 Central Ave. #B, Chino, California 91710 **Tel:** 1 909 464-1200
Web site: http://www.anapr.com/category/the-weekly-news/
Freq: Fri
Advertising Sales Manager: Diane Armijo; **Editor:** Sarah Armijo
Profile: The Weekly News is a weekly newspaper providing Local and Community News coverage to the residents of the communities of Walnut, Diamond Bar, Chino Hills, Rowland Heights and Phillips Ranch, CA.
Language (s): English
COMMUNITY NEWSPAPER

Weekly News Publishing
231788

Owner: Suburban Publishing
Editorial: 10 1st Ave, Peabody, Massachusetts 1960 **Tel:** 1 978 532-5880
Email: editor@weeklynews.net **Web site:** http://www.weeklynews.net
Circ: 20000 Not Audited
Circulation Manager: Jim Downey; **Editor:** Jeff Shmase
Profile: Weekly News Publishing is a community newspaper publisher serving the communities of Peabody, MA and Lynnfield, MA with the Peabody (MA) Weekly News and the Winfield (MA) Weekly News.
Language (s): English
COMMUNITY NEWSPAPER

The Weekly Sentinel
745460

Editorial: 952 Post Rd Unit 10, Wells, Maine 04090-4142 **Tel:** 1 207 646-8448
Email: editor@theweeklysentinel.com **Web site:** http://www.theweeklysentinel.com
Freq: Fri; **Circ:** 37962
Circulation Manager: Dan Brennan
Profile: The Weekly Sentinel is a community newspaper for the residents of Wells, ME and the surrounding communities.
Language (s): English
Ad Rate: Full Page Mono 12.00
Currency: United States Dollars
COMMUNITY NEWSPAPER

Weekly Surge
438857

Editorial: 914 Frontage Rd E, Myrtle Beach, South Carolina 29577-6700 **Tel:** 1 843 443-2462
Email: staff@weeklysurge.com **Web site:** http://www.weeklysurge.com
Freq: Thu; **Circ:** 20000 Not Audited
Advertising Sales Manager: Diana Zipko
Profile: Weekly Surge is an alternative newspaper serving the residents of Myrtle Beach, SC. The paper includes arts & entertainment, news, local events, politics and lifestyle information.
Language (s): English
Ad Rate: Full Page Mono 25.00
Ad Rate: Full Page Colour 12.06
Currency: United States Dollars
COMMUNITY NEWSPAPER

The Weekly View
584772

Owner: Eastside Voice Community News Media, Inc.
Editorial: 195 N Shortridge Rd Ste D, Indianapolis, Indiana 46219-8909 **Tel:** 1 317 356-2222
Web site: http://www.weeklyview.net
Freq: Fri; **Circ:** 20000
Advertising Sales Manager: Jeanne Dixon
Profile: The Weekly View is a weekly community newspaper serving neighborhoods in Eastern Indianapolis. Each edition includes local news stories, columns, a calendar of events, puzzles and games and comics. Special sections include school zone, financial focus, senior lifestyle and health and fitness. The publication launched in March 2009.
Language (s): English
Ad Rate: Full Page Mono 14.00
Currency: United States Dollars
COMMUNITY NEWSPAPER

The Weekly Villager
154143

Owner: Villager Newspapers
Editorial: 8088 Main St, Garrettsville, Ohio 44231-1214 **Tel:** 1 330 527-5761
Email: news@weeklyvillager.com **Web site:** http://www.weeklyvillager.com
Freq: Thu; **Circ:** 10000 Not Audited
Profile: The Weekly Villager is a free, weekly newspaper serving the communities of Garretsville, Newton Falls, Burton and Middlefield, OH. It covers local news, events, entertainment and features.
Language (s): English
Ad Rate: Full Page Mono 7.50
Currency: United States Dollars
COMMUNITY NEWSPAPER

The Weirs Times
22272

Owner: Weirs Publishing Co., Inc.
Editorial: 515 Endicott St N, Laconia, New Hampshire 03246-1725 **Tel:** 1 603 366-8463
Email: sales@weirs.com **Web site:** http://www.weirs.com
Freq: Thu; **Circ:** 30000 Not Audited
Advertising Sales Manager: Debra Bennett; **Publisher:** Robert Lawton; **Editor:** Brendan Smith
Profile: The Weirs Times is a local newspaper written for residents of Laconia, NH. The newspaper covers local news, sports, business, entertainment, and events.
Language (s): English
Ad Rate: Full Page Mono 12.30
Currency: United States Dollars
COMMUNITY NEWSPAPER

Welch News
14845

Owner: Moffitt Newspapers
Editorial: 125 Wyoming St, Welch, West Virginia 24801-2220 **Tel:** 1 304 436-3144
Email: welchnews@frontiernet.net
Freq: Fri; **Circ:** 5672 Not Audited
Advertising Sales Manager: Melissa McKinney; **Circulation Manager:** Tom Molin; **Publisher & Editor:** Greg Spinella
Profile: Welch News is a local newspaper that is published for residents of Welch, WV. The publication covers local news, sports and events.
Language (s): English
Ad Rate: Full Page Mono 8.68
Currency: United States Dollars
COMMUNITY NEWSPAPER

Welch Publishing Company
24666

Owner: Welch (Matt)
Editorial: 117 E 2nd St, Perrysburg, Ohio 43551-2102 **Tel:** 1 419 874-4491
Email: editor@perrysburg.com **Web site:** http://perrysburg.com
Circ: 35125
Editor: Deb Buker; **Circulation Manager:** Sharon Terdoest
Profile: Welch Publishing Company, of Perrysburg, OH, publishes local newspapers in the state of Ohio, including: the Perrysburg Messenger Journal; Rossford Record Journal; Holland-Springfield Journal, and Point and Shoreland Journal.
Language (s): English
COMMUNITY NEWSPAPER

The Wendover Times
382625

Owner: Croasmun Publishing
Editorial: 335 E Airport Way, Wendover, Utah 84083 **Tel:** 1 435 665-2563
Email: news@wendovertimes.com **Web site:** http://www.wendovertimes.com
Freq: Fri; **Circ:** 6700 Not Audited
Editor, Publisher & Owner: Deeanna Croasmun
Profile: The Wendover Times is a weekly newspaper serving residents of Wendover, West Wendover, Oasis, Weels, Elko and Spring Creek, UT. It contains community news, events, sports, school information and features of interest to local residents. Advertising deadlines are on Wednesdays at 5pm MT.
Language (s): English
Ad Rate: Full Page Mono 7.46
Currency: United States Dollars
COMMUNITY NEWSPAPER

West 10 Newspapers
621738

Owner: West 10 Newspapers
Editorial: 2850 Stage Village Cv Ste 5, Bartlett, Tennessee 38134-4682 **Tel:** 1 901 388-1500
Circ: 40000
Editor: Carolyn Bahm; **Advertising Sales Manager:** Vikki Clark; **Editor:** Graham Sweeney
Language (s): English
COMMUNITY NEWSPAPER

West Central Publishing
24743

Editorial: 206 George St, Saint Marys, West Virginia 26170-1024 **Tel:** 1 304 684-2424
Email: news@oracleandleader.com **Web site:** http://oracleandleader.com
Circ: 13000
Language (s): English
COMMUNITY NEWSPAPER

West Essex Tribune
20202

Owner: Chuck (Jennifer)
Editorial: 495 S Livingston Ave, Livingston, New Jersey 07039-4327 **Tel:** 1 973 992-1771
Email: tribuneeditorial@verizon.net **Web site:** http://www.westessextribune.net
Freq: Thu; **Circ:** 7000 Not Audited
Publisher: Jennifer Cone Chciuk; **Editor:** Nancy Dinar
Profile: West Essex Tribune is written for residents of Livingston, New Jersey. Press releases are excepted if they have subject matter having to do with Livingston.
Language (s): English
Ad Rate: Full Page Mono 13.10
Currency: United States Dollars
COMMUNITY NEWSPAPER

West Georgia Newspapers
25705

Owner: Paxton Media Group
Editorial: 604A Alabama Ave S, Bremen, Georgia 30110-2302 **Tel:** 1 770 537-2434
Circ: 14600 Not Audited
Editor: Bruce Browning; **Circulation Manager:** John Knoll
Language (s): English
COMMUNITY NEWSPAPER

West Hartford News
26929

Owner: Journal Register Company
Editorial: 386 Main St Fl 4, Middletown, Connecticut 06457-3360 **Tel:** 1 860 294-0157
Email: westhartfordnews@ctcentral.com **Web site:** http://www.westhartfordnews.com
Freq: Thu; **Circ:** 13000 Not Audited
Editor: Viktoria Sundquist
Profile: West Hartford News is a weekly newspaper for residents of West Hartford, CT.
Language (s): English
Ad Rate: Full Page Mono 15.65
Currency: United States Dollars
COMMUNITY NEWSPAPER

West Nebraska Register
22223

Editorial: 2708 Old Fair Rd, Grand Island, Nebraska 68803-5221 **Tel:** 1 308 382-4660
Web site: http://register.gidiocese.org
Freq: Semi-Monthly; **Circ:** 18000 Not Audited
Publisher: William Deninger; **Editor:** Mary Parlin
Profile: West Nebraska Register is written for Catholics in Grand Island, NE. It covers local news as well as organizational news from the Diocese of Grand Island.
Language (s): English
Ad Rate: Full Page Mono 8.56
Currency: United States Dollars
COMMUNITY NEWSPAPER

West Of
585338

Owner: Chambers (Lorne)
Editorial: 811 Savannah Hwy Ste 2, Charleston, South Carolina 29407-7284 **Tel:** 1 843 766-9378
Email: publisher@westof.net **Web site:** http://www.westof.net
Freq: Wed; **Circ:** 25000
Publisher & Editor: Lorne Chambers
Profile: West Of is a free, weekly newspaper that serves the West Ashley community of Charleston, SC. It covers local news, opinions, schools, arts & entertainment, dining and sports as well as features a calendar of events.
Language (s): English
Ad Rate: Full Page Mono 5.23
Currency: United States Dollars
COMMUNITY NEWSPAPER

West Orange Times & Observer
18771

Editorial: 720 S Dillard St, Winter Garden, Florida 34787-3908 **Tel:** 1 407 656-2121
Email: aqrhode@wotimes.com **Web site:** http://www.thewestorangetimes.com
Freq: Thu; **Circ:** 9500 Not Audited
Publisher and Editor: Dawn Willis
Profile: West Orange Times in Winter Garden, FL is a weekly newspaper that covers local news and events for residents of West Orange County, FL.
Language (s): English
Ad Rate: Full Page Mono 12.00
Currency: United States Dollars
COMMUNITY NEWSPAPER

West Point Publishing
408184

Tel: 1 209 293-7482
Circ: 8000 Not Audited
Publisher, Editor & Advertising Sales Manager: Rick Torgerson
Language (s): English
Ad Rate: Full Page Colour 11.50
Currency: United States Dollars
COMMUNITY NEWSPAPER

West Seattle Herald Inc.
25062

Owner: Robinson Newspapers
Editorial: 14006 1St Ave S Suite B, Burien, Washington 98168-3402 **Tel:** 1 206 932-0300

Email: wseditor@robinsonnews.com **Web site:** http://www.westseattleherald.com
Circ: 15200 Not Audited
Publisher: Gerald Robinson; **Editor:** Ken Robinson
Language (s): English
COMMUNITY NEWSPAPER

West Sherburne Tribune 21396
Editorial: 29 Lake St S, Big Lake, Minnesota 55309-4588 **Tel:** 1 763 263-3602
Email: editor@westsherburnetribune.net **Web site:** http://www.westsherburnetribune.com
Freq: Sat; **Circ:** 12370 Not Audited
Advertising Sales Manager: Sue Emberland; **Publisher & Editor:** Gary Meyer
Profile: West Sherburne Tribune is written for residents of Sherburne County, MN in the Big Lake area. Deadlines are on Thursdays by noon CT.
Language (s): English
Ad Rate: Full Page Mono 10.10
Currency: United States Dollars
COMMUNITY NEWSPAPER

West Side Community News 22324
Owner: Community Papers, Inc.
Editorial: 608 S Vine St, Indianapolis, Indiana 46241-0815 **Tel:** 1 317 241-7363
Email: commnews@communitypapers.net
Freq: Wed; **Circ:** 25000 Not Audited
Editor and Publisher: Jackie Deppe
Profile: West Side Community News is published weekly for the residents of Indianapolis, IN and surrounding areas. The newspaper covers local news, sports and community events. Deadlines for the publications are on Fridays at noon CT.
Language (s): English
Ad Rate: Full Page Mono 19.00
Currency: United States Dollars
COMMUNITY NEWSPAPER

West Side Star 490369
Owner: GateHouse Media Inc.
Editorial: 165 Missouri Blvd, Ste 4, Laurie, Missouri 65038 **Tel:** 1 573 374-3100
Email: newsroom@lakesunonline.com **Web site:** http://www.lakenewsonline.com
Freq: Wed; **Circ:** 7000 Not Audited
Circulation Manager: Mike Valko; **Community News Editor:** Amy Wilson
Profile: West Side Star is a weekly community newspaper for the residents of Laurie, MO. It covers local news, sports, opinion, lifestyle, events and real estate.
Language (s): English
Ad Rate: Full Page Mono 6.00
Currency: United States Dollars
COMMUNITY NEWSPAPER

West Springfield Record 19458
Owner: Gill (Marie)
Editorial: 516 Main St, West Springfield, Massachusetts 01089-3973 **Tel:** 1 413 736-1587
Email: wsrecord@comcast.net
Freq: Thu; **Circ:** 5500 Not Audited
Editor: Thomas Coburn; **Editor:** Jack Farrell
Profile: West Springfield Record is published weekly for the residents of West Springfield, MA and surrounding areas. The newspaper covers local news and community events.
Language (s): English
Ad Rate: Full Page Mono 4.50
Currency: United States Dollars
COMMUNITY NEWSPAPER

West Suburban Journal 383006
Owner: Trottie Publishing Inc.
Editorial: 9930 Derby Ln Ste 101, Westchester, Illinois 60154-3770 **Tel:** 1 708 344-5975
Web site: http://www.westsuburbanjournal.com
Freq: Thu; **Circ:** 10000 Not Audited
Circulation Manager: Mike Lamb; **Publisher:** Nicole Trottie
Profile: West Suburban Journal is a free, weekly newspaper that serves residents of the near and far west Chicago suburbs. It features hard-hitting news, profiles and entertainment stories.
Language (s): English
Ad Rate: Full Page Mono 15.27
Currency: United States Dollars
COMMUNITY NEWSPAPER

West Valley View 21428
Owner: West Valley View Inc.
Editorial: 1050 E Riley Dr, Avondale, Arizona 85323-2002 **Tel:** 1 623 535-8439
Email: news1@westvalleyview.com **Web site:** http://www.westvalleyview.com
Freq: 2 Times/Week; **Circ:** 72243 Not Audited
Profile: West Valley View is written for the residents of Litchfield Park, AZ and surrounding areas including Avondale, Buckeye, Goodyear and Tolleson, AZ. The newspaper covers local news and community events. Deadlines are on Fridays before issue date.
Language (s): English
Ad Rate: Full Page Mono 43.12
Currency: United States Dollars
COMMUNITY NEWSPAPER

The West Volusia Beacon 21832
Owner: Mustard Seed Publishing Inc.
Editorial: 110 W New York Ave, Deland, Florida 32720-5416 **Tel:** 1 386 734-4622
Email: info@beacononlinenews.com **Web site:** http://www.beacononlinenews.com
Freq: Mon; **Circ:** 20000 Not Audited
Circulation Manager: Vicki Duckett
Profile: The West Volusia Beacon is a local newspaper serving West Volusia County, FL. It provides the local community with information on news, events, sports and weather.
Language (s): English
Ad Rate: Full Page Mono 16.25
Currency: United States Dollars
COMMUNITY NEWSPAPER

West Windsor & Plainsboro News 537801
Editorial: 12 Roszel Rd Ste C205, Princeton, New Jersey 08540-6234 **Tel:** 1 609 243-9119
Web site: http://www.wwpinfo.com
Freq: Bi-Weekly; **Circ:** 12000
Publisher & Editor: Richard Rein
COMMUNITY NEWSPAPER

The Westchester County Press 20299
Owner: Blackwell (Sandra)
Tel: 1 914 684-0006
Email: westchestercountypress@yahoo.com
Freq: Thu; **Circ:** 12500 Not Audited
Publisher & Editor: Sandra Blackwell
Profile: The Westchester County Press is a local weekly newspaper serving Westchester County, NY. It covers local news and events, personalities, arts & entertainment, sports and travel. The paper is distributed to churches, community centers and county office buildings.
Language (s): English
Ad Rate: Full Page Mono 12.00
Currency: United States Dollars
COMMUNITY NEWSPAPER

Western Recorder 22777
Owner: Kentucky Baptist Convention
Editorial: 13420 Eastpoint Centre Dr, Louisville, Kentucky 40223-4160 **Tel:** 1 502 489-3535
Web site: http://www.westernrecorder.org
Freq: Tue; **Circ:** 25000 Not Audited
Editor: Todd Deaton; **Circulation Manager:** Karen Martin
Profile: Western Recorder is written for Baptists and Christians in Kentucky. It covers Christian issues, church issues and mission reports.
Language (s): English
Ad Rate: Full Page Mono 30.00
Currency: United States Dollars
COMMUNITY NEWSPAPER

Western States Weeklies Inc. 24773
Owner: Hagerty (Sara)
Editorial: 6153 Fairmount Ave Ste 220, San Diego, California 92120-3436 **Tel:** 1 619 280-2985
Email: editor@navydispatch.com **Web site:** http://www.navydispatch.com
Circ: 35000 Not Audited
Publisher & Editor: Sara Hagerty; **Advertising Sales Manager:** Brenda Pressior
Profile: Western States Weeklies Inc. in San Diego, CA is a weekly community newspaper publisher serving the Navy communities of San Diego, Ventura, Long Beach, Mira Mesa and Scripps Ranch, CA.
Language (s): English
COMMUNITY NEWSPAPER

Westminster Herald 18657
Owner: Thomas (Lloyd)
Editorial: 5789 Westminster Blvd, Westminster, California 92683-3541 **Tel:** 1 714 893-4501
Email: westmherald@aol.com **Web site:** http://westminsterheraldnews.com
Freq: Thu; **Circ:** 5000 Not Audited
Editor: Lloyd Thomas
Profile: Westminster Herald is a daily newspaper covering the Westminster, CA area, including Garden Grove, Los Alamitos and Huntington Beach. The publication covers local news, government, business, lifestyle, daily updates, and sports. The newspaper covers national events, if they have an impact on the readership.
Language (s): English
Ad Rate: Full Page Mono 9.80
Currency: United States Dollars
COMMUNITY NEWSPAPER

Westmoreland News 28911
Owner: Lakeway Publishers, Inc.
Editorial: 15692 Kings Hwy, Montross, Virginia 22520 **Tel:** 1 804 493-8096
Email: wmnoffice@lcs.net **Web site:** http://www.westmorelandnews.net
Freq: Thu; **Circ:** 7412 Not Audited
Advertising Sales Manager: Janice Bryant; **Circulation Manager:** Stephanie Sanford; **Editor:** Beth Spindler; **Publisher:** Mosby Wigginton
Language (s): English
Ad Rate: Full Page Mono 12.20
Currency: United States Dollars
COMMUNITY NEWSPAPER

The Weston Democrat 21278
Owner: Billeter, (Robert)
Editorial: 306 Main Ave, Weston, West Virginia 26452-2046 **Tel:** 1 304 269-1600
Email: news@westondemocrat.com **Web site:** http://www.westondemocrat.com
Freq: Wed; **Circ:** 7000 Not Audited
Publisher & Editor: Robert Billeter
Profile: The Weston Democrat is a local weekly newspaper written for local residents in West Virginia. Features include local politics updates, news, and event information from the community.
Language (s): English
Ad Rate: Full Page Mono 4.14
Currency: United States Dollars
COMMUNITY NEWSPAPER

Westside Gazette 18785
Owner: Henry Sr. (Bobby R.)
Editorial: 545 NW 7th Ter, Fort Lauderdale, Florida 33311-8140 **Tel:** 1 954 525-1489
Email: wgazette@thewestsidegazette.com **Web site:** http://www.thewestsidegazette.com
Freq: Thu; **Circ:** 44704 Not Audited
Publisher: Bobby Henry; **Editor:** Pamela Henry-Lewis; **Circulation Manager:** Elizabeth Miller; **Advertising Sales Manager:** Charles Mosely
Profile: Westside Gazette is a weekly newspaper offering insight into news and events that affect African-Americans in Broward County, FL.
Language (s): English
Ad Rate: Full Page Mono 32.87
Currency: United States Dollars
COMMUNITY NEWSPAPER

Westside News Inc. 24811
Owner: Ryan (Keith)
Editorial: 1776 Hilton Parma Corners Rd, Spencerport, New York 14559-9501 **Tel:** 1 585 352-3411
Web site: http://www.westsidenewsny.com/
Circ: 33065 Not Audited
Editor: Evelyn Dow; **Advertising Sales Manager:** Karen Fien; **Circulation Manager:** Don Griffin; **Publisher:** Keith Ryan
Profile: Westside News in Spencerport, NY is a community newspaper publisher whose publications include the Suburban News North Edition; the Suburban News West Edition; the Suburban News South Edition; and the Hamlin-Clarkson Herald.
Language (s): English
COMMUNITY NEWSPAPER

Westside Story Newspaper 24125
Owner: WJ Allen Multimedia Productions, Inc.
Editorial: 577 N D St, Ste 112H, San Bernardino, California 92401 **Tel:** 1 909 384-8131
Email: mail@westsidestorynewspaper.com **Web site:** http://www.westsidestorynewspaper.com
Freq: Thu; **Circ:** 7500 Not Audited
Circulation Manager: Rah-Mann Allen; **Publisher:** Wallace Allen; **Editor:** Lita Pezant
Profile: Westside Story Newspaper is written for the African American community of San Bernardino, CA. Send all press releases via e-mail.
Language (s): English
Ad Rate: Full Page Mono 28.00
Currency: United States Dollars
COMMUNITY NEWSPAPER

Westside Weekly 354973
Owner: Johnson (Tyree)
Editorial: 6253 Pine St, Philadelphia, Pennsylvania 19143-1027 **Tel:** 1 215 474-7411
Email: westsidepa@aol.com **Web site:** http://www.westsidepa.com
Freq: Weekly; **Circ:** 15000 Not Audited
Editor & Publisher: Tyree Johnson
Profile: Westside Weekly is a community newspaper written for the residents of West Philadelphia.
Language (s): English
Ad Rate: Full Page Mono 15.00
Currency: United States Dollars
COMMUNITY NEWSPAPER

Westword 21311
Owner: Voice Media Group
Editorial: 969 Broadway, Denver, Colorado 80203-2705 **Tel:** 1 303 296-7744
Email: editorial@westword.com **Web site:** http://www.westword.com
Freq: Thu; **Circ:** 62520 Not Audited
Editor: Patricia Calhoun; **Publisher:** Scott Tobias
Profile: Westword is a weekly alternative newspaper started to inform young, active people of Denver. Every week, the new edition is distributed to college classrooms, coffeehouses, corporate offices and at the state capitol. It generally does not accept press releases, unless it is of particular interest to the local audience. Contact the editorial department for further inquiries.
Language (s): English
Ad Rate: Full Page Mono 43.70
Ad Rate: Full Page Colour 46.23
Currency: United States Dollars
COMMUNITY NEWSPAPER

Wetzel Chronicle 21266
Owner: Ogden Newspapers
Editorial: 1100 3rd St, New Martinsville, West Virginia 26155-1500 **Tel:** 1 304 455-3300
Email: editor@wetzelchronicle.com **Web site:** http://www.wetzelchronicle.com
Freq: Wed; **Circ:** 6400 Not Audited
Advertising Sales Manager: Tammy Bucy; **Publisher:** Brian Clutter; **Editor:** Amy Witschey; **Circulation Manager:** Diann Wright
Profile: Wetzel Chronicle is written for the residents of Wetzel County, WV, which borders on the Ohio River. It covers local news and event information. Deadlines are on Fridays.
Language (s): English
Ad Rate: Full Page Mono 6.23
Currency: United States Dollars
COMMUNITY NEWSPAPER

Wharton Co. Newspapers, Inc. 20978
Owner: Wharton County Newspapers
Editorial: 115 W Burleson St, Wharton, Texas 77488-5003 **Tel:** 1 979 532-8840
Web site: http://www.journal-spectator.com
Circ: 6025
Advertising Sales Manager: Ricki Boyd; **News Editor:** Barry Halvorson; **Publisher & Editor:** Bill Wallace
Language (s): English
Ad Rate: Full Page Mono 7.00
Currency: United States Dollars
COMMUNITY NEWSPAPER

The Wheel 22437
Owner: Military Newspapers of Virginia
Editorial: 213 Calhoun Dr, Fort Eustis, Virginia 23604-1645 **Tel:** 1 757 878-4920
Email: wheel5@militarynews.com **Web site:** http://www.forteustiswheel.com
Freq: Thu; **Circ:** 10500
Publisher: Laura Baxter; **Editor:** Zach Shelby
Profile: The Wheel is a military newspaper in Fort Eustis, VA. The paper covers military news, community news and sports.
Language (s): English
Ad Rate: Full Page Mono 9.68
Currency: United States Dollars
COMMUNITY NEWSPAPER

Wheel/Herald 19711
Owner: Beers (Randy)
Tel: 1 507 836-8726
Email: wheelherald@gmail.com **Web site:** http://wheelherald.com
Freq: Mon; **Circ:** 7200 Not Audited
Editor and Publisher: Randy Beers
Profile: Wheel-Herald is a weekly newspaper for residents of Murray County, MN.
Language (s): English
Ad Rate: Full Page Mono 7.90
Currency: United States Dollars
COMMUNITY NEWSPAPER

White County News 24329
Owner: Community Newspapers Inc.
Editorial: 13 E Jarrard St, Cleveland, Georgia 30528 **Tel:** 1 706 865-4718
Email: press@whitecountynews.net **Web site:** http://www.whitecountynews.net
Freq: Thu; **Circ:** 6400 Not Audited
Publisher & Editor: Billy Chism
Profile: White County News Telegraph is written for residents of White County, GA. The paper covers news, sports, television listings, family news and other vital information about what's going on in and around White County. Deadlines are on Mondays by 5pm ET.
Language (s): English
Ad Rate: Full Page Mono 13.10
Currency: United States Dollars
COMMUNITY NEWSPAPER

White Mountain Publishing Co. 25192
Owner: Kramer Publications
Editorial: 3191 S White Mountain Rd, Show Low, Arizona 85901-7409 **Tel:** 1 928 537-5721
Email: postmaster@wmicentral.com **Web site:** http://www.wmicentral.com
Circ: 25174 Not Audited
Profile: White Mountain Publishing Co. publishes the White Mountain Independent for the Show Low, Pinetop-Lakeside, Snowflake-Taylor, Springville-Eager, St. Johns, Heber/Overgaard, AZ areas, including Local and Community News coverage for the local Navajo and Apache communities.
Language (s): English
COMMUNITY NEWSPAPER

Whitesburg Mountain Eagle 19388
Editorial: 41 N Webb St, Whitesburg, Kentucky 41858-7324 **Tel:** 1 606 633-2252
Email: mtneagle@bellsouth.net **Web site:** http://themountaineagle.com
Freq: Wed; **Circ:** 5500 Not Audited
Editor: Ben Gish; **Advertising Sales Manager:** Freddy Oakes
Profile: Whitesburg Mountain Eagle is a local newspaper written for the residents of Letcher County, KY.
Language (s): English
Ad Rate: Full Page Mono 7.50
Ad Rate: Full Page Colour 23.32
Currency: United States Dollars
COMMUNITY NEWSPAPER

Whitewater Publications, Inc. 24557
Editorial: 531 Main St, Brookville, Indiana 47012-1407 **Tel:** 1 765 647-4221
Email: info@whitewaterpub.com
Circ: 6250 Not Audited
Editor: John Estridge; **Advertising Sales Manager:** Melissa Lilly; **Publisher:** Gary Wolf
Language (s): English
COMMUNITY NEWSPAPER

Whitman-Hanson Express 615464
Tel: 1 781 293-0420
Web site: http://whitmanhansonexpress.com
Freq: Weekly
Editor: Tracy Seelye

Profile: Covers local news in the towns of Whitman & Hanson, Massachusetts.
Language (s): English
Ad Rate: Full Page Colour 850.00
Currency: United States Dollars
COMMUNITY NEWSPAPER

Wilkes-Barre/Scranton Independent Gazette 843936
Tel: 1 570 266-8086
Email: social@wilkesbarrescrantonig.com **Web site:** http://wilkesbarrescrantonig.com/
Freq: Weekly
Publisher: Lou Jasikoff
Profile: The Wilkes-Barre/Scranton Independent Gazette is a a community newspaper composed of local news, commentary, letters to the editor, classifieds, puzzles and press releases.
Language (s): English
COMMUNITY NEWSPAPER

Willamette Week 20524
Owner: City of Roses Newspaper Co.
Editorial: 2220 NW Quimby St, Portland, Oregon 97210-2624 **Tel:** 1 503 243-2122
Email: news@wweek.com **Web site:** http://www.wweek.com
Freq: Wed; **Circ:** 70000 Not Audited
Editor: Aaron Mesh; **Advertising Sales Manager:** Jane Smith; **Editor & Publisher:** Mark Zusman
Profile: Willamette Week is a weekly publication for the residents of Portland, OR and the surrounding areas. The readership tends to be younger, based on the liberal news and views in the newspaper. Half of the publication deals with local news while the other half deals with local arts and culture. Deadlines for the publication are 10 days prior to the issue date.
Language (s): English
Ad Rate: Full Page Mono 39.96
Ad Rate: Full Page Colour 3700.00
Currency: United States Dollars
COMMUNITY NEWSPAPER

Willapa Harbor Herald 21139
Owner: Flannery Publications
Editorial: 305 S Fork Rd, Raymond, Washington 98577-9598 **Tel:** 1 360 942-3466
Email: theherald@flannerypubs.com **Web site:** http://www.flannerypubs.com
Freq: Wed; **Circ:** 5300 Not Audited
Advertising Sales Manager: Gina Kolhaje; **Editor:** George Kunke; **Publisher:** Patrick Myers
Profile: Willapa Harbor Herald is written for residents of Pacific County, WA. The newspaper covers local news, events, sports, entertainment and arts. Deadlines are at 5pm PT on Fridays.
Language (s): English
Ad Rate: Full Page Mono 7.00
Currency: United States Dollars
COMMUNITY NEWSPAPER

Willgratten Publications 24570
Owner: Willgratten Publications LLC
Editorial: 407 Lincoln St, Wamego, Kansas 66547-1631 **Tel:** 1 785 456-2602
Email: office@wamegonews.com **Web site:** http://www.wamegotimes.com
Circ: 23105 Not Audited
Editor & Publisher: Tim Hobbs
Profile: Willgratten Publications produces the Wamego Times and Smoke Signal community newspapers.
Language (s): English
COMMUNITY NEWSPAPER

Williams Publishing Company 25209
Editorial: 107 N Main St, Greensboro, Georgia 30642-1143 **Tel:** 1 706 453-7988
Circ: 6200 Not Audited
Advertising Sales Manager: Beth Lyons; **Publisher:** Carey Williams
Language (s): English
COMMUNITY NEWSPAPER

Williamson County Sun, Inc. 24706
Owner: Thurmond (Clark)
Editorial: 707 S Main St, Georgetown, Texas 78626-5700 **Tel:** 1 512 930-4824
Email: letters@countysun.com **Web site:** http://www.wilcosun.com
Circ: 21800 Not Audited
Language (s): English
COMMUNITY NEWSPAPER

Williamson Herald 377461
Owner: CMD Publishing LLC
Editorial: 1117 Columbia Ave, Franklin, Tennessee 37064-3616 **Tel:** 1 615 790-6465
Email: news@williamsonherald.com **Web site:** http://www.williamsonherald.com
Freq: Thu; **Circ:** 10000 Not Audited
Publisher: Derby Jones
Profile: Williamson Herald is a local newspaper serving residents of Williamson County, TN. The paper covers local news, lifestyle stories and sports. Deadlines are on Mondays at noon ET.
Language (s): English
Ad Rate: Full Page Mono 14.00
Currency: United States Dollars
COMMUNITY NEWSPAPER

Williston Observer 22220
Owner: Williston Publishing & Promotions LLC
Editorial: 300 Cornerstone Dr Ste 330, Williston, Vermont 05495-4045 **Tel:** 1 802 879-4839
Email: editor@willistonobserver.com **Web site:** http://www.willistonobserver.com
Freq: Thu; **Circ:** 7000 Not Audited
Editor: Stephanie Choate
Profile: Williston Observer, also referred to as the Whistle, is a free publication written for residents of Williston, Richmond, and Saint George, VT. It contains local stories about news, business, and education. Deadlines are noon ET on Fridays before issue date.
Language (s): English
Ad Rate: Full Page Mono 7.20
Currency: United States Dollars
COMMUNITY NEWSPAPER

Wilmington Journal 20026
Editorial: 412 S 7th St, Wilmington, North Carolina 28401-5214 **Tel:** 1 910 762-5502
Email: wilmjourn@aol.com **Web site:** http://www.wilmingtonjournal.com
Freq: Thu; **Circ:** 10000 Not Audited
Publisher & Editor: Mary Alice Thatch
Profile: Wilmington Journal is a weekly newspaper written for residents of Wilmington, NC. The newspaper covers local and national news. Deadlines are at 5pm ET on the Tuesday before issue date.
Language (s): English
Ad Rate: Full Page Mono 20.00
Ad Rate: Full Page Colour 1207.00
Currency: United States Dollars
COMMUNITY NEWSPAPER

Wilson County News 21994
Owner: WCN Inc.
Editorial: 1012 C St, Floresville, Texas 78114-2224 **Tel:** 1 830 216-4519
Email: reader@wcn-online.com **Web site:** http://www.wilsoncountynews.com
Freq: Wed; **Circ:** 11000 Not Audited
Editor: Nannette Kilbey-Smith; **Publisher:** Elaine Kolodziej
Profile: Wilson County News's editorial mission is to provide accurate and fair news and information to the community. The paper is written for residents of Wilson County, TX. Deadlines for Wilson County News are noon CT, Thursday before issue date.
Language (s): English
Ad Rate: Full Page Mono 11.75
Currency: United States Dollars
COMMUNITY NEWSPAPER

Wilson Post 20768
Owner: MainStreet Media, LLC
Editorial: 216 Hartman Dr, Lebanon, Tennessee 37087-1516 **Tel:** 1 615 444-6008
Email: news@wilsonpost.com **Web site:** http://www.wilsonpost.com
Freq: Fri; **Circ:** 9200 Not Audited
Publisher: David Gould
Profile: Wilson Post is written for residents of Wilson County, TN. Deadlines are at noon CT on Tuesdays before the issue date.
Language (s): English
Ad Rate: Full Page Mono 9.85
Currency: United States Dollars
COMMUNITY NEWSPAPER

Wimberley View 28391
Owner: San Marcos Publishing, L.P.
Editorial: 101 FM 3237 Ste A, Wimberley, Texas 78676-5371 **Tel:** 1 512 847-2202
Email: wimberleyview@gmail.com **Web site:** http://wimberleyview.com
Freq: Thu; **Circ:** 5200 Not Audited
Profile: Wimberley View is a weekly newspaper that provides News and Information for the residents of Wimberley, Texas.
Language (s): English
Ad Rate: Full Page Mono 7.98
Currency: United States Dollars
COMMUNITY NEWSPAPER

Windsor Beacon 18715
Owner: Gannett Co. Inc.
Editorial: 425 Main St, Windsor, Colorado 80550-5129 **Tel:** 1 970 686-9646
Email: editor@windsorbeacon.com **Web site:** http://www.windsorbeacon.com
Freq: Sun; **Circ:** 7300 Not Audited
Editor and Publisher: Kathy Jack-Romero
Profile: Windsor (CO) Beacon is a twice-weekly newspaper that covers local news and events.
Language (s): English
Ad Rate: Full Page Mono 7.14
Currency: United States Dollars
COMMUNITY NEWSPAPER

Windsor Journal Weekly 26910
Owner: Acorn Media Services, LLC
Editorial: 1406 Main St., East Hartford, Connecticut 6108 **Tel:** 1 860 289-6468
Email: editor@thewindsorjournal.com **Web site:** http://www.thewindsorjournal.com
Freq: Fri; **Circ:** 5000
Editor: John Karas
Profile: The Windsor Journal Weekly is a weekly community newspaper containing local news, business, sports, weather, features, lifestyle, entertainment and events, serving the residents of Windsor, CT.
Language (s): English
Ad Rate: Full Page Mono 14.62
Currency: United States Dollars
COMMUNITY NEWSPAPER

The Windy City Word 72247
Editorial: 5090 W Harrison St, Chicago, Illinois 60644-5141 **Tel:** 1 773 378-0261
Email: windycityword02@yahoo.com **Web site:** http://www.windycityword.com
Freq: Thu; **Circ:** 20000 Not Audited
Editor: Jocelyn Denson; **Publisher:** Mary Denson
Profile: The Windy City Word is written for the residents of Chicago's West Side.
Language (s): English
Ad Rate: Full Page Mono 45.00
Currency: United States Dollars
COMMUNITY NEWSPAPER

Winfield American 154609
Owner: Region Communications Inc.
Editorial: 7590 E 109th Ave, Winfield, Indiana 46307-8631
Email: news@winfieldamerican.com **Web site:** http://www.winfieldamerican.com
Freq: Fri; **Circ:** 5000 Not Audited
Editor & Publisher: Mike Kucic
Profile: Winfield American is a community newspaper serving Winfield, IN and the surrounding Crown Point, IN area, including local news and community events.
Language (s): English
Ad Rate: Full Page Mono 40.00
Currency: United States Dollars
COMMUNITY NEWSPAPER

Wingspread 86756
Owner: Hearst Corporation (The)
Editorial: 1150 5th St E, Randolph Afb, Universal City, Texas 78150-4401 **Tel:** 1 210 652-5760
Email: randolphpublicaffairs@us.af.mil **Web site:** http://www.mysanantonio.com/news/local/communities/article/Randolph-Wingspread-4752528.php
Freq: Fri; **Circ:** 10725 Not Audited
Profile: Wingspread is a weekly military newspaper serving the military and civilian community at Randolph Air Force Base in Texas. It covers news and issues relevant to the people at the base, which itself is known as the "Showplace of the Air Force" due to its extensive and famous training school for pilots. The base is the headquarters of the U.S. Air Force's Education and Training command and home to the 12th Flying Training Wing, the 19th Air Force, the Air Force Personnel center, the Recruiting Service headquarters, the Air Force Services Agency and the Air Force Management Engineering Agency. Stories and photographs for publication may be faxed, e-mailed or turned in on a disc. It is published by Prime Time Military Newspapers in San Antonio, TX, where all of it's corporate staff are located. Deadlines are on Thursdays at noon CT.
Language (s): English
Ad Rate: Full Page Mono 19.06
Currency: United States Dollars
COMMUNITY NEWSPAPER

Winnebago Indian News 754760
Editorial: 100 Bluff Ave, Winnebago, Nebraska 68071-9787 **Tel:** 1 402 878-3221
Email: winnebagoindiannews@yahoo.com **Web site:** http://www.winnebagotribe.com/winnebago_indian_news.html
Freq: Bi-Weekly
Editor: Jerome Lapointe
Profile: Winnebago Indian News is a bi-weekly newspaper offering news and information for the Winnebago Tribe of Nebraska.
Language (s): English
Ad Rate: Full Page Mono 7.00
Currency: United States Dollars
COMMUNITY NEWSPAPER

Winona Post 21761
Editorial: 64 E 2Nd St, Winona, Minnesota 55987-3409 **Tel:** 1 507 452-1262
Email: winpost@winonapost.com **Web site:** http://www.winonapost.com
Freq: Sun; **Circ:** 23782 Not Audited
Editor: Frances Edstrom; **Publisher:** John Edstrom; **News Editor:** Sarah Squires; **Circulation Manager:** Mary Veraguth
Profile: Winona Post is written for surrounding communities of Winona, MN. It provides residents with information on news and events of interest to the local communities. Deadlines for the Wednesday edition are on the Monday prior to the issue date at noon CT. Deadlines for the Sunday edition are on the Thursday prior to the issue date at noon CT.
Language (s): English
Ad Rate: Full Page Mono 18.27
Currency: United States Dollars
COMMUNITY NEWSPAPER

Winston-Salem Chronicle 20027
Owner: Consolidated Media
Editorial: 617 N Liberty St, Winston Salem, North Carolina 27101-2912 **Tel:** 1 336 722-8624
Email: news@wschronicle.com **Web site:** http://www.wschronicle.com
Freq: Thu; **Circ:** 10000 Not Audited
Publisher: Ernest Pitt
Profile: Winston-Salem Chronicle is written for African-American community of Forsyth County, NC. Deadlines are at 5pm ET on Mondays.
Language (s): English
Ad Rate: Full Page Mono 16.20
Currency: United States Dollars
COMMUNITY NEWSPAPER

The Winter Texan Times 778332
Owner: Brunson (James)
Editorial: 1217 N Conway Ave, Mission, Texas 78572-4112 **Tel:** 1 956 580-7800
Email: news@wintertexantimes.com **Web site:** http://www.wintertexantimes.com
Freq: Weekly; **Circ:** 25000
Community News Editor: Kathy Olivarez
Profile: The Winter Texan Times is distributed free of charge to Mobile Home and RV Parks Valleywide, from Mission to Brownsville, including the following: Mission - McAllen - Pharr - San Juan - Alamo - Edinburg - Donna - Weslaco - Mercedes La Feria - Harlingen - San Benito - Los Fresnos - Port Isabel - South Padre Island - Brownsville.
Language (s): English
Ad Rate: Full Page Mono 30.00
Currency: United States Dollars
COMMUNITY NEWSPAPER

Wisconsin Newspress, Inc. 24735
Owner: Johanson (Christie)
Editorial: 113 E Mill St, Plymouth, Wisconsin 53073-1703 **Tel:** 1 920 893-6411
Email: reply@plymouth-review.com **Web site:** http://www.plymouth-review.com
Circ: 32405 Not Audited
Editor: Emmitt Feldner; **Editor:** Jeff Pederson
Profile: Wisconsin Newspress Inc. in Plymouth, WI publishes The Sheboygan Falls News, The Review and The Beacon.
Language (s): English
COMMUNITY NEWSPAPER

Wise County Messenger 22265
Editorial: 115 S Trinity St, Decatur, Texas 76234-1819 **Tel:** 1 940 627-5987
Email: news@wcmessenger.com **Web site:** http://www.wcmessenger.com
Freq: Sun; **Circ:** 7015 Not Audited
Advertising Sales Manager: Lisa Davis; **Editor:** Brian Knox
Profile: Wise County Messenger is a local newspaper written for the residents of Wise County, TX. The publication covers local news, events and sports. Deadlines are on Tuesdays at 8am CT for the Thursday edition and on Fridays at 8am CT for the Sunday edition.
Language (s): English
Ad Rate: Full Page Mono 6.80
Currency: United States Dollars
COMMUNITY NEWSPAPER

The Witness 21911
Owner: Archdiocese of Dubuque
Editorial: 1229 Mount Loretta Ave, Dubuque, Iowa 52003-7826 **Tel:** 1 563 588-0556
Email: dbqcwo@arch.pvt.k12.ia.us **Web site:** http://www.dbqarch.org
Freq: Sun; **Circ:** 11970 Not Audited
Advertising Manager: Bret Fear; **Publisher:** Michael Jackels; **Circulation Manager:** Cathy White
Profile: The Witness serves the Catholic Diocese of Dubuque, IA. Its editorial mission is to inform people of news from Rome and the Pope. Deadlines are on Mondays at noon CT.
Language (s): English
Ad Rate: Full Page Mono 12.95
Currency: United States Dollars
COMMUNITY NEWSPAPER

WNS Publications 25270
Owner: Komlanc Jr. (Anthony)
Editorial: 100 E Main St, Morrison, Illinois 61270 **Tel:** 1 815 772-7244
Email: sentinel@whitesidesentinel.com **Web site:** http://www.whitesidesentinel.com
Circ: 5500 Not Audited
Editor: Jerry Lindsey; **Publisher:** Sue Patten; **Circulation Manager:** Marilyn Vegter
Profile: WNS Publications is a community newspaper publisher serving the residents of Davenport, IA, Rock Island and Moline, IL.
Language (s): English
COMMUNITY NEWSPAPER

Womack Publishing 324766
Owner: Womack Newspapers Inc.
Editorial: 206 E Main St, Jamestown, North Carolina 27282-9532 **Tel:** 1 336 841-4933
Email: jamestownnews@northstate.net **Web site:** http://www.womacknewspapers.com/jamestownnews
Circ: 9000 Not Audited
Language (s): English
COMMUNITY NEWSPAPER

Wood Land Publishing Inc. 25170
Editorial: 2404 Park Ave, Pearland, Texas 77581-4234 **Tel:** 1 281 485-7501
Web site: http://myreporternews.com
Circ: 12500 Not Audited
Editor: David Davis; **Circulation Manager:** Randy Emmons
Language (s): English
COMMUNITY NEWSPAPER

The Woodford Sun 19386
Editorial: 184 S Main St, Versailles, Kentucky 40383-1214 **Tel:** 1 859 873-4131
Email: news@woodfordsun.com **Web site:** http://www.woodfordsun.com
Freq: Weekly; **Circ:** 5600 Not Audited
Advertising Sales Manager: Jennifer Cardwell; **Publisher:** Ben Chandler; **Circulation Manager:** Patricia Osterloh
Profile: Woodford Sun is written for residents of Versailles, Midway and Woodford County, KY.
Language (s): English
Ad Rate: Full Page Mono 9.70

Currency: United States Dollars
COMMUNITY NEWSPAPER

Woodmen Edition 600885

Owner: Walter Publishing Co.
Editorial: 620 Southpointe Ct Ste 235, Colorado Springs, Colorado 80906-3861 **Tel:** 1 719 578-5112
Email: hannah@gazettecommunitynews.com **Web site:** http://www.waltpub.com
Freq: Weekly; **Circ:** 16000
Advertising Sales Manager: Jenny Hillstrom
Profile: Contains community news for Colorado Springs, CO area residents.
Language (s): English
Ad Rate: Full Page Mono 13.75
Currency: United States Dollars
COMMUNITY NEWSPAPER

Woodside Herald 21580

Editorial: 4311 Greenpoint Ave, Sunnyside, New York 11104-2605 **Tel:** 1 718 729-3772
Email: SSabba@WoodsideHerald.com **Web site:** http://www.woodsideherald.com
Freq: Fri; **Circ:** 16000 Not Audited
Publisher & Editor: Sherilyn Sabba
Profile: Woodside Herald is written for residents of Sunnyside, Woodside and Long Island City, NY. Deadlines are on Mondays at 5pm ET.
Language (s): English
Ad Rate: Full Page Mono 18.00
Currency: United States Dollars
COMMUNITY NEWSPAPER

Worcester Mag 21857

Owner: Holden Landmark Co.
Editorial: 72 Shrewsbury St, Worcester, Massachusetts 01604-4625 **Tel:** 1 508 749-3166
Email: editor@worcestermag.com **Web site:** http://worcestermag.com
Freq: Thu; **Circ:** 30500 Not Audited
Advertising Sales Manager: Helen Linnehan; **Publisher:** Kathy Real; **Circulation Manager:** Thomas Signa
Profile: Worcester Mag is a weekly local newspaper of Worcester Publishing Ltd. The publication covers a mix of investigative reporting, issue analysis, personality profiles and opinion columns for readers in the Worcester, MA community. The newspaper also reaches readers in central Massachusetts and some Boston suburbs. Regular features include news, opinion, in-depth cover stories, an arts & entertainment section containing dedicated music, culture and film/video pages and a comprehensive events calendar.
Language (s): English
Ad Rate: Full Page Colour 2960.00
Currency: United States Dollars
COMMUNITY NEWSPAPER

The World 22188

Owner: Phillips (Deborah) and Hass (Gary)
Editorial: 403 US Route 302, Barre, Vermont 05641-2272 **Tel:** 1 802 479-2582
Email: editor@vt-world.com **Web site:** http://www.vt-world.com
Freq: Wed; **Circ:** 18500 Not Audited
Editor: Laura Rappold; **Advertising Sales Mahager:** Kay Roberts
Profile: The World is published weekly for the residents of Barre, VT and surrounding areas. The publication provides information about local news and community events.
Language (s): English
Ad Rate: Full Page Mono 12.00
Currency: United States Dollars
COMMUNITY NEWSPAPER

Worldwest Ltd., Liability Co. 25210

Owner: Worldwest LLC
Editorial: 708 N Beeline Hwy, Payson, Arizona 85541 **Tel:** 1 928 474-5251
Email: editor@payson.com **Web site:** http://www.paysonroundup.com
Circ: 11000 Not Audited
Editor: Pete Aleshire; **Circulation Manager:** Patty Behm; **Publisher:** John Naughton
Language (s): English
COMMUNITY NEWSPAPER

Worrall Community Newspapers 25521

Owner: Worrall Community Newspapers Inc.
Editorial: 1291 Stuyvesant Ave, Union, New Jersey 07083-3823 **Tel:** 1 908 686-7700
Email: editorial@thelocalsource.com **Web site:** http://www.localsource.com
Circ: 24550 Not Audited
Advertising Sales Manager: Steven DuBois; **Editor:** Stacey Eaton; **Editor:** Yael Katzwer; **Publisher:** David Worrall
Profile: Worrall Community Newspapers is a community newspaper publisher in Union, NJ.
Language (s): English
COMMUNITY NEWSPAPER

Wright County Journal-Press 19602

Owner: McDonnell (J.P.)
Editorial: 108 Central Ave, Buffalo, Minnesota 55313-1521 **Tel:** 1 763 682-1221
Email: business@thedrummer.com **Web site:** http://www.thedrummer.com
Freq: Thu; **Circ:** 5600 Not Audited
Editor: J.P. McDonnell; **Advertising Sales Manager:** Jim McDonnell
Profile: The Wright County Journal-Press is written for the residents of Buffalo, MN.
Language (s): English
Ad Rate: Full Page Mono 9.72
Currency: United States Dollars
COMMUNITY NEWSPAPER

Wyalusing Rocket-Courier 20604

Owner: W. David Keeler
Editorial: 196 State St, Wyalusing, Pennsylvania 18853 **Tel:** 1 570 746-1217
Email: rocket@epix.net **Web site:** http://www.rocket-courier.com
Freq: Weekly; **Circ:** 5000 Not Audited
Circulation Manager: Nancy Keeler; **Publisher & Editor:** W. David Keeler
Profile: Wyalusing Rocket-Courier is a local weekly newspaper whose editorial mission is to report news, analysis, and features to the community. The newspaper reports on happenings in the courts, school districts, government, law enforcement, and ongoing community events. Wyalusing Rocket-Courier is written for residents of Bradford, Wyoming, and Susquehanna County, PA.
Language (s): English
Ad Rate: Full Page Mono 13.00
Currency: United States Dollars
COMMUNITY NEWSPAPER

Wyandotte County Business News 863292

Owner: Lewis Legal News Inc
Tel: 1 913 422-8232
Email: notices@wyandottecountylegalnews.com
Web site: http://www.wybiznews.com
Freq: Weekly
Profile: Wyandotte County Business News is a local source for local, state, and national news covering Politics, Government, Business, Law, Society, Religion and Sports, and well as Business news including new homeowners, foreclosures and mortgages, new business, credit, and law news.
Language (s): English
COMMUNITY NEWSPAPER

Wynne Progress Inc. 25441

Editorial: 702 Falls Blvd N, Wynne, Arkansas 72396-2209 **Tel:** 1 870 238-2375
Email: news@wynneprogressinc.com
Circ: 27000 Not Audited
Publisher: David Boger; **Editor:** David Owens
Profile: Wynne Progress Inc. providing news to the community of Wynne, AR.
Language (s): English
COMMUNITY NEWSPAPER

The Yadkin Ripple 20021

Owner: Civitas Media
Editorial: 115 Jackson St, Yadkinville, North Carolina 27055 **Tel:** 1 336 679-2341
Email: editor@yadkinripple.com **Web site:** http://www.yadkinripple.com
Freq: Thu; **Circ:** 5000 Not Audited
Profile: The Yadkin Ripple provides local news coverage for the Yadkinville, NC area.
Language (s): English
Ad Rate: Full Page Mono 6.60
Currency: United States Dollars
COMMUNITY NEWSPAPER

Yated Ne'Eman 22028

Editorial: 53 Olympia Ln, Monsey, New York 10952-2829 **Tel:** 1 845 369-1600
Email: editor@yated.com **Web site:** http://www.yated.com
Freq: Wed; **Circ:** 33000 Not Audited
Publisher: Pinchos Lipschultz; **Editor:** Avi Yishai
Profile: Yated Ne'Eman is a newspaper written for the Haredi Jewish community in and around Monsey, NY.
Language (s): English
Ad Rate: Full Page Mono 6.25
Currency: United States Dollars
COMMUNITY NEWSPAPER

Yelp & Yosemite Sun Newspapers 377561

Owner: Lucenup Media
Editorial: 30651 Holiday Dr, Coarsegold, California 93614 **Tel:** 1 559 658-5419
Web site: http://www.theyelp.com
Circ: 10000 Not Audited
Language (s): English
COMMUNITY NEWSPAPER

YES! Weekly 324614

Owner: Womack Newspapers Inc.
Editorial: 5500 Adams Farm Ln Ste 204, Greensboro, North Carolina 27407-7059 **Tel:** 1 336 316-1231
Email: publisher@yesweekly.com **Web site:** http://www.yesweekly.com
Freq: Wed; **Circ:** 43000 Not Audited
Publisher: Charles Womack
Profile: YES! Weekly in Greensboro, NC is an alternative newspaper that focuses on the cultural, political and artistic aspects of the Triad, which includes High Point and Winston-Salem, NC. Targeted to young professionals, it strives to be the conscience of the community, a recorder of history, a voice for all citizens and an advocate of the good. Deadlines are on Mondays.
Language (s): English
Ad Rate: Full Page Mono 30.00
Currency: United States Dollars
COMMUNITY NEWSPAPER

Yevreiski Mir 217324

Editorial: 1100 Coney Island Ave, Brooklyn, New York 11230-2342 **Tel:** 1 718 434-0900
Web site: http://www.evreimir.com
Freq: Tue; **Circ:** 14000 Not Audited
Advertising Sales Manager: Sergei Burmin; **Publisher & Editor:** Aryeh Katzin
Profile: Yevreiski Mir is a community newspaper written for Russian-speaking Jewish residents of Brooklyn, NY and the surrounding areas.
Language (s): Russian
Ad Rate: Full Page Mono 6.72
Currency: United States Dollars
COMMUNITY NEWSPAPER

Yountville Sun 816623

Tel: 1 707 944-5676
Email: news@yountvillesun.com **Web site:** http://www.yountvillesun.com
Freq: Weekly; **Circ:** 5000
Editor & Publisher: Sharon Stensaas
Profile: Yountville Sun is a weekly community newspaper serving Yountville, Oakville, Rutherford, and unincorporated Napa Valley, CA.
Language (s): English
Ad Rate: Full Page Mono 12.85
Currency: United States Dollars
COMMUNITY NEWSPAPER

Yucaipa/Calimesa News Mirror 30133

Owner: Century Group (The)
Editorial: 35154 Yucaipa Blvd, Yucaipa, California 92399-4339 **Tel:** 1 909 797-9101
Email: news@newsmirror.net **Web site:** http://www.newsmirror.net
Freq: Fri; **Circ:** 21304 Not Audited
Advertising Sales Manager: Larry Williams
Profile: Yucaipa/Calimesa News Mirror is a weekly newspaper serving residents of Yucaipa, Calimesa and Oak Glen, CA. It emphasizes local news and covers breaking news, crimes, public announcements and civic events.
Language (s): English
Ad Rate: Full Page Mono 18.50
Currency: United States Dollars
COMMUNITY NEWSPAPER

Zion-Benton News 19139

Owner: United Communications Corp.
Editorial: 2711 Sheridan Rd Ste 202, Zion, Illinois 60099-2650 **Tel:** 1 847 746-9000
Email: zion@kenoshanews.com **Web site:** http://www.zion-bentonnews.com
Freq: Thu; **Circ:** 21800 Not Audited
Circulation Manager: Tony Decesaro; **Publisher:** Frank Misureli; **Editor:** Mona Shannon
Profile: Zion-Benton News is a community newspaper for the residents of Beach Park, Winthrop Harbor and Zion, IL.
Language (s): English
Ad Rate: Full Page Mono 10.75
Currency: United States Dollars
COMMUNITY NEWSPAPER

Uruguay

Time Difference: GMT -3
National Telephone Code: 598
Continent: The Americas
Capital: Montevideo

Newspapers

Acción 378064

Editorial: Artigas 352, Mercedes 75000
Tel: 598 53 22236
Email: diarioaccion@adinet.com.uy
Freq: Daily
Director: Fernando Fernández
Profile: Accion is a daily newspaper serving Mercedes, Uruguay and the surrounding area. The newspaper circulates in the departments of Soriano, Río Negro and Colonia. The paper is published in Spanish.
Language (s): Spanish
DAILY NEWSPAPER

Actualidad 378129

Editorial: Garibaldi 539, Las Piedras 90200
Tel: 598 36 45358
Email: actualid@adinet.com.uy
Freq: Weekly
Director: Sergio Guerrero
Profile: Semanario con circulación en las localidades de:Las Piedras, La Paz, Progreso, Juanicó, Los Cerrillos, Sauce, Canelones y parte de la Ciudad de la Costa.Edición de 24 páginas color.Director: Sergio Guerrero.Fecha de Aparición: 27368
Language (s): Spanish
DAILY NEWSPAPER

Arequita 378078

Editorial: Unavailable, Minas
Email: arequit@adinet.com.uy **Web site:** http://www.galeon.com/arequita/
Freq: Weekly
Director: Alvaro Rodríguez Días
Profile: Semanario Independiente. Minas, Lavalleja, República Oriental del Uruguay. DIRECTOR: Álvaro Rodríguez Díaz. REDACTOR RESPONSABLE: Luis María Rodríguez Bentancour. SECRETARIO DE REDACCIÓN y DISEÑO: Luis Rodríguez Díaz
Language (s): Spanish
DAILY NEWSPAPER

Avisos Clasificados (El País) 378198

Editorial: Av. 18 de Julio 1489, Montevideo 11200
Tel: 598 2 4002141
Email: avisos@elpaisclasific.com.uy **Web site:** http://gallito.elpais.com.uy
Freq: Weekly
Director: Eduardo Sheck
Profile: Semanario de avisos clasificados de oferta y demanda de bienes y servicios. Se publica cada domingo con El País.
Language (s): Spanish
DAILY NEWSPAPER

Batoví 378110

Editorial: Juan Ortiz 300, Tacuarembó 45000
Tel: 598 63 23900
Email: semanariobatovi@adinet.com.uy **Web site:** http://www.batovi.com.uy
Freq: Daily
Profile: Semanario que sale los viernes y circula en las localidades de : Tacuarembó, Paso de los Toros, Achar, Curtina, Ansina, San Gregorio de Polanco yTambores. Fecha de Aparición: 30195
Language (s): Spanish
DAILY NEWSPAPER

Búsqueda 378205

Editorial: Av. Uruguay 1146, Montevideo 11200
Tel: 598 2 9021300
Email: busquedaonline@busqueda.com.uy **Web site:** http://www.busqueda.com.uy
Freq: Weekly
Director: Pilar Perrier
Profile: Semanario independiente de gran prestigio e influencia en los ámbitos políticos, económicos y culturales del país. Distribución nacional. Su público objetivo son las clases media alta y alta. Fecha de Aparición: 1972
Language (s): Spanish
DAILY NEWSPAPER

Cambio 378139

Editorial: Unavailable, Salto 50000 **Tel:** 598 73 35045
Email: otlas@adinet.com.uy **Web site:** http://www.diariocambiodigital.com.uy
Freq: Daily
Director: Carlos F. Artía
Profile: Circula en las localidades de : Salto, Bella Unión.Edición de 24 páginas.Director: Carlos F. Artía. Fecha de Aparición: 30834
Language (s): Spanish
DAILY NEWSPAPER

Carta Popular 378204

Editorial: Fernandez Crespo 2106, Montevideo
Tel: 598 2 9290410
Freq: Weekly
Language (s): Spanish
DAILY NEWSPAPER

Centenario 378104

Editorial: Artigas 1324, Cardona 75200
Tel: 598 53 69224
Web site: http://www.centenario.com.uy
Freq: Weekly
Profile: Tri semanario que sale los días: lunes miércoles y sábados.Edición de 20 páginas.Circula en las localidades de : Cardona, Florencio Sánchez, Cortinas, Santa Catalina, Ombúes de Lavalle, Miguelete y Rodó. Fecha de Aparición: 11067
Language (s): Spanish
DAILY NEWSPAPER

Crónicas 378203

Editorial: 484 Buenos Aires, Primer Piso, Oficina 4, Montevideo 11000 **Tel:** 598 2 915-6511
Email: cronicas@cronicas.com.uy **Web site:** http://www.cronicas.com.uy
Freq: Weekly
Editor: Oscar Cestau
Profile: Crónicas es un semanario que brinda información sobre la Economía, Política, Agro, Sociedad, Seguros en Uruguay. Crónicas is a weekly publication that provides coverage of Economy, Politics, Agriculture, Society Insurance in Uruguay.
Language (s): Spanish
DAILY NEWSPAPER

Diario Atlas 378285

Editorial: 18 de Julio 664, Melo 37000
Tel: 598 64 23726
Email: atlasmel@adinet.com.uy
Freq: Bi-Monthly
Director: Zelmar Paggiola
Profile: Edición de 12 páginas.Director: Zelmar Paggiola. Fecha de Aparición: 31190
Language (s): Spanish
DAILY NEWSPAPER

Diario Correo de Punta del Este 378287

Editorial: Unavailable, Maldonado 2000
Tel: 598 42 235633
Email: info@diariocorreo.com **Web site:** http://www.diariocorreo.com

Freq: Weekly
Language (s): Spanish
DAILY NEWSPAPER

Diario Crónicas 378114
Editorial: Eusebio Gimenez 695, Mercedes 75000
Tel: 598 53 25310
Email: diariocronicas@adinet.com.uy **Web site:** http://www.diariocronicas.com.uy
Freq: Weekly
Director: Ricardo Nolé Laguno
Profile: Edición de 16 páginas, color.Circula en las localidades de : Departamentos de Soriano, Río Negro, Colonia.Director: Ricardo Nolé Laguno. Fecha de Aparición: 30021
Language (s): Spanish
DAILY NEWSPAPER

Diario Helvecia 378214
Editorial: Colon 1117, Nueva Helvecia 70.201
Tel: 598 55 44031
Email: helvecia@adinet.com.uy **Web site:** http://www.colonia-suiza.com.uy/helvecia.htm
Freq: Weekly
Director: Alfredo Stutz
Profile: Circula en las localidades de : Nueva Helvecia, Colonia Valdense, Rosario, Ecilda Paullier, Cufré y Balnearios.Edición de 16 páginas.Director: Alfredo Stutz. Fecha de Aparición: 5149
Language (s): Spanish
DAILY NEWSPAPER

Diario la Unión 378081
Editorial: Florencio Sanchez 569, Minas 30000
Tel: 598 44 22065
Email: decano@chasque.net **Web site:** http://www.lavalleja.com/noticias/marco_news.htm
Freq: Daily
Director: Hugo Vázquez Ortiz
Profile: Diario vespertino de la capital departamental de Lavalleja.Redactor Responsable: Hugo Vázquez Ortiz.Edición de 16 páginas.
Language (s): Spanish
DAILY NEWSPAPER

Ecos 378281
Editorial: Dr. Pedro E. Ferrer 1644, Castillos
Tel: 598 47 59600
Freq: Daily
Director: Julio A. Bianchi Coello
Profile: Circula en las localidades de : Rocha, Castillos, Lascano, Chuy, La Paloma, Cebollatí, La Coronilla, La Pedrera.Edición de 26 páginas. Director:Julio A. Bianchi Coello. Fecha de Aparición: 33229
Language (s): Spanish
DAILY NEWSPAPER

Ecos Regionales de Durazno 378217
Editorial: Fructuoso Rivera 364, Durazno 97000
Tel: 598 36 22146
Email: ecossrl@adinet.com.uy
Freq: Daily
Director: Ricardo Ariel López
Profile: Circula en las localidades de: Departamentos de Durazno, Flores y Paso de los Toros.Edición de 32 páginas.Director: Ricardo Ariel López. Fecha de Aparición: 34831
Language (s): Spanish
DAILY NEWSPAPER

Ecos Regionales de Trinidad 378147
Editorial: Luis Alberto de Herrera 812, Trinidad 85000
Tel: 598 36 44666
Email: ecossrl@adinet.com.uy
Director: Ricardo Ariel López
Profile: Bi semanario que sale los martes y viernes.Edición de 32 páginas.Circula en las localidades de : Departamentos de Flores, Durazno y Paso de los Toros.Director: Ricardo Ariel López. Fecha de Aparición: 34831
Language (s): Spanish
DAILY NEWSPAPER

El Acontecer 378216
Editorial: Artigas 374, Durazno 97000
Tel: 598 36 24416
Email: acontece@adinet.com.uy
Freq: Bi-Monthly
Director: Carlos Román Fernández
Profile: Circula en las localidades del departamento de Durazno.Edición de 20 páginas, color.Director: Carlos Román Fernández. Fecha de Aparición: 31427
Language (s): Spanish
DAILY NEWSPAPER

El Avisador 378128
Editorial: Dr. Catalina 181, Tacuarembó 45000
Tel: 598 63 24411
Email: diario@avisador.com.uy **Web site:** http://www.avisador.com.uy
Freq: Daily
Profile: Director: Jorge W. Carozo Redactor Responsable:Jorge Carozo Barcelona.Circula en las localidades de : Tacuarembó, Rivera, San Gregorio, Ansina y Curtina. Fecha de Aparición: 31048
Language (s): Spanish
DAILY NEWSPAPER

El Correo 378208
Editorial: Unavailable, Maldonado
Tel: 598 42 235633
Email: gallardo@adinet.com.uy **Web site:** http://www.diariocorreo.com
Freq: Weekly
Director: María Palmira Rodriguez
Profile: Sale de lunes a viernes y circula en el departamento de maldonado.Edición de 12 páginas.Director: María Palmira Rodríguez. Fecha de Aparición: 34043
Language (s): Spanish
DAILY NEWSPAPER

El Diario Médico 378249
Editorial: Antonio Maria Fernandez 765, Florida
Tel: 598 35 23833
Email: saludhoy@adinet.com.uy **Web site:** http://www.smu.org.uy/publicaciones/eldiariomedico/
Freq: Monthly
Director: Elbio Alvarez
Profile: Tabloide mensual dedicado al acontecer médico.Redactor Responsable:Prof. Elbio D. Álvarez.
Language (s): Spanish
DAILY NEWSPAPER

El Eco de Colonia 378212
Editorial: Ruta 21 1630, Colonia **Tel:** 598 52 21395
Email: elecosrl@adinet.com.uy
Freq: Monthly
Director: Daniel Roselli
Profile: Semanario que sale los sábados.Tiene cobertura departamental.Director: Daniel Roselli.Edición de 20 páginas. Fecha de Aparición: 37919
Language (s): Spanish
DAILY NEWSPAPER

El Eco de Palmira 378134
Editorial: Unavailable, Nueva Palmira 70101
Tel: 598 54 46815
Email: elecosrl@adinet.com.uy **Web site:** http://www.nuevapalmira.net/eleco
Freq: Daily
Director: Nancy Banchero
Profile: Circula en las localidades de: Nueva Palmira, Carmelo y zona rural de influencia.Edición de 24 páginas.Directora: Nancy Banchero.
Language (s): Spanish
DAILY NEWSPAPER

El Este 378093
Editorial: Zorrilla 70, Rocha **Tel:** 598 47 22099
Email: info@diarioeleste.com **Web site:** http://www.diarioeleste.com
Freq: Daily
Director: José Carlos Cardoso
Profile: Matutino capitalino del departamento de Rocha.Director: José Carlos Cardozo.Edición de 16 páginas.Circula en las localidades de : Rocha, Castillos, Lascano, Chuy, La Paloma, Cebollatí, La Coronilla y La Pedrera. Fecha de Aparición: 16674
Language (s): Spanish
DAILY NEWSPAPER

El Heraldo 378146
Editorial: Independencia 825, Florida 94000
Tel: 598 35 22229
Email: marino9753@hotmail.com **Web site:** http://www.elheraldo.com.uy
Freq: Daily
Director: Alvaro Riva Rey
Profile: Edición de 20 páginas, color.Director: Alvaro Riva Rey. Fecha de Aparición: 6974
Language (s): Spanish
DAILY NEWSPAPER

El Mundo y sus Comarcas 378276
Editorial: Hector Miranda 87, Santa Lucía 90700
Tel: 598 33 46022
Email: rlegnani@adinet.com.uy
Freq: Weekly
Director: Eduardo Pi
Profile: Quincenario que sale los días jueves.Con cobertura en el departamento de Canelones.Edición: 10 páginas. Director:Eduardo Pi. Fecha de Aparición: 34335
Language (s): Spanish
DAILY NEWSPAPER

El Nuevo Rionegrense 378246
Editorial: 25 de agosto 3118, Fray Bentos 65000
Tel: 598 56 22210
Email: elrione@adinet.com.uy
Freq: Monthly
Director: Félix Omar Rovelli
Profile: Bi Semanario (miércoles y sábado), circula en las localidades de : Fray Bentos, Young y Nuevo Berlin.Edición de 8 páginas.Director: Félix Omar Rovelli. Fecha de Aparición: 37469
Language (s): Spanish
DAILY NEWSPAPER

El Pueblo 378103
Editorial: Luis A. De Herrera 479, Santa Lucía 90700
Tel: 598 33 46151
Email: diarioelpueblo@hotmail.com
Freq: Monthly
Director: Gilda Caputi
Profile: Semanario que sale los dias miércoles.Circula en las localidades de: Santa Lucía, Canelones y zonas cercanas. Edición 8 páginas. Director:Gilda Caputi. Fecha de Aparición: 7868
Language (s): Spanish
DAILY NEWSPAPER

El Pueblo 378133
Editorial: 18 de Julio 151, Salto 50000
Tel: 598 73 34133
Email: dipueblo@adinet.com.uy **Web site:** http://www.diarioelpueblo.com.uy
Freq: Daily
Director: Walter Martínez
Profile: Diario de información local.Circula en las localidades de: Salto, Belén, Constitución, Artigas y Bella Unión.Edición de 32 páginas, color.Director: Walter Martínez. Fecha de Aparición: 20515
Language (s): Spanish
DAILY NEWSPAPER

El Sol 378211
Editorial: Fosalva 614, Colonia 70000
Tel: 598 52 26017
Email: monteric@adinet.com.uy
Freq: Daily
Director: Ricardo Montenegro
Profile: Circula en las localidades de: Colonia y zonas cercanas. Director: Ricardo Montenegro.Edición de 30 páginas. Fecha de Aparición: 30939
Language (s): Spanish
DAILY NEWSPAPER

El Telégrafo 378130
Editorial: 18 de Julio 1027, Paysandú 60000
Tel: 598 72 24605
Email: correo@eltelegrafo.com **Web site:** http://www.eltelegrafo.com
Freq: Daily
Director: Fernando Baccaro
Profile: Edición de 28 páginas, color.Circula en las localidades de : Paysandú, Salto, Young, Mercedes y Tacuarembó.Director: Fernando Baccaro. Fecha de Aparición: 3835
Language (s): Spanish
DAILY NEWSPAPER

Hechos 378076
Editorial: Buxareo Oribe 2478, San Ramón 90600
Tel: 598 31 22142
Email: shechos@adinet.com.uy
Freq: Daily
Director: Jorge Zitto Ferré
Profile: Semanario que sale los ías viernes.Circula en las localidades de : San Ramón, Santa Rosa, San Baustista, Castellanos, Tala, Fray Marcos y Chamizo.Edición: 14 páginas. Director:Jorge Zitto Ferré. Fecha de Aparición: 31321
Language (s): Spanish
DAILY NEWSPAPER

Hoy Canelones 378206
Editorial: Tomas Berreta 207, Canelones 90000
Tel: 598 33 24386
Email: hoycanel@adinet.com.uy **Web site:** http://www.hoycanelones.com.uy
Freq: Daily
Director: Julio Britos Bide
Profile: Diario local que cubre el área de de la ciudad de canelones y aledaños en forma diaria. Se dedica a las noticias de orden local y nacional. Cubre el área nacional en la modalidad de sucscripción y envío.Director: Julio Britos Bide.Diario: Lunes a Sábado. Edición: 24 páginas en color. Fecha de Aparición: 29779
Language (s): Spanish
DAILY NEWSPAPER

Irupe 378303
Editorial: Asencio 1341, Dolores 75100
Tel: 598 53 42134
Email: Irupe21@adinet.com.uy
Freq: Daily
Director: Miguel Pose
Profile: Circula en las localidades de : Dolores, Cañada Nieto, Villa Soriano y Mercedes.Edición de 12 páginas.Director: Miguel Pose. Fecha de Aparición: 22883
Language (s): Spanish
DAILY NEWSPAPER

Jornada 378071
Editorial: Brasil 1262, Rivera 40000
Tel: 598 62 23991
Email: jornada@adinet.com.uy
Freq: Daily
Director: Neiva Zampayo de Gaal
Profile: De circulación departamental.Edición de 12 páginas.Directora: Neiva Zampayo de Gaál. Fecha de Aparición: 31217
Language (s): Spanish
DAILY NEWSPAPER

La Colonia 378254
Editorial: Gral. Flores 317, Colonia 70000
Tel: 598 52 22580
Web site: http://www.portalcolonia.com
Freq: Daily
Director: Juan Carlos Puppo
Profile: Bi semanario que circula en las localidades de:Colonia y alrededores, El General, Real de San Carlos y zonas rurales de influencia.Director: Juan Carlos Puppo. Edición de 36 páginas. Fecha de Aparición: 532
Language (s): Spanish
DAILY NEWSPAPER

La Democracia 378209
Editorial: 18 de Julio 25, San Carlos 20000
Tel: 598 42 250321
Freq: Daily
Director: Raúl José Arias
Profile: Sale de lunes a sábado y circula en las localidades de : San Carlos, Maldonado, Punta del Este, zonas de la costa, Piriápolis y Pan de Azúcar. Edición de 24 páginas.Director: Raúl José Arias. Fecha de Aparición: 8266
Language (s): Spanish
DAILY NEWSPAPER

La Diaria 412407
Editorial: Juan Paullier 1235, Montevideo
Tel: 598 2 4012100
Email: ladiaria@ladiaria.com.uy **Web site:** http://www.ladiaria.com.uy
Freq: Daily
General Manager: Damian Osta
Profile: Nuevo periódico joven, que trata temas de actualidad como una mirada seria y renovada. Secciones: política, cultura, internacional, sociedad, economía, deportes y humor. Tiene contenido gratuito a través de su página web. Exite la opción de suscribirse por $220 pesos mensuales, € 15 o US$ 18 para la versión en PDF para el exterior.
Language (s): Spanish
DAILY NEWSPAPER

La Juventud 378201
Editorial: Nueva York 1326, Montevideo
Email: juvnetud@chasque.net **Web site:** http://chasque.apc.org/juventud/
Freq: Monthly
Profile: Diario de izquierda idetificado con el Frente Amplio.
Language (s): Spanish
DAILY NEWSPAPER

La Noticia 378086
Editorial: Garzon 450, Artigas 55000
Tel: 598 77 25091
Email: lnoticia@adinet.com.uy **Web site:** http://www.publimatic.com/diariolanoticia
Freq: Daily
Director: Ricardo Pedrón
Profile: Circula en las localidades de: Artigas, Bella Unión, Tomás Gomensoro y Baltasar Brum.Edición de 12 páginas, color.Director: Ricardo Pedrón. Fecha de Aparición: 32295
Language (s): Spanish
DAILY NEWSPAPER

La Tribuna 378123
Editorial: Manuel Oribe 452, Paso De Los Toros 45100 **Tel:** 598 66 42268
Email: latribuna@pasodelostoros.com **Web site:** http://www.pasodelostoros.com/latribuna/
Freq: Weekly
Director: Iris Andrada
Profile: Circula en las localidades de : Paso de los Toros, Tacuarembó, Achar, San Gregorio de Polanco, Salto, Rivera, Durazno y Centenario.Edición de 20 páginas, color.Director: Iris Andrada de Andrada. Fecha de Aparición: 19977
Language (s): Spanish
DAILY NEWSPAPER

Norte 378051
Editorial: San Martin 711, Rivera 40000
Tel: 598 62 35676
Email: norte1@adinet.com.uy
Freq: Weekly
Director: María del Carmen Pereira Soares de Araujo
Profile: Circula en las localidades de : Rivera, Tacuarembó, Tranqueras, Minas de Corrales, Vichadero, Cerro Pelado, Paso de los Toros.Edición de 22 páginas.Directora: María del Carmen Pereira Soáres de Araújo. Fecha de Aparición: 19836
Language (s): Spanish
DAILY NEWSPAPER

El Observador 378197
Editorial: Cuareim 2052, Montevideo 11800
Tel: 598 2 9247000
Web site: http://www.elobservador.com.uy/
Freq: Daily
Director: Ricardo Peirano
Profile: Matutino de alcance nacional.Tendencia liberal. Afín católico. De consumo de clases media, media alta y alta. Fecha de Aparición: 33878
Language (s): Spanish
DAILY NEWSPAPER

Opción Veintiuno 378261
Editorial: Ciganda 720, San José **Tel:** 598 34 29353
Freq: Daily
Director: Gabriel Reyes Montes
Profile: Semanario que sale los viernes.Es de circulaciónen todo el departamento y consta de 20 páginas en color.Director: Gabriel Reyes Montes. Fecha de Aparición: 36588
Language (s): Spanish
DAILY NEWSPAPER

Orejano 378085
Editorial: Dionisio Oribe 1388, Treinta Y Tres 33000
Tel: 598 45 24512
Freq: Weekly
Director: Damián Blanco
Profile: Semanario que sale los viernes de cobertura departamental.Edición de 12 páginas.Director: Damián Blanco. Fecha de Aparición: 35156
Language (s): Spanish
DAILY NEWSPAPER

El País 378251
Editorial: Zelmar Michelini (diario), Plaza Cagancha 1162 (administracion) 1287, Montevideo
Tel: 598 2 9020115

Uruguay

Web site: http://www.elpais.com.uy
Freq: Daily; **Circ:** 30000
Language (s): Spanish
DAILY NEWSPAPER

Patria   378314
Editorial: Av. Rivera 2476, 5 1, Montevideo
Tel: 598 2 9080250
Email: semanariopatria@gmail.com **Web site:** http://www.patria.com.uy
Freq: Weekly
Profile: Semanario que publica el Partido Nacional
Language (s): Spanish
DAILY NEWSPAPER

Prensa Rosarina   378138
Editorial: Boulevar Jose E. Rodo 433, Rosario 70200
Tel: 598 55 22390
Email: prensaro@adinet.com.uy
Freq: Daily
Profile: Bi semanario.Circula en las localidades de : Rosario, Colonia Valdense, Nueva Helvecia, Cufré, Colonia Española, Balnearios. Fecha de Aparición: 28357
Language (s): Spanish
DAILY NEWSPAPER

Primera Hora   378210
Editorial: 25 de Mayo 488, San José
Tel: 598 34 21598
Email: primerah@adinet.com.uy
Freq: Daily
Director: Wilson Ramírez
Profile: Circula en las localidades de : San José, Ecilda Paullier, Villa Rodríguez, Libertad, Rincón de la Bolsa, Playa Pascual.Director:Wilson Ramírez.Edición de 16 páginas. Fecha de Aparición: 36368
Language (s): Spanish
DAILY NEWSPAPER

Progreso al Día   378065
Editorial: Unavailable, Progreso 9300
Tel: 598 36 89592
Email: proaldia@adinet.com.uy
Freq: Weekly
Director: Javier Peraza Bártora
Profile: Semanario (sábado) con circulación en las localidades de Progreso, Juanicó y Canelón Chico. Edición: 16 páginas. Director:Jorge Javier Peraza Bartora. Fecha de Aparición: 33390
Language (s): Spanish
DAILY NEWSPAPER

Que hacemos hoy   378116
Editorial: Unavailable, Punta Del Este
Email: redaccion@quehacemoshoy.com.uy **Web site:** http://www.quehacemoshoy.com.uy
Freq: Weekly
Profile: Semanario de Punta del Este.
Language (s): Spanish
DAILY NEWSPAPER

Que Hacemos Hoy   378315
Editorial: Marsella 1234, Punta Del Este
Tel: 598 42 489117
Freq: Bi-Monthly
Language (s): Spanish
DAILY NEWSPAPER

La República   378196
Editorial: Garibaldi 2597, Montevideo
Tel: 598 2 4873565
Email: avisos@diariolarepublica.net **Web site:** http://www.republica.com.uy
Freq: Daily; **Circ:** 10000
Editor: Gustavo Carbajal; **Director:** Federico Fassano
Language (s): Spanish
DAILY NEWSPAPER

San José Hoy   378284
Editorial: Sarandi 786, San José **Tel:** 598 34 23189
Email: sanjose@adinet.com.uy **Web site:** http://www.sanjoseonline.com
Freq: Monthly
Director: Mirtana López
Profile: Tri semanario: lunes miércoles y viernes.De circulación local.Directora: Mirtana López.Edición de 20 páginas. Fecha de Aparición: 33215
Language (s): Spanish
DAILY NEWSPAPER

Santa Clara   378268
Editorial: Unavailable, Santa Clara De Olimar 37007
Tel: 598 46 45084
Freq: Weekly
Director: Ruben Medina
Profile: Circula en las localidades de : Santa Clara de Olimar y zonas cercanas.Edición de 8 páginas.Director: Ruben Medina. Fecha de Aparición: 22867
Language (s): Spanish
DAILY NEWSPAPER

Semanario Brecha   378199
Editorial: Av.Uruguay 844, Montevideo 11200
Tel: 598 2 9000388
Email: hola@brecha.com.uy **Web site:** http://www.brecha.com.uy
Freq: Weekly
Director: Mónica Wellington

Profile: Semanario de línea editorial de izquierda. Sucesor del legendario semanario Marcha. Fecha de Aparición: 1985
Language (s): Spanish
DAILY NEWSPAPER

Semanario de Acá   378077
Editorial: Roosvelt 730, Mercedes **Tel:** 598 53 22999
Freq: Daily
Director: Juan Manuel Delpino
Profile: Semanario que sale los sábados.Circula en las localidades de : Mercedes, Palmitas y Dolores. Edición de 16 páginas.Director: Juan Manuel Delpino. Fecha de Aparición: 37926
Language (s): Spanish
DAILY NEWSPAPER

Semanario Minuano   378057
Editorial: Carabajal 513, Minas 30000
Tel: 598 44 23554
Email: sepe16@hotmail.com
Freq: Daily
Director: Fernando Bonhomme
Profile: Semanario que sale los viernes, tiene cobertura departamental.Edición de 16 páginas.Director: Fernando Bonhomme. Fecha de Aparición: 34243
Language (s): Spanish
DAILY NEWSPAPER

Semanario Realidad   378296
Editorial: Unavailable, Punta Del Este
Tel: 598 42 494730
Freq: Daily
Language (s): Spanish
DAILY NEWSPAPER

Serrano   378121
Editorial: Washington Beltran 480, Minas 30000
Tel: 598 44 24100
Email: serrano@adinet.com.uy
Freq: Daily
Director: Juan Caraballo
Profile: Diario que sale de lunes a sábado, de alcance departamental.Edición de 20 páginas, color.Director: Juan Caraballo. Fecha de Aparición: 31229
Language (s): Spanish
DAILY NEWSPAPER

Tiempo   378247
Editorial: Treinta y Tres 1080, Pando 91000
Tel: 598 29 20222
Email: diariotiempo@hotmail.com
Freq: Daily
Director: Daniel Mesa
Profile: Edición de 6 páginas. Cubre la zona este del departamento. Director: Daniel Mesa. Fecha de Aparición: 30724
Language (s): Spanish
DAILY NEWSPAPER

Tri Semanario Profesional 378290
Editorial: 18 de Julio 997, Melo 37000
Tel: 598 64 29750
Freq: Daily
Director: Alejandro Olmedo
Profile: Trisemanario de 12 páginas.Director: Alejandro Olmedo. Fecha de Aparición: 35632
Language (s): Spanish
DAILY NEWSPAPER

Tribuna Popular   378266
Editorial: El Fanal 410, Río Branco 37100
Tel: 598 67 52103
Email: comtri@adinet.com.uuy
Freq: Daily
Director: Claudina Gonzalez
Profile: Semanario que sale los días viernes.Edición de 20 páginas.Circula en las localidades de: Rio Branco y Yaguarón.Director: Claudina González Fecha de Aparición: 31367
Language (s): Spanish
DAILY NEWSPAPER

Últimas Noticias   378299
Editorial: Paysandu 1179, Montevideo
Tel: 598 2 9020452
Email: redaccion@ultimasnoticias.com.uy **Web site:** http://www.ultimasnoticias.com.uy
Freq: Daily
Language (s): Spanish
DAILY NEWSPAPER

Vamos   378213
Editorial: Defensa 310, Juan Lacaze 70.001
Tel: 598 58 63218
Email: vamos@adinet.com.uy
Freq: Weekly
Director: Raúl Collazo
Profile: Circula en las localidades de : Juan Lacaze y zona de influencia. Sale los viernes.Edición de 14 páginas.Director: Juan Cervantes.Edición de 22 páginas.Director: Raúl Collazo. Fecha de Aparición: 30504
Language (s): Spanish
DAILY NEWSPAPER

Verdad   378126
Editorial: Jose Pedro Varela 2170, Tarariras 70002
Tel: 598 57 43530
Email: semanarioverdad@adinet.com.uy
Freq: Weekly
Director: Pablo Caledón

Profile: Sale los días viernes.Circula en las localidades de : Tarariras, Colonia Miguelete, Semillero, Estanzuela Edición de 24 páginas.Director: Pablo Celedón Vergara.Fecha de Aparición: 20944
Language (s): Spanish
DAILY NEWSPAPER

Visión Ciudadana   378322
Editorial: Treinta y Tres 427, San José 80000
Tel: 598 34 30988
Email: visionciudadana@adinet.com.uy
Freq: Weekly
Director: Jorge Scagni Gandini
Profile: Tri semanario que sale los días martes, jueves y sábados.Circula en las localidades de : San José, Ecilda Paullier, Villa Rodríguez, Libertad, Peraza, Puntas de Valdez, Capurro.Director: Jorge Scagni Gandini Montes. Edición de 16 páginas. Fecha de Aparición: 37978
Language (s): Spanish
DAILY NEWSPAPER

News Service/Syndicate

Agencia France Presse   380833
Editorial: Unavailable, Montevideo
Tel: 598 2 71202576
Web site: http://www.afp.com
Language (s): Spanish
NEWS SERVICE/SYNDICATE

COMCOSUR   380835
Editorial: Proyectada 17 metros 5192 E, Montevideo 11400 **Tel:** 598 2 408-1650
Email: comcosur@comcosur.com.uy **Web site:** http://nuevo.comcosur.org
Profile: COMCOSUR tiene carácter sub-regional abarca iniciativas de comunicación participativa en los países del Cono Sur, a las que busca conectar con otras iniciativas similares en América Latina y Europa. Los países de la subregión son Chile, Bolivia, Paraguay, Argentina, Brasil y Uruguay.
Language (s): Spanish
NEWS SERVICE/SYNDICATE

IPS Agencia de Noticias   380837
Editorial: J.C. Gomez 1445, Montevideo
Tel: 598 2 916-4397
Email: latam@ipslatam.net **Web site:** http://www.ipsnoticias.net
Director: Joaquin Costanzo
Language (s): Spanish
NEWS SERVICE/SYNDICATE

Uzbekistan

Time Difference: GMT +5
National Telephone Code: 998
Continent: Asia
Capital: Tashkent

Newspapers

Narodnoye slovo   564985
Editorial: ul. Matbuotchilar 32, Tashkent
Tel: 998 3712 233 15 22
Email: info@narodnoeslovo.uz **Web site:** http://www.narodnoeslovo.uz
Freq: Daily
Profile: National newspaper covering official parliament and president's documentation, legal information, social and cultural issues.
Language (s): Russian
DAILY NEWSPAPER

Uzbekistan Ovozi   218473
Owner: Narodnaya Partya Uzbekistana
Editorial: ul. Matbuotchilar 32, Tashkent 700000
Tel: 998 71 13 36 545
Email: uzbovozi@sarkor.uz **Web site:** http://www.uzbekistonovozi.uz
Freq: 2 Times/Week; **Circ:** 12000 Publisher's Statement
Editor-in-Chief: Safar Ostanov
Profile: Newspaper focusing on national and international news, business, politics, culture and sport.
Language (s): Uzbek (Northern)
DAILY NEWSPAPER

News Service/Syndicate

INTER-PRESS   491800
Editorial: ul. Navoi 13, Tashkent 100011
Tel: 998 97 55 09 55
Email: book@interpress.uz **Web site:** http://www.interpress.uz
Profile: Information agency dealing with national news, specializing in newspapers and magazines' national subscription, book trade and library fund formation.
Language (s): Uzbek (Northern)
NEWS SERVICE/SYNDICATE

Press-uz.info   497872
Editorial: ul. Navoi 16, Tashkent
Tel: 998 371 14 42 506
Email: admin@press-uz.info **Web site:** http://www.press-uz.info
Editor In Chief: Akhror Djobbarov
Profile: Political, socio-economical information on Uzbekistan. The information resources of IA Press-uz.info on the internet are provided in Uzbek, Russian and English.
Language (s): Uzbek (Northern)
NEWS SERVICE/SYNDICATE

Uzbekistan National News Agency   353742
Editorial: ul. Buyuk Turon 41, Tashkent 700047
Tel: 998 71 13 31 622
Email: pochta@uza.uz **Web site:** http://uza.uz
Editor: Golib Hasanov
Profile: National Information Agency of Uzbekistan (UzA) is the official source of information and a leading news agency of the country.
Language (s): English
NEWS SERVICE/SYNDICATE

Community Newspaper

Pravda Vostoka   564986
Editorial: ul. Matboutchilar 32, Tashkent 700000
Tel: 998 71 133 15 20
Email: info@pv.uz **Web site:** http://www.pv.uz
Circ: 10000
Profile: National weekly covering economical, business, financial, social and cultural issues.
Language (s): Russian
COMMUNITY NEWSPAPER

Vanuatu

Time Difference: GMT +11
National Telephone Code: 678
Continent: Oceania
Capital: Port Vila

Newspapers

The Ni-Vanuatu   538564
Owner: Moses Stevens
Email: thenivanuatu@vanuatu.com.vu **Web site:** http://cometo.vu/news/frontpage.htm
Freq: Daily
Editor/Publisher: Moses Steven
Language (s): English
DAILY NEWSPAPER

Vanuatu Daily Post   538557
Owner: Trading Post Ltd
Editorial: PO Box 1292, Port Vila, Vanuatu
Tel: 678 23 111
Email: news@dailypost.vu **Web site:** http://dailypost.vu
Freq: Daily; **Circ:** 3000 Publisher's Statement
Publisher: Marc Neil-Jones
Profile: National newspaper covering general news and current affairs in Vanuatu including business, politics, economy, gossip, sports, entertainment and travel.
Language (s): English
DAILY NEWSPAPER

The Vanuatu Independent   538738
Owner: The Independent Foundation
Editorial: BP 1555, Port Vila, Vanuatu
Tel: 678 29 999
Email: news@independent.vu **Web site:** http://independent.vu
Advertising Manager: Valerie Byrne; **Editor:** Tony Wilson
Profile: Provide independent and balanced news & information to citizens and inhabitants of Vanuatu.
Language (s): English
Ad Rate: Full Page Colour 70200.00
Currency: Vanuatu Vatu
DAILY NEWSPAPER

Vanuatu News Online   538558
Owner: Port Vila Presse
Editorial: PO Box 637, Port Vila, Vanuatu
Tel: 678 27 676
Email: publisher@news.vu **Web site:** http://presse.com.vu
Freq: Daily
Editor: Mark Lowen
Profile: Site provides online news service for Vanuatu.
Language (s): English
DAILY NEWSPAPER

Venezuela

Time Difference: GMT -4
National Telephone Code: 58
Continent: The Americas
Capital: Caracas

Newspapers

2001 161214
Owner: Bloque Editorial de Armas
Editorial: Final Avenida San Martin con Avenida La Paz, Edificio Bloque De Armas Piso 6, Caracas
Tel: 58 212 406-4111
Email: 2001@dearmas.com **Web site:** http://www.2001.com.ve
Freq: Daily; **Circ:** 150000 Not Audited
Editor: Jorge Collazo; **Editor:** José Feijoo
Profile: Tabloid-sized covering national and world news, politics, economics, features, opinion, social issues and sport.
Language (s): Spanish
DAILY NEWSPAPER

Diario Vea 413502
Owner: Diario Vea
Editorial: Av. Fuerzas Armadas, Esquina de Cristo Arizmendi, San Agustin del Norte, Edificio Diario Vea, local #98, Caracas **Tel:** 58 212 578 39 09
Web site: http://www.diariovea.com.ve
Freq: Daily; **Circ:** 80000 Not Audited
Director: Guillermo García Ponce; **Editor in Chief:** Mercedes Ortuño; **Editor in Chief:** Argelio Perez
Language (s): Spanish
DAILY NEWSPAPER

El Informador (Venezuela) 413498
Owner: Diario El Informador C.A.
Editorial: Carrera 21 esquina calle 23, Edificio El Informador, Barquisimeto (lara) **Tel:** 58 251 231-1811
Email: informador@elinformador.com.ve **Web site:** http://www.elinformador.com.ve
Freq: Daily; **Circ:** 45000 Not Audited
Editor: Erick Espinoza; **Director:** Mauricio Gómez; **Editor in Chief:** Jeovanny Villamizar
Profile: Covers regional and national news.
Language (s): Spanish
DAILY NEWSPAPER

El Mundo 160821
Owner: Grupo Últimas Noticias, C.A.
Editorial: Cadena Capriles, Plaza el Panteon, Torre la Prensa, Caracas **Tel:** 58 212 240-9841
Email: cmundo@cadena-capriles.com **Web site:** http://www.elmundo.com.ve
Freq: Daily; **Circ:** 33731 Not Audited
Director: Omar Lugo; **Editor in Chief:** Gregorio Yepez
Profile: Newspaper covering national and world news, economics, opinion, community, social, sport, events, country profiles and entertainment.
Language (s): Spanish
DAILY NEWSPAPER

La Nación 160822
Owner: Editorial Torbes
Editorial: Calle 4 entre Carreras 6 y 7, Edificio La Nacion, La Concordia, San Cristobal (táchira)
Tel: 58 2763462178
Email: redaccion@lanacion.com.ve **Web site:** http://www.lanacion.com.ve
Freq: Daily; **Circ:** 30000 Not Audited
Editor: Gustavo Carrillo; **Editor in Chief:** Omaira Labrador; **Editor:** Augusto Medina; **Editor:** Gloria Niño de Cortes; **Editor:** Leidy Zafra
Profile: Newspaper covering national and world news, politics, economics, features, opinion, social issues and sport.
Language (s): Spanish
DAILY NEWSPAPER

El Nacional 156977
Owner: CA Editoria El National
Editorial: Avenida Principal de los Cortijos de Lourdes con 3ra Transversal, Edificio El Nacional frente a la Coca Cola FEMSA. CP 1071-A, Caracas
Tel: 58 212 203-3168
Web site: http://www.el-nacional.com
Freq: Daily; **Circ:** 254000 Not Audited
Editor: Patricia Espadaro; **President & Publisher:** Miguel Enrique Otero
Profile: Newspaper covering national and international news, politics, economics, finance, business, culture and sport.
Language (s): Spanish
DAILY NEWSPAPER

El Norte 418248
Owner: Diario El Norte
Editorial: Avenida Intercomunal Jorge Rodriguez, Sector Las Garzas. Grupo UP, Barcelona (anzoategui)
Tel: 58 281 286 24 84
Email: diarioelnorte@elnorte.com.ve **Web site:** http://www.elnorte.com.ve
Freq: Daily; **Circ:** 60000 Not Audited
Editor: Edgar Alfaro; **Editor:** Gina Mistaje
Language (s): Spanish
DAILY NEWSPAPER

Notitarde 160824
Owner: Editorial Notitarde C.A
Editorial: Avenida Boyaca 98 #107-148, Sector Las Flores, Carabobo **Tel:** 58 241 850 16 66
Email: redaccion@notitarde.com **Web site:** http://www.notitarde.com
Freq: Daily; **Circ:** 80000 Not Audited
Editor in Chief: Luis Borja; **Editor:** Maria Julia Melendez; **Editor:** Marleni Pina
Profile: Newspaper covering national and international news, politics, economics, finance, business, culture and sport.
Language (s): Spanish
DAILY NEWSPAPER

Panorama 160989
Owner: CA Diario Panorama
Editorial: Avenida 15 No.95 - 60, Maracaibo
Tel: 58 261 721 10 00
Email: redaccion@panodi.com **Web site:** http://www.panodi.com
Freq: Daily; **Circ:** 120000 Not Audited
Director: Luis Cañón; **Editor:** Anaida Larreal; **Editor:** Heilet Morales; **Editor in Chief:** Lolimar Suárez
Profile: Newspaper covering national and international news, politics, economics, finance, business, culture and sport.
Language (s): Spanish
DAILY NEWSPAPER

El Periodiquito 418249
Owner: Editorial Mara
Editorial: Calle Paez Este N 178, Maracay (aragua)
Tel: 58 243 232 14 22
Email: elperiodiquito@gmail.com **Web site:** http://www.elperiodiquito.com
Freq: Daily; **Circ:** 100000 Not Audited
News Editor: Ana Maria Campos; **Editor in Chief:** Yosseline Luna; **Publicity Manager:** Mauri Rengel; **Editor:** Rafael Rodriguez-Rendon
Profile: National newspaper.
Language (s): Spanish
DAILY NEWSPAPER

El Progreso 418246
Owner: Diario El Progreso
Editorial: Calle Vidal con Urbina, Sector Negro Primero, Estado Bolívar, Aptdo 8001, Bolívar
Tel: 58 285 654 71 54
Email: publiprogres@cantv.net **Web site:** http://www.diarioelprogreso.com
Freq: Daily; **Circ:** 30000 Not Audited
Editor in Chief: Karen Mejias
Language (s): Spanish
DAILY NEWSPAPER

Región 409805
Owner: Editora de Región Oriente
Editorial: Calle Bonpland, Edificio Region, detras de la Avenida Gran Mariscal, Cumaná (sucre)
Tel: 58 293 441 00 71
Email: regionoriente@cantv.net **Web site:** http://www.diarioregion.com.ve
Freq: Daily; **Circ:** 53360 Not Audited
Director: Yndira Linneth Lugo; **President:** Germán Marcano Barrios; **Editor:** Luis Marcano Barrios
Profile: Covers news of the west region of Venezuela.
Language (s): Spanish
DAILY NEWSPAPER

Tal Cual 412081
Owner: Editorial La Mosca Analfabeta C.A.
Editorial: Romulo Gallego Edificio Pascal B Piso 1 Oficina 3, Caracas **Tel:** 58 212 710 82 53
Email: hbecerra@talcualdigital.com **Web site:** http://www.talcualdigital.com
Freq: Daily; **Circ:** 45000 Not Audited
Editor: Héctor Becerra; **Editor in Chief:** Alejandro Botía; **Editor:** Carmen Mendez; **President:** Teodoro Petkoff
Profile: National Newspaper.
Language (s): Spanish
DAILY NEWSPAPER

Últimas Noticias 160987
Owner: Grupo Últimas Noticias
Editorial: Ultimas Noticias, Cadena Capriles, Plaza el Panteon, Torre la Prensa, Caracas 1192
Tel: 58 212 596-1911
Web site: http://www.ultimasnoticias.com.ve
Freq: Daily; **Circ:** 142039 Not Audited
News Editor: Hilda Carmona; **Editor:** Hugo Chávez; **Director:** Eleazar Díaz Rangel; **Editor:** Jesús Duran; **Editor:** Hercilia Garnica; **Editor:** Desiree Lozano; **Editor:** Adela Medina
Profile: Newspaper covering national and world news, politics, economics, features, opinion, social issues and sport.
Language (s): Spanish
DAILY NEWSPAPER

El Universal 160812
Owner: Grupo El Universal
Editorial: Avenida Urdaneta Esquina de Animas, Urbanizacion La Candelaria, Edif El Universal, Caracas **Tel:** 58 212 505-2290
Email: erojas@eluniversal.com **Web site:** http://www.eluniversal.com
Freq: Daily; **Circ:** 86281 Not Audited
Editor: Richard Delgado; **Editor:** Ernesto Ecarri; **Editor:** María Angela Lando; **Editor:** Amalia LLorca; **Editor in Chief:** Elides Rojas
Profile: Newspaper covering national and international news, economics, politics, sport, social, culture, travel and classified advertising.
Language (s): Spanish
DAILY NEWSPAPER

La Verdad 159007
Owner: Sinergia Editorial, Diario La Verdad, CA
Editorial: Avenida 13 con calle 82 y 83, Maracaibo (zulia) **Tel:** 58 261 798 13 59
Email: noticias@laverdad.com **Web site:** http://www.laverdad.com
Freq: Daily; **Circ:** 215000 Not Audited
Publicity Manager: Gabriela Acacio; **Editor:** Enrique Peña; **Editor:** Luis Pérez; **Editor:** Sheila Urdaneta
Profile: A metropolitan newspaper in four parts which includes, economy, sports, politics and city information.
Language (s): Spanish
DAILY NEWSPAPER

Community Newspaper

Correio de Venezuela 412312
Owner: Editorial Correio C.A.
Editorial: Av. Principal de las Mercedes, referencia Banco Plaza, Edificio Centro Vectorial, piso 3, Caracas **Tel:** 58 2129932026
Email: correio.prensa@gmail.com **Web site:** http://www.correiodevenezuela.com
Freq: Weekly; **Circ:** 11000 Not Audited
Director: Aleixo Vieira; **Manager:** Carla Vieira
Profile: Newspaper of the Portuguese community in Venezuela and it is written in Portuguese language.
Language (s): Portuguese
COMMUNITY NEWSPAPER

El Nuevo País 230006
Owner: El Nuevo País
Editorial: Pinto Santarosalia, Edificio Nuevo País No 44, Caracas **Tel:** 58 212 545 73 46
Email: elnuevopais1@gmail.com
Freq: Daily; **Circ:** 45000 Not Audited
Editor in Chief: Luis Camacho; **Editor in Chief:** Francisco Orta
Profile: Newspaper covering national and world news, politics, economics, features, opinion, social issues and sport.
Language (s): Spanish
COMMUNITY NEWSPAPER

Quinto Dia 230788
Owner: MC Master Communication CA
Editorial: Avenida principal de los Ruices con Avenida Romulo Gallegos, Res. Los Almendros Nivel Mezzanina, Oficina 05, Los Ruices, Caracas
Tel: 58 212 237 98 09
Email: redaccion@quintodia.com **Web site:** http://www.quintodia.com
Freq: Weekly; **Circ:** 150000 Not Audited
Editor in Chief: Carlos Croes
Profile: Newspaper featuring national and international news, business and economy, current affairs, sport and culture.
Language (s): Spanish
COMMUNITY NEWSPAPER

La Razón 222233
Owner: CA Diario La Razón
Editorial: Avenida Urdaneta esquina Urapal, Edificio Valores Sotano A La Candelaria, Caracas
Tel: 58 212 578 31 43
Email: larazon@cantv.net
Freq: Sun; **Circ:** 150000 Not Audited
Editor in Chief: Carlos Diaz
Profile: Broadsheet covering national and international news, politics, economics, finance, business, culture and sport.
Language (s): Spanish
COMMUNITY NEWSPAPER

Vietnam

Time Difference: GMT +7
National Telephone Code: 84
Continent: Asia
Capital: Hanoi

Newspapers

Binh Dinh 460116
Editorial: People's Committee of Binh Dinh, 84 Pham Hung, Quy Nhon, Binh Dinh **Tel:** 84 56 821867
Web site: http://www.baobinhdinh.com.vn
Freq: 2 Times/Week; **Circ:** 4001 Not Audited
Editor in Chief: Nguyen Hung Do
Profile: Covers local and national news.
Language (s): Vietnamese
DAILY NEWSPAPER

Business Weekly 459677
Editorial: Lien minh Hop tac xa Viet Nam, 77 Nguyen Thai Hoc, Hanoi **Tel:** 84 46 6728543
Email: info@bandoanhnghiep.com.vn **Web site:** http://www.baodoanhnghiep.com.vn
Freq: Weekly; **Circ:** 32801 Not Audited
Editor in Chief: Pham Le Tan Phong
Profile: Covers current affairs and news.
Language (s): Vietnamese
DAILY NEWSPAPER

Economy And The Urban Areas 460132
Editorial: People's Committee of Hanoi City, 21 Huynh Thuc Khang Street, Dong Da District, Hanoi
Tel: 84 043 7732198
Email: ktdtonline@gmail.com **Web site:** http://www.ktdt.com.vn
Freq: Weekly; **Circ:** 10001 Not Audited
Profile: Covers the economy in Vietnam's big cities.
Language (s): Vietnamese
DAILY NEWSPAPER

Hai Phong 459667
Editorial: People's Committee of Hai Phong City, 8 Da Nang st., Ngo Quyen dist., Hai Phong
Tel: 84 31 3852806
Email: haiphongdientu@vnn.vn **Web site:** http://www.baohaiphong.com.vn
Freq: Daily; **Circ:** 15001 Not Audited
Editor in Chief: Trong Nghia Le
Profile: Covers current local, national and international news topics.
Language (s): Vietnamese
DAILY NEWSPAPER

Lao Dong 459670
Editorial: Lao Dong Newspaper, 15/167 Tay Son - Dong Da, Hanoi **Tel:** 84 43 5330304
Email: webmaster@laodong.vn **Web site:** http://www.laodong.com.vn
Freq: Daily; **Circ:** 80001 Not Audited
Profile: Covers all current news topics nationally, locally and internationally.
Language (s): Vietnamese
DAILY NEWSPAPER

Liberation Saigon 459666
Editorial: Bao Sai Gon Giai Phong, 399 Hong Bang, Ward 14, Dist. 5, Quan 3, Thanh Pho, Ho Chi Minh City **Tel:** 84 8 3929409
Email: sggponline@sggp.org.vn **Web site:** http://www.sggp.org.vn
Freq: Daily; **Circ:** 130001 Not Audited
Editor in Chief: The Tuyen Tran
Profile: Covers a variety of topics from business to sports and from a local to international range. Also publishes a Chinese edition.
Language (s): Mandarin
DAILY NEWSPAPER

New Hanoi 459665
Editorial: Bao Hanoimoi, 44 Le Thai To Street, Hoan Kiem, Hanoi **Tel:** 84 43 8253067
Web site: http://www.hanoimoi.com.vn
Freq: Daily; **Circ:** 50001 Not Audited
Editor in Chief: To Quang Phan
Profile: Covers a wide range of news and business news. Also includes both local and international topics.
Language (s): Vietnamese
DAILY NEWSPAPER

Nhan Dan Newspaper 459663
Editorial: Nhan Dan Newspaper (Bao Nhan Dan), 71 Hang Trong Street, Hoan Kiem District, Hanoi
Tel: 84 438254231
Email: toasoan@nhandan.org.vn **Web site:** http://www.nhandan.org.vn
Freq: Daily; **Circ:** 180001 Not Audited
Editor in Chief: The Huynh Dinh
Profile: Covers current issues and news.
Language (s): Vietnamese
DAILY NEWSPAPER

People's Army 459664
Editorial: People's Army Newspaper, No.7 Phan Dinh Phung Street, Hanoi **Tel:** 84 43 7471748
Email: webmaster@qdnd.vn **Web site:** http://www.qdnd.vn
Freq: Daily; **Circ:** 25001 Not Audited
Editor in Chief: Le Phuc Nguyen
Profile: Covers news and politics and Vietnamese Army affairs.
Language (s): Vietnamese
DAILY NEWSPAPER

People's Army Weekly 459267
Editorial: People's Army Newspaper, No.7 Phan Dinh Phung Street, Hanoi - **Tel:** 84 4 37471748
Email: dientubqd@gmail.com **Web site:** http://www.qdnd.vn
Freq: Weekly; **Circ:** 40003 Not Audited
Editor in Chief: Le Phuc Nguyen
Profile: Covers a variety of topics including army news.
Language (s): Vietnamese
DAILY NEWSPAPER

Saigon Times Daily 156951
Editorial: Saigon Times Group, 35 Nam Ky Khoi Nghia Street, District 1, Ho Chi Minh City
Tel: 848 8295936
Email: daily@thesaigontimes.vn **Web site:** http://english.thesaigontimes.vn/Home
Freq: Daily; **Circ:** 20001 Not Audited
Editor in Chief: Tran Thi Ngoc Hue
Profile: Covers policies and national issues and the future of the country.
Language (s): English
DAILY NEWSPAPER

Vietnam Economic Times 459678
Editorial: Vietnam Economic Times, 96 Hoang Quoc Viet, Cau Giay District, Hanoi **Tel:** 84 43 7552060

Vietnam

Email: editor@vneconomy.vn **Web site:** http://vneconomy.vn
Freq: Daily; **Circ:** 43001 Not Audited
Editor in Chief: Nguyen Cat Dao
Profile: Covers all things dealing with Vietnam and it's economy in a Vietnamese and English edition. Also covers economic and business trends.
Language (s): English
DAILY NEWSPAPER

Vietnam Investment Review
459674
Editorial: Ministry of Planning & Investment, 47 Quan Thanh Street, Hanoi **Tel:** 84 43 8450537
Email: vir.hn@vir.com.vn **Web site:** http://www.vir.com.vn
Freq: Weekly; **Circ:** 25000 Not Audited
Editor in Chief: Anh Tuan Nguyen
Profile: Covers all financial and investment topics including banking and trading (import-export).
Language (s): English
DAILY NEWSPAPER

Vietnam News
459669
Editorial: Vietnam News Agency, 11 Tran Hung Dao, Hanoi **Tel:** 84 43 9332316
Email: vnnews@vnagency.com.vn **Web site:** http://vietnamnews.vnagency.com.vn
Freq: Daily; **Circ:** 30001 Not Audited
Profile: Covers all news in Vietnam and Internationally as well.
Language (s): English
DAILY NEWSPAPER

The Workers Newspaper
460139
Editorial: 14 Cach Mang Thang 8, Ho Chi Minh City, District 1, Ho Chi Minh City **Tel:** 84 83 9306262
Email: toasoan@nld.com.vn **Web site:** http://www.nld.com.vn
Freq: 2 Times/Week; **Circ:** 60001 Not Audited
Editor in Chief: Danh Phuong Do
Profile: Covers issues for the working class and union workers of Ho Chi Minh City.
Language (s): Vietnamese
DAILY NEWSPAPER

News Service/Syndicate

Vietnam News Agency
467596
Owner: Vietnam News Agency,
Editorial: Vietnam News Agency, 79 Ly Thuong Kiet Str., Hanoi **Tel:** 84 438 255443
Email: btk@vnanet.vn **Web site:** http://news.vnanet.vn
Freq: Daily
General Manager: Mai Huong Tran
Profile: News service covering a range of current issues locally and internationally.
Language (s): English
NEWS SERVICE/SYNDICATE

Virgin Islands (British)

Time Difference: GMT -4
National Telephone Code: 1 284
Continent: The Americas
Capital: Road Town (Tortola)

Community Newspaper

The Island Sun
224397
Owner: Sun Enterprises (BVI) Ltd
Editorial: 112 Main St, Tortola 1110
Tel: 1 2844942476
Email: issun@candwbvi.net **Web site:** http://www.islandsun.com
Freq: Sat; **Circ:** 3600 Not Audited
Editor & Publisher: Vernon Pickering
Profile: Island Sun is a weekly newspaper serving the British Virgin Islands. It covers local and Caribbean news, events, sports and features. Deadlines are Mondays at 1pm AST.
Language (s): English
Ad Rate: Full Page Mono 79.00
Currency: United States Dollars
COMMUNITY NEWSPAPER

Virgin Islands (USA)

Time Difference: GMT -4
National Telephone Code: 1 340
Continent: The Americas
Capital: Charlotte Amalie (St Thomas)

Newspapers

The Virgin Islands Daily News
73286
Owner: Times-Shamrock Communications
Editorial: 9155 Estate Thomas, Saint Thomas 802
Tel: 1 340 774-8772
Email: dailynews@vipowernet.net **Web site:** http://www.virginislandsdailynews.com
Freq: Daily; **Circ:** 16500 Not Audited
Publisher: Jason Robbins
Profile: The Virgin Islands Daily News is a source of information for news, sports, entertainment and events in St. Thomas, St. Croix, St. John and the British Islands of Tortola and Virgin Gorda in the Virgin Islands.
Language (s): English
Ad Rate: Full Page Mono 33.00
Ad Rate: Full Page Colour 300.00
Currency: United States Dollars
DAILY NEWSPAPER

Community Newspaper

St. John Tradewinds Newspaper
330949
Tel: 1 340 776-6496
Email: info@tradewinds.vi **Web site:** http://www.tradewinds.vi
Freq: Weekly; **Circ:** 3000 Not Audited
News Editor: Jaime Elliott; **Publisher & Editor:** MaLinda Nelson
Profile: Weekly newspaper.
Language (s): English
Ad Rate: Full Page Mono 14.00
Currency: United States Dollars
COMMUNITY NEWSPAPER

Yemen

Time Difference: GMT +3
National Telephone Code: 967
Continent: Asia
Capital: Sana'a

Newspapers

14th October
475016
Owner: October Corporation for Press
Editorial: PO Box 5487, Ma'alla, Aden
Tel: 967 2 242660
Email: ansam2593_l_@hotmail.com
Freq: Daily; **Circ:** 26000 Rate Card
Advertising Manager: Bassam Thabet
Profile: 14th October is a government-owned, Arabic daily newspaper covering local and international news, business and sport. It was first published in 1968.
Language (s): Arabic
DAILY NEWSPAPER

Al Ayyam
493049
Owner: Al Ayyam Printing, Publishing, Advertising and Distribution House
Editorial: PO Box 648, Crater, Aden
Tel: 967 2 259164
Email: editor@al-ayyam.info **Web site:** http://www.al-ayyam.info
Freq: Daily; **Circ:** 76000 Publisher's Statement
News Editor: Saeed Bagash; **General Manager & Editor in Chief:** Bashraheel Bashraheel; **Advertising Manager:** Abdullah Ubaid
Profile: Al Ayyam (The Days) is a newspaper covering national and international news, current affairs, politics, business and sport. The newspaper

launched in 1958 and is aimed at local and expatriate Arabs in Yemen.
Language (s): Arabic
Ad Rate: Full Page Mono 1500.00
Currency: United States Dollars
DAILY NEWSPAPER

Al Methaq
493340
Owner: Al Moatamar Al Shaabi Al Aaam
Editorial: PO Box 3777, Al Zubeiry, Sana'a
Tel: 967 1 466128
Email: editor@almethaq.net **Web site:** http://www.almethaq.net
Freq: Weekly; **Circ:** 15000 Publisher's Statement
Financial & Advertising Manager: Jamal Abd-Elhameed; **Editor in Chief:** Mohammed An'naam
Profile: Al Methaq is a weekly Arabic newspaper covering national and international news, current affairs, politics, business and sport. It launched in 1982 and is published on Mondays.
Language (s): Arabic
DAILY NEWSPAPER

Al Thawrah
156802
Owner: Al Thawra Press, Printing & Publishing
Editorial: PO Box 1475, Airport Road, Sana'a
Tel: 967 1 321532
Email: al-thawrah@y.net.ye **Web site:** http://www.althawranews.net
Freq: Daily; **Circ:** 22000 Publisher's Statement
Office Manager: Eiad Al Mosemi; **Advertising Manager:** Saleh Al Qobati; **News Manager:** Abdulmalek Al Shara'bi
Profile: Al Thawrah is a daily newspaper covering national and international news, politics, business, culture, society and sport. The newspaper launched in 1962.
Language (s): Arabic
Ad Rate: Full Page Mono 3300.00
Ad Rate: Full Page Colour 4950.00
Currency: United States Dollars
DAILY NEWSPAPER

Al Wahdah
492701
Owner: Al Thawra Press, Printing & Publishing
Editorial: PO Box 8973, Airport Highway, Sana'a
Tel: 967 1 323443
Email: alwahda@y.net.ye
Freq: Weekly; **Circ:** 8000 Publisher's Statement
Editor In Chief: Hasan Abdelwares; **Head of News:** Abdullah Al Qadhi; **Advertising Manager:** Saleh Al Qobati
Profile: Al Wahdah is a bi-weekly newspaper covering national and international news, current affairs, politics, business and sport. It launched in 1990.
Language (s): Arabic
DAILY NEWSPAPER

Yemen Observer
225904
Owner: Yemen Observer Publishing House
Editorial: PO Box 19183, Police Academy Street, Sana'a **Tel:** 967 1 505466
Email: info@yobserver.com **Web site:** http://www.yemenobserver.com
Freq: 3 Times/Week; **Circ:** 12000 Rate Card
Editor in Chief: Abdul-Aziz Oudah; **CEO & Publisher:** Faris Sanabani; **Advertising Manager:** Shezaan Syed
Profile: Yemen Observer is an English newspaper covering local and regional news, politics, business, culture and sport. The newspaper launched in 1996 and is published three times a week (Saturdays, Mondays and Wednesdays).
Language (s): English
Ad Rate: Full Page Mono 800.00
Ad Rate: Full Page Colour 1500.00
Currency: United States Dollars
DAILY NEWSPAPER

News Service/Syndicate

Yemen News Agency
491396
Owner: Yemen News Agency
Editorial: PO Box 881, Jameat Al Dowal Al Arabia Street, Sana'a **Tel:** 967 1 250085
Email: yemensb98@gmail.com **Web site:** http://www.sabanews.net
Profile: Yemen News Agency is the official news agency of Yemen and covers government news and issues of national importance.
Language (s): Arabic
NEWS SERVICE/SYNDICATE

Zambia

Time Difference: GMT +2
National Telephone Code: 260
Continent: Africa
Capital: Lusaka

Newspapers

The Mast
224414
Owner: Post Newspapers Ltd
Editorial: 36 Bwinjimfumu Rd. Rhodespark, Private bag E 352, Lusaka **Tel:** 260 211 231092
Freq: Daily; **Circ:** 45000 Not Audited
Managing Director: Fred M'membe
Profile: Newspaper covering regional, national and international news and current affairs including politics, business, economics, lifestyle and sport.
Language (s): English
DAILY NEWSPAPER

Times of Zambia
156717
Owner: Post Newspapers Ltd
Editorial: P.O.Box 30394, Freedom Way, Lusaka
Tel: 260 211 229076
Email: times@zamtel.zm **Web site:** http://www.times.co.zm
Freq: Daily; **Circ:** 14000
Profile: Newspaper covering national and international news and current affairs including politics, economics, business, entertainment and sports.
Language (s): English
DAILY NEWSPAPER

Zambia Daily Mail
217927
Owner: Zambia Daily Mail
Editorial: PO Box 31421, Lusaka
Email: editor@daily-mail.co.zm **Web site:** http://www.daily-mail.co.zm
Freq: Daily; **Circ:** 15000
Editor in Chief: Sheikh Chifuwe
Profile: Newspaper focusing on national and international news, politics, business, entertainment and sports.
Language (s): English
DAILY NEWSPAPER

Zimbabwe

Time Difference: GMT +2
National Telephone Code: 263
Continent: Africa
Capital: Harare

Newspapers

The Herald
156777
Owner: Zimbabwe Newspapers Limited
Editorial: PO Box 396, Harare **Tel:** 263 4 79 57 71
Email: theherald@zimpapers.co.zw **Web site:** http://www.herald.co.zw
Freq: Daily; **Circ:** 90000
Editor: Ceasar Zvayi
Profile: Daily newspaper covering regional, national and international news and current affairs including politics, business, entertainment and sports.
Language (s): English
DAILY NEWSPAPER

The Sunday Mail
156778
Owner: Zimbabwe Newspapers (1980) Ltd
Editorial: PO Box 396, Harare **Tel:** 263 4 70 43 76
Email: sundaymail@zimpapers.co.zw **Web site:** http://www.sundaymail.co.zw
Freq: Sun
Editor: Mabasa Sasa
Profile: Weekly newspaper covering news and current affairs in Zimbabwe and across the world including business, politics, economics, sports and culture.
Language (s): English
DAILY NEWSPAPER

Willings Volume 2
Section 3

World Broadcast
Radio & Television stations & networks, listed by country

Afghanistan

Radio

Arman FM 467712
Editorial: ARMAN FM, PO Box 1045, Kabul
Web site: http://www.arman.fm
AM RADIO STATION

Albania

Radio

Radio Tirana 290971
Editorial: Rr. Ismail Qemali 11, Tirane
Tel: 355 4 22 24 81.
Email: edamerepeza@yahoo.it
Web site: http://rtsh.sil.at
RADIO NETWORK

Top Albania Radio 605741
Editorial: QNK, Blv Deshmoret e Kombit, Tirana
Tel: 355 42 247492.
Email: contact@topalbaniaradio.com
Web site: http://www.topalbaniaradio.com
Profile: National radio station in Albania covering general entertainment.
RADIO NETWORK

Television

Vizion Plus 492833
Editorial: Rr. Don Bosko Nr.5, Tirane
Tel: 355 4 225 84 88.
Email: info@vizionplus.tv
Web site: http://www.vizionplus.tv
Profile: A national TV station transmitting news, local production (entertainment, social, political programs, movies, sports, documentaries and series).
TELEVISION STATION

Algeria

Radio

Radio Algérienne - Chaine 1 386851
Owner: La Radio Algérienne
Editorial: 21 Boulevard des Martyrs, Algiers
Tel: 213 21 483790.
Email: radioalgerie@gmail.com
Web site: http://www.radioalgerie.dz
Profile: Chaine 1 (Channel 1) is a state-owned national radio station broadcasting round the clock in Arabic. Besides four full news bulletins and hourly news summaries, programmes include educational, cultural, information and entertainment broadcasting. It launched in 1986.
FM RADIO STATION

Radio Algérienne - Chaine 2 393328
Owner: La Radio Algérienne
Editorial: 21 Boulevard des Martyrs, Algiers
Tel: 213 21 483790.
Email: radioalgerie@gmail.com
Web site: http://www.radioalgerie.dz
Profile: Chaine 2 (Channel 2) is a state-owned national radio station broadcasting round the clock in the Tamazight (Berber) language. The station launched in 1986 and aims to promote Algerian national culture and the people's cultural heritage.
FM RADIO STATION

Radio Algérienne - Chaine 3 393329
Owner: La Radio Algérienne
Editorial: 21, Boulevard des Martyrs, Algiers
Tel: 213 21 483790.
Email: se.directiongeneral@gmail.com
Web site: http://www.radioalgerie.dz/chaine3
Profile: Chaine 3 (Channel 3) is a state-owned national radio station broadcasting for 21-hrs a day in French. The station launched in 1986, and broadcasts music, entertainment and information programmes tackling daily topical issues.
FM RADIO STATION

Television

Algérie 1 405479
Owner: L'Enterprise Nationale de Télévision
Editorial: PO Box 184, 21, Boulevard des Martyrs, Algiers 16000 **Tel:** 213 21 602300.
Email: dinfo.entv@gmail.com
Web site: http://www.entv.dz
Profile: Algérie 1, also known as ENTV, is a state-owned television channel broadcasting entertainment, news and films 24 hours a day. The channel launched in 1962 and broadcasts terrestrially in Algeria.
TELEVISION STATION

Algérie 3 404288
Owner: L'Enterprise Nationale de Télévision
Editorial: PO Box 184, 21, Boulevard des Martyrs, Algiers 16000 **Tel:** 213 21 602300.
Email: dinfo.entv@gmail.com
Web site: http://www.entv.dz
Profile: Algérie 3, also known as Thalitha TV, is a state-owned television station broadcasting entertainment, news and films 24 hours a day. Launched in 2002, the station broadcasts free-to-air on satellite.
TELEVISION STATION

Algérie 4 652273
Owner: L'Enterprise Nationale de Télévision
Editorial: PO Box 184, 21, Boulevard des Martyrs, Algiers 16000 **Tel:** 213 21 239870.
Email: dinfo.entv@gmail.com
Web site: http://www.entv.dz
Profile: Algérie 4 is a state-owned television station broadcasts films, news and general programmes. Launched in 2009, the channel is aimed at the Amazigh population of Algeria.
TELEVISION STATION

Algérie 5 652270
Owner: L'Enterprise Nationale de Télévision
Editorial: Centre Club des Pins, Algiers
Tel: 213 21 374121.
Email: aouadi@entv.dz
Web site: http://www.entv.dz
Profile: Algérie 5 is a state-owned television station broadcasting Islamic programmes presented by Algerian Muslim scholars. Launched in 2009, the channel was formerly called Al Qoran Al Kareem Channel Algérie.
TELEVISION STATION

Canal Algérie 404289
Owner: L'Enterprise Nationale de Télévision
Editorial: PO Box 184, 21, Boulevard des Martyrs, Algiers 16000 **Tel:** 213 21 239919.
Email: webmaster@canalalgerie.dz
Web site: http://www.entv.dz
Profile: Canal Algérie, also known as Algérie 2, is a state-owned television channel broadcasting entertainment, news and films 24-hours a day. The channel launched in 1994 and broadcasts free-to-air on satellite.
TELEVISION STATION

American Samoa

Radio

KKHJ-FM 387608
Owner: South Seas Broadcasting Inc.
Tel: 684 6337793.
Web site: http://www.khjradio.com
Profile: Provides daily news, sports, and live programs.
FM RADIO STATION

WVUV-FM 628188
Owner: Shannon J. Cummings
Tel: 1 684 633-7793.
Web site: http://www.wvuv.com
FM RADIO STATION

Television

KVZK-TV 387607
Owner: American Samoa Government
Tel: 684 6334191.
Profile: Covers socio-economic and entertainment news.
TELEVISION STATION

Angola

Radio

Radio Ecclesia 290980
Editorial: Street Commander Papal brief, N. 118, Luanda **Tel:** 244 2443041.
Email: recclesia@recclesia.org
Web site: http://www.recclesia.org
AM RADIO STATION

Anguilla

Radio

Radio Anguilla 290848
Editorial: PO Box 60, The Valley **Tel:** 264 4972218.
Email: radioaxa@anguillanet.com
Web site: http://www.radioaxa.com
Profile: Provides news and live music, playing country, hip hop, socca, calypso and other rhythms.
RADIO NETWORK

Antigua & Barbuda

Radio

Observer Radio 91.1FM 290994
Tel: 268 4819105.
Email: voice@antiguaobserver.com
Web site: http://www.antiguaobserver.com
Profile: Plays Calipso, Soca, Reggaeton. Provides daily news, sports, radio call-in programs in which the audience interacts.
RADIO NETWORK

Argentina

Radio

La 100 (FM 99.9) 371271
Editorial: Mansilla 2668, Capital Federal C1425BDP
Tel: 54 11 41260100.
Email: la100@la100.com.ar
Web site: http://www.la100.com.ar
Profile: Si bien a la mañana tiene algún programa de noticias, la radio apuesta decididamente a la música pop del momento.
RADIO NETWORK

Cadena Eco (AM 1220) 371278
Editorial: Av. Rivadavia 10561, Capital Federal 1408
Tel: 54 11 56311220.
Web site: http://www.cadenaeco.com.ar
Profile: AM de la ciudad de Buenos Aires con programación de información general.
RADIO NETWORK

Concepto (AM 1050) 371264
Editorial: Maipu 267, Capital Federal 1084
Tel: 54 11 41361050.
Email: opaino@conceptoam.com.ar
Web site: http://www.conceptoam.com.ar
Profile: Radio AM de Capital Federal con magazines, espectáculos, novedades, entrevistas y muy buena música. Con cobertura nacional.
RADIO NETWORK

Continental (AM 590) 371265
Editorial: Rivadavia 835, Capital Federal C1002AAG
Tel: 54 11 43384250.
Email: rrpp@continental.com.ar
Web site: http://www.continental.com.ar
Profile: Una de las radios más escuchada en el país. Tiene una importante cadena de filiales en el interior. Los programas son convencionales. Fecha de Aparición: 28 de septiembre de 1969
RADIO NETWORK

Del Plata (AM 1030) 371266
Editorial: Olleros 3551, Capital Federal C1427BNE
Tel: 54 11 45357070.
Email: rrhh@ideasdelsur.com.ar
Web site: http://www.amdelplata.com
Profile: Una de las radios más escuchadas en el país. Tiene una importante cadena de filiales en el interior. Los programas son convencionales. Fecha de Aparición: 4 de marzo de 1969
RADIO NETWORK

FM Provincia (FM 89.9) 371260
Editorial: Calle 60 826, La Plata 1900
Tel: 54 221 4519696.
Web site: http://www.radioprovincia.gba.gov.ar
Profile: Es la FM de Radio Provincia AM 1270 de la Ciudad de La Plata. Emite programación local.
RADIO NETWORK

La Red (AM 910) 371269
Editorial: Av. Paseo Colon 505, Capital Federal C1063ACF **Tel:** 54 11 5032-0400.
Email: info@radiolared.com.ar
Web site: http://www.laredonline.com.ar
Profile: Es la radio de Torneos y Competenecias que, si bien en un origen intentó cubrir en su totalidad la actualidad deportiva, luego se posicionó entre las radios líderes cuando decidió ampliar su programación con contenidos de actualidad general. Fecha de Aparición: 1 de abril de 1991
RADIO NETWORK

Lagos (FM 93.5) 371279
Editorial: Unavailable, San Miguel - Gba Oeste
Email: jlagos@radiolagos.com.ar
Web site: http://www.radiolagos.com.ar
Profile: FM con programación de información general.
RADIO NETWORK

Libertad (AM 11240) 371277
Editorial: Unavailable, Capital Federal
Email: mensajes@cadenauno.com.ar
Web site: http://www.cdenauno.com.ar
Profile: AM de la ciudad de Buenos Aires con programación de información general.
RADIO NETWORK

Los 40 principales (FM 105.5) 371263
Editorial: Rivadavia 835, Capital Federal C1002AAG
Tel: 54 11 43384250.
Email: internet@boxpublicidad.es
Web site: http://www.los40principales.com.ar
Profile: Como su nombre lo indica emite los hit del momento del Pop y del Rock. Es la radio de los rankings de los 40 principales.
RADIO NETWORK

LV3 Cadena 3 (FM 106.9) 371262
Editorial: Alvear 139, Cordoba X5000EAC
Tel: 54 351 5260597.
Email: info@cadena3.com.ar
Web site: http://www.cadena3.com.ar
Profile: Es una de las FM más escuchada de la ciudad de Córdoba. Retransmite la programación de Radio Córdoba.
RADIO NETWORK

María (FM 101.5) 371261
Editorial: Unavailable, Cordoba 5000
Tel: 54 351 4443999.
Web site: http://www.radiomaria.org.ar
Profile: Radio María Argentina es un medio de comunicación para la evangelización. Su objetivo es la difusión del mensaje evangélico de gozo y esperanza, y la promoción de las personas en su realidad cultural, conforme al espíritu de la Iglesia Católica Apostólica
RADIO NETWORK

Mega (FM 98.3) 371270
Editorial: Uriarte 1899, Buenos Aires C1414DAU
Tel: 54 11 48338800.
Email: mega@mega983.com.ar
Web site: http://www.mega983.com.ar/
Profile: Es una de las radios más escuchada y la única que pasa música rock nacional. Su programación es puramente musical.
RADIO NETWORK

Mitre (AM 790) 371272
Editorial: Mansilla 2668, Buenos Aires C1425BDP
Tel: 54 11 57771500.
Email: info@radiomitre.com.ar
Web site: http://www.radiomitre.com.ar
Profile: Es líder en noticias, con un prestigioso equipo de conductores y periodistas. Es una radio que goza de buena credibilidad. En su programación general, la emisora distribuye contenidos con énfasis en la información, los deportes y el entretenimiento. Fecha de Aparición: 16 de agosto de 1925
RADIO NETWORK

Provincia (AM 1270) 371259
Editorial: Calle 53 810, La Plata 1900
Tel: 54 221 4247305.
Web site: http://www.radioprovincia.gba.gov.ar
Profile: AM de la ciudad de La Plata con programas de información general. Fecha de Aparición: 18 de febrero de 1937
RADIO NETWORK

Radio 10 (AM 710) 371274
Editorial: Uriarte 1899, Capital Federal C1414DAU
Tel: 54 11 48338800.
Web site: http://www.radio10.com.ar
Profile: Es la AM más escuchada. Tiene un estilo sensacionalista e impactante, y busca adquirir el lenguaje de la calle y más generalizado.
RADIO NETWORK

Radio Nacional Buenos Aires (AM 870) 371273
Editorial: Maipu 555, Capital Federal C1006ACE
Tel: 54 11 43259100.
Email: portal@radionacional.gov.ar
Web site: http://www.radionacional.com.ar/
Profile: Es la radio perteneciente al Estado Nacional. Fomenta la cultura y las tradiciones argentinas. Fecha de Aparición: 6 de julio de 1937
RADIO NETWORK

Radio Nacional Clásica (FM 96.7) 371275
Editorial: Maipu 555, Capital Federal C1006ACE
Tel: 54 11 43228944.
Email: clasica@radionacional.gov.ar
Web site: http://www.radionacional.gov.ar
Profile: La música y las artes, las críticas y los comentarios, las noticias y los protagonistas de la identidad Nacional Argentina. Fecha de Aparición: Febrero de 2000
RADIO NETWORK

Radio Nacional Folklórica (FM 98.7) 371276
Editorial: Maipu 555, Capital Federal C1006ACE
Tel: 54 11 43259100.
Email: portal@radionacional.gov.ar
Web site: http://www.radionacional.gov.ar
Profile: Un lugar para la divulgación del género y la cultura popular, donde el protagonismo musical está acompañado con la recreación de los relatos, los personajes y la mística del acervo tradicional del país.
RADIO NETWORK

Rivadavia (AM 630) 371267
Editorial: Arenales 2467, Capital Federal C1124AAM
Tel: 54 11 5219-4760.
Email: info@rivadavia.com.ar
Web site: http://www.rivadavia.com.ar

Profile: Se destaca por no pertenecer a ningún grupo de medios. Mantiene independencia accionaria con respecto a las grandes corporaciones. Fecha de Aparición: 24 de julio de 1958
RADIO NETWORK

Rock & Pop (FM 95.9) 371268
Editorial: Gral. Ramon Freire 962, Capital Federal C1426AVT **Tel:** 54 11 40108200.
Email: valeria.podesta@rpmb.com.ar
Web site: http://www.fmrockandpop.com
Profile: Como su nombre lo indica es la radio del Rock and Roll de la actualidad. También presenta programas de información con una interpretación crítica juvenil de la realidad. Fecha de Aparición: 16 de enero de 1985
RADIO NETWORK

Television

América 2 375375
Editorial: Fitz Roy 1650, Capital Federal C1414CHX
Tel: 54 11 50322222.
Email: americanoticias@america2.com.ar
Web site: http://www.america2.com.ar
Profile: Presenta varios programas periodísticos, deportivos y algunos Reality Shows. No tiene programas para chicos.
TELEVISION NETWORK

América 24 375388
Editorial: Fitz Roy 1650, Capital Federal C1414CHX
Tel: 54 11 50322222.
Email: america24@america2.com.ar
Profile: Transmite noticias en vivo las 24 horas.
TELEVISION NETWORK

America Sports 375376
Editorial: Honduras 5637, Capital Federal 1414
Tel: 54 11 47785421.
Web site: http://www.amsports.com.ar
Profile: Es la señal de deportes de Pramer. Desde el fútbol al automovilismo, pasando por el rugby, el golf, el esquí y los deportes extremos. Emite, en exclusivo, motociclismo de velocidad y motocross, box nacional e internacional, automovilismo, fútbol de salón,
TELEVISION NETWORK

Canal 13 375378
Owner: Arte Radiotelevisivo Argentino S.A.
Editorial: Lima 1261, Capital Federal C1138ACA
Tel: 54 11 4305-0013.
Email: eltrecetv@artear.com
Web site: http://www.eltrecetv.com.ar
Profile: Pelea el primer puesto del rating de TV. Presenta varios programas de ficción. Fecha de Aparición: 1 de Octubre de 1960
TELEVISION NETWORK

Canal 26 375369
Editorial: Av. Provincias Unidas 2860, San Justo 1754
Tel: 54 11 44820091.
Email: canal26@telecentro.com.ar
Web site: http://www.canal26.com.ar/
Profile: Es una señal satelital y de aire(UHF) que llega a toda la Argentina a través de 700 cableoperadores que la reciben por medio del satélite INTELSAT 806. En Buenos Aires y Gran Buenos Aires mediante CABLEVISION, MULTICANAL, TELECENTRO, DIRECTV Y TELERED. Ad
TELEVISION NETWORK

Canal 5 Noticias (C5N) 513160
Editorial: Fitz Roy 1940, Capital Federal 1414
Tel: 54 11 48993737.
Email: comercial@c5n.com
Web site: http://www.infobae.com/c5n/index.html
Profile: Canal de noticias de cable. Fecha de Aparición: Agosto de 2007
TELEVISION NETWORK

Canal 7 Argentina 375380
Owner: Radio y Televisión Argentina S.E.
Editorial: Av. Figueroa Alcorta 2977, Capital Federal C1425CKI **Tel:** 54 11 48082500.
Email: comercial@tvpublica.com.ar
Web site: http://www.tvpublica.com.ar
Profile: Es el canal de aire de propiedad estatal que llega a todo el país. No tiene programas de ficción, es el que emite más noticieros y programas de interés general.
TELEVISION NETWORK

Canal 9 375382
Editorial: Dorrego 1782, Capital Federal C1414CKZ
Tel: 54 11 41199999.
Email: info@canal9.com.ar
Web site: http://www.canal9.com.ar
Profile: Canal 9, considerado como el canal decano de la televisión privada, nace el 9 de junio de l960 con el slogan "los esperamos el 9, a las 9 y por el 9", poniendo en el aire una programación especial de 4 horas y en una época que solamente un 38 de la poblac Fecha de Aparición: 9 de julio de 1960
TELEVISION NETWORK

Canal á 375383
Editorial: Bonpland 1745, Capital Federal C1414CMU
Tel: 54 11 47785427.
Email: jczulueta@pramer.tv
Web site: http://www.canalaonline.com
Profile: Canal dedicado al arte y a los espectáculos. Desde la Argentina, llega a toda América Latina. Informa sobre todo lo que sucede en el mundo acerca de los estrenos de cine, teatro, grandes exposiciones, recitales y conciertos, lanzamientos de CD y libros, d
TELEVISION NETWORK

Canal Rural Satelital 375384
Editorial: Honduras 5940, Capital Federal C1414BNL
Tel: 54 11 47774200.
Email: elrural@elrural.com
Web site: http://www.elrural.com/
Profile: Noticieros y programación de interés para productores del campo, y transmisión de documentales temáticas, como por ejemplo: los distintos procesos de producción agroalimentarios. Desde su nacimiento, se ha convertido en un vínculo entre las temáticas del
TELEVISION NETWORK

Cosmopolitan TV 375386
Editorial: Bonpland 1745, Capital Federal C1414CMU
Tel: 54 11 47785420.
Email: cosmopolitan@pramer.tv
Web site: http://www.cosmopolitan.tv
Profile: Canal dedicado a la mujer, líder en Latinoamérica. Presenta una programación para la mujer moderna. Fecha de Aparición: 1 de Julio de 2002
TELEVISION NETWORK

Crónica TV 375387
Editorial: Riobamba 280, Capital Federal C1025ABF
Tel: 54 11 49530297.
Email: cronicatv@cronicatv.com.ar
Web site: http://www.cronicatv.com.ar
Profile: Transmite noticias en vivo las 24 horas, esa es su única programación. Tiene un marcado estila sensacionalista. Pelea el primer puesto del rating en señales de cable. Fecha de Aparición: 1 de enero de 199
TELEVISION NETWORK

El Garage TV 513159
Editorial: Sir Alexander Fleming 2845, Capital Federal
Tel: 54 11 4836.
Email: info@elgarage.com
Web site: http://www.elgarage.com
Profile: Primer canal de habla hispana dedicado al mundo del motor Fecha de Aparición: Agosto de 2005
TELEVISION NETWORK

elgourmet.com 375379
Editorial: Bonpland 1745, Capital Federal C1414CMU
Tel: 54 11 47785451.
Email: elgourmet@pramer.tv
Web site: http://www.elgourmet.com
Profile: Es una señal que trata sobre el mundo de la cocina y su entorno: cocina exquisita, bebidas incomparables, lugares exóticos, historias cautivantes y los finos detalles de la vida. Se posiciona como el canal de los amantes de la buena vida. (Fuente: Pramer) Fecha de Aparición: 1 de julio de 2000
TELEVISION NETWORK

ESPN 375389
Editorial: Maipu 939, Capital Federal C1006ACM
Tel: 54 11 50310800.
Email: ignacio.x.cabanillas@espn.com
Web site: http://www.espndeportes.com
Profile: Programación deportiva local e internacional y selección de noticias deportivas y programas de información en español, incluyendo SportsCenter, el noticiero deportivo líder en el mundo. ESPN está posicionado como el mayor proveedor internacional de progra
TELEVISION NETWORK

FOX Sports 375392
Editorial: Balcarce 510, Capital Federal 1064
Tel: 54 11 4103-1100.
Web site: http://www.foxsports.com.ar
Profile: Cadena deportiva que transmite en español a toda Latinoamérica. Transmite todo tipo de especialidad deportiva.
TELEVISION NETWORK

Magazine 375393
Editorial: Lima 1261, Capital Federal C1138ACA
Tel: 54 11 43701109.
Email: infocomercial@artear.com.ar
Web site: http://www.comercial.artear.com.ar/info/magazine/index.htm
Profile: Señal de interés general con producciones sobre moda, espectáculos, arte, política, turismo, actualidad, música, deportes y muchas otras actividades que tienen que ver con la cultura. (Fuente: Artear)
TELEVISION NETWORK

MTV 375394
Editorial: Av. del Libertador 498, Capital Federal C1001ABR **Tel:** 54 11 45100600.
Web site: http://www.mtvla.com
Profile: Emite los videos musicales del momento de cantantes más famosos de Latinoamérica y del resto del mundo. Los conductores son de hable hispana. La programación musical se complementa con información del mundo del espectáculo. Y por su puesto transmite los r
TELEVISION NETWORK

Sólo Tango 375390
Editorial: Pje Carlos Gardel 3200, Capital Federal C1215AAB **Tel:** 54 11 4862.
Web site: http://www.tangocity.com
Profile: La primera señal televisiva satelital dedicada exclusivamente a la difusión del tango a nivel nacional e internacional. Orquestas, solistas, bailarines, clases, espectáculos, personajes, anécdotas, entrevistas... Todo el ayer, el hoy y el futuro del tango
TELEVISION NETWORK

Telefé 375370
Editorial: Pavon 2444, Capital Federal C1248AAT
Tel: 54 11 49419331.
Web site: http://www.telefe.com
Profile: Emite varios programas de ficción, novelas, Reality Show. No tiene programas periodístico, ni deportivos.
TELEVISION NETWORK

TN - Todo Noticias 375371
Editorial: Lima 1261, Capital Federal C1138ACA
Tel: 54 11 43050013.
Email: mensajes@tn.com.ar
Web site: http://www.tn.com.ar
Profile: Canal de noticias durante las 25Hs. Número uno de audiencia por cable.
TELEVISION NETWORK

TyC Sports 375372
Editorial: Av. San Juan 1132, Capital Federal C1147AAW **Tel:** 54 11 43003800.
Email: libero@tycsports.com.ar
Web site: http://www.tycsports.com.ar
Profile: Es la señal de deportes nacional más vista la Argentina. Presenta un programación variada de eventos deportivos y programas de análisis y opinión. El principal rasgo que distingue a TyC Sports, es la variedad de eventos deportivos de origen nacional e int Fecha de Aparición: 3 de Septiembre de 1994
TELEVISION NETWORK

Utilísima Satelital 375373
Editorial: Piedras 1080, Capital Federal 1070
Tel: 54 11 43005270.
Email: utilisimasatelital@speedy.com.ar
Web site: http://www.utilisima.com.ar
Profile: Canal dedicado a la mujer, líder en la Argentina. Se posiciona como el espacio útil de la mujer. Y cuenta con una amplia variedad de ofertas en su programación, es especial se destacan los programas de manualidades. Fecha de Aparición: 6 de octubre de 1984
TELEVISION NETWORK

Volver 375374
Editorial: Lima 1261, Capital Federal C1138ACA
Tel: 54 11 43701424.
Email: correovolver@artear.com.ar
Web site: http://www.volver.com.ar
Profile: Es el archivo más importante de la televisión argentina, con material de todas las épocas, y es a la vez, el canal con más películas nacionales en su poder. Es una señal ciento por ciento argentina, intenta conservar la memoria audiovisual de nuestro país Fecha de Aparición: 1 de Agosto de 1994
TELEVISION NETWORK

Armenia

Radio

Impulse 518567
Editorial: 19 Hanjanyana Str., 6 floor, Yerevan 375001
Tel: 374 10 54 12 73.
Email: impuls@impuls.am
Web site: http://www.impuls.am
Profile: Dedicated to analytical, political, social and ethnic issues and broadcasts classical and ethnic Armenian music.
RADIO NETWORK

Television

Armenian Second TV Channel 316308
Editorial: G-3 3/1, Achapniak, Yerevan 375088
Tel: 374 10 39 88 31.
Email: h2@tv.am
Web site: http://www.tv.am
Profile: Armenian Second TV-Channel is the biggest private TV-Channel in the whole region of Armenia and in Nagorno-Karabakh. Contains informational-analytical programs, talk-shows, entertaining, music, sports programs, soap operas and Hollywood latest films.
TELEVISION STATION

Public TV of Armenia 316309
Editorial: 26 Gevorg Hovsepyan St., Nork, Yerevan 47
Tel: 374 10 65 15 00.
Email: diana@armtv.com
Web site: http://www.armtv.com
Profile: Armenian Public Television has largest coverage in Armenia with a choice of cultural, entertainment, sports programmes, films and documentaries.
TELEVISION STATION

Australia

Radio

101.7 WS-FM Classic Hits 289584
Owner: Australian Radio Network
Editorial: 3 Byfield Street, North Ryde NSW 2113
Tel: 61 2 8899 9888.
Email: info@wsfm.com.au
Web site: http://www.wsfm.com.au
Profile: Adult classic hits music station.
RADIO NETWORK

4KQ 287748
Owner: Australian Radio Network
Editorial: 444 Logan Road, Stones Corner QLD 4151
Tel: 61 7 3394 0693.
Email: info@4kq.com.au
Web site: http://www.4kq.com.au
Profile: The home of 'Good Times & Great Classic Hits', 4KQ began broadcasting on the 7th of May 1947.
AM RADIO STATION

612 ABC Brisbane 287788
Owner: Australian Broadcasting Corporation (ABC)
Editorial: 114 Grey Street, Brisbane QLD 4101
Tel: 61 7 3377 5222.
Email: radio.612@abc.net.au
Web site: http://www.abc.net.au/brisbane
Profile: Brisbane's premier talk radio station, broadcasting live on air, online, on digital radio and on mobiles to the greater Brisbane region. Every day, their team of experienced presenters and producers brings Brisbane's latest news and information and the best entertainment the region has to offer.
FM RADIO STATION

666 ABC Canberra 287815
Owner: Australian Broadcasting Corporation (ABC)
Editorial: Cnr Northbourne & Wakefield Avenues, Dickson ACT 2602 **Tel:** 61 2 6275 4555.
Email: act.news@abc.net.au
Web site: http://www.abc.net.au/canberra
Profile: 666 ABC Canberra is the leading radio and online station in the national capital region.
FM RADIO STATION

702 ABC Sydney 287771
Owner: Australian Broadcasting Corporation (ABC)
Editorial: Level 2, ABC Centre, 700 Harris Street, Ultimo NSW 2007 **Tel:** 61 2 8333 1234.
Email: 702@your.abc.net.au
Web site: http://www.abc.net.au/sydney
Profile: 702 ABC Sydney offers the latest news and information, views, comedy, music, entertainment, and sport. The station - Sydney's major source of local, national, and international stories - draws on the full resources of ABC News and Current Affairs correspondents worldwide.
FM RADIO STATION

720 ABC Perth 287829
Owner: Australian Broadcasting Corporation (ABC)
Editorial: 30 Fielder Street, East Perth WA 6004
Tel: 61 8 9220 2700.
Email: 720perth@your.abc.net.au
Web site: http://www.abc.net.au/perth
Profile: 720 ABC Perth, broadcasts high quality, relevant and entertaining radio programs to the Perth metro area, reflecting the issues, opinions and concerns of a well-informed Western Australian audience.
FM RADIO STATION

891 ABC Adelaide 287737
Owner: Australian Broadcasting Corporation (ABC)
Editorial: 85 North East Road, Collinswood SA 5081
Tel: 61 8 8343 4000.
Email: sanews@your.abc.net.au
Web site: http://www.abc.net.au/adelaide
Profile: Based in Collinswood, 891 ABC Adelaide provides a local radio and internet service for South Australia.
FM RADIO STATION

936 ABC Hobart 288707
Owner: Australian Broadcasting Corporation (ABC)
Editorial: 1-7 Liverpool Street, Hobart TAS 7000
Tel: 61 3 6235 3333.
Email: tasmania.news@abc.net.au
Web site: http://www.abc.net.au/hobart
Profile: ABC Local Radio for southern Tasmania.
RADIO NETWORK

96 FM 288565
Owner: Australian Radio Network
Editorial: Level 1, 169 Hay Street, East Perth WA 6004 **Tel:** 61 8 9220 1400.
Email: info@96fm.com.au
Web site: http://www.96fm.com.au
Profile: Commercial FM radio station broadcasting in Perth, Western Australia owned by the Australian Radio Network since January 2015.
FM RADIO STATION

97.3 FM 290394
Owner: Australian Radio Network
Editorial: 444 Logan Road, Stones Corner QLD 4120
Tel: 61 7 3421 4973.
Email: info@973fm.com.au
Web site: http://www.973fm.com.au
Profile: Plays popular music from the 80s, 90s, and today aimed at a female audience of 24-44 years old.
RADIO NETWORK

Australia

ABC Classic FM 291080
Owner: Australian Broadcasting Corporation (ABC)
Editorial: PO Box 9994, Melbourne VIC 3001
Tel: 61 1300 766 282.
Email: classicfm@your.abc.net.au
Web site: http://www.abc.net.au/classic
Profile: Australia's only national classical music radio network, on more than one hundred frequencies, and around the world via online streaming.
FM RADIO STATION

ABC Local Radio 472234
Owner: Australian Broadcasting Corporation (ABC)
Editorial: 700 Harris Street, Ultimo NSW 2007
Tel: 61 2 8333 2619.
Email: patrick.rhianna@abc.net.au
Web site: http://www.abc.net.au/radio/localradio
RADIO NETWORK

ABC NewsRadio 291220
Owner: Australian Broadcasting Corporation (ABC)
Editorial: 700 Harris Street, PO Box 9994, Ultimo NSW 2007 **Tel:** 61 2 8333 5094.
Email: newsradio.media@your.abc.net.au
Web site: http://www.abc.net.au/newsradio
Profile: Rolling format of news, current affairs, finance, business, politics, technology & sport; broadcasts Federal Parliament when its sitting.
RADIO NETWORK

ABC Radio Australia 291221
Owner: Australian Broadcasting Corporation (ABC)
Editorial: Level 1, 700 Harris Street, Ultimo NSW 2007
Tel: 61 2 8333 1500.
Email: browning.daniel@abc.net.au
Web site: http://www.radioaustralia.net.au/international
Profile: National radio network featuring news, arts and music.
RADIO NETWORK

FM 104.7 Canberra 288661
Owner: Australian Radio Network
Editorial: Bellenden Street, Gungahlin ACT 2615
Tel: 61 2 6123 4104.
Email: news@canberrafm.com.au
Web site: http://www.fm1047.com.au
Profile: Contemporary music station, with talk, interviews and competition. Target audience: 18-34 yrs. Editorial material accepted: specialist topics, please send to Production Manager. First broadcast:1988
RADIO NETWORK

Gold 104.3 FM 290747
Owner: Australian Radio Network
Editorial: Level 2, 21-31 Goodwood Street, Richmond VIC 3121 **Tel:** 61 3 9420 1043.
Email: melnews@arn.com.au
Web site: http://www.gold1043.com.au
Profile: Classic hits metropolitan radio station.
RADIO NETWORK

Mix 102.3 289813
Owner: Australian Radio Network
Editorial: 201 Tynte Street, North Adelaide SA 5006
Tel: 61 8 8300 1000.
Email: info@mix1023.com.au
Web site: http://www.mix1023.com.au
Profile: A blend of adult contemporary and solid gold music favourites. 24 hour news, contests and on-air personalities. Targets 25-54 year olds with most appeal to 30-49 years and household shoppers.Editorial material accepted: specialist topics please send to producer/ news room Formerly known as Radio 5AD.
RADIO NETWORK

Mix 106.3 288660
Owner: Australian Radio Network
Editorial: Bellenden Street, Gungahlin ACT 2912
Tel: 61 2 6242 0860.
Email: news@canberrafm.com.au
Web site: http://www.mix106.com.au
Profile: Adult contemporary, music and entertainment. News via Prime TV local newsroom. Year First Broadcast: 1988 Audience Figure: 106,000 Mon - Sun (Source: AC Neilson Survey 2 2000) Target Audience: 35-49 yrs.The Newsroom Phone, 02 6242 0860, is the best point of contact for after hours, it's diverted onto messagebank which is checked frequently.
RADIO NETWORK

Radio Australia 291054
Owner: Australian Broadcasting Corporation (ABC)
Editorial: ABC Southbank Centre, Southbank Boulevard, South Melbourne VIC 3205
Tel: 61 3 9626 1500.
Email: english@ra.abc.net.au
Web site: http://www.abc.net.au/ra
Profile: International shortwave, satellite and cable service of the ABC broadcasting in English, Indonesian, Cambodian, Pidgin (PNG), Vietnamese and Mandarin with a focus on Asia and the Pacific. To listen to the programme must have a shortwave radio. Satellite, Internet and Re-broadcast. Year first broadcast: 1940 Target audience: Asia-Pacific. Editorial material accepted in: English.
RADIO NETWORK

Triple J 291222
Owner: Australian Broadcasting Corporation (ABC)
Editorial: Level 1, 700 Harris Street, Ultimo NSW 2007
Tel: 61 2 8333 2905.
Email: triplejradio@your.abc.net.au
Web site: http://www.abc.net.au/triplej
Profile: National youth radio network. Editorial material accepted: specialist topics please send to News Editor.NOTE: There is no specific Triple J News Director. Preferred format for email: attachments should not exceed 4 meg
RADIO NETWORK

Television

ABC 3 652282
Owner: Australian Broadcasting Corporation (ABC)
Editorial: 700 Harris Street, Ultimo NSW 2007
Tel: 61 2 8333 4441.
Email: tvnews@news.abc.net.au
Web site: http://www.abc.net.au/abc3/
Profile: ABC3 is the digital TV channel created for young people of Australia, aged 6 to 15 years old.
TELEVISION STATION

ABC Channel 2 NSW 316549
Owner: Australian Broadcasting Corporation (ABC)
Editorial: 700 Harris Street, Ultimo NSW 2007
Tel: 61 2 8333 1500.
Email: tvnews@news.abc.net.au
Web site: http://www.abc.net.au
Profile: Regional television service with State news, current affairs and sport, with production and transmission centres in all States and Territories.
TELEVISION STATION

ABC Channel 2 QLD 316577
Owner: Australian Broadcasting Corporation (ABC)
Editorial: GPO Box 9994, Brisbane QLD 4001
Tel: 61 7 3377 5222.
Email: news.qld@abc.net.au
Web site: http://www.abc.net.au
Profile: National Television Network - QLD, with a local news service and local as well as national programming.
TELEVISION NETWORK

ABC Channel 2 SA 316554
Owner: Australian Broadcasting Corporation (ABC)
Editorial: 85 North East Road, Collinswood SA 5081
Tel: 61 8 8343 4000.
Email: sanews@your.abc.net.au
Web site: http://www.abc.net.au/adelaide/news
Profile: National Television Network - SA, with a local news service and local as well as national programming.
TELEVISION NETWORK

ABC Channel 2 TAS 317069
Owner: Australian Broadcasting Corporation (ABC)
Editorial: 1-7 Liverpool Street, Hobart TAS 7000
Tel: 61 3 6235 3333.
Email: tasmania.news@abc.net.au
Web site: http://www.abc.net.au/news/tas
Profile: National Television Network - TAS, with a local news service and local as well as national programming.
TELEVISION NETWORK

ABC Channel 2 VIC 316570
Owner: Australian Broadcasting Corporation (ABC)
Editorial: ABC Southbank Centre, Level 3, 120 - 130 Southbank Boulevard, Southbank VIC 3006
Tel: 61 3 9626 1500.
Email: tvnews.abcvic@abc.net.au
Web site: http://www.abc.net.au/news/vic/
Profile: National Television Network - VIC, with a local news service and local as well as national programming.
TELEVISION NETWORK

ABC Channel 2 WA 316530
Owner: Australian Broadcasting Corporation (ABC)
Editorial: 30 Fielder Street, East Perth WA 6004
Tel: 61 8 9220 2700.
Email: tvperth@your.abc.net.au
Web site: http://www.abc.net.au/news/wa/
Profile: National Television Network for WA, with a local news service and local as well as national programming.
TELEVISION NETWORK

ABC News 24 697518
Owner: Australian Broadcasting Corporation (ABC)
Editorial: 700 Harris Street, Ultimo NSW 2007
Tel: 61 2 8333 3685.
Email: abcnews24@your.abc.net.au
Web site: http://www.abc.net.au/news
Profile: ABC News 24 is Australia's most watched news channel and provides live, continuous news coverage of breaking stories from Australia and around the world.
TELEVISION STATION

ABC Television NT 316829
Owner: Australian Broadcasting Corporation (ABC)
Editorial: 1 Cavenagh Street, Darwin NT 0800
Tel: 61 8 8943 3222.
Email: tlozek.eric@abc.net.au
Web site: www.abc.net.au/tv
Profile: It screens repeated ABC news and current affairs programs, ABC news, bulletin stories and some reporting, childrens programming, music documentaries and state football.
TELEVISION STATION

NITV (National Indigenous Television) 543653
Owner: NITV (National Indigenous Television) PTY LTD
Editorial: 14 Herbert Street, Artarmon, Sydney NSW 2064
Email: comments@sbs.com.au
Web site: http://www.sbs.com.au/nitv
Profile: Australia's 24hr TV service dedicated to Indigenous News, Current Affairs, Documentaries, Sports and Films.
TELEVISION STATION

Austria

Television

ATV 316096
Owner: ProSiebenSat.1 PULS 4
Editorial: Aspernbrückengasse 2, Wien 1020
Tel: 43 1 213640.
Email: atv@atv.at
Web site: http://www.atv.at
Profile: ATV ist ein privater Fernsehsender in Österreich, welcher neben Nachrichten auch Dokumentationen, Infotainment, Shows und Serien bietet. ATV is a private television station in Austria, which offers news and documentaries, infotainment, shows and series.
TELEVISION STATION

ORF 2 923677
Owner: Österreichischer Rundfunk ORF
Editorial: Würzburggasse 30, Wien 1136
Tel: 43 1 87878 0.
Web site: http://tv.orf.at/
Profile: ORF 2 ist der zweite öffentlich-rechtliche TV-Kanal des ORF, welcher vor allem Kultursendungen mit Bezug auf Österreich bietet, sowie auch Nachrichten. Das Programm besteht vor allem aus Informationssendungen, enhält aber auch Unterhaltungs-Shows. ORF 2 is the second public TV channel by the ORF, which mainly offers cultural programs with a focus on Austria, as well as news. The program consists primarily of information programs, but also contains entertainment shows.
TELEVISION STATION

ORF eins 775663
Owner: Österreichischer Rundfunk ORF
Editorial: Würzburggasse 30, Wien 1136
Tel: 43 1 87878 0.
Web site: http://tv.orf.at/
Profile: ORF eins, oder auch ORF 1, ist ein öffentlich-rechtlicher TV-Sender des ORF, welcher neben Nachrichten, vor allem Informationssendungen, aber auch Unterhaltung bietet. ORF eins, or ORF 1, is a public service television channel by the ORF, which offers news, information programs, as well as entertainment.
TELEVISION STATION

Azerbaijan

Radio

Radio Antenn 101 FM 446161
Owner: Independent teleradiocompany Antenn
Editorial: 1 Sharifzade Street, Baku AZ 1138
Tel: 994 12 43 37 101.
Web site: http://antenn.az
Profile: Broadcasts news, political programmes and music.
RADIO NETWORK

Television

AZ TV 446171
Editorial: 1 M. Huseyn, Baku AZ1011
Tel: 994 12 49 23 807.
Email: webmaster@aztv.az
Web site: http://www.aztv.az
Profile: Covers current events in Azerbaijan – politics, economics, public life, sport, cultural events and weather.
TELEVISION STATION

Bahamas

Radio

91.1 Talk City 850081
Owner: Caribbean New Media Group
Tel: 1 868 622-4141.
Email: talkcity91fm@gmail.com
Web site: http://www.talkcity91fm.com
Profile: The station's format is talk. They also feature local music and culture and acts from Trinidad & Tobago and the Caribbean.
FM RADIO STATION

i95.5 850077
Owner: One Caribbean Media
Editorial: 47 Tragerete Road, Newtown, Port Of Spain
Tel: 1 868 628-4955.
Web site: http://i955fm.com
Profile: i95.5 FM is a commercial station owned by One Caribbean Media. The format of the station is gospel and urban music. Their target audience is gospel music listeners, ages 18 to 64, in the Newtown, Trinidad & Tobago area. The station airs locally at 95.5 FM.
FM RADIO STATION

Television

CNC3 Television 850065
Owner: Guardian Media Limited
Editorial: 22-24 St Vincent Street, Port Of Spain
Tel: 1 868 623-8870.
Web site: http://www.cnc3.co.tt
Profile: CNC3 Television features news and entertainment programming.
TELEVISION STATION

Gayelle Television 849954
Owner: Fabien (Errol)
Editorial: 43 Eastern Main Road, Port Of Spain
Tel: 1 868 221-8832.
Email: gayelletv@gmail.com
Web site: http://www.gayelletv.com
Profile: Gayelle Television offers local and Caribbean programming.
TELEVISION STATION

ZNS TV 13 316295
Editorial: Harcourt Rusty Bethel Dr, Nassau
Tel: 1 242 502-3800.
Email: znsnews@gmail.com
Web site: http://www.znsbahamas.com
Profile: Television channel presenting information about national news, sports, and entertainment.
TELEVISION NETWORK

Bahrain

Radio

98.4 Shabab FM 714174
Owner: Bahrain Radio & Television Corporation
Editorial: PO Box 194, Isa Town **Tel:** 973 17 788353.
Email: bahrainfm@iaa.gov.bh
Web site: http://www.iaa.bh
Profile: 98.4 Shabab FM is a youth-orientated radio station broadcasting cultural, social, educational and entertainment programmes. It airs on 98.4 FM and launched in February 2010.
FM RADIO STATION

Bahrain 93.3 FM 714289
Owner: Bahrain Radio & Television Corporation
Editorial: PO Box 194, Isa Town **Tel:** 973 17 682696.
Email: bahrainfm@iaa.gov.bh
Web site: http://www.iaa.bh
Profile: Bahrain 93.3 FM is a national radio station broadcasting music, news, entertainment and cultural programmes. It launched in 2001.
FM RADIO STATION

Radio Bahrain 102.3 FM 381038
Owner: Bahrain Radio & Television Corporation
Editorial: PO Box 194, Isa Town **Tel:** 973 17 871371.
Email: alnaar12@yahoo.com
Web site: http://www.iaa.bh
Profile: Radio Bahrain 102.3 FM broadcasts major local events and news in Bahrain, as well as locally produced drama serials, educational and cultural programmes. It launched in 1955 and airs on 102.3 FM, MW 801, MW 612 and MW 1458.
FM RADIO STATION

Radio Bahrain 96.5 FM 381039
Owner: Bahrain Radio & Television Corporation
Editorial: PO Box 702, Isa Town, Manama
Tel: 973 17 871562.
Email: bahrainfm@hotmail.com
Web site: http://www.iaa.bh
Profile: Radio Bahrain 96.5 FM is the English radio station of the Bahrain Radio & Television Corporation, and broadcasts music and entertainment 24-hours a day with local and international news every hour. It launched in 1977 and broadcasts on 96.5 FM and 99.5 FM.
FM RADIO STATION

Your FM 104.2 500865
Owner: Your FM 104.2
Editorial: PO Box 76024, Office 13, Building 618, Manama **Tel:** 973 17 369370.
Email: pr@yourfm.bh
Web site: http://www.yourfm.bh
Profile: Your FM 104.2 is an independent, commercial radio station broadcasting Asian music and programmes to Bahrain and the Eastern province of Saudi Arabia. The station launched in June 2012, replacing Radio Voice 104.2 which had broadcast on the same frequency since 2007. The station airs 20 hours of Hindi programming and four hours of Malayalam programming daily on 104.2 FM.
FM RADIO STATION

Television

Bahrain TV
375345
Owner: Bahrain Radio & Television Corporation
Editorial: PO Box 1075, Al Istiglal Highway, Isa Town
Tel: 973 17 871525.
Email: news@brtc.gov.bh
Web site: http://www.iaa.bh
Profile: Bahrain TV is a state-owned television channel broadcasting local and international news, current affairs, documentaries, educational programmes, entertainment series and films 24-hours a day. The channel launched in 1973.
TELEVISION STATION

Channel 55
508639
Owner: Bahrain Radio & Television Corporation
Editorial: PO Box 1075, Al Istiglal Highway, Isa Town
Tel: 973 17 871309.
Email: news@brtc.gov.bh
Web site: http://www.iaa.bh
Profile: Channel 55 is a state-owned television station broadcasting news and general entertainment programmes. The channel launched in 1978.
TELEVISION STATION

Bangladesh

Television

ATN Bangla
458947
Editorial: WASA Bhaban (1st Floor), 98 Kazi Nazrul Islam Avenue, Kawran Bazar, Dhaka 1215
Tel: 880 28111207.
Email: atn@dhaka.agni.com
Web site: http://www.atnbangla.tv
Profile: Covers of news and general interests.
TELEVISION STATION

Ekattor TV
896931
Editorial: 57 Sohrawardi Avenue, Baridhara, Dhaka 1212 Tel: 880 9669-710000.
Email: ekattortv@gmail.com
Web site: http://www.ekattor.tv
Profile: Launched in June 2012, serves as the first full high-definition news and current affairs television service available 24/7 in Bangladesh.
TELEVISION NETWORK

Barbados

Radio

Caribbean Broadcasting Corporation (Radio)
291029
Editorial: PO Box 900, The Pine, St. Michael, Bridgetown BB11000 Tel: 1 246 467-5400.
Email: nca@cbc.bb
Web site: http://www.cbc.bb
Profile: Provides news, life music shows. 98.1 FM targets teenagers and provides interviews and top music 94.7FM plays Caribbean music. 100.7 FM provides general government information and provides community service coverage.
RADIO NETWORK

Voice of Barbados
290923
Editorial: River Road, Bridgetown Tel: 246 4341790.
Email: vob@starcomnetwork.net
Web site: http://www.vob929.com
Profile: VOB presents interactive programs related to socio-economic issues related to the Barbadians lifestyle. Transmits sports, surveys, regional and business news on the frequency 92.9 FM.
RADIO NETWORK

Belgium

Radio

RTBF
583011
Owner: RTBF
Editorial: Boulevard Auguste Reyers, 52, BBR 100, Bruxelles 1044 Tel: 32 2 737 48 81.
Email: rtbf.info@rtbf.be
Web site: http://www.rtbf.be
Profile: National network of the Radio Television Belge Francophone.
RADIO NETWORK

RTBF - Classic 21
583012
Owner: RTBF
Tel: 32 6532 7111.
Email: classic21@rtbf.be
Web site: http://www.classic21.be
Profile: Belgian classic rock radio, owned by national RTBF media group and based in Mons.
RADIO NETWORK

RTBF - International
583013
Owner: RTBF
Editorial: Boulevard Reyers, 52, BRR 016, Bruxelles 1044 Tel: 32 2737 21 11.
Web site: http://www.rtbfi.be
Profile: Belgian international, shortwave radio station, available in Europe and Central Africa. Owned by RTBF.
RADIO NETWORK

RTBF - La Première
583014
Owner: RTBF
Editorial: Boulevard Auguste Reyers, 52, BRR 020, Bruxelles 1044 Tel: 32 2 737 21 11.
Email: lpdirection@rtbf.be
Web site: http://www.rtbf.be/lapremiere
Profile: National radio station covering news and current affairs including politics, economics, culture, sports and entertainment.
RADIO NETWORK

RTBF - Pure FM
583016
Owner: RTBF
Tel: 32 2737 27 76.
Email: purefm@rtbf.be
Web site: http://www.rtbf.be/purefm/
Profile: Young audience orientated radio, owned by national media group RTBF.
RADIO NETWORK

RTBF - VivaCité
583017
Owner: RTBF
Tel: 32 6532 71 01.
Email: vivacite@rtbf.be
Web site: http://www.rtbf.be/vivacite/
Profile: Belgian public service radio station, owned by national media company RTBF.
RADIO NETWORK

Television

Canal Z
310944
Owner: Roularta Media Group
Editorial: 50, rue de la Fusee, Bruxelles 1130
Tel: 32 2 702 70 91.
Email: info@canalz.be
Web site: http://www.canalz.be
Profile: Television channel focusing on economics and finance (French Edition).
TELEVISION STATION

Kanaal Z
316160
Owner: RMG - ROULARTA MEDIA GROUP
Editorial: Medialaan 1, Vilvoorde 1800
Tel: 32 2 255 37 08.
Email: info@z-nieuws.be
Web site: http://kanaalz.knack.be/
Profile: Kanaal Z / Canal Z are managed by NV Belgian Business Television, which was set by Brussels-listed Roularta Media Group. Kanaal Z / Canal Z are broadcasting 24 hours a day news about companies, economy and finances. Local Translation: Televisiezender met informatie over wat er reilt en zeilt op financieel-economisch gebied. Tijdens de week worden het journaal en het aansluitend beursgesprek om het half uur herhaald. Met in het weekend programma's als "Z Hebdo" en "Trends TV" . (AANVULLENDE INFORMATIE: Wat advertentiemogelijkheden betreft, 30 sec kosten 5500,00 Eur. Eveneens promoties naargelang de hoeveelheid, goede klant, ... Geïnteresserden kunnen telefoneren naar 02/4675859.)
TELEVISION STATION

TV-Brussel
316887
Tel: 32 2702 87 30.
Email: nieuws@tvbrussel.be
Web site: http://www.tvbrussel.be
Profile: tvbrussel is a Dutch-speaking channel which believes in an international approach to a multicultural city. And so all our programmes are subtitled in French and English.
TELEVISION STATION

VTM - Vlaamse Televisie Maatschappij
316157
Owner: VLAAMSE MEDIA MAATSCHAPPIJ
Editorial: Medialaan 1, Vilvoorde 1800
Tel: 32 2255 3211.
Email: hetnieuws@vtm.be
Web site: http://www.vtm.be
Profile: National broadcaster, market leader in information and entertainment, focusing on Flemish productions. "Family" channel.
TELEVISION STATION

Belize

Television

Channel 5 Belize
316428
Editorial: 2882 Coney Dr, Belize City
Tel: 501 2233745.
Email: gbtv@btl.net
Web site: http://www.channel5belize.com
Profile: Local television station broadcasting news and original entertainment shows.
TELEVISION NETWORK

Channel Seven
316263
Editorial: 73 Albert Street, Belize City
Tel: 501 2235589.
Email: tvseven@btl.net
Web site: http://www.7newsbelize.com
Profile: Provides social, political, and sport news.
TELEVISION NETWORK

Bermuda

Radio

1450AM Gold
290921
Editorial: 94 Reid St., Hamilton HM FX
Tel: 1 441 292-0050.
Email: 1450gold@vsbbermuda.com
Web site: http://www.vsbbermuda.com/1450-am-gold.html
Profile: Plays music from the 40s, 50s, and 60s. Provides talk shows, daily and weather news from Bermuda.
RADIO NETWORK

MIX 106FM
290922
Editorial: 94 Reid St, Hamilton HM FX Tel: 1 441 292-0050.
Email: mix106@vsbbermuda.com
Web site: http://www.vsbbermuda.com/mix-106-fm.html
Profile: Plays today's music including urban, country, hip hop. Provides daily news twice a day.
RADIO NETWORK

Television

VSB TV-11
316449
Editorial: 94 Reid St, Hamilton HM FX Tel: 1 441 276-1111.
Email: news@vsbbermuda.com
Web site: http://www.vsbbermuda.com
Profile: Broadcasts local daily news. Presentes different programming including entertainment shows.
TELEVISION NETWORK

Bhutan

Radio

Bhutan Broadcasting Service Radio
290935
Editorial: PO Box 101, Thimphu Tel: 975 2 32 35 80.
Email: bbs@bbs.com.bt
Web site: http://www.bbs.com.bt
RADIO NETWORK

Television

Bhutan Broadcasting Service TV
316412
Editorial: PO Box 101, Thimphu Tel: 975 2 32 35 80.
Email: md@bbs.com.bt
Web site: http://www.bbs.com.bt
TELEVISION STATION

Bolivia

Radio

Radio Fides
381074
Editorial: Calle Jenaro Sanjines 799 Esquina Sucre, CP 9143, La Paz Tel: 591 2 240 6363.
Email: prensa@radiofides.com
Web site: http://www.radiofides.com
Profile: Catholic Radio Station covers national news and social programs in which the radio fundraises in benefit of people with low income. Plays Bolivian national music.
RADIO NETWORK

Radio Panamericana
290913
Editorial: Edificio 16 de Julio Piso 9, Oficina 902 El Prado, La Paz Tel: 591 2 231 3980.
Email: pana@panamericana.bo
Web site: http://www.panamericana.bo
Profile: Broadcasts daily news and sports. Plays Surcos Bolivianos and traditional Bolivian music and rhythms.
RADIO NETWORK

Channel Seven

P.A.T.
316264
Editorial: Posnansky 1069, Miraflores, La Paz
Tel: 591 2 222 4422.
Email: info@red-pat.com
Web site: http://www.red-pat.com
Profile: Television network broadcasting a variety of cultural, entertainment programs and the news shows.
TELEVISION NETWORK

Television

Bosnia-Herzegovina

Radio

BH Radio 1
290893
Editorial: Bulevar Mese Selimovica 12, Sarajevo 71000 Tel: 387 33 255 220.
Email: radio1@bhrt.ba
Web site: http://www.bhrt.ba/bhr1
Profile: National radio station broadcasting news, music, religious and social programmes 24 hours a day.
RADIO NETWORK

Television

BHT 1
316372
Editorial: Bulevar Mese Selimovica 12, Sarajevo 71000 Tel: 387 33 65 04 52.
Web site: http://www.bhrt.ba
Profile: Bosnian national TV station broadcasting on the territory of the whole country.
TELEVISION STATION

Botswana

Radio

RB1
518566
Owner: Department of Broadcasting Services
Editorial: Department of Broadcasting Services, Private Bag 60, Gaborone Tel: 267 365 30 00.
Email: newsroom@btv.gov.bw
Web site: http://www.btv.gov.bw
Profile: National radio station covering general news and current affairs.
RADIO NETWORK

Brazil

Radio

Rádio Disney
795006
Owner: Grupo Estado
Editorial: Av Celestino Bourroul, 100-2M, Sao Paulo 02710-000 Tel: 55 11 2108-6742.
Web site: http://radiodisney.disney.com.br
FM RADIO STATION

Rádio Eldorado
795005
Owner: Grupo Estado
Editorial: Av Celestino Bourroul, 100-2M, Sao Paulo 02710-000 Tel: 55 11 2108-6472.
Web site: http://www.territorioeldorado.limao.com.br
FM RADIO STATION

Rádio Estadão FM
795002
Owner: Grupo Estado
Editorial: Av Celestino Bourroul, 100-2M, Sao Paulo 02710-000 Tel: 55 11 3856-2122.
Web site: http://radio.estadao.com.br
FM RADIO STATION

Sistema Difusora de Comunicação
471779
Editorial: Av. Camboa, 120, Camboa, São Luís 65020-260 Tel: 55 9832143000.
Email: jornalismo@sistemadifusora.com.br
Web site: http://www.sistemadifusora.com.br
Profile: O Sistema Difusora de Comunicação, é composto por um complexo de emissoras de TVs e Rádios e uma rede de retransmissoras espalhadas em todo o Estado do Maranhão. O Sistema oferece aos telespectadores entretenimento e informação e aos empresários e agências excelentes oportunidades de negócios. Com uma programação local extensa, o Sistema Difusora de Comunicação cumpre sua missão de informar e entreter o público telespectador e ouvinte, sempre levando em consideração, os costumes e tradições culturais da região onde atua, e com isso, estabelecendo uma integração com a comunidade, além de retransmitir a programação do SBT - Sistema Brasileiro de Televisão a quem está afiliado.
RADIO NETWORK

Brazil

Sistema Globo de Rádio 471778
Editorial: Rua do Russel, 434, Gloria, Rio De Janeiro 22210-010 **Tel:** 55 2125558282.
Email: cbnrio@cbn.com.br
Web site: http://globonoar.globo.com
RADIO NETWORK

Television

MTV Brasil 310950
Owner: Editora Abril S.A.
Editorial: Av. Professor Alfonso Bovero, 52, Sumaré, Sao Paulo 01254-000 **Tel:** 55 11 3871-7100.
Email: mtv.responde@mtvbrasil.com.br
Web site: http://www.mtv.com.br
Profile: Launched in 1990, MTV Brasil offers music, entertainment and news targeting teenagers and young adults.
TELEVISION NETWORK

Record News 728826
Editorial: Rua da Varzea, 240, Barra Funda, Sao Paulo 01140-080 **Tel:** 55 11 33004101.
Web site: http://www.recordnewstv.com.br
Profile: Launched in 2007, Record News is the first 24-hour free-to-air terrestrial news channel in Brazil.
TELEVISION NETWORK

Rede Bandeirantes 316423
Owner: Grupo Bandeirantes de Comunicação
Editorial: Rua Radiantes 13, Morumbi, Sao Paulo 05699-900 **Tel:** 55 11 3131-1313.
Email: cat@band.com.br
Web site: http://www.band.com.br
Profile: Offers news, art and entertainment shows. Rede Bandeirantes (Bandeirantes Network), officially nicknamed Band or Band Network, is a television network from Brazil, based in São Paulo. Part of the Grupo Bandeirantes de Comunicação (Bandeirantes Communications Group), it aired for the first time in 1967. Currently, is the fourth TV network in Brazil by the ratings.
TELEVISION NETWORK

Rede Brasil de Televisão 730675
Editorial: Alameda Uapes, 313, Planalto Paulista, Sao Paulo 4067-030 **Tel:** 55 21 5078-5900.
Web site: http://www.rbtv.com.br
Profile: Launched in 2007, offers news and entertainment.
TELEVISION NETWORK

Rede CNT 725731
Owner: Grupo Empresarial Organizações Martinez
Editorial: Rua Francisco Caron, 29, Pilarzinho, Curitiba 82120-200 **Tel:** 55 41 2129-7250.
Web site: http://redecnt.com.br
TELEVISION NETWORK

Rede Gazeta 727339
Owner: Fundação Cásper Libero
Editorial: Av. Paulista, 900, Cerqueira César, Sao Paulo 01310-940 **Tel:** 55 11 3170-5945.
Web site: http://www.tvgazeta.com.br/
TELEVISION NETWORK

Rede Globo 316422
Owner: Organizações Globo
Editorial: Rua Lopes Quintas, 303, Jardim Botânico, Rio De Janeiro 22460-010 **Tel:** 55 21 2540-2307.
Web site: http://redeglobo.globo.com
Profile: The Globo Television Network is a national broadcast television network providing a range of general entertainment fare. Launched by media mogul Roberto Marinho on April 26, 1965. It is owned by media conglomerate Organizações Globo, being by far the largest of its holdings. Globo is currently the largest commercial television network of Latin America and the third largest in the world[not in citation given], behind only CBS and NBC, being watched by an estimate of 120 million people daily.
TELEVISION NETWORK

Rede Internacional de Televisão 728618
Owner: Igreja Internacional da Graça de Deus
Editorial: Estrada dos Bandeirantes, 1000, Taguara, Rio De Janeiro 22710-112 **Tel:** 55 21 3344-5959.
Web site: http://www.rittv.com.br
Profile: Founded in 1999, Rede Internacional de Televisão (The International Network, in English) better known as RIT is a Brazilian television religious channel. Offers children's programs, worship, music and news.
TELEVISION NETWORK

Rede NGT de Televisão 725582
Owner: Rede NGT - Nova Geração de Televisão
Editorial: Av. Magalhaes de Castro, 420, Butanta, Sao Paulo 05502-000 **Tel:** 55 11 2827-2600.
Email: noticias@redengt.com.br
Web site: http://www.redengt.com.br
Profile: Launched October 8, 2003 and offers arts and entertainment, sports and news.
TELEVISION NETWORK

Rede Record de Televisão 471838
Owner: Rádio e Televisão Record S/A
Editorial: Rua da Varzea, 240, Barra Funda, Sao Paulo 01140-080 **Tel:** 55 11 2184-5473.
Web site: http://rederecord.r7.com
Profile: Offers arts, entertainment and news. Rede Record currently is Brazil's second largest television network. With 57 years of uninterrupted transmission, it is also the oldest TV network in the country.
TELEVISION NETWORK

RedeTV! 727792
Editorial: Av. Presidente Kennedy, 2869, Vila Sao José, Osasco 06298-190 **Tel:** 55 11 3306-1000.
Web site: http://www.redetv.com.br
Profile: Offers News and Entertainment. Formed in 1999 using part of Rede Manchete structure. RedeTV! started its transmissions on November 15, 1999. It was the first network worldwide to be broadcast in 3D.
TELEVISION NETWORK

SBT 316425
Owner: Sistema Brasileiro de Televisão
Editorial: Avenida das Comunicacões 4, Jaragua, Osasco, Sao Paulo 06278-905 **Tel:** 55 11 3687-3000.
Email: jornalpauta@sbt.com.br
Web site: http://www.sbt.com.br
Profile: Offers a variety of news, art & entertainment shows. The network first aired in 1981, and its headquarters are based in Osasco. SBT is owned by Silvio Santos, a popular Brazilian TV host. Its studios are located in São Paulo.
TELEVISION NETWORK

TV Brasil 724258
Owner: Empresa Brasil de Comunicação S.A.
Editorial: SCRN 702/703 Bloco B, Edifício Radiobras, Brasilia 70323-900 **Tel:** 55 61 3799-5324.
Email: pauta@ebc.com.br
Web site: http://www.tvbrasil.org.br
Profile: Offers news, arts and entertainment shows. Brazilian non-profit public broadcasting television network launched on December 2, 2007. It was the first launched by the federal government.
TELEVISION NETWORK

TV Câmara 725373
Owner: Câmara dos Deputados
Editorial: Palacio do Congresso Nacional, Praca dos Três Poderes, Brasilia 70160-900 **Tel:** 55 61 3216-1602.
Email: jornalismo@camara.gov.br
Web site: http://www.tv.camara.gov.br
Profile: Offers broadcasting activities and news from the Brazilian Chamber of Deputies.
TELEVISION NETWORK

TV Cultura 724838
Owner: Fundação Padre Anchieta
Editorial: Rua Cenno Sbrighi, 378, Sao Paulo 05036-900 **Tel:** 55 11 2182-3546.
Email: chefiadereportagem@tvcultura.com.br
Web site: http://www3.tvcultura.com.br
Profile: TV Cultura (Portuguese: Culture TV) is Brazilian television network headquartered in São Paulo and a part of Fundação Padre Anchieta. It focuses on cultural and education subjects but also has sports as entertainment options.
TELEVISION NETWORK

TV Senado 725418
Owner: Senado Federal
Editorial: Senado Federal, Praca dos Três Poderes, Brasilia 70165-900 **Tel:** 55 61 3303-3198.
Email: tv@senado.gov.br
Web site: http://www.senado.gov.br/tv
Profile: Offers broadcasting activity and news from the Brazilian Senate. It was created in 1996 by the Brazilian Senate.The channel broadcasts 24h from the Senate.
TELEVISION NETWORK

Brunei

Television

Radio Televisyen Brunei 653617
Owner: Radio Televisyen Brunei
Tel: 673 2243111 127.
Email: manap_hjadam@rtb.gov.bn
Web site: http://www.rtb.gov.bn
Profile: Government run media service projecting the national image at regional and international levels.
TELEVISION STATION

Bulgaria

Radio

Bulgarian National Radio 433965
Editorial: 4 Dragan Tsankov Blvd, Sofia 1040
Tel: 359 2 933 65 49.
Email: newsroom@bnr.bg
Web site: http://bnr.bg
Profile: National state radio of Bulgaria. Main part of it is Radio Bulgaria, which is a main source of information to the million people outside the Bulgarian borders.
RADIO NETWORK

Fresh 433966
Owner: Emmis Bulgaria Group
Editorial: 51 Jerusalem Blvd, Business building, Sofia
Tel: 359 2 976 74 99.
Email: office@radiofresh.bg
Web site: http://www.radiofresh.bg
Profile: National radio network Fresh is a musical radio of CHR format (Contemporary Hit Radio). Our radio is for modern hits with audience of young people aged 15-30.
RADIO NETWORK

Television

Bulgarian National Television 316369
Editorial: 29 San Stefano St, Sofia 1504
Tel: 359 2 9444 999.
Email: news@bnt.bg
Web site: http://www.bnt.bg
Profile: Bulgarian National Television is the first national television.
TELEVISION STATION

Burundi

Radio

Radio Isanganiro 406380
Owner: Radio Isanganiro
Editorial: 27 Avenue de l'Amitie, Bujumbara
Tel: 257 22 25 03 11.
Email: isanganiro@isanganiro.org
Web site: http://www.isanganiro.org
Profile: National radio station covering general news and current affairs including politics, cultural, social and freedom of speech issues.
RADIO NETWORK

Radio Nationale du Burundi 291037
Editorial: 12 Avenue 13 Octobre, Bujumbara
Tel: 257 22 22 35 85.
Email: rtnb@rtnb.bi
Web site: http://www.rtnb.bi
Profile: National radio of Burundi covering current affairs, sports, politics and general information.
RADIO NETWORK

Television

Television Nationale du Burundi 316351
Editorial: 12 Avenue 13 Octobre, Bujumbara
Tel: 257 22 22 35 85.
Email: rtnb@rtnb.bi
Web site: http://www.rtnb.bi
Profile: National television of Burundi covering current affairs, politics, sports and general information.
TELEVISION STATION

Cambodia

Television

National Television of Cambodia (TVK) 468420
Editorial: National Television Kampuchea (TVK), #62 Preah Monivoing Boulevard, Sangkat Sras Chork, Khan Daun Penh, Phnom Penh 12201
Tel: 855 023 426761.
Email: tvk@camnet.com.kh
Web site: http://www.tvk.gov.kh
Profile: TVK became known in English as the National Television of Cambodia. TVK has broadcast its programmes both regionally and globally by satellite.
TELEVISION STATION

Cameroon

Television

Cameroon Radio Television 316353
Editorial: BP 16344, Yaoundé **Tel:** 237 22 21 40 77.
Email: crtvweb@iccnet.cm
Web site: http://www.crtv.cm
Profile: National Radio and Television of Cameroon covering current affairs, sport, politics and broadcasting entertainment.
TELEVISION STATION

Canada

Radio

Bell Media Radio 86052
Owner: Bell Media
Editorial: 250 Richmond St W, Toronto, Ontario M5V 1W4 **Tel:** 1 416 384-4163.
Email: bellmediacommunications@bellmedia.ca
Web site: http://www.bellmedia.ca
Profile: Bell Media Radio is a music and entertainment syndication service owned by Bell Media. It produces and customizes radio features and infomercials upon request.
RADIO NETWORK

CBAF-FM 47584
Owner: Société Radio-Canada
Editorial: 250 Av Universite, Moncton, New Brunswick E1C 5K3 **Tel:** 1 506 853-6666.
Web site: http://radio-canada.ca/acadie
Profile: CBAF-FM is a non-commercial station owned by Société Radio-Canada. The format of the station is variety. CBAF-FM broadcasts to the Moncton, New Brunswick area at 88.5 FM.
FM RADIO STATION

CBAF-FM-15 837071
Editorial: 430 University Ave, Charlottetown, Prince Edward Island C1A 4N6 **Tel:** 1 902 629-6400.
FM RADIO STATION

CBA-FM 47585
Owner: Canadian Broadcasting Corp.
Editorial: 250 University Avenue, Moncton, New Brunswick E1C 8N8 **Tel:** 1 506 853-6630.
Web site: http://www.cbc.ca/nb
Profile: CBA-FM is a non-commercial station owned by the Canadian Broadcasting Corp. The station is a part of the Radio 2 network and its format is classical, jazz, world music, and live music of all types. CBA-FM broadcasts to the Moncton, NB area at 95.5 FM.
FM RADIO STATION

CBAL-FM 47596
Owner: Société Radio-Canada
Editorial: 250 Universite Ave, Moncton, New Brunswick E1C 5K3 **Tel:** 1 506 853-6666.
Web site: http://www.radio-canada.ca/Acadie
Profile: CBAL-FM is a non-commercial station owned by Societe Radio-Canada. The format of the station is classical and jazz. CBAL-FM broadcasts to Moncton, New Brunswick at 98.3 FM.
FM RADIO STATION

CBAM-FM 47262
Owner: Canadian Broadcasting Corp.
Editorial: 250 Universite Ave, Moncton, New Brunswick E1C 5K3 **Tel:** 1 506 853-6630.
Web site: http://www.cbc.ca/nb
Profile: CBAM-FM is a commercial station owned by the Canadian Broadcasting Corp. The format of the station is news and talk. CBAM-FM broadcasts to the Moncton, NB area at 106.1 FM.
FM RADIO STATION

CBAX-FM 612583
Owner: Canadian Broadcasting Corporation
Editorial: 5600 Sackville St, Halifax, Nova Scotia B3J 1L2 **Tel:** 1 902 420-8311.
Web site: http://www.cbc.ca/ns
Profile: CBAX-FM is a non-commercial station owned by the Canadian Broadcasting Corporation. The format for the station is classical, jazz, world, and folk music. CBAX-FM broadcasts to the Halifax, NS area at 91.5 FM.
FM RADIO STATION

CBBS-FM (CBC Radio 2 Sudbury 90.1) 83091
Owner: Canadian Broadcasting Corp.
Editorial: 15 MacKenzie St, Sudbury, Ontario P3C 4Y1 **Tel:** 1 705 688-3200.
Email: sudburynews@cbc.ca
Web site: http://www.cbc.ca/sudbury
Profile: CBBS-FM is a non-commercial station owned by the Canadian Broadcasting Corp. The format of the station is music. CBBS-FM broadcasts to the Sudbury, Ontario area on 90.1 FM.
FM RADIO STATION

CBBX-FM 83161
Owner: Société Radio-Canada
Editorial: 15 MacKenzie St, Sudbury, Ontario P3C 4Y1 **Tel:** 1 705 688-3200.
Web site: http://radio-canada.ca/ontario
Profile: CBBX-FM is a non-commercial station owned by the Societe Radio-Canada. The format of the station is variety. CBBX-FM broadcasts to the Sudbury, Ontario area at 90.9 FM.
FM RADIO STATION

CBC Radio One 70309
Owner: Canadian Broadcasting Corp.
Editorial: 205 Wellington St W, Toronto, Ontario M5V 3G7- **Tel:** 1 416 205-3311.
Web site: http://www.cbc.ca/radio
Profile: CBC Radio One airs the CBC network's news and current affairs programming. CBC serves as Canada's largest cultural institution, aiming to touch the lives of the country's citizens on a daily basis. Owned by all Canadians, CBC has a heritage as the nation's supplier of Canadian cultural content.

CBC Radio One is a member of the Canadian Press Gallery.
RADIO NETWORK

CBC Radio One - Edmonton Bureau
70621
Editorial: 123 Edmonton City Centre, 10062-102 Avenue, Edmonton, Alberta T5J 2Y8 **Tel:** 1 780 468-7500.
Email: newsedmonton@cbc.ca
Web site: http://www.cbc.ca/edmonton
Profile: The CBC Radio One bureau in Edmonton, Alberta.
RADIO NETWORK

CBC Radio One - Halifax Bureau
70623
Editorial: 6940 Mumford Road, Suite 100, Halifax, Nova Scotia B3L 0B7 **Tel:** 1 902 420-4100.
Web site: http://www.cbc.ca/ns
Profile: Halifax, Nova Scotia bureau of CBC Radio One.
RADIO NETWORK

CBC Radio One - Montreal Bureau
70624
Editorial: 1400 Rene-Levesque Blvd Est, Montreal, Quebec H2L 2M2 **Tel:** 1 514 597-6000.
Web site: http://www.cbc.ca/montreal
Profile: CBC Radio One Montreal bureau.
RADIO NETWORK

CBC Radio One - New York Bureau
151870
Editorial: 747 3rd Ave Ste 8C, New York, New York 10017-2803 **Tel:** 1 212 546-0506.
Profile: New York Bureau of CBC Radio One.
RADIO NETWORK

CBC Radio One - Ottawa Bureau
70620
Editorial: 181 Queen St, Ottawa, Ontario K1P 1K9 **Tel:** 1 613 288-6000.
Email: cbcnewsottawa@cbc.ca
Web site: http://www.cbc.ca/ottawa
RADIO NETWORK

CBC Radio One - Regina Bureau
70625
Editorial: 2440 Broad St, Regina, Saskatchewan S4P 4A1 **Tel:** 1 306 347-9540.
Web site: http://www.cbc.ca/sask
Profile: CBC Radio One Regina, Saskatchewan bureau.
RADIO NETWORK

CBC Radio One - Vancouver Bureau
70622
Editorial: 700 Hamilton St, Vancouver, British Columbia V6B 2R5 **Tel:** 1 604 662-6000.
Email: cbcnewsvancouver@cbc.ca
Web site: http://www.cbc.ca/bc
Profile: CBC Radio One Vancouver, British Columbia bureau.
RADIO NETWORK

CBC Radio One - Washington Bureau
151984
Editorial: 529 14th St NW Ste 500, Washington, District Of Columbia 20045-1501 **Tel:** 1 202 383-2900.
Profile: Washington Bureau of CBC Radio One.
RADIO NETWORK

CBC Radio Two
363819
Owner: Canadian Broadcasting Corp.
Editorial: 700 Hamilton St, Vancouver, British Columbia V6B 2R5 **Tel:** 1 416 205-3311.
Web site: http://www.cbc.ca/radio2
Profile: CBC Radio Two airs the CBC network's music and fine arts programming. CBC serves as Canada's largest cultural institution, aiming to touch the lives of the country's citizens on a daily basis. Owned by all Canadians, CBC has a heritage as the nation's supplier of Canadian cultural content.
RADIO NETWORK

CBC-AM
47329
Owner: Canadian Broadcasting Corp.
Editorial: 825 Riverside Dr West, Windsor, Ontario N9A 5K9 **Tel:** 1 519 255-3411.
Email: windsor@cbc.ca
Web site: http://www.cbc.ca/windsor
AM RADIO STATION

CBCK-FM
781193
Owner: Canadian Broadcasting Corp.
Tel: 1 613 288-6485.
Email: cbcnewsottawa@cbc.ca
Web site: http://www.cbc.ca/ottawa
Profile: CBCK-FM is a non-commercial radio station owned by Canadian Broadcasting Corp. The format of the station is news and talk. CBCK-FM broadcasts to the Kingston, ON at 107.5 FM.
FM RADIO STATION

CBCL-FM (CBC London 93.5)
83088
Owner: Canadian Broadcasting Corp.
Editorial: 208 Piccadilly St Unit 4, London, Ontario N6A 1S1 **Tel:** 1 519 667-1990.
Web site: http://www.cbc.ca/

Profile: CBCL-FM is a non-commercial station owned by Canadian Broadcasting Corp. The format of the station is news and talk. CBCL-FM broadcasts to London, Ontario area at 93.5 FM.
FM RADIO STATION

CBCS-FM (CBC Radio One Sudbury 99.9)
47626
Owner: Canadian Broadcasting Corp.
Editorial: 15 MacKenzie St, Sudbury, Ontario P3C 4Y1 **Tel:** 1 705 688-3200.
Email: sudburynews@cbc.ca
Web site: http://www.cbc.ca/sudbury
Profile: CBCS-FM is a non-commercial station owned by the Canadian Broadcasting Corp. The format of the station is news and talk. CBCS-FM broadcasts to the Sudbury, Ontario area on 99.9 FM.
FM RADIO STATION

CBCT-FM (CBC Radio One Charlottetown)
83089
Owner: Canadian Broadcasting Corp.
Editorial: 430 University Ave, Charlottetown, Prince Edward Island C1A 4N6 **Tel:** 1 902 629-6400.
Web site: http://www.cbc.ca/pei
Profile: CBCT-FM is a non-commercial station owned by Canadian Broadcasting Corp. The format of the station is news and talk programming. CBCT-FM broadcasts to the Charlottetown, Prince Edward Island area at 96.1 FM.
FM RADIO STATION

CBCV-FM
83090
Owner: Canadian Broadcasting Corp.
Editorial: 780 Kings Rd, Victoria, British Columbia V8T 5A2 **Tel:** 1 222 111-3333.
Email: victoria@cbc.ca
Web site: http://www.cbc.ca/bc
Profile: CBCV-FM is a non-commercial station owned by the Canadian Broadcasting Corp. The format of the station is news and talk. CBCV-FM broadcasts to the Victoria, British Columbia area at 90.5 FM.
FM RADIO STATION

CBCX-FM
612739
Owner: Société Radio-Canada
Editorial: 1724 Westmount Blvd NW, Calgary, Alberta T2N 3G7 **Tel:** 1 403 521-6000.
Email: cbcx@radio-canada.ca
Web site: http://www.radio-canada.ca/espace_musique
Profile: CBCX-FM is a non-commercial station owned by Société Radio-Canada. The format for the station is classical, jazz, world, and folk music. CBCX-FM broadcasts to the Calgary, AB area at 89.7 FM.
FM RADIO STATION

CBDB-AM
610587
Owner: Canadian Broadcasting Corp.
Editorial: 3103 3rd Ave, Whitehorse, Yukon Territory Y1A 1E5 **Tel:** 1 867 668-8400.
Email: cbcnorth@cbc.ca
Web site: http://www.cbc.ca/north
Profile: CBDB-AM is a non-commercial radio station owned by the Canadian Broadcasting Corp. The station serves as the CBC Radio One affiliate for adult listeners throughout Watson Lake, Yukon Territory, and airs locally on 990 AM.
AM RADIO STATION

CBDC-AM
610609
Owner: Canadian Broadcasting Corp.
Editorial: 3103 3rd Ave, Whitehorse, Yukon Territory Y1A 1E5 **Tel:** 1 867 668-8400.
Email: cbcnorth@cbc.ca
Web site: http://www.cbc.ca/north
Profile: CBDC-AM is a non-commercial radio station owned by the Canadian Broadcasting Corp. The station serves as the CBC Radio One affiliate for adult listeners throughout Mayo, Yukon Territory, and airs locally on 1230 AM.
AM RADIO STATION

CBDD-AM
610613
Owner: Canadian Broadcasting Corp.
Editorial: 3103 3rd Ave, Whitehorse, Yukon Territory Y1A 1E5 **Tel:** 1 867 668-8400.
Email: cbcnorth@cbc.ca
Web site: http://www.cbc.ca/north
Profile: CBDD-AM is a non-commercial radio station owned by the Canadian Broadcasting Corp. The station serves as the CBC Radio One affiliate for adult listeners throughout Elsa, Yukon Territory, and airs locally on 560 AM.
AM RADIO STATION

CBDF-FM
610640
Owner: Canadian Broadcasting Corp.
Editorial: 3103 3rd Ave, Whitehorse, Yukon Territory Y1A 1E5 **Tel:** 1 867 668-8400.
Email: cbcnorth@cbc.ca
Web site: http://www.cbc.ca/north
Profile: CBDF-FM is a non-commercial radio station owned by the Canadian Broadcasting Corp. The station serves as the CBC Radio One affiliate for adult listeners throughout Haines Junction, Yukon Territory, and airs locally on 103.5 FM.
FM RADIO STATION

CBD-FM
47641
Owner: Canadian Broadcasting Corp.
Editorial: 560 Main St, Saint John, New Brunswick E2K 1J5 **Tel:** 1 506 632-7745.
Web site: http://www.cbc.ca/nb
Profile: CBD-FM is a non-commercial station owned by Canadian Broadcasting Corp. The format of the

station is news and talk. CBD-FM broadcasts to the Saint John, Canada area at 91.3 FM.
FM RADIO STATION

CBDK-AM
610617
Owner: Canadian Broadcasting Corp.
Editorial: 3103 3rd Ave, Whitehorse, Yukon Territory Y1A 1E5 **Tel:** 1 867 668-8400.
Email: cbcnorth@cbc.ca
Web site: http://www.cbc.ca/north
Profile: CBDK-AM is a non-commercial radio station owned by the Canadian Broadcasting Corp. The station serves as the CBC Radio One affiliate for adult listeners throughout Teslin, Yukon Territory, and airs locally on 940 AM.
AM RADIO STATION

CBDL-FM
610638
Owner: Canadian Broadcasting Corp.
Editorial: 3103 3rd Ave, Whitehorse, Yukon Territory Y1A 1E5 **Tel:** 1 867 668-8400.
Email: cbcnorth@cbc.ca
Web site: http://www.cbc.ca/north
Profile: CBDL-FM is a non-commercial radio station owned by the Canadian Broadcasting Corp. The station serves as the CBC Radio One affiliate for adult listeners throughout Destruction Bay and Burwash Landing, Yukon Territory, and airs locally on 105.1 FM.
FM RADIO STATION

CBDM-AM
610620
Owner: Canadian Broadcasting Corp.
Editorial: 3103 3rd Ave, Whitehorse, Yukon Territory Y1A 1E5 **Tel:** 1 867 668-8400.
Email: cbcnorth@cbc.ca
Web site: http://www.cbc.ca/north
Profile: CBDM-AM is a non-commercial radio station owned by the Canadian Broadcasting Corp. The station serves as the CBC Radio One affiliate for adult listeners throughout Beaver Creek, Yukon Territory, and airs locally on 690 AM.
AM RADIO STATION

CBDN-AM
610642
Owner: Canadian Broadcasting Corp.
Editorial: 3103 3rd Ave, Whitehorse, Yukon Territory Y1A 1E5 **Tel:** 1 867 668-8400.
Email: cbcnorth@cbc.ca
Web site: http://www.cbc.ca/north
Profile: CBDN-AM is a non-commercial radio station owned by the Canadian Broadcasting Corp. The station serves as the CBC Radio One affiliate for adult listeners throughout Dawson City, Yukon Territory, and airs locally on 560 AM.
AM RADIO STATION

CBDQ-FM
47389
Owner: Canadian Broadcasting Corp.
Editorial: 500 Vanier, Labrador City, Newfoundland A2V 2W7 **Tel:** 1 709 944-3616.
Web site: http://www.cbc.ca/nl
Profile: CBDQ-FM is a non-commercial station owned by Canadian Broadcasting Corp. The target audience of the station is adults, ages 18 to 64. CBDQ-FM broadcasts to the Labrador City, Newfoundland area at 96.3 FM.
FM RADIO STATION

CBDX-AM
610625
Owner: Canadian Broadcasting Corp.
Editorial: 3103 3rd Ave, Whitehorse, Yukon Territory Y1A 1E5 **Tel:** 1 867 668-8400.
Email: cbcnorth@cbc.ca
Web site: http://www.cbc.ca/north
Profile: CBDX-AM is a non-commercial radio station owned by the Canadian Broadcasting Corp. The station serves as the CBC Radio One affiliate for adult listeners throughout Swift River, Yukon Territory, and airs locally on 970 AM.
AM RADIO STATION

CBEF-AM
47350
Owner: Société Radio-Canada
Editorial: 825 promenade Riverside West, Windsor, Ontario N9A 5K9 **Tel:** 1 416 205-2887.
Email: tjontario@radio-canada.ca
Web site: http://www.radio-canada.ca/regions/ontario/index.shtml
Profile: CBEF-AM is a commercial station owned by Societe Radio-Canada. The format of the station is variety. CBEF-FM broadcasts to Windsor, Ontario at 540 AM. CBEF-AM plays 33 hours of Franco-Ontarian programming from CJBC-AM in Toronto; all other programming comes from the Radio-Canada headquarters in Montreal.
AM RADIO STATION

CBE-FM
47633
Owner: Canadian Broadcasting Corp.
Editorial: 825 Riverside Drive West, Windsor, Ontario N9A 5K9 **Tel:** 1 519 255-3411.
Email: windsor@cbc.ca
Web site: http://www.cbc.ca/windsor
FM RADIO STATION

CBEG-FM
47692
Owner: Canadian Broadcasting Corp.
Editorial: 825 Riverside Drive West, Windsor, Ontario N9A5K9 **Tel:** 1 519 255-3411.
Email: windsor@cbc.ca
Web site: http://www.cbc.ca/windsor
FM RADIO STATION

CBEW-FM
47366
Owner: Canadian Broadcasting Corp.
Editorial: 825 Riverside Drive West, Windsor, Ontario N9A 5K9 **Tel:** 1 519 255-3411.
Email: windsor@cbc.ca
Web site: http://www.cbc.ca/windsor
Profile: CBEW-FM is a non-commercial station owned by the Canadian Broadcasting Corporation. The format of the station is news. CBEW-FM broadcasts to the Windsor, Ontario area at 97.5 FM.
FM RADIO STATION

CBF-FM (Ici Radio-Canada Première Montréal 95.1)
47616
Owner: Société Radio-Canada
Editorial: 1400 Boul Rene-Levesque E, Montreal, Quebec H2L 2M2- **Tel:** 1 514 597-6000.
Web site: http://ici.radio-canada.ca/grandmontreal
Profile: CBF-FM is a non-commercial station owned by Société Radio-Canada. The format of the station is news and talk. CBF-FM broadcasts to the Montreal area at 95.1 FM. CBF-FM has a transmitter of 5,460 watts broadcasting to the Saint-Donat, Quebec area at 89.7 FM.
FM RADIO STATION

CBF-FM-10
612029
Owner: Société Radio-Canada
Editorial: 1335, rue King Ouest, Sherbrooke, Quebec J1J 2B8 **Tel:** 1 819 620-0000.
Web site: http://www.radio-canada.ca/regions/estrie/index.shtml
Profile: CBF-FM-10 is a French-language non-commercial station owned by Société Radio-Canada. The format for the station is news and talk. CBF-FM-10 broadcasts to the Sherbrooke area at 101.1 FM.
FM RADIO STATION

CBF-FM-8
658984
Owner: Société Radio-Canada
Editorial: 225 Rue des Forges Bureau 101, Trois-Rivieres, Quebec G9A 2G7 **Tel:** 1 819 694-0114.
Email: tjmauricie@radio-canada.ca
Web site: http://www.radio-canada.ca/regions/mauricie
Profile: CBF-FM-8 is a public station owned by Société Radio-Canada. The format for the station is news and talk. CBF-FM-8 broadcasts to the Mauricie - Centre-du-Québec area at 96.5 FM.
FM RADIO STATION

CBFX-FM
83162
Owner: Société Radio-Canada
Editorial: 1400 boul Rene-Levesque Est, Montreal, Quebec H2L 2M2 **Tel:** 1 514 597-6000.
Web site: http://radio-canada.ca/espace_musique
Profile: CBFX-FM is a non-commercial station owned by Societe Radio-Canada. The format of the station is variety. CBFX-FM broadcasts to the Montreal area at 100.7 FM.
FM RADIO STATION

CBGA-FM
47360
Owner: Société Radio-Canada
Editorial: 303 Av Saint-Jerôme, Matane, Quebec G4W 3A8 **Tel:** 1 418 566-2349.
Email: nouvelles.matane@radio-canada.ca
Web site: http://ici.radio-canada.ca/gaspesie-iles-de-la-madeleine
Profile: CBGA-FM is a non-commercial station owned by Societe Radio-Canada. The format of the station is news and talk. CBGA-FM broadcasts to Matane, Quebec at 102.1 FM.
FM RADIO STATION

CBG-AM
47305
Owner: Canadian Broadcasting Corp.
Editorial: 98 Sullivan Ave, Gander, Newfoundland A1V 1S2 **Tel:** 1 709 256-4311.
Web site: http://www.cbc.ca/nl
Profile: CBG-AM is a non-commercial station owned by Canadian Broadcasting Corp. The format of the station is news and talk. The target audience of the station is adults, ages 18 to 64. CBDQ-FM broadcasts to the Gander, Newfoundland and Labrador area at 1400 AM.
AM RADIO STATION

CBHA-FM (CBC Radio One Halifax)
47684
Owner: Canadian Broadcasting Corp.
Editorial: 6940 Mumford Road, Suite 100, Halifax, Nova Scotia B3L 0B7 **Tel:** 1 902 420-4100.
Email: cbcns@cbc.ca
Web site: http://www.cbc.ca/news/canada/nova-scotia
Profile: CBHA-FM is a non-commercial radio station owned by the Canadian Broadcasting Corp. The format of the station news and information. The station broadcasts to the Halifax, NS area at 90.5 FM.
FM RADIO STATION

CBH-FM
47552
Owner: Canadian Broadcasting Corp.
Editorial: 5600 Sackville St, Halifax, Nova Scotia B3J 1L2 **Tel:** 1 902 420-8311.
Web site: http://www.cbc.ca/ns
Profile: CBH-FM is a non-commercial station owned by the Canadian Broadcasting Corp. The format of the station is classical music. CBH-FM broadcasts to the Halifax, Nova Scotia area at 102.7 FM.
FM RADIO STATION

CBI-AM
47196
Owner: Canadian Broadcasting Corp.
Editorial: 500 George St Suite 120, Sydney, Nova Scotia B1P 1K6 **Tel:** 1 902 563-4100.
Email: radionewscb@cbc.ca

Web site: http://www.cbc.ca/ns
Profile: CBI-AM is a non-commercial station owned by the Canadian Broadcasting Corp. The format of the station is news and talk. CBI-AM broadcasts to the Sydney, Nova Scotia area on 1140 AM.
AM RADIO STATION

CBI-FM 47558
Owner: Canadian Broadcasting Corp.
Editorial: 500 George Street, Suite 120, Sydney, Nova Scotia B1P 1K6 **Tel:** 1 902 563-4100.
Email: radionews@sydney.cbc.ca
Web site: http://www.cbc.ca/ns
Profile: CBI-FM is a non-commercial station owned by the Canadian Broadcasting Corp. The format of the station is variety, a combination of news, talk and regional music programming. CBI-FM broadcasts to the Sydney, Nova Scotia area area at 105.1 FM.
FM RADIO STATION

CBJ (ICI Radio-Canada FM 93.7) 47548
Owner: Société Radio-Canada
Editorial: 500 Rue des Sagueneens, Chicoutimi, Quebec G7H 6N4 **Tel:** 1 418 696-6666.
Email: saguenay@radio-canada.ca
Web site: http://www.radio-canada.ca/regions/saguenay-lac/index.shtml
Profile: CBJ-FM is a non-commercial station owned by Société Radio-Canada. The format of the station is news and talk. CBJ-FM broadcasts to Chicoutimi, Quebec at 93.7 FM.
FM RADIO STATION

CBJX-FM 83160
Owner: Société Radio-Canada
Editorial: 500 rue des Sagueneens, Chicoutimi, Quebec G7H 6N4 **Tel:** 1 418 696-6600.
Web site: http://www.radio-canada.ca/espace_musique
Profile: CBJX-FM is a non-commercial station owned by Societe Radio-Canada. The format of the station is classical and jazz. CBJX-FM broadcasts to Chicoutimi, Quebec at 100.9 FM.
FM RADIO STATION

CBK-AM 47210
Owner: Canadian Broadcasting Corp.
Editorial: 2440 Broad St, Regina, Saskatchewan S4P 0A5 **Tel:** 1 306 347-9691.
Email: sasknews@cbc.ca
Web site: http://www.cbc.ca/news/canada/saskatchewan
Profile: CBK-AM is a non-commercial station owned by the Canadian Broadcasting Corp. The format of the station is variety. The station broadcasts to the Regina, Saskatchewan area at 540 AM.
AM RADIO STATION

CBKF-FM 47486
Owner: Société Radio-Canada
Editorial: 2440 Broad St, Regina, Saskatchewan S4P 0A5 **Tel:** 1 306 347-9540.
Email: saskatchewan@radio-canada.ca
Web site: http://ici.radio-canada.ca/saskatchewan
Profile: CBKF-FM is a non-commercial station owned by Societe Radio-Canada. The format of the station is variety. CBKF-FM broadcasts to the Regina, Saskatchewan area at 97.7 FM.
FM RADIO STATION

CBK-FM 47655
Owner: Canadian Broadcasting Corp.
Editorial: 2440 Broad St, Regina, Saskatchewan S4P 0A5 **Tel:** 1 306 347-9540.
Web site: http://www.cbc.ca/sask
Profile: CBK-FM is a non-commercial station owned by the Canadian Broadcasting Corporation. The format of the station is news and talk. CBK-FM broadcasts to the Regina, Saskatchewan area at 102.5 FM.
FM RADIO STATION

CBKS-FM 238305
Owner: Canadian Broadcasting Corp.
Editorial: 2440 Broad St, Regina, Saskatchewan S4P 0A5 **Tel:** 1 306 956-7400.
Email: sasknews@cbc.ca
Web site: http://www.cbc.ca/sask
Profile: CBKS-FM is a non-commercial station owned by the Canadian Broadcasting Corp. The format of the station is variety including classical music. CKBS-FM broadcasts throughout the Saskatoon, Saskatchewan area at 105.5 FM.
FM RADIO STATION

CBLA-FM 83092
Owner: Canadian Broadcasting Corp.
Editorial: 205 Wellington St W, Toronto, Ontario M5V 3G7 **Tel:** 1 416 205-3311.
Web site: http://www.cbc.ca/toronto
Profile: CBLA-FM is a non-commercial station owned by the Canadian Broadcasting Corp. The format of the station is news and talk. CBLA-FM broadcasts to the Toronto area at 99.1 FM.
FM RADIO STATION

CBL-FM 47528
Owner: Canadian Broadcasting Corp.
Editorial: 205 Wellington St W, Toronto, Ontario M5V 3G7 **Tel:** 1 416 205-3311.
Web site: http://www.cbc.ca/radiotwo
FM RADIO STATION

CBLL-FM 47632
Owner: Canadian Broadcasting Corp.
Editorial: 205 Wellington St W, Room 1A-101B, Toronto, Ontario M5V 3G7 **Tel:** 1 416 205-3311.
Web site: http://www.cbc.ca/toronto
FM RADIO STATION

CBME-FM 47683
Owner: Canadian Broadcasting Corp.
Editorial: 1400 Boul Rene-Levesque E, Montreal, Quebec H2L 2M2 **Tel:** 1 514 597-6000.
Web site: http://www.cbc.ca/montreal
Profile: CBME-FM is a non-commercial station owned by the Canadian Broadcasting Corp. The format for the station is news and talk. CBME-FM broadcasts to the Montreal area at 88.5 FM.
FM RADIO STATION

CBM-FM 47578
Owner: Canadian Broadcasting Corp.
Editorial: 1400 Rene Levesque E, Montreal, Quebec H2L 2M2 **Tel:** 1 514 597-6665.
Web site: http://www.cbc.ca/radio2
FM RADIO STATION

CBMR-FM 47680
Owner: Canadian Broadcasting Corp.
Tel: 1 416 205-3311.
Web site: http://www.radio-canada.ca/radio
FM RADIO STATION

CBN-AM 47318
Owner: Canadian Broadcasting Corp.
Editorial: 95 University Ave, St. John's, Newfoundland A1B 1Z4 **Tel:** 1 709 576-5000.
Web site: http://www.cbc.ca/nl
Profile: CBN-AM is a non-commercial station owned by the Canadian Broadcasting Corp. The format of the station is news and talk. CBN-AM broadcasts to the Saint John's, NL area at 640 AM.
AM RADIO STATION

CBN-FM 47634
Owner: Canadian Broadcasting Corp.
Editorial: 342-44 Duckworth St, St. John's, Newfoundland A1C 1H5 **Tel:** 1 709 576-5225.
Web site: http://www.cbc.ca/nl/
Profile: CBN-FM is a commercial station owned by Canadian Broadcasting Corp. The format of the station is variety. CBN-FM broadcasts to St. John's, Newfoundland at 106.9 FM.
FM RADIO STATION

CBOF-FM 152404
Owner: CBC/ Radio-Canada
Editorial: 181 Queen St, Ottawa, Ontario K1P 1K9
Tel: 1 613 288-6000.
Email: nouvelles.ottawagatineau@radio-canada.ca
Web site: http://www.radio-canada.ca/ottawa-gatineau
Profile: CBOF-FM is a non-commercial station owned by CBC/ Radio-Canada. The format of the station is news and talk. CBOF-FM broadcasts to the Ottawa, Ontario area at 90.7 FM.
FM RADIO STATION

CBO-FM (CBC Radio One Ottawa 91.5) 47516
Owner: Canadian Broadcasting Corp.
Editorial: 181 Queen St, Ottawa, Ontario K1P 1K9
Tel: 1 613 288-6445.
Email: cbcnewsottawa@cbc.ca
Web site: http://www.cbc.ca/ottawa
Profile: CBO-FM is a non-commercial station owned by Canadian Broadcasting Corp. The format of the station is news and talk. CBO-FM broadcasts to the Ottawa, Ontario area at 91.5 FM.
FM RADIO STATION

CBON-FM (Ici Radio-Canada Première Ontario) 47620
Owner: Société Radio-Canada
Editorial: 15 MacKenzie St, Sudbury, Ontario P3C 4Y1 **Tel:** 1 705 688-3200.
Email: infocbon@radio-canada.ca
Web site: http://ici.radio-canada.ca/ontario/nordontario
Profile: CBON-FM est une station non-commerciale, une propriété de Radio-Canada. Le contenu présentée par la station est l'actualité et des discussions. CBON-FM est diffusée à Sudbury, en Ontario au 98.1 FM. Radio-Canada a plus de 20 tours qui retransmet le signal de CBON-FM à travers le Nord de l'Ontario.

CBON-FM is a non-commercial station owned by Societe Radio-Canada. The format of the station is news and talk. CBON-FM broadcasts to the Sudbury, Ontario area at 98.1 FM. Radio-Canada has over 20 towers that retransmit CBON-FM's signal across northern Ontario.
FM RADIO STATION

CBOQ-FM (CBC Radio 2 Ottawa 103.3) 47515
Owner: Canadian Broadcasting Corp.
Editorial: 181 Queen St, Ottawa, Ontario K1P 1K9
Tel: 1 613 288-6000.
Email: cbcnewsottawa@cbc.ca
Web site: http://www.cbc.ca/ottawa
Profile: CBOQ-FM is a non-commercial station owned by the Canadian Broadcasting Corp. The format of the station is variety. CBOQ-FM broadcasts to the Ottawa, Ontario area at 103.3 FM.
FM RADIO STATION

CBQF-AM 610628
Owner: Canadian Broadcasting Corp.
Editorial: 3103 3rd Ave, Whitehorse, Yukon Territory Y1A 1E5 **Tel:** 1 867 668-8400.
Email: cbcnorth@cbc.ca
Web site: http://www.cbc.ca/north
Profile: CBQF-AM is a non-commercial radio station owned by the Canadian Broadcasting Corp. The station serves as the CBC Radio One affiliate for adult listeners throughout Carmacks, Yukon Territory, and airs locally on 990 AM.
AM RADIO STATION

CBQJ-AM 610630
Owner: Canadian Broadcasting Corp.
Editorial: 3103 3rd Ave, Whitehorse, Yukon Territory Y1A 1E5 **Tel:** 1 867 668-8400.
Email: cbcnorth@cbc.ca
Web site: http://www.cbc.ca/north
Profile: CBQJ-AM is a non-commercial radio station owned by the Canadian Broadcasting Corp. The station serves as the CBC Radio One affiliate for adult listeners throughout Ross River, Yukon Territory, and airs locally on 990 AM.
AM RADIO STATION

CBQK-FM 610634
Owner: Canadian Broadcasting Corp.
Editorial: 3103 3rd Ave, Whitehorse, Yukon Territory Y1A 1E5 **Tel:** 1 867 668-8400.
Email: cbcnorth@cbc.ca
Web site: http://www.cbc.ca/north
Profile: CBQK-FM is a non-commercial radio station owned by the Canadian Broadcasting Corp. The station serves as the CBC Radio One affiliate for adult listeners throughout Faro, Yukon Territory, and airs locally on 105.1 FM.
FM RADIO STATION

CBQL-FM 47679
Owner: Canadian Broadcasting Corp.
Editorial: 213 East Miles St, Thunder Bay, Ontario P7C 1J5 **Tel:** 1 807 625-5000.
Email: thunderbay@cbc.ca
Web site: http://www.cbc.ca/thunderbay
FM RADIO STATION

CBQN-FM 47678
Owner: Canadian Broadcasting Corp.
Editorial: 213 East Miles St, Thunder Bay, Ontario P7C 1J5 **Tel:** 1 807 625-5000.
Email: thunderbay@cbc.ca
Web site: http://www.cbc.ca/thunderbay
FM RADIO STATION

CBQP-FM 47677
Owner: Canadian Broadcasting Corp.
Editorial: 213 East Miles St, Thunder Bay, Ontario P7C 1J5 **Tel:** 1 807 625-5000.
Email: thunderbay@cbc.ca
Web site: http://www.cbc.ca/thunderbay
FM RADIO STATION

CBQR-FM 47877
Owner: Canadian Broadcasting Corp.
Tel: 1 867 645-2244.
Web site: http://cbc.ca/north
Profile: CBQR-FM is a non-commercial station owned by Canadian Broadcasting Corp. The format of the station is variety. CBQR-FM broadcasts to the Rankin Inlet, Northwest Territories area at 105.1 FM.
FM RADIO STATION

CBQS-FM 47676
Owner: Canadian Broadcasting Corp.
Editorial: 213 Miles St East, Thunder Bay, Ontario P7C 1J5 **Tel:** 1 807 625-5000.
Email: thunderbay@cbc.ca
Web site: http://www.cbc.ca/thunderbay
FM RADIO STATION

CBQT-FM 47652
Owner: Canadian Broadcasting Corp.
Editorial: 213 Miles St East, Thunder Bay, Ontario P7C 1J5 **Tel:** 1 807 625-5001.
Email: thunderbay@cbc.ca
Web site: http://www.cbc.ca/thunderbay
Profile: CBQT-FM is a non-commercial station owned by the Canadian Broadcasting Corp. The format of the station is news and talk. CBQT-FM broadcasts to the Thunder Bay, Ontario region at 88.3 FM.
FM RADIO STATION

CBQX-FM 47675
Owner: Canadian Broadcasting Corp.
Editorial: 213 Miles St East, Thunder Bay, Ontario P7C 1J5 **Tel:** 1 807 625-5000.
Email: thunderbay@cbc.ca
Web site: http://www.cbc.ca/thunderbay
FM RADIO STATION

CBR-AM 47166
Owner: Canadian Broadcasting Corp.
Editorial: 1724 Westmount Blvd NW, Calgary, Alberta T2N 3G7 **Tel:** 1 403 521-6000.
Web site: http://www.cbc.ca/calgary
Profile: CBR-AM is a non-commercial radio station owned by the Canadian Broadcasting Corp. The format of the station is news and talk. CBR-AM broadcasts to the Calgary, AB area on 1010 AM.
AM RADIO STATION

CBR-FM 47461
Owner: Canadian Broadcasting Corp.
Editorial: 1724 Westmount Blvd NW, Calgary, Alberta T2N 3G7 **Tel:** 1 403 521-6222.
Web site: http://www.cbc.ca/calgary
FM RADIO STATION

CBRX-FM 83159
Owner: Société Radio-Canada
Editorial: 273 rue St-Jean Baptiste, Rimouski, Quebec G5L 4J8 **Tel:** 1 418 723-2217.
Web site: http://ici.radio-canada.ca/est-du-quebec/
Profile: CBRX-FM is a non-commercial station owned by Societe Radio-Canada. The format of the station is classical, jazz and news. CBRX-FM broadcasts to the Rimouski, Quebec area at 101.5 FM.
FM RADIO STATION

CBSI-FM (ICI Première Côte-Nord) 47604
Owner: Société Radio-Canada
Editorial: 350 Rue Smith Bureau 30, Sept-Iles, Quebec G4R 3X2 **Tel:** 1 418 968-0720.
Email: cbsi@radio-canada.ca
Web site: http://www.radio-canada.ca/cote-nord
Profile: CBSI-FM est la station non-commerciale, propriété de la Société de Radio-Canada. Le style de la station est axée sur les nouvelles et les discussions. CBSI-FM est diffusé à Sept-îles, au Québec à 98.1 FM.

CBSI-FM is a non-commercial station owned by Societe Radio-Canada. The format of the station is news and talk. CBSI-FM broadcasts to the Sept-Iles, Quebec area at 98.1 FM.
FM RADIO STATION

CBT-AM 47303
Owner: Canadian Broadcasting Corp.
Editorial: 2 Harris Ave, Grand Falls-Windsor, Newfoundland A2A 2Y2 **Tel:** 1 709 489-2102.
Email: centralmorning@cbc.ca
Web site: http://www.cbc.ca/nl
Profile: CBT-AM is a non-commercial station owned by Canadian Broadcasting Corp. The format of the station is variety. CBT-AM broadcasts to the Grand Falls-Windsor, Newfoundland and Labrador area at 540 AM.
AM RADIO STATION

CBTK-FM 47650
Owner: Canadian Broadcasting Corp.
Editorial: 243 Lawrence Ave, Kelowna, British Columbia V1Y 6L2 **Tel:** 1 250 861-3781.
Email: daybreakkelowna@cbc.ca
Web site: http://www.cbc.ca/bc
FM RADIO STATION

CBUA-FM 610633
Owner: Canadian Broadcasting Corp.
Editorial: 3103 3rd Ave, Whitehorse, Yukon Territory Y1A 1E5 **Tel:** 1 867 668-8400.
Email: cbcnorth@cbc.ca
Web site: http://www.cbc.ca/north
Profile: CBUA-FM is a non-commercial radio station owned by the Canadian Broadcasting Corp. The station serves as the CBC Radio One affiliate for adult listeners throughout Atlin, British Columbia, and airs locally on 90.1 FM.
FM RADIO STATION

CBU-AM 47150
Owner: Canadian Broadcasting Corp.
Editorial: 700 Hamilton St, Vancouver, British Columbia V6B 2R5 **Tel:** 1 604 662-6000.
Email: cbcnewsvancouver@cbc.ca
Web site: http://www.cbc.ca/bc
Profile: CBU-AM is a non-commercial radio station owned by the Canadian Broadcasting Corp. The format of the station is news and public affairs programming. CBU-AM broadcasts throughout the Vancouver, British Columbia area at 690 AM.
AM RADIO STATION

CBUF-FM (Radio-Canada Première Vancouver) 47449
Owner: Société Radio-Canada
Editorial: 775 Rue Cambie, Vancouver, British Columbia V6B 0L8 **Tel:** 1 604 662-6135.
Web site: http://www.radio-canada.ca/regions/colombie-Britannique
Profile: CBUF-FM is a non-commercial station owned by Societe Radio-Canada. The format of the station is news and talk. CBUF-FM broadcasts to the Vancouver, British Columbia area at 97.7 FM.
FM RADIO STATION

CBU-FM (CBC Radio One Vancouver) 47448
Owner: Canadian Broadcasting Corp.
Editorial: 700 Hamilton St, Vancouver, British Columbia V6B 2R5 **Tel:** 1 604 662-6000.
Web site: http://www.cbc.ca/bc
Profile: CBU-FM is a non-commercial station owned by Canadian Broadcasting Corp. The format of the station is a variety of musical genres, news, and public affairs programming. CBU-FM broadcasts to the Vancouver, British Columbia area at 105.7 FM.
FM RADIO STATION

CBUX-FM 612619
Owner: Société Radio-Canada
Editorial: 700 Hamilton St, PO Box 4600, Vancouver, British Columbia V6B 4A2 **Tel:** 1 604 662-6000.
Web site: http://www.radio-canada.ca/espace_musique
Profile: CBUX-FM is a non-commercial station owned by Société Radio-Canada. the format for the station is classical, jazz, world, and folk music.

CBUX-FM broadcasts to the Vancouver, BC area at 90.9 FM.
FM RADIO STATION

CBVE-FM 47606
Owner: Canadian Broadcasting Corp.
Editorial: 888 St-Jean Street, Quebec, Quebec G1K 9L4 **Tel:** 1 418 691-3620.
Web site: http://www.cbc.ca/montreal
Profile: CBVE-FM is a non-commercial station owned by the Canadian Broadcasting Corporation. The format of the station is talk. CBVE-FM broadcasts to the Quebec area at 104.7 FM.
FM RADIO STATION

CBV-FM 47566
Owner: Société Radio-Canada
Editorial: 888 Rue Saint-Jean, Quebec, Quebec G1R 5H6- **Tel:** 1 418 656-8557.
Email: nouvelles.quebec@radio-canada.ca
Web site: http://ici.radio-canada.ca/quebec
Profile: CBV-FM is a non-commercial radio station owned by Societe Radio-Canada. The format of the station is news and talk. CBV-FM broadcasts to the Quebec area at 106.3 FM.
FM RADIO STATION

CBVX-FM 47774
Owner: Société Radio-Canada
Editorial: 888 Rue Saint-Jean, Quebec, Quebec G1R 5H6- **Tel:** 1 418 654-1341.
Profile: CBVX-FM is a non-commercial station owned by Societe Radio-Canada. The format of the station is classical and jazz. CBVX-FM broadcasts to the Quebec area at 95.3 FM.
FM RADIO STATION

CBW-AM 47253
Owner: Canadian Broadcasting Corp.
Editorial: 541 Portage Ave, Winnipeg, Manitoba R3B 2G1 **Tel:** 1 204 788-3222.
Email: talkback@cbc.ca
Web site: http://www.cbc.ca/manitoba
Profile: CBW-AM is a commercial station owned by the Canadian Broadcasting Corp. The format of the station is news and talk. CBW-AM broadcasts to the Winnipeg, Manitoba area at 990 AM.
AM RADIO STATION

CBW-FM 47499
Owner: Canadian Broadcasting Corp.
Editorial: 541 Portage Ave, Winnipeg, Manitoba R3B 2G1 **Tel:** 1 204 788-3222.
Email: talkback@cbc.ca
Web site: http://www.cbc.ca/manitoba
Profile: CBW-FM is a non-commercial station owned by the Canadian Broadcasting Corp. The format of the station is variety. CBW-FM broadcasts to the Winnipeg, Manitoba area on 98.3 FM
FM RADIO STATION

CBWK-FM 47498
Owner: Canadian Broadcasting Corp.
Editorial: 7 Selkirk Ave, Thompson, Manitoba R8N 0M4 **Tel:** 1 204 677-1682.
Email: north@cbc.ca
Web site: http://www.cbc.ca/manitoba
Profile: CBWK-FM is a non-commercial station owned by the Canadian Broadcasting Corp. The format of the station is news and talk. CBWK-FM broadcasts to Thompson, Manitoba area at 100.9 FM.
FM RADIO STATION

CBX-AM 47174
Owner: Canadian Broadcasting Corp.
Editorial: 123 Edmonton City Centre NW, Edmonton, Alberta T5J 2Y8 **Tel:** 1 780 468-7401.
Email: cbx.edmonton@cbc.ca
Web site: http://www.cbc.ca/edmonton
Profile: CBX-AM is a non-commercial station owned by the Canadian Broadcasting Corp. The format of the station is talk and news. CBX-AM broadcasts to the Edmonton, Alberta area on 740 AM.
AM RADIO STATION

CBX-FM 47471
Owner: Canadian Broadcasting Corp.
Editorial: 123 Edmonton City Centre NW, Edmonton, Alberta T5J 2Y8 **Tel:** 1 780 468-7500.
Email: cbx.edmonton@cbc.ca
Web site: http://www.cbc.ca/edmonton
Profile: CBX-FM is a non-commercial station owned by the Canadian Broadcasting Corp. The station's format is variety. CBX-FM broadcasts to the Edmonton, Alberta area at 90.9 FM.
FM RADIO STATION

CBY-AM 47307
Owner: Canadian Broadcasting Corp.
Editorial: 162 Premier Drive, Corner Brook, Newfoundland A2H 6G1 **Tel:** 1 709 637-1178.
Email: cbrookradio@cbc.ca
Web site: http://www.cbc.ca/nl
Profile: CBY-AM is a non-commercial station owned by Canadian Broadcasting Corp. The format of the station is news and talk. The target audience of the station is adults, ages 18 to 64. CBY-AM broadcasts to the west coast of Newfoundland at 990 AM.
AM RADIO STATION

CBYG-FM 47651
Owner: Canadian Broadcasting Corp.
Editorial: 890 Victoria Street, Prince George, British Columbia V2L 5PI **Tel:** 1 250 562-6701.
Web site: http://www.cbc.ca/bc
FM RADIO STATION

CBZF-FM 47673
Owner: Canadian Broadcasting Corp.
Editorial: 1160 Regent St, Fredericton, New Brunswick E3B 3Z1 **Tel:** 1 506 451-4000.
Web site: http://www.cbc.ca/nb
FM RADIO STATION

CBZ-FM 47597
Owner: Canadian Broadcasting Corp.
Editorial: 1160 Regent St, Fredericton, New Brunswick E3B 5G4 **Tel:** 1 506 451-4000.
Web site: http://www.cbc.ca/nb
FM RADIO STATION

CFAB-AM 47387
Owner: Maritime Broadcasting System Ltd.
Editorial: 169-A Water St, Windsor, Nova Scotia B0N 2T0 **Tel:** 1 902 798-2111.
Email: newsroom@avrnetwork.com
Web site: http://www.avrnetwork.com
Profile: CFAB-AM is a commercial station owned by Maritime Broadcasting System Ltd. The format of the station is classic country. CFAB-AM broadcasts to the Windsor, Nova Scotia area at 1450 AM.
AM RADIO STATION

CFAC-AM 47167
Owner: Rogers Communications Inc.
Editorial: 2723 37 Ave NE, Calgary, Alberta T1Y 5R8-
Tel: 1 403 246-9696.
Email: fan960@rci.rogers.com
Web site: http://www.sportsnet.ca/960
Profile: CFAC-AM is a commercial station owned by Rogers Communications Inc. The format of the station is sports and talk. CFAC-AM broadcasts to the Calgary, Alberta area at 960 AM.
AM RADIO STATION

CFAD-FM 588214
Owner: Salmo Community Radio
Editorial: 6919 Highway 3, Salmo, British Columbia V0G 1Z0 **Tel:** 1 250 357-2299.
Email: info@salmofm.ca
Web site: http://www.salmofm.ca/Home.aspx
Profile: CFAD-FM is a non-commercial station owned by Salmo Community Radio. The format of the station is variety. CFAD-FM broadcasats to the Salmo, British Columbia area at 92.1 FM.
FM RADIO STATION

CFAI-FM 47672
Owner: Coopérative des Montagnes Ltee
Editorial: 165 boulevard Hebert, 7ieme etage, Edmundston, New Brunswick E3V 2S8
Tel: 1 506 737-5060.
Email: radio@cfai.fm
Web site: http://www.cfai.fm
Profile: CFAI-FM is a non-commercial station owned by La Coopérative des Montagnes Ltee. The format of the station is easy listening. CFAI-FM broadcasts in the Edmunston, New Brunswick area at 101.1 FM.
FM RADIO STATION

CFAK-FM 588223
Owner: Université de Sherbrooke(L')
Editorial: 2500 boul. de l'Universite suite G3, Sherbrooke, Quebec J1K 2R1 **Tel:** 1 819 821-8000 62693.
Email: info.cfak883@usherbrooke.ca
Profile: CFAK-FM est la radio étudiante de l'Université de Sherbrooke. La station diffuse sur le 88,3FM. En plus de donner de l'information sur l'Université, les activités et la vie étudiante, la station propose une programmation musical très variée.

CFAK-FM is the student radio station of the Université de Sherbrooke on 88, 3 FM. The station is offering a large variety of music styles besides the normal informations on the University, student activities and lifestyle.
FM RADIO STATION

CFAM-AM 47242
Owner: Golden West Broadcasting Ltd.
Editorial: 200-125 Center Ave, Altona, Manitoba R0G 0B0 **Tel:** 1 204 324-6464.
Email: info@goldenwestradio.com
Web site: http://www.cfamradio.com
Profile: CFAM-AM is a commercial station owned by Golden West Broadcasting Ltd. The format of the station is variety. CFAM-AM broadcasts to the Altona, Manitoba area at 950 AM.
AM RADIO STATION

CFAN-FM 47309
Owner: Maritime Broadcasting System Ltd.
Editorial: 396 Pleasant St, Miramichi, New Brunswick E1V 1X3 **Tel:** 1 506 622-3311.
Email: cfannews@mbsradio.com
Web site: http://www.993theriver.com
Profile: CFAN-FM is a commercial station owned by Maritime Broadcasting System Ltd. The format of the station is hot adult contemporary. CFAN-FM broadcast to Miramichi, New Brunswick at 99.3 FM.
FM RADIO STATION

CFAR-AM 47249
Owner: Arctic Radio (1982) Ltd.
Editorial: 316 Green St, Flin Flon, Manitoba R8A 0H2
Tel: 1 204 687-3469.
Email: cfar@arcticradio.ca
Web site: http://www.arcticradio.ca
Profile: CFAR-AM is a commercial station owned by Arctic Radio (1982) Ltd. The format of the station is adult contemporary music. CFAR-AM broadcasts in the Flin Flon, Manitoba area at 590 AM.
AM RADIO STATION

CFAX-AM 47161
Owner: Bell Media
Editorial: 1420 Broad St, Victoria, British Columbia V8W 2B1 **Tel:** 1 250 386-1070.
Email: cfaxnews@cfax1070.com
Web site: http://www.cfax1070.com
Profile: CFAX-AM is a commercial station owned by Bell Media. The format of the station is news and talk. CFAX-AM broadcasts to the Victoria, British Columbia area at 1070 AM.
AM RADIO STATION

CFBC-AM 47259
Owner: Maritime Broadcasting System Ltd.
Editorial: 226 Union St, Saint John, New Brunswick E2L 1B1 **Tel:** 1 506 658-5100.
Email: mailbag@k100.ca
Web site: http://www.cfbc.am/
Profile: CFBC-AM is a commercial station owned by the Maritime Broadcasting System Ltd. The format of the station is classic country. CFBC-AM broadcasts in the Saint John, New Brunswick area at 930 AM.
AM RADIO STATION

CFBG-FM 47671
Owner: Vista Broadcast Group
Editorial: 50-2 Balls Dr, Bracebridge, Ontario P1L 1T1
Tel: 1 705 645-2218.
Email: moose995.news@moosefm.com
Web site: http://www.moosefm.com/cfbg
Profile: CFBG-FM is a commercial station owned by the Vista Broadcast Group. The format of the station is hot adult contemporary. CFBG-FM broadcasts in the Bracebridge, Ontario area at 99.5 FM.
FM RADIO STATION

CFBI-FM 502451
Owner: Cambridge Bay Communications Society
Tel: 1 867 983-3232.
Profile: CFBI-FM is a non-commercial station owned by the Cambridge Bay Communications Society. The format of the station is variety. CFBI-FM broadcasts to the Cambridge Bay, Nunavut area at 97.7 FM.
FM RADIO STATION

CFBK-FM 47479
Owner: Vista Broadcast Group
Editorial: 7 John Street, Huntsville, Ontario P1H 1H2
Tel: 1 705 789-4461.
Email: moose1055.news@moosefm.ca
Web site: http://moosefm.com/cfbks
Profile: CFBK-FM is a commercial radio station owned by Vista Broadcast Group. The format of the station is adult contemporary music. CFBK-FM broadcasts to the Huntsville, ON area at 105.5 FM.
FM RADIO STATION

CFBL-FM 47857
Owner: Wawatay Native Communications Society
Tel: 1 807 363-1056.
Web site: http://www.wawataynews.ca/radio
Profile: CFLB-FM is a commercial station owned by the Wawatay Native Communications Society. The format is talk and its programming is in English and Oji-Cree, a local language. CFLB-FM broacasts to the Bearskin Lake, Ontario area at 89.9 FM.
FM RADIO STATION

CFBO-FM 546060
Owner: Radio Beausejour Inc.
Editorial: Cornwall 51, Shediac, New Brunswick E4P 8T8 **Tel:** 1 506 532-0080.
Email: cfbo@cfbo.ca
Web site: http://www.cfbo.ca
Profile: CFBO-FM is French-language commercial station owned by Radio Beausejour. The format of the station is adult contemporary. CFBO-FM broadcasts to the Dieppe, New Brunswick area at 90.7 FM.
FM RADIO STATION

CFBR-FM 47473
Owner: Bell Media
Editorial: 18520 Stony Plain Rd NW Suite 100, Edmonton, Alberta T5S 2E2 **Tel:** 1 780 486-2800.
Web site: http://www.thebearrocks.com
Profile: CFBR-FM is a commercial station owned by Bell Media. The format of the station is rock/album-oriented rock music. CFBR-FM broadcasts in the Edmonton, AB area at 100.3 FM.
FM RADIO STATION

CFBS-FM Blanc-Sablon 89.9 & 93.1 47814
Owner: Radio Blanc-Sablon Inc.
Editorial: 1193 Boul Docteur Camille Marcoux, Lourdes-de-Blanc-Sablon, Quebec G0G 1W0
Tel: 1 418 461-2445.
Email: cfbs@globetrotter.net
Web site: http://cfbsradio.net
Profile: CFBS-FM est une station non-commerciale, une propriété de Radio Blanc-Sablon Inc. Le genre musical de la station est variée. CBFS-FM est diffusé à Lourdes-de-Blanc-Sablon, au Québec aux fréquences 89.9 FM et 93.1 FM.

CFBS-FM is a non-commercial station owned by Radio Blanc-Sablon Inc. The format for the station is variety. CFBS-FM broadcasts to the Lourdes-de-Blanc-Sablon, Quebec area at 89.9 FM and 93.1 FM.
FM RADIO STATION

CFBT-FM 81208
Owner: Bell Media
Editorial: 500-969 Robson St 500, Vancouver, British Columbia V6Z 1X5 **Tel:** 1 604 871-9000.
Email: heydj@thebeat.com
Web site: http://www.iheartradio.ca/virginradio/vancouver
Profile: CFBT-FM is a commercial station owned by Bell Media. The format of the station is rhythmic Top 40/CHR. CFBT-FM broadcasts to the Vancouver, British Columbia area at 94.5 FM.
FM RADIO STATION

CFBU-FM 47821
Owner: Brock University Student Radio
Editorial: 30 Ontario St., St Catharines, Ontario L2R 7M3 **Tel:** 1 905 346-2644.
Email: pd@cfbu.ca
Web site: http://www.cfbu.ca
Profile: CFBU-FM is a non-commercial station owned by the Brock University Student Radio, Inc. The format of the station is variety. CFBU-FM broadcasts to Saint Catharines, Ontario at 103.7 FM
FM RADIO STATION

CFBV-AM (The Moose Smithers) 47143
Owner: Vista Broadcast Group Inc.
Editorial: 1139 Queen St, Smithers, British Columbia V0J 2N0 **Tel:** 1 250 847-2521.
Email: pgnews@vistaradio.ca
Web site: http://www.mybulkleylakesnow.com/
Profile: CFBV-AM (The Moose Smithers) is a commercial station owned by Vista Broadcast Group Inc. It's a local Radio station playing the Bulkley Valley and Lakes Biggest Variety! CFBV-AM broadcasts to Smithers, British Columbia at 870 AM.
AM RADIO STATION

CFBW-FM 281688
Owner: Bluewater Community Radio Inc.
Editorial: 267 10th Street, Hanover, Ontario N4N 1P1
Tel: 1 519 364-0200.
Email: bluewaterradio@on.aibn.com
Web site: http://www.bluewaterradio.ca
FM RADIO STATION

CFBX-FM 588192
Owner: Kamloops Campus/Community Radio Society
Editorial: 900 McGill Rd, House 8, Kamloops, British Columbia V2C 5N3 **Tel:** 1 250 377-3988.
Email: radio@tru.ca
Web site: http://www.thex.ca
Profile: CFBX-FM is a non-commercial station owned by Kamloops Campus/Community Radio Society. The format of the station is variety. CFBX-FM broadcasts to the Kamloops, British Columbia area at 92.5 FM.
FM RADIO STATION

CFCA-FM 47495
Owner: Bell Media
Editorial: 255 King St N Suite 207, Waterloo, Ontario N2J 4V2 **Tel:** 1 519 884-4470.
Email: news@koolfm.com
Web site: http://kitchener.virginradio.ca/
Profile: CFCA-FM is a commercial station owned by Bell Media. The format of the station is Top 40/CHR. CFCA-FM broadcasts to Waterloo, Ontario at 105.3 FM.
FM RADIO STATION

CFCB-AM (570 VOCM) 47306
Owner: Newfoundland Capital Corporation Limited
Editorial: 345 O'Connell Dr, Corner Brook, Newfoundland A2H 7V3 **Tel:** 1 709 634-4570.
Email: onair@cfcbradio.com
Web site: http://vocm.com/network-stations/cfcb
Profile: CFCB-AM is a commercial station owned by Newfoundland Capital Corporation Limited. The format of the station is classic country. CFCB-AM broadcasts to the Corner Brook, Newfoundland area at 570 AM.
AM RADIO STATION

CFCH-FM 588295
Owner: Chase and District Community Radio Society
Editorial: 320 Shepherd St, Chase, British Columbia V0E 1M0 **Tel:** 1 250 679-2800.
Profile: CFCH-FM is a non-commercial station owned by Chase and District Community Radio Society. The format is a variety of eclectic music and

programming. CFCH-FM broadcasts to the Chase, British Columbia area at 103.5 FM.
FM RADIO STATION

CFCO-AM 47200
Owner: Blackburn Radio Inc.
Editorial: 117 Keil Drive South, Chatham, Ontario N7M 3H3 **Tel:** 1 519 354-2200.
Email: info@country929.com
Web site: http://www.country929.com
Profile: CFCO-AM is a commercial radio station owned by Blackburn Radio Inc. The format of the station is contemporary country. CFCO-AM broadcasts to the Chatham, Ontario area at 630 AM.
AM RADIO STATION

CFCO-FM 238308
Owner: Blackburn Radio Inc.
Editorial: 117 Keil Drive South, Chatham, Ontario N7M 3H3 **Tel:** 1 519 352-3000.
Email: info@country929.com
Web site: http://www.630cfco.com
Profile: CFCO-FM is a commercial station owned by Blackburn Radio Inc. The format of the station is contemporary ountry. CFCO-FM broadcasts to the Chatham, Ontario area at 92.9 FM.
FM RADIO STATION

CFCP-FM (98.9 The GOAT FM) 47110
Owner: Vista Broadcast Group Inc.
Editorial: 201A-910 Fitzgerald Ave 201A, Courtenay, British Columbia V9N 2R5 **Tel:** 1 250 334-2421.
Web site: http://www.mycomoxvalleynow.com
Profile: CFCP-FM (98.9 The GOAT FM) is a commercial station owned by Vista Broadcast Group Inc. The format of the station is classic rock. CFCP-FM broadcasts to Courtenay, British Columbia at 98.9 FM.
FM RADIO STATION

CFCR-FM 47670
Owner: Community Radio Society of Saskatoon
Editorial: 267 3rd Ave South, Saskatoon, Saskatchewan S7K 2H4 **Tel:** 1 306 664-6678.
Email: cfcr@cfcr.ca
Web site: http://www.cfcr.ca
Profile: CFCR-FM is a non-commercial station owned by Community Radio Society of Saskatoon. The format for the station is variety. CFCR-FM broadcasts to the Saskatoon, Saskatchewan area at 90.5 FM.
FM RADIO STATION

CFCV-FM 47811
Owner: Newfoundland Capital Corporation Limited
Editorial: 345 O'Connell Dr, Corner Brook, Newfoundland AZH 7E5 **Tel:** 1 709 634-4570.
FM RADIO STATION

CFCW-AM 47175
Owner: Newfoundland Capital Corporation Limited
Editorial: 2394 West Edmonton Mall, 8882-170 Street, Edmonton, Alberta T5T 4M2 **Tel:** 1 780 468-3939.
Email: news@cfcw.com
Web site: http://www.cfcw.com
Profile: CFCW-AM is a commercial station owned by Newfoundland Capital Corporation Limited. The format of the station is country music. CFCW-AM broadcasts to the Edmonton, Alberta area at 790 AM.
AM RADIO STATION

CFCW-FM 396995
Owner: Newfoundland Capital Corporation Limited
Editorial: 5708-48 Ave, Camrose, Alberta T4V 0K1
Tel: 1 780 672-8255.
Email: feedback@981camfm.com
Web site: http://www.981camfm.com
Profile: CFCW-FM is a commercial station owned by Newfoundland Capital Corporation Limited. The format for the station is classic hits. CFCW-FM broadcasts to the Camrose, Alberta area at 98.1 FM.
FM RADIO STATION

CFCY-FM 47369
Owner: Maritime Broadcasting System Ltd.
Editorial: 5 Prince St, Charlottetown, Prince Edward Island C1A 4P4 **Tel:** 1 902 892-1066.
Email: news@cfcy.pe.ca
Web site: http://www.cfcy.fm
Profile: CFCY-FM is a commercial station owned by Maritime Broadcasting System Ltd. The format of the station is classic country music. CFCY-FM broadcasts to the Charlottetown, Prince Edward Island area at 95.1 FM.
FM RADIO STATION

CFDA-FM 47871
Owner: Réseau des Appalaches
Editorial: 55 rue St-Jean Baptiste, Victoriaville, Quebec G6P 4E1 **Tel:** 1 819 752-5545.
Email: plaisir1019@attractionradio.ca
Web site: http://plaisir1019.com/
Profile: CFDA-FM is a commercial station owned by Réseau des Appalaches. The format of the station is hot adult contemporary. CFDA-FM broadcasts to the Victoriaville, Quebec area at 101.9 FM.
FM RADIO STATION

CFDL-FM 47686
Owner: Newfoundland Capital Corporation Limited
Editorial: 345 O'Connell Dr, Corner Brook, Newfoundland A2H 7E5 **Tel:** 1 709 634-4570.
Profile: CFDL-FM is a commercial station owned by Newfoundland Capital Corporation Limited. The format of the station is classic and contemporary country. CFDL-FM broadcasts to the Corner Brook, Newfoundland area at 97.9 FM.
FM RADIO STATION

CFDM-FM 586193
Owner: Flying Dust First Nation
Tel: 1 306 236-1445.
Email: cfdmradio@hotmail.com
Web site: http://cfdm.sasktelwebhosting.com
Profile: CFDM-FM is a non-commercial station owned by Flying Dust First Nation. The format of the station is variety of community radio. CFDM-FM broadcasts to Meadow Lake, Saskatchewan and surrounding areas at 105.7 FM.
FM RADIO STATION

CFDV-FM 394596
Owner: Jim Pattison Broadcast Group(The)
Editorial: 2840 Brenner Avenue, 2nd Floor, Red Deer, Alberta T4R 1M9 **Tel:** 1 403 343-7105.
Email: rock@1067thedrive.fm
Web site: http://www.1067thedrive.fm
Profile: CFDV-FM is a commercial station owned by The Jim Pattison Broadcast Group. The format is classic rock. CFDV-FM broadcasts to the Red Deer, Alberta area at 106.7 FM.
FM RADIO STATION

CFEI-FM (Boom FM 106.5) 47696
Owner: Bell Media
Editorial: 2596 Boul Casavant O, Saint-Hyacinthe, Quebec J2S 7R8 **Tel:** 1 450 774-6486.
Email: receptioncfei@astral.com
Web site: http://www.iheartradio.ca/boom/boom-106-5
Profile: CFEI-FM (Boom FM 106.5) est une station de radio commerciale sous la propriété de Bell Media. Cette station vise un public plus mature. CFEI-FM est situé à Saint-Hyacinthe, Québec. CFEI-FM is a commercial station owned by Bell Media. The format of the station is oldies. CFEI-FM broadcasts to the Saint-Hyacinthe, Quebec area at 106.5 FM.
FM RADIO STATION

CFEL-FM (BLVD 102.1 Québec) 47605
Owner: LeClerc Communications
Editorial: 505-815 Boul Lebourgneuf 505, Quebec, Quebec G2J 0C1 **Tel:** 1 418 682-8433.
Email: nouvelles@blvd.fm
Web site: http://www.blvd.fm
Profile: CFEL-FM is a commercial station owned by LeClerc Communications. The format of the station is hot adult contemporary. CFEL-FM broadcasts to the Quebec, Quebec area at 102.1 FM.
FM RADIO STATION

CFEP-FM 503960
Owner: Seaside Broadcasting Org.
Editorial: 1540 Shore Rd, Eastern Passage, Nova Scotia b3g 1m5 **Tel:** 1 902 469-9231.
Email: wharrett@seasidefm.com
Web site: http://www.seasidefm.com
Profile: CFEP-FM is a commercial station owned by Seaside Broadcasting Org. The format is easy listening. CFEP-FM broadcasts to the Eastern Passage, Nova Scotia area at 105.9 FM.
FM RADIO STATION

CFEX-FM 443593
Owner: Harvard Broadcasting
Editorial: 400, 255-17th Ave SW, Calgary, Alberta T2S 2T8 **Tel:** 1 403 670-0210.
Web site: http://www.x929.ca
Profile: CFEX-FM is a commercial station owned by Harvard Broadcasting. The format of the station is rock alternative. CFEX-FM broadcasts to the Calgary, Alberta area at 92.9 FM.
FM RADIO STATION

CFFB-AM 47103
Owner: Canadian Broadcasting Corp.
Tel: 1 867 979-6100.
Email: nunavut@cbc.ca
Web site: http://cbc.ca/north
Profile: CFFB-AM is a non-commercial station owned by the Canadian Broadcasting Corp. The format of the station is news and talk. CFFB-AM broadcasts to Iqalui, Nunavut at 1230 AM.
AM RADIO STATION

CFFF-FM 47838
Owner: Trent Radio
Editorial: 715 George St North, Peterborough, Ontario K9H 3T2 **Tel:** 1 705 741-4011.
Email: info@trentradio.ca
Web site: http://www.trentradio.ca
Profile: CFFF-FM is a non-commercial station owned by Trent Radio. The format of the station is variety. CFFF-FM broadcasts to the Peterborough, Ontario area at 92.7 FM.
FM RADIO STATION

CFFM-FM 47697
Owner: Vista Broadcast Group Inc.
Editorial: 83 S First Ave, Williams Lake, British Columbia V2G 1H4 **Tel:** 1 250 392-6551.
Email: cariboonews@reachthecariboo.com
Web site: http://www.therushfm.ca
Profile: CFFM-FM is a commercial station owned by the Vista Broadcast Group Inc. The format of the station is adult album alternative. CFFM-FM broadcasts to the Williams Lake, British Columbia area at 97.5 FM.
FM RADIO STATION

CFFR-AM 47169
Owner: Rogers Communications Inc.
Editorial: 2723 37 Ave NE Suite 240, Calgary, Alberta T1Y 5R8 **Tel:** 1 403 291-0000.
Email: news660@rogers.com
Web site: http://www.660news.com
Profile: CFFR-AM is a commercial station owned by Rogers Communications Inc. The format of the station is all news. CFFR-AM broadcasts to the Calgary, Alberta area at 660 AM.
AM RADIO STATION

CFGB-FM 47593
Owner: Canadian Broadcasting Corp.
Editorial: 12 Loring Dr, Goose Bay, Newfoundland A0P 1C0 **Tel:** 1 709 896-2911.
Email: labradormorning@cbc.ca
Web site: http://www.cbc.ca/nl
Profile: CFGB-FM is a non-commercial station owned by Canadian Broadcasting Corp. The format of the station is new and talk. CFGB-FM broadcasts to the Happy Valley - Goose Bay, Newfoundland and Labrador area at 89.5 FM.
FM RADIO STATION

CFGE-FM 245115
Owner: Cogeco
Editorial: 4020, boul de Portland, Sherbrooke, Quebec J1L 2V6 **Tel:** 1 819 822-0937.
Web site: http://www.rythmefm.com/estrie
Profile: CFGE-FM is a commercial station owned by Cogeco. The format of the station is adult contemporary. CFGE-FM broadcasts to the Sherbrooke, Quebec area at 93.7 FM.
FM RADIO STATION

CFGL-FM (Rythme FM 105.7) 83102
Owner: Cogeco
Editorial: 2830 Boul Saint-Martin E Bureau 100, Laval, Quebec H7E 5A1 **Tel:** 1 450 664-4647.
Web site: http://www.rythmefm.com/montreal
Profile: CFGL-FM est une station commerciale appartenant à Cogeco. Le format de la station est adulte contemporain. CFGL-FM est diffusé dans le Grand Montréal au 105.7 FM. En tant que station phare de Rythme FM, plusieurs emissions sont rediffusées dans les autres stations du Québec.

CFGL-FM is a commercial station owned by Cogeco. The format of the station is adult contemporary. CFGL-FM broadcasts to Greater Montreal at 105.7 FM. As the flagship station of Rythme FM, many of the station's programs are syndicated throughout Quebec.
FM RADIO STATION

CFGN-AM 47298
Owner: Newfoundland Capital Corporation Limited
Editorial: 345 O'Connell Dr, Corner Brook, Newfoundland A2H 7V3 **Tel:** 1 709 634-4570.
Profile: CFGN-AM is a commercial station owned by Newfoundland Capital Corporation Limited. The format of the station is classic country. CFLN-AM broadcasts to the Corner Brook, Newfoundland area at 1230 AM.
AM RADIO STATION

CFGO-AM (TSN Radio 1200) 47294
Owner: Bell Media
Editorial: 87 George St, Ottawa, Ontario K1N 9H7-
Tel: 1 613 750-1200.
Web site: http://www.iheartradio.ca/tsn/tsn-ottawa
Profile: CFGO-AM is a commercial station owned by Bell Media. The format of the station is sports. CFGO-AM broadcasts to the Ottawa area at 1200 AM.
AM RADIO STATION

CFGP-FM 47841
Owner: Rogers Communications Inc.
Editorial: #200, 9835 101 Ave SUN Bldg, Grande Prairie, Alberta T8V 5V4 **Tel:** 1 780 539-9700.
Email: comments@rock977.ca
Web site: http://www.rock977.ca
Profile: CFGP-FM is a commercial station owned by Rogers Communications Inc. The format of the station is rock. CFGP-FM broadcasts to the Grande Prairie, Alberta area at 97.7 FM.
FM RADIO STATION

CFGQ-FM 47468
Owner: Corus Entertainment Inc.
Editorial: 170-200 Barclay Parade SW 170, Eau Claire Market, Calgary, Alberta T2P 4R5 **Tel:** 1 403 716-6500.
Web site: http://www.q107fm.ca
Profile: CFGQ-FM is a commercial station owned by Corus Entertainment Inc. The format of the station is classic rock. CFGQ-FM broadcasts in the Calgary, AB area at 107.3 FM.
FM RADIO STATION

CFGT-FM 47328
Owner: RNC Media
Editorial: 460 Rue Sacre-Coeur O Bureau 200, Alma, Quebec G8B 1L9 **Tel:** 1 418 662-6888.
Web site: http://www.alma.planeteradio.ca
Profile: CFGT-FM is a commercial station owned by RNC Media. The format for the station is adult contemporary. CFGT-AM broadcasts to the Alma, Quebec area at 104.5 FM.
FM RADIO STATION

CFGW-FM 83110
Owner: Harvard Broadcasting
Editorial: 120 Smith St E Fl 4TH, Yorkton, Saskatchewan S3N 3V3 **Tel:** 1 306 782-9410.
Email: ykt-reception@harvardbroadcasting.com
Web site: http://www.foxonline.ca
Profile: CFGW-FM is a commercial station owned by Harvard Broadcasting. The format of the station is hot adult contemporary. CFGW-FM broadcasts to the Yorkton, Saskatchewan area at 94.1 FM.
FM RADIO STATION

CFGX-FM 47527
Owner: Blackburn Radio Inc.
Editorial: 1415 London Road, Sarnia, Ontario N7S 1P6 **Tel:** 1 519 542-5500.
Web site: http://www.foxfm.com
Profile: CFGX-FM is a commercial station owned by Blackburn Radio Inc. The format of the station is adult contemporary. CFGX-FM broadcasts to Sarnia, Ontario at 99.9 FM.
FM RADIO STATION

CFHK-FM (Fresh Radio 103.1) 47695
Owner: Corus Entertainment Inc.
Editorial: 380 Wellington St Rm 222, London, Ontario N6A 5B5 **Tel:** 1 519 931-6000.
Web site: http://www.1031freshfm.ca
Profile: CFHK-FM is a commercial station owned by Corus Entertainment Inc. The format of the station is adult contemporary. CFHK-FM broadcasts to London, Ontario at 103.1 FM.
FM RADIO STATION

CFID-FM 382940
Owner: Radio Acton
Editorial: 1185 Rue St. Andre, Acton Vale, Quebec J0H 1A0 **Tel:** 1 450 546-1037.
Email: redaction@radio-acton.com
Web site: http://www.radio-acton.com
Profile: CFID-FM is a non-commercial station owned by Radio Acton. The format of the station is variety. CFID-FM broadcasts to Acton Vale, Quebec at 103.7 FM.
FM RADIO STATION

CFIF-FM (The Moose Iroquois Falls 101.1) 610933
Owner: Vista Broadcast Group
Tel: 1 705 272-6467.
Email: moose981@moosefm.com
Web site: http://www.moosefm.com
Profile: CFIF-FM is a commercial station owned by Vista Broadcast Group. The format of the station is lite rock. CFIF-FM broadcasts in the Iroquois Falls, ON area at 101.1 FM.
FM RADIO STATION

CFIM-FM 47648
Owner: Diffusion Communautaire des Iles Inc.
Editorial: 1172 chemin Laverniere, Etang-du-Nord, Cap-Aux-Meules, Quebec G4T 1R3 **Tel:** 1 418 986-5233.
Email: administration@cfim.ca
Web site: http://www.cfim.ca
Profile: CFIM-FM est une station francophone communautaire détenue par Diffusion communautaire des Iles inc. La station diffuse sur Cap-aux-Meules et sa région sur le 92,7FM.

CFIM-FM is commercial station owned by Diffusion communautaire des Iles inc. CFIM-FM broadcasts to Cap-aux-Meules, Quebec at 92.7 FM.
FM RADIO STATION

CFIN-FM (Passion FM) 47649
Owner: Radio Bellechasse
Editorial: 201 Rue Claude-Bilodeau, Lac-Etchemin, Quebec G0R 1S0 **Tel:** 1 418 625-3737.
Web site: http://passion-fm.com
Profile: CFIN-FM présente une programmation variée s'adressant aux habitants de Lac-Etchemin et des environs sur le 100,5FM.

CFIN-FM is a non-commercial station owned by Radio Bellechasse. The format of the station is variety. CFIN-FM broadcasts to the Lac-Etchemin, Quebec area at 100.5 FM.
FM RADIO STATION

CFIS-FM 553355
Owner: Prince George Community Radio Society
Editorial: 2880 15th Ave, Prince George, British Columbia V2M 1T1 **Tel:** 1 250 563-2347.
Email: mail@cfisfm.com
Web site: http://www.cfisfm.com
Profile: CFIS-FM is a non-commercial station owned by Prince George Community Radio Society. The format of the station is oldies. CFIS-FM broadcasts to the Prince George, BC area at 93.1 FM.
FM RADIO STATION

CFIT-FM 472367
Owner: Golden West
Editorial: 105 main st. north, unit 30, Airdrie, Alberta t4b 0r3 **Tel:** 1 403 217-1061.
Email: airdrienews@goldenwestradio.com
Web site: http://discoverairdrie.com
Profile: CFIT-FM is a commercial station owned by Golden West Broadcasting Ltd. The format is hot adult contemporary. CFIT-FM broadcasts to the Airdrie, Alberta area at 106.1 FM.
FM RADIO STATION

CFIX-FM (Rouge Saguenay 96.9) 47815
Owner: Bell Media
Editorial: 267 Rue Racine E Etage 2E, Chicoutimi, Quebec G7H 1S5 **Tel:** 1 418 543-9797.
Web site: http://saguenay.rougefm.ca
Profile: CFIX-FM est une station commencial de Bell Media. Le format de la station est Top40 CHR. CFIX-FMdiffuse ses émissions à Chicoutimi, Québec (96.9 FM). Le titre d'appel est Rouge FM 96.9. Le public ciblé de la station est les adultes, âgés entre 18 et 64 ans.

CJAB-FM is a commercial station owned by Bell Media. The format of the station is Top 40/CHR. CFIX-FM broadcasts to the Chicoutimi, Quebec area at 96.9 FM. The tagline is Rouge FM 96.9. The target audience of the station is adults, ages 18 to 64. CFIX-FM broadcasts to the Chicoutimi, Quebec area at 96.9 FM.
FM RADIO STATION

CFJB-FM (Rock 95) 47509
Owner: Central Ontario Broadcasting
Editorial: 431 Huronia Rd Unit 10, Barrie, Ontario L4N 9B3 **Tel:** 1 705 725-7304.
Web site: http://www.rock95.com
Profile: CFJB-FM is a commercial station owned by Central Ontario Broadcasting. The format of the station is classic rock. CFJB-FM broadcasts to the Barrie, Ontario area at 95.7 FM.
FM RADIO STATION

CFJL-FM 391057
Owner: Evanov Communications
Editorial: 520 Corydon Ave, Winnipeg, Manitoba R3L 0P1 **Tel:** 1 204 477-1221.
Email: info@jewel101.com
Web site: http://www.jewelradio.com/new/101
Profile: CFJL-FM is a commercial station owned by Evanov Communications. The format of the station is soft AC. CFJL-FM broadcasts to the Winnipeg, Manitoba area at 100.7 FM.
FM RADIO STATION

CFJO-FM 47600
Owner: Réseau des Appalaches
Editorial: 55, rue Saint-Jean-Baptiste, Victoriaville, Quebec G6P 4E1 **Tel:** 1 819 752-2785.
Email: info@o973.com
Web site: http://www.o973.com
Profile: CFJO-FM is a commercial radio station owned by Reseau des Appalaches. The format of the station is adult contemporary. CFJO-FM broadcasts to Victoriaville, Quebec at 97.3 FM.
FM RADIO STATION

CFJR-FM (JR 104.9) 47192
Owner: Bell Media
Editorial: 601 Stewart Blvd, Brockville, Ontario K6V 5T4 **Tel:** 1 613 345-1666.
Web site: http://www.1049jrfm.com
Profile: CFJR-FM is a commercial station owned by Bell Media. The format of the station is adult contemporary. CFJR-FM broadcasts to the Brockville, Ontario area at 104.9 FM.
FM RADIO STATION

CFJU-FM 47793
Owner: Radio Communautaire des Hauts-Plateaux Inc.
Tel: 1 506 235-9000.
Email: cfjufm@rogers.com
Web site: http://www.cfjufm.com
Profile: CFJU-FM is a non-commercial station owned by Radio Communautaire des Hauts-Plateaux Inc. The format of the station is variety. CFJU-FM broadcasts to the Kedgwick, New Brunswick area at 90.1 FM.
FM RADIO STATION

CFLC-FM 47694
Owner: Newfoundland Capital Corporation Limited
Editorial: 345 O'Connell Drive, Corner Brook, Newfoundland A2H 7E5 **Tel:** 1 709 634-4570.
Email: info@bigland.fm
Web site: http://www.bigland.fm
Profile: CFLC-FM is a commercial station owned by Newfoundland Capital Corporation Limited. The format of the station is country. CFLC-FM broadcasts to the Churchill Falls, Labrador area at a frequency of 97.9 FM.
FM RADIO STATION

CFLG-FM (104.5 Fresh Radio) 47465
Owner: Corus Entertainment Inc.
Editorial: 709 Cotton Mill St, Cornwall, Ontario K6H 7K7- **Tel:** 1 613 932-5180.
Web site: http://www.1045freshfm.com
Profile: CFLG-FM (104.5 Fresh Radio) is a commercial station owned by Corus Entertainment Inc. The format of the station is hot adult contemporary. CFLG-FM broadcasts to the Cornwall, Ontario area at 104.5 FM.
FM RADIO STATION

CFLM-FM 47286
Owner: CFLM Radio Haute Mauricie Inc.
Editorial: 537 Rue Commerciale, La Tuque, Quebec G9X 3A7 **Tel:** 1 819 523-4575.
Web site: http://www.fm971.ca
Profile: CFLM-FM is a commercial station owned by CFLM Radio Haute Mauricie Inc. The format of the station is Adult Contemporary. CFLM-FM broadcasts to the La Tuque, Quebec area at 97.1 FM.
FM RADIO STATION

CFLN-FM 47383
Owner: Newfoundland Capital Corporation Limited
Editorial: 345 O'Connell Dr, Corner Brook, Newfoundland A2H 7V3 **Tel:** 1 709 634-4570.
Email: info@bigland.fm
Web site: http://www.bigland.fm
Profile: CFLN-FM is a commercial station owned by Newfoundland Capital Corporation Limited. The format of the station is adult contemporary. CFLN-FM broadcasts to the Happy Valley Goose Bay, Newfoundland area at 97.9 FM.
FM RADIO STATION

CFLO-FM 47693
Owner: Sonème (2007) Inc.
Editorial: 456 Rue du Pont, Mont-Laurier, Quebec J9L 2R9 **Tel:** 1 819 623-6610.
Email: nouvelles@cflo.ca
Web site: http://www.cflo.ca
Profile: CFLO-FM est un station radiophonique de Sonème (2007) Inc. CFLO-FM couvre Mont-Laurier et ses environs sur le 104,7FM.

CFLO-FM is a commercial station owned by Sonème (2007) Inc. The format of the station is adult contemporary. CFLO-FM broadcasts to the Mont-Laurier, Quebec area at 104.7 FM.
FM RADIO STATION

CFLT-FM 47182
Owner: Rogers Media Inc.
Editorial: 6080 Young Street, Ste 911, Halifax, Nova Scotia B3K 5L2 **Tel:** 1 902 493-7200.
Email: news957@rogers.com
Web site: http://www.lite929.com
Profile: CFLT-FM is a commercial station owned by Rogers Media Inc. The format of the station is lite rock music. CFLT-FM broadcasts to the Halifax, Nova Scotia area at 92.9 FM.
FM RADIO STATION

CFLW-AM 47382
Owner: Newfoundland Capital Corporation Limited
Editorial: 391 Kenmount Rd, St. John's, Newfoundland A1B 3P9 **Tel:** 1 709 726-5590.
Email: feedback@vocm.com
Web site: http://www.vocm.com
Profile: CFLW-AM is a transmitter located in Wabush, Newfoundland that simulcasts the programming of CFLN-AM. It is owned by Newfoundland Capital Corporation Limited. CFLW-AM broadcasts to the Wabush, Newfoundland area at 1340 AM. The stations are part of NewCap's VOCM brand.
AM RADIO STATION

CFLX-FM (La radio communautaire de l'Estrie 95.5) 47569
Owner: Radio Communautaire de l'Estrie
Editorial: 67 Rue Wellington N, Sherbrooke, Quebec J1H 5A9 **Tel:** 1 819 566-2787.
Email: commentaires@cflx.qc.ca
Web site: http://www.cflx.qc.ca
Profile: CFLX-FM est une station non-commerciale appartenant à Radio Communautaire de l'Estrie. Le genre de la station est adulte contemporain. CFLX-FM est diffusé à Sherbrooke, dans la région de Québec au 95.5 FM.

CFLX-FM is a non-commercial station owned by Radio Communautaire de l'Estrie. The format of the station is adult contemporary. CFLX-FM broadcasts to the Sherbrooke, Quebec area 95.5 FM.
FM RADIO STATION

CFLY-FM 47480
Owner: Bell Media
Editorial: 993 Princess St Suite 10, Kingston, Ontario K7L 1H3 **Tel:** 1 613 544-1380.
Email: heydeejay@983flyfm.com
Web site: http://www.983flyfm.com/
Profile: CFLY-FM is a commercial station owned by Bell Media. The format of the station is adult contemporary music. CFLY-FM broadcasts to the Kingston, Ontario area at 98.3 FM.
FM RADIO STATION

CFLZ-FM (101.1 Juice FM) 47507
Owner: Vista Broadcast Group
Editorial: 4673 Ontario Ave, Niagara Falls, Ontario L2E 3R1 **Tel:** 1 905 356-6710.
Web site: http://1011.juicefm.ca/
Profile: CFLZ-FM (101.1 Juice FM) is a commercial station owned by Vista Broadcast Group. The format of the station is Top 40/CHR. CKEY-FM broadcasts to the Niagara Falls, Ontario area at 101.1 FM.
FM RADIO STATION

CFMB-AM 47269
Owner: Evanov Radio
Editorial: 5877 Av Papineau, Montreal, Quebec H2G 2W3 **Tel:** 1 514 483-2362.
Email: info@cfmb.ca
Web site: http://www.cfmb.ca
Profile: CFMB-FM est une propriété d'Evanov Radio, diffusant sur Montréal au 1280 AM. La station offre une programmation unique et originale en seize langues.

CFMB-AM a commercial station owned by Evanov Radio.The station offers a unique and original programming in sixteen languages. CFMB-AM broadcasts on Montreal at 1280 AM.
AM RADIO STATION

CFMC-FM 47490
Owner: Rawlco Radio Ltd.
Editorial: 715 Saskatchewan Cres W, Saskatoon, Saskatchewan S7M 5V7 **Tel:** 1 306 934-2222.
Web site: http://www.c95.com
Profile: CFMC-FM is a commercial station owned by Rawlco Radio Ltd. The format of the station is hot adult contemporary. CFMC-FM broadcasts to Saskatoon, Saskatchewan at 95.1 FM.
FM RADIO STATION

CFMF-FM 47865
Owner: Diffusion Fermont
Editorial: 20 Place Daviault, Fermont, Quebec G0G 1J0 **Tel:** 1 418 287-5147.
Email: dp@diffusionfermont.ca
Web site: http://www.cfmf.ca
Profile: CFMF-FM is a commercial station owned by Diffusion Fermont. The format of the station is Top 40/CHR. CFMF-FM broadcasts to Fermont, Quebec at 103.1 FM.
FM RADIO STATION

CFMG-FM 47665
Owner: Bell Media
Editorial: 18520 Stony Plain Rd NW, Edmonton, Alberta T5S 1A8 **Tel:** 1 780 435-1049.
Web site: http://edmonton.virginradio.ca
Profile: CFMG-FM is a commercial station owned by Bell Media. The format of the station is Top 40/CHR. CFMG-FM broadcasts to Edmonton, Alberta at 104.9 FM.
FM RADIO STATION

CFMH-FM 83165
Owner: Campus Radio St. John Inc.
Editorial: T.J. Condon Student Centre, 100 Tucker Park Road, Saint John, New Brunswick E2L 4L5
Tel: 1 506 648-5667.
Email: cfmh@unbsj.ca
Web site: http://www.localfm.ca
Profile: CFMH-FM is a non-commercial station owned by Campus Radio St. John Inc. The format for the station is college variety. CFMH-FM broadcasts to the Saint John, New Brunswick area at 107.3 FM.
FM RADIO STATION

CFMI-FM 47441
Owner: Corus Entertainment Inc.
Editorial: 700 Georgia St W, Vancouver, British Columbia V7Y 1K8 **Tel:** 1 604 331-2808.
Email: info@rock101.com
Web site: http://www.rock101.com
Profile: CFMI-FM is a commercial station owned by Corus Entertainment Inc. The format of the station is classic rock music. CFMI-FM broadcasts to the Vancouver, BC area at 101.1 FM.
FM RADIO STATION

CFMJ-AM (Talk Radio AM640) 47288
Owner: Corus Entertainment Inc.
Editorial: 25 Dockside Dr, corus quay, Toronto, Ontario M5A 0B5 **Tel:** 1 416 479-7000.
Email: newstip@640toronto.com
Web site: http://globalnews.ca/radio/640toronto/
Profile: CFMJ-AM (Talk Radio AM640) is a commercial station owned by Corus Entertainment Inc. The format of the station is news and talk. AM640 broadcasts in the greater Toronto, Ontario area.
AM RADIO STATION

CFMK-FM 47484
Owner: Corus Entertainment Inc.
Editorial: 170 Queen St, Kingston, Ontario K7K 1B2
Tel: 1 613 544-2340.
Web site: http://www.963bigfm.com
Profile: CFMK-FM is a commercial station owned by Corus Entertainment Inc. The format of the station is classic rock. CFMK-FM broadcasts to Kingston, Ontario at 96.3 FM.
FM RADIO STATION

CFML-FM 83128
Owner: BC Institute of Technology
Editorial: 3700 Willingdon Ave, BC Institute of Technology Bldg SE-10, Burnaby, British Columbia V5G 3H2 **Tel:** 1 604 432-8510.
Email: sales@evolution1079.com
Web site: http://www.evolution1079.com
Profile: CFML-FM is a non-commercial station owned by the BC Institute of Technology. The format of the station is AAA-Adult Album Alternative. CFML-FM broadcasts to the Burnaby, British Columbia area at 107.9 FM. The station is student-run.
FM RADIO STATION

CFMM-FM 47485
Owner: Jim Pattison Broadcast Group(The)
Editorial: 1316 Central Ave, Prince Albert, Saskatchewan S6V 7R4 **Tel:** 1 306 763-7421.
Web site: http://www.power99fm.com
Profile: CFMM-FM is a commercial station owned by Jim Pattison Broadcast Group. The format of the station is adult contemporary. CFMM-FM broadcasts to the Prince Albert, Saskatchewan area at 99.1 FM.
FM RADIO STATION

CFMQ-FM 47691
Owner: HB Communications Inc.
Editorial: 635 Prince Street, Hudson Bay, Saskatchewan S0E 0Y0 **Tel:** 1 306 865-3065.
Email: cfmq@sasktel.net
Profile: CFMQ-FM is a commercial station owned by HB Communications Inc. CFMQ-FM's format is variety. CFMQ-FM broadcasts to Hudson Bay, Saskatchewan at 98.1 FM.
FM RADIO STATION

CFMU-FM 47690
Owner: McMaster Students' Union
Editorial: McMaster University Rm B119, MUSC Student Centre, Hamilton, Ontario L8S 4S4
Tel: 1 905 525-9140.
Email: cfmuprod@msu.mcmaster.ca
Web site: http://cfmu.mcmaster.ca
Profile: CFMU-FM is a commercial station owned by the McMaster Students' Union. The format for the

station is variety. CFMU-FM broadcasts to the Hamilton, Ontario area at 93.3 FM.
FM RADIO STATION

CFMV-FM (Bleu 96.3) 444963
Owner: Radio du Golfe Inc.
Editorial: 141 Rue Commerciale O Apt 101, Chandler, Quebec G0C 1K0 **Tel:** 1 418 689-0963.
Email: direction@bleufm.ca
Web site: http://bleufm.ca
Profile: CFMV-FM est une station de radio commerciale, une propriété de Radio du Golfe Inc. Le format de la station est la discussion. CFMV-FM est diffusé à Chandler, Québec au 96.3 FM.

CFMV-FM is a commercial station owned by Radio du Golfe Inc. The format of the station is talk. CFMV-FM broadcasts to the Chandler, Quebec area at 96.3 FM.
FM RADIO STATION

CFMX-FM (The New Classical 103.1) 690412
Owner: ZoomerMedia Limited
Editorial: 1 Queen St Suite 101, Cobourg, Ontario K9A 1M8 **Tel:** 1 905 372-4366.
Email: cfmx@primus.ca
Web site: http://www.classical963fm.com
Profile: CFMX-FM is a commercial station owned by ZoomerMedia Limited. The format of the station is classical. CFMX-FM broadcasts to the Cobourg, Ontario area at 103.1 FM.
FM RADIO STATION

CFMY-FM 47884
Owner: Jim Pattison Broadcast Group(The)
Editorial: 10 Boundary Rd SE, Redcliff, Alberta T0J 2P0- **Tel:** 1 403 548-8282.
Email: my96fm@jpbg.com
Web site: http://www.my96fm.com
Profile: CFMY-FM is a commercial station owned by The Jim Pattison Broadcast Group. The format is hot adult contemporary. CFMY-FM broadcasts in the Redcliff, Alberta area at 96.1 FM.
FM RADIO STATION

CFMZ-FM (The New Classical 96.3) 47464
Owner: ZoomerMedia Limited
Editorial: 550 Queen St W Suite 205, Toronto, Ontario M5V 2B5 **Tel:** 1 416 367-5353.
Email: info@classical963fm.com
Web site: http://www.classical963fm.com
Profile: CFMZ-FM is a commercial station owned by ZoomerMedia Limited. The format of the station is classical. CFMX-FM broadcasts to the Toronto area at 96.3 FM.
FM RADIO STATION

CFNA-FM (Country 99 FM) 501917
Owner: Vista Broadcast Group Inc.
Editorial: 102-5316 54 Ave 102, Bonnyville, Alberta T9N 2C9 **Tel:** 1 780 573-1745.
Web site: http://www.mylakelandnow.com
Profile: CFNA-FM is a commercial station owned by Vista Broadcast Group Inc. The format for the station is country. CFNA-FM broadcasts to the Bonnyville, Alberta area at 99.7 FM.
FM RADIO STATION

CFNC-AM 47381
Owner: Cross Lake Radio Committee
Tel: 1 204 676-2331.
Profile: CFNC-AM is a commercial station owned by Cross Lake Radio Committee. The format of the station is variety. CFNC-AM broadcasts to the Cross Lake, Manitoba area at 1490 AM.
AM RADIO STATION

CFND-FM 588433
Owner: Ecole Notre-Dame
Editorial: 581, rue Ouimet, St-Jerome, Quebec J5Z 1R3 **Tel:** 1 450 432-4472 5763.
Email: radionotredame@edu.csrdn.qc.ca
Web site: http://www.csrdn.qc.ca/notre-dame/canvas2.asp?pageid=78
Profile: CFND-FM is a non-commericial station owned by Ecole Notre-Dame. The format of the station is children. The target audience of the station is children, ages 2 to 12. CFND-FM broadcasts to the Saint-Jerome, Quebec area at 101.9 FM.
FM RADIO STATION

CFNI-AM (1240 Coast AM) 47128
Owner: Vista Broadcast Group Inc.
Editorial: 7035 A Market Street, Port Hardy, British Columbia V0N 2P0 **Tel:** 1 250 949-6500.
Web site: http://www.mytriportnow.com
Profile: CFNI-AM (1240 Coast AM) is a commercial station owned by Vista Broadcast Group Inc. The format of the station is adult contemporary. CFNI-AM broadcasts to the Port Hardy, British Columbia area at 1240 AM.
AM RADIO STATION

CFNJ-FM 47689
Owner: Radio Nord-Joli Inc.
Editorial: 245 Rue Beauvilliers, St-Gabriel-de-Brandon, Quebec J0K 2N0 **Tel:** 1 450 835-3437.
Email: info@cfnj.net
Web site: http://www.cfnj.net
Profile: CFNJ-FM est une radio de Radio Nord-Joli Inc. La station diffuse sur St-Gabriel-de-Brandon à la fréquence 99.1FM. La programmation est un mélange de radio parlée et de musique folklorique, traditionnelle et country.

CFNJ-FM is a commercial station owned by Radio Nord-Joli Inc. The format of the station is a variety of music and talk. CFNJ-FM broadcasts to the St-Gabriel-de-Brandon, Quebec area at 99.1 FM.
FM RADIO STATION

CFNN-FM 47687
Owner: Newfoundland Capital Corporation Limited
Editorial: 345 O'Connell Dr, Corner Brook, Newfoundland A2H 7E5 **Tel:** 1 709 634-4570.
Email: onair@cfcbradio.com
Web site: http://www.cfcbradio.com
Profile: CFNN-FM is a commercial station owned by Newfoundland Capital Corporation Limited. The format of the station is classic country. CFNN-AM broadcasts to the Corner Brook, Newfoundland area at 97.9 FM.
FM RADIO STATION

CFNO-FM 47506
Owner: North Superior Broadcasting Ltd.
Editorial: 93 Evergreen Drive, Marathon, Ontario P0T 2E0 **Tel:** 1 807 229-1010.
Web site: http://www.cfno.fm
Profile: CFNO-FM is a commercial station owned by North Superior Broadcasting Ltd. The format of the station is adult contemporary music. CFNO-FM broadcasts to the Marathon, Ontario area at 93.1 FM.
FM RADIO STATION

CFNR-FM 83148
Owner: Northern Native Broadcasting Terrace
Editorial: 4562B Queensway Dr, Terrace, British Columbia V8G 3X6 **Tel:** 1 250 638-8137.
Email: reception@classicrockcfnr.ca
Web site: http://cfnrfm.ca/
FM RADIO STATION

CFNW-AM 47379
Owner: Newfoundland Capital Corporation Limited
Editorial: 345 O'Connell Dr, Corner Brook, Newfoundland A2H 7V3 **Tel:** 1 709 634-4570.
Profile: CFNW-AM is a commercial station owned by Newfoundland Capital Corporation Limited. The format of the station is classic country. CFNW-AM broadcasts to the Corner Brook, Newfoundland area at 790 AM.
AM RADIO STATION

CFNY-FM (102.1 The Edge) 47455
Owner: Corus Entertainment Inc.
Editorial: 25 Dockside Dr, corus quay, Toronto, Ontario M5A 0B5 **Tel:** 1 416 479-7000.
Email: info@edge.ca
Web site: http://www.edge.ca
Profile: CFNY-FM is a commercial station owned by Corus Entertainment Inc. The format of the station is rock alternative. CFNY-FM broadcasts throughout the Toronto metro area at 102.1 FM.
FM RADIO STATION

CFOB-FM (The Border 93.1) 47212
Owner: Arcadia Broadcasting
Editorial: 210 Scott St, Fort Frances, Ontario P9A 1G7 **Tel:** 1 807 274-5390.
Email: news@931theborder.ca
Web site: http://931theborder.ca
Profile: CFOB-FM is a commercial station owned by Arcadia Broadcasting. The format of the station is adult contemporary. CFOB-FM broadcasts in the Fort Frances, Ontario area at 93.1 FM.
FM RADIO STATION

CFOM-FM (M FM 102.9) 47846
Owner: Cogeco
Editorial: 1305, chemin Ste-Foy - 4e etage, Quebec, Quebec G1S 4Y5 **Tel:** 1 418 694-1029.
Web site: http://www.1029quebec.fm
Profile: CFOM-FM is a commercial station owned by Cogeco. The format for the station is adult contemporary. CFOM-FM broadcasts to the Sainte-Foy, Quebec area at 102.9 FM.
FM RADIO STATION

CFOR-FM 83152
Owner: Radio CFOR
Editorial: 139 Principale Sud., Maniwaki, Quebec J9E 1Z8 **Tel:** 1 819 441-0993.
Email: cfor993@b2b2c.ca
Web site: http://www.cforfm.com
Profile: CFOR-FM is a commercial station owned by Radio CFOR. The format of the station is classic rock. CFOR-FM broadcasts to the Maniwaki, Quebec area at 99.3 FM.
FM RADIO STATION

CFOS-AM (560 CFOS) 47297
Owner: Bayshore Broadcasting Corp.
Editorial: 270 Ninth Street East, Owen Sound, Ontario N4K 1N7 **Tel:** 1 519 376-2030.
Web site: http://www.560cfos.ca
Profile: CFOS-AM is a commercial station owned by Bayshore Broadcasting Corp. The format of the station is oldies music and talk. CFOS-AM broadcasts throughout the Owen Sound, Ontario area at 560 AM.
AM RADIO STATION

CFOU-FM 47805
Owner: Université du Québec à Trois-Rivières(L')
Editorial: 3351 Boulevard des Forges, Pavillon Nérée-Beauchemin, Trois-Rivieres, Quebec G9A 5H7
Tel: 1 819 376-5184.
Email: progcfou@uqtr.ca
Web site: http://www.cfou.ca
Profile: CFOU-FM is a non-commercial station owned by the Université du Québec à Trois-Rivières. The format of the station is variety. CFOU-FM broadcasts to Trois-Rivières, Quebec at 89.1 FM.
FM RADIO STATION

CFOX-FM 47450
Owner: Corus Entertainment Inc.
Editorial: 700 West Georgia, Suite 2000, Vancouver, British Columbia V7Y 1K9 **Tel:** 1 604 684-7221.
Web site: http://www.cfox.com
Profile: CFOX-FM is a commercial station owned Corus Entertainment Inc. The format of the station is rock alternative. CFOX-FM broadcasts in the Vancouver, BC area at 99.3 FM.
FM RADIO STATION

CFOZ-FM 47659
Owner: Newfoundland Broadcasting Co. Ltd.
Editorial: 446 Logy Bay Rd, St. John's, Newfoundland A1A 5C6 **Tel:** 1 709 726-2922.
Email: ozfm@ozfm.com
Web site: http://www.ozfm.com
FM RADIO STATION

CFPA-FM 47831
Owner: Vista Broadcast Group Inc.
Editorial: 7035 A Market Street, Port Hardy, British Columbia V0N 2P0 **Tel:** 1 250 949-6500.
Email: onair@theport.ca
Web site: http://coastamradio.ca
Profile: CFPA-FM is a commercial station owned by Vista Broadcast Group Inc. The format of the station is adult contemporary. CFPA-FM broadcasts in the Port Hardy, British Columbia area at 100.3 FM.
FM RADIO STATION

CFPG-FM (Peggy 99.1 - Feel Good Winnipeg) 155616
Owner: Corus Entertainment Inc.
Editorial: 1440 Jack Blick Ave Suite 200, Winnipeg, Manitoba R3G 0L4 **Tel:** 1 204 786-2471.
Web site: http://www.peggy991.com
Profile: CFPG-FM is a commercial station owned by Corus Entertainment Inc. The format of the station is new and they are hiring new people now. CFPG-FM broadcasts to the Winnipeg, Manitoba area at 99.1 FM.
FM RADIO STATION

CFPL-AM 47225
Owner: Corus Entertainment Inc.
Editorial: 380 Wellington Street, Room 222, London, Ontario N6A 5B5 **Tel:** 1 519 931-6000.
Web site: http://www.am980.ca
Profile: CFPL-AM is a commercial station owned by Corus Entertainment Inc. The format of the station is news, sports and talk. CFPL-AM broadcasts throughout the London, Ontario area at 980 AM. To send a general e-mail to the station please see the comment form on their website.
AM RADIO STATION

CFPL-FM (London's Best Rock FM96) 47434
Owner: Corus Entertainment Inc.
Editorial: 380 Wellington St Rm 222, London, Ontario N6A 5B5 **Tel:** 1 519 931-6000.
Web site: http://www.fm96.com
Profile: CFPL-FM is a commercial station owned by Corus Entertainment Inc. The format of the station is album-oriented rock. CFPL-FM broadcasts to London, Ontario at 95.9 FM.
FM RADIO STATION

CFPR-AM 47134
Owner: Canadian Broadcasting Corp.
Editorial: 1-222 3rd Ave W 1, Prince Rupert, British Columbia V8J 1L1 **Tel:** 1 250 624-2161.
Email: daybreaknorth@cbc.ca
Web site: http://cbc.ca/bc
Profile: CFPR is a Canadian radio station, airing at 860 AM in Prince Rupert, British Columbia. It is part of the CBC Radio One network. The station covers regional and national news.
AM RADIO STATION

CFPS-FM (98 The Beach) 363741
Owner: Bayshore Broadcasting Corp.
Editorial: 382 Goderich St, Port Elgin, Ontario N0H 2C1 **Tel:** 1 519 832-9800.
Email: info@98thebeach.ca
Web site: http://www.98thebeach.ca
Profile: CFPS-FM is a commercial station owned by Bayshore Broadcasting Corporation. The format of the station is adult contemporary. The station's tagline is "98 The Beach." CFPS-FM broadcasts to the Port Elgin, Ontario area at 97.9 FM.
FM RADIO STATION

CFPV-FM 521106
Owner: McBride Communications & Media Inc.
Editorial: 10760 Fundy Drive, Richmond, British Columbia V7E 5K7 **Tel:** 1 604 220-8393.
Email: info@cfpvfm.com
Web site: http://www.cfpvfm.com
Profile: CFPV-FM is a commercial station owned by McBride Communications & Media Inc. The format of the station is classic rock. CFPV-FM broadcasts to the Pemberton, British Columbia area at 98.9 FM.
FM RADIO STATION

CFPW-FM 545365
Owner: Vista Broadcast Group Inc.
Editorial: 101-7074 Westminster St 101, Powell River, British Columbia V8A 1C5 **Tel:** 1 604 485-4207.
Web site: http://www.mypowellrivernow.com
Profile: CFPW-FM is a commercial station owned by Vista Broadcast Group Inc. The format of the station is Adult Contemporary. CFPW-FM broadcasts to the Powell River, British Columbia area at 95.7 FM.
FM RADIO STATION

CFQK-FM 359182
Owner: Dougall Media
Editorial: 87 Hill St N, Thunder Bay, Ontario P7A 5V6
Tel: 1 807 346-2600.
Email: energy@energyfm.fm
Web site: http://www.energyfm.fm
Profile: CFQK-FM is a commercial station owned by Dougall Media. The format of the station is adult contemporary. CFQK-FM broadcasts to the Thunder Bay, Ontario area at 104.5 FM.
FM RADIO STATION

CFQM-FM 47583
Owner: Maritime Broadcasting System Ltd.
Editorial: 1000 St George Blvd, Moncton, New Brunswick E1E 4M7- **Tel:** 1 506 858-1220.
Web site: http://www.1039maxfm.com
Profile: CFQM-FM is a commercial station owned by the Maritime Broadcasting System Ltd. The format of the station is classic hits. CFQM-FM broadcasts throughout the Moncton, New Brunswick area at 103.9 FM.
FM RADIO STATION

CFQX-FM 47496
Owner: Jim Pattison Broadcast Group (The)
Editorial: 177 Lombard Avenue, 3rd Floor, Winnipeg, Manitoba R3B 0W5 **Tel:** 1 204 944-1031.
Email: psa@hotqx.com
Web site: http://www.qx104fm.com
Profile: CFQX-FM is a commercial station owned by Astral Media. The format of the station is contemporary country. CFQX-FM broadcasts to the Winnipeg, Manitoba area at 104.1 FM.
FM RADIO STATION

CFRA-AM (580 CFRA) 47295
Owner: Bell Media
Editorial: 87 George St, Ottawa, Ontario K1N 9H7-
Tel: 1 613 789-2486 4252.
Email: news@cfra.com
Web site: http://www.iheartradio.ca/580-cfra
Profile: CFRA-AM is a commercial station owned by Bell Media. The format of the station is news and talk. CFRA-AM broadcasts to the Ottawa, Ontario area at 580 AM.
AM RADIO STATION

CFRB-AM 47331
Owner: Bell Media
Editorial: 250 Richmond St W Fl THIRD, Toronto, Ontario M5V 1W4 **Tel:** 1 416 924-5711.
Email: news@newstalk1010.com
Web site: http://www.iheartradio.ca/newstalk-1010
Profile: CFRB-AM is a commercial station owned by Bell Media. The format of the station is news and talk. CFRB-AM broadcasts to the Toronto area at 1010 AM. CFRB-AM is a member of the Canadian Press Gallery.
AM RADIO STATION

CFRC-FM 47493
Owner: Radio Queen's University
Editorial: Queen's University Lower Carruthers Hall, Kingston, Ontario K7L 3N6 **Tel:** 1 613 533-2121.
Email: cfrc@ams.queensu.ca
Web site: http://www.cfrc.ca
Profile: CFRC-FM is a non-commercial station owned by Radio Queen's University. The format of the station is variety. CFRC-FM broadcasts to the Kingston, Ontario area at 101.9 FM.
FM RADIO STATION

CFRE-FM 83129
Owner: University of Toronto
Editorial: 3359 Mississauga Rd N R#131, University of Toronto at Mississauga, Mississauga, Ontario L5L 1C6 **Tel:** 1 905 369-0504.
Email: staff@cfreradio.com
Web site: http://www.cfreradio.com
Profile: CFRE-FM is a college station owned by the University of Toronto. The station airs at 91.9 in the Mississauga, Ontario area.
FM RADIO STATION

CFRG-FM
585530

Owner: Association communautaire fransaskoise de Gravelbourg
Tel: 1 306 648-2374.
Email: cfrg@sasktel.net
Web site: http://cfrg.ca
FM RADIO STATION

CFRH-FM
47624

Owner: Radio-Huronie FM Communautaire Inc.
Editorial: 63 rue Main, Penetanguishene, Ontario L9M 2G3 **Tel:** 1 705 549-3116.
Email: vaguefm@vaguefm.ca
Web site: http://vaguefm.ca
Profile: CFRH-FM is a non-commercial station owned by Radio-Huronie FM Communautaire Inc. The format of the station is adult contemporary. CFRH-FM broadcasts to the Penetanguishene, Ontario area at 88.1 FM
FM RADIO STATION

CFRI-FM
475942

Owner: Vista Broadcast Group Inc.
Editorial: 1-11002 104 Ave 1, Grande Prairie, Alberta T8V 7W5- **Tel:** 1 780 357-1047.
Web site: http://1047.2dayfm.ca
Profile: CFRI-FM is a commercial station owned by Vista Broadcast Group Inc. The format of the station is classic rock. CFRI-FM broadcasts to the Grande Prairie, Alberta area at 104.7 FM.
FM RADIO STATION

CFRK-FM
377206

Owner: Newfoundland Capital Corporation Limited
Editorial: 495 Prospect St., Fredericton, New Brunswick E3B 9M4 **Tel:** 1 506 455-0923.
Web site: http://www.thenewhot923.com
Profile: CFRK-FM is a commercial station owned by Newfoundland Capital Corporation Limited. The format of the station is Top 40/ CHR. CFRK-FM broadcasts to the Fredericton, New Brunswick area at 92.3 FM.
FM RADIO STATION

CFRM-FM
475434

Owner: Timmermans (Craig)
Editorial: 10 Campbell St E, Little Current, Ontario P0P 1K0 **Tel:** 1 705 368-1419.
Email: radio@manitoulin.net
Web site: http://www.theislandfm.com
Profile: CFRM-FM is a commercial station owned by Craig Timmermans. The format for the station is contemporary country. CFRM-FM broadcasts to the Little Current, Ontario area at 100.7 FM.
FM RADIO STATION

CFRN-AM
47176

Owner: Belll Media
Editorial: 18520 Stony Plain Rd NW Suite 100, Edmonton, Alberta T5S 2E2 **Tel:** 1 780 486-2800.
Web site: http://www.tsn.ca/radio/edmonton-1260
Profile: CFRN-AM is a commercial station owned by Bell Media. The format of the station is sports and talk. CFRN-AM broadcasts to the Edmonton, Alberta area at 1260 AM.
AM RADIO STATION

CFRO-FM
47452

Owner: Vancouver Co-Operative Radio
Editorial: 110-360 Columbia St, Vancouver, British Columbia V6A 4J1 **Tel:** 1 604 684-8494.
Email: cfro-psa@coopradio.org
Web site: http://www.coopradio.org
Profile: CFRO-FM is a non-commercial radio station owned by Vancouver Co-Op Radio. The format of the station is news, talk, and multi-cultural programming. CFRO-FM broadcasts in the Vancouver, British Columbia area at 102.7 FM.
FM RADIO STATION

CFRP-FM
47414

Owner: Radio Port-Cartier Inc.
Editorial: 907, rue de Puyjalon, Baie-Comeau, Quebec G5C 1N3 **Tel:** 1 418 589-3771.
Email: chlcfm97@globetrotter.net
Web site: http://www.chlc.com
Profile: CFRP-FM is a commercial station owned by Radio Port-Cartier Inc. The format of the station is Hot Adult Contemporary. CFRP-FM broadcasts to Forestville, Quebec at 100.5 FM.
FM RADIO STATION

CFRQ-FM
47549

Owner: Newfoundland Capital Corporation Limited
Editorial: 3770 Kempt Rd, Halifax, Nova Scotia B3K 4X8- **Tel:** 1 902 453-4004.
Email: halifaxnews@newcap.ca
Web site: http://www.q104.ca
Profile: CFRQ-FM is a commercial station owned by Newfoundland Capital Corporation Limited. The format of the station is classic rock. CFRQ-FM broadcasts to Halifax, Nova Scotia at 104.3 FM.
FM RADIO STATION

CFRT-FM
363726

Owner: Association des francophones du Nunavut
Editorial: 981 Nunavut Drive, Iqaluit, Nunavut X0A 0H0 **Tel:** 1 867 979-4606.
Web site: http://www.cfrt.ca
Profile: CFRT-FM is a non-commercial station owned by the Association des francophones du Nunavut. The format of the station is variety. CFRT-FM broadcasts to the Iqaluit, Nunavut area at 107.3 FM.
FM RADIO STATION

CFRU-FM
47698

Owner: University of Guelph
Editorial: Level 2 Univ Ctr Univ of Guelph, Guelph, Ontario N1G2W1 **Tel:** 1 519 824-4120.
Email: programming@cfru.ca
Web site: http://www.cfru.ca
Profile: CFRU-FM is a non-commercial station owned by the University of Guelph. The format is college and community variety. CFRU-FM broadcasts to the Guelph, Ontario area at 93.3 FM.
FM RADIO STATION

CFRV-FM
47482

Owner: Rogers Communications Inc.
Editorial: 1015 3rd Avenue South, Lethbridge, Alberta T1J 0J3 **Tel:** 1 403 328-1077.
Email: theriver@rci.rogers.com
Web site: http://www.1077theriver.ca
Profile: CFRV-FM is a commercial radio station owned by Rogers Communications Inc. The format of the station is adult contemporary. CFRV-FM broadcasts to the Lethbridge, Alberta area at 107.7 FM.
FM RADIO STATION

CFRW-AM (TSN 1290 Winnipeg)
47254

Owner: Bell Media
Editorial: 1445 Pembina Hwy, Winnipeg, Manitoba R3T 5C2 **Tel:** 1 204 477-5120.
Email: tsngo@bellmedia.ca
Web site: http://www.tsn.ca/winnipeg
Profile: CFRW-AM is a commercial station owned by Bell Media. The format of the station is sports. CFRW-AM broadcasts throughout the Winnipeg, Manitoba area at 1290 AM.
AM RADIO STATION

CFRY-AM
47250

Owner: Golden West Broadcasting Ltd.
Editorial: 350 River Rd, Portage La Prairie, Manitoba R1N 3V6 **Tel:** 1 204 239-5111.
Web site: http://www.cfryradio.ca
Profile: CFRY (920 AM) is a simulcasting radio station that broadcasts country music. Licensed to Portage la Prairie, Manitoba, the station serves the Central Plains region of Manitoba.
AM RADIO STATION

CFRY-FM
47843

Owner: Golden West Broadcasting Ltd.
Editorial: 350 River Rd, Portage La Prairie, Manitoba R1N 3V6 **Tel:** 1 204 239-5111.
Web site: http://www.cfryradio.ca
Profile: CFRY-FM is a commercial station owned by Golden West Broadcasting Ltd. The format of the station is country music. CFRY-FM broadcasts in Portage la Prairie, Manitoba area at 93.1 FM.
FM RADIO STATION

CFSF-FM
689845

Owner: Vista Broadcast Group
Editorial: 130-204 King St, Sturgeon Falls, Ontario P2B 1R7 **Tel:** 1 705 753-6776.
Email: sturgeonmoose993@moosefm.com
Web site: http://www.moosefm.com/cfsf
Profile: CFSF-FM is a commercial station owned by Vista Broadcast Group. The format for the station is English and French Top 40/CHR. CFSF-FM broadcasts to the Sturgeon Falls, Ontario area at 99.3 FM.
FM RADIO STATION

CFSL-AM
47238

Owner: Golden West Broadcasting Ltd.
Editorial: 305 Souris Ave, Weyburn, Saskatchewan S4H 0C6 **Tel:** 1 306 848-1190.
Email: am1190@goldenwestradio.com
Web site: http://am1190radio.com/
Profile: CFSL-AM is a commercial radio station owned by Golden West Broadcasting Ltd. The format of the station is country. CFSL-AM broadcasts to the Weyburn, Saskatchewan area at 1190 AM.
AM RADIO STATION

CFSR-FM
47116

Owner: Rogers Communications Inc.
Editorial: 46167 Yale Road, Unit 309, Chilliwack, British Columbia V2P 2P2 **Tel:** 1 604 795-5711.
Email: starnews@starfm.rogers.com
Web site: http://www.starfm.com
FM RADIO STATION

CFSX-AM
47326

Owner: Newfoundland Capital Corporation Limited
Editorial: 60 West Street, Stephenville, Newfoundland A2N 1C6 **Tel:** 1 709 643-2191.
Email: cfsx@vocm.com
Web site: http://www.cfsxradio.com
Profile: CFSX-AM is a commercial station owned by Newfoundland Capital Corporation Limited. The format of the station is news, talk and classic country. CFSX-AM broadcasts to the Stephenville, Newfoundland area at 870 AM.
AM RADIO STATION

CFTA-FM
768708

Owner: Tantramar Community Radio Society
Editorial: 141-S Victoria St. E., Amherst, Nova Scotia B4H 1X9 **Tel:** 1 902 660-1079.
Email: cfta@eastlink.ca
Web site: http://www.tantramarfm.ca
Profile: CFTA-FM is an independent commercial station owned by Tantramar Community Radio Society. The format of the station is community news, talk, and local music. CFTA-FM broadcasts to the

Amherst, Nova Scotia area at a frequency of 107.9 FM.
FM RADIO STATION

CFTE-AM
47151

Owner: Bell Media
Editorial: 500-969 Robson St 500, Vancouver, British Columbia V6Z 1X5 **Tel:** 1 604 871-9000.
Web site: http://tsn1410.ca
Profile: CFTE-AM is a commercial station owned by Bell Media. The format of the station is sports. CFTE-AM broadcasts to the Vancouver, British Columbia area at 1410 AM.
AM RADIO STATION

CFTH-FM
47700

Owner: Harrington Community Radio
Tel: 1 418 795-3349.
Web site: http://www.cfthradio.com
FM RADIO STATION

CFTK-AM
47145

Owner: Bell Media
Editorial: 4625 Lazelle Ave, Terrace, British Columbia V8G 1S4 **Tel:** 1 250 635-6316.
Web site: http://terrace.myezrock.com/
Profile: CFTK-AM is a commercial station owned by Bell Media. The format of the station is hot adult contemporary. CFTK-AM broadcasts to the Terrace, British Columbia area at 590 AM.
AM RADIO STATION

CFTL-FM
47832

Owner: Ayamowin Communications Society
Editorial: Big Trout First Nations Office, Big Trout Lake, Ontario P0V 1G0 **Tel:** 1 807 537-2260.
FM RADIO STATION

CFTR-AM (680 NEWS)
47343

Owner: Rogers Communications Inc.
Editorial: 1 Ted Rogers Way Fl 5TH, Toronto, Ontario M4Y 3B7 **Tel:** 1 416 413-3930.
Email: news680@rogers.com
Web site: http://www.680news.com
Profile: CFTR-AM is a commercial station owned by Rogers Communications Inc. The format is news programming. CFTR-AM broadcasts to the Toronto, ON area at 680 AM. CFTR-AM is a member of the Canadian Press Gallery.
AM RADIO STATION

CFTX-FM
396805

Owner: RNC Media
Editorial: 171A Rue Jean-Proulx, Gatineau, Quebec J8Z 1W5 **Tel:** 1 819 770-9650.
Web site: http://www.capitalerock.ca
Profile: CFTX-FM is a commercial station owned by RNC Media Inc. The format of the station is rock. CFTX-FM broadcasts to the Gatineau, Quebec area at 96.5 FM.
FM RADIO STATION

CFUR-FM
588197

Owner: Education Alternative Radio Society
Editorial: 3333 University, Prince George, British Columbia V2N 4Z9 **Tel:** 1 250 960-7664.
Email: news@cfur.ca
Web site: http://www.cfur.ca
Profile: CFUR-FM is a non-commercial station owned by Education Alternative Radio Society. The format of the station is variety. CFUR-FM broadcasts to the Prince George, British Columbia area at 88.7 FM.
FM RADIO STATION

CFUT-FM
528603

Owner: La Radio Campus Communautaire Francophone de Shawinigan Inc.
Editorial: 540 Av Broadway, Shawinigan, Quebec G9N 1M3 **Tel:** 1 819 537-0911.
Email: dg@radioshawinigan.com
Web site: http://www.radioshawinigan.com
Profile: CFUT-FM is a non-commercial station owned by La Radio Campus Communautaire Francophone de Shawinigan Inc. The format of the station is variety. CFUT-FM broadcasts to the Shawinigan, Quebec area at 91.1 FM.
FM RADIO STATION

CFUV-FM
47699

Owner: University of Victoria Student Radio Society
Tel: 1 250 721-8702.
Email: cfuvpsa@uvic.ca
Web site: http://cfuv.uvic.ca
Profile: CFUV-FM is a commercial station owned by University of Victoria Student Radio Society. The format of the station is variety. CFUV-FM broadcasts to the Victoria, British Columbia area at 101.9 FM.
FM RADIO STATION

CFVD-FM
47701

Owner: Radio Dégelis Inc
Editorial: 654 6e rue Est, Degelis, Quebec G5T 1Y1 **Tel:** 1 418 853-3370.
Email: cfvd@fm95.ca
Web site: http://www.fm95.ca
Profile: CFVD-FM is a commercial station owned by Radio Dégelis Inc. The format of the station is Top 40/CHR music. CFVD-FM broadcasts in the Degelis, Quebec area at 95.5 FM.
FM RADIO STATION

CFVM-FM
47354

Owner: Bell Media
Editorial: 111 Av Gaetan-Archambault, Amqui, Quebec G5J 2K1 **Tel:** 1 418 629-2025.
Web site: http://amqui.rougefm.ca

Profile: CFVM-FM is a commercial station owned by Bell Media. The format of the station is adult contemporary. CFVM-FM broadcasts to the Amqui, Quebec area at 99.9 FM.
FM RADIO STATION

CFVR-FM
514112

Owner: Harvard Broadcasting
Editorial: 9904 Franklin Ave., Fort McMurray, Alberta T9H 2K5 **Tel:** 1 780 791-0103.
Email: mixnews@mix1037fm.com
Web site: http://www.mix1037fm.com
Profile: CFVR-FM is a commercial station owned by Harvard Broadcasting. The format for the station is hot adult contemporary. CFVR-FM broadcasts to the Fort McMurray, Alberta area at 103.7 FM.
FM RADIO STATION

CFWC-FM (FaithFM 93.9)
342192

Owner: 1486781 Ontario Limited
Editorial: 271 Greenwich St, Brantford, Ontario N3S 2X9 **Tel:** 1 519 759-2339.
Email: info@brant939.faithfm.org
Web site: http://www.brantford.faithfm.org
Profile: CFWC-FM (FaithFM 93.9) is a commercial station owned by 1486781 Ontario Limited. The format for the station is Christian. CFWC-FM broadcasts to the Brantford, Ontario area at 93.9 FM.
FM RADIO STATION

CFWD-FM
526028

Owner: Harvard Broadcasting
Editorial: 105 21st St E Suite 200, Saskatoon, Saskatchewan S7K 0B3 **Tel:** 1 306 653-9630.
Email: heyyou@cruzfm.com
Web site: http://www.cruzfm.com
Profile: CFWD-FM is a commercial station owned by Harvard Broadcasting. The format of the station is Classic Hits. CFWD-FM broadcasts to the Saskatoon, Saskatchewan area at 96.3 FM.
FM RADIO STATION

CFWE-FM
47702

Owner: Aboriginal Multi-Media Society
Editorial: 13245 146 Street, Edmonton, Alberta T5L 4S8 **Tel:** 1 780 447-2393.
Email: info@cfweradio.ca
Web site: http://www.cfweradio.ca
Profile: CFWE-FM is a commercial radio station owned by the Aboriginal Multi-Media Society. The format of the station is a mix of Aboriginal and country music, as well as talk. CFWE-FM broadcasts to Edmonton, Alberta at 98.5 FM.
FM RADIO STATION

CFWF-FM
47830

Owner: Harvard Broadcasting
Editorial: 1900 Rose Street, Regina, Saskatchewan S4P 0A9 **Tel:** 1 306 546-6200.
Web site: http://www.thewolfrocks.com
Profile: CFWF-FM is a commercial station owned by Harvard Broadcasting. The format of the station is rock/album-oriented rock. CFWF-FM broadcasts to the Regina, Saskatchewan area at 104.9 FM.
FM RADIO STATION

CFWH-FM
47100

Owner: Canadian Broadcasting Corp.
Editorial: 3103 3rd Ave, Whitehorse, Yukon Territory Y1A 1E5 **Tel:** 1 867 668-8400.
Email: cbcnorth@cbc.ca
Web site: http://www.cbc.ca/north
Profile: CFWH-FM is a non-commercial radio station owned by the Canadian Broadcasting Corp. The format of the station is a variety of news, talk and information. CFWH-FM broadcasts throughout Whitehorse, Yukon Territory at 94.5.
FM RADIO STATION

CFWM-FM
47721

Owner: Bell Media
Editorial: 1445 Pembina Hwy, Winnipeg, Manitoba R3T 5C2 **Tel:** 1 204 477-5120.
Web site: http://www.999bobfm.com
Profile: CFWM-FM is a commercial station owned by Bell Media. The format of the station is adult hits music. CFWM-FM broadcasts in the Winnipeg, Manitoba area at 99.9 FM.
FM RADIO STATION

CFXE-FM
47181

Owner: Newfoundland Capital Corporation Limited
Editorial: 2nd Floor, 422-50th Street, Edson, Alberta T7E 1T1 **Tel:** 1 780 723-4461.
Email: news@theeagle.ca
Web site: http://www.theeagle.ca
Profile: CFXE-FM is a commercial station owned by Newfoundland Capital Corporation Limited. The format of the station is classic hits. CFXE-FM broadcasts to the Edson, Alberta area at 94.3 FM.
FM RADIO STATION

CFXG-AM
536661

Owner: Newfoundland Capital Corporation Limited
Editorial: 422 50th Street, Edson, Alberta T7E 1V8 **Tel:** 1 780 723-4461.
Email: news@theeagle.ca
Web site: http://www.theeagle.ca
Profile: CFXG-AM is a commercial station owned by Newfoundland Capital Corporation Limited. The format of the station is classic hits. CFXG-AM broadcasts to the Grande Cache, Alberta area at 1230 AM.
AM RADIO STATION

Canada

CFXG-FM
801069

Owner: Newcap Radio
Editorial: 422-50th Street 2nd floor, Edson, Alberta T7E 1T1
Email: news@theeagle.ca
Web site: http://www.theeagle.ca
Profile: CFXG-FM is a commercial station owned by Newcap Radio. The format of the station is classic hits. CFXG-FM broadcasts to Grande Cache at 93.3.
FM RADIO STATION

CFXH-FM
394760

Owner: Newfoundland Capital Corporation Limited
Editorial: 2nd Floor, 422-50th Street, Edson, Alberta T7E 1T1 **Tel:** 1 780 723-4461.
Email: feedback@theeagle.ca
Web site: http://www.theeagle.ca
Profile: CFXH-FM is a commercial station owned by Newfoundland Capital Corporation Limited. The format for the station is classic hits. CFXH-FM broadcasts to the Hinton, Alberta area at 97.5 FM.
FM RADIO STATION

CFXJ-FM
83142

Owner: Newcap Radio
Editorial: 2 St. Clair Ave W Fl 20TH, Toronto, Ontario M4V 1L5 **Tel:** 1 416 482-0973.
Web site: http://www.935themove.com/
Profile: CFXJ-FM is a commercial station owned by Newcap Radio. The format for the station is urban contemporary. CFXJ-FM broadcasts to the Toronto area at 93.5 FM.
FM RADIO STATION

CFXL-FM
139785

Owner: Newfoundland Capital Corporation Limited
Editorial: 1110 Centre St NE Suite 100, Calgary, Alberta T2E 2R2 **Tel:** 1 403 271-6366.
Email: feedback@xl103calgary.com
Web site: http://www.xl103calgary.com
Profile: CFXL-FM is a commercial station owned by Newfoundland Capital Corporation Limited. The format of the station is classic hits. CFXL-FM broadcasts to the Calgary, Alberta area at 103.1 FM.
FM RADIO STATION

CFXM-FM
83105

Owner: Coopérative de travail de la radio de Granby
Editorial: 135 Rue Principale Bureau 35, Granby, Quebec J2G 2V1 **Tel:** 1 450 372-5105.
Email: nouvelles@m105.ca
Web site: http://www.m105.ca
Profile: CFXM-FM est une station de la Coopérative de travail de la radio de Granby. La station diffuse sur Granby et sa région sur le 104.9FM.

CFXM-FM is a commercial station owned by the Coopérative de travail de la radio de Granby. The format of the station is adult contemporary. CFXM-FM broadcasts to the Granby, Quebec area at 104.9 FM.
FM RADIO STATION

CFXN-FM
412059

Owner: Vista Broadcast Group
Editorial: 118 Main St E, North Bay, Ontario P1B 1A8 **Tel:** 1 705 475-9991.
Email: moose1063.news@moosefm.com
Web site: http://www.moosefm.com/cfxn
Profile: CFXN-FM is a commercial station owned by Vista Broadcast Group. The format of the station is adult hits. CFXN-FM broadcasts to the North Bay, ON area at 106.3 FM.
FM RADIO STATION

CFXO-FM
504739

Owner: Golden West Broadcasting Ltd.
Editorial: 11-5th Avenue SE, High River, Alberta T1V 1G2 **Tel:** 1 403 652-2472.
Web site: http://www.sun99radio.com
Profile: CFXO-FM is a commercial station owned by Golden West Broadcasting Ltd. The format for the station is contemporary country music. CFXO-FM broadcasts to the High River, Alberta area at 99.7 FM.
FM RADIO STATION

CFXP-FM
47390

Owner: Newfoundland Capital Corporation Limited
Editorial: 422 50th, 2nd FL, Edson, Alberta T7E 1T1
Tel: 1 780 723-4461.
Email: feedback@theeagle.ca
Web site: http://www.theeagle.ca
Profile: CFXP-FM is a commercial station owned by Newfoundland Capital Corporation Limited. The format of the station is hot adult contemporary. CFXP-FM broadcasts to the Edson, AB area at 95.5 FM.
FM RADIO STATION

CFXU-FM
47425

Owner: St. Francis Xavier University
Tel: 1 902 867-2410.
Email: cfxu@stfx.ca
Web site: http://www.radiocfxu.ca
Profile: CFXU-FM is a non-commercial station owned by St. Francis Xavier University. The format is variety. CFXU-FM broadcasts to the Antigonish, Nova Scotia area at 93.3 FM.
FM RADIO STATION

CFXW-FM
394764

Owner: Newfoundland Capital Corporation Limited
Editorial: 5118 50th Street, Whitecourt, Alberta T7S 1A1 **Tel:** 1 780 778-5101.
Web site: http://www.therig.ca
Profile: CFXW-FM is a commercial station owned by Newfoundland Capital Corporation Limited. The format for the station is classic rock. CFXW-FM broadcasts to the Whitecourt, Alberta area at 96.7 FM.
FM RADIO STATION

CFXY-FM
47314

Owner: Bell Media
Editorial: 206 Rookwood Ave, Fredericton, New Brunswick E3B 2M2 **Tel:** 1 506 454-2444.
Email: frederictonnewsteam@bellmedia.ca
Web site: http://www.foxrocks.ca
Profile: CFXY-FM is a commercial station owned by Bell Media. The format of the station is rock music. CFXY-FM broadcasts to the Fredericton, New Brunswick area at 105.3 FM. Twitter handle: twitter.com/105thefox
FM RADIO STATION

CFYK-FM
47104

Owner: Canadian Broadcasting Corp.
Editorial: 5002 Forrest Dr, Yellowknife, Northwest Territories X1A 2A9 **Tel:** 1 867 920-5400.
Email: cbcnorth@cbc.ca
Web site: http://www.cbc.ca/north
Profile: CFYK-FM is a non-commercial station owned by the Canadian Broadcasting Corp. The format of the station is news and talk. CFYK-FM broadcasts to the Yellowknife, Northwest Territories area at 98.9 FM.
FM RADIO STATION

CFYM-AM
47202

Owner: Golden West Broadcasting Ltd.
Editorial: 404 12 Ave E, Bay A, Kindersley, Saskatchewan S0L 1S0 **Tel:** 1 306 463-2692.
Email: cjymnews@goldenwestradio.com
Web site: http://www.cjym.com
Profile: CFYM-AM is a commercial station owned by Golden West Broadcasting Ltd. The format of the station is classic hits. CFYM-AM broadcasts to the Rosetown, Saskatchewan area at 1210 AM.
AM RADIO STATION

CFYT-FM
810461

Owner: Dawson City Community Radio Society
Tel: 1 867 993-5152.
Email: cfytradio@gmail.com
Web site: http://www.cfyt.ca
Profile: CFYT-FM is a community station owned by the Dawson City Community Radio Society. The format of the station is variety. CFYT-FM broadcasts to the Dawson City, Yukon Territory area at 96.7 FM.
FM RADIO STATION

CFYX-FM
502444

Owner: Groupe Radio Simard
Editorial: 158 Rue Saint-Germain O, Rimouski, Quebec G5L 4B7 **Tel:** 1 418 722-2848.
Web site: http://cfyxrimouski.com/
Profile: CFYX-FM est une station radiophonique propriété du Groupe Radio Simard qui diffuse des émissions parlées et de la musique de format adulte contemporain. CFYX-FM diffuse sur la bande 93.3FM sur Rimouski et les environs.

CFYX-FM is a commercial station owned by Groupe Radio Simard. The format of the station is Hot Adult Contemporary and talk. CFYX-FM broadcasts to the Rimouski, Quebec area at 93.3 FM.
FM RADIO STATION

CFZM-AM
47290

Owner: ZoomerMedia Limited
Editorial: 70 Jefferson Ave, Toronto, Ontario M6K 1Y4 **Tel:** 1 416 367-5353.
Email: gene@zoomerradio.ca
Web site: http://www.zoomerradio.ca
Profile: CFZM-AM is a commercial station owned by ZoomerMedia Limited. The format of the station is adult standards. CFZM-AM broadcasts to the Toronto area at 740 AM. To send a general e-mail to the station please use the online contact form on their website.
AM RADIO STATION

CFZN-FM
393969

Owner: Vista Broadcast Group
Editorial: 152 Highland Street, Box 960, Upper level, Haliburton, Ontario K0M 1S0 **Tel:** 1 705 457-3897.
Email: moose935.news@moosefm.com
Web site: http://moosefm.com/cfzn/
Profile: CFZN-FM is a commercial station owned by the Vista Broadcast Group. The format for the station is classic rock. CFZN-FM broadcasts to the Haliburton, Ontario area at 93.5 FM.
FM RADIO STATION

CFZZ-FM (Boom FM 104.1)
47601

Owner: Bell Media
Editorial: 104 Richelieu, St-Jean-sur-Richelieu, Quebec J3B 6X3 **Tel:** 1 450 346-0104.
Web site: http://www.boomfm.com
Profile: CFZZ-FM is a French-language commercial station owned by Bell Media. The format of the station is oldies. CFZZ-FM broadcasts to the Saint-Jean-sur-Richelieu, Quebec area at 104.1 FM.
FM RADIO STATION

CHAA-FM (La radio allumée 103.3)
47555

Owner: Radio Communautaire de la Rive-Sud Inc.(La)
Editorial: 91 Rue Saint-Jean, Longueuil, Quebec J4H 2W8 **Tel:** 1 450 646-6800.
Email: info@fm1033.ca
Web site: http://www.fm1033.ca
Profile: CHAA-FM est une station de radio non-commerciale, une propriété de La Radio Communautaire de la Rive-Sud Inc. Le format de la station est le variété. CHAA-FM est diffusé à Longueil, Québec au 103.3 FM.

CHAA-FM is a non-commercial station owned by La Radio Communautaire de la Rive-Sud Inc. The format of the station is variety. CHAA-FM broadcasts to the Longueuil, Quebec area at 103.3 FM.
FM RADIO STATION

CHAB-AM
47207

Owner: Golden West Broadcasting Ltd.
Editorial: 1704 Main St N, Moose Jaw, Saskatchewan S6J 1L4 **Tel:** 1 306 694-0800.
Email: mjnews@goldenwestradio.com
Web site: http://www.chabradio.com
Profile: CHAB-AM is a commercial station owned by Golden West Broadcasting Ltd. The format of the station is classic hits music. CHAB-AM broadcasts to the Moose Jaw, Saskatchewan area at 800 AM.
AM RADIO STATION

CHAD-FM
231772

Owner: Chetwynd Communications Society
Editorial: 4612 N Access Rd #102, Chetwynd, British Columbia V0C 1J0 **Tel:** 1 250 788-9452.
Email: news@peacefm.ca
Web site: http://www.peacefm.ca
Profile: CHAD-FM is a non-commercial station owned by Chetwynd Communications Society. The format of the station is full service and variety. CHAD-FM broadcasts to the Chetwynd, British Columbia area at 104.1 FM.
FM RADIO STATION

CHAI-FM
47547

Owner: Radio Communautaire Inc.(La)
Editorial: 25 boul St-Francis, Chateauguay, Quebec J6J 1Y2 **Tel:** 1 450 698-3131.
Email: chai@videotron.ca
Web site: http://www.1019fm.net
Profile: CHAI-FM is a non-commercial station owned by La Radio Communautaire Inc. The format for the station is adult contemporary. WIXO-FM broadcasts to the Chateauguay, Quebec area at 101.9 FM.
FM RADIO STATION

CHAK-AM
47102

Owner: Canadian Broadcasting Corp.
Editorial: Bag Service #8, 155 MacKenzie Road, Inuvik, Northwest Territories X0E 0T0 **Tel:** 1 867 777-7615.
Email: cbcnorth@cbc.ca
Web site: http://cbc.ca/north
Profile: CHAK-AM is a non-commercial station owned by the Canadian Broadcasting Corp. The format of the station is variety. CHAK-AM broadcasts to the Inuvik, Northwest Territories area at 860 AM.
AM RADIO STATION

CHAM-AM
47216

Owner: Bell Media
Editorial: 883 Upper Wentworth St Suite 401, Hamilton, Ontario L9A 4Y6 **Tel:** 1 905 574-1150.
Web site: http://www.funny820.com
Profile: CHAM-AM is a commercial station owned by Bell Media. The format of the station is comedy. CHAM-AM broadcasts in the Hamilton, Ontario area at 820 AM.
AM RADIO STATION

CHAS-FM (Kiss 100.5)
47654

Owner: Rogers Communications Inc.
Editorial: 642 Great Northern Rd, Sault Ste. Marie, Ontario P6B 4Z9 **Tel:** 1 705 759-9200.
Web site: http://www.kisssoo.com
Profile: CHAS-FM is a commercial station owned by Rogers Communications Inc. The format of the station is adult contemporary. CHAS-FM broadcasts to the Sault Ste. Marie, Ontario area at 100.5 FM.
FM RADIO STATION

CHAT-FM
394652

Owner: Jim Pattison Broadcast Group(The)
Editorial: 10 Boundary Rd SE, Redcliff, Alberta T0J 2P0- **Tel:** 1 403 548-8282.
Email: chat945@jpbg.ca
Web site: http://www.chat945.com
Profile: CHAT-FM is a commercial station owned by The Jim Pattison Broadcast Group. The format is contemporary country. CHAT-FM broadcasts to the Redcliff, Alberta area at 94.5 FM.
FM RADIO STATION

CHAY-FM
47510

Owner: Corus Entertainment Inc.
Editorial: 1125 Bayfield St North, Barrie, Ontario L4N 4S5 **Tel:** 1 705 737-3511.
Email: news@931freshradio.ca
Web site: http://www.931freshradio.ca
Profile: CHAY-FM is a commercial radio station owned by Corus Entertainment Inc. The format of the station is adult contemporary. CHAY-FM broadcasts to the Barrie, Ontario area at 93.1 FM.
FM RADIO STATION

CHBD-FM
521856

Owner: Bell Media
Editorial: 4303 Albert St Suite 100, Regina, Saskatchewan S4S 3R6 **Tel:** 1 306 337-2850.
Web site: http://www.bigdog927.com
Profile: CHBD-FM is a commercial station owned by Bell Media. The format of the station is contemporary country. CHBD-FM broadcasts to Regina, Saskatchewan at 92.7 FM.
FM RADIO STATION

CHBE-FM
62195

Owner: Bell Media
Editorial: 1420 Broad Street, Victoria, British Columbia V8W 2B1 **Tel:** 1 250 382-1073.
Web site: http://www.1073kool.fm
Profile: CHBE-FM is a commercial station owned by Bell Media. The format of the station is hot adult contemporary. CHBE-FM broadcasts to the Victoria, British Columbia area at 107.3 FM.
FM RADIO STATION

CHBI-FM
586216

Owner: The Burnt Islands Economic Development Board
Editorial: 74 Main St, Burnt Islands, Newfoundland A0M 1B0 **Tel:** 1 709 698-3110.
Email: chbi95.7fm@hotmail.com
Web site: http://www.burntislandsnl.ca
Profile: CHBI-FM is a non-commercial station owned by The Burnt Islands Economic Development Board. The format of the station is variety. CHBI-FM broadcasts to the Burnt Islands, Newfoundland area at 95.7 FM.
FM RADIO STATION

CHBM-FM
47625

Owner: Newcap Radio
Editorial: 2 St. Clair Ave W Fl 2ND, Toronto, Ontario M4V 1L5 **Tel:** 1 416 482-0973.
Email: info@boom973.com
Web site: http://www.boom973.com
Profile: CHBM-FM is a commercial station owned by Newcap Radio. The format of the station is classic hits. CHBM-FM broadcasts to the Toronto area at 97.3 FM.
FM RADIO STATION

CHBN-FM
363745

Owner: Rogers Communications Inc.
Editorial: 5915 Gateway Blvd NW, Edmonton, Alberta T6H 2H3 **Tel:** 1 780 423-2005.
Web site: http://www.thebounce.ca
Profile: CHBN-FM is a commercial radio station owned by Rogers Communications Inc. The format of the station is Top 40/CHR. CHBN-FM broadcasts to the Edmonton, Alberta area at 91.7 FM.
FM RADIO STATION

CHBO-FM
810772

Owner: Golden West Broadcasting Ltd.
Editorial: 640 10th St, Humboldt, Saskatchewan S0K 2A0 **Tel:** 1 855 476-0155.
Web site: http://www.bolt1075fm.com
Profile: CHBO-FM is a commercial station owned by Golden West Broadcasting Ltd. The format of the station is adult hits. CHBO-FM broadcasts to the Humboldt, Saskatchewan area at a frequency of 107.5 FM.
FM RADIO STATION

CHBV-AM 47430
Owner: Vista Broadcast Group
Editorial: 1940 3rd Avenue, Prince George, British Columbia V2M 1G7 **Tel:** 1 250 564-2524.
Web site: http://www.thevalleywolf.ca
AM RADIO STATION

CHBW-FM 47882
Owner: Jim Pattison Broadcast Group(The)
Editorial: 4814B-49th Street, Rocky Mountain House, Alberta T4T 1S8 **Tel:** 1 403 844-9450.
Email: onair@b94.ca
Web site: http://b94.ca
Profile: CHBW-FM is a commercial station owned by The Jim Pattison Broadcast Group. The format is adult hits. CHBW-FM broadcasts to the Rocky Mountain House, Alberta area at 93.9 FM.
FM RADIO STATION

CHBZ-FM 47757
Owner: Jim Pattison Broadcast Group(The)
Editorial: 19-9th Ave South, Cranbrook, British Columbia V1C 2L9 **Tel:** 1 250 426-2224.
Email: news@thedrivefm.ca
Web site: http://www.b104.ca
Profile: CHBZ-FM is a commercial station owned by The Jim Pattison Broadcast Group. The format of the station is contemporary country music. CHBZ-FM broadcasts in the Cranbrook, British Columbia area at 104.7 FM.
FM RADIO STATION

CHCD-FM (98.9 myFM) 47787
Owner: My Broadcasting Corporation
Editorial: 55 Park Rd, Simcoe, Ontario N3Y 4J9
Tel: 1 519 426-7700.
Email: news989@myfmradio.ca
Web site: http://www.norfolktoday.ca
Profile: CHCD-FM is a commercial station owned by My Broadcasting Corporation. The format of the station is adult contemporary music. CHCD-FM broadcasts in the Simcoe, Ontario area at 98.9 FM.
FM RADIO STATION

CHCM-AM 47300
Owner: Steele Communications
Editorial: Ville Marie Drive, Marystown, Newfoundland A0E 2M0 **Tel:** 1 709 279-2560.
Profile: CHCM-AM is a commercial radio station owned by the Steele Communications. The format is contemporary country music. CHCM-AM broadcasts in the Marystown, Newfoundland area at 740 AM.
AM RADIO STATION

CHCQ-FM 83086
Owner: Starboard Communications Ltd.
Editorial: 497 Dundas St W, Belleville, Ontario K8P 1B6 **Tel:** 1 613 966-0955.
Email: news@cool100.ca
Web site: http://www.cool100.ca
Profile: CHCQ-FM is a commercial station owned by Starboard Communications Ltd. The format for the station is contemporary country. CHCQ-FM broadcasts to the Belleville, Ontario area at 100.1 FM.
FM RADIO STATION

CHCR-FM 553376
Owner: Homegrown Community Radio
Editorial: 14 Lake St., Unit A, Killaloe, Ontario K0J 2A0 **Tel:** 1 613 757-0657.
Email: radio@chcr.org
Web site: http://www.chcr.org
Profile: CHCR-FM is a commercial station owned by Homegrown Community Radio. The format of the station is variety. CHCR-FM broadcasts to the Killaloe, Ontario area at 102.9 FM.
FM RADIO STATION

CHDI-FM 387552
Owner: Rogers Communications Inc.
Editorial: 5915 Gateway Blvd NW, Edmonton, Alberta T6H 2H3 **Tel:** 1 780 423-2005.
Web site: http://www.sonic1029.com
Profile: CHDI-FM is a commercial station owned by Rogers Communications Inc. The format of the station is rock/album-oriented rock. CHDI-FM broadcasts to the Edmonton, Alberta area at 102.9 FM.
FM RADIO STATION

CHDR-FM 47111
Owner: Jim Pattison Broadcast Group(The)
Editorial: 19 9th Ave S, Cranbrook, British Columbia V1C 2L9 **Tel:** 1 250 426-2224.
Email: news@thedrivefm.ca
Web site: http://www.thedrivefm.ca
Profile: CHDR-FM is a commercial station owned by The Jim Pattison Broadcast Group. The format of the station is classic rock music. CHDR-FM broadcasts to Cranbrook, British Columbia at 102.9 FM.
FM RADIO STATION

CHED-AM 47177
Owner: Corus Entertainment Inc.
Editorial: 5204 84 St NW, Edmonton, Alberta T6E 5N8
Tel: 1 780 440-6300.
Email: chednews@630ched.com
Web site: http://www.630ched.com
Profile: CHED-AM is a commercial station owned by Corus Entertainment Inc. The format of the station is news, talk and sports. CHED-AM broadcasts to the Edmonton, Alberta area at 630 AM.
AM RADIO STATION

CHEF-FM (Radio Matagami 99.9) 383019
Owner: Radio Matagami
Editorial: 110 Boul Matagami, Matagami, Quebec J0Y 2A0 **Tel:** 1 819 739-9990.
Email: chef99fm@lino.com
Profile: CHEF-FM est une station de radio commerciale, une propriété de Radio Matagami. Le format de la station est adulte contemporain. CHEF-FM est diffusé à Matagami, au Québec à 99.9 FM.

CHEF-FM is a commercial station owned by Radio Matagami. The format of the station is adult contemporary. CHEF-FM broadcasts to Matagami, Quebec at 99.9 FM.
FM RADIO STATION

CHEQ-FM 47808
Owner: Attraction Radio
Editorial: 373, route Cameron, Ste-Marie-de-Beauce, Quebec G6E 3E2 **Tel:** 1 418 387-1013.
Web site: http://www.fm1015.ca
Profile: CHEQ-FM is a commercial station owned by Attraction Radio. The format of the station is a mix of adult contemporary. CHEQ-FM broadcasts to the Ste-Marie-de-Beauce, Quebec area at 101.5 FM.
FM RADIO STATION

CHER-FM 47198
Owner: Maritime Broadcasting System Ltd.
Editorial: 318 Charlotte St, Sydney, Nova Scotia B1P 1C8 **Tel:** 1 902 564-5596.
Email: news@capebretonradio.com
Web site: http://www.983maxfm.com
Profile: CHER-FM is a commercial station owned by the Maritime Broadcasting System Ltd. The format of the station is classic hits. CHER-FM broadcasts in the Sydney, Nova Scotia area at 98.3 FM.
FM RADIO STATION

CHES-FM (Erin Radio 91.7) 557833
Owner: Erin Community Radio Inc
Editorial: P.O. Box 1080, Erin, Ontario **Tel:** 1 519 833-9300.
Email: info@erinradio.org
Web site: http://www.erinradio.org
Profile: CHES-FM (Erin Radio 91.7) is a non-commercial radio station owned by Erin Radio Membership. The format for the station is community radio. CHES-FM broadcasts to the Erin, Ontario area at 91.7 FM.
FM RADIO STATION

CHET-FM 47833
Owner: Chetwynd Communications Society
Editorial: 4612 N Access Rd #102, Chetwynd, British Columbia V0C 1J0 **Tel:** 1 250 788-9452.
Email: news@peacefm.ca
Web site: http://www.peacefm.ca
Profile: CHET-FM is a non-commercial station owned by Chetwynd Communications Society. The format of the station is variety. CHET-FM broadcasts to the Chetwynd, British Columbia area at 94.5 FM.
FM RADIO STATION

CHEY-FM (Rouge FM Mauricie 94,7) 47589
Owner: Bell Media
Editorial: 1500 Rue Royale Bureau 260, Trois-Rivieres, Quebec G9A 6J4 **Tel:** 1 819 378-1023.
Email: nouvelles.mauricie.radio@bellmedia.ca
Web site: http://mauricie.rougefm.ca/
Profile: CHEY-FM (Rouge FM Mauricie 94,7) est une station de radio commerciale appartenant à Bell Media. Le format de sa programmation est musicale et parlée. Elle est diffusée sur la fréquence 94.7 à Trois-Rivières.

CHEY-FM (Rouge FM Mauricie 94,7) is a commercial station owned by Bell Media. The format of the station is adult contemporary. It broadcasts to the Trois-Rivieres, Quebec area at 94.7 FM.
FM RADIO STATION

CHEZ-FM (106.1 CHEZ) 47519
Owner: Rogers Communications Inc.
Editorial: 2001 Thurston Dr, Ottawa, Ontario K1G 6C9
Tel: 1 613 736-2001.
Email: ottawanewsroom@ottawaradio.rogers.com
Web site: http://www.chez106.com
Profile: CHEZ-FM is a commercial station owned by Rogers Communications Inc. The format of the station is classic rock music. CHEZ-FM's broadcasts to Ottawa, Ontario and surrounding communities at 106.1 FM.
FM RADIO STATION

CHFA-FM 47178
Owner: Société Radio-Canada
Editorial: 10062-102 Avenue, Suite 123 Edmonton City Centre, Edmonton, Alberta T5J 2Y8
Tel: 1 780 468-7500.
Email: nouvelles.alberta@radio-canada.ca
Web site: http://ici.radio-canada.ca/alberta
Profile: CHFA-FM is a non-commercial station owned by Société Radio-Canada. The format for the station is news and talk. CHFA-FM broadcasts to the Edmonton, Alberta area at 90,1 FM.
FM RADIO STATION

CHFG-FM (Mistissini 101.1) 83124
Owner: James Bay Cree Communications Society
Editorial: 23 Petawabano Street, Chisasibi, Quebec G0W 1C0 **Tel:** 1 819 855-2527.
Email: creeradio@hotmail.com
Web site: http://www.creeradio.com
Profile: CHFG-FM est une station commercial, une propriété de James Bay Cree Communications Society. Le format de la station est le variété. CHFG-FM est diffusé à Mistissini, au Québec à 101.1 FM.

CHFG-FM is a commercial station owned by the James Bay Cree Communications Society. The format of the station is variety. CHFG-FM broadcast to the Mistssini, Quebec area at 101.1 FM.
FM RADIO STATION

CHFI-FM 47531
Owner: Rogers Communications Inc.
Editorial: 1 Ted Rogers Way, Toronto, Ontario M4Y 3B7 **Tel:** 1 416 935-8298.
Email: chfi@rci.rogers.com
Web site: http://www.chfi.com
Profile: CHFI-FM is a commercial station owned by Rogers Communications Inc. The format is Soft Rock/Soft AC. CHFI-FM broadcasts to the Toronto area at 98.1 FM.
FM RADIO STATION

CHFM-FM 47635
Owner: Rogers Communications Inc.
Editorial: 2723 37 Ave NE Suite 240, Calgary, Alberta T1Y 5R8 **Tel:** 1 403 246-9696.
Web site: http://www.kiss959.com/
Profile: CHFM-FM is a commercial station owned by Rogers Communications Inc. The format for the station is lite rock. CHFM-FM broadcasts to the Calgary, Alberta area at 95.9 FM.
FM RADIO STATION

CHFN-FM 784631
Owner: Chippewas of Nawash Unceded First Nation
Editorial: 67 Community Centre Rd, RR#5, Wiarton, Ontario N0H 2T0 **Tel:** 1 519 534-1003.
Email: chfn@ymail.com
Web site: http://www.nawash.ca/index.cfm?page=link_chfn
Profile: CHFN-FM is a non-commercial station owned by Chippewas of Nawash Unceded First Nation. The format of the station is variety. CHFN-FM broadcasts to Wiarton, ON adt 100.1 FM.
FM RADIO STATION

CHFT-FM 539418
Owner: Harvard Broadcasting
Editorial: 9904 Franklin Ave, Fort McMurray, Alberta T9H 2K5 **Tel:** 1 780 791-0103.
Web site: http://1005cruzfm.com
Profile: CHFT-FM is a commercial station owned by Harvard Broadcasting. The format of the station is adult hits. CHFT-FM broadcasts to the Fort McMurray, Alberta area at 100.5 FM.
FM RADIO STATION

CHFX-FM 47554
Owner: Maritime Broadcasting System Ltd.
Editorial: 5121 Sackville St, 3rd Floor, Halifax, Nova Scotia B3J 1K1 **Tel:** 1 902 422-1651.
Email: chfxnews@chfxradio.com
Web site: http://www.fx1019.ca
Profile: CHFX-FM is a commercial station owned by the Maritime Broadcasting System Limited. The format of the station is contemporary country. CHFX-FM broadcasts to the Halifax, Nova Scotia area at 101.9 FM.
FM RADIO STATION

CHGA-FM (Maniwaki 97.3) 47580
Owner: Radio Communautaire de la Haute Gatineau
Editorial: 163 Rue Laurier, Maniwaki, Quebec J9E 2K6 **Tel:** 1 819 449-9730.
Email: chga@chga.fm
Web site: http://chga.fm
Profile: CHGA-FM est une station de radio francophone appartenant à Radio Communautaire de la Haute Gatineau. Le format de la station est le variété. CHGA-FM est diffusée à Maniwaki, Québec au 97.3 FM.

CHGA-FM is a commercial station owned by Radio Communautaire de la Haute Gatineau. The format of the station is variety. CHGA-FM broadcasts to Maniwaki, Quebec area at 97.3 FM.
FM RADIO STATION

CHGB-FM (97.7 The Beach) 472287
Owner: Bayshore Broadcasting Corp.
Editorial: 9937 Hwy 26, Collingwood, Ontario L9Y 3Z3
Tel: 1 705 422-0970.
Email: news@977thebeach.ca
Web site: http://www.977thebeach.ca
Profile: CHGB-FM is a commercial station owned by Bayshore Broadcasting Corp. The format for the station is adult contemporary. CHGB-FM broadcasts to the Wasaga Beach, Ontario area at 97.7 FM.
FM RADIO STATION

CHGK-FM 155271
Owner: Vista Broadcast Group Inc.
Editorial: 376 Romeo St S, Stratford, Ontario N5A 4T9- **Tel:** 1 519 271-2450.
Email: news@fm1077stratford.com
Web site: http://www.fm1077stratford.com
Profile: CHGK-FM is a commercial station owned by Vista Broadcast Group Inc. The format of the station is adult contemporary. CHGK-FM broadcasts to the Stratford, Ontario area at 107.7 FM.
FM RADIO STATION

CHGO-FM 70726
Owner: RNC Media
Editorial: 1729 3e Av, Val-d'Or, Quebec J9P 1W3
Tel: 1 819 825-0010.
Email: live@abitibi.capitalerock.ca
Web site: http://www.abitibi.capitalerock.ca/
Profile: CHGO-FM est une station de RNC Média, diffusant sur Val-d'Or et sa région au 104,3 FM. On y diffuse de la musique rock classique.

CHGO-FM is a commercial station owned by RNC Media. The format of the station is rock. CHGO-FM broadcasts to the Val d'Or, Quebec area at 104.3 FM.
FM RADIO STATION

CHHA-AM 585908
Owner: San Lorenzo Latin American Community Center
Editorial: 22 Wenderly Dr, Toronto, Ontario M6B 2N9-
Tel: 1 416 785-8729.
Web site: http://www.sanlorenzo.ca/english/Voces_Latinas_1610_AM.html
Profile: CHHA-AM is a non-commercial station owned by San Lorenzo Latin American Community Center. The format is Hispanic variety. CHHA-AM broadcasts to the Toronto area at 1610 AM.
AM RADIO STATION

CHHO-FM - (Maskinonge 103.1) 588160
Owner: La Coopérative de solidarité radio communautaire de la MRC de Maskinongé
Editorial: 50-A rue de la Fabrique, Saint-Leon-le-Grand, Quebec J0K 2W0 **Tel:** 1 819 228-1001.
Web site: http://www.1031fm.ca
Profile: CHHO-FM est une station de radio francophone non-commerciale, une propriété de La Coopérative de solidarité radio communautaire de la MRC de Maskinongé. Le format de la station est le variété. CHHO-FM est diffusée Saint-Leon-le-Grand, au Québec à 103.1.

CHHO-FM is a non-commericial French-language station owned by La Coopérative de solidarité radio communautaire de la MRC de Maskinongé. The format of the station is variety. CHHO-FM broadcasts to Saint-Leon-le-Grand, Quebec at 103.1.
FM RADIO STATION

CHHR-FM 591409
Owner: Newcap Radio
Editorial: 20-11151 Horseshoe Way 20, Richmond, British Columbia V7A 4S5 **Tel:** 1 604 241-2100.
Web site: http://www.lg1043.com
Profile: CHHR-FM is a commercial station owned by Newcap Radio. The format of the station is adult standards/nostalgia. CHHR-FM broadcasts to the Vancouver, British Columbia area at 104.3 FM.
FM RADIO STATION

CHIC-FM 553377
Owner: Communications CHIC
Editorial: 120, Rue 9e, Rouyn-Noranda, Quebec J9X 2B6 **Tel:** 1 819 797-4242.
Email: 887@chicfm.org
Web site: http://www.chicfm.org
Profile: CHIC-FM is a commercial station owned by Communications CHIC. The format for the station is French contemporary Christian. CHIC-FM broadcasts to the Rouyn-Noranda, Quebec area at 88.7 FM.
FM RADIO STATION

CHIK-FM (Énergie Québec 98.9) 47574
Owner: Bell Media
Editorial: 900 Place D'Youville Etage 1ER, Quebec, Quebec G1R 3P7 **Tel:** 1 418 687-9900.
Email: nouvelles.quebec.radio@bellmedia.ca
Web site: http://www.iheartradio.ca/energie/energie-quebec/
Profile: CHIK-FM (Énergie Québec 98.9) est une station de radio commerciale appartenant à Bell Media. Son format est de type Top40 et parlée. CHIK-FM (Énergie Québec 98.9) is a commercial station owned by Bell Media. The format for the station is Top 40/CHR. CHIK-FM broadcasts to the Quebec City area at 98.9 FM.
FM RADIO STATION

CHIM-FM 83093
Owner: Celestial Sound
Editorial: Celestial Sound, 226 Delnite Road, Timmins, Ontario P4N 7C2 **Tel:** 1 705 264-2150.
Email: chimfm@vianet.ca
Web site: http://www.chimfm.com

Profile: CHIM-FM is a non-commercial station owned by Celestial Sound. The format of the station is contemporary Christian. CHIM-FM broadcasts to Timmins, Ontario at 102.3 FM.
FM RADIO STATION

CHIN-AM 47344
Owner: Radio 1540 Ltd.
Editorial: 622 College St, Suite 400, Toronto, Ontario M6G 1B6 **Tel:** 1 416 531-9991.
Email: info@chinradio.com
Web site: http://www.chinradio.com
Profile: CHIN-AM is a commercial station owned by Radio 1540 Ltd. The format of the station is multi-lingual news and talk. CHIN-AM broadcasts to the Toronto area at 1540 AM.
AM RADIO STATION

CHIN-FM 47534
Owner: Radio 1540 Ltd.
Editorial: 622 College St Suite 400, Toronto, Ontario M6G 1B4 **Tel:** 1 416 531-9991.
Email: info@chinradio.com
Web site: http://www.chinradio.com
Profile: CHIN-FM is a commercial station owned by Radio 1540 Ltd. The format of the station is variety. CHIN-FM broadcasts to Toronto and southern Ontario at 100.7 FM.
FM RADIO STATION

CHIP-FM 47615
Owner: Radio Communautaire du Pontiac Inc.
Editorial: 138 Principale St, Fort-Coulonge, Quebec J0X 1V0 **Tel:** 1 819 683-3155.
Email: news@chipfm.com
Web site: http://www.chipfm.com
Profile: CHIP-FM est une radio communautaire bilingue détenue par Radio Communautaire du Pontiac. La programmation variée est diffusée sur la fréquence 101,7 pour Fort-Coulonge et les environs. Le site web est fourni en français et anglais.

CHIP-FM is a commercial bilingual station owned by Radio Communautaire du Pontiac Inc. The format of the station is variety. CHIP-FM broadcasts to Fort-Coulonge, Quebec at 101.7 FM. The web site is in french and english.
FM RADIO STATION

CHIQ-FM (The Drive 94.3) 47500
Owner: Jim Pattison Broadcast Group (The)
Editorial: 1445 Pembina Hwy, Winnipeg, Manitoba R3T 5C2 **Tel:** 1 204 477-5120.
Web site: http://www.fab943.com
Profile: CHIQ-FM is a commercial station owned by Bell Media. The format of the station is classic hits music. CHIQ-FM broadcasts to the Winnipeg, Manitoba area at 94.3 FM.
FM RADIO STATION

CHJM-FM (Mix 99.7) 47568
Owner: Groupe Radio Simard
Editorial: 11760 3e Ave, Saint-Georges, Quebec G5Y 1V4 **Tel:** 1 418 227-0997.
Email: nouvelles@radiobeauce.com
Web site: http://www.mix997.com
Profile: CHJM-FM est une station commerciale, une propriété de Groupe Radio Simard. La formule de la station est contemporain adulte. CHJM-FM est diffusé à Saint-Georges, dans la région de Québec. La fréquence est 99.7 FM.

CHJM-FM is a commercial station owned by Groupe Radio Simard. The format for the station is adult contemporary. CHJM-FM broadcasts to the Saint-Georges, Quebec area at 99.7 FM.
FM RADIO STATION

CHJX-FM 342191
Owner: Sound of Faith Broadcasting
Editorial: 254 Adelaide St S, London, Ontario N5Z 3L1 **Tel:** 1 519 679-9882.
Email: inspirefm@gmail.com
Web site: http://www.london.faithfm.org
Profile: CHJX-FM is a commercial station owned by Sound of Faith Broadcasting. The format of the station is contemporary Christian. CHJX-FM broadcasts to the London, Ontario area at 105.9 FM.
FM RADIO STATION

CHKF-FM 47870
Owner: Fairchild Radio Group Ltd.
Editorial: 2723 37th Ave NE, Suite 109, Calgary, Alberta T1Y 5R8 **Tel:** 1 403 717-1940.
Email: news@fm947.com
Web site: http://www.fm947.com
Profile: CHKF-FM is a commercial station owned by the Fairchild Radio Group Ltd. The format of the station is multi-lingual and multi-ethnic music, news, entertainment, lifestyle, and general interest talk. CHKF-FM broadcasts to Calgary, Alberta at 94.7 FM.
FM RADIO STATION

CHKG-FM 47837
Owner: Fairchild Radio Group Ltd.
Editorial: 4151 Hazelbridge Way, Richmond, British Columbia V6X 4J7- **Tel:** 1 604 295-1234.
Email: news@am1470.com
Web site: http://www.fm961.com
Profile: CHKG-FM is a commercial station owned by the Fairchild Radio Group Ltd. The format of the station is ethnic music, news, and talk. CHKG-FM broadcasts to Vancouver, British Columbia at 96.1 FM.
FM RADIO STATION

CHKS-FM 47869
Owner: Blackburn Radio Inc.
Editorial: 1415 London Road, Sarnia, Ontario N7S 1P6 **Tel:** 1 519 542-5500.
Email: rock@k106fm.com
Web site: http://www.k106fm.com
FM RADIO STATION

CHKT-AM 47421
Owner: Fairchild Radio Group Ltd.
Editorial: 151 Esna Park Dr Unit 26-29, Markham, Ontario L3R 3B1 **Tel:** 1 905 415-6265.
Email: news@am1430.com
Web site: http://www.am1430.com
Profile: CHKT-AM is a commercial station owned by Fairchild Radio Group Ltd. The format of the station is international variety. CHKT-AM broadcasts to Richmond Hill, Ontario at 1430 AM.
AM RADIO STATION

CHKX-FM (KX94-7 New Country FM) 83087
Owner: Durham Radio Inc.
Editorial: 589 Upper Wellington St, Hamilton, Ontario L9A 3P8 **Tel:** 1 905 388-8911.
Email: news@kx947.fm
Web site: http://www.kx947.fm
Profile: CHKX-FM is a commerical station owned by Durham Radio Inc. The format of the station is contemporary country. CHKX-FM broadcasts to the Hamilton, Ontario area at 94.7 FM.
FM RADIO STATION

CHLB-FM 47780
Owner: Jim Pattison Broadcast Group(The)
Editorial: 401 Mayor Magrath Drive, Lethbridge, Alberta T1J 3L8 **Tel:** 1 403 329-0955.
Email: info@country95.fm
Web site: http://www.country95.fm
Profile: CHLB-FM is a commercial station owned by The Jim Pattison Broadcast Group. The format is classic and contemporary country. CHLB-FM broadcasts to Lethbridge, Alberta at 95.5 FM.
FM RADIO STATION

CHLC-FM 47813
Owner: Radio Port-Cartier Inc.
Editorial: 907 Rue de Puyjalon, Baie-Comeau, Quebec G5C 1N3 **Tel:** 1 418 589-3771.
Email: chlcfm97@globetrotter.net
Web site: http://www.chlc.com
Profile: CHLC-FM is a commercial station owned by Radio Port-Cartier Inc. The format of the station is Hot Adult Contemporary. CHLC-FM broadcasts to the Baie-Comeau, Quebec area at 97.1 FM.
FM RADIO STATION

CHLI-FM 588221
Owner: Rossland Radio Coop
Editorial: 1807 Columbia Ave, Rossland, British Columbia V0G 1Y0 **Tel:** 1 250 362-0080.
Email: radio@rosslandradio.com
Web site: http://www.rosslandradio.com
Profile: CHLI-FM is non-commercial station owned by Rossland Radio Corp. The format of the station is variety. CHLI-FM broadcasts to the Rossland, British Columbia area at 101.1 FM.
FM RADIO STATION

CHLK-FM 492911
Owner: (Perkin) Brian & Norm Wright
Editorial: 43 Wilson St W, Perth, Ontario K7H 2N3
Tel: 1 613 264-8811.
Email: events@lake88.ca
Web site: http://www.lake88.ca
Profile: CHLK-FM is a commercial station owned by Norm Wright and Brian Perkin. The format of the station is adult contemporary. CHLK-FM broadcasts to the Perth, Ontario area at 88.1 FM.
FM RADIO STATION

CHLM-FM 83163
Owner: Société Radio-Canada
Editorial: 70 Av Principale, Rouyn-Noranda, Quebec J9X 4P2 **Tel:** 1 819 762-8155.
Email: abitibi@radio-canada.ca
Web site: http://ici.radio-canada.ca/abitibi-temiscamingue/
Profile: CHLM-FM is a non-commercial station owned by Societe Radio-Canada. The format of the station is news/talk. CHLM-FM broadcasts to the Rouyn-Noranda, Quebec area at 90.7 FM.
FM RADIO STATION

CHLQ-FM 47636
Owner: Maritime Broadcasting System Ltd.
Editorial: 5 Prince Street, Charlottetown, Prince Edward Island C1A 4P4 **Tel:** 1 902 892-1066.
Web site: http://q93.fm
Profile: CHLQ-FM is a commercial station owned by the Maritime Broadcasting System Ltd. The format of the station is classic rock. CHLQ-FM broadcasts to the Charlottetown, Prince Edward Island area at 93.1 FM.
FM RADIO STATION

CHLS-FM 586062
Owner: Radio Lillooet Society
Editorial: #415 Main Street, Lillooet, British Columbia V0K 1V0 **Tel:** 1 250 256-2113.
Email: station@radiolillooet.ca
Web site: http://radiolillooet.ca
FM RADIO STATION

CHLX-FM (WOW! 97.1) 139537
Owner: RNC Media
Tel: 1 819 770-1040.
Web site: https://wowfm.ca/planete/chlx
Profile: CHLX-FM is a commercial station owned by RNC Media. CHLX-FM broadcasts to the Gatineau, Quebec area at 97.1 FM. CHLX-FM's tagline is "WOW! 97.1"
FM RADIO STATION

CHLY-FM 588194
Owner: Radio Malaspina Society
Editorial: 34 Victorica Cres. #2, Nanaimo, British Columbia V9R 5B8 **Tel:** 1 250 716-3410.
Email: news@chly.ca
Web site: http://www.chly.ca
Profile: CHLY-FM is a non-commercial station owned by Radio Malaspina Society. The format of the station is variety. CHLY-FM broadcasts to the Nanaimo, British Columbia at 101.7 FM.
FM RADIO STATION

CHMA-FM 47719
Owner: Attic Broadcasting Co. Ltd.
Editorial: 62 York St, Sackville, New Brunswick E4L 1E2 **Tel:** 1 506 364-2221.
Email: chma@mta.ca
Web site: http://www.mta.ca/chma
Profile: CHMA-FM is a non-commercial station owned by Attic Broadcasting Co. Ltd. The format of the station is college variety. CHMA-FM broadcasts to the Sackville, New Brunswick area at 106.9 FM.
FM RADIO STATION

CHMB-AM 47152
Owner: Mainstream Broadcasting Corp.
Editorial: 1200 W 73rd Avenue, Suite 100, Vancouver, British Columbia V6P 6G5 **Tel:** 1 604 263-1320.
Email: adm@am1320.com
Web site: http://www.am1320.com
Profile: CHMB-AM is a commercial station owned by the Mainstream Broadcasting Corp. The format of the station is ethnic and multicultural music and talk. CHMB-AM broadcasts to the Vancouver, BC area at 1320 AM.
AM RADIO STATION

CHME-FM 83153
Owner: Radio Essipit/Haute Cote-Nord Inc.
Editorial: 34 de la Reserve, Les Escoumins, Quebec G0T 1K0 **Tel:** 1 418 233-2700.
Email: chme@b2b2c.ca
Web site: http://chme949.com
Profile: CHME-FM is a commercial station owned by Radio Essipit/Haute Cote-Nord Inc. The format of the station is news, talk and rock/album-oriented rock. CHME-FM broadcasts to the Les Escoumins, Quebec area at 94.9 FM.
FM RADIO STATION

CHMJ-AM 47155
Owner: Corus Entertainment Inc.
Editorial: 700 Georgia St W Suite 2000, Vancouver, British Columbia V7Y 1K8 **Tel:** 1 604 331-2844.
Email: am730traffic@corusent.com
Web site: http://www.am730.ca
Profile: CHMJ-AM is a commercial station owned by Corus Entertainment Inc. The format of the station is talk. CHMJ-AM broadcasts to the Vancouver, British Columbia area at 730 AM.
AM RADIO STATION

CHML-AM (AM 900) 47217
Owner: Corus Entertainment Inc.
Editorial: 875 Main St W, Hamilton, Ontario L8S 4P9
Tel: 1 905 521-9900.
Email: news@900chml.com
Web site: http://www.900chml.com
Profile: CHML-AM (AM 900) is a commercial station owned by Corus Entertainment Inc. The format of the station is news and talk. CHML-AM broadcasts to the Hamilton, Ontario area at 900 AM.
AM RADIO STATION

CHMM-FM 490409
Owner: MacKenzie Area Community Radio Society
Editorial: 86 Centennial, MacKenzie, British Columbia V0J 2C0 **Tel:** 1 250 997-6277.
Email: chmm1035@chmm.ca
Web site: http://www.chmm.ca
Profile: CHMM-FM is a non-commercial station owned by MacKenzie Area Community Radio Society. The format for the station is hot adult contemporary. CHMM-FM broadcasts to the MacKenzie, British Columbia area at 103.5 FM.
FM RADIO STATION

CHMN-FM 47823
Owner: Rogers Communications Inc.
Editorial: 749 Railway Ave, Canmore, Alberta T1W 1P2 **Tel:** 1 403 678-2222.
Web site: http://www.mountainfm.ca
Profile: CHMN-FM is a commercial station owned by Rogers Communications Inc. The format of the station is hot adult contemporary. CHMN-FM broadcasts to the Canmore, Alberta area at 106.5 FM.
FM RADIO STATION

CHMO-AM 47230
Owner: James Bay Broadcasting Corp.
Editorial: 28 First St, Moosonee, Ontario P0L 1Y0
Tel: 1 705 336-2466.
Email: jbbtcorp@onlink.net
Profile: CHMO-AM is a non-commercial station owned by James Bay Broadcasting Corp. The format of the station is classic country. CHMO-AM broadcasts to the Moosonee, Ontario at area 1450 AM.
AM RADIO STATION

CHMP-FM (98,5 fm Montréal) 83140
Owner: Cogeco
Editorial: 800 Rue de la Gauchetiere O Bureau 1100, Montreal, Quebec H5A 1K6 **Tel:** 1 514 789-0985.
Web site: http://www.985fm.ca
Profile: CHMP-FM est une station radiophonique francophone de Cogeco où on diffuse principalement de l'information et des émissions parlées. CHMP-FM diffuse sur le 98,5FM dans la grande région de Montréal.

CHMP-FM is a commercial station owned by Cogeco. The format of the station is news and talk. CHMP-FM broadcasts to the Montreal area at 98,5 FM.
FM RADIO STATION

CHMR-FM 47718
Owner: Memorial University Students Union
Editorial: University Center, Rm 4C 2009 2nd Fl, St. John's, Newfoundland A1C 5S7 **Tel:** 1 709 737-4777.
Email: chmr@mun.ca
Web site: http://www.chmr.ca
Profile: CHMR-FM is a college station owned by Memorial University Students Union. The format of the station is variety. CHMR-FM broadcasts to the St. John's, Newfoundland area at 93.5 FM.
FM RADIO STATION

CHMS-FM 47283
Owner: Vista Broadcast Group
Editorial: 30674 Hwy 28 E, Bancroft, Ontario K0L 1C0
Tel: 1 613 332-1423.
Email: moose977.news@moosefm.com
Web site: http://www.moosefm.com/chms/index.php
Profile: CHMS-FM is a commercial station owned by the Vista Broadcast Group. The format of the station is adult contemporary music. CHMS-FM broadcasts to Bancroft, Ontario at 97.7 FM.
FM RADIO STATION

CHMT-FM (The Moose Timmins 93.1) 83112
Owner: Vista Broadcast Group
Editorial: 49 Cedar St S, Timmins, Ontario P4N 2G5
Tel: 1 705 267-6070.
Email: moose931.news@moosefm.com
Web site: http://www.moosefm.com/chmt
Profile: CHMT-FM is a commercial station owned by Vista Broadcast Group. The format for the station is Top 40/CHR. CHMT-FM broadcasts to the Timmins, Ontario area at 93.1 FM.
FM RADIO STATION

CHMX-FM 47487
Owner: Harvard Broadcasting
Editorial: 1900 Rose St., Regina, Saskatchewan S4P 0A9 **Tel:** 1 306 546-6200.
Web site: http://www.my921.ca

Profile: CHMX-FM is a commercial station owned by Harvard Broadcasting. The format of the station is hot AC. CHMX-FM broadcasts to the Regina, Saskatchewan area at 92.1 FM.
FM RADIO STATION

CHMY-FM (96.1 myFM) 281625
Owner: My Broadcasting Corporation
Editorial: 321B Raglan St S, Renfrew, Ontario K7V 1R6 **Tel:** 1 613 432-6936.
Email: news@myfmradio.ca
Web site: http://www.renfrewtoday.ca
Profile: CHMY-FM is a commercial station owned by My Broadcasting Corporation. The format of the station is adult contemporary. CHMY-FM broadcasts to the Renfrew, Ontario area at 96.1 FM. It is also simulcast to the Arnprior, Ontario area at 107.7 FM.
FM RADIO STATION

CHMZ-FM 521100
Owner: McBride Communications & Media Inc.
Editorial: 10760 Fundy Dr, Richmond, British Columbia V7E 5K7 **Tel:** 1 604 220-8393.
Profile: CHMZ-FM is owned and operated by McBride Communications & Media Inc. The format of the station is classic rock. CHMZ-FM broadcasts to the Ucluelet, British Columbia area at 90.1 FM.
FM RADIO STATION

CHNC-FM 47287
Owner: Cooperative des travailleurs CHNC
Editorial: 153 Boul Gerard-D.-Levesque, New Carlisle, Quebec G0C 1Z0 **Tel:** 1 418 752-2215.
Email: radiochnc@globetrotter.net
Web site: http://www.radiochnc.com
Profile: CHNC-FM is a commercial station owned by Cooperative des travailleurs CHNC. The format of the station is Adult Contemporary. CHNC-FM broadcasts to the New Carlisle, Quebec area at 610 AM.
FM RADIO STATION

CHNI-FM 409081
Owner: Newcap Radio
Editorial: 137 Market Square, Saint John, New Brunswick E2L 4Z6 **Tel:** 1 506 635-6500.
Web site: http://rock889.ca
Profile: CHNI-FM is a commercial station owned by Newcap Radio. The format of the station is classic rock music. CHNI-FM broadcasts to the Saint John, New Brunswick area at 88.9 FM.
FM RADIO STATION

CHNL-AM (Radio NL 610) 47118
Owner: Newfoundland Capital Corporation Limited
Editorial: 611 Lansdowne St, Kamloops, British Columbia V2C 1Y6 **Tel:** 1 250 372-2292.
Email: nlnews@radionl.com
Web site: http://www.radionl.com
Profile: CHNL-AM is a commercial station owned by Newfoundland Capital Corporation Limited. The format of the station is news, talk and sports. CHNL-AM broadcasts to Kamloops, British Columbia at 610 AM.
AM RADIO STATION

CHNO-FM (Rewind 103.9) 47338
Owner: Newfoundland Capital Corporation Limited
Editorial: 493B Barrydowne Rd, Sudbury, Ontario P3A 3T4 **Tel:** 1 705 560-8323.
Email: news@rewind1039.ca
Web site: http://rewind1039.ca
Profile: CHNO-FM is a commercial station owned by Newfoundland Capital Corporation Limited. The format of the station is classic hits. The station broadcasts to the Sudbury, Ontario area at 103.9.
FM RADIO STATION

CHNS-FM 47184
Owner: Maritime Broadcasting System
Editorial: 90 Lovett Lake Court- Suite 101, Halifax, Nova Scotia B3S 0H6 **Tel:** 1 902 422-1651.
Web site: http://www.899thewave.fm
Profile: CHNS-FM is a commercial station owned by the Maritime Broadcasting System Ltd. The format of the station is classic hits. CHNS-FM broadcasts to the Halifax, Nova Scotia area at 89.9 FM.
FM RADIO STATION

CHNV-FM 47839
Owner: Vista Broadcast Group Inc.
Editorial: 312 Hall St, Nelson, British Columbia V1L 1Y8 **Tel:** 1 250 352-1902.
Web site: http://1035.juicefm.ca
Profile: CHNV-FM is a commercial station owned by Vista Broadcast Group Inc. The format of the station is adult album alternative. CHNV-FM broadcasts to Nelson, British Columbia at 103.5 FM.
FM RADIO STATION

CHOA-FM 47637
Owner: Cogeco Media
Editorial: 380 Av Murdoch, Rouyn-Noranda, Quebec J9X 1G5 **Tel:** 1 819 762-0744.
Web site: http://www.rythmefm.com/abitibi
Profile: CHOA-FM is a commercial station owned by Cogeco Media. The format of the station is adult contemporary. CHOA-FM broadcasts to Rouyn-Noranda, Quebec and surrounding communities at 96.5 FM.
FM RADIO STATION

CHOC-FM (Saint-Rémi 104.9) 586478
Owner: La Radio Communautaire Intergeneration
Editorial: 93 Rue Lachapelle E, Saint-Remi, Quebec J0L 2L0 **Tel:** 1 450 454-5500.
Email: studio@chocfm.com
Web site: http://chocfm.com
Profile: CHOC-FM est une station de radio non-communautaire francophone, une propriété de La Radio Communautaire Intergeneration. Le format de la station est le variété. CHOC-FM est diffusé à Saint-Rémi, Québec au 104.9 FM.

CHOC-FM is a non-commercial French-language radio station owned by La Radio Communautaire Intergeneration. The format of the station is variety. CHOC-FM broadcasts to Saint-Rémi, Quebec at 104.9 FM.
FM RADIO STATION

CHOD-FM 47716
Owner: Radio Communautaire Cornwall-Alexandria Inc.
Editorial: 1111 chemin Montreal, Suite 202, Cornwall, Ontario K6H 1E1 **Tel:** 1 613 936-2463.
Email: chodfm@chodfm.ca
Web site: http://www.chodfm.ca
Profile: CHOD-FM is a commercial station owned by Radio Communautaire Cornwall-Alexandria Inc. The format of the station is French Lite Rock/Lite AC music. CHOD-FM broadcasts to the Cornwall, Ontario area at 92.1 FM.
FM RADIO STATION

CHOE-FM 47715
Owner: Communications Matane Inc.(Les)
Editorial: 800, avenue du Phare Ouest, Matane, Quebec G4W 1V7 **Tel:** 1 418 562-8181.
Email: choefm@globetrotter.net
Web site: http://www.choefm.com
Profile: CHOE-FM is a commercial station owned by Les Communications Matane Inc. The format of the station is top 40/CHR. CHOE-FM broadcasts to Matane, Quebec at 95.3 FM.
FM RADIO STATION

CHOI-FM (Radio X 98.1) 47573
Owner: RNC Media
Editorial: 1134 Grande Allee O Bureau 300, Quebec, Quebec G1S 1E5 **Tel:** 1 418 687-9810.
Web site: https://www.radiox.com/
Profile: CHOI-FM (Radio X 98.1) est une station de radio commerciale francophone, une propriété de RNC Media. Le format de la station est le rock alternatif and les discussions. CHOI-FM est diffusé dans la ville du Québec, au Québec à 98.1 FM.

CHOI-FM (Radio X 98,1) is a commercial French-language station owned by RNC Media. The format of the station is rock alternative and talk. CHOI-FM broadcasts to the Quebec City area at 98.1 FM.
FM RADIO STATION

CHOK 103.9 FM 584335
Owner: Blackburn Radio Inc.
Editorial: 1415 London Rd, Sarnia, Ontario N7S 1P6 **Tel:** 1 519 542-5500.
Web site: http://www.blackburnradio.com
Profile: CHOK 103.9 FM is a commerical station owned by Blackburn Radio Inc. The format of the station is adult contemporary. CHOK-FM broadcasts to the Sarnia, ON area at 103.9 FM.
FM RADIO STATION

CHOK 1070 AM 47241
Owner: Blackburn Radio Inc.
Editorial: 1415 London Rd, Sarnia, Ontario N7S 1P6 **Tel:** 1 519 542-5500.
Web site: http://www.chok.com
Profile: CHOK 1070 AM is a commercial station owned by Blackburn Radio Inc. The format of the station is adult contemporary. CHOK-AM broadcasts to the Sarnia, Ontario area at 1070 AM.
AM RADIO STATION

CHOM-FM 47598
Owner: Bell Media
Editorial: 1717 Boul Rene-Levesque E, Montreal, Quebec H2L 4T3 **Tel:** 1 514 529-3200.
Email: receptionmontreal1717@bellmedia.ca
Web site: http://www.iheartradio.ca/chom
Profile: CHOM-FM est une station radiophonique de Bell Media qui diffuse de la musique rock classique. Elle diffuse sur le Grand Montréal sur le 97.7FM.

CHOM-FM is a commercial station owned by Bell Media. The format of the station is classic rock. CHOM-FM broadcasts to the Montreal area at 97.7 FM.
FM RADIO STATION

CHON-FM 47435
Owner: Northern Native Broadcasting Yukon
Editorial: 4230-A 4th Ave, Suite 6, Whitehorse, Yukon Territory Y1A 1K1 **Tel:** 1 867 668-6629.
Email: nnby@nnby.net
Web site: http://www.nnby.net
Profile: CHON-FM is a commercial station owned by Northern Native Broadcasting Yukon. The format of the station is variety. CHON-FM broadcasts to the Whitehorse, Yukon Territory area at 98.1 FM.
FM RADIO STATION

CHOO-FM 588844
Owner: Golden West Broadcasting Ltd.
Editorial: 105 S. Railway Ave, Drumheller, Alberta T0J 0Y6 **Tel:** 1 403 823-9936.
Web site: http://995drumfm.com
Profile: CHOO-FM is a commercial station owned by Golden West Broadcasting Ltd. The format of the station is a variety of news, pop, rock and adult contemporary music. CHOO-FM broadcasts to the Drumheller, Alberta area at 99.5 FM.
FM RADIO STATION

CHOQ-FM 411955
Owner: Coopérative Radiophonique de Toronto(La)
Editorial: 425 Rue Adelaide O Bureau 302, Toronto, Ontario M5V 3C1 **Tel:** 1 416 599-2666.
Email: info@choqfm.ca
Web site: http://www.choqfm.ca
Profile: CHOQ-FM is a French-language non-commercial station owned by La Coopérative Radiophonique de Toronto. The format of the station is variety. CHOQ-FM broadcasts to the Toronto area at 105.1 FM.
FM RADIO STATION

CHOR-FM 47376
Owner: Bell Media
Editorial: 9901 Main St, Suite 200, Summerland, British Columbia V0H 1Z0 **Tel:** 1 250 492-2800.
Web site: http://summerland.myezrock.com/index.aspx
Profile: CHOR-FM is a commercial station owned by Bell Media. The format of the station is Adult Contemporary. CHOR-FM broadcasts to Summerland, British Columbia and surrounding communities at 98.5 FM.
FM RADIO STATION

CHOS-FM 47657
Owner: Newfoundland Broadcasting Co. Ltd.
Editorial: 446 Logy Bay Rd, St. John's, Newfoundland A1A 5C6 **Tel:** 1 709 726-2922.
Email: ozfm@ozfm.com
Web site: http://www.ozfm.com
FM RADIO STATION

CHOU-AM (Radio Moyen-Orient 1450) 588461
Owner: Radio Moyen-Orient du Canada
Editorial: 11876 Rue de Meulles, Montreal, Quebec H4J 2E6 **Tel:** 1 514 790-0002.
Email: pdg@1450am.ca
Web site: http://www.1450am.ca
Profile: CHOU-AM est une station de radio commerciale, une propriété de Radio Moyen-Orient du Canada. La format de la station est le variété. CHOU-AM est diffusé dans la région de Montréal au 1450 AM. L'auditoire ciblé de la station est les auditeurs, âgés de 13 à 100 ans.

CHOU-AM is a commercial station owned by Radio Moyen-Orient du Canada. The format for the station is variety. CHOU-AM broadcasts to the Montreal area at 1450 AM. The target audience of the station is listeners, ages 13 to 100.
AM RADIO STATION

CHOW-FM (Radio Boréale 105.3) 691896
Owner: Radio Boréale
Editorial: 43 1re Av E, Amos, Quebec J9T 1H2 **Tel:** 1 819 732-6991.
Email: info@radioboreale.com
Web site: http://www.radioboreale.com
Profile: CHOW-FM est une station de radio commerciale, une propriété de Radio Boréale. Le format de la station est le variété. CHOW-FM est diffusé à Amos, au Québec à 105.3 FM.

CHOW-FM is a commercial radio station owned by Radio Boréale. The format for the station is variety. CHOW-FM broadcasts to the Amos, Quebec area at 105.3 FM.
FM RADIO STATION

CHOX-FM 47599
Owner: Groupe Radio Simard
Editorial: 601, 1re Rue Poire Bureau 50, La Pocatiere, Quebec G0R 1Z0 **Tel:** 1 418 856-1310.
Email: chox@chox97.com
Web site: http://www.chox97.com/chox
Profile: CHOX-FM is a commercial station owned by Groupe Radio Simard. The format of the station is contemporary pop and rock music. CHOX-FM broadcasts to the La Pocatiere, Quebec area at 97.5 FM.
FM RADIO STATION

CHOY-FM 83127
Owner: Maritime Broadcasting System Ltd.
Editorial: 1000 St George Blvd, Moncton, New Brunswick E1E 4M7- **Tel:** 1 506 384-2469.
Web site: http://choix999.com
Profile: CHOY-FM is a commercial station owned by Maritime Broadcasting System Ltd. The format of the station is country. CHOY-FM broadcasts to the Moncton, New Brunswick area at 99.9 FM.
FM RADIO STATION

CHOZ-FM 47592
Owner: Newfoundland Broadcasting Co. Ltd.
Editorial: 446 Logy Bay Road, St. John's, Newfoundland A1C 5S2 **Tel:** 1 709 726-2922.
Email: ntv@ntv.ca
Web site: http://www.ozfm.com
Profile: CHOZ-FM is a commercial station owned by the Newfoundland Broadcasting Co. Ltd. The format of the station is top 40/CHR. CHOZ-FM broadcasts to Saint John's, Newfoundland and surrounding communities at 94.7 FM.
FM RADIO STATION

CHPB-FM (The Moose Cochrane 98.1) 281682
Owner: Vista Broadcast Group
Editorial: 171 6th Ave, Cochrane, Ontario P1L 1C0 **Tel:** 1 705 272-6467.
Email: moose981@moosefm.com
Web site: http://www.moosefm.com/chpb
Profile: CHPB-FM is a commercial station owned by Vista Broadcast Group. The format of the station is lite rock. The station is broadcast to the Cochrane, ON area at 98.1 FM.
FM RADIO STATION

CHPD-FM 588449
Owner: Aylmer & Area Inter-Mennonite Community
Editorial: 16 Talbot Street, Aylmer, Ontario N5H 1H4 **Tel:** 1 519 773-8555.
Email: radio@debrigj.org
Profile: CHPD-FM is a non-commercial station owned by Aylmer & Area Inter-Mennonite Community. The format of the station is ethnic variety including programming in German, Spanish and English. CHPD-FM broadcasts to the Mennonite, Ontario area at 105.9 FM.
FM RADIO STATION

CHPK-FM 908777
Editorial: 222 58 Ave SW Suite 600, Calgary, Alberta T2H 2S3 **Tel:** 1 403 536-3866.
Web site: http://953thepeak.com
Profile: CHPK-FM is a commercial station owned by The Jim Pattinson Group. The format of the station is AAA. CHPK-FM broadcasts locally at 101.5 FM.
FM RADIO STATION

CHPQ-FM 414096
Owner: Jim Pattison Broadcast Group(The)
Editorial: 166 E Island Hwy, Parksville, British Columbia V9P 2H3 **Tel:** 1 250 248-4211.
Email: info@thelounge999.com
Web site: http://www.thelounge999.com
Profile: CHPQ-FM is a commercial station owned by The Jim Pattison Broadcast Group. The format of the station is adult standards. CHPQ-FM broadcasts to the Parksville, British Columbia at 99.9 FM.
FM RADIO STATION

CHPR-FM 47713
Owner: RNC Media
Editorial: 11 rue Argenteuil, Lachute, Quebec J8H 1X8 **Tel:** 1 450 562-8862.
Web site: http://planetelov.ca
Profile: CHPR-FM is a commercial station owned by RNC Media. The format of the station is adult contemporary. CHPR-FM broadcasts to Lachute, Quebec at 102.1 FM.
FM RADIO STATION

CHQC-FM 515500
Owner: Coopérative radiophonique – La Brise de la Baie
Editorial: 67 chemin Ragged Point, Saint John, New Brunswick E2K 5C3 **Tel:** 1 506 643-6996.
Email: animateurs@chqc.ca
Web site: http://www.chqc.ca
FM RADIO STATION

CHQM-FM (QMFM 103.5) 47453
Owner: Bell Media
Editorial: 500-969 Robson St 500, Vancouver, British Columbia V6Z 1X5 **Tel:** 1 604 871-9000.
Web site: http://www.qmfm.com
Profile: CHQM-FM is a commercial station owned by Bell Media. The format of the station is Lite Rock/Lite AC music. CHQM-FM broadcasts to the Vancouver, British Columbia area at 103.5 FM.
FM RADIO STATION

CHQR-AM 47171
Owner: Corus Entertainment Inc.
Editorial: 170-200 Barclay Parade SW 170, Calgary, Alberta T2P 4R5 **Tel:** 1 403 716-6500.
Web site: http://www.newstalk770.com/
Profile: CHQR-AM is a commercial station owned by Corus Entertainment. The format of the station is news, talk and sports. CHQR-AM broadcasts to the Calgary, Alberta area at 770 AM.
AM RADIO STATION

CHQT-AM 47179
Owner: Corus Entertainment Inc.
Editorial: 5204 84 St NW, Edmonton, Alberta T6E 5N8 **Tel:** 1 780 440-6300.
Email: news@inews880.com
Web site: http://www.inews880.com
Profile: CHQT-AM is a commercial station owned by Corus Entertainment. The format of the station is

news. CHQT-AM broadcasts to Edmonton, Alberta and its environs at 880 AM.
AM RADIO STATION

CHQX-FM 75479
Owner: Jim Pattison Broadcast Group (The)
Editorial: 1316-900 Central Ave 1316, Prince Albert, Saskatchewan S6V 4V3 **Tel:** 1 306 763-7421.
Web site: http://www.mix101fm.com
Profile: CHQX-FM is a commercial station owned by The Jim Pattison Broadcast Group. The format of the station is album-oriented rock music. CHQX-FM broadcasts to the Prince Albert, Saskatchewan area at 101.5 FM.
FM RADIO STATION

CHRB-AM 47131
Owner: Golden West Broadcasting Ltd.
Editorial: 11-5th Ave SE, High River, Alberta T1V 1G2
Tel: 1 403 652-2472.
Web site: http://www.am1140radio.com
Profile: CHRB-AM is a commercial station owned by Golden West Broadcasting. The format of the station is a variety of Christian, gospel and contemporary country music, inspirational programming and local and agricultural news. CHRB-AM broadcasts to High River, Alberta and its environs at 1140 AM.
AM RADIO STATION

CHRD-FM 47881
Owner: Bell Media
Editorial: 2070 rue St-Georges, Drummondville, Quebec J2C 5G6 **Tel:** 1 819 474-1892.
Web site: http://drummondville.rougefm.ca
Profile: CHRD-FM is a commercial station owned by Bell Media. The format of the station is adult contemporary. CHRD-FM broadcasts to Drummondville, Quebec at 105.3 FM.
FM RADIO STATION

CHRE-FM 47520
Owner: Bell Media
Editorial: 12 Yates Street, St Catharines, Ontario L2R 5R2 **Tel:** 1 905 688-1057.
Web site: http://www.1057ezrock.com
Profile: CHRE-FM is a commercial station owned by Bell Media. The format of the station is easy listening. CHRE-FM broadcasts to St. Catharines, Ontario and surrounding communities at 105.7 FM. Twitter handle: twitter.com/1057ezrock
FM RADIO STATION

CHRI-FM 47712
Owner: Christian Hit Radio Inc.
Editorial: 1010 Thomas Spratt Place, Suite 3, Ottawa, Ontario K1G 5L5 **Tel:** 1 613 247-1440.
Email: chri@chri.ca
Web site: http://www.chri.ca
Profile: CHRI-FM is a commercial station owned by Christian Hit Radio Inc. The format of the station is contemporary Christian music and religious talk. CHRI-FM broadcasts to Ottawa, Ontario and its environs at 99.1 FM.
FM RADIO STATION

CHRK-FM 531232
Owner: NewCap Radio
Editorial: 5 Detheridge Drive, Sydney, Nova Scotia B1L 1B8 **Tel:** 1 902 270-1019.
Email: reception@giant1019.com
Web site: http://www.giant1019.com
Profile: CHRK-FM is a commercial station owned by NewCap Radio. The format of the station is Top 40/CHR. CHRK-FM broadcasts to the Sydney, Nova Scotia area at 101.9 FM.
FM RADIO STATION

CHRL-FM 47282
Owner: RNC Media
Editorial: 568 boul St-Joseph, Roberval, Quebec G8H 2K6 **Tel:** 1 418 275-1831.
Web site: http://roberval.planeteradio.ca
Profile: CHRL-FM is a commercial station owned by RNC Media. The format of the station is adult contemporary. CHRL-FM broadcasts to the Roberval, Quebec area at 99.5 FM.
FM RADIO STATION

CHRM-FM 47279
Owner: Communications Matane Inc.(Les)
Editorial: 800 Av du Phare O, Matane, Quebec G4W 1V7 **Tel:** 1 418 562-4141.
Email: choefm@globetrotter.net
Web site: http://www.plaisir1053.com
Profile: CHRM-FM is a commercial station owned by Les Communications Matane Inc. The format of the station is adult contemporary. CHRM-FM broadcasts to Matane, Quebec at 105.3 FM.
FM RADIO STATION

CHRW-FM 47711
Owner: University of Western Ontario
Editorial: University of Western Ontario, Bldg Rm 250, London, Ontario N6A 3K7 **Tel:** 1 519 661-3601.
Email: news@chrwradio.com
Web site: http://chrwradio.ca
Profile: CHRW-FM is a non-commercial station owned by the University of Western Ontario. The format of the station is college variety. CHRW-FM broadcasts to London, Ontario at 94.9 FM.
FM RADIO STATION

CHRX-FM 47842
Owner: Bell Media
Editorial: 10532 Alaska Rd, Fort St. John, British Columbia V1J 1B3 **Tel:** 1 250 785-6634.
Email: peacenews@astral.com
Web site: http://www.peacesunfm.com
Profile: CHRX-FM is a commercial station owned by Bell Media. The format of the station is Top 40/CHR music. CHRX-FM broadcasts to the Fort St. John, British Columbia area at 98.5 FM.
FM RADIO STATION

CHRY-FM 47710
Owner: CHRY Community Radio Inc.
Editorial: York University 4700 Keele St, Room #413 Student Centre, Toronto, Ontario M3J 1P3
Tel: 1 416 736-5293.
Email: chrynews@yorku.ca
Web site: http://www.chry.fm
Profile: CHRY-FM is a non-commercial college station owned by CHRY Community Radio Inc. The format of the station is variety. CHRY-FM broadcasts to the Toronto area at 105.5 FM.
FM RADIO STATION

CHSB-FM 578941
Owner: Bedford Baptist Church
Editorial: 158 Rocky Lake Dr, Bedford, Nova Scotia B4A 2S7 **Tel:** 1 902 835-5966.
Profile: CHSB-FM is a non-commerical station owned by Bedford Baptist Church. The format of the station is religious and Christian programming. CHSB-FM broadcasts to the Bedford, NS area at 99.3 FM.
FM RADIO STATION

CHSJ-FM 47794
Owner: Acadia Broadcasting Ltd.
Editorial: 2000-58 King St 2000, Saint John, New Brunswick E2L 1G4 **Tel:** 1 506 633-3323.
Email: mail@country94.ca
Web site: http://www.country94.ca
Profile: CHSJ-FM is a commercial station owned by Acadia Broadcasting Ltd. The format of the station is classic country music. CHSJ-FM broadcasts to the Saint John, New Brunswick area at 94.1 FM.
FM RADIO STATION

CHSL-FM 47392
Owner: Newfoundland Capital Corporation Limited
Editorial: 221 3rd Ave NW, Slave Lake, Alberta T0G 2A1 **Tel:** 1 780 849-2569.
Email: news@lakefm.ca
Web site: http://www.lakefm.ca
Profile: CHSL-FM is a commercial station owned by Newfoundland Capital Corporation Limited. The format of the station is classic hits. CHSL-FM broadcasts to the Slave Lake, Alberta area at 92.7 FM.
FM RADIO STATION

CHSM-AM 47364
Owner: Golden West Broadcasting Ltd.
Editorial: 105-32 Brandt St 105, Steinbach, Manitoba R5G 2J7 **Tel:** 1 204 326-3737.
Email: info@goldenwestradio.com
Web site: http://www.steinbachonline.com/radio/am1250
Profile: CHSM-AM is a commercial station owned by Golden West Broadcasting Ltd. The format of the station is easy listening music. CHSM-AM broadcasts to Steinbach, Manitoba and its environs at 1250 AM.
AM RADIO STATION

CHSN-FM 83109
Owner: Golden West Broadcasting Ltd.
Editorial: 200-1236 5th Street, Estevan, Saskatchewan S4A 0Z6 **Tel:** 1 306 634-1280.
Web site: http://www.sun102radio.com
Profile: CHSN-FM is a commercial station owned by Golden West Broadcasting Ltd. The format for the station is adult contemporary. CHSN-FM broadcast to the Estevan, Saskatchewan area at 102.3 FM.
FM RADIO STATION

CHSP-FM 47149
Owner: Newfoundland Capital Corporation Limited
Editorial: 201-4341 50th Ave, Saint Paul, Alberta T0A 3A3 **Tel:** 1 780 645-4425.
Web site: http://www.977thespur.com
Profile: CHSP-FM is a commercial station owned by Newfoundland Capital Corporation Limited. The format of the station is contemporary country music. CHSP-FM broadcasts to St. Paul, Alberta area at 97.7 FM.
FM RADIO STATION

CHSR-FM 47709
Owner: CHSR Broadcasting Inc.
Editorial: 21 Pacey Drive, Room 223, Fredericton, New Brunswick E3B 5A3 **Tel:** 1 506 453-4985.
Email: feedback@chsrfm.ca
Web site: http://www.chsrfm.ca
Profile: CHSR-FM is a commercial station owned by CHSR Broadcasting Inc. The format of the station is variety. CHSR-FM broadcasts to the University of New Brunswick in Fredericton, New Brunswick at 97.9 FM.
FM RADIO STATION

CHST-FM (102.3 JACK FM) 83096
Owner: Rogers Communications Inc.
Editorial: 1 Communications Rd, London, Ontario N6J 4Z1 **Tel:** 1 519 690-0102.
Web site: http://www.1023jackfm.com
Profile: CHST-FM (102.3 JACK FM) is a commercial station owned by Rogers Communications Inc. The format of the station is adult hits. CHST-FM broadcasts to the London, Ontario area at 102.3 FM.
FM RADIO STATION

CHSU-FM 47778
Owner: Bell Media
Editorial: 435 Bernard Ave, Kelowna, British Columbia V1Y 6N8 **Tel:** 1 250 860-8600.
Email: info@thesun.net
Web site: http://www.thesun.net
Profile: CHSU-FM is a commercial station owned by Bell Media. The format of the station is Top 40/CHR. CHSU-FM broadcasts to the Kelowna, British Columbia area at 99.9 FM.
FM RADIO STATION

CHTD-FM 83144
Owner: Acadia Broadcasting Ltd.
Editorial: 112 Milltown Boulevard, Saint Stephen, New Brunswick E3L 1G6 **Tel:** 1 506 466-1000.
Email: tidenews@radioabl.ca
Web site: http://www.thetide.ca
Profile: CHTD-FM is a commercial station owned by Acadia Broadcasting Ltd. The format of the station is contemporary country. CHTD-FM broadcasts to the Saint Stephen, New Brunswick area at 98.1.
FM RADIO STATION

CHTK-FM 47135
Owner: Bell Media
Editorial: 215 Cow Bay Rd Suite 230, Prince Rupert, British Columbia V8J 1A2 **Tel:** 1 250 635-6316.
Email: webmaster@themixbc.com
Web site: http://www.princerupert.myezrock.com
Profile: CHTK-FM is a commercial station owned by Bell Media. The format of the station is adult hits. CHTK-AM broadcasts to Prince Rupert, British Columbia at 560 AM.
FM RADIO STATION

CHTM-AM 47252
Owner: Arctic Radio (1982) Ltd.
Editorial: 103 Cree Road, Thompson, Manitoba R8N 0B9 **Tel:** 1 204 778-7361.
Email: chtm@arcticradio.ca
Web site: http://www.thompsononline.ca
Profile: CHTM-AM is a commercial station owned by Arctic Radio (1982) Ltd. The format of the station is adult contemporary. CHTM-AM broadcasts to the Thompson, Manitoba area at 610 AM.
AM RADIO STATION

CHTN-FM 47363
Owner: Newfoundland Capital Corporation Limited
Editorial: 90 University Ave, Ste 320, Charlottetown, Prince Edward Island C1A 4K9 **Tel:** 1 902 569-1003.
Email: news@ocean100.com
Web site: http://www.ocean100.com
Profile: CHTN-FM is a commercial station owned by Newfoundland Capital Corporation Limited. The format for the station is classic hits. CHTN-FM broadcasts to Charlottetown, Prince Edward Island and its environs at 100.3 FM.
FM RADIO STATION

CHTO-AM (AM1690) 588293
Owner: Canadian Hellenic Toronto Radio Inc.
Editorial: 437 Danforth Ave Suite 300, Toronto, Ontario M4K 1P1 **Tel:** 1 416 465-1112.
Email: info@am1690.ca
Web site: http://www.am1690.ca
Profile: CHTO-AM (AM1690) is a commercial station owned by Canadian Hellenic Toronto Radio Inc. The format of the station is ethnic variety, programming is predominantly Greek. CHTO-AM (AM1690) broadcasts to the Toronto area at 1690 AM.
AM RADIO STATION

CHTT-FM 47162
Owner: Rogers Communications Inc.
Editorial: 817 Fort St, Victoria, British Columbia V8W 1H6 **Tel:** 1 250 382-0900.
Web site: http://www.1031jackfm.ca
Profile: CHTT-FM is a commercial station owned by Rogers Communications Inc. The format of the station is adult hits. CHTT-FM broadcasts to Victoria, British Columbia at 103.1 FM.
FM RADIO STATION

CHTZ-FM (97.7 HTZ-FM) 47521
Owner: Bell Media
Editorial: 12 Yates St, St Catharines, Ontario L2R 5R2
Tel: 1 905 688-0977.
Web site: http://www.iheartradio.ca/977htzfm
Profile: CHTZ-FM (97.7 HTZ-FM) is a commercial station owned by Bell Media. The format of the station is classic and contemporary rock music. CHTZ-FM broadcasts to St. Catharines, Ontario and surrounding communities at 97.7 FM.
FM RADIO STATION

CHUB-FM 70479
Owner: Jim Pattison Broadcast Group(The)
Editorial: 2840 Bremner Avenue, 2nd Floor, Red Deer, Alberta T4R 1M9 **Tel:** 1 403 343-7105.
Email: heydj@big105.fm
Web site: http://www.big105.fm
Profile: CHUB-FM is a commercial station owned by The Jim Pattison Broadcast Group. The format is Top 40/CHR. CHUB-FM broadcasts to Red Deer, Alberta and surrounding communities at 105.5 FM.
FM RADIO STATION

CHUC-FM (Classic Rock 107.9) 47203
Owner: My Broadcasting Corporation
Editorial: 7805 Telephone Rd, Cobourg, Ontario K9A 4L3 **Tel:** 1 905 372-5401.
Web site: http://classicrock1079.ca
Profile: CHUC-FM is a commercial station owned by My Broadcasting Corporation. The format of the station is classic rock. CHUC-FM broadcasts to the Cobourg, Ontario area at 107.9 FM.
FM RADIO STATION

CHUK-FM (Mashteuiatsh 107.3) 409168
Owner: Corporation Mediatique Teuehikan
Editorial: 1491 Rue Ouiatchouan, Mashteuiatsh, Quebec G0W 2H0 **Tel:** 1 418 275-4684.
Email: chuk@chukfm.ca
Web site: http://www.chukfm.ca
Profile: CHUK-FM est une station de radio commerciale, une propriété de Corporation mediatique Teuehikan. Le format de la station est le variété. CHUK-FM est diffusé à Mashteuiatsh, au Québec à 107.3 FM. Le site Internet est en présentement en reconstruction

CHUK-FM is a commercial station owned by Corporation Mediatique Teuehikan. The format of the station is variety. CHUK-FM broadcasts to the Mashteuiatsh, Quebec area at 107.3 FM. The website is in reconstruction.
FM RADIO STATION

CHUM-AM (TSN 1050) 47345
Owner: Bell Media
Editorial: 299 Queen St W, Toronto, Ontario M5V 2Z5- **Tel:** 1 416 870-1050.
Email: tsngo@bellmedia.ca
Web site: http://www.tsn.ca/radio/toronto-1050
Profile: CHUM-AM is a commercial station owned by Bell Media. The format of the station is sports. CHUM-AM broadcasts to the Toronto area at 1050 AM.
AM RADIO STATION

CHUM-FM 47535
Owner: Bell Media
Editorial: 299 Queen St W, Toronto, Ontario M5V 2Z5- **Tel:** 1 416 925-6666.
Web site: http://www.iheartradio.ca/chum-fm
Profile: CHUM-FM is a commercial station owned by Bell Media. The format of the station is hot adult contemporary. CHUM-FM broadcasts to the Toronto area at 104.5 FM.
FM RADIO STATION

CHUO-FM 47708
Owner: Radio Ottawa
Editorial: 65 University Pvt., Suite 0038, Ottawa, Ontario K1N 9A5 **Tel:** 1 613 562-5965.
Email: info@chuo.fm
Web site: http://www.chuo.fm
Profile: CHUO-FM is a non-commercial station owned by Radio Ottawa. The format of the station is variety. CHUO-FM broadcasts to Ottawa, Ontario at 89.1 FM.
FM RADIO STATION

CHUP-FM 521734
Owner: Rawlco Radio Ltd.
Editorial: 6807 Railway St SE Suite 110, Calgary, Alberta T2H 2V6 **Tel:** 1 403 385-4000.
Email: fun@up977.com
Web site: http://www.up977.com
Profile: CHUP-FM is a commercial station owned by Rawlco Radio Ltd. The format for the station is adult contemporary. CHUP-FM broadcasts to the Calgary, Alberta area at 97.7 FM.
FM RADIO STATION

CHUR-FM 47836
Owner: Rogers Communications Inc.
Editorial: 743 Main St E, North Bay, Ontario P1B 1C2
Tel: 1 705 474-2000.
Web site: http://www.kissnorthbay.com
Profile: CHUR-FM is a commercial station owned by Rogers Communications Inc. The format of the station is Top 40/CHR. CHUR-FM broadcasts to North Bay, Ontario and surrounding communities at 100.5 FM.
FM RADIO STATION

CHVD-FM (Planète 100.3) 47864
Owner: RNC Media
Editorial: 1975 Boul Wallberg, Dolbeau-Mistassini, Quebec G8L 1J5 **Tel:** 1 418 276-3333.
Email: infodolbeaumistassini@rncmedia.ca
Web site: http://dolbeau-mistassini.planeteradio.ca
Profile: CHVD-FM est une station de radio commerciale, une propriété de RNC Media. Le format de la station est adulte contemporain. CHVD-FM est diffusé à Dolbeau-Mistassini, Québec au 100.3 FM

CHVD-FM is commercial station owned by RNC Media. The format of the station is adult contemporary. CHVD-FM broadcasts to the Dolbeau-Mistassini, Quebec area at 100.3 FM.
FM RADIO STATION

CHVN-FM 83103
Owner: Golden West Broadcasting Ltd.
Editorial: 1-741 St. Mary's Rd 1, Winnipeg, Manitoba R2M 3N5 **Tel:** 1 204 452-9602.
Web site: http://www.chvnradio.com
Profile: CHVN-FM is commercial station owned by Golden West Broadcasting Ltd. The format of the station is contemporary Christian music and religious talk. CHVN-FM broadcasts to the Winnipeg, Manitoba area at 95.1 FM.
FM RADIO STATION

CHVO-FM 47308
Owner: Newfoundland Capital Corporation Limited
Editorial: 1 CHVO Drive, Carbonear, Newfoundland A1Y 1A2 **Tel:** 1 709 726-5590.
Email: info@kixxcountry.ca

Web site: http://www.kixxcountry.ca
Profile: CHVO-FM is a commercial station owned by Newfoundland Capital Corporation Limited. The format of the station is country. CHVO-FM broadcasts to the Carbonear, Newfoundland area at 103.9 FM.
FM RADIO STATION

CHVR-FM 47788

Owner: Bell Media
Editorial: 595 Pembroke St E, Pembroke, Ontario K8A 3L7 **Tel:** 1 613 735-9670.
Email: star96@bellmedia.ca
Web site: http://www.star96.ca
Profile: CHVR-FM is a commercial station owned by Bell Media. The format of the station is contemporary country. CHVR-FM broadcasts to the Pembroke, Ontario area at 96.7 FM. Twitter handle: www.twitter.com/Star96FM
FM RADIO STATION

CHWC-FM (104.9 The Beach) 503271

Owner: Bayshore Broadcasting Corp.
Editorial: 300 Suncoast Dr E Unit E, Goderich, Ontario N7A 4N7 **Tel:** 1 519 612-1149.
Email: news@1049thebeach.ca
Web site: http://www.1049thebeach.ca
Profile: CHWC-FM is a commercial station owned by Bayshore Broadcasting Corp. The format of the station is adult contemporary. CHWC-FM broadcasts to the Goderich, Ontario area at 104.9 FM.
FM RADIO STATION

CHWE-FM 768706

Owner: Evanov Radio Group
Editorial: 520 Corydon Ave, Winnipeg, Manitoba R3L 0P1 **Tel:** 1 204 477- 1221.
Email: info@energy106.ca
Web site: http://www.energy106.ca
Profile: CHWE-FM is a commercial station owned by Evanov Radio Group. The format of the station is Top 40/CHR. CHWE-FM broadcasts to the Winnipeg, Manitoba area at a frequency of 106.1 FM.
FM RADIO STATION

CHWF-FM 47123

Owner: Jim Pattison Broadcast Group(The)
Editorial: 4550 Wellington Road, Nanaimo, British Columbia V9T 2H3 **Tel:** 1 250 758-1131.
Email: info@1069thewolf.com
Web site: http://www.1069thewolf.com
Profile: CHWF-FM is a commercial station owned by The Jim Pattison Broadcast Group. The format of the station is classic rock/rock alternative. CHWF-FM broadcasts to the Nanaimo, British Columbia area at 106.9 FM.
FM RADIO STATION

CHWK-FM 564858

Owner: Fabmar Communications Ltd.
Editorial: 46167 Yale Rd, Chilliwack, British Columbia V2P 2P2- **Tel:** 1 604 795-2429.
Email: info@895thedrive.com
Web site: http://www.895thedrive.com
Profile: CHWK-FM is a commercial station owned by Fabmar Communications Ltd. The format of the station is rock music. CHWK-FM broadcasts to the Chilliwack, BC area at 89.5 FM.
FM RADIO STATION

CHWV-FM 83145

Owner: Acadia Broadcasting Ltd.
Editorial: 2000-58 King St 2000, Saint John, New Brunswick E2L 1G4 **Tel:** 1 506 633-3323.
Email: mail@thewave.ca
Web site: http://www.thewave.ca
Profile: CHWV-FM is a commercial radio station owned by Acadia Broadcasting Ltd. The format of the station is hot adult contemporary music. CHWV-FM broadcasts to Saint John, New Brunswick at 97.3 FM.
FM RADIO STATION

CHXL-FM 585880

Owner: Okanese First Nation
Tel: 1 306 334-3331.
Email: psa@creekfm.com
Web site: http://www.creekfm.com
Profile: CHXL-FM is a non-commercial station owned by O.K. Creek Radio Station Inc. The format of the station is variety. CHXL-FM broadcasts to the Balcarres, Saskatchewan area at 95.3 FM.
FM RADIO STATION

CHXX-FM (POP 100.9) 498240

Owner: RNC Media
Editorial: 1134 Grande Allee O Suite 300, Quebec, Quebec G1S 1E5 **Tel:** 1 418 670-1009.
Email: studio@pop1009.ca
Web site: http://www.pop1009.ca/
Profile: POP 100,9 (CHXX-FM) est une station radiophonique de RNC Média. CHXX-FM diffuse sur la ville de Québec et ses environs sur la fréquence 100,9 FM. Le format musical est de la musique pop des années '70, '80 et '90.

POP 100,9 (CHXX-FM) is a commercial station owned by RNC Media. CHXX-FM broadcasts to the Quebec City area at 100.9 FM. Pop music from '70, '80 and '90 is aired on CHXX-FM.
FM RADIO STATION

CHYC-FM (Le loup 98.9) 83111

Owner: LE5 Communications Inc.
Editorial: 336 Rue Pine Suite 301, Sudbury, Ontario P3C 1X8 **Tel:** 1 705 222-8306.
Web site: http://www.leloupfm.com/Sudbury
Profile: CHYC-FM est une station de radio commerciale, une propriété de Le5 Communications Inc. Le format de la station est adulte contemporain francophone. CHYC-FM diffuse son contenu à Timmins, en Ontario au 98.9 FM.

CHYC-FM is a commercial station owned by Le5 Communications Inc. The format of the station is hot adult contemporary french music. CHYC-FM broadcasts to Sudbury, Ontario at 98.9 FM.
FM RADIO STATION

CHYF 88.9 FM (Gimaa Radio) 703700

Owner: GIMA Radio
Editorial: 15 Highway 551, M'Chigeeng, Ontario P0P 1G0 **Tel:** 1 705 282-8955.
Email: GimaaGC@gmail.com
Web site: http://www.gimaaradio.com
Profile: CHYF 88.9 FM is a non-profit station owned by GIMA Radio. The format for the station is variety. CHYF-FM broadcasts to the M'Chigeeng, Ontario area at 88.9 FM.
FM RADIO STATION

CHYK-FM (Le Loup 104.1) 47374

Owner: Le5 Communications Inc.
Editorial: 136 Troisieme Avenue, Timmins, Ontario P4N 1C6 **Tel:** 1 705 269-8307.
Web site: http://www.leloupfm.com/Timmins
Profile: CHYK-FM est une station de radio commerciale, une propriété de Le5 Communications Inc. Le format de la station est adulte contemporain. CHYK-FM diffuse son contenu à Timmins, en Ontario AU 104.1 FM.

CHYK-FM is a commercial station owned by Le5 Communications Inc. The format of the station is hot adult contemporary. CHYK-FM broadcasts to Timmins, Ontario at 104.1 FM.
FM RADIO STATION

CHYM-FM 47497

Owner: Rogers Communications Inc.
Editorial: 305 King St West, Kitchener, Ontario N2G 4E4 **Tel:** 1 519 743-2611.
Email: news570@rogers.com
Web site: http://www.chymfm.com
Profile: CHYM-FM is a commercial station owned by Rogers Communications Inc. The format of the station is adult contemporary. CHYM-FM broadcasts to the Kitchener, Ontario area at 96.7 FM.
FM RADIO STATION

CHYR-FM 47501

Owner: Blackburn Radio Inc.
Editorial: 100 Talbot St East, Leamington, Ontario N8H 1L3 **Tel:** 1 519 326-6171.
Web site: http://www.mix967.ca
Profile: CHYR-FM is a commercial station owned by Blackburn Radio Inc. The format of the station is hot adult contemporary. CHYR-FM broadcasts to Leamington, Ontario at 96.7 FM.
FM RADIO STATION

CHYZ-FM (94.3) 83125

Owner: Université Laval(L')
Editorial: Universite Laval, 2305 rue de l'Universite, Local 0236 Pavillon Maurice Pollack, Quebec, Quebec G1V 0A6 **Tel:** 1 418 656-7007.
Email: chyz@public.ulaval.ca
Web site: http://www.chyz.ca
Profile: CHYZ-FM est une station de radio non-commerciale, une propriété de l'Université Laval, à Québec. Le format de la station est la radio étudiante et le variété. CHYZ-FM est diffusée dans la ville de Québec au 94.3 FM.

CHYZ-FM is a non-commercial station owned by the Université Laval, Quebec city. The format of the station is college variety. CHYZ-FM broadcasts to Quebec City at 94.3 FM.
FM RADIO STATION

CIAM-FM 558548

Owner: Care Radio Broadcasting Association
Editorial: 4709 River Road, Fort Vermilion, Alberta T0H 1N0 **Tel:** 1 780 927-2426.
Email: news@ciamradio.com
Web site: http://www.ciam.ciamradio.com
Profile: CIAM-FM is a non-commercial station owned by Care Radio Broadcasting Association. The station broadcasts to the northern Alberta region. The format of the station is religious.
FM RADIO STATION

CIAO-AM 47186

Owner: Evanov Radio Group
Editorial: 5312 Dundas St West, Toronto, Ontario M9B 1B2 **Tel:** 1 416 213-1035.
Email: info@evanovradio.com
Web site: http://www.am530.ca
Profile: CIAO-AM is a commercial station owned by Evanov Radio Group. The format of the station is news and talk as well as ethnic and multicultural music. CIAO-AM broadcasts to the Toronto area at 530 AM.
AM RADIO STATION

CIAU-FM 382953

Owner: CIAU-FM Radio
Editorial: 143 Joliet, Radisson, Quebec J0Y 2X0
Tel: 1 819 638-7033.
Email: ciaufm@lino.com
Web site: http://www.ciaufm.ca
Profile: CIAU-FM is a commercial station owned by CIAU-FM Radio. The format of the station is variety. WIXO-FM broadcasts to the Radisson, Quebec area at 103.1 FM.
FM RADIO STATION

CIAX-FM 541388

Owner: La Radio Communautaire de Windsor et Region Inc.
Editorial: 49 6e Av, Windsor, Quebec J1S 1T2
Tel: 1 819 845-2692.
Email: info@ciaxfm.net
Web site: http://www.ciaxfm.net
Profile: CIAX-FM is a non-commercial station owned by La Radio Communautaire de Windsor et Region Inc. The format of the station is variety. CIAX-FM broadcasts to the Windsor, Quebec area at 98.3 FM.
FM RADIO STATION

CIAY-FM 342183

Owner: Board of Bethany Pentecostal Tabernacle
Editorial: 91806 Alaska Highway, Whitehorse, Yukon Territory Y1A 5B7 **Tel:** 1 867 393-2429.
Email: info@lifewhitehorse.com
Web site: http://lifewhitehorse.com
Profile: CIAY-FM is a commercial station owned by Board of Bethany Pentecostal Tabernacle. The format of the station is Christian Contemporary. CIAY-FM broadcasts to the Whitehorse, Yukon Territory area at 100.7 FM.
FM RADIO STATION

CIBH-FM 83098

Owner: Jim Pattison Broadcast Group(The)
Editorial: 166 E Island Hwy, Parksville, British Columbia V9P 2H3 **Tel:** 1 250 248-4211.
Email: info@885thebeach.com
Web site: http://www.885thebeach.com
Profile: CIBH-FM is a commercial station owned by The Jim Pattison Broadcast Group. The format of the station is adult contemporary music. CIBH-FM broadcasts to the Parksville, British Columbia area at 88.5 FM.
FM RADIO STATION

CIBK-FM 132214

Owner: Bell Media
Editorial: 1110 Centre St NE Suite 300, Calgary, Alberta T2E 2R2 **Tel:** 1 403 240-5800.
Web site: http://www.iheartradio.ca/virginradio/calgary
Profile: CIBK-FM is a commercial station owned by Bell Media. The format of the station is Top 40/CHR. CIBK-FM broadcasts to the Calgary, Alberta area at 98.5 FM. Beginning June 30, 2010, CIBK-FM will take on Virgin Radio branding.
FM RADIO STATION

CIBL-FM 47613

Owner: Radio Communautaire Francophone de Montréal Inc.(La)
Editorial: 2 Ste-Catherine St Est, Suite 201, Montreal, Quebec H2X 1K4 **Tel:** 1 514 526-2581.
Email: direction@cibl1015.com
Web site: http://www.cibl1015.com
Profile: CIBL-FM est une radio indépendante de format variété basée à Montréal.

CIBL-FM is a non-commercial station owned by La Radio Communautaire Francophone de Montréal Inc. The format of the station is variety. CIBL-FM broadcasts to Montreal at 101.5 FM.
FM RADIO STATION

CIBM-FM 47707

Owner: Groupe Radio Simard
Editorial: 64 Rue de L'Hotel-De-Ville, Riviere-du-Loup, Quebec G5R 1L5 **Tel:** 1 418 867-1071.
Web site: http://www.cibm107.com/cibm
Profile: CIBM-FM est une radio du Groupe Radio Simard. On y entend de la musique de type pop-rock et l'auditoire visé est les hommes et les femmes de 18-49 ans. La station diffuse sur Rivière-du-Loup et les environs au 107.1FM.

CIBM-FM is a commercial station owned by Groupe Radio Simard. The format of the station is Lite Rock/Lite AC. CIBM-FM broadcasts to the Rivière-du-Loup, Quebec area at 107.1 FM.
FM RADIO STATION

CIBN-FM 47844

Owner: Bufalows Broadcasting Co.
Editorial: 1224 Peterson Box 38, Buffalo Narrows, Saskatchewan S0M 0J0 **Tel:** 1 306 235-4722.
Email: buflo@sasktel.net
FM RADIO STATION

CIBO-FM (Senneterre 100.5) 47570

Owner: Radio Communautaire de Senneterre Inc.(La)
Editorial: 121 1re Rue E, Senneterre, Quebec J0Y 2M0 **Tel:** 1 819 737-2222.
Email: cibo.fm@cableamos.com
Profile: CIBO-FM est une station de radio commerciale francophone, une propriété de La Radio Communautaire de Senneterre Inc. Le format de la station est adulte contemporain. CIBO-FM est diffusé à Senneterre, Québec au 100.5 FM.

CIBO-FM is a commercial French-language station owned by La Radio Communautaire de Senneterre Inc. The format of the station is adult contemporary. CIBO-FM broadcasts to the Senneterre, Quebec area at 100.5 FM.
FM RADIO STATION

CIBQ-FM 47165

Owner: Newcap Radio
Editorial: 403 2 Ave W Unit 8, Brooks, Alberta T1R 0S3 **Tel:** 1 403 362-3418.
Email: info@realcountrybrooks.ca
Web site: http://www.realcountrybrooks.ca/
Profile: CIBQ-FM is a commercial station owned by Newcap Radio. The format of the station is country music. CIBQ-FM broadcasts to Brooks, Alberta and surrounding communities at 105.7 FM.
FM RADIO STATION

CIBU-FM (Classic Rock 94.5) 355101

Owner: Blackburn Radio Inc.
Editorial: 215 Carling Terrace, Wingham, Ontario N0G 2W0 **Tel:** 1 519 357-1310.
Email: info@945thebull.ca
Web site: http://www.945thebull.ca
Profile: CIBU-FM is a commercial station owned by Blackburn Radio Inc. The format of the station is rock alternative music. CIBU-FM broadcasts in the Wingham, Ontario area at 94.5.
FM RADIO STATION

CIBW-FM 47706

Owner: Jim Pattison Broadcast Group(The)
Editorial: 5164-52 Avenue, Drayton Valley, Alberta T7A 1V3 **Tel:** 1 780 542-9290.
Email: jocks@bigwestcountry.ca
Web site: http://www.bigwestcountry.ca
Profile: CIBW-FM is a commercial station owned by The Jim Pattison Broadcast Group. The format is country and easy listening music. CIBW-FM broadcasts to Drayton Valley, Alberta and its environs at 92.9 FM.
FM RADIO STATION

CIBX-FM 47705

Owner: Bell Media
Editorial: 206 Rookwood Ave, Fredericton, New Brunswick E3B 2M2 **Tel:** 1 506 451-9111.
Email: frederictonnewsteam@bellmedia.ca
Web site: http://www.capitalfm.ca
Profile: CIBX-FM is a commercial station owned by Bell Media. The format of the station is adult contemporary. CIBX-FM broadcasts to the Fredericton, New Brunswick area at 106.9 FM. Twitter handle: www.twitter.com/1069_CapitalFM
FM RADIO STATION

CICF-FM 47159

Owner: Bell Media
Editorial: 2800 31 St, Vernon, British Columbia V1T 5H4 **Tel:** 1 250 545-9222.
Email: reception@thesunonline.ca
Web site: http://www.thesunonline.ca
Profile: CICF-FM is a commercial radio station owned by Bell Media. The format of the station is hot adult comtemporary. CICF-FM broadcasts to Vernon, British Columbia at 105.7 FM.
FM RADIO STATION

CICR-FM 586040

Owner: Parrsboro Radio Society
Editorial: 396 Upper Main St, Parrsboro, Nova Scotia B0M 1S0 **Tel:** 1 902 216-0042.
Email: parrsborocommunityradio@hotmail.com
Web site: http://www.parrsborocommunityradio.ca
Profile: CICR-FM is a non-commercial station owned by Parrsboro Radio Society. The format of the station is a mix of classic hits and country music. CICR-FM broadcasts to the Parrsboro, Nova Scotia area at 99.1 FM.
FM RADIO STATION

CICS-FM 543865

Owner: Larche Communications Inc.
Editorial: 60 Elm St, Sudbury, Ontario P3C 1R8
Tel: 1 705 671-7330.
Email: news@kicx917.com
Web site: http://www.kicx917.com
Profile: CICS-FM is a commercial station owned by Larche Communications Inc. The format of the station is contemporary country. CICS-FM broadcasts to Sudbury, Ontario at 91.7 FM.
FM RADIO STATION

CICV-FM 599218

Owner: Cowichan Valley Community Radio Society
Editorial: 37 Wellington St. West, Trans Canada Trail Blvd., Lake Cowichan, British Columbia V0R 2G0
Tel: 1 250 749-6635.
Email: admin@cicv.ca
Web site: http://www.cvcradio.ca
Profile: CICV-FM is a non-commercial station owned by Cowichan Valley Community Radio Society. The format of the station is community news. CICV-FM

broadcasts to the Lake Cowichan, British Columbia area at 98.7 FM.
FM RADIO STATION

CICW-FM 791252
Owner: Centre Wellington Radio
Editorial: 198 St Andrew St W Suite 200, Fergus, Ontario N1M 1N7 **Tel:** 1 122 63839290.
Email: info@thegrand929.com
Web site: http://www.thegrand929.com
Profile: CICW-FM is a non-commercial station owned by Centre Wellington Radio. The format of the station is adult contemporary. CICW-FM broadcasts to Wellington, ON at 92.9 FM.
FM RADIO STATION

CICX-FM (KICX New Country 105.9) 47513
Owner: Larche Communications Inc.
Editorial: 7 Progress Dr RR 1, Orillia, Ontario L3V 6H1 **Tel:** 1 705 722-5429.
Email: news@kicxfm.com
Web site: http://kicx106.com
Profile: CICX-FM is a commercial station owned by Larche Communications Inc. The format of the station is contemporary country. CICX-FM broadcasts to Orillia, Ontario at 105.9 FM.
FM RADIO STATION

CICY-FM 238327
Owner: Native Communications, Inc.
Editorial: 1507 Inkster Blvd, Winnipeg, Manitoba R2X 1R2 **Tel:** 1 204 772-8255.
Email: info@ncifm.com
Web site: http://www.ncifm.com
Profile: CICY-FM is a commercial station owned by Native Communications, Inc. (NCI). The format of the station is aboriginal language news and programming. CICY-FM broadcasts to Selkirk, Manitoba and its environs at 105.5 FM.
FM RADIO STATION

CICZ-FM (The Dock 104,1) 47704
Owner: Larche Communications Inc.
Editorial: 355 Cranston Crescent, Midland, Ontario L4R 4L3 **Tel:** 1 705 720-1991.
Email: events@thedockfm.com
Web site: http://www.1041thedock.com
Profile: CICZ-FM is a commercial station owned by Larche Communications Inc. The format of the station is Classic Rock and Classic Hits. CICZ-FM broadcasts in the Midland, Ontario area at 104.1 FM.
FM RADIO STATION

CIDC-FM 47512
Owner: Evanov Radio Group
Editorial: 5312 Dundas St West, Toronto, Ontario M9B 1B2 **Tel:** 1 416 213-1035.
Email: info@z1035.com
Web site: http://www.z1035.com
Profile: CIDC-FM is a commercial station owned by Evanov Radio Group. The format of the station is Top 40/CHR music. CIDC-FM broadcasts to the Toronto area at 103.5 FM.
FM RADIO STATION

CIDG-FM (101.9 DAWG FM) 689367
Owner: Torres Media
Editorial: 380 Hunt Club Rd Suite 203, Ottawa, Ontario K1V 1C1 **Tel:** 1 613 730-1019.
Email: info@dawgfm.com
Web site: http://www.dawgfm.com
Profile: CIDG-FM is a commercial station owned by Torres Media. The format for the station is blues. CIDG-FM broadcasts to the Ottawa, Ontario and Gatineau, Quebec area at 101.9 FM.
FM RADIO STATION

CIDI-FM 585889
Owner: RCM Media
Editorial: 305B Knowlton Road, Knowlton, Quebec J0E 1V0 **Tel:** 1 450 242-9873.
Web site: http://cidi991.com/
Profile: CIDI-FM is a non-commercial station owned by RCM Media. The format of the station is variety. CIDI-FM broadcasts to the Knowlton, Quebec area at 99.1 FM.
FM RADIO STATION

CIDO-FM 585868
Owner: Creston Community Radio Society
Tel: 1 250 402-6772.
Email: info@crestonradio.ca
Web site: http://www.crestonradio.ca
Profile: CIDO-FM is a non-commercial station owned by Creston Community Radio Society. The format of the station is variety. CIDO-FM broadcasts to the Creston, British Columbia area at 97.7 FM.
FM RADIO STATION

CIDR-FM (93.9 The River) 47560
Owner: Bell Media
Editorial: 1640 Ouellette Ave, Windsor, Ontario N8X 1L1- **Tel:** 1 519 258-8888.
Web site: http://www.939theriverradio.com
Profile: CIDR-FM is a commercial station owned by Bell Media.The format of the station is AAA-Adult Album Alternative. CIDR-FM broadcasts to Windsor, Ontario at 93.9 FM.
FM RADIO STATION

CIEL-FM 47810
Owner: Groupe Radio Simard
Editorial: 64 Rue de L'Hotel-De-Ville, Riviere-du-Loup, Quebec G5R 1L5 **Tel:** 1 418 862-8241.
Email: info@ciel103.com
Web site: http://www.ciel103.com/ciel
Profile: CIEL-FM is a commercial radio station owned by Groupe Radio Simard. The format of the station is adult contemporary. CIEL-FM broadcasts to the Riviere-du-Loup, Quebec area at 103.7 FM.
FM RADIO STATION

CIEU-FM 47619
Owner: Diffusion Communautaire Baie-des-Chaleurs
Editorial: 1645 Boul Perron Est, Carleton, Quebec G0C 1J0 **Tel:** 1 418 364-7094.
Email: administration@cieufm.com
Web site: http://www.cieufm.com
Profile: CIEU-FM is a French-language commercial station owned by Diffusion Communautaire Baie-des-Chaleurs. The format of the station is variety. CIEU-FM broadcasts to the Carleton, Quebec area at 94.9 FM.
FM RADIO STATION

CIFA-FM 47749
Owner: Association Radio Clare (L')
Tel: 1 902 769-2432.
Email: info@cifafm.ca
Web site: http://www.cifafm.ca
Profile: CIFA-FM is a non-commercial station owned by L'Association Radio Clare. The format of the station is variety. CIFA-FM broadcasts to the Saulnierville, Nova Scotia area at 104.1 FM.
FM RADIO STATION

CIFM-FM 47438
Owner: Jim Pattison Broadcast Group(The)
Editorial: 460 Pemberton Terrace, Kamloops, British Columbia V2C 1T5 **Tel:** 1 250 372-3322.
Email: info@98.3cifm.com
Web site: http://www.98.3cifm.com
Profile: CIFM-FM is a commercial station owned by The Jim Pattison Broadcast Group. The format of the station is album-oriented rock music. CIFM-FM broadcasts to Kamloops, British Columbia at 98.3 FM.
FM RADIO STATION

CIFX-FM 154810
Owner: Mix FM Inc.
Editorial: 37 George Street, Lewisporte, Newfoundland A0G 3A0 **Tel:** 1 709 535-6000.
Profile: CIFX-FM is a commercial station owned by Mix FM Inc. The format of the station is Hot AC. CIFX-FM broadcasts to the Lewisporte, Newfoundland area at 93.7 FM.
FM RADIO STATION

CIGB-FM(Énergie Mauricie 102,3) 47588
Owner: Bell Media
Editorial: 1500 Rue Royale Bureau 260, Trois-Rivieres, Quebec G9A 6J4 **Tel:** 1 819 378-1023.
Email: nouvelles.mauricie.radio@bellmedia.ca
Web site: http://mauricie.radionrj.ca
Profile: CIGB-FM(Énergie Mauricie 102,3) est une station de radio commerciale appartenant à Bell Media. Son format est de type Top40 et parlée. CIGB-FM(Énergie Mauricie 102,3) is a commercial station owned by Bell Media. The format of the station is Top 40/CHR. CIGB-FM broadcasts to the Trois-Rivières, Quebec area at 102.3 FM.
FM RADIO STATION

CIGL-FM 47451
Owner: Quinte Broadcasting Co. Ltd.
Editorial: 10 South Front St, Belleville, Ontario K8N 2Y3 **Tel:** 1 613 969-5555.
Email: info@mix97.com
Web site: http://www.mix97.com
Profile: CIGL-FM is a commercial station owned by Quinte Broadcasting Co. Ltd. The format of the station is hot adult contemporary music. CIGL-FM broadcasts to Belleville, Ontario at 97.1 FM.
FM RADIO STATION

CIGM-FM 47339
Owner: Newfoundland Capital Corporation Limited
Editorial: 493B Barrydowne Rd, Sudbury, Ontario P3A3T4 **Tel:** 1 705 560-8323.
Email: info@hot935.ca
Web site: http://www.hot935.ca
Profile: CIGM-FM is a commerical station owned by Newfoundland Capital Corporation Limited. The format is Top 40. The station airs at 93.5 FM in the Sudbury, Ontario area.
FM RADIO STATION

CIGO-FM 47194
Owner: MacEachern Broadcasting Ltd.
Editorial: 609 Church Street, Suite 201, Port Hawkesbury, Nova Scotia B9A 2X4 **Tel:** 1 902 625-1220.
Email: news@1015thehawk.com
Web site: http://www.1015thehawk.com
Profile: CIGO-FM is a commercial station owned by MacEachern Broadcasting Ltd. The format of the station is adult contemporary. CIGO-FM broadcasts to the Port Hawkesbury, Nova Scotia area at 101.5 FM.
FM RADIO STATION

CIGV-FM 47442
Owner: Newfoundland Capital Corporation
Editorial: 125 Nanaimo Ave W, Penticton, British Columbia V2A 1N2 **Tel:** 1 250 493-6767.
Web site: http://okanagancountry.com
Profile: CIGV-FM is a commercial station owned by Newfoundland Capital Corporation. The format of the station is adult contemporary and contemporary country. CIGV-FM broadcasts to Penticton, British Columbia at 100.7 FM.
FM RADIO STATION

CIHO-FM 47602
Owner: Radio MF Charlevoix Inc.
Editorial: 315 Ch Cartier, St-Hilarion, Quebec G0A 3V0 **Tel:** 1 418 457-3333.
Email: studio@cihofm.com
Web site: http://www.cihofm.com
Profile: CIHO-FM est une radio communautaire, détenue par Radio MF Charlevoix Inc. Avec une programmation variée, la station diffuse sur St-Hilarion et les environs au 96.3FM.

CIHO-FM is a community radio station owned by Radio MF Charlevoix Inc. The format of the station is variety. CIHO-FM broadcasts to the St-Hilarion, Quebec area at 96.3 FM.
FM RADIO STATION

CIHR-FM 399942
Owner: Byrnes Communications Inc.
Editorial: 223 Norwich Ave, Woodstock, Ontario N4S 3V8 **Tel:** 1 519 537-8400.
Web site: http://www.heartfm.ca
Profile: CIHR-FM is a commercial station owned by Byrnes Communications Inc. The format of the station is adult contemporary. CIHR-FM broadcasts to the Woodstock, Ontario area at 104.7 FM.
FM RADIO STATION

CIHS-FM 342203
Owner: Dhillon (David)
Editorial: 5222 - 50 Avenue, Wetaskiwin, Alberta T9A 0S8 **Tel:** 1 780 361-0245.
Email: mail@cihsfm.net
Web site: http://www.cihsfm.net
Profile: CIHS-FM is a commercial station owned by David Dhillon. The format of the station is religious, gospel and classic country. CIHS-FM broadcasts to the Wetaskiwin, AB area at 93.5 FM.
FM RADIO STATION

CIHT-FM 139541
Owner: Newfoundland Capital Corporation Limited
Editorial: 6 Antares Dr Unit 100, phase 1, Ottawa, Ontario K2E 8A9 **Tel:** 1 613 723-8990.
Email: news@hot899.com
Web site: http://www.hot899.com
Profile: CIHT-FM is a commercial station owned by Newfoundland Capital Corporation Limited. The format of the station is Top 40/CHR music. CIHT-FM broadcasts to Ottawa, Ontario area at 89.9 FM.
FM RADIO STATION

CIHW-FM (Radio communautaire de Wendake 100.3) 553380
Owner: Radio Huron-Wendat
Editorial: 545 rue Thomas Martin, Wendake, Quebec G0A 4V0 **Tel:** 1 418 843-3937.
Email: cihw@megaquebec.net
Web site: http://www.cihw.org
Profile: CIHW-FM est une station de radio non-commerciale, une propriété de Radio Huron-Wendat et membre de SOCAM. Le format de la station est le variété. CIHW-FM est diffusé à Wendake, Québec à 100.3.

CIHW-FM is a non-commerciale radio station owned by Radio Huron-Wendat and a member of SOCAM. The format of the station is variety. CIHW-FM broadcasts to Wendake, Quebec at 100.3 FM.
FM RADIO STATION

CIJK-FM (89.3 K-Rock) 535349
Owner: Newfoundland Capital Corporation Limited
Editorial: 8794 Commercial St Suite 3, New Minas, Nova Scotia B4N 3C5 **Tel:** 1 902 365-8930.
Email: info@893krock.com
Web site: http://893krock.com
Profile: CIJK-FM is a commercial station owned by Newfoundland Capital Corporation Limited. The format of the station is classic rock. CIJK-FM broadcasts to the New Minas, Nova Scotia area at 89.3 FM.
FM RADIO STATION

CIKI-FM 47653
Owner: Bell Media
Editorial: 287 Rue Pierre-Saindon Bureau 502, Rimouski, Quebec G5L 9A7 **Tel:** 1 418 724-2323.
Email: receptionrimouski@astral.com
Web site: http://www.radionrj.ca/rimouski
Profile: CIKI-FM is a commercial station owned by Bell Media. The format of the station is Top 40/CHR. CIKI-FM broadcasts to the Rimouski, Quebec area at 98.7 FM.
FM RADIO STATION

CIKR-FM [K-Rock 105.7] 83138
Owner: Rogers Communications Inc.
Editorial: 863 Princess St Suite 301, Kingston, Ontario K7L 5N4 **Tel:** 1 613 549-1057.
Web site: http://www.krock1057.ca
Profile: CIKR-FM is a commercial station owned by Rogers Communications Inc. The format of the station is rock/album-oriented rock. CIKR-FM broadcasts to the Kingston, Ontario area at 105.7 FM.
FM RADIO STATION

CIKT-FM 458804
Owner: Jim Pattison Broadcast Group
Editorial: 8716 108 St Suite 104, Grande Prairie, Alberta T8V 4C7 **Tel:** 1 780 882-6612.
Email: events@q99live.com
Web site: http://www.q99live.com
Profile: CIKT-FM is a commercial station owned by Jim Pattison Broadcast Group. The format of the station is adult hits. CIKT-FM broadcasts to the Grande Prairie, Alberta area at 98.9 FM.
FM RADIO STATION

CIKX-FM 47879
Owner: Bell Media
Editorial: 399 Broadway Blvd, Grand Falls, New Brunswick E3Z 2K5 **Tel:** 1 506 473-9393.
Email: k93@bellmedia.ca
Web site: http://www.k93.ca
Profile: CIKX-FM is a commercial station owned by Bell Media. The format of the station is hot adult contemporary music. CIKX-FM broadcasts in the Grand Falls, New Brunswick area at 93.5 FM.
FM RADIO STATION

CIKZ-FM (Country 106.7) 217481
Owner: Rogers Communications Inc.
Editorial: 305 King St W Suite 1101, 11th floor, Kitchener, Ontario N2G 1B9 **Tel:** 1 519 743-2611.
Web site: http://www.country1067.com
Profile: CIKZ-FM is a commercial station owned by Rogers Communications Inc. The format of the station is New Country music. CIKZ-FM broadcasts to Kitchener, Ontario at 106.7 FM.
FM RADIO STATION

CILB-FM 509742
Owner: Newfoundland Capital Corporation Limited
Editorial: 10107 102 Ave., Suite 201, Lac La Biche, Alberta T0A 2C0 **Tel:** 1 780 623-3744.
Web site: http://www.1035bigdog.com
Profile: CILB-FM is a commercial station owned by Newfoundland Capital Corporation Limited. The format of the station is classic hits. CILB-FM broadcasts to the Lac La Biche, Alberta area at 103.5 FM.
FM RADIO STATION

CILE-FM 47748
Owner: Radio Télévision Communautaire Havre-Saint-Pierre(La)
Editorial: 992 rue du Bouleau, Havre-St-Pierre, Quebec G0G 1P0 **Tel:** 1 418 538-2451.
Email: nouvelles@cilemf.com
Web site: http://www.cilemf.com
Profile: CILE-FM est propriété de La Radio Télévision Communautaire Havre-Saint-Pierre. Elle offre une programmation variée et diffuse sur Havre-Saint-Pierre et ses environs sur la fréquence 95.1FM.

CILE-FM is a commercial station owned by La Radio Télévision Communautaire Havre-Saint-Pierre. The format of the station is variety. CILE-FM broadcasts to Havre-St-Pierre, Quebec at 95.1 FM.
FM RADIO STATION

CILG-FM 235350
Owner: Golden West Broadcasting Ltd.
Editorial: 1704 Main St N, Moose Jaw, Saskatchewan S6J 1L4 **Tel:** 1 306 694-0800.
Email: country100@goldenwestradio.com
Web site: http://www.discovermoosejaw.com/radio/country-100
Profile: CILG-FM is a commercial station owned by Golden West Broadcasting Ltd. The format of the station is classic country. CILG-FM broadcasts to the Moose Jaw, Saskatchewan area at 100.7 FM.
FM RADIO STATION

CILK-FM 47439

Owner: Bell Media
Editorial: 435 Bernard Ave, Kelowna, British Columbia V1Y 6N8 **Tel:** 1 250 860-8600.
Email: kelownainfo@myezrock.com
Web site: http://kelowna.myezrock.com
Profile: CILK-FM is a commercial station owned by Bell Media. The format of the station is soft rock/ soft ac. CILK-FM broadcasts to Kelowna, British Columbia at 101.5 FM.
FM RADIO STATION

CILM-FM (Rythme FM Saguenay 98.3) 47356

Owner: Cogeco Media
Editorial: 345 Rue Racine E, Chicoutimi, Quebec G7H 1S8 **Tel:** 1 418 545-2577.
Email: nouvelles@ckrs.ca
Web site: http://www.rythmefm.com/saguenay
Profile: CILM-FM est une station de radio commerciale, une propriété de Cogeco Media. Le format de la station est les classiques musicales et les vieux succès. CILM-FM est diffusé à Chicoutimi, Québec au 98.3 FM.

CILM-FM is a commercial station owned by Cogeco Media. The format of the station is classic hits and oldies. CILM-FM broadcasts to the Chicoutimi, Quebec area at 98.3 FM.
FM RADIO STATION

CILQ-FM (Q107) 47511

Owner: Corus Entertainment Inc.
Editorial: 25 Dockside Dr, corus quay, Toronto, Ontario M5A 0B5 **Tel:** 1 416 479-7000.
Web site: http://www.q107.com
Profile: CILQ-FM (Q107) is a commercial station owned by Corus Entertainment Inc. The format of the station is classic rock. CILQ-FM broadcasts to the Toronto, ON area at 107.1 FM.
FM RADIO STATION

CILR-FM 598943

Owner: Newfoundland Capital Corporation Limited
Editorial: 5026-50th St., Lloydminster, Alberta T9V 1P3 **Tel:** 1 780 875-3321.
Profile: CILR-FM is a non-commercial station owned by Newfoundland Capital Corporation Limited. The format of the station is tourist information. CILR-FM broadcasts to the Lloydminster, Alberta area at 98.9 FM.
FM RADIO STATION

CILS-FM 578688

Owner: Societe radio communautaire Victoria
Editorial: 200-535 Yates St., Victoria, British Columbia V8W 2Z6 **Tel:** 1 250 220-4139.
Email: radio@francocentre.com
Web site: http://www.cilsfm.ca
FM RADIO STATION

CILT-FM 47860

Owner: Golden West Broadcasting Ltd.
Editorial: 105-32 Brandt St, Steinbach, Manitoba R5G 2J7 **Tel:** 1 204 346-0000.
Email: info@goldenwestradio.com
Web site: http://www.mix967radio.com
Profile: CILT-FM is a commercial station owned by Golden West Broadcasting Ltd. The format of the station is Lite Rock/Lite AC music. CILT-FM broadcasts to the Steinbach, Manitoba area at 96.7 FM.
FM RADIO STATION

CILU (102.7 FM) 588290

Owner: Lakehead University
Editorial: 707 Oliver Rd, Thunder Bay, Ontario P7B 2H8 **Tel:** 1 807 343-8881.
Email: info@luradio.ca
Web site: http://www.luradio.ca
Profile: CILU (102.7 FM) is a commerical station owned by Lakehead University. The format of the station is campus radio. CILU-FM broadcasts to the Thunder Bay, Ontario area at 102.7 FM.
FM RADIO STATION

CILV-FM 382301

Owner: Newfoundland Capital Corporation Limited
Editorial: 6 Antares Dr, Ottawa, Ontario K2E 8A9- **Tel:** 1 613 688-8888.
Web site: http://www.live885.com
Profile: CILV-FM is a commercial station owned by Newfoundland Capital Corporation Limited. The format of the station is adult album alternative. CILV-FM broadcasts to the Ottawa, Ontario area at 88.5 FM.
FM RADIO STATION

CIMB-FM (Pessamit 95.1) 83120

Owner: Radio Ntetemuk Inc(La)
Editorial: 8 Rue Laletaut, Betsiamites, Quebec G0H 1B0 **Tel:** 1 418 567-4642.
Email: betradio@globetrotter.net
Web site: http://www.cimb.fm
Profile: CIMB-FM est une station non-commerciale, une propriété de La Radio Ntetemuk Inc. Le format de la station est le Talk. CIMB-FM est diffusée à Betsiamites, Québec au 95.1 FM.

CIMB-FM is a non-commercial station owned by La Radio Ntetemuk Inc. The format of the station is talk. CIMB-FM broadcasts to Betsiamites, Quebec at 95.1 FM.
FM RADIO STATION

CIME-FM 47567

Owner: Cogeco
Editorial: 300 Rue Marie-Victorin Suite 102, St-Jerome, Quebec J7Y 2G8 **Tel:** 1 450 431-2463.
Email: nouvelles@cime.fm
Web site: http://www.cime.fm
Profile: CIME-FM is a commercial station owned by Cogeco. The format of the station is adult contemporary. CIME-FM broadcasts to St-Jerome, Quebec at 103.9 FM.
FM RADIO STATION

CIMF-FM (Rouge FM 94.9) 47551

Owner: Bell Media
Editorial: 15 Rue Taschereau, Gatineau, Quebec J8Y 2V6 **Tel:** 1 819 243-5555.
Web site: http://gatineau.rougefm.ca
Profile: CIMF-FM est une station de radio commerciale, une propriété de Bell Média. Le format de la station est adulte contemporain. CIMF-FM est diffusée à Gatineau, au Québec à 94.9 FM.

CIMF-FM is a commercial station owned by Bell Media. The format of the station is adult contemporary. CIMF-FM broadcasts to the Gatineau, Quebec area at 94.9 FM.
FM RADIO STATION

CIMG-FM 47492

Owner: Golden West Broadcasting Ltd.
Editorial: 134 Central Avenue North, Swift Current, Saskatchewan S9L 0L1 **Tel:** 1 306 773-4605.
Email: eaglecontrol@goldenwestradio.com
Web site: http://www.eagle94.ca
Profile: CIMG-FM is a commercial radio station owned by Golden West Broadcasting Inc. The format of the station is classic hits. CIMG-FM broadcasts to Swift Current, Saskatchewan and its environs at 94.1 FM.
FM RADIO STATION

CIMJ-FM 47469

Owner: Corus Entertainment Inc.
Editorial: 75 Speedvale Ave E, Guelph, Ontario N1E 6M3 **Tel:** 1 519 824-7000.
Email: news@cjoy.com
Web site: http://www.magic106.com
Profile: CIMJ-FM is a commercial station owned by Corus Entertainment Inc. The format of the station is hot adult contemporary music. CIMJ-FM broadcasts to East Guelph, Ontario at 106.1-FM.
FM RADIO STATION

CIML-FM 47798

Owner: Makkovik Radio Society Inc.
Editorial: 59 Anderson St, Makkovik, Newfoundland A0P 1J0 **Tel:** 1 709 923-2327.
Profile: CIML-FM is a non-commercial station owned by Makkovik Radio Society Inc. The format of the station is variety. CIML-FM broadcasts to the Makkovik, Newfoundland area at 99.5 FM.
FM RADIO STATION

CIMM-FM 521095

Owner: McBride Communications & Media Inc.
Editorial: 10760 Fundy Dr, Richmond, British Columbia V7E 5K7 **Tel:** 1 604 220-8393.
Profile: CIMM-FM is owned and operated by McBride Communications & Media Inc. The format of the station is classic hits. CIMM-FM broadcasts to the Richmond, British Columbia area at 99.5 FM.
FM RADIO STATION

CIMO-FM (ÉNERGIE Sherbrooke 106.1) 47559

Owner: Bell Media
Editorial: 2185 Rue King O, Sherbrooke, Quebec J1J 2G2 **Tel:** 1 819 347-1414.
Web site: http://www.sherbrooke.radioenergie.ca/
Profile: CIMO-FM est une station de radio commerciale, une propriété de Bell Media. Le format de la station est la musique, le Top 40. CIMO-FM est diffusé à Sherbrooke, Québec au 106.1 FM.

CIMO-FM is a commercial station owned by Bell Media. The format of the station is Top 40/CHR. CIMO-FM broadcasts to the Sherbrooke, Quebec area at 106.1 FM.
FM RADIO STATION

CIMS-FM 47791

Owner: Cooperative Radio Restigouche Ltee.(La)
Editorial: 1991 Ave des Pionniers, Balmoral, New Brunswick E8E 2W7 **Tel:** 1 506 826-1040.
Email: info@cimsfm.ca
Web site: http://www.cimsfm.ca
Profile: CIMS-FM is a non-commercial station owned by La Cooperative Radio Restigouche Ltee. The format of the station is variety. CIMS-FM broadcasts to the Balmoral, New Brunswick area at 103.9 FM.
FM RADIO STATION

CIMX-FM 47621

Owner: Bell Media
Editorial: 1640 Ouellette Ave, Windsor, Ontario N8X 1L1- **Tel:** 1 519 258-8888.
Email: programming@89Xradio.com
Web site: http://www.89xradio.com
Profile: CIMX-FM is a commercial station owned by Bell Media. The format of the station is rock alternative music. CIMX-FM broadcasts to Windsor, Ontario at 88.7 FM.
FM RADIO STATION

CIMY-FM (104.9 myFM) 390877

Owner: My Broadcasting Corporation
Editorial: 84 Isabella St Fl 2ND, Pembroke, Ontario K8A 5S5 **Tel:** 1 613 735-6936.
Email: news@myfmradio.ca
Web site: http://www.pembroketoday.ca
Profile: CIMY-FM is a commercial station owned by My Broadcasting Corporation. The format of the station is adult contemporary. CIMY-FM broadcasts to the Pembroke, Ontario area at 104.9 FM.
FM RADIO STATION

CINA-AM 577745

Owner: Ray, Neeti
Editorial: 1515 Britannia Road East, Suite 315, Mississauga, Ontario L4W 4K1 **Tel:** 1 416 777-1650.
Email: info@cinaradio.com
Web site: http://www.cinaradio.com
Profile: CINA-AM is a commercial station owned by Neeti Ray. The format of the station is a variety with a focus on Bollywood hits and Indo-Pakistani programming. CINA-AM broadcasts to the Mississauga, ON area at 1650 AM.
AM RADIO STATION

CINB-FM 363725

Owner: New Song Communications Ministries Ltd.
Editorial: 37 Hanover, Saint John, New Brunswick e2l 3xl **Tel:** 1 506 657-9600.
Email: staff@newsongfm.com
Web site: http://www.newsongfm.com
Profile: CINB-FM is a non-commercial station owned by New Song Communications Ministries Ltd. The format of the station is contemporary Christian. CINB-FM broadcasts to the Saint John, New Brunswick area at 96.1 FM.
FM RADIO STATION

CINC-FM 47746

Owner: Native Communications Inc.
Editorial: 1507 Inkster Boulevard, Winnipeg, Manitoba R2X 1R2 **Tel:** 1 204 772-8255.
Email: info@ncifm.com
Web site: http://www.ncifm.com
Profile: CINC-FM is a commercial station owned by Native Communications Inc. The format of the station is aboriginal language news and programming. CINC-FM broadcasts to the Thompson, Manitoba area at 96.3 FM. CICY-FM is a commercial station owned by Native Communications, Inc. (NCI). The format of the station is aboriginal language news and programming.
FM RADIO STATION

CIND-FM (Indie88) 879184

Owner: Central Ontario Broadcasting
Editorial: 20 Hanna Ave, Toronto, Ontario M6K 0B7 **Tel:** 1 416 588-7595.
Email: questions@indie88.com
Web site: http://indie88.com/
Profile: CIND-FM (Indie88) is a commercial station owned by Central Ontario Broadcasting. The format for the station is indie/alternative rock. CIND-FM broadcasts to the Toronto, Ontario area at 88.1 FM.
FM RADIO STATION

CING-FM (95.3 Fresh Radio) 47462

Owner: Corus Entertainment Inc.
Editorial: 875 Main St W, Hamilton, Ontario L8S 4P9 **Tel:** 1 905 521-9900.
Email: info@953freshradio.ca
Web site: http://www.953freshradio.ca
Profile: CING-FM is a commercial station owned by Corus Entertainment Inc. The format of the station is Hot AC. CING-FM broadcasts to Toronto at 95.3 FM.
FM RADIO STATION

CINN-FM (91.1 FM) 47745

Owner: Radio de l'Epinette Noire Inc.
Editorial: 1004 rue Prince, Hearst, Ontario P0L 1N0 **Tel:** 1 705 372-1011.
Web site: http://cinn911.com
Profile: CINN-FM (91.1 FM) est une station de radio non-commerciale possédée par Radio de l'Épinette Noire Inc. Le format de la station est variété. CINN-FM diffuse dans la région d'Hearst en Ontario à 91.1 FM.

CINN-FM (91.1 FM) is a non-commercial station owned by Radio de l'Épinette Noire Inc. The format of the station is variety. CINN-FM broadcasts to the Hearst, Ontario area at 91.1 FM.
FM RADIO STATION

CINQ-FM (Radio centre-ville) 47611

Owner: Radio Centre-Ville
Editorial: 5212 boul St-Laurent, 2e etage, Montreal, Quebec H2T 1S1 **Tel:** 1 514 495-2597.
Email: cinqfm@radiocentreville.com
Web site: http://www.radiocentreville.com
Profile: CINQ-FM is a non-commercial station owned by Radio Centre-Ville. The format of the station is variety. CINQ-FM broadcasts to the Montreal, Quebec area at 102.3 FM.
FM RADIO STATION

CINU-FM 604548

Owner: Hope FM Ministries Ltd
Editorial: 217 Harmony Ridge Rd, Truro, Nova Scotia B6L 3P4 **Tel:** 1 902 843-4673.
Email: hopefmministries@eastlink.ca
Web site: http://www.hoperadio.ca
FM RADIO STATION

CIOC-FM 47744

Owner: Rogers Communications Inc.
Editorial: 817 Fort St, Victoria, British Columbia V8W 1H6 **Tel:** 1 250 382-0900.
Web site: http://www.ocean985.com
Profile: CIOC-FM is a commercial station owned by Rogers Communications Inc. The format of the station is adult contemporary. CIOC-FM broadcasts to Victoria, British Columbia at 98.5 FM.
FM RADIO STATION

CIOG-FM 812035

Owner: International Harvesters for Christ Evangelistic Association Inc.
Editorial: 101 Ilsley Ave Unit 3, Dartmouth, Nova Scotia B3B 1S8 **Tel:** 1 902 468-8854.
Email: harvestersoffice@gmail.com
Web site: http://www.ciogfm.com
Profile: CIOG-FM is a commercial station owned by International Harvesters for Christ Evangelistic Association Inc. The format of the station is Contemporary Christian music. CIOG-FM broadcasts to the Charlottetown, Prince Edward Island, Canada area 93.9 FM.
FM RADIO STATION

CIOI-FM (The Hawk 101.5) 83143

Owner: Mohawk College Radio Co.
Editorial: 135 Fennell Ave E Rm GF11, Hamilton, Ontario L9A 1S2 **Tel:** 1 905 575-2175.
Web site: http://www.1015thehawk.ca
Profile: CIOI-FM is a commercial station owned by Mohawk College Radio Co. The format for the station is college variety. CIOI-FM broadcasts to the Hamilton, Ontario area at 101.5 FM.
FM RADIO STATION

CIOK-FM 47564

Owner: Maritime Broadcasting System Ltd.
Editorial: 226 Union St, Saint John, New Brunswick E2L 1B1 **Tel:** 1 506 658-5100.
Email: mailbag@k100.ca
Web site: http://www.k100.ca
Profile: CIOK-FM is a commercial station owned by Maritime Broadcasting System Ltd. The format of the station is top 40/CHR. CIOK-FM broadcasts to Saint John, New Brunswick and surrounding communities at 100.5 FM.
FM RADIO STATION

CION-FM 47743

Owner: Fondation Radio Galilee
Editorial: 3196 Chemin Sainte-Foy, Sainte-Foy, Quebec G1X 1R4 **Tel:** 1 418 659-9090.
Email: cionfm@radiogalilee.com
Web site: http://www.radiogalilee.com
Profile: CION-FM est une radio religieuse francophone de la Fondation radio Galilée. La station diffuse sur la ville de Québec sur la fréquence 90.9FM.

CION-FM is a non-commercial radio station owned by the Fondation Radio Galilee. The format of the station is religious. CION-FM broadcasts to the Quebec area at 90.9 FM.
FM RADIO STATION

CIOO-FM 47595

Owner: Bell Media
Editorial: 2900 Agricola St, Halifax, Nova Scotia B3K 6A7 **Tel:** 1 902 453-2524.
Email: c100fm@bellmedia.ca
Web site: http://www.c100fm.com
Profile: CIOO-FM commercial station owned by Bell Media. The format of the station is hot adult contemporary. CIOO-FM broadcasts to Halifax, Nova Scotia at 100.1 FM.
FM RADIO STATION

CIOR-AM 47373

Owner: Bell Media
Editorial: 5-130 Harold Ave, Princeton, British Columbia V0X 1W0 **Tel:** 1 250 492-2800.
Profile: CIOR-AM is a commercial station owned by Bell Media. The format of the station is easy listening music. CIOR-AM broadcasts to Penticton, British Columbia at 1400 AM. The station airs CKOR-AM's programming.
AM RADIO STATION

CIOT-FM 586201
Owner: Wilderness Ministries, Inc.
Tel: 1 306 862-2468.
Email: info@lighthousefm.ca
Web site: http://www.lighthousefm.ca
Profile: CIOT-FM is a non-commercial station owned by Wilderness Ministries, Inc. The format of the station is gospel and religious music. CIOT-FM broadcasts to the Nipawin, Saskatchewan area at 104.1 FM.
FM RADIO STATION

CIOZ-FM 47741
Owner: Newfoundland Broadcasting Co. Ltd.
Editorial: 446 Logy Bay Rd, St. John's, Newfoundland A1C 5S2 **Tel:** 1 709 726-2922.
Email: ozfm@ozfm.com
Web site: http://www.ozfm.com
FM RADIO STATION

CIPC-FM (Radioactive 99.1) 47807
Owner: Radio Port-Cartier Inc.
Editorial: 365 Boul Laure, Sept-Iles, Quebec G4R 1X2 **Tel:** 1 418 968-2472.
Email: cipc991@laradioactive.com
Web site: http://www.laradioactive.com
Profile: CIPC-FM is a commercial station owned by Radio Port-Cartier Inc. The format of the station is Top 40/CHR. CIPC-FM broadcasts to Port-Cartier, Quebec at 99.1 FM.
FM RADIO STATION

CIPI-FM 47799
Owner: Sipisishk Communications Inc.
Editorial: 49 Lavoie St., Beauval, Saskatchewan S0M 0G0 **Tel:** 1 306 288-2222.
Email: cipi@sasktel.net
Web site: http://www.cipiradio.com
FM RADIO STATION

CIPU-FM 791261
Owner: Lnusipuk Communication Information Net
Editorial: 529 Church St, Indian Brook, Micmac, Nova Scotia B0N1W0 **Tel:** 1 902 236-3636.
Email: shubiefm@gmail.com
Web site: http://shubiefm.com
Profile: CIPU-FM is a non-commercial station owned by Lnusipuk Communication Information Net. The format of the station is variety. CIPU-FM broadcasts to Mic Mac, NS at 97.1 FM.
FM RADIO STATION

CIQB-FM 47661
Owner: Corus Entertainment Inc.
Editorial: 1125 Bayfield Street N, Barrie, Ontario L4M 4S5 **Tel:** 1 705 726-1011.
Email: news@b101fm.com
Web site: http://www.b101fm.com
Profile: CIQB-FM is a commercial station owned by Corus Entertainment Inc. The format of the station is hot adult contemporary music. CIQB-FM broadcasts to Barrie, Ontario at 101.1 FM.
FM RADIO STATION

CIQC-FM (99.7 2day FM) 47107
Owner: Vista Broadcast Group Inc.
Editorial: 470 13th Ave, Campbell River, British Columbia V9W 7J4- **Tel:** 1 250 287-7106.
Web site: http://mycampbellrivernow.com
Profile: CIQC-FM (99.7 2day FM) is a commercial station owned by Vista Broadcast Group Inc. The format of the station is Contemporary Hits.
FM RADIO STATION

CIQM-FM 47503
Owner: Bell Media
Editorial: 743 Wellington Rd, London, Ontario N6C 4R5- **Tel:** 1 519 686-2525.
Web site: http://www.iheartradio.ca/virginradio/london
Profile: CIQM-FM is a commercial station owned by Bell Media. The format of the station is hot AC music. CIQM-FM broadcasts to the London, Ontario area at 97.5 FM.
FM RADIO STATION

CIRA-FM 47739
Owner: Société Radio-Ville-Marie Inc.
Editorial: 4020, rue St-Ambroise, Suite 199, Montreal, Quebec H4C 2C7 **Tel:** 1 514 382-3913.
Email: info@radiovm.com
Web site: http://www.radiovm.com
Profile: CIRA-FM is a non-commercial station owned by Société Radio-Ville-Marie Inc. The format of the station is religious. CIRA-FM broadcasts to the Montreal area at 91.3 FM.
FM RADIO STATION

CIRK-FM 47475
Owner: Newfoundland Capital Corporation Limited
Editorial: 2394 West Edmonton Mall, 8882-170 Street, Edmonton, Alberta T5T 4M2 **Tel:** 1 780 437-4996.
Email: news@cfcw.com
Web site: http://www.k97.ca
Profile: CIRK-FM is a commercial station owned by Newfoundland Capital Corporation Limited. The format of the station is classic rock music. CIRK-FM broadcasts to Edmonton, Alberta and area at 97.3 FM.
FM RADIO STATION

CIRR-FM (Proud 103.9 FM) 468602
Owner: Evanov Radio Group
Editorial: 5312 Dundas St W, Toronto, Ontario M9B 1B3 **Tel:** 1 416 213-1035.
Email: info@evanovradio.com
Web site: http://www.proudfm.com
Profile: CIRR-FM is a commercial station owned by Rainbow Media Group Inc. The format of the station is adult contemporary and talk. CIRR-FM broadcasts to the Toronto area at 103.9 FM.
FM RADIO STATION

CIRV-FM (Radio International 88.9 fm) 47537
Owner: CIRC Radio Inc.
Editorial: 1087 Dundas St W, Toronto, Ontario M6J 1W9 **Tel:** 1 416 537-1088.
Email: info@cirvfm.com
Web site: http://www.cirvfm.com
Profile: CIRV-FM is a commercial station owned by CIRC Radio Inc. The format of the station is news and talk. CIRV-FM broadcasts to Toronto, ON at 88.9 FM.
FM RADIO STATION

CIRX-FM 47444
Owner: Vista Broadcast Group Inc.
Editorial: 1940 3rd Ave, Prince George, British Columbia V2M 1G7 **Tel:** 1 250 564-2524.
Web site: http://94.thegoatrocks.ca
Profile: CIRX-FM is a commercial radio station owned by the Vista Broadcast Group Inc. The format of the station is world class rock. CIRX-FM broadcasts to the Prince George, British Columbia area at 94.3 FM.
FM RADIO STATION

CISC-FM 47735
Owner: Rogers Media Inc.
Editorial: 40147 Glenalder Pl Unit 202, Squamish, British Columbia V8B 0G2 **Tel:** 1 604 892-1021.
Email: news@mountainfm.com
Web site: http://www.mountainfm.com
Profile: CISC-FM is a commercial station owned by Rogers Media Inc. The format for the station is hot adult contemporary. CISC-FM broadcasts to the Gibsons, British Columbia at 107.5 FM. CISC FM rebroadcasts the signal from CISQ FM. JL.
FM RADIO STATION

CISL-AM 47140
Owner: Newcap Radio
Editorial: 20-11151 Horseshoe Way 20, Richmond, British Columbia V7A 4S5 **Tel:** 1 604 2722100.
Web site: http://www.am650radio.com
Profile: CISL-AM is a commercial station owned by Newcap Radio. The format of the station is adult standards. CISL-AM broadcasts to Richmond, British Columbia at 650 AM.
AM RADIO STATION

CISM-FM 47737
Owner: Communication du Versant Nord Ltd.
Editorial: 2332 Boul Edouard-Montpetit Bureau C-1509, Montreal, Quebec H3C 3J7 **Tel:** 1 514 343-7511.
Email: info@cism893.ca
Web site: http://www.cism.umontreal.ca
Profile: CISM-FM est une radio communautaire de Communication du Versant Nord Ltd. Les genres musicaux sont diversifiés. CISM-FM diffuse au 89.3FM sur Montréal.

CISM-FM is a non-commercial station owned by Communication du Versant Nord Ltd. The format of the station is rock alternative. CISM-FM broadcasts to Montreal at 89.3 FM.
FM RADIO STATION

CISN-FM 47476
Owner: Corus Entertainment Inc.
Editorial: 5204 84 St NW, Edmonton, Alberta T6E 5N8 **Tel:** 1 780 440-6300.
Email: info@cisnfm.com
Web site: http://www.cisnfm.com
Profile: CISN-FM is a commercial station owned by Corus Entertainment. The format of the station is contemporary country music. CISN-FM broadcasts to the Edmonton, Alberta area at 103.9 FM.
FM RADIO STATION

CISO-FM (Sunshine 89) 737639
Owner: Bayshore Broadcasting Corp.
Editorial: 490 W St N Suite 2, Orillia, Ontario L3V 5E8 **Tel:** 1 705 325-9786.
Email: info@sunshine89.ca
Web site: http://www.sunshine89.ca
Profile: CISO-FM is a commercial station owned by Bayshore Broadcasting Corporation. The format of the station is adult contemporary. CISO-FM broadcasts to the Twin Lakes District on 89.1.
FM RADIO STATION

CISP-FM 47736
Owner: Rogers Media Inc.
Editorial: 40147 Glenalder Pl Unit 202, Squamish, British Columbia V8B 0G2 **Tel:** 1 604 892-1021.
Email: news@mountainfm.com
Web site: http://www.mountainfm.com
Profile: CISP-FM is a commercial station owned by Rogers Media Inc. The format for the station is hot adult contemporary. CISP-FM broadcasts to the Pemberton, British Columbia at 104.5 FM.
FM RADIO STATION

CISQ-FM 47446
Owner: Rogers Communications Inc.
Editorial: 40147 Glenalder Place, Unit 202, Squamish, British Columbia V8B 0G2 **Tel:** 1 604 892-1021.
Email: news@mountainfm.com
Web site: http://www.mountainfm.com
Profile: CISQ-FM is a commercial station owned by Rogers Communications Inc. The format of the station is hot adult contemporary music. CISQ-FM broadcasts to Squamish, BC area at 107.1 FM. CISQ simulcasts to CISW FM, CISC FM, CISP FM and CIEG FM. JL.
FM RADIO STATION

CISS-FM 47522
Owner: Rogers Communications Inc.
Editorial: 2001 Thurston Dr, Ottawa, Ontario K1G 6C9 **Tel:** 1 613 736-2001.
Email: ottawanewsroom@ottawaradio.rogers.com
Web site: http://www.1053kissfm.com
Profile: CISS-FM is a commercial station owned by Rogers Communications Inc. The format of the station is Top 40/CHR music. CISS-FM broadcasts to the Ottawa, Ontario area at 105.3 FM.
FM RADIO STATION

CISW-FM 47734
Owner: Rogers Media Inc.
Editorial: 40147 Glenalder Pl Unit 202, Squamish, British Columbia V8B 0G2 **Tel:** 1 604 892-1021.
Email: news@mountainfm.com
Web site: http://www.mountainfm.com
Profile: CISW-FM is a commercial station owned by Rogers Media Inc. The format of the station is hot adult contemporary. CISW-FM broadcasts to Whistler, British Columbia at 102.1 FM. CISW-FM rebroadscasts CISQ FM. JL.
FM RADIO STATION

CITA-FM 342193
Owner: International Harvesters for Christ Evangelistic Association Inc.
Editorial: 101 Ilsey Avenue, Unit 3, Dartmouth, Nova Scotia B3B 1S8 **Tel:** 1 902 468-8854.
Email: info@cjlufm.com
Web site: http://www.citafm.com
FM RADIO STATION

CITE-FM (Rouge FM Montreal 107.3) 47603
Owner: Bell Media
Editorial: 1717 Boul Rene-Levesque E, Montreal, Quebec H2L 4T3 **Tel:** 1 514 529-3229.
Email: nouvelles.montreal@bellmedia.ca
Web site: http://www.iheartradio.ca/rouge-fm/rouge-fm-montreal/
Profile: CITE-FM (Rouge 107.3) est une station de radio commerciale de Bell Media. La formule de la station est adulte contemporain. CITE-FM (Rouge 107.3) est diffusé dans la région de Montréal.

CITE-FM (Rouge 107.3) is a commercial radio station owned by Bell Media. The format of the station is adult contemporary. CITE-FM broadcasts to the Montréal area at 107.3 FM.
FM RADIO STATION

CITE-FM-1 (Rouge Sherbrooke 102.7) 610840
Owner: Bell Media
Editorial: 2185 Rue King O Bureau 200, Sherbrooke, Quebec J1J 2G2 **Tel:** 1 819 566-6655.
Web site: http://estrie.rougefm.ca
Profile: CITE-FM-1 est une station de radio commerciale francophone, une propriété de Bell Media. Le format de la station est adulte contemporain. CITE-FM-1 est diffusé à Sherbrooke, Québec à 102.7 FM.

CITE-FM-1 is a French-language commercial station owned by Bell Media. The format of the station is adult contemporary. CITE-FM-1 broadcasts to Sherbrooke, Quebec at 102.7 FM.
FM RADIO STATION

CITF-FM (Rouge FM Québec 107.5) 47610
Owner: Bell Media
Editorial: 900 Place D'Youville Etage 1ER, Quebec, Quebec G1R 3P7 **Tel:** 1 418 527-3232.
Web site: http://www.iheartradio.ca/rouge-fm/rouge-fm-quebec
Profile: CITF-FM (Rouge FM Québec 107.5) est une station de radio commerciale appartenant à Bell Media. Son format est de type musicale. CITF-FM (Rouge FM Québec 107.5) is a French-language commercial station owned by Bell Media. The format of the station is adult contemporary. CITF-FM broadcasts to the Quebec area at 107.5 FM.
FM RADIO STATION

CITI-FM 47502
Owner: Rogers Communications Inc.
Editorial: 4-166 Osborne St, Winnipeg, Manitoba R3L 1Y8 **Tel:** 1 204 788-3400.
Web site: http://www.92citifm.ca
Profile: CITI-FM is a commercial radio station owned by Rogers Communications Inc. The format of the station is classic rock. CITI-FM broadcasts to Winnipeg, Manitoba at 92.1 FM.
FM RADIO STATION

CITR-FM 47454
Owner: Student Radio Society of U.B.C.
Editorial: 6138 Sub Blvd Rm 233, Vancouver, British Columbia V6T 2A5 **Tel:** 1 604 822-1242.
Email: news@citr.ca
Web site: http://www.citr.ca
Profile: CITR-FM is a non-commercial station owned by the Student Radio Society of U.B.C. The format of the station is variety. CITR-FM broadcasts to the Vancouver, British Columbia area at 101.9 FM.
FM RADIO STATION

CITU-FM 586050
Owner: Co-opérative Radio Richmond Limitée(La)
Editorial: 3435 Route 206, Petit de Grat, Nova Scotia B0E 2L0 **Tel:** 1 902 226-0981.
Profile: CITU-FM is a commercial station owned by La Co-opérative de Radio Richmond Limitée. The format for the station is country and folk. CITU-FM broadcasts to the Petit-de-Grat, Nova Scotia area at 104.1 FM.
FM RADIO STATION

CIUP-FM 382998
Owner: Jim Pattison Broadcast Group(The)
Editorial: 9894 42 Ave NW, Edmonton, Alberta T6E 5V5 **Tel:** 1 780 433-7877.
Email: contactus@up993.com
Web site: http://www.up993.com
Profile: CIUP-FM is a commercial station owned by The Jim Pattison Broadcast Group. The format of the station is soft rock. CIUP-FM broadcasts to the Edmonton, Alberta area at 99.3 FM.
FM RADIO STATION

CIUR-FM 614942
Owner: Native Communications Inc.
Editorial: 1507 Inkster Blvd, 2nd fl, Winnipeg, Manitoba R2X 1R2 **Tel:** 1 204 772-8255.
Email: info@rhythm1047.com
Web site: http://nowcountry.fm
Profile: CIUR-FM is a commercial station owned by Native Communications Inc. The format of the station is county music. CIUR-FM broadcasts to the Winnipeg, Manitoba area at 104.7 FM.
FM RADIO STATION

CIUT-FM 47627
Owner: University of Toronto Community Radio
Editorial: 89.5 Tower Road, Toronto, Ontario M5S 0A2 **Tel:** 1 416 978-0909.
Email: communications@ciut.fm
Web site: http://www.ciut.fm
Profile: CIUT-FM is a non-commercial station owned by the University of Toronto Community Radio. The format is a variety of music, news, and talk programming. CIUT-FM broadcasts to the University of Toronto and the broader Toronto community at 89.5 FM.
FM RADIO STATION

CIVH-AM 47158
Owner: Vista Broadcast Group Inc.
Editorial: 150 West Columbia, Vanderhoof, British Columbia V0J 3A0 **Tel:** 1 250 567-4914.
Email: thewolf@hwy16.com
Web site: http://thevalleywolf.ca
Profile: CIVH-AM is a commercial station owned by Vista Broadcast Group Inc. The format for the station is contemporary country. CIVH-AM broadcasts to the Vanderhoof, British Columbia area at 1340 AM.
AM RADIO STATION

CIVL-FM 564793
Owner: University of the Fraser Valley
Editorial: 33844 King Road, Abbotsford, British Columbia V2S 7M8 **Tel:** 1 604 851-6306.
Email: info@civl.ca
Web site: http://www.civl.ca
Profile: CIVL-FM is a non-commercial station owned by University College of the Fraser Valley. The format of the station is variety. CIVL-FM broadcasts to the Abbotsford, BC area at 88.5 FM.
FM RADIO STATION

CIVR-FM 363733
Owner: Association franco-culturelle de Yellowknife
Editorial: 5016 48 Street, Yellowknife, Northwest Territories X1A 1N3 **Tel:** 1 867 766-5172.
Email: societeradiotaiga@gmail.com
Web site: http://www.radiotaiga.com
Profile: CIVR-FM is a non-commercial station owned by Association franco-culturelle de Yellowknife. The format of the station is variety. CIVR-FM broadcasts to the Yellowknife, Northwest Territories area at 103.5 FM.
FM RADIO STATION

CIWS-FM 583997
Owner: Whistle Community Radio
Editorial: 6379 Main St, Stouffville, Ontario L4A 1G4 **Tel:** 1 905 640-0311.
Email: admin@whistleradio.com
Web site: http://www.whistleradio.com
Profile: CIWS-FM is a non-profit station owned by Whistle Community Radio. The format of the station

is variety. CIWS-FM broadcasts to the Stouffville, ON area at 102.7 FM.
FM RADIO STATION

CIWW-AM (1310 NEWS) 47296
Owner: Rogers Communications Inc.
Editorial: 2001 Thurston Dr, Ottawa, Ontario K1G 6C9
Tel: 1 613 736-2001.
Email: tips1310@rogers.com
Web site: http://www.1310news.com
Profile: CIWW-AM is a commercial station owned by Rogers Communications Inc. The format of the station is news. CIWW-AM broadcasts to the Ottawa, Ontario area at 1310 AM.
AM RADIO STATION

CIXF-FM 598931
Owner: Newfoundland Capital Corporation Limited
Editorial: 403 2nd Ave West, Unit 8, Brooks, Alberta T1R 0S3 **Tel:** 1 403 362-3418.
Email: theone@newcap.ca
Web site: http://www.the1brooks.com
Profile: CIXF-FM is a commercial station owned by Newfoundland Capital Corporation Limited. The format of the station is adult contemporary. CIXF-FM broadcasts to Brooks, Alberta and surrounding communities at 101.1 FM.
FM RADIO STATION

CIXK-FM (Mix 106.5) 47543
Owner: Bayshore Broadcasting Corp.
Editorial: 270 Ninth Street East, Owen Sound, Ontario N4K 1N7 **Tel:** 1 519 376-2030.
Email: info@mix1065.ca
Web site: http://www.mix106.ca
Profile: CIXK-FM is a commercial station owned by Bayshore Broadcasting Corp. The format of the station is adult contemporary. CIXK-FM broadcasts to the Owen Sound, Ontario area at 106.5 FM.
FM RADIO STATION

CIXL-FM 47348
Owner: R.B. Communications Ltd.
Editorial: 860 Forks Road W, Welland, Ontario L3B 5R6 **Tel:** 1 905 732-4433.
Email: info@giantfm.com
Web site: http://www.giantfm.com
Profile: CIXL-FM is a commercial station owned by R.B. Communications Ltd. The format of the station is classic rock. CIXL-FM broadcasts to the St. Catharines-Niagara, Ontario area at 91.7 FM.
FM RADIO STATION

CIXM-FM 430428
Owner: Fabmar Communications Ltd.
Editorial: 4912A 50th Avenue, Whitecourt, Alberta T7S 1N9 **Tel:** 1 780 706-1053.
Email: info@xm105fm.com
Web site: http://www.xm105fm.com
Profile: CIXM-FM is a commercial station owned by Fabmar Investments Ltd. The format of the station is country. CIXM-FM broadcasts to the Whitecourt, Alberta area at 105.3 FM.
FM RADIO STATION

CIXN-FM 83136
Owner: Joy FM Network Inc.
Editorial: 1010 Hanwell Road, Suite 10, Fredericton, New Brunswick E3B 6A4 **Tel:** 1 506 454-9600.
Email: welcome@joyfm.ca
Web site: http://www.joyfm.ca
Profile: CIXN-FM is a commercial station owned by Joy FM Network Inc. The format of the station is contemporary Christian. CIXN-FM broadcasts to Fredericton, New Brunswick at 96.5 FM.
FM RADIO STATION

CIXX-FM 47504
Owner: Radio Fanshawe Inc.
Editorial: 1001 Fanshawe College Blvd., London, Ontario N5V 5R6 **Tel:** 1 519 453-2810.
Web site: http://www.1069thex.com
Profile: CIXX-FM is a commercial station owned by Radio Fanshawe Inc. The format of the station is urban contemporary music. CIXX-FM broadcasts to the London, Ontario area at 106.9 FM.
FM RADIO STATION

CIYM-FM (Oldies 100.9) 670667
Owner: My Broadcasting Corporation
Editorial: 6 Oliphant Rd Unit 5, Brighton, Ontario K0K 1H0 **Tel:** 1 613 475-6936.
Email: news1009@myfmradio.ca
Web site: http://www.brightontoday.ca
Profile: CIYM-FM is a commercial station owned by My Broadcasting Corporation. The format for the station is oldies. CIYM-FM broadcasts to the Brighton, Ontario area at 100.9 FM.
FM RADIO STATION

CIYN-FM (95.5 myFM) 507723
Owner: My Broadcasting Corporation
Editorial: 756 Queen St, Kincardine, Ontario N2Z 2Y2
Tel: 1 519 396-7770.
Email: 955news@myfmradio.ca
Web site: http://www.shorelinetoday.ca
Profile: CIYN-FM is a commercial station owned by My Broadcasting Corporation. The format for the station is classic hits. CIYN-FM broadcasts to the Kincardine, Ontario area at 95.5 FM.
FM RADIO STATION

CIZL-FM 47488
Owner: Rawlco Radio Ltd.
Editorial: 210-2401 Saskatchewan Dr, Regina, Saskatchewan S4P 4H8 **Tel:** 1 306 525-0000.
Web site: http://www.z99.com
Profile: CIZL-FM is a commercial station owned by Rawlco Radio Ltd. The format for the station is adult contemporary. CIZL-FM broadcasts to the Regina, Saskatchewan area at 98.9 FM.
FM RADIO STATION

CIZZ-FM 47483
Owner: Newfoundland Capital Corporation Limited
Editorial: 4920 59th St, Red Deer, Alberta T4N 2N1
Tel: 1 403 343-1303.
Email: news@zedfm.com
Web site: http://www.zed99.com
Profile: CIZZ-FM is a commercial station owned by Newfoundland Capital Corporation Limited. The format for the station is rock. CIZZ-FM broadcasts to the Red Deer, Alberta, area at 98.9 FM.
FM RADIO STATION

CJAB-FM (Énergie Saguenay 94.5) 47550
Owner: Bell Media
Editorial: 267 Rue Racine E, 2e etage, Chicoutimi, Quebec G7H 1S5 **Tel:** 1 418 545-9450.
Web site: http://www.saguenay.radioenergie.ca/
Profile: CJAB-FM est une station commerciale de Bell Media. Le format de la station est Top40 CHR. CJAB-FM diffuse ses émissions à Chicoutimi, Québec (94.5 FM).

CJAB-FM is a commercial station owned by Bell Media. The format of the station is Top 40/CHR. CJAB-FM broadcasts to the Chicoutimi, Quebec area at 94.5 FM.
FM RADIO STATION

CJAD-AM 47359
Owner: Bell Media
Editorial: 1717 Boul Rene-Levesque E, Montreal, Quebec H2L 4T3- **Tel:** 1 514 989-2523.
Email: yourstory@cjad.com
Web site: http://www.iheartradio.ca/cjad
Profile: CJAD-AM is a commercial station owned by Bell Media. The format of the station is news and talk. CJAD-AM broadcasts to the Montreal area at 800 AM.
AM RADIO STATION

CJAG-FM 586209
Owner: Athabasca Hotel
Tel: 1 780 852-7789.
Web site: http://www.cjagjasper.com
Profile: CJAG-FM is a commercial station owned by Athabasca Hotel. The format of the station is rock music. CJAG-FM broadcasts to the Jasper, Alberta area at 92.3 FM.
FM RADIO STATION

CJAI-FM 585879
Owner: Amherst Island Public Radio
Editorial: 5830 Front Road, Stella, Ontario K0H 2S0
Tel: 1 613 384-8282.
Email: air@cjai.ca
Web site: http://www.cjai.ca
Profile: CJAI-FM is a non-commercial station owned Amherst Island Public Radio. The format of the station is a variety of eclectic public radio. CJAI-FM broadcasts to Stella, Ontario area at 92.1 FM.
FM RADIO STATION

CJAM-FM 47803
Owner: University of Windsor, Student Media Corp.
Editorial: c/o University of Windsor, Univ Centre 401 Sunset Ave, Windsor, Ontario N9B 3P4
Tel: 1 519 971-3606.
Web site: http://www.cjam.ca
Profile: CJAM-FM is a non-commmercial station owned by the University of Windsor, Student Media Corp. The format is a college variety. CJAM-FM broadcasts to the University of Windsor and the surrounding communities in Windsor, Ontario at 99.1 FM.
FM RADIO STATION

CJAN-FM (Asbestos 99.3) 47327
Owner: Radio Plus BMD Inc
Editorial: 1 Rue Hilaire, Asbestos, Quebec J1T 0A3
Tel: 1 819 879-0993.
Email: info@fm993.ca
Web site: http://www.fm993.ca
Profile: CJAN-FM est une station de radio francophone commerciale appartenant à Radio Plus BMD Inc. Le format de la station est adulte contemporain. CJAN-FM est diffusé à Asbestos, Québec au 99.3 FM.

CJAN-FM is a commercial French-language station owned by Radio Plus BMD Inc. The format of the station is adult contemporary. CJAN-FM broadcasts to the Asbestos, Quebec area at 99.3 FM.
FM RADIO STATION

CJAQ-FM 238959
Owner: Rogers Communications Inc.
Editorial: 2723 37 Ave NE Suite 240, Calgary, Alberta T1Y 5R8 **Tel:** 1 403 250-9797.
Web site: http://www.jackfm.ca
Profile: CJAQ-FM is a commercial station owned by Rogers Communications Inc. The format of the station is adult hits. CJAQ-FM broadcasts to Calgary, Alberta at 96.9 FM.
FM RADIO STATION

CJAR-FM 47371
Owner: Arctic Radio (1982) Ltd.
Editorial: 133rd St. W, The Pas, Manitoba R9A 1R7
Tel: 1 204 623-5307.
Email: cjar@arcticradio.ca
Web site: http://www.thepasonline.com
Profile: CJAR-FM is a commercial station owned by Arctic Radio (1982) Ltd. The format of the station is variety. CJAR-FM broadcasts to The Pas, Manitoba area at 102.9 FM.
AM RADIO STATION

CJAS-FM (Radio 93.5) 83119
Owner: CJAS Radio Communautaire St. Augustin
Tel: 1 418 947-2239.
Email: cjasradio93.5@gmail.com
Web site: http://www.cjasradio.ca
Profile: CJAS-FM is a commercial station owned by CJAS Radio Communautaire St. Augustin. The format of the station is variety. CJAS-FM broadcasts to the St-Augustin, Quebec area at 93.5 FM.
FM RADIO STATION

CJAT-FM 70727
Owner: Bell Media
Editorial: 1560 2nd Avenue, Trail, British Columbia V1R 1M4 **Tel:** 1 250 368-5510.
Web site: http://kootenays.myezrock.com
Profile: CJAT-FM is a commercial station owned by Bell Media. The format for the station is hot adult contemporary music. CJAT-FM broadcasts to the Trail, British Columbia area at 95.7 FM.
FM RADIO STATION

CJAV-FM 47127
Owner: Jim Pattison Broadcast Group(The)
Editorial: 3296 Third Ave, Port Alberni, British Columbia V9Y 4E1 **Tel:** 1 250 723-2455.
Email: info@933thepeak.com
Web site: http://www.933thepeak.com
Profile: CJAV-AM is a commercial station owned by The Jim Pattison Broadcast Group. The format of the station is adult contemporary. CJAV-AM broadcasts to the Port Alberni, British Columbia area at 93.3 FM.
FM RADIO STATION

CJAW-FM 528856
Owner: Golden West Broadcasting Ltd.
Editorial: 1704 Main Street North, Moose Jaw, Saskatchewan S6J 1L4 **Tel:** 1 306 694-0800.
Email: mjnews@goldenwestradio.com
Web site: http://www.discovermoosejaw.com
Profile: CJAW-FM is a commercial station owned by Golden West Broadcasting Ltd. The format of the station is adult contemporary. CJAW-FM broadcasts to the Moose Jaw, Saskatchewan area at 103.9 FM.
FM RADIO STATION

CJAX-FM 47458
Owner: Rogers Communications Inc.
Editorial: 2440 Ash St, Vancouver, British Columbia V5Z 4J6 **Tel:** 1 604 872-2557.
Web site: http://www.jackfm.com
Profile: CJAX-FM is a commercial radio station owned by Rogers Communications Inc. The format of the station is adult hits. CJAX-FM broadcasts to Vancouver, British Columbia at 96.9 FM.
FM RADIO STATION

CJAY-FM 47466
Owner: Bell Media
Editorial: 300-1110 Centre St NE 300, Calgary, Alberta T2E 2R2 **Tel:** 1 403 240-5800.
Web site: http://www.iheartradio.ca/cjay92
Profile: CJAY-FM is a commercial station owned by Bell Media. The format of the station is classic rock. CJAY-FM broadcasts to the Calgary, Alberta area at 92.1 FM.
FM RADIO STATION

CJBB-FM 83117
Owner: Woods (Boyd)
Editorial: 50 Third Street, Englehart, Ontario P0J 1H0
Tel: 1 705 544-1121.
Email: cjbbradio@gmail.com
Profile: CJBB-FM is a commercial station owned by Boyd Woods. The format is adult contemporary. CJBB-FM broadcasts to the Englehart, Ontario area at 103.2 FM.
FM RADIO STATION

CJBC-AM (Ici Radio-Canada Première Ontario) 47330
Owner: Société Radio-Canada
Editorial: 205 Wellington St W Bureau 5G506, Toronto, Ontario M5V 3G7 **Tel:** 1 416 205-2887.
Email: tjontario@radio-canada.ca
Web site: http://radio-canada.ca/regions/ontario
Profile: CJBC-AM is a non-commercial station owned by Societe Radio-Canada. The format of the station is news/talk. CJBC-AM broadcasts to Toronto at 860 AM. CBJC-AM is a member of the Canadian Press Gallery.
AM RADIO STATION

CJBC-FM (Ici Musique) 47732
Owner: Société Radio-Canada
Editorial: 205 Wellington St W, Toronto, Ontario M5V 3G7 **Tel:** 1 416 205-3311.
Web site: http://www.icimusique.ca
Profile: CJBC-FM is a non-commercial station owned by Société Radio-Canada. The format of the station is classical, jazz and adult contemporary. CJBC-FM broadcasts to the Toronto area at 90.3 FM. CBJC-FM is a member of the Canadian Press Gallery.
FM RADIO STATION

CJBE-FM (Radio Anticosti 90.1) 83118
Owner: Radio Communautaire d'Anticosti Inc.
Editorial: 4A Rue Savoy, Port-Menier, Ile d'Anticosti, Quebec G0G 2Y0 **Tel:** 1 418 535-0292.
Email: radioanticosti@gmail.com
Profile: CJBE-FM est une station de radio non-commerciale francophone, une propriété de Radio Communautaire d'Anticosti Inc. Le format de la station est le variété. CJBE-FM est diffusé à l'Île d'Anticosti, Québec au 90.5 FM. La station n'a pas de site Internet.

CJBE-FM is a non-commercial French-Language station owned by Radio Communautaire d'Anticosti Inc. The format of the station is variety. CJBE-FM broadcasts to the Ile d'Anticosti, Quebec region at 90.5 FM. The station doesn't have a Website.
FM RADIO STATION

CJBK-AM 47226
Owner: Astral Media
Editorial: 743 Wellington Road South, London, Ontario N6C 4R5 **Tel:** 1 519 686-2525.
Email: mailbag@cjbk.com
Web site: http://www.cjbk.com
Profile: CJBK-AM is a commercial station owned by Astral Media. The format of the station is news, talk and sports programming. CJBK-AM broadcasts to the London, Ontario area at 1290 AM.
AM RADIO STATION

CJBP-FM 685093
Owner: Stillwater Broadcasting Ltd
Editorial: 290 Davidson St., Neepawa, Manitoba R0J 1H0 **Tel:** 1 204 476-2669.
Email: news@cj97radio.com
Web site: http://cj97radio.com
Profile: CJBP-FM is a commercial station owned by Stillwater Broadcasting Ltd. The format is country. The station airs in the Neepawa, Manitoba area at 97.1FM.
FM RADIO STATION

CJBQ-AM 47180
Owner: Quinte Broadcasting Co. Ltd.
Editorial: 10 South Front St, Belleville, Ontario K8N 2Y3 **Tel:** 1 613 969-5555.
Email: news@cjbq.com
Web site: http://www.cjbq.com
Profile: CJBQ-AM is a commercial station owned by Quinte Broadcasting Co. Ltd. The format of the station is classic country and talk. CJBQ-AM broadcasts to the Belleville, Ontario area at 800 AM.
AM RADIO STATION

CJBR-FM 47571
Owner: Societe Radio-Canada
Editorial: 185 Boul Rene-Lepage E, Rimouski, Quebec G5L 1P2 **Tel:** 1 418 723-2217.
Email: nouvelles.rimouski@radio-canada.ca
Web site: http://www.radio-canada.ca/regions/bas-st-laurent
Profile: CJBR-FM is a non-commercial station owned by Societe Radio-Canada. The format of the station is news and talk. CJBR-FM broadcasts to the Rimouski, Quebec area at 89.1 FM.
FM RADIO STATION

CJBX-FM 47505
Owner: Astral Media
Editorial: 743 Wellington Rd, London, Ontario N6C 4R5- **Tel:** 1 519 686-2525.
Web site: http://www.bx93.com
Profile: CJBX-FM is a commercial station owned by Astral Media. The format of the station is contemporary country music. CJBX-FM broadcasts to the London, Ontario area at 92.7 FM.
FM RADIO STATION

CJBZ-FM 70481
Owner: Jim Pattison Broadcast Group(The)
Editorial: 401 Mayor Magrath Drive, Lethbridge, Alberta T1J 3L8 **Tel:** 1 403 394-9300.
Email: news@country95.fm
Web site: http://www.b93.fm
Profile: CJBZ-FM is a commercial station owned by The Jim Pattison Broadcast Group. The format is top 40/CHR. CJBZ-FM broadcasts to the Lethbridge, Alberta area at 93.3 FM.
FM RADIO STATION

CJCA-AM 47410
Owner: Touch Canada Broadcasting (2006) Inc.
Editorial: 5316 Calgary Trail, Edmonton, Alberta T6H 4J8 **Tel:** 1 780 466-4930.
Email: 105.9@shinefm.com
Web site: http://www.am930thelight.com
Profile: CJCA-AM is a commercial station owned by Touch Canada Broadcasting Inc. The format of the station is religious. CJCA-AM broadcasts to the Edmonton, Alberta area at 930 AM.
AM RADIO STATION

CJCB-AM 47214
Owner: Maritime Broadcasting System Ltd.
Editorial: 318 Charlotte St, Sydney, Nova Scotia B1P 1C8 **Tel:** 1 902 564-5596.
Email: news@capebretonradio.com
Web site: http://www.cjcbradio.com
Profile: CJCB-AM is a commercial station owned by the Maritime Broadcasting System Ltd. The format for the station is country music. CJCB-AM broadcasts to the Sydney, Nova Scotia area at 1270 AM.
AM RADIO STATION

CJCD-FM 70509
Owner: Vista Broadcast Group Inc.
Editorial: 5114 49 St, Yellowknife, Northwest Territories X1A 1P8 **Tel:** 1 867 920-4663.
Web site: http://cjcd.moosefm.com
Profile: CJCD-FM is a commercial station owned by Vista Broadcast Group Inc. The format of the station is adult contemporary. CJCD-FM broadcasts to the Yellowknife, Northwest Territories area at 100.1 FM.
FM RADIO STATION

CJCH-FM 47185
Owner: Bell Media
Editorial: 2900 Agricola St, Halifax, Nova Scotia B3K 6A7 **Tel:** 1 902 453-2524.
Web site: http://www.halifax.virginradio.ca
Profile: CJCH-FM is a commercial station owned by Bell Media. The format of the station is Top 40/CHR. CJCH-FM broadcasts to the Halifax, Nova Scotia area at 101.3 FM.
FM RADIO STATION

CJCI-FM 47130
Owner: Vista Broadcast Group Inc.
Editorial: 2977 Ferry Ave Unit 101, Prince George, British Columbia V2N 1L3 **Tel:** 1 250 564-2524.
Web site: http://www.myprincegeorgenow.com/country-97-fm
Profile: CJCI-FM is a commercial station owned by the Vista Broadcast Group Inc. The format of the station is contemporary country and rock music. CJCI-FM broadcasts to the Prince George, British Columbia area at 97.3 FM.
FM RADIO STATION

CJCJ-FM (CJ104) 47260
Owner: Astral Media
Editorial: 131 Queen St Unit 2, Woodstock, New Brunswick E7M 2M8 **Tel:** 1 506 325-3030.
Email: cj104@astral.com
Web site: http://www.cj104.com
Profile: CJCJ-FM (CJ104) is a commercial station owned by Astral Media. The format of the station is adult contemporary. CJCJ-FM (CJ104) broadcasts to the Woodstock, New Brunswick area at 104.1 FM.
FM RADIO STATION

CJCL-AM 47346
Owner: Rogers Communications Inc.
Editorial: 1 Ted Rogers Way, Toronto, Ontario M4Y 3B7 **Tel:** 1 416 935-0590.
Email: contact@fan590.com
Web site: http://www.sportsnet.ca/590
Profile: CJCL-AM is a commercial station owned by Rogers Communications Inc. The format is sports. CJCL-AM broadcasts to the Toronto area at 590 AM.
AM RADIO STATION

CJCQ-FM 83149
Owner: Jim Pattison Broadcast Group(The)
Editorial: 1711-100 Street, North Battleford, Saskatchewan S9A 0W7 **Tel:** 1 306 445-2477.
Web site: http://www.q98.ca
Profile: CJCQ-FM is a commercial station owned by The Jim Pattison Broadcast Group. The format of the station is adult contemporary. CJCQ-FM broadcasts to the North Battleford, Saskatchewan area at 97.9 FM.
FM RADIO STATION

CJCS-AM 47333
Owner: Vista Broadcast Group
Editorial: 376 Romeo St S, Stratford, Ontario N5A 4T9- **Tel:** 1 519 271-2450.
Email: news@cjcsradio.com
Web site: http://www.cjcsradio.com
Profile: CJCS-AM is a commercial station owned by Vista Broadcast Group. The format of the station is classic hits and oldies music. CJCS-AM broadcasts to the Stratford, Ontario area at 1240 AM.
AM RADIO STATION

CJCV-FM 793847
Owner: Corus Radio
Editorial: 1440 Jack Blick Ave. Unit 200, Winnipeg, Manitoba R3G 0L4 **Tel:** 1 204 786-2471.
Web site: http://www.991freshfm.com
Profile: CJCV-FM is a commercial station owned by Corus Radio. The format of the station is hot AC. CJCV-FM broadcasts to the Winnipeg, Manitoba at 99.1 FM.
FM RADIO STATION

CJCW-AM 47409
Owner: Maritime Broadcasting System Ltd.
Editorial: 6 Marble Street, Sussex, New Brunswick E4E 5M2 **Tel:** 1 506 432-2529.
Email: cjcw@mbsradio.com
Web site: http://www.590cjcw.com
Profile: CJCW-AM is commercial station owned by Maritime Broadcasting System Ltd. The format for the station is Jack FM/adult hits. CJCW-AM broadcasts to the Sussex, New Brunswick area at 590 AM.
AM RADIO STATION

CJCY-FM 535794
Owner: Clear Sky Radio Inc.
Editorial: 1865 Dunmore Road S.E., Suite 104, Medicine Hat, Alberta T1A 1Z8 **Tel:** 1 403 488-4684.
Email: news@cjcyfm.com
Web site: http://www.cjcyfm.com
Profile: CJCY-FM is a commercial station owned by Clear Sky Radio Inc. The format of the station is classic hits. CJCY-FM broadcasts to the Medicine Hat, Alberta area at 102.1 FM.
FM RADIO STATION

CJDC-AM 47112
Owner: Bell Media
Editorial: 901 102 Ave, Dawson Creek, British Columbia V1G 2B6 **Tel:** 1 250 782-3341.
Web site: http://www.cjdccountry.com
Profile: CJDC-AM is a commercial station owned by Bell Media. The format of the station is classic country. CJDC-AM broadcasts to the Dawson Creek, British Columbia area at 890 AM.
AM RADIO STATION

CJDJ-FM 83151
Owner: Rawlco Radio Ltd.
Editorial: 715 Saskatchewan Cres West, Saskatoon, Saskatchewan S7M 5V7 **Tel:** 1 306 934-2222.
Email: rock102@rawlco.com
Web site: http://www.rock102rocks.com
Profile: CJDJ-FM is a commercial station owned by Rawlco Radio Ltd. The format of the station is classic rock. CJDJ-FM broadcasts to the Saskatoon, Saskatchewan area at 102.1 FM.
FM RADIO STATION

CJDL-FM (Country 107.3) 47341
Owner: Tillsonburg Broadcasting Ltd.
Editorial: 77 Broadway St, Tillsonburg, Ontario N4G 3P5 **Tel:** 1 519 842-4281.
Email: info@easy101.com
Web site: http://www.country1073.ca
Profile: CJDL-FM is a commercial station owned by Tillsonburg Broadcasting Ltd. The format of the station is country. CJDL-FM broadcasts to the Tillsonburg, Ontario area at 107.3 FM.
FM RADIO STATION

CJDM-FM 47618
Owner: Bell Media
Editorial: 2070 Rue Raphael-Nolet, Drummondville, Quebec J2C 5G6 **Tel:** 1 819 475-1480.
Web site: http://www.drummondville.radioenergie.ca
Profile: CJDM-FM is a commercial station owned by Bell Media. The format of the station is Top 40/CHR. CJDM-FM broadcasts to the Drummondville, Quebec area at 92.1 FM.
FM RADIO STATION

CJDR-FM 47385
Owner: Jim Pattison Broadcast Group(The)
Editorial: 19 9th Ave S, Cranbrook, British Columbia V1C 2L9 **Tel:** 1 250 426-2224.
Email: news@thedrivefm.ca
Web site: http://www.thedrivefm.ca
Profile: CJDR-FM is a commercial station owned by The Jim Pattison Broadcast Group. The format of the station is classic rock. CJDR-FM broadcasts to the Fernie, British Columbia area at 99.1 FM.
FM RADIO STATION

CJDV-FM (Dave Rocks 107.5) 47873
Owner: Corus Entertainment Inc.
Editorial: 50 Sportsworls Crossing Rd, Unit 210, Kitchener, Ontario N2P 0A4 **Tel:** 1 519 772-1212.
Email: mornings@davefm.com
Web site: http://www.davefm.com
Profile: CJDV-FM is a commercial station owned by Corus Entertainment Inc. The format of the station is rock. CJDV-FM broadcasts to the Cambridge, Ontario area at 107.5 FM.
FM RADIO STATION

CJEB-FM 324791
Owner: Cogeco Media
Editorial: 1350 Rue Royale, 12e bureau 1200 etage, Trois-Rivieres, Quebec G9A 4J4 **Tel:** 1 819 691-1001.
Web site: http://www.rythmefm.com/mauricie
Profile: CJEB-FM is a French-language commercial station owned by Cogeco Media. The format of the station is adult contemporary. CJEB-FM broadcasts to the Trois-Rivières, Quebec area at 100.1 FM.
FM RADIO STATION

CJEC-FM (WKND 91.9 Québec) 156599
Owner: LeClerc Communications
Editorial: 815 Boul Lebourgneuf Suite 505, Quebec, Quebec G2J 0C1 **Tel:** 1 418 682-8433.
Email: nouvelles@wknd.fm
Web site: http://www.wknd.fm
Profile: CJEC-FM (WKND 91.9 Québec) est une station de radio commerciale de Leclerc Communications Inc. Le format de la station est adulte-contemporain. CJEF-FM diffuse dans la région de Québec (91.9 FM).

CJEC-FM (WKND 91.9 Québec) is a commercial station owned by Leclerc Comunications, Inc. The format for the station is adult contemporary. CJEC-FM broadcasts to the Quebec City area at 91.9 FM.
FM RADIO STATION

CJED-FM (105.1 2day FM) 152836
Owner: Vista Radio Limited
Editorial: 4673 Ontario Avenue, Niagara Falls, Ontario L2E 3R1 **Tel:** 1 905 356-6710.
Web site: http://1051.2dayfm.ca
Profile: CJED-FM (105.1 2day FM) is a commercial station owned by Vista Radio Limited. The format of the station is CHR/Top 40. CJED-FM broadcasts to the Niagara Region in Southern Ontario at 105.1 (CJED-FM).
FM RADIO STATION

CJEG-FM 404001
Owner: Newfoundland Capital Corporation Limited
Editorial: 4816 50th Avenue, Bonnyville, Alberta T9N 2G4 **Tel:** 1 780 812-3058.
Web site: http://www.1013koolfm.com
Profile: CJEG-FM is a commercial station owned by Newfoundland Capital Corporation Limited. The format of the station is adult contemporary. CJEG-FM broadcasts to the Bonnyville, Alberta area at 101.3 FM.
FM RADIO STATION

CJEL-FM 83108
Owner: Golden West Broadcasting Ltd.
Editorial: 277A 1st St, Winkler, Manitoba R6W 4A6 **Tel:** 1 204 331-9300.
Email: info@goldenwestradio.com
Web site: http://www.eagle935fm.com
Profile: CJEL-FM is a commercial station owned by Golden West Broadcasting. The format for the station is adult contemporary. CJEL-FM broadcasts to the Winkler, Manitoba area at 93.5 FM.
FM RADIO STATION

CJEM-FM 47880
Owner: Radio Edmunston Inc.
Editorial: 64, rue Rice, Edmundston, New Brunswick E3V 1T2 **Tel:** 1 506 735-3351.
Email: cjem@cjemfm.com
Web site: http://www.cjemfm.com
Profile: CJEM-FM is a commercial station owned by Radio Edmunston Inc. The format for the station is adult contemporary. CJEM-FM broadcasts to the Edmunston, New Brunswick area at 92.7 FM.
FM RADIO STATION

CJET-FM 47246
Owner: Rogers Communications Inc.
Editorial: 6A Beckwith Street North, Smiths Falls, Ontario K7A 2B1 **Tel:** 1 613 283-4630.
Email: ottawanewsroom@rci.rogers.com
Web site: http://www.923jackfm.com
Profile: CJET-FM is a commercial station owned by Rogers Communications Inc. The format is adult hits. CJET-FM broadcasts to the Smith Falls, Ontario area at 92.3 FM.
FM RADIO STATION

CJEU-AM (Radio Jeunesse 1670) 618697
Owner: Radio Jeunesse du Canada
Editorial: 855 Boul de la Gappe Piece 310, studio de la maison de la culture, Gatineau, Quebec J8T 8H9 **Tel:** 1 819 243-6226.
Email: info@radioenfant.ca
Web site: http://radiojeunesse.ca/
Profile: CJEU-AM est une station de radio non-commerciale, une propriété de Radio Jeunesse du Canada. La formule de la station est la programmation jeunesse. CJEU-AM est diffusé à Gatineau, au Québec à 1670 AM.

CJEU-AM is a non-commercial station owned by La Fondation Radio-Enfant. The format of the station is children's programming. CJEU-AM broadcasts to the Gatineau, Quebec area at 1670 AM.
AM RADIO STATION

CJEV-AM 47420
Owner: Newfoundland Capital Corporation Limited
Editorial: 13213 20th Ave, Blairmore, Alberta T0K 0E0 **Tel:** 1 403 562-2806.
Web site: http://www.mountainradiofm.com
Profile: CJEV-AM is a commercial station owned by Newfoundland Capital Corporation Limited. The format of the station is contemporary country. CJEV-AM broadcasts to the Blairmore, Alberta area at 1340 AM.
AM RADIO STATION

CJFM-FM (Virgin Radio Montréal 96 FM) 584151
Owner: Bell Media
Editorial: 1717 Boul Rene-Levesque E, Montreal, Quebec H2L 4T3 **Tel:** 1 514 790-9696.
Web site: http://www.iheartradio.ca/virginradio/montreal/
Profile: CJFM-FM est une station de Bell Media dont le format musical est adulte contemporain. CJFM-FM diffuse sur le 95.9 FM à Montréal.

CJFM-FM is a commercial station owned by Bell Media. The format of the station is hot adult contemporary. CJFM-FM broadcasts to the Montreal area at 95.9 FM.
FM RADIO STATION

CJFO-FM (94.5 Unique FM) 719156
Owner: La Radio Communautaire Francophone d'Ottawa
Editorial: 245 Av McArthur, Ottawa, Ontario K1L 6P3 **Tel:** 1 613 745-5529.
Web site: http://uniquefm.ca
Profile: CJFO-FM (94.5 Unique FM) is a radio station in Ottawa aimed specifically at the francophone population in the area. The focus of the station will be primarily local featuring local news, arts, and local talent.
FM RADIO STATION

CJFW-FM 47447
Owner: Astral Media
Editorial: 4625 Lazelle Ave, Terrace, British Columbia V8G 1S4 **Tel:** 1 250 635-6316.
Web site: http://www.cjfw.ca
Profile: CJFW-FM is a commercial station owned by Astral Media. The format of the station is classic country and contemporary country. CJFW-FM broadcasts to the Terrace, British Columbia area at 103.1 FM.
FM RADIO STATION

CJFX-FM 47261
Owner: Atlantic Broadcasters Ltd.
Editorial: 85 Kirk St, Antigonish, Nova Scotia B2G 1Y7 **Tel:** 1 902 863-4580.
Email: 989xfm@989xfm.ca
Web site: http://www.989xfm.ca
Profile: CJFX-FM is a commercial station owned by Atlantic Broadcasters Ltd. The format of the station is hot adult contemporary. CJFX-FM broadcasts to the Antigonish, Nova Scotia area at 98.9 FM.
FM RADIO STATION

CJFY-FM 342414
Owner: Miramichi Communications
Editorial: 401 Main St, Blackville, New Brunswick E9B 1T3 **Tel:** 1 506 843-2208.
Email: staff@liferadio.ca
Web site: http://www.liferadio.ca
Profile: CJFY-FM is a commercial station owned by Miramichi Communications. The format of the station is contemporary Christian. CJFY-FM broadcasts to the Blackville, New Brunswick area at 107.7 FM.
FM RADIO STATION

CJGM-FM (99.9 myFM) 775730
Owner: My Broadcasting Corporation
Editorial: 110 Kate Street, Gananoque, Ontario K7G 2M7 **Tel:** 1 613 382-6936.
Email: news999@myfmradio.ca
Web site: http://www.gananoquenow.ca
Profile: CJGM-FM is a commercial station owned by My Broadcasting Corporation. The format of the station is adult contemporary. CJGM-FM broadcasts to the Gananoque/Kingston, ON area at 99.9 FM.
FM RADIO STATION

CJGX-AM 47240
Owner: Harvard Broadcasting
Editorial: 120 Smith St E Fl 4TH, Yorkton, Saskatchewan S3N 3V3- **Tel:** 1 306 782-2256.
Email: ykt-reception@harvardbroadcasting.com
Web site: http://www.gx94radio.com
Profile: CJGX-AM is a commercial station owned by Harvard Broadcasting. The format of the station is country music. CJGX-AM broadcasts to the Yorktown, Saskatchewan area at 940 AM.
AM RADIO STATION

CJHD-FM 585882
Owner: Jim Pattison Broadcast Group(The)
Editorial: 1711-100 Street, North Battleford, Saskatchewan S9A 0W7 **Tel:** 1 306 445-2477.
Web site: http://933therock.ca
Profile: CJHD-FM is a commercial station owned by The Jim Pattison Broadcast Group. The format of the station is rock music. CJHD-FM broadcasts to the North Battleford, Saskatchewan area at 93.3 FM.
FM RADIO STATION

CJHK-FM 697119
Owner: Acadia Broadcasting Ltd.
Editorial: 135 North St, Bridgewater, Nova Scotia B4V 8Z8 **Tel:** 1 902 543-2401.
Web site: http://hankfm.ca
Profile: CJHK-FM is a commercial station owned by Acadia Broadcasting Ltd. The format for the station is contemporary country music. The station broadcasts at 100.7 FM in the Bridgewater, Nova Scotia area.
FM RADIO STATION

CJHL-FM 47819
Owner: Hopedale Inuit Community Gov't
Editorial: 1 Sitsik, Hopedale, Newfoundland A0P 1G0 **Tel:** 1 709 933-3808.
Profile: CJHL-FM is a non-commercial station owned by Hopedale Inuit Community Gov't. The format of the station is variety. CJHL-FM broadcasts to the Hopedale, Newfoundland area at 89.9 FM.
FM RADIO STATION

CJHQ-FM 810722
Owner: Columbia Basin Alliance for Literacy
Editorial: Nakusp, British Columbia
Email: tunein@thearrow107.com
Web site: http://thearrow107.com
Profile: CJHQ-FM is a commercial station owned by Columbia Basin Alliance for Literacy. The format of the station is variety, including a wide range of music and spoken word content. CJHQ-FM broadcasts to the Nakusp, British Columbia area at 107.1 FM.
FM RADIO STATION

CJHR-FM 554768
Owner: Valley Heritage Radio
Editorial: 3009 Burnstown, Renfrew, Ontario K7V 4H4
Tel: 1 613 432-9873.
Email: info@valleyheritageradio.ca
Web site: http://www.valleyheritageradio.ca
Profile: CJHR-FM is a commercial station owned by Valley Haritage Radio. The station airs a country and easy listening format at 98.7 FM in the Renfrew, Ontario area.
FM RADIO STATION

CJIJ-FM 553381
Owner: Membertou Radio Association Inc.
Editorial: 111 Membertou St, Membertou, Nova Scotia B1S 2M9 **Tel:** 1 902 562-0009.
Email: c99@membertou.ca
FM RADIO STATION

CJIT-FM 83155
Owner: Les Productions Du Temps Perdu, Inc.
Editorial: 5605 Rue Papineau, Lac-Megantic, Quebec G6B 0C8 **Tel:** 1 819 583-0663.
Web site: http://www.cjitfm.com
Profile: CJIT-FM est une propriété de Les productions du temps perdu Inc. La station radiophonique francophone diffuse au 106.7FM sur Lac-Mégantic.

CJIT-FM is a commercial station owned by Les Productions Du Temps Perdu, Inc. The format of the station is easy listening. CJIT-FM broadcasts to Lac-Megantic, Quebec at 106.7 FM.
FM RADIO STATION

CJIV-FM 342357
Owner: Way of Life Broadcasting
Editorial: 16640 Highway 17 W, Dryden, Ontario P8N 2Y7 **Tel:** 1 807 216-6811.
Web site: http://www.cjiv973.net
Profile: CJIV-FM is a non-commercial station owned by Way of Life Broadcasting. The format is religious and airs at 97.3 in the Dryden, Ontario area.
FM RADIO STATION

CJJC-FM 488974
Owner: 1010 56012 Saskatchewan Ltd.
Editorial: 395 Riverview Road, Yorkton, Saskatchewan S3N 3V6 **Tel:** 1 306 786-7625.
Email: rocktalk@therock985.ca
Web site: http://www.therock985.ca
Profile: CJJC-FM is a commercial station owned by 1010 56012 Saskatchewan Ltd. The format for the station is contemporary Christian. CJJC-FM broadcasts to the Yorkton, Saskatchewan area at 98.5 FM.
FM RADIO STATION

CJJJ-FM 588440
Owner: Assiniboine Community College
Editorial: 1430 Victoria Ave, Brandon, Manitoba R7A 2A9 **Tel:** 1 204 725-8700.
Email: campusradio@assiniboine.net
Web site: http://cj-106.assiniboine.net
Profile: CJJJ-FM is a commerical station owned by Assiniboine Community College. The format of the station is variety. CJJJ-FM broadcasts to the Brandon, Manitoba area at 106.5 FM.
FM RADIO STATION

CJJM-FM 689846
Owner: Vista Broadcast Group
Editorial: 50 Gray Street, Espanola, Ontario P5E 1G1
Tel: 1 705 869-0578.
Web site: http://www.moosefm.com/cjjm
Profile: CJJM-FM is a commercial station owned by Vista Broadcast Group. The format for the station is Classic Hits. CJJM-FM broadcasts to the Espanola, Ontario area at 99.3 FM.
FM RADIO STATION

CJJR-FM 47456
Owner: Jim Pattison Broadcast Group(The)
Editorial: 1401 W 8th Ave, Suite 300, Vancouver, British Columbia V6H 1C9 **Tel:** 1 604 731-7772.
Email: cjjr@jrfm.com
Web site: http://www.jrfm.com
Profile: CJJR-FM is a commercial station owned by The Jim Pattison Broadcast Group. The format for the station is contemporary country. CJJR-FM broadcasts to the Vancouver, British Columbia area at 93.7 FM.
FM RADIO STATION

CJKC-FM (Country 103.1) 412358
Owner: Newfoundland Capital Corporation Limited
Editorial: 611 Lansdowne St, Kamloops, British Columbia V2C 1Y6 **Tel:** 1 250 571-1031.
Email: nlnews@radionl.com
Web site: http://www.country103.ca
Profile: CJKC-FM is a commercial station owned by Newfoundland Capital Corporation Limited. The format of the station is contemporary country. CJKC-FM broadcasts to the Kamloops, British Columbia area at 103.1 FM.
FM RADIO STATION

CJKK-FM 47731
Owner: Newfoundland Broadcasting Co. Ltd.
Editorial: 446 Logy Bay Road, St. John's, Newfoundland A1C 5S2 **Tel:** 1 709 726-2922.
Email: ozfm@ozfm.com
Web site: http://www.ozfm.com
Profile: CJKK-FM is a commercial station owned by Newfoundland Broadcasting Co. Ltd. The format of the station is Top 40/CHR. CJKK-FM broadcasts to the St. John's, Newfoundland area at 105.3 FM.
FM RADIO STATION

CJKL-FM (101.5) 47222
Owner: Connelly Communications Corp.
Editorial: 5 Kirkland Street, Kirkland Lake, Ontario P2N 3J4 **Tel:** 1 705 567-3366.
Email: cjkl@cjklfm.com
Web site: http://www.cjklfm.com
Profile: CJKL-FM is a commercial station owned by Connelly Communications Corp. The format for the station is hot adult contemporary. CJKL-FM broadcasts to the Kirkland Lake, Ontario area at 101.5 FM. .
FM RADIO STATION

CJKR-FM 47508
Owner: Corus Entertainment Inc.
Editorial: 20-1440 Jackblick Ave, Winnipeg, Manitoba R3G 0L4 **Tel:** 1 204 786-2471.
Web site: http://www.975bigfm.com
Profile: CJKR-FM is a commercial station owned by Corus Entertainment Inc. The format for the station is classic rock. CJKR-FM broadcasts to the Winnipeg, Manitoba area at 97.5 FM.
FM RADIO STATION

CJKX-FM (KX96 New Country FM) 47663
Owner: Durham Radio Inc.
Editorial: 1200 Airport Blvd, Oshawa, Ontario L1J 8P5
Tel: 1 905 571-0949.
Email: newsroom@kx96.fm
Web site: http://www.kx96.fm
Profile: CJKX-FM is a commercial station owned by Durham Radio Inc. The format for the station is contemporary country music. CJKX-FM broadcasts to the Ajax, Ontario area at 95.9 FM.
FM RADIO STATION

CJLA-FM 47553
Owner: RNC Media
Editorial: 11 rue Argenteuil, Lachute, Quebec J8H 1X8 **Tel:** 1 450 562-8862.
Web site: http://www.planetelov.ca
Profile: CJLA-FM is a commercial station owned by RNC Media. The format of the station is adult contemporary. CJLA-FM broadcasts to the Lachute, Quebec area at 104.9 FM.
FM RADIO STATION

CJLF-FM 83168
Owner: Trust Communications Ministries
Editorial: 115 Bell Farm Rd Suite 111, Barrie, Ontario L4M 5G1 **Tel:** 1 705 735-3370.
Web site: http://www.lifeonline.fm
Profile: CJLF-FM is a commercial station owned by Trust Communications Ministries. The format is contemporary Christian. CJLF-FM broadcasts to the Barrie, Ontario area at 100.3 FM.
FM RADIO STATION

CJLL-FM (CHIN Ottawa) 155727
Owner: Radio 1540 Ltd.
Editorial: 1391 Wellington St W, Ottawa, Ontario K1Y 2X1 **Tel:** 1 613 244-0979.
Email: chinottawa@chinradio.com
Web site: http://chinradioottawa.com
Profile: CJLL-FM is a commercial station owned by Radio 1540 Ltd. The format of the station is variety. CJLL-FM broadcasts to the Ottawa, Ontario area at 97.9 FM.
FM RADIO STATION

CJLM-FM 47607
Owner: Coop. Radio-diffusion FM de Lanaudiere
Editorial: 540 rue St-Thomas, Joliette, Quebec J6E 3R4 **Tel:** 1 450 756-1035.
Email: radio@m1035fm.com
Web site: http://www.m1035fm.com
Profile: CJLM-FM is a commercial station owned by the Coop. Radio-diffusion FM de Lanaudiere. The format for the station is adult contemporary. CJLM-FM broadcasts to Joliette, Quebec at 103.5 FM.
FM RADIO STATION

CJLO-AM (1690) 83104
Owner: Concordia Students' Broadcasting Corp.
Editorial: 7141 Sherbrooke St W, PO Box 430 Cc Rm, Montreal, Quebec H4B 1R6 **Tel:** 1 514 848-8663.
Email: feedback@cjlo.com
Web site: http://www.cjlo.com
Profile: CJLO-AM is a non-commercial station owned by Concordia Students' Broadcasting Corp. The format for the station is variety. CJLO-AM broadcasts to the Montreal, Quebec area at 1690 AM.
AM RADIO STATION

CJLP-FM 47426
Owner: Réseau des Appalaches
Editorial: 327 rue Labbe, Thetford Mines, Quebec G6G 1Z2 **Tel:** 1 418 335-7533.
Email: info@passionrock.com
Web site: http://www.passionrock.com
Profile: CJLP-FM is a commercial station owned by Réseau des Appalaches. The format of the station is soft/lite adult contemporary. CJLP-FM broadcasts to Thetford Mines, Quebec at 107.1 FM.
FM RADIO STATION

CJLR-FM 47730
Owner: Missinipi Broadcasting Corp.
Editorial: 712 Finlayson St, La Ronge, Saskatchewan S0J 1L0 **Tel:** 1 306 425-4003.
Email: news@mbcradio.com
Web site: http://www.mbcradio.com
Profile: CJLR-FM is a commercial station owned by Missinipi Broadcasting Corp. The format of the station is adult contemporary. CJLR-FM broadcasts to the La Ronge, Saskatchewan area at 89.9 FM.
FM RADIO STATION

CJLS-FM (Y95 95.5 FM) 47638
Owner: Acadia Broadcasting Ltd
Editorial: 201-328 Main St 201, Yarmouth, Nova Scotia B5A 1E4 **Tel:** 1 902 742-7175.
Email: cjls@radioabl.ca
Web site: http://www.cjls.com
Profile: CJLS-FM is a commercial station owned by Acadia Broadcasting Ltd. The format of the station is adult contemporary. CJLS-FM broadcasts to the Yarmouth, Nova Scotia area at 95.5 FM.
FM RADIO STATION

CJLT-FM 342188
Owner: Vista Radio
Editorial: 206-1741 Dunmore Rd SE 206, Medicine Hat, Alberta T1A 1Z8 **Tel:** 1 403 529-9599.
Email: studio@937praisefm.com
Web site: http://937praisefm.com
Profile: CJLT-FM is a commercial station owned by Vista Radio. The format of the station is religious programming and contemporary Christian. CJLT-FM broadcasts to the Medicine Hat, Alberta area at 93.7 FM.
FM RADIO STATION

CJLU-FM 537065
Owner: International Harvesters for Christ Evangelistic Association Inc.
Editorial: 101 Ilsley Ave Unit 3, Dartmouth, Nova Scotia B3B 1S8 **Tel:** 1 902 468-8854.
Email: info@cjlufm.com
Web site: http://www.cjlufm.com
Profile: CJUL-FM is a commercial station owned by International Harvesters for Christ Evangelistic Association Inc. The format of the station is Contemporary Christian music. CJLU-FM broadcasts to the Halifax and Annapolis Valley areas in Nova Scotia Canada at 93.9 FM.
FM RADIO STATION

CJLV-AM 498277
Owner: Radio Humsafar Inc.
Editorial: 2040, Autoroute Laval, Laval, Quebec H7S 2M9 **Tel:** 1 450 680-1570.
Email: info@1570ampluslaval.com
Web site: http://www.1570ampluslaval.com
Profile: CJLV-AM is a commercial station owned byRadio Humsafar Inc. The format of the station is classic hits and oldies. CJLV-AM broadcasts to the Laval, Quebec area at 1570 AM.
AM RADIO STATION

CJLX-FM 47729
Owner: Loyalist College Radio Inc.
Editorial: Wallbridge-Loyalist Road, Belleville, Ontario K8N 4Z2 **Tel:** 1 613 966-0923.
Email: contact@91x.fm
Web site: http://www.91x.fm
Profile: CJLX-FM is a non-commercial station owned by Loyalist College Radio Inc. The format of the station is a rock alternative. CJLX-FM broadcasts to the Belleville, Ontario area at 91.3 FM.
FM RADIO STATION

CJLY-FM 554755
Owner: Kootenay Cooperative Radio
Editorial: 308a Hall St, Nelson, British Columbia V1L 1Y8 **Tel:** 1 250 352-9600.
Email: admin@kootenaycoopradio.com
Web site: http://www.cjly.org
Profile: CJLY is owned by Kootenay Cooperative Radio. The station broadcasts at a frequency of 93.5 FM to Nelson, British Columbia. The station is a community based format and volunteer run.
FM RADIO STATION

CJMB-FM (Extra 90.5) 554698
Owner: My Broadcasting Corporation
Editorial: 360 George St N Unit 1, Peterborough, Ontario K9H 7E7 **Tel:** 1 705 876-7773.
Email: newsptbo@mbcmedia.ca
Web site: http://www.extrapeterborough.ca
Profile: CJMB-FM is a commercial station owned by My Broadcasting Corporation. The format of the station is talk and sports. CJMB-FM broadcasts to the Peterborough, Ontario area at 90.5 FM.
FM RADIO STATION

CJMC-FM 47809
Owner: Radio du Golfe Inc.
Editorial: 170 boulevard Ste-Anne Est, Ste-Anne-des-Monts, Quebec G4V 1N1 **Tel:** 1 418 763-5522.
Web site: http://bleufm.ca/fm
Profile: CJMC-FM is a commercial station owned by Radio du Golf Inc. The format of the station is Adult Contemporary. CJMC-FM broadcasts to the Ste-Anne-des-Monts, Quebec area at 100.3 FM.
FM RADIO STATION

CJMD-FM 621049
Owner: Radio Communautaire de Lévis(La)
Editorial: 20 Duplessis St, Levis, Quebec G6V 2L1
Tel: 1 418 903-1911.
Web site: http://969fm.ca/
Profile: CJMD-FM is a non-commercial radio station owned by La Radio Communautaire de Lévis. The format for the station is variety. CJMD-FM broadcasts to the Lévis, Quebec area at 96.9 FM.
FM RADIO STATION

CJME-AM 47211
Owner: Rawlco Radio Ltd.
Editorial: 210-2401 Saskatchewan Dr 210, Regina, Saskatchewan S4P 4H8 **Tel:** 1 306 525-0000.
Web site: http://cjme.com/
Profile: CJME-AM is a commercial station owned by Rawlco Radio Ltd. The format of the station is news and talk. CJME-AM broadcasts to the Regina, Saskatchewan area at 980 AM.
AM RADIO STATION

CJMF-FM (FM 93) 47581
Owner: Cogeco Diffusion Inc.
Editorial: 1305 chemin Ste-Foy, Suite 402, Quebec, Quebec G1S 4Y5 **Tel:** 1 418 687-9330.
Email: info@fm93.com
Web site: http://www.fm93.com
Profile: CJMF-FM is a commercial station owned by Cogeco. The format of the station is classic rock and talk. CJMF-FM broadcasts to the Quebec City area at 93.3 FM.
FM RADIO STATION

CJMG-FM 47443
Owner: Astral Media
Editorial: 33 Carmi Ave, Penticton, British Columbia V2A 3G4 **Tel:** 1 250 492-2800.
Email: bcnews@astral.com
Web site: http://www.sunonline.ca
Profile: CJMG-FM is a commercial station owned by Astral Media. The format of the station is hot adult contemporary. CJMG-FM broadcasts to the Penticton, Britsh Columbia area at 97.1 FM.
FM RADIO STATION

CJMI-FM (105.7 myFM) 445519
Owner: My Broadcasting Corporation
Editorial: 85 Zimmerman Ave Unit 1, Strathroy, Ontario N7G 0A3 **Tel:** 1 519 246-6936.
Email: news1057@myfmradio.ca
Web site: http://www.strathroytoday.ca
Profile: CJMI-FM is a commercial station owned by My Broadcasting Corporation. The format of the station is adult contemporary. CJMI-FM broadcasts to the Strathroy, Ontario area at 105.7 FM.
FM RADIO STATION

CJMJ-FM (Majic Ottawa 100.3) 47529
Owner: Bell Media
Editorial: 87 George St, Ottawa, Ontario K1N 9H7-
Tel: 1 613 789-2486.
Web site: http://www.majic100.com
Profile: CJMJ-FM is a commercial station owned by Bell Media. The format of the station is easy listening music. CJMJ-FM broadcasts to the Ottawa, Ontario area at 100.3 FM.
FM RADIO STATION

CJMK-FM 75737
Owner: Saskatoon Media Group
Editorial: 366 3rd Ave S, Saskatoon, Saskatchewan S7K 1M5 **Tel:** 1 306 244-1975.
Email: cool@98cool.ca
Web site: http://98cool.ca
Profile: CJMK-FM is a commercial station owned by Saskatoon Media Group. The format of the station is adult contemporary. CJMK-FM broadcasts to the Saskatoon, Saskatchewan area at 98.3 FM.
FM RADIO STATION

CJMM-FM (ÉNERGIE 99.1 Rouyn) 47639
Owner: Astral Media
Editorial: 191 Av Murdoch, Rouyn-Noranda, Quebec J9X 1E3 **Tel:** 1 819 797-2566.
Web site: http://www.radionrj.ca/rouyn
Profile: CJMM-FM est la radio commercial, une propriété de Bell Média. CJMM-FM est diffusé à Rouyn, dans la région de Québec au 99.1.

CJMM-FM is a commercial station owned by Bell Media. CJMM-FM broadcasts to the Rouyn, Quebec area at 99.1.
FM RADIO STATION

CJMO-FM 47582
Owner: Newfoundland Capital Corporation Limited
Editorial: 27 Arsenault Court, Moncton, New Brunswick E1E 4J8 **Tel:** 1 506 858-5525.
Email: c103@c103.com
Web site: http://www.c103.com
Profile: CJMO-FM is a commercial station owned by Newfoundland Capital Corporation Limited. The format for the station is classic rock music. CJMO-

FM broadcasts to the Moncton, New Brunswick area at 103.1 FM.
FM RADIO STATION

CJMP-FM 579378
Owner: Powell River Community Radio Society
Editorial: 4476A Marine Ave, Powell River, British Columbia V8A 2K2 **Tel:** 1 604 485 0088.
Email: prcrs09@gmail.com
Web site: http://blog.cjmp.ca
Profile: CJMP-FM is a non-commercial station owned byPowell River Community Radio Society. The format of the station is variety. CJMP-FM broadcasts to the Powell River, BC area at 90.1 FM.
FM RADIO STATION

CJMQ-FM 47812
Owner: Radio Bishop's Inc.
Editorial: 184 Queen St, Sherbrooke, Quebec J1M 1J9 **Tel:** 1 819 822-1838.
Email: cjmqnews@yahoo.ca
Web site: http://www.cjmq.fm
Profile: CJMQ-FM est une station radio anglophone communautaire proposant une programmation musicale variée, diffusant sur le 88.9FM. Elle rejoint la ville de SHerbrooke et un partie dse Cantons de l'Est.

CJMQ-FM is a non-commercial station owned by Radio Bishop's Inc. It is an english speaking community station. The format of the station is variety. CJMQ-FM broadcasts to the Sherbrooke, Quebec area at 88.9 FM.
FM RADIO STATION

CJMR-AM 47292
Owner: Whiteoaks Communications Group Limited
Editorial: 284 Church St, Oakville, Ontario L6J 7N2
Tel: 1 905 271-1320.
Email: contact@cjmr1320.ca
Web site: http://www.cjmr1320.ca
Profile: CJMR-AM is a commercial station owned by Whiteoaks Communications Group Limited. The format of the station is variety. CJMR-AM broadcasts to the Oakville, Ontario area at 1320 AM.
AM RADIO STATION

CJMS-AM 83116
Owner: Medialex
Editorial: 143 Saint-Pierre, Saint Constant, Quebec J5A 2G9 **Tel:** 1 450 900-2567.
Web site: http://www.cjms1040.com
Profile: CJMS-AM is a commercial station owned by Medialex. The format of the station is classic country. CJMS-AM broadcasts to the Saint Constant, Quebec area at 1040 AM.
AM RADIO STATION

CJMV-FM (ÉNERGIE 102.7 Val-d'Or) 47640
Owner: Bell Media
Editorial: 1610 3e Av, Val-d'Or, Quebec J9P 1V8
Tel: 1 819 825-2568.
Email: nouvelles.abitibi@bellmedia.ca
Web site: http://www.valdor.radioenergie.ca
Profile: CJMV-FM est la radio commercial, une propriété de Bell Média. CJMV-FM est diffusé à Val-d'Or, dans la région de Québec au 102.7.

CJMV-FM is a commercial station owned by Bell Media. CJMV-FM broadcasts to the Val-d'Or, Quebec area at 102.7.
FM RADIO STATION

CJMX-FM 47523
Owner: Rogers Communications Inc.
Editorial: 880 LaSalle Blvd, Sudbury, Ontario P3A 1X5
Tel: 1 705 566-4480.
Web site: http://www.ezrocksudbury.com
Profile: CJMX-FM is a commercial station owned by Rogers Communications Inc. The format of the station is adult contemporary. CJMX-FM broadcasts to the Sudbury, Ontario area at 105.3 FM.
FM RADIO STATION

CJNB-AM 47208
Owner: Jim Pattison Broadcast Group (The)
Editorial: 1711- 100 St, North Battleford, Saskatchewan S9A OW7 **Tel:** 1 306 445-2477.
Web site: http://www.cjnb.com/
Profile: CJNB-AM is a commercial station owned by The Jim Pattison Broadcast Group. The format for the station is contemporary country. CJNB-AM broadcasts to the North Battleford, Saskatchewan area at 1050 AM.
AM RADIO STATION

CJNC-FM 70511
Owner: Norway House First Nations Communications
Editorial: 250 Kistapinanih, Norway House, Manitoba R0B 1B0 **Tel:** 1 204 359-6775.
Profile: CJNC-FM is a commercial station owned by Norway House First Nations Communications. The format of the station is variety. CJNC-FM broadcasts to the Norway House, Manitoba area at 97.9 FM.
FM RADIO STATION

CJNE-FM 561441
Owner: CJNE-FM Radio Inc.
Tel: 1 306 862-9478.
Email: pro.cjne@sasktel.net
Web site: http://www.cjnefm.com
Profile: CJNE-FM is a commercial station owned by CJNE-FM Radio Inc. The format of the station is classic rock and oldies. CJNE-FM broadcasts to the Nipawin, Saskatchewan area at 94.7 FM.
FM RADIO STATION

CJNG-FM 610056
Owner: Radio touristique de Québec inc.(La)
Editorial: 20 Rue des Grisons, Quebec, Quebec G1R 4M7 **Tel:** 1 418 527-4444.
Email: lm@netcreation.ca
Web site: http://sortirfm.com/english.html
Profile: CJNG-FM is an English-language tourist radio station for the Quebec City, Chaudière-Appalaches and Charlevoix regions of Quebec. CJNG-FM broadcasts at 89.7 FM. Its French-language sister station, CKJF-FM, broadcasts at 106.9 FM.
FM RADIO STATION

CJNI-FM 363274
Owner: Rogers Broadcasting Ltd.
Editorial: 6080 Young Street, Suite 911, Halifax, Nova Scotia B3K 5L2 **Tel:** 1 902 493-7200.
Email: news957@rogers.com
Web site: http://www.news957.com
Profile: CJNI-FM is a commercial station owned by Rogers Communications Inc. The format of the station is news and talk. CJNI-FM broadcasts to the Halifax, Nova Scotia area at 95.7 FM.
FM RADIO STATION

CJNS-FM 47204
Owner: Jim Pattison Broadcast Group(The)
Editorial: 225 Centre Ave Box 1660, Meadow Lake, Saskatchewan S9X 1H2 **Tel:** 1 306 236-6494.
Profile: CJNS-FM is a commercial station owned by The Jim Pattison Broadcast Group. The format of the station is contemporary country music. CJNS-FM broadcasts to the Meadow Lake, Saskatchewan area at 102.3 FM.
FM RADIO STATION

CJNW-FM 607063
Owner: Harvard Broadcasting
Editorial: 5241 Calgary Trail, Suite 700 center 105, Edmonton, Alberta T6H 5GB **Tel:** 1 780 435-3023.
Web site: http://www.hot107.ca
Profile: CJNW-FM is a commercial station owned by Harvard Broadcasting. The format of the station is Top 40/CHR. The station broadcasts to the Edmonton, AB area at 107.1 FM.
FM RADIO STATION

CJOA-FM 342209
Owner: Thunder Bay Christian Radio
Editorial: 63 Carrie St Rm 42, Thunder Bay, Ontario P7A 4J2 **Tel:** 1 807 344-9525.
Email: fm95@cjoa.ca
Web site: http://www.cjoa.ca
Profile: CJOA-FM is a non-commercial station owned by Thunder Bay Christian Radio. The format is religious. The station airs at 95.1 FM in Thunder Bay, Ontario.
FM RADIO STATION

CJOB-AM 47255
Owner: Corus Entertainment Inc.
Editorial: 930 Portage Ave, Winnipeg, Manitoba R3G 0P8- **Tel:** 1 204 786-2471.
Email: cjobnews@corusent.com
Web site: http://www.cjob.com
Profile: CJOB-AM is a commercial station owned by Corus Entertainment Inc. The format of the station is news, talk and sports. CJOB-AM broadcasts to the Winnipeg, Manitoba area at 680 AM.
AM RADIO STATION

CJOC-FM 489151
Owner: Clear Sky Radio Inc.
Editorial: 220 Third Avenue S, Suite 400, Lethbridge, Alberta T1J 0G9 **Tel:** 1 403 388-2910.
Email: info@cjocfm.com
Web site: http://www.cjocfm.com
Profile: CJOC-FM is a commercial station owned by Clear Sky Radio Inc. The format of the station is classic hits. CJOC-FM broadcasts to the Lethbridge, Alberta area at 94.1 FM.
FM RADIO STATION

CJOI-FM 47275
Owner: Bell Media
Editorial: 287 Rue Pierre-Saindon Bureau 502, Rimouski, Quebec G5L 9A7 **Tel:** 1 418 723-2323.
Web site: http://rimouski.rougefm.ca
Profile: CJOI-FM is a commercial station owned by Bell Media. The format of the station is adult contemporary. CJOI-FM broadcasts to the Rimouski, Quebec area at 102.9 FM.
FM RADIO STATION

CJOJ-FM 47658
Owner: Starboard Communications Ltd.
Editorial: 497 Dundas St W, Belleville, Ontario K8P 1B6 **Tel:** 1 613 966-0955.
Email: news@955hitsfm.ca
Web site: http://www.955hitsfm.ca
Profile: CJOJ-FM is a commercial station owned by Starboard Communications Ltd. The format for the station is classic hits. CJOJ-FM broadcasts to the Belleville, Ontario area at 95.5 FM.
FM RADIO STATION

CJOK-FM 47779
Owner: Rogers Communications Inc.
Editorial: 9912 Franklin Ave, Fort McMurray, Alberta T9H 2K5- **Tel:** 1 780 743-2246.
Email: rock979.news@rci.rogers.com
Web site: http://www.country933.com
Profile: CJOK-FM is a commercial station owned by Rogers Communications Inc. The format of the station is contemporary country. CJOK-FM broadcasts to the Fort McMurray, Alberta area at 93.3 FM.
FM RADIO STATION

CJOR-AM 77601
Owner: Astral Media
Editorial: 33 Carmi Avenue, Penticton, British Columbia V2A 3G4 **Tel:** 1 250 492-2800.
Email: bcnews@astral.com
Web site: http://www.osoyoos.myezrock.com
Profile: CJOR-AM is a commercial radio station owned by Astral Media. The format of the station is adult contemporary. CJOR-AM broadcasts to the Penticton, British Columbia area at 1240 AM. CJOR-AM is a transmitter for CKOR-AM.
AM RADIO STATION

CJOS-FM (The Dock 92.3) 695970
Owner: Larche Communications Inc.
Editorial: 787 9th Ave E, Owen Sound, Ontario N4K 3E6 **Tel:** 1 519 470-7626.
Web site: http://www.923thedock.com
Profile: CJOS-FM is a commercial station owned by Larche Communications Inc. The format for the station is classic rock. CJOS-FM broadcasts to the Owen Sound and Grey-Bruce, Ontario area at 92.3 FM.
FM RADIO STATION

CJOT-FM (Boom 99.7) 688891
Owner: Corus Entertainment Inc.
Editorial: 1504 Merivale Rd, Ottawa, Ontario K2E 6Z5
Tel: 1 613 225-1069.
Web site: http://www.boom997.com
Profile: CJOT-FM (Boom 99.7) is a commercial station owned by Corus Entertainment Inc. The format for the station is soft rock/soft AC. CJOT-FM's tagline is "Boom 99.7."
FM RADIO STATION

CJOY-AM 47215
Owner: Corus Entertainment Inc.
Editorial: 75 Speedvale Ave East, Guelph, Ontario N1E 6M3 **Tel:** 1 519 824-7000.
Email: studio@cjoy.com
Web site: http://www.cjoy.com
Profile: CJOY-AM is a commercial station owned by Corus Entertainment Inc. The format for the station is oldies. CJOY-AM broadcasts to the East Guelph, Ontario area at 1460 AM.
AM RADIO STATION

CJOZ-FM 47660
Owner: Newfoundland Broadcasting Co. Ltd.
Editorial: 446 Logy Bay Rd, St. John's, Newfoundland A1A 5C6 **Tel:** 1 709 726-2922.
Email: ntv@ntv.ca
Web site: http://www.ozfm.com
Profile: CJOZ-FM is a commercial station owned by Newfoundland Broadcasting Co. Ltd. The format of the station is top 40/CHR. CJOZ-FM broadcasts to St. John's, NF at 92.1 FM.
FM RADIO STATION

CJPG-FM 239134
Owner: Golden West Broadcasting Ltd.
Editorial: 350 River Road, Portage La Prairie, Manitoba R1N 3V6 **Tel:** 1 204 239-5111.
Email: info@goldenwestradio.com
Web site: http://www.mix965fm.com
FM RADIO STATION

CJPN-FM 47792
Owner: Radio Fredericton Inc.
Editorial: 715 Rue Priestman, Fredericton, New Brunswick E3B 5W7 **Tel:** 1 506 454-2576.
Email: cjpn@live.ca
Web site: http://www.cjpn.ca
Profile: CJPN-FM is a commercial station owned by Radio Fredericton Inc. The format of the station is variety. CJPN-FM broadcasts in the Fredericton, New Brunswick area at 90.5 FM.
FM RADIO STATION

CJPR-FM 47164
Owner: Newfoundland Capital Corporation Limited
Editorial: 13-213 20th Ave, Blairmore, Alberta T0K 0E0 **Tel:** 1 403 562-2806.
Web site: http://www.mountainradiofm.com
Profile: CJPR-FM is a commercial station owned by Newfoundland Capital Corporation Limited. The format for the station is contemporary country. CJPR-FM broadcasts to the Blairmore, Alberta area at 94.9 FM.
FM RADIO STATION

CJPT-FM (BOB 103.7) 47459
Owner: Bell Media
Editorial: 601 Stewart Blvd, Brockville, Ontario K6V 5T4 **Tel:** 1 613 345-1666.
Web site: http://www.bob.fm
Profile: CJPT-FM is a commercial station owned by Bell Media. The format of the station is adult hits. CJPT-FM broadcasts to Brockville, Ontario at 103.7 FM.
FM RADIO STATION

CJPX-FM 128727
Owner: Groupe Musique Greg
Editorial: 124 Ch du Chenal-Lemoyne, parc jean lle notre dame, Montreal, Quebec H3C 6J6
Tel: 1 514 871-0995.
Profile: CJPX-FM is a commercial station owned by Groupe Musique Greg. The format of the station is classical. CJPX-FM broadcasts to Montreal, Quebec at 99.5.
FM RADIO STATION

CJQM-FM 47524
Owner: Rogers Communications Inc.
Editorial: 642 Great Northern Rd, Sault Ste. Marie, Ontario P6B 4Z9 **Tel:** 1 705 759-9200.
Web site: http://www.country1043.com
Profile: CJQM-FM is a commercial station owned by Rogers Communications Inc. The format for the station is contemporary country. CJQM-FM broadcasts to the Sault Ste. Marie, Ontario area at 104.3 FM.
FM RADIO STATION

CJQQ-FM 47628
Owner: Rogers Communications Inc.
Editorial: 260 Second Ave, Timmins, Ontario P4N 8A4
Tel: 1 705 264-2351.
Web site: http://www.921rock.ca/
Profile: CJQQ-FM is a commercial station owned by Rogers Communications Inc. The format of the station is classic rock. CJQQ-FM broadcasts to Timmins, Ontario at 92.1 FM.
FM RADIO STATION

CJRB-AM 47368
Owner: Golden West Broadcasting Ltd.
Tel: 1 204 324-6464.
Email: info@goldenwestradio.com
Profile: CJRB-AM is a commercial station owned by Golden West Broadcasting Ltd. The format for the station is a mix of adult contemporary and agricultural. CJRB-AM broadcasts to the Boissevain, Manitoba area at 1220 AM.
AM RADIO STATION

CJRD-FM 585886
Owner: Radio Drummond
Editorial: 161 Rue Marchand, c.p. 801, Drummondville, Quebec J2C 4N3 **Tel:** 1 819 474-2573.
Profile: CJRD-FM is a non-commercial station owned by Radio Drummond. The format of the station is variety. CJRD-FM broadcasts to the Drummondville, Quebec area at 88.9 FM.
FM RADIO STATION

CJRG-FM (Gaspé 94.5) 47612
Owner: Radio Gaspésie Inc.
Editorial: 162 Rue Jacques-Cartier, Gaspe, Quebec G4X 1M9 **Tel:** 1 418 368-3511.
Email: accueil@radiogaspesie.ca
Web site: http://www.radiogaspesie.ca
Profile: CJRG-FM est une station de radio commerciale, une propriété de Radio Gaspésie Inc. Le format de la station est adulte contemporain. CJRG-FM est diffusée à Gaspé, au Québec à 94.5 FM.

CJRG-FM is a commercial station owned by Radio Gaspésie Inc. The format of the station is adult contemporary. CJRG-FM broadcasts to the Gaspé, Quebec area at 94.5 FM.
FM RADIO STATION

CJRI-FM 562120
Owner: Faithway Communications, Inc.
Editorial: 151 Main St, Fredericton, New Brunswick E3A 1C6 **Tel:** 1 506 472-0947.
Email: cjrifm@gmail.com
Web site: http://www.cjrifm.com
Profile: CJRI-FM is a commercial station owned by Faithway Communications, Inc. The format of the station is Southern Gospel. CJRI-FM broadcasts to the Fredericton, New Brunswick area at a frequency of 104.5 FM.
FM RADIO STATION

CJRJ-AM 445459
Owner: I.t. Productions Ltd.
Editorial: 110-3060 Norland Ave 110, Burnaby, British Columbia V5B 3A6 **Tel:** 1 604 299-1727.
Email: info@spiceradio1200am.com
Web site: http://spiceradio1200am.com
Profile: CJRJ-AM is a commercial station owned by I.t. Productions Ltd. The format of the station is South Asian top 40/CHR. CJRJ-AM broadcasts to the Burnaby, British Columbia area at 1200 AM.
AM RADIO STATION

CJRL-FM 89.5 The Lake 47220
Owner: Acadia Broadcasting Ltd.
Editorial: 301 First Ave S, Kenora, Ontario P9N 1W2
Tel: 1 807 468-3181.
Web site: http://895thelake.ca/
Profile: CJRL-FM is a commercial station owned by Acadia Broadcasting Ltd. The format of the station is

adult contemporary. CJRL-FM broadcasts to the Kenora, Ontario area at 89.5 FM.
FM RADIO STATION

CJRM-FM 47862
Owner: Radio Communautaire Francophone du Labrador
Editorial: 308 Hudson Drive, Labrador City, Newfoundland A2V 1L5 **Tel:** 1 709 944-7600.
Email: cjrm@crrstv.net
Profile: CJRM-FM is a non-commercial station owned by Radio Communautaire Francophone du Labrador. The format of the station is variety. CJRM-FM broadcasts to the Labrador City, Newfoundland area at 97.3 FM.
FM RADIO STATION

CJRQ-FM 47525
Owner: Rogers Communications Inc.
Editorial: 880 Lasalle Blvd, Sudbury, Ontario P3A 1X5 **Tel:** 1 705 566-4480.
Web site: http://www.q92rocks.com
Profile: CJRQ-FM is a commercial station owned by Rogers Communications Inc. The format for the station is album-oriented rock. CJRQ-FM broadcasts to Sudbury, Ontario at 92.7 FM.
FM RADIO STATION

CJRS-AM 472740
Owner: Radio Shalom
Editorial: 4835, Côte Ste-Catherine, Ste 2, Montreal, Quebec H3W 1M4 **Tel:** 1 514 738-8350.
Email: info@radio-shalom.ca
Web site: http://www.radio-shalom.ca
Profile: CJRS-AM is a non-commercial station owned by Radio Shalom. The format of the station is talk. CJRS-AM broadcasts to the Montreal area at 1650 AM.
AM RADIO STATION

CJRT-FM (Jazz 91.1) 47623
Owner: CJRT-FM Inc.
Editorial: 4 Pardee Ave Unit 100, Toronto, Ontario M6K 3H5 **Tel:** 1 416 595-0404.
Email: info@jazz.fm
Web site: http://www.jazz.fm
Profile: CJRT-FM is a non-commercial station owned by CJRT-FM Inc. The format of the station is jazz. CJRT-FM broadcasts to the Toronto area at 91.1 FM.
FM RADIO STATION

CJRW-FM 47311
Owner: Maritime Broadcasting System Ltd.
Editorial: 763 Water St East, Summerside, Prince Edward Island C1N 4J3 **Tel:** 1 902 436-2202.
Web site: http://www.spud.fm
Profile: CJRW-FM is a commercial station owned by the Maritime Broadcasting System Ltd. The format of the station is classic hits. CJRW-FM broadcasts to the Summerside, Prince Edward Island area at 102.1 FM.
FM RADIO STATION

CJRX-FM 47132
Owner: Rogers Communications Inc.
Editorial: 1015 3rd Ave South, Lethbridge, Alberta T1J 0J3 **Tel:** 1 403 320-1220.
Email: rock106@rci.rogers.com
Web site: http://www.rock106.ca
Profile: CJRX-FM is a commercial station owned by Rogers Communications Inc. The format for the station is rock alternative. CJRX-FM broadcasts to the Lethbridge, Alberta area at 106.7 FM.
FM RADIO STATION

CJRY-FM 474996
Owner: Touch Canada Broadcasting (2006) Inc.
Editorial: 5316 Calgary Trail, Edmonton, Alberta T6H 4J8 **Tel:** 1 780 466-4930.
Web site: http://am930thelight.com
Profile: CJRY-FM is a commerical station owned by Touch Canada Broadcasting (2006) Inc. The format of the station is contemporary Christian. CJRY-FM broadcasts to the Edmonton, Alberta area at 105.9 FM.
FM RADIO STATION

CJSA-FM (Canadian Multicultural Radio 101.3) 588291
Owner: Canadian Multicultural Radio
Editorial: 306 Rexdale Blvd, Suite 1, Toronto, Ontario M9W 1R6 **Tel:** 1 416 593-9300.
Email: info@cmr.fm
Web site: http://www.cmr.fm
Profile: CJSA-FM is a commerical station owned by Canadian Multicultural Radio. The format of the station is ethnic variety. CJSA-FM broadcasts to the Toronto area at 101.3 FM.
FM RADIO STATION

CJSB-FM 553383
Owner: Stillwater Broadcasting Ltd
Editorial: 513 Main Street, Swan River, Manitoba R0L 1Z0 **Tel:** 1 204 734-6484.
Email: news@cj104radio.com
Web site: http://www.cj104radio.com
Profile: CJSB-FM is a commercial station owned by Stillwater Broadcasting Ltd. The station airs a variety format at 104.5 FM in the Swan River, Manitoba area.
FM RADIO STATION

CJSD-FM 47629
Owner: CJSD Inc.
Editorial: 87 N Hill Street, Thunder Bay, Ontario P7A 5V6 **Tel:** 1 807 346-2600.
Email: rock@rock94.com
Web site: http://www.rock94.com
Profile: CJSD-FM is a commercial station owned by CJSD Inc. The format for the station is classic rock and rock alternative. CJSD-FM broadcasts to the Thunder Bay, Ontario area at 94.3 FM.
FM RADIO STATION

CJSE-FM 47817
Owner: Radio Beausejour Inc.
Editorial: Cornwall 51, Shediac, New Brunswick E4P 8T8 **Tel:** 1 506 532-0080.
Email: cjse@cjse.ca
Web site: http://www.cjse.ca
Profile: CJSE-FM is a commercial station owned by Radio Beausejour Inc. The format of the station is country music. CJSE-FM broadcasts in the Shediac, New Brunswick area at 89.5 FM.
FM RADIO STATION

CJSF-FM 47878
Owner: Simon Fraser Campus Radio Society
Editorial: Simon Fraser University, 8888 University Drive TC 216, Burnaby, British Columbia V5A 1S6 **Tel:** 1 778 782-3727.
Email: cjsfmgr@sfu.ca
Web site: http://www.cjsf.ca
Profile: CJSF-FM is a non-commercial station owned by the Simon Fraser Campus Radio Society. The format of the station is college variety. CJSF-FM broadcasts to the Burnaby, British Columbia area at 90.1 FM.
FM RADIO STATION

CJSI-FM 47827
Owner: Touch Canada Broadcasting (2006) Inc.
Editorial: 4510 Macleod Trail South, Suite 100, Calgary, Alberta T2G 0A4 **Tel:** 1 403 276-1111.
Web site: http://www.cjsi.ca
Profile: CJSI-FM is a commercial station owned by Touch Canada Broadcasting. The format for the station is contemporary Christian. CJSI-FM broadcasts to the Calgary, Alberta area at 88.9 FM.
FM RADIO STATION

CJSL-AM 47201
Owner: Golden West Broadcasting Ltd.
Editorial: 200-1236 5th Street, Estevan, Saskatchewan S4A 0Z6 **Tel:** 1 306 634-1280.
Email: cj1280@goldenwestradio.com
Web site: http://www.cj1280radio.com
Profile: CJSL-AM is a commercial station owned by Golden West Broadcasting Ltd. The format for the station is contemporary country. CJSL-AM broadcasts to the Estevan, Saskatchewan area at 1280 AM.
AM RADIO STATION

CJSN-AM 47235
Owner: Golden West Broadcasting Ltd.
Editorial: 407 Centre St, Shaunavon, Saskatchewan S0N 2M0 **Tel:** 1 306 297-2671.
Email: cjsn@goldenwestradio.com
Profile: CJSN-AM is a commercial station owned by Golden West Broadcasting Ltd. The format for the station is classic country. CJSN-AM broadcast to the Shaunavon, Saskatchewan area at 1490 AM.
AM RADIO STATION

CJSO-FM 47726
Owner: Radio Diffusion Sorel-Tracy Inc.
Editorial: 52 Rue du Roi, Sorel-Tracy, Quebec J3P 4M7 **Tel:** 1 450 743-2772.
Email: studio@cjso.ca
Web site: http://www.fm1017.ca
Profile: CJSO-FM is a commercial station owned by Radio Diffusion Sorel-Tracy Inc. The format of the station is adult contemporary. CJSO-FM broadcasts to Sorel-Tracy, Quebec at 101.7 FM.
FM RADIO STATION

CJSP-FM 529377
Owner: Blackburn Radio Inc.
Editorial: 100 Talbot St E, Leamington, Ontario N8H 1L3 **Tel:** 1 519 326-6171.
Web site: http://country959.com
Profile: CJSP-FM is a commercial station owned by Blackburn Radio Inc. The format of the station is Country. CJSP-FM broadcasts to the Leamington, Ontario area at 92.7 FM.
FM RADIO STATION

CJSQ-FM 510017
Owner: Groupe Musique Greg
Editorial: 2525 Boul Laurier, Quebec, Quebec G1V 2L2 **Tel:** 1 418 650-9270.
Email: cjsq@radioclassique.ca
Web site: http://www.radioclassique.ca
Profile: CJSQ-FM is a commercial station owned by Groupe Musique Greg. The format of the station is classical. CJSQ-FM broadcasts to the Quebec, QC area at 92.7 FM.
FM RADIO STATION

CJSR-FM 47725
Owner: First Alberta Campus Radio Association
Editorial: University of Alberta, SUB Lower Level Room 009, Edmonton, Alberta T6G 2J7
Tel: 1 780 492-2577 228.
Email: news@cjsr.com
Web site: http://www.cjsr.com
Profile: CJSR-FM is a non-commercial station owned by First Alberta Campus Radio Association. The format for the station is variety. CJSR-FM broadcasts to the Edmonton, Alberta area at 88.5 FM.
FM RADIO STATION

CJSS-FM (Boom 101.9) 47883
Owner: Corus Entertainment Inc.
Editorial: 709 Cotton Mill St, Cornwall, Ontario K6H 7K7- **Tel:** 1 613 932-5180.
Web site: http://www.boom1019.com
Profile: CJSS-FM (Boom 101.9) is a commercial station owned by Corus Entertainment Inc. The format of the station is classic hits. CJSS-FM broadcasts to the Cornwall, Ontario area at 101.9 FM.
FM RADIO STATION

CJSU-FM (89.7 Juice FM) 47113
Owner: Vista Broadcast Group Inc.
Editorial: 4-5380 Trans-Canada Hwy 4, Duncan, British Columbia V9L 6W4 **Tel:** 1 250 746-0897.
Web site: http://www.mycowichanvalleynow.com
Profile: CJSU-FM (89.7 Juice FM) is a commercial station owned by Vista Broadcast Group Inc. The format for the station is Hot AC/Modern AC. CJSU-FM broadcasts to the Duncan, British Columbia area at 89.7 FM.
FM RADIO STATION

CJSW-FM 47724
Owner: University of Calgary Student Radio Society
Editorial: University of Calgary, Rm 312 MacEwan Hall, Calgary, Alberta T2N 1N4 **Tel:** 1 403 220-3902.
Email: news@cjsw.com
Web site: http://www.cjsw.com
Profile: CJSW-FM is a non-commercial station owned by the University of Calgary Student Radio Society. The format of the station is variety. CJSW-FM broadcasts to Calgary, Alberta at 90.9 FM.
FM RADIO STATION

CJTB-FM (Radio Basse-Côte-Nord 93.1) 383122
Owner: Radio communataire Tête-à-la-Baleine
Editorial: 152 rue de la Salle, bureau 10, Tete a la Baleine, Quebec G0G 2W0 **Tel:** 1 418 242-2974.
Email: cjtb@globetrotter.net
Profile: CJTB-FM est une station de radio communautaire, une propriété de Radio communataire Tête-à-la-Baleine. Le format de la station est le variété. CJTB-FM est diffusé à Tête-à-la-Baleine, au Québec à 93.1.

CJTB-FM is a community radio station owned by Radio communataire Tête-à-la-Baleine. The format of the station is variety. CJTB-FM broadcasts to Tête-à-la-Baleine, Quebec at 93.1 FM.
FM RADIO STATION

CJTK-FM 47818
Owner: Eternacom Inc.
Editorial: 2150 La Salle Blvd, Sudbury, Ontario P3C 2A7 **Tel:** 1 705 674-2585.
Email: mail@kfmradio.ca
Web site: http://www.kfmradio.ca
Profile: CJTK-FM is a commercial station owned by Eternacom Inc. The format of the station is contemporary Christian music. CJTK-FM broadcasts to the Sudbury, Ontario area at 95.5 FM. CJTK-FM has two transmitters. CJTK-FM-1 broadcasts at 103.5 FM in North Bay, Ontario. CJTK-FM-2 broadcasts at 102.1 FM to the Manitoulin/Little Current, Ontario area.
FM RADIO STATION

CJTN-FM 47347
Owner: Quinte Broadcasting Co. Ltd.
Editorial: 10 S. Front St, 4th fl, Belleville, Ontario K8N 2Y3 **Tel:** 1 613 969-5555.
Web site: http://www.rock107.ca
Profile: CJTN-FM is a commercial station owned by Quinte Broadcasting Co. Ltd. The format of the station is classic rock. CJTN-FM broadcasts to the Trenton, Ontario area at 107.1 FM.
FM RADIO STATION

CJTR-FM 153489
Owner: Radius Communications Inc.
Editorial: 301-1102 8th Ave 301, Regina, Saskatchewan S4R 1C9- **Tel:** 1 306 525-7274.
Email: radius@cjtr.ca
Web site: http://www.cjtr.ca
Profile: CJTR-FM is a commercial station owned by Radius Communications Inc. The format of the station is variety. CJTR-FM broadcasts to the Regina, Saskatchewan area at 480 AM.
FM RADIO STATION

CJTT-FM (104.5) 47231
Owner: Connelly Communications Corp.
Editorial: 55 Whitewood Ave, New Liskeard, Ontario P0J 1P0 **Tel:** 1 705 647-7334.
Email: cjtt@cjttfm.com
Web site: http://www.cjttfm.com
Profile: CJTT-FM is a commercial station owned by Connelly Communications Corp. The format of the station is adult contemporary music. CJTT-FM broadcasts to the New Liskeard, Ontario area at 104.5 FM.
FM RADIO STATION

CJTW-FM 363758
Owner: Sound of Faith Broadcasting
Editorial: 659 King St E Suite 207, Kitchener, Ontario N2G 2M4 **Tel:** 1 519 575-9090.
Email: info@faithfm.org
Web site: http://www.faithfm.org
Profile: CJTW-FM is a commercial station owned by Sound of Faith Broadcasting. The format is contemporary Christian. CJTW-FM broadcasts to the Kitchener, Ontario area at 94.3 FM.
FM RADIO STATION

CJUC-FM 811963
Owner: Utilities Consumers Group
Editorial: Yukon Arts Centre, College Drive, Whitehorse, Yukon Territory Y1A 5X9 **Tel:** 1 867 667-8577.
Email: mail@cjucfm.com
Web site: http://cjucfm.com
Profile: CJUC-FM is a non-commercial station owned by Utilities Consumers Group. The format of the station is community radio. CJUC-FM broadcasts to the Whitehorse, Yukon Territory, Canada area at a frequency of 92.5 FM.
FM RADIO STATION

CJUI-FM 553494
Owner: Vista Broadcast Group Inc.
Editorial: 1729 Gordon Dr, Kelowna, British Columbia V1Y 3H3 **Tel:** 1 250 980-9009.
Web site: http://1039.juicefm.ca
Profile: CJUI-FM is a commercial station owned by Vista Broadcast Group Inc. The format for the station is classic hits. CJUI-FM broadcasts to the Kelowna, BC area at 103.9 FM.
FM RADIO STATION

CJUK-FM (Magic 99.9 Thunder Bay) 83085
Owner: Arcadia Broadcasting
Editorial: 180 Park Av Suite 200, Thunder Bay, Ontario P7B 6J4 **Tel:** 1 807 344-2000.
Email: magic@magic999.ca
Web site: http://www.magic999.ca
Profile: CJUK-FM is a commercial station owned by Arcadia Broadcasting. The format of the station is hot adult contemporary. CJUK-FM broadcasts to the Thunder Bay, Ontario area at 99.9 FM.
FM RADIO STATION

CJUM-FM 83169
Owner: University of Manitoba Students Union
Editorial: University Centre Room #308, University of Manitoba, Winnipeg, Manitoba R3T 2N2
Tel: 1 204 474-7027.
Email: cjum@cjum.com
Web site: http://www.umfm.com
Profile: CJUM-FM is a non-commercial station owned by University of Manitoba Students Union. The format is college variety. CJUM-FM broadcasts to the Winnipeg, Manitoba area at 101.5 FM.
FM RADIO STATION

CJUV-FM 409621
Owner: Golden West Broadcasting Ltd.
Editorial: 4725 49B Ave, Lacombe, Alberta T4L 1K1
Tel: 1 403 786-0194.
Email: news@sunny94.com
Web site: http://www.sunny94.com
Profile: CJUV-FM is a commercial station owned by Golden West Broadcasting Ltd.. The format of the station is classic hits. CJUV-FM broadcasts to the Lacombe, Alberta area at 94.1 FM.
FM RADIO STATION

CJVA-AM 47316
Owner: Radio-Acadie Ltd.
Editorial: 195 rue Main, Bathurst, New Brunswick E2A 1A7 **Tel:** 1 506 546-4600.
Email: superstation@ckle.fm
Web site: http://www.ckle.fm
Profile: CJVA-AM is a commercial station owned by Radio-Acadie Ltd. The format for the station is adult contemporary. CJVA-AM broadcasts to the Bathurst, New Brunswick area at 810 AM.
AM RADIO STATION

CJVB-AM 47154
Owner: Fairchild Radio Group Ltd.
Editorial: 4151 Hazelbridge Way, Unit 2090, Richmond, British Columbia V6X 4J7 **Tel:** 1 604 295-1234.
Email: news@am1470.com
Web site: http://www.am1470.com
Profile: CJVB-AM is a commercial station owned by the Fairchild Radio Group Ltd. The format of the station is variety. CJVB-FM broadcasts to the Vancouver, British Columbia area at 1470 AM.
AM RADIO STATION

CJVD-FM 689479
Owner: Yves Sauvé
Editorial: 2555, rue Dutrisac, Local RC-08 A, Vaudreuil-Dorion, Quebec J7V 7E6 **Tel:** 1 514 790-1001.
Email: info@cjvd.ca
Web site: http://www.cjvd.ca
Profile: CJVD-FM is a commercial station owned by Yves Sauvé. The format for the station is adult contemporary. CJVD-FM broadcasts to the Vaudreuil-Dorion, Quebec area.
FM RADIO STATION

CJVR-FM 83106
Owner: Fabmar Investments Ltd.
Editorial: 611 Main Street North, Melfort, Saskatchewan S0E 1A0 **Tel:** 1 306 752-2587.
Email: news@cjvr.com
Web site: http://www.yourtownnews.ca/news/97
Profile: CJVR-FM is a commercial station owned by Fabmar Investments Ltd. The format of the station is contemporary country. CJVR-FM broadcasts to the Melfort, Saskatchewan area at 105.1 FM.
FM RADIO STATION

CJWA-FM 83150
Owner: Labbe Media Corp.
Editorial: 96 Broadway Avenue, Wawa, Ontario P0S 1K0 **Tel:** 1 705 856-4555.
Email: jjamfmnews@bellnet.ca

Profile: CJWA-FM is a commercial station owned by Labbe Media Corp. The format of the station is adult contemporary. CJWA-FM broadcasts to Wawa, Ontario at 107.1 FM.
FM RADIO STATION

CJWF-FM 610069
Owner: Blackburn Radio Inc.
Editorial: 2090 Wyandotte St E, Windsor, Ontario N8Y 5B2 **Tel:** 1 519 944-4400.
Email: news.windsor@blackburnradio.com
Web site: http://country959.com
Profile: CJWF-FM is a commercial station owned by Blackburn Radio Inc. The format for the station is contemporary country. CJWF-FM broadcasts to the Windsor, ON area at 95.9 FM.
FM RADIO STATION

CJWI-AM (CPAM Radio Union 1410) 387384
Owner: CPAM Radio Union
Editorial: 3390 Boul Cremazie E Etage 2EME, Montreal, Quebec H2A 1A4 **Tel:** 1 514 790-2726.
Email: info@cpam1410.com
Web site: http://www.cpam1410.com
Profile: CJWI-AM est une station de radio commerciale, une propriété de CPAM Radio Union. Le format de la station est le variété. CJWI-AM est diffusé dans la région de Montréal à 1410 AM.

CJWI-AM is a commercial station owned by CPAM Radio Union. The format of the station is variety. CJWI-AM broadcasts to the Montreal area at 1410 AM.
AM RADIO STATION

CJWL-FM 390882
Owner: Evanov Radio Group
Editorial: 127 York Street, Ottawa, Ontario K1N 5T4 **Tel:** 1 613 241-9850.
Email: info@985thejewel.com
Web site: http://www.985thejewel.com/985/
Profile: CJWL-FM is a commercial station owned by Evanov Radio Group. The format of the station is easy listening. CJWL-FM broadcasts to the Ottawa, Ontario area at 98.5 FM.
FM RADIO STATION

CJWT-FM 546257
Owner: Wawatay Native Communications Society
Editorial: 135 Pine Street, Timmins, Ontario P4N 2K3 **Tel:** 1 705 360-4556.
Email: editor@wawatay.on.ca
Web site: http://www.wawataynews.ca
Profile: CJWT-FM is a commercial station owned by the Wawatay Native Communications Society. The format is a variety of content offered in English, Cree Oji and Ojibway. CJWT-FM broadcast to the Timmins, Ontario area at 106.7 FM.
FM RADIO STATION

CJWV-FM (Oldies 96.7) 758812
Owner: My Broadcasting Corporation
Editorial: 360 George St N Unit 1, Peterborough, Ontario K9H 7E7 **Tel:** 1 705 876-7773.
Email: newsptbo@mbcmedia.ca
Web site: http://www.oldies967.ca
Profile: CJWV-FM is a commercial station owned by My Broadcasting Corporation. The format of the station is Oldies. CJWV-FM broadcasts to the Peterborough area at 96.7 FM.
FM RADIO STATION

CJWW-AM 47233
Owner: Saskatoon Media Group
Editorial: 366 3rd Avenue S, Saskatoon, Saskatchewan S7K 1M5 **Tel:** 1 306 244-1975.
Email: cjwwnews@sasktel.net
Web site: http://www.cjwwradio.com
Profile: CJWW-AM is a commercial station owned by Saskatoon Media Group. The format of the station is classic country. CJWW-AM broadcasts to the Saskatoon, Saskatchewan area at 600 AM.
AM RADIO STATION

CJXK-FM 47413
Owner: Newfoundland Capital Corporation Limited
Editorial: B-5412 55 Street, Cold Lake, Alberta T9M 1R5 **Tel:** 1 780 594-2459.
Email: news@k-rock953.com
Web site: http://www.953krock.com
Profile: CJXK-FM is a commercial station owned by Newfoundland Capital Corporation Limited. The format for the station is classic rock. CJXK-FM broadcasts to the Cold Lake, Alberta area at 95.3 FM.
FM RADIO STATION

CJXL-FM 83146
Owner: Newfoundland Capital Corporation Limited
Editorial: 27 Arsenault Court, Moncton, New Brunswick E1E 4J8 **Tel:** 1 506 858-5525.
Email: xl96@xl96.com
Web site: http://www.xl96.com
Profile: CJXL-FM is a commercial station owned by Newfoundland Capital Corporation Limited. The format for the station is contemporary country music. CJXL-FM broadcasts to Moncton, New Brunswick at 96.9 FM.
FM RADIO STATION

CJXX-FM 47188
Owner: Jim Pattison Broadcast Group(The)
Editorial: 9817 101st Avenue, Suite 202, Grande Prairie, Alberta T8V 0X6 **Tel:** 1 780 532-0840.
Email: general@bigcountryxx.com
Web site: http://www.bigcountryxx.com
Profile: CJXX-FM is a commercial station owned by The Jim Pattison Broadcast Group. The format is classic country. CJXX-FM broadcasts to the Grande Prairie, Alberta area at 93.1 FM.
FM RADIO STATION

CJXY-FM (Y108) 47472
Owner: Corus Entertainment Inc.
Editorial: 875 Main St W Suite 900, Hamilton, Ontario L8S 4R1 **Tel:** 1 905 521-9900.
Web site: http://www.y108.ca
Profile: CJXY-FM (Y108) is a commercial station owned by Corus Entertainment Inc. The format of the station is rock/album-oriented rock. CJXY-FM broadcasts to the Hamilton, Ontario area at 107.9 FM.
FM RADIO STATION

CJYC-FM 47563
Owner: Maritime Broadcasting System Ltd.
Editorial: 226 Union St, Saint John, New Brunswick E2L 1B1 **Tel:** 1 506 658-5100.
Email: mailbag@k100.ca
Web site: http://kool98.fm
Profile: CJYC-FM is a commercial station owned by Maritime Broadcasting System Ltd. The format of the station is classic hits. CJYC-FM broadcasts to the Saint John, New Brunswick area at 98.9 FM.
FM RADIO STATION

CJYE-AM (Joy Radio) 83097
Owner: Whiteoaks Communications Group Limited
Editorial: 284 Church St, broadcast centre, Oakville, Ontario L6J 7N2 **Tel:** 1 905 845-2821.
Email: contact@joy1250.ca
Web site: http://www.joy1250.ca
Profile: CJYE-AM is a non-commercial station owned by Whiteoaks Communications Group Limited. The format is Christian. CJYE-AM broadcasts to the Oakville, Ontario area at 1250 AM.
AM RADIO STATION

CJYM-AM 47228
Owner: Golden West Broadcasting Ltd.
Editorial: 208 Highway 4 North, Rosetown, Saskatchewan S0L 2V0 **Tel:** 1 306 882-2686.
Email: cjymnews@goldenwestradio.com
Web site: http://www.cjym.com
Profile: CJYM-AM is a commercial station owned by Golden West Broadcasting Ltd. The format of the station is classic hits. CFYM-AM broadcasts in the Rosetown, Saskatchewan area at 1330 AM.
AM RADIO STATION

CJYQ-AM 47319
Owner: Newfoundland Capital Corporation Limited
Editorial: 391 Kenmount Rd, St. John's, Newfoundland A1B 3P9 **Tel:** 1 709 726-5590.
Email: radionewfoundland@vocm.com
Web site: http://www.thisisnewfoundlandlabrador.ca
Profile: CJYQ-FM is a commercial station owned by Newfoundland Capital Corporation Limited. The format of the station is variety. CJYQ-FM broadcasts to the St. John's, Newfoundland area at 930 AM.
AM RADIO STATION

CJZN-FM 47163
Owner: Jim Pattison Broadcast Group(The)
Editorial: 2750 Quadra St, Top Floor, Victoria, British Columbia V8T 4E8 **Tel:** 1 250 475-6611.
Web site: http://www.thezone.fm
Profile: CJZN-FM is a commercial station owned by The Jim Pattison Broadcast Group. The format of the station is rock alternative. CJZN-FM broadcasts to the Victoria, British Columbia area at 91.3 FM.
FM RADIO STATION

CKAC-AM Radio Circulation 730 47277
Owner: Cogeco
Editorial: 800 Rue de la Gauchetiere O Bureau 1100, Montreal, Quebec H5A 1K6 **Tel:** 1 514 787-0730.
Web site: http://www.radiocirculation.net
Profile: CKAC-AM est une station de Cogeco qui ne diffuse que des bulletins météo et l'état de la circulation. La station diffuse sur la ville de Montréal sur le 730AM.

CKAC-AM is a commercial station owned by Cogeco. The format of the station is traffic and weather. CKAC-AM broadcasts to the Montreal area at 730 AM.
AM RADIO STATION

CKAD-AM 47405
Owner: Maritime Broadcasting System Ltd.
Editorial: 29 Oakdene Ave, Kentville, Nova Scotia B4N 1H5 **Tel:** 1 902 825-3429.
Email: newsroom@avrnetwork.com
Web site: http://www.avrnetwork.com
Profile: CKAD-AM is a commercial station owned by Maritime Broadcasting System Ltd. The format of the station is classic country. CKAD-AM broadcasts to the Middleton, Nova Scotia area at 1350 AM.
AM RADIO STATION

CKAG-FM (100.1) 628101
Owner: Société de communication Ikito Pikogan Ltée(La)
Editorial: 30, rue David Kistabish, Pikogan, Quebec J9T 3A3 **Tel:** 1 819 727-3237.
Email: ckagfm@cableamos.com
Web site: http://www.ckagfm.com
Profile: CKAG-FM est la station de radio communautaire, une propriété de La Société de communication Ikito Pikogan Ltée. Le genre de la station est varié. CKAF-FM est diffusé à Pikogan, dans la région de Québec à 100.1 FM. On diffuse les émissions du lundi au vendredi dans la journée seulement, soit de 10h à 17h.

CKAG-FM is a community radio station owned by La Société de communication Ikito Pikogan Ltée. The format for the station is variety. CKAG-FM broadcasts to the Pikogan, Quebec area at 100.1 FM. They broadcast Mon - Fri daytime only.
FM RADIO STATION

CKAJ-FM 47845
Owner: Cooperative des Artisans Radio-Soleil
Editorial: 3877 Boulevard Harvey, 2e étage, Jonquiere, Quebec G7X 0A6 **Tel:** 1 418 546-2525.
Email: ckaj@ckaj.org
Web site: http://www.ckaj.org
Profile: CKAJ-FM est la propriété de La radio communautaire du Saguenay et le format musical est country-folk et vieilles chansons. CKAJ-FM couvre Jonquière et sa région sur le 92.5FM. La station accorde une grande place aux talents locaux et régionaux.

CKAJ-FM is a commercial station owned by La radio communautaire du Saguenay. The format of the station is classic country and oldies. CKAJ-FM broadcasts to the Jonquiere, Quebec area at 92.5 FM. The station give a lot of air time to local and regional talent.
FM RADIO STATION

CKAP-FM (The Moose Kapuskasing 100.9) 47219
Owner: Vista Broadcast Group
Editorial: 22 Queen St Unit 2A, Kapuskasing, Ontario P5N 1G8 **Tel:** 1 705 335-2379.
Email: moose1009@moosefm.com
Web site: http://www.moosefm.com/ckap
Profile: CKAP-FM is a commercial station owned by Vista Broadcast Group. The format of the station is adult contemporary music. CKAP-FM broadcasts to the Kapuskasing, Ontario area at 100.9 FM.
FM RADIO STATION

CKAT-AM 47433
Owner: Rogers Communications Inc.
Editorial: 743 Main St E, North Bay, Ontario P1B 1C2 **Tel:** 1 705 474-2000.
Email: nbnews@rci.rogers.com
Web site: http://www.country600.com
Profile: CKAT-AM is a commercial station owned by Rogers Communications Inc. The format of the station is contemporary country and sports. CKAT-AM broadcasts to North Bay, Ontario at 600 AM.
AM RADIO STATION

CKAY-FM (91.7 Coast FM) 498312
Owner: Vista Radio
Editorial: 1-1877 Field Rd 1, 1, Sechelt, British Columbia V0N 3A1 **Tel:** 1 604 741-9170.
Web site: http://www.mycoastnow.com
Profile: CKAY-FM (91.7 Coast FM) is a commercial station owned by Vista Radio. The format of the station is adult contemporary. CKAY-FM broadcasts to the Sechelt, British Columbia area at 91.7 FM.
FM RADIO STATION

CKBA-FM 47404
Owner: New Cap Radio
Editorial: #1 4902-49 Street, Athabasca, Alberta T9S 1C2 **Tel:** 1 780 675-5301.
Web site: http://www.941theriver.ca
Profile: CKBA-FM is a commercial station owned by New Cap Radio. The format of the station is adult contemporary music. CKBA-FM broadcasts to the Athabasca, Alberta area at 94.1 FM.
FM RADIO STATION

CKBC-FM 47268
Owner: Bell Media
Editorial: 640 St. Peter Ave Unit 1, Bathurst, New Brunswick E2A 2Y7 **Tel:** 1 506 547-1360.
Email: maxnews@bellmedia.ca
Web site: http://www.max1049.ca
Profile: CKBC-FM is a commercial station owned by Bell Media. The format of the station is adult contemporary music. CKBC-FM broadcasts in Bathurst, New Brunswick at 104.9 FM.
FM RADIO STATION

CKBD-FM 458233
Owner: Clear Sky Radio
Editorial: 400-220 3 Ave S 400, Lethbridge, Alberta T1J 0G9 **Tel:** 1 403 388-2910.
Web site: http://www.981thebridge.ca
Profile: CKBD-FM is a commercial station owned by Clear Sky Radio.. The format of the station is modern rock. CKBD-FM broadcasts to the Lethbridge, Alberta area at 98.1 FM.
FM RADIO STATION

CKBE-FM 47577
Owner: Cogeco
Editorial: 800 Rue de la Gauchetiere O Bureau 1100, Montreal, Quebec H5A 1M1 **Tel:** 1 514 767-9250.
Web site: http://www.925thebeat.ca
Profile: CKBE-FM is a commercial station owned by Cogeco. The format of the station is adult contemporary. CKBE-FM broadcasts to the Montreal area at 92.5 FM.
FM RADIO STATION

CKBI-AM 47209
Owner: Jim Pattison Broadcast Group (The)
Editorial: 1316-900 Central Ave 1316, Prince Albert, Saskatchewan S6V 4V3 **Tel:** 1 306 763-7421.
Web site: http://www.900ckbi.com
Profile: CKBI-AM is a commercial station owned by The Jim Pattison Broadcast Group. The format of the station is classic country. CKBI-AM broadcasts to the Prince Albert, Saskatchewan area at 900 AM.
AM RADIO STATION

CKBL-FM 47664
Owner: Saskatoon Media Group
Editorial: 366 3rd Avenue S, Saskatoon, Saskatchewan S7K 1M5 **Tel:** 1 306 244-1975.
Email: cjwwnews@sasktel.net
Web site: http://www.929thebullrocks.com
Profile: CKBL-FM is a commercial station owned by Saskatoon Media Group. The format of the station is contemporary country. CKBL-FM broadcasts to the Saskatoon, Saskatchewan area at 92.9 FM.
FM RADIO STATION

CKBN-FM (Rive-Sud 90.5) 535224
Owner: Cooperative de solidarite radio communautaire Nicolet-Yamask
Editorial: 127-10275, ch Leblanc, Becancour, Quebec G0X 1B0 **Tel:** 1 819 294-2526.
Email: information@ckbn.ca
Web site: http://www.ckbn.ca
Profile: CKBN-FM est une station de radio non-commerciale, une propriété de la Coopérative de solidarité radio communautaire Nicolet-Yamaska/ Bécancour. Le format de la station est le variété. CKBN-FM est diffusé à Bécancour, au Québec à 90.5 FM.

CKBN-FM is a non-commercial station owned by the Cooperative de solidarite radio communautaire Nicolet-Yamaska/Becancour. The format of the station is variety. CKBN-FM broadcasts to the Becancour, Quebec area at 90.5 FM.
FM RADIO STATION

CKBT-FM (The Beat 91.5) 217314
Owner: Corus Entertainment Inc.
Editorial: 50 Sportsworld Crossing Rd, Unit 210, Kitchener, Ontario N2P 0A4 **Tel:** 1 519 772-1212.
Email: info@915thebeat.com
Web site: http://www.915thebeat.com
Profile: CKBT-FM is a commercial station owned by Corus Entertainment Inc. The format for the station is Top 40/CHR. CKBT-FM broadcasts to the Kitchener, Ontario area at 91.5 FM.
FM RADIO STATION

CKBW-FM 47643
Owner: Acadia Broadcasting Ltd.
Editorial: 135 North Street, Bridgewater, Nova Scotia B4V 2V7 **Tel:** 1 902 543-2401.
Email: ckbwnews@radioabl.ca
Web site: http://www.ckbw.ca
Profile: CKBW-FM is a commercial station owned by Acadia Broadcasting Ltd. The format of the station is adult contemporary music. CKBW-FM broadcasts to the Bridgewater, Nova Scotia area at 98.1 FM.
FM RADIO STATION

CKBX-AM 47403
Owner: Vista Broadcast Group Inc.
Editorial: 260 3rd Street, 100 Mile House, British Columbia V0K 2E0 **Tel:** 1 250 395-3848.
Email: cariboonews@reachthecariboo.com

Web site: http://www.mycariboonow.com/country-840-am/
Profile: CKBX-AM is a commercial station owned by Vista Broadcast Group Inc. The format of the station is classic country. CKBX-AM broadcasts to 100 Mile House, BC at 840 AM.
AM RADIO STATION

CKBY-FM (Country Ottawa 101.1) 47532
Owner: Rogers Communications Inc.
Editorial: 2001 Thurston Dr, Ottawa, Ontario K1G 6C9
Tel: 1 613 736-2001.
Email: ottawanewsroom@ottawaradio.rogers.com
Web site: http://www.country1011.com
Profile: CKBY-FM is a commercial station owned by Rogers Communications Inc. The format of the station is contemporary country. CKBY-FM broadcasts to Ottawa, Ontario at 101.1 FM.
FM RADIO STATION

CKBZ-FM 47117
Owner: Jim Pattison Broadcast Group(The)
Editorial: 460 Pemberton Terr, Kamloops, British Columbia V2C 1T5 **Tel:** 1 250 372-3322.
Web site: http://www.b100.ca
Profile: CKBZ-FM is a commercial station owned by The Jim Pattison Broadcast Group. The format of the station is adult contemporary music. CKBZ-FM broadcasts to the Kamloops, Britsh Columbia area ast 100.1 FM.
FM RADIO STATION

CKCB-FM 47782
Owner: Corus Entertainment Inc.
Editorial: 1400 26 Hwy, Collingwood, Ontario L9Y 4W2 **Tel:** 1 705 446-9510.
Email: general@thepeakfm.com
Web site: http://www.thepeakfm.com
Profile: CKCB-FM is a commercial station owned by Corus Entertainment Inc. The format of the station is adult contemporary. CKCB-FM broadcasts to the Collingwood, Ontario area at 95.1 FM.
FM RADIO STATION

CKCE-FM (101.5 Kool FM) 458796
Owner: Jim Pattison Broadcast Group(The)
Editorial: 222 58 Ave SW Suite 600, Calgary, Alberta T2H 2S3 **Tel:** 1 403 536-3866.
Web site: http://kool1015.ca
Profile: CKCE-FM is a commercial station owned by Jim Pattison Broadcast Group. The format of the station is hot adult contemporary. CKCE-FM broadcasts to the Calgary, Alberta area at 101.5 FM.
FM RADIO STATION

CKCH-FM (New Country 103.5) 536834
Owner: Martin (Barry)
Editorial: 500 Kings Rd Suite 300, Sydney, Nova Scotia B1S 1B1 **Tel:** 1 902 563-1035.
Email: info@newcountry1035.com
Web site: http://newcountry1035.ca/
Profile: CKCH-FM is a commercial station owned by Barry Martin. NewCap Broadcasting Ltd. also has a stake in the station. The format of the station is contemporary country. CKCH-FM broadcasts to the Sydney, Nova Scotia area at 103.1 FM.
FM RADIO STATION

CKCI-FM 560387
Owner: Points Eagle Radio
Editorial: 9111 W Ipperwash Rd, Unit 6 RR #2, Forest, Ontario N0N 1J0 **Tel:** 1 519 786-3883.
Email: info@eaglecountry.ca
Web site: http://www.eaglecountry.ca
Profile: CKCI-FM is a commercial station owned by Points Eagle Radio. The format of the station is contemporary country, classic rock and oldies. CKCI-FM broadcasts to the Sarnia, Ontario area at 103.3 FM.
FM RADIO STATION

CKCK-FM 153491
Owner: Rawlco Radio Ltd.
Editorial: 210-2401 Saskatchewan Dr, Regina, Saskatchewan S4P 4H8 **Tel:** 1 306 525-0000.
Web site: http://www.jackfmregina.com
Profile: CKCK-FM is a commercial station owned by Rawlco Radio Ltd.The format for the station is adult hits. CKCK-FM broadcasts to the Regina, Saskatchewan area at 94.5 FM.
FM RADIO STATION

CKCL-FM 238428
Owner: Golden West Broadcasting Ltd.
Editorial: 2-20 St.Mary's Rd 2, Winnipeg, Manitoba R2H 1H1 **Tel:** 1 204 256-2525.
Email: info@classic107.com
Web site: http://www.classic107.com
Profile: CFEQ-FM is a commercial station owned by Golden West Broadcasting Ltd. The format of the station is Classical and Jazz. CKCL-FM broadcasts to the Winnipeg, Manitoba area at 107.1 FM.
FM RADIO STATION

CKCM-AM 47302
Owner: Steele Communications
Editorial: 35 Grenfell Heights, Grand Falls-Windsor, Newfoundland A2A 2K2 **Tel:** 1 709 489-2192.
Email: grandfallswindsor@vocm.com
Web site: http://www.vocm.com
Profile: CKCM-AM is a commercial station owned by Steele Communications. The format is classic and contemporary country music, news and talk. CKCM-AM broadcasts to the Grand Falls-Windsor, Newfoundland area at 620 AM.
AM RADIO STATION

CKCN-FM (Pur 94.1) 47776
Owner: Radio Sept-Iles Inc.
Editorial: 365 Boul Laure, Sept-Iles, Quebec G4R 1X2
Tel: 1 418 962-3838.
Email: ckcn941@Purfm.com
Web site: http://www.le941.com
Profile: CKCN-FM (Pur 94.1) est une station de radio commerciale, propriété de Radio Sept-Îles Inc. Le genre de musique de la station est adulte contemporain. CKCN-FM est diffusé à Sept-Îles, Québec.

CKCN-FM (Pur 94.1) is a commercial station owned by Radio Sept-Iles Inc. The format of the station is adult contemporary. CKCN-FM broadcasts to Sept-Iles, Quebec.
FM RADIO STATION

CKCQ-FM 47137
Owner: Vista Radio Ltd.
Editorial: 502-410 Kinchant St 502, Quesnel, British Columbia V2J 7J5 **Tel:** 1 250 992-7046.
Email: cariboonews@vistaradio.ca
Web site: http://www.mycariboonow.com/
Profile: CKCQ-FM is a commercial station owned by Vista Radio Ltd. The format of the station is contemporary country and Southern rock. CKCQ-FM broadcasts to Quesnel, British Columbia at 100.3 FM.
FM RADIO STATION

CKCR-FM 47402
Owner: Bell Media
Tel: 1 250 837-2149.
Email: info@myezrock.com
Web site: http://wwww.revelstoke.myezrock.com
Profile: CKCR-FM is a commercial station owned by Bell Media. The format of the station is Lite Rock/Lite AC. CKCR-FM broadcasts to the Revelstoke, British Columbia area at 106.1 FM.
FM RADIO STATION

CKCU-FM (93.1) 47536
Owner: CKCU Radio Carleton Inc.
Editorial: 1125 Colonel by Dr Rm 517, university centre, Ottawa, Ontario K1S 5R1 **Tel:** 1 613 520-2898.
Email: info@ckcufm.com
Web site: http://www.ckcufm.com
Profile: CKCU-FM is a non-commercial station owned by CKCU Radio Carleton Inc. The format of the station is variety. CKCU-FM broadcasts to Ottawa, Ontario at 93.1 FM.
FM RADIO STATION

CKCV-FM 47834
Owner: Newfoundland Broadcasting Co. Ltd.
Editorial: 446 Logy Bay Rd., St. John's, Newfoundland A1C 5S2 **Tel:** 1 709 726-2922.
Email: ntv@ntv.ca
Web site: http://www.ozfm.com
FM RADIO STATION

CKCW-FM 47312
Owner: Maritime Broadcasting System Ltd.
Editorial: 1000 St George Blvd, Moncton, New Brunswick E1E 4M7 **Tel:** 1 506 858-1220.
Web site: http://www.k945.ca
Profile: CKCW-FM is a commercial station owned by Maritime Broadcasting System Ltd. The format for the station is hot adult contemporary. CKCW-FM broadcasts to the Moncton, New Brunswick area at 94.5 FM.
FM RADIO STATION

CKDG-FM 47614
Owner: Canadian Hellenic Cable Radio Ltd.
Editorial: 4865 Jean-Talon Ouest, Montreal, Quebec H4P 1W7 **Tel:** 1 514 273-2481.
Email: info@mikefm.ca
Web site: http://www.mikefm.ca
Profile: CKDG-FM is a commercial station owned by Canadian Hellenic Cable Radio Ltd. The format for the station is Jack FM-Adult Hits. CKDG-FM broadcasts to the Montreal area at 105.1 FM.
FM RADIO STATION

CKDH-FM 47265
Owner: Maritime Broadcasting System Ltd.
Editorial: #38 Highway 6, Amherst, Nova Scotia B4H 3Y4 **Tel:** 1 902 667-3875.
Email: ckdh@ckdh.net
Web site: http://www.ckdh.net
Profile: CKDH-FM is a commercial station owned by Maritime Broadcasting System Ltd. The format of the station is easy listening music. CKDH-FM broadcasts to Amherst, Nova Scotia at 101.7 FM.
FM RADIO STATION

CKDJ-FM 47723
Owner: Algonquin College
Editorial: Algonquin Col 1385 Woodroffe Avenue, Room N-101, Ottawa, Ontario K2G 1V8
Tel: 1 613 727-4723.
Email: pihlaid@algonquincollege.com
Web site: http://www.ckdj.net
Profile: CKDJ-FM is a commercial station owned by Algonquin College. The format of the station is alternative hip hop. CKDJ-FM broadcasts to the Ottawa, Ontario area at 107.9 FM.
FM RADIO STATION

CKDK-FM 47545
Owner: Corus Entertainment Inc.
Editorial: 380 Wellington Street, Room 222, London, Ontario N6A 5B5 **Tel:** 1 519 931-6000.
Web site: http://www.more1039.ca
Profile: CKDK-FM is a commercial station owned by Corus Entertainment Inc. The format of the station is classic hits. CKDK-FM broadcasts in the Woodstock, Ontario area at 103.9 FM.
FM RADIO STATION

CKDM-AM 47248
Owner: Dauphin Broadcasting Company Ltd.
Editorial: 27 3rd Ave NE, Dauphin, Manitoba R7N 0Y5
Tel: 1 204 638-3230.
Email: ckdm.news@730ckdm.com
Web site: http://www.730ckdm.com
Profile: CKDM-AM is a commercial station owned by Dauphin Broadcasting. The format of the station is news and country music. CKDM-AM broadcasts to Dauphin, Manitoba and surrounding communities at 730 AM.
AM RADIO STATION

CKDO-AM (1580 AM) 47293
Owner: Durham Radio Inc.
Editorial: 1200 Airport Blvd Suite 207, Oshawa, Ontario L1J 8P5 **Tel:** 1 905 571-0949.
Email: newsroom@kx96.fm
Web site: http://www.ckdo.ca
Profile: CKDO-AM is a commercial station owned by Durham Radio Inc. The format of the station is oldies. CKDO-AM broadcasts to the Oshawa, Ontario area at 1580 AM. CKDO-AM airs programming on CKDO-FM.
AM RADIO STATION

CKDO-FM (107.7 FM) 359183
Owner: Durham Radio Inc.
Editorial: 1200 Airport Blvd Suite 207, Oshawa, Ontario L1J 8P5 **Tel:** 1 905 571-0949.
Email: newsroom@kx96.fm
Web site: http://www.ckdo.ca
Profile: CKDO-FM is a commercial station owned by Durham Radio Inc. The format of the station is oldies. CKDO-FM broadcasts to Oshawa, Ontario at 107.7 FM. CKDO-FM airs CKDO-AM's programming.
FM RADIO STATION

CKDQ-AM 47173
Owner: Newfoundland Capital Corporation Limited
Editorial: 515 Highway 10 East, Drumheller, Alberta T0J 0Y0 **Tel:** 1 403 823-3384.
Email: q91@newcap.ca
Web site: http://www.q91country.com
Profile: CKDQ-AM is a commercial station owned by Newfoundland Capital Corporation Limited. The format of the station is contemporary country music. CKDQ-AM broadcasts to Drumheller, Alberta and its environs at 910 AM.
AM RADIO STATION

CKDR-FM (92.7 Dryden) 47205
Owner: Arcadia Broadcasting
Editorial: 122 King St, Dryden, Ontario P8N 1C2
Tel: 1 807 223-2355.
Email: ckdr@radioabl.ca
Web site: http://www.ckdr.net
Profile: CKDR-FM is a commercial station owned by Arcadia Broadcasting. The format of the station is adult contemporary. CKDR-FM broadcasts to Dryden, Ontario at 92.7 FM.
FM RADIO STATION

CKDU-FM 47642
Owner: CKDU-FM Society
Editorial: Dalhousie University, 6136 University Ave 4th Floor, Halifax, Nova Scotia B3H 4J2
Tel: 1 902 494-6479.
Email: info@ckdu.ca
Web site: http://www.ckdu.ca
Profile: CKDU-FM is a non-commercial station owned by CKDU-FM Society. The format of the station is variety. CKDU-FM broadcasts to the Halifax, Nova Scotia area at 88.1 FM.
FM RADIO STATION

CKDV-FM 47133
Owner: Jim Pattison Broadcast Group(The)
Editorial: 1810 3rd Ave, 2nd Floor, Prince George, British Columbia V2M 1G4 **Tel:** 1 250 564-8861.
Web site: http://www.993thedrive.com
Profile: CKDV-FM is a commercial station owned by The Jim Pattison Broadcast Group. The format of the station is classic rock. CKDV-FM broadcasts to the Prince George, British Columbia area at 99.3 FM.
FM RADIO STATION

CKDX-FM 47662
Owner: Evanov Radio Group
Editorial: 5312 Dundas St W, Toronto, Ontario M9B 1B3 **Tel:** 1 416 213-1035.
Web site: http://www.jewelradio.com
Profile: CKDX-FM is a commercial station owned by Evanov Radio Group. The format of the station is adult standards. CKDX-FM broadcasts to the Toronto area at 88.5 FM.
FM RADIO STATION

CKDY-AM 47401
Owner: Maritime Broadcasting System Ltd.
Editorial: 53 Sydney St, Digby, Nova Scotia B0V 1A0
Tel: 1 902 245-2111.
Email: newsroom@avrnetwork.com
Web site: http://www.avrnetwork.com
Profile: CKDY-AM is a commercial station owned by Maritime Broadcasting System Ltd. The format of the station is classic country. CKDY-AM broadcasts to the Digby, Nova Scotia area at 1420 AM.
AM RADIO STATION

CKDY-FM 47795
Owner: Maritime Broadcasting System Ltd.
Editorial: 53 Sydney St, Digby, Nova Scotia B0V 1A0
Tel: 1 902 245-2111.
Email: newsroom@avrnetwork.com
Web site: http://www.avrnetwork.com
FM RADIO STATION

CKEA-FM (95.7 CRUZ FM) 705645
Owner: Harvard Broadcasting
Editorial: 104-5241 Calgary Trail NW 104, Edmonton, Alberta T6H 5G8 **Tel:** 1 780 435-3023.
Web site: http://www.957cruzfm.ca
Profile: CKEA-FM is a commercial station owned by Harvard Broadcasting. The format for the station is adult Hits. CKEA-FM broadcasts to the Edmonton, Alberta are at 95.7 FM.
FM RADIO STATION

CKEC-FM 47190
Owner: Hector Broadcasting Co. Ltd.
Editorial: 84 Provost St, New Glasgow, Nova Scotia B2H 2P4 **Tel:** 1 902 752-4200.
Email: info@ecfm.ca
Web site: http://www.ecfm.ca
Profile: CKEC-FM is a commercial station owned by Hector Broadcasting Co. Ltd. The format of the station is adult contemporary. CKEC-FM broadcasts to the New Glasgow, Nova Scotia area at 94.1 FM.
FM RADIO STATION

CKEN-FM 47187
Owner: Maritime Broadcasting System Ltd.
Editorial: 29 Oakdene Ave, Kentville, Nova Scotia B4N 1H5 **Tel:** 1 902 678-2111.
Email: newsroom@avrnetwork.com
Web site: http://www.avrnetwork.com
Profile: CKEN-FM is a commercial station owned by Maritime Broadcasting System Ltd. The format of the station is classic and contemporary country. CKEN-FM broadcasts to the Kentville, Nova Scotia area at 97.7 FM.
FM RADIO STATION

CKER-FM 47772
Owner: Rogers Communications Inc.
Editorial: 10212 Jasper Ave, Edmonton, Alberta T5J 5A3 **Tel:** 1 780 424-2222.
Web site: http://www.worldfm.ca
Profile: CKER-FM is a commercial station owned by Rogers Communications Inc. The format of the station is a variety of music, news, public affairs, religion, and general interest talk programs broadcast in multiple languages. CKER-FM broadcasts to Edmonton, AB area at 101.7 FM.
FM RADIO STATION

CKFG-FM 778485
Owner: Intercity Broadcasting
Editorial: 34 Kern Rd, Toronto, Ontario M3B 1T1
Tel: 1 416 498-4987.
Web site: http://g987fm.com
Profile: CKFG-FM is a commercial station owned by Intercity Broadcasting. The format for the station is urban adult contemporary. CKFG-FM broadcasts to the Toronto, Ontario area at 98.7 FM.
FM RADIO STATION

CKFI-FM 432461
Owner: Golden West Broadcasting Ltd.
Editorial: 134 Central Avenue North, Swift Current, Saskatchewan S9H 0L1 **Tel:** 1 306 773-4605.
Web site: http://magic97radio.ca
Profile: CKFI-FM is a commercial station owned by Golden West Broadcasting Ltd. The format for the station is adult contemporary. CKFI-FM broadcasts to the Swift Current, Saskatchewan area at 97.1 FM.
FM RADIO STATION

CKFM-FM (99.9 Virgin Radio) 47539
Owner: Bell Media
Editorial: 299 Queen St W, Toronto, Ontario M5V 2Z5- **Tel:** 1 416 384-8000.
Web site: http://www.iheartradio.ca/virginradio/toronto
Profile: CKFM-FM (99.9 Virgin Radio) is a commercial station owned by Bell Media. The format of the station is Top 40/CHR. CKFM-FM broadcasts to the Toronto area at 99.9 FM.
FM RADIO STATION

CKFR-AM 47119
Owner: Bell Media
Editorial: 435 Bernard Ave, Kelowna, British Columbia V1Y 6N8 **Tel:** 1 250 860-8600.
Email: info@am1150.ca
Web site: http://www.am1150.ca
Profile: CKFR-AM is a commercial station owned by Bell Media. The format of the station is news, talk and sports. CKFR-AM broadcasts to the Kelowna, British Columbia area at 1150 AM.
AM RADIO STATION

CKFT-FM 877326
Owner: Golden West Broadcasting Ltd.
Editorial: 9940-99th Avenue, Fort Saskatchewan, Alberta **Tel:** 780 997 1079.
Web site: http://fortsaskonline.com
FM RADIO STATION

CKFU-FM 358835
Owner: Moose Communications
Editorial: 10423 101st Avenue, Fort St. John, British Columbia V1J 2B7 **Tel:** 1 250 787-7100.
Email: reception@moosefm.ca
Web site: http://energeticcity.ca/moosefm

Profile: CKFU-FM is a commercial station owned by Moose Communications. The format of the station is contemporary country. CKFU-FM broadcasts to the Fort St. John, BC area at 100.1 FM.
FM RADIO STATION

CKFX-FM 47722
Owner: Rogers Communications Inc.
Editorial: 743 Main St E, North Bay, Ontario P1B 1C2
Tel: 1 705 474-2000.
Email: thefox@foxradio.ca
Web site: http://www.foxradio.ca
Profile: CKFX-FM is a commercial station owned by Rogers Communications Inc. The format of the station is rock/album-oriented rock. CKFX-FM broadcasts to the North Bay, Ontario area at 101.9 FM.
FM RADIO STATION

CKGA-AM 47304
Owner: Newfoundland Capital Corporation Limited
Tel: 1 709 651-3650.
Email: ckxdnews@vocm.com
Web site: http://www.vocm.com
Profile: CKGA-AM is a commercial radio station owned by Newfoundland Capital Corporation Limited. The format of the station is classic country music. CKGA-AM broadcasts to Gander, Newfoundland and surrounding communities at 650 AM.
AM RADIO STATION

CKGB-FM 47332
Owner: Rogers Communications Inc.
Editorial: 260 Second Ave, Timmins, Ontario P4N 8A4
Tel: 1 705 264-2351.
Web site: http://www.kisstimmins.com/
Profile: CKGB-FM is a commercial station owned by Rogers Communications Inc. The format of the station is adult contemporary. CKGB-FM broadcasts to Timmins, Ontario at 99.3 FM.
FM RADIO STATION

CKGC-FM 811980
Owner: Northern Lights Entertainment Inc.
Tel: 1 877 445-2547.
Email: 1035capitalfm@gmail.com
Web site: http://www.1035capitalfm.ca
Profile: CKGC-FM is a commercial station owned by Northern Lights Entertainment Inc. The format of the station is classic hits with an emphasis on rock music. CKGC-FM broadcasts locally to the Iqaluit, NU, Canada area at a frequency of 103.5 FM.
FM RADIO STATION

CKGE-FM (The Rock 94.9) 47514
Owner: Durham Radio Inc.
Editorial: 1200 Airport Blvd Suite 207, Oshawa, Ontario L1J 8P5 **Tel:** 1 905 571-0949.
Email: newsroom@kx96.fm
Web site: http://www.therock.fm
Profile: CKGE-FM is a commercial radio station owned by Durham Radio Inc. The format of the station is album-oriented rock. CKGE-FM broadcasts to Oshawa, Ontario at 94.9 FM.
FM RADIO STATION

CKGF-FM 47115
Owner: Vista Broadcast Group Inc.
Editorial: 1101A 4th St, Castlegar, British Columbia V1N 2A8 **Tel:** 1 250 365-7600.
Email: news@mountainfm.net
Web site: http://www.mykootenaynow.com
Profile: CKGF-FM is a commercial station owned by Vista Broadcast Group Inc. The format of the station is classic rock. CKGF-FM broadcasts to the Castlegar, British Columbia area at 96.7 FM.
FM RADIO STATION

CKGL-AM 47223
Owner: Rogers Communications Inc.
Editorial: 305 King St West, 11th Floor, Kitchener, Ontario N2G 4E4 **Tel:** 1 519 743-2611.
Email: news570@rogers.com
Web site: http://www.570news.com
Profile: CKGL-AM is a commercial station owned by Rogers Communications Inc. The format of the station is news and talk. CKGL-AM broadcasts to the Kitchener, Ontario area at 570 AM.
AM RADIO STATION

CKGM-AM (TSN Sports Montreal 690) 47317
Owner: Bell Media
Editorial: 1717 Boul Rene-Levesque E, Montreal, Quebec H2L 4T3- **Tel:** 1 514 931-4487.
Email: live@tsn690.ca
Web site: http://www.iheartradio.ca/tsn/tsn-montreal
Profile: CKGM-AM is a commercial station owned by Bell Media. The format of the station is sports. CKGM-AM broadcasts to the Montreal area at 690 AM.
AM RADIO STATION

CKGN-FM (89,7 FM) 47783
Owner: Radio Communautaire KapNord Inc.
Editorial: 77 Brunelle Rd N, Kapuskasing, Ontario P5N 2M1 **Tel:** 1 705 335-5915.
Email: ckgn-fm@nt.net
Web site: http://www.ckgn.ca
Profile: CKGN-FM est une station de radio non-commerciale, une propriété de Radio Communautaire KapNord Inc. Le format de la station est le variété. CKGN-FM diffuse son contenu à Kapuskasing, en Ontario au 89.7 FM.

CKGN-FM is a non-commercial station owned by Radio Communautaire KapNord Inc. The format of the station is variety. CKGN-FM broadcasts to the Kapuskasing, Ontario area at 89.7 FM.
FM RADIO STATION

CKGR-FM 47399
Owner: Astral Media
Editorial: 825 10th Ave S, Golden, British Columbia V0A 1H0 **Tel:** 1 250 344-7177.
Email: webmaster@myezrock.com
Web site: http://golden.myezrock.com
Profile: CKGR-FM is a commercial station owned by Astral Media. The format of the station is soft rock/ soft AC. CKGR-FM broadcasts to Golden, British Columbia at 106.3 FM.
FM RADIO STATION

CKGS-FM (Rythme FM Saguenay 105.5) 695345
Owner: Cogeco Media
Editorial: 345 Rue Racine E, Chicoutimi, Quebec G7H 1S8 **Tel:** 1 418 545-2577.
Web site: http://www.rythmefm.com/saguenay
Profile: CKGS-FM is a commercial station owned by Cogeco Media. The format of the station is adult contemporary. CKGS-FM broadcasts to the La Baie, Quebec area at 105.5 FM.
FM RADIO STATION

CKGW-FM (UCB Canada) 506377
Owner: UCB
Editorial: 40 Centre St, Chatham, Ontario N7M 5W3
Tel: 1 519 351-1118.
Web site: http://www.ucbchathamkent.com
Profile: CKGW-FM is a commercial station owned by UCB. The format is adult contemporary music. CKGW-FM broadcasts to the Chatham-Kent, Ontario area at 89.3 FM.
FM RADIO STATION

CKGY-FM 47146
Owner: Newcap Radio
Editorial: 4920 59 St, Red Deer, Alberta T4N 2N1
Tel: 1 403 343-1170.
Email: news@kgcountry.ca
Web site: http://www.kgcountry.ca
Profile: CKGY-FM is a commercial station owned by Newfoundland Capital Corporation Limited. The format of the station is contemporary country. CKGY-FM broadcasts to Red Deer, Alberta at 95.5 FM.
FM RADIO STATION

CKHA-FM 585885
Owner: Vista Broadcast Group
Editorial: 739 Mountain St., Haliburton, Ontario K0M 1S0 **Tel:** 1 705 457-9603.
Email: canoefm@bellnet.ca
Web site: http://www.canoefm.com
Profile: CKHA-FM is a non-commercial station owned by Vista Broadcast Group. The format of the station is variety. CKHA-FM broadcasts to the Haliburton, Ontario area at 100.9 FM.
FM RADIO STATION

CKHC-FM 83114
Owner: Humber College
Editorial: 205 Humber College Blvd, Humber College, Toronto, Ontario M9W 5L7 **Tel:** 1 416 675-6622.
Email: radiohumber@humber.ca
Web site: http://www.radio.humber.ca
Profile: CKHC-FM is a non-commercial station owned by Humber College. The format of the station is variety. CKHC-FM broadcasts to the Toronto area at 96.9 FM.
FM RADIO STATION

CKHJ-AM 47586
Owner: Bell Media
Editorial: 206 Rookwood Ave, Fredericton, New Brunswick E3B 2M2 **Tel:** 1 506 451-9111.
Web site: http://www.khj.ca
Profile: CKHJ-AM is a commercial station owned by Bell Media. The format of the station is contemporary country. CKHJ-AM broadcasts to Fredericton, New Brunswick area at 1260 AM.
AM RADIO STATION

CKHK-FM 529157
Owner: Evanov Radio Group
Editorial: 1320 Main Street East, Hawkesbury, Ontario K6A 1C5 **Tel:** 1 613 872-1077.
Email: info@1077thejewel.com
Web site: http://www.evanovradio.com
Profile: CKHK-FM is a commercial station owned by the Evanov Radio Group. The format of the station is easy listening. CKHK-FM broadcasts to the Hawkesbury, Ontario area at 107.7 FM.
FM RADIO STATION

CKHL-FM 47417
Owner: Peace River Broadcasting Corp.
Tel: 1 780 926-4530.
Email: news@ylcountry.com
Web site: http://www.ylcountry.com
Profile: CKHL-AM is a commercial station owned by Peace River Broadcasting Corp. The format of the station is classic country music. The station airs locally at 102.1 FM.
FM RADIO STATION

CKHT-FM (The Moose Hearst 94.5) 610668
Owner: Vista Broadcast Group
Editorial: 22 Queen St Unit 2A, Kapuskasing, Ontario P5N 1G8 **Tel:** 1 705 335-2379.
Email: moose1009@moosefm.com
Web site: http://www.moosefm.com/ckap
Profile: CKHT-FM is a commercial radio station owned by Vista Broadcast Group. The format of the station is adult contemporary music. The target audience of the station is adults, ages 18 to 64 throughout Hearst, Ontario. CKHT-FM is broadcast locally on 94.5 FM.
FM RADIO STATION

CKHY-FM 697865
Owner: Evanov Radio Group
Editorial: 5527 Cogswell St, Halifax, Nova Scotia B3J 1R2 **Tel:** 1 902 429-1035.
Email: info@live105.ca
Web site: http://www.live105.ca
Profile: CKHY-FM is a commercial station owned by Evanov Radio Group. The format for the station is modern rock. CKHY-FM broadcasts to the greater Halifax, Nova Scotia area at 105.1 FM.
FM RADIO STATION

CKHZ-FM (Hot Country 103.5 FM) 412044
Owner: Evanov Radio Group
Editorial: 5527 Cogswell St, Halifax, Nova Scotia B3J 1R2 **Tel:** 1 902 429-1035.
Web site: http://www.hotcountry1035.com
Profile: CKHZ-FM is a commercial station owned by Evanov Radio Group. The format for the station is Hot Country. CKHZ-FM broadcasts to the Halifax, Nova Scotia area at 103.5 FM.
FM RADIO STATION

CKIA-FM 47608
Owner: Radio Basse-Ville Inc.
Editorial: 335 Rue Saint-Joseph E Bureau 200, Quebec, Quebec G1K 3B4 **Tel:** 1 418 529-9026.
Web site: http://www.ckiafm.org/accueil
Profile: CKIA-FM is a non-commercial station owned by Radio Basse-Ville Inc. The format of the station is French adult contemporary. CKIA-FM broadcasts to the Quebec City, Quebec area at 88.3 FM.
FM RADIO STATION

CKIK-FM 596015
Owner: Harvard Broadcasting
Editorial: 103-6751 52 Ave 103, Red Deer, Alberta T4N 4K8 **Tel:** 1 403 358-3100.
Email: admin@laradiogroup.com
Web site: http://www.kraze1013.com
Profile: CKIK-FM is a commercial station owned by Harvard Broadcasting. The format of the station is Top 40. CKIK-FM broadcasts to the Red Deer, Alberta area at 101.3 FM.
FM RADIO STATION

CKIM-AM 47398
Owner: Steele Communications
Editorial: 35 Grenfell Hts, Grand Falls-Windsor, Newfoundland A2A 1W3 **Tel:** 1 709 489-2192.
Email: grandfallswindsor@vocm.com
Web site: http://www.vocm.com
Profile: Re-broadcasts shows originally aired on VOCM-AM.
AM RADIO STATION

CKIQ-FM 554776
Owner: Northern Lights Entertainment Inc.
Tel: 1 877 445-2547.
Email: icefmiqaluit@gmail.com
Web site: http://www.icefm.ca
FM RADIO STATION

CKIR-AM 47397
Owner: Astral Media
Editorial: 825 10th Ave South, Golden, British Columbia V0A 1H0 **Tel:** 1 250 3447177.
Email: info@myezrock.com
Web site: http://www.golden.myezrock.com
Profile: CKIR-AM is a commercial station owned by Bell Media. The format of the station is easy listening. CKIR-AM broadcasts to Golden, British Columbia at 870 AM.
AM RADIO STATION

CKIS-FM 47538
Owner: Rogers Communications Inc.
Editorial: 1 Ted Rogers Way, Toronto, Ontario M4Y 3B7 **Tel:** 1 416 935-8392.
Web site: https://twitter.com/Kiss925
Profile: CKIS-FM is a commercial station owned by Rogers Communications Inc. The format is Top 40/ CHR. CKIS-FM broadcasts to Toronto at 92.5 FM.
FM RADIO STATION

CKIX-FM 47591
Owner: Newfoundland Capital Corporation Limited
Editorial: 391 Kenmount Road, St. John's, Newfoundland A1B 3M7 **Tel:** 1 709 726-5590.
Email: hitsmail@991hitsfm.com
Web site: http://www.991hitsfm.com
Profile: CKIX-FM is a commercial station owned by Newfoundland Capital Corporation Limited. The format of the station is Top 40/CHR. CKIX-FM broadcasts to Saint John's, Newfoundland and surrounding communities at 99.1 FM.
FM RADIO STATION

CKIZ-FM 83156
Owner: Jim Pattison Broadcast Group(The)
Editorial: 3313 - 32nd Avenue, Vernon, British Columbia V1T 2M7 **Tel:** 1 250 545-2141.
Email: 1075kiss@gmail.com
Web site: http://www.1075kiss.com
Profile: CKIZ-FM is a commercial station owned by Jim Pattison Broadcast Group. The format of the station is adult contemporary. CKIZ-FM broadcasts to the Vernon, British Columbia area at 107.5 FM.
FM RADIO STATION

CKJF-FM 39756
Owner: Radio touristique de Québec inc.(La)
Editorial: 20 Rue des Grisons, Quebec, Quebec G1R 4M7 **Tel:** 1 418 527-4444.
Web site: http://sortirfm.com
Profile: CKJF-FM is a French-language tourist radio station for the Quebec City, Chaudière-Appalaches and Charlevoix regions of Quebec. CKJF-FM broadcasts at 106.9 FM. Its English-language sister station, CJNG-FM, broadcasts at 89.7 FM.
FM RADIO STATION

CKJH-AM 83107
Owner: Fabmar Investments Ltd.
Editorial: 611 Main Street North, Melfort, Saskatchewan S0E 1A0 **Tel:** 1 306 752-2587.
Email: info@yourtownnews.ca
Web site: http://www.ck750.com
Profile: CKHJ-AM is a commercial station owned by Fabmar Investments Ltd. The format of the station is oldies. CKHJ-AM broadcasts to the Melfort, Saskatchewan area at 750 AM.
AM RADIO STATION

CKJJ-FM 597806
Owner: UCB
Editorial: 214 Pinnacle St Fl 2, Belleville, Ontario K8N 3A6 **Tel:** 1 866 388-4488.
Web site: http://www.ucbcanada.com
Profile: CKJJ-FM is a commercial station owned by UCB. The format is adult contemporary Christian music. CKJJ-FM broadcasts to the Belleville, Ontario area at 102.3 FM.
FM RADIO STATION

CKJM-FM 47760
Owner: Cooperative Radio Cheticamp Ltee.
Editorial: 15584 Cabot Trail, Cheticamp, Nova Scotia B0E 1H0 **Tel:** 1 902 224-1242.
Email: info@ckjm.ca
Web site: http://www.ckjm.ca
Profile: CKJM-FM is a non-commercial station owned by Cooperative Radio Cheticamp Ltee. The format of the station is variety. CKJM-FM broadcasts to the Cheticamp, Nova Scotia area at 106.1 FM.
FM RADIO STATION

CKJN-FM 489147
Owner: Vista Broadcast Group
Editorial: 282 Argyle St S Unit 4, Caledonia, Ontario N3W 1K8 **Tel:** 1 289 284-1070.
Email: moose929@moosefm.com
Web site: http://www.moosefm.com/ckjn
Profile: CKJN-FM is a commercial station owned by Vista Broadcast Group. The format for the station is easy listening. CKJN-FM broadcasts to the Haldimand, ON area at 92.9 FM.
FM RADIO STATION

CKJR-AM 47199
Owner: Newfoundland Capital Corporation Limited
Editorial: 5214A 50th Avenue, Wetaskiwin, Alberta T9A 0S8 **Tel:** 1 780 352-0144.
Web site: http://www.w1440.com
Profile: CKJR-AM is a commercial station owned by Newfoundland Capital Corporation Limited. The format of the station is oldies. CKJR-AM broadcasts to Wetaskiwin, Alberta and its environs at 1440 AM.
AM RADIO STATION

CKJS-AM 47256
Owner: Evanov Communications
Editorial: 520 Corydon Ave, Winnipeg, Manitoba R3L 0P1 **Tel:** 1 204 477-1221.
Email: info@ckjs.com
Web site: http://www.ckjs.com
Profile: CKJS-AM is a commercial station owned by Evanov Communications. The format of the station is multilingual station serving various ethnic groups. CKJS-AM broadcasts to Winnipeg, Manitoba at 810 AM.
AM RADIO STATION

CKJX-FM 533540
Owner: CAB-K Broadcasting Ltd.
Editorial: #6-4526 49 Avenue, Olds, Alberta T4H 1A4
Tel: 1 403 586-7625.
Web site: http://www.rock104.ca
Profile: CKJX-FM is a commercial station owned by CAB-K Broadcasting Ltd. The format of the station is rock/album-oriented rock. CKJX-FM broadcasts to the Olds, Alberta area at 104.5 FM.
FM RADIO STATION

CKKC-FM 47759
Owner: Astral Media
Editorial: 513 C Front Street, Nelson, British Columbia V1L 4B4 **Tel:** 1 250 352-5510.
Email: webmaster@myezrock.com
Web site: http://kootenays.myezrock.com
Profile: CKKC-FM is a commercial station owned by Astral Media. The format of the station is adult contemporary. CKKC-FM broadcasts to the Trail, British Columbia area at 106.9 FM.
FM RADIO STATION

CKKL-FM 47540
Owner: Bell Media
Editorial: 87 George St, Ottawa, Ontario K1N 9H7-
Tel: 1 613 789-2486.
Web site: http://www.newcountry94.com
Profile: CKKL-FM is a commercial station owned by Bell Media. The format of the station is contemporary

country. CKKL-FM broadcasts to the Ottawa, Ontario area at 93.9 FM.
FM RADIO STATION

CKKN-FM 47758
Owner: Jim Pattison Broadcast Group(The)
Editorial: 1810 3rd Ave, 2nd Floor, Prince George, British Columbia V2M 1G4 **Tel:** 1 250 564-8861.
Web site: http://www.1013theriver.com
Profile: CKKN-FM is a commercial station owned by The Jim Pattison Broadcast Group. The format of the station is hot adult contemporary. CKKN-FM broadcasts to Prince George, British Columbia at 101.3 FM.
FM RADIO STATION

CKKO-FM 556850
Owner: Newfoundland Capital Corporation
Editorial: 1601 Bertram St, Kelowna, British Columbia V1Y 2G5 **Tel:** 1 250 861-5963.
Email: publicservice@k963.fm
Web site: http://www.k963.fm
Profile: CKKO-FM is a commercial station owned by Newfoundland Capital Corporation. The format of the station is classic rock. CKKO-FM broadcasts to the Kelowna, Ontario area at 96.3 FM.
FM RADIO STATION

CKKQ-FM 47460
Owner: Jim Pattison Broadcast Group(The)
Editorial: 2750 Quadra St, Top Floor, Victoria, British Columbia V8T 4E8 **Tel:** 1 250 475-0100.
Email: news@theq.fm
Web site: http://www.theq.fm
Profile: CKKQ-FM is a commercial station owned by The Jim Pattison Broadcast Group. The format of the station is rock/album-oriented rock. CKKQ-FM broadcasts to Victoria, British Columbia at 100.3 FM.
FM RADIO STATION

CKKS-FM (KISS 104.9) 63219
Owner: Rogers Communications Inc.
Editorial: 2440 Ash St, Vancouver, British Columbia V5Z 4J6 **Tel:** 1 604 877-6357.
Web site: http://www.kissradio.ca
Profile: CKKS-FM is a commercial station owned by Rogers Communications Inc. The format of the station is Top 40. CKKS-FM broadcasts to the Vancouver, British Columbia area at 104.9 FM.
FM RADIO STATION

CKKV-FM 809544
Owner: Vista Broadcast Group
Editorial: 4 Industrial Rd unit#3, Kemptville, Ontario K0G 1J0 **Tel:** 1 613 258-1786.
Web site: http://www.fm975kemptville.com
Profile: CKKV-FM is a commercial station owned by Vista Broadcast Group. The format for the station is adult contemporary. CKKV-FM broadcasts to the Kemptville, ON area at 97.5 FM.
FM RADIO STATION

CKKW-FM 47224
Owner: Bell Media
Editorial: 255 King St North, Suite 207, Waterloo, Ontario N2J 4V2 **Tel:** 1 519 884-4470.
Web site: http://www.kfun995.com
Profile: CKKW-FM is a commercial station owned by Bell Media. The format of the station is adult hits. CKKW-FM broadcasts to Waterloo, Ontario at 99.5 FM.
FM RADIO STATION

CKKX-FM 47781
Owner: Peace River Broadcasting Corp.
Editorial: 9807 100th Ave, Peace River, Alberta T8S 1T5 **Tel:** 1 780 624-2535.
Email: news@ylcountry.com
Web site: http://www.kix106.net
Profile: CKKX-FM is a commercial radio station owned by Peace River Broadcasting Corp. The format of the station is adult contemporary music. CKKX-FM broadcasts to Peace River, Alberta and surrounding communities at 106.1 FM.
FM RADIO STATION

CKKY-FM 47195
Owner: Newfoundland Capital Corporation Limited
Editorial: 1037 2 Ave Fl 2ND, Wainwright, Alberta T9W 1K7 **Tel:** 1 780 842-4311.
Web site: http://www.krock1019.com/
Profile: CKKY-FM is a commercial station owned by Newfoundland Capital Corporation Limited. The format of the station is rock music. CKKY-FM broadcasts to Wainwright, Lloydminster, Vermillion and its environs at 101.9 FM.
FM RADIO STATION

CKLC-FM 47183
Owner: Bell Media
Editorial: 993 Princess St, Ste 10, Kingston, Ontario K7L 1H3 **Tel:** 1 613 544-1380.
Email: onair@989thedrive.com
Web site: http://www.989thedrive.com
Profile: CKLC-FM is a commercial station owned by Bell Media. The format of the station is AAA-Adult Album Alternative. CKLC-FM broadcasts to the Kingston, Ontario area at 98.9 FM.
FM RADIO STATION

CKLD-FM (Passion Rock 105.5 FM) 47777
Owner: Réseau des Appalaches
Editorial: 327 Rue Labbe, Thetford Mines, Quebec G6G 1Z2 **Tel:** 1 418 335-7533.
Email: redaction@passionrock.com
Web site: http://www.passionrock.com
Profile: CKLD-FM is a commercial station owned by Réseau des Appalaches. The format of the station is soft and lite adult contemporary. CKLD-FM broadcasts to Thetford Mines, Quebec at 105.5 FM.
FM RADIO STATION

CKLE-FM 47631
Owner: Radio-Acadie Ltd.
Editorial: 195 rue Main, Bathurst, New Brunswick E2A 1A7 **Tel:** 1 506 546-4600.
Email: superstation@ckle.fm
Web site: http://www.ckle.fm
Profile: CKLE-FM is a commercial station owned by Radio-Acadie Ltd. The format of the station is adult contemporary. CKLE-FM broadcasts in the Bathurst, New Brunswick area at 92.9 FM.
FM RADIO STATION

CKLF-FM 70710
Owner: Riding Mountain Broadcasting Ltd.
Editorial: 624 14th Street East, Brandon, Manitoba R7A 7E1 **Tel:** 1 204 726-8888.
Email: starfm@starfmradio.com
Web site: http://www.starfmradio.com
Profile: CKLF-FM is a commercial station owned by Riding Mountain Broadcasting Ltd. The format of the station is hot adult contemporary. CKLF-FM broadcasts to Brandon, Manitoba at 94.7 FM.
FM RADIO STATION

CKLG-FM 47703
Owner: Rogers Communications Inc.
Editorial: 40147 Glenalder Pl Unit 202, Squamish, British Columbia V8B 0G2 **Tel:** 1 604 892-1021.
Email: news@mountainfm.com
Web site: http://www.mountainfm.com
Profile: CKLG-FM is a commercial station owned by Rogers Communications Inc. The format of the station is hot adult contemporary. CKLG-FM broadcasts to the Squamish, British Columbia area at 107.5 FM.
FM RADIO STATION

CKLH-FM 47474
Owner: Bell Media
Editorial: 883 Upper Wentworth St Suite 401, Hamilton, Ontario L9A 4Y6 **Tel:** 1 905 574-1150.
Web site: http://www.iheartradio.ca/k-lite
Profile: CKLH-FM is a commercial station owned by Bell Media. The format of the station is Lite Rock/Lite AC. CKLH-FM broadcasts to the Hamilton, Ontario area at 102.9 FM.
FM RADIO STATION

CKLJ-FM 231466
Owner: CAB-K Broadcasting Ltd.
Editorial: 6-4526 49 Avenue, Olds, Alberta T4H 1A4 **Tel:** 1 403 556-2628.
Email: cklj@telus.net
Web site: http://www.ckfm.ca
Profile: CKLJ-FM is a commercial station owned by CAB-K Broadcasting Ltd. The format of the station is classic country. CKLJ-FM broadcasts to the Olds, Alberta area at 96.5 FM.
FM RADIO STATION

CKLM-FM (106.1 The Goat) 153482
Owner: Vista Radio Ltd.
Editorial: 5012 – 494th Street, Lloydminster, Alberta T9V 0K2 **Tel:** 1 780 875-5400.
Web site: http://www.mylloydminsternow.com
Profile: CKLM-FM (106.1 The Goat) is a commercial station owned by Vista Radio Ltd. The format is classic rock. CKLM-FM broadcasts to Lloydminster, Alberta at 106.1 FM.
FM RADIO STATION

CKLO-FM 761878
Owner: Blackburn Radio
Editorial: 700 Richmond St unit 101, London, Ontario N6A 5C7 **Tel:** 1 519 679-8680.
Web site: http://www.981freefm.ca
Profile: CKLO-FM is a commercial station owned by Blackburn Radio. The format of the station album alternative. CKLO-FM broadcasts to the London, Ontario area at 98.1 FM.
FM RADIO STATION

CKLP-FM 47546
Owner: Vista Broadcast Group
Editorial: 60 James St, Parry Sound, Ontario P2A 1T5 **Tel:** 1 705 746-2163.
Email: moose1033@moosefm.com
Web site: http://www.moosefm.com/cklp
Profile: CKLP-FM is a commercial station owned by the Vista Broadcast Group. The format of the station is easy listening. CKLP-FM broadcasts to Parry Sound, Ontario at 103.3 FM.
FM RADIO STATION

CKLQ-AM 47245
Owner: Riding Mountain Broadcasting Ltd.
Editorial: 624 14th St East, Brandon, Manitoba R7A 7E1 **Tel:** 1 204 726-8888.
Email: qcountry@cklq.mb.ca
Web site: http://www.cklq.com
Profile: CKLQ-AM is a commercial station owned by Riding Mountain Broadcasting Ltd. The format of the station is classic country. CKLQ-AM broadcasts to Brandon, Manitoba at 880 AM.
AM RADIO STATION

CKLR-FM 47861
Owner: Jim Pattison Broadcast Group(The)
Editorial: 801 B-29th St, Courtenay, British Columbia V9N 7Z5 **Tel:** 1 250 703-2200.
Email: info@973theeagle.com
Web site: http://www.973theeagle.com
Profile: CKLR-FM a commercial station owned by The Jim Pattison Broadcast Group. The format of the station is classic hits. CKLR-FM broadcasts to Courtenay, British Columbia and the surrounding area at 97.3 FM.
FM RADIO STATION

CKLS-AM 47357
Owner: RNC Media
Editorial: 200 ave Laurier ouest, bureau 250, Montreal, Quebec H2T 2N8 **Tel:** 1 514 871-0919.
Profile: CKLS-FM is a commercial station owned by CKLS Inc. The format of the station is rock. CKLS-FM broadcasts to La Sarre, Quebec at 1240 AM.
AM RADIO STATION

CKLU-FM 83139
Owner: Laurentian Student & Community Radio Corp.
Editorial: Laurentian University, 935 Ramsey Lake Road, Sudbury, Ontario P3E 2C6 **Tel:** 1 705 673-6538.
Email: traffic@cklu.ca
Web site: http://www.cklu.ca
Profile: CKLU-FM is a non-commercial station owned by Laurentian Student & Community Radio Corp. The format of the station is college variety. CKLU-FM broadcasts to the Laurentian University campus and local community of Sudbury, Ontario at 96.7 FM.
FM RADIO STATION

CKLW-AM (AM 800) 47351
Owner: Bell Media
Editorial: 1640 Ouellette Ave, Windsor, Ontario N8X 1L1- **Tel:** 1 519 258-8888.
Email: newscentre@am800cklw.com
Web site: http://www.iheartradio.ca/am800
Profile: CKLW-AM (AM 800) is a commercial station owned by Bell Media. The format of the station is news and talk. CKLW-AM broadcasts to Windsor, Ontario at 800 AM.
AM RADIO STATION

CKLX-FM (91.9 Sports) 363724
Owner: RNC Media
Editorial: Montreal, Quebec **Tel:** 1 514 790-0919.
Web site: http://919sport.ca
Profile: CKLX-FM is a commercial station owned by RNC Media. The format of the station is sports talk. CKLX-FM broadcasts to the Montreal area at 91.9 FM.
FM RADIO STATION

CKLY-FM 47775
Owner: Bell Media
Editorial: 249 Kent St West, Lindsay, Ontario K9V 2Z3 **Tel:** 1 705 324-9103.
Email: bob@919bobfm.com
Web site: http://www.919bobfm.com
Profile: CKLY-FM is a commercial station owned by Bell Media. The format of the station is adult hits. CKLY-FM broadcasts to the Lindsay, Ontario area at 91.9 FM.
FM RADIO STATION

CKLZ-FM 47440
Owner: Jim Pattison Broadcast Group(The)
Editorial: 3805 Lakeshore Rd, Kelowna, British Columbia V1W 3K6 **Tel:** 1 250 763-1047.
Email: newsroom@power104.fm
Web site: http://www.power104.fm
Profile: CKLZ-FM is a commercial station owned by The Jim Pattison Broadcast Group. The format of the station is rock alternative music. CKLZ-FM broadcasts to Kelowna, British Columbia and surrounding communities at 104.7 FM.
FM RADIO STATION

CKMA-FM 533866
Owner: Radio MirAcadie Inc.
Editorial: 300 chemin Beaverbrook, Miramichi, New Brunswick E1V 1A1 **Tel:** 1 506 624-9370.
Email: ckma@ckma.ca
Web site: http://www.ckma.ca
Profile: CKMA-FM is a non-commercial station owned by Radio MirAcadie Inc. The format of the station is variety. CKMA-FM broadcasts to the Miramichi, New Brunswick area at 93.7 FM.
FM RADIO STATION

CKMB-FM (107.5 Kool FM) 83101
Owner: Central Ontario Broadcasting
Editorial: 431 Huronia Rd Unit 10, Barrie, Ontario L4N 9B3 **Tel:** 1 705 725-7304.
Web site: http://www.1075koolfm.com
Profile: CKMB-FM (107.5 Kool FM) is a commercial station owned by Central Ontario Broadcasting. The format of the station is hot adult contemporary music. CKMB-FM broadcasts to the Barrie, Ontario area at 107.5 FM.
FM RADIO STATION

CKMF-FM (ÉNERGIE 94.3 Montreal) 47646
Owner: Bell Media
Editorial: 1717 Boul Rene-Levesque E, Montreal, Quebec H2L 4T3 **Tel:** 1 514 529-3200.
Email: infoFR@iheartradio.ca
Web site: http://www.iheartradio.ca/energie/energie-montreal
Profile: CKMF-FM est une station de radio commerciale, une propriété de Bell Media. Le format de la station est Top 40/CHR. CKMF-FM est diffusé à Montréal à 94.3 FM.

CKMF-FM is a commercial station owned by Bell Media. The format of the station is Top 40/CHR. CKMF-FM broadcasts to Montreal at 94.3 FM.
FM RADIO STATION

CKMH-FM 521871
Owner: Rogers Media Inc.
Editorial: 7 Strachan Bay, Suite 107, Medicine Hat, Alberta T1B 4Y2 **Tel:** 1 403 548-7581.
Web site: http://www.rock1053.ca
Profile: CKMH-FM is a commercial station owned by Rogers Media Inc. The format is rock/album-oriented rock. CKMH-FM broadcasts to the Medicine Hat, Alberta area at 105.3 FM.
FM RADIO STATION

CKMM-FM 47756
Owner: Bell Media
Editorial: 1445 Pembina Hwy, Winnipeg, Manitoba R3T 5C2 **Tel:** 1 204 477-5120.
Web site: http://winnipeg.virginradio.ca
Profile: CKMM-FM is a commercial station owned by Astral Media. The format of the station is Top 40/ CHR. CKMM-FM broadcasts to Winnipeg, Manitoba at 103.1 FM.
FM RADIO STATION

CKMN-FM (96.5) 47755
Owner: Radio Communautaire du Comte Ltd.(La)
Editorial: 323 Montee Industrielle, Rimouski, Quebec G5M 1A7 **Tel:** 1 418 722-2566.
Email: info@ckmn.fm
Web site: http://www.ckmn.fm
Profile: CKMN-MF est une station commerciale de La Radio Communautaire du Comté Ltd. Elle diffuse surtout de la musique Country et folk. CKMN-FM rayonne dans la grande Région de Rimouski au 96.5 FM.

CKMN-FM is a commercial station owned by La Radio Communautaire du Comte Ltd. The format of the station is Folk and Country. CKMN-FM broadcasts to Rimouski, Quebec at 96.5 FM.
FM RADIO STATION

CKMP-FM 450664
Owner: Newfoundland Capital Corporation Limited
Editorial: 1110 Centre Street NE, Suite 100, Calgary, Alberta T2E 2R2 **Tel:** 1 403 271-6366.
Web site: http://www.ampradiocalgary.com
Profile: CKMP-FM is a commercial station owned by Newfoundland Capital Corporation Limited. The format of the station is Top 40/CHR. CKMP-FM broadcasts to the Calgary, Alberta area at 90.3 FM.
FM RADIO STATION

CKMQ-FM 47407
Owner: Merritt Broadcasting Ltd.
Editorial: 201-2196 Quilchena Ave, Merritt, British Columbia V1K 1B8 **Tel:** 1 250 378-4288.
Email: info@q101.ca
Web site: http://q101.ca
Profile: CKMQ-FM is a commercial station owned by Merritt Broadcasting Ltd. The format for the station is adult contemporary. CKMQ-FM broadcasts to the Merritt, British Columbia area at 101.1 FM.
FM RADIO STATION

CKMS-FM 47754
Owner: Corporation of Radio Waterloo Inc.
Editorial: 142 Waterloo St, Waterloo, Ontario N2J 1Y2 **Tel:** 1 519 886-2567.
Email: cooperative@soundfm.ca
Web site: http://soundfm.ca
Profile: CKMS-FM is a non-commercial campus community radio station. The station is located in Waterloo, Ontario and broadcasts at a frequency of 100.3. The station plays independent and alternative music. CKMS-FM is funded by a co-op of programmers and volunteer run.
FM RADIO STATION

CKMW-AM 47243
Owner: Golden West Broadcasting Ltd.
Editorial: 277A 1st St., Winkler, Manitoba R6W 4A6 **Tel:** 1 204 331-9300.
Email: info@goldenwestradio.com
Web site: http://www.ckmwradio.com
Profile: CKMW-AM is a commercial station owned by Golden West Broadcasting. The format of the station is contemporary country music. CKMW-AM

broadcasts to Winkler, Manitoba and surrounding communities at 1570 AM.
AM RADIO STATION

CKMX-AM   47168
Owner: Bell Media
Editorial: 300-1110 Centre St NE 300, Calgary, Alberta T2E 2R2 **Tel:** 1 403 240-5800.
Web site: http://www.iheartradio.ca/funny/funny-1060
Profile: CKMX-AM is a commercial station owned by Bell Media. The format of the station is comedy. CKMX-AM broadcasts to Calgary, Alberta at 1060 AM.
AM RADIO STATION

CKNA-FM   83099
Owner: Radio Communautaire CKNA Inc.(La)
Editorial: 29 Chemin d'en Haut, Edifice Municipale, Natashquan, Quebec G0G 2E0 **Tel:** 1 418 726-3284.
Email: ckna@globetrotter.net
Web site: http://pages.globetrotter.net/ckna
Profile: CKNA-FM is a non-commercial station operated by La Radio Communautaire CKNA Inc. The format of the station is variety. CKNA-FM broadcasts to Natashquan, Quebec at 104.1 FM.
FM RADIO STATION

CKNB-AM   47267
Owner: Maritime Broadcasting System Ltd.
Editorial: 74 Water Street, Campbellton, New Brunswick E3N 1B1 **Tel:** 1 506 753-4415.
Email: cknb@mbsradio.com
Web site: http://www.95cknb.ca
Profile: CKNB-AM is a commercial station owned by Maritime Broadcasting System Ltd. The format of the station is variety. CKNB-AM broadcasts to Campbellton, New Brunswick and its environs at 950 AM.
AM RADIO STATION

CKNG-FM   47477
Owner: Corus Entertainment Inc.
Editorial: 5204 84 St NW, Edmonton, Alberta T6E 5N8 **Tel:** 1 780 469-6992.
Web site: http://www.925freshradio.ca
Profile: CKNG-FM is a commercial radio station owned by Corus Entertainment. The format of the station is adult contemporary. CKNG-FM broadcasts to the Edmonton, Alberta area at 92.5 FM.
FM RADIO STATION

CKNI-FM   409071
Owner: Acadia Broadcasting Ltd.
Editorial: 220-1600 Main St 220, jones lake place office complex 220, Moncton, New Brunswick E1E 1G5 **Tel:** 1 506 857-1922.
Email: info@919thebend.ca
Web site: http://www.919thebend.ca
Profile: CKNI-FM is a commercial station owned by Acadia Broadcasting Ltd. The format of the station is adult contemporary. CKNI-FM broadcasts to the Moncton, New Brunswick area at 91.9 FM.
FM RADIO STATION

CKNL-FM   47114
Owner: Bell Media
Editorial: 10532 Alaska Rd, Fort St. John, British Columbia V1J 1B3 **Tel:** 1 250 785-6634.
Web site: http://www.1015thebear.com
Profile: CKNL-FM is a commercial station owned by Bell Media. The format of the station is classic rock. CKNL-FM broadcasts to the Fort St. John, British Columbia area at 101.5 FM.
FM RADIO STATION

CKNO-FM   652975
Owner: Jim Pattison Broadcast Group(The)
Editorial: 9894 42 Ave NW Suite 102, Edmonton, Alberta T6E 5V5 **Tel:** 1 780 433-7877.
Email: controlroom@1023nowradio.com
Web site: http://1023nowradio.com
Profile: CKNO-FM is a commercial station owned by The Jim Pattison Broadcast Group. The format of the station is hot adult contemporary. CKNO-FM broadcasts to the Edmonton, Alberta area at 102.3 FM.
FM RADIO STATION

CKNR-FM   47668
Owner: Vista Broadcast Group
Editorial: 144 Ontario Ave, Elliot Lake, Ontario P5A 1Y3 **Tel:** 1 705 848-3608.
Email: moose941@moosefm.com
Web site: http://www.moosefm.com/cknr
Profile: CKNR-FM is a commercial station owned by Vista Broadcast Group. The format of the station is adult contemporary music. CKNR-FM broadcasts to Elliot Lake, Ontario and its environs at 94.1 FM.
FM RADIO STATION

CKNW-AM   47124
Owner: Corus Entertainment Inc.
Editorial: 700 Georgia St W Suite 2000, Vancouver, British Columbia V7Y 1K8 **Tel:** 1 604 331-2711.
Email: nwnews@cknw.com
Web site: http://www.cknw.com
Profile: CKNW-AM is a commercial station owned by Corus Entertainment Inc. The format of the station is news, talk and sports. CKNW-AM broadcasts to Vancouver, British Columbia and its environs at 980 AM.
AM RADIO STATION

CKNX-AM (920)   47352
Owner: Blackburn Radio Inc.
Editorial: 215 Carling Terrace, Wingham, Ontario N0G 2W0 **Tel:** 1 519 357-1310.
Email: news@cknxradio.com
Web site: http://www.am920.ca
Profile: CKNX-AM is a commercial station owned by Blackburn Radio Inc. The format of the station is contemporary country music. CKNX-AM broadcasts to Wingham, Ontario and surrounding communities at 920 AM.
AM RADIO STATION

CKNX-FM (The One 101.7)   47544
Owner: Blackburn Radio Inc.
Editorial: 215 Carling Terrace, Wingham, Ontario N0G 2W0 **Tel:** 1 519 357-1310.
Email: news@cknxradio.com
Web site: http://www.1017theone.ca
Profile: CKNX-FM is a commercial station owned by Blackburn Radio Inc. The format of the station is adult contemporary. CKNX-FM broadcasts to Wingham, Ontario and surrounding communities at 101.7 FM.
FM RADIO STATION

CKOA-FM   508943
Owner: Coastal Community Cooperative Ltd.
Editorial: 106 Reserve St, Glace Bay, Nova Scotia B1A 4W5 **Tel:** 1 902 849-4301.
Email: news@coastalradio.ca
Web site: http://www.coastalradio.ca
Profile: CKOA-FM is a commercial, non-profit station owned by Coastal Community Cooperative Ltd. The format for the station is a variety of local music programming, news and sports. CKOA-FM broadcasts to the Glace Bay, Nova Scotia area at 89.7 FM.
FM RADIO STATION

CKOB-FM   47321
Owner: Cogeco
Editorial: 1350 Rue Royale Bureau 1200, Trois-Rivieres, Quebec G9A 4J4 **Tel:** 1 819 374-3556.
Email: nouvelles@1069fm.net
Web site: http://www.fm1069.ca
Profile: CKOB-FM is a commercial station owned by Cogeco. The format of the station is classic hits and oldies music. CKOB-FM broadcasts to the Trois-Rivieres, Quebec area at 106.9 FM.
FM RADIO STATION

CKOC-AM (TSN 1150 Hamilton)
                                                        47218
Owner: Bell Media
Editorial: 883 Upper Wentworth St, Hamilton, Ontario L9A 4Y6- **Tel:** 1 905 574-1150.
Web site: http://www.tsn.ca/radio/hamilton-1150
Profile: CKOC-AM is a commercial station owned by Bell Media. The format of the station is sports. CKOC-AM broadcasts to the Hamilton, Ontario area at 1150 AM.
AM RADIO STATION

CKOD-FM   47666
Owner: Torres Media
Editorial: 129 Rue Alexandre Suite 200, Salaberry-de-Valleyfield, Quebec J6S 3K5 **Tel:** 1 450 373-0103.
Web site: https://www.max103.com
Profile: CKOD-FM est une propriété de Torres Media et diffuse sur Salaberry-de-Valleyfield et ses environs à la fréquence 103.1FM.

_____
_____
_____
_____
_____
_____
_____
_____
_____
_____
_____
_____
_____
_____

CKOD-FM is a commercial station owned by Torres Media. The format of the station is adult contemporary. CKOD-FM broadcasts to Salaberry-de-Valleyfield, Quebec at 103.1 FM.
FM RADIO STATION

CKOE-FM   342204
Owner: Houssen Broadcasting
Editorial: 3030 Mountain Road, Moncton, New Brunswick E1G 2W8 **Tel:** 1 506 384-1009.
Email: info@ckoefm.com
Web site: http://www.ckoefm.com
Profile: CKOE-FM is a commercial station owned by Houssen Broadcasting. The format of the station is contemporary Christian. CKOE-FM broadcasts to the Moncton, New Brunswick area at 107.3 FM.
FM RADIO STATION

CKOF-FM   47411
Owner: Cogeco
Editorial: 150 Rue D'Edmonton, Gatineau, Quebec J8Y 3S6 **Tel:** 1 819 561-8801.
Web site: http://www.fm1047.ca
Profile: CKOF-FM is a commercial station owned by Cogeco. The format of the station is talk. CKOF-FM broadcasts to the Gatineau, Quebec area at 104.7 FM.
FM RADIO STATION

CKOI-FM (Montreal 96.9)   47587
Owner: Cogeco
Editorial: 800 Rue de la Gauchetiere O Bureau 1100, place bonaventure, Montreal, Quebec H5A 1M1 **Tel:** 1 514 789-2564.
Email: communiqueCKOI@cogecomedia.com
Web site: http://www.ckoi.com
Profile: CKOI-FM est une station de radio commerciale appartenant à Cogeco. Le format de la station est Top 40/CHR. CKOI-FM est diffusé à Montréal, au 96.6 FM.

_____

CKOI-FM is a commercial station owned by Cogeco. The format of the station is Top 40/CHR. CKOI-FM broadcasts to Montreal at 96.9 FM.
FM RADIO STATION

CKOK-AM   47416
Owner: Okalakatiget Society
Editorial: 94 Middlepath Rd, Nain, Newfoundland A0P 1L0 **Tel:** 1 709 922-2187.
Email: okradio@oksociety.com
Web site: http://www.oksociety.com
Profile: CKOK-AM is a non-commercial station owned by The Okalakatiget Society. The format for the station is variety. CKOK-AM broadcasts to Nain, Newfoundland at 610 AM.
AM RADIO STATION

CKOL-FM   585876
Owner: Campbellford Area Radio Association
Editorial: 15 Raglan St South, Campbellford, Ontario K0L 1L0 **Tel:** 1 705 653-1089.
Email: ckol-radio@bell.net
Web site: http://ckol.webs.com
Profile: CKOL-FM is a non-commercial station owned by Campbellford Area Radio Association. The format of the station is variety. CKOL-FM broadcasts to the Campbellford, Ontario area at 93.7 FM.
FM RADIO STATION

CKOM-AM   47491
Owner: Rawlco Radio Ltd.
Editorial: 715 Saskatchewan Cres W, Saskatoon, Saskatchewan S7M 5V7 **Tel:** 1 306 934-2222.
Email: iwitness@rawlco.com
Web site: http://newstalk650.com
Profile: CKOM-AM is a commercial radio station owned by Rawlco Radio Ltd. The format of the station is news and talk. CKOM-AM broadcasts to Saskatoon, Saskatchewan at 650 AM.
AM RADIO STATION

CKON-FM (97.3)   47753
Owner: Community of Akwesasne
Editorial: 22 Hiltop Dr., Suite 2, Akwesasne, Quebec H0M 1A0 **Tel:** 1 613 575-2100.
Email: ckonfm@yahoo.com
Web site: http://www.ckonfm.com
Profile: CKON-FM is a commercial station owned by the Community of Akwesasne. The format of the station is contemporary country. CKON-FM broadcasts to Cornwall, Ontario at 97.3 FM.
FM RADIO STATION

CKOR-AM   47126
Owner: Astral Media
Editorial: 33 Carmi Ave, Penticton, British Columbia V2A 3G4 **Tel:** 1 250 492-2800.
Email: bcnews@astral.com
Web site: http://www.penticton.myezrock.com
Profile: CKOR-AM is a commercial radio station owned by Astral Media. The format of the station is easy listening music. CKOR-AM broadcasts to Penticton, British Columbia at 800 AM.
AM RADIO STATION

CKOT-FM (Easy 101 FM)   47526
Owner: Tillsonburg Broadcasting Ltd.
Editorial: 77 Broadway St, Tillsonburg, Ontario N4G 3P5 **Tel:** 1 519 842-4281.
Email: info@easy101.com
Web site: http://www.easy101.com
Profile: CKOT-FM is a commercial station owned by Tillsonburg Broadcasting Ltd. The format is adult standards music. CKOT-FM broadcasts to Tillsonburg, Ontario and surrounding communities at 101.3 FM.
FM RADIO STATION

CKOY-FM   47272
Owner: Cogeco
Editorial: 4020 Boul de Portland, Sherbrooke, Quebec J1L 2V6 **Tel:** 1 819 822-0937.
Web site: http://www.fm1077.ca
Profile: CKOY-FM est une station francophone de Cogeco sur le 107,7FM qui diffuse sur Sherbrooke et les environs.

_____
_____
_____
_____

_____
_____
_____
_____

CKOY-FM is a French-language commercial station owned by Cogeco. The format of the station is Top 40/CHR. CKOY-FM broadcasts to the Sherbrooke, Quebec area at 107.7 FM.
FM RADIO STATION

CKOZ-FM   47656
Owner: Newfoundland Broadcasting Co. Ltd.
Editorial: 446 Logy Bay Rd, St. John's, Newfoundland A1A 5C6 **Tel:** 1 709 726-2922.
Email: ozfm@ozfm.com
Web site: http://www.ozfm.com
FM RADIO STATION

CKPC-AM (1380)   47189
Owner: Evanov Radio Group
Editorial: 571 West St, Brantford, Ontario N3R 7C5 **Tel:** 1 519 759-1000.
Web site: http://www.am1380.ca
Profile: CKPC-AM is a commercial station owned by Evanov Radio Group. The format is classic country and news. CKPC-AM broadcasts to the Brantford, Ontario area at 1380 AM.
AM RADIO STATION

CKPC-FM (The Jewel 92)   47457
Owner: Evanov Radio Group
Editorial: 571 West St, Brantford, Ontario N3R 7C5 **Tel:** 1 519 759-1000.
Web site: http://www.jewel92.com
Profile: CKPC-FM is a commercial station owned by Evanov Communications Inc. The format of the station is soft adult contemporary. CKPC-FM broadcasts to the Brantford, Ontario area at 92.1 FM.
FM RADIO STATION

CKPE-FM (The Cape 94.9)   47561
Owner: Maritime Broadcasting System Ltd.
Editorial: 318 Charlotte St, Sydney, Nova Scotia B1P 1C8 **Tel:** 1 902 564-5596.
Email: news@capebretonradio.com
Web site: http://thecape949.com
Profile: CKPE-FM is a commercial station owned by the Maritime Broadcasting System Ltd. The format of the station is Adult Contemporary. CKPE-FM broadcasts to Sydney, Nova Scotia and surrounding communities at 94.9 FM.
FM RADIO STATION

CKPK-FM   556738
Owner: Jim Pattison Broadcast Group(The)
Editorial: 1401 8th Ave W, Vancouver, British Columbia V6H 1C9- **Tel:** 1 604 731-6111.
Email: thepeak@thepeak.fm
Web site: http://www.thepeak.fm
Profile: CKPK-FM is a commercial station owned by The Jim Pattison Broadcast Group. The format of the station is adult album alternative. CKPK-FM broadcasts to the Vancouver, British Columbia area at 102.7 FM.
FM RADIO STATION

CKPM-FM   845846
Owner: McBride Communications & Media
Editorial: 2-99 Moray St 2, Port Moody, British Columbia V3H 3M2- **Tel:** 1 604 917-0197.
Email: info@ckpmfm.com
Web site: http://ckpmfm.com/
Profile: CKPM-FM is a commercial station owned by McBride Communications & Media. The format for the station is Adult Album Alternative. CKPM-FM broadcasts to the Port Moody area at 98.7 FM.
FM RADIO STATION

CKPR-FM (Thunder Bay 91.5)
                                                        47340
Owner: H.F. Dougall Company Limited
Editorial: 87 Hill St N, Thunder Bay, Ontario P7A 5V6 **Tel:** 1 807 346-2600.
Email: news@dougallmedia.com
Web site: http://www.ckpr.com
Profile: CKPR-FM is a commercial station owned by H.F. Dougall Company Limited. The format of the station is adult contemporary. CKPR-FM broadcasts to Thunder Bay, Ontario at 91.5 FM.
FM RADIO STATION

CKPT-FM (Energy 99.7)   47236
Owner: Bell Media
Editorial: 59 George St N, Peterborough, Ontario K9J 3G2 **Tel:** 1 705 742-8844.
Email: energy997@bellmedia.ca
Web site: http://www.energy997.ca
Profile: CKPT-FM is a commercial station owned by Bell Media. The format of the station is hot adult contemporary. CKPT-FM broadcasts to the Peterborough, Ontario area at 99.7 FM.
FM RADIO STATION

CKQB-FM (JUMP! 106.9)   47667
Owner: Corus Entertainment Inc.
Editorial: 1504 Merivale Rd, Ottawa, Ontario K2E 6Z5 **Tel:** 1 613 225-1069.
Web site: http://www.jumpradio.ca

Profile: CKQB-FM (JUMP! 106.9) is a commercial station owned by Corus Entertainment Inc. The station airs a Top 40/CHR format. CKQB-FM broadcasts to Ottawa, Ontario and surrounding communities at 106.9 FM.
FM RADIO STATION

CKQC-FM 47645
Owner: Rogers Communications Inc.
Editorial: 318-31935 S Fraser Way, Abbotsford, British Columbia V2T 5N7 **Tel:** 1 604 853-4756.
Web site: http://www.country1071.com
Profile: CKQC-FM is a commercial station owned by Rogers Communications Inc. The format of the station is contemporary country. CKQC-FM broadcasts to the Abbotsford, British Columbia area at 107.1 FM.
FM RADIO STATION

CKQK-FM 411124
Owner: Newfoundland Capital Corporation Limited
Editorial: 90 University Avenue, Suite 320, Charlottetown, Prince Edward Island C1A 4K9
Tel: 1 902 569-1003.
Web site: http://www.hot1055fm.com
Profile: CKQK-FM is a commercial station owned by Newfoundland Capital Corporation Limited. The format of the station is Top 40/CHR. CKQK-FM broadcasts to the Charlottetown, Prince Edward Island area at 105.5 FM.
FM RADIO STATION

CKQM-FM (Country 105) 47533
Owner: Bell Media
Editorial: 59 George St N, Peterborough, Ontario K9J 3G2 **Tel:** 1 705 742-8844.
Email: country105@bellmedia.ca
Web site: http://www.iheartradio.ca/country-105/
Profile: CKQM-FM is a commercial station owned by Bell Media. The format of the station is classic country. CKQM-FM broadcasts to the Peterborough, Ontario area at 105.1 FM.
FM RADIO STATION

CKQQ-FM 47120
Owner: Jim Pattison Broadcast Group(The)
Editorial: 3805 Lakeshore Rd, Kelowna, British Columbia V1W 3K6 **Tel:** 1 250 762-3331.
Email: theq@q103.ca
Web site: http://www.q1031.ca
Profile: CKQQ-FM is a commercial station owned by The Jim Pattison Broadcast Group. The format of the station is hot adult contemporary. CKQQ-FM broadcasts to the Kelowna, British Columbia area at 103.1 FM.
FM RADIO STATION

CKQR-FM 70516
Owner: Vista Broadcast Group Inc.
Editorial: 1101A 4th St, Castlegar, British Columbia V1N 2A8 **Tel:** 1 250 365-7600.
Web site: http://kootenay.thegoatrocks.ca
Profile: CKQR-FM is commercial station owned by Vista Broadcast Group Inc. The format of the station is classic rock. CKQR-FM broadcasts to the Castlegar, British Columbia area at 99.3 FM.
FM RADIO STATION

CKQV-FM (Q104) 363740
Owner: Golden West Broadcasting Ltd.
Editorial: 619 Lakeview Dr, Kenora, Ontario P9N 3P6
Tel: 1 807 468-1045.
Web site: http://www.kenoraonline.com
Profile: CKQV-FM (Q104) is a commercial station owned by Golden West Broadcasting Ltd. The format of the station is hot adult contemporary. CKQV-FM broadcasts to the Kenora, Ontario area at 103.3 FM.
FM RADIO STATION

CKRA-FM 47478
Owner: Newfoundland Capital Corporation Limited
Editorial: 2394 West Edmonton Mall, 8882-170 Street, Edmonton, Alberta T5T 4M2 **Tel:** 1 780 437-4996.
Web site: http://www.963capitalfm.com
Profile: CKRA-FM is a commercial station owned by Newfoundland Capital Corporation Limited. The station's format is classic hits. CKRA-FM broadcasts to the Edmonton, AB area at 96.3 FM.
FM RADIO STATION

CKRB-FM (Cool 103.5) 47867
Owner: Groupe Radio Simard
Editorial: 11760 3e Av, Saint-Georges, Quebec G5Y 1V4 **Tel:** 1 418 228-1460 228.
Email: nouvelles@radiobeauce.com
Web site: http://www.coolfm.biz
Profile: CKRB-FM est une station commerciale, une propriété de Groupe Radio Simard. La formule de la station est contemporain adulte. CKRB-FM est diffusé à Saint-Georges, dans la région de Québec. La fréquence est 103.5 FM.

CKRB-FM is a commercial station owned by Groupe Radio Simard. The format of the station is adult contemporary. CKRB-FM broadcasts to the Saint-Georges, Quebec area at 103.5 FM.
FM RADIO STATION

CKRC-FM 450003
Owner: Golden West Broadcasting Ltd.
Editorial: 305 Souris Avenue, Weyburn, Saskatchewan S4H 2K2 **Tel:** 1 306 848-1190.
Email: magic103@goldenwestradio.com
Web site: http://www.discoverweyburn.com
Profile: CKRC-FM is a commercial station owned by Golden West Broadcasting Ltd. The format of the station is classic hits. CKRC-FM broadcasts to the Weyburn, Saskatchewan area at 103.5 FM.
FM RADIO STATION

CKRD-FM 756238
Owner: Touch Canada Broadcasting Inc
Editorial: 37464 Hwy 2, Red Deer, Alberta T4E 1B9
Tel: 1 403 356-9052.
Email: 90.5@shinefm.com
Web site: http://www.ckrd.ca
Profile: CKRD-FM is a commercial station owned by Touch Canada Broadcasting Inc. The format of the station is contemporary Christian. CKRD-FM broadcasts to the Red Deer area at 90.5.
FM RADIO STATION

CKRH-FM 506269
Owner: Cooperative Radio-Halifax-Metro Limitee
Editorial: 5527 Rue Cogswell, Halifax, Nova Scotia B3J 1R2 **Tel:** 1 902 490-2574.
Email: info@ckrhfm.ca
Web site: http://www.ckrhfm.ca
Profile: CKRH-FM is a non-commercial station owned by Cooperative Radio-Halifax-Metro Limitee. The format of the station is variety. CHRH-FM broadcasts to the Halifax, Nova Scotia area at 98.5 FM. It reaches the French population of the regional municipality of Halifax as well as listeners in the central region of the province of Nova Scotia. It
FM RADIO STATION

CKRI-FM 696096
Owner: Harvard Broadcasting
Editorial: F-3617 50th Avenue, Red Deer, Alberta T4N 3Y5 **Tel:** 1 403 346-8051.
Web site: http://www.theriverfm.ca
Profile: CKRI-FM is a commercial radio station owned by Harvard Broadcasting. The format for the station is adult contemporary. CKRI-FM broadcasts to the Red Deer, Alberta area at 100.7 FM.
FM RADIO STATION

CKRK-FM 47751
Owner: Kahnawake Broadcasting Service
Tel: 1 450 638-1313.
Email: programming@k103radio.com
Web site: http://k103radio.com/
Profile: CKRK-FM est une radio communautaire diffusant sur le 103.7FM pour les gens de Kahnawake et sa région. Le style musical est vairé, donnant dans le country le week-end.

CKRK-FM is a community station owned by the Kahnawake Broadcasting Service. The format of the station is variety. CKRK-FM broadcasts to the Kahnawake, Quebec (south suburban Montreal) area at 103.7 FM.
FM RADIO STATION

CKRL-FM 47572
Owner: CKRL MF 89.1 Inc.
Editorial: 405 3e Av, Quebec, Quebec G1L 2W2
Tel: 1 418 640-2575.
Web site: http://www.ckrl.qc.ca
Profile: CKRL-FM is a non-commercial station owned by CKRL MF 89.1 Inc. The format of the station is variety. CKRL-FM broadcasts to the Quebec City area at 89.1 FM.
FM RADIO STATION

CKRM-AM 47227
Owner: Harvard Broadcasting
Editorial: 1900 Rose St., Regina, Saskatchewan S4P 0A9 **Tel:** 1 306 546-6200.
Web site: http://www.620ckrm.com
Profile: CKRM-AM is a commercial station owned by Harvard Broadcasting. The format of the station is country music, sports, news and talk. CKRM-AM broadcasts to the Regina, Saskatchewan area at 620 AM.
AM RADIO STATION

CKRO-FM 47750
Owner: Radio Peninsule Inc.
Editorial: 142 Route 113, Pokemouche, New Brunswick E8P 1K7 **Tel:** 1 506 336-9706.
Email: info@ckro.ca
Web site: http://www.ckro.ca
Profile: CKRO-FM is a commercial station owned by Radio Peninsule Inc. The format of the station is variety. CKRO-FM broadcasts to the Pokemouche, New Brunswick area at 97.1 FM.
FM RADIO STATION

CKRP-FM 47769
Owner: ACFA Riviere-La-Paix
Editorial: 308 Rue Principale, Falher, Alberta T0H 1M0
Tel: 1 780 837-2346.
Email: ckrp_fm@yahoo.ca
Web site: http://www.acfa-ckrp.ca
Profile: CKRP-FM is a commercial station owned by ACFA Riviere-La-Paix. The format of the station is adult contemporary. CKRP-FM broadcasts to Falher, Alberta at 95.7 FM.
FM RADIO STATION

CKRU-FM 47239
Owner: Corus Entertainment Inc.
Editorial: 159 King St, Peterborough, Ontario K9J 2R8
Tel: 1 705 748-6101.
Web site: http://www.1005freshradio.ca
Profile: CKRU-FM is a commercial station owned by Corus Entertainment Inc. The format of the station is oldies. CKRU-FM broadcasts to Peterborough, Ontario area at 100.5 FM.
FM RADIO STATION

CKRV-FM (The River 97.5) 47647
Owner: Newfoundland Capital Corporation Limited
Editorial: 611 Lansdowne St, Kamloops, British Columbia V2C 1Y6 **Tel:** 1 250 372-2197.
Email: nlnews@radionl.com
Web site: http://www.ckrv.com
Profile: CKRV-FM is a commercial station owned by Newfoundland Capital Corporation Limited. The format of the station is hot adult contemporary music. CKRV-FM broadcasts to Kamloops, British Columbia and its environs at 97.5 FM.
FM RADIO STATION

CKRW-FM 47101
Owner: Klondike Broadcasting Company Ltd.
Editorial: 203-4103 4th Ave, Whitehorse, Yukon Territory Y1A 1H6 **Tel:** 1 867 668-6100.
Email: admin@ckrw.com
Web site: http://www.ckrw.com
Profile: CKRW-FM is a commercial station owned by Klondike Broadcasting Ltd. The format of the station is adult contemporary. CKRW-FM broadcasts to the Whitehorse, Yukon Territory area at 96.1 FM.
FM RADIO STATION

CKRX-FM 506391
Owner: Bell Media
Editorial: 5152 Liard St., Fort Nelson, British Columbia V0C 1R0 **Tel:** 1 250 774-2525.
Web site: http://www.1023thebear.com
Profile: CKRX-FM is a commercial station owned by Belll Media. The format for the station is rock music. CKRX-FM broadcasts to the Ft. Nelson, British Columbia area at 102.3 FM.
FM RADIO STATION

CKRY-FM 47470
Owner: Corus Entertainment Inc.
Editorial: 170-200 Barclay Parade SW 170, eau claire market 170, Calgary, Alberta T2P 4R5 **Tel:** 1 403 716-6500.
Web site: http://www.country105.com
Profile: CKRY-FM is a commercial station owned by Corus Entertainment Inc. The format of the station is contemporary country. CKRY-FM broadcasts to Calgary, Alberta at 105.1 FM.
FM RADIO STATION

CKSA-FM 47138
Owner: Newfoundland Capital Corporation Limited
Editorial: 5026 50 St, Lloydminster, Alberta T9V 1P3
Tel: 1 780 875-3321.
Email: lloyd@newcap.ca
Web site: http://www.959lloydfm.com
Profile: CKSA-FM is a commercial station owned by Newfoundland Capital Corporation Limited. The format of the station is classic country. CKSA-FM broadcasts to the Lloydminster, Alberta area at 95.9 FM.
FM RADIO STATION

CKSB-AM 47251
Owner: Société Radio-Canada
Editorial: 607 rue Langevin, Saint-Boniface, Manitoba R2H 2W2 **Tel:** 1 204 788-3235.
Email: manitoba@radio-canada.ca
Web site: http://radio-canada.ca/regions/manitoba
Profile: CKSB-AM is a non-commercial station owned by Société Radio-Canada. The format for the station is variety. CKSB-AM broadcasts to the Winnipeg, Manitoba area at 1050 AM.
AM RADIO STATION

CKSB-FM 612503
Owner: Société Radio-Canada
Editorial: 607, rue Langevin, Saint-Boniface, Manitoba R2H 2W2 **Tel:** 1 204 788-3235.
Email: manitoba@radio-canada.ca
Web site: http://www.radio-canada.ca/espace_musique
Profile: CKSB-FM is a non-commercial station owned by Société Radio-Canada. The format for the station is classical, jazz, world, and folk music. CKSB-FM broadcasts to the Winnipeg, MB area at 89.9 FM.
FM RADIO STATION

CKSG-FM (myStar FM 93.3) 231463
Owner: My Broadcasting Corporation
Editorial: 7805 Telephone Rd., Cobourg, Ontario K9A 4J7 **Tel:** 1 905 372-5401.
Email: news933@myfmradio.ca
Web site: http://www.gonorthumberland.ca
Profile: CKSG-FM is a commercial station owned by My Broadcasting Corporation. The format for the station is adult contemporary. CKSG-FM broadcasts to the Cobourg, Ontario area at 93.3 FM.
FM RADIO STATION

CKSJ-FM 231379
Owner: Coast Broadcasting Ltd
Editorial: 95 Bonaventure Ave Suite 201, St. John's, Newfoundland A1B 2X5 **Tel:** 1 709 754-6748.
Email: onair@coast1011.com
Web site: http://www.coast1011.com
Profile: CKSJ-FM is a commercial station owned by Coast Broadcasting Ltd. The format for the station is adult contemporary. CKSJ-FM broadcasts to the St. John's, Newfoundland area at 101.1 FM.
FM RADIO STATION

CKSL-AM 47229
Owner: Astral Media
Editorial: 743 Wellington Road South, London, Ontario N6C 4R5 **Tel:** 1 519 686-2525.
Email: mailbag@am1410.ca
Web site: http://www.funny1410.ca
Profile: CKSL-AM is a commercial radio station owned by Astral Media. The format of the station is comedy. CKSL-AM broadcasts to London, Ontario at 1410 AM.
AM RADIO STATION

CKSQ-FM 47191
Owner: Newcap Radio
Editorial: 4812A 50 Ave, Stettler, Alberta T0C 2L2
Tel: 1 403 742-1400.
Email: Q933@newcap.ca
Web site: http://www.q933.ca
Profile: CKSQ-FM is a commercial station owned by Newcap Radio. The format of the station is contemporary country. CKSQ-FM broadcasts to the Stettler, Alberta area at 93.3FM.
FM RADIO STATION

CKSR-FM 47106
Owner: Rogers Communications Inc.
Editorial: 46167 Yale Rd, Unit 309, Chilliwack, British Columbia V2P 2N2 **Tel:** 1 604 795-5711.
Email: starnews@starfm.rogers.com
Web site: http://www.starfm.com
Profile: CKSR-FM is a commercial station owned by Rogers Communications Inc. The format of the station is adult contemporary. CKSR-FM broadcasts to Chilliwack, British Columbia at 98.3 FM.
FM RADIO STATION

CKSS-FM 47767
Owner: Newfoundland Broadcasting Co. Ltd.
Editorial: 446 Logy Bay Road, St. John's, Newfoundland A1C 5S2 **Tel:** 1 709 726-2922.
Email: ntv@ntv.ca
Web site: http://www.ozfm.com
FM RADIO STATION

CKST-AM 47156
Owner: Bell Media
Editorial: 500-969 Robson St 500, Vancouver, British Columbia V6Z 1X5 **Tel:** 1 604 280-8326.
Web site: http://www.tsnradiovancouver.ca
Profile: CKST-AM is a commercial station owned by Bell Media. The format of the station is sports. CKST-AM broadcasts to the Vancouver, British Columbia area at 1040 AM.
AM RADIO STATION

CKSW-AM 47237
Owner: Golden West Broadcasting Ltd.
Editorial: 134 Central Avenue North, Swift Current, Saskatchewan S9H 0L1 **Tel:** 1 306 773-4605.
Email: scnews@goldenwestradio.com
Web site: http://www.ckswradio.ca
Profile: CKSW-AM is a commercial station owned by Golden West Broadcasting Ltd. The format of the station is classic country music. CKSW-AM broadcasts to the Swift Current, Saskatchewan area at 570 AM.
AM RADIO STATION

CKSY-FM 47463
Owner: Blackburn Radio Inc.
Editorial: 117 Keil Drive South, Chatham, Ontario N7M 3H3 **Tel:** 1 519 354-2200.
Email: info@943cksy.com
Web site: http://943cksy.com
Profile: CKSY-FM is a commercial station owned by Blackburn Radio Inc. The format of the station is adult contemporary. CKSY-FM broadcasts to Chatham, Ontario at 94.3 FM.
FM RADIO STATION

CKTB-AM 47334
Owner: Bell Media
Editorial: 12 Yates St, St Catharines, Ontario L2R 5R2
Tel: 1 905 684-1174.
Email: newsroom@610cktb.com
Web site: http://www.610cktb.com
Profile: CKTB-AM is a commercial station owned by Bell Media. The format of the station is news and talk. CKTB-AM broadcasts to the St. Catharines, Ontario area at 610 AM. Twitter handle: twitter.com/610CKTB
AM RADIO STATION

CKTF-FM 47609
Owner: Bell Media
Editorial: 15 Rue Taschereau, Gatineau, Quebec J8Y 2V6 **Tel:** 1 819 243-5555.
Web site: http://www.gatineau.radioenergie.ca/
Profile: CKTF-FM is a commercial station owned by Bell Media. The format of the station is Top 40/CHR.

CKTF-FM broadcasts to the Gatineau, Quebec area at 104.1 FM.
FM RADIO STATION

CKTG-FM 47789
Owner: Acadia Broadcasting Ltd.
Editorial: 180 Park Ave Suite 200, Thunder Bay, Ontario P7B 6J4 **Tel:** 1 807 344-2000.
Email: country@country1053.ca
Web site: http://country1053.ca
Profile: CKTG-FM is a commercial station owned by Acadia Broadcasting Ltd. The format of the station is contemporary country. CKTG-FM broadcasts to the Thunder Bay, Ontario area at 105.3 FM.
FM RADIO STATION

CKTI-FM 489472
Owner: Points Eagle Radio
Editorial: 9111 W Ipperwash Rd, Unit 6 RR #2, Forest, Ontario N0N 1J0 **Tel:** 1 519 786-3883.
Email: info@eaglecountry.ca
Web site: http://www.eaglecountry.ca
Profile: CKTI-FM is a commercial station owned by Point's Eagle Radio. The format of the station is contemporary country, classic rock and oldies. CKTI-FM broadcasts to the Kettle Point, Ontario area at 107.7 FM.
FM RADIO STATION

CKTK-FM (EZ Rock 97.7 FM) 47121
Owner: Bell Media
Editorial: 4625 Lazelle Ave, Terrace, British Columbia V8G 1S4 **Tel:** 1 250 635-6316.
Web site: http://www.iheartradio.ca/ez-rock/ez-rock-kitimat
Profile: CKTK-FM is a commercial station owned by Bell Media. The format of the station is hot adult contemporary. CKTK-FM broadcasts to Terrace, British Columbia and surrounding communities at 101.9 FM.
FM RADIO STATION

CKTO-FM 47594
Owner: Bell Media
Editorial: 187 Industrial Ave, Truro, Nova Scotia B2N 6V3 **Tel:** 1 902 893-6060.
Email: truronewsroom@bellmedia.ca
Web site: http://www.bigdog1009.ca
Profile: CKTO-FM is a commercial station owned by Bell Media. The format of the station is adult contemporary. CKTO-FM broadcasts to Truro, Nova Scotia at 100.9 FM.
FM RADIO STATION

CKTP-FM 155497
Owner: CKTP Radio Inc.
Editorial: 150 Cliffe Street, Box R13, Fredericton, New Brunswick E3A 0A1 **Tel:** 1 506 474-2795.
Email: info@957thewolf.ca
Web site: http://cktpradio.com
Profile: CKTP-FM is a commercial station owned by CKTP Radio Inc. The format of the station is rock and blues. CKTP-FM broadcasts to the Fredericton, New Brunswick area at 95.7 FM.
FM RADIO STATION

CKTY-FM 47315
Owner: Astral Media
Editorial: 187 Industrial Ave, Truro, Nova Scotia B2N 6V3 **Tel:** 1 902 893-6060.
Email: truronewsroom@bellmedia.ca
Web site: http://www.catcountry995.ca
FM RADIO STATION

CKUA-AM 47370
Owner: CKUA Radio Foundation
Editorial: 9804 Jasper Ave NW Fl 4TH, Edmonton, Alberta T5J 0C5 **Tel:** 1 780 428-7595.
Email: newsfeed949@yahoo.com
Web site: http://www.ckua.com
Profile: CKUA-AM is a commercial station owned by CKUA Radio Foundation. The format for the station is variety. CKUA-AM broadcasts to the Edmonton, Alberta area at 580 AM.
AM RADIO STATION

CKUA-FM 47876
Owner: CKUA Radio Foundation
Editorial: 9804 Jasper Ave NW, Edmonton, Alberta T5J 0C5 **Tel:** 1 780 428-7595.
Web site: http://www.ckua.com
Profile: CKUA-FM is a non-commercial station owned by CKUA Radio Foundation. The station features an eclectic mix of music including jazz, blues, pop, world music, folk, country and classical. CKUA-FM broadcasts to listeners throughout Edmonton, Alberta at 94.9 FM.
FM RADIO STATION

CKUE-FM 70484
Owner: Blackburn Radio Inc.
Editorial: 2090 Wyandotte St E, Windsor, Ontario N8Y 5B2 **Tel:** 1 519 944-4400.
Email: info@canadasrock.ca
Web site: http://windsor.coolradio.ca
Profile: CKUE-FM is a commercial station owned by Blackburn Radio Inc. The format of the station is classic rock. CKUE-FM broadcasts to the Windsor, Ontario area at 95.1 FM.
FM RADIO STATION

CKUJ-FM (Kuujjuaq 97.3) 47785
Owner: Société Kuujjuamiut
Editorial: Kuujjuaq, Quebec **Tel:** 1 819 964-2921.
Profile: CKUJ-FM is a commercial station owned by Société Kuujjuamiut. The format for the station is variety. CKUJ-AM broadcasts to Kuujjuaq, Quebec area at 97.3 FM.
FM RADIO STATION

CKUL-FM 47565
Owner: Newfoundland Capital Corporation Limited
Editorial: 3770 Kempt Rd, Halifax, Nova Scotia B3K 4X8- **Tel:** 1 902 453-4004.
Web site: http://www.mix965.ca/
Profile: CKUL-FM is a commercial station owned by Newfoundland Capital Corporation Limited. The format of the station is Hot AC. CKUL-FM broadcasts to Halifax, Nova Scotia at 96.5 FM.
FM RADIO STATION

CKUM-FM 47766
Owner: Medias Acadiens Universitaires Inc.(Les)
Editorial: Centre Etudiant 2e etage, Universite de Moncton, Moncton, New Brunswick E1A 3E9
Tel: 1 506 858-4485.
Web site: http://ckum935.com
Profile: CKUM-FM is a commercial station owned by Les Medias Acadiens Universitaires Inc. The format of the station is Top 40/CHR. CKUM-FM broadcasts to the Moncton, New Brunswick area at 93.5 FM.
FM RADIO STATION

CKUT-FM 47575
Owner: McGill Radio Inc.
Editorial: 3647 University Street, 2nd Floor, Montreal, Quebec H3A 2B3 **Tel:** 1 514 448-4041 8992.
Email: news@ckut.ca
Web site: http://www.ckut.ca
Profile: CKUT-FM is a non-commercial station owned by McGill Radio Inc. The format for the station is college variety. CKUT-FM broadcasts to the Montreal, Quebec area at 90.3 FM.
FM RADIO STATION

CKUV-FM 156601
Owner: Golden West Broadcasting Ltd.
Editorial: 42 McRay St., 2nd Floor, Okotoks, Alberta T1S 1B7 **Tel:** 1 403 995-9611.
Email: foothillsnews@goldenwestradio.com
Web site: http://theeagle1009.com
Profile: CKUV-FM is a commercial station owned by Golden West Broadcasting Ltd. The format of the station is classic hits music. CKUV-FM broadcasts to the High River, Alberta area at 100.9 FM.
FM RADIO STATION

CKUW-FM 83135
Owner: Winnipeg Campus Community Radio Society
Editorial: 515 Portage Rm #4CM11, University of Winnipeg, Winnipeg, Manitoba R3B 2E9
Tel: 1 204 786-9782.
Email: ckuwnews@rocketmail.com
Web site: http://www.ckuw.ca
Profile: CKUW-FM is a non-commercial station owned by the Winnipeg Campus Community Radio Society. The format is college variety. CKUW-FM broadcasts to the University of Winnipeg and the surrounding community of Winnipeg, Manitoba at 95.9 FM. Twitter Handle: http://twitter.com/ckuw
FM RADIO STATION

CKVH-FM 47393
Owner: Newfoundland Capital Corporation Limited
Editorial: 4833 52 Ave, High Prairie, Alberta T0G 1E0
Tel: 1 780 523-5120.
Email: news@prairiefm.ca
Web site: http://www.prairiefm.ca
Profile: CKVH-FM is a commercial station owned by Newfoundland Capital Corporation Limited. The format of the station is classic hits. CKVH-FM broadcasts to the High Prairie, Alberta area at 93.5 FM.
FM RADIO STATION

CKVI-FM 585870
Owner: KCVI Educational Radio Station Inc.
Editorial: 235 Frontenac St., Room 119, Kingston, Ontario K7L 3S7 **Tel:** 1 613 544-7864.
Email: ckvi@limestone.on.ca
Web site: http://www.thecave.ca
Profile: CKVI-FM is a non-commercial station owned by KCVI Educational Radio Station Inc. The format of the station is variety. CKVI-FM broadcasts to the Kingston, Ontario area at 91.9 FM.
FM RADIO STATION

CKVL-FM (LaSalle 100.1) 585881
Owner: La radio communautaire de LaSalle
Editorial: 55 Av Dupras, 3rd fl, Lasalle, Quebec H8R 4A8 **Tel:** 1 514 360-2585.
Email: info@100-1fm.com
Web site: http://www.100-1fm.com
Profile: CKVL-FM est une station non-commerciale, une propriété de La radio communautaire de LaSalle. Le format de la station est le variété. CKVL-FM est diffusée à LaSalle, Quebec au 100.1 FM.

CKVL-FM is a non-commercial station owned by La radio communautaire de LaSalle. The format of the station is variety. CKVL-FM broadcasts to the LaSalle, Quebec area at 100.1 FM.
FM RADIO STATION

CKVM-FM 47806
Owner: Radio Temiscamingue Inc.
Editorial: 62 Rue Sainte-Anne, Ville-Marie, Quebec J9V 2B7 **Tel:** 1 819 629-2710.
Email: ckvm@ckvmfm.com
Web site: http://http.www.ckvm.qc.ca
Profile: CKVM-FM est une radio commerciale de Radio Témiscamingue Inc. La station diffuse sur Ville-Marie et ses environs à la fréquence 93.2FM.

CKVM-FM is a commercial station owned by Radio Temiscamingue Inc. The format of the station is adult contemporary. CKVM-FM broadcasts to the Ville-Marie, Quebec area at 93.1 FM.
FM RADIO STATION

CKVO-AM 47322
Owner: NewCap Broadcasting
Editorial: 391 Kenmount Rd, St. John's, Newfoundland A1B 3P9 **Tel:** 1 709 726-5590.
Web site: http://www.vocm.com
Profile: CKVO-AM is a commercial station owned by NewCap Broadcasting. The format of the station is country music. CKVO-AM broadcasts to the St. John's, NL area at 710 AM.
AM RADIO STATION

CKVX-FM 588463
Owner: Golden West Broadcasting Ltd.
Editorial: 404 12 Ave E, Kindersley, Saskatchewan S0L 1S0 **Tel:** 1 306 463-2692.
Web site: http://www.mix1049fm.ca
Profile: CKVX-FM is a commerical station owned by Golden West Broadcasting Ltd. The format of the station is adult contemporary. CKVX-FM broadcasts to the Kindersley, Saskatchewan area at 104.9 FM.
FM RADIO STATION

CKWB-FM 47197
Owner: Newfoundland Capital Corporation Limited
Editorial: 17-10030 106 Street, Westlock, Alberta T7P 2K4 **Tel:** 1 780 349-4421.
Web site: http://www.realcountrywestlock.ca
Profile: CKWB-FM is a commercial station owned by Newfoundland Capital Corporation Limited. The format of the station is contemporary country. CKWB-FM broadcasts in the Westlock, Alberta area at 97.9 FM.
FM RADIO STATION

CKWE-FM (Maniwaki 103.9) 588431
Owner: Mohawk Nation Radio
Editorial: 3 chemin Kikinamage Mikan, Maniwaki, Quebec J9E 3C9 **Tel:** 1 819 449-5097.
Email: ckwe.radio@gmail.com
Profile: CKWE-FM est une station commercial, une propriété de Mohawk Nation Radio. Le format de la station est le variété. CKWE-FM est diffusée à Maniwaki, Québec au 103.9 FM. La programmation de la station est en anglais, français et en algonquin.

CKWE-FM is a commercial station owned by Mohawk Nation Radio. The format of the station is variety. CKWE-FM broadcasts to the Maniwaki, Quebec area at 103.9 FM. The station has programming in English, French and Algonquin.
FM RADIO STATION

CKWF-FM 47530
Owner: Corus Entertainment Inc.
Editorial: 159 King St, Peterborough, Ontario K9J 2R8
Tel: 1 705 748-6101.
Email: info@thewolf.ca
Web site: http://www.thewolf.ca
Profile: CKWF-FM is a commercial station owned by Corus Entertainment Inc. The format of the station is rock/album-oriented rock. CKWF-FM broadcasts to the Peterborough, Ontario area at 101.5 FM.
FM RADIO STATION

CKWL-AM 47391
Owner: Vista Broadcast Group Inc.
Editorial: 83 First Ave S, Williams Lake, British Columbia V2G 1H4 **Tel:** 1 250 392-6551.
Email: cariboonews@vistaradio.ca
Web site: http://www.mycariboonow.com
Profile: CKWL-AM is a commercial station owned by Vista Broadcast Group Inc. The format of the station is contemporary country and Southern rock. CKWL-AM broadcasts to the Williams Lake, British Columbia area at 570 AM.
AM RADIO STATION

CKWM-FM 47556
Owner: Maritime Broadcasting System Ltd.
Editorial: 29 Oakdene Ave, Kentville, Nova Scotia B4N 1H5 **Tel:** 1 902 678-2111.
Email: magic949@magic949.ca
Web site: http://www.magic949.ca
Profile: CKWM-FM is commercial station owned by Maritime Broadcasting System Ltd. The format of the station is adult contemporary and classic hits. CKWM-FM broadcasts to Kentville, Nova Scotia and surrounding communities at 94.9 FM.
FM RADIO STATION

CKWR-FM 47622
Owner: Wired World Inc.
Editorial: 375 University Avenue East, Waterloo, Ontario N2K 3M7 **Tel:** 1 519 886-9870.
Email: general@ckwr.com
Web site: http://www.ckwr.com
Profile: CKWR-FM is a commercial station owned by Wired World Inc. The format of the station is adult contemporary and multicultural programming. CKWR-FM broadcasts to Waterloo, Ontario at 98.5 FM.
FM RADIO STATION

CKWS-FM 47221
Owner: Corus Entertainment Inc.
Editorial: 170 Queen St, Kingston, Ontario K7K 1B2
Tel: 1 613 544-2340.
Email: newswatch@corusent.com
Web site: http://www.ckwsfm.com
Profile: CKWS-FM is a commercial station owned by Corus Entertainment Inc. The format of the station is classic hits. CKWS-FM broadcasts to the Kingston, Ontario area at 104.3 FM.
FM RADIO STATION

CKWT-FM (Wawatay Radio Network 89.9 FM) 47874
Owner: Wawatay Native Communications Society
Tel: 1 807 737-2951.
Web site: http://www.wawatay.on.ca
Profile: CKWT-FM is a non-commercial station owned by Wawatay Native Communications Society. The format for the station is news. CKWT-FM broadcasts to the Sioux Lookout, Ontario area at 89.9 FM.
FM RADIO STATION

CKWV-FM 47765
Owner: Jim Pattison Broadcast Group(The)
Editorial: 4550 Wellington Road, Nanaimo, British Columbia V9T 2H3 **Tel:** 1 250 758-1131.
Email: info@1023thewave.com
Web site: http://www.1023thewave.com
Profile: CKWV-FM is a commercial station owned by The Jim Pattison Broadcast Group. The format of the station is adult contemporary. CKWV-FM broadcasts to the Nanaimo, British Columbia area at 102.3 FM.
FM RADIO STATION

CKWW-AM (AM 580) 47335
Owner: Bell Media
Editorial: 1640 Ouellette Ave, Windsor, Ontario N8X 1L1- **Tel:** 1 519 258-8888.
Web site: http://www.iheartradio.ca/am-580
Profile: CKWW-AM (AM 580) is a commercial station owned by Bell Media. The format of the station is oldies. CKWW-AM broadcasts to Windsor, Ontario and the Detroit area at 580 AM.
AM RADIO STATION

CKWX-AM (News 1130) 47157
Owner: Rogers Communications Inc.
Editorial: 2440 Ash St, Vancouver, British Columbia V5Z 4J6 **Tel:** 1 604 873-2599.
Email: news1130@news1130.rogers.com
Web site: http://www.news1130.com
Profile: CKWX-AM (News 1130) is a commercial radio station owned by Rogers Communications Inc. The format of the station is news, talk and sports programming. CKWX-AM broadcasts to the Vancouver, BC area at 1130 AM.
AM RADIO STATION

CKWY-FM 355361
Owner: Newfoundland Capital Corporation Limited
Editorial: 1037 2nd Ave, 2nd Floor, Wainwright, Alberta T9W 1K7 **Tel:** 1 780 842-4311.
Web site: http://www.waynefm.com
Profile: CKWY-FM is a commercial station owned by Newfoundland Capital Corporation Limited. The format of the station is adult contemporary. CKWY-FM broadcasts to Wainwright, Alberta and its environs at 93.7 FM.
FM RADIO STATION

CKXA-FM 70480
Owner: Astral Media
Editorial: 2940 Victoria Ave, Brandon, Manitoba R7B 3Y3 **Tel:** 1 204 728-1150.
Email: psabrandon@astral.com
Web site: http://www.101thefarm.ca/
Profile: CKXA-FM is a commercial station owned by Astral Media. The format of the station is classic country. CKXA-FM broadcasts in the Brandon, Manitoba area at 101.1 FM.
FM RADIO STATION

CKXC-FM 47796
Owner: Rogers Communications Inc.
Editorial: 863 Princess St Suite 301, Kingston, Ontario K7L 5N4 **Tel:** 1 613 549-1057.
Web site: http://www.country935.ca
Profile: CKXC-FM is a commercial station owned by Rogers Communications Inc. The format of the station is contemporary country. CKXC-FM broadcasts to the Kingston, Ontario area at 93.5 FM.
FM RADIO STATION

CKXD-FM 83147
Owner: Newfoundland Capital Corporation Limited
Editorial: 105 Roe Ave, Gander, Newfoundland A1V 1X2 **Tel:** 1 709 651-3650.
Email: ckxdnews@vocm.com
Web site: http://www.987krock.com
Profile: CKXD-FM is a commercial station owned by Newfoundland Capital Corporation Limited. The format of the station is classic rock. CKXD-FM broadcasts to the Gander, Newfoundland area at 98.7 FM.
FM RADIO STATION

CKX-FM 47494
Owner: Bell Media
Editorial: 2940 Victoria Ave, Brandon, Manitoba R7B 3Y3 **Tel:** 1 204 728-1150.
Email: brandonnews@astral.com
Web site: http://www.kx96online.com
Profile: CKX-FM is a commercial station owned by Bell Media. The format of the station is album-oriented rock. CKX-FM broadcasts to Brandon, Manitoba at 96.1 FM.
FM RADIO STATION

CKXG-FM 47301
Owner: Steele Communications
Editorial: 35-A Grenfell Heights, Grand Falls-Windsor, Newfoundland A2A 2K2 **Tel:** 1 709 489-2192.
Email: grandfallswindsor@vocm.com
Profile: CKXG-FM is a commercial station owned by Steele Communications. The format is adult contemporary. The station airs at 102.3 FM in the Grand Falls-Windsor, Newfoundland area.
FM RADIO STATION

CKXL-FM 47764
Owner: La Radio Communautaire du Manitoba Inc.
Editorial: 340 boul Provencher, Saint-Boniface, Manitoba R2H 0G7 **Tel:** 1 204 233-4243.
Email: info@envol91.mb.ca
Web site: http://www.envol91.mb.ca
Profile: CKXL-FM is a non-commercial station owned by La Radio Communautaire du Manitoba Inc. The format of the station is variety. CKXL-FM broadcasts to the Saint-Boniface, Manitoba area at 91.1 FM.
FM RADIO STATION

CKXM-FM (90.5 myFM) 603146
Owner: My Broadcasting Corporation
Editorial: 145 Thames Rd W Unit 6, Exeter, Ontario N0M 1S3 **Tel:** 1 519 235-3000.
Email: news905@myfmradio.ca
Web site: http://www.exetertoday.ca
Profile: CKXM-FM is a commercial station owned by My Broadcasting Corporation. The format of the station is adult contemporary. CKXM-FM's tagline is "MyFM." CKXM-FM broadcasts to the Exeter, Ontario area at 90.5 FM.
FM RADIO STATION

CKXO-FM 47408
Owner: RNC Media
Editorial: 568 boul St Joseph, Roberval, Quebec G8H 2K6 **Tel:** 1 418 275-1831.
Web site: http://chibougamau.planeteradio.ca
FM RADIO STATION

CKXR-FM 47141
Owner: Bell Media
Editorial: 360 Ross St, Salmon Arm, British Columbia V1E 4N2 **Tel:** 1 250 832-2161.
Email: webmaster@myezrock.com
Web site: http://www.salmonarm.myezrock.com
Profile: CKXR-FM is a commercial station owned by Bell Media. The format of the station is adult contemporary music. CKXR-FM broadcasts to the Salmon Arm, British Columbia area at 91.5 FM.
FM RADIO STATION

CKXS-FM (99.1 FM) 605591
Owner: Five Amigos Broadcasting Inc.
Editorial: 520 James St, Wallaceburg, Ontario N8A 2N9 **Tel:** 1 519 627-0007.
Email: news@ckxsfm.com
Web site: http://www.ckxsfm.com
Profile: CKXS-FM is a commercial station owned by Five Amigos Broadcasting Inc. The format of the station is adult contemporary. CKXS-FM broadcasts to the Wallaceburg, ON area at 99.1 FM.
FM RADIO STATION

CKXU-FM 83100
Owner: CKXU Radio Society
Editorial: SU-164 University Drive West, University of Lethbridge, Lethbridge, Alberta T1K 3M4
Tel: 1 403 329-2335.
Email: manager@ckxu.com
Web site: http://www.ckxu.com
Profile: CKXU-FM is a non-commercial college station owned by CKXU Radio Society. The format of the station is college variety. CKXU-FM broadcast to the Lethbridge, Alberta area at 88.3 FM.
FM RADIO STATION

CKXX-FM 47773
Owner: Newfoundland Capital Corporation Limited
Editorial: 345 O'Connell Dr, Corner Brook, Newfoundland A2H 7V3 **Tel:** 1 709 634-4570.
Email: cfcb.news@vocm.com
Web site: http://www.k-rock1039.com
Profile: CKXX-FM is a commercial station owned by Newfoundland Capital Corporation Limited. The format of the station is classic rock. CKXX-FM broadcasts to the Corner Brook, Newfoundland area at 103.9 FM.
FM RADIO STATION

CKYC-FM (Country 93) 83084
Owner: Bayshore Broadcasting Corp.
Editorial: 270 Ninth Street East, Owen Sound, Ontario N4K 5P5 **Tel:** 1 519 376-2030.
Email: country93@bayshorebroadcasting.ca
Web site: http://www.country93.ca
Profile: CKYC-FM is a commercial station owned by Bayshore Broadcasting Corp. The format for the station is contemporary country. CKYC-FM broadcasts to the Owen Sound, Ontario area at 93.7 FM.
FM RADIO STATION

CKYE-FM 558841
Owner: South Asian Broadcasting
Editorial: #201 8383A 128th St, Surrey, British Columbia V3W 4G1 **Tel:** 1 604 598-9311.
Email: info@redfm.ca
Web site: http://www.redfm.ca
Profile: CKYE-FM is a commercial station owned by South Asian Broadcasting. The format of the station is variety, featuring ethnic and multicultural programming. CKYE-FM broadcasts to the Vancouver, British Columbia area at 93.1 FM.
FM RADIO STATION

CKY-FM 47280
Owner: Rogers Communications Inc.
Editorial: 166 Osborne Street, Unit 4, Winnipeg, Manitoba R3L 1Y8 **Tel:** 1 204 788-3400.
Web site: http://www.102clearfm.com
Profile: CKY-FM is a commercial station owned by Rogers Communications Inc. The format of the station is adult contemporary music. CKY-FM broadcasts in the Winnipeg, Manitoba area at 102.3 FM.
FM RADIO STATION

CKYK-FM (KYK 95.7 Radio X Saguenay) 47763
Owner: RNC Media
Editorial: 345 Rue des Sagueneens Loc 160, Chicoutimi, Quebec G7H 6T1 **Tel:** 1 418 543-8912.
Web site: http://www.kykradiox.com
Profile: CKYK-FM KYK 95.7 Radio X Saguenay est une station commerciale, détenue par RNC Média. Le genre de la station est rock. CKYK-FM est diffusé au Saguenay, Québec à 95.7 FM.

CKYK-FM KYK 95.7 Radio X Saguenay is a commercial station owned by RNC Media. The format of the station is rock. CKYK-FM broadcasts to Saguenay, Quebec at 95.7 FM.
FM RADIO STATION

CKYL-AM 47144
Owner: Peace River Broadcasting Corp.
Tel: 1 780 624-2535.
Email: news@ylcountry.com
Web site: http://www.ylcountry.com
Profile: CKYL-AM is a commercial station owned by Peace River Broadcasting Corp. The format of the station is classic country music. CKYL-AM broadcasts throughout Peace River, Alberta at 610 AM.
AM RADIO STATION

CKYM-FM (88.7 myFM) 502014
Owner: My Broadcasting Corporation
Editorial: 20 Market Sq, Napanee, Ontario K7R 1J3
Tel: 1 613 354-4554.
Email: news887@myfmradio.ca
Web site: http://www.napaneetoday.ca
Profile: CKYM-FM is a commercial station owned by My Broadcasting Corporation. The format of the station is adult contemporary. CKYM-FM broadcasts to the Napanee, Ontario area at 88.7 FM.
FM RADIO STATION

CKYQ-FM 47762
Owner: 176100 Canada Inc.
Editorial: 1646 Av Saint-Laurent, Plessisville, Quebec G6L 2P6 **Tel:** 1 819 362-3737.
Email: studio@kyqfm.com
Web site: http://kyqfm.com/
Profile: CKYQ-FM est un radio d'Attraction Radio proposant un format adulte contemporain, diffusant sur le 95.7 pour les gens de Plessisville et des environs.

CKYQ-FM is a commercial station owned by Attraction Radio. The format of the station is hot adult contemporary. CKYQ-FM broadcasts to Plessisville, Quebec at 95.7 FM.
FM RADIO STATION

CKYX-FM 47481
Owner: Rogers Communications Inc.
Editorial: 9912 Franklin Ave, Fort McMurray, Alberta T9H 2K5- **Tel:** 1 780 743-2246.
Web site: http://www.rock979.ca
Profile: CKYX-FM is a commercial station owned by Rogers Communications Inc. The format of the station is classic rock and rock/album oriented. CKYX-FM broadcasts to the Fort McMurray, Alberta area at 97.9 FM.
FM RADIO STATION

CKZZ-FM (Z95.3) 47445
Owner: Newcap Radio
Editorial: 20-11151 Horseshoe Way 20, Richmond, British Columbia V7A 4S5 **Tel:** 1 604 241-2100.
Web site: http://www.z953.ca
Profile: CKZZ-FM is a commercial station owned by Newcap Radio. The format of the station is hot adult contemporary. CKZZ-FM broadcasts to the Richmond, British Columbia area at 95.3 FM.
FM RADIO STATION

Corus Radio Network 70308
Editorial: 25 Dockside Dr, corus quay, Toronto, Ontario M5A 0B5 **Tel:** 1 416 479-7000.
Web site: http://www.corusent.com
Profile: Network featuring programming and specials revolving around the world of rock music and its personalities. The network specializes in premier properties for radio, nationally sponsored, major market coverage, created, produced and distributed coast to coast.
RADIO NETWORK

CPWA-FM 446017
Owner: CPWA, Inc.
Editorial: 62 Nassau St, Toronto, Ontario M5T 1M2
Tel: 1 416 596-1566.
Email: asasdo1@bellnet.ca
Web site: http://www.asasdoatlantico.com
Profile: CPWA-FM is a commercial station owned by CPWA, Inc. The format of the station is news, talk, sports and ethnic programming. CPWA-FM broadcasts to the Toronto area at 90.7 FM.
FM RADIO STATION

CRFM-FM 83130
Owner: Canadore College
Editorial: 100 College Dr, Canadore College, North Bay, Ontario P1B 8K9 **Tel:** 1 705 474-7601.
Web site: http://www.thepanther.ca
Profile: CRFM-FM is a non-commercial college station owned by Canadore College. The format of the station is Top 40/CHR. CRFM-FM broadcasts to the North Bay, Ontario area at a frequency of 89.9 FM.
FM RADIO STATION

CRNC-FM 83131
Owner: Niagara College
Editorial: 300 Woodlawn Road, Niagara College, Welland, Ontario L3C 7L3 **Tel:** 1 905 735-2211.
Web site: http://www.broadcasting.niagaracollege.ca
Profile: CRNC-FM is a non-commercial station owned by Niagara College. The format of the station is variety. CRNC-FM broadcasts to the Welland, Ontario area at 90.1 FM.
FM RADIO STATION

CSCR-FM (Fusion Radio 90.3 FM) 83132
Owner: SCCR Inc.
Editorial: 1265 Military Trail, sl 213, Toronto, Ontario M1C 1A4 **Tel:** 1 416 287-7051.
Email: info@fusionradio.ca
Web site: http://www.fusionradio.ca
Profile: CSCR-FM (Fusion Radio 90.3 FM) is a non-commercial station owned by SCCR Inc. The format of the station is variety. CSCR-FM broadcasts to the Scarborough, Ontario area at 90.3 FM.
FM RADIO STATION

Fairchild Radio Network 139314
Owner: Fairchild Radio Ltd.
Editorial: 135 E Beaver Creek Road, Unit 8, Richmond Hill, Ontario L4B 1E2 **Tel:** 1 905 763-3350.
Web site: http://www.fairchildradio.com
Profile: Fairchild Media Group's Chinese language radio operations across the country offer their audiences a varied fare of news and talk radio to serial mini dramas and pop music. Full service radio network programming in more than 18 languages. Offers over 90 hours of Chinese programs every week, featuring a wide array of formats ranging from news, current affairs, everyday information talk show, entertainment, music, and more.
RADIO NETWORK

ICI Musique 83164
Owner: Société Radio-Canada
Editorial: 1400 Boul Rene-Levesque E, Montreal, Quebec H2L 2M2- **Tel:** 1 514 597-6000.
Email: liaison@radio-canada.ca
Profile: Ici Musique est le réseau musical français de Radio-Canada. Il s'agit d'une société publique créée par la Loi sur la radiodiffusion du Parlement canadien. Radio-Canada Réseau Espace Musique propose une grande variété de programmes musicaux, presque tous canadiens et sans publicité commerciale. Ici Musique is the French music network of Radio-Canada. It is a publicly-owned corporation established by the Canadian Parliament's Broadcasting Act. Radio-Canada Réseau Espace Musique features a wide variety of musical programming, nearly all Canadian and free of commercial advertising.
RADIO NETWORK

ICI Radio-Canada Première 70636
Owner: Société Radio-Canada
Editorial: 1400 Boul Rene-Levesque E, Montreal, Quebec H2L 2M2- **Tel:** 1 514 597-6000.
Email: nouvelles@radio-canada.ca
Web site: http://ici.radio-canada.ca/premiere
Profile: Ici Radio-Canada Première est le seul réseau francophone à offrir une programmation entièrement canadienne à heure de grande écoute. Le réseau de radio francophone découle de l'adoption de la Loi sur la radiodiffusion par le parlement canadien. La programmation offerte par le réseau tente d'être le reflet de la réalité et de la diversité canadienne en plus de fournir de l'information sur des sujets et nouvelles pertinents.

Ici Radio-Canada Première is the only French language network offering a predominantly Canadian primetime schedule. The French radio network was established as a result of the Canadian Parliament's Broadcasting Act. The network's programming tells stories reflecting the reality and diversity of Canada and provides information about relevant and interesting news and issues.
RADIO NETWORK

ICI Radio-Canada Première - Charlottetown Bureau 364372
Editorial: 430 Av University, Charlottetown, Prince Edward Island C1A 4N6 **Tel:** 1 902 629-6400.
Web site: http://ici.radio-canada.ca/acadie/ile-du-prince-edouard
Profile: Charlottetown Bureau for Radio-Canada Réseau La Première Chaîne.
RADIO NETWORK

ICI Radio-Canada Première - Chicoutimi Bureau 364382
Editorial: 500 Rue des Sagueneens, Chicoutimi, Quebec G7H 6N4 **Tel:** 1 418 696-6600.
Web site: http://www.radio-canada.ca/regions/saguenay-lac/index.shtml
RADIO NETWORK

ICI Radio-Canada Première - Edmonton Bureau 70640
Editorial: 125 Edmonton City Centre NW, Edmonton, Alberta T5J 2Y8 **Tel:** 1 780 468-7500.
Web site: http://www.radio-canada.ca/regions/alberta
RADIO NETWORK

ICI Radio-Canada Première - Matane Bureau 364375
Editorial: 155 Rue Saint-Sacrement, Matane, Quebec G4W 1Y9 **Tel:** 1 418 562-0290.
Web site: http://www.radio-canada.ca/regions/gaspesie-lesiles/index.shtml
RADIO NETWORK

ICI Radio-Canada Première - Moncton Bureau 70637
Editorial: 250 avenue Universite, Moncton, New Brunswick E1C 8N8 **Tel:** 1 506 853-6666.
Email: infoacadie@radio-canada.ca
Web site: http://www.radio-canada.ca/atlantique
RADIO NETWORK

ICI Radio-Canada Première - Ottawa Bureau 364376
Editorial: 181 Rue Queen, Ottawa, Ontario K1P 1K9
Tel: 1 613 288-6000.
Email: nouvelles.ottawagatineau@radio-canada.ca
Web site: http://www.radio-canada.ca/regions/ottawa/index.shtml
Profile: Ottawa bureau for Radio-Canada La Première Chaîne.
RADIO NETWORK

ICI Radio-Canada Première - Quebec Bureau 70638
Editorial: 888 Boul. St-Jean, Quebec, Quebec G1R 5H6 **Tel:** 1 418 654-1341.
Web site: http://www.radio-canada.ca/regions/quebec
Profile: Quebec bureau of Radio-Canada's La Première Chaîne.
RADIO NETWORK

ICI Radio-Canada Première - Regina Bureau 70642
Editorial: 2440 Broad St, Regina, Saskatchewan S4P 0A5 **Tel:** 1 306 347-9540.
Web site: http://www.radio-canada.ca/regions/saskatchewan
RADIO NETWORK

ICI Radio-Canada Première - Rimouski Bureau 364380
Editorial: 273 Rue Saint-Jean-Baptiste O, Rimouski, Quebec G5L 4J7 **Tel:** 1 418 723-2217.
Email: nouvelles.rimouski@radio-canada.ca
Web site: http://www.radio-canada.ca/regions/bas-st-laurent/index.shtml
RADIO NETWORK

ICI Radio-Canada Première - Rouyn-Noranda Bureau 364381
Editorial: 70 Av Principale, Rouyn-Noranda, Quebec J9X 4P2 **Tel:** 1 819 762-8155.
Email: abitibi@radio-canada.ca
Web site: http://www.radio-canada.ca/regions/abitibi/index.shtml
RADIO NETWORK

ICI Radio-Canada Première - Saint-Boniface Bureau 70641
Editorial: 607 Rue Langevin, Winnipeg, Manitoba R2H 2W2 **Tel:** 1 204 788-3235.
Email: manitoba@radio-canada.ca
Web site: http://www.radio-canada.ca/regions/manitoba
RADIO NETWORK

ICI Radio-Canada Première - Sept-Iles Bureau 364384
Editorial: 350 Rue Smith Bureau 30, Sept-Iles, Quebec G4R 3X2 **Tel:** 1 418 968-0720.
Email: cbsi@radio-canada.ca
Web site: http://www.radio-canada.ca/regions/cote-nord/index.shtml
Profile: Radio-Canada Réseau La Première Chaîne - Sept-Iles Bureau est le bureau de Radio-Canada à Sept-Îles.

Radio-Canada Réseau La Première Chaîne - Sept-Iles Bureau is the bureau of Radio-Canada at Sept-Îles.
RADIO NETWORK

ICI Radio-Canada Première - Sherbrooke Bureau 364379
Editorial: 1335 Rue King O, Sherbrooke, Quebec J1J 2B8 **Tel:** 1 819 620-0000.
Web site: http://www.radio-canada.ca/regions/estrie/index.shtml
RADIO NETWORK

ICI Radio-Canada Première - Sudbury Bureau 364385
Editorial: 15 Rue MacKenzie, Sudbury, Ontario P3C 4Y1 **Tel:** 1 705 688-3200.
Web site: http://www.radio-canada.ca/regions/ontario/index.shtml
RADIO NETWORK

ICI Radio-Canada Première - Toronto Bureau 364386
Editorial: 205 Rue Wellington O, Toronto, Ontario M5V 3G7 **Tel:** 1 416 205-3700.
Email: tjontario@radio-canada.ca
Web site: http://www.radio-canada.ca/regions/ontario/index.shtml
Profile: Toronto bureau for Radio-Canada La Première Chaîne.
RADIO NETWORK

ICI Radio-Canada Première - Trois-Rivieres Bureau 364387
Editorial: 225 Rue des Forges Suite 101, Trois-Rivieres, Quebec G9A 2G7 **Tel:** 1 819 694-0114.
Web site: http://www.radio-canada.ca/regions/mauricie/index.shtml
RADIO NETWORK

ICI Radio-Canada Première - Vancouver Bureau 70639
Editorial: 700 Hamilton St, Vancouver, British Columbia V6B 2R5 **Tel:** 1 604 662-6000.
Email: tjcb@radio-canada.ca
Web site: http://www.radio-canada.ca/regions/colombie-Britannique
Profile: Radio-Canada Réseau La Première Chaîne bureau for British Columbia and Yukon.
RADIO NETWORK

ICI Radio-Canada Première - Windsor Bureau 706336
Editorial: 825 Riverside Dr O, Windsor, Ontario N9A 5K9 **Tel:** 1 519 255-3508.
Web site: http://www.radio-canada.ca/regions/ontario/index.shtml
Profile: Windsor, Ontario bureau for Radio-Canada Réseau La Première Chaîne.
RADIO NETWORK

Radio-Canada International 153169
Owner: Canadian Broadcasting Corp.
Editorial: 1400 Boul Rene-Levesque E, level b, Montreal, Quebec H2L 2M2 **Tel:** 1 514 597-7500.
Web site: http://www.rcinet.ca
Profile: Radio-Canada International est un réseau radio qui produit une grande variété de programmes quotidiens et hebdomadaires en anglais, français, espagnol, russe, ukrainien, portugais, mandarin et arabe. On diffuse également une sélection des programmes de CBC/Radio-Canada.

Radio-Canada International is a radio network that broadcasts a full range of daily and weekly programs in English, French, Spanish, Russian, Ukrainian, Portuguese, Mandarin and Arabic. It also broadcasts a selection of CBC/Radio-Canada programs.
RADIO NETWORK

SiriusXM Canada 377173
Owner: Sirius XM Canada Holdings Inc.
Editorial: 135 Liberty St, 4th fl, Toronto, Ontario M6K 1A7 **Tel:** 1 416 408-6000.
Web site: http://siriusxm.ca
Profile: SiriusXM Canada is a Sirius XM Canada is a Canadian radio broadcasting company, which operates as a Canadian affiliate of Sirius XM Radio. SiriusXM Canada is a digital audio platform that offers commercial-free music, sports, news, talk, entertainment and weather.
RADIO NETWORK

VOAR-AM 47299
Owner: Seventh-Day Adventist Church
Editorial: 1041 Topsail, Mt. Pearl, Newfoundland A1N 5E9 **Tel:** 1 709 745-8627.
Email: voar@voar.org
Web site: http://www.voar.org
Profile: VOAR-AM is a non-commercial station owned by the Seventh-Day Adventist Church. The format is contemporary Christian. VOAR-AM broadcasts to the Mt. Pearl, Newfoundland area at 1210 AM.
AM RADIO STATION

VOCM-AM 47324
Owner: Newfoundland Capital Corporation Limited
Editorial: 391 Kenmount Rd, St. John's, Newfoundland A1B 3P9 **Tel:** 1 709 726-5590.
Email: feedback@vocm.com
Web site: http://www.vocm.com
Profile: VOCM-AM is a commercial station owned by Newfoundland Capital Corporation Limited. The format of the station is news and talk. VOCM-AM broadcasts to Saint John's, Newfoundland at 590 AM.
AM RADIO STATION

VOCM-FM 47590
Owner: Newfoundland Capital Corporation Limited
Editorial: 391 Kenmount Rd, St. John's, Newfoundland A1B 3P9 **Tel:** 1 709 726-5590.
Email: email@krockrocks.com
Web site: http://www.k-rock975.com
Profile: VOCM-FM is a commercial station owned by Newfoundland Capital Corporation Limited. The format of the station is classic rock. VOCM-FM broadcasts to the Saint John's, Newfoundland area at 97.5 FM.
FM RADIO STATION

VOWR-AM 47325
Owner: Wesley United Church Radio Broadcasting
Editorial: 101 Patrick St., St. John's, Newfoundland A1E 5T9 **Tel:** 1 709 579-9233.
Email: vowr@vowr.org
Web site: http://www.vowr.org
Profile: VOWR-AM is a non-commercial station owned by Wesley United Church Radio Broadcasting. The format is variety and can be heard at 800 AM in the St. John's, Newfoundland area.
AM RADIO STATION

WLYK-FM 43265
Owner: Roger Radio
Editorial: 863 Princess Street, Ste 301, Kingston, Ontario K7L 5N4 **Tel:** 1 613 549-1057.
Web site: http://www.1027thelake.com
Profile: WLYK-FM is a commercial station owned by Roger Radio. The format of the station is adult contemporary. WLYK-FM broadcasts to the Watertown, NY area at 102.7 FM.
FM RADIO STATION

WTOR-AM (770AM) 36814
Owner: Birach Broadcasting Corp.
Editorial: 600 The East Mall Suite 400, Toronto, Ontario M9B 4B1 **Tel:** 1 248 557-3500.
Web site: http://www.birach.com/wtor.html
Profile: WTOR-AM is a commercial station owned by Birach Broadcasting Corp. The format of the station is variety, featuring ethnic brokered programming. WTOR-AM broadcasts to the Toronto, ON area at 770 AM.
AM RADIO STATION

Television

CBAFT-TV 33182
Owner: Société Radio-Canada
Editorial: 165 Rue Main Bureau 15, Moncton, New Brunswick E1C 1B8 **Tel:** 1 506 853-6666.
Email: infoacadie@radio-canada.ca
Web site: http://www.radio-canada.ca/Acadie
Profile: CBAFT-TV is the Radio-Canada affiliate for the Moncton, New Brunswick market. The station is owned by Societe Radio-Canada. CBAFT-TV broadcasts locally on channel 11.
TELEVISION STATION

CBAT-TV 33238
Owner: Canadian Broadcasting Corp.
Editorial: 1160 Regent St, Fredericton, New Brunswick E3B 3Z1 **Tel:** 1 506 451-4000.
Web site: http://www.cbc.ca/nb
Profile: CBAT-TV is a commercial television station owned by the Canadian Broadcasting Corp. CBAT-TV airs locally on channels 3 and 14.
TELEVISION STATION

CBC Television Network 63597
Owner: Canadian Broadcasting Corp.
Editorial: 250 Front St W, Toronto, Ontario M5V 3G5- **Tel:** 1 416 205-3311.
Email: yournews@cbc.ca
Web site: http://www.cbc.ca/television
Profile: The CBC serves as Canada's largest cultural institution, aiming to touch the lives of the country's citizens on a daily basis. Owned by all Canadians, the CBC has a heritage as the nation's supplier of Canadian cultural content and its nationwide presence sets the standard for excellence in Canadian broadcasting.
TELEVISION NETWORK

CBC Television Network - Calgary Bureau 231202
Editorial: 1724 Westmount Blvd NW, Calgary, Alberta T2N 3G7 **Tel:** 1 403 521-6000.
Email: calgarynewstips@cbc.ca
Web site: http://www.cbc.ca/calgary
TELEVISION NETWORK

CBC Television Network - Edmonton Bureau 70613
Editorial: 123 Edmonton City Centre, 10062-102 Ave, Edmonton, Alberta T5J 2Y8 **Tel:** 1 780 468-5555.
Email: cbx.edmonton@cbc.ca
Web site: http://www.cbc.ca/edmonton
TELEVISION NETWORK

CBC Television Network - Halifax Bureau 70616
Editorial: 6940 Mumford Road, Halifax, Nova Scotia B3L 0B7 **Tel:** 1 902 420-4100.
Email: cbcns@cbc.ca
Web site: http://www.cbc.ca/ns
Profile: Halifax, Nova Scotia bureau of the Canadian Broadcast Corp.
TELEVISION NETWORK

CBC Television Network - Los Angeles Bureau 623603
Editorial: 6255 W Sunset Blvd Ste 1500, Los Angeles, California 90028-7416
Web site: http://www.cbc.ca
TELEVISION NETWORK

CBC Television Network - Montreal Bureau 70619
Editorial: 1400 Rene-Levesque Blvd E Suite B96-50, Montreal, Quebec H2L 2M2 **Tel:** 1 514 597-6371.
Email: cbcnewsmontreal@cbc.ca
Web site: http://www.cbc.ca/montreal
Profile: It is the Montreal office for CBC Television Network.
TELEVISION NETWORK

CBC Television Network - New York Bureau 151987
Editorial: 745 3rd Ave, Ste 8C, New York, New York 10017 **Tel:** 1 212 546-0500.
TELEVISION NETWORK

CBC Television Network - Newfoundland and Labrador Bureau 70617
Tel: 1 709 576-5100.
Web site: http://www.cbc.ca/nl
Profile: Newfoundland and Labrador bureau of the CBC Television Network.
TELEVISION NETWORK

CBC Television Network - Ottawa Bureau 70612
Editorial: 181 Queen St, Ottawa, Ontario K1P 1K9 **Tel:** 1 613 288-6000.
Email: cbcnewsottawa@cbc.ca
Web site: http://www.cbc.ca/ottawa
Profile: CBC's Parliamentary Bureau in Ottawa, Ontario.
TELEVISION NETWORK

CBC Television Network - Vancouver Bureau 70614
Editorial: 700 Hamilton St, Vancouver, British Columbia V6B 2R5 **Tel:** 1 604 662-6000.
Email: cbcnewsvancouver@cbc.ca
Web site: http://www.cbc.ca/bc
Profile: CBC Television Vancouver, British Columbia bureau.
TELEVISION NETWORK

CBC Television Network - Washington Bureau 151988
Editorial: 529 14th St NW, Ste 500529, Washington, District Of Columbia 20045 **Tel:** 1 202 383-2900.
TELEVISION NETWORK

CBC Television Network - Winnipeg Bureau 70615
Editorial: 541 Portage Ave, Winnipeg, Manitoba R3B 2G1 **Tel:** 1 204 788-3222.
Email: radio893@cbc.ca
Web site: http://www.cbc.ca/manitoba
Profile: Manitoba bureau of the CBC Television.
TELEVISION NETWORK

CBC Television Network - Yellowknife Bureau 70618
Editorial: 5002 Forrest Drive, Yellowknife, Northwest Territories X1A 2N2 **Tel:** 1 867 920-5400.
Email: cbcnorth@cbc.ca
Web site: http://www.cbc.ca/north
TELEVISION NETWORK

CBCT-TV (CBC Television PEI) 33193
Owner: Canadian Broadcasting Corp.
Editorial: 430 University Ave, Charlottetown, Prince Edward Island C1A 4N6 **Tel:** 1 902 629-6400.
Web site: http://www.cbc.ca/news/canada/prince-edward-island
Profile: CBCT-TV is the CBC affiliate for the Charlottetown, Prince Edward Island market. The station is owned by Canadian Broadcasting Corp. CBCT-TV broadcasts locally on channel 13.
TELEVISION STATION

CBEFT-TV (Radio-Canada Windsor) 33294
Owner: Société Radio-Canada
Editorial: 825 Riverside Dr W, Windsor, Ontario N9A 5K9 **Tel:** 1 519 255-3572.
Email: iciontario-grp@radio-canada.ca
Web site: http://ici.radio-canada.ca/ontario/Windsor/
Profile: CBEFT-TV is a transmitter located in Windsor, Ontario, that simulcasts the programming of CBOFT-TV, the Radio-Canada affiliate in Ottawa, Ontario. It is owned by the Societe Radio Canada. CBEFT-TV airs locally on channel 54.
TELEVISION STATION

CBET-TV (CBC Windsor) 33194
Owner: Canadian Broadcasting Corp.
Editorial: 825 Riverside Dr W, Windsor, Ontario N9A 5K9 **Tel:** 1 519 255-3411.
Web site: http://www.cbc.ca/windsor
Profile: CBET-TV is the CBC affiliate for the Windsor, Ontario market. The station is owned by the Canadian Broadcasting Corp. CBET-TV broadcasts locally on channel 9.
TELEVISION STATION

CBFT-TV (Radio-Canada Montréal) 33199
Owner: Société Radio-Canada
Editorial: 1400 Boul Rene Levesque E, Montreal, Quebec H2L 2M2 **Tel:** 1 514 597-6000.
Web site: http://www.radio-canada.ca/montreal
Profile: CBFT-TV est une station affiliée de Radio-Canada à Montréal. La station est une propriété de Radio-Canada. CBFT-TV diffuse localement sur le canal 2.

CBFT-TV is the Radio-Canada affiliate for the Montreal market. The station is owned by Societe Radio-Canada. CBFT-TV airs locally on channel 2.
TELEVISION STATION

CBHT-TV (CBC Television Halifax) 33189
Owner: Canadian Broadcasting Corp.
Editorial: 7067 Chebucto Rd Suite 100, Halifax, Nova Scotia B3L 4R5 **Tel:** 1 902 420-4350.
Email: cbcns@cbc.ca
Web site: http://www.cbc.ca/ns
Profile: CBHT-TV is the CBC affiliate for the Halifax, Nova Scotia market. The station is owned by the Canadian Broadcasting Corp. CBHT-TV broadcasts locally on channel 3.
TELEVISION STATION

CBKFT-TV 83248
Owner: Société Radio-Canada
Editorial: 2440 Broad St, Regina, Saskatchewan S4P 0A5 **Tel:** 1 306 347-9540.
Email: saskatchewan@radio-canada.ca
Web site: http://www.radio-canada.ca/regions/saskatchewan
Profile: CBKFT-TV is the Radio-Canada affiliate for the Regina, Saskatchewan market. The station is owned by Societe Radio-Canada. CBKFT-TV broadcasts locally on channel 13.
TELEVISION STATION

CBKF-TV 33289
Owner: Canadian Broadcasting Corp.
Editorial: 2440 Broad St, Regina, Saskatchewan S4P 0A5 **Tel:** 1 306 347-9540.
Email: sasknews@cbc.ca
Web site: http://www.cbc.ca/sask
Profile: CBKF-TV is the CBC affiliate for the Regina, Saskatchewan market. The station is owned by the Canadian Broadcasting Corp. CBKF-TV airs locally on channel 4.
TELEVISION STATION

CBKT-TV 33136
Owner: Canadian Broadcasting Corp.
Editorial: 2440 Broad St, Regina, Saskatchewan S4P 4A1 **Tel:** 1 306 347-9540.
Email: sasknews@cbc.ca
Web site: http://www.cbc.ca/sask
Profile: CBKT-TV is the CBC affiliate for the Regina, Saskatchewan market. The station is owned by Canadian Broadcasting Corp. CBKT-TV broadcasts locally on channel 9.
TELEVISION STATION

CBLFT-TV (Radio-Canada Toronto) 397587
Owner: Société Radio-Canada
Editorial: 205 Rue Wellington O, Toronto, Ontario M5V 3G7 **Tel:** 1 416 205-2887.
Web site: http://www.radio-canada.ca/regions/ontario
Profile: CBLFT-TV is the Télévision de Radio-Canada affiliate for the Toronto market. The station is owned by Societe Radio-Canada. CBLFT-TV broadcasts locally on channel 12.
TELEVISION STATION

CBLN-TV (CBC-London) 445496
Owner: Canadian Broadcasting Corp.
Editorial: 250 Front Street, Toronto, Ontario M5V 3G5 **Tel:** 1 416 205-3311.
Email: tonews@cbc.ca
Web site: http://www.cbc.ca/toronto
Profile: CBLN-TV is the CBC affiliate serving the London, ON area. The station is owned by the Canadian Broadcasting Corp. CBLN-TV broadcasts locally on channel 26 and syndicates CBC Newsworld programming.
TELEVISION STATION

CBLT-TV (CBC Toronto) 33207
Owner: Canadian Broadcasting Corp.
Editorial: 250 Front Street, Toronto, Ontario M5V 3G5 **Tel:** 1 416 205-6309.
Email: tonews@cbc.ca
Web site: http://www.cbc.ca/toronto
Profile: CBLT-TV is the CBC affiliate serving the Toronto market. The station is owned by Canadian Broadcasting Corp. CBLT-TV broadcasts locally on channel 25.
TELEVISION STATION

CBMT-TV (CBC Montreal) 33185
Owner: Canadian Broadcasting Corp.
Editorial: 1400 Rene-Levesque Blvd E, Montreal, Quebec H2L 2M2 **Tel:** 1 514 597-6000.
Web site: http://www.cbc.ca/news/canada/montreal
Profile: CBMT-TV is the CBC affiliate for the Montreal market. The station is owned by the Canadian Broadcasting Corp. CBMT-TV broadcasts locally on channel 6.
TELEVISION STATION

CBNT-TV 33198
Owner: Canadian Broadcasting Corp.
Editorial: 95 University Ave, St. John's, Newfoundland A1B 1Z4 **Tel:** 1 709 576-5000.
Web site: http://www.cbc.ca/news/canada/newfoundland-labrador
Profile: CBNT-TV is the CBC affiliate for the St. John's, Newfoundland market. The station is owned by Canadian Broadcasting Corp. CBNT-TV broadcasts locally on channel 8.
TELEVISION STATION

CBOFT-TV (Radio-Canada Ottawa-Gatineau) 33216
Owner: Société Radio-Canada
Editorial: 181 Queen St, Ottawa, Ontario K1P 1K9 **Tel:** 1 613 288-6000.
Email: nouvelles.ottawagatineau@radio-canada.ca
Web site: http://ici.radio-canada.ca/ottawa-gatineau
Profile: CBOFT-TV est une station de télévision affiliée de Radio-Canada, basée à Ottawa. La station est une propriété de la Société de Radio-Canada. CBOFT-TV est diffusé localement sur le canal 9.

CBOFT-TV is the Societe Radio-Canada affiliate serving the Ottawa, Ontario market. The station is owned by Societe Radio-Canada. CBOFT-TV airs locally on channel 9.
TELEVISION STATION

CBOT-TV (CBC Ottawa) 33218
Owner: Canadian Broadcasting Corp.
Editorial: 181 Queen St, Ottawa, Ontario K1P 1K9 **Tel:** 1 613 288-6000.
Email: cbcnewsottawa@cbc.ca
Web site: http://www.cbc.ca/news/canada/ottawa
Profile: CBOT-TV is the CBC affiliate for the Ottawa, Ontario market. The station is owned by the Canadian Broadcasting Corp. CBOT-TV broadcasts locally on channel 4.
TELEVISION STATION

CBRT-TV (CBC Calgary) 33162
Owner: Canadian Broadcasting Corp.
Editorial: 1724 Westmount Blvd NW, Calgary, Alberta T2N 3G7 **Tel:** 1 403 521-6000.
Email: calgarynewstips@cbc.ca
Web site: http://www.cbc.ca/calgary
Profile: CBRT-TV(CBC Calgary) is the CBC affiliate for the Calgary, Alberta market. The station is owned by Canadian Broadcasting Corp. CBRT-TV broadcasts locally on channel 9.
TELEVISION STATION

CBUFT-DT (Radio-Canada Colombie-Britannique/Yukon) 33167
Owner: Société Radio-Canada
Editorial: 775 Rue Cambie, Vancouver, British Columbia V6B 0L8 **Tel:** 1 604 662-6135.
Web site: http://ici.radio-canada.ca/colombie-britannique-et-yukon
Profile: CBUFT-DT (Radio-Canada Colombie-Britannique/Yukon) est une station affiliée à la Société Radio-Canada couvrant le territoire de la Colombie-Britannique et du Yukon.

CBUFT-DT (Radio-Canada Colombie-Britannique/Yukon) is the Societe Radio-Canada affiliate serving the Vancouver, British Columbia area and Yukon. CBUFT-DT airs locally on channel 26.
TELEVISION STATION

CBUT-TV (CBC Vancouver) 33166
Owner: Canadian Broadcasting Corp.
Editorial: 700 Hamilton St, Vancouver, British Columbia V6B 2R5 **Tel:** 1 604 662-6000.
Email: cbcnewsvancouver@cbc.ca
Web site: http://www.cbc.ca/news/canada/british-columbia
Profile: CBUT-TV is the CBC affiliate for the Vancouver, British Columbia market. The station is owned by Canadian Broadcasting Corp. CBUT-TV broadcasts locally on channel 2. Press releases and story ideas should be directed to the assignment desk.
TELEVISION STATION

CBVT-TV (ICI Radio-Canada Québec) 133687
Owner: Société Radio-Canada
Editorial: 888 Rue Saint-Jean, Quebec, Quebec G1R 5H6- **Tel:** 1 418 654-1341.
Email: nouvelles.quebec@radio-canada.ca
Web site: http://radio-canada.ca/quebec
Profile: CBVT-TV est une station affiliée de Radio-Canada desservant la ville de Québec. La station est une propriété de la Société Radio-Canada. CBVT-TV est diffusée localement sur le canal 11.

CBVT-TV is the Radio-Canada affiliate serving the Quebec City area. The station is owned by Societe Radio-Canada. CBVT-TV broadcasts locally on channel 11.
TELEVISION STATION

CBWFT-TV 33229
Owner: Société Radio-Canada
Editorial: 541 Avenue Portage, Winnipeg, Manitoba R3B 2G1 **Tel:** 1 204 788-3235.
Email: manitoba@radio-canada.ca
Web site: http://radio-canada.ca/regions/manitoba
Profile: CBWFT-TV is the Radio-Canada-Reseau TV affiliate serving the Winnipeg, Manitoba area. The station is owned by Societe Radio-Canada. CBWFT-TV broadcasts locally on channel 3.
TELEVISION STATION

CBWT-TV 33228
Owner: Canadian Broadcasting Corp.
Editorial: 541 Portage Ave, Winnipeg, Manitoba R3B 2G1 **Tel:** 1 204 788-3222.
Web site: http://www.cbc.ca/manitoba
Profile: CBWT-TV is the CBC affiliate for the Winnipeg, Manitoba market. The station is owned by the Canadian Broadcasting Corp. CBWT-TV broadcasts locally on channel 6.
TELEVISION STATION

CBXFT-TV (Ici Radio-Canada Alberta) 33158
Owner: Société Radio-Canada
Editorial: 10062-102 Avenue, Suite 123 Edmonton City Centre, Edmonton, Alberta T5J 2Y8 **Tel:** 1 780 468-7500.
Web site: http://radio-canada.ca/regions/alberta
Profile: CBXFT-TV is the Radio-Canada affiliate for the Edmonton, Alberta market. The station is owned by Societe Radio-Canada. CBXFT-TV broadcasts locally on channel 11.
TELEVISION STATION

CBXT-TV (CBC Edmonton) 33156
Owner: Canadian Broadcasting Corp.
Editorial: Ste 123 Edmonton City Centre, 10062 102nd Ave, Edmonton, Alberta T5J 2Y8 **Tel:** 1 780 468-7500.
Email: cbx.edmonton@cbc.ca
Web site: http://www.cbc.ca/edmonton
Profile: CBXT-TV is the CBC affiliate for the Edmonton, Alberta market. The station is owned by the Canadian Broadcasting Corp. CBXT-TV broadcasts locally on channel 5.
TELEVISION STATION

CBYT-TV 33201
Owner: Canadian Broadcasting Corp.
Editorial: 162 Premier Drive, Corner Brook, Newfoundland A2H 6G1 **Tel:** 1 709 634-3141.
Email: cbrookradio@cbc.ca
Web site: http://www.cbc.ca/nl
Profile: CBYT-TV is a transmitter located in Corner Brook, Newfoundland that simulcasts the programming of CBNT-TV in St. John's, Newfoundland. It is owned by Canadian Broadcasting Corp. CBYT-TV broadcasts locally on channel 5.
TELEVISION STATION SATELLITE

CFAP-TV (V Media Québec) 33184
Owner: Remstar Corporation
Editorial: 330 rue Saint-Vallier E, Bureau 335, Quebec, Quebec G9K 9C5 **Tel:** 1 418 624-2222.
Email: cv@vtele.ca
Web site: http://vtele.ca
Profile: CFAP-TV est une station affiliée de V Média pour la ville de Québec. La station est une propriété de Remstar Corporation. CFAP-TV est diffusée localement sur le canal 2.

CFAP-TV is the V affiliate for the Quebec City market. The station is owned by Remstar Corporation. CFAP-TV broadcasts locally on channel 2.
TELEVISION STATION

CFCF-TV (CTV News Montreal) 33211
Owner: Bell Media
Editorial: 1205 Papineau Ave, Montreal, Quebec H2K 4R2 **Tel:** 1 514 273-6311.
Email: cfcfassignment@ctv.ca
Web site: http://montreal.ctvnews.ca
Profile: CFCF-TV is the CTV affiliate for the Montreal market. The station is owned by Bell Media. CFCF-TV broadcasts locally on channel 12. All press releases and story ideas should be sent to the news department's e-mail address or faxed.
TELEVISION STATION

CFCL-TV (CTV Timmins) 33222
Owner: Bell Media
Editorial: 681 Pine St N, Timmins, Ontario P4N 7L6 **Tel:** 1 705 264-4211.
Email: tonews@cbc.ca
Web site: http://www.cbc.ca/toronto
Profile: CFCL-TV (CBLT7-TV) is the CTV affiliate for the Timmins, Ontario market. The station is owned by Bell Media. CFCL-TV broadcasts locally on channel 6. The station rebroadcasts CBLT-TV programming.
TELEVISION STATION

CFCM-TV (TVA Québec) 33225
Owner: Quebecor Media Inc.
Editorial: 1000 Av Myrand, Quebec, Quebec G1V 2W3 **Tel:** 1 418 688-9330.
Email: nouvelles.quebec@tva.ca
Web site: http://www.tvanouvelles.ca/regional/quebec
Profile: CFCM-TV est une station de télévision affiliée de TVA à Québec. La station est une propriété de Québécor Media Inc. CFCM-TV est diffusé localement sur le canal 4.

CFCM-TV is the TVA network affiliate for the Quebec City market. The station is owned by Quebecor Media Inc. CFCM-TV broadcasts locally on channel 4.
TELEVISION STATION

CFCNL-TV 716584
Owner: Bell Media
Editorial: 640 13 St N, Lethbridge, Alberta T1H 2S8 **Tel:** 1 403 329-3644.
Email: lethbridgenews@bellmedia.ca
Web site: http://calgary.ctvnews.ca/ctvlethbridge
Profile: CFCNL-TV is the CTV affiliate for the Lethbridge market. The station is owned by Bell Media. CFCNL-TV broadcasts locally on channel 13. This station is the CFCN-TV transmitter in Lethbridge.
TELEVISION STATION

CFCN-TV 33160
Owner: Bell Media
Editorial: 80 Patina Rise SW, Calgary, Alberta T3H 2W4- **Tel:** 1 403 240-5600.
Email: calgarynews@ctv.ca
Web site: http://calgary.ctvnews.ca
Profile: CFCN-TV is the CTV affiliate for the Calgary, Alberta; southern Alberta; and southeastern British Columbia market. The station is owned by Bell Media. CFCN-TV broadcasts locally on channel 3.
TELEVISION STATION

CFEM-TV (TVA Abitibi-Témiscamingue) 33177
Owner: RNC Media Inc.
Editorial: 380 Murdoch Ave, Rouyn-Noranda, Quebec J9X 1G5 **Tel:** 1 819 762-0744.
Web site: http://www.tvaabitibi.ca/
Profile: CFEM-TV est une station affiliée de TVA en Abitibi-Témiscamingue. La station est une propriété de RNC Media Inc. CFEM-TV est diffusé localement sur le canal 10.

CFEM-TV is the TVA affiliate for the the Rouyn-Noranda, Quebec area. The station is owned by RNC Media. CFEM-TV airs locally on channel 10.
TELEVISION STATION

CFER-TV (TVA Est-du-Québec) 33139
Owner: Quebecor Media Inc.
Editorial: 465 Boul Sainte-Anne, Rimouski, Quebec G5M 1G1 **Tel:** 1 418 722-6011.
Email: nouvelles@cfer.tva.ca
Web site: http://tva.canoe.ca/stations/cfer
Profile: CFER-TV est une station de télévision affiliée de TVA à Rimouski. La station est une propriété de Quebecor Media Inc. CFER-TV diffuse localement sur le canal 11.

CFER-TV is the TVA affiliate for the Rimouski, Quebec market. The station is owned by Quebecor Media Inc. CFER-TV broadcasts locally on channel 11.
TELEVISION STATION

CFGS-TV (V Media Gatineau) 33145
Owner: RNC Media
Editorial: 171A Rue Jean-Proulx, Gatineau, Quebec J8Z 1W5 **Tel:** 1 819 770-1040.
Web site: http://www.vgatineau.ca/
Profile: CFGS-TV est une station affiliée de V Media à Gatineau. La station est une propriété de RNC Média. CFGS-TV est diffusé localement sur le canal 34. CFGS-TV produit ses propres bulletins de nouvelles et la programmation est celle de V.

CFGS-TV is the TQS affiliate serving the Gatineau, Quebec area. The station is owned by RNC Média. CFGS-TV airs locally on channel 34. CFGS-TV produces its own local newscasts and gets other programming from V.
TELEVISION STATION

CFJC-TV 33137
Owner: Jim Pattison Broadcast Group(The)
Editorial: 460 Pemberton Terr, Kamloops, British Columbia V2C 1T5 **Tel:** 1 250 372-3322.
Email: news@cfjctoday.com
Web site: http://cfjctoday.com/
Profile: CFJC-TV is an independent station serving the Kamloops, British Columbia market. The station is owned by The Jim Pattison Broadcast Group. CFJC-TV broadcasts locally on channel 7. On September 1, 2012 CFJC-TV will begin airing some content from CITY-TV.
TELEVISION STATION

CFJP-TV (V Media Montréal) 33210
Owner: Remstar Corporation
Editorial: 85, rue St-Paul Ouest, Montreal, Quebec H2Y 3V4 **Tel:** 1 514 390-6100.
Profile: CFJP-TV est la station de télévision affiliée de Groupe V Media à Montréal. La station est une propriété de Remstar Corporation. CFJP-TV diffuse son contenu localement sur le canal 35.

CFJP-TV is the V affiliate serving the Montreal area. The station is owned by Remstar Corporation. CFJP-TV broadcasts locally on channel 35.
TELEVISION STATION

CFKM-TV (V Média Trois-Rivières) 33172
Owner: Remstar Corporation
Editorial: 926 Rue Notre Dame Centre, Trois-Rivieres, Quebec G9A 4W8 **Tel:** 1 819 565-9232.
Web site: http://noovo.ca/
Profile: CFKM-TV est la station affilié de V Télé à Trois-Rivières. La station est une propriété de Remstar Corporation. CFKM-TV est diffusé localement sur le canal 16.

CFKM-TV is the V affiliate for the Trois-Rivieres, Quebec market. The station is owned by Remstar Corporation. CFKM-TV broadcasts locally on channel 16.
TELEVISION STATION

CFKS-TV (V Media Sherbrooke) 33213
Owner: Remstar Corporation
Editorial: 3720 boulevard Industriel, Sherbrooke, Quebec J1L 1Z9 **Tel:** 1 819 565-9232.
Profile: CFKS-TV est une station de télévision affiliée de V à Sherbrooke. La station est une propriété de Remstar Corporation. CFKS-TV est diffusée localement sur le canal 30. CFKS-TV n'a pas de division nouvelles.

CFKS-TV is the V affiliate for the Sherbrooke, Quebec market. The station is owned by Remstar Corporation. CFKS-TV broadcasts locally on channel 30. CFKS-TV has no news division.
TELEVISION STATION

CFMT-TV (Rogers Media-OMNI-1) 33209
Owner: Rogers Media Inc.
Editorial: 33 Dundas St E, Toronto, Ontario M5B 1B8- **Tel:** 1 416 764-3005.
Email: news@omnitv.ca
Web site: http://www.omnitv.ca/ontario
Profile: CFMT-TV, also known as OMNI.1, is an independent station for the Toronto market. The station is owned by Rogers Media Inc. CFMT-TV broadcasts locally on channel 47.
TELEVISION STATION

CFPL-TV (CTVNews-London) 33169
Owner: Bell Media
Editorial: 1 Communications Rd, London, Ontario N6J 4Z1 **Tel:** 1 519 686-8810.
Email: londonnews@ctv.ca
Web site: http://london.ctvnews.ca
Profile: CFPL-TV is the CTV affiliate for the London, Ontario market. The station is owned by Bell Media. CFPL-TV broadcasts locally on channel 10.
TELEVISION STATION

CFQC-TV 33171
Owner: Bell Media
Editorial: 216 First Ave North, Saskatoon, Saskatchewan S7K 3W3 **Tel:** 1 306 665-8600.
Email: cfqcnews@ctv.ca
Web site: http://saskatoon.ctv.ca
Profile: CFQC-TV is the CTV affiliate for the Saskatoon, Saskatchewan market. The station is owned by Bell Media. CFQC-TV broadcasts locally on channel 8.
TELEVISION STATION

CFRE-TV (Global Television Regina) 33277
Owner: Corus Entertainment Inc.
Editorial: 370 Hoffer Dr, Regina, Saskatchewan S4N 7A4 **Tel:** 1 306 775-4000.
Email: regina@globalnews.ca
Web site: http://www.globalregina.com
Profile: CFRE-TV is the Global Television affiliate for the Regina, Saskatchewan market. The station is owned by Corus Entertainment Inc.. CFRE-TV broadcasts locally on channel 11.
TELEVISION STATION

CFRN-TV (CTV Edmonton) 33153
Owner: Bell Media
Editorial: 18520 Stony Plain Rd NW, Edmonton, Alberta T5S 1A8 **Tel:** 1 780 483-3311.
Email: cfrnnewsassignment@ctv.ca
Web site: http://edmonton.ctv.ca
Profile: CFRN-TV is the CTV affiliate for the Edmonton, Alberta market. The station is owned by Bell Media. CFRN-TV airs locally on channel 2.
TELEVISION STATION

CFRS-TV (V Média Saguenay) 33202
Owner: Remstar Corporation
Editorial: 2303 Sir Wilfrid Laurier, Jonquiere, Quebec G7X 5Z2 **Tel:** 1 418 542-4551.
Email: cv@vtele.ca
Profile: CFRS-TV est une station affiliée de V AU Saguenay. La station est une propriété de Remstar Corporation. CFRS-TV diffuse localement sur le canal 4.

CFRS-TV is the V affiliate for the Jonquiere, Quebec market. The station is owned by Remstar Corporation. CFRS-TV broadcasts locally on channel 4.
TELEVISION STATION

CFSK-TV (Global Television Saskatoon) 33276
Owner: Corus Entertainment Inc.
Editorial: 218 Robin Cres, Saskatoon, Saskatchewan S7L 7C3 **Tel:** 1 306 665-6969.
Email: saskatoon@globalnews.ca
Web site: http://globalnews.ca/saskatoon
Profile: CFSK-TV is the Global Television affiliate for the Saskatoon, Saskatchewan market. The station is owned by Corus Entertainment Inc. CFSK-TV broadcasts locally on channel 4.
TELEVISION STATION

CFSO-TV 812005
Owner: McCarthy (Corey)
Editorial: 810 2nd Street West, Cardston, Alberta TOK OKO **Tel:** 1 403 448-0432.
Email: news@channel32.ca
Web site: http://www.channel32.ca
Profile: CFSO-TV is an independent station for the Cardston, Alberta market. The station is owned by Corey McCarthy. The station airs community-related news and public affairs programming. CFSO-TV broadcasts locally on channel 32.
TELEVISION STATION

CFTK-TV 33132
Owner: Bell Media
Editorial: 4625 Lazelle Ave, Terrace, British Columbia V8G 1S4 **Tel:** 1 250 635-6316.
Web site: http://www.cftktv.com
Profile: CFTK-TV is the CTV affiliate for the Terrace, British Columbia market. The station is owned by Bell Media. CFTK-TV broadcasts locally on channel 3.
TELEVISION STATION

CFTM-TV (TVA Montréal) 33186
Owner: Quebecor Media Inc.
Editorial: 1600 Boul de Maisonneuve E, Montreal, Quebec H2L 4P2- **Tel:** 1 514 526-9251.
Email: nouvelles@tva.ca
Web site: http://www.tvanouvelles.ca/regional/montreal
Profile: CFTM-TV est une station affiliée de TVA à Montréal. La station est une propriété de Québécor Média Inc. CFTM-TV est diffusé localement sur le Canal 10.

CFTM-TV is the TVA affiliate for the Montreal market. The station is owned by Quebecor Media Inc. CFTM-TV broadcasts locally on channel 10.
TELEVISION STATION

CFTO-TV (CTV Toronto) 33208
Owner: Bell Media
Editorial: 9 Channel Nine Crt, Toronto, Ontario M1S 4B5- **Tel:** 1 416 384-5000.
Email: torontodesk@ctv.ca
Web site: http://toronto.ctvnews.ca
Profile: CFTO-TV is the CTV affiliate for the Toronto market. The station is owned by Bell Media. CFTO-TV broadcasts locally on channel 9.
TELEVISION STATION

CFTU-TV (Canal Savoir Montréal) 612290
Owner: Corporation pour l'Avancement des Nouvelles Applications des Langages Ltée
Editorial: 2200 Rue Sainte-Catherine E Etage 1ER, Montreal, Quebec H2K 2J1 **Tel:** 1 514 509-2222.
Email: info@canalsavoir.tv
Web site: http://www.canalsavoir.tv
Profile: CFTU-TV est une station affiliée du Canal Savoir à Montréal. La station est une station non-commerciale, une propriété de la Corporation pour l'Avancement des Nouvelles Applications des Langages Ltée (CANAL). CFTU-TV est diffusée localement sur le canal 29.

CFTU-TV is the Canal Savoir affiliate in the Montreal market. The station is a non-commercial station owned by the Corporation pour l'Avancement des Nouvelles Applications des Langages Ltée (CANAL). CFTU-TV broadcasts locally on channel 29.
TELEVISION STATION

CFTV-TV (Canadian Radio-television and Telecommunications Commission) 616581
Owner: Southshore Broadcasting Inc.
Editorial: 3165 South Talbot Rd., Leamington, Ontario N0R 1B0 **Tel:** 1 519 839-3434.
Web site: http://www.cftvdt.net
Profile: CFTV-TV is an independent station for the Leamington, Ontario market. The station is owned by Southshore Broadcasting Inc. CFTV-TV broadcasts locally on channel 34.
TELEVISION STATION

CFVS-TV (V Média Val d'Or) 33178
Owner: RNC Media
Editorial: 1729 3e Av, Val-d'Or, Quebec J9P 1W3 **Tel:** 1 819 825-0010.
Email: nouvelles@rncmedia.ca
Web site: http://www.rncmedia.ca
Profile: CFVS-TV est une station de télévision affiliée de V Média à Val d'or. La station est une propriété de RNC Media. CFVS-TV diffuse son contenu localement sur le canal 25.

CFVS-TV is the V Tele affiliate for the Val-d'Or, Quebec market. The station is owned by RNC Media. CFVS-TV broadcasts locally on channel 25.
TELEVISION STATION

CFYK-TV 33234
Owner: Canadian Broadcasting Corp.
Editorial: 5002 Forrest Drive, Yellowknife, Northwest Territories X1A 2N2 **Tel:** 1 867 920-5400.
Email: cbcnorth@cbc.ca
Web site: http://www.cbc.ca/north
Profile: CFYK-TV is a CBC affiliate for the Yellowknife, Northwest Territories area. The station is owned by the Canadian Broadcasting Corporation. The station broadcasts locally on channel 10.
TELEVISION STATION

CHAN-TV (Global BC) 33274
Owner: Corus Entertainment Inc.
Editorial: 7850 Enterprise St, Burnaby, British Columbia V5A 1V7 **Tel:** 1 604 420-2288.
Email: tips@GlobalTVBC.com
Web site: http://www.globalnews.ca/bc
Profile: CHAN-TV (Global BC) is the Global Television affiliate for Burnaby, British Columbia. The station is owned by Corus Entertainment Inc. CHAN-TV broadcasts locally on channel 8.
TELEVISION STATION

CHAT-TV 33147
Owner: Jim Pattison Broadcast Group(The)
Editorial: 10 Boundary Rd SE, Redcliff, Alberta T0J 2P0- **Tel:** 1 403 548-8282.
Email: chatnews@jpbg.ca
Web site: http://www.chattelevision.ca
Profile: CHAT-TV is an independent station for the Medicine Hat, Alberta market. The station is owned by The Jim Pattison Broadcast Group. CHAT-TV broadcasts locally on channel 6. On September 1, 2012 CHAT-TV will begin airing some content from CITY-TV.
TELEVISION STATION

CHAU-TV (TVA Carleton) 33175
Owner: Tele Inter-Rives Ltee.
Editorial: 349 Boul Perron, Carleton, Quebec G0C 1J0 **Tel:** 1 418 364-3344.
Email: info@chautva.com
Web site: http://www.chautva.com
Profile: CHAU-TV est une station affiliée de TVA à Carleton, Québec. La station est une propriété de Tele Inter-Rives Ltee. CHAU-TV est diffusé localement sur le canal 5.

CHAU-TV is the TVA affiliate for the Carleton, Quebec market. The station is owned by Tele Inter-Rives Ltee. CHAU-TV broadcasts locally on channel 5.
TELEVISION STATION

CHBC-TV (Global News Okanagan) 33135
Owner: Corus Entertainment Inc.
Editorial: 342 Leon Ave, Kelowna, British Columbia V1Y 6J2- **Tel:** 1 250 762-4535.
Email: okanagan@globalnews.ca
Web site: http://globalnews.ca/okanagan
Profile: CHBC-TV (Global News Okanagan) is the Global Television affiliate for the Kelowna, British Columbia market. The station is owned by Corus Entertainment Inc. CHBC-TV broadcasts locally on channel 13. **All press releases should be send via okanagan@globalnews.ca
TELEVISION STATION

CHBX-TV (CTV Sault Ste. Marie) 33196
Owner: Bell Media
Editorial: 119 East St, Sault Ste. Marie, Ontario P6A 3C7 **Tel:** 1 705 759-8232.
Email: newsforthenorth@ctv.ca
Web site: http://northernontario.ctvnews.ca
Profile: CHBX-TV is the CTV affiliate for the Sault Ste. Marie, Ontario market. The station is owned by Bell Media. CHBX-TV broadcasts locally on channel 2.
TELEVISION STATION

CHCH-TV (Channel Zero-Hamilton) 33143
Owner: Channel Zero Inc.
Editorial: 163 Jackson St W, Hamilton, Ontario L8P 0A8 **Tel:** 1 905 522-1101.
Email: contact@chch.com
Web site: http://www.chch.com
Profile: CHCH-TV is an independent superstation for the Ontario market. The station is owned by Channel Zero Inc. CHCH-TV broadcasts in Hamilton on channel 11. CHCH-TV is a member of the Canadian Press Gallery.
TELEVISION STATION

CHCO-TV 778302
Owner: Charlotte Community Television
Editorial: 24 Reed Ave, Unit #2, Saint Andrews, New Brunswick E5B 1A1 **Tel:** 1 506 529-8826.
Email: local@chco.tv
Web site: http://www.chco.tv
Profile: CHCO-TV or Charlotte Community Television is an independent local television station based in St. Andrews, New Brunswick. CHCO-TV broadcasts on channel 26 to local residents.
TELEVISION STATION

CHEK-TV 33163
Owner: CHEK Media Group
Editorial: 780 Kings Road, Victoria, British Columbia V8T 5A2 **Tel:** 1 250 383-2435.
Email: tips@cheknews.ca
Web site: http://www.cheknews.ca
Profile: CHEK-TV an independent station for the Victoria, British Columbia market. The station is owned by CHEK Media Group. CHEK-TV broadcasts to the Victoria, British Columbia area on channel 6.
TELEVISION STATION

CHEM-TV (TVA Trois-Rivières) 33174
Owner: Quebecor Media Inc.
Editorial: 3625 rue Chanoine-Moreau, Trois-Rivieres, Quebec G8Y 5N6 **Tel:** 1 819 376-8880.
Email: nouvelles@chem.tva.ca
Web site: http://www.tvanouvelles.ca/regional/mauricie
Profile: CHEM-TV est une station de télévision affiliée de TVA à Trois-Rivières. La station est une propriété de Québécor Média Inc. CHEM-TV est diffusée localement sur le canal 8.

CHEM-TV is the TVA affiliate for the Trois-Rivieres, Quebec market. The station is owned by Quebecor Media Inc. CHEM-TV broadcasts locally on channel 8.
TELEVISION STATION

CHEX2-TV (Global-Durham) 525777
Owner: Corus Entertainment Inc.
Editorial: 10 Simcoe St N, Oshawa, Ontario L1G 4R8 **Tel:** 1 905 434-2421.
Email: studio12news@corusent.com
Web site: http://www.channel12.ca
Profile: CHEX-TV2 is the CTV affiliate for the Oshawa, Ontario market. The station is owned by Corus Entertainment Inc. CHEX-TV2 broadcasts locally on channel 12.
TELEVISION STATION

CHEX-TV (Global-Peterborough) 33195
Owner: Corus Entertainment Inc.
Editorial: 743 Monaghan Rd, Peterborough, Ontario K9J 5K2 **Tel:** 1 705 742-0451.
Email: newswatch@chextv.com
Web site: http://www.chextv.com
Profile: CHEX-TV is the CTV affiliate for the Peterborough, Ontario market. The station is owned by Corus Entertainment Inc. CHEX-TV broadcasts locally on channel 12. CHEX-TV airs CTV programming including news, sports and entertainment.
TELEVISION STATION

CHFD-TV (Global-Thunder Bay) 33214
Owner: Dougall Media
Editorial: 87 Hill St N, Thunder Bay, Ontario P7A 5V6 **Tel:** 1 807 346-2600.
Email: news@dougallmedia.com
Profile: CHFD-TV is the CTV affiliate for the Thunder Bay, Ontario market. The station is owned by Dougall Media. CHFD-TV broadcasts locally on channel 4.
TELEVISION STATION

CHIN-TV 63283
Owner: Lombardi(Lenny)
Editorial: 622 College St Suite 400, Toronto, Ontario M6G 1B4 **Tel:** 1 416 531-9991.
Email: chintv@chinradio.com
Web site: http://www.chinradio.com
Profile: CHIN-TV is an independent station for the Toronto market. The station is owned by Lenny Lombardi. CHIN-TV broadcasts locally on channel 7.
TELEVISION STATION

CHLF-TV (TFO) 63284
Owner: Office des télécommunications éducatives de langue francaise de l'Ontario(L')
Editorial: 21 College St Etage 6E, Toronto, Ontario M9V 1H5 **Tel:** 1 416 968-3536.
Email: vos_questions@tfo.org
Web site: http://www.tfo.org
Profile: CHLF-TV is an independent station for the Toronto market. The station is owned by GroupeMédia TFO with the Office des télécommunications éducatives de langue francaise de l'Ontario (OTÉLFO). CHLF-TV is broadcast locally on channel 19.
TELEVISION STATION

CHLT-TV (TVA Sherbrooke) 33154
Owner: Quebecor Media Inc.
Editorial: 3330 Rue King O, Sherbrooke, Quebec J1L 1C9 **Tel:** 1 819 565-7777.
Email: nouvelles.sherbrooke@tva.ca
Web site: http://tvasherbrooke.com/
Profile: CHLT-TV est une station de télévision de TVA à Sherbrooke. La station est une propriété de Québécor Média Inc. CHLT-TV diffuse localement sur le canal 7.

CHLT-TV is the TVA affiliate for the Sherbrooke, Quebec market. The station is owned by Quebecor Media Inc. CHLT-TV broadcasts locally on channel 7.
TELEVISION STATION

CHMG-TV (Télé-Mag Québec) 83471
Owner: TeleMag Quebec
Editorial: 2700 Rue Jean-Perrin Bureau 120, Quebec, Quebec G2C 1S9 **Tel:** 1 418 670-9078.
Email: info@tele-mag.tv
Web site: http://www.tele-mag.tv
Profile: CHMG-TV est une station de télévision commerciale, une propriété de Télé-mag Quebec. CHMG-TV est diffusé sur le canal 10 dans la ville de Québec.

CHMG-TV is a commercial station owned by TeleMag Quebec. CHMG-TV broadcasts on channel 10 in the Quebec City region.
TELEVISION STATION

CHMI-TV 33230
Owner: Rogers Media Inc.
Editorial: 8 Forks Market Road, Winnipeg, Manitoba R3C 4Y3 **Tel:** 1 204 947-9613.
Email: citytvwinnipegfeedback@rci.rogers.com
Web site: http://www.citytv.com/winnipeg
Profile: CHMI-TV is branded as part of the CityTV family offering local news programming for the Winnipeg, Manitoba market. The station is owned by Rogers Media Inc. CHMI-TV broadcasts locally on channel 13.
TELEVISION STATION

CHNM-TV (OMNI BC) 151128
Owner: Rogers Media Inc.
Editorial: 180 2nd Ave W, Vancouver, British Columbia V5Y 3T9 **Tel:** 1 604 678-3800.
Email: news@omnibc.ca
Web site: http://www.omnitv.ca/bc/en/
Profile: CHNM-TV is an independent station for the Vancouver, British Columbia market. The station is owned by Rogers Media Inc.. CHNM-TV broadcasts locally on channel 8.
TELEVISION STATION

CHNU-TV 83251
Owner: ZoomerMedia Limited
Editorial: 5668 192 St Suite 204, Surrey, British Columbia V3S 2V7 **Tel:** 1 604 576-6880.
Email: audience@joytv.ca
Web site: http://www.joytv.ca
Profile: CHNU-TV is a Christian-based television station for the Surrey, British Columbia market. The station is owned by ZoomerMedia Limited. CHNU-TV broadcasts locally on channel 66.
TELEVISION STATION

CHOT-TV (TVA Gatineau) 33144
Owner: RNC Media
Editorial: 171A Rue Jean-Proulx, Gatineau, Quebec J8Z 1W5 **Tel:** 1 819 770-1040.
Email: chot@rncmedia.ca
Web site: http://www.tvagatineau.ca
Profile: CHOT-TV est une station de télévision affiliée de TVA à Gatineau. La station est une propriété de TNC Media. CHOT-TV est diffusé localement sur le canal 40.

CHOT-TV is the TVA affiliate serving the Gatineau, Quebec area. The station is owned by RNC Media. CHOT-TV broadcasts locally on channel 40.
TELEVISION STATION

CHRO-TV (CTV Two Ottawa) 33217
Owner: Bell Media
Editorial: 87 George St, Ottawa, Ontario K1N 9H7- **Tel:** 1 613 789-0606.
Email: ctvottawa@ctv.ca
Web site: http://ctvottawamorning.ca

Section 3 World Broadcast

Profile: CHRO-TV is the CTV. affiliate for the Ottawa, Ontario market. The station is owned by Bell Media. CHRO-TV broadcasts locally on channel 43.
TELEVISION STATION

CHWI-TV(CTVNews-Windsor)
33155
Owner: Bell Media
Editorial: 300 Ouellette Ave, Windsor, Ontario N9A 7B4- **Tel:** 1 519 977-7432.
Email: windsorcontact@ctv.ca
Web site: http://windsor.ctvnews.ca
Profile: CHWI-TV is the CTV affiliate for the Windsor, Ontario market. The station is owned by Bell Media. CHWI-TV broadcasts locally on channel 60.
TELEVISION STATION

CICA-TV (TVO) 33149
Owner: TVOntario
Editorial: 2180 Yonge St, Toronto, Ontario M4S 2B9
Tel: 1 416 484-2600.
Email: asktvo@tvo.org
Web site: http://www.tvo.org
Profile: CICA-TV is an independent station for the Toronto market. The station is owned by TVOntario. CICA-TV broadcasts locally on channel 19.
TELEVISION STATION

CICC-TV 33270
Owner: Bell Media
Editorial: 95 Broadway St E, Yorkton, Saskatchewan S3N 0L1 **Tel:** 1 306 786-8400.
Email: cicc@ctv.ca
Web site: http://regina.ctvnews.ca/yorkton
Profile: CICC-TV is the CTV affiliate for the Yorktown, Saskatchewan market. CICC-TV is owned by Bell Media. CICC-TV broadcasts locally on channel 10.
TELEVISION STATION

CICT-TV (Global Television Calgary) 33159
Owner: Corus Entertainment Inc.
Editorial: 222 23 St NE, Calgary, Alberta T2E 7N2
Tel: 1 403 235-7777.
Email: calgary@globalnews.ca
Web site: http://www.globaltvcalgary.com
Profile: CICT-TV is the Global Television affiliate for the Calgary, Alberta market. The station is owned by Corus Entertainment Inc.. CICT-TV broadcasts locally on channel 2.
TELEVISION STATION

CIHF-TV (Global Halifax) 33190
Owner: Corus Entertainment Inc.
Editorial: 2110 Gottingen St, Halifax, Nova Scotia B3K 3B3 **Tel:** 1 902 481-7400.
Email: halifax@globalnews.ca
Web site: http://globalnews.ca/halifax
Profile: CIHF-TV, the Global affiliate for the Dartmouth, Nova Scotia market. The station is owned by Corus Entertainment Inc. CIHF-TV broadcasts locally on channel 8.
TELEVISION STATION

CIII-TV (Global News Toronto)
33205
Owner: Corus Entertainment Inc.
Editorial: 81 Barber Greene Rd, Toronto, Ontario M3C 2A2- **Tel:** 1 416 446-5460.
Email: newstips@globaltv.com
Web site: http://globalnews.ca/toronto
Profile: CIII-TV, also known as Global Toronto, is a local, commercial television station owned by Corus Entertainment Inc. The station serves as the Global Television affiliate, serving viewers throughout the Toronto area. The station airs locally on channels 6 and 41.
TELEVISION STATION

CIIT-DT (HopeTV) 389932
Owner: ZoomMedia Limited
Editorial: 64 Jefferson Ave, Toronto, Ontario M6K 1Y4
Tel: 1 416 368-3194.
Email: audience@hopetelevision.ca
Web site: http://www.hopetelevision.ca/
Profile: CIIT-DT (HopeTV) is an independent station for the Winnipeg, Manitoba market. The station is owned by ZoomMedia Limited. CIIT-DT (HopeTV) broadcasts locally on channel 35.
TELEVISION STATION

CIMC-TV (Telile Community TV)
811962
Owner: Telile
Editorial: 17 Conney's Lane, Arichat, Nova Scotia B0E 1A0 **Tel:** 1 902 226-1928.
Email: telile@telile.tv
Web site: http://www.telile.tv
Profile: CIMC-TV (Telile Community TV) is an independent station for the Arichat, Nova Scotia market. The station airs community-related and public affairs programming.
TELEVISION STATION

CIMT-TV (TVA Rivière-du-loup)
33161
Owner: Télé Inter-Rives Ltée
Editorial: 15 Rue de la Chute, Riviere-du-Loup, Quebec G5R 5B7 **Tel:** 1 418 867-1341.
Email: nousjoindre@cimt.ca
Web site: http://www.cimt.ca
Profile: CIMT-TV est une station affiliée de TVA à Rivière-du-Loup, Québec. La station est une propriété de Télé Inter-Rives Ltée. CIMT-TV est diffusé localement au canal 9.

CIMT-TV is the TVA affiliate for the Rivière-du-Loup, Quebec market. The station is owned by Télé Inter-Rives Ltée. CIMT-TV broadcasts locally on channel 9.
TELEVISION STATION

CIPA-TV 33140
Owner: Bell Media
Editorial: 22 10th St W, Prince Albert, Saskatchewan S6V 3A5 **Tel:** 1 306 763-3041.
Email: cipanews@ctv.ca
Web site: http://saskatoon.ctvnews.ca/prince-albert
Profile: CIPA-TV is the CTV affiliate for the Prince Albert, Saskatchewan market. The station is owned by Bell Media. CIPA-TV broadcasts locally on channel 6.
TELEVISION STATION

CISA-TV (Global Lethbridge)
33236
Owner: Corus Entertainment Inc.
Editorial: 1401 28 St N, Lethbridge, Alberta T1H 6H9
Tel: 1 403 327-1521.
Email: lethbridge@globalnews.ca
Web site: http://www.globallethbridge.com
Profile: CISA-TV is the Global Television network affiliate for the Lethbridge, Alberta market. The station is owned by Corus Entertainment Inc. CISA-TV broadcasts locally on channel 7.
TELEVISION STATION

CITL-TV 33148
Owner: Newcap Radio
Editorial: 5026 50 St, Lloydminster, Alberta T9V 1P3
Tel: 1 780 875-3321.
Email: tvnews@newcap.ca
Web site: http://www.citltv.ca/
Profile: Newcap Television operates CKSA and CITL broadcasting from Lloydminster, Alberta.
TELEVISION STATION

CITO-TV (CTVNews-Northern Ontario Timmins) 33224
Owner: Bell Media
Editorial: 681 Pine St N, Timmins, Ontario P4N 7L6
Tel: 1 705 264-4211.
Email: newsforthenorth@ctv.ca
Web site: http://northernontario.ctvnews.ca/timmins
Profile: CITO-TV is the CTV affiliate for the Timmins, Ontario market. The station is owned by Bell Media. CITO-TV broadcasts locally on channel 3.
TELEVISION STATION

CITS-TV (YES-TV) 33296
Owner: Crossroads Television Systems
Editorial: 1295 N Service Road, Burlington, Ontario L7R 4X5 **Tel:** 1 905 331-7333.
Email: contactus@ctstv.com
Web site: http://www.ctstv.com
Profile: CITS-TV is an independent station serving the Burlington, Ontario market. The station is owned by Crossroads Television Systems. CITS-TV broadcasts locally on channel 36.
TELEVISION STATION

CITV-TV (Global Edmonton) 33152
Owner: Corus Entertainment Inc.
Editorial: 5325 Allard Way NW, Edmonton, Alberta T6H 5B8 **Tel:** 1 780 436-1250.
Email: edmonton@globalnews.ca
Web site: http://www.globaltvedmonton.com
Profile: CITV-TV is the Global Television network affiliate for the Edmonton, Alberta market. The station is owned by Corus Entertainment Inc.. CITV-TV broadcasts locally on channel 13.
TELEVISION STATION

CITY-TV (CityNews-Toronto)
33206
Owner: Rogers Media Inc.
Editorial: 33 Dundas St E, Toronto, Ontario M5B 1B8-
Tel: 1 416 599-2489.
Email: news.to@citynews.ca
Web site: http://www.citynews.ca/
Profile: CITY-TV is the City affiliate of the Toronto market. The station is owned by Rogers Media Inc. CITY-TV broadcasts locally on channel 57. CITY-TV reaches about 11.4 million people daily.
TELEVISION STATION

CIVA-TV (Télé-Québec Abitibi-Témiscamingue) 33180
Owner: Société de télédiffusion du Québec(La)
Editorial: 689 3e Av Suite 201, Val-d'Or, Quebec J9P 1S7 **Tel:** 1 819 874-5132.
Web site: http://www.telequebec.tv
Profile: CIVA-TV est une station affiliée de Télé-Québec en Abitibi-Témiscamingue. La station est une propriété de La Société de télédiffusion du Québec. CIVA-TV est transmit localement sur le canal 8.

CIVA-TV is the Tele-Quebec affiliate for the Abitibi-Témiscamingue market. The station is owned by La Société de télédiffusion du Québec. CIVA-TV broadcasts locally on channel 8.
TELEVISION STATION

CIVB-TV (Télé-Québec Rimouski) 377695
Owner: Société de télédiffusion du Québec(La)
Editorial: 79 Rue de l'evêche Est, Rimouski, Quebec G5L 1X7 **Tel:** 1 418 727-3743.
Email: bureau.rimouski@telequebec.tv
Web site: http://www.telequebec.tv
Profile: CIVB-TV est une station affiliée de Télé-Québec du Bas-St-Laurent. La station est une propriété de La Société de télédiffusion du Québec. CIVB-TV est diffusé localemet sur la canal 22.

CIVB-TV is the Télé-Québéc affiliate for the Bas-St-Laurent, QC market. The station is owned by La Société de télédiffusion du Québec. CIVB-TV broadcasts locally on channel 22.
TELEVISION STATION

CIVC-TV (Télé-Québec Trois-Rivière) 377707
Owner: Société de télédiffusion du Québec(La)
Editorial: 1350 Rue Royale Bureau 201, Trois-Rivieres, Quebec G9A 4J4 **Tel:** 1 819 371-6752.
Email: info@telequebec.tv
Web site: http://www.telequebec.tv
Profile: CIVC-TV est une station affiliée de Télé-Québec à Trois-Rivière. La station est une propriété de La Société de télédiffusion du Québec. CIVC-TV est diffusée localement au canal 45.

CIVC-TV is the Télé-Québec affiliate at Trois-Rivière, a region of Quebec. The station is owned by La Société de télédiffusion du Québec. CIVC-TV broadcasts locally on channel 45.
TELEVISION STATION

CIVG-TV (Télé-Québec Côte-Nord) 377698
Owner: Société de télédiffusion du Québec(La)
Editorial: 410 Av Evangeline, Sept-Iles, Quebec G4R 2N5 **Tel:** 1 418 964-8240.
Email: info@telequebec.tv
Web site: http://www.telequebec.tv
Profile: CIVG-TV est une station affiliée de Télé-Québec sur la Côte-Nord. La station est une propriété de La Société de Télédiffusion du Québec. CIVG-TV est diffusé localement sur le canal 22.

CIVG-TV is the Télé-Québec affiliate for the Côte-Nord, Quebec market. The station is owned by La Société de Télédiffusion du Québec. CIVG-TV broadcasts locally on channel 22.
TELEVISION STATION

CIVI-TV (CTV Two Vancouver Island) 78211
Owner: Bell Media
Editorial: 1420 Broad St, Victoria, British Columbia V8W 2B1 **Tel:** 1 250 381-2484.
Email: islandnews@ctv.ca
Web site: http://vancouverisland.ctvnews.ca/
Profile: CIVI-TV (CTV Two Vancouver Island) is the CTV affiliate serving the markets of Victoria, Nanaimo and Vancouver in British Columbia. The station is owned by Bell Media. The station airs locally on cable 12.
TELEVISION STATION

CIVK-TV (Télé-Québec Gaspésie) 377701
Owner: Société de télédiffusion du Québec(La)
Editorial: 436 Boul Perron, Carleton, Quebec G0C 1J0 **Tel:** 1 418 364-7025.
Email: info@telequebec.tv
Web site: http://www.telequebec.tv
Profile: CIVK-TV est une station affiliée en Gaspésie-Îles-de-la-Madeleine. La station est une propriété de La Société de télédiffusion du Québec. CIVK-TV est diffusée localement au canal 11.

CIVK-TV is the Télé-Québec affiliate for the Gaspésie-Îles-de-la-Madeleine. The station is owned by La Société de télédiffusion du Québec. CIVK-TV broadcasts locally on channel 11.
TELEVISION STATION

CIVM-TV (Télé-Québec Montréal) 33191
Owner: Société de télédiffusion du Québec(La)
Editorial: 1000 Rue Fullum, Montreal, Quebec H2K 3L7 **Tel:** 1 514 521-2424.
Email: info@telequebec.tv
Web site: http://www.telequebec.tv
Profile: CIVM-TV est une station affiliée pour le marché du Grand Montréal. La station est une propriété par La Société de télédiffusion du Québec. CIVM-TV est diffusé localement sur le canal 17.

CIVM-TV is the Tele-Quebec affiliate for the Greater Montreal market. The station is owned by La Société de télédiffusion du Québec. CIVM-TV broadcasts locally on channel 17.
TELEVISION STATION

CIVO-TV (Télé-Québec Outaouais) 377709
Owner: Société de télédiffusion du Québec(La)
Editorial: 170 Rue de L'Hôtel-De-Ville, 7eme étage, bureau 7.100, Gatineau, Quebec J8X 4C2
Tel: 1 819 772-3471.
Email: info@telequebec.tv
Web site: http://www.telequebec.tv
Profile: CIVO-TV est une station affiliée de Télé-Québec en Outaouais. La station est une propriété de La Société de télédiffusion du Québec. CIVO-TV est retransmit localement au canal 11.

CIVO-TV is the Télé-Québec affiliate for the Outaouais. The station is owned by La Société de télédiffusion du Québec. CIVO-TV broadcasts locally on channel 11.
TELEVISION STATION

CIVQ-TV (Télé-Québec Capitale-Nationale – Chaudière-Appalaches) 377710
Owner: Société de télédiffusion du Québec(La)
Editorial: 270 Ch Sainte-Foy, Quebec, Quebec G1R 1T3 **Tel:** 1 418 643-5303.
Email: bureau.quebec@telequebec.tv
Web site: http://www.telequebec.tv
Profile: CIVQ-TV est une station affilié de Télé-Québec pour la Capitale-Nationale (Québec) et Chaudière-Appalaches. La station est une propriété de La Société de télédiffusion du Québec. CIVQ-TV est diffusé localement au canal 15.

CIVQ-TV is the Télé-Québec affiliate for the Greater Quebec City and the Chaudière-Appalaches market. The station is owned by La Société de télédiffusion du Québec. CIVQ-TV broadcasts locally on channel 15.
TELEVISION STATION

CIVS-TV (Télé-Québec Estrie-Montérégie) 377700
Owner: Société de télédiffusion du Québec(La)
Editorial: 200 Rue Belvedere N RC 2, Sherbrooke, Quebec J1H 4A9 **Tel:** 1 819 820-3436.
Email: bureau.sherbrooke@telequebec.tv
Web site: http://www.telequebec.tv
Profile: CIVS-TV est une station affiliée pour Télé-Québec pour L'Estrie-Montérégie. La station est une propriété de La Société de télédiffusion du Québec. CIVS-FM est diffusé localement au canal 24.

CIVS-TV is the Télé-Québec affiliate for the Eastern Townships, Quebec market. The station is owned by La Société de télédiffusion du Québec. CIVS-TV broadcasts locally on channel 24.
TELEVISION STATION

CIVT-TV (CTV News Vancouver Island) 63285
Owner: Bell Media
Editorial: 969 Robson St, Vancouver, British Columbia V6Z 1X5- **Tel:** 1 604 608-2868.
Email: bcnews@ctv.ca
Web site: http://bc.ctvnews.ca
Profile: CIVT-TV (CTV News Vancouver Island) is the CTV affiliate serving the Vancouver, British Columbia area. The station is owned by Bell Media. CIVT-TV broadcasts locally on channel 32. For news tips, story ideas and press releases send an email at bcassign@ctv.ca
TELEVISION STATION

CIVV-TV (Télé-Québec Saguenay) 377711
Owner: Société de télédiffusion du Québec(La)
Editorial: 3788 Rue de la Fabrique, pavillon joseph-angers, Jonquiere, Quebec G7X 3P4 **Tel:** 1 418 695-8152.
Email: info@telequebec.tv
Web site: http://www.telequebec.tv
Profile: CIVV-TV est une station affiliée de Télé-Québec au Saguenay-Lac-St-Jean. La station est une propriété de La Société de télédiffusion du Québec. CIVV-TV est retransmit localement au canal 8.

CIVV-TV is the Télé-Québec affiliate for the Saguenay-Lac-St-Jean. The station is owned by La Société de télédiffusion du Québec. CIVV-TV broadcasts locally on channel 8.
TELEVISION STATION

CJBR-TV (ICI Radio-Canada Télévision Est-du-Québec) 33286
Owner: Société Radio-Canada
Editorial: 273 Rue Saint-Jean-Baptiste O, Rimouski, Quebec G5L 4J7 **Tel:** 1 418 723-2217.
Email: cjbr@radio-canada.ca
Web site: http://www.radio-canada.ca/est-du-quebec/
Profile: CJBR-TV est une station affiliée de Radio-Canada pour l'Est-du-Québec. La station est une propriété de Société de Radio-Canada. CJBR-TV est diffusé localement sur le canal 2.

CJBR-TV is the Radio-Canada affiliate serving the Rimouski, Quebec area. The station is owned by Société Radio-Canada. CJBR-TV broadcasts locally on channel 2.
TELEVISION STATION

CJCB-TV (CTV Atlantic Sydney/Cape Breton NS) 33192
Owner: Bell Media
Editorial: 1283 George St, Sydney, Nova Scotia B1P 1N7 **Tel:** 1 902 562-5511.
Email: atlanticnews@bellmedia.ca
Web site: http://atlantic.ctvnews.ca
Profile: CJCB-TV is the CTV affiliate for the Sydney, Nova Scotia market. The station is owned by Bell Media. CJCB-TV broadcasts locally on channel 4.
TELEVISION STATION

CJCH-DT (CTV Atlantic Halifax NS) 33187
Owner: Bell Media
Editorial: 2885 Robie St, Halifax, Nova Scotia B3K 5Z4 **Tel:** 1 902 453-4000.
Email: atlanticnews@bellmedia.ca
Web site: http://atlantic.ctv.ca
Profile: CJCH-DT is the CTV affiliate for the Halifax, Nova Scotia market. The station is owned by Bell Media. CJCH-DT broadcasts on digital channel 48 (UHF).
TELEVISION STATION

CJCN-TV 33254
Owner: Newfoundland Broadcasting Co. Ltd.
Editorial: 446 Logy Bay Rd, St. John's, Newfoundland A1A 5C6 **Tel:** 1 709 722-5015.
Email: ntv@ntv.ca
Web site: http://www.ntv.ca
TELEVISION STATION

Canada

CJCO-TV (OMNI Calgary) 545858
Owner: Rogers Media Inc.
Editorial: 535 7 Ave SW, Calgary, Alberta T2P 0Y4
Tel: 1 403 508-3542.
Web site: http://www.omniab.ca
Profile: CJCO-TV is an independent station for the Calgary, Alberta market. The station is owned by Rogers Media Inc. CJCO-TV broadcasts locally on channel 38.
TELEVISION STATION

CJDC-TV 33141
Owner: Astral Media
Editorial: 901-102nd Avenue, Dawson Creek, British Columbia V1G 2B6 **Tel:** 1 250 782-3341.
Email: peacereception@astral.com
Web site: http://www.cjdctv.com
Profile: CJDC-TV is the CBC affiliate in Dawson Creek, British Columbia. The station is owned by Astral Media. CJDC-TV broadcasts locally on channel 5.
TELEVISION STATION

CJEO-TV 545859
Owner: Rogers Media Inc.
Editorial: 10212 Jasper Ave NW, Edmonton, Alberta T5J 5A3 **Tel:** 1 780 424-2222.
Web site: http://www.omniab.ca
Profile: CJEO-TV is an independent station for the Edmonton, Alberta market. The station is owned by Rogers Media Inc. CJEO-TV broadcasts locally on channel 56.
TELEVISION STATION

CJIC-TV (CBC-Sault Ste. Marie) 33197
Owner: Canadian Broadcasting Corp.
Editorial: 250 Front St, Toronto, Ontario M5V 3G5
Tel: 1 416 205-6309.
Email: tonews@cbc.ca
Web site: http://www.cbc.ca/toronto
Profile: CBLT5-TV is a local, commercial television station owned by Canadian Broadcasting Corp. The station serves as the CBC affiliate for Sault-Sainte Marie, and Ontario. CBLT5-TV airs locally on channel 11. There is no physical station or staff located in Sault Ste. Marie, Ontario.
TELEVISION STATION

CJIL-TV 63286
Owner: Miracle Channel Association(The)
Editorial: 450 31 St N, Lethbridge, Alberta T1H 3Z3
Tel: 1 403 380-3399.
Web site: http://www.miraclechannel.ca
Profile: CJIL-TV is a commercial television station for the Lethbridge, Alberta area. The station is owned by The Miracle Channel Association. CJIL-TV broadcasts locally on channel 17.
TELEVISION STATION

CJMT-TV (Rogers Media-OMNI-2) 154570
Owner: Rogers Media Inc.
Editorial: 33 Dundas St E, Toronto, Ontario M5B 1B8-
Tel: 1 416 260-0047.
Web site: http://www.omnitv.ca/ontario
Profile: CJMT-TV is an independent station for the Toronto, ON market. The station is owned by Rogers Media Inc. CJMT-TV broadcasts locally on channel 69.
TELEVISION STATION

CJNT-TV (CITY TV Montreal) 33253
Owner: Rogers Communications
Editorial: 1200 McGill College ave, bur. 800, Montreal, Quebec H3K 1G6 **Tel:** 1 514 599-2489.
Web site: http://www.citytv.com/montreal
Profile: CJNT-TV is owned by Rogers Communications. CJNT-TV broadcasts locally on channel 62. On June 4, 2012 CJNT-TV will start airing some content from CITY-TV.
TELEVISION STATION

CJOH-TV (CTV Ottawa) 33173
Owner: Bell Media
Editorial: 87 George St, Ottawa, Ontario K1N 9H7-
Tel: 1 613 224-1313.
Email: ctvottawa@ctv.ca
Web site: http://ottawa.ctvnews.ca
Profile: CJOH-TV is the CTV affiliate for the Ottawa, Ontario market. The station is owned by Bell Media. The station's tagline is CTV Ottawa. CJOH-TV broadcasts locally on channel 13.
TELEVISION STATION

CJOM-TV 33252
Owner: Newfoundland Broadcasting Co. Ltd.
Editorial: 446 Logy Bay Rd, St. John's, Newfoundland A1A 5C6 **Tel:** 1 709 722-5015.
Email: ntv@ntv.ca
Web site: http://www.ntv.ca
Profile: Local television station broadcasting in the St. John's area.
TELEVISION STATION

CJON-TV 33200
Owner: Newfoundland Broadcasting Co. Ltd.
Editorial: 446 Logy Bay Rd, St. John's, Newfoundland A1A 5C6 **Tel:** 1 709 722-5015.
Email: news@ntv.ca
Web site: http://ntv.ca
Profile: CJON-TV is the CTV affiliate for the St. John's, Newfoundland market. The station is owned by Newfoundland Broadcasting Co. Ltd. CJON-TV broadcasts locally on channel 6.
TELEVISION STATION

CJPM-TV (TVA Saguenay) 33188
Owner: Quebecor Media Inc.
Editorial: 1 rue Mont Ste-Claire, Chicoutimi, Quebec G7H 5G3 **Tel:** 1 418 549-2576.
Email: nouvelles.cjpm@tva.ca
Web site: http://www.tvanouvelles.ca/regional/saguenay-lac-saint-jean
Profile: CJPM-TV est une station de télévision affiliée de TVA au Saguenay. La station est une propriété de Quebecor Media Inc. CJPM-TV est diffusé localement sur le canal 6.

CJPM-TV is the TVA affiliate for the Chicoutimi, Quebec market. The station is owned by Quebecor Media Inc. CJPM-TV broadcasts locally on channel 6.
TELEVISION STATION

CJWB-TV 33250
Owner: Newfoundland Broadcasting Co. Ltd.
Editorial: 446 Logy Bay Rd, St. John's, Newfoundland A1A 5C6 **Tel:** 1 709 722-5015.
Email: ntv@ntv.ca
Web site: http://www.ntv.ca
TELEVISION STATION

CJWN-TV 33249
Owner: Newfoundland Broadcasting Co. Ltd.
Editorial: 446 Logy Bay Rd, St. John's, Newfoundland A1A 5C6 **Tel:** 1 709 722-5015.
Email: news@ntv.ca
Web site: http://www.ntv.ca
Profile: Offers news updates, entertainment and sports. Their tagline is Canada's Superstation.
TELEVISION STATION

CKAL-TV 63289
Owner: Rogers Media Inc.
Editorial: 535 7 Ave SW, Calgary, Alberta T2P 0Y4
Tel: 1 403 508-2222.
Web site: http://www.citytv.com/calgary
Profile: CKAL-TV is the CityTV Calgary affiliate for the Calgary, Alberta market. The station is owned by Rogers Media Inc. CKAL-TV broadcasts locally on channel 5.
TELEVISION STATION

CKCD-TV 33246
Owner: Bell Media
Editorial: Campbellton, New Brunswick
Tel: 1 506 857-2600.
Email: news@ctv.ca
Web site: http://atlantic.ctv.ca
Profile: CKCD-TV is the CTV affiliate for the Campbellton, New Brunswick market. The station is owned by Bell Media. CKCD-TV broadcasts locally on channel 7. CKCD-TV is a rebroadcaster of CKCW-TV (CTV Atlantic Moncton). It retransmits the programs of CKCW-TV.
TELEVISION STATION

CKCK-TV 33133
Owner: Bell Media
Editorial: 1 Highway East, Regina, Saskatchewan S4P 3E5 **Tel:** 1 306 569-2000.
Email: ckcknews@ctv.ca
Web site: http://www.regina.ctv.ca
Profile: CKCK-TV is the CTV affiliate for the Regina, Saskatchewan market. The station is owned by Bell Media. CKCK-TV broadcasts locally on channel 2.
TELEVISION STATION

CKCO-TV (CTV Kitchener) 33219
Owner: Bell Media
Editorial: 864 King St W, Kitchener, Ontario N2G 1E8
Tel: 1 519 578-1313.
Email: news@kitchener.ctv.ca
Web site: http://kitchener.ctvnews.ca
Profile: CKCO-TV is the CTV affiliate for the Kitchener, Ontario market. The station is owned by Bell Media. CKCO-TV broadcasts locally on channel 13.
TELEVISION STATION

CKCS-TV 505379
Owner: Crossroads Television Systems
Editorial: Atrium 1, 839 5th Ave SW, Ste 100B, Calgary, Alberta T2P 3C8 **Tel:** 1 403 263-3191.
Web site: http://www.ctstv.com
Profile: CKCS-TV is the CTS television affiliate for the Calgary, Alberta market. The station is owned by Crossroads Television Systems. CKCS-TV broadcasts locally on channel 32.
TELEVISION STATION

CKCW-DT (CTV Atlantic Moncton NB) 33183
Owner: Bell Media
Editorial: 191 Halifax St, Moncton, New Brunswick E1C 9R7 **Tel:** 1 506 857-2600.
Email: ckcw@ctv.ca
Web site: http://atlantic.ctv.ca
Profile: CKCW-DT is the CTV affiliate for the Moncton, New Brunswick market. The station is owned by Bell Media. CKCW-DT broadcasts on digital channel 29 (UHF). Former call sign was CKCW-TV and former analog channel was 2 (1954-2011).
TELEVISION STATION

CKEM-TV 63288
Owner: Rogers Media Inc.
Editorial: 10212 Jasper Ave, Edmonton, Alberta T5J 5A3 **Tel:** 1 780 424-2222.
Email: newsdesk@citytv.com
Web site: http://www.citytv.com/edmonton
Profile: CKEM-TV is the CityTV affiliate for the Edmonton, Alberta market. The station is owned by Rogers Media Inc. CKEM-TV broadcasts locally on channel 51.
TELEVISION STATION

CKES-TV 505387
Owner: Crossroads Television Systems
Editorial: 5330 Calgary Trail, Edmonton, Alberta T6H 4J8 **Tel:** 1 780 433-3118.
Email: contactus@ctstv.com
Web site: http://www.ctstv.com
Profile: CKES-TV is the CTS television affiliate for the Edmonton, Alberta market. The station is owned by Crossroads Television Systems. CKES-TV airs locally on channel 45.
TELEVISION STATION

CKLT-DT (CTV Atlantic Saint John NB) 231781
Owner: Bell Media
Editorial: 12 Smythe Street, Suite 3, Saint John, New Brunswick E2L 5G5 **Tel:** 1 506 658-1010.
Email: cklt@ctv.ca
Web site: http://atlantic.ctv.ca
Profile: CKLT-DT is the CTV affiliate for the Saint John, New Brunswick market. The station is owned by Bell Media. CKLT-DT broadcasts on digital channel 9.
TELEVISION STATION

CKMI-TV (Global Television Montreal) 33235
Owner: Corus Entertainment Inc.
Editorial: 1010, Rue Ste-Catherine Ouest, Bureau 200, Montreal, Quebec H3B 5L1 **Tel:** 1 514 521-4323.
Email: montreal@globalnews.ca
Web site: http://www.globalmontreal.com
Profile: CKMI-TV is a Global Television Network affiliate for the Montreal market. The station is owned by Corus Entertainment Inc. CKMI-TV broadcasts locally on channel 46.
TELEVISION STATION

CKND-TV (Global Winnipeg) 33227
Owner: Corus Entertainment Inc.
Editorial: 201 Portage Ave, 30th floor, Winnipeg, Manitoba R3B 3K6 **Tel:** 1 204 233-3304.
Email: winnipeg@globalnews.ca
Web site: http://www.globalwinnipeg.com
Profile: CKND-TV is the Global Television Network affiliate for the Winnipeg, Manitoba market. The station is owned by Corus Entertainment Inc. CKND-TV broadcasts locally on channel 9.
TELEVISION STATION

CKNY-TV (CTV News-Northern Ontario) 33223
Owner: Bell Media
Editorial: 245 Oak St E, North Bay, Ontario P1B 8P8
Tel: 1 705 476-3111.
Email: newsforthenorth@ctv.ca
Web site: http://northernontario.ctvnews.ca
Profile: CKNY-TV is the CTV affiliate for the North Bay, Ontario market. The station is owned by Bell Media. CKNY-TV broadcasts locally on channel 10.
TELEVISION STATION

CKPG-TV 33134
Owner: Jim Pattison Broadcast Group(The)
Editorial: 1810 3rd Ave Fl 2ND, Prince George, British Columbia V2M 1G4 **Tel:** 1 250 564-8861.
Email: ckpgnews@ckpg.com
Web site: http://www.ckpg.com
Profile: CKPG-TV is an independent station for the Prince George, British Columbia market. The station is owned by The Jim Pattison Broadcast Group. CKPG-TV broadcasts locally on channel 2. .
TELEVISION STATION

CKPR-TV (CTV-Thunder Bay) 33215
Owner: Dougall Media
Editorial: 87 Hill St N, Thunder Bay, Ontario P7A 5V6
Tel: 1 807 346-2600.
Email: news@dougallmedia.com
Web site: http://www.ckprthunderbay.com/
Profile: CKPR-TV is the CBC affiliate for the Thunder Bay, Ontario market. The station is owned by Dougall Media. CKPR-TV broadcasts locally on channel 2.
TELEVISION STATION

CKRN-TV (Radio-Canada Abitibi-Temiscamingue) 33181
Owner: RNC Media
Editorial: 70 Av Principale, Rouyn-Noranda, Quebec J9X 4P2 **Tel:** 1 819 762-0744.
Web site: http://www.rncmedia.ca
Profile: CKRN-TV est une station de télévision affiliée de Radio-Canada en Abitibi-Témiscamingue. La station est une propriété de RNC Media. CKRN-TV est diffusé localement sur le canal 4.

CKRN-TV is the Radio-Canada Reseaux Television affiliate for the Abitibi-Témiscamingue, Quebec area. The station is owned by RNC Media. CKRN-TV airs locally on channel 4.
TELEVISION STATION

CKRT-TV (Radio-Canada Rivière-du-Loup) 33157
Owner: Télé Inter-Rives Ltée
Editorial: 15 Rue de la Chute, Riviere-du-Loup, Quebec G5R 5B7 **Tel:** 1 418 867-8080.
Email: nouvelles@ckrt.ca
Web site: http://www.ckrt.ca
Profile: CKRT-TV est une station affiliée de Radio-Canada pour Rivière-du-loup, Québec. La station est une propriété de Télé Inter-Rives Ltée. CKRT-TV est diffusé localement au canal 7.

CKRT-TV is the Radio-Canada affiliate for the Riviere-du-Loup, Quebec market. The station is owned by Télé Inter-Rives Ltée. CKRT-TV broadcasts locally on channel 7.
TELEVISION STATION

CKSA-TV 33150
Owner: Newfoundland Capital Corporation Limited
Editorial: 5026 50th St, Lloydminster, Alberta T9V 1P3
Tel: 1 780 875-3321.
Email: tvnews@newcap.ca
Web site: http://www.newcaptv.com
Profile: CKSA-TV is the CBC affiliate for the Lloydminster, Alberta market. The station is owned by Newfoundland Capital Corporation Limited. CKSA-TV airs locally on channel 2.
TELEVISION STATION

CKSH-TV (Radio-Canada Estrie) 33212
Owner: Société Radio-Canada
Editorial: 1335 Rue King O, Sherbrooke, Quebec J1J 2B8 **Tel:** 1 819 620-0000.
Email: estrie@radio-canada.ca
Web site: http://www.radio-canada.ca/estrie
Profile: CKSH-TV est une station de télévision de Radio-Canada à Sherbooke. La station est une propriété de la Société de Radio-Canada. CKSH-TV est diffusée localement sur la canal 9.

CKSH-TV is the Radio-Canada affiliate for the Sherbrooke, Quebec market. The station is owned by Société Radio-Canada. CKSH-TV broadcasts locally on channel 9.
TELEVISION STATION

CKTM-TV (Radio-Canada Mauricie) 33176
Owner: Société Radio-Canada
Editorial: 225 Rue des Forges Suite 101, Trois-Rivieres, Quebec G9A 2G7 **Tel:** 1 819 694-0114.
Email: tjmauricie@radio-canada.ca
Web site: http://www.radio-canada.ca/regions/mauricie
Profile: CKTM-TV est une station affiliée de Radio-Canada à Trois-Rivières. La station est une propriété de la Société de Radio-Canada. CKTM-TV est diffusé localement sur le canal 13.

CKTM-TV is an affiliate of Radio-Canada for the Trois-Rivieres, Quebec area. The station is owned by Societe Radio-Canada. CKTM-TV broadcasts locally on channel 13.
TELEVISION STATION

CKTV-TV (Radio-Canada Saguenay-Lac-Saint-Jean) 33204
Owner: Société Radio-Canada
Editorial: 500 Rue des Sagueneens, Chicoutimi, Quebec G7H 6N4 **Tel:** 1 418 696-6600.
Email: saguenay@radio-canada.ca
Web site: http://radio-canada.ca/saguenay-lac-saint-jean
Profile: CKTV-TV est la station affiliée de Radio-Canada au Saguenay-Lac-Saint-Jean. La station est une propriété de la Société de Radio-Canada. CKTV-TV est diffusé localement sur le canal 12.

CKTV-TV is the Radio-Canada affiliate for the Saguenay, Quebec area. The station is owned by Société Radio-Canada. CKTV-TV broadcasts locally on channel 12. Les bulletins de nouvelles sont produits localement à la station.
TELEVISION STATION

CKVR-TV 33170
Owner: Bell Media
Editorial: 33 Beacon Rd, Barrie, Ontario L4N 9J9
Tel: 1 705 734-3300.
Email: barrienews@ctv.ca
Web site: http://ctvbarrie.ca
Profile: CKVR-TV is the CTV affiliate for the Barrie, Ontario market. The station is owned by Bell Media. CKVR-TV broadcasts locally on channel 3.
TELEVISION STATION

CKVU-TV (CityTV Vancouver) 33165
Owner: Rogers Media Inc.
Editorial: 180 2nd Ave W, Vancouver, British Columbia V5Y 3T9 **Tel:** 1 604 876-1344.
Email: news@btvancouver.ca
Web site: http://www.citytv.com/vancouver
Profile: CKVU-TV is branded as part of the CityTV family offering local news programming for the Vancouver, British Columbia market. The station is owned by Rogers Media Inc. CKVU-TV broadcasts locally on channel 10.
TELEVISION STATION

CKWS-TV (CTV-Kingston) 33142
Owner: Corus Entertainment Inc.
Editorial: 170 Queen St, Kingston, Ontario K7K 1B2
Tel: 1 613 544-2340.
Email: newswatch@corusent.com
Web site: http://www.ckwstv.com
Profile: CKWS-TV is the CTV affiliate for the Kingston, Ontario market. The station is owned by Corus Entertainment Inc. CKWS-TV broadcasts locally on channel 11.
TELEVISION STATION

CKY-TV 33226
Owner: Bell Media
Editorial: 400-345 Graham Ave 400, Winnipeg, Manitoba R3C 5S6 **Tel:** 1 204 788-3300.
Email: winnipegnews@ctv.ca
Web site: http://winnipeg.ctvnews.ca
Profile: CKY-TV is the CTV affiliate for the Winnipeg, Manitoba region. The station is owned by Bell Media. CKY-TV broadcasts locally on channel 7.
TELEVISION STATION

CRRS-TV 83442
Owner: Community Recreation Rebroad. Service Association
Editorial: 208 Amherst Ave, Labrador City, Newfoundland A2V 2Y5 **Tel:** 1 709 944-7676.
Email: info@crrstv.net
Web site: http://www.crrstv.net
Profile: Local television station.
TELEVISION STATION

CTV Atlantic 152066
Owner: Bell Media
Editorial: 2885 Robie St, Halifax, Nova Scotia B3K 5Z4 **Tel:** 1 902 453-4000.
Email: cjch@ctv.ca
Web site: http://atlantic.ctvnews.ca
Profile: CTV Atlantic is a network of four television stations in the Canadian Maritimes, owned and operated by the CTV Television Network, a division of Bell Media. The four CTV Atlantic stations are CJCH-DT in Halifax, Nova Scotia, CJCB-TV in Sydney, Nova Scotia, CKCW-DT in Moncton, New Brunswick and CKLT-DT in Saint John, New Brunswick.
TELEVISION NETWORK

CTV Atlantic - Fredericton Bureau 152067
Owner: Bell Media
Editorial: 206 Rookwood Ave, Fredericton, New Brunswick E3B 2M2 **Tel:** 1 506 459-1010.
Profile: CTV Atlantic - Fredericton Bureau is the television network bureau of CTV in Fredericton, New Brunswick.
TELEVISION NETWORK

CTV Atlantic - Moncton Bureau 152068
Owner: Bell Media
Editorial: 191 Halifax St, Moncton, New Brunswick E1C 9R7 **Tel:** 1 506 857-2610.
Email: ckcw@ctv.ca
Profile: CTV Atlantic - Moncton Bureau is the television network bureau of CTV in Moncton, New Brunswick.
TELEVISION NETWORK

CTV Atlantic - Saint John Bureau 152069
Owner: Bell Media
Editorial: 1 Germain St, Saint John, New Brunswick E2L 4V1 **Tel:** 1 506 636-6068.
Profile: CTV Atlantic - Saint John Bureau is the television network bureau of CTV in Saint John, New Brunswick.
TELEVISION NETWORK

CTV Television Network 63598
Owner: Bell Media
Editorial: 9 Channel Nine Crt, Toronto, Ontario M1S 4B5- **Tel:** 1 416 332-5000.
Email: news@ctv.ca
Web site: http://www.ctv.ca
Profile: CTV Television Network is owned by Bell Media, Canada's largest private broadcaster and premier multimedia company. The network offers a wide range of quality news, sports, information and entertainment programming that reaches 99% of English-speaking Canadians. It has the number one national newscast, and is the number one choice for primetime viewing.
TELEVISION NETWORK

CTV Television Network - Washington Bureau 231342
Editorial: 1717 Desales St Nw, Suite 354, Washington, District Of Columbia 20036-4401 **Tel:** 1 202 775-0356.
TELEVISION NETWORK

E! Entertainment Television (NBCUniversal-Canada) 526199
Owner: Bell Media
Editorial: 299 Queen St W, Toronto, Ontario M5V 2Z5- **Tel:** 1 416 384-5000.
Email: eonline@bellmedia.ca
Web site: http://ca.eonline.com
Profile: In Canada, the E! network broadcasts into the major markets of Vancouver, British Columbia; Toronto; Calgary, Alberta and Edmonton, Alberta.
TELEVISION NETWORK

Fairchild Television Network 70632
Editorial: 35 E Beaver Creek Road, Unit 8, Richmond Hill, Ontario L4B 1B3 **Tel:** 1 905 889-8090.
Email: newstor@fairchildtv.com
Web site: http://www.fairchildtv.com
Profile: Twenty-one hours a day, seven days a week, Fairchild TV provides the Chinese audience with the information they need in their own language. Fairchild is carried on cable in Toronto and throughout Southern Ontario, in Montreal, Vancouver, Calgary and Edmonton and also on the nationwide direct-to-home satellite services. Every day, Fairchild TV produces newscasts covering local and international news from a Chinese-Canadian perspective. It also broadcasts same-day satellite news programs from Hong Kong.
TELEVISION NETWORK

Fairchild Television Network - Calgary Bureau 70633
Editorial: 2723-37 Avenue NE, Suite 130, Calgary, Alberta T1Y 5R8 **Tel:** 1 403 571-3187.
Email: info@fairchildtv.com
Web site: http://www.fairchildtv.com
TELEVISION NETWORK

Fairchild Television Network - Richmond Bureau 70634
Owner: Fairchild Television Ltd.
Editorial: 4151 Hazelbridge Way, aberdeen centre, Richmond, British Columbia V6X 4J7 **Tel:** 1 604 295-1313.
Email: info@fairchildtv.com
Web site: http://www.fairchildtv.com
TELEVISION NETWORK

Global Television Network 63595
Owner: Corus Entertainment
Editorial: 81 Barber Greene Rd, Toronto, Ontario M3C 2A2- **Tel:** 1 416 446-5460.
Email: newstips@globaltv.com
Web site: http://www.globaltv.com
Profile: Global Television Network, owned by Corus Entertainment, is a national television network serving viewers throughout Canada. The network provides a wide variety of programming, ranging from hard news to entertainment. Global Television offers a programming mix aimed at viewers primarily in the 18 to 49 age bracket. The Global Television Network is a member of the Canadian Press Gallery.
TELEVISION NETWORK

Global Television Network - Burnaby Bureau 620987
Editorial: 7850 Enterprise St, Burnaby, British Columbia V5A 1V7 **Tel:** 1 604 420-2288.
Email: tips@globaltvbc.com
Web site: http://globalnews.ca/bc
TELEVISION NETWORK

Global Television Network - Calgary Bureau 620998
Editorial: 222 23 Ave NE, Calgary, Alberta T2E 1V7 **Tel:** 1 403 235-7777.
Email: calgary@globalnews.ca
TELEVISION NETWORK

Global Television Network - Edmonton Bureau 620648
Editorial: 5325 Allard Way NW, Edmonton, Alberta T6H 5B8 **Tel:** 1 780 436-1250.
Email: edmonton@globalnews.ca
Web site: http://globalnews.ca/edmonton
Profile: Edmonton, Alberta bureau of the Global Television Network.
TELEVISION NETWORK

Global Television Network - Halifax Bureau 151905
Editorial: 2110 Gottingen St, Halifax, Nova Scotia B3K 3B3 **Tel:** 1 902 481-7400.
Email: halifax@globalnews.ca
Web site: http://globalnews.ca/halifax
TELEVISION NETWORK

Global Television Network - Lethbridge Bureau 619638
Editorial: 1401 28 St N, Lethbridge, Alberta T1H 6H9 **Tel:** 1 403 327-1507.
Email: lethbridge@globalnews.ca
Web site: http://globalnews.ca/lethbridge
TELEVISION NETWORK

Global Television Network - Montreal Bureau 619651
Editorial: 1010, rue Sainte-Catherine, bureau 200, Montreal, Quebec H3B 5L1 **Tel:** 1 514 521-4323.
Email: montreal@globalnews.ca
Web site: http://globalnews.ca/montreal
Profile: Global Television Network - Montreal Bureau is the the Global News Bureau for the Montreal market.
TELEVISION NETWORK

Global Television Network - Regina Bureau 619337
Editorial: 370 Hoffer Dr, Regina, Saskatchewan S4N 7A4 **Tel:** 1 306 775-4000.
Email: regina@globalnews.ca
Web site: http://globalnews.ca/regina
TELEVISION NETWORK

Global Television Network - Saskatoon Bureau 619391
Editorial: 218 Robin Cres, Saskatoon, Saskatchewan S7L 7C3 **Tel:** 1 306 978-6397.
Email: saskatoon@globalnews.ca
Web site: http://globalnews.ca/saskatoon
TELEVISION NETWORK

Global Television Network - Winnipeg Bureau 619399
Editorial: 201 Portage Ave, Winnipeg, Manitoba R3B 3K6 **Tel:** 1 204 235-8545.
Email: winnipeg@globalnews.ca
Web site: http://globalnews.ca/winnipeg
TELEVISION NETWORK

Nickelodeon Canada 606409
Owner: Corus Entertainment Inc.
Editorial: 25 Dockside Dr, corus quay, Toronto, Ontario M5A 0B5 **Tel:** 1 416 479-7000.
Web site: http://www.nickcanada.com
Profile: This specialty cable network provides programming geared toward children, teens and their parents. It is based off the the programming from Nickelodeon in United States. The network also includes exclusive programs to Canadian kids and features a line-up of award-winning properties, from current live-action comedies and animated favorites to classic hits.
TELEVISION NETWORK

Talentvision (FairechildTV-Toronto) 139334
Editorial: 35 E Beaver Creek Road, Unit 8, Richmond Hill, Ontario L4B 1B3 **Tel:** 1 905 889-8090.
Email: prgtor@fairchildtv.com
Web site: http://www.fairchildtv.com
Profile: Launched in June 1998, Talentvision is a national network serving the Mandarin community of Canada. The network has regional stations in British Columbia and Ontario, and is distributed via cable and Direct-to-Home satellite services. The network boasts 18 hours of Mandarin programs a day, 7 days a week.
TELEVISION NETWORK

La Télévision de Radio-Canada 83249
Owner: Société Radio-Canada
Editorial: 1400 Boul Rene-Levesque E, Montreal, Quebec H2L 2M2- **Tel:** 1 514 597-6000.
Email: nouvelles@radio-canada.ca
Web site: http://ici.radio-canada.ca/tele
Profile: La Télévision de Radio-Canada est l'équivalence de CBC Television Network. Ce réseau est le service de télévision principal francophone de CBC. Il est transmit partout à travers le Canada. La Télévision de Radio-Canada est un membre de la Galerie de presse canadienne.

La Télévision de Radio-Canada is the French equivalent of the CBC Television Network. It is the main French-language television service of the CBC. It broadcasts in all Canadian provinces. La Télévision de Radio-Canada is a member of the Canadian Press Gallery.
TELEVISION NETWORK

TVA 573792
Owner: Quebecor Media Inc.
Editorial: 1600 boulevard Maisonneuve Est, Montreal, Quebec H2L 4P2 **Tel:** 1 514 526-9251.
Email: nouvelles@tva.ca
Web site: http://tva.canoe.ca
Profile: TVA est un réseau de télévision, une propriété de Québécor Média Inc. TVA crée, produit et met en onde des émissions de divertissement, de nouvelles et d'affaires publiques.

TVA is a Television Network, owned by Quebecor Media Inc. TVA creates, produces and airs shows in the areas of entertainment, news and public affairs.
TELEVISION NETWORK

UmeedTV Network 897296
Editorial: 363A-6830 Av du Parc 363A, Montreal, Quebec H3N 1W7 **Tel:** 1 514 495-6699.
Email: info@umeedtv.com
Web site: http://www.umeedtv.com
Profile: A multicultural television network presenting news and entertainment that represents the South Asian community.
TELEVISION NETWORK

V 577713
Owner: Remstar Corporation
Editorial: 355, rue Ste-Catherine Ouest, Bureau 100, Montreal, Quebec H3B 1A5 **Tel:** 1 514 390-6100.
Web site: http://noovo.ca
Profile: V est un réseau de télévision francophone avec différentes stations affiliées à travers le Québec. Le nom "V" est une réflexion du nouveau divertissement du réseau : Vedettes, Vitesse, Victoires, Voyages, Vice ou Vérité. V a changé de nom le 31 août 2009. Le nom qui le précédait TQS (Télévision Quatre Saisons).

V is a French-language television network with stations and affiliates throughout Quebec. The name, "V," is a reflection of the new entertainment focus of the network: Vedettes (Stars), Vitesse (Speed), Victoires (Victories), Voyages (Trips) and Vice ou Vérité (Vice or Truth). V changed its name from TQS (Télévision Quatre Saisons) on August 31, 2009.
TELEVISION NETWORK

Cable

ABC Spark 788773
Owner: Corus Entertainment Inc.
Editorial: 25 Dockside Dr, corus quay, Toronto, Ontario M5A 0B5 **Tel:** 1 416 479-7000.
Email: info@abcsparkcanada.com
Web site: http://www.abcspark.ca
Profile: ABC Spark offers fun, light-hearted programming with a twist for kids, teens, and adults. The channel features original series and movies, major theatrical releases, and repurposed programming from the ABC Television Network. ABC Spark officially launched on March 26, 2012.
CABLE NETWORK

Aboriginal Peoples Television Network 83237
Editorial: 339 Portage Ave, Winnipeg, Manitoba R3B 2C3 **Tel:** 1 204 947-9331.
Email: info@aptn.ca
Web site: http://www.aptn.ca
Profile: A network that provides Indigenous people the opportunity to share their stories with the rest of the world on a television outlet dedicated to Aboriginal programming. Through documentaries, news magazines, dramas, entertainment specials, children's series, cooking shows and education programs, APTN offers all Canadians a window into the remarkably diverse worlds of Indigenous peoples in Canada and throughout the world. Headquartered in Winnipeg, Manitoba, APTN offers an unprecedented opportunity for Aboriginal producers, directors, actors, writers and media professionals to create innovative, reflective and relevant programming for Canadian viewers.
CABLE NETWORK

Aboriginal Peoples Television Network - Montreal Bureau 701134
Editorial: 1819 Boul Rene-Levesque O Bureau 300, Montreal, Quebec H3H 2P5 **Tel:** 1 514 495-6424.
Email: info@aptn.ca
Web site: http://aptnnews.ca/
Profile: The Montreal Bureau of Aboriginal Peoples Television Network.
CABLE NETWORK

Aboriginal Peoples Television Network - North Vancouver Bureau 701141
Editorial: 210-1999 Marine Dr 210, North Vancouver, British Columbia V7P 3J3 **Tel:** 1 604 986-9843.
Email: info@aptn.ca
Web site: http://aptnnews.ca/tag/british-columbia/
Profile: Vancouver Bureau of Aboriginal Peoples Television Network.
CABLE NETWORK

Aboriginal Peoples Television Network - Ottawa Bureau 701132
Editorial: 45 O'Connor St Suite 880, Ottawa, Ontario K1P 1A4 **Tel:** 1 613 567-1550.
Profile: The APTN's Ottawa Bureau. Aboriginal Peoples Television Network (APTN) is a network that provides Indigenous people the opportunity to share their stories with the rest of the world on a television outlet dedicated to Aboriginal programming.
CABLE NETWORK

Action 83178
Owner: Corus Entertainment Inc
Editorial: 121 Bloor St E Fl SUITE, 15th b1, Toronto, Ontario M4W 3M5 **Tel:** 1 416 967-0022.
Email: feedback@showcase.ca
Web site: http://www.action-tv.ca
Profile: Network which features smash-hit movies with spies and tough guys, adventurers and kung-fu masters. Showcase Action programs include some of the world's greatest heroes like Arnold Schwarzenegger, Sylvester Stallone, Jackie Chan, Bruce Willis and Steve McQueen. Programming includes classic action series and sexy late-night programming.
CABLE NETWORK

Addik TV 363154
Owner: Groupe TVA Inc.
Editorial: 1600 Boul de Maisonneuve E, Montreal, Quebec H2L 4P2- **Tel:** 1 514 526-9251.
Email: relations.auditoire@tva.ca
Web site: http://www.addik.tv
Profile: Addik TV, auparavant Mystère, est un réseau de chaînes spécialisées francophones, une propriété de Groupe TVA Inc. On présente des films et des séries, pendant toute la journée, 24H sur 24. La programmation inclut 2 différents genres: fantaisie, crime, action et mystère.

Addik TV, formerly Mystère, is a French-language cable network owned by Groupe TVA Inc. It offers movies and series twenty-four hours a day. Its programming includes four different genres: fantasy, crime, action and mystery.
CABLE NETWORK

Al Al Jazeera English - Toronto Bureau 685425
Owner: Al Jazeera Network
Editorial: Toronto, Ontario **Tel:** 1 416 941-8107.
Email: america@aljazeera.net
Web site: http://www.aljazeera.com
Profile: The Al Jazeera English - Toronto Bureau launched in June 2010.
CABLE NETWORK

AMI Television 771744
Owner: Accessible Media Inc.
Editorial: 1090 Don Mills Rd, Toronto, Ontario M3C 3R6 **Tel:** 1 416 422-4222.
Email: amitele@ami.ca
Web site: http://www.ami.ca
Profile: AMI (Accessible Media Inc.) Television broadcasts popular movies and TV shows in open described closed-captioned format for people who are blind, vision-impaired, deaf or hard of hearing.
CABLE NETWORK

Canada

Animal Planet 83239
Owner: Bell Media
Editorial: 9 Channel Nine Crt, Toronto, Ontario M1S 4B5- **Tel:** 1 416 332-5000.
Email: comments@animalplanet.ca
Web site: http://www.animalplanet.ca
Profile: Animal Planet lets viewers see Earth from a wilder perspective. The world's weirdest, wildest and most wonderful creatures take charge of Animal Planet Canada in the most entertaining and engaging ways. From the most perilous encounters with nature's fiercest predators to the pets we bring into our own family, all creatures big and small are the undeniable stars of Animal Planet.
CABLE NETWORK

Asian Television Network 83193
Owner: Asian Television Network International Limited
Editorial: 330 Cochrane Drive, Markham, Ontario L3R 8E4 **Tel:** 1 905 948-8199.
Email: atn@asiantelevision.com
Web site: http://www.asiantelevision.com
Profile: Programming is geared to people of the South East Asian communities who come from India, Pakistan, Sri Lanka, South Africa, East Africa, Trinidad, Surinam and Guyana. The network reaches Canada, the U.S. and the Caribbean.
CABLE NETWORK

AUX TV 692447
Owner: GlassBOX Television Inc.
Editorial: 2196 Dunwin Dr., Mississauga, Ontario L5L 1C7 **Tel:** 1 905 828-2483.
Email: info@aux.tv
Web site: http://www.aux.tv
Profile: Offers music videos and music-related programming to a Canadian audience. First launched on an Internet-television model and then as a show on BITE TV, the channel subsequently launched in October 2009.
CABLE NETWORK

BBC Kids 363625
Owner: Corus Entertainment Inc.
Editorial: 4355 Mathissi Pl, Burnaby, British Columbia V5G 4S8 **Tel:** 1 604 431-3222.
Email: kids@knowledge.ca
Web site: http://www.bbckids.ca
Profile: BBC Kids brings viewers children's programming from across the U.K. and around the world. The network features programs specifically aimed at preschoolers, school-aged children and teenagers. To contact this network please use the online contact form located in the "Contact us" section of the website.
CABLE NETWORK

BNN/Business News Network 83195
Owner: Bell Media
Editorial: 299 Queen St W, Toronto, Ontario M5V 2Z5- **Tel:** 1 416 384-8000.
Web site: http://www.bnn.ca
Profile: Business News Network (BNN) is Canada's only business and financial news network, and is currently available in about 4.5 million Canadian homes. Its editorial team features business journalists, entrepreneurs and financial professionals that deliver up-to-the-minute business news, commentary and interviews with leading business newsmakers.
CABLE NETWORK

BNN/Business News Network - Calgary Bureau 550474
Editorial: 80 Patina Rise SW, Calgary, Alberta T3H 2W4- **Tel:** 1 403 240-5600.
Web site: http://www.bnn.ca
Profile: Calgary Bureau of BNN/Business News Network.
CABLE NETWORK

bold 363603
Owner: Canadian Broadcasting Corp.
Editorial: 205 Wellington St W, Toronto, Ontario M5V 3G7 **Tel:** 1 416 205-3311.
Web site: http://www.cbc.ca/bold
Profile: bold is a network of the performing arts, drama, comedy and world championship sports.
CABLE NETWORK

The Brand New One 76152
Owner: ZoomerMedia Limited
Editorial: 171 East Liberty Street, Suite 230, Toronto, Ontario M6K 3P6 **Tel:** 1 416 368-3194.
Email: audience@onebodymindspirit.com
Web site: http://www.onebodymindspiritlove.com
Profile: The Brand New One brings viewers progressive programming from Canada and around the world on natural health, personal growth, new ideas and intriguing possibilities, each of them opening up options for recharging lives and helping viewers reach their maximum potential.
CABLE NETWORK

Bravo! 154405
Owner: Bell Media
Editorial: 299 Queen St W, Toronto, Ontario M5V 2Z5- **Tel:** 1 416 591-7400.
Email: bravomail@bravo.ca
Web site: http://www.bravo.ca
Profile: Bravo! is dedicated to entertaining, stimulating and enlightening viewers who have a taste for complex television. Bravo! delivers a wide array of fine arts programming, balancing longer-form structured shows and shorter pieces that appear in a more random way as "flow" to create a fluid mix of distinctive music, dance, opera, drama, literature, cinema, visual art, the art of television and the art of talk.
CABLE NETWORK

Cable Public Affairs Channel 83221
Owner: CPAC (Cable Public Affairs Channel)
Editorial: 45 O'Connor St Suite 1750, Ottawa, Ontario K1P 1A4 **Tel:** 1 613 567-2722.
Email: comments@cpac.ca
Web site: http://www.cpac.ca
Profile: Launched in 1992. Bilingual English-French, commercial-free coverage of Canadian public affairs issues and live broadcasts of the House of Commons and Standing Committees. Also includes coverage of current events in Canadian politics. CPAC is Canada's top source of parliamentary, political and public affairs programming. CPAC's French title is La Chaîne d'affaires publiques par câble.
CABLE NETWORK

Canal Savoir 612281
Owner: Corporation pour l'Avancement des Nouvelles Applications des Langages Ltée (CANAL)
Editorial: 2200, rue Ste-Catherine Est, 1er étage, Montreal, Quebec H2K 2J1 **Tel:** 1 514 509-2222.
Email: info@canalsavoir.tv
Web site: http://www.canalsavoir.tv
Profile: Canal Savoir est une organisation à but non-lucratif dédié aux échanges de connaissance. La station fait son possible pour s'assurer que la programmation soit éducative afin que les auditeurs apprennent des choses. C'est dans le but de promouvoir l'acquisition de connaissance.

Canal Savoir is a nonprofit organisation dedicated to spreading knowledge. The station strives to be sure its programming is educational to ensure its viewers are learning. It is trying to promote a desire to gain knowledge.
CABLE NETWORK

Cartoon Network (Canada) 816358
Owner: Corus Entertainment
Editorial: 25 Dockside Dr, corus quay, Toronto, Ontario M5A 0B5
Web site: http://www.cartoonnetwork.ca
Profile: The 24-hour network is devoted to providing cartoon and animation programming. Drawing from the world's largest cartoon library, Cartoon Network showcases unique original cartoon ventures. The network offers cable service in original, acquired and classic entertainment for youth and families. The channel is owned by Corus Entertainment in Canada.
CABLE NETWORK

Casa 577841
Owner: Quebecor Media
Editorial: 1600 Boul de Maisonneuve E, Montreal, Quebec H2L 4P2 **Tel:** 1 514 526-9251.
Email: relations.auditoire@tva.ca
Web site: http://www.casatv.ca
Profile: Casa offre aux télespectateurs québécois ce qui se fait de mieux dans monde du "comment faire". Le réseau propose une programmation québécoise et venant d'ailleurs qui se concentre sur la cuisine, la décoration, la renovation et le design d'intérieur.

Casa gives Quebecois viewers what's best in the world of "how-to." The network offers Quebecois and foreign programming focusing on the topics of cooking, home decorating, renovation and interior design.
CABLE NETWORK

CBC News Network 80831
Owner: Canadian Broadcasting Corp.
Editorial: 205 Wellington St W, Toronto, Ontario M5V 3G7- **Tel:** 1 416 205-3311.
Web site: http://www.cbc.ca/news
Profile: CBC News Network (CBC NN) is a 24-hour cable news and information service with a special emphasis on round-the-clock national news, live coverage, in-depth specials and award-winning documentaries. CBC News Network is a member of the Canadian Press Gallery.
CABLE NETWORK

CMT Canada 83203
Owner: Corus Entertainment Inc.
Editorial: 25 Dockside Dr, corus quay, Toronto, Ontario M5A 0B5 **Tel:** 1 416 479-7000.
Web site: http://www.cmt.ca
Profile: CMT Canada combines an engaging, entertaining blend of music videos with programs that focus on country artists and their music. CMT provides viewers with the latest news and information as well as videos, artist performances and appearances.
CABLE NETWORK

Comedy Gold 697097
Owner: Bell Media
Editorial: 299 Queen St W, Toronto, Ontario M5V 2Z5- **Tel:** 1 416 384-8000.
Email: comedygoldfeedback@bellmedia.ca
Web site: http://www.comedygold.ca
Profile: Features ground-breaking and iconic comedic series from 1970s, 1980s and 1990s.
CABLE NETWORK

The Comedy Network 83223
Owner: Bell Media
Editorial: 299 Queen St W, Toronto, Ontario M5V 2Z5- **Tel:** 1 416 384-8000.
Email: TheComedy.Network@bellmedia.ca
Web site: http://www.thecomedynetwork.ca
Profile: Canada's first-and-only specialty comedy service, The Comedy Network airs comedy of all kinds, 24 hours-a-day, across multiple platforms, including a revolutionary broadband service at thecomedynetwork.ca. Launched in October 1997, The Comedy Network broadcasts, uncut and uncensored, an eclectic mix of scripted, stand-up, sketch, improv, and animated comedy. Also featured are topical comedy talk shows, game shows and classic situation comedies.
CABLE NETWORK

Commonwealth Broadcasting Network (CBN) 617755
Owner: Asian Television Network International Limited
Editorial: 130 Pony Dr, Newmarket, Ontario L3Y 7B6
Tel: 1 905 836-6460.
Email: atn@asiantelevision.com
Web site: http://asiantelevision.com/atncbnp.htm
Profile: Commonwealth Broadcasting Network features live cricket coverage, cricket news and highlights, as well as local news and events for the Caribbean and South Asian communities across Canada.
CABLE NETWORK

Cosmopolitan TV 521437
Owner: Corus Entertainment Inc.
Editorial: Corus Quay, 25 Dockside, Toronto, Ontario M5A 0B5 **Tel:** 1 416 479-7000.
Email: info@cosmotv.ca
Web site: http://www.cosmotv.ca
Profile: Targeting women 18 to 34, CosmoTV programming runs the gamut from comedies and dramas to relationship and reality programming. Like the magazine, the focus for Cosmopolitan TV is men, sex and relationships, packed with the kind of information that best girlfriends share over drinks.
CABLE NETWORK

CP24 83213
Owner: Bell Media
Editorial: 299 Queen St W, Toronto, Ontario M5V 2Z5- **Tel:** 1 416 384-2400.
Email: breakingnews@cp24.com
Web site: http://www.cp24.com
Profile: CP24 is Canada's first and only 24-hour local news channel. CP24's enriched screen provides nine simultaneous and continuous streams of information to meet the demands of today's most sophisticated news consumer.
CABLE NETWORK

Crime + Investigation 83208
Owner: Corus Entertainment Inc.
Editorial: 121 Bloor St E Suite B1, Toronto, Ontario M4W 3M5 **Tel:** 1 416 967-1174.
Email: feedback@crimeandinvestigation.ca
Web site: http://www.crimeandinvestigation.ca/
Profile: Crime + Investigation is a cable network specializing in mystery-related programming, including dramas, documentaries and series. Its shows include spine-tingling thrillers and horror stories, police dramas, and the best Movies of the Week. Formerly known as Mystery.
CABLE NETWORK

CTV News Channel 80830
Owner: Bell Media
Editorial: 9 Channel Nine Crt, Toronto, Ontario M1S 4B5- **Tel:** 1 416 384-5000.
Email: news@ctv.ca
Web site: http://www.ctvnews.ca/ctv-news-channel
Profile: CTV News Channel is Canada's only national headline news service providing Canadians with up-to-the-minute news. With a perspective that is distinctly Canadian, CTV News Channel offers both quality and immediacy with reports from around the world. A part of the CTV News family, CTV News Channel draws on the resources of CTV's national, international and local news operations, including 21 stations across the country, as well as nine foreign and seven domestic network news bureaus. CTV News Channel is a member of the Canadian Press Gallery.
CABLE NETWORK

CTV News Channel - Montreal Bureau 696839
Owner: Bell Media
Editorial: 1205 Av Papineau, Montreal, Quebec H2K 4R2 **Tel:** 1 514 273-6311.
Email: montrealnews@ctv.ca
Web site: http://montreal.ctvnews.ca
Profile: The Montreal Bureau of CTV News Channel.
CABLE NETWORK

CTV News Channel - Ottawa Bureau 696838
Editorial: 87 George St, Ottawa, Ontario K1N 9H7-
Tel: 1 613 224-1313.
Email: ctvottawa@ctv.ca
Web site: http://ottawa.ctvnews.ca
Profile: Ottawa bureau of CTV News Channel.
CABLE NETWORK

CTV News Channel - Washington Bureau 696840
Editorial: 1717 Desales St Nw Suite 354, Washington, District Of Columbia 20036-4401 **Tel:** 1 202 775-0356.
CABLE NETWORK

DejaView 83206
Owner: Corus Entertainment Inc.
Editorial: 121 Bloor St E Fl SUITE, 15th b1, Toronto, Ontario M4W 3M5 **Tel:** 1 416 967-0022.
Email: contactus@globaltv.ca
Web site: http://www.dejaviewtv.ca
Profile: A destination for television's ultimate classics from the '70s and '80s. With familiar favorites including The Cosby Show, Who's the Boss, All In the Family, through to Three's Company, Roseanne and other classic sitcoms. Network helps viewers relive the early years of television.
CABLE NETWORK

Discovery Canada 697172
Owner: Bell Media
Editorial: 9 Channel Nine Crt, Toronto, Ontario M1S 4B5- **Tel:** 1 416 332-5000.
Email: comments@discovery.ca
Web site: http://www.discovery.ca
Profile: Showcases the world's most dynamic people and places, culture, science and natural history programming.
CABLE NETWORK

Discovery Channel (Canada) 70669
Owner: Bell Media
Editorial: 9 Channel Nine Crt, Toronto, Ontario M1S 4B5- **Tel:** 1 416 332-5000.
Email: comments@discovery.ca
Web site: http://www.discovery.ca
Profile: Bold and leading edge, while information and entertaining, Discovery Channel is Canada's leading source for factual programming, as it puts a new spin on exploring adventure, science and technology. This award-winning channel covers the scientific beat, from animals to the animalistic side of humanity, from the sea to space, and the latest in innovation.
CABLE NETWORK

Discovery Science 83234
Owner: Bell Media
Editorial: 9 Channel Nine Court, Toronto, Ontario M1S 4B5 **Tel:** 1 416 332-5000.
Email: comments@discovery.ca
Web site: http://www.sciencechannel.ca
Profile: Discovery Science brings science to an accessible and easy-to-understand level, revealing entertaining facts and relevant applications in daily life. The show delves into the idiosyncrasies of technology and science and introduces the people behind them.
CABLE NETWORK

DIY Network Canada 609247
Owner: Corus Entertainment Inc.
Editorial: 121 Bloor St E Suite B1, Toronto, Ontario M4W 3M5 **Tel:** 1 416 967-1174.
Email: feedback@diy.ca
Web site: http://www.diy.ca
Profile: DIY Network Canada, launched on October 19, 2009, offers Canadians all they need to know about home improvement. Its programs and experts offer creative projects for do-it-yourself enthusiasts, from small-scale fix-it jobs to major home renovations.
CABLE NETWORK

documentary 83204
Owner: Canadian Broadcasting Corp.
Editorial: 205 Wellington St W, Toronto, Ontario M5V 3G7 **Tel:** 1 416 205-3311.
Web site: http://www.cbc.ca/documentarychannel
Profile: documentary is a digital television station devoted to showing the best documentaries from Canada and around the world.
CABLE NETWORK

DTOUR 83205
Owner: Corus Entertainment Inc.
Editorial: 121 Bloor St E, Toronto, Ontario M4W 3M5
Tel: 1 416 967-1174.
Email: feedback@dtourtv.com
Web site: http://www.dtourtv.com
Profile: Programming features drama and entertainment.
CABLE NETWORK

Dusk 83200
Owner: Corus Entertainment Inc.
Editorial: Corus Quay, 25 Dockside Drive, Toronto, Ontario M5A 0B5 **Tel:** 1 416 479-7000.
Email: info@dusktv.ca
Web site: http://www.dusktv.ca
Profile: Dusk features non-stop thrills and chills with horror and thriller movies, series and magazine-style shows focusing on the genre. The channel showcases modern-day classics, "teen screamers" and cultish B-movies. Includes new shows, old favorites and obscure programs never before seen on television.
CABLE NETWORK

ESPN Classic 83236
Owner: Bell Media
Editorial: 9 Channel Nine Court, Toronto, Ontario M1S 4B5 **Tel:** 1 416 332-5000.
Web site: http://www.tsn.ca/classic
Profile: ESPN Classic Canada features great individual performances, controversial victories, huge upsets, momentous comebacks and unforgettable team dynasties. ESPN Classic has encore broadcasts of the most cherished classic games and moments from the world of sports. The network has all the bases covered with baseball, hockey, football, golf, wrestling, boxing, soccer, tennis, skating, Reel Classics sports movies and much more.
CABLE NETWORK

EuroWorld Sport 697541
Owner: TLN Telelatino Network Inc.
Editorial: 5125 Steeles Avenue West, Toronto, Ontario M9L 1R5 **Tel:** 1 416 744-8200.
Email: info@tlntv.com
Web site: http://legacy.tlntv.com/soccerspecials/EuroWorldSports
Profile: Offers around-the-clock coverage of top-league soccer games, including all FIFA tournaments, the UEFA Europa League and Ligue 1 matches.
CABLE NETWORK

Évasion 83194
Owner: Groupe Serdy
Editorial: 619 Rue Le Breton, Longueuil, Quebec J4G 1R9 **Tel:** 1 450 672-0052.
Email: info@groupeserdy.com
Web site: http://www.evasion.tv
Profile: Évasion est une chaîne de television spécialisée francophone dédiée au voayge, au tourisme et à l'aventure.

Évasion is a French-language specialty television channel devoted to travel, tourism and adventure.
CABLE NETWORK

Family Channel 70677
Owner: DHX Media Ltd.
Editorial: 181 Bay St Suite 100, Toronto, Ontario M5J 2T3 **Tel:** 1 416 956-2030.
Email: info@family.ca
Web site: http://www.family.ca
Profile: Family Channel is a premium, commercial-free network offering the best in family television entertainment in approximately 5.4 million homes across Canada. Programming includes series, movies and specials aimed at a family audience.
CABLE NETWORK

Fashion Television Channel 77132
Owner: Bell Media
Editorial: 299 Queen St W, Toronto, Ontario M5V 2Z5- **Tel:** 1 416 591-7400.
Email: fashiontelevision@ctv.ca
Web site: http://www.fashiontelevision.com
Profile: Network provides a sexy look at art, architecture, photography and design. It's a fast-paced collage focusing on people's changing lifestyles, sexual attitudes and social conscience, as well as beauty, fitness and health. The Fashion Channel is Canada's first and only 24-hour English language fashion channel dedicated to the world of art, architecture, photography and design, with a celebration of style.
CABLE NETWORK

The Fight Network 658758
Owner: Fight Media Inc.
Editorial: 171 East Liberty St Suite 230, Toronto, Ontario M6K 3P6 **Tel:** 1 416 987-2456.
Web site: http://www.thefightnetwork.com
Profile: Features several varieties of combat sports: Mixed martial arts, boxing, wrestling, kick boxing and other sports.
CABLE NETWORK

Food Network Canada 83175
Owner: Corus Entertainment Inc.
Editorial: 121 Bloor St E Suite B1, Toronto, Ontario M4W 3M5 **Tel:** 1 416 967-1174.
Email: feedback@foodtv.ca
Web site: http://www.foodnetwork.ca
Profile: 24-hour cable network dedicated to good food and good times. The network airs a variety of taped and live programs dealing with cooking, health, nutrition and food. Shows emphasize unique recipes, cooking tips and techniques, and feature famous personalities in the cooking world.
CABLE NETWORK

FX Canada 780099
Owner: Rogers Media Inc.
Editorial: 1 Mount Pleasant Rd, Toronto, Ontario M4Y 2Y5 **Tel:** 1 416 935-8294.
Email: Viewerrelations@rci.rogers.com
Web site: http://www.fxcanada.ca
Profile: FX Canada is a digital specialty channel that delivers critically-acclaimed dramas and hit comedies, including FX original series American Horror Story, Wilfred, The League, Lights Out, Terriers and Sons of Anarchy. Delivering compelling entertainment to Canadians, FX Canada's unique content also features movies, and original Canadian programming.
CABLE NETWORK

FXX Canada 905401
Owner: Rogers Media
Editorial: 1 Mount Pleasant Rd, Toronto, Ontario M4Y 2Y5-
Web site: http://www.fxnowcanada.ca
Profile: FXX is a Canadian English-language digital cable specialty channel devoted primarily to scripted comedies for young adults. It launched in Canada on April 1, 2014.
CABLE NETWORK

FYITV 83174
Owner: Corus Entertainment Inc.
Editorial: 121 Bloor Street B1, Ste B1, Toronto, Ontario M4W 3M5 **Tel:** 1 416 967-1174.
Email: feedback@fyitv.ca
Web site: http://www.fyitv.ca
Profile: FYI TV features lifestyle programming, with a mix of reality, culinary, home renovation and makeover series.
CABLE NETWORK

G4 Canada 83230
Owner: Rogers Communications Inc.
Editorial: 545 Lakeshore Boulevard West, Toronto, Ontario M5V 1A3 **Tel:** 1 416 260-0060.
Email: info@g4tv.ca
Web site: http://www.g4tv.ca
Profile: G4 Canada is Canada's only 24-hour television channel dedicated to using technology as a backdrop to entertain, amaze, and engage viewers, by showcasing the latest trends, products and events. G4 Canada is targeted towards young adults. All press releases, pitches and other submissions should be directed to the mailing address.
CABLE NETWORK

Game TV 788783
Owner: The GameTV Corporation
Editorial: 184 Pearl St. Suite 302, Toronto, Ontario M5H 1L5 **Tel:** 1 416 593-0915.
Web site: http://www.igametv.com
Profile: For Canadians who love to play and watch games, GameTV provides viewers with a wide range of winning programming and online options including classic game shows, reality programming, non-sports gaming and game-related movies and documentaries.
CABLE NETWORK

Global News: BC 1 853769
Owner: Corus Entertainment Inc.
Editorial: 7850 Enterprise St, Burnaby, British Columbia V5A 1V7 **Tel:** 1 604 420-2288.
Email: tips@globaltvbc.com
Web site: http://globalnews.ca/bc/program/bc-1
Profile: British Columbia's first 24 hour news channel. A regional, English-language specialty channel Category B service offering a mix of local and regional news, traffic, weather, business, sports and entertainment information devoted to serving residents of British Columbia
CABLE NETWORK

Global Reality Channel 684792
Owner: Corus Entertainment Inc.
Editorial: 121 Bloor St W Suite 200, Toronto, Ontario M5S 1P7 **Tel:** 1 416 967-1174.
Web site: http://www.globalreality.ca
Profile: Offers reality television programs 24/7.
CABLE NETWORK

Grace Television Network 664274
Owner: World Impact Ministries
Editorial: 89 St Paul St, St Catharines, Ontario L2R 3M3 **Tel:** 1 905 346-4828.
Email: info@gracetelevision.net
Web site: http://www.gracetelevision.net
Profile: Targets Canadian Christians. Features Christian programming from around the world, as well as new content from Canadian and international producers.
CABLE NETWORK

The H2 83210
Owner: Corus Entertainment Inc.
Editorial: 25 Ontario St, Toronto, Ontario M5A 4L6 **Tel:** 1 416 601-0010.
Web site: http://www.history.ca/h2-shows/
Profile: H2 is a specialty television edicated to airing historic and non-historical programming of military, science, and technology interest. Formerly known as The Cave and MenTV
CABLE NETWORK

HBO Canada 552658
Owner: Corus Entertainment/Astral Media Inc.
Editorial: 25 Dockside Dr, corus quay, Toronto, Ontario M5A 0B5 **Tel:** 1 416 479-7000.
Web site: http://www.hbocanada.com
Profile: HBO Canada is a multiplex channel offered at no additional charge to customers who subscribe to The Movie Network or Movie Central. The service also offers more than 200 hours of library titles and first-run HBO original films, comedy specials, documentaries, live concerts and sporting events previously unavailable in Canada. HBO Canada rounds out its offering with Canadian films and series. The cable channel does not accept any pitches and is commercial-free.
CABLE NETWORK

HGTV Canada 317558
Owner: Corus Entertainment Inc.
Editorial: 121 Bloor St E Suite B1, Toronto, Ontario M4W 3M5 **Tel:** 1 416 967-1174.
Email: feedback@hgtv.ca
Web site: http://www.hgtv.ca
Profile: Cable network with national distribution focusing on an array of home, lifestyle, decorating, gardening, hobbies and craft-related topics. Broadcasts a potpourri of original and exclusive programming hosted by experts in these various fields. Programming aired on HGTV Canada is developed by Corus Entertainment Inc. and changes quarterly. Viewers are advised to check the channel's Web site for the most updated schedules.
CABLE NETWORK

HIFI 721228
Owner: Blue Ant Media
Editorial: 130 Merton St Suite 200, Toronto, Ontario M4S 1A4 **Tel:** 1 416 646-4434.
Email: feedback@blueantmedia.ca
Web site: http://www.hifi.ca
Profile: HIFI is owned and operated by Blue Ant Media, Canada's leading HD broadcaster. The channel explores and celebrates the cultural treasures that enrich our lives. From quirky pieces of pop culture to priceless vestiges of human civilization in the world's finest museums; from iconic films picked for their originality to classic concerts by the legends who shaped music this channel is where everything that stirs your passion can be found.
CABLE NETWORK

History Television 70679
Owner: Corus Entertainment Inc.
Editorial: 121 Bloor St E Suite 1500, Toronto, Ontario M4W 3M5 **Tel:** 1 416 967-1174.
Email: media@canwest.com
Web site: http://www.history.ca
Profile: History Television chronicles the past with a range of documentaries, historical reenactments, motion pictures and mini-series dealing with significant figures, events and inventions.
CABLE NETWORK

HPItv 788785
Owner: Woodbine Entertainment Group
Editorial: 555 Rexdale Boulevard, Toronto, Ontario M9W 5L2
Email: hpi@WoodbineEntertainment.com
Web site: http://www.horseplayerinteractive.com
Profile: HPItv broadcasts live thoroughbred and standardbred racing, from tracks across North America and the world.
CABLE NETWORK

ICI ARTV 83245
Owner: Société Radio-Canada/ARTE France
Editorial: 1400 Boul Rene-Levesque E Bureau A-53-1, Montreal, Quebec H2L 2M2 **Tel:** 1 514 597-3636.
Email: auditoire@artv.ca
Web site: http://www.artv.ca
Profile: ICI ARTV est une chaîne de television francophone présentant une programmation d'arts, sans pause, du Canada et partout autour du monde. On présente des performances, des films, des documentaires, de la musique, des drames et des designs, et ce, 24 heures sur 24.

ARTV is a French-language cable television channel featuring non-stop arts programming from Canada and around the world. It offers performances, movies, documentaries, music, dramas and design, twenty four hours a day.
CABLE NETWORK

ICI EXPLORA 800787
Owner: Canadian Broadcasting Corp.
Editorial: 1400 Boul Rene-Levesque E Suite A, 76-80, Montreal, Quebec H2L 2M2
Email: info.explora@radio-canada.ca
Web site: http://ici.exploratv.ca
Profile: ICI EXPLORA livre une expérience télévisuelle plus grande que nature en plongeant dans les mondes fascinants que sont la santé, la science, la nature et l'environnement. La chaîne vise ceux qui aiment découvrir de nouvelles choses.

ICI EXPLORA delivers a larger-than-life viewing experience as it delves into the fascinating worlds of health, science, nature and the environment. The channel is aimed at inquiring minds who like to discover new things.
CABLE NETWORK

The Independent Film Channel 83180
Owner: Corus Entertainment Inc.
Editorial: 121 Bloor St E Suite 1500, Toronto, Ontario M4W 3M5 **Tel:** 1 416 967-1174.
Email: ifccanada@shawmedia.ca
Web site: http://www.ifctv.ca
Profile: The Independent Film Channel(IFC) is Canada's first English-language specialty television service dedicated to the world of filmmakers. IFC presents a rich schedule of cutting-edge and creative films, providing a new avenue of exhibition for Canadian films.
CABLE NETWORK

Investigation Discovery 83240
Owner: Bell Media
Editorial: 9 Channel Nine Crt, Toronto, Ontario M1S 4B5- **Tel:** 1 416 332-5000.
Email: comments@investigationdiscovery.ca
Web site: http://www.investigationdiscovery.ca
Profile: Fact-based channel offering insight into the real-life world of investigation, exploration of the latest forensic analysis and true stories that piece together the dramatic puzzles of human nature. Expands on these themes by touching on some less common areas of investigation, including the paranormal and modern mysteries.
CABLE NETWORK

LCN/Le Canal Nouvelles 83226
Owner: Groupe TVA Inc.
Editorial: 1600 Boul de Maisonneuve E, Montreal, Quebec H2L 4P2- **Tel:** 1 514 526-9251.
Email: lcn@tva.ca
Web site: http://tvanouvelles.ca
Profile: LCN/Le Canal Nouvelles Online est un réseau de nouvelles en continue francophone, une propriété du Groupe TVA Inc. Les émissions sont enregistrées dans les bureaux de TVA, à Montréal. On offre aux téléspectateurs des nouvelles 24 heures sur 24, avec les nouvelles qui défilent au bas de l'écran.

Le Canal Nouvelles (LCN) is a 24-hour Canadian French language cable news television channel owned by Groupe TVA Inc. It broadcasts from TVA headquarters in Montreal. It offers viewers continuous, updated news coverage, 24 hours a day, with headlines scrolling at the bottom of the screen.
CABLE NETWORK

Leafs TV 619287
Owner: Maple Leaf Sports & Entertainment
Editorial: 50 Bay Street, Suite 500, Toronto, Ontario M5J 2L2 **Tel:** 1 416 815-5400.
Email: leafstv@mapleleafsports.com
Web site: http://mapleleafs.nhl.com/club/page.htm?id=42121
Profile: Leafs TV is a Canadian specialty cable network owned by Maple Leafs Sports & Entertainment. Features programming revolving around the Toronto Maple Leafs National Hockey League team including broadcasts of games, pre- and post-game shows, and more.
CABLE NETWORK

Lifetime Canada 83179
Owner: Corus Entertainment Inc.
Editorial: 121 Bloor St E Suite B1, Toronto, Ontario M4W 3M5 **Tel:** 1 416 967-0022.
Email: feedback@mylifetimetv.ca
Web site: http://www.mylifetimetv.ca
Profile: Lifetime Canada specializes in star-studded movies with a bold female attitude. The network offers chick flicks for fabulous women of all ages. Viewers enjoy hit movies with favorite stars including Cameron Diaz, Tom Cruise, Julia Roberts, Penelope Cruz, John Cusack and Marilyn Monroe. Programming also includes great series and critically acclaimed premieres. Formerly called Showcase Diva
CABLE NETWORK

MétéoMédia 83244
Owner: Pelmorex Media, Inc.
Editorial: 1755 boul Rene-Levesque Est, Bureau 251, Montreal, Quebec H2K 4P6 **Tel:** 1 514 597-1700.
Web site: http://www.meteomedia.com
Profile: MétéoMédia is a 24-hour French-language cable television channel owned by Pelmorex Media, Inc. It features continuous, up-to-the-minute reports on weather conditions throughout the world, occasional weather-related feature specials, and regional, local and national forecasts.
CABLE NETWORK

Moi & Cie 750625
Owner: Groupe TVA
Editorial: 1600 Boul de Maisonneuve E, Montreal, Quebec H2L 4P2- **Tel:** 1 514 526-9251.
Web site: http://tv.moietcie.ca
Profile: Moi & Cie est une propriété de Groupe TVA. Cette chaîne s'oriente sur une programmation féminine, comme la mode et la beauté.

Moi & Cie is owned by Groupe TVA. This channel is geared towards women with programs on fashion and beauty.
CABLE NETWORK

Movieola-The Short Film Channel 363621
Owner: Channel Zero Inc.
Editorial: 2844 Dundas St West, Toronto, Ontario M6P 1Y7 **Tel:** 1 416 492-1595.
Email: info@movieola.ca
Web site: http://www.movieola.ca
Profile: This cable network is devoted entirely to short films. From drama to comedy, and animation to documentaries, all films are between 30 seconds and 40 minutes in length. Programming includes film festival winners, cult classics and late night features. Billing itself as "A Feature Film Experience in a Fraction of the Time," Movieola is a one-of-a-kind network.
CABLE NETWORK

MovieTime 83209
Owner: Corus Entertainment Inc.
Editorial: 121 Bloor St E, ste b1 suite 1500, Toronto, Ontario M4W 3M5 **Tel:** 1 416 967-1174.
Email: contactus@globaltv.ca
Web site: http://www.movietimetv.ca
Profile: MovieTime is the digital channel destination for big-ticket movies seven days a week. With over 250 movie titles each month and back to back movies on the weekend, MovieTime offers movie lovers unparalleled access to an extensive collection of favorite hits. During the week, viewers can enjoy favorite series in the mornings and during prime time, with movies filling the schedule in the afternoons and throughout the night. From adventure-packed blockbusters to definitive movie moments, MovieTime has a star-studded, jam-packed line-up that satisfies viewers' cravings for hit movies.
CABLE NETWORK

MTV Canada 83196
Owner: Bell Media
Editorial: 299 Queen St W, Toronto, Ontario M5V 2Z5- **Tel:** 1 416 384-2000.
Email: feedback@mtv.ca
Web site: http://www.mtv.ca
Profile: MTV Canada is a Canadian programmed and managed business wholly owned by Bell Media. MTV offers a distinctly Canadian interpretation of the MTV brand across multiple platforms, including a revolutionary broadband service, MTV Overdrive, and across an MTV-branded analogue specialty service that delivers innovative lifestyle, talk and documentary programming with a commitment to 71 percent Canadian programming in prime time.
CABLE NETWORK

MTV2 in Canada 354785
Owner: Bell Media
Editorial: 299 Queen St W, Toronto, Ontario M5V 2Z5- **Tel:** 1 416 591-7400.
Email: feedback@mtv.ca
Web site: http://www.mtv2.ca

Profile: MTV2 in Canada feeds viewers' needs for the latest in everything from movies and music to video games, fashion, technology, sports and more.
CABLE NETWORK

MUCH 83217
Owner: Bell Media
Editorial: 299 Queen St W, Toronto, Ontario M5V 2Z5- **Tel:** 1 416 870-6824.
Email: contactmuch@bellmedia.ca
Web site: http://www.much.com
Profile: Much is live to air approximately eight hours daily from the network's headquarters in downtown Toronto, with programs showcasing exclusive live performances and interviews from today's hottest musical artists and celebrity guests. In addition, the network's specialty programming focuses on the latest music-related news and information.
CABLE NETWORK

MusiMax 83232
Owner: Groupe V Media
Editorial: 355 Rue Sainte-Catherine O, Montreal, Quebec H3B 1A5 **Tel:** 1 514 284-7587.
Email: auditoire@musimax.com
Web site: http://www.musimax.com
Profile: MusiMax is a French-language cable television channel owned by Groupe V Media. MusiMax broadcasts concerts, documentaries, films and other music-based programs.
CABLE NETWORK

MusiquePlus 83233
Owner: V Media Group
Editorial: 355 Rue Sainte-Catherine O, Montreal, Quebec H3B 1A5 **Tel:** 1 514 284-7587.
Web site: http://www.musiqueplus.com
Profile: MusiquePlus is a French-language cable music television channel owned by V Media Group. It is the sister network of MusiMax and MuchMusic. The channel airs music videos, numerous special features, documentaries and films about the music industry in addition to celebrity interviews and profiles.
CABLE NETWORK

National Geographic Channel 83176
Owner: Corus Entertainment Inc.
Editorial: 121 Bloor St E Suite B1, Toronto, Ontario M4W 3M5 **Tel:** 1 416 967-0022.
Email: pressroom@ngs.org
Web site: http://natgeotv.com/ca
Profile: A national cable network providing a range of feature programming derived from the world of the National Geographic Society. The network features "experience" television, with programming in travel, adventure, exploration, natural history, science, culture and news. Aimed at people who are curious and interested in the world around them.
CABLE NETWORK

NBA TV Canada 619280
Owner: Maple Leaf Sports & Entertainment
Editorial: 40 Bay St Suite 400, Toronto, Ontario M5J 2X2 **Tel:** 1 416 815-5500.
Web site: http://www.nba.com/nbatvcanada
Profile: NBA TV Canada s a cable specialty network owned by Maple Leaf Sports & Entertainment. The network features programming related to the National Basketball Association, with a particular emphasis on the Toronto Raptors.
CABLE NETWORK

New Tang Dynasty Television 849004
Owner: New Tang Dynasty Television Canada
Editorial: 420 Consumers Rd, Toronto, Ontario M2J 1P8 **Tel:** 1 416 787-1577.
Web site: http://www.ntdtv.ca
Profile: New Tang Dynasty Television is a non-profit general interest Chinese language channel. It airs a unique programming mix of news, cultural shows, educational programs, sports and entertainment. NTD Television Canada officially launched on March 28, 2012.
CABLE NETWORK

NHL Network 83224
Owner: National Hockey League
Editorial: 9 Channel Nine Court, Toronto, Ontario M1S 4B5 **Tel:** 1 416 332-5000.
Web site: http://www.nhl.com
Profile: NHL Network has round-the-clock hockey programming, offering viewers the most complete and in-depth hockey coverage including news, information and extended highlights from the National Hockey League. To contact the channel use the online contact form located in the contact us section of the website.
CABLE NETWORK

Nuevo Mundo TV 533450
Editorial: 4119 Blvd. St. Laurent, Suite 200, Montreal, Quebec H2W 1Y7 **Tel:** 1 514 543-7904.
Email: info@nuevomundotv.com
Web site: http://www.nuevomundotv.com
Profile: Nuevo Mundo TV's mission is to satisfy the communications needs of the Spanish speaking community in Canada and the lovers of the Hispanic culture.
CABLE NETWORK

Oasis 721198
Owner: Blue Ant Media
Editorial: 130 Merton St Suite 200, Toronto, Ontario M4S 1A4 **Tel:** 1 416 646-4434.
Email: feedback@blueantmedia.ca
Web site: http://www.oasishd.ca
Profile: Oasis is owned and operated by Blue Ant Media, Canada's leading HD broadcaster. The channel is the first nature channel committed to continuous programming, showcasing the endless beauty of the natural world. The channel lets viewers explore, reflect and embrace the essence of our exquisite planet, with stories woven together from the finest Canadian and international documentary programming available.
CABLE NETWORK

Odyssey Television Network 618054
Owner: Maniatakos(Peter)
Editorial: 437 Danforth Ave, Ste 300, Toronto, Ontario M4K 1P1 **Tel:** 1 416 462-1200.
Email: info@odysseytv.ca
Web site: http://www.odysseytv.ca
Profile: Odyssey Television Network is a Greek-language broadcaster that airs programming, which targets the Greek-Canadian community. Programming is a mix of local productions and of shows from popular networks in Greece.
CABLE NETWORK

OLN/Outdoor Life Network 70678
Owner: Rogers Media Television
Editorial: 545 Lake Shore Blvd W, Toronto, Ontario M5V 1A3 **Tel:** 1 416 260-0047.
Email: info@oln.ca
Web site: http://oln.ca
Profile: OLN/Outdoor Life Network fills a unique niche in the specialty television landscape, attracting viewers with an adventurous spirit and a passion for the great outdoors in Canada. From skateboarding to sailing to road trips and shipwrecks, OLN celebrates all aspects of outdoor recreation, conservation, wilderness and adventure programming.
CABLE NETWORK

Ontario Parliament Network Broadcasting & Recording Service 363575
Owner: Ontario Legislative Assembly
Editorial: Legislative Assembly, Rm.453, Queen's Park, Toronto, Ontario M7A1A2 **Tel:** 1 416 325-7900.
Web site: http://ontla.on.ca
Profile: The network carries all proceedings of the Ontario Legislative Assembly. Sessions are broadcast live and also rebroadcast twice in the evening.
CABLE NETWORK

OUTtv 363526
Owner: OUTtv Network Inc.
Editorial: 53 6th Ave E, Vancouver, British Columbia V5T 1J3 **Tel:** 1 604 874-4300.
Web site: http://www.outtv.ca
Profile: OUTtv is a GLBT (gay, lesbian, bisexual and transgender) television network that provides news, information and entertainment to viewers 24/7. Canadian Gay-owned and operated, OUTtv has the best in GBLT popular movies and comedies from around the world including Canadian and international dramas, arts programming, biographies and variety shows. OUTtv has more original programming than any other digital channel in Canada. OUTtv provides up-to-date in-house GLBT news programming, live call-in shows, current affairs, documentaries, health and fitness, lifestyle, finance, relationships, music, cooking and travel for GLBT and gay-positive viewers.
CABLE NETWORK

OWN: The Oprah Winfrey Network 621113
Owner: Corus Entertainment Inc.
Editorial: Corus Quay, 25 Dockside Drive, Toronto, Ontario M5A 0B5 **Tel:** 1 416 479-7000.
Email: info@owntv.ca
Web site: http://www.owntv.ca
Profile: OWN: The Oprah Winfrey Show is the network of self-discovery, connecting people to each other and to their greatest potential. The programming includes a mix of nonfiction, short form programming, movies, documentaries and acquisitions. In the United States, OWN is a joint venture between Oprah Winfrey and Discovery Communications and launched on January 1, 2011 in the United States. OWN has a licensing agreement with Corus Entertainment to broadcast in Canada that began March 1, 2011 and replaced VIVA.
CABLE NETWORK

PHSN 624470
Owner: The Canadian Health Media network
Editorial: 150 Ferrand Drive, Suite 800, Toronto, Ontario M3C 3E5 **Tel:** 1 416 486-0110.
Web site: http://www.phsn.ca
Profile: PHSN is a national television network featuring customized content that is organized into short, themed segments allowing patients to enjoy worthwhile programming and yet engage and disengage in a manner suited to the environment. PHSN can be seen in the waiting rooms of health care professionals across Canada. The company is dedicated to engaging viewers with customized information and entertainment programming. Content is both in-house and advertiser-generated. Content is 95% produced by PHSN and 5% from News Canada. Programs are 30 minutes long consisting of 90 second segments. Each ad is run once every 30 minutes.
CABLE NETWORK

Prise 2 509207
Owner: Groupe TVA Inc.
Editorial: 1600 Boulevard de Maisonneuve Est, Montreal, Quebec H2L 4P2 **Tel:** 1 514 526-9251.
Email: relations.auditoire@tva.ca
Web site: http://prise2.canoe.ca
Profile: Presents the classics of Quebecois and American television and film.
CABLE NETWORK

RDI/Le Réseau de l'information 70691
Owner: Societe Radio-Canada
Editorial: 1400, boul. Rene-Levesque, Montreal, Quebec H2L 2M2 **Tel:** 1 514 597-7734.
Email: rdicomm@radio-canada.ca
Web site: http://www.radio-canada.ca/rdi
Profile: RDI/Le Réseau de l'information est un chaîne de télévision d'information continu francophone de la Société Radio-Canada. RDI est un équivalent de CBC News Network. RDI offre une couverture en direct d'événements majeurs, des bulletins de nouvelles à chaque 30 minutes, des nouvelles du sports et sur la finance ainsi que des programmes d'informations sur divers sujets.

RDI/Le Réseau de l'Information is a 24-hour Canadian French-language cable news television channel operated by CBC/Radio-Canada. RDI is the French-language equivalent of CBC News Network. RDI provides live coverage of major events, newscasts every 30 minutes, sports and financial news as well as informational programs on a wide range of topics.
CABLE NETWORK

RDS - Le Réseau des Sports 83242
Owner: Bell Media
Editorial: 1755 Boul Rene-Levesque E Bureau 300, Montreal, Quebec H2K 4P6 **Tel:** 1 514 599-2244.
Email: medias@rds.ca
Web site: http://www.rds.ca
Profile: RDS - Le Réseau des Sports est un chaîne de nouvelles sportives en contitnue francophone, une propriété de Bell Media. On y diffuse les matchs d'événements sportifs ainsi que des émissions sur le sport. RDS a été crée en septembre 1989.

RDS - Le Réseau des Sports is a 24-hour French language, all-sports cable channel owned by Bell Media. It broadcasts games as well as sport-related shows. RDS launched in September 1989.
CABLE NETWORK

RDS 2 809553
Owner: Bell Media
Editorial: 1755 Boul Rene-Levesque E Bureau 300, Montreal, Quebec H2K 4P6 **Tel:** 1 514 599-2244.
Email: info@rds.com
Web site: http://www.rds2.ca
Profile: RDS 2 est la chaîne de nouvelles sportives francophone, une propriété de Bell Media.

RDS 2 is a French language all sports cable channel owned by Bell Media.
CABLE NETWORK

RDS INFO 489112
Owner: Bell Media
Editorial: 1755 Boul Rene-Levesque E Bureau 300, Montreal, Quebec H2K 4P6 **Tel:** 1 514 599-2244.
Email: medias@rds.ca
Web site: http://www.rds.ca/ris
Profile: RDS Info présente les dernières nouvelles de l'actualité sportives, comme le hockey, football, baseball et sur les sports amateurs. RDS Info comprend les émissions Sports 30, 30 Midi et 30 Magazine. C'est complémentaire à la programmation présentée sur RDS - Le Réseau des Sports.

RDS Info features the latest sports headlines as well as hockey, football, baseball and amateur sports. RDS Info includes the show called Sports 30, 30 Midi and 30 Magazine. It complements the programming that is featured on RDS - Le Reseau des Sports.
CABLE NETWORK

The Score 83227
Owner: Score Media Inc.
Editorial: 500 King St W Fl 4TH, Toronto, Ontario M5V 1L9 **Tel:** 1 416 679-8812.
Email: hello@thescore.com
Web site: http://www.thescore.com
Profile: Score Media is a media company committed to delivering interactive and authentic sports entertainment. Created in 1997 in response to the growing desire for increased participation in the consumption of sports, the Company has now established itself as the home for hardcore sports fans. Score Media's primary asset, The Score Television Network ("The Score"), is a national specialty television service providing sports news, information, highlights and live event programming in more than 6.6 million homes across Canada.
CABLE NETWORK

Shopping Channel 83246
Owner: Rogers Media Inc.
Editorial: 59 Ambassador Dr, Mississauga, Ontario L5T 2P9 **Tel:** 1 905 362-2020.
Web site: http://www.theshoppingchannel.com
Profile: The Shopping Channel is a home shopping channel on cable television. It is owned and operated by Rogers Media.
CABLE NETWORK

Showcase 83177
Owner: Corus Entertainment Inc.
Editorial: 121 Bloor St E Suite B1, Toronto, Ontario M4W 3M5 **Tel:** 1 416 967-0022.
Email: media@canwest.com
Web site: http://www.showcase.ca
Profile: Showcase offers viewers a chance to catch some of the best critically acclaimed TV programming. Showcase gives viewers a chance to catch some of the biggest blockbuster titles in all genres, including dramas, comedies and thrillers.
CABLE NETWORK

Silver Screen Classics 431616
Owner: Channel Zero Inc.
Editorial: 2844 Dundas St West, Toronto, Ontario M6P 1Y7 **Tel:** 1 416 492-1595.
Email: info@silverscreenclassics.com
Web site: http://www.silverscreenclassics.com
Profile: Silver Screen Classics brings viewers motion pictures which have stood the test. From silent classics to twelve-chapter serials; from gritty film noir to splashy musical extravaganzas; from timeless melodramas to madcap screwball comedies, the network inspires, entertains and enthralls viewers.
CABLE NETWORK

SKY TG24 Canada 697535
Owner: TLN Telelatino Network Inc.
Editorial: 5125 Steeles Ave W, Toronto, Ontario M9L 1R5 **Tel:** 1 416 744-8200.
Email: info@tlntv.com
Web site: http://www.tlntv.com/tln_SkyTGEnglishAbout.aspx
Profile: All-news, information and talk channel in Italian, primarily a simulcast of the Italian SKY TG24, with some added Canadian content.
CABLE NETWORK

Slice 70671
Owner: Corus Entertainment Inc.
Editorial: 121 Bloor St E Suite B1, Toronto, Ontario M4W 3M5 **Tel:** 1 416 967-0022.
Email: media@canwest.com
Web site: http://www.slice.ca
Profile: Geared toward women, this network offers lifestyle entertainment programming about the people, places and experiences that make the journey of life worthwhile and interesting.
CABLE NETWORK

Smithsonian Channel 721220
Owner: Blue Ant Media
Editorial: 130 Merton St Suite 200, Toronto, Ontario M4S 1A4 **Tel:** 1 416 646-4434.
Email: feedback@blueantmedia.ca
Web site: http://www.smithsonianchannel.ca
Profile: Smithsonian Channel is owned and operated by Blue Ant Media.. The channel celebrates ideas, perspectives, and ways of life around the world, by bringing your family smart compelling documentaries and commercial free films that will inspire and engage its audience.
CABLE NETWORK

Sony Entertainment Television Asia 658752
Owner: Sony Entertainment Television Asia
Editorial: 115 Gordon Baker, Toronto, Ontario M2H 3R6 **Tel:** 1 416 619-5797.
Email: viewer_infoCAN@spe.sony.com
Web site: http://www.setasia.tv
Profile: Features contemporary programming tailored to South Asian tastes and sensibilities. Reaching the upscale, economically active 18 to 49 year-old age group.
CABLE NETWORK

SPACE 70681
Owner: Bell Media
Editorial: 299 Queen St W, Toronto, Ontario M5V 2Z5- **Tel:** 1 416 384-8000.
Email: space@space.ca
Web site: http://www.space.ca
Profile: SPACE is a national cable-delivered English-language, science fiction, fact, speculation and fantasy channel owned and operated by Bell Media, available 24 hours.
CABLE NETWORK

Sportsnet One 698775
Owner: Rogers Media Inc.
Editorial: 1 Mount Pleasant Rd, 7th fl, Toronto, Ontario M4Y 2Y5 **Tel:** 1 416 764-6000.
Email: assignment@sportsnet.ca
Web site: http://www.sportsnet.ca
Profile: National sports channel available across Canada and featuring primarily high-definition content from the Toronto Raptors, the NBA, the Toronto Blue Jays, the Seattle Mariners, Major League Baseball and Barclay's Premier League Soccer.
CABLE NETWORK

Sundance Channel (Canada) 83219
Owner: Corus Entertainment Inc.
Editorial: Corus Quay, 25 Dockside Drive, Toronto, Ontario M5A 0B5 **Tel:** 1 416 479-6785.
Email: info@sundancechannel.ca
Web site: http://www.sundancechannel.ca
Profile: Sundance Channel (Canada) offers movie enthusiasts, movie fans, creative and socially-engaged audiences a lineup of award-winning, diverse and engaging movies. The network presents the best in feature films, festival-selected shorts, documentaries and innovative, original series.
CABLE NETWORK

Super Écran 83188
Owner: Bell Media
Editorial: 1800 Av McGill College Bureau 1600, Montreal, Quebec H3A 3J6 **Tel:** 1 514 939-5090.
Email: auditoire@superecran.com
Web site: http://www.superecran.com
Profile: Super Écran is a French-language television network owned by Bell Media. It broadcasts the French version of popular movies 24 hours a day, as well as comedy shows and exclusive series. Super Écran's tagline is "La Télé des Cinévores."
CABLE NETWORK

Télémagino 600898
Owner: DHX Media Ltd.
Editorial: 181 Bay St Suite 100, Toronto, Ontario M5J 2T3
Web site: http://www.familyjr.ca
Profile: Télémagino is the brand name for DHX Television's preschool programs in French. The target age for this segment of the channel is children from age 2.
CABLE NETWORK

TELETOON 83231
Owner: Astral Media Inc./Corus Entertainment
Editorial: Corus Quay, 25 Dockside Drive, Toronto, Ontario M5A 0B5 **Tel:** 1 416 956-2060.
Email: info@teletoon.com
Web site: http://www.teletoon.com
Profile: The only Canadian 24-hour network devoted to providing cartoon and animation programming. Intended for audiences of all ages, the network broadcasts a variety of classic cartoon series and characters, new cartoons, original productions and animated feature films. Includes English and French-language services.
CABLE NETWORK

TLN en Español 697538
Owner: TLN Telelatino Network Inc.
Editorial: 5125 Steeles Avenue West, Toronto, Ontario M9L 1R5 **Tel:** 1 416 744-8200.
Email: info@tlntv.com
Web site: http://www.tlntv.com/EspanolAcerca.aspx?video=GenericSpanish09.flv
Profile: TLN en Español complements TLN Telelatino with 100% Spanish-language programming. TLN includes movies, telenovelas, variety shows, sports, news and more.
CABLE NETWORK

TLN Telelatino 83250
Owner: TLN Telelatino Network Inc.
Editorial: 5125 Steeles Avenue West, Toronto, Ontario M9L 1R5 **Tel:** 1 416 744-8200.
Email: info@tlntv.com
Web site: http://www.tlntv.com
Profile: TLN means the best coverage of soccer from Italy and Latin America. TLN also is the source for drama, intrigue, and romance portioned out in steamy installments on telenovelas. The network is also known for cryptically bizarre game shows. TLN serves as Canada's window into Hispanic and Italian cultures.
CABLE NETWORK

Travel + Escape 77078
Owner: Blue Ant Media
Editorial: 130 Merton Street Suite 200, Mississauga, Ontario M4S 1A4 **Tel:** 1 416 646-4434.
Email: feedback@blueantmedia.ca
Web site: http://www.travelandescape.ca
Profile: Travel + Escape is the ultimate destination for escapist entertainment. The network seduces viewers with compelling stories that highlight the most exotic and luxurious experiences the world has to offer.
CABLE NETWORK

Treehouse TV 70690
Owner: Corus Entertainment Inc.
Editorial: Corus Quay, 25 Dockside Drive, Toronto, Ontario M5A 0B5 **Tel:** 1 416 479-7000.
Email: info@treehousetv.com
Web site: http://www.treehousetv.com
Profile: Treehouse TV is the only national, specialty network in North America dedicated to providing suitable programming to pre-schoolers, age six years and younger. Launched in 1997, Treehouse is now available in over six million Canadian households. Treehouse offers a unique television environment that reflects the interests and developmental levels of this age group. Treehouse is owned by Corus Entertainment, a Canadian based media and entertainment company.
CABLE NETWORK

TSN 70682
Owner: Bell Media
Editorial: 9 Channel Nine Crt, Toronto, Ontario M1S 4B5- **Tel:** 1 416 332-5000.
Email: sdesk@tsn.ca
Web site: http://www.tsn.ca
Profile: TSN (The Sports Network), a division of Bell Media, sets the Canadian sports broadcasting standard. TSN's flagship news program, SportsCentre, was voted the number one source for sports news by sports fans from across the country. TSN's comprehensive broadcast schedule also includes the NHL, international hockey, the Olympic Games, CFL, NFL, golf, curling, NASCAR, iFormula One, IRL auto racing, baseball, basketball, tennis, soccer, boxing and figure skating. The network's slogan is "Canada's Sports Leader."
CABLE NETWORK

TSN2 543950
Owner: CTVglobemedia Inc.
Editorial: 9 Channel Nine Crt, Toronto, Ontario M1S 4B5- **Tel:** 1 416 332-5000.
Email: sdesk@tsn.ca
Web site: http://www.tsn.ca/tsn2
Profile: TSN2 is a 24-hour sports digital network which features more than 800 hours of live events.
CABLE NETWORK

TV5 Québec Canada 154456
Owner: TV5 Québec Canada
Editorial: 1755 boulevard Rene-Levesque Est, Bureau 101, Montreal, Quebec H2K 4P6 **Tel:** 1 514 522-5322.
Email: info@tv5.ca
Web site: http://www.tv5.ca
Profile: TV5 Québec Canada is a cable network that offers French-speaking programs produced in Europe and Africa, as well as in Canada. The programs include news, movies, travel, entertainment, documentaries, reports, debates and interviews. TV5 Québec Canada reaches 6.3 million households in Canada through cable and satellite, 4.1 million of which live out of Québec. TV5 Québec Canada is partnered with TV5, a global television network.
CABLE NETWORK

TVA Sports 776490
Owner: Quebecor Media
Editorial: 1600 boul. Maisonneuve Est, Montreal, Quebec H2L 4P2 **Tel:** 1 514 526-9251.
Email: tvasportsmtl@tva.ca
Web site: http://tvasports.ca
Profile: TVA Sports est un chaîne de TVA, présentant les nouvelles du sports, les résultats sportifs ainsi que des analyses.

TVA Sports is a cable channel featuring sports news, results and analyses.
CABLE NETWORK

VICELAND 83228
Owner: Vice Network Canada Inc.
Editorial: 204-360 Dufferin St 204, Toronto, Ontario M6K 1Z8 **Tel:** 1 416 596-6638.
Web site: http://www.vice.com/en_ca
Profile: Launched on February 29, 2016, VICELAND focuses on lifestyle-oriented documentary and reality series targeting millennials, leveraging the resources of Vice's verticals with new original series, and reruns of existing Vice web series. Formerly called Bio/The Biography Channel.
CABLE NETWORK

VisionTV 584256
Owner: ZoomerMedia Limited
Editorial: 171 East Liberty Street, Suite 230, Toronto, Ontario M6K 3P6 **Tel:** 1 416 368-3194.
Email: visiontv@visiontv.ca
Web site: http://www.visiontv.ca
Profile: VisionTV presents inspirational, insightful and original programming that celebrates diversity and promotes understanding among people of different faiths and cultures. VisionTV's lineup consists of faith programming presented by groups of various religious denominations, including Catholics, Protestants, Muslims, Sikhs and Hindus.
CABLE NETWORK

VoicePrint 83241
Owner: Accessible Media Inc.
Editorial: 1090 Don Mills Rd, Ste 200, Toronto, Ontario M3C 3R6 **Tel:** 1 416 422-4222.
Email: info@accessiblemedia.com
Web site: http://www.voiceprintcanada.com
Profile: VoicePrint is a free 24-hour news and information audio service. VoicePrint was established in 1990 to bring full-text audio recordings from more than 600 publications to all Canadians, but particularly those who can't access this information due to blindness or vision restrictions, learning or physical disability, low literacy skills or aging. Every day, volunteers record full-length articles, columns and feature reports related to news, sports, health, entertainment, science and more. VoicePrint is delivered via satellite and cable to 8.3 million homes throughout Canada.
CABLE NETWORK

W Movies 78265
Owner: Corus Entertainment Inc.
Editorial: Corus Quay, 25 Dockside Drive, Toronto, Ontario M4A 0B5 **Tel:** 1 416 479-7000.
Web site: http://www.wnetwork.com/Movies/WMovies.aspx
Profile: W Movies is the go-to destination for women seeking smart, fun and engaging films. The network features Hollywood hits, Canadian films and critically-acclaimed TV movies. W Movies will showcase films for and about women, with genres ranging from romance and comedy to drama and suspense.
CABLE NETWORK

W Network 83199
Owner: Corus Entertainment Inc.
Editorial: 25 Dockside Dr, corus quay, Toronto, Ontario M5A 0B5 **Tel:** 1 416 479-7000.
Email: comments@wnetwork.com
Web site: http://www.wnetwork.com
Profile: W Network is a compelling and contemporary television network, committed to bringing Canadian women the best entertainment that television has to offer through distinctive programming. W Network is for women all day, every day and strives to make its 24-hour programming as unique and diverse as the women who watch it. The target demographics are women, ages 25 to 54.
CABLE NETWORK

The Weather Network 70683
Owner: Pelmorex Media, Inc.
Editorial: 2655 Bristol Cir, Oakville, Ontario L6H 7W1
Tel: 1 905 829-1159.
Email: twnweb@pelmorex.com
Web site: http://www.theweathernetwork.com
Profile: The Weather Network and its French language counterpart, Meteomedia, are Canada's round-the-clock local, regional, national and international weather service. The network is available on basic cable, direct to home and on the Internet. There were 13.4 million viewers nationally in 2014.
CABLE NETWORK

World Fishing Network 695282
Owner: Insight Sports Ltd.
Editorial: 184 Pearl St Suite 302, Toronto, Ontario M5H 1L5 **Tel:** 1 416 593-0915.
Web site: http://www.insightsports.com
Profile: World Fishing Network is the only 24/7 television network dedicated to all segments of fishing with programming that covers instruction, tips, tournaments, travel, food, boating, outdoor lifestyle and more.
CABLE NETWORK

YOOPA 653749
Owner: Québécor Média
Editorial: 1600 Boul de Maisonneuve E, Montreal, Quebec H2L 4P2- **Tel:** 1 514 526-9251.
Email: jeunesse@tva.ca
Web site: http://www.yoopa.ca/statique/yoopa-tv
Profile: YOOPA est une chaîne spécialisée qui se consacre aux enfants (de 2 à 6 ans) et à leurs parents.

YOOPA is a fun and educational, specialty television channel, which invites children, ages two to six, to discover a friendly, colorful and contemporary visual universe.
CABLE NETWORK

YTV Canada 70674
Owner: Corus Entertainment Inc.
Editorial: 25 Dockside Dr, corus quay, Toronto, Ontario M5A 0B5 **Tel:** 1 416 479-7000.
Email: info@ytv.com
Web site: http://www.ytv.com
Profile: This specialty cable network provides programming geared toward children, teens, and their parents. The network is seen in over 11 million Canadian households and is aimed at audiences aged 2 to 17 and their families.
CABLE NETWORK

Cape Verde

Radio

Radio Cape Verde 313693
Owner: Radiotelevisão de Cabo Verde
Tel: 238 2 60 52 00.
Email: tcv@rtc.cv
Web site: http://www.rtc.cv/rcv
Profile: Radio Cape Verde (RCV) is the national radio station of Cape Verde, broadcasting news and entertainment.
RADIO NETWORK

Television

RTP África 381455
Tel: 238 261 13 15.
Email: rtpacv2@cvtelecom.cv
Web site: http://www.rtp.pt
Profile: Cape Verde foreign office of RTP África, reporting on news, current affairs and entertainment.
TELEVISION STATION

Televisão Cape Verde 381454
Owner: Radiotelevisão de Cabo Verde
Tel: 238 260 50 00.
Email: tcv@rtc.cv
Web site: http://www.rtc.cv/tcv
Profile: Televisão Cape Verde (TCV) is the national television station of Cape Verde, broadcasting news and entertainment.
TELEVISION STATION

Cayman Islands

Radio

ZFKC-FM 776612
Owner: Government of the Cayman Islands
Tel: 1 345 949-7799.
Email: rcnews@gov.ky
Web site: http://www.radiocayman.gov.ky
Profile: ZFKC-FM is a non-commercial radio station owned by the Government of the Cayman Islands. The format of the station is news and talk. ZFKC-FM broadcasts to the Cayman Islands at 89.9.
FM RADIO STATION

ZFKZ-FM 776608
Owner: Government of the Cayman Islands
Tel: 1 345 949-7799.
Email: rcnews@gov.ky
Web site: http://www.radiocayman.gov.ky
Profile: ZFKZ-FM is a non-commercial radio station owned by the Government of the Cayman Islands. The format of the station is a mixture of pop, soca, Latin, reggae, religious and Caribbean music. ZFKZ-FM broadcasts to the Cayman Islands at 105.3 FM.
FM RADIO STATION

ZFZZ-FM 901951
Owner: Hurley's Entertainment Corporation Limited
Tel: +1 345 945-1166.
Web site: http://www.z99.ky
Profile: Z99 (99.9 FM) is a radio station in the Cayman Islands in the British West Indies. The station is owned by Hurley's Entertainment Corporation. Station format is Contemporary Hit Radio. Hurley's Entertainment Corporation Limited was founded in 1992 by Randy L. Merren. Z99FM was the first commercial radio station in the Cayman Islands. It began broadcasting as ZFZZ, issued under the British call sign system, in May 1992. The station's most recent license was issued on 11 December, 2003.
FM RADIO STATION

Television

Cayman 27 776211
Owner: Weststar Television
Tel: 1 345 745-2739.
Email: news@cayman27.com.ky
Web site: http://www.cayman27.com.ky
Profile: Cayman 27 provides the Cayman Islands community with news, sports, and entertainment. The station is owned by Weststar Television. Cayman 27 broadcasts locally on channel 27.
TELEVISION STATION

China

Radio

China National Radio 405443
Editorial: China National Radio, 2 Fuxingmenwai Dajie, Beijing 100866 **Tel:** 86 1086093114.
Email: 4008000088@cnr.cn
Web site: http://www.cnr.cn
Profile: Broadcasts information online.
AM RADIO STATION

China Radio International Chinese Channel 467834
Editorial: China Radio International, Jia 16 Shijingshanlu, Beijing 100040 **Tel:** 86 1068892571.
Web site: http://www.chinabroadcast.cn
Profile: Covers the news and cultural issues.
AM RADIO STATION

Cable

China Central Television (CCTV 1) 458949
Editorial: China Central Television, 11 Fuxinglu, Beijing 100859 **Tel:** 86 10 68509505.
Web site: http://www.cctv.com
Profile: China Central Television is the national television station of the People's Republic of China. CCTV 1 is the Variety Channel which provides news, and entertainment and culture programmes.
CABLE NETWORK

China Central Television (CCTV 10) 458902
Editorial: China Central Television, 11 Fuxinglu, Beijing 100859 **Tel:** 86 10 68509505.
Web site: http://www.cctv.com
Profile: China Central Television is a national television station of People's Republic of China. CCTV-10 (Science and Education Channel) aims to popularize modern science and technology, promote modern education theories and show cultural heritabe in China and around the world.
CABLE NETWORK

Colombia

Radio

Radio Guatapurí 467698
Editorial: Calle 17 #15-67, Valledupar
Tel: 57 55713872.
Email: radioguatapuri@gmail.com
Web site: http://www.radioguatapuri.com
Profile: Transmits daily news. The programming includes politic, economy, science and technology, health and cultural topics. Plays Vallenatos, Boleros, and Romantic music through the frequency 740 AM.
AM RADIO STATION

Colombia

Television

Associated Press Television News
468161
Editorial: Transversal 21 No 96-17, Bogota 571
Tel: 57 16001984.
Web site: http://www.aptn.com
Profile: Associated Press Television News, APTV, is the international division of the American Press, AP. AP delivers breaking global news, sports, entertainment, technology and human video content to broadcasters through the APTV service.
TELEVISION NETWORK

Canal Caracol
407771
Editorial: Calle 103 No. 69B-43, Bogota
Tel: 57 1 643 0430.
Web site: http://www.caracoltv.com
Profile: National TV network broadcasting news, sports, cultural and entertainment programs.
TELEVISION NETWORK

Caracol Televisión
468327
Editorial: Calle 103 #69 B-43, Bogota
Tel: 57 16430430.
Email: latino@caracoltv.com.co
Web site: http://www.canalcaracol.com
Profile: TV station.
TELEVISION STATION

Telecafé
468337
Editorial: Carrera 19 A #43-02, Manizales
Tel: 57 68727100.
Email: telecafenoticias@telecafe.tv
Web site: http://www.telecafe.tv
Profile: This TV channel airs three news programs that are independently produced. These other programs are UN Noticias, TVA Noticias and Noticias 1A.
TELEVISION STATION

Cook Islands

Radio

KC FM - Radio Ikurangi
539173
Owner: David Schmidt
Editorial: PO Box 521, Rarotonga, Cook Islands
Tel: 682 23203.
Email: mariana@oyster.net.ck
RADIO NETWORK

Radio Cook Islands
539172
Owner: Elijah Communications Ltd
Editorial: PO Box 126, Rarotonga, Cook Islands
Tel: 682 29 460.
Email: jeanne@oyster.net.ck
Web site: http://www.radio.co.ck
Profile: Immediate, comprehensive and responsive source of news for the whole of the Cook Islands, overseas Cook Islanders and visitors interested in staying in touch with the country.
RADIO NETWORK

Television

Cook Islands Television
539196
Owner: Elijah Communications Ltd
Editorial: PO Box 126, Rarotonga, Cook Islands
Tel: 682 29 460.
Email: watchus@citv.co.ck
Web site: http://cookislandstelevision.com
TELEVISION STATION

Cuba

Radio

Radio Habana Cuba
393336
Editorial: Infanta no 105 esq.a 25, Centro Habana, CP 6240, Habana Tel: 53 7 87 76 533.
Email: radiohc@enet.cu
Web site: http://www.radiohc.cu
Profile: Provides daily news. Plays current popular music, Salsa, and Ballads.
RADIO NETWORK

Radio Rebelde
291148
Editorial: Edificio del ICRT, Calle 23 #258 e/ L y M, Vedado, Habana CP 10600 Tel: 53 78313514.
Web site: http://www.radiorebelde.com.cu
Profile: Provides daily news. Provides different type of music in Spanish and English.
RADIO NETWORK

Radio Reloj
291144
Editorial: Calle 23 #258 e/ L y M, Vedado, Habana CP 10400 Tel: 53 78384226.
Web site: http://www.radioreloj.co/notiweb/
Profile: National radio providing 24 hours of general news. Covers Cuban and the world news.
RADIO NETWORK

Radio Sancti Spíritus
392879
Editorial: Circunvalacion s/n, Olivos 1, Sancti Spíritus
Tel: 53 41328373.
Web site: http://www.radiosanctispiritus.cu
Profile: Broadcasts daily news, cultural and educational live shows.
FM RADIO STATION

Cyprus

Radio

Kiss FM
535061
Editorial: Diogenous 1, Engomi, Nicosia 1501
Tel: 357 22 74 44 64.
Email: kissfm89@phileleftheros.com
Web site: http://www.kissfm.com.cy
Profile: National radio station broadcasting news and pop music.
RADIO NETWORK

Czech Republic

Television

?T1 - ?eská televize
403570
Owner: ?eská televize
Editorial: Divacke centrum, Kavi hory, Prague 140 70
Tel: 420 261 131 111.
Email: info@ceskatelevize.cz
Web site: http://www.ceskatelevize.cz/ct1
Profile: Nationwide channel broadcasting 24 hours a day.
TELEVISION STATION

?T2 - ?eská televize
403567
Owner: ?eská televize
Editorial: Divacke centrum, Kaví hory, Prague 14070
Tel: 420 261131111.
Email: info@ceskatelevize.cz
Web site: http://www.ceskatelevize.cz/ct2
Profile: ?T2 is a nationwide statutory family channel in the Czech Republic broadcasting 24 hours a day. This TV channel provides documentaries, films and TV series from the Czech Republic and abroad.
TELEVISION STATION

Denmark

Radio

DR P4 Bornholm
290401
Owner: DR
Editorial: akirkebyvej 52, Rønne 3700
Tel: 45 56 94 37 00.
Email: bornholm@dr.dk
Web site: http://www.dr.dk/bornholm
Profile: DR P4 Bornholm is a regional radio station in the region of Bornholm.
RADIO NETWORK

DR P4 Esbjerg
475229
Owner: DR
Editorial: DR Syd, H.P. Hanssensgade 9-11, Aabenraa 6200 Tel: 45 73 33 79 99.
Email: esbjerg@dr.dk
Web site: http://www.dr.dk/Regioner/Esbjerg
Profile: DR P4 Esbjerg is a part of DR Syd. DR Syd are based in Aabenraa and they air the regional channels P4 Syd and P4 Esbjerg from there.
RADIO NETWORK

DR P4 Fyn
290387
Owner: DR
Editorial: Lille Tornbjerg Vej 10, Odense 5220
Tel: 45 63 15 77 00.
Email: fyn@dr.dk
Web site: http://www.dr.dk/fyn
Profile: DR P4 Fyn is a regional radio channel produced by DR Fyn.
RADIO NETWORK

DR P4 København
290402
Owner: DR
Editorial: Emil Holms Kanal 20, Copenhagen 999
Tel: 45 35 20 68 58.
Email: kbh@dr.dk
Web site: http://www.dr.dk/kbh
Profile: DR P4 København is a regional radio station that airs P4 Morgen, P4 Eftermiddag, P4 Weekend, Mig & Monica, regional news and traffic.
RADIO NETWORK

DR P4 Midt & Vest
290403
Owner: DR
Editorial: Vestergade 1, Holstebro 7500
Tel: 45 96 10 75 00.
Email: vest@dr.dk
Web site: http://www.dr.dk/vest
Profile: DR P4 Midt & Vest is a Danish regional radio station for Midt- and Vestjylland.
RADIO NETWORK

DR P4 Nordjylland
290380
Owner: Danmarks Radio
Editorial: Fredrik Bajers Vej 9, Aalborg 9220
Tel: 45 96 35 76 00.
Email: nord@dr.dk
Web site: http://www.dr.dk/nord
Profile: P4 Nordjylland is DR's editorial office in Aalborg. They provide daily news to listerners in the regions Hjørring, Frederikshavn, Jammerbugt, Brønderslev, Aalborg, Rebild, Vesthimmerland, Mariagerfjord and Læsø.
RADIO NETWORK

DR P4 Østjylland
290378
Owner: DR
Editorial: Olof Palmes Alle 10-12, Århus 8200
Tel: 45 87 39 70 00.
Email: p4aarhus@dr.dk
Web site: http://www.dr.dk/p4aarhus
Profile: DR P4 Østjylland is a regional radio station that provides news for the region around Århus.
RADIO NETWORK

DR P4 Sjælland
290404
Owner: DR
Editorial: Vadestedet 1, Næstved 4700
Tel: 45 55 75 34 00.
Email: sjaelland@dr.dk
Web site: http://www.dr.dk/p4sjaelland/
Profile: DR P4 Sjælland is a regional radio station that provides news from the areas Midt-, Vest- and Sydsjællandske as well as Lolland and Falster.
RADIO NETWORK

DR P4 Syd
290381
Owner: DR
Editorial: H.P. Hanssensgade 9-11, Aabenraa 6200
Tel: 45 73 33 79 99.
Email: syd@dr.dk
Web site: http://www.dr.dk/p4syd
Profile: DR P4 Syd is a regional radio station that provides news for Syd- and Sønderjylland.
RADIO NETWORK

DR P4 Trekanten
290379
Owner: DR
Editorial: Den hvide Facet 1, 4. sal, Vejle 7100
Tel: 45 76 41 78 00.
Email: trekanten@dr.dk
Web site: http://www.dr.dk/p4trekanten
Profile: DR P4 Trekanten is a regional radio station that provides news for the areas Hedensted, Vejle, Fredericia, Billund and Kolding.
RADIO NETWORK

Radio24syv
844441
Owner: Berlingske People A/S
Editorial: Vester Farimagsgade 41, Copenhagen 1606
Tel: 45 31 24 72 47.
Email: nyhedsredaktionen@radio24syv.dk
Web site: http://www.radio24syv.dk
Profile: Radio24syv is a Danish public service radio station covering news and debate radio.
RADIO NETWORK

Skala fm
289821
Owner: Radio Skala ApS
Editorial: Dalbygade 40, Kolding 6000
Tel: 45 70 21 62 19.
Email: studiet@skala.dk
Web site: http://www.skalafm.dk
Profile: Skala fm is the largest commercial radio station in the south of Denmark.
FM RADIO STATION

Television

DK4
434737
Owner: DK4
Editorial: Radmandsgade 55, Copenhagen 2200
Tel: 45 70 25 35 35.
Email: post@dk4.dk
Web site: http://www.dk4.dk
TELEVISION NETWORK

Frederiksberg Lokal TV
475240
Editorial: Allegade 12, Frederiksberg 2000
Tel: 45 32 17 09 00.
Email: info@frederiksberglokal-tv.dk
Web site: http://frederiksberglokal-tv.dk/
Profile: Frederiksberg Lokal TV is a local television station that airs reports from Frederiksberg and Copenhagen.
TELEVISION STATION

Kanal 4
492820
Owner: Discovery Networks Danmark
Editorial: H.C. Andersen Boulevard 1, København V 1553 Tel: 45 70 10 10 10.
Email: infodk@discovery.com
Web site: http://www.kanal4.dk
Profile: Kanal 4 is a Danish TV station covering news and entertainment.
TELEVISION STATION

TV 2
316068
Owner: TV 2 / Danmark
Editorial: TV 2 Kvægtorvet, Rugaardsvej 25, Odense 5100 Tel: 45 65 91 91 91.
Email: tv2@tv2.dk
Web site: http://www.tv2.dk
Profile: TV 2 is a publicly owned television network in Denmark based in Odense. TV 2 has six subsidiary stations known as TV 2 Zulu, targeted at the youth; TV 2 Charlie, oriented towards older audiences; TV 2 News, a 24-hour news channel; TV 2 Film; TV 2 Sport; and TV 2 Fri, a leisure and hobby channel as well as an internet-based pay-per-view channel TV 2 Sputnik.
TELEVISION NETWORK

TV 2 Charlie
492819
Owner: TV 2 Networks
Editorial: TV 2 Teglholmen, Teglholm Allé 16, Copenhagen DK-1711 Tel: 45 39 75 75 75.
Email: charlie@tv2.dk
Web site: http://programmer.tv2.dk/tv-2-charlie
Profile: TV 2 Charlie is a Danish tv-channel produced by TV 2 covering entertainment.
TELEVISION NETWORK

TV 2 Lorry
317216
Owner: TV 2 / Danmark
Editorial: Allegade 7-9, Frederiksberg 2000
Tel: 45 38 38 55 55.
Email: redaktion@tv2lorry.dk
Web site: http://www.tv2lorry.dk/
Profile: TV 2 Lorry is a regional television station with regional news from the Capital region.
TELEVISION NETWORK

TV 2 Zulu
316441
Owner: TV 2 / DANMARK
Editorial: TV 2 Kvægtorvet, Rugaardsvej 25, Odense 5100 Tel: 45 65 91 91 91.
Email: zulu@tv2.dk
Web site: http://www.zulu.dk
Profile: TV 2 Zulu is a Danish TV-channel covering general entertainment aimed at the young public between 15-30. The channel belongs to the TV 2 network.
TELEVISION NETWORK

TV 2; Midt-Vest
316639
Owner: TV 2 / DANMARK
Editorial: Sovej 2, Holstebro 7500
Tel: 45 96 12 12 12.
Email: redaktionen@tvmidtvest.dk
Web site: http://www.tvmidtvest.dk/
Profile: TV 2; Midt-Vest is a regional tv-station under TV 2 covering Midt- and Vestjylland.
TELEVISION NETWORK

TV3
310886
Owner: TV3 Danmark / MTG TV
Editorial: Strandlodsvej 30, Copenhagen 2300
Tel: 45 77 30 55 00.
Email: tv3@viasat.dk
Web site: http://www.tv3.dk
Profile: TV3 Denmark is a Danish commercial television station. It is one of the channels owned by the Viasat Corporation. The channels shows a lot of American and British shows.
TELEVISION STATION

Djibouti

Television

Radiodiffusion Télévision de Djibouti - RTD
316302
Editorial: 1 Avenue Saint Laurent du Var, BP 97, Djibouti Tel: 253 35 22 94.
Email: rtd@intnet.dj
Web site: http://www.rtd.dj
Profile: National television and radio broadcasting from its office in Djibouti and focusing on national and international news, current affairs, politics, economics, culture and entertainment.
TELEVISION STATION

Dominica

Radio

DBS Radio
381086
Tel: 767 4483282.
Email: dbsmanager@dbcradio.net
Web site: http://www.dbcradio.net
Profile: Provides daily news shows and plays different types of music.
RADIO NETWORK

Voice of Life Radio
381085
Editorial: PO Box 205, Madrelle Loubiere
Tel: 767 4487017.
Email: volradio@cwdom.dm
Web site: http://www.voiceoflife.com
Profile: Christian radio playing gospel music.
RADIO NETWORK

Dominican Republic

Radio

La Nota Diferente
402169
Editorial: Teleantillas #2 de Fillo, Autopista Duarte, Km 71/2, Santo Domingo Tel: 809 5677751.

Web site: http://www.tele-antillas.tv/
Profile: Broadcasts entertainment and cultural programs. Provides daily news.
RADIO NETWORK

Television

CDN TV 402256
Editorial: Calle Defillo no. 4, Los Prados, Santo Domingo **Tel:** 1 809 683-8100.
Email: redaccion@cdn.com.do
Web site: http://www.cdn.com.do/envivo
Profile: Broadcasts daily news, sports, cooking and health programs.
TELEVISION NETWORK

Color Vision 402257
Editorial: Corporacion Dominicana de Radio y Television, C/A, Emilio A. Morel, esq Luís Perez, ensanche la FE, Santo Domingo **Tel:** 809 5665875.
Email: luismundovision@gmail.com
Web site: http://www.colorvision.com.do
Profile: Covers the national territory of Dominican Republic. Broadcasts daily news, sports, entertainment and programs with live shows related to health and life styles. On Saturdays transmits a children's program.
TELEVISION NETWORK

Teleantillas 402247
Owner: Grupo Corripio
Editorial: Autopista Duarte, km 7 1/2, Santo Domingo
Tel: 809 5677751.
Email: webmaster@tele-antillas.tv
Web site: http://www.tele-antillas.tv
Profile: Broadcasts entertainment, educational, and informative programs. Transmits daily news, sports, international soap-operas and musical shows.
TELEVISION NETWORK

Ecuador

Radio

Alfa Radio 736057
Owner: CRTV
Editorial: Km 4 1/2 Av. Juan Tanca Marengo junto a RTS canal 4, Guayaquil **Tel:** 593 4 3810049.
Web site: http://www.alfa.com.ec/
Profile: Alfa Radio is a commercial station owned by CRTV. The station air Top 40 music. Alfa Radio broadcasts to the Guayaquil, Ecuador area on 104.1 FM.
FM RADIO STATION

Antena 1 289036
Editorial: Heroes de Verdeloma 9-15, Cuenca
Tel: 593 7 284 9215.
Email: radio@antenaunofm.net
Web site: http://www.antenaunofm.net
FM RADIO STATION

CRE Satelital 733522
Owner: Compañia de Radio y Televisión, SA
Editorial: Boyaca 642 y Padre Solano Edificio El Torreon 8 Piso, Guayaquil 593 **Tel:** 59 34 42560900.
Email: cre@cre.com.ec
Web site: http://www.cre.com.ec
Profile: CRE Satelital is a Spanish satellite radio service located in Guayquil, Guayas, Ecuador that broadcasts across Ecuador. It broadcasts primarily news and sports news, with 70 percent of its current programming dedicated to sports news.
RADIO NETWORK

FM 88.5 Radio Activa 290880
Editorial: Avenida Miguel Cordero y Av. Paucarbamba esquina, Edificio Work Center 5to Piso, Oficina 508, Cuenca (azuay) **Tel:** 593 72814688.
Email: radio@cadenactiva.com
Web site: http://www.cadenactiva.com
Profile: Plays Pop, Rock, Ballads, Urban music in Spanish and English. Also broadcasts soccer programs.
RADIO NETWORK

JC Radio 290881
Editorial: Av. Isabela Catolica No. 833 y Luis Cordero, Quito **Tel:** 593 2 255 4401.
Email: labruja@jcradio.com.ec
Web site: http://www.jcradio.com.ec
Profile: Provides music, sport, tourism news, and call-in programs in which the audience participates and interacts. Targets a youth audience.
RADIO NETWORK

Mix 99.3 733477
Owner: Servidinadica
Editorial: Av J Tanca Marengo Km1 al lado de Almacen Grayman, entrando por India, Guayaquil
Tel: 593 4 2682271.
Email: gye@servidinamica.com
FM RADIO STATION

Radio Activa 735875
Owner: Radio Zaracay
Editorial: Calle George Town y Rio Yamboya, Santo Domingo **Tel:** 593 2 2763900.
Email: radioactiva.maspositiva@gmail.com
Web site: http://www.zaracayradio.com
Profile: Radio Activa is a commercial station owned by Radio Zaracay. The station airs a variety of music, news, agriculture news, culture, and education. It broadcasts to the Santo Domingo de los Colores, Ecuador area on 99.7 FM.
FM RADIO STATION

Radio Alfa Musical 736062
Editorial: Hermano Miguel 10-68 y Gran Colombia, 2do piso, Cuenca **Tel:** 593 7 2838451.
Email: radioalfa1140am@gmail.com
AM RADIO STATION

Radio Ambato 736069
Owner: Radio Ambato
Editorial: Calle Sucre N-09-42 y Passaje Rodo, Quito
Tel: 593 3 242-1602.
Email: radioambato@radioambato.com.ec
Web site: http://www.radioambato.com.ec
Profile: Radio Ambato is a commercial radio station owned by Radio Ambato. The station air sports news and some general news. Radio Ambato broadcasts to the Ambato, Ecuador area on 930 AM.
AM RADIO STATION

Radio America 736077
Editorial: Olmedo 974 y Velasco, Ibarra (imbabura)
Tel: 593 6 2641742.
Web site: http://www.americaestereo.com/
FM RADIO STATION

Radio Amiga 410976
Owner: EDIASA
Editorial: Avenida Metropolitana Eloy Alfaro, 1.1/2 vía a Manta, Aptdo. 13-01-050, Portoviejo (manabi)
Tel: 593 5 293 3777.
Email: cabinaamiga@radioamiga.ec
Web site: http://www.eldiario.com.ec
Profile: Alternate news and music from 7:00 AM until 8:00 PM. Every hour the programming includes micronews.
FM RADIO STATION

Radio Antena 3 733665
Editorial: Cordova E/ 9 de Octubre y Pedro Carbo Edif. San Francisco 300 Piso 12 Ofic 1201, Guayaquil 593 **Tel:** 59 34 2560610.
Email: antena3@radioantena3.com
Web site: http://www.radioantena3.com
Profile: Radio Antena 3 is a commercial station in Guayaquil, Ecuador. The format of the station is Hispanic adult contemporary, and broadcasts at 91.7 FM. The target audience of the station is adults, ages 18 to 64.
FM RADIO STATION

Radio Canela 736538
Editorial: Via Proano, Cdad Macas, Quito
Tel: 593 7 2701387.
FM RADIO STATION

Radio Caravana Guayaquil 733678
Editorial: Av Juan Tanca Marengo Km 3, Guayaquil 593 **Tel:** 593 4 2889666.
Email: info@radiocaravana.com
Web site: http://www.radiocaravana.com
Profile: Radio Caravana Guayaquil is a commercial station in Guayaquil, Ecuador. The format of the station is Spanish sports news and talk. The target audience of the station is adults, ages 18 to 64. Radio Caravana broadcasts to the Guayaquil, Ecuador area at 750 AM.
AM RADIO STATION

Radio Caravana Quito 736343
Editorial: Pasaje A OE 513 y Vasco de Contreras, Quito **Tel:** 593 2 2442951.
Web site: http://www.radiocaravana.com
Profile: Radio Carvana Quito is a commercial station. The format of the station is sports, news and talk. Radio Caravana Quito broadcasts to the Quito, Ecuador area at 610 AM. The station airs Radio Carvana Guayaquil's programming.
AM RADIO STATION

Radio Casa de la Cultura 736354
Owner: Casa de la Cultura
Editorial: 6 de Diciembre N16-224 y Patria, Quito
Tel: 593 2 2223392.
Email: info@cce.org.ec
Web site: http://www.cce.org.ec
AM RADIO STATION

Radio Católica Nacional de Ecuador 409564
Editorial: Av. America, 1830, Mercadillo, Quito 17-03-540 **Tel:** 593 2 255 8916.
Email: noticias1@radiocatolica.org.ec
Web site: http://www.radiocatolica.org.ec
Profile: Broadcasts educational and cultural programs including shows in a Catholic context. Plays different music genres.
RADIO NETWORK

Radio Cenit 736363
Editorial: Av. Quito 806 y 9 de Octubre piso 11 Ofc. #1104, Guayaquil **Tel:** 593 4 2282076.
Email: radio-cenit-guayaquil@hotmail.com
Profile: Radio Cenit is a commercial station. The station airs a variety of music and news. Radio Cenit broadcasts to the Guayaquil, Ecuador area on 1300 AM.
AM RADIO STATION

Radio Centro 97.7 733483
Tel: 593 4 228-0500.
Email: noticiero_elobservador@hotmail.com
Web site: http://www.radiocentro.com.ec
Profile: Radio Centro is a commercial station. The format of the station is adult contemporary, romantic and pop music. Radio Centro broadcasts in the Guayaquil, Ecuador area at 97.7 FM.
FM RADIO STATION

Radio Colón 733898
Owner: ServiDinamica S.A.
Editorial: Juan Tanca Marengo Km.2.5, Guayaquil 593 **Tel:** 59 34 2682271.
Email: escucha@radiocolon.ec
Profile: Radio Colón is a Spanish commercial station owned by ServiDinamica S.A. The format of the station is news and variety. The target audience of the station is adults, ages 18 to 64. It broadcasts to Guayaquil, Ecuador at 92.9 FM.
FM RADIO STATION

Radio Cóndor 738963
Editorial: Km 8.5 via Daule, lotizacion San Francisco, Av. Primera y calle 4ta, Guayaquil
Tel: 593 4 2250528.
Email: radio.condor@hotmail.com
Profile: Radio Cóndor is a commercial station in Guayaquil, Ecuador. The format of the station is news, talk, and variety. Radio Cóndor broadcasts to Guayaquil, Ecuador at 1140 AM. The target audience of the station is adults, ages 18 to 64.
AM RADIO STATION

Radio Constelación 737685
Editorial: Calle Latacunga y Av. Quito 136, Quito
Tel: 593 2 2751397.
Email: ventas@radioconstelacionfm.com
Web site: http://www.radioconstelacionfm.com
Profile: Radio Constelación is a commercial station in Quito, Ecuador. The format of the station is top 40/ CHR, classic hits, and variety. Radio Constelación broadcasts to Quito, Ecuador at 99.3 FM. The target audience for the station is adults, ages 18 to 54.
FM RADIO STATION

Radio Cristal 733941
Editorial: 1407-1409 Luque J and Antepara, Guayaquil 593 **Tel:** 593 4 253160.
Email: rcristal@ecua.net.ec
Profile: Radio Cristal is a Spanish commercial station with a format of primarily news and talk, with some variety. The target audience of the station is adults, ages 18 to 64. The station broadcasts to Guayaquil, Ecuador at 870 AM.
AM RADIO STATION

Radio Cristal 736142
Editorial: Avs. de la Prensa N60-22 Y Del Maestro, Quito **Tel:** 593 2 2595219.
Email: noticias@amcristal.com
Profile: Radio Cristal is a commercial station in Quito, Ecuador. The format of the station is news, talk, adult hits, and variety. Radio Cristal broadcasts to Quito, Ecuador at 1380 AM. The target audience of the station is adults, ages 18 to 64.
AM RADIO STATION

Radio El Mercurio 735253
Editorial: Av. de las Americas y Francisco Azcazubi, esq, Quito **Tel:** 593 7 4095684.
Email: radio@radioelmercurio.com
Web site: http://www.radioelmercurio.com.ec
Profile: Radio El Mercurio is a commercial station in Quito, Ecuador. The format of the station is news, sports, and variety. Radio El Mercurio broadcasts to Quito, Ecuador at 1200 AM.
AM RADIO STATION

Radio Eres 735864
Editorial: Av. Amazonas N35-89 y Corea, 4to piso, Edif. Amazonas 4000, Quito **Tel:** 593 2 2255999.
Email: contacto@radioeres.com
Web site: http://www.radioeres.com
FM RADIO STATION

Radio Estrella 735912
Owner: Radio Estrella Ecuador
Editorial: Cdla. Mirador del Norte, Mz. 21 Solar 12, Guayaquil **Tel:** 593 4 2235230.
Email: radioestrella_921@hotmail.com
Web site: http://www.radioestrella.com.ec
Profile: Radio Estrella is a commercial station owned by Radio Estrella Ecuador. The format for the station is classic hits and top 40 CHR. Radio Estrella broadcasts to Guayaquil, Ecuador at 92.1 FM. The target audience is adults, agres 18 to 64.
FM RADIO STATION

Radio Forever 733893
Owner: Forever Music Radio
Editorial: Jose Alevedra y Francisco de Orellana, Edificio Ralio Piso 3, Guayaquil 593
Tel: 59 34 2690328.
Email: forever@radioforever925.com
Web site: http://www.radioforever925.com
Profile: Radio Forever is a Spanish commercial station owned by Forever Music Radio. The format of the station is news and classic hits. It broadcasts to Guayaquil, Ecuador at 92.5 FM. The target audience of the station is adults, ages 18 to 64.
FM RADIO STATION

Radio Francisco Stereo 734919
Owner: Francisco Stereo
Editorial: Cuenca No. 477 y Sucre Bajos, Convento de San Francisco, Quito **Tel:** 593 2 2289365.
Email: franciscolaradio@gmail.com
Web site: http://www.franciscostereo.com
Profile: Radio Francisco Stereo is a commercial station owned by Francisco Stereo. The format of the station is Religious news and talk. Radio Francisco Stereo broadcasts to Quito, Ecuador at 102.5 FM.
FM RADIO STATION

Radio Francisco Stereo 734921
Owner: Francisco Stereo
Tel: 593 2 2289365.
Email: franciscolaradio@gmail.com
Web site: http://www.franciscostereo.com
Profile: Radio Francisco Stereo is a commercial station owned by Francisco Stereo. The format of the station is Religious news and talk. Radio Francisco Stereo broadcasts to Guayaquil, Ecuador at 106.9 FM.
FM RADIO STATION

Radio Fuego 737721
Editorial: Cdla. Kennedy Norte, Mz 1008 villa #21, Guayaquil **Tel:** 593 4 2682985.
Email: noticiero@radiofuego.com
Web site: http://www.hot106fuego.com
Profile: Radio Fuego is a commercial station in Guayaquil, Ecuador. The format of the station is top 40 CHR and classic hits. Radio Fuego broadcasts to the Guayaquil, Ecuador area at 106.5 FM. The target audience for the station is adults, ages 18 to 54.
FM RADIO STATION

Radio Gitana 737728
Owner: Gitana FM S.A.
Editorial: Av 12 de Octubre N24-402 y Cordero, Casilla 17-01-2105, Quito **Tel:** 593 2 2529205.
Email: ventas@gitana.com.ec
Web site: http://www.gitana.com.ec
Profile: Radio Gitana is a commercial station owned by Gitana FM S.A. The format of the station is classic hits and top 40 CHR. Radio Gitana broadcasts to the Quito, Ecuador area at 94.9 FM.
FM RADIO STATION

Radio HCJB-2 733533
Owner: HCJB Global
Editorial: Chambers 301entre 5 de Junio y Domingo Comin, Guayaquil 593 **Tel:** 59 34 244-0759.
Email: miradio@hcjb2.org
Web site: http://www.hcjb2.org
Profile: Radio HCJB-2 is a radio station owned by HCJB Global. The format of the station is Christian and religious music and talk, and broadcasts to the Guayaquil, Guayas, Ecuador area at 102.5 FM.
FM RADIO STATION

Radio i99 733664
Owner: Radio i99
Tel: 593 4 2680877.
Web site: http://www.i99.com.ec
Profile: Radio i99 is a commercial station owned by Radio i99. The format of the station is hot AC. Radio i99 broadcasts to the Guayaquil, Ecuador area at 98.9 FM.
FM RADIO STATION

Radio Imperio 734135
Editorial: Calle 7 de Octubre y Decima Septima, Edf.Pedro Pablo, 2do Piso, Guayaquil
Tel: 59 35 2753497.
Email: radioimperiopog@yahoo.es
Web site: http://www.radioimperioquevedo.com
Profile: Radio Imperio is a Spanish commercial, station in Quevedo, Ecuador. The format of the station is news, talk, and variety. The target, audience of the station is adults, ages 18 to 64. Radio, Imperio broadcasts to Quevedo, Ecuador at 101.9 FM.
FM RADIO STATION

Radio Iris 738014
Editorial: Portete E10-334 Y Faustino Sarmiento, Quito **Tel:** 593 2 2275747.
Email: marisa6_66@hotmail.com
Profile: Radio Iris is a commercial station in Quito, Ecuador. The format of the station is news, talk and variety. Radio Iris broadcasts to Quito, Ecuador at 530 AM. The target audience for the station is adults, ages 18-64.
AM RADIO STATION

Radio Jesús del Gran Poder 735299
Owner: Francisco Stereo
Editorial: Cuenca No. 477 y Sucre Bajos, Convento de San Francisco, Quito **Tel:** 593 2 2289365.
Email: franciscolaradio@gmail.com
Web site: http://www.franciscostereo.com
Profile: Radio Jesús del Gran Poder is a commercial station owned by Francisco Stereo. The format of the station is Religious news and talk. Radio Jesús del Gran Poder broadcasts to Quito, Ecuador at 670 AM.
AM RADIO STATION

Radio Kiss 734361
Owner: ServiDinamica S.A.
Editorial: Juan Tanca Marengo Km 2 1/2, Guayaquil
Tel: 59 34 2682271.
Email: admin@kissfm.ec
Web site: http://www.kissfm.ec
Profile: Radio Kiss is a commercial station owned by ServiDinamica S.A. The format of the station is Top 40 CHR. The target audience of the station is adults,

Ecuador

ages 18 to 64. Radio Kiss broadcasts to Guayaquil, Ecuador at 90.9 FM.
FM RADIO STATION

Radio La Estación 738927
Editorial: Kennedy Norte, Av. Luis Orrantia y calle Victor Hugo Sicouret, Esquina solar 22 y 23, edif. Rafermartz 2do. piso, Guayaquil **Tel:** 593 4 2682311.
Web site: http://www.laestacion.fm
Profile: Radio La Estación is a commercial station in Guayaquil, Ecuador. The format of the station is top 40 CHR, classic hits, news, and talk. Radio La Estación broadcasts to Guayaquil, Ecuador at 101.3 FM. The target audience for the station is adults, ages 18 to 64.
FM RADIO STATION

Radio La Prensa 733643
Owner: Radio La Prensa TV. S.A.
Editorial: Cdla. Adace: Av. Constitucion y Av. De las Americas (junto a TC Television), Guayaquil
Tel: 593 4 2288094.
Email: info@radiolaprensatvsa.com
Web site: http://www.radiolaprensatvsa.com/
Profile: Radio La Prensa is a commercial station owned by Radio La Prensa TV. S.A. The format of the station is classical music, and some variety music such as jazz and tango, along with news. Radio La Prensa broadcasts to the Guayaquil, Ecuador area at 100.1 FM.
FM RADIO STATION

Radio La Rumbera 736096
Owner: Enrique Gallegos Custode
Editorial: Manuel Camacho 143 y Portete, sector Estadio Olimpico Atahualpa, Quito
Tel: 593 2 2442178.
Email: lahoraclave@hotmail.com
Web site: http://www.radiolarumbera.com
Profile: Radio La Rumbera is a commercial station owned by Enrique Gallegos. The station airs a variety of music. La Rumbera broadcasts to the Quito, Ecuador area at 99.7 FM.
FM RADIO STATION

Radio Majestad 89.7 738022
Editorial: 6 de Diciembre 3981 y Checoslovaquia, Quito **Tel:** 593 2 2269918.
Web site: http://www.radiomajestad.com
Profile: Radio Majestad 89.7 is a commercial station owned by Radio Majestad. The format of the station is top 40 CHR classic hits news and talk. Radio Majestad broadcasts to Quito, Ecuador at 89.7 FM. The target audience for the station is adults, ages 18 to 64.
FM RADIO STATION

Radio Mas Candela 734367
Owner: ServiDinamica S.A.
Editorial: Juan Tanca Marengo Km 2.5, Guayaquil
Tel: 59 34 2682271.
Email: admin@servidinamica.com
Profile: Radio Mas Candela is a commercial station owned by ServiDinamica S.A. The format of the station is variety and Top 40 CHR. Radio Mas Candela broadcasts to Guayaquil, Ecuador at 96.9 FM.
FM RADIO STATION

Radio Morena 734040
Owner: Radio Morena S.A
Editorial: Av. Quito 1200 y Aguirre, esquina Edificio Radio Morena, Guayaquil **Tel:** 593 4 2519000.
Email: radiomorena640@hotmail.com
Web site: http://www.radiomorena640.com/
Profile: Radio Morena is a commercial station owned by Radio Morena S.A. The format of the station is talk and news. Radio Morena broadcasts to the Guayaquil, Ecuador area at 640 AM.
AM RADIO STATION

Radio Nuevo Tiempo 734205
Owner: Unión Ecuatoriana de la Iglesia Adventista del Séptimo Día
Editorial: Tulcan 901 y Hurtado, Guayaquil
Tel: 593 4 2371211.
Email: nuevotiempo@adventistas.ec
Web site: http://adventistas.ec/
Profile: Radio Tiempo Nuevo is owned by Unión Ecuatoriana de la Iglesia Adventista del Séptimo Día. The station airs Christian programming, music, and news. Radio Tiempo Nuevo broadcasts to the area on 97.3 FM.
FM RADIO STATION

Radio Once Q 734319
Owner: Radio Cadena Musical Uno
Editorial: Velez 905 y 6 de Marzo, Edificio Forum, Piso 25 Suite #8, Guayaquil **Tel:** 593 4 2323171.
Web site: http://www.radio11q.com.ec
Profile: Radio Once Q a is a commercial station owned by Radio Cadena Musical Uno. The format of the station is oldies. Radio Once Q broadcasts to the Guayaquil, Ecuador area at 104.9 FM.
FM RADIO STATION

Radio Onda Cero 734373
Owner: ServiDinamica S.A.
Editorial: Juan Tanca Marengo Km 2.5, Guayaquil
Tel: 59 34 2682271.
Email: admin@servidinamica.com
Profile: Radio Onda Cero is a commercial station owned by ServiDinamica S.A. The format of the station is hip hop. Radio Onda Cero broadcasts to Guayaquil, Ecuador at 96.1 FM.
FM RADIO STATION

Radio Onda Positiva 738029
Owner: Radio Onda Positiva
Editorial: Cosme Renella y Av. de las Americas, Edif. La Espanola P.2, Of. 8, Guayaquil
Tel: 593 4 2396002.
Web site: http://www.radioondapositiva.com
Profile: Radio Onda Positiva is a commercial station owned by Radio Onda Positiva. The format of the station is top 40 CHR, news, and talk. Radio Onda Positiva broadcasts to Guayaquil, Ecuador at 94.1 FM. The target audience of the station is adults, ages 18 to 64.
FM RADIO STATION

Radio Ondas Azuayas 287710
Editorial: Heroes de Verdeloma 9-15, Cuenca (azuay)
Tel: 593 7 2831975.
Email: radioondasazuayas@gmail.com
Web site: http://www.ondasazuayas.com
Profile: Radio Ondas Azuayas is a commercial station in Cuenca, Ecuador. The format of the station is news, talk, variety and sports. Radio Ondas Azuayas broadcasts to Cuenca, Ecuador at 1110 AM. The target audience for the station is all ages.
AM RADIO STATION

Radio Pasión 734479
Owner: ServiDinamica S.A.
Editorial: Juan Tanca Marengo Km 2.5, Guayaquil
Tel: 59 34 2682271.
Email: admin@servidinamica.com
Profile: Radio Pasión is a commercial station owned by ServiDinamica S.A. The format of the station is Smooth AC and Variety. Radio Pasión broadcasts to Guayaquil, Ecuador at 96.5 FM.
FM RADIO STATION

Radio Publica de Ecuador 736884
Owner: U.S. Embassy in Ecuador
Editorial: San Salvador E6-49 Y Eloy Alfaro, Quito
Tel: 593 3 970800.
Web site: http://www.radiopublica.info
Profile: Radio Publica de Ecuador is a commercial station owned by the U.S. Embassy in Ecuador. The format of the station is politics, human rights, news, and talk. Radio Publica de Ecuador broadcasts to the Quito, Ecuador area at 100.9 FM. The target audience of the station is adults, ages 18 to 64.
FM RADIO STATION

Radio Punto Rojo 734141
Owner: Extra Radio S.A.
Editorial: Av. 9 de Octubre #1904 y Esmeraldas, Edif. Florida Piso 10, Guayaquil **Tel:** 59 34 2289922.
Web site: http://www.radiopuntorojo.com
Profile: Radio Punto Rojo is a commercial station owned by Extra Radio S.A. The format of the station is news, talk, and variety. The target audience of the station is adults, ages 18 to 64. Radio Punta Rojo broadcasts to the Guayaquil, Ecuador area at 89.7 FM.
FM RADIO STATION

Radio Quito 736337
Owner: Editores Ecuatorianos S.A.
Editorial: Av. Coruna 2104 and Whimper, Edf. Aragones, P.9. Ecuador, Quito **Tel:** 593 2 2508301.
Email: info@ecuadoradio.com
Web site: http://www.radioquito.ec
Profile: Radio Quito is a commercial station owned by Editores Ecuatorianos S.A. The format of the station is news, talk, sports, and variety. Radio Quito broadcasts to the Quito, Ecuador area at 760 AM.
AM RADIO STATION

Radio Romance 734145
Owner: Extra Radio S.A.
Editorial: Av. 9 de Octubre #1904 y Esmeraldas, Edif. Florida Piso 10, Guayaquil **Tel:** 59 34 2290577.
Web site: http://www.radioromance.com
Profile: Radio Romance is a Spanish commercial station owned by Extra Radio S.A. The format of the station is news, talk, and Smooth AC. Radio Romance broadcasts to the Guayaquil, Ecuador area at 90.1 FM.
FM RADIO STATION

Radio Rumba 734493
Editorial: Chimborazo 115 y Velez, 1er. Piso, Guayaquil **Tel:** 593 4 2328012.
Email: rumba107@radiorumba.fm
Web site: http://www.radiorumba.fm
Profile: Radio Rumba is a Spanish commercial station in Ecuador. The format of the station is variety and Top 40 CHR. The target audience of the station is adults, ages 18 to 64.
FM RADIO STATION

Radio Sonorama 735635
Owner: Sonorama S.A.
Editorial: Moscu 378 y Republica del Salvador, Quito
Tel: 593 2 2442697.
Email: noticias@sonorama.com.ec
Web site: http://www.sonorama.com.ec
Profile: Radio Sonorama features news, sports, talk, and top 40 CHR. Radio Sonorama broadcasts nationally to Ecuador. The target audience is adults, ages 18 to 54. The tagline of the station is "La Gran Señal Nacional".
RADIO NETWORK

Radio Tropicana 733875
Owner: Medios Y Proyectos
Editorial: Hurtado 212 y Machala, Edificio FURNAS 4 Piso, Guayaquil 593 **Tel:** 59 34 2511758.
Email: info@radiotropicana.com.ec
Web site: http://www.radiotropicana.com.ec
Profile: Radio Tropicana is a Spanish commerical station owned by Medios Y Proyectos. The format of the station is news, talk and classical. Radio Tropicana broadcasts to Guayaquil, Ecuador at 540 AM.
AM RADIO STATION

Radio Universal 733498
Tel: 593 4 2448410.
Email: radiouniversalguayaquil@hotmail.com
Web site: http://es.justin.tv/radiouniversalguayaquil
Profile: Radio Universal is a commercial station. The format of the station is a variety of music, as well as news and sports. Radio Universal broadcasts in the Guayaquil, Ecuador area at 1270 AM.
AM RADIO STATION

Radio Uno 734321
Owner: Radio Cadena Musical Uno
Tel: 593 4 2323171.
Web site: http://www.radio11q.com.ec
Profile: Radio Uno is a commercial station owned by Radio Cadena Musical Uno. The format of the station is romantic music. Radio Uno broadcasts in the Guayaquil, Ecuador area at 580 AM.
AM RADIO STATION

Radio Vigía 738907
Owner: Policía Nacional del Ecuador
Editorial: Av. Amazonas N53 113 y Japon, Quito
Tel: 593 2 254-4869.
Email: dnctsv.administracioncaja@policiaecuador.gob.ec
Profile: Radio Vigía is a non-commercial radio station owned by Policía Nacional del Ecuador. The format of the station is news. Radio Vigía broadcasts to Quito, Ecuador at 840 AM. The target audience of the station is adults, ages 18 to 64.
AM RADIO STATION

Radio Visión 735575
Editorial: Francisco Arizaga Luque N34-229 y Federico Paez, Quito **Tel:** 593 2 2260315.
Email: ventas@radiovision.com.ec
Web site: http://www.radiovision.com.ec
Profile: Radio Visión is a commercial station in Quito Ecuador. The format of the station is news, talk, and variety. Radio Visión broadcasts to Quito, Ecuador at 91.7 FM.
FM RADIO STATION

Radio Zaracay 735874
Owner: Radio Zaracay
Editorial: Av. Quito 1424 y Psaje. Aguavil, Quito
Tel: 593 2 2750140.
Email: radiozaracay@hotmail.com
Web site: http://zaracayradio.com/home.html
Profile: Radio Zaracay is a commercial station owned by Radio Zaracay. The station airs a variety of music. It broadcasts to the Quito, Ecuador area on 100.5 FM.
FM RADIO STATION

Teleradio 1350 733673
Owner: Teleradio AM
Editorial: Kennedy Norte Calle Flores Perez MZ 504 Condominio Colon 1er Piso, Guayaquil
Tel: 593 4 2680696.
Web site: http://www.teleradio.am/
Profile: Teleradio 1350 is a commercial station owned by Teleradio AM. The format of the station is news and sports talk. Teleradio 1350 broadcasts to the Guayaquil, Ecuador area at 1350 AM.
AM RADIO STATION

La Voz de Tomebamba 735922
Owner: Radio La Voz
Editorial: Benigno Malo 15-91, Cuenca
Tel: 593 7 2842000.
Email: info@lavozdeltomebamba.com
Web site: http://www.lavozdeltomebamba.com
Profile: La Voz de Tomebamba is a commercial station owned by Radio La Voz. The format is news, talk, sports and variety. La Voz de Tomebamba broadcasts to Cuenca, Ecuador at 102.1 FM. The target audience for the station is adults, ages 18 to 64. The station's tagline is "Nace de todas las voces".
FM RADIO STATION

Egypt

Radio

Al Aghani Radio 715930
Owner: Egypt Radio & Television Union (ERTU)
Editorial: PO Box 1186, Egyptian Radio & TV Building, Cairo **Tel:** 20 2 2577 6078.
Email: ern.news@yahoo.com
Web site: http://www.ertu.org
Profile: Al Aghani Radio broadcasts Arabic music and entertainment news on 105.8 FM and 90.9 FM. The station launched in 2000 and is operated by state-owned public broadcaster, the Egypt Radio & Television Union (ERTU).
FM RADIO STATION

El Bernameg Al-Aam Egypt 774752
Owner: Egypt Radio & Television Union (ERTU)
Editorial: PO Box 1186, Egyptian Radio & TV Building, Cairo **Tel:** 20 2 2578 4124.
Email: aly_tv@yahoo.com
Web site: http://www.ertu.org
Profile: El Bernameg Al-Aam Egypt, also known as Iza'at Al Gomhuriya Al Masriya Al Arabiya, is a radio station broadcasting music, news and entertainment programmes. The station launched in 1934 and is operated by state-owned public broadcaster, the Egypt Radio & Television Union (ERTU).
FM RADIO STATION

Al Quraan Al-Kareem 77475
Owner: Egypt Radio & Television Union (ERTU)
Editorial: PO Box 1186, Egyptian Radio & TV Building, Cairo **Tel:** 20 2 2577 5104.
Email: qurankareem@gmail.com
Web site: http://www.ertu.org
Profile: Al Quraan Al-Kareem is a radio station broadcasting Quranic recitals and religious programmes on 98.2 FM. The station launched in 1964 and is operated by state-owned public broadcaster, the Egypt Radio & Television Union (ERTU).
FM RADIO STATION

Radio Misr 88.7FM 71493
Owner: Egypt News Center
Editorial: PO Box 1186, Corniche El Nil, Cairo 11511
Tel: 20 2 2578 5893.
Email: info@radio-masr.com
Web site: http://www.radio-masr.com
Profile: Radio Misr 88.7FM is a radio station broadcasting news, politics and sports programmes on 88.7 FM. The station launched in 2009 and is operated by state-owned public broadcaster, the Egypt Radio & Television Union (ERTU).
FM RADIO STATION

Sout Al Arab 71429
Owner: Egypt Radio & Television Union (ERTU)
Editorial: PO Box 1186, 3rd Floor, Egyptian Radio & TV Building, Cairo 11511 **Tel:** 20 2 2578 9421.
Email: lamia_radio@yahoo.com
Web site: http://www.ertu.org
Profile: Sout Al Arab is a radio station broadcasting news, society, culture, art, sport and music programmes on 483 AM. The station launched in 1953 and is operated by state-owned public broadcaster, the Egypt Radio & Television Union (ERTU).
AM RADIO STATION

Television

CNBC Arabia - Cairo Office 434614
Owner: Middle East Business News
Editorial: 4 Galaa Street, 7th Floor, Dohat Maspeero Building, Cairo **Tel:** 20 2 2574 8100.
Email: yassein.elgohary@cnbcarabia.com
Web site: http://www.cnbcarabia.com
Profile: CNBC Arabia is a television station broadcasting regional and international business and financial news 24-hours a day. The Cairo bureau covers business news from Egypt for the Dubai-based channel.
TELEVISION NETWORK

Nile News 378046
Owner: Egypt Radio & Television Union (ERTU)
Editorial: Egypt TV & Radio Union, PO Box 1186, Cairo 11511 **Tel:** 20 2 2577 9144.
Email: nilenewsoffice@yahoo.com
Web site: http://www.nile.eg
Profile: Nile News is a free-to-air television station broadcasting news, political programmes, current affairs and documentaries. The channel launched in 1998.
TELEVISION STATION

Nile TV International 375333
Owner: Egypt Radio & Television Union (ERTU)
Editorial: Egypt Radio & TV Union, PO Box 1186, Cairo 11511 **Tel:** 20 2 2579 9358.
Email: nilenewsoffice@yahoo.com
Web site: http://www.nileinternational.net
Profile: Nile TV International is a television station broadcasting entertainment programmes, films, serials, sports and tourism programmes, news & current affairs, talk shows, French cinema, culture and lifestyle programmes. The channel launched in 1994.
TELEVISION STATION

ONTV 445216
Owner: Hawa Ltd.
Editorial: Mezzanine Floor, 35 Abu El Feda Street, Cairo 11211 **Tel:** 20 2 2737 4202.
Email: feedback@hawaltd.com
Web site: http://www.ontveg.com
Profile: ONTV is a free-to-air television station broadcasting news, talk shows, serials and sitcoms 24-hrs a day. Formerly called OTV, the television station launched in 2007.
TELEVISION STATION

Al Tahrir TV 768136
Owner: Al Tahrir Satellite Channel
Editorial: Building 12, Egyptian Media Production City, Cairo **Tel:** 20 122 564 5990.
Email: mohamedkhedr72@gmail.com
Profile: Al Tahrir TV is a television station broadcasting political, social and cultural programmes, as well as drama series. It launched in 2011 and broadcasts free-to-air on satellite.
TELEVISION STATION

Estonia

Television

ETV Eesti Televisioon 316168
Owner: Eesti Rahvusringhääling
Editorial: Gonsiori 27, Tallinn 15029
Tel: 372 6 28 41 00.
Email: ak@err.ee
Web site: http://etv.err.ee
Profile: National Estonian television, broadcasting different kinds of programs, news and films.
TELEVISION STATION

Fiji

Radio

Fiji Broadcasting Corporation 538706
Owner: Fiji Broadcasting Corporation Ltd
Editorial: PO Box 334, Suva, Fiji Islands
Tel: 679 3220 934.
Email: fbcnews@fbc.com.fj
Web site: http://www.fbc.com.fj
Profile: The Fiji Broadcasting Corporation is Fiji's national radio broadcasting service.
RADIO NETWORK

Television

Fiji TV 538719
Owner: Fiji Television Limited
Editorial: 20 Gorrie Street, Suva, Fiji Islands
Tel: 679 330 5100.
Web site: http://fijione.tv
Profile: Fiji Television is Fiji's premier television service provider, providing television services to the Fiji Islands, Papua New Guinea and other Pacific Island countries.
TELEVISION STATION

Finland

Radio

Ålands Radio och TV Ab 291209
Owner: Ålands Radio och TV Ab
Editorial: PB 140/alandsvagen 24, Mariehamn AX-22101 **Tel:** 358 18 26 060.
Email: redaktion@radiotv.ax
Web site: http://www.radiotv.ax/
Profile: Company for production of radio and distribution of radio and TV emissions on the Åland/Ahvenanmaa Islands between Finland and Sweden. Landskapsägt aktiebolag med ansvar för produktion av radio och distribution av radio och TV på Åland.
RADIO NETWORK

Helsingin Lähiradio 288783
Editorial: Hameentie 32, Helsinki 530
Tel: 358 9 70 13 300.
Email: lahi.radio@kara.inet.fi
Web site: http://www.kansanradioliitto.fi
Profile: Radio station by the People's Radio Union. Kansan radioliiton radiolähetys. Nykyinen nimi: Helsigin Lähiradio. Regular features: Part of Lähiradio KSL.
FM RADIO STATION

Iskelmä Janne 288757
Editorial: Hopunkatu 1, Sastamala 38200
Tel: 358 10 229 0400.
Web site: http://www.radiomedia.fi/radiokanavat/mediakortit/iskelma-janne
Profile: Regional radio station in Forssa, Hattula, Hämeenlinna, Janakkala and Lammi. Iskelmä Janne on 20 vuotta kuuntelijoitaan palvellut paikallisradio. Iskelmä Janne tavoittaa 31000 eri kuuntelijaa viikossa ja 13000 päiväkuuntelijaa. Janne on aikuisväestölle suunnattu radiokanava, jonka kuuntelijoista 67 % on yli 45 -vuotiaita. 24 % on 24 – 44 -vuotiaita.
FM RADIO STATION

Iskelmä Oikea Asema 288847
Owner: Kevyt Kanava Oy
Editorial: Sammonkatu 16 A, Kuopio 70500
Tel: 358 17 28 96 700.
Email: toimitus@oikeaasema.fi
Web site: http://www.oikeaasema.fi
Profile: Local radio station in Kuopio and Varkaus. Kuopiossa taajuudella 96,7 MHz, Iisalmessa taajuudella 89,5 MHz ja Varkaudessa taajuudella 92,7 MHz toimiva paikallisradio. (Previously known as: Radio Salminen Kuopio).
FM RADIO STATION

Iskelmä Oikea Asema Iisalmi 288766
Owner: Pohjois-Savon Paikallisradio Oy
Editorial: Pohjolankatu 5, Iisalmi 74100
Tel: 358 17 28 96 700.
Email: toimitus@oikeaasema.fi
Web site: http://www.oikeaasema.fi
Profile: Radio channel active in Iisalmi, Siilinjärvi and Vehmasjärvi. Iisalmessa, Siilinjärvellä ja Vehmasjärvellä toimiva radiokanava.
FM RADIO STATION

Iskelmä Oikea Asema Varkaus 288774
Owner: Kevyt Kanava Oy
Editorial: Pirnankatu 4, Varkaus 78200
Tel: 358 17 38 92 701.
Email: toimitus@oikeaasema.fi
Web site: http://www.radiomedia.fi/radioasemat/mediakortit/fi_FI/iskelma_oikea_asema_varkaus/
Profile: Local radio station with news from Varkaus and surroundings. Varkauden paikallisradio. Previous title: Radio Varkaus
FM RADIO STATION

Iskelmä Pohjanmaa 288764
Owner: SBS Finland Oy
Editorial: Puistotie 2, Lapua 62100
Tel: 358 6 42 32 900.
Web site: http://www.iskelma.fi/paikallissivut/pohjanmaa
Profile: Radio frequences: Kurikka 92,3 MHz, Seinäjoki 96,9 MHz, Lapua 96,9 MHz, Ähtäri 97,8 MHz, Alajärvi 104,3 MHz, Kokkola - Pietarsaari 105,9MHz, Vaasa/kaapeli 104,3 MHz, Pyhävuori, Kristiinankaupunki 105,1 MHz.
FM RADIO STATION

Iskelmä Rex 288884
Editorial: PL 928/ Malmikatu 5 B II krs, Joensuu 80101 **Tel:** 358 10 23 11 800.
Email: toimitus@radiorex.fi
Web site: http://www.radiorex.fi
Profile: News and music radio channel in northern Carelia. Local Translation: Rex on uutis- ja musiikkiradio, joka toimii Pohjois-Karjalan alueella. Alternative Title: Radio Joensuu Also known by the name Radio Joensuu and Iskelmä Joensuu.
FM RADIO STATION

Iskelmä Sastamala 289902
Editorial: Iskelma Sastamala/Alueviesti, Hopunkatu 1, Sastamala 38200 **Tel:** 358 10 22 90 400.
Email: iskelma@alueviesti.fi
Web site: http://iskelmasastamala.palvelut.alueviesti.fi/
Profile: Radio channel in Suodenniemi, Kiikoinen, Mouhijärvi, Äetsä, Vammala, Huittinen, Punkalaidun and Vampula. Local Translation: Taajuudella 101,2 MHz toimiva radiokanava Suodenniemellä, Kiikoisissa, Mouhijärvellä, Äetsässä, Vammalassa, Huittisissa, Punkalaitumella ja Vampulassa. Requested not to receive any press material by fax.
FM RADIO STATION

Iskelmä Satakunta 288762
Editorial: Kappelikuja 3, Huittinen 32700
Tel: 358 2 55 54 291.
Email: toimitus@iskelmasatakunta.fi
Web site: http://www.iskelmasatakunta.fi
Profile: Local radio station in Huittinen, Harjavalta and Köyliö. Lähinnä Huittisissa, Harjavallassa ja Köyliössä toimiva paikallisradio. Previous title: Radio West
FM RADIO STATION

Iskelmäradio 290857
Owner: SBS Finland Oy
Editorial: Kehrasaari B 5, Tampere 33200
Tel: 358 20 74 74 100.
Email: toimitus@iskelma.fi
Web site: http://www.iskelma.fi
Profile: Iskelmämusiikin radiokanava, jolla on paikallista mainosmyyntiä eri puolilla Suomea. Radio channel focusing on light dance music. Aimed mainly at middle-aged people.
RADIO NETWORK

Järviradio 289465
Owner: Järviseudun Paikallisradio Oy
Editorial: Kiertotie 5, Alajärvi 62900
Tel: 358 500 557 234.
Email: jr@jarviradio.fi
Web site: http://www.jarviradio.fi
Profile: Järviradion lähetykset kuuluvat Pohjanmaan ja Keski-Suomen alueilla. Regional radio station in central Finland and Ostrobothnia.
FM RADIO STATION

Kiss 837419
Owner: Bauer Media Oy
Editorial: Tallberginkatu 1 C, Helsinki 180
Web site: http://www.kiss.fi
Profile: Kiss on viihde-, musiikki ja lifestylesisältöä tuottava radiokanava. Kiss is a radio station producing music, entertainment and lifestyle content.
FM RADIO STATION

Loop 912795
Editorial: Sanomatalo, Toolonlahdenkatu 2 PL 15, Helsinki 89 **Tel:** 358 10 800 106.
Email: studio@loop.fi
Web site: http://www.loop.fi/
Profile: Loop on suomalainen, Nelonen Median omistama radiokanava, jonka ohjelmisto perustuu vahvasti menevään, nopeatempoiseen musiikkiin ja tiukkoihin soittolistoihin. Kanava soittaa pääosin hiphoppia, R&B:tä ja dancea. Sen lupaus on "Enemmän musiikkia, vähemmän puhetta"
RADIO NETWORK

NRJ (Radio Energy) Helsinki 291213
Owner: NRJ Finland Oy
Editorial: Kiviaidankatu 2 i (4. krs), Helsinki 210
Tel: 358 50 502 1033.
Web site: http://www.nrj.fi
Profile: NRJ, virallisesti Radio NRJ Finland Oy, on 1995 Suomessa toimintansa aloittanut valtakunnallinen kaupallinen radiokanava. NRJ on yksityinen, valtakunnallinen radioasema, jonka kuuluvuusalueella asuu noin 4,4 miljoonaa suomalaista. NRJ started to broadcast in Finland in 1995. It is a private radio channel with coverage of 4,4 million people in Finland.
RADIO NETWORK

Radio Auran Aallot 289753
Editorial: Lansikaari 15, Turku 20240
Tel: 358 2 26 93 905.
Email: info@auranaallot.fi
Web site: http://www.auranaallot.fi
Profile: Radio station in the Turku region. Local Translation: Turun seudulla toimiva paikallisradio.
FM RADIO STATION

Radio City 787426
Owner: SBS Finland Oy
Editorial: Tallberginkatu 1 C, Helsinki 180
Tel: 358 40 56 98 176.
Email: toimitus@radiocity.fi
Web site: http://www.radiocity.fi
Profile: Rock radio station aired in Helsinki region covering music, news programmes as well as sports. Helsinkiläinen rock-radiokanava.
FM RADIO STATION

Radio City Jyväskylä 288829
Owner: SBS Finland Oy
Editorial: PL 480/ Vainonkatu 26 A, Jyväskylä 40101
Tel: 358 20 35 23 52.
Email: toimitus@radiocity.fi
Web site: http://www.radiocity.fi/jyvaskyla
Profile: Local editorial of Radio City in Jyväskylä run by SBS Broadcasting. Local Translation: Radio Cityn Jyväskylän paikallistoimitus. Previously listed as Radio Jyväskylä.
FM RADIO STATION

Radio City Tampere 288758
Owner: SBS Finland Oy
Editorial: PL 957/ Kehrasaari B porras, 5 krs, Tampere 33101 **Tel:** 358 40 56 98 176.
Email: toimitus@radiocity.fi
Web site: http://www.radiocity.fi/tampere
Profile: Radio with programmes for the Pirkanmaa region around Tampere. Local Translation: Radio lähettää ohjelmaa Pirkanmaan alueella taajuudella 95,7 MHz. Previously listed as Radio 957.
FM RADIO STATION

Radio City Turku 288760
Owner: SBS Finland Oy
Editorial: Lantinen Rantakatu 53, 2 krs, Turku 20100
Tel: 358 40 56 98 176.
Email: toimitus@radiocity.fi
Web site: http://www.radiocity.fi/turku
Profile: Radio City local editorial in Turku. Radio Cityn Turun aluetoimitus. Previously listed as Radio Sata.
FM RADIO STATION

Radio Dei 625843
Editorial: Ilmalankuja 2 I, Helsinki 240
Tel: 358 9 75 14 45 11.
Email: info@radiodei.fi
Web site: http://www.radiodei.fi
Profile: Description: Osavaltakunnallinen kristillinen radiokanava. Kanavan pääkuuluvuusalueet ovat Helsinki, Hämeenlinna, Joensuu, Jyväskylä, Kokkola, Kuopio, Kouvola, Lohja, Lahti, Lappeenranta, Mikkeli, Oulu, Pori, Rovaniemi, Savonlinna, Seinäjoki, Tampere ja Turku. Partly national radio channel covering religion and Christian issues. Paikallistoimitukset Turussa ja Pohjanmaalla.
FM RADIO STATION

Radio Dei Pohjanmaa 625477
Editorial: Koulukatu 13 C, 2 krs., Seinäjoki 60100
Tel: 358 6 21 40 300.
Email: toimitus.pohjanmaa@radiodei.fi
Web site: http://www.radiodei.fi
Profile: Kristillisen radiokanava Radio Dein paikallistoimitus Pohjanmaalla. Ostrobothnia local editorial of the Christian radio channel Radio Dei.
FM RADIO STATION

Radio Dei Turku 625872
Editorial: Kalastajankatu 1 B, Turku 20100
Tel: 358 2 46 99 800.
Email: toimitus.turku@radiodei.fi
Web site: http://www.radiodei.fi
Profile: Kristillisen radiokanava Radio Dein Turun paikallistoimitus. Turku local editorial of the Christian radio channel Radio Dei.
FM RADIO STATION

Radio Groove FM & Metro FM 291031
Owner: Nelonen Media
Editorial: Toolonlahdenkatu 2, Sanoma 89
Email: studiogroove@groovefm.fi
Web site: http://www.groovefm.fi/
Profile: Radio channel with jazz and blues music that can be heard in the Internet. No e-mails allowed to their address info@groovefm.fi Metro FM is their sister channel.
RADIO NETWORK

Radio Helsinki 290730
Editorial: Tyopajankatu 2 a 1, rakennus 5, Helsinki 580
Email: palaute@radiohelsinki.fi
Web site: http://www.radiohelsinki.fi
Profile: Helsinki radio channel on 98,5 MHz, but it can also be heard nation-wide over the Internet. Radio Helsinki kuuluu Helsingissä taajuudella 98,5 MHz.
FM RADIO STATION

Radio Kajaus 288768
Editorial: PL 230/ Kauppakatu 21, 4 krs., Kajaani 87101 **Tel:** 358 8 62 99 57.
Email: kajaus.toimitus@radiokajaus.fi
Web site: http://www.radiokajaus.fi
Profile: Local radio station in Kajaani, Sotkamo, Hyrynsalmi and Kuhmo. Local Translation: Kainuun Paikallisradio Oy:n radiokanava Kajaanissa, Sotkamossa, Hyrynsalmella ja Kuhmossa.
FM RADIO STATION

Radio Moreeni 288781
Editorial: Kalevantie 4, Tampereen Yliopisto 33014
Tel: 358 3 35 51 69 46.
Email: moreeni@uta.fi
Web site: http://moreeni.uta.fi
Profile: Radio broadcasting at 98.4 MHz by the University of Tampere. People in Tampere of age 20-65. Local Translation: Tampereen Yliopiston radio 98.4 MHz, kaapelissa 101.5 MHz.
FM RADIO STATION

Radio Nova 291152
Owner: Bauer Media
Editorial: Tallberginkatu 1 C, Helsinki 180
Tel: 358 10 300 7227.
Email: toimitus@radionova.fi
Web site: http://www.radionova.fi
Profile: Bauermedian omistama valtakunnallinen radiokanava. Kattaa myös Radio Helmen ja Sävelradion verkkolähetykset. A National radio channel owned by Bauer Media. Broadcasts also Radio Helmi online well as podcasts from Sävelradio.
RADIO NETWORK

Radio Pooki 290174
Editorial: Ollinkalliontie 3, Raahe 92100
Tel: 358 8 21 18 200.
Email: toimitus@radiopooki.fi
Web site: http://www.radiopooki.fi
Profile: Finnish radio station for Finnish people. Frequences: Oulu 88.0 MHz, Kemi/Tornio 89.5 MHz, Raahe 94.8 MHz, Ylivieska 95.5 MHz, Kalajoki 101.0 MHz, Nivala 100.5 MHz, Haapavesi 103.3 Mhz, Haapajärvi 95.0 MHz, Kokkola 89.3 MHz. Radio Pooki on kotimainen radioasema, joka lähettää ohjelmaa viikon jokaisena päivänä. Radio Pooki tekee ohjelmaa paikallisista, alueellisista ja valtakunnallisista asioista elämän eri osa-alueilta ihmisläheisellä tavalla, eli suomalaiselta ihmiseltä suomalaiselle ihmiselle. Musiikki: kotimainen iskelmä- ja tanssimusiikkia eri vuosikymmeniltä. Taajuudet: Oulu 88.0 MHz, Kemi/Tornio 89.5 MHz, Raahe 94.8 MHz, Ylivieska 95.5 MHz, Kalajoki 101.0 MHz, Nivala 100.5 MHz, Haapavesi 103.3 MHz, Haapajärvi 95.0 MHz, Kokkola 89.3 MHz. Kaapeleissa 90.5 MHz ja Oulun kaapelissa 89.9 MHz.
FM RADIO STATION

Radio Pori 288761
Editorial: Itapuisto 3, Pori 28100
Tel: 358 44 59 02 550.
Email: toimitus@radiopori.fi
Web site: http://www.radiopori.fi
Profile: Radio channel active in Pori, Luvia, Nakkila, Noormarkku and Ulvila. Age 25-50. Local Translation: Porissa, Luvialla, Nakkilassa, Noormarkussa ja Ulvilassa kuuluva radioasema.
FM RADIO STATION

Radio Ramona 288763
Editorial: Itakatu 5, Rauma 26100
Tel: 358 440 933 933.
Email: ramona@radioramona.fi
Web site: http://www.radioramona.fi
Profile: Radio-Ramona lähettää ohjelmaa Raumalla, Eurassa, Kodisjoella, Lapissa, Eurajoella, Pyhärannassa ja Laitilassa. Ramonan musiikkilinja keskittyy kotimaiseen pop- ja rockmusiikkiin, höystettynä ulkomaalaisilla klassikoilla. Musiikkivalikoima on räätälöity 25-55-vuotiaiden mieltymysten mukaisesti, ja ydinkohderyhmään kuuluvatkin aikuiset, 35-55-vuotiaat raumanseutulaiset. Radio channel in Rauma, Eura, Kodisjoki, Lappi, Eurajoki, Pyhäranta and Laitila.
FM RADIO STATION

Radio Robin Hood 288769
Editorial: Itainen Rantakatu 64, Turku 20810
Tel: 358 2 27 73 666.
Email: info@radiorobinhood.fi
Web site: http://www.radiorobinhood.fi
Profile: Local multilingual radio station in Turku on frequency 91,5 MHz. Local Translation: Radio Robin Hood on monikielinen turkulainen radioasema taajuudella 91,5 MHz.
FM RADIO STATION

Radio Rock 291215
Owner: Nelonen Media
Editorial: Toolonlahdenkatu 2, Sanoma 89
Tel: 358 10 80 121.
Email: uutiset@radioaalto.fi
Web site: http://www.radiorock.fi
Profile: Radio Rock on rock-musiikin radiokanava. Radio Rock is a radio channel focusing on rock music.
RADIO NETWORK

Radio SUN 288759
Editorial: Ideaparkinkatu 4, Lempäälä 37570
Tel: 358 43 217 0645.
Email: toimitus@radiosun.fi
Web site: http://www.radiosun.fi
Profile: Local radio station in Hämeenkyrö, Ikaalinen, Jämijärvi, Viljakkala, Parkano and Kankaanpää. Local Translation: Hämeenkyrössä, Ikaalisissa, Jämijärvellä, Viljakkalassa, Parkanossa ja Kankaanpäässä toimiva paikallisradio. Previous title: Radio Satahäme (Previously known as: Radio Satahäme).
FM RADIO STATION

Radio Vaasa 288885
Editorial: PL 371/ Hovioikeudenpuistikko 16, Vaasa 65101 **Tel:** 358 6 32 03 910.
Email: toimitus@radiovaasa.fi
Web site: http://www.radiovaasa.fi
Profile: Regional radio station with general-interest for listeners in Vaasa and its surroundings. Local Translation: Vaasassa ja sen ympäristökunnissa kuuluva radioasema, jonka lähetystaajuus on 99,5 MHz.
FM RADIO STATION

Radio Voima 290813
Editorial: PL 80/ Aleksanterinkatu 10, Lahti 15101
Tel: 358 3 75 75 986.
Email: toimitus@radiovoima.fi
Web site: http://www.radiovoima.fi
Profile: Radio station in Lahti, Asikkala, Heinola, Nastola, Sysmä, Hollola, Hämeenkoski, Orimattila, Kärkölä, Hartola, Joutsa, Padasjoki and Kuhmoinen. Lahdessa, Asikkalassa, Heinolassa, Nastolassa, Sysmässä, Hollolassa, Hämeenkoskella, Orimattilassa, Kärkölässä, Hartolassa, Joutsassa, Padasjoella ja Kuhmoisissa kuuluva radioasema. Previously known as: Radio 99 and Radio Ysiysi Incorporating: Päijänneradio
FM RADIO STATION

Spirit FM 290226
Owner: Radio Satellite Finland Oy
Editorial: Bulevardi 10 C 26, Helsinki 120
Tel: 358 9 34 36 340.
Email: info@spiritfm.fi
Web site: http://spiritfm.fi
Profile: Radio channel for the Russian/English speaking minority in the Helsinki region and southeast Finland. No press releases into info@spiritfm.fi or tiedote@spiritfm.fi Russian travellers and tourists coming to Finland. Local Translation: Helsingin venäjänkielisen/ englanninkielisen vähemmistön radiokanava kuuluu myös itäisellä Uudellamaalla ja Kymenlaaksossa. Previous title: Radio Sputnik
FM RADIO STATION

SR EKOT ; Helsingfors 625876
Editorial: Stora Robertsgatan 43 C 39, Helsingfors 120 **Tel:** 358 9 60 42 02.
Email: jenny.roosqvist@sr.se
Web site: http://sverigesradio.se/nyheter/
Profile: Baltic and Finnish correspondent for Swedish Radio SR Ekot.
RADIO NETWORK

Steel FM 290286
Editorial: Strandgrand 2, Mariehamn 22100
Tel: 358 18 16 200.
Email: mail@steelfm.net
Web site: http://www.steelfm.net
Profile: Commercial radio channel with music, entertainment and news. Local Translation: Ålands tredje radiokanal med musik, nyheter och underhållning.
FM RADIO STATION

Svenska Yle 291211
Owner: Yleisradio
Editorial: PB 83, Rundradion 24 **Tel:** 358 9 1480 5185.
Email: justnu@yle.fi
Web site: http://svenska.yle.fi/
Profile: Svenska Yle on Yleisradion ruotsinkielinen uutispalvelu. Svenska Yle is a Swedish language news service for the Finnish Broadcasting Company Yleisradio/Rundradion.
RADIO NETWORK

Tuotantoyksikkö Kantti 288755
Editorial: PL 99/ Kotkankallionkatu 12, Kuopio 70101
Tel: 358 17 24 78 900.
Email: toimitus@kantti.net
Web site: http://www.kantti.net
Profile: Radio for educational purposes about science, culture and schools. Local Translation: Pohjois-Savossa kuuluva tiede- ja opintoradio tieteen, kulttuurin ja opetuksen väelle.
FM RADIO STATION

YLE Åboland 288776
Editorial: PB 400/ Auragatan 8, Åbo 20101
Tel: 358 2 27 17 859.
Email: aboland@yle.fi
Web site: http://svenska.yle.fi/aboland
Profile: Turussa sijaitseva Ylen ruotsinkielinen toimitus. Description: Turku regional office of Yle's Swedish speaking news service. Rundradions Radio Vegas Åboredaktion.
RADIO NETWORK

Yle Åboland Kimito 288800
Editorial: Redaktorsstigen 2, Kimito 25700
Tel: 358 2 42 17 77.
Email: monica.forssell@yle.fi
Web site: http://www.yle.fi/vega
Profile: Local correspondent in Kimito for Radio Vega Åboland. Local Translation: Description: Local correspondent in Kimito for Radio Vega Åboland. Kimitos lokalkorrespondent för Radio Vega Åboland.
RADIO NETWORK

Yle Hämeenlinna 288787
Editorial: Viipurintie 4 E, Hämeenlinna 13200
Tel: 358 3 54 46 969.
Email: hameenlinna@yle.fi
Web site: http://yle.fi/alueet/hame
Profile: Regional radio in Hämeenlinna, Forssa and Riihimäki by national broadcasting company Yleisradio. Ylen Hämeenlinnan toimitus. This radio station is also in charge of regional tv-news called Hämeen tv-alueuutiset. Alternative Title: Hämeen tv-alueuutiset
RADIO NETWORK

YLE Hämeenlinna Forssan toimitus 288788
Editorial: Hameentie 7 II krs, Forssa 30100
Tel: 358 3 42 21 521.
Email: hameenlinna@yle.fi
Web site: http://yle.fi/uutiset/hameenlinna/
Profile: Forssa regional office of Yleisradio regional radio channel Radio Hämeenlinna. Yleisradion Hämeenlinnan toimituksen Forssan paikallistoimisto.
RADIO NETWORK

YLE Huvudstadsregionen 288812
Editorial: PB 87/ Radiogatan 5 A, Rundradion 24
Tel: 358 9 14 80 37 02.
Email: vega.huvudstadsregionen@yle.fi
Web site: https://svenska.yle.fi/vega
Profile: Helsinki regional office of Radio Vega. Radio Vegas redaktion om huvudstadsregionen. Previously listed as YLE Radio Vega Mellannyland.
RADIO NETWORK

YLE Joensuu 290048
Editorial: PL 206/ Kirkkokatu 20, Joensuu 80101
Tel: +358 13 51 07 450.
Email: joensuu@yle.fi
Web site: http://yle.fi/uutiset
Profile: Regional radio station in Joensuu, Koli, Kiihtelysvaara and Kerimäki. Joensuussa, Kolilla, Kiihtelysvaarassa ja Kerimäellä kuuluva Yleisradion alueradio.
RADIO NETWORK

YLE Jyväskylä 314042
Editorial: PL3/Kauppakatu 33, Jyväskylä 40101
Tel: 358 14 44 58 243.
Email: jyvaskyla@yle.fi
Web site: http://www.yle.fi/uutiset/jyvaskyla
Profile: Jyväskylä regional office of the national broadcasting company Yleisradio for radio news. Local Translation: Description: Jyväskylä regional office of the national broadcasting company Yleisradio for radio news. Radion uutistoimituksen Jyväskylän aluetoimisto.
RADIO NETWORK

Yle Kajaani 288801
Owner: Yleisradio
Editorial: PL 111/ Lonnrotinkatu 14 B, Kajaani 87101
Tel: 358 8 61 98 80 60.
Email: kajaani@yle.fi
Web site: http://yle.fi/alueet/kainuu
Profile: Kajaani office of Yleisradio regional radio channel Kainuun Radio. Yleisradion Kainuun Radion Kajaanin toimisto.
RADIO NETWORK

Yle Kemi 288797
Editorial: Tietokatu 3, toinen kerros, Kemi 94600
Tel: 358 16 33 57 400.
Email: kemi@yle.fi
Web site: http://yle.fi
Profile: Regional radio channel in Kemi owned by national broadcasting company Yleisradio. Kemillä toimiva paikallinen Yleisradion radioasema.
RADIO NETWORK

Yle Kokkola 288805
Editorial: PL 1000/ Rantakatu 16, Kokkola 67101
Tel: 358 6 21 98 100.
Email: kokkola@yle.fi
Web site: http://yle.fi
Profile: Radio channel active in Kruunupyy, Haapavesi and Kokkola. Kruunupyyssä, Haapavedellä ja Kokkolassa toimiva Yleisradion alueradiokanava.
RADIO NETWORK

Yle Kotka 288793
Owner: Yleisradio
Editorial: Ruotsinsalmenkatu 12, Kotka 48100
Tel: 358 5 81 37 300.
Email: kotka@yle.fi
Web site: http://yle.fi/uutiset/kotka/
Profile: Kotka regional office of Yleisradio Yleisradion Kotkan aluetoimisto.
RADIO NETWORK

Yle Kouvola 288792
Owner: Yleisradio
Editorial: Salpausselankatu 40, Kouvola 45100
Tel: 358 5 81 37 300.
Email: kotka@yle.fi
Web site: http://yle.fi/uutiset/18-198551
Profile: Kouvola office of regional radio station Kotkan Radio. Yleisradion Kotkan toimituksen Kouvolan toimisto.
RADIO NETWORK

Yle Kuopio 288778
Editorial: PL 99/ Kotkankallionkatu 12, Kuopio 70101
Tel: 358 17 247 8901.
Email: kuopio@yle.fi
Web site: http://yle.fi/uutiset/kuopio/
Profile: Kuopio office of Yleisradio regional radio station Radio Savo. Yleisradion Radio Savon Kuopion toimitus. Incorporating: Itä-Suomen alueelliset TV-uutiset
RADIO NETWORK

Yle Lahti 288786
Owner: Yleisradio
Editorial: PL 120/ Aleksanterinkatu 8, Lahti 15111
Tel: 358 3 46 86 900.
Email: lahti@yle.fi
Web site: http://yle.fi/alueet/lahti
Profile: Regional radio station in Lahti serviced by national broadcasting company Yleisradio. Yleisradion Lahden alueradio.
RADIO NETWORK

Yle Lappeenranta 288791
Editorial: PL 100/ Kristiinankatu 11 A, Lappeenranta 53101 **Tel:** 358 5 63 031.
Email: lappeenranta@yle.fi
Web site: http://yle.fi/uutiset/lappeenranta/
Profile: Lappeenrannan Radio on yksi Radio Suomen (YLE) maakuntaradioista. Incorporating regional tv news channel Kaakkois-Suomen alueelliset tv-uutiset. National broadcasting company Yleisradio regional radio station in Lappeenranta.
RADIO NETWORK

Yle Mikkeli 288790
Owner: Yleisradio
Editorial: PL 361/ Vilhonkatu 11, Mikkeli 50101
Tel: 358 15 41 57 70.
Email: mikkeli@yle.fi
Web site: http://yle.fi/uutiset/mikkeli/
Profile: The Mikkeli regional radio station by national broadcasting company Yleisradio. Yleisradion Mikkelin aluetoimisto Etelä-Savossa. The name of the TV-station is Itä-Suomen TV-uutiset.
RADIO NETWORK

Yle Mikkeli Savonlinnan toimitus 288789
Editorial: Olavinkatu 24, Savonlinna 57130
Tel: 358 15 41 57 70.
Email: mikkeli@yle.fi
Web site: http://yle.fi/mikkeli
Profile: Savonlinna office of YLE Mikkeli. YLE Mikkelin Savonlinnan-toimitus. PR Accepted in: Finnish
RADIO NETWORK

Yle Österbotten 290101
Editorial: Box 1000/ Aborrvagen 20, Vasa 65101
Tel: 358 6 229 8549.
Email: osterbotten@yle.fi
Web site: http://svenska.yle.fi//osterbotten
Profile: YLE Österbottenin pääkonttori Vaasassa. Ruotsinkielistä Yleisradion tarjoamaa ohjelmaa. The main office of YLE Österbotten. Programs for the Swedish-speaking society in Finland.
RADIO NETWORK

YLE Österbotten Jakobstad 288845
Editorial: Box 1000/ Radhusgatan 11, Jakobstad 68601 **Tel:** 358 6 32 00 200.
Email: radiovega.osterbotten@yle.fi
Web site: http://svenska.yle.fi//osterbotten
Profile: Jakobstad local office of the Österbotten regional office of Radio Vega. Local Translation: Description: Jakobstad local office of the Österbotten regional office of Radio Vega. Radio Vega Österbottens Jakobstadsredaktion.
RADIO NETWORK

YLE Österbotten Karleby 288777
Editorial: PB 1000/ Strandgatan 16, Karleby 67101
Tel: 358 6 32 00 200.
Email: osterbotten@yle.fi
Web site: http://svenska.yle.fi//osterbotten
Profile: Karleby local office of Ostrobothnia regional office of Radio Vega. Local Translation: Description: Karleby local office of Ostrobothnia regional office of Radio Vega. Radio Vega Österbottens Karlebyredaktion.
RADIO NETWORK

YLE Österbotten Kristinestad 687085
Tel: 358 6 22 12 830.
Email: osterbotten@yle.fi
Web site: http://svenska.yle.fi//osterbotten
Profile: Kristinestad local office of Radio Vega Österbotten. Local Translation: Radio Vega Österbottens Kristinestadredaktion.
RADIO NETWORK

YLE Östnyland 288780
Editorial: Kramaregatan 2, Borgå 6100
Tel: 358 19 66 18 810.
Email: ostnyland@yle.fi
Web site: http://www.yle.fi/vega
Profile: Eastern Uusimaa regional office of Radio Vega. Local Translation: Description: Eastern Uusimaa regional office of Radio Vega. Radio Vegas redaktion för östra Nyland.
RADIO NETWORK

Yle Oulu 289841
Owner: Yleisradio
Editorial: PL 277/ Sepankatu 20, Oulu 90101
Tel: 358 8 53 73 800.
Email: oulu@yle.fi
Web site: http://yle.fi/uutiset/oulu/
Profile: Regional radio station of Radio Suomi and national broadcasting company Yleisradio. Radio Suomen ja Yleisradion alueradio ja Pohjois-Suomen tv-alueuutiset . Alternative title: Radio Suomi Oulu. Incorporating: Pohjois-Suomen tv-alueuutiset Alternative Title: Radio Suomi Oulu
RADIO NETWORK

YLE Pori 288799
Editorial: PL 113/ Mikonkatu 4 D, Pori 28101
Tel: 358 2 555 7950.
Email: pori@yle.fi
Profile: Yleisradio regional editorial in Pori. Yleisradion Porin alueradiokanava.
RADIO NETWORK

Yle Puhe 291197
Owner: Yleisradio
Editorial: PL 78, Yleisradio 24 **Tel:** 358 9 14 801.
Email: yle.puhe@yle.fi
Web site: http://www.yle.fi/puhe
Profile: Kanava on Yleisradion asiapuheradio, jossa käsitellään uutisasioita päiväsaikaan sekä soitetaan musiikkia öisin. National broadcasting company Yleisradio's radio channel delivers news during daytime and music during nights.
RADIO NETWORK

YLE Radio 1 291214
Owner: Yleisradio
Editorial: PL 8/ Radiokatu 5, Yleisradio 24
Tel: 358 9 14 801.
Email: yle.radio1@yle.fi
Web site: http://www.yleradio1.fi
Profile: YLE Radio 1 on kulttuurin, asiapuheen ja radiodraaman sekä klassisen musiikin, jazzin ja kansanmusiikin radiokanava 24 tuntia vuorokaudessa. Yle Radio 1 is a national radio channel concentrating on culture and music.
RADIO NETWORK

Yle Radio Suomi 314266
Owner: Yleisradio
Editorial: PL 8/ Radiokatu 5, Yleisradio 24
Tel: 358 9 14 801.
Email: radio.suomi@yle.fi
Web site: http://www.yle.fi/radiosuomi
Profile: Ekologiasta, luonnosta, puutarhasta, naisista, kirjallisuudesta, kuluttamisesta, ruoasta ja lääketieteestä kertovia radio-ohjelmia Radio Suomessa. Radio Suomi programmes about ecology, nature, gardening, women, literature, consumer-affairs, food and medicine.
RADIO NETWORK

YLE Radio Suomi Ajantasa 291217
Owner: Yleisradio
Editorial: PL 8/ Radiokatu 5, Yleisradio 24
Tel: 358 9 14 801.
Email: radio.suomi@yle.fi
Web site: http://yle.fi/radiosuomi
Profile: Governmentally owned broadcasting company Yleisradio national radio channel. 30-year-olds and older. Yleisradion valtakunnallinen radiokanava. Readers: 30-year-olds and older. Alternative Title: YLE Radio Suomi
RADIO NETWORK

Yle Radio Suomi Helsinki 288811
Editorial: PL 3/ Uutiskatu 5, Yleisradio 24
Tel: 358 9 1480 3148.
Email: helsinki@yle.fi
Web site: http://yle.fi/uutiset/helsinki/
Profile: Yleisradion Helsingin aluetoimitus ja Ylen aikainen radio. Helsinki regional and Ylen aikainen radio channel editorial for the national broadcasting company Yleisradio. Alternative Title: Uudenmaan tv-alueuutiset
RADIO NETWORK

YLE Radio Ylen läntinen 288814
Editorial: PL 86/ Laurinkatu 57 A, Lohja 8101
Tel: 358 19 31 81 00.
Email: lohja@yle.fi
Web site: http://yle.fi/alueet/helsinki
Profile: Western Uusimaa regional radio channel. Länsi-Uusimaan radiokanava palvelee Karjaan, Tammisaaren, Hangon ja Lohjan asukkaita.
RADIO NETWORK

Yle Rovaniemi 289774
Owner: Yleisradio
Editorial: PL 8113/ Jorma Etontie 8, Rovaniemi 96101
Tel: 358 16 33 06 000.
Email: rovaniemi@yle.fi
Web site: http://yle.fi/alueet/lappi
Profile: Ylen Lapin toimitus tekee arkisin radiolähetyksiä ja televisiossa TV2:lla näkyvät Yle Uutiset Pohjois-Suomesta. YLE Lappi Rovaniemi office of national broadcasting company Yleisradio.
RADIO NETWORK

YLE Saamen radio 288808
Editorial: PL 38/ Menesjarventie 2, Inari 99871
Tel: 358 16 67 57 500.
Email: sami.radio@yle.fi
Web site: http://yle.fi/sapmi
Profile: Radio channel on three different Sami/ Lappish languages. It works in co-operation with Norway and Sweden. Lähettää ohjelmaa omalla kanavalla kolmella saamen kielellä: pohjois-, inarin- ja koltansaameksi. Toimii koko Saamenmaan alueella

läheisessä päivittäisessä yhteistyössä Ruotsin ja Norjan saamelaisradioitten kanssa. The tv desk is called Saamenkieliset tv-uutiset. Alternative Title: Yle Saamen Radio Inari
RADIO NETWORK

YLE Saamen Radio Utsjoki 371217
Editorial: Unavailable, Utsjoki 99980
Tel: 358 16 67 57 500.
Email: sami.radio@yle.fi
Web site: http://www.yle.fi/samiradio
Profile: Utsjoki regional office of YLE/Sámi Radio. Local Translation: Description: Utsjoki regional office of YLE/Sámi Radio. Sámi Radion Utsjoen aluetoimisto.
RADIO NETWORK

YLE Seinäjoki 288806
Owner: Yleisradio
Editorial: PL 1000/ Marttilantie 24, Seinäjoki 60101
Tel: 358 6 21 18 400.
Email: pohjanmaa@yle.fi
Web site: http://yle.fi/alueet/pohjanmaa
Profile: Seinäjoki office of regional radio station Pohjanmaan Radio. Yleisradion Pohjanmaan Radion Seinäjoen aluetoimitus.
RADIO NETWORK

YLE Tampere 288785
Editorial: PL 110 /Vuolteenkatu 20, 3 krs., Tampere 33101 **Tel:** 358 3 34 56 111.
Email: tampere@yle.fi
Web site: http://yle.fi/alueet/tampere
Profile: Tampere local radio station by national broadcasting company Yleisradio. Yleisradion Tampereen paikallisradio.
RADIO NETWORK

YLE Turku 288775
Editorial: PL 400/ Aurakatu 8, 7 krs, Turku 20101
Tel: 358 2 27 09 00.
Email: turku@yle.fi
Web site: http://yle.fi/uutiset
Profile: Turku local radio station of national broadcasting company Yleisradio. Yleisradion Turun paikallisradio. Incorporates regional tv desk Lounais-Suomen tv-alueuutiset.
RADIO NETWORK

Yle Uutiset Radiouutiset 291208
Editorial: PL 3/ Radiokatu 5, Yleisradio 24
Tel: 358 9 14 801.
Email: uutiset@yle.fi
Web site: http://yle.fi/uutiset
Profile: Yle Uutisten Radiouutiset seuraa kotimaan ja maailman menoa ympäri vuorokauden, viikon jokaisena päivänä. Uutiset tiiviissä paketissa tasatunnein sekä taustoittavina lähetyksinä arkisin viisi kertaa päivässä. Lisäksi lauantai- ja sunnuntailähetykset. Ylen radiouutiset tuottaa uutiset kaikille Yleisradion suomenkielisille radiokanaville. Kotikanavana on Radio Suomi. News desk of national broadcast company Yleisradio produces news for all Finnish-speaking radio channels of the company. Radio Suomi acts as the home channel.
RADIO NETWORK

Yle Vaasa 288804
Owner: Yleisradio
Editorial: PL 1000/ Ahventie 20, Vaasa 65101
Tel: 358 6 22 981.
Email: pohjanmaa@yle.fi
Web site: http://yle.fi/alueet/pohjanmaa
Profile: Vaasa office of regional radio station Pohjanmaan Radio. Yleisradion ja Pohjanmaan Radion Vaasan aluetoimitus. Pohjanmaan Uutiset is the regional tv-station based on the same editorial office. Alternative Title: Pohjanmaan alueelliset tv-uutiset
RADIO NETWORK

YLE Västnyland 290051
Editorial: PB 33/Gustav Wasas gata 8 A, Ekenäs 10601 **Tel:** 358 19 26 48 846.
Email: vastnyland@yle.fi
Web site: http://www.yle.fi/vega
Profile: Western Uusimaa regional office for Radio Vega. Local Translation: Description: Western Uusimaa regional office for Radio Vega. Radio Vegas västnyländska redaktion för Karis, Ekenäs, Hangö, Pojo och Ingå.
RADIO NETWORK

YLE Vega 291218
Editorial: PB 83, Rundradion 24 **Tel:** 358 9 14 801.
Email: nyheter@yle.fi
Web site: http://www.yle.fi/vega
Profile: Radio Vega on YLEn ruotsinkielinen radiokanava. Radio Vega bjuder bland annat på regionala program, nyheter en gång i timmen och musik för en vuxen smak. National broadcasting company Yleisradio Swedish-speaking radio channel Radio Vega offers regional news, news once an hour and music for adults.
RADIO NETWORK

YLE Venäjänkielinen toimitus 291005
Owner: Yleisradio
Editorial: YLE Uutiset Venajankielinen toimitus PL 3, Yleisradio 24 **Tel:** 358 9 14 801.
Email: heidi.zidan@yle.fi
Web site: http://yle.fi/uutiset/novosti/
Profile: Yleisradion venäjänkieliset uutiset. News in Russian presented by national Finnish broadcasting company Yleisradio.
RADIO NETWORK

YLE X3M 288772
Editorial: PB 13/ Radiogatan 5, Helsingfors 240
Tel: 358 9 14 801.
Email: justnu@yle.fi
Web site: http://www.yle.fi/extrem
Profile: Radio channel by national broadcasting company Yleisradio for the whole Finnish coastline, where Swedish-speakers live. Young, Swedish-speaking people. Local Translation: Radio EXtrem är Rundradions, svenskspråkiga ungdomsprogramblock. Address to the regional editor in Turku: PB 400, 20101 TURKU. Telephone: 358 2-21 570, fax 358 2-27 17 850.
FM RADIO STATION

YLEX 291210
Owner: Yleisradio
Editorial: PL 17/ Radiokatu 5 D, Yleisradio 24
Tel: 358 9 14 801.
Web site: http://www.yle.fi/ylex
Profile: YLEX on lähinnä nuorelle yleisölle tarkoitettu Yleisradion valtakunnallinen radiokanava. YLEX is a youngish national radio channel of national broadcasting company Yleisradio.
RADIO NETWORK

Television

Fox 625581
Owner: Family Channel Oy
Editorial: Mikonkatu 17A, Helsinki 100
Tel: 358 20 7644 600.
Web site: http://foxtv.fi
Profile: Itsenäinen ja riippumaton viihdepainotteinen antenni- ja kaapeliverkossa näkyvä ilmaiskanava. Independent digital and cable free TV channel specialising in entertainment. Previously listed as SuomiTV.
TELEVISION NETWORK

Kutonen 316147
Owner: SBS Media Group Finland
Editorial: Discovery Networks Finland Oy, Tallberginkatu 1 C, 7. krs, Helsinki 180
Tel: 358 20 7 870 850.
Email: Info_DNF@discovery.com
Web site: http://www.kutonen.fi/
Profile: Maksuton viihdekanava, jonka pääpaino on sarjoissa, urheilussa, elokuvissa ja musiikkiohjelmissa. Kanavan pääkohderyhmää ovat 15-44-vuotiaat katsojat. Digital-TV focusing on entertainment, sports, series, films and music. Aimed at anyone aged 15 to 44 years.
TELEVISION STATION

MoonTV.fi 845805
Web site: http://moontv.fi
Profile: Verkossa toimiva Tv-kanava. Web TV network. palaute@moontv.fi
TELEVISION NETWORK

MTV 586110
Owner: MTV Oy
Editorial: Ilmalankatu 2, Mtv 33 **Tel:** 358 10 300 300.
Email: uutiset@mtv.fi
Web site: http://www.mtv.fi
Profile: MTV:n johtajisto, päälliköt ja ohjelmahankinta. Myös digitalinen kanava. The management of national TV company MTV. The company also has a digital TV channel with the same editorial board as the actual TV channel.
TELEVISION NETWORK

MTV Aluetoimitus Itä-Suomi 316585
Owner: MTV Media
Editorial: Viestintätoimisto Lehtiniemi Oy, Kokontie 10, Joensuu 80230
Email: keimo.lehtiniemi@mtv.fi
Web site: http://www.mtv.fi
Profile: The national tv-channel MTV3 Itä-Suomi office. Local Translation: MTV3-Itä-Suomi toimitus.
TELEVISION NETWORK

MTV Finland (Music TV) 359881
Editorial: Kaisaniemenkatu 3 B 20-21, Helsinki 100
Tel: 358 20 74 24 440.
Email: info@musictelevision.fi
Web site: http://www.musictelevision.fi
Profile: Suomen Music Television. Finnish section of Nordic Music Television. Target Audience: Young, urban people of age 15-30.
TELEVISION NETWORK

MTV Sport 586157
Owner: MTV Media
Editorial: Ilmalantori 2, Mtv 33 **Tel:** 358 10 30 03 00.
Email: uutiset@mtv.fi
Web site: http://www.mtv.fi/sport
Profile: Sports news at national TV channel MTV3. MTV3-kanavan urheilutoimitus.
TELEVISION NETWORK

MTV Uutiset 586156
Owner: MTV Media
Editorial: Ilmalankatu 2, Mtv 33 **Tel:** 358 10 30 03 00.
Email: uutiset@mtv.fi
Web site: http://www.mtv.fi/uutiset
Profile: MTV3-kanavan uutistoimitus. The news desk of national tv channel MTV3.
TELEVISION NETWORK

Nelonen Media 316084
Owner: Sanoma Media Finland Oy
Editorial: Toolonlahdenkatu 2, Helsinki 89
Tel: 358 9 45 451.
Email: uutiset@nelonen.fi
Web site: http://www.nelonen.fi/
Profile: Nelonen on suomalainen valtakunnallinen, kaupallinen televisiokanava. Kaupallisena kanavana Nelonen rahoittaa toimintansa kokonaisuudessaan mainostuloilla ja on osa Nelonen Media - liiketoimintayksikköä, joka kuuluu Sanoma-konsernin sähköisen viestinnän liiketoimintaryhmään, Sanoma Media Finlandiin. Nelonen on Suomen toiseksi tavoittavin mainosmedia. Nelonen (Four) is a Finnish commercial TV channel. Much of its programming is Australian, American, British, and European shows, with Finnish captions. Its main market is the 25-44 demographic. Nelonen has 9 sister channels: Nelonen HD, Jim, Nelonen Prime, Nelonen Nappula, Nelonen Maailma, Nelonen Pro 1, Nelonen Pro 2, Liv and Hero.
TELEVISION NETWORK

Nelonen Pro 316093
Owner: Sanoma Media Finland Oy
Editorial: Toolonlahdenkatu 2, Helsinki 89
Tel: 358 9 45 451.
Web site: http://www.nelonenpro.fi
Profile: Digitaalinen urheilukanava, jonka omistaa Sanoma Entertainment (Nelonen Media). Urheilukanava (UTV) on suomalainen urheiluun erikoistunut TV-kanava jonka ohjelmistoon kuuluu myös kansainvälisiä urheiluohjelmia. Digital sports channel (The Finnish Sport Television Company Ltd.) owned by Sanoma Entertainment (Channel Four Finland) offerring a wide range of programmes consisting of Finnish sports combined with selected international programmes. No generic email address. Previously listed as Urheilukanava.
TELEVISION NETWORK

Sub 586160
Owner: MTV Oy
Editorial: Ilmalankatu 2, Mtv 33 **Tel:** 358 10 30 03 00.
Web site: http://www.sub.fi
Profile: Sub on valtakunnallinen digi-televisiokanava. Sub is a digital TV channel.
TELEVISION NETWORK

Svenska Yle Nyheter och aktualiteter 316099
Editorial: PB 83, Rundradion 24 **Tel:** 358 9 1480 4752.
Email: nyheter@yle.fi
Web site: http://svenska.yle.fi/nyheter/
Profile: YLEn ruotsinkieliset tv-uutiset. YLE's TV-news in Swedish by national broadcasting company Yleisradio (Finnish) / Rundradion (Swedish).
TELEVISION NETWORK

Svenska Yle Sporten 315322
Owner: Yleisradio
Editorial: PB 82/ Radiogatan 5, Rundradion 24
Tel: 358 9 14 801.
Email: svenskasporten@yle.fi
Web site: http://svenska.yle.fi/nyheter/sport.php
Profile: Sports section for different sports programmes in Swedish-speaking TV and radio. Rundradions svenska sportredaktion omfattar Sportmagasinet, Idrottsbiten, Sportradion och Xtrem-sport. Previously listed as FST5 Sportredaktionen.
TELEVISION NETWORK

Swedish Television Helsinki 316473
Editorial: Sjokaptensvagen 9, Helsingfors 890
Email: hasse.svens@svt.se
Web site: http://www.svt.se/nyheter
Profile: Helsinki and Baltic states local correspondent for Swedish Television in Sweden.
TELEVISION NETWORK

TSTV 316589
Owner: TS-yhtymä
Editorial: Lansikaari 15, Turku 20240
Tel: 358 2 26 93 311.
Email: ts.uutiset@ts.fi
Web site: http://www.ts.fi/tstv
Profile: Local TV station broadcasting in the Turku region. Previously listed as Turku TV Local Translation: TS-Yhtymän paikallinen tv-asema Turussa. Their fax number is 358 2-26 93 505, but e-mails are preferred
TELEVISION STATION

TV5 Finland 829322
Owner: SBS Finland Oy
Editorial: Esterinportti 2, Helsinki 240
Tel: 358 20 78 70 850.
Email: info@sbstv.fi
Web site: http://www.tv5.fi
Profile: Description: Kanavapaikalla 10 näkyvä maksuton TV5 on viihdekanava, jonka ohjelmisto koostuu pääasiassa elokuvista, 5D-dokumenteista ja sarjoista. TV5 ja TV Kutonen ovat osa SBS Mediaa ja saksalaista ProSiebenSat.1 Media AG –konsernia. Free entertainment channels mainly covering films, 5D documentaries and series. Part of SBS Media and German ProSiebenSat.1 Media AG Group. Readers: Kanavan pääkohderyhmä on 15-44-vuotiaat. Main target group consists of anyone between 15 and 44 years old.
TELEVISION STATION

Wave 100 710285
Owner: Tampereen Kaupunkitelevisio Oy
Editorial: Hameenkatu 27 B, Tampere 33200
Email: kari.pusa@wave100.fi
Web site: http://www.wave100.fi
Profile: Paikallistelevisiokanava Tampereen seudulla. Local television channels in Tampere region. Start year: 2010
TELEVISION STATION

Yle Asia 316098
Editorial: PL 79, Yleisradio 24 **Tel:** 358 9 14 801.
Email: yle.uutiset@yle.fi
Web site: http://tv1.yle.fi/ohjelmat/ajankohtaisohjelmat
Profile: Current-affairs programmes produced by national broadcasting company Yleisradio for its television and radio service (including programmes such as A-Plus, A-Zoom and A-talk). Ylen asia- ja ajankohtaisohjelmat sekä televisiossa, verkossa että radiossa (mukaan lukien A-Plus, A-Zoom ja A-talk). No faxes are allowed to their fax number 358 9-14 15 01
TELEVISION NETWORK

Yle Kulttuuri ja Viihde 315752
Owner: Yleisradio
Editorial: PL 10, Yleisradio 24 **Tel:** 358 9 14 801.
Email: yle.kulttuuri@yle.fi
Web site: http://www.yle.fi/kulttuuri
Profile: Culture programmes in YLE. YLEn kulttuuriohjelmat ja toimitus The address to the production company is Ikoni & Indeksi Oy, PL 50, 00024 YLEISRADIO.
TELEVISION NETWORK

YLE Lapset ja Nuoret 315719
Editorial: Tohlopinranta 31, Tampere 33270
Tel: 358 3 34 56 111.
Email: pikkukakkonen@yle.fi
Web site: http://yle.fi/lapset/
Profile: YLE:n TV2:n lastenohjelmien tuotantoryhmä. Production board of children's programmes for Yleisradio TV2.
TELEVISION NETWORK

YLE Oppiminen ja ympäristö 315286
Editorial: PL 90, Yleisradio 24 **Tel:** 358 9 14 801.
Email: yle.uutiset@yle.fi
Web site: http://oppiminen.yle.fi
Profile: Educational TV-programmes presented in Yleisradio TV1. YLEn opetusohjelmat.
TELEVISION NETWORK

Yle Teema & Fem 316091
Editorial: PB 76, Yle i Helsingfors, Helsingfors 24
Tel: 358 9 14801.
Email: svenska@yle.fi
Web site: http://svenska.yle.fi/fem
Profile: Ylen ruotsinkieliset uutiset ja ohjelmat. Tämän lisäksi suomeksi dokumenteille, elokuville ja musiikille omistautuva YLEn teemallinen kulttuurikanava. YLE's digital channel that contains culture, education and science programmes. Also Yle's Swedish speaking service/National digital tv-station with programmes in Swedish. Previously listed as YLE Teema & Yle Fem. No releases allowed to email: yleinfo@yle.fi
TELEVISION NETWORK

YLE Viihdeohjelmat 315939
Editorial: PL 196/ Tohlopinranta 31, Tampere 33101
Tel: 358 3 34 56 111.
Web site: http://tv2.yle.fi/etusivu
Profile: Entertainment programme production team of Yleisradio TV2. Yleisradion TV2:n viihdeohjelmien toimituskunta.
TELEVISION NETWORK

Yleisradio Oy Ab 316294
Editorial: Radiokatu 5, Helsinki 240 **Tel:** 358 9 14 801.
Web site: http://www.yle.fi
Profile: Yleisradion TV-toimialan johtajisto. The management of the TV section of national broadcasting company Yleisradio. Broadcast also on Youtube: www.youtube.com/yle. No releases allowed to email: yleinfo@yle.fi
TELEVISION NETWORK

France

Radio

Africa N°1 291122
Owner: AFRICA N°1
Editorial: 33 rue du Faubourg-Saint-Antoine, Paris 75011 **Tel:** +33 1 55 07 58 01.
Email: africa@africa1.com
Web site: http://www.africa1.com
Profile: International and national radio station focussing on African interest, culture and community. Local Translation: Radio panafricaine qui émet en ondes courtes et en FM sur toute l'Afrique. 1ère radio africaine francophone. Diffusion internationale par Eutelsat AB3 Canalsatellite + Satellite Astra sur toute l'Europe + Internet.
RADIO NETWORK

Arte Radio 613636
Owner: ARTE
Editorial: 8 rue Marceau, Issy-Les-Moulineaux CEDEX 9 **Tel:** +33 1 5500 7777.
Email: contacts@arte-radio.com
Web site: http://www.arteradio.com
Profile: Depuis 2002, ARTE Radio est la radio web d'ARTE France, la branche française de la chaîne culturelle européenne. C'est une radio de création "à la demande" qui propose des centaines de courts et

France

moyens métrages à écouter à volonté, gratuitement et sans publicité : reportages, fictions, documentaires, créations sonores, feuilletons, chroniques...
RADIO NETWORK

Beur FM Paris 106.7 309599
Editorial: Beur FM, BP 249, Paris 75524 **Tel:** +33 8 9268 1067.
Email: redaction@beurfm.net
Web site: http://www.beurfm.net
Profile: Satellite radio covering Europe, Morocco, Algeria and Tunisia. Local Translation: Radio généraliste des maghrébins de France, média de toutes les expressions culturelles. Infos spectacles, théâtre et littérature franco-maghrébine, actualité musicale des artistes et interprètes franco-maghrébins, cinéma, loisirs, sorties... Fréquences : Paris/Ile-de-France 106.7, Aix/Marseille 92.6, Grenoble 97.8, Nimes/Alès 104.6, Rouen 98.7, Saint-Etienne 94.3, Bourges/Vierzon 89.1, Le Mans 102.9, Toulon 98.2, Valenciennes 97.4.
RADIO NETWORK

CHERIE FM 291229
Owner: GROUPE NRJ
Editorial: GROUPE NRJ, 22 rue Boileau, Paris 75016
Tel: 33 01 40 71 40 00.
Web site: http://www.cheriefm.fr
Profile: Jours et Heures d'Emission : Quotidien 24 h/ 24. Zone Géographique d'Emission : France. Orientation Thématique : Culture, féminin. Diffusion : Journaux d'informations, émissions culturelles.
RADIO NETWORK

Europe 1 291230
Owner: Lagardère Active
Editorial: 26 bis, rue Francois 1er, Paris 75008
Tel: 33 1 44 31 90 00.
Email: courrier@europe1.fr
Web site: http://www.europe1.fr
Profile: National radio station covering news and current affairs including music, culture and sports.
RADIO NETWORK

France Culture 291124
Editorial: 116 avenue du President-Kennedy, Paris 75220 CEDEX 16 **Tel:** 33 1 56 40 22 22.
Web site: http://www.radiofrance.fr
Profile: National radio station focusing on culture including news, current affairs and entertainment. Local Translation: Chaîne de création, de connaissance et de réflexion, France Culture est unique dans le paysage radiophonique européen.
RADIO NETWORK

FUN RADIO 291233
Editorial: 20 rue Bayard, Paris 75008
Tel: 33 01 40 70 48 48.
Web site: http://www.funradio.fr
Profile: Jours et Heures d'Emission : 7j/7 - 24h/24. Zone Géographique d'Emission : France - Belgique. Orientation Thématique : Musique
RADIO NETWORK

I>Tele La Radio 615880
Owner: CANAL+
Editorial: 6 allee de la Deuxieme D.B., Paris 75015
Tel: +33 1 4114 5353.
Web site: http://www.goomradio.fr/radio/itele-la-radio
Profile: Local Translation: Version radio de la chaine d'information en continu I>Télé avec un journal toutes les quinze minutes ainsi que des chroniques réalisées par des journalistes de la chaîne.
RADIO NETWORK

Mauritius Radio Station 290959
Owner: Mauritius Broadcasting Corporation
Editorial: Mauritius Broadcasting Corporation, 1 Louis Pasteur Street, Forest Side **Tel:** 230 602 12 69.
Email: mbcnews@mbc.intnet.mu
Web site: http://mbc.intnet.mu
Profile: National radio station focussing on news, current affairs, music, sport and weather.
RADIO NETWORK

Le Mouv' 291198
Owner: RADIO FRANCE
Editorial: 116, avenue du president Kennedy, cedex 16, Paris 75220 **Tel:** +33 1 56 40 22 22.
Web site: http://www.lemouv.com
Profile: Young radio of mainly pop music. Local Translation: Le Mouv', la r@dio : l'esprit rock. 70 % musiques + 30 % news / sans pub / 100 % pure radio (colorant rock très naturel) / à consommer sans modération. Parce que générations des réseaux, adeptes de l'internet comme des sports de glisse, épris d'éthique, habitants lucides d'une petite planète, les plus jeunes manifestent de solides facultés d'adaptation : Le Mouv', la r@dio pour écouter ce qu'ils ont à dire et faire entendre. Pour ceux qui se cherchent une culture résistante, des boussoles et des systèmes de navigation efficaces : Le Mouv', l'autre r@dio pour dénicher les talents de demain, démêler l'info de l'intox, construire un dialogue attentif et respectueux. Sur CanalSatellite, RDS, DAB, TPS et sur le réseau câble numérique de la Lyonnaise de Câble et de France Télécom. Cible : 15-35 ans. Fréquences : Aix-en-Provence 96.8, Ajaccio 92.0, Angers 103.0, Brest 94.0, Clermont-Ferrand 97.5, Dijon 88.9, Lille 91.0, Lyon 87.8, Marseille 96.4, Nantes 96.1, Nice 101.1, Paris 92.1, Rennes 107.3, Rouen 95.8, Toulouse 95.2, Valence 100.7.
RADIO NETWORK

NRJ Tahiti 555773
Owner: Groupe Hersant Media Polynesie
Web site: http://nrj.pf
RADIO NETWORK

RADIO APAL 94.9 - 98.1 589094
Editorial: 8 rue Pierre-et-Marie-Curie, Fort-De-France 97200
Email: radio-apal@orange.fr
Profile: Local Translation: Radio locale de la Martinique.
FM RADIO STATION

Radio France 291238
Owner: Radio France
Editorial: 116 avenue du President-Kennedy, Paris 75016 **Tel:** 33 1 56 40 29 07.
Email: mediateur@radiofrance.com
Web site: http://www.radiofrance.fr
Profile: National radio station focussing on news, current affairs, culture and entertainment.
RADIO NETWORK

Radio France Internationale - RFI 742080
Owner: France Médias Monde
Editorial: 116 avenue du President Kennedy, Paris 75762 **Tel:** 33 1 56 40 12 12.
Web site: http://www.rfi.fr
Profile: International radio station focusing on news and current affairs including national and international interest, practical information, music, economics, sport, culture, science, health and medical, youth interest, women's interest and European issues.
RADIO NETWORK

RADIO MEDIA TROPICAL GUADELOUPE 88.1 559417
Owner: RADIO MEDIA TROPICAL GUADELOUPE 88.1
Editorial: 32 residence Belcourt UB 01, Baie-Mahault 97122 **Tel:** 0590 5 90 25 90 03.
Email: mediatropicalguadeloupe@hotmail.com
Web site: http://www.mediatropicalguadeloupe.com
Profile: Local Translation: Radio de référence des Français d'Outre-Mer. Rubriques : infos pratiques, rendez-vous artistiques, hit parade, recettes tropicales...
FM RADIO STATION

RADIO SALAZES 106.6 - 100.2 590055
Editorial: Rue de l'Amiral-Lacaze, Saint-Denis
Email: radio@salazes-fm.com
Web site: http://www.salazes-fm.com
Profile: Local Translation: Radio indépendante de la Réunion.
FM RADIO STATION

RCI (RADIO CARAIBES INTERNATIONAL) MARTINIQUE 544378
Owner: GROUPE RCI
Editorial: 2 boulevard de la Marne, BP 1111, Fort-De-France 97248 **Tel:** 0596 5 96 63 72 66.
Email: redaction-martinique@radiocaraibes.com
Web site: http://www.radiocaraibes.com
Profile: Local Translation: Radio locale martiniquaise : diffusion des programmes 24h/24 (programmes Europe 1 de minuit à 5h du matin). Fréquences : Diamant / Nord Atlantique 91.2, Lorrain / Macouba 92.6, Fort-de-France / Grand-Rivière 98.7, Prêcheur / St Pierre 98.9, Sud 103.0 et Nord 104.6
FM RADIO STATION

RFM 291062
Editorial: 28 rue Francois 1er, Paris 75008
Tel: 33 01 42 32 20 00.
Email: eric.halimi@rfm.fr
Web site: http://www.rfm.fr
Profile: Jours et Heures d'Emission : 7j/7, 24h/24. Zone Géographique d'Emission : France. Orientation Thématique : radios musicales adultes, 'Le meilleur de la musique'. Diffusion : Flash d'informations, chroniques.
RADIO NETWORK

RMC 291127
Owner: RMC INFO
Editorial: 12 rue d'Oradour-sur-Glane, Paris 75740
Tel: 33 1 71 19 11 91.
Email: lsaigre@rmc.fr
Web site: http://rmc.bfmtv.com
Profile: National radio station focusing on general interest.
RADIO NETWORK

RTL 291018
Owner: RTL
Editorial: 22. rue Bayard, Paris 75008
Tel: 33 1 40 70 40 70.
Email: contact.antenne@rtl.fr
Web site: http://www.rtl.fr
Profile: National and international radio station focussing on news and current affairs including culture, sports, music and entertainment.
RADIO NETWORK

Television

France Télévisions 316247
Owner: FRANCE TELEVISIONS
Editorial: 7 Esplanade Henri-de-France, Paris 75015
Tel: 33 1 56 22 60 00.
Web site: http://www.francetelevisions.fr
Profile: National public television network.
TELEVISION NETWORK

Mauritius TV 316346
Editorial: Mauritius Broadcasting Corporation, 1 Louis Pasteur Street, Forest Side **Tel:** 230 602 12 23.
Email: mbcnews@mbc.intnet.mu
Web site: http://mbc.intnet.mu
Profile: National TV station focussing on news, current affairs, entertainment, culture, sports and weather forecast.
TELEVISION STATION

Nouvelle Calédonie 1ère 555100
Owner: France Télévisions
Editorial: 1 rue du General Leclerc, BP G3, Paris 98848 **Tel:** 33 687 2 39 99 9.
Email: infonc2@francetv.fr
Web site: http://www.rfo.fr
Profile: Journaux d'actualités, magazines d'information, débats, sports, émissions diverses : musique, ethnologie, histoire, croyances, traditions... Local office of the overseas national public TV channel focussing on regional and local news, sport, entertainment, music, ethology, history, faith and traditions.
TELEVISION STATION

RFO GUADELOUPE 317051
Owner: RFO
Editorial: Morne-Bernard-Destrellan, BP 180, Baie-Mahault 97122
Web site: http://www.rfo.fr
Profile: Regional TV and radio station focussing on regional interest, news, sport, magazines, music, ethology, history, faith and traditions.
TELEVISION STATION

RFO GUYANE 317052
Owner: RFO
Editorial: Avenue Le Grand-Boulevard, ZAD Moulin-à-Vent, Remire-Montjoly 97354CEDEX
Tel: 594 5 94 25 6700.
Web site: http://www.rfo.fr
Profile: Local office of the overseas national public TV channel focussing on regional and local news, sport, entertainment, music, ethology, history, faith and traditions.
TELEVISION STATION

RFO MARTINIQUE 317053
Editorial: La Clairiere, BP 662, Fort-De-France Cedex 97263
Web site: http://www.rfo.fr
Profile: Local office of the overseas national public TV channel focussing on regional and local news, sport, entertainment, music, ethology, history, faith and traditions.
TELEVISION STATION

RFO MAYOTTE 654836
Owner: RFO
Tel: 269 2 69 60 80 41.
Web site: http://www.rfo.fr
Profile: Local office of the overseas national public TV channel focussing on regional and local news, sport, entertainment, music, ethology, history, faith and traditions.
TELEVISION STATION

RFO New Caledonia 539199
Owner: RFO (rŽseau france outre-mer)
Editorial: BP G3, Noumea 98848
Profile: National TV station in New Caledonia covering local news.
TELEVISION STATION

RFO REUNION 317056
Owner: RFO
Editorial: 1 rue Jean-Chatel, Messagerie 9, Saint-Denis 97716
Web site: http://www.rfo.fr
Profile: Local office of the overseas national public TV channel focussing on regional and local news, sport, entertainment, music, ethology, history, faith and traditions.
TELEVISION STATION

RFO SAINT PIERRE ET MIQUELON 317057
Web site: http://www.rfo.fr
Profile: Local office of the overseas national public TV channel focussing on regional and local news, sport, entertainment, music, ethology, history, faith and traditions.
TELEVISION STATION

RFO WALLIS ET FUTUNA 317058
Editorial: Mata Utu - Pointe Matala, Pacifique Sud, Iles De Wallis-Et-Futuna **Tel:** 681 7 22 02 0.
Web site: http://www.rfo.fr
Profile: Regional TV and radio station focussing on regional interest, news, sport, magazines, music, ethology, history, faith and traditions. Local Translation: Télévision et radio régionales. Journaux d'actualités, sports, émissions diverses : musique, ethnologie, histoire, croyances, traditions...
TELEVISION STATION

Georgia

Radio

Fortuna 653840
Editorial: 2 Marshal Gelovani Avenue, Tbilisi 179
Tel: 995 22 38 30 30.
Email: tamara@fortuna.ge
Web site: http://www.fortuna.ge
Profile: Format of this station is Golden Hits. Fortuna's music library represents the best of the native and world's pop and classical music. The news is broadcasted at the beginning of each hour, after a classical music. The slogan of Radio Fortuna is - "The Best Hits and the Latest Information".
FM RADIO STATION

Fortuna+ 653839
Editorial: 2 Marshal Gelovani Avenue, Tbilisi 179
Tel: 995 22 38 30 30.
Email: tamara@fortuna.ge
Web site: http://www.fortunaplus.ge
Profile: The format of this station is a certain mixture of EHR and Dance formats, that gives it a big popularity.
FM RADIO STATION

Hereti FM 653858
Tel: 995 254 23 766.
Email: office@heretifm.com
Web site: http://www.heretifm.com
Profile: Provides best music of all times and modern hits, hourly news on local and international events, special programs and talk-shows. Ratio of news and entertainment programmes is 50-50% .
FM RADIO STATION

Hit FM 616840
Tel: 995 32 55 10 14.
Email: radio@hitfm.ge
Web site: http://www.hitfm.ge
Profile: Broadcasts contemporary Russian and Georgian hits combined with entertainment programmes and news.
FM RADIO STATION

Television

Adjara TV 654247
Tel: 995 222 74 370.
Email: info@adjaratv.ge
Web site: http://www.adjaratv.ge
Profile: Regional TV channel in Georgia which broadcasts via satellite.
TELEVISION STATION

Germany

Radio

horads - Hochschulradio Stuttgart 809040
Web site: http://www.horads.de
RADIO NETWORK

Gibraltar

Radio

GBC Radio Gibraltar 290995
Owner: Gibraltar Broadcasting Corporation
Editorial: Broadcasting House, 18 South Barrack Road, Gibraltar GX11 1AA **Tel:** 350 200 48995.
Email: radiogibraltar@gbc.gi
Web site: http://www.radiogibraltar.gi
Profile: National radio station covering regional, national and international news and current affairs including music and entertainment.
RADIO NETWORK

Television

GBC Television 316331
Owner: Gibraltar Broadcasting Corporation
Editorial: Broadcasting House, 18 South Barrack Road, Gibraltar GX11 1AA **Tel:** 350 200 79760.
Email: television@gbc.gi
Web site: http://www.gbc.gi
Profile: National television station covering regional, national and international news and current affairs including sports and entertainment.
TELEVISION STATION

Guam

Radio

KGUM-AM 342409
Owner: Sorensen Pacific Broadcasting
Editorial: 111 Chalan Santo Papa, Ste 800, Hagatna 96910 **Tel:** 671 4775700.
Web site: http://www.k57.com
AM RADIO STATION

KGUM-FM 342408
Owner: Sorensen Pacific Broadcasting
Editorial: 111 Chalan Santo Papa, Ste 800, Agana 96910 **Tel:** 671 4775700.
Web site: http://www.sorensenmediagroup.com/thekat
Profile: KGUM-FM is a commercial station owned by Sorensen Pacific Broadcasting. The format of the station is Hot AC. KGUM-FM broadcasts to the Dededo, GU area at 105.1.
FM RADIO STATION

KPRG-FM 290984
Owner: Guam Educational Radio Foundation
Editorial: 303 University Drive, UOG Station, Mangilao 96923 **Tel:** 671 7348930.
Web site: http://www.kprgfm.com
Profile: KPRG-FM 89.3 is the public radio broadcast station of the Guam Educational Radio Foundation. It is an NPR/National Public Radio affiliate.
FM RADIO STATION

KSDA-FM 290965
Owner: Good News Broadcasting Corp.
Editorial: 290 Chalan Palasyo, Agaña Heights 96910
Tel: 671 4725732.
Email: mail@joy92.net
Web site: http://www.joy92.net
FM RADIO STATION

KUAM-AM 587041
Owner: Pacific Telestations Inc.
Editorial: 600 Harmon Loop, Dededo 96912
Tel: 1 671 637-5826.
Email: newsdirector@kuam.com
Web site: http://www.kuam.com
Profile: KUAM-AM is a commercial station owned by Pacific Telestations Inc. The format of the station is island music from different pacific islands. KUAM-AM broadcasts to the Dededo, Guam area at 630 AM.
AM RADIO STATION

KZGZ-FM 342442
Owner: Sorensen Pacific Broadcasting
Tel: 671 4775700.
Email: JB@power98.com
Web site: http://www.power98.com
FM RADIO STATION

Television

KUAM-TV 316409
Owner: Pacific Telestations Inc.
Editorial: 600 Harmon Loop, Dededo 96912
Tel: 671 6375826.
Email: newsdirector@kuam.com
Web site: http://www.kuam.com
Profile: The outlet offers RSS (Really Simple Syndication) and a digital Podcast.
TELEVISION STATION

Guyana

Television

CNS Television Channel 6 316259
Editorial: 43 Robb and Wellington Streets, Georgetown **Tel:** 592 2261834.
Email: sharma@cns6.tv
Web site: http://www.cns6.tv
Profile: Television channel providing community news through a variety of shows related to cultural, music, and films.
TELEVISION NETWORK

Guyana Television Broadcasting Company 316260
Editorial: Homestretch Avenue, D'Urban Park, Georgetown **Tel:** 592 2 27 15 66.
Email: feedback@ncnguyana.com
Web site: http://www.ncnguyana.com
Profile: Broadcasts educational, cultural, and entertainment programs for both the urban and the rural areas of the Guyana.
TELEVISION NETWORK

Haiti

Radio

Radio Antilles Internationale 747732
Owner: Radio Tele Antilles
Editorial: 175, Rue du Centre, Port-Au-Prince
Web site: http://www.radioteleantilleshaiti.com
Profile: Radio Antilles Internationale is a radio station focusing on news.
FM RADIO STATION

Radio Nationale d'Haiti 747881
Owner: Television Nationale d'Haiti
Editorial: 174, Rue Magasin de l'etat, Port-Au-Prince
Tel: 011 509 22 23 7932.
Profile: Radio Nationale d'Haiti is a government owned and run radio station in Port-au-Prince Haiti.
RADIO NETWORK

Television

PVS Antenne 747852
Owner: Raynald Delerme
Editorial: 137 Rue Monseigneur Guilloux, Port-Au-Prince **Tel:** 011 509 222-1277.
Profile: PVS Antenne is a private French language television station that primarily covers news events and stories.
TELEVISION STATION

Television Nationale D'Haiti 747741
Owner: Television Nationale D'Haiti
Editorial: 13400 Delmas., Port-Au-Prince
Tel: 011 509 246-0200.
Email: haitipaw@hotmail.fr
Web site: http://haitipaw.kif.fr
Profile: This station is a government owned television station. Its covers news stories as well as various other cultural topics.
TELEVISION NETWORK

Trans-America 747868
Owner: Hébert Pelissier
Editorial: Ruelle Rogers, Gonaives
Profile: Trans-America is a television station that primarily covers news.
TELEVISION STATION

Holy See (Vatican City)

Radio

Radio Vaticana 437157
Owner: Radio Vaticana
Editorial: Palazzo Pio, Piazza Pia, 3, Rome 120
Tel: 39 06 69883551.
Email: english@vatiradio.va
Web site: http://www.radiovaticana.va
Profile: Radio station covering news and current affairs through the eyes of the Christian church.
RADIO NETWORK

Honduras

Radio

Radio HRN La Voz de Honduras 290871
Owner: Emisoras Unidas SA Honduras
Editorial: Blvd. Suyapa, Colonia Florencia Sur, contiguo a la Corporacion Televicentro, Apartado Postal 642, Tegucigalpa **Tel:** 504 2325178.
Web site: http://www.emisorasunidas.net
Profile: Broadcasts daily news, sports, and cultural programming.
RADIO NETWORK

Indonesia

Television

BBC Indonesia 520293
Editorial: Deutsche Bank, Lantai 15, Jl. Imam Bonjol No.80, Jakarta 10310 **Tel:** 62 21 39831635.
Email: indonesian@bbc.co.uk
Web site: http://www.bbc.co.uk/indonesia
Profile: Covers local, national, and international news, as well as economic and political issues.
TELEVISION NETWORK

Iran

Radio

IRIB World Service 381043
Owner: Islamic Republic Of Iran Broadcasting (IRIB)
Editorial: PO Box 19395-6767, 2nd Floor, Jam-e-Jam Building, Tehran **Tel:** 98 21 2201 3720.
Email: english@parstoday.com
Web site: http://parstoday.com/en
Profile: IRIB World Service, also known as English Radio of the Islamic Republic of Iran, is an international radio station broadcasting the recitation of Quranic verses, news, political commentaries, different series and features on special occasions. The station was established in 1956 with the aim of familiarising world nations with Iran's history and culture, as well as its different regions and historical sites. It is operated by state-owned public broadcaster, Islamic Republic Of Iran Broadcasting (IRIB), and generates around 180 minutes of programming each day in the form of recorded programmes, live news, commentaries and news reports.
AM RADIO STATION

Television

Al Alam News Network 378048
Owner: Islamic Republic Of Iran Broadcasting (IRIB)
Editorial: PO Box 19615-885, Vali-Asr Street, Tehran
Tel: 98 21 2216 8720.
Email: info@alalam.ir
Web site: http://www.alalam.ir
Profile: Al Alam News Network is a state-owned television station broadcasting news and current affairs programmes in Arabic for 24-hours a day. The channel launched in 2003.
TELEVISION STATION

Amouzesh TV 653810
Owner: Islamic Republic Of Iran Broadcasting (IRIB)
Editorial: No. 33, Eastern Shahid Atefi Str., Tehran
Tel: 98 21 2204 4958.
Email: info@tv7.ir
Web site: http://www.tv7.ir
Profile: Amouzesh TV is a state-owned television station broadcasting cultural and educational programmes. The channel launched in 1999.
TELEVISION STATION

Azarbaijan-e Sharqi TV 654377
Owner: Islamic Republic Of Iran Broadcasting (IRIB)
Editorial: PO Box 4444, IRIB East Azarbaijan Center, Bahman 29th Boulevard, Tabriz 5166617466
Tel: 98 411 330 3041.
Email: web@tabriz.irib.ir
Web site: http://tabriz.irib.ir
Profile: Azarbaijan-e Sharqi TV is a state-owned, regional television station broadcasting youth, family, children's and sports programmes in the East Azarbaijan province of Iran. The chanel launched in 2000.
TELEVISION STATION

Channel 1 653802
Owner: Islamic Republic Of Iran Broadcasting (IRIB)
Editorial: PO Box 19395-1351, 10th Floor, Toleed Building, Tehran **Tel:** 98 21 2204 0420.
Email: sima1@irib.ir
Web site: http://www.tv1.ir
Profile: Channel 1 is a state-owned television station broadcasting children's shows, drama series, Iranian movies, talk shows and news. The channel launched in 1966.
TELEVISION STATION

Channel 2 653803
Owner: Islamic Republic Of Iran Broadcasting (IRIB)
Editorial: PO Box 15875-6874, Channel 2 Sima, Tehran **Tel:** 98 21 8867 8860.
Email: sima2@irib.ir
Web site: http://www.tv2.ir
Profile: Channel 2 is a state-owned television station broadcasting news and entertainment programmes, including mini-series, comedies, movies, children's shows and talk shows. The channel launched in 1970.
TELEVISION STATION

Channel 3 653809
Owner: Islamic Republic Of Iran Broadcasting (IRIB)
Editorial: PO Box 19395-3334, No. 12, Tehran
Tel: 98 21 2204 0092.
Email: sima3@irib.ir
Web site: http://www.tv3.ir
Profile: Channel 3 is a state-owned television station broadcasting major Iranian sport events, mini-series, comedies, and movies. The channel launched in 1993.
TELEVISION STATION

Channel 4 653805
Owner: Islamic Republic Of Iran Broadcasting (IRIB)
Editorial: PO Box 19395-6767, No.22 Mahnaz Str., Tehran **Tel:** 98 21 2621 5600.
Email: sima4@irib.ir
Web site: http://www.tv4.ir
Profile: Channel 4 is a state-owned television station broadcasting documentaries, academic conferences, interviews with scholars, artistic movies, plays and philosophical discussions. The channel launched in 1996.
TELEVISION STATION

Iran News Network 654379
Owner: Islamic Republic Of Iran Broadcasting (IRIB)
Editorial: PO Box 19395-1351, Jam-e-Jam Street, Tehran **Tel:** 98 21 2201 3911.
Email: pr@irinn.ir
Web site: http://www.irinn.ir
Profile: Iran News Network (IRINN) is a free-to-air satellite channel broadcasting news and current affairs, as well as political, sports, science and medical programmes. The station launched in 1999.
TELEVISION STATION

Jam-e-Jam 1 653806
Owner: Islamic Republic Of Iran Broadcasting (IRIB)
Editorial: No. 10, 18th Street Garbi, Saadat-Abad, Tehran 1997855533 **Tel:** 98 21 2207 9381.
Email: jjtv@irib.ir
Web site: http://www.jjtvn.ir
Profile: Jam-e-Jam 1 is a state-owned television station broadcasting social, religious, cultural, literary, political, news, current affairs, sports and entertainment programmes. Launched in 1997, the free-to-air satellite channel is aimed at Iranian expatriates and Persian speakers in Europe, parts of Asia and the Middle East.
TELEVISION STATION

Jam-e-Jam 2 653807
Owner: Islamic Republic Of Iran Broadcasting (IRIB)
Editorial: No. 10, 18th Street Garbi, Saadat-Abad, Tehran 1997855533 **Tel:** 98 21 2207 9381.
Email: jjtv@irib.ir
Web site: http://www.jjtvn.ir
Profile: Jam-e-Jam 2 is a state-owned television station broadcasting Iranian movies, TV series, children's programmes, major Iranian sporting events and news. The free-to-air satellite channel is aimed at Iranian expatriates and Persian speakers in Europe, the USA and Canada.
TELEVISION STATION

Jam-e-Jam 3 653808
Owner: Islamic Republic Of Iran Broadcasting (IRIB)
Editorial: No. 10, 18th Street Garbi, Saadat-Abad, Tehran 1997855533 **Tel:** 98 21 2207 9381.
Email: jjtv@irib.ir
Web site: http://www.jjtvn.ir
Profile: Jam-e-Jam 3 is a state-owned television station broadcasting entertainment, news, sports, Islamic and children's programmes. Launched in 2002, the free-to-air satellite channel is aimed at Iranian expatriates and Persian speakers in the Indian subcontinent, Pakistan, Afghanistan and the Pacific.
TELEVISION STATION

Press TV 653847
Owner: Press TV
Editorial: PO Box 19977-66411, 24 East 2nd Street, Block 6, Tehran **Tel:** 98 21 2306 6170.
Email: info@presstv.ir
Web site: http://www.presstv.com
Profile: Press TV is a state-owned television station broadcasting news and current affairs programmes, specifically focusing on the Middle East. The channel launched in 2007.
TELEVISION STATION

Sahar Universal Network 378043
Owner: Islamic Republic Of Iran Broadcasting (IRIB)
Editorial: PO Box 19395-6767, Jame-e-Jam Street, Tehran **Tel:** 98 21 2216 2887.
Email: reportage_sahar1@yahoo.com
Web site: http://www.sahartv.ir
Profile: Sahar Universal Network is a bouquet of television stations broadcasting religious, social and cultural programmes in seven languages. Launched in 1997, the free-to-air satellite network is aimed at viewers around the world.
TELEVISION STATION

Tehran TV 617529
Owner: Islamic Republic Of Iran Broadcasting (IRIB)
Editorial: PO Box 19978-54469, Saadat Abad Street, Tehran 7388-19395 **Tel:** 98 21 2351 1000.
Email: s_moghiseh@irib.ir
Web site: http://www.tv5.ir
Profile: Tehran TV, also known as Channel 5, is a regional television station broadcasting movies, local news, political, cultural, social, Islamic and youth programmes in the province of Tehran. The channel launched in 1995.
TELEVISION STATION

Iraq

Radio

Alrasheed FM 402165
Owner: Al Rasheed Media Services
Editorial: Al Masbah Area, Baghdad
Tel: 964 7901 704722.
Email: alrasheedfm@yahoo.com
Web site: http://www.alrasheedmedia.com
Profile: Alrasheed FM is a radio station broadcasting entertainment, news, Arabic and foreign pop music, and live programmes. It launched in 2004 and broadcasts on 91.5 FM.
FM RADIO STATION

Dar Al-Salam Radio 371226
Owner: Iraqi Islamic Party
Editorial: Al Rabee Street, Al Jama'a Area, Baghdad
Tel: 964 790 194 6621.
Email: dsir_2003@yahoo.com

Iraq

Profile: Dar Al-Salam Radio is the radio station of the Iraqi Islamic Party and broadcasts news, religious, cultural, social, political and entertainment programmes. It launched in 2003 and broadcasts on 91.0 FM and 1116 MW.
FM RADIO STATION

Al Forqan Radio 417348
Owner: Iraqi Media Network
Editorial: Iraqi Media Network Building, King Faisal Roundabout, Baghdad **Tel:** 964 1 537 2354.
Web site: http://www.imn.iq
Profile: Al Forqan Radio is an Islamic radio station broadcasting Holy Quran recitals and religious programmes on 92.5 FM. Originally called Holy Quran Radio, the station launched in 2009 and is operated by state-owned public broadcaster, Iraqi Media Network.
FM RADIO STATION

Al Hoda 89.7 FM 586882
Owner: Dar Al Hoda for Culture & Media
Editorial: Baghdad Street, Karbala
Tel: 964 780 103 3238.
Email: al-hodaonline@al-hodaonline.com
Web site: http://www.al-hodaonline.com
Profile: Al Hoda 89.7 FM is an Arabic radio station broadcasting Islamic programmes. It launched in 2005 and broadcasts on 89.7 FM.
FM RADIO STATION

Al Hurria FM 750770
Owner: Safwat Al Iraq
Editorial: PO Box 3303, Al Jadiriyah, Baghdad 10070
Tel: 964 7704 425615.
Email: info@alhurria.fm
Web site: http://www.alhurria.fm
Profile: Al Hurria FM (Freedom FM) is a radio station broadcasting news, pop music and entertainment programmes. The radio station broadcasts on 97.7 FM and was launched by the Patriotic Union of Kurdistan (PUK) in 2003.
FM RADIO STATION

Radio Al Iraqia 417349
Owner: Iraqi Media Network
Editorial: Iraqi Media Network Building, King Faisal Roundabout, Baghdad **Tel:** 964 1 537 2423.
Email: aliraqea_imn2009@yahoo.com
Web site: http://www.imn.iq
Profile: Radio Al Iraqia is a national radio station broadcasting news, social, cultural and children's programmes. Originally called Shahrazad Radio, the station launched in 2006 and transmits on 103.3 FM and 105.2 FM. It is owned by Iraqi Media Network, the state-owned public broadcaster.
FM RADIO STATION

Radio Al Mustaqbal 381048
Owner: Iraqi National Accord
Editorial: PO Box 1843, Baghdad
Tel: 964 790 126 0521.
Email: aliamustafaz@yahoo.com
Profile: Radio Al Mustaqbal, also known as Sawt Al Wifaq Al Watani, is the radio station of the Iraqi National Accord political party and broadcasts music, news, and political talk shows. Launchedi in 1996, it transmits on 95.5 FM and 1305 AM.
FM RADIO STATION

Radio Dijla 381049
Owner: Tigris Media Ltd
Editorial: House 2, Street 60, Area 110 (Kadi Mohammad), Sulaimaniyah **Tel:** 964 7707 705831.
Email: post@radiodijla.com
Web site: http://www.radiodijla.com
Profile: Radio Dijla is a talk radio station which combines news and entertainment programmes with the opinions of listeners who phone in to air their grievances. The station launched in April 2004 and broadcasts on 88.3 FM (Baghdad), 88.5 FM (Basra), 94.0 FM (Mosul), 95.7 FM (Erbil), 95.7 FM (Kirkuk) and 93.0 FM (Suleimaniya).
FM RADIO STATION

Radio Nawa 381075
Owner: Nawa Establishment
Editorial: Radio Nawa Building, Kursat, Sulaimaniyah
Tel: 964 53 328 8581.
Email: info@radionawa.com
Web site: http://www.radionawa.com
Profile: Radio Nawa is a radio station broadcasting news, music and programmes in Arabic and Kurdish for 24-hrs a day. It launched in 2005 and transmits on 89.7 FM (Kalar, Deyala), 89.9 FM (Baghdad, Babel), 90.6 FM (Sulaimaniyah), 92.6 FM (Erbil), 102.5 FM (Duhok) and 92.0 FM (Basra).
FM RADIO STATION

Republic of Iraq Radio 417350
Owner: Iraqi Media Network
Editorial: Iraqi Media Network Building, King Faisal Roundabout, Baghdad **Tel:** 964 1 537 2360.
Email: editor@imn.iq
Web site: http://www.imn.iq
Profile: Republic of Iraq Radio (RIR) is a national radio station broadcasting local news, sports reports and social programmes. It launched in 1936 and is owned by Iraqi Media Network, the state-owned public broadcaster. It transmits on 98.3 FM.
FM RADIO STATION

Sumer FM 554250
Owner: Alsumaria Iraqi Satellite TV Network
Editorial: Al Masbah Street, Karada Kharej, Baghdad
Tel: 964 1 719 5910.
Email: sumerfm@sumerfm.com
Web site: http://www.sumerfm.com
Profile: Sumer FM is a radio station broadcasting music, entertainment, social, cultural and sports programmes. It launched in 2004 and broadcasts on 99.8 FM (Baghdad), 91.8 FM (Basra), 98.2 FM (Erbil), 92.8 FM (Sulaimaniyah), 99.9 FM (Dohuk) and 105.8 FM (Diwaniya).
FM RADIO STATION

UR FM 396543
Owner: UR Radio Broadcasting LLC
Editorial: 113 Abu Nuash Street, Baghdad
Tel: 964 771 777 5366.
Email: info@urradio.fm
Web site: http://urradio.fm
Profile: UR FM is a radio station broadcasting pop music, entertainment and news programmes 24-hrs a day. The station launched in December 2005 and broadcasts on 98.9 FM in Baghdad and 97.9 FM in Basra. It is aimed at Iraqi listeners aged 15-40 years old.
FM RADIO STATION

Voice of Iraq 381055
Owner: Voice of Iraq
Editorial: PO Box 74143, Baghdad
Tel: 964 1 523 9628.
Email: voiceiraq@yahoo.com
Web site: http://www.voiraq.com
Profile: Voice of Iraq is a national radio station broadcasting talk shows and discussion programmes. The station launched in 2003 and broadcasts on 93.0 FM and 1180 MW.
AM RADIO STATION

Television

Ahlulbayt Satellite Channel 525418
Owner: Ahlulbayt TV
Editorial: Imam Al Hussein Grand Mosque Complex, Qeblat Al Hussien Street, Karbala
Tel: 964 770 621 9999.
Email: ahlulbayt@ahlulbayt.com
Web site: http://www.ahlulbayt.com
Profile: Ahlulbayt Satellite Channel is a free-to-air television station broadcasting cultural and Islamic-related programmes, with special emphasis on the Prophet and his household. The channel launched in 2005.
TELEVISION STATION

Aldiyar Satellite Channel 416965
Owner: Aldiyar Sat
Editorial: Karadet Mariam, Near Jumhouria Bridge, Baghdad **Tel:** 964 1 538 4180.
Email: diyarsat@hotmail.com
Web site: http://www.aldiyarsat.net
Profile: Aldiyar Satellite Channel is a free-to-air television station broadcasting Iraqi news and cultural programmes, as well as dramas, talk shows, music, documentaries, children's programmes, films, series, sports and entertainment programmes for 18-hours a day (9am-3am). The channel launched in 2004.
TELEVISION STATION

Almasar Satellite Channel 525413
Owner: Almasar TV
Editorial: Al Fardoss Place, Baghdad
Tel: 964 790 168 5660.
Email: abdm02@hotmail.com
Web site: http://www.almasar.tv
Profile: Almasar Satellite Channel is a free-to-air television station broadcasting local news and current affairs, political talk shows, as well as cultural and social programmes about family and women's issues for 24-hours a day. The channel launched in 2004.
TELEVISION STATION

Alrasheed TV 402245
Owner: Al Rasheed Media Services
Editorial: Al Qadsia, Baghdad **Tel:** 964 780 195 3167.
Email: t_b_b1956@yahoo.com
Web site: http://www.alrasheedmedia.com
Profile: Alrasheed TV is a general entertainment channel broadcasting entertainment and news programmes, as well as Arabic and foreign films. The channel launched in 2004 and broadcasts free-to-air on satellite.
TELEVISION STATION

Beladi Satellite Channel 416964
Owner: Beladi Satellite Channel
Editorial: NH 909, Street 52, 412, Karada, Baghdad
Tel: 964 790 111 3022.
Email: beladi_tv@yahoo.com
Web site: http://www.beladitv.tv
Profile: Beladi Satellite Channel is a free-to-air television station broadcasting news reports, talk shows, documentaries and current affairs programmes. It launched in 2004.
TELEVISION STATION

Al Forat TV 391111
Owner: Al Forat Information Co.
Editorial: D 903-S 10-B, Karadda, Baghdad
Tel: 964 1 718 8394.
Email: info@alforattv.com
Web site: http://www.alforatnews.com
Profile: Al Forat TV is a free-to-air television station broadcasting news, political, religious and general entertainment programmes for 22-hrs a day. The channel launched in 2004.
TELEVISION STATION

Iraqiya Sports TV 417370
Owner: Iraqi Media Network
Editorial: Iraqi Media Network Building, King Faisal Roundabout, Baghdad **Tel:** 964 1 537 2423.
Email: info@imn.iq
Profile: Iraqiya Sports TV is a state-owned television station broadcasting local and international sports programmes for 18-hours a day. The channel launched in 2005.
TELEVISION STATION

Iraqiya TV 1 417368
Owner: Iraqi Media Network
Editorial: Iraqi Media Network Building, King Faisal Roundabout, Baghdad **Tel:** 964 1 537 2351.
Email: aliraqea_imn2009@yahoo.com
Web site: http://www.imn.iq
Profile: Iraqiya TV 1 is a state-owned television station broadcasting news, entertainment and public interest programmes. The channel launched in 2003 and broadcasts terrestrially in Iraq and free-to-air on satellite.
TELEVISION STATION

Al Iraqiya TV 2 654380
Owner: Iraqi Media Network
Editorial: Iraqi Media Network Building, King Faisal Roundabout, Baghdad **Tel:** 964 1 537 2351.
Email: iraqiatv@imn.iq
Profile: Al Iraqiya TV 2 is a state-owned television station broadcasting Islamic programmes and Quranic recitals, as well as cultural and women's programmes. The channel launched in 2007 and was formerly called Al Forqan TV.
TELEVISION STATION

Ishtar TV 769334
Owner: Ishtar Broadcasting Cooperation
Editorial: Mahlat 24/414, Hadyab Street, Erbil
Tel: 964 66 225 1132.
Email: info@ishtartv.com
Web site: http://www.ishtartv.com
Profile: Ishtar TV is a television station broadcasts news, culture and art programmes. The channel launched in 2007 and broadcasts free-to-air on satellite.
TELEVISION STATION

NRT TV 774746
Owner: Nalia Radio & Television (NRT)
Editorial: German Village, Sulaimaniyah
Tel: 964 53 323 9014.
Email: info@nrttv.com
Web site: http://www.nrttv.com
Profile: NRT TV is an independent Kurdish news and current affairs channel. It launched in 2011 and broadcasts free-to-air on satellite.
TELEVISION STATION

Al Salam TV 769330
Owner: Al Salam TV
Editorial: Al Kazemia City, Baghdad
Tel: 964 790 396 6848.
Email: mail@tvalsalam.tv
Web site: http://www.tvalsalam.tv
Profile: Al Salam TV is a free-to-air satellite channel broadcasting news, politics, entertainment, culture, society and Islamic programmes. The station launched in 2005.
TELEVISION STATION

Israel

Radio

Kol Israel 840512
Owner: Israel Broadcasting Authority
Editorial: 21 Heleni HaMalka, PO 1082, Jerusalem 91010 **Tel:** 972 1 599 509 510.
Email: radiodirector@iba.org.il
Web site: http://www.iba.org.il
Profile: National radio station covering news and current affairs.
RADIO NETWORK

Reshet Bet 840513
Owner: Israel Broadcasting Authority
Editorial: 21 Heleni HaMalka, PO 1082, Jerusalem 91010 **Tel:** 97 1 599 509 510.
Email: bet@iba.org.il
Web site: http://www.iba.org.il
Profile: National radio station covering news and current affairs.
RADIO NETWORK

Television

Arutz 1 Mabat 903148
Owner: Israel Broadcasting Authority
Editorial: 15 Tora Mizion, P.O.Box 7139, Jerusalem 91071 **Tel:** 972 2 5301333.
Email: mabat@iba.org.il
Web site: http://www.iba.org.il
Profile: National television station covering national and international news and current affairs.
TELEVISION STATION

Arutz 10 903145
Owner: Arutz 10
Editorial: 53 Derech Hashalom street, Givatayim 53454 **Tel:** 972 77 6101000.
Email: rikuz@10.tv
Web site: http://www.nana10.co.il
Profile: National television station covering national and international news and current affairs.
TELEVISION STATION

Arutz 2 903143
Owner: Israel Broadcasting Authority
Editorial: 12 Raul Vallenberg Street, P.O.Box 58151, Tel-Aviv 61580 **Tel:** 972 3 7676000.
Email: info@mako.co.il
Web site: http://www.mako.co.il
Profile: National television station covering national and international news and current affairs.
TELEVISION STATION

Israel Plus 583802
Editorial: 6 Meytav Street, Tel Aviv 67898
Tel: 972 3 6232999.
Web site: http://www.israel-plus.tv
Profile: National TV station (9 channel) broadcasting news, films, series and entertainment in Russian language.
TELEVISION STATION

Italy

Radio

Ciao Radio 534581
Owner: Dinamica Sas
Editorial: Via dei Fornaciai, 24, Bologna 40129
Tel: 39 051 4187476.
Email: ciaoradio@ciaoradio.com
Web site: http://www.ciaoradio.it
Profile: Regional radio station covering music and news.
RADIO NETWORK

InBlu 428677
Owner: News Press Spa
Editorial: Piazza Carbonari, 3, Milano 20125
Tel: 39 02 693121.
Email: redazione.mi@blusat2000.it
Web site: http://www.radioinblu.it
Profile: Radio station covering catholic news.
RADIO NETWORK

R101 428674
Owner: Gruppo Finelco SpA
Editorial: Via Ventura, 3, Milano 20134
Tel: 39 02 210831.
Email: centralino.r101@mediaset.it
Web site: http://www.r101.it
Profile: Radio station covering adult contemporary music and news.
FM RADIO STATION

Radio 105 291167
Owner: Gruppo Finelco SpA
Editorial: Largo Donegani, 1, Milano 20121
Tel: 39 02 6596116.
Email: fabrizioratiglia@105.net
Web site: http://www.105.net
Profile: National radio founded in 1976, broadcasting music and entertainment programs for youn adults.
FM RADIO STATION

Radio 24 428679
Owner: Gruppo 24 ORE
Editorial: Via Monte Rosa, 91, Milano 20149
Tel: 39 02 30221.
Email: info@radio24.it
Web site: http://www.radio24.ilsole24ore.com
Profile: National radio station founded in 1999 and owned by 24 Ore group.
FM RADIO STATION

Radio Alex 428680
Owner: Nuova Factory srl
Editorial: Via Marsala, 20, Alessandria 15100
Tel: 39 0131 443593.
Email: redazione@radioalex.it
Web site: http://www.radioalex.it
Profile: Radio station covering regional news and music in the Alessandria region.
RADIO NETWORK

Radio Capital 437159
Owner: Gruppo Ed. L'Espresso SpA
Editorial: Via Cristoforo Colombo, 90, Roma 147
Tel: 39 06 492324117.
Email: segreteria_capital@capital.it
Web site: http://www.capital.it
Profile: Radio station covering news and entertainment including music classic hits and talk shows.
FM RADIO STATION

Radio Cuore 291036
Owner: Radio Cuore di Dessì M.L. & C. Sas
Editorial: Via Carpaccio, 26, Oristano Or 9170
Tel: 39 0783 31 02 21.
Email: redazione@radiocuore.net
Web site: http://www.radiocuore.net
Profile: Regional radio station.
FM RADIO STATION

Radio Deejay 428676
Owner: Gruppo Ed. L'Espresso SpA
Editorial: Via Andrea Massena, 2, Milano 20145
Email: redazione@deejay.it
Web site: http://www.deejay.it
Profile: Radio station covering news, contemporary music and entertainment.
FM RADIO STATION

Radio Italia 291162
Owner: Mediaset / Fininvest SpA
Editorial: Viale Europa, 49, Cologno Monzese Mi 20093 **Tel:** 39 02 254441.
Email: redazione@radioitalia.it
Web site: http://www.radioitalia.it
Profile: National radio station covering news and entertainment including Italian music, concerts and events.
FM RADIO STATION

Radio Kiss Kiss 508606
Editorial: Via Sgambati, 61, Napoli 80131
Tel: 39 081 546 1212.
Email: info@kisskiss.it
Web site: http://www.kisskiss.it
Profile: Radio station covering news and contemporary music.
FM RADIO STATION

Radio Monte Carlo 291164
Owner: Gruppo Finelco SpA
Editorial: Via Principe Amedeo, 2, Milano 20121
Tel: 39 02 231521.
Email: rmc@radiomontecarlo.net
Web site: http://www.radiomontecarlo.net
Profile: Regional radio station.
RADIO NETWORK

RADIO MORABEZA 508593
Editorial: Via dell'Umiltà, 83/C, Roma 187
Tel: 39 06 675911.
Web site: http://www.studiomorabeza.com
RADIO NETWORK

RADIO NAZIONALE BULGARA 508601
Editorial: via dell'Umiltà, 83/C, Roma 187
Tel: 39 06 675911.
Web site: http://www.bulgaria-italia.com
RADIO NETWORK

Radio Popolare 428673
Owner: Radio Popolare Errepi SpA
Editorial: Via Ollearo, 5, Milano 20155
Tel: 39 02 392411.
Email: radiopop@radiopopolare.it
Web site: http://www.radiopopolare.it
Profile: Regional radio station.
RADIO NETWORK

Radio Radicale 291165
Editorial: Via Principe Amedeo, 2, Rome 185
Tel: 39 06 488781.
Email: redazione@radioradicale.it
Web site: http://www.radioradicale.it
Profile: Radio station covering government, politics and parliamentary debates and decisions.
FM RADIO STATION

Rai - Giornale Radio Rai 437155
Owner: RAI - Radiotelevisione Italiana SpA
Editorial: Via Asiago, 10, Roma 195
Tel: 39 06 33172188.
Email: grr@rai.it
Web site: http://www.rai.it
Profile: News program of the RAI network, covering news and current affairs for the main radio stations of the group.
RADIO NETWORK

Rai - Radio 1 - L'Economia in Tasca 508566
Owner: RAI - Radiotelevisione Italiana SpA
Editorial: Viale Mazzini, 14, Rome 195
Tel: 39 06 33172075.
Email: economiaintasca@rai.it
Web site: http://www.radio.rai.it/radio1/economiaintasca
Profile: Radio show covering regional economy, business and finance.
FM RADIO STATION

Rai - Radio 2 - Decanter 578153
Owner: RAI - Radiotelevisione Italiana SpA
Editorial: Via Asiago, 10, Roma 195
Email: decanter@rai.it
Web site: http://www.decanter.rai.it
Profile: Radio show covering food and gastronomy.
FM RADIO STATION

Rai GR Parlamento 727151
Owner: Rai - Radiotelevisione Italiana Spa
Editorial: Viale Mazzini, 14, Roma 195
Tel: 39 06 33174146.
Email: grparlamento@rai.it
Web site: http://www.grparlamento.rai.it
Profile: Government-owned radio station that covers the Italian government and its institutions.
FM RADIO STATION

Rai International 437156
Owner: Radiotelevisione Italiana Spa
Editorial: Viale Mazzini, 14, Roma 195
Tel: 39 06 33172264.
Email: raiinternational@rai.it
Web site: http://www.raitalia.it
Profile: International radio station covering regional, national and international news and current affair including government, politics, economy, business, finance, entertainment and sports.
FM RADIO STATION

Rai IsoRadio 508548
Owner: RAI - Radiotelevisione Italiana SpA
Editorial: L.go Villy de Luca, 4 - Pal. G2 - Saxa Rubra, Roma 188 **Tel:** 39 06 33176609.
Email: isoradio@rai.it
Web site: http://www.isoradio.rai.it
Profile: Radio station covering traffic information including news and entrainment.
FM RADIO STATION

Rai Radio 1 - La Radio ne parla 508560
Owner: RAI - Radiotelevisione Italiana SpA
Editorial: Largo Villy De Luca, 4, Roma 188
Tel: 39 800 055103.
Email: laradioneparla@rai.it
Web site: http://www.laradioneparla.rai.it
Profile: Radio program covering a variety of public and social issues, featuring discussion with listeners who call in.
FM RADIO STATION

Rai Radio 1 - Radio anch'io 508549
Owner: RAI - Radiotelevisione Italiana SpA
Editorial: Largo Villy De Luca, 4, Roma 188
Tel: 39 06 3368 0021.
Email: radioanchio@rai.it
Web site: http://www.radioanchio.rai.it
Profile: Radio program covering in-depth news and current affairs.
FM RADIO STATION

Rai Radio 1 - Zapping 508551
Owner: RAI - Radiotelevisione Italiana SpA
Editorial: Viale Mazzini, 14, Roma 195
Tel: 39 06 33542301.
Email: zapping@rai.it
Web site: http://www.zapping.rai.it
Profile: Radio show covering national and international news and current affairs.
FM RADIO STATION

Rai Radio 3 - Fahrenheit 508554
Owner: Rai - Radiotelevisione Italiana Spa
Editorial: Via Asiago, 10, Roma 195
Tel: 39 06 3701450.
Email: fahre@rai.it
Web site: http://www.fahre.rai.it
Profile: Radio show covering books and literature.
FM RADIO STATION

Rai Radio 3 - Hollywood Party 508555
Owner: RAI - Radiotelevisione Italiana SpA
Editorial: Via Asiago, 10, Roma 195
Tel: 39 06 3226297.
Email: hollywoodparty@rai.it
Web site: http://www.hollywoodparty.rai.it
Profile: Radio show covering film, cinema and celebrities.
FM RADIO STATION

Rai Radio 3 - Prima Pagina 508553
Owner: RAI - Radiotelevisione Italiana SpA
Editorial: Via Asiago, 10, Roma 195
Tel: 39 06 3219932.
Email: primapagina@rai.it
Web site: http://www.primapagina.rai.it
Profile: Radio program covering news and current affairs.
FM RADIO STATION

Rai Radio 3 - Suite 508556
Owner: Rai - Radiotelevisione Italiana Spa
Editorial: Via Asiago, 10, Roma 195
Tel: 39 06 3242841.
Email: radio3-suite@rai.it
Web site: http://www.radio3suite.rai.it
Profile: Radio program covering music, performing arts, dance, concert, classical, culture, art, architecture, poetry, photography, museum and art exhibition.
FM RADIO STATION

RTL 102.5 437158
Owner: RTL 102.5 Hit Radio Srl
Editorial: Via Piemonte, 61, Cologno Monzese 20093
Tel: 39 02 250961.
Email: fulvio.giuliani@rtl.it
Web site: http://www.rtl.it
Profile: National radio station covering news and entertainment.
FM RADIO STATION

RTVA - Canal Sur 508568
Owner: Radio y Televisión de Andalucía
Editorial: via dell'Umiltà, 83/C, Roma 187
Tel: 39 06 675911.
Email: comunicacion@rtva.es
Web site: http://www.canalsur.es
Profile: Regional radio station.
RADIO NETWORK

Virgin Radio 523240
Owner: Gruppo Finelco SpA
Editorial: Largo Donegani, 1, Milano 20121
Tel: 39 02 6596116.
Email: info@virginradio.it
Web site: http://www.virginradio.it
Profile: National radio station covering news and music.
FM RADIO STATION

VOA 508588
Editorial: Via dell'Umiltà, 83/c, Roma 187
Tel: 39 06 675911.
Web site: http://www.voanews.com
Profile: Radio network covering international news and current affairs.
RADIO NETWORK

Television

Rai - London Bureau 627951
Owner: RAI - Radiotelevisione Italiana SpA
Editorial: 4 Millbank, London, England SW1P 3XR
Tel: 44 207 4091683.
Email: raitvlondon@rai.it
Web site: http://www.rai.it
Profile: Foreign bureau of Rai, the public radio and TV network.
TELEVISION NETWORK

Rai - Paris Bureau 311111
Owner: RAI - Radiotelevisione Italiana SpA
Editorial: 15 rue Cognacq-Jay, Paris 75007
Tel: 33 1 56 52 51 50.
Email: raiparis@rai.it
Web site: http://www.rai.it
Profile: Foreign bureau of Rai, the public radio and TV network.
TELEVISION NETWORK

Japan

Radio

ARD German Radio - Tokyo Bureau 537655
Editorial: ARD, Denenchofu 39-2, 3-chome, Ota-ku, Tokyo 145-0071 **Tel:** 81 3 3721-5151.
Email: ard.radio.tokyo@ndr.de
Profile: Acts as a bureau for a German public broadcast station.
RADIO NETWORK

Nippon Broadcasting System 468063
Editorial: Nippon Broadcasting System, 1-9-3 Yuraku-cho, Tokyo 100-8439 **Tel:** 81 332 871111.
Web site: http://www.1242.com
Profile: Nippon Broadcasting System is a portal site which writes about the radio program and events information on Nippon Broadcasting System.
RADIO NETWORK

Radio Nikkei 467727
Owner: Nikkei Radio Broadcasting Corporation
Editorial: Nikkei Radio Broadcasting Corporation, 1-9-15, Akasaka Minato-ku, Tokyo 107-8373
Tel: 81 335838151.
Email: hensei@radionikkei.jp
Web site: http://www.radionikkei.jp
Profile: Broadcasts a variety of programs such as music, songs, economics, gamble, and medical.
AM RADIO STATION

Tokyo FM Broadcasting (FM Tokyo/TFM) 467728
Owner: TOKYO FM Broadcasting Co., Ltd.
Editorial: TOKYO FM Broadcasting Co., Ltd. 1-7, Kojimachi, Chiyoda-ku, Tokyo 102-8080
Tel: 81 332210080.
Email: webmaster@tfm.co.jp
Web site: http://www.tfm.co.jp
Profile: FM Tokyo is one of radio stations in Japan which supports the development of events such as digital, Internet, mobile and broadband.
AM RADIO STATION

Television

Asahi Broadcasting Corporation (ABC) 493633
Editorial: Asahi Broadcasting Corporation, 1-1-30 Fukushima, Fukushima-ku, Osaka 553-8503
Tel: 81 664 585321.
Web site: http://asahi.co.jp/
Profile: Asahi Broadcasting Corporation (ABC) is a major broadcaster in Japan, airing entertainment, sports and news programs. Subsidiary TV Asahi Music publishes music as a tie-in to the company's programming.
TELEVISION NETWORK

CBS News 468134
Editorial: CBS Interactive Inc., 3-29-1 KandaJinbo-cho, Tokyo 101-0051 **Tel:** 81 335 871861.
Web site: http://www.cbsnews.com
Profile: CBS News provides breaking world news and commentary in the U.S. and around the world.
TELEVISION NETWORK

Fuji Television Network(CX) 468184
Editorial: Fuji Television Network, 2-4-8, Daiba, Minato-ku, Tokyo 137-8088 **Tel:** 81 355 008888.
Web site: http://www.fujitv.co.jp
Profile: Fuji News Network(FNN) is Japan's most powerful news-gathering organization, with offices at each of the 28 affiliated stations of the Fuji Network System(FNS) throughout Japan.
TELEVISION NETWORK

Nippon Hoso Kyokai/NHK 468186
Owner: Japan Broadcasting Corporation
Editorial: 2-2-1, Jinnan, Shibuya-ku, Tokyo 150-8001
Tel: 81 334 651111.
Web site: http://www.nhk.or.jp
Profile: Serves as Japan's only public broadcaster, funded by fees received from TV viewers. Delivers a wide range of impartial, high-quality programs, both at home and abroad.
TELEVISION NETWORK

Nippon Television Network Corporation 316290
Editorial: Nippon Television Network Corporation, 1-6-1 Higashishinbashi, Minato-ku, Tokyo 105-7444
Tel: 81 362 151111.
Web site: http://www.ntv.co.jp
Profile: Nippon Television Network Corporation is one of major television network in Japan. It has a viewer rating of 8.
TELEVISION NETWORK

R-TV Asia 468135
Editorial: Thomson Reuters, 30/F Akasaka Biz Tower, 5-3-1, Akasaka, Minato-ku, Tokyo 107-6330
Tel: 81 364 411200.
Web site: http://www.thomsonreuters.com
Profile: Thomson Reuters is the world's leading source of intelligent information for businesses and professionals. Thomson Reuters combine industry expertise with innovative technology to deliver critical information to leading decision makers in the financial, legal, tax and accounting, healthcare, science and media markets, powered by the world's most trusted news organization.
TELEVISION NETWORK

Television Asahi 468183
Editorial: Television Asahi, 6-9-1, Roppongi, Minato-ku, Tokyo 106-8001 **Tel:** 81 364 061111.
Email: webmaster@tv-asahi.co.jp
Web site: http://www.tv-asahi.co.jp
Profile: Television Asahi is a major television network in Japan.
TELEVISION NETWORK

Tokyo Hoso 468182
Editorial: Tokyo Broadcasting System, Inc. 5-3-6, Akasaka, Minato-ku, Tokyo 107-8006
Tel: 81 337 461111.
Email: houtoku@best.tbs.co.jp
Web site: http://www.tbs.co.jp
Profile: (TBS) is one of the major commercial terrestrial networks in Japan and the only one which provides both television and radio broadcasting services.
TELEVISION NETWORK

TV Tokyo - New York Bureau 504048
Editorial: 1325 Avenue of the Americas Ste 2402, New York, New York 10019-6055 **Tel:** 1 212 261-6430.
Web site: http://www.tv-tokyo.co.jp/corporation/
Profile: New York bureau of TV Tokyo.
TELEVISION NETWORK

TV Tokyo(TX) 468185
Editorial: 4-3-12, Toranomon, Minato-ku, Tokyo 105-8012 **Tel:** 81 334 321212.
Web site: http://www.tv-tokyo.co.jp
Profile: Provides a steady stream of sound, reliable programs covering a variety of topics.
TELEVISION NETWORK

Kazakhstan

Radio

Kazakhskoye Radio 530304
Owner: RTRK Kazakhstan
Editorial: ul. Zheltoksan 177, Almaty 50013
Tel: 7 727 26 11 999.
Email: radio@kazakstan.kz
Web site: http://kazakstan.kz/rus/radio
Profile: National radio station with socio-political end entertainment programmes.
RADIO NETWORK

Television

Kazakhstan 530305
Owner: RTRK Kazakhstan
Editorial: ul. Zheltoksan 175, Almaty 50013
Tel: 7 727 27 21 336.
Email: kaztv@kazakstan.kz
Web site: http://kazakstan.kz/rus/tv

Kazakhstan

Profile: National TV station with informative and entertaining programmes, series and films.
TELEVISION STATION

TV 31 Kanal
492830
Owner: Mediaholding 31 Kanal
Editorial: Ulica Tazhibayevoy 155, Almaty 50060
Tel: 7 727 25 05 601.
Email: 31@31.kz
Web site: http://www.31.kz
Profile: National informative-analytical and entertaining TV station.
TELEVISION STATION

Kenya

Television

CNBC Africa - Kenya Bureau
514059
Owner: CNBC Africa
Editorial: 19th Floor, Ambank House, University Way, Nairobi **Tel:** 254 20 225 2150.
Web site: http://www.cnbcafrica.com
Profile: Breaking news, multimedia, videos, reviews and opinion on African business, finance, private equity, real estate, infrastructure and more.
TELEVISION STATION

KBC - Kenya Broadcasting Corporation
323882
Editorial: Harry Thuku Road, Nairobi 100
Tel: 254 20 2223757.
Email: md@kbc.co.ke
Web site: http://www.kbc.co.ke
Profile: Kenya Broadcasting Corporation (KBC) is the state-run media organisation of Kenya. It broadcasts in English and Swahili, as well as in most local languages of Kenya. The corporation started its life in 1928 when Kenya was a British colony. In 1964, when Kenya became an independent country, the corporation's name was changed to Voice of Kenya. In 1989, the Kenyan parliament reverted the corporation's name from Voice of Kenya to Kenya Broadcasting Corporation. Kenya Broadcasting Corporation offers the following radio and television services: Public Service Radios National Kiswahili Service(Radio Taifa) National English Service Regional Eastern Service transmitting in Somali, Borana, Rendile, Burji and Turkana Regional Central Service transmitting in Meru, Embu and Kamba Regional Western Service transmitting in Kuria, Teso, Luhya, Suba and Pokot Commercial Radio Music and Entertainment, Venus FM transmitting to major urban areas of Nairobi, Mombasa, Nakuru, Nyeri, Eldoret and Kisumu. Coro FM transmitting to Nairobi and Mount Kenya Region on 102.3 and 99.5 MGHZ Pwani FM transmitting to coast region on 103.1 MGHZ Nosim FM transmitting to Narok and its environs on 90.5 MGHZ Minto FM transmitting to Kisii and its environs on 101.7 MGHZ Kitwek FM transmitting to Eldoret on 92.9 MGHZ and other areas on 98.0 MGHZ Mayienga FM transmitting to Kisumu and its environs on 93.5 MGHZ Television Services Free to air KBC channel 1
TELEVISION STATION

Kuwait

Radio

Kuwait FM
381068
Owner: Ministry of Information, Kuwait
Editorial: PO Box 193, Safat 13002
Tel: 965 2241 8730.
Email: arabicfm@radio.gov.kw
Web site: http://www.media.gov.kw
Profile: Kuwait FM is a state-owned radio station broadcasting modern Arabic songs 24-hours a day. It launched in 1995 and transmits on 103.7 FM.
FM RADIO STATION

Radio Kuwait - Classical Arabic Music Station
554817
Owner: Ministry of Information, Kuwait
Editorial: PO Box 193, Safat 13002
Tel: 965 2232 6268.
Email: ramilovera@gmail.com
Web site: http://www.media.gov.kw
Profile: Radio Kuwait's Classical Arabic Music Station plays local, Gulf and classical Arabic songs for 24-hrs a day, in addition to live broadcast of youth-orientated programmes. This station launched in July 1993 and broadcasts on 87.9 FM.
FM RADIO STATION

Radio Kuwait - Main Arabic Programme
554200
Owner: Ministry of Information, Kuwait
Editorial: PO Box 193, Safat 13002
Tel: 965 2245 1288.
Email: s_r_1955@yahoo.com
Web site: http://www.media.gov.kw
Profile: Radio Kuwait's Main Arabic Programme is a state-owned radio station broadcasting drama, news, entertainment, literary, scientific, family and children's programmes 24-hrs a day, in addition to programmes developed in cooperation with authorities and

ministries in the country. The station launched in 1951 and broadcasts on 89.5 FM.
FM RADIO STATION

Radio Kuwait - Second Arabic Programme
554201
Owner: Ministry of Information, Kuwait
Editorial: PO Box 193, Safat 13002
Tel: 965 2244 2684.
Email: a13aa@hotmail.com
Web site: http://www.media.gov.kw
Profile: Radio Kuwait's Second Arabic Programme is a state-owned radio station broadcasting programmes of local character, in addition to songs, musical and guidance programmes. The station launched in 1964 and broadcasts for 15 hours per day, from 07:00 to 00:00, on 97.5 FM. Programmes are designed to be relevant to issues of concern to society, and include prominent activities and services undertaken by institutions and authorities, with particular focus on serving local heritage and folklore.
FM RADIO STATION

Kyrgyzstan

Radio

AvtoRadio Bishkek
291180
Editorial: ul. Ahunbaeva 119 A, Bishkek 720055
Tel: 996 312 901009.
Email: autoradio@infotel.kg
Web site: http://www.avtoradio.ru
Profile: National radio station with music and news. Broadcasts 60% of music in Russian language and 40% international.
FM RADIO STATION

Hit FM Kyrgyzstan
291179
Editorial: Prospekt Chui 36 (13th floor), Bishkek 720065 **Tel:** 996 312 68 10 56.
Email: news@hitfm.kg
Web site: http://hitfm.kg
Profile: National radio station with news and pop music.
RADIO NETWORK

Television

KTRK
492813
Editorial: Pr. Molodaya Gvardia 58, Bishkek 720040
Tel: 996 312 392 238.
Email: alatoo@ntrk.kg
Web site: http://www.ktrk.kg
Profile: National state TV station with news, documentaries, films and entertainment.
TELEVISION STATION

Laos

Radio

Lao National Radio
467718
Editorial: Lao National Radio, Ban Srisakate Village, Phynam Road, P.O. Box 310, Vientiane
Tel: 856 21 243250.
Email: laonradio@lnr.org.la
Web site: http://www.lnr.org.la
Profile: Covers news and other topics for Laos.
AM RADIO STATION

Television

Lao National Television
468359
Tel: 856 21 710067.
Email: laotv1@gmail.com
Web site: http://www.tnl.gov.la
Profile: Covers of news and general interests.
Address: Lao National Television, P.O. Box 5635 Sivilay Village, Saythany District Vientiane, Laos
TELEVISION STATION

Latvia

Television

TV3 Latvia
316452
Editorial: Dzelzavas iela 120G, Riga LV–1021
Tel: 371 67479100.
Email: pasts@skaties.lv
Web site: http://skaties.lv/tv3
Profile: National TV station broadcasting via Viaset 3 satellite and received throughout Latvia.
TELEVISION STATION

TV5 Riga
316451
Editorial: Dzelzavas iela 120G, Riga 1021
Tel: 371 6 7479100.
Email: info@tv5.lv
Web site: http://tv5.skaties.lv

Profile: National TV station focusing on news and reality shows, also broadcasting films and TV series in Russian language.
TELEVISION STATION

Lesotho

Radio

Radio Lesotho
291001
Editorial: PO Box 552, Maseru 100, Maseru
Tel: 266 22 32 33 71.
Web site: http://www.radiolesotho.co.ls
Profile: Talk shows based on Current Affairs, Information and educational programmes relating to agriculture, health, women's issues, law, culture and magazine programmes with music, news and sports.
RADIO NETWORK

Libya

Radio

Al Aan FM
824479
Owner: Tower Media Middle East FZLLC
Editorial: PO Box 500765, Building 1, Dubai
Tel: 971 4 427 7880.
Email: samer.hamza@alaan.tv
Web site: http://www.alaan.fm
Profile: Al Aan FM is a radio station broadcasting news, music and entertainment programmes. It launched in 2011 and broadcasts on 105.3 FM in Libya and 96.6, 96.9, 96.3 and 97.6 FM in Syria.
FM RADIO STATION

LibyanaHits FM
873542
Editorial: Alnafaq Street, Alhadaeq, Benghazi
Tel: 218 91 830 0100.
Email: info@libyanahits.fm
Web site: http://www.libyanahits.fm
Profile: LibyanaHits FM is a radio station broadcasting music and entertainment. The station launchedin 2011 and broadcasts to Benghazi and the surrounding area on 100.1 FM.
FM RADIO STATION

Tripoli FM 102.5
842965
Owner: Araam Ltd
Editorial: Tojara' Area, Tripoli **Tel:** 218 21 729 7779.
Email: info@tripolifm.ly
Web site: http://www.tripolifm.ly
Profile: Tripoli FM 102.5 is an entertainment radio station broadcasting English music, as well as entertainment, culture and society programmes. The station launched in 2011 and broadcasts on 102.5 FM.
FM RADIO STATION

Liechtenstein

Radio

Radio Liechtenstein
529311
Owner: Radio Liechtenstein
Editorial: Dorfstr. 24, Triesen 9495 **Tel:** 423 399 1313.
Email: redaktion@radio.li
Web site: http://www.radio.li
Profile: Radiosender für Liechtenstein mit Nachrichten, Musik und regionalen Informationen. Radio station for Liechtenstein with news, music and regional information.
RADIO NETWORK

Lithuania

Radio

Lietuvos Radijas
290929
Editorial: S. Konarskio 49, Vilnius LT-03123
Tel: 370 5 23 63 000.
Email: lrzinios@lrt.lt
Web site: http://www.lrt.lt
Profile: Public non profit making radio station, broadcasting across the whole of Lithuania. Offers a variety of informative and musical programmes.
RADIO NETWORK

Ziniu radijas
289326
Editorial: A. Smetonos g. 6, Vilnius 1115
Tel: 370 5 24 31 430.
Email: bluras@ziniuradijas.lt
Web site: http://www.ziniuradijas.lt
Profile: National radio station covering political, economical, cultural and sport news.
RADIO NETWORK

Television

BTV
316460
Editorial: seskins g. 20, Vilnius LT-07156
Tel: 370 5 2431058.
Web site: http://btv.alfa.lt
Profile: National TV station broadcasting form Vilnius and covering 80% of Lithuania.
TELEVISION STATION

Lietuvos Televizija
316450
Editorial: S. Konarskio 49, Vilnius LT- 03123
Tel: 370 5 23 63 209.
Email: lrt@lrt.lt
Web site: http://www.lrt.lt
Profile: State owned national television station, providing a variety of informative and general programmes.
TELEVISION STATION

Macedonia

Radio

Kanal 77
458724
Editorial: Josif Kovacev 18, Stip 2000
Tel: 389 32 39 77 07.
Email: kanal77@kanal77.com.mk
Web site: http://www.kanal77.com.mk
Profile: National radio station focussing on news and current affairs, music and fun.
RADIO NETWORK

Malaysia

Television

RTM 1
468372
Editorial: RTM, Dept. Of Broadcasting, Angkasapuri, Kuala Lumpur 50614 **Tel:** 603 2282 5333.
Web site: http://www.rtm.gov.my
Profile: Family programming, educational programs in Malay and English.
TELEVISION STATION

RTM 2
468373
Editorial: RTM, Dept. Of Broadcasting, Angkasapuri, Kuala Lumpur 50614 **Tel:** 60 322887355.
Web site: http://www.rtm.gov.my
Profile: Government run Malaysian TV station.
TELEVISION STATION

Maldives

Television

Television Maldives
362735
Editorial: Buruzu magu, Male 20-24
Tel: 960 332 31 05.
Email: info@tvm.gov.mv
Web site: http://www.tvm.gov.mv
Profile: National TV station focussing on news, current affairs, entertainment and sport.
TELEVISION STATION

Malta

Radio

Radju Malta
291040
Owner: Public Service Broadcaster
Editorial: 75 St. Luke's Road, G'mangia MSD 09
Tel: 356 21 225051.
Email: info@tvm.com.mt
Web site: http://tvm.com.mt
Profile: Radju Malta is the radio station of PBS Ltd, the public service broadcaster of Malta.
RADIO NETWORK

Television

TVM - Television Malta
316328
Owner: Public Broadcasting Services
Editorial: 75 St. Luke's Road, G'mangia PTA 1022
Tel: 356 22 91 3100.
Email: info@pbs.com.mt
Web site: http://www.tvm.com.mt
Profile: National television station of Malta operated by Public Broadcasting Services and covering general news and current affairs including sports, economics, entertainment, magazines and teleshopping.
TELEVISION STATION

Section 3 World Broadcast

Marshall Islands

Radio

V7AB Radio Marshalls 668762
Owner: RMI Government
Email: gazette@ntamar.net
RADIO NETWORK

Mexico

Radio

Radio Educacion 593526
Editorial: Angel Urraza No. 622 Col. del Valle., Mexico City, Distrito Federal 3100 **Tel:** 52 55 41551050.
Email: contacto@radioeducacion.edu.mx
Web site: http://www.radioeducacion.edu.mx
Profile: Radio Educacion is a decentralized body of the Ministry of Education, coordinated by the National Council for Culture and the Arts, whose substantive work is to promote and disseminate expressions educational, cultural and artistic Mexico through the radio.
RADIO NETWORK

Radio Fórmula 571250
Editorial: Privada de Horacio 10, Col. Chapultepec, Mexico City, Distrito Federal 11560
Tel: 52 55 52792200.
Email: formula_noticias@hotmail.com
Web site: http://radioformula.com.mx
RADIO NETWORK

RTV - Radio 732135
Editorial: Cerro de la Galaxia s/n Col. Unidad del Bosqu, Xalapa, Veracruz **Tel:** 52 228 8423500.
Web site: http://rtv.org.mx
RADIO NETWORK

XEITE-AM 844347
Owner: Grupo Radio Capital
Editorial: Montes Urales No. 425, 2 Piso, Lomas De Chapultepec, Mexico City, Distrito Federal C.P. 06600 **Tel:** 52 55 30993000.
Web site: http://gruporadiocapital.mx/xeite
Profile: Audience: 2,294,740
AM RADIO STATION

Television

Azteca Deportes 844551
Editorial: Periferico Sur 4121, Col. Fuentes del Pedregal, Mexico City, Distrito Federal CP 14141
Tel: 52 55 1720-1313.
Web site: http://www.aztecadeportes.com
Profile: Azteca deportes is a division of Azteca America, which broadcasts sports events from the Azteca America television network. Its headquarters are in Mexico City, Distrito Federal.
TELEVISION NETWORK

Enlace 733897
Editorial: Av. San Jeronimo #137 Col. San Angel, Del Alvaro Obregon, Mexico City, Distrito Federal 1000
Tel: 52 55 55507222.
Web site: http://www.enlacemexicotv.com
Profile: Broadcasts Christian programming, musical shows, and educational programs. Transmits live and interview shows.
TELEVISION NETWORK

Ritmoson Latino 827396
Editorial: Av. Chapultepec #18, Col. Doctores, Col. Cuauhtemoc, Distrito Federal 6724 **Tel:** 52 55 5224-5657.
Email: ritmosonlatino@ritmosonlatino.com
Web site: http://ritmoson.tv
Profile: The network features Latin music, artists and news in the music industry.
TELEVISION NETWORK

RTV - Radio Televisión de Veracruz 732137
Editorial: Cerro de la Galaxia s/n Col. Unidad del Bosqu, Xalapa, Veracruz **Tel:** 52 228 8423500.
Web site: http://rtv.org.mx
Profile: Programación de radio y TV, Noticias de Veracruz, México y el mundo, radio y televisión por Internet.
TELEVISION NETWORK

Televisa 594259
Editorial: Av. Chapultepec #18, Col. Doctores, Col. Cuauhtemoc, Distrito Federal 6724
Tel: 52 55 52245000.
Email: mesadeinformacion@televisa.com.mx
Web site: http://noticieros.televisa.com/us
Profile: Televisa is the largest media company in the Spanish-speaking world and a major participant in the international entertainment business. It has interests in television production and broadcasting, production of pay-television networks, international distribution of television programming, direct-to-home satellite services, cable television and telecommunication services, magazine publishing and distribution, radio production and broadcasting,

professional sports and live entertainment, feature-film production and distribution, the operation of an internet portal, and gaming.
TELEVISION NETWORK

TV Azteca 612180
Editorial: Periferico Sur 4121, Col Fuentes del Pedregal, Delegacion Tlalpan, Mexico City, Distrito Federal 14141 **Tel:** 52 55 17201313.
Email: aztecanoticias@tvazteca.com.mx
Web site: http://www.azteca.com
Profile: TV Azteca es la cadena de noticias y entretenimiento de México.
TELEVISION NETWORK

XHIJ-TV 238267
Owner: Arnoldo Cabada De La O
Editorial: Blvd. Manuel Gomez Morin 8388, Senecu, 32470 Las Colonias, Ciudad Juarez, Chihuahua
Tel: 52 656 648-3743.
Email: vmares@canal44.com
Web site: http://www.canal44.com
Profile: XHIJ-TV conocido como Canal 44, es una filial en español de Cadenatres que sirven el área metropolitana de Ciudad Juárez-El Paso-Las Cruces. La estación tiene licencia para Ciudad Juárez y difunde localmente en el canal 44. La estación ofrece la programación hispana. XHIJ-TV known as Canal 44, is a Spanish-language affiliate of cadenatres serving the Ciudad Juárez-El Paso-Las Cruces metropolitan area. The station is licensed to Ciudád Juarez and broadcasts locally on channel 44. The station provides Hispanic programming.
TELEVISION STATION

Cable

Cablemas 440531
Editorial: Sevilla No 4, Juarez, Distrito Federal, Mexico City, Distrito Federal 6600
Tel: 52 55 52076606.
Email: phernandezc@cablemas.com.mx
Web site: http://www.cablemas.com
CABLE NETWORK

Cablevisión 440532
Editorial: Av. Chapultepec No. 28-2 Piso, Doctores, Queretaro, Queretaro, Queretaro 6724
Tel: 52 55 57093333.
Email: servicio.clientes@cablevision.net.mx
Web site: http://www.esmas.com/cablevision/
CABLE NETWORK

Canal 22 611911
Owner: Television Metropolitana S.A. de C.V.
Editorial: Atletas N.2, Edificio Pedro Infante, Colonia COuntry CLub, Delegacion Coyoacan, Mexico City, Distrito Federal 4220 **Tel:** 52 55 5544-9022.
Email: internacional@canal22.org.mx
Web site: http://www.canal22.org.mx
CABLE NETWORK

Canal Once 610976
Owner: Instituto Politecnico Nacional
Editorial: Prolongacion Carpio 475 Col. Casco de Sto. Tomas, Mexico City, Distrito Federal 11340
Tel: 52 55 53561111.
Email: info@canalonce.ipn.mx
Web site: http://www.canalonce.mx/
CABLE NETWORK

Grupo Megacable 440534
Editorial: Lazaro Cardenas No. 1694, Del Fresno, Guadalajara, Jalisco C.P. 44140 **Tel:** 52 33 9690-0000.
Web site: http://www.megacable.com.mx
CABLE NETWORK

Multimedios Televisión 735586
Owner: Grupo Multimedios
Editorial: Tennyson No. 80, Col Polanco, Mexico City, Distrito Federal 11570 **Tel:** 52 55 51404900.
Web site: http://www.multimedios.tv
CABLE NETWORK

Mvs Tv Networks 440535
Editorial: Blvd.puerto Aereo No. 486, Moctezuma 2a. Seccion, Distrito Federal, Mexico City, Distrito Federal 15530 **Tel:** 52 55 57648262.
Email: orivas@mvs.com
Web site: http://www.mvs.com.mx
CABLE NETWORK

PCTV 440536
Editorial: Calzada del Hueso 10, Coyoacan, Mexico City, Distrito Federal 4850 **Tel:** 52 55 3098-2300.
Email: webmaster@pctv.mx
Web site: http://www.pctv.com.mx
CABLE NETWORK

Sony Pictures Televisión 440537
Editorial: Prolg. Pase De La Reforma No. 600 P.h., Santa Fe Pena Blanca, Distrito Federal, Mexico City, Distrito Federal 1210 **Tel:** 52 55 52582799.
Email: mariana_mendoza@spe.sony.com
CABLE NETWORK

Television Mexiquense 734716
Owner: Estado de Mexico
Editorial: Av. Estado de Mexico Oriente No.1701, Colonia Llano Grande, Mexico City, Distrito Federal C.P. 52148 **Tel:** 52 722 275-4792.
Web site: http://www.radioytvmexiquense.mx

Profile: Founded in 1984.
CABLE NETWORK

Warner Channel 440539
Editorial: Homero No. 203, 1 Piso, Ofc. 3, Chapultepec Morales, Distrito Federal, Mexico City, Distrito Federal 11560 **Tel:** 52 55 52552080.
CABLE NETWORK

Micronesia

Radio

V6AI Radio Yap 668759
Owner: FSM Telecommunications Corporation
Tel: 691 350 2174.
Email: petergar@mail.fm
FM RADIO STATION

V6AJ Radio Kosrae 668757
Owner: FSM Telecommunications Corporation
Tel: 691 370 3040.
Email: kosraebroadcast@yahoo.com
Web site: http://telecom.fm
FM RADIO STATION

V6AK Radio Chuuk 668756
Owner: FSM Telecommunications Corporation
Tel: 691 330 2596.
Profile: V6AK radio broadcasts daily from 6 am to 12 am.
RADIO NETWORK

Voice of Pohnpei V6AH 668758
Owner: FSM Telecommunications Corporation
Tel: 691 320 2296.
Profile: Provides news, views and interviews of special interest to all Pohnpei residents.
FM RADIO STATION

Monaco

Radio

RADIO ETHIC (WEB RADIO) 690513
Editorial: 5 avenue Princesse-Alice, Monaco 98000
Tel: 377 9 33 07 48 2.
Email: info@radioethic.com
Web site: http://www.radioethic.com
Profile: Local Translation: Webradio dédiée au développement durable et aux valeurs humaines. Rubriques : Vert'Ethic, Solidar'Ethic, Eco'Ethic, Vie'Ethic, News'Ethic. A noter également des retransmissions de conférences sur ces sujets, ainsi que des interviews de personnalités dans la rubrique 'L'Invité'.
RADIO NETWORK

Riviera Radio 290203
Owner: RIVIERA RADIO MONACO 106.3
Editorial: 10-12 quai Antoine-1er, Monaco 98000
Tel: 377 979 794 75.
Email: info@rivieraradio.mc
Web site: http://www.rivieraradio.mc
Profile: Regional radio station focussing on general interest, international and regional news (BBC) and music. Broadcasted in English.
FM RADIO STATION

Television

TMC 317061
Owner: GROUPE AB
Editorial: 6 bis quai Antoine-1er, Monaco 98000
Tel: 377 9 31 51 41 5.
Web site: http://www.tmc.tv
Profile: TV cable/satellite channel focussing on general interest including movies, entertainment, TV series, sport, magazines, reviews and documentaries. Local Translation: Diffusée par câble, satellite et en hertzien (PACA), ADSL, et sur le réseau TNT (canal 10), sa programmation est celle d'une chaîne généraliste familiale. Films grand public, séries inédites, sports, émissions, reportages et documentaires pour tous les publics.
TELEVISION STATION

Montenegro

Radio

Antena M 472235
Editorial: Djoka Mirasevia 59, Podgorica 81 000
Tel: 382 20 66 42 84.
Email: redakcija@antenam.net
Web site: http://antenam.net
Profile: Broadcasts news, cultural programmes and music.
RADIO NETWORK

Radio Corona 439222
Editorial: Jovana Tomasevica Street, G-9, Bar
Tel: 382 85 31 77 17.
Email: mcorona@cg.yu
Web site: http://www.corona-radio.com
Profile: Radio Station broadcasting music and news throughout Montenegro and in southern parts of Europe.
RADIO NETWORK

Radio Kotor 469221
Editorial: Stari grad (zgrada SO), Kotor 85330
Email: radio.kotor@cg.yu
Web site: http://radiokotor.info.mn
Profile: Regional radio station from Kotor town.
FM RADIO STATION

Television

Pink M 519969
Owner: Pink Media Group
Editorial: Bulevar Ivana Crnojevia br.97, Podgorica 81000 **Tel:** 382 81 40 35 11.
Email: redakcija@pinkm.cg.yu
Web site: http://www.pinkm.com
Profile: Pink M is a part of Pink Media Group based in Beograd and covers the whole territory of Republic of Montenegro, broadcasting news, entertainment programmes and music.
TELEVISION STATION

TV Budva 469239
Editorial: Stari grad, Budva 85310 **Tel:** 382 33 454-894.
Email: tv@rtvbudva.me
Web site: http://www.rtvbudva.me
Profile: Broadcasts regional political and cultural news, documentaries and entertainment programmes.
TELEVISION STATION

Montserrat

Radio

ZJB Radio Montserrat 290924
Tel: 664 4912885.
Email: zjb@gov.ms
Web site: http://www.zjb.gov.ms
Profile: Transmits news related to Montserrat, the Caribbean, and the world. The ZJB radio also provides entertainment through contest and chat shows.
RADIO NETWORK

Television

PTV 316456
Tel: 664 4915110.
Email: deedge@candw.ms
Profile: Local television station providing information about daily news and entertainment.
TELEVISION NETWORK

Morocco

Radio

Chaîne Inter 774878
Owner: Société Nationale de Radiodiffusion et de Télévision
Editorial: PO Box 1042, 1, rue El Brihi, Rabat 10000
Tel: 212 537 685100.
Email: lemediateur@snrt.ma
Web site: http://www.chaineinter.ma
Profile: Chaîne Inter is the international radio station of state-owned public broadcaster Société Nationale de Radiodiffusion et de Télévision (SNRT). The station broadcasts music and news, as well as politics, business, family, society and entertainment programmes in French, Spanish and English. It launched in March 2009 and broadcasts on various FM frequencies across the country including 90.0 FM (Casablanca), 87.9 FM (Rabat), 94.2 FM (Agadir) and 91.8 FM (Tanger).
FM RADIO STATION

Al Idaa Al Amazighia 774567
Owner: Société Nationale de Radiodiffusion et de Télévision
Editorial: PO Box 1042, 1, rue El Brihi, Rabat 10000
Tel: 212 537 685100.
Email: tamazight@snrt.ma
Web site: http://www.alidaa-alamazighia.ma
Profile: Al Idaa Al Amazighia is a Berber radio station broadcasting news, music, culture and entertainment programmes. It was launched by state-owned public broadcaster Société Nationale de Radiodiffusion et de Télévision in 1938 and broadcasts on 95.3 FM (Casablanca), 104.6 FM (Rabat), 97.5 FM (Agadir), 98.3 FM (Afroud), 94.5 FM (Al Rachidia) and 101.9 FM (Meknes and Fes).
FM RADIO STATION

Morocco

Al Idaa Al Watania 668465
Owner: Société Nationale de Radiodiffusion et de Télévision
Editorial: PO Box 1042, 1 rue El Brihi, Rabat 10000
Tel: 212 537 685100.
Email: secdirad@yahoo.fr
Web site: http://www.alidaa-alwatania.ma
Profile: Al Idaa Al Watania is a state-owned, national radio station broadcasting entertainment programmes and music. Formerly called Al Maghribia Radio, it was launched in 1928 and broadcasts on various FM frequencies across Morocco.
FM RADIO STATION

Radio Agadir 472226
Owner: Société Nationale de Radiodiffusion et de Télévision
Editorial: Avenue Hassan II, Agadir 80000
Tel: 212 528 840305.
Email: anaghmas@yahoo.fr
Web site: http://www.snrt.ma
Profile: Radio Agadir is a state-owned, regional radio station broadcasting music and news bulletins. The station launched in 1972 and broadcasts in Arabic and the regional Amazigh language on 87.9 FM in the Agadir area of Morocco.
FM RADIO STATION

Radio Casablanca 472225
Owner: Société Nationale de Radiodiffusion et de Télévision
Editorial: Hay al Ousra, Negala Street, Ain Chock, Casablanca **Tel:** 212 522 522632.
Email: radregcas@yahoo.fr
Web site: http://www.snrt.ma
Profile: Radio Casablanca is a state-owned, regional radio station broadcasting music and news bulletins. It launched in 1928 and broadcasts on 98.6 FM in the Casablanca area of Morocco.
FM RADIO STATION

Radio Dakhla 472224
Owner: Société Nationale de Radiodiffusion et de Télévision
Editorial: PO Box 37, 21, Avenue Imlili, Dakhla
Tel: 212 528 897341.
Email: rtmdak2006@yahoo.fr
Web site: http://www.radiolaayoune.ma/Radiodakhla/
Profile: Radio Dakhla is a state-owned, regional radio station broadcasting music and news bulletins in Arabic and the regional Hassani language. It launched in 1980 and broadcasts on 91.8 FM in the Dakhla area of Morocco.
FM RADIO STATION

Radio Fes 472223
Owner: Société Nationale de Radiodiffusion et de Télévision
Editorial: Boulevard Moulay Ahmed Loukili, Fes
Tel: 212 535 623050.
Email: essafi2@yahoo.fr
Web site: http://www.radiofes.ma
Profile: Radio Fes is a state-owned, regional radio station broadcasting music and news bulletins in Arabic and the regional Amazigh language. It launched in 1961 and transmits on 98.4 FM in the Fes area of Morocco.
FM RADIO STATION

Radio Laâyoune 472222
Owner: Société Nationale de Radiodiffusion et de Télévision
Editorial: PO Box 459, Laayoune 70000
Tel: 212 528 893363.
Email: zazamed2@yahoo.fr
Web site: http://www.radiolaayoune.ma
Profile: Radio Laâyoune is a state-owned, regional radio station broadcasting music and news bulletins. It launched in 1976 and broadcasts on 91.1 FM in the Laâyoune area of Morocco.
FM RADIO STATION

Radio Marrakech 472221
Owner: Société Nationale de Radiodiffusion et de Télévision
Editorial: 40 rue de Yougoslavie, Marrakech
Tel: 212 524 447945.
Email: snrtmarrakech@yahoo.fr
Web site: http://www.radio-marrakech.net
Profile: Radio Marrakech is a state-owned, regional radio station broadcasting music and news bulletins in the Marrakech area of Morocco. The station launched in 1968 and broadcasts on 91.7 FM.
FM RADIO STATION

Radio Meknes 472220
Owner: Société Nationale de Radiodiffusion et de Télévision
Editorial: Rue Okba Ibn Nafie, Place Al Andalouss (Ahouaz Meknes), Meknes **Tel:** 212 535 527203.
Email: snrtmeknes@gmail.com
Web site: http://www.snrt.ma
Profile: Radio Meknes is a state-owned, regional radio station broadcasting music and news bulletins. It launched in 2007 and broadcasts on 92.5 FM in the Meknes area of Morocco.
FM RADIO STATION

Radio Mohammed VI du Saint Coran 668503
Owner: Société Nationale de Radiodiffusion et de Télévision
Editorial: PO Box 1042, 1, rue El Brihi, Rabat 10000
Tel: 212 537 685100.
Email: secdirad@yahoo.fr
Web site: http://www.idaatmohammedassadiss.ma
Profile: Radio Mohammed VI du Saint Coran is a radio station broadcasting religious programmes and discussions about Islam and the Holy Quran. It launched in 2004 and broadcasts on 94.2 FM (Rabat and Laayoune), 98.6 FM (Casablanca), 91.7 FM (Marrakech) and 96.1 FM (Oujda).
FM RADIO STATION

Radio Oujda 472219
Owner: Société Nationale de Radiodiffusion et de Télévision
Editorial: Avenue Omar Errifi, Oujda
Tel: 212 536 682317.
Email: hafid63@hotmail.fr
Web site: http://www.snrt.ma
Profile: Radio Oujda is a regional radio station broadcasting music and news bulletins. The station launched in 1962 and broadcasts on 96.1 FM in the Oujda region of Morocco.
FM RADIO STATION

Radio Tanger 472218
Owner: Société Nationale de Radiodiffusion et de Télévision
Editorial: PO Box 404, 33, Avenue Le Prince Moulay Abdellah, Tangiers **Tel:** 212 539 321680.
Email: radio_tanger@yahoo.fr
Web site: http://www.radiotanger.ma
Profile: Radio Tanger is a state-owned, regional radio station broadcasting music and news bulletins. The station launched in 1946 and broadcasts on 88.7 FM and 104.0 FM in the Tanger (Tangiers) region of Morocco.
FM RADIO STATION

Radio Tetouan 472217
Owner: Société Nationale de Radiodiffusion et de Télévision
Editorial: 30, Avenue Mohamed V, Tetouan
Tel: 212 539 963697.
Email: radiotetouan@gmail.com
Web site: http://www.snrt.ma
Profile: Radio Tetouan is a state-owned, regional radio station broadcasting music and news programmes in Arabic and the Amazigh language (Tarifit). Launched in 1984, it broadcasts on 100.2 FM in the Tetouan region of Morocco.
FM RADIO STATION

Television

Aflam TV 656984
Owner: Société Nationale de Radiodiffusion et de Télévision
Editorial: PO Box 1042, 1 rue El Brihi, Rabat 10000
Tel: 212 537 685100.
Email: mfaddou@yahoo.fr
Web site: http://www.aflamtv.ma
Profile: Aflam TV (Films TV) is a state-owned television channel broadcasting Moroccan and foreign films, as well as programmes about the Moroccan film industry. It launched in 2008 and brpoadcasts terrestrially within Morocco.
TELEVISION STATION

Al Aoula 655108
Owner: Société Nationale de Radiodiffusion et de Télévision
Editorial: 1, rue El Brihi, Rabat 10000
Tel: 212 537 685100.
Email: lemediateur@snrt.ma
Web site: http://www.alaoula.ma
Profile: Al Aoula, also known as Channel 1, is a state-owned general entertainment channel broadcasting cultural programmes, magazine programmes, films, sport and news for 17-hours a day. The station launched in 1962 and broadcasts free-to-air on satellite.
TELEVISION STATION

Arrabia 655110
Owner: Société Nationale de Radiodiffusion et de Télévision
Editorial: 1, rue El Brihi, Rabat 10000
Tel: 212 537 685100.
Email: marialatifi@hotmail.com
Web site: http://www.arrabia.ma
Profile: Arrabia, also known as Channel 4, is a state-owned educational channel broadcasting teaching programmes, cultural magazine programmes and movies. The station launched in 2005 and broadcasts terrestrially in Morocco and free-to-air on satellite.
TELEVISION STATION

Arriyadia 490488
Owner: Société Nationale de Radiodiffusion et de Télévision
Editorial: Rue Michael Nouima, Casablanca
Tel: 212 529 025520.
Email: arryadia@arryadia.com
Web site: http://www.arryadia.com
Profile: Arriyadia, also known as Channel 3, is a state-owned sports channel broadcasting local and international sports programmes. Launched in 2006, the station broadcasts terrestrially in Morocco and free-to-air on satellite.
TELEVISION STATION

Assadissa 655109
Owner: Société Nationale de Radiodiffusion et de Télévision
Editorial: 1, rue El Brihi, Rabat 10000
Tel: 212 537 685100.
Email: assadissa@snrt.ma
Web site: http://www.assadissatv.ma
Profile: Assadissa, also known as Channel 6, is a state-owned television station broadcasting religious programmes with the aim of bringing Islam to a wider audience. The channel launched in 2005 and broadcasts terrestrially in Morocco and free-to-air on satellite.
TELEVISION STATION

Al Maghribia TV 654916
Owner: Société Nationale de Radiodiffusion et de Télévision
Editorial: PO Box 1042, 1 rue El Brihi, Rabat 10000
Tel: 212 537 685100.
Email: mrinid@yahoo.fr
Web site: http://www.almaghribia-tv.ma
Profile: Al Maghribia TV, also known as Channel 5, is a state-owned, general entertainment channel aimed at Moroccans living abroad. The station launched in 2004 and broadcasts free-to-air on satellite.
TELEVISION STATION

Tamazight TV 692153
Owner: Société Nationale de Radiodiffusion et de Télévision
Editorial: 1, rue El Brihi, Rabat 10000
Tel: 212 537 661735.
Email: tamazight@snrt.ma
Web site: http://www.tamazight-tv.ma
Profile: Tamazight TV is a state-owned television station broadcasting political, business, sport, religion and entertainment programmes. The station launched in 2010 and is aimed at the Berber population of Morocco.
TELEVISION STATION

TV Laâyoune 655100
Owner: Société Nationale de Radiodiffusion et de Télévision
Editorial: PO Box 550, 1 rue Zerktouni, Laayoune 70000 **Tel:** 212 528 892767.
Email: tvregional@gmail.com
Web site: http://www.snrt.ma
Profile: TV Laâyoune, also known as Television Regionale De Laâyoune, is a state-owned regional news and entertainment channel. Launched in 2004, the station is aimed at viewers in the Laayoune area of southern Morocco and broadcasts terrestrially and also free-to-air on satellite.
TELEVISION STATION

Mozambique

Television

Televisao De Mocambique (TVM) 316139
Editorial: Av 25 de Setembro, N 154, Caixa Postal 2675, Maputo - **Tel:** 258 21 30 81 17.
Email: redaccao@tvm.co.mz
Web site: http://www.tvm.co.mz
TELEVISION STATION

Namibia

Television

Namibian Broadcasting Corporation - NBC 410693
Owner: Namibian Broadcasting Corporation
Editorial: Cullinan St. Northern Industrial, Windhoek
Tel: 264 61 291 3101.
Email: pr@nbc.na
Web site: http://www.nbc.na
Profile: Public broadcaster of Namibia covering regional, national and international news, current affairs and entertainment.
TELEVISION NETWORK

Nauru

Radio

Radio Pasifik Nauru, Triple 9 FM 538709
Owner: University of the South Pacific
Editorial: Private Bag, Post Office, Republic Of Nauru
Tel: 674 444 3744.
Email: lauti_a@usp.ac.fj
Web site: http://usp.ac.fj/index.php?id=usp_nauru_home
Profile: Radio Pasifik Nauru, Triple 9 FM, began broadcasting on 2 April. It is a sister station to USP's main student and community radio station.
RADIO NETWORK

Nepal

Radio

Image FM 97.9 467874
Owner: Image Group of Companies
Editorial: Image Group of Companies, Image Complex, P.O. Box 5566, Panipokharir, Kathmandu
Tel: 977 14006555.
Email: imagefm@imagechannels.com
Web site: http://www.imagechannels.com
Profile: Provides information, entertainment and news updates.
AM RADIO STATION

Radio Nepal 467869
Owner: Radio Broadcasting Service
Editorial: Radio Broadcasting Service (Radio Nepal), G.P.O. Box. No. 634, Singha Durbar, Kathmandu
Tel: 977 14211649.
Email: news@radionepal.org
Web site: http://www.radionepal.org
Profile: Covers news and music.
AM RADIO STATION

Television

Nepal Television 468491
Owner: Nepal Television Corporation
Editorial: Nepal Television Corporation, Singha Durbar, P.O. Box 3826, Kathmandu
Tel: 977 14220348.
Email: neptv@vishnu.ccsl.com.np
Web site: http://www.explorenepal.com
Profile: Covers of news and general interests.
TELEVISION STATION

Cable

High Himalayan Sky Cable TV 458955
Owner: High Himalayan Sky Cable TV Co. (P) Ltd.
Editorial: High Himalayan Sky Cable TV Co. (P) Ltd., Dhara Tole, Boudha, Kathmandu **Tel:** 977 14477845.
Email: highhimalayan@yahoo.com
Profile: Covering news and general interests.
CABLE NETWORK

Nicaragua

Television

Telenica Canal 8 410983
Editorial: Mansion Teodolinda 1c al sur, 1/2c abajo, Managua **Tel:** 505 22665021.
Web site: http://www.telenica.com.ni
Profile: Provides daily news, soap operas, touristic and cultural programs.
TELEVISION NETWORK

Nigeria

Television

Bloomberg TV Africa 874967
Owner: Optima Media International
Editorial: Africa Head Office, 35 Oladipo Bateye Street, Lagos **Tel:** 234 1 775 5486.
Web site: http://bloomafrica2013.mmsite.co.uk
Profile: Bloomberg TV Africa is a Pan-African TV station broadcasting business and financial news.
TELEVISION STATION

CNBC Africa - Nigeria Bureau 514060
Owner: CNBC Africa
Editorial: 5th Floor, Left Wing, River State Complex, Plot 83, Ralph Shodeinde Street, Abuja
Tel: 234 9 234 40 76.
Web site: http://www.cnbcafrica.com
Profile: Regional bureau covering breaking news, multimedia, videos, reviews and opinion on African business, finance, private equity, real estate, infrastructure and more.
TELEVISION STATION

Niue

Radio

Radio Sunshine 538711
Owner: Broadcasting Corporation of Niue (BCN)
Editorial: PO Box 68, Alofi, Niue **Tel:** 683 4026.
Email: sunshine@mail.gov.nu
RADIO NETWORK

Television

Television Niue 538722
Owner: Broadcasting Corporation of Niue (BCN)
Editorial: PO Box 68, Alofi, Niue **Tel:** 683 4026.
Email: gm.bcn@mail.gov.nu
TELEVISION STATION

Norfolk Island

Radio

Norfolk Island Broadcasting Service 291003
Editorial: PO Box 456, New Cascade Road, Norfolk Island 2899 **Tel:** 672 32 21 37.
Email: manager@radio.gov.nf
Web site: http://www.norfolkisland.gov.nf
Profile: Norfolk Island Radio (community radio on 1566AM and 89.9) plus rebroadcasts of several Australian stations.
RADIO NETWORK

Northern Mariana Islands

Radio

KRSI-FM 472322
Owner: Sorensen Pacific Broadcasting
Tel: 1 6702357996.
Web site: http://www.sorensenmediagroup.com
Profile: Provides local news, entertainment, live music including raggae and other island's rhytms.
FM RADIO STATION

Norway

Radio

Beiarradioen 290183
Editorial: Moldjord, Moldjord 8110
Tel: 47 75 56 83 10.
Email: post@beiarradioen.no
Web site: http://www.beiarradioen.no/
Profile: Beiarradioen is a local radio station covering Beiarn.
FM RADIO STATION

Bygderadio Vest 287907
Editorial: Bygderadio Vest AS, Doktorvegen 1, Volda 6101 **Tel:** 47 70 07 85 00.
Email: red@bygderadiovest.no
Web site: http://bygderadiovest.no
Profile: Bygderadio Vest is a radio station covering the 7 municipalities; Volda, Ørsta, Hareid, Herøy, Ulstein, Sande and Vannylven.
FM RADIO STATION

Gimlekollen Radio 287914
Editorial: Gimlekollen Mediesenter, Bergtoras vei 120, Kristiansand 4604 **Tel:** 47 38 14 51 00.
Email: post@gimra.no
Web site: http://www.gimra.no
Profile: Gimlekollen Radio is a radio station that offers a Christian, modern morning broadcast, ecclesiastical magazine programs and preaching programs.
FM RADIO STATION

Guovdageainnu Lagasradio 670735
Editorial: Bredbuktnesveien 8, Kautokeino 9520
Tel: 47 78 48 53 00.
Email: glr@glr.no
Web site: http://www.glr.no
Profile: GLR is defined as a Sami local radio. They use both languages during transmission. All GLRs broadcasts defined as local content.
FM RADIO STATION

Hallo Kragerø 289853
Editorial: Frydenborgveien 4, Kragerø 3770
Tel: 47 35 98 00 00.
Web site: http://www.hallokragero.no
Profile: Hallo Kragerø is a local Christian radio station. The editorial office can be contacted via a form on the website: http://www.hallokragero.no/kontakt
FM RADIO STATION

Håpets Røst 287919
Editorial: Restaurationsveien 1, Hundvåg 4085
Tel: 47 51 86 12 26.
Email: movaag@online.no
Web site: http://www.haapetsrost.no
Profile: Håpets Røst is a Christian radio station in Stavanger.
FM RADIO STATION

Hjalarhornet Radio 323500
Editorial: Seljord **Tel:** 47 35 05 20 05.
Email: post@hjalar.no
Web site: http://www.hjalar.no
Profile: Hjalarhornet Radio is a local radio station for Kviteseid, Nissedal and Seljord. Sending music, together with press releases, local news, local advertising and broadcasts in the evenings.
FM RADIO STATION

JærRadioen 287921
Editorial: Strandgaten 119 B, Sandnes 4307
Tel: 47 51 97 92 00.
Email: post@jaerradioen.no
Web site: http://www.jaerradioen.no
Profile: Jærradioen is a local radio station sending live across Jæren every day. Covering news, sports, weather, and traffic, in addition to music.
FM RADIO STATION

Kiss 287992
Editorial: Jernbanetorget 4, Oslo 154
Email: hei@kissradio.no
Web site: http://www.radioplay.no/kiss
Profile: KISS is a commercial radio station covering news, entertainment and music. The Radio Station was previously owned by SBS Discovery and called Radio 1. The name changed to KISS when the new owner Bauer Media took over 1 january 2016.
FM RADIO STATION

Kontakt Radio 287923
Editorial: Peder Bogens gate 4, Sandefjord
Tel: 47 33 46 22 22.
Web site: http://www.kontaktradio.no/
Profile: Kontakt Radio is Sandefjords oldest local radio and had its first broadcast on 15 feb.1985. The radio station is controlled by Samel Sandefjord, the Pentecostal Church in New Town. Contact via form: http://www.kontaktradio.no/kontakt-oss.html
FM RADIO STATION

Nærkanalen 289251
Editorial: Gammelveien 1, Ørnes 8150
Tel: 47 75 72 05 50.
Email: post@narkanalen.no
Web site: http://www.narkanalen.no
Profile: Nærkanalen is a local radio station for Meloy, Rødøy and Gildeskål municipalities. In addition, areas further south in Helgeland can receive broadcasts.
FM RADIO STATION

Narvik Studentradio 289223
Editorial: Lodve Langes Gate 2, Narvik 8505
Tel: 47 76 96 64 51.
Web site: https://nsr.samfunnet.no/
Profile: Wishes not to receive any press material. Narvik Studentradio is a local radio station broadcasting on the FM band in the Narvik area as well as online on the web site.
FM RADIO STATION

NB Radio 289196
Editorial: Vestregate 9, Arendal, Færvik 4836
Tel: 47 37 02 20 66.
Web site: http://www.nbradio.no/Default.aspx
Profile: Wishes not to receive press releases. NB Radio is a local radio station in Arendal.
FM RADIO STATION

Nea Radio Røros 289230
Owner: Nea Radio
Editorial: Oslovn 14, Røros 7461 **Tel:** 47 72 41 44 00.
Email: nr-roros@nearadio.no
Web site: http://www.nearadio.no
Profile: Nea Radio's local office in Røros.
FM RADIO STATION

Nea Radio Tydal/Selbu 287928
Owner: Nea Radio
Editorial: Mediahuset, Selbu 7580
Tel: 47 73 81 74 00.
Email: nr-selbu@nearadio.no
Web site: http://www.nearadio.no
Profile: Nea Radio's local office in Tydal/Selbu.
FM RADIO STATION

Norea Hope 290255
Owner: Norea Mediemisjon
Tel: 47 38 14 50 20.
Email: post@norea.no
Web site: http://norea.no/
Profile: Norea Hope is a radio station playing the latest and greatest of Christian pop and rock - all day. Broadcasted by the Christian organization Norea Mediemisjon.
FM RADIO STATION

NRJ 289773
Owner: NRJ Norge AS
Editorial: Akersgata 73, Oslo 180 **Tel:** 47 22 79 75 00.
Email: nrj@nrj.no
Web site: http://www.nrj.no/
Profile: NRJ is one of the most popular radio stations in Norway with the biggest hits. They play the latest songs. NRJ Group was established in 1998 in Norway and has radio stations in more than twenty countries within Europe.
FM RADIO STATION

NRK Mp3 527206
Owner: NRK
Editorial: Pb 8500 Majorstuen, Oslo 340
Tel: 47 23 04 70 00.
Email: mp3@nrk.no
Web site: http://www.nrk.no/mp3/
Profile: NRK mP3 is a music channel for those who like music. They offer commercial-free music radio 24 hours every day of the year. You can hear mP3 on FM radio in the largest cities in the country, as well as DAB +, Digital satellite, cable, in apps and Internet radio.
RADIO NETWORK

NRK P1; P.I.L.S. 449878
Owner: NRK
Editorial: Postboks 8500 Majorstuen, Oslo 340
Email: info@nrk.no
Web site: http://radio.nrk.no/serie/p-i-l-s
Profile: P.I.L.S. is a show with stories about the most popular artists and the latest music. The hosts is Finn Tokvam and Bård Ose.
RADIO NETWORK

NRK Radio News Desk 289190
Owner: Norsk Rikskringkasting As Avd Oslo
Editorial: Pb 8500 Majorstuen, Oslo 340
Tel: 47 23 04 70 00.
Email: 03030@nrk.no
Web site: http://www.nrk.no/nyheter/
Profile: The news desk of NRK covering international and regional news in NRK radio.
RADIO NETWORK

NRK Radiosporten 289231
Owner: Norsk Rikskringkasting As Avd Oslo
Editorial: Bjornstjerne Bjornsons Plass 1, Marienlyst, Oslo 340 **Tel:** 47 23 04 70 00.
Email: sporten@nrk.no
Web site: http://radio.nrk.no/direkte/sport
Profile: NRK Sport is a brand name for sports produced by the sports department of Norwegian Broadcasting Corporation (NRK). They produce most national sports broadcasts on television, radio and new media.
RADIO NETWORK

NRK Rogaland 287939
Owner: Norsk Rikskringkasting
Editorial: Hafrsfjord **Tel:** 47 51 72 72 72.
Email: rogaland@nrk.no
Web site: http://www.nrk.no/rogaland
Profile: The District Office of NRK Rogaland. Covering local and national news via Internet, Radio and TV.
RADIO NETWORK

NRK Sápmi 289199
Owner: Norsk Rikskringkasting As Avd Oslo
Editorial: Mari Boine geaidnu 12, Karasjok 9730
Tel: 47 78 46 92 00.
Email: sapmi@nrk.no
Web site: http://www.nrk.no/samiradio
Profile: NRK Sápmi is the Sami indigenous division of Norway's largest media company, NRK, the Norwegian Broadcasting Corporation.
RADIO NETWORK

NRK Trøndelag 289189
Owner: Norsk Rikskringkasting As Avd Oslo
Editorial: Otto Nielsensvei 2, Trondheim 7005
Tel: 47 73 88 12 00.
Email: trondelag@nrk.no
Web site: http://www.nrk.no/trondelag
Profile: The District Office of NRK Trøndelag. Covering local and national news via Internet, Radio and TV.
RADIO NETWORK

P4 Radio Hele Norge 289566
Owner: P4 Radio Hele Norge ASA
Editorial: Postboks 817, Lillehammer 2626
Tel: 47 61 24 84 44.
Email: p4@p4.no
Web site: http://www.p4.no
Profile: P4 Radio Hele Norge is Norway's largest commercial and private radio station.
FM RADIO STATION

P5 Radio 670731
Owner: P5 Radio Halve Norge AS
Editorial: Akersgata 73, Oslo 180 **Tel:** 47 23 000 000.
Email: p5@p5.no
Web site: http://www.p5.no
Profile: P5 Radio is P4s local radio channels. They air in Oslo, Bergen, Trondheim, Stavanger and Østfoldbyene. The channel provides local- and national news as well as weather forecasts and music hits.
FM RADIO STATION

P7 Klem 289200
Owner: Radio Melodi Norge AS
Editorial: Akersgata 73, Oslo 180 **Tel:** 47 23 00 00 00.
Email: post@p7klem.no
Web site: http://www.p7klem.no/
Profile: P7 Klem is a local radio station in Oslo, playing "funny favorites".
FM RADIO STATION

P7 Kystradioen 287924
Owner: Kystradioen AS
Editorial: Skjenet 2, Straume 5354
Tel: 47 55 62 62 66.
Email: post@kystradioen.no
Web site: http://www.kystradioen.no
Profile: P7 Kystradioen is a local, christian radio station covering Bergen and Hordaland.
FM RADIO STATION

Radio 102 289973
Owner: Haugesunds Avis
Editorial: Karmsundgt. 74, Haugesund 5506
Tel: 47 52 720 102.
Email: post@radio102.no
Web site: http://www.radio102.no
Profile: Radio102 is a local radio station covering Karmøy, Haugesund and Haugalandet.
FM RADIO STATION

Radio Alta 287990
Owner: Mediehuset Altaposten/Nordavis AS
Editorial: Mediehuset Altaposten, Labyrinten 5, Alta 9510 **Tel:** 47 78 45 67 00.
Email: redaksjonen@altaposten.no
Web site: http://www.altaposten.no/lokalt/radioalta/article6417865.ece
Profile: "Radio Alta" is a local Radio Station covering Alta. Established in 1984.
FM RADIO STATION

Radio Askøy 290159
Owner: Askøy Nærradiolag
Editorial: Kleppevegen 75 (Torvgarden), Kleppestø 5300 **Tel:** 47 56 14 60 02.
Email: radioaskoy@hotmail.com
Web site: http://www.radioaskoy.no
Profile: Radio Askøy is a local local radio staion covering Askøy. Also available online.
FM RADIO STATION

Radio Atlantic 289192
Owner: Radio Atlantic Ryfylkeradioen AS
Editorial: Sandnes **Tel:** 47 51 97 92 00.
Email: post@radioatlantic.no
Web site: http://www.radioatlantic.no
Profile: Radio Atlantic is sending live every single day, with coverage from Sauda in the north to Stavanger, Sandnes and Jæren in the south.
FM RADIO STATION

Radio Bø 290102
Owner: Radio Bø Ba
Tel: 47 76 11 40 50.
Email: post@radiobo.no
Web site: http://www.radiobo.no
Profile: Radio Bø is a local radio station covering Andøy, Bø and Sortland.
FM RADIO STATION

Radio DSF 287984
Owner: Norges Samemisjon Hovedkontoret
Editorial: Suomageaidnu 18, Karasjohka, Unavailable 9730 **Tel:** +47 73 87 62 50.
Email: radio.dsf@samemisjonen.no
Web site: http://www.radiodsf.no/
Profile: Radio DSF is a christian, bilingual (Sami and Norwegian) local radio for inner Finnmark. The radio also broadcasts in Finnish and Russian.
FM RADIO STATION

Radio E6 287985
Owner: Medieselskapet OPP AS
Editorial: Inge Krokanns veg 11, Oppdal 7340
Tel: 47 72 42 20 80.
Email: perroar@opp.no
Web site: http://www.opp.no/
Profile: Radio E6 is a regional radio station owned by the local newspaper Opp. Covering news, culture, sports, politics and music.
FM RADIO STATION

Radio Exact 287980
Owner: Exact Media AS
Editorial: Gronnegata 64 – inngang Seminargata, Hamar 2317 **Tel:** 47 62 51 96 30.
Email: red@exact24.no
Web site: http://www.exact24.no
Profile: Radio Exact are a regional radio station airing in the municipalities of Hamar, Ringsaker and Stange. Radio Exact covers local news, features, interviews and reports.
FM RADIO STATION

Radio Fana 287987
Owner: Nesttun Indremisjon
Tel: 47 55 52 75 30.
Email: post@radiofana.net
Web site: http://nesttunbedehus.no
Profile: Radio Fana is a local radio station covering Bergen. Target group is interested in the bible and christianity.
FM RADIO STATION

Radio Fitjar 371194
Owner: Radio Fitjar
Editorial: Fitjar Bedehus, Fitjar
Web site: http://www.fitjar-bedehus.no/radio.htm
Profile: Radio Fitjar is a christian local radio station on Fitjar (on the island Stord in Sunnhordland). Radio Fitjar have the Bible and the Evangelical Christians values as basis for their activities.
FM RADIO STATION

Radio Folgefonn 287973
Owner: Radio Folgefonn
Editorial: Tyssedalsvegen 4, Odda 5750
Tel: 47 53 64 44 44.
Email: post@radiofolgefonn.no
Web site: http://www.radiofolgefonn.no
Profile: Radio Folgefonn is a local radio station in Odda, covering the areas; Ulvik, Voss Ullensvang, Eidfjord, Granvin, Jondal, Kvam and parts of Kvinnherad.
FM RADIO STATION

Norway

Radio Gnisten 287976
Owner: Norsk Luthersk Misjonssamband Bergen Krets
Editorial: Sigurdsgate 6, Bergen 5015
Tel: 47 55 90 48 00.
Email: radiognisten@nlm.no
Web site: http://www.radiognisten.no
Profile: Radio Sparkle is a regional, christian radio station covering the area from Kvinnherad in the south to Byrknesøyna in the north. They send cases from Norway and Christian missionary, religious stories, devotional, and Christian music.
FM RADIO STATION

Radio Grenland 333607
Owner: Grenlandsradioen AS
Editorial: Postboks 1543, Downtown, Porsgrunn 3902
Tel: 47 35 93 03 33.
Email: post@radiogrenland.no
Web site: http://www.radiogrenland.no
Profile: Radio Grenland sends live across Grenland every day. Covering local news, sports, weather, traffic and news reports, in addition to music. Covering Grenland, Skien, Porsgrunn, Bamble and Siljan.
FM RADIO STATION

Radio Grimstad 289680
Owner: Radio Grimstad AS
Editorial: Storgata 37, Grimstad 4876
Tel: 47 37 04 30 99.
Email: post@radiogrimstad.no
Web site: http://www.radiogrimstad.no
Profile: Radio Grimstad is a regional radio station for Grimstad, focusing on local news and daily newscasts. The channel broadcasts magazine shows and entertainment programs daily, geared towards locals.
FM RADIO STATION

Radio Hallingdal 287979
Owner: Radio Hallingdal BA
Tel: 47 32 08 91 11.
Email: post@radiohallingdal.no
Web site: http://www.radiohallingdal.no
Profile: Radio Hallingdal is a regional radio station which cover an area from Krøderen in the S. East to Krøderud in the N. West. News, entertainment and culture is the profile for the station. National news, but equally important is local news and involving the 'locals'.
FM RADIO STATION

Radio Harstad 287981
Owner: Radio Harstad
Editorial: Verftsgata 7, Harstad 9504
Tel: 47 77 06 14 30.
Email: post@radioharstad.no
Web site: http://www.radioharstad.no
Profile: Radio Harstad is the only youth-controlled radio station in Norway. It is young people themselves who sets the agenda, what will be sent and content of broadcasts.
FM RADIO STATION

Radio Haugaland 287982
Owner: Radio Haugaland og underleverandører
Editorial: Haraldsgaten 110, Haugesund 5501
Tel: 47 52 71 72 73.
Email: post@radioh.no
Web site: http://www.radiohaugaland.no
Profile: Radio Haugaland is a local radio station covering Haugalandet and Sunnhordland.
FM RADIO STATION

Radio Kongsvinger 287946
Editorial: Markedsvegen 1, Kongsvinger 2212
Tel: 47 62 88 24 00.
Email: studio@radiokongsvinger.no
Web site: http://www.radiokongsvinger.no
Profile: Radio Kongsvinger is a local radio station covering Kongsvinger in Hedmark.
FM RADIO STATION

Radio Kvinesdal 290196
Owner: Radio Kvinesdal AL
Editorial: Elveveien 1, Kvinesdal 4480
Tel: 47 38 35 81 00.
Email: post@radiokvinesdal.no
Web site: http://www.radiokvinesdal.no
Profile: Radio Kvinesdal is a local radio station broadcasting in Kvinesdal, Flekkefjord, Hægebostad and Sirda. Covering local news, entertainment and music.
FM RADIO STATION

Radio L 289203
Owner: Radio L Lillesand Nærradio AS
Editorial: Svabekk 5, Lillesand 4790
Tel: 47 37 27 26 00.
Email: post@radio-l.no
Web site: http://radio-l.com/
Profile: Radio L is a local radio station covering Birkenes and Lillesand.
FM RADIO STATION

Radio Latin-Amerika 289185
Owner: Radio Latin-Amerika.
Editorial: Maridalsveien 3, Oslo 178
Tel: 47 22 11 04 45.
Email: post@radiolatinamerika.no
Web site: http://www.radiolatinamerika.no/
Profile: Radio Latin-Amerika is a radio station for people in Norway with a Latin America background or interest.
FM RADIO STATION

Radio Loland 323494
Owner: Radio Loland AL
Editorial: Venneslamoen 10, Vennesla 4700
Tel: 47 38 13 96 00.
Email: post@radiololand.no
Web site: http://www.radiololand.no
Profile: Radio Loland is a local radio station covering Vennesla, Iveland, Søgne and Songdalen Municipality. Radio Loland are focusing on local news and entertainment.
FM RADIO STATION

Radio Luster 323524
Owner: Radio Luster AL
Editorial: Pyramiden, Gaupne 6868
Tel: 47 57 68 14 10.
Email: post@radioluster.org
Web site: http://radioluster.no/
Profile: Radio Luster is a local radio station covering Luster and Sogndal.
FM RADIO STATION

Radio Lyngdal 287950
Owner: Radio Lyngdal AL
Editorial: Kirkeveien 219, Lyngdal 4580
Tel: 47 38 34 31 90.
Email: post@radio-lyngdal.no
Web site: http://www.radio-lyngdal.no
Profile: Radio Lyngdal is a local radio station covering Lister, Lyngdal and Farsund.
FM RADIO STATION

Radio Melbu 323537
Editorial: Postboks 193, Chr Frederiksensgate 24, Melbu **Tel:** 47 76 15 80 00.
Email: radio.melbu@trollfjord.no
Web site: http://www.radiomelbu.no
Profile: Radio Melbu is a local radio station in the Hadsel municipality. Covering local news, music and entertainment.
FM RADIO STATION

Radio Metro 572599
Editorial: 21st Venture AS, AAkersgata 45, Oslo 158
Tel: 47 21 55 59 19.
Email: redaksjonen@radiometro.no
Web site: http://www.radiometro.no
Profile: Radio Metro is playing music from the 60s and forward. Broadcasted in Oslo, Romerike, Follo, Indre Østfold, Gjøvik, Lillehammer, Hønefoss and Drammen.
FM RADIO STATION

Radio Midt-Østerdal 289197
Editorial: amot Kulturhus, Rena, Rena 2451 **Tel:** +47 62 44 15 51.
Email: einar.ofstaas@gmail.com
Web site: http://www.radioamot.no
Profile: Radio Midt-Østerdal is a local radio station covering Åmot, Stor-Elvdal and Rendalen.
FM RADIO STATION

Radio Modum 289201
Editorial: Folkvangveien 4, Geithus 3360
Tel: 47 32 78 31 10.
Email: post@radiomodum.no
Web site: http://www.radiomodum.no
Profile: Radio Modum is a local radio station covering Modum, Sigdal and Krødsherad.
FM RADIO STATION

Radio New Life Ålesund 289265
Editorial: Postbox 9114, Ålesund 6023
Tel: 47 70 14 16 60.
Email: post@newlifeaalesund.no
Web site: http://www.newlifeaalesund.no/radio.php
Profile: Radio New life is a local radio station covering Ålesund region. Broadcasted by the christian organization "New Life".
FM RADIO STATION

Radio Nordkapp 287955
Editorial: Storgata 9, Honningsvåg 9750
Tel: 47 78 47 70 80.
Web site: http://www.radionordkapp.no
Profile: Radio Nordkapp is a local radio station for Nordkapp. The channel broadcasts on the FM network and also offers radio on the Internet. Covering local and national news, sports, culture and music. Radio Nordkapp AL is a cooperative whose purpose is to provide local news and be promoter of local culture built on journalistic principles.
FM RADIO STATION

Radio Nord-Salten 290063
Editorial: Hamarøy **Tel:** 47 75 77 83 12.
Email: post@radionordsalten.no
Web site: http://www.radionordsalten.no
Profile: Radio Nord-Salten is a regional radio station sending from Steigen, Tysfjord and Hamarøy. Radio Nord-Salten sends on frequencies for Småtindan, Hamlot, Drag, Botnheia, Kjøpsvik and Vinkenes.
FM RADIO STATION

Radio Nordsjø 323560
Editorial: Sandnes **Tel:** 47 51 97 92 00.
Email: post@radionordsjo.no
Web site: http://www.radionordsjo.no
Profile: Radio Nordsjø is a regional radio station in Dalane broadcasting live every day. Reporting on local news, sports, weather, traffic and music.
FM RADIO STATION

Radio Norge 313680
Editorial: Jernbanetorget 4a, Oslo 154 **Tel:** 47 07270.
Email: redaksjon@radionorge.com
Web site: http://www.radionorge.com
Profile: RadioNorge covers at least 90% of the norwegian population through FM. The channel delivers commercial radio on nationwide basis.
FM RADIO STATION

Radio Øksnes 323538
Tel: 47 76 11 94 00.
Email: studio@radiooksnes.no
Web site: http://www.radiooksnes.no
Profile: Radio Øksnes is a local radio station covering the municipality with news, music and entertainment.
FM RADIO STATION

Radio Øst 287956
Editorial: Pb 14, Råde 1641 **Tel:** 47 69 29 42 42.
Email: redaksjonen@radio-ost.no
Web site: http://www.radio-ost.no
Profile: Radio Øst is a radio station covering east Norway.
FM RADIO STATION

Radio P5 289191
Editorial: Akersgata 73, Oslo 180 **Tel:** 47 23 00 00 00.
Email: p5@p5.no
Web site: http://www.p5.no
Profile: P5 is Norway's big city channel for hit music in Oslo, Bergen, Trondheim, Stavanger and Østfoldbyene.
FM RADIO STATION

Radio Revolt 323559
Editorial: Singsakerbakken 2E, Trondheim 7030
Tel: 47 400 44 908.
Email: tips@studentmediene.no
Web site: https://radiorevolt.no/
Profile: Radio Revolt (formerly known as Studentradion i Trondheim) is a student radio station in Trondheim, Norway.
FM RADIO STATION

Radio Rjukan 287957
Editorial: Saheimsveien 30, Rjukan 3661
Tel: 47 35 08 24 20.
Email: post@radiorjukan.no
Web site: http://www.radiorjukan.no
Profile: Radio Rjukan is a local radio station covering Rjukan, Tinn and Hjartdal.
FM RADIO STATION

Radio Røst 287959
Editorial: Radhuset, Røst 8064 **Tel:** 47 76 09 64 25.
Email: tor.andreassen@rost.kommune.no
Web site: http://www.radiorost.no/
Profile: Radio Røst is a local radio station in Røst on frequency 100.8 MHz. Every Tuesday radio bingo is hosted. The radio is also used at various other occasions such as Puffin Festival, Cancer Campaign, Summer Radio.
FM RADIO STATION

Radio Sandefjord 290832
Editorial: Andebuveien 74, Sem 3170
Tel: 47 333 78 555.
Web site: http://www.radiosandefjord.no
Profile: Radio Sandefjord is a regional radio station that provides local news, sports, weather, traffic and news reports, as well as music.
FM RADIO STATION

Radio Sandnes 289652
Editorial: Strandgaten 119 B, Sandnes 4307
Tel: 47 51 97 92 00.
Email: post@radiosandnes.no
Web site: http://www.radiosandnes.no
Profile: Radio Sandnes is a regional radio station providing local and national news, traffic, gossip as well as music.
FM RADIO STATION

Radio Skjeberg 371189
Editorial: Skjeberg Folkehoyskole, Oldtidsveien 35, Skjeberg 1745 **Tel:** 47 69 11 65 60.
Email: radioskjeberg@ostfoldfk.no
Web site: http://www.skjeberg.fhs.no/
Profile: Radio Skjeberg is a rehearsal radio for students of radio and television journalism at Skjeberg Folkehøyskole. The content is mainly regional from the regions of Moss, Halden, Sarpsborg and Fredrikstad.
FM RADIO STATION

Radio Sør 289249
Editorial: Vesterveien 2, Kristiansand 4613
Tel: 47 38 00 64 04.
Email: studio@radiosor.no
Web site: http://www.radiosor.no
Profile: Radio Sør is a commercial and independent chain of local radio stations. The radio station has its headquarters and studio in Kristiansand and subdivisions in Mandal (Radio Sør Lindesnes) and Lillesand (Radio Sør Lillesand).
FM RADIO STATION

Radio Sotra 289800
Editorial: Straume **Tel:** 47 56 31 36 60.
Email: redaksjon@radiosotra.no
Web site: http://www.radiosotra.no
Profile: Radio Sotra is a local radio station covering Fjell, Sund and Øygarden.
FM RADIO STATION

Radio Sunnmøre 287960
Editorial: Radio Sunnmøre, Vasstrandvegen 1, Ålesund 6011 **Tel:** 47 70 15 41 00.
Email: post@radiosunnmore.no
Web site: http://radiosunnmore.no
Profile: Radio Sunnmøre is a christian radio station covering the Sunnmøre region.
FM RADIO STATION

Radio Tønsberg 28796
Editorial: Radio Tonsberg AS, Andebuveien 74, Sem 3171 **Tel:** 47 33 37 85 55.
Email: post@radiotonsberg.no
Web site: http://www.radiotonsberg.no
Profile: Radio Tønsberg is a local radio station covering the Tønsberg region in southern Norway.
FM RADIO STATION

Radio Toten 28982
Editorial: Nysethvegen 6, Raufoss 2830
Tel: 47 611 94 800.
Email: post@radiototen.no
Web site: http://www.radiototen.no
Profile: Radio Toten is a local radio for western- and eastern Toten.
FM RADIO STATION

Radio Tromsø 32352
Editorial: Tromsø **Tel:** 47 77 69 00 00.
Email: studio@radiotromso.no
Web site: http://www.radiotromso.no
Profile: Radio Tromsø is a regional radio station broadcasting music and other entertainment.
FM RADIO STATION

Radio Trøndelag 85470
Tel: +47 74 83 95 95.
Email: tips@radiotrondelag.no
Web site: http://www.radiomt.no
Profile: Radio Trøndelag is one of the largest local radio stations in Norway, covering 24 municipalities in North and South Trondelag.
FM RADIO STATION

Radio Vest-Telemark 37110
Editorial: Rauland **Tel:** 47 35 06 29 20.
Email: studio@radiovt.no
Web site: http://www.radiovt.no
Profile: Radio Vest-Telemark is a local radio station covering Vinje, Tokke and Fyresdal with the head office in Rauland.
FM RADIO STATION

RadioNordvest 28793
Editorial: Spjelkavikveien 132, Ålesund 6010
Tel: 47 70 17 44 44.
Email: post@radionordvest.no
Web site: http://radionordvest.no/
Profile: RadioNordvest is a local radio station in Ålesund.
FM RADIO STATION

radiOrakel 28791
Editorial: Pilestredet 30c, Oslo 166
Tel: 47 23 32 69 60.
Email: redaktor@radiorakel.no
Web site: http://www.radiorakel.no
Profile: radiOrakel is a local radio station in Oslo directed at women. They mix music with journalism, innovative comedy and investigate news/reportage.
FM RADIO STATION

RadiOs 28966
Editorial: oyro 37, Os 5202 **Tel:** 47 56 30 14 30.
Email: redaksjonen@radios.no
Web site: http://www.radios.no
Profile: RadiOs is a local radio station covering Os, Fusa, Samnanger and Austevoll.
FM RADIO STATION

Studentradioen i Bergen 28796
Editorial: Parkveien 1, Bergen 5007
Tel: 47 55 45 51 29.
Email: kontakt@srib.no
Web site: http://www.srib.no
Profile: Studentradioen i Bergen is the oldest local radio station in Bergen. Every week Bergen Student Radio broadcasts 119 hours of commercial free radio, with live shows every day from 7am – 2pm, and both live shows, replays and podcasts in the evening from 9pm.
FM RADIO STATION

Valdres Radio 28797
Owner: Valdres Radio AL
Editorial: Skrautvalsvegen 85, Fagernes 2901
Tel: 47 61 35 99 70.
Email: valdresrad@gmail.com
Web site: http://www.valdresradio.com/
Profile: Valdres Radio is a local radio station in Fagernes. The station broadcasts various kind of the latest pop- and folk music and news, from monday to saturday.
FM RADIO STATION

Television

ES-TV 316225
Owner: Nordisk Kristen Kringkasting
Editorial: Klostergata 29, Moss 1532
Tel: 47 21 00 49 00.
Email: post@ev-s.no
Web site: http://www.evangeliesenteret.no/es-tv
Profile: ES-TV sends Christian programs with a mission to send positive belifes to as many people as possible. ES-TV broadcasts to the whole Norway and

arge parts of Europe. Houst is Lise Karlsen and Bjørn Gjellum
TELEVISION STATION

Fem 505989
Editorial: Nydalen alle, Oslo 484 **Tel:** 47 21 02 20 00.
Email: tvnorge@tvnorge.no
Web site: http://www.fem.no/
Profile: Fem is a channel for entertainment that includes drama, movies, documentaries, entertainment news and lifestyle. For those who are interested in movies, drama, documentaries and lifestyle.
TELEVISION STATION

NRK Sport 527212
Owner: Norsk Rikskringkasting As Avd Oslo
Editorial: Bjornstjørne Bjornsons Plass 1, Marienlyst, Oslo 340 **Tel:** 47 23 04 70 00.
Email: sporten@nrk.no
Web site: http://www.nrk.no/sport/
Profile: NRK Sport is a brand name for sports produced by the sports department of Norwegian Broadcasting Corporation (NRK). They produce most national sports broadcasts on television, radio and new media.
TELEVISION NETWORK

NRK Super 512003
Owner: Norsk Rikskringkasting As Avd Oslo
Editorial: Bjornstjørne Bjornsons Plass 1, Marienlyst, Oslo 340 **Tel:** 47 23 04 70 00.
Email: supernytt@nrk.no
Web site: http://www.nrksuper.no
Profile: NRK Super is a Norwegian TV and radio channel aimed at children, run by the Norwegian Broadcasting Corporation (NRK). The channel airs the news program Supernytt amongst others. NRK Super is NRK's channel for children. It provides TV, radio and content online.
TELEVISION NETWORK

TV Norge 316228
Editorial: Postboks 4800 Nydalen, Oslo 484
Tel: 47 21 02 20 00.
Email: tvnorge@tvnorge.no
Web site: http://www.tvnorge.no
Profile: TVNorge is a Norwegian TV- channel. The channel started in 1988. It was the first financed Tv channel in Norway, The channel goes out to 88,9 procent of the Norwegian viewers and is the third biggest Tv channel in the country.
TELEVISION STATION

TV Visjon Norge 315269
Editorial: ovre Eikervei 126, Drammen 3048
Tel: 47 32 21 13 00.
Email: mail@visjonnorge.com
Web site: http://www.visjonnorge.com
Profile: TV Visjon Norge is a christian tv-channel covering Scandinavia.
TELEVISION STATION

TV2 316177
Editorial: Nostegaten 72, Pb 7222, Bergen 5020
Tel: 47 915 02255.
Email: tips@tv2.no
Web site: http://www.tv2.no
Profile: TV 2 is Norway's largest commercial TV channel. TV 2 is part of the media group TV 2, involving both television, internet, mobile and new interactive platforms. Mediehuset TV 2 is behind a number of established brands such as TV2, TV2 Nyhetskanalen, TV 2 Sportkanalen, TV 2 Zebra, TV 2 Bliss, TV2 Humor, TV 2 Sumo, TV2.no and TV2 Mobil.
TELEVISION STATION

TV3 316226
Editorial: Pb TV3 Youngstorget, Oslo 28
Tel: 47 22 99 00 33.
Email: info@mtgtv.no
Web site: http://www.tv3.no
Profile: TV3 Norway is a Norwegian subsidiary to MTG-owned TV3 Sweden which broadcasts from London via satellite to a large part of the Norwegian cable television networks.
TELEVISION STATION

Viasat Sport 527210
Editorial: Akersgata 73, Oslo 180 **Tel:** 47 22 99 00 33.
Email: sport@viasatsport.no
Web site: http://www.viasat.no/sport
Profile: Viasat Sport in Norway has exclusive coverage of Formula One, MotoGP, NFL, National Hockey League (NHL), the KHL international ice hockey league and the annual Ice Hockey World Championship, as well as cycling and boxing.
TELEVISION STATION

Oman

Radio

Radio Oman 90.4 FM 291153
Owner: Public Authority for Radio and Television (PART)
Editorial: PO Box 1130, Media City, Muscat 113
Tel: 968 24 943353.
Email: feedback@oman-radio.gov.om
Web site: http://www.part.gov.om
Profile: Radio Oman 90.4 FM is a state-owned radio station broadcasting English news and entertainment programmes for 16-hours per day (6am to 12am). It launched on 15 December 1975 and broadcasts on 90.4 FM (Muscat and Salalah) and 91.3 FM (Thumrait).
FM RADIO STATION

Radio Sultanate of Oman 381056
Owner: Public Authority for Radio and Television (PART)
Editorial: PO Box 1130, Media City, Muscat 100
Tel: 968 24 943426.
Email: feedback-rd@oman-radio.gov.om
Web site: http://part.gov.om/omanradio
Profile: Radio Sultanate of Oman broadcasts Arabic news and entertainment programmes for 24-hrs a day. The station launched in 1970 and broadcasts on 98.8 FM and 100.0 FM.
FM RADIO STATION

Al Shabab Radio 417629
Owner: Public Authority for Radio and Television (PART)
Editorial: PO Box 1130, Media City, Muscat 113
Tel: 968 24 943500.
Email: shababb_2012@hotmail.com
Web site: http://part.gov.om/shababradio
Profile: Al Shabab Radio is a youth-orientated radio station broadcasting entertainment programmes, as well as live coverage of festivals, national and cultural events. The state-owned station launched in 2003 and broadcasts on 100.0 FM, 98.5 FM and 94.5 FM.
FM RADIO STATION

Television

Majan TV 656973
Owner: Halley Studios
Editorial: PO Box 1825, Al Azeeba 130
Tel: 968 24 596464.
Email: majan-tv@omantel.net.om
Web site: http://www.majan-tv.com
Profile: Majan TV is a television station broadcasting entertainment programmes and drama serials. The channel launched in 2009 and broadcasts free-to-air on satellite.
TELEVISION STATION

Oman TV 375334
Owner: Public Authority for Radio and Television (PART)
Editorial: PO Box 1130, Media City, Muscat 113
Tel: 968 24 603222.
Email: omantvnews@gmail.com
Web site: http://www.part.gov.om
Profile: Oman TV is a state-owned television station broadcasting films, sport, entertainment, local events and news. The channel launched in 1974 and broadcasts terrestrially in Oman and free-to-air on satellite.
TELEVISION STATION

Oman TV2 608706
Owner: Public Authority for Radio and Television (PART)
Editorial: PO Box 1130, Media City, Muscat 113
Tel: 968 24 693115.
Email: presstv@oman-tv.gov.om
Web site: http://www.part.gov.om
Profile: Oman TV2 is a state-owned television channel primarily focusing on sports programmes, but also broadcasts drama series and movies in English and Arabic. The channel launched in 2006 and broadcasts terrestrially in Oman and free-to-air on satellite.
TELEVISION STATION

Qatar TV - Oman bureau 734152
Owner: Qatar Media Corporation
Editorial: PO Box 108, Dohat al Adab Steet, Muscat 133 **Tel:** 968 24 483962.
Email: badar-tv@hotmail.com
Web site: http://www.qtv.qa
Profile: Qatar TV is a state-owned television channel broadcasting entertainment and news programmes. The Oman bureau opened in 2008 and covers news from the Sultanate for the Doha-based channel.
TELEVISION NETWORK

Pakistan

Radio

Radio Pakistan (Pakistan Broadcasting Corporation) 467855
Editorial: National Broadcasting House, G-5 Constitutional Avenue, Islamabad 44000
Tel: 92 519208772.
Email: cnoreporting@gmail.com
Web site: http://www.radio.gov.pk
Profile: Covers topics for a Pakistan audience.
AM RADIO STATION

Television

ARY OneWorld 559003
Editorial: ARY Communication, 6th Floor Madaina City Mall, Abdullah Haroon Road, Karachi
Tel: 92 215657315.
Web site: http://www.aryoneworld.net
Profile: Current affair programs with prominent Pakistani journalists are the strength of ARY One World. Its program mix covers all the genres of news & infotainment, and most of its programs are presented by top international anchors such as P.J. Mir, Javed Malik, Ayaz Amir, Faeza Dawood, Kashif Abaasi and Asima Shirazi. ARY One World is one of the first dedicated international news channels in Pakistan. It has exclusive correspondents in almost all major capitals around the globe, a network of over 500 reporters and correspondents in Pakistan, and major international networks as exclusive partners for the exchange of news, information and other technical facilities. The channel also maintains a rich archive library with exclusive footage.
TELEVISION NETWORK

Pakistan Television Corporation (PTV) 468223
Editorial: Federal TV Complex, Constitution Avenue, Islamabad 44000 **Tel:** 92 519208651.
Email: ptvgq@hotmail.com
Web site: http://www.ptv.com.pk
Profile: National television stations gov't controlled. broadcast news, sports, entertainments, health & lifestyle news
TELEVISION NETWORK

Cable

JAAG TV 458943
Editorial: CNBC Pakistan Karachi Head Office, Techno City Corporate Towers 13/F, Karachi 74000
Tel: 92 21111262275.
Email: info@jaagtv.com
Web site: http://jaag.tv
Profile: Formerly known as CNBC Pakistan, covers frontline news and current affairs in Pakistan with hourly bulletins and various programming features.
CABLE NETWORK

Palau

Television

PNCC Digital TV 310937
Editorial: PO Box 39, Koror 96940 **Tel:** 680 587 35 15.
Email: pncc@palaunet.com
Web site: http://www.palaunet.com
Profile: Offers over 46 channels of entertainment, movies, news, music, educational, and children's programming in our Basic Service, including two local channels.
TELEVISION STATION

Panama

Radio

Omega Stereo 417347
Editorial: Calle G, El Cangrejo, Edificio Don Isaac Planta Baja, Apartado 6-4632, El Dorado
Tel: 507 2692237.
Email: omegaste@omegastereo.com
Web site: http://www.omegastereo.com
Profile: Presents daily news, analysis, and music including pop and ballads targeting an audience between 18 and 50 years old.
FM RADIO STATION

Radio Hogar 333621
Editorial: Via Cinquentanario No 9 y Av. Jose Matilde Perez, Apdo. 0834-00102, Panama **Tel:** 507 2700142.
Email: radiohogar@cableonda.net
Web site: http://www.radiohogar.org
Profile: Provides Catholic news, cultural and educational programs. Includes two daily news broadcasts in the morning and in the afternoon. Plays classic music.
AM RADIO STATION

Radio KW Continente 290398
Editorial: Primer Alto, Via Argentina, Edificio Carillon Mezanine, Apdo. 0816-07920, Panama
Tel: 507 2645711.
Web site: http://www.kwcontinente.com
Profile: Informative radio broadcasts news and opinion shows.
FM RADIO STATION

Radio Mia 290395
Editorial: Calle 50 y Via Brasil, Edificio Plaza 50 Piso 6, Apdo. 5117, Zona 5, Panama **Tel:** 507 2630946.
Email: radiomia1@cableonda.net
Web site: http://www.radiomiapanama.com/
Profile: Provides daily news, sport programs, interviews, radial magazine, and music. Radio Mia 96.7 FM.
FM RADIO STATION

Radio Veraguas 290397
Editorial: Calle 9na Norte Santiago Canto del Llano Via Panamericana, Santiago de Veraguas, Santiago
Tel: 507 9587060.
Email: rveraguas@pa.inter.net
Profile: The radio station has two frequencies AM and FM, the AM transmits cultural, religious, and educational programs, the FM transmits news, interviews, and music.
FM RADIO STATION

RPC Radio 290396
Owner: MEDCOM Corporation
Editorial: Av. 12 de Octubre, Edificio MEDCOM, 1 piso, Apdo. 082700116, Zona 8, Panama
Tel: 507 3906700.
Web site: http://www.rpcradio.com
Profile: Provides daily news, interviews, sports. Plays national and international music.
FM RADIO STATION

Television

Canal 4 RPC 333895
Editorial: Corporacion Medcom SA, Av. 12 de Octubre, Apdo. 0827-00116, Panama
Tel: 507 390 6700.
Email: kchalmers@medcom.com.pa
Web site: http://www.rpctv.com/
Profile: National TV station broadcasting entertainment, sports, and news for Panama.
TELEVISION NETWORK

FETV Canal 5 316431
Editorial: Via Ricardo J. Alfaro, detras del Edificio de Postgrado de la USMA, Apdo. 0819-02874, El Dorado Panamá **Tel:** 507 230 8000.
Email: comentarios@fetv.org
Web site: http://www.fetv.org
Profile: Educational and cultural TV channel focusing on the values and traditions of Panama citizens.
TELEVISION NETWORK

Telemetro Canal 13 316433
Editorial: Corporacion Medcom Panama SA, Av. 12 de Octubre, Apdo. 0827-00116, Panama
Tel: 507 390 6700.
Web site: http://www.telemetro.com
Profile: National TV broadcasting news, comedies, and movies for Panama. Telemetro targets adults and Tele 7 targets children and youths. Tele 7 is a childrens network that provides children programming from 7am until 8pm. After 8 pm Tele 7 broadcasts programs for mothers.
TELEVISION NETWORK

TVN - Canal 2 316432
Editorial: Via Simon Bolivar, Transismica, Panama
Tel: 507 2793711.
Email: tvn@tvn-2.com
Web site: http://www.tvn-2.com
Profile: Presents daily news and broadcasts cultural and entertainment programs including soap operas.
TELEVISION NETWORK

Papua New Guinea

Radio

FM100 Rural Radio 539178
Editorial: Telikom Technology Haus, 2 Floor, Waigani Drive, 4 mile, 121, Papua New Guinea
Tel: 675 300 4300.
Email: info@fm100.com.pg
Web site: http://www.fm100.com.pg
Profile: FM100 broadcasts 24 hours a day starting from 5am till 1am on manual broadcasting mode which means the on-air announcer is behind the console. From 12am to 6am commercials are played in between songs.
RADIO NETWORK

NBC National Radio of Papua New Guinea 539177
Editorial: PO Box 1359, Boroko, Papua New Guinea
Tel: 675 32 55 233.
Email: info@nbc.com.pg
Web site: http://nbc.com.pg
Profile: National Broadcasting Corporation (NBC) is established and funded by the Parliament of PNG to provide a national radio service for Papua New Guinea.
RADIO NETWORK

PNG FM Ltd 539175
Owner: PNG FM Ltd
Editorial: PO Box 774, Port Moresby, Papua New Guinea **Tel:** 675 320 1996.
Email: pngfmnews@naufm.com.pg
Web site: http://pngvillage.com.pg
Profile: PNG government-owned with two AM networks: Karai (national) and Kundu (provincial) and one FM commercial station Kalang.
RADIO NETWORK

Television

EMTV 539197
Owner: Fiji Television
Editorial: PO Box 443, Boroko, Papua New Guinea
Tel: 675 325 7322.
Web site: http://emtv.com.pg
TELEVISION STATION

Paraguay

Radio

Radio Nacional del Paraguay
290295
Editorial: Cuarta 241 entre Yegros e Iturde, Asuncion
Tel: 595 21 390374.
Web site: http://www.rnpy.com
Profile: Transmits in two frequencies. The FM plays every 30 minutes traditional Paraguayan music convined with international and latin music. The AM, ZPU Radio Nacional del Paraguay plays traditional Paraguayan music.
FM RADIO STATION

Radio UNO 650 AM
291175
Owner: Multimedia S.A.
Editorial: Grupo Multimedia SA, Avenida Mariscal Lopez 2948, Asuncion **Tel:** 595 21 603400.
Email: prensa650@mm.com.py
Web site: http://www.radiouno.com.py
Profile: Provides news, sports, interviews, chat, health shows, and life programs. Multimedia S.A. owns also Radio Popular 103.1 FM and Diario Popular that covers news from Paraguay and Argentina.
RADIO NETWORK

Television

SNT - Sistema Nacional de Televisión
409985
Editorial: Television Cerro Cora SA., Avda. Carlos A. Lopez 572, 1135, Asuncion **Tel:** 595 21 421744.
Email: info@snt.com.py
Web site: http://www.snt.com.py
Profile: Broadcasts daily news, entertainment, including films and documentaries.
TELEVISION NETWORK

Peru

Radio

Radio RPP Noticias
291051
Owner: Grupo RPP
Editorial: Grupo RPP SA, Av. Paseo de la Republica 3866, San Isidro, Lima **Tel:** 51 1 215 0200.
Email: editor@gruporpp.com.pe
Web site: http://www.rpp.com.pe
Profile: Radio Nacional provides 24 hours of news. The programming includes political, cultural, economic, health and entertainment news.
RADIO NETWORK

Philippines

Radio

Radio Mindanao Network
468035
Owner: Radio Mindanao Network, Inc.
Editorial: 4F State Condominium 1, Salcedo St. Legaspi Village, Guadalupe, Makati City
Tel: 63 2 815 8304.
Email: admin@rmn.ph
Web site: http://www.rmn.ph
Profile: Launched in 1952, broadcasts as one of the largest radio networks in the Philippines.
RADIO NETWORK

Television

ABS-CBN Broadcasting Corporation
316405
Owner: ABS-CBN Interactive Inc.
Editorial: Sgt. E.A. Esguerra Ave, Quezon City 1103
Tel: 632 415-2272.
Email: feedback@abs-cbn.com
Web site: http://www.abs-cbn.com
Profile: Provides news and entertainment television programming.
TELEVISION NETWORK

Poland

Radio

Polskie Radio Czwórka - Program 4
493326
Editorial: al. Niepodlegoci, 77/85, Warszawa 00-977
Tel: 48 22 645 99 44.
Email: czworka@polskieradio.pl
Web site: http://www.polskieradio.pl/10, Czworka
Profile: National radio station targeting young audiences with news and music.
RADIO NETWORK

Polskie Radio Dwójka - Program 2
493328
Editorial: al. Niepodlegoci 77/85, Warszawa 00-977
Tel: 48 22 645 98 04.
Email: dwojka@polskieradio.pl
Web site: http://www.polskieradio.pl/8, Dwojka
Profile: National radio station with news, literature, jazz and classical music programs.
RADIO NETWORK

Polskie Radio Trójka - Program 3
493329
Editorial: ul. Myliwiecka, 39205, Warszawa 00-977
Tel: 48 22 645 55 47.
Email: reportertrojki@polskieradio.pl
Web site: http://www.polskieradio.pl/9, Trojka
Profile: National radio station with news, cultural programs and music.
RADIO NETWORK

Radio Rock
622394
Editorial: ul. Czerska 8/10, Warszawa 00-732
Tel: 48 22 44 44 024.
Web site: http://rockradio.tuba.pl
Profile: A network of radio stations located in all major cities in Poland.
RADIO NETWORK

Radio Vox FM
622395
Editorial: ul. Jubilerska, 10, Warszawa 04-190
Tel: 48 22 516 47 03.
Email: warszawa@voxfm.pl
Web site: http://www.voxfm.pl
Profile: A network of radio stations located all over Poland.
RADIO NETWORK

Radio Z?ote Przeboje
622396
Editorial: ul. Czerska 8/10, Warszawa 00-732
Tel: 48 22 555 51 00.
Email: kontakt@zloteprzeboje.pl
Web site: http://zloteprzeboje.tuba.pl
Profile: A network of radio stations based in 18 major cities of Poland.
RADIO NETWORK

Radio Zet
493330
Editorial: ul. urawia 8, Warszawa 00-503
Tel: 48 22 583 33 82.
Email: radiozet@radiozet.pl
Web site: http://www.radiozet.pl
Profile: National radio station with news, music, culture, competitions.
RADIO NETWORK

RMF FM
493325
Editorial: al. Waszyngtona 1, Krakow 30-204
Tel: 48 12 425 22 52.
Email: redakcja@rmf.fm
Web site: http://www.rmf.fm
Profile: National radio station with news, music and topic programs.
RADIO NETWORK

Television

Polsat
493335
Owner: Telewizja Polsat SA
Editorial: ul. Ostrobramska 77, Warszawa 04-175
Tel: 48 22 514 40 00.
Email: biuro@polsat.com.pl
Web site: http://www.polsat.pl
Profile: Polsat TV started to broadcast December 5, 1992. Polsat, the first commercial television station in Poland, broke the monopoly of public television and blazed the trail for next independent commercial television projects in Poland.
TELEVISION STATION

Polsat News
657062
Editorial: ul. Ostrobramska 77, Warszawa 04-175
Tel: 48 22 514 43 34.
Email: redakcja@polsatnews.pl
Web site: http://www.polsatnews.pl
Profile: News TV station covering domestic and foreign news and events.
TELEVISION STATION

Portugal

Radio

Antena 1
425965
Owner: Rádio Difusão Portuguesa
Editorial: Av. Marechal Gomes da Costa, 37, Lisboa 1849-030 **Tel:** 351 213 820 000.
Email: antena1@rtp.pt
Web site: tv1.rtp.pt/antena1
Profile: Generalist radio station. Special emphasis on Portuguese and international news, entertainment, sports latest headlines and Portuguese music promoting. Radio frequency available on 95.7 FM (Monsanto brodcasting station). National. Local Translation: Estação radiofónica destinada à generalidade dos ouvintes. As suas principais componentes são a actualidade nacional e internacional; o entretenimento, com predominância para a música portuguesa; a divulgação de temas de relevância socio-cultural e a actualidade desportiva, com grande destaque para o futebol profissional. Frequência disponível em 95.7 FM (Emissor de Monsanto). Também dispõe de emissão online.
RADIO NETWORK

Antena 2
425966
Owner: Rádio Difusão Portuguesa
Editorial: Av. Marechal Gomes da Costa, 37, Lisboa 1849-030 **Tel:** 351 213 820 000.
Email: rdp.antena2@rtp.pt
Web site: antena2.rtp.pt
Profile: Radio station whose main purpose is promoting culture, specially the Portuguese cultural scenery. Poetry, music (from jazz to ethnic, but with special emphasis on classical and erudite music), interviews, programs dedicated to the Portuguese language, documentaries, popular traditions, live classical music concerts produced by Antena 2. Radio frequency available on 94.4 FM (Monsanto broadcasting station). National. Local Translation: Estação de rádio da rede RTP - Rádio e Televisão de Portugal, cuja programação é baseada em música clássica e programas culturais. A Antena 2 tem os seus tipos de música organizados por "tons". Assim, são estes os tons que podemos ouvir nesta estação: tons recentes; tons do mundo; tons de voz; tons antigos; tons conhecidos; tons de jazz; tons ao vivo; tons das ideias; tons da noite e outros tons. Transmite música erudita, jazz, fado, notícias e magazines culturais. Frequência disponível em 94.4 FM (Emissor de Monsanto). Também dispõe de emissão online. Phone: +351 213 820 015
RADIO NETWORK

Antena 3
425967
Owner: Rádio Difusão Portuguesa
Editorial: Av. Marechal Gomes da Costa, 37, Lisboa 1849-030 **Tel:** 351 213 820 000.
Email: antena3@rtp.pt
Web site: ww1.rtp.pt/antena3
Profile: National radio station with a strong identity and a juvenile attitude. Antena 3 represents one third of the Portuguese teenagers radio listening preferences. News and current affairs, humor programmes and music. Radio frequency available on 100.3 FM (Monsanto broadcasting station). National. Mainly youngsters. Local Translation: Rádio de cobertura nacional. A Antena 3 é o canal jovem da RDP, destinado a um universo que representa mais de um terço da escuta de Rádio em Portugal. Com uma forte identidade própria, acompanha a evolução da mentalidade juvenil, proporcionando a melhor música jovem e os acontecimentos marcantes da actualidade. Frequência disponível em 100.3 FM (Emissor de Monsanto). Também dispõe de emissão online.
RADIO NETWORK

Renascença
291285
Owner: R/com
Editorial: R. Ivens, 14, Lisboa 1249-108
Tel: 351 213 239 200.
Email: mail@rr.pt
Web site: rr.sapo.pt
Profile: National generalist radio station, with Catholic orientation. Latest news reports with permanent update, music, listener's participation and opinion, religious programmes, open discussion programmes, interviews and comments by recognized Portuguese personalities on current events and Portuguese cultural promotion characterize this well-known station. Radio frequency available on 105.8 FM. Also available online. General population, but mainly listeners aged between 35 to 55 years old and being part of the A, B and C1 targets. Local Translation: Estação de rádio nacional, de cariz generalista e inspiração católica, pertencente à Igreja católica. É essencialmente composta por programas de informação - notícias, debates, entrevistas, entre outros. Frequência disponível em 105.8 FM no Continente e em 95.2 MHz nos Açores. Dispõe de emissão online. Estabeleceu um protocolo com a ARIC, na área de cedência de conteúdos e formação profissional. Eleita pelo estudo "Marcas de Confiança 2011" (Selecções do Reader's Digest), como uma das estações de rádio em que os portugueses mais confiam.
RADIO NETWORK

TSF
291041
Owner: Rádio Notícias, Produções e Publicidade, S.A.
Editorial: Edificio Altejo, R. 3 da Matinha, 3 Piso - Sala 301, Lisboa 1900-823 **Tel:** 351 218 612 500.
Email: tsf@tsf.pt
Web site: www.tsf.pt
Profile: National radio station dedicated mainly to national and international news report services, being updated every thirty minutes. Sports and economy/ business news, stock market info, weather and traffic reports, chronicles and opinion programmes with special guests and several interactive programmes. National. General population. Local Translation: Estação de carácter informativo e noticioso, composta por notícias nacionais e internacionais referentes à actualidade política, à economia, ao desporto, às artes, entre outros. Contem crónicas e programas de debate e opinião e ainda vários programas interactivos. Eleito em 2010 como uma das marcas de media com melhor reputação em Portugal. A Reportagem TSF "Missão Haiti" foi galardoada com o Prémio Internacional de Jornalismo Rei de Espanha.
RADIO NETWORK

Puerto Rico

Radio

Alfa Rock
291146
Editorial: PO Box 9024188, San Juan PR 00902-4188
Tel: 1 787 726-6144.
Email: alfa@alfarock.com
Web site: http://www.alfarock.com
Profile: Ralf Perez Ramirez is the General Manager to whom press releases should be addressed.
RADIO NETWORK

Russia

Radio

Radio Mayak
291174
Editorial: 5 ul. Yamskogo Polya 19-21, Moskva 125040 **Tel:** 7 495 950-67-67.
Email: box@radiomayak.ru
Web site: http://www.radiomayak.ru
Profile: The oldest public information and music station broadcasting around the clock.
RADIO NETWORK

Television

Domashniy
679859
Editorial: ul. Pravdy 15a, Moskva 125124
Tel: 7 495 785 63 33.
Email: info@domashny.ru
Web site: http://tv.domashniy.ru
Profile: National TV channel for the whole family with films and programmes on health, home decoration, cooking, children care, etc. Targets women in the age group 35 - 45.
TELEVISION STATION

NTV Russia
679294
Editorial: ul. A. Koroleva 12, Moskva 127427
Tel: 7 495 725 53 83.
Email: info@ntv.ru
Web site: http://www.ntv.ru
Profile: National TV station with news, films, series, sports and entertainment programmes.
TELEVISION STATION

Peretz
679854
Owner: STS Media
Tel: 7 495 785-63-47.
Email: post@peretz.ru
Web site: http://peretz.ru
Profile: National TV informative-entertaining channel covering detective issues and criminal investigations, action films and thrillers, documentary and comedy programmes.
TELEVISION STATION

Piyaty Kanal
679654
Owner: TRK Peterburg
Editorial: ul. Chapygina 6, str. 2, Sankt Peterburg 197376 **Tel:** 7 812 335-15-64.
Email: news@5-tv.ru
Web site: http://www.5-tv.ru
Profile: National TV station based in St. Petersburg with cultural, political and entertainment programmes.
TELEVISION STATION

Rossiya 1
679167
Owner: VGTRK
Editorial: 5 ul. Yamskogo Polya 22, Moskva
Tel: 7 495 232 63 33.
Email: pr@rfn.ru
Web site: http://russia.tv
Profile: National TV station covering 98,5% of Russia and broadcasting news, sports, entertainment, films and series.
TELEVISION STATION

Rossiya 24
679757
Owner: VGTRK
Editorial: 5 ul. Yamskogo Polya 22, Moskva
Tel: 7 495 221 94 81.
Email: vesti24@vesti.ru
Web site: http://www.vesti.ru
Profile: National and international 24/7 Russian-language news channel covering major national and international events with a Russian perspective and a focus on domestic issues with a broad and impartial outline of life in all of Russia's regions from its European enclave of Kaliningrad to Vladivostok in the Far East.
TELEVISION STATION

Sport
679851
Owner: VGTRK
Tel: 7 495 955 83 88.
Email: info@sportbox.ru
Web site: http://news.sportbox.ru
Profile: National TV channel entirely dedicated to sports.
TELEVISION STATION

Telekanal Kultura 679141
Owner: VGTRK
Editorial: ul. Malaya Nikitinskaya 24, Moskva 123995
Tel: 7 495 780 56 01.
Email: press@tv-culture.ru
Web site: http://www.tvkultura.ru
Profile: National TV station with cultural programmes: theatre, music, cinema, literature and history.
TELEVISION STATION

Rwanda

Radio

Radio Rwanda 327166
Owner: RBA - Rwanda Broadcasting Agency (former ORINFOR)
Editorial: KG 550 St, P.O Box 83, Kigali
Tel: 250 252 572 276.
Email: radiorwanda@rba.co.rw
Web site: http://rba.co.rw/radiyo
Profile: National radio station covering regional, national and international news and current affairs including politics, economics, society, entertainment, sports and culture.
RADIO NETWORK

Television

Rwanda TV 316352
Owner: RBA - Rwanda Broadcasting Agency (former ORINFOR)
Editorial: KG 550 St, P.O Box 83, Kigali
Tel: 250 252 572 276.
Email: info@rba.co.rw
Web site: http://www.rba.co.rw/tv
Profile: National television station covering regional, national and international news and current affairs including politics, economics, society, entertainment, sports and culture.
TELEVISION STATION

Saint Helena

Radio

Saint FM 537539
Owner: St. Helena Media Productions Ltd.
Editorial: 2nd Floor, Association Hall, Main street, South Atlantic Ocean STHL 1ZZ **Tel:** 290 26 60.
Email: fm@cwimail.sh
Web site: http://www.saint.fm
RADIO NETWORK

Saint Kitts and Nevis

Radio

VON Voice of Nevis 291079
Tel: 1 8694691616.
Email: vonradio@sisterisles.kn
Web site: http://www.vonradio.com
Profile: Transmits talk shows, news, and provides life coverage of cultural programs, political programs and conferences. Plays hip hop, rock, R&B, reggae.
RADIO NETWORK

Saint Lucia

Television

Helen Television System 316223
Editorial: PO Box 621, Castries **Tel:** 1758 45 22 693.
Email: radio@htsstlucia.com
Web site: http://www.htsstlucia.com
TELEVISION NETWORK

Saint Vincent and the Grenadines

Radio

Hot97 SVG 834881
Owner: RadioActive Ltd
Editorial: RadioActive/Hot 97.1 FM, Moulton Mayers Building, Higginson St, Kingstown **Tel:** 1 784 452-9797.
Email: hot97ad@gmail.com
Web site: http://www.hot97svg.com
Profile: Hot97 SVG is a commercial station owned by RadioActive Ltd, airing in Saint Vincent and the

---

Grenadines. The format of the station is urban contemporary. Hot97 SVG broadcasts to the area at 97.1 FM. The target audience of the station is listeners, ages 18 to 54. The station's tagline is "Hot 97.1".
FM RADIO STATION

Television

SVG TV 411385
Editorial: Dorsetshire Hill, PO Box 617, Kingstown
Tel: 1 7844561078.
Email: svgbcnews@vincysurf.com
Web site: http://www.svgbc.com
Profile: Presents news, sports, and entertainment programming.
TELEVISION NETWORK

Samoa

Radio

K-Roq FM96.1 291108
Editorial: PO Box 762, Apia
Email: info@fmradio.ws
Web site: http://www.fmradio.ws
RADIO NETWORK

Magik 98.1 FM 290986
Editorial: PO Box 762, Apia
Email: sales@fmradio.ws
RADIO NETWORK

Radio Polynesia 538699
Owner: Radio Polynesia Ltd
Editorial: PO Box 762, Apia, Samoa
Email: corey@fmradio.ws
Web site: http://fmradio.ws
Profile: Provides news and music broadcasting in English and Samoan.
RADIO NETWORK

Talofa 88.5 & 99.9 FM 291030
Editorial: P O Box 762, Apia
Email: info@fmradio.ws
Web site: http://www.fmradio.ws
Profile: Talofa FM Samoa's most popular radio station playing latest Samoan music.
RADIO NETWORK

Television

SBC TV 1 538721
Owner: Samoa Broadcasting Corporation
Editorial: Mulinuu, Apia, Samoa
Email: mhuch69@yahoo.com
TELEVISION STATION

San Marino

Television

San Marino RTV 375327
Tel: 378 0549 88 20 17.
Email: redazione@sanmarinortv.sm
Web site: http://www.sanmarinortv.sm
Profile: National radio and television of the republic of San Marino.
TELEVISION STATION

Sao Tome & Principe

Radio

Radio Nacional de São Tomé e Principe 386855
Editorial: Avenida Marginal 12 Julho, Caixa Postal 44, São Tomé **Tel:** 239 223 836.
Email: rnstp@cstome.net
Web site: http://radionacional.st
RADIO NETWORK

Television

RTP África 386946
Editorial: Caixa Postal 855, São Tomé
Tel: 239 223 613.
Email: arquivo@rtp.pt
Web site: http://www.rtp.pt
TELEVISION STATION

Televisão Santomense 386945
Editorial: Caixa Postal 420, São Tomé
Tel: 239 221 493.
Email: tvs@cstome.net
TELEVISION STATION

Senegal

Radio

Dakar FM 290944
Owner: Radiodiffusion Télévision Sénégalaise
Editorial: BP 1765, Dakar **Tel:** 221 33 849 13 13.
Email: rts@rts.sn
Web site: http://live.rts.sn
Profile: Radio station covering local news and current affairs including music, entertainment and sport.
FM RADIO STATION

Radio Senegal International - RSI 290943
Owner: Radiodiffusion Télévision Sénégalaise
Editorial: BP 1765, Dakar **Tel:** 221 33 849 13 13.
Email: rts@rts.sn
Web site: http://www.rts.sn
Profile: International radio station covering national and international news and current affairs including music, entertainment and sport.
FM RADIO STATION

Radiodiffusion Télévision Sénégalaise - RTS 291111
Owner: Radiodiffusion Télévision Sénégalaise
Editorial: BP 1765, Dakar **Tel:** 221 33 849 13 13.
Email: rts@rts.sn
Web site: http://www.rts.sn
Profile: National television of Senegal covering regional, national and international news and current affairs including politics, economics, society, culture, entertainment and sport.
RADIO NETWORK

Television

RTS 1 316340
Owner: Radiodiffusion Télévision Sénégalaise
Editorial: BP 1765, Dakar BP 1765
Tel: 221 33 849 13 13.
Email: rts@rts.sn
Web site: http://www.rts.sn
Profile: National TV station of Senegal covering regional, national and international news and current affairs including culture, society, entertainment and sport.
TELEVISION STATION

Seychelles

Radio

Paradise FM 288827
Editorial: PO Box 321, Victoria, Mahe
Tel: 248 28 96 00.
Email: paradise.fm@sbc.sc
Web site: http://www.sbc.sc
Profile: Local radio station broadcasting in the Seychelles with news, events and music.
FM RADIO STATION

Slovakia

Radio

Rádio Slovensko 668853
Owner: Rozhlas a televízia Slovenska
Editorial: Mýtna 1, Bratislava 81755
Tel: 421 2 60611111.
Email: slovensko@rtvs.sk
Web site: http://slovensko.rtvs.sk
Profile: Rádio Slovensko is a national radio station broadcasting current news, information about traffic and weather conditions, current affairs programs, interviews with interesting people, live broadcasts of sporting and other events.
FM RADIO STATION

Solomon Islands

Radio

Paua FM 538701
Owner: Communications Fiji Ltd
Editorial: Honiara, Solomon Islands **Tel:** 677 38 984.
Email: pacafm@welcam.solomon.com.sb
RADIO NETWORK

Radio Hapi Lagun 291075
Editorial: PO Box 78, Gizo
Email: sibcnews@solomon.com.sb
Web site: http://www.sibconline.com.sb
FM RADIO STATION

Radio Happy Isles 290962
Editorial: PO Box 654, Honiara **Tel:** 677 20 051.
Email: sibcnews@solomon.com.sb
RADIO NETWORK

Radio Temotu 290963
Editorial: PO Box 46, Lata
Email: sibcnews@solomon.com.sb
Web site: http://www.sibconline.com.sb
FM RADIO STATION

Solomon Islands Broadcasting Corporation (SIBC) 538702
Owner: Solomon Islands Broadcasting Corporation (SIBC)
Editorial: PO Box 654, Honiara, Solomon Islands
Tel: 677 20051.
Email: sibcnews@solomon.com.sb
Web site: http://sibconline.com.sb
Profile: SIBC is a public service broadcaster which facilitates educational programs, recording and promotion of local music and the unity of diverse cultures in a scattered island nation.
RADIO NETWORK

Wantok FM 96.3 290964
Editorial: PO Box 654, Honiara **Tel:** 677 29 600.
Email: sibcnews@solomon.com.sb
Web site: http://www.sibconline.com.sb
RADIO NETWORK

South Africa

Television

Africa News Network 7 (ANN7) 882730
Tel: 27 11 5421222.
Email: ann7online@ann7.com
Web site: http://www.ann7.com
TELEVISION STATION

Business Day TV 701983
Owner: Business Day TV
Editorial: Avusa House, 4 Biermann Avenue, Rosebank, Johannesburg 2169
Email: news@bdtv.co.za
Web site: http://www.businessdaytv.co.za
Profile: BusinessDay TV is the South Africa's business & markets channel.
TELEVISION STATION

CNBC Africa 510036
Owner: CNBC Africa
Editorial: 5th Floor, The Hudson, No. 30 Hudson Street, De Waterkant, Cape Town 8001
Tel: 27 21 421 74 50.
Email: feedback@cnbcafrica.com
Web site: http://www.cnbcafrica.com
TELEVISION STATION

eNCA (eNews Channel Africa) 863357
Editorial: 5 Summit Road, Dunkeld West, Johannesburg 2196 **Tel:** 27 11 537 9300.
Email: info@enca.com
Web site: http://www.enca.com
Profile: eNews Channel Africa is South Africa's 24-hour news service with live reports, breaking news, sports, weather, entertainment, financial and business updates, along with a host of topical current affairs shows.
TELEVISION STATION

e-TV 316348
Owner: AZoM.com Pty Ltd
Editorial: PO Box 12124, Mill Street, Gardens 8010
Tel: 27 21 481 45 00.
Email: info@etv.co.za
Web site: http://www.etv.co.za
TELEVISION STATION

SABC 1 316336
Owner: AZoM.com Pty Ltd
Editorial: Private Bag 41, Auckland Park 2006
Tel: 27 11 7146296.
Email: news@sabc.co.za
Web site: http://www.sabc1.co.za
Profile: National television station covering sport, drama, entertainment and religious programming.
TELEVISION STATION

SABC 2 316334
Owner: AZoM.com Pty Ltd
Editorial: Private Bag X41, Auckland Park 2006, Johannesburg **Tel:** 27 11 71 49 111.
Web site: http://www.sabc2.co.za
Profile: National television station broadcasting kids programmes, entertainment, comedy and drama.
TELEVISION STATION

South Africa

SABC 3 316335
Editorial: Private Bag X41, Auckland Park 2006
Tel: 27 11 71 46 100.
Web site: http://www.sabc3.co.za/sabc/home/sabc3
Profile: Television station broadcasting news, sport and drama.
TELEVISION STATION

SABC News 882733
Editorial: Johannesburg **Tel:** 27 11 714 6173.
Web site: http://www.sabc.co.za
Profile: SABC News brings you the latest news from around South Africa and the world, together with multimedia from the SABC's three TV and 18 radio stations.
TELEVISION NETWORK

SuperSport 760725
Tel: 27 11 6866000.
Email: info@supersport.co.za
Web site: http://www.supersport.com
TELEVISION NETWORK

Spain

Radio

Cadena Dial 291243
Editorial: Gran Via 32, 7 planta, Madrid E-28013
Tel: 34 91 34 70 740.
Email: jmgarciam@unionradio.es
Web site: http://www.cadenadial.com
Profile: 78 stations affiliated.
RADIO NETWORK

M80 Radio 291245
Editorial: Gran Via, 32, 7 planta, Madrid 28013
Tel: 34 913 47 08 07.
Email: aalvarez@m80radio.com
Web site: http://www.m80radio.com
Profile: Regional radio network covering general news and current affairs.
RADIO NETWORK

Onda Cero 291246
Owner: Atresmedia
Editorial: C/ Fuerteventura, 12, San Sebastian de los Reyes, Madrid 28703 **Tel:** 34 91 436 64 00.
Email: webmaster@ondacero.es
Web site: http://www.ondacero.es
Profile: National radio station covering news and current affairs and entertainment.
RADIO NETWORK

Radio 3 828257
Owner: RTVE
Editorial: Casa de la Radio, Avda. Radio Television, 4, Madrid 28223 **Tel:** 34 91 346 10 00.
Email: webradio3@rtve.es
Web site: http://www.rtve.es/radio/radio3
Profile: Radio station covering music and culture.
RADIO NETWORK

Radio Cadena Top 291244
Editorial: Calle Manuel Silvela 9, Madrid E-28010
Tel: 34 91 44 75 300.
Email: info@topradio.es
Web site: http://www.topradio.es
Profile: Pop music station. 30 stations affiliated.
RADIO NETWORK

Radio Intereconomía 288511
Owner: Intereconomia
Editorial: Calle Modesto Lafuente, 42, Madrid 28010
Tel: 34 91 432 77 66.
Email: comunicacion@intereconomia.com
Web site: http://www.intereconomia.com/oir-intereconomia-radio
Profile: Radio station broadcasting classical music and economic information.
FM RADIO STATION

Radio Nacional de España - RNE 291248
Editorial: Casa de la Radio, Avda. Radio Television, 4, Madrid 28223 **Tel:** 34 91 346 10 00.
Email: areaeconomia.rne@rtve.es
Web site: http://www.rtve.es/radio
Profile: National radio station covering general news and current affairs including entertainment, politics, economics and culture.
RADIO NETWORK

Radio Santander 288394
Editorial: Pasaje de Pena 2 Int., 7 planta, Santander E-39008 **Tel:** 34 942 31 95 95.
Email: informativos@radiosantander.com
Web site: http://www.radiosantander.com
Profile: Radio Santander is a news radio station in Spain.
FM RADIO STATION

Talk Radio Europe 714361
Owner: Talk Radio Europe
Editorial: Centro Comercial La Colonia, San Pedro de Alcantara, Málaga 29670 **Tel:** 34 952 799 953.
Email: info@talkradioeurope.com
Web site: http://www.talkradioeurope.com
Profile: Radio station providing the English speaking communities on the Costas of southern Spain with a range of first class talk programmes, and a judicious mix of music, all matching the eclectic and sophisticated tastes of our listeners.
FM RADIO STATION

Television

Antena 3 Televisión 362743
Editorial: Avda. Isla Graciosa, 13, San Sebastian De Los Reyes (madrid) 28700 **Tel:** 34 91 62 30 500.
Email: nacional@antena3tv.es
Web site: http://www.antena3.com
Profile: National TV station covering news and current affairs, culture and entertainment.
TELEVISION STATION

Radio Televisión Española - RTVE 871874
Owner: Radio Televisión Española - RTVE
Editorial: Casa de la Radio, Avda. Radio Television, 4, Madrid 28223 **Tel:** 34 91 346 10 00.
Email: instituto.direccion@rtve.es
Web site: http://www.rtve.es
Profile: National TV and Radio network.
TELEVISION NETWORK

RTV 2 658610
Tel: 34 91 346 80 00.
Email: rtve.dircom@rtve.es
Web site: http://www.rtve.es
Profile: Second channel of the Spain national TV station TVE.
TELEVISION STATION

TVE 316072
Owner: RTVE
Editorial: C/ Avenida Radio Television, 4, Madrid 28223 **Tel:** 34 91 34 64 000.
Email: rtve.dircom@rtve.es
Web site: http://www.rtve.es/television
Profile: National television station covering general news and current affairs including society, entertainment and documentaries.
TELEVISION STATION

Suriname

Radio

ABC Radio 290872
Editorial: Maystraat 52, Paramaribo
Tel: 597 011597464555.
Email: ampies@sr.net
Web site: http://www.abcsuriname.com
Profile: Plays different type of music and provides news and entertainment shows.
RADIO NETWORK

Television

ABC TV 330818
Editorial: Maystraat 57, Paramaribo
Tel: 597 011597434247.
Email: ampies@sr.net
Web site: http://www.abcsuriname.com
Profile: Provides daily news, cultural and special entertainment programs targeting youth.
TELEVISION NETWORK

ATV-Suriname 316430
Owner: Algemene Televisie Verzorging(ATV)
Editorial: Van het Hogerhuysstraat 58-60, Paramaribo
Tel: 597 404-611.
Email: news@atv.sr
Web site: http://www.atv.sr
Profile: ATV-Suriname provides educational and entertainment programming in Suriname.
TELEVISION NETWORK

STVS 316429
Editorial: Letitia Vriesdelaan 5, Paramaribo
Tel: 597 011597473032.
Email: info@stvs.sr
Web site: http://www.parbo.com/stvs
Profile: Television station presenting local and international news. The programming includes children and sport shows.
TELEVISION NETWORK

Sweden

Radio

Bandit Rock 106.3 327141
Editorial: MTG Radio, Ringvagen 52, Stockholm 118 67 **Tel:** 46 8 56 27 20 00.
Email: ina.jonsson@mtgradio.se
Web site: http://www.bandit.se
Profile: Bandit Rock 106.3 producerar kommersiell musikradio med inriktning på aktuell rockmusik. Bandit Rock spelar en blandning av rockmusik med fokus på modern, alternativ rock blandat med låtar från förr som håller än idag. Bandit gör även musikdrivna nischprogram för lyssnare som gillar speciella genrer. Stationen har funnits sedan 2004 och är sedan 2010 ett nätverk.
FM RADIO STATION

Guldkanalen 498556
Editorial: Klagerupsvagen 16, Staffanstorp 245 44
Tel: 46 46 25 27 52.
Web site: http://www.guldkanalen.se
Profile: Kommersiella radiostationen Guldkanalen är Skånes lokala radiostation som bjuder på musik dygnet runt. De riktar sig till en vuxen målgrupp och syftar på att de spelar de stora hitsen från 60-talet fram till idag, samtidigt som de blandar med Svensktoppslåtar och nya låtar. Nås via formulär på hemsidan: http://guldkanalen.se/kontakt/
FM RADIO STATION

Lugna Favoriter 288521
Editorial: MTG Radio, Ringvagen 52, Stockholm 118 67 **Tel:** 46 8 56 27 20 00.
Web site: http://www.lugnafavoriter.com
Profile: Önskar ej motta pressutskick. Lugna Favoriter är en kommersiell radiostation som främst spelar lugn populärmusik. Stationens primära utbud är musik och stationen spelar en konsekvent blandning av familjära och populära låtar med tyngd på 1980- och 1990-talen. Under morgonsändningarna finns även lokala nyheter, trafikinformation och väderuppdateringar.
FM RADIO STATION

Mix Megapol 289269
Editorial: Gjorwellsgatan 30, Stockholm 112 60
Tel: 46 8 45 03 300.
Email: info@mixmegapol.com
Web site: http://www.radioplay.se/mixmegapol
Profile: Mix Megapol är ett kommersiellt nätverk av radiostationer som spelar en blandning av 1980-, 1990- och 2000-tals-musik ("Mer musik - bättre blandning"). I dag sänder Mix Megapol i 36 koncessionsområden i Sverige och på Åland och når 91% av Sveriges befolkning. Radiosändningarna kan också höras på www.radioplay.se samt även i mobilappen Radio Play. Nätverket ingår i tyska Bauer Media Group.
FM RADIO STATION

NRJ 289034
Editorial: Bauer Media Group, Gjorwellsgatan 30, Stockholm 100 26 **Tel:** 46 8 56 27 20 00.
Email: daillou.axelsson@bauermedia.se
Web site: http://www.radioplay.se/nrj
Profile: NRJ är en radiokanal som når 70 procent av Sveriges befolkning. Stationen spelar hits non stop för unga vuxna.
FM RADIO STATION

Rix FM 289026
Editorial: Soder Malarstrand 31, Stockholm 118 25
Tel: 46 85 62 72 000.
Web site: http://www.ilikeradio.se/rixfm/
Profile: Rix FM är en kommersiell, underhållningsradiokanal som spelar "bäst musik just nu", sänder talkshows och håller tävlingar.
FM RADIO STATION

Rockklassiker 289516
Editorial: Gjorwellsgatan 30 (DN-huset), Stockholm 112 60 **Tel:** 46 8 45 03 303.
Web site: http://www.radioplay.se/rockklassiker
Profile: Rockklassiker är en kommersiell radiostation och Sveriges största rockstation med alla klassiska rockhits från 70-talet till 2000-talets början! Stationen hette tidigare Klassiska hits men bytte år 1999 namn till Rockklassiker. Kanalen sänder i Borgholm, Borlänge, Gotland, Hedemora, Kalmar, Kungsbacka, Lidköping, Malmö/Lund, Skellefteå, Stockholm, Sundsvall, Sävsjö, Veberöd, Värnamo och Örnsköldsvik. Kontaktas via formulär på hemsidan: http://www.radioplay.se/rockklassiker/kontakt
FM RADIO STATION

Sveriges Radio - Sameradion 911133
Editorial: Sveriges Radio Sameradion, osterleden 21, Kiruna 981 24 **Tel:** 46 98 07 50 20.
Email: sameradion@sverigesradio.se
Web site: http://sverigesradio.se/sameradion/
Profile: Sameradion är en egen kanal i Sveriges Radio som sänder på fyra olika språk; sydsamiska, lulesamiska, nordsamiska och svenska. Redaktionen sänder nyheter, aktualiteter, kultur, sport, underhållning, debatt, barnradio och ungdomsradio. Sameradion sänder 2 timmar och 25 minuter varje vardag i P2. Utöver det kan man även höra 1 timme på söndag i P2 och 15 minuter 2 gånger per vecka i P4-Jämtland samt 24 timmar på Sveriges Radio Sápmi. Sedan 2015 har Sameradion och SVT Sápmi slått ihop sina verksamheter helt i Kiruna, med en gemensam chef och en arbetsledare.
RADIO NETWORK

Sveriges Radio - Sisuradio 291016
Editorial: Oxenstiernsgatan 20, Stockholm 105 10
Tel: 46 8 78 42 400.
Email: sisuradio@sverigesradio.se
Web site: http://www.sverigesradio.se/sisuradio
Profile: Sisuradio är Sveriges Radios finskspråkiga kanal. Kanalen sänder allt från nyheter till underhållning på finska och tornedalsfinska - 16 timmar om dagen. Kanalen erbjuder även fyra timmar i veckan på svenska. Sisuradio is a Finnish Radio Station in Sweden broadcasting news and entertainment everyday.
RADIO NETWORK

Sveriges Radio P1 845453
Owner: Sveriges Radio AB
Editorial: Sveriges Radio P1, Oxenstiernsgatan 20, Stockholm 105 10 **Tel:** 46 87 84 50 00.
Web site: http://sverigesradio.se/P1
Profile: Sveriges Radio P1 är rikskanalen som ger fördjupning. P1 är den talade kanalen. P1 är kanalen för kvalificerade nyheter. Och det är definitivt P1 du ska lyssna på om det är vetenskap, dokumentärer, film, konst, teater, litteratur eller livsåskådningsfrågor som intresserar dig. Vill ej motta utskick!
RADIO NETWORK

Sveriges Radio P2 Musik 862897
Editorial: Radiohuset, Oxenstiernsgatan 20, Stockholm 105 10 **Tel:** 46 8 78 45 000.
Web site: http://sverigesradio.se/sida/tabla.aspx?programid=2562
Profile: Sveriges Radio P2 är en rikstäckande kanal med ett dubbelt uppdrag: dels att sända musikprogram inom konstmusik, jazz och folkmusik. Dels att sända program på andra språk än svenska. P2 associeras ofta med klassisk musik och det är mycket riktigt en radiokanal där du hör konstmusik från alla tidsåldrar. P2 sänder även improvisationsmusik (t ex jazz), traditionsmusik och gränsöverskridande musik du inte kan höra i någon annan FM-kanal. P2 är Sveriges i särklass största livescen för klassiskt, folkmusik och jazz.
RADIO NETWORK

Sveriges Radio P3 863229
Editorial: Radiohuset, Oxenstiernsgatan 20, Stockholm 105 10 **Tel:** 46 8 78 45 000.
Web site: http://www.sverigesradio.se/p3
Profile: Sveriges Radio P3 producerar radio som innehåller musik, underhållning, samhälle och kultur. P3 är radio för och av unga människor i Sverige.
RADIO NETWORK

Sveriges Radio P4 845457
Editorial: Sveriges Radio P4, Oxenstiernsgatan 20, Stockholm 105 10 **Tel:** 46 8 78 49 500.
Email: p4stockholm@sverigesradio.se
Web site: http://sverigesradio.se/p4
Profile: Sveriges Radio P4 är en radiokanal som täcker hela Sverige, och drivs av Sveriges Radio. Den startades 1987 och vänder sig till en vuxen publik. P4 är Sveriges Radios mest lyssnade kanal, och används under dagtid av de 25 lokala radiostationer som sänder lokalt över en viss region. Under kvällar, nätter och helger sänds nationella program i kanalen, eller så sker då samsändningar med P3 då de båda är populärkanaler. Programmen i P4 handlar ofta om det svenska samhället och lokala händelser, eller om nationella fenomen i Sverige och omvärlden, men till skillnad från P1 spelas även musik (oftast populärmusik).
RADIO NETWORK

Sveriges Radio P4 Blekinge 289701
Editorial: Hogabersgatan 3, Karlskrona 371 34
Tel: 46 455 36 68 00.
Email: nyheter.blekinge@sverigesradio.se
Web site: http://www.sverigesradio.se/blekinge
Profile: I P4 Blekinge hör du lokala nyheter, lokala aktualiteter och lokal kultur. En heltäckande, angelägen kanal för regionen.
RADIO NETWORK

Sveriges Radio P4 Blekinge - Sporten 289936
Editorial: Hogabersgatan 3, Karlskrona 371 34
Tel: 46 455 36 68 00.
Web site: http://sverigesradio.se/sida/gruppsida.aspx?programid=21&grupp=3824
Profile: Sportredaktionen på Sveriges Radio Blekinge. Önskar ej motta pressutskick.
RADIO NETWORK

Sveriges Radio P4 Dalarna 290683
Editorial: P4 Dalarna, Sveriges Radio, Engelbrektsgatan 27 B, Falun 791 60
Tel: 46 23 77 77 00.
Email: dalanytt@sverigesradio.se
Web site: http://www.sverigesradio.se/dalarna
Profile: P4 Dalarna gör angelägen lokal radio för dalfolket, på plats när det händer. I deras program och nyheter hör man ämnen som berör, alltid dagsaktuella och alltid med Dalarna i centrum.
RADIO NETWORK

Sveriges Radio P4 Dalarna - Klartext 290720
Editorial: P4 Dalarna, Sveriges Radio, Engelbrektsgatan 27B, Falun 791 60
Tel: 46 23 77 77 50.
Email: klartext@sverigesradio.se
Web site: http://sverigesradio.se/sida/default.aspx?programid=493
Profile: Klartext är ett nyhetsprogram på lätt svenska i Sveriges Radio P4. Varje vardagskväll berättar Klartext om nyheter inom politik, ekonomi, utrikeshändelser och mycket annat. Programmet är för de som vill höra om nyheter på ett lite lugnare sätt och med enkla ord. Programmet sänds vardagar 18.55-19:00 i P4 och 20:55-21:00 i P1.
RADIO NETWORK

Sveriges Radio P4 Dalarna - Sportredaktionen 290721
Editorial: P4 Dalarna, Sveriges Radio, Engelbrektsgatan 27 B, Falun 791 60
Tel: 46 23 77 77 30.
Email: sporten.dalarna@sverigesradio.se
Web site: http://sverigesradio.se/sida/gruppsida.aspx?programid=22&grupp=3825

Profile: Sportredaktionen på Sveriges Radio Dalarna.
RADIO NETWORK

Sveriges Radio P4 Gävleborg
290681
Owner: Förvaltningsstiftelsen för SVT AB, SR AB, UR AB
Editorial: P4 Gavleborg, Nygatan 29, 3tr, Gävle 801 04 **Tel:** 46 26 66 65 00.
Email: p4gavleborg@sverigesradio.se
Web site: http://www.sverigesradio.se/gavleborg
Profile: P4 Gävleborg är en radiokanal som sänder lokala och regionala nyheter, sport, kultur och nöje över Gästrikland och Hälsingland.
RADIO NETWORK

Sveriges Radio P4 Gävleborg - Bollnäs
289727
Editorial: Vaggatan 13, Bollnäs 821 42
Tel: 46 26 66 65 80.
Email: info.gavleborg@sverigesradio.se
Web site: http://www.sverigesradio.se/gavleborg
Profile: Sveriges Radio P4 Gävleborgs redaktion i Bollnäs. Lokala nyheter.
RADIO NETWORK

Sveriges Radio P4 Gävleborg - Nyhetsredaktionen
562270
Editorial: P4 Gavleborg, Nygatan 29 3tr, Gävle 801 04
Tel: 46 26 66 65 31.
Email: nyheterna.gavleborg@sverigesradio.se
Web site: http://sverigesradio.se/sida/default.aspx?programid=99
Profile: Lokala nyhetssändningar i Gävleborg. P4 Gävleborg är en radiokanal som sänder lokala och regionala nyheter över Gästrikland och Hälsingland.
RADIO NETWORK

Sveriges Radio P4 Gävleborg - Sportredaktionen
570335
Owner: Förvaltningsstiftelsen för SVT AB, SR AB, UR AB
Editorial: P4 Gavleborg, Nygatan 29 3tr, Gävle 801 04
Tel: 46 26 66 65 00.
Email: nyheterna.gavleborg@sverigesradio.se
Web site: http://sverigesradio.se/sida/gruppsida.aspx?programid=24&grupp=3827
Profile: Sportredaktionen på Sveriges Radio Gävleborg. Lokal sport från Gävleborg i radion och på webben, från elit till amatör.
RADIO NETWORK

Sveriges Radio P4 Göteborg
290673
Editorial: P4 Sveriges Radio Goteborg, Pumpgatan 2, Goteborg 405 13 **Tel:** 46 31 83 76 00.
Email: P4goteborg@sverigesradio.se
Web site: http://sverigesradio.se/goteborg
Profile: Sveriges Radio Göteborg gör inte bara radio för P4 Radio Göteborg utan också för rikskanalerna P1, P2, P3, Ekot, P7 Sisuradion och P4 Riks. Totalt är de drygt 100 medarbetare som jobbar för Sveriges Radio Göteborg. Några av våra många programrubriker är Christer i P3, Morronpasset i P3, Kvällspasset, Ring P1, Språket, Mitt i musiken, Kaliber med flera. Dessutom till exempel Radioteater och Sport.
RADIO NETWORK

Sveriges Radio P4 Göteborg; Sportredaktionen
289934
Owner: Förvaltningsstiftelsen för SVT AB, SR AB, UR AB
Editorial: Sveriges Radio P4 Goteborg, Pumpgatan 2, Goteborg 405 13 **Tel:** 46 31 83 76 00.
Email: p4goteborg@sverigesradio.se
Web site: http://sverigesradio.se/sida/gruppsida.aspx?programid=25&grupp=3828
Profile: Sportredaktionen på Sveriges Radio Göteborg.
RADIO NETWORK

Sveriges Radio P4 Gotland 912470
Editorial: Sveriges Radio Gotland, ostra Hansegatan 28, Visby 621 24 **Tel:** 46 498 75 00 00.
Email: info.gotland@sverigesradio.se
Web site: http://www.sverigesradio.se/gotland
Profile: P4 Gotland bevakar det som händer på och omkring Gotland, med nyheter, intervjuer och reportage.
RADIO NETWORK

Sveriges Radio P4 Gotland - Nyhets- & programredaktion
317155
Editorial: Sveriges Radio Gotland, ostra Hansegatan 28, Visby 621 24 **Tel:** 46 498 75 00 00.
Email: gotlandsnytt@sverigesradio.se
Web site: http://sverigesradio.se/gotland
Profile: P4 Gotland bevakar det som händer på och omkring Gotland, med nyheter, intervjuer och reportage.
RADIO NETWORK

Sveriges Radio P4 Gotland - Sportredaktionen
570336
Editorial: Sveriges Radio Gotland, ostra Hansegatan 28, Visby 621 24 **Tel:** 46 498 75 00 00.
Email: gotlandssporten@sverigesradio.se
Web site: http://sverigesradio.se/sida/gruppsida.aspx?programid=94&grupp=3826
Profile: Sveriges Radio P4 Gotlands sportredaktion. De bevakar gotländska idrottsprestationer i många olika sammanhang. Ofta sänder de direkt.
RADIO NETWORK

Sveriges Radio P4 Halland 572601
Editorial: Sveriges Radio P4 Halland, Kopmansgatan 41, Halmstad 302 32 **Tel:** 46 35 17 27 00.
Email: p4halland@sverigesradio.se
Web site: http://sverigesradio.se/halland/
Profile: Sveriges Radio P4 Halland är en regional radiokanal som sänder nyheter och aktuella program för invånarna.
RADIO NETWORK

Sveriges Radio P4 Halland - Nyhetsredaktionen
290675
Editorial: Sveriges Radio P4 Halland, Kopmansgatan 41, Halmstad 302 32 **Tel:** 46 35 17 27 00.
Email: nyheter.halland@sverigesradio.se
Web site: http://www.sverigesradio.se/halland
Profile: Sveriges Radio P4 Halland nyhetsredaktion sänder lokala nyhetssändningar för Halland.
RADIO NETWORK

Sveriges Radio P4 Halland - Sportredaktionen
572600
Editorial: Sveriges Radio P4 Halland, Kopmansgatan 41, Halmstad 302 32 **Tel:** 46 35 17 27 00.
Email: sporten.halland@sverigesradio.se
Web site: http://sverigesradio.se/sida/gruppsida.aspx?programid=26&grupp=3829
Profile: Sportredaktionen på Sveriges Radio Halland.
RADIO NETWORK

Sveriges Radio P4 Halland - Varberg
290656
Editorial: Otto Torells gata 14, Varberg 432 44
Email: nyheter.halland@sverigesradio.se
Web site: http://www.sverigesradio.se/halland
Profile: Sveriges Radio P4 Hallands lokalredaktion i Varberg.
RADIO NETWORK

Sveriges Radio P4 Jämtland
572811
Editorial: Lingonvagen 21, Östersund 831 62
Tel: 46 63 16 06 00.
Email: p4jamtland@sverigesradio.se
Web site: http://sverigesradio.se/jamtland
Profile: Sveriges Radio P4 Jämtland sänder lokalradio i Jämtlandsregionen. I P4 Jämtland hör du lokala nyheter, aktualiteter, väderprognoser, sport och kultur.
RADIO NETWORK

Sveriges Radio P4 Jämtland - Nyhetsredaktionen
290678
Editorial: Lingonvagen 21, Östersund 831 62
Tel: 46 63 16 06 32.
Email: nyheter.jamtland@sverigesradio.se
Web site: http://sverigesradio.se/sida/avsnitt?programid=78
Profile: Nyhetsredaktionen på Sveriges Radio Jämtland.
RADIO NETWORK

Sveriges Radio P4 Jämtland - Sportredaktionen
572812
Editorial: Lingonvagen 21, Östersund 831 62
Tel: 46 63 16 06 00.
Email: sport.jamtland@sverigesradio.se
Web site: http://sverigesradio.se/sida/gruppsida.aspx?programid=27&grupp=3830
Profile: Sportredaktionen på Sveriges Radio Jämtland.
RADIO NETWORK

Sveriges Radio P4 Jönköping
290672
Editorial: Barnarpsgatan 35 D, Jönköping 553 16
Tel: 46 36 21 56 600.
Email: p4jonkoping@sverigesradio.se
Web site: http://www.sverigesradio.se/jonkoping
Profile: P4 Jönköping Sveriges Radio bevakar Jönköpings län. Nyheterna, sporten och kulturen. I P4 Jönköping Sveriges Radio hör du lokala nyheter, lokala aktualiteter och lokal kultur för Jönköpings län.
RADIO NETWORK

Sveriges Radio P4 Jönköping - Sportredaktionen
845154
Editorial: Sveriges Radio Jonkoping, Besoksadress: Barnarpsgatan 35 D, Jönköping 551 92
Tel: 46 36 215 66 00.
Email: sport.jkpg@sverigesradio.se
Web site: http://sverigesradio.se/sida/gruppsida.aspx?programid=28&grupp=3831
Profile: Sportredaktionen på Sveriges Radio Jönköping.
RADIO NETWORK

Sveriges Radio P4 Jönköping - Värnamo
317129
Editorial: Jonkopingsvagen 43 B, Värnamo 331 34
Tel: 46 36 21 56 660.
Email: p4jonkoping@sverigesradio.se
Web site: http://www.sverigesradio.se/jonkoping
Profile: Sveriges Radio P4 Jönköpings lokalredaktion i Värnamo.
RADIO NETWORK

Sveriges Radio P4 Kalmar 573486
Editorial: Norra vagen 22, Kalmar 392 34
Tel: 46 480 45 80 00.
Email: p4kalmar@sverigesradio.se
Web site: http://sverigesradio.se/kalmar/
Profile: Sveriges Radio P4 Kalmar bevakar hela Kalmar län och ger lokala nyheter och program.
RADIO NETWORK

Sveriges Radio P4 Kalmar - Sportredaktionen
371212
Editorial: Norra vagen 22, Kalmar 392 34
Tel: 46 480 45 80 00.
Email: sport.kalmar@sverigesradio.se
Web site: http://sverigesradio.se/sida/gruppsida.aspx?programid=30&grupp=3832
Profile: Sportredaktionen på Sveriges Radio Kalmar bevakar lokal sport.
RADIO NETWORK

Sveriges Radio P4 Kristianstad
573703
Editorial: Gasverksgatan 2, Kristianstad 291 54
Tel: 46 44 77 51 200.
Email: nyheterna.kristianstad@sverigesradio.se
Web site: http://sverigesradio.se/kristianstad/
Profile: Sveriges Radios lokala radio för Kristianstad. P4 Kristianstad hör du lokala nyheter, lokala aktualiteter och lokal kultur. Nyheter från östra och norra Skåne.
RADIO NETWORK

Sveriges Radio P4 Kristianstad - Nyhetsredaktionen
290197
Editorial: Sveriges Radio Kristianstad, Gasverksgatan 2, Kristianstad 291 54 **Tel:** 46 44 77 51 200.
Email: nyheterna.kristianstad@sverigesradio.se
Web site: http://sverigesradio.se/sida/avsnitt?programid=101
Profile: Nyhetsredaktionen på Sveriges Radio Kristianstad.
RADIO NETWORK

Sveriges Radio P4 Kristianstad - Simrishamn
290652
Editorial: Sveriges Radio Kristianstad, Jarnvagsgatan 5, Simrishamn 272 32 **Tel:** 46 414 14 655.
Email: nyheterna.kristianstad@sverigesradio.se
Web site: http://www.sverigesradio.se/kristianstad
Profile: Sveriges Radio P4 Kristianstads lokalredaktion i Simrishamn.
RADIO NETWORK

Sveriges Radio P4 Kristianstad - Sportredaktionen
573701
Editorial: Sveriges Radio Kristianstad, Gasverksgatan 2, Kristianstad 291 54 **Tel:** 46 44 77 51 200.
Email: sporten.kristianstad@sverigesradio.se
Web site: http://sverigesradio.se/sida/gruppsida.aspx?programid=29&grupp=3833
Profile: Sportredaktionen på Sveriges Radio Kristianstad.
RADIO NETWORK

Sveriges Radio P4 Kronoberg
290680
Editorial: Vastergatan 1, Växjo **Tel:** 46 470 72 60 00.
Email: p4kronoberg@sverigesradio.se
Web site: http://www.sverigesradio.se/kronoberg
Profile: P4 Kronoberg är en radiokanal för nyheter, sport och underhållning med anknytning till Kronoberg.
RADIO NETWORK

Sveriges Radio P4 Kronoberg - Nyhetsredaktionen
845348
Editorial: Vastergatan 1, Växjo 352 30
Tel: 46 470 72 60 50.
Email: nyheter.kronoberg@sverigesradio.se
Web site: http://www.sverigesradio.se/kronoberg
Profile: Sveriges Radio Kronobergs nyhetsredaktion.
FM RADIO STATION

Sveriges Radio P4 Kronoberg - Sportredaktionen
577599
Editorial: Vastergatan 1, Växjo 352 30
Tel: 46 470 72 60 00.
Email: sporten.kronoberg@sverigesradio.se
Web site: http://sverigesradio.se/sida/gruppsida.aspx?programid=31&grupp=3834
Profile: Sportredaktionen på Sveriges Radio Kronoberg.
FM RADIO STATION

Sveriges Radio P4 Malmö 371205
Editorial: Balzarsgatan 16, Malmo 211 01
Tel: 46 40 666 55 00.
Email: p4malmohus@sverigesradio.se
Web site: http://www.sverigesradio.se/malmo
Profile: Sveriges Radio Malmö. Kanalledning och personal som jobbar med lokalt sända program för alla skåningar, speciellt alla i västra, mellersta och södra Skåne.
FM RADIO STATION

Sveriges Radio P4 Malmö - Nyhetsredaktionen
811881
Editorial: Baltzarsgatan 16, Malmo 211 01
Tel: 46 40 666 55 00.
Email: news.malm@sverigesradio.se
Web site: http://sverigesradio.se/malmo/
Profile: Nyhetsredaktionen på Sveriges Radio P4 Malmö. Redaktionen sänder lokala nyheter som rör och berör Skånes 33 kommuner.
FM RADIO STATION

Sveriges Radio P4 Malmö - Sportredaktionen
371215
Editorial: Balzarsgatan 16, Malmo 211 01
Tel: 46 40 666 55 00.
Email: sporten.malm@sverigesradio.se
Web site: http://sverigesradio.se/sida/gruppsida.aspx?programid=32&grupp=3835
Profile: Sportredaktionen på Sveriges Radio P4 Malmö.
FM RADIO STATION

Sveriges Radio P4 Malmö/ Sveriges Radio P4 Kristianstad - Helsingborg
811863
Editorial: Drottninggatan 72 A, Helsingborg 252 21
Tel: 46 42 13 33 00.
Email: nordvast@sverigesradio.se
Web site: http://sverigesradio.se/malmo/
Profile: Sveriges Radio P4 Malmös lokalredaktion i Helsingborg.
FM RADIO STATION

Sveriges Radio P4 Norrbotten
290677
Editorial: Nygatan 3, Luleå 971 71
Tel: 46 920 27 53 00.
Email: p4norrbotten@sverigesradio.se
Web site: http://sverigesradio.se/norrbotten/
Profile: Sveriges Radios lokala och regionala nyheter i Norrbotten. Sveriges Radio P4 har redaktioner i Luleå, Piteå, Arvidsjaur, Pajala, Gällivare och Kiruna.
FM RADIO STATION

Sveriges Radio P4 Norrbotten - Gällivare
290660
Editorial: Box 264, Industrigatan 4, Gällivare 982 31
Tel: 46 970 789 70.
Email: nyheter.norrbotten@sverigesradio.se
Web site: http://sverigesradio.se/sida/gruppsida.aspx?programid=98&grupp=3592
Profile: Sveriges Radio P4 Norrbottens lokalredaktion i Gällivare. För närvarande obemannad.
FM RADIO STATION

Sveriges Radio P4 Norrbotten - Nyhetsredaktionen
289634
Editorial: Nygatan 3, Luleå 971 71
Tel: 46 920 27 53 50.
Email: nyheter.norrbotten@sverigesradio.se
Web site: http://www.sverigesradio.se/norrbotten
Profile: Regionala och lokala nyheter från Sveriges Radio P4 Norrbotten.
FM RADIO STATION

Sveriges Radio P4 Norrbotten - Pajala/Meänraatio
371200
Editorial: Medborgarvagen 3, Pajala 984 31
Tel: 46 978 27 78 00.
Web site: http://sverigesradio.se/sida/gruppsida.aspx?programid=98&grupp=3598
Profile: Sveriges Radio P4 Norrbottens lokalredaktion i Pajala. Redaktionen sänder på tornedalsfinska och vänder sig främst till tornedalingar och finländare i Norrbotten och Finland. Önskar ej motta pressutskick.
RADIO NETWORK

Sveriges Radio P4 Norrbotten - Sportredaktionen
290789
Editorial: Nygatan 3, Luleå 971 71
Tel: 46 920 27 53 70.
Email: sporten.norrbotten@sverigesradio.se
Web site: http://sverigesradio.se/sida/gruppsida.aspx?programid=33&grupp=3836
Profile: Sportredaktionen på Sveriges Radio P4 Norrbotten.
RADIO NETWORK

Sveriges Radio P4 Örebro 371204
Editorial: Vastra Bangatan 15, Orebro 701 80
Tel: 46 19 19 20 00.
Email: p4orebro@sverigesradio.se
Web site: http://sverigesradio.se/orebro
Profile: Sveriges Radio P4 Örebro sänder lokala nyheter, aktualiteter och kultur i regionen.
RADIO NETWORK

Sveriges Radio P4 Örebro - Sport
910931
Editorial: Vastra Bangatan 15, Orebro 701 80
Tel: 46 19 19 20 00.
Email: nyheter.orebro@sverigesradio.se
Web site: http://sverigesradio.se/sida/gruppsida.aspx?programid=44&grupp=3847
Profile: Sveriges Radio P4 Örebros sportredaktion.
RADIO NETWORK

Sveriges Radio P4 Östergötland
289941
Editorial: Vastgotegatan 13 A, Norrköping 601 07
Tel: 46 11 49 54 100.
Email: nyheter.ostg@sverigesradio.se
Web site: http://www.sverigesradio.se/ostergotland
Profile: P4 Östergötland sänder lokala nyheter, underhållning och kultur i regionen.
RADIO NETWORK

Sveriges Radio P4 Östergötland - Linköping
290669
Editorial: Apotekaregatan 13 D, Linköping 582 24
Tel: 46 11 49 54 100.
Email: nyheter.ostg@sr.se

Sweden

Web site: http://www.sverigesradio.se/ostergotland
Profile: Sveriges Radio P4 Östergötlands lokalredaktion i Linköping.
RADIO NETWORK

Sveriges Radio P4 Östergötland - Sport 910941
Editorial: Vastgotegatan 13 A, Norrköping 601 07
Tel: 46 11 49 54 100.
Email: sport.ostg@sverigesradio.se
Web site: http://sverigesradio.se/sida/gruppsida.aspx?programid=45&grupp=3848
Profile: Sveriges Radio P4 Östergötlands sportredaktion.
RADIO NETWORK

Sveriges Radio P4 Sjuhärad 290682
Editorial: P4 Sjuharad Sveriges Radio, Katrinedalsgatan 22, Borås 501 13
Tel: 46 33 17 75 00.
Email: p4sjuharad@sverigesradio.se
Web site: http://www.sverigesradio.se/sjuharad
Profile: Sveriges Radio P4 Sjuhärad är en lokal kanal i Sveriges Radio P4. Når trakterna runt Borås, Falköping, Alingsås.
RADIO NETWORK

Sveriges Radio P4 Sjuhärad - Sportredaktionen 290724
Owner: Sveriges Radio AB
Editorial: P4 Sjuharad Sveriges Radio, Box 27, Borås 501 13 **Tel:** 46 33 17 75 00.
Email: sporten.sjuharad@sr.se
Web site: http://sverigesradio.se/sida/gruppsida.aspx?programid=34&grupp=3839
Profile: Sveriges Radio P4 Sjuhärads sportredaktion.
RADIO NETWORK

Sveriges Radio P4 Skaraborg 579198
Editorial: Norra Bergvagen 4, Skövde
Tel: 46 500 77 30 00.
Email: p4.skaraborg@sverigesradio.se
Web site: http://www.sverigesradio.se/skaraborg
Profile: Sveriges Radio P4 Skaraborg levererar lokala nyheter i Skaraborg.
RADIO NETWORK

Sveriges Radio P4 Skaraborg - Nyhetsredaktionen 290797
Editorial: Norra Bergvagen 4, Skövde
Tel: 46 500 77 30 10.
Email: nyheterna.skaraborg@sverigesradio.se
Web site: http://www.sverigesradio.se/skaraborg
Profile: Sveriges Radio P4 Skaraborgs nyhetsredaktion.
RADIO NETWORK

Sveriges Radio P4 Skaraborg - Sportredaktionen 371216
Editorial: Norra Bergvagen 4, Skövde
Tel: 46 500 77 30 00.
Email: sporten.skaraborg@sverigesradio.se
Web site: http://sverigesradio.se/sida/gruppsida.aspx?programid=35&grupp=3840
Profile: Sveriges Radio P4 Skaraborgs sportredaktion.
RADIO NETWORK

Sveriges Radio P4 Sörmland 289494
Editorial: Rademachergatan 1, Eskilstuna 632 21
Tel: 46 16 16 16 00.
Email: p4sormland@sverigesradio.se
Web site: http://sverigesradio.se/sormland/
Profile: Sveriges Radio P4 Sörmland presenterar regionala nyheter, aktualiteter, kultur och livsstilsfrågor tillsammans med bred radiounderhållning i form av både klassiker och nysatsningar. Sveriges Radio P4 Sörmland har redaktioner i Eskilstuna och i Nyköping.
RADIO NETWORK

Sveriges Radio P4 Sörmland - Nyhetsredaktionen 915120
Editorial: Rademachergatan 1, Eskilstuna 632 21
Tel: 46 16 16 16 00.
Email: sormland@sverigesradio.se
Web site: http://sverigesradio.se/sormland/
Profile: Nyhetsredaktionen på Sveriges Radio P4 Sörmland.
RADIO NETWORK

Sveriges Radio P4 Sörmland - Nyköping 290663
Editorial: Sankt Annegatan 4, Nyköping 611 34
Tel: 46 16 16 16 00.
Email: sormland@sverigesradio.se
Web site: http://www.sverigesradio.se/sormland
Profile: Sveriges Radio P4 Sörmlands lokalredaktion i Nyköping.
RADIO NETWORK

Sveriges Radio P4 Sörmland - Sportredaktionen 581257
Editorial: Rademachergatan 1, Eskilstuna 632 21
Tel: 46 16 16 16 00.
Email: sport.sormland@sverigesradio.se
Web site: http://sverigesradio.se/sida/gruppsida.aspx?programid=37&grupp=3841
Profile: Sportredaktionen på Sveriges Radio P4 Sörmland.
RADIO NETWORK

Sveriges Radio P4 Stockholm 371203
Editorial: Oxenstiernsgatan 20, Stockholm
Tel: 46 8 784 95 00.
Email: p4stockholm@sverigesradio.se
Web site: http://www.sverigesradio.se/stockholm
Profile: Sveriges Radio P4 Stockholm är Stockholms största radiokanal. Kanalen levererar lokala nyheter, sport och kultur.
RADIO NETWORK

Sveriges Radio P4 Stockholm - Nyhetsredaktionen 559138
Editorial: Oxenstiernsgatan 20, Stockholm 105 10
Tel: 46 8 784 95 00.
Email: news.sth@sverigesradio.se
Web site: http://www.sverigesradio.se/stockholm
Profile: Nyhetsredaktionen för Sveriges Radio P4 Radio Stockholm. De sänder lokala nyheter från Stockholmregionen.
RADIO NETWORK

Sveriges Radio P4 Stockholm - Sportredaktionen 578138
Editorial: Sveriges Radio P4 Radio Stockholm, Oxenstiernsgatan 20, Stockholm 105 10
Tel: 46 8 78 49 500.
Email: stockholmsnytt@sverigesradio.se
Web site: http://sverigesradio.se/sida/gruppsida.aspx?programid=36&grupp=3837
Profile: Sportredaktionen på Sveriges Radio P4 Stockholm.
RADIO NETWORK

Sveriges Radio P4 Uppland 583059
Editorial: Bredgrand 7, Uppsala **Tel:** 46 18 17 40 00.
Email: p4uppland@sverigesradio.se
Web site: http://www.sverigesradio.se/uppland
Profile: Sveriges Radio P4 Uppland bevakar Uppland/Uppsala län och levererar lokala nyheter, viktiga samhällsfrågor och underhållning. Redaktionen granskar makten, bevakar sporten och följer kulturlivet. Sveriges Radio P4 Uppland producerar även riksprogram som Kossornas Planet, P4 Dokumentär och Karlavagnen.
RADIO NETWORK

Sveriges Radio P4 Uppland - Nyhetsredaktionen 290041
Editorial: Box 1552, Bredgrand 7, Uppsala 751 45
Tel: 46 18 17 40 00.
Email: upplandsnytt@sverigesradio.se
Web site: http://www.sverigesradio.se/uppland
Profile: Sveriges Radio P4 Upplands nyhetsredaktionen; Upplandsnytt.
RADIO NETWORK

Sveriges Radio P4 Uppland - Sportredaktionen 911067
Editorial: Bredgrand 7, Uppsala 751 45
Tel: 46 18 17 40 00.
Email: sporten.uppland@sverigesradio.se
Web site: http://sverigesradio.se/sida/gruppsida.aspx?programid=38&grupp=3842
Profile: Sveriges Radio P4 Upplands sportredaktion.
RADIO NETWORK

Sveriges Radio P4 Värmland 289971
Editorial: Verkstadsgatan 20, Karlstad 652 19
Tel: 46 54 777 26 00.
Email: p4varmland@sverigesradio.se
Web site: http://www.sverigesradio.se/varmland
Profile: Sveriges Radio P4 Värmland levererar lokala nyheter, lokala aktualiteter och lokal kultur för Värmland.
RADIO NETWORK

Sveriges Radio P4 Värmland - Sportredaktionen 911081
Editorial: Verkstadsgatan 20, Karlstad 652 19
Tel: 46 54 777 26 00.
Email: sporten.varmland@sverigesradio.se
Web site: http://sverigesradio.se/sida/gruppsida.aspx?programid=39&grupp=3843
Profile: Sveriges Radio P4 Värmlands sportredaktion.
RADIO NETWORK

Sveriges Radio P4 Värmland - Torsby 290664
Editorial: Alstigen 8C, Torsby 685 34
Tel: 46 54 777 26 00.
Email: p4varmland@sverigesradio.se
Web site: http://www.sverigesradio.se/varmland
Profile: Sveriges Radio P4 Värmlands lokalredaktion i Torsby.
RADIO NETWORK

Sveriges Radio P4 Väst 578467
Editorial: P4 Vast Sveriges Radio, Sodergatan 11, Uddevalla 451 40 **Tel:** 46 522 67 00 00.
Email: nyheter.vast@sverigesradio.se
Web site: http://www.sverigesradio.se/vast
Profile: Sveriges Radio P4 Radio Väst levererar nyheter samt lokalt sända program i norra Bohuslän, Dalsland, Trollhättan, Vänersborg och Lilla Edet.
RADIO NETWORK

Sveriges Radio P4 Väst - Åmål 323468
Editorial: Norra Langgatan 26, Åmål 662 30
Tel: 46 522 67 00 00.
Email: nyheter.vast@sverigesradio.se
Web site: http://sverigesradio.se/sida/gruppsida.aspx?programid=125&grupp=3610
Profile: Sveriges Radio P4 Västs lokalredaktion i Åmål.
RADIO NETWORK

Sveriges Radio P4 Väst - Sport 578466
Editorial: P4 Vast Sveriges Radio, Sodergatan 11, Uddevalla 451 40 **Tel:** 46 522 67 00 00.
Email: sporten.vast@sverigesradio.se
Web site: http://sverigesradio.se/avsnitt?programid=41
Profile: Sportredaktionen på Sveriges Radio P4 Väst.
RADIO NETWORK

Sveriges Radio P4 Västerbotten 290676
Editorial: Mariehemsvagen 4, Umeå 906 15
Tel: 46 90 17 17 00.
Email: p4vasterbotten@sverigesradio.se
Web site: http://www.sverigesradio.se/vasterbotten
Profile: Sveriges Radio P4 Västerbotten sänder lokala nyheter och radioprogram i regionen. De har även lokalredaktioner i Lycksele och Skellefteå.
RADIO NETWORK

Sveriges Radio P4 Västerbotten - Lycksele 290666
Editorial: Storgatan 29, Box 103, Lycksele 921 31
Email: lycksele@sverigesradio.se
Web site: http://www.sverigesradio.se/vasterbotten
Profile: Sveriges Radio P4 Västerbottens lokalredaktion i Lycksele.
RADIO NETWORK

Sveriges Radio P4 Västerbotten - Skellefteå 290667
Editorial: Stationsgatan 9, Skellefteå 931 23
Tel: 46 91 08 87 55.
Email: skelleftea@sverigesradio.se
Web site: http://www.sverigesradio.se/vasterbotten
Profile: Sveriges Radio P4 Västerbottens lokalredaktion i Skellefteå.
RADIO NETWORK

Sveriges Radio P4 Västerbotten - Sport 911098
Editorial: Mariehemsvagen 4, Umeå 906 15
Tel: 46 90 17 17 00.
Email: sporten.vbtn@sverigesradio.se
Web site: http://sverigesradio.se/sida/gruppsida.aspx?programid=42&grupp=3844
Profile: Sveriges Radio P4 Västerbottens sportredaktion.
RADIO NETWORK

Sveriges Radio P4 Västernorrland 371207
Editorial: Kronvagen 18, Sundsvall 851 79
Tel: 46 60 19 03 00.
Email: p4vasternorrland@sverigesradio.se
Web site: http://www.sverigesradio.se/vasternorrland
Profile: Sveriges Radio P4 Västernorrland levererar lokala nyheter, aktualiteter och kultur i regionen.
RADIO NETWORK

Sveriges Radio P4 Västernorrland - Örnsköldsvik 290670
Editorial: Strandgatan 15, Örnsköldsvik 891 33
Tel: 46 66 01 39 45.
Email: p4vasternorrland@sverigesradio.se
Web site: http://www.sverigesradio.se/vasternorrland
Profile: Sveriges Radio P4 Västernorrlands lokalredaktion i Örnsköldsvik.
RADIO NETWORK

Sveriges Radio P4 Västernorrland - Sport 911113
Editorial: Kronvagen 18, Sundsvall 851 79
Email: sport.vasternorrland@sverigesradio.se
Web site: http://sverigesradio.se/sida/gruppsida.aspx?programid=40&grupp=3845
Profile: Sveriges Radio P4 Västernorrlands sportredaktion.
RADIO NETWORK

Sveriges Radio P4 Västmanland 290674
Editorial: Master Ahls Gata 6, Västerås 721 22
Tel: 46 21 49 52 500.
Email: p4vastmanland@sverigesradio.se
Web site: http://www.sverigesradio.se/vastmanland
Profile: Sveriges Radio P4 Västmanland levererar lokala och regionala nyheter för Västmanland. De sänder även i delar av Södermanland och Örebro län.
RADIO NETWORK

Sveriges Radio P4 Västmanland - Sport 911121
Editorial: Master Ahls Gata 6, Västerås 721 22
Tel: 46 21 49 52 500.
Email: sporten.vstm@sverigesradio.se
Web site: http://sverigesradio.se/sida/gruppsida.aspx?programid=43&grupp=3846
Profile: Sveriges Radio P4 Västmanlands sportredaktion.
RADIO NETWORK

Vinyl FM 288512
Editorial: Stockholm
Email: info@vinyl107.se
Web site: http://www.radioplay.se/vinylfm
Profile: Kommersiell, musikbaserad radiostation. Sänder främst musik från 60-, 70- och 80-tal, lokala nyheter med väderprognoser samt trafikinformation.
FM RADIO STATION

Television

Axess TV 498405
Editorial: Jakobsbergsgatan 2, 6 tr, Stockholm 111 44
Tel: 46 87 88 50 50.
Email: info@axess.se
Web site: http://www.axess.se/tv
Profile: Axess Television är en svenskproducerad frikanal via det digitala marknätet, digital kabel-tv och via Telia. Axess erbjuder aktuell svensk och internationell idédebatt inom samhällsvetenskap och humaniora. Axess TV sänder program inom kultur, samhälle och vetenskap. Utbudet består av egenproducerade program och utvalda internationella produktioner.
TELEVISION STATION

C More 364848
Editorial: C More Entertainment AB, Tegeluddsvagen 3-5, Stockholm 115 84
Email: info@cmore.se
Web site: http://www.cmore.se
Profile: C More (tidigare CANAL+) visar filmer, sport och serier. De visar de senaste storfilmerna från Hollywood, svenska favoriter och fascinerande dokumentärer. Man hittar även världens bästa serier från bland andra HBO, NBC och Sony. Serierna visas på C More dagen efter USA-premiären. Kanalen visar direktsänd sport från bland annat Allsvenskan, Elitserien, La Liga och Serie A samt massor av tennis, fighting, motorsport och ridsport. C More har ca 1 000 000 abonnerande hushåll i Norden. De erbjuder totalt 20 kanaler, varav 6 filmkanaler, 1 seriekanal, 9 sportkanaler, och 4 HD-kanaler för sport respektive film/serier.
TELEVISION STATION

C More - Sportredaktionen 827274
Editorial: C More Entertainment AB, Tegeluddsvagen 3-5, Stockholm 115 84
Email: info@cmore.se
Web site: http://www.cmore.se
Profile: C More (tidigare CANAL+) sportkanaler direktsänder de stora internationella och nationella ligorna, framför allt inom fotboll, hockey och motorsport. Bland ligorna återfinns La Liga, Elitserien i hockey, Allsvenskan, Serie A, holländska fotbollsligan, IndyCar, STCC och Elitserien i speedway.
TELEVISION STATION

Eurosport Television AB 310890
Editorial: Sturegatan 2, Sundbyberg 172 24
Tel: 46 85 06 61 000.
Web site: http://www.eurosport.se/
Profile: Redaktionen önskar ej motta pressutskick. Eurosport Television AB är Europas största sportkanal. Sänder på 19 språk till 240 miljoner tittare i 54 länder. Eurosportgruppen består av TV-kanalerna Eurosport, Eurosport 2 och Eurosportnews samt eurosport.com och Eurosport Mobile. Nordiska huvudkontoret ligger i Sundbyberg. Där arbetar ett tjugotal personer med produktion, annonsförsäljning, distribution, marknadsarbete och pressinformation. I Norden är cirka 270 frilanskommentatorer knutna till Eurosport.
TELEVISION STATION

Kanal 11 828740
Editorial: Discovery Networks Sweden, Radmansgatan 42, Stockholm 114 99
Tel: 46 8 52 05 55 55.
Email: calle.jansson@sbstv.se
Web site: http://www.kanal11play.se/
Profile: Kanal 11 (fd. TV11) är en kanal för de som älskar tv och underhållning. Dygnet runt blandar de internationella underhållningsformat med drama, långfilm, en massa humor och de mest omtalade realityserierna. Kanal 11 lanserades som TV11 i januari 2011 av TV4-gruppen, men togs sedan i juni 2013 över av SBS TV och fick senare samma år ett namnbyte till Kanal 11.
TELEVISION STATION

Kanal 5 364875
Editorial: Radmansgatan 42, Stockholm 114 99
Tel: 46 85 20 55 555.
Email: kanal5@discovery.com
Web site: http://www.kanal5play.se
Profile: Kanal 5 är en rikstäckande kommersiell TV-kanal som funnits sedan 1989. Kanalen visar svenska underhållningsprogram, amerikanska serierna och sitcomserier.
TELEVISION STATION

Kanal 9 498509
Editorial: Radmansgatan 42, Stockholm 114 99
Tel: 46 8 52 05 55 55.
Email: kanal9@discovery.com
Web site: http://www.dplay.se/kanal9/
Profile: Kanal 9 sänder serier, långfilmer och dokumentärer tillsammans med sport och galor. Kanal 9 ingår i Discovery Networks Sweden.
TELEVISION STATION

SVT AB 375322
Editorial: Oxenstiernsgatan 26-34, Stockholm 105 10
Tel: 46 8 78 40 000.

Web site: http://www.svt.se
Profile: För pressutskick, använd SVT:s underredaktioner. SVT (Sveriges Television Aktiebolag) ansvarar för public service-produktionen i Sverige. SVT sänder en mix av programgenrer: nyhets- och samhällsprogram, nöje, drama, barnprogram, sport, utländska program och minioritetsprogram med mera. SVT (Sveriges Television Aktiebolag) is the public service television in Sweden, the equivalent of British BBC.
TELEVISION NETWORK

SVT Allmän-tv-divisionen 375318
Editorial: Oxenstiernsgatan 26-34, Stockholm 105 10
Tel: 46 8 78 40 000.
Web site: http://www.svt.se
Profile: För pressutskick, använd SVT Allmän-tv-divisionen:s underredaktioner. SVT:s enhet för programproduktion inom områdena drama, barn och ungdom och underhållning. Public service. SVT Allmän TV-divisionen finns på fyra orter i Sverige: Stockholm, Umeå, Malmö och Göteborg.
TELEVISION NETWORK

SVT Allmän-tv-divisionen - Vetenskap 316803
Editorial: Sveriges Television, Oxenstiernsgatan 26-34, Stockholm 105 10 Tel: 46 8 78 40 000.
Email: vetenskap@svt.se
Web site: http://www.svt.se/nyheter/vetenskap
Profile: SVT's Vetenskapsredaktion gör Vetenskapsmagasinet, Vetenskapens värld samt vetenskapsnyheter på webben.
TELEVISION NETWORK

SVT Barnkanalen 834419
Editorial: Oxenstiernsgatan 26-34, Stockholm 105 10
Tel: 46 8 78 40 000.
Email: barnkanalen@svt.se
Web site: http://www.svt.se/barn
Profile: SVTs barnkanal med program för barn och ungdom. "Vi vill att du som barn, ungdom och vuxen ska känna att du kan få behållning av det som visas på SVT Barnkanalen. Sedan är inte alla program till för alla tittare. En del program lämpar sig bättre för yngre barn och del för litet äldre. Men en sak du kan vara helt säker på: du kommer aldrig att trilla in i ett extrainsatt Rapport, eller något annat program som i första hand riktar sig till vuxna. Och du slipper reklamen. Det är många olika åldrar som vi ska finnas till för. Och behoven varierar mycket beroende på vilken tid i livet man är i. Trots det finns det vissa grundläggande saker som är viktiga i alla åldrar. Det vill vi ta tillvara på och värna om."
TELEVISION NETWORK

SVT Göteborg 375452
Editorial: Pumpgatan 2, Goteborg 417 55
Tel: 46 31 83 70 00.
Web site: http://www.svt.se/nyheter/lokalt/vast/
Profile: SVT Göteborg producerar regionala nyheter till hela västsverige, Göteborg, Bohuslän, Halland, Dalsland, Västergötland samt producerar nationella program i allmän-tv-avdelningen. I Göteborg har allmän-tv-avdelningen (ATV) två programavdelningar: Drama/Samhälle och Nöje/Fakta. För fler medarbetare, se diverse program.
TELEVISION NETWORK

SVT Kunskapskanalen 375329
Editorial: Oxenstiernsgatan 26-34, Stockholm 105 10
Tel: 46 8 78 40 000.
Email: info@kunskapskanalen.se
Web site: http://www.kunskapskanalen.se
Profile: Kunskapskanalen sänder utbildnings- och folkbildningsprogram varje dag mellan 09-01. Kunskapskanalen är en fri-tv-kanal som alla public service-kanaler och finns överallt - i marknät, på satellit och via kabel- och bredbandsnät. Kunskapskanalen ingår i Public Service-utbudet och är ett samarbete mellan SVT och UR.
TELEVISION NETWORK

SVT Nyheter Dalarna 317145
Editorial: Box 212, Myntgatan 45, Falun 791 25
Tel: 46 23 76 50 00.
Email: dalarna@svt.se
Web site: http://www.svt.se/nyheter/regionalt/dalarna/
Profile: SVT Nyheter Dalarna är en regional tv-station som sänder program och nyheter rörande Dalarna. SVT Dalarna har också sänt och producerat mängder av tv-program, däribland Trafikmagasinet, Café Falun, Nyhetstecken, Jakttid, Packat & klart.
TELEVISION NETWORK

SVT Nyheter Örebro 375456
Editorial: Fabriksgatan 18, Orebro 701 84
Tel: 46 19 35 35 35.
Email: orebro@svt.se
Web site: http://www.svt.se/nyheter/regionalt/orebro
Profile: SVT Nyheter Örebro (fd. Tvärsnytt) är ett regionalt nyhetsprogram på Sveriges Television som täcker Örebro län.
TELEVISION NETWORK

SVT Nyheter Västmanland 317142
Editorial: Kopparbergsvagen 6, Västerås 722 13
Tel: 46 21 15 04 00.
Email: vastmanland@svt.se
Web site: http://www.svt.se/nyheter/regionalt/vastmanland/
Profile: SVT Nyheter Västmanland är sedan april 2015 en egen redaktion som sänder regionala nyheter. De tillhörde tidigare Tvärsnytt i Örebro.
TELEVISION NETWORK

SVT Nyhetsdivisionen 375315
Editorial: Sveriges Television AB Nyhetsdivisionen, Oxenstiernsgatan 26-34, Stockholm 105 10
Tel: 46 87 84 00 00.
Email: svtnyheter@svt.se
Web site: http://www.svt.se/nyheter
Profile: SVT:s Nyhetsdivision. Inom Nyhetsdivisionen samlas hela SVT:s nyhets- och sportutbud för alla kanaler och tjänster och divisionen är indeland i tre underdivisioner; Riksnyheter (utrike, Rapport, Aktuellt, Samhälle, Agenda, SVT forum), Regionala Nyheter (11 regionala redaktioner, Finska redaktionen, Sapmi, SVT teckenspråk), och Sport. SVT:s nyhetsverksamhet finns utspridd på 28 orter över hela Sverige. Sveriges Television (SVT) is the Swedish public service television company with the widest range of programming of all TV companies in Sweden.
TELEVISION NETWORK

SVT Nyhetsdivisionen - Uutiset / Finska redaktionen 375476
Editorial: SVT / Uutiset, TH-E22, Stockholm 105 10
Tel: 46 8 784 74 35.
Email: uutiset@svt.se
Web site: http://www.svt.se/nyheter/uutiset/
Profile: Uutiset är SVT:s finskspråkiga nyhetsprogram som sänds varje vardag på SVT och finns på SVT Play.
TELEVISION NETWORK

SVT Sápmi 316813
Editorial: Sveriges Radio Sameradion & SVT Sapm, Box 225 981 24, Kiruna, Kiruna 981 38
Tel: 46 980 750 00.
Email: oddasat@svt.se
Web site: http://www.svtplay.se/oddasat
Profile: Sveriges Radio Sameradion & SVT Sápmi sänder de bästa samiska nyheterna.
TELEVISION NETWORK

SVT Sport 375458
Editorial: Oxenstiernsgatan 26-34, Stockholm 105 10
Tel: 46 8 784 76 10.
Email: svtsport@svt.se
Web site: http://www.svt.se/sport
Profile: Sveriges Televisions sportredaktion. SVT's sports editorial section.
TELEVISION NETWORK

SVT Sundsvall 375474
Editorial: Nya Hamngatan 2, Sundsvall 851 80
Tel: 46 60 19 01 90.
Email: vasternorrland@svt.se
Web site: http://www.svt.se/nyheter/lokalt/vasternorrland/
Profile: SVT Sundsvall är ett av SVT's regionala kontor för public service beläget i Sundsvall, Västernorrland.
TELEVISION NETWORK

SVT Teckenspråk 290123
Owner: Sveriges Television AB
Editorial: Myntgatan 45, Falun 791 25
Tel: 46 23 76 51 13.
Email: nyhetstecken@svt.se
Web site: https://www.svt.se/nyheter/amne/Teckenspr%C3%A5ksv%C3%A4rlden
Profile: SVT Teckenspråk sänder tv-program på teckenspråk - såväl barnprogram som nyheter och kultur- och samhällsprogram. Redaktionen är tvåspråkig och har teckenspråk som huvudspråk och svenska som andraspråk. SVT Teckenspråk broadcast television programs in sign language.
TELEVISION NETWORK

SVT Umeå 316790
Editorial: Box 6094, Formvagen 14, Umeå 906 03
Tel: 46 90 17 50 00.
Email: vasterbotten@svt.se
Web site: http://www.svt.se/nyheter/lokalt/vasterbotten/
Profile: SVT Umeå är Sveriges Televisions avdelning i Umeå, och är huvudproducent för SVT Nord.
TELEVISION NETWORK

SVT Växjö 317164
Editorial: Framtidsvagen 16, Växjo 351 96
Tel: 46 470 77 87 00.
Email: smaland@svt.se
Web site: http://www.svt.se/nyheter/lokalt/smaland/
Profile: SVT Växjö är ett av SVT's regionala kontor för public service i Småland.
TELEVISION NETWORK

TV3 Sverige AB 316077
Editorial: Ringvagen 52, Stockholm 118 67
Tel: 46 8 56 24 10 01.
Web site: http://mtgsverige.se/tv3/
Profile: TV3 Sverige AB är en rikstäckande kommersiell TV-kanal som sänder utländska serier, långfilmer, sport samt egenproducerade program. Önskar ej motta pressutskick.
TELEVISION STATION

TV4 AB 316076
Editorial: Tegeluddsvagen 3-5, Stockholm 115 79
Tel: 46 8 45 94 000.
Web site: http://www.tv4.se
Profile: Önskar ej motta pressutskick. TV4 är TV4-Gruppens flaggskepp och huvudkanal. Kanalen startade den 15 september 1990 och har sedan dess levererat underhållning, nyheter, sport, barnprogram, filmer, samhällsprogram och mycket mer till hela svenska folket. Vissa av TV4:s populära program sänds i HD-kvalitet i en egen HD-kanal, TV4 HD. TV4-Gruppens verksamhet består i huvudsak av ett stort antal tv-kanaler, vissa finansierade via reklam, vissa via abonnemang, samt ett stort antal webbplatser. Gruppens verksamhet omfattar också TV4 Sverige som producerar lokal-tv, samt text-tv, mobila tjänster, licensieringsverksamhet med mera. TV4 is a commercially financed TV-channel. It is the largest commercially financed channel in Sweden.
TELEVISION STATION

TV4 AB - Sjuan 375363
Editorial: Tegeluddsvagen 3-5, Stockholm 115 79
Tel: 46 8 45 94 000.
Web site: http://www.sjuan.se
Profile: Sjuan är en digitalt distribuerad TV-kanal, systerkanal till TV4, med inriktning på nischade featureprogram, sport samt lättare underhållning. Sjuan hette tidigare TV4 Plus.
TELEVISION NETWORK

TV4 AB - TV12 915372
Editorial: Tegeluddsvagen 3-5, Stockholm 115 79
Tel: 46 8 45 94 000.
Web site: http://www.tv4play.se/kanaler/tv12
Profile: TV12 är en bred kanal med fokus på livsstil och sport. Medan livsstilsprogram inom inredning och hälsa sätter sin prägel på kanalen under vardagarna fylls helgtablån av ett starkt sportutbud.
TELEVISION NETWORK

TV4 AB - TV4 Fakta 827778
Editorial: Tegeluddsvagen 3-5, Stockholm 115 79
Tel: 46 8 459 40 00.
Email: press@tv4.se
Web site: https://www.tv4play.se/kanaler/tv4-fakta
Profile: TV4 Fakta är en digitalkanal som är inriktad på moderna dokumentärer. Kanalen är den enda svenska kanalen som sänder enbart dokumentärer dygnet runt och den distribueras av samtliga större tv-leverantörer.
TELEVISION STATION

TV6 498501
Editorial: BOX 17115, Ringvagen 52, Stockholm 104 62 Tel: 46 8 562 023 00.
Email: redaktionen@tv6.se
Web site: http://www.tv6.se
Profile: TV6 är en underhållningskanal som kan ses över 6 miljoner svenskar. TV6 är en del av det fria digitala marknätet och kan tas emot gratis av alla med hjälp av en digitalbox för marknätet. TV6 ingår i de flesta kabelleverantörers basutbud, liksom i Boxers och Viasats. Kanalen sänder utländska serier, långfilmer, sport samt egenproduktion. TV6 ägs av Viasat Broadcasting UK Ltd.
TELEVISION STATION

TV8 316056
Editorial: Ringvagen 52, Stockholm 118 67
Tel: 46 8 56 20 23 00.
Web site: https://www.viafree.se/
Profile: TV8 är en rikstäckande kommersiell TV-kanal. TV8 sänder serier, dokumentärer, reality, sport och gameshows. Kanalen finansieras med hjälp av abonnemangsintäkter, reklam och sponsring.
TELEVISION STATION

UR 375365
Editorial: Sveriges Utbildningsradio AB, Oxenstiernsgatan 34, Stockholm 105 10
Tel: 46 8 784 40 00.
Email: kundtjanst@ur.se
Web site: http://www.ur.se
Profile: Kunskapsföretaget UR är ett av tre public service-bolag i Sverige tillsammans med Sveriges Radio och SVT. Deras uppdrag är att producera utbildnings- och folkbildningsprogram från förskola till högskola och därmed bredda, förstärka och komplettera andras utbildningsinsatser. De har också uppdraget att producera program för grupper som annars inte syns och hörs så ofta, som språkliga och etniska minoriteter samt för funktionshindrade. UR är ett fristående bolag som driver Kunskapskanalen tillsammans med SVT samt sänder i SVT:s samt Sveriges Radios kanaler.
TELEVISION NETWORK

UR - Samtiden 827151
Editorial: Sveriges Utbildningsradio AB, Oxenstiernsgatan 34, Stockholm 105 10
Tel: 46 8 784 00 00.
Email: samtiden@ur.se
Web site: http://www.ur.se/
Profile: Den publicistiska idén med UR Samtiden är att ge tittaren helheten. De sänder får mängder av föreläsningar och seminarier från såväl populärvetenskapliga som mer specialiserade lärosäten. Över hela Sverige pågår debatter och samtal. Varje dag, året om, sänder Samtiden samtal från Sverige om vår tid - oavsett om det handlar om ny forskning, kulturdebatt eller om hur vi lever tillsammans. Vi har sänt några av världens främsta (Dalai Lama, Tony Blair, Herta Müller) så väl som de som bara är kända inom sitt mycket snäva specialområde. Programmet sänds vardagar mellan klockan 14.00 - 17.00, helger 9:00-15:00.
TELEVISION NETWORK

Viasat Sport 621931
Editorial: Ringvagen 52, Stockholm 104 62
Tel: 46 73 699 23 18.
Email: fredrik.johansson@viasat.se
Web site: http://www.viasatsport.se
Profile: Viasat Sport är en kanal inom det ledande internationella mediebolaget Modern Times Group MTG AB. Viasat Sport är Viasats tjänst som erbjuder höjdpunkter från bland annat Premier League, Champions League, NHL, Hockey Allsvenskan, Formula1 och PGA.
TELEVISION STATION

Switzerland

Television

SRF 1 316485
Owner: Schweizer Radio und Fernsehen
Editorial: Fernsehstr. 1-4, Zurich 8052
Tel: 41 44 3056611.
Email: srf@srf.ch
Web site: http://www.srf.ch
Profile: SRF 1 ist der nationale, deutschsprachige, öffentlich-rechtliche Fernsehsender des SRF. Neben Nachrichten präsentiert der Sender Informationssendungen, sowie auch Unterhaltung. 1 SRF is the national public television station of the SRF in German. In addition to news of the station offers information programs, as well as entertainment.
TELEVISION STATION

SRF 2 776997
Owner: Schweizer Rundfunk und Fernsehen
Editorial: Fernsehstr. 1, Zurich 8052
Tel: 41 44 3056611.
Email: srf@srf.ch
Web site: http://www.srf.ch
Profile: SRF 2 ist der zweite TV-Kanal des SRF, welcher sich vor allem an ein jüngeres Publikum richtet. Zum Programm gehören vor allem Filme, Serien und Sport, aber auch ein Anteil von Informations- und Nachrichtenformaten. SRF 2 is the second television channel of the SRF, which is primarily aimed at a younger audience. The program includes mainly movies, series and sports, but also a share of information and news formats.
TELEVISION STATION

TeleZüri 544400
Owner: AZ Medien AG
Editorial: Redaktion TeleZüri, Heinrichstr. 267, Zurich 8005 Tel: 41 44 447 24 24.
Email: redaktion@telezueri.ch
Web site: http://www.telezueri.ch
Profile: TeleZüri ist eine privater, schweizer Fernsehsender für die Region Zürich mit Nachrichten, Informationssendungen und Unterhaltung. TeleZüri is a private, Swiss TV station for the area Zürich with news, information programs and entertainment.
TELEVISION STATION

Syria

Television

Syria Drama Channel 656986
Owner: General Organisation of Radio and TV
Editorial: Sahat Al Omaween, Damascus
Tel: 963 11 225 0963.
Email: drama@rtv.gov.sy
Web site: http://www.rtv.gov.sy
Profile: Syria Drama Channel is a state-owned television channel broadcasting films and drama serials. The station launched in 2009 and broadcasts free-to-air on satellite.
TELEVISION STATION

Syria TV - Channel 1 375337
Owner: General Organisation of Radio and TV
Editorial: General Organisation of Radio & TV Building, Omawyeen Square, Damascus
Tel: 963 11 222 8500.
Email: salehmaan@hotmail.com
Web site: http://www.rtv.gov.sy
Profile: Channel 1 of Syria TV is a state-owned television station broadcasting entertainment, news and drama programmes. The channel launched in 1960 and broadcasts terrestrially in Syria and free-to-air on satellite.
TELEVISION STATION

Syria TV - Channel 2 608753
Owner: General Organisation of Radio and TV
Editorial: General Organisation of Radio & TV Building, Omayad Square, Damascus
Tel: 963 11 222 8500.
Email: e-naser@scs-net.org
Web site: http://www.rtv.gov.sy
Profile: Channel 2 of Syria TV is a state-owned television station broadcasting documentaries and sports programmes. The channel launched in 1985 and broadcasts terrestrially in Syria.
TELEVISION STATION

Tajikistan

Television

Tojikiston TV 536643
Editorial: Bekhzod 25, Dushanbe
Email: info@1tv.tj
Web site: http://tvt.tj
Profile: National TV station with political and analytical programmes, entertainment, films and sports.
TELEVISION STATION

Tajikistan

TV Safina 536094
Editorial: ul. Bukhoro 43, Dushanbe
Tel: 992 372 27 80 29.
Email: info@safina.tj
Web site: http://www.safina.tj
Profile: National TV station providing informative, cultural-entertaining and sports programmes.
TELEVISION STATION

Thailand

Radio

GGNews Network 468067
Editorial: GG News Network Grp, 459 Soi Ladprao 48, Ladprao Rd, Samsennok, Huaykwang, Bangkok 10310 **Tel:** 66 26934777 600.
Web site: http://www.ggnews.co.th
Profile: Covers business news.
RADIO NETWORK

Nation Radio 394051
Editorial: Nation Group, 1854 Bangna-Trad Road (KM 4.5), Bangna, Bangkok 10260
Tel: 66 23383333 2704.
Email: lekkungs@hotmail.com
Web site: http://www.nationradioonline.com
Profile: News and general interest programming
AM RADIO STATION

T-News Radio 620461
Owner: Multimedia Group
Editorial: Multimedia Group, 50/33, Moo 5, Pracharat 1 Rd., Talad Kwan, Muang, Nontaburi 11000
Tel: 66 25254242 108.
Email: nantita@tnews.co.th
Web site: http://www.tnews.co.th
Profile: Covers of news and general interests.
RADIO NETWORK

Television

Nagoya Television - Bangkok Bureau 468198
Owner: TV Asahi Corporation
Editorial: TV Asahi Corporation, 93/1 Dietham Tower, Wireless Rd., Lumpini, Patumwan, Bangkok 10330
Tel: 66 22543134.
Profile: Covers of news and general interests.
TELEVISION NETWORK

Thai PBS 526159
Owner: Thai Public Broadcasting Service
Editorial: Thai Public Broadcasting Service, 1010 Chinnawatra Tower 3, 13/F, Viphawadee-Rangsit Rd., Jatujak, Bangkok 10900 **Tel:** 66 27911000 1622.
Email: program@thaipbs.or.th
Web site: http://www.thaipbs.or.th/
Profile: Focuses on news and general interests.
TELEVISION NETWORK

TV Asahi - Bangkok Bureau 468197
Editorial: 93/1 Dietham Tower, Wireless Road, Lumpini, Patumwan, Bangkok 10330
Tel: 66 22543134.
Email: tv-asahi@inet.co.th
Web site: http://www.tv-asahi.co.jp
Profile: Covers of news and general interests.
TELEVISION NETWORK

Togo

Radio

Kanal FM 289319
Editorial: Immeuble DECAMPOS, Avenue de la Nouvelle Marche, Lome **Tel:** 228 22 21 33 74.
Email: kanalfm@cafe.tg
Profile: Regional radio station focussing on music, news, current affairs, politics, economics and sports.
FM RADIO STATION

Nana FM 289815
Editorial: Bld du 13 janvier, Angle rue Biblos Night Club, Lome **Tel:** 228 22 20 12 02.
Email: nana_tg@yahoo.fr
Web site: http://radionanafm.info
Profile: Regional radio station focussing on music, news, current affairs, entertainment and sports.
FM RADIO STATION

Television

TV2 316834
Editorial: BP 13100, Lome **Tel:** 228 22 51 49 93.
Email: contact@tv2togo.tv
Web site: http://tv2togo.tv/site
Profile: TV station covering from Lomé to Palimero and focussing on national and regional news, current affairs, entertainment, culture and sports.
TELEVISION STATION

TVT - Télévision Togolaise 316138
Editorial: Rue des Medias, Quartier Administratif, Lome **Tel:** 228 22 21 53 57.
Email: televisiontogolaise@yahoo.fr
Web site: http://www.tvt.tg
Profile: National TV station focussing on entertainment, news, politics, economics, society, health, culture and sports.
TELEVISION STATION

Tonga

Radio

Millennium Radio 2000 (A3V) 538703
Editorial: A3V Radio 2000, PO Box 838, Kingdom Of Tonga **Tel:** 676 25 891.
Profile: A3V The Millenium Radio 2000 broadcasts popular music format in the Kingdom of Tonga on FM89.1.
RADIO NETWORK

Radio Tonga 1 (A3Z) 538700
Owner: Tonga Broadcasting Commission
Editorial: Fasi, Nuku'alofa, Kingdom Of Tonga
Tel: 676 23 556.
Email: nanisefifita@yahoo.com
Web site: http://radiotonga.com
Profile: Provides best Tongan and English languages' music.
RADIO NETWORK

Television

TV Tonga 538720
Owner: Tonga Broadcasting Corporation
Editorial: Nuku'alofa, Tonga **Tel:** 676 23 555.
Email: eamanaki@tonga-broadcasting.com
Web site: http://tonga-broadcasting.com
Profile: Tonga Broadcasting Commission (TBC) is the first Broadcasting which began operations in 1961.
TELEVISION STATION

Turkey

Television

ATV 821108
Owner: Çal?k Holding
Editorial: Barbaros Bulvar. No: 153, Cam Han, Istanbul **Tel:** 90 216 474 20 20.
Email: iletisim@atv.com.tr
Web site: http://www.atv.com.tr
Profile: atv (Actual Television) is a nationwide TV channel in Turkey, founded in 1993.
TELEVISION STATION

NTV Spor 527475
Owner: Do?u? Yay?n Grubu Anonim ?irketi
Editorial: Ahi Evran Cad. No: 4, Maslak, Istanbul 34398 **Tel:** 90 212 335 00 00.
Email: ntvspor@ntvspor.net
Web site: http://www.ntvspor.net
TELEVISION STATION

Turkmenistan

Television

Türkmenistan TV 316404
Editorial: Ulica Navoi 5, Ashgabat 744000
Tel: 993 12 39 25 20.
Email: tvkm@online.tm
TELEVISION STATION

Turks and Caicos Islands

Radio

Radio Turks & Caicos 290979
Editorial: PO Box 69, Grand Turk **Tel:** 649 9462007.
Email: rtc@tciway.tc
Web site: http://www.rtc.tc
Profile: Local radio station broadcasting news, sports, health and music shows.
RADIO NETWORK

Tuvalu

Radio

Radio Tuvalu 538707
Owner: Tuvalu Media Corporation
Editorial: Private Mail Bag, Vaiaku, Tuvalu
Tel: 688 20 138.
Email: meltaape@yahoo.co.ck
Profile: Radio Tuvalu broadcasts on Funafuti, the capital of Tuvalu in the Central Pacific.
RADIO NETWORK

Television

Tuvalu-news.tv 316408
Editorial: Tuvalu Media Corporation, Private Mail Bag, Funafuti
Email: media@tuvalu.tv
Profile: Tuvalu ISP is the first ISP here in Tuvalu. This ISP is under the Tuvalu Government and is operated under the department of ICT (Information Communication and Transportation), off the Ministry of Communication Transportation and Tourism.
TELEVISION NETWORK

Ukraine

Radio

Radio EC 291044
Editorial: Kyiv **Tel:** 380 44 499-10-12.
Email: sales@radiocorp.com.ua
Web site: http://radioec.com.ua
Profile: National radio network broadcasting news and pop music.
RADIO NETWORK

Radio Svoboda Ukraine 290974
Editorial: Ukrainskaya Redaksya Radio Svoboda, Hreshatik 19a, Kiev 10011 **Tel:** 380 44 490 29 00.
Web site: http://www.radiosvoboda.org
Profile: Radio Svoboda is a part of Radio Free Europe with the head office in Washington, USA.
RADIO NETWORK

Television

ICTV 657139
Editorial: ul. Pankovskaya 11, Kiev 1033
Tel: 380 44 288 1919.
Email: site@ictv.ua
Web site: http://ictv.ua
Profile: ICTV has got a priority in the information broadcast with information programs Facts, Business Facts, the final analytical news project Facts of the week with Oksana Sokolova. Recently, a cohort of IT projects become Facts. Outcome of the day - informative-analytical program, which summarizes and analyzes most of the day resonant events and their impact on the further development of the country.
TELEVISION STATION

Inter 657142
Editorial: ul. Dmytrivska 30, Kiev 1054
Tel: 380 44 490 67 65.
Email: pr@inter.ua
Web site: http://inter.ua
Profile: Inter TV Channel is the Ukrainian national broadcaster since 20th of October 1996. During all that time it has managed to hold the leading position in the domestic television market. Its position Inter holds due to the wisely chosen conception of family channel, which considers needs of all social and age groups in Ukraine.
TELEVISION STATION

Inter+ 657158
Editorial: ul. Dmytrivska 30, Kiev 1054
Tel: 380 44 490 67 65.
Email: interplus@interplus.tv
Web site: http://interplus.ua
Profile: The international television channel Inter+ started broadcasting on January 13th, 2003. It represents an international license-cleared version of Inter, the leading Ukrainian TV channel seasoned with the best projects of other Ukrainian TV production companies.
TELEVISION STATION

NTN TV 657149
Editorial: ul. Degtyarevskaya 48, Kiev 4112
Tel: 380 44 206 03 03.
Email: ntn@ntn.tv
Web site: http://ntn.ua
Profile: NTN - a general format broadcasting station. NTN technical coverage is 88.3% of the country. It's 88 cities with populations over 50 thousand people. In 83 cities and towns of Ukraine television programs are included in packages of cable operators.
TELEVISION STATION

Pershiy Diloviy Kanal 657154
Editorial: ul. Yakira 13b, Kiev 4119
Tel: 380 44 207 47 17.
Email: office@tv1.com.ua
Web site: http://fbc.net.ua
Profile: First Business TV is a specialized business television, which provides business news and analytical information round the clock, 7 days a week.
TELEVISION STATION

Strana Sovietov kanal 657152
Editorial: ul. Kanatnaya 83, office 419/1, Odessa 65107 **Tel:** 380 48 714 85 61.
Email: personal@glas.odessa.ua
Web site: http://www.glasweb.com
Profile: The Land of the Soviets TV seeks to convey as much useful information to each viewer and create a good mood among the audience. Programs reflect all aspects of our lives: spiritual, intellectual, social, cultural, political and economic-financial. This multiplicity is due to diverse interests of the audience of the channel.
TELEVISION STATION

United Arab Emirates

Radio

104.8 Channel 4 FM 362467
Owner: Ajman Independent Studios LLC
Editorial: PO Box 55137, Level 21, Damac Business Tower, Dubai **Tel:** 971 4 567 0444.
Email: info@channel4fm.com
Web site: http://www.channel4fm.com
Profile: 104.8 Channel 4 FM is a commercial radio station broadcasting contemporary English music 24-hours a day with news on the top of the hour. Launched in 1997, the station broadcasts on 104.8 FM and forms part of the Channel 4 Radio Network, a wholly owned subsidiary of Ajman Independent Studios LLC.
FM RADIO STATION

105.4 FM Radio Spice 430890
Owner: V3 Media Solutions FZ LLC
Editorial: PO Box 8372, Office 8, 1st Floor, Dubai
Tel: 971 4 339 1110.
Email: mail@radiospicefm.com
Web site: http://www.radiospicefm.com
Profile: 105.4 FM Radio Spice is a radio station broadcasting entertainment programmes, hit music, news, business, sport and competitions. Launched in 2006, the station is aimed at Hindi-speaking expatriates in the UAE and broadcasts on 105.4 FM.
FM RADIO STATION

107.8 Al Rabia FM 362455
Owner: Ajman Independent Studios LLC
Editorial: PO Box 442, Ajman **Tel:** 971 6 703 8001.
Email: ammgroup@emirates.net.ae
Web site: http://www.alrabiafm.com
Profile: 107.8 Al Rabia FM is a radio station broadcasting contemporary Arabic music along with news on the top of the hour and financial, sports news and traffic updates every half hour. Launched in 2001, the station is aimed at Arabic-speaking listeners aged 22-34 years. It broadcasts on 107.8 FM and forms part of the Channel 4 Radio Network, a wholly owned subsidiary of Ajman Independent Studios LLC.
FM RADIO STATION

89.1 Radio 4FM 362462
Owner: Ajman Independent Studios LLC
Editorial: PO Box 442, Ajman **Tel:** 971 6 703 8008.
Email: info@radio4fm.com
Web site: http://www.radio4fm.com
Profile: 89.1 Radio 4FM is a radio station broadcasting contemporary hit music 24-hours a day with news on the hour. Launched in 1999, the station is aimed at Hindi-speaking listeners aged 22-34 years. It broadcasts on 89.1 FM and forms part of the Channel 4 Radio Network, a wholly owned subsidiary of Ajman Independent Studios LLC.
FM RADIO STATION

Abu Dhabi Classic FM 610350
Owner: Abu Dhabi Media
Editorial: PO Box 3966, Abu Dhabi
Tel: 971 2 445 9999.
Email: andrew.hosie@abudhabiclassicfm.ae
Web site: http://www.adradio.ae/abudhabiclassicfm
Profile: Abu Dhabi Classic FM is a radio station broadcasting classical, jazz & world music. It broadcasts on 91.6 FM in Abu Dhabi, 87.9 FM in Dubai and 105.2 FM in Al Ain. The station plays well-known, mainstream, popular and accessible classical music during the day, special programming dedicated to jazz fans during the evenings, and then chill out music into the early hours. The station launched on 23 October 2009 and is owned by Abu Dhabi Media, the media division of the Abu Dhabi government, and forms part of the company's Abu Dhabi Radio Network.
FM RADIO STATION

Abu Dhabi Qur'an Kareem 381050
Owner: Abu Dhabi Media
Editorial: PO Box 3966, Abu Dhabi Media Building, Abu Dhabi **Tel:** 971 2 414 5535.
Email: adquran@admedia.ae
Web site: http://www.qurankareem.ae
Profile: Abu Dhabi Qur'an Kareem is a religious radio station broadcasting Quranic recitals and religious programmes. Launched in 1979, the station

broadcasts on 98.1 FM. It is owned by Abu Dhabi Media, the media division of the Abu Dhabi government, and forms part of the company's Abu Dhabi Radio Network.
FM RADIO STATION

Abu Dhabi Radio 381047
Owner: Abu Dhabi Media
Editorial: PO Box 3966, Abu Dhabi
Tel: 971 2 445 9999.
Email: abdulla.alzaabi@admedia.ae
Web site: http://www.adradio.ae/abudhabiradio
Profile: Abu Dhabi Radio is a radio station broadcasting classic Arabic music and news programmes. The station launched in 1969 and airs on 90.0 FM. It is owned by Abu Dhabi Media, the media division of the Abu Dhabi government, and forms part of the company's Abu Dhabi Radio Network.
FM RADIO STATION

All India Radio (Prasar Bharati) - Middle East bureau 828882
Owner: All India Radio
Editorial: PO Box 6999, Office 422, Tower 2, Dubai
Tel: 971 4 227 2767.
Email: dubainewsairdd@gmail.com
Web site: http://www.newsonair.com
Profile: Middle East bureau of All India Radio (AIR), India's National Public Service Broadcaster, which was established in 1936 to inform, educate and entertain the masses. The Middle East bureau is located in Dubai and provides news content from the region to All India Radio's home service, which comprises 277 radio stations located across India and reaches nearly 92% of the country's area and 99.19 % of its total population, with programming in 23 languages and 146 dialects.
RADIO NETWORK

Al Arabiya 99 FM 362465
Owner: Arabian Radio Network
Editorial: PO Box 502012, Office 103, Building 2, Dubai **Tel:** 971 4 391 2000.
Email: nmajid@arn.ae
Web site: http://alarabiya99.ae
Profile: Al Arabiya 99 FM is a radio station broadcasting hit music, chat and competitions. The station launched in 2001 and broadcasts on 99.0 FM.
FM RADIO STATION

Asianet Radio 657 AM 381065
Owner: Star Asianet Middle East FZ LLC
Editorial: PO Box 62787, Villa 10, Boutique Offices, Dubai **Tel:** 971 4 391 4151.
Email: asianetd@yahoo.com
Web site: http://www.asianetradio.me
Profile: Asianet Radio 657 AM is a radio station broadcasting infotainment, news and music 24-hours a day. The station launched in 2000 and broadcasts on 657 AM.
AM RADIO STATION

City 101.6 FM 362460
Owner: Arabian Radio Network
Editorial: PO Box 502012, Office 103-104, Building 2, Dubai **Tel:** 971 4 391 2000.
Email: info@city1016.ae
Web site: http://www.city1016.ae
Profile: City 101.6 FM is a radio station broadcasting hit music, news, talk shows and entertainment programmes. It launched in 2002 and airs on 101.6 FM.
FM RADIO STATION

Dubai 92 362468
Owner: Arabian Radio Network
Editorial: PO Box 502012, Building BS-16, Dubai
Tel: 971 4 435 4700.
Email: info@dubai92.ae
Web site: http://dubai92.com
Profile: Dubai 92 is a radio station broadcasting hit music from the 80s, 90s and current day, as well as event coverage, news, weather and traffic updates. The station launched in 2004 and is aimed at the 18-35 year-old expat community. It broadcasts on 92.0 FM.
FM RADIO STATION

Dubai Eye 103.8 FM 381037
Owner: Arabian Radio Network
Editorial: PO Box 502012, Building BS-16, Dubai
Tel: 971 4 435 4700.
Email: englishnews@arn.ae
Web site: http://www.dubaieye1038.com
Profile: Dubai Eye 103.8 FM is a talk radio station broadcasting news, current affairs, business, sports and lifestyle programmes for 24-hours a day. Launched in 2004, the station airs on 103.8 FM.
FM RADIO STATION

Dubai Radio 776621
Owner: Dubai Media Incorporated
Editorial: PO Box 835, Oud Metha Road, Next to Rashid Hospital, Dubai **Tel:** 971 4 307 7922.
Email: dubaifm@dmi.ae
Web site: http://www.dcn.ae/dubairadio
Profile: Dubai Radio is a radio station broadcasting music, entertainment and chat shows. It launched in 2011 and airs on 93.0 FM. The station is owned by the government of Dubai through its Dubai Media Incorporated division.
FM RADIO STATION

Emarat FM 381072
Owner: Abu Dhabi Media
Editorial: PO Box 3966, Abu Dhabi
Tel: 971 2 445 9999.
Email: info@adradio.ae
Web site: http://www.adradio.ae/emaratfm
Profile: Emarat FM is a national radio station broadcasting entertainment, live programmes and music. It launched in 1995 and is owned by the Government of Abu Dhabi through its Abu Dhabi Media division. The station broadcasts on 95.8 FM (Abu Dhabi), 94.9 FM (Al Ain), 97.1 FM (Dubai & Sharjah), 88.5 FM (Ras Al Khaimah) and 103.9 FM (Fujairah).
FM RADIO STATION

Fujairah 92.6 430889
Owner: Fujairah Media FZ LLC
Editorial: PO Box 4422, 16th-20th Floor, Creative Tower, Fujairah **Tel:** 971 9 223 1515.
Email: info@926.fm
Web site: http://www.926.fm
Profile: Fujairah 92.6 is a news-orientated radio station re-broadcasting news from BBC Arabic, as well as producing its own local news and programmes. The station launched in 2006 and broadcasts on 92.6 FM.
FM RADIO STATION

Gold 101.3 FM 688165
Owner: Ajman Independent Studios LLC
Editorial: PO Box 442, Ajman TV Building, Ajman
Tel: 971 6 703 8003.
Email: info@gold1013fm.com
Web site: http://www.gold1013fm.com
Profile: Gold 101.3 FM is a radio station broadcasting contemporary Malayalam hit music and entertainment. Launched in 2010, the station is aimed at Malayalam speakers in the UAE. It broadcasts on 101.3 FM and forms part of the Channel 4 Radio Network, a wholly owned subsidiary of Ajman Independent Studios LLC.
FM RADIO STATION

Hit 96.7 FM 362463
Owner: Arabian Radio Network
Editorial: PO Box 502012, Office 103-104, Building 2, Dubai **Tel:** 971 4 455 5888.
Email: hitfmnews@arnonline.com
Web site: http://www.hit967.ae
Profile: Hit 96.7 FM is a radio station broadcasting hit music from South India, news, talk shows and other entertainment programmes. Launched in 2004, the station is aimed at South Indian expatriates in the UAE and broadcasts on 96.7 FM.
FM RADIO STATION

Al Khaleejiya 100.9 FM 362466
Owner: Arabian Radio Network
Editorial: PO Box 502012, Office 103-104, CNN Building, Dubai **Tel:** 971 4 391 2000.
Email: mohd@arn.ae
Web site: http://www.1009.ae
Profile: Al Khaleejiya 100.9 FM is a radio station broadcasting Khaleeji (Gulf) music, news, talk shows and entertainment programmes. Launched in 2003, the station is aimed at UAE and GCC nationals and broadcasts on 100.9 FM.
FM RADIO STATION

MBC FM 362456
Owner: MBC Group
Editorial: PO Box 72627, MBC Building, Dubai
Tel: 971 4 391 9999.
Email: mohammad.alkurdi@mbc.net
Web site: http://www.mbc.net/mbcfm
Profile: MBC FM is a Pan Arab radio station broadcasting Khaleeji (Gulf) music, entertainment, competitions and news 24-hours a day. Launched in 1994, the station broadcasts on various FM frequencies in Saudi Arabia, 92.0 FM in Qatar and 101.9 FM in Bahrain.
FM RADIO STATION

Noor Dubai 93.9 FM 381036
Owner: Dubai Media Incorporated
Editorial: PO Box 835, Dubai **Tel:** 971 4 307 7930.
Email: muhsen.hassan@dmi.ae
Web site: http://www.dcn.ae/noordubai
Profile: Noor Dubai 93.9 FM is an Islamic-oriented station broadcasting news, talk and social issues relating to youths in the Emirates. The station launched on 9 May 2006 and broadcasts on 93.9 FM. It is owned by the government of Dubai through its Dubai Media Incorporated division.
FM RADIO STATION

Panorama FM 362457
Owner: MBC Group
Editorial: PO Box 72627, MBC Building, Dubai
Tel: 971 4 391 9999.
Email: ahossnyt@yahoo.com
Web site: http://www.mbc.net/panoramafm
Profile: Panorama FM is a radio station broadcasting contemporary Arabic music, entertainment programming, competitions and on-the-hour news 24-hours a day. Launched in 2003, the station broadcasts on various FM frequencies in Saudi Arabia, 88.6 FM in Baghdad and 103.0 FM in Bahrain.
FM RADIO STATION

Radio Asia 362459
Owner: Radio Asia Network
Editorial: PO Box 4300, Dolphin Recording Studio, Ras Al Khaimah **Tel:** 971 7 228 4660.
Email: admin@radioasia.ae
Web site: http://www.radioasiauae.com
Profile: Radio Asia is a radio station broadcasting news, current affairs and entertainment programmes. Launched in 1994, the station is aimed at South Asian expatriates in the GCC and broadcasts on 1269 AM.
AM RADIO STATION

Radio Mirchi UAE 798754
Owner: Abu Dhabi Media
Editorial: PO Box 63, Al Ittihad Bulding, Mohamed Bin Khalifa Street, Abu Dhabi **Tel:** 971 2 414 5516.
Email: feedback@radiomirchiuae.ae
Web site: http://www.radiomirchiuae.ae
Profile: Radio Mirchi UAE is a radio station broadcasting Indian music, news from Bollywood and entertainment programmes. It launched in February 2012 as a joint venture between Radio Mirchi in India and Abu Dhabi Media. The station targets Hindi-speakers in the UAE and broadcasts on 88.8 FM (Dubai), 97.3 FM (Abu Dhabi) & 95.6 FM (Al Ain). Radio Mirchi was launched in India in 2001 by Entertainment Network (India) Limited and operates in 32 cities across the country.
FM RADIO STATION

Radio Shoma 93.4 774776
Owner: Arabian Radio Network
Editorial: PO Box 502012, Office 103-104, Building 2, Dubai **Tel:** 971 4 391 2000.
Email: info@radioshoma934.ae
Web site: http://radioshoma934.ae
Profile: Radio Shoma 93.4 is a radio station broadcasting Persian music, entertainment, culture, business and sports programmes. Launched in 2011, the station is aimed at Iranian expatriates in the UAE and broadcasts on 93.4 FM.
FM RADIO STATION

Sharjah FM 381034
Owner: Sharjah Media Corporation
Editorial: PO Box 111, Quran Roundabout, Sharjah
Tel: 971 6 501 1111.
Email: info@smc.ae
Web site: http://www.smc.ae
Profile: Sharjah FM is a regional radio station broadcasting religious, cultural and educational programmes 24-hours a day in the emirate of Sharjah. Launched on 31 August 1972, it is owned by the government of Sharjah's media division, Sharjah Media Corporation, and broadcasts on 94.4 FM (Sharjah), 107.6 FM (Khor Fakkan and Dibba) and 107.7 FM (Kalba).
FM RADIO STATION

Star FM 594027
Owner: Abu Dhabi Media
Editorial: PO Box 3966, Abu Dhabi
Tel: 971 2 445 9999.
Email: info@starfm.ae
Web site: http://www.starfm.ae
Profile: Star FM is a youth-orientated radio station broadcasting a mixture of English and Arabic songs, interspersed with light entertainment, news updates and listener-generated content. The station launched in 2009 and broadcasts on 92.4 FM (Abu Dhabi), 99.9 FM (Dubai) and 100.1 FM (Al Ain). It is owned by Abu Dhabi Media, the media division of the Abu Dhabi government, and forms part of the company's Abu Dhabi Radio Network.
FM RADIO STATION

Suno 1024 774766
Owner: Radio Asia Network
Editorial: PO Box 31876, Office 1602, Al Shafar Tower 1, Dubai **Tel:** 971 4 453 4950.
Email: admin@radioasia.ae
Web site: http://www.suno1024.com
Profile: Suno 1024 is a radio station broadcasting hit music from South Asia. It launched in 2011 and broadcasts on 102.4 FM.
FM RADIO STATION

Tag 91.1 855242
Owner: Arabian Radio Network
Editorial: PO Box 502012, Building BS-16, Dubai
Tel: 971 4 435 4700.
Email: louisec@arn.ae
Web site: http://www.tag911.ae
Profile: Tag 91.1 is a radio station broadcasting Filipino music, news and entertainment. Launched in March 2013, the station is aimed at the Filipino community in the UAE and broadcasts on 91.1 FM.
FM RADIO STATION

Virgin Radio Dubai 521696
Owner: Arabian Radio Network
Editorial: PO Box 502012, Building BS-16, Dubai
Tel: 971 4 435 4700.
Email: info@arn.ae
Web site: http://www.virginradiodubai.com
Profile: Virgin Radio Dubai is a radio station broadcasting hit music, chat and competitions. The station launched in 2008 and broadcasts on 104.4 FM.
FM RADIO STATION

Zayed Radio for Qura'an 769415
Owner: Fujairah Culture & Media Authority
Editorial: PO Box 7444, Fujairah Tower, Fujairah
Tel: 971 9 222 6645.
Email: zuriaqat@zayedquran.gov.ae
Web site: http://www.zayedquran.gov.ae
Profile: Zayed Radio for Qura'an is a radio station broadcasting Quranic recitals and religious programmes. It launched in 2009 and broadcasts on 97.6 FM. The station is owned by the government of Fujairah through its Fujairah Culture & Media Authority division.
FM RADIO STATION

United States of America

Radio

3ABN/Three Angels Broadcasting Network 62767
Editorial: 3391 Charley Good Rd, West Frankfort, Illinois 62896-5815 **Tel:** 1 618 627-4651.
Email: mail@3abn.org
Web site: http://www.3abn.org
Profile: Round-the-clock Christian lifestyle network presenting news, music and talk programs to a worldwide audience, through traditional broadcasting and over the Internet. Three Angels Broadcasting Network's (3ABN) programming is designed to reach into the hearts and lives of the listeners, addressing their everyday problems and most urgent needs.
RADIO NETWORK

ABC News Radio - Glendale Bureau 821807
Editorial: 500 Circle Seven Dr, Glendale, California 91201-2331 **Tel:** 1 818 553-5500.
Web site: http://abcnewsradioonline.com
RADIO NETWORK

ABC News Radio - Washington Bureau 46990
Editorial: 1717 Desales St NW, Washington, District Of Columbia 20036-4401 **Tel:** 1 202 222-7300.
RADIO NETWORK

ABC News Radio Network 774857
Owner: Walt Disney Co.
Editorial: 47 W 66th St, St. #211, New York, New York 10023-6201 **Tel:** 1 212 456-5100.
Email: radio@abc.com
Web site: http://abcradio.com
Profile: ABC News Radio provides comprehensive news programming as the nation's largest commercial radio news organization. It features the day's top national and international breaking news stories and political coverage. The network is owned by Walt Disney Co. and distributed by Skyview Networks.
RADIO NETWORK

ABC Sports Radio 774860
Editorial: 125 W End Ave, New York, New York 10023-6387
Web site: http://abcnewsradioonline.com/sports-news
Profile: A sports blog hosted by ABC News Radio.
RADIO NETWORK

Advanced Radio Network 281893
Editorial: 18165 NW 62nd Ct, Miami Gardens, Florida 33015-4405 **Tel:** 1 305 824-9000.
Email: advanced@graveline.com
Web site: http://www.advancedradionetwork.com
Profile: Distributor of Into Tomorrow with Dave Graveline, the listener interactive network radio show covering the latest in consumer electronics and technology.
RADIO NETWORK

Ag Radio Network 740047
Owner: Learfield Communications, Inc.
Tel: 1 315 896-4750.
Email: agradionet@aol.com
Web site: http://www.jlfarmakis.com/Radio/AgRadioNetwork/tabid/94/Default.aspx
RADIO NETWORK

AgNet West 827677
Owner: AgNet West Media, LLC
Editorial: 12822 E Rialto Ave, Sanger, California 93657-9221 **Tel:** 1 559 797-4081.
Email: office@agnetwest.com
Web site: http://agnetwest.com
Profile: Serves stations in California and the western region with news, weather and programming that relates to the region's agricultural industries.
REGIONAL RADIO NETWORKS

Agrinet Farm Radio Network 46927
Editorial: 104 Radio Rd, Powells Point, North Carolina 27966-9601 **Tel:** 1 252 491-2414.
Email: info@agrinetradio.com
Web site: http://www.agrinet.com
Profile: Distributes agriculture and farm reports to 150 stations across the United States. The network provides international, national and regional agricultural news, weather and markets.
RADIO NETWORK

Alabama Radio Network 139847
Editorial: 600 Beacon Pkwy W Ste 400, Birmingham, Alabama 35209-3118 **Tel:** 1 205 439-9600.
Web site: http://www.arnnet.com
Profile: The Alabama Radio Network provides hourly newscasts from 6:30am through 6:30pm Central Time, six days a week. Each newscast is four minutes long, including commercial break, and is repeated at :55 past the hour and the top of the hour. The newscasts are formatted so that stations can take a three minute version (two minutes of content plus a 60-second network commercial) or a four minute version (with another minute of content after the commercial).
REGIONAL RADIO NETWORKS

United States of America

Alaska Public Radio Network 155910
Owner: Alaska Public Telecommunications Inc.
Editorial: 3877 University Dr, Anchorage, Alaska 99508-4676 **Tel:** 1 907 550-8400.
Email: news@aprn.org
Web site: http://www.alaskapublic.org
Profile: APRN provides balanced news and information, builds bridges of communication between urban and rural Alaska and promotes Alaska's cultures, regions and ethnic diversity. The network is especially committed to informing and empowering Alaska's Native peoples. APRN serves 90 percent of Alaska's vast geography (90,000 Alaskans listen each week in over 250 communities).
REGIONAL RADIO NETWORKS

American Ag Network 47068
Editorial: 2501 13th Ave S Ste 201, Fargo, North Dakota 58103-3601 **Tel:** 1 701 237-5000.
Email: americanagnetwork@gmail.com
Web site: http://www.americanagnetwork.com
Profile: Distributes international, national, and regional farm news stories as well as weather, and grain and livestock market analysis to 40 affiliates in North and South Dakota.
REGIONAL RADIO NETWORKS

American Family Radio 46926
Owner: American Family Association
Editorial: 107 Park Gate Dr, Tupelo, Mississippi 38801-3010 **Tel:** 1 662 844-8888.
Email: comments@afr.net
Web site: https://afr.net
Profile: American Family Radio supplies Christian-oriented radio programming to Southern and Midwestern states. The network has approximately 40 professional broadcasters, news and engineer personnel who combine their knowledge and skills to provide the very finest in Christian radio. PSAs should be directed to the network's main e-mail address.
RADIO NETWORK

American Forces Network Broadcast Center 518658
Editorial: 23755 Z St, Riverside, California 92518-2077 **Tel:** 1 951 413-2351.
Email: contactus@myafn.net
Web site: http://myafn.dodmedia.osd.mil
Profile: American Forces Network Broadcast Center (AFN-BC) operates and provides multi-channel broadcast quality radio and television services and expanded internal information products to all Department of Defense members and their families stationed overseas, on contingency operations, and onboard Navy ships around the world. All entertainment, news, sports and information programming is acquired and distributed by AFN based on the popularity of programs within the specific Department of Defense audience demographics, the unique interests of military audiences and AFN scheduling needs.
RADIO NETWORK

American Public Media 281563
Editorial: 480 Cedar St, Saint Paul, Minnesota 55101-2217 **Tel:** 1 651 290-1500.
Web site: http://www.americanpublicmedia.org
Profile: American Public Media is the national production and distribution arm of Minnesota Public Radio, one of the nation's premier public radio organizations.
RADIO NETWORK

American Urban Radio Networks 46971
Editorial: 960 Penn Ave Fl 4, Pittsburgh, Pennsylvania 15222-3818 **Tel:** 1 412 456-4000.
Email: information@aurn.com
Web site: http://www.aurn.com
Profile: AURN is the only African American owned network radio company in the United States. It is the largest network reaching urban America. With more than 300 weekly shows, AURN reaches an estimated 20 million listeners. Through four programming networks and one marketing division, American Urban Radio Networks reaches more African Americans than any other medium in America and produces more urban programming than all other broadcasting companies combined. American Urban Radio Networks broadcasts news, entertainment, sports and information programming to more than 400 radio stations nationwide. AURN's SPM Urban Network specializes in the creation, implementation and execution of national promotions and fully integrated marketing programs. It is the only African American broadcaster with a bureau in the White House. AURN has offices in New York, Pittsburgh, Atlanta, Chicago, Detroit, Los Angeles and Washington, D.C.
RADIO NETWORK

Animal Radio Network 154994
Owner: Animal Radio Network LLC
Editorial: 699 Paula St, Morro Bay, California 93442-1773 **Tel:** 1 805 772-1314.
Email: postmaster@animalradio.com
Profile: Animal Radio, according to Arbitron radio ratings, provides the most-listened-to animal programming in the United States. The two-hour celebration of our pets is hosted by veteran air-talent Hal Abrams and Judy Francis.
RADIO NETWORK

Arizona News Radio 825530
Editorial: 14605 N Airport Dr Ste 370, Scottsdale, Arizona 85260-2491 **Tel:** 1 480 503-8700.
Email: aznews@skyviewsat.com
Web site: http://www.skyviewsatellite.com
Profile: The network provides news to radio stations across Arizona.
REGIONAL RADIO NETWORKS

Arkansas Radio Network 47033
Owner: Cumulus Media Inc
Editorial: 700 Wellington Hills Rd, Little Rock, Arkansas 72211-2026 **Tel:** 1 501 401-0228.
Profile: The Arkansas Radio Network, ARN, is the oldest statewide radio network in Arkansas, providing Arkansas stations with local news, agriculture, sports, special programming and weather seven days a week to hometown radio stations across the region.
REGIONAL RADIO NETWORKS

Associated Press Broadcast 46972
Editorial: 1100 13th St NW Ste 500, Washington, District Of Columbia 20005-4051 **Tel:** 1 202 641-9710.
Email: tvplanning@ap.org
Web site: http://www.ap.org/products-services/radio
Profile: AP Broadcast Radio offers coverage of news, sports, business news, political news, technology news, entertainment, and weather. News, analysts and experts should first be pitched to local or regional bureaus before the national network.
RADIO NETWORK

Associated Press Broadcast - Albany Bureau 781377
Editorial: 645 Albany Shaker Rd, Albany, New York 12211-1158 **Tel:** 1 518 458-7821.
Email: apalbany@ap.org
RADIO NETWORK

Associated Press Broadcast - Los Angeles Bureau 47000
Editorial: 221 S Figueroa St Fl 3, Los Angeles, California 90012-2524 **Tel:** 1 000 213-5555.
Email: losangeles@ap.org
RADIO NETWORK

Associated Press Broadcast - New York Bureau 46993
Editorial: 450 W 33rd St Fl 14, New York, New York 10001-2626 **Tel:** 1 212 621-1524.
Profile: Send all pitches by mail. The bureau does not accept faxes.
RADIO NETWORK

Associated Press Broadcast - Pittsburgh Bureau 151504
Editorial: 11 Stanwix St, Ste 1020, Pittsburgh, Pennsylvania 15222 **Tel:** 1 412 281-3747.
Email: appittsburgh@ap.org
RADIO NETWORK

BARN 735880
Editorial: 51294 WCR 76, Briggsdale, Colorado 80611 **Tel:** 1 970 656-3489.
Email: barnmedia40@gmail.com
Web site: http://www.barnmedia.net
Profile: The network offers accurate and factual information regarding agriculture and issues concerning producers and the agriculture sector.
RADIO NETWORK

BBN/Bible Broadcasting Network 150813
Editorial: 11530 Carmel Commons Blvd, Charlotte, North Carolina 28226-3976 **Tel:** 1 704 523-5555.
Email: bbn@bbnmedia.org
Web site: http://www.bbnradio.org
Profile: BBN/Bible Broadcasting Network's mission is to share the Word of God around the world. The network operates AM and FM radio stations in 14 countries that reach over 200 million people in six languages.
RADIO NETWORK

BizTalkRadio 46914
Owner: Center Post Holdings
Editorial: 810 E Abram St, Arlington, Texas 76010-1277 **Tel:** 1 817 274-1609.
Email: info@biztalkradio.com
Web site: http://biztalkradio.com/
Profile: This business, financial and lifestyle all-talk programming network is delivered via satellite, 24-hours a day. The BizTalkRadio spotlights everything from personal finance to dining and home improvement. Send PSAs to the network via the main e-mail or fax and they will be distributed to the appropriate person. Press releases and guest pitches may also be sent to the network's main e-mail address. Books, videos and samples may be sent to the network by mail.
RADIO NETWORK

Black Radio Network 46910
Editorial: 375 5th Ave, New York, New York 10016-3323 **Tel:** 1 212 686-6850.
Email: news@blackradionetwork.com
Web site: http://www.blackradionetwork.com
Profile: Radio network distributed to affiliates serving black and other minority communities throughout the United States and providing reports and news on issues affecting African-Americans. The network also specializes in news of interest to Hispanics, Asians, Native Americans and women.
RADIO NETWORK

Bloomberg Radio Network 46985
Owner: Bloomberg L.P.
Editorial: 731 Lexington Ave, New York, New York 10022-1331 **Tel:** 1 212 617-5560.
Email: nydesk@bloomberg.net
Web site: http://www.bloomberg.com/audio
Profile: Bloomberg Radio provides live updates on world and national news as well as the latest in business news 24 hours a day. The network distributes news and information throughout North America. Bloomberg provides syndicated reports to more than 750 radio stations around the nation. Outside of the United States, the outlet delivers news in the local languages of the countries where they broadcast. Bloomberg Radio currently offers programming in English, French, German, Japanese, Spanish and Portuguese. The assignment desk should ONLY be contacted to notify the department of serious business news stories about publicly traded companies. Bloomberg Radio Network has over 1.2 million listeners.
RADIO NETWORK

Bloomberg Radio Network - Boston Bureau 376546
Editorial: 100 Summer St, Boston, Massachusetts 02110-2106 **Tel:** 1 617 210-4600.
RADIO NETWORK

Bloomberg Radio Network - Washington Bureau 47025
Editorial: 1399 New York Ave NW Fl 11, Washington, District Of Columbia 20005-4749 **Tel:** 1 202 624-1800.
RADIO NETWORK

Blue Funk Broadcasting 217836
Editorial: 428 Broadway St, New Haven, Indiana 46774 **Tel:** 1 260 493-7279.
Email: comments@bluefunkbroadcasting.com
Web site: http://www.bluefunkbroadcasting.com
Profile: Syndicates the Ric Bratton Show, This Week in America with Ric Bratton, and Boomer and Company.
RADIO NETWORK

Bott Radio Network 46946
Editorial: 10550 Barkley St Ste 100, Overland Park, Kansas 66212-1824 **Tel:** 1 913 642-7770.
Web site: http://www.bottradionetwork.com
Profile: Bott Radio Network provides a wide range of spiritual and religious programming to affiliates across the United States. The network's stated purpose is to serve the Lord's people and to help strengthen each Christian family in its listening audience. The network encourages each listener to walk more closely with the Lord. Its stations broadcast Bible teachings and Christian news and information programming across America. Do not send PSAs to the network.
RADIO NETWORK

Brownfield Ag News 47060
Owner: Learfield Communications, Inc.
Editorial: 505 Hobbs Rd, Jefferson City, Missouri 65109-5788 **Tel:** 1 573 893-5700.
Email: info@brownfieldnetwork.com
Web site: http://brownfieldagnews.com
Profile: The Brownfield Network is America's largest farm network, producing agribusiness news, markets and weather for more than 300 radio stations in Illinois, Indiana, Iowa, Michigan, Missouri, Minnesota, Nebraska, Ohio, South Dakota and Wisconsin.
REGIONAL RADIO NETWORKS

Buzz Radio Network 504525
Owner: Signal Media Inc.
Editorial: 2400 Cottondale Ln, Little Rock, Arkansas 72202-2020 **Tel:** 1 501 661-1037.
Web site: http://www.1037thebuzz.com
Profile: The Buzz Radio Network syndicates KABZ-FM's on-air line-up to several stations in Arkansas.
REGIONAL RADIO NETWORKS

CBS News Radio 46975
Owner: CBS Radio
Editorial: 1271 Avenue of the Americas Fl 44, New York, New York 10020-1401 **Tel:** 1 212 975-4321.
Web site: http://www.cbsradio.com
Profile: CBS News Radio provides the latest in news, sports and entertainment programming. The network features a wide variety of news and public affairs programming, including news on the hour, breaking news and feature programs. The network is merging with Entercom Communications. The sale is expected to close during the second half of 2017, pending FCC approval. The network changed named from CBS Radio Network to CBS News Radio in August 2017.
RADIO NETWORK

CBS News Radio - Orlando Bureau 821891
Editorial: 13816 Valleybrooke Ln, Orlando, Florida 32826-2642 **Tel:** 1 407 823-8747.
RADIO NETWORK

CBS News Radio - Washington Bureau 46995
Editorial: 2020 M St NW, Washington, District Of Columbia 20036-3304 **Tel:** 1 202 457-4321.
Profile: The bureau no longer uses faxes at all and does not accept any unsolicited press material.
RADIO NETWORK

CBS Sports Radio Network 823513
Owner: CBS Radio
Editorial: 1271 Avenue of the Americas, New York, New York 10020-1300 **Tel:** 1 212 649-9600.
Web site: http://radio.cbssports.com
Profile: Radio network offering all sports programming, and features news updates. Westwood One is the network's exclusive distributor and content is produced by CBS Radio and CBS Sports. CBS Sports Radio launched on January 2, 2013. The network reaches over 10 million listeners.
RADIO NETWORK

CMT Radio Network 87820
Editorial: 330 Commerce St, Nashville, Tennessee 37201 **Tel:** 1 615 335-8400.
Web site: http://www.cmt.com/music/radio
Profile: CMT Radio Network is a comprehensive network of news and music tailored to country music stations. CMT Radio Network features exclusive access to CMT talent, show prep, audio cuts and news and information from CMT. Affiliates also get exclusive live interviews and celebrity one-on-ones, CMT concerts and live events. The network is owned and operated by Westwood One.
RADIO NETWORK

CNBC Radio Network 922802
Editorial: 900 Sylvan Ave, Englewood Cliffs, New Jersey 07632-3312 **Tel:** 1 201 735-2622.
RADIO NETWORK

CNN en Español Radio 46939
Owner: Time Warner Inc.
Editorial: 1 Cnn Ctr NW, Atlanta, Georgia 30303-2762 **Tel:** 1 404 827-1220.
Web site: http://www.cnnenespanol.com/radio/
Profile: Full-service Spanish language radio network providing radio affiliates in the United States and throughout Latin America with the latest information in news, sports, business and entertainment. The network offers a menu of actualities and reports in closed-circuit news feeds, which are produced using the network's own Latin American resources, CNN's nine domestic and 20 international bureaus, and radio and television affiliates.
RADIO NETWORK

Colorado Public Radio 831269
Editorial: 7409 S Alton Ct, Centennial, Colorado 80112-2301 **Tel:** 1 303 871-9191.
Web site: http://www.cpr.org
Profile: The network provides in-depth news, information, entertainment and music for people in Colorado.
REGIONAL RADIO NETWORKS

Compass Media Networks 584639
Editorial: 32 Elm Pl, Ste 3N, Rye, New York 10580-2972 **Tel:** 1 914 600-5099.
Web site: http://compassmedianetworks.com
Profile: Debuted in January 2009 with the mission of providing outstanding representation and marketing services to the best brands and programs in national radio.
RADIO NETWORK

Cox Radio Inc. 46951
Owner: Cox Enterprises, Inc.
Editorial: 6205 Peachtree Dunwoody Rd NE, Atlanta, Georgia 30328-4524 **Tel:** 1 404 892-8227.
Email: cxr.info@cox.com
Web site: http://www.coxmediagroup.com
Profile: Cox Radio Inc. is one of the largest radio broadcasting companies in the United States based on revenues. Cox Radio Inc. owns, operates or provides sales and marketing services to 80 stations in 18 markets. In 15 of its 18 markets, Cox Radio Inc. operates three or more stations.
RADIO NETWORK

CRN Digital Talk Radio 837407
Owner: Cable Radio Network, Inc.
Editorial: 10487 Sunland Blvd, Sunland, California 91040-1905 **Tel:** 1 818 352-7152.
Web site: http://www.crntalk.com
Profile: CRN Digital Talk Radio is a 24-hour nationally syndicated radio network. Launched in 1983, CRN can also be heard worldwide via the Internet at www.crni.net. The network is made up of six digital radio channels: CRN1, CRN2, CRN3, CRN4, CRN5, and CRN6.
RADIO NETWORK

Crystal Media Networks 135731
Editorial: 7201 Wisconsin Ave, Ste 780, Bethesda, Maryland 20814-4879 **Tel:** 1 240 223-0850.
Web site: http://www.crystalmedianetworks.com
Profile: National radio network providing programming to radio stations nationwide in various genres, including sports, nostalgia, entertainment and finance. The network is a leading independent creator, producer and distributor of creative entertainment and music-related radio programs and a supplier of marketing and promotional services to the radio industry. Crystal produces, syndicates and/or reps to more than 2,300 radio station affiliates nationwide.
RADIO NETWORK

CSN International Radio Network 46958
Owner: CSN International
Editorial: 4002 N 3300 E, Twin Falls, Idaho 83301 **Tel:** 1 800 357-4226.
Email: feedback@csnradio.com
Web site: http://www.csnradio.com

Profile: Producer of religious and Christian programming for a national audience. CSN International is a non-profit organization, an outreach of Calvary Chapel of Twin Falls. The network broadcasts programming that faithfully follows sound Biblical teaching and anointed praise and worship music 24 hours a day to communities throughout the United States and the world.
RADIO NETWORK

C-SPAN Radio 402952
Editorial: 400 N Capitol St NW, Ste 650, Washington, District Of Columbia 20001 **Tel:** 1 202 737-3220.
Email: radio@c-span.org
Web site: http://www.c-span.org
Profile: C-SPAN Radio offers commercial-free public affairs programming 24 hours a day. Listeners hear live coverage from Washington, D.C. of important congressional hearings, key speeches from national leaders, along with archival recordings of presidential tapes, military memoirs and judicial proceedings from both contemporary times and before the advent of television. C-SPAN Radio should not be contacted via fax. General inquiries may be sent via the main e-mail address.
RADIO NETWORK

Cumulus Media Networks 46968
Owner: Cumulus Media Inc.
Editorial: 3280 Peachtree Rd NE Ste 2300, Atlanta, Georgia 30305-2455 **Tel:** 1 404 949-0700.
Web site: http://www.cumulus.com
Profile: Headquartered in Atlanta, G.A., Cumulus Media Networks is a national radio network with approximately 460 stations in 90 cities. It broadcasts five full-service news networks, ABC News Radio, Radio Disney, ESPN Radio, music, talk and information programming, 10 ABC Radio 24-Hour formats and daily and weekly long and short form programming.
RADIO NETWORK

Cumulus Media Networks en Espanol 592497
Owner: Cumulus Media Inc
Editorial: 2 Alhambra Plz, Coral Gables, Florida 33134-5202 **Tel:** 1 305 567-2271.
Web site: http://adsales.cumulusmedianetworks.com/tag/Hispanic
Profile: Cumulus Media Networks en Espanol is a recognized leader in Spanish-language programming. With a presence in 28 of the top 30 Hispanic DMAs and the only two Hispanic RADAR rated networks, Cumulus Media Networks en Espanol reaches more than 10 million Hispanic listeners in an average week across 131 Spanish language radio stations in the United States. Programming includes Latino superstars and megabrands.
RADIO NETWORK

Deutsche Welle Radio Washington Bureau 618014
Owner: Deutsche Welle
Editorial: 2000 M St NW Ste 335, Washington, District Of Columbia 20036-3307 **Tel:** 1 202 785-5730.
Web site: http://www.dw-world.de
Profile: Deutsche Welle Radio (DW Radio) is Germany's international news and information broadcaster. DW Radio's Washington bureau produces segments of shows and occasionally an entire show, all of which are then broadcast from the headquarters in Germany.
RADIO NETWORK

Entertainment Radio Network 816194
Editorial: 231 SW I St, Grants Pass, Oregon 97526-2814 **Tel:** 1 541 471-1479.
Email: info@ernlive.com
Web site: http://www.ernlive.com
Profile: Entertainment Radio Network (ERN) is aligned with many popular magazines, including Motor Trend, Hot Rod, Motorcyclist, Popular Science among others, and bringing them to life. Programming is listener interactive and provides more information, insight and content outside of the print/digital publications.
RADIO NETWORK

Envision Networks 564426
Editorial: 3733 Park East Dr, Cleveland, Ohio 44122-4338 **Tel:** 1 216 831-3761.
Web site: http://www.envisionradio.com
Profile: Independently owned affiliate relations company. It supplies all types of programming and services for radio including news (www.virtualnewscenter.com) and weather, morning show prep, short-form vignettes, live syndicated morning shows, long-form weekend programming, comedy services, remote broadcasts and event programming, off-air tools and web content, album releases and artist specials. It is also offering Spanish language news reports.
RADIO NETWORK

ESPN Deportes Radio Network 594287
Owner: Walt Disney Co.
Editorial: 2 Alhambra Plz, Coral Gables, Florida 33134-5202 **Tel:** 1 305 567-2270.
Web site: http://espndeportes.espn.go.com
Profile: ESPN Deportes is a radio network dedicated to broadcasting sports-related programming 24/7 in the Spanish language. The channel broadcasts transmissions made in different ESPN studios in North America.
RADIO NETWORK

ESPN Radio Network 46917
Owner: Walt Disney Co.
Editorial: 545 Middle St, Bristol, Connecticut 06010-8413 **Tel:** 1 860 766-2000.
Email: radio@espn.com
Web site: http://espn.go.com/espnradio
Profile: The ESPN Radio Network features the latest sports information and personality-driven commentary and talk. The network spotlights the exclusive national radio broadcast rights to Major League baseball, NBA basketball games during the regular season and the playoffs, and the Bowl Championship Series in college football. News, scores and updates are provided in conjunction with the vast resources of the ESPN cable television network.
RADIO NETWORK

Family Life Network 613054
Owner: Family Life Ministries Inc.
Editorial: 7634 Campbell Creek Road, Box 506, Bath, New York 14810-7612 **Tel:** 1 607 776-4151.
Web site: http://www.fln.org/radio-network
Profile: Network features radio programming that shares Christ through music, biblical teaching, and creative communication. Music ranges from inspirational to adult contemporary to southern gospel. Teaching programs that offer instruction from well-respected pastors and teachers. Family Life also has news and public affairs programming that keeps listeners informed from a Biblical perspective.
RADIO NETWORK

Family Life Radio 48052
Owner: Family Life Communications, Inc.
Editorial: 7355 N Oracle Rd, Tucson, Arizona 85704-6325 **Tel:** 1 520 742-6976.
Web site: http://www.myflr.org
Profile: Family Life Radio delivers inspirational, Christ-centered Christian music with relevant, Bible-based programs all focused on communicating Christ's love and hope. Family Life Radio connects personally with its listeners through live broadcasts and community events, and works in partnership with area churches and ministries.
RADIO NETWORK

Family Stations Radio Network 46945
Owner: Family Stations Inc.
Editorial: 290 Hegenberger Rd, Oakland, California 94621-1436 **Tel:** 1 510 568-6200.
Email: familyradio@familyradio.com
Web site: http://www.familyradio.org
Profile: Family Stations Radio Network is a Christian nonprofit, nondenominational, educational organization that produces and broadcasts Christian programming and music around the world.
RADIO NETWORK

Farmhouse Media LLC 740074
Editorial: 2400 E Highland Dr Fl 4, Jonesboro, Arkansas 72401-6213 **Tel:** 1 870 931-7500.
Web site: http://www.agwatchnetwork.com
Profile: AgWatch Network provides a daily source for agriculture news updates of regional, national, livestock & poultry, and market reports for Arkansas, Kentucky, Mississippi, Missouri and Tennessee.
RADIO NETWORK

First Oklahoma Ag 47069
Owner: iHeartMedia Inc.
Editorial: 1900 NW Expressway Ste 1000, Oklahoma City, Oklahoma 73118-1854 **Tel:** 1 405 858-1458.
Web site: http://www.aghub.net/main.html
Profile: Serves 42 stations in Oklahoma with farm and agriculture news and market reports.
REGIONAL RADIO NETWORKS

Florida News Network 47037
Owner: iHeartMedia Inc.
Editorial: 2500 Maitland Center Pkwy, Maitland, Florida 32751-7224 **Tel:** 1 407 916-7810.
Email: help@frn.com
Web site: http://www.fnnonline.net
Profile: Provides news, lawn & gardening, and entertainment programming to affiliates in Florida. One- to four-minute business, sports and state newscasts are produced throughout weekdays.
REGIONAL RADIO NETWORKS

Florida Public Radio Network 47090
Editorial: 1600 Red Barber Plz, Tallahassee, Florida 32310-6068 **Tel:** 1 850 487-3086.
Email: newsroom@wfsu.org
Web site: http://www.wfsu.org
Profile: Serves 13 FM public radio stations throughout the state of Florida. Provides a variety of news, information and entertainment programming.
REGIONAL RADIO NETWORKS

FOX News Radio Network 46959
Owner: Fox News Channel (21st Century Fox) and Premiere Networks
Editorial: 1211 Avenue of the Americas, New York, New York 10036-8701 **Tel:** 1 212 301-3000.
Web site: http://radio.foxnews.com
Profile: FOX News Radio features news, sports and entertainment actualities produced for radio, along with breaking news coverage from FOX News Channel. Pitch stories to the assignment desk by e-mail. Only call the assignment desk with breaking news of national interest.
RADIO NETWORK

FOX News Radio Network - Los Angeles Bureau 821889
Editorial: 2044 Armacost Ave, Los Angeles, California 90025-6113 **Tel:** 1 310 571-2000.
RADIO NETWORK

FOX Sports Radio Network 62905
Owner: Premiere Radio Networks
Editorial: 15260 Ventura Blvd Ste 400, Sherman Oaks, California 91403-5300 **Tel:** 1 818 377-5300.
Web site: http://foxsportsradio.iheart.com
Profile: FOX Sports Radio Network is a 24-hour radio network that provides sports programming to affiliates nationwide. FOX Sports Radio Network is a division of Premiere Radio Networks, in connection with FOX Sports and FOX Sports Net.
RADIO NETWORK

GAB Network 794633
Owner: Kovas Communications
Editorial: 2100 Lee St, Evanston, Illinois 60202-1539 **Tel:** 1 847 475-1590.
Email: info@gabradionetwork.com
Web site: http://gabradionetwork.com
Profile: GAB Network (Global American Broadcasting) was formed in 2000 to provide satellite and production services to the growing population of program syndicaters. Global American Broadcasting Network Inc was founded by Dr. Gene Hood and Ronald Crider.
RADIO NETWORK

Georgia Farm Radio Network 390909
Owner: Georgia Farm Bureau
Editorial: 1620 Bass Rd, Macon, Georgia 31210-6503 **Tel:** 1 866 217-7603.
Web site: http://www.gfrn.net
Profile: GFRN, Georgia's largest agriculture network with 54 stations, features the latest daily Georgia agribusiness news, market, commodity information and analysis.
REGIONAL RADIO NETWORKS

Georgia News Network 47038
Owner: iHeartMedia Inc.
Editorial: 1819 Peachtree Rd NE Ste 700, Atlanta, Georgia 30309-1849 **Tel:** 1 404 875-8080.
Web site: http://www.georgianewsnetwork.com
Profile: News programming distributed to 120 stations in the southern United States.
REGIONAL RADIO NETWORKS

Georgia Public Broadcasting Radio 47091
Editorial: 260 14th St NW, Atlanta, Georgia 30318-5360 **Tel:** 1 404 685-2400.
Email: news@gpb.org
Web site: http://www.gpb.org
Profile: Since 1984, Georgia's 17-station public radio network has been a source of classical and jazz music as well as NPR news. GPB Radio has made a name for itself by producing and broadcasting award-winning local news and public affairs programming and feature programming.
REGIONAL RADIO NETWORKS

GLR Networks 877678
Editorial: 5000 SW 75th Ave Fl 4, Miami, Florida 33155-4488
Email: info@glrnetworks.com
Web site: http://glrnetworks.com
Profile: The network provides Spanish language radio stations in the USA with news services, sports, entertainment and community programming, as well as a variety of musical formats.
RADIO NETWORK

Head On Radio Network 617825
Editorial: 1038 N Eisenhower Dr, Pmb 318, Beckley, West Virginia 25801-3116 **Tel:** 1 304 658-3333.
Web site: http://headonradionetwork.com
Profile: The Head On Radio Network is a national broadcast radio network providing a range of Liberal talk programming.
RADIO NETWORK

HIA Radio Network 797989
Editorial: 10540 Marty St Ste 240, Overland Park, Kansas 66212-2596 **Tel:** 1 913 385-2224.
Web site: http://hiaradio.com
RADIO NETWORK

Hispanic Communications Network 46916
Owner: Hispanic Communications Network, Inc.
Editorial: 50 F St NW Fl 8, Washington, District Of Columbia 20001-1530 **Tel:** 1 202 360-4107.
Email: press@hcnmedia.com
Web site: http://www.hcnmedia.com
Profile: Hispanic Communications Network (formerly known as the Hispanic Radio Network) produces and syndicates Spanish-language radio programs aimed at educating and informing the Hispanic population. These programs are broadcast throughout the USA on more than 200 popular Spanish language radio stations.
RADIO NETWORK

Hodgson Media 46918
Editorial: 28840 County Road R, Brush, Colorado 80723 **Tel:** 1 970 842-2902.
Email: office@hodgsonmedia.com
Web site: http://www.hodgsonmedia.com
Profile: The network provides comprehensive and frequent reports on the livestock and agricultural markets, in addition to farm and agricultural news and information.
RADIO NETWORK

I*ON Weather Radio Network 47084
Tel: 1 973 983-8222.
Email: research@ionweather.com
Web site: http://www.ionweather.com
Profile: The network provides weather programming, including forecasts and severe weather alerts, to stations in six states on the East Coast.
REGIONAL RADIO NETWORKS

Icon Radio Network 586802
Editorial: 6625 Lenox Park Dr Ste 110, Memphis, Tennessee 38115-4434 **Tel:** 1 888 510-4266.
Web site: http://www.iconradionetwork.com
Profile: Network syndicates the Ben Ferguson Show, and launched in May 2009.
RADIO NETWORK

Illinois News Network Radio 944587
Editorial: 190 S La Salle St Ste 1630, Chicago, Illinois 60603-3470 **Tel:** 1 312 346-5700.
Web site: https://www.ilnews.org
Profile: Regional news reporting service that covers public policies that affect the residents of Illinois.
REGIONAL RADIO NETWORKS

Illinois Radio Network 47041
Owner: Saga Communications
Editorial: Press Room, Illinois State Capitol, Springfield, Illinois 62706 **Tel:** 1 312 943-6363.
Email: newsirn@sbcglobal.net
Web site: http://www.illinoisradionetwork.com
Profile: Illinois Radio Network (IRN) is a statewide radio network covering news and sports in Illinois. The network is affiliated with over 40 stations in Illinois.
REGIONAL RADIO NETWORKS

Indianapolis Motor Speedway Radio Network 153420
Editorial: 4555 W 16th St, Indianapolis, Indiana 46222-2513 **Tel:** 1 317 492-6596.
Email: imsradio@brickyard.com
Web site: http://www.imsproductions.tv
Profile: Network providing live coverage of the Indy Racing League (IRL) IndyCar Series racing and qualifications, plus a weekly talk show featuring IRL news, as well as interviews with drivers, owners and track officials. The Network covers 16 IRL races each year, including the Indianapolis 500, plus it carries NASCAR's Brickyard 400 and associated programing. The IMS Radio Network is a division of IMS Productions.
RADIO NETWORK

Inland Empire News Radio Network 512047
Owner: Inland Empire News Radio
Editorial: 5225 Canyon Crest Dr, Riverside, California 92507-6301 **Tel:** 1 951 369-3900.
Email: inlandnewstoday@sbcglobal.net
Web site: http://www.inlandnewstoday.com
Profile: Inland Empire News Radio Network broadcasts local news, traffic reports and public affairs programming to radio affiliates in Riverside, Big Bear and San Bernardino Counties in Southern California. The network welcomes same day news, press releases and PSAs as long as they focus on the Southern California area. The network prefers PSAs and releases be sent via e-mail, one week in advance.
REGIONAL RADIO NETWORKS

Iowa Public Radio 535531
Owner: State of Iowa
Editorial: 2111 Grand Ave Ste 100, Des Moines, Iowa 50312-5393 **Tel:** 1 800 861-8000.
Email: news@iowapublicradio.org
Web site: http://www.iowapublicradio.org
Profile: Iowa Public Radio is the result of a merge of the three Regents' university-licensed stations into a statewide network. It was originally established by The Board of Regents of the State of Iowa to oversee public radio operations at the three Regents' universities at the end of 2004. Iowa Public Radio includes WOI-AM and WOI-FM at Iowa State University, WSUI-AM and KSUI-FM at the University of Iowa, and KUNI-FM and KHKE-FM at the University of Northern Iowa.
REGIONAL RADIO NETWORKS

Irish Radio Network 74261
Owner: Flannelly Promotions Ltd.
Editorial: 515 Madison Ave, Fl 11, New York, New York 10022 **Tel:** 1 212 935-0606.
Email: info@irishradio.com
Web site: http://www.irishradio.com
Profile: The Irish Radio Network is the preeminent broadcast source of topical issues and entertainment, aimed at over 44 million Americans of Irish ancestry.
RADIO NETWORK

Jefferson Public Radio Network 354582
Editorial: 1250 Siskiyou Blvd, Ashland, Oregon 97520 **Tel:** 1 541 552-6301.
Email: jprinfo@sou.edu
Web site: http://www.ijpr.org
Profile: Jefferson Public Radio Network distributes news, public affairs and business programming as well as jazz and classical music throughout the state

of Oregon and adjacent states. The mission of the network is to provide cultural programming that celebrates the human experience.
REGIONAL RADIO NETWORKS

KAAA-AM 37165
Owner: Cameron Broadcasting Inc.
Editorial: 2350 Miracle Mile Ste 300, Bullhead City, Arizona 86442-7505 **Tel:** 1 928 763-5586.
Web site: http://www.talkatoz.com
Profile: KAAA-AM is a commercial station owned by Cameron Broadcasting Inc. The format of the station is news and talk programming. KAAA-AM broadcasts to the Bullhead City, AZ area at 1230 AM.
AM RADIO STATION

KAAB-AM 39508
Owner: WRD Entertainment Inc.
Editorial: 920 Harrison St, Batesville, Arkansas 72501-6949 **Tel:** 1 870 793-4196.
Profile: KAAB-AM is a commercial station owned by WRD Entertainment Inc. The format of the station is classic hits music. KAAB-AM broadcasts to the Batesville, AR area at 1130 AM.
AM RADIO STATION

KAAK-FM 45844
Owner: Cherry Creek Radio
Editorial: 914 13th Ave S, Great Falls, Montana 59405-4406 **Tel:** 1 406 761-7600.
Web site: http://www.k99fm.net
Profile: KAAK-FM is a commercial station owned by Cherry Creek Radio. The format for the station is hot adult contemporary. KAAK-FM broadcasts to the Great Falls, MT area at 98.9 FM.
FM RADIO STATION

KAAM-AM 35044
Owner: DJRD Broadcasting LLC
Editorial: 3201 Royalty Row, Irving, Texas 75062-4943 **Tel:** 1 972 445-1700.
Email: kaam@kaamradio.com
Web site: http://www.kaamradio.com
Profile: KAAM-AM is a commercial station owned by DJRD Broadcasting LLC. The format of the station is adult standards. KAAM-AM broadcasts to the Dallas-Fort Worth area at 770 AM.
AM RADIO STATION

KAAN-AM 38477
Owner: Alpha Media
Editorial: 1212 S 25th St, Bethany, Missouri 64424-2602 **Tel:** 1 660 425-6380.
Web site: http://www.northwestmoinfo.com
Profile: KAAN-AM is a commercial station owned by Alpha Media. The format of the station is oldies. KAAN-AM broadcasts to the Bethany, MO at 870 AM.
AM RADIO STATION

KAAN-FM 45849
Owner: Alpha Media
Editorial: Highway 69 South, Bethany, Missouri 64424 **Tel:** 1 660 425-6380.
Web site: http://www.northwestmoinfo.com
Profile: KAAN-FM is a commercial station owned by Alpha Media. The format of the station is country music. KAAN-FM broadcasts to the Kansas City, MO area at 95.5 FM.
FM RADIO STATION

KAAP-FM 43731
Owner: Cherry Creek Radio
Editorial: 231 N Wenatchee Ave, Wenatchee, Washington 98801-2009 **Tel:** 1 509 665-6565.
Email: newswenatchee@cherrycreekradio.com
Web site: http://www.applefm.com
Profile: KAAP-FM is a commercial station owned by Cherry Creek Radio. The format of the station is adult contemporary music. KAAP-FM broadcasts to the Wenatchee, WA area at 99.5 FM.
FM RADIO STATION

KAAQ-FM 45796
Owner: Eagle Radio Inc.
Editorial: 1210 W 10th St, Alliance, Nebraska 69301-2804 **Tel:** 1 308 762-1400.
Web site: http://www.panhandlepost.com
Profile: KAAQ-FM is a commercial station owned by Eagle Radio Inc. The format of the station is contemporary country. KAAQ-FM broadcasts to the Alliance, NE area at 105.9 FM.
FM RADIO STATION

KAAR-FM 41091
Owner: Cherry Creek Radio
Editorial: 750 Dewey Blvd, Butte, Montana 59701-3200 **Tel:** 1 406 494-1030.
Web site: http://www.925kaar.com
Profile: KAAR-FM is a commercial station owned by Cherry Creek Radio. The format for the station is contemporary country. KAAR-FM broadcasts to the Butte, MT area at 92.5 FM.
FM RADIO STATION

KAAT-FM 45842
Owner: Casa Media Partners, LLC
Editorial: 320 W Bedford Ave, Ste 201, Fresno, California 93711 **Tel:** 1 559 436-1031.
Profile: KAAT-FM is a commercial station owned by Casa Media Partners, LLC. The format of the station is Hispanic programming. KAAT-FM broadcasts to the Oakhurst, CA area at 103.1 FM.
FM RADIO STATION

KAAY-AM 34859
Owner: Cumulus Media Inc
Editorial: 700 Wellington Hills Rd, Little Rock, Arkansas 72211-2026 **Tel:** 1 501 401-0200.
Web site: http://www.1090kaay.com
Profile: KAAY-AM is a commercial station owned by Cumulus Media Inc. The format of the station is Christian talk. KAAY-AM broadcasts to the Little Rock, AR area at 1090 AM.
AM RADIO STATION

KAAZ-FM 42891
Owner: iHeartMedia Inc.
Editorial: 2801 Decker Lake Dr, Salt Lake City, Utah 84119-2330 **Tel:** 1 801 908-1300.
Web site: http://www.rock1065.com
Profile: KAAZ-FM is a commercial station owned by iHeartMedia Inc. The format of the station is Rock. KOSY-FM broadcasts to the Salt Lake City area at 106.5 FM.
FM RADIO STATION

KAAZ-FM 45918
Owner: Appaloosa Broadcasting
Editorial: 302 S 2nd St Ste 204, Laramie, Wyoming 82070-3650 **Tel:** 1 307 745-5208.
Profile: KAAZ-FM is a commercial station owned by Appaloosa Broadcasting. The format of the station is rock. KAAZ-FM broadcasts to the Laramie, WY area at 98.7 FM.
FM RADIO STATION

KABC-AM 36366
Owner: Cumulus Media Inc
Editorial: 8965 Lindblade St, Culver City, California 90232-2438 **Tel:** 1 310 840-4900.
Email: kabcpress@gmail.com
Web site: http://www.kabc.com
Profile: KABC-AM is a commercial station owned by Cumulus Media Inc. The format of the station is news and talk. KABC-AM broadcasts to the Los Angeles area at 790 AM.
AM RADIO STATION

KABD-FM 134133
Owner: Dakota Broadcasting, LLC
Editorial: 426 N Highway 281 Ste 4, Aberdeen, South Dakota 57401-1864 **Tel:** 1 605 725-5551.
Web site: http://www.dakotabroadcasting.com
FM RADIO STATION

KABF-FM 41095
Owner: Arkansas Broadcasting Foundation
Editorial: 2101 Main St, Little Rock, Arkansas 72206-1527 **Tel:** 1 501 372-6119.
Web site: http://www.kabf.org
Profile: KABF-FM is a non-commercial community station owned by the Arkansas Broadcasting Foundation. The format of the station is variety. KABF-FM broadcasts to the Little Rock, AR area at 88.3 FM.
FM RADIO STATION

KABG-FM 42336
Owner: American General Media
Editorial: 4125 Carlisle Blvd NE, Albuquerque, New Mexico 87107-4806 **Tel:** 1 505 878-0980.
Web site: http://www.big985.com
Profile: KABG-FM is a commercial station owned by American General Media. The format of the station is classic hits. KABG-FM broadcasts to the Albuquerque, NM area at 98.5 FM.
FM RADIO STATION

KABI-AM 37166
Owner: Rocking M Radio
Editorial: 200 N Broadway St, Abilene, Kansas 67410-2647 **Tel:** 1 785 823-1111.
Web site: http://www.kabiabilene.com
Profile: KABI-AM is a commercial station owned by Rocking M Radio. The format of the station is adult standards. KABI-AM broadcasts to the Abilene, KS area at 1560 AM.
AM RADIO STATION

KABQ-AM 34860
Owner: iHeartMedia Inc.
Editorial: 5411 Jefferson St NE Ste 100, Albuquerque, New Mexico 87109-3485 **Tel:** 1 505 830-6400.
Web site: http://www.abqtalk.com
Profile: KABQ-AM is a commercial station owned by iHeartMedia Inc. The format of the station is talk. KABQ-AM broadcasts to the Albuquerque, NM area at 1350 AM.
AM RADIO STATION

KABQ-FM 156589
Owner: iHeartMedia Inc.
Editorial: 5411 Jefferson St NE Ste 100, Albuquerque, New Mexico 87109-3485 **Tel:** 1 505 830-6400.
Web site: http://www.classiccountry1047.com
Profile: KABQ-FM is a commercial station owned by iHeartMedia Inc. The format of the station is classic country. KABQ-FM broadcasts to the Albuquerque, NM area at 104.7 FM.
FM RADIO STATION

KABU-FM 44534
Owner: Dakota Circle Tipi, Inc.
Editorial: 7889 Highway 57, Saint Michael, North Dakota 58370-9000 **Tel:** 1 701 766-4095.
Web site: http://kabu.radio.net
FM RADIO STATION

KABW-FM 87113
Owner: Doud Media Group LLC
Editorial: 1500 Industrial Blvd Ste 200, Abilene, Texas 79602-8063 **Tel:** 1 325 437-9596.
Web site: http://www.wolfabilene.com/
Profile: KABW-FM is a commercial station owned by Doud Media Group LLC. The format of the station is country. KABW-FM broadcasts in the Abilene, TX area at 95.1 FM.
FM RADIO STATION

KABX-FM 44779
Owner: Mapleton Radio, LLC
Editorial: 1020 W Main St, Merced, California 95340-4521 **Tel:** 1 209 723-2191.
Web site: http://www.975kabx.com
Profile: KABX-FM is a commercial station owned by Mapleton Radio, LLC. The format of the station is adult contemporary. KABX-FM broadcasts to the Merced, Ca area at 97.5 FM.
FM RADIO STATION

KABZ-FM 40997
Owner: Signal Media Inc.
Editorial: 2400 Cottondale Ln, Little Rock, Arkansas 72202 **Tel:** 1 501 661-1037.
Web site: http://www.1037thebuzz.com
Profile: KABZ-FM is a commercial station owned by Signal Media Inc. The format of the station is sports. KABZ-FM broadcasts in the Little Rock, AR area at 103.7 FM.
FM RADIO STATION

KACC-FM 41676
Owner: Alvin Community College
Editorial: 3110 Mustang Rd, Alvin, Texas 77511-4807 **Tel:** 1 281 756-3766.
Web site: http://www.kaccradio.com
Profile: KACC-FM is a non-commercial station owned by Alvin Community College. The format of the station is rock/album-oriented rock. KACC-FM broadcasts to the Alvin, TX area at 89.7 FM.
FM RADIO STATION

KACH-AM 36098
Owner: White(Alan & Nelada)
Editorial: 1633 N Radio Station Rd, Preston, Idaho 83263-4706 **Tel:** 1 208 852-1340.
Email: kach@kachradio.com
Web site: http://www.kachradio.com
Profile: KACH-AM is a commercial station owned by Alan & Nelada White. The format of the station is adult contemporary. KACH-AM broadcasts to the Preston, ID area at 1340 AM.
AM RADIO STATION

KACI-AM 38478
Owner: Bicoastal Media LLC
Editorial: 719 E 2Nd St, The Dalles, Oregon 97058-2417 **Tel:** 1 541 296-2211.
Web site: http://www.gorgeradio.com
Profile: KACI-AM is a commercial station owned by Bicoastal Media LLC. The format of the station is news and talk. KACI-AM broadcasts to The Dalles, OR area at 1300 AM.
AM RADIO STATION

KACI-FM 45839
Owner: Bicoastal Media LLC
Editorial: 719 E 2Nd St Ste 203, The Dalles, Oregon 97058-2417 **Tel:** 1 541 296-2211.
Web site: http://www.935kaci.com
Profile: KACI-FM is a commercial station owned by Bicoastal Media LLC. The format of the station is classic hits music. KACI-FM broadcasts to the Portland, OR area at 97.7 FM.
FM RADIO STATION

KACL-FM 43230
Owner: Townsquare Media, Inc.
Editorial: 4303 Memorial Hwy, Mandan, North Dakota 58554-4711 **Tel:** 1 701 250-6602.
Web site: http://www.cool987fm.com
Profile: KACL-FM is a commercial station owned by Townsquare Media, Inc. The format of the station is classic hits. KACL-FM broadcasts to the Minot-Bismarck, ND area at 98.7 FM.
FM RADIO STATION

KACO-FM 43575
Owner: Perry Publishing & Broadcasting Inc.
Editorial: 115 W Broadway St, Anadarko, Oklahoma 73005-2805 **Tel:** 1 405 247-6682.
Email: kperry@kvsp.com
Web site: http://www.superstarcountry985.com
Profile: KACO-FM is a commercial station owned by Perry Publishing & Broadcasting Inc. The format of the station is country music. KACO-FM broadcasts to the Anadarko, OK area at 98.5 FM.
FM RADIO STATION

KACQ-FM 43821
Owner: Witcher(Ronald K.)
Editorial: 505 N Key Ave, Lampasas, Texas 76550-1850 **Tel:** 1 512 556-6193.
Email: management@lampasasradio.com
Web site: http://www.lampasasradio.com
FM RADIO STATION

KACT-AM 38969
Owner: Zia Broadcasting
Editorial: 2125 N US Highway 385, Andrews, Texas 79714-9106 **Tel:** 1 432 523-2845.
Email: kact1055@windstream.net
Web site: http://www.kactradio.com
Profile: KACT-AM is a commercial station owned by Zia Broadcasting. The format of the station is talk. KACT-AM broadcasts to the Andrews, TX area at 1360 AM. Send PSAs and press submissions to the station via the main e-mail or mail.
AM RADIO STATION

KACT-FM 4630
Owner: Zia Broadcasting
Editorial: 2125 N US Highway 385, Andrews, Texas 79714 **Tel:** 1 432 523-2845.
Email: kact1055@windstream.net
Web site: http://www.kactradio.com
Profile: KACT-FM is a commercial station owned by Zia Broadcasting. The format of the station is country. KACT-FM broadcasts to the Odessa-Midland, Texas area at a frequency of 105.5 FM. Send PSAs and press submissions to the station via the main e-mail or mail.
FM RADIO STATION

KACV-FM 3952
Owner: Amarillo College
Editorial: 2408 S Jackson St, Amarillo, Texas 79109 **Tel:** 1 806 371-5222.
Email: kacvfm90@actx.edu
Web site: http://www.kacvfm.org
Profile: KACV-FM is a non-commercial station owned by Amarillo College. The format of the station is variety. KACV-FM broadcasts to the Amarillo, TX area at 89.9 FM.
FM RADIO STATION

KACY-FM 4448
Owner: Tornado Alley Communications LLC
Editorial: 106 N Summit St, Arkansas City, Kansas 67005 **Tel:** 1 620 442-1102.
Email: studio@1025theriver.com
Web site: http://1025theriver.com
Profile: KACY-FM is a commercial station owned by Tornado Alley Communications LLC. The format of the station is classic hits. KACY-FM broadcasts to the Arkansas City, KS area at 102.5 FM.
FM RADIO STATION

KACZ-FM 23837
Owner: Manhattan Broadcasting
Editorial: 2414 Casement Rd, Manhattan, Kansas 66502 **Tel:** 1 785 776-1350.
Web site: http://www.z963.com
Profile: KACZ-FM is a commercial station owned by Manhattan Broadcasting. The format of the station is Top 40/CHR music. KACZ-FM broadcasts in the Manhattan, KS area at 96.3 FM.
FM RADIO STATION

KADA-AM 3905
Owner: Chickasaw Nation
Editorial: 1019 N Broadway Ave, Ada, Oklahoma 74820 **Tel:** 1 580 332-1212.
Email: score@cableone.net
Web site: http://www.kadaradio.net
Profile: KADA-AM is a commercial station owned by Chickasaw Nation. The format of the station is sports and talk. KADA-AM broadcasts in the Ada, OK area adults at 1230 AM.
AM RADIO STATION

KADA-FM 4638
Owner: Chickasaw Nation
Editorial: 1019 N Broadway Ave, Ada, Oklahoma 74820-2036 **Tel:** 1 580 436-1616.
Email: kada@cableone.net
Web site: http://www.kadaradio.net
Profile: KADA-FM is a commercial station owned by Chickasaw Nation. The format of the station is adult contemporary music. KADA-FM broadcasts to the Ada, OK area at 99.3 FM.
FM RADIO STATION

KADI-AM 3612
Owner: Vision Communications Inc.
Editorial: 5431 W Sunshine St, Brookline Station, Missouri 65619-9433 **Tel:** 1 417 831-0995.
Email: traffickadi@gmail.com
Web site: http://www.1340kadi.com
Profile: KADI-AM is a commercial station owned by Vision Communications Inc. The format of the station is Conservative news talk. KADI-AM broadcasts to the Brookline Station, MO area at 1340 AM.
AM RADIO STATION

KADI-FM 41757
Owner: Vision Communications Inc.
Editorial: 5431 W Sunshine St, Brookline Station, Missouri 65619-9433 **Tel:** 1 417 831-0995.
Web site: http://www.99hitfm.com
Profile: KADI-FM is a commercial station owned by Vision Communications Inc. The format of the station is contemporary Christian music. KADI-FM broadcasts to the Springfield, MO area at 99.5 FM.
FM RADIO STATION

KADL-FM 518278
Owner: Armada Media Corp.
Tel: 1 308 882-4209.
Email: kadl@highplainsradio.net
Web site: http://plainsreporter.k2radio.net
Profile: KADL-FM is a commercial station owned by Armada Media Corp. The format of the station is oldies music. KADL-FM broadcasts to the Lincoln, NE area at 102.9 FM.
FM RADIO STATION

KADR-AM 38482
Owner: Design Homes Inc.
Editorial: 24493 Highway 128, Elkader, Iowa 52043-8038 **Tel:** 1 563 245-1400.
Email: kctn@alpinecom.net

Profile: KADR-AM is a commercial station owned by Design Homes Inc. The format of the station is adult contemporary and oldies. KADR-AM broadcasts to the Cedar Rapids, IA area at 1400 AM.
AM RADIO STATION

KADS-AM 37005
Owner: Paragon Communications Inc.
Editorial: 220 S Pioneer Rd, Elk City, Oklahoma 73644-4926 **Tel:** 1 580 225-9696.
Email: kecoproduction@cableone.net
Web site: http://www.thesportsanimal.com
Profile: KADS-AM is a commercial station owned by Paragon Communications Inc. The format of the station is sports. KADS-AM broadcasts to the Elk City, OK area at 1240 AM.
AM RADIO STATION

KADU-FM 43822
Owner: Heartland Christian Broadcasters Inc.
Editorial: 4090 Highway 11, International Falls, Minnesota 56649 **Tel:** 1 218 285-7398.
Email: studio@psalmfm.org
Web site: http://www.psalmfm.org
Profile: KADU-FM is a non-commercial station owned by Heartland Christian Broadcasters Inc. The format of the station is contemporary Christian. KADU-FM broadcasts to Hibling, MN at 90.1 FM.
FM RADIO STATION

KADV-FM 41122
Owner: Central Valley Christian Academy
Editorial: 1300 S Woodland St, Visalia, California 93277-4214 **Tel:** 1 855 427-7664.
Email: info@mypromisefm.org
Web site: http://www.mypromisefm.com
Profile: KADV-FM is a non-commercial station owned by Central Valley Christian Academy. The format of the station is Christian music and teachings. KADV-FM broadcasts to the Ceres, CA area at 90.5 FM. This station mostly simulcasts from KARM-FM.
FM RADIO STATION

KAEH-FM 43817
Owner: Casa Media Partners, LLC
Editorial: 650 S E St Ste. 4, San Bernardino, California 92408-1902 **Tel:** 1 909 381-0969.
Web site: http://lamaquina1009.com
Profile: KAEH-FM is a commercial station owned by Casa Media Partners, LLC. The format of the station is regional Mexican programming. KAEH-FM broadcasts to the San Bernardino, CA area at 100.9 FM.
FM RADIO STATION

KAFC-FM 44537
Owner: Christian Broadcasting Inc.
Editorial: 6401 E Northern Lights Blvd, Anchorage, Alaska 99504-3312 **Tel:** 1 907 222-4826.
Email: info@kafc.org
Web site: http://www.kafc.org
Profile: KAFC-FM is a commercial station owned by the Christian Broadcasting Inc. The format of the station is contemporary Christian music. KAFC-FM broadcasts in the Anchorage, AK area at 93.7 FM.
FM RADIO STATION

KAFE-FM 44796
Owner: Saga Communications
Editorial: 2219 Yew Street Rd, Bellingham, Washington 98229-8855 **Tel:** 1 360 734-9790.
Email: kafe@kafe.com
Web site: http://www.kafe.com
Profile: KAFE-FM is a commercial station owned by Saga Communications, dba Cascade radio Group. The format of the station is Lite Rock/Lite AC music. KAFE-FM broadcasts to the Bellingham, WA area at 104.1 FM.
FM RADIO STATION

KAFF-AM 37168
Owner: Great Circle Media
Editorial: 1117 W Route 66, Flagstaff, Arizona 86001-6213 **Tel:** 1 928 774-5231.
Email: news@kaff.com
Web site: http://www.country935.com
Profile: KAFF-AM is a commercial station owned by Guyann Corp. The format of the station is classic country. KAFF-AM broadcasts in the Flagstaff, AZ area at 930 AM.
AM RADIO STATION

KAFF-FM 44557
Owner: Great Circle Media
Editorial: 1117 W Route 66, Flagstaff, Arizona 86001-6213 **Tel:** 1 928 774-5231.
Email: news@kaff.com
Web site: http://www.kaff.com
Profile: KAFF-FM is a commercial station owned by Guyann Corp. The format of the station is contemporary country music. KAFF-FM broadcasts to the Flagstaff, AZ area at 92.9 FM.
FM RADIO STATION

KAFM-FM 44535
Owner: Grand Valley Public Radio Co. Inc.
Editorial: 1310 Ute Ave, Grand Junction, Colorado 81501-4620 **Tel:** 1 970 241-8801.
Web site: http://www.kafmradio.org
Profile: KAFM-FM is a non-commercial station owned by Grand Valley Public Radio Co. Inc. The format of the station is variety. KAFM-FM broadcasts to the Grand Junction, CO area at 88.1 FM.
FM RADIO STATION

KAFR-FM 43791
Owner: American Family Association
Editorial: 107 Park Gate Dr, Tupelo, Mississippi 38801-3010 **Tel:** 1 662 844-8888.
Email: comments@afr.net
Web site: http://www.afr.net
Profile: KAFR-FM is a non-commercial station owned by American Family Association. The format of the station is contemporary Christian music and talk. KAFR-FM broadcasts to the Willis, TX area at 88.3 FM.
FM RADIO STATION

KAFX-FM 42935
Owner: Townsquare Media, LLC
Editorial: 1216 S 1st St, Lufkin, Texas 75901-4716 **Tel:** 1 936 639-4455.
Web site: http://www.kfox95.com
Profile: KAFX-FM is a commercial station owned by Townsquare Media, LLC. The format of the station is contemporary hits radio. KAFX-FM broadcasts to the Lufkin, TX area at 95.5 FM.
FM RADIO STATION

KAFY-AM 475986
Owner: Favorita Broadcasting(La)
Editorial: 4043 Geer Rd, Hughson, California 95326-9798 **Tel:** 1 209 883-8760.
Email: lafavorita@lafavorita.net
Web site: http://www.lafavorita.net
Profile: KAFY-AM is a commercial station owned by La Favorita Broadcasting. The format of the station is Hispanic religious. KAFY-AM broadcasts to the Hughson, CA area at 1100 AM.
AM RADIO STATION

KAGB-FM 589688
Owner: Pacific Media Group
Editorial: 75-5852 Alii Dr Ste B1, Lagoon Tower, Kailua Kona, Hawaii 96740-1310 **Tel:** 1 808 329-6633.
Email: support@kaparadio.com
Web site: http://www.kaparadio.com
Profile: KAGB-FM is a commercial station owned by Pacific Media Group. The format of the station is Hawaiian AC. The station airs locally in the Kona, HI area at 99.1 FM.
FM RADIO STATION

KAGC-AM 34861
Owner: Bryan Broadcasting
Editorial: 2700 Rudder Freeway South, Suite 5000, College Station, Texas 77845 **Tel:** 1 979 695-9595.
Email: christianfamilyradio@yahoo.com
Web site: http://www.kagcradio.com
Profile: KAGC-AM is a commercial station owned by Bryan Broadcasting. The format of the station is religious programming. KAGC-AM broadcasts to the College Station, TX area at 1510 AM.
AM RADIO STATION

KAGE-AM 37169
Owner: Leighton Enterprises Inc.
Editorial: 752 Bluffview Cir, Winona, Minnesota 55987-2515 **Tel:** 1 507 452-4000.
Web site: http://www.winonaradio.com
Profile: KAGE-AM is a commercial station owned by Leighton Enterprises Inc. The format of the station is country music. KAGE-AM broadcasts to the Winona, MN area at 1380 AM.
AM RADIO STATION

KAGG-FM 41748
Owner: iHeartMedia Inc.
Editorial: 1716 Briarcrest Dr Ste 150, Bryan, Texas 77802-2776 **Tel:** 1 979 268-9696.
Web site: http://www.aggie96.com
Profile: KAGG-FM is a commercial station owned by iHeartMedia Inc. The format of the station is country music. KAGG-FM broadcasts to the Bryan, TX area at 96.1 FM.
FM RADIO STATION

KAGH-AM 37170
Owner: Ashley County Broadcasters
Editorial: 117 E Wellfield Road, Crossett, Arkansas 71635 **Tel:** 1 870 364-2181.
Email: kagh@windstream.net
Web site: http://www.crossettradio.com
Profile: KAGH-AM is a commercial statio owned by Ashley County Broadcasters. The format of the station is Classic Hits. KAGH-AM broadcasts to the Crossett, AR area at 800 AM.
AM RADIO STATION

KAGH-FM 44559
Owner: Ashley County Broadcasters
Editorial: 117 E Wellfield Road, Crossett, Arkansas 71635 **Tel:** 1 870 364-2182.
Email: kagh@windstream.net
Web site: http://www.crossettradio.com
Profile: KAGH-FM is a commercial station owned by Ashley County Broadcasters. The format of the station is contemporary country. KAGH-FM broadcasts to the Crossett, AR area at 104.9 FM.
FM RADIO STATION

KAGI-AM 36832
Owner: State of Oregon
Editorial: 1250 Siskiyou Blvd, Ashland, Oregon 97520-5001 **Tel:** 1 541 552-6301.
Email: jprinfo@sou.edu
Web site: http://www.ijpr.org
Profile: KAGI-AM is a non-commercial station owned by State of Oregon. The format of the station is news and talk. KAGI-AM broadcasts to the Grant Pass, OR area at 930 AM.
AM RADIO STATION

KAGJ-FM 39631
Owner: Snow College
Editorial: 150 College Ave, Ephraim, Utah 84627 **Tel:** 1 435 283-7425.
Web site: http://www.snow.edu/~kage/
Profile: KAGJ-FM is a non-commercial station owned by Snow College. The format of the station is rock alternative music. KAGJ-FM broadcasts to the Ephraim, UT area area at 89.5 FM.
FM RADIO STATION

KAGL-FM 42571
Owner: Noalmark Broadcasting Corp.
Editorial: 2525 N West Ave, El Dorado, Arkansas 71730 **Tel:** 1 870 863-6126.
Email: newsroom@totalradio.us
Web site: http://www.eagle933.com
Profile: KAGL-FM is a commercial station owned by Noalmark Broadcasting Corp. The format of the station is classic rock. KAGL-FM broadcasts to the El Dorado, AR area at 93.3 FM.
FM RADIO STATION

KAGM-FM 41553
Owner: American General Media
Editorial: 4125 Carlisle Blvd NE, Albuquerque, New Mexico 87107-4806 **Tel:** 1 505 878-0980.
Web site: http://power1067.com
Profile: KAGM-FM is a commercial station owned by American General Media. The format of the station is urban contemporary. KAGM-FM broadcasts to the Albuquerque, NM area at 106.7 FM.
FM RADIO STATION

KAGO-AM 37171
Owner: Basin Mediactive, LLC
Editorial: 404 Main St Ste 4, Klamath Falls, Oregon 97601-6021 **Tel:** 1 541 882-8833.
Email: news@mybasin.com
Web site: http://www.mybasin.com
Profile: KAGO-AM is a commercial station owned by Basin Mediactive, LLC. The format of the station is news and talk. KAGO-AM broadcasts in the Klamath Falls, OR area at 1150 AM.
AM RADIO STATION

KAGO-FM 44560
Owner: Basin Mediactive, LLC
Editorial: 404 Main St Ste 4, Klamath Falls, Oregon 97601-6021 **Tel:** 1 541 882-8833.
Email: news@mybasin.com
Web site: http://www.99-5therock.com
Profile: KAGO-FM is a commercial station owned by Basin Mediactive, LLC. The format of the station is rock music. KAGO-FM broadcasts to the Klamath Falls, OR area at 99.5 FM.
FM RADIO STATION

KAGY-AM 34862
Owner: Spotlight Broadcasting of New Orleans LLC
Editorial: 409 Duke St, Morgan City, Louisiana 70380-3518 **Tel:** 1 985 384-1430.
Email: kagyradio@gmail.com
Web site: http://www.kagyradio.com
Profile: KAGY-AM is a commercial station owned by Spotlight Broadcasting of New Orleans LLC. The format of the station is variety. KAGY-AM broadcasts to the New Orleans, LA - Gulf Coast area at 1510 AM.
AM RADIO STATION

KAHE-FM 44613
Owner: Rocking M Radio
Editorial: 2601 Central Ave, Village Plaza, Ste. C, Dodge City, Kansas 67801-6200 **Tel:** 1 620 225-8080.
Web site: http://mykansasradio.todayinkansas.com
Profile: KAHE-FM is a commercial station owned by Rocking M Radio. The format of the station is oldies music. KAHE-FM broadcasts to the Dodge City, KS area at 95.5 FM.
FM RADIO STATION

KAHI-AM 36217
Owner: KAHI Corporation
Editorial: 985 Lincoln Way Ste 103, Auburn, California 95603-5255 **Tel:** 1 530 885-5636.
Email: info@kahi.com
Web site: http://www.kahi.com
Profile: KAHI-AM is a commercial station owned by KAHI Corporation. The format of the station is variety. KAHI-AM's target audience is listeners, ages 13 to 100, in the Sacramento, CA area. The station airs locally at 950 AM. KAHI-AM's tagline is "KAHI 950 AM" and their slogan is "The Voice of the Foothills." The station also streams on their website 24/7. Please send press releases to the attention of the news director via fax. The station accepts 30 and 60 second PSAs in CD format.
AM RADIO STATION

KAHL-AM 36988
Owner: San Antonio Radio Works
Editorial: 8023 Vantage Dr, Ste 840, San Antonio, Texas 78230 **Tel:** 1 210 341-1310.
Email: info@call1310.com
Web site: http://www.call1310.com
Profile: KAHL-AM is a commercial station owned by San Antonio Radio Works. The format of the station is adult standards. KAHL-AM broadcasts to the San Antonio area at 1310 AM.
AM RADIO STATION

KAHM-FM 44561
Owner: Southwest Broadcasting
Editorial: 510 Henry St, Prescott, Arizona 86301-2670 **Tel:** 1 928 445-7800.
Email: prescott@kahm.info
Web site: http://www.kahm.info
Profile: KAHM-FM is a commercial station owned by Southwest Broadcasting. The format of the station is easy listening music. KAHM-FM broadcasts to the Phoenix area at 102.1 FM.
FM RADIO STATION

KAHR-FM 41187
Owner: Eagle Bluff Enterprises
Editorial: 932 County Road 448, Poplar Bluff, Missouri 63901-9018 **Tel:** 1 573 686-3700.
Email: frn@tcmax.net
Web site: http://todaysbesthits.com
Profile: KAHR-FM is a commercial station owned by Eagle Bluff Enterprises. The format of the station is Jack FM - Adult Hits. KAHR-FM broadcasts to the Poplar Bluff, MO area at 96.7 FM.
FM RADIO STATION

KAHS-AM 36847
Owner: Catholic Radio Network
Editorial: 1612 SE River Rd, El Dorado, Kansas 67042-8602 **Tel:** 1 316 320-1360.
Email: kahs@kahs.kscoxmail.com
Web site: http://www.1360kahs.com
Profile: KAHS-AM is a commercial station owned by Catholic Radio Network. The format of the station is religious, featuring Catholic programming. KAHS-AM broadcasts to the El Dorado, KS area at 1360 AM.
AM RADIO STATION

KAHU-FM 716935
Owner: Hawaii Public Radio
Editorial: 738 Kaheka St, Honolulu, Hawaii 96814-3726 **Tel:** 1 808 928-8988.
Web site: http://hawaiipublicradio.org
Profile: KAHU-FM is a non-commercial station owned by Hawaii Public Radio. The format of the station is variety. The station broadcasts at a frequency of 91.7 FM to the Ka'u community. The station has requested to not be part of any distribution list and does not accept press releases. KAHU-AM is an NPR/National Public Radio affiliate.
FM RADIO STATION

KAHZ-AM 35009
Owner: Multicultural Radio Broadcasting Inc.
Editorial: 747 E Green St, Pasadena, California 91101-2145 **Tel:** 1 626 844-1600.
Web site: http://www.am1300.com
Profile: KAHZ-AM is a commercial station owned by Multicultural Radio Broadcasting Inc. The format of the station is Chinese news and talk. KAHZ-AM broadcasts to the greater Los Angeles area at 1300 AM.
AM RADIO STATION

KAIC-FM 523719
Owner: Calvary Chapel of Tuscon
Tel: 1 602 997-4434.
Email: phoenix@kloveair1.com
Web site: http://www.air1.com
Profile: KAIC-FM is a non-commercial station owned by Calvary Chapel of Tuscon and Educational Media Foundation. The format of the station is contemporary Christian. KAIC-FM broadcasts to the Tucson, AZ area at 88.9 FM.
FM RADIO STATION

KAIM-FM 44562
Owner: Salem Media Group, Inc.
Editorial: 1160 N King St Fl 2, Honolulu, Hawaii 96817-3307 **Tel:** 1 808 533-0065.
Web site: http://www.thefishhawaii.com
Profile: KAIM-FM is a commercial station owned by Salem Media Group, Inc. The format of the station is contemporary Christian. KAIM-FM broadcasts to the Honolulu area at 95.5 FM.
FM RADIO STATION

KAIQ-FM 328171
Owner: Entravision Communications Corp.
Editorial: 1220 Broadway, Ste 600, Lubbock, Texas 79401 **Tel:** 1 806 763-6051.
Web site: http://www.tricolor955.com
Profile: KAIQ is owned by Entravision Communications. It's format is Hispanic. It broadcasts locally on 95.5 FM.
FM RADIO STATION

KAIR-AM 39330
Owner: KNZA, Inc.
Editorial: 200 N 5th St, Atchison, Kansas 66002-2413 **Tel:** 1 913 367-1470.
Email: kairradio@gmail.com
Web site: http://kairfm.com
Profile: KAIR-AM is a commercial station owned by KNZA, Inc. The format of the station is classic country. KAIR-AM broadcasts to the Atchison, KS area at 1470 AM.
AM RADIO STATION

KAIR-FM 46689
Owner: KNZA, Inc.
Editorial: 200 N 5th St, Atchison, Kansas 66002 **Tel:** 1 913 367-1470.
Email: kairradio@gmail.com
Web site: http://www.kairfm.com
Profile: KAIR-FM is a commercial station owned by KNZA, Inc. The format of the station is contemporary country music. KAIR-FM broadcasts to the Atchison, KS, area at 93.7 FM.
FM RADIO STATION

KAJA-FM 46266
Owner: iHeartMedia Inc.
Editorial: 6222 W Interstate 10, San Antonio, Texas 78201-2013 **Tel:** 1 210 736-9700.
Web site: http://www.kj97.com

Profile: KAJA-FM is a commercial station owned by iHeartMedia Inc. The format for the station is contemporary country. KAJA-FM broadcasts to the San Antonio area at 97.3 FM.
FM RADIO STATION

KAJC-FM 558870
Owner: Calvary Chapel Monmouth-Independence
Editorial: 1399 Monmouth St, Independence, Oregon 97351-1126 **Tel:** 1 503 837-1000.
Email: kajc@kajcfm.com
Web site: http://www.kajcfm.org
Profile: KAJC-FM is a non-commercial station owned by Calvary Chapel Monmouth-Independence. The format of the station is Contemporary Christian music and Christian teaching programming. KAJC-FM broadcasts to the Salem, OR area at 90.1 FM.
FM RADIO STATION

KAJE-FM 43492
Owner: Convergent Broadcasting
Editorial: 615 N Upper Broadway St Ste 105, Corpus Christi, Texas 78401-0703 **Tel:** 1 361 814-3800.
Web site: http://www.mycountry1073.com
Profile: KAJE-FM is a commercial station owned by Convergent Broadcasting. The format of the station is Classic Country. KAJE-FM broadcasts to the Corpus Christi, TX area at 107.3 FM.
FM RADIO STATION

KAJM-FM 41197
Owner: Sierra H Broadcasting, Inc.
Editorial: 1710 E Indian School Rd Ste 205, Phoenix, Arizona 85016-5957 **Tel:** 1 480 994-9100.
Web site: http://www.mega1043.com
Profile: KAJM-FM is a commercial station owned by Sierra H Broadcasting, Inc. The format of the station is rhythmic oldies music. KAJM-FM broadcasts in the Scottsdale, AZ area at 104.3 FM.
FM RADIO STATION

KAJN-FM 42945
Owner: Agape Broadcasting Foundation Inc.
Editorial: 110 W 3rd St, Crowley, Louisiana 70526
Tel: 1 337 783-1560.
Email: barryt@kajn.com
Web site: http://www.kajn.com
Profile: KAJN-FM is a commercial station owned by Agape Broadcasting Foundation Inc. The format of the station is contemporary Christian music, news and talk. KAJN-FM broadcasts to Lafayette, LA at 102.9 FM.
FM RADIO STATION

KAJO-AM 38715
Owner: Grants Pass Broadcasting Corp.
Editorial: 888 Rogue River Hwy, Grants Pass, Oregon 97527-5209 **Tel:** 1 541 476-6608.
Email: news@kajo.com
Web site: http://www.kajo.com
Profile: KAJO-AM is a commercial station owned by Grants Pass Broadcasting Corp. The format of the station is adult standards music and talk. KAJO-AM broadcasts in the Grants Pass, OR area at 1270 AM.
AM RADIO STATION

KAJR-FM 503903
Owner: RM Broadcasting LLC
Editorial: 75153 Merle Dr Ste G, Palm Desert, California 92211-5197 **Tel:** 1 760 568-4550.
Web site: http://959theoasis.com
Profile: KAJR-FM is a commercial station owned by RM Broadcasting LLC. The format of the station is Lite AC. KAJR-FM broadcasts to the Palm Springs, CA area at 95.9 FM.
FM RADIO STATION

KAJX-FM 41098
Owner: Roaring Fork Public Radio Inc.
Editorial: 110 E Hallam St Ste 134, Aspen, Colorado 81611-1467 **Tel:** 1 970 920-9000.
Email: news@aspenpublicradio.org
Web site: http://www.aspenpublicradio.org
Profile: KAJX-FM is a non-commercial station owned by Roaring Fork Public Radio Inc. The format of the station is news, classical and jazz. KAJX-FM broadcasts to the Aspen, CO area at 91.5 FM.
FM RADIO STATION

KAKC-AM 38309
Owner: iHeartMedia Inc.
Editorial: 2625 S Memorial Dr, Tulsa, Oklahoma 74129-2601 **Tel:** 1 918 388-5100.
Web site: http://www.1300thebuzz.com/main.html
Profile: KAKC-AM is a commercial station owned by iHeartMedia Inc. The format of the station is sports. KAKC-AM broadcasts to the Tulsa, OK area at 1300 AM.
AM RADIO STATION

KAKJ-FM 43535
Owner: Delta Force II Radio
Editorial: 700 W Martin Luther King Jr Dr, Ste 2, West Helena, Arkansas 72390 **Tel:** 1 870 572-9506.
Email: force2@sbcglobal.net
Web site: http://www.force2radio.com
Profile: KAKJ-FM is a commercial station owned by Delta Force II Radio. The format of the station is oldies, blues and gospel. KAKJ-FM broadcasts to the West Helena, AR area at 105.3 FM.
FM RADIO STATION

KAKK-AM 37367
Owner: De La Hunt Broadcasting
Editorial: Highway 34 West, Walker, Minnesota 56470
Tel: 1 218 547-4000.
Web site: http://www.kkradionetwork.com
Profile: KAKK-AM is a commercial station owned by De La Hunt Broadcasting. The format of the station is oldies. KAKK-AM broadcasts to the Walker, MN area at 1570 AM.
AM RADIO STATION

KAKN-FM 41766
Owner: Assn. of Free Lutheran Congregations Mission Corp.
Editorial: Mile 2 Alaska Peninsula Highway, Naknek, Alaska 99633-9999 **Tel:** 1 907 246-7492.
Email: kakn@kakn.org
Web site: http://www.kaknradio.org
Profile: KAKN-FM is a commercial station owned by Assn. of Free Lutheran Congregations Mission Corp. The format of the station is contemporary Christian and gospel music. KAKN-FM broadcasts to the Naknek, AK area at 100.9 FM.
FM RADIO STATION

KAKQ-FM 39541
Owner: iHeartMedia Inc.
Editorial: 546 9th Ave, Fairbanks, Alaska 99701-4902
Tel: 1 907 450-1000.
Email: kakq@iheartmedia.com
Web site: http://101magic.iheart.com
Profile: KAKQ-FM is a commercial station owned by iHeartMedia Inc. The format for the station is hot adult contemporary. KAKQ-FM broadcasts to the Fairbanks, AK area at 101.1 FM.
FM RADIO STATION

KAKS-FM 42254
Owner: Hog Radio, Inc.
Editorial: 2250 W Sunset Ave Ste 3, Springdale, Arkansas 72762-5187 **Tel:** 1 479 303-2034.
Web site: http://espn995.com/
Profile: KAKS-FM is a commercial station owned by Hog Radio, Inc. The format of the station is sports. KAKS-FM broadcasts to the Fayetteville, AR area at 99.5 FM.
FM RADIO STATION

KAKT-FM 42917
Owner: Mapleton Radio, LLC
Editorial: 1438 Rossanley Dr, Medford, Oregon 97501-1751 **Tel:** 1 541 779-1550.
Web site: http://www.thewolf1051.com
Profile: KAKT-FM is a commercial station owned by Mapleton Radio, LLC. The format of the station is country music. KAKT-FM broadcasts in the Medford, OR area at 105.1 FM.
FM RADIO STATION

KALC-FM 42239
Owner: Entercom Communications Corp.
Editorial: 4700 S Syracuse St, Ste 1050, Denver, Colorado 80237 **Tel:** 1 303 967-2700.
Web site: http://www.alice1059.com
Profile: KALC-FM is a commercial station owned by Entercom Communications Corp. The format of the station is hot adult contemporary. KALC-FM broadcasts to the Denver area at 105.9 FM.
FM RADIO STATION

KALD-FM 599026
Owner: Houston Christian Broadcasters
Editorial: 2424 South Blvd, Houston, Texas 77098-5110 **Tel:** 1 713 520-5200.
Email: email@khcb.org
Web site: http://www.khcb.org
Profile: KALD-FM is a non-commercial station owned by Houston Christian Broadcasters. The format of the station is Christian programming and music. KALD-FM broadcasts to the Caldwell, TX area at 91.9 FM.
FM RADIO STATION

KALE-AM 39080
Owner: Ingstad Radio Washington, LLC
Editorial: 4304 W 24th Ave Ste 200, Kennewick, Washington 99338-2320 **Tel:** 1 509 783-0783.
Web site: http://www.1061morefm.com
Profile: KALE-AM is a commercial station owned by Ingstad Radio Washington, LLC. The format of the station is adult contemporary. KALE-AM broadcasts to the Kennewick, WA area at 960 AM.
AM RADIO STATION

KALF-FM 41818
Owner: Mapleton Radio, LLC
Editorial: 1459 Humboldt Rd Ste D, Chico, California 95928-9100 **Tel:** 1 530 899-3600.
Web site: http://www.957thewolfonline.com
Profile: KALF-FM is a commercial station owned by Mapleton Radio, LLC. The format of the station is country music. KALF-FM broadcasts to the Chico, CA area at 95.7 FM.
FM RADIO STATION

KALI-AM 34863
Owner: Multicultural Radio Broadcasting Inc.
Editorial: 747 E Green St Fl 4, Pasadena, California 91101-2145 **Tel:** 1 626 993-6067.
Web site: http://www.kali900am.com/
Profile: KALI-AM is a commercial station owned by Multicultural Radio Broadcasting Inc. The format of the station Spanish religious. KALI-AM broadcasts to the Pasadena, CA area at 900 AM. The station does not accept press releases.
AM RADIO STATION

KALI-FM 40056
Owner: Multicultural Radio Broadcasting Inc.
Editorial: 747 E Green St Fl 4, Pasadena, California 91101-2145 **Tel:** 1 626 844-8882.
Web site: http://www.saigonradio.com
Profile: KALI-FM is a commerical station owned by Multicultural Radio Broadcasting Inc. The format of the station is primarily adult standards, and features a variety of ethnic and multicultural programming, most of it being Vietnamese. The format of the station is primarily adult standards, and features a variety of ethnic and multicultural programming, most of it being Vietnamese. KALI-FM broadcasts to the Pasadena, CA area at 106.3 FM.
FM RADIO STATION

KALK-FM 40978
Owner: East Texas Broadcasting Inc.
Editorial: Highway 67 West 1 Mile, Mount Pleasant, Texas 75455 **Tel:** 1 903 577-9770.
Web site: http://www.easttexasradio.com
Profile: KALK-FM is a commercial station owned by East Texas Broadcasting Inc. The format of the station is adult hits. KALK-FM broadcasts to the Mount Pleasant, TX area at 97.7 FM.
FM RADIO STATION

KALL-AM 38613
Owner: Broadway Media
Editorial: 9256 S State St, Sandy, Utah 84070-2604
Tel: 1 801 956-4121.
Web site: http://espn700sports.com/
Profile: KALL-AM is a commercial station owned by Broadway Media Group. The format of the station is sports. KALL-AM broadcasts to the Salt Lake City area at 700 AM.
AM RADIO STATION

KALM-AM 36462
Owner: E-Communications, LLC
Editorial: Highway 63 North, Thayer, Missouri 65791
Tel: 1 417 264-7211.
Email: kkountry@kkountry.com
Web site: http://www.am1290thegift.com
Profile: KALM-AM is a commercial station owned by E-Communications, LLC. The format of the station is gospel. KALM-AM broadcasts to the Thayer, MO area at 1290 AM.
AM RADIO STATION

KALP-FM 46736
Owner: Alpine Radio, LLC
Editorial: 500 E Hendryx Ave, Alpine, Texas 79830-2108 **Tel:** 1 432 837-2144.
Email: alpinetxradio@gmail.com
Web site: http://www.bigbendradio.com
Profile: KALP-FM is a commercial station owned by Alpine Radio, LLC. The format of the station is country. KALP-FM broadcasts to the Alpine, TX area at 92.7 FM.
FM RADIO STATION

KALQ-FM 44563
Owner: Community Broadcasting Co.
Editorial: 292 Santa Fe Ave, Alamosa, Colorado 81101-2810 **Tel:** 1 719 589-6644.
Web site: http://www.kgiwkalq.com
Profile: KALQ-FM is a commercial station owned by Community Broadcasting Co. The format of the station is country. KALQ-FM broadcasts to the Alamosa, CO area at 93.5 FM.
FM RADIO STATION

KALS-FM 41799
Owner: Hi-Line Radio Fellowship Inc
Editorial: 106 Cooperative Way Ste 102, Kalispell, Montana 59901-9506 **Tel:** 1 406 752-5257.
Email: onair@ynop.org
Web site: http://www.ynop.org
FM RADIO STATION

KALV-AM 34864
Owner: MM & K of Alva, Inc.
Editorial: Highway 281 North, Alva, Oklahoma 73717
Tel: 1 580 327-1430.
Email: kalvradio@yahoo.com
Profile: KALV-AM is a commercial station owned by MM & K of Alva, Inc. The format of the station is oldies. KALV-AM broadcasts to the Alva, OK area at 1430 AM.
AM RADIO STATION

KALV-FM 44380
Owner: CBS Radio
Editorial: 840 N Central Ave, Phoenix, Arizona 85004-2003 **Tel:** 1 602 452-1000.
Web site: http://live1015phoenix.cbslocal.com/
Profile: KALV-FM is a commercial station owned by CBS Radio. The format of the station is Top 40/CHR. KALV-FM broadcasts in the Phoenix area at 101.5 FM.
FM RADIO STATION

KALZ-FM 39637
Owner: iHeartMedia Inc.
Editorial: 83 E Shaw Ave Ste 150, Fresno, California 93710-7622 **Tel:** 1 559 230-4300.
Web site: http://www.powertalk967.com
Profile: KALZ-FM is a commercial station owned by IHeart Media and Entertainment. The format of the station is news and talk. KALZ-FM broadcasts to the Fresno, CA, area at 96.7 FM.
FM RADIO STATION

KAMA-AM 36344
Owner: Univision Communications Inc.
Editorial: 2211 E Missouri Ave Ste 300, El Paso, Texas 79903-3837 **Tel:** 1 915 544-9797.
Web site: http://univisionamerica.univision.com
Profile: KAMA-AM is commercial station owned by Univision Communications Inc. The format of the station is Hispanic news and talk. KAMA-AM broadcasts to the El Paso, TX area at 750 AM.
AM RADIO STATION

KAMA-FM 86339
Owner: Univision Communications Inc.
Editorial: 5100 Southwest Fwy, Houston, Texas 77056-7308 **Tel:** 1 713 965-2400.
Web site: http://www.univision.com/houston/kama
Profile: KAMA-FM is a commercial station owned by Univision Communications Inc. The format is Hispanic hits. KAMA-FM broadcasts to the Houston area at 104.9 FM.
FM RADIO STATION

KAMB-FM 39526
Owner: Central Valley Broadcasting
Editorial: 90 E 16th St, Merced, California 95340
Tel: 1 209 723-1015.
Email: kamb@celebrationradio.com
Web site: http://www.celebrationradio.com
Profile: KAMB-FM is a non-commercial station owned by Central Valley Broadcasting. The format of the station is contemporary Christian music and talk. KAMB-FM broadcasts in the Merced, CA area at 101.5 FM.
FM RADIO STATION

KAMD-FM 43036
Owner: Radio Works Inc.
Editorial: 612 Fairview Rd SW, Camden, Arkansas 71701-6554 **Tel:** 1 870 836-9567.
Email: radioworks@cablelynx.com
Web site: http://www.yesradioworks.com/k97
Profile: KAMD-FM is a commercial station owned by Radio Works Inc. The format of the station is adult contemporary music. KAMD-FM broadcasts in the Camden, AR area at 97.1 FM.
FM RADIO STATION

KAMI-AM 37175
Owner: Community Broadcasting, Inc.
Editorial: 1007 Plum Creek Pkwy, Lexington, Nebraska 68850-2621 **Tel:** 1 308 324-2371.
Web site: http://krvn.com
Profile: KAMI-AM is a commercial station owned by Community Broadcasting, Inc. The station airs a classic country music format. KAMI-AM broadcasts to the Cozad, Nebraska area at a frequency of 1580 AM.
AM RADIO STATION

KAMJ-FM 44360
Owner: Sudbury Broadcasting Group
Editorial: 125 S 2nd St, Blytheville, Arkansas 72315
Tel: 1 870 762-2093.
FM RADIO STATION

KAML-AM 34865
Owner: SIGA Broadcasting Corp.
Editorial: 1568 County Road 345, Kenedy, Texas 78119-5229 **Tel:** 1 830 583-2990.
Email: kaml990am@gmail.com
Web site: http://ww.kaml990.com
Profile: KAML-AM is a commercial station owned by SIGA Broadcasting Corp. The format for the station is country. KAML-AM broadcasts to the Kenedy, TX area at 990 AM.
AM RADIO STATION

KAML-FM 46204
Owner: Legend Communications
Editorial: 2810 Southern Dr, Gillette, Wyoming 82718-9369 **Tel:** 1 307 686-2242.
Email: news@basinsradio.com
Web site: http://www.basinsradio.com
Profile: KAML-FM is a commercial station owned by Legend Communications. The format of the station is hot adult contemporary. KAML-FM broadcasts to the Gillette, WY area at 97.3 FM.
FM RADIO STATION

KAMO-FM 44216
Owner: Cumulus Media Inc.
Editorial: 4209 N Frontage Rd, Fayetteville, Arkansas 72703-5002 **Tel:** 1 479 521-5566.
Web site: http://www.nashfm943.com
Profile: KAMO-FM is a commercial station owned by Cumulus Media Inc. The format of the station is country music. KAMO-FM broadcasts to the Fayetteville, AR area at 94.3 FM.
FM RADIO STATION

KAMP-FM 44755
Owner: CBS Radio
Editorial: 5670 Wilshire Blvd Ste 200, Los Angeles, California 90036-5657
Web site: http://amp.cbslocal.com
Profile: KAMP-FM is a commercial station owned by CBS Radio. The format of the station is Top 40/CHR. KAMP-FM broadcasts to the Los Angeles area at 97.1 FM. KAMP-FM does not wish to be contacted for pitches or press releases.
FM RADIO STATION

KAMQ-AM 39285
Owner: Hughes Broadcasting
Editorial: 1609 Radio Blvd, Carlsbad, New Mexico 88220 **Tel:** 1 575 887-7563.
Web site: http://www.carlsbadradio.com
Profile: KAMQ-AM is a commercial station owned by Hughes Broadcasting. The format of the station is sports. KAMQ-AM broadcasts to the Carlsbad, NM area at 1240 AM.
AM RADIO STATION

KAMS-FM 42809
Owner: E-Communications, LLC
Editorial: Highway 63 North, Thayer, Missouri 65791
Tel: 1 417 264-7211.
Email: news@kkountry.com

Web site: http://www.kkountry.com
Profile: KAMS-FM is a commercial station owned by E-Communications, LLC. The format of the station is contemporary country. KAMS-FM broadcasts to the Thayer, MO area at 95.1 FM.
FM RADIO STATION

KAMX-FM 40924
Owner: Entercom Communications Corp.
Editorial: 4301 Westbank Dr, 3rd Fl, Austin, Texas 78746-6568 **Tel:** 1 512 327-9595.
Web site: http://www.mix947.com
Profile: KAMX-FM is a commercial station owned by Entercom Communications Corp. The format of the station is hot adult contemporary. KAMX-FM broadcasts to the Austin, TX area at 94.7 FM.
FM RADIO STATION

KAMY-FM 42584
Owner: Family Life Communciations, Inc.
Editorial: 7355 N Oracle Rd, Tucson, Arizona 85704-6325 **Tel:** 1 520 742-6976.
Web site: http://www.myflr.org
Profile: KAMY-FM is a non-commercial station owned by Family Life Communications. The format of the station is Christian programming and music. KAMY-FM broadcasts to the Lubbock, TX area at 90.1 FM.
FM RADIO STATION

KAMZ-FM 87777
Owner: Tahoka Radio LLC
Editorial: 4821 73rd St, Lubbock, Texas 79424-2105
Tel: 1 806 416-4080.
Profile: KAMZ-FM is a commercial station owned by Tahoka Radio LLC. The format of the station is regional Mexican. KAMZ-FM broadcasts to the Lubbock, TX area at 103.5 FM. The station has no main e-mail.
FM RADIO STATION

KANA-AM 39312
Owner: Butte Broadcasting Inc.
Editorial: 105 Main St, Anaconda, Montana 59711-2251 **Tel:** 1 406 563-8011.
Email: mail@kbowkopr.com
Profile: KANA-AM is a commercial station owned by Butte Broadcasting Inc. The format for the station is classic hits. KANA-AM broadcasts to the Anaconda, MT area at 580 AM.
AM RADIO STATION

KAND-AM 36351
Owner: New Century Broadcasting
Editorial: 701 S Main St Ste 1340, Corsicana, Texas 75110-7228 **Tel:** 1 903 874-7421.
Email: mail@kandradio.com
Web site: http://www.kandradio.com
Profile: KAND-AM is a commercial station owned by New Century Broadcasting. The format is country. KAND-AM broadcasts to the Corsicana, TX area at 1340 AM.
AM RADIO STATION

KANE-AM 34866
Owner: Coastal Broadcasting of Larose Inc.
Editorial: 107 W Main St, New Iberia, Louisiana 70560-3732 **Tel:** 1 337 365-3434.
Email: kane@kane1240.com
Web site: http://www.kane1240.com
Profile: KANE-AM is a commercial station owned by Coastal Broadcasting of Larose Inc. The format of the station is variety. KANE-AM broadcasts to the Lafayette, LA area at 1240 AM.
AM RADIO STATION

KANI-AM 34867
Owner: Martin Broadcasting
Editorial: 215 E Milam St, Wharton, Texas 77488
Tel: 1 979 532-4141.
Email: kaniam1500@yahoo.com
Profile: KANI-AM is a commercial station owned by Martin Broadcasting. The format of the station is gospel music and religious talk programming. KANI-AM broadcasts to the Wharton, TX area at 1500 AM.
AM RADIO STATION

KANN-AM 34868
Owner: Faith Communications Corp.
Editorial: 2201 S 6th St, Las Vegas, Nevada 89104-2962 **Tel:** 1 702 731-5452.
Email: info@sosradio.net
Web site: http://www.sosradio.net
Profile: KANN-AM is a non-commercial station owned by Faith Communications Corp. The format of the station is contemporary Christian music. KANN-AM broadcasts to the Syracuse, UT, area at 1120 AM.
AM RADIO STATION

KANO-FM 70039
Owner: Hawaii Public Radio
Editorial: 738 Kaheka St Ste 101, Honolulu, Hawaii 96814-3726 **Tel:** 1 808 955-8821.
Email: Mail@hawaiipublicradio.org
Web site: http://www.hawaiipublicradio.org
Profile: KANO-FM is a non-commercial station owned by Hawaii Public Radio. The format of the station is news, talk, and classical music. KANO-FM broadcasts to the Honolulu, HI area at 91.1 FM.
FM RADIO STATION

Kansas Agriculture Network 47046
Editorial: 1210 SW Executive Dr, Topeka, Kansas 66615-3850 **Tel:** 1 785 272-3456.
Web site: http://kansasagnetwork.com
Profile: Provides agriculture news, weather, and markets to all 105 counties across Kansas. Their team of broadcasters includes two NAFB members with over 40 years of agricultural experience.
REGIONAL RADIO NETWORKS

Kansas Information Network 47047
Editorial: 1210 SW Executive Dr, Topeka, Kansas 66615-3850 **Tel:** 1 785 272-3456.
Web site: http://www.radionetworks.com
Profile: Provides live newscasts with weather and sports to 38 affiliate stations across the state of Kansas.
REGIONAL RADIO NETWORKS

KANS-FM 44169
Owner: Kansas Radio Inc.
Editorial: 918 Graham St, Emporia, Kansas 66801
Tel: 1 620 343-9393.
Email: thewave@ksradio.com
Web site: http://www.ksradio.com
Profile: KANS-FM is a commercial station owned by Kansas Radio Inc. The format of the station is Lite Rock/Lite AC music. KANS-FM broadcasts in the Emporia, KS area at 99.5 FM.
FM RADIO STATION

KANY-FM 521457
Owner: La Estación De La Familia
Editorial: 1520 Simpson Ave, Aberdeen, Washington 98520-4708 **Tel:** 1 206 439-1188.
Email: laestaciondelafamilia@gmail.com
Web site: http://laestaciondelafamilia.org
Profile: KANY-FM is a commercial station owned by La Estación De La Familia. The format of the station is Spanish Contemporary Christian. KANY-FM broadcasts to the Aberdeen, WA area at 93.7 FM.
FM RADIO STATION

KANZ-FM 41189
Owner: Kanza Society Inc.
Editorial: 210 N 7th St, Garden City, Kansas 67846
Tel: 1 620 275-7444.
Email: hppr@hppr.org
Web site: http://www.hppr.org
Profile: KANZ-FM is a non-commercial station owned by Kanza Society Inc. The format of the station is news and classical. KANZ-FM broadcasts to the Garden City, KS area at 91.1 FM.
FM RADIO STATION

KAOC-FM 44042
Owner: Simmons Media Group
Editorial: 1403 3Rd St, Langdon, North Dakota 58249-2232 **Tel:** 1 701 256-1080.
Web site: http://www.maverick105fm.com
Profile: KAOC-FM is a commercial station owned by Simmons Media Group. The format of the station is contemporary country. KAOC-FM broadcasts to the Langdon, ND area at 105.1 FM.
FM RADIO STATION

KAOI-AM 38572
Owner: Visionary Related Entertainment
Editorial: 1900 Main St, Wailuku, Hawaii 96793-1900
Tel: 1 808 244-9145.
Email: kaoi@kaoi.net
Web site: http://kaoi1110.com
Profile: KAOI-AM is commercial station owned by Visionary Related Entertainment. The format of the station is news, talk and sports. KAOI-AM broadcasts to the Wailuku, HI area at 1110 AM.
AM RADIO STATION

KAOI-FM 45933
Owner: Visionary Related Entertainment, LLC
Editorial: 1900 Main St, Wailuku, Hawaii 96793-1900
Tel: 1 808 244-9145.
Email: kaoi@kaoi.com
Web site: http://kaoifm.com
Profile: KAOI-FM is a commercial station owned by Visionary Related Entertainment, LLC. The format of the station is AAA-Adult Album Alternative and Classic Rock. KAOI-FM broadcasts to the Wailuku, HI area at 95.1 FM.
FM RADIO STATION

KAOK-AM 34869
Owner: Cumulus Media Inc.
Editorial: 425 Broad St, Lake Charles, Louisiana 70601-4225 **Tel:** 1 337 439-3300.
Web site: http://www.kaok.com
Profile: KAOK-AM is a commercial station owned by Cumulus Media Inc. The format of the station is news and talk. KAOK-AM broadcasts to the Lake Charles, LA area at 1400 AM.
AM RADIO STATION

KAOL-AM 38892
Owner: Kanza Inc.
Editorial: 102 N Mason St, Carrollton, Missouri 64633-2159 **Tel:** 1 660 542-0404.
Web site: http://kaolradio.com
Profile: KAOL-AM is a commercial station owned by Kanza Inc. The format of the station is classic country. KAOL-AM broadcasts to the Carrollton, MO area at 1410 AM.
AM RADIO STATION

KAOS-FM 39528
Owner: Evergreen State College
Editorial: 2700 Evergreen Pkwy Nw, Olympia, Washington 98505-0001 **Tel:** 1 360 867-6895.
Email: kaos@evergreen.edu
Web site: http://www.kaosradio.org
Profile: KAOS-FM is a non-commercial station owned by Evergreen State College. The format of the station is variety. KAOS-FM broadcasts to the Olympia, WA area at 89.3 FM.
FM RADIO STATION

KAOX-FM 232130
Owner: Simmons Media Group
Editorial: 436 Fossil Butte Dr, Kemmerer, Wyoming 83101 **Tel:** 1 307 877-4422.
FM RADIO STATION

KAOY-FM 410883
Owner: New West Broadcasting
Editorial: 74-5615 Lunia St., suite az, Kailua-Kona, Hawaii 96740 **Tel:** 1 808 935-5461.
Web site: http://www.kwxx.com
Profile: KAOY-FM is a commercial station owned by New West Broadcasting. The format of the station is a variety of Hawaiian music. KAOY-FM broadcasts to the Kona, HI at 101.5 FM.
FM RADIO STATION

KAPA-FM 45752
Owner: Pacific Media Group
Editorial: 75-5852 Alii Dr Ste B1, Kailua Kona, Hawaii 96740-1310 **Tel:** 1 808 329-6633.
Email: studio@kaparadio.com
Web site: http://www.kaparadio.com
Profile: KAPA-FM is a commercial station owned by Pacific Media Group. The format of the station is Hawaiian AC. KAPA-FM's target audience is listeners, ages 18 to 64, in the Hilo, HI area. The station airs locally at 100.3 FM.
FM RADIO STATION

KAPB-FM 42908
Owner: Three Rivers Radio Company
Editorial: 520 Chester St, Marksville, Louisiana 71351-2844 **Tel:** 1 318 253-9331.
Email: kapbfm977@gmail.com
Profile: KAPB-FM is a commercial station owned by Three Rivers Radio Company. The format of the station is country. KAPB-FM broadcasts to the Marksville, LA area at 97.7 FM.
FM RADIO STATION

KAPE-AM 37355
Owner: Withers Broadcasting of Missouri, LLC
Editorial: 901 S Kingshighway St, Cape Girardeau, Missouri 63703-8003 **Tel:** 1 573 339-7000.
Email: news@withersradio.net
Web site: http://kaperadio1550.com
Profile: KAPE-AM is a commercial station owned by Withers Broadcasting of Missouri, LLC. The format of the station is talk. KAPE-AM broadcasts to the Cape Girardeau, MO area at 1550 AM.
AM RADIO STATION

KAPL-AM 36835
Owner: Applegate Media Inc.
Editorial: 7590 Highway 238, Jacksonville, Oregon 97530-9140 **Tel:** 1 541 899-5275.
Email: staff@kaplradio.com
Web site: http://www.kaplradio.org
Profile: KAPL-AM is a non-commercial station owned by the Applegate Media Inc. The format of the station is religious talk and music. KAPL-AM broadcasts in the Jacksonville, OR area at 1300 AM.
AM RADIO STATION

KAPN-FM 45873
Owner: Brazos Valley Communications LLC
Editorial: 1240 E Villa Maria Rd, Bryan, Texas 77802-2519 **Tel:** 1 979 776-1240.
Web site: http://www.oldies1073online.com
Profile: KAPN-FM is a commercial station owned by Brazos Valley Communications LLC. The format of the station is oldies. KAPN-FM broadcasts to the Brenham, TX area at 107.3 FM.
FM RADIO STATION

KAPR-AM 38462
Owner: Sonora Broadcasting, LLC
Editorial: 2031 N. Sculpture Springs Rd., Douglas, Arizona 85713 **Tel:** 1 520 790-2440.
Web site: http://www.kvoi.com
Profile: KAPR-AM is a commercial station owned by Sonora Broadcasting, LLC. The format of the station is talk. KAPR-AM broadcasts to the Tucson, AZ area at 930 AM.
AM RADIO STATION

KAPS-AM 34870
Owner: J & J Broadcasting, Inc.
Editorial: 2029 Freeway Dr, Mount Vernon, Washington 98273-5470 **Tel:** 1 360 424-0660.
Email: kapsradio@gmail.com
Web site: http://www.kapsradio.com
Profile: KAPS-AM is a commercial station owned by J & J Broadcasting, Inc. The format of the station is contemporary country. KAPS-AM broadcasts to the Seattle area at 660 AM.
AM RADIO STATION

KAPW-FM 86092
Owner: Reynolds Radio Inc.
Editorial: 212 Old Grande Blvd, Tyler, Texas 75703-4226 **Tel:** 1 903 581-5259.
Email: spots@theblaze.cc
Web site: http://mega993.com
Profile: KAPW-FM is a commercial station owned by Reynolds Radio Inc. The format is Spanish CHR. KAPW-FM broadcasts to the Tyler, TX area at 99.3 FM.
FM RADIO STATION

KAQA-FM 43453
Owner: Kekahu Foundation Inc.
Editorial: 4520D Hanalei Plantation Rd, Princeville, Hawaii 96722-5420 **Tel:** 1 808 826-7774.
Email: kkcr@kkcr.org
Web site: http://www.kkcr.org
Profile: KAQA-FM is a non-commercial station owned by Kekahu Foundation Inc. The format of the station is variety. KAQA-FM broadcasts to the Princeville, HI area at 90.9 FM.
FM RADIO STATION

KARB-FM 46386
Owner: Eastern Utah Broadcasting
Editorial: 1899 N. Carbonville Rd, Price, Utah 84501
Tel: 1 435 637-1167.
Web site: http://www.castlecountryradio.com
Profile: KARB-FM is a commercial station owned by Eastern Utah Broadcasting. The format of the station is contemporary country. KARB-FM broadcasts to the Salt Lake City area at 98.3 FM.
FM RADIO STATION

KARI-AM 34871
Owner: Way Broadcasting Inc.
Editorial: 4840 Lincoln Rd, Blaine, Washington 98230-9602 **Tel:** 1 360 371-5500.
Email: info@kari55.com
Web site: http://www.kari55.com
Profile: KARI-AM is a commercial station owned by Way Broadcasting Inc. The format of the station is gospel and religious programming. KARI-AM broadcasts to the Blaine, WA area at 550 AM.
AM RADIO STATION

KARL-FM 41912
Owner: KMHL Broadcasting Corp.
Editorial: 1414 E College Dr, Marshall, Minnesota 56258-2027 **Tel:** 1 507 532-2282.
Email: kmhlradio@gmail.com
Web site: http://1051karl.com
Profile: KARL-FM is a commercial station owned by KMHL Broadcasting Corp. The format of the station is contemporary country music. KARL-FM broadcasts to the Marshall, MN area at 105.1 FM.
FM RADIO STATION

KARM-FM 41443
Owner: Harvest Broadcasting Company, Inc.
Editorial: 1300 S Woodland St, Visalia, California 93277-4214 **Tel:** 1 559 627-5276.
Email: info@mypromisefm.com
Web site: http://www.mypromisefm.com
Profile: KARM-FM is a non-commercial station owned by Harvest Broadcasting Company, Inc. The format of the station is Christian teaching. KARM-FM broadcasts to the Visalia, CA area at 89.7 FM.
FM RADIO STATION

KARN-AM 39429
Owner: Cumulus Media Inc
Editorial: 700 Wellington Hills Rd, Little Rock, Arkansas 72211-2026 **Tel:** 1 501 401-0200.
Web site: http://www.sportsanimal920.com
Profile: KARN-AM is a commercial station owned by Cumulus Media Inc. The format of the station is sports. KARN-AM broadcasts in the Little Rock, AR area at 920 AM
AM RADIO STATION

KARN-FM 46812
Owner: Cumulus Media Inc
Editorial: 700 Wellington Hills Rd, Little Rock, Arkansas 72211-2026 **Tel:** 1 501 401-0200.
Web site: http://www.newsradio1029.com
Profile: KARN-FM is a commercial station owned by Cumulus Media Inc. The format of the station is news and talk. KARN-FM broadcasts to the Little Rock, AR area at 102.5 FM.
FM RADIO STATION

KARP-FM 44724
Owner: Iowa City Broadcasting Co.
Editorial: 20132 Highway 15 N, Hutchinson, Minnesota 55350-5642 **Tel:** 1 320 587-2140.
Email: info@karpradio.com
Web site: http://www.karpradio.com
Profile: KARP-FM is a commercial station owned by Iowa City Broadcasting Co.The format of the station is classic country. KARP-FM broadcasts to the Hutchinson, MN area at 106.9 FM.
FM RADIO STATION

KARS-AM 38915
Owner: American General Media
Editorial: 4125 Carlisle Blvd NE, Albuquerque, New Mexico 87107-4806 **Tel:** 1 505 878-0980.
Web site: http://www.area1029.com
Profile: KARS-AM is a commercial station owned by American General Media. The format of the station is a modern rock. KARS-AM broadcasts to the Belen, NM area at 840 AM.
AM RADIO STATION

KARS-FM 376371
Owner: Townsquare Media
Editorial: 600 Main St, Windsor, Colorado 80550-5133 **Tel:** 1 970 674-2700.
Web site: http://www.rock1029.com
Profile: KARS-FM is a commercial station owned by Townsquare Media. The format of the station is rock/album oriented rock. KARS-FM broadcasts in the Cheyenne, WY area with a booster in Fort Collins, CO at 102.9 FM.
FM RADIO STATION

KART-AM 37176
Owner: Lee Family Broadcasting
Editorial: 47 N 100 W, Jerome, Idaho 83338-5403
Tel: 1 208 324-8181.
Email: traffic@leeradio.net
Profile: KART-AM is a commerical station owned by Lee Family Broadcasting. The format of the station is country music. KART-AM broadcasts to the Jerome, ID area at 1400 AM.
AM RADIO STATION

KARV-AM 39476
Owner: KERM Inc.
Editorial: 201 W 2nd St, Russellville, Arkansas 72801
Tel: 1 479 968-1184.
Email: karv_kyel@yahoo.com
Profile: KARV-AM is a commercial station owned by KERM Inc. The format of the station is news and talk. KARV-AM broadcasts in the Russellville, AR, area at 610 AM.
AM RADIO STATION

KARV-FM 46865
Owner: KERM Inc.
Editorial: 201 W 2nd St, Russellville, Arkansas 72801-5003 **Tel:** 1 479 968-1184.
Email: karv_kyel@yahoo.com
Profile: KARV-FM is a commercial station owned by KERM Inc. The format of the station is news and talk. KARV-FM broadcasts to the Ola, AR, area at 101.3 FM.
FM RADIO STATION

KARX-FM 41992
Owner: Cumulus Media Inc.
Editorial: 301 S Polk St Ste 100, Amarillo, Texas 79101-1404 **Tel:** 1 806 342-5200.
Email: karx957@hotmail.com
Web site: http://www.957nashicon.com
Profile: KARX-FM is a commercial station owned by Cumulus Media Inc. The format of the station is Country. KARX-FM broadcasts to the Amarillo, TX area at 95.7 FM.
FM RADIO STATION

KARY-FM 43713
Owner: New Northwest Broadcasters LLC
Editorial: 1200 Chesterly Dr, Ste 160, Yakima, Washington 98902 **Tel:** 1 509 248-2900.
Web site: http://www.cherryfm.com
Profile: KARY-FM is owned by New Northwest Broadcasters. The format of the station is oldies. KARY-FM broadcasts to the Yakima, WA area at 100.9 FM.
FM RADIO STATION

KARZ-FM 39554
Owner: KMHL Broadcasting Corp.
Editorial: 1414 E College Dr, Marshall, Minnesota 56258-2027 **Tel:** 1 507 532-2282.
Email: kmhlradio@gmail.com
Web site: http://1075karz.com
Profile: KARZ-FM is a commercial station owned by KMHL Broadcasting Corp. The format of the station is rock. KARZ-FM broadcasts to the Marshall, MN area at 107.5 FM.
FM RADIO STATION

KASA-AM 34872
Owner: Herrera(Moises)
Editorial: 1445 W Baseline Rd, Phoenix, Arizona 85041-7010 **Tel:** 1 602 276-4241.
Profile: KASA-AM is a commercial station owned by Moises Herrera. The format of the station is Hispanic Christian programming. KASA-AM broadcasts in the Phoenix area at 1540 AM.
AM RADIO STATION

KASE-FM 42130
Owner: iHeartMedia Inc.
Editorial: 3601 S Congress Ave, Austin, Texas 78704-7250 **Tel:** 1 512 684-7300.
Web site: http://www.kase101.com
Profile: KASE-FM is a commercial station owned by iHeartMedia Inc. The format of the station is contemporary country music. KASE-FM broadcasts to the Austin, TX area at 100.7 FM.
FM RADIO STATION

KASF-FM 39531
Owner: Adams State College
Editorial: 208 Edgemont Blvd, Alamosa, Colorado 81101-2320 **Tel:** 1 719 587-7830.
Email: kasf909fm@gmail.com
Web site: http://blogs.adams.edu/kasf
Profile: KASF-FM is a non-commercial station owned by Adams State College. The format of the station is college variety. KASF-FM broadcasts to the Alamosa, CO area at 90.9 FM.
FM RADIO STATION

KASH-FM 43522
Owner: iHeartMedia Inc.
Editorial: 800 E Dimond Blvd Ste 3-370, Anchorage, Alaska 99515-2058 **Tel:** 1 907 522-1515.
Email: news@650keni.com
Web site: http://kashcountry1075.iheart.com
Profile: KASH-FM is a commercial station owned by iHeartMedia Inc. The format of the station is contemporary country music. KASH-FM broadcasts to the Anchorage, AK area at 107.5 FM.
FM RADIO STATION

KASI-AM 37177
Owner: iHeartMedia Inc.
Editorial: 415 Main St, Ames, Iowa 50010-6099
Tel: 1 515 232-1430.
Web site: http://www.1430kasi.com
Profile: KASI-AM is a commercial station owned by iHeartMedia Inc. The format of the station is news, sports and talk. KASI-AM broadcasts to the Ames, IA area at 1430 AM.
AM RADIO STATION

KASL-AM 34873
Owner: Cook Brothers Broadcasting, LLC
Editorial: 2208 W Main St, Newcastle, Wyoming 82701-2331 **Tel:** 1 307 746-4433.
Email: kasl@kaslradio.com
Web site: http://www.kaslradio.com
Profile: KASL-AM is a commercial station owned by Cook Brothers Broadcasting, LLC. The format of the station is classic country. KASL-AM broadcasts to the Newcastle, WY area at 1240 AM.
AM RADIO STATION

KASM-AM 39318
Owner: StarCom LLC
Editorial: 35223 238th Ave, Albany, Minnesota 56307-9798 **Tel:** 1 320 845-2184.
Email: kasm1150am@albanytel.com
Web site: http://www.kasmwqpm.com
Profile: KASM-AM is a commercial station owned by StarCom LLC. The format of the station is agricultural and talk. KASM-AM broadcasts in the St. Cloud, MN area at 1150 AM.
AM RADIO STATION

KASO-AM 36728
Owner: Minden Broadcasting, LLC
Editorial: 410 Lakeshore Dr, Minden, Louisiana 71055-2139 **Tel:** 1 318 377-1240.
Email: mark@kbef.com
Web site: http://www.kbef.com
Profile: KASO-AM is commercial station owned by Minden Broadcasting, LLC. The format of the station is mainstream country. KASO-AM broadcasts to the Minden, LA area at 1240 AM.
AM RADIO STATION

KASR-FM 44916
Owner: Creative Sports Media Inc.
Editorial: 1072 Markham St Ste 300, Conway, Arkansas 72032-4310 **Tel:** 1 501 327-6611.
Email: kasr@mail.com
Web site: http://www.kasrfm.com
Profile: KASR-FM is a non-commercial station owned by Creative Sports Media Inc. The format of the station is sports. KASR-FM broadcasts to the Conway, AR area at 92.7 FM.
FM RADIO STATION

KASS-FM 42479
Owner: Mount Rushmore Broadcasting Inc.
Editorial: 218 N Wolcott St, Casper, Wyoming 82601-1923 **Tel:** 1 307 265-1984.
Email: mrbnews@wyoming.com
Profile: KASS-FM is a commercial station owned by Mount Rushmore Broadcasting Inc. The format for the station is rock. KASS-FM broadcasts to the Casper, WY area at 106.9 FM.
FM RADIO STATION

KAST-AM 38970
Owner: Ohana Media Group
Editorial: 285 SW Main Ct, Ste 200, Warrenton, Oregon 97146-9457 **Tel:** 1 503 861-6620.
Web site: http://www.kast1370.com
Profile: KAST-AM is a commercial station owned by Ohana Media Group. The format of the station is news and talk. KAST-AM broadcasts in the Astoria, OR area at 1370 AM.
AM RADIO STATION

KATA-AM 37178
Owner: Bicoastal Media LLC
Editorial: 5640 S Broadway St, Eureka, California 95503-6905 **Tel:** 1 707 442-2000.
Email: eurekanews@bicoastalmedia.com
Web site: http://www.kata1340.com
Profile: KATA-AM is a commercial station owned by Bicoastal Media LLC. The format of the station is sports. KATA-AM broadcasts to the Eureka, CA area at 1340 AM.
AM RADIO STATION

KATB-FM 42980
Owner: Christian Broadcasting Inc.
Editorial: 6401 E Northern Lights Blvd, Anchorage, Alaska 99504-3312 **Tel:** 1 907 333-5282.
Web site: http://www.katb.org
Profile: KATB-FM is a non-commercial station owned by Christian Broadcasting Inc. The format of the station is Christian. KATB-FM broadcasts to the Anchorage, AK area at 89.3 FM.
FM RADIO STATION

KATC-FM 44857
Owner: Cumulus Media Inc
Editorial: 6805 Corporate Dr, Colorado Springs, Colorado 80919-1976 **Tel:** 1 719 593-2700.
Web site: http://www.catcountry951.com
Profile: KATC-FM is a commercial station owned by Cumulus Media Inc. The format of the station is contemporary country. KATC-FM broadcasts to the Colorado Springs, CO area at 95.1 FM.
FM RADIO STATION

KATD-AM 36346
Owner: Multicultural Radio Broadcasting Inc.
Editorial: 44 Gough St Ste 301, San Francisco, California 94103-5424 **Tel:** 1 415 978-5378.
Email: kiqi1010@gmail.com
Web site: http://www.kiqi1010am.com
Profile: KATD-AM is a commercial station owned by Multicultural Radio Broadcasting Inc. The format of the station is Hispanic. KATD-AM broadcasts to the San Francisco area at 990 AM.
AM RADIO STATION

KATE-AM 37179
Owner: Alpha Media
Editorial: 1633 W Main St, Albert Lea, Minnesota 56007-1868 **Tel:** 1 507 373-2338.
Web site: http://www.myalbertlea.com/2015/02/09/kate-1450-am/
Profile: KATE-AM is a commercial station owned by Alpha Media. The format of the station is talk. KATE-AM broadcasts to the Rochester, MN and Mason City, IA areas at 1450 AM.
AM RADIO STATION

KATF-FM 44565
Owner: Radio Dubuque Inc.
Editorial: 1055 University Ave, Dubuque, Iowa 52001-6154 **Tel:** 1 563 690-0800.
Email: katfm@katfm.com
Web site: http://www.katfm.com
Profile: KATF-FM is a commercial station owned by Radio Dubuque Inc. The format for the station is Adult contemporary music. KATF-FM broadcasts to the Cedar Rapids, IA area at 92.9 FM.
FM RADIO STATION

KATG-FM 813712
Owner: American Family Association
Tel: 1 662 844-8888.
Web site: http://www.afr.net
Profile: KATG-FM is a non-commercial station owned by American Family Association. The format of the station is Christian talk and teaching. KATG-FM broadcasts to the Elkhart, TX area at a frequency of 88.1 FM.
FM RADIO STATION

KATH-AM 36132
Owner: La Promesa Foundation
Editorial: 8828 N Stemmons Fwy Ste 106, Dallas, Texas 75247-3720 **Tel:** 1 214 951-0132.
Web site: http://grnonline.com
Profile: KATH-AM is a commercial station owned by La Promesa Foundation. The format of the station is religious. KATH-AM broadcasts to the Dallas area at 1000 AM.
AM RADIO STATION

KATI-FM 42934
Owner: Zimmer Radio Group
Editorial: 3109 S 10 Mile Dr, Jefferson City, Missouri 65109 **Tel:** 1 573 893-5696.
Web site: http://www.943kat.com
Profile: KATI-FM is a commercial station owned by Zimmer Radio Group. The format of the station is contemporary country music. KATI-FM broadcasts to the Jefferson City, MO area at 94.3 FM.
FM RADIO STATION

KATJ-FM 45903
Owner: El Dorado Broadcasting
Editorial: 12370 Hesperia Rd, Victorville, California 92395-7719 **Tel:** 1 760 241-1313.
Web site: http://www.katcountry1007.com
Profile: KATJ-FM is a commercial station owned by El Dorado Broadcasting. The format of the station is country music. KATJ-FM broadcasts to the Victorville, CA area at 100.7 FM.
FM RADIO STATION

KATK-AM 37180
Owner: Hughes Broadcasting
Editorial: 1609 Radio Blvd, Carlsbad, New Mexico 88220 **Tel:** 1 575 887-7563.
Web site: http://www.carlsbadradio.com
Profile: KATK-AM is a commercial station owned by Hughes Broadcasting. The format of the station is classic hits. KATK-AM broadcasts to the Carlsbad, NM area at 740 AM.
AM RADIO STATION

KATK-FM 44566
Owner: Hughes Broadcasting
Editorial: 1609 Radio Blvd, Carlsbad, New Mexico 88220-6427 **Tel:** 1 575 885-2151.
Web site: http://www.carlsbadradio.com
Profile: KATK-FM is a commercial station owned by Hughes Broadcasting. The format of the station is country. KATK-FM broadcasts to the Carlsbad, NM area at 92.1 FM.
FM RADIO STATION

KATL-AM 34874
Owner: Star Printing Co.
Editorial: 818 Main St, Miles City, Montana 59301
Tel: 1 406 234-7700.
Email: katlradio@katlradio.com
Web site: http://www.katlradio.com
Profile: KATL-AM is a commercial station owned by Star Printing Co. The format of the station is adult contemporary music. KATL-AM broadcasts in the Miles City, MT area at 770 AM.
AM RADIO STATION

KATM-FM 44576
Owner: Cumulus Media Inc
Editorial: 3127 Transworld Dr #270, Stockton, California 95206-4988 **Tel:** 1 209 507-8500.
Web site: http://www.katm.com
Profile: KATM-FM is a commercial station owned by Cumulus Media Inc. The format of the station is country music. KATM-FM broadcasts in the Modesto, CA area at 103.3 FM.
FM RADIO STATION

KATO-AM 38946
Owner: McMurray Communications Inc.
Editorial: 3335 W 8th St, Thatcher, Arizona 85552
Tel: 1 928 428-1230.
Email: traffic@mcmurrayradio.com
Web site: http://www.mysouthernaz.com
Profile: KATO-AM is a commercial station owned by McMurray Communications Inc. The format of the station is news and talk. KATO-AM broadcasts in the Safford, AZ area at 1230 AM.
AM RADIO STATION

KATO-FM 523609
Owner: Radio Mankato
Editorial: 59346 Madison Ave, Mankato, Minnesota 56001-8518 **Tel:** 1 507 345-4537.
Email: news@ktoe.com
Web site: http://www.radiomankato.com
FM RADIO STATION

KATP-FM 40078
Owner: Townsquare Media, LLC
Editorial: 6214 SW 34th Ave, Amarillo, Texas 79109-4006 **Tel:** 1 806 355-9777.
Web site: http://blakefm.com
Profile: KATP-FM is a commercial station owned by Townsquare Media, LLC. The format of the station is contemporary country. KATP-FM broadcasts to the Amarillo, TX, area at 101.9 FM.
FM RADIO STATION

KATQ-AM 38971
Owner: Radio Int'l/KATQ Broadcast Association Inc.
Editorial: 112 E 3rd Ave, Plentywood, Montana 59254-2223 **Tel:** 1 406 765-1480.
Email: katq@nemont.net
Web site: http://www.katqradio.com
Profile: KATQ-AM is a commercial station owned by Radio Int'l/KATQ Broadcast Association Inc. The format of the station is classic country. KATQ-AM broadcasts to the Plentywood, MT area at 1070 AM.
AM RADIO STATION

KATQ-FM 46308
Owner: Radio Int'l/KATQ Broadcast Association Inc.
Editorial: 112 E 3rd Ave, Plentywood, Montana 59254-2223 **Tel:** 1 406 765-1480.
Email: katq@nemont.net
Web site: http://www.katqradio.com
Profile: KATQ-FM is a commercial station owned by Radio Int'l/KATQ Broadcast Assoc. Inc. The format of the station is classic rock. KATQ-FM broadcasts in the Plentywood, MT area at 100.1 FM.
FM RADIO STATION

KATR-FM 45663
Owner: Media Logic LLC
Editorial: 519 W Main St, Sterling, Colorado 80751-3059 **Tel:** 1 970 521-2732.
Email: medialogic@kci.net
Web site: http://www.katcountry983.com
Profile: KATR-FM is a commercial station owned by Media Logic LLC. The format of the station is contemporary country. KATR-FM broadcasts to the Denver area at 98.3 FM.
FM RADIO STATION

KATS-FM 44567
Owner: Townsquare Media, LLC
Editorial: 4010 Summitview Ave, Yakima, Washington 98908-2966 **Tel:** 1 509 972-3461.
Email: katsfm@gmail.com
Web site: http://www.katsfm.com
Profile: KATS-FM is a commercial station owned by Townsquare Media, LLC. The format of the station is rock/album-oriented rock. KATS-FM broadcasts to the Yakima, WA area at 94.5 FM.
FM RADIO STATION

KATT-FM 42070
Owner: Cumulus Media Inc
Editorial: 4045 NW 64th St Ste 600, Oklahoma City, Oklahoma 73116-2607 **Tel:** 1 405 848-0100.
Web site: http://www.katt.com
Profile: KATT-FM is a commercial station owned by Cumulus Media Inc. The format of the station is rock music. KATT-FM broadcasts to the Oklahoma City area at 100.5 FM.
FM RADIO STATION

KATW-FM 39535
Owner: Pacific Empire Radio Corp.
Editorial: 403 Capitol St, Lewiston, Idaho 83501-1815
Tel: 1 208 743-6564.
Email: wecare@catfm.com
Web site: http://www.catfm.com
Profile: KATW-FM is a commercial station owned by Pacific Empire Radio Corp. The format of the station is hot adult contemporary music. KATW-FM broadcasts to the Lewiston, ID area at 101.5 FM.
FM RADIO STATION

KATX-FM 44630
Owner: High Plains Radio Network
Editorial: 2900 W Washington St, Stephenville, Texas 76401-3734 **Tel:** 1 254 629-2621.
Email: katx@hpnetwork.com
Web site: http://www.katxradio.com
Profile: KATX-FM is an commercial station owned by High Plains Radio Network. The format of the station is classic rock. ATX-FM broadcasts to the Eastland, TX area at 97.7 FM.
FM RADIO STATION

KATY-FM
41182
Owner: All Pro Broadcasting Inc.
Editorial: 27431 Enterprise Cir W, Temecula, California 92590-4833 **Tel:** 1 951 506-1222.
Web site: http://www.1013themix.com/
Profile: KATY-FM is a commercial station owned by All-Pro Broadcasting Inc. The format of the station is adult contemporary music. KATY-FM broadcasts to the Temecula, CA area at 101.3 FM.
FM RADIO STATION

KATZ-AM
37181
Owner: iHeartMedia Inc.
Editorial: 1001 Highlands Plaza Dr W Ste 200, Saint Louis, Missouri 63110-1337 **Tel:** 1 314 333-8000.
Web site: http://hallelujah1600.iheart.com
Profile: KATZ-AM is a commercial station owned by iHeartMedia Inc. The format of the station is gospel music. KATZ-AM broadcasts to the St. Louis area at 1600 AM.
AM RADIO STATION

KAUJ-FM
45766
Owner: Simmons Broadcasting, Inc.
Editorial: 856 W 12th St, Grafton, North Dakota 58237-2120 **Tel:** 1 701 352-0431.
Web site: http://www.myborderland.com/
Profile: KAUJ-FM is a commercial station owned by the Simmons Broadcasting, Inc. The format of the station is Classic Rock. KAUJ-FM broadcasts to the Fargo, ND area at 100.9 FM.
FM RADIO STATION

KAUM-FM
45992
Owner: Baum(James G.)
Editorial: West Highway 80, Colorado City, Texas 79512 **Tel:** 1 325 728-5530.
Email: kvmckaum@sbcglobal.net
Web site: http://www.tsnradio.com
Profile: KAUM-FM is a commercial station owned by James G. Baum. The format of the station is country music. KAUM-FM broadcasts in the Colorado City, TX area at 107.1 FM.
FM RADIO STATION

KAUR-FM
39536
Owner: Minnesota Public Radio
Editorial: 2001 S Summit Ave 2001 Smt S, Sioux Falls, South Dakota 57197-0001 **Tel:** 1 605 274-4388.
Web site: http://kaur.augie.edu
FM RADIO STATION

KAUS-AM
37182
Owner: Alpha Media
Editorial: 18431 State Highway 105, Austin, Minnesota 55912-6147 **Tel:** 1 507 437-7666.
Web site: http://www.myaustinminnesota.com
Profile: KAUS-AM is a commercial station owned by Alpha Media. The format of the station is news, sports and talk. KAUS-AM broadcasts to the Austin, MN area at 1480 AM.
AM RADIO STATION

KAUS-FM
44570
Owner: Alpha Media
Editorial: 18431 State Highway 105, Austin, Minnesota 55912-6147 **Tel:** 1 507 437-7666.
Web site: http://www.myaustinminnesota.com
Profile: KAUS-FM is a commercial station owned by Alpha Media. The format of the station is country music. KAUS-FM broadcasts to the Austin, MN area at 99.9 FM.
FM RADIO STATION

KAVA-AM
133445
Owner: Latino Communications
Editorial: 600 Grant St, Ste 600, Denver, Colorado 80203 **Tel:** 1 303 733-5266.
Profile: KAVA-AM is a commercial station owned by Latino Communications. The format of the station is news/talk. KAVA-AM broadcasts to the Denver area at 1480 AM.
AM RADIO STATION

KAVL-AM
38346
Owner: RZ Radio LLC
Editorial: 552 East Avenue K4, Lancaster, California 93535 **Tel:** 1 661 942-1121.
Profile: KAVL-AM is a commercial station owned by RZ Radio LLC. The format of the station is sports. KAVL-AM broadcasts in the Lancaster, CA area at 610 AM.
AM RADIO STATION

KAVP-AM
828197
Owner: Western Slope Communications
Editorial: 751 Horizon Ct Ste 225, Grand Junction, Colorado 81506-8767 **Tel:** 1 970 241-6460.
Email: production@wscradio.net
Web site: http://wscradio.net
Profile: KAVP-AM is a commercial station owned by Western Slope Communications. The format of the station is sports/talk. KAVP-AM broadcasts to the Grand Junction-Montrose, CO area at 1450 AM.
AM RADIO STATION

KAVV-FM
39537
Owner: Stereo 97 Inc.
Editorial: 156 W 5th St, Benson, Arizona 85602-6508 **Tel:** 1 520 290-9797.
Web site: http://www.cavefm.com
Profile: KAVV-FM is a commercial station owned by Stereo 97 Inc. The format of the station is country. KAVV-FM broadcasts to the Tucson, AZ area at 97.7 FM.
FM RADIO STATION

KAVW-FM
43446
Owner: American Family Association
Editorial: 107 Park Gate Dr, Tupelo, Mississippi 38801-3010 **Tel:** 1 662 844-8888.
Email: comments@afr.net
Web site: http://www.afr.net
Profile: KAVW-FM is the Tupelo, Mississippi American Family Radio station.
FM RADIO STATION

KAWC-AM
39054
Owner: Arizona Western College
Editorial: 2020 S Avenue 8 E, Yuma, Arizona 85365-6900 **Tel:** 1 928 344-7690.
Email: info@kawc.org
Web site: http://www.kawc.org
Profile: KAWC-AM is a non-commercial station owned by Arizona Western College. The format of the station is variety. KAWC-AM broadcasts to the Yuma, AZ area at 1320 AM. KAWC-AM is an NPR affiliate.
AM RADIO STATION

KAWC-FM
46395
Owner: Arizona Western College
Editorial: 2020 S Avenue 8 E, Yuma, Arizona 85365-6900 **Tel:** 1 928 344-7690.
Email: info@kawc.org
Web site: http://www.kawc.org
Profile: KAWC-FM is a non-commercial station owned by Arizona Western College. The format of the station is news and talk. KAWC-FM broadcasts in the Yuma, AZ area at 88.9 FM.
FM RADIO STATION

KAWL-AM
37183
Owner: Nebraska Rural Radio Association
Editorial: 1309 Road 11, York, Nebraska 68467-7513 **Tel:** 1 402 362-4433.
Web site: http://1049maxcountry.com/
Profile: KAWL-AM is a commercial station owned by Nebraska Rural Radio Association. The format of the station is oldies. KAWL-AM broadcasts to the Lincoln, NE area at 1370 AM.
AM RADIO STATION

KAWO-FM
44756
Owner: Townsquare Media, LLC
Editorial: 827 E Park Blvd Ste 100, Boise, Idaho 83712-7783 **Tel:** 1 208 344-6363.
Web site: http://www.wow1043.com
Profile: KAWO-FM is a commercial station owned by Townsquare Media, LLC. The format of the station is contemporary country. KAWO-FM broadcasts to the Boise, ID area at 104.3 FM.
FM RADIO STATION

KAWW-AM
37075
Owner: Crain Media Group LLC
Editorial: 111 N Spring St, Searcy, Arkansas 72143-7712 **Tel:** 1 501 268-7123.
Email: production@crainmedia.com
Web site: http://www.crainmedia.com
Profile: KAWW-AM is a commercial station owned by Crain Media Group LLC. The format of the station is news, talk and sports. KAWW-AM broadcasts in the Heber Springs, AR area at 1370 AM.
AM RADIO STATION

KAWZ-FM
41096
Owner: CSN International
Editorial: 4002 N 3300 E, Twin Falls, Idaho 83301-0354 **Tel:** 1 208 734-2049.
Email: feedback@csnradio.com
Web site: http://www.csnradio.com
Profile: KAWZ-FM is a non commercial station owned by Calvary Chapel Twin Falls. The format of the station is religious music and talk. KAWZ-FM broadcasts in the Twin Falls, ID area at 89.9 FM.
FM RADIO STATION

KAXA-FM
810185
Owner: Thomas Gebhart's Reddog Media
Editorial: 874 Harper Rd, Kerrville, Texas 78028-2984 **Tel:** 1 830 896-8380.
Email: buck@thebuck1037.com
Web site: http://www.thebuck1037.com
Profile: KAXA-FM is a commercial station owned by Thomas Gebhart's Reddog Media. The format of the station is classic rock music, featuring sounds from the 50s, 60s and 70s. KAXA-FM broadcasts to the Kerrville, TX area at a frequency of 103.7 FM.
FM RADIO STATION

KAXE-FM
41183
Owner: Northern Community Radio Inc.
Editorial: 260 NE 2nd St, Grand Rapids, Minnesota 55744-2864 **Tel:** 1 218 326-1234.
Email: comments@kaxe.org
Web site: http://kaxe.org/#stream/0
Profile: KAXE-FM is a non-commercial station owned by Northern Community Radio Inc. The format of the station is variety. KAXE-FM broadcasts in the Grand Rapids, MN area at 91.7 FM.
FM RADIO STATION

KAXL-FM
42629
Owner: Skyride Unlimited Inc.
Editorial: 110 S Montclair St, Ste 205, Bakersfield, California 93309 **Tel:** 1 661 832-2800.
Email: kaxl@kaxl.com
Web site: http://www.kaxl.com
Profile: KAXL-FM's format is Contemporary Christian/ Inspirational. Their target audience is 18-54.
FM RADIO STATION

KAYD-FM
45681
Owner: Cumulus Media Inc.
Editorial: 755 S 11th St Ste 102, Beaumont, Texas 77701-3723 **Tel:** 1 409 833-9421.
Web site: http://www.nashfm1017.com
Profile: KAYD-FM is a commercial station owned by Cumulus Media Inc. The format of the station is country music. KAYD-FM broadcasts to the Beaumont, TX area at 101.7 FM.
FM RADIO STATION

KAYE-FM
39538
Owner: Northern Oklahoma College
Editorial: 1220 E Grand Ave, Tonkawa, Oklahoma 74653-4022 **Tel:** 1 580 628-6446.
Web site: http://www.noc.edu
Profile: KAYE-FM is a non-commercial station owned by Northern Oklahoma College. The format of the station is rock alternative. KAYE-FM broadcasts to the Tonkawa, OK area at 90.7 FM.
FM RADIO STATION

KAYH-FM
502466
Owner: Bott Broadcasting Co.
Editorial: 2201 S Thompson St, Ste C7, Springdale, Arkansas 72764 **Tel:** 1 479 750-7893.
Web site: http://www.bottradionetwork.com
Profile: KAYH-FM is a non-commercial station owned by Bott Broadcasting Co. The format of the station is Christian. KAYH-FM broadcasts to Fayetteville, AR and its surrounding areas at 89.3 FM.
FM RADIO STATION

KAYL-AM
37184
Owner: Community First Broadcasting
Editorial: 910 Flindt Dr, Storm Lake, Iowa 50588-3204 **Tel:** 1 712 732-3520.
Email: production@stormlakeradio.com
Web site: http://www.stormlakeradio.com
Profile: KAYL-AM is a commercial station owned by Community First Broadcasting. The format of the station is Spanish Adult Hits. KAYL-AM broadcasts to the Storm Lake, IA area at 990 AM.
AM RADIO STATION

KAYL-FM
44572
Owner: Community First Broadcasting
Editorial: 606 1/2 Lake Ave, Storm Lake, Iowa 50588-1875 **Tel:** 1 712 732-3520.
Email: production@stormlakeradio.com
Web site: http://www.stormlakeradio.com/
Profile: KAYL-FM is a commercial station owned by Community First Broadcasting. The format of the station is adult contemporary music. KAYL-FM broadcasts to the Storm Lake, IA area at 101.7 FM.
FM RADIO STATION

KAYO-FM
579332
Owner: Morris Communications
Editorial: 5431 E Mayflower Ln Ste 3, Wasilla, Alaska 99654-7891 **Tel:** 1 907 631-0493.
Web site: http://www.countrylegends1009.com
Profile: KAYO-FM is a commercial station owned by Morris Communications. The format of the station is classic country. KAYO-FM broadcasts to the Wasilla, AK area at 100.9.
FM RADIO STATION

KAYQ-FM
39540
Owner: Valkyrie Broadcasting Inc.
Editorial: 1649 Commercial St, Warsaw, Missouri 65355-3060 **Tel:** 1 660 438-7343.
Email: kayqtraffic@embarqmail.com
Profile: KAYQ-FM is a commercial station owned by Valkyrie Broadcasting Inc. The format of the station is classic country. KAYQ-FM broadcasts to the Warsaw, MO area at 97.1 FM.
FM RADIO STATION

KAYS-AM
39060
Owner: Eagle Radio Inc.
Editorial: 2300 Hall St, Hays, Kansas 67601-3062 **Tel:** 1 785 625-2578.
Email: haysnews@eagleradio.net
Web site: http://www.kaysradio.com
Profile: KAYS-AM is a commercial station owned by Eagle Radio Inc. The format of the station is Oldies, Sports and Classic Hits . KAYS-AM's target audience is adults, ages 35 to 100, in the Hays, KS area. The station airs locally on 1400 AM. KAYS-AM's tagline is "KAYS Radio 1400 AM." The station newscasts air at the top of each hour, CT.
AM RADIO STATION

KAYX-FM
46881
Owner: Bott Broadcasting Co.
Editorial: 111 W Main St, Richmond, Missouri 64085-1709 **Tel:** 1 816 470-9925.
Web site: http://www.bottradionetwork.com
Profile: KAYX-FM is a commercial station owned by Bott Broadcasting Co. The format of the station is Christian and religious programming. KAYX-FM broadcasts to the Richmond, MO area at 92.5 FM.
FM RADIO STATION

KAZA-AM
34877
Owner: Radio Fiesta Corporation
Editorial: 1820 Cochrane Rd, Morgan Hill, California 95037-9029 **Tel:** 1 805 928-1030.
Web site: http://radiovidaabundante.com
Profile: KAZA-AM is a commercial station owned by Radio Fiesta Corporation. The format of the station is Hispanic contemporary Christian and religious music. KAZA-AM broadcasts to the San Jose, CA area at 1290 AM.
AM RADIO STATION

KAZC-FM
44275
Owner: South Central Oklahoma Christian Broadcasting Inc.
Editorial: 20750 State Hwy 1W, Ada, Oklahoma 74820-5421 **Tel:** 1 580 332-0902.
Email: email@thegospelstation.com
Web site: http://www.thegospelstation.com
Profile: KAZC-FM is a non-commercial station owned by South Central Oklahoma Christian Broadcasting Inc. The format of the station is gospel. KAZC-FM broadcasts to the Ada, OK area at 88.3 FM.
FM RADIO STATION

KAZE-FM
73566
Owner: Reynolds Radio Inc.
Editorial: 212 Old Grande Blvd Ste B100, Tyler, Texas 75703-4201
Email: spots@theblaze.cc
Web site: http://www.theblaze.fm
Profile: KAZE-FM is a commercial station owned by Reynolds Radio Inc. The format of the station is urban contemporary. KAZE-FM broadcasts to Tyler, TX area at 106.9 FM and is a simulcast of KBLZ-FM.
FM RADIO STATION

KAZF-FM
317993
Owner: Bernal(Paulino)
Editorial: 4501 N McColl Rd, McAllen, Texas 78504-2431 **Tel:** 1 956 781-5528.
Web site: http://nuevaradiocristiana.com
Profile: KAZF-FM is a commercial station owned by Paulino Bernal. The format of the station is Hispanic contemporary Christian programming. KAZF-FM broadcasts to the McAllen, TX area at 91.9 FM.
FM RADIO STATION

KAZG-AM
39177
Owner: Hubbard Radio, LLC
Editorial: 4343 E Camelback Rd Ste 200, Phoenix, Arizona 85018-2756 **Tel:** 1 480 941-1007.
Web site: http://kazg1440.com
Profile: KAZG-AM is a commercial station owned by Hubbard Radio, LLC. The format of the station is oldies. KAZG-AM broadcasts to the Phoenix area at 1440 AM.
AM RADIO STATION

KAZI-FM
41124
Owner: Austin Community Radio
Editorial: 8906 Wall St Ste 203, Austin, Texas 78754-4542 **Tel:** 1 512 836-9544.
Web site: http://www.kazifm.org
Profile: KAZI-FM is a commercial station owned by Austin Community Radio. The format of the station is variety. KAZI-FM broadcasts to the Austin, TX community at 88.7 FM.
FM RADIO STATION

KAZM-AM
34878
Owner: Tabback Broadcasting Company
Editorial: 3400 W State Route 89A, Sedona, Arizona 86336-4914 **Tel:** 1 928 282-4154.
Email: news@kazmradio.com
Web site: http://www.kazmradio.com
Profile: KAZM-AM is a commercial station owned by the Tabback Broadcasting Company. The format of the station is news, talk and sports. KAZM-AM broadcasts to the Phoenix area at 780 AM.
AM RADIO STATION

KAZN-AM
36043
Owner: Multicultural Radio Broadcasting Inc.
Editorial: 747 E Green St, Pasadena, California 91101-2145 **Tel:** 1 626 568-1300.
Web site: http://www.am1300.com
Profile: KAZN-AM is a commercial station owned by Multicultural Radio Broadcasting Inc. The format of the station is a variety of Chinese music and talk. KAZN-AM broadcasts to the Pasadena, CA area at 1300 AM.
AM RADIO STATION

KAZR-FM
39646
Owner: Saga Communications
Editorial: 1416 Locust St, Des Moines, Iowa 50309-3014 **Tel:** 1 515 280-1350.
Web site: http://www.lazer1033.com
Profile: KAZR-FM is a commercial station owned by Saga Communications. The format of the station is rock music. KAZR-FM broadcasts to the Des Moines, IA area at 103.3 FM.
FM RADIO STATION

KAZX-FM
217814
Owner: iHeartMedia Inc.
Editorial: 200 E Broadway, Farmington, New Mexico 87401-6418 **Tel:** 1 505 325-1716.
Web site: http://www.star1029.com
Profile: KAZX-FM is a commercial station owned by iHeartMedia Inc. The format of the station is Top 40/ CHR music. KAZX-FM broadcasts to the Farmington, NM area at 102.9 FM.
FM RADIO STATION

KAZY-FM
393974
Owner: Appaloosa Broadcasting
Editorial: 1600 Van Lennen Ave, Cheyenne, Wyoming 82001-4636 **Tel:** 1 307 638-8921.
Email: news@radiowyo.com
Web site: http://www.937kazy.com
Profile: KAZY-FM is a commercial station owned by Appaloosa Broadcasting. The format of the station is rock. KAZY-FM broadcasts to the Laramie, WY area at 93.7 FM.
FM RADIO STATION

KBAA-FM
238562

Owner: Adelante Media Group
Editorial: 500 Media Pl, Sacramento, California 95815-3733 **Tel:** 1 916 216-3712.
Profile: KBAA-FM is a commercial station owned by Adelante Media Group. The format of the station is Spanish AC. KBAA-FM broadcasts to the Grass Valley, CA area at 103.3 FM.
FM RADIO STATION

KBAC-FM
43826

Owner: Hutton Broadcasting, LLC
Editorial: 2502 Camino Entrada Ste C, Santa Fe, New Mexico 87507-4911 **Tel:** 1 505 471-1067.
Web site: http://www.santafe.com/kbac
Profile: KBAC-FM is a commercial station owned by Hutton Broadcasting, LLC. The format of the station is adult album alternative music. KBAC-FM broadcasts to the Santa Fe, NM area at 98.1 FM.
FM RADIO STATION

KBAD-AM
38720

Owner: Lotus Communications Corp.
Editorial: 8755 W Flamingo Rd, Las Vegas, Nevada 89147-8667 **Tel:** 1 702 876-1460.
Email: lotussignup@yahoo.com
Web site: http://www.werlv.com
Profile: KBAD-AM is a commercial station owned by Lotus Communications Corp. The format of the station is sports. KBAD-AM broadcasts in the Las Vegas area at 920 AM.
AM RADIO STATION

KBAI-AM
34884

Owner: Saga Communications
Editorial: 2219 Yew Street Rd, Bellingham, Washington 98229-8855 **Tel:** 1 360 734-9790.
Web site: http://989kbay.com
Profile: KBAI-AM is a commercial station owned by Saga Communications. The format of the station is classic hits. KBAI-AM broadcasts to the Bellingham, WA area at 930 AM. The station's slogan is, "Re-live your favorites every day."
AM RADIO STATION

KBAM-AM
39319

Owner: Bicoastal Media LLC
Editorial: 1130 14th Ave, Longview, Washington 98632-3017 **Tel:** 1 360 425-1500.
Web site: http://www.kbamcountry.com
Profile: KBAM-AM is a commercial station owned by Bicoastal Media LLC. The format of the station is country music. KBAM-AM broadcasts in the Portland, OR area at 1270 AM.
AM RADIO STATION

KBAQ-FM
42099

Owner: Maricopa Community Colleges
Editorial: 2323 W 14th St, Tempe, Arizona 85281-6948 **Tel:** 1 480 833-1122.
Email: news@rioradio.org
Web site: http://www.kbaq.org
Profile: KBAQ-FM is a non-commercial station owned by Maricopa Community Colleges. The format of the station is classical music. KBAQ-FM broadcasts to the Tempe, AZ area at 89.5 FM.
FM RADIO STATION

KBAR-AM
39213

Owner: Lee Family Broadcasting
Editorial: 120 S 300 W, Rupert, Idaho 83350-9667
Tel: 1 208 436-4757.
Profile: KBAR-AM is a commercial station owned by Lee Family Broadcasting. The primary format of the station is news/talk, and it also airs oldies music. KBAR-AM broadcasts to the Twin Falls area in Idaho at a frequency of 1230 AM.
AM RADIO STATION

KBAR-FM
41326

Owner: Victoria RadioWorks Inc.
Editorial: 3613 N Main St, Victoria, Texas 77901-2607
Tel: 1 361 579-6499.
Profile: KBAR-FM is a commercial station owned by Victoria RadioWorks Inc. The format of the station is rock music. KBAR-FM broadcasts to the Victoria, TX area at 100.9 FM.
FM RADIO STATION

KBAT-FM
41220

Owner: Townsquare Media, Inc.
Editorial: 11300 State Highway 191 Bldg 2, Midland, Texas 79707-1367 **Tel:** 1 432 563-5636.
Email: contact@kbat.com
Web site: http://www.kbat.com
Profile: KBAT-FM a commercial station owned by Townsquare Media, Inc. The format of the station is rock music. KBAT-FM broadcasts to the Midland, TX area at 99.9 FM.
FM RADIO STATION

KBAY-FM
43242

Owner: Alpha Media
Editorial: 190 Park Center Plz Ste 200, San Jose, California 95113-2223 **Tel:** 1 408 287-5775.
Web site: http://www.kbay.com
Profile: KBAY-FM is a commercial station owned by Alpha Media. The format of the station is Classic Hits. KBAY-FM broadcasts to the San Francisco area at 94.5 FM.
FM RADIO STATION

KBAZ-FM
46359

Owner: Townsquare Media, LLC
Editorial: 3250 S Reserve St Ste 200, Missoula, Montana 59801-8236 **Tel:** 1 406 728-9300.
Web site: http://www.963theblaze.com
Profile: KBAZ-FM is a commercial station owned by Townsquare Media, LLC. The format of the station is rock alternative. KBAZ-FM broadcasts to the Missoula, MT area at 96.3 FM.
FM RADIO STATION

KBBD-FM
42145

Owner: Mapleton Communications LLC
Editorial: 1601 E 57th Ave, Spokane, Washington 99223-6623 **Tel:** 1 509 448-1000.
Web site: http://www.1039bobfm.com
Profile: KBBD-FM is a a commercial station owned by Mapleton Communications LLC. The format of the station is Adult Hits.
FM RADIO STATION

KBBE-FM
46104

Owner: Davies Communications Inc.
Editorial: 411 E Euclid St, McPherson, Kansas 67460-4417 **Tel:** 1 620 241-1504.
Email: news@midkansasradio.com
Web site: http://www.midkansasonline.com
Profile: KBBE-FM is a commercial station owned by Davies Communication Inc. The format of the station is oldies and classic hits music. KBBE-FM broadcasts to the McPherson, KS area at 96.7 FM.
FM RADIO STATION

KBBG-FM
41539

Owner: Afro-American Community Broadcasting Inc
Editorial: 918 Newell St, Waterloo, Iowa 50703-2720
Tel: 1 319 234-1515.
Web site: http://www.kbbgfm.org
Profile: KBBG-FM is a non-commercial station owned by Afro-American Community Broadcasting Inc. The format of the station is educational. KBBG-FM broadcasts to the Cedar Rapids, IA area at 88.1 FM.
FM RADIO STATION

KBBI-AM
36057

Owner: Kachemak Bay Broadcasting Inc.
Editorial: 3913 Kachemak Way, Homer, Alaska 99603
Tel: 1 907 235-7721.
Email: dorle@kbbi.org
Web site: http://www.kbbi.org
Profile: KBBI-AM is a non-commercial station owned by Kachemak Bay Broadcasting Inc. The format of the station is variety. KBBI-AM broadcasts to the Homer, AK area at 890 AM.
AM RADIO STATION

KBBK-FM
45916

Owner: NRG Media LLC
Editorial: 4343 O St, Lincoln, Nebraska 68510
Tel: 1 402 475-4567.
Web site: http://www.b1073.com
Profile: KBBK-FM is a commercial station owned by NRG Media. The format of the station is hot adult contemporary. KBBK-FM broadcasts to the Lincoln, NE area at 107.3 FM.
FM RADIO STATION

KBBM-FM
86078

Owner: Cumulus Media Inc.
Editorial: 503 Old 63 N, Columbia, Missouri 65201-6305 **Tel:** 1 573 449-4141.
Web site: http://www.nashfm100.com
Profile: KBBM-FM is a commercial station owned by Cumulus Media Inc. The format of the station is contemporary country. KBBM-FM broadcasts to the Columbia, MO area at 100.1 FM.
FM RADIO STATION

KBBN-FM
45840

Owner: Custer County Broadcasting Inc.
Editorial: Highway 2 and Callaway Road, Broken Bow, Nebraska 68822 **Tel:** 1 308 872-5881.
Email: info@sandhillsexpress.com
Web site: http://www.kbbn.com
Profile: KBBN-FM is a commercial station owned by Custer County Broadcasting Inc. The format of the station is classic rock. KBBN-FM broadcasts to the Broken Bow, NE area at 95.3 FM.
FM RADIO STATION

KBBO-AM
36982

Owner: New Northwest Broadcasters LLC
Editorial: 1200 Chesterly Dr Ste 160, Yakima, Washington 98902-7345 **Tel:** 1 509 248-2900.
Web site: http://www.thefanyakima.com/
Profile: KBBO-AM is a commercial station owned by New Northwest Broadcasters LLC. The format of the station is sports. KBBO-AM broadcasts in the Yakima, WA area at 980 AM.
AM RADIO STATION

KBBO-FM
43369

Owner: Ohana Media Group
Editorial: 833 Gambell St, Anchorage, Alaska 99501-3756 **Tel:** 1 907 344-4045.
Web site: http://www.921bob.fm
Profile: KBBO-FM is a commercial station owned by Ohana Media Group. The format of the station is adult hits. KBBO-FM broadcasts to the Anchorage, AK area at 92.1 FM.
FM RADIO STATION

KBBQ-FM
44377

Owner: Cumulus Media Inc.
Editorial: 4209 N Frontage Rd, Fayetteville, Arkansas 72703-5002 **Tel:** 1 479 452-0681.
Web site: http://www.1027thevibe.com
Profile: KBBQ-FM is a commercial station owned by Cumulus Media Inc. The format of the station is rhythmic Top 40/CHR. KBBQ-FM broadcasts to Fort Smith, AR area at 102.7 FM.
FM RADIO STATION

KBBR-AM
38890

Owner: Bicoastal Media LLC
Editorial: 320 Central Ave Ste 519, Coos Bay, Oregon 97420-2241 **Tel:** 1 541 267-2121.
Web site: http://www.1340kbbr.com
Profile: KBBR-AM is a commercial station owned by Bicoastal Media LLC. The format of the station is progressive news and talk. KBBR-AM broadcasts to the Coos Bay, OR area at 1340 AM. The station prefers to be contacted via its contact form found here: http://www.1340kbbr.com/page.php?page_id=83.
AM RADIO STATION

KBBS-AM
39430

Owner: Legend Communications
Email: kbbs@vcn.com
Web site: http://tunein.com/radio/KBBS-1450-s31639
Profile: KBBS-AM is a commercial station owned by Legend Communications. The format of the station is classic country. KBBS-AM broadcasts to the Buffalo, WY area at 1450 AM.
AM RADIO STATION

KBBT-FM
44221

Owner: Univision Communications Inc.
Editorial: 12451 Network Blvd Ste 140, San Antonio, Texas 78249-3336 **Tel:** 1 210 610-4141.
Web site: http://www.thebeatsa.com
Profile: KBBT-FM is a commercial station owned by Univision Communications Inc. The format for the station is urban contemporary. KBBT-FM broadcasts to the San Antonio area at 98.5 FM.
FM RADIO STATION

KBBU-FM
44202

Owner: Adelante Media Group
Editorial: 500 Media Pl, Sacramento, California 95815-3733 **Tel:** 1 209 248-4303.
Profile: KBBU-FM is a commercial station owned by Adelante Media Group. The format of the station is regional Mexican. KBBU-FM broadcasts to the Modesto, CA area at 93.9.
FM RADIO STATION

KBBW-AM
34879

Owner: Williams(Steve)
Editorial: 1019 Washington Ave, Waco, Texas 76701-1256 **Tel:** 1 254 757-1010.
Email: info@1010kbw.com
Web site: http://www.kbbw.com
Profile: KBBW-AM is a commercial station owned by Steve Williams. The format of the station is Christian talk. KBBW-AM broadcasts to the Waco, TX area at 1010 AM.
AM RADIO STATION

KBBX-FM
42781

Owner: Flood Communications
Editorial: 11128 John Galt Blvd Ste 25, Omaha, Nebraska 68137-2385 **Tel:** 1 402 884-0968.
Web site: http://www.lobo977.com
Profile: KBBX-FM is a commercial station owned by Flood Communications. The format of the station is regional Mexican. KBBX-FM broadcasts to Omaha, NE at 97.7 FM.
FM RADIO STATION

KBBY-FM
42753

Owner: Cumulus Media Inc.
Editorial: 1376 Walter St, Ventura, California 93003-5658 **Tel:** 1 805 642-8595.
Web site: http://www.b951.com
Profile: KBBY-FM is a commercial station owned by Cumulus Media Inc. The format of the station is adult contemporary music. KBBY-FM broadcasts to the Ventura, CA area at 95.1 FM.
FM RADIO STATION

KBBZ-FM
44575

Owner: Bee Broadcasting Inc.
Editorial: 2432 US Highway 2 E, Kalispell, Montana 59901-2310 **Tel:** 1 406 755-8700.
Email: b98@kbbz.com
Web site: http://www.kbbz.com
Profile: KBBZ-FM is a commercial station owned by Bee Broadcasting, Inc. The format of the station is classic rock. KBBZ-FM broadcasts to the Kalispell, MT area at 98.5 FM.
FM RADIO STATION

KBCE-FM
39543

Owner: JWBP Broadcasting, LLC
Editorial: 1605 Murray St Ste 111, Alexandria, Louisiana 71301-6875 **Tel:** 1 318 445-0800.
Web site: http://www.b102jamz.com
Profile: KBCE-FM is a commercial station owned by JWBP Broadcasting, LLC. The format of the station is urban adult contemporary music. KBCE-FM broadcasts to the Alexandria, LA area at 102.3 FM.
FM RADIO STATION

KBCH-AM
39283

Owner: Yaquina Bay Communications Inc.
Editorial: 800 SE Highway 101 Ste C, Lincoln City, Oregon 97367-2755 **Tel:** 1 541 265-2266.
Email: news@ybcradio.com
Web site: http://www.kbcham.com
Profile: KBCH-AM is a commercial station owned by Yaquina Bay Communications Inc. The format of the station is adult standards music, news and talk. KBCH-FM broadcasts to Lincoln City, OR at 1400 AM.
AM RADIO STATION

KBCK-AM
3615

Owner: Toole(Robert Cummings)
Editorial: 302 Missouri Ave, Deer Lodge, Montana 59722-1077 **Tel:** 1 406 846-1100.
Email: bobsatriver@gmail.com
Profile: KBCK-AM is a commercial station owned by Robert Cummings Toole. The format of the station is classic and country. KBCK-AM broadcasts to the Deer Lodge, MT area at 1400 AM.
AM RADIO STATION

KBCL-AM
3488

Owner: Barnabas Center Ministries
Editorial: 316 Gregg St, Shreveport, Louisiana 71104-5186 **Tel:** 1 318 861-1070.
Email: kbcl_radio@bellsouth.net
Web site: http://www.kbclthebridge.com
Profile: KBCL-AM is a commercial station owned by Barnabas Center Ministries. The format of the station is Christian talk programming. KBCL-AM broadcasts to the Shreveport, LA area at 1070 AM.
AM RADIO STATION

KBCN-FM
4261

Owner: Pearson Broadcasting
Editorial: 101 Bluebird St, Harrison, Arkansas 72601-1908 **Tel:** 1 870 743-1157.
Web site: http://www.espnarkansas.net
Profile: KBCN-FM is a commercial station owned by Pearson Broadcasting. The format of the station is sports talk. KBCN-FM is the ESPN Radio affiliate for the Harrison, AR area and broadcasts locally at 104.3 FM.
FM RADIO STATION

KBCO-FM
4278

Owner: iHeartMedia Inc.
Editorial: 4695 S Monaco St, Denver, Colorado 80237-3525 **Tel:** 1 303 444-5600.
Web site: http://www.kbco.com
Profile: KBCO-FM is a commercial station owned by iHeartMedia Inc. The format of the station is adult album alternative. KBCO-FM broadcasts to the Boulder, CO area at 97.3 FM.
FM RADIO STATION

KBCQ-AM
3692

Owner: Majestic Communications
Editorial: 5206 W 2nd St, Roswell, New Mexico 88201-8839 **Tel:** 1 575 622-6450.
Web site: https://www.majesticradio.net
Profile: KBCQ-AM is a commercial station owned by Majestic Communications. The format of the station is classic hits. KBCQ-AM broadcasts to the Roswell, NM area at 1230 AM.
AM RADIO STATION

KBCQ-FM
4612

Owner: Majestic Communications
Editorial: 5206 W 2nd St, Roswell, New Mexico 88201-8839 **Tel:** 1 575 622-6450.
Web site: http://www.q971fm.com
Profile: KBCQ-FM is a commercial station owned by Majestic Communications. The format of the station is Top 40/CHR music. KBCQ-FM broadcasts to the Roswell, NM area at 97.1 FM.
FM RADIO STATION

KBCR-AM
3944

Owner: Cool Radio, LLC
Editorial: 2110 Mount Werner Cir, Steamboat Springs, Colorado 80487-9009 **Tel:** 1 970 879-2270.
Web site: http://www.kbcr.com
Profile: KBCR-AM is a commercial station owned by Cool Radio, LLC. The format of the station is local talk. KBCR-AM broadcasts to the Steamboat Springs, CO area at 1230 AM.
AM RADIO STATION

KBCR-FM
4683

Owner: Cool Radio, LLC
Editorial: 2110 Mount Werner Rd, Steamboat Springs, Colorado 80487 **Tel:** 1 970 879-2270.
Email: kbcr@nctelecom.net
Web site: http://www.kbcr.com
Profile: KBCR-FM is a commercial station owned by Cool Radio, LLC. The format of the station is classic and contemporary country. KBCR-FM broadcasts to the Steamboat Springs, CO area at 96.9 FM.
FM RADIO STATION

KBCS-FM
3954

Owner: Bellevue Community College
Editorial: 3000 Landerholm Cir Se, Bellevue, Washington 98007-6406 **Tel:** 1 425 564-2427.
Email: office@kbcs.fm
Web site: http://www.kbcs.fm
Profile: KBCS-FM is a non-commercial station owned by Bellevue Community College. The format of the station is variety. KBCS-FM broadcasts to the Bellevue, WA area at 91.3 FM.
FM RADIO STATION

KBCU-FM
4384

Owner: Bethel College
Editorial: 300 E 27th St, North Newton, Kansas 67117-8061 **Tel:** 1 316 284-5273.
Email: kbcu@bethelks.edu
Web site: http://www.bethelks.edu/kbcu
FM RADIO STATION

KBCV-AM
408456

Owner: Bott Broadcasting Co.
Editorial: 500 W Main St Ste 103A, Branson, Missouri 65616-2862 **Tel:** 1 417 336-1570.
Web site: http://www.bottradionetwork.com

Profile: KBCV-AM is a non-commercial station owned by Bott Broadcasting Co. The format of the station is religious and talk. KBCV-AM broadcasts to Branson, MO and surrounding areas at 1570 AM.
AM RADIO STATION

KBCY-FM
39949
Owner: Cumulus Media Inc.
Editorial: 2525 S Danville Dr, Abilene, Texas 79605
Tel: 1 325 793-9700.
Web site: http://www.kbcy.com
Profile: KBCY-FM is a commercial station owned by Cumulus Media Inc. The format of the station is country. KBCY-FM broadcasts to the Abilene, TX area at a frequency of 99.7.
FM RADIO STATION

KBDB-FM
44749
Owner: Forks Broadcasting, Inc.
Editorial: 260 Cedar Ave, Forks, Washington 98331-9605 **Tel:** 1 360 374-6233.
Email: news@forksbroadcasting.com
Web site: http://www.twilight967.com
Profile: KBDB-FM is a commercial station owned by Forks Broadcasting, Inc. The format of the station is adult contemporary. KBDB-FM broadcasts to the Forks, WA area at 96.7 FM.
FM RADIO STATION

KBDN-FM
43838
Owner: Bicoastal Media LLC
Editorial: 320 Central Ave, Ste 519, Coos Bay, Oregon 97420 **Tel:** 1 541 267-2121.
Email: southcoastpsa@bicoastalmedia.com
Web site: http://www.kbdn.com
Profile: KBDN-FM is a commercial station owned by Bicoastal Media LLC. The format of the station is country. KBDN-FM broadcasts to the Coos Bay, OR area at 96.5 FM.
FM RADIO STATION

KBDR-FM
42086
Owner: R Communications, LLC
Editorial: 107 Calle Del Norte Ste 212, Laredo, Texas 78041-9120 **Tel:** 1 956 725-1000.
Web site: http://www.laley1005.com
Profile: KBDR-FM is a commercial station owned by Border Media Partners LLC. The format of the station is Regional Mexican. KBDR-FM broadcasts to the Loredo, TX area on 100.5 FM.
FM RADIO STATION

KBDS-FM
44529
Owner: Radio Campesina Bakersfield, Inc.
Editorial: 6313 Schirra Ct Ste 313, Bakersfield, California 93313-2174 **Tel:** 1 661 837-0745.
Web site: http://www.campesina.com
Profile: KBDS-FM is a commercial station owned by Radio Campesina Bakersfield, Inc. The format of the station is rhythmic CHR. KBDS-FM broadcasts to the Bakersfield, CA area at 103.9 FM.
FM RADIO STATION

KBDV-FM
535556
Owner: Baldridge-Dumas Communications Inc.
Editorial: 605 San Antonio Ave, Many, Louisiana 71449-3018 **Tel:** 1 318 256-0555.
Email: producetion@bdcradio.com
Web site: http://bdcradio.com
Profile: KBDV-FM is a commercial station owned by Baldridge-Dumas Communications Inc. The format of the station is adult contemporary. KBDV-FM broadcasts to the Shreveport, LA area at 92.7 FM.
FM RADIO STATION

KBDY-FM
620171
Owner: Toga Radio, LLC
Editorial: 106 N First St, Saratoga, Wyoming 82331
Tel: 1 307 326-8642.
Email: traffic@bigfoot99.com
Profile: KBDY-FM is a commercial station owned by Toga Radio LLC. The format of the station is country. KBDY-FM broadcasts to the Saratoga, WY at 102.1 FM. The station does not air PSAs, but does accept local community event announcements via email to traffic@bigfoot99.com.
FM RADIO STATION

KBDZ-FM
42802
Owner: Donze Communications Inc.
Editorial: 122 Perry Plz Ste D, Perryville, Missouri 63775-4203 **Tel:** 1 573 547-8005.
Email: kbdz@suntimesnews.com
Web site: http://www.classicrock931.com/
Profile: KBDZ-FM is a commercial station owned by Donze Communications Inc. The format of the station is Classic Rock. KBDZ-FM broadcasts to the Perryville, MO area at 93.1 FM.
FM RADIO STATION

KBEA-FM
42201
Owner: Townsquare Media
Editorial: 1229 Brady St, Davenport, Iowa 52803-4616 **Tel:** 1 563 326-2541.
Web site: http://www.b100.net
Profile: KBEA-FM is a commercial station owned by Townsquare Media. The format of the station is Top 40/CHR. The station broadcasts to the Davenport, IA area at 99.7 FM.
FM RADIO STATION

KBEB-FM
43195
Owner: iHeartMedia Inc.
Editorial: 1545 River Park Dr Ste 500, Sacramento, California 95815-4693 **Tel:** 1 916 929-5325.
Web site: http://thebullsacramento.iheart.com
Profile: KBEB-FM is a commercial station owned by iHeartMedia Inc. The format of the station is Country. KBEB-FM broadcasts to the Sacramento, CA area at 92.5 FM. The target audience is ages 18 to 54.
FM RADIO STATION

KBEC-AM
34881
Owner: Tuck (Faye and Richard)
Editorial: 711 Ferris Ave, Waxahachie, Texas 75165-2585 **Tel:** 1 972 923-1390.
Email: info@kbec.com
Web site: http://www.kbec.com
Profile: KBEC-AM is a commercial station owned by Phillips (Jim). The format of the station is country, specifically Classic Texas music. KBEC-AM broadcasts to the Waxahachie, TX area at 1390 AM.
AM RADIO STATION

KBED-AM
37243
Owner: Cumulus Media Inc.
Editorial: 755 S 11th St Ste 102, Beaumont, Texas 77701-3723 **Tel:** 1 409 951-2500.
Web site: http://www.sportsradiobeaumont.com/
Profile: KBED-AM is a commercial station owned by Cumulus Media Inc. The format of the station is Sports. KBED-AM broadcasts to the Beaumont, TX area at 1510 AM.
AM RADIO STATION

KBEE-FM
46425
Owner: Cumulus Media Inc
Editorial: 434 W Bearcat Dr, Salt Lake City, Utah 84115-2520 **Tel:** 1 801 485-6700.
Web site: http://www.b987.com
Profile: KBEE-FM is a commercial station owned by Cumulus Media Inc. The format for the station is adult contemporary. KBEE-FM broadcasts to the Salt Lake City area at 98.7 FM.
FM RADIO STATION

KBEL-AM
37189
Owner: Brute Force Radio LLC
Editorial: 813 E Lincoln Rd, Idabel, Oklahoma 74745-7816 **Tel:** 1 580 286-6642.
Email: kbel967@yahoo.com
Web site: http://kbelradio.com
Profile: KBEL-AM is a commercial station owned by Brute Force Radio LLC. The format of the station is news/talk. KBEL-AM broadcasts to the Idabel, OK area at 1240 AM.
AM RADIO STATION

KBEL-FM
44952
Owner: Brute Force Radio LLC
Editorial: 813 E Lincoln Rd, Idabel, Oklahoma 74745-7816 **Tel:** 1 580 286-6642.
Email: kbel967@yahoo.com
Web site: http://www.kbelradio.com
Profile: KBEL-FM is a commercial station owned by Brute Force Radio LLC. The format of the station is country music. KBEL-FM broadcasts to the Idabel, OK area at 96.7 FM.
FM RADIO STATION

KBEQ-FM
44237
Owner: Steel City Media
Editorial: 508 Westport Rd, Kansas City, Missouri 64111-3012 **Tel:** 1 816 753-4000.
Web site: http://www.q104kc.com
Profile: KBEQ-FM is a commercial station owned by Steel City Media. The format of the station is contemporary country music. KBEQ-FM broadcasts to the Kansas City, MO area on 104.3 FM.
FM RADIO STATION

KBER-FM
46774
Owner: Cumulus Media Inc
Editorial: 434 Bearcat Dr, Salt Lake City, Utah 84115
Tel: 1 801 485-6700.
Web site: http://www.kber.com
Profile: KBER-FM is a commercial station owned by Cumulus Media Inc. The format of the station is rock/album-oriented rock. KBER-FM broadcasts to the Salt Lake City area at 101.1 FM.
FM RADIO STATION

KBES-FM
43848
Owner: Bet Nahrain Inc.
Tel: 1 209 538-4130.
Web site: http://wordpress.betnahrain.org
Profile: KBES-FM is a commercial station owned by Bet Nahrain Inc. The format of the station is Assyrian variety. KBES-FM broadcasts to the Los Angeles area at 89.5 FM.
FM RADIO STATION

KBET-AM
492800
Owner: Royce International Broadcasting Corporation
Editorial: 6725 Via Austi Pkwy Fl 2, Las Vegas, Nevada 89119-3507 **Tel:** 1 760 341-0123.
Web site: http://790talknow.com
Profile: KBET-AM is a commercial station owned by Royce International (dba Silver State Broadcasting, LLC). The format of the station is Conservative talk programming. KBET-AM broadcasts to the Las Vegas area at 790 AM.
AM RADIO STATION

KBEV-FM
46848
Owner: Dead-Air Broadcasting Co.
Editorial: 610 N Montana St, Dillon, Montana 59725-3353 **Tel:** 1 406 683-2800.
Email: deadair@kdbm-kbev.com
Web site: http://www.kdbm-kbev.com/
FM RADIO STATION

KBEW-AM
39316
Owner: KBEW, Inc.
Editorial: 705 E Leland Pkwy, Blue Earth, Minnesota 56013 **Tel:** 1 507 526-2181.
Email: kbew@bevcomm.net
Profile: KBEW-AM is a commercial station owned by KBEW, Inc. The format of the station is oldies music. KBEW-AM broadcasts to the Blue Earth, MN area at 1560 AM.
AM RADIO STATION

KBEW-FM
46670
Owner: KBEW, Inc.
Editorial: 705 E Leland Pkwy, Blue Earth, Minnesota 56013 **Tel:** 1 507 526-2181.
Email: kbew@bevcomm.net
Profile: KBEW-FM is a commercial station owned by KBEW, Inc. The format of the station is country music. KBEW-FM broadcasts to the Blue Earth, MN area at 98.1 FM.
FM RADIO STATION

KBEX-FM
44975
Owner: Viva Media, LLC
Editorial: 500 S Polk St Ste 110, Amarillo, Texas 79101-2318 **Tel:** 1 806 242-0877.
Web site: http://www.lapoderosa961.com
Profile: KBEX-FM is a commercial station owned by Viva Media, LLC. The format of the station is regional Mexican. KBEX-FM broadcasts to the Dalhart, TX area at 96.1 FM.
FM RADIO STATION

KBEY-FM
42720
Owner: Victory Publishing Company, Ltd.
Editorial: 2108 US Highway 281 Ste A, Marble Falls, Texas 78654-4361 **Tel:** 1 830 693-5551.
Web site: http://www.kbeyfm.com
Profile: KBEY-FM is a commercial station owned by Two Way Communications, LLC. The format of the station is classic country. KBEY-FM broadcasts to the Austin, TX area at 103.9 FM.
FM RADIO STATION

KBEZ-FM
39547
Owner: E.W. Scripps Co.
Editorial: 4590 E 29th St, Tulsa, Oklahoma 74114-6208 **Tel:** 1 918 743-7814.
Web site: http://www.929thedrive.com
Profile: KBEZ-FM is a commercial station owned by E.W. Scripps Co. The format of the station is classic hits. KBEZ-FM broadcasts to the Tulsa, OK area at 92.9 FM. The station's slogan is, "Tulsa's classic hits."
FM RADIO STATION

KBFB-FM
41747
Owner: Urban One, Inc.
Editorial: 13760 Noel Rd Ste 1100, Dallas, Texas 75240-1383 **Tel:** 1 972 331-5400.
Web site: http://thebeatdfw.com
Profile: KBFB-FM is a commercial station owned by Urban One, Inc. The format of the station is rhythmic Top 40/CHR music. KBFB-FM broadcasts to the Dallas area at 97.9 FM.
FM RADIO STATION

KBFC-FM
44577
Owner: Forrest City Broadcasting Co.
Editorial: 501 E Broadway St, Forrest City, Arkansas 72335-3801 **Tel:** 1 870 633-1252.
Email: radio@arkansas.net
Web site: http://arkradio.com
Profile: KBFC-FM is a commercial station owned by Forrest City Broadcasting Co. The format of the station is classic and contemporary country. KBFC-FM broadcasts to the Forrest City, AR area at 93.5 FM.
FM RADIO STATION

KBFF-FM
44977
Owner: Alpha Media
Editorial: 1211 SW 5th Ave Ste 600, Portland, Oregon 97204-3706 **Tel:** 1 503 243-7595.
Web site: http://www.live955.com
Profile: KBFF-FM is a commercial station owned by Alpha Media. The format of the station is Hot AC. KBFF-FM broadcasts to the Portland, OR area at 95.5 FM.
FM RADIO STATION

KBFI-AM
34883
Owner: Blue Sky Broadcasting Inc.
Editorial: 6821 Main St Ste 5, Bonners Ferry, Idaho 83805-8552 **Tel:** 1 208 263-0953.
Profile: KBFI-AM is a commercial station owned by Blue Sky Broadcasting. The format of the station is news, sports and talk. KBFI-AM broadcast to the Sandpoint, ID area at 1450 AM.
AM RADIO STATION

KBFL-AM
36185
Owner: Meyer Communications
Editorial: 3000 E Chestnut Expy, Springfield, Missouri 65802-2528 **Tel:** 1 417 862-3751.
Web site: http://www.kbflfm.com
Profile: KBFL-AM is a commercial station owned by Meyer Communications. The format of the station is smooth jazz. KBFL-AM broadcasts to the Springfield, MO area at 1060 AM.
AM RADIO STATION

KBFL-FM
39548
Owner: Meyer Communications
Editorial: 3000 E Chestnut Expy, Springfield, Missouri 65802-2528 **Tel:** 1 417 862-3751.
Email: manager@radiospringfield.com
Web site: http://www.kbflfm.com
Profile: KBFL-FM is a commercial station owned by Meyer Communications. The format of the station is adult standards. KBFL-FM broadcasts to the Springfield, MO area at 99.9 FM.
FM RADIO STATION

KBFM-FM
39549
Owner: iHeartMedia Inc.
Editorial: 901 E Pike Blvd, Weslaco, Texas 78596-4937 **Tel:** 1 956 973-9202.
Web site: http://www.wild104.net
Profile: KBFM-FM is a commercial station owned by iHeartMedia Inc. The format of the station is Top 40/CHR music. KBFM-FM broadcasts to the Weslaco, TX area at 104.1 FM.
FM RADIO STATION

KBFO-FM
63916
Owner: Armada Media Corp.
Editorial: 3304 S Highway 281, Aberdeen, South Dakota 57401-8792 **Tel:** 1 605 229-3632.
Email: aberdeenproduction@hubcityradio.com
Web site: http://www.hubcityradio.com/point
Profile: KBFO-FM is a commercial station owned by Armada Media Corp. The format of the station is hot adult contemporary. KBFO-FM broadcasts to the Aberdeen, SD area at 106.7 FM.
FM RADIO STATION

KBFP-AM
38510
Owner: iHeartMedia Inc.
Editorial: 1100 Mohawk St Ste 280, Bakersfield, California 93309-7417 **Tel:** 1 661 322-9929.
Web site: http://comedy800.iheart.com
Profile: KBFP-AM is a commercial station owned by iHeartMedia Inc. The format of the station is comedy. KBFP-AM broadcasts to the Bakersfield, CA area at 800 AM.
AM RADIO STATION

KBFP-FM
39609
Owner: iHeartMedia Inc.
Editorial: 1100 Mohawk St Ste 280, Bakersfield, California 93309-7417 **Tel:** 1 661 322-9929.
Web site: http://lapreciosa1053.iheart.com
Profile: KBFP-FM is a commercial station owned by iHeartMedia Inc. The format of the station is Hispanic oldies. KBFP-FM broadcasts to the Bakersfield, CA area at 105.3 FM.
FM RADIO STATION

KBFS-AM
39460
Owner: Ultimate Caps, Inc.
Editorial: 707 Harding St, Belle Fourche, South Dakota 57717-1402 **Tel:** 1 605 892-2571.
Web site: http://www.kbfs.com
Profile: KBFS-AM is a commercial station owned by Ultimate Caps, Inc. The format of the station is farm, talk, sports and country music. KBFS-AM broadcasts to the Belle Fourche, SD area at 1450 AM.
AM RADIO STATION

KBFX-FM
44722
Owner: iHeartMedia Inc.
Editorial: 800 E Dimond Blvd Ste 3-370, Anchorage, Alaska 99515-2058 **Tel:** 1 907 522-1515.
Web site: http://1005thefox.iheart.com
Profile: KBFX-FM is a commercial station owned by iHeartMedia Inc. The format of the station is classic rock music. KBFX-FM broadcasts to the Anchorage, AK area at 100.5 FM.
FM RADIO STATION

KBGB-FM
831260
Owner: Crain Media Group, LLC
Editorial: 111 N Spring St, Searcy, Arkansas 72143-7712 **Tel:** 1 501 268-7123.
Web site: http://www.crainmedia.com
Profile: KBGB-FM is a commercial station owned by Crain Media Group, LLC. The format of the station is contemporary country. KBGB-FM broadcasts to the Kensett, AR area at a frequency of 105.7 FM.
FM RADIO STATION

KBGG-AM
38416
Owner: Cumulus Media Inc
Editorial: 4143 109th St, Urbandale, Iowa 50322-7925
Tel: 1 515 331-9200.
Web site: http://martyandmiller.com
Profile: KBGG-AM is a commercial station owned by Cumulus Media Inc. The format of the station is talk/sports. KBGG-AM broadcasts to the Des Moines, IA area at 1700 AM.
AM RADIO STATION

KBGL-FM
73621
Owner: Hull Broadcasting
Editorial: 1200 Baker Ave, Great Bend, Kansas 67530-4523 **Tel:** 1 620 792-3647.
Web site: http://www.kbglfm.com
Profile: KBGL-FM is a commercial station owned by Hull Broadcasting. The format of the station is CHR. KBGL-FM broadcasts to the Great Bend, KS area on 106.9 FM.
FM RADIO STATION

KBGN-AM
35844
Owner: Wilson(Nelson & Karen)
Editorial: 3303 E Chicago St, Caldwell, Idaho 83605
Tel: 1 208 459-3635.
Email: kbgn@kbgnradio.com
Web site: http://www.kbgnradio.com
Profile: KBGN-AM is a commercial station owned by Nelson and Karen Wilson. The format of the station is Christian music and talk. KBGN-AM broadcasts to the Caldwell, ID area at 1060 AM.
AM RADIO STATION

KBGO-FM 39797
Owner: iHeartMedia Inc.
Editorial: 314 W State Highway 6, Waco, Texas 76712-3971 **Tel:** 1 254 776-3900.
Web site: http://www.oldies95online.com
Profile: KBGO-FM is a commercial station owned by iHeartMedia Inc. The format of the station is oldies. KBGO-FM broadcasts to the Waco, TX area at 95.7 FM.
FM RADIO STATION

KBGX-FM 238624
Owner: Mahalo Broadcasting
Editorial: 74-5605 Luhia St, Ste B7, Kailua Kona, Hawaii 96740 **Tel:** 1 808 329-8090.
Email: info@lava105.com
Web site: http://www.lava105.com
Profile: KBGX-FM is a commercial station owned by Maholo Broadcasting. The format for the station is oldies. KBGX-FM broadcasts to Kailua Kona, HI area at 105.3 FM.
FM RADIO STATION

KBGZ-FM 556934
Owner: Ruby Radio Corp.
Tel: 1 775 777-1196.
Email: news@rubyradio.fm
Web site: http://www.bigcountry.fm
Profile: KBGZ-FM is a commercial station owned by Ruby Radio Corp. The format of the station is contemporary country. KBGZ-FM broadcasts to the Spring Creek, NV area at a frequency of 103.9 FM.
FM RADIO STATION

KBHB-AM 37148
Owner: Homeslice Media Group
Editorial: 1612 Junction Ave Ste 1, Sturgis, South Dakota 57785-2166 **Tel:** 1 605 347-4455.
Email: info@kbhbradio.com
Web site: http://www.kbhbradio.com
Profile: KBHB-AM is a commercial station owned by New Rushmore Radio. The format of the station is an eclectic mix of country music, news and agriculture reporting. KBHB-AM broadcasts to the Rapid City, SD area at 810 AM.
AM RADIO STATION

KBHC-AM 37190
Owner: Southwest Arkansas Radio
Editorial: 1513 S 4th St, Nashville, Arkansas 71852-3012 **Tel:** 1 870 845-3601.
Email: operations@southwestarkansasradio.com
Web site: http://www.southwestarkansasradio.com
Profile: KBHC-AM is a commercial station owned by Southwest Arkansas Radio. The format of the station is regional Mexican music. KBHC-AM broadcasts to the Nashville, AR area at 1260 AM.
AM RADIO STATION

KBHI-FM 514108
Owner: Dana Withers
Editorial: 1 Industrial Dr., Sikeston, Missouri 63801-2943 **Tel:** 1 573 471-2000.
Email: kbxb@withersradio.net
Web site: http://rock107.fm
Profile: KBHI-FM is a commercial station owned by Dana Withers. The format of the station is rock music. KBHI-FM broadcasts to the Sikeston, MO area at 107.1 FM.
FM RADIO STATION

KBHL-FM 41421
Owner: Christian Heritage Broadcasting
Editorial: 402 E Pike St, Osakis, Minnesota 56360-8346 **Tel:** 1 320 859-3000.
Email: mail@praisefm.org
Web site: http://www.praisefm.org
Profile: KBHL-FM is a non-commercial station owned by Christian Heritage Broadcasting. The format of the station is contemporary Christian music. KBHL-FM broadcasts in the Osakis, MN area at 103.9 FM.
FM RADIO STATION

KBHP-FM 45767
Owner: Hubbard Broadcasting Inc.
Editorial: 502 Beltrami Ave NW, Bemidji, Minnesota 56601-3010 **Tel:** 1 218 444-1500.
Web site: http://www.kb101fm.com
Profile: KBHP-FM is a commercial station owned by Hubbard Broadcasting Inc. The format of the station is country music. KBHP-FM broadcasting in the Bemidji, MN area at 101.1 FM.
FM RADIO STATION

KBHR-FM 43129
Owner: Parallel Broadcasting Inc.
Editorial: 649 W Country Club, Big Bear City, California 92314 **Tel:** 1 909 584-5247.
Email: news@kbhr933.com
Web site: http://www.kbhr933.com
Profile: KBHR-FM is a commercial station owned by Parallel Broadcasting Inc. The format of the station is adult album alternative. KBHR-FM broadcasts to the Big Bear City, CA area at 93.3 FM.
FM RADIO STATION

KBHT-FM 44984
Owner: M & M Broadcasters
Editorial: 5501 Bagby Ave, Waco, Texas 76711-2300 **Tel:** 1 254 772-0930.
Web site: http://www.mymagic1045.com
Profile: KBHT-FM is a commercial station owned by M & M Broadcasters. The format of the station is urban adult contemporary. KBHT-FM broadcasts to the Waco, TX area at 104.5 FM.
FM RADIO STATION

KBHW-FM 41180
Owner: Heartland Christian Broadcasters Inc.
Editorial: 4090 Highway 11, International Falls, Minnesota 56649 **Tel:** 1 218 285-7398.
Email: studio@psalmfm.org
Web site: http://www.psalmfm.org
Profile: KBHW-FM is a non-commercial station owned by Heartland Christian Broadcasters Inc. The format of the station is contemporary Christian music. KBHW-FM broadcasts to the International Falls, MN area at 99.5 FM.
FM RADIO STATION

KBHZ-FM 42912
Owner: Christian Heritage Broadcasting
Editorial: 402 E Pike St, Osakis, Minnesota 56360-8346 **Tel:** 1 320 859-3000.
Email: mail@praisefm.org
Web site: http://praisefm.org
Profile: KBHZ-FM is a non-commercial station owned by Christian Heritage Broadcasting. The format of the station is contemporary Christian music and talk. KBHZ-FM broadcasts to the Osakis, MN area at 91.9 FM.
FM RADIO STATION

KBIB-AM 36047
Owner: Hispanic Community College
Editorial: 290 N Santa Clara Rd, Marion, Texas 78124-2047 **Tel:** 1 830 914-2083.
Web site: http://kbibradio.org
Profile: KBIB-AM is a non-commercial station owned by Hispanic Community College. The format of the station is Hispanic religious programming. KBIB-AM broadcasts to the Marion, TX area at 1000 AM.
AM RADIO STATION

KBIC-FM 46837
Owner: Christian Ministries of the Valley Inc.
Editorial: 2720 W Business 83, Weslaco, Texas 78596-1225 **Tel:** 1 956 968-7777.
Email: informacion@radiovida.com
Web site: http://www.radiovida.com
Profile: KBIC-FM is a commercial station owned by Christian Ministries of the Valley Inc. The format of the station is Hispanic religious programming. KBIC-FM broadcasts to the Weslaco, TX area at 105.7 FM.
FM RADIO STATION

KBIE-FM 46723
Owner: Flood Communications
Editorial: 814 Central Ave, Nebraska City, Nebraska 68410-2409 **Tel:** 1 402 873-3348.
Email: b103@b103.fm
Web site: http://www.bigappleradio.am
Profile: KBIE-FM is a commercial station owned by Flood Communications. The format of the station is contemporary country music. KBIE-FM broadcasts to the Auburn, NE area at 103.1 FM.
FM RADIO STATION

KBIF-AM 34885
Owner: Gore-Overgaard Broadcasting Inc.
Editorial: 3401 W Holland Ave, Fresno, California 93722-4197 **Tel:** 1 559 222-0900.
Email: kbif@900kbif.com
Web site: http://900kbif.com
Profile: KBIF-AM is a commercial station owned by Gore-Overgaard Broadcasting Inc. The format of the station is Asian and Indian variety. KBIF-AM broadcasts to the Fresno, CA area at 900 AM.
AM RADIO STATION

KBIG-FM 39553
Owner: iHeartMedia Inc.
Editorial: 3400 W Olive Ave Ste 550, Burbank, California 91505-5544 **Tel:** 1 818 559-2252.
Web site: http://1043myfm.iheart.com
Profile: KBIG-FM is a commercial station owned by iHeartMedia Inc. The format of the station is hot adult contemporary. KBIG-FM broadcasts to the Los Angeles area at 104.3 FM.
FM RADIO STATION

KBIK-FM 44700
Owner: My Town Media, Inc.
Editorial: 309 N Penn Ave, Independence, Kansas 67301-3325 **Tel:** 1 620 331-3000.
Web site: http://www.indy1029.com
Profile: KBIK-FM is a commercial station owned by My Town Media, Inc. The format is contemporary country. KBIK-FM broadcasts to the Independence, KS area at 102.9 FM.
FM RADIO STATION

KBIM-FM 44578
Owner: Noalmark Broadcasting Corp.
Editorial: 1301 N Main St, Roswell, New Mexico 88201-5013 **Tel:** 1 575 623-9100.
Web site: http://kbimradio.com/
Profile: KBIM-FM is a commercial station owned by Noalmark Broadcasting Corp. The format of the station is contemporary country. KBIM-FM broadcasts to the Roswell, NM area at 94.9 FM.
FM RADIO STATION

KBIQ-FM 42882
Owner: Salem Media Group, Inc.
Editorial: 7150 Campus Dr Ste 150, Colorado Springs, Colorado 80920-3157 **Tel:** 1 719 531-5438.
Web site: http://www.kbiqradio.com
Profile: KBIQ-FM is a commercial station owned by Salem Media Group, Inc. The format of the station is contemporary Christian. KBIQ-FM broadcasts to the Colorado Springs, CO area at 102.7 FM.
FM RADIO STATION

KBIU-FM 44579
Owner: Cumulus Media
Editorial: 425 Broad St, Lake Charles, Louisiana 70601-4225 **Tel:** 1 337 439-3300.
Web site: http://www.kbiu.com
Profile: KBIU-FM is a commercial station owned by Cumulus Media. The format of the station is Rhythmic CHR. KBIU-FM broadcasts to the Lake Charles, LA area at a frequency of 103.3 FM.
FM RADIO STATION

KBIZ-AM 37192
Owner: Ottumwa Radio.
Editorial: 416 E Main St, Ottumwa, Iowa 52501-3026 **Tel:** 1 641 684-5563.
Web site: http://www.kbizam.com
Profile: KBIZ-AM is a commercial station owned by Ottumwa Radio. The format for the station is talk. KBIZ-AM broadcasts to the Ottumwa, IA/Kirksville, MO area at 1240 AM.
AM RADIO STATION

KBJA-AM 318636
Owner: United Broadcasting Company, Inc.
Editorial: 10348 S Redwood Rd, South Jordan, Utah 84095-9339 **Tel:** 1 801 254-7699.
Email: super@kbja1640.com
Web site: http://www.kbja1640.com
Profile: KBJA-AM is a commercial station owned by United Broadcasting Company, Inc. The format of the station is talk and news. KBJA-AM broadcasts to the South Jordan, UT area at 1640 AM.
AM RADIO STATION

KBJD-AM 37125
Owner: Salem Media Group, Inc.
Editorial: 3131 S Vaughn Way Ste 601, Aurora, Colorado 80014-3510 **Tel:** 1 303 750-5687.
Email: news@710knus.com
Web site: http://www.1650radioluz.com
Profile: KBJD-AM is a commercial station owned by Salem Media Group, Inc. The format of the station is Spanish Christian. KBJD-AM broadcasts to the Aurora, CO area at 1650 AM.
AM RADIO STATION

KBJK-FM 43877
Owner: Huth Broadcasting Inc.
Editorial: 2654 Cramer Ln, Chico, California 95928-8838 **Tel:** 1 530 592-4299.
Profile: KBJK-FM is a commercial station owned by Huth Broadcasting. The format for the station is adult hits. KBJK-FM broadcasts to the Chico, CA area at 100.3 FM.
FM RADIO STATION

KBJM-AM 34886
Owner: Media Associates Inc.
Editorial: 500 1st Ave E, Lemmon, South Dakota 57638-1506 **Tel:** 1 605 374-5747.
Email: kbjm1400@sdplains.com
Web site: http://kbjm.com
Profile: KBJM-AM is a commercial station owned by Media Associates Inc. The format of the station is classic country. KBJM-AM broadcasts to the Lemmon, SD area at 1400 AM.
AM RADIO STATION

KBJS-FM 41241
Owner: Shivery(Bob)
Editorial: 406 Nacogdoches St, Jacksonville, Texas 75766-2440 **Tel:** 1 903 586-5257.
Email: info@kbjs.org
Web site: http://www.kbjs.org
Profile: KBJS (90.3 FM) is a radio station broadcasting a Christian Radio/Talk format with Family Programming, News & Information from a Christian perspective. It is licensed to Jacksonville, Texas, the station serves the Tyler-Longview area. The station is currently owned by East Texas Media Association, Inc. The station can be emailed through the website.
FM RADIO STATION

KBJT-AM 38818
Owner: KBJT, Inc.
Editorial: 303 N Spring St, Fordyce, Arkansas 71742-3317 **Tel:** 1 870 352-7137.
Email: kbjt@coatesmedia.com
Web site: http://www.kbjtkq.com
Profile: KBJT-AM is a commercial station owned by KBJT, Inc. The format of the station is news and talk. KBJT-AM broadcasts in the Fordyce, AR area at 1590 AM.
AM RADIO STATION

KBKB-AM 37193
Owner: Pritchard Broadcasting Co.
Editorial: 610 N 4th St Ste 300, Burlington, Iowa 52601-5059 **Tel:** 1 319 752-5402.
Email: news@burlingtonradio.com
Web site: http://www.bigcountry1031.com
Profile: KBKB-AM is a commercial station owned by Pritchard Broadcasting Co. The format of the station is Sports. KBKB-AM broadcasts to the Burlington, IA area at 1360 AM.
AM RADIO STATION

KBKB-FM 44580
Owner: Titan Broadcasting LLC
Editorial: 610 N 4th St Ste 310, Burlington, Iowa 52601-5059 **Tel:** 1 319 752-2701.
Email: production@titanburlington.com
Web site: http://www.1017thebull.com
Profile: KBKB-FM is a commercial station owned by Titan Broadcasting LLC. The format of the station is country. KBKB-FM broadcasts to the Burlington, IA area at 107.1 FM.
FM RADIO STATION

KBKG-FM 45827
Owner: Adkins(Jim)
Editorial: 501 Bryan Ave, Corning, Arkansas 72422-3262 **Tel:** 1 870 857-6646.
Email: lite93fm@isainet.com
Web site: http://www.moremusic93.com
Profile: KBKG-FM is a commercial station owned by Jim Adkins. The format of the station is classic hits. KBKG-FM broadcasts to the Corning, AR area at 93.5 FM.
FM RADIO STATION

KBKK-FM 43987
Owner: Mapleton Communications
Editorial: 92 W Shamrock Ave, Pineville, Louisiana 71360-6435 **Tel:** 1 318 487-1035.
Email: dixie@lagniappebroadcasting.com
Web site: http://www.1055kbuck.com
Profile: KBKK-FM is a commercial station owned by Opus Broadcasting of Alexandria, LLC. The format of the station is country music. KBKK-FM broadcasts to the Alexandria, LA area at 105.5 FM.
FM RADIO STATION

KBKL-FM 42586
Owner: Townsquare Media, Inc.
Editorial: 315 Kennedy Ave, Grand Junction, Colorado 81501-7552 **Tel:** 1 970 242-7788.
Email: kool1079@cumulus.com
Web site: http://kool1079.com
Profile: KBKL-FM is a commercial station owned by Townsquare Media, Inc. The format of the station is oldies music. KBKL-FM broadcasts in the Grand Junction, CO area at 107.9 FM.
FM RADIO STATION

KBKR-AM 37194
Owner: Pacific Empire Communications
Editorial: 2510 Cove Ave, La Grande, Oregon 97850-3911 **Tel:** 1 541 963-4121.
Web site: http://supertalknews.com/
Profile: KBKR-AM is a commercial station owned by Pacific Empire Communications. The format of the station is talk. KLBM-AM broadcasts in the La Grande, OR area at 1490 AM and is a simulcast of KLBM-AM. The station prefers to be contacted via its contact from here: http://supertalknews.com/contact-us/.
AM RADIO STATION

KBKS-FM 44875
Owner: iHeartMedia Inc.
Editorial: 645 Elliott Ave W #400, Seattle, Washington 98119-3911 **Tel:** 1 206 494-2000.
Email: pd@kissfmseattle.com
Web site: http://www.kissfmseattle.com
Profile: KBKS-FM is a commercial station owned by iHeartMedia Inc. The format of the station is Top 40/CHR. KBKS-FM broadcasts to the Seattle area at 106.1 FM.
FM RADIO STATION

KBKW-AM 37185
Owner: Jodesha Broadcasting Inc.
Editorial: 1520 Simpson Ave, Aberdeen, Washington 98520-4708 **Tel:** 1 360 533-3000.
Email: news@kbkw.com
Web site: http://www.kbkw.com
Profile: KBKW-AM is a commercial station owned by Jodesha Broadcasting Inc. The format of the station is news and talk. KBKW-AM broadcasts to the Aberdeen, WA area at 1450 AM.
AM RADIO STATION

KBKY-FM 87140
Owner: KM Communications Inc.
Editorial: 1850 Yosemite Pkwy, Merced, California 95341-5213 **Tel:** 1 209 726-1351.
Profile: KBKY-FM is a commercial station owned by KM Communications Inc. The format of the station is Spanish religious. KBKY-FM broadcasts to the Merced, CA area at 94.1 FM.
FM RADIO STATION

KBKZ-FM 760132
Owner: Phillips Broadcasting Inc
Editorial: 100 Fisher Dr, Trinidad, Colorado 81082-3919 **Tel:** 1 719 846-3355.
Email: kcrt@comcast.net
Web site: http://www.kcrtradio.com/kbkz
Profile: KBKZ-FM is a commercial station owned by Phillips Broadcasting Inc. The format of the station is contemporary country. KBKZ-FM broadcasts to the Trinidad, CO area at 96.5 FM.
FM RADIO STATION

KBLA-AM 34920
Owner: Multicultural Radio Broadcasting Inc.
Editorial: 12145 Woodruff Ave, Downey, California 90241-5605 **Tel:** 1 626 844-8882.
Web site: http://www.radiozion.net/
Profile: KBLA-AM is a commercial station owned by Multicultural Radio Broadcasting Inc. The format of the station is Spanish religious. KBLA-AM broadcasts to the Los Angeles area at 1580 AM. The station does not accept press releases.
AM RADIO STATION

KBLB-FM 79653
Owner: Hubbard Broadcasting Inc.
Editorial: 13225 Dogwood Dr, Baxter, Minnesota 56425-8669 **Tel:** 1 218 828-1244.
Email: B933@hubbardradio.com
Web site: http://www.todaysbestcountry.com

Profile: KBLB-FM is a commercial station owned by Hubbard Broadcasting Inc. The format of the station is contemporary country music. KBLB-FM broadcasts in the Minneapolis area at 93.3 FM.
FM RADIO STATION

KBLC-FM 552127
Owner: Houston Christian Broadcasters
Editorial: 2424 South Blvd, Houston, Texas 77098-5110 **Tel:** 1 713 520-5200.
Email: email@khcb.org
Web site: http://www.khcb.org
Profile: KBLC-FM is non-commercial station owned by Houston Christian Broadcasters. The format of the station is Christian music and religious talk. KBLC-FM broadcasts to the Fredericksburg Houston area at 91.5 FM and simulcasts on KHCB-FM.
FM RADIO STATION

KBLD-FM 43770
Owner: Calvary Chapel of Tri-Cities
Editorial: 10611 W Clearwater Ave, Kennewick, Washington 99336-8621 **Tel:** 1 509 619-7007.
Email: kbldthetree@gmail.com
Web site: http://www.kbld.com
Profile: KBLD-FM is a non-commercial station owned by Calvary Chapel of Tri-Cities. The format of the station is Christian music and talk. KBLD-FM broadcasts in the Kennewick, WA area at 91.7 FM.
FM RADIO STATION

KBLE-AM 34887
Owner: Sacred Heart Radio
Editorial: 7357 148th Ave NE, Redmond, Washington 98052-4148 **Tel:** 1 425 867-2340.
Email: info@sacredheartradio.org
Web site: http://www.sacredheartradio.org
Profile: KBLE-AM is a non-commercial station owned by Sacred Heart Radio. The format of the station is religious. KBLE-AM broadcasts to the Kirkland, WA area at 1050 AM.
AM RADIO STATION

KBLG-AM 38546
Owner: Connoisseur Media LLC
Editorial: 2075 Central Ave, Billings, Montana 59102
Tel: 1 406 248-7777.
Web site: http://www.kblg910.com
Profile: KBLG-AM is a commercial station owned by Connoisseur Media LLC. The format of the station is news, talk and sports. KBLG-AM broadcasts in the Billings, MT area at 910 AM.
AM RADIO STATION

KBLJ-AM 39276
Owner: Cherry Creek Radio
Editorial: 116 Dalton Ave, La Junta, Colorado 81050
Tel: 1 719 384-5456.
Email: kblj@secom.net
Web site: http://www.cherrycreekradio.com
Profile: KBLJ-AM is a commercial station owned by Cherry Creek Radio. The format of the station is oldies. KBLJ-AM broadcasts to the La Junta, CO area at 1400 AM.
AM RADIO STATION

KBLL-FM 44582
Owner: Cherry Creek Radio
Editorial: 110 E Broadway St, Helena, Montana 59601-4232 **Tel:** 1 406 442-6620.
Email: ebaker@cherrycreekradio.com
Web site: http://www.995kbllfm.com
Profile: KBLL-FM is a commercial station owned by Cherry Creek Radio. The format of the station is country music. KBLL-FM broadcasts in the Helena, MT area at 99.5 FM.
FM RADIO STATION

KBLP-FM 41129
Owner: South Central Broadcasting & Advertising
Editorial: 204 S Main St, Lindsay, Oklahoma 73052-5634 **Tel:** 1 405 756-4438.
Web site: http://www.kblpradio.com
Profile: KBLP-FM is a commercial station owned by South Central Oklahoma Broadcasting & Advertising. The format of the station is country music. KBLP-FM broadcasts to the Oklahoma City area at 105.1 FM.
FM RADIO STATION

KBLQ-FM 45700
Owner: Cache Valley Radio Inc.
Editorial: 810 W 200 N, Logan, Utah 84321
Tel: 1 435 752-1390.
Email: kblq@cvradio.com
Web site: http://www.q92.fm
Profile: KBLQ-FM is a commercial station owned by Cache Valley Radio Inc. The format of the station is adult contemporary music. KBLQ-FM broadcasts to the Salt Lake City area at 92.9 FM.
FM RADIO STATION

KBLR-FM 64001
Owner: Walnut Radio, LLC
Editorial: 5011 Capitol Ave, Omaha, Nebraska 68132-2921 **Tel:** 1 402 342-2000.
Profile: KBLR-FM is a commercial station owned by Walnut Radio, LLC.The format of the show is country music. KBLR-FM broadcasts to the Blair, NE area at 97.3 FM.
FM RADIO STATION

KBLS-FM 42064
Owner: Morris Communications
Editorial: 200 N Broadway St, Abilene, Kansas 67410-2647 **Tel:** 1 785 263-3422.
Web site: http://www.sunny1025.com
Profile: KBLS-FM is a commercial station owned by Morris Communications. The format of the station is adult contemporary music. KBLS-FM broadcasts in the Salina, KS area at 102.5 FM.
FM RADIO STATION

KBLU-AM 37197
Owner: El Dorado Broadcasting
Editorial: 755 W 28th St, Yuma, Arizona 85364
Tel: 1 928 344-4980.
Web site: http://www.kbluam.com
Profile: KBLU-AM is a commercial station owned by El Dorado Broadcasting. The format of the station is news, sports and talk. KBLU-AM broadcasts to the Yuma, AZ area at 560 AM.
AM RADIO STATION

KBLX-FM 42261
Owner: Entercom Communications Corp.
Editorial: 201 3rd St Ste 1200, San Francisco, California 94103-3143 **Tel:** 1 415 777-0965.
Email: kblxcomments@entercom.com
Web site: http://www.kblx.com
Profile: KBLX-FM is a commercial station owned by Entercom Communications Corp.. The format of the station is urban adult contemporary music. KBLX-FM broadcasts to the San Francisco area at 102.9 FM.
FM RADIO STATION

KBLZ-FM 73564
Owner: Reynolds Radio Inc.
Editorial: 212 Old Grande Blvd Ste B100, Tyler, Texas 75703-4201 **Tel:** 1 903 581-5259.
Web site: http://www.theblaze.fm
Profile: KBLZ is a commercial station owned by Reynolds Radio Inc. The format of the station is urban contemporary music. KBLZ-FM broadcasts to Tyler, TX at 102.7 FM.
FM RADIO STATION

KBMB-AM 81023
Owner: Entravision Communications Corp.
Editorial: 501 N 44th St Ste 425, Phoenix, Arizona 85008-6587 **Tel:** 1 602 776-1400.
Web site: http://www.espnradio710am.com
Profile: KBMB-AM is a commercial station owned by Entravision Communications Corp. The format of the station is Hispanic sports programming. KBMB-AM broadcasts to the Phoenix area at 710 AM.
AM RADIO STATION

KBME-AM 37084
Owner: iHeartMedia Inc.
Editorial: 2000 West Loop S Ste 300, Houston, Texas 77027-3510 **Tel:** 1 713 212-8000.
Web site: http://www.sports790.com
Profile: KBME-AM is a commercial station owned by iHeartMedia Inc. The format of the station is sports. KBME-AM broadcasts to the Houston area at 790 AM.
AM RADIO STATION

KBMG-FM 328199
Owner: Alpha Media
Editorial: 2722 S Redwood Rd, Salt Lake City, Utah 84119-8409 **Tel:** 1 801 908-8777.
Web site: http://www.adelantemediagroup.com
Profile: KBMG-FM is a commercial station owned by Alpha Media. The format of the station is Bilingual Top 40/CHR. KBMG-FM broadcasts to the Salt Lake City area at 106.3 FM.
FM RADIO STATION

KBMI-FM 44286
Owner: Cherry Creek Radio
Editorial: 110 E Broadway St, Helena, Montana 59601-4232 **Tel:** 1 406 442-6620.
Email: ebaker@cherrycreekradio.com
Web site: http://www.theb104.com
Profile: KBMI-FM is a commercial station owned by Cherry Creek Radio. The format of the station is hot adult contemporary. KBMI-FM broadcasts in the Helena, MT area at 104.1 FM.
FM RADIO STATION

KBMO-AM 37198
Owner: Headwaters Media
Tel: 1 320 235-1194.
Email: info@kkln.com
Profile: KBMO-AM is a commercial station owned by Headwaters Media. The format of the station is adult standards. KBMO-AM broadcasts to the Benson, MN area at 1290 AM.
AM RADIO STATION

KBMP-FM 457296
Owner: Bott Broadcasting Co.
Editorial: 10550 Barkley St Ste 100, Overland Park, Kansas 66212-1824 **Tel:** 1 913 642-7770.
Web site: http://www.bottradionetwork.com
Profile: KBMP-FM is a commercial station owned by Bott Broadcasting Co. The format of the station is religious programming. KBMP-FM broadcasts to the Overland Park, KS area at 90.5 FM.
FM RADIO STATION

KBMQ-FM 842418
Owner: Media Ministries, Inc.
Editorial: 130 N. 2nd Street, Ste. C, Monroe, Louisiana 71201-6749 **Tel:** 1 318 387-1230.
Email: info@kbmq.org
Web site: http://www.kbmq.org
Profile: KBMQ-FM is a non-commercial station owned by Media Ministries, Inc. The format of the station is Contemporary Christian. KBMQ-FM broadcasts to the Monroe, LA area at a frequency of 88.7 FM.
FM RADIO STATION

KBMR-AM 36995
Owner: iHeartMedia Inc.
Editorial: 3500 E Rosser Ave, Bismarck, North Dakota 58501-3376 **Tel:** 1 701 255-1234.
Web site: http://www.kbmr.com
Profile: KBMR-AM is a commercial station owned by iHeartMedia Inc. The format of the station is country music. KBMR-AM broadcasts to the Bismarck, ND area at 1130 AM.
AM RADIO STATION

KBMS-AM 35887
Owner: Christopher Bennett Broadcasting Co.
Tel: 1 360 699-1881.
Web site: http://www.kbmsradio.com
Profile: KBMS-AM is a commercial station owned by Christopher Bennett Broadcasting Co. The format of the station is urban adult contemporary. KBMS-AM broadcasts to the Vancouver, WA area at 1480 AM.
AM RADIO STATION

KBMV-FM 44584
Owner: E-Communications LLC.
Editorial: 10 Court Sq, West Plains, Missouri 65775-3444 **Tel:** 1 417 255-2548.
Email: eckman@centurytel.net
Web site: http://khomthetrain.com
Profile: KBMV-FM is a commercial station owned by E-Communications LLC. The format of the station is Christian music and talk. KBMV-FM broadcasts to the Springfield, MO area at 107.1 FM.
FM RADIO STATION

KBMW-AM 39344
Owner: James Ingstad Broadcast Group
Editorial: 605 Dakota Ave, Wahpeton, North Dakota 58075-4331 **Tel:** 1 701 642-8747.
Email: studio@kbmwam.com
Web site: http://www.kbmwam.com
Profile: KBMW-AM is a commercial station owned by James Ingstad Broadcast Group. The format of the station is country. KBMW-AM broadcasts to the Wahpeton, ND area at 1450 AM.
AM RADIO STATION

KBMX-FM 42518
Owner: Townsquare Media, LLC
Editorial: 14 E Central Entrance, Duluth, Minnesota 55811 **Tel:** 1 218 727-4500.
Web site: http://www.mix108.com
Profile: KBMX-FM is a commercial station owned by Townsquare Media, LLC. The format of the station is hot adult contemporary. KBMX-FM broadcasts to the Duluth, MN area at 107.7 FM.
FM RADIO STATION

KBNA-FM 44585
Owner: Univision Communications Inc.
Editorial: 2211 E Missouri Ave Ste 300, El Paso, Texas 79903-3837 **Tel:** 1 915 544-9797.
Web site: http://kbna975.univision.com
Profile: KBNA-FM is a commercial station owned by Univision Communications Inc. The format of the station is regional Mexican. KBNA-FM broadcasts to the El Paso, TX area at 97.5 FM.
FM RADIO STATION

KBND-AM 38431
Owner: Combined Communications, Inc.
Editorial: 63088 NE 18th St Ste 200, Bend, Oregon 97701-7102 **Tel:** 1 541 382-5263.
Email: talk@kbnd.com
Web site: http://www.kbnd.com
Profile: KBND-AM is a commercial station owned by Combined Communications. The format for the station is news and talk. KBND-AM broadcasts to the Bend, OR area at 1110 AM.
AM RADIO STATION

KBNH-AM 39451
Owner: Harney County Radio, LLC
Editorial: 69470 S Egan Rd, Burns, Oregon 97720-2537 **Tel:** 1 541 573-2055.
Profile: KBNH-AM is a commercial station owned by Harney County Radio, LLC. The format of the station is classic country with a mix of hits from every decade. KBNH-AM broadcasts to the Burns, OR area at 1230 AM.
AM RADIO STATION

KBNJ-FM 41554
Owner: World Radio Network, Inc.
Editorial: 3766 Saturn Rd, Corpus Christi, Texas 78413-1915 **Tel:** 1 361 855-0975.
Email: dj@kbnj.org
Web site: http://www.kbnj.org
Profile: KBNJ-FM is a non-commercial station owned by World Radio Network, Inc. The format is contemporary Christian music and talk. KBNJ-FM broadcasts in the Corpus Christi, TX area at 91.7 FM.
FM RADIO STATION

KBNL-FM 41551
Owner: Inspiracom
Editorial: 1620 E Plum St, Laredo, Texas 78043-1023
Tel: 1 956 724-9090.
Email: kbnl@inspiracom.org
Web site: http://www.kbnl.org
Profile: KBNL-FM is a non-commercial station owned by Inspiracom. The format is contemporary Christian and Hispanic. KBNL-FM broadcasts to the Laredo, TX area at 89.9 FM.
FM RADIO STATION

KBNN-AM 37342
Owner: Alpha Media
Editorial: 18553 Gentry Rd, Lebanon, Missouri 65536-5748 **Tel:** 1 417 532-9111.
Web site: http://www.myozarksonline.com
Profile: KBNN-AM is a commercial station owned by Alpha Media. The format of the station is news and talk. KBNN-AM broadcasts in the Lebanon, MO area at 750 AM.
AM RADIO STATION

KBNO-AM 38424
Owner: Latino Communications
Editorial: 600 S Grant St Ste 600, Denver, Colorado 80209-4146 **Tel:** 1 303 733-5266.
Web site: http://quebueno1280.com/
Profile: KBNO-AM is a commercial station owned by Latino Communications. The format of the station is Hispanic programming. KBNO-AM broadcasts to the Denver area at 1280 AM.
AM RADIO STATION

KBNP-AM 35804
Owner: Second Amendment Foundation
Editorial: 278 SW Arthur St, Portland, Oregon 97201-4745 **Tel:** 1 503 223-6769.
Email: kbnp@kbnp.com
Web site: http://www.kbnp.com
Profile: KBNP-AM is a commercial station owned by Second Amendment Foundation. The format of the station is business talk. KBNP-AM broadcasts to Portland, OR, at 1410 AM.
AM RADIO STATION

KBNR-FM 39556
Owner: World Radio Network, Inc.
Editorial: 901 Mexico Blvd, Brownsville, Texas 78520
Tel: 1 956 542-6933.
Email: kbnr@lwrn.org
Web site: http://www.radiokbnr.org
Profile: KBNR-FM is a non-commercial station owned by World Radio Network, Inc. The format is Hispanic religious talk and music. KBNR-FM broadcasts to the Brownsville, TX area at 88.3 FM.
FM RADIO STATION

KBNU-FM 43062
Owner: MBM Radio Uvalde LLC
Editorial: 1400 Batesville Road, Uvalde, Texas 78801
Tel: 1 830 278-3693.
Web site: http://rcommunications.com
Profile: KBNU-FM is a commercial station owned by MBM Radio Uvalde LLC. The format of the station is rock. KBNU-FM broadcasts to the San Antonio area at 93.9 FM.
FM RADIO STATION

KBNV-FM 70462
Owner: American Family Association
Editorial: 107 Parkgate Dr, Tupelo, Mississippi 38801
Tel: 1 662 844-8888.
Email: comments@afr.net
Web site: http://www.afr.net
FM RADIO STATION

KBNW-AM 543258
Owner: Horizon Broadcasting Group
Editorial: 854 NE 4th St, Bend, Oregon 97701-4711
Tel: 1 541 383-3825.
Email: news@horizonbroadcastinggroup.com
Web site: http://www.kbnwnews.com
Profile: KBNW-AM is a commerical station owned by Horizon Broadcast Group. The format for the station is news and talk. KBNW-AM broadcasts to the Bend, OR area at 1340 AM.
AM RADIO STATION

KBOA-AM 38382
Owner: Pollack Broadcasting Co.
Editorial: 1303 Southwest Drive, Kennett, Missouri 63857 **Tel:** 1 573 888-4616.
Web site: http://www.kboaradio.com
Profile: KBOA-AM is a commercial station owned by Pollack Broadcasting Co. The format of the station is adult standards. KBOA-AM broadcasts to the Kennett, MO area at 1540 AM.
AM RADIO STATION

KBOA-FM 45745
Owner: Pollack Broadcasting Co.
Editorial: 1303 Southwest Drive, Kennett, Missouri 63857 **Tel:** 1 573 888-4616.
Email: ktmo@semoradio.com
Web site: http://www.kboaradio.com
Profile: KBOA-FM is a commercial station owned by Pollack Broadcasting Co. The format of the station is hot adult contemporary music. KBOA-FM broadcasts to the Kennett, MO area at 105.5 FM.
FM RADIO STATION

KBOB-AM 39048
Owner: Townsquare Media
Editorial: 1229 Brady St, Davenport, Iowa 52803-4616 **Tel:** 1 563 326-2541.
Profile: KBOB-AM is a commercial station owned by Townsquare Media. The format of the station is classic country. KBOB-AM broadcasts to the Davenport, IA area at 1170 AM.
AM RADIO STATION

KBOB-FM 43362
Owner: Townsquare Media
Editorial: 1229 Brady St, Davenport, Iowa 52803-4616 **Tel:** 1 563 326-2541.
Web site: http://1049thehawk.com
Profile: KBOB-FM is a commercial station owned by Townsquare Media. The format of the station is

contemporary country music. KBOB-FM broadcasts to the Davenport, IA area at 104.9 FM.
FM RADIO STATION

KBOC-FM 42578

Owner: Liberman Broadcasting Inc.
Editorial: 2410 Gateway Dr, Irving, Texas 75063-2727
Tel: 1 972 652-2900.
Web site: http://la983.estrellatv.com
Profile: KBOC-FM is a commercial station owned by Liberman Broadcasting Inc. The format of the station is Spanish Hits. KBOC-FM broadcasts to the Dallas area at 98.3 FM.
FM RADIO STATION

KBOD-FM 42516

Owner: KTLO, LLC
Editorial: 620 Highway 5 N, Mountain Home, Arkansas 72653-3012 **Tel:** 1 870 425-3101.
Web site: http://www.ktlo.com
Profile: KBOD-FM is a commercial station owned by KTLO, LLC. The format of the station is country. KBOD-FM broadcasts to the Harrison, AR area at 99.7 FM.
FM RADIO STATION

KBOE-FM 44810

Owner: Jomast Corp.
Editorial: Hwy 63 North, Oskaloosa, Iowa 52577-9113
Tel: 1 641 673-3493.
Email: contact@kboeradio.com
Web site: http://www.kboeradio.com
Profile: KBOE-FM is a commercial station owned by Jomast Corp. The format of the station is contemporary country. KBOE-FM broadcasts to the Oskaloosa, IA area at 104.9 FM.
FM RADIO STATION

KBOI-AM 37202

Owner: Cumulus Media Inc
Editorial: 1419 W Bannock St, Boise, Idaho 83702-5234 **Tel:** 1 208 336-3670.
Email: 670@kboi.com
Web site: http://www.670kboi.com
Profile: KBOI-AM is a commercial station owned by Cumulus Media Inc. The format of the station is news, talk and sports. KBOI-AM broadcasts to the Boise, ID area at 670 AM.
AM RADIO STATION

KBON-FM 43292

Owner: Marx (Rose Ann)
Editorial: 109 S 2nd St, Eunice, Louisiana 70535
Tel: 1 337 546-0007.
Email: 101.1@kbon.com
Web site: http://www.kbon.com
Profile: KBON-FM is a commercial station owned by Rose Ann Marx. The format of the station is classic country. KBON-FM broadcasts in the Lafayette, LA area at 101.1 FM.
FM RADIO STATION

KBOO-FM 39557

Owner: KBOO Foundation
Editorial: 20 SE 8th Ave, Portland, Oregon 97214-1257 **Tel:** 1 503 231-8032.
Web site: http://www.kboo.fm
Profile: KBOO-FM is a non-commercial station owned by KBOO Foundation. The format of the station is variety. KBOO-FM broadcasts to the Portland, OR area at 90.7 FM.
FM RADIO STATION

KBOS-FM 45814

Owner: iHeartMedia Inc.
Editorial: 83 E Shaw Ave Ste 150, Fresno, California 93710-7622 **Tel:** 1 559 230-4300.
Web site: http://www.b95forlife.com
Profile: KBOS-FM is a commercial station owned by IHeart Media and Entertainment. The format of the station is rhythmic Top 40/CHR. KBOS-FM broadcasts to the Fresno, CA area at 94.9 FM.
FM RADIO STATION

KBOT-FM 42581

Owner: Leighton Enterprises Inc.
Editorial: 1340 Richwood Rd, Detroit Lakes, Minnesota 56501-6903 **Tel:** 1 218 847-5624.
Email: studio@catchthewave1041.com
Web site: http://www.catchthewave1041.com
Profile: KBOT-FM is a commercial station owned by Leighton Enterprises Inc. The format of the station is adult contemporary. KBOT-FM broadcasts in the Detroit Lakes, MN area at 104.1 FM.
FM RADIO STATION

KBOV-AM 38305

Owner: Great Country Broadcasting Inc.
Editorial: South Highway 395, Bishop, California 93514 **Tel:** 1 760 873-6325.
Email: kibskbov@yahoo.com
Web site: http://www.kibskbov.com
Profile: KBOV-AM is a commercial station owned by Great Country Broadcasting Inc. The format of the station is classic hits. KBOV-AM broadcasts to the Bishop, CA area at 1230 AM.
AM RADIO STATION

KBOW-AM 39056

Owner: Butte Broadcasting Inc.
Editorial: 660 Dewey Blvd, Butte, Montana 59701-3218 **Tel:** 1 406 494-7777.
Email: mail@kbowkopr.com
Web site: http://www.kbow550.net
Profile: KBOW-AM is a commercial station owned by Butte Broadcasting Inc. The format for the station is country music, news and sports. KBOW-AM broadcasts to the Butte, MT area at 550 AM.
AM RADIO STATION

KBOX-FM 39559

Owner: American General Media
Editorial: 2325 Skyway Dr, Santa Maria, California 93455-1137 **Tel:** 1 805 922-1041.
Web site: http://www.1041pirateradio.com
Profile: KBOX-FM is a commercial station owned by American General Media. The format of the station is adult hits. KBOX-FM broadcasts to the Santa Barbara, CA area at 104.1 FM.
FM RADIO STATION

KBOY-FM 42282

Owner: Mapleton Radio, LLC
Editorial: 1438 Rossanley Dr, Medford, Oregon 97501-1751 **Tel:** 1 541 779-1550.
Web site: http://www.957kboy.com
Profile: KBOY-FM is a commercial station owned by Mapleton Radio, LLC. The format of the station is classic rock music. KBOY-FM broadcasts in the Medford, OR area at 95.7 FM.
FM RADIO STATION

KBOZ-AM 37203

Owner: Reier Broadcasting Company Inc.
Editorial: 5445 Johnson Rd, Bozeman, Montana 59718-8333 **Tel:** 1 406 587-9999.
Email: themarketleader@kboz.com
Web site: http://www.kboz.com
Profile: KBOZ-AM is a commercial station owned by Reier Broadcasting Co., Inc. The format of the station is news and talk. KBOZ-AM broadcasts in the Bozeman, MT area at 1090 AM.
AM RADIO STATION

KBOZ-FM 46450

Owner: Reier Broadcasting Company Inc.
Editorial: 5445 Johnson Rd, Bozeman, Montana 59718-8333 **Tel:** 1 406 587-9999.
Email: themarketleader@kboz.com
Web site: http://www.kboz.com
Profile: KBOZ-FM is a commercial station owned by the Reier Broadcasting Co., Inc. The format of the station is country music. KBOZ-FM broadcasts in the Bozeman, MT area at 99.9 FM.
FM RADIO STATION

KBPA-FM 44645

Owner: Emmis Communications Corp.
Editorial: 8309 N Interstate 35, Austin, Texas 78753-5720 **Tel:** 1 512 832-4000.
Web site: http://www.1035bobfm.com
Profile: KBPA-FM is a commercial station owned by Emmis Communications Corp. The format of the station is adult hits. KBPA-FM broadcasts to the Austin, TX area at 103.5 FM.
FM RADIO STATION

KBPC-FM 39550

Owner: ALlied Broadcasting KBPC, LLC
Tel: 1 936 544-9350.
Email: news@kbpcfm.com
Web site: http://www.kbpcfm.com
Profile: KBPC-FM is a commercial station owned by Arlied Broadcasting and operated by Allied Broadcasting. The format of the station is country music. KBPC-FM broadcasts to the East Texas area at 93.5 FM.
FM RADIO STATION

KBPI-FM 46695

Owner: iHeartMedia Inc.
Editorial: 4695 S Monaco St, Denver, Colorado 80237-3525 **Tel:** 1 303 713-8000.
Web site: http://www.kbpi.com
Profile: KBPI-FM is a commercial station owned by iHeartMedia Inc. The format of the station is rock. KBPI-FM broadcasts to the Denver area at 106.7 FM.
FM RADIO STATION

KBPN-FM 310458

Owner: Minnesota Public Radio
Editorial: 501 W College Dr, #402, Brainerd, Minnesota 56401 **Tel:** 1 218 829-1072.
Email: newsroom@mpr.org
Web site: http://minnesota.publicradio.org/radio/stations/kbpnkbpr
Profile: KBPN-FM is a non-commercial station owned by Minnesota Public Radio. The station of the station is news and talk. KBPN-FM broadcasts to the Brainerd, MN area at 88.3 FM.
FM RADIO STATION

KBPR-FM 41132

Owner: Minnesota Public Radio
Editorial: 501 W College Dr, #402, Brainerd, Minnesota 56401 **Tel:** 1 218 829-1072.
Email: newsroom@mpr.org
Web site: http://minnesota.publicradio.org/radio/stations/kbpnkbpr/
Profile: KBPR-FM is a non-commercial station owned by Minnesota Public Radio. The format of the station is classical. KBPR-FM broadcasts to the Brainerd, MN area at 90.7 FM.
FM RADIO STATION

KBPY-FM 740867

Owner: Chadrad Communications, Inc
Editorial: 226 Bordeaux St, Chadron, Nebraska 69337-2393 **Tel:** 1 308 432-5545.
Email: kbpy@chadrad.com
Profile: KBPY-FM is a commercial station owned by Chadrad Communications, Inc. The format of the station is rock/album-oriented rock. KBPY-FM is licensed to the Hay Springs, NE area broadcasting at a frequency of 107.7 FM.
FM RADIO STATION

KBQB-FM 42535

Owner: Results Radio Group
Editorial: 856 Manzanita Ct, Chico, California 95926
Tel: 1 530 342-2200.
Email: friendsofbob@927bobfm.com
Web site: http://www.927bobfm.com
Profile: KBQB-FM is a commercial station owned by Results Radio Group. The format of the station is adult hits. KBQB-FM broadcasts to the Chico, CA area at 92.7 FM.
FM RADIO STATION

KBQI-FM 44079

Owner: iHeartMedia Inc.
Editorial: 5411 Jefferson St NE Ste 100, Albuquerque, New Mexico 87109-3485 **Tel:** 1 505 830-6400.
Web site: http://www.bigi1079.com
Profile: KBQI-FM is a commercial station owned by iHeartMedia Inc. The format of the station is contemporary country. KBQI-FM broadcasts to the Albuquerque, NM area at 107.9 FM.
FM RADIO STATION

KBRB-AM 37205

Owner: Sandhills Broadcasting
Editorial: 122 E 2nd St, Ainsworth, Nebraska 69210
Tel: 1 402 387-1400.
Email: kbrb@sscg.net
Web site: http://www.kbrbradio.com
Profile: KBRB-AM is a commercial station owned by Sandhills Broadcasting. The format of the station is country. KBRB-AM broadcasts to the Ainsworth, NE area at 1400 AM.
AM RADIO STATION

KBRB-FM 44588

Owner: Sandhills Broadcasting
Editorial: 122 E 2nd St, Ainsworth, Nebraska 69210
Tel: 1 402 387-1400.
Email: kbrb@sscg.net
Web site: http://www.kbrbradio.com
Profile: KBRB-FM is a commercial station owned by Sandhills Broadcasting. The format of the station is classic rock. KBRB-FM broadcasts to the Ainsworth, NE area at 92.7 FM.
FM RADIO STATION

KBRC-AM 34889

Owner: J & J Broadcasting, Inc.
Editorial: 2029 Freeway Dr, Mount Vernon, Washington 98273-5470 **Tel:** 1 360 424-0660.
Email: kbrcradio@gmail.com
Web site: http://www.kbrcradio.com
Profile: KBRC-AM is a commercial station owned by J & J Broadcasting, Inc. The format of the station is classic hits. KBRC-AM broadcasts to the Mount Vernon, WA area at 1430 AM.
AM RADIO STATION

KBRD-AM 36557

Owner: BJ & Skip's For The Music Foundation
Editorial: 1849 Abernethy Rd NE, Olympia, Washington 98516-3710 **Tel:** 1 360 491-6800.
Email: kbrdpsa@gmail.com
Web site: http://www.apikai.com/kbrd
Profile: KBRD-AM is a non-commercial station owned by BJ & Skip's For The Music Foundation. The format of the station is adult standards. KBRD-AM broadcasts to the Olympia, WA area at 680 AM. Please note that they do NOT accept PSAs from outside of Thurston County, WA.
AM RADIO STATION

KBRE-FM 42914

Owner: Mapleton Radio, LLC
Editorial: 1020 W Main St, Merced, California 95340-4521 **Tel:** 1 209 723-2191.
Email: kbre@radiomerced.com
Web site: http://www.925thebear.com
Profile: KBRE-FM is a commercial station owned by Mapleton Radio, LLC. The format of the station is rock music. KBRE-FM broadcasts to the Merced, CA area at 105.7 FM.
FM RADIO STATION

KBRF-AM 37207

Owner: Lakes Radio
Editorial: 728 Western Ave, Fergus Falls, Minnesota 56537-1095 **Tel:** 1 218 736-7596.
Email: contactus@lakesradio.net
Web site: http://www.lakesradio.net
Profile: KBRF-AM is a commercial station owned by Lakes Radio. The format of the station is news and talk. KBRF-AM broadcasts to the Fergus Falls, MN area at 1250 AM.
AM RADIO STATION

KBRG-FM 43244

Owner: Univision Communications Inc.
Editorial: 50 Fremont St, San Francisco, California 94105-2278 **Tel:** 1 888 808-1003.
Web site: http://www.univision.com/san-francisco/kbrg
Profile: KBRG-FM is a commercial station owned by Univision Communications Inc. The format of the station is Spanish Adult Hits. KBRG-FM broadcasts to the San Francisco area at 100.3 FM.
FM RADIO STATION

KBRI-AM 38324

Owner: East Arkansas Broadcasters Inc.
Editorial: 1501 S. Main St., Wynne, Arkansas 72021
Tel: 1 870 734-1570.
Profile: KBRI-AM is a commercial station owned by East Arkansas Broadcasters Inc. The format of the station is country. KBRI-AM broadcasts to the Wynne, AR area at 1570 AM.
AM RADIO STATION

KBRJ-FM 44726

Owner: Alpha Media
Editorial: 301 Arctic Slope Ave Ste 200, Anchorage, Alaska 99518-3035 **Tel:** 1 907 344-9622.
Web site: http://www.kbrj.com
Profile: KBRJ-FM is a commercial station owned by Alpha Media. The format of the station is country. KBRJ-FM broadcasts to the Anchorage, AK area at 104.1 FM.
FM RADIO STATION

KBRK-AM 37208

Owner: Alpha Media
Editorial: 227 22nd Ave S, Brookings, South Dakota 57006-2827 **Tel:** 1 605 692-1430.
Email: info@brookingsradio.com
Web site: http://www.brookingsradio.com
Profile: KBRK-AM is a commercial station owned by Alpha Media. The format of the station is adult standards. KBRK-AM broadcasts to the Brookings, SD area at 1430 AM.
AM RADIO STATION

KBRK-FM 46006

Owner: Alpha Media
Editorial: 227 22nd Ave S, Brookings, South Dakota 57006-2827 **Tel:** 1 605 692-1430.
Email: info@brookingsradio.com
Web site: http://www.brookingsradio.com
Profile: KBRK-FM is a commercial station owned by Alpha Media. The format of the station is adult contemporary. KBRK-FM broadcasts to the Brookings, SD area at 93.7 FM.
FM RADIO STATION

KBRL-AM 38557

Owner: Armada Media Corp.
Editorial: 1811 W O St, McCook, Nebraska 69001-4268 **Tel:** 1 308 345-5400.
Email: production@highplainsradio.net
Web site: http://www.highplainsradio.net
Profile: KBRL-AM is a commercial station owned by Armada Media Corp. The format of the station is talk. KBRL-AM broadcasts to the McCook, NE area at 98.5 FM.
AM RADIO STATION

KBRN-AM 39406

Owner: Hill Country Broadcasting Corp
Editorial: 4501 N McColl Street, McAllen, Texas 78505 **Tel:** 1 956 781-5528.
Web site: http://radioformulasa.com
Profile: KBRN-AM is a commercial radio station owned and operated by Hill Country Broadcasting Corp. The format of the station is Hispanic religious programming. KBRN-AM Broadcasts to the Kerrville, TX area at 1500 AM.
AM RADIO STATION

KBRQ-FM 39710

Owner: iHeartMedia Inc.
Editorial: 314 W State Highway 6, Waco, Texas 76712-3971 **Tel:** 1 254 776-3900.
Web site: http://www.1025thebear.com
Profile: KBRQ-FM is a commercial station owned by iHeartMedia Inc. The format of the station is rock. KBRQ-FM broadcasts to the Waco, TX area at 102.5 FM.
FM RADIO STATION

KBRT-AM 34891

Owner: Crawford Broadcasting Co.
Editorial: 3183 Airway Ave Ste D, Costa Mesa, California 92626-4611 **Tel:** 1 714 754-4450.
Email: kbrt@sbcglobal.net
Web site: http://www.kbrt740.com
Profile: KBRT-AM is a commercial station owned by Crawford Broadcasting Co. The format of the station is Christian talk. KBRT-AM broadcasts in the Costa Mesa, CA area at 740 AM.
AM RADIO STATION

KBRU-FM 39618

Owner: iHeartMedia Inc.
Editorial: 1900 NW Expressway Ste 1000, Oklahoma City, Oklahoma 73118-1854 **Tel:** 1 405 858-1400.
Web site: http://www.947thebrew.com
Profile: KBRU-FM is a commercial station owned by iHeartMedia Inc. The format of the station is classic rock. KBRU-FM broadcasts to the Oklahoma City area at 94.7 FM.
FM RADIO STATION

KBRV-AM 38401

Owner: Old West Media, Inc.
Editorial: 225 S Main St, Soda Springs, Idaho 83276-1627 **Tel:** 1 208 547-2400.
Web site: http://mylocalradio.com/sodasprings
Profile: KBRV-AM is a commercial station owned by Old West Media, Inc. The format of the station is classic and contemporary country music. KBRV-AM broadcasts to the Salt Lake City area at 800 AM.
AM RADIO STATION

KBRW-AM 36022

Owner: Silakkuagvik Communications Inc.
Editorial: 1695 Okpik St, Barrow, Alaska 99723-9999
Tel: 1 907 852-6811.
Email: gm@kbrw.org
Web site: http://www.kbrw.org
Profile: KBRW-AM is a non-commercial station owned by Silakkuagvik Communications Inc. The

format of the station is variety. KBRW-AM broadcasts to Barrow, AK at 680 AM.
AM RADIO STATION

KBRW-FM 235318
Owner: Silakkuagvik Communications Inc.
Editorial: 1695 Okpik St, Barrow, Alaska 99723-9999
Tel: 1 907 852-6811.
Email: gm@kbrw.org
Web site: http://www.kbrw.org
Profile: KBRW-FM is a non-commercial station owned by Silakkuagvik Communications, Inc. The format of the station is talk. KBRW-FM broadcasts to Barrow, AK at 91.9 FM.
FM RADIO STATION

KBRX-AM 37209
Owner: Ranchland Broadcasting Co.
Editorial: 251 N Jefferson St, Oneill, Nebraska 68763
Tel: 1 402 336-1612.
Email: news@kbrx.com
Web site: http://www.kbrx.com
Profile: KBRX-AM is a commercial station owned by Ranchland Broadcasting Co. The format of the station is oldies. KBRX-AM broadcasts to the Oneill, NE area at 1350 AM.
AM RADIO STATION

KBRX-FM 44591
Owner: Ranchland Broadcasting Co.
Editorial: 251 N Jefferson St, Oneill, Nebraska 68763
Tel: 1 402 336-1612.
Email: news@kbrx.com
Web site: http://www.kbrx.com
Profile: KBRX-FM is a commercial station owned by Ranchland Broadcasting Co. The format of the station is classic country. KBRX-FM broadcasts to the Oneill, NE area at 102.9 FM.
FM RADIO STATION

KBRY-FM 923922
Owner: Mid Nebraska Broadcasting
Editorial: 1309 Road 11, York, Nebraska 68467-7513
Tel: 1 402 362-4433.
Profile: KBRY-FM is a commercial station owned by Mid Nebraska Broadcasting. The format of the station is country. The station broadcasts locally to the Sargent, NE area at 92.3 FM.
FM RADIO STATION

KBRZ-AM 35842
Owner: Sangeet Radio
Tel: 1 832 327-1000.
Email: info@sangeetradio.com
Web site: http://www.sangeetradio.com
Profile: KBRZ-AM is a commercial station owned by Sangeet Radio. The format of the station is Desi Music. KBRZ-AM broadcasts to the Houston area at 1460 AM.
AM RADIO STATION

KBRZ-FM 825154
Owner: Aleluya Broadcasting Network
Editorial: 1722 Treble Dr, Humble, Texas 77338-5253
Tel: 1 281 446-5725.
Email: info@radioaleluya.org
Web site: http://radioaleluya.org
Profile: KBRZ-FM is a non-commercial station owned by Aleluya Broadcasting Network. The format of the station is Spanish Contemporary Christian. KBRZ-FM broadcasts to the Victoria, TX area at 89.3 FM.
FM RADIO STATION

KBSN-AM 37210
Owner: KSEM Inc.
Editorial: 2241 W Main St, Moses Lake, Washington 98837-2826 **Tel:** 1 509 765-3441.
Profile: KBSN-AM is a commercial station owned by KSEM Inc. The format of the station is news, talk and sports. The station airs in the Moses Lake, WA area on 1470 AM.
AM RADIO STATION

KBSO-FM 44504
Owner: Championship Communications
Editorial: 701 Benys Rd, Corpus Christi, Texas 78408-2215
Email: info@badlandsfm.com
Web site: http://badlandsfm.com
Profile: KBSO-FM is a commercial station owned by Championship Communications. The format of the station is country. KBSO-FM broadcasts to the Corpus Christi, TX area at 94.7 FM.
FM RADIO STATION

KBSR-AM 36137
Owner: Sun Mountain Inc.
Editorial: Rr 1, Hardin, Montana 59034-9801
Tel: 1 406 665-2828.
Web site: http://www.bigskyradio.net
Profile: KBSR-AM is a commercial station owned by Sun Mountain Inc. The format of the station is news, talk and sports. KBSR-AM broadcasts to the Billings, MT area at 1490 AM.
AM RADIO STATION

KBST-AM 38927
Owner: Rhattigan Broadcasting
Editorial: 608 Johnson St, Big Spring, Texas 79720-2851 **Tel:** 1 432 267-6391.
Email: news@kbst.com
Web site: http://kbestmedia.com/the-mighty-1490-kbst-am
Profile: KBST-AM is a commercial station owned by Rhattigan Broadcasting. The format of the station is news, talk and sports. KBST-AM broadcasts to the Big Spring, TX area at 1490 AM.
AM RADIO STATION

KBST-FM 46270
Owner: Rhattigan Broadcasting
Editorial: 608 Johnson St, Big Spring, Texas 79720-2851 **Tel:** 1 432 267-6391.
Email: office@kbst.com
Web site: http://kbestmedia.com/
Profile: KBST-FM is a commercial station owned by Rhattigan Broadcasting. The format of the station is contemporary country. KBST-FM broadcasts to the Big Spring, TX area at 95.7 FM.
FM RADIO STATION

KBSZ-AM 39174
Owner: 1TV.com, Inc.
Editorial: 4301 N 75th St Ste 105, Scottsdale, Arizona 85251-3501 **Tel:** 1 480 319-6565.
Web site: http://funny1260am.com
Profile: KBSZ-AM is a commercial station owned by 1TV.com, Inc. The format of the station is comedy. KBSZ-AM broadcasts to the Apache Junction, AZ area at 1260 AM.
AM RADIO STATION

KBTA-AM 37211
Owner: WRD Entertainment Inc.
Editorial: 920 Harrison St Ste C, Batesville, Arkansas 72501-6949 **Tel:** 1 870 793-4196.
Web site: http://995hitsnow.com
Profile: KBTA-AM is a commercial station owned by WRD Entertainment Inc. The format of the station is sports. KBTA-AM broadcasts in the Batesville, AR area at 1340 AM.
AM RADIO STATION

KBTA-FM 46903
Owner: WRD Entertainment Inc.
Editorial: 920 Harrison St Ste C, Batesville, Arkansas 72501-6949 **Tel:** 1 870 793-4196.
Web site: http://995hitsnow.com
Profile: KBTA-FM is a commercial station owned by WRD Entertainment Inc. The format of the station is adult contemporary. KBTA-FM broadcasts to the Batesville, AR area at 99.5 FM.
FM RADIO STATION

KBTC-AM 63564
Owner: Media Professionals, Inc.
Editorial: 17647 Highway B, Houston, Missouri 65483
Tel: 1 417 967-3353.
Web site: http://bigcountry99.com
Profile: KBTC-AM is a commercial station owned by Media Professionals, Inc. The format of the station is sports and talk. KBTC-AM broadcasts to the Houston, MO area at 1250 AM.
AM RADIO STATION

KBTE-FM 154053
Owner: Alpha Media
Editorial: 33 Briercroft Office Park, Lubbock, Texas 79412-3020 **Tel:** 1 806 762-3000.
Web site: http://www.1049thebeat.com
Profile: KBTE-FM is a commercial station owned by Alpha Media The format for the station is urban contemporary music. KBTE-FM broadcasts to the Lubbock, TX, area at 104.9 FM.
FM RADIO STATION

KBTK-FM 704506
Owner: Grenax Broadcasting
Editorial: 2409 N 4Th St Ste 101, Flagstaff, Arizona 86004-3735 **Tel:** 1 928 779-1177.
Web site: http://www.bigtalkerradio.com
Profile: KBTK-FM is a commercial station owned by Grenax Broadcasting. The format of the station is news and talk. KBTK-FM broadcasts to the Flagstaff, AZ area at 105.1 FM.
FM RADIO STATION

KBTM-AM 37212
Owner: East Arkansas Broadcasters Inc.
Editorial: 407 W Parker Rd, Jonesboro, Arkansas 72404-8408 **Tel:** 1 870 932-8400.
Profile: KBTM-AM is a commercial station owned by East Arkansas Broadcasters Inc. The format of the station is news, sports and talk. KBTM-AM broadcasts to the Jonesboro, AR area at 1230 AM.
AM RADIO STATION

KBTN-AM 39437
Owner: American Media Investments
Editorial: 2510 W 20th St, Joplin, Missouri 64804-0216 **Tel:** 1 417 451-1420.
Email: kbtnam@att.net
Web site: http://kbtnradio.com
Profile: KBTN-AM is a commercial station owned by American Media Investments. The format of the station is country. KBTN-AM broadcasts to the Neosho, MO area at 1420 AM.
AM RADIO STATION

KBTN-FM 46822
Owner: American Media Investments
Editorial: 2510 W 20Th St, Joplin, Missouri 64804-0216 **Tel:** 1 417 781-1313.
Email: production@ami-joplin.com
Web site: http://kbtnradio.com
Profile: KBTN-FM is a commercial station owned by American Media Investments. The format of the station is classic country music. KBTN-FM broadcasts in the Joplin, MO area at 99.7 FM.
FM RADIO STATION

KBTO-FM 39561
Owner: Programmers Broadcasting Inc.
Editorial: 1120 Highway 5 NE, Bottineau, North Dakota 58318-7100 **Tel:** 1 701 228-5151.
Email: sunnyradio@hotmail.com
Web site: http://sunny1019fm.com
Profile: KBTO-FM is a commercial station owned by Programmers Broadcasting Inc. The format of the station is country music. KBTO-FM broadcasts to the Minot-Bismarck, ND area at 101.9 FM.
FM RADIO STATION

KBTQ-FM 46549
Owner: Univision Communications Inc.
Editorial: 200 S 10th St Ste 600, McAllen, Texas 78501-4869 **Tel:** 1 956 631-5499.
Web site: http://961masvariednd.com
Profile: KBTQ-FM is a commercial station owned by Univision Communications Inc. The format of the station is Hispanic oldies and romantic music. KBTQ-FM broadcasts to the McAllen, TX, area at 96.1 FM.
FM RADIO STATION

KBTS-FM 44506
Owner: KBEST Media, LLC
Editorial: 608 Johnson St, Big Spring, Texas 79720-2851 **Tel:** 1 432 267-6391.
Email: kbstnews@kbst.com
Web site: http://kbestmedia.com/943-the-fuse
Profile: KBTS-FM is a commercial station owned by KBEST Media, LLC. The format of the station is hot adult contemporary music. KBTS-FM broadcasts to the Big Spring, TX area at 94.3 FM.
FM RADIO STATION

KBTT-FM 46459
Owner: Alpha Media
Editorial: 208 N Thomas Dr, Shreveport, Louisiana 71107-6520 **Tel:** 1 318 222-3122.
Web site: http://www.kbtt.fm
Profile: KBTT-FM is a commercial station owned by Access.1 Communications Corp. The format of the station is urban contemporary. KBTT-FM broadcasts to the Shreveport, LA area at 103.7 FM.
FM RADIO STATION

KBUA-FM 43835
Owner: Liberman Broadcasting Inc.
Editorial: 1845 W Empire Ave, Burbank, California 91504-3402 **Tel:** 1 818 729-5300.
Web site: http://aquisuena.estrellatv.com
Profile: KBUA-FM is a commercial station owned by Liberman Broadcasting Inc. The format of the station is regional Mexican music. KBUA-FM broadcasts to the greater Los Angeles area at 94.3 FM.
FM RADIO STATION

KBUB-FM 43254
Owner: Better Living Ministries
Editorial: 910 Main St, Brownwood, Texas 76801
Tel: 1 325 646-5993.
Email: kpsmfm@gmail.com
Web site: http://www.kpsm.net
Profile: KBUB-FM is a non-commercial station owned by Better Living Ministries. The format of the station is southern gospel. KBUB-FM broadcasts to the Brownwood, TX area at 90.3 FM.
FM RADIO STATION

KBUC-FM 44548
Owner: R Communications, LLC
Editorial: 1201 N Jackson Rd Ste 900, McAllen, Texas 78501-5764 **Tel:** 1 956 992-8895.
Web site: http://supertejano1021.com
Profile: KBUC-FM is a commercial station owned by R Communications, LLC. The format of the station features Tejano music. KBUC-FM broadcasts to the McAllen, TX area at 102.1 FM.
FM RADIO STATION

KBUD-FM 355341
Owner: Flinn Broadcasting Corp.
Tel: 1 901 375-9324.
Web site: http://theradiophantom.com
Profile: KBUD-FM is a commercial station owned by Flinn Broadcasting Corp. The format of the station is adult hits. KBUD-FM broadcasts to the Oxford, MS area at 102.1 FM.
FM RADIO STATION

KBUE-FM 46748
Owner: Liberman Broadcasting Inc.
Editorial: 1845 W Empire Ave, Burbank, California 91504-3402 **Tel:** 1 818 729-5300.
Web site: http://aquisuena.estrellatv.com
Profile: KBUE-FM is a commercial station owned by Liberman Broadcasting Inc. The format of the station is regional Mexican music. KBUE-FM broadcasts to the Los Angeles area at 105.5 FM.
FM RADIO STATION

KBUF-AM 38381
Owner: Armada Media Corp.
Editorial: 1402 E Kansas Ave, Garden City, Kansas 67846-5806 **Tel:** 1 620 276-2366.
Email: production@wksradio.com
Web site: http://www.westernkansasnews.com
Profile: KBUF-AM is a commercial station owned by Armada Media Corp. The format of the station is talk. KBUF-AM broadcasts in the Garden City, KS area at 1030 AM.
AM RADIO STATION

KBUK-FM 44777
Owner: KBUK Radio, Inc.
Editorial: 511 FM 155 South, La Grange, Texas 78945
Tel: 1 979 968-3173.
Email: kvlgkbuk@kvlgkbuk.com
Web site: http://www.kvlgkbuk.com
Profile: KBUK-FM is a commercial station owned by KBUK Radio, Inc. The format of the station is classic country music. KBUK-FM broadcasts to the La Grange, TX area at 104.9 FM.
FM RADIO STATION

KBUL-AM 38882
Owner: Townsquare Media, LLC
Editorial: 27 N 27th St, Billings, Montana 59101-2357
Tel: 1 406 248-7827.
Web site: http://newstalk955.com
Profile: KBUL-AM is a commercial station owned by Townsquare Media, LLC. The format of the station is news and talk. KBUL-AM broadcasts in the Billings, MT area at 970 AM.
AM RADIO STATION

KBUL-FM 39562
Owner: Cumulus Media Inc
Editorial: 595 E Plumb Ln, Reno, Nevada 89502-3503
Tel: 1 775 789-6700.
Web site: http://www.kbul.com
Profile: KBUL-FM is a commercial station owned by Cumulus Media Inc. The format of the station is country. KBUL-FM broadcasts to the Reno, NV area at 98.1 FM.
FM RADIO STATION

KBUN-AM 38404
Owner: Hubbard Broadcasting Inc.
Editorial: 502 Beltrami Ave NW, Bemidji, Minnesota 56601-3010 **Tel:** 1 218 444-1500.
Web site: http://kbunsportsradio.com/
Profile: KBUN-AM is a commercial station owned by Hubbard Broadcasting Inc. The format of the station is sports. KBUN-AM broadcasts to the Bemidji, MN area at 1450 AM.
AM RADIO STATION

KBUN-FM 528542
Owner: Hubbard Broadcasting Inc.
Editorial: 502 Beltrami Ave NW, Bemidji, Minnesota 56601-3010 **Tel:** 1 218 444-1500.
Web site: http://www.kbunam.com/home.html
Profile: KBUN-FM is a commercial station owned by Hubbard Broadcasting Inc. The format of the station is Sports. KBUN-FM broadcasts to the Minneapolis area at 104.5 FM.
FM RADIO STATION

KBUR-AM 37213
Owner: Pritchard Broadcasting Corp.
Editorial: 610 N 4th St Ste 300, Burlington, Iowa 52601-5059 **Tel:** 1 319 752-5402.
Email: info@kbur.com
Web site: http://www.kbur.com
Profile: KBUR-AM is a commercial station owned by Pritchard Broadcasting Corp. The format of the station is news and talk. KBUR-AM broadcasts to the Burlington, IA area at 1490 AM.
AM RADIO STATION

KBUS-FM 44592
Owner: East Texas Broadcasting Inc.
Editorial: 2810 Pine Mill Rd, Paris, Texas 75460
Tel: 1 903 785-1068.
Web site: http://www.easttexasradio.com
Profile: KBUS-FM is a commercial station owned by East Texas Broadcasting Inc. The format of the station is classic rock music. KBUS-FM broadcasts to the Paris, TX area at 101.9 FM.
FM RADIO STATION

KBUT-FM 41089
Owner: Crested Butte Mountain Educ. Radio Inc.
Editorial: 508 Maroon Ave, Crested Butte, Colorado 81224 **Tel:** 1 970 349-5225.
Email: kbut@kbut.org
Web site: http://www.kbut.org
Profile: KBUT-FM is a commercial station owned by Crested Butte Mountain Educ. Radio Inc. The format of the station is college variety. KBUT-FM broadcasts to the Crested Butte, CO area at 90.3 FM.
FM RADIO STATION

KBUX-FM 231109
Owner: Burdette(Maude J.)
Editorial: 16031 Camel Dr, Quartzsite, Arizona 85346
Tel: 1 928 927-5111.
Email: kbuxradio@hotmail.com
Web site: http://kbuxradio.tripod.com
Profile: KBUX-FM is a commercial station owned by Maude Burdette. The format of the station is variety. KBUX-FM brodcasts to the Quartzsite, AZ area at 94.3 FM.
FM RADIO STATION

KBUY-AM 39172
Owner: Walton Stations of New Mexico, Inc.
Editorial: 1096 Mechem Dr Ste 230, Ruidoso, New Mexico 88345-7071 **Tel:** 1 575 258-2222.
Email: production@kwes.net
Web site: http://www.kwes.net
Profile: KBUY-AM is a commercial station owned by Walton Stations of New Mexico, Inc. The format of the station is Classic hits. KBUY-AM broadcasts to the Ruidoso, NM area at 1360 AM.
AM RADIO STATION

United States of America

KBUZ-FM 43840
Owner: American Family Association
Editorial: 2800 SW Wanamaker Rd Ste 196, Topeka, Kansas 66614-4293 **Tel:** 1 662 844-8888.
Email: comments@afr.net
Web site: http://www.afa.net
Profile: KBUZ-FM is a non-commercial station owned by the American Family Association. The format of the station is contemporary Christian. KBUZ-FM broadcasts to the Topeka, KS area at 90.3 FM.
FM RADIO STATION

KBVA-FM 41901
Owner: La Zeta 957 Co.
Editorial: 2323 S Old Missouri Rd, Springdale, Arkansas 72764-7470 **Tel:** 1 479 787-6411.
Email: kbva@variety1065.com
Web site: http://www.variety1065.com
Profile: KBVA-FM is a commercial station owned by La Zeta 957 Co. The format of the station is classic hits. KBVA-FM broadcasts to the Fayetteville, AR area at 106.5 FM.
FM RADIO STATION

KBVB-FM 43409
Owner: Midwest Communications Inc.
Editorial: 1020 25th St S, Fargo, North Dakota 58103-2312 **Tel:** 1 701 237-5346.
Web site: http://www.bob95fm.com
Profile: KBVB-FM is a commercial station owned by Midwest Communications Inc. The format of the station is contemporary country music. KBVB-FM broadcasts to the Fargo, ND area at 95.1 FM.
FM RADIO STATION

KBVC-FM 43091
Owner: Alpha Media
Editorial: 7600 County Road 120, Salida, Colorado 81201-9423 **Tel:** 1 719 539-2575.
Web site: http://www.kbvcfm.com
Profile: KBVC-FM is a commercial station owned by Alpha Media. The format of the station is country. KBVC-FM broadcasts to the Salida, CO area at 104.1 FM.
FM RADIO STATION

KBVM-FM 41336
Owner: Catholic Broadcasting Northwest, Inc.
Editorial: 5000 N Willamette Blvd, Portland, Oregon 97203-5743 **Tel:** 1 503 285-5200.
Email: info@kbvm.fm
Web site: http://www.kbvm.fm
Profile: KBVM-FM is a non-commercial station owned by Catholic Broadcasting Northwest, Inc. The format of the station is Catholic programming. KBVM-FM broadcasts in the Portland, OR area at 88.3 FM.
FM RADIO STATION

KBVR-FM 39564
Owner: State of Oregon
Editorial: 210 Memorial Union E, Corvallis, Oregon 97331 **Tel:** 1 541 737-6323.
Web site: http://www.kbvr.com
FM RADIO STATION

KBWA-FM 408510
Owner: WAY Media Inc.
Editorial: 1707 Main St, Ste 302, Longmont, Colorado 80501 **Tel:** 1 303 702-9293.
Web site: http://kxwa.wayfm.com
Profile: KBWA-FM is a commercial station owned by WAY Media Inc. The format of the station is contemporary Christian. KBWA-FM broadcasts to the Brush, CO area on 89.1 FM.
FM RADIO STATION

KBWC-FM 44313
Owner: Wiley College
Editorial: 711 Wiley Ave, Marshall, Texas 75670-5151 **Tel:** 1 903 927-3307.
Web site: https://www.wileyc.edu/kbwcprogram
Profile: KBWC-FM is a commercial station owned by Wiley College. The format of the station is gospel, R&B oldies and urban contemporary. KBWC-FM broadcasts to the Marshall, TX area at 91.1 FM.
FM RADIO STATION

KBWD-AM 37214
Owner: Brown County Broadcasting Co.
Editorial: 300 Carnegie St, Brownwood, Texas 76801-7222 **Tel:** 1 325 646-3505.
Email: upfront@koxe.com
Web site: http://www.koxe.com
Profile: KBWD-AM is a commercial station owned by Brown County Broadcasting Co. The format of the station is adult contemporary. KBWD-AM broadcasts to the Brownwood, TX area at 1380 AM.
AM RADIO STATION

KBWS-FM 39565
Owner: Armada Media Corp.
Editorial: 509 Veterans Ave, Sisseton, South Dakota 57262 **Tel:** 1 605 698-3471.
Email: kbwsstudio@venturecomm.net
Web site: http://www.bigstoneradio.com
Profile: KBWS-FM is a commercial station owned by Armada Media Corp. The format of the station is country. KBWS-FM broadcasts to the Sisseton, SD area at a frequency of 102.9 FM.
FM RADIO STATION

KBWX-FM 44569
Owner: iHeartMedia Inc.
Editorial: 1001 Highlands Plaza Dr W, Saint Louis, Missouri 63110-1337 **Tel:** 1 314 333-8000.
Web site: http://www.wild1049stl.com
Profile: KBWX-FM is a commercial station owned by iHeartMedia Inc. The format of the station is Top 40/CHR. KBWX-FM broadcasts to the St. Louis area at 100.3 FM.
FM RADIO STATION

KBXB-FM 44899
Owner: Withers Broadcasting of Southeast Missouri, LLC
Editorial: 1 Industrial Dr., Sikeston, Missouri 63801-2943 **Tel:** 1 573 471-2000.
Email: kbxb@withersradio.net
Web site: http://www.b979.net
Profile: KBXB-FM is a commercial station owned by Withers Broadcasting of Southeast Missouri, LLC. The format of the station is classic country. KBXB-FM broadcasts to Sikeston, MO at 97.9 FM.
FM RADIO STATION

KBXI-FM 44764
Owner: Chaparral Broadcasting Inc.
Editorial: 1140 W. Highway 22, Jackson, Wyoming 83301 **Tel:** 1 307 733-2120.
Email: psa@mojo925.com
Web site: http://www.mojo925.com/
Profile: KBXI-FM is a commercial station owned by Chaparral Broadcasting Inc. The format of the station is hybrid of classic rock and adult hits music. KBXI-FM broadcasts in the Park City, MT area at 92.5 FM.
FM RADIO STATION

KBXL-FM 46350
Owner: Inspirational Family Radio
Editorial: 1440 S Weideman Ave, Boise, Idaho 83709-1450 **Tel:** 1 208 377-3790.
Email: info@myfamilyradio.com
Web site: http://www.941thevoice.com
Profile: KBXL-FM is a commercial station owned by Inspirational Family Radio. The format of the station is religious talk. KBXL-FM broadcasts to the Boise, ID area at 94.1 FM.
FM RADIO STATION

KBXR-FM 42181
Owner: Cumulus Media Inc.
Editorial: 503 Old 63 N, Columbia, Missouri 65201-6305 **Tel:** 1 573 449-4141.
Web site: http://www.bxr.com
Profile: KBXR-FM is a commercial station owned by Cumulus Media Inc. The format of the station is adult album alternative music. KBXR-FM broadcasts to the Columbia, MO area at 102.3 FM.
FM RADIO STATION

KBXT-FM 43067
Owner: Brazos Valley Communications LLC
Editorial: 1240 E Villa Maria Rd, Bryan, Texas 77802-2519 **Tel:** 1 979 776-1240.
Web site: http://www.1019thebeatfm.com
Profile: KXBT-FM is a commercial station owned by Brazos Valley Communications LLC. The format of the station is urban contemporary. KXBT-FM broadcasts to the Bryan, TX area on 101.9 FM.
FM RADIO STATION

KBXX-FM 39648
Owner: Urban One, Inc.
Editorial: 24 Greenway Plz Ste 900, Houston, Texas 77046-2418 **Tel:** 1 713 623-2108.
Web site: http://theboxhouston.com
Profile: KBXX-FM is a commercial station owned by Urban One, Inc. The format of the station is rhythmic Top 40/CHR music. KBXX-FM broadcasts in the Houston area at 97.9 FM.
FM RADIO STATION

KBYB-FM 44453
Owner: Texarkana Radio Center Licenses, LLC
Editorial: 615 Olive St, Texarkana, Texas 75501-5512 **Tel:** 1 903 793-4671.
Web site: http://1017hotfm.com
Profile: KBYB-FM is a commercial station owned by Texarkana Radio Center Licenses, LLC. The format of the station is contemporary country. KBYB-FM broadcasts to the Texarkana, TX area at 101.7 FM.
FM RADIO STATION

KBYG-AM 35846
Owner: Pappajohn (David)
Editorial: 2801 Wasson Rd, Big Spring, Texas 79720-6412 **Tel:** 1 432 263-5294.
Web site: http://www.kbygradio.com
Profile: KBYG-AM is a commercial station owned by David Pappajohn. The format of the station is oldies. KBYG-AM broadcasts to the Big Spring, TX area at 1400 AM.
AM RADIO STATION

KBYN-FM 43609
Owner: Favorita Broadcasting(La)
Editorial: 4043 Geer Rd, Hughson, California 95326-9798 **Tel:** 1 209 883-8760.
Email: lafavorita@lafavorita.net
Web site: http://www.lafavorita.net
Profile: KBYN-FM is a commercial station owned by La Favorita Broadcasting. The format of the station is regional Mexican. KBYN-FM broadcasts to the Arnold, CA area at 95.9 FM.
FM RADIO STATION

KBYR-AM 37090
Owner: Ohana Media Group, LLC.
Editorial: 1399 W 34th Ave Ste 202, Anchorage, Alaska 99503-3659 **Tel:** 1 907 344-4045.
Web site: http://www.kbyr.com
Profile: KBYR-AM is a commercial station owned by Ohana Media Group, LLC. The format of the station is news and talk. KBYR-AM broadcasts to the Anchorage, AK area at 700 AM.
AM RADIO STATION

KBYZ-FM 46561
Owner: Townsquare Media, Inc.
Editorial: 4303 Memorial Hwy, Mandan, North Dakota 58554-4711 **Tel:** 1 701 250-6602.
Web site: http://www.965thefox.com
Profile: KBYZ-FM is a commercial station owned by Townsquare Media, Inc. The format of the station is classic rock. KBYZ-FM broadcasts to the Mandan, ND area at 96.5 FM.
FM RADIO STATION

KBZD-FM 42715
Owner: My Home Team Media
Editorial: 2505 Lakeview Dr Ste 302B, Amarillo, Texas 79109-1527 **Tel:** 1 806 355-1044.
Web site: http://fun997.com
Profile: KBZD-FM is a commercial station owned by My Home Team Media. The format of the station is hot adult contemporary. KBZD-FM broadcasts to the Amarillo, TX area at 99.7 FM.
FM RADIO STATION

KBZE-FM 41608
Owner: Hubcast Broadcasting Inc.
Editorial: 1320 Victor II Blvd, Morgan City, Louisiana 70380-1360 **Tel:** 1 985 385-6266.
Email: kbze.kfra@gmail.com
Web site: http://www.kbze.com
Profile: KBZE-FM is a commercial station owned by Hubcast Broadcasting Inc. The format of the station is urban contemporary. KBZE-FM broadcasts to the Baton Rouge, LA area at 105.9 FM.
FM RADIO STATION

KBZM-FM 44336
Owner: Orion Media, LLC
Editorial: 8274 Huffine Ln, Bozeman, Montana 59718-8118 **Tel:** 1 406 582-1045.
Web site: http://www.montanassuperstation.com
Profile: KBZM-FM is a commercial station owned by Orion Media, LLC. The format of the station is classic rock. KBZM-FM broadcasts to the Big Sky, MT area at a frequency of 104.7 FM.
FM RADIO STATION

KBZN-FM 42836
Owner: Capitol Broadcasting
Editorial: 257 E 200 S, Ste 400, Salt Lake City, Utah 84111 **Tel:** 1 801 364-9836.
Email: comments@kbzn.com
Web site: http://www.kbzn.com
Profile: KBZN-FM is a commercial station owned by Capitol Broadcasting. The format of the station is adult contemporary. KBZN-FM broadcasts to the Salt Lake City area at 97.9 FM.
FM RADIO STATION

KBZO-AM 35093
Owner: Entravision Communications Corp.
Editorial: 6502 Caprock Dr, Lubbock, Texas 79412-3712 **Tel:** 1 806 763-6051.
Web site: http://www.espn1460am.com
Profile: KBZO-AM is a commercial station owned by Entravision Communications Corp. The format of the station is Spanish sports. KBZO-AM broadcasts to the Lubbock, TX area on 1460 AM.
AM RADIO STATION

KBZQ-FM 41984
Owner: Fritsch Jr.(William Richard)
Editorial: 2332 SW Lee Blvd., Lawton, Oklahoma 73505 **Tel:** 1 580 357-9950.
Email: kbzq@sbcglobal.net
Web site: http://www.hitsandfavorites.com
Profile: KBZQ-FM is a commercial station owned by William Richard Fritsch Jr. The format of the station is adult contemporary music. KBZQ-FM broadcasts to the Lawton, OK area at 99.5 FM.
FM RADIO STATION

KBZS-FM 39951
Owner: Townsquare Media, LLC
Editorial: 2525 Kell Blvd Ste 200, Wichita Falls, Texas 76308-1008 **Tel:** 1 940 763-1111.
Web site: http://www.1063thebuzz.com
Profile: KBZS-FM is a commercial station owned by Townsquare Media, LLC. The format of the station is rock music. KBZS-FM broadcasts to the Wichita Falls, TX area at 106.3 FM.
FM RADIO STATION

KBZT-FM 41002
Owner: Entercom Communications Corp.
Editorial: 1615 Murray Canyon Rd Ste 710, San Diego, California 92108-4321 **Tel:** 1 619 297-9595.
Web site: http://www.fm949sd.com
Profile: KBZT-FM is a commercial station owned by Entercom Communications Corp. The format of the station is rock alternative music. KBZT-FM broadcasts to the San Diego area at 94.9 FM.
FM RADIO STATION

KBZU-FM 46690
Owner: Cumulus Media
Editorial: 500 4th St NW Fl 5, Albuquerque, New Mexico 87102-5324 **Tel:** 1 505 767-6700.
Web site: http://www.963nashicon.com
Profile: KBZU-FM is a commercial station owned by Cumulus Media. The format of the station is country music. KBZU-FM broadcasts to the Albuquerque, NM area at 96.3 FM.
FM RADIO STATION

KBZY-AM 3489
Owner: Capital Broadcasting Inc.
Editorial: 2659 Commercial St SE Ste 204, Salem, Oregon 97302-4496 **Tel:** 1 503 362-1490.
Web site: http://www.kbzy.com
Profile: KBZY-FM is a commercial station owned by Capital Broadcasting Inc. The format of the station is oldies music. KBZY-AM broadcasts to the Salem, OR, area at 1490 AM.
AM RADIO STATION

KBZZ-AM 3928
Owner: Americom Broadcasting
Editorial: 961 Matley Ln Ste 120, Reno, Nevada 89502-2119 **Tel:** 1 775 829-1964.
Web site: http://thebuzzreno.com
Profile: KBZZ-AM is a commercial station owned by Americom Broadcasting. The format for the station is talk. KBZZ-AM broadcasts to the Reno, NV area at 1270 AM.
AM RADIO STATION

KCAA-AM 23140
Owner: Broadcast Management Services Inc.
Editorial: 254 Carousel Mall, San Bernardino, California 92401 **Tel:** 1 909 885-8502.
Web site: http://www.kcaaradio.com
Profile: KCAA-AM is a commercial station owned by Broadcast Management Services Inc. The format of the station is talk. KCAA-AM broadcasts to the San Bernardino, CA area at 1050 AM.
AM RADIO STATION

KCAB-AM 3930
Owner: East Arkansas Broadcasters Inc.
Editorial: 2705 E Parkway Dr, Russellville, Arkansas 72802-2006 **Tel:** 1 479 968-6816.
Email: news@rivervalleyradio.com
Web site: http://www.rivertalk980.com
Profile: KCAB-AM is a commercial station owned by East Arkansas Broadcasters Inc. The format of the station is news, talk and sports. KCAB-AM broadcasts to the Russellville, AR area at 980 AM.
AM RADIO STATION

KCAD-FM 4310
Owner: iHeartMedia Inc.
Editorial: 11291 39th St SW, Dickinson, North Dakota 58601-9206 **Tel:** 1 701 227-1876.
Web site: http://kc99country.iheart.com
Profile: KCAD-FM is a commercial station owned by iHeartMedia Inc. The format of the station is contemporary country. KCAD-FM broadcasts to the Dickinson, ND area at 99.1 FM.
FM RADIO STATION

KCAJ-FM 4383
Owner: North Country Media, LLC.
Editorial: 107 Center St W, Roseau, Minnesota 56751-1022 **Tel:** 1 218 463-0161.
Email: info@wild102fm.com
Web site: http://www.wild102fm.com
Profile: KCAJ-FM is a commercial station owned byNorth Country Media, LLC. The format of the station is Top 40/CHR, news and sports. KCAJ-FM broadcasts to the Roseau, MN area at 102.2 FM.
FM RADIO STATION

KCAL-AM 3583
Owner: Lazer Broadcasting Corp.
Editorial: 1950 S Sunwest Ln Ste 302, San Bernardino, California 92408-3227 **Tel:** 1 909 384-9750.
Profile: KCAL-AM is a commercial station owned by Lazer Broadcasting. The format of the station is Spanish oldies. KCAL-AM broadcasts to San Bernardino, CA at 1410 AM.
AM RADIO STATION

KCAL-FM 4094
Owner: Anaheim Broadcasting Corp.
Editorial: 1940 Orange Tree Ln, Ste 200, Redlands, California 92374 **Tel:** 1 909 793-3554.
Web site: http://www.kcalfm.com
Profile: KCAL-FM is a commercial station owned by Anaheim Broadcasting Corp. The format of the station is rock music. KCAL-FM broadcasts to the Redlands, CA area at 96.7 FM.
FM RADIO STATION

KCAM-AM 34894
Owner: Northern Light Network
Editorial: Mile 187 Glenn Highway, Glennallen, Alaska 99588 **Tel:** 1 907 822-5226.
Email: kcam@kcam.org
Web site: http://www.kcam.org
AM RADIO STATION

KCAP-AM 3739
Owner: Cherry Creek Radio
Editorial: 110 E Broadway St, Helena, Montana 59601-4232 **Tel:** 1 406 442-6620.
Email: ebaker@cherrycreekradio.com
Web site: https://950kcap.com
Profile: KCAP-AM is a commercial station owned by Cherry Creek Radio. The format of the station is news/talk. KCAP-AM broadcasts to the Helena, MT area at 950 AM.
AM RADIO STATION

KCAQ-FM 43284
Owner: Gold Coast Broadcasting, LLC
Editorial: 2284 S Victoria Ave, Ventura, California 93003-6641 **Tel:** 1 805 289-1400.
Email: kvtanews@yahoo.com
Web site: http://www.q1047.com

Profile: KCAQ-FM is a commercial station owned by Gold Coast Broadcasting, LLC. The format of the station is Top 40. KCAQ-FM broadcasts to the Ventura, CA area at 104.7 FM.
FM RADIO STATION

KCAR-AM 39118
Owner: American Media Investments
Editorial: 203 N Locust St, Clarksville, Texas 75426-3024 **Tel:** 1 903 427-3861.
Email: kool985@cebridge.net
Profile: KCAR-AM is a commercial station owned by American Media Investments. The format of the station is country music. KCAR-AM broadcasts to the Clarksville, TX area at 1350 AM.
AM RADIO STATION

KCAR-FM 44365
Owner: American Media Investments
Editorial: 2510 W 20th St, Joplin, Missouri 64804-0216 **Tel:** 1 417 781-1313.
Email: production@ami-joplin.com
Web site: http://star1043joplin.com
Profile: KCAR-FM is a commercial station owned by American Media Investments. The format of the station is Hot AC. KCAR-FM broadcasts to the Joplin, MO area at 104.3 FM.
FM RADIO STATION

KCAT-AM 34895
Owner: Mondy(Elijah)
Editorial: 1207 W 6th Ave, Pine Bluff, Arkansas 71601-3927 **Tel:** 1 870 534-5001.
Web site: http://kcatam.com
Profile: KCAT-AM is a commercial station owned by Elijah Mondy. The format of the station is gospel. KCAT-AM broadcasts in the Pine Bluff, AR at 1340 AM.
AM RADIO STATION

KCAW-FM 41919
Owner: Raven Radio Foundation Inc.
Editorial: 2 Lincoln St, Sitka, Alaska 99835-7538
Tel: 1 907 747-5877.
Email: news@kcaw.org
Web site: http://www.kcaw.org
Profile: KCAW-FM is non-commercial station owned by Raven Radio Foundation Inc. The format of the station is variety. KCAW-FM broadcasts to the Sitka, AK area at 104.7 FM.
FM RADIO STATION

KCBC-AM 35806
Owner: Crawford Broadcasting Co.
Editorial: 10948 Cleveland Ave, Oakdale, California 95361-9709 **Tel:** 1 209 847-0770.
Email: kcbcpsa@velociter.net
Web site: http://www.770kcbc.com
Profile: KCBC-FM is a non-commercial station owned by Crawford Broadcasting Co. The format of the station is Christian music and talk. KCBC-FM broadcasts to the Sacramento area at 770 AM.
AM RADIO STATION

KCBF-AM 39049
Owner: Last Frontier Mediactive, LLC
Editorial: 529 5th Ave, Fairbanks, Alaska 99701-4749
Tel: 1 907 451-5910.
Email: lfm@fbxradio.com
Web site: http://www.820sports.com
Profile: KCBF-AM is a commercial station owned by Last Frontier Mediactive, LLC. The format of the station is sports. KCBF-AM broadcasts in the Fairbanks, AK area at 880 AM.
AM RADIO STATION

KCBI-FM 39567
Owner: First Dallas Media, Inc.
Editorial: 750 N Saint Paul St Ste 1050, Dallas, Texas 75201-3236 **Tel:** 1 817 792-3800.
Email: kcbi@kcbi.org
Web site: http://www.kcbi.org
Profile: KCBI-FM is a non-commercial station owned by First Dallas Media, Inc. The format of the station is Christian music, talk and teaching. KCBI-FM broadcasts to the Dallas area at 90.9 FM.
FM RADIO STATION

KCBL-AM 38444
Owner: iHeartMedia Inc.
Editorial: 83 E Shaw Ave Ste 150, Fresno, California 93710-7622 **Tel:** 1 559 243-4300.
Web site: http://www.foxsportsradio1340.com
Profile: KCBL-AM is a commercial station owned by iHeart Media and Entertainment. The format of the station is sports. KCBL-AM broadcasts to the Fresno, CA area at 1340 AM.
AM RADIO STATION

KCBN-FM 779148
Owner: First Dallas Media, Inc.
Editorial: 11 Ryan Plaza Dr., Arlington, Texas 76011
Tel: 1 325 655-6917.
Web site: http://www.kcbinet.org
Profile: KCBN-FM is a non-commercial station owned by First Dallas Media, Inc. The format of the station is Christian teaching and Contemporary Christian music. KCBN-FM broadcasts to the Hamilton, TX area at a frequency of 107.7 FM.
FM RADIO STATION

KCBQ-AM 36446
Owner: Salem Media Group, Inc.
Editorial: 9255 Towne Centre Dr Ste 535, San Diego, California 92121-3038 **Tel:** 1 858 535-1210.
Web site: http://am1170theanswer.com
Profile: KCBQ-FM is a commercial station owned by Salem Media Group, Inc. The format of the station is news and conservative talk. KCBQ-FM broadcasts to the San Diego area at 1170 AM. Station does not accept PSAs.
AM RADIO STATION

KCBS-AM 36367
Owner: CBS Radio
Editorial: 865 Battery St Fl 3, San Francisco, California 94111-1503 **Tel:** 1 415 765-4000.
Email: kcbsnewsdesk@cbs.com
Web site: http://sanfrancisco.cbslocal.com
Profile: KCBS-AM is a commercial station owned by CBS Radio. The format of the station is news. KCBS-AM broadcasts to the San Francisco area at 740 AM.
AM RADIO STATION

KCBS-FM 46744
Owner: CBS Radio
Editorial: 5901 Venice Blvd, Los Angeles, California 90034-1708 **Tel:** 1 323 937-9331.
Email: jack@931jackfm.com
Web site: http://931jackfm.cbslocal.com
Profile: KCBS-FM is a commercial station owned by CBS Radio. The format of the station is an eclectic mix of adult hits. KCBS-FM broadcasts to the Los Angeles area at 93.1 FM.
FM RADIO STATION

KCBX-FM 39568
Owner: KCBX Inc.
Editorial: 4100 Vachell Ln, San Luis Obispo, California 93401-8113 **Tel:** 1 805 549-8855.
Email: news@kcbx.org
Web site: http://www.kcbx.org
Profile: KCBX-FM is a non-commercial station owned by KCBX Inc. The format of the station is news and jazz. KCBX-FM broacasts to the San Luis Obispo, CA area at 90.1 FM.
FM RADIO STATION

KCCB-AM 38456
Owner: Adkins(Jim)
Editorial: 501 Bryan Ave, Corning, Arkansas 72422-3262 **Tel:** 1 870 857-6646.
Email: lite93fm@isainet.com
Profile: KCCB-AM is a commercial station owned by Jim Adkins. The format of the station is jazz. KCCB-AM broadcasts to the Corning, AR area at 1260 AM.
AM RADIO STATION

KCCC-AM 34896
Owner: Compass Enterprise Inc.
Editorial: 930 N Canal St, Carlsbad, New Mexico 88220-5110 **Tel:** 1 575 887-5521.
Profile: KCCC-AM is a commercial station owned by Compass Enterprise Inc. The format of the station is oldies. KCCC-AM broadcasts to the Albuquerque, NM area at 930 AM.
AM RADIO STATION

KCCD-FM 42012
Owner: Minnesota Public Radio
Editorial: 901 8th St S, Moorhead, Minnesota 56562
Tel: 1 218 287-0666.
Email: newsroom@mpr.org
Web site: http://www.mpr.org
Profile: KCCD-FM is a non-commercial station owned by Minnesota Public Radio. The format of the station is news and talk programming. KCCD-FM broadcasts to the Moorhead, MN area at 90.3 FM.
FM RADIO STATION

KCCK-FM 39569
Owner: Kirkwood Community College
Editorial: 6301 Kirkwood Blvd SW, Cedar Rapids, Iowa 52404-5260 **Tel:** 1 319 398-5446.
Email: psa@kcck.org
Web site: http://www.kcck.org
Profile: KCCK-FM is a non-commercial station owned by Kirkwood Community College. The format for the station is jazz. KCCK-FM broadcasts to the Cedar Rapids, IA area at 88.3 FM.
FM RADIO STATION

KCCL-FM 39675
Owner: Results Radio Group
Editorial: 298 Commerce Cir, Sacramento, California 95815-4212 **Tel:** 1 916 576-7333.
Web site: http://1015khits.com/
Profile: KCCL-FM is a commercial station owned by Results Radio Group. The format of the station is classic hits. KXCL-FM broadcasts to the Sacramento, CA area at 101.5 FM.
FM RADIO STATION

KCCM-FM 39570
Owner: Minnesota Public Radio
Editorial: 901 8th St S, Moorhead, Minnesota 56562
Tel: 1 218 287-0666.
Email: newsroom@mpr.org
Web site: http://minnesota.publicradio.org/radio/stations/kccdkccm/
Profile: KCCM-FM is a non-commercial station owned by Minnesota Public Radio. The format of the station is classical music. KCCM-FM broadcasts to the Moorhead, MN area at 91.1 FM.
FM RADIO STATION

KCCN-FM 45910
Owner: Summit Media Broadcasting LLC
Editorial: 900 Fort Street Mall Ste 700, Honolulu, Hawaii 96813-3701 **Tel:** 1 808 536-2728.
Web site: http://www.kccnfm100.com
Profile: KCCN-FM is a commercial owned by Summit Media Broadcasting LLC. The format of the station is Hawaiian Contemporary Hits. KCCN-FM broadcasts to the Honolulu, HI area at 100.3 FM.
FM RADIO STATION

KCCQ-FM 44596
Owner: iHeartMedia Inc.
Editorial: 415 Main St, Ames, Iowa 50010-6099
Tel: 1 515 232-1430.
Web site: http://www.now1051.com/main.html
Profile: KCCQ-FM is a commercial station owned by iHeartMedia Inc. The format of the station is Hot AC. KCCQ-FM broadcasts to the Ames, IA area at 105.1 FM.
FM RADIO STATION

KCCR-AM 39268
Owner: Riverfront Broadcasting
Editorial: 106 W Capitol Ave, Pierre, South Dakota 57501-2018 **Tel:** 1 605 224-1240.
Email: news@todayskccr.com
Web site: http://www.todayskccr.com
Profile: KCCR-AM is a commercial station owned by Riverfront Broadcasting. The format of the station is classic hits music and talk. KCCR-AM broadcasts to the Pierre, SD area at 1240 AM.
AM RADIO STATION

KCCS-FM 546294
Owner: Colorado College
Editorial: 912 N Weber St, Colorado Springs, Colorado 80903-2921 **Tel:** 1 719 473-4801.
Email: news@krcc.org
Web site: http://www.krcc.org
Profile: KCCS-FM is a non-commercial station owned by Colorado College. The format of the station is variety. KCCS-FM broadcasts to the Colorado Springs, CO area at 91.7 FM.
FM RADIO STATION

KCCT-AM 37139
Owner: Davila Broadcasting
Editorial: 701 Benys Rd, Corpus Christi, Texas 78408-2215 **Tel:** 1 361 289-0999.
Email: texasradiocc@gmail.com
Web site: http://www.texasradiocc.com/
Profile: KCCT-AM is a commercial station owned by Davila Broadcasting. The format of the station is news, talk and classic country. KCCT-AM broadcasts to the Corpus Christi, TX area at 1150 AM.
AM RADIO STATION

KCCV-AM 39232
Owner: Bott Broadcasting Co.
Editorial: 10550 Barkley St Ste 112, Overland Park, Kansas 66212-1824 **Tel:** 1 913 642-7600.
Email: kccv@bottradionetwork.com
Web site: http://www.bottradionetwork.com
Profile: KCCV-AM is a commercial station owned by Bott Broadcasting Co. The format of the station is religious and Christian programming. KCCV-FM broadcasts to the Overland Park, KS area at 760 AM.
AM RADIO STATION

KCCV-FM 46598
Owner: Bott Broadcasting Co.
Editorial: 10550 Barkley St, Ste 112, Overland Park, Kansas 66212 **Tel:** 1 913 642-7600.
Email: kccv@bottradionetwork.com
Web site: http://www.bottradionetwork.com
Profile: KCCV-FM is a commercial station owned by Bott Broadcasting Co. The format of the station is religious and Christian programming. KCCV-FM broadcasts to the Kansas City, MO, area at 92.3 FM.
FM RADIO STATION

KCCY-AM 36586
Owner: iHeartMedia Inc.
Editorial: 106 W 24th St, Pueblo, Colorado 81003-2408 **Tel:** 1 719 545-2080.
Web site: http://www.foxsportspueblo.com
Profile: KCCY-AM is a commercial station owned by iHeartMedia Inc. The format of the station is sports. KCCY-AM broadcasts to the Pueblo, CO area at 1350 AM.
AM RADIO STATION

KCCY-FM 39571
Owner: iHeartMedia Inc.
Editorial: 2864 S Circle Dr Ste 150, Colorado Springs, Colorado 80906-4128 **Tel:** 1 719 540-9200.
Web site: http://www.y969.com
Profile: KCCY-FM is a commercial station owned by iHeartMedia Inc. The format of the station is contemporary country. KCCY-FM broadcasts to the Colorado Springs, CO area at 96.9 FM.
FM RADIO STATION

KCDA-FM 39572
Owner: iHeartMedia Inc.
Editorial: 808 E Sprague Ave, Spokane, Washington 99202-2126 **Tel:** 1 509 242-2400.
Web site: http://www.1031kcda.com
Profile: KCDA-FM is a commercial station owned by iHeartMedia Inc. The format of the station is hot adult contemporary music. KCDA-FM broadcasts to the Spokane, WA area at 103.1 FM.
FM RADIO STATION

KCDD-FM 42579
Owner: Cumulus Media Inc.
Editorial: 2525 S Danville Dr, Abilene, Texas 79605-6414 **Tel:** 1 325 793-9700.
Web site: http://www.power103.com
Profile: KCDD-FM is a commercial station owned by Cumulus Media Inc. The format of the station is Top 40/CHR music. KCDD-FM broadcasts in the Abilene, TX area at 103.7 FM.
FM RADIO STATION

KCDQ-FM 45828
Owner: Desert West Air Ranchers Corp.
Editorial: 500 E Fry Blvd Ste L10, Sierra Vista, Arizona 85635-1840 **Tel:** 1 520 459-8201.
Email: info@kkyz.com
Web site: http://kcdq.com
FM RADIO STATION

KCDU-FM 42901
Owner: Mapleton Radio, LLC
Editorial: 60 Garden Ct Ste 300, Monterey, California 93940-5370 **Tel:** 1 831 658-5200.
Email: thebeach1017@yahoo.com
Web site: http://www.1017thebeach.com
Profile: KCDU-FM is a commercial station owned by Mapleton Radio, LLC. The format of the station is Top 40/CHR. KCDU-FM broadcasts to the Monterey, CA area at 101.7 FM.
FM RADIO STATION

KCDV-FM 46820
Owner: Bayview Communications Inc.
Editorial: 112 Forestry Way, Cordova, Alaska 99574
Tel: 1 907 424-3796.
Email: email@cordovaradio.com
Web site: http://www.cordovaradio.com
Profile: KCDV-FM is a commercial station owned by Bayview Communications Inc. The format of the station is adult contemporary music. KCDV-AM broadcasts in Cordova, AK area at 100.9 FM.
FM RADIO STATION

KCDX-FM 43686
Owner: Desert West Air Ranchers Corp.
Editorial: 500 E Fry Blvd, Ste L10, Sierra Vista, Arizona 85635 **Tel:** 1 520 459-8201.
Email: info@kkyz.com
Web site: http://www.kcdx.com
Profile: KCDX-FM is a commercial station owned by Desert West Air Ranchers Corp. The format of the station is classic rock. KCDX-FM broadcasts to the Sierra Vista, AZ area at 103.1 FM.
FM RADIO STATION

KCDY-FM 46642
Owner: Hughes Broadcasting
Editorial: 1609 Radio Blvd, Carlsbad, New Mexico 88220-6427 **Tel:** 1 575 887-7563.
Web site: http://www.carlsbadradio.com
Profile: KCDY-FM is a commercial station owned by Hughes Broadcasting. The format of the station is adult contemporary music. KCDY-FM broadcasts to the Carlsbad, NM area at 104.1 FM.
FM RADIO STATION

KCDZ-FM 41125
Owner: Morongo Basin Broadcasting Corp.
Editorial: 6448 Hallee Rd Ste 5, Joshua Tree, California 92252-1908 **Tel:** 1 760 366-8471.
Email: z1077fm@gmail.com
Web site: http://z1077fm.com
Profile: KCDZ-FM is a commercial station owned by Morongo Basin Broadcasting Corp. The format of the station is adult contemporary and Top 40/CHR. KCDZ-FM broadcasts to the Joshua Tree, CA area at 107.7 FM.
FM RADIO STATION

KCEC-FM 133727
Owner: Campesina Network(La)
Editorial: 670 E 32nd St Ste 12A, Yuma, Arizona 85365-3558 **Tel:** 1 928 782-5995.
Web site: http://campesina.net/yuma
Profile: KCEC-FM is a commercial station owned by La Campesina Network. The format of the station is Hispanic. KCEC-FM broadcasts to the Yuma, AZ area on 104.5 FM.
FM RADIO STATION

KCED-FM 39573
Owner: Centralia College
Editorial: 600 Centralia College Blvd, Centralia, Washington 98531-4035 **Tel:** 1 360 736-9391 243.
Web site: http://www.centralia.edu/kced
FM RADIO STATION

KCEE-AM 39490
Owner: Good News Radio Broadcasting Inc.
Editorial: 3222 S Richey Ave, Tucson, Arizona 85713-5498 **Tel:** 1 520 790-2440.
Email: info@690kcee.com
Web site: http://www.690kcee.com
Profile: KCEE-AM is a commercial station owned by Good News Radio Broadcasting Inc. The format of the station is adult standards. KCEE-AM broadcasts to the Tucson, AZ area at 690 AM.
AM RADIO STATION

KCEG-AM 814235
Owner: Cutforth (Timothy)
Editorial: 516 Main St, Walsenburg, Colorado 81089-2036
Email: production@socoradio.com
Web site: http://www.kceg780.com
Profile: KCEG-AM is a commercial station owned by Cutforth (Timothy) and operated by SOCO Radio. The format of the station is classic country. KCEG-AM broadcasts to the Colorado Springs, CO area at a frequency of 780 AM.
AM RADIO STATION

KCEP-FM 41097
Owner: Economic Opportunity Board of Clark County
Editorial: 330 W Washington Ave, Las Vegas, Nevada 89106-3327 **Tel:** 1 702 648-0104.
Email: info@kcepfm.com
Web site: http://power88lv.com

Profile: KCEP-FM is a non-commercial station owned by the Economic Opportunity Board of Clark County. The format of the station is urban contemporary music. KCEP-FM broadcasts to the Las Vegas area at 88.1 FM.
FM RADIO STATION

KCEU-FM 736137
Owner: College of Eastern Utah
Editorial: 451 E 400 N, Price, Utah 84501-2626
Tel: 1 435 613-5668.
Web site: http://upr.org
Profile: KCEU-FM is a non-commercial station owned by College of Eastern Utah. The format of the station is alternative rock. KCEU-FM broadcasts at 89.7 FM to the Price, Utah area. Simulcast of KUSU-FM.
FM RADIO STATION

KCEZ-FM 41102
Owner: Results Radio Group
Editorial: 856 Manzanita Ct, Chico, California 95926-2369 **Tel:** 1 530 342-2200.
Web site: http://www.power102radio.com
Profile: KCEZ-FM is a commercial station owned by Results Radio Group. The format of the station is Top 40/CHR. KCEZ-FM broadcasts to the Chico, CA area at 102.1 FM.
FM RADIO STATION

KCFA-FM 43830
Owner: Favorita Broadcasting(La)
Editorial: 4043 Geer Rd, Hughson, California 95326
Tel: 1 209 883-8760.
Email: lafavorita@lafavorita.net
Web site: http://www.lafavorita.net
Profile: KCFA-FM is a commercial station owned by La Favorita Broadcasting. The format of the station is regional Mexican music. KCFA-FM broadcasts in the Hughson, CA area at 106.1 FM.
FM RADIO STATION

KCFB-FM 41137
Owner: Minnesota Christian Broadcasters Inc.
Editorial: 31287 Brunes St, Pequot Lakes, Minnesota 56472-2761 **Tel:** 1 218 568-4422.
Email: info@theword.mn
Web site: http://theword.mn
Profile: KCFB-FM is a non-commercial station owned by Minnesota Christian Broadcasters Inc. The format of the station is Christian teaching and music. KCFB-FM broadcasts to the St. Cloud, MN area at 91.5 FM.
FM RADIO STATION

KCFI-AM 36963
Owner: Coloff Media
Editorial: 721 Shirley St, Cedar Falls, Iowa 50613-1513 **Tel:** 1 319 277-1918.
Web site: http://cruisin1250.com
Profile: KCFI-AM is a commercial station owned by Coloff Media (Fife Communication Company, LLC). The format for the station is oldies. KCFI-AM broadcasts to the Waterloo, IA area at 1250 AM.
AM RADIO STATION

KCFJ-AM 39288
Owner: EDI Media
Editorial: 1773 W San Bernardino Rd Bldg C31-34, West Covina, California 91790-1049 **Tel:** 1 530 233-3570.
Email: englishradio@edimediainc.com
Web site: http://www.edimediainc.com/en/index.php?option=com_content&view=article&id=76&Itemid=113
Profile: KCFJ-AM is a commercial station owned by EDI Media. The format of the station is adult standards. KCFJ-AM broadcasts to the Alturas, CA area at 570 AM.
AM RADIO STATION

KCFM-AM 39147
Owner: Coast Broadcasting Inc.
Editorial: 4480 Highway 101, Florence, Oregon 97439
Tel: 1 541 997-9136.
Email: radiowaves@kcst.com
Web site: http://www.kcst.com
Profile: KCFM-AM is a commercial station owned by Coast Broadcasting Inc. The format of the station is adult standards. KCFM-AM broadcasts to the Eugene, OR area at 1250 AM.
AM RADIO STATION

KCFN-FM 41230
Owner: American Family Association
Editorial: 720 N Murray St, Wichita, Kansas 67212-4166 **Tel:** 1 662 884-8888.
Email: kcfn@afr.net
Web site: http://www.afa.net/radio
Profile: KCFN-FM is a non-commercial station owned by American Family Association. The format of the station is contemporary Christian. KCFN-FM broadcasts in the Wichita, KS area at 91.1 FM.
FM RADIO STATION

KCFO-AM 34899
Owner: Friendship Broadcasting, L.P.
Editorial: 5800 E Skelly Dr Ste 150, Tulsa, Oklahoma 74135-6416 **Tel:** 1 918 622-0970.
Email: studio@kcfo.com
Web site: http://www.kcfo.com
Profile: KCFO-AM is a commercial station owned by Friendship Broadcasting, L.P. The format of the station is religious programming and talk. KCFO-AM broadcasts to the Tulsa, OK area at 970 AM. KCFO's slogan is "Talk You Can Trust."
AM RADIO STATION

KCFP-FM 43829
Owner: Public Broadcasting of Colorado Inc.
Editorial: 7409 S Alton Ct, Centennial, Colorado 80112 **Tel:** 1 303 871-9191.
Email: info@cpr.org
Web site: http://www.cpr.org
Profile: KCFP-FM is a non-commercial station owned by Public Broadcasting of Colorado Inc. The format of the station is news and classical. KCFP-FM broadcasts to the Centennial, CO area at 91.9 FM. The station is a simulcast of KVOD-FM.
FM RADIO STATION

KCFR-FM 538169
Owner: Public Broadcasting of Colorado Inc.
Editorial: 7409 S Alton Ct, Centennial, Colorado 80112-2301 **Tel:** 1 303 871-9191.
Email: info@cpr.org
Web site: http://www.cpr.org
Profile: KCFR-FM is a non-commercial station owned by Public Broadcasting of Colorado Inc. The format of the station is news and talk programming. KCFR-FM broadcasts to the Denver area at 90.1 FM.
FM RADIO STATION

KCFV-FM 39576
Owner: St. Louis Community College
Editorial: 3400 Pershall Rd, Saint Louis, Missouri 63135 **Tel:** 1 314 513-4463.
Web site: http://www.stlcc.edu/kcfv
Profile: KCFV-FM is a non-commercial station owned by St. Louis Community College. The format of the station is rhythmic Top 40/CHR music. KCFV-FM broadcasts to the St. Louis area at 89.5 FM.
FM RADIO STATION

KCFX-FM 39577
Owner: Cumulus Media Inc.
Editorial: 5800 Foxridge Dr, 6th Fl, Mission, Kansas 66202-2333 **Tel:** 1 913 514-3000.
Web site: http://www.kcfx.com
Profile: KCFX-FM is a commercial station owned by Cumulus Media Inc. The format of the station is classic rock. KCFX-FM broadcasts to the Kansas, MO area at 101.1 FM.
FM RADIO STATION

KCFY-FM 41899
Owner: Relevant Media Inc.
Editorial: 1921 S Rail Ave, Yuma, Arizona 85365
Tel: 1 928 341-9730.
Email: kcfy@kcfyfm.com
Web site: http://www.kcfyfm.com
Profile: KCFY-FM is a non-commercial station owned by Relevant Media Inc. The format of the station is contemporary Christian. KCFY-FM broadcasts to the Yuma, AZ area at 88.1 FM.
FM RADIO STATION

KCGB-FM 44597
Owner: Bicoastal Media LLC
Editorial: 1190 22nd St, Hood River, Oregon 97031
Tel: 1 541 386-1511.
Web site: http://www.gorgeradio.com
Profile: KCGB-FM is a commercial station owned by Bicoastal Media LLC. The format of the station is hot adult contemporary music. KCGB-FM broadcasts to the Portland, OR area at 105.5 FM.
FM RADIO STATION

KCGL-FM 155774
Owner: Legend Communications
Editorial: 1949 Mountain View Dr, Cody, Wyoming 82414 **Tel:** 1 307 578-5000.
Email: news@bhrnwy.com
Web site: http://www.mybighornbasin.com
FM RADIO STATION

KCGM-FM 39578
Owner: Prairie Communications Inc.
Editorial: 20 Main St, Scobey, Montana 59263
Tel: 1 406 487-2293.
Email: kcgm@nemont.net
Profile: KCGM-FM is a commercial station owned by Prairie Communications Inc. The format of the station is country. KCGM-FM broadcasts to the Minot-Bismarck, ND area at 95.7 FM.
FM RADIO STATION

KCGN-FM 41424
Owner: Christian Heritage Broadcasting
Editorial: 402 E Pike St, Osakis, Minnesota 56360-8346 **Tel:** 1 320 859-3000.
Email: mail@praisefm.org
Web site: http://www.praisefm.org
Profile: KCGN-FM is a non-commercial station owned by Christian Heritage Broadcasting. The format of the station is contemporary Christian programming. KCGN-FM broadcasts in the Osakis, MN area at 101.5 FM.
FM RADIO STATION

KCGQ-FM 45785
Owner: Max Media
Editorial: 324 Broadway St, Cape Girardeau, Missouri 63701-7331 **Tel:** 1 573 335-8291.
Email: realrock@riverradio.net
Web site: http://www.realrock993.com
Profile: KCGQ-FM is a commercial station owned by the Max Media. The format of the station is rock/album-oriented rock. KCGQ-FM broadcasts to the Cape Girardeau, MO area at 99.3 FM.
FM RADIO STATION

KCGS-AM 34900
Owner: Kiefer Retirement Services
Editorial: 208 Battle St, Marshall, Arkansas 72650-9440 **Tel:** 1 870 448-5567.
Email: kcgsam@windstream.net
Web site: http://www.kcgsam.com
Profile: KCGS-AM is a commercial station owned by Kiefer Retirement Services. The format of the station is talk. KCGS-AM broadcasts to the Marshall, AR area at 960 AM.
AM RADIO STATION

KCGY-FM 46498
Owner: Townsquare Media, LLC
Editorial: 3525 Soldier Springs Rd, Laramie, Wyoming 82070-9017 **Tel:** 1 307 745-4888.
Web site: http://www.Y95country.com
Profile: KCGY-FM is a commercial station owned by Townsquare Media, LLC. The format of the station is classic and contemporary country music. KCGY-FM broadcasts to the Laramie, WY area at 95.1 FM.
FM RADIO STATION

KCHA-AM 37217
Owner: Coloff Media
Editorial: 207 N Main St, Charles City, Iowa 50616-2016 **Tel:** 1 641 394-1000.
Email: kcha@kchanews.com
Web site: http://www.kchaam.com
Profile: KCHA-AM is a commercial station owned by Coloff Media. The format of the station is oldies. KCHA-AM broadcasts to the Charles City, IA area at 1580 AM.
AM RADIO STATION

KCHA-FM 44598
Owner: Coloff Media
Editorial: 207 N Main St, Charles City, Iowa 50616-2016 **Tel:** 1 641 228-1000.
Email: kcha@kchanews.com
Web site: http://kchanews.com
Profile: KCHA-FM is a commercial station owned by Coloff Media. The format of the station is adult contemporary. KCHA-FM broadcasts to the Charles City, IA area at 95.9 FM.
FM RADIO STATION

KCHE-AM 38457
Owner: J&J Radio Corp.
Editorial: 201 S 5th St, Cherokee, Iowa 51012-1731
Tel: 1 712 225-2511.
Email: kche1@ncn.net
Web site: http://www.kcheradio.com
Profile: KCHE-AM is a commercial station owned by J&J Radio Corp. The format of the station is adult standards. KCHE-AM broadcasts to the Cherokee, IA area at 1440 AM.
AM RADIO STATION

KCHE-FM 45826
Owner: J&J Radio Corp.
Editorial: 201 S 5th St, Cherokee, Iowa 51012-1731
Tel: 1 712 225-2511.
Email: news@kcheradio.com
Web site: http://www.kcheradio.com
Profile: KCHE-FM is a commercial station owned by the J&J Radio Corp. The format of the station is adult contemporary. KCHE-FM broadcasts to the Cherokee, IA area at 92.1 FM.
FM RADIO STATION

KCHH-FM 41139
Owner: Townsquare Media, LLC
Editorial: 27 N 27Th St, Billings, Montana 59101-2357
Tel: 1 406 248-7827.
Web site: http://www.newsradio95.com
Profile: KCHH-FM is a commercial station owned by Townsquare Media, LLC. The format of the station is news/talk. KCHH-FM broadcasts in the Billings, MT area at 95.5FM.
FM RADIO STATION

KCHI-AM 37218
Owner: Leatherman Communications Inc.
Editorial: 421 Washington St, Chillicothe, Missouri 64601-2521 **Tel:** 1 660 646-4173.
Web site: http://www.kchi.com
Profile: KCHI-AM is a commercial station owned by Leatherman Communications Inc. The format of the station is classic hits. KCHI-AM broadcasts to the Kansas City, MO area at 1010 AM.
AM RADIO STATION

KCHI-FM 44599
Owner: Leatherman Communications Inc.
Editorial: 421 Washington St, Chillicothe, Missouri 64601-2521 **Tel:** 1 660 646-4173.
Web site: http://www.kchi.com
Profile: KCHI-FM is a commercial station owned by Leatherman Communications Inc. The format of the station is classic hits. KCHI-FM broadcasts to the Kansas City, MO area at 98.5 FM.
FM RADIO STATION

KCHJ-AM 34901
Owner: Lotus Communications Corp.
Editorial: 5100 Commerce Dr, Bakersfield, California 93309-0684 **Tel:** 1 661 327-9711.
Web site: http://www.elgallito.com
Profile: KCHJ-AM is a commercial station owned by Lotus Communications Corp. The format of the station is Hispanic oldies. KCHJ-AM broadcasts to the Bakersfield, CA area at 1010 AM.
AM RADIO STATION

KCHK-AM 38662
Owner: Ingstad Brothers Broadcasting, LLC
Editorial: 25821 Langford Ave, New Prague, Minnesota 56071-8864 **Tel:** 1 952 758-2571.
Email: production@kchkradio.net
Web site: http://www.kchkradio.net
Profile: KCHK-AM is a commercial station owned by Ingstad Brothers Broadcasting, LLC. The primary format of the station is country. KCHK-AM broadcasts to the New Prague, MN area at a frequency of 1350 AM.
AM RADIO STATION

KCHK-FM 46015
Owner: Ingstad Brothers Broadcasting, LLC
Editorial: 25821 Langford Ave, New Prague, Minnesota 56071-8864 **Tel:** 1 952 758-2571.
Web site: http://www.kchkradio.net/listen-live-kchk
Profile: KRDS-FM is a commercial station owned by Ingstad Brothers Broadcasting, LLC. The primary format of the station is oldies. KRDS-FM broadcasts to the St. Paul, MN area at 95.5 FM.
FM RADIO STATION

KCHL-AM 36117
Owner: Martin Broadcasting
Editorial: 1211 W Hein Rd, San Antonio, Texas 78220-3301 **Tel:** 1 210 333-0050.
Web site: http://www.kchl.org
Profile: KCHL-AM is a commercial station owned by Martin Broadcasting. The format of the station is gospel music. KCHL-AM broadcasts to the San Antonio area at 1480 AM.
AM RADIO STATION

KCHQ-FM 434270
Owner: Rich Broadcasting, LLC
Editorial: 1406 Commerce Way, Idaho Falls, Idaho 83401-1233 **Tel:** 1 208 233-1133.
Web site: http://www.rivercountryfm.com
Profile: KCHQ-FM is a commercial station owned by Rich Broadcasting, LLC. The format of the station is contemporary country music. KCHQ-FM broadcasts to the eastern Idaho and western Wyoming areas at 102.1 FM.
FM RADIO STATION

KCHR-AM 34902
Owner: South Missouri Broadcasting Co. Inc.
Editorial: 205 E Commercial St, Charleston, Missouri 63834-1731 **Tel:** 1 573 683-6044.
Profile: KCHR-AM is a commercial station owned by South Missouri Broadcasting Co. Inc. The format of the station is oldies. KCHR-AM broadcasts to the Charleston, MO area at 1350 AM.
AM RADIO STATION

KCHS-AM 34903
Owner: GPK Media, LLC
Editorial: 1747 E 3rd Ave, Truth or Consequences, New Mexico 87901-2042 **Tel:** 1 575 894-2400.
Email: kchs@gpkmedia.com
Web site: http://www.gpkmedia.com
Profile: KCHS-AM is a commercial station owned by GPK Media, LLC. The format of the station is country and gospel. KCHS-AM broadcasts to the Truth or Consequences, NM area at 1400 AM.
AM RADIO STATION

KCHU-AM 36023
Owner: Terminal Radio Inc.
Editorial: 128 Pioneer Drive, Valdez, Alaska 99686
Tel: 1 907 835-4665.
Email: news@kchu.org
Web site: http://www.kchu.org
Profile: KCHU-AM is a non-commercial station owned by Terminal Radio Inc. The format of the station is variety. KATB-FM broadcasts to the Valdez, AK area at 770 AM.
AM RADIO STATION

KCHW-FM 961542
Owner: Northeast Washington Community Radio Guild
Tel: 1 509 935-6627.
Web site: http://www.kchw.org
Profile: KCHW-FM is a non-commercial station owned by Northeast Washington Community Radio Guild. The format of the station is community radio. The station broadcasts to the Chewelah, Washington area at 102.7 FM.
FM RADIO STATION

KCHX-FM 41657
Owner: ICA Radio
Editorial: 1330 E 8th St Ste 207, Odessa, Texas 79761-4731 **Tel:** 1 432 563-9102.
Web site: http://quebuena106.com
Profile: KCHX-FM is a commercial station owned by ICA Radio. The format of the station is Regional Mexican. KCHX-FM broadcasts to the Odessa, TX area at 106.7 FM.
FM RADIO STATION

KCHZ-FM 43160
Owner: Cumulus Media Inc.
Editorial: 5800 Foxridge Dr Ste 600, Mission, Kansas 66202-2335 **Tel:** 1 913 514-3000.
Web site: http://www.957thevibe.com
Profile: KCHZ-FM is a commercial station owned by Cumulus Media Inc. The format of the station is rhythmic Top 40/CHR music. KCHZ-FM broadcasts to the Kansas City, MO area at 95.7 FM.
FM RADIO STATION

KCID-AM 39471
Owner: SNL Radio, LLC
Editorial: 5601 Cassia St, Boise, Idaho 83705-1836
Tel: 1 208 344-4774.
Web site: http://www.salyluzradio.com
Profile: KCID-AM is a commercial station owned by SNL Radio, LLC. The format of the station is Spanish Catholic. KCID-AM broadcasts to the Boise, ID area at 1490 AM.
AM RADIO STATION

KCIE-FM 43845
Owner: Jicarilla Apache Nation
Editorial: AIE Building, Narrow Gauge Road, Dulce, New Mexico 87528 **Tel:** 1 575 759-3681.
Web site: http://www.kcieradio.com
Profile: KCIE-FM a non-commercial station owned by Jicarilla Apache Nation. The format of the station is a mixed variety of music and talk. KCIE-FM broadcasts to the Albuquerque, NM area at 90.5 FM.
FM RADIO STATION

KCII-AM 37219
Owner: M & H Broadcasting
Editorial: 110 E Main St, Washington, Iowa 52353-2043 **Tel:** 1 319 653-2113.
Email: news@kciiradio.com
Web site: http://www.kciiradio.com
Profile: KCII-AM is a commercial station owned by M & H Broadcasting. The format of the station is adult contemporary music and news. KCII-AM broadcasts to the Cedar Rapids, IA area at 1380 AM.
AM RADIO STATION

KCII-FM 44600
Owner: M & H Broadcasting
Editorial: 110 E Main St, Washington, Iowa 52353-2043 **Tel:** 1 319 653-2113.
Email: kcii@kciiradio.com
Web site: http://www.kciiradio.com
Profile: KCII-FM is a commercial station owned by M & H Broadcasting. The format of the station is adult contemporary. KCII-FM broadcasts to the Cedar Rapids, IA area at 106.1 FM.
FM RADIO STATION

KCIL-FM 44512
Owner: My Home Team Media
Editorial: 120 Prevost Dr, Houma, Louisiana 70364-2338 **Tel:** 1 985 851-1020.
Web site: http://www.c967.com
Profile: KCIL-FM is a commercial station owned by My Home Team Media, LLC. The format of the station is contemporary country. KCIL-FM broadcasts to the southern Louisiana area at 96.7.
FM RADIO STATION

KCIM-AM 38361
Owner: Carroll Broadcasting Co.
Editorial: 1119 East Plaza Dr, Carroll, Iowa 51401-3838 **Tel:** 1 712 792-4321.
Email: kcim@carrollbroadcasting.com
Web site: http://www.1380kcim.com
Profile: KCIM-AM is commercial station owned by Carroll Broadcasting Co. The format of the station is classic hits and news. KCIM-AM broadcasts to the Carroll, IA area at 1380 AM.
AM RADIO STATION

KCIN-FM 72922
Owner: Cherry Creek Radio
Editorial: 750 Ridgeview Dr Ste 204, St George, Utah 84770-2697 **Tel:** 1 435 673-3579.
Web site: http://www.bigkickincountry.com
Profile: KCIN-FM is a commercial station owned by Cherry Creek Radio. The format of the station is contemporary country. KCIN-FM broadcasts to the Cedar City, UT area at 94.9 FM.
FM RADIO STATION

KCIR-FM 41131
Owner: Faith Communications Corp.
Editorial: 1446 Filer Ave E, Twin Falls, Idaho 83301-4121 **Tel:** 1 702 731-5452.
Email: info@sosradio.net
Web site: http://www.sosradio.net
Profile: KCIR-FM is non-commercial station owned by Faith Communications Corp. The format of the station is contemporary Christian music. KCIR-FM broadcasts in the Twin Falls, ID area at 90.7 FM.
FM RADIO STATION

KCIS-AM 38688
Owner: Crista Ministries
Editorial: 19319 Fremont Ave N, Shoreline, Washington 98133 **Tel:** 1 206 546-7350.
Email: news@kcisradio.com
Web site: http://www.kcisradio.com
Profile: KCIS-AM is a commercial station owned by Crista Ministries. The format of the station is religious and Christian programming. KCIS-AM broadcasts to the Seattle area at 630 AM.
AM RADIO STATION

KCIV-FM 41100
Owner: Bott Broadcasting Co.
Editorial: 1031 15th St, Ste 1, Modesto, California 95354 **Tel:** 1 209 524-8999.
Email: kciv@bottradionetwork.com
Web site: http://www.bottradionetwork.com
Profile: KCIV-FM is a commercial station owned by Bott Broadcasting Co. The format of the station is religious and Christian programming. KCIV-FM broadcasts to the Modesto, CA area at 99.9 FM.
FM RADIO STATION

KCIX-FM 42265
Owner: Townsquare Media, LLC
Editorial: 827 E Park Blvd Ste 100, Boise, Idaho 83712-7783 **Tel:** 1 208 344-6363.
Web site: http://mix106radio.com
Profile: KCIX-FM is a commercial station owned by Townsquare Media, LLC. The format of the station is hot adult contemporary. KCIX-FM broadcasts to the Boise, ID area at 105.9 FM.
FM RADIO STATION

KCJB-AM 38857
Owner: iHeartMedia Inc.
Editorial: 1000 20th Ave SW, Minot, North Dakota 58701-6447 **Tel:** 1 701 852-4646.
Web site: http://www.kcjb910.com
Profile: KCJB-AM is a commercial station owned by iHeartMedia Inc. The format of the station is classic country music. KCJB-AM broadcasts in the Minot, ND area at 910 AM.
AM RADIO STATION

KCJC-FM 42256
Owner: East Arkansas Broadcasters Inc.
Editorial: 2705 E Parkway Dr, Russellville, Arkansas 72802-2006 **Tel:** 1 479 968-6816.
Email: news@rivervalleyradio.com
Web site: http://www.rivercountrykcjc.com
Profile: KCJC-FM is a commercial station owned by East Arkansas Broadcasters Inc. The format of the station is country. KCJC-FM broadcasts in Russellville, AR at 102.3 FM.
FM RADIO STATION

KCJF-FM 358820
Owner: MOR Media Inc.
Editorial: 400 Tower Dr, Paragould, Arkansas 72450-4891 **Tel:** 1 870 236-7627.
Web site: http://www.irocknea.com/
Profile: KCJF-FM is a commercial station owned by MOR Media Inc. The format of the station is rock. KCJF-FM broadcasts to the Jonesboro, AR area at 103.9 FM.
FM RADIO STATION

KCJJ-AM 35800
Owner: River City Radio Inc.
Editorial: 845 Quarry Rd Ste 120, Coralville, Iowa 52241-2206 **Tel:** 1 319 354-1242.
Email: kcjjam@gmail.com
Web site: http://www.1630kcjj.com
Profile: KCJJ-AM is a commercial station owned by River City Radio Inc. The format for the station is hot adult contemporary and talk. KCJJ-AM broadcasts to the Cedar Rapids, IA area at 1630 AM.
AM RADIO STATION

KCJK-FM 75706
Owner: Cumulus Media Inc.
Editorial: 5800 Foxridge Dr Fl 6, Mission, Kansas 66202-2347 **Tel:** 1 913 514-3000.
Web site: http://www.x1051kc.com/
Profile: KCJK-FM is a commercial station owned by Cumulus Media Inc. The format of the station is Kansas City's alternative music. KCJK-FM broadcasts to the Mission, MO area at 105.1 FM.
FM RADIO STATION

KCKC-FM 43420
Owner: Steel City Media
Editorial: 508 Westport Rd Ste 202, Kansas City, Missouri 64111-3019 **Tel:** 1 816 753-4000.
Web site: http://kc1021.com
Profile: KCKC-FM is a commercial station owned by Steel City Media. The format of the station is adult contemporary. KCKC-FM broadcasts to the Kansas City, MO area at 102.1 FM.
FM RADIO STATION

KCKK-AM 153418
Owner: Hunt Broadcasting
Editorial: 1032 S Union Blvd, Lakewood, Colorado 80228-3373 **Tel:** 1 303 989-3920.
Web site: http://www.937therock.com
Profile: KCKK-AM is a commercial station owned by Hunt Broadcasting. The format of the station is adult hits. KCKK-AM broadcasts to the Denver area at 1510 AM.
AM RADIO STATION

KCKL-FM 46505
Owner: Lake Country Radio LP
Editorial: 11125 State Highway 31 W, Malakoff, Texas 75148-7158 **Tel:** 1 903 489-1238.
Email: tcrum@kcklfm.com
Web site: http://www.kcklfm.com
Profile: KCKL-FM is a commercial station owned by Lake Country Radio LP. The format of the station is contemporary country music. KCKL-FM broadcasts in the Malakoff, TX area at 95.9 FM.
FM RADIO STATION

KCKM-AM 35108
Owner: Kickin' Country Broadcasting Inc.
Editorial: 1200 S Stockton Ave, Monahans, Texas 79756 **Tel:** 1 432 943-2588.
Email: kckm1330@aol.com
Web site: http://www.kckm1330.com
Profile: KCKM-AM is a commercial station owned by Kickin' Country Broadcasting Inc. The format of the station is classic country. KCKM-AM broadcasts to the Monahans, TX area at 1330 AM.
AM RADIO STATION

KCKN-AM 235286
Owner: Radio Visión Cristiana Management
Tel: 1 973 881-8700.
Email: 1020kckn@gmail.com
Web site: http://www.radiovision.net
Profile: KCKN-AM is a commercial station owned by Radio Visión Cristiana Management. The format of the station is Hispanic and religious programming. KCKN-AM broadcasts to the Roswell, NM area at 1020 AM.
AM RADIO STATION

KCKX-AM 35884
Owner: La Unica Broadcasting Company
Editorial: 1665 James St, Woodburn, Oregon 97071-3475 **Tel:** 1 503 981-9400.
Email: info@lapantera940.com
Web site: http://www.espn1460deportes.com
Profile: KCKX-AM is a commercial station owned by the La Unica Broadcasting Company. The format of the station is Hispanic sports. KCKX-AM broadcasts to the Woodburn, OR area at 1460 AM.
AM RADIO STATION

KCKY-AM 86632
Owner: Herrera(Moises)
Editorial: 1445 W Baseline Rd, Phoenix, Arizona 85041 **Tel:** 1 602 276-4241.
Profile: KCKY-AM is a commercial station owned by Moises Herrera. The format of the station is Hispanic Christian programming. KCKY-AM broadcasts in the Phoenix area at 1150 AM.
AM RADIO STATION

KCLB-FM 44422
Owner: Morris Communications
Editorial: 1321 N Gene Autry Trl, Palm Springs, California 92262-5473 **Tel:** 1 760 322-7890.
Email: studio@937kclb.com
Web site: http://www.937kclb.com
Profile: KCLB-FM is a commercial station owned by Morris Communications. The format of the station is rock alternative music. KCLB-FM broadcasts to the Palm Springs, CA area at 93.7 FM.
FM RADIO STATION

KCLD-FM 44602
Owner: Leighton Enterprises Inc.
Editorial: 619 W Saint Germain St, Saint Cloud, Minnesota 56301-3640 **Tel:** 1 320 251-1450.
Web site: http://www.1047kcld.com
Profile: KCLD-FM is a commercial station owned by Leighton Enterprises Inc. The format of the station is Top 40/CHR music. KCLD-FM broadcasts in the Saint Cloud, MN area at 104.7 FM. Send any press materials to the station's program director.
FM RADIO STATION

KCLE-AM 35801
Owner: M&M Broadcasters Ltd.
Editorial: 919 N Main St, Cleburne, Texas 76033-3853
Tel: 1 817 645-6643.
Web site: http://www.sports1460espn.com
Profile: KCLE-AM is a commercial station owned by M&M Broadcasters Ltd. The format of the station is country music. KCLE-AM broadcasts to the Cleburne, TX area at 1460 AM.
AM RADIO STATION

KCLF-AM 36291
Owner: New World Broadcasting Co.
Editorial: 803 Parent St, New Roads, Louisiana 70760-2215 **Tel:** 1 225 638-6821.
Web site: http://www.kclf1500am.com
Profile: KCLF-AM is a commercial station owned by New World Broadcasting Co. The format of the station is variety. KCLF-AM broadcasts to the New Roads, LA area at 1500 AM.
AM RADIO STATION

KCLH-FM 44194
Owner: Midwest Family Broadcasting
Editorial: 201 State St, La Crosse, Wisconsin 54601
Tel: 1 608 782-1230.
Email: email@classichits947.com
Web site: http://www.classichits947.com
Profile: KCLH-FM is a commercial station owned by Midwest Family Broadcasting. The format of the station is classic hits. KCLH-FM broadcasts in the La Crosse, WI area at 94.7 FM.
FM RADIO STATION

KCLI-AM 36630
Owner: Wright Broadcasting Systems
Editorial: 10040 Highway 54, Weatherford, Oklahoma 73096-3021 **Tel:** 1 580 772-5939.
Web site: http://www.newstalk1320.com
AM RADIO STATION

KCLI-FM 42569
Owner: Wright Broadcasting Systems
Editorial: 10040 Highway 54, Weatherford, Oklahoma 73096-3021 **Tel:** 1 580 772-5939.
Email: news@wrightwradio.com
Web site: http://www.newstalkkcli.com
Profile: KCLI-FM is a commercial station owned by Wright Broadcasting Systems. The format of the station is news and talk. KCLI-FM broadcasts to Oklahoma City at 99.3 FM.
FM RADIO STATION

KCLK-AM 37220
Owner: Pacific Empire Radio Corp.
Editorial: 1859 5th Ave, Clarkston, Washington 99403-1401 **Tel:** 1 208 743-6564.
Email: wecare@catfm.com
Profile: KCLK-AM is a commercial station owned by Pacific Empire Radio Corp. The format of the station is sports. KCLK-AM broadcasts to the Spokane, WA area at 1430 AM.
AM RADIO STATION

KCLK-FM 44603
Owner: Pacific Empire Radio Corp.
Editorial: 403 Capital St, Lewiston, Idaho 83501-1815
Tel: 1 208 743-6564.
Email: wecare@catfm.com
Web site: http://catfm01.businesscatalyst.com
Profile: KCLK-FM is a commercial station owned by Pacific Empire Radio Corp. The format of the station is oldies music. KCLK-FM broadcasts to the Spokane, WA area at 94.1 FM.
FM RADIO STATION

KCLL-FM 42719
Owner: Foster Communications Co. Inc.
Editorial: 2824 Sherwood Way, San Angelo, Texas 76901-3514 **Tel:** 1 325 949-3333.
Web site: http://www.kcll-fm.com
Profile: KCLL-FM is a commercial station owned by Foster Communications Co. Inc. The format of the station is oldies music. KCLL-FM broadcasts to San Angelo, TX at 100.1 FM.
FM RADIO STATION

KCLN-AM 37221
Owner: Prairie Communications LLP
Editorial: 1853 442nd Ave, Clinton, Iowa 52732-8748
Tel: 1 563 243-1390.
Web site: http://www.1390kcln.wix.com
Profile: KCLN-AM is a commercial station owned by Prairie Communications LLP. The format of the station is adult standards. KCLN-AM broadcasts to the Clinton, IA area at 1390 AM.
AM RADIO STATION

KCLQ-FM 45823
Owner: Pearson Broadcasting
Editorial: 18785 Finch Rd, Lebanon, Missouri 65536-7812 **Tel:** 1 417 532-2962.
Web site: http://www.1079thecoyote.com
Profile: KCLQ-FM is a commercial station owned by Pearson Broadcasting. The format of the station is contemporary country. KCLQ-FM broadcasts to the Lebanon, MO area at 107.9 FM.
FM RADIO STATION

KCLR-FM 41623
Owner: Zimmer Radio Group
Editorial: 3215 Lemone Industrial Blvd, Columbia, Missouri 65201-8248 **Tel:** 1 800 449-5257.
Email: clear99@zrgmail.com
Web site: http://www.clear99.com
Profile: KCLR-FM is a commercial station owned by Zimmer Radio Group. The format of the station is contemporary country music. KCLR-FM broadcasts to the Columbia, MO area at 99.3 FM.
FM RADIO STATION

KCLT-FM 39582
Owner: Delta Force II Radio
Editorial: 700 W Martin Luther King Jr Dr, Ste 2, West Helena, Arkansas 72390 **Tel:** 1 870 572-9506.
Email: force2@sbcglobal.net
Web site: http://www.force2radio.com
Profile: KCLT-FM is a commercial station owned by Delta Force II Radio. The format of the station is urban contemporary, blues and gospel. KCLT-FM broadcasts to the West Helena, AR area at 104.9 FM.
FM RADIO STATION

KCLV-AM 38823
Owner: Zia Broadcasting
Editorial: 710 CR K, Clovis, New Mexico 88101-9149
Tel: 1 575 763-4401.
Email: kclv@allsups.com
Profile: KCLV-AM is a commercial station owned by Zia Broadcasting. The format of the station is sports. KCLV-AM broadcasts to the Clovis, NM area at 1240 AM.
AM RADIO STATION

KCLV-FM 46159
Owner: Zia Broadcasting
Editorial: 710 CR K, Clovis, New Mexico 88101-9149
Tel: 1 575 763-4401.
Email: kclv@allsups.com
Profile: KCLV-FM is a commercial station owned by Zia Broadcasting. The format of the station is contemporary country music. KCLV-FM broadcasts to the Clovis, NM area at 99.1 FM.
FM RADIO STATION

KCLW-AM 36067
Owner: Lasting Value Broadcasting Group
Editorial: 115 N Rice St, Hamilton, Texas 76531
Tel: 1 254 386-8804.
Web site: http://www.kclw.com
Profile: KCLW-AM is a commercial station owned by Lasting Value Broadcasting Group. The format of the station is classic country. KCLW-AM broadcasts to the Hamilton, TX area at 900 AM.
AM RADIO STATION

KCLX-AM 39003
Owner: Inland Northwest Broadcasting
Editorial: 1114 N Almon St, Moscow, Idaho 83843-8507 **Tel:** 1 208 882-2551.
Email: psa@inlandradio.com
Profile: KCLX-AM is a commercial station owned by Inland Northwest Broadcasting. The format of the station is classic country. KCLX-AM broadcasts to the Moscow, ID area at 1450 AM.
AM RADIO STATION

KCLY-FM 46769
Owner: Taylor Communications
Editorial: 1815 Meadowlark Rd, Clay Center, Kansas 67432 **Tel:** 1 785 632-5661.
Email: news@kclyradio.com
Web site: http://www.kclyradio.com
Profile: KCLY-FM is a commercial station owned by Taylor Communications. The format of the station is adult contemporary and adult standards music. KCLY-FM broadcasts to the Clay Center, KS area at 100.9 FM.
FM RADIO STATION

KCLZ-FM 779569
Owner: Copper Mountain Broadcasting
Tel: 1 760 362-4264.
Web site: http://www.937kclb.com/
Profile: KCLZ-FM is a commercial station owned by Copper Mountain Broadcasting. The format of the station is Rock. KCLZ-FM broadcasts to the Twentynine Palms, CA area at a frequency of 95.5 FM.
FM RADIO STATION

KCMB-FM 41171
Owner: Elkhorn Media Group
Editorial: 1009 Adams Ave Ste C, La Grande, Oregon 97850-2667 **Tel:** 1 541 963-3405.
Web site: http://www.1047kcmb.com
Profile: KCMB-FM is a commercial station owned by Elkhorn Media Group. The format of the station is country. KCMB-FM broadcasts to the La Grande, OR area at 104.7 FM.
FM RADIO STATION

KCMC-AM 38474
Owner: Texarkana Radio Center Licenses, LLC
Editorial: 615 Olive St, Texarkana, Texas 75501-5512 **Tel:** 1 903 793-4671.
Profile: KCMC-AM is a commercial station owned by Texarkana Radio Center Licenses, LLC. The format of the station is classic hits. KCMC-AM broadcasts to the Texarkana, TX area at 940 AM.
AM RADIO STATION

KCME-FM 41113
Owner: Cheyenne Mountain PB House Inc.
Editorial: 1921 N Weber St, Colorado Springs, Colorado 80907-6903 **Tel:** 1 719 578-5263.
Email: gm@kcme.org
Web site: http://www.kcme.org
Profile: KCME-FM is a non-commercial station owned by Cheyenne Mountain PB House Inc. The format of the station is classical music. KCME-FM broadcasts to the Colorado Springs, CO area at 88.7 FM.
FM RADIO STATION

KCMH-FM 43327
Owner: Christian Broadcasting Group of Mountain Home Inc.
Editorial: 126 S Church St, Mountain Home, Arkansas 72653-3828 **Tel:** 1 870 425-2525.
Web site: http://www.kcmhradio.org
Profile: KCMH-FM is a non-commercial station owned by Christian Broadcasting Group of Mountain Home Inc. The format of the station is Christian and religious. KCMH-FM broadcasts to Mountain Home, AR at 91.5 FM.
FM RADIO STATION

KCMI-FM 41138
Owner: Christian Media, Inc.
Editorial: 209 E 15th St, Scottsbluff, Nebraska 69361-3176 **Tel:** 1 308 632-5264.
Email: contact@kcmifm.com
Web site: http://www.kcmifm.com
Profile: KCMI-FM is a commercial station owned by Christian Media, Inc. The format of the station is contemporary Christian music and religious talk. KCMI-FM broadcasts in the Scottsbluff, NE area at 96.9 FM
FM RADIO STATION

KCML-FM 43983
Owner: Leighton Enterprises Inc.
Editorial: 619 W Saint Germain St, Saint Cloud, Minnesota 56301-3640 **Tel:** 1 320 251-1450.
Web site: http://999morefm.com
Profile: KCML-FM is a commercial station owned by Leighton Enterprises Inc. The format of the station is Lite Rock/Lite AC music. KCML-FM broadcasts to the St. Cloud, MN area at 99.9 FM. Send any press materials to the station's program director.
FM RADIO STATION

KCMO-AM 38640
Owner: Cumulus Media Inc.
Editorial: 5800 Foxridge Dr Fl 6, Mission, Kansas 66202-2347 **Tel:** 1 913 514-3000.
Web site: http://www.kcmotalkradio.com/
Profile: KCMO-AM is a commercial station owned by Cumulus Media Inc. The format of the station is news and talk. KCMO-AM broadcasts to the Kansas City, MO area at 710 AM.
AM RADIO STATION

KCMO-FM 45993
Owner: Cumulus Media Inc.
Editorial: 5800 Foxridge Dr Fl 6, Mission, Kansas 66202-2347 **Tel:** 1 913 514-3000.
Email: news@710kcmo.com
Web site: http://www.949kcmo.com
Profile: KCMO-FM is a commercial station owned by Cumulus Media Inc. The format for the station is classic hits. KCMO-FM broadcasts to the Kansas City, MO area at 94.9 FM.
FM RADIO STATION

KCMP-FM 42630
Owner: Minnesota Public Radio
Editorial: 480 Cedar St, Saint Paul, Minnesota 55101-2217 **Tel:** 1 651 290-1500.
Email: 893dj@mpr.org
Web site: http://www.mpr.org/listen/stations/knowksjn
Profile: KCMP-FM is a non-commercial station owned by Minnesota Public Radio. The format of the station is adult album alternative with a significant playlist of local music. KCMP-FM broadcasts to the St. Paul, MN area at 89.3 FM.
FM RADIO STATION

KCMQ-FM 46782
Owner: Zimmer Radio Group
Editorial: 3215 Lemone Industrial Blvd Ste 200, Columbia, Missouri 65201-8248 **Tel:** 1 573 875-1099.
Email: kcmq@zrgmail.com
Web site: http://www.kcmq.com
Profile: KCMQ-FM is a commercial station owned by the Zimmer Radio Group. The format of the station is classic rock music. KCMQ-FM broadcasts in the Columbia, MO area at 96.7 FM.
FM RADIO STATION

KCMR-FM 41136
Owner: T L C Broadcasting Corp.
Editorial: 316 N Federal Ave, Mason City, Iowa 50401-3212 **Tel:** 1 641 424-9300.
Email: kcmr@kcmrfm.com
Web site: http://www.kcmrfm.com
FM RADIO STATION

KCMS-FM 46040
Owner: Crista Ministries
Editorial: 19319 Fremont Ave N, Shoreline, Washington 98133-3800 **Tel:** 1 206 546-7350.
Email: comments@spirit1053.com
Web site: http://www.spirit1053.com
Profile: KCMS-FM is a commercial station owned by Crista Ministries. The format of the station is contemporary Christian music. KCMS-FM broadcasts to the Seattle area at 105.3 FM.
FM RADIO STATION

KCMT-FM 88105
Owner: Lotus Communications Corp.
Editorial: 3871 N Commerce Dr, Tucson, Arizona 85705-2983 **Tel:** 1 520 407-4500.
Web site: http://www.kcmt.com
Profile: KCMT-FM is a commercial station owned by Lotus Communications Corp. The format of the station is regional Mexican music. KCMT-FM broadcasts to the Tucscon, AZ area at 92.1 FM.
FM RADIO STATION

KCMX-AM 38973
Owner: Mapleton Radio, LLC
Editorial: 1438 Rossanley Dr, Medford, Oregon 97501 **Tel:** 1 541 779-1550.
Web site: http://www.kcmxam.com
Profile: KCMX-AM is a commercial station owned by Mapleton Radio, LLC. The format of the station is news and talk. KCMX-AM broadcasts to the Medford, OR area at 880 AM.
AM RADIO STATION

KCMX-FM 46310
Owner: Mapleton Radio, LLC
Editorial: 1438 Rossanley Dr, Medford, Oregon 97501-1751 **Tel:** 1 541 779-1550.
Web site: http://www.lite102.com
Profile: KCMX-FM is a commercial station owned by Mapleton Radio, LLC. The format of the station is Lite Rock/Lite AC. KCMX-FM broadcasts to the Medford, OR area at 101.9 FM.
FM RADIO STATION

KCMY-AM 39313
Owner: Evans Broadcasting
Editorial: 1960 Idaho St, Carson City, Nevada 89701-5306 **Tel:** 1 775 884-8000.
Email: prod@991fmtalk.com
Profile: KCMY-AM is a commercial station owned by Evans Broadcasting. The format of the station is classic country. KCMY-AM broadcasts to the Reno, NV area at 1300 AM.
AM RADIO STATION

KCNA-FM 41610
Owner: Opus Broadcasting Systems Inc.
Editorial: 511 Rossanley Dr, Medford, Oregon 97501-1771 **Tel:** 1 541 772-0322.
Web site: http://www.1027thedrive.com
Profile: KCNA-FM is a commercial station owned by Opus Broadcasting Systems Inc. The format of the station is classic hits music. KCNA-FM broadcasts to the Medford, OR area at 102.7 FM.
FM RADIO STATION

KCNB-FM 521915
Owner: Eagle Communications
Editorial: 331 Main St, Chadron, Nebraska 69337 **Tel:** 1 308 432-2060.
Profile: KCNB-FM is a commercial station owned by Eagle Communications. The format of the station is adult contemporary. KCNB-FM broadcasts to the Chadron, NE area at 94.7 FM.
FM RADIO STATION

KCND-FM 41130
Owner: Prairie Public Broadcasting Inc.
Editorial: 1814 N 15th St, Bismarck, North Dakota 58501 **Tel:** 1 701 224-1700.
Email: info@prairiepublic.org
Web site: http://www.prairiepublic.org
Profile: KCND-FM is a non-commercial station owned by Prairie Public Broadcasting Inc. The format of the station is news, classical and jazz music. KCND-FM broadcasts to the Bismarck, ND area at 90.5 FM.
FM RADIO STATION

KCNI-AM 38480
Owner: Custer County Broadcasting Inc.
Editorial: West Hwy 2, Broken Bow, Nebraska 68822 **Tel:** 1 308 872-5881.
Email: info@sandhillsexpress.com
Web site: http://www.kbbn.com/kcni.php
Profile: KCNI-AM is a commercial station owned by Custer County Broadcasting Inc. The format of the station is country. KCNI-AM broadcasts to the Broken Bow, NE area at 1280 AM.
AM RADIO STATION

KCNO-FM 46641
Owner: EDI Media
Editorial: 1773 W San Bernardino Rd Bldg C31, West Covina, California 91790-1049 **Tel:** 1 530 233-3570.
Email: englishradio@edimediainc.com
Web site: http://www.edimediainc.com/en/index.php?option=com_content&view=article&id=75&Itemid=112
Profile: KCNO-FM is a commercial station owned by EDI Media. The format of the station is classic country. KCNO-FM broadcasts to the Alturas, CA area at 94.5 FM.
FM RADIO STATION

KCNP-FM 613299
Owner: Chickasaw Nation
Editorial: 100 W 13th St Ste 220, Ada, Oklahoma 74820-6445 **Tel:** 1 580 272-5267.
Email: kcnp@chickasaw.net
Web site: http://www.kcnpradio.org
Profile: KCNP-FM is a non-commercial station owned by Chickasaw Nation. The format of the station is community radio, a variety of news, folk, jazz and ethnic programming. KCNP-FM broadcasts to Ada, OK and surrounding areas at 89.5 FM.
FM RADIO STATION

KCNQ-FM 41103
Owner: QAB Media LLC
Editorial: 14 Sierra Dr, Kernville, California 93238-1006 **Tel:** 1 760 376-4500.
Web site: http://www.kernriverradio.com
Profile: KCNQ-FM is a commercial station owned by QAB Media LLC. The format of the station is country. KCNQ-FM broadcasts to the Kernville, CA area at 102.5 FM.
FM RADIO STATION

KCNR-AM 36626
Owner: Free Fire Radio
Editorial: 1326 Market St, Redding, California 96001-0610 **Tel:** 1 530 605-4565.
Web site: http://www.kcnr1460.com
Profile: KCNR-AM is owned by Free Fire Radio. The format for the station is talk. KCNR-AM broadcasts to Shasta, CA and surrounding areas at 1460 AM.
AM RADIO STATION

KCNT-FM 39586
Owner: Central Community College
Editorial: 550 Technical Blvd, Hastings, Nebraska 68901-8362 **Tel:** 1 402 461-2581.
Web site: http://www.cccneb.edu/programs/mart/broadcasting.html
Profile: KCNT-FM is a non-commercial station owned by Central Community College. The format of the station is variety. KCNT-FM broadcasts to the Hastings, NE area at 88.1 FM.
FM RADIO STATION

KCNV-FM 155128
Owner: Nevada Public Radio
Editorial: 1289 S Torrey Pines Dr, Las Vegas, Nevada 89146-1004 **Tel:** 1 702 258-9895.
Email: info@classical897.org
Web site: http://www.classical897.org
Profile: KCNV-FM is a non-commercial station owned by Nevada Public Radio. The format of the station is classical music. KCNV-FM broadcasts to the Las Vegas area at 89.7 FM.
FM RADIO STATION

KCNW-AM 34907
Owner: Wilkins Communication Networks Inc.
Editorial: 4535 Metropolitan Ave, Kansas City, Kansas 66106-2551 **Tel:** 1 913 384-1380.
Email: kcnw@wilkinsradio.com
Web site: http://www.wilkinsradio.com
Profile: KCNW-AM is a commercial station owned by Wilkins Communication Networks Inc. and licensed by Kansas City Radio Inc. The format of the station is religious talk. KCNW-AM broadcasts to the Kansas City, KS area at 1380 AM.
AM RADIO STATION

KCNY-FM 45831
Owner: Crain Media Group LLC
Editorial: 1825 E Oak St Ste 103, Conway, Arkansas 72032-5957 **Tel:** 1 501 932-0825.
Email: production@crainmedia.com
Web site: http://www.y107fm.com
Profile: KCNY-FM is a commercial station owned by Crain Media Group LLC. The format of the station is contemporary country music. KCNY-FM broadcasts in the Searcy, AR area at 107.1 FM.
FM RADIO STATION

KCNZ-AM 34898
Owner: Coloff Media
Editorial: 721 Shirley St, Cedar Falls, Iowa 50613-1513 **Tel:** 1 319 277-1918.
Web site: http://www.kcnzam.com
Profile: KCNZ-AM is a commercial station owned by Coloff Media. The format of the station is sports. KCNZ-AM broadcasts to the Cedar Falls, IA area at 1650 AM.
AM RADIO STATION

KCOB-AM 37222
Owner: Alpha Media
Editorial: 1801 N 13th Ave E, Newton, Iowa 50208-1308 **Tel:** 1 641 792-5262.
Email: radioinfo@alphamediausa.com
Web site: http://myiowainfo.com
Profile: KCOB-AM is a commercial station owned by Alpha Media. The format of the station is oldies. KCOB-AM broadcasts to the Netwon, IA area at 1280 AM.
AM RADIO STATION

KCOB-FM 44758
Owner: Alpha Media
Editorial: 1801 N 13th Ave E, Newton, Iowa 50208-1308 **Tel:** 1 641 792-5262.
Email: radioinfo@alphamediausa.com
Web site: http://www.myiowainfo.com
Profile: KCOB-FM is a commercial station owned by Alpha Media. The format of the station is country music. KCOB-FM broadcasts to the Newton, IA area at 95.9 FM.
FM RADIO STATION

KCOG-AM 38730
Owner: KCOG, Inc.
Editorial: 402 N 12th St, Centerville, Iowa 52544-1718 **Tel:** 1 641 437-4242.
Email: kmgofm@lisco.com
Profile: KCOG-AM is a commercial station owned by KCOG, Inc. The format of the station is classic hits. KCOG-AM broadcasts to the Centerville, IA area at 1400 AM.
AM RADIO STATION

KCOH-FM 608383
Owner: A Better Broadcasting
Editorial: 5011 Almeda Rd, Houston, Texas 77004-5975 **Tel:** 1 713 803-2987.
Web site: http://www.kcohradio.com
Profile: KCOH-FM is a commercial station owned by A Better Broadcasting. The format of the station is urban contemporary. KCOH-FM broadcasts to Houston, TX and surrounding areas at 92.9 FM HD2.
FM RADIO STATION

KCOL-AM 37223
Owner: iHeartMedia Inc.
Editorial: 4270 Byrd Dr, Loveland, Colorado 80538-7074 **Tel:** 1 970 461-2560.
Email: 600kcol@iheartmedia.com
Web site: http://600kcol.iheart.com
Profile: KCOL-AM is a commercial station owned by iHeartMedia Inc. The format of the station is news, sports and talk. KCOL-AM broadcasts to the Fort Collins, CO area at 600 AM.
AM RADIO STATION

KCOL-FM 46809
Owner: iHeartMedia Inc.
Editorial: 2885 Interstate 10 E, Beaumont, Texas 77702-1001 **Tel:** 1 409 896-5555.
Email: requests@cool925.com
Web site: http://cool925.iheart.com
Profile: KCOL-FM is a commercial station owned by iHeartMedia Inc. The format of the station is classic hits. KCOL-FM broadcasts to the Beaumont, TX area at 92.5 FM.
FM RADIO STATION

KCOM-AM 34909
Owner: Cherry Creek Radio
Editorial: 218 N Austin St, Comanche, Texas 76442-2429 **Tel:** 1 325 356-3090.
Email: 943theox@gmail.com
Web site: http://www.kyoxfm.com/
Profile: KCOM-AM is a commercial station owned by Cherry Creek Radio. The format of the station is classic country and religious. KCOM-AM broadcasts to the Comanche, TX area at 1550 AM.
AM RADIO STATION

KCOR-AM 39114
Owner: Univision Communications Inc.
Editorial: 12451 Network Blvd Ste 140, San Antonio, Texas 78249-3336 **Tel:** 1 210 610-4300.
Web site: http://univisionamerica.com
Profile: KCOR-AM is a commercial station owned by Univision Communications Inc. The format of the station is Hispanic news and talk. KCOR-AM broadcasts to the San Antonio area at 1350 AM.
AM RADIO STATION

KCOW-AM 38428
Owner: Eagle Radio Inc.
Editorial: 1210 W 10th St, Alliance, Nebraska 69301-2804 **Tel:** 1 308 762-1400.
Web site: http://www.kcowradio.com
Profile: KCOW-AM is a commercial station owned by Eagle Radio Inc. The format of the station is classic hits. KCOW-AM broadcasts to the Alliance, NE area at 1400 AM.
AM RADIO STATION

KCOX-AM
37531

Owner: Cross Texas Media Inc.
Editorial: 1408 E Gibson St, Jasper, Texas 75951-5123 **Tel:** 1 409 384-4500.
Web site: https://www.1027ktxj.com/home-12.html
Profile: KCOX-AM is a commercial station owned by Cross Texas Media Inc. The format of the station is conservative talk. KCOX-AM broadcasts in the Jasper, TX area at 1350 AM.
AM RADIO STATION

KCOZ-FM
39922

Owner: College of the Ozarks
Editorial: College Of The Ozarks, Point Lookout, Missouri 65726-9999 **Tel:** 1 417 334-6411.
Email: jones@cofo.edu
Web site: http://www.cofo.edu
Profile: KCOZ-FM is a non-commercial station owned by College of the Ozarks. The format of the station is contemporary Christian music. KCOZ-FM broadcasts to the Point Lookout, MO area at 91.7 FM.
FM RADIO STATION

KCPI-FM
44607

Owner: Alpha Media
Editorial: 1633 W Main St, Albert Lea, Minnesota 56007-1868 **Tel:** 1 507 373-2338.
Email: 949thebreeze@digity.me
Web site: http://www.myalbertlea.com
Profile: KCPI-FM is a commercial station owned by Alpha Media. The format of the station is adult contemporary music. KCPI-FM broadcasts to the Albert Lea, MN area at 94.9 FM.
FM RADIO STATION

KCPS-AM
35895

Owner: Sandcastle Entertainment
Editorial: 205 S Gear Ave, West Burlington, Iowa 52655-1009 **Tel:** 1 319 754-6698.
Email: kcps@aol.com
Web site: http://www.kcpsradio.com
Profile: KCPS-AM is a commercial station owned by Sandcastle Entertainment. The format of the station is talk and sports. KCPS-AM broadcasts to the Burlington, IA area at 1150 AM.
AM RADIO STATION

KCPW-FM
42597

Owner: Wasatch Public Media
Editorial: 210 E 400 S Ste 7, Salt Lake City, Utah 84111-2849 **Tel:** 1 801 359-5279.
Email: news@kcpw.org
Web site: http://www.kcpw.org
Profile: KCPW-FM is a non-commercial station owned by Wasatch Public Media. The format of the station is news and talk. KCPW-FM broadcasts to the Salt Lake City area at 88.3 FM.
FM RADIO STATION

KCQL-AM
38822

Owner: iHeartMedia Inc.
Editorial: 200 E Broadway, Farmington, New Mexico 87401-6418 **Tel:** 1 505 325-1716.
Web site: http://www.foxsports1340.com
Profile: KCQL-AM is a commercial station owned by iHeartMedia Inc. The format of the station is sports. KCQL-AM broadcasts to the Farmington, NM area at 1340 AM.
AM RADIO STATION

KCQQ-FM
41629

Owner: iheartMedia Inc.
Editorial: 3535 E Kimberly Rd, Davenport, Iowa 52807-2583 **Tel:** 1 563 344-7000.
Web site: http://q106online.iheart.com/
Profile: KCQQ-FM is a commercial station owned by iheartMedia Inc. The format of the station is classic rock music. KCQQ-FM broadcasts to the Davenport, IA area at 106.5 FM.
FM RADIO STATION

KCRB-FM
41557

Owner: Minnesota Public Radio
Editorial: 405A Beltrami Ave NW, Bemidji, Minnesota 56601 **Tel:** 1 218 751-8864.
Email: newsroom@mpr.org
Web site: http://minnesota.publicradio.org
Profile: KCRB-FM is a non-commercial station owned by Minnesota Public Radio. The format of the station is classical. KCRB-FM broadcasts to the Bemidji, MN area at 88.5 FM.
FM RADIO STATION

KCRC-AM
37224

Owner: Chisholm Trail Broadcasting
Editorial: 316 E Willow Rd, Enid, Oklahoma 73701-1514 **Tel:** 1 580 237-1390.
Web site: http://www.ctbsports.com
Profile: KCRC-AM is a commercial station owned by Chisholm Trail Broadcasting. The format of the station is sports. KCRC-AM broadcasts to the Enid, OK area at 1390 AM.
AM RADIO STATION

KCRE-FM
44608

Owner: Bicoastal Media LLC
Editorial: 1345 Northcrest Dr, Crescent City, California 95531-2322 **Tel:** 1 707 464-9561.
Email: kcre@bicoastalmedia.com
Web site: http://www.kcrefm.com
Profile: KCRE-FM is a commercial station owned by Bicoastal Media LLC. The format of the station is adult contemporary. KCRE-FM broadcasts to the Crescent City, CA area at 94.3 FM.
FM RADIO STATION

KCRF-FM
46640

Owner: Yaquina Bay Communications Inc.
Editorial: 906 SW Alder St, Newport, Oregon 97365-4712 **Tel:** 1 541 265-2266.
Email: news@ybcradio.com
Web site: http://www.kcrffm.com
Profile: KCRF-FM is a commercial station owned by Yaquina Bay Communications Inc. The format of the station is classic rock music. KCRF-FM broadcasts in the Newport, OR area at 96.7 FM.
FM RADIO STATION

KCRH-FM
44304

Owner: Chabot-Las Positas Community College
Editorial: 25555 Hesperian Blvd, Hayward, California 94545-2447 **Tel:** 1 510 723-6954.
Email: kcrhradio@gmail.com
Web site: http://www.kcrhradio.com
Profile: KCRH-FM is a non-commercial station owned by Chabot-Las Positas Community College. The format of the station is variety. KCRH-FM broadcasts to the Hayward, CA area at 89.9 FM.
FM RADIO STATION

KCRK-FM
44610

Owner: North Country Broadcasting
Editorial: 187 Mantz Rickey Rd, Colville, Washington 99114-9562 **Tel:** 1 509 684-5031.
Email: news@kcvl.com
Web site: http://www.kcvl.com
Profile: KCRK-FM is a commercial station owned by North Country Broadcasting. The format of the station is adult contemporary. KCRK-FM broadcasts to the Spokane, WA area at 92.1 FM.
FM RADIO STATION

KCRL-FM
44170

Owner: Community Broadcasting, Inc.
Editorial: 10550 Barkley St Ste 100, Overland Park, Kansas 66212-1824 **Tel:** 1 800 875-1903.
Profile: KCRL-FM is a commercial station owned by Community Broadcasting, Inc. The format of the station is Christian programming. KCRL-FM broadcasts to the St. Louis, MO area at 90.3 FM.
FM RADIO STATION

KCRN-AM
39004

Owner: First Dallas Media, Inc.
Editorial: 750 N Saint Paul St Ste 1050, Dallas, Texas 75201-3236
Profile: KCRN-AM is a non-commercial station owned by First Dallas Media Inc. The format of the station is contemporary Christian music and religious programming. KCRN-AM broadcasts to the San Angelo, TX area at 1340 AM.
AM RADIO STATION

KCRO-AM
34911

Owner: Salem Media Group, Inc.
Editorial: 11717 Burt St Ste 202, Omaha, Nebraska 68154-1500 **Tel:** 1 402 422-1600.
Web site: http://www.kcro.com
Profile: KCRO-AM is a commercial station owned by Salem Media Group, Inc. The format of the station is Christian talk. KCRO-AM broadcasts to the Omaha, NE area at 660 AM.
AM RADIO STATION

KCRR-FM
39656

Owner: Waterloo Broadcasting
Editorial: 501 Sycamore St Ste 300, Waterloo, Iowa 50703-4651 **Tel:** 1 319 833-4800.
Email: kcrr@kcrr.com
Web site: http://www.kcrr.com
Profile: KCRR-FM is a commercial station owned by Cumulus Media Inc. The format for the station is classic rock. KCRR-FM broadcasts to the Cedar Rapids, IA area at 97.7 FM.
FM RADIO STATION

KCRS-AM
38828

Owner: ICA Radio
Editorial: 1330 E 8th St, Ste 207, Odessa, Texas 79761 **Tel:** 1 432 563-9102.
Email: newstalkkcrs@icabroadcasting.com
Web site: http://www.newstalkkcrs.com
Profile: KCRS-AM is a commercial station owned by ICA Radio. The format of the station is news and talk. KCRS-AM broadcasts to the Odessa, TX area at 550 AM.
AM RADIO STATION

KCRS-FM
46156

Owner: ICA Radio
Editorial: 1330 E 8th St, Ste 207, Odessa, Texas 79761 **Tel:** 1 432 563-9102.
Web site: http://www.1033kissfm.net
Profile: KCRS-FM is a commercial station owned by ICA Radio. The format of the station is Top 40/CHR. KCRS-FM broadcasts to the Odessa, TX area at 103.3 FM.
FM RADIO STATION

KCRT-AM
38987

Owner: Phillips Broadcasting Inc.
Editorial: 100 Fisher Dr, Trinidad, Colorado 81082
Tel: 1 719 846-3355.
Email: kcrt@comcast.net
Web site: http://www.kcrtradio.com
Profile: KCRT-AM is a commercial station owned by Phillips Broadcasting Inc. The format of the station is country. KCRT-AM broadcasts to the Trinidad, CO area at 1240 AM.
AM RADIO STATION

KCRT-FM
46326

Owner: Phillips Broadcasting Inc.
Editorial: 100 Fisher Dr, Trinidad, Colorado 81082
Tel: 1 719 846-3355.
Email: kcrt@comcast.net
Web site: http://www.kcrtradio.com
Profile: KCRT-FM is a commercial station owned by Phillips Broadcasting Inc. The format of the station is classic rock. KCRT-FM broadcasts to the Trinidad, CO area at 92.5 FM.
FM RADIO STATION

KCRV-AM
38868

Owner: Pollack Broadcasting Co.
Editorial: 717 Highway 84, Caruthersville, Missouri 63830 **Tel:** 1 573 333-1370.
Email: kcrvradio@att.net
Web site: http://www.kcrvradio.com/am
Profile: KCRV-AM is a commercial station owned by Pollack Broadcasting Co. The format of the station is classic country. KCRV-AM broadcasts to the Caruthersville, MO area at 1370 AM.
AM RADIO STATION

KCRV-FM
46205

Owner: Pollack Broadcasting Co.
Tel: 1 573 888-4616.
Email: kcrv@semoradio.com
Web site: http://pollackcompanies.net
Profile: KCRV-FM is a commercial station owned by Pollack Broadcasting Co. The format of the station is classic hits. KCRV-FM broadcasts to the Caruthersville, MO area at 105.1 FM.
FM RADIO STATION

KCRW-FM
39589

Owner: Santa Monica College
Editorial: 1900 Pico Blvd, Santa Monica, California 90405-1628 **Tel:** 1 310 450-5183.
Email: mail@kcrw.org
Web site: http://www.kcrw.com
Profile: KCRW-FM is a non-commercial station owned by Santa Monica College. The format of the station is college variety. KCRW-FM broadcasts to the Santa Monica, CA area at 89.9 FM.
FM RADIO STATION

KCRX-AM
36049

Owner: Casarez Jr.(Rosendo)
Editorial: 200 W 1st St Ste 801, Roswell, New Mexico 88203-4679 **Tel:** 1 575 622-1432.
Email: kcrx1430@hotmail.com
Web site: http://kcrx.tripod.com
Profile: KCRX-AM is a commercial station owned by Rosendo Casarez, Jr. The format of the station is classic hits. KCRX-AM broadcasts to the Roswell, NM area at 1430 AM.
AM RADIO STATION

KCRX-FM
46861

Owner: Ohana Media Group
Editorial: 285 SW Main Ct, Ste 200, Warrenton, Oregon 97146-9457 **Tel:** 1 503 861-6620.
Web site: http://www.kcrx1023.com
Profile: KCRX-FM is a commercial station owned by Ohana Media Group. The format of the station is classic rock music. KCRX-FM broadcasts in the Astoria, OR area at 102.3 FM.
FM RADIO STATION

KCRZ-FM
43559

Owner: Momentum Broadcasting LP
Editorial: 1401 W Caldwell Ave, Visalia, California 93277-7725 **Tel:** 1 559 553-1500.
Email: studio@z1049.com
Web site: http://www.hitz1049.com
Profile: KCRZ-FM is a commercial station owned by Momentum Broadcasting LP. The format of the station is hot adult contemporary. KCRZ-FM broadcasts to the Visalia, CA area at 104.9 FM.
FM RADIO STATION

KCSF-AM
36992

Owner: Cumulus Media Inc
Editorial: 6805 Corporate Dr Ste 130, Colorado Springs, Colorado 80919-1977 **Tel:** 1 719 593-2700.
Web site: http://www.xtrasports1300.com
Profile: KCSF-AM is a commercial station owned by Cumulus Media Inc. The format of the station is sports talk. KCSF-AM broadcasts to the Colorado Springs, CO area at 1300 AM.
AM RADIO STATION

KCSH-FM
44299

Owner: Lifetalk Radio Inc.
Editorial: 11070 Hwy 10, Ste B, Ellensburg, Washington 98926 **Tel:** 1 509 964-2061.
Web site: http://www.lifetalk.net
Profile: KCSH-FM is a non-commercial station owned by Lifetalk Radio Inc. The format of the station is religious. KCSH-FM broadcasts to the Ellensburg, WA area at 88.9 FM.
FM RADIO STATION

KCSI-FM
45696

Owner: Hawkeye Communications
Editorial: 1991 Ironwood Ave, Red Oak, Iowa 51566-3204 **Tel:** 1 712 623-2584.
Email: kcsi@kcsifm.com
Web site: http://www.kcsifm.com
Profile: KCSI-FM is a commercial station owned by Hawkeye Communications. The format of the station is contemporary country music. KCSI-FM broadcasts to the Omaha, NE area at 95.3 FM.
FM RADIO STATION

KCSJ-AM
37128

Owner: iHeartMedia Inc.
Editorial: 106 W 24th St, Pueblo, Colorado 81003-2408 **Tel:** 1 719 545-2080.
Web site: http://www.590kcsj.com
Profile: KCSJ-AM is a commercial station owned by iHeartMedia Inc. The format of the station is news and talk. KCSJ-AM broadcasts to the Pueblo, CO area at 590 AM.
AM RADIO STATION

KCSM-FM
39593

Owner: San Mateo County Comm. College Dist.
Editorial: 1700 W Hillsdale Blvd, San Mateo, California 94402 **Tel:** 1 650 574-6586.
Email: info@kcsm.net
Web site: http://www.kcsm.org
Profile: KCSM-FM is a commercial station owned by San Mateo County Comm. College Dist. The format of the station is jazz. KCSM-FM broadcasts to the San Mateo, CA area at 91.1 FM.
FM RADIO STATION

KCSP-AM
154853

Owner: Entercom Communications Corp.
Editorial: 7000 Squibb Rd, Mission, Kansas 66202-3233 **Tel:** 1 913 744-3600.
Web site: http://www.610sports.com
Profile: KCSP-AM is a commercial station owned by Entercom Communications Corp. The format of the station is sports. KCSP-AM broadcasts to the Kansas City, MO area at 610 AM.
AM RADIO STATION

KCSP-FM
41700

Owner: Western Inspirational Broadcasters Inc.
Editorial: 6363 US Highway 50 E, Carson City, Nevada 89701 **Tel:** 1 775 883-5647.
Email: info@pilgrimradio.com
Web site: http://www.pilgrimradio.com
Profile: KCSP-FM is a non-commercial station owned by Western Inspirational Broadcasters Inc. The format of the station is contemporary Christian programming. KCSP-FM broadcasts to the Carson City, NV area at 90.3 FM.
FM RADIO STATION

KCSR-AM
34912

Owner: Chadrad Communications Inc.
Editorial: 226 Bordeaux St, Chadron, Nebraska 69337-2393 **Tel:** 1 308 432-5545.
Email: kcsr@chadrad.com
Web site: http://www.chadrad.com
Profile: KCSR-AM is a commercial station owned by Chadrad Communications Inc. The format of the station is country music, news and sports. KCSR-AM broadcasts to the Chadron, NE area at 610 AM.
AM RADIO STATION

KCST-FM
46488

Owner: Coast Broadcasting Inc.
Editorial: 4480 Highway 101, Florence, Oregon 97439
Tel: 1 541 997-9136.
Email: radiowaves@kcst.com
Web site: http://www.kcst.com
Profile: KCST-FM is a commercial station owned by Coast Broadcasting Inc. The format of the station is adult contemporary. KCST-FM broadcasts to the Florence, OR area at 106.9 FM.
FM RADIO STATION

KCSU-FM
39596

Owner: Rocky Mountain Student Media Corp.
Tel: 1 970 491-7611.
Email: news@kcsufm.com
Web site: http://www.kcsufm.com
Profile: KCSU-FM is a non-commercial station owned by Rocky Mountain Student Media Corp. The format of the station is variety. KCSU-FM broadcasts to the Fort Collins, CO area at 90.5 FM.
FM RADIO STATION

KCTA-AM
36692

Owner: Broadcasting Corp./Southwest
Editorial: 1602 S Brownlee Blvd, Corpus Christi, Texas 78404-3134 **Tel:** 1 361 882-7711.
Email: kctapsa@yahoo.com
Web site: http://www.kctaradio.com
Profile: KCTA-AM is a commercial station owned by Broadcasting Corp./Southwest. The format of the station is Christian music and talk. KCTA-AM broadcasts to the Corpus Christi, TX area at 1030 AM.
AM RADIO STATION

KCTE-AM
37143

Owner: Union Broadcasting Inc.
Editorial: 6721 W 121st St, Overland Park, Kansas 66209-2003 **Tel:** 1 913 344-1500.
Email: info@810whb.com
Web site: http://www.1510.com
Profile: KCTE-AM is a commercial station owned by Union Broadcasting Inc. The format of the station is talk and sports. KCTE-AM broadcasts in the Kansas City, MO, area at 1510 AM.
AM RADIO STATION

KCTN-FM
45845

Owner: Design Homes Inc.
Editorial: 24493 Highway 128, Elkader, Iowa 52043-8038 **Tel:** 1 563 245-1400.
Email: kctn@alpinecom.net
Web site: http://www.kctn.com
Profile: KCTN-FM is a commercial station owned by Design Homes Inc. The format for the station is contemporary country. KCTN-FM broadcasts to the Elkader, IA area at 100.1 FM.
FM RADIO STATION

United States of America

KCTR-FM 46228
Owner: Townsquare Media, LLC
Editorial: 27 N 27th St, 23rd Floor Crowne Plaza, Billings, Montana 59101-2357 **Tel:** 1 406 248-7827.
Web site: http://catcountry1029.com
Profile: KCTR-FM is a commercial station owned by Townsquare Media, LLC. The format of the station is country music. KCTR-FM broadcasts to the Billings, MT area at 102.9 FM.
FM RADIO STATION

KCTT-FM 40998
Owner: Mountain Lakes Broadcasting Inc.
Editorial: 620 Highway 5 N, Mountain Home, Arkansas 72653 **Tel:** 1 870 425-3101.
Email: news@ktlo.com
Web site: http://www.ktlo.com
Profile: KCTT-FM is a commercial station owned by Mountain Lakes Broadcasting Inc. The format of the station is classic hits. KCTT-FM broadcasts to the Mountain Home, AR area at 101.7 FM.
FM RADIO STATION

KCTX-AM 34913
Owner: Boles Broadcasting Co.
Editorial: 1111 16th St NW, Childress, Texas 79201-3417 **Tel:** 1 940 937-6316.
Email: kctxradio@gmail.com
Profile: KCTX-AM is a commercial station owned by Boles Broadcasting Co. The format of the station is oldies and talk. KCTX-AM broadcasts to the Childress, TX area at 1510 AM.
AM RADIO STATION

KCTX-FM 39928
Owner: Boles Broadcasting Co.
Editorial: 1111 16th Street NW, Childress, Texas 79201-3417 **Tel:** 1 940 937-6316.
Email: kctxradio@gmail.com
Profile: KCTX-FM is a commercial station owned by Boles Broadcasting Co. The format of the station is classic and contemporary country music. KCTX-FM broadcasts to the Amarillo, TX area at 96.1 FM.
FM RADIO STATION

KCTY-AM 37512
Owner: Wayne Radio Works
Editorial: 85592 574th Ave, Wayne, Nebraska 68787-7043 **Tel:** 1 402 375-3700.
Profile: KCTY-AM is a commercial station owned by Wayne Radio Works. The format of the station is hot adult contemporary. KCTY-AM broadcasts to the Wayne, NE area at 1590 AM.
AM RADIO STATION

KCUA-FM 518337
Owner: Evans Broadcasting
Editorial: 2242 E 1000 S, Roosevelt, Utah 84066-4554 **Tel:** 1 435 722-5011.
Email: radio@ubtanet.com
Web site: http://www.mybasinradio.com
Profile: KCUA-FM is a commercial station owned by Evans Broadcasting. The format of the station is classic rock. KCUA-FM broadcasts to the Naples, UT area at 92.5 FM.
FM RADIO STATION

KCUB-AM 38415
Owner: Cumulus Media Inc
Editorial: 575 W Roger Rd, Tucson, Arizona 85705-2616 **Tel:** 1 520 887-1000.
Email: studio@1290amthesource.com
Web site: http://www.1290amthesource.com
Profile: KCUB-AM is a commercial station owned by Cumulus Media Inc. The format of the station is sports and talk. KCUB-AM broadcasts to the Tucson, AZ area at 1290 AM.
AM RADIO STATION

KCUE-AM 39022
Owner: Q Media Group, LLC
Editorial: 474 Guernsey Ln, Red Wing, Minnesota 55066 **Tel:** 1 651 388-7151.
Profile: KCUE-AM is a commercial station owned by Q Media Group, LLC. The format of the station is classic country. KCUE-AM broadcasts in the Minneapolis area at 1250 AM. The station operates under an LMA with Sorenson Broadcasting.
AM RADIO STATION

KCUL-FM 46314
Owner: Access.1 Communications Corp.
Editorial: 210 S Broadway Ave Ste 100, Tyler, Texas 75702-7353 **Tel:** 1 903 581-9966.
Web site: http://lainvasora.fm
Profile: KCUL-FM is a commercial station owned by Access.1 Communications Corp. The format of the station is regional Mexican music. KCUL-FM broadcasts to the Shreveport, LA area at 92.3 FM.
FM RADIO STATION

KCUP-AM 38411
Owner: Agpal Broadcasting Inc.
Editorial: 145 N Coast Hwy Ste D, Newport, Oregon 97365-3165 **Tel:** 1 541 265-5000.
Email: bossbusiness@actionnet.net
Web site: http://www.kcup.net
Profile: KCUP-AM is a commercial station owned by Agpal Broadcasting Inc. The format of the station is news and talk. KCUP-AM broadcasts to the Newport, OR area at 1230 AM.
AM RADIO STATION

KCUZ-AM 37227
Owner: Cochise Broadcasting LLC
Editorial: 301 E US Highway 70, #B, Safford, Arizona 85546 **Tel:** 1 928 428-0916.

Web site: http://www.saffordradio.com
Profile: KCUZ-AM is a commercial station owned by Cochise Broadcasting LLC. The format of the station is classic rock. KCUZ-AM broadcasts to the Safford, AZ area at 1490 AM.
AM RADIO STATION

KCVI-FM 42592
Owner: Riverbend Communications LLC
Editorial: 400 W Sunnyside Rd, Idaho Falls, Idaho 83402-4613 **Tel:** 1 208 523-3722.
Web site: http://www.kbear.fm
Profile: KCVI-FM is a commercial station owned by Riverbend Communications LLC. The format of the station is rock. KCVI-FM broadcasts to the Idaho Falls, ID area at 101.5 FM.
FM RADIO STATION

KCVL-AM 37228
Owner: North Country Broadcasting
Editorial: 187 Mantz Rickey Rd, Colville, Washington 99114-9562 **Tel:** 1 509 684-5031.
Email: news@kcvl.com
Web site: http://www.kcvl.com
Profile: KCVL-AM is a commercial station owned by North Country Broadcasting. The format of the station is contemporary country music. KCVL-AM broadcasts to the Spokane, WA area at 1240 AM.
AM RADIO STATION

KCVM-FM 73914
Owner: Coloff Media
Editorial: 721 Shirley St, Cedar Falls, Iowa 50613-1513 **Tel:** 1 319 277-1918.
Email: themix@935themix.com
Web site: http://935themix.com
Profile: KCVM-FM is a commercial station owned by Coloff Media. The format of the station is adult contemporary. KCVM-FM broadcasts to the Cedar Falls, IA area at 93.5 FM.
FM RADIO STATION

KCVN-FM 45694
Owner: Bott Broadcasting Co.
Editorial: 233 S 13th St Ste 1520, Lincoln, Nebraska 68508-2003 **Tel:** 1 402 465-8850.
Email: kcvn@bottradionetwork.com
Web site: http://www.bottradionetwork.com
Profile: KCVN-FM is a commercial station owned by Bott Broadcasting Co. The format of the station is religious. KCVN-FM broadcasts to the Lincoln, NE area at 104.5 FM.
FM RADIO STATION

KCVR-AM 36726
Owner: Entravision Communications Corp.
Editorial: 6820 Pacific Ave Ste 3A, Stockton, California 95207-2631 **Tel:** 1 209 474-0154.
Web site: http://www.maria989.com
Profile: KCVR-AM is a commercial station owned by Entravision Communications Corp. The format of the station is Hispanic adult hits. KCVR-AM broadcasts to the Stockton, CA area at 1570 AM.
AM RADIO STATION

KCVR-FM 82632
Owner: Entravision Communications Corp.
Editorial: 6820 Pacific Ave Ste 3A, Stockton, California 95207-2631 **Tel:** 1 209 474-0154.
Web site: http://www.maria989.com
Profile: KCVR-FM is a commercial station owned by Entravision Communications Corp. The format of the station is Hispanic adult hits. KCVR-FM broadcasts in Stockton, CA area at 98.9 FM.
FM RADIO STATION

KCVS-FM 43347
Owner: VCY America Inc.
Editorial: 3434 W Kilbourn Ave, Milwaukee, Wisconsin 53208-3313 **Tel:** 1 414 935-3000.
Email: kcvs@vcyamerica.org
Web site: http://www.vcyamerica.org
Profile: KCVS-FM is a non-commercial station owned by VCY America Inc. The format of the station is religious. KCVS-FM broadcasts to the Milwaukee area at 91.7 FM.
FM RADIO STATION

KCVT-FM 43871
Owner: Bott Broadcasting Co.
Editorial: 534 S Kansas Ave, Ste 930, Topeka, Kansas 66603 **Tel:** 1 785 233-9250.
Email: kcvt@bottradionetwork.com
Web site: http://www.bottradionetwork.com
Profile: KCVT-FM is a commercial station owned by Bott Broadcasting Co. The format of the station is Christian news, music and talk. KCVT-FM broadcasts in the Topeka, KS area at 92.5 FM.
FM RADIO STATION

KCVV-AM 35069
Owner: Radio Santisimo
Editorial: 1909 7th St, Sacramento, California 95811-7007 **Tel:** 1 916 442-7389.
Email: kcvv1240am@radiosantisimosacramento.com
Web site: http://www.radiosantisimosacramento.com
Profile: KCVV-AM is a commercial station owned by Radio Santisimo. The format of the station is Spanish-language Catholic programming. KCVV-AM broadcasts to Sacramento, CA, at 1240 AM.
AM RADIO STATION

KCVW-FM 43675
Owner: Bott Broadcasting Co.
Editorial: 209 N Meridian Rd, Newton, Kansas 67114-5102 **Tel:** 1 620 663-0943.
Email: kcvw@bottradionetwork.com

Web site: http://www.bottradionetwork.com
Profile: KCVW-FM is a commercial station owned by Bott Broadcasting Co. The format of the station is religious and Christian programming. KCVW-FM broadcasts to the Newton, KS area at 94.3 FM.
FM RADIO STATION

KCWB-FM 924736
Owner: Legend Communications
Editorial: 1949 Mountain View Dr, Cody, Wyoming 82414-4932 **Tel:** 1 307 578-5000.
Web site: http://www.mybighornbasin.com
Profile: KCWB-FM is a commercial station owned by Legend Communications. The format of the station is classic country. KCWB-FM broadcasts locally at 92.1 FM.
FM RADIO STATION

KCWC-FM 39600
Owner: Central Wyoming College
Editorial: 2660 Peck Ave, Riverton, Wyoming 82501-2215 **Tel:** 1 307 855-2268.
Web site: https://www.cwc.edu/what/rustler-radio
Profile: KCWC-FM is a non-commercial station owned by Central Wyoming College. The format of the station is variety. KCWC-FM broadcasts to the Riverton, WY area at 88.1 FM.
FM RADIO STATION

KCWD-FM 46381
Owner: Dowdy Broadcasting, Inc.
Editorial: 600 S Pine St, Harrison, Arkansas 72601-5828 **Tel:** 1 870 741-1402.
Email: info@kcwdradio.com
Web site: http://www.kcwdradio.com
Profile: KCWD-FM is a commercial station owned by Dowdy Broadcasting, Inc. The format of the station is classic hits. KCWD-FM broadcasts to the Harrison, AR area at 96.1 FM.
FM RADIO STATION

KCWJ-AM 37002
Owner: KCWJ, Inc.
Editorial: 18920 E Valley View Pkwy Ste C, Independence, Missouri 64055-7020 **Tel:** 1 816 795-6826.
Email: gregharris@kcwj.org
Web site: http://www.realcountry1030am.com
Profile: KCWJ-AM is a commercial station owned by KCWJ, Inc. The format of the station is Classic Country. KCWJ-AM broadcasts to the Kansas City, MO area at 1030 AM.
AM RADIO STATION

KCWM-AM 35060
Owner: Hondo Communications
Editorial: 1605 Avenue K, Hondo, Texas 78861-1838 **Tel:** 1 830 741-5296.
Email: kcwm@aol.com
Web site: http://www.kcwm.net
Profile: KCWM-AM is a commercial station owned by Hondo Communications. The format of the station is classic country. KCWM-AM broadcasts to the Hondo, TX area at 1460 AM.
AM RADIO STATION

KCWN-FM 42868
Owner: Crown Broadcasting Inc.
Editorial: 304 Oskaloosa St, Pella, Iowa 50219-2122 **Tel:** 1 641 628-9999.
Email: kcwn@kcwnfm.org
Web site: http://www.kcwnfm.org
Profile: KCWN-FM is a commercial station owned by Crown Broadcasting Inc. The format of the station is contemporary Christian music. KCWN-FM broadcasts to the Pella, IA area at 99.9 FM.
FM RADIO STATION

KCWR-FM 41297
Owner: Owens Productions Inc.(Buck)
Editorial: 3223 N Sillect Ave, Bakersfield, California 93308-6332 **Tel:** 1 661 326-1011.
Email: kuzznews@buckowens.com
Profile: KCWR-FM is a commercial station owned by Buck Owens Productions Inc. The format of the station is classic country music. The station broadcasts to the Bakersfield, CA area at 107.1 FM.
FM RADIO STATION

KCXL-AM 36838
Owner: Alpine Broadcasting Corp.
Editorial: 310 S La Frenz Rd, Liberty, Missouri 64068 **Tel:** 1 816 576-7800.
Email: kcxl@kc.rr.com
Web site: http://www.kcxl.com
Profile: KCXL-AM is a commercial station owned by Alpine Broadcasting Corp. The format of the station is talk and variety. KCXL-AM broadcasts to the Liberty, MO area at 1140 AM.
AM RADIO STATION

KCXR-FM 41906
Owner: ABS Communications
Editorial: 2448 E 81st St Ste 5500, Tulsa, Oklahoma 74137-4201 **Tel:** 1 918 492-2660.
Email: kxoj@kxoj.com
Profile: KCXR-FM is a commercial station owned by ABS Communications. The format of the station is contemporary Christian rock and CHR. KCXR-FM broadcasts to the Tulsa, OK area at 100.3 FM. Send all PSAs to the main email.
FM RADIO STATION

KCXY-FM 41559
Owner: Radio Works Inc.
Editorial: 612 Fairview Rd SW, Camden, Arkansas 71701-6554 **Tel:** 1 870 836-9567.
Email: camdenradio@hotmail.com

Web site: http://yesradioworks.com/y95
Profile: KCXY-FM is a commercial station owned by Radio Works Inc. The format of the station is country music. KCXY-FM broadcasts to the Camden, AR area at 95.3 FM.
FM RADIO STATION

KCYE-FM 40967
Owner: Beasley Broadcast Group
Editorial: 2920 S Durango Dr, Las Vegas, Nevada 89117-4412 **Tel:** 1 702 730-0300.
Web site: http://www.kcye.com
Profile: KCYE-FM is a commercial station owned by Beasley Broadcast Group. The format of the station is country. KCYE-FM broadcasts to the Las Vegas area at 102.7 FM.
FM RADIO STATION

KCYK-AM 37267
Owner: MonsterMedia LLC
Editorial: 949 S Avenue B, Yuma, Arizona 85364-3440 **Tel:** 1 928 782-4321.
Web site: http://www.monstermediayuma.com/
Profile: KCYK-AM is a commercial station owned by MonsterMedia LLC. The format of the station is country. KCYK-AM broadcasts in the Yuma, AZ area at 1400 AM.
AM RADIO STATION

KCYL-AM 34915
Owner: Witcher(Ronald K.)
Editorial: 505 N Key Ave, Lampasas, Texas 76550 **Tel:** 1 512 556-6193.
Email: management@lampasasradio.com
Web site: http://www.lampasasradio.com
AM RADIO STATION

KCYN-FM 44066
Owner: Moab Communications LLC
Editorial: 1030 Bowling Alley Ln, Moab, Utah 84532-3048 **Tel:** 1 435 259-1035.
Email: kcyn@kcynfm.com
Web site: http://www.kcynfm.com
Profile: KCYN-FM is a commercial station owned by Moab Communications LLC. The format of the station is contemporary country. KCYN-FM broadcasts to the Salt Lake City area at 97.1 FM.
FM RADIO STATION

KCYS-FM 43119
Owner: Dave's Broadcasting Corp.
Editorial: 1324 N Holladay Dr, Seaside, Oregon 97138-7132 **Tel:** 1 503 717-9643.
Email: kcys@gowebway.com
Profile: KCYS-FM is a commercial station owned by Dave's Broadcasting Corp. The format of the station is contemporary country music. KCYS-FM broadcasts to the Seaside, OR area at 96.5 FM.
FM RADIO STATION

KCYY-FM 46144
Owner: Cox Media Group, Inc.
Editorial: 8122 Datapoint Dr, San Antonio, Texas 78229-3272 **Tel:** 1 210 615-5400.
Email: psa@coxinc.com
Web site: http://www.y100fm.com
Profile: KCYY-FM is a commercial station owned by Cox Media Group, Inc. The format of the station is country. KCYY-FM broadcasts to the San Antonio area at 100.3 FM.
FM RADIO STATION

KCZE-FM 41769
Owner: Coloff Media
Editorial: 207 N Main St, Charles City, Iowa 50616-2016 **Tel:** 1 641 228-1000.
Web site: http://www.951thebull.com
Profile: KCZE-FM is a commercial station owned by Coloff Media. The format of the station is contemporary country. KCZE-FM broadcasts to the Charles City, IA area at 95.1 FM.
FM RADIO STATION

KCZO-FM 46778
Owner: Bernal(Paulino)
Editorial: 4501 N McColl Rd, McAllen, Texas 78504-2431 **Tel:** 1 956 686-6382.
Web site: http://nuevaradiocristiana.com
Profile: KCZO-FM is a non-commercial station owned by Paulino Bernal. The format of the station is Hispanic contemporary Christian music. KCZO-FM broadcasts to the McAllen, TX area at 92.1 FM.
FM RADIO STATION

KCZQ-FM 41765
Owner: Mega Media Ltd.
Editorial: 116 1st Ave W, Cresco, Iowa 52136 **Tel:** 1 563 547-1000.
Email: superc@iowatelecom.net
FM RADIO STATION

KCZZ-AM 36663
Owner: Reyes Media Group
Editorial: 1701 S 55th St, Kansas City, Kansas 66106-2241 **Tel:** 1 913 287-1480.
Web site: http://reyesmediagroup.com
Profile: KCZZ-AM is a commercial station owned by Reyes Media Group. The format of the station is Hispanic Top 40/CHR. KCZZ-AM broadcasts to the Kansas City, KS area at 1480 AM.
AM RADIO STATION

KDAA-FM 44605
Owner: Mahaffey Enterprises Inc.
Editorial: 1505 Soest Rd, Rolla, Missouri 65401-3709 **Tel:** 1 573 364-2525.
Email: kznnpsa@yahoo.com

Web site: http://www.resultsradioonline.com
FM RADIO STATION

KDAC-AM 34917
Owner: Bicoastal Media LLC
Editorial: 140 N Main St, Lakeport, California 95453 **Tel:** 1 707 263-6113.
Email: kukinews@bicoastalmedia.com
Profile: KDAC-AM is a commercial station owned by Bicoastal Media LLC. The format of the station is regional Mexican. KDAC-AM broadcasts to the Ukiah, CA area at 1230 AM.
AM RADIO STATION

KDAE-AM 36765
Owner: Worship Center of Kingsville(The)
Editorial: 929 N Padre Island Dr, Corpus Christi, Texas 78406-1911 **Tel:** 1 361 299-1980.
Web site: http://www.radiolibertad.net
Profile: KDAE-AM is a commercial station owned by The Worship Center of Kingsville. The format of the station is Hispanic religious programming. KDAE-AM broadcasts to the Corpus Christi, TX area at 1590 AM.
AM RADIO STATION

KDAG-FM 42773
Owner: iHeartMedia Inc.
Editorial: 200 E Broadway, Farmington, New Mexico 87401-6418 **Tel:** 1 505 325-1716.
Web site: http://www.bigdog969.com
Profile: KDAG-FM is a commercial station owned by iHeartMedia Inc. The format of the station is classic rock music. KDAG-FM broadcasts to the Albuquerque, NM area at 96.9.
FM RADIO STATION

KDAK-AM 34918
Owner: Robert Ingstad Broadcast Group
Editorial: 1255 7th St S, Carrington, North Dakota 58421-2411 **Tel:** 1 701 652-3151.
Web site: http://www.newsdakota.com
Profile: KDAK-AM is a commercial station owned by Robert Ingstad Broadcast Group. The format of the station is country music. KDAK-AM broadcasts to the Carrington, ND area at 1600 AM.
AM RADIO STATION

KDAL-AM 38906
Owner: Midwest Communications Inc.
Editorial: 11 E Superior St Ste 380, Duluth, Minnesota 55802-3016 **Tel:** 1 218 722-4321.
Web site: http://www.kdal610.com
Profile: KDAL-AM is a commercial station owned by Midwest Communications Inc. The format for this station is news and talk. KDAL-AM broadcasts in the Duluth, MN, area at 610 AM.
AM RADIO STATION

KDAL-FM 46249
Owner: Midwest Communications Inc.
Editorial: 11 E Superior St Ste 380, Duluth, Minnesota 55802-3016 **Tel:** 1 218 722-4321.
Web site: http://my957.com
Profile: KDAL-FM is a commercial station owned by Midwest Communications Inc. The format of the station is adult contemporary. KDAL-FM broadcasts in the Duluth, MN area at 95.7 FM.
FM RADIO STATION

KDAM-FM 695474
Owner: Riverfront Broadcasting
Editorial: 202 W 2Nd St, Yankton, South Dakota 57078-4317 **Tel:** 1 605 665-7892.
Web site: http://www.kdam.fm
Profile: KDAM-FM is a commercial station owned by Riverfront Broadcasting. The format of the station is rock. KDAM-FM broadcasts to the Yankton, SD area at 94.3 FM.
FM RADIO STATION

KDAP-AM 38810
Owner: Goodman (Alex)
Editorial: 2031 N Sulphur Springs Rd, Douglas, Arizona 85607-7207 **Tel:** 1 520 364-3484.
Email: kdapfm@yahoo.com
Profile: KDAP-AM is a commercial station owned by Alex Goodman. The format of the station is Hispanic religious programming. KDAP-AM broadcasts to the Douglas, AZ area at 1450 AM.
AM RADIO STATION

KDAP-FM 46173
Owner: Henderson (Howard)
Editorial: 2031 N Sulphur Springs Rd, Douglas, Arizona 85607 **Tel:** 1 520 364-3484.
Email: kdapfm@yahoo.com
Profile: KDAP-FM is a commercial station owned by Henderson (Howard). The format of the station is contemporary country music. KDAP-FM broadcasts to the Tucson, AZ area at 96.5 FM.
FM RADIO STATION

KDAR-FM 39602
Owner: Salem Media Group, Inc.
Editorial: 500 E Esplanade Dr Ste 1500, Oxnard, California 93036-0571 **Tel:** 1 805 485-8881.
Web site: http://www.kdar.com
Profile: KDAR-FM is a commercial station owned by Salem Media Group, Inc. The format of the station is religious talk. KDAR-FM broadcasts to the Oxnard, CA area at 98.3 FM.
FM RADIO STATION

KDAT-FM 43373
Owner: Townsquare Media, LLC
Editorial: 425 2nd St SE Fl 4, Cedar Rapids, Iowa 52401-1819 **Tel:** 1 319 365-9431.
Email: kdat@kdat.com
Web site: http://www.kdat.com
Profile: KDAT-FM is a commercial station owned by Townsquare Media, LLC. The format of the station is Lite Rock/Lite AC. KDAT-FM broadcasts to the Cedar Rapids, IA area at 104.5 FM.
FM RADIO STATION

KDAY-FM 44498
Owner: Meruelo Group
Editorial: 5055 Wilshire Blvd, Los Angeles, California 90036-6100 **Tel:** 1 323 337-1600.
Web site: http://www.935kday.com
Profile: KDAY-FM is a commercial station owned by Meruelo Group. The format of the station is classic hip hop music. DAY-FM broadcasts to the Los Angeles area at 93.5 FM.
FM RADIO STATION

KDAZ-AM 34921
Owner: Pan American Broadcasting Company, Inc.
Editorial: 820 Candelaria Rd NE, Albuquerque, New Mexico 87107-2121 **Tel:** 1 505 345-1991.
Email: info@am730kdaz.com
Web site: http://am730kdaz.com
Profile: KDAZ-AM is a non-commercial station owned by Pan American Broadcasting Company, Inc. The format of the station is religious talk programming. KDAZ-AM broadcasts to the Albuquerque, NM area at 730 AM.
AM RADIO STATION

KDBB-FM 46908
Owner: MKS Broadcasting Inc.
Editorial: 804 S Saint Joe Dr, Park Hills, Missouri 63601-2427 **Tel:** 1 573 431-1000.
Email: news@b104fm.com
Web site: http://www.b104fm.com
Profile: KDBB-FM is a commercial station owned by MKS Broadcasting Inc. The format of the station is adult album alternative. KDBB-FM broadcasts to the Park Hills, MO area at 104.3 FM.
FM RADIO STATION

KDB-FM 41831
Owner: Santa Monica College
Editorial: 414 E Cota St, Santa Barbara, California 93101-1624 **Tel:** 1 213 225-7400.
Email: pressrelease@kusc.org
Web site: http://www.kusc.org
Profile: KDB-FM is a commercial station owned by Santa Monica College. The format of the station is classical. KDB-FM broadcasts to the Santa Barbara, CA area at 93.7 FM.
FM RADIO STATION

KDBH-FM 44612
Owner: Baldridge-Dumas Communications Inc.
Editorial: 400 Jefferson St, Natchitoches, Louisiana 71457-4634 **Tel:** 1 318 352-9696.
Email: production@bdcradio.com
Web site: http://www.bdcradio.com
Profile: KDBH-FM is a commercial station owned by Baldridge-Dumas Communications Inc. The format of the station is contemporary country music. KDBH-FM broadcasts to the Natchitoches, LA area at 97.5 FM.
FM RADIO STATION

KDBI-FM 396691
Owner: Adelante Media Group
Editorial: 3307 Caldwell Blvd, Nampa, Idaho 83651-6402 **Tel:** 1 208 463-2900.
Web site: http://www.latinosoloexitos.com
Profile: KDBI-FM is a commercial station owned by Adelante Media Group. The format of the station is Bilingual Top 40/CHR. KDBI-FM broadcasts to the Nampa, ID area at 106.3 FM.
FM RADIO STATION

KDBL-FM 41410
Owner: Townsquare Media, LLC
Editorial: 4010 Summitview Ave, Yakima, Washington 98908-2966 **Tel:** 1 509 972-3461.
Web site: http://www.929thebull.com
Profile: KDBL-FM is a commercial station owned by Townsquare Media, LLC. The format of the station is contemporary country music. KDBL-FM broadcasts to the Yakima, WA area at 92.9 FM.
FM RADIO STATION

KDBM-AM 37233
Owner: Dead-Air Broadcasting Co.
Editorial: 610 N Montana St, Dillon, Montana 59725-3353 **Tel:** 1 406 683-2800.
Email: deadair@kdbm-kbev.com
Web site: http://www.kdbmkbev.com
Profile: KDBM-AM is a commercial station owned by Dead-Air Broadcasting Co. The format for the station is country. KDBM-AM broadcasts to the Dillon, MT area at 1490 AM.
AM RADIO STATION

KDBN-FM 713976
Owner: KSUN Community Radio
Editorial: 398 Arroyo Dr, Parachute, Colorado 81635-9200 **Tel:** 1 970 285-2246.
Web site: http://ksunradio.org
Profile: KDBN-FM is a commercial station owned by KSUN Community Radio. The format of the station is classic rock. KDBN-FM broadcasts to the Parachute, CO area at 101.1 FM.
FM RADIO STATION

KDBR-FM 42300
Owner: Bee Broadcasting Inc.
Editorial: 2432 US Highway 2 E, Kalispell, Montana 59901-2310 **Tel:** 1 406 755-8700.
Email: thebear@beebroadcasting.com
Web site: http://www.kdbr.com
Profile: KDBR-FM is a commercial station owned by Bee Broadcasting Inc. The format of the station is contemporary country. KDBR-FM broadcasts to the Kalispell, MT area at 106.7 FM.
FM RADIO STATION

KDBS-AM 37229
Owner: Cenla Broadcasting Inc.
Editorial: 1115 Texas Ave, Alexandria, Louisiana 71301 **Tel:** 1 318 445-1234.
Web site: http://www.espn1410.com
Profile: KDBS-AM is a commercial station owned by Cenla Broadcasting Inc. The format of the station is sports. KDBS-AM broadcasts to the Alexandria, LA area at 1410 AM.
AM RADIO STATION

KDBX-FM 61907
Owner: Alpha Media
Editorial: 227 22nd Ave S, Brookings, South Dakota 57006-2827 **Tel:** 1 605 692-9125.
Email: kjjqnews@brookings.net
Web site: http://www.brookingsradio.com
Profile: KDBX-FM is a commercial station owned by Alpha Media. The format of the station is classic country. KDBX-FM broadcasts to the Brookings, SD area at 107.1 FM.
FM RADIO STATION

KDCC-AM 39311
Owner: Dodge City Community College
Editorial: 3004 N 14th Ave, Dodge City, Kansas 67801 **Tel:** 1 620 225-6783.
Web site: http://www.dc3.edu
Profile: KDCC-AM is a non-commercial station owned by Dodge City Community College. The format of the station is sports. KDCC-AM broadcasts to the Dodge City, KS area at 1550.
AM RADIO STATION

KDCD-FM 42075
Owner: Four R Broadcasting
Editorial: 3434 Sherwood Way, San Angelo, Texas 76901-3531 **Tel:** 1 325 947-5323.
Web site: http://www.lonestar929.com
Profile: KDCD-FM is a commercial station owned by Four R Broadcasting. The format for the station is classic country. KDCD-FM broadcasts to the San Angelo, TX area at 92.9 FM.
FM RADIO STATION

KDCE-AM 34922
Owner: Rio Chama Broadcasting
Editorial: 403 W Pueblo Dr, Espanola, New Mexico 87532-2530 **Tel:** 1 505 753-2201.
Email: production@kdceradio.com
Web site: http://www.kdceradio.com
Profile: KDCE-AM is a commercial station owned by Rio Chama Broadcasting. The format of the station is Latin music and Spanish news and talk. KDCE-AM broadcasts to the Albuquerque, NM area at 950 AM.
AM RADIO STATION

KDCQ-FM 43853
Owner: Bay Cities Building Company Inc.
Editorial: 3120 Broadway Ave, North Bend, Oregon 97459-2223 **Tel:** 1 541 269-0929.
Email: info@kdcq.com
Web site: http://www.kdcq.com
Profile: KDCQ-FM is a commercial station owned by Bay Cities Building Company Inc. The format of the station is classic hits music. KDCQ-FM broadcasts to the North Bend, OR area at 92.9 FM.
FM RADIO STATION

KDCR-FM 39603
Owner: Dordt College
Editorial: 498 4th Ave NE, Sioux Center, Iowa 51250 **Tel:** 1 712 722-0885.
Email: kdcr@dordt.edu
Web site: http://www.kdcr.dordt.edu
Profile: KDCR-FM is a non-commercial station owned by Dordt College. The format of the station is Christian music and talk. KDCR-FM broadcasts to the Sioux Center, IA area at 88.5 FM.
FM RADIO STATION

KDCZ-FM 156040
Owner: Townsquare Media
Editorial: 122 4th St SW, Rochester, Minnesota 55902-3320 **Tel:** 1 507 286-1010.
Web site: http://therockofrochester.com
Profile: KDCZ-FM is a commercial station owned by Townsquare Media. The format of the station is rock. KDCZ-FM broadcasts to the Rochester, MN area at 103.9 FM.
FM RADIO STATION

KDDB-FM 42270
Owner: Ohana Broadcast Company LLC
Editorial: 1000 Bishop St Ste 200, Honolulu, Hawaii 96813-4203 **Tel:** 1 808 947-1500.
Web site: http://www.1027dabomb.net
Profile: KDDB-FM is a commercial station owned by Ohana Broadcast Company LLC. The format of the station is rhythmic Top 40/CHR. KDDB-FM broadcasts to the Honolulu area on 102.7.
FM RADIO STATION

KDDD-AM 38784
Owner: PBI, LLC
Editorial: 408 N Dumas Ave, Dumas, Texas 79029-2445 **Tel:** 1 806 983-5704.
Email: kflp@kflp.net
Web site: http://www.allagnews.com
Profile: KDDD-AM is a commercial station owned by PBI, LLC. The format of the station is farm and agriculture. KDDD-AM broadcasts to the Dumas-Amarillo, TX area at 800 AM.
AM RADIO STATION

KDDD-FM 46124
Owner: PBI, LLC
Editorial: 408 N Dumas Ave, Dumas, Texas 79029 **Tel:** 1 806 935-4141.
Email: kddd@cableone.net
Web site: http://www.kddd953fm.com
Profile: KDDD-FM is a commercial station owned by PBI, LLC. The format of the station is oldies. KDDD-FM broadcasts to the Dumas, TX area at 95.3 FM.
FM RADIO STATION

KDDG-FM 46683
Owner: StarCom LLC
Editorial: 35223 238th Ave, Albany, Minnesota 56307-9798 **Tel:** 1 320 845-2184.
Web site: http://www.mybobcountry.com
Profile: KDDG-FM is a commercial station owned by StarCom LLC. The format of the station is classic country. KDDG-FM broadcasts to the Albany, MN area at 105.5 FM.
FM RADIO STATION

KDDK-FM 43900
Owner: Radio and Investments, Inc.
Editorial: 11724 Industriplex Blvd Bldg A2, Baton Rouge, Louisiana 70809-5162 **Tel:** 1 225 636-5568.
Email: kddk1055@att.net
Web site: http://www.kddkfm.com
Profile: KDDK-FM is a commercial station owned by Radio and Investments, Inc. The format of the station is tropical Spanish. KDDK-FM broadcasts to the Addis, LA area at a frequency of 105.5 FM.
FM RADIO STATION

KDDQ-FM 43854
Owner: Perry Publishing & Broadcasting Inc.
Editorial: 1701 W Pine Ave, Duncan, Oklahoma 73533 **Tel:** 1 580 355-1050.
Web site: http://www.perry-pub-broadcasting.com/kddq/
FM RADIO STATION

KDDR-AM 36169
Owner: Ingstad Family Media
Editorial: 412 Main Ave, Oakes, North Dakota 58474-1600 **Tel:** 1 701 742-2187.
Email: kddrstudio@drtel.net
Web site: http://www.newsdakota.com
Profile: KDDR-AM is a commercial station owned by Ingstad Family Media. The format of the station is country music. KDDR-AM broadcasts to the Oakes, ND area at 1220 AM.
AM RADIO STATION

KDDS-FM 44573
Owner: Bustos Media, LLC
Editorial: 1400 W Main St, Auburn, Washington 98001-5230 **Tel:** 1 253 735-9700.
Web site: http://kdds.lagranderadio.com
Profile: KDDS-FM is a commercial station owned by Bustos Media, LLC. The format of the station is Hispanic programming. KDDS-FM broadcasts to the Olympia, WA area at 99.3 FM. Contact the station via the online form.
FM RADIO STATION

KDDX-FM 39641
Owner: Duhamel Broadcasting
Editorial: 2827 E Colorado Blvd, Spearfish, South Dakota 57783-9703 **Tel:** 1 605 642-5747.
Web site: http://www.xrock.fm
Profile: KDDX-FM is a commercial station owned by Duhamel Broadcasting. The format of the station is rock. KDDX-FM broadcasts to the Spearfish, SD area at 101.1 FM.
FM RADIO STATION

KDEC-AM 38466
Owner: Decorah Broadcasting Inc.
Editorial: 110 Highland Dr, Decorah, Iowa 52101-1102 **Tel:** 1 563 382-4251.
Email: kdec@kdecradio.net
Web site: http://kdecradio.net
Profile: KDEC-AM is a commercial station owned by Decorah Broadcasting Inc. The format of the station is adult standards, easy listening and news. KDEC-AM broadcasts to the Cedar Rapids, IA area at 1240 AM.
AM RADIO STATION

KDEC-FM 45824
Owner: Decorah Broadcasting Inc.
Editorial: 110 Highland Dr, Decorah, Iowa 52101-1102 **Tel:** 1 563 382-4251.
Email: kdec@kdecradio.net
Web site: http://kdecradio.net
Profile: KDEC-FM is a commercial station owned by Decorah Broadcasting Inc. The format for the station is adult album alternative. KDEC-FM broadcasts to the Cedar Rapids, IA area at 100.5 FM.
FM RADIO STATION

KDEM-FM 44615
Owner: Luna County Broadcasting
Editorial: 1700 S Gold Ave, Deming, New Mexico 88030-5839 **Tel:** 1 575 546-9011.
Email: radio@demingradio.com
Web site: http://www.demingradio.com
Profile: KDEM-FM is a commercial station owned by Luna County Broadcasting. The format of the station is adult contemporary music. KDEM-FM broadcasts to the Albuquerque, NM area at 94.3 FM.
FM RADIO STATION

KDEP-FM 598659
Owner: Alexandra Communications Inc.
Editorial: 170 3rd St, Tillamook, Oregon 97141-9489 **Tel:** 1 503 842-4422.
Web site: http://www.tillamookradio.com
Profile: KDEP-FM is a commercial station owned by Alexandra Communications Inc. The format is adult contemporary. KDEP-FM broadcasts to the Tillamook, OR at 105.5 FM.
FM RADIO STATION

KDES-FM 46751
Owner: Alpha Media
Editorial: 1321 N Gene Autry Trl, Palm Springs, California 92262-5473 **Tel:** 1 760 322-7890.
Web site: http://www.985thebull.com
Profile: KDES-FM is a commercial station owned by Alpha Media. The format of the station is oldies. KDES-FM broadcasts to the Palm Springs, CA area at 98.5 FM.
FM RADIO STATION

KDET-AM 38625
Owner: Center Broadcasting Company Inc.
Editorial: 307 San Augustine St, Center, Texas 75935-3937 **Tel:** 1 936 598-3304.
Email: news@cbcradio.com
Web site: http://www.cbc-radio.com
Profile: KDET-AM is a commercial station owned by Center Broadcasting Company Inc. The format for the station is talk. KDET-AM broadcasts to the Shreveport, LA, area at 930 AM.
AM RADIO STATION

KDEW-FM 43260
Owner: Arkansas County Broadcasters Inc.
Editorial: 1818 S Buerkle St, Stuttgart, Arkansas 72160-5804 **Tel:** 1 870 673-1595.
Email: kdew973@yahoo.com
Web site: http://www.country973.com
Profile: KDEW-FM is a commercial station owned by Arkansas County Broadcasters Inc. The format of the station is contemporary country. KDEW-FM broadcasts to the Stuttgart, AR area at 97.3 FM.
FM RADIO STATION

KDEX-AM 37230
Owner: Dexter Broadcasting Inc.
Editorial: 20487 State Highway 114, Dexter, Missouri 63841 **Tel:** 1 573 624-3545.
Email: kdex1@sbcglobal.net
Profile: KDEX-AM is a commercial station owned by Dexter Broadcasting Inc. The format of the station is contemporary country. KDEX-AM broadcasts to the Dexter, MO area at 102.3 FM.
AM RADIO STATION

KDEX-FM 44616
Owner: Dexter Broadcasting Inc.
Editorial: 20487 State Highway 114, Dexter, Missouri 63841 **Tel:** 1 573 624-3545.
Email: kdex1@sbcglobal.net
Profile: KDEX-FM is a commercial station owned by Dexter Broadcasting Inc. The format of the station is country music. KDEX-FM broadcasts in the Dexter, MO area at 102.3 FM.
FM RADIO STATION

KDEY-FM 62239
Owner: Meruelo Group
Editorial: 5055 Wilshire Blvd Ste 720, Los Angeles, California 90036-6107
Profile: KDEY-FM is a commercial station owned by Meruelo Group. The format of the station is Urban Contemporary. KDEY-FM broadcasts to the Inland Empire, CA area at 93.5 FM. The station's slogan is, "The I.E.'s #1 for Hip -Hop and R&B."
FM RADIO STATION

KDEZ-FM 505252
Owner: Townsquare Media, Inc.
Editorial: 5100 S Tennis Ln, Sioux Falls, South Dakota 57108-2212 **Tel:** 1 605 361-0300.
Web site: http://www.easy1001.com
Profile: KDEZ-FM is a commercial station owned by Townsquare Media, Inc. The format of the station is adult contemporary. KDEZ-FM broadcasts to the Sioux Falls, SD area at 100.1 FM.
FM RADIO STATION

KDFC-FM 41116
Owner: Classical Public Radio Network, LLC
Tel: 1 415 546-8710.
Email: feedback@kdfc.com
Web site: http://www.kdfc.com
Profile: KDFC-FM is a non-commercial station owned by Classical Public Radio Network, LLC. The format of the station is classical music. KDFC-FM broadcasts to the Angwin, CA and Napa Valley areas at 89.9 FM.
FM RADIO STATION

KDFM-FM 44105
Owner: Bernal(Paulino)
Editorial: 4501 N McColl Rd, McAllen, Texas 78504-2431 **Tel:** 1 956 686-6382.
Web site: http://www.nuevaradiocristiana.com
Profile: KDFM-FM is a commercial station owned by Paulino Bernal. The format of the station is Hispanic contemporary Christian music. KDFM-FM broadcasts to the McAllen, TX area at 103.3 FM.
FM RADIO STATION

KDFO-FM 45868
Owner: iHeartMedia Inc.
Editorial: 1100 Mohawk St Ste 280, Bakersfield, California 93309-7417 **Tel:** 1 661 322-9929.
Web site: http://985thefox.iheart.com
Profile: KDFO-FM is a commercial station owned by iHeartMedia Inc. The format of the station is classic rock. KDFO-FM broadcasts to the Bakersfield, CA area at 98.5 FM.
FM RADIO STATION

KDFR-FM 41087
Owner: Family Stations Inc.
Editorial: 2350 NE 44th Ct, Des Moines, Iowa 50317-2835 **Tel:** 1 515 262-0449.
Email: kdfrpa@gmail.com
Web site: http://www.familyradio.com
Profile: KDFR-FM is a non-commercial station owned by Family Stations Inc. The format of the station is religion. KDFR-FM broadcasts to the Des Moines, IA area at 91.3 FM.
FM RADIO STATION

KDFT-AM 35990
Owner: Multicultural Radio Broadcasting Inc.
Editorial: 5801 Marvin D Love Fwy Ste 409, Dallas, Texas 75237-2319 **Tel:** 1 972 572-1540.
Web site: http://www.kdft540.com
Profile: KDFT-AM is a commercial station owned by Multicultural Radio Broadcasting Inc. The format of the station is Hispanic religious programming. KDFT-AM broadcasts to the Dallas area at 540 AM.
AM RADIO STATION

KDGE-FM 40923
Owner: iHeartMedia Inc.
Editorial: 14001 Dallas Pkwy Ste 300, Dallas, Texas 75240-7369 **Tel:** 1 214 866-8000.
Web site: http://star1021.iheart.com
Profile: KDGE-FM is a commercial station owned by iHeart Media Inc. The format of the station is Hot AC. KDGE-FM broadcasts to the Dallas area at 102.1 FM.
FM RADIO STATION

KDGL-FM 42842
Owner: Morris Communications
Editorial: 1321 N Gene Autry Trl, Palm Springs, California 92262 **Tel:** 1 760 322-7890.
Web site: http://www.theeagle1069.com
Profile: KDGL-FM is a commercial station owned by Morris Communications. The format of the station is classic hits music. KDGL-FM broadcasts to the Palm Springs, CA area at 106.9 FM.
FM RADIO STATION

KDGO-AM 39393
Owner: American General Media
Editorial: 1911 Main Ave Ste 100, Durango, Colorado 81301-5079 **Tel:** 1 970 247-1240.
Web site: http://www.kdgoam.com
Profile: KDGO-AM is a commercial station owned by American General Media. The format of the station is news and talk. KDGO-AM broadcasts to the Albuquerque, NM area at 1240 AM.
AM RADIO STATION

KDGS-FM 42244
Owner: Entercom Communications Corp.
Editorial: 2120 N Woodlawn St Ste 352, Wichita, Kansas 67208-1881 **Tel:** 1 316 685-2121.
Web site: http://www.power935.com
Profile: KDGS-FM is a commercial station owned by Entercom Communications Corp. The format of the station is rhythmic Top 40/CHR music. KDGS-FM broadcasts to the Wichita, KS area at 93.5 FM.
FM RADIO STATION

KDHL-AM 37231
Owner: Townsquare Media, LLC
Editorial: 601 Central Ave N, Faribault, Minnesota 55021-4307 **Tel:** 1 507 334-0061.
Web site: http://www.kdhlradio.com
Profile: KDHL-AM is a commercial station owned by Townsquare Media, LLC. The format of the station is country music. KDHL-AM broadcasts to the Faribault, MN area at 920 AM.
AM RADIO STATION

KDHN-AM 38953
Owner: Hometown Radio Network
Editorial: 704 W Cleveland St, Dimmitt, Texas 79027-3108 **Tel:** 1 806 647-4161.
Email: kdhn1470twister@outlook.com
Web site: http://www.kdhnradio.com/#
Profile: KDHN-AM is a commercial station owned by Hometown Radio Network. The format of the station is country. KDHN-AM broadcasts to the Dimmitt, TX area at 1470 AM.
AM RADIO STATION

KDHX-FM 41202
Owner: Double Helix Corporation
Editorial: 3524 Washington Ave, Saint Louis, Missouri 63103-1019 **Tel:** 1 314 664-3955.
Email: spam@kdhx.org
Web site: http://www.kdhx.org
Profile: KDHX-FM is a non-commercial station owned by Double Helix Corporation. The format of the station is a variety of music and talk. KDHX-FM broadcasts to the St. Louis area at 88.1 FM.
FM RADIO STATION

KDIA-AM 36760
Owner: Baybridge Communications
Editorial: 3260 Blume Dr Ste 520, Richmond, California 94806-5715 **Tel:** 1 510 222-4242.
Web site: http://www.kdia.com
Profile: KDIA-AM is a non-commercial station owned by Baybridge Communications. The format of the station is Christian talk. KDIA-AM broadcasts in the Richmond, CA area at 1640 AM.
AM RADIO STATION

KDIC-FM 39604
Owner: Trustees of Grinnell College
Editorial: 1115 8th Ave, Grinnell, Iowa 50112-1553 **Tel:** 1 641 269-3335.
Email: kdicfm@grinnell.edu
Web site: http://kdic.grinnell.edu
Profile: KDIC-FM is a non-commercial station owned by Trustees of Grinnell College. The format of the station is variety. KDIC-FM broadcasts to the Grinnel, IA area at 88.5 FM.
FM RADIO STATION

KDIO-AM 39461
Owner: Armada Media Corp.
Editorial: 47 2nd St NW, Ortonville, Minnesota 56278 **Tel:** 1 320 839-2581.
Web site: http://www.bigstoneradio.com
Profile: KDIO-AM is a commercial station owned by Armada Media Corp. The format of the station is classic country music and talk. KDIO-AM broadcasts to the Ortonville, MN area at 1350 AM.
AM RADIO STATION

KDIS-FM 42042
Owner: Salem Media Group, Inc.
Editorial: 415 N McKinley St Ste 610, Little Rock, Arkansas 72205-3168 **Tel:** 1 501 404-6560.
Email: info@faithtalk995.com
Web site: http://faithtalk995.com
Profile: KDIS-FM a commercial station owned by Salem Media Group, Inc. The format of the station is Christian talk programming. KDIS-FM broadcasts to the Little Rock, AR area at 99.5 FM.
FM RADIO STATION

KDIX-AM 34924
Owner: Starrdak Inc.
Editorial: 119 2nd Ave W, Dickinson, North Dakota 58601 **Tel:** 1 701 225-5133.
Email: kdix@kdix.net
Web site: http://www.kdix.net
Profile: KDIX-AM is a commercial station owned by Starrdak Inc. The format of the station is classic hits. KDIX-AM broadcasts to the Dickinson, ND area at 1230 AM.
AM RADIO STATION

KDIZ-AM 35871
Owner: Salem Media Group, Inc.
Editorial: 2110 Cliff Rd, Eagan, Minnesota 55122-3522 **Tel:** 1 651 405-8800.
Web site: http://twincitieswellnessradio.com
Profile: KDIZ-AM is a commercial station owned by Salem Media Group, Inc. KDIZ-AM broadcasts to the Minneapolis-St Paul, MN area at 1570 AM.
AM RADIO STATION

KDJE-FM 41614
Owner: iHeartMedia Inc.
Editorial: 10800 Colonel Glenn Rd, Little Rock, Arkansas 72204-8017 **Tel:** 1 501 217-5000.
Email: jeffcage@iheartmedia.com
Web site: http://edgelittlerock.iheart.com
Profile: KDJE-FM is a commercial station owned by iHeartMedia Inc. The format of the station is rock alternative. KDJE-FM broadcasts to the Little Rock, AR area at 100.3 FM.
FM RADIO STATION

KDJI-AM 39284
Owner: Petracom
Editorial: 1838 Commerce Dr Ste A, Lakeside, Arizona 85929-7008 **Tel:** 1 928 532-3232.
Web site: http://www.970kvm.com
Profile: KDJI-AM is a commercial station owned by Petracom. The format of the station is news and talk. KDJI-AM broadcasts in the Phoenix area at 1270 AM.
AM RADIO STATION

KDJK-FM 607059
Owner: Cumulus Media Inc
Editorial: 3127 Transworld Dr #270, Stockton, California 95206-4988 **Tel:** 1 209 507-8500.
Email: thehawk@104thehawk.com
Web site: http://www.104thehawk.com
Profile: KDJK-FM is a commercial station owned by Cumulus Media Inc. The format of the station is classic rock music. KDJK-FM broadcasts in the Mariposa, CA area at 103.9 FM.
FM RADIO STATION

KDJM-FM 553015
Owner: Rocking M Radio
Editorial: 641 W Cloud St, Salina, Kansas 67401-5618 **Tel:** 1 785 8272100.
Email: info@rockingmradio.com
Web site: http://rockingmradio.todayinkansas.com/kdjm-101-7
Profile: KDJM-FM is a commercial station owned by Rocking M Radio. The format of the station is classic country. KJDM-FM broadcasts to the Salina, KS area at a frequency of 101.7 FM.
FM RADIO STATION

KDJR-FM 44543
Owner: Family Worship Center Church, Inc.
Editorial: 8919 World Ministries Ave, Baton Rouge, Louisiana 70810-9006 **Tel:** 1 225 768-3288.
Email: info@jsm.org
Web site: http://www.jsm.org
Profile: KDJR-AM is a non-commercial station owned by Family Worship Center Church, Inc. The format of the station is religious. KDJR-FM broadcasts to the Baton Rouge, LA area at 100.1 FM.
FM RADIO STATION

KDJS-AM 39164
Owner: Iowa City Broadcasting Co.
Editorial: 730 Highway 71 NE, Willmar, Minnesota 56201 **Tel:** 1 320 231-1600.
Web site: http://www.k-musicradio.com
Profile: KDJS-AM is a commercial station owned by Iowa City Broadcasting Co. The format of the station is oldies. KDJS-AM broadcasts to the Willmar, MN area at 1590 AM.
AM RADIO STATION

KDJS-FM 46520
Owner: Iowa City Broadcasting Co.
Editorial: 730 Highway 71 NE, Willmar, Minnesota 56201 **Tel:** 1 320 231-1600.
Web site: http://www.k-musicradio.com
Profile: KDJS-FM is a commercial station owned by Iowa City Broadcasting Co. The format of the station is country music. KDJS-FM broadcasts to the Willmar, MN area at 95.3 FM.
FM RADIO STATION

KDJW-AM 35906
Owner: Dale Artho
Editorial: 701 S Pierce St, Ste 101, Amarillo, Texas 79101-2428 **Tel:** 1 806 350-1360.
Email: stval@kdjw.org
Web site: http://www.kdjw.org
Profile: KDJW-AM is a commercial station owned by Dale Artho. The format of the station is Catholic talk programming. KDJW-AM broadcasts to the Amarillo, TX area at 1360 AM.
AM RADIO STATION

KDKA-AM 34925
Owner: CBS Radio
Editorial: 651 Holiday Dr, Foster Plz Bldg 5, Pittsburgh, Pennsylvania 15220-2740 **Tel:** 1 412 353-1300.
Email: radionews@kdka.com
Web site: http://pittsburgh.cbslocal.com/station/newsradio-1020-kdka/
Profile: KDKA-AM is a commercial station owned by CBS Radio. The format of the station is news and talk programming. KDKA-AM broadcasts to the Pittsburgh area at 1020 AM.
AM RADIO STATION

KDKA-FM 40156
Owner: CBS Radio
Editorial: 651 Holiday Dr Ste 2, Pittsburgh, Pennsylvania 15220-2740 **Tel:** 1 412 920-9400.
Web site: http://pittsburgh.cbslocal.com/station/93-7-the-fan/
Profile: KDKA-FM is a commercial station owned by CBS Radio. The format of the station is sports. KDKA-FM broadcasts to the Pittsburgh area at 93.7 FM.
FM RADIO STATION

KDKB-FM 42018
Owner: Hubbard Radio, LLC
Editorial: 1167 W Javelina Ave, Mesa, Arizona 85210-5936 **Tel:** 1 602 629-8660.
Web site: http://altaz933.com
Profile: KDKB-FM is a commercial station owned by Hubbard Radio, LLC. The format of the station is alternative rock music. KDKB-FM broadcasts to the Mesa, AZ area at 93.3 FM.
FM RADIO STATION

KDKD-AM 37232
Owner: Goodradio.TV LLC
Editorial: 2201 N Antioch St, Clinton, Missouri 64735-1119 **Tel:** 1 660 885-6141.
Web site: http://www.kdkd.net
Profile: KDKD-AM is a commercial station owned by Goodradio.TV LLC. The format of the station is oldies music. KDKD-AM broadcasts to the Clinton, MO area at 1280 AM.
AM RADIO STATION

KDKD-FM 44618
Owner: Goodradio.TV LLC
Editorial: 2201 N Antioch St, Clinton, Missouri 64735-1119 **Tel:** 1 660 885-6141.
Email: production@kdkd.net
Web site: http://www.kdkd.net
Profile: KDKD-FM is commercial station owned by Goodradio.TV LLC. The format of the station is contemporary country music. KDKD-FM broadcasts to the Kansas City, MO area at 95.3 FM.
FM RADIO STATION

KDKK-FM 44829
Owner: De La Hunt Broadcasting
Editorial: Highway 34 East, Park Rapids, Minnesota 56470 **Tel:** 1 218 732-3306.
Email: kprmkdkk@unitelc.com
Web site: http://www.kkradionetwork.com
Profile: KDKK-FM is a commercial station owned by De La Hunt Broadcasting. The format of the station is

adult standards music. KDKK-FM in the Park Rapids, MN area at 97.5 FM.
FM RADIO STATION

KDKN-FM 872925
Owner: Dockins Broadcast Group
Editorial: 235 Business Hh, Piedmont, Missouri 63957-9410 **Tel:** 1 573 223-4518.
Email: fdj@dockinsbroadcastgroup.com
Web site: http://www.thezonerocks.com
Profile: KDKN-FM is a commercial station owned by Dockins Broadcast Group. The format of the station is alternative rock music. KDKN-FM broadcasts to the Poplar Bluff, MO area at a frequency of 106.7 FM.
FM RADIO STATION

KDKR-FM 43937
Owner: Penfold Communications, Inc.
Editorial: 5617 Diamond Oaks Dr S Ste 200, Fort Worth, Texas 76117-2804 **Tel:** 1 817 831-9130.
Web site: http://www.kdkr.org
Profile: KDKR-FM is a non-commercial station owned by Penfold Communications, Inc. The format of the station is Christian talk and music programming. KDKR-FM broadcasts to the Fort Worth, TX area at 91.3 FM.
FM RADIO STATION

KDKS-FM 44093
Owner: Access.1 Communications Corp.
Editorial: 208 N Thomas Dr, Shreveport, Louisiana 71107-6520 **Tel:** 1 318 222-3122.
Web site: http://www.kdks.fm
Profile: KDKS-FM is a commercial station owned by Access.1 Communications Corp. The format of the station is urban adult contemporary. KDKS-FM broadcasts to the Shreveport, LA area at 102.1 FM.
FM RADIO STATION

KDKT-AM 34970
Owner: Digital Syndicate Network LLC
Editorial: 850 County 21, Beulah, North Dakota 58523-9566 **Tel:** 1 701 873-2215.
Email: info@foxsports1410.com
Web site: http://www.foxsports1410.com
Profile: KDKT-AM is a commercial station owned by Digital Syndicate Network LLC. The format of the station is sports. KDKT-AM broadcasts in the Beulah, ND area at 1410 AM.
AM RADIO STATION

KDLD-FM 135577
Owner: Entravision Communications Corp.
Editorial: 5700 Wilshire Blvd Ste 250, Los Angeles, California 90036-3647 **Tel:** 1 323 900-6100.
Web site: http://www.joseradio.com
Profile: KDLD-FM is a commercial station owned by Entravision Communications Corp. The format of the station is Spanish Adult Hits. KDLD-FM broadcasts to the greater Los Angeles area at 103.1 FM.
FM RADIO STATION

KDLE-FM 43736
Owner: Entravision Communications Corp.
Editorial: 5700 Wilshire Blvd Ste 250, Los Angeles, California 90036-3647 **Tel:** 1 323 900-6100.
Web site: http://www.joseradio.com
Profile: KDLE-FM is a commercial station owned by Entravision Communications Corp. The format of the station is Spanish Adult Hits. KDLE-FM broadcasts to the Newport Beach, CA area at 103.1 FM and simulcasts the programming of KDLD-FM.
FM RADIO STATION

KDLF-AM 37274
Owner: Latin World Broadcasting
Editorial: 900 8th St, Boone, Iowa 50036-2920
Tel: 1 515 287-0055.
Profile: KDLF-AM is a commercial station owned by Latin World Broadcasting. The format of the station is Hispanic. Christian and religious talk. KDLF-AM broadcasts to the Boone, IA area at 1260 AM.
AM RADIO STATION

KDLK-FM 46451
Owner: Forum Broadcasting Inc.
Editorial: 107 Center Dr, Del Rio, Texas 78840-3015
Tel: 1 830 775-9583.
Email: travis@klto.net
Web site: http://www.kdlk.com
Profile: KDLK-FM is a commercial station owned by Forum Broadcasting Inc. The format of the station is contemporary country music. KDLK-FM broadcasts to the Del Rio, TX area at 94.1 FM.
FM RADIO STATION

KDLL-FM 43847
Owner: Pickle Hill Public Broadcasting
Editorial: 14896 Kenai Spur Hwy, Kenai, Alaska 99611-7014 **Tel:** 1 907 283-8433.
Web site: http://www.kdll.org
Profile: KDLL-FM is a non-commercial station owned by Pickle Hill Public Broadcasting. The format of the station is news and talk programming. KDLL-FM broadcasts to the Kenai, AK area at 91.9 FM.
FM RADIO STATION

KDLM-AM 36641
Owner: Leighton Enterprises Inc.
Editorial: 1340 Richwood Rd, Detroit Lakes, Minnesota 56501-6903 **Tel:** 1 218 847-5624.
Web site: http://www.kdlmradio.com
Profile: KDLM-AM is a commercial station owned by Leighton Enterprises Inc. The format of the station is news, talk, and sports. KDLM-AM broadcasts to the Detroit Lakes, MN area at 1340 AM.
AM RADIO STATION

KDLO-FM 39606
Owner: Alpha Media
Editorial: 921 9th Ave SE, Watertown, South Dakota 57201-4960 **Tel:** 1 605 886-8444.
Email: kwatnews@digity.me
Web site: http://www.gowatertown.net
Profile: KDLO-FM is a commercial station owned by Alpha Media. The format of the station is classic country. KDLO-FM broadcasts to the Watertown, SD area at and 96.9 FM.
FM RADIO STATION

KDLR-AM 37234
Owner: Double Z Broadcasting Inc.
Editorial: 320 Walnut St W, Devils Lake, North Dakota 58301-3506 **Tel:** 1 701 662-2161.
Web site: http://www.lrradioworks.com/kdlr
Profile: KDLR-AM is a commercial station owned by Double Z Broadcasting Inc. The format of the station is country music and news. KDLR-AM broadcasts to the Devils Lake, ND area at 1240 AM.
AM RADIO STATION

KDLS-AM 37235
Owner: M&M Broadcasting, Inc.
Tel: 1 515 465-5357.
Email: kniakrls@kniakrls.com
Web site: http://raccoonvalleyradio.com
Profile: KDLS-AM is a commercial station owned by M&M Broadcasting, Inc. The format of the station is oldies. KDLS-AM broadcasts to the Perry, IA, area at 1310 AM.
AM RADIO STATION

KDLS-FM 44619
Owner: Latin Broadcasting Company
Editorial: 950 Office Park Rd Ste 212, West Des Moines, Iowa 50265-2548 **Tel:** 1 515 278-4117.
Email: laley105@yahoo.com
Profile: KDLS-FM is a commercial station owned by Latin Broadcasting Company. The format of the station is Regional Mexican. KDLS-FM broadcasts to the Perry, IA area at a frequency of 105.5 FM.
FM RADIO STATION

KDLW-FM 43025
Owner: American General Media
Editorial: 4125 Carlisle Blvd NE, Albuquerque, New Mexico 87107-4806 **Tel:** 1 505 878-0980.
Web site: http://z1063.com
Profile: KDLW-FM is a commercial station owned by American General Media. The format of the station is Top 40/CHR. KDLW-FM broadcasts to the Albuquerque, NM area at 106.3 FM.
FM RADIO STATION

KDLX-FM 41964
Owner: Visionary Related Entertainment
Editorial: 1900 Main St, Wailuku, Hawaii 96793-1900
Tel: 1 808 244-9145.
Email: kaoi@kaoi.net
Web site: http://kdlx943.com
FM RADIO STATION

KDLY-FM 46506
Owner: Kenney(Joseph R. and Andrea L.)
Editorial: 1530 Main St, Lander, Wyoming 82520-2658 **Tel:** 1 307 332-5683.
Email: radio1@wyoming.com
Web site: http://www.kdlykove.com
Profile: KDLY-FM is a commercial station owned by Joseph R. and Andrea L. Kenney. The format for the station is classic hits. KDLY-FM broadcasts to the Casper-Riverton, WY area at 97.5 FM.
FM RADIO STATION

KDMA-AM 37236
Owner: Iowa City Broadcasting Co.
Editorial: 4454 Highway 212, Montevideo, Minnesota 56265-4539 **Tel:** 1 320 269-8815.
Email: kdmaprod@radiokdma.com
Profile: KDMA-AM is a commercial station owned by Iowa City Broadcasting Co.. The format of the station is country music. KDMA-AM broadcasts in the Montevideo, MN area at 1460 AM.
AM RADIO STATION

KDMG-FM 42117
Owner: Pritchard Broadcasting Co.
Editorial: 610 N 4th Street, Suite 300, Burlington, Iowa 52601 **Tel:** 1 319 752-5402.
Email: mail@bigcountry1031.com
Web site: http://www.bigcountry1031.com
Profile: KDMG-FM is a commercial station owned by Pritchard Broadcasting Co. The format of the station is country. KDMG-FM broadcasts to the Burlington, IA area at 103.1 FM.
FM RADIO STATION

KDMO-AM 38682
Owner: Petersen(Ronald L.)
Editorial: 221 E 4th St, Carthage, Missouri 64836-1629 **Tel:** 1 417 358-7953.
Email: news@cbcradio.com
Profile: KDMO-AM is a commercial station owned by Ronald L. Petersen. The format of the station is adult standards. KDMO-AM broadcasts to the Carthage, MO area at 1490 AM.
AM RADIO STATION

KDMS-AM 37237
Owner: El Dorado Broadcasting
Editorial: 1904 W Hillsboro St, El Dorado, Arkansas 71730-6806 **Tel:** 1 870 863-5121.
Email: klbqfm@yahoo.com
Web site: http://kdms1290.com
Profile: KDMS-AM is a commercial station owned by El Dorado Broadcasting. The format of the station is gospel music and country. KDMS-AM broadcasts in the El Dorado, AR area at 1290 AM.
AM RADIO STATION

KDMX-FM 39771
Owner: iHeartMedia Inc.
Editorial: 14001 Dallas Pkwy Ste 300, Dallas, Texas 75240-7369 **Tel:** 1 214 866-8000.
Email: psa@ccdallas.com
Web site: http://1029now.iheart.com
Profile: KDMX-FM is a commercial station owned by iHeartMedia Inc. The format of the station is hot adult contemporary. KDMX-FM broadcasts to the Dallas area at 102.9 FM.
FM RADIO STATION

KDND-FM 43201
Owner: Entercom Communications Corp.
Editorial: 5345 Madison Ave, Sacramento, California 95841-3141 **Tel:** 1 916 334-7777.
Web site: http://www.endonline.com
Profile: KDND-FM is a commercial station owned by Entercom Communications Corp. The format of the station is Top 40/CHR. KDND-FM broadcasts to the Sacramento, CA area at 106.5 FM.
FM RADIO STATION

KDNE-FM 43855
Owner: Doane College Board of Trustees
Editorial: 1014 Boswell Ave, Crete, Nebraska 68333
Tel: 1 402 826-8677.
Email: kdne@doane.edu
Web site: http://www.doane.edu/FacStaff/Media/KDNE
Profile: KDNE-FM is a non-commercial station owned by Doane College Board of Trustees. The format of the station is variety. KDNE-FM broadcasts to the Crete, NE area at 91.9 FM.
FM RADIO STATION

KDNG-FM 682523
Owner: KUTE Inc.
Editorial: 123 Capote Drive, Ignacio, Colorado 81137
Tel: 1 970 563-0255.
Web site: http://www.ksut.org
Profile: KDNG-FM is a non-commercial station owned by KUTE Inc. The format of the station is variety. KDNG-FM broadcasts to the Durango, CO area at 89.3 FM.
FM RADIO STATION

KDNI-FM 41514
Owner: Northwestern College
Editorial: 1101 E Central Entrance, Duluth, Minnesota 55811 **Tel:** 1 218 722-6700.
Web site: http://www.life973.com
Profile: KDNI-FM is a non-commercial station owned by Northwestern College. The format of the station is Christian talk. KDNI-FM broadcasts in the Duluth, MN area at 90.5 FM.
FM RADIO STATION

KDNK-FM 43156
Owner: Carbondale Community Access Radio
Editorial: 76 S 2nd St, Carbondale, Colorado 81623
Tel: 1 970 963-0139.
Web site: http://www.kdnk.org
Profile: KDNK-FM is a commercial station owned by Carbondale Community Access Radio. The format of the station is variety. KDNK-FM broadcasts to the Carbondale, CO area at 88.1 FM.
FM RADIO STATION

KDNN-FM 45867
Owner: iHeartMedia Inc.
Editorial: 650 Iwilei Rd Ste 400, Honolulu, Hawaii 96817-5319 **Tel:** 1 808 550-9200.
Web site: http://www.island985.com
Profile: KDNN-FM is a commercial station owned by iHeartMedia Inc. The format for the station is a variety of Hawaiian and reggae music. KDNN-FM broadcasts to the Honolulu area at 98.5 FM.
FM RADIO STATION

KDNO-FM 399933
Owner: Edwards Communications LLC
Editorial: 603 E Pershing Ave, Riverton, Wyoming 82501-3605 **Tel:** 1 307 856-2251.
Web site: http://www.wrrnetwork.com/kdno
Profile: KDNO-FM is a commercial station owned by CarJim LLC. The format of the station is country music. KDNO-FM broadcasts to the Casper, WY area at 101.7 FM.
FM RADIO STATION

KDNS-FM 42583
Owner: Dierking Communications
Editorial: 1937 Highway 24, Glen Elder, Kansas 67446-9461 **Tel:** 1 785 545-3220.
Email: kdnskzdy@nckcn.com
Web site: http://kdcountry94.com
Profile: KDNS-FM is a commercial station owned by Dierking Communications. The format of the station is country music. KDNS-FM broadcasts to the Downs, KS area at 94.1 FM.
FM RADIO STATION

KDNW-FM 42056
Owner: Northwestern College
Editorial: 1101 E Central Entrance, Duluth, Minnesota 55811 **Tel:** 1 218 722-6700.
Web site: http://www.life973.com
Profile: KDNW-FM is a non-commercial station owned by Northwestern College. The format of the station is contemporary Christian music and talk. KDNW-FM broadcasts to the Duluth, MN area at 97.3 FM.
FM RADIO STATION

KDOE-FM 445515
Owner: Payne Radio Group
Editorial: 1600 W Jackson St, Hugo, Oklahoma 74743
Tel: 1 580 326-2555.
Web site: http://kdoe1023.com
Profile: KDOE-FM is a commercial station owned by Payne Radio Group. The format for the station is adult contemporary. KDOE-FM broadcasts to the Antlers, OK area at 102.3 FM.
FM RADIO STATION

KDOG-FM 45843
Owner: Radio Mankato
Editorial: 59346 Madison Ave, Mankato, Minnesota 56001-8518 **Tel:** 1 507 345-4537.
Email: news@ktoe.com
Web site: http://www.hot967.fm
Profile: KDOG-FM is a commercial station owned by Radio Mankato. The format of the station is Top 40/CHR. KDOG-FM broadcasts in the Mankato, MN area at 96.7 FM.
FM RADIO STATION

KDOK-AM 37530
Owner: Chalk Hill Communications, LLC
Tel: 1 903 643-7711.
Web site: http://www.kdokradio.com
Profile: KDOK-AM is a commercial station owned by Chalk Hill Communications, LLC. The format of the station is classic hits. KDOK-AM broadcasts to the Tyler, TX area at 1240 AM.
AM RADIO STATION

KDOM-AM 37238
Owner: Results Broadcasting, Inc.
Editorial: 1450 Highway 60 71 N, Windom, Minnesota 56101-2025 **Tel:** 1 507 831-3908.
Email: kdomnews@windomnet.com
Web site: http://www.kdomradio.com
Profile: KDOM-AM is a commercial station owned by Results Broadcasting, Inc. The format of the station is country music. KDOM-AM broadcasts to the Minneapolis area at 1580 AM.
AM RADIO STATION

KDOM-FM 44620
Owner: Southwestern Minnesota Radio, Inc.
Editorial: 1450 Highway 60 71 N, Windom, Minnesota 56101 **Tel:** 1 507 831-3908.
Email: kdomnews@windomnet.com
Web site: http://www.kdomradio.com
Profile: KDOM-FM is a commercial station owned by Southwestern Minnesota Radio, Inc. The format of the station is country music. KDOM-FM broadcasts to the Minneapolis area at 94.3 FM.
FM RADIO STATION

KDON-FM 46795
Owner: iHeartMedia Inc.
Editorial: 903 N Main St, Salinas, California 93906-3912 **Tel:** 1 831 755-8181.
Web site: http://www.kdon.com
Profile: KDON-FM is a commercial station owned by iHeartMedia Inc. The format of the station is rhythmic Top 40/CHR music. KDON-FM broadcasts to the Salinas, CA area at 102.5 FM.
FM RADIO STATION

KDOT-FM 46749
Owner: Lotus Communications Corp.
Editorial: 2900 Sutro St, Reno, Nevada 89512-1616
Tel: 1 775 329-9261.
Web site: http://www.kdot.com
Profile: KDOT-FM is a commercial station owned by Lotus Communications Corp. The format of the station is rock. KDOT-FM broadcasts to the Reno, NV area at 104.5 FM.
FM RADIO STATION

KDOV-FM 43057
Owner: UCB USA Inc.
Editorial: 2070 Milligan Way, Medford, Oregon 97504-5894 **Tel:** 1 541 776-5368.
Email: thedove@thedove.us
Web site: http://www.thedove.us/radio
Profile: KDOV-FM is a non-commercial station owned by UCB USA Inc. The format of the station is contemporary Christian music and talk programming. KDOV-FM broadcasts in the Medford, OR area at 91.7 FM.
FM RADIO STATION

KDOW-AM 36525
Owner: Salem Media Group, Inc.
Editorial: 39650 Liberty St, Fremont, California 94538-2223 **Tel:** 1 510 713-1100.
Email: comments@kdow.biz
Web site: http://www.kdow.biz
Profile: KDOW-AM is a commercial station owned by Salem Media Group, Inc. The format of the station is business talk. KDOW-AM broadcasts to the San Francisco and San Jose, CA markets at 1220 AM.
AM RADIO STATION

KDQN-AM 37239
Owner: Bunyard Broadcasting
Editorial: 921 W Collin Raye Dr, De Queen, Arkansas 71832-2025 **Tel:** 1 870 642-2446.
Email: numberonecountry@yahoo.com
Web site: http://www.kdqn.net
Profile: KDQN-AM is a commercial station owned by Bunyard Broadcasting. The format of the station is

Hispanic music and news. KDQN-AM broadcasts to the De Queen, AR area at 1390 AM.
AM RADIO STATION

KDQN-FM 44621
Owner: Bunyard Broadcasting
Editorial: 921 W Collin Raye Dr, De Queen, Arkansas 71832 **Tel:** 1 870 642-2446.
Email: numberonecountry@yahoo.com
Web site: http://www.kdqn.net
Profile: KDQN-FM is a commercial station owned by Bunyard Broadcasting. The format for the station is country music. KDQN-FM broadcasts to the Shreveport, LA area at 92.1 FM.
FM RADIO STATION

KDRB-FM 44759
Owner: iHeartMedia Inc.
Editorial: 2141 Grand Ave, Des Moines, Iowa 50312-5303 **Tel:** 1 515 245-8900.
Web site: http://www.thebusfm.com
Profile: KDRB-FM is a commercial station owned by iHeartMedia Inc. The format of the station is adult hits. KDRB-FM broadcasts in the Des Moines, IA area at 100.3 FM.
FM RADIO STATION

KDRF-FM 41579
Owner: Cumulus Media Inc
Editorial: 500 4th St NW, 5th Floor, Albuquerque, New Mexico 87102-5324 **Tel:** 1 505 767-6700.
Email: ed@ed.fm
Web site: http://www.ed.fm
Profile: KDRF-FM is a commercial station owned by Cumulus Media Inc. The format of the station is adult hits. KDRF-FM broadcasts to the Albuquerque, NM area at 103.3 FM.
FM RADIO STATION

KDRK-FM 44622
Owner: Mapleton Communications LLC
Editorial: 1601 E 57th Ave, Spokane, Washington 99223 **Tel:** 1 509 448-1000.
Email: themountain937@yahoo.com
Web site: http://www.937themountain.com
Profile: KDRK-FM is a commercial station owned by Mapleton Communications LLC. The format of the station is contemporary country. KDRK-FM broadcasts to the Spokane, WA area at 93.7 FM.
FM RADIO STATION

KDRM-FM 44623
Owner: KSEM Inc.
Editorial: 2241 W Main St, Moses Lake, Washington 98837 **Tel:** 1 509 765-3441.
Profile: KDRM-FM is a commercial station owned by KSEM Inc. The format of the station is hot adult contemporary. KDRM-FM broadcasts to the Spokane, WA area at 99.3 FM.
FM RADIO STATION

KDRO-AM 34927
Owner: Benne Media
Editorial: 301 S Ohio Ave, Sedalia, Missouri 65301 **Tel:** 1 660 826-5005.
Email: bennemedia@bennemedia.com
Web site: http://www.kdro.com
Profile: KDRO-AM is a commercial station owned by Benne Media. The format of the station is classic country music. KDRO-AM broadcasts to the Kansas City, MO area at 1490 AM.
AM RADIO STATION

KDRS-AM 38458
Owner: MOR Media Inc.
Editorial: 400 Tower Dr, Paragould, Arkansas 72450-4891 **Tel:** 1 870 236-7627.
Web site: http://www.irocknea.com/
Profile: KDRS-AM is a commercial station owned by MOR Media Inc. The format of the station is Hot AC. KDRS-AM broadcasts to the Paragould, AR area at 1490 AM.
AM RADIO STATION

KDRS-FM 45822
Owner: MOR Media Inc.
Editorial: 400 Tower Dr, Paragould, Arkansas 72450 **Tel:** 1 870 236-7627.
Web site: http://www.neajackfm.com
Profile: KDRS-FM is a commercial station owned by MOR Media Inc. The format of the station is Jack FM. KDRS-FM broadcasts to the Paragould, AR area at 107.1 FM.
FM RADIO STATION

KDRX-FM 809893
Owner: MBM Radio Del Rio, LLC
Tel: 1 830 703-6704.
Web site: http://www.outlaw1069.com
Profile: KDRX-FM is a commercial station owned by MBM Radio Del Rio, LLC. The format of the station is Regional Mexican. KDRX-FM broadcasts to the Del Rio, TX area at a frequency of 106.9 FM.
FM RADIO STATION

KDRY-AM 34928
Owner: KDRY Radio Inc.
Editorial: 16414 San Pedro Ave Ste 575, San Antonio, Texas 78232-2311 **Tel:** 1 210 545-1100.
Email: am1100@kdry.com
Web site: http://www.kdry.com
Profile: KDRY-AM is a commercial station owned by KDRY Radio Inc. The format of the station is religious programming. KDRY-AM broadcasts to the San Antonio area at 1100 AM.
AM RADIO STATION

KDSJ-AM 34929
Owner: Goldrush Broadcasting Co.
Editorial: 745 Main St, Deadwood, South Dakota 57732-1015 **Tel:** 1 605 578-1826.
Email: kdsj@vastbb.net
Web site: http://www.kdsj980.com
Profile: KDSJ-AM is a commercial station owned by Goldrush Broadcasting Co. The format of the station is oldies. KDSJ-AM broadcasts to the Deadwood, SD area at a frequency of 980 AM.
AM RADIO STATION

KDSK-AM 35003
Owner: KD Radio Inc.
Editorial: 733 E Roosevelt Ave, Grants, New Mexico 87020-2113 **Tel:** 1 505 285-5598.
Web site: http://www.kdsk.com
Profile: KDSK-AM is a commercial station owned by the KD Radio Inc.. The format of the station is oldies. KDSK-AM broadcasts to the Albuquerque, NM area at 1240 AM. The station does not accept pitches.
AM RADIO STATION

KDSK-FM 43222
Owner: KD Radio Inc.
Editorial: 733 E Roosevelt Ave, Grants, New Mexico 87020-2113 **Tel:** 1 505 285-5598.
Web site: http://www.kdsk.com
Profile: KDSK-FM is a commercial station owned by KD Radio Inc. The format of the station is oldies. KDSK-FM broadcasts to the Grants, NM area at 92.7 FM. The station does not accept pitches.
FM RADIO STATION

KDSN-AM 37240
Owner: M&J Radio, Corp
Editorial: 1530 Ridge Rd, Denison, Iowa 51442-1172 **Tel:** 1 712 263-3141.
Email: info@kdsnradio.com
Web site: http://www.kdsnradio.com
Profile: KDSN-AM is a commercial station owned byM&J Radio, Corp. The format of the station is country music. KDSN-AM broadcasts to the Denison, IA area at 1530 AM.
AM RADIO STATION

KDSN-FM 44624
Owner: M&J Radio, Corp
Editorial: 1530 Ridge Rd, Denison, Iowa 51442-1172 **Tel:** 1 712 263-3141.
Email: info@kdsnradio.com
Web site: http://www.kdsnradio.com
Profile: KDSN-FM is a commercial station owned by M&J Radio, Corp. The format of the station is adult contemporary music. KDSN-FM broadcasts to the Denison, IA area at 107.1 FM.
FM RADIO STATION

KDSP-FM 364670
Owner: Colorado Public Radio
Editorial: 7409 S Alton Ct, Centennial, Colorado 80112-2301 **Tel:** 1 303 871-9191.
Web site: http://denversports760.iheart.com/
Profile: KDSP-FM is a non-commercial station owned by Colorado Public Radio. The format of the station is sports. KDSP-FM broadcasts to the Denver area at 102.3 FM.
FM RADIO STATION

KDSR-FM 41193
Owner: Stephen Marks Enterprises
Editorial: 910 E Broadway, Williston, North Dakota 58801 **Tel:** 1 701 572-4478.
Email: kdsr@nemont.net
Profile: KDSR-FM is a commercial station owned by Stephen Marks Enterprises. The format of the station is adult hits music. KDSR-FM broadcasts to the Williston, ND area at 101.1 FM.
FM RADIO STATION

KDSS-FM 41092
Owner: Coates Broadcasting Inc.
Editorial: 466 Aultman St, Ely, Nevada 89301-1551 **Tel:** 1 775 289-6474.
Email: kdssfm@sbcglobal.net
Profile: KDSS-FM is a commercial station owned by Coates Broadcasting Inc. The format of the station is country. KDSS-FM broadcasts to the Salt Lake City area at 92.7 FM.
FM RADIO STATION

KDST-FM 40042
Owner: Design Homes Inc.
Editorial: 1931 20th Ave SE, Dyersville, Iowa 52040-9571 **Tel:** 1 563 875-8193.
Email: kdst993@iowatelecom.net
Web site: http://www.realcountryonline.com
Profile: KDST-FM is a commercial station owned by Design Homes Inc. The format of the station is classic country. KDST-FM broadcasts to the Dyersville, IA area at 99.3 FM.
FM RADIO STATION

KDTD-AM 35880
Owner: Reyes Media Group
Editorial: 1701 S 55th Street, Kansas City, Missouri 66106 **Tel:** 1 913 287-1480.
Web site: http://www.lagrand1340kc.com
Profile: KDTD-AM is a commercial station owned by Reyes Media Group. The format of the station is regional Mexican music. KDTD-AM broadcasts to the Kansas City, MO area at 1340 AM.
AM RADIO STATION

KDTH-AM 37241
Owner: Radio Dubuque Inc.
Editorial: 1055 University Ave, Dubuque, Iowa 52001-6154 **Tel:** 1 563 690-0800.
Email: kdth@kdth.com
Web site: http://www.kdth.com
Profile: KDTH-AM is a commercial station owned by Radio Dubuque Inc. The format of the station is adult standards music, news and talk programming. KDTH-AM broadcasts to the Dubuque, IA area at 1370 AM.
AM RADIO STATION

KDTR-FM 349606
Owner: Spanish Peaks Broadcasting, Inc.
Editorial: 2425 W Central Ave Ste 203, Missoula, Montana 59801-6402 **Tel:** 1 406 721-6800.
Web site: http://www.trail1033.com
Profile: KDTR-FM is a commercial station owned by Spanish Peaks Broadcasting, Inc., which does business as The Montana Radio Company, LLC. The format of the station is adult album alternative. KDTR-FM broadcasts to the Missoula, MT area at 103.3 FM.
FM RADIO STATION

KDUC-FM 46482
Owner: Dos Costas Communications Corp.
Editorial: 29000 Radio Rd, Barstow, California 92311-1648 **Tel:** 1 760 256-2121.
Email: doscostas@yahoo.com
Profile: KDUC-FM is a commercial station owned by Dos Costas Communications Corp. The format of the station is rhythmic Top 40/CHR music. KDUC-FM broadcasts to the Barstow, CA area at 94.3 FM.
FM RADIO STATION

KDUK-FM 46720
Owner: Bicoastal Media LLC
Editorial: 1500 Valley River Dr Ste 350, Eugene, Oregon 97401-2163 **Tel:** 1 541 485-1120.
Web site: http://www.kduk.com
Profile: KDUK-FM is a commercial station owned by Bicoastal Media LLC. The format of the station is Top 40/CHR music. KDUK-FM broadcasts in the Eugene, OR at 104.7 FM.
FM RADIO STATION

KDUN-AM 36633
Owner: Sand & Sea Broadcasting LLC
Editorial: 136 N 7th St, Reedsport, Oregon 97467-1503 **Tel:** 1 541 271-1030.
Email: psa@kdunam.com
Web site: http://www.kdune.com
Profile: The station prefers to be contacted via its contact form: http://www.kdunam.com/contacts.html.
AM RADIO STATION

KDUR-FM 39612
Owner: Fort Lewis College
Editorial: 1000 Rim Drive Ft Lewis College, Durango, Colorado 81301-3911 **Tel:** 1 970 247-7634.
Email: kdur@fortlewis.edu
Web site: http://www.kdur.org
Profile: KDUR-FM is a non-commercial station owned by Fort Lewis College. The format for the station is free-form. KDUR-FM broadcasts to the Durango, CO area at 91.9 FM.
FM RADIO STATION

KDUS-AM 38649
Owner: Hubbard Radio, LLC
Editorial: 1100 N 52nd St, Phoenix, Arizona 85008-3432 **Tel:** 1 602 629-8660.
Web site: http://nbcsportsradioam1060.com
Profile: KDUS-AM is a commercial station owned by Hubbard Radio, LLC. The format of the station is sports. KDUS-AM broadcasts in the Tempe, AZ area at 1060 AM.
AM RADIO STATION

KDUT-FM 73462
Owner: Adelante Media Group
Editorial: 2722 S Redwood Rd Ste 1, Salt Lake City, Utah 84119-8410 **Tel:** 1 801 908-8777.
Web site: http://adelantemediagroup.com
Profile: KDUT-FM is a commercial station owned by Adelante Media Group. The format of the station is regional Mexican. KDUT-FM broadcasts to the Salt Lake City area at 102.3 FM.
FM RADIO STATION

KDUX-FM 45848
Owner: Morris Communications
Editorial: 1308 Coolidge Rd, Aberdeen, Washington 98520-6317 **Tel:** 1 360 533-1320.
Web site: http://www.kdux.com
Profile: KDUX-FM is a commercial station owned by Morris Communications. The format of the station is classic rock music. KDUX-FM broadcasts to the Aberdeen, WA area at 104.7 FM.
FM RADIO STATION

KDUZ-AM 37242
Owner: Iowa City Broadcasting Co.
Editorial: 20132 Highway 15 N, Hutchinson, Minnesota 55350 **Tel:** 1 320 587-2140.
Email: news@kduz.com
Web site: http://www.kduz.com
Profile: KDUZ-AM is a commercial station owned by Iowa City Broadcasting Co. The format of the station is news, talk and classic country music. KDUZ-AM broadcasts in the Hutchinson, MN area at 1260 AM.
AM RADIO STATION

KDVA-FM 74129
Owner: Entravision Communications Corp.
Editorial: 501 N 44th St, Ste 425, Phoenix, Arizona 85008 **Tel:** 1 602 776-1400.
Web site: http://www.josephoenix.com
Profile: KDVA-FM is a commercial station owned by Entravision Communications Corp. The format of the station is Hispanic adult hits. KDVA-FM broadcasts to the Phoenix area at 106.9 FM.
FM RADIO STATION

KDVL-FM 44625
Owner: Double Z Broadcasting Inc.
Editorial: 320 Walnut St W, Devils Lake, North Dakota 58301-3506 **Tel:** 1 701 662-2161.
Web site: http://www.lrradioworks.com
Profile: KDVL-FM is a commercial station owned by Double Z Broadcasting Inc. The format of the station is oldies music. KDVL-FM broadcasts to the Fargo, ND area at 102.5 FM.
FM RADIO STATION

KDVV-FM 42756
Owner: Cumulus Media Inc.
Editorial: 825 S Kansas Ave, Ste 100, Topeka, Kansas 66612 **Tel:** 1 785 272-2122.
Web site: http://www.v100rocks.com
Profile: KDVV-FM is a commercial station owned by Cumulus Media Inc. The format of the station is rock. KDVV-FM broadcasts to the Topeka, KS area at a frequency of 100.3 FM.
FM RADIO STATION

KDWA-AM 34931
Owner: K & M Broadcasting Inc.
Editorial: 514 Vermillion St, Hastings, Minnesota 55033 **Tel:** 1 651 437-1460.
Email: news@kdwa.com
Web site: http://www.kdwa.com
Profile: KDWA-AM is a commercial station owned by K&M Broadcasting Inc. The format of the station is news, sports and talk. KDWA-FM broadcasts to the Hastings, MN area at 1460 AM.
AM RADIO STATION

KDWB-FM 42167
Owner: iHeartMedia Inc.
Editorial: 1600 Utica Ave S Ste 400, Minneapolis, Minnesota 55416-1480 **Tel:** 1 952 417-3000.
Web site: http://www.kdwb.com
Profile: KDWB-FM is a commercial station owned by iHeartMedia Inc. The format of the station is Top 40/CHR music. KDWB-FM broadcasts to the Minneapolis area at 101.3 FM.
FM RADIO STATION

KDWG-FM 839376
Editorial: 710 S Atlantic St, Dillon, Montana 59725-3511 **Tel:** 1 406 683-7156.
Email: kdwg@umwestern.edu
Web site: http://streamdb6web.securenetsystems.net/v5/KDWG
Profile: KDWG-FM is a non-commercial college station owned by The University of Montana - Western. The format of the station is variety. KDWG-FM broadcasts to the Dillon, MT area at a frequency of 90.9 FM.
FM RADIO STATION

KDWN-AM 34932
Owner: Beasley Broadcast Group
Editorial: 2920 S Durango Dr, Las Vegas, Nevada 89117-4412 **Tel:** 1 702 730-0300.
Email: email@bbgi.com
Web site: http://www.kdwn.com
Profile: KDWN-AM is a commercial station owned by Beasley Broadcast Group. The format of the station is sports, news and talk. KDWN-AM broadcasts to the Las Vegas area at 720 AM.
AM RADIO STATION

KDWY-FM 232129
Owner: SLC Divestiture Trust I
Editorial: 436 Fossil Butte Dr, Kemmerer, Wyoming 83101
Profile: KDWY-FM is a commercial station owned by SLC Divestiture Trust I. The format of the station is classic country. KDWY-FM broadcasts to the Kemmerer, WY area at 105.3 FM.
FM RADIO STATION

KDWZ-FM 44998
Owner: Midwest Communications Inc.
Editorial: 11 E Superior St Ste 380, Duluth, Minnesota 55802-3016 **Tel:** 1 218 722-4321.
Web site: http://dukefmduluth.com/
Profile: KDWZ-FM is a commercial station owned by Midwest Communications Inc. The format of the station is Classic Country. KDWZ-FM broadcasts to the Duluth, MN area at 102.5 FM.
FM RADIO STATION

KDXA-FM 41793
Owner: iHeartMedia Inc.
Editorial: 2141 Grand Ave, Des Moines, Iowa 50312-5303 **Tel:** 1 515 245-8900.
Web site: http://www.alt1063.com/main.html
Profile: KDXA-FM is a commercial station owned by iHeartMedia Inc. The format of the station is Modern Rock. KDXA-FM broadcasts to the Des Moines, IA area at 106.3 FM.
FM RADIO STATION

KDXE-AM 36596
Owner: Simmons Media Group
Editorial: 515 S 700 E Ste 1C, Salt Lake City, Utah 84102-2802 **Tel:** 1 801 524-2600.

Profile: KDXE-AM is a commercial station owned by Simmons Media Group. The format of the station is Spanish AC. KDXE-AM broadcasts to the Little Rock, AR area at 1380 AM.
AM RADIO STATION

KDXT-FM 521792
Owner: Western Rockies Radio Inc.
Editorial: 2600 S Garfield St, Missoula, Montana 59801-7709 Tel: 1 406 541-1071.
Web site: https://www.kdxttheranch.com
Profile: KDXT-FM is a commercial station owned by Western Rockies Radio Inc. The format of the station is classic country. KDXT-FM broadcasts to the Missoula, MT area at 97.9 FM.
FM RADIO STATION

KDXU-AM 37244
Owner: Cherry Creek Radio
Editorial: 750 Ridgeview Dr, St George, Utah 84770 Tel: 1 435 673-3579.
Web site: http://www.newstalk890.com
Profile: KDXU-AM is a commercial station owned by Cherry Creek Radio. The format of the station is news and talk. KDXU-AM broadcasts to the Salt Lake City area at 890 AM.
AM RADIO STATION

KDXY-FM 39616
Owner: Saga Communications
Editorial: 314 Union St, Jonesboro, Arkansas 72401 Tel: 1 870 933-8800.
Web site: http://www.thefox1049.com
Profile: KDXY-FM is a commercial station owned by Saga Communications. The format of the station is contemporary country. KDXY-FM broadcasts to the Jonesboro, AR at 104.9 FM.
FM RADIO STATION

KDYA-AM 36842
Owner: Bay Bridge Communications
Editorial: 3260 Blume Dr, Ste 520, Richmond, California 94806 Tel: 1 510 222-4242.
Email: sales@gospel1190.net
Web site: http://www.gospel1190.net
Profile: KDYA-AM is a commercial station owned by Bay Bridge Communications. The format of the station is gospel. KDYA-AM broadcasts to the Richmond, CA area at 1190 AM.
AM RADIO STATION

KDYK-AM 35964
Owner: Bustos Media, LLC
Editorial: 706 Butterfield Rd, Yakima, Washington 98901-2021 Tel: 1 509 457-1000.
Profile: KDYK-AM is a commercial station owned by Bustos Media, LLC. The format of the station is Spanish Adult Hits. KDYK-AM broadcasts to the Yakima, WA area at 1020 AM.
AM RADIO STATION

KDYM-AM 37462
Owner: Adelante Media Group
Editorial: 706 Butterfield Rd, Yakima, Washington 98901 Tel: 1 509 457-1000.
Profile: KDYM-AM is a commercial station owned by Adelante Media Group. The format of the station is Spanish AC. KDYM-AM broadcasts to the Yakima, WA area at 1210 AM.
AM RADIO STATION

KDYN-AM 37245
Owner: Ozark Communications Inc.
Editorial: 9331 Puddin Ridge Rd, Ozark, Arkansas 72949 Tel: 1 479 667-4567.
Email: kdyn@centurytel.net
Web site: http://www.kdyn.com
Profile: KDYN-AM is a commercial station owned by Ozark Communications Inc. The format of the station is classic country. KDYN-AM broadcasts to the Ozark, AR area at 1540 AM.
AM RADIO STATION

KDYN-FM 44628
Owner: Ozark Communications Inc.
Editorial: 9331 Puddin Ridge Rd, Ozark, Arkansas 72949 Tel: 1 479 667-4567.
Email: kdyn@centurytel.net
Web site: http://www.kdyn.com
Profile: KDYN-FM is a commercial station owned by Ozark Communications Inc. The format of the station is classic country music. KDYN-FM broadcasts to the Ozark, AR area at 96.7 FM.
FM RADIO STATION

KDZA-FM 42110
Owner: iHeartMedia Inc.
Editorial: 2864 S Circle Dr Ste 300, Colorado Springs, Colorado 80906-4131 Tel: 1 719 540-9200.
Web site: http://www.z1079rocks.com
Profile: KDZA-FM is a commercial station owned by iHeartMedia Inc. The format of the station is classic rock. KDZA-FM broadcasts to the Pueblo, CO area at 107.9 FM.
FM RADIO STATION

KDZN-FM 43728
Owner: Magic Air Communications
Editorial: 210 S Douglas St, Glendive, Montana 59330 Tel: 1 406 377-3377.
Email: kxgnkdzn@midrivers.com
Web site: http://www.kxgn.com
Profile: KDZN-FM is a commercial station owned by Magic Air Communications. The format of the station is contemporary country music. KDZN-FM broadcasts to the Glendive, MT area at 96.5 FM.
FM RADIO STATION

KDZZ-FM 524473
Owner: Townsquare Media
Editorial: 122 4th St SW, Rochester, Minnesota 55902-3320 Tel: 1 507 286-1010.
Web site: http://www.zrock1077.com
Profile: KDZZ-FM is a commercial station owned by Townsquare Media. The format of the station is rock. KDZZ-FM broadcasts to the Rochester, MN area at 107.7 FM.
FM RADIO STATION

KEAG-FM 42284
Owner: Alpha Media
Editorial: 301 Arctic Slope Ave Ste 200, Anchorage, Alaska 99518-3035 Tel: 1 907 344-9622.
Web site: http://www.kool973.com
Profile: KEAG-FM is a commercial station owned by Alpha Media. The format of the station is oldies music. KEAG-FM broadcasts to the Anchorage, AK area at 97.3 FM.
FM RADIO STATION

KEAN-FM 44629
Owner: Townsquare Media, LLC
Editorial: 3911 S 1st St, Abilene, Texas 79605 Tel: 1 325 676-7711.
Web site: http://www.keanradio.com
Profile: KEAN-FM is a commercial station owned by Townsquare Media, LLC. The format of the station is contemporary country music. KEAN-FM broadcasts to the Abliene, TX area at 105.1 FM.
FM RADIO STATION

KEAR-AM 38685
Owner: Family Stations Inc.
Editorial: 290 Hegenberger Rd, Oakland, California 94621-1436 Tel: 1 510 568-6200.
Email: info@familyradio.org
Web site: http://www.familyradio.com
Profile: KEAR-AM is a non-commercial station owned by Family Stations Inc. The format of the station is religious. KEAR-AM broadcasts to the greater San Francisco Bay area at 610 AM.
AM RADIO STATION

KEAZ-FM 135477
Owner: Crain Media Group LLC
Editorial: 111 N Spring St, Searcy, Arkansas 72143-7712 Tel: 1 501 268-7123.
Web site: http://www.myz100.com
Profile: KEAZ-FM is a commercial station owned by Crain Media Group LLC. The format of the station is adult contemporary. KEAZ-FM broadcasts to the Searcy, AR area at 100.7 FM.
FM RADIO STATION

KEBC-AM 36731
Owner: Tyler Media Group Inc.
Editorial: 400 E Britton Rd, Oklahoma City, Oklahoma 73114-7515 Tel: 1 405 616-5500.
Web site: http://www.kokcradio.com
Profile: KEBC-AM is a commercial station owned by Tyler Media Group Inc. The format of the station is talk. KEBC-AM broadcasts to the Oklahoma City area locally at 1560 AM.
AM RADIO STATION

KEBE-AM 38486
Owner: Waller Broadcasting
Tel: 1 903 643-7711.
Email: kzqxfm@aol.com
Web site: http://kzqx.com
Profile: KEBE-AM is a commercial station owned by Waller Broadcasting. The format of the station is adult standards/nostalgia. KEBE-AM broadcasts to the Jacksonville, TX area at 1400 AM.
AM RADIO STATION

KEBR-FM 43470
Owner: Family Stations Inc.
Editorial: 290 Hegenberger Rd, Oakland, California 94621-1436 Tel: 1 510 568-6200.
Web site: http://www.familyradio.com
Profile: KEBR-FM is a non-commercial station owned by Family Stations Inc. The format of the station is religious. KEBR-FM broadcasts to the Sacramento, CA, area at 88.1 FM.
FM RADIO STATION

KEBT-FM 43755
Owner: American General Media
Editorial: 1400 Easton Dr Ste 144-B, Bakersfield, California 93309-9412 Tel: 1 661 328-1410.
Web site: http://www.969lacaliente.com
Profile: KEBT-FM is a commercial station owned by American General Media. The format of the station is regional Mexican. KEBT-FM broadcasts to the Bakersfield, CA area at 96.9 FM.
FM RADIO STATION

KECH-FM 41196
Owner: Rich Broadcasting, LLC.
Editorial: 201 S Main St, Hailey, Idaho 83333-8406 Tel: 1 208 788-7118.
Email: kech95@richbroadcasting.com
Web site: http://www.kech95fm.com/
Profile: KECH-FM is a commercial station owned by Rich Broadcasting, LLC. The format of the station is classic rock and album-oriented rock. KECH-FM broadcasts to the Ketchum, ID area at 95.3 FM.
FM RADIO STATION

KECO-FM 39619
Owner: Paragon Communications Inc.
Editorial: 220 S Pioneer Rd, Elk City, Oklahoma 73644 Tel: 1 580 225-9696.
Email: kecoproduction@cableone.net
Web site: http://www.kecofm.com
Profile: KECO-FM is a commercial station owned by Paragon Communications Inc. The format of the station is classic and contemporary country music. KECO-FM broadcasts to the Elk City, OK area at 96.5 FM.
FM RADIO STATION

KECR-AM 36460
Owner: Family Stations Inc.
Editorial: 11865 Moreno Ave, Lakeside, California 92040-1110 Tel: 1 619 390-3481.
Email: info@familyradio.org
Web site: http://familyradio.com
Profile: KECR-AM is a non-commercial station owned by Family Stations Inc. The format of the station is religious. KECR-AM broadcasts to the Lakeside, CA area at 910 AM.
AM RADIO STATION

KEDA-AM 34934
Owner: D&E Broadcasting
Editorial: 1246 W Laurel Ste 100, San Antonio, Texas 78201-6431 Tel: 1 210 226-5254.
Email: kedaradio@yahoo.com
Web site: http://www.kedaradio.com
Profile: KEDA-AM is a commercial station owned by D&E Broadcasting. The format of the station is Hispanic programming. KEDA-AM broadcasts to the San Antonio area at 1540 AM.
AM RADIO STATION

KEDB-FM 43389
Owner: Honey Creek Broadcasting
Editorial: 402 N 12th St, Centerville, Iowa 52544-1718 Tel: 1 641 856-3996.
Email: kmgofm@lisco.net
Web site: http://www.kedb.fm
Profile: KEDB-FM is a commercial station owned by Honey Creek Broadcasting. The format of the station is oldies. KEDB-FM broadcasts to the Chariton, IA area at 105.3 FM.
FM RADIO STATION

KEDG-FM 83676
Owner: Lagniappe Broadcasting
Editorial: 92 W Shamrock Ave, Pineville, Louisiana 71360-6435 Tel: 1 318 487-1035.
Web site: http://www.sunny1069fm.com
Profile: KEDG-FM is a commercial station owned by Lagniappe Broadcasting. The format of the station is adult contemporary. KEDG-FM broadcasts to the Alexandria, LA area at 106.9 FM.
FM RADIO STATION

KEDJ-FM 44657
Owner: Lee Family Broadcasting
Editorial: 47 N 100 W, Jerome, Idaho 83338-5403 Tel: 1 208 324-8181.
Web site: http://www.1031theedge.com
Profile: KEDJ-FM is a commercial station owned by Lee Family Broadcasting. The format of the station is rock. KEDJ-FM broadcasts to the Jerome, ID area at 103.1 FM.
FM RADIO STATION

KEDO-AM 37248
Owner: Bicoastal Media LLC
Editorial: 1130 14th Ave, Longview, Washington 98632-3017 Tel: 1 360 425-1500.
Web site: http://www.kedoam.com
Profile: KEDO-AM is a commercial station owned by Bicoastal Media. The format of the station is news and talk. KEDO-AM broadcasts to the Portland, OR area at 1400 AM.
AM RADIO STATION

KEDT-FM 39720
Owner: South Texas Public Broadcasting
Editorial: 4455 S Padre Island Dr, Ste 38, Corpus Christi, Texas 78411 Tel: 1 361 855-2213.
Web site: http://www.kedt.org
Profile: KEDT-FM is a non-commercial station owned by South Texas Public Broadcasting. The format of the station is classical and jazz. KEDT-FM broadcasts to the Corpus Christi, TX area at 90.3 FM.
FM RADIO STATION

KEEH-FM 76082
Owner: Upper Columbia Media
Editorial: 3715 S Grove Rd, Spokane, Washington 99224-6090 Tel: 1 509 527-2991.
Web site: http://www.plr.org
Profile: KEEH-FM is a non-commercial station owned by Upper Columbia Media. The format of the station is contemporary Christian music. KEEH-FM broadcasts to the Spokane, WA area at 104.9 FM.
FM RADIO STATION

KEEL-AM 39334
Owner: Townsquare Media, LLC
Editorial: 6341 Westport Ave, Shreveport, Louisiana 71129-2415 Tel: 1 318 688-1130.
Web site: http://710keel.com
Profile: KEEL-AM is a commercial station owned by Townsquare Media, LLC. The format of the station is news and talk. KEEL-AM broadcasts to the Shreveport, LA area at 710 AM. The station focuses on local news only and does not wish to receive any guest pitches whatsoever.
AM RADIO STATION

KEEP-FM 44345
Owner: Hill Country Broadcasting, LLC
Editorial: 210 Woodcrest St, Fredericksburg, Texas 78624-2529 Tel: 1 830 997-2197.
Email: hillcountrybroadcasting@gmail.com
Web site: http://www.texasrebelradio.com
Profile: KEEP-FM is a commercial station owned by Hill Country Broadcasting, LLC. The format of the station is country. KEEP-FM broadcasts to the Bandera, TX area at 103.1 FM.
FM RADIO STATION

KEES-AM 34935
Owner: Salt of the Earth Broadcasting
Editorial: 2737 S Broadway Ave, Tyler, Texas 75701-5413 Tel: 1 903 526-1330.
Email: kgldradio@yahoo.com
Web site: http://www.kgld.org
Profile: KEES-AM is a commercial station owned by Salt of the Earth Broadcasting. The format of the station is urban gospel. KEES-AM broadcasts to the Tyler, Texas area at 1430 AM.
AM RADIO STATION

KEEY-FM 44632
Owner: iHeartMedia Inc.
Editorial: 1600 Utica Ave S Ste 400, Saint Louis Park, Minnesota 55416-1480 Tel: 1 952 417-3000.
Web site: http://www.k102.com
Profile: KEEY-FM is a commercial station owned by iHeartMedia Inc. The format of the station is contemporary country. KEEY-FM broadcasts to the Minneapolis area at 102.1 FM.
FM RADIO STATION

KEEZ-FM 41037
Owner: Alpha Media
Editorial: 1807 Lee Blvd, North Mankato, Minnesota 56003-2633 Tel: 1 507 345-4646.
Web site: http://www.myz99.com
Profile: KEEZ-FM is a commercial station owned by Alpha Media. The format of the station is hot adult contemporary music. KEEZ-FM broadcasts to the Mankato, MN area at 99.1 FM.
FM RADIO STATION

KEFH-FM 44410
Owner: Alliance Broadcast Communications
Editorial: 207 South Sulley, Clarendon, Texas 79226-0370 Tel: 1 806 874-2296.
Email: kefh@kool993.net
Web site: http://www.kefh.net
Profile: KEFH-FM is a commercial station owned by Alliance Broadcast Communications. The format of the station is classic hits and some regular oldies music. KEFH-FM broadcasts to the Clarendon, TX area at 99.3 FM.
FM RADIO STATION

KEFR-FM 41374
Owner: Family Stations Inc.
Editorial: 13306 Jefferson St, Le Grand, California 95333 Tel: 1 209 389-4659.
Email: info@familyradio.org
Web site: http://www.familyradio.com
Profile: KFRB-FM is a non-commercial station owned by Family Station Inc. The format of the station is religious music and talk. KFRB-FM broadcasts in the Le Grand, CA at 89.9 FM.
FM RADIO STATION

KEFX-FM 43087
Owner: CSN International
Editorial: 4002 N 3300 E, Twin Falls, Idaho 83301-0354 Tel: 1 208 734-2049.
Email: feedback@csnradio.com
Web site: http://www.csnradio.com
Profile: KEFX-FM is a non-commercial station owned by CSN International. The format of the station is Christian rock. KEFX-FM broadcasts to the Twin Falls, ID area at 88.9 FM.
FM RADIO STATION

KEGA-FM 155387
Owner: Broadway Media
Editorial: 50 W Broadway Ste 200, Salt Lake City, Utah 84101-2024 Tel: 1 801 524-2600.
Web site: http://www.1015theeagle.com
Profile: KEGA-FM is a commercial station owned by Broadway Media. The format of the station is country. KEGA-FM broadcasts to the Salt Lake City area at 105.1 FM.
FM RADIO STATION

KEGH-FM 44431
Owner: SLC Divestiture Trust II
Editorial: 314 S Redwood Rd, Salt Lake City, Utah 84104-3536 Tel: 1 801 524-2600.
Web site: http://www.larazamedia.com/
Profile: KEGH-FM is a commercial station owned by SLC Divestiture Trust II. The format of the station is Regional Mexican. KEGH-FM broadcasts to the Salt Lake City area on 107.1 FM.
FM RADIO STATION

KEGI-FM 41192
Owner: Saga Communications
Editorial: 314 Union St, Jonesboro, Arkansas 72401-2815 Tel: 1 870 933-8800.
Web site: http://www.eagle1005.com
Profile: KEGI-FM is a commercial station owned by Saga Communications. The format of the station is rock music. KEGI-FM broadcasts to the Jonesboro, AR area at 100.5 FM.
FM RADIO STATION

KEGK-FM 139317
Owner: SMAHH Communications, LLC
Editorial: 64 Broadway N, Fargo, North Dakota 58102-4934 Tel: 1 701 356-1156.
Email: studio@youreagle1069.com
Web site: http://www.youreagle1069.com
Profile: KEGK-FM is a commercial station owned by SMAHH Communications, LLC. The format of the

station is classic hits. KEGK-FM broadcasts to the Fargo, ND area at 106.9 FM.
FM RADIO STATION

KEGL-FM 39621
Owner: iHeartMedia Inc.
Editorial: 14001 Dallas Pkwy Ste 300, Dallas, Texas 75240-7369 **Tel:** 1 214 866-8000.
Web site: http://www.kegl.com
Profile: KEGL-FM is a commercial station owned by iHeartMedia Inc. The format of the station is rock alternative. KEGL-FM broadcasts to the Dallas area at 97.1 FM.
FM RADIO STATION

KEGX-FM 46171
Owner: Ingstad Radio Washington, LLC
Editorial: 4304 W 24Th Ave Suite 200, Kennewick, Washington 99338-2320 **Tel:** 1 509 783-0783.
Web site: http://www.eagle1065.com
Profile: KEGX-FM is a commercial station owned by Ingstad Radio Washington, LLC. The format of the station is classic rock. KEGX-FM broadcasts to Kennewick, WA area at 106.5.
FM RADIO STATION

KEGY-FM 39712
Owner: CBS Radio
Editorial: 8033 Linda Vista Rd, San Diego, California 92111-5108 **Tel:** 1 858 571-7600.
Web site: http://energy1037.cbslocal.com
Profile: KEGY-FM is a commercial station owned by CBS Radio. The format of the station is a mix of Top 40/CHR. KEGY-FM broadcasts to the San Diego area at 103.7 FM.
FM RADIO STATION

KEHK-FM 42830
Owner: Cumulus Media Inc.
Editorial: 1200 Executive Pkwy Ste 440, Eugene, Oregon 97401-2169 **Tel:** 1 541 284-8500.
Web site: http://www.starfm1023.com
Profile: KEHK-FM is a commercial station owned by Cumulus Media Inc. The format of the station is adult contemporary. KEHK-FM broadcasts to the Eugene, OR area at a frequency of 102.3 FM.
FM RADIO STATION

KEIB-AM 37319
Owner: iHeartMedia Inc.
Editorial: 3400 W Olive Ave Ste 550, Burbank, California 91505-5544 **Tel:** 1 818 559-2252.
Web site: http://patriotla.iheart.com
Profile: KEIB-AM is a commercial station owned by iHeartMedia Inc. The format of the station is news talk. KEIB-AM broadcasts to the Los Angeles area on 1150 AM.
AM RADIO STATION

KEII-AM 39070
Owner: Riverbend Communications LLC
Editorial: 400 W Sunnyside Rd, Idaho Falls, Idaho 83402-4613 **Tel:** 1 208 523-3722.
Web site: http://www.eastidahonews.com
Profile: KEII-AM is a commercial station owned by Riverbend Communications LLC. The format of the station is news and talk. KEII-AM broadcasts to the Idaho Falls, ID area at 630 AM.
AM RADIO STATION

KEIN-AM 39442
Owner: Munson Radio Inc.
Editorial: 3313 15th St #F, Black Eagle, Montana 59414-1090 **Tel:** 1 406 761-1310.
Email: z93@mpiwifi.com
Profile: KEIN-AM is a commercial station owned by Munson Radio Inc. The format of the station is adult standards music. KEIN-AM broadcasts in the Great Falls, MT area at 1310 AM.
AM RADIO STATION

KEIR-AM 36777
Owner: Riverbend Communications LLC
Editorial: 400 W Sunnyside Rd, Idaho Falls, Idaho 83402-4613 **Tel:** 1 208 785-1400.
Web site: http://www.eastidahonews.com
Profile: KEIR-AM is a commercial station owned by Riverbend Communications LLC. The format of the station is talk. KEIR-AM broadcasts to the Idaho Falls, ID area at 1260 AM.
AM RADIO STATION

KEJJ-FM 42173
Owner: J.H. Rees.
Editorial: 219 N Iowa St, Gunnison, Colorado 81230-2478 **Tel:** 1 970 641-4000.
Email: gunnisonradio@gmail.com
Profile: KEJJ-AM is a commercial station owned by J.H. Rees. The format of the station is oldies. KEJJ-AM broadcasts to the Denver area at 98.3 FM.
FM RADIO STATION

KEJL-AM 37612
Owner: Noalmark Broadcasting Corp.
Editorial: 1423 W Bender Blvd, Hobbs, New Mexico 88240-9252 **Tel:** 1 575 393-1551.
Web site: http://www.hobbsradio.com
Profile: KEJL-AM is a commercial station owned by Noalmark Broadcasting Corp. The format of the station is news and talk. KEJL-AM broadcasts to the Hobbs, NM area at 1110 AM.
AM RADIO STATION

KEJO-AM 37277
Owner: Bicoastal Media LLC
Editorial: 2840 Marion St SE, Albany, Oregon 97322-3978 **Tel:** 1 541 926-8628.

Web site: http://www.kejoam.com
Profile: KEJO-AM is a commercial station owned by Bicoastal Media LLC. The format of the station is sports and talk programming. KEJO-AM broadcasts to the Albany, OR area at 1240 AM.
AM RADIO STATION

KEJS-FM 128157
Owner: Ramar Communications Inc.
Editorial: 9800 University Ave, Lubbock, Texas 79423-5302 **Tel:** 1 806 745-3434.
Email: sports@doublet1043.com
Web site: http://www.doublet1043.com
Profile: KEJS-FM is a commercial station owned by Ramar Communications Inc. The format of the station is tejano. KEJS-FM broadcasts to the Lubbock, TX area at 104.3 FM.
FM RADIO STATION

KEJY-AM 36066
Owner: Eureka Broadcasting Inc.
Editorial: 1101 Marsh Rd, Eureka, California 95501-1574 **Tel:** 1 707 442-5744.
Profile: KEJY-AM is a commercial station owned by Eureka Broadcasting Inc. The format of the station is Spanish Adult Hits. KEJY-AM broadcasts to the Eureka, CA area at 790 AM.
AM RADIO STATION

KEKA-FM 44634
Owner: Eureka Broadcasting Inc.
Editorial: 1101 Marsh Rd, Eureka, California 95501-1574 **Tel:** 1 707 442-5744.
Web site: http://www.keka101.com
Profile: KEKA-FM is a commercial station owned by Eureka Broadcasting Inc. The format of the station is classic country. KEKA-FM broadcasts to the Eureka, CA area at 101.5 FM.
FM RADIO STATION

KEKB-FM 39622
Owner: Townsquare Media, Inc.
Editorial: 315 Kennedy Ave, Grand Junction, Colorado 81501-7552 **Tel:** 1 970 242-7788.
Web site: http://www.kekbfm.com
Profile: KEKB-FM is a commercial station owned by Townsquare Media, Inc. The format for the station is country. KEKB-FM broadcasts to the Grand Junction-Montrose, CO area at 99.9 FM.
FM RADIO STATION

KEKO-FM 476772
Owner: Cadena Radio Luz Inc.(La)
Editorial: 2702 Pine St, Laredo, Texas 78046-6225 **Tel:** 1 956 726-4738.
Profile: KEKO-FM is a commercial station owned by La Cadena Radio Luz Inc. The format of the station is Hispanic religious programming. The station airs locally on 101.7 FM.
FM RADIO STATION

KELA-AM 37249
Owner: Bicoastal Media LLC
Editorial: 1635 S Gold St, Centralia, Washington 98531-8950 **Tel:** 1 360 736-3321.
Web site: http://www.kelaam.com
Profile: KELA-AM is a commercial station owned by Bicoastal Media LLC. The format of the station is news, talk and sports. KELA-AM broadcasts to the Centralia, WA area at 1470 AM.
AM RADIO STATION

KELD-AM 37250
Owner: Noalmark Broadcasting Corp.
Editorial: 2525 N West Ave, El Dorado, Arkansas 71730 **Tel:** 1 870 862-1400.
Email: newsroom@totalradio.us
Web site: http://www.totalradio.com/keldam.htm
Profile: KELD-AM is a commercial station owned by Noalmark Broadcasting Corp. The format of the station is sports. KELD-AM broadcasts to the El Dorado, AR, area at 1400 AM.
AM RADIO STATION

KELD-FM 44416
Owner: Noalmark Broadcasting Corp.
Editorial: 2525 N West Ave, El Dorado, Arkansas 71730-3120 **Tel:** 1 870 863-6126.
Email: newsroom@totalradio.us
Web site: http://www.keldfm.com
Profile: KELD-FM is a commercial station owned by Noalmark Broadcasting Corp. The format of the station is news and talk. KELD-FM broadcasts to the El Dorado, AR area at 106.5 FM.
FM RADIO STATION

KELE-AM 39412
Owner: Ozark Media Inc.
Editorial: 800 Hubbard St, Mountain Grove, Missouri 65711-9441 **Tel:** 1 417 926-4650.
Email: production@925thegrove.com
Web site: http://925thegrove.com
Profile: KELE-AM is a commercial station owned by Ozark Media Inc. The format of the station is news and talk. KELE-AM broadcasts to the Mountain Grove, MO area at 1360 AM.
AM RADIO STATION

KELE-FM 46787
Owner: Ozark Media Inc.
Editorial: 800 Hubbard St, Mountain Grove, Missouri 65711-9441 **Tel:** 1 417 926-4650.
Web site: http://www.925thegrove.com
Profile: KELE-FM is a commercial station owned by Ozark Media Inc. The format of the station is contemporary country. KELE-FM broadcasts to the Mountain Grove, MO area at 92.5 FM.
FM RADIO STATION

KELI-FM 39624
Owner: Townsquare Media
Editorial: 1301 S Abe St, San Angelo, Texas 76903-7245 **Tel:** 1 325 655-7161.
Web site: http://todaysi987.com/
Profile: KELI-FM is a commercial station owned by Westwood One- Hot AC. The format of the station is Hot AC . KELI-FM broadcasts to the San Angelo, TX area at 98.7 FM.
FM RADIO STATION

KELK-AM 37251
Owner: Elko Broadcasting Company
Editorial: 1800 Idaho St, Elko, Nevada 89801-4031 **Tel:** 1 775 738-1240.
Email: production@elkoradio.com
Web site: http://www.elkoradio.com
Profile: KELK-AM is a commercial station owned by Elko Broadcasting Company. The format of the station is adult contemporary. KELK-AM broadcasts to the Elko, NV area at 1240 AM.
AM RADIO STATION

KELN-FM 44635
Owner: Eagle Radio Inc.
Editorial: 1301 E 4th St, North Platte, Nebraska 69101 **Tel:** 1 308 532-1120.
Web site: http://www.mix97one.com
Profile: KELN-FM is a commercial station owned by Eagle Radio Inc. The format of the station is adult contemporary music. KELN-FM broadcasts in the North Platte, NE area at 97.1 FM.
FM RADIO STATION

KELO-AM 37252
Owner: Midwest Communications
Editorial: 500 S Phillips Ave, Sioux Falls, South Dakota 57104-6825 **Tel:** 1 605 331-5350.
Web site: http://kelo.com/
Profile: KELO-AM is a commercial station owned by Midwest Communications. The format of the station is news and talk. KELO-AM broadcasts in the Sioux Falls, SD area at 1320 AM.
AM RADIO STATION

KELO-FM 44636
Owner: Midwest Communications
Editorial: 500 S Phillips Ave, Sioux Falls, South Dakota 57104-6825 **Tel:** 1 605 331-5350.
Web site: http://www.kelofm.com
Profile: KELO-FM is a commercial station owned by Midwest Communications. The format of the station is adult contemporary music. KELO-FM broadcasts in the Sioux Falls, SD area at 92.5 FM.
FM RADIO STATION

KELP-AM 36677
Owner: McClatchey(Arnie)
Editorial: 6900 Commerce Ave, El Paso, Texas 79915-1102 **Tel:** 1 915 779-0016.
Web site: http://www.kelpradio.com
Profile: KELP-AM is a commercial station owned by Arnie McClatchey. The format of the station is religious music and talk. KELP-AM broadcasts to the El Paso, TX area at 1590 AM.
AM RADIO STATION

KELQ-FM 44088
Owner: Midwest Communications
Editorial: 500 S Phillips Ave, Sioux Falls, South Dakota 57104-6825 **Tel:** 1 605 331-5350.
Web site: http://kelo.com
Profile: KELQ-FM is a commercial station owned by Midwest Communications. The format of the station is news/talk. KELQ-FM broadcasts to the Sioux Falls, SD area at 107.9 FM.
FM RADIO STATION

KELY-AM 38926
Owner: Ely Radio LLC
Tel: 1 702 418-0433.
Web site: http://www.trueoldieschannel.com
Profile: KELY-AM is a commercial station owned by Ely Radio LLC. The format of the station is oldies. KELY-AM broadcasts to the Ely, NV area at 1230 AM.
AM RADIO STATION

KEMX-FM 41931
Owner: ABS Communications, Inc.
Editorial: 2448 E 81st St Ste 5500, Tulsa, Oklahoma 74137-4201 **Tel:** 1 918 492-2660.
Email: kxoj@kxoj.com
Web site: http://www.kxoj.com
Profile: KEMX-FM is a commercial station owned by ABS Communications, Inc. The format of the station is contemporary Christian. KEMX-FM broadcasts to the Tulsa, OK area at 94.5 FM. Send PSAs to the main email.
FM RADIO STATION

KENA-AM 37253
Owner: Ouachita Broadcasting Inc.
Editorial: 1600 Reine St S, Mena, Arkansas 71953 **Tel:** 1 479 394-1450.
Email: menaradio@allegiance.tv
Profile: KENA-AM is a commercial station owned by Ouachita Broadcasting Inc. The format of the station is gospel music. KENA-AM broadcasts to the Mena, AR area at 1450 AM.
AM RADIO STATION

KENA-FM 44932
Owner: Ouachita Broadcasting Inc.
Editorial: 1600 Reine St S, Mena, Arkansas 71953-3728 **Tel:** 1 479 394-1450.
Email: menaradio@aol.com

Profile: KENA-FM is a commercial station owned by Ouachita Broadcasting Inc. The format of the station is contemporary country. KENA-FM broadcasts to the Mena, AR area at 102.1 FM.
FM RADIO STATION

KENC-FM 69697
Owner: Community Radio for Northern Colorado
Editorial: 1901 56th Ave Ste 200, Greeley, Colorado 80634-2950 **Tel:** 1 970 378-2579.
Email: news@kunc.org
Web site: http://www.kunc.org
Profile: KENC-FM is a non-commercial station owned by Community Radio for Northern Colorado. The format of the station is news/talk. KUNC-FM broadcasts to the Greeley, CO are at 90.7 FM.
FM RADIO STATION

KEND-FM 4259.
Owner: Pecos Valley Broadcasting Company
Editorial: 317 W Quay Ave, Artesia, New Mexico 88210-2158 **Tel:** 1 575 746-2751.
Email: info@pvbcradio.com
Web site: http://www.kendfm.com
Profile: KEND-FM is a commercial station owned by Pecos Valley Broadcasting Company. The format of the station is classic hits. KEND-FM broadcasts to the Roswell, NM area at 106.5 FM.
FM RADIO STATION

KENI-AM 37610
Owner: iHeartMedia Inc.
Editorial: 800 E Dimond Blvd Ste 3-370, Anchorage, Alaska 99515-2058 **Tel:** 1 907 522-1515.
Email: news@650keni.com
Web site: http://650keni.iheart.com
Profile: KENI-AM is a commercial station owned by iHeartMedia Inc. The format of the station is news and talk programming. KENI-FM broadcasts to the Anchorage, AK area at 650 AM.
AM RADIO STATION

KENN-AM 36697
Owner: American General Media
Editorial: 212 W Apache St, Farmington, New Mexico 87401-6235 **Tel:** 1 505 327-4449.
Web site: http://www.kennradio.com
Profile: KENN-AM is a commercial station owned by American General Media. The format of the station is news and talk. KENN-AM broadcasts in the Farmington, NM area at 1390 AM.
AM RADIO STATION

KENO-AM 37255
Owner: Lotus Communications Corp.
Editorial: 8755 W Flamingo Rd, Las Vegas, Nevada 89147-8667 **Tel:** 1 702 876-1460.
Email: lotussignup@yahoo.com
Web site: http://www.lvsportsnetwork.com
Profile: KENO-AM is a commercial station owned by Lotus Communications Corp. The format of the station is Hispanic sports. KENO-AM broadcasts to the Las Vegas area at 1490 AM.
AM RADIO STATION

KENR-FM 354598
Owner: Townsquare Media, LLC
Editorial: 3250 S Reserve St Ste 200, Missoula, Montana 59801-8236 **Tel:** 1 406 728-9300.
Web site: http://www.1075zoofm.com
Profile: KENR-FM is a commercial station owned by Townsquare Media, LLC. The format of the station is adult contemporary. KENR-FM broadcasts to the Missoula, MT area at 107.5 FM.
FM RADIO STATION

Kentucky Ag-Net 47049
Owner: iHeartMedia Inc.
Editorial: 4000 #1 Radio Dr, Louisville, Kentucky 40218 **Tel:** 1 502 479-2222.
Email: whasnews@iheartmedia.com
Web site: http://www.kentuckynewsnetwork.com
Profile: Supplies various stations in Kentucky with state news, farm news, market briefs, and local, regional and national farming news.
REGIONAL RADIO NETWORKS

Kentucky News Network 47050
Owner: iHeartMedia Inc.
Editorial: 4000 #1 Radio Dr, Louisville, Kentucky 40218 **Tel:** 1 502 479-2200.
Email: whasnews@iheartmedia.com
Web site: http://www.kentuckynewsnetwork.com
Profile: Generates news and sports programming for 85 stations in Kentucky.
REGIONAL RADIO NETWORKS

KEOJ-FM 43761
Owner: KXOJ, Inc.
Editorial: 2448 E 81st St Ste 5500, Tulsa, Oklahoma 74137-4201 **Tel:** 1 918 492-2660.
Email: kxoj@kxoj.com
Web site: http://www.kxoj.com
Profile: KEOJ-FM is a commercial station owned by KXOJ, Inc. The format for the station is contemporary christian/inspirational. KEOJ-FM broacasts to the Tulsa, OK area at 101.1 FM. Send PSAs to the main email.
FM RADIO STATION

KEOK-FM 44638
Owner: Payne Radio Group
Editorial: 5686 S Muskogee Ave, Tahlequah, Oklahoma 74464-5487 **Tel:** 1 918 456-2511.
Email: info@lakescountry1021.com
Web site: http://www.lakescountry1021.com
Profile: KEOK-FM is a commercial station owned by Payne Radio Group. The format of the station is

contemporary country. KEOK-FM broadcasts to the Tulsa, OK area at 102.1 FM.
FM RADIO STATION

KEPC-FM 39630
Owner: Pikes Peak Community College
Editorial: 5675 S Academy Blvd, Colorado Springs, Colorado 80906 **Tel:** 1 719 502-3128.
Email: kepc@ppcc.edu
Web site: http://www.ppcc.edu/kepc
Profile: KEPC-FM is a non-commercial station owned by Pikes Peak Community College. The format of the station is adult album alternative. KEPC-FM broadcasts to the Colorado Springs, CO area at 89.7 FM.
FM RADIO STATION

KEPD-FM 44655
Owner: Adelman Broadcasting Inc.
Editorial: 731 Balsam St, Ridgecrest, California 93555-3510 **Tel:** 1 760 371-1700.
Web site: http://www.juanfm1049.com
Profile: KEPD-FM is a commercial station owned by Adelman Broadcasting Inc. The format of the station is Spanish Adult Hits. KEPD-FM broadcasts to the Ridgecrest, CA area at 104.9 FM.
FM RADIO STATION

KEPI-FM 43143
Owner: World Radio Network, Inc.
Editorial: 2477 El Indio Hwy, Eagle Pass, Texas 78852-5538 **Tel:** 1 830 757-0887.
Email: kepi@inspiracom.org
Web site: http://www.887kepi.org
Profile: KEPI-FM is a commercial station owned by World Radio Network, Inc. The format is contemporary Christian. KEPI-FM broadcasts to the San Antonio area at 88.7 FM.
FM RADIO STATION

KEPN-AM 37487
Owner: Bonneville International Corp.
Editorial: 7800 E Orchard Rd Ste 400, Greenwood Village, Colorado 80111-2599 **Tel:** 1 303 321-0950.
Web site: http://1600thezone.com
Profile: KEPN-AM is commercial station owned by Bonneville International Corp. The format of the station is sports. KEPN-AM broadcasts to the Denver area at 1600 AM.
AM RADIO STATION

KEPS-AM 39199
Owner: MBM Radio LLC
Editorial: 127 Kilowatt Dr, Eagle Pass, Texas 78852-3397 **Tel:** 1 830 773-9247.
Web site: http://www.tejanoymas1270.com/
Profile: KEPS-AM is a commercial station owned by MBM Radio LLC (dba R Communications). The format of the station is Tejano music. KEPS-AM broadcasts to the Eagle Pass, TX area at 1270 AM.
AM RADIO STATION

KEPX-FM 43144
Owner: World Radio Network, Inc.
Editorial: 2477 El Indio Hwy, Eagle Pass, Texas 78852 **Tel:** 1 830 757-0895.
Email: kepx@lwm.org
Web site: http://www.kepx.org
Profile: KEPX-FM is non-commercial station owned by World Radio Network, Inc. The format is Hispanic religious. KEPX-FM broadcasts to the San Antonio, TX area at 89.5 FM.
FM RADIO STATION

KEQB-FM 42053
Owner: McKenzie River Broadcasting
Editorial: 925 Country Club Rd Ste 200, Eugene, Oregon 97401-2271
Profile: KEQB-FM is a commercial station owned by McKenzie River Broadcasting. The format of the station is regional Mexican music. KEQB-FM broadcasts in the Newport, OR area at 97.7 FM.
FM RADIO STATION

KERA-FM 39632
Owner: North Texas Public Broadcasting
Editorial: 3000 Harry Hines Blvd, Dallas, Texas 75201-1012 **Tel:** 1 214 871-1390.
Email: kerafm@kera.org
Web site: http://www.kera.org
Profile: KERA-FM is a non-commercial station owned by North Texas Public Broadcasting. The format of the station is news and talk programming. KERA-FM broadcasts to the Dallas area at 90.1 FM.
FM RADIO STATION

KERB-AM 38501
Owner: Bernal(Paulino)
Editorial: 4501 N McColl Rd, McAllen, Texas 78504-2431 **Tel:** 1 956 686-6382.
Web site: http://www.nuevaradiocristiana.com
Profile: KERB-AM is a commercial station owned by Paulino Bernal. The format of the station is Hispanic contemporary Christian programming. KERB-AM broadcasts to the McAllen, TX area at 600 AM.
AM RADIO STATION

KERB-FM 45863
Owner: Bernal(Paulino)
Editorial: 4501 N McColl Rd, McAllen, Texas 78504-2431 **Tel:** 1 956 686-6382.
Web site: http://nuevaradiocristiana.com
Profile: KERB-FM is a non-commercial station owned by Paulino Bernal. The format of the station is Hispanic contemporary Christian programming. KERB-FM broadcasts to the McAllen, TX area at 105.7 FM.
FM RADIO STATION

KERG-FM 786701
Owner: Christian Ministries of the Valley, Inc.
Tel: 1 956 968-7777.
Email: informacion@radiovida.com
Web site: http://www.radiovida.com
Profile: KVGE-FM is a commercial station owned by Christian Ministries of the Valley, Inc. The format of the station is Hispanic Christian programming. KVGE-FM broadcasts to the Escobares, TX area at a frequency of 104.7 FM.
FM RADIO STATION

KERI-AM 38438
Owner: American General Media
Editorial: 1400 Easton Dr Ste 144B, Bakersfield, California 93309-9412 **Tel:** 1 661 328-1410.
Profile: KERI-AM is a commercial station owned by American General Media. The format of the station is Christian music and talk. KERN-AM broadcasts to the Bakersfield, CA area at 1410 AM.
AM RADIO STATION

KERL-FM 561377
Owner: Caldwell Media LLC
Editorial: 2758 Highway 64, Wynne, Arkansas 72396-4061 **Tel:** 1 870 318-7354.
Profile: KERL-FM is a commercial station owned by Caldwell Media LLC. The format of the station is classic rock. KERL-FM broadcasts to the Wynne, AR at 99.3 FM.
FM RADIO STATION

KERM-FM 44639
Owner: Kath Broadcasting, LLC
Editorial: 7060 Radio Rd, Torrington, Wyoming 82240-8467 **Tel:** 1 307 532-2158.
Email: news@kgoskerm.com
Web site: http://kgoskerm.com
Profile: KERM-FM is a commercial station owned by Kath Broadcasting, LLC. The format of the station is country music. KERM-FM broadcasts in the Torrington, WY area at 98.3 FM.
FM RADIO STATION

KERN-AM 34937
Owner: American General Media
Editorial: 1400 Easton Dr Ste 144B, Bakersfield, California 93309-9412 **Tel:** 1 661 328-1410.
Web site: http://www.kernradio.com
Profile: KERN-AM is a commercial station owned by American General Media. The format of the station is news and talk. KERN-AM broadcasts to the Bakersfield, CA area at 1180 AM.
AM RADIO STATION

KERP-FM 128765
Owner: Rocking M Radio
Editorial: 2601 Central Ave Ste C, Dodge City, Kansas 67801-6212 **Tel:** 1 620 225-8080.
Web site: http://www.mykansasradio.com
Profile: KERP-FM is a commercial station owned by Rocking M Radio. The format of the station is contemporary country. KERP-FM broadcasts to the Dodge City, KS area at 96.3 FM.
FM RADIO STATION

KERR-AM 37257
Owner: Anderson Radio Broadcasting Inc.
Editorial: 36581 N Reservoir Rd, Polson, Montana 59860-8471 **Tel:** 1 406 883-5255.
Email: news@andersonbroadcasting.com
Web site: http://750kerr.com
Profile: KERR-AM is a commercial station owned by Anderson Radio Broadcasting Inc. The format of the station is classic country. KERR-AM broadcasts to the Polson, MT area at 750 AM.
AM RADIO STATION

KERU-FM 43876
Owner: Escuela de la Raza Unida
Editorial: 137 N Broadway, Blythe, California 92225-1607 **Tel:** 1 760 922-2582.
Email: keru885@yahoo.com
Web site: http://www.radiobilingue.org
Profile: KERU-FM is a commercial station owned by Escuela de la Raza Unida. The format of the station is Hispanic and educational programming. KERU-FM broadcasts in the Blythe, CA area at 88.5 FM.
FM RADIO STATION

KERV-AM 38808
Owner: Revolution Broadcast Co.
Editorial: 2125 Sidney Baker St, Kerrville, Texas 78028-2551 **Tel:** 1 830 896-1230.
Email: contact@revfm.rocks
Web site: http://revfmradio.com
Profile: KERV-AM is a commercial station owned by Revolution Broadcast Co. The format of the station is talk. KERV-AM broadcasts to the Kerrville, TX area at 1230 AM.
AM RADIO STATION

KERX-FM 42162
Owner: Pearson Broadcasting
Editorial: 1912 Church St, Barling, Arkansas 72923-2305 **Tel:** 1 479 484-7285.
Web site: http://www.espnarkansas.net
Profile: KERX-FM is a commercial station owned by Pearson Broadcasting. The format of the station is sports. KERX-FM broadcasts to the Barling, AR area at 95.3 FM.
FM RADIO STATION

KESA-FM 41175
Owner: Northeast Oklahoma Broadcast Network, Inc.
Editorial: 175 Sanctuary Rd, Eureka Springs, Arkansas 72632-9216 **Tel:** 1 479 253-9001.
Email: kesa@okradiostation.com
Profile: KESA-FM is a commercial station owned by Northeast Oklahoma Broadcast Network, Inc. The format of the station is adult contemporary. KESA-FM broadcasts to the Eureka Springs, AR at a frequency of 100.9 FM.
FM RADIO STATION

KESJ-AM 37351
Owner: Eagle Communications
Editorial: 4104 Country Ln, Saint Joseph, Missouri 64506-4921 **Tel:** 1 816 233-8881.
Profile: KESJ-AM is a commercial station owned by Eagle Communications. The format of the station is sports. KESJ-AM broadcasts to the Saint Joseph, MO area at 1550 AM.
AM RADIO STATION

KESM-AM 37258
Owner: Wildwood Communications Inc.
Editorial: 200 Radio Ln, El Dorado Springs, Missouri 64744-1957 **Tel:** 1 417 876-2741.
Email: kesm@kesmradio.com
Web site: http://kesmradio.com
Profile: KESM-AM is a commercial station owned by Wildwood Communications Inc. The format of the station is classic country. KESM-AM broadcasts to the El Dorado Springs, MO area at 1580 AM.
AM RADIO STATION

KESM-FM 44640
Owner: Wildwood Communications Inc.
Editorial: 200 Radio Ln, El Dorado Springs, Missouri 64744-1957 **Tel:** 1 417 876-2741.
Email: kesm@kesmradio.com
Web site: http://www.kesmradio.com
Profile: KESM-FM is a commercial station owned by Wildwood Communications Inc. The format of the station is country music. KESM-FM broadcasts to the El Dorado Spring, MO area at 105.5 FM.
FM RADIO STATION

KESN-FM 83355
Owner: Cumulus Media
Editorial: 3090 Olive St Ste 400, Dallas, Texas 75219-7640 **Tel:** 1 214 526-2400.
Web site: http://www.kesn1033.com
Profile: KESN-FM is a commercial station owned by Walt Disney Co. and operated by Cumulus Media. The format of the station is sports. KESN-FM broadcasts to the Dallas area at 103.3 FM.
FM RADIO STATION

KESO-FM 43867
Owner: R Communications
Editorial: 1201 N Jackson Rd Ste 900, McAllen, Texas 78501-5764 **Tel:** 1 956 992-8895.
Web site: http://clublaley1025.com
Profile: KESO-FM is a commercial station owned by R Communications. The format of the station is Hispanic. KESO-FM broadcasts to the South Padre Island, TX area at 92.7 FM.
FM RADIO STATION

KESP-AM 37312
Owner: Cumulus Media Inc
Editorial: 3127 Transworld Dr #270, Stockton, California 95206-4988 **Tel:** 1 209 507-8500.
Web site: http://www.sportsradio970.com
Profile: KESP-AM is a commercial station owned by Cumulus Media Inc. The format of the station is sports. KESP-AM broadcasts in the Modesto, CA area at 970 AM.
AM RADIO STATION

KESQ-AM 38817
Owner: Gulf-California Broadcast Co.
Editorial: 42650 Melanie Pl, Palm Desert, California 92211-5170 **Tel:** 1 760 340-7000.
Profile: KESQ-AM is a commercial station owned by Gulf-California Broadcast Co. The format of the station is Regional Mexican music. KESQ-AM broadcasts to the Palm Desert, CA area at 1400 AM.
AM RADIO STATION

KESR-FM 44021
Owner: Results Radio Group
Editorial: 1588 Charles Dr, Redding, California 96003 **Tel:** 1 530 244-9700.
Web site: http://www.1071bobfm.com
Profile: KESR-FM is a commercial station owned by Results Radio Group. The format of the station is Jack FM-Adult Hits. KESR-FM broadcasts to the Redding, CA area at 107.1 FM.
FM RADIO STATION

KESS-FM 46832
Owner: Univision Communications Inc.
Editorial: 7700 John W Carpenter Fwy Fl 1, Dallas, Texas 75247-4829 **Tel:** 1 214 525-0400.
Web site: http://lajefadallas.univision.com
Profile: KESS-FM is a commercial station owned by Univision Communications Inc. The format of the station is Regional Mexican. KESS-FM broadcasts to the Dallas area at 107.1 FM.
FM RADIO STATION

KEST-AM 36383
Owner: Multicultural Radio Broadcasting Inc.
Editorial: 44 Gough St Ste 301, San Francisco, California 94103-5424 **Tel:** 1 415 978-5378.
Email: kest1450@sbcglobal.net
Web site: http://www.kestradio.com
Profile: KEST-AM is a commercial station owned by Multicultural Radio Broadcasting Inc. The format of the station variety featuring multicultural programming. KEST-AM broadcasts to the San Francisco area at 1450 AM.
AM RADIO STATION

KESZ-FM 39634
Owner: iHeartMedia Inc.
Editorial: 4686 E Van Buren St Ste 300, Phoenix, Arizona 85008-6967 **Tel:** 1 602 374-6000.
Web site: http://kez999.iheart.com
Profile: KESZ-FM is a commercial station owned by iHeartMedia Inc. The format of the station is adult contemporary music. KESZ-FM broadcasts in the Phoenix area at 99.9 FM.
FM RADIO STATION

KETT-FM 542441
Owner: Armada Media
Editorial: 307 E 4th St, North Platte, Nebraska 69101-6903 **Tel:** 1 308 532-3344.
Profile: KETT-FM is a commercial station owned by Armada Media. The format of the station is rock. KETT-FM broadcasts to the Scottsbluff, NE area at 99.3 FM.
FM RADIO STATION

KETX-FM 44642
Owner: Livingston Telcom Supply, Inc.
Editorial: 115 Radio Rd, Livingston, Texas 77351-7702 **Tel:** 1 936 327-8916.
Web site: http://www.923theeagle.com
Profile: KETX-FM is a commercial station owned by Livingston Telcom Supply, Inc. The format of the station is classic hits. KETX-FM broadcasts in the Livingston, TX area at 92.3 FM.
FM RADIO STATION

KEUG-FM 43798
Owner: McKenzie River Broadcasting
Editorial: 925 Country Club Rd, Ste 200, Eugene, Oregon 97401 **Tel:** 1 541 484-9400.
Web site: http://www.1055bobfm.com
Profile: KEUG-FM is a commercial station owned by McKenzie River Broadcasting. The format of the station is adult hits. KEUG-FM broadcasts to the Eugene, OR area at 105.5 FM.
FM RADIO STATION

KEUN-AM 39133
Owner: Tri-Parish Broadcasting Co.
Editorial: 1237 E Ardoin St, Eunice, Louisiana 70535-6848 **Tel:** 1 337 457-3041.
Profile: KEUN-AM is a commercial station owned by Tri-Parish Broadcasting Co. The format of the station is talk. KEUN-AM broadcasts to the Lafayette, LA area at 1490 AM.
AM RADIO STATION

KEUN-FM 46483
Owner: Tri-Parish Broadcasting Co.
Editorial: 1237 E Ardoin St, Eunice, Louisiana 70535-6848 **Tel:** 1 337 457-3041.
Profile: KEUN-FM is a commercial station owned by Tri-Parish Broadcasting Co. The format of the station is contemporary country. KEUN-FM broadcasts to the Lafayette, LA area at 105.5.
FM RADIO STATION

KEVT-AM 35052
Owner: One Mart, Corp.
Editorial: 2919 E Broadway Blvd Ste 330, Tucson, Arizona 85716-5301 **Tel:** 1 520 272-0105.
Web site: http://www.powertalk1210.com
Profile: KEVT-AM is a commercial station owned by One Mart, Corp. The format of the station is not available. KEVT-AM broadcasts to the Tuscon, AZ area at 1210 AM. The station will start to broadcast its new format on March 1, 2014.
AM RADIO STATION

KEWB-FM 41223
Owner: Results Radio Group
Editorial: 1588 Charles Dr, Redding, California 96003-1459 **Tel:** 1 530 244-9700.
Web site: http://www.power94radio.com
Profile: KEWB-FM is a commercial station owned by Results Radio Group. The format of the station is rhythmic Top 40/CHR. KEWB-FM broadcasts to the Redding, CA area at 94.7 FM.
FM RADIO STATION

KEWF-FM 44689
Owner: BMG Billings
Editorial: 222 N 32nd St Fl 10, Billings, Montana 59101-1973 **Tel:** 1 406 238-1000.
Web site: http://www.985thewolf.com
Profile: KEWF-FM is a commercial station owned by BMG Billings. The format is contemporary country. The station airs int he Billings, MT area at 98.5FM.
FM RADIO STATION

KEWI-AM 37035
Owner: Saline River Media
Editorial: 115 S Main St, Benton, Arkansas 72015-4329 **Tel:** 1 501 778-6677.
Profile: KEWI-AM is a commercial station owned by Saline River Media. The format of the station is primarily news/talk. KEWI-AM broadcasts to the Benton, AR area at 690 AM.
AM RADIO STATION

KEWL-FM 43109
Owner: American Media Investments
Editorial: 1323 College Dr, Texarkana, Texas 75503-3531 **Tel:** 1 903 793-1109.
Email: kool@ami-texarkana.com
Web site: http://www.alwayskool.com
Profile: KEWL-FM is a commercial station owned by American Media Investments. The format for the station is classic hits music. KEWL-FM broadcasts to the Texarkana, TX area at 95.1 FM.
FM RADIO STATION

KEXA-FM 46162
Owner: Wolfhouse Radio Group Inc.
Editorial: 548 E Alisal St, Salinas, California 93905-2760 **Tel:** 1 831 757-1910.
Profile: KEXA-FM is a commercial station owned by Wolfhouse Radio Group Inc. The format of the station is Spanish Christian. KEXA-FM broadcasts to the Salinas, CA area at 93.9 FM.
FM RADIO STATION

KEX-AM 38669
Owner: iHeartMedia Inc.
Editorial: 13333 SW 68th Pkwy Ste 310, Tigard, Oregon 97223-8304 **Tel:** 1 503 323-6400.
Email: newstips@1190kex.com
Web site: http://1190kex.iheart.com
Profile: KEX-AM is a commercial station owned by iHeartMedia Inc. The format of the station is news and talk. KEX-AM broadcasts in the Portland, OR area at 1190 AM.
AM RADIO STATION

KEXL-FM 615091
Owner: WJAG Inc.
Editorial: 309 Braasch Ave, Norfolk, Nebraska 68701-4113 **Tel:** 1 402 371-0780.
Web site: http://www.literock97.com
Profile: KEXL-FM is a commercial station owned by WJAG Inc. The format of the station is Lite Rock/Lite AC. KEXL-FM broadcasts to Norfolk, NE and surrounding areas at 97.5 FM.
FM RADIO STATION

KEXO-AM 38801
Owner: Townsquare Media, Inc.
Editorial: 315 Kennedy Ave, Grand Junction, Colorado 81501-7552 **Tel:** 1 970 242-7788.
Web site: http://1230espn.com
Profile: KEXO-AM is a commercial station owned by Townsquare Media, Inc. The format for the station is sports. KEXO-AM broadcasts to the Grand Junction-Montrose, CO area at 1230 AM.
AM RADIO STATION

KEXS-AM 34938
Owner: Catholic Radio Network
Editorial: 201 N Industrial Park Rd, Excelsior Springs, Missouri 64024 **Tel:** 1 816 630-1090.
Email: kexs1090am@gmail.com
Web site: http://www.thecatholicradionetwork.com
Profile: KEXS-AM is a commercial station owned by Catholic Radio Network. The format of the station is religious Catholic programming and music. KEXS-AM broadcasts to the Kansas City, MO area at 1090 AM.
AM RADIO STATION

KEXS-FM 537102
Owner: Catholic Radio Network
Editorial: 201 N Industrial Park Rd, Excelsior Springs, Missouri 64024-1736 **Tel:** 1 816 630-1090.
Email: info@thecatholicradionetwork.com
Web site: http://www.thecatholicradionetwork.com
Profile: KEXS-FM is a commercial station owned by Catholic Radio Network. The format of the station is religious Catholic programming and music. KEXS-FM broadcasts to the Kansas City, MO area at 106.1 FM.
FM RADIO STATION

KEXX-FM 44361
Owner: Riviera Broadcast Group
Editorial: 4745 N 7th St Ste 410, Phoenix, Arizona 85014-3669 **Tel:** 1 602 648-9800.
Web site: http://trendingradio.com
Profile: KEXX-FM is a commercial station owned by Riviera Broadcast Group. The format of the station is Hot AC. KEXX-FM broadcasts to the Phoenix area at 103.9 FM.
FM RADIO STATION

KEYA-FM 235366
Owner: KEYA Inc.
Tel: 1 701 477-5686.
Email: keya@utma.com
Web site: http://keya.utma.com/885
Profile: KEYA-FM is a non-commercial station owned by KEYA Inc. The format of the station is variety. KEYA-FM broadcasts to the Minot-Bismarck, ND area at 88.5 FM.
FM RADIO STATION

KEYB-FM 41562
Owner: Altus FM Inc.
Editorial: 808 N Main St, Altus, Oklahoma 73521-3116 **Tel:** 1 580 482-1555.
Email: keyb@keyb.net
Web site: http://www.keyb.net
Profile: KEYB-FM is a commercial station owned by Altus FM Inc. The format is of the station is country music. KEYB-FM broadcasts to the Altus, OK area at 107.9 FM.
FM RADIO STATION

KEYE-AM 37262
Owner: Perryton Radio Inc.
Editorial: Perryton, Texas **Tel:** 1 806 435-5458.
Email: mail@keye.net
Web site: http://www.keye.net
Profile: KEYE-AM is a commercial station owned by Perryton Radio Inc. The format of the station is classic country and talk. KEYE-AM broadcasts to the Perryton, TX area at 1400 AM.
AM RADIO STATION

KEYE-FM 44644
Owner: Perryton Radio Inc.
Editorial: Highway 15 West, Perryton, Texas 79070
Tel: 1 806 435-5458.
Email: keye@keye.net
Web site: http://www.keye.net
Profile: KEYE-FM is a commercial station owned by Perryton Radio Inc.. The format of the station is adult contemporary. KEYE-FM broadcasts to the Perryton, TX area at 93.7 FM.
FM RADIO STATION

KEYF-FM 45954
Owner: Mapleton Communications LLC
Editorial: 1601 E 57th Ave, Spokane, Washington 99223 **Tel:** 1 509 448-1000.
Web site: http://www.1011fmspokane.com
Profile: KEYF-FM is a commercial station owned by Mapleton Communications LLC. The format of the station is classic hits. KEYF-FM broadcasts to the Spokane, WA area on 101.1 FM.
FM RADIO STATION

KEYG-AM 38579
Owner: Wheeler Broadcasting Inc.
Editorial: 58053 Spokane BLVD NE, Grand Coulee, Washington 99133 **Tel:** 1 509 633-2020.
Email: keygprod@aol.com
Web site: http://www.keyg937.com
Profile: KEYG-AM is a commercial station owned by Wheeler Broadcasting Inc. The format of the station is contemporary country. KEYG-AM broadcasts to the Spokane, WA area 1490 AM.
AM RADIO STATION

KEYG-FM 45943
Owner: Wheeler Broadcasting Inc.
Editorial: #1 Radio Road, Grand Coulee, Washington 99133 **Tel:** 1 509 633-2020.
Email: keygprod@aol.com
Web site: http://www.kxa937.com/keygfm.html
Profile: KEYG-FM is a commercial station owned by Wheeler Broadcasting Inc. The format of the station is classic hits. KEYG-FM broadcasts to the Grand Coulee, WA area at 98.5 FM.
FM RADIO STATION

KEYH-AM 36487
Owner: Liberman Broadcasting Inc.
Editorial: 3000 Bering Dr, Houston, Texas 77057-5708 **Tel:** 1 713 315-3400.
Profile: KEYH-AM is a commercial station owned by Liberman Broadcasting Inc. The format of the station is Hispanic music. KEYH-AM broadcasts to the Houston area at 850 AM.
AM RADIO STATION

KEYJ-FM 43759
Owner: Townsquare Media, LLC
Editorial: 3911 S 1st St, Abilene, Texas 79605-1639
Tel: 1 325 676-7711.
Email: keyj@keyj.com
Web site: http://www.keyj.com
Profile: KEYJ-FM is a commercial station owned by Townsquare Media, LLC. The format of the station is rock/album-oriented music. KEYJ-FM broadcasts to the Abilene, TX area at 107.9 FM.
FM RADIO STATION

KEYL-AM 39025
Owner: Prairie Broadcasting Inc.
Editorial: 221 Central Ave, Long Prairie, Minnesota 56347 **Tel:** 1 320 732-2164.
Email: hotrodfm@rea-alp.com
Web site: http://www.kxdlhotrodradio.com
Profile: KEYL-AM is a commercial station owned byPrairie Broadcasting Inc. The format of the station is classic country. KEYL-AM broadcasts to the Long Prairie, MN area at 1400 FM.
AM RADIO STATION

KEYN-FM 43460
Owner: Entercom Communications Corp.
Editorial: 2120 N Woodlawn St, Ste 352, Wichita, Kansas 67208 **Tel:** 1 316 685-2121.
Web site: http://www.keyn.com
Profile: KEYN-FM is a commercial station owned by Entercom Inc. The format of the station is classic hits. KEYN-FM broadcasts to the Wichita, KS area at 103.7 FM.
FM RADIO STATION

KEYS-AM 37265
Owner: Malkan Interactive Communications
Editorial: 2117 Leopard St, Corpus Christi, Texas 78408 **Tel:** 1 361 882-7411.
Web site: http://www.espncorpus.com
Profile: KEYS-AM is a commercial station owned by Malkan Interactive Communications. The format of the station is sports/talk. KEYS-AM broadcasts to the Corpus Christi, TX area at 1440 AM.
AM RADIO STATION

KEYU-FM 41246
Owner: Midessa Broadcasting Limited Partnership
Tel: 1 800 776-1070.
Web site: http://www.myflr.org
Profile: KEYU-FM is a non-commercial station owned by Midessa Broadcasting Limited Partnership. The format of the station is Contemporary Christian. The station broadcasts to the Amarillo, TX area at 102.9 FM.
FM RADIO STATION

KEYW-FM 41674
Owner: Townsquare Media, LLC
Editorial: 2621 W A St, Pasco, Washington 99301-4702 **Tel:** 1 509 547-9791.
Web site: http://www.keyw.com
Profile: KEYW-FM is a commercial station owned by Townsquare Media, LLC. The format of the station is hot adult contemporary. KEYW-FM broadcasts to the Pasco, WA area at 98.3 FM.
FM RADIO STATION

KEYY-AM 34940
Owner: Biblical Ministries Worldwide
Editorial: 307 S 1600 W, Provo, Utah 84601-3932
Tel: 1 801 374-5210.
Email: mail@keyradio.org
Web site: http://www.keyy.com
Profile: KEYY-AM is a non-commercial station owned by Biblical Ministries Worldwide. The format of the station is religious. KEYY-AM broadcasts to the Provo, UT area at 1450 AM.
AM RADIO STATION

KEYZ-AM 37266
Owner: Cherry Creek Radio
Editorial: 410 6th St E, Williston, North Dakota 58801-5552 **Tel:** 1 701 572-5371.
Web site: http://www.keyzradio.com
Profile: KEYZ-AM is a commercial station owned by Cherry Creek Radio. The format of the station is primarily news, with some classic country. KEYZ-AM's target audience is adults, ages 35 to 100, in the Williston, ND area, covering Williston/Minot/Dickinson . The airs locally at 660 AM
AM RADIO STATION

KEZA-FM 41561
Owner: iHeartMedia Inc.
Editorial: 2049 E Joyce Blvd Ste 101, Fayetteville, Arkansas 72703-6395 **Tel:** 1 479 582-1079.
Web site: http://magic1079.iheart.com
Profile: KEZA-FM is a commercial station owned by iHeartMedia Inc. The format of the station is adult contemporary. KEZA-FM broadcasts to the Fayetteville, AR area at 107.9 FM.
FM RADIO STATION

KEZE-FM 44026
Owner: Queen B Inc.
Editorial: 500 W Boone Ave, Spokane, Washington 99201-2404 **Tel:** 1 509 324-4200.
Web site: http://www.hot969.com
Profile: KEZE-FM is a commercial station owned by Queen B Inc. The format of the station is urban contemporary/Top 40. KEZE-FM broadcasts to the Spokane, WA area at 96.9 FM.
FM RADIO STATION

KEZJ-AM 36959
Owner: SNL Radio, LLC
Editorial: 630 Falls Ave, Twin Falls, Idaho 83301-3300
Email: info@saltandlightradio.com
Web site: http://salyluzradio.com
Profile: KEZJ-AM is a non-commercial station owned by Salt & Light Radio (SNL Radio). The format of the station is Spanish religious. KESJ-AM broadcasts to the Twin Falls, ID area at 1450 AM.
AM RADIO STATION

KEZJ-FM 42154
Owner: Townsquare Media, LLC
Editorial: 415 Park Ave, Twin Falls, Idaho 83301
Tel: 1 208 733-7512.
Web site: http://www.kezj.com
Profile: KEZJ-FM is a commercial station owned by Townsquare Media, LLC. The format is contemporary country music. The station broadcasts to the Twin Falls, Idaho area 95.7 FM.
FM RADIO STATION

KEZK-FM 43525
Owner: CBS Radio
Editorial: 1220 Olive St Fl 3, Saint Louis, Missouri 63103-2324 **Tel:** 1 314 621-2345.
Web site: http://fresh1025.radio.com
Profile: KEZK-FM is a commercial station owned by CBS Radio. The format of the station is Adult Contemporary. KEZK-FM broadcasts to the St. Louis area at 102.5 FM.
FM RADIO STATION

KEZM-AM 34942
Owner: Merchant Broadcasting Inc.
Editorial: 113 E Napoleon St, Sulphur, Louisiana 70663-3313 **Tel:** 1 337 527-3611.
Email: kezm1310am@structurex.net
Web site: http://www.kezmonline.com/
Profile: KEZM-AM is a commercial station owned by Merchant Broadcasting Inc. The format of the station is sports. KEZM-AM broadcasts to the Sulphur, LA area at 1310 AM.
AM RADIO STATION

KEZN-FM 39638
Owner: CBS Radio
Editorial: 72915 Parkview Dr, Palm Desert, California 92260 **Tel:** 1 760 340-9383.
Web site: http://www.ez103.com
Profile: KEZN-FM is a commercial station owned by CBS Radio. The format of the station is adult contemporary. KEZN-FM broadcasts to the Palm Desert, CA area at 103.1 FM.
FM RADIO STATION

KEZO-FM 44647
Owner: E.W. Scripps Co.
Editorial: 10714 Mockingbird Dr, Omaha, Nebraska 68127-1942 **Tel:** 1 402 592-5300.
Web site: http://www.z92.com
Profile: KEZO-FM is a commercial station owned by E.W. Scripps Co. The format of the station is rock. KEZO-FM broadcasts to the Omaha, NE area at 92.3 FM.
FM RADIO STATION

KEZP-FM 42576
Owner: Opus Broadcasting of Alexandria, LLC
Editorial: 92 W Shamrock Ave, Pineville, Louisiana 71360-6435 **Tel:** 1 318 487-1035.
Profile: KEZP-FM is a commercial station owned by Opus Broadcasting of Alexandria, LLC. The format of the station is Christian AC. KEZP-FM broadcasts to the Alexandria, LA area at 104.3 FM.
FM RADIO STATION

KEZR-FM 39639
Owner: Alpha Media
Editorial: 190 Park Center Plz Ste 200, San Jose, California 95113-2223 **Tel:** 1 408 287-5775.
Web site: http://mymix1065.com
Profile: KEZR-FM is a commercial station owned by Alpha Media. The format of the station is hot adult contemporary. KEZR-FM broadcasts to the San Jose, CA area at 106.5 FM.
FM RADIO STATION

KEZS-FM 46596
Owner: Max Media
Editorial: 324 Broadway St, Cape Girardeau, Missouri 63701-7331 **Tel:** 1 573 335-8291.
Email: realrock@riverradio.net
Web site: http://www.k103fm.com
Profile: KEZS-FM is a commercial station owned by Max Media. The format of the station is contemporary country. KEZS-FM broadcasts to the Cape Girardeau, MO area at 102.9 FM.
FM RADIO STATION

KEZW-AM 38388
Owner: Entercom Communications Corp.
Editorial: 4700 S Syracuse St Ste 1050, Denver, Colorado 80237-2713 **Tel:** 1 303 967-2700.
Web site: http://www.cruisin1430.com
Profile: KEZW-AM is a commercial station owned by Entercom Communications Corp. The format of the station is oldies. KEZW-AM broadcasts to the Denver area at 1430 AM.
AM RADIO STATION

KEZX-AM 87569
Owner: Opus Broadcasting Systems Inc.
Editorial: 511 Rossanley Dr, Medford, Oregon 97501-1771 **Tel:** 1 541 772-0322.
Web site: http://www.sportsradio730.com
Profile: KEZX-AM is a non-commercial station owned by Opus Broadcasting Systems Inc. The format of the station is sports. KEZX-AM broadcasts to the Medford, OR area at 730 AM.
AM RADIO STATION

KEZY-AM 36387
Owner: Hi-Favor Broadcasting LLC
Editorial: 136 S Oak Knoll Ave, Ste 202, Pasadena, California 91101 **Tel:** 1 626 356-4230.
Web site: http://www.nuevavida.com
Profile: KEZY-AM is a commercial station owned by Hi-Favor Broadcasting LLC. The format of the station is Hispanic and religious. KEZY-AM broadcasts to the Pasadena, CA area at 1240 AM.
AM RADIO STATION

KFAB-AM 37269
Owner: iHeartMedia Inc.
Editorial: 5010 Underwood Ave, Omaha, Nebraska 68132-2236 **Tel:** 1 402 561-2000.
Web site: http://www.kfab.com
Profile: KFAB-AM is a commercial station owned by iHeartMedia Inc. The format of the station is news and talk. KFAB-AM broadcasts in the Omaha, NE area at 1110 AM.
AM RADIO STATION

KFAI-FM 39642
Owner: Fresh Air Inc.
Editorial: 1808 Riverside Ave, Minneapolis, Minnesota 55454 **Tel:** 1 612 341-3144.
Email: newsdepartment@kfai.org
Web site: http://www.kfai.org
Profile: KFAI-FM is a non-commercial station owned by Fresh Air Inc. The format of the station is variety. KFAI-FM broadcasts to the Minneapolis area at 90.3 FM.
FM RADIO STATION

KFAL-AM 3905
Owner: Zimmer Radio Group
Editorial: 1805 Westminster Ave, Fulton, Missouri 65251-1067 **Tel:** 1 800 455-1099.
Email: kfal@zrgmail.com
Web site: http://www.kfalthebig900.com
Profile: KFAL-AM is a commercial station owned by Zimmer Radio Group. The format of the station is country music. KFAL-AM broadcasts in the Fulton, MO area at 900 AM.
AM RADIO STATION

KFAN-AM 37573
Owner: iHeartMedia Inc.
Editorial: 1530 Greenview Dr SW Ste 200, Rochester, Minnesota 55902-4327 **Tel:** 1 507 288-3888.
Web site: http://www.fan1270.com
Profile: KFAN-AM is a commercial station owned by iHeartMedia Inc. The format of the station is sports. KFAN-AM broadcasts to the Rochester, MN area at 1270 AM.
AM RADIO STATION

KFAN-FM 46448
Owner: Hill Country Broadcasting, LLC
Editorial: 210 Woodcrest St, Fredericksburg, Texas 78624-2529 **Tel:** 1 830 997-2197.
Email: hillcountrybroadcasting@gmail.com
Web site: http://www.texasrebelradio.com
Profile: KFAN-FM is a commercial station owned by Hill Country Broadcasting, LLC. The format of the station is adult album alternative. KFAN-FM broadcasts to the Fredericksburg, TX area at 107.9 FM.
FM RADIO STATION

KFAQ-AM 38434
Owner: E.W. Scripps Co.
Editorial: 4590 E 29th St, Tulsa, Oklahoma 74114-6208 **Tel:** 1 918 743-7814.
Web site: http://www.1170kfaq.com
Profile: KFAQ-AM is a commercial station owned by the E.W. Scripps Co. The format of the station is news and talk. KFAQ-AM broadcasts to the Tulsa, OK area at 1170 AM.
AM RADIO STATION

KFAR-AM 38453
Owner: Last Frontier Mediactive, LLC
Editorial: 819 1st Ave Ste A, Fairbanks, Alaska 99701-4449 **Tel:** 1 907 451-5910.
Web site: http://www.kfar660.com
Profile: KFAR-AM is a commercial station owned by Last Frontier Mediactive, LLC. The format of the station is news/talk. KFAR-AM broadcasts locally to the Fairbanks, AK area at 660 AM.
AM RADIO STATION

KFAT-FM 44376
Owner: Ohana Media Group
Editorial: 833 Gambell St, Anchorage, Alaska 99501-3756 **Tel:** 1 907 344-4045.
Web site: http://www.kfat929.com
Profile: KFAT-FM is a commercial station owned by Ohana Media Group. The format of the station is Top 40/CHR. KFAT-FM broadcasts to the Anchorage, AK area at a frequency of 92.9 FM.
FM RADIO STATION

KFAV-FM 43298
Owner: Kaspar Broadcasting Co.
Editorial: 1217 N State Highway 47, Warrenton, Missouri 63383-1330 **Tel:** 1 636 377-2300.
Email: kwrekfav@socket.net
Web site: http://www.kfav.com
Profile: KFAV-FM is a commercial station owned by Kaspar Broadcasting Co. The format of the station is contemporary country music. KFAV-FM broadcasts to the St. Louis area at 99.9 FM.
FM RADIO STATION

KFAX-AM 34944
Owner: Salem Media Group, Inc.
Editorial: 39650 Liberty St Ste 340, Fremont, California 94538-2227 **Tel:** 1 510 713-1100.
Email: comments@kfax.com
Web site: http://www.kfax.com
Profile: KFAX-AM is a commercial station owned by Salem Media Group, Inc. The format of the station is Christian talk. KFAX-AM broadcasts to the San Francisco and San Jose, CA markets at 1100 AM. Please submit PSAs via their website.
AM RADIO STATION

KFAY-AM 39091
Owner: Cumulus Media Inc.
Editorial: 4209 N Frontage Rd, Fayetteville, Arkansas 72703-5002 **Tel:** 1 479 521-5566.
Email: newstalk1030@cumulus.com
Web site: http://www.newstalk1030.com
Profile: KFAY-AM is a commercial station owned by Cumulus Media Inc. The format of the station is news and talk. KFAY-AM broadcasts to the Fayetteville, AR area at 1030 AM.
AM RADIO STATION

KFBC-AM 36209
Owner: Montgomery Broadcasting
Editorial: 1806 Capitol Ave, Cheyenne, Wyoming 82001-4530 **Tel:** 1 307 634-4461.
Web site: http://kfbcradio.com
Profile: KFBC-AM is a commercial radio station owned by Montgomery Broadcasting. The format of the station is sports. KFBC-AM broadcasts to the Cheyenne, WY area at 1240 AM.
AM RADIO STATION

KFBD-FM 44650
Owner: Digity
Editorial: 313 Old Route 66, Saint Robert, Missouri 65584 **Tel:** 1 573 336-4913.
Email: news.kfbd@alphamediausa.com
Web site: http://www.myozarksonline.com/
Profile: KFBD-FM is a commercial station owned by Digity. The format of the station is adult contemporary. KFBD-FM broadcasts to the Springfield, MO, area at 97.9 FM.
FM RADIO STATION

KFBK-AM 37270
Owner: iHeartMedia Inc.
Editorial: 1545 River Park Dr Ste 500, Sacramento, California 95815-4693 **Tel:** 1 916 929-5325.
Email: kfbknews@iheartmedia.com
Web site: http://kfbk.iheart.com
Profile: KFBK-AM is a commercial station owned by iHeartMedia Inc. The format of the station is news and talk. KFBK-AM broadcasts to the Sacramento, CA area at 1530 AM.
AM RADIO STATION

KFBK-FM 44556
Owner: iHeartMedia Inc.
Editorial: 1545 River Park Dr Ste 500, Sacramento, California 95815-4693 **Tel:** 1 916 929-5325.
Email: kfbknews@iheartmedia.com
Web site: http://kfbk.iheart.com
Profile: KFBK-FM is a commercial station owned by iHeartMedia Inc. The format of the station is news/talk. KFBK-FM broadcasts to the Sacramento, CA area at 93.1 FM. The station simulcasts KFBK-AM 1530.
FM RADIO STATION

KFBN-FM 43805
Owner: Fargo Baptist Church
Editorial: 3303 23rd Ave S, Fargo, North Dakota 58103-6277 **Tel:** 1 701 232-5500.
Email: heaven887@cableone.net
Web site: http://www.kfbn.org
Profile: KFBN-FM is a non-commercial station owned by Fargo Baptist Church. The format of the station is gospel music and religious programming. KFBN-FM broadcasts to the Fargo, ND area at 88.7 FM.
FM RADIO STATION

KFBT-FM 39773
Owner: iHeartMedia Inc.
Editorial: 83 E Shaw Ave Ste 150, Fresno, California 93710-7622 **Tel:** 1 559 230-4300.
Web site: http://www.thebeat1037.com
Profile: KFBT-FM is a commercial station owned by IHeart Media and Entertainment. The format of the station is urban contemporary, more specifically "Gen-X Rhythmic." KFBT-FM broadcasts to the Fresno, CA area at 103.7 FM.
FM RADIO STATION

KFBW-FM 86301
Owner: iHeartMedia Inc.
Editorial: 13333 SW 68th Pkwy Ste 310, Tigard, Oregon 97223-8304 **Tel:** 1 503 323-6400.
Web site: http://1059thebrew.iheart.com
Profile: KFBW-FM is a commercial station owned by iHeartMedia Inc. The format of the station is classic rock. KFBW-FM broadcasts to the Portland, OR area at 105.9 FM.
FM RADIO STATION

KFBX-AM 38427
Owner: iHeartMedia Inc.
Editorial: 546 9th Ave, Fairbanks, Alaska 99701-4902 **Tel:** 1 907 450-1000.
Email: kfbx@iheartmedia.com
Web site: http://970kfbx.com
Profile: KFBX-AM is a commercial station owned by iHeartMedia Inc. The format of the station is talk. KFBX-AM broadcasts in the Fairbanks, AK area at 970 AM.
AM RADIO STATION

KFBZ-FM 73347
Owner: Entercom Communications Corp.
Editorial: 2120 N Woodlawn St, Ste 352, Wichita, Kansas 67208 **Tel:** 1 316 685-2121.
Web site: http://www.1053thebuzz.com
Profile: KFBZ-FM is a commercial station owned by Entercom Communications Corp. The format of the station is hot adult contemporary. KFBZ-FM broadcasts to the Wichita, KS area at 105.3 FM.
FM RADIO STATION

KFCD-AM 128057
Owner: Bernard Radio
Editorial: 12900 Preston Rd Ste 201, Dallas, Texas 75230-1380 **Tel:** 1 972 354-1990.
Web site: http://www.kfcd990.com/
Profile: KFCD-AM is a commercial station owned by Bernard Radio and operated by Principle Broadcasting, LLC. The format of the station is Spanish Religious. KFCD-AM broadcasts to the Dallas area at 990 AM.
AM RADIO STATION

KFCF-FM 39643
Owner: Fresno Free College Foundation
Editorial: 1449 N Wishon Ave, Fresno, California 93728 **Tel:** 1 559 233-2221.
Web site: http://www.kfcf.org
Profile: KFCF-FM is a non-commercial station owned by the Fresno Free College Foundation. The format of the station is variety. KFCF-FM broadcasts in the Fresno, CA area at 88.1 FM.
FM RADIO STATION

KFCM-FM 39644
Owner: KFCM Inc.
Editorial: 11 FM 101 Rd, Hardy, Arkansas 72542-0458 **Tel:** 1 870 856-3249.
Email: hometownradio@centurytel.net
Profile: KFCM-FM is a commercial station owned by KFCM Inc. The format of the station is oldies. KFCM-FM broadcasts to the Hardy, AR area at 98.3 FM.
FM RADIO STATION

KFCO-FM 394882
Owner: Max Media of Colorado
Editorial: 3033 S Parker Rd Ste 700, Aurora, Colorado 80014-2923 **Tel:** 1 303 872-1500.
Web site: http://flo1071.com
Profile: KFCO-FM is a commercial station owned by Max Media of Colorado. The format of the station is rhythmic oldies. KFCO-FM broadcasts to the Aurora, CO area at 107.1 FM.
FM RADIO STATION

KFCW-FM 445518
Owner: Edwards Communications LLC
Editorial: 1002 N 8th St W, Riverton, Wyoming 82501-2427 **Tel:** 1 307 856-2922.
Profile: KFCW-FM is a commercial station owned by Edwards Communications. The format of the station is classic rock. KFCW-FM broadcasts to the Riverton, WY area at 93.1 FM.
FM RADIO STATION

KFDI-FM 44651
Owner: Kiel Media Group, LLC
Editorial: 4200 N Old Lawrence Rd, Wichita, Kansas 67219-3211 **Tel:** 1 316 838-9141.
Email: news@kfdi.com
Web site: http://www.kfdi.com
Profile: KFDI-FM is a commercial station owned by Kiel Media Group, LLC. The format of the station is contemporary country. KFDI-FM broadcasts to the Wichita, KS area at 101.3 FM.
FM RADIO STATION

KFEB-FM 44160
Owner: Eagle Bluff Enterprises
Editorial: 932 County Road 448, Poplar Bluff, Missouri 63901-9018 **Tel:** 1 573 686-3700.
Email: frn@tcmax.net
Web site: http://foxradionetwork.com
Profile: KFEB-FM is a commercial station owned by Eagle Bluff Enterprises. The format of the station is Top 40/CHR. KFEB-FM broadcasts to the Poplar Bluff, MO area at 107.5 FM.
FM RADIO STATION

KFEG-FM 334525
Owner: Wynne Broadcasting Co.
Editorial: 1338 Oregon Ave, Klamath Falls, Oregon 97601-6540 **Tel:** 1 541 882-4656.
Email: webmaster@klamathradio.com
Web site: http://www.klamathradio.com
Profile: KFEG-FM is a commercial station owned by Wynne Broadcasting Co. The format of the station is classic rock. KFEG-FM broadcasts to the Klamath Falls, OR area at a frequency of 104.7 FM.
FM RADIO STATION

KFEL-AM 36938
Owner: Kansas City Catholic Network, Inc.
Editorial: 3003 N Elizabeth St Ste D, Pueblo, Colorado 81008-1153 **Tel:** 1 816 630-1090.
Web site: http://www.thecatholicradionetwork.com
Profile: KFEL-AM is a commercial station owned by Kansas City Catholic Network, Inc. The format of the station is religious. KFEL-AM broadcasts to the Pueblo, Co area at 970 AM.
AM RADIO STATION

KFEQ-AM 39125
Owner: Eagle Communications
Editorial: 4104 Country Ln, Saint Joseph, Missouri 64506-4921 **Tel:** 1 816 233-8881.
Web site: http://www.680kfeq.com
Profile: KFEQ-AM is a commercial station owned by Eagle Communications. The format of the station is news and talk. KFEQ-AM broadcasts to the Saint Joseph, MO area at 680 AM.
AM RADIO STATION

KFEZ-FM 813926
Owner: Magnus (Edward)
Editorial: 516 Main St, Walsenburg, Colorado 81089-2036
Email: production@socoradio.com
Web site: http://easy1013.com
Profile: KFEZ-FM is a commercial station owned by Magnus (Edward) and operated by SOCO Radio. The format of the station is soft adult contemporary. KFEZ-FM broadcasts to the Greater Southern Colorado area at a frequency of 101.3 FM.
FM RADIO STATION

KFFA-AM 37272
Owner: Delta Broadcasting
Editorial: 1360 Radio Dr, Helena, Arkansas 72342 **Tel:** 1 870 338-8361.
Email: kffa@arkansas.net
Web site: http://www.kffa.com
Profile: KFFA-AM is a commercial station owned by Delta Broadcasting. The format of the station is classic country and blues. KFFA-AM broadcasts to the Helena, AR area at 1360 AM.
AM RADIO STATION

KFFA-FM 44609
Owner: Delta Broadcasting
Editorial: 1360 Radio Dr, Helena, Arkansas 72342 **Tel:** 1 870 338-8331.
Email: kffa@arkansas.net
Web site: http://www.kffa.com
Profile: KFFA-FM is a commercial station owned by Delta Broadcasting. The format of the station is adult contemporary. KFFA-FM broadcasts to the Helena, AR area at 103.1 FM.
FM RADIO STATION

KFFB-FM 41224
Owner: Freedom Broadcasting, Inc.
Editorial: 12080 Edgemont Rd, Shirley, Arkansas 72153 **Tel:** 1 501 723-4850.
Email: kffb@kffb.com
Web site: http://www.kffb.com
Profile: KFFB-FM is a commercial station owned by Freedom Broadcasting, Inc. The format of the station is adult standards music. KFFB-FM broadcasts to the Shirley, AR area at 106.1 FM.
FM RADIO STATION

KFFF-FM 41794
Owner: iHeartMedia Inc.
Editorial: 5010 Underwood Ave, Omaha, Nebraska 68132-2236 **Tel:** 1 402 561-2000.
Web site: http://www.wolfradio933.com
Profile: KFFF-FM is a commercial station owned by iHeartMedia Inc. The format of the station is classic country. KFFF-FM broadcasts to the Omaha, NE area at 93.3 FM.
FM RADIO STATION

KFFG-FM 39673
Owner: Cumulus Media Inc.
Editorial: 750 Battery St Fl 3, San Francisco, California 94111-1523 **Tel:** 1 415 819-9568.
Web site: http://www.kfog.com
Profile: KFFG-FM is a commercial station owned by Cumulus Media Inc. The format of the station is adult album alternative. KFFG-FM broadcasts to the San Jose area at 97.7 FM.
FM RADIO STATION

KFFK-AM 36989
Owner: Butler Broadcasting
Editorial: 1780 W Holly St, Fayetteville, Arkansas 72703 **Tel:** 1 479 582-3776.
Profile: KFFK-AM is a commercial station owned by Butler Broadcasting. The format of the station is sports. KFFK-AM broadcasts in the Fayetteville, AR area at 1390 AM.
AM RADIO STATION

KFFM-FM 46136
Owner: Townsquare Media, LLC
Editorial: 4010 Summitview Ave, Yakima, Washington 98908-2966 **Tel:** 1 509 972-3461.
Web site: http://www.kffm.com
Profile: KFFM-FM is a commercial station owned by Townsquare Media, LLC. The format of the station is Rhythmic Top 40 music. KFFM-FM broadcasts to the Yakima, WA area at 107.3 FM.
FM RADIO STATION

KFFN-AM 37173
Owner: E.W. Scripps Co.
Editorial: 7280 E Rosewood St, Tucson, Arizona 85710-1350 **Tel:** 1 520 722-5486.
Web site: http://www.espntucson.com
Profile: KFFN-AM is a commercial station owned by E.W. Scripps Co. The format of the station is sports. KFFN-AM broadcasts in the Tucson, AZ area at 1490 AM.
AM RADIO STATION

KFFX-FM 42918
Owner: Emporia Radio Stations Inc.
Editorial: 1420 C Of E Dr, Emporia, Kansas 66801 **Tel:** 1 620 342-1400.
Email: kvoe@kvoe.com
Web site: http://www.kvoe.com
Profile: KFFX-FM is a commercial station owned by Emporia Radio Stations Inc. The format of the station is hot adult contemporary music. KFFX-FM broadcasts in the Emporia, KS at 104.9 FM
FM RADIO STATION

KFGE-FM 44550
Owner: NRG Media LLC
Editorial: 4343 O St, Lincoln, Nebraska 68510-1753 **Tel:** 1 402 475-4567.
Email: news@klin.com
Web site: http://www.froggy981.com
Profile: KFGE-FM is a commercial station owned by NRG Media LLC. The format of the station is country. KFGE-FM broadcasts to the Lincoln, NE area at 98.1 FM.
FM RADIO STATION

KFGI-FM 46662
Owner: Red Rock Radio Corporation
Editorial: 305 W Washington St, Brainerd, Minnesota 56401-2923 **Tel:** 1 218 828-9994.
Email: kkinradio@embarqmail.com
Web site: http://www.kkinradio.com/samfm.htm
Profile: KFGI-FM is a commercial station owned by Red Rock Radio Corp. The format of the station is adult hits. KFGI-FM's target audience is adults, ages 18 to 54, in the Minneapolis- St. Paul, MN area.
FM RADIO STATION

KFGO-AM 37273
Owner: Midwest Communications
Editorial: 1020 25th St S, Fargo, North Dakota 58103-2312 **Tel:** 1 701 237-5346.
Email: kfgo.news@mwcradio.com
Web site: http://www.kfgo.com
Profile: KFGO-AM is a commercial station owned by Midwest Communications. The format of the station is news, talk and sports. KFGO-AM broadcasts to the Fargo, ND area at 790 AM.
AM RADIO STATION

KFGY-FM 44859
Owner: Sonoma Media Group
Editorial: 1410 Neotomas Ave, Santa Rosa, California 95405-7533 **Tel:** 1 707 543-0100.
Web site: http://www.froggy929.com
Profile: KFGY-FM is a commercial station owned by Sonoma Media Group. The format of the station is contemporary country. KGFY-FM broadcasts to the Santa Rosa, CA area at 92.9 FM.
FM RADIO STATION

KFH-AM 38372
Owner: Entercom Communications Corp.
Editorial: 2120 N Woodlawn St, Ste 352, Wichita, Kansas 67208 **Tel:** 1 316 685-2121.
Email: letters@kfhradio.com
Web site: http://www.kfhradio.com
Profile: KFH-AM is a commercial station owned by Entercom Communications Corp. The format of the station is sportstalk programming. KFH-AM broadcasts to the Wichita, KS area at 1240 AM.
AM RADIO STATION

KFHC-FM 862993
Owner: St. Gabriel Communications, LTD
Editorial: 705 Douglas St Ste 238, Sioux City, Iowa 51101-1043 **Tel:** 1 712 224-5342.
Email: fhcradio@fhcradio.com
Web site: http://www.fhcradio.com
Profile: KFHC-FM is a non-commercial station owned by St. Gabriel Communications, LTD. The format of the station is Catholic teaching. KFHC-FM broadcasts to the Ponca, NE area at a frequency of 88.1 FM. The station is a Catholic radio station and has no interest in other programming.
FM RADIO STATION

KFH-FM 45734
Owner: Entercom Communications Corp.
Editorial: 2120 N Woodlawn St, Ste 352, Wichita, Kansas 67208 **Tel:** 1 316 685-2121.
Email: letters@kfhradio.com
Web site: http://www.kfhradio.com
Profile: KFH-FM is a commercial station owned by Entercom Communications Corp. The format of the station is sportstalk programming. KFH-FM broadcasts to Wichita, KS area at 98.7 FM.
FM RADIO STATION

KFHL-FM 418476
Owner: Mary V. Harris Foundation
Editorial: 2600 Kenwood Rd, Bakersfield, California 93306-3427 **Tel:** 1 800 617-9673.
Web site: http://www.kfhlradio.com
Profile: KFHL-FM is a non-commercial station owned by Mary V. Harris Foundation. The format of the station is religious. KFHL-FM broadcasts to the Bakersfield, CA area at 91.7 FM.
FM RADIO STATION

KFIA-AM 36329
Owner: Salem Media Group, Inc.
Editorial: 1425 River Park Dr Ste 520, Sacramento, California 95815-4524 **Tel:** 1 916 924-0710.
Web site: http://www.kfia.com
Profile: KFIA-AM is a commercial station owned by Salem Media Group, Inc. The format of the station is religious talk. KFIA-AM broadcasts to the Sacramento, CA area at 710 AM.
AM RADIO STATION

KFI-AM 39292
Owner: iHeartMedia Inc.
Editorial: 3400 W Olive Ave Ste 550, Burbank, California 91505-5544 **Tel:** 1 818 559-2252.
Email: kfiassignmentdesk@iheartmedia.com
Web site: http://kfiam640.iheart.com
Profile: KFI-AM is a commercial station owned by iHeartMedia Inc. The format of the station is news and talk. KFI-AM broadcasts to the Los Angeles area at 640 AM. The station does not accepts PSAs.
AM RADIO STATION

KFIG-AM 37099
Owner: Ostlund(John Edwards)
Editorial: 1415 Fulton St, Fresno, California 93721-1609 **Tel:** 1 559 497-5118.
Web site: http://1430espn.com
Profile: KFIG-AM is a commercial station owned by John Edwards Ostlund. The format of the station is sports. KFIG-AM broadcasts to the Fresno, CA area at 940 AM.
AM RADIO STATION

KFIL-AM 37275
Owner: Townsquare Media
Editorial: 300 Saint Paul St SW, Preston, Minnesota 55965-1097 **Tel:** 1 507 765-3856.
Web site: http://www.kfilradio.com
Profile: KFIL-AM is a commercial station owned by Townsquare Media. The format of the station is country and talk. KFIL-AM broadcasts to the Preston, MN area at 1060 AM.
AM RADIO STATION

KFIL-FM 44654
Owner: Cumulus Media Inc.
Editorial: 300 Saint Paul St SW, Preston, Minnesota 55965-1097 **Tel:** 1 507 765-3856.
Web site: http://www.kfilradio.com
Profile: KFIL-FM is a commercial station owned by Cumulus Media Inc. The format of the station is classic country. KFIL-FM broadcasts in the Preston, MN area at 103.1 FM.
FM RADIO STATION

KFIN-FM 46616
Owner: East Arkansas Broadcasters Inc.
Editorial: 407 W Parker Rd, Jonesboro, Arkansas 72404 **Tel:** 1 870 932-1079.
Email: kfin@kfin.com
Web site: http://www.kfin.com
Profile: KFIN-FM is a commercial station owned by East Arkansas Broadcasters Inc. The format of the station is contemporary country. KFIN-FM broadcasts to the Jonesboro, AR area at 107.9 FM.
FM RADIO STATION

KFIO-AM 38598
Owner: Mapleton Communications LLC
Editorial: 1601 E 57th Ave, Spokane, Washington 99223-6623 **Tel:** 1 509 448-1000.
Profile: KFIO-AM is a commercial station owned by Mapleton Communications. The format of the station is adult standards. KFIO-AM broadcasts to the Spokane, WA area at a frequency of 1050 AM.
AM RADIO STATION

KFIR-AM 36640
Owner: Radio Fiesta Network LLC
Editorial: 28041 Pleasant Valley Rd, Sweet Home, Oregon 97386 **Tel:** 1 541 367-5117.
Email: info@kfir720am.com
Web site: http://www.kfir720am.com
Profile: KFIR-AM is a commercial station owned by Radio Fiesta Network LLC. The format of the station is primarily talk. KFIR-AM broadcasts to the Sweet Home, OR area at 720 AM.
AM RADIO STATION

KFIS-FM 81504
Owner: Salem Media Group, Inc.
Editorial: 6400 SE Lake Rd Ste 350, Portland, Oregon 97222-2189 **Tel:** 1 503 786-0600.
Email: contactus@1041thefish.com
Web site: http://www.1041thefish.com
Profile: KFIS-FM is a commercial station owned by Salem Media Group, Inc. The format of the station is contemporary Christian music. KFIS-FM broadcasts to the Portland, OR area at 104.1 FM.
FM RADIO STATION

KFIT-AM 35907
Owner: Martin Broadcasting
Editorial: 110 Wild Basin Rd, West Lake Hills, Texas 78746-3339 **Tel:** 1 512 328-8400.
Email: darrellemartin@yahoo.com
Web site: http://gospel1060.com
Profile: KFIT-AM is a commercial station owned by Martin Broadcasting. The format of the station is gospel music and Hispanic religious programming. KFIT-AM broadcasts to the Austin, TX area at 1060 AM.
AM RADIO STATION

KFIV-AM 38502
Owner: iHeartMedia Inc.
Editorial: 2121 Lancey Dr, Modesto, California 95355-3036 **Tel:** 1 209 551-1306.
Web site: http://powertalk1360.iheart.com
Profile: KFIV-AM is a commercial station owned by iHeartMedia Inc. The format of the station is news and talk. KFIV-AM broadcasts to the Modesto, CA area at 1360 AM.
AM RADIO STATION

KFIX-FM 44167
Owner: Hull Broadcasting
Editorial: 2300 Hall St, Hays, Kansas 67601-3062
Tel: 1 785 625-2578.
Email: haysnews@eagleradio.net
Web site: http://www.kfix.com
Profile: KFIX-FM is a commercial station owned by Hull Broadcasting. The format of the station is classic rock music. KFIX-FM broadcasts to the Hays, KS area at 96.9 FM.
FM RADIO STATION

KFIZ-AM 38553
Owner: RBH Enterprises Inc.
Editorial: 254 Winnebago Dr, Fond du Lac, Wisconsin 54935-2447 **Tel:** 1 920 921-1071.
Web site: http://www.kfiz.com
Profile: KFIZ-AM is a commercial station owned by RBH Enterprises Inc. The format of the station is news, sports and talk. KFIZ-AM broadcasts to the Fond Du Lac, WI area at 1450 AM.
AM RADIO STATION

KFJB-AM 39183
Owner: Marshalltown Broadcasting Inc.
Editorial: 123 W Main St, Marshalltown, Iowa 50158-5860 **Tel:** 1 641 753-3361.
Email: news@marshalltownbroadcasting.com
Web site: http://www.1230kfjb.com
Profile: KFJB-AM is a commercial station owned by Marshalltown Broadcasting Inc. The format of the station is news and talk. KFJB-AM broadcasts in the Marshalltown, IA area at 1230 AM.
AM RADIO STATION

KFJC-FM 39645
Owner: Foothill- De Anza Community College
Editorial: 12345 S El Monte Rd, Los Altos Hills, California 94022-4504 **Tel:** 1 650 949-7260.
Email: info@kfjc.org
Profile: KFJC-FM is a non-commercial station owned by Foothill- De Anza Community College. The format of the station is variety, including alternative and underground music. KFJC-FM broadcasts to the Los Altos Hills, CA area at 89.7 FM.
FM RADIO STATION

KFJZ-AM 34947
Owner: SIGA Broadcasting Corp.
Editorial: 1320 N Shepherd Dr, Houston, Texas 77008-3752 **Tel:** 1 713 868-5559.
Profile: KFJZ-AM is a commercial station owned by SIGA Broadcasting Corp. The format of the station is Hispanic Christian. KFJZ-AM broadcasts in the Dallas area at AM 870.
AM RADIO STATION

KFKA-AM 36113
Owner: Broadcast Media
Editorial: 820 11th Ave, Greeley, Colorado 80631
Tel: 1 970 356-1310.
Email: info@1310kfka.com
Web site: http://www.1310kfka.com
Profile: KFKA-AM is a commercial station owned by Broadcast Media. The station's format is news, sports and talk. KFKA-AM broadcasts to the Greely, CO area at 1310 AM.
AM RADIO STATION

KFKF-FM 43517
Owner: Steel City Media
Editorial: 508 Westport Rd Ste 202, Kansas City, Missouri 64111-3019 **Tel:** 1 816 753-4000.
Web site: http://www.kfkf.com
Profile: KFKF-FM is a commercial station owned by Steel City Media. The format of the station is contemporary country music. KFKF-FM broadcasts to the Kansas City, MO at 94.1 FM.
FM RADIO STATION

KFKX-FM 43703
Owner: Hastings College
Editorial: 710 N Turner Ave, Hastings, Nebraska 68901-7621 **Tel:** 1 402 461-7342.
Email: kfkx@hastings.edu
Web site: http://hcmediaonline.org/index.cfm
Profile: KFKX-FM is a commercial station owned by Hastings College. The format of the station is primarily rock alternative. KFKX-FM broadcasts to the Hastings, NE area at 90.1 FM.
FM RADIO STATION

KFLB-AM 39082
Owner: Family Life Communications, Inc.
Editorial: 7355 N Oracle Rd, Tucson, Arizona 85704-6325 **Tel:** 1 520 742-6976.
Web site: http://www.myflr.org
Profile: KFLB-AM is a non-commercial station owned by Family Life Radio. The format of the station is contemporary Christian. KFLB-AM broadcasts to the Odessa, TX area at 920 AM.
AM RADIO STATION

KFLB-FM 382871
Owner: Family Life Radio
Editorial: 808 Tower Dr Ste 6, Odessa, Texas 79761-4243 **Tel:** 1 520 742-6976.
Web site: http://www.myflr.org
Profile: KFLB-FM is a non-commercial station owned by Family Life Radio. The format of the station is contemporary Christian. KFLB-FM broadcasts to the Stanton, TX area at 88.1 FM.
FM RADIO STATION

KFLC-AM 39469
Owner: Univision Communications Inc.
Editorial: 7700 John W Carpenter Fwy Fl 1, Dallas, Texas 75247-4829 **Tel:** 1 214 920-4977.
Web site: http://univisionamerica.com
Profile: KFLC-AM is a commercial station owned by Univision Communications Inc. The format of the station is Hispanic news and talk programming. KFLC-AM broadcasts to the Dallas area at 1270 AM.
AM RADIO STATION

KFLD-AM 37422
Owner: Townsquare Media, LLC
Editorial: 2621 W A St, Pasco, Washington 99301-4702 **Tel:** 1 509 547-9791.
Web site: http://www.newstalk870.am
Profile: KFLD-AM is a commercial station owned by Townsquare Media, LLC. The format of the station is news, talk and sports. KFLD-AM broadcasts to the Pasco, WA area at 870 AM.
AM RADIO STATION

KFLF-FM 610982
Owner: Fresh Life Church, Inc.
Editorial: 120 2nd St E, Kalispell, Montana 59901-4533 **Tel:** 1 406 257-3339.
Web site: http://www.freshliferadio.com
Profile: KFLF-FM is a non-commercial station owned by Fresh Life Church, Inc. The format of the station is religious programming. KFLF-FM broadcasts to the Somers, MT area at 91.3 FM.
FM RADIO STATION

KFLG-AM 38338
Owner: Cameron Broadcasting Inc.
Editorial: 2350 Miracle Mile Ste 300, Bullhead City, Arizona 86442-7505 **Tel:** 1 928 763-5586.
Web site: http://www.talkatoz.com
Profile: KFLG-AM is a commercial station owned by Cameron Broadcasting Inc. The format of the station is adult standards. KFLG-AM broadcasts to the Bullhead City, AZ area at 1000 AM.
AM RADIO STATION

KFLG-FM 45006
Owner: Cameron Broadcasting Inc.
Editorial: 2350 Miracle Mile Ste 300, Bullhead City, Arizona 86442-7505 **Tel:** 1 928 763-5586.
Web site: http://www.kflg947.com
Profile: KFLG-FM is a commercial station owned by Cameron Broadcasting Inc. The format of the station is country music. KFLG-FM broadcasts in the Bullhead City, AZ area at 94.7 FM.
FM RADIO STATION

KFLI-FM 518593
Owner: Flinn Broadcasting Corp.
Editorial: 929 Eastline Rd, Searcy, Arkansas 72143-8341 **Tel:** 1 501 268-1047.
Web site: http://www.cool1047.com
Profile: KFLI-FM is a commercial station owned by Flinn Broadcasting Corp. The format of the station is classic hits. KFLI-FM broadcasts to the Searcy, AR area at 104.7 FM.
FM RADIO STATION

KFLN-AM 34948
Owner: Newell Broadcasting
Editorial: 3584 Highway 7, Baker, Montana 59313
Tel: 1 406 778-3371.
Email: kfln@midrivers.com
Web site: http://newellbroadcasting.com
AM RADIO STATION

KFLP-AM 37345
Owner: Ricketts(Anthony L.)
Editorial: 201 W California St, Floydada, Texas 79235-2700 **Tel:** 1 806 983-5704.
Email: kflp@kflp.net
Web site: http://www.allagnews.com
Profile: KFLP-AM is a commercial station owned by Anthony L. Ricketts. The format of the station is agricultural. KFLP-AM broadcasts to the Floydada, TX area at 900 AM.
AM RADIO STATION

KFLP-FM 44715
Owner: Ricketts(Anthony L.)
Editorial: 201 W California St, Floydada, Texas 79235-2700 **Tel:** 1 806 983-5704.
Email: kflp@kflp.net
Web site: http://www.1061flipfm.com
Profile: KFLP-FM is a commercial station that is owned by Anthony L. Ricketts. The format of the station is contemporary country music. KFLP-FM broadcasts to the Floydada, TX area at 106.1 FM.
FM RADIO STATION

KFLQ-FM 41235
Owner: Family Life Broadcasting, Inc.
Editorial: 300 S Lea Ave, Roswell, New Mexico 88203-4562 **Tel:** 1 505 296-9100.
Web site: http://www.myflr.org
Profile: KFLQ-FM is a non-commercial station owned by Family Life Broadcasting, Inc. The format of the station is religious music and talk. KFLQ-FM broadcasts to the Albuquerque, NM area at 91.5 FM.
FM RADIO STATION

KFLR-FM 41716
Owner: Family Life Broadcasting, Inc.
Editorial: 7355 N Oracle Rd, Tucson, Arizona 85704-6325 **Tel:** 1 520 742-6976.
Web site: http://myflr.org
Profile: KFLR-FM is a non-commercial station owned by Family Life Broadcasting, Inc. The format of the station is religious, family-oriented programming. KFLR-FM broadcasts to the Phoenix area at 90.3 FM.
FM RADIO STATION

KFLS-AM 38824
Owner: Wynne Broadcasting Co.
Editorial: 1338 Oregon Ave, Klamath Falls, Oregon 97601-6540 **Tel:** 1 541 882-4656.
Web site: http://www.klamathradio.com
Profile: KFLS-AM is a commercial station owned by Wynne Broadcasting Co. The format of the station is news, talk and sports. KFLS-AM broadcasts to the Klamath Falls, OR area at 1450 AM.
AM RADIO STATION

KFLS-FM 46674
Owner: Wynne Broadcasting Co.
Editorial: 1338 Oregon Ave, Klamath Falls, Oregon 97601-6540 **Tel:** 1 541 882-4656.
Email: webmaster@klamathradio.com
Web site: http://www.klamathradio.com
Profile: KFLS-FM is a commercial station owned by Wynne Broadcasting Co. The format of the station is contemporary country. KFLS-FM broadcasts to the Klamath Falls, OR area at a frequency of 96.5.
FM RADIO STATION

KFLT-AM 34950
Owner: Family Life Radio
Editorial: 7355 N Oracle Rd Ste 102, Tucson, Arizona 85704-6326 **Tel:** 1 520 742-6976.
Web site: http://www.myflr.org
Profile: KFLT-AM is a non-commercial station owned by Family Life Radio. The format of the station is contemporary Christian. KFLT-AM broadcasts to the Tuscon, AZ area at 830 AM.
AM RADIO STATION

KFLW-FM 42625
Owner: Ozark Media Inc.
Editorial: 555 Marshall Dr, Saint Robert, Missouri 65584-5601 **Tel:** 1 573 336-5359.
Email: manager@ozarkmedia.com
Web site: http://www.kflw989.com
Profile: KFLW-FM is a commercial station owned by Ozark Media Inc.. The format of the station is hot adult contemporary music. KFLW-FM broadcasts to the Saint Robert, MO area at 98.9 FM.
FM RADIO STATION

KFLX-FM 42223
Owner: Grenax Broadcasting
Editorial: 2409 N 4th St, Ste 101, Flagstaff, Arizona 86004-3735 **Tel:** 1 928 779-1177.
Web site: http://www.rewindmymusic.com
Profile: KFLX-FM is a commercial station owned by Grenax Broadcasting. The format of the station is hot adult contemporary. KFLX-FM broadcasts to the Flagstaff, AZ area at 104.1 FM.
FM RADIO STATION

KFLY-FM 44633
Owner: Bicoastal Media LLC
Editorial: 1500 Valley River Dr Ste 350, Eugene, Oregon 97401-2163 **Tel:** 1 541 485-1120.
Email: eugenepsa@bicoastalmedia.com
Web site: http://www.kflyfm.com
Profile: KFLY-FM is a commercial station owned by Bicoastal Media LLC. The format of the station is rock alternative music. KFLY-FM broadcasts to the Eugene, OR area at 101.5 FM.
FM RADIO STATION

KFMA-FM 41870
Owner: Lotus Communications Corp.
Editorial: 3871 N Commerce Dr, Tucson, Arizona 85705-2983 **Tel:** 1 520 407-4500.
Web site: http://www.kfma.com
Profile: KFMA-FM is a commercial station owned by Lotus Communications Corp. The format of the station is rock alternative music. KFMA-FM broadcasts to the Tucson, AZ area at 102.1 FM.
FM RADIO STATION

KFMB-AM 37278
Owner: Midwest Television Inc.
Editorial: 7677 Engineer Rd, San Diego, California 92111-1515 **Tel:** 1 858 571-8888.
Email: webmaster@kfmb.com
Web site: http://www.760kfmb.com
Profile: KFMB-AM is a commercial station owned by Midwest Television Inc. The format for the station is news and talk. KFMB-AM broadcasts to the San Diego area at 760 AM.
AM RADIO STATION

KFMB-FM 44658
Owner: Midwest Television Inc.
Editorial: 7677 Engineer Rd, San Diego, California 92111-1515 **Tel:** 1 858 292-7600.
Email: radiopromotions@kfmb.com
Web site: http://www.kfmbfm.com/
Profile: KFMB-FM is a commercial station owned by Midwest Television Inc. The format of the station is Rock. KFMB-FM broadcasts to the San Diego area at 100.7 FM.
FM RADIO STATION

KFMC-FM 44659
Owner: Woodward Broadcasting, Inc.
Editorial: 1371 W Lair Rd, Fairmont, Minnesota 56031-2320 **Tel:** 1 507 235-5595.
Email: info@ksum.com
Web site: http://www.kfmc.com
Profile: KFMC-FM is a commercial station owned by Woodward Broadcasting, Inc. The format for the station is classic rock. KFMC-FM broadcasts to the Fairmont, MN area at 106.5 FM.
FM RADIO STATION

KFMD-FM 815080
Owner: Hog Radio, Inc.
Editorial: 2250 W Sunset Ave Ste 3, Springdale, Arkansas 72762-5187 **Tel:** 1 479 303-2034.
Web site: http://www.classichits1015.com
Profile: KFMD-FM is a commercial station owned by Hog Radio, Inc. The format of the station is classic hits. KFMD-FM broadcasts to the Fayetteville, AR area at a frequency of 101.5 FM.
FM RADIO STATION

KFMF-FM 39647
Owner: Mapleton of Chico, LLC
Editorial: 1459 Humboldt Rd Ste D, Chico, California 95928-9100 **Tel:** 1 530 899-3600.
Web site: http://939thehippo.com/
Profile: KFMF-FM is a commercial station owned by Mapleton of Chico, LLC. The format of the station is classic rock. KFMF-FM broadcasts to the Chico, CA area at 93.9 FM.
FM RADIO STATION

KFMI-FM 44660
Owner: Bicoastal Media LLC
Editorial: 5640 S Broadway St, Eureka, California 95503-6905 **Tel:** 1 707 442-2000.
Email: eurekanews@bicoastalmedia.com
Web site: http://www.power963.com
Profile: KFMI-FM is a commercial station owned by Bicoastal Media LLC. The format of the station is hot adult contemporary. KFMI-FM broadcasts to the Eureka, CA area at 96.3 FM.
FM RADIO STATION

KFMJ-FM 43841
Owner: Rhyner, (Steven L.)
Editorial: 516 Stedman St, Ketchikan, Alaska 99901-6629 **Tel:** 1 907 247-3699.
Web site: http://www.kfmjradio.com
Profile: KFMJ-FM is a commercial station owned by Steve L. Rhyner. The format of the station is oldies and talk. KFMJ-FM's target audience is listeners, ages 35 to 100 in the Ketchikan, AK area. The station airs locally on 99.9 FM.
FM RADIO STATION

KFMK-FM 43988
Owner: Crista Broadcasting
Editorial: 3600 N Capital of Texas Hwy Ste A200, Austin, Texas 78746-3219 **Tel:** 1 512 329-4400.
Email: info@SPIRIT1059.com
Web site: http://www.spirit1059.com
Profile: KFMK-FM is a commercial station owned by Crista Broadcasting. The format of the station is contemporary Christian. KFMK-FM broadcasts to the Austin, TX area at 105.9 FM.
FM RADIO STATION

KFML-FM 46109
Owner: Little Falls Radio Corp.
Editorial: 16405 Haven Rd, Little Falls, Minnesota 56345-6400 **Tel:** 1 320 632-5414.
Email: news@fallsradio.com
Web site: http://www.fallsradio.com
Profile: KFML-FM is a commercial station owned by Little Falls Radio Corp. The format of the station is hot adult contemporary. KFML-FM broadcasts to the Little Falls, MN area at 94.1 FM.
FM RADIO STATION

KFMM-FM 44661
Owner: Cochise Broadcasting LLC
Editorial: 301 E US Highway 70, #B, Safford, Arizona 85546 **Tel:** 1 928 428-0916.
Email: info@kkyz.com
Web site: http://www.saffordradio.com
Profile: KFMM-FM is a commercial station owned by Cochise Broadcasting LLC. The format of the station is classic rock. KFMM-FM broadcasts to the Phoenix area at 99.1 FM.
FM RADIO STATION

KFMN-FM 41239
Owner: FM 97 Associates
Editorial: 1860 Leleiona St, Lihue, Hawaii 96766-9000 **Tel:** 1 808 246-1197.
Email: frontdesk@fm97radio.com
Web site: http://kauaifm97.com
Profile: KFMN-FM is a commercial station owned by FM 97 Associates. The format of the station is adult contemporary. KFMN-FM broadcasts to the Greater Lihue, HI area at a frequency of 96.9 FM.
FM RADIO STATION

KFMO-AM 39494
Owner: MKS Broadcasting Inc.
Editorial: 804 S Saint Joe Dr, Park Hills, Missouri 63601-2427 **Tel:** 1 573 431-1000.
Web site: http://www.kfmo.com
Profile: KFMO-AM is a commercial station owned by MKS Broadcasting Inc. The format of the station is news, talk and sports. KFMO-AM broadcasts to the Park Hills, MO area at 1240 AM.
AM RADIO STATION

KFMQ-FM 43185
Owner: iHeartMedia Inc.
Editorial: 1632 S Second St, Gallup, New Mexico 87301-5836 **Tel:** 1 505 863-9391.
Web site: http://www.kfmqrock1061.com
Profile: KFMQ-FM is a commercial station owned by iHeartMedia Inc. The format of the station is rock music. KFMQ-FM broadcasts to the Albuquerque, NM area at 106.1 FM.
FM RADIO STATION

KFMT-FM 46576
Owner: Walnut Radio, LLC
Editorial: 118 E 5th St, Fremont, Nebraska 68025-5022 **Tel:** 1 402 721-1340.
Web site: http://myfremontradio.com
Profile: KFMT-FM is a commercial station owned by Walnut Radio, LLC. The format of the station is classic rock. KFMT-FM broadcasts to the Fremont, NE area at 105.5.
FM RADIO STATION

KFMU-FM 39650
Owner: NRC Broadcasting
Editorial: 2955 Village Dr, Steamboat Springs, Colorado 80487-2143 **Tel:** 1 970 879-5368.
Web site: http://alwaysmountaintime.com/kfmu
Profile: KFMU-FM is a commercial station owned by NRC Broadcasting. The format of the station is adult album alternative. KFMU-FM broadcasts to the Steamboat Springs, CO area at 105.5 FM.
FM RADIO STATION

KFMW-FM 44662
Owner: NRG Media LLC
Editorial: 514 Jefferson St, Waterloo, Iowa 50701-5422 **Tel:** 1 319 234-2200.
Web site: http://www.rock108.com
Profile: KFMW-FM is a commercial station owned by NRG Media LLC. The format for the station is rock. KFMW-FM broadcasts to the Cedar Rapids, IA area at 107.9 FM.
FM RADIO STATION

KFMX-FM 46312
Owner: Townsquare Media, LLC
Editorial: 4413 82nd St, Ste 300, Lubbock, Texas 79424 **Tel:** 1 806 798-7078.
Web site: http://www.kfmx.com
Profile: KFMX-FM is a commercial station owned by Townsquare Media, LLC. The format of the station is rock. KFMX-FM broadcasts to the Lubbock, TX area at 95.4 FM.
FM RADIO STATION

KFMZ-AM 37297
Owner: Best Broadcast Group
Editorial: 107 S Main St, Brookfield, Missouri 64628-2101 **Tel:** 1 660 258-3383.
Email: kzbk@shighway.com
Web site: http://www.kzbkradio.com
Profile: KFMZ-AM is a commercial station owned by Best Broadcast Group. The format of the station is hot adult contemporary. KFMZ-AM broadcasts to the Brookfield, MO area at 1470 AM.
AM RADIO STATION

KFNC-FM 41993
Owner: Gow Media Inc.
Editorial: 5353 W Alabama St Ste 415, Houston, Texas 77056-5942 **Tel:** 1 713 479-5300.
Web site: http://www.espn975.com
Profile: KFNC-FM is a commercial station owned by Gow Media. The format of the station is sports. KFNC-FM broadcasts to the Houston area at 97.5 FM.
FM RADIO STATION

KFNN-AM 34981
Owner: CRC Broadcasting Co.
Editorial: 8145 E Evans Rd Ste 8, Scottsdale, Arizona 85260-3645 **Tel:** 1 602 241-1510.
Email: producer1510@moneyradio.com
Web site: http://www.moneyradio1510.com
Profile: KFNN-AM is a commercial station owned by CRC Broadcasting Co. The format of the station is financial news and talk. KFNN-AM broadcasts to the Phoenix area on 1510 AM.
AM RADIO STATION

KFNO-FM 41951
Owner: Family Stations Inc.
Editorial: 706 W Herndon Ave, Fresno, California 93650-1033 **Tel:** 1 800 543-1495.
Email: familyradio@familyradio.org
Web site: http://www.familyradio.com
Profile: KFNO-FM is a commercial station owned by Family Stations Inc. The format of the station is Christian programming. KFNO-FM broadcasts to the Fresno, CA area at 90.3 FM.
FM RADIO STATION

KFNQ-AM 37480
Owner: CBS Radio
Editorial: 1000 Dexter Ave N Ste 100, Seattle, Washington 98109-3577 **Tel:** 1 206 805-1090.
Web site: http://seattle.cbslocal.com/category/sports
Profile: KFNQ-AM is commercial station owned by CBS Radio. The format of the station is sports. KFNQ-AM broadcasts in the Seattle area at 1090 AM.
AM RADIO STATION

KFNS-FM 46889
Owner: Viper Broadcasting, LLC
Editorial: 30 Tower St, Moscow Mills, Missouri 63362-1139 **Tel:** 1 636 695-2300.
Web site: http://viperrocks.com
Profile: KFNS-FM is a commercial station owned by Viper Broadcasting, LLC. The format of the station is rock. KFNS-FM broadcasts to the St. Louis and Moscow Mills areas at 100.7 FM.
FM RADIO STATION

KFNV-FM 44663
Owner: Radio Group(The)
Editorial: 917 Ee Wallace Blvd S, Ferriday, Louisiana 71334-3503 **Tel:** 1 318 757-4200.
Email: kfnv@bellsouth.net
Profile: KFNV-FM is a commercial station owned by The Radio Group. The format of the station is classic hits music. KFNV-FM broadcasts to the Ferriday, LA area at 107.1 FM.
FM RADIO STATION

KFNW-AM 37280
Owner: Northwestern College
Editorial: 5702 52nd Ave S, Fargo, North Dakota 58104 **Tel:** 1 701 282-5910.
Email: kfnw@kfnw.org
Web site: http://www.kfnw.org
Profile: KFNW-AM is a non-commercial station owned by Northwestern College. The format of the station is contemporary Christian music and talk. KFNW-AM broadcasts to the Fargo, ND area at 1200 AM.
AM RADIO STATION

KFNW-FM 44664
Owner: Northwestern College
Editorial: 5702 52nd Ave S, Fargo, North Dakota 58104-5605 **Tel:** 1 701 282-5910.
Email: kfnw@kfnw.org
Web site: http://www.life979.com
Profile: KFNW-FM is a non-commercial station owned by Northwestern College. The format of the station is contemporary Christian music and talk. KFNW-FM broadcasts to the Fargo, ND area at 97.9 FM.
FM RADIO STATION

KFNX-AM 36602
Owner: Premiere Broadcasting
Editorial: 2001 N 3rd St Ste 102, Phoenix, Arizona 85004-1495 **Tel:** 1 602 277-1100.
Web site: http://www.1100kfnx.com
Profile: KFNX-AM is a commercial station owned by Premiere Broadcasting. The format of the station is news and talk. KFNX-AM broadcasts in the Phoenix area at 1100 AM.
AM RADIO STATION

KFNY-AM 35802
Owner: iHeartMedia Inc.
Editorial: 2030 Iowa Ave Ste A, Riverside, California 92507-7412 **Tel:** 1 951 684-1991.
Web site: http://newstalk1440.iheart.com
Profile: KFNY-AM is a commercial station owned by iHeartMedia Inc. The format of the station is news/talk. KFNY-AM broadcasts to the Riverside, CA area at 1440 AM.
AM RADIO STATION

KFOG-FM 46268
Owner: Cumulus Media Inc.
Editorial: 750 Battery St Fl 3, San Francisco, California 94111-1523 **Tel:** 1 415 995-6800.
Web site: http://www.kfog.com
Profile: KFOG-FM is a commercial station owned by Cumulus Media Inc. The format of the station is adult album alternative. KFOG-FM broadcasts to the San Francisco area at 104.5 FM.
FM RADIO STATION

KFOO-FM 44772
Owner: iHeartMedia Inc.
Editorial: 645 Elliott Ave W Ste 400, Seattle, Washington 98119-3911 **Tel:** 1 206 494-2000.
Web site: http://alt1029.iheart.com
Profile: KFOO-FM is a commercial station owned by iHeartMedia Inc. The format of the station is Alternative Rock. KFOO-FM broadcasts to the Centralia, WA area at 102.9 FM.
FM RADIO STATION

KFOR-AM 38533
Owner: Alpha Media
Editorial: 3800 Cornhusker Hwy, Lincoln, Nebraska 68504-1533 **Tel:** 1 402 466-1234.
Web site: http://www.kfor1240.com
Profile: KFOR-AM is a commercial station owned by Alpha Media. The format of the station is news and talk. KFOR-AM broadcasts to the Lincoln, NE area at 1240 AM.
AM RADIO STATION

KFOX-AM 426615
Owner: HK Media, Inc.
Editorial: 4525 Wilshire Blvd Fl 3, Los Angeles, California 90010-3845 **Tel:** 1 323 935-0606.
Web site: http://www.radioseoul1650.com
Profile: KFOX-AM is a commercial station owned by HK Media, Inc. The format for the station is Korean programming. KFOX-AM broadcasts to the Los Angeles area at 1650 AM.
AM RADIO STATION

KFPT-AM 38811
Owner: Fat Dawgs 7 Broadcasting LLC
Editorial: 351 W Cromwell Ave, Fresno, California 93711-6115 **Tel:** 1 559 447-3570.
Profile: KFPT-AM is a commercial station owned by Fat Dawgs 7 Broadcasting LLC. The format of the station is sports. KFPT-AM broadcasts to the Fresno, CA area at 790 AM.
AM RADIO STATION

KFPW-AM 37067
Owner: Pharis Broadcasting Inc.
Editorial: 321 N Greenwood Ave Ste 201, Fort Smith, Arkansas 72901-3453 **Tel:** 1 479 288-1047.
Web site: http://www.sportshog1031.com
Profile: KFPW-AM is a commercial station owned by Pharis Broadcasting Inc. The format of the station is news and talk. KFPW-AM broadcasts to the Fort Smith, AR area at 1230 AM.
AM RADIO STATION

KFPW-FM 43181
Owner: Pharis Broadcasting Inc.
Editorial: 321 N Greenwood Ave Ste 201, Fort Smith, Arkansas 72901-3453 **Tel:** 1 479 288-1047.
Web site: http://www.sportshog1031.com
Profile: KFPW-FM is a commercial radio station owned by Pharis Broadcasting Inc. The format of the station is rock. KFPW-FM broadcasts to the Fort Smith, AR area on 94.5 FM.
FM RADIO STATION

KFQD-AM 37281
Owner: Alpha Media
Editorial: 301 Arctic Slope Ave Ste 200, Anchorage, Alaska 99518-3035 **Tel:** 1 907 344-9622.
Email: news@kfqd.com
Web site: http://www.kfqd.com
Profile: KFQD-AM is a commercial station owned by Alpha Media. The format of the station is news and talk. KFQD-AM broadcasts to the Anchorage, AK area at 750 AM.
AM RADIO STATION

KFRA-AM 36855
Owner: Hubcast Broadcasting Inc.
Editorial: 1320 Victor II Blvd, Morgan City, Louisiana 70380-1360 **Tel:** 1 985 385-6266.
Email: kbze.kfra@gmail.com
Web site: http://www.kbze.com
Profile: KFRA-AM is a commercial station owned by Hubcast Broadcasting Inc. The format of the station is urban adult contemporary. KFRA-AM broadcasts to the Morgan City, LA area at 1390 AM.
AM RADIO STATION

KFRB-FM 43870
Owner: Family Stations Inc.
Tel: 1 805 363-5576.
Email: info@familyradio.org
Web site: http://www.familyradio.com
FM RADIO STATION

KFRC-FM 39617
Owner: CBS Radio
Editorial: 865 Battery St Fl 2, San Francisco, California 94111-1503 **Tel:** 1 415 392-1069.
Email: kcbsnewsdesk@cbs.com
Web site: http://www.kcbs.com
Profile: KFRC-FM is a commercial station owned by CBS Radio. The format of the station is news. KFRC-FM broadcasts to the San Francisco area at 106.9 FM.
FM RADIO STATION

KFRG-FM 41829
Owner: CBS Radio
Editorial: 900 E Washington St Ste 315, Colton, California 92324-8182 **Tel:** 1 909 825-9525.
Web site: http://kfrog.radio.com
Profile: KFRG-FM is a commercial station owned by CBS Radio. The format of the station is country. KFRG-FM broadcasts to the San Bernardino, CA area at 95.1 FM.
FM RADIO STATION

KFRH-FM 39882
Owner: Royce International Broadcasting Corporation
Editorial: 73733 Fred Waring Dr Ste 201, Palm Desert, California 92260-2591 **Tel:** 1 702 546-5000.
Email: james@1043now.com
Web site: http://www.1043now.com
Profile: KFRH-FM is a commercial station owned by Royce International Broadcasting Corporation. The format of the station is Top 40/CHR. KFRH-broadcasts to the Las Vegas area at 104.3 FM.
FM RADIO STATION

KFRM-AM 39396
Owner: Taylor Communications
Editorial: 1815 Meadowlark Rd, Clay Center, Kansas 67432-8201 **Tel:** 1 785 632-5661.
Email: news@kfrm.com
Web site: http://www.kfrm.com
Profile: KFRM-AM is a commercial station owned by Taylor Communications. The format of the station is agricultural, news, sports, and talk. KFRM-AM broadcasts to Clay Center, KS area at 550 AM.
AM RADIO STATION

KFRN-AM 34951
Owner: Family Stations Inc.
Editorial: 11865 Moreno Ave, Lakeside, California 92040-1110 **Tel:** 1 800 797-7579.
Email: familyradio@familyradio.org
Web site: http://www.familyradio.com
Profile: KFRN-AM is a non-commercial station owned by Family Stations Inc. The format of the station is religious programming. KFRN-AM broadcasts to the Long Beach, CA area at 1280 AM.
AM RADIO STATION

KFRO-AM 38327
Owner: RCA Broadcasting
Tel: 1 903 663-9800.
Profile: KFRO-AM is a commercial station owned by RCA Broadcasting. The format of the station is sports. KFRO-AM broadcasts to the Longview, TX area at 1370 AM.
AM RADIO STATION

KFRO-FM 45686
Owner: Waller Broadcasting
Editorial: 3400 W Marshall Ave Ste 307, Longview, Texas 75604-5048 **Tel:** 1 903 663-2477.
Web site: http://www.mybreezefm.com
Profile: KFRO-FM is a commercial station owned by Waller Broadcasting. The format of the station is Top 40/CHR. KFRO-FM broadcasts to the Jacksonville, TX area at 95.3 FM.
FM RADIO STATION

KFRQ-FM 39625
Owner: Entravision Communications Corp.
Editorial: 801 N Jackson Rd, McAllen, Texas 78501
Tel: 1 956 661-6000.
Email: kfrq@hiline.net
Web site: http://www.q945rocks.com
Profile: KFRQ-FM is a commercial station owned by Entravision Communications Corp. The format of the station is rock. KFRQ-FM broadcasts to the McAllen, TX area at 94.5 FM.
FM RADIO STATION

KFRR-FM 42628
Owner: One Putt Broadcasting
Editorial: 1066 E Shaw Ave, Fresno, California 93710-7807 **Tel:** 1 559 230-0104.
Web site: http://www.newrock1041.fm
Profile: KFRR-FM is a commercial station owned by One Putt Broadcasting. The format of the station is rock alternative. KFRR-FM broadcasts to the Fresno, CA area at 104.1 FM.
FM RADIO STATION

KFRU-AM 39145
Owner: Cumulus Media Inc.
Editorial: 503 Old 63 N, Columbia, Missouri 65201-6305 **Tel:** 1 573 449-4141.
Web site: http://www.kfru.com
Profile: KFRU-AM is a commercial station owned by Cumulus Media Inc. The format of the station is news and talk. KFRU-AM broadcasts in the Columbia, MO area at 1400 AM.
AM RADIO STATION

KFRX-FM 39563
Owner: Alpha Media
Editorial: 3800 Cornhusker Hwy, Lincoln, Nebraska 68504-1533 **Tel:** 1 402 466-1234.
Web site: http://www.kfrxfm.com
Profile: KFRX-FM is a commercial station owned by Alpha Media. The format of the station is Top 40/CHR. KFRX-FM broadcasts to the Lincoln, NE area at 106.3 FM.
FM RADIO STATION

KFRZ-FM 44525
Owner: Wagonwheel Communications Corp.
Editorial: 40 Shoshone Ave, Green River, Wyoming 82935-5321 **Tel:** 1 307 875-6666.
Email: audio@theradionetwork.net
Web site: http://www.theradionetwork.net
Profile: KFRZ-FM is a commercial station owned by Wagonwheel Communications Corp. The format of the station is classic and contemporary country music. KFRZ-FM broadcasts to the Salt Lake City area at 92.1 FM.
FM RADIO STATION

KFSA-AM 36603
Owner: Fred H. Baker
Editorial: 5111 Rogers Ave Ste 650, Fort Smith, Arkansas 72903-2096 **Tel:** 1 749 785-2526.
Email: production@kisr.net
Web site: http://www.kisr.net
Profile: KFSA-AM is a commercial station owned by Fred H. Baker. The format of the station is top 40/CHR. KFSA-AM broadcasts in the Fort Smith, AR area at 950 area.
AM RADIO STATION

KFSD-AM 37427
Owner: Astor Broadcast Group
Editorial: 2888 Loker Ave E Ste 211, Carlsbad, California 92010-6685 **Tel:** 1 760 729-1000.
Email: astorbroadcasting@gmail.com
Web site: http://www.financialnewsandtalk.com
Profile: KFSD-AM is a commercial station owned by Astor Broadcast Group (North County Broadcasting Corporation). The format of the station is business news and talk. KFSD-AM broadcasts to the Inland Empire area of Southern California at 1450 AM.
AM RADIO STATION

KFSG-AM 395480
Owner: Multicultural Radio Broadcasting Inc.
Editorial: 3463 Ramona Ave Ste 15, Sacramento, California 95826-3827 **Tel:** 1 916 456-3288.
Profile: KFSG-AM is a commercial station owned by Multicultural Radio Broadcasting Inc. The format of the station is variety, including multicultural programming. KFSG-AM broadcasts to the Sacramento, CA area on 1690 AM.
AM RADIO STATION

KFSH-FM 44648
Owner: Salem Media Group, Inc.
Editorial: 701 N Brand Blvd Ste 550, Glendale, California 91203-1235 **Tel:** 1 714 796-4458.
Email: marissa@thefishla.com
Web site: http://www.thefishla.com
Profile: KFSH-FM is a commercial station owned by Salem Media Group, Inc. The format of the station is contemporary Christian. KFSH-FM broadcasts to the Los Angeles area at 95.9 FM.
FM RADIO STATION

KFSI-FM 41238
Owner: Faith Sound, Inc.
Editorial: 4016 28th St SE, Rochester, Minnesota 55904 **Tel:** 1 507 289-8585.
Email: shine@kfsi.org
Web site: http://www.kfsi.org
FM RADIO STATION

KFSK-FM 41237
Owner: Narrows Broadcasting
Editorial: 404 N 2nd St, Petersburg, Alaska 99833-9999 **Tel:** 1 907 772-3808.
Web site: http://www.kfsk.org
Profile: KFSK-FM is a non-commercial station owned by Narrows Broadcasting. The format of the station is variety. KFSK-FM broadcasts to Petersburg, AK at 100.9 FM.
FM RADIO STATION

KFSO-FM 44666
Owner: iHeartMedia Inc.
Editorial: 83 E Shaw Ave Ste 150, Fresno, California 93710-7622 **Tel:** 1 559 230-4300.
Web site: http://lapreciosa929.com
Profile: KFSO-FM is a commercial station owned by Clear Channel Media and Entertainment. The format of the station is Hispanic oldies. KFSO-FM's broadcasts to the Fresno, CA area at 92.9 FM.
FM RADIO STATION

KFSP-AM 37616
Owner: Radio Mankato
Editorial: 59346 Madison Ave, Mankato, Minnesota 56001-8518 **Tel:** 1 507 345-4537.
Email: news@ktoe.com
Web site: http://www.radiomankato.com
Profile: KFSP-AM is a commercial station owned by Radio Mankato. The format of the station is sports and news. KFSP-AM broadcasts to the North Mankato, MN area at 1230 AM.
AM RADIO STATION

KFST-AM 37282
Owner: Fort Stockton Radio Co., Inc.
Editorial: 954 S US Highway 385, Fort Stockton, Texas 79735 **Tel:** 1 432 336-2228.
Email: kfst@sbcglobal.net
Profile: KFST-AM is commercial station owned by Fort Stockton Radio Co., Inc. The format of the station is adult contemporary. KFST-AM broadcasts to the Fort Stockton, TX area at 860 AM.
AM RADIO STATION

KFST-FM 44667
Owner: Fort Stockton Radio Co., Inc.
Editorial: 954 S US Highway 385, Fort Stockton, Texas 79735 **Tel:** 1 432 336-2228.
Email: kfst@sbcglobal.net
Profile: KFST-FM is a commercial station owned by Fort Stockton Radio Co., Inc. The format of the station is country and Hispanic music. KFST-FM broadcasts in the Fort Stockton, TX area at 94.3 FM.
FM RADIO STATION

KFSZ-FM 774844
Owner: Great Circle Media
Editorial: 1117 W Route 66, Flagstaff, Arizona 86001-6213 **Tel:** 1 928 774-5231.
Web site: http://www.hits1061.com
Profile: KFSZ-FM is a commercial station owned by Great Circle Media. The format of the station is Top 40/CHR. KFSZ-FM broadcasts to the Flagstaff, AZ at a frequency of 106.1 FM.
FM RADIO STATION

KFTA-AM 37187
Owner: Lee Family Broadcasting
Editorial: 120 S 300 W, Rupert, Idaho 83350-9667
Tel: 1 208 324-8181.
Email: traffic@leeradio.net
Profile: KFTA-AM is a commercial station owned by Lee Family Broadcasting. The format of the station is Regional Mexican music. KFTA-AM broadcasts to the Rupert, ID area at a frequency of 970 AM.
AM RADIO STATION

KFTE-FM 42246
Owner: Townsquare Media, LLC
Editorial: 1749 Bertrand Dr, Lafayette, Louisiana 70506-2054 **Tel:** 1 337 233-6000.
Web site: http://www.planet1051.com
Profile: KFTE-FM is a commercial station owned by Townsquare Media, LLC. The format of the station rock music. KFTE-FM broadcasts to the Lafayette, LA area at 105.1 FM.
FM RADIO STATION

KFTG-FM 43660
Owner: Aleyua Christian Broadcasting
Editorial: 1600 Pasadena Blvd, Pasadena, Texas 77502-2404 **Tel:** 1 713 589-1460.
Email: fm@radioaleluya.org
Web site: http://radioaleluya.org
Profile: KFTG-FM is a commercial station owned by Aleluya Christian Broadcasting. The format of the station is Hispanic contemporary Christian. KFTG-FM broadcasts to the Pasadena, TX area at 88.1 FM.
FM RADIO STATION

KFTK-FM 42312
Owner: Emmis Communications Corp.
Editorial: 800 Saint Louis Union Sta, Saint Louis, Missouri 63103-2296 **Tel:** 1 314 231-9710.
Web site: http://www.971talk.com
Profile: KFTK-FM is a commercial station owned by Emmis Communications Corp. The format of the station is news and talk. KFTK-FM broadcasts to the St. Louis area at 97.1 FM.
FM RADIO STATION

KFTM-AM 39155
Owner: Media Logic LLC
Editorial: 16041 US Highway 34, Fort Morgan, Colorado 80701 **Tel:** 1 970 867-5674.
Email: kftm@medialogicradio.com
Web site: http://www.kftm.net
Profile: KFTM-AM is a commercial station owned by Media Logic LLC. The format of the station is adult contemporary music. KFTM-AM broadcasts to the Fort Morgan, CO area at 1400 AM.
AM RADIO STATION

KFTT-FM 537781
Owner: Mad Dog Wireless Inc.
Editorial: 2068 McCulloch Blvd N, Lake Havasu City, Arizona 86403-6712 **Tel:** 1 928 855-1051.
Web site: http://www.maddog.net
Profile: KFTT-FM is a commercial station owned by Mad Dog Wireless Inc. The format of the station is oldies. KFTT-FM broadcasts to the Lake Havasu City, AZ area at 107.7 FM.
FM RADIO STATION

KFTX-FM 40956
Owner: Quality Broadcasting
Editorial: 1520 S Port Ave, Corpus Christi, Texas 78405 **Tel:** 1 361 883-5987.
Web site: http://www.kftx.com
Profile: KFTX-FM is a commercial station owned by Quality Broadcasting. The format of the station is country. KFTX-FM broadcasts to the Corpus Christi, TX area at 97.5 FM.
FM RADIO STATION

KFTZ-FM 41236
Owner: Riverbend Communications LLC
Editorial: 400 W Sunnyside Rd, Idaho Falls, Idaho 83402-4613 **Tel:** 1 208 523-3722.
Email: onair@z103.fm
Web site: http://www.z103.fm
Profile: KFTZ-FM is a commercial station owned by Riverbend Communications LLC. The format of the station is Top 40/CHR music. KFTZ-FM broadcasts to the Idaho Falls, ID area at 103.3 FM.
FM RADIO STATION

KFUN-AM 3856
Owner: Baca Broadcasting LLC
Tel: 1 505 425-6766.
Web site: http://kfunsugsq.itm-staging.com
Profile: KFUN-AM is a commercial station owned by Baca Broadcasting LLC. The format of the station is country and Spanish tejano music. KFUN-AM broadcasts to the Las Vegas, NM area at 1230 AM.
AM RADIO STATION

KFUO-AM 3868
Owner: Lutheran Church-Missouri Synod
Editorial: 1333 S Kirkwood Rd, Saint Louis, Missouri 63122-7226 **Tel:** 1 314 965-9000.
Email: kfuo@kfuo.org
Web site: http://kfuo.org
Profile: KFUO-AM is a non-commercial station owned by the Lutheran Church-Missouri Synod. The format of the station is religious music and talk. KFUO-AM broadcasts to the St. Louis area at 850 AM.
AM RADIO STATION

KFUT-AM 3637
Owner: Morris Communications
Editorial: 1321 N Gene Autry Trl, Palm Springs, California 92262 **Tel:** 1 760 322-7890.
Web site: http://www.1270kfut.com
Profile: KFUT-AM is a commercial station owned by Morris Communications. The format of the station is Spanish-language news, talk and sports programming. KFUT-AM broadcasts to the Palm Springs, CA area at 1270 AM.
AM RADIO STATION

KFVR-FM 51562
Owner: Greeley Broadcasting Corp.
Editorial: 2099 U.S. Hwy W, Ste 130-A, Pueblo, Colorado 81008 **Tel:** 1 719 253-3777.
Profile: KFVR-FM is a commercial station owned by Greeley Broadcasting Corp. The format for the station is classic rock. KFVR-FM broadcasts to the Crescent City, California area at 94.7 FM.
FM RADIO STATION

KFWB-AM 3693
Owner: Lotus Communications Corp.
Editorial: 5670 Wilshire Blvd Ste 200, Los Angeles, California 90036-5657
Web site: https://www.980lameramera.com
Profile: KFWB-AM is a commercial station owned by Lotus Communications Corps. The format of the station is Regional Mexican music. KFWB-AM broadcasts to the Los Angeles area at 980 AM.
AM RADIO STATION

KFWR-FM 4328
Owner: LKCM Radio Group LP
Editorial: 201 Main St, Fort Worth, Texas 76102-3105
Tel: 1 817 332-0959.
Email: contactus@theranchradio.com
Web site: http://www.959theranch.com
Profile: KFWR-FM is a commercial station owned by LKCM Radio Group LP. The format of the station is country music. KFWR-FM broadcasts to the Dallas area at 95.9 FM.
FM RADIO STATION

KFXD-AM 3671
Owner: Townsquare Media, LLC
Editorial: 827 E Park Blvd Ste 100, Boise, Idaho 83712-7783 **Tel:** 1 208 344-6363.
Web site: http://630thefan.com
Profile: KFXD-AM is a commercial station owned by Townsquare Media, LLC. The format of the station is sports/talk. KFXD-AM broadcasts to the Boise, ID area at 630 AM.
AM RADIO STATION

KFXE-FM 556854
Owner: Radio Ranch Ltd.
Editorial: 3505 Fredericksburg Rd, Kerrville, Texas 78028-9272 **Tel:** 1 830 896-4990.
Web site: http://www.96gun.com/
Profile: KFXE-FM is a commercial station owned by Radio Ranch Ltd. The format of the station is contemporary country. KFXE-FM broadcasts to the Kerryville, TX area at 96.5 FM.
FM RADIO STATION

KFXI-FM 4094
Owner: DFWU Inc.
Editorial: 1101 N Broadway St, Marlow, Oklahoma 73055-1123 **Tel:** 1 580 658-9292.
Email: kfxi92@att.net
Web site: http://www.kfxi.com
Profile: KFXI-FM is a commercial station owned by DFWU Inc. The format of the station is country music. KFXI-FM broadcasts in the Marlow, OK area at 92.1 FM.
FM RADIO STATION

KFXJ-FM 42432
Owner: Kiel Media Group, LLC
Editorial: 4200 N Old Lawrence Rd, Wichita, Kansas 67219-3211 **Tel:** 1 316 838-9141.
Email: news@kfdi.com
Web site: http://www.1045thefox.com
Profile: KFXJ-FM is a commercial station owned by Kiel Media Group, LLC.The format of the station is

classic rock. KFXJ-FM broadcasts to the Wichita, KS area at 104.5 FM.
FM RADIO STATION

KFXN-AM 37086
Owner: MMTC Broadcasting LLC
Editorial: 1088 Payne Ave, Saint Paul, Minnesota 55130-3739 **Tel:** 1 651 810-6412.
Web site: http://hmongradioam690.com/
Profile: KFXN-AM is a commercial station owned by MMTC Broadcasting LLC. The format of the station is Asian American news, music and talk programming, specifically Hmong and Lao American. KFXN-AM broadcasts in the Minneapolis area at 690 AM.
AM RADIO STATION

KFXN-FM 42250
Owner: iHeartMedia Inc.
Editorial: 1600 Utica Ave S Ste 400, Saint Louis Park, Minnesota 55416-1480 **Tel:** 1 952 417-3000.
Web site: http://kfan.iheart.com
Profile: KFXN-FM is a commercial station owned by iHeartMedia Inc. The format for the station is sports.KFXN-FM broadcasts to the Minneapolis area at 100.3 FM.
FM RADIO STATION

KFXR-AM 36045
Owner: iHeartMedia Inc.
Editorial: 14001 Dallas Pkwy Ste 300, Dallas, Texas 75240-7369 **Tel:** 1 214 866-8000.
Email: psa@ccdallas.com
Web site: http://www.1190talkradio.com/main.html
Profile: KFXR-AM is a commercial station owned by iHeartMedia Inc. The format of the station is talk. KFXR-AM broadcasts to the Dallas area at 1190 AM.
AM RADIO STATION

KFXR-FM 43186
Owner: iHeartMedia Inc.
Editorial: 1632 S Second St, Gallup, New Mexico 87301-5836 **Tel:** 1 505 863-9391.
Profile: KFXR-FM is a commercial station owned by iHeartMedia Inc. The format of the station is country. KFXR-FM broadcasts to the Gallup, NM area at 107.3 FM.
FM RADIO STATION

KFXS-FM 43579
Owner: New Rushmore Radio
Editorial: 660 Flormann St, Ste 100, Rapid City, South Dakota 57701 **Tel:** 1 605 343-6161.
Web site: http://www.foxradio.com
Profile: KFXS-FM is a commercial station owned by New Rushmore Radio. The format of the station is classic rock. KFXS-FM broadcasts to the Rapid City, SD area at 100.3 FM.
FM RADIO STATION

KFXX-AM 38706
Owner: Entercom Communications Corp.
Editorial: 0700 SW Bancroft St, Portland, Oregon 97239-4226 **Tel:** 1 503 223-1441.
Web site: http://www.1080thefan.com
Profile: KFXX-AM is a commercial station owned by Entercom Communications Corp. The format of the station is sports. KFXX-AM broadcasts to the Portland, OR area at 1080 AM.
AM RADIO STATION

KFXZ-AM 41419
Owner: Delta Media Corporation
Editorial: 3501 NW Evangeline Trwy, Carencro, Louisiana 70520-6240 **Tel:** 1 337 896-1600.
Profile: KFXZ-FM is a commercial station Delta Media Corporation. The format of the station is Regional Mexican. KFXZ-AM broadcasts to the Lafayette, LA area at 1520 AM.
AM RADIO STATION

KFXZ-FM 46235
Owner: Delta Media Corporation
Editorial: 3501 NW Evangeline Trwy, Carencro, Louisiana 70520-6240 **Tel:** 1 337 896-1600.
Web site: http://www.z1059.com
Profile: KFXZ-FM is a commercial station owned by Delta Media Corporation. The format of the station is urban adult contemporary, soul and R&B. KFXZ-FM broadcasts to the Lafayette, LA area at 105.9 FM.
FM RADIO STATION

KFYI-AM 37283
Owner: iHeartMedia Inc.
Editorial: 4686 E Van Buren St Ste 300, Phoenix, Arizona 85008-6967
Web site: http://kfyi.iheart.com
Profile: KFYI-AM is a commercial station owned by iHeartMedia Inc. The format of the station is news and talk programming. KFYI-AM broadcasts to the Phoenix area at 550 AM. They COVER PHOENIX-AREA LOCAL NEWS. They only accept PHOENIX-SPECIFIC news story suggestions. They are ONLY INTERESTED in news releases that are SPECIFIC to PHOENIX. Talk show hosts on their station DO NOT have access to the newsroom's e-mail account. They may have to be reached via their online contact forms for inquiries related to their coverage in the Phoenix area ONLY.
AM RADIO STATION

KFYN-AM 39146
Owner: Vision Media Group
Editorial: 506 N Main St, Bonham, Texas 75418-3718
Tel: 1 903 583-3151.
Web site: http://1420thewarrior.com
Profile: KFYN-AM is a commercial station owned by Vision Media Group. The format of the station is classic country music. KFYN-AM broadcasts to the Bonham, TX area at 1420 AM.
AM RADIO STATION

KFYO-AM 38436
Owner: Townsquare Media, LLC
Editorial: 4413 82nd St Ste 300, Lubbock, Texas 79424-3366 **Tel:** 1 806 798-7078.
Email: news@kfyo.com
Web site: http://www.kfyo.com
Profile: KFYO-AM is a commercial station owned by Townsquare Media, LLC. The format of the station is news and talk. KFYO-AM broadcasts to the Lubbock, TX area at 790 AM.
AM RADIO STATION

KFYR-AM 39350
Owner: iHeartMedia Inc.
Editorial: 3500 E Rosser Ave, Bismarck, North Dakota 58501-3376 **Tel:** 1 701 255-1234.
Email: kfyr@iheartmedia.com
Web site: http://www.kfyr.com
Profile: KFYR-AM is a commercial station owned by iHeartMedia Inc. The format of the station is news and talk. KFYR-AM broadcasts to the Bismarck, ND area at 550 AM.
AM RADIO STATION

KFYV-FM 42775
Owner: Gold Coast Radio, LLC
Editorial: 2284 S Victoria Ave, Ventura, California 93003-6641 **Tel:** 1 805 289-1400.
Web site: http://www.live1055.fm
Profile: KFYV-FM is a commercial station owned by Gold Coast Radio, LLC. The format of the station is Top 40/CHR. KFYV-FM broadcasts to the Ventura, CA area at 105.5 FM.
FM RADIO STATION

KFYZ-FM 43649
Owner: Rincon Broadcasting
Editorial: 414 E Cota St, Santa Barbara, California 93101 **Tel:** 1 805 879-8300.
Web site: http://z945fm.com/main.php
Profile: KFYZ-FM is a commercial station owned by Rincon Broadcasting. The format of the station is Top 40/CHR. KFYZ-FM broadcasts to the Santa Barbara, CA area at 107.7 FM.
FM RADIO STATION

KFZO-FM 46858
Owner: Univision Communications Inc.
Editorial: 7901 John W Carpenter Fwy, Dallas, Texas 75247-4832 **Tel:** 1 214 920-4977.
Web site: http://maximadallas.univision.com
Profile: KFZO-FM is a commercial station owned by Univision Communications Inc. The format of the station is Spanish adult contemporary. KFZO-FM broadcasts to the Dallas area at 99.1 FM.
FM RADIO STATION

KFZX-FM 40020
Owner: ICA Radio
Editorial: 1330 E 8th St Ste 207, Odessa, Texas 79761-4731 **Tel:** 1 432 563-9102.
Web site: http://classicrock102.net
Profile: KFZX-FM is a commercial station owned by ICA Radio. The format of the station is classic rock. KFZX-FM broadcasts to the Odessa, TX area at 102.1 FM.
FM RADIO STATION

KGA-AM 37284
Owner: Mapleton Communications LLC
Editorial: 1601 E 57th Ave, Spokane, Washington 99223-6623 **Tel:** 1 509 448-1000.
Web site: http://www.1510kga.com
Profile: KGA-AM is a commercial station owned by Mapleton Communications LLC. The format of the station is sports. KGA-AM broadcasts to the Spokane, WA area at 1510AM.
AM RADIO STATION

KGAB-AM 39417
Owner: Townsquare Media, LLC
Editorial: 1912 Capitol Ave Ste 300, Cheyenne, Wyoming 82001-3659 **Tel:** 1 307 632-4400.
Web site: http://www.kgab.com
Profile: KGAB-AM is a commercial station owned by Townsquare Media, LLC. The format of the station is talk. The station is broadcast to the Cheyenne, WY area at 650 AM.
AM RADIO STATION

KGAC-FM 41575
Owner: Minnesota Public Radio
Editorial: 206 S Broadway, Ste 735, Rochester, Minnesota 55904 **Tel:** 1 507 282-0910.
Email: newsroom@mpr.org
Web site: http://minnesota.publicradio.org/radio/stations/kngakgac
Profile: KGAC-FM tries to inform, enrich and nourish audiences, assisting them to engage effectively as citizens, enhance their lives, expand their perspectives and strengthen their communities.
FM RADIO STATION

KGAF-AM 34952
Owner: First IV Media, Inc.
Editorial: 401 N Radio Hill Rd, Gainesville, Texas 76240-7635 **Tel:** 1 940 665-5546.
Email: info@1580kgaf.com
Web site: http://www.1580kgaf.com
Profile: KGAF-AM is a commercial station owned by Steve Eberhart. The format of the station is oldies. KGAF-AM broadcasts to the Gainesville, TX area at 1580 AM.
AM RADIO STATION

KGAK-AM 36205
Owner: KRJG Broadcasting Co.
Editorial: 401 E Coal Ave, Gallup, New Mexico 87301-6001 **Tel:** 1 505 863-4444.
Profile: KGAK-AM is a commercial station owned by KRJG Broadcasting Co. The format of the station is mixed variety of news and country music. KGAK-AM broadcasts to the Albuquerque, NM area at 1330 AM. The station broadcasts only in the Navajo language.
AM RADIO STATION

KGAL-AM 36314
Owner: EADS Broadcasting Corp.
Editorial: 36991 Kgal Dr, Lebanon, Oregon 97355
Tel: 1 541 451-5425.
Email: kgal@kgal.com
Web site: http://www.kgal.com
Profile: KGAL-AM is a commercial station owned by EADS Broadcasting Corp. The format of the station is news, sports and talk. KGAL-AM broadcasts to the Albany, OR area at 1580 AM.
AM RADIO STATION

KGAM-FM 44513
Owner: Lazer Broadcasting
Editorial: 1020 W Main St, Merced, California 95340-4521 **Tel:** 1 209 723-2191.
Profile: KGAM-FM is a commercial station owned by Lazer Broadcasting. The format of the station is Regional Mexican. KGAM-FM broadcasts to the Fresno-Visalia, CA area at 106.3 FM.
FM RADIO STATION

KGAP-FM 46467
Owner: American Media Investments
Editorial: 1323 College Dr, Texarkana, Texas 75503-3531 **Tel:** 1 903 793-1100.
Profile: KGAP-FM is a commercial station owned by American Media Investments. The format of the station is classic hits music. KGAP-FM broadcasts to the Texarkana, TX area at 98.5 FM.
FM RADIO STATION

KGAS-AM 39143
Owner: Hanszen Broadcast Group
Editorial: 215 S Market St, Carthage, Texas 75633-2623 **Tel:** 1 903 693-6668.
Email: news@kgasradio.com
Web site: http://www.easttexastoday.com
Profile: KGAS-AM is a commercial station owned by Hanszen Broadcast Group. The format for the station is sports and talk programming. KGAS-AM broadcasts to the Shreveport, LA area at 1590 AM.
AM RADIO STATION

KGAS-FM 46490
Owner: Hanszen Broadcast Group
Editorial: 215 S Market St, Carthage, Texas 75633-2623 **Tel:** 1 903 693-6668.
Email: info@kgasradio.com
Web site: http://www.easttexastoday.com
Profile: KGAS-FM is a commercial station owned by Hanszen Broadcast Group. The format of the station is country music. KGAS-FM broadcasts to the Shreveport, LA area at 104.3 FM.
FM RADIO STATION

KGBA-AM 39179
Owner: Voice of International Christian Evangelism Inc. (The)
Editorial: 605 W State St, El Centro, California 92243-2943 **Tel:** 1 760 352-9860.
Email: espanol@kgba.org
Web site: http://espanol.kgba.org
Profile: KGBA-AM is a non-commercial station owned by The Voice of International Christian Evangelism Inc. The format of the station is Hispanic and contemporary Christian. KGBA-AM broadcasts to the El Centro, CA area at 1490 AM.
AM RADIO STATION

KGBA-FM 39654
Owner: Voice of International Christian Evangelism Inc. (The)
Editorial: 605 W State St, El Centro, California 92243-2943 **Tel:** 1 760 352-9860.
Email: kgba@kgba.org
Web site: http://www.kgba.org
Profile: KGBA-FM is a non-commercial station owned by The Voice of International Christian Evangelism Inc. The format of the station is contemporary Christian. KGBA-FM broadcasts to the El Centro, CA area at 100.1 FM.
FM RADIO STATION

KGBB-FM 44188
Owner: Adelman Broadcasting Inc.
Editorial: 42010 50th St W, Quartz Hill, California 93536-3509 **Tel:** 1 661 718-1552.
Email: contact@adelmanbroadcasting.com
Web site: http://www.bobfm1039.com
Profile: KGBB-FM is a commercial station owned by Adelman Broadcasting Inc. The format of the station is Jack FM-Adult Hits. KGBB-FM broadcasts to the Ridgecrest, CA area at 103.9 FM.
FM RADIO STATION

KGBC-AM 34953
Owner: SIGA Broadcasting Corp.
Editorial: 1302 N Shepherd Dr, Houston, Texas 77008-3752 **Tel:** 1 713 868-5559.
Email: signbroadcasting@gmail.com
Web site: http://www.sigabroadcasting.com
Profile: KGBC-AM is a commercial station owned by SIGA Broadcasting Corp and in an LMA with Pacific Media International. The format of the station is variety of music, news, ethnic programming and Chinese Radio. KGBC-AM broadcasts to the Houston and Galveston, TX areas at 1540 AM.
AM RADIO STATION

KGB-FM 44434
Owner: iHeartMedia Inc.
Editorial: 9660 Granite Ridge Dr Ste 100, San Diego, California 92123-2689 **Tel:** 1 858 292-2000.
Web site: http://www.101kgb.com
Profile: KGB-FM is a commercial station owned by iHeartMedia Inc. The format of the station is classic rock music. KGB-FM broadcasts to the San Diego area at 101.5 FM.
FM RADIO STATION

KGBI-FM 39655
Owner: Salem Media Group, Inc.
Editorial: 11717 Burt St Ste 202, Omaha, Nebraska 68154-1500 **Tel:** 1 402 422-1600.
Web site: http://www.thefishomaha.com
Profile: KGBI-FM is a commercial station owned by Salem Media Group, Inc. The format of the station is contemporary Christian music. KGBI-FM broadcasts to the Omaha, NE at 100.7 FM.
FM RADIO STATION

KGBN-AM 37448
Owner: Korean Gospel Broadcasting Network
Editorial: 621 S Virgil Ave Ste 400, Los Angeles, California 90005-4043 **Tel:** 1 213 381-1190.
Email: am1190@igbc.net
Web site: http://www.igbc.net
Profile: KGBN-AM is a commercial station owned by Korean Gospel Broadcasting Network. The format of the station is Korean language Christian programming. KGBN-AM broadcasts to the Los Angeles area at 1190 AM.
AM RADIO STATION

KGBR-FM 41227
Owner: St. Marie Communications Inc.
Editorial: 29795 Ellensburg Ave, #H, Gold Beach, Oregon 97444 **Tel:** 1 541 247-7211.
Web site: http://www.kgbr.com
FM RADIO STATION

KGBT-AM 39201
Owner: Univision Communications Inc.
Editorial: 200 S 10Th St Ste 600, McAllen, Texas 78501-4869 **Tel:** 1 956 631-5499.
Web site: http://univisionamerica.com
Profile: KGBT-AM is a commercial station owned by Univision Communications Inc. The format of the station is Spanish news and talk. KGBT-AM broadcasts to the Rio Grande Valley area in Texas at 1530 AM.
AM RADIO STATION

KGBT-FM 43766
Owner: Univision Communications Inc.
Editorial: 200 S 10th St, Ste 600, McAllen, Texas 78501-4869 **Tel:** 1 956 631-5499.
Web site: http://kgbt985.univision.com
Profile: KGBT-FM is a commercial station owned by Univision Communications Inc. The format of the station is regional Mexican. KGBT-FM broadcasts to the McAllen, TX area at 98.5 FM.
FM RADIO STATION

KGBX-FM 42886
Owner: iHeartMedia Inc.
Editorial: 1856 S Glenstone Ave, Springfield, Missouri 65804-2303 **Tel:** 1 417 890-5555.
Email: kgbx@kgbx.com
Web site: http://www.kgbx.com
Profile: KGBX-FM is a commercial station owned by iHeartMedia Inc. The format for the station is adult contemporary. KGBX-FM broadcasts to the Springfield, MO area at 105.9 FM.
FM RADIO STATION

KGCB-FM 43875
Owner: Educational Media Foundation
Editorial: 5700 W Oaks Blvd, Rocklin, California 95765-3719 **Tel:** 1 928 776-0909.
Web site: http://www.klove.com/
Profile: KGCB-FM is a commercial station owned by Educational Media Foundation. The format of the station is contemporary Christian music and religious programming. KGCB-FM broadcasts to the Phoenix area at 90.9 FM.
FM RADIO STATION

KGCD-FM 395242
Owner: Praise Network, Inc. (The)
Tel: 1 785 694-2877.
Profile: KGCD-FM is a non-commercial station owned by The Praise Network, Inc. The format of the station is contemporary Christian. KGCD-FM broadcasts to the Wray, CO area at 89.1 FM.
FM RADIO STATION

KGCR-FM 41574
Owner: Praise Network(The)
Editorial: 3410 Road 66, Brewster, Kansas 67732-8907 **Tel:** 1 785 694-2877.
Email: kgcr@kgcr.org
Web site: http://www.praisenetwork.info/kger
Profile: KGCR-FM is a non-commercial station owned by the Praise Network. The format of the station is religious and contemporary Christian programming. KGCR-FM broadcasts to the Brewster, KS area at 107.7 FM.
FM RADIO STATION

KGCX-FM
242128

Owner: Sidney Community Broadcasting
Editorial: 213 2nd Ave SW, Sidney, Montana 59270-4019 **Tel:** 1 406 433-5429.
Email: kgcxeagle@midrivers.com
Profile: KGCX-FM is a commercial station owned by Sidney Community Broadcasting, a subsidiary of The Marks Radio Group. The format of the station is classic rock. KGCX-FM broadcasts to the Sidney, MT area at a frequency of 93.1 FM.
FM RADIO STATION

KGDC-AM
39304

Owner: Two Hearts Communications LLC
Editorial: 30 W Main St Ste 303, Walla Walla, Washington 99362-2872 **Tel:** 1 509 525-7878.
Web site: http://www.kgdcradio.com
Profile: KGDC-AM is a commercial station owned by Two Hearts Communications LLC. The format of the station is news and talk. KGDC-AM broadcasts to the Walla Walla, WA area at 1320 AM.
AM RADIO STATION

KGDN-FM
43031

Owner: Read Broadcasting
Tel: 1 509 783-8600.
Email: kgdn@kgdn.com
Web site: http://www.kgdn.com
Profile: KGDN-FM is a commercial station owned by Read Broadcasting. The format of the station is religious and Christian programming. KGDN-FM broadcasts to the Pasco, WA area at 101.3 FM.
FM RADIO STATION

KGED-AM
74882

Owner: Compass Broadcasting, Inc
Editorial: 2171 Ralph Ave, Stockton, California 95206-3625 **Tel:** 1 559 233-8803.
Email: my1680am@gmail.com
Web site: http://www.my1680.com/
Profile: KGED-AM is a commercial station owned by Compass Broadcasting, Inc. The format of the station is Christian talk. KGED-AM broadcasts to the Fresno, CA area at 1680 AM.
AM RADIO STATION

KGEM-AM
37285

Owner: Salt & Light Radio, Inc.
Editorial: 5601 W Cassia St, Boise, Idaho 83705-1836 **Tel:** 1 208 344-4774.
Email: info@saltandlightradio.com
Web site: http://www.saltandlightradio.com
Profile: KGEM-AM is a commercial station owned by Salt & Light Radio, Inc.The format of the station is religious. KGEM-AM broadcasts to the Boise, ID area at 1140 AM.
AM RADIO STATION

KGEN-AM
39457

Owner: JA Ventures, Inc.
Editorial: 323 E San Joaquin Ave, Tulare, California 93274-4130 **Tel:** 1 559 686-1370.
Profile: KGEN-AM is a commercial station owned by JA Ventures, Inc. The format of the station is regional Mexican music. KGEN-AM broadcasts in the Tulare, CA area at 1370 AM.
AM RADIO STATION

KGEN-FM
46843

Owner: JA Ventures, Inc.
Editorial: 323 E San Joaquin Ave, Tulare, California 93274-4130 **Tel:** 1 559 686-1370.
Profile: KGEN-FM is a commercial station owned by JA Ventures, Inc. The format of the station is Hispanic. KGEN-FM broadcasts in the Tulare, CA area.
FM RADIO STATION

KGEO-AM
37286

Owner: American General Media
Editorial: 1400 Easton Dr Ste 144B, Bakersfield, California 93309-9412 **Tel:** 1 661 328-1410.
Profile: KGEO-AM is a commercial station owned by American General Media. The format of the station is news/talk. KGEO-AM broadcasts to the Bakersfield, CA area at 1230 AM.
AM RADIO STATION

KGFF-AM
34956

Owner: Citizen Band Potawatomi Tribe of OK Inc
Editorial: 1570 Gordon Cooper Dr, Shawnee, Oklahoma 74801-9000 **Tel:** 1 405 273-4390.
Email: 1450kgff@gmail.com
Web site: http://www.kgff.com
Profile: KGFF-AM is a commercial station owned by Citizen Band Potawatomi Tribe of OK Inc. The format of the station is oldies. KGFF-AM broadcasts to the Oklahoma City area at 1450 AM.
AM RADIO STATION

KGFJ-FM
43894

Owner: CSN International
Editorial: 4002 N 3300 E, Twin Falls, Idaho 83301-0354 **Tel:** 1 208 734-2049.
Email: feedback@csnradio.com
Web site: http://www.csnradio, com
Profile: KGFJ-FM is a non-commercial station owned by Calvary Chapel of Twin Falls, Inc. The format of the station is religious teaching. KGFJ-FM broadcasts to the Belt, MT area at a frequency of 88.1 FM.
FM RADIO STATION

KGFK-AM
38949

Owner: Leighton Enterprises Inc.
Editorial: 1185 9th St NE, Thompson, North Dakota 58278-9343 **Tel:** 1 701 746-5266.
Web site: http://www.957theforks.com

Profile: KGFK-AM is a commercial station owned by Leighton Enterprises Inc. The format of the station is adult contemporary. KGFK-AM broadcasts to the Thompson, ND area at 1590 AM.
AM RADIO STATION

KGFL-AM
37287

Owner: King-Sullivan Radio
Editorial: 360 Main St, Clinton, Arkansas 72031
Tel: 1 501 745-4474.
Email: kgflkhpq@artelco.com
Web site: http://www.kgflam.com
Profile: KGFL-AM is a commercial station owned by King-Sullivan Radio. The format of the station is oldies. KGFL-AM broadcasts to the Clinton, AR area at 1110 AM.
AM RADIO STATION

KGFM-FM
44668

Owner: American General Media
Editorial: 1400 Easton Dr Ste 144B, Bakersfield, California 93309-9412 **Tel:** 1 661 328-1410.
Email: listeners@kgfm.com
Web site: http://www.kgfm.com
Profile: KGFM-FM is a commercial station owned by American General Media. The format of the station is Lite Rock/Lite AC. KGFM-FM broadcasts to the Bakersfield, CA area at 101.5 FM.
FM RADIO STATION

KGFN-FM
793608

Owner: Radio Goldfield Broadcasting, Inc.
Tel: 1 775 485-9923.
Email: radiogoldfield@hotmail.com
Web site: http://www.kgfn.org
Profile: KGFN-FM is a non-commercial station owned by Radio Goldfield Broadcasting, Inc. The format of the station is country. KGFN-FM broadcasts to the Goldfield, NV area in Esmeralda County at a frequency of 89.1 FM.
FM RADIO STATION

KGFT-FM
42599

Owner: Salem Media Group, Inc.
Editorial: 7150 Campus Dr Ste 150, Colorado Springs, Colorado 80920-3157 **Tel:** 1 719 531-5438.
Email: mgoodyear@kbiqradio.com
Web site: http://www.kgftradio.com
Profile: KGFT-FM is a commercial station owned by Salem Media Group, Inc. The format of the station is Christian programming. KGFT-FM broadcasts to the Colorado Springs, CO area at 100.7 FM.
FM RADIO STATION

KGFW-AM
37288

Owner: NRG Media LLC
Editorial: 2223 Central Ave, Kearney, Nebraska 68847-5346 **Tel:** 1 308 698-2100.
Web site: http://www.kgfw.com
Profile: KGFW-AM is a commercial station owned by NRG Media LLC. The format of the station is news, sports and talk. KGFW-AM broadcasts to the Kearney, NE area at 1340 AM.
AM RADIO STATION

KGFX-AM
38496

Owner: James River Broadcasting
Editorial: 214 W Pleasant Dr, Pierre, South Dakota 57501 **Tel:** 1 605 224-8686.
Web site: http://www.dakotaradiogroup.com
Profile: KGFX-AM is a commercial station owned by James River Broadcasting. The format of the station is news, talk and country. KGFX-AM broadcasts to the Pierre, SD area at 1060 AM.
AM RADIO STATION

KGFX-FM
45871

Owner: James River Broadcasting
Editorial: 214 W Pleasant Dr, Pierre, South Dakota 57501 **Tel:** 1 605 224-8686.
Web site: http://www.dakotaradiogroup.com/
Profile: KGFX-FM is a commercial station owned by James River Broadcasting. The format of the station is hot adult contemporary. KGFX-FM broadcasts to the Pierre, SD area at 92.7 FM.
FM RADIO STATION

KGFY-FM
40008

Owner: Mahaffey Enterprises Inc.
Editorial: 408 E Thomas Ave, Stillwater, Oklahoma 74075-2648 **Tel:** 1 405 372-7800.
Email: stillwaterradio@coxinet.net
Web site: http://www.stillwaterradio.net
Profile: KGFY-FM is a commercial station owned by Mahaffey Enterprises Inc. The format of the station is country music. KGFY-FM broadcasts to Oklahoma City at 105.5 FM.
FM RADIO STATION

KGGF-AM
37289

Owner: SEK Media, Inc
Editorial: 306 W 8th St, Coffeyville, Kansas 67337-5829 **Tel:** 1 620 251-3800.
Email: news@kggfradio.com
Web site: http://kggfradio.com/
Profile: KGGF-AM is a commercial station owned by SEK Media, Inc. The format of the station is news and talk. KGGF-AM broadcasts to the Tulsa, OK area at 690 AM.
AM RADIO STATION

KGGF-FM
43358

Owner: SEK Media, Inc
Editorial: 306 W 8th St, Coffeyville, Kansas 67337-5829 **Tel:** 1 620 251-3800.
Email: news@kggfradio.com
Web site: http://kggfradio.com/

Profile: KGGF-FM is a commercial station owned by SEK Media, Inc. The format of the station is classic hits. KGGF-FM broadcasts to the Tulsa, OK area at 104.1 FM.
FM RADIO STATION

KGGI-FM
46446

Owner: iHeartMedia Inc.
Editorial: 2030 Iowa Ave #100, Riverside, California 92507-7415 **Tel:** 1 951 684-1991.
Web site: http://991kggi.iheart.com
Profile: KGGI-FM is a commercial station owned by iHeartMedia Inc. The format of the station is Top 40/CHR. KGGI-FM broadcasts to the Riverside, CA area at 99.1 FM.
FM RADIO STATION

KGGL-FM
44627

Owner: Cherry Creek Radio
Editorial: 1600 North Ave W Ste 101, Missoula, Montana 59801-5500 **Tel:** 1 406 721-9300.
Web site: http://www.eagle93.com
Profile: KGGL-FM is a commercial station owned by Cherry Creek Radio. The format of the station is contemporary country music. KGGL-FM broadcasts to the Missoula, MT area at 93.3 FM.
FM RADIO STATION

KGGM-FM
44369

Owner: Diebel(Kenneth W.)
Editorial: 1204 Highway 80, Delhi, Louisiana 71232-7502 **Tel:** 1 318 878-8255.
Web site: http://www.kggmfm.com
Profile: KGGM-FM is a commercial station owned by Kenneth W. Diebel. The format of the station is southern gospel music. KGGM-FM broadcasts to the Delhi, LA area at 93.5 FM.
FM RADIO STATION

KGGO-FM
42298

Owner: Cumulus Media Inc
Editorial: 4143 109th St, Urbandale, Iowa 50322-7925 **Tel:** 1 515 331-9200.
Web site: http://www.kggo.com
Profile: KGGO-FM is a commercial station owned by Cumulus Media Inc. The format of the station is classic rock music. KGGO-FM broadcasts to the Des Moines, IA area at 94.5 FM.
FM RADIO STATION

KGGR-AM
36048

Owner: Mortenson Broadcasting Co.
Editorial: 5787 S Hampton Rd, Ste 285, Dallas, Texas 75232 **Tel:** 1 972 572-5447.
Web site: http://www.kggram.com
Profile: KGGR-AM is a commercial station owned by the Mortenson Broadcasting Co. The format of the station is gospel music and religious programming. KGGR-AM broadcasts to the Dallas area at 1040 AM.
AM RADIO STATION

KGGS-AM
851028

Owner: Steckline Communications
Editorial: 609 E Kansas Plz, Garden City, Kansas 67846-5767 **Tel:** 1 620 276-3251.
Web site: http://www.kiulradio.com
Profile: KGGS-AM is a commercial station owned by Steckline Communications. The format of the station is sports. The station airs locally in the Garden City, KS area at 1340 AM.
AM RADIO STATION

KGHE-FM
758935

Owner: Grays Harbor Institute
Editorial: 717 Lincoln St, Hoquiam, Washington 98550-1457 **Tel:** 1 360 580-4001.
Web site: http://www.ghinstitute.org
Profile: KGHE-FM is a non-commercial community radio station owned by Grays Harbor Institute. The format of the station is variety. KGHE-FM broadcasts to the Elma, WA area at a frequency of 89.1 FM.
FM RADIO STATION

KGHL-AM
37290

Owner: BMG Billings
Editorial: 222 N 32nd St Fl 10, Billings, Montana 59101-1973 **Tel:** 1 406 238-1000.
Web site: http://www.mighty790.com
Profile: KGHL-AM is a commercial station owned by BMG Billings. The format for the station is classic country. KGHL-AM broadcasts to the Billings, MT area at 790 AM.
AM RADIO STATION

KGHM-AM
37608

Owner: iHeartMedia Inc.
Editorial: 1900 NW Expressway, Oklahoma City, Oklahoma 73118-1802 **Tel:** 1 405 840-5271.
Web site: http://www.1340thegame.com/main.html
Profile: KGHM-AM is a commercial station owned by iHeartMedia Inc. The format of the station is sports talk. KGHM-AM broadcasts to the Oklahoma City area at 1340.
AM RADIO STATION

KGHR-FM
43872

Owner: TCHSB Inc.
Editorial: 160 Warrior Drive, Tuba City, Arizona 86045-0160 **Tel:** 1 928 283-6271.
Email: kghrpublic@ymail.com
Web site: http://www.kghr.net
Profile: KGHR-FM is a commercial station owned by TCHSB Inc. The format of the station is variety. KGHR-FM broadcasts to the Tuba City, AZ area at 91.3 FM.
FM RADIO STATION

KGHS-AM
37292

Owner: Red Rock Radio Corp.
Editorial: 519 3rd St, International Falls, Minnesota 56649-2317 **Tel:** 1 218 283-3481.
Email: production@ksdmradio.com
Web site: http://www.ksdmradio.com
Profile: KGHS-AM is a commercial station owned by Red Rock Radio Corp. The format of the station is oldies music. KGHS-FM broadcasts to the International Falls, MN area at 1230 AM.
AM RADIO STATION

KGHY-FM
593204

Owner: CCS Radio, Inc.
Editorial: 12021 Palmbeach St, Houston, Texas 77034-3814 **Tel:** 1 409 299-3339.
Email: dj@thegospelhiway.org
Web site: http://www.thegospelhiway.org
Profile: KGHY-FM is a commercial station owned by CCS Radio, Inc. The format of the station is gospel music. KGHY-FM airs locally on 88.5 FM.
FM RADIO STATION

KGIM-AM
39443

Owner: Armada Media Corp.
Editorial: 13541 386th Ave, Aberdeen, South Dakota 57401 **Tel:** 1 605 229-3632.
Email: aberdeenproduction@hubcityradio.com
Web site: http://www.hubcityradio.com
Profile: KGIM-AM is a commercial station owned by Armada Media Corp. The format of the station is sports. KGIM-AM broadcasts to the Aberdeen, SD area at 1420 AM.
AM RADIO STATION

KGIM-FM
46115

Owner: Armada Media Corp.
Editorial: 3304 S Highway 281, Aberdeen, South Dakota 57401-8792 **Tel:** 1 605 229-3632.
Email: aberdeenproduction@hubcityradio.com
Web site: http://www.hubcityradio.com
Profile: KGIM-FM is a commercial station owned by Armada Media Corp. The format of the station is contemporary country. KGIM-FM broadcasts to the Aberdeen, SD area at 103.7 FM.
FM RADIO STATION

KGIR-AM
38417

Owner: Mississippi River Radio
Editorial: 324 Broadway St, Cape Girardeau, Missouri 63701-7331 **Tel:** 1 573 335-8291.
Web site: http://www.kgir.com
Profile: KGIR-AM is a commercial station owned by Mississippi River Radio. The format of the station is sports. KGIR-AM broadcasts to the Cape Girardeau, MO area at 1220 AM.
AM RADIO STATION

KGIW-AM
37293

Owner: Community Broadcasting Co.
Editorial: 292 Santa Fe Ave, Alamosa, Colorado 81101-2810 **Tel:** 1 719 589-6644.
Web site: http://www.kgiw1450.com/
Profile: KGIW-AM is a commercial station owned by Community Broadcasting Co. The format of the station is adult contemporary. KGIW-AM broadcasts to the Alamosa, CO area at 1450 AM.
AM RADIO STATION

KGKL-AM
37294

Owner: Townsquare Media
Editorial: 1301 S Abe St, San Angelo, Texas 76903-7245 **Tel:** 1 325 655-7161.
Web site: http://960kgkl.com
Profile: KGKL-AM is a commercial station owned by Townsquare Media. The format of the station is news, sports and talk. KGKL-AM broadcasts to the San Angelo, TX area at 960 AM.
AM RADIO STATION

KGKL-FM
44670

Owner: Townsquare Media
Editorial: 1301 S Abe St, San Angelo, Texas 76903-7245 **Tel:** 1 325 655-7161.
Email: kgkl975@aol.com
Web site: http://www.975kgkl.com
Profile: KGKL-FM is a commercial station owned by Townsquare Media. The format of the station is contemporary country. KGKL-FM broadcasts to the San Angelo, TX area at 97.5 FM.
FM RADIO STATION

KGKS-FM
44165

Owner: Max Media
Editorial: 324 Broadway St, Cape Girardeau, Missouri 63701-7331 **Tel:** 1 573 335-8291.
Email: realrock@riverradio.net
Web site: http://www.kgks.com
Profile: KGKS-FM is a commercial station owned by Max Media. The format of the station is classic hits. KGKS-FM broadcasts to the Cape Girardeau, MO area at 93.9 FM.
FM RADIO STATION

KGLB-AM
37458

Owner: Iowa City Broadcasting Co.
Editorial: 911 Hennepin Ave N, Glencoe, Minnesota 55336-2931 **Tel:** 1 320 269-8815.
Profile: KGLB-AM is a commercial station owned by Iowa City Broadcasting Co. The format of the station is classic country. KGLB-AM broadcasts to the Minneapolis area at 1310 AM.
AM RADIO STATION

KGLC-FM
45893
Owner: Northeast Oklahoma Broadcasting Network
Editorial: 1 N Main St, Miami, Oklahoma 74354-6322
Tel: 1 918 542-1818.
Email: kglc-kvis@okradiostation.com
Profile: KGLC-FM is a commercial station owned by Northeast Oklahoma Broadcasting Network. The format for the station is adult contemporary. KGLC-FM broadcasts to the Miami, OK area at 100.9 FM.
FM RADIO STATION

KGLD-AM
39148
Owner: Salt of the Earth Broadcasting
Editorial: 2737 S Broadway Ave, Ste 101, Tyler, Texas 75701 **Tel:** 1 903 526-1330.
Email: kgldradio@yahoo.com
Web site: http://www.kgld.org
Profile: KGLD-AM is a commercial station owned by Salt of the Earth Broadcasting. The format of the station is gospel. KGLD-AM broadcasts to the Tyler, TX area at 1330 AM.
AM RADIO STATION

KGLE-AM
34959
Owner: Friends of Christian Radio Inc.
Editorial: 86 Seven Mile Dr, Glendive, Montana 59330-9406 **Tel:** 1 406 377-3331.
Email: kgle@midrivers.com
Web site: http://www.kgle.org
Profile: KGLE-AM is a commercial station owned by Friends of Christian Radio Inc. The format of the station is religious. KGLE-AM broadcasts to the Glendive, MT area at 590 AM.
AM RADIO STATION

KGLI-FM
46175
Owner: iHeartMedia Inc.
Editorial: 1113 Nebraska St, Sioux City, Iowa 51105-1438 **Tel:** 1 712 258-5595.
Web site: http://kg95.iheart.com
Profile: KGLI-FM is a commercial station owned by iHeartMedia Inc. The format of the station is hot adult contemporary music. KGLI-FM broadcasts to the Sioux City, IA area at 95.5 FM.
FM RADIO STATION

KGLK-FM
39713
Owner: Cox Media Group, Inc.
Editorial: 1990 Post Oak Blvd Ste 2300, Houston, Texas 77056-3847 **Tel:** 1 713 963-1200.
Web site: http://www.houstonseagle.com
Profile: KGLK-FM is a commercial station owned by Cox Media Group, Inc. The format of the station is classic hits. KGLK-FM broadcasts to the Houston area at 107.5 FM.
FM RADIO STATION

KGLM-FM
46668
Owner: Butte Broadcasting Inc.
Editorial: 105 Main St, Anaconda, Montana 59711-2251 **Tel:** 1 406 563-8011.
Email: mail@kbowkopr.com
Profile: KGLM-FM is a commercial station owned by Butte Broadcasting Inc. The format of the station is hot adult contemporary music. The station is aired in Anaconda, MT on 97.7 FM.
FM RADIO STATION

KGLN-AM
38376
Owner: MBC Grand Broadcasting Inc.
Editorial: 1360 E Sherwood Dr, Grand Junction, Colorado 81501-7546 **Tel:** 1 970 254-2100.
Profile: KGLN-AM is a commercial station owned by MBC Grand Broadcasting Inc. The format of the station is news and talk. KGLN-AM broadcasts to the Glenwood Springs, CO area at 980 AM.
AM RADIO STATION

KGLO-AM
39184
Owner: Alpha Media
Editorial: 341 S Yorktown Pike, Mason City, Iowa 50401-4533 **Tel:** 1 641 423-1300.
Web site: http://www.kglonews.com/
AM RADIO STATION

KGLP-FM
43873
Owner: Gallup Public Radio, Inc.
Editorial: 705 Gurley Ave, Gallup, New Mexico 87301-6979 **Tel:** 1 505 863-7626.
Email: kglpradio@kglp.org
Web site: http://www.kglp.org
Profile: KGLP-FM is a non-commercial station owned by Gallup Public Radio, Inc. The format for the station is variety. KGLP-FM broadcasts to the Albuquerque, NM area at 91.7 FM.
FM RADIO STATION

KGLX-FM
41229
Owner: iHeartMedia Inc.
Editorial: 1632 S Second St, Gallup, New Mexico 87301-5836 **Tel:** 1 505 863-9391.
Web site: http://991kglx.com
Profile: KGLX-FM is a commercial station owned by iHeart Media Inc. The format of the station is contemporary country. KGLX-FM broadcasts to the Gallup, NM area at 99.1 FM.
FM RADIO STATION

KGME-AM
70359
Owner: iHeartMedia Inc.
Editorial: 4686 E Van Buren St Ste 300, Phoenix, Arizona 85008-6967 **Tel:** 1 602 374-6000.
Web site: http://foxsports910.iheart.com
Profile: KGME-AM is a commercial station owned by iHeartMedia Inc. The format of the station is sports. KGME-AM broadcasts to the Phoenix area at 910 AM.
AM RADIO STATION

KGMI-AM
39014
Owner: Saga Communications
Editorial: 2219 Yew Street Rd, Bellingham, Washington 98229 **Tel:** 1 360 734-9790.
Email: kgmi@kgmi.com
Web site: http://www.kgmi.com
Profile: KGMI-AM is a commercial station owned by Saga Communications. The format of the station is news and talk. KGMI-AM broadcasts to the Bellingham, WA area at 790 AM.
AM RADIO STATION

KGMN-FM
39658
Owner: New West Broadcasting
Editorial: 812 E Beale St, Kingman, Arizona 86401-5925 **Tel:** 1 928 753-9100.
Web site: http://www.kgmn.net
Profile: KGMN-FM is a commercial station owned by New West Broadcasting. The format of the station is contemporary country music. KGMN-FM broadcasts in the Phoenix area at 101.1 FM.
FM RADIO STATION

KGMO-FM
44671
Owner: Withers Broadcasting of Missouri, LLC
Editorial: 901 S Kingshighway St, Cape Girardeau, Missouri 63703-8003 **Tel:** 1 573 339-7000.
Email: news@withersradio.net
Web site: http://www.kgmo.com
Profile: KGMO-FM is a commercial station owned by Withers Broadcasting of Missouri LLC. The format of the station is classic rock. KGMO-FM broadcasts to the Cape Girardeau, MO area at 100.7 FM.
FM RADIO STATION

KGMS-AM
235174
Owner: Good News Radio Broadcasting Inc.
Editorial: 3222 S Richey Ave, Tucson, Arizona 85713
Tel: 1 520 790-2440.
Email: info@kvoi.com
Web site: http://www.kgms.com
Profile: KGMS-AM is a commercial station owned by Good News Radio Broadcasting Inc. The format of the station is religious programming. KGMS-AM broadcasts to the Tucson, AZ area at 940 AM.
AM RADIO STATION

KGMT-AM
38845
Owner: Siebert Communications Inc.
Editorial: 414 4th St, Fairbury, Nebraska 68352
Tel: 1 402 729-3382.
Profile: KGMT-AM is a commercial station owned by Siebert Communications Inc. The format of the station is oldies. KGMT-AM broadcasts to the Fairbury, NE area at 1310 AM.
AM RADIO STATION

KGMX-FM
43048
Owner: High Desert Broadcasting LLC
Editorial: 570 E Avenue Q9, Palmdale, California 93550-4655 **Tel:** 1 661 947-3107.
Email: psa@highdesertbroadcasting.com
Web site: http://www.kmix1063.com
Profile: KGMX-FM-FM is a commercial station owned by High Desert Broadcasting LLC. The format of the station is adult contemporary. KGMX-FM broadcasts to the Antelope Valley area at 106.3 FM.
FM RADIO STATION

KGMY-AM
38597
Owner: iHeartMedia Inc.
Editorial: 1856 S Glenstone Ave, Springfield, Missouri 65804-2303 **Tel:** 1 417 890-5555.
Web site: http://www.1400foxsports.com/main.html
Profile: KGMY-AM is a commercial station owned by iHeartMedia Inc. The format of the station is sports. KGMY-AM broadcasts in the Springfield, MO area at 1400 AM.
AM RADIO STATION

KGMZ-FM
43364
Owner: Entercom Communications Corp.
Editorial: 201 3rd St Ste 1200, San Francisco, California 94103-3143 **Tel:** 1 415 957-0957.
Web site: http://www.957thegame.com
Profile: KGMZ-FM is a commercial station owned by Entercom Communications Corp. The format of the station is sports. KGMZ-FM broadcasts to the San Francisco area at 95.7 FM.
FM RADIO STATION

KGNB-AM
37295
Owner: New Braunfels Communications Inc
Editorial: 1540 Loop 337, New Braunfels, Texas 78130-3352 **Tel:** 1 830 625-7311.
Email: newsdesk@kgnb.am
Web site: http://radionb.com
Profile: KGNB-AM is a commercial station owned by New Braunfels Communications Inc. The format of the station is classic country and talk. KGNB-AM broadcasts to the New Braunfels, TX area at 1420 AM.
AM RADIO STATION

KGNC-AM
37296
Owner: Morris Communications
Editorial: 3505 Olsen Blvd, Ste 117, Amarillo, Texas 79109 **Tel:** 1 806 355-9801.
Email: kgnc@kgnc.com
Web site: http://www.kgncam.com
Profile: KGNC-AM is a commercial station owned by Morris Communications. The format for the station is news and talk. KGNC-AM broadcasts to the Amarillo, TX area at 710 AM.
AM RADIO STATION

KGNC-FM
44672
Owner: Morris Communications
Editorial: 3505 Olsen Blvd, Ste 117, Amarillo, Texas 79109 **Tel:** 1 806 355-9801.
Email: kgnc@kgnc.com
Web site: http://www.kgncfm.com
Profile: KGNC-FM is a commercial station owned by Morris Communications. The format of the station is country music. KGNC-FM broadcasts to Amarillo, TX at 97.9 FM.
FM RADIO STATION

KGNN-FM
39434
Owner: Missouri River Christian Broadcasting
Tel: 1 636 239-0400.
Email: info@goodnewsvoice.org
Web site: http://www.goodnewsvoice.org
Profile: KGNN-FM is a non-commercial station owned by Missouri River Christian Broadcasting. The format of the station is religious programming. KGNN-FM broadcasts to the Washington, MO area at 90.3 FM.
FM RADIO STATION

KGNO-AM
37298
Owner: Rocking M Radio
Editorial: 2601 Central Ave Ste C, Dodge City, Kansas 67801-6212 **Tel:** 1 620 225-8080.
Email: rockingmproduction@gmail.com
Web site: http://mykansasradio.com
Profile: KGNO-AM is a commercial station owned by Rocking M Radio. The format of the station is classic country and talk. KGNO-AM broadcasts to the Dodge City, KS area at 1370 AM.
AM RADIO STATION

KGNR-FM
43874
Owner: Life Broadcasting Inc.
Editorial: 166 SE Dayton St, John Day, Oregon 97845
Tel: 1 541 575-1840.
Email: contact@kgnr.org
Web site: http://www.kgnr.org
FM RADIO STATION

KGNT-FM
75954
Owner: Frandsen Media Company, LLC
Editorial: 810 W 200 N, Logan, Utah 84321-3726
Tel: 1 435 752-1390.
Web site: http://www.kool.fm
Profile: KGNT-FM is a commercial station owned by Frandsen Media Company, LLC. The format of the station is oldies. KGNT-FM broadcasts to the Salt Lake City area at 99.1 FM.
FM RADIO STATION

KGNU-AM
35973
Owner: Boulder Community Broadcast Association, Inc.
Editorial: 4700 Walnut St, Boulder, Colorado 80301-2538 **Tel:** 1 303 449-4885.
Email: news@kgnu.org
Web site: http://www.kgnu.org
Profile: KGNU-AM is a non-commercial station owned by Boulder Community Broadcast Association, Inc. The format of the station is variety. KGNU-AM broadcasts to the Denver area at 1390 AM. Use the station's news department email address for contact information for author requests. Please submit PSAs through the website.
AM RADIO STATION

KGNU-FM
41219
Owner: Boulder Community Broadcast Association, Inc.
Editorial: 4700 Walnut St, Boulder, Colorado 80301-2538 **Tel:** 1 303 449-4885.
Email: news@kgnu.org
Web site: http://www.kgnu.org
Profile: KGNU-FM is a non-commercial station owned by Boulder Community Broadcast Association, Inc. The format of the station is variety. KGNU-FM broadcasts to the Boulder, CO area at 88.5 FM. Use the station's news department email address for contact information for author requests. Please submit PSAs through the website.
FM RADIO STATION

KGNV-FM
46818
Owner: Missouri River Christian Broadcasting
Tel: 1 636 239-0400.
Web site: http://www.goodnewsvoice.org
Profile: KGNV-FM is a non-commercial station owned by Missouri River Christian Broadcasting. The format of the station is religious programming. KGNV-FM broadcasts to the Washington, MO area at 89.9 FM.
FM RADIO STATION

KGNW-AM
35349
Owner: Salem Media Group, Inc.
Editorial: 2201 6th Ave Ste 1500, Seattle, Washington 98121-1840 **Tel:** 1 206 443-8200.
Email: webmaster@kgnw.com
Web site: http://thewordseattle.com
Profile: KGNW-AM is a commercial station owned by Salem Media Group, Inc. The format of the station is religious music and Christian conservative talk. KGNW-AM broadcasts to the Seattle area at 820 AM.
AM RADIO STATION

KGNZ-FM
41418
Owner: Christian Broadcasting Co.
Editorial: 542 Butternut St, Abilene, Texas 79602
Tel: 1 325 673-3045.
Email: studio@kgnz.com
Web site: http://www.kgnz.com
Profile: KGNZ-FM is a non-commercial station owned by the Christian Broadcasting Co. The format of the station is contemporary Christian music and talk. KGNZ-FM broadcasts in the Abilene, TX area at 88.1 FM.
FM RADIO STATION

KGO-AM
34961
Owner: Cumulus Media Inc
Editorial: 750 Battery St Fl 2, San Francisco, California 94111-1524 **Tel:** 1 415 216-1300.
Email: producers@kgoradio.com
Web site: http://www.kgoradio.com
Profile: KGO-AM is a commercial station owned by Cumulus Media Inc. The format of the station is talk. The station does news briefs at the top and bottom of the hour throughout the weekday. KGO-AM broadcasts to the San Francisco area at 810 AM.
AM RADIO STATION

KGOE-AM
37460
Owner: Bicoastal Media LLC
Editorial: 5640 S Broadway St, Eureka, California 95503-6905 **Tel:** 1 707 442-2000.
Email: eurekanews@bicoastalmedia.com
Web site: http://www.kgoe1480.com
Profile: KGOE-AM is a commercial station owned by Bicoastal Media LLC. The format for the station is news, talk and sports. KGOE-AM broadcasts to the Eureka, CA area at 1480 AM.
AM RADIO STATION

KGOL-AM
35915
Owner: Entravision Communications Corp.
Editorial: 5353 W Alabama St Ste 450, Houston, Texas 77056-5922 **Tel:** 1 713 349-9880.
Web site: http://espndeporteshouston.com
Profile: KGOL-AM is a commercial station owned by Entravision Communications Corp. The format of the station is Hispanic sports. KGOL-AM broadcasts to the Houston area at 1180 AM.
AM RADIO STATION

KGON-FM
42706
Owner: Entercom Communications Corp.
Editorial: 0700 SW Bancroft St, Portland, Oregon 97239-4226 **Tel:** 1 503 223-1441.
Web site: http://www.kgon.com
Profile: KGON-FM is a commercial station owned by Entercom Communications Corp. The format of the station is classic rock music. KGON-FM broadcasts to the Portland, OR area at 92.3 FM.
FM RADIO STATION

KGOR-FM
44673
Owner: iHeartMedia Inc.
Editorial: 5010 Underwood Ave, Omaha, Nebraska 68132-2236 **Tel:** 1 402 561-2000.
Web site: http://www.kgor.com
Profile: KGOR-FM is a commercial station owned by iHeartMedia Inc. The format of the station is oldies. KGOR-FM broadcasts to the Omaha, NE area at 99.9 FM.
FM RADIO STATION

KGOS-AM
37299
Owner: Kath Broadcasting, LLC
Editorial: 7060 Radio Rd, Torrington, Wyoming 82240-8467 **Tel:** 1 307 532-2158.
Email: news@kgoskerm.com
Web site: http://kgoskerm.com
Profile: KGOS-AM is a commercial station owned by Kath Broadcasting, LLC. The format of the station is country. KGOS-AM broadcasts to the Torrington, WY area at 1490 AM.
AM RADIO STATION

KGOT-FM
44674
Owner: iHeartMedia Inc.
Editorial: 800 E Dimond Blvd Ste 3-370, Anchorage, Alaska 99515-2058 **Tel:** 1 907 522-1515.
Web site: http://kgot.iheart.com/
Profile: KGOT-FM is a commercial station owned by iHeartMedia Inc. The format of the station is Top 40/CHR. KGOT-FM broadcasts to the Anchorage, AK area at 101.3 FM.
FM RADIO STATION

KGOW-AM
36843
Owner: Gow Communications, LLC
Editorial: 5353 W Alabama St Ste 415, Houston, Texas 77056-5942 **Tel:** 1 713 479-5300.
Web site: http://www.ysr1560.com
Profile: KGOW-AM is a commercial station owned by Gow Communications, LLC. The format of the station is sports. KGOW-AM broadcasts to the Houston area at 1560 AM, and is the flagship station for Sporting News Radio Network.
AM RADIO STATION

KGOZ-FM
42622
Owner: Par Broadcast Group
Editorial: 804 Main St, Trenton, Missouri 64683-2044
Tel: 1 660 359-2727.
Email: news@kttn.com
Web site: http://www.kgozfm.com
Profile: KGOZ-FM is a commercial station owned by Par Broadcast Group. The format of the station is contemporary country. KGOZ-FM broadcasts to the Trenton, MO area at 101.7 FM.
FM RADIO STATION

KGPQ-FM 43338
Owner: Pines Broadcasting
Editorial: 279 Midway Rte, Monticello, Arkansas 71655-8605 **Tel:** 1 870 367-6854.
Email: pines.radio@sbcglobal.net
Profile: KGPQ-FM is a commercial station owned by Pines Broadcasting. The format of the station is adult contemporary. KGPQ-FM broadcasts to the Monticello, AR area at 99.9 FM.
FM RADIO STATION

KGPZ-FM 43864
Owner: Latto Northland and Broadcasting, Inc.
Editorial: 504 NW 1st Ave Ste 290, Grand Rapids, Minnesota 55744-2668 **Tel:** 1 218 326-7427.
Email: kgpz@paulbunyan.net
Web site: http://www.kgpzfm.com
Profile: KGPZ-FM is a commercial station owned by Latto Northland and Broadcasting, Inc. The format of the station is country music. KGPZ-FM broadcasts to the Grand Rapids, MN area at 96.1 FM.
FM RADIO STATION

KGRA-FM 41084
Owner: M&M Broadcasting, Inc.
Editorial: 1610 N Lincoln Street, Knoxville, Iowa 50138 **Tel:** 1 641 842-3161.
Web site: http://raccoonvalleyradio.com/kg98-98-9-fm-kgra/
Profile: KGRA-FM is a commercial station owned by M&M Broadcasting, Inc. The format of the station is country music. KGRA-FM broadcasts to the Jefferson, IA area at 98.9 FM.
FM RADIO STATION

KGRB-FM 43695
Owner: Lazer Broadcasting
Editorial: 500 Media Pl, Sacramento, California 95815-3733 **Tel:** 1 916 216-3712.
Profile: KGRB-FM is a commercial station owned by Adelante Media Group. The format of the station is regional Mexican. KGRB-FM broadcasts to the Sacramento, CA area at 94.3 FM.
FM RADIO STATION

KGRC-FM 39660
Owner: Staradio Corp.
Editorial: 329 Maine St, Quincy, Illinois 62301
Tel: 1 217 224-4102.
Email: real929@staradio.com
Web site: http://www.real929.com
Profile: KGRC-FM is a commercial station owned by Starradio Corp. The format of the station is Lite Rock/Lite AC. KGRC-FM broadcasts to the Quincy, IL area at 92.9 FM.
FM RADIO STATION

KGRD-FM 41601
Owner: Praise Network(The)
Editorial: 128 S 4th St, Oneill, Nebraska 68763
Tel: 1 402 336-3886.
Web site: http://www.goodnewsgreatmusic.org
Profile: KGRD-FM is a non-commercial station owned by The Praise Network. The format of the station is Contemporary Christian. KGRD-FM broadcasts to the Oneill, NE area at 105.3 FM.
FM RADIO STATION

KGRE-AM 35916
Owner: NRC Broadcasting
Editorial: 800 8th Ave Ste 304, Greeley, Colorado 80631-1190 **Tel:** 1 970 356-1452.
Email: kgre@msn.com
Web site: http://www.tigrecolorado.com
Profile: KGRE-AM is a commercial station owned by NRC Broadcasting. The format of the station is Hispanic. KGRE-AM broadcasts to the Greeley, CO area at 1450 AM.
AM RADIO STATION

KGRG-AM 36839
Owner: Green River Community College
Editorial: 12401 SE 320th St, Auburn, Washington 98092 **Tel:** 1 253 833-9111.
Email: programming@kgrg.com
Web site: http://www.kgrg1.com
Profile: KGRG-AM is a non-commercial station owned by Green River Community College. The format of the station is a mix of rock alternative and classic rock. KGRG-AM broadcasts to the Auburn, WA area at 1330 AM.
AM RADIO STATION

KGRG-FM 39661
Owner: Green River Community College
Editorial: 12401 SE 320th St, Auburn, Washington 98092 **Tel:** 1 253 833-9111.
Email: programming@kgrg.com
Web site: http://www.kgrg.com
Profile: KGRG-FM is a non-commercial station owned by Green River Community College. The format of the station is rock alternative. KGRG-FM broadcasts to the Auburn, WA area at 89.9 FM.
FM RADIO STATION

KGRN-AM 35979
Owner: Good Radio
Editorial: 909 1/2 Main St, Grinnell, Iowa 50112-2174
Tel: 1 641 236-6106.
Email: radioinfo@alphamediausa.com
Web site: http://www.myiowainfo.com
Profile: KGRN-AM is commercial station owned by Good Radio. The format of the station is adult contemporary. KGRN-AM broadcasts to the Grinnell, IA area at 1410 AM.
AM RADIO STATION

KGRO-AM 37301
Owner: Hughes(Jim)
Editorial: 1701 1/2 N Banks St, Pampa, Texas 79065
Tel: 1 806 669-6809.
Email: production@kgrokomxradio.com
Web site: http://www.kgrokomxradio.com
Profile: KGRO-AM is a commercial station owned by Jim Hughes. The format of the station is adult contemporary. KGRO-AM broadcasts to the Pampa, TX area at 1230 AM.
AM RADIO STATION

KGRR-FM 43865
Owner: Radio Dubuque Inc.
Editorial: 1055 University Ave, Dubuque, Iowa 52001-6154 **Tel:** 1 563 690-0800.
Web site: http://www.973therock.com
Profile: KGRR-FM is a commercial station owned by Radio Dubuque Inc. The format of the station is rock. KGRR-FM broadcasts to the Dubuque, IA area at 97.3 FM.
FM RADIO STATION

KGRS-FM 44675
Owner: Titan Broadcasting LLC
Editorial: 610 N 4th St Ste 310, Burlington, Iowa 52601-5059 **Tel:** 1 319 752-2701.
Email: production@titanburlington.com
Web site: http://www.thenewmix.com
Profile: KGRS-FM is a commercial station owned by Titan Broadcasting LLC. The format of the station is hot adult contemporary. KGRS-FM broadcasts to the Burlington, IA area at 107.3 FM.
FM RADIO STATION

KGRT-FM 44676
Owner: Adams Radio Group
Editorial: 1355 California Ave, Las Cruces, New Mexico 88001-4130 **Tel:** 1 575 525-9298.
Web site: http://kgrt.com/
Profile: KGRT-FM is a commercial station owned by Adams Radio Group. The format of the station is contemporary country. KGRT-FM broadcasts to the Las Cruces, NM area at 103.9 FM.
FM RADIO STATION

KGRV-AM 34962
Owner: Pacific Cascade Communications Corp.
Editorial: 196 SE Main St, Winston, Oregon 97496
Tel: 1 541 679-8185.
Email: info@kgrv700.net
Web site: http://www.kgrv700.net
AM RADIO STATION

KGRW-FM 43562
Owner: Tejas Broadcasting
Editorial: 2505 Lakeview Dr Ste 302B, Amarillo, Texas 79109-1527 **Tel:** 1 806 355-1044.
Profile: KGRW-FM is a commercial station owned by Tejas Broadcasting. The format of the station is Hispanic. KGRW-FM broadcasts to the Amarillo, TX area at 104.3 FM.
FM RADIO STATION

KGRZ-AM 37303
Owner: Cherry Creek Radio
Editorial: 1600 North Ave W Ste 101, Missoula, Montana 59801-5500 **Tel:** 1 406 728-1450.
Profile: KGRZ-AM is a commercial station owned by Cherry Creek Radio. The format of the station is sports. KGRZ-AM broadcasts to the Missoula, MT area at 1450 AM.
AM RADIO STATION

KGSL-FM 44558
Owner: Leighton Enterprises Inc.
Editorial: 752 Bluffview Cir, Winona, Minnesota 55987-2515 **Tel:** 1 507 452-4000.
Web site: http://www.winonaradio.com
Profile: KGSL-FM is a commercial station owned by Leighton Enterprises Inc. The format of the station is adult contemporary. KGSL-FM broadcasts to the Winona, MN area at 95.3 FM.
FM RADIO STATION

KGSO-AM 35072
Owner: Steckline Communications
Editorial: 1632 S Maize Rd, Wichita, Kansas 67209
Tel: 1 316 721-8484.
Web site: http://www.kgso.com
Profile: KGSO-AM is a commercial station owned by Steckline Communications. The format of the station is sports. KGSO-AM broadcasts to Wichita, KS, at 1410 AM.
AM RADIO STATION

KGSR-FM 41577
Owner: Emmis Communications Corp.
Editorial: 8309 N Interstate 35, Austin, Texas 78753-5720 **Tel:** 1 512 832-4000.
Email: community@kgsr.com
Web site: http://www.kgsr.com
Profile: KGSR-FM is a commercial station owned by Emmis Communications Corp. The format of the station is adult album alternative music. KGSR-FM broadcasts to the Austin, TX area at 93.3 FM.
FM RADIO STATION

KGST-AM 39346
Owner: Lotus Communications Corp.
Editorial: 1110 E Olive Ave, Fresno, California 93728-3535 **Tel:** 1 559 497-1100.
Email: production@lotusfresno.com
Web site: http://www.espn1600am.com
Profile: KGST-AM is a commercial station owned by Lotus Broadcasting Corp. The format of the station is Mexican Hispanic sports programming. KGST-AM broadcasts to the Fresno, CA area at 1600 AM.
AM RADIO STATION

KGSX-FM 42414
Owner: Univision Communications Inc.
Editorial: 12451 Network Blvd Ste 140, San Antonio, Texas 78249-3336 **Tel:** 1 210 610-4300.
Email: lakalle951@radio.univision.com
Web site: http://951sanantonio.univision.com
Profile: KGSX-FM is a commercial station owned by Univision Communications Inc. The format of the station is Hispanic contemporary hits. KGSX-FM broadcasts to the San Antonio area at 95.1 FM.
FM RADIO STATION

KGTK-AM 37147
Owner: KITZ Radio Inc.
Editorial: 1700 Se Mile Hill Dr Ste 243, Port Orchard, Washington 98366-3507 **Tel:** 1 360 876-1400.
Email: info@kitz1400.com
Web site: http://www.kitz1400.com
Profile: KGTK-AM is a commercial station owned by KITZ Radio Inc. The format of the station is business talk and sports. KGTK-AM broadcasts to the Bellevue, WA area at 920 AM.
AM RADIO STATION

KGTL-AM 37304
Owner: Peninsula Communications Inc.
Editorial: 66060 Diamond Ridge Rd, Homer, Alaska 99603-9229 **Tel:** 1 907 235-6000.
Email: kwavefm@xyz.net
Profile: KGTL-AM is a commercial station owned by Peninsula Communications Inc. The format of the station is adult standards and talk. KGTL-AM broadcasts to the Homer, AK area at 620 AM.
AM RADIO STATION

KGTM-FM 87466
Owner: Rich Broadcasting
Editorial: 1406 Commerce Way, Idaho Falls, Idaho 83401-1233 **Tel:** 1 208 524-5900.
Web site: http://www.ezrockradio.com
Profile: KGTM-FM is a commercial station owned by Rich Broadcasting. The format of the station is adult contemporary. KGTM-FM broadcasts to the Idaho Falls, ID area at 98.1 FM.
FM RADIO STATION

KGTO-AM 37305
Owner: Perry Publishing & Broadcasting Inc.
Editorial: 7030 S Yale Ave Ste 302, Tulsa, Oklahoma 74136-5722 **Tel:** 1 918 494-9886.
Web site: http://thetouch1050.com
Profile: KGTO-AM is a commercial station owned by Perry Publishing & Broadcasting Inc. The format of the station is R&B oldies. KGTO-AM broadcasts to the Tulsa, OK area at 1050 AM.
AM RADIO STATION

KGTW-FM 45799
Owner: Alaska Broadcast Communications Inc.
Editorial: 526 Stedman St, Ketchikan, Alaska 99901-6629 **Tel:** 1 907 225-2193.
Web site: http://ketchikanradio.com
Profile: KGTW-FM is a commercial station owned by Alaska Broadcast Communications Inc. The format of the station is contemporary country. KGTW-FM broadcasts to the Ketchikan, AK area at 106.7 FM.
FM RADIO STATION

KGUA-FM 818453
Owner: Native Media Resource Center
Editorial: 35501 S Highway 1 Unit 50, Gualala, California 95445-9548 **Tel:** 1 707 884-4883.
Web site: http://nativemediaresourcecenter.org
Profile: KGUA-FM is a non-commercial community station owned by Native Media Resource Center. The format of the station is variety with a focus on Native American news/information and issues in Mendocino County and the Northern tip of Sonoma County. KGUA-FM broadcasts to the Gualala, CA area at 88.3 FM.
FM RADIO STATION

KGU-AM 36336
Owner: Salem Media Group, Inc.
Editorial: 1160 N King St, Honolulu, Hawaii 96817-3307 **Tel:** 1 808 533-0065.
Web site: http://www.760kgu.biz
Profile: KGU-AM is a commercial station owned by Salem Media Group, Inc. The format of the station is business talk. KGU-AM broadcasts to the Honolulu area at 760 AM.
AM RADIO STATION

KGU-FM 43694
Owner: Salem Media Group, Inc.
Editorial: 1160 N King St Fl 2, Honolulu, Hawaii 96817-3307 **Tel:** 1 808 533-0065.
Web site: http://www.995theword.com
Profile: KGU-FM is a commercial station owned by Salem Media Group, Inc. The format of the station is Religious. KGU-FM broadcasts to the Honolulu area at 99.5 FM.
FM RADIO STATION

KGVA-FM 43910
Owner: Fort Belknap College
Editorial: Chippewa and 1st St, Harlem, Montana 59526 **Tel:** 1 406 353-4656.
Email: kgvaradiostation@yahoo.com
Web site: http://www.kgvafm.org
FM RADIO STATION

KGVE-FM 39665
Owner: Caleb Corp.
Editorial: 1 W 3rd St, Grove, Oklahoma 74344
Tel: 1 918 786-2211.
Profile: KGVE-FM is a commercial station owned by Caleb Corp. The format of the station is country. KGVE-FM broadcasts to the Tulsa, OK area at 99.3 FM.
FM RADIO STATION

KGVL-AM 37306
Owner: Hunt County Radio, LLC
Editorial: 1517 Wolfe City Dr, Greenville, Texas 75401-2111 **Tel:** 1 903 455-1400.
Profile: KGVL-AM is a commercial station owned by Hunt County Radio, LLC. The format of the station is Classic Country. KGVL-AM broadcasts to the Greenville, TX area at 1400 AM.
AM RADIO STATION

KGVO-AM 34963
Owner: Townsquare Media, LLC
Editorial: 3250 S Reserve St Ste 200, Missoula, Montana 59801-8236 **Tel:** 1 406 728-9300.
Web site: http://newstalkkgvo.com
Profile: KGVO-AM is a commercial station owned by Townsquare Media, LLC. The format of the station is news and talk. KGVO-AM broadcasts to the Missoula, MT area at 1290 AM.
AM RADIO STATION

KGVO-FM 507466
Owner: Townsquare Media, LLC
Editorial: 3250 S Reserve St Ste 200, Missoula, Montana 59801-8236 **Tel:** 1 406 728-9300.
Email: kgvonewsroom@townsquaremedia.com
Web site: http://newstalkkgvo.com
Profile: KGVO-FM is a commercial station owned by Townsquare Media, LLC. The format is news talk. KGVO-FM broadcasts to the Missoula, MT area at 101.5 FM. The station is a simulcast of KGVO-AM.
FM RADIO STATION

KGVY-AM 34964
Owner: KGVY LLC
Editorial: 1510 W Camino Antigua, Sahuarita, Arizona 85629 **Tel:** 1 520 399-1000.
Email: kgvynews@kgvy1080.com
Web site: http://www.kgvy1080.com
Profile: KGVY-AM is a commercial station owned by KGVY LLC. The format of the station is adult standards. KGVY-AM broadcasts to the Tucson, AZ area at 1080 AM.
AM RADIO STATION

KGWA-AM 38750
Owner: Williams Broadcasting LLC
Editorial: 1710 W Willow Rd Ste 300, Enid, Oklahoma 73703-2432 **Tel:** 1 580 234-4230.
Email: production@kofm.com
Web site: http://www.kgwanews.com/
Profile: KGWA-AM is a commercial station owned by Williams Broadcasting LLC. The format of the station is news and talk. KGWA-AM broadcasts to the Oklahoma City area at 960 AM.
AM RADIO STATION

KGWT-FM 821093
Owner: Hispanic Target Media, Inc.
Editorial: 1524 S Interstate 35, Austin, Texas 78704-8931 **Tel:** 1 602 283-3293.
Email: hispanictargetmedia@gmail.com
Web site: http://www.hispanictargetmedia.info/
Profile: KGWT-FMis a commercial station owned by Hispanic Target Media, Inc. The format of the station is Hispanic music. KGWT-FM broadcasts locally to the George West, TX area at a frequency of 93.5 FM.
FM RADIO STATION

KGWY-FM 39666
Owner: Legend Communications
Editorial: 2810 Southern Dr, Gillette, Wyoming 82718
Tel: 1 307 686-2242.
Email: news@basinsradio.com
Web site: http://www.basinsradio.com
Profile: KGWY-FM is a commercial station owned by Legend Communications. The format of the station is country. KGWY-FM broadcasts to the Denver area at 100.7 FM.
FM RADIO STATION

KGYM-AM 34910
Owner: KZIA Inc.
Editorial: 1110 26th Ave SW, Cedar Rapids, Iowa 52404-3430 **Tel:** 1 319 363-2061.
Email: info@kgymradio.com
Web site: http://www.kgymradio.com
Profile: KGYM-AM is a commercial station owned by KZIA Inc. The format of the station is sports. KGYM-AM broadcasts to the Cedar Rapids, IA area at 1600 AM.
AM RADIO STATION

KGYN-AM 34965
Owner: Steckline Communications
Editorial: 2300 N Lelia St, Guymon, Oklahoma 73942-2840 **Tel:** 1 580 338-1210.
Email: kgyn@kgynradio.com
Web site: http://www.kgynradio.com
Profile: KGYN-AM is a commercial station owned by Steckline Communications. The format of the station is classic country and news. KGYN-AM broadcasts to the Guymon, OK area at 1210 AM.
AM RADIO STATION

KHAC-AM 34966
Owner: Western Indian Ministries
Editorial: Highway 264, 02C Hilltop Drive, HC33 Box 40, Gallup, New Mexico 87301 **Tel:** 1 505 371-5587.
Email: khac@westernindian.org
Web site: http://khac.westernindian.net
Profile: KHAC-AM is a commercial station owned by Western Indian Ministries. The format of the station is contemporary Christian. KHAC-AM broadcasts to the Rock, AZ area at 880 AM.
AM RADIO STATION

KHAK-FM 42744
Owner: Townsquare Media, LLC
Editorial: 425 2nd St SE Fl 4, Cedar Rapids, Iowa 52401-1819 **Tel:** 1 319 365-3698.
Email: khak@khak.com
Web site: http://www.khak.com
Profile: KHAK-FM is a commercial station owned by Townsquare Media, LLC. The format of the station is contemporary country. KHAK-FM broadcasts to the Cedar Rapids, IA area at 98.1 FM.
FM RADIO STATION

KHAM-FM 551890
Owner: Coloff Media
Editorial: 18643 360th St, Forest City, Iowa 50436-7491 **Tel:** 1 641 585-1073.
Profile: KHAM-FM is a commercial station owned by Coloff Media. The format of the station is adult contemporary. KHAM-FM broadcasts to the Forest City, IA area at 103.1 FM.
FM RADIO STATION

KHAP-FM 42637
Owner: Family Stations Inc.
Editorial: 290 Hegenberger Rd, Oakland, California 94621-1436 **Tel:** 1 510 568-6200.
Web site: http://www.familyradio.com
Profile: KHAP-FM is a non-commercial station owned by Family Stations Inc. The format of the station is religious. KEAR-AM broadcasts to the Chico, CA area at 89.1 FM.
FM RADIO STATION

KHAQ-FM 70200
Owner: Armada Media Corp.
Editorial: 307 E 4th St, North Platte, Nebraska 69101-6903 **Tel:** 1 308 532-3344.
Email: production@huskeradio.com
Profile: KHAQ-FM is a commercial station owned by Armada Media Corp. The format of the station is classic rock. KHAQ-FM broadcasts to the McCook, NE area at 98.5 FM.
FM RADIO STATION

KHAR-AM 37307
Owner: Alpha Media
Editorial: 301 Arctic Slope Ave, Anchorage, Alaska 99518-3035 **Tel:** 1 907 344-9622.
Web site: http://www.khar590.com
Profile: KHAR-AM is a commercial station owned by Alpha Media. The format of the station is sports. KHAR-AM broadcasts to the Anchorage, AK area at 590 AM.
AM RADIO STATION

KHAS-AM 34967
Owner: Platte River Radio, Inc.
Editorial: 500 E J St, Hastings, Nebraska 68901-7113 **Tel:** 1 402 463-1230.
Email: khaskics@khasradio.com
Web site: http://www.hastingslink.com
Profile: KHAS-AM is a commercial station owned by Platte River Radio, Inc. The format of the station is news, talk and AC music. KHAS-AM broadcasts to the Hastings, NE area at 1230 AM.
AM RADIO STATION

KHAT-AM 38559
Owner: Appaloosa Broadcasting
Editorial: 302 S 2nd St Ste 204, Laramie, Wyoming 82070-3650 **Tel:** 1 307 745-5208.
Profile: KHAT-AM is a commercial station owned by Appaloosa Broadcasting. The format of the station is sports. KHAT-AM broadcasts to the Laramie, WY area on 1210 AM.
AM RADIO STATION

KHAY-FM 44678
Owner: Cumulus Media Inc.
Editorial: 1376 Walter St, Ventura, California 93003-5658 **Tel:** 1 805 642-8595.
Web site: http://www.khay.com
Profile: KHAY-FM is a commercial station owned by the Cumulus Media Inc. The format of the station is country music. KHAY-FM broadcasts to the Ventura, CA area at 100.7 FM.
FM RADIO STATION

KHAZ-FM 46382
Owner: Eagle Radio Inc.
Editorial: 2300 Hall St, Hays, Kansas 67601-3062 **Tel:** 1 785 625-2578.
Email: haysnews@eagleradio.net
Web site: http://www.99kzcountry.com
Profile: KHAZ-FM is a commercial station owned by Eagle Radio Inc. The format of the station is country. KHAZ-FM broadcasts to the Hays, KS area at 99.5 FM.
FM RADIO STATION

KHBC-FM 604220
Owner: Resonate Hawaii, LLC
Editorial: 688 Kinoole St Ste 112, Hilo, Hawaii 96720-3868 **Tel:** 1 208 837-4104.
Web site: http://www.hawaiiswave.com
Profile: KHBC-FM is a commercial station owned by Resonate Hawaii, LLC. The format for the station is Hot AC. KHBC-FM broadcasts to the Hilo area at 92.7 FM.
FM RADIO STATION

KHBM-AM 37308
Owner: Pines Broadcasting
Editorial: 279 Midway Rte, Monticello, Arkansas 71655-8605 **Tel:** 1 870 367-6854.
Email: pines.radio@sbcglobal.net
Profile: KHBM-AM is a commercial station owned by Pines Broadcasting. The format of the station is adult standards music. KHBM-AM broadcasts in the Monticello, AR area at 1430 AM.
AM RADIO STATION

KHBM-FM 44679
Owner: Pines Broadcasting
Editorial: 279 Midway Rte, Monticello, Arkansas 71655-8605 **Tel:** 1 870 367-6854.
Email: pines.radio@sbcglobal.net
Profile: KHBM-FM is a commercial station owned by Pines Broadcasting. The format of the station is classic rock. KHBM-FM broadcasts to the Monticello, AR area at 93.7 FM.
FM RADIO STATION

KHBR-AM 36011
Owner: KHBR Radio Inc.
Editorial: 335 Country Club Rd, Hillsboro, Texas 76645 **Tel:** 1 254 582-3431.
Email: info@khbrhillsboro.com
Web site: http://hillsbororeporter.com
Profile: KHBR-AM is a commercial station owned by KHBR Radio Inc. The format of the station is classic country music. KHBR-AM broadcasts to the Hillsboro, TX, area at 1560 AM.
AM RADIO STATION

KHBT-FM 39667
Owner: NRG Media LLC
Editorial: 2196 Montana Ave, Humboldt, Iowa 50548-8625 **Tel:** 1 515 332-4100.
Email: thebolt@977thebolt.com
Web site: http://www.977thebolt.com
Profile: KHBT-FM is a commercial station owned by NRG Media LLC. The format of the station is adult contemporary music. KHBT-FM broadcasts to the Humboldt, IA at 97.7 FM.
FM RADIO STATION

KHBW-FM 86811
Owner: Houston Christian Broadcasters
Editorial: 2424 South Blvd, Houston, Texas 77098-5110 **Tel:** 1 713 520-5200.
Email: email@khcb.org
Web site: http://www.khcb.org/index.html
Profile: KHBW-FM is a non-commercial station owned by Houston Christian Broadcasters. The format of the station is Christian music and religious talk. KHBW-FM broadcasts to the Brownwood, TX area at 91.7 FM.
FM RADIO STATION

KHBZ-FM 44682
Owner: KHOZ LLC
Editorial: 1111 Radio Ave, Harrison, Arkansas 72601-2516 **Tel:** 1 870 741-2301.
Web site: http://www.947thebrew.com
Profile: KHBZ-FM is a commercial station owned by KHOZ LLC. The format of the station is contemporary country. KHBZ-FM broadcasts to the Harrison, AR area at 102.9 FM.
FM RADIO STATION

KHCA-FM 41804
Owner: KHCA Inc.
Editorial: 103 N 3rd St, Ste A, Manhattan, Kansas 66502 **Tel:** 1 785 537-9595.
Email: angel95fm@hotmail.com
Web site: http://www.angel95fm.com
Profile: KHCA-FM is a non-commercial station owned by KHCA Inc. The format of the station is contemporary Christian music and talk. KHCA-FM broadcasts to the Manhattan, KS area at 95.3 FM.
FM RADIO STATION

KHCB-AM 38769
Owner: Houston Christian Broadcasters
Editorial: 2424 South Blvd, Houston, Texas 77098-5110 **Tel:** 1 713 520-5200.
Email: email@khcb.org
Web site: http://www.khcb.org
Profile: KHCB-AM is a non-commercial station owned by Houston Christian Broadcasters. The format of the station is Hispanic Christian programming. KHCB-AM broadcasts to the Houston area at 1400 AM.
AM RADIO STATION

KHCB-FM 46135
Owner: Houston Christian Broadcasters
Editorial: 2424 South Blvd, Houston, Texas 77098 **Tel:** 1 713 520-5200.
Email: email@khcb.org
Web site: http://www.khcb.org
Profile: KHCB-FM is non-commercial station owned by Houston Christian Broadcasters. The format of the station is Christian music and religious talk. KHCB-FM broadcasts to the Houston area at 105.7 FM.
FM RADIO STATION

KHCC-FM 39668
Owner: Hutchinson Community College
Editorial: 815 N Walnut St Ste 300, Hutchinson, Kansas 67501-6389 **Tel:** 1 620 662-6646.
Email: comments@radiokansas.org
Web site: http://www.radioks.org
Profile: KHCC-FM is a non-commercial station owned by Hutchinson Community College. The format of the station is news and classical music. KHCC-FM broadcasts to the Wichita, KS area at 90.1 FM.
FM RADIO STATION

KHCD-FM 41040
Owner: Hutchinson Community College
Editorial: 815 N Walnut St, Ste 300, Hutchinson, Kansas 67501 **Tel:** 1 620 662-6646.
Email: comments@radiokansas.org
Web site: http://www.radiokansas.org
Profile: KHCD-FM is a non-commercial station owned by Hutchinson Community College. The format of the station is news and classical music. KHCD-FM broadcasts to the Wichita, KS area at 90.1 FM.
FM RADIO STATION

KHCM-AM 36203
Owner: Salem Media Group, Inc.
Editorial: 1160 N King St, Honolulu, Hawaii 96817-3307 **Tel:** 1 808 533-0065.
Profile: KHCM-AM is a commercial station owned by Salem Media Group, Inc. The format of the station is Chinese programming with blocks of English variety programming. KHCM-AM broadcasts to the Honolulu area at 880 AM.
AM RADIO STATION

KHCM-FM 529741
Owner: Salem Media Group, Inc.
Editorial: 1160 N King St Fl 2, Honolulu, Hawaii 96817-3307 **Tel:** 1 808 533-0065.
Web site: http://www.975countrykhem.com
Profile: KHCM-FM is a commercial station owned by Salem Media Group, Inc. The format for the station is classic and contemporary country music. KHCM-FM broadcasts to the Honolulu area at 97.5 FM.
FM RADIO STATION

KHCS-FM 43893
Owner: Prairie Avenue Gospel Center
Editorial: 2341 N Duane Rd, Palm Springs, California 92262-3102 **Tel:** 1 760 864-9620.
Email: khcs@juno.com
Web site: http://www.joy92.org
Profile: KHCS-FM is a non-commercial station owned by Prairie Avenue Gospel Center. The format of the station is Christian programming. KHCS-FM broadcasts to the Palm Springs, CA area at 91.7 FM.
FM RADIO STATION

KHCT-FM 42252
Owner: Hutchinson Community College
Editorial: 815 N Walnut St Ste 300, Hutchinson, Kansas 67501-6389 **Tel:** 1 620 662-6646.
Email: comments@radiokansas.org
Web site: http://www.radiokansas.org
Profile: KHCT-FM is a non-commercial station owned by Hutchinson Community College. The format of the station is news and classical music. KHCT-FM broadcasts to the Wichita, KS area at 90.9 FM.
FM RADIO STATION

KHDC-FM 41290
Owner: Radio Bilingue Inc.
Editorial: 161 Main St, Ste 4, Salinas, California 93901 **Tel:** 1 831 757-8039.
Web site: http://www.radiobilingue.org
Profile: KHDC-FM is a non-commercial station owned by Radio Bilingue Inc. The format of the station is Hispanic variety. KHDC-FM broadcasts to the Salinas, CA area at 90.9 FM.
FM RADIO STATION

KHDK-FM 426578
Owner: Pritchard Broadcasting Co.
Editorial: 610 N 4th St Ste 300, Burlington, Iowa 52601-5059 **Tel:** 1 319 758-0973.
Web site: http://www.hot973online.com
Profile: KHDK-FM is a commercial station owned by Pritchard Broadcasting Co. The format of the station is Top 40/CHR. KHDK-FM broadcasts to the Des Moines, IA area at 97.3 FM.
FM RADIO STATION

KHDN-AM 36180
Owner: Sun Mountain Inc.
Editorial: Rr 1, Hardin, Montana 59034-9801 **Tel:** 1 406 665-2828.
Web site: http://www.bigskyradio.net
Profile: KHDN-AM is a commercial station owned by Sun Mountain Inc. The format of the station is talk. KHDN-AM broadcasts in the Hardin, MT area at 1230 AM.
AM RADIO STATION

KHDR-FM 134140
Owner: Highway Radio Inc.
Editorial: 1611 E Main St, Barstow, California 92311 **Tel:** 1 760 256-0326.
Email: highwayradio@highwayradio.com
Web site: http://www.highwayrock.com
Profile: KHDR-FM is a commercial station owned by Highway Radio Inc. The format of the station is rock music. KHDR-FM broadcasts to the Barstow, CA area at 96.9 FM.
FM RADIO STATION

KHDV-FM 560556
Owner: Mountain Broadcasting
Editorial: 725 Strand Ave, Missoula, Montana 59801-5710 **Tel:** 1 406 542-1025.
Email: info@mtnbdc.com
Web site: http://mountain1079.com/
Profile: KHDV-FM is a commercial station owned by Mountain Broadcasting. The format of the station is oldies. KHDV-FM broadcasts to the Darby, MT area at 107.9 FM.
FM RADIO STATION

KHEY-AM 38692
Owner: iHeartMedia Inc.
Editorial: 4045 N Mesa St, El Paso, Texas 79902-1526 **Tel:** 1 915 351-5400.
Web site: http://www.khey1380.com
Profile: KHEY-AM is a commercial station owned by iHeartMedia Inc. The format of the station is sports. KHEY-AM broadcasts to the El Paso, TX area at 1380 AM.
AM RADIO STATION

KHEY-FM 46045
Owner: iHeartMedia Inc.
Editorial: 4045 N Mesa St, El Paso, Texas 79902-1526 **Tel:** 1 915 351-5400.
Email: khey963fm@yahoo.com
Web site: http://www.khey.com
Profile: KHEY-FM is a commercial station owned by Clear iHeartMedia Inc. The format of the station is country music. KHEY-FM broadcasts to the El Paso, TX area at 96.3 FM.
FM RADIO STATION

KHFI-FM 41753
Owner: iHeartMedia Inc.
Editorial: 3601 S Congress Ave Bldg F, Austin, Texas 78704-7280 **Tel:** 1 512 684-7300.
Web site: http://www.967kissfm.com
Profile: KHFI-FM is a commercial station owned by iHeartMedia Inc. The format of the station is Top 40/CHR music. KHFI-FM broadcasts to the Austin, TX area at 96.7 Kiss FM.
FM RADIO STATION

KHFM-FM 74426
Owner: American General Media
Editorial: 4125 Carlisle Blvd NE, Albuquerque, New Mexico 87107-4806 **Tel:** 1 505 878-0980.
Web site: http://www.classicalkhfm.com
Profile: KHFM-FM is a commercial station owned by American General Media. The format of the station is classical music. KHFM-FM broadcasts to the Albuquerque, NM area at 95.5 FM.
FM RADIO STATION

KHFX-AM 37048
Owner: SIGA Broadcasting Corp.
Editorial: 1302 N Shepherd Dr, Houston, Texas 77008-3752 **Tel:** 1 713 868-5559.
Profile: KHFX-AM is a commercial station owned by SIGA Broadcasting Corp. The format of the station is Spanish Religious. KHFX-AM broadcasts to the Cleburne, TX area at 1140 AM.
AM RADIO STATION

KHGC-FM 762319
Owner: Cherry Creek Radio
Editorial: 110 E Broadway St, Helena, Montana 59601-4232 **Tel:** 1 406 442-4490.
Email: ebaker@cherrycreekradio.com
Profile: KHGC-FM is a commercial station owned by Cherry Creek Radio. The format of the station is classic country. The station airs locally at 98.5 FM.
FM RADIO STATION

KHGE-FM 39727
Owner: iHeartMedia Inc.
Editorial: 83 E Shaw Ave Ste 150, Fresno, California 93710-7622 **Tel:** 1 559 230-4300.
Web site: http://www.1027thewolf.com
Profile: KHGE-FM is a commercial station owned by iHeartMedia Inc. The format of the station is contemporary country music. KHGE-FM broadcasts to the Fresno, CA area at 102.7 FM.
FM RADIO STATION

KHGG-AM 34945
Owner: Pharis Broadcasting Inc.
Editorial: 321 N Greenwood Ave, Fort Smith, Arkansas 72901-3453 **Tel:** 1 479 288-1047.
Web site: http://www.sportshog1031.com
Profile: KHGG-AM is a commercial station owned by Pharis Broadcasting Inc. The format of the station is sports. KHGG-AM broadcasts to the Fort Smith, AR area at 1580 AM.
AM RADIO STATION

KHGG-FM 42417
Owner: Pharis Broadcasting Inc.
Editorial: 321 N Greenwood Ave, Fort Smith, Arkansas 72901-3453 **Tel:** 1 479 288-1047.
Web site: http://www.sportshog1031.com
Profile: KHGG-FM is a commercial station owned by Pharis Broadcasting Inc. The format of the station is sports. KHGG-FM broadcasts to the Greenwood, AR area at 103.1 FM.
FM RADIO STATION

KHGZ-AM 38870
Owner: MLS Broadcasting
Editorial: 180 Highway 70 E Ste 11, Glenwood, Arkansas 71943-8810 **Tel:** 1 870 356-2151.
Web site: http://caddocountryradio.com
Profile: KHGZ-AM is a commercial station owned by MLS Broadcasting. The format of the station is country. KHGZ-AM broadcasts in the Glenwood, AR area at 670 AM.
AM RADIO STATION

KHHK-FM 44210
Owner: New Northwest Broadcasters LLC
Editorial: 1200 Chesterly Dr, Ste 160, Yakima, Washington 98902 **Tel:** 1 509 248-2900.
Web site: http://www.newhot997.com
Profile: KHHK-FM is a commercial station owned by New Northwest Broadcasters LLC. The format of the station is urban contemporary music. KHHK-FM broadcasts to the Yakima, WA area at 99.7 FM.
FM RADIO STATION

KHHL-FM 687533
Owner: Alpha Media
Editorial: 4050 Eisenhauer Rd, San Antonio, Texas 78218-3409 **Tel:** 1 210 654-5100.
Profile: KHHL-FM is a commercial station owned by Alpha Media. The format of the station is Spanish Sports. KHHL-FM broadcasts to the San Antonio and Karnes City, TX areas at 103.1.
FM RADIO STATION

KHHM-FM 43836
Owner: Entravision Communications Corp.
Editorial: 1436 Auburn Blvd, Sacramento, California 95815-2745 **Tel:** 1 916 646-4000.
Web site: http://www.hot1035radio.com
Profile: KHHM-FM is a commercial station owned by Entravision Communications Corp. The format of the station is Top 40/CHR. KHHM-FM broadcasts to the Sacramento, CA area at 103.5 FM.
FM RADIO STATION

KHHO-AM 36738
Owner: iHeartMedia Inc.
Editorial: 645 Elliott Ave W Ste 400, Seattle, Washington 98119-3911 **Tel:** 1 206 494-2000.
Web site: http://sportsradiokjr.iheart.com
Profile: KHHO-AM is a commercial station owned by iHeartMedia Inc. The format of the station is sports. KHHO-AM broadcasts to the Tacoma, WA area at 850 AM.
AM RADIO STATION

KHHZ-FM 46702
Owner: Deer Creek Broadcasting
Editorial: 2654 Cramer Ln, Chico, California 95928
Tel: 1 530 894-4818.
Web site: http://www.khhz.com
Profile: KHHZ-FM is a commercial station owned by Deer Creek Broadcasting. The format of the station is Hispanic programming. KHHZ-FM broadcasts to the Chico, CA area at 97.7 FM.
FM RADIO STATION

KHIB-FM 43941
Owner: Houston Christian Broadcasters
Editorial: 2424 South Blvd, Houston, Texas 77098
Tel: 1 713 520-5200.
Email: email@khcb.org
Web site: http://www.khcb.org
Profile: KHIB-FM is a non-commercial station owned by Houston Christian Broadcasters. The format of the station is Christian programming. KHIB-FM broadcasts to the Austin, TX area at 88.5 FM.
FM RADIO STATION

KHIG-AM 36054
Owner: Pilgrim Communications
Editorial: 5050 Edison Ave Ste 218, Colorado Springs, Colorado 80915-3540 **Tel:** 1 719 591-1064.
Web site: http://letstalkpot.com
Profile: KHIG-AM is a commercial station owned by Pilgrim Communications and operated by SOCO Radio. The format of the station is marijuana talk. Programming also includes alternative medicine, yoga and related subjects. KHIG-AM broadcasts to the Boulder, CO area at 1580 AM.
AM RADIO STATION

KHII-FM 151547
Owner: Southern New Mexico Radio Foundation
Editorial: 3001 N Florida Ave, Alamogordo, New Mexico 88310-8711 **Tel:** 1 575 437-0917.
Email: kupr917@yahoo.com
Profile: KHII-FM is a non-commercial community radio station owned by Southern New Mexico Radio Foundation. The format of the station is Southern Gospel and Contemporary Country. KHII-FM broadcasts to the Alamogordo, New Mexico area at a frequency of 88.9 FM.
FM RADIO STATION

KHIL-AM 36849
Owner: KZLZ LLC
Editorial: 900 W Pattie Rd, Willcox, Arizona 85643-3404 **Tel:** 1 520 384-4626.
Web site: http://www.xwave1049.com
Profile: KHIL-AM is a commercial station owned by KZLC LLC. The format of the station is contemporary country. KHIL-AM broadcasts to the Tucson, AZ area at 1250 AM.
AM RADIO STATION

KHIP-FM 44201
Owner: Mapleton Radio, LLC
Editorial: 60 Garden Ct, Ste 300, Monterey, California 93940 **Tel:** 1 831 658-5200.
Web site: http://www.thehippo.com
FM RADIO STATION

KHIT-AM 39379
Owner: Lotus Communications Corp.
Editorial: 2900 Sutro St, Reno, Nevada 89512-1616
Tel: 1 775 329-9261.
Profile: KHIT-AM is a commercial station owned by Lotus Communications Corp. The format of the station is Spanish sports. KHIT-AM broadcasts to the Reno, NV area at 1450 AM.
AM RADIO STATION

KHIT-FM 42531
Owner: Lotus Communications Corp.
Editorial: 1110 E Olive Ave, Fresno, California 93728
Tel: 1 559 497-1100.
Email: production@lotusfresno.com
Web site: http://www.exitos1071.com
Profile: KHIT-FM is a commercial station owned by Lotus Communications Corp. The format of the station is Spanish AC. KHIT-FM broadcasts to the Fresno, CA area at 107.1 FM.
FM RADIO STATION

KHIX-FM 86848
Owner: Ruby Radio Corp.
Editorial: 1750 Manzanita Dr Ste 1, Elko, Nevada 89801-1600 **Tel:** 1 775 777-1196.
Web site: http://www.mix96.fm
Profile: KHIX-FM is a commercial station owned by Ruby Radio Corp. The format of the station is hot adult contemporary. KHIX-FM broadcasts to the Elko, NV area at 96.7 FM.
FM RADIO STATION

KHJ-AM 39377
Owner: Liberman Broadcasting Inc.
Editorial: 1845 W Empire Ave, Burbank, California 91504-3402 **Tel:** 1 818 729-5300.
Web site: http://laranchera.estrellatv.com
Profile: KHJ-AM is a commercial station owned by Liberman Broadcasting Inc. The format of the station is Hispanic music. KHJ-AM broadcasts to the Los Angeles area at 930 AM.
AM RADIO STATION

KHJM-FM 670661
Owner: Covenant Network
Editorial: 4424 Hampton Ave, Saint Louis, Missouri 63109-2232 **Tel:** 1 314 752-7000.
Web site: http://www.covenantnet.net
Profile: KHJM-FM is a non-commercial station owned by Covenant Network. The format of the station is religious music and talk. KHJM-FM broadcasts to the Dexter, MO area at 89.1 FM.
FM RADIO STATION

KHJZ-FM 46792
Owner: iHeartMedia Inc.
Editorial: 650 Iwilei Rd Ste 400, Honolulu, Hawaii 96817-5319 **Tel:** 1 808 550-9200.
Profile: KHJZ-FM is a commercial station owned by iHeartMedia Inc. The format of the station is Top 40/ Rhythmic. KHJZ-FM's target audience is adults, ages 18 to 54, in the Honolulu area. The station airs locally 93.9 FM. Newscasts air between the hours of 6am and 10am, HST.
FM RADIO STATION

KHKA-AM 37538
Owner: Blow Up, LLC
Editorial: 1088 Bishop St Ste LL2, Honolulu, Hawaii 96813-3113 **Tel:** 1 808 536-3624.
Web site: http://nbcsportsradiohawaii.com
Profile: KHKA-AM is a commercial station owned by Blow Up, LLC. The format of the station is sports. KHKA-AM broadcasts to the Honolulu area at 1500 AM.
AM RADIO STATION

KHKI-FM 39607
Owner: Cumulus Media Inc
Editorial: 4143 109th St, Urbandale, Iowa 50322-7925
Tel: 1 515 331-9200.
Web site: http://www.nashfm973.com
Profile: KHKI-FM is a commercial station owned by Cumulus Media Inc. The format of the station is contemporary country. KHKI-FM broadcasts to the Urbandale, IA area at 97.3 FM.
FM RADIO STATION

KHKK-FM 43448
Owner: Cumulus Media Inc
Editorial: 3127 Transworld Dr #270, Stockton, California 95206-4988 **Tel:** 1 209 507-8500.
Email: thehawk@104thehawk.com
Web site: http://www.104thehawk.com
Profile: KHKK-FM is a commercial station owned by Cumulus Media Inc. The format of the station is classic rock music. KHKK-FM broadcasts in the Modesto, CA area at 104.1 FM.
FM RADIO STATION

KHKM-FM 44347
Owner: Cherry Creek Radio
Editorial: 1600 North Ave W, Ste 101, Missoula, Montana 59801 **Tel:** 1 406 728-5000.
Profile: KHKM-FM is a commercial station owned by Cherry Creek Radio. The format of the station is classic country. KHKM-FM broadcasts to the Missoula, MT area at 98.7 FM.
FM RADIO STATION

KHKN-FM 43585
Owner: iHeartMedia Inc.
Editorial: 10800 Colonel Glenn Rd, Little Rock, Arkansas 72204-8017 **Tel:** 1 501 217-5000.
Email: tom@949tomfm.com
Web site: http://big949.iheart.com/
Profile: KHKN-FM is a commercial station owned by iHeartMedia Inc. The format of the station is classic hits. KHKN-FM broadcasts to the Little Rock, AR area at 94.9 FM.
FM RADIO STATION

KHKR-AM 39305
Owner: Cherry Creek Radio
Editorial: 750 W. Ridge View Dr., Ste 204, St George, Utah 84770-2697 **Tel:** 1 435 673-3579.
Profile: KHKR-AM is a commercial station owned by Cherry Creek Radio. The format of the station is classic country. KHKR-AM broadcasts to the St. George, UT area at 1210 AM.
AM RADIO STATION

KHKS-FM 39816
Owner: iHeartMedia Inc.
Editorial: 14001 Dallas Pkwy Ste 300, Dallas, Texas 75240-7369 **Tel:** 1 214 866-8000.
Web site: http://www.1061kissfm.com
Profile: KHKS-FM is a commercial station owned by iHeartMedia Inc. The format of the station is Top 40/ CHR. KHKS-FM broadcasts to the Dallas area at 106.1 FM.
FM RADIO STATION

KHKV-FM 43746
Owner: Houston Christian Broadcasters
Editorial: 2424 South Blvd, Houston, Texas 77098-5110 **Tel:** 1 713 520-5200.
Web site: http://www.khcb.org
Profile: KHKV-FM is a commercial station owned by Houston Christian Broadcasters. The format of the station is Hispanic Christian programming. KHKV-FM broadcasts to the Houston area at 91.1 FM.
FM RADIO STATION

KHKX-FM 40016
Owner: Brazos Communications West, LLC
Editorial: 3303 N Midkiff Rd Ste 115, Midland, Texas 79705-4860 **Tel:** 1 432 520-9912.
Web site: http://www.kicks99.net
Profile: KHKX-FM is a commercial station owned by Brazos Communications West, LLC. The format of the station is contemporary country. KHKX-FM broadcasts to the Midland, TX area at 99.1 FM.
FM RADIO STATION

KHKZ-FM 46261
Owner: iHeartMedia Inc.
Editorial: 901 E Pike Blvd, Weslaco, Texas 78596-4937 **Tel:** 1 956 973-9202.
Web site: http://www.hotkiss1063.com
Profile: KHKZ-FM is a commercial station owned by iHeartMedia Inc. The format of the station is hot adult contemporary music. KHKZ-FM broadcasts to the Weslaco, TX area at 106.3 FM.
FM RADIO STATION

KHLA-FM 44710
Owner: Townsquare Media, LLC
Editorial: 900 N Lake Shore Dr, Lake Charles, Louisiana 70601-2120 **Tel:** 1 337 433-1641.
Web site: http://929thelake.com
Profile: KHLA-FM is a commercial station owned by Townsquare Media, LLC. The format of the station is classic hits. KHLA-FM broadcasts to the Lake Charles, LA area at 92.9 FM.
FM RADIO STATION

KHLB-FM 359467
Owner: III & W Broadcasting
Editorial: 105 N. Spring Street, Mason, Texas 76826
Tel: 1 325 347-1025.
Email: info@khlb1025.com
Web site: http://www.khlb1025.com
Profile: KHLB-FM is a commercial station owned by III & W Broadcasting. The station broadcasts to the Mason, TX area at 102.5.
FM RADIO STATION

KHLL-FM 43863
Owner: Gilliland(Dan)
Editorial: 704 Trenton St, Ste C, West Monroe, Louisiana 71291 **Tel:** 1 318 323-5994.
Email: mail@hillradio.com
Web site: http://www.hillradio.com
Profile: KHLL-FM is a commercial station owned by Dan Gilliland. The format of the station is contemporary Christian music. KHLL-FM broadcasts in the Monroe, LA area at 100.9 FM.
FM RADIO STATION

KHLO-AM 39110
Owner: Pacific Media Group
Editorial: 913 Kanoelehua Ave, Hilo, Hawaii 96720-5116 **Tel:** 1 808 961-0651.
Web site: http://www.espnhawaii.com
Profile: KHLO-AM is a commercial station owned by Pacific Media Group. The format of the station is sports. KHLO-AM broadcasts to the Hilo, HI area at 850 AM.
AM RADIO STATION

KHLR-FM 40069
Owner: Signal Media of Arkansas, Inc
Editorial: 2400 Cottondale Ln, Little Rock, Arkansas 72202-2020 **Tel:** 1 501 664-9410.
Web site: http://1067theride.com/
Profile: KHLR-FM is a commercial station owned by Signal Media of Arkansas, Inc. The format of the station is Country. KHLR-FM broadcasts in the Little Rock, AR area at 106.7 FM.
FM RADIO STATION

KHLS-FM 44681
Owner: Sudbury Broadcasting Group
Editorial: 125 S 2nd St, Blytheville, Arkansas 72315-3413 **Tel:** 1 870 762-2093.
Web site: http://www.thundercountry963.com
Profile: KHLS-FM is a commercial station owned by Sudbury Broadcasting Group. The format of the station is contemporary country. KHLS-FM broadcasts to the Blytheville, AR area at 96.3 FM.
FM RADIO STATION

KHLT-FM 42979
Owner: Air Capitol Media Group
Editorial: 2120 N Woodlawn St, Wichita, Kansas 67208-1847
Email: local@litewichita.com
Web site: http://www.litewichita.com
Profile: KHLT-FM is a commercial station owned by Air Capitol Media Group. The format is Adult Contemporary music. KHLT-FM broadcasts to the Wichita, KS area at 99.7 FM.
FM RADIO STATION

KHMB-FM 43879
Owner: R & M Broadcasting
Editorial: 203 Fairview Rd, Crossett, Arkansas 71635
Tel: 1 870 364-4700.
Email: qlite@arkansas.net
Web site: http://www.qliteradio.com
Profile: KHMB-FM is a commercial station owned by R & M Broadcasting. The format of the station is lite rock and adult contemporary. KHMB-FM broadcasts to the Crossett, AR area at 99.5 FM.
FM RADIO STATION

KHMC-FM 43878
Owner: Lopez(Minerva)
Editorial: 2001 E Sabine St Ste 101, Victoria, Texas 77901-5648 **Tel:** 1 361 575-9533.
Email: majictejano@yahoo.com
Web site: http://www.majic95fm.com
Profile: KHMC-FM is a commercial station owned by Minerva Lopez. The format of the station is Hispanic music. KHMC-FM broadcasts in the Victoria, TX area at 95.9 FM.
FM RADIO STATION

KHMD-FM 42426
Owner: Houston Christian Broadcasters
Editorial: Mansfield, Louisiana **Tel:** 1 713 520-5200.
Email: email@khcb.org
Web site: http://www.khcb.org
Profile: KHMD-FM is a non-commercial station owned by Houston Christian Broadcasters. The format of the station is Christian music and religious talk. KHMD-FM broadcasts to the Mansfield, LA area at 104.7 FM.
FM RADIO STATION

KHMO-AM 37309
Owner: Townsquare Media
Editorial: 119 N 3rd St, Hannibal, Missouri 63401-3501 **Tel:** 1 573 221-3450.
Web site: http://khmoradio.com
Profile: KHMO-AM is a commercial station owned by Townsquare Media. The format of the station is news and talk. KHMO-AM broadcasts to the Quincy, IL area at 1070 AM.
AM RADIO STATION

KHMX-FM 39722
Owner: CBS Radio
Editorial: 24 Greenway Plz Ste 1900, Houston, Texas 77046-2428 **Tel:** 1 713 881-5100.
Web site: http://mix965houston.cbslocal.com
Profile: KHMX-FM is a commercial station owned by CBS Radio. The format of the station is hot adult contemporary music. KHMX-FM broadcasts to the Houston area at 96.5 FM.
FM RADIO STATION

KHMY-FM 42825
Owner: Eagle Communications
Editorial: 825 N Main St, Hutchinson, Kansas 67501-4605 **Tel:** 1 620 662-4486.
Email: khmy@cox.net
Web site: http://www.khmyfm.com
Profile: KHMY-FM is a commercial station owned by Eagle Radio Inc. The format of the station is adult contemporary. KHMY-FM broadcasts to the Hutchinson, KS area at 93.1 FM.
FM RADIO STATION

KHNC-AM 36433
Owner: American Freedom Network
Tel: 1 970 587-5175.
Email: Info@1360am.co
Web site: http://www.americanewsnet.com
Profile: KHNC-AM is a commercial station owned by American Freedom Network. The format of the station is news and talk programming. KHNC-AM broadcasts to the Johnstown, CO area at 1360 AM.
AM RADIO STATION

KHND-AM 34969
Owner: Three Way Broadcasting Inc.
Editorial: 718 Lincoln Ave, Harvey, North Dakota 58341-1520 **Tel:** 1 701 324-4848.
Email: traffic@khnd1470.com
Web site: http://www.khnd1470.com
Profile: KHND-AM is a commercial station owned by Three Way Broadcasting Inc. The format of the station is adult contemporary. KHND-AM broadcasts to the Harvey, ND area at 1470 AM.
AM RADIO STATION

KHNK-FM 43860
Owner: Bee Broadcasting Inc.
Editorial: 2432 US Highway 2 E, Kalispell, Montana 59901 **Tel:** 1 406 755-8700.
Email: hank@myhank.com
Web site: http://www.myhank.com
Profile: KHNK-FM is a commercial station owned by Bee Broadcasting, Inc. The format of the station is

country music. KHNK-FM broadcasts in the Kalispell, MT area at 95.9 FM.
FM RADIO STATION

KHNR-AM 37172
Owner: Salem Media Group, Inc.
Editorial: 1160 N King St, Honolulu, Hawaii 96817-3307 **Tel:** 1 808 533-0065.
Email: info@khnr.com
Web site: http://www.khnr.com
Profile: KHNR-AM is a commercial station owned by Salem Media Group, Inc. The format of the station is news and talk. KHNR-AM broadcasts to the Honolulu area at 690 AM.
AM RADIO STATION

KHNS-FM 41933
Owner: Lynn Canal Broadcasting
Editorial: #1 Theater Drive, Haines, Alaska 99827-1109 **Tel:** 1 907 766-2020.
Email: news@khns.org
Web site: http://www.khns.org
Profile: KHNS-FM is a non-commercial station owned by Lynn Canal Broadcasting. The format of the station is free-form, with a wide variety of musical styles, ranging from classic rock to reggae. KHNS-FM broadcasts to Haines, AK at 102.3 FM.
FM RADIO STATION

KHOB-AM 36884
Owner: American Asset Management Inc.
Editorial: 1000 E Sanger St, Hobbs, New Mexico 88240-4547 **Tel:** 1 575 392-9292.
Email: espnsw@gmail.com
Web site: http://www.espnsouthwest.com
Profile: KHOB-AM is a commercial station owned by American Asset Management Inc. The format is sports. KHOB-AM airs in the Hobbs, NM area at 1390 AM.
AM RADIO STATION

KHOJ-AM 34977
Owner: Covenant Network
Editorial: 4424 Hampton Ave, Saint Louis, Missouri 63109-2232 **Tel:** 1 314 752-7000.
Email: covenantnetwork@juno.com
Web site: http://www.covenantnet.net
Profile: KHOJ-AM is a non-commercial station owned by Covenant Network. The format of the station is religious music and talk. KHOJ-AM broadcasts to the St. Louis area at 1460 AM.
AM RADIO STATION

KHOK-FM 39670
Owner: Eagle Radio Inc.
Editorial: 1200 Baker Ave, Great Bend, Kansas 67530-4523 **Tel:** 1 620 792-3647.
Web site: http://www.khokfm.com
Profile: KHOK-FM is a commercial station owned by Eagle Radio Inc. The format of the station is contemporary country. KHOK-FM broadcasts to the Great Bend, KS area at 100.7 FM.
FM RADIO STATION

KHOL-FM 532199
Owner: Jackson Hole Community Radio
Editorial: 265 S Cache St, Jackson, Wyoming 83001-8690 **Tel:** 1 307 733-4030.
Web site: http://www.jhcr.org
Profile: KHOL-FM is a non-commercial station owned by Jackson Hole Community Radio. The format for the station is variety. KHOL-FM broadcasts to the Jackson, WY area at 89.1 FM. The station does not accept pitches and does not wish to be contacted.
FM RADIO STATION

KHOM-FM 39891
Owner: E-Communications, LLC
Editorial: 10 Court Sq, West Plains, Missouri 65775-3444 **Tel:** 1 417 255-2548.
Email: eckman@centurytel.net
Web site: http://khomthetrain.com
Profile: KHOM-FM is a commercial station owned by E-Communications, LLC. The format of the station is classic hits of the 60s, 70s and 80s. KHOM-FM broadcasts to the Springfield, MO area at 100.9 FM.
FM RADIO STATION

KHOP-FM 39605
Owner: Cumulus Media Inc
Editorial: 3127 Transworld Dr #270, Stockton, California 95206-4988 **Tel:** 1 209 507-8500.
Web site: http://www.khop.com
Profile: KHOP-FM is commercial station owned by Cumulus Media Inc. The format of the station is Top 40/CHR. KHOP-FM broadcasts to the Oakdale, CA area at 95.1 FM.
FM RADIO STATION

KHOS-FM 43366
Owner: Foster Charitable Foundation, Inc.
Editorial: 680 Highway 277 South, Sonora, Texas 76950 **Tel:** 1 325 387-3553.
Email: khoskyxx@verizon.net
Web site: http://www.revfmradio.com
Profile: KHOS-FM is a commerical station owned by Foster Charitable Foundation, Inc.. The format of the station is classic country. KHOS-FM broadcasts to the Sonora, TX area at 92.1 FM.
FM RADIO STATION

KHOT-AM 38541
Owner: Immaculate Heart Radio
Editorial: 3256 Penryn Rd Ste 100, Loomis, California 95650-8052 **Tel:** 1 916 535-0500.
Email: programming@ihradio.org
Web site: http://ihradio.org
Profile: KHOT-AM is a non-commercial station owned by Immaculate Heart Radio. The format of the station is religious. KHOT-AM broadcasts to the Fresno, CA area at 1250 AM.
AM RADIO STATION

KHOT-FM 43165
Owner: Univision Communications Inc.
Editorial: 6006 S 30th St, Phoenix, Arizona 85042-4802 **Tel:** 1 602 308-7900.
Web site: http://www.univision.com/arizona/khot
Profile: KHOT-FM is a commercial station owned by Univision Communications Inc. The format of the station is regional Mexican. KHOT-FM broadcasts to the Phoenix area at 105.9 FM.
FM RADIO STATION

KHOV-FM 44386
Owner: Univision Communications Inc.
Editorial: 6006 S 30th St, Phoenix, Arizona 85042-4802 **Tel:** 1 602 308-7900.
Web site: http://www.univision.com/arizona/kqmr
Profile: KHOV-FM is a commercial station owned by Univision Communications Inc. The format of the station is Spanish Urban. KHOV-FM broadcasts to the Phoenix area at 95.7 FM.
FM RADIO STATION

KHOW-AM 38677
Owner: iHeartMedia Inc.
Editorial: 4695 S Monaco St, Denver, Colorado 80237-3525 **Tel:** 1 303 713-8000.
Web site: http://khow.iheart.com
Profile: KHOW-AM is a commercial station owned by iHeartMedia Inc. The format of the station is talk. KHOW-AM broadcasts to the Denver area at 630 AM.
AM RADIO STATION

KHOY-FM 41914
Owner: Laredo Catholic Communications Inc.
Editorial: 1901 Corpus Christi St, Laredo, Texas 78043-3308 **Tel:** 1 956 722-4167.
Email: khoy@khoy.org
Web site: http://www.khoy.org
Profile: KHOY-FM is a non-commercial station owned by Laredo Catholic Communications Inc. The format of the station is Hispanic religious programming and easy listening. KHOY-FM broadcasts to the Laredo, TX area at 88.1 FM.
FM RADIO STATION

KHOZ-AM 37310
Owner: KHOZ LLC
Editorial: 1111 Radio Ave, Harrison, Arkansas 72601-2516 **Tel:** 1 870 741-2301.
Email: khozradio@khoz.com
Web site: http://www.1029thez.com
Profile: KHOZ-AM is a commercial station owned by KHOZ LLC. The format of the station is nostalgia music. KHOZ-AM broadcasts to the Harrison, AR area at 900 AM.
AM RADIO STATION

KHPA-FM 39671
Owner: Sudbury Broadcasting Group
Editorial: 1600 S Elm St, Hope, Arkansas 71801 **Tel:** 1 870 777-8868.
Email: khpafm@supercountry105.com
Web site: http://www.supercountry105.com
Profile: KHPA-FM is a commercial station owned by Sudbury Broadcasting Group. The format of the station is contemporary country. KHPA-FM broadcasts to the Hope, AR area at 104.9 FM.
FM RADIO STATION

KHPE-FM 44683
Owner: Extra Mile Media Inc.
Editorial: 34545 Highway 20 SE, Albany, Oregon 97322-9731 **Tel:** 1 541 926-2233.
Email: events@hope1079.com
Web site: http://www.hope1079.com
Profile: KHPE-FM is a commercial station owned by Extra Mile Inc. The format of the station is contemporary Christian music. KHPE-FM broadcasts to the Albany, OR area at 107.9 FM.
FM RADIO STATION

KHPO-FM 475354
Owner: Houston Christian Broadcasters
Editorial: 2424 South Blvd, Houston, Texas 77098 **Tel:** 1 713 520-5200.
Email: email@khcb.org
Web site: http://www.khcb.org
Profile: KHPO-FM is a non-commercial station owned by Houston Christian Broadcasters. The format of the station is Christian programming and music. KHPO-FM broadcasts to the Austin, TX area at 91.9 FM.
FM RADIO STATION

KHPQ-FM 44684
Owner: King-Sullivan Radio
Editorial: 360 Main St, Clinton, Arkansas 72031 **Tel:** 1 501 745-4474.
Email: kgflkhpq@artelco.com
Web site: http://www.khpq.com
Profile: KHPQ-FM is a commercial station owned by King-Sullivan Radio. The format of the station is contemporary country. KHPQ-FM broadcasts to the Clinton, AR area at 92.1 FM.
FM RADIO STATION

KHPR-FM 39672
Owner: Hawaii Public Radio
Editorial: 738 Kaheka St Ste 101, Honolulu, Hawaii 96814-3726 **Tel:** 1 808 955-8821.
Email: mail@hawaiipublicradio.org
Web site: http://www.hawaiipublicradio.org
Profile: KHPR-FM is a non-commercial station owned by Hawaii Public Radio. The format of the station is news and classical music. KHPR-FM broadcasts to the Honolulu area at 88.1 FM.
FM RADIO STATION

KHPT-FM 43979
Owner: Cox Radio, Inc.
Editorial: 1990 Post Oak Blvd, Ste 2300, Houston, Texas 77056 **Tel:** 1 713 963-1200.
Web site: http://www.houstonseagle.com
Profile: KHPT-FM is a commercial station owned by Cox Radio, Inc. The format of the station is classic hits. KHPT-FM broadcasts to the Houston area at 106.9 FM. The station airs KGLK-FM's programming
FM RADIO STATION

KHPY-AM 35929
Owner: Van Voorhis (D.L.)
Editorial: 24490 Sunnymead Blvd, Moreno Valley, California 92553-7734 **Tel:** 1 951 247-5479.
Web site: http://www.elsembrador.org
Profile: KHPY-AM is a non-commercial station owned by Van Voorhis (D.L.). The format of the station is Hispanic religious. KHPY-AM broadcasts to the Moreno Valley, CA area at 1670 AM.
AM RADIO STATION

KHQN-AM 34971
Owner: Howell(Robyn)
Editorial: 1043 E 2620 N, Provo, Utah 84604-4108 **Tel:** 1 800 776-1913.
Web site: http://khqnradio.com
Profile: KHQN-AM is a commercial station owned by Robyn Howell. The format of the station is news, sports and talk. KHQN-AM broadcasts to the Salt Lake City area at 1480 AM.
AM RADIO STATION

KHQT-FM 39532
Owner: Adams Radio Group
Editorial: 1355 California Ave, Las Cruces, New Mexico 88001-4130 **Tel:** 1 575 525-9298.
Email: production@arglc.com
Web site: http://www.hot103.fm
Profile: KHQT-FM is a commercial station owned by Adams Radio Group. The format of the station is Top 40/CHR. KHQT-FM broadcasts to the Las Cruces, NM area at 103.1 FM.
FM RADIO STATION

KHRD-FM 86115
Owner: Results Radio Group
Editorial: 1588 Charles Dr, Redding, California 96003-1459 **Tel:** 1 530 244-9700.
Web site: http://www.red1031.com
Profile: KHRD-FM is a commercial station owned by Results Radio Group. The format of the station is classic rock. KHRD-FM broadcasts to the Redding, CA area at 103.1 FM.
FM RADIO STATION

KHRK-FM 606882
Owner: Noalmark Broadcasting Corp.
Editorial: 208 Buena Vista Rd, Hot Springs, Arkansas 71913-8208 **Tel:** 1 501 525-4600.
Web site: http://www.realrock1015.com
Profile: KHRK-FM is a commercial station owned by Noalmark Broadcasting Corp. The format of the station is active rock music KHRK-FM broadcasts to the Hot Springs, AR area at 101.5.
FM RADIO STATION

KHRO-AM 156390
Owner: Entravision Communications Corp.
Editorial: 5426 N Mesa St, El Paso, Texas 79912-5421 **Tel:** 1 915 581-1126.
Web site: http://www.fox1150.com
Profile: KHRO-AM is a commercial station owned by Entravision Communications Corp. The format of the station is oldies. KHRO-AM broadcasts to the El Paso, TX area on 1150 AM.
AM RADIO STATION

KHRQ-FM 392857
Owner: Highway Radio Inc.
Editorial: 1611 E Main St, Barstow, California 92311 **Tel:** 1 760 256-0326.
Email: highwayradio@highwayradio.com
Web site: http://www.highwayrock.com
Profile: KHRQ-FM is a commercial station owned by Highway Radio Inc. The format of the station is rock music. KHRQ-FM broadcasts to the Baker, CA area at 94.9 FM.
FM RADIO STATION

KHRS-FM 539235
Owner: Radio Mankato
Editorial: 59346 Madison Ave, Mankato, Minnesota 56001-8518 **Tel:** 1 507 345-4537.
Email: news@ktoe.com
Web site: http://www.kxlp941.com
Profile: KHRS-FM is a commercial station owned by Radio Mankato. The format of the station is classic rock. KHRS-FM broadcasts to the Mankato, MN area at 105.9 FM.
FM RADIO STATION

KHRT-AM 38717
Owner: Faith Broadcasting
Editorial: 3600 County Road 19 S, Minot, North Dakota 58701 **Tel:** 1 701 852-3789.
Email: khrt@srt.com
Web site: http://www.khrt.com
Profile: KHRT-AM is a commercial station owned by Faith Broadcasting. The format of the station is gospel music and religious programming. KHRT-AM broadcasts to the Minot, ND area at 1320 AM.
AM RADIO STATION

KHRT-FM 46071
Owner: Faith Broadcasting
Editorial: 3600 County Road 19 S, Minot, North Dakota 58701 **Tel:** 1 701 852-3789.
Email: khrt@srt.com
Web site: http://www.khrt.com
Profile: KHRT-FM is a commercial station owned by Faith Broadcasting. The format of the station is contemporary Christian. KHRT-AM broadcasts to the Minot-Bismarck, ND area at 106.9 FM.
FM RADIO STATION

KHSL-FM 43021
Owner: Deer Creek Broadcasting
Editorial: 2654 Cramer Ln, Chico, California 95928 **Tel:** 1 530 345-0021.
Web site: http://www.1035theblaze.com
Profile: KHSL-FM is a commercial station owned by Deer Creek Broadcasting. The format of the station is classic country. KHSL-FM broadcasts in the Chico, CA area at 103.5 FM.
FM RADIO STATION

KHSN-AM 38581
Owner: W-7 Broadcasting
Editorial: 320 Central Ave, Ste 519, Coos Bay, Oregon 97420 **Tel:** 1 541 267-2121.
Web site: http://www.khsn1230.com
Profile: KHSN-AM is a commercial station owned by W-7 Broadcasting. The format of the station is sports. KHSN-AM broadcasts to the Coos Bay, OR area at 1230 AM.
AM RADIO STATION

KHSS-FM 41287
Owner: Two Hearts Communications LLC
Editorial: 30 W Main St Ste 303, Walla Walla, Washington 99362-2872 **Tel:** 1 509 525-7878.
Email: comments@khssradio.com
Web site: http://www.khssradio.com
Profile: KHSS-FM is a commercial station owned by Two Hearts Communications LLC. The format of the station is religious talk. KHSS-FM broadcasts to the Walla Walla, WA area at 100.7 FM.
FM RADIO STATION

KHST-FM 42615
Owner: My Town Media, Inc.
Editorial: 412 N Locust St, Pittsburg, Kansas 66762-4014 **Tel:** 1 620 232-5993.
Web site: http://www.mycountry1017.com/site/
Profile: KHST-FM is a commercial station owned by My Town Media, Inc. The format is classic hits. The station airs in the Pittsburg, KS area at 101.7 FM.
FM RADIO STATION

KHTB-FM 39715
Owner: Cumulus Media Inc
Editorial: 434 W Bearcat Dr, Salt Lake City, Utah 84115-2520 **Tel:** 1 801 485-6700.
Web site: http://www.alt1019.com/
Profile: KHTB-FM is a commercial station owned by Cumulus Media Inc. The format of the station is classic hits music. KHTB-FM broadcasts to the Salt Lake City area at 101.9 FM.
FM RADIO STATION

KHTB-FM 43496
Owner: Cumulus Media Inc
Editorial: 434 W Bearcat Dr, Salt Lake City, Utah 84115-2520 **Tel:** 1 801 485-6700.
Web site: http://www.949zrock.com
Profile: KHTB-FM is a commercial station owned by Cumulus Media Inc. The format of the station is alternative rock. KHTB-FM broadcasts to the Salt Lake City area at 94.9 FM.
FM RADIO STATION

KHTE-FM 43303
Owner: Crain Media Group LLC
Editorial: 415 N McKinley St Ste 700, Little Rock, Arkansas 72205-3041 **Tel:** 1 501 404-6560.
Web site: http://965fmtheanswer.com
Profile: KHTE-FM is a commercial station owned by Crain Media Group LLC and operated by Salem Media Group. The format of the station is Conservative Talk. KHTE-FM broadcasts to the Little Rock, AR area at 96.5 FM.
FM RADIO STATION

KHTH-FM 42289
Owner: Sonoma Media Group
Editorial: 1410 Neotomas Ave, Santa Rosa, California 95405-7533 **Tel:** 1 707 543-0100.
Web site: http://www.hot1017online.com
Profile: KHTH-FM is a commercial station owned by Sonoma Media Group. The station's format is Top 40/CHR. KHTH-FM broadcasts to the San Francisco area at 101.7 FM.
FM RADIO STATION

KHTI-FM 44046
Owner: All Pro Broadcasting Inc.
Editorial: 242 E Airport Dr Ste 106, San Bernardino, California 92408-3408 **Tel:** 1 909 890-5904.
Web site: http://www.hot1039.com
Profile: KHTI-FM is a commercial station owned by All Pro Broadcasting Inc. The format is rhythmic contemporary. KHTI-FM broadcasts to the San Bernardino, CA area at 103.9 FM.
FM RADIO STATION

KHTK-AM 37457
Owner: CBS Radio
Editorial: 5244 Madison Ave, Sacramento, California 95841-3004 **Tel:** 1 916 338-9200.
Web site: http://sacramento.cbslocal.com/station/cbs-sports-1140
Profile: KHTK-AM is a commercial station owned by CBS Radio. The format of the station is sports. KHTK-AM broadcasts to the Sacramento, CA area at 1140 AM.
AM RADIO STATION

KHTN-FM 39920
Owner: Alpha Media
Editorial: 510 W 19th St, Merced, California 95340-4705 **Tel:** 1 209 723-2191.
Email: hot1047email@aol.com
Web site: http://www.hot1047fm.com
Profile: KHTN-FM is a commercial station owned by Mapleton Communications LLC. The format of the station is rhythmic Top 40/CHR. KHTN-FM broadcasts to the Merced, CA area at 104.7 FM.
FM RADIO STATION

KHTO-FM 42045
Owner: US Stations, LLC
Editorial: 125 Corporate Ter, Hot Springs, Arkansas 71913-7248 **Tel:** 1 501 525-9700.
Web site: http://www.myhotsprings.com
Profile: KHTO-FM is a commercial station owned by US Stations, LLC. The format of the station is top 40/CHR. KHTO-FM broadcasts to the Hot Springs, AR area at 96.7 FM.
FM RADIO STATION

KHTP-FM 43028
Owner: Entercom Communications Corp.
Editorial: 1100 Olive Way, Seattle, Washington 98101-1873 **Tel:** 1 206 233-1037.
Web site: http://www.hot1037seattle.com
Profile: KHTP-FM is a commercial station owned by Entercom Communications Corp. The format of the station is rhythmic hot adult contemporary. KHTP-FM broadcasts to the Seattle area at 103.7 FM.
FM RADIO STATION

KHTQ-FM 46299
Owner: Queen B Inc.
Editorial: 504 E Sherman Ave, Coeur D Alene, Idaho 83814 **Tel:** 1 208 664-9271.
Web site: http://www.rock945.com
Profile: KHTQ-FM is a commercial station owned by Queen B Inc. The format of the station is rock music. KHTQ-FM broadcasts to the Spokane, WA area at 94.5 FM.
FM RADIO STATION

KHTR-FM 44842
Owner: Radio Palouse Inc.
Editorial: 1101 Old Wawawai Road, Pullman, Washington 99163 **Tel:** 1 509 332-6551.
Email: info@pullmanradio.com
Web site: http://www.pullmanradio.com
Profile: KHTR-FM is a commercial station owned by Radio Palouse Inc. The format of the station is classic hits. KHTR-FM broadcasts to the Spokane, WA area at 104.3 FM.
FM RADIO STATION

KHTS-AM 36156
Owner: Jeri Lyn Broadcasting Inc.
Editorial: 27225 Camp Plenty Rd Ste 8, Santa Clarita, California 91351-2654 **Tel:** 1 661 298-1220.
Email: info@hometownstation.com
Web site: http://www.hometownstation.com
Profile: KHTS-AM is a commercial station owned by Jeri Lyn Broadcasting Inc. The format of the station is adult contemporary music and talk. KHTS-AM broadcasts to Santa Clarita and Lancaster, CA at 1220 AM.
AM RADIO STATION

KHTS-FM 43301
Owner: iHeartMedia Inc.
Editorial: 9660 Granite Ridge Dr Ste 100, San Diego, California 92123-2689 **Tel:** 1 858 292-2000.
Web site: http://channel933.iheart.com
Profile: KHTS-FM is a commercial station owned by iHeartMedia Inc. The format of the station is Top 40/CHR music. KHTS-FM broadcasts to the San Diego area at 93.3 FM.
FM RADIO STATION

KHTT-FM 39539
Owner: E.W. Scripps Co.
Editorial: 4590 E 29th St, Tulsa, Oklahoma 74114-6208 **Tel:** 1 918 743-7814.
Web site: http://www.khits.com
Profile: KHTT-FM is a commercial station owned by E.W. Scripps Co. The format of the station is Top 40/CHR. KHTT-FM broadcasts to the Tulsa, OK area at 106.9 FM.
FM RADIO STATION

KHTY-AM 36526
Owner: iHeartMedia Inc.
Editorial: 1100 Mohawk St Ste 280, Bakersfield, California 93309-7417 **Tel:** 1 661 322-9929.
Web site: http://foxsports970am.iheart.com
Profile: KHTY-AM is a commercial station owned by iHeartMedia Inc. The format of the station is sports. KHTY-AM broadcasts to the Bakersfield, CA, area at 970 AM.
AM RADIO STATION

KHUB-AM 39222
Owner: Walnut Radio, LLC
Editorial: 118 E 5th St, Fremont, Nebraska 68025-5022 **Tel:** 1 402 721-1340.
Profile: KHUB-AM is a commercial station owned by Walnut Radio, LLC. The format of the station is news and talk. KHUB-AM broadcasts to the Fremont, NE area at 1340 AM.
AM RADIO STATION

KHUM-FM 42869
Owner: Lost Coast Communications
Editorial: 1400 Main St Ste 104, Ferndale, California 95536-9459 **Tel:** 1 707 786-5104.
Email: info@khum.com
Web site: http://www.khum.com
Profile: KHUM-FM is a commercial station owned by Lost Coast Communications. The format for the station is adult album alternative. KHUM-FM broadcasts to the Ferndale, CA area at 104.7 FM.
FM RADIO STATION

KHUT-FM 44685
Owner: Eagle Communications
Editorial: 825 N Main St, Hutchinson, Kansas 67501-4605 **Tel:** 1 620 662-4486.
Email: khut.studio@eagleradio.net
Web site: http://www.hutchinsonscountrystation.com
Profile: KHUT-FM is commercial station owned by Eagle Radio Inc. The format of the station is contemporary country. KHUT-FM broadcasts to Hutchinson, KS area at 102.9 FM.
FM RADIO STATION

KHVH-AM 38507
Owner: iHeartMedia Inc.
Editorial: 650 Iwilei Rd Ste 400, Honolulu, Hawaii 96817-5319 **Tel:** 1 808 550-9200.
Web site: http://www.khvhradio.com
Profile: KHVH-AM is a commercial station owned by iHeartMedia Inc. The format of the station is news and talk. KHVH-AM broadcasts to the Honolulu area at 830 AM.
AM RADIO STATION

KHVL-AM 38982
Owner: HEH Communications LLC
Editorial: 622 Interstate 45 S, Huntsville, Texas 77340-6433 **Tel:** 1 936 295-2651.
Email: ksamnews@yahoo.com
Web site: http://www.khvl.com
Profile: KHVL-AM is a commercial station owned by HEH Communications LLC. The format of the station is classic hits. KHVL-AM broadcasts to the Huntsville, TX area at 1490 AM.
AM RADIO STATION

KHVN-AM 38671
Owner: Mortenson Broadcasting Co.
Editorial: 5787 S Hampton Rd Ste 285, Dallas, Texas 75232-2290 **Tel:** 1 214 331-5486.
Email: khvncommunitycalendar@yahoo.com
Web site: http://www.khvnam.com
Profile: KHVN-AM is a commercial station owned by Mortenson Broadcasting Co. The format of the station is gospel music and religious programming. KHVN-AM broadcasts to the Dallas area at 970 AM.
AM RADIO STATION

KHWI-FM 526683
Owner: Resonate Hawaii, LLC
Editorial: 688 Kinoole St Ste 112, Hilo, Hawaii 96720-3868 **Tel:** 1 808 959-5700.
Web site: http://www.hawaiiswave.com
Profile: KHWI-FM is a commercial station owned by Resonate Hawaii, LLC. The format for the station is Hot AC. KHWI-FM broadcasts to the Honolulu area at 92.1 FM.
FM RADIO STATION

KHWL-FM 821483
Owner: Wolfpack Media, LLC
Editorial: 102 W Broadway St, Altus, Oklahoma 73521-3802 **Tel:** 1 580 482-5495.
Email: sales@khowl.fm
Web site: http://khowl.fm
Profile: KHWL-FM is a commercial station owned by Wolfpack Media, LLC. The format of the station is rock. KHWL-FM broadcasts to the Lone Wolf, OK area at a frequency of 98.7 FM.
FM RADIO STATION

KHWY-FM 42017
Owner: Highway Radio Inc.
Editorial: 1611 E Main St, Barstow, California 92311 **Tel:** 1 760 256-0326.
Email: highwayradio@highwayradio.com
Web site: http://www.thehighwaystations.com
Profile: KHWY-FM is a commercial station owned by Highway Radio Inc. The format of the station is dance music. KHWY-FM broadcasts to the Barstow, CA area at 98.9 FM.
FM RADIO STATION

KHXS-FM 41257
Owner: Cumulus Media Inc.
Editorial: 2525 S Danville Dr, Abilene, Texas 79605 **Tel:** 1 325 793-9700.
Web site: http://www.102thebear.com
Profile: KHXS-FM is a commercial station owned by Cumulus Media Inc. The format of the station is Classic Rock music. KHXS-FM broadcasts in the Abilene, TX area at 102.7 FM.
FM RADIO STATION

KHXT-FM 44910
Owner: Townsquare Media, LLC
Editorial: 1749 Bertrand Dr, Lafayette, Louisiana 70506-2054 **Tel:** 1 337 233-6000.
Web site: http://www.1079ishot.com
Profile: KHXT-FM is a commercial station owned by Townsquare Media, LLC. The format of the station is rhythmic Top 40/CHR. KHXT-FM broadcasts to the Lafayette, LA area at 107.9 FM.
FM RADIO STATION

KHYI-FM 42225
Owner: Metro Broadcasters-Texas, Inc.
Editorial: 12225 Greenville Ave Ste 359, Dallas, Texas 75243-2089 **Tel:** 1 972 633-0953.
Web site: http://www.khyi.com
Profile: KHYI-FM is a commercial station owned by the Metro Broadcasters-Texas, Inc. The format of the station is country music. KHYI-FM broadcasts to the Allen, TX area at 95.3 FM.
FM RADIO STATION

KHYL-FM 42302
Owner: iHeartMedia Inc.
Editorial: 1545 River Park Dr Ste 500, Sacramento, California 95815-4693 **Tel:** 1 916 929-5325.
Email: sacramentopsas@iheartmedia.com
Web site: http://v1011fm.iheart.com
Profile: KHYL-FM is a commercial station owned by iHeartMedia Inc. The format of the station is urban oldies. KHYL-FM broadcasts to the Sacramento, CA area at 101.1 FM.
FM RADIO STATION

KHYM-FM 43632
Owner: Great Plains Christian Radio
Editorial: 909 W Carthage, Meade, Kansas 67864 **Tel:** 1 620 873-2991.
Email: khym@khym.org
Web site: http://www.khym.org
Profile: KHYM-FM is a non-commercial station owned by Great Plains Christian Radio. The format of the station is gospel music and religious talk. KHYM-FM broadcasts to the Meade, KS area at 103.9 FM.
FM RADIO STATION

KHYT-FM 42103
Owner: Cumulus Media Inc
Editorial: 575 W Roger Rd, Tucson, Arizona 85705 **Tel:** 1 520 887-1000.
Web site: http://www.khit1075.com
Profile: KHYT-FM is a commercial station owned by Cumulus Media Inc. The format of the station is classic hits. KHYT-FM broadcasts to the Tucson, AZ area at 107.5 FM.
FM RADIO STATION

KHYX-FM 867103
Owner: Ruby Radio Corp.
Editorial: 530 Melarkey St Ste 201, Winnemucca, Nevada 89445-3168 **Tel:** 1 775 625-1027.
Web site: http://mix1027.fm
Profile: KHYX-FM is a commercial station owned by Ruby Radio Corp. The format of the station is Hot AC. KHYX-FM broadcasts to the Winnemucca, NV area at a frequency of 102.7 FM.
FM RADIO STATION

KHYZ-FM 40049
Owner: Highway Radio Inc.
Editorial: 1611 E Main St, Barstow, California 92311-3239 **Tel:** 1 760 256-0326.
Email: highwayradio@highwayradio.com
Web site: http://www.thehighwaystations.com
Profile: KHYZ-FM is a commercial station owned by Highway Radio Inc. The format of the station is dance music. KHYZ-FM broadcasts to Mountain Pass, CA and the surrounding area at 99.7FM.
FM RADIO STATION

KHZR-FM 43380
Owner: Gateway Creative Broadcasting, Inc
Editorial: 13358 Manchester Rd Ste 100, Des Peres, Missouri 63131-1730 **Tel:** 1 314 909-8569.
Email: info@joyfmonline.org
Web site: http://boost1019.com
Profile: KHZR-FM is a non-commercial station owned by Gateway Creative Broadcasting, Inc. The format of the station is Christian CHR. KHZR-FM broadcasts to the St. Louis area at 97.7 FM.
FM RADIO STATION

KIAI-FM 46533
Owner: Alpha Media
Editorial: 341 S Yorktown Pike, Mason City, Iowa 50401-4533 **Tel:** 1 641 423-1300.
Web site: http://www.discovernorthiowa.com
Profile: KIAI-FM is a commercial station owned by Alpha Media. The format of the station is classic and contemporary country. KIAI-FM broadcasts to the Rochester, MN, and Mason City, IA areas at 93.9 FM.
FM RADIO STATION

KIAK-FM 45850
Owner: iHeartMedia Inc.
Editorial: 546 9th Ave, Fairbanks, Alaska 99701-4902 **Tel:** 1 907 450-1000.
Email: kiak@iheartmedia.com
Web site: http://kiak.iheart.com
Profile: KIAK-FM is a commercial station owned by iHeartMedia Inc. The format for the station is contemporary country. KIAK-FM broadcasts to the Fairbanks, AK area at 102.5 FM.
FM RADIO STATION

KIAM-AM 36058
Owner: Voice for Christ Ministries Inc.
Editorial: 409 East 1st St, Nenana, Alaska 99760-0474 **Tel:** 1 907 832-5426.
Email: alaskaradio@vfcm.org
Web site: http://www.vfcm.org
Profile: KIAM-AM is a commercial station owned by Voice for Christ Ministries Inc. The format of the station is Christian music and talk. KIAM-AM broadcasts to Nenana, AK 630 AM.
AM RADIO STATION

KIAQ-FM 39870
Owner: Alpha Media
Editorial: 200 N 10th St, Fort Dodge, Iowa 50501-3925 **Tel:** 1 515 955-5656.
Web site: http://www.yourfortdodge.com
Profile: KIAQ-FM is a commercial station owned by Alpha Media. The format of the station is contemporary country music. KIAQ-FM broadcasts to the Fort Dodge, IA area at 96.9 FM.
FM RADIO STATION

KIBB-FM 429769
Owner: Connoisseur Media LLC
Editorial: 1938 N Woodlawn St Ste 150, Wichita, Kansas 67208-1929 **Tel:** 1 316 558-8800.
Web site: http://www.971bobfm.com
Profile: KIBB-FM is a commercial station owned by Connoisseur Media LLC. The format of the station is Country. KIBB-FM broadcasts to the Wichita, KS area at 97.1 FM.
FM RADIO STATION

KIBC-FM 43884
Owner: Burney Educ. Broadcasting Foundation
Editorial: 20410 Marquette St, Burney, California 96013 **Tel:** 1 530 335-5422.
Web site: http://www.kibcfm.org
Profile: KIBC-FM is a non-commercial station owned by Burney Educ. Broadcasting Foundation. The format of the station is gospel music and religious programming. KIBC-FM broadcasts to the Burney, CA area at 90.5 FM.
FM RADIO STATION

KIBG-FM 519208
Owner: Anderson Radio Broadcasting Inc.
Editorial: 36581 N Reservoir Rd, Polson, Montana 59860-8471 **Tel:** 1 406 883-5255.
Email: news@andersonbroadcasting.com
Web site: http://www.thebig100.com
Profile: KIBG-FM is a commercial station owned by Anderson Radio Broadcasting Inc. The format of the station is classic hits. KIBG-FM airs to the Polson, MT area at 100.7 FM.
FM RADIO STATION

KIBR-FM 46719
Owner: Blue Sky Broadcasting Inc.
Editorial: 327 S Marion Ave, Sandpoint, Idaho 83864-1723 **Tel:** 1 208 263-2179.
Profile: KIBR-FM is a commercial station owned by Blue Sky Broadcasting Inc. The format of the station is country music. KIBR-FM broadcasts to the Spokane, WA area at 102.5 FM.
FM RADIO STATION

KIBS-FM 45665
Owner: Great Country Broadcasting Inc.
Editorial: South Highway 395, Bishop, California 93514 **Tel:** 1 760 873-6324.
Email: kibskbov@yahoo.com
Web site: http://www.kibskbov.com
Profile: KIBS-FM is a commercial station owned by Great Country Broadcasting Inc. The format of the station is country music. KIBS-FM broadcasts to the Bishop, CA area at 100.7 FM.
FM RADIO STATION

KIBT-FM 43114
Owner: iHeartMedia Inc.
Editorial: 2864 S Circle Dr Ste 300, Colorado Springs, Colorado 80906-4131 **Tel:** 1 719 540-9200.
Web site: http://www.beatcolorado.com
Profile: KIBT-FM is a commercial station owned by iHeartMedia Inc. The format of the station is rhythmic Top 40/CHR. KIBT-FM broadcasts to the Colorado Springs, CO area at 96.1 FM.
FM RADIO STATION

KIBX-FM 238649
Owner: Spokane Public Radio Inc.
Editorial: 2319 N Monroe St, Spokane, Washington 99205-4548 **Tel:** 1 509 328-5729.
Email: kpbx@kpbx.org
Web site: http://www.kpbx.org
FM RADIO STATION

KIBZ-FM 42329
Owner: Alpha Media
Editorial: 3800 Cornhusker Hwy, Lincoln, Nebraska 68504-1533 **Tel:** 1 402 466-1234.
Email: blaze@kibz.com
Web site: http://www.kibz.com
Profile: KIBZ-FM is a commercial station owned by Alpha Media. The format of the station is rock/album-oriented rock. KIBZ-FM broadcasts to the Lincoln, NE area at 104.1 FM.
FM RADIO STATION

KICB-FM 42297
Owner: Iowa Central Community College
Editorial: 1 Triton Cir, Fort Dodge, Iowa 50501-5730 **Tel:** 1 515 576-6049.
Web site: http://881thepoint.com

Profile: KICB-FM is a non-commercial station owned by Iowa Central Community College. The format of the station is adult album alternative. KICB-FM broadcasts to the Fort Dodge, IA area at 88.1 FM.
FM RADIO STATION

KICD-AM 37313
Owner: Saga Communications
Editorial: 2600 Highway Blvd, Spencer, Iowa 51301-2140 **Tel:** 1 712 262-1240.
Email: rlong@spencerradiogroup.com
Web site: http://www.kicdam.com
Profile: KICD-AM is a commercial station owned by Saga Communications. The format of the station is news and talk. KICD-AM broadcasts to the Spencer, IA area at 1240 AM.
AM RADIO STATION

KICD-FM 44686
Owner: Saga Communications
Editorial: 2600 Highway Blvd, Spencer, Iowa 51301-2140 **Tel:** 1 712 262-1240.
Web site: http://www.cd1077fm.com
Profile: KICD-FM is a commercial station owned by Saga Communications. The format of the station is country music. KICD-FM roadcasts to the Spencer, IA area at 107.7 FM.
FM RADIO STATION

KICE-AM 37300
Owner: Gross Communications Co.
Editorial: 345 SW Cyber Dr Ste 101-103, Bend, Oregon 97702-1045 **Tel:** 1 541 388-3300.
Web site: http://sportsradio1065and940.com
Profile: KICE-AM is a commercial station owned by Gross Communications Co. The format of the station is sports. KICE-AM broadcasts to the Bend, OR area at 940 AM.
AM RADIO STATION

KICK-FM 44688
Owner: Townsquare Media
Editorial: 408 N 24th St, Quincy, Illinois 62301-3254 **Tel:** 1 217 223-5292.
Email: kickfm@hqradio.com
Web site: http://979kickfm.com
Profile: KICK-FM is a commercial station owned by Townsquare Media. The format of the station is contemporary country music. KICK-FM broadcasts to the Quincy, IL area at 97.9 FM.
FM RADIO STATION

KICM-FM 39970
Owner: Keystone Broadcasting Corp
Editorial: 661 1st Ave NW, Ardmore, Oklahoma 73401-4569 **Tel:** 1 580 226-9797.
Web site: http://kicm.com
Profile: KICM-FM is a commercial station owned by Keystone Broadcasting Corp. The format of the station is contemporary country music. KICM-FM broadcasts to the Ardmore, OK area at 97.7 FM.
FM RADIO STATION

KICR-FM 518217
Owner: Blue Sky Broadcasting Inc.
Editorial: 327 S Marion Ave, Sandpoint, Idaho 83864-1723 **Tel:** 1 208 263-2179.
Profile: KICR-FM is a commercial station owned by Blue Sky Broadcasting Inc. The format of the station is contemporary country. KICR-FM broadcasts to the Sandpoint, ID area at 102.3 FM.
FM RADIO STATION

KICS-AM 36831
Owner: Platte River Radio, Inc.
Editorial: 500 E J St, Hastings, Nebraska 68901 **Tel:** 1 402 462-5101.
Email: generalmanager@espnsuperstation.com
Web site: http://espnsuperstation.com
Profile: KICS-AM is a commercial station owned by Platte River Radio, Inc. The format of the station is sports. KICS-FM broadcasts in the Hastings, NE area at 1550 AM.
AM RADIO STATION

KICT-FM 39677
Owner: Kiel Media Group, LLC
Editorial: 4200 N Old Lawrence Rd, Wichita, Kansas 67219-3211 **Tel:** 1 316 838-9141.
Email: news@kfdi.com
Web site: http://www.t95.com
Profile: KICT-FM is a commercial station owned by Kiel Media Group, LLC. The format of the station is rock. KICT-FM broadcasts to the Wichita, KS area at 95.1 FM.
FM RADIO STATION

KICX-FM 45917
Owner: Armada Media Corp.
Editorial: 1811 W O St, McCook, Nebraska 69001-4268 **Tel:** 1 308 345-5400.
Email: production@highplainsradio.net
Web site: http://www.highplainsradio.net/kicx-96-1/
Profile: KICX-FM is a commercial station owned by Armada Media Corp. The format of the station is adult contemporary. KICX-FM broadcasts to the McCook, NE area at 98.5 FM.
FM RADIO STATION

KICY-AM 37314
Owner: Arctic Broadcasting Association
Editorial: 408 W D St, Nome, Alaska 99762-0820 **Tel:** 1 907 443-2213.
Email: office@kicy.org
Web site: http://www.kicy.org
Profile: KICY-AM is a commercial station owned by Arctic Broadcasting Association. The format of the station is gospel and religion. KICY-AM broadcasts to the Nome, AK area at 850 AM.
AM RADIO STATION

KICY-FM 44687
Owner: Arctic Broadcasting Association
Editorial: 408 W D St, Nome, Alaska 99762-0820 **Tel:** 1 907 443-2213.
Email: office@kicy.org
Web site: http://www.kicy.org
Profile: KCIY-FM is a commercial station owned by KICY-FM. The format is gospel and religous music. The station airs at 100.3FM in the Nome, AK area.
FM RADIO STATION

KID-AM 37315
Owner: Rich Broadcasting, LLC
Editorial: 1406 Commerce Way, Idaho Falls, Idaho 83401 **Tel:** 1 208 524-5900.
Web site: http://590kid.com
Profile: KID-AM is a commercial station owned by Rich Broadcasting, LLC. The format of the station is news and talk. KID-AM broadcasts to the Idaho Falls, ID area at 590 AM.
AM RADIO STATION

KIDD-AM 39378
Owner: Alpha Media
Editorial: 5 Harris Ct Bldg C, Monterey, California 93940-5751 **Tel:** 1 831 649-0969.
Web site: http://www.espn630.com
Profile: KIDD-AM is a commercial station owned by Alpha Media. The format of the station is classical. KIDD-AM broadcasts to the Monterey, CA area at 630 AM.
AM RADIO STATION

KIDE-FM 41282
Owner: Hoopa Valley Tribe
Editorial: Hoopa Valley Shopping Ctr Hwy 96, Hoopa, California 95546 **Tel:** 1 530 625-4245.
Web site: http://kidefm.org/
Profile: KIDE-FM is a non-commercial station owned by Hoopa Valley Tribe. The format of the station is variety, Native American programming. KIDE-FM broadcasts in the Hoopa Valley Indian Reservation, CA at 91.3 FM.
FM RADIO STATION

KID-FM 44646
Owner: Rich Broadcasting, LLC
Editorial: 1406 Commerce Way, Idaho Falls, Idaho 83401-1233 **Tel:** 1 208 524-5900.
Email: ty@richbroadcasting.com
Web site: http://www.rivercountryfm.com
Profile: KID-FM is a commercial station owned by Rich Broadcasting, LLC. The format of the station is country music. KID-FM broadcasts in the Idaho Falls, ID area at 96.1 FM.
FM RADIO STATION

KIDG-FM 500947
Owner: Rich Broadcasting, LLC
Editorial: 1406 Commerce Way, Idaho Falls, Idaho 83401-1233 **Tel:** 1 208 233-1133.
Web site: http://www.590kid.com
Profile: KIDG-FM is a commercial station owned by Rich Broadcasting, LLC. The format of the station is news talk. KIDG-FM broadcasts to the Pocatello, ID area at 92.1 FM.
FM RADIO STATION

KIDI-FM 46634
Owner: Emerald Wave Media
Editorial: 718 E Chapel St, Santa Maria, California 93454-4524 **Tel:** 1 805 928-4334.
Email: traffic@emeraldwavemedia.com
Web site: http://www.labuena.fm
Profile: KIDI-FM is a commercial station owned by Emerald Wave Media. The format of the station is regional Mexican. KIDI-FM broadcasts to the Santa Maria, CA area at 105.1 FM.
FM RADIO STATION

KIDJ-FM 42811
Owner: Rich Broadcasting, Inc.
Editorial: 544 N Arthur Ave, Pocatello, Idaho 83204-3002 **Tel:** 1 208 529-6926.
Web site: http://590kid.com
Profile: KIDJ-FM is a commercial station owned by Rich Broadcasting, Inc. The format of the station is News/Talk. KQEZ-FM broadcasts to the Idaho Falls, ID area at 106.3 FM.
FM RADIO STATION

KIDN-FM 43885
Owner: NRC Broadcasting
Editorial: 2955 Village Dr, Steamboat Springs, Colorado 80487-2143 **Tel:** 1 970 879-5368.
Web site: http://alwaysmountaintime.com/kidn
Profile: KIDN-FM is a commercial station owned by NRC Broadcasting. The format of the station is Hot AC. KIDN-FM broadcasts to the Steamboat Springs, CO area on 95.5 FM.
FM RADIO STATION

KIDO-AM 37316
Owner: Townsquare Media, LLC
Editorial: 827 E Park Blvd Ste 100, Boise, Idaho 83712-7783 **Tel:** 1 208 344-6363.
Web site: http://www.kidoam.com
Profile: KIDO-AM is a commercial station owned by Townsquare Media, LLC. The format of the station is news and talk. KIDO-AM broadcasts to the Boise, ID area at 580 AM.
AM RADIO STATION

KIDR-AM 36660
Owner: En Familia, Inc.
Editorial: 3015 N 33rd Dr, Phoenix, Arizona 85017-5204 **Tel:** 1 602 234-8998.
Email: info@enfamilia.com
Web site: http://www.enfamilia.com
Profile: KIDR-AM is a commercial station owned by En Familia, Inc. The format of the station is Spanish talk. KIDR-AM broadcasts to the Phoenix area at 740 AM.
AM RADIO STATION

KIFG-AM 37317
Owner: Times Citizen Communications
Editorial: 406 Stevens St, Iowa Falls, Iowa 50126-2214 **Tel:** 1 641 648-2521 360.
Email: kifg@iafalls.com
Web site: http://www.kifgradio.com
Profile: KIFG-AM is a commercial station owned by Times Citizen Communications. The format of the station is classic hits. KIFG-AM broadcasts to the Iowa Falls, IA area at 1510 AM.
AM RADIO STATION

KIFG-FM 44690
Owner: Times Citizen Communications
Editorial: 406 Stevens st., Iowa Falls, Iowa **Tel:** 1 641 648-2521 360.
Email: kifg@iafalls.com
Web site: http://www.kifgradio.com
Profile: KIFG-FM is a commercial station owned by Times Citizen Communications. The format of the station is classic hits. KIFG-FM broadcasts to the Des Moines, IA area at 95.3 FM.
FM RADIO STATION

KIFM-AM 36658
Owner: Entercom Communications Corp.
Editorial: 5345 Madison Ave, Sacramento, California 95841-3141 **Tel:** 1 916 334-7777.
Email: writeus@espn1320.net
Web site: http://espn1320.net
Profile: KIFM-AM is a commercial station owned by Entercom Communications Corp. The format for the station is sports. KIFM-AM broadcasts to the Sacramento, CA area at 1320 AM.
AM RADIO STATION

KIFS-FM 43097
Owner: Bicoastal Media LLC
Editorial: 3624 Avion Dr, Medford, Oregon 97504 **Tel:** 1 541 772-4170.
Web site: http://www.107kiss.com
Profile: KIFS-FM is a commercial station owned by Bicoastal Media LLC. The format of the station is Top 40/CHR music. KIFS-FM broadcasts to the Medford, OR area at 107.5 FM.
FM RADIO STATION

KIFT-FM 43368
Owner: NRC Broadcasting
Editorial: 130 Ski Hill Rd, Ste 240, Breckenridge, Colorado 80424 **Tel:** 1 970 453-2234.
Web site: http://www.lift106.com
Profile: KIFT-FM is a commercial station owned by NRC Broadcasting. The format of the station is Top 40. KIFT-FM is licensed to Kremmling, CO and broadcasts to Summit, Grand and Eagle counties at 106.3 FM.
FM RADIO STATION

KIFW-AM 38939
Owner: Alaska Broadcast Communications Inc.
Editorial: 611 Lake St, Sitka, Alaska 99835-7402 **Tel:** 1 907 747-5439.
Email: kifw@abcstations.com
Web site: http://www.sitkaradio.com
Profile: KIFW-AM is a commercial station owned by Alaska Broadcast Communications Inc. The format of the station is adult contemporary music. KIFW-AM broadcasts to the Sitka, AK area at 1230 AM.
AM RADIO STATION

KIFX-FM 46364
Owner: Evans Broadcasting
Editorial: RR 2 Box 2384, 2242 E 1000 S, Roosevelt, Utah 84066-9523 **Tel:** 1 435 722-5011.
Email: radio@ubtanet.com
Web site: http://www.stormpc.com/fox/foxlink.htm
Profile: KIFX-FM is a commercial station owned by Evans Broadcasting. The format of the station is adult contemporary. KIFX-FM broadcasts to the Salt Lake City area at 98.5 FM.
FM RADIO STATION

KIGL-FM 43480
Owner: iHeartMedia Inc.
Editorial: 2049 E Joyce Blvd Ste 101, Fayetteville, Arkansas 72703-6395 **Tel:** 1 479 973-9339.
Web site: http://www.933theeagle.com
Profile: KIGL-FM is a commercial station owned by iHeartMedia Inc. The format of the station is classic rock. KIGL-FM broadcasts to the Fayetteville, AR area at 93.3 FM.
FM RADIO STATION

KIGN-FM 42549
Owner: Townsquare Media, LLC
Editorial: 1912 Capitol Ave Ste 300, Cheyenne, Wyoming 82001-3659 **Tel:** 1 307 632-4400.
Web site: http://www.kingfm.com
Profile: KIGN-FM is a commercial station owned by Townsquare Media, LLC. The format of the station is rock music. KIGN-FM broadcasts in the Cheyenne, WY area at 101.9 FM.
FM RADIO STATION

KIHK-FM 43597
Owner: Community First Broadcasting, LLC
Editorial: 128 20th St SE, Sioux Center, Iowa 51250 **Tel:** 1 712 722-1090.
Email: ksou@siouxcountyradio.com
Web site: http://www.ksoufm.com
Profile: KIHK-FM is a commercial station owned by Community First Broadcasting, LLC. The format of the station is classic country. KIHK-FM broadcasts to the Sioux Center, IA area at 106.9 FM.
FM RADIO STATION

KIHM-AM 36411
Owner: Immaculate Heart Radio
Tel: 1 888 887-7120.
Email: programming@ihradio.org
Web site: http://ihradio.org
Profile: KIHM-AM is a non-commercial station owned by Immaculate Heart Radio. The format of the station is religious. KIHM-AM broadcasts in the Reno, NV area at 920 AM.
AM RADIO STATION

KIHP-AM 36050
Owner: Immaculate Heart Radio
Editorial: 2800 N 44th St Ste 125, Phoenix, Arizona 85008-1569 **Tel:** 1 916 535-0500.
Email: programming@ihradio.org
Web site: http://ihradio.com
Profile: KIHP-AM is a commercial station owned by Immaculate Heart Radio. The format of the station is religious and catholic programming. KIHP-AM broadcasts in the Phoenix area at 1310 AM.
AM RADIO STATION

KIHR-AM 37318
Owner: Bicoastal Media LLC
Editorial: 1190 22Nd St, Hood River, Oregon 97031-9669 **Tel:** 1 541 386-1511.
Web site: http://www.kihramfm.com
Profile: KIHR-AM is a commercial station owned by Bicoastal Media LLC. The format of the station is contemporary country music. KIHR-AM broadcasts to the Portland, OR area at 1340 AM.
AM RADIO STATION

KIHU-AM 36262
Owner: Immaculate Heart Radio
Editorial: 3256 Penryn Rd Ste 100, Loomis, California 95650-8052 **Tel:** 1 916 535-0500.
Email: programming@ihradio.org
Web site: http://ihradio.com
Profile: KIHU-FM is a non-commercial station owned by Immaculate Heart Radio. The format is Catholic programming. KIHU-AM broadcasts to the Park City, UT area at 1010 AM.
AM RADIO STATION

KIIC-FM 46755
Owner: Waveguide Communications Inc
Editorial: 7 Benton Ave E, Ste 1, Albia, Iowa 52531 **Tel:** 1 641 932-2112.
Web site: http://www.kiicradio.com
Profile: KIIC-FM is a commercial station owned by Waveguide Communications Inc. The format of the station is country. KIIC-FM broadcasts to the Albia, IA area at 96.7 FM.
FM RADIO STATION

KIID-AM 36520
Owner: Punjabi American Media LLC
Editorial: 3750 McKee Rd Ste B, San Jose, California 95127-2000 **Tel:** 1 408 272-5200.
Email: info@punjabiradiousa.com
Web site: http://punjabiradiousa.com
AM RADIO STATION

KIIM-FM 45782
Owner: Cumulus Media Inc
Editorial: 575 W Roger Rd, Tucson, Arizona 85705 **Tel:** 1 520 887-1000.
Web site: http://www.kiimfm.com
Profile: KIIM-FM is a commercial station owned by Cumulus Media Inc. The format of the station is contemporary country. KIIM-FM broadcasts to the Tucson, AZ area at 99.5 FM.
FM RADIO STATION

KIIS-FM 44691
Owner: iHeartMedia Inc.
Editorial: 3400 W Olive Ave Ste 550, Burbank, California 91505-5544 **Tel:** 1 818 559-2252.
Web site: http://kiisfm.iheart.com
Profile: KIIS-FM is a commercial station owned by iHeartMedia Inc. The format of the station is Top 40/CHR. KIIS-FM broadcasts to the Los Angeles area at 102.7 FM.
FM RADIO STATION

KIIX-AM 36758
Owner: iHeartMedia Inc.
Editorial: 4270 Byrd Dr, 1410 Kiix Country C/O Iheartmedia, Loveland, Colorado 80538-7074 **Tel:** 1 970 461-2560.
Web site: http://www.kiixcountry.com/main.html
Profile: KIIX-AM is a commercial station owned by iHeartMedia Inc. The format of the station is Classic Country. KIIX-AM broadcasts to the Denver area at 1410 AM.
AM RADIO STATION

KIIZ-FM 42229
Owner: iHeartMedia Inc.
Editorial: 314 W State Highway 6, Waco, Texas 76712-3971 **Tel:** 1 254 776-3900.
Web site: http://www.kiiz.com/main.html

Profile: KIIZ-FM is a commercial station owned by iHeartMedia Inc. The format of the station is urban contemporary. KIIZ-FM broadcasts to the Killeen, TX area at 92.3 FM.
FM RADIO STATION

KIJN-AM 37320
Owner: Unido Para Christo, Inc.
Editorial: 205 9th St, Farwell, Texas 79325-5653
Tel: 1 806 481-3318.
Email: kijn@email.com
Web site: http://www.myjesusradio.com
Profile: KIJN-AM is a commercial station owned by Unido Para Christo, Inc. The format of the station is religious programming and Hispanic. KIJN-AM broadcasts to the Farwell, TX area at 1060 AM.
AM RADIO STATION

KIJN-FM 44692
Owner: Top of Texas Educational Broadcasting Foundation
Tel: 1 806 359-8855.
Web site: http://www.kingdomkeysradio.org
Profile: KIJN-FM is a commercial station owned by Top of Texas Educational Broadcasting Foundation. The format of the station is religious teaching. KIJN-FM broadcasts to the Farwell, TX area at 92.3 FM.
FM RADIO STATION

KIJV-AM 37321
Owner: Dakota Communications, Ltd.
Editorial: 1726 Dakota Ave S, Huron, South Dakota 57350-4024 **Tel:** 1 605 352-1933.
Email: production@kokk.com
Web site: http://www.performance-radio.com
Profile: KIJV-AM is a commercial station owned by Dakota Communications, Ltd. The format of the station is CHR. KIJV-AM broadcasts to the Huron, SD area at 1340 AM.
AM RADIO STATION

KIKC-AM 37322
Owner: Miles City Forsyth Broadcasting Inc.
Tel: 1 406 346-2711.
Email: kikc@rangeweb.net
Web site: http://kikcradio.com/
Profile: KIKC-AM is a commercial station owned by Miles City Forsyth Broadcasting Inc. The format of the station is classic country. KIKC-AM broadcasts in the Forsyth, MT area at 1250 AM.
AM RADIO STATION

KIKC-FM 44693
Owner: Miles City Forsyth Broadcasting Inc.
Tel: 1 406 346-2711.
Email: kikc@rangeweb.net
Web site: http://kikcradio.com/
Profile: KIKC-FM is a commercial station owned by Miles City Forsyth Broadcasting Inc. The format of the station is contemporary country music. KIKC-FM broadcasts to the Forsyth, MT area at 101.3 FM.
FM RADIO STATION

KIKD-FM 43232
Owner: Carroll Broadcasting Co.
Editorial: 1119 Plaza Dr, Carroll, Iowa 51401-3838
Tel: 1 712 792-4321.
Web site: http://carrollbroadcasting.com
Profile: KIKD-FM is a commercial station owned by Carroll Broadcasting Co. The format of the station is contemporary country music. KIKD-FM broadcasts to the Carrol, IA area at 106.7 FM.
FM RADIO STATION

KIKF-FM 80883
Owner: STARadio Corp.
Editorial: 1300 Central Ave W, Great Falls, Montana 59404-3971 **Tel:** 1 406 761-2800.
Email: audiogf@staradio.com
Web site: http://www.1049wolf.com
Profile: KIKF (104.9 FM) is a radio station broadcasting a Country music format. Licensed to Cascade, Montana, USA, the station serves the Great Falls area. The station is currently owned by STARadio Corporation.
FM RADIO STATION

KIKI-AM 39415
Owner: iHeartMedia Inc.
Editorial: 650 Iwilei Rd Ste 400, Honolulu, Hawaii 96817-5319 **Tel:** 1 808 550-9200.
Web site: http://www.kikiradio.com
Profile: KIKI-AM is a commercial station owned by iHeartMedia Inc. The format for the station is sports. KIKI-AM broadcasts to the Honolulu area at 990 AM.
AM RADIO STATION

KIKK-AM 37323
Owner: CBS Radio
Editorial: 24 Greenway Plz, Houston, Texas 77046-2401 **Tel:** 1 713 881-5100.
Web site: http://houston.cbslocal.com/station/talk-650
Profile: KIKK-AM is commercial station owned by CBS Radio. The format of the station is news, talk and sports. KIKK-AM broadcasts to the Houston area at 650 AM.
AM RADIO STATION

KIKN-FM 42596
Owner: Townsquare Media, Inc.
Editorial: 5100 S Tennis Ln, Sioux Falls, South Dakota 57108-2212 **Tel:** 1 605 361-0300.
Web site: http://www.kikn.com
Profile: KIKN-FM is a commercial station owned by Townsquare Media, Inc. The format of the station is classic country. KIKN-FM broadcasts to the Sioux Falls, SD area at 100.5 FM.
FM RADIO STATION

KIKO-AM 38797
Owner: 1TV.Com, Inc.
Editorial: 4501 Broadway, Miami, Arizona 85539-3800
Tel: 1 928 425-4471.
Web site: http://kikonews.tumblr.com
Profile: KIKO-AM is a commercial station owned by 1TV.Com, Inc. The format of the station is primarily oldies. KIKO-AM broadcasts to the Miami, AZ area at 1340 AM.
AM RADIO STATION

KIKO-FM 46140
Owner: 1TV.Com, Inc.
Editorial: 4501 Broadway, Miami, Arizona 85539-3800
Tel: 1 928 425-4471.
Web site: http://oldies1340am.com
Profile: KIKO-FM is a commercial station owned by 1TV.Com, Inc. The format of the station is Oldies. KIKO-FM broadcasts to the Miami, AZ area at 97.3 FM
FM RADIO STATION

KIKR-AM 38972
Owner: Cumulus Media Inc.
Editorial: 755 S 11th St Ste 102, Beaumont, Texas 77701-3723 **Tel:** 1 409 951-2500.
Web site: http://www.sportsradiobeaumont.com/
Profile: KIKR-AM is a commercial station owned by Cumulus Media Inc. The format of the station is Sports. KIKR-AM broadcasts to the Beaumont, TX area at 1450 AM.
AM RADIO STATION

KIKS-FM 44695
Owner: Iola Broadcasting Inc.
Editorial: 2221 S State St, Iola, Kansas 66749
Tel: 1 620 365-3151.
Email: radiostation@iolaradio.com
Web site: http://www.iolaradio.com
Profile: KIKS-FM is a commercial station owned by Iola Broadcasting Inc. The format of the station is contemporary country. KIKS-FM broadcasts to the Iola, KS area at 99.3 FM.
FM RADIO STATION

KIKT-FM 44696
Owner: Hunt County Broadcasting, LLC
Editorial: Cooper, Texas **Tel:** 1 903 455-1400.
Web site: http://www.935thecoyote.com
Profile: KIKT-FM is a commercial station owned by Hunt County Broadcasting, LLC. The format of the station is contemporary country. KIKT-FM broadcasts to the Cooper, TX area at 93.5 FM.
FM RADIO STATION

KIKV-FM 39682
Owner: Hubbard Broadcasting Inc.
Editorial: 604 3rd Ave W, Alexandria, Minnesota 56308-2669 **Tel:** 1 320 762-2154.
Email: 100.7@kikvfm.com
Web site: http://www.kikvradio.com
Profile: KIKV-FM is a commercial station owned by Hubbard Broadcasting. The format of the station is classic country. KIKV-FM broadcasts to the Alexandria, MN area at 100.7 FM.
FM RADIO STATION

KIKX-FM 43116
Owner: Locally Owned Radio, LLC
Editorial: 21361 Highway 30, Twin Falls, Idaho 83301-0197 **Tel:** 1 208 735-8300.
Web site: http://www.1047bobfm.com
Profile: KIKX-FM is a commercial station owned by Locally Owned Radio, LLC. The format of the station is adult hits. KIKX-FM broadcasts to the Twin Falls, ID area at 104.7 FM. The station's slogan is, "We Play Anything."
FM RADIO STATION

KIKZ-AM 37325
Owner: Gaines County Broadcasting
Editorial: 105 Nw 11Th St, Seminole, Texas 79360-3301 **Tel:** 1 432 758-5878.
Email: kikz-ksem@bajabb.com
Web site: http://www.kikzksem.ws
Profile: KIKZ-AM is a commercial station owned by Gaines County Broadcasting. The format of the station is country and Hispanic music. KIKZ broadcasts to the Seminole, TX area at 1250 AM.
AM RADIO STATION

KILI-FM 41273
Owner: Lakota Communications Inc.
Tel: 1 605 867-5002.
Web site: http://www.kiliradio.org/
Profile: KILI-FM is a non-commercial station owned by Lakota Communications Inc. The format of the station is variety. KILI-FM broadcasts to the Rapid City, SD area at 90.1 FM.
FM RADIO STATION

KILJ-AM 37326
Owner: Dennison(Paul and Joyce)
Editorial: 2411 Radio Dr, Mount Pleasant, Iowa 52641-8207 **Tel:** 1 319 385-8728.
Email: kiljradio@kilj.com
Web site: http://www.kilj.com
Profile: KILJ-AM is a commercial station owned by Paul and Joyce Dennison. The format of the station is classic country music. KILJ-AM broadcasts to the Mount Pleasant, IA area at 1130 AM.
AM RADIO STATION

KILJ-FM 44697
Owner: Dennison(Paul and Joyce)
Editorial: 2411 Radio Dr, Mount Pleasant, Iowa 52641-8207 **Tel:** 1 319 385-8728.
Email: kiljradio@kilj.com
Web site: http://www.kilj.com
Profile: KILJ-FM is a commercial station owned by Paul and Joyce Dennison. The format of the station is adult standards. KILJ-FM broadcasts to the Mount Pleasant, IA area at 105.5 FM.
FM RADIO STATION

KILO-FM 39684
Owner: Bahakel Communications
Editorial: 1805 E Cheyenne Rd, Colorado Springs, Colorado 80905-2868 **Tel:** 1 719 634-4896.
Email: kilostudio@kilo943.com
Web site: http://www.kilo943.com
Profile: KILO-FM is a commercial station owned by Bahakel Communications. The format of the station is rock. KILO-FM broadcasts to the Colorado Springs, CO area at 94.3 FM.
FM RADIO STATION

KILR-AM 37327
Owner: Jacobson Broadcasting Companies Inc.
Editorial: 3875 150th St, Estherville, Iowa 51334-7517
Tel: 1 712 362-2644.
Email: kilr@yourstarnet.net
Profile: KILR-AM is a commercial station owned by Jacobson Broadcasting Companies Inc. The format for the station is talk. KILR-AM broadcasts to the Estherville, IA area at 1070 AM.
AM RADIO STATION

KILR-FM 44698
Owner: Jacobson Broadcasting Companies Inc.
Editorial: 3875 150th St, Estherville, Iowa 51334-7517
Tel: 1 712 362-2644.
Email: kilrradio@hotmail.com
Web site: http://kilrradio.com/
Profile: KILR-FM is a commercial station owned by Jacobson Broadcasting Companies Inc. The format of the station is country. KILR-FM broadcasts to the Estherville, IA area at 95.9 FM.
FM RADIO STATION

KILT-AM 37329
Owner: CBS Radio
Editorial: 24 Greenway Plz, Houston, Texas 77046-2401 **Tel:** 1 713 881-5100.
Email: houstonpsa@cbsradio.com
Web site: http://houston.cbslocal.com
Profile: KILT-AM is a commercial station owned by CBS Radio. The format of the station is sports. KILT-AM broadcasts to the Houston area at 610 AM.
AM RADIO STATION

KILT-FM 44699
Owner: CBS Radio
Editorial: 24 Greenway Plz Ste 1900, Houston, Texas 77046-2428 **Tel:** 1 713 881-5100.
Web site: http://thebull.cbslocal.com
Profile: KILT-FM is a commercial station owned by CBS Radio. The format of the station is contemporary country. KILT-FM broadcasts to the Houston area at 100.3 FM.
FM RADIO STATION

KILX-FM 444843
Owner: Ouachita Broadcasting Inc.
Editorial: 921 W Collin Raye Dr, De Queen, Arkansas 71832-2025 **Tel:** 1 870 642-2440.
Email: 102thegoodpath@gmail.com
Profile: KILX-FM is a commercial station owned by Ouachita Broadcasting Inc. The format for the station is hot adult contemporary. KILX-FM broadcasts to the Mena, AR area at 104.1 FM.
FM RADIO STATION

KIML-AM 38869
Owner: Legend Communications
Editorial: 2810 Southern Dr, Gillette, Wyoming 82718
Tel: 1 307 686-2242.
Email: news@basinsradio.com
Web site: http://www.basinsradio.com
Profile: KIML-AM is a commercial station owned by Legend Communications. The format of the station is news, talk and sports. KIML-AM broadcasts to the Gillette, WY area at 1270 AM.
AM RADIO STATION

KIMM-AM 36915
Owner: Flasen Publishing
Editorial: 11 Main St, Rapid City, South Dakota 57701-2831 **Tel:** 1 605 342-1150.
Web site: http://kimmradio.net/
Profile: KIMM-AM is a commercial station owned by Flasen Publishing. The format of the station is news/talk. KIMM-AM broadcasts to the Rapid City, SD area at 1150 AM.
AM RADIO STATION

KIMN-FM 42271
Owner: Wilks Broadcast Group
Editorial: 720 S Colorado Blvd Ste 1200N, Denver, Colorado 80246-1947 **Tel:** 1 303 832-5665.
Web site: http://www.mix100.com
Profile: KIMN-FM is a commercial station owned by Kroenke Sports & Entertainment. The format of the station is hot adult contemporary. KIMN-FM broadcasts to the Denver area at 100.3 FM.
FM RADIO STATION

KIMO-FM 80364
Owner: The Montana Radio Company, LLC.
Editorial: 100 W Lyndale Ave Ste B, Helena, Montana 59601-2999 **Tel:** 1 406 442-6645.
Email: mo@montanaradio.com
Web site: http://www.mightymo.com/home.html
Profile: KIMO-FM (107.3 FM) is a commercial radio station located in Townsend, Montana and serves the Helena area. KIMO airs a country music format and is owned by The Montana Radio Company.
FM RADIO STATION

KIMP-AM 36950
Owner: East Texas Broadcasting Inc.
Editorial: Highway 67 West 1 Mile, Mount Pleasant, Texas 75455 **Tel:** 1 903 577-9770.
Web site: http://easttexasradio.com
Profile: KIMP-AM is a commercial station owned by East Texas Broadcasting Inc. The format of the station is Spanish Adult Hits. KIMP-AM broadcasts to the Mount Pleasant, TX area at 960 AM.
AM RADIO STATION

KIMX-FM 235284
Owner: Appaloosa Broadcasting
Editorial: 302 S 2nd St Ste 204, Laramie, Wyoming 82070-3650 **Tel:** 1 307 745-5208.
Email: imixwyoming@gmail.com
Web site: http://www.planet967.com
Profile: KIMX-FM is a commercial station owned by Appaloosa Broadcasting. The format of the station is Top 40/CHR. KIMX-FM broadcasts to the Laramie, WY area at 96.9 FM.
FM RADIO STATION

KIMY-FM 41278
Owner: South Central Oklahoma Christian Broadcasting Inc.
Editorial: 20750 State Hwy 1W, Ada, Oklahoma 74820-5424 **Tel:** 1 580 332-0902.
Email: email@thegospelstation.com
Web site: http://www.thegospelstation.com
Profile: KIMY-FM is a commercial station owned by South Central Oklahoma Christian Broadcasting Inc. The format of the station is gospel music. KIMY-FM broadcasts in the Watonga, OK area at 93.9 FM.
FM RADIO STATION

KINA-AM 39331
Owner: Eagle Radio Inc.
Editorial: 1825 S Ohio St, Salina, Kansas 67401-6601
Tel: 1 785 825-4631.
Profile: KINA-AM is a commercial station owned by Eagle Radio Inc. The format of the station is news, talk and sports. KINA-AM broadcasts to the Salina, KS area at 910 AM.
AM RADIO STATION

KINB-FM 80887
Owner: The Last Bastion Station Trust, LLC
Editorial: 7725 W Britton Rd Ste B, Oklahoma City, Oklahoma 73132-1508 **Tel:** 1 405 848-0100.
Profile: KINB-FM is a commercial station owned by The Last Bastion Station Trust, LLC. The format of the station is sports. KINB-FM broadcasts locally to the Kingfisher, OK area at 105.3 FM.
FM RADIO STATION

KIND-AM 37330
Owner: My Town Media, Inc.
Editorial: 309 N Penn Ave, Independence, Kansas 67301-3325 **Tel:** 1 620 331-3000.
Web site: http://mytown-media.com
Profile: KIND-AM is a commercial station owned by My Town Media, Inc. The format of the station is classic hits. KIND-AM broadcasts to the Independence, KS area at 1010 AM.
AM RADIO STATION

KIND-FM 687906
Owner: My Town Media, Inc.
Editorial: 309 N Penn Ave, Independence, Kansas 67301-3325 **Tel:** 1 620 331-3000.
Web site: http://mytown-media.com
Profile: KIND-FM is a commercial station owned by My Town Media, Inc. The format of the station is Hot AC. KBIP-FM broadcasts to the Elk City, KS area at 94.9 FM.
FM RADIO STATION

KINE-AM 36572
Owner: Cotton Broadcasting
Editorial: 2209 N Padre Island Dr, Corpus Christi, Texas 78408-2432 **Tel:** 1 361 289-8877.
Profile: KINE-AM is a commercial station owned by Cotton Broadcasting. The format of the station is Hispanic religious programming. KINE-AM broadcasts to the Corpus Christi, TX area at 95.7 FM.
AM RADIO STATION

KINE-FM 41578
Owner: Summit Media Broadcasting LLC
Editorial: 900 Fort Street Mall, Honolulu, Hawaii 96813-3721 **Tel:** 1 808 536-2728.
Web site: http://www.hawaiian105.com
Profile: KINE-FM is commercial station owned by Summit Media Broadcasting LLC. The format of the station is adult contemporary. KINE-FM broadcasts to the Honolulu area at 105.1 FM.
FM RADIO STATION

KING-FM 42686
Owner: Classic Radio Inc.
Editorial: 10 Harrison St, Ste 100, Seattle, Washington 98109-4554 **Tel:** 1 206 691-2981.
Email: feedback@king.org
Web site: http://www.king.org

Profile: KING-FM is a commercial station owned by Classic Radio Inc. The format of the station is classical music. KING-FM broadcasts to Seattle at 98.1 FM.
FM RADIO STATION

KINI-FM 41581
Owner: St. Francis Mission
Editorial: 100 S Main St, Saint Francis, South Dakota 57572-0419 **Tel:** 1 605 747-2291.
Email: kinifm@gwtc.net
Web site: http://www.kinifm.com
Profile: KINI-FM is a non-commercial station owned by St. Francis Mission. The format of the station is variety. KINI-FM broadcasts to the Saint Francis, SD area at 96.1 FM.
FM RADIO STATION

KINK-FM 43243
Owner: Alpha Media
Editorial: 1211 SW 5th Ave Fl 6, Portland, Oregon 97204-3735 **Tel:** 1 503 517-6000.
Web site: http://kink.fm
Profile: KINK-FM is a commercial station owned by Alpha Media. The format of the station is adult album alternative music. KINK-FM broadcasts to the Portland, OR area on 101.9 FM.
FM RADIO STATION

KINL-FM 46551
Owner: R Communication Group
Editorial: 127 Kilowatt Dr, Eagle Pass, Texas 78852-3397 **Tel:** 1 830 773-9247.
Email: newsep@rcommunications.com
Web site: http://www.power927.net
Profile: KINL-FM is a commercial station owned by R Communications Group. The station's format is hot adult contemporary. KINL-FM broadcasts to the Eagle Pass, TX area at 92.7 FM.
FM RADIO STATION

KINN-AM 38487
Owner: Burt Broadcasting Inc.
Editorial: 501 S Florida Ave, Alamogordo, New Mexico 88310 **Tel:** 1 575 434-1414.
Email: burtbroadcasting@bbiradio.net
Web site: http://www.1270kinn.net
Profile: KINN-AM is a commercial station owned by Burt Broadcasting Inc. The format of the station is talk. KINN-AM broadcasts to the Albuquerque, NM area at 1270 AM.
AM RADIO STATION

KINO-AM 34975
Owner: Sunflower Communications Inc.
Tel: 1 928 289-3364.
Email: kinoradio@cableone.net
Profile: KINO-AM is a commercial station owned by Sunflower Communications Inc. The format of the station is classic country. KINO-AM broadcasts to the Winslow, AZ area at 1230 AM.
AM RADIO STATION

KINT-FM 46573
Owner: Entravision Communications Corp.
Editorial: 5426 N Mesa St, El Paso, Texas 79912-5421 **Tel:** 1 915 581-1126.
Web site: http://www.jose939.com
Profile: KINT-FM is a commercial station owned by Entravision Communications Corp. The format of the station is Regional Mexican. KINT-FM broadcasts to the El Paso, TX, area at 93.9 FM.
FM RADIO STATION

KINX-FM 841612
Owner: STARadio Corp.
Editorial: 1300 Central Ave, Great Falls, Montana 59401-3834 **Tel:** 1 406 761-2800.
Email: audiogf@staradio.com
Profile: KINX-FM is a commercial station owned by STARadio Corp. The format of the station is news and talk. The station airs locally at 102.7 FM.
FM RADIO STATION

KINY-AM 37331
Owner: Alaska-Juneau Communications
Editorial: 3161 Channel Dr Ste 2, Juneau, Alaska 99801-7866 **Tel:** 1 907 586-3630.
Email: news@abcstations.com
Web site: http://www.kinyradio.com
Profile: KINY-AM is a commercial station owned by Alaska-Juneau Communications. The station's primary format is news/talk/sports. The station airs adult contemporary music programming weekday evenings, Saturday evenings. Sunday mornings feature jazz and blues music. KINY-AM broadcasts to the Juneau, AK area at 800 AM.
AM RADIO STATION

KINZ-FM 44076
Owner: My Town Media, Inc.
Editorial: 702 N Plummer Ave, Chanute, Kansas 66720-1463 **Tel:** 1 620 431-3700.
Web site: http://www.kinz.biz
Profile: KINZ-FM is a commercial station owned by My Town Media, Inc. The format of the station is classic rock music. KINZ-FM broadcasts to the Chanute, KS area at 95.3 FM.
FM RADIO STATION

KIOA-FM 44626
Owner: Saga Communications
Editorial: 1416 Locust St, Des Moines, Iowa 50309-3014 **Tel:** 1 515 280-1350.
Web site: http://www.kioa.com
Profile: KIOA-FM is a commercial station owned by Saga Communications. The format of the station is oldies music. KIOA-FM broadcasts to the Des Moines, IA area at 93.3 FM.
FM RADIO STATION

KIOC-FM 39685
Owner: iHeartMedia Inc.
Editorial: 2885 Interstate 10 E, Beaumont, Texas 77702-1001 **Tel:** 1 409 896-5555.
Web site: http://bigdog106.iheart.com
Profile: KIOC-FM is a commercial station owned by iHeartMedia Inc. The format of the station is rock. KIOC-FM broadcasts to the Beaumont, TX area at 106.1 FM.
FM RADIO STATION

KIOD-FM 40071
Owner: GI Family Radio
Editorial: 106 W 8th St, McCook, Nebraska 69001-3508 **Tel:** 1 308 345-1981.
Email: production@krgi.com
Web site: http://www.coyote105.com/KIOD/index.htm
Profile: KIOD-FM is a commercial station owned by GI Family Radio. The format of the station is country. KIOD-FM broadcasts to the McCook, NE area at 105.3 FM.
FM RADIO STATION

KIOI-FM 39686
Owner: iHeartMedia Inc.
Editorial: 340 Townsend St, San Francisco, California 94107-1633 **Tel:** 1 415 538-1013.
Web site: http://1013.iheart.com
Profile: KIOI-FM is a commercial station owned by iHeartMedia Inc. The format of the station is hot adult contemporary. KIOI-FM broadcasts to the San Francisco area at 101.3 FM.
FM RADIO STATION

KIOK-FM 46426
Owner: Ingstad Radio Washington, LLC
Editorial: 4304 W 24Th Ave Suite 200, Kennewick, Washington 99338-2320 **Tel:** 1 509 783-0783.
Web site: http://www.949thewolfpack.com
Profile: KIOK-FM is a commercial station owned by Ingstad Radio Washington, LLC. The format of the station is classic and contemporary country. KIOK-FM broadcasts to the Kennewick, WA area at 94.9 FM.
FM RADIO STATION

KIOL-AM 37324
Owner: Iola Broadcasting Inc.
Editorial: 2221 S State St, Iola, Kansas 66749
Tel: 1 620 365-3151.
Email: radiostation@iolaradio.com
Web site: http://www.iolaradio.com
Profile: KIOL-AM is a commercial station owned by Iola Broadcasting Inc. The format of the station is talk. KIOL-AM broadcasts to the Iola, KS area at 1370 AM.
AM RADIO STATION

KION-AM 39418
Owner: iHeartMedia Inc.
Editorial: 903 N Main St, Salinas, California 93906-3912 **Tel:** 1 831 755-8181.
Web site: http://powertalk1460.iheart.com
Profile: KION-AM is a commercial station owned by iHeartMedia Inc. The format for the station is news and talk. KION-AM broadcasts to the Salinas, CA area at 1460 AM.
AM RADIO STATION

KIOO-FM 42746
Owner: Momentum Broadcasting LP
Editorial: 617 W Tulare Ave, Visalia, California 93277-2552 **Tel:** 1 559 553-1500.
Web site: http://www.997classicrock.com
Profile: KIOO-FM is a commercial station owned by Momentum Broadcasting LP. The format of the station is classic rock. KIOO-FM broadcasts to the Visalia, CA area at 99.7 FM.
FM RADIO STATION

KIOT-FM 42769
Owner: Univision Communications Inc.
Editorial: 8009 Marble Ave NE, Albuquerque, New Mexico 87110-7901 **Tel:** 1 505 262-1142.
Web site: http://www.coyote1025.com/
Profile: KIOT-FM is a commercial station owned by Univision Communications Inc. The format of the station is classic rock music. KIOT-FM broadcasts to the Albuquerque, NM area at 102.5 FM.
FM RADIO STATION

KIOU-AM 34904
Owner: Capital City Radio Corp.
Editorial: 2438 E Texas St Ste 7, Bossier City, Louisiana 71111-3737 **Tel:** 1 318 752-2115.
Web site: http://wilkinsradio.com/kiou-1480am-shreveport-la
AM RADIO STATION

KIOW-FM 39688
Owner: Pilot Knob Broadcasting Inc.
Editorial: 18643 360th St, Forest City, Iowa 50436
Tel: 1 641 585-1073.
Email: kiow@kiow.com
Web site: http://www.kiow.com
Profile: KIOW-FM is a commercial station owned by Pilot Knob Broadcasting Inc. The format of the station is variety. KIOW-FM broadcasts to the Forest City, IA area at 107.3 FM.
FM RADIO STATION

KIOZ-FM 43184
Owner: iHeartMedia Inc.
Editorial: 9660 Granite Ridge Dr Ste 100, San Diego, California 92123-2689 **Tel:** 1 858 292-2000.
Web site: http://www.rock1053.com
Profile: KIOZ-FM is a commercial station owned by iHeartMedia Inc. The format of the station is rock. KIOZ-FM broadcasts to the San Diego area at 105.3 FM.
FM RADIO STATION

KIPA-AM 35989
Owner: Resonate Hawaii, LLC
Editorial: 688 Kinoole St, Hilo, Hawaii 96720-3877
Tel: 1 808 959-5700.
Profile: KIPA-AM is a commercial station owned by Resonate Hawaii, LLC. The format for the station is news and talk. KIPA-AM broadcasts to the Hilo area at 1060 AM.
AM RADIO STATION

KIPO-FM 46405
Owner: Hawaii Public Radio
Editorial: 738 Kaheka St Ste 101, Honolulu, Hawaii 96814-3726 **Tel:** 1 808 955-8821.
Email: mail@hawaiipublicradio.org
Web site: http://www.hawaiipublicradio.org
Profile: KIPO-FM is a non-commercial station owned by Hawaii Public Radio. The format of the station is jazz and news. KIPO-FM broadcasts to the Honolulu area at 89.3 FM.
FM RADIO STATION

KIPR-FM 42125
Owner: Cumulus Media Inc
Editorial: 700 Wellington Hills Rd, Little Rock, Arkansas 72211-2026 **Tel:** 1 501 401-0200.
Web site: http://www.power923.com
Profile: KIPR-FM is a commercial station owned by Cumulus Media Inc. The format of the station is urban contemporary music. KIPR-FM broadcasts to the Little Rock, AR area at 92.3 AM.
FM RADIO STATION

KIQI-AM 34976
Owner: Multicultural Radio Broadcasting Inc.
Editorial: 44 Gough St Ste 301, San Francisco, California 94103-5424 **Tel:** 1 415 978-5378.
Email: kiqi1010@gmail.com
Web site: http://www.kiqi1010am.com
Profile: KIQI-AM is a commercial station owned by Multicultural Radio Broadcasting Inc. The format of the station is Hispanic news and talk. KIQI-AM broadcasts to the San Francisco area at 1010 AM.
AM RADIO STATION

KIQK-FM 46277
Owner: Haugo Broadcasting Inc.
Editorial: 3601 Canyon Lake Dr Ste 1, Rapid City, South Dakota 57702-3901 **Tel:** 1 605 343-0888.
Email: news@haugobroadcasting.com
Web site: http://www.kick104.com
Profile: KIQK-FM is a commercial station owned by Haugo Broadcasting Inc. The format of the station is country. KIQK-FM broadcasts to the Rapid City, SD area at 104.1 FM.
FM RADIO STATION

KIQO-FM 39689
Owner: American General Media
Editorial: 3620 Sacramento Dr, San Luis Obispo, California 93401-7215 **Tel:** 1 805 781-2750.
Email: news@americangeneralmedia.com
Web site: http://www.q1045fm.com
Profile: KIQO-FM is a commercial station owned by American General Media. The format of the station is oldies. KIQO-FM broadcasts to the San Luis Obispo, CA area at 104.5 FM.
FM RADIO STATION

KIQX-FM 39691
Owner: Four Corners Broadcasting LLC
Editorial: 190 Turner Dr, Durango, Colorado 81303-8231 **Tel:** 1 970 259-4444.
Email: fcb@frontier.net
Profile: KIQX-FM is a commercial station owned by Four Corners Broadcasting LLC. The format of the station is adult contemporary music. KIQX-FM broadcasts to the Durango, CO area at 101.3 FM.
FM RADIO STATION

KIRC-FM 39912
Owner: One Ten Broadcasting Group Inc.
Editorial: 2 E Main St, Shawnee, Oklahoma 74801-6904 **Tel:** 1 405 878-1803.
Email: kirc1059@aol.com
Web site: http://kirc1059.com
Profile: KIRC-FM is a commercial station owned by One Ten Broadcasting Group Inc. The format of the station is classic country music. KIRC-FM broadcasts to the Shawnee, OK area at 105.9 FM.
FM RADIO STATION

KIRK-FM 43940
Owner: Moberly/Macon License Co., LLC
Editorial: 300 W Reed St, Moberly, Missouri 65270
Tel: 1 660 263-1500.
Email: kresnews@regionalradio.com
Web site: http://www.centralmoinfo.com
Profile: KIRK-FM is a commercial station owned by Moberly/Macon License Co., LLC. The format of the station is Classic Hits. KIRK-FM broadcasts to the Moberly, MO area at 99.9 FM.
FM RADIO STATION

KIRN-AM 35121
Owner: Lotus Communications Corp.
Editorial: 3301 Barham Blvd Ste 300, Los Angeles, California 90068-1477 **Tel:** 1 323 851-5476.
Web site: http://www.670amkirn.com/
Profile: KIRN-AM is a commercial station owned by Lotus Communications Corp. The format of the station is Iranian music and talk. The station broadcasts to the Los Angeles area at 670 AM.
AM RADIO STATION

KIRO-AM 39088
Owner: Bonneville International Corp.
Editorial: 1820 Eastlake Ave E, Seattle, Washington 98102-3711 **Tel:** 1 206 726-7000.
Web site: http://mynorthwest.com/category/sports
Profile: KIRO-AM is a commercial station owned by Bonneville International Corp. The format of the station is sports. KIRO-AM broadcasts to the Seattle area at 710 AM.
AM RADIO STATION

KIRO-FM 45931
Owner: Bonneville International Corp.
Editorial: 1820 Eastlake Ave E, Seattle, Washington 98102-3711 **Tel:** 1 206 726-7000.
Email: newsdesk@973kiro.com
Web site: http://www.kiroradio.com
Profile: KIRO-FM is a commercial station owned by Bonneville International Corp. The format of the station is news and talk. KIRO-FM broadcasts to the Seattle area at 97.3 FM.
FM RADIO STATION

KIRQ-FM 524391
Owner: Locally Owned Radio, LLC
Editorial: 21361 Highway 30, Twin Falls, Idaho 83301-0197 **Tel:** 1 208 735-8300.
Web site: http://www.irock1051.com
Profile: KIRQ-FM is a commercial station owned by Locally Owned Radio, LLC. The format for the station is rock alternative. KIRQ-FM broadcasts to the Twin Falls, ID area at 105.1 FM. The station's slogan is, "A Better Mix of Music."
FM RADIO STATION

KIRV-AM 34978
Owner: Centro Cristiano Vida Abundante, Inc.
Editorial: 121 W Alvin Ave, Santa Maria, California 93458-3002 **Tel:** 1 805 406-9157.
Web site: http://www.radiovidaabundante.com
Profile: KIRV-AM is a non-commercial station owned by Centro Cristiano Vida Abundante, Inc. The format for the station is Spanish religious programming. KIRV-AM broadcasts to the Fresno, CA area at 1510 AM.
AM RADIO STATION

KIRX-AM 37333
Owner: KIRX Inc.
Editorial: 1308 N Baltimore St, Kirksville, Missouri 63501-2509 **Tel:** 1 660 665-3781.
Email: kirx@cableone.net
Web site: http://www.1450kirx.com
Profile: KIRX-AM is a commercial station owned by KIRX Inc. The format for the station is news, talk and oldies. KIRX-AM broadcasts to the Kirksville, MO area at 1450 AM.
AM RADIO STATION

KISC-FM 45682
Owner: iHeartMedia Inc.
Editorial: 808 E Sprague Ave, Spokane, Washington 99202-2126 **Tel:** 1 509 242-2400.
Web site: http://www.literockkiss.com
Profile: KISC-FM is a commercial station owned by iHeartMedia Inc. The format of the station is Lite Rock/Lite AC. KISC-FM broadcasts to the Spokane, WA area at 98.1 FM.
FM RADIO STATION

KISD-FM 44751
Owner: Christensen Broadcasting
Editorial: 608 State Highway 30, Pipestone, Minnesota 56164 **Tel:** 1 507 825-4282.
Email: kisd@kisdradio.com
Web site: http://www.kisdradio.com/kisd
Profile: KISD-FM is a commercial station owned by Christensen Broadcasting. The format of the station is oldies. KISD-FM broadcasts to the Pipestone, MN area at 98.7 FM.
FM RADIO STATION

KISF-FM 41457
Owner: Univision Communications Inc.
Editorial: 6767 W Tropicana Ave Ste 102, Las Vegas, Nevada 89103-4755 **Tel:** 1 702 284-6400.
Web site: http://www.univision.com
Profile: KISF-FM is a commercial station owned by Univision Communications Inc. The format of the station is regional Mexican. KISF-FM broadcasts to the Las Vegas area at 103.5 FM.
FM RADIO STATION

KISL-FM 43857
Owner: Catalina Island Performing Arts Foundation
Editorial: 707 Crescent Ave, Avalon, California 90704
Tel: 1 310 510-7469.
Email: kisl887@gmail.com
Web site: http://www.kisl.org
FM RADIO STATION

KISM-FM 46347
Owner: Saga Communications
Editorial: 2219 Yew Street Rd, Bellingham, Washington 98229-8855 **Tel:** 1 360 734-9790.
Email: kism@kism.com

Web site: http://www.kism.com
Profile: KISM-FM is a commercial station owned by Saga Communications. The format of the station is classic rock. KISM-FM broadcasts to the Bellingham, WA area at 92.9 FM.
FM RADIO STATION

KISN-FM 42303
Owner: Townsquare Media, LLC
Editorial: 125 W Mendenhall St Ste 1, Bozeman, Montana 59715-3500 **Tel:** 1 406 586-2343.
Web site: http://bozemanskissfm.com
Profile: KISN-FM is a commercial station owned by Townsquare Media, LLC. The format of the station is Top 40/CHR music. KISN-FM broadcasts to the Bozeman, MT area at 96.7 FM.
FM RADIO STATION

KISO-FM 39620
Owner: iHeartMedia Inc.
Editorial: 5010 Underwood Ave, Omaha, Nebraska 68132-2236 **Tel:** 1 402 561-2000.
Web site: http://www.961kissonline.com
Profile: KISO-FM is a commercial station owned by iHeartMedia Inc. The format of the station is top 40/CHR. KISO-FM broadcasts to the Omaha, NE area at 96.1 FM.
FM RADIO STATION

KISQ-FM 44555
Owner: iHeartMedia Inc.
Editorial: 340 Townsend St, San Francisco, California 94107-1633 **Tel:** 1 415 538-1013.
Web site: http://981thebreeze.iheart.com
Profile: KISQ-FM is a commercial station owned by iHeartMedia Inc. The format of the station is Soft AC. KISQ-FM broadcasts to the San Francisco area at 98.1 FM.
FM RADIO STATION

KISR-FM 42810
Owner: Baker Broadcasting
Editorial: 5111 Rogers Ave Ste 650, Fort Smith, Arkansas 72903-2096 **Tel:** 1 479 785-2526.
Email: production@kisr.net
Web site: http://www.kisr.net
Profile: KISR-FM is a commercial station owned by Baker Broadcasting. The format of the station is Top 40/CHR music. KISR-FM broadcasts to the Fort Smith, AR area at 93.7 FM.
FM RADIO STATION

KISS-FM 46039
Owner: Cox Media Group, Inc.
Editorial: 8122 Datapoint Dr Ste 600, San Antonio, Texas 78229-3446 **Tel:** 1 210 615-5400.
Email: psa@coxinc.com
Web site: http://www.kissrocks.com
Profile: KISS-FM is a commercial station owned by Cox Media Group, Inc. The format of the station is rock/album-oriented rock. KISS-FM broadcasts to the San Antonio area at 99.5 FM.
FM RADIO STATION

KIST-FM 46738
Owner: Rincon Broadcasting
Editorial: 414 E Cota St, Santa Barbara, California 93101 **Tel:** 1 805 879-8300.
Web site: http://www.radiobronco.com
Profile: KIST-FM is a commercial station owned by Rincon Broadcasting. The format of the station is regional Mexican. KIST-FM broadcasts to the Santa Barbara, CA area at 107.7 FM.
FM RADIO STATION

KISV-FM 45807
Owner: American General Media
Editorial: 1400 Easton Dr Ste 144B, Bakersfield, California 93309-9412 **Tel:** 1 661 328-1410.
Email: news@kernradio.com
Web site: http://www.hot941.com
Profile: KISV-FM is a commercial station owned by American General Media. The format of the station is urban contemporary. KISV-FM broadcasts to the Bakersfield, CA area at 94.1 FM.
FM RADIO STATION

KISW-FM 39693
Owner: Entercom Communications Corp.
Editorial: 1100 Olive Way, Ste 1650, Seattle, Washington 98101 **Tel:** 1 206 233-1037.
Email: hairclub@kisw.com
Web site: http://www.kisw.com
Profile: KISW-FM is a commercial station owned by Entercom Communications Corp. The format of the station is rock and rock alternative music. KISW-FM broadcasts to the Seattle area at 99.9 FM.
FM RADIO STATION

KISX-FM 41611
Owner: Townsquare Media, LLC
Editorial: 3810 Brookside Dr, Tyler, Texas 75701-9420 **Tel:** 1 903 581-0606.
Web site: http://www.hot1073jamz.com
Profile: KISX-FM is a commercial station owned by Townsquare Media, LLC. The format of the station is urban adult contemporary music. KISX-FM broadcasts in the Tyler, TX, area at 107.3 FM.
FM RADIO STATION

KISY-FM 961701
Owner: McCutchen, Tracy
Editorial: 2644 Lamar Ave, Paris, Texas 75460-4847
Tel: 1 903 513-4149.
Profile: KISY-FM is a commercial station owned by Tracy McCutchen. The format of the station is Top 40/CHR. KISY-FM broadcasts to the Paris, TX area at a frequency of 92.7 FM.
FM RADIO STATION

KISZ-FM 41823
Owner: American General Media
Editorial: 212 W Apache St, Farmington, New Mexico 87401-6235 **Tel:** 1 505 327-4449.
Web site: http://www.kisscountry.net
Profile: KISZ-FM is a commercial station owned by American General Media. The format of the station is country music. KISZ-FM broadcasts to the Albuquerque, NM area at 97.9 FM.
FM RADIO STATION

KIT-AM 37334
Owner: Townsquare Media, LLC
Editorial: 4010 Summitview Ave Ste 200, Yakima, Washington 98908-2966 **Tel:** 1 509 972-3461.
Web site: http://www.1280kitam.com
Profile: KIT-AM is a commercial station owned by Townsquare Media, LLC. The format of the station is news, sports and talk. KIT-AM broadcasts to the Yakima, WA area at 1280 AM.
AM RADIO STATION

KITF-FM 721283
Owner: Minnesota Public Radio
Tel: 1 651 290-1500.
Email: newsroom@mpr.org
Web site: http://www.mpr.org/listen/stations/kitf
Profile: KITF-FM is a non-commercial station owned by Minnesota Public Radio. The format of the station is news. KITF-FM broadcasts to the International Falls, MN area at a frequency of 88.3 FM.
FM RADIO STATION

KITH-FM 87065
Owner: Hochman Hawaii Four, Inc.
Editorial: 4334 Rice St Ste 206, Lihue, Hawaii 96766-1801 **Tel:** 1 808 246-4444.
Web site: http://www.hhawaiimedia.com
Profile: KITH-FM is a commercial station owned by Hochman Hawaii Four, Inc. The format of the station is Island music. KITH-FM broadcasts to the Kauai, HI area at 98.9 FM.
FM RADIO STATION

KITI-AM 39364
Owner: Premier Broadcasters, Inc.
Editorial: 1133 Kresky Ave, Centralia, Washington 98531-3773 **Tel:** 1 360 736-1355.
Email: newsroom@live95.com
Web site: http://www.1420kiti.com
Profile: KITI-AM is a commercial station owned by Premier Broadcasters, Inc. The format of the station is oldies and classic hits music. KITI-AM broadcasts to the Centralia, WA area at 1420 AM.
AM RADIO STATION

KITI-FM 46725
Owner: Premier Broadcasters, Inc.
Editorial: 1133 Kresky Ave, Centralia, Washington 98531-3773 **Tel:** 1 360 736-1355.
Email: newsroom@live95.com
Web site: http://www.live95.com
Profile: KITI-FM is a commercial station owned by Premier Broadcasters, Inc. The format of the station is hot adult contemporary and Top 40. KITI-FM broadcasts to the Centralia, WA area at 95.1 FM.
FM RADIO STATION

KITN-FM 44490
Owner: Absolute Communications (dba Radio Werks)
Editorial: 28779 County Highway 35, Worthington, Minnesota 56187-6322 **Tel:** 1 507 376-9350.
Email: info@myradioworks.net
Web site: http://rockitfm.com
Profile: KITN-FM is a commercial station owned by Absolute Communications (dba Radio Werks). The format of the station is Classic Rock. KITN-FM broadcasts to the Worthington, MN area at 93.5 FM.
FM RADIO STATION

KITO-FM 46605
Owner: Stephens Media Group
Editorial: 2448 E 81st St Ste 5500, Tulsa, Oklahoma 74137-4201 **Tel:** 1 918 492-2660.
Email: onair@sportsanimalradio.com
Web site: http://sportsanimalradio.com
Profile: KITO-FM is a commercial station owned by Stephens Media Group. The format of the station is sports. KITO-FM broadcasts to the Vinita, OK area at 96.1 FM.
FM RADIO STATION

KITS-FM 39695
Owner: CBS Radio
Editorial: 865 Battery St, San Francisco, California 94111-1503 **Tel:** 1 415 402-6700.
Web site: http://live105.cbslocal.com
Profile: KITS-FM is a commercial station owned by CBS Radio. The format of the station is rock alternative. KITS-FM broadcasts to the San Francisco area at 105.3 FM.
FM RADIO STATION

KITT-FM 45770
Owner: Jackson Hole Community Radio
Editorial: 213 E 2nd S, Soda Springs, Idaho 83276-1411 **Tel:** 1 208 547-2500.
Profile: KITT-FM is a commercial station owned by Jackson Hole Community Radio. The format of the station is contemporary country. KITT-FM broadcasts to the Soda Springs, ID area at 100.1 FM.
FM RADIO STATION

KITX-FM 39696
Owner: Payne Radio Group
Editorial: 1600 W Jackson St, Hugo, Oklahoma 74743-5653 **Tel:** 1 580 326-2555.
Email: k955@neto.com
Web site: http://www.k955.com
Profile: KITX-FM is a commercial station owned by Payne Radio Group. The format of the station is country music. KITX-FM broadcasts in the Hugo, OK area at 95.5 FM.
FM RADIO STATION

KITZ-AM 36867
Owner: KITZ Radio, Inc.
Editorial: 1700 SE Mile Hill Dr, Ste 243, Port Orchard, Washington 98366 **Tel:** 1 360 876-1400.
Email: info@kitz1400.com
Web site: http://www.kitz1400.com
Profile: KITZ-AM is a commercial station owned by KITZ Radio, Inc. The format of the station is business talk and sports. KITZ-AM broadcasts to the Port Orchard, WA area at 1400 AM.
AM RADIO STATION

KIUL-AM 36682
Owner: Steckline Communications
Editorial: 609 E Kansas Plz, Garden City, Kansas 67846-5767 **Tel:** 1 620 276-3251.
Web site: http://www.kiulradio.com
Profile: KIUL-AM is a commercial station owned by Steckline Communications. The format of the station is news, sports and talk. KIUL-AM broadcasts to Garden City, KS area at 1240 AM.
AM RADIO STATION

KIUN-AM 39274
Owner: Pecos Radio Co, Inc.
Editorial: 316 S Cedar St, Pecos, Texas 79772-3211
Tel: 1 432 445-2498.
Email: kiun@valornet.com
Web site: http://www.98xfm.com
Profile: KIUN-AM is a commercial station owned by Pat Parker. The format of the station is Hispanic and classic country. KIUN-AM broadcasts to the Pecos, TX area at 1400 AM.
AM RADIO STATION

KIUP-AM 37335
Owner: Four Corners Broadcasting LLC
Editorial: 190 Turner Dr Unit G, Durango, Colorado 81303-8231 **Tel:** 1 970 259-4444.
Email: fcb@frontier.net
Web site: http://www.radiodurango.com
Profile: KIUP-AM is a commercial station owned by Four Corners Broadcasting LLC. The format of the station is sports. KIUP-AM broadcasts to the Durango, CO area at 930 AM.
AM RADIO STATION

KIVA-AM 37124
Owner: Vanguard Media, LLC
Editorial: 1213 San Pedro Dr NE, Albuquerque, New Mexico 87110-6725 **Tel:** 1 505 899-5029.
Profile: KIVA-AM is a commercial station owned by Vanguard Media, LLC. The format of the station is oldies. KIVA-AM broadcasts to the Albuquerque, NM area at 1600 AM.
AM RADIO STATION

KIVM-FM 794875
Owner: La Promesa Foundation
Tel: 1 210 821-5050.
Web site: http://grnonline.info
Profile: KIVM-FM is a non-commercial station owned by La Promesa Foundation. The format of the station is religious with a focus on Catholic programming. KIVM-FM broadcasts to the Fredericksburg, TX area at a frequency of 91.1 FM.
FM RADIO STATION

KIVY-AM 37336
Owner: Hunt Broadcasting
Editorial: 102 S 5th St, Crockett, Texas 75835-2037
Tel: 1 936 544-2171.
Email: kivy@kivy.com
Web site: http://www.kivy.com
Profile: KIVY-AM is a commercial station owned by Hunt Broadcasting. The format of the station is adult standards, news and talk. KIVY-AM broadcasts to the Crockett, TX area at 1290 AM.
AM RADIO STATION

KIVY-FM 44705
Owner: Hunt Broadcasting
Editorial: 102 S 5th St, Crockett, Texas 75835
Tel: 1 936 544-2171.
Email: spots@kivy.com
Web site: http://www.kivy.com
Profile: KIVY-FM is a commercial station owned by Hunt Broadcasting. The format of the station is country music. KIVY-FM broadcasts to the Crockett, TX area at 92.7 FM.
FM RADIO STATION

KIWA-AM 37337
Owner: Sheldon Broadcasting Co. Inc.
Editorial: 411 9th St, Sheldon, Iowa 51201
Tel: 1 712 324-2597.
Email: newstips@kiwaradio.com
Web site: http://www.kiwaradio.com
Profile: KIWA-AM is a commercial station owned by Sheldon Broadcasting Co. Inc. The format of the station is country. KIWA-AM broadcasts to the Sheldon, IA area at 1550 AM.
AM RADIO STATION

KIWA-FM 44706
Owner: Sheldon Broadcasting Co. Inc.
Editorial: 411 9th St, Sheldon, Iowa 51201
Tel: 1 712 324-2597.
Email: newstips@kiwaradio.com
Web site: http://www.kiwa-fm.com
Profile: KIWA-FM is a commercial station owned by Sheldon Broadcasting Co. Inc. The format of the station is classic rock. KIWA-FM broadcasts to the Sheldon, IA area at 105.3 FM.
FM RADIO STATION

KIWI-FM 43474
Owner: Lotus Communications Corp.
Editorial: 5100 Commerce Dr, Bakersfield, California 93309-0684 **Tel:** 1 661 327-9711.
Web site: http://www.radiolobo.com
Profile: KIWI-FM is a commercial station owned by Lotus Communications Corp. The format of the station is Hispanic programming. KIWI-FM broadcasts to the Bakersfield, CA area at 102.9 FM.
FM RADIO STATION

KIWR-FM 41463
Owner: Iowa Western Community College
Editorial: 2700 College Rd, Council Bluffs, Iowa 51503 **Tel:** 1 712 325-3254.
Email: 897theriver@iwcc.edu
Web site: http://www.897theriver.com
Profile: KIWR-FM is a non-commercial station owned by Iowa Western Community College. The format of the station is rock alternative. KIWR-FM broadcasts to the Omaha, NE area at 89.7 FM.
FM RADIO STATION

KIXA-FM 46871
Owner: El Dorado Broadcasting
Editorial: 12370 Hesperia Rd, Ste 16, Victorville, California 92395 **Tel:** 1 760 241-1313.
Web site: http://www.thefox1065.com
Profile: KIXA-FM is a commercial station owned by El Dorado Broadcasting. The format of the station is classic rock. KIXA-FM broadcasts to Victorville, CA area at 106.5 FM.
FM RADIO STATION

KIXB-FM 44574
Owner: Noalmark Broadcasting Corp.
Editorial: 2525 N West Ave, El Dorado, Arkansas 71730-3120 **Tel:** 1 870 863-6126.
Email: newsroom@totalradio.us
Web site: http://www.kix1033.com
Profile: KIXB-FM is a commercial station owned by Noalmark Broadcasting Corp. The format of the station is classic country. KIXB-FM broadcasts to the El Dorado, AR area at 103.3 FM.
FM RADIO STATION

KIXF-FM 42237
Owner: Highway Radio Inc.
Editorial: 1611 E Main St, Barstow, California 92311
Tel: 1 760 256-0326.
Email: highwayradio@highwayradio.com
Web site: http://www.highwaycountry.com
Profile: KIXF-FM is a commercial station owned by Highway Radio Inc. The format of the station is country music. KIXF-FM broadcasts to the Baker, CA area at 101.5 FM.
FM RADIO STATION

KIXI-AM 39008
Owner: Hubbard Radio, LLC
Editorial: 3650 131st Ave SE Ste 550, Bellevue, Washington 98006-1334 **Tel:** 1 425 562-8964.
Email: info@kixi.com
Web site: http://www.kixi.com
Profile: KIXI-AM is a commercial station owned by Hubbard Radio, LLC. The format of the station is adult standards. KIXI-AM broadcasts to the Bellevue, WA area at 880 AM.
AM RADIO STATION

KIXL-AM 34980
Owner: Starboard Media Foundation Inc.
Editorial: 11615 Angus Rd Ste 102, Austin, Texas 78759-4064 **Tel:** 1 920 884-1460.
Email: info@relevantradio.com
Web site: http://www.relevantradio970.com
Profile: KIXL-AM is a non-commercial station owned by Starboard Media Foundation Inc. The format of the station is religious talk. KIXL-AM broadcasts to the Austin, TX area at 970 AM.
AM RADIO STATION

KIXN-FM 43858
Owner: Noalmark Broadcasting Corp.
Editorial: 619 N Turner St, Hobbs, New Mexico 88240-8232 **Tel:** 1 575 397-4969.
Email: mail@1radiosquare.com
Web site: http://www.1radiosquare.com
Profile: KIXN-FM is a commercial station owned by Noalmark Broadcasting Corp. The format of the station is country. KIXN-FM broadcasts to the Hobbs, NM area at 102.9 FM.
FM RADIO STATION

KIXO-FM 39898
Owner: DFWU Inc.
Editorial: 1101 N Broadway St, Marlow, Oklahoma 73055-1123 **Tel:** 1 580 658-9292.
Email: kfxl92@att.net
Web site: http://www.kixoradio.com/
Profile: KIXO-FM is a commercial station owned by DFWU Inc. The format of the station is country music. KIXO-FM broadcasts to the Marlow, OK area at 106.1 FM.
FM RADIO STATION

KIXQ-FM 42732
Owner: Zimmer Radio Group
Editorial: 2702 E 32nd St, Joplin, Missouri 64804
Tel: 1 417 624-1025.
Web site: http://www.kix1025.com
Profile: KIXQ-FM is a commercial station owned by Zimmer Radio Group. The format of the station is country music. KIXQ-FM broadcasts to the Joplin, MO area at 102.5 FM.
FM RADIO STATION

KIXS-FM 41046
Owner: Townsquare Media, LLC
Editorial: 107 N Star Dr, Victoria, Texas 77904-2082
Tel: 1 361 573-0777.
Web site: http://www.kixs.com
Profile: KIXS-FM is a commercial station owned by Townsquare Media, LLC. The format for the station is contemporary country. KIXS-FM broadcasts to the Victoria, TX area at 107.9 FM.
FM RADIO STATION

KIXT-FM 796384
Owner: Prophecy Media Group, LLC (dba Waco Entertainment Group, LLC)
Editorial: 6401 Cobbs Dr, Waco, Texas 76710-2536
Tel: 1 254 772-6104.
Web site: http://kix1067.com
Profile: KIXT-FM is a commercial station owned by Prophecy Media Group, LLC (dba Waco Entertainment Group, LLC). The format of the station is contemporary country. KIXT-FM broadcasts to the Waco, TX area at a frequency of 106.7 FM.
FM RADIO STATION

KIXW-AM 38998
Owner: El Dorado Broadcasting
Editorial: 12370 Hesperia Rd Ste 16, Victorville, California 92395-5808 **Tel:** 1 760 241-1313.
Web site: http://www.talk960.com
Profile: KIXW-AM is a commercial station owned by El Dorado Broadcasting. The format of the station is talk. KIXW-AM broadcasts to Victorville, CA area at 960 AM.
AM RADIO STATION

KIXW-FM 43636
Owner: Highway Radio Inc.
Editorial: 1611 E Main St, Barstow, California 92311
Tel: 1 760 256-0326.
Email: highwayradio@highwayradio.com
Web site: http://www.highwaycountry.com
Profile: KIXW-FM is a commercial station owned by Highway Radio Inc. The format of the station is country music. KIXW-FM broadcasts to the Barstow, CA area at 107.3 FM.
FM RADIO STATION

KIXX-FM 46387
Owner: Alpha Media
Editorial: 921 9th Ave SE, Watertown, South Dakota 57201-4960 **Tel:** 1 605 886-9696.
Email: kwatnews@digity.me
Web site: http://www.gowatertown.net
Profile: KIXX-FM is a commercial station owned by Alpha Media. The format of the station is hot adult contemporary. KIXX-FM broadcasts to the Watertown, SD area at 96.1 FM.
FM RADIO STATION

KIXY-FM 46402
Owner: Foster Communications Co. Inc.
Editorial: 2824 Sherwood Way, San Angelo, Texas 76901-3514 **Tel:** 1 325 949-2112.
Email: advertising@kixyfm.com
Web site: http://www.kixyfm.com
Profile: KIXY-FM is commercial station owned by Foster Communications Co. Inc. The format of the station is Top 40/CHR. KIXY-FM broadcasts to the San Angelo, TX area at 94.7 FM.
FM RADIO STATION

KIXZ-AM 38830
Owner: Townsquare Media, LLC
Editorial: 6214 SW 34th Ave, Amarillo, Texas 79109-4006 **Tel:** 1 806 355-9777.
Web site: http://voiceofamarillo.com
Profile: KIXZ-AM is a commercial station owned by Townsquare Media, LLC. The format of the station is news and talk. KIXZ-AM broadcasts to the Amarillo, TX area at 940 AM.
AM RADIO STATION

KIXZ-FM 42111
Owner: iHeartMedia Inc.
Editorial: 808 E Sprague Ave, Spokane, Washington 99202-2126 **Tel:** 1 509 242-2400.
Web site: http://www.kix961.com
Profile: KIXZ-FM is a commercial station owned by iHeartMedia Inc. The format of the station is Country. KIXZ-FM broadcasts to the Spokane, WA area at 96.1 FM.
FM RADIO STATION

KIYK-FM 44995
Owner: Cherry Creek Radio
Editorial: 750 Ridgeview Dr, St George, Utah 84770-2665 **Tel:** 1 435 673-3579.
Profile: KIYK-FM is a commercial station owned by Cherry Creek Radio. The format of the station is hot adult contemporary music. KIYK-FM broadcasts to the St. George, UT area at 107.3 FM.
FM RADIO STATION

KIYS-FM 44594
Owner: East Arkansas Broadcasters, Inc
Editorial: 407 W Parker Rd, Jonesboro, Arkansas 72404-8408 **Tel:** 1 870 934-5000.
Web site: http://www.kissjonesboro.com
Profile: KIYS-FM is a commercial station owned by East Arkansas Broadcasters, Inc. The format of the station is Top 40/CHR. KRLW-FM broadcasts to the Pocahontas, AR area at 101.7 FM.
FM RADIO STATION

KIYU-AM 689258
Owner: Big River Public Broadcasting Corp.
Editorial: 165 Tiger Freeway, Galena, Alaska 99714
Tel: 1 907 656-1488.
Email: office@kiyu.com
Web site: http://www.kiyu.com
Profile: KIYU-AM is a non-commercial station owned by Big River Public Broadcasting Corp. The format of the station is variety. KIYU-AM's target audience is adults, ages 13 to 100, in the Galena, AK area. The station airs locally at 910 AM.
AM RADIO STATION

KIYU-FM 36024
Owner: Big River Public Broadcasting Corp.
Editorial: 165 Tiger Freeway, Galena, Alaska 99714
Tel: 1 907 656-1488.
Email: office@kiyu.com
Web site: http://www.kiyu.com
Profile: KIYU-FM is a non-commercial station owned by Big River Public Broadcasting Corp. The format of the station is variety. KIYU-FM broadcasts to the Fairbanks, AK area at 97.1 FM.
FM RADIO STATION

KIYX-FM 83675
Owner: Queen B Radio of Wisconsin
Editorial: 51 Means Dr, Platteville, Wisconsin 53818-3829 **Tel:** 1 608 349-2021.
Web site: http://www.superhits106.com
Profile: KIYX-FM is a commercial station owned by Queen B Radio of Wisconsin. The format is classic hits.
FM RADIO STATION

KIZN-FM 41849
Owner: Cumulus Media Inc
Editorial: 1419 W Bannock St, Boise, Idaho 83702-5234 **Tel:** 1 208 336-3670.
Email: kissin92@kizn.com
Web site: http://www.kizn.com
Profile: KIZN-FM is a commercial station owned by Cumulus Media Inc. The format of the station is contemporary country. KIZN-FM broadcasts to the Boise, ID area at 92.3 FM.
FM RADIO STATION

KIZS-FM 43325
Owner: iHeartMedia Inc.
Editorial: 2625 S Memorial Dr, Tulsa, Oklahoma 74129-2601 **Tel:** 1 918 388-5100.
Web site: http://tulsa.lapreciosa.com
Profile: KIZS-FM is a commercial station owned by iHeartMedia Inc. The format of the station is Hispanic oldies. KIZS-FM broadcasts to the Tulsa, OK area at 101.5 FM.
FM RADIO STATION

KIZZ-FM 39698
Owner: iHeartMedia Inc.
Editorial: 1000 20th Ave SW, Minot, North Dakota 58701-6447 **Tel:** 1 701 852-4646.
Web site: http://www.z94radio.com
Profile: KIZZ-FM is a commercial station owned by iHeartMedia Inc. The format of the station is Top 40/ CHR. KIZZ-FM broadcasts to the Minot-Bismarck, ND area at 93.7 FM.
FM RADIO STATION

KJAA-AM 35913
Owner: Globecasting, Inc.
Editorial: 5734 S McKinney Ave, Globe, Arizona 85501-4361 **Tel:** 1 928 425-7186.
Web site: http://www.jukebox1240.com
Profile: KJAA-AM is a commercial station owned by Globecasting, Inc. The format of the station is oldies. KJAA-AM broadcasts to the Globe, AZ area at 1240 AM.
AM RADIO STATION

KJAC-FM 41580
Owner: Front Range Sports Network, LLC
Editorial: 10200 E Girard Ave Bldg B, Denver, Colorado 80231-5500 **Tel:** 1 800 443-5862.
Email: comment@coloradosound.org
Web site: http://coloradosound.org
Profile: KJAC-FM is a commercial station owned byFront Range Sports Network, LLC. The format of the station is Adult Album Alternative. KJAC-FM broadcasts to the Denver area at 105.5 FM.
FM RADIO STATION

KJAE-FM 46415
Owner: Pene Broadcasting Inc.
Editorial: 101 Lees Ln, Leesville, Louisiana 71446-3643 **Tel:** 1 337 239-3402.
Email: swapshop@kjae935.com
Web site: http://www.kjae935.com
FM RADIO STATION

KJAK-FM 39699
Owner: Williams Broadcasting Corp.
Tel: 1 806 745-6677.
Email: kjak@kjak.com
Web site: http://www.kjak.com
Profile: KJAK-FM is a commercial station owned by Williams Broadcasting Corp. The format of the station is Christian music and talk. KJAK-FM broadcasts in the Lubbock, TX area at 92.7 FM.
FM RADIO STATION

KJAM-AM 37339
Owner: Alpha Media
Editorial: 101 S Egan Ave, Madison, South Dakota 57042-2841 **Tel:** 1 605 256-4514.
Email: kjamonair@digity.me
Web site: http://www.amazingmadison.com
Profile: KJAM-AM is a commercial station owned by Alpha Media. The format of the station is classic hits. KJAM-FM broadcasts to the Madison, SD area at 1390 AM.
AM RADIO STATION

KJAM-FM 44708
Owner: Digity Media
Editorial: 101 S Egan Ave, Madison, South Dakota 57042-2841 **Tel:** 1 605 256-4514.
Email: kjamonair@digity.me
Web site: http://www.amazingmadison.com
Profile: KJAM-FM is a commercial station owned by Digity Media. The format of the station is comtemporary country. KJAM-FM broadcasts to the Madison, SD area at 103.1 FM.
FM RADIO STATION

KJAN-AM 36149
Owner: Wireless Communications Corp.
Editorial: North Olive St, Atlantic, Iowa 50022
Tel: 1 712 243-3920.
Email: kjannews@metc.net
Web site: http://www.kjan.com
Profile: KJAN-AM is a commercial station owned by Wireless Communications Corp. The format of the station is adult contemporary. KJAN-AM broadcasts to the Atlantic, IA area at 1220 AM.
AM RADIO STATION

KJAQ-FM 42890
Owner: CBS Radio
Editorial: 1000 Dexter Ave N Ste 100, Seattle, Washington 98109-3577 **Tel:** 1 206 805-0965.
Web site: http://jackseattle.cbslocal.com
Profile: KJAQ-FM is a commercial station owned by CBS Radio. The format of the station is Jack FM-Adult Hits. KJAQ-FM broadcasts to the Seattle market at 96.5 FM.
FM RADIO STATION

KJAS-FM 43862
Owner: Rayburn Broadcasting Co.
Editorial: 765 Hemphill St, Jasper, Texas 75951
Tel: 1 409 384-2626.
Email: sales@kjas.com
Web site: http://www.kjas.com
Profile: KJAS-FM is a commercial station owned by Rayburn Broadcasting Co. The format of the station is adult contemporary. KJAS-FM broadcasts to the Jasper, TX area at 107.3 FM.
FM RADIO STATION

KJAV-FM 606068
Owner: R Communications
Editorial: 1201 N Jackson Rd, McAllen, Texas 78501-5760 **Tel:** 1 956 992-8895.
Web site: http://www.valleyjack.com
Profile: KJAV-FM is a commercial station owned by R Communications. The format of the station is adult hits. KJAV-FM broadcasts to the McAllen, TX area at 104.9.
FM RADIO STATION

KJAX-FM 44553
Owner: Rich Broadcasting, LLC.
Editorial: 1140 Hwy 22, Jackson, Wyoming 83001-9401 **Tel:** 1 307 733-2120.
Web site: http://kjaxcountry.com/
Profile: KJAX-FM is a commercial station owned by Rich Broadcasting, LLC. The format of the station is classic country. KJAX-FM broadcasts to the Jackson, WY area at 93.5 FM.
FM RADIO STATION

KJAY-AM 34982
Owner: Powell(Trudi)
Editorial: 5030 S River Rd, West Sacramento, California 95691 **Tel:** 1 916 371-5101.
Profile: KJAY-AM is a commercial station owned by Trudi Powell. The format of the station is variety. KJAY-AM broadcasts to the Sacramento, CA area at 1430 AM.
AM RADIO STATION

KJBN-AM 35893
Owner: Joshua Community Development Corp.
Editorial: 1800 Maple St, North Little Rock, Arkansas 72114-2838 **Tel:** 1 501 791-1000.
Email: programs@kjbnradio.com
Profile: KJBN-AM is a commercial station owned by Joshua Community Development Corp. The format of the station is contemporary Christian. KJBN-AM broadcasts to the Little Rock, AR area at 1050 AM.
AM RADIO STATION

KJBX-FM 41750
Owner: Saga Communications
Editorial: 314 Union St, Jonesboro, Arkansas 72401-2815 **Tel:** 1 870 933-8800.
Web site: http://www.themix1067.com
Profile: KJBX-FM is a commercial station owned by Saga Communications. The format of the station is adult contemporary. KJBX-FM broadcasts to Jonesboro, AR area at 106.7 FM.
FM RADIO STATION

KJBZ-FM 39701
Owner: Guerra Enterprises
Editorial: 6402 N Bartlett Ave Ste 1, Laredo, Texas 78041-6453 **Tel:** 1 956 726-9393.
Email: livewire@krrg.com
Web site: http://z93laredo.com
Profile: KJBZ-FM is a commercial radio station owned by Guerra Enterprises. The format for the station is Tejano music. KJBZ-FM broadcasts to the Laredo, TX, area at 92.7 FM.
FM RADIO STATION

KJCE-AM 38798
Owner: Entercom Communications Corp.
Editorial: 4301 Westbank Dr Fl 3, Austin, Texas 78746-6568 **Tel:** 1 512 493-6370.
Email: news@talk1370.com
Web site: http://www.talkradio1370am.com
Profile: KJCE-AM is a commercial station owned by Entercom Communications Corp. The format of the station is talk. KJCE-AM broadcasts to the Austin, TX area at 1370 AM.
AM RADIO STATION

KJCG-FM 763536
Owner: Hi-Line Radio Fellowship
Editorial: 317 1st St, Havre, Montana 59501-3505
Tel: 1 406 265-5845.
Email: ynop@ynop.org
Web site: http://www.ynop.org
Profile: KJCG-FM is a non-commercial station owned by Hi-Line Radio Fellowship. The format of the station is contemporary Christian. The station airs locally at 88.3 FM. KJCG-FM airs KXEI-FM's programming.
FM RADIO STATION

KJCK-AM 37340
Owner: Eagle Communications
Editorial: 1030 Southwind Ct, Junction City, Kansas 66441-2601 **Tel:** 1 785 762-5525.
Email: office@eagleradio.net
Web site: http://www.kjck.com
Profile: KJCK-AM is a commercial station owned by Eagle Communications. The format of the station is news and talk. KJCK-AM broadcasts to the Junction City, KS area at 1420 AM.
AM RADIO STATION

KJCK-FM 44709
Owner: Eagle Communications, Inc.
Editorial: 1030 South Wind, Junction City, Kansas 66441 **Tel:** 1 785 762-5525.
Email: powerhits@eagleradio.net
Web site: http://www.powerhits975.com
Profile: KJCK-FM is a commercial station owned by Eagle Communications, Inc. The format of the station is Top 40/CHR music. KJCK-FM broadcasts to the Junction City, KS area at 97.5 FM.
FM RADIO STATION

KJCR-AM 36264
Owner: Agnus Dei Communications
Editorial: 941 Grand Ave, Billings, Montana 59102-3301 **Tel:** 1 406 294-5250.
Web site: http://www.kjcrradio.com
Profile: KJCR-AM is a commercial station owned by Agnus Dei Communications. The format of the station is Catholic talk programming. KJCR-AM broadcasts to the Billings, MT area at 1240 AM.
AM RADIO STATION

KJCS-FM 43312
Owner: Radio Licensing
Editorial: 1407 N University Dr Ste C, Nacogdoches, Texas 75961-4265 **Tel:** 1 936 564-2900.
Email: info@103thebull.com
Web site: http://www.103thebull.com
Profile: KJCS-FM is a commercial station owned by Radio Licensing. The format of the station is classic country. KJCS-FM broadcasts to the Nacogdoches, TX area at 103.3 FM.
FM RADIO STATION

KJCU-FM 558878
Owner: Calvary Chapel of Costa Mesa, Inc.
Editorial: 900 N Main St, Fort Bragg, California 95437-3021 **Tel:** 1 707 961-6252.
Web site: http://www.ccfortbragg.com
Profile: KJCU-FM is a non-commercial station owned by Calvary Chapel of Costa Mesa, Inc. The format of the station is Christian music and religious programming. KJCU-FM broadcasts to the Ft.Bragg, CA area at 89.9 FM.
FM RADIO STATION

KJDJ-AM 37521
Owner: Centro Cristiano Vida Abundante, Inc.
Editorial: 121 W Alvin Ave, Santa Maria, California 93458-3002 **Tel:** 1 805 928-1030.
Web site: http://www.radiovidaabundante.com
Profile: KJDJ-AM is a non-commercial station owned by Centro Cristiano Vida Abundante, Inc. The format of the station is Spanish religious programming. KJDJ-AM broadcasts to the San Luis Obispo, CA area at a frequency of 1030 AM.
AM RADIO STATION

KJDL-FM 46021
Owner: Walker Broadcasting and Communications Inc.
Editorial: 1500 Broadway Ste 115, Lubbock, Texas 79401-3117 **Tel:** 1 806 712-1053.
Web site: http://www.thereddirtrebel.com
Profile: KJDL-FM is a commercial station owned by Walker Broadcasting and Communications Inc. The

format of the station is country. KJDL-FM broadcasts to the Lubbock, TX area at 105.3 FM.
FM RADIO STATION

KJDX-FM 44902
Owner: Sierra Broadcasting Corp.
Editorial: 3015 Johnstonville Rd, Susanville, California 96130-8739 **Tel:** 1 530 257-2121.
Email: radioinfo@theradionetwork.com
Web site: http://www.sierradailynews.com/kjdx.html
Profile: KJDX-FM is a commercial station owned by Sierra Broadcasting Corp. The format of the station is contemporary country. KJDX-FM broadcasts to the Susanville, CA area at 93.3 FM.
FM RADIO STATION

KJDY-AM 34985
Owner: Elkhorn Media Group
Editorial: 413 NW Bridge St, John Day, Oregon 97845-1134 **Tel:** 1 541 575-1400.
Email: events@elkhornmediagroup.com
Web site: http://www.myeasternoregon.com
Profile: KJDY-AM is a commercial station owned by Elkhorn Media Group. The format of the station is country music. KJDY-AM broadcasts to John Day, OR and the surrounding area on 1400 AM. The station simulcasts on KJDY-FM.
AM RADIO STATION

KJDY-FM 242180
Owner: Elkhorn Media Group
Editorial: 413 NW Bridge St, John Day, Oregon 97845-1134 **Tel:** 1 541 575-1400.
Email: events@elkhornmediagroup.com
Web site: http://www.myeasternoregon.com
Profile: KJDY-FM is a commercial station owned by Elkhorn Media Group. The format for the station is classic and contemporary country. KJDY-FM broadcasts to the John Day, OR area at 94.5 FM.
FM RADIO STATION

KJEE-FM 42603
Owner: Evans(James)
Editorial: 302 W Carrillo St, #B, Santa Barbara, California 93101 **Tel:** 1 805 962-4588.
Email: kjee929@aol.com
Web site: http://www.kjee.com
Profile: KJEE-FM is a commercial station owned by James Evans. The format of the station is rock alternative. KJEE-FM broadcasts to the Santa Barbara, CA area at 92.9 FM.
FM RADIO STATION

KJEF-AM 37341
Owner: Townsquare Media, LLC
Editorial: 900 N Lake Shore Dr, Lake Charles, Louisiana 70601-2120 **Tel:** 1 337 433-1641.
Web site: http://www.cajunradio.com
Profile: KJEF-AM is a commercial station owned by Townsquare Media, LLC. The format of the station is cajun and country music. KJEF-AM broadcasts to Lafayette, LA area at 1290 AM.
AM RADIO STATION

KJEL-FM 44702
Owner: Alpha Media
Editorial: 18553 Gentry Rd, Lebanon, Missouri 65536-5748 **Tel:** 1 417 532-9111.
Email: kjel@regionalradio.com
Web site: http://www.myozarksonline.com
Profile: KJEL-FM is a commercial station owned by Alpha Media. The format of the station is country music. KJEL-FM broadcasts in the Lebanon, MO area at 103.7 FM.
FM RADIO STATION

KJET-FM 85946
Owner: Jodesha Broadcasting Inc.
Editorial: 1520 Simpson Ave, Aberdeen, Washington 98520-4708 **Tel:** 1 360 533-3000.
Email: news@kbkw.com
Web site: http://www.1057thejet.com/
Profile: KJET-FM is a commercial station owned by Jodesha Broadcasting Inc. The format of the station is hot adult contemporary. KJET-FM broadcasts to the Seattle area at 105.7 FM.
FM RADIO STATION

KJEZ-FM 39703
Owner: Max Media
Editorial: 1015 W Pine St, Poplar Bluff, Missouri 63901-4839 **Tel:** 1 573 785-0881.
Email: z95@riverradio.net
Web site: http://www.z95thebone.net
Profile: KJEZ-FM is a commercial station owned by Max Media. The format of the station is rock music. KJEZ-FM broadcasts in the Poplar Bluff, MO area at 94.5 FM.
FM RADIO STATION

KJFA-FM 45805
Owner: Univision Communications Inc.
Editorial: 8009 Marble Ave NE, Albuquerque, New Mexico 87110-7901 **Tel:** 1 505 254-7100.
Web site: http://kjfa.univision.com
Profile: KJFA-FM is a commercial station owned by Univision Communications Inc. The format of the station is regional Mexican. KJFA-FM broadcasts to the Albuquerque, NM area at 101.3 FM.
FM RADIO STATION

KJFF-AM 34984
Owner: Goodradio.TV LLC
Editorial: 1026 Scenic Dr, Festus, Missouri 63028-1146 **Tel:** 1 636 937-7642.
Web site: http://www.mymoinfo.com/kjff-straight-talk-1400-fm/8959720
Profile: KJFF-AM is a commercial station owned by Goodradio.TV LLC. The format of the station is news and talk. KJFF-AM broadcasts to the Festus, MO area at 1400 AM.
AM RADIO STATION

KJFM-FM 41121
Owner: Foxfire Communications Inc.
Editorial: 615 Georgia St, Louisiana, Missouri 63353 **Tel:** 1 573 324-0303.
Email: kjfmradioeagle102@yahoo.com
Web site: http://www.kjfmeagle102.net
Profile: KJFM-FM is a commercial station owned by Foxfire Communications Inc. The format of the station is contemporary country music. KJFM-FM broadcasts to the Louisiana, MO area at 102.1 FM.
FM RADIO STATION

KJFX-FM 44439
Owner: One Putt Broadcasting
Editorial: 1066 E Shaw Ave, Fresno, California 93710-7807 **Tel:** 1 559 230-0104.
Web site: http://www.957thefox.com
Profile: KJFX-FM is a commercial station owned by One Putt Broadcasting. The format of the station is classic rock. KJFX-FM broadcasts to the Fresno, CA area at 95.7 FM.
FM RADIO STATION

KJGT-FM 823179
Owner: Jagerita Radio
Editorial: 7575 Corporate Way #B, Eden Prairie, Minnesota 55344-2022 **Tel:** 1 800 810-5559.
Email: kjgt@newmail.kinshipradio.org
Web site: http://www.kjgt.org/
Profile: KJGT-FM is a commercial station owned by Jagerita Radio. The format of the station is verity. KJGT-FM broadcasts in the Minneapolis-St. Paul, MN area at 88.3 FM.
FM RADIO STATION

KJHL-FM 563241
Owner: Great Plains Christian Radio
Editorial: 909 W Carthage St, Meade, Kansas 67864-6406 **Tel:** 1 620 873-2991.
Email: kjil@kjil.com
Web site: http://www.kjil991.com
Profile: KJHL-FM is a non-commercial station owned by Great Plains Christian Radio. The format of the station is contemporary Christian music and religious programming. KJHL-FM broadcasts to the Boise City, OK area at 90.9 FM.
FM RADIO STATION

KJHM-FM 394881
Owner: Max Media of Colorado
Editorial: 3033 S Parker Rd, Aurora, Colorado 80014-2910 **Tel:** 1 303 872-1500.
Web site: http://www.jammin1015.com
Profile: KJHM-FM is a commercial station owned by Max Media of Colorado. The format of the station is rhythmic hot adult contemporary. KJHM-FM broadcasts to the Aurora, CO area at 101.5 FM.
FM RADIO STATION

KJIC-FM 39705
Owner: Community Radio, Inc.
Editorial: 8315 County Road 198, Alvin, Texas 77511 **Tel:** 1 281 824-1228.
Email: kjic@kjic.org
Web site: http://www.kjic.org
Profile: KJIC-FM is a non-commercial station owned by Community Radio, Inc. The format of the station is gospel music. KJIC-FM broadcasts to the Alvin, TX area at 90.5 FM.
FM RADIO STATION

KJIL-FM 42572
Owner: Great Plains Christian Radio
Editorial: 909 W Carthage, Meade, Kansas 67864 **Tel:** 1 620 873-2991.
Email: kjil@kjil.com
Web site: http://www.kjil991.com
Profile: KJIL-FM is a non-commercial station owned by Great Plains Christian Radio. The format of the station is contemporary Christian music and religious programming. KJIL-FM broadcasts to the Meade, KS area at 99.1 FM.
FM RADIO STATION

KJIM-AM 36298
Owner: Allen Productions(Bob Mark)
Editorial: 4367 Woodlawn Rd, Denison, Texas 75021 **Tel:** 1 903 893-1197.
Email: kjim1500am@verizon.net
Profile: KJIM-AM is a commercial station owned by Bob Mark Allen Productions. The format of the station is adult standards. KJIM-AM broadcasts to the Denison, TX area on 1500 AM.
AM RADIO STATION

KJIN-AM 38591
Owner: My Home Team Media
Editorial: 120 Prevost Dr, Houma, Louisiana 70364-2338 **Tel:** 1 985 851-1020.
Profile: KJIN-AM is a commercial station owned by My Home Team Media, LLC. The format of the station is regional Mexican music. KJIN-AM broadcasts to the Houma, LA area at 1490 AM.
AM RADIO STATION

KJIR-FM 70292
Owner: Believer's Broadcasting Corp.
Editorial: 220 N 6th St, Quincy, Illinois 62301 **Tel:** 1 217 221-9410.
Email: thecross@kjir.org
Web site: http://www.kjir.org
FM RADIO STATION

KJIW-FM 44341
Owner: Mondy(Elijah)
Editorial: 204 Moore St, Helena, Arkansas 72342-3438 **Tel:** 1 870 338-2700.
Web site: http://www.kjiwfm.com
Profile: KJIW-FM is a commercial station owned by Elijah Mondy. The format for the station is Christian and religious programming and gospel music. KJIW-FM broadcasts to the Helena, AR area at 94.5 FM.
FM RADIO STATION

KJJD-AM 35112
Owner: Rodriguez-Gallegos Broadcasting Corp.
Editorial: 624 Main St, Longmont, Colorado 80501-4970 **Tel:** 1 303 651-1199.
Email: secretaria1170@yahoo.com
Profile: KJJD-AM is a commercial station owned by Rodriguez-Gallegos Broadcasting Corp. The format of the station is Hispanic programming. KJJD-AM broadcasts to the Longmont, CO area at 1170 AM.
AM RADIO STATION

KJJJ-FM 42598
Owner: Greeley(Steven M.)
Editorial: 1845 McCulloch Blvd N Ste A14, Lake Havasu City, Arizona 86403-6777 **Tel:** 1 928 855-9336.
Email: office@myradiocentral.com
Web site: http://www.kjjjfm.com
Profile: KJJJ-FM is a commercial station owned by Steven M. Greeley. The format of the station is country. KJJJ-FM broadcasts to Lake Havasu City, AZ at 102.3 FM.
FM RADIO STATION

KJJK-AM 38608
Owner: Results Radio Group
Editorial: 728 Western Ave, Fergus Falls, Minnesota 56537-1095 **Tel:** 1 218 736-7596.
Email: contactus@lakesradio.net
Web site: http://family1020.net/family/family.htm
Profile: KJJK-AM is commercial station owned by Results Radio Group. The format of the station is contemporary Christian. KJJK-AM broadcasts to the Fergus Falls, ND area at 1020 AM.
AM RADIO STATION

KJJK-FM 45960
Owner: Results Radio Group
Editorial: 728 Western Ave, Fergus Falls, Minnesota 56537-1095 **Tel:** 1 218 736-7596.
Email: contactus@lakesradio.net
Web site: http://www.lakesradio.net
Profile: KJJK-FM is a commercial station owned by Results Radio Group. The format of the station is contemporary country music. KJJK-FM broadcasts to the Fergus Falls, ND area at 96.5 FM.
FM RADIO STATION

KJJP-FM 41859
Owner: Kanza Society Inc.
Editorial: 104 Sw 6Th Ave Suite B-4, Amarillo, Texas 79101-2324 **Tel:** 1 806 367-9088.
Email: hppr@hppr.org
Web site: http://www.hppr.org
Profile: KJJP-FM is a non-commercial station owned by Kanza Society Inc. The format of the station is news and classical. KJJP-FM broadcasts to the Amarillo, TX area at 105.7 FM.
FM RADIO STATION

KJJQ-AM 38461
Owner: Alpha Media
Editorial: 227 22nd Ave S, Brookings, South Dakota 57006-2827 **Tel:** 1 605 692-9125.
Email: kjjqnews@brookings.net
Web site: http://www.brookingsradio.com
Profile: KJJQ-AM is a commercial station owned by Alpha Media. The format is classic country. The station airs in the Brookings, SD area at 910 AM.
AM RADIO STATION

KJJR-AM 37343
Owner: Bee Broadcasting Inc.
Editorial: 2432 US Highway 2 E, Kalispell, Montana 59901-2310 **Tel:** 1 406 755-8700.
Email: kjjr@beebroadcasting.com
Web site: http://www.beebroadcasting.com
Profile: KJJR-AM is a commercial station owned by Bee Broadcasting Inc. The format of the station is news and talk. KJJR-AM broadcasts to the Kalispell, MT area at 880 AM.
AM RADIO STATION

KJJS-FM 876925
Owner: Hispanic Target Media, Inc.
Editorial: 1201 US Highway 16, Zapata, Texas 78076-3690 **Tel:** 1 866 761-3393.
Email: hispanictargetmedia@gmail.com
Web site: http://www.hispanictargetmedia.info
Profile: KJJS-FM is a commercial station owned by Hispanic Target Media, Inc. The format of the station is Hispanic music. KJJS-FM broadcasts locally to the Zapata, TX area at a frequency of 103.9 FM.
FM RADIO STATION

KJJY-FM 45783
Owner: Cumulus Media Inc
Editorial: 4143 109th St, Urbandale, Iowa 50322-7925 **Tel:** 1 515 331-9200.
Web site: http://www.kjjy.com
Profile: KJJY-FM is a commercial station owned by Cumulus Media Inc. The format of the station is country music. KJJY-FM broadcasts to the Des Moines, IA area at 92.5 FM.
FM RADIO STATION

KJJZ-FM 42544
Owner: Marker Broadcasting
Editorial: 75153 Merle Dr Ste G, Palm Desert, California 92211-5197 **Tel:** 1 760 568-4550.
Web site: http://959theoasis.com/
Profile: KJJZ-FM is a commercial station owned by Marker Broadcasting. The format of the station is classic rock. KJJZ-FM broadcasts to the Palm Springs, CA area at 95.9 FM.
FM RADIO STATION

KJKE-FM 394929
Owner: Tyler Media Group Inc.
Editorial: 400 E Britton Rd, Oklahoma City, Oklahoma 73114-7515 **Tel:** 1 405 616-5500.
Web site: http://www.jakefm.com
Profile: KJKE-FM is a commercial station owned by Tyler Media Group Inc. The format of the station is contemporary country. KJKE-FM broadcasts to the Oklahoma City area at 93.3 FM.
FM RADIO STATION

KJKJ-FM 39707
Owner: iHeartMedia Inc.
Editorial: 505 University Ave, Grand Forks, North Dakota 58203-3545 **Tel:** 1 701 746-1417.
Web site: http://www.kjkj.com
Profile: KJKJ-FM is a commercial station owned by iHeartMedia Inc. The format of the station is rock music. KJKJ-FM broadcasts to the Grand Forks, ND area at 107.5 FM.
FM RADIO STATION

KJKK-FM 87380
Owner: CBS Radio
Editorial: 4131 N Central Expy Ste 1000, Dallas, Texas 75204-2121 **Tel:** 1 214 525-7000.
Email: jack@cbsradio.com
Web site: http://www.jackontheweb.com
Profile: KJKK-FM is a commercial station owned by CBS Radio. The format of the station is adult hits. KJKK-FM broadcasts to the Dallas area at 100.3 FM. The station has no on air personalities.
FM RADIO STATION

KJKS-FM 45925
Owner: Pacific Media Group
Editorial: 311 Ano St, Kahului, Hawaii 96732-1304 **Tel:** 1 808 877-5566.
Email: support@kjksfm.com
Web site: http://www.kissfmmaui.com
Profile: KJKS-FM is a commercial station owned by Pacific Media Group. The format of the station is adult contemporary. KJKS-FM is licensed to Maui, HI and broadcasts locally at 99.9 FM.
FM RADIO STATION

KJLF-FM 535298
Owner: Hi-Line Radio Fellowship
Editorial: 317 1st St, Havre, Montana 59501-3505 **Tel:** 1 406 265-5845.
Email: ynop@ynop.org
Web site: http://www.ynop.org
Profile: KJLF-FM is a non-commercial station owned by Hi-Line Radio Fellowship. The format of the station is contemporary Christian music and religious. KJLF-FM broadcasts to the Havre, MT area at 90.5 FM.
FM RADIO STATION

KJLH-FM 39708
Owner: Taxi Productions Inc.
Editorial: 161 N La Brea Ave, Inglewood, California 90301-1707 **Tel:** 1 310 330-2200.
Email: production@kjlhradio.com
Web site: http://www.kjlhradio.com
Profile: KJLH-FM is a commercial station owned by Taxi Productions Inc. The format is urban adult contemporary. KJLH-FM broadcasts to the Los Angeles area at 102.3 FM.
FM RADIO STATION

KJLO-FM 46442
Owner: Holladay Broadcasting Co.
Editorial: 1109 Hudson Ln, Monroe, Louisiana 71201-6003 **Tel:** 1 318 388-2323.
Web site: http://www.kjlo.com
Profile: KJLO-FM is a commercial station owned by Holladay Broadcasting Co. The format of the station is country music. KJLO-FM broadcasts to the Monroe, LA area at 104.1 FM.
FM RADIO STATION

KJLS-FM 39709
Owner: Eagle Radio Inc.
Editorial: 2300 Hall St, Hays, Kansas 67601-3062 **Tel:** 1 785 625-2578.
Email: haysnews@eagleradio.net
Web site: http://www.mix103fm.com
Profile: KJLS-FM is a commercial station owned by Eagle Radio Inc. The format of the station is Top 40/CHR. KJLS-FM broadcasts to the Hutchinson, KS area at 103.3 FM.
FM RADIO STATION

KJLT-AM 38455
Owner: Tri-State Broadcasting Association, Inc.
Editorial: 201 S Bailey Ave, North Platte, Nebraska 69101-5406 **Tel:** 1 308 532-5515.
Email: kjlt@kjlt.org
Web site: http://www.kjlt.org
AM RADIO STATION

KJLT-FM 45821
Owner: Tri-State Broadcasting Association, Inc.
Editorial: 201 S Bailey Ave, North Platte, Nebraska 69101-5406 **Tel:** 1 308 532-5515.
Email: kjlt@kjlt.org

Web site: http://www.kjlt.org
Profile: KJLT-FM is a non-commercial station owned by Tri-State Broadcasting Association, Inc. The format of the station is Contemporary Christian. KJLT-FM is licensed to North Platte, NE and broadcasts at a frequency of 94.9 FM, with a translator on 95.7 FM.
FM RADIO STATION

KJLY-FM 41090
Owner: Minn.-Iowa Christian Broadcasting
Editorial: 12089 380th Ave, Blue Earth, Minnesota 56013 **Tel:** 1 507 526-3233.
Email: kjly@kjly.com
Web site: http://www.kjly.com
Profile: KJLY-FM is a non-commercial station owned by Minn.-Iowa Christian Broadcasting. The format of the station is Christian talk and music. KJLY-FM broadcasts to the Minneapolis area at 104.5 FM.
FM RADIO STATION

KJMA-FM 40018
Owner: La Promesa Foundation
Editorial: 1905 10th St, Floresville, Texas 78114-2767 **Tel:** 1 210 579-9844.
Web site: http://grnonline.com
Profile: KJMA-FM is a non-commercial station owned by La Promesa Foundation. The format of the station is religion with a focus on Catholic programming. KJMA-FM broadcasts to Wilson County, TX residents and the South and Central areas of the state locally at 89.7 FM.
FM RADIO STATION

KJMB-FM 41837
Owner: Blythe Radio Inc.
Editorial: 681 N 4th St, Blythe, California 92225 **Tel:** 1 760 922-7143.
Email: kjmbfm@hotmail.com
Web site: http://www.kjmbfm.com
Profile: KJMB-FM is a commercial station owned by Blythe Radio Inc. The format of the station is adult contemporary. KJMB-FM broadcasts to Blythe, CA at 100.3 FM.
FM RADIO STATION

KJMC-FM 44472
Owner: Minority Communications Inc.
Editorial: 1169 25th St, Des Moines, Iowa 50311-4207 **Tel:** 1 515 279-1811.
Web site: http://www.kjmcfm.org
Profile: KJMC-FM is a non-commercial station owned by Minority Communications Inc. The format of the station is urban contemporary music. KJMC-FM broadcasts to the Des Moines, IA area at 89.3 FM.
FM RADIO STATION

KJMD-FM 46672
Owner: Pacific Media Group
Editorial: 311 Ano St, Kahului, Hawaii 96732-1304 **Tel:** 1 808 877-5566.
Email: studio@dajam983.com
Web site: http://www.dajam983.com
Profile: KJMD-FM is a commercial station owned by Pacific Media Group. The format of the station is Rhythmic CHR. KJMD-FM broadcasts to the Kahului, HI area at 98.3 FM.
FM RADIO STATION

KJMH-FM 44166
Owner: Townsquare Media, LLC
Editorial: 900 N Lake Shore Dr, Lake Charles, Louisiana 70601-2120 **Tel:** 1 337 433-1641.
Web site: http://www.107jamz.com
Profile: KJMH-FM is a commercial station owned by Townsquare Media, LLC. The format of the station is urban adult contemporary. KJMH-FM broadcasts to the Lake Charles, LA area at 107.5 FM.
FM RADIO STATION

KJMJ-AM 36331
Owner: Radio Maria Inc.
Editorial: 601 Washington St, Alexandria, Louisiana 71301 **Tel:** 1 318 561-6145.
Email: info.usa@radiomaria.org
Web site: http://www.radiomaria.us
Profile: KJMJ-AM is a commercial station owned by Radio Maria Inc. The format of the station is Catholic and religious programming. KJMJ-AM broadcasts to the Shreveport, LA area at 580 AM.
AM RADIO STATION

KJMK-FM 43274
Owner: Zimmer Radio, Inc.
Editorial: 2702 E 32nd St, Joplin, Missouri 64804 **Tel:** 1 417 624-1025.
Web site: http://www.939classichits.com
Profile: KJMK-FM is a commercial station owned by Zimmer Radio, Inc. The format of the station is classic hits. KJMK-FM broadcasts to the Joplin, MO area at 93.9 FM.
FM RADIO STATION

KJML-FM 43434
Owner: American Media Investments
Editorial: 2510 W 20th St, Joplin, Missouri 64804-0216 **Tel:** 1 417 624-1071.
Web site: http://www.rock1071.com
Profile: KJML-FM is a commercial station owned by American Media Investments. The format of the station is rock. KJML-FM broadcasts to the Joplin, MO area at 107.1 FM.
FM RADIO STATION

KJMM-FM 42893
Owner: Perry Publishing & Broadcasting Inc.
Editorial: 7030 S Yale Ave, Ste 302, Tulsa, Oklahoma 74136-5722 **Tel:** 1 918 494-9886.
Email: spots@kjmm.com
Web site: http://www.kjmm.com
Profile: KJMM-FM is a commercial station owned by Perry Publishing & Broadcasting Inc. The format is urban contemporary. KJMM-FM broadcasts to the Tulsa, OK area at 105.3 FM.
FM RADIO STATION

KJMN-FM 46335
Owner: Entravision Communications Corp.
Editorial: 1907 Mile High Stadium West Cir, Denver, Colorado 80204-1908 **Tel:** 1 303 832-0050.
Web site: http://www.jose921.com
Profile: KJMN-FM is a commercial station owned by Entravision Communications Corp. The format of the station is Hispanic adult hits. KJMN-FM broadcasts to the Denver area at 92.1 FM.
FM RADIO STATION

KJMO-FM 417854
Owner: Cumulus Media Inc.
Editorial: 1002 Diamond Rdg Ste 400, Jefferson City, Missouri 65109-7902 **Tel:** 1 573 893-5100.
Web site: http://www.kjmo.com
Profile: KJMO-FM is a commercial station owned by Cumulus Media Inc. The format of the station is oldies music. KJMO-FM broadcasts to the Jefferson City, MO area at 97.5 FM.
FM RADIO STATION

KJMQ-FM 502176
Owner: Hochman Hawaii Four, Inc.
Editorial: 4334 Rice St, Ste 206, Lihue, Hawaii 96766 **Tel:** 1 808 246-4444.
Email: jamz@hhawaiimedia.com
Web site: http://www.hhawaiimedia.com
Profile: KJMQ-FM is a commercial station owned by Hochman Hawaii Four, Inc. The format of the station is Top 40/CHR music. KJMQ-FM broadcasts to the Kauai, HI area at 98.1 FM.
FM RADIO STATION

KJMS-FM 46292
Owner: iHeartMedia Inc.
Editorial: 2650 Thousand Oaks Blvd Ste 4100, Memphis, Tennessee 38118-2451 **Tel:** 1 901 259-1300.
Web site: http://www.myv101.com
Profile: KJMS-FM is a commercial station owned by iHeartMedia Inc. The format of the station is urban adult contemporary music. KJMS-FM broadcasts to the Memphis, TN area at 101.1 FM.
FM RADIO STATION

KJMT-FM 772129
Owner: Malvern Entertainment Corporation
Editorial: 223 Russell St, Mountain Home, Arkansas 72653-3665 **Tel:** 1 870 425-4971.
Email: news@mountaintalk97.com
Web site: http://www.mountaintalk97.com
Profile: KJMT-FM is a commercial station owned by Malvern Entertainment Corporation. The format of the station is news talk. The station airs locally at 97.1 FM.
FM RADIO STATION

KJMX-FM 42198
Owner: Bicoastal Media LLC
Editorial: 320 Central Ave, Ste 519, Coos Bay, Oregon 97420 **Tel:** 1 541 271-3300.
Web site: http://www.kjmxfm.com
Profile: KJMX-FM is a commercial station owned by Bicoastal Media LLC. The format of the station is classic rock. KJMX-FM broadcasts to the Coos Bay, OR area at 99.5 FM.
FM RADIO STATION

KJMY-FM 42888
Owner: iHeartMedia Inc.
Editorial: 2801 Decker Lake Dr, Salt Lake City, Utah 84119-2330 **Tel:** 1 801 908-1300.
Web site: http://www.my995fm.com
Profile: KJMY-FM is a commercial station owned by iHeartMedia Inc. The format of the station is adult contemporary. KJMY-FM broadcasts to the Salt Lake City area at 99.5 FM.
FM RADIO STATION

KJMZ-FM 46628
Owner: Perry Publishing & Broadcasting Inc.
Editorial: 1525 SE Flower Mound Rd, Lawton, Oklahoma 73501 **Tel:** 1 580 355-1050.
Web site: http://www.kjmz.com
Profile: KJMZ-FM is a commercial station owned by Perry Publishing & Broadcasting Inc. The format of the station is urban contemporary music. KJMZ-FM broadcasts to the Lawton, OK area at 97.9 FM.
FM RADIO STATION

KJNA-FM 43355
Owner: Little River Radio Co.
Editorial: 1791 N 2nd St, Jena, Louisiana 71342 **Tel:** 1 318 992-4155.
Email: kjnafm@hotmail.com
Profile: KJNA-FM is a commercial station owned by Little River Radio Co. The format of the station is country music. KJNA-FM broadcasts to the Jena, LA area at 102.7 FM.
FM RADIO STATION

KJNO-AM 38548
Owner: Alaska Broadcast Communications Inc.
Editorial: 3161 Channel Dr Ste 2, Juneau, Alaska 99801-7866 **Tel:** 1 907 586-3630.
Email: news@abcstations.com
Web site: http://www.kinyradio.com
Profile: KJNO-AM is a commercial station owned by Alaska Broadcast Communications Inc. The format of the station is sports programming. KJNO-AM broadcasts to the Ketchikan, AK area at 630 AM.
AM RADIO STATION

KJNP-AM 38488
Owner: Evangelistic Alaska Missionary Fellowship
Tel: 1 907 488-2216.
Email: kjnp@mosquitonet.com
Web site: http://www.mosquitonet.com/~kjnp
Profile: KJNP-AM is a non-commercial station owned by Evangelistic Alaska Missionary Fellowship. The format of the station is gospel and country. KJNP-AM broadcasts to the North Pole, AK area at 1170 AM.
AM RADIO STATION

KJNP-FM 45846
Owner: Evangelistic Alaska Missionary Fellowship
Tel: 1 907 488-2216.
Email: kjnpnews@yahoo.com
Web site: http://www.mosquitonet.com/~kjnp
Profile: KJNP-FM is a non-commercial station owned by Evangelistic Alaska Missionary Fellowship. The format for the station is classical and religious. KJNP-FM broadcasts to the North Pole, AK area at 100.3 FM.
FM RADIO STATION

KJNY-FM 46829
Owner: Mad River Radio
Editorial: 728 7th St Ste 2A, Eureka, California 95501-1158 **Tel:** 1 707 445-3699.
Web site: http://www.991kissfm.com
Profile: KJNY-FM is a commercial station owned by Mad River Radio. The format of the station is Top 40/CHR. KJNY-FM broadcasts to the Eureka, CA area at 99.1 FM.
FM RADIO STATION

KJOE-FM 42433
Owner: Christensen Broadcasting
Editorial: 2660 Broadway Ave, Slayton, Minnesota 56172-1353 **Tel:** 1 507 836-6125.
Email: kjoe@kjoeradio.com
Web site: http://www.kjoeradio.com/kjoe
Profile: KJOE-FM is a commercial station owned by Christensen Broadcasting. The format of the station is country music. KJOE-FM broadcasts to the Pipestone, MN area at 106.1 FM.
FM RADIO STATION

KJOJ-FM 46427
Owner: Liberman Broadcasting Inc.
Editorial: 3000 Bering Dr, Houston, Texas 77057-5708 **Tel:** 1 713 315-3400.
Web site: http://houston.laraza.fm
Profile: KJOJ-FM is a commercial station owned by Liberman Broadcasting Inc. The format of the station is regional Mexican music. KJOJ-FM broadcasts to the Houston area at 103.3 FM.
FM RADIO STATION

KJOK-FM 840205
Owner: Altus FM Inc.
Editorial: 808 N Main St, Altus, Oklahoma 73521-3116 **Tel:** 1 580 482-1555.
Web site: http://www.keyb.net
Profile: KJOK-FM is a commercial station owned by Altus FM Inc. The format of the station is classic rock music. The station is aired locally on 102.7 FM in Altus, OK.
FM RADIO STATION

KJOL-AM 74623
Owner: United Ministries
Editorial: 1354 E Sherwood Dr, Grand Junction, Colorado 81501-7546 **Tel:** 1 970 254-5565.
Email: info@kjol.org
Web site: http://www.kjol.org
Profile: KJOL-AM is a non-commercial station owned by United Ministries. The format of the station is religious. KJOL-AM broadcasts to the Grand Junction, CO area at a frequency of 620 AM.
AM RADIO STATION

KJOL-FM 42575
Owner: United Ministries
Editorial: 1354 E Sherwood Dr, Grand Junction, Colorado 81501-7546 **Tel:** 1 970 254-5565.
Email: info@kjol.org
Web site: http://www.kjol.org
Profile: KJOL-FM is a non-commercial station owned by United Ministries. The format of the station is religious. KJOL-FM broadcasts to the Montrose, CO area at a frequency of 91.9.
FM RADIO STATION

KJON-AM 37481
Owner: Chatham Hill Foundation, Inc.
Editorial: 8828 N Stemmons Fwy Ste 106, Dallas, Texas 75247-3720 **Tel:** 1 214 951-0132.
Web site: http://grnonline.com
Profile: KJON-AM is a commercial station owned by Chatham Hill Foundation, Inc. The format of the station is Hispanic/Christian programming. KJON-AM broadcasts to the Dallas area at 850 AM.
AM RADIO STATION

KJOP-AM 36088
Owner: Immaculate Heart Radio
Editorial: 3256 Penryn Rd Ste 100, Loomis, California 95650-8052 **Tel:** 1 916 535-0500.
Email: programming@ihradio.org
Web site: http://ihradio.org
Profile: KJOP-AM is a non-commercial station owned by Immaculate Heart Radio. The format of the station is religious. KJOP-AM broadcasts to the Fresno, CA area at 1240 AM.
AM RADIO STATION

KJOT-FM 44713
Owner: E.W. Scripps Co.
Editorial: 5257 W Fairview Ave Ste 260, Boise, Idaho 83706-1766 **Tel:** 1 208 344-3511.
Web site: http://www.varietyrocks.com
Profile: KJOT-FM is a commercial station owned by E.W. Scripps Co. The format of the station is variety of rock and adult hits music. KJOT-FM broadcasts to the Boise, ID area at 105.1 FM.
FM RADIO STATION

KJOV-FM 62625
Owner: Great Plains Christian Radio
Editorial: 909 W Carthage, Meade, Kansas 67864 **Tel:** 1 620 873-2991.
Email: kjil@kjil.com
Web site: http://www.kjil991.com
Profile: KJOV-FM is a non-commercial station owned by Great Plains Christian Radio. The format of the station is contemporary Christan music. KJOV-FM broadcasts to the Woodward, OK area at 90.7 FM.
FM RADIO STATION

KJOX-AM 37188
Owner: Ingstad (James D.)
Editorial: 1200 Chesterly Dr, Ste 160, Yakima, Washington 98902 **Tel:** 1 509 248-2900.
Profile: KJOX-AM is a commercial station owned by Ingstad (James D.). The format of the station is sports. KJOX-AM broadcasts to the Yakima, WA area at 1340 AM.
AM RADIO STATION

KJOY-FM 43887
Owner: Cumulus Media Inc
Editorial: 3127 Transworld Dr #270, Stockton, California 95206-4988 **Tel:** 1 209 507-8500.
Web site: http://www.993kjoy.com
Profile: KJOY-FM is a commercial station owned by Cumulus Media Inc. The format of the station is adult contemporary. KJOY-FM broadcasts to the Stockton, CA area at 99.3 FM.
FM RADIO STATION

KJOZ-AM 39081
Owner: Next Level Communications
Editorial: 397 N Sam Houston Pkwy E Ste 475, Houston, Texas 77060-2496 **Tel:** 1 832 456-5569.
Email: fm@radioaleluya.org
Web site: http://kjozradio.com
Profile: KJOZ-AM is a commercial station owned by Next Level Communications. The format of the station is progressive talk, news and sports. KJOZ-AM broadcasts to the Houston area at 880 AM.
AM RADIO STATION

KJPG-AM 88207
Owner: Immaculate Heart Radio
Editorial: 1550 N Fresno St, Fresno, California 93703-3711 **Tel:** 1 916 535-0500.
Email: programming@ihradio.org
Web site: http://ihradio.org
Profile: KJPG-AM is a commercial station owned by Immaculate Heart Radio. The format of the station is religious programming. KJPG-AM broadcasts to the Bakersfield, CA area at 1050 AM.
AM RADIO STATION

KJPW-AM 36578
Owner: Alpha Media
Editorial: 313 Old Route 66, Saint Robert, Missouri 65584 **Tel:** 1 573 336-4913.
Email: news.kfbd@alphamediausa.com
Web site: http://www.myozarksonline.com
Profile: KJPW-AM is a commercial station owned by Alpha Media. The format of the station is talk programming. KJPW-AM broadcasts to the Waynesville, MO area at 1390 AM.
AM RADIO STATION

KJPW-FM 43290
Owner: Alpha Media
Editorial: 313 Old Route 66, Saint Robert, Missouri 65584 **Tel:** 1 573 336-4913.
Email: news.kfbd@alphamediausa.com
Web site: http://www.myozarksonline.com
Profile: KJPW-FM is a commercial station owned by Alpha Media. The format of the station is talk programming. KJPW-FM broadcasts to the Saint Roberts, MO area at 102.3 FM.
FM RADIO STATION

KJR-AM 38430
Owner: iHeartMedia Inc.
Editorial: 645 Elliott Ave W Ste 400, Seattle, Washington 98119-3911 **Tel:** 1 206 494-2000.
Web site: http://sportsradiokjr.iheart.com
Profile: KJR-AM is a commercial station owned by iHeartMedia Inc. The format of the station is sports. KJR-AM broadcasts to the Seattle area at 950 AM.
AM RADIO STATION

KJRB-AM 39358
Owner: Mapleton Communications LLC
Editorial: 1601 E 57th Ave, Spokane, Washington 99223-6623 **Tel:** 1 509 448-1000.
Web site: http://www.790kjrb.com
Profile: KJRB-AM is a commercial station owned by Mapleton Communications LLC. The format of the station is Classic Rock. KJRB-AM broadcasts to the Spokane, WA area at 790 AM and 94.1 FM. The station's slogan is, "The Rock You Know."
AM RADIO STATION

KJR-FM 45798
Owner: iHeartMedia Inc.
Editorial: 645 Elliott Ave W Ste 400, Seattle, Washington 98119-3911 **Tel:** 1 206 494-2000.
Web site: http://957thejet.iheart.com
Profile: KJR-FM is a commercial station owned by iHeartMedia Inc. The format of the station is classic hits. KJR-FM broadcasts to the Seattle area at 95.7 FM.
FM RADIO STATION

KJRG-AM 37104
Owner: Bott Broadcasting Co.
Editorial: 209 N Meridian Rd, Newton, Kansas 67114 **Tel:** 1 316 283-4592.
Email: kjrg@bottradionetwork.com
Web site: http://www.bottradionetwork.com
Profile: KJRG-AM is a commercial station owned by Bott Broadcasting Co. The format of the station is religious programming. KJRG-AM broadcasts to the Newton, KS area at 950 AM.
AM RADIO STATION

KJRV-FM 407956
Owner: Performance Radio
Editorial: 1726 Dakota Ave S, Huron, South Dakota 57350 **Tel:** 1 605 352-1933.
Web site: http://www.bigjimrocks.com
Profile: KJRV-FM is a commercial station owned by Performance Radio. The format of the station is classic rock. KJRV-FM broadcasts to the Huron, SD area at 93.3 FM.
FM RADIO STATION

KJSK-AM 38966
Owner: Alpha Media
Editorial: 1418 25th St, Columbus, Nebraska 68601-2820 **Tel:** 1 402 564-2866.
Email: kjsk@megavision.com
Web site: http://www.mycentralnebraska.com
Profile: KJSK-AM is a commercial station owned by Alpha Media. The format of the station is news, sports and talk. KJSK-AM broadcasts to the Columbus, NE area at 900 AM.
AM RADIO STATION

KJSM-FM 43818
Owner: Family Worship Center Church, Inc.
Editorial: 8919 World Ministries Ave, Baton Rouge, Louisiana 70810-9006 **Tel:** 1 225 768-3288.
Email: info@jsm.org
Web site: http://www.jsm.org
FM RADIO STATION

KJSN-FM 45865
Owner: iHeartMedia Inc.
Editorial: 2121 Lancey Dr, Modesto, California 95355-3036 **Tel:** 1 209 551-1306.
Web site: http://sunny102fm.iheart.com
Profile: KJSN-FM is a commercial station owned by iHeartMedia Inc. The format of the station is adult contemporary music. KJSN-FM broadcasts to the Modesto, CA area at 102.3 FM.
FM RADIO STATION

KJSR-FM 39947
Owner: Cox Media Group, Inc.
Editorial: 7136 S Yale Ave Ste 500, Tulsa, Oklahoma 74136-6358 **Tel:** 1 918 493-3434.
Web site: http://www.1033theeagle.com
Profile: KJSR-FM is a commercial station owned by Cox Media Group, Inc. The format of the station is classic rock. KJSR-FM broadcasts to the Tulsa, OK area at 103.3 FM.
FM RADIO STATION

KJTA-FM 444962
Owner: Family Life Radio
Editorial: 1700 N 2nd St, Flagstaff, Arizona 86004-5008 **Tel:** 1 520 742-6976.
Web site: http://www.myflr.org
FM RADIO STATION

KJTF-FM 728869
Owner: Tri-State Broadcasting Association
Tel: 1 308 532-5515.
Email: kjlt@kjlt.org
Web site: http://www.kjlt.org
Profile: KJTF-FM is a non-commercial station owned by Tri-State Broadcasting Association. The format of the station is southern gospel. KJTF-FM broadcasts to the North Platte, NE area at a frequency of 89.3.
FM RADIO STATION

KJTH-FM 217735
Owner: Love Station Inc.(The)
Editorial: 6600 W Highway 60, Ponca City, Oklahoma 74601-7926 **Tel:** 1 580 767-1400.
Email: mail@thehousefm.com
Web site: http://www.thehousefm.com
Profile: KJTH-FM is a non-commercial station owned by The Love Station, Inc. The format of the station is contemporary Christian music. KJTH-FM broadcasts to the Ponca City, OK area at 89.7 FM.
FM RADIO STATION

KJTV-AM 39144
Owner: Ramar Communications Inc.
Editorial: 9800 University Ave, Lubbock, Texas 79423-5302 **Tel:** 1 806 745-3434.
Web site: http://www.am9501007fm.com
Profile: KJTV-AM is a commercial station owned by Ramar Communications Inc. The format of the station is news, sports and talk. KJTV-AM broadcasts to the Lubbock, TX area at 950 AM.
AM RADIO STATION

KJTX-FM 41650
Owner: Wisdom Ministries Inc.
Editorial: 3607 Gilmer Rd, Longview, Texas 75604 **Tel:** 1 903 759-1243.
Email: kjtxlr@juno.com
Web site: http://www.kjtx1045fm.com
Profile: KJTX-FM is a commercial station owned by Wisdom Ministries Inc. The format for the station is contemporary Christian and gospel music. KJTX-FM broadcasts to the Longview, TX area at 104.5 FM.
FM RADIO STATION

KJTY-FM 41093
Owner: Family Life Communications, Inc.
Editorial: 7355 N Oracle Rd, Tucson, Arizona 85704-6325 **Tel:** 1 520 742-6976.
Web site: http://www.myflr.org
Profile: KJTY-FM is a non-commercial station owned by Family Life Radio. The format of the station is contemporary Christian and relgious programming. KJTY-FM broadcasts to the Topeka, KS area at 88.1 FM.
FM RADIO STATION

KJUG-FM 45904
Owner: Momentum Broadcasting LP
Editorial: 1401 W Caldwell Ave, Visalia, California 93277-7725 **Tel:** 1 559 553-1500.
Email: studio@kjug.com
Web site: http://www.kjug.com
Profile: KJUG-FM is a commercial station owned by Momentum Broadcasting LP. The format for the station is contemporary country. KJUG-AM broadcasts to the Visalia, CA area at 106.7 FM.
FM RADIO STATION

KJUL-FM 349910
Owner: Summit American Inc.
Editorial: 150 Spectrum Blvd, Las Vegas, Nevada 89101 **Tel:** 1 702 258-0285.
Web site: http://www.kjul1047.com
Profile: KJUL-FM is a commercial station owned by Summit American Inc. The format of the station is adult standards. KJUL-FM broadcasts to the Las Vegas area at 104.7 FM.
FM RADIO STATION

KJVC-FM 43553
Owner: Hunt (Leon)
Editorial: 805 Polk St, Mansfield, Louisiana 71052-2413 **Tel:** 1 318 871-5582.
Email: kjvc@kjvcfm.com
Web site: http://www.kjvcfm.com
Profile: KJVC-FM is a commercial station owned by Leon Hunt. The format of the station is contemporary country music. KJVC-FM broadcasts in the Logansport, LA area at 92.7 FM.
FM RADIO STATION

KJWL-FM 42570
Owner: Ostlund(John Edwards)
Editorial: 1415 Fulton St, Fresno, California 93721-1609 **Tel:** 1 559 497-5118.
Web site: http://993now.fm
Profile: KJWL-FM is a commercial station owned by John Edwards Ostlund. The format of the station is adult contemporary. KJWL-FM broadcasts to the Fresno, CA area at 99.3 FM.
FM RADIO STATION

KJWM-FM 623924
Owner: VSS Catholic Communications Inc.
Editorial: 5829 N 60th St, Omaha, Nebraska 68104-1140 **Tel:** 1 402 571-0200.
Email: kvss@kvss.com
Web site: http://www.kvss.com
Profile: KJWM-FM is a non-commercial station owned by VSS Catholic Communications Inc. The format of the station is Catholic and religious programming. KJWM-FM broadcasts to the Grand Island, NE area at 91.5 FM.
FM RADIO STATION

KJXJ-FM 42623
Owner: Brazos Valley Communications LLC
Editorial: 1240 E Villa Maria Rd, Bryan, Texas 77802-2519 **Tel:** 1 979 776-1240.
Web site: http://www.espnaggieland1039.com
Profile: KJXJ-FM is a commercial station owned by Brazos Valley Communications LLC. The format of the station is sports. KJXJ-FM broadcasts to the Waco, TX area at 103.9 FM.
FM RADIO STATION

KJXK-FM 44911
Owner: Alpha Media
Editorial: 4050 Eisenhauer Rd, San Antonio, Texas 78218-3409 **Tel:** 1 210 654-5100.
Web site: http://www.jackfmsa.com
Profile: KJXK-FM is a commercial station owned by Alpha Media. The format of the station is adult hits. KJXK-FM broadcasts to the San Antonio area at 102.7 FM.
FM RADIO STATION

KJXX-AM 36031
Owner: W. Russell Withers
Editorial: 901 S Kingshighway St, Cape Girardeau, Missouri 63703-8003 **Tel:** 1 573 339-7000.
Email: news@withersradio.net
Web site: http://www.1170kjxx.com
Profile: KJXX-AM is a commercial station owned by W Russell Withers. The format of the station is contemporary Christian and adult standards music. KJXX-AM broadcasts to the Cape Girardeau, MO; Paducah, KY; and Harrisburg, IL areas at 1170 AM.
AM RADIO STATION

KJYE-AM 34930
Owner: United Ministries
Editorial: 1354 E Sherwood Dr, Grand Junction, Colorado 81501-7546 **Tel:** 1 970 254-5565.
Email: info@kjol.org
Web site: http://www.kjol.org
Profile: KJYE-AM is a non-commercial station owned by United Ministries. The format of the station is religious programming. KJYE-AM broadcasts to the Delta, CO area at 1400 AM.
AM RADIO STATION

KJYE-FM 45896
Owner: MBC Grand Broadcasting Inc.
Editorial: 1360 E Sherwood Dr, Grand Junction, Colorado 81501-7546 **Tel:** 1 970 254-2100.
Email: 92.3thevault@gmail.com
Web site: http://www.thevault923.com
Profile: KJYE-FM is a commercial station owned by MBC Grand Broadcasting Inc. The format of the station is classic hits. KJYE-FM broadcasts to the Grand Junction, CO area at 92.3 FM.
FM RADIO STATION

KJYL-FM 42590
Owner: Minn-Iowa Christian Broadcasting
Editorial: 103 W Broadway St, Eagle Grove, Iowa 50533-1701 **Tel:** 1 515 448-4588.
Email: kjyl@newmail.kinshipradio.org
Web site: http://www.kjyl.org
Profile: KJYL-FM is a non-commercial station owned by Minn-Iowa Christian Broadcasting. The format of the station is gospel music and religious programming. KJYL-FM broadcasts to the Des Moines, IA area at 100.7 FM.
FM RADIO STATION

KJYO-FM 46468
Owner: iHeartMedia Inc.
Editorial: 1900 NW Expressway Ste 1000, Oklahoma City, Oklahoma 73118-1854 **Tel:** 1 405 840-5271.
Web site: http://www.kj103fm.com
Profile: KJYO-FM is a commercial station owned by iHeartMedia Inc. The format of the station is Top 40/ CHR music. KJYO-FM broadcasts to the Oklahoma City area at 102.7 FM.
FM RADIO STATION

KJZA-FM 63029
Owner: St. Paul Bible College
Editorial: 2719 S Dw Ranch Rd, Kingman, Arizona 86401-8611 **Tel:** 1 928 541-1008.
Email: kjzafm@yahoo.com
Web site: http://www.kjza.org
Profile: KJZA-FM is a non-commercial station owned by St. Paul Bible College. The format of the station is jazz and news. KJZA-FM broadcasts to the Prescott, AZ area at 89.5 FM.
FM RADIO STATION

KJZY-FM 42953
Owner: Redwood Empire Stereocasters
Editorial: 3392 Mendocino Ave, Santa Rosa, California 95403-2213 **Tel:** 1 707 528-4434.
Email: jazznotes@kjzy.com
Web site: http://www.kjzy.com
Profile: KJZY-FM is a commercial station owned by Redwood Empire Stereocasters. The format of the station is smooth AC. KJZY-FM broadcasts to the San Francisco area at 93.7 FM.
FM RADIO STATION

KJZZ-FM 39714
Owner: Maricopa Community Colleges
Editorial: 2323 W 14th St, Tempe, Arizona 85281-6948 **Tel:** 1 480 834-5627.
Email: news@rioradio.org
Web site: http://www.kjzz.org
Profile: KJZZ-FM is a commercial station owned by Maricopa Community Colleges. The format of the station is news and jazz. KJZZ-FM broadcasts to the Tempe, AZ area at 91.5 FM.
FM RADIO STATION

KKAA-AM 38905
Owner: Family Stations Inc.
Editorial: 290 Hegenberger Rd, Oakland, California 94621-1436 **Tel:** 1 510 568-6200.
Web site: http://www.familyradio.com
Profile: KKAA-AM is a commercial station owned by Family Stations Inc. The format of the station is religious programming. KKAA-FM broadcasts to the Aberdeen, SD area at 1560 AM.
AM RADIO STATION

KKAJ-FM 46058
Owner: LKCM Radio Group LP
Editorial: 1205 Northglen St, Ardmore, Oklahoma 73401-1202 **Tel:** 1 580 226-0421.
Email: news@sokradio.com
Web site: http://www.kkaj.com
Profile: KKAJ-FM is a commercial station owned by LKCM Radio Group LP. The format of the station is contemporary country music. KKAJ-FM broadcasts to the Ardmore, OK area at 95.7 FM.
FM RADIO STATION

KKAL-FM 43506
Owner: American General Media
Editorial: 3620 Sacramento Dr, San Luis Obispo, California 93401-7215 **Tel:** 1 805 781-2750.
Email: news@americangeneralmedia.com
Web site: http://www.krush925.com
Profile: KKAL-FM is a commercial station owned by American General Media. The format of the station is hot adult contemporary. KKAL-FM broadcasts in the San Luis Obispo, CA area at 92.5 FM.
FM RADIO STATION

KKAM-AM 38974
Owner: Townsquare Media, LLC
Editorial: 4413 82nd St Ste 300, Lubbock, Texas 79424-3366 **Tel:** 1 806 798-7078.
Web site: http://1340thefan.com
Profile: KKAM-AM is a commercial station owned by Townsquare Media, LLC. The format of the station is sports. KKAM-AM broadcasts to the Lubbock, TX area at 1340 AM.
AM RADIO STATION

KKAN-AM 37344
Owner: S-Y Communications
Editorial: 205 F St, Phillipsburg, Kansas 67661-1943 **Tel:** 1 785 543-2151.
Email: radio@kkankqma.com
Web site: http://www.kkankqma.com
Profile: KKAN-AM is a commercial station owned by S-Y Communications. The format of the station is adult standards. KKAN-AM broadcasts to the Phillipsburg, KS area at 1490 AM.
AM RADIO STATION

KKAQ-AM 38799
Owner: Iowa City Broadcasting Co.
Editorial: 1433 Main Ave N, Thief River Falls, Minnesota 56701 **Tel:** 1 218 681-4900.
Email: ktrf@mncable.net
Web site: http://www.trfradio.com/
Profile: KKAQ-AM is a commercial station owned by Iowa City Broadcasting Co. The format of the station is classic country. KKAQ-AM broadcasts to the Thief River Falls, MN area at 1460 AM.
AM RADIO STATION

KKAT-AM 39402
Owner: Cumulus Media Inc
Editorial: 434 Bearcat Dr, Salt Lake City, Utah 84115 **Tel:** 1 801 485-6700.
Web site: http://utahsbigtalker.com
Profile: KKAT-AM is a commercial station owned by Cumulus Media Inc. The format for the station is news and talk. KKAT-AM broadcasts to the Salt Lake City area at 860 AM.
AM RADIO STATION

KKBA-FM 41754
Owner: Malkan Interactive Communications
Editorial: 2117 Leopard St, Corpus Christi, Texas 78408-3925 **Tel:** 1 361 883-3516.
Web site: http://www.927kbay.com
Profile: KKBA-FM is a commercial station owned by Malkan Interactive Communications. The format of the station is rhythmic adult contemporary. KKBA-FM broadcasts to the Corpus Christi, TX area at 92.7 FM.
FM RADIO STATION

KKBB-FM 42402
Owner: Alpha Media
Editorial: 3651 Pegasus Dr Ste 107, Bakersfield, California 93308-6836 **Tel:** 1 661 393-1900.
Web site: http://www.groove993.com
Profile: KKBB-FM is a commercial station owned by Alpha Media. The format of the station is R&B oldies. KKBB-FM broadcasts to the Bakersfield, CA area at 99.3 FM.
FM RADIO STATION

KKBC-FM 44581
Owner: Pacific Empire Communications
Editorial: 2510 Cove Ave, La Grande, Oregon 97850 **Tel:** 1 541 523-4431.
Web site: http://yourboomerradio.com
Profile: KKBC-FM is a commercial station owned by Pacific Empire Communications. The format of the station is oldies music. KKBC-AM broadcasts to the La Grande, OR area at 95.3 FM.
FM RADIO STATION

KKBD-FM 42947
Owner: iHeartMedia Inc.
Editorial: 311 Lexington Ave, Fort Smith, Arkansas 72901-3842 **Tel:** 1 479 782-8888.
Web site: http://www.bigdog959.com
Profile: KKBD-FM is a commercial station owned by iHeartMedia Inc. The format of the station is classic rock. KKBD-FM broadcasts to the Fort Smith, AR area at 95.9 FM.
FM RADIO STATION

KKBE-AM 37191
Owner: Noalmark Broadcasting Corp.
Editorial: 1301 N Main St, Roswell, New Mexico 88201-5013 **Tel:** 1 575 623-9100.
Email: kevin@kbimradio.com
Profile: KKBE-AM is a commercial station owned by Noalmark Broadcasting Corp. The format of the station is Top 40. KKBE-AM broadcasts to the Roswell, NM area at 910 AM.
AM RADIO STATION

KKBG-FM 46457
Owner: Pacific Media Group
Editorial: 913 Kanoelehua Ave, Hilo, Hawaii 96720-5116 **Tel:** 1 808 961-0651.
Email: support@kbigfm.com
Web site: http://www.kbigfm.com
Profile: KKBG-FM is a commercial station owned by Pacific Media Group. The format of the station is adult contemporary. KKBG-FM broadcasts to the Hilo, HI area at 97.9 FM.
FM RADIO STATION

KKBI-FM 41111
Owner: JDC Radio Inc.
Editorial: 108 N Broadway St, Broken Bow, Oklahoma 74728-3934 **Tel:** 1 580 584-3388.
Email: kkbi@pine-net.com
Web site: http://www.kkbifm.com
Profile: KKBI-FM is a commercial station owned by JDC Radio Inc. The format of the station is contemporary country. KKBI-FM broadcasts to the Broken Bow, OK area at 106.1 FM.
FM RADIO STATION

KKBJ-AM 37346
Owner: R.P. Broadcasting
Editorial: 2115 Washington Ave S, Bemidji, Minnesota 56601-8918 **Tel:** 1 218 751-7777.
Email: news@kkbj.com
Web site: http://www.kkbjam.com
Profile: KKBJ-AM is a commercial station owned by R.P. Broadcasting. The format of the station is news and talk. KKBJ-AM broadcasts in the Minneapolis area at 1360 AM.
AM RADIO STATION

KKBJ-FM 44716
Owner: R.P. Broadcasting
Editorial: 2115 Washington Ave S, Bemidji, Minnesota 56601 **Tel:** 1 218 751-7777.
Email: news@kkbj.com
Web site: http://www.kkbj.com
Profile: KKBJ-FM is a commercial station owned by R.P. Broadcasting. The format of the station is hot adult contemporary music. KKBJ-FM broadcasts to the Bemidji, MN area at 103.7 FM.
FM RADIO STATION

KKBL-FM 44717
Owner: Eagle Broadcasting Inc.
Editorial: 126 S Jefferson Ave, Aurora, Missouri 65605-1635 **Tel:** 1 417 235-6041.
Email: kkbl@radiotalon.com
Web site: http://www.radiotalon.com
Profile: KKBL-FM is a commercial station owned by Eagle Broadcasting Inc. The format of the station is rock music. KKBL-FM broadcasts to the Monett, MO area at 95.9 FM.
FM RADIO STATION

KKBN-FM 39716
Owner: Clarke Broadcasting Corp.
Editorial: 342 S Washington St, Sonora, California 95370 **Tel:** 1 209 533-1450.
Web site: http://www.kkbnfm.com
Profile: KKBN-FM is a commercial station owned by Clarke Broadcasting Corp. The format of the station is contemporary country. KKBN-FM broadcasts to the Sonora, CA area at 93.5 FM.
FM RADIO STATION

KKBO-FM 563538
Owner: Radio Bismarck, LLC.
Editorial: 3128 E Broadway Ave, Bismarck, North Dakota 58501-5033 **Tel:** 1 701 751-8000.
Profile: KKBO-FM is a commercial station owned by Radio Bismarck, LLC. The format of the station is country. KKBO-FM broadcasts to the Bismarck, ND area at 105.9 FM.
FM RADIO STATION

KKBQ-FM 44403
Owner: Cox Media Group, Inc.
Editorial: 1990 Post Oak Blvd Ste 2300, Houston, Texas 77056-3847 **Tel:** 1 713 963-1200.
Web site: http://www.thenew93q.com
Profile: KKBQ-FM is a commercial station owned by Cox Media Group, Inc. The format of the station is contemporary country music. KKBQ-FM broadcasts to the Houston area at 92.9 FM.
FM RADIO STATION

KKBR-FM 40070
Owner: Town Square Media
Editorial: 27 N 27th St, Billings, Montana 59101-2357 **Tel:** 1 406 248-7827.
Web site: http://popcrush971.com
Profile: KKBR-FM is a commercial station owned by Town Square Media. The format of the station is Top 40/CHR. KKBR-FM broadcasts in the Billings, MT area at 97.1 FM.
FM RADIO STATION

KKBS-FM 40980
Owner: MLS Communications Inc.
Editorial: 3001 N Highway 64, Guymon, Oklahoma 73942 **Tel:** 1 580 338-5493.
Email: kkbs@kkbs.com
Web site: http://www.kkbs.com
Profile: KKBS-FM is a commercial station owned by MLS Communications Inc. The format of the station is rock. KKBS-FM broadcasts to the Guymon, OK area at 92.7 FM.
FM RADIO STATION

KKBZ-FM 46706
Owner: Lotus Communications Corp.
Editorial: 1110 E Olive Ave, Fresno, California 93728 **Tel:** 1 559 497-1100.
Web site: http://www.1051theblaze.com
Profile: KKBZ-FM is a commercial station owned by Lotus Communications Corp. The format of the station is classic rock. KKBZ-FM broadcasts to the Fresno, CA area at 105.1 FM.
FM RADIO STATION

KKCB-FM 45033
Owner: Townsquare Media, LLC
Editorial: 14 E Central Entrance, Duluth, Minnesota 55811 **Tel:** 1 218 727-4500.
Web site: http://www.kkcb.com
Profile: KKCB-FM is a commercial station owned by Townsquare Media, LLC. The format of the station is country music. KKCB-FM broadcasts to the Duluth, MN area at 105.1 FM.
FM RADIO STATION

KKCD-FM 41803
Owner: E.W. Scripps Co.
Editorial: 10714 Mockingbird Dr, Omaha, Nebraska 68127-1942 **Tel:** 1 402 592-5300.
Web site: http://www.cd1059.com
Profile: KKCD-FM is a commercial station owned by the E.W. Scripps Co. The format of the station is classic rock. KKCD-FM broadcasts to the Omaha, NE area at 105.9 FM.
FM RADIO STATION

KKCH-FM 43581
Owner: NRC Broadcasting
Editorial: 182 Avon Rd, Ste 240, Avon, Colorado 81620-9999 **Tel:** 1 970 949-0140.
Web site: http://www.mountainjackfm.com
Profile: KKCH-FM is a commercial station owned by NRC Broadcasting. The format of the station is adult hits. KKCH-FM broadcasts to the Avon, CO area at 92.7 FM.
FM RADIO STATION

KKCI-FM 46351
Owner: Rocking M Radio
Editorial: 3023 W 31st St, Goodland, Kansas 67735 **Tel:** 1 785 899-2309.
Email: kloe@st-tel.net
Web site: http://www.kloe.com
Profile: KKCI-FM is a commercial station owned by Rocking M Radio. The format of the station is classic rock. KKCI-FM broadcasts to the Goodland, KS area at 102.5 FM.
FM RADIO STATION

KKCJ-FM 559562
Owner: Calvary Chapel of Albuquerque
Editorial: 4001 Osuna Rd NE, Albuquerque, New Mexico 87109-4422 **Tel:** 1 505 344-9146.
Email: studio@star88.fm
Web site: http://star88.fm
Profile: KKCJ-FM is a non-commerical station owned by Calvary Chapel of Albuquerque. The format of the station is Christian contemporary. KKCJ-FM broadcasts to the Cannon AFB, NM area at 90.7 FM. It's sister station is KLYT-FM and they share the same staff.
FM RADIO STATION

KKCK-FM 44718
Owner: KMHL Broadcasting Corp.
Editorial: 1414 E College Dr, Marshall, Minnesota 56258-2027 **Tel:** 1 507 532-2282.
Email: kmhlradio@gmail.com
Web site: http://997kkck.com
Profile: KKCK-FM is a commercial station owned by KMHL Broadcasting Corp. The format of the station is Top 40/CHR music. KKCK-FM broadcasts in the Minneapolis area at 99.7 FM.
FM RADIO STATION

KKCL-FM 41253
Owner: Townsquare Media, LLC
Editorial: 4413 82nd St Ste 300, Lubbock, Texas 79424-3366 **Tel:** 1 806 798-7078.
Web site: http://awesome98.com/
Profile: KKCL-FM is a commercial station owned by Townsquare Media, LLC. The format of the station is classic hits. KKCL-FM broadcasts to the Lubbock, TX area at 98.1 FM.
FM RADIO STATION

KKCM-FM 46391
Owner: Copper Mountain Broadcasting
Editorial: 68474 Twentynine Palms Highway, Twentynine Palms, California 92277 **Tel:** 1 760 362-4264.
Email: coppermountainbroadcasting@yahoo.com
Profile: KKCM-FM is a commercial station owned by Copper Mountain Broadcasting. The format of the station is contemporary country. KKCM-FM broadcasts to the Palm Springs, CA area at 92.1 FM.
FM RADIO STATION

KKCN-FM 44179
Owner: Townsquare Media
Editorial: 1301 S Abe St, San Angelo, Texas 76903-7245 **Tel:** 1 325 655-7161.
Web site: http://www.103kkcn.com
Profile: KKCN-FM is a commercial station owned by Townsquare Media. The format of the station is contemporary country. KKCN-FM broadcasts to the San Angelo, TX area at 103.1 FM.
FM RADIO STATION

KKCQ-AM 38760
Owner: Pine to Prairie Broadcasting Inc.
Editorial: 35006 US Highway 2 SE, Fosston, Minnesota 56542-9404 **Tel:** 1 218 435-1919.
Email: info@kkcqradio.com
Web site: http://rjbroadcasting.com
Profile: KKCQ-AM is a commercial station owned by Pine to Prairie Broadcasting Inc. The format of the station is talk programming and oldies music. KKCQ-AM broadcasts to the Fosston, MN area at 1480 AM.
AM RADIO STATION

KKCQ-FM 518289
Owner: Pine to Prairie Broadcasting Inc.
Editorial: 35006 US Highway 2 SE, Fosston, Minnesota 56542-9404 **Tel:** 1 218 435-1919.
Email: info@kkcqradio.com
Web site: http://rjbroadcasting.com
Profile: KKCQ-FM is a commercial station owned by Pine to Prairie Broadcasting Inc. The format of the station is contemporary country. KKCQ-FM broadcasts to the Fosston, MN area at 96.7 FM.
FM RADIO STATION

KKCR-FM 43452
Owner: Kekahu Foundation Inc.
Editorial: 4520D Hanalei Plantation Rd, Princeville, Hawaii 96722-5420 **Tel:** 1 808 826-7774.
Email: kkcr@kkcr.org
Web site: http://www.kkcr.org
Profile: KKCR-FM is a non-commercial station owned by Kekahu Foundation Inc. The format of the station is variety. KKCR-FM broadcasts to the Hanalei, HI area at 90.9 FM.
FM RADIO STATION

KKCT-FM 42180
Owner: Townsquare Media, Inc.
Editorial: 4303 Memorial Hwy, Mandan, North Dakota 58554-4711 **Tel:** 1 701 250-6602.
Web site: http://www.hot975fm.com
Profile: KKCT-FM is a commercial station owned by Townsquare Media, Inc. The format of the station is Top 40/CHR music. KKCT-FM broadcasts to the Bismarck, ND area at 97.5 FM.
FM RADIO STATION

KKCW-FM 39717
Owner: iHeartMedia Inc.
Editorial: 13333 SW 68th Pkwy Ste 310, Tigard, Oregon 97223-8304 **Tel:** 1 503 323-6400.
Web site: http://www.k103.com
Profile: KKCW-FM is a commercial station owned by iHeartMedia Inc. The format of the station is adult contemporary music. KKCW-FM broadcasts to the Portland, OR area at 103.3 FM.
FM RADIO STATION

KKCY-FM 41118
Owner: Results Radio Group
Editorial: 1479 Sanborn Rd, Yuba City, California 95993-6042 **Tel:** 1 530 673-2200.
Web site: http://www.kkcy.com
Profile: KKCY-FM is a commercial station owned by Results Radio Group. The format of the station is classic country. KKCY-FM broadcasts to the Yuba City, CA area at 103.1 FM.
FM RADIO STATION

KKDA-AM 37348
Owner: SKR Partners, LLC
Editorial: 2356 Glenda Ln, Dallas, Texas 75229-3317 **Tel:** 1 972 620-6296.
Web site: http://dknet730.com/
Profile: KKDA-AM is a commercial station owned by SKR Partners, LLC. The format of the station Korean language programming. KKDA-AM broadcasts to the Grand Prairie, TX area at 730 AM.
AM RADIO STATION

KKDA-FM 44720
Owner: Service Broadcasting Corp.
Editorial: 621 NW 6th St, Grand Prairie, Texas 75050-5555 **Tel:** 1 972 263-9911.
Web site: http://www.myk104.com
Profile: KKDA-FM is a commercial station owned by Service Broadcasting Corp. The format of the station is urban contemporary music. KKDA-FM broadcasts to the Dallas area at 104.5 FM.
FM RADIO STATION

KKDC-FM 238707
Owner: Four Corners Broadcasting LLC
Editorial: 310 Railroad St, Dolores, Colorado 81323 **Tel:** 1 970 259-4444.
Web site: http://www.radiodolores.com
Profile: KKDC-FM is a commercial station owned by Four Corners Broadcasting LLC. The format of the station is classic rock. KKDC-FM broadcasts to the Dolores, CO area at 93.3 FM.
FM RADIO STATION

KKDD-AM 39098
Owner: iHeartMedia Inc.
Editorial: 2030 Iowa Ave #100, Riverside, California 92507-7415 **Tel:** 1 951 684-1991.
Web site: http://lapreciosa1290.iheart.com
Profile: KKDD-AM is a commercial station owned by iHeartMedia Inc. The format of the station is Regional Mexican. KKDD-AM broadcasts to the San Bernardino-Riverside CA metro area at 1290 AM.
AM RADIO STATION

KKDG-FM 46764
Owner: American General Media
Editorial: 1911 Main Ave, Durango, Colorado 81301-5078 **Tel:** 1 970 247-1240.
Web site: http://99xdurango.com
Profile: KKDG-FM is a commercial station owned by American General Media. The format of the station is hot adult contemporary. KKDG-FM broadcasts to the Durango, CO area at 99.7 FM.
FM RADIO STATION

KKDM-FM 42883
Owner: iHeartMedia Inc.
Editorial: 2141 Grand Ave, Des Moines, Iowa 50312-5303 **Tel:** 1 515 245-8900.
Web site: http://www.1075kissfm.com
Profile: KKDM-FM is a commercial station owned by iHeartMedia Inc. The format of the station is Top 40/CHR music. KKDM-FM broadcasts to the Des Moines, IA area at 107.5 FM.
FM RADIO STATION

KKDO-FM 42726
Owner: Entercom Communications Corp.
Editorial: 5345 Madison Ave, Sacramento, California 95841-3141 **Tel:** 1 916 334-7777.
Email: feedback@radio947.net
Web site: http://www.radio947.net
Profile: KKDO-FM is a commercial station owned by Entercom Communications Corp. The format of the station is rock alternative. KKDO-FM broadcasts to the Sacramento, CA area at 94.7 FM.
FM RADIO STATION

KKDQ-FM 46138
Owner: Iowa City Broadcasting Co.
Editorial: 1433 Main Ave N, Thief River Falls, Minnesota 56701 **Tel:** 1 218 681-4900.
Email: jock@mncable.net
Web site: http://www.trfradio.com
Profile: KKDQ-FM is a commercial station owned by Iowa City Broadcasting Co. The format of the station is country music. KKDQ-FM broadcasts in the Thief River Falls, MN area at 99.3 FM.
FM RADIO STATION

KKDV-FM 42772
Owner: Alpha Media
Editorial: 7901 Stoneridge Dr Ste 525, Pleasanton, California 94588-3656 **Tel:** 1 925 944-6300.
Web site: http://www.kkdv.com
Profile: KKDV-FM is a commercial station owned by Alpha Media. The format of the station is adult contemporary. KKDV-FM broadcasts in the San Francisco, CA area at 92.1 FM.
FM RADIO STATION

KKDY-FM 39719
Owner: Central Ozark Radio Network Inc.
Editorial: 983 E US Highway 160, West Plains, Missouri 65775-4801 **Tel:** 1 417 256-3131.
Email: news@ozarkradionetwork.com
Web site: http://www.kkdy.com
Profile: KKDY-FM is a commercial station owned by Central Ozark Radio Network Inc. The format of the station is contemporary country music. KKDY-FM broadcasts to the Springfield, MO area at 102.5 FM.
FM RADIO STATION

KKEA-AM 38549
Owner: Blow Up LLC
Editorial: 900 Fort Street Mall Ste 700, Honolulu, Hawaii 96813-3701 **Tel:** 1 808 536-3624.
Web site: http://www.espn1420am.com
Profile: KKEA-AM is a commercial station owned by Blow Up LLC. The format of the station is sports. KKEA-AM broadcasts to the Honolulu area at 1420 AM.
AM RADIO STATION

KKED-FM 39971
Owner: iHeartMedia Inc.
Editorial: 546 9th Ave, Fairbanks, Alaska 99701-4902 **Tel:** 1 907 450-1000.
Email: theedge@iheartmedia.com
Web site: http://1047theedge.iheart.com
Profile: KKED-FM is a commercial station owned by iHeartMedia Inc. The format of the station is alternative rock music. KKED-FM broadcasts to the Fairbanks, AK area at 104.7 FM.
FM RADIO STATION

KKEG-FM 46438
Owner: Cumulus Media Inc.
Editorial: 4209 N Frontage Rd, Fayetteville, Arkansas 72703-5002 **Tel:** 1 479 521-5566.
Web site: http://www.983thekeg.com
Profile: KKEG-FM is a commercial station owned by Cumulus Media Inc. The format of the station is alternative and modern rock music. KKEG-FM broadcasts to the Fayetteville, AR area at 98.3 FM.
FM RADIO STATION

KKEN-FM 44865
Owner: Perry Publishing & Broadcasting Inc.
Editorial: 1701 W Pine Ave, Duncan, Oklahoma 73533 **Tel:** 1 580 355-1050.
Web site: http://perrybroadcasting.net
Profile: KKEN-FM is a commercial station owned by Perry Publishing & Broadcasting Inc. The format of the station is classic country. KKEN-FM broadcasts to the Duncan, OK area at 97.1 FM.
FM RADIO STATION

KKEQ-FM 46113
Owner: Pine to Prairie Broadcasting Inc.
Editorial: 35006 US Highway 2 SE, Fosston, Minnesota 56542-9404 **Tel:** 1 218 435-1071.
Web site: http://www.yourqfm.com
Profile: KKEQ-FM is a commercial station owned by Pine to Prairie Broadcasting Inc. The format of the

station is contemporary Christian music. KKEQ-FM broadcasts to the Fosston, MN area at 107.1 FM.
FM RADIO STATION

KKEX-FM 42955
Owner: Cache Valley Radio Inc.
Editorial: 810 W 200 N, Logan, Utah 84321
Tel: 1 435 752-1390.
Email: kkex@cvradio.com
Web site: http://www.kix96fm.com
Profile: KKEX-FM is a commercial station owned by Cache Valley Radio Inc. The format of the station is contemporary country. KKEX-FM broadcasts to the Salt Lake City area at 96.7 FM.
FM RADIO STATION

KKEZ-FM 46231
Owner: Alpha Media
Editorial: 200 N 10th St, Fort Dodge, Iowa 50501-3925 **Tel:** 1 515 955-5656.
Web site: http://www.yourfortdodge.com
Profile: KKEZ-FM is a commercial station owned by the Alpha Media. The format of the station is hot adult contemporary music. KKEZ-FM broadcasts to the Fort Dodge, IA area at 94.5 FM.
FM RADIO STATION

KKFD-FM 45895
Owner: Alpha Media USA
Editorial: 57 1/2 S Court St, Fairfield, Iowa 52556-3287 **Tel:** 1 641 472-4191.
Web site: http://www.exploreseiowa.com
Profile: KKFD-FM is a commercial station owned by Alpha Media USA. The format of the station is classic hits. KKFD-FM broadcasts to the Fairfield, IA area at 95.9 FM.
FM RADIO STATION

KKFG-FM 46160
Owner: iHeartMedia Inc.
Editorial: 200 E Broadway, Farmington, New Mexico 87401-6418 **Tel:** 1 505 325-1716.
Web site: http://www.kool1045.com
Profile: KKFG-FM is a commercial station owned by iHeartMedia Inc. The format of the station is classic hits. KKFG-FM broadcasts to the Farmington, NM area at 104.5 FM.
FM RADIO STATION

KKFI-FM 41596
Owner: Midcoast Radio Project Inc.
Editorial: 3901 Main St, Kansas City, Missouri 64111-2290 **Tel:** 1 816 931-3122.
Web site: http://www.kkfi.org
Profile: KKFI-FM is a non-commercial station owned by Midcoast Radio Project Inc. The format of the station is variety programming. KKFI-FM broadcasts to the Kansas City, MO area at 90.1 FM.
FM RADIO STATION

KKFM-FM 39721
Owner: Cumulus Media Inc
Editorial: 6805 Corporate Dr, Ste 130, Colorado Springs, Colorado 80919-1977 **Tel:** 1 719 593-2700.
Web site: http://www.kkfm.com
Profile: KKFM-FM is a commercial station owned by Cumulus Media Inc. The format of the station is classic rock. KKFM-FM broadcasts to the Colorado Springs, CO area at 98.1 FM.
FM RADIO STATION

KKFN-FM 38702
Owner: Bonneville International Corp.
Editorial: 7800 E Orchard Rd Ste 400, Greenwood Village, Colorado 80111-2599 **Tel:** 1 303 321-0950.
Web site: http://www.1043thefan.com
Profile: KKFN-FM is a commercial station owned by Bonneville International Corp. The format of the station is sports. KKFN-FM broadcasts to the Greenwood Village, CO area at 104.3 FM.
FM RADIO STATION

KKFR-FM 44721
Owner: Riviera Broadcast Group
Editorial: 4745 N 7th St Ste 410, Phoenix, Arizona 85014-3669 **Tel:** 1 602 648-9800.
Web site: http://www.power983.com
Profile: KKFR-FM is a commercial station owned by Riviera Broadcast Group. The format of the station is urban contemporary music. KKFR-FM broadcasts to the Phoenix area at 98.3 FM. KKFR-FM is in an LMA with Sun City Communications.
FM RADIO STATION

KKFS-FM 39798
Owner: Salem Media Group, Inc.
Editorial: 1425 River Park Dr Ste 520, Sacramento, California 95815-4524 **Tel:** 1 916 924-0710.
Email: info@1039thefish.com
Web site: http://www.1039thefish.com
Profile: KKFS-FM is a commercial station owned by Salem Media Group, Inc. The format of the station is contemporary Christian. KKFS-FM broadcasts to the Sacramento, CA area at 103.9 FM.
FM RADIO STATION

KKFT-FM 41310
Owner: Evans Broadcasting
Editorial: 1960 Idaho St, Carson City, Nevada 89701-5306 **Tel:** 1 775 884-8000.
Email: prod@991fmtalk.com
Web site: http://www.991fmtalk.com
Profile: KKFT-FM is a commercial station owned by Evans Broadcasting. The format of the station is talk. KKFT-FM broadcasts to the Carson City, NV, area at 99.1 FM.
FM RADIO STATION

KKGB-FM 39957
Owner: Cumulus Media Inc.
Editorial: 425 Broad St, Lake Charles, Louisiana 70601-4225 **Tel:** 1 337 439-3300.
Web site: http://www.kkgb.com
Profile: KKGB-FM is a commercial station owned by Cumulus Media Inc. The format of the station is rock music. KKGB-FM broadcasts to the Lake Charles, LA area at 101.3 FM.
FM RADIO STATION

KKGL-FM 39735
Owner: Cumulus Media Inc
Editorial: 1419 W Bannock St, Boise, Idaho 83702-5234 **Tel:** 1 208 336-3670.
Web site: http://www.kkgl.com
Profile: KKGL-FM is a commercial station owned by Cumulus Media Inc. The format of the station is classic rock music. KKGL-FM broadcasts to the Boise, ID area at 96.9 FM.
FM RADIO STATION

KKGM-AM 232081
Owner: Mortenson Broadcasting Co.
Editorial: 5787 S Hampton Rd Ste 285, Dallas, Texas 75232-2290 **Tel:** 1 214 337-5700.
Web site: http://www.kkgmam.com
Profile: KKGM-AM is a commercial station owned by Mortenson Broadcasting Co. The format of the station is Southern and Bluegrass Gospel. KKGM-AM broadcasts to the Dallas area at 1630 AM.
AM RADIO STATION

KKGO-FM 45982
Owner: Mount Wilson FM Broadcasters
Editorial: 1500 Cotner Ave, Los Angeles, California 90025-3303 **Tel:** 1 310 478-5540.
Email: mail@gocountry105.com
Web site: http://mountwilsoninc.com
Profile: KKGO-FM is a commercial station owned by Mount Wilson FM Broadcasters. The format for the station is contemporary country. KKGO-FM broadcasts to the Los Angeles area at 105.1 FM.
FM RADIO STATION

KKGQ-FM 44454
Owner: Envision Broadcast Group
Editorial: 4200 N Old Lawrence Rd, Wichita, Kansas 67219-3211 **Tel:** 1 316 838-9141.
Web site: http://www.q92wichita.com
Profile: KKGQ-FM is a commercial station owned by Envision Broadcast Group. The format of the station is Hot AC. KKGQ-FM broadcasts to the Wichita, KS area at 92.3 FM.
FM RADIO STATION

KKGR-AM 37025
Owner: KKGR Inc.
Editorial: 1400 11th Ave, Helena, Montana 59601-4516 **Tel:** 1 406 443-5237.
Email: kgr@mt.net
Profile: KKGR-AM is a commercial station owned by KKGR Inc. The format of the station is oldies. KKGR-AM broadcasts to the Helena, MT area at 680 AM.
AM RADIO STATION

KKHA-FM 489515
Owner: Tomlinson-Leis Communications L.P.
Editorial: 1713 7th St, Bay City, Texas 77414-5005
Tel: 1 979 323-7771.
Email: news@kkhafm.com
Web site: http://www.yoursoutheasttexas.com
Profile: KKHA-FM is a commercial station owned by Tomlinson-Leis Communications L.P. The format of the station is classic hits. KKHA-FM broadcasts to the Bay City, TX area at 92.5 FM.
FM RADIO STATION

KKHB-FM 43477
Owner: Bicoastal Media LLC
Editorial: 5640 S Broadway St, Eureka, California 95503-6905 **Tel:** 1 707 442-2000.
Email: eurekanews@bicoastalmedia.com
Web site: http://www.cool1055.com
Profile: KKHB-FM is a commercial station owned by Bicoastal Media LLC. The format of the station is oldies. KKHB-FM broadcasts to the Eureka, CA area at 105.5 FM.
FM RADIO STATION

KKHH-FM 44694
Owner: CBS Radio
Editorial: 24 Greenway Plz Ste 1900, Houston, Texas 77046-2428 **Tel:** 1 713 881-5100.
Web site: http://957thespot.cbslocal.com
Profile: KKHH-FM is a commercial station owned by CBS Radio. The format of the station is Adult Hits. KKHH-FM broadcasts to the Houston area at 95.7 FM.
FM RADIO STATION

KKHK-FM 42707
Owner: Mapleton Communications LLC
Editorial: 60 Garden Ct, Ste 300, Monterey, California 93940 **Tel:** 1 831 658-5200.
Email: bob@955bobfm.com
Web site: http://www.955bobfm.com
Profile: KKHK-FM is a commercial station owned by Mapleton Communications LLC. The format of the station is adult hits. KKHK-FM broadcasts to the Monterey, CA area at 95.5 FM.
FM RADIO STATION

KKHQ-FM 44799
Owner: Waterloo Broadcasting
Editorial: 501 Sycamore St Ste 300, Waterloo, Iowa 50703-4651 **Tel:** 1 319 833-4800.
Web site: http://www.q923.net
Profile: KKHQ-FM is a commercial station owned by Townsquare Media. The format of the station is Top 40/CHR. KKHQ-FM broadcasts to the Waterloo, IA area at 92.3 FM.
FM RADIO STATION

KKHR-FM 41120
Owner: Canfin Enterprises Inc.
Editorial: 402 Cypress St, Ste 510, Abilene, Texas 79601 **Tel:** 1 325 672-5442.
Web site: http://www.radioabilene.com
Profile: KKHR-FM is a commercial station owned by Canfin Enterprises Inc. The format of the station is Hispanic Top 40/CHR. KKHR-FM broadcasts to the Abilene, TX area at 106.3 FM.
FM RADIO STATION

KKHT-FM 42896
Owner: Salem Media Group, Inc.
Editorial: 6161 Savoy Dr Ste 1200, Houston, Texas 77036-3363 **Tel:** 1 713 260-3600.
Email: comments@kkht.com
Web site: http://www.kkht.com
Profile: KKHT-FM is a commercial station owned by Salem Media Group, Inc. The format of the station is religious programming. KKHT-FM broadcasts in the Houston area at 100.7 FM.
FM RADIO STATION

KKIA-FM 39678
Owner: Community First Broadcasting
Editorial: 910 Flindt Dr, Storm Lake, Iowa 50588-3204
Tel: 1 712 732-3520.
Email: production@stormlakeradio.com
Web site: http://www.stormlakeradio.com
Profile: KKIA-FM is a commercial station owned by Community First Broadcasting. The format of the station is contemporary country. KKIA-FM broadcasts to the Sioux City, IA area at 92.9 FM.
FM RADIO STATION

KKID-FM 39781
Owner: Wheeler (Dave & Carroll)
Editorial: 1415 Forum Dr, Rolla, Missouri 65401-2508
Tel: 1 573 364-4433.
Email: kkid929fm@kkid929fm.com
Web site: http://www.kkid929fm.com
Profile: KKID-FM is a commercial station owned by Dave and Carroll Wheeler. The format of the station is classic rock music. KKID-FM broadcasts to the Springfield, MO area at 92.9 FM.
FM RADIO STATION

KKIM-AM 34988
Owner: American General Media
Editorial: 4125 Carlisle Blvd NE, Albuquerque, New Mexico 87107-4806 **Tel:** 1 505 878-0980.
Web site: http://www.wilkinsradio.com/our-stations/kkim-1000am-albuquerque-nm
Profile: KKIM-AM is a non-commercial station owned by the American General Media. The format of the station is religious talk. KKIM-AM broadcasts to the Albuquerque, NM area at 1000 AM.
AM RADIO STATION

KKIN-AM 37350
Owner: Red Rock Radio Corp.
Editorial: 37208 US Highway 169, Aitkin, Minnesota 56431 **Tel:** 1 218 927-2344.
Email: kkinradio@embarqmail.com
Web site: http://www.kkinradio.com
Profile: KKIN-AM is a commercial station owned by Red Rock Radio Corp. The format of the station is adult standards music. KKIN-AM broadcasts to the Aitkin, WI area at 94.3 FM.
AM RADIO STATION

KKIN-FM 44649
Owner: Red Rock Radio Corp.
Tel: 1 218 927-2100.
Email: kkinradio@embarqmail.com
Web site: http://www.kkinradio.com
Profile: KKIN-FM is a commercial station owned by Red Rock Radio Corp. The format of the station is country music. KKIN-FM broadcasts in the Aitkin, MN area at 93.4 FM.
FM RADIO STATION

KKIQ-FM 39723
Owner: Alpha Media
Editorial: 7901 Stoneridge Dr Ste 525, Pleasanton, California 94588-3656 **Tel:** 1 925 455-4500.
Email: programming@kkiq.com
Web site: http://www.kkiq.com
Profile: KKIQ-FM is a commercial station owned by the Alpha Media. The format of the station is adult contemporary music. KKIQ-FM broadcasts to the Pleasanton, CA area at 101.7 FM.
FM RADIO STATION

KKIS-FM 42956
Owner: KSRM, Inc.
Editorial: 40960 K-Beach Rd, Kenai, Alaska 99611
Tel: 1 907 283-8700.
Email: rken18@radiokenai.com
Web site: http://www.radiokenai.com
Profile: KKIS-FM is a commercial station owned by KSRM, Inc. The format of the station is hot adult contemporary. KKIS-FM broadcasts to the Kenai, AK area at 96.5 FM.
FM RADIO STATION

KKIT-FM 363394
Owner: DMC Broadcasting Inc.
Editorial: 125 Camino De La Merced Apt A, Taos, New Mexico 87571-5131 **Tel:** 1 575 758-4491.
Web site: http://www.radiointaos.com
Profile: KKIT-FM is a commercial station owned by DMC Broadcasting Inc. The format of the station is adult hits music. KKIT-FM broadcasts to the Taos, NM area on 95.9 FM.
FM RADIO STATION

KKIX-FM 3972
Owner: iHeartMedia Inc.
Editorial: 2049 E Joyce Blvd Ste 101, Fayetteville, Arkansas 72703-6395 **Tel:** 1 479 521-0104.
Web site: http://kix104.iheart.com
Profile: KKIX-FM is a commercial station owned by iHeartMedia Inc. The format of the station is classic country. KKIX-FM broadcasts to the Fayetteville, AR area at 103.9 FM.
FM RADIO STATION

KKJG-FM 41104
Owner: American General Media
Editorial: 3620 Sacramento Dr, San Luis Obispo, California 93401-7215 **Tel:** 1 805 781-2750.
Email: news@americangeneralmedia.com
Web site: http://www.jugcountry.com
Profile: KKJG-FM is a commercial station owned by American General Media. The format of the station is contemporary country. KKJG-FM broadcasts to the San Luis Obispo, CA area at 98.1 FM.
FM RADIO STATION

KKJK-FM 409218
Owner: Legacy Communications, LLC
Editorial: 3205 W North Front St, Grand Island, Nebraska 68803-4024 **Tel:** 1 308 381-1430.
Email: production@krgi.com
Web site: http://newsacrossnebraska.com
Profile: KKJK-FM is a commercial station owned by Legacy Communications, LLC (dba GI Family Radio). The format of the station is Top 40/CHR. KKJK-FM broadcasts to the Grand Island, NE area at 103.1 FM.
FM RADIO STATION

KKJL-AM 36228
Owner: San Luis Obispo Broadcasting Inc.
Editorial: 51 Zaca Ln #90, San Luis Obispo, California 93401-7399 **Tel:** 1 805 543-9400.
Email: info@kjewel.net
Web site: http://www.kjewel.net
Profile: KKJL-AM is a commercial station owned by San Luis Obispo Broadcasting Inc. The format of the station is adult standards music. KKJL-AM broadcasts in the San Luis Obispo, CA area at 1400 AM.
AM RADIO STATION

KKJM-FM 43861
Owner: Gabriel Communications
Editorial: 1310 2nd St N, Sauk Rapids, Minnesota 56379 **Tel:** 1 320 251-1780.
Email: friends@spirit929.com
Web site: http://www.spirit929.com
Profile: KKJM-FM is a commercial station owned by Gabriel Communications. The format of the station is contemporary Christian. KKJM-FM broadcasts to the Minneapolis area at 92.9 FM.
FM RADIO STATION

KKJO-FM 44891
Owner: Eagle Communications
Editorial: 4104 Country Ln, Saint Joseph, Missouri 64506-4921 **Tel:** 1 816 233-8881.
Web site: http://www.kjo1055.com
Profile: KKJO-FM is a commercial station owned by Eagle Communications. The format of the station is hot adult contemporary music. KKJO-FM broadcasts in the St. Joseph, MO area at 105.5 FM.
FM RADIO STATION

KKJQ-FM 45743
Owner: Armada Media Corp.
Editorial: 1402 E Kansas Ave, Garden City, Kansas 67846-5806 **Tel:** 1 620 276-2366.
Email: production@wksradio.com
Web site: http://www.westernkansasnews.com
Profile: KKJQ-FM is a commercial station owned by Armada Media Corp. The format of the station is classic country. KKJQ-FM broadcasts to the Garden City, KS area at 97.3 FM.
FM RADIO STATION

KKKJ-FM 514365
Owner: Wynne Broadcasting Co.
Editorial: 1338 Oregon Ave, Klamath Falls, Oregon 97601-6540 **Tel:** 1 541 882-4656.
Email: webmaster@klamathradio.com
Web site: http://www.klamathradio.com
Profile: KKKJ-FM is a commercial station owned by Wynne Broadcasting Co. The format of the station is Top 40/CHR. KKKJ-FM broadcasts to the Klamath Falls, OR area at 105.5 FM.
FM RADIO STATION

KKLA-FM 42851
Owner: Salem Media Group, Inc.
Editorial: 701 N Brand Blvd Ste 550, Glendale, California 91203-1235 **Tel:** 1 818 956-5552.
Email: info@kkla.com
Web site: http://www.kkla.com
Profile: KKLA-FM is a commercial station owned by Salem Media Group, Inc. The format of the station is Christian talk. KKLA-FM broadcasts to the Los Angeles area at 99.5 FM.
FM RADIO STATION

KKLD-FM 42929
Owner: Yavapai Broadcasting
Editorial: 3405 E State Route 89A, Bldg A, Cottonwood, Arizona 86326 **Tel:** 1 928 634-2286.
Email: kkld@myradioplace.com

Web site: http://www.kkld.com
Profile: KKLD-FM is a commercial station owned by Yavapai Broadcasting. The format of the station is classic hits. KKLD-FM broadcasts to the Cottonwood, AZ area at 95.9 FM.
FM RADIO STATION

KKLE-AM 35812
Owner: Johnson Enterprises Inc.
Editorial: 338 South Kley Dr, Wellington, Kansas 67152 **Tel:** 1 620 326-3341.
Email: kley@sutv.com
Web site: http://www.kkle.com
Profile: KKLE-AM is a commercial station owned by Johnson Enterprises Inc. The format of the station is sports. KKLE-AM broadcasts to the Wellington, KS area at 1550 AM.
AM RADIO STATION

KKLF-AM 37098
Owner: Claro Communications, Ltd.
Editorial: 13725 Montfort Dr Ste 340, Dallas, Texas 75240-4455 **Tel:** 1 214 526-7400.
Web site: http://www.kick-am.com
Profile: KKLF-AM is a commercial station owned by Volt Radio, LLC. The format of the station is comedy radio. KKLF-AM broadcasts to the Dallas area at 1700 AM.
AM RADIO STATION

KKLH-FM 42915
Owner: Midwest Family Stations
Editorial: 2453 E Elm St, Springfield, Missouri 65802-2868 **Tel:** 1 417 886-5677.
Web site: http://www.1047thecave.com
Profile: KKLH-FM is a commercial station owned by Midwest Family Stations. The format of the station is classic rock. KKLH-FM broadcasts to the Springfield, MO area on 104.7 FM.
FM RADIO STATION

KKLI-FM 41808
Owner: iHeartMedia Inc.
Editorial: 2864 S Circle Dr Ste 300, Colorado Springs, Colorado 80906-4131 **Tel:** 1 719 540-9200.
Web site: http://sunny1063online.iheart.com
Profile: KKLI-FM is a commercial station owned by iHeartMedia Inc. The format of the station is Lite Rock/Lite AC. KKLI-FM broadcasts to the Colorado Springs, CO area at 106.3 FM.
FM RADIO STATION

KKLL-AM 36333
Owner: New Life Evangelistic Center, Inc
Editorial: 831 Moffit Street, Joplin, Missouri 64801-3571 **Tel:** 1 417 781-1100.
Web site: http://www.newlifeevangelisticcenter.org
Profile: KKLL-AM is a commercial station owned by the New Life Evangelistic Center. The format of the station is contemporary Christian talk and gospel. KKLL-AM broadcasts to the Joplin, MO area at 1100 AM.
AM RADIO STATION

KKLN-FM 41386
Owner: Headwaters Media
Editorial: 1605 South 1st St, Kandi Mall, Willmar, Minnesota 56201-4234 **Tel:** 1 320 235-1194.
Email: info@kkln.com
Web site: http://www.kkln.com
Profile: KKLN-FM is a commercial station owned by Headwaters Media. The format of the station is rock music. KKLN-FM broadcasts to the Willmar, MN area at 94.1 FM.
FM RADIO STATION

KKLO-AM 34914
Owner: Vision Communications, Inc.
Editorial: 481 Muncie Rd, Leavenworth, Kansas 66048-4947 **Tel:** 1 913 276-0555.
Web site: http://1410kklo.com/
Profile: KKLO-AM is a commercial station owned by Vision Communications, Inc. The format of the station is talk. KKLO-AM broadcasts to the Kansas City, MO, metro area at 1410 AM.
AM RADIO STATION

KKLR-FM 44961
Owner: Max Media
Editorial: 1015 W Pine St, Poplar Bluff, Missouri 63901-4839 **Tel:** 1 573 785-0881.
Email: clear94@riverradio.net
Web site: http://www.clear94.com
Profile: KKLR-FM is a commercial station owned by Max Media. The format of the station is contemporary country music. KKLR-FM broadcasts to the Poplar Bluff, MO, area at 94.5 FM.
FM RADIO STATION

KKLS-AM 37352
Owner: Homeslice Media Group
Editorial: 660 Flormann St Ste 100, Rapid City, South Dakota 57701-4688 **Tel:** 1 605 343-6161.
Web site: http://www.kkls.net
Profile: KKLS-AM is a commercial station owned by New Rushmore Radio. The format of the station is adult contemporary. KKLS-AM broadcasts to the Rapid City, SD area at 920 AM.
AM RADIO STATION

KKLS-FM 44725
Owner: Townsquare Media, Inc.
Editorial: 5100 S Tennis Ln, Sioux Falls, South Dakota 57108-2212 **Tel:** 1 605 361-0300.
Web site: http://www.hot1047.com
Profile: KKLS-FM is a commercial station owned by Townsquare Media, Inc. The format of the station is Top 40/CHR music. KKLS-FM broadcasts to the Sioux Falls, SD area at 104.7 FM.
FM RADIO STATION

KKLX-FM 44637
Owner: Legend Communications
Editorial: 1340 Radio Dr, Worland, Wyoming 82401-8700 **Tel:** 1 307 347-3231.
Email: kwor@bhrnwy.com
Web site: http://www.mybighornbasin.com
Profile: KKLX-FM is a commercial station owned by Legend Communications. The format for the station is hot adult contemporary. KKLX-FM broadcasts to the Worland, WY area at 96.1 FM.
FM RADIO STATION

KKLZ-FM 43167
Owner: Beasley Broadcast Group
Editorial: 2920 S Durango Dr, Las Vegas, Nevada 89117-4412 **Tel:** 1 702 730-0300.
Web site: http://www.963kklz.com
Profile: KKLZ-FM is a commercial station owned by Beasley Broadcast Group. The format of the station is classic hits. KKLZ-FM broadcasts to the Las Vegas area at 96.3 FM.
FM RADIO STATION

KKMA-FM 46216
Owner: Powell Broadcasting Co.
Editorial: 2000 Indian Hills Dr, Sioux City, Iowa 51104 **Tel:** 1 712 239-2100.
Web site: http://www.kool995.com
Profile: KKMA-FM is a commercial station owned by Powell Broadcasting Co. The format of the station is classic hits. KKMA-FM broadcasts to the Sioux City, IA area at 99.5 FM.
FM RADIO STATION

KKMC-AM 34989
Owner: Monterey County Broadcasters Inc.
Editorial: 30 E San Joaquin St, Ste 105, Salinas, California 93901 **Tel:** 1 831 424-5562.
Web site: http://www.kkmc.com
Profile: KKMC-AM is a commercial station owned by Monterey County Broadcasters Inc. The format of the station is Christian talk. KKMC-AM broadcasts to the Salinas, CA area at 880 AM.
AM RADIO STATION

KKMG-FM 42048
Owner: Cumulus Media Inc
Editorial: 6805 Corporate Dr, Ste 130, Colorado Springs, Colorado 80919 **Tel:** 1 719 593-2700.
Web site: http://www.989magicfm.com
Profile: KKMG-FM is a commercial station owned by Cumulus Media Inc. The format of the station is Top 40/CHR. KKMG-FM broadcasts to the Colorado Springs, CO area at 98.9 FM.
FM RADIO STATION

KKMI-FM 39614
Owner: Pritchard Broadcasting Co.
Editorial: 610 N 4th St Ste 300, Burlington, Iowa 52601-5059 **Tel:** 1 319 752-5402.
Email: 935kkmi@935kkmi.com
Web site: http://935kkmi.com
Profile: KKMI-FM is a commercial station owned by Pritchard Broadcasting Co. The format of the station is adult contemporary. KKMI-FM broadcasts to the Burlington, IA area at 93.5 FM.
FM RADIO STATION

KKMJ-FM 46139
Owner: Entercom Communications Corp.
Editorial: 4301 Westbank Dr Fl 3, Austin, Texas 78746-6568 **Tel:** 1 512 327-9595.
Web site: http://www.majic.com
Profile: KKMJ-FM is a commercial station owned by Entercom Communications Corp. The format of the station is adult contemporary music. KKMJ-FM broadcasts to the Austin, TX area at 99.5 FM.
FM RADIO STATION

KKMK-FM 44701
Owner: New Rushmore Radio
Editorial: 660 Flormann St, Ste 100, Rapid City, South Dakota 57701-4688 **Tel:** 1 605 343-6161.
Web site: http://www.newrushmoreradio.com/kkmk
Profile: KKMK-FM is a commercial station owned by New Rushmore Radio. The format of the station is hot adult contemporary. KKMK-FM broadcasts to the Rapid City, SD area at 93.9 FM.
FM RADIO STATION

KKMO-AM 34990
Editorial: 2201 6th Ave Ste 1500, Seattle, Washington 98121-1840 **Tel:** 1 206 436-7851.
Email: traffic@elrey1360seattle.com
Web site: http://www.elrey1360seattle.com
Profile: KKMO-AM is a commercial station owned by Salem Media Group, Inc. The format of the station is regional Mexican. KKMO-AM broadcasts to the Seattle area at 1360 AM.
AM RADIO STATION

KKMR-FM 396814
Owner: Univision Communications Inc.
Editorial: 6006 S 30th St, Phoenix, Arizona 85042-4802 **Tel:** 1 602 308-7900.
Web site: http://www.univision.com/arizona/komr
Profile: KKMR-FM is a commercial station owned by Univision Communications Inc. The format of the station is Spanish Adult Hits. KKMR-FM broadcasts to the Phoenix area at 106.5 FM.
FM RADIO STATION

KKMS-AM 135238
Owner: Salem Media Group, Inc.
Editorial: 2110 Cliff Rd, Eagan, Minnesota 55122-3522 **Tel:** 1 651 405-8800.
Email: comments@kkms.com
Web site: http://www.am980themission.com
Profile: KKMS-AM is a commercial station owned by Salem Media Group, Inc. The format of the station is religious talk. KKMS-AM broadcasts to the Minneapolis area at 980 AM.
AM RADIO STATION

KKMT-FM 44843
Owner: Anderson Radio Broadcasting Inc.
Editorial: 36581 N Reservoir Rd, Polson, Montana 59860-8471 **Tel:** 1 406 883-5255.
Email: news@andersonbroadcasting.com
Web site: http://750kerr.com
Profile: KKMT-FM is a commercial station owned by Anderson Radio Broadcasting. The format of the station is classic country music. KKMT-FM broadcasts in the Polson, MT area at 92.3 FM.
FM RADIO STATION

KKMV-FM 44781
Owner: Lee Family Broadcasting
Editorial: 120 S 300 W, Rupert, Idaho 83350-9667 **Tel:** 1 208 436-4757.
Web site: http://kat106.com
Profile: KKMV-FM is a commercial station owned by Lee Family Broadcasting. The format of the station is country music. KKMV-FM broadcasts to the Rupert, ID area at a frequency of 106.1 FM.
FM RADIO STATION

KKMX-FM 42574
Owner: Brooke Communications Inc.
Editorial: 1445 W Harvard Ave, Roseburg, Oregon 97471 **Tel:** 1 541 672-6641.
Web site: http://www.541radio.com
Profile: KKMX-FM is a commercial station owned by Brooke Communications Inc. The format of the station is adult contemporary. KKMX-FM broadcasts to the Roseburg, OR area at 104.5 FM.
FM RADIO STATION

KKMY-FM 42939
Owner: iHeartMedia Inc.
Editorial: 2885 Interstate 10 E, Beaumont, Texas 77702-1001 **Tel:** 1 409 896-5555.
Web site: http://www.kiss1045fm.com
Profile: KKMY-FM is a commercial station owned by iHeartMedia Inc. The format of the station is Top 40/Rhythmic contemporary music. KKMY-FM broadcasts to the Beaumont, TX area at 104.5 FM.
FM RADIO STATION

KKND-FM 41638
Owner: Cumulus Media Inc
Editorial: 201 Saint Charles Ave Ste 201, New Orleans, Louisiana 70170-1017 **Tel:** 1 504 581-7002.
Web site: http://www.power1029.com
Profile: KKND-FM is a commercial station owned by Cumulus Media Inc. The format of the station is rhythmic urban contemporary. KKND-FM broadcasts to New Orleans at 102.9 FM.
FM RADIO STATION

KKNE-AM 324713
Owner: Summit Media Broadcasting LLC
Editorial: 900 Fort Street Mall Ste 700, Honolulu, Hawaii 96813-3701 **Tel:** 1 808 275-1000.
Web site: http://www.am940hawaii.com
Profile: KKNE-AM is a commercial station owned by Summit Media Broadcasting LLC. The format of the station is variety. KKNE-AM broadcasts to the Honolulu area at 940 AM.
AM RADIO STATION

KKNG-FM 43670
Owner: WPA Radio LLC
Editorial: 5101 S Shields Blvd, Oklahoma City, Oklahoma 73129-3217 **Tel:** 1 405 601-6380.
Email: info@okcatholicbroadcasting.com
Web site: http://okcatholicbroadcasting.com
Profile: KKNG-FM is a commercial station owned by the WPA Radio LLC. The format of the station is Catholic programming. KKNG-FM broadcasts to the Oklahoma City area at 97.3 FM.
FM RADIO STATION

KKNI-AM 562452
Owner: Kenai Broadcasting, LLC
Editorial: 851 E Westpoint Dr Ste 301, Wasilla, Alaska 99654-7183 **Tel:** 1 907 373-0222.
Web site: http://www.1430hometownradio.com
Profile: KKNI-AM is a commercial station owned by Kenai Broadcasting, LLC. The format of the station is news/talk and oldies. KKNI-AM broadcasts to the Wasilla, AK area at 1430 AM.
AM RADIO STATION

KKNM-FM 527418
Owner: Tejas Broadcasting
Editorial: 2505 Lakeview Dr Ste 302B, Amarillo, Texas 79109-1527 **Tel:** 1 806 355-1044.
Profile: KKNM-FM is a commercial station owned by Tejas Broadcasting. The format of the station is classic country. KKNM-FM broadcasts to the Amarillo, TX area at 96.5 FM.
FM RADIO STATION

KKNN-FM 46179
Owner: Townsquare Media, Inc.
Editorial: 315 Kennedy Ave, Grand Junction, Colorado 81501-7552 **Tel:** 1 970 242-7788.
Web site: http://www.95rockfm.com
Profile: KKNN-FM, is a commercial station owned by Townsquare Media, Inc. The format of the station is rock. KKNN-FM broadcasts to the Grand Junction, CO area at 95.1 FM.
FM RADIO STATION

KKNO-AM 35886
Owner: Blakes Enterprises(Robert)
Editorial: 980 Avenue A, Marrero, Louisiana 70072-3228 **Tel:** 1 504 347-7775.
Web site: http://kkno750.com
Profile: KKNO-AM is a commercial station owned by Robert Blakes Enterprises. The format of the station is gospel music. KKNO-AM broadcasts locally to the New Orleans area at 750 AM.
AM RADIO STATION

KKNS-AM 128304
Owner: El Camino Communications, LLC
Editorial: 1606 Central Ave SE, Albuquerque, New Mexico 87106-4478 **Tel:** 1 505 255-5015.
Email: vcamino@elcaminoradio.com
Web site: http://www.elcaminoradio.com
Profile: KKNS-AM is a commercial station owned by El Camino Communications, LLC. The format of the station is regional Mexican. KKNS-AM broadcasts to the Albuquerque, NM area at 1310 AM.
AM RADIO STATION

KKNT-AM 36482
Owner: Salem Media Group, Inc.
Editorial: 2425 E Camelback Rd Ste 570, Phoenix, Arizona 85016-4250 **Tel:** 1 602 955-9600.
Web site: http://www.960thepatriot.com
Profile: KKNT-AM is a commercial station owned by Salem Media Group, Inc. The format of the station is news and talk. KKNT-AM broadcasts to the Phoenix area at 960 AM.
AM RADIO STATION

KKNU-FM 42257
Owner: McKenzie River Broadcasting
Editorial: 925 Country Club Rd, Ste 200, Eugene, Oregon 97401 **Tel:** 1 541 484-9400.
Email: bearfox@kknu.com
Web site: http://www.kknu.com
Profile: KKNU-FM is a commercial station owned by McKenzie River Broadcasting. The format for the station is contemporary country. KKNU-FM broadcasts to the Eugene, OR area at 93.3 FM.
FM RADIO STATION

KKNW-AM 38696
Owner: Hubbard Radio, LLC
Editorial: 3650 131st Ave SE Ste 550, Bellevue, Washington 98006-1334 **Tel:** 1 425 562-8219.
Email: kknwlistener@1150kknw.com
Web site: http://1150kknw.com
Profile: KKNW-AM is a commercial station owned by Hubbard Radio, LLC. The format of the station is alternative news and talk. KKNW-AM broadcasts to the Seattle area at 1150 AM.
AM RADIO STATION

KKNX-AM 36284
Owner: Willamette Broadcasting
Editorial: 1142 Willagillespie Rd Ste 28, Eugene, Oregon 97401-6723 **Tel:** 1 541 342-1012.
Web site: http://www.radio84.com
Profile: KKNX-AM is a commercial station owned by Willamette Broadcasting. The format of the station is oldies. KKNX-AM broadcasts to the Eugene, OR area at 840 AM.
AM RADIO STATION

KKOA-FM 43451
Owner: Mahalo Broadcasting
Editorial: 74-5605 Luhia St Ste B7, Kailua Kona, Hawaii 96740-1678 **Tel:** 1 808 329-8090.
Email: info@koacountry.com
Web site: http://www.koacountry.com
Profile: KKOA-FM is a commercial station owned by Mahalo Broadcasting. The format of the station is contemporary country. KKOA-FM broadcasts to the Kailua Kona, HI area at 107.7.
FM RADIO STATION

KKOB-AM 38802
Owner: Cumulus Media Inc
Editorial: 500 4th St NW, Albuquerque, New Mexico 87102-5324 **Tel:** 1 505 767-6700.
Email: newsroom@770kkob.com
Web site: http://www.770kkob.com
Profile: KKOB-AM is a commercial station owned by Cumulus Media Inc. The format of the station is news and talk. KKOB-AM broadcasts to the Albuquerque, NM area at 770 AM.
AM RADIO STATION

KKOB-FM 46176
Owner: Cumulus Media Inc
Editorial: 500 4th St NW Fl 5, Albuquerque, New Mexico 87102-5324 **Tel:** 1 505 767-6700.
Web site: http://www.kobfm.com
Profile: KKOB-FM is a commercial station owned by Cumulus Media Inc. The format of the station is Top 40/CHR. KKOB-FM broadcasts to the Albuquerque, NM area at 93.3 FM.
FM RADIO STATION

KKOH-AM 38783
Owner: Cumulus Media Inc
Editorial: 595 E Plumb Ln, Reno, Nevada 89502 **Tel:** 1 775 789-6700.
Email: info@kkoh.com
Web site: http://www.kkoh.com
Profile: KKOH-AM is a commercial station owned by Cumulus Media Inc. The format of the station is news

and talk. KKOH-AM broadcasts to the Reno, NV area at 780 AM.
AM RADIO STATION

KKOJ-AM 39258
Owner: Community First Broadcasting
Tel: 1 507 847-5400.
Email: info@kkoj.com
Web site: http://www.kkoj.com
Profile: KKOJ-AM is a commercial station owned by Community First Broadcasting. The format of the station is classic hits. KKOJ-AM broadcasts to the Minneapolis area at 1190 AM.
AM RADIO STATION

KKOK-FM 44727
Owner: Iowa City Broadcasting Co.
Editorial: 46671 State Highway 28, Morris, Minnesota 56267-4508 **Tel:** 1 320 589-3131.
Email: kmrskkok@fedtel.net
Web site: http://www.kmrskkok.com
Profile: KKOK-FM is a commercial station owned by the Iowa City Broadcasting Co. The format of the station is contemporary country music. KKOK-FM broadcasts in the Morris, MN area at 95.7 FM.
FM RADIO STATION

KKOL-AM 36621
Owner: Salem Media Group, Inc.
Editorial: 2201 6th Ave Ste 1500, Seattle, Washington 98121-1840 **Tel:** 1 206 443-8200.
Email: webmaster@kgnw.com
Web site: http://www.kkol.com
Profile: KKOL-AM is a commercial station owned by Salem Media Group, Inc. The format of the station is business news and talk. KKOL-AM broadcasts to the Seattle area at 1300 AM.
AM RADIO STATION

KKOL-FM 42739
Owner: Salem Media Group, Inc.
Editorial: 1160 N King St Fl 2, Honolulu, Hawaii 96817-3307 **Tel:** 1 808 533-0065.
Web site: http://www.oldies1079honolulu.com
Profile: KKOL-FM is a commercial station owned by Salem Media Group, Inc. The format of the station is oldies. KKOL-FM broadcasts to the Honolulu area at 107.9 FM.
FM RADIO STATION

KKON-AM 37353
Owner: Pacific Media Group
Editorial: 75-5852 Alii Dr. Suite B1 & B2, Lagoon Tower, Kailua-Kona, Hawaii 96740 **Tel:** 1 808 961-0651.
Web site: http://www.espnhawaii.com
Profile: KKON-AM is a commercial station owned by Pacific Media Group. The format of the station is sports. KKON-AM broadcasts to the Kona, HI area at 790 AM.
AM RADIO STATION

KKOO-AM 38983
Owner: Idaho Co., Inc.
Editorial: 5660 E Franklin Rd, Nampa, Idaho 83687-8173 **Tel:** 1 541 889-8651.
Web site: http://www.kkooradio.com
Profile: KKOO-AM is a commercial station owned by FM Idaho Co., Inc (dba Armstrong Radio Group). The format of the station is oldies. KKOO-AM broadcasts to the Boise, ID area at 1380 AM.
AM RADIO STATION

KKOR-FM 44816
Owner: Main Street Broadcasting Inc.
Editorial: 255 Cedardale Dr SE, Owatonna, Minnesota 55060-4425 **Tel:** 1 507 444-9224.
Email: booth@krue92.com
Web site: http://www.kowzonline.com
Profile: KKOR-FM is a commercial station owned by Main Street Broadcasting Inc. The format of the station is country. KKOR-FM broadcasts to the Owatonna, MN area at 92.1 FM.
FM RADIO STATION

KKOT-FM 45733
Owner: Alpha Media
Editorial: 1418 25th St, Columbus, Nebraska 68601-2820 **Tel:** 1 402 564-2866.
Web site: http://www.mycentralnebraska.com
Profile: KKOT-FM is a commercial station owned by Alpha Media The format of the station is classic hits. KKOT-FM broadcasts to the Columbus, NE area at 93.5 FM.
FM RADIO STATION

KKOV-AM 36192
Owner: Pamplin Broadcasting-Washington, Inc.
Editorial: 6605 Se Lake Rd, Portland, Oregon 97222-2161 **Tel:** 1 503 223-4321.
Profile: KKOV-AM is a commercial station owned by Pamplin Broadcasting-Washington, Inc. The format of the station is adult standards. KKOV-AM broadcasts to the Portland, OR area at 1550 AM.
AM RADIO STATION

KKOW-AM 38778
Owner: American Media Investments
Editorial: 1162 E Highway 126, Pittsburg, Kansas 66762 **Tel:** 1 620 231-7200.
Web site: http://www.kkowam.com
Profile: KKOW-AM is a commercial station owned by American Media Investments. The format of the station is country music. KKOW-AM broadcasts in the Pittsburg, KS, area at 860 AM.
AM RADIO STATION

KKOW-FM 46131
Owner: American Media Investments
Editorial: 1162 E Highway 126, Pittsburg, Kansas 66762-8712 **Tel:** 1 620 231-7200.
Web site: http://www.kkowfm.com
Profile: KKOW-FM is a commercial station owned by American Media Investments. The format of the station is contemporary country music. KKOW-FM broadcasts to the Pittsburg, KS, area at 96.9 FM.
FM RADIO STATION

KKOY-AM 37354
Owner: My Town Media, Inc.
Editorial: 702 N Plummer Ave, Chanute, Kansas 66720-1463 **Tel:** 1 620 431-3700.
Profile: KKOY-AM is a commercial station owned by My Town Media, Inc. The format of the station is sports and country. KKOY-AM broadcasts to the Chanute, KS area at 1460 AM.
AM RADIO STATION

KKOY-FM 44845
Owner: My Town Media, Inc.
Editorial: 702 N Plummer Ave, Chanute, Kansas 66720 **Tel:** 1 620 431-3700.
Web site: http://kkoy.com
Profile: KKOY-FM is a commercial station owned by My Town Media, Inc. The format of the station is top 40/CHR KKOY-FM broadcasts in the Chanute, KS area at 105.5 FM.
FM RADIO STATION

KKOZ-AM 38689
Owner: Corum Industries Inc.
Editorial: 303 SE 2nd Avenue, Ava, Missouri 65608
Tel: 1 417 683-4191.
Email: news@kkoz.com
Web site: http://www.kkoz.com
Profile: KKOZ-AM is a commercial station owned by Corum Industries Inc. The format of the station is news/talk. KKOZ-AM broadcasts to the Ava, MO area at 1430 AM.
AM RADIO STATION

KKOZ-FM 46042
Owner: Corum Industries Inc.
Editorial: 303 Southeast 2nd Avenue, Ava, Missouri 65608-0386 **Tel:** 1 417 683-4191.
Email: news@kkoz.com
Web site: http://www.kkoz.com
Profile: KKOZ-FM is a commercial station owned by Corum Industries Inc. The format of the station is news/talk. KKOZ-FM broadcasts to the Springfield, MO area at 92.1 FM.
FM RADIO STATION

KKPK-FM 43461
Owner: Cumulus Media Inc
Editorial: 6805 Corporate Dr, Ste 130, Colorado Springs, Colorado 80919 **Tel:** 1 719 593-2700.
Web site: http://www.929peakfm.com
Profile: KKPK-FM is a commercial station owned by Cumulus Media Inc. The format of the station is adult contemporary. KKPK-FM broadcasts to the Colorado Springs, CO area at 92.9 FM.
FM RADIO STATION

KKPL-FM 43617
Owner: Townsquare Media, LLC
Editorial: 600 Main St, Windsor, Colorado 80550-5133 **Tel:** 1 970 674-2700.
Web site: http://www.999thepoint.com
Profile: KKPL-FM is a commercial station owned by Townsquare Media, LLC. The format of the station is Hot AC. KKPL-FM broadcasts to the Denver area at 99.9 FM.
FM RADIO STATION

KKPN-FM 42381
Owner: Convergent Broadcasting
Editorial: 615 N Upper Broadway St Ste 105, Corpus Christi, Texas 78401-0703 **Tel:** 1 361 814-3800.
Web site: http://planet1023.com
Profile: KKPN-FM is a commercial station owned by Convergent Broadcasting. The format of the station is Top 40/CHR. KKPN-FM broadcasts in Corpus Christi, TX area at 102.3 FM.
FM RADIO STATION

KKPR-FM 217826
Owner: Platte River Radio, Inc.
Editorial: 403 E 25th St, Kearney, Nebraska 68847
Tel: 1 308 236-9900.
Email: generalmanager@kkpr.com
Web site: http://www.kkpr.com
Profile: KKPR-FM is a commercial station owned by Platte River Radio, Inc. The format of the station is classic hits. KKPR-FM broadcasts to the Kearney, NE area at 98.9 FM.
FM RADIO STATION

KKPS-FM 42118
Owner: Entravision Communications Corp.
Editorial: 801 N Jackson Rd, McAllen, Texas 78501-9306 **Tel:** 1 956 661-6000.
Web site: http://995lanueva.com
Profile: KKPS-FM is a commercial station owned by Entravision Communications Corp. The format of the station is regional Mexican. KKPS-FM broadcasts to the McAllen, TX, area at 99.5 FM.
FM RADIO STATION

KKPT-FM 42764
Owner: Signal Media Inc.
Editorial: 2400 Cottondale Ln, Little Rock, Arkansas 72202-2020 **Tel:** 1 501 664-9410.
Web site: http://www.point941.com
Profile: KKPT-FM is a commercial station owned by Signal Media Inc. The format of the station is classic rock music. KKPT-FM broadcasts in the Little Rock, AR area at 94.1 FM.
FM RADIO STATION

KKPZ-AM 36406
Owner: Crawford Broadcasting Co.
Editorial: 9700 SE Eastview Dr, Happy Valley, Oregon 97086-6975 **Tel:** 1 503 242-1950.
Email: info@kkpz.com
Web site: http://www.kkpz.com
Profile: KKPZ-AM is a commercial station owned by Crawford Broadcasting Co. The format of the station is Christian music and programming. KKPZ-AM broadcasts to the Portland, OR area at 1400 AM.
AM RADIO STATION

KKQQ-FM 45825
Owner: Alpha Media
Editorial: 227 22nd Ave S, Brookings, South Dakota 57006-2827 **Tel:** 1 605 692-9125.
Email: kjjqnews@brookings.net
Web site: http://www.kcountry102.com
Profile: KKQQ-FM is a commercial station owned by Alpha Media. The format of the station is country music. KKQQ-FM broadcasts to the Brookings, SD area at 102.3 FM.
FM RADIO STATION

KKQY-FM 43322
Owner: Eagle Radio Inc.
Editorial: 2300 Hall St, Hays, Kansas 67601-3062
Tel: 1 785 625-2578.
Email: haysnews@eagleradio.net
Web site: https://www.hayspost.com/1019thebull
Profile: KKQY-FM is a commercial station owned by Eagle Radio Inc. The format of the station is contemporary country music. KKQY-FM broadcasts to Hays, KS at 101.9 FM.
FM RADIO STATION

KKRB-FM 42859
Owner: Wynne Broadcasting Co.
Editorial: 1338 Oregon Ave, Klamath Falls, Oregon 97601-6540 **Tel:** 1 541 882-4656.
Email: webmaster@klamathradio.com
Web site: http://www.klamathradio.com
Profile: KKRB-FM is a commercial station owned by Wynne Broadcasting Co. The format of the station is soft rock. KKRB-FM broadcasts to the Klamath Falls, OR area at a frequency of 106.9 FM.
FM RADIO STATION

KKRC-FM 42957
Owner: Tom Ingstad Broadcast Group
Editorial: 4454 Highway 212, Montevideo, Minnesota 56265-4539 **Tel:** 1 320 269-8815.
Email: kdmaprod@radiokdma.com
Profile: KKRC-FM is a commercial station owned by Iowa City Broadcasting Co. The format of the station is oldies music. KKRC-FM broadcasts to the Montevideo, MN area at 93.9 FM.
FM RADIO STATION

KKRE-FM 475413
Owner: Altus FM Inc.
Editorial: 808 N Main St, Altus, Oklahoma 73521-3116 **Tel:** 1 580 482-1555.
Email: keyb@keyb.net
Web site: http://www.keyb.net
Profile: KKRE-FM is a commercial station owned by Altus FM Inc. The format of the station is oldies music. KKRE-FM broadcasts to the Altus, OK area at 92.5 FM.
FM RADIO STATION

KKRF-FM 42565
Owner: M&M Broadcasting, Inc.
Tel: 1 515 523-7107.
Email: kniakrls@kniakrls.com
Web site: http://raccoonvalleyradio.com
Profile: KKRF-FM is a commercial station owned by M&M Broadcasting, Inc. The format of the station is country music. KKRF-FM broadcasts to the Stuart, IA area at 107.9 FM.
FM RADIO STATION

KKRG-FM 43781
Owner: Univision Communications Inc.
Editorial: 8009 Marble Ave NE, Albuquerque, New Mexico 87110-7901 **Tel:** 1 505 254-7100.
Web site: http://www.univision.com/content/channel.jhtml?chid=10014&schid=10027
Profile: KKRG-FM is a commercial station owned by Univision Communications Inc. The format of the station is Spanish adult contemporary. KKRG-FM broadcasts to the Albuquerque, NM area at 105.1 FM.
FM RADIO STATION

KKRK-FM 901229
Owner: The Montana Radio Company, LLC.
Editorial: 100 W Lyndale Ave Ste B, Helena, Montana 59601-2999 **Tel:** 1 406 442-6645.
Profile: KKRK-FM is a commercial station owned by Montana Radio Company (The). The format of the station is rock music and broadcasts to the Helena, MT area at a frequency of 106.5 FM.
FM RADIO STATION

KKRL-FM 44729
Owner: Carroll Broadcasting Co.
Editorial: 1119 East Plaza Dr, Carroll, Iowa 51401-3838 **Tel:** 1 712 792-4321.
Email: 937kkrl@carrollbroadcasting.com
Web site: http://carrollbroadcasting.com
Profile: KKRL-FM is a commercial station owned by Carroll Broadcasting Co. The format of the station is hot adult contemporary music. KKRL-FM broadcasts to the Carroll, IA area at 93.7 FM.
FM RADIO STATION

KKRQ-FM 44730
Owner: iHeartMedia Inc.
Editorial: 1 Stephen Atkins Dr, Iowa City, Iowa 52240-8021 **Tel:** 1 319 354-9500.
Email: news@kxic.com
Web site: http://www.kkrq.com
Profile: KKRQ-FM is a commercial station owned by iHeartMedia Inc. The format of the station is classic rock music. KKRQ-FM broadcasts to the Cedar Rapids, IA area at 100.7 FM.
FM RADIO STATION

KKRS-FM 44085
Owner: Penfold Communications, Inc.
Editorial: 12720 W Sunset Hwy, Ste C, Airway Heights, Washington 99001-9410 **Tel:** 1 509 244-5577.
Email: kkrs973fm@hotmail.com
Profile: KKRS-FM is a non-commercial station owned by Penfold Communications, Inc. The station airs a religious format in the Airway Heights, WA area at 97.3 FM.
FM RADIO STATION

KKRT-AM 37264
Owner: MCC Radio, LLC
Tel: 1 509 663-5186.
Web site: http://www.kkrt.com
Profile: KKRT-AM is a commercial station owned by MCC Radio, LLC. The format of the station is sports. KKRT-AM broadcasts to the Moses Lake, WA area at 900 AM.
AM RADIO STATION

KKRV-FM 44985
Owner: Morris Communications
Editorial: 1124 N Miller St, Wenatchee, Washington 98801-1541 **Tel:** 1 509 663-5186.
Email: johnw@kkrv.com
Web site: http://www.kkrv.com
Profile: KKRV-FM is a commercial station owned by Morris Communications. The format of the station is country. KKRV-FM broadcasts to the Seattle area at 104.7 FM.
FM RADIO STATION

KKRX-AM 35086
Owner: Perry Publishing & Broadcasting Inc.
Editorial: 1525 SE Flower Mound Rd, Lawton, Oklahoma 73501-6325 **Tel:** 1 580 355-1050.
Web site: http://kkrx.com
Profile: KKRX-AM is a commercial station owned by Perry Publishing & Broadcasting Inc. The format of the station is Urban AC. KKRX-AM broadcasts to the Lawton, OK area at 1380 AM.
AM RADIO STATION

KKRZ-FM 46022
Owner: iHeartMedia Inc.
Editorial: 13333 SW 68th Pkwy Ste 310, Tigard, Oregon 97223-8304 **Tel:** 1 503 323-6400.
Web site: http://z100portland.iheart.com
Profile: KKRZ-FM is a commercial station owned by iHeartMedia Inc. The format of the station Top 40/CHR music. KKRZ-FM broadcasts to the Portland, OR area at 100.3 FM.
FM RADIO STATION

KKSA-AM 39068
Owner: Foster Communications Co. Inc.
Editorial: 2824 Sherwood Way, San Angelo, Texas 76901-3514 **Tel:** 1 325 949-3333.
Web site: http://www.kksa-am.com
Profile: KKSA-AM is a commercial station owned by Foster Communications Co. Inc. The format for the station is news, talk and sports. KKSA-AM broadcasts to the San Angelo, TX area at 1260 AM.
AM RADIO STATION

KKSD-FM 43608
Owner: Alpha Media
Editorial: 921 9th Ave SE, Watertown, South Dakota 57201-4960 **Tel:** 1 605 882-1480.
Email: kwatnews@digity.me
Web site: http://www.gowatertown.net
Profile: KKSD-FM is a commercial station owned by Alpha Media. The format of the station is classic hits. KKSD-FM broadcasts to the Watertown, SD area 104.3 FM.
FM RADIO STATION

KKSE-AM 544549
Owner: KSE Radio Ventures
Editorial: 4700 S Syracuse St Ste 1050, Denver, Colorado 80237-2713 **Tel:** 1 303 631-1430.
Web site: http://www.altitudesports950.com/
Profile: KKSE-AM is a commercial station owned by KSE Radio Ventures. The format of the station is Sports. KKSE-AM broadcasts to the Denver area at 950 AM.
AM RADIO STATION

KKSF-AM 62044
Owner: iHeartMedia Inc.
Editorial: 340 Townsend St, San Francisco, California 94107-1633 **Tel:** 1 415 356-5500.
Web site: http://talk910.iheart.com
Profile: KKSF-AM is a commercial station owned by iHeartMedia Inc.. The format of the station is talk. KKSF-AM broadcasts to the San Francisco area at 910 AM.
AM RADIO STATION

KKSI-FM 41792
Owner: O-Town Communications, Inc.
Editorial: 416 E Main St, Ottumwa, Iowa 52501-3026
Tel: 1 641 684-5563.
Email: info@ottumwaradio.com
Web site: http://www.kissclassicrock.com
Profile: KKSI-FM is a commercial station owned by O-Town Communications, Inc. The format of the station is classic rock. KKSI-FM broadcasts to the Ottumwa, IA area at a frequency of 101.5 FM.
FM RADIO STATION

KKSM-AM 36509
Owner: Palomar Community College
Editorial: 1140 W Mission Rd, San Marcos, California 92069-1415 **Tel:** 1 760 744-1150 2183.
Web site: http://www.palomar.edu/kksm
Profile: KKSM-AM is a non-commercial college station owned by Palomar Community College. The format of the station is college variety. KKSM-AM broadcasts to the San Marcos, CA area at AM 1320.
AM RADIO STATION

KKSP-FM 46669
Owner: Salem Media Group
Editorial: 415 N McKinley St Ste 700, Little Rock, Arkansas 72205-3041 **Tel:** 1 501 219-1919.
Web site: http://www.933fmthefish.com
Profile: KKSP-FM is a commercial station owned by Salem Media Group. The format of the station is Contemporary Christian. KKSP-FM broadcasts to the Little Rock, AR area at 93.3 FM.
FM RADIO STATION

KKSR-FM 43385
Owner: Ingstad Radio Washington, LLC
Editorial: 4304 W 24th Ave Ste 200, Kennewick, Washington 99338-2320 **Tel:** 1 509 783-0783.
Web site: http://www.cities957.com
Profile: KKSR-FM is a commercial station owned by Ingstad Radio Washington, LLC. The format of the station is classic hits. KKSR-FM broadcasts to the Kennewick, WA area at 95.7 FM.
FM RADIO STATION

KKSS-FM 39729
Owner: Univision Communications Inc.
Editorial: 8009 Marble Ave NE, Albuquerque, New Mexico 87110-7901 **Tel:** 1 505 254-7100.
Web site: http://www.univision.com/albuquerque/kkss
Profile: KKSS-FM is a commercial station owned by Univision Communications Inc. The format of the station is rhythmic Top 40/CHR music. KKSS-FM broadcasts to the Albuquerque, NM area at 97.3 FM.
FM RADIO STATION

KKST-FM 42000
Owner: Cenla Broadcasting Inc.
Editorial: 1115 Texas Ave, Alexandria, Louisiana 71301 **Tel:** 1 318 445-1234.
Web site: http://www.kiss987.fm
Profile: KKST-FM is a commercial station owned by Cenla Broadcasting Inc. The format of the station is urban contemporary music. KKST-FM broadcasts to the Alexandria, LA area at 98.7 FM.
FM RADIO STATION

KKSW-FM 44763
Owner: Great Plains Media
Editorial: 3125 W 6th St, Lawrence, Kansas 66049-3101 **Tel:** 1 785 843-1320.
Web site: http://www.1059kissfm.com
Profile: KKSW-FM is a commercial station owned by Great Plains Media. The format of the station is Top 40/CHR. KKSW-FM broadcasts to the Lawrence, KS area at 105.9 FM.
FM RADIO STATION

KKSY-FM 45387
Owner: iHeartMedia Inc.
Editorial: 600 Old Marion Rd NE, Cedar Rapids, Iowa 52402-2159 **Tel:** 1 319 395-0530.
Web site: http://www.965kisscountry.com
Profile: KKSY-FM is a commercial station owned by iHeartMedia Inc. The format of the station is contemporary country music. KKSY-FM broadcasts in the Cedar Rapids, IA area at 96.5 FM.
FM RADIO STATION

KKTC-FM 42546
Owner: DMC Broadcasting Inc.
Editorial: 125A Camino De La Merced Ste A, Taos, New Mexico 87571-5119 **Tel:** 1 575 758-4491.
Web site: http://www.kktctruecountry.com
Profile: KKTC-FM is a commercial station owned by DMC Broadcasting Inc. The format of the station is contemporary country music. KKTC-FM broadcasts to the Taos, NM area at 99.9 FM.
FM RADIO STATION

KKTK-AM 37514
Owner: Freed AM Corp.
Editorial: 3446 Summerhill Rd #B, Texarkana, Texas 75503-3560 **Tel:** 1 903 255-7938.
Email: espnradio1400@aol.com
Web site: http://www.foxsportstexarkana.com
Profile: KKTK-AM is a commercial station owned by Freed AM Corp.. The format of the station is sports. KKTK-AM broadcasts to the Texarkana area at 1400 AM.
AM RADIO STATION

KKTL-AM 62809
Owner: Townsquare Media, LLC
Editorial: 150 Nichols Ave, Casper, Wyoming 82601-1816 **Tel:** 1 307 266-5252.
Web site: http://am1400espn.com/
Profile: KKTL-AM is a commercial station owned by Townsquare Media, LLC. The format for the station is talk and sports. KKTL-AM broadcasts to the Casper-Riverton, WY area at 1400 AM.
AM RADIO STATION

KKTS-FM 45847
Owner: Douglas Broadcasting Inc.
Editorial: 247 N Russell Ave, Douglas, Wyoming 82633-2315 **Tel:** 1 307 358-3636.
Email: kkts@kktyonline.com
Web site: http://www.kktyonline.com
Profile: KKTS-FM is a commercial station owned by Douglas Broadcasting Inc. The format of the station is Hot AC. KKTS-FM airs locally at 99.3 FM to the Douglas, WY area.
FM RADIO STATION

KKTU-FM 44940
Owner: Lahontan Valley Broadcasting
Editorial: 1155 Gummow Dr, Fallon, Nevada 89406
Tel: 1 775 423-2243.
Email: kvlv@phonewave.net
Profile: KKTU-FM is a commercial station owned by Lahontan Valley Broadcasting. The format of the station is adult contemporary. KKTU-FM broadcasts to the Fallon, NV area at 99.5 FM.
FM RADIO STATION

KKTX-AM 429888
Owner: iHeartMedia Inc.
Editorial: 501 Tupper Ln, Corpus Christi, Texas 78417-9736 **Tel:** 1 361 289-0111.
Web site: http://1360kktx.iheart.com
Profile: KKTX-AM is a commercial station owned by iHeartMedia Inc. The format of the station is news, talk and sports. KKTX-AM broadcasts to the Corpus Christi, TX area at 1360 AM.
AM RADIO STATION

KKTX-FM 44731
Owner: Townsquare Media, LLC
Editorial: 3810 Brookside Dr, Tyler, Texas 75701-9420 **Tel:** 1 903 581-0606.
Web site: http://www.classicrock961.com
Profile: KKTX-FM is a commercial station owned by Townsquare Media, LLC. The format of the station is classic rock music. KKTX-FM broadcasts to the Tyler, TX area at 96.1 FM.
FM RADIO STATION

KKTY-AM 38479
Owner: Douglas Broadcasting Inc.
Editorial: 247 N Russell Ave, Douglas, Wyoming 82633-2315 **Tel:** 1 307 358-3636.
Email: kkty@kktyonline.com
Web site: http://www.kktyonline.com
Profile: KKTY-AM is a commercial station owned by Douglas Broadcasting Inc. The format for the station is oldies. KKTY-AM broadcasts to the Casper-Riverton, WY area at 1470 AM.
AM RADIO STATION

KKTY-FM 750085
Owner: Douglas Broadcasting Inc.
Editorial: 247 N Russell Ave, Douglas, Wyoming 82633-2315 **Tel:** 1 307 358-3636.
Email: kkty@kktyonline.com
Web site: http://kktyonline.com
Profile: KKTY-FM is a commercial station owned by Douglas Broadcasting Inc. The format for the station is Country. KKTY-AM broadcasts to the Casper-Riverton, WY area at 99.3 FM.
FM RADIO STATION

KKTZ-FM 39730
Owner: Mac Partners
Editorial: 2352 Highway 62 E Business, Mountain Home, Arkansas 72653-6847 **Tel:** 1 870 492-6022.
Web site: http://www.twinlakesradio.com/
Profile: KKTZ-FM is a commercial station owned by Mac Partners. The format of the station is adult contemporary. KKTZ-FM broadcasts to the Mountain Home, AR area at 107.5 FM.
FM RADIO STATION

KKUA-FM 41595
Owner: Hawaii Public Radio
Editorial: 738 Kaheka St, Honolulu, Hawaii 96814-3726 **Tel:** 1 808 955-8821.
Email: mail@hawaiipublicradio.org
Web site: http://www.hawaiipublicradio.org
Profile: KKUA-FM is a non-commercial station owned by Hawaii Public Radio. The format of the station is news, talk, and classical music. KKUA-FM broadcasts to the Honolulu area at 90.7 FM.
FM RADIO STATION

KKUP-FM 43305
Owner: Assurance Sciences Foundation
Editorial: 1241 Franklin Mall, Santa Clara, California 95050-4806 **Tel:** 1 408 260-2999.
Email: webmeister@kkup.org
Web site: http://www.kkup.org
Profile: KKUP-FM is a non-commercial station owned by Assurance Sciences Foundation. The format of the station is variety. KKUP-FM broadcasts to the Santa Clara, CA area at 91.5 FM.
FM RADIO STATION

KKUS-FM 41637
Owner: Access.1 Communications Corp.
Editorial: 210 S Broadway Ave Ste 100, Tyler, Texas 75702-7353 **Tel:** 1 903 581-9966.
Web site: http://www.theranch.fm/
Profile: KKUS-FM is a commercial station owned by Access.1 Communications Corp. The format of the station is classic country. KKUS-FM broadcasts to Tyler, TX at 104.1 FM.
FM RADIO STATION

KKUT-FM 354584
Owner: Sanpete County Broadcasting Co.
Editorial: 1600 W 500 N, Manti, Utah 84642-5503
Tel: 1 435 835-7301.
Web site: http://www.937skyfm.com
Profile: KKUT-FM is a commercial station owned by Sanpete County Broadcasting Co. The format of the station is country music. KKUT-FM broadcasts to the Richfield, UT area at 93.7 FM.
FM RADIO STATION

KKUU-FM 46007
Owner: Morris Communications
Editorial: 1321 N Gene Autry Trl, Palm Springs, California 92262 **Tel:** 1 760 322-7890.
Web site: http://www.927kkuu.com
Profile: KKUU-FM is a commercial station owned by Morris Communications. The format of the station is rhythmic Top 40/CHR. KKUU-FM broadcasts to the Los Angeles area at 92.7 FM.
FM RADIO STATION

KKVR-FM 556848
Owner: Radio Ranch Ltd.
Editorial: 3505 Fredericksburg Rd, Kerrville, Texas 78028-9272 **Tel:** 1 830 896-4990.
Email: psa@ranchradiogroup.com
Profile: KKVR-FM is a commercial station owned by Radio Ranch Ltd. The format of the station is oldies KKVR-FM broadcasts to the Kerryville, TX area at 106.1 FM.
FM RADIO STATION

KKVU-FM 349769
Owner: Spanish Peaks Broadcasting, Inc.
Editorial: 2425 W Central Ave Ste 203, Missoula, Montana 59801-6402 **Tel:** 1 406 721-6800.
Web site: http://www.u1045.com
Profile: KKVU-FM is a commercial station owned by Spanish Peaks Broadcasting, Inc., doing business as The Montana Radio Company, LLC. The format of the station is Top 40/CHR. KKVU-FM broadcasts to the Missoula, MT area at 104.5 FM.
FM RADIO STATION

KKVV-AM 35883
Owner: Vegas Broadcasters Inc.(Las)
Editorial: 3185 S Highland Dr Ste 13, Las Vegas, Nevada 89109-1029 **Tel:** 1 702 731-5588.
Web site: http://www.kkvv.com
Profile: KKVV-AM is a commercial station owned by Las Vegas Broadcasters Inc. The format of the station is Christian talk. KKVV-AM broadcasts to the Las Vegas area at 1060 AM.
AM RADIO STATION

KKWD-FM 39726
Owner: Cumulus Media Inc
Editorial: 4045 NW 64th St Ste 600, Oklahoma City, Oklahoma 73116-2607 **Tel:** 1 405 848-0100.
Web site: http://www.wild1049hd.com
Profile: KKWD-FM is a commercial station owned by Cumulus Media Inc. The format of the station is rhythmic Top 40/CHR music. KKWD-FM broadcasts to the Oklahoma City area at 104.9 FM.
FM RADIO STATION

KKWF-FM 46435
Owner: Entercom Communications Corp.
Editorial: 1100 Olive Way, Seattle, Washington 98101-1873 **Tel:** 1 206 233-1037.
Email: frontdeskmp@entercom.com
Web site: http://www.seattlewolf.com
Profile: KKWF-FM is a commercial station owned by Entercom Communications Corp. The format of the station is country. KKWF-FM broadcasts to the Seattle area at 100.7 FM.
FM RADIO STATION

KKWK-FM 46817
Owner: Goodradio.TV LLC
Editorial: 607 E Platte Clay Way, Cameron, Missouri 64429-8825 **Tel:** 1 816 632-6661.
Web site: http://www.northwestmoinfo.com
Profile: KKWK-FM is a commercial station owned by Goodradio.TV LLC. The format of the station is classic hits. KKWK-FM broadcasts to the Kansas City, MO area at 100.1 FM.
FM RADIO STATION

KKWQ-FM 41114
Owner: Border Broadcasting
Editorial: 113 A Lake St Center, Warroad, Minnesota 56763 **Tel:** 1 218 386-3024.
Email: kq92@mncable.net
Web site: http://www.kq92.com
Profile: KKWQ-FM is a commercial station owned by Border Broadcasting. The format of the station is contemporary country music. KKWQ-FM broadcasts to the Warroad, MN area at 92.5 FM.
FM RADIO STATION

KKWS-FM 39731
Owner: Hubbard Broadcasting Inc.
Editorial: 201 Jefferson St S, Wadena, Minnesota 56482-1531 **Tel:** 1 218 631-1803.
Web site: http://www.superstationk106.com
Profile: KKWS-FM is a commercial station owned by Hubbard Broadcasting Inc.The format of the station is contemporary country music. KKWS-FM broadcasts to Wadena, MN at 105.9 FM.
FM RADIO STATION

KKXA-AM 778392
Owner: North Sound Media
Editorial: 2707 Colby Ave Ste 1380, Everett, Washington 98201-3568 **Tel:** 1 425 304-1381.
Email: info@1520kxa.com
Web site: http://www.1520kxa.com
Profile: KKXA-AM is a commercial station owned by CAAM Partnership (Andy Skotdal). The format of the station is classic country. KAAM-AM broadcasts to the Snohomish, WA area at a frequency of 1520 AM.
AM RADIO STATION

KKXK-FM 44733
Owner: Cherry Creek Radio
Editorial: 106 Rose Ln, Montrose, Colorado 81401-3823 **Tel:** 1 970 249-4546.
Email: 94kix@cherrycreekmedia.com
Web site: http://94kix.com
Profile: KKXK-FM is a commercial station owned by Cherry Creek Radio. The format for the station is contemporary country. KKXK-FM broadcasts to the Grand Junction-Montrose, CO area at 94.1 FM.
FM RADIO STATION

KKXL-AM 37356
Owner: iHeartMedia Inc.
Editorial: 505 University Ave, Grand Forks, North Dakota 58203-3545 **Tel:** 1 701 775-0575.
Web site: http://www.1440kkxl.com
Profile: KKXL-AM is a commercial station owned by iHeartMedia Inc. The format of the station is sports. KKXL-AM broadcasts to the Grand Forks, ND area at 1440 AM.
AM RADIO STATION

KKXL-FM 44734
Owner: iHeartMedia Inc.
Editorial: 505 University Ave, Grand Forks, North Dakota 58203-3545 **Tel:** 1 701 775-0575.
Web site: http://xl93.iheart.com
Profile: KKXL-FM is a commercial station owned by iHeartMedia Inc. The format of the station is Top 40/CHR music. KKXL-FM broadcasts to the Grand Forks, ND area at 92.9 FM.
FM RADIO STATION

KKXS-FM 239081
Owner: Results Radio Group
Editorial: 1588 Charles Dr, Redding, California 96003
Tel: 1 530 244-9700.
Web site: http://xs961.com
Profile: KKXS-FM is a commercial station owned by Results Radio Group. The format of the station is sports. KKXS-FM broadcasts to the Redding, CA area at 96.1 FM.
FM RADIO STATION

KKXT-FM 40011
Owner: North Texas Public Broadcasting
Editorial: 3000 Harry Hines Blvd, Dallas, Texas 75201-1012 **Tel:** 1 214 871-1390.
Web site: http://kxt.org
Profile: KKXT-FM is a non-commercial station owned by North Texas Public Broadcasting. The format of the station is adult album alternative. KKXT-FM broadcasts in the Dallas area at 91.7 FM.
FM RADIO STATION

KKXX-AM 39481
Owner: Butte Broadcasting Inc.
Editorial: 1363 Longfellow Ave, Chico, California 95926 **Tel:** 1 530 894-7325.
Email: info@kkxx.net
Web site: http://www.kkxx.net
AM RADIO STATION

KKXX-FM 42850
Owner: American General Media
Editorial: 1400 Easton Dr Ste 144B, Bakersfield, California 93309-9412 **Tel:** 1 661 328-1410.
Web site: http://www.hits931fm.com
Profile: KKXX-FM is a commercial station owned by American General Media. The format of the station is Top 40/CHR. KKXX-FM broadcasts to the Bakersfield, CA area at 93.1 FM.
FM RADIO STATION

KKYA-FM 44736
Owner: Riverfront Broadcasting
Editorial: 202 W 2nd St, Yankton, South Dakota 57078-4317 **Tel:** 1 605 665-7892.
Email: production@kk93.com
Web site: http://www.kk93.com
Profile: KKYA-FM is a commercial station owned by Riverfront Broadcasting. The format of the station is country. KKYA-FM broadcasts to the Yankton, SD area at 93.1 FM.
FM RADIO STATION

KKYN-FM 45774
Owner: Rhattigan Broadcasting
Editorial: 3218 Quincy St, Plainview, Texas 79072-1906 **Tel:** 1 806 293-2771.
Web site: http://www.kickinkountry1069.com
Profile: KKYN-FM is a commercial station owned by Rhattigan Broadcasting. The format of the station is country music. KKYN-FM broadcasts to the Plainview, TX area at 106.9 FM.
FM RADIO STATION

KKYR-FM 44811
Owner: Townsquare Media, LLC
Editorial: 2324 Arkansas Blvd, Texarkana, Arkansas 71854-2016 **Tel:** 1 870 772-3771.
Web site: http://www.kkyr.com
Profile: KKYR-FM is a commercial station owned by Townsquare Media, LLC. The format of the station is

country, featuring contemporary and classic hits. KKYR-FM broadcasts to the Texarkana, AR area at 102.5 FM.
FM RADIO STATION

KKYS-FM 39732
Owner: iHeartMedia Inc.
Editorial: 1716 Briarcrest Dr Ste 150, Bryan, Texas 77802-2776 **Tel:** 1 979 846-5597.
Web site: http://www.mix1047.com
Profile: KKYS-FM is a commercial station owned by iHeartMedia Inc. The format of the station is hot adult contemporary. KKYS-FM broadcasts to the Bryan, TX area at 104.7 FM.
FM RADIO STATION

KKYX-AM 38793
Owner: Cox Media Group, Inc.
Editorial: 8122 Datapoint Dr, Ste 600, San Antonio, Texas 78229-3446 **Tel:** 1 210 615-5400.
Web site: http://www.kkyx.com
Profile: KKYX-AM is a commercial station owned by Cox Media Group, Inc. The format of the station is country. KKYX-AM broadcasts to the San Antonio area at 680 AM.
AM RADIO STATION

KKYZ-FM 42948
Owner: Cochise Broadcasting LLC
Editorial: 500 E Fry Blvd Ste L10, Sierra Vista, Arizona 85635-1840 **Tel:** 1 520 459-8201.
Email: info@kkyz.com
Web site: http://www.kkyz.com
Profile: KKYZ-FM is a commercial station owned by Cochise Broadcasting, LLC. The format of the station is oldies music. KKYZ-FM broadcasts to the Tucson, AZ area at 101.7 FM.
FM RADIO STATION

KKZN-AM 39336
Owner: iHeartMedia Inc.
Editorial: 4695 S Monaco St, Denver, Colorado 80237-3525 **Tel:** 1 303 713-8000.
Web site: http://denversports760.iheart.com
Profile: KKZN-AM is a commercial station owned by iHeartMedia Inc. The format of the station is talk. KKZN-AM broadcasts to the Denver area at 760 AM.
AM RADIO STATION

KKZQ-FM 475342
Owner: High Desert Broadcasting LLC
Editorial: 570 E Avenue Q9, Palmdale, California 93550 **Tel:** 1 661 947-3107.
Web site: http://www.edge100.com
Profile: KKZQ-FM is a commercial station owned by High Desert Broadcasting LLC. The format of the station is rock alternative. KKZQ-FM broadcasts to the Palmdale, CA area at 100.1 FM.
FM RADIO STATION

KKZX-FM 46360
Owner: iHeartMedia Inc.
Editorial: 808 E Sprague Ave, Spokane, Washington 99202-2126 **Tel:** 1 509 242-2400.
Web site: http://www.kkzx.com
Profile: KKZX-FM is a commercial station owned by iHeartMedia Inc. The format of the station is classic rock. KKZX-FM broadcasts to the Spokane, WA area at 98.9 FM.
FM RADIO STATION

KKZY-FM 44402
Owner: Hubbard Broadcasting Inc.
Editorial: 502 Beltrami Ave NW, Bemidji, Minnesota 56601-3010 **Tel:** 1 218 444-1500.
Email: news@pbbroadcasting.com
Web site: http://www.kzyfm955.com/home.html
Profile: KKZY-FM is a commercial station owned by Hubbard Broadcasting Inc. The format of the station is adult contemporary music. KKZY-FM broadcasts to Bemidji, MN at 95.5 FM.
FM RADIO STATION

KLAA-AM 36106
Owner: LAA1 LLC
Editorial: 2000 E Gene Autry Way, Anaheim, California 92806-6143 **Tel:** 1 714 940-2500.
Web site: http://www.am830klaa.com
Profile: KLAA-AM is a commercial station owned by LAA1 LLC. The format of the station is sports. KLAA-AM broadcasts to the Anaheim, CA area at 830 AM.
AM RADIO STATION

KLAA-FM 43507
Owner: Mapleton Communications
Editorial: 92 W Shamrock Ave, Pineville, Louisiana 71360-6435 **Tel:** 1 318 487-1035.
Email: la103contest@gmail.com
Web site: http://www.la103.com
Profile: KLAA-FM is a commercial station owned by Opus Broadcasting of Alexandria, LLC. The format of the station is country music. KLAA-FM broadcasts in the Pineville, LA area at 103.5 FM.
FM RADIO STATION

KLAC-AM 38302
Owner: iHeartMedia Inc.
Editorial: 3400 W Olive Ave Ste 550, Burbank, California 91505-5544 **Tel:** 1 818 559-2252.
Web site: http://am570lasports.iheart.com
Profile: KLAC-AM is a commercial station owned by iHeartMedia Inc. The format of the station is sports. KLAC-AM broadcasts to the Los Angeles area at 570 AM.
AM RADIO STATION

KLAD-AM 37357
Owner: Basin Mediactive, LLC
Editorial: 404 Main St Ste 4, Klamath Falls, Oregon 97601-6021 **Tel:** 1 541 882-8833.
Email: news@mybasin.com
Web site: http://www.mybasin.com
Profile: KLAD-AM is a commercial station owned by Basin Mediactive, LLC. The format of the station is sports talk. KLAD-AM broadcasts to the Klamath Falls, OR area at 960 AM.
AM RADIO STATION

KLAD-FM 44737
Owner: Basin Mediactive, LLC
Editorial: 404 Main St Ste 4, Klamath Falls, Oregon 97601-6021 **Tel:** 1 541 882-8833.
Email: news@mybasin.com
Web site: http://www.mybasin.com
Profile: KLAD-FM is a commercial station owned by New Northwest Broadcasters LLC. The format of the station is country music. KLAD-FM broadcasts to the Klamath Falls, OR area at 92.5 FM.
FM RADIO STATION

KLAK-FM 41101
Owner: Digity LLC
Editorial: 1700 Redbud Blvd Ste 185, McKinney, Texas 75069-3270 **Tel:** 1 972 542-9755.
Email: community@975klak.com
Web site: http://www.975klak.com
Profile: KLAK-FM is a commercial station owned by Digity LLC. The format of the station is adult contemporary music. KLAK-FM broadcasts in the Denison, TX area at 97.5 FM.
FM RADIO STATION

KLAL-FM 43345
Owner: Cumulus Media Inc
Editorial: 700 Wellington Hills Rd, Little Rock, Arkansas 72211 **Tel:** 1 501 401-0200.
Web site: http://www.alice1077.com
Profile: KLAL-FM is a commercial station owned by Cumulus Media Inc. The format of the station is Top 40/CHR. KLAL-FM broadcasts to the Little Rock, AR area at 107.7 FM.
FM RADIO STATION

KLAM-AM 39436
Owner: Bayview Communications Inc.
Editorial: 112 Forestry Way, Cordova, Alaska 99574 **Tel:** 1 907 424-3796.
Email: email@cordovaradio.com
Web site: http://www.cordovaradio.com
Profile: KLAM-AM is a commercial station owned by Bayview Communications Inc. The format of the station is classic hits. KLAM-AM broadcasts to the Anchorage, AK area at 1450 AM.
AM RADIO STATION

KLAN-FM 46194
Owner: Glasgow Broadcasting Corp.
Editorial: 504 2nd Ave S, Glasgow, Montana 59230 **Tel:** 1 406 228-9336.
Email: kltz@kltz.com
Web site: http://www.kltz.com
Profile: KLAN-FM is a commercial station owned by Glascow Broadcasting Corp. The format of the station is adult contemporary. KLAN-FM broadcasts to the Glasgow, MT area at 93.5 FM.
FM RADIO STATION

KLAQ-FM 46526
Owner: Townsquare Media, LLC
Editorial: 4180 N Mesa St, El Paso, Texas 79902 **Tel:** 1 915 544-8864.
Web site: http://www.klaq.com
Profile: KLAQ-FM is a commercial station owned by Townsquare Media, LLC. The format of the station is rock music. KLAQ-FM broadcasts to the El Paso, TX area at 95.5 FM.
FM RADIO STATION

KLAR-AM 34993
Owner: Faith & Power Communications
Editorial: 3320 Anna Ave, Laredo, Texas 78040-1070 **Tel:** 1 956 723-1300.
Email: radiopoder1300@gmail.com
Web site: http://www.radiopoder1300.com/
Profile: KLAR-AM is a commercial station owned by Faith & Power Communications. The format of the station is Hispanic religious programming. KLAR-AM broadcasts to the Laredo, TX area at 1300 AM.
AM RADIO STATION

KLAT-AM 39230
Owner: Univision Communications Inc.
Editorial: 5100 Southwest Fwy, Houston, Texas 77056-7308 **Tel:** 1 713 407-1415.
Web site: http://univisionamerica.com
Profile: KLAT-AM is a commercial station owned by Univision Communications Inc. The format of the station is Hispanic news and talk programming. KLAT-AM broadcasts to the Houston area at 1010 AM.
AM RADIO STATION

KLAV-AM 34941
Owner: Lotus Broadcasting Corp
Editorial: 8755 W Flamingo Rd, Las Vegas, Nevada 89147-8667 **Tel:** 1 702 876-1230.
Web site: http://www.lacalientelv.com/
Profile: KLAV-AM is a commercial station owned by Lotus Broadcasting Corp. The format of the station is news and talk. KLAV-AM broadcasts to the Las Vegas area at 1230 AM.
AM RADIO STATION

KLAW-FM 39733
Owner: Townsquare Media, LLC
Editorial: 626 SW D Ave, Lawton, Oklahoma 73501 **Tel:** 1 580 581-3600.
Email: lawtonpsa@townsquaremedia.com
Web site: http://www.klaw.com
Profile: KLAW-FM is a commercial station owned by Townsquare Media, LLC. The format of the station is country music. KLAW-FM broadcasts to the Lawton, OK area at 101.3 FM.
FM RADIO STATION

KLAX-FM 43443
Owner: Spanish Broadcasting System
Editorial: 10281 W Pico Blvd, Los Angeles, California 90064-2674 **Tel:** 1 310 229-3200.
Web site: http://www.979laraza.com
Profile: KLAX-FM is a commercial station owned by Spanish Broadcasting System. The format of the station is regional Mexican music. KLAX-FM broadcasts to the Los Angeles area at 97.9 FM.
FM RADIO STATION

KLAY-AM 36184
Owner: Huntington(Clay)
Editorial: 10025 Lakewood Dr SW Ste B, Tacoma, Washington 98499-3878 **Tel:** 1 253 581-0324.
Email: klay1180@blarg.net
Web site: http://www.klay1180.com
Profile: KLAY-AM is a commercial station owned by Clay Huntington. The format of the station is news and talk. KLAY-AM broadcasts to the Tacoma, WA area at 1180 AM.
AM RADIO STATION

KLAZ-FM 44738
Owner: Noalmark Broadcasting Corp.
Editorial: 208 Buena Vista Rd, Hot Springs, Arkansas 71913-8208 **Tel:** 1 501 525-4600.
Email: spots@klaz.com
Web site: http://www.klaz.com
Profile: KLAZ-FM is a commercial station owned by Noalmark Broadcasting Corp. The format of the station is Top 40/CHR. KLAZ-FM broadcasts to the Hot Springs, AR area at 105.9 FM.
FM RADIO STATION

KLBB-AM 36286
Owner: Endurance Broadcasting LLC
Editorial: 104 Main St N, Stillwater, Minnesota 55082-5076 **Tel:** 1 651 439-5006.
Web site: http://www.klbbradio.com
Profile: KLBB-AM is a commercial station owned by Endurance Broadcasting LLC. The format of the station is adult standards music. KLBB-AM broadcasts to the Stillwater, MN area at 1220 AM.
AM RADIO STATION

KLBC-FM 44739
Owner: Mid-Continental Broadcasting, LLC
Editorial: 1418 N 1st Ave, Durant, Oklahoma 74701-2812 **Tel:** 1 580 924-3100.
Web site: http://www.klbcfm.com
Profile: KLBC-FM is a commercial station owned by Mid-Continental Broadcasting, LLC. The format of the station is country music. KLBC-FM broadcasts in the Durant, OK area at 106.3 FM.
FM RADIO STATION

KLBJ-AM 39071
Owner: Emmis Communications Corp.
Editorial: 8309 N Interstate 35, Austin, Texas 78753-5720 **Tel:** 1 512 832-4000.
Email: newsroom@emmisaustin.com
Web site: http://www.newsradioklbj.com
Profile: KLBJ-AM is a commercial station owned by Emmis Communications Corp. The format of the station is news, sports and talk. KLBJ-AM broadcasts to the Austin, TX area at 590 AM.
AM RADIO STATION

KLBJ-FM 46404
Owner: Emmis Communications Corp.
Editorial: 8309 N Interstate 35, Austin, Texas 78753-5720 **Tel:** 1 512 832-4000.
Email: community@klbjfm.com
Web site: http://www.klbjfm.com
Profile: KLBJ-FM is a commercial station owned by Emmis Communications Corp. The format of the station is rock. KLBJ-FM broadcasts to the Austin, TX area at 93.7 FM.
FM RADIO STATION

KLBL-FM 46203
Owner: US Stations, LLC
Editorial: 125 Corporate Ter, Hot Springs, Arkansas 71913-7248 **Tel:** 1 501 525-9700.
Email: info@usstations.com
Web site: http://www.myhotsprings.com/?pid=624708
Profile: KLBL-FM is a commercial station owned by US Stations, LLC. The format of the station is classic country. KLBL-FM broadcasts to the Hot Springs, AR and surrounding areas at 104.5 FM.
FM RADIO STATION

KLBM-AM 38377
Owner: Pacific Empire Communications
Editorial: 2510 Cove Ave, La Grande, Oregon 97850-3911 **Tel:** 1 541 963-4121.
Web site: http://supertalknews.com
Profile: KLBM-AM is a commercial station owned by Pacific Empire Communications. The format of the station is talk. KLBM-AM broadcasts in the La Grande, OR area at 1450 AM and simulcasts on KBKR-AM.
AM RADIO STATION

KLBN-FM 46172
Owner: Lotus Communications Corp.
Editorial: 1110 E Olive Ave, Fresno, California 93728-3535 **Tel:** 1 559 497-1100.
Email: production@lotusfresno.com
Web site: http://www.1019labuena.com
Profile: KLBN-FM is a commercial station owned by Lotus Communications Corp. The format of the station is regional Mexican. KLBN-FM broadcasts to the Fresno, CA area at 101.9 FM.
FM RADIO STATION

KLBQ-FM 44740
Owner: El Dorado Broadcasting
Editorial: 1904 W Hillsboro St, El Dorado, Arkansas 71730-6806 **Tel:** 1 870 863-5121.
Email: klbqfm@yahoo.com
Web site: http://realamericancountry987.com
Profile: KLBQ-FM is a commercial station owned by El Dorado Broadcasting. The format of the station is classic and contemporary country. KLBQ-FM broadcasts to the El Dorado, AR area at 98.7 FM.
FM RADIO STATION

KLBS-AM 39245
Owner: Ethnic Radio of Los Banos
Editorial: 401 Pacheco Blvd, Los Banos, California 93635 **Tel:** 1 209 826-0578.
Email: pr@klbs.com
Web site: http://www.klbs.com
Profile: KLBS-AM is a commercial station owned by Ethnic Radio of Los Banos. The format of the station is Portuguese news, talk, and music. KLBS-AM broadcasts in the Los Banos, CA area at 1330 AM.
AM RADIO STATION

KLBU-FM 155883
Owner: Hutton Broadcasting, LLC
Editorial: 2502 Camino Entrada, Santa Fe, New Mexico 87507-4911 **Tel:** 1 505 471-1067.
Web site: http://www.santafe.com/juan
Profile: KLBU-FM is a commercial station owned by Hutton Broadcasting, LLC. The format of the station is Spanish Adult Hits. KLBU-FM broadcasts to the Santa Fe, NM area at 102.9 FM.
FM RADIO STATION

KLCA-FM 46715
Owner: Americom Broadcasting
Editorial: 961 Matley Ln, Ste 120, Reno, Nevada 89502 **Tel:** 1 775 829-1964.
Web site: http://www.alice965.com
Profile: KLCA-FM is a commercial station owned by Americom Broadcasting. The format of the station is hot adult contemporary. KLCA-FM broadcasts to the Reno, NV area at 96.5 FM.
FM RADIO STATION

KLCB-AM 38472
Owner: Lincoln County Broadcasters Inc.
Editorial: 251 W Cedar St, Libby, Montana 59923-2610 **Tel:** 1 406 293-6234.
Email: klcb@frontiernet.net
Web site: http://klcb-ktny.com
Profile: KLCB-AM is commercial station owned by Lincoln County Broadcasters Inc. The format of the station is contemporary country music. KLCB-AM broadcasts to the Libby, MT area at 1230 AM.
AM RADIO STATION

KLCC-FM 39734
Owner: Lane Community College
Editorial: 136 W 8th Ave, Eugene, Oregon 97401-2940 **Tel:** 1 541 463-6000.
Email: news@klcc.org
Web site: http://www.klcc.org
Profile: KLCC-FM is a non-commercial station owned by Lane Community College. The format of the station is variety. KLCC-FM broadcasts to the Eugene, OR area at 89.7 FM.
FM RADIO STATION

KLCE-FM 46400
Owner: Riverbend Communications LLC
Editorial: 400 W Sunnyside Rd, Idaho Falls, Idaho 83402-4613 **Tel:** 1 208 528-3722.
Web site: http://www.klce.com
Profile: KLCE-FM is a commercial station owned by Riverbend Communications LLC. The format of the station is adult contemporary music. KLCE-FM broadcasts to the Idaho Falls, ID area at 97.3 FM.
FM RADIO STATION

KLCH-FM 324656
Owner: Q Media Group, LLC
Editorial: 474 Guernsey Ln, Red Wing, Minnesota 55066-7448 **Tel:** 1 651 388-7151.
Web site: http://lakehits95.com
Profile: KLCH-FM is a commercial station owned by Q Media Group, LLC. The format of the station is oldies. KLCH-FM broadcasts to the Red Wing, MN area at 94.9 FM.
FM RADIO STATION

KLCI-FM 45478
Owner: Milestone Radio
Editorial: 14443 Armstrong Blvd NW, Anoka, Minnesota 55303-7284 **Tel:** 1 763 450-7777.
Web site: http://www.mybobcountry.com
Profile: KLCI-FM is a commercial station owned by Milestone Radio. The format of the station is classic country music. KLCI-FM broadcasts to the Princeton, MN area at 106.1 FM.
FM RADIO STATION

KLCK-AM 39293
Owner: Haystack Broadcasting, Inc
Editorial: 620 E 3Rd St, The Dalles, Oregon 97058-2506 **Tel:** 1 541 296-9102.
Web site: http://klck1400.com
Profile: KLCK-AM is a commercial station owned by Haystack Broadcasting, Inc. The format of the station s talk. KLCK-AM broadcasts to The Dalles, OR area at 1400 AM.
AM RADIO STATION

KLCL-AM 39263
Owner: Townsquare Media, LLC
Editorial: 900 N Lake Shore Dr, Lake Charles, Louisiana 70601-2120 **Tel:** 1 337 433-1641.
Web site: http://cajunradio.net
Profile: KLCL-AM is a commercial station owned by Townsquare Media, LLC. The format of the station is classic country. KLCL-AM broadcasts to the Lake Charles, LA area at 1470 AM.
AM RADIO STATION

KLCM-FM 44741
Owner: Montana Broadcast Communications Inc.
Editorial: 620 NE Main St, Lewistown, Montana 59457-2021 **Tel:** 1 406 535-3441.
Email: traffic@kxlo-klcm.com
Web site: http://www.kxlo-klcm.com
Profile: KLCM-FM is a commercial station owned by Montana Broadcast Communications Inc. The format of the station is classic and modern rock. KLCM-FM broadcasts to the Lewistown, MT area at 95.9 FM.
FM RADIO STATION

KLCN-AM 37358
Owner: Sudbury Broadcasting Group
Editorial: 125 S 2nd St, Blytheville, Arkansas 72315-3413 **Tel:** 1 870 762-2093.
Profile: KLCN-AM is a commercial station owned by Sudbury Broadcasting Group. The format of the station is news and talk. KLCN-AM broadcasts to the Blytheville, AR area at 910 AM.
AM RADIO STATION

KLCV-FM 43886
Owner: Bott Broadcasting Co.
Editorial: 233 S 13th St Ste 1520, Lincoln, Nebraska 68508-2003 **Tel:** 1 402 465-8850.
Email: klcv@bottradionetwork.com
Web site: http://www.bottradionetwork.com
Profile: KLCV-FM is a commercial station owned by Bott Broadcasting Co. The format of the station is Christian news and talk. KLCV-FM broadcasts to the Lincoln, NE area at 88.5 FM.
FM RADIO STATION

KLCY-FM 44929
Owner: Ashley Communications
Editorial: 2425 N Vernal Ave, Vernal, Utah 84078-9587 **Tel:** 1 435 789-1059.
Web site: http://www.klcy.com
Profile: KLCY-FM is a commercial station owned by Ashley Communications. The format of the station is country. KLCY-FM broadcasts to the Salt Lake City area at 105.9 FM.
FM RADIO STATION

KLCZ-FM 579331
Owner: Lewis & Clark State College
Editorial: 500 8th Ave, Lewiston, Idaho 83501-2691 **Tel:** 1 208 792-2418.
Web site: http://www.klcz.com
Profile: KLCZ-FM is a non-commercial station owned by Lewis & Clark State College. The format of the station is variety. KLCZ-FM broadcasts to the Lewiston, ID area at 88.9 FM.
FM RADIO STATION

KLDC-AM 35004
Owner: Crawford Broadcasting Co.
Editorial: 2821 S Parker Rd Ste 1205, Aurora, Colorado 80014-2708 **Tel:** 1 303 433-5500.
Web site: http://www.1220kldc.com
Profile: KLDC-AM is a commercial station owned by Crawford Broadcasting Co. The format of the station is gospel music. KLDC-AM broadcasts to the Denver area at 1220 AM.
AM RADIO STATION

KLDG-FM 42545
Owner: Seward County Broadcasting Co.
Editorial: 1410 N Western Ave, Liberal, Kansas 67901 **Tel:** 1 620 624-3891.
Web site: http://www.kscb.net
Profile: KLDG-FM is a commercial station owned by Seward County Broadcasting Co. The format of the station is contemporary country music. KLDG-FM broadcasts to the Liberal, KS area at 102.7 FM.
FM RADIO STATION

KLDJ-FM 42224
Owner: Townsquare Media, LLC
Editorial: 14 E Central Entrance, Duluth, Minnesota 55811 **Tel:** 1 218 727-4500.
Web site: http://www.kool1017.com
Profile: KLDJ-FM is a commercial station owned by Townsquare Media, LLC. The format of the station is classic hits. KLDJ-FM broadcasts to the Duluth, MN area at 101.7 FM.
FM RADIO STATION

KLDR-FM 46069
Owner: Grants Pass Broadcasting Corp.
Editorial: 888 Rogue River Hwy, Grants Pass, Oregon 97527-5209 **Tel:** 1 541 474-7292.
Email: kldr@kldr.com
Web site: http://www.kldr.com
Profile: KLDR-FM is a commercial station owned by Grants Pass Broadcasting Corp. The format of the station is hot adult contemporary. KLDR-FM broadcasts to the Grants Pass, OR area at 98.3 FM.
FM RADIO STATION

KLDZ-FM 41806
Owner: Bicoastal Media LLC
Editorial: 3624 Avion Dr, Medford, Oregon 97504 **Tel:** 1 541 772-4170.
Web site: http://www.kool103.net
Profile: KLDZ-FM is a commercial station owned by Bicoastal Media LLC. The format of the station is oldies. KLDZ-FM broadcasts to the Medford, OR area at 103.5 FM.
FM RADIO STATION

KLEA-AM 37359
Owner: Lea County Broadcasting
Editorial: Country Club Road, Lovington, New Mexico 88260 **Tel:** 1 575 396-2244.
Profile: KLEA-AM is a commercial station owned by Lea County Broadcasting. The format of the station is classic country. KLEA-AM broadcasts to the Lovington, NM area at 630 AM.
AM RADIO STATION

KLEA-FM 44742
Owner: Lea County Broadcasting
Editorial: 1 Country Club Road, Lovington, New Mexico 88260-0877 **Tel:** 1 575 396-2244.
Web site: http://www.oldies1017.com
Profile: KLEA-FM is a commercial station owned by Lea County Broadcasting. The format of the station is oldies music. KLEA-AM broadcasts to the Albuquerque, NM area at 101.7 FM.
FM RADIO STATION

KLEB-AM 39501
Owner: Coastal Broadcasting of Larose Inc.
Editorial: 11603 Highway 308, Larose, Louisiana 70373 **Tel:** 1 985 798-7792.
Email: klrz@viscom.net
Web site: http://www.klrzfm.com
Profile: KLEB-AM is a commercial station owned by Coastal Broadcasting of Larose Inc. The format of the station is oldies music. KLEB-AM broadcasts to the New Orleans area at 1600 AM.
AM RADIO STATION

KLEE-AM 37360
Owner: O-Town Communications, Inc.
Editorial: 416 E Main St, Ottumwa, Iowa 52501-3026 **Tel:** 1 641 684-5563.
Email: info@ottumwaradio.com
Web site: http://www.1480KLEE.com
Profile: KLEE-AM is a commercial station owned by O-Town Communications, Inc. The format for the station is oldies. KLEE-AM broadcasts to the Ottumwa, IA area at 1480 AM.
AM RADIO STATION

KLEF-FM 41597
Owner: Chinook Concert Broadcasters Inc.
Editorial: 4700 Business Park Blvd, Anchorage, Alaska 99503-7176 **Tel:** 1 907 522-1018.
Email: klef@klef.com
Web site: http://www.klef.com
Profile: KLEF-FM is a commercial station owned by Chinook Concert Broadcasters Inc. The format of the station is classical. KLEF-FM broadcasts to the Anchorage, AK area at 98.1 FM.
FM RADIO STATION

KLEM-AM 38876
Owner: Powell Broadcasting Co.
Editorial: 37 2nd Ave NW, Le Mars, Iowa 51031-3529 **Tel:** 1 712 546-4121.
Email: klemnews@powellbroadcasting.com
Web site: http://www.klem1410.com
Profile: KLEM-AM is a commercial station owned by Powell Broadcasting Co. The format of the station is adult contemporary music. KLEM-AM broadcasts in the Sioux City, IA area at 1410 AM.
AM RADIO STATION

KLEN-FM 39737
Owner: Townsquare Media, LLC
Editorial: 1912 Capitol Ave Ste 300, Cheyenne, Wyoming 82001-3659 **Tel:** 1 307 632-4400.
Web site: http://www.1063cowboycountry.com
Profile: KLEN-FM is a commercial station owned by Townsquare Media, LLC. The format for the station is contemporary country. KLEN-FM broadcasts to the Cheyenne, WY area at 106.3 FM.
FM RADIO STATION

KLEO-FM 42317
Owner: Pacific Media Group
Editorial: 75-5852 Alii Dr Ste B1, Lagoon Tower, Kailua Kona, Hawaii 96740-1310 **Tel:** 1 808 961-0651.
Web site: http://www.kbigfm.com
Profile: KLEO-FM is a commercial station owned by Pacific Media Group. The format of the station is adult contemporary music. KLEO-FM broadcasts to the Hilo, HI area at 106.1 FM.
FM RADIO STATION

KLER-AM 37361
Owner: Central Idaho Broadcasting
Editorial: 981 Upper Fords Creek Rd, Orofino, Idaho 83544-6217 **Tel:** 1 208 476-5702.
Email: klerproduction@kler-radio.com
Profile: KLER-AM is a commercial station owned by Central Idaho Broadcasting. The format of the station is contemporary country music. KLER-AM broadcasts to the Spokane, WA area at 1300 AM.
AM RADIO STATION

KLER-FM 44743
Owner: Central Idaho Broadcasting
Editorial: 981 Upper Fords Creek Rd, Orofino, Idaho 83544-6217 **Tel:** 1 208 476-5702.
Email: klerproduction@koze.com
Profile: KLER-FM is a commercial station owned by Central Idaho Broadcasting. The format of the station is adult contemporary music. KLER-FM broadcasts to the Orofino, ID, area at 95.1 FM.
FM RADIO STATION

KLES-FM 39519
Owner: Casa Media Partners, LLC
Editorial: 152101 W County Road 12, Prosser, Washington 99350-7265 **Tel:** 1 509 786-1310.
Profile: KLES-FM is a commercial station owned by Casa Media Partners, LLC. The format of the station is regional Mexican. KLES-FM broadcasts to the Prosser, WA area at 101.7 FM.
FM RADIO STATION

KLEX-AM 39493
Owner: Bott Broadcasting Co.
Editorial: 111 W Main St, Richmond, Missouri 64085 **Tel:** 1 816 470-9925.
Email: kayx@bottradionetwork.com
Web site: http://www.bottradionetwork.com
AM RADIO STATION

KLEY-AM 38320
Owner: Johnson Enterprises Inc.
Editorial: 338 S Kley Dr, Wellington, Kansas 67152 **Tel:** 1 620 326-3341.
Email: kley@sutv.com
Web site: http://www.kleyam.com
Profile: KLEY-AM is a commercial station owned by Johnson Enterprises Inc. The format of the station is sports. KLEY-AM broadcasts to the Wellington, KS area at 1130 AM.
AM RADIO STATION

KLEY-FM 63999
Owner: Alpha Media
Editorial: 4050 Eisenhauer Rd, San Antonio, Texas 78218-3409 **Tel:** 1 210 654-5100.
Web site: http://www.vidasanantonio.com
Profile: KLEY-FM is a commercial station owned by Alpha Media. The format of the station is regional Mexican. KLEY-FM broadcasts to the San Antonio area at 95.7 FM.
FM RADIO STATION

KLEZ-FM 821274
Owner: Pueblo Broadcasting Group, LLC
Editorial: 516 Main St, Walsenburg, Colorado 81089-2036 **Tel:** 1 877 842-6336.
Email: production@socoradio.com
Web site: http://power1033.com
Profile: KLEZ-FM is a commercial station owned by Pueblo Broadcasting Group, LLC and operated by SOCO Radio. The format of the station is Top 40/ CHR. KLEZ-FM broadcasts to the Pueblo County, Colorado area at a frequency of 103.3 FM.
FM RADIO STATION

KLFC-FM 61932
Owner: Mountaintop Broadcasting Inc.
Editorial: 205 W Atlantic St, Branson, Missouri 65616 **Tel:** 1 417 334-5532.
Email: 881fm@klfcradio.com
Web site: http://www.klfcradio.com
Profile: KLFC-FM is a non-commercial station owned by Mountaintop Broadcasting Inc. The format of the station is contemporary Christian. KLFC-FM broadcasts to the Branson, MO area at 88.1 FM.
FM RADIO STATION

KLFD-AM 36437
Owner: Mid-Minnesota Media LLC
Editorial: 234 N Sibley Ave, Litchfield, Minnesota 55355 **Tel:** 1 320 693-3281.
Email: news@klfd1410.com
Web site: http://www.klfd1410.com
Profile: KLFD-AM is a commercial station owned by Mid-Minnesota Media LLC. The format of the station is variety. KLDF-AM broadcasts to the Litchfield, MN area at 1410 AM.
AM RADIO STATION

KLFE-AM 36436
Owner: Salem Media Group, Inc.
Editorial: 2201 6th Ave Ste 1500, Seattle, Washington 98121-1840 **Tel:** 1 206 443-8200.
Web site: http://am1590theanswer.com
Profile: KLFE-AM is a commercial station owned by Salem Media Group, Inc. The format of the station is talk. KLFE-AM broadcasts to the Seattle area at 1590 AM.
AM RADIO STATION

KLFF-FM 42865
Owner: Logos Broadcasting Corp.
Editorial: 560 Higuera St Ste G, San Luis Obispo, California 93401-3850 **Tel:** 1 805 541-4343.
Web site: http://life893.com
Profile: KLFF-FM is a non-commercial station owned by Logos Broadcasting Corp. The format of the station is contemporary Christian. KLFF-FM broadcasts to the San Luis Obispo, CA area at 89.3 FM.
FM RADIO STATION

KLFM-FM 43053
Owner: Cherry Creek Radio
Editorial: 914 13th Ave S, Great Falls, Montana 59405-4406 **Tel:** 1 406 761-7600.
Email: kmon560@cherrycreekradio.com
Profile: KLFM-FM is a commercial station owned by Cherry Creek Radio. The format of the station is classic hits. KLFM-FM broadcasts to the Great Falls, MT at 92.9 FM.
FM RADIO STATION

KLFX-FM 42670
Owner: iHeartMedia Inc.
Editorial: 100 W Central Texas Expy Ste 306, Harker Heights, Texas 76548-2080 **Tel:** 1 254 699-5000.
Web site: http://www.1073rocks.com
Profile: KLFX-FM is a commercial station that is owned by iHeartMedia Inc. The station's format is rock music. KLFX-FM broadcasts to the Waco, TX area at 107.3 FM.
FM RADIO STATION

KLGA-FM 46088
Owner: NRG Media LLC
Editorial: 2102 80th Ave, Algona, Iowa 50511-7134 **Tel:** 1 515 295-2475.
Web site: http://www.algonaradio.com
Profile: KLGA-FM is a commercial station owned by NRG Media LLC. The format of the station is adult contemporary. KLGA-FM broadcasts to the Algona, IA area at 92.7 FM.
FM RADIO STATION

KLGD-FM 46680
Owner: Vance Communications, LLC
Editorial: 209 S Danville Dr, Abilene, Texas 79605-1464 **Tel:** 1 325 437-5590.
Web site: http://klgd.fm/
Profile: KLGD-FM is a commercial station owned byVance Communications, LLC. The format of the station is classic country music. KLGD-FM broadcasts to the Abilene, TX area at 106.9 FM.
FM RADIO STATION

KLGL-FM 852075
Owner: Mid-Utah Radio Inc.
Editorial: 1600 W 500 N, Manti, Utah 84642-5503 **Tel:** 1 435 835-7301.
Web site: http://midutahradio.com/klgl
Profile: KLGL-FM is a commercial station owned by Mid-Utah Radio Inc. The format of the station is classic hits. KLGL-FM broadcasts to the Salina, UT area at a frequency of 94.5 FM.
FM RADIO STATION

KLGN-AM 37196
Owner: Cache Valley Radio Inc.
Editorial: 810 W 200 N, Logan, Utah 84321-3726 **Tel:** 1 435 752-1390.
Web site: http://www.1390klgn.com
Profile: KLGN-AM is a commercial station owned by Cache Valley Radio Inc. The format of the station is soft AC. KLGN-AM broadcasts to the Salt Lake City area at 1390 AM.
AM RADIO STATION

KLGO-AM 35087
Owner: Genuine Austin Radio
Editorial: 912 S Capital of Texas Hwy Ste 400, West Lake Hills, Texas 78746-6176 **Tel:** 1 512 416-1100.
Web site: http://hornfm.com/
Profile: KLGO-AM is a commercial station owned by Genuine Austin Radio. The format of the station is sports. KLGO-AM broadcasts to the Austin, TX area at 1260 AM. The tagline is "The Horn 104.9 FM/1260 AM."
AM RADIO STATION

KLGR-AM 37362
Owner: Alpha Media
Editorial: 639 W Bridge St, Redwood Falls, Minnesota 56283-1503 **Tel:** 1 507 637-2989.
Email: klgr@alphamediausa.com
Web site: http://www.myklgr.com
Profile: KLGR-AM is a commercial station owned by Alpha Media. The format of the station is classic country. KLGR-AM broadcasts to the Redwood Falls, MN area at 1490 AM.
AM RADIO STATION

KLGR-FM 44744
Owner: Alpha Media
Editorial: 639 W Bridge St, Redwood Falls, Minnesota 56283-1503 **Tel:** 1 507 637-2989.
Email: klgr@alphamediausa.com
Web site: http://www.myklgr.com
Profile: KLGR-FM is a commercial station owned by Alpha Media. The format of the station is adult contemporary. KLGR-FM broadcasts to the Redwood Falls, MN area at 97.7 FM.
FM RADIO STATION

KLGT-FM 46813
Owner: Legend Communications
Editorial: 324 Coffeen Ave, Sheridan, Wyoming 82801-4809 **Tel:** 1 307 672-2690.
Email: klgt@vcn.com
Web site: http://www.bighornmountainradio.com
Profile: KLGT-FM is a commercial station owned by Legend Communications. The format of the station is hot country. KLGT-FM broadcasts to the Buffalo, WY area at 92.9 FM.
FM RADIO STATION

KLGZ-AM 38746
Owner: NRG Media LLC
Editorial: 2102 80th Ave, Algona, Iowa 50511-7134
Tel: 1 515 295-2475.
Web site: http://algonaradio.com
Profile: KLGZ-AM is a commercial station owned by NRG Media LLC . The format for the station is Contemporary music. KLGZ-AM broadcasts to the Algona, IA area at 1600 AM.
AM RADIO STATION

KLHB-FM 39694
Owner: Tejas Broadcasting
Editorial: 1733 S Brownlee Blvd, Corpus Christi, Texas 78404-3018 **Tel:** 1 361 883-1600.
Web site: http://1055espn.com
Profile: KLHB-FM is a commercial station owned by Tejas Broadcasting. The format of the station is sports. KMJR-FM broadcasts in the Corpus Christi, TX area at 105.5 FM.
FM RADIO STATION

KLHI-FM 42985
Owner: Pacific Media Group
Editorial: 311 Ano St, Kahului, Hawaii 96732-1304
Tel: 1 808 877-5566.
Email: studio@native925.com
Web site: http://www.native925.com
Profile: KLHI-FM is a commercial station owned by Pacific Media Group. The format of the station is contemporary island hits. KLHI-FM broadcasts to the Honolulu area at 92.5 FM.
FM RADIO STATION

KLHT-AM 34996
Owner: Calvary Chapel Honolulu
Editorial: 98-1016 Komo Mai Dr, Aiea, Hawaii 96701-1927 **Tel:** 1 808 524-1040.
Email: klhtradio@gmail.com
Web site: http://www.calvarychapel.org/honolulu/
AM RADIO STATION

KLID-AM 34997
Owner: Browning Skidmore Broadcasting Inc.
Editorial: 43 Ripple Ln, Poplar Bluff, Missouri 63901-7057 **Tel:** 1 573 714-1871.
Web site: http://www.klidsports.com
Profile: KLID-AM is a commercial station owned by Browning Skidmore Broadcasting Inc. The format of the station is Sports. KLID-AM broadcasts to the Poplar Bluff, MO area at 1340 AM. Dexter MO and Corning AR area at 1340 AM.—— our format is News talk with local, regional and national sports. We are in a mostly republican area and a high church area
AM RADIO STATION

KLIF-AM 39064
Owner: Cumulus Media Inc.
Editorial: 3090 Olive Street West Victory Plaza, Suite 400, Dallas, Texas 75219 **Tel:** 1 214 526-2400.
Web site: http://www.klif.com
Profile: KLIF-AM is a commercial station owned by Cumulus Media Inc. The format of the station is talk programming. KLIF-AM broadcasts to the Dallas area at 570 AM.
AM RADIO STATION

KLIF-FM 43072
Owner: Cumulus Media Inc.
Editorial: 3090 Olive St Ste 400, Dallas, Texas 75219-7640 **Tel:** 1 214 526-7400.
Web site: http://www.hot933hits.com
Profile: KLIF-FM is a commercial station owned by Cumulus Media Inc. The format of the station is Top 40/CHR. KLIF-FM broadcasts to the Dallas area at 93.3 FM.
FM RADIO STATION

KLIK-AM 36772
Owner: Cumulus Media Inc.
Editorial: 1002 Diamond Rdg Ste 400, Jefferson City, Missouri 65109-7902 **Tel:** 1 573 893-5100.
Web site: http://www.klik1240.com
Profile: KLIK-AM is a commercial station owned by Cumulus Media Inc. The format of the station is news and talk. KLIK-AM broadcasts in the Jefferson City, MO area at 1240 AM.
AM RADIO STATION

KLIL-FM 41115
Owner: Cajun Broadcasting
Editorial: 10365 Hwy 1, Moreauville, Louisiana 71355
Tel: 1 318 985-2929.
Email: klil@kricket.net
Profile: KLIL-FM is a commercial station owned by Cajun Broadcasting. The format of the station is oldies music. KLIL-FM broadcasts to the Moreauville, LA, area at 92.1 FM.
FM RADIO STATION

KLIN-AM 38554
Owner: NRG Media LLC
Editorial: 4343 O St, Lincoln, Nebraska 68510-1753
Tel: 1 402 475-4567.
Email: news@klin.com
Web site: http://www.klin.com
Profile: KLIN-AM is a commercial station owned by NRG Media LLC. The format of the station is news, sports and talk. KLIN-AM broadcasts to the Lincoln, NE area at 1400 AM.
AM RADIO STATION

KLIO-AM 37271
Owner: E.W. Scripps Co.
Editorial: 4200 N Old Lawrence Rd, Wichita, Kansas 67219-3211 **Tel:** 1 316 838-9141.
Web site: http://www.classiccountry923.com
Profile: KLIO-AM is a commercial station owned by the E.W. Scripps Co. The format of the station is classic country. KLIO-AM broadcasts to the Wichita, KS area at 1070 AM.
AM RADIO STATION

KLIP-FM 42541
Owner: Holladay Broadcasting Co.
Editorial: 1109 Hudson Ln, Monroe, Louisiana 71201-6003 **Tel:** 1 318 388-2323.
Email: la105monroeradio@gmail.com
Web site: http://www.la105.com
Profile: KLIP-FM is a commercial station owned by Holladay Broadcasting Co. The format of the station is classic hits music. KLIP-FM broadcasts in the Monroe, LA area at 105.3 FM.
FM RADIO STATION

KLIQ-FM 74565
Owner: Platte River Radio, Inc.
Editorial: 500 E J St, Hastings, Nebraska 68901
Tel: 1 402 463-1230.
Email: thebreeze@kliqfm.com
Web site: http://www.kliqfm.com
Profile: KLIQ-FM is a commercial station owned by Platte River Radio, Inc. The format of the station is Lite Rock/Lite AC music. KLIQ-FM broadcasts to the Hastings, NE area at 94.5 FM.
FM RADIO STATION

KLIR-FM 46302
Owner: Alpha Media
Editorial: 1418 25th St, Columbus, Nebraska 68601-2820 **Tel:** 1 402 564-2866.
Email: colproduction@digity.me
Web site: http://www.mycentralnebraska.com
Profile: KLIR-FM is a commercial station owned by Alpha Media. The format of the station is adult contemporary. KLIR-FM broadcasts to the Columbus, Nebraska area at 101.1 FM.
FM RADIO STATION

KLIT-FM 153378
Owner: Nueva Cadena Radio Luz Inc. (La)
Editorial: 2702 Pine St, Laredo, Texas 78046-6225
Tel: 1 956 726-4738.
Profile: KLIT-FM is a commercial station owned by La Nueva Cadena Radio Luz Inc. The format of the station is Hispanic contemporary Christian. The station airs in the Laredo, TX area at 93.3 FM.
FM RADIO STATION

KLIV-AM 39089
Owner: Empire Broadcasting Systems Corp.
Editorial: 750 Story Rd, San Jose, California 95122-2604 **Tel:** 1 408 293-8030.
Email: news@kliv.com
Web site: http://www.kliv.com
Profile: KLIV-AM is a commercial station owned by Empire Broadcasting Systems Corp. The format of the station is country music. KLIV-AM broadcasts to the San Jose, CA area at 1590 AM.
AM RADIO STATION

KLIX-AM 37363
Owner: Townsquare Media, LLC
Editorial: 415 Park Ave, Twin Falls, Idaho 83301-7752
Tel: 1 208 733-7512.
Email: topstory@townsquaremedia.com
Web site: http://www.newsradio1310.com
Profile: KLIX-AM is a commercial station owned by Townsquare Media, LLC. The format of the station is news and talk. KLIX-AM broadcasts to the Twin Falls, ID area at 1310 AM.
AM RADIO STATION

KLIX-FM 44745
Owner: Townsquare Media, LLC
Editorial: 415 Park Ave, Twin Falls, Idaho 83301-7752
Tel: 1 208 733-7512.
Web site: http://www.kool965.com
Profile: KLIX-FM is a commercial station owned by Townsquare Media, LLC. The format of the station is oldies. KLIX-FM broadcasts to the Twin Falls, ID area at 96.5 FM.
FM RADIO STATION

KLIZ-AM 37364
Owner: Hubbard Broadcasting Inc.
Editorial: 13225 Dogwood Dr, Baxter, Minnesota 56425-8669 **Tel:** 1 218 828-1244.
Email: production@brainerd.net
Web site: http://www.kliz.com
Profile: KLIZ-AM is a commercial station owned by Hubbard Broadcasting Inc. The format of the station is sports talk. KLIZ-AM broadcasts in the Minneapolis area at 1380 AM.
AM RADIO STATION

KLIZ-FM 44746
Owner: Hubbard Broadcasting Inc.
Editorial: 13225 Dogwood Dr, Baxter, Minnesota 56425-8669 **Tel:** 1 218 828-1244.
Email: kliz_1075@hotmail.com
Web site: http://www.theloon.com
Profile: KLIZ-FM is a commercial station owned by Hubbard Broadcasting Inc. The format of the station is classic rock. KLIZ-FM broadcasts in the Brainerd, MN area at 107.5 FM.
FM RADIO STATION

KLJA-FM 41846
Owner: Univision Communications Inc.
Editorial: 10801-2 N Mopac Expy, Austin, Texas 78759-5973 **Tel:** 1 512 381-1077.
Web site: http://www.univision.com/content/channel.jhtml?chid=10032&schid=10045
Profile: KLJA-FM is a commercial station owned by Univision Communications Inc. The format of the station is regional Mexican. KLJA-FM broadcasts to the Austin, TX area at 107.7 FM.
FM RADIO STATION

KLJR-FM 40963
Owner: Lazer Broadcasting Corp.
Editorial: 200 S A St Ste 400, Oxnard, California 93030-5723 **Tel:** 1 805 240-2070.
Email: lazerbroadcasting@radiolazer.com
Web site: http://www.radiolazer.com
Profile: KLJR-FM is a commercial station owned by Lazer Broacasting Corp. The format of the station is Spanish adult hits. KLJR-FM broadcasts to the Santa Barbara, CA area at 96.7 FM.
FM RADIO STATION

KLJT-FM 42435
Owner: Waller Broadcasting
Editorial: 3400 W Marshall Ave Ste 307, Longview, Texas 75604-5048 **Tel:** 1 903 663-2477.
Email: jjo@mybreezefm.com
Web site: http://www.mybreezefm.com
Profile: KLJT-FM is a commercial station owned by Waller Broadcasting. The format of the station is hot adult contemporary. KLJT-FM broadcasts to the Jacksonville, TX area at 102.3 FM.
FM RADIO STATION

KLJY-FM 46038
Owner: Gateway Creative Broadcasting, Inc
Editorial: 13358 Manchester Rd Ste 100, Des Peres, Missouri 63131-1730 **Tel:** 1 314 909-8569.
Web site: http://joyfmonline.org
Profile: KLJY-FM is a non-commercial station owned by Gateway Creative Broadcasting, Inc. The format of the station is Contemporary Christian and talk. The station airs locally on 99.1 FM.
FM RADIO STATION

KLJZ-FM 44712
Owner: MonsterMedia LLC
Editorial: 949 S Avenue B, Yuma, Arizona 85364-3440
Tel: 1 928 782-4321.
Email: todaysbestmusic@z93yuma.com
Web site: http://www.z93yuma.com
Profile: KLJZ-FM is a commercial station owned by MonsterMedia LLC. The format of the station is hot adult contemporary music. KLJZ-FM broadcasts in the Yuma, AZ area at 93.1 FM.
FM RADIO STATION

KLKC-AM 37365
Owner: Southeast Kansas Independent Living (SKIL)
Editorial: 1812 Main St, Parsons, Kansas 67357-3366
Tel: 1 620 421-6400.
Web site: http://www.sekinfo.com
Profile: KLKC-AM is a commercial station owned by Southeast Kansas Independent Living (SKIL). The format of the station is talk and sports. KLKC-AM broadcasts to the Parsons, KS area at 1540 AM.
AM RADIO STATION

KLKC-FM 44747
Owner: Southeast Kansas Independent Living (SKIL)
Editorial: 1812 Main St, Parsons, Kansas 67357-3366
Tel: 1 620 421-6400.
Web site: http://www.sekinfo.com
Profile: KLKC-FM is a commercial station owned by Southeast Kansas Independent Living (SKIL). The format of the station is adult hits. KLKC-FM broadcasts to the Parsons, KS area at 93.5 FM.
FM RADIO STATION

KLKK-FM 40066
Owner: Coloff Media
Editorial: 201 N Federal Ave, Mason City, Iowa 50401-3209 **Tel:** 1 641 421-7744.
Email: fox@klkkfm.com
Web site: http://www.klkkfm.com
Profile: KLKK-FM is a commercial station owned by Coloff Media. The format of the station is classic rock. KLKK-FM broadcasts to the Mason City, IA, area at 103.7 FM.
FM RADIO STATION

KLKL-FM 40932
Owner: Access.1 Communications Corp.
Editorial: 208 N Thomas Dr, Shreveport, Louisiana 71107-6520 **Tel:** 1 318 222-3122.
Web site: http://www.klkl.fm
Profile: KLKL-FM is a commercial station owned by the Access.1 Communications Corp. The format of the station is oldies. KLKL-FM broadcasts to the Shreveport, LA area at 95.7 FM.
FM RADIO STATION

KLKO-FM 44748
Owner: Elko Broadcasting Company
Editorial: 1800 Idaho St, Elko, Nevada 89801-4031
Tel: 1 775 738-1240.
Email: traffic@elkoradio.com
Web site: http://www.elkoradio.com
Profile: KLKO-FM is a commercial station owned by Elko Broadcasting Company. The format of the station is adult hits. KLKO-FM broadcasts to the Salt Lake City area at 93.7 FM.
FM RADIO STATION

KLKS-FM 411500
Owner: Red Rock Radio Corp.
Editorial: 305 W Washington St, Brainerd, Minnesota 56401-2923 **Tel:** 1 218 828-9994.
Email: kkinradio@embarqmail.com
Web site: http://www.kkinradio.com/klks.html
Profile: KLKSJ-FM is a non-commercial station owned by Red Rock Radio Corp. The format of the station is classic hits. KLKS-FM broadcasts to the Brainerd Lakes, MN area at 100.1 FM.
FM RADIO STATION

KLKY-FM 874827
Owner: Jacobs Radio Programming, LLC
Editorial: 2617 W Falls Ave, Kennewick, Washington 99336-3002 **Tel:** 1 509 302-9874.
Web site: http://www.urockfm.com
Profile: KLKY-FM is a commercial station owned by Jacobs Radio Programming, LLC. The format of the station is classic rock. The station airs locally at 96.1 FM.
FM RADIO STATION

KLLA-AM 37366
Owner: Pene Broadcasting Inc.
Editorial: 101 Lees Ln, Leesville, Louisiana 71446
Tel: 1 337 239-3403.
Email: swapshop@kjae935.com
Web site: http://www.kjae935.com
Profile: KLLA-AM is a commercial station owned by Pene Broadcasting Co. Inc. The format of the station is oldies. KLLA-AM broadcasts to the Leesville, LA area at 1570 AM.
AM RADIO STATION

KLLB-AM 35139
Owner: United Security Financial Inc.
Editorial: 1510 S Richards St, Salt Lake City, Utah 84115-5350 **Tel:** 1 801 487-0247.
Email: kllbam@yahoo.com
Profile: KLLB-AM is a commercial station owned by United Security Financial Inc. The format of the station is gospel music. KLLB-AM broadcasts in the Salt Lake City area.
AM RADIO STATION

KLLC-FM 42792
Owner: CBS Radio
Editorial: 865 Battery St Fl 3, San Francisco, California 94111-1503 **Tel:** 1 415 765-4097.
Email: studio@radioalice.com
Web site: http://radioalice.cbslocal.com
Profile: KLLC-FM is a commercial station owned by CBS Radio. The format of the station is hot adult contemporary music. KLLC-FM broadcasts to the San Francisco area at 97.3 FM.
FM RADIO STATION

KLLE-FM 41719
Owner: Univision Communications Inc.
Editorial: 601 W Univision Plz, Fresno, California 93704-1092 **Tel:** 1 559 430-8500.
Web site: http://www.univision.com/fresno/klle
Profile: KLLE-FM is a commercial station owned by Univision Communications Inc. The format of the station is Regional Mexican. KLLE-FM broadcasts to the Fresno, CA market at 107.9 FM.
FM RADIO STATION

KLLK-AM 38806
Owner: Bicoastal Media LLC
Editorial: 140 N Main St, Lakeport, California 95453-4815 **Tel:** 1 707 263-6113.
Email: ukiah@bicoastalspots.com
Profile: KLLK-AM is a commercial station owned by Bicoastal Media LLC. The format for the station is Hispanic music. KLLK-AM broadcasts to the San Francisco area at 1250 AM.
AM RADIO STATION

KLLL-FM 43890
Owner: Alpha Media
Editorial: 33 Briercroft Office Park, Lubbock, Texas 79412-3020 **Tel:** 1 806 762-3000.
Email: info@klll.com
Web site: http://www.klll.com
Profile: KLLL-FM is a commercial station owned by Alpha Media. The format of the station is contemporary country. KLLL-FM broadcasts to the Lubbock, TX area at 96.3 FM.
FM RADIO STATION

KLLP-FM 42452
Owner: Rich Broadcasting, LLC
Editorial: 1406 Commerce Way, Idaho Falls, Idaho 83401-1233 **Tel:** 1 208 233-1133.
Web site: http://www.star985.com
Profile: KLLP-FM is a commercial station owned by Rich Broadcasting, LLC. The format of the station is hot adult contemporary. KLLP-FM broadcasts to the Pocatello, ID area at 98.5 FM.
FM RADIO STATION

KLLY-FM 45926
Owner: Alpha Media
Editorial: 3651 Pegasus Dr Ste 107, Bakersfield, California 93308-6836 **Tel:** 1 661 393-1900.
Web site: http://www.energy953.com
Profile: KLLY-FM is a commercial station owned by Alpha Media. The format of the station is Top 40/CHR. KLLY-FM broadcasts to the Bakersfield, CA area at 95.3 FM.
FM RADIO STATION

KLLZ-FM 86767
Owner: Hubbard Broadcasting Inc.
Editorial: 502 Beltrami Ave NW, Bemidji, Minnesota 56601-3010 **Tel:** 1 218 444-1500.
Email: news@pbbroadcasting.com
Web site: http://www.z99fm.com
Profile: KLLZ-FM is a commercial station owned by Hubbard Broadcasting Inc. The format of the station is classic rock music. KLLZ-FM broadcasts to Bemidji, MN at 99.1 FM.
FM RADIO STATION

KLMA-FM
42245

Owner: Ojeda Broadcasting Inc.
Editorial: 108 S Willow St, Hobbs, New Mexico 88240-6733 **Tel:** 1 575 391-9650.
Email: klmafm@yahoo.com
Web site: http://www.klmaradio.com
Profile: KLMA-FM is a commercial station owned by Ojeda Broadcasting Inc. The format of the station is regional Mexican music. KLMA-FM broadcasts in the Hobbs, NM area at 96.5 FM.
FM RADIO STATION

KLMG-FM
44973

Owner: Lazer Broadcasting
Editorial: 500 Media Pl, Sacramento, California 95815-3733 **Tel:** 1 916 368-6300.
Web site: http://www.latino979.com
Profile: KLMG-FM is a commercial station owned by Lazer Broadcasting. The format of the station is Bilingual Top 40/CHR. KLMG-FM broadcasts to the Jackson, CA area at 97.9 FM.
FM RADIO STATION

KLMJ-FM
40022

Owner: CD Broadcasting Inc.
Editorial: 1509 4th St NE, Hampton, Iowa 50441-1106 **Tel:** 1 641 456-5656.
Email: radio@radioonthego.com
Web site: http://www.klmj.com
Profile: KLMJ-FM is a commercial station owned by CD Broadcasting Inc. The format of the station is a blend of country and farm news. KLMJ-FM broadcasts to the Hampton, IA area at 104.9 FM.
FM RADIO STATION

KLMM-FM
43510

Owner: Lazer Broadcasting Corp.
Editorial: 312 E Mill St, #302, Santa Maria, California 93454 **Tel:** 1 805 928-9796.
Email: lazerbroadcasting@radiolazer.com
Web site: http://www.radiolazer.com
Profile: KLMM-FM is a commercial station owned by Lazer Broadcasting Corp. The format of the station is Regional Mexican. KLMM-FM broadcasts to the Santa Maria/Lompoc, CA area at a frequency of 94.1 FM.
FM RADIO STATION

KLMP-FM
40010

Owner: Bethesda Christian Broadcasting
Editorial: 1853 Fountain Plaza Dr, Rapid City, South Dakota 57702 **Tel:** 1 605 342-6822.
Email: klmp@klmp.com
Web site: http://www.klmp.com
Profile: KLMP-FM is a non-commercial station owned by Bethesda Christian Broadcasting. The format of the station is religious music and talk. KLMP-FM broadcasts to the Rapid City, SD area on 88.3 FM.
FM RADIO STATION

KLMR-AM
37368

Owner: Cherry Creek Radio
Editorial: 7350 US Highway 50, Lamar, Colorado 81052-9563 **Tel:** 1 719 336-2206.
Web site: http://www.myhometeamsports.com/KLMR.html
Profile: KLMR-AM is a commercial station owned by Cherry Creek Radio. The format of the station is classic country. KLMR-AM broadcasts to the Lamar, CO area at 920 AM.
AM RADIO STATION

KLMR-FM
44889

Owner: Cherry Creek Radio
Editorial: 7350 US Highway 50, Lamar, Colorado 81052-9563 **Tel:** 1 719 336-2206.
Web site: http://www.myhometeamsports.com/KLMR.html
Profile: KLMR-FM is a commercial station owned by Cherry Creek Radio. The format of the station is classic hits. KLMR-FM broadcasts to the Lamar, CO area at 93.5 FM.
FM RADIO STATION

KLMS-AM
39171

Owner: Alpha Media
Editorial: 3800 Cornhusker Hwy, Lincoln, Nebraska 68504-1533 **Tel:** 1 402 466-1234.
Web site: http://www.espn1480.com
Profile: KLMS-AM is a commercial station owned by Alpha Media. The format of the station is sports. KLMS-AM broadcasts to the Lincoln, NE area at 1480 AM.
AM RADIO STATION

KLMX-AM
35000

Owner: Jim and Melva McCollum
Tel: 1 575 374-2555.
Web site: http://klmx.us
Profile: KLMX-AM is a commercial station owned by Jim and Melva McCollum. The format of the station is classic country. KLMX-AM broadcasts to the Clayton, NM area at 1450 AM.
AM RADIO STATION

KLMY-FM
88317

Owner: Ohana Media Group
Editorial: 285 SW Main Ct, Warrenton, Oregon 97146-9456 **Tel:** 1 503 861-6620.
Web site: http://www.ilovemy997.com
Profile: KLMY-FM is a commercial station owned by Ohana Media Group. The format of the station is Hot AC. KLMY-FM broadcasts to the Astoria, OR area at 99.7 FM.
FM RADIO STATION

KLNC-FM
42627

Owner: NRG Media LLC
Editorial: 4343 O St, Lincoln, Nebraska 68510-1753 **Tel:** 1 402 475-4567.
Email: comments@1053wow.com
Web site: http://www.1053wow.com
Profile: KLNC-FM is a commercial station owned by NRG Media LLC. The format of the station is classic hits. KLNC-FM broadcasts to the Lincoln, NE area at 105.3 FM.
FM RADIO STATION

KLNG-AM
35001

Owner: Wilkins Communication Networks Inc.
Editorial: 120 S 35th St, Ste 2, Council Bluffs, Iowa 51501 **Tel:** 1 712 323-0100.
Email: klng@wilkinsradio.com
Web site: http://www.wilkinsradio.com
Profile: KLNG-AM is a commercial station owned by Wilkins Communication Networks Inc. The format of the station is Christian talk. KLNG-AM broadcasts to the Omaha, NE area at 1560 AM.
AM RADIO STATION

KLNO-FM
62257

Owner: Univision Communications Inc.
Editorial: 7700 John W Carpenter Fwy Fl 1, Dallas, Texas 75247-4829
Web site: http://www.univision.com/musica
Profile: KLNO-FM is a commercial station owned by Univision Communications Inc. The format of the station is regional Mexican. KLNO-FM broadcasts to the Dallas area at 94.1 FM.
FM RADIO STATION

KLNR-FM
586714

Owner: Nevada Public Radio
Editorial: 1289 S Torrey Pines Dr, Las Vegas, Nevada 89146-1004 **Tel:** 1 702 258-9895.
Email: info@knpr.org
Web site: http://www.knpr.org
Profile: KLNR-FM is a non-commercial station owned by Nevada Public Radio. The format of the station is news and talk. KLNR-FM broadcasts to the Las Vegas area at 91.7 FM.
FM RADIO STATION

KLNV-FM
43782

Owner: Univision Communications Inc.
Editorial: 600 W Broadway Ste 2150, San Diego, California 92101-3389 **Tel:** 1 619 235-0600.
Web site: http://www.univision.com/san-diego/klnv
Profile: KLNV-FM is a commercial station owned by Univision Communications. The format of the station is regional Mexican music. KLNV-FM broadcasts to the San Diego area at 106.5 FM.
FM RADIO STATION

KLNZ-FM
42233

Owner: Entravision Communications Corp.
Editorial: 501 N 44th St Ste 425, Phoenix, Arizona 85008-6587 **Tel:** 1 602 776-1400.
Web site: http://www.tricolor1035.com
Profile: KLNZ-FM is a commercial station owned by Entravision Communications Corp. The format of the station is regional Mexican music. KLNZ-FM broadcasts to the Phoenix area at 103.5 FM.
FM RADIO STATION

KLOA-AM
37369

Owner: Adelman Broadcasting Inc.
Editorial: 731 Balsam St, Ridgecrest, California 93555-3510 **Tel:** 1 760 371-1700.
Web site: http://www.adelmanbroadcasting.com
Profile: KLOA-AM is a commercial station owned by Adelman Broadcasting Inc. The format of the station is oldies. KLOA-AM broadcasts to the Ridgecrest, CA area at 1240 AM.
AM RADIO STATION

KLO-AM
36376

Owner: KLO Broadcasting Co.
Editorial: 257 E 200 S Ste 400, Salt Lake City, Utah 84111-2073 **Tel:** 1 801 364-9836.
Email: comments@kloradio.com
Web site: http://www.kloradio.com
Profile: KLO-AM is a commercial station owned by KLO Broadcasting Co. The format of the station is talk. KLO-AM broadcasts to the Salt Lake City area at 1430 AM.
AM RADIO STATION

KLOB-FM
42464

Owner: Entravision Communications Corp.
Editorial: 41601 Corporate Way, Palm Desert, California 92260-1971 **Tel:** 1 760 341-5837.
Web site: http://www.jose947.com
Profile: KLOB-FM is a commercial station owned by Entravision Communications Corp. The format of the station is Regional Mexican. KLOB-FM broadcasts to the Palm Desert, CA area at 94.7 FM.
FM RADIO STATION

KLOC-AM
39389

Owner: Favorita Broadcasting(La)
Editorial: 4043 Geer Rd, Hughson, California 95326 **Tel:** 1 209 883-8760.
Profile: KLOC-AM is a commercial station owned by La Favorita Broadcasting. The format of the station is regional Mexican. KLOC-AM broadcasts to Modesto, CA area at 1370.
AM RADIO STATION

KLOE-AM
39021

Owner: Melia Communications Inc.
Editorial: 3023 W 31st St, Goodland, Kansas 67735-9098 **Tel:** 1 785 899-2309.
Web site: http://nwksradio.com/kloe-730am
Profile: KLOE-AM is a commercial station owned by Melia Communications Inc. The format of the station is news, talk and sports. KLOE-AM broadcasts to the Goodland, KS area at 730 AM.
AM RADIO STATION

KLOG-AM
38954

Owner: Washington Interstate Broadcasting Inc
Editorial: 506 W Cowlitz Way, Kelso, Washington 98626-1177 **Tel:** 1 360 636-0110.
Web site: http://www.klog.com
Profile: KLOG-AM is a commercial station owned by Washington Interstate Broadcasting Inc. The format for the station is sports. KLOG-AM broadcasts to the Kelso, WA area at 1490 AM.
AM RADIO STATION

KLOH-AM
37370

Owner: Christensen Broadcasting
Editorial: 608 State Highway 30, Pipestone, Minnesota 56164 **Tel:** 1 507 825-4282.
Email: kloh@klohradio.com
Web site: http://www.klohradio.com
Profile: KLOH-AM is a commercial station owned by Christensen Broadcasting. The format of the station is country music, talk and news. KLOH-AM broadcasts to the Pipestone, MN area at 1050 AM.
AM RADIO STATION

KLOK-AM
36538

Owner: Principle Broadcasting Network, LLC
Editorial: 2905 S King Rd, San Jose, California 95122-1518 **Tel:** 1 408 440-0851.
Email: desi1170am@aol.com
Web site: http://www.klok1170am.com
Profile: KLOK-AM is a commercial station owned by Principle Broadcasting Network, LLC. The station airs a variety of news, music and talk South Asian programming. KLOK-AM broadcasts to the San Francisco Bay area at 1170 AM.
AM RADIO STATION

KLOK-FM
45878

Owner: Entravision Communications Corp.
Editorial: 67 Garden Ct, Monterey, California 93940-5302 **Tel:** 1 831 333-9735.
Web site: http://www.tricolor995.com
Profile: KLOK-FM is a commercial station owned by Entravision Communications Corp. The format of the station is Regional Mexican. KLOK-FM broadcasts to the Monterey/Salinas, CA area at a frequency of 99.5 FM.
FM RADIO STATION

KLOL-FM
46741

Owner: CBS Radio
Editorial: 24 Greenway Plz Ste 1900, Houston, Texas 77046-2428 **Tel:** 1 713 881-5100.
Web site: http://klol.radio.com
Profile: KLOL-FM is a commercial station owned by CBS Radio. The format of the station is Hurban. KLOL-FM broadcasts to the Houston area on 101.1 FM.
FM RADIO STATION

KLOO-AM
38775

Owner: Bicoastal Media LLC
Editorial: 2840 Marion St SE, Albany, Oregon 97322-3978 **Tel:** 1 541 926-8628.
Web site: http://www.klooam.com
Profile: KLOO-AM is a commercial station owned by Bicoastal Media LLC. The format of the station is news and talk. KLOO-AM broadcasts to the Albany, OR area at 1340 AM.
AM RADIO STATION

KLOO-FM
46121

Owner: Bicoastal Media LLC
Editorial: 2840 Marion St SE, Albany, Oregon 97322-3978 **Tel:** 1 541 926-8628.
Web site: http://www.kloofm.com
Profile: KLOO-AM is a commercial station owned by Bicoastal Media LLC. The format of the station is classic rock. KLOO-AM broadcasts to Albany, OR at 106.3 FM.
FM RADIO STATION

KLOQ-FM
46675

Owner: Mapleton Radio, LLC
Editorial: 1020 W Main St, Merced, California 95340-4521 **Tel:** 1 209 723-2191.
Web site: http://www.radiolobo987.com
Profile: KLOQ-FM is a commercial station owned by Mapleton Radio, LLC. The format of the station is Hispanic. KLOQ-FM broadcasts to Merced, CA at 98.7 FM.
FM RADIO STATION

KLOR-FM
39744

Owner: Team Radio LLC
Editorial: 122 N 3rd St, Ponca City, Oklahoma 74601-4326 **Tel:** 1 580 762-9930.
Email: klor@eteamradio.com
Web site: http://www.eteamradio.com
Profile: KLOR-FM is a commercial station owned by Team Radio LLC. The format of the station is classic hits. KLOR-FM broadcasts to the Oklahoma City area at 99.3 FM.
FM RADIO STATION

KLOS-FM
46646

Owner: Cumulus Media Inc
Editorial: 8944 Lindblade St, Culver City, California 90232-2439 **Tel:** 1 310 840-4900.
Web site: http://www.955klos.com
Profile: KLOS-FM is a commercial station owned by Cumulus Media Inc. The format of the station is classic rock. KLOS-FM broadcasts to the Los Angeles area at 95.5 FM.
FM RADIO STATION

KLOU-FM
43440

Owner: iHeartMedia Inc.
Editorial: 1001 Highlands Plaza Dr W Ste 200, Saint Louis, Missouri 63110-1337 **Tel:** 1 314 333-8000.
Email: klou@iheartmedia.com
Web site: http://klou.iheart.com
Profile: KLOU-FM is a commercial station owned by iHeartMedia Inc. The format of the station is oldies. KLOU-FM broadcasts to the St. Louis area at 103.3 FM.
FM RADIO STATION

KLOW-FM
874650

Owner: Vision Media Group, Inc.
Editorial: 2654 Lamar Ave, Paris, Texas 75460-4847 **Tel:** 1 903 783-9890.
Web site: http://www.989thehotfm.com
Profile: KLOW-FM is a commercial station owned by Vision Media Group, Inc. The format of the station is Top 40/CHR. KCYY-FM broadcasts to the Paris, TX, Northeast Texas nad South East Oklahoma areas at 98.9 FM.
FM RADIO STATION

KLOZ-FM
39736

Owner: Benne Media
Editorial: 160 Highway 42, Kaiser, Missouri 65047-2011 **Tel:** 1 573 348-1958.
Web site: http://www.mix927.com/
Profile: KLOZ-FM is a commercial station owned by Benne Media. The format of the station is hot adult contemporary music. KLOZ-FM broadcasts to the Kaiser, MO area at 92.7 FM.
FM RADIO STATION

KLPF-AM
34983

Owner: La Promesa Foundation
Tel: 1 888 784-3476.
Web site: http://www.grnonline.com
Profile: KLPF-AM is a non-commercial station owned by La Promesa Foundation. The format of the station is religious programming with a Catholic emphasis. KLPF-AM broadcasts to the Midland, TX area at 1150 AM.
AM RADIO STATION

KLPW-AM
37372

Owner: Broadcast Properties
Editorial: 6501 Highway Bb, Washington, Missouri 63090-6085 **Tel:** 1 636 583-5155.
Email: news@klpw.com
Web site: http://www.klpw.com
Profile: KLPW-AM is a commercial station owned by Broadcast Properties. The format of the station is news and talk. KLPW-AM broadcasts to the Washington, MO area at 1220 AM.
AM RADIO STATION

KLPW-FM
44753

Owner: Marathon Media Group, LLC
Editorial: 5988 Mid Rivers Mall Dr Ste 136, Saint Peters, Missouri 63304-8303 **Tel:** 1 314 808-3870.
Profile: KLPW-FM is a commercial station owned by Marathon Media Group, LLC. The format of the station is sports. KLPW-FM broadcasts in the Elsberry, MO area at 101.7 FM.
FM RADIO STATION

KLPX-FM
46273

Owner: Lotus Communications Corp.
Editorial: 3871 N Commerce Dr, Tucson, Arizona 85705-2983 **Tel:** 1 520 407-4500.
Web site: http://www.klpx.com
Profile: KLPX-FM is a commercial station owned by Lotus Communications Corp. The format of the station is classic rock. KLPX-FM broadcasts in the Tucson, AZ area at 96.1 FM.
FM RADIO STATION

KLPZ-AM
35002

Owner: Learn Broadcasting (Keith Douglas)
Editorial: 816 W 6th St, Parker, Arizona 85344-4501 **Tel:** 1 928 669-9274.
Email: info@klpz1380.com
Web site: http://www.klpz1380.com
Profile: KLPZ-AM is commercial station owned by Keith Douglas Learn. The format of the station is classic country and talk. KLPZ-AM broadcasts to the Phoenix area at 1380 AM.
AM RADIO STATION

KLQB-FM
42765

Owner: Univision Communications Inc.
Editorial: 2233 W North Loop Blvd, Austin, Texas 78756-2324 **Tel:** 1 512 372-1043.
Web site: http://www.univision.com/austin/klqb
Profile: KLQB-FM is a commercial station owned by Univision Communications Inc. The format of the station is regional Mexican. KXBT-FM broadcasts to the Austin, TX area at 104.3 FM.
FM RADIO STATION

KLQL-FM
44754

Owner: Alpha Media
Editorial: 1140 150th Ave, Luverne, Minnesota 56156-4215 **Tel:** 1 507 283-4444.
Email: luverneinfo@alphamediausa.com
Web site: http://www.k101fm.net/
Profile: KLQL-FM is a commercial station owned by Alpha Media. The format of the station is country music. KLQL-FM broadcasts to the Luverne, MN area at 101.1 FM.
FM RADIO STATION

KLQP-FM 39746
Owner: Lac Qui Parle Broadcasting Co.
Editorial: 623 W 3rd St, Madison, Minnesota 56256-1325 **Tel:** 1 320 598-7301.
Email: klqpfm@farmerstel.net
Web site: http://www.klqpfm.com
Profile: KLQP-FM is a commercial station owned by Lac Qui Parle Broadcasting Co. The format of the station is a mix of classic country and classic hits. KLQP-FM broadcasts to the Madison, MN area at 92.1 FM.
FM RADIO STATION

KLQV-FM 43783
Owner: Univision Communications Inc.
Editorial: 600 W Broadway Ste 2150, San Diego, California 92101-3389 **Tel:** 1 619 235-0600.
Web site: http://www.1029masvariedad.univision.com
Profile: KLQV-FM is a commercial station owned by Univision Communications Inc. The format of the station is Hispanic oldies and adult hits. KLQV-FM broadcasts to the San Diego area at 102.9 FM.
FM RADIO STATION

KLRG-AM 36082
Owner: Kinlow (Joel, J.)
Editorial: 6400 Scott Hamilton Dr, Little Rock, Arkansas 72209-8538 **Tel:** 1 727 441-3311.
Web site: http://www.tantalk1340.com
Profile: KLRG-AM is a commercial station owned by Joel J. Kinlow. The format of the station is news and talk. KLRG-AM broadcasts in the Little Rock, AR area at 880 AM.
AM RADIO STATION

KLRK-AM 37483
Owner: M & M Broadcasters
Editorial: 5501 Bagby Ave, Waco, Texas 76711-2300 **Tel:** 1 254 772-0930.
Web site: http://party1013.com
Profile: KLRK-AM is a commercial station owned by M & M Broadcasters. The format of the station is adult contemporary. KLRK-AM broadcasts to the Waco, TX area at 1590 AM.
AM RADIO STATION

KLRR-FM 45797
Owner: Combined Communications, Inc.
Editorial: 63088 18th St Ste 200, Bend, Oregon 97701-7102 **Tel:** 1 541 389-1088.
Email: clear@clear1017.fm
Web site: http://1017.fm
Profile: KLRR-FM is a commercial station owned by Combined Communications. The format of the station is adult album alternative music. KLRR-FM broadcasts to the Bend, OR area at 101.7 FM.
FM RADIO STATION

KLRZ-FM 46892
Owner: Coastal Broadcasting of Larose Inc.
Editorial: 11603 Highway 308, Larose, Louisiana 70373-6013 **Tel:** 1 985 798-7792.
Email: klrz@viscom.net
Web site: http://www.klrzfm.com
Profile: KLRZ-FM is a commercial station owned by Coastal Broadcasting of Larose Inc. The format of the station is Sports and Talk. The target audience is listeners ages 13 to 100. KLRZ-FM broadcasts to the Larose, LA area at 100.3 FM. The station's slogan is "The Rajun Cajun."
FM RADIO STATION

KLSC-FM 44394
Owner: Max Media
Editorial: 324 Broadway St, Cape Girardeau, Missouri 63701-7331 **Tel:** 1 573 335-8291.
Email: realrock@riverradio.net
Web site: http://www.929theriver.com
Profile: KLSC-FM is a commercial station owned by Max Media. The format of the station is sports. KLSC-FM broadcasts to the Cape Girardeau, MO area at a frequency of 92.9 FM.
FM RADIO STATION

KLSD-AM 37096
Owner: iHeartMedia Inc.
Editorial: 9660 Granite Ridge Dr Ste 100, San Diego, California 92123-2689 **Tel:** 1 858 292-2000.
Web site: http://1360sports.iheart.com
Profile: KLSD-AM is a commercial station owned by iHeartMedia Inc. The format of the station is sports. KLSD-AM broadcasts to the San Diego area at 1360 AM.
AM RADIO STATION

KLSE-FM 39748
Owner: Minnesota Public Radio
Editorial: 206 S Broadway, Ste 735, Rochester, Minnesota 55904 **Tel:** 1 507 282-0910.
Email: newsroom@mpr.org
Web site: http://minnesota.publicradio.org/radio/stations/kzseklse/
Profile: KLSE-FM is a non-commercial station owned by Minnesota Public Radio. The format of the station is news/talk programming. KLSE-FM broadcasts to the Rochester, MN area at 91.7 FM.
FM RADIO STATION

KLSK-FM 153938
Owner: Flinn Broadcasting Corp.
Editorial: 1601 2nd Ave N Ste 528, Great Falls, Montana 59401-3289 **Tel:** 1 406 727-8200.
Web site: http://www.klove.com
Profile: KLSK-FM is in an LMA with Educational Media Foundation. The format of the station is christian music. KLSK-FM broadcasts to the Great Falls, MT area at 100.3 FM.
FM RADIO STATION

KLSM-FM 45817
Owner: Debut Broadcasting Inc.
Editorial: 1601 N Frontage Rd #E, Vicksburg, Mississippi 39180-5149 **Tel:** 1 601 636-2340.
Web site: http://khits1045.com
Profile: KLSM-FM is a commercial station owned by Debut Broadcasting Inc. The format of the station is adult hits. KLSM-FM broadcasts to the Vicksburg, MS area at 104.5 FM.
FM RADIO STATION

KLSQ-AM 36319
Owner: Univision Communications Inc.
Editorial: 6767 W Tropicana Ave Ste 102, Las Vegas, Nevada 89103-4755 **Tel:** 1 702 284-6400.
Web site: http://univisionamerica.com
Profile: KLSQ-AM is a commercial station owned by Univision Communications Inc. The format is Spanish news and talk. KLSQ-AM broadcasts to the Las Vegas area on 870 AM.
AM RADIO STATION

KLSR-FM 44343
Owner: Davis Broadcast Company, Inc
Editorial: 114 N 7th St, Memphis, Texas 79245-2808 **Tel:** 1 806 259-3511.
Web site: http://www.klsr105.com
Profile: KLSR-FM is a commercial station owned by Davis Broadcast Company, Inc. The format of the station is country. KLSR-FM broadcasts to the Memphis, TX area at a frequency of 105.3.
FM RADIO STATION

KLSS-FM 46298
Owner: Alpha Media
Editorial: 341 S Yorktown Pike, Mason City, Iowa 50401-4533 **Tel:** 1 641 423-1300.
Web site: http://www.mystar106.com
Profile: KLSS-FM is a commercial station owned by Alpha Media. The format of the station is adult contemporary. KLSS-FM broadcasts to the Mason City, IA area at 106.1 FM.
FM RADIO STATION

KLSW-FM 39764
Owner: Queen Cities Broadcasting LLC
Editorial: 553 Roosevelt Ave, Enumclaw, Washington 98022-2990 **Tel:** 1 214 969-9977.
Web site: http://www.classichitsq1045.com
Profile: KLSW-FM is a commercial station owned by Queen Cities Broadcasting LLC. The format of the station is classic hits. KLSW-FM broadcasts to Enumclaw, WA area at 104.5 FM.
FM RADIO STATION

KLSZ-FM 43346
Owner: Cumulus Media Inc.
Editorial: 4209 N Frontage Rd, Fayetteville, Arkansas 72703-5002 **Tel:** 1 479 452-0681.
Web site: http://www.1007nashicon.com
Profile: KLSZ-FM is a commercial station owned by Cumulus Media Inc. The format of the station is country music. KLSZ-FM broadcasts to the Fort Smith, AR area at 100.7 FM.
FM RADIO STATION

KLTA-FM 39752
Owner: Radio FM Media
Editorial: 2720 7th Ave S, Fargo, North Dakota 58103-8710 **Tel:** 1 701 237-4500.
Web site: http://www.big987.com
Profile: KLTA-FM is a commercial station owned by Radio FM Media. The format of the station is adult contemporary music. KLTA-FM broadcasts to the Fargo, ND area at 98.7 FM.
FM RADIO STATION

KLTC-AM 36600
Owner: iHeartMedia Inc.
Editorial: 11291 39th St SW, Dickinson, North Dakota 58601-9206 **Tel:** 1 701 227-1876.
Web site: http://www.1460kltc.com/main.html
Profile: KLTC-AM is a commercial station owned by iHeartMedia Inc. The format of the station is country. KLTC-AM broadcasts to the Dickinson, ND area at 1460 AM.
AM RADIO STATION

KLTD-FM 42966
Owner: Townsquare Media, Inc.
Editorial: 608 Moody Ln, Temple, Texas 76504-2952 **Tel:** 1 254 773-5252.
Web site: http://www.k1017fm.com
Profile: KLTD-FM is a commercial station owned by Townsquare Media, Inc. The format of the station is classic hits. KLTD-FM broadcasts to the Temple, TX area at 101.7 FM.
FM RADIO STATION

KLTE-FM 42527
Owner: Bott Broadcasting Co.
Editorial: 3 Crown Dr #100, Kirksville, Missouri 63501-2549 **Tel:** 1 660 627-5583.
Email: klte@bottradionetwork.com
Web site: http://www.bottradionetwork.com
Profile: KLTE-FM is a commercial station owned by Bott Broadcasting Co. The format of the station is Christian talk programming. KLTE-FM broadcasts to the Kirksville, MO area at 107.9 FM.
FM RADIO STATION

KLTF-AM 38754
Owner: Little Falls Radio Corp.
Editorial: 16405 Haven Rd, Little Falls, Minnesota 56345-6400 **Tel:** 1 320 632-2992.
Email: news@fallsradio.com
Web site: http://www.fallsradio.com
Profile: KLTF-AM is a commercial station owned by Little Falls Radio Corp. The format of the station is news, sports, and talk. KLTF-AM broadcasts to the Little Falls, MN area at 960 AM.
AM RADIO STATION

KLTG-FM 43657
Owner: Tejas Broadcasting
Editorial: 1733 S Brownlee Blvd, Corpus Christi, Texas 78404-3018 **Tel:** 1 361 883-1600.
Email: beach965@gmail.com
Web site: http://thebeach965fm.com
Profile: KLTG-FM is a commercial station owned by Tejas Broadcasting. The format of the station is hot adult contemporary music. KLTG-FM broadcasts to the Corpus Christi, TX area at 96.5 FM.
FM RADIO STATION

KLTH-FM 42104
Owner: iHeartMedia Inc.
Editorial: 13333 SW 68th Pkwy Ste 310, Tigard, Oregon 97223-8304 **Tel:** 1 503 323-6400.
Web site: http://1067theeagle.iheart.com
Profile: KLTH-FM is a commercial station owned by iHeartMedia Inc. The format of the station is classic hits. KLTH-FM broadcasts to the Portland, OR area at 106.7 FM.
FM RADIO STATION

KLTI-AM 36555
Owner: Best Broadcast Group
Editorial: 32968 US Highway 63, Macon, Missouri 63552-4535 **Tel:** 1 660 385-1560.
Email: klti@mcmsys.com
Web site: http://www.kltiradio.com
Profile: KLTI-AM is a commercial station owned by Best Broadcast Group. The format for the station is classic country. KLTI-AM broadcasts to the Ottumna, IA-Kirksville, MO area at 1560 AM.
AM RADIO STATION

KLTI-FM 39640
Owner: Saga Communications
Editorial: 1416 Locust St, Des Moines, Iowa 50309-3014 **Tel:** 1 515 280-1350.
Web site: http://www.lite1041.com
Profile: KLTI-FM is a commercial station owned by Saga Communications. The format of the station is adult contemporary. KLTI-FM broadcast to Des Moines, IA at 104.1 FM.
FM RADIO STATION

KLTN-FM 43705
Owner: Univision Communications Inc.
Editorial: 5100 Southwest Fwy, Houston, Texas 77056-7308 **Tel:** 1 713 965-2400.
Web site: http://www.univision.com/houston/kltn
Profile: KLTN-FM is a commercial station owned by Univision Communications Inc. The format of the station is Mexican regional music. KLTN-FM broadcasts to the Houston area at 102.9 FM.
FM RADIO STATION

KLTO-AM 39104
Owner: Forum Broadcasting Inc.
Editorial: 107 Center Dr, Del Rio, Texas 78840-3015 **Tel:** 1 830 775-9583.
Web site: http://www.latino1230.com
Profile: KLTO-AM is a commercial station owned by Forum Broadcasting Inc. The format of the station is Hispanic Top 40/CHR. KLTO-AM broadcasts to the Del Rio, TX area at 1230 AM.
AM RADIO STATION

KLTR-FM 41247
Owner: La Grange Broadcasting
Editorial: 530 W Main St, Brenham, Texas 77833-3663 **Tel:** 1 979 836-9411.
Email: litefm941@yahoo.com
Web site: http://www.litefm941.com
Profile: KLTR-FM is a commercial station owned by La Grange Broadcasting. The format of the station is Lite Rock/Lite AC. KLTR-FM broadcasts to the Brenham, TX area at 94.1 FM.
FM RADIO STATION

KLTT-AM 63991
Owner: Crawford Broadcasting Co.
Editorial: 2821 S Parker Rd Ste 1205, Aurora, Colorado 80014-2720 **Tel:** 1 303 481-1800.
Email: kltt@crawfordbroadcasting.com
Web site: http://www.670kltt.com
Profile: KLTT-AM is a commercial station owned by Crawford Broadcasting Co. The format of the station is Christian talk. KLTT-AM broadcasts to the Denver area at 670 AM.
AM RADIO STATION

KLTU-FM 358742
Owner: Good News Radio Broadcasting Inc.
Editorial: 3222 S Richey Ave, Tucson, Arizona 85713 **Tel:** 1 520 790-2440.
Web site: http://www.klove.com
Profile: KLTU-FM is a commercial station owned by Good News Radio Broadcasting Inc. The format of the station is contemporary Christian. KLTU-FM broadcasts to the Mammoth, AZ area at 88.1 FM. The programming comes from the K-Love Network.
FM RADIO STATION

KLTW-FM 46484
Owner: Horizon Broadcasting Group
Editorial: 854 NE 4th St, Bend, Oregon 97701-4711 **Tel:** 1 541 383-3825.
Email: news@horizonbroadcastinggroup.com
Web site: http://www.957myfm.com
Profile: KLTW-FM is a commercial station owned by Horizon Broadcasting Group. The format for the station is AC. KLTW-FM broadcasts to the Bend, OR area at 95.7 FM.
FM RADIO STATION

KLTX-AM 34954
Owner: Hi-Favor Broadcasting LLC
Editorial: 136 S Oak Knoll Ave Ste 202, Pasadena, California 91101-2624 **Tel:** 1 626 356-4230.
Web site: http://www.nuevavida.com
Profile: KLTX-AM is a commercial radio station owned by Hi-Favor Broadcasting LLC. The format of the station is Spanish religious music. KLTX-AM broadcasts to the Pasadena, CA area on 1390 AM.
AM RADIO STATION

KLTY-FM 41399
Owner: Salem Media Group, Inc.
Editorial: 6400 N Belt Line Rd Ste 120, Irving, Texas 75063-6065 **Tel:** 1 972 870-9949.
Email: onair@klty.com
Web site: http://www.klty.com
Profile: KLTY-FM is a commercial station owned by Salem Media Group, Inc. The format of the station is contemporary Christian music. KLTY-FM broadcasts to the Dallas area at 94.9 FM.
FM RADIO STATION

KLTZ-AM 38855
Owner: Glasgow Broadcasting Corp.
Editorial: 504 2nd Ave S, Glasgow, Montana 59230 **Tel:** 1 406 228-9336.
Email: kltz@kltz.com
Web site: http://www.kltz.com
Profile: KLTZ-AM is a commercial station owned by Glasgow Broadcasting Corp. The format of the station is classic country. KLTZ-AM broadcasts to the Great Falls, MT area at 1240 AM.
AM RADIO STATION

KLUA-FM 42534
Owner: Pacific Media Group
Editorial: 75-5852 Alii Dr Ste B1, Lagoon Tower, Kailua Kona, Hawaii 96740-1310 **Tel:** 1 808 961-0651.
Email: studio@kaparadio.com
Web site: http://www.nativefm.com
Profile: KLUA-FM is a commercial station owned by Pacific Media Group. The format of the station is dance. The station airs locally at 93.9 FM.
FM RADIO STATION

KLUB-FM 42285
Owner: Townsquare Media, LLC
Editorial: 107 N Star Dr, Victoria, Texas 77904-2082 **Tel:** 1 361 573-0777.
Web site: http://classicrock1069.com
Profile: KLUB-FM is a commercial station owned by Townsquare Media, LLC. The format for the station is classic rock. KLUB-FM broadcasts to the Victoria, TX area at 106.9 FM.
FM RADIO STATION

KLUC-FM 45765
Owner: CBS Radio
Editorial: 7255 S Tenaya Way Ste 100, Las Vegas, Nevada 89113-1900 **Tel:** 1 702 253-9800.
Web site: http://www.kluc.com
Profile: KLUC-FM is a commercial station owned by CBS Radio. The format of the station is urban contemporary. KLUC-FM broadcasts to the Las Vegas area at 98.5 FM.
FM RADIO STATION

KLUE-FM 80997
Owner: Stratemeyer Media
Editorial: 203 S Main St, Poplar Bluff, Missouri 63901-5831 **Tel:** 1 573 778-1219.
Web site: http://www.kluefm.com
Profile: KLUE-FM is a commercial station owned by Stratemeyer Media. The format of the station is hot adult contemporary. KLUE-FM broadcasts to the Poplar Bluff, MO area at 103.5 FM.
FM RADIO STATION

KLUH-FM 41773
Owner: David Craig Ministries Inc.
Editorial: 1165 County Road 307, Poplar Bluff, Missouri 63901-4887 **Tel:** 1 573 686-1663.
Email: info@dcmliferadio.org
Web site: http://www.dcmliferadio.org/
Profile: KLUH-FM is a non-commercial station David Craig Ministries Inc. The format of the station is contemporary Christian. KLUH-FM broadcasts to the Poplar Bluff, MO area at 90.3 FM.
FM RADIO STATION

KLUK-FM 44951
Owner: Cameron Broadcasting Inc.
Editorial: 2350 Miracle Mile Ste 300, Bullhead City, Arizona 86442-7505 **Tel:** 1 928 763-5586.
Web site: http://www.lucky98fm.com
Profile: KLUK-FM is a commercial station owned by Cameron Broadcasting Inc. The format of the station is classic rock. KLUK-FM broadcasts to the Bullhead City, AZ area at 97.9 FM
FM RADIO STATION

KLUN-FM
42982
Owner: Lazer Broadcasting Corp.
Editorial: 1427 Pine St Ste 3, Paso Robles, California 93446-1766 **Tel:** 1 805 226-7578.
Email: lazerbroadcasting@radiolazer.com
Web site: http://www.radiolazer.com
Profile: KLUN-FM is a commercial station owned by Lazer Broadcasting Corp. The format of the station is Regional Mexican. KLUN-FM is licensed to Paso Robles, CA and broadcasts to the San Luis Obispo, CA area at a frequency of 103.1 FM.
FM RADIO STATION

KLUP-AM
38687
Owner: Salem Media Group, Inc.
Editorial: 9601 McAllister Fwy Ste 1200, San Antonio, Texas 78216-4695 **Tel:** 1 210 344-8481.
Email: contact_us@kslr.com
Web site: http://930amtheanswer.com
Profile: KLUP-AM is a commercial station owned by Salem Media Group, Inc. The format of the station is talk. KLUP-AM broadcasts to the San Antonio area at 930 AM.
AM RADIO STATION

KLUR-FM
39758
Owner: Cumulus Media Inc.
Editorial: 4302 Call Field Rd, Wichita Falls, Texas 76308-2534 **Tel:** 1 940 691-2311.
Web site: http://www.klur.com
Profile: KLUR-FM is a commercial station owned by Cumulus Media Inc. The format of the station is contemporary country music. KLUR-FM broadcasts to the Wichita Falls, TX area at 99.9 FM.
FM RADIO STATION

KLUV-FM
39759
Owner: CBS Radio
Editorial: 4131 N Central Expy Ste 1200, Dallas, Texas 75204-2123 **Tel:** 1 214 525-7000.
Web site: http://kluv.cbslocal.com
Profile: KLUV-FM is a commercial station owned by CBS Radio. The format is classic hits. KLUV-FM broadcasts to the Dallas area at 98.7 FM.
FM RADIO STATION

KLUX-FM
41240
Owner: Diocesan Telecomms. Corp.
Editorial: 1200 Lantana St, Corpus Christi, Texas 78407 **Tel:** 1 361 289-2487.
Email: klux@goccn.org
Web site: http://www.klux.org
Profile: KLUX-FM is a non-commercial station owned by Diocesan Telecomms. Corp. The format of the station is easy listening and religion. KLUX-FM broadcasts to the Corpus Christi, TX area at 89.5 FM.
FM RADIO STATION

KLVE-FM
44757
Owner: Univision Communications Inc.
Editorial: 5999 Center Dr, Los Angeles, California 90045-8901 **Tel:** 1 310 846-2800.
Web site: http://www.univision.com/los-angeles/klve
Profile: KLVE-FM is a commercial station owned by Univision Communications Inc. The format of the station is Hispanic adult contemporary music. The station airs in the Glendale, CA area on 107.5 FM.
FM RADIO STATION

KLVF-FM
45920
Owner: Baca Broadcasting LLC
Editorial: One Radio Heights, Las Vegas, New Mexico 87701 **Tel:** 1 505 425-6766.
Profile: KLVF-FM is a commercial station owned by Baca Broadcasting LLC. The format of the station is adult contemporary music. KLVF-FM broadcasts to the Albuquerque, NM area at 100.7 FM.
FM RADIO STATION

KLVI-AM
38758
Owner: iHeartMedia Inc.
Editorial: 2885 Interstate 10 E, Beaumont, Texas 77702-1001 **Tel:** 1 409 896-5555.
Web site: http://klvi.iheart.com
Profile: KLVI-AM is a commercial station owned by iHeartMedia Inc. The format of the station is news, talk and sports. KLVI-AM broadcasts to the Beaumont, TX area at 560 AM.
AM RADIO STATION

KLVJ-FM
43018
Owner: Educational Media Foundation
Editorial: 9710 Scranton Rd Ste 200, San Diego, California 92121-1744 **Tel:** 1 858 678-0102.
Profile: KLVJ-FM is a commercial station owned by Educational Media Foundation. The format of the station is contemporary christian music. KLVJ-FM broadcasts to the San Diego area at 102.1 FM.
FM RADIO STATION

KLVL-AM
36268
Owner: SIGA Broadcasting Corp.
Editorial: 6161 Savoy Dr Ste 1140, Houston, Texas 77036-3323 **Tel:** 1 713 787-9922.
Web site: http://klvl1480.com/
Profile: KLVL-AM is a commercial station owned by SIGA Broadcasting Corp. The format of the station features a mix of South Asian music, news and talk programming. KLVL-AM broadcasts to the Houston area at 1480 AM.
AM RADIO STATION

KLVO-FM
46257
Owner: American General Media
Editorial: 4125 Carlisle Blvd NE, Albuquerque, New Mexico 87107-4806 **Tel:** 1 505 878-0980.
Web site: http://lainvasora977.com
Profile: KLVO-FM is a commercial station owned by American General Media. The format of the station is Regional Mexican. KLVO-FM broadcasts to the Albuquerque, NM area at 97.7 FM.
FM RADIO STATION

KLVQ-AM
39152
Owner: Lake Country Radio LP
Editorial: 11125 State Highway 31 W, Malakoff, Texas 75148-7158 **Tel:** 1 903 489-1238.
Email: tcrum@kcklfm.com
Web site: http://www.kcklfm.com/klvq/
Profile: KLVQ-AM is a commercial station owned by Lake Country Radio LP. The format of the station is contemporary Christian. KLVQ-AM broadcasts to Malakoff, TX area at 1410 AM.
AM RADIO STATION

KLVT-AM
38668
Owner: Cute Boots Broadcasting, LLC
Editorial: 611 N West Ave, Levelland, Texas 79336-3930 **Tel:** 1 806 894-3134.
Email: klvtradio@gmail.com
Web site: http://www.hprnetwork.com
Profile: KLVT-AM is a commercial station owned by Cute Boots Broadcasting, LLC. The format of the station is news, talk and sports. KLVT-AM broadcasts to the Levelland, TX area at 1230 AM. The station's programming is not pitchable and does not accept press releases, interview requests, or any related information.
AM RADIO STATION

KLVV-FM
42041
Owner: Love Station Inc.(The)
Editorial: 6600 W Highway 60, Ponca City, Oklahoma 74601-7926 **Tel:** 1 580 767-1600.
Email: mail@klvv.com
Web site: http://www.klvv.com
Profile: KLVV-FM is a non-commercial station owned by The Love Station, Inc. The format of the station is contemporary Christian. KLVV-FM broadcasts to the Ponca City, OK area at 88.7 FM.
FM RADIO STATION

KLWB-FM
800417
Owner: Delta Media Corporation
Editorial: 3500 Nw Evangeline Trwy, Carencro, Louisiana 70520-6240 **Tel:** 1 337 896-1600.
Email: 1037thegame@gmail.com
Web site: http://1037thegame.com
Profile: KLWB-FM is a commercial station owned by Delta Media Corporation. The format of the station is sports/talk. KSLO-FM broadcasts to the Lafayette, LA area at a frequency of 103.7 FM.
FM RADIO STATION

KLWN-AM
37373
Owner: Great Plains Media
Editorial: 3125 W 6th St, Lawrence, Kansas 66049-3101 **Tel:** 1 785 843-1320.
Web site: http://www.klwn.com
Profile: KLWN-AM is a commercial station owned by Great Plains Media. The format of the station is news, sports and talk programming. KLWN-AM broadcasts to the Lawrence, KS area at 1320 AM.
AM RADIO STATION

KLXH-FM
40047
Owner: Educational Media Foundation
Editorial: 120 Prevost Dr, Houma, Louisiana 70364-2338
Profile: KLXH-FM is owned by the Education Media Foundation. It broadcasts to theMouma/Thibodaux area at 106.3.
FM RADIO STATION

KLXI-FM
44953
Owner: Treasure Valley Broadcasting
Editorial: 556 Highway 95, Weiser, Idaho 83672-5722
Profile: KLXI-FM is a commercial station owned by he Educational Media Foundation. The format of the station is Contemporary Christian. KLXI-FM broadcasts to the Boise, ID area at 99.5 FM. The station's slogan is, "Positive and Encouraging."
FM RADIO STATION

KLXK-FM
46340
Owner: MediaNews Group Inc.
Editorial: 114 E Elm St, Breckenridge, Texas 76424-3613 **Tel:** 1 254 559-6543.
Web site: http://www.lakecountryradio.net
Profile: KLXK-FM is a commercial station owned by MediaNews Group Inc. The format of the station is country music. KLXK-FM broadcasts in the Breckenridge, TX area at 93.5 FM.
FM RADIO STATION

KLXQ-FM
62092
Owner: US Stations, LLC
Editorial: 125 Corporate Ter, Hot Springs, Arkansas 71913-7248 **Tel:** 1 501 525-9700.
Email: info@usstations.com
Web site: http://www.myhotsprings.com
Profile: KLXQ-FM is a commercial station owned by US Stations, LLC. The format of the station is classic rock. KLXQ-FM broadcasts to the Hot Springs, AR area at 101.9 FM.
FM RADIO STATION

KLXR-AM
135293
Owner: Quinn(Michael)
Editorial: 1326 Market St, Redding, California 96001 **Tel:** 1 530 244-5082.
Email: klxr1230@yahoo.com
Profile: KLXR-AM is a commercial station owned by Michael Quinn. The format of the station is adult standards music. KLXR-FM broadcasts to the Redding, CA area on 1230 AM.
AM RADIO STATION

KLXS-FM
46624
Owner: Riverfront Broadcasting
Editorial: 106 W Capitol Ave, Pierre, South Dakota 57501-2018 **Tel:** 1 605 224-0095.
Email: production@todayskccr.com
Web site: http://pierrecountry.com
Profile: KLXS-FM is a commercial station owned by Riverfront Broadcasting. The format of the station is contemporary country. KLXS-FM broadcasts to the Pierre, SD area at 95.3 FM.
FM RADIO STATION

KLXX-AM
39207
Owner: Townsquare Media, Inc.
Editorial: 4303 Memorial Hwy, Mandan, North Dakota 58554-4711 **Tel:** 1 701 250-6602.
Web site: http://www.supertalk1270.com
Profile: KLXX-AM is a commercial station owned by Townsquare Media, Inc. The format of the station is news and talk. KLXX-AM broadcasts to the Bismarck, ND area at 1270 AM.
AM RADIO STATION

KLYC-AM
34916
Owner: Celebrate Life Media, LLC
Editorial: 1975 NE Colvin Ct, McMinnville, Oregon 97128-8404 **Tel:** 1 503 472-1260.
Web site: http://klyc.us/
Profile: KLYC-AM is a commercial station owned by Celebrate Life Media, LLC. The format of the station is oldies. KLYC-AM broadcasts to the McMinnville, OR area at 1260 AM.
AM RADIO STATION

KLYD-FM
154931
Owner: Snyder Broadcasting Co.
Editorial: 2301 Avenue R, Snyder, Texas 79549-1919 **Tel:** 1 325 573-9322.
Email: news@ksnyradio.com
Web site: http://bigstarradiogroup.com
Profile: KLYD-FM is a commercial station owned by Snyder Broadcasting Co. The format of the station is rock alternative. KLYD-FM broadcasts to the Snyder, TX area at 98.9 FM.
FM RADIO STATION

KLYK-FM
44760
Owner: Bicoastal Media LLC
Editorial: 1130 14th Ave, Longview, Washington 98632-3017 **Tel:** 1 360 425-1500.
Web site: http://www.klykradio.com
Profile: KLYK-FM is a commercial station owned by Bicoastal Media LLC. The format of the station is hot adult contemporary music. KLYK-FM broadcasts to the Portand, OR area at 94.5 FM.
FM RADIO STATION

KLYQ-AM
39031
Owner: Townsquare Media, LLC
Editorial: 320 N 1st St, Hamilton, Montana 59840-3516 **Tel:** 1 406 728-9300.
Email: contact@klyq.com
Web site: http://www.klyq.com
Profile: KLYQ-AM is a commercial station owned by Townsquare Media, LLC. The format of the station is oldies. KLYQ-AM broadcasts to the Hamilton, MT area at 1240 AM.
AM RADIO STATION

KLYR-AM
37374
Owner: Forrester Partnership
Editorial: Highway 64 West, Clarksville, Arkansas 72830 **Tel:** 1 479 754-3092.
Web site: http://www.klyr.com
Profile: KLYR-AM is commercial station owned by Forrester Partnership. The format of the station is classic country. KLYR-AM broadcasts in Clarksville, AR area at 1360 AM.
AM RADIO STATION

KLYR-FM
44761
Owner: Forrester Partnership
Editorial: Highway 64 West, Clarksville, Arkansas 72830 **Tel:** 1 479 754-3092.
Web site: http://www.klyr.com
Profile: KLYR-FM is a commercial station owned by Forrester Partnership. The format of the station is classic country. KLYR-FM broadcasts to the Clarksville, AR area at 92.7 FM.
FM RADIO STATION

KLYT-FM
41109
Owner: Calvary Chapel of Albuquerque, Inc.
Editorial: 4001 Osuna Rd NE, Albuquerque, New Mexico 87109-4422 **Tel:** 1 505 344-9146.
Web site: http://star88.fm
Profile: KLYT-FM is a non-commercial station owned by Calvary Chapel of Albuquerque, Inc. The format of the station is contemporary Christian rock and pop music. KLYT-FM broadcasts to the Albuquerque, NM area at 88.3 FM.
FM RADIO STATION

KLYV-FM
44762
Owner: Townsquare Media
Editorial: 5490 Saratoga Rd, Asbury, Iowa 52002-2593 **Tel:** 1 563 557-1040.
Web site: http://www.y105music.com
Profile: KLYV-FM is a commercial station owned by Townsquare Media. The format for the station is Top 40/CHR. KLYV-FM broadcasts to the Cedar Rapids, IA area at 105.3 FM.
FM RADIO STATION

KLYY-FM
41157
Owner: Entravision Communications Corp.
Editorial: 5700 Wilshire Blvd Ste 250, Los Angeles, California 90036-3647 **Tel:** 1 323 900-6100.
Web site: http://www.jose975.com
Profile: KLYY-FM is a commercial station owned by Entravision Communications Corp. The format of the station is regional mexican. KLYY-FM broadcasts locally to the Los Angeles area at 97.5 FM.
FM RADIO STATION

KLZA-FM
43984
Owner: KNZA, Inc.
Editorial: 1602 Stone St, Falls City, Nebraska 68355 **Tel:** 1 402 245-6010.
Email: sunny1013fm@hotmail.com
Web site: http://www.sunny1013.com
Profile: KLZA-FM is a commercial station owned by KNZA, Inc. The format of the station is adult contemporary. KLZA-FM broadcasts to the Falls City, NE area at 101.3 FM.
FM RADIO STATION

KLZ-AM
36116
Owner: Crawford Broadcasting Co.
Editorial: 2821 S Parker Rd Ste 1205, Aurora, Colorado 80014-2720 **Tel:** 1 303 433-5500.
Email: 4crawford@gmail.com
Web site: http://www.560thesource.com
Profile: KLZ-AM is a commercial station owned by Crawford Broadcasting Co. The format of the station is talk. KLZ-AM broadcasts to the Denver area at 560 AM.
AM RADIO STATION

KLZK-FM
42580
Owner: Barton Broadcasting Co.
Editorial: 1607 13th St, Lubbock, Texas 79401-3830 **Tel:** 1 806 747-5951.
Email: kejsfm@kejsfm.com
Web site: http://www.kejsfm.com
Profile: KLZK-FM is a commercial station owned by Barton Broadcasting Co. The format of the station is Tejano music. The station airs to the Lubbock, TX area at 106.5 FM.
FM RADIO STATION

KLZS-AM
39153
Owner: Eugene Comedy Radio, LLC
Editorial: 471 S A St, Springfield, Oregon 97477-5402
Web site: http://piratecomedynetwork.com
Profile: KLZS-AM is a commercial station owned by Eugene Comedy Radio, LLC. The format of the station is comedy. KLZS-AM broadcasts to the Euguene, OR area on 1450 AM.
AM RADIO STATION

KLZT-FM
42127
Owner: Emmis Communications Corp.
Editorial: 8309 N Interstate 35, Austin, Texas 78753-5720 **Tel:** 1 512 481-1071.
Web site: http://www.1071laz.com
Profile: KLZT-FM is a commercial station owned by Emmis Communications Corp. The format of the station is regional Mexican. KLZT-FM broadcasts in the Austin, TX area at 107.1 FM.
FM RADIO STATION

KLZX-FM
87126
Owner: Cache Valley Radio Inc.
Editorial: 810 W 200 N, Logan, Utah 84321 **Tel:** 1 435 752-1390.
Email: klzx@cvradio.com
Web site: http://www.klzxfm.com
Profile: KLZX-FM is a commercial station owned by Cache Valley Radio Inc. The format of the station is classic rock. KLZX-FM broadcasts to the Salt Lake City area at 99.9 FM.
FM RADIO STATION

KLZZ-FM
46083
Owner: Townsquare Media, LLC
Editorial: 640 Lincoln Ave SE, Saint Cloud, Minnesota 56304-1024 **Tel:** 1 320 251-4422.
Web site: http://www.1037theloon.com
Profile: KLZZ-FM is a commercial station owned by Townsquare Media, LLC. The format of the station is classic rock music. KLZZ-FM broadcasts to the Saint Cloud, MN area at 103.7 FM.
FM RADIO STATION

KMA-AM
38887
Owner: May Broadcasting
Editorial: 209 N Elm St, Shenandoah, Iowa 51601 **Tel:** 1 712 246-5270.
Email: news@kmaland.com
Web site: http://www.kma960.com
Profile: KMA-AM is a commercial station owned by May Broadcasting. The format of the station is talk. KMA-AM broadcasts to the Shenandoah, IA area at 960 AM.
AM RADIO STATION

KMAD-FM
43645
Owner: Digity LLC
Editorial: 1800 Teague Dr Ste 300, Sherman, Texas 75090-2654 **Tel:** 1 903 463-6800.
Web site: http://www.madrock1025.com
Profile: KMAD-FM is a commercial station owned by Digity LLC. The format of the station is rock/album oriented rock. KMAD-FM broadcasts to Denison, TX and surrounding areas at 102.5 FM.
FM RADIO STATION

United States of America

KMA-FM 46230
Owner: May Broadcasting
Editorial: 209 N Elm St, Shenandoah, Iowa 51601-1139 **Tel:** 1 712 246-5270.
Email: kmaradio@kmaland.com
Web site: http://www.kmaland.com
Profile: KMA-FM is a commercial station owned by May Broadcasting. The format of the station is adult contemporary music. KMA-FM broadcasts to the Shenandoah, IA area at 99.1 FM.
FM RADIO STATION

KMAG-FM 46271
Owner: iHeartMedia Inc.
Editorial: 311 Lexington Ave, Fort Smith, Arkansas 72901-3842 **Tel:** 1 479 782-8888.
Web site: http://www.kmag991.com
Profile: KMAG-FM is a commercial station owned by iHeartMedia Inc. The format of the station is classic country. KMAG-FM broadcasts to the Fort Smith, AR area at 99.1 FM.
FM RADIO STATION

KMAJ-AM 38622
Owner: Cumulus Media Inc.
Editorial: 825 S Kansas Ave Ste 100, Topeka, Kansas 66612-1233 **Tel:** 1 785 272-2122.
Web site: http://www.kmaj1440.com
Profile: KMAJ-AM is a commercial station owned by Cumulus Media Inc. The format of the station is news, talk, and sports. KMAJ-AM broadcasts to the Topeka, KS area at 1440 AM.
AM RADIO STATION

KMAJ-FM 46761
Owner: Cumulus Media Inc.
Editorial: 825 S Kansas Ave Ste 100, Topeka, Kansas 66612-1233 **Tel:** 1 785 272-2122.
Web site: http://www.kmaj.com
Profile: KMAJ-FM is a commercial station owned by Cumulus Media Inc. The format of the station is adult contemporary music. KMAJ-FM broadcasts to the Topeka, KS area at 107.7 FM.
FM RADIO STATION

KMAK-FM 41774
Owner: Smith(Richard)
Tel: 1 559 891-1515.
Email: kmakfm@kmakfm.com
Web site: http://www.kmakfm.com
Profile: KMAK-FM is a commercial station owned by Richard Smith. The format of the station is regional Mexican. KMAK-FM broadcasts to the Fresno, CA area at 100.3 FM.
FM RADIO STATION

KMAL-AM 37151
Owner: Mississippi River Radio
Editorial: 324 Broadway St, Cape Girardeau, Missouri 63701-7331 **Tel:** 1 573 335-8291.
Web site: http://www.1470kmal.com
Profile: KMAL-AM is a commercial station owned by Mississippi River Radio. The format of the station is sports. KMAL-AM broadcasts to the Cape Girardeau, MO area at a frequency of 1470 AM.
AM RADIO STATION

KMAM-AM 37375
Owner: Bates County Broadcasting Co.
Editorial: 800 E Nursery St, Butler, Missouri 64730-1771 **Tel:** 1 660 679-4191.
Web site: http://www.921kmoe.com
Profile: KMAM-AM is a commercial station owned by Bates County Broadcasting Co. The format of the station is country. KMAM-AM broadcasts to the Butler, MO area at 1530 AM.
AM RADIO STATION

KMAN-AM 37376
Owner: Manhattan Broadcasting
Editorial: 2414 Casement Rd, Manhattan, Kansas 66502 **Tel:** 1 785 776-1350.
Email: news@1350kman.com
Web site: http://www.1350kman.com
Profile: KMAN-AM is commercial station owned by Manhattan Broadcasting. The format of the station is news, talk, and sports programming. KMAN-AM broadcasts to the Manhattan, KS area on 1350 AM.
AM RADIO STATION

KMAQ-AM 37377
Owner: Maquoketa Broadcasting, Co.
Editorial: 129 N Main St, Maquoketa, Iowa 52060-2256 **Tel:** 1 563 652-2426.
Email: kmaq@kmaq.com
Web site: http://www.kmaq.com
Profile: KMAQ-AM is a commercial station owned by Maquoketa Broadcasting, Co.. The format of the station is country. KMAQ-AM broadcasts to the Maquoketa, IA area at 1230 AM.
AM RADIO STATION

KMAQ-FM 44765
Owner: Voy(Dennis W.)
Editorial: 129 N Main St, Maquoketa, Iowa 52060-2256 **Tel:** 1 563 652-2426.
Email: kmaq@kmaq.com
Web site: http://www.kmaq.com
Profile: KMAQ-FM is a commercial station owned by Dennis W. Voy. The format of the station is adult contemporary. KMAQ-FM broadcasts to the Maquoketa, IA area at 95.1 FM.
FM RADIO STATION

KMAR-FM 42909
Owner: Boeuf River Broadcasting Co.
Editorial: 1823 Highway 618, Winnsboro, Louisiana 71295 **Tel:** 1 318 435-5141.
Email: kmarfm@bellsouth.net
Profile: KMAR-FM is a commercial station owned by Boeuf River Broadcasting Co. The format of the station is contemporary country. KMAR-FM broadcasts to the Winnsboro, LA area at 95.9 FM.
FM RADIO STATION

KMAS-AM 35005
Owner: Olympic Broadcasting Inc.
Editorial: 210 W Cota St, Shelton, Washington 98584-2264 **Tel:** 1 360 426-1030.
Email: kmasnews@kmas.com
Web site: http://www.ifiberonenewsradio.com
Profile: KMAS-AM is a commercial station owned by Olympic Broadcasting Inc. The format of the station is news/talk. KMAS-AM broadcasts to the Seattle area at 1030 AM.
AM RADIO STATION

KMAT-FM 483789
Owner: Cordell Communications, Inc
Editorial: 2424 South Blvd, Houston, Texas 77098-5110 **Tel:** 1 713 520-5200.
Email: amistad@radioamistad.net
Web site: http://www.khcb.org
Profile: KMAT-FM is a non-commercial station owned by Cordell Communications, Inc. The format of the station is Hispanic Christian programming. KMAT-FM broadcasts to the Seadrift/Port O'Connor, TX area at 105.1 FM.
FM RADIO STATION

KMAV-FM 46407
Owner: KMSR, Inc.
Editorial: 1000 Main St W, Mayville, North Dakota 58257-1036 **Tel:** 1 701 786-2335.
Email: news@kmav.com
Web site: http://www.kmav.com
Profile: KMAV-FM is a commercial station owned by KMSR, Inc. The format of the station is country music. KMAV-FM broadcasts to the Mayville, ND area at 105.5 FM.
FM RADIO STATION

KMAX-AM 39466
Owner: Inland Northwest Broadcasting
Editorial: 1114 N Almon St, Moscow, Idaho 83843-8507 **Tel:** 1 208 882-2551.
Profile: KMAX-AM is a commercial station owned by Inland Northwest Broadcasting. The format of the station is news, sports and talk. KMAX-AM broadcasts to the Moscow, ID area at 840 AM.
AM RADIO STATION

KMAX-FM 136706
Owner: Townsquare Media, LLC
Editorial: 600 Main St, Windsor, Colorado 80550-5133 **Tel:** 1 970 674-2700.
Web site: http://943loudwire.com
Profile: KMAX-FM is a commercial station owned by Townsquare Media, LLC. The format of the station is classic rock. KMAX-FM broadcasts to the Windsor, CO area at 94.3 FM.
FM RADIO STATION

KMBI-AM 37378
Owner: Moody Bible Institute
Editorial: 5408 S Freya St, Spokane, Washington 99223-7114 **Tel:** 1 509 448-2555.
Email: radiomoody@moody.edu
Web site: http://www.radiomoody.org/escucha
Profile: KMBI-AM is a non-commercial station owned by Moody Bible Institute. The format of the station is Spanish-language religious. KMBI-AM broadcasts to the Spokane, WA area at 1330 AM.
AM RADIO STATION

KMBI-FM 44766
Owner: Moody Bible Institute
Editorial: 5408 S Freya St, Spokane, Washington 99223-7114 **Tel:** 1 509 448-2555.
Email: kmbi@moody.edu
Web site: http://www.moodyradionorthwest.fm
Profile: KMBI-FM is a non-commercial station owned by the Moody Bible Institute. The format of the station is religious. KMBI-FM broadcasts to the Spokane, WA area at 107.9 FM.
FM RADIO STATION

KMBL-AM 35006
Owner: Foster Charitable Foundation, Inc.
Editorial: 214 Pecan St, Junction, Texas 76849-4141
Tel: 1 325 446-3371.
Email: chuck@krvl.com
Web site: http://www.kmblam.com
Profile: KMBL-AM is a commercial station owned by Foster Charitable Foundation, Inc.. The format of the station is classic country. KMBL-AM broadcasts to the Junction, TX area at 1450 AM.
AM RADIO STATION

KMBQ-FM 41665
Owner: Spirit of Alaska Broadcasting Inc.
Editorial: 851 E Westpoint Dr Ste 301, Wasilla, Alaska 99654-7183 **Tel:** 1 907 373-0222.
Web site: http://www.kmbq.com
Profile: KMBQ-FM is a commercial station owned by Spirit of Alaska Broadcasting Inc. The format of the station is adult contemporary. KMBQ-FM broadcasts to the Wasilla, AK area at 99.7 FM.
FM RADIO STATION

KMBR-FM 44848
Owner: Cherry Creek Radio
Editorial: 750 Dewey Blvd, Butte, Montana 59701-3200 **Tel:** 1 406 494-1030.
Email: prodbutte@cherrycreekradio.com
Web site: http://www.955kmbr.com
FM RADIO STATION

KMBX-AM 38515
Owner: Entravision Communications Corp.
Editorial: 67 Garden Ct, Monterey, California 93940-5302 **Tel:** 1 831 373-6767.
Profile: KMBX-AM is a commercial station owned by Entravision Communications Corp. The format of the station is Hispanic religious. KMBX-AM broadcasts to the Monterey, CA area at 700 AM.
AM RADIO STATION

KMBZ-AM 39387
Owner: Entercom Communications Corp.
Editorial: 7000 Squibb Rd, Mission, Kansas 66202-3233 **Tel:** 1 913 744-3600.
Web site: http://www.kmbz.com
Profile: KMBZ-AM is a commercial station owned by Entercom Communications Corp. The format of the station is talk programming. KMBZ-AM broadcasts to the Kansas City, MO area at 980 AM.
AM RADIO STATION

KMBZ-FM 42165
Owner: Entercom Communications Corp.
Editorial: 7000 Squibb Rd, Mission, Kansas 66202-3233 **Tel:** 1 913 744-3600.
Email: news@kmbz.com
Web site: http://www.kmbz.com
Profile: KMBZ-FM is a commercial station owned by Entercom Communications Corp. The format of the station is news/talk. KMBZ-FM broadcasts to the Westwood, KS, area at 98.1 FM.
FM RADIO STATION

KMCD-AM 38460
Owner: Alpha Media USA
Editorial: 57 S Court St, Fairfield, Iowa 52556
Tel: 1 641 472-4191.
Email: news@fairfieldiowaradio.com
Web site: http://www.fairfieldiowaradio.com
Profile: KMCD-AM is a commercial station owned by Alpha Media USA. The format for the station is classic country. KMCD-AM broadcasts to the Ottumna, IA, Kirksville, MO area at 1570 AM.
AM RADIO STATION

KMCH-FM 41902
Owner: Coloff Media
Editorial: 212 E Main St, Manchester, Iowa 52057-1733 **Tel:** 1 563 927-6249.
Email: mix947@kmch.com
Web site: http://www.kmch.com
Profile: KMCH-FM is a commercial station owned by Coloff Media. The format of the station is adult contemporary and country music. KMCH-FM broadcasts to the Cedar Rapids, IA area at 94.7 FM.
FM RADIO STATION

KMCK-FM 39763
Owner: Cumulus Media Inc.
Editorial: 4209 N Frontage Rd, Fayetteville, Arkansas 72703-5002 **Tel:** 1 479 521-5566.
Web site: http://www.power1057.com
Profile: KMCK-FM is a commercial station owned by Cumulus Media Inc. The format of the station is Top 40/CHR music, consisting of contemporary pop and rock. KMCK-FM broadcasts to the Fayetteville, AR area at 105.7 FM.
FM RADIO STATION

KMCM-FM 39857
Owner: Brazos Communications West, LLC
Editorial: 3303 N Midkiff Rd Ste 115, Midland, Texas 79705-4860 **Tel:** 1 432 520-9912.
Web site: http://www.97gold.com
Profile: KMCM-FM is a commercial station owned by Brazos Communications West, LLC. The format of the station is classic hits music. KMCM-FM broadcasts in the Midland, TX, area at 96.9 FM.
FM RADIO STATION

KMCN-FM 44604
Owner: Prairie Communications LLP
Editorial: 1853 442nd Ave, Clinton, Iowa 52732-8748
Tel: 1 563 243-1390.
Web site: http://www.mac947.wix.com
Profile: KMCN-FM is a commercial station owned by Prairie Communications LLP. The format of the station is adult hits. KMCN-FM broadcasts to the Clinton, IA, area at 94.7 FM.
FM RADIO STATION

KMCO-FM 45668
Owner: Southeastern Oklahoma Radio, LLC
Editorial: 1801 E Electric Ave, McAlester, Oklahoma 74501-3824 **Tel:** 1 918 426-1050.
Email: info@mcalesterradio.com
Web site: http://www.mcalesterradio.com
Profile: KMCO-FM is a commercial station owned by Southeastern Oklahoma Radio, LLC. The format of the station is country music. KMCO-FM broadcasts to the McAlester, OK area at 101.3 FM.
FM RADIO STATION

KMCR-FM 39765
Owner: Best Broadcast Group
Editorial: 205 E Norman St, Montgomery City, Missouri 63361-1437 **Tel:** 1 573 564-2275.
Email: kmcr@socket.net
Web site: http://www.kmcrradio.com
Profile: KMCR-FM is a commercial station owned by Best Broadcast Group. The format of the station is adult contemporary music. KMCR-FM broadcasts to the Montgomery City, MO area at 103.9 FM.
FM RADIO STATION

KMCS-FM 46756
Owner: Prairie Communications LLP
Editorial: 3218 Mulberry Ave, Muscatine, Iowa 52761-2319 **Tel:** 1 563 263-2442.
Email: requests@vintage931.com
Web site: http://vintage931.com
Profile: KMCS-FM is a commercial station owned by Prairie Communications LLP. The format of the station is classic rock and blues. KMCS-FM broadcasts to the Muscatine, IA area at 93.1 FM.
FM RADIO STATION

KMCV-FM 450687
Owner: Bott Broadcasting Co.
Editorial: 1701 N Bishop Ave Ste 15, Rolla, Missouri 65401-2229 **Tel:** 1 573 308-1616.
Web site: http://www.bottradionetwork.com
Profile: KMCV-FM is a non-commercial station owned by Bott Broadcasting Co. The format of the station is religious and Christian programming. KMCV-FM broadcasts to the Rolla, MO area at 89.9 FM.
FM RADIO STATION

KMCX-FM 39766
Owner: iHeartMedia Inc.
Editorial: 113 W 4th St, Ogallala, Nebraska 69153-2508 **Tel:** 1 308 284-3633.
Web site: http://kmcx.iheart.com
Profile: KMCX-FM is a commercial station owned by iHeartMedia Inc.The format of the station is contemporary country music. KMCX-FM broadcasts to the Ogallala, NE area at 106.5 FM.
FM RADIO STATION

KMDL-FM 39767
Owner: Townsquare Media, LLC
Editorial: 1749 Bertrand Dr, Lafayette, Louisiana 70506-2054 **Tel:** 1 337 233-6000.
Web site: http://www.973thedawg.com
Profile: KMDL-FM is a commercial station owned by Townsquare Media, LLC. The format of the station is contemporary country music. KMDL-FM broadcasts to the Lafayette, LA area at 97.3 FM.
FM RADIO STATION

KMDO-AM 37379
Owner: Fort Scott Broadcasting Co., Inc.
Editorial: 2 N National Ave, Fort Scott, Kansas 66701-1307 **Tel:** 1 620 223-4500.
Profile: KMDO-AM is a commercial station owned by Fort Scott Broadcasting Co., Inc. The format of the station is Adult Hits. KMDO-AM broadcasts to the Fort Scott, KS area at 1600 AM.
AM RADIO STATION

KMDR2-FM 883719
Owner: Mad River Radio
Editorial: 728 7th St Ste 2A, Eureka, California 95501-1158 **Tel:** 1 707 445-3699.
Web site: http://www.1067theedgefm.com
Profile: KMDR2-FM is owned by Mad River Radio. The format for the station is rock music. KMDR2-FM broadcasts to the Eureka, CA on 106.7 FM. Digital radio technology is used by AM and FM radio stations, via a digital signal embedded in their analog signal, to transmit audio and data.
FM RADIO STATION

KMDX-FM 44127
Owner: Four R Broadcasting
Editorial: 3434 Sherwood Way, San Angelo, Texas 76901-3531 **Tel:** 1 325 947-1061.
Web site: http://www.1061mdx.com
Profile: KMDX-FM is a commercial station owned by Four R Broadcasting. The format of the station is Rhythmic AC. KMDX-FM broadcasts to the San Angelo, TX area at 106.1 FM.
FM RADIO STATION

KMDY-FM 440615
Owner: Cornerstone Community Radio Inc.
Editorial: 521 Main St, Carthage, Illinois 62321-1338
Tel: 1 217 357-3000.
Email: kmdy@adams.net
Web site: http://www.kmdy.org
FM RADIO STATION

KMDZ-FM 238250
Owner: Sangre de Cristo Broadcasting Inc.
Editorial: 304 S Grand Ave, Las Vegas, Nevada 87701
Tel: 1 505 426-1967.
Profile: KMDZ-FM is a commercial station owned by Sangre de Cristo Broadcasting Inc. The format of the station is adult hits-Jack-FM. KMDZ-FM broadcasts to the Las Vegas area at 96.7 FM.
FM RADIO STATION

KMED-AM 37380
Owner: Bicoastal Media LLC
Editorial: 3624 Avion Dr, Medford, Oregon 97504
Tel: 1 541 772-4170.
Web site: http://www.kmed.com
Profile: KMED-AM is a commercial station owned by Bicoastal Media LLC. The format of the station is news and talk programming. KMED-AM broadcasts to the Medford, OR area at 1440 AM.
AM RADIO STATION

KMEL-FM 39768
Owner: iHeartMedia Inc.
Editorial: 340 Townsend St Ste 4, San Francisco, California 94107-1698 **Tel:** 1 415 538-1013.
Web site: http://kmel.iheart.com
Profile: KMEL-FM is a commercial station owned by iHeartMedia Inc. The format of the station is urban contemporary music. KMEL-FM broadcasts to the San Francisco area at 106.1 FM.
FM RADIO STATION

KMEM-FM 39769
Owner: Tri-Rivers Broadcasting Company, Inc.
Editorial: 650 N Clay St, Memphis, Missouri 63555-1618 **Tel:** 1 660 465-7225.
Email: email@kmemfm.com
Web site: http://www.kmemfm.com
Profile: KMEM-FM is a commercial station owned by Tri-Rivers Broadcasting Company, Inc. The format of the station is country music. KMEM-FM broadcasts to the Memphis, MO area at 100.5 FM.
FM RADIO STATION

KMER-AM 35007
Owner: Broadway Media LS, LLC
Editorial: 436 Fossil Butte Dr, Kemmerer, Wyoming 83101 **Tel:** 1 307 877-4422.
Profile: KMER-AM is a commercial station owned by Broadway Media LS, LLC. The format of the station is oldies. KMER-AM broadcasts to the Kemmerer, WY area on 940 AM.
AM RADIO STATION

KMET-AM 36527
Owner: Sunset Broadcasting Inc.
Editorial: 700 E Redlands Blvd, Ste U, Redlands, California 92373 **Tel:** 1 951 402-5305.
Email: kmet1490talkradio@yahoo.com
Web site: http://www.kmet1490am.com
Profile: KMET-AM is a commercial station owned by Sunset Broadcasting Inc. The format of the station is news, talk and sports. KMET-AM broadcasts to the Banning, CA area at 1490 AM.
AM RADIO STATION

KMEZ-FM 42797
Owner: Cumulus Media Inc
Editorial: 201 Saint Charles Ave, Ste 201, New Orleans, Louisiana 70170 **Tel:** 1 504 581-7002.
Web site: http://www.oldschool1067.com
Profile: KMEZ-FM is a commercial station owned by Cumulus Media Inc. The format of the station is urban adult contemporary. KMEZ-FM broadcasts to the New Orleans area at 106.7 FM.
FM RADIO STATION

KMFA-FM 39770
Owner: Capitol Broadcasting Association, Inc.
Editorial: 3001 N Lamar Blvd Ste 100, Austin, Texas 78705-2033 **Tel:** 1 512 476-5632.
Email: info@kmfa.org
Web site: http://www.kmfa.org
Profile: KMFA-FM is a non-commercial station owned by Capitol Broadcasting Association, Inc. The format of the station is classical music. KMFA-FM broadcasts to the Austin, TX area at 89.5 FM.
FM RADIO STATION

KMFG-FM 43544
Owner: Midwest Communications Inc.
Editorial: 807 W 37th St, Hibbing, Minnesota 55746-2839 **Tel:** 1 218 263-7531.
Web site: http://mwcradio.com/station/70/
Profile: KMFG-FM is a commercial station owned by Midwest Communications Inc. The format of the station is classic rock music. KMFG-FM broadcasts in the Hibbing, MN area at 102.9 FM.
FM RADIO STATION

KMFR-AM 234961
Owner: Pearsall Radioworks Ltd.
Editorial: 8023 Vantage Dr Ste 840, San Antonio, Texas 78230-4771 **Tel:** 1 888 522-7437.
Email: info@call1310.com
Web site: http://www.call1310.com
Profile: KMFR-AM is a commercial station owned by Pearsall Radioworks, LTD. The format of the station is classic rock.KMFR-AM broadcasts to the San Antonio area at 1280 AM.
FM RADIO STATION

KMFX-AM 38935
Owner: Q Media, LLC
Editorial: 474 Guernsey Ln, Red Wing, Minnesota 55066-7448 **Tel:** 1 651 388-7151.
Profile: KMFX-AM is a commercial station owned by Q Media, LLC. The format of the station is classic country. KMFX-AM broadcasts to the Wabasha, MN area at a frequency of 1190 AM.
AM RADIO STATION

KMFX-FM 46286
Owner: iHeartMedia Inc.
Editorial: 1530 Greenview Dr SW Ste 200, Rochester, Minnesota 55902-4327 **Tel:** 1 507 288-3888.
Web site: http://www.1025thefox.com
Profile: KMFX-FM is a commercial station owned by iHeartMedia Inc. The format of the station is contemporary country. KMFX-FM broadcasts to the Rochester, MN area on 102.5 FM.
FM RADIO STATION

KMFY-FM 46178
Owner: Lamke Broadcasting, Inc.
Editorial: 507 SE 11th St, Grand Rapids, Minnesota 55744 **Tel:** 1 218 999-5699.
Email: info@kozyradio.com
Web site: http://www.kmfyradio.com
Profile: KMFY-FM is a commercial station owned by Lamke Broadcasting, Inc. The format of the station is adult contemporary and lite rock. KMFY-FM broadcasts locally to the Grand Rapids, MN area at a frequency of 96.9 FM.
FM RADIO STATION

KMGA-FM 46251
Owner: Cumulus Media Inc
Editorial: 500 4th St NW Fl 5, Albuquerque, New Mexico 87102-5324 **Tel:** 1 505 767-6700.
Email: studio@995magicfm.com
Web site: http://www.995magicfm.com
Profile: KMGA-FM is a commercial station owned by Cumulus Media Inc. The format of the station is adult contemporary. KMGA-FM broadcasts to the Albuquerque, NM area at 99.5 FM.
FM RADIO STATION

KMGC-FM 43566
Owner: Radio Works Inc.
Editorial: 612 Fairview Rd SW, Camden, Arkansas 71701 **Tel:** 1 870 836-9567.
Email: radioworks@cablelynx.com
Web site: http://www.magic104online.com
Profile: KMGC-FM is a commercial station owned by Radio Works Inc. The format of the station is urban contemporary music. KMGC-FM broadcasts to the Camden, AR area at 104.5 FM.
FM RADIO STATION

KMGE-FM 46504
Owner: McKenzie River Broadcasting
Editorial: 925 Country Club Rd, Ste 200, Eugene, Oregon 97401 **Tel:** 1 541 484-9400.
Web site: http://www.kmge.fm
Profile: KMGE-FM is a commercial station owned by McKenzie River Broadcasting. The format of the station is adult contemporary music. KMGE-FM broadcasts to the Eugene, OR area at 94.5 FM.
FM RADIO STATION

KMGI-FM 45832
Owner: Idaho Wireless Corp.
Editorial: 544 N Arthur Ave, Pocatello, Idaho 83204-3002 **Tel:** 1 208 233-2121.
Profile: KMGI-FM is a commercial station owned by Idaho Wireless Corp.The format of the station is rock music. KMGI-FM broadcasts to the Pocatello, ID area at 102.5 FM.
FM RADIO STATION

KMGJ-FM 43692
Owner: MBC Grand Broadcasting Inc.
Editorial: 1360 E Sherwood Dr, Grand Junction, Colorado 81501-7546 **Tel:** 1 970 254-2100.
Web site: http://www.931magic.com
Profile: KMGJ-FM is a commercial station owned by MBC Grand Broadcasting Inc. The format of the station is adult contemporary. KMGJ-FM broadcasts to the Grand Junction, CO area at 93.1 FM.
FM RADIO STATION

KMGK-FM 40077
Owner: Branstock Communications Inc.
Editorial: 12 1st St SE, Glenwood, Minnesota 56334-1619 **Tel:** 1 320 634-5358.
Email: traffic@kmgk1071.com
Web site: http://www.kmgk1071.com
Profile: KMGK-FM is a commercial station owned by Branstock Communications Inc. The format of the station is smooth AC. KMGK-FM broadcasts to the Glenwood, MN area at 107.1 FM.
FM RADIO STATION

KMGL-FM 39772
Owner: Tyler Media, LLC
Editorial: 400 E Britton Rd, Oklahoma City, Oklahoma 73114-7515 **Tel:** 1 405 478-5104.
Web site: http://www.magic104.com
Profile: KMGL-FM is a commercial station owned by Tyler Media, LLC. The format of the station is adult contemporary music. KMGL-FM broadcasts to the Oklahoma City area at 104.1 FM.
FM RADIO STATION

KMGM-FM 44767
Owner: Iowa City Broadcasting Co.
Editorial: 4454 Highway 212, Montevideo, Minnesota 56265-4539 **Tel:** 1 320 269-8815.
Email: kdmaprod@radiokdma.com
Profile: KMGM-FM is a commercial station owned by Iowa City Broadcasting Co. The format of the station is classic rock music. KMGM-FM broadcasts to the Montevideo, MN area at 105.5 FM.
FM RADIO STATION

KMGN-FM 41460
Owner: Great Circle Media
Editorial: 1117 W Route 66, Flagstaff, Arizona 86001-6213 **Tel:** 1 928 774-5231.
Email: news@kaff.com
Web site: http://www.939themountain.com
Profile: KMGN-FM is a commercial station owned by the Guyann Corp. The format of the station is rock. KMGN-FM broadcasts to the Flagstaff, AZ area at 93.9 FM.
FM RADIO STATION

KMGO-FM 46085
Owner: KMGO Inc.
Editorial: 402 N 12th St, Centerville, Iowa 52544-1718 **Tel:** 1 641 856-3996.
Email: kmgofm@lisco.net
Web site: http://www.kmgo.com
Profile: KMGO-FM is a commercial station owned by KMGO Inc. The format of the station is contemporary country. KMGO-FM broadcasts to the Cedar Rapids, IA area at 98.7 FM.
FM RADIO STATION

KMGV-FM 43419
Owner: Cumulus Media
Editorial: 1071 W Shaw Ave, Fresno, California 93711-3702 **Tel:** 1 559 490-9800.
Web site: http://www.mega979.com
Profile: KMGV-FM is a commercial station owned by Cumulus Media. The format of the station is rhythmic oldies music. KMGV-FM broadcasts to the Fresno, CA area at 97.9 FM.
FM RADIO STATION

KMGW-FM 44438
Owner: Townsquare Media, LLC
Editorial: 4010 Summitview Ave, Yakima, Washington 98908-2966 **Tel:** 1 509 972-3461.
Web site: http://mega993online.com/
Profile: KMGW-FM is a commercial station owned by Townsquare Media, LLC. The format of the station is rhythmic oldies. KMGW-FM broadcasts to the Yakima, WA area at 99.3 FM.
FM RADIO STATION

KMGX-FM 41715
Owner: Gross Communications Co.
Editorial: 345 SW Cyber Dr Ste 101-103, Bend, Oregon 97702-1045 **Tel:** 1 541 388-3300.
Web site: http://www.themix1007.com
Profile: KMGX-FM is a commercial station owned by Gross Communications Co. The format of the station is Lite Rock/Lite AC music. KMGX-FM broadcasts to the Bend, OR area at 100.7 FM.
FM RADIO STATION

KMGZ-FM 39774
Owner: Broadco of Texas Inc.
Editorial: 1421 NW Great Plains Blvd Ste C, Lawton, Oklahoma 73505-2843 **Tel:** 1 580 536-9530.
Web site: http://www.kmgz.com
Profile: KMGZ-FM is a commercial station owned by Broadco of Texas Inc. The format of the station is hot adult contemporary music. KMGZ-FM broadcasts in the Lawton, OK area. at 95.3 FM.
FM RADIO STATION

KMHA-FM 41459
Owner: Ft. Berthold Communications
Editorial: 601 Lodge Rd, New Town, North Dakota 58763-9400 **Tel:** 1 701 627-3333.
Web site: http://www.nv1.org/kmhastations.html
Profile: KMHA-FM is a non-commercial station owned by Ft. Berthold Communications. The format of the station is variety. KMHA-FM broadcasts to the New Town, ND area at 91.3 FM.
FM RADIO STATION

KMHD-FM 41469
Owner: Oregon Public Broadcasting
Editorial: 7140 SW MacAdam Ave, Portland, Oregon 97219-3013 **Tel:** 1 503 244-9900.
Web site: http://www.opb.org/kmhd
Profile: KMHD-FM is a non-commercial station owned by Oregon Public Broadcasting. The format of the station is jazz and blues music. KMHD-FM broadcasts to the Portland, OR area at 89.1 FM.
FM RADIO STATION

KMHK-FM 43449
Owner: Townsquare Media, LLC
Editorial: 27 N 27th St Fl 23, Billings, Montana 59101-2357 **Tel:** 1 406 248-7827.
Web site: http://kmhk.com
Profile: KMHK-FM is a commercial station owned by Townsquare Media, LLC. The format of the station is classic rock music. KMHK-FM broadcasts in Billings, MT area at 103.7 FM.
FM RADIO STATION

KMHL-AM 37382
Owner: KMHL Broadcasting Corp.
Editorial: 1414 E College Dr, Marshall, Minnesota 56258-2027 **Tel:** 1 507 532-2282.
Email: kmhlradio@gmail.com
Web site: http://www.marshallradio.net
Profile: KMHL-AM is a commercial station owned by KMHL Broadcasting Corp. The format of the station is news, talk, sports and variety music. KMHL-AM broadcasts in the Marshall, MN area at 1400 AM.
AM RADIO STATION

KMHM-FM 338556
Owner: Southern Gospetality LLC
Editorial: RR 1 Box 266E, Marble Hill, Missouri 63764-9713 **Tel:** 1 573 238-1041.
Email: kmhm1041@clas.net
Web site: http://mysoutherngospel.net
Profile: KMHM-FM is a commercial station owned by Southern Gospetality LLC. The format of the station is gospel. KMHM-FM broadcasts to the Marble Hill, MO area at 104.1 FM.
FM RADIO STATION

KMHR-AM 37349
Owner: First Western, Inc.
Editorial: 624 3rd St S, Nampa, Idaho 83651-3840 **Tel:** 1 208 463-1900.
Profile: KMHR-AM is a commercial station owned by First Western, Inc. The format of the station is southern gospel. KMHR-AM airs in the Nampa, ID area at 950 AM.
AM RADIO STATION

KMHT-AM 36438
Owner: Hanszen Broadcast Group
Editorial: 2323 Jefferson Ave, Marshall, Texas 75670-1281 **Tel:** 1 903 923-8000.
Email: info@kmhtradio.com
Web site: http://www.easttexastoday.com
Profile: KMHT-AM is a commercial station owned by Hanszen Broadcast Group. The format of the station is sports. KMHT-AM broadcasts to the Marshall, TX area at 1450 AM.
AM RADIO STATION

KMHT-FM 46732
Owner: Hanszen Broadcast Group
Editorial: 2323 Jefferson Ave, Marshall, Texas 75670-1281 **Tel:** 1 903 923-8000.
Email: info@kmhtradio.com
Web site: http://www.easttexastoday.com
Profile: KMHT-FM is a commercial station owned by Hanszen Broadcast Group. The format of the station is country. KMHT-FM broadcasts to the Marshall, TX area at 103.9 FM.
FM RADIO STATION

KMHX-FM 43428
Owner: Sonoma Media Group
Editorial: 1410 Neotomas Ave, Santa Rosa, California 95405-7533 **Tel:** 1 707 543-0100.
Web site: http://www.mix1049fm.com
Profile: KMHX-FM is a commercial station owned by Sonoma Media Group. The format of the station is hot adult contemporary music. KMHX-FM broadcasts to the Santa Rosa, CA area at 104.9 FM.
FM RADIO STATION

KMIA-AM 36324
Owner: Bustos Media, LLC
Editorial: 1400 W Main St, Auburn, Washington 98001-5230 **Tel:** 1 253 735-9700.
Web site: http://kmia.lazetaradio.com
Profile: KMIA-AM is a commercial station owned by Bustos Media, LLC. The format of the station is Bilingual Top 40/CHR. KMIA-AM broadcasts to the Seattle, WA area at 1210 AM.
AM RADIO STATION

KMIC-AM 35132
Owner: Daij Media, LLC
Editorial: 1600 Pasadena Blvd, Pasadena, Texas 77502-2404 **Tel:** 1 713 589-1336.
Email: info@radioaleluya.org
Web site: http://radioaleluya.org
Profile: KMIC-AM is a commercial station owned by the Daij Media, LLC. The format of the station is Spanish religious. KMIC-AM broadcasts to the Houston area on 1590 AM.
AM RADIO STATION

KMIL-FM 235220
Owner: Centex Broadcasting
Editorial: 901 E 1st St, Cameron, Texas 76520-3404 **Tel:** 1 254 697-6633.
Email: kmil@kmil.com
Web site: http://www.kmil.com
Profile: KMIL-FM is a commercial station owned by Centex Broadcasting. The format of the station is contemporary country music. KMIL-FM broadcasts to the Cameron, TX area at 105.1 FM.
FM RADIO STATION

KMIN-AM 39328
Owner: KD Radio Inc.
Editorial: 733 E Roosevelt Ave, Grants, New Mexico 87020-2113 **Tel:** 1 505 285-5598.
Web site: http://www.kmin980.com
Profile: KMIN-AM is a commercial station owned by KD Radio Inc. The format of the station is country music. KMIN-AM broadcasts to the Grants, NM area at 980 AM. The station does not accept pitches.
AM RADIO STATION

KMIQ-FM 43297
Owner: Cotton Broadcasting
Editorial: 2209 N Padre Island Dr, Corpus Christi, Texas 78408-2432 **Tel:** 1 361 289-8877.
Profile: KMIQ-FM is a commercial station owned by Cotton Broadcasting. The format of the station is Hispanic programming. KMIQ-FM broadcasts to the Corpus Christi, TX area at 104.9 FM.
FM RADIO STATION

KMIS-AM 37383
Owner: Pollack Broadcasting Co.
Editorial: 1303 Southwest Drive, Kennett, Missouri 63857 **Tel:** 1 573 888-4616.
Email: monte@semoradio.com
Web site: http://www.kmisradio.com
Profile: KMIS-AM is a commercial station owned by Pollack Broadcasting Co. The format of the station is sports. KMIS-AM broadcasts to the Kennett, MO area at 1050 AM.
AM RADIO STATION

KMIS-FM 543931
Owner: Pollack Broadcasting Co.
Editorial: 1303 Southwest Drive, Kennett, Missouri 63857 **Tel:** 1 573 888-4616.
Email: monte@semoradio.com
Profile: KMIS-FM is a commercial station owned by Pollack Broadcasting Co. The format of the station is sports. KMIS-FM broadcasts to the Malden, MO area at 103.9 FM.
FM RADIO STATION

KMIT-FM 39776
Owner: Saga Communications
Editorial: 501 S Ohlman St, Mitchell, South Dakota 57301 **Tel:** 1 605 996-9667.
Email: news@kmit.com
Web site: http://www.kmit.com
Profile: KMIT-FM is a commercial station owned by Saga Communications. The format of the station is contemporary country. KMIT-FM broadcasts to the Mitchell, SD area at 105.9 FM.
FM RADIO STATION

KMIX-FM 42949
Owner: Entravision Communications Corp.
Editorial: 6820 Pacific Ave Ste 3A, Stockton, California 95207-2631 **Tel:** 1 209 474-0154.
Web site: http://www.tricolor1009.com
Profile: KMIX-FM is a commercial station owned by Entravision Communications Corp. The format of the station is Regional Mexican. KMIX-FM broadcasts to the Stockton, CA area at 100.9 FM.
FM RADIO STATION

KMIY-FM 46055
Owner: iHeartMedia Inc.
Editorial: 3202 N Oracle Rd, Tucson, Arizona 85705-3820 **Tel:** 1 520 618-2100.
Web site: http://www.my929.com
Profile: KMIY-FM is a commercial station owned by iHeartMedia Inc. The format of the station is Hot AC. KMIY-FM broadcasts to the Tuscon, AZ area at 92.9 FM.
FM RADIO STATION

KMJ-AM 38990
Owner: Cumulus Media
Editorial: 1071 W Shaw Ave, Fresno, California 93711-3702 **Tel:** 1 559 490-5800.
Web site: http://www.kmjnow.com
Profile: KMJ-AM is a commercial station owned by Cumulus Media. The format of the station is news and talk. KMJ-AM broadcasts to the Fresno, CA area at 580 AM.
AM RADIO STATION

KMJB-FM 781429
Owner: Western Inspirational Broadcasters
Editorial: 6363 Us Highway 50 E, Carson City, Nevada 89701-1410 **Tel:** 1 775 883-5647.
Email: info@pilgrimradio.com
Web site: http://www.pilgrimradio.com
Profile: KCSP-FM is a non-commercial station owned by Western Inspirational Broadcasters Inc. The format of the station is Christian programming. The station airs locally at 89.1 FM in Hudson, WY, as well as the Riverton and Lander areas, also in Wyoming
FM RADIO STATION

KMJC-AM 37589
Owner: State of Oregon
Editorial: 1250 Siskiyou Blvd, Ashland, Oregon 97520-5001 **Tel:** 1 541 552-6301.
Email: jprinfo@sou.edu
Web site: http://www.ijpr.org
Profile: KMJC-AM is a non commercial station owned by State of Oregon. The format of the station is news and talk. KMJC-AM broadcasts to the Redding, CA area at 620 AM.
AM RADIO STATION

KMJE-FM 43083
Owner: Results Radio Group
Editorial: 861 Gray Ave, Yuba City, California 95991-3613 **Tel:** 1 530 673-2200.
Web site: http://1015khits.com/
Profile: KMJE-FM is a commercial station owned by Results Radio Group. The format of the station is Spanish Hits. KMJE-FM broadcasts to the Yuba City, CA area at 92.1 FM.
FM RADIO STATION

KMJ-FM 39718
Owner: Cumulus Media
Editorial: 1071 W Shaw Ave, Fresno, California 93711-3702 **Tel:** 1 559 490-5800.
Web site: http://www.kmjnow.com
Profile: KMJ-FM is a commercial station owned by Cumulus Media. The format of the station is news and talk. KMJ-FM broadcasts to the Fresno, CA area on 105.9 FM.
FM RADIO STATION

KMJI-FM 39529
Owner: Townsquare Media, LLC
Editorial: 2324 Arkansas Blvd, Texarkana, Arkansas 71854-2016 **Tel:** 1 870 772-3771.
Web site: http://www.magic933.com
Profile: KMJI-FM is a commercial station owned by Townsquare Media, LLC. The format of the station is hot adult contemporary. KMJI-FM broadcasts to the Texarkana, AR area at 93.3 FM.
FM RADIO STATION

KMJJ-FM 39587
Owner: Cumulus Media Inc.
Editorial: 270 Plaza Loop, Cumulus Broadcast Center, Bossier City, Louisiana 71111-4389
Tel: 1 318 549-8500.
Web site: http://www.997kmjj.com
Profile: KMJJ-FM is a commercial station owned by Cumulus Media Inc. The format of the station is urban contemporary music. KMJJ-FM broadcasts to the Shreveport, LA area at 99.7 FM.
FM RADIO STATION

KMJK-FM 39756
Owner: Cumulus Media Inc.
Editorial: 5800 Foxridge Dr, Ste 600, Mission, Kansas 66202 **Tel:** 1 913 514-3000.
Web site: http://www.magic1073.com
Profile: KMJK-FM is a commercial station owned by Cumulus Media Inc. The format of the station is urban adult contemporary music. KMJK-FM broadcasts to the Kansas City, MO area at 107.3 FM.
FM RADIO STATION

KMJM-AM 37081
Owner: iHeartMedia Inc.
Editorial: 600 Old Marion Rd NE, Cedar Rapids, Iowa 52402-2159 **Tel:** 1 319 395-0530.
Web site: http://1360kmjm.iheart.com
Profile: KMJM-AM is a commercial station owned by iHeartMedia Inc. The format of the station is country. KMJM-AM broadcasts to the Cedar Rapids, IA area at 1360 AM.
AM RADIO STATION

KMJM-FM 40160
Owner: iHeartMedia Inc.
Editorial: 1001 Highlands Plaza Dr W, Saint Louis, Missouri 63110-1337 **Tel:** 1 314 333-8000.
Email: kmjm@iheartmedia.com
Web site: http://www.kmjm.com
Profile: KMJM-FM is a commercial station owned by iHeartMedia Inc. The format of the station is urban adult contemporary music. KMJM-FM broadcasts to the St. Louis area at 100.3 FM.
FM RADIO STATION

KMJO-FM 217743
Owner: Midwest Communications
Editorial: 1020 25th St S, Fargo, North Dakota 58103-2312 **Tel:** 1 701 237-5346.
Web site: http://dukefmfargo.com
Profile: KMJO-FM is a commercial station owned by Midwest Communications. The format of the station is country. KMJO-FM broadcasts to the Fargo, ND area at 104.7 FM.
FM RADIO STATION

KMJQ-FM 39777
Owner: Urban One, Inc.
Editorial: 24 Greenway Plz Ste 900, Houston, Texas 77046-2418 **Tel:** 1 713 623-2108.
Web site: http://myhoustonmajic.hellobeautiful.com
Profile: KMJQ-FM is a commercial station owned by Urban One, Inc. The format of the station is urban adult contemporary music. KMJQ-FM broadcasts to the Houston area at 102.1 FM.
FM RADIO STATION

KMJR-FM 42591
Owner: Tejas Broadcasting
Editorial: 1733 S Brownlee Blvd, Corpus Christi, Texas 78404-3018 **Tel:** 1 361 883-1600.
Web site: http://lacaliente983.com
Profile: KMJR-FM is a commercial station owned by Tejas Broadcasting. The format of the station is regional Mexican music. KMJR-FM broadcasts in the Corpus Christi, TX area at 98.3 FM.
FM RADIO STATION

KMJV-FM 42524
Owner: Wolfhouse Radio Group Inc.
Editorial: 548 E Alisal St, Salinas, California 93905
Tel: 1 831 757-1910.
Profile: KMJV-FM is a commercial station owned by Wolfhouse Radio Group Inc. The format of the station is Hispanic, featuring regional Mexican music. The station airs locally on 106.3 FM.
FM RADIO STATION

KMJX-FM 39778
Owner: iHeartMedia Inc.
Editorial: 10800 Colonel Glenn Rd, Little Rock, Arkansas 72204-8017 **Tel:** 1 501 217-5000.
Web site: http://www.1051thewolf.com
Profile: KMJX-FM is a commercial station owned by iHeartMedia Inc. The format of the station is country. KMJX-FM broadcasts to the Little Rock, AR area at 105.1 FM.
FM RADIO STATION

KMKF-FM 44769
Owner: Manhattan Broadcasting
Editorial: 2414 Casement Rd, Manhattan, Kansas 66502-6633 **Tel:** 1 785 776-1350.
Email: news@1350kman.com
Web site: http://www.purerock.com
Profile: KMKF-FM is a commercial station owned by Manhattan Broadcasting. The format of the station is rock music. KMKF-FM broadcasts in the Manhattan, KS area at 101.5 FM.
FM RADIO STATION

KMKK-FM 450667
Owner: Ohana Broadcast Company LLC
Editorial: 1000 Bishop St Ste 200, Honolulu, Hawaii 96813-4203 **Tel:** 1 808 947-1500.
Web site: http://ohanabroadcast.com
Profile: KMKK-FM is a commercial station owned by Ohana Broadcast Company LLC. The format of the station is a variety of ethnic Hawaiian programming. KMKK-FM broadcasts to the Kaunakakai, HI area at 102.3 FM, but is based in Wailuku, HI.
FM RADIO STATION

KMKO-FM 501765
Owner: Alpha Media
Editorial: 1807 Lee Blvd, North Mankato, Minnesota 56003-2633 **Tel:** 1 507 345-4646.
Email: studio@957kmko.com
Web site: http://www.957therockstation.com
Profile: KMKO-FM is a commercial station owned by Alpha Media. The format of the station is AAA. KMKO-FM broadcasts to Mankato, MN area at 95.7 FM.
FM RADIO STATION

KMKS-FM 39779
Owner: Sandlin Broadcasting Co. Inc.
Editorial: 2309 5th St, Bay City, Texas 77414-6220
Tel: 1 979 244-4242.
Email: kmks@kmks.com
Web site: http://www.kmks.com
Profile: KMKS-FM is a commercial station owned by Sandlin Broadcasting Co. The format of the station is contemporary country music. KMKS-FM broadcasts to the Matagorda, TX area at 102.5 FM.
FM RADIO STATION

KMKT-FM 44230
Owner: Digity LLC
Editorial: 1800 Teague Dr Ste 300, Sherman, Texas 75090-2654 **Tel:** 1 903 463-6800.
Web site: http://931kmkt.com
Profile: KMKT-FM is a commercial station owned by Digity LLC. The format of the station is contemporary country music. KMKT-FM broadcasts in the Denison, TX area at 93.1 FM. The station does not produce its own news.
FM RADIO STATION

KMKX-FM 62649
Owner: Radio Millennium LLC
Editorial: 1100 Hastings Rd, #B, Ukiah, California 95482-7101 **Tel:** 1 707 462-4389.
Email: info@maxrock.com
Web site: http://www.maxrock.com
Profile: KMKX-FM is a commercial station owned by Radio Millennium LLC. The format of the station is classic rock. KMKX-FM broadcasts to the San Francisco area at 93.5 FM.
FM RADIO STATION

KMKY-AM 34923
Owner: Radio Mirchi Inc
Editorial: 963 Industrial Rd Ste I, San Carlos, California 94070-4146 **Tel:** 1 650 637-8800.
Web site: http://radio.disney.go.com/music/yourstation/sanfrancisco/index.html
Profile: KMKY-AM is a commercial station owned by Radio Mirchi Inc.
AM RADIO STATION

KMLA-FM 43085
Owner: Gold Coast Radio, LLC
Editorial: 355 S A St, Oxnard, California 93030-5823
Tel: 1 805 385-5656.
Email: kmla@lam1037.com
Web site: http://www.lam1037.com
Profile: KMLA-FM is a commercial station owned by Gold Coast Radio, LLC. The format of the station is regional Mexican music. KMLA-FM broadcasts to the Los Angeles area at 103.7 FM.
FM RADIO STATION

KMLB-AM 39096
Owner: Holladay Broadcasting Co.
Editorial: 1109 Hudson Ln, Monroe, Louisiana 71201-6003 **Tel:** 1 318 388-2323.
Email: talk540@bayou.com
Web site: http://talk540.com
Profile: KMLB-AM is commercial station owned by Holladay Broadcasting Co. The format of the station is news, talk, and sports. KMLB-AM broadcasts in the Monroe, LA area at 540 AM.
AM RADIO STATION

KMLE-FM 39780
Owner: CBS Radio
Editorial: 840 N Central Ave, Phoenix, Arizona 85004-2003 **Tel:** 1 602 452-1000.
Web site: http://kmle1079.cbslocal.com
Profile: KMLE-FM is a commercial station owned by CBS Radio. The format of the station is contemporary country. KMLE-FM broadcasts to the Phoenix area at 107.9 FM.
FM RADIO STATION

KMLK-FM 72057
Owner: Noalmark Broadcasting Corp.
Editorial: 2525 N West Ave, El Dorado, Arkansas 71730 **Tel:** 1 870 863-6126.
Web site: http://www.totalradio.com/kmlk.htm
Profile: KMLK-FM is a commercial station owned by Noalmark Broadcasting Corp. The format of the station is urban adult contemporary. KMLK-FM broadcasts to the El Dorado, AR area at 101.5 FM.
FM RADIO STATION

KMLO-FM 43996
Owner: James River Broadcasting
Editorial: 214 W Pleasant Dr, Pierre, South Dakota 57501 **Tel:** 1 605 224-8686.
Web site: http://www.dakotaradiogroup.com
Profile: KMLO-FM is a commercial station owned by James River Broadcasting. The format of the station is classic country. KMLO-FM broadcasts to the Pierre, SD area at 100.7 FM.
FM RADIO STATION

KMME-FM 46567
Owner: Catholic Broadcasting Northwest, Inc
Editorial: 835 E Park St, Eugene, Oregon 97401-2909
Tel: 1 503 285-5200.
Profile: KMME-FM is a non-commercial station owned by Catholic Broadcasting Northwest, Inc. The format of the station is religious specifically Catholic programming. KMME-FM broadcasts to the Eugene and Springfield areas in Oregon at 100.5 FM.
FM RADIO STATION

KMMG-FM 44860
Owner: Bustos Media, LLC
Editorial: 706 Butterfield Rd, Yakima, Washington 98901-2021 **Tel:** 1 509 457-1000.
Profile: KMMG-FM is a commercial station owned by Bustos Media, LLC. The format of the station is Bilingual Top 40/CHR. KMMG-FM broadcasts to the Yakima, WA, area at 96.7 FM.
FM RADIO STATION

KMMJ-AM 39057
Owner: Praise Network(The)
Editorial: 723 Turtle Beach, Marquette, Nebraska 68854 **Tel:** 1 888 920-5665.
Email: kmmj@kmmj.org
Web site: http://www.kmmj.org
Profile: KMMJ-AM is a non-commercial station owned by The Praise Network. The format of the station is religious music and religious talk. KMMJ-AM broadcasts to the Marquette, NE area at 750 AM.
AM RADIO STATION

KMMM-AM 36918
Owner: Rocking M Radio
Editorial: 30129 E US Highway 54, Pratt, Kansas 67124-8304 **Tel:** 1 620 672-5581.
Web site: http://themighty1290am.com
Profile: KMMM-AM is a commercial station owned by Rocking M Radio. The format of the station is classic hits. KMMM-AM broadcasts to the Pratt, KS area at 1290 AM.
AM RADIO STATION

KMMO-AM 37384
Owner: Missouri Valley Broadcasting Inc.
Editorial: Highway 65 North, Marshall, Missouri 65340
Tel: 1 660 886-7422.
Email: news@kmmo.com
Web site: http://www.kmmo.com
Profile: KMMO-AM is a commercial station owned by Missouri Valley Broadcasting Inc. The format of the station is classic country. KMMO-AM broadcasts to the Kansas City, MO area at 1300 AM.
AM RADIO STATION

KMMO-FM 44771
Owner: Missouri Valley Broadcasting Inc.
Editorial: 1070 Lexington Ave., Marshall, Missouri 65340 **Tel:** 1 660 886-7422.
Web site: http://www.kmmo.com
Profile: KMMO-FM is a commercial station owned by Missouri Valley Broadcasting Inc. The format of the station is classic country music. KMMO-FM broadcasts to the Kansas City, MO, area at 102.9 FM.
FM RADIO STATION

KMMQ-AM 39353
Owner: NRG Media LLC
Editorial: 5011 Capitol Ave, Omaha, Nebraska 68132-2921 **Tel:** 1 402 342-2000.
Web site: http://1020lanueva.com
Profile: KMMQ-AM is a commercial station owned by NRG Media LLC. The format of the station is regional Mexican. KMMQ-AM broadcasts to the Omaha, NE, area at 1020 AM.
AM RADIO STATION

KMMR-FM 41162
Owner: Kielb(Gregory & Claudette)
Editorial: 140 S 2nd Ave E, Malta, Montana 59538-9069 **Tel:** 1 406 654-2472.
Email: kmmrfm@itstriangle.com
Web site: http://kmmrfm.com
Profile: KMMR-FM is a commercial station owned by Gregory & Claudette Kielb. The format for the station is contemporary country and classics. KMMR-FM broadcasts to the Malta, MT area at 100.1 FM.
FM RADIO STATION

KMMS-AM 38665
Owner: Townsquare Media, LLC
Editorial: 125 W Mendenhall St Ste 1, Bozeman, Montana 59715-3500 **Tel:** 1 406 586-2343.
Email: kmmsam@gmail.com
Web site: http://www.kmmsam.com
Profile: KMMS-AM is a commercial station owned by Townsquare Media, LLC. The format of the station is news, talk and sports. KMMS-AM broadcasts in the Bozeman, MT area at 1450 AM.
AM RADIO STATION

KMMS-FM 46019
Owner: Townsquare Media, LLC
Editorial: 125 W Mendenhall St Ste 1, Bozeman, Montana 59715-3500 **Tel:** 1 406 586-2343.
Web site: http://www.mooseradio.com
Profile: KMMS-FM is a commercial station owned by Townsquare Media, LLC. The format for the station is adult album alternative. KMMS-FM broadcasts to the Bozeman, MT area at 95.1 FM.
FM RADIO STATION

KMMT-FM 39782
Owner: Digerness(Dave & Maryann)
Editorial: 94 Laurel Mountain Road, Mammoth Lakes, California 93546 **Tel:** 1 760 934-8888.
Email: kmmtradioworks@yahoo.com
Web site: http://www.kmmtradio.com
Profile: KMMT-FM is a commercial station owned by Dave and Maryann Digerness. The format of the station is Adult Top 40. KMMT-FM broadcasts to the Mammoth Lakes, CA area at 106.5 FM.
FM RADIO STATION

KMMX-FM 40962

Owner: Alpha Media
Editorial: 33 Briercroft Office Park, Lubbock, Texas 79412-3020 **Tel:** 1 806 762-3000.
Web site: http://www.mix100.net
Profile: KMMX-FM is a commercial station owned by Alpha Media. The format of the station is hot adult contemporary music. KMMX-FM broadcasts to the Lubbock, TX area at 100.3 FM.
FM RADIO STATION

KMMY-FM 578341

Owner: Will Payne
Editorial: 1600 W Jackson St, Hugo, Oklahoma 74743-5653 **Tel:** 1 580 326-2555.
Email: info@myrock965.com
Web site: http://www.myrock965.com
Profile: KMMY-FM is a commercial station owned by Will Payne. The format of the station is active rock. KMMY-FM broadcasts to the Soper, OK area at 96.5 FM.
FM RADIO STATION

KMMZ-FM 43641

Owner: PERMIAN BASIN BROADCASTING, LLC
Editorial: 12200 Service Road East, Odessa, Texas 79760 **Tel:** 1 432 563-2266.
Email: traffic@lacalienteonline.com
Web site: http://www.lacalienteonline.com
Profile: KMMZ-FM is a commercial station owned by PERMIAN BASIN BROADCASTING, LLC. The format of the station is regional Mexican. KMMZ-FM broadcasts to the Odessa, TX area on 101.3 FM.
FM RADIO STATION

KMNA-FM 431873

Owner: Casa Media Partners, LLC
Editorial: 152101 W County Road 12, Prosser, Washington 99350-7265 **Tel:** 1 509 786-1310.
Profile: KMNA-FM is a commercial station owned by Casa Media Partners, LLC. The format of the station is regional Mexican. KMNA-FM broadcasts to the Prosser, WA area at 98.7 FM.
FM RADIO STATION

KMNB-FM 42819

Owner: CBS Radio
Editorial: 625 2nd Ave S, Minneapolis, Minnesota 55402-1912 **Tel:** 1 612 339-1029.
Web site: http://buzn1029.cbslocal.com
Profile: KMNB-FM is a commercial station owned by CBS Radio. The format of the station is contemporary country music. KMNB-FM broadcasts to the Minneapolis area at 102.9 FM.
FM RADIO STATION

KMND-AM 37385

Owner: Townsquare Media, Inc.
Editorial: 11300 State Highway 191 Bldg 2, Midland, Texas 79707-1367 **Tel:** 1 432 563-9300.
Web site: http://espnwesttexas.com
Profile: KMND-AM is a commercial station owned by Townsquare Media, Inc. The format of the station is sports. KMND-AM broadcasts to the Midland, TX area at 1510 AM.
AM RADIO STATION

KMNS-AM 39279

Owner: iHeartMedia Inc.
Editorial: 1113 Nebraska St, Sioux City, Iowa 51105-1438 **Tel:** 1 712 258-5595.
Web site: http://www.620kmns.com
Profile: KMNS-AM is a commercial station owned by iHeartMedia Inc. The format of the station is sports. KMNS-AM broadcasts to the Sioux City, IA area at 620 AM. They do not accept press releases since they get everything for FOX Sports Network.
AM RADIO STATION

KMNT-FM 354777

Owner: Bicoastal Media LLC
Editorial: 1635 S Gold St, Centralia, Washington 98531 **Tel:** 1 360 736-3321.
Email: kmntryan@gmail.com
Web site: http://www.kmnt.com
Profile: KMNT-FM is a commercial station owned by Bicoastal Media LLC. The format of the station is country. KMNT-FM broadcasts to the Centralia, WA area at 104.3 FM.
FM RADIO STATION

KMNV-AM 36652

Owner: Davidson Media Group
Editorial: 3003 27th Ave S Ste 400, Minneapolis, Minnesota 55406-1914 **Tel:** 1 612 354-3282.
Web site: http://laraza1400.com
Profile: KMNV-AM is a commercial station owned by Davidson Media Group. The format of the station is regional Mexican music. KMNV-AM broadcasts to the Edina, MN area at 1400 AM.
AM RADIO STATION

KMNY-AM 35814

Owner: Multicultural Radio Broadcasting Inc.
Editorial: 5801 Marvin D Love Fwy Ste 409, Dallas, Texas 75237-2319 **Tel:** 1 972 572-1540.
Profile: KMNY-AM is a commercial station owned by Multicultural Radio Broadcasting Inc. The format of the station is Spanish programming. KMNY-AM broadcasts to the Dallas area at 1360 AM.
AM RADIO STATION

KMOC-FM 39783

Owner: Christian Service Foundation Inc.
Editorial: 1040 W Wenonah Blvd, Wichita Falls, Texas 76309 **Tel:** 1 940 767-3303.
Email: kmocfm@wf.net
Web site: http://www.kmocfm.com
Profile: KMOC-FM is a non-commercial station owned by The Christian Service Foundation Inc. The format of the station is contemporary Christian music. KMOC-FM broadcasts to the Wichita Falls, TX area at 89.5 FM.
FM RADIO STATION

KMOD-FM 45669

Owner: iHeartMedia Inc.
Editorial: 2625 S Memorial Dr, Tulsa, Oklahoma 74129-2601 **Tel:** 1 918 388-5100.
Web site: http://www.kmod.com
Profile: KMOD-FM is a commercial station owned by iHeartMedia Inc. The format is rock. KMOD-FM broadcasts to the Tulsa, OK area at 97.5 FM.
FM RADIO STATION

KMOE-FM 44773

Owner: Bates County Broadcasting Co.
Editorial: 800 E Nursery St, Butler, Missouri 64730 **Tel:** 1 660 679-4191.
Email: fm92@embarqmail.com
Web site: http://www.921kmoe.com
Profile: KMOE-FM is a commercial station owned by Bates County Broadcasting Co. The format of the station is classic country music. KMOE-FM broadcasts to the Kansas City, MO area at 92.1 FM.
FM RADIO STATION

KMOG-AM 35010

Owner: Farrell Enterprises LLC
Editorial: 500 E Tyler Pkwy, Payson, Arizona 85541-3276 **Tel:** 1 928 474-5214.
Email: news@1420kmog.com
Web site: http://www.rimcountryradio.com
Profile: KMOG-AM is a commercial station owned by Farrell Enterprises LLC. The format of the station is country. KMOG-AM broadcasts to the Payson, AZ area at 1420 AM and 103.3 FM.
AM RADIO STATION

KMOJ-FM 39784

Owner: State of Minnesota
Editorial: 2123 W Broadway Ave Ste 200, Minneapolis, Minnesota 55411-1870 **Tel:** 1 612 377-0594.
Email: info@kmojfm.com
Web site: http://www.kmojfm.com
Profile: KMOJ-FM is a non-commercial station owned by the State of Minnesota. The format of the station is a Urban Contemporary. KMOJ-FM broadcasts to the Minneapolis area at 89.9 FM.
FM RADIO STATION

KMOK-FM 44774

Owner: Ida-Vend Communications Group
Editorial: 805 Stewart Ave, Lewiston, Idaho 83501-4709 **Tel:** 1 208 746-5056.
Profile: KMOK-FM is a commercial station owned by Ida-Vend Communications Group. The format of the station is Top 40 music. KMOK-FM broadcasts to the Spokane, WA area at 106.9 FM.
FM RADIO STATION

KMOM-FM 514641

Owner: Dakota Broadcasting, LLC
Editorial: 426 N Highway 281 Ste 4, Aberdeen, South Dakota 57401-1864 **Tel:** 1 605 725-5551.
Web site: http://www.dakotabroadcasting.com
Profile: KMOM-FM is a commercial station owned by Dakota Broadcasting, LLC. The format is country music. KMOM-FM broadcasts to the Aberdeen, SD area at 105.5 FM.
FM RADIO STATION

KMON-AM 37386

Owner: Cherry Creek Radio
Editorial: 914 13th Ave S, Great Falls, Montana 59405-4406 **Tel:** 1 406 761-7600.
Web site: http://www.kmonam.com
Profile: KMON-AM is a commercial station owned by Cherry Creek Radio. The format of the station is country music. KMON-AM broadcasts in the Great Falls, MT area at 560 AM.
AM RADIO STATION

KMON-FM 44775

Owner: Cherry Creek Radio
Editorial: 914 13th Ave S, Great Falls, Montana 59405-4406 **Tel:** 1 406 761-7600.
Email: kmon560@cherrycreekradio.com
Web site: http://www.maxcountry945.com
Profile: KMON-FM is a commercial station owned by Cherry Creek Radio. The format of the station is contemporary and classic country music. KMON-FM broadcasts to the Great Falls, MT area at 94.5 FM.
FM RADIO STATION

KMOO-FM 42697

Owner: Hightower (Ingrid)
Editorial: 2065 N Us Highway 69, Mineola, Texas 75773-3731 **Tel:** 1 903 569-3823.
Email: news@kmoo.com
Web site: http://www.kmoo.com
Profile: KMOO-FM is a commercial station owned by Ingrid Hightower. The format of the station is contemporary country. KMOO-FM broadcasts to the Mineola, TX area at 99.9 FM.
FM RADIO STATION

KMOQ-FM 39555

Owner: American Media Investments
Editorial: 2510 W 20th St, Joplin, Missouri 64804 **Tel:** 1 417 781-1313.
Web site: http://www.mynewliferadio.com
Profile: KMOQ-FM is a commercial station owned by American Media Investments. The format of the station is contemporary Christian and broadcasts to the Joplin, MO area at 105.3 FM.
FM RADIO STATION

KMOU-FM 43034

Owner: Majestic Communication
Editorial: 5206 W 2nd St, Roswell, New Mexico 88201-8839 **Tel:** 1 575 622-6450.
Email: kmou@roswellradio.org
Profile: KMOU-FM is a commercial station owned by Majestic Communication. The format of the station is country music. KMOU-FM broadcasts to the Roswell, NM area at 104.7 FM.
FM RADIO STATION

KMOX-AM 36661

Owner: CBS Radio
Editorial: 1220 Olive St Fl 3, Saint Louis, Missouri 63103-2324 **Tel:** 1 314 444-3234.
Email: kmoxnews@kmox.com
Web site: http://stlouis.cbslocal.com
Profile: KMOX-AM is a commercial station owned by CBS Radio. The format of the station is news, sports and talk. KMOX-AM broadcasts to the St. Louis area at 1120 AM.
AM RADIO STATION

KMOZ-AM 38506

Owner: Bott Broadcasting Co.
Editorial: 1701 N Bishop Ave Ste 15, Rolla, Missouri 65401-2229 **Tel:** 1 573 647-6285.
Email: kmoz@bottradionetwork.com
Web site: http://www.bottradionetwork.com
Profile: KMOZ-AM is a commercial station owned by Bott Broadcasting Co. The format of the station is Christian talk. KMOZ-AM broadcasts in the Rolla, MO area at 1590 AM.
AM RADIO STATION

KMOZ-FM 61870

Owner: MBC Grand Broadcasting Inc.
Editorial: 1360 E Sherwood Dr, Grand Junction, Colorado 81501-7546 **Tel:** 1 970 254-2100.
Web site: http://www.themoose923.com/
Profile: KMOZ-FM is a commercial station owned by MBC Grand Broadcasting Inc. The format of the station is country. KMOZ-FM broadcasts to the Grand Junction, CO area at 100.7 FM.
FM RADIO STATION

KMPA-FM 43677

Owner: Waller Broadcasting
Editorial: 3400 W Marshall Ave Floor 3, Longview, Texas 75604-5035 **Tel:** 1 903 663-2477.
Web site: http://www.kompafm.com
Profile: KMPA-FM is a commercial station owned by Waller Broadcasting. The format of the station is Spanish Contemporary. KMPA-FM broadcasts to the Longview, TX, area at 103.1 FM.
FM RADIO STATION

KMPB-FM 538872

Owner: Wren Communications, Inc.
Tel: 1 970 378-2579.
Email: comment@kunc.org
Web site: http://www.kunc.org
Profile: KMPB-FM is a non-commercial station owned by Wren Communications, Inc. The format of the station is a variety of news and music programming. KMPB-FM broadcasts to the Summit County area in Colorado at 90.7 FM.
FM RADIO STATION

KMPC-AM 36662

Owner: P & Y Broadcasting Corp.
Editorial: 3700 Wilshire Blvd Ste 1020, Los Angeles, California 90010-3006 **Tel:** 1 213 487-1300.
Email: info@radiokorea.com
Web site: http://www.radiokorea.com
Profile: KMPC-AM is a commercial station owned by P & Y Broadcasting Corp. The format of the station is Korean language programming. KMPC-AM broadcasts to the Greater Los Angeles, CA area at 1540 AM.
AM RADIO STATION

KMPG-AM 35011

Owner: Promo Radio Corp.
Tel: 1 831 728-1520.
Email: kmpgradiobonita@yahoo.com
Web site: http://www.kmpgradiobonita.com/#
Profile: KMPG-AM is a commercial station owned by Promo Radio Corp. The format of the station is regional Mexican. KMPG-AM broadcasts to the Hollister, CA area at 1520 AM.
AM RADIO STATION

KMPH-AM 521794

Owner: Immaculate Heart Radio
Tel: 1 916 535-0500.
Email: programming@ihradio.org
Web site: http://ihradio.com
Profile: KMPH-AM is a non-commercial station owned by Immaculate Heart Radio. The format of the station is Catholic radio. KMPH-AM broadcasts to the Modesto, CA area at 840 AM.
AM RADIO STATION

KMPO-FM 41875

Owner: Radio Bilingue Inc.
Editorial: 5005 E Belmont Ave, Fresno, California 93727 **Tel:** 1 559 455-5777.
Web site: http://www.radiobilingue.org
Profile: KMPO-FM is a non-commercial station owned by Radio Bilingue Inc. The format of the station is Hispanic, featuring a variety of music and talk programming. KMPO-FM's target audience is Hispanic listeners in the Modesto, CA area. KMPO-FM airs at 88.7 FM and is a simulcast of KSJV-FM in Fresno, CA.
FM RADIO STATION

KMPR-FM 41458

Owner: Prairie Public Broadcasting
Editorial: 1814 N 15th St, Bismarck, North Dakota 58501-2025 **Tel:** 1 701 241-6900.
Web site: http://www.prairiepublic.org/radio
Profile: KMPR-FM is owned by Prairie Public Broadcasting. It is a non-commercial station with a classical and news/talk format that airs locally to the Minot, ND area at 88.9 FM.
FM RADIO STATION

KMPS-FM 43377

Owner: CBS Radio
Editorial: 1000 Dexter Ave N, Seattle, Washington 98109-3582 **Tel:** 1 206 805-0941.
Web site: http://kmps.cbslocal.com
Profile: KMPS-FM is a commercial station owned by CBS Radio. The format of the station is contemporary country. KMPS-FM broadcasts to the Seattle area at 94.1 FM.
FM RADIO STATION

KMPT-AM 39226

Owner: Townsquare Media, LLC
Editorial: 3250 S Reserve St, Missoula, Montana 59801-8236 **Tel:** 1 406 728-9300.
Email: newsroom@townsquaremedia.com
Web site: http://930kmpt.com
Profile: KMPT-AM is a commercial station owned by Townsquare Media, LLC. The format of the station is progressive talk. KMPT-AM broadcasts to the Missoula, MT area at 930 AM.
AM RADIO STATION

KMQA-FM 41026

Owner: Casa Media Partners, LLC
Editorial: 1450 E Bardsley Ave, Tulare, California 93274-5805 **Tel:** 1 559 687-3170.
Profile: KMQA-FM is a commercial station owned by Casa Media Partners, LLC. The format of the station is Hispanic programming. KMQA-FM broadcasts to the Tulare, CA area at 100.5 FM.
FM RADIO STATION

KMRB-AM 82630

Owner: Multicultural Radio Broadcasting Inc.
Editorial: 747 E Green St, Ste 208, Pasadena, California 91101 **Tel:** 1 626 773-1430.
Web site: http://www.am1430.net
Profile: KMRB-AM is a commercial station owned by Multicultural Radio Broadcasting Inc. The format of the station is variety. KMRB-AM broadcasts to the Pasadena, CA area at 1430 AM.
AM RADIO STATION

KMRC-AM 37134

Owner: Spotlight Broadcasting of New Orleans LLC
Editorial: 409 Duke St, Morgan City, Louisiana 70380-3518 **Tel:** 1 985 384-1430.
Web site: http://www.kmrcradio.com
Profile: KMRC-AM is a commercial station owned by Spotlight Broadcasting of New Orleans LLC. The format of the station is variety, including Lousiana swamp pop and ethnic Cajun music. KMRC-AM broadcasts to the Morgan City, LA area at 1430 AM.
AM RADIO STATION

KMRF-AM 36706

Owner: New Life Evangelistic Center
Editorial: 3208 State Highway Oo, Marshfield, Missouri 65706-2480 **Tel:** 1 314 421-3020.
Web site: http://www.hereshelpnetwork.org
Profile: KMRF-AM is a commercial station owned by New Life Evangelistic Center, Inc. The format of the station is religious. KMRF-AM broadcasts to the Greater Springfield, MO area at a frequency of 1510 AM.
AM RADIO STATION

KMRJ-FM 44014

Owner: Marker Broadcasting
Editorial: 75153 Merle Dr Ste G, Palm Desert, California 92211-5197 **Tel:** 1 760 568-4550.
Email: jammin995@markerbroadcasting.com
Web site: http://www.jammin995fm.com
Profile: KMRJ-FM is a commercial station owned by Marker Broadcasting. The format of the station is Rhythmic AC. KMRJ-FM broadcasts to the Palm Springs, CA area at 99.5 FM.
FM RADIO STATION

KMRK-FM 41956

Owner: ICA Radio
Editorial: 1330 E 8th St, Ste 207, Odessa, Texas 79761 **Tel:** 1 432 563-9102.
Web site: http://www.mycountry961.com
Profile: KMRK-FM is a commercial station owned by ICA Radio. The format of the station is country. KMRK-FM broadcasts to the Odessa, TX area at 96.1 FM.
FM RADIO STATION

KMRN-AM 39433

Owner: Cameron/Bethany Licence Co., LLC
Editorial: 607 E Platte Clay Way, Cameron, Missouri 64429-8825 **Tel:** 1 816 632-6661.
Web site: http://www.northwestmoinfo.com
Profile: KMRN-AM is a commercial station owned by Cameron/Bethany Licence Co., LLC. The format of the station is country. KMRN-AM broadcasts to the Cameron, MO, area on 1360 AM.
AM RADIO STATION

United States of America

KMRQ-FM 39905
Owner: iHeartMedia Inc.
Editorial: 2121 Lancey Dr, Modesto, California 95355-3036 Tel: 1 209 551-1306.
Web site: http://rock967.iheart.com
Profile: KMRQ-FM is a commercial station owned by iHeartMedia Inc. The format of the station is alternative rock. KMRQ-FM broadcasts to the Modesto, CA area at 96.7 FM.
FM RADIO STATION

KMRR-FM 42604
Owner: Saga Communications
Editorial: 2600 Highway Blvd, Spencer, Iowa 51301-2140 Tel: 1 712 262-3300.
Web site: http://more1049.com
Profile: KMRR-FM is a commercial station owned by Saga Communications. The format of the station is adult contemporary. KMRR-FM broadcasts to the Spencer, IA area at a frequency of 104.9 FM.
FM RADIO STATION

KMRS-AM 37388
Owner: Iowa City Broadcasting Co.
Editorial: 46671 State Highway 28, Morris, Minnesota 56267-4508 Tel: 1 320 589-3131.
Email: kmrskkok@fedtel.net
Web site: http://www.kmrskkok.com
Profile: KMRS-AM is a commercial station owned by Iowa City Broadcasting Co. The format of the station is local news, talk, and sports. KMRS-AM broadcasts to the Morris, MN area at 1230 AM.
AM RADIO STATION

KMRV-AM 37397
Owner: Wennes Communications Stations, Inc.
Editorial: 14 W Main St, Waukon, Iowa 52172-1638 Tel: 1 563 568-3476.
Email: knei@kneiradio.com
Web site: http://www.kmrvradio.com/
Profile: KMRV-AM is a commercial station owned by Wennes Communications Stations, Inc. The format for the station is Oldies. KMRV-AM broadcasts to the Waukon, IA area at 1160 AM.
AM RADIO STATION

KMRX-FM 39697
Owner: Noalmark Broadcasting Corp.
Editorial: 2525 N West Ave, El Dorado, Arkansas 71730 Tel: 1 870 863-6126.
Web site: http://www.totalradio.com/96x.htm
Profile: KMRX-FM is a commercial station owned by Noalmark Broadcasting Corp. The format of the station is adult contemporary. KMRX-FM broadcasts to the El Dorado, AR area at 96.1 FM.
FM RADIO STATION

KMRY-AM 36263
Owner: Sellers Broadcasting Inc.
Editorial: 1957 Blairs Ferry Rd NE, Cedar Rapids, Iowa 52402-5891 Tel: 1 319 393-1450.
Web site: http://www.kmryradio.com
Profile: KMRY-AM is a commercial station owned by Sellers Broadcasting Inc. The format for the station is Classic Hits. KMRY-AM broadcasts to the Cedar Rapids, IA area at 1450 AM.
AM RADIO STATION

KMRZ-FM 542133
Owner: Big Thickett Broadcasting Co., Inc. dba WYO Radio
Editorial: 2717 Yellowstone Rd, Rock Springs, Wyoming 82901-3261 Tel: 1 307 362-3793.
Email: wyoradio@wyoradio.com
Web site: http://www.wyoradio.com
Profile: KMRZ-FM is a commercial station owned by Big Thickett Broadcasting Co., Inc. dba WYO Radio. The format for the station is Top 40/CHR. KMRZ-FM broadcasts to the Salt Lake City area at 106.7 FM.
FM RADIO STATION

KMSA-FM 39785
Owner: Colorado Mesa University
Editorial: 1100 North Ave, Grand Junction, Colorado 81501-3122 Tel: 1 970 248-1442.
Web site: http://www.coloradomesa.edu/mass-communication/student-media.html
Profile: KMSA-FM is a non-commercial station owned by Colorado Mesa University. The format of the station is rock alternative music. KMSA-FM broadcasts in the Grand Rapids, CO area at 91.3 FM.
FM RADIO STATION

KMSD-AM 36736
Owner: Armada Media Corp.
Editorial: 15096 SD Highway 15, Milbank, South Dakota 57252-5954 Tel: 1 605 432-5516.
Email: kmsd@tnics.com
Web site: http://bigstoneradio.com
Profile: KMSD-AM is a commercial station owned by Armada Media Corp. The format of the station is classic hits. KMSD-AM broadcasts to the Milbank, SD area at 1510 AM.
AM RADIO STATION

KMSE-FM 658193
Owner: Minnesota Public Radio
Editorial: 480 Cedar St, Saint Paul, Minnesota 55101-2217 Tel: 1 651 290-1500.
Email: 893dj@mpr.org
Web site: http://www.mpr.org/listen/stations/kzseklse
FM RADIO STATION

KMSO-FM 39787
Owner: Mountain Broadcasting
Editorial: 725 Strand Ave, Missoula, Montana 59801 Tel: 1 406 542-1025.
Email: info@mtnbdc.com
Web site: http://www.moclub.com
Profile: KMSO-FM is a commercial station owned by Mountain Broadcasting. The format of the station is hot adult contemporary music. KMSO-FM broadcasts to the Missoula, MT area at 102.5 FM.
FM RADIO STATION

KMSR-AM 38976
Owner: KMSR, Inc.
Editorial: 1000 Main St W, Mayville, North Dakota 58257-1036 Tel: 1 701 786-2335.
Email: news@kmav.com
Web site: http://www.kmav.com
Profile: KMSR-AM is a commercial station owned by KMSR, Inc. The format of the station is sports. KMSR-AM broadcasts to the Mayville, ND area at 1520 AM.
AM RADIO STATION

KMSW-FM 128101
Owner: Bicoastal Media LLC
Editorial: 719 E 2nd St, The Dalles, Oregon 97058 Tel: 1 541 296-2211.
Web site: http://www.gorgeradio.com
Profile: KMSW-FM is a commercial station owned by Bicoastal Media LLC. The format of the station is classic rock music. KMSW-FM broadcasts in the Portland, OR area at 92.7 FM.
FM RADIO STATION

KMTA-AM 38329
Owner: Custer County Broadcasting Inc.
Editorial: 508 Main St, Miles City, Montana 59301-3019 Tel: 1 406 234-5626.
Web site: http://www.kyuskmta.com
Profile: KMTA-AM is a commercial station owned by Custer County Broadcasting Inc., dba Marks Group Inc. The format of the station is oldies. KMTA-AM broadcasts in the Miles City, MT area at 1050 AM.
AM RADIO STATION

KMTB-FM 41462
Owner: Southwest Arkansas Radio
Editorial: 1513 S 4th St, Nashville, Arkansas 71852 Tel: 1 870 845-3601.
Email: swarkradio@hotmail.com
Web site: http://www.southwestarkansasradio.com
Profile: KMTB-FM is a commercial station owned by Southwest Arkansas Radio. The format of the station is contemporary country. KMTB-FM broadcasts to the Nashville, AR area at 99.5 FM.
FM RADIO STATION

KMTI-AM 37389
Owner: Barton(Douglas L.)
Editorial: 500 North 1600 West, Manti, Utah 84642 Tel: 1 435 835-7301.
Email: news@kmtiradio.com
Web site: http://www.midutahradio.com/kmti
Profile: KMTI-AM is a commercial station owned by Douglas L. Barton. The format of the station is country. KMTI-AM broadcasts to the Manti, UT area at 650 AM.
AM RADIO STATION

KMTK-FM 235423
Owner: Combined Communications, Inc.
Editorial: 63088 NE 18th St Ste 200, Bend, Oregon 97701-7102 Tel: 1 541 382-5263.
Email: country@mountain997.com
Web site: http://www.997thebull.com
Profile: KMTK-FM is a commercial station owned by Combined Communications. The format of the station is contemporary country music. KMTK-FM broadcasts to the Bend, OR area at 99.7 FM.
FM RADIO STATION

KMTL-AM 35805
Owner: Domerese(George)
Editorial: 301 Brookswood Rd Unit 208, Sherwood, Arkansas 72120-4200 Tel: 1 501 835-1554.
Email: kmtl760am@sbcglobal.net
Web site: http://KMTL760AM.com
Profile: KMTL-AM is a commercial station owned by George Domerese. The format of the station is gospel and religious programming. KMTL-AM broadcasts to the Sherwood, AR area at 760 AM.
AM RADIO STATION

KMTN-FM 46572
Owner: Rich Broadcasting, LLC.
Editorial: 1140 State Highway 22, Jackson, Wyoming 83001-9401 Tel: 1 307 733-2120.
Email: fish@richbroadcasting.com
Web site: http://kmtnthemountain.com/
Profile: KMTN-FM is a commercial station owned by Rich Broadcasting, LLC. The format of the station is adult album alternative. KMTN-FM broadcasts to the Jackson, WY area at 96.9 FM.
FM RADIO STATION

KMTS-FM 45730
Owner: Colorado West Broadcasting Inc.
Editorial: 3230 S Glen Ave Unit B2, Glenwood Springs, Colorado 81601-4284 Tel: 1 970 945-9124.
Email: kmts@kmts.com
Web site: http://www.kmts.com
Profile: KMTS-FM is a commercial station owned by Colorado West Broadcasting Inc. The format of the station is country. KMTS-FM broadcasts to the Denver area at 99.1 FM.
FM RADIO STATION

KMTT-AM 45756
Owner: Entercom Communications Corp.
Editorial: 0700 SW Bancroft St, Portland, Oregon 97239-4226 Tel: 1 503 223-1441.
Web site: http://www.1080thefan.com/pages/17659677.php
Profile: KMTT-AM is a commercial station owned by Entercom Communications Corp. The format of the station is sports. KMTT-AM broadcasts to the Portland, OR area at 910 AM.
AM RADIO STATION

KMTX-FM 44776
Owner: The Montana Radio Company, LLC.
Editorial: 100 W Lyndale Ave Ste B, Helena, Montana 59601-2999 Tel: 1 406 442-6645.
Email: kmtx@montanaradio.com
Web site: http://www.kmtxfm.com
Profile: KMTX-FM is a commercial station owned by Montana Radio Company (The). The format for the station is adult contemporary. KMTX-FM broadcasts to the Helena, MT area at 105.3 FM.
FM RADIO STATION

KMTY-FM 44935
Owner: Armada Media Corp.
Editorial: 613 4th Ave, Holdrege, Nebraska 68949-2202 Tel: 1 308 995-4020.
Email: kmty@highplainsradio.net
Web site: http://www.kmtyfm.com/
Profile: KMTY-FM is a commercial station owned by Armada Media Corp. The format of the station is adult hits. KMTY-FM broadcasts to the Lincoln, NE area at 97.7 FM.
FM RADIO STATION

KMUC-FM 40037
Owner: University of Missouri
Editorial: 409 Jesse Hall, University of Missouri, Columbia, Missouri 65211-1310
Web site: http://kmuc.org
Profile: KMUC-FM is a commercial station owned by University of Missouri. The format of the station is classical music. KMUC-FM broadcasts to the Columbia, MO area at 90.5 FM.
FM RADIO STATION

KMUD-FM 43307
Owner: Redwood Community Radio Inc.
Editorial: 1144 Redway Dr, Redway, California 95560 Tel: 1 707 923-2513.
Email: news@kmud.org
Web site: http://www.kmud.org
Profile: KMUD-FM is a non-commercial station owned by Redwood Community Radio Inc. The format for the station is variety. KMUD-FM broadcasts to the Redway, CA area at 91.1 FM.
FM RADIO STATION

KMUN-FM 41461
Owner: Tillicum Foundation
Editorial: 1445 Exchange St, Astoria, Oregon 97103-3818 Tel: 1 503 325-0010.
Email: kmun@kmun.org
Web site: http://www.kmun.org
Profile: KMUN-FM is a non-commercial station owned by the Tillicum Foundation. The format of the station is variety. KMUN-FM broadcasts to the Astoria, OR area at 91.9 FM.
FM RADIO STATION

KMUZ-FM 786465
Owner: Willamette Information, News and Entertainment Service
Editorial: 1313 Mill St Se, Salem, Oregon 97301-6307 Tel: 1 503 967-5689.
Email: info@kmuz.org
Web site: http://www.KMUZ.org
Profile: KMUZ-FM is a non-commercial community radio station owned by Willamette Information, News and Entertainment Service. The format of the station is variety. KMUZ-FM broadcasts to the Willamette Valley area in Oregon at a frequency of 88.5 FM.
FM RADIO STATION

KMVA-FM 45758
Owner: Riviera Broadcast Group
Editorial: 4747 N 7th St Ste 424, Phoenix, Arizona 85014-3663 Tel: 1 602 648-9800.
Web site: http://trendingradio.com
Profile: KMVA-FM is a commercial station owned by Riviera Broadcast Group. The format of the station is Hot AC. KMVA-FM broadcasts to the Phoenix market at 97.5 FM AND 103.9 FM.
FM RADIO STATION

KMVE-FM 44398
Owner: High Desert Broadcasting LLC
Editorial: 570 E Avenue Q9, Palmdale, California 93550-4655 Tel: 1 661 947-3107.
Web site: http://www.classictop401069.com
Profile: KMVE-FM is a commercial station owned by High Desert Broadcasting LLC. The format of the station is classic hits music. KMVE-FM broadcasts to the Palmdale, CA area at 106.9 FM.
FM RADIO STATION

KMVG-AM 36485
Owner: Catholic Radio Network
Editorial: 201 N Industrial Park Rd, Excelsior Springs, Missouri 64024-1736 Tel: 1 816 630-1090.
Web site: http://www.thecatholicradionetwork.com/
Profile: KMVG-AM is a commercial station owned by Catholic Radio Network. The format of the station is gospel music. KMVG-AM broadcasts to the Kansas City, MO area at 890 AM.
AM RADIO STATION

KMVI-AM 39314
Owner: Pacific Media Group
Editorial: 311 Ano St, Kahului, Hawaii 96732-1304 Tel: 1 808 877-5566.
Email: studio@espnmaui.com
Web site: http://www.espn550.com
Profile: KMVI-AM is a commercial station owned by Pacific Media Group. The format of the station is sports. KMVI-AM broadcasts to the Maui, HI area at 900 AM.
AM RADIO STATION

KMVK-FM 42152
Owner: CBS Radio
Editorial: 4131 N Central Expy, STE 1000, Dallas, Texas 75204-2102 Tel: 1 214 525-7000.
Web site: http://lagrande1075.cbslocal.com
Profile: KMVK-FM is a commercial station owned by CBS Radio. The format of the station is Regional Mexican music. KMVK-FM broadcasts to the Dallas area at 107.5 FM.
FM RADIO STATION

KMVL-AM 39427
Owner: Hunt Broadcasting
Editorial: 102 W Main St, Madisonville, Texas 77864-1905 Tel: 1 936 348-9200.
Email: spots@kmvl.net
Web site: http://www.kmvl.net
Profile: KMVL-AM is a commercial station owned by Hunt Broadcasting. The format of the station is adult standards. KMVL-AM broadcasts to the Madisonville, TX area at 1220 AM.
AM RADIO STATION

KMVL-FM 46796
Owner: Hunt Broadcasting
Editorial: 102 W Main St, Madisonville, Texas 77864-1905 Tel: 1 936 348-9200.
Email: spots@kmvl.net
Web site: http://www.kmvl.net
Profile: KMVL-FM is a commercial station owned by Hunt Broadcasting. The format of the station is country. KMVL-FM broadcasts to the Madisonville, TX area at 100.5 FM.
FM RADIO STATION

KMVN-FM 44430
Owner: Alaksa Integrated Media
Editorial: 4700 Business Park Blvd Ste 44, Anchorage, Alaska 99503-7176 Tel: 1 907 522-1018.
Email: info@movin1057.com
Web site: http://www.movin1057.com
Profile: KMVN-FM is a commercial station owned by Alaksa Integrated Media. The format of the station is lite rock/lite ac. KMVN-FM broadcasts to the Anchorage, AK area at 105.7 FM.
FM RADIO STATION

KMVP-AM 36812
Owner: Farmworker Educational Network Inc.
Editorial: 3321 N 116th Dr, Avondale, Arizona 85392-3828 Tel: 1 623 533-3213.
Web site: http://www.gospel860.com
Profile: KMVP-AM is a commercial station owned by Farmworker Educational Network Inc. and in an LMA with AIM Broadcasting. The format of the station is gospel. KMVP-AM broadcasts to the Phoenix area on 860AM.
AM RADIO STATION

KMVQ-FM 46037
Owner: CBS Radio
Editorial: 865 Battery St Fl 2, San Francisco, California 94111-1503 Tel: 1 415 391-9970.
Web site: http://997now.cbslocal.com
Profile: KMVQ-FM is a commercial station owned by CBS Radio. The format of the station is top 40/CHR. KMVQ-AM broadcasts to the San Francisco area at 99.7 FM.
FM RADIO STATION

KMVR-FM 46254
Owner: Bravo Mic Communications, LLC
Editorial: 101 Perkins Dr, Las Cruces, New Mexico 88005-3295 Tel: 1 575 527-1111.
Web site: http://www.mymagic105.com
Profile: KMVR-FM is a commercial station owned by Bravo Mic Communications, LLC. The format of the station is hot adult contemporary music. KMVR-FM broadcasts to the Las Cruces, NM area at 104.9 FM.
FM RADIO STATION

KMVX-FM 44792
Owner: The Radio People
Editorial: 1107 Hudson Ln, Monroe, Louisiana 71201-6033 Tel: 1 318 388-2323.
Web site: http://www.mix1019.net
Profile: KMVX-FM is a commercial station owned by The Radio People. The format of the station is Urban AC. KMVX-FM broadcasts in the Monroe, LA area at 101.9 FM.
FM RADIO STATION

KMWB-FM 506217
Owner: New West Broadcasting
Editorial: 74-5615 Luhia St Ste A2, Kailua Kona, Hawaii 96740-1680 Tel: 1 808 935-5461.
Web site: http://www.b97hawaii.com
Profile: KMWB-FM is a commercial station owned by New West Broadcasting. The format of the station is classic hits. KMWB-FM broadcasts to the Hilo, HI area at 93.1 FM. The station simulcasts KNWB-FM.
FM RADIO STATION

KMWX-FM 43604
Owner: Townsquare Media, LLC
Editorial: 3911 S 1st St, Abilene, Texas 79605
Tel: 1 325 676-7711.
Web site: http://www.mymix92.com
Profile: KMWX-FM is a commercial station owned by Townsquare Media, LLC. The format of the station is adult contemporary music. KMWX-FM broadcasts to the Abilene, TX area at 92.5 FM.
FM RADIO STATION

KMWY-FM 689390
Owner: Moody Bible Institute
Editorial: 5408 S Freya St, Spokane, Washington 99223-7114 **Tel:** 1 509 448-2555.
Email: kmbi@moody.edu
Web site: http://www.moodyradionw.fm
Profile: KMWY-FM is a non-commercial station owned by Moody Bible Institute. The format of the station is religious. KMWY-FM broadcasts to the Jackson, WY area at 91.1 FM.
FM RADIO STATION

KMXA-AM 39001
Owner: Entravision Communications Corp.
Editorial: 1907 Mile High Stadium West Cir, Denver, Colorado 80204-1908 **Tel:** 1 303 832-0050.
Web site: http://www.superestrella1090.com
Profile: KMXA-AM is a commercial station owned by Entravision Communications Corp. The format of the station is Spanish romantica. KMXA-AM broadcasts to the Denver area at 1090 AM.
AM RADIO STATION

KMXA-FM 43052
Owner: iHeartMedia Inc.
Editorial: 1000 20th Ave SW, Minot, North Dakota 58701-6447 **Tel:** 1 701 852-4646.
Web site: http://mix999fm.iheart.com
Profile: KMXA-FM is a commercial station owned by iHeartMedia Inc. The format of the station is hot adult contemporary. KMXA-FM broadcasts to the Minot-Bismarck, ND area at 99.9 FM.
FM RADIO STATION

KMXB-FM 40048
Owner: CBS Radio
Editorial: 7255 S Tenaya Way Ste 100, Las Vegas, Nevada 89113-1900 **Tel:** 1 702 257-9400.
Web site: http://mix941fm.cbslocal.com
Profile: KMXB-FM is a commercial station owned by CBS Radio. The format of the station is hot adult contemporary. KMXB-FM broadcasts to the Las Vegas area at 94.1 FM.
FM RADIO STATION

KMXC-FM 44823
Owner: Townsquare Media, Inc.
Editorial: 5100 S Tennis Ln Ste 200, Sioux Falls, South Dakota 57108-2271 **Tel:** 1 605 361-0300.
Web site: http://www.mix97-3.com
Profile: KMXC-FM is a commercial station owned by Townsquare Media, Inc. The format of the station is hot adult contemporary. KMXC-FM broadcasts to the Sioux Falls, SD area at 97.3 FM.
FM RADIO STATION

KMXE-FM 42222
Owner: Silver Rock Communications Inc
Editorial: 9 S Broadway Ave, Red Lodge, Montana 59068-9365 **Tel:** 1 406 446-1199.
Email: fm99office@gmail.com
Web site: http://www.fm99mtn.com
Profile: KMXE-FM is a commercial station owned by Silver Rock Communications. The station airs locally on 99.3 FM. The format of the station is oldies, and the target audience is listeners, ages 35 to 100, in the Red Lodge, MT-area.
FM RADIO STATION

KMXF-FM 42001
Owner: iHeartMedia Inc.
Editorial: 2049 E Joyce Blvd Ste 101, Fayetteville, Arkansas 72703-6395 **Tel:** 1 479 582-1079.
Web site: http://hotmix1019.iheart.com
Profile: KMXF-FM is a commercial station owned by iHeartMedia Inc. The format of the station is Top 40/CHR. KMXF-FM broadcasts to the Fayetteville, AR area at 101.9 FM.
FM RADIO STATION

KMXG-FM 41021
Owner: iHeartMedia Inc.
Editorial: 3535 E Kimberly Rd, Davenport, Iowa 52807-2583 **Tel:** 1 563 344-7000.
Web site: http://www.mix96online.com
Profile: KMXG-FM is a commercial station owned by iHeartMedia Inc. The format of the station is adult contemporary music. KMXG-FM broadcasts to the Davenport, IA area at 96.1 FM.
FM RADIO STATION

KMXH-FM 42150
Owner: JWBP Broadcasting, LLC
Editorial: 1605 Murray St Ste 111, Alexandria, Louisiana 71301-6875 **Tel:** 1 318 445-0800.
Web site: http://www.mix939.fm
Profile: KMXH-FM is a commercial station owned by JWBP Broadcasting, LLC. The format of the station is rhythmic contemporary. KMXH-FM broadcasts to the Alexandria, LA area at a frequency of 93.3 FM.
FM RADIO STATION

KMXI-FM 45731
Owner: Deer Creek Broadcasting
Editorial: 2654 Cramer Ln, Chico, California 95928
Tel: 1 530 345-0021.
Web site: http://www.kmxi.com
Profile: KMXI-FM is a commercial station owned by Deer Creek Broadcasting. The format of the station is adult contemporary. KMXI-FM broadcasts to the Chico, CA area at 95.1 FM.
FM RADIO STATION

KMXJ-FM 43620
Owner: Townsquare Media, LLC
Editorial: 6214 SW 34th Ave, Amarillo, Texas 79109-4006 **Tel:** 1 806 355-9777.
Web site: http://www.mix941kmxj.com
Profile: KMXJ-FM is a commercial station owned by Townsquare Media, LLC. The format of the station is adult contemporary. KMXJ-FM broadcasts to the Amarillo, TX area at 94.1 FM.
FM RADIO STATION

KMXK-FM 42033
Owner: Townsquare Media, LLC
Editorial: 640 Lincoln Ave SE, Saint Cloud, Minnesota 56304-1024 **Tel:** 1 320 251-4422.
Web site: http://www.mix949.com
Profile: KMXK-FM is a commercial station owned by Townsquare Media, LLC. The format of the station is hot adult contemporary music. KMXK-FM broadcasts in the St. Cloud, MN area.
FM RADIO STATION

KMXL-FM 46035
Owner: Petersen(Ronald L.)
Editorial: 221 E 4th St, Carthage, Missouri 64836-1629 **Tel:** 1 417 358-2648.
Email: news@cbciradio.com
Web site: http://www.951mikefm.com
Profile: KMXL-FM is a commercial station owned by Ronald L. Petersen. The format of the station is adult hits. KMXL-FM broadcasts to the Carthage, MO area at 95.1 FM.
FM RADIO STATION

KMXN-FM 40073
Owner: Great Plains Media
Editorial: 3125 W 6th St, Lawrence, Kansas 66049
Tel: 1 785 843-1320.
Web site: http://www.bull929.com
Profile: KMXN-FM is a commercial station owned by Great Plains Media. The format of the station is contemporary country. KMXN-FM broadcasts in the Lawrence, KS area at 92.9 FM.
FM RADIO STATION

KMXO-AM 133717
Owner: Silva (Ray)
Editorial: 604 N 2nd St, Merkel, Texas 79536
Tel: 1 325 928-3060.
Email: kmxo@yahoo.com
Profile: KMXO-AM is a commercial station owned by Silva (Ray R). The format of the station is Hispanic religious. KMXO-AM broadcasts to the Merkel, TX area at 1500 AM.
AM RADIO STATION

KMXP-FM 43436
Owner: iHeartMedia Inc.
Editorial: 4686 E Van Buren St Ste 300, Phoenix, Arizona 85008-6967 **Tel:** 1 602 374-6000.
Web site: http://mix969.iheart.com
Profile: KMXP-FM is a commercial station owned by iHeartMedia Inc. The format of the station is hot adult contemporary music. KMXP-FM broadcasts to the Phoenix area at 96.9 FM.
FM RADIO STATION

KMXR-FM 39930
Owner: iHeartMedia Inc.
Editorial: 501 Tupper Ln, Corpus Christi, Texas 78417-9736 **Tel:** 1 361 289-0111.
Web site: http://big939.iheart.com
Profile: KMXR-FM is a commercial station owned by iHeartMedia Inc. The format of the station is oldies music. KMXR-FM broadcasts to the Corpus Christi, TX area at 93.9 FM.
FM RADIO STATION

KMXS-FM 42547
Owner: Morris Communications
Editorial: 301 Arctic Slope Ave, Ste 200, Anchorage, Alaska 99518 **Tel:** 1 907 344-9622.
Email: winner@kmxs.com
Web site: http://www.kmxs.com
Profile: KMXS-FM is a commercial station owned by Morris Communications. The format of the station is hot adult contemporary. KMXS-FM broadcasts to the Anchorage, AK area at 103.1 FM.
FM RADIO STATION

KMXT-FM 41682
Owner: Kodiak Island Broadcasting Co., Inc.
Editorial: 620 Egan Way, Kodiak, Alaska 99615-6487
Tel: 1 907 486-3181.
Email: gm@kmxt.org
Web site: http://www.kmxt.org
Profile: KMXT-FM is a non-commercial station owned by Kodiak Island Broadcasting Co., Inc. The format of the station is a variety of music, news, and talk. KMXT-FM broadcasts to Kodiak Island and the Alaska Peninsula at 100.1 FM.
FM RADIO STATION

KMXV-FM 39749
Owner: Steel City Media
Editorial: 508 Westport Rd Ste 202, Kansas City, Missouri 64111-3019 **Tel:** 1 816 753-4000.
Web site: http://www.mix93.com
Profile: KMXV-FM is a commercial station owned by Steel City Media. The format of the station is Top 40/CHR music. KMXV-FM broadcasts to the Kansas City, MO area at 93.3 FM.
FM RADIO STATION

KMXX-FM 41781
Owner: Entravision Communications Corp.
Editorial: 1803 N Imperial Ave, El Centro, California 92243-1333 **Tel:** 1 760 482-7777.
Web site: http://www.tricolor993.com
Profile: KMXX-FM is a commercial station owned by Entravision Communications Corp. The format for the station is Spanish. KMXX-FM broadcasts to the El Centro, CA area at 99.3 FM.
FM RADIO STATION

KMXY-FM 43177
Owner: Townsquare Media, Inc.
Editorial: 315 Kennedy Ave, Grand Junction, Colorado 81501-7552 **Tel:** 1 970 242-7788.
Web site: http://www.mix1043fm.com
Profile: KMXY-FM is a commercial station owned by Townsquare Media, Inc. The format of the station is hot adult contemporary music. KMXY-FM broadcasts to the Grand Junction, CO area at 104.3 FM.
FM RADIO STATION

KMXZ-FM 44714
Owner: E.W. Scripps Co.
Editorial: 7280 E Rosewood St, Tucson, Arizona 85710-1350 **Tel:** 1 520 722-5486.
Web site: http://www.mixfm.com
Profile: KMXZ-FM is a commercial station owned by E.W. Scripps Co. The format of the station is adult contemporary. KMXZ-FM broadcasts to the Tucson, AZ area at 94.9 FM.
FM RADIO STATION

KMYC-AM 36357
Owner: Huth Broadcasting Inc.
Editorial: 2654 Cramer Ln, Chico, California 95928-8838 **Tel:** 1 530 592-4299.
Profile: KMYC-AM is a commercial station owned by Huth Broadcasting Inc. The format of the station is news, sports and talk. KMYC-AM broadcasts in the Chico, CA at 1410 AM.
AM RADIO STATION

KMYI-FM 44090
Owner: iHeartMedia Inc.
Editorial: 9660 Granite Ridge Dr Ste 100, San Diego, California 92123-2689 **Tel:** 1 858 292-2000.
Web site: http://star941fm.iheart.com
Profile: KMYI-FM is a commercial station owned by iHeartMedia Inc. The format for the station is hot adult contemporary. KMYI-FM broadcasts to the San Diego area at 94.1 FM.
FM RADIO STATION

KMYK-FM 44986
Owner: Viper Communications Inc.
Editorial: 5715 Osage Beach Pkwy, Osage Beach, Missouri 65065-3030 **Tel:** 1 573 348-2772.
Email: info@krmsradio.com
Web site: http://www.935rocksthelake.com
Profile: KMYK-FM is a commercial station owned by Viper Communications Inc. The format of the station is classic rock. KMYK-FM broadcasts to the Osage Beach, MO area at 93.5 FM.
FM RADIO STATION

KMYO-FM 779772
Owner: Univision Communications Inc.
Editorial: 12451 Network Blvd Ste 140, San Antonio, Texas 78249-3336 **Tel:** 1 210 616-4300.
Web site: http://www.myyo951.com
Profile: KMYO-FM is a commercial station owned by Univision Communications Inc. The format of the station is classic hip hop. The station broadcasts to the San Antonio, Texas area at a frequency of 95.1 FM.
FM RADIO STATION

KMYT-FM 69897
Owner: iHeartMedia Inc.
Editorial: 27349 Jefferson Ave Ste 116, Temecula, California 92590-5610 **Tel:** 1 951 296-9050.
Web site: http://www.kmyt945.com
Profile: KMYT-FM is a commercial station owned by Clear iHeartMedia Inc. The format of the station is AAA. KMYT-FM broadcasts to the Temecula, CA area at 94.5 FM.
FM RADIO STATION

KMYX-FM 42678
Owner: Campesina Network(La)
Editorial: 6313 Schirra Ct, Bakersfield, California 93313-2174 **Tel:** 1 661 837-0745.
Web site: http://campesina.net/bakersfield
Profile: KMYX-FM is a commercial station owned by La Campesina Network. The format of the station is regional Mexican. KMYX-FM broadcasts to the Bakersfield, CA area at 92.5 FM.
FM RADIO STATION

KMYY-FM 39791
Owner: Opus Media Partners
Editorial: 1200 N 18th St Ste D, Monroe, Louisiana 71201-5449 **Tel:** 1 318 387-3922.
Email: 923thewolf@lagniappebroadcasting.com
Web site: http://realcountry923.com
Profile: KMYY-FM is a commercial station owned by Opus Media Partners. The format of the station is country music. KMYY-FM broadcasts in the Monroe, LA area at 92.3 FM.
FM RADIO STATION

KMYZ-FM 43633
Owner: Stephens Media Group
Editorial: 2448 E 81st St Ste 5500, Tulsa, Oklahoma 74137-4201 **Tel:** 1 918 492-2660.
Email: studio@edgetulsa.com
Web site: http://edgetulsa.com/
Profile: KMYZ-FM is a commercial station owned by Stephens Media Group. The format of the station is rock alternative. KMYZ-FM broadcasts to the Tulsa, OK area at 104.5 FM. Send all PSAs to kxoj@kxoj.com.
FM RADIO STATION

KMZA-FM 42294
Owner: KNZA, Inc.
Tel: 1 785 336-6166.
Email: kmza@bbwi.net
Web site: http://www.kmzafm.com
Profile: KMZA-FM is a commercial station owned by KNZA, Inc. The format of the station is contemporary country music. KMZA-FM broadcasts in the Seneca, KS area at 92.1 FM.
FM RADIO STATION

KMZE-FM 42460
Owner: FM 92 Broadcasters, Inc.
Editorial: 2728 Williams Ave Ste R, Woodward, Oklahoma 73801-5841 **Tel:** 1 580 256-3692.
Email: k101@k101online.com
Web site: http://www.z92online.com
Profile: KMZE-FM is a commercial station owned by FM 92 Broadcasters, Inc. The format of the station is news talk and sports. KMZE-FM broadcasts to Oklahoma City, OK area at 92.1 FM.
FM RADIO STATION

KMZN-AM 37201
Owner: Jomast Corp.
Tel: 1 641 673-3493.
Email: news@kboeradio.com
Web site: http://www.kboeradio.com
Profile: KMZN-AM is a commercial station owned by Jomast Corp. The format of the station is country. KMZN-AM broadcasts to the Oskaloosa, IA area at 740 AM.
AM RADIO STATION

KMZQ-AM 545171
Owner: Kemp Broadcasting
Editorial: 3999 Las Vegas Blvd S, Las Vegas, Nevada 89119-1001 **Tel:** 1 702 736-6161.
Web site: http://www.670theq.com
Profile: KMZQ-AM is a commercial station owned by Kemp Broadcasting. The format of the station is sports. KMZQ-AM broadcasts to the Las Vegas market at 670 AM.
AM RADIO STATION

KMZQ-FM 555273
Owner: Kemp Broadcasting
Editorial: 3999 Las Vegas Blvd S, Las Vegas, Nevada 89119-1001 **Tel:** 1 702 736-6161.
Web site: http://1069theq.com
Profile: KMZQ-FM is a commercial station owned by Kemp Broadcasting. The format for the station is Hot AC. KMZQ-FM broadcasts to the Las Vegas area at 99.3 FM.
FM RADIO STATION

KMZU-FM 46224
Owner: Kanza Inc.
Editorial: 102 N Mason St, Carrollton, Missouri 64633-2159 **Tel:** 1 660 542-0404.
Email: news@kmzu.com
Web site: http://www.kmzu.com
Profile: KMZU-FM is a commercial station owned by Kanza Inc. The format of the station is contemporary country music and agricultural programming. KMZU-FM broadcasts to the Kansas City, MO area at 100.7 FM.
FM RADIO STATION

KMZZ-FM 43615
Owner: Claro Communications Ltd.
Editorial: 1734 N. Padre Island Dr, Corpus Christi, Texas 78405 **Tel:** 1 361 299-6000.
Profile: KMZZ-FM is a commercial station owned by Claro Communications Ltd. The format of the station is regional Mexican. KMZZ-FM broadcasts to the Corpus Christi, TX area at 106.9 FM.
FM RADIO STATION

KNAB-AM 37391
Owner: KNAB Inc.
Editorial: 17534 County Road 49, Burlington, Colorado 80807 **Tel:** 1 719 346-8600.
Email: knab@centurytel.net
Web site: http://www.knabradio.com
Profile: KNAB-AM is a commercial station owned by KNAB Inc. The format of the station is adult standards. KNAB-AM broadcasts to the Burlington, CO area at 1140 AM.
AM RADIO STATION

KNAB-FM 44780
Owner: KNAB Inc.
Editorial: 17534 County Road 49, Burlington, Colorado 80807-9350 **Tel:** 1 719 346-8600.
Email: info@knabradio.com
Web site: http://knabradio.com
Profile: KNAB-FM is a commercial station owned by KNAB Inc. The format of the station is classic country. KNAB-FM broadcasts to the Denver, CO area at 104.1 FM.
FM RADIO STATION

United States of America

KNAF-AM 39101
Owner: Hill Country Broadcasting, LLC
Editorial: 210 Woodcrest St, Fredericksburg, Texas 78624-2529 **Tel:** 1 830 997-2197.
Email: hillcountrybroadcasting@gmail.com
Web site: http://www.texasrebelradio.com
Profile: KNAF-AM is a commercial station owned by Hill Country Broadcasting, LLC. The format of the station is classic country. KNAF-AM broadcasts to the San Antonio area at 910 AM.
AM RADIO STATION

KNAF-FM 334807
Owner: Hill Country Broadcasting, LLC
Editorial: 210 Woodcrest St, Fredericksburg, Texas 78624-2529 **Tel:** 1 830 997-2197.
Email: knattradingpost@gmail.com
Web site: http://www.texasrebelradio.com
Profile: KNAF-FM is a commercial station owned by Hill Country Broadcasting, LLC. The format of the station is classic and contemporary country. KNAF-FM broadcasts to the San Antonio area at 105.7 FM.
FM RADIO STATION

KNAH-FM 543272
Owner: Champlin Broadcasting
Editorial: 4045 NW 64th St Ste 306, Oklahoma City, Oklahoma 73116-2616 **Tel:** 1 405 456-0760.
Email: hank@crankhank.com
Web site: http://www.crankhank.com
Profile: KNAH-FM is a commercial station owned by Champlin Broadcasting. The format of the station is classic country. KNAH-FM broadcasts to the Oklahoma City area at 99.7 FM.
FM RADIO STATION

KNAI-FM 519460
Owner: Campesina Network(La)
Editorial: 1440 E Washington St Ste 200, Phoenix, Arizona 85034-1192 **Tel:** 1 602 269-3121.
Email: info@campesinainfo.com
Web site: http://www.campesina.com
Profile: KNAI-FM is a commercial station owned by La Campesina Network. The format of the station is regional Mexican. KNAI-FM broadcasts to the Phoenix area at 88.3 FM.
FM RADIO STATION

KNAM-AM 696540
Owner: MBC Grand Broadcasting Inc.
Editorial: 1360 E Sherwood Dr, Grand Junction, Colorado 81501-7546 **Tel:** 1 970 254-2100.
Web site: http://www.theteam1340.com
Profile: KNAM-AM is a commercial station owned by MBC Grand Broadcasting Inc. The format of the station is sports. KNAM-AM broadcasts to the Grand Junction, CO area at 1490 AM.
AM RADIO STATION

KNAS-FM 44782
Owner: Southwest Arkansas Radio
Editorial: 1513 S 4th St, Nashville, Arkansas 71852-3012 **Tel:** 1 870 845-3601.
Email: operations@southwestarkansasradio.com
Web site: http://www.southwestarkansasradio.com
Profile: KNAS-FM is a commercial station owned by Southwest Arkansas Radio. The format of the station is sports and talk. KNAS-FM broadcasts to the Nashville, AR area at 105.5 FM.
FM RADIO STATION

KNBA-FM 43086
Owner: Koahnic Broadcast Corp.
Editorial: 3600 San Jeronimo Ct, Ste 480, Anchorage, Alaska 99508 **Tel:** 1 907 793-3500.
Email: feedback@knba.org
Web site: http://www.knba.org
Profile: KNBA-FM is a non-commercial station owned by Koahnic Broadcast Corp. The format of the station is variety. KNBA-FM broadcasts to the Anchorage, AK area at 90.3 FM.
FM RADIO STATION

KNBB-FM 86715
Owner: Communications Capital Managers II of Louisiana LLC
Editorial: 500 N Monroe St, Ruston, Louisiana 71270-3835 **Tel:** 1 318 255-5000.
Email: espn977@gmail.com
Web site: http://www.espn977.com
Profile: KNBB-FM is a commercial station owned by Communications Capital Managers II of Louisiana LLC. The format of the station is sports. KNBB-FM broadcasts to the Ruston, LA area at 97.7 FM.
FM RADIO STATION

KNBJ-FM 42459
Owner: Minnesota Public Radio
Editorial: 405A Beltrami Ave NW, Bemidji, Minnesota 56601 **Tel:** 1 218 751-8864.
Email: newsroom@mpr.org
Web site: http://www.mpr.org
Profile: KNBJ-FM is a non-commercial station owned by Minnesota Public Radio. The format of the station is news and talk. KNBJ-FM broadcasts to the Bemidji, MN area at 91.3 FM.
FM RADIO STATION

KNBR-AM 38925
Owner: Cumulus Media Inc.
Editorial: 750 Battery St Fl 3, San Francisco, California 94111-1523 **Tel:** 1 415 995-6800.
Email: sports@knbr.com
Web site: http://www.knbr.com
Profile: KNBR-AM is a commercial station owned by Cumulus Media Inc. The format of the station is

sports. KNBR-AM broadcasts to the San Francisco area at 680 AM.
AM RADIO STATION

KNBT-FM 44783
Owner: New Braunfels Communications Inc
Editorial: 1540 Loop 337, New Braunfels, Texas 78130-3352 **Tel:** 1 830 625-7311.
Web site: http://knbt.fm
Profile: KNBT-FM is a commercial station owned by New Braunfels Communications Inc. The format of the station is classic country music. KNBT-FM broadcasts to the San Antonio area at 92.1 FM.
FM RADIO STATION

KNBX-FM 603118
Owner: KCBX Inc.
Editorial: 4100 Vachell Ln, San Luis Obispo, California 93401-8113 **Tel:** 1 805 549-8855.
Email: news@kcbx.org
Web site: http://www.kcbx.org
Profile: KNBX-FM is a non-commercial station owned by KCBX Inc. The format is classical and jazz music, news and talk. KNBX-FM broadcasts to the San Ardo, CA area at 91.7 FM.
FM RADIO STATION

KNBY-AM 38582
Owner: Sudbury Broadcasting Group
Editorial: 2025 McLarty Dr, Newport, Arkansas 72112-4822 **Tel:** 1 870 523-5891.
Email: legends@rivercountry967.com
Profile: KNBY-AM is a commercial station owned by Sudbury Broadcasting Group. The format of the station is oldies with a focus on 1970s classics. KNBY-AM broadcasts in the Newport, AR area at 1280 AM.
AM RADIO STATION

KNBZ-FM 44426
Owner: Armada Media Corp.
Editorial: 3304 S Highway 281, Aberdeen, South Dakota 57401-8792 **Tel:** 1 605 229-3632.
Email: aberdeenproduction@hubcityradio.com
Web site: http://www.hubcityradio.com
Profile: KNBZ-FM is a commercial station owned by Armada Media Corp. The format of the station is adult hits. KNBZ-FM broadcasts to the Aberdeen, SD area at 97.7 FM.
FM RADIO STATION

KNCB-AM 35015
Owner: MIS Broadcasting, Inc.
Editorial: 17525 Highway 1, Vivian, Louisiana 71082-9526 **Tel:** 1 318 375-5622.
Email: kncbradio@gmail.com
Web site: http://www.thesportsrebel.com
Profile: KNCB-AM is a commercial station owned by MIS Broadcasting, Inc. The format of the station is classic sports and news. KNCB-AM broadcasts to the Vivian, LA area at 1320 AM.
AM RADIO STATION

KNCB-FM 331238
Owner: MIS Broadcasting, Inc.
Editorial: 17525 Highway 1, Vivian, Louisiana 71082-9526 **Tel:** 1 318 375-5622.
Email: kncbradio@gmail.com
Web site: http://www.caddocountry.net
Profile: KNCB-FM is a commercial station owned by MIS Broadcasting, Inc. The format of the station is a mix of classic and contemporary country music. KNCB-FM broadcasts to the Vivian, LA area at 105.3 FM.
FM RADIO STATION

KNCI-FM 44853
Owner: CBS Radio
Editorial: 5244 Madison Ave, Sacramento, California 95841-3004 **Tel:** 1 916 338-9200.
Web site: http://kncifm.cbslocal.com
Profile: KNCI-FM is a commercial station owned by CBS Radio. The format of the station is contemporary country. KNCI-FM broadcasts to the Sacramento, CA area at 105.1 FM.
FM RADIO STATION

KNCK-AM 37392
Owner: KNCK Inc.
Tel: 1 785 243-1414.
Web site: http://www.ncktoday.com
Profile: KNCK-AM is a commercial station owned by KNCK Inc. The format of the station is oldies. KNCK-AM broadcasts to the Concordia, KS area at 1390 AM.
AM RADIO STATION

KNCK-FM 44601
Owner: KNCK Inc.
Editorial: 1390 West 11th Ave., Concordia, Kansas 66901 **Tel:** 1 785 243-1414.
Web site: http://www.ncktoday.com
Profile: KNCK-FM is a commercial station owned by KNCK Inc. The format of the station is hot adult contemporary. KNCK-FM broadcasts to the Concordia, KS area at 94.9 FM.
FM RADIO STATION

KNCM-FM 43337
Owner: Minnesota Public Radio
Editorial: 480 Cedar St, Saint Paul, Minnesota 55101-2217 **Tel:** 1 651 290-1500.
Email: newsroom@mpr.org
Web site: http://www.mpr.org/listen/stations/knowksjn
Profile: KNCM-FM is a non-commercial station owned by Minnesota Public Radio. The format of the

station is classical. KNCM-FM broadcasts to the Appleton, MN area at 88.5 FM.
FM RADIO STATION

KNCN-FM 39793
Owner: iHeartMedia Inc.
Editorial: 501 Tupper Lane Radio Plaza, Corpus Christi, Texas 78417-9736 **Tel:** 1 361 289-0111.
Web site: http://www.c101.com
Profile: KNCN-FM is a commercial station owned by iHeartMedia Inc. The format of the station is album-oriented rock music. KNCN-FM broadcasts to the Corpus Christi, TX area at 101.3 FM.
FM RADIO STATION

KNCO-AM 37393
Owner: Nevada County Broadcasters Inc.
Editorial: 1255 E Main St, Grass Valley, California 95945-5766 **Tel:** 1 530 272-3424.
Email: news@knco.com
Web site: http://www.knco.com
Profile: KNCO-AM is a commercial station owned by Nevada County Broadcasters Inc. The format of the station is news and talk. KNCO-AM broadcasts in the Grass Valley, CA area at 830 AM.
AM RADIO STATION

KNCO-FM 44784
Owner: Nevada County Broadcasters Inc.
Editorial: 1255 E Main St, Grass Valley, California 95945-5766 **Tel:** 1 530 272-3424.
Email: news@knco.com
Web site: http://www.mystarradio.com
Profile: KNCO-FM is a commercial station owned by Nevada County Broadcasters Inc. The format of the station is adult contemporary. KNCO-FM broadcasts to the Grass Valley, CA area at 94.3 FM.
FM RADIO STATION

KNCQ-FM 41149
Owner: Results Radio Group
Editorial: 1588 Charles Dr, Redding, California 96003-1459 **Tel:** 1 530 244-9700.
Email: resultsradio@sbcglobal.net
Web site: http://www.q97country.com
Profile: KNCQ-FM is a commercial station owned by Results Radio Group. The format of the station is contemporary country. KNCQ-FM broadcasts to the Redding, CA area at 97.3 FM.
FM RADIO STATION

KNCR-AM 80928
Owner: Del Rosario Talpa Inc.
Editorial: 428 C St, Eureka, California 95501 **Tel:** 1 707 725-9363.
Email: kncr@lanueva1090.com
Profile: KNCR-AM is a commercial station owned by Del Rosario Talpa Inc. The format of the station is regional Mexican. KNCR-AM broadcasts to the Eureka, CA area at 1090 AM.
AM RADIO STATION

KNCT-FM 39794
Owner: Central Texas College
Editorial: Highway 190 West, Killeen, Texas 76541 **Tel:** 1 254 526-1176.
Email: knct.music@knct.org
Web site: http://www.knct.org
Profile: KNCT-FM is a non-commercial station owned by Central Texas College. The format of the station is easy listening music. KNCT-FM broadcasts to the Killeen, TX area at 91.3 FM.
FM RADIO STATION

KNCU-FM 70140
Owner: Yaquina Bay Communications Inc.
Editorial: 906 SW Alder St, Newport, Oregon 97365-4712 **Tel:** 1 541 265-2266.
Email: news@ybcradio.com
Profile: KNCU-FM is a commercial station owned by Yaquina Bay Communications Inc. The format of the station is country music. KNCU-FM broadcasts in the Newport, OR area at 92.7 FM. The station's target audience is adults, ages 18 to 64. The station's slogan is, "Where The Music And 'U' Make The Difference."
FM RADIO STATION

KNCW-FM 46408
Owner: North Cascades Broadcasting
Editorial: 320 Emery Dr, Omak, Washington 98841-9237 **Tel:** 1 509 826-0100.
Email: news@komw.net
Web site: http://www.komw.net
Profile: KNCW-FM is a commercial station owned by North Cascades Broadcasting. The format of the station is country music. KNCW-FM broadcasts to the Spokane, WA area at 92.7 FM.
FM RADIO STATION

KNCY-AM 37394
Owner: Flood Communications
Editorial: 814 Central Ave, Nebraska City, Nebraska 68410-2409 **Tel:** 1 402 873-3348.
Email: b103@b103.fm
Web site: http://www.bigappleradio.am
Profile: KNCY-AM is a commercial station owned by Riverfront Broadcasting. The format of the station is news, sports, and classic hits. KNCY-AM broadcasts to the Nebraska City, NE area at 1600 AM.
AM RADIO STATION

KNDA-FM 42731
Owner: Rodriguez(Pat & Jessie)
Editorial: 2001 Saratoga Blvd, Corpus Christi, Texas 78417-3416 **Tel:** 1 361 653-1030.
Web site: http://1029dabomb.com

Profile: KNDA-FM is a commercial station owned by Pat and Jessie Rodriquez. The format of the station is rhythmic Top 40/CHR music. KNDA-FM broadcasts to the Corpus Christi, TX area at 102.9 FM.
FM RADIO STATION

KNDC-AM 35016
Owner: Schweitzer Media
Editorial: 505 2nd Ave S, Hettinger, North Dakota 58639-7028 **Tel:** 1 701 567-2421.
Email: kndc1490@ndsupernet.com
Web site: http://www.kndcradio.com
Profile: KNDC-AM is a commercial station owned by Schweitzer Media. The format of the station is contemporary country. KNDC-AM broadcasts to the Hettinger, ND area at 1490 AM.
AM RADIO STATION

KNDD-FM 41893
Owner: Entercom Communications Corp.
Editorial: 1100 Olive Way, Seattle, Washington 98101-1873 **Tel:** 1 206 285-7625.
Web site: http://www.1077theend.com
Profile: KNDD-FM is a commercial station owned by Entercom Communications Corp. The format of the station is rock alternative. KNDD-FM broadcasts to the Seattle area at 107.7 FM.
FM RADIO STATION

KNDE-FM 45923
Owner: Bryan Broadcasting
Editorial: 2700 Earl Rudder Fwy S, Ste 5000, College Station, Texas 77845 **Tel:** 1 979 846-1150.
Email: radio@knde.com
Web site: http://www.candy95.com
Profile: KNDE-FM is a commercial station owned by Bryan Broadcasting. The format of the station is Top 40/CHR. KNDE-FM broadcasts to the College Station, TX area at 95.1 FM.
FM RADIO STATION

KNDI-AM 35017
Owner: Geronimo Broadcasting LLC
Editorial: 1734 S King St, Honolulu, Hawaii 96826-2068 **Tel:** 1 808 946-2844.
Email: kndiradio@hawaii.rr.com
Web site: http://www.kndi.com
Profile: KNDI-AM is a commercial station owned by Geronimo Broadcasting LLC. The format of the station is variety. KNDI-AM broadcasts to the Honolulu area at 1270 AM.
AM RADIO STATION

KNDK-AM 38922
Owner: Simmons Media Group
Editorial: 1403 3rd St, Langdon, North Dakota 58249-2232 **Tel:** 1 701 256-1080.
Email: kndkmw@utma.com
Web site: http://www.maverick105fm.com
Profile: KNDK-AM is a commercial station owned by Simmons Media Group. The format of the station is classic country and talk. KNDK-AM broadcasts to the Langdon, ND area at 1080 AM.
AM RADIO STATION

KNDK-FM 46264
Owner: KNDK, Inc.
Editorial: 1403 3rd St, Langdon, North Dakota 58249-2232 **Tel:** 1 701 256-1080.
Email: kndkmw@utma.com
Profile: KNDK-FM is a commercial station owned by KNDK, Inc. The format of the station is classic rock. KNDK-FM broadcasts to the Langdon, ND area at 95.7 FM.
FM RADIO STATION

KNDN-AM 38819
Owner: Basin Broadcasting Company
Editorial: 1515 W Main St, Farmington, New Mexico 87401-3837 **Tel:** 1 505 325-1996.
Profile: KNDN-AM is a commercial station owned by Basin Broadcasting Company. The format of the station is a variety of music, news and talk. KNDN-AM broadcasts to the Farmington, NM area at 960 AM.
AM RADIO STATION

KNDR-FM 41150
Owner: Central Dakota Enterprises Inc.
Editorial: 1400 3rd St NE, Mandan, North Dakota 58554-3611 **Tel:** 1 701 663-2345.
Email: production.kndr@midconetwork.com
Web site: http://www.kndr.fm
Profile: KNDR-FM is a non-commercial station owned by Central Dakota Enterprises Inc. The format of the station is contemporary Christian music. KNDR-FM broadcasts to the Mandan, ND area at 104.7 FM.
FM RADIO STATION

KNDY-AM 37395
Owner: Dierking Communications
Editorial: 937 Jayhawk Rd, Marysville, Kansas 66508 **Tel:** 1 785 562-2361.
Email: kndy@bluevalley.net
Web site: http://www.kndyradio.com
Profile: KNDY-AM is a commercial station owned by Dierking Communications. The format of the station is country music. KNDY-AM broadcasts in the Marysville, KS area at 1570 AM.
AM RADIO STATION

KNDY-FM 44785
Owner: Dierking Communications
Editorial: 937 Jayhawk Rd, Marysville, Kansas 66508 **Tel:** 1 785 562-2361.
Email: kndy@bluevalley.net
Web site: http://www.kndyradio.com

Profile: KNDY-FM is a commercial station owned by Dierking Communications. The format of the station is country music. KNDY-FM broadcasts in the Marysville, KS area at 95.5 FM.
FM RADIO STATION

KNDZ-FM 609563
Owner: Pacific Cascade Communications Corp.
Editorial: 1139 Hartnell Ave, Redding, California 96002-2113 **Tel:** 1 530 222-4455.
Email: info@kvip.org
Web site: http://www.kvip.org
Profile: KNDZ-FM is a non-commercial station owned by Pacific Cascade Communications Corp. The format of the station is Christian and inspirational talk. The station broadcasts to the McKinleyville, CA area at 89.3 FM.
FM RADIO STATION

KNEA-AM 35018
Owner: East Arkansas Broadcasters Inc.
Editorial: 403 W Parker Rd, Jonesboro, Arkansas 72404-8408 **Tel:** 1 870 932-8400.
Profile: KNEA-AM is a commercial station owned by East Arkansas Broadcasters Inc. The format of the station is news and talk. KNEA-AM broadcasts to the Jonesboro, AR area on 970 AM.
AM RADIO STATION

KNEB-AM 37396
Owner: Nebraska Rural Radio Association
Editorial: 1928 E Portal Pl, Scottsbluff, Nebraska 69361-2727 **Tel:** 1 308 632-7121.
Web site: http://www.kneb.com
Profile: KNEB-AM is a commercial station owned by Nebraska Rural Radio Association. The format for the station is talk and sports. KNEB-AM broadcasts to the Cheyenne, WY, Scottsbluff, NE area at 960 AM.
AM RADIO STATION

KNEB-FM 44786
Owner: Nebraska Rural Radio Association
Editorial: 1928 E Portal Pl, Scottsbluff, Nebraska 69361-2727 **Tel:** 1 308 632-7121.
Web site: http://www.kneb.com
Profile: KNEB-FM is a commercial station owned by Nebraska Rural Radio Association. The format of the station is contemporary country. KNEB-FM broadcasts to the Cheyenne, WY, Scottsbluff, NE area at 94.1 FM.
FM RADIO STATION

KNEC-FM 44324
Owner: Media Logic LLC
Tel: 1 970 848-2302.
Email: knec100.9@gmail.com
Web site: http://www.medialogicradio.com/index.html
Profile: KNEC-FM is a commercial station owned by Media Logic LLC. The format of the station is adult contemporary music. KNEC-FM broadcasts to the Yuma, CO area at 100.9 FM.
FM RADIO STATION

KNED-AM 38308
Owner: Southeastern Oklahoma Radio, LLC
Editorial: 1801 E Electric Ave, McAlester, Oklahoma 74501 **Tel:** 1 918 426-1050.
Email: info@mcalesterradio.com
Web site: http://www.mcalesterradio.com
Profile: KNED-AM is a commercial station owned by Southeastern Oklahoma Radio, LLC. The format of the station is classic country. KNED-AM broadcasts to the McAlester, OK area at 1150 AM.
AM RADIO STATION

KNEI-FM 44787
Owner: Wennes Communications Stations, Inc.
Editorial: 14 W Main St, Waukon, Iowa 52172
Tel: 1 563 568-3476.
Email: knei@kneiradio.com
Web site: http://www.kneiradio.com
Profile: KNEI-FM is a commercial station owned by Wennes Communications Stations, Inc. The format for the station is country. KNEI-FM broadcasts to the Waukon, IA, area at 103.5 FM.
FM RADIO STATION

KNEK-AM 36936
Owner: Cumulus Media Inc
Editorial: 202 Galbert Rd, Lafayette, Louisiana 70506-1806 **Tel:** 1 337 232-1311.
Web site: http://www.knek.com
Profile: KNEK-AM is a commercial station owned by Cumulus Media Inc. The format of the station is urban adult contemporary music. KNEK-AM broadcasts to the Lafayette, LA area at 1190 AM.
AM RADIO STATION

KNEK-FM 44049
Owner: Cumulus Media Inc
Editorial: 202 Galbert Rd, Lafayette, Louisiana 70506
Tel: 1 337 232-1311.
Web site: http://www.knek.com
Profile: KNEK-FM is a commercial station owned by Cumulus Media Inc. The format of the station is urban adult contemporary music. KNEK-FM broadcasts to the Lafayette, LA area at 104.7 FM.
FM RADIO STATION

KNEL-AM 37398
Owner: Farris Broadcasting
Editorial: 117 S Blackburn St, Brady, Texas 76825-4504 **Tel:** 1 325 597-2119.
Email: knel@airmail.net
Web site: http://www.knelradio.com
Profile: KNEL-AM is a commercial station owned by Farris Broadcasting. The format for the station is oldies. KNEL-AM broadcasts to the Brady, TX area at 1490 AM.
AM RADIO STATION

KNEL-FM 44707
Owner: Farris Broadcasting
Editorial: 117 S Blackburn St, Brady, Texas 76825-4504 **Tel:** 1 325 597-2119.
Email: knel@airmail.net
Web site: http://www.knelradio.com
Profile: KNEL-FM is a commercial station owned by Farris Broadcasting. The format for the station is classic country. KNEL-FM broadcasts to the San Angelo, TX area at 95.3 FM.
FM RADIO STATION

KNEM-AM 38570
Owner: Harbit Communications
Editorial: 414 E Walnut St, Nevada, Missouri 64772
Tel: 1 417 667-3113.
Email: news@knemknmo.com
Web site: http://www.knemknmo.com
Profile: KNEM-AM is a commercial station owned by Harbit Communications. The format of the station is contemporary country music. KNEM-AM broadcasts to the Nevada, MO area at 1240 AM.
AM RADIO STATION

KNEN-FM 39795
Owner: Red Beacon Communications LLC
Editorial: 214 N 7th St Ste 1, Norfolk, Nebraska 68701-4086 **Tel:** 1 402 371-0100.
Email: ncn@newschannelnebraska.com
Web site: http://newschannelnebraska.com
Profile: KNEN-FM is a commercial station owned by Red Beacon Communications LLC. The format of the station is classic hits. KNEN-FM broadcasts to the Norfolk, NE area at 94.7 FM.
FM RADIO STATION

KNEO-FM 42983
Owner: Sky High Broadcasting Corp.
Editorial: 10827 E Highway 86, Neosho, Missouri 64850-7052 **Tel:** 1 417 451-5636.
Email: kneo@kneo.org
Web site: http://www.kneo.org
Profile: KNEO-FM is a non-commercial station owned by Sky High Broadcasting Corp. The format of the station is religious. KNEO-FM broadcasts to the Joplin, MO area at 91.7 FM.
FM RADIO STATION

KNES-FM 39796
Owner: J & J Communications Inc.
Editorial: 627 W Commerce St, Fairfield, Texas 75840-1425 **Tel:** 1 903 389-5637.
Email: texas99@texas99.com
Web site: http://www.kxas99-1.com
Profile: KNES-FM is a commercial station owned by J & J Communications Inc. The format of the station is country music. KNES-FM broadcasts to the Fairfield, TX area at 99.1 FM.
FM RADIO STATION

KNET-AM 37399
Owner: Tomlinson-Leis Communications L.P.
Editorial: 800 W Palestine Ave, Palestine, Texas 75801 **Tel:** 1 903 729-6077.
Email: news@kyyk.com
Web site: http://www.youreasttexas.com
Profile: KNET-AM is a commercial station owned by Tomlinson-Leis Communications L.P. The format of the station is news and talk. KNET-AM broadcasts to the Palestine, TX area at 1450 AM.
AM RADIO STATION

KNEU-AM 39039
Owner: Evans Broadcasting
Editorial: 2242 E 1000 S, Roosevelt, Utah 84066-9523
Tel: 1 435 722-5011.
Email: radio@ubtanet.com
Web site: http://www.stormpc.com/fox/CntryLink.htm
Profile: KNEU-AM is a commercial station owned by Evans Broadcasting. The format of the station is country. KNEU-AM broadcasts to the Roosevelt, UT area at 1250 AM.
AM RADIO STATION

KNEV-FM 46123
Owner: Cumulus Media Inc
Editorial: 595 E Plumb Ln, Reno, Nevada 89502-3503
Tel: 1 775 789-6700.
Web site: http://www.955thevibe.com/
Profile: KNEV-FM is a commercial station owned by Cumulus Media Inc. The format of the station is rhythmic oldies. KNEV-FM broadcasts in the Reno, NV area at 95.5 FM.
FM RADIO STATION

KNEW-AM 37167
Owner: iHeartMedia Inc.
Editorial: 340 Townsend St, San Francisco, California 94107-1633
Web site: https://www.iheart.com/live/bloomberg-960-301
Profile: KNEW-AM is a commercial station owned by iHeartMedia Inc. The format of the station is talk. KNEW-AM broadcasts in the San Francisco area at 960 AM.
AM RADIO STATION

KNEX-FM 46574
Owner: R Communications, LLC
Editorial: 307 E 8th St, Del Rio, Texas 78840-3823
Tel: 1 956 775725-1000.
Email: info@rcommunications.com
Web site: http://www.hot1061.com
Profile: KNEX-FM is a commercial station owned by MBM Radio LLC (dba R Communications). The format of the station is Top 40/CHR. KNEX-FM broadcasts to the Laredo, TX area at 106.1 FM.
FM RADIO STATION

KNFL-AM 38924
Owner: Impact Radio
Editorial: 1910 University Dr, Boise, Idaho 83725-0001 **Tel:** 1 208 426-3663.
Web site: http://www.espnboise.com
Profile: KNFL-AM is a commercial station owned by Impact Radio. The station format is sports KNFL-AM broadcasts to the Boise, ID area at 730 AM.
AM RADIO STATION

KNFM-FM 44788
Owner: Townsquare Media, Inc.
Editorial: 11300 State Highway 191 Bldg 2, Midland, Texas 79707-1367 **Tel:** 1 432 563-5636.
Web site: http://www.lonestar92.com
Profile: KNFM-FM is a commercial station owned by Townsquare Media, Inc. The format of the station is contemporary country music. KNFM-FM broadcasts in the Midland, TX area at 92.3 FM.
FM RADIO STATION

KNFO-FM 42984
Owner: NRC Broadcasting
Editorial: 402 Aspen Airport Business Ctr, Ste D, Aspen, Colorado 81611 **Tel:** 1 970 544-9100.
Web site: http://www.kspnradio.com
Profile: KNFO-FM is a commercial station owned by NRC Broadcasting. The format of the station is news, sports and talk. KNFO-FM broadcasts to the Aspen, CO area at 106.1 FM.
FM RADIO STATION

KNFT-AM 38714
Owner: SkyWest Media, LLC
Editorial: 1560 N Corbin St, Silver City, New Mexico 88061-6526 **Tel:** 1 575 388-1958.
Profile: KNFT-AM is a commercial station owned by SkyWest Media, LLC. The format of the station is oldies music and talk. KNFT-AM broadcasts to the Silver City, NM area at 950 AM.
AM RADIO STATION

KNFT-FM 46068
Owner: SkyWest Media, LLC
Editorial: 1560 N Corbin St, Silver City, New Mexico 88061-6526 **Tel:** 1 575 538-3396.
Email: events@silverradio.com
Profile: KNFT-FM is a commercial station owned by SkyWest Media, LLC. The format of the station is country. KNFT-FM broadcasts to the Silver City, NM area at 102.9 FM.
FM RADIO STATION

KNFX-FM 41932
Owner: iheartMedia Inc.
Editorial: 1716 Briarcrest Dr Ste 150, Bryan, Texas 77802-2776 **Tel:** 1 979 268-9696.
Web site: http://995thefox.iheart.com
Profile: KNFX-FM is a commercial station owned by iheartMedia Inc. The format of the station is classic rock. KNFX-FM broadcasts to the Bryan, TX area at 99.5 FM.
FM RADIO STATION

KNGA-FM 42026
Owner: Minnesota Public Radio
Editorial: 1530 Greenview Dr SW Ste 215, Rochester, Minnesota 55902-4327 **Tel:** 1 507 292-8630.
Email: newsroom@mpr.org
Web site: http://www.mpr.org/listen/stations/kngakgac
Profile: KNGA-FM is a non-commercial station owned by Minnesota Public Radio. The format of the station is news and talk. KNGA-FM broadcasts to the Rochester, MN, Mason City, IA area at 91.7 FM.
FM RADIO STATION

KNGL-AM 38753
Owner: Davies Communications Inc.
Editorial: 411 E Euclid St, McPherson, Kansas 67460
Tel: 1 620 241-1504.
Email: news@midkansasradio.com
Web site: http://www.midkansasradio.com
Profile: KNGL-AM is a commercial station owned by Davies Communications Inc. The format of the station is talk. KNGL-AM broadcasts to the McPherson, KS area at 1540 AM.
AM RADIO STATION

KNGN-AM 36046
Owner: Kansas Nebraska Good News Broadcasting Corp.
Editorial: 38005 Road 717, McCook, Nebraska 69001-7217 **Tel:** 1 308 345-2006.
Web site: http://www.kngn.org
Profile: KNGN-AM is a commercial station owned by Kansas Nebraska Good News Broadcasting Corp. The format of the station is religious programming. KNGN-AM broadcasts to the McCook, NE area at 1360 AM.
AM RADIO STATION

KNGT-FM 46618
Owner: Townsquare Media, LLC
Editorial: 900 N Lake Shore Dr, Lake Charles, Louisiana 70601-2120 **Tel:** 1 337 433-1641.
Web site: http://www.gator995.com
Profile: KNGT-FM is a commercial station owned by Townsquare Media, LLC. The format of the station is classic country. KNGT-FM broadcasts to the Lake Charles, LA area at 99.5 FM.
FM RADIO STATION

KNHT-FM 62181
Owner: State of Oregon
Editorial: 1250 Siskiyou Blvd, Ashland, Oregon 97520-5001 **Tel:** 1 541 552-6301.
Email: jprinfo@sou.edu
Web site: http://www.ijpr.org
Profile: KNHT-FM is a non-commercial station owned by State of Oregon. The format of the station is news and classical music. KNHT-FM broadcasts to the Eureka, CA area at 107.3 FM.
FM RADIO STATION

KNIA-AM 37400
Owner: M & H Broadcasting Inc.
Editorial: 1610 N Lincoln St, Knoxville, Iowa 50138
Tel: 1 641 842-3161.
Email: kniakrls@kniakrls.com
Web site: http://www.kniakrls.com
Profile: KNIA-AM is a commercial station owned by M & H Broadcasting Inc. The format of the station is country music. KNIA-AM broadcasts to the Knoxville, IA area at 1320 AM.
AM RADIO STATION

KNID-FM 44789
Owner: Chisholm Trail Broadcasting
Editorial: 316 E Willow Rd, Enid, Oklahoma 73701
Tel: 1 580 237-1390.
Web site: http://www.knid.com
Profile: KNID-FM is a commercial station owned by Chisholm Trail Broadcasting. The format of the station is country music. KNID-FM broadcasts to the Oklahoma City area at 107.1 FM
FM RADIO STATION

KNIH-AM 35026
Owner: Immaculate Heart Radio
Editorial: 3256 Penryn Rd Ste 100, Loomis, California 95650-8052 **Tel:** 1 916 535-0500.
Email: programming@ihradio.org
Web site: http://ihradio.com
Profile: KNIH-AM is a commercial station owned by Immaculate Heart Radio. The format of the station is Catholic radio programming. KNIH-AM broadcasts to the Las Vegas area at 970 AM.
AM RADIO STATION

KNIM-AM 37401
Owner: Nodaway Broadcasting Corp
Editorial: 1618 S Main St, Maryville, Missouri 64468-2612 **Tel:** 1 660 582-2151.
Email: traffic@nowadaybroadcasting.com
Web site: http://www.971thevill.com
Profile: KNIM-AM is a commercial station owned by Nodaway Broadcasting Corp. The format of the station is country. KNIM-AM broadcasts to the Maryville, MO area at 1580 AM.
AM RADIO STATION

KNIN-FM 44499
Owner: Townsquare Media, LLC
Editorial: 2525 Kell Blvd Ste 200, Wichita Falls, Texas 76308-1008 **Tel:** 1 940 763-1111.
Web site: http://www.929nin.com
Profile: KNIN-FM is a commercial station owned by Townsquare Media, LLC. The format of the station is Top 40/CHR. KNIN-FM broadcasts to the Wichita Falls, TX area at 92.9 FM.
FM RADIO STATION

KNIS-FM 39801
Owner: Western Inspirational Broadcasters Inc.
Editorial: 6363 US Highway 50 E, Carson City, Nevada 89701 **Tel:** 1 775 883-5647.
Email: info@pilgrimradio.com
Web site: http://www.pilgrimradio.com
Profile: KNIS-FM is a non-commercial station owned by Western Inspirational Broadcasters Inc. The format of the station is contemporary Christian programming. KNIS-FM broadcasts to the Carson City, NV area at 91.3 FM.
FM RADIO STATION

KNIV-FM 153063
Owner: MAV Media, LLC
Editorial: 385 Ironwood Dr, Salt Lake City, Utah 84115-2912 **Tel:** 1 801 990-8424.
Web site: http://www.mipreferidafm.com
Profile: KNIV-FM is a commercial station owned by MAV Media, LLC. The format of the station is Regional Mexican. KNIV-FM is licensed to Lyman, WY and broadcasts to the Salt Lake City area at 104.7 FM.
FM RADIO STATION

KNIX-FM 43980
Owner: iHeartMedia Inc.
Editorial: 4686 E Van Buren St, Phoenix, Arizona 85008-6959 **Tel:** 1 602 374-6000.
Web site: http://knixcountry.iheart.com
Profile: KNIX-FM is a commercial station owned by iHeartMedia Inc. The format of the station is country. KNIX-FM broadcasts to the Phoenix area at 102.5 FM.
FM RADIO STATION

KNKK-FM 134045
Owner: Cameron Broadcasting Inc.
Editorial: 2350 Miracle Mile, Bullhead City, Arizona 86442-7505 **Tel:** 1 928 763-5586.
Web site: http://www.cameronbroadcasting.com/
Profile: KNKK-FM is a commercial station owned by Cameron Broadcasting Inc. The format of the station is hot adult contemporary. KNKK-FM broadcasts to the Bullhead City, AZ area at 107.1 FM.
FM RADIO STATION

KNKT-FM 42251
Owner: Calvary Chapel of Albuquerque, Inc.
Editorial: 4001 Osuna Rd NE, Albuquerque, New Mexico 87109-4422 **Tel:** 1 505 344-9146.
Email: knkt@calvaryabq.org
Web site: http://www.knkt.com
Profile: KNKT-FM is a commercial station owned by Calvary Chapel of Albuquerque, Inc. The format of the station is religious and contemporary Christian. KNKT-FM broadcasts to the Albuquerque, NM area at 107.1 FM.
FM RADIO STATION

KNLB-FM 42502
Owner: Advance Ministries
Editorial: 510 Acoma Blvd N, Lake Havasu City, Arizona 86403-4838 **Tel:** 1 928 855-9110.
Email: info@knlb.com
Web site: http://www.knlb.com
Profile: KNLB-FM is a non-commercial station owned by Advance Ministries. The format of the station is Contemporary Christian and Inspirational. KNLB-FM broadcasts to Lake Havasu City, AZ at 91.1 FM.
FM RADIO STATION

KNLE-FM 39802
Owner: Ixoye Productions Inc.
Editorial: 12703 Research Blvd Ste 222, Austin, Texas 78759-4321 **Tel:** 1 512 996-8336.
Web site: http://knle.org
Profile: KNLE-FM is a commercial station owned by Ixoye Productions Inc. The format of the station is contemporary Christian. KNLE-FM broadcasts to the Austin, TX area at 88.1 FM.
FM RADIO STATION

KNLF-FM 43219
Owner: Trumbo(Ron)
Editorial: 440 Lawrence St, Quincy, California 95971 **Tel:** 1 530 283-4145.
Email: rtrumbo@gmail.com
Web site: http://www.knlfradio.com
Profile: KNLF-FM is a commercial station owned by Ron Trumbo. The format of the station is Christian programming, sports and talk. KNLF-FM broadcasts to the Quincy, CA area at 95.9 FM.
FM RADIO STATION

KNLG-FM 44192
Owner: New Life Evangelistic Center
Editorial: 9810 State Road Ae, New Bloomfield, Missouri 65063 **Tel:** 1 573 896-5945.
Web site: http://www.hereshelpnet.org
Profile: KNLG-FM is a non-commercial station owned by New Life Evangelistic Center. The format of the station is gospel. KNLG-FM broadcasts to the New Bloomfield, MO area at 90.3 FM.
FM RADIO STATION

KNLH-FM 44282
Owner: New Life Evangelistic Center, Inc.
Editorial: 1411 Locust St, Saint Louis, Missouri 63103 **Tel:** 1 314 421-3020.
Web site: http://www.hereshelpnetnetwork.org
Profile: KNLH-FM is a non-commercial station owned by New Life Evangelistic Center, Inc. The format of the station is contemporary Christian and gospel music. KNLH-FM broadcasts to the St. Louis area at 89.5 FM.
FM RADIO STATION

KNLP-FM 43715
Owner: New Life Evangelistic Center, Inc.
Editorial: 2319 Highway 8, Potosi, Missouri 63664 **Tel:** 1 573 438-4403.
Web site: http://www.hereshelpnetwork.org
Profile: KNLP-FM is a non-commercial station owned by New Life Evangelistic Center, Inc. The format of the station is gospel and contemporary Christian programming. KNLP-FM broadcasts to the Potosi, MO area at 89.7 FM.
FM RADIO STATION

KNLR-FM 39803
Owner: Cowan(Terry A.)
Editorial: 30 SE Bridgeford Blvd, Bend, Oregon 97702-1460 **Tel:** 1 541 389-8873.
Email: info@knlr.com
Web site: http://www.knlr.com
Profile: KNLR-FM is a commercial station owned by Terry A. Cowan. The format of the station is contemporary Christian and religious programming. KNLR-FM broadcasts to the Bend, OR area at 95.7 FM.
FM RADIO STATION

KNLV-AM 37402
Owner: Sandhills Advertising Corp.
Editorial: 205 S 16th St, Ord, Nebraska 68862 **Tel:** 1 308 728-3263.
Email: knlvnews@yahoo.com
Web site: http://www.knlvradio.com
Profile: KNLV-AM is a commercial station owned by Sandhills Advertising Corp. The format of the station is oldies music, agricultural news and information. KNLV-AM broadcasts to the Ord, NE area at 1060 AM.
AM RADIO STATION

KNLV-FM 44791
Owner: Sandhills Advertising Corp.
Editorial: 205 S 16th St, Ord, Nebraska 68862-1709 **Tel:** 1 308 728-3263.
Email: knlvnews@yahoo.com
Web site: http://www.knlvradio.com
Profile: KNLV-FM is a commercial station owned by Sandhills Advertising Corp. The format of the station is contemporary country music. KNLV-FM broadcasts to the Ord, NE area at 103.9 FM.
FM RADIO STATION

KNLX-FM 543129
Owner: Cowan(Terry A.)
Editorial: 30 SE Bridgeford Blvd, Bend, Oregon 97702-1460 **Tel:** 1 541 389-8873.
Email: info@knlr.com
Web site: http://www.knlr.com
Profile: KNLX-FM is a commercial station owned by Terry A. Cowan. The format of the station is contemporary Christian programming. KNLX-FM broadcasts to the Bend, OR area at 104.9 FM.
FM RADIO STATION

KNMB-FM 518256
Owner: MTD Inc.
Editorial: 1086 Mechem Dr, Ruidoso, New Mexico 88345-7029 **Tel:** 1 575 258-9922.
Email: mtdradio@mtdradio.com
Profile: KNMB-FM is a commercial station owned by MTD Inc. The format of the station is Hot AC. KNMB-FM broadcasts to the Ruidoso, NM area at 96.7 FM.
FM RADIO STATION

KNMI-FM 39805
Owner: Navajo Ministries, Inc.
Editorial: 2103 W Main St, Farmington, New Mexico 87401-3220 **Tel:** 1 505 327-4357.
Email: email@verticalradio.org
Web site: http://www.verticalradio.org
Profile: KNMI-FM is a non-commercial station owned by Navajo Ministries, Inc. The format of the station is contemporary Christian music. KNMI-FM broadcasts to the Farmington, NM area at 88.9 FM.
FM RADIO STATION

KNML-AM 39335
Owner: Cumulus Media Inc
Editorial: 500 4th St NW, Albuquerque, New Mexico 87102-5324 **Tel:** 1 505 767-6700.
Web site: http://www.610thesportsanimal.com
Profile: KNML-AM is a commercial station owned by Cumulus Media Inc. The format of the station is sports. KNML-AM broadcasts to the Albuquerque, NM area at 610 AM.
AM RADIO STATION

KNMO-FM 45929
Owner: Harbit Communications
Editorial: 414 E Walnut St, Nevada, Missouri 64772 **Tel:** 1 417 667-3113.
Email: news@knemknmo.com
Web site: http://www.knemknmo.com
Profile: KNMO-FM is a commercial station owned by Harbit Communications. The format of the station is contemporary country. KNMO-FM broadcasts to the Nevada, MO area at a frequency of 97.5 FM.
FM RADIO STATION

KNMX-AM 35019
Owner: Sangre de Cristo Broadcasting Inc.
Editorial: 304 S Grand Ave, Las Vegas, New Mexico 87701-3873 **Tel:** 1 505 426-1967.
Email: news@sdcradio.com
Web site: http://www.sdcradio.com/knmx-home
Profile: KNMX-AM is a commercial station owned by Sangre de Cristo Broadcasting Inc. The format of the station is variety programming. KNMX-AM broadcasts to the Las Vegas, NM area at 540 AM.
AM RADIO STATION

KNMZ-FM 43601
Owner: WP Broadcasting LLC
Editorial: 119 N Canyon Rd, Alamogordo, New Mexico 88310-5910 **Tel:** 1 575 437-1505.
Email: knmz@snmradio.com
Web site: http://www.snmradio.com
Profile: KNMZ-FM is a commercial station owned by WP Broadcasting LLC. The format of the station is sports. KNMZ-FM broadcasts to the Alamogordo, NM area at 103.7 FM.
FM RADIO STATION

KNNB-FM 41156
Owner: White Mountain Apache Tribe
Editorial: 103 W. Flatcoe Rd., Whiteriver, Arizona 85941 **Tel:** 1 928 338-5229.
Email: knnb@wmat.nsn.us
Web site: http://www.nv1.org/knnb.html
Profile: KNNB-FM is a non-commercial station owned by the White Mountain Apache Tribe. The format of the station is a variety of programming. KNNB-FM broadcasts to the Whiteriver, AZ area at 88.1 FM.
FM RADIO STATION

KNND-AM 39212
Owner: Reiten Communications, LLC
Editorial: 321 E Main St, Cottage Grove, Oregon 97424-2032 **Tel:** 1 541 942-2468.
Email: knnd@knnd.com
Web site: http://www.knnd.com
Profile: KNND-AM is a commercial station owned by Reiten Communications, LLC. The format of the station is Classic Country. KNND-AM broadcasts to the Cottage Grove, OR area at 1400 AM.
AM RADIO STATION

KNNG-FM 45936
Owner: Media Logic LLC
Editorial: 16041 US Highway 34, Fort Morgan, Colorado 80701-4105 **Tel:** 1 970 522-1607.
Email: medialogicradio@kci.net
Web site: http://www.1047knng.com/index.html
Profile: KNNG-FM is a commercial station owned by Media Logic, LLC. The format of the station is talk. KNNG-FM broadcasts to the Sterling, CO area at 104.7 FM.
FM RADIO STATION

KNNK-FM 43998
Owner: High Plains Radio Network
Editorial: 207 S 25 Mile Ave, Hereford, Texas 79045-6015 **Tel:** 1 806 363-1005.
Email: knnk@wtrt.net
Web site: http://www.knnkradio.com
Profile: KNNK-FM is a commercial station owned by High Plains Radio Network.The format of the station is religious, news, and talk. KNNK-FM broadcasts to the Amarillo, TX area at 100.5 FM.
FM RADIO STATION

KNNR-AM 128119
Owner: Flinn Broadcasting Corp.
Editorial: 10580 N McCarran Blvd Ste 115, Reno, Nevada 89503-1896 **Tel:** 1 0155 2632100.
Email: lamejor@lamejor.com.mx
Web site: http://www.lamejor.com.mx/#!/cadena/home
Profile: KNNR-AM is a commercial station owned by Flinn Broadcasting Corp. The station broadcasts to the Reno, NV area at 1400 AM, and the format if Regional Mexican music. The station's slogan is, "¡Aqui Nomás!"
AM RADIO STATION

KNNS-AM 238282
Owner: Rocking M Radio
Editorial: 5501 10th St, Great Bend, Kansas 67530-6319 **Tel:** 1 620 792-7108.
Web site: http://centralkansasradio.com
Profile: KNNS-AM is a commercial station owned by Rocking M Radio. The format of the station is talk. KNNS-AM broadcasts to the Great Bend, KS area at 1510 AM.
AM RADIO STATION

KNNW-FM 41177
Owner: Opus Media Partners
Editorial: 1200 N 18th St Ste D, Monroe, Louisiana 71201-5449 **Tel:** 1 318 387-3922.
Web site: http://www.1031nowfm.com
Profile: KNNW-FM is a commercial station owned by Opus Media Partners. The format of the station is Top 40/CHR music. KNNW-FM broadcasts in the Monroe, LA area at 103.1 FM.
FM RADIO STATION

KNOB-FM 87637
Owner: JYH Broadcasting
Editorial: 3565 Standish Ave, Santa Rosa, California 95407-8139 **Tel:** 1 707 588-0707.
Email: psadirector@winecountryradio.net
Web site: http://www.96xonline.com
Profile: KNOB-FM is a commercial station owned by JYH Broadcasting. The format of the station is alternative rock. KNOB-FM broadcasts to the Santa Rosa, CA area at 96.7 FM.
FM RADIO STATION

KNOC-AM 37403
Owner: North Face Broadcasting LLC
Editorial: 213 Renee St, Natchitoches, Louisiana 71457-6225 **Tel:** 1 318 354-4000.
Profile: KNOC-AM is a commercial station owned by North Face Broadcasting LLC. The format of the station is Urban AC. KNOC-AM broadcasts to the Natchitoches, LA area at 1450 AM.
AM RADIO STATION

KNOD-FM 39806
Owner: Wireless Communications Corp.
Editorial: 902 Chatburn Ave, Harlan, Iowa 51537 **Tel:** 1 712 755-3883.
Email: knodnews@harlannet.com
Web site: http://www.knodfm.com
Profile: KNOD-FM is a commercial station owned by Wireless Communications Corp. The format of the station is oldies music. KNOD-FM broadcasts to the Harlan, IA area at 105.3 FM.
FM RADIO STATION

KNOG-FM 43142
Owner: World Radio Network, Inc.
Editorial: 150 W 1st St, Nogales, Arizona 85621-1486 **Tel:** 1 520 287-5206.
Email: knog@lwrn.org
Web site: http://www.knog.org
Profile: KNOG-FM is a non-commercial station owned by the World Radio Network, Inc. The format for the station is Hispanic contemporary Christian. KNOG-FM broadcasts to the Tuscon, AZ area at 91.7 FM.
FM RADIO STATION

KNOM-AM 39390
Owner: KNOM Radio Mission, Inc.
Editorial: 107 W 3rd Ave, Nome, Alaska 99762 **Tel:** 1 907 443-5221.
Email: hotline@knom.org
Web site: http://www.knom.org
Profile: KNOM-AM is a non-commercial station owned by the KNOM Radio Mission, Inc. The format of the station is a wide variety of music. KNOM-AM broadcasts to the Nome, AK at 780 AM.
AM RADIO STATION

KNOM-FM 46762
Owner: KNOM Radio Mission, Inc.
Editorial: 107 W 3rd Ave, Nome, Alaska 99762 **Tel:** 1 907 443-5221.
Web site: http://www.knom.org
Profile: KNOM-FM is a non-commercial radio station owned by the KNOM Radio Mission, Inc. The format of the station is religious programming. KNOM-FM broadcasts in the Nome, AK area at 96.1 FM.
FM RADIO STATION

KNON-FM 39808
Owner: Agape Broadcasting Foundation Inc.
Editorial: 11311 N. Central Expressway, Ste 105, Dallas, Texas 75243 **Tel:** 1 214 828-9500.
Email: news@knon.org
Web site: http://www.knon.org
Profile: KNON-FM is a commercial station owned by Agape Broadcasting Foundation Inc. The format of the station is variety. KNON-FM broadcasts to the Dallas area at 89.3 FM.
FM RADIO STATION

KNOR-FM 80889
Owner: Liberman Broadcasting Inc.
Editorial: 2410 Gateway Dr, Irving, Texas 75063-2727 **Tel:** 1 972 652-2900.
Web site: http://larazadallas.estrellatv.com
Profile: KNOR-FM is a commercial station owned by Liberman Broadcasting Inc. The format of the station is regional Mexican. KNOR-FM broadcasts to the Colleyville, TX area at 93.7 FM.
FM RADIO STATION

KNOT-AM 37405
Owner: Flagstaff Radio, Inc.
Editorial: 3741 Karicio Ln, Prescott, Arizona 86303-6829 **Tel:** 1 928 776-0909.
Email: info@arizonashine.org
Web site: http://arizonashine.org/
Profile: KNOT-AM is a commercial station owned by Flagstaff Radio, Inc. The format of the station is Contemporary Christian. KNOT-AM broadcasts to the Prescott, AZ area at 1450 AM.
AM RADIO STATION

KNOU-FM 39873
Owner: Emmis Communications Corp.
Editorial: 800 Saint Louis Union Sta, Saint Louis, Missouri 63103-2296 **Tel:** 1 314 621-4106.
Web site: http://www.now963.com
Profile: KNOU-FM is a commercial station owned by Emmis Communications Corp. The format of the station is Top 40. KNOU-FM broadcasts to the St. Louis area at 96.3 FM.
FM RADIO STATION

KNOW-FM 46275
Owner: Minnesota Public Radio
Editorial: 480 Cedar St, Saint Paul, Minnesota 55101-2217 **Tel:** 1 651 290-1500.
Email: newsroom@mpr.org
Web site: http://www.mpr.org/listen/stations/knowksjn
Profile: KNOW-FM is a non-commercial station owned by Minnesota Public Radio. The format of the station is news and talk. KNOW-FM broadcasts to the St. Paul, MN area at 91.1 FM.
FM RADIO STATION

KNOX-AM 37406
Owner: Leighton Enterprises Inc.
Editorial: 1185 9th St NE, Thompson, North Dakota 58278-9343 **Tel:** 1 701 775-4611.
Email: live@knoxradio.com
Web site: http://www.knoxradio.com
Profile: KNOX-AM is a commercial station owned by Leighton Enterprises Inc. The primary format of the station is news and talk. KNOX-AM broadcasts to the Thompson, ND area at 1310 AM.
AM RADIO STATION

KNOZ-FM 821557
Owner: Rocky III Investments, Inc.
Editorial: 203 Grand Ave, Grand Junction, Colorado 81501-7816 **Tel:** 1 970 609-1200.
Email: news@knozfm.com
Web site: http://knozfm.com
Profile: KNOZ-FM is a commercial station owned by Rocky III Investments, Inc. The format of the station is news talk. KNOZ-FM broadcasts to the Grand Junction, CO and surrounding areas at 97.7 FM.
FM RADIO STATION

KNPQ-FM 518954
Owner: Eagle Radio Inc.
Editorial: 1301 E 4th St, North Platte, Nebraska 69101-4302 **Tel:** 1 308 532-1120.
Web site: http://www.northplattepost.com
Profile: KNPQ-FM is a commercial station owned by Eagle Radio Inc. The format of the station is country music. KNPQ-FM broadcasts to the North Platte, NE area at 107.3 FM.
FM RADIO STATION

KNPR-FM 39809
Owner: Nevada Public Radio
Editorial: 1289 S Torrey Pines Dr, Las Vegas, Nevada 89146-1004 **Tel:** 1 702 258-9895.
Email: info@knpr.org
Web site: http://www.knpr.org
Profile: KNPR-FM is a non-commercial station owned by Nevada Public Radio. The format of the station is news and talk. KNPR-FM broadcasts to the Las Vegas area at 89.5 FM.
FM RADIO STATION

KNPT-AM 38304
Owner: Yaquina Bay Communications Inc.
Editorial: 906 SW Alder St, Newport, Oregon 97365-4712 **Tel:** 1 541 265-2266.
Email: news@ybcradio.com
Web site: http://www.knptam.com
Profile: KNPT-AM is a commercial station owned by Yaquina Bay Communications Inc. The format of the

station is news and talk. KNPT-AM broadcasts in the Newport, OR area at 1310 AM.
AM RADIO STATION

KNRB-FM 44833
Owner: Family Worship Center Church, Inc.
Editorial: Highway 43 S, Atlanta, Texas 78888
Tel: 1 225 768-3224.
Email: onair@jsm.org
Web site: http://www.jsm.org
Profile: KNRB-FM is a non-commercial station owned by Family Worship Center Church, Inc. The format of the station is religious. KNRB-FM broadcasts to Atlanta, TX at 100.1 FM.
FM RADIO STATION

KNRG-FM 44466
Owner: La Grange Broadcasting
Editorial: 325 Radio Ln, Columbus, Texas 78934-3235 **Tel:** 1 979 732-5766.
Email: kulmradio@yahoo.com
Web site: http://www.923knrg.com
Profile: KNRG-FM is a commercial station owned by La Grange Broadcasting. The format of the station is country music. KNRG-FM broadcasts in the Columbus, TX area at 92.3 FM.
FM RADIO STATION

KNRJ-FM 44022
Owner: Sierra H Broadcasting, Inc.
Editorial: 1710 E Indian School Rd Ste 205, Phoenix, Arizona 85016-5957 **Tel:** 1 480 994-9100.
Web site: http://www.azthebeat.com
Profile: KNRJ-FM is a commercial station owned by Sierra H Broadcasting, Inc. The format of the station is classic hip hop and urban contemporary. KNRJ-FM broadcasts to the Scottsdale, AZ area at 101.1 FM.
FM RADIO STATION

KNRK-FM 46430
Owner: Entercom Communications Corp.
Editorial: 0700 SW Bancroft St, Portland, Oregon 97239 **Tel:** 1 503 223-1441.
Web site: http://www.947.fm
Profile: KNRK-FM is a commercial station owned by Entercom Communications Corp. The format of the station is rock alternative music. KNRK-FM broadcasts to the Portland, OR area at 94.7 FM.
FM RADIO STATION

KNRO-AM 37311
Owner: Mapleton of Redding, LLC
Editorial: 3360 Alta Mesa Dr, Redding, California 96002-2831 **Tel:** 1 530 226-9500.
Web site: http://www.foxsportsradio1670.com/
Profile: KNRO-AM is a commercial station owned by Mapleton of Redding, LLC. The format of the station is sports. KNRO-AM broadcasts to the Redding, CA area at 1670 AM.
AM RADIO STATION

KNRQ-FM 39692
Owner: Cumulus Media
Editorial: 1200 Executive Pkwy Ste 440, Eugene, Oregon 97401-2169 **Tel:** 1 541 284-8500.
Web site: http://www.nrq.com
Profile: KXPC-FM is a commercial station owned by Cumulus Media. The format of the station is rock music. KXPC-FM broadcasts to the Portland, OR area at 103.7 FM.
FM RADIO STATION

KNRS-AM 36696
Owner: iHeartMedia Inc.
Editorial: 2801 Decker Lake Dr, Salt Lake City, Utah 84119-2330 **Tel:** 1 801 908-1300.
Web site: http://knrs.iheart.com
Profile: KNRS-AM is a commercial station owned by iHeartMedia Inc. The format of the station is news/ talk. KNRS-AM broadcasts to the Salt Lake City area at 570 AM.
AM RADIO STATION

KNRS-FM 43023
Owner: iHeartMedia Inc.
Editorial: 2801 Decker Lake Dr, Salt Lake City, Utah 84119-2330 **Tel:** 1 801 908-1300.
Web site: http://knrs.iheart.com
Profile: KNRS-FM is a commercial station owned by iHeartMedia Inc. The format of the station is talk. KNRS-FM broadcasts to the Salt Lake City area at 105.7 FM.
FM RADIO STATION

KNRV-AM 36323
Owner: New Radio Venture, Inc.
Editorial: 1582 S Parker Rd Ste 204, Denver, Colorado 80231-2716 **Tel:** 1 303 696-5967.
Web site: http://www.onda1150am.com
Profile: KNRV-AM is a commercial station owned by New Radio Venture, Inc. The format of the station is Hispanic news and talk. KNRV-AM broadcasts to the Aurora, CO area at 1150 AM.
AM RADIO STATION

KNRX-FM 44510
Owner: Townsquare Media
Editorial: 1301 S Abe St, San Angelo, Texas 76903-7245 **Tel:** 1 325 655-7161.
Web site: http://965therock.com
Profile: KNRX-FM is a commercial station owned by Townsquare Media. The format of the station is classic rock. KNRX-FM broadcasts to the San Angelo, TX, area at 96.5 FM.
FM RADIO STATION

KNRY-AM 35021
Owner: Mount Wilson FM Broadcasters
Editorial: 5 Harris Ct Ste B, Monterey, California 93940-5751 **Tel:** 1 831 324-0375.
Email: reception@mountwilsoninc.com
Web site: http://knry1240.com
Profile: KNRY-AM is a commercial station owned by Mount Wilson FM Broadcasters. The format of the station is adult standards. KNRY-AM broadcasts to the Monterey, CA area at 1240 AM.
AM RADIO STATION

KNSG-FM 42717
Owner: kmhl broadcasting group
Editorial: 110 W Central St, Springfield, Minnesota 56087-1404 **Tel:** 1 507 532-2282.
Email: kmhlradio@gmail.com
Profile: KNSG-FM is a commercial station owned by kmhl broadcasting group. The format of the station is adult comtemporary. KNSG-FM broadcasts to the Mankato, MN area at 94.7 FM.
FM RADIO STATION

KNSH-AM 38803
Owner: Cumulus Media Inc.
Editorial: 301 S Polk St Ste 100, Amarillo, Texas 79101-1404 **Tel:** 1 806 342-5200.
Profile: KNSH-AM is a commercial station owned by Cumulus Media Inc. The format of the station is talk. KNSH-AM broadcasts to the Amarillo, TX area at 1550 AM.
AM RADIO STATION

KNSI-AM 37407
Owner: Leighton Enterprises Inc.
Editorial: 619 W Saint Germain St, Saint Cloud, Minnesota 56301-3640 **Tel:** 1 320 251-1450.
Web site: http://www.knsiradio.com
Profile: KNSI-AM is a commercial station owned by Leighton Enterprises Inc. The format of the station is news and talk. KNSI-AM broadcasts to the St. Cloud, MN area at 1450 AM. Send any press materials to the station's program director.
AM RADIO STATION

KNSJ-FM 868342
Owner: Activist San Diego
Editorial: 4246 Wightman St, San Diego, California 92105-2618 **Tel:** 1 619 283-1100.
Email: info@knsj.org
Web site: http://knsj.org
Profile: KNSJ-FM is a non-commercial station owned by Activist San Diego. The format of the station features a variety of news and local music. KNSJ-FM broadcasts to the San Diego area at a frequency of 89.1 FM.
FM RADIO STATION

KNSP-AM 35023
Owner: Hubbard Broadcasting Inc.
Editorial: 201 Jefferson St S, Wadena, Minnesota 56482-1531 **Tel:** 1 218 631-1803.
Web site: http://www.superstationk106.com
Profile: KNSP-AM is a commercial station owned by Hubbard Broadcasting Inc.The format of the station is country music. KNSP-AM broadcasts to Wadena, MN at 1430 AM.
AM RADIO STATION

KNSR-FM 41528
Owner: Minnesota Public Radio
Editorial: 300 Wimmer Hall St John's Univ, Collegeville, Minnesota 56321-9999 **Tel:** 1 320 363-7702.
Email: newsroom@mpr.org
Web site: http://minnesota.publicradio.org
Profile: KNSR-FM is a non-commercial station owned by Minnesota Public Radio. The format of the station is news and talk. KNSR-FM broadcasts in the Collegeville, MN area at 88.9 FM.
FM RADIO STATION

KNSS-AM 37038
Owner: Entercom Communications Corp.
Editorial: 2120 N Woodlawn St Ste 352, Wichita, Kansas 67208-1881 **Tel:** 1 316 685-2121.
Email: news@knssradio.com
Web site: http://www.knssradio.com
Profile: KNSS-AM is a commercial station owned by Entercom Communications Corp. The format of the station is news and talk. KNSS-AM broadcasts in the Wichita, KS area at 1330 AM.
AM RADIO STATION

KNST-AM 38826
Owner: iHeartMedia Inc.
Editorial: 3202 N Oracle Rd, Tucson, Arizona 85705-3820 **Tel:** 1 520 618-2100.
Web site: http://www.knst.com
Profile: KNST-AM is a commercial station owned by iHeartMedia Inc. The format of the station is news and talk. KNST-AM broadcasts to the Tucson, AZ area at 790 AM.
AM RADIO STATION

KNSW-FM 39883
Owner: Minnesota Public Radio
Editorial: 1450 Collegeway, Worthington, Minnesota 56187-3024 **Tel:** 1 507 372-2904.
Email: newsroom@mpr.org
Web site: http://www.mpr.org/listen/stations/knswkrsw
Profile: KNSW-FM is a non-commercial station owned by Minnesota Public Radio. The format of the station is news and talk. KNSW-FM broadcasts to the Worthington, MN area at 91.7 FM.
FM RADIO STATION

KNTE-FM 86668
Owner: Liberman Broadcasting Inc.
Editorial: 3000 Bering Dr, Houston, Texas 77057-5708 **Tel:** 1 713 315-3400.
Web site: http://www.elnorteenlinea.com
Profile: KNTE-FM is a commercial station owned by Liberman Broadcasting Inc. The format of the station is Regional Mexican. KNTE-FM broadcasts to the Bay City, TX area at a frequency of 101.7 FM.
FM RADIO STATION

KNTH-AM 36886
Owner: Salem Media Group, Inc.
Editorial: 6161 Savoy Dr Ste 1200, Houston, Texas 77036-3363 **Tel:** 1 713 260-3600.
Email: comments@1070knth.com
Web site: http://am1070theanswer.com
Profile: KNTH-AM is a commercial station owned by Salem Media Group, Inc. The format of the station is news and talk. KNTH-AM broadcasts to the Houston area at 1070 AM.
AM RADIO STATION

KNTI-FM 39810
Owner: Bicoastal Media LLC
Editorial: 140 N Main St, Lakeport, California 95453-4815 **Tel:** 1 707 263-6113.
Web site: http://www.knti.com
Profile: KNTI-FM is a commercial station owned by Bicoastal Media LLC. The format of the station is adult album alternative. KNTI-FM broadcasts to the Lakeport, CA area at 99.5 FM.
FM RADIO STATION

KNTN-FM 42473
Owner: Minnesota Public Radio
Editorial: 901 8th St S, Moorhead, Minnesota 56562
Tel: 1 218 287-0666.
Email: newsroom@mpr.org
Web site: http://minnesota.publicradio.org
Profile: KNTN-FM is non-commercial station owned by Minnesota Public Radio. The format of the station is news and talk programming. KNTN-FM broadcasts to the Moorhead, MN area at 102.7 FM.
FM RADIO STATION

KNTR-AM 86124
Owner: Greeley(Steven M.)
Editorial: 1845 McCulloch Blvd N Ste A14, Lake Havasu City, Arizona 86403-6777 **Tel:** 1 928 855-9336.
Email: office@myradiocentral.com
Web site: http://kntrtalk.com
Profile: KNTR-AM is a commercial station owned by Steven M. Greely. The format of the station is sports. KNTR-AM broadcasts to Phoenix area at 980 AM.
AM RADIO STATION

KNTS-AM 36865
Owner: Salem Media Group, Inc.
Editorial: 2201 6th Ave Ste 1500, Seattle, Washington 98121-1840 **Tel:** 1 206 443-8200.
Email: info@radioluzseattle.com
Web site: http://www.radioluzseattle.com
Profile: KNTS-AM is a commercial station owned by Salem Media Group, Inc. The format of the station is Hispanic religious talk. KNTS-AM broadcasts to the Seattle area at 1680 AM.
AM RADIO STATION

KNTX-AM 37036
Owner: Henderson Broadcasting Co. LP
Editorial: 7704 FM 1758, State Highway 59 N, Bowie, Texas 76230 **Tel:** 1 940 872-2288.
Email: onair@kntxradio.com
Web site: http://www.kntxradio.com
Profile: KNTX-AM is a commercial station owned by Henderson Broadcasting Co. LP. The format of the station is oldies music. KNTX-AM broadcasts in the Bowie, TX area at 1410 AM.
AM RADIO STATION

KNTY-FM 43612
Owner: Entravision Communications Corp.
Editorial: 1436 Auburn Blvd, Sacramento, California 95815-2745 **Tel:** 1 916 646-4000.
Web site: http://www.1019thewolf.com
Profile: KNTY-FM is a commercial station owned by Entravision Communications Corp. The format of the station is contemporary country music. KNTY-FM broadcasts to the Sacramento, CA area at 107.1 FM.
FM RADIO STATION

KNUE-FM 40996
Owner: Townsquare Media, LLC
Editorial: 3810 Brookside Dr, Tyler, Texas 75701-9420 **Tel:** 1 903 581-0606.
Web site: http://knue.com
Profile: KNUE-FM is a commercial station owned by Townsquare Media, LLC. The format of the station is classic and contemporary country. KNUE-FM broadcasts to the Tyler, TX area at 101.5 FM.
FM RADIO STATION

KNUI-AM 38569
Owner: Pacific Media Group
Editorial: 311 Ano St, Kahului, Hawaii 96732-1304
Tel: 1 808 877-5566.
Web site: http://knuimaui.com
Profile: KNUI-AM is a commercial station owned by the Pacific Media Group. The format for the station is news and talk. KNUI-AM broadcasts to the Maui, HI area at 550 AM.
AM RADIO STATION

KNUJ-AM 39382
Owner: Ingstad Brothers Broadcasting, LLC
Editorial: 317 N Minnesota St, New Ulm, Minnesota 56073-1876 **Tel:** 1 507 359-2921.
Email: news@knuj.net
Web site: http://www.knuj.net
Profile: KNUJ-AM is a commercial station owned by Ingstad Brothers Broadcasting, LLC. The format for the station is classic country. KNUJ-AM broadcasts to the New Ulm, MN area at 860 AM.
AM RADIO STATION

KNUJ-FM 46753
Owner: Ingstad Brothers Broadcasting, LLC
Editorial: 317 N Minnesota St, New Ulm, Minnesota 56073-1876 **Tel:** 1 507 359-2921.
Email: knuj@knuj.net
Web site: http://www.knuj.net
Profile: KNUJ-FM is a commercial station owned by Ingstad Brothers Broadcasting, LLC. The format for the station is adult hits. KNUJ-FM broadcasts to the New Ulm, MN area at 107.3 FM.
FM RADIO STATION

KNUQ-FM 42987
Owner: Visionary Related Entertainment, Inc
Editorial: 1900 Main St, Wailuku, Hawaii 96793-1900
Tel: 1 808 244-9145.
Email: kaoi@kaoi.net
Web site: http://q103maui.com
Profile: KNUQ-FM is a commercial station owned by Visionary Related Entertainment, Inc. The format of the station is variety featuring roots, rock and reggae music. KNUQ-FM is licensed to the Paauilo, Hawaii area and broadcasts at a frequency of 103.9 FM.
FM RADIO STATION

KNUS-AM 36439
Owner: Salem Media Group, Inc.
Editorial: 3131 S Vaughn Way Ste 601, Aurora, Colorado 80014-3510 **Tel:** 1 303 750-5687.
Email: news@salemdenver.com
Web site: http://www.710knus.com
Profile: KNUS-AM is a commercial station owned by Salem Media Group, Inc. The format of the station is news and talk programming. KNUS-AM broadcasts to the Aurora, CO area at 710 AM.
AM RADIO STATION

KNUV-AM 37074
Owner: New Radio Venture, Inc.
Editorial: 1582 S Parker Rd, Ste 204, Denver, Colorado 80231-2716 **Tel:** 1 602 759-1914.
Profile: KNUV-AM is a commercial station owned by New Radio Venture, Inc. The format of the station is Spanish-language talk. KNUV-AM broadcasts to the Phoenix area at 1190 AM.
AM RADIO STATION

KNUZ-FM 46789
Owner: La Grange Broadcasting
Editorial: 705 S Live Oak St, San Saba, Texas 76877-6023 **Tel:** 1 325 372-5225.
Email: knuz@sansabaradio.com
Web site: http://www.sansabaradio.com
Profile: KNUZ-FM is a commercial station owned by La Grange Broadcasting. The format of the station is classic country. KNUZ-FM broadcasts to the San Saba, TX area at 106.1 FM.
FM RADIO STATION

KNVO-FM 42526
Owner: Entravision Communications Corp.
Editorial: 801 N Jackson Rd, McAllen, Texas 78501
Tel: 1 956 661-6000.
Web site: http://www.jose1011.com
Profile: KNVO-FM is a commercial station owned by Entravision Communications Corp. The format of the station is Hispanic Top 40/CHR. KNVO-FM broadcasts to the McAllen, TX area at 101.1 FM.
FM RADIO STATION

KNVR-AM 39413
Owner: Henderson(Roy)
Editorial: 705 S Live Oak St, San Saba, Texas 76877
Tel: 1 325 372-5225.
Email: knuz@sansabaradio.com
Web site: http://www.sansabaradio.com
Profile: KNVR-AM is a commercial station owned by Roy Henderson. The format of the station is adult standards. KNVR-AM broadcasts to the Waco, TX area at 1410 AM.
AM RADIO STATION

KNWA-AM 39059
Owner: Dowdy Broadcasting, Inc.
Editorial: 600 S Pine St, Harrison, Arkansas 72601-5828 **Tel:** 1 870 741-1402.
Email: info@knwaradio.com
Web site: http://knwaradio.com
Profile: KNWA-AM is a commercial station owned by Dowdy Broadcasting, Inc. The format of the station is Conservative talk. KNWA-AM broadcasts to the Harrison, AR area at 1600 AM.
AM RADIO STATION

KNWB-FM 42986
Owner: New West Broadcasting
Editorial: 1145 Kilauea Ave, Hilo, Hawaii 96720-4203
Tel: 1 808 935-5461.
Web site: http://www.b97hawaii.com
Profile: KNWB-FM is a commercial station owned by New West Broadcasting. The format of the station is classic hits. KNWB-FM broadcasts to the Hilo, HI area at 97.1 FM. The station simulcasts with KMWB-FM.
FM RADIO STATION

KNWC-AM 37408
Owner: Northwestern College
Editorial: 6300 S Tallgrass Ave, Sioux Falls, South Dakota 57108-8107 **Tel:** 1 605 339-1270.
Email: knwc@knwc.org
Web site: http://www.knwc.org
Profile: KNWC-AM is a non-commercial station owned by Northwestern College. The format of the station is religious. KNWC-AM broadcasts to the Sioux Falls, SD area at 1270 AM.
AM RADIO STATION

KNWC-FM 44795
Owner: Northwestern College
Editorial: 6300 South Tallgrass Ave, Sioux Falls, South Dakota 57108-8107 **Tel:** 1 605 339-1270.
Email: knwc@knwc.org
Web site: http://www.knwc.org
Profile: KNWC-FM is a non-commercial station owned by Northwestern College. The format of the station is contemporary Christian. KNWC-FM broadcasts to the Sioux Falls, SD area 96.5 FM.
FM RADIO STATION

KNWH-AM 39061
Owner: Morris Communications
Editorial: 1321 N Gene Autry Trl, Palm Springs, California 92262 **Tel:** 1 760 322-7890.
Web site: http://www.knewsradio.com
AM RADIO STATION

KNWI-FM 46727
Owner: Northwestern College
Editorial: 3737 Woodland Ave, Suite 111, Des Moines, Iowa 50266 **Tel:** 1 515 327-1071.
Email: info@life1071.com
Web site: http://www.life1071.com
Profile: KNWI-FM is a non-commercial station owned by Northwestern College. The format of the station is contemporary Christian. KNWI-FM broadcasts to the Des Moines, IA area at 107.1 FM.
FM RADIO STATION

KNWM-FM 43881
Owner: Northwestern College
Editorial: 3737 Woodland Ave, Ste 111, Des Moines, Iowa 50266 **Tel:** 1 515 327-1071.
Email: info@life1071.com
Web site: http://www.life1071.com
Profile: KNWM-FM is a non-commercial station owned by Northwestern College. The format of the station is contemporary Christian. KNWM-FM broadcasts to the Des Moines, IA area at 96.1 FM.
FM RADIO STATION

KNWQ-AM 38653
Owner: Morris Communications
Editorial: 1321 N Gene Autry Trl, Palm Springs, California 92262-5473 **Tel:** 1 760 322-7890.
Web site: http://www.943knews.com
Profile: KNWQ-AM is a commercial station owned by Morris Communications. The format of the station is news and talk. KNWQ-AM broadcasts to the Palm Springs, CA area at 1140 AM.
AM RADIO STATION

KNWS-AM 37409
Owner: Northwestern College
Editorial: 4880 Texas St, Waterloo, Iowa 50702-4742 **Tel:** 1 319 296-1975.
Email: info@life1019.com
Web site: http://www.life1019.com
Profile: KNWS-AM is a non-commercial station owned by Northwestern College. The format of the station is religious programming. KNWS-AM broadcasts to the Cedar Rapids, IA area at 1090 AM.
AM RADIO STATION

KNWS-FM 44797
Owner: Northwestern College
Editorial: 4880 Texas St, Waterloo, Iowa 50702-4742 **Tel:** 1 319 296-1975.
Email: info@life1019.com
Web site: http://www.life1019.com
Profile: KNWS-FM is a non-commercial station owned by Northwestern College. The format of the station is contemporary Christian. KNWS-FM broadcasts to the Cedar Rapids, IA area at 101.9 FM.
FM RADIO STATION

KNWZ-AM 342309
Owner: Alpha Media
Editorial: 1321 N Gene Autry Trl, Palm Springs, California 92262-5473 **Tel:** 1 760 322-7890.
Web site: http://www.943knews.com
Profile: KNWZ-AM is a commercial station owned by Alpha Media. The format of the station is news and talk. KNWZ-AM broadcasts to the Coachella, CA area at 970 AM.
AM RADIO STATION

KNX-AM 39376
Owner: CBS Radio
Editorial: 5670 Wilshire Blvd Ste 200, Los Angeles, California 90036-5657 **Tel:** 1 323 569-1070.
Email: knxnews@cbsradio.com
Web site: http://losangeles.cbslocal.com/station/knx-1070
Profile: KNX-AM is a commercial station owned by CBS Radio. The format of the station is news. KNX-AM broadcasts in the Los Angeles area at 1070 AM.
AM RADIO STATION

KNXN-AM 238342
Owner: Good News Radio Broadcasting Inc.
Editorial: 3222 S Richey Ave, Tucson, Arizona 85713 **Tel:** 1 520 790-2440.
Email: info@kvoi.com
Web site: http://www.kgms.com
Profile: KNXN-AM is a commercial station owned by Good News Radio Broadcasting Inc. The format of the station is religious programming. KNXN-AM broadcasts to the Sierra Nevada, AZ area at 1470 AM.
AM RADIO STATION

KNXR-FM 39815
Owner: Linder Radio Group
Editorial: 1620 Greenview Dr SW, Rochester, Minnesota 55902-4319 **Tel:** 1 507 285-5697.
Web site: http://mn975.com/
Profile: KNXR-FM is a commercial station owned by Linder Radio Group. The format of the station is Classic Hits. KNXR-FM broadcasts to the Rochester, MN, Mason City, IA area at 97.5 FM.
FM RADIO STATION

KNXX-FM 44467
Owner: Guaranty Broadcasting
Editorial: 929 Government St Ste B, Baton Rouge, Louisiana 70802-6034 **Tel:** 1 225 388-9898.
Web site: http://www.1045espn.com
Profile: KNXX-FM is a commercial station owned by Guaranty Broadcasting. The format of the station is sports. KNXX-FM broadcasts to the Baton Rouge, LA area at 104.9 FM.
FM RADIO STATION

KNYE-FM 489868
Owner: Karen Jackson
Editorial: 1230 Dutch Ford St, Pahrump, Nevada 89048-9105 **Tel:** 1 775 537-6100.
Web site: http://www.knye.com
Profile: KNYE-FM is a commercial station owned by Karen Jackson. The format of the station is oldies music and talk. KNYE-FM broadcasts to the Pahrump, NV area at 95.1 FM.
FM RADIO STATION

KNYN-FM 44812
Owner: Frandsen (M. Kent)
Editorial: 1044 Main St Ste B, Evanston, Wyoming 82930-3480 **Tel:** 1 307 789-8116.
Email: knyn@k-9radio.com
Web site: http://k-9radio.com
Profile: KNYN-FM is a commercial station owned by Frandsen (M. Kent). The format of the station is contemporary country. The station is broadcasts to the Evanston, WY area at 103.9 FM.
FM RADIO STATION

KNZA-FM 41158
Owner: KNZA, Inc.
Editorial: 1828 US Highway 73, Hiawatha, Kansas 66434 **Tel:** 1 785 547-3461.
Email: knzanews@yahoo.com
Web site: http://www.knzafm.com
Profile: KNZA-FM is a commercial station owned by KNZA, Inc. The format of the station is contemporary country music. KNZA-FM broadcasts in the Hiawatha, KS are at 103.9 FM.
FM RADIO STATION

KNZR-AM 38568
Owner: Alpha Media
Editorial: 3651 Pegasus Dr Ste 107, Bakersfield, California 93308-6836 **Tel:** 1 661 393-1900.
Web site: http://www.knzr.com
Profile: KNZR-AM is a commercial station owned by Alpha Media. The format of the station is news and talk. KNZR-AM broadcasts to the Bakersfield, CA area at 1560 AM.
AM RADIO STATION

KNZR-FM 42946
Owner: Alpha Media
Editorial: 3651 Pegasus Dr Ste 107, Bakersfield, California 93308-6836 **Tel:** 1 661 393-1900.
Web site: http://www.knzr.com
Profile: KNZR-FM is a commercial station owned by Alpha Media. The format of the station is news and talk. KNZR-FM broadcasts to the Bakersfield, CA area at 97.7 FM. The station is a simulcast of KNZR-AM.
FM RADIO STATION

KNZS-FM 429768
Owner: Ad Astra Per Aspera Broadcasting, Inc.
Editorial: 10 E 5th Ave, Hutchinson, Kansas 67501-6201 **Tel:** 1 620 665-5758.
Web site: http://www.adastraradio.com/knzs.php
Profile: KNZS-FM is a commercial station owned by Ad Astra Per Aspera Broadcasting, Inc. The format for the station is classic rock. KNZS-FM broadcasts to the Wichita-Hutchinson, KS area at 100.3 FM.
FM RADIO STATION

KNZZ-AM 38534
Owner: MBC Grand Broadcasting Inc.
Editorial: 1360 E Sherwood Dr, Grand Junction, Colorado 81501-7546 **Tel:** 1 970 254-2100.
Email: news@gjradio.com
Web site: http://www.1100knzz.com
Profile: KNZZ-AM is a commercial station owned by MBC Grand Broadcasting Inc. The format of the station is news and talk. KNZZ-AM broadcasts in the Grand Junction, CO area at 1100 AM.
AM RADIO STATION

KOA-AM 39000
Owner: iHeartMedia Inc.
Editorial: 4695 S Monaco St, Denver, Colorado 80237-3525 **Tel:** 1 303 713-8000.
Email: denvernewsroom@iheartmedia.com
Web site: http://koanewsradio.iheart.com
Profile: KOA-AM is a commercial station owned by iHeartMedia Inc. The format of the station is news, sports, and talk. KOA-AM broadcasts in the Denver area at 850 AM.
AM RADIO STATION

KOAC-AM 36377
Owner: Oregon Public Broadcasting
Editorial: 7140 Sw Macadam Ave, Portland, Oregon 97219-3013 **Tel:** 1 503 244-9900.
Email: opbnews@opb.org
Web site: http://www.opb.org
AM RADIO STATION

KOAI-FM 43685
Owner: Riviera Broadcasting
Editorial: 4745 N 7th St Ste 410, Phoenix, Arizona 85014-3669 **Tel:** 1 602 648-9800.
Web site: http://theoasisphoenix.com
Profile: KOAI-FM is a commercial station owned by Riviera Broadcasting. The format of the station is AC. KOAI-FM broadcasts to the Phoenix area at 95.1 FM.
FM RADIO STATION

KOAK-AM 37410
Owner: Hawkeye Communications
Editorial: 1991 Ironwood Ave, Red Oak, Iowa 51566-3204 **Tel:** 1 712 623-2584.
Email: kcsi@kcsifm.com
Web site: http://www.kcsifm.com
Profile: KOAK-AM is a commercial station owned by Hawkeye Communications. The format of the station is contemporary country. KOAK-AM broadcasts to the Red Oak, IA area at 1080 AM.
AM RADIO STATION

KOAL-AM 39051
Owner: Eastern Utah Broadcasting
Editorial: 1899 N. Carbonville Road, Price, Utah 84501 **Tel:** 1 435 637-1167.
Email: news@koal.net
Web site: http://www.castlecountryradio.com
Profile: KOAL-AM is a commercial station owned by Eastern Utah Broadcasting. The format of the station is news, sports and talk. KOAL-AM broadcasts to the Salt Lake City area at 750 AM.
AM RADIO STATION

KOAN-AM 36710
Owner: IBEW Local 1547 Investments, LLC
Editorial: 4700 Business Park Blvd Bldg E, Anchorage, Alaska 99503-7176 **Tel:** 1 907 522-1018.
Web site: http://www.1080koan.com
Profile: KOAN-AM is a commercial station owned by IBEW Local 1547 Investments, LLC and managed by Alaska Integrated Media. The format of the station is Sports. KOAN-AM broadcasts to the Anchorage, AK area at 1080 AM.
AM RADIO STATION

KOAS-FM 85983
Owner: Beasley Broadcast Group
Editorial: 2920 S Durango Dr, Las Vegas, Nevada 89117-4412 **Tel:** 1 702 730-0300.
Web site: http://www.oldschool1057.com/
Profile: KOAS-FM is a commercial station owned by Beasley Broadcast Group. The format of the station is rhythmic oldies. KOAS-FM broadcasts to the Las Vegas area at 105.7 FM.
FM RADIO STATION

KOAZ-AM 36029
Owner: Isleta Radio Co. (Whitman, Martha)
Editorial: 809 Wellesley Dr NE, Albuquerque, New Mexico 87106-1936 **Tel:** 1 505 899-5029.
Web site: http://1037theoasis.com
Profile: KOAZ-AM is a commercial station owned by Isleta Radio Co. (Whitman, Martha). The format of the station is smooth jazz. KOAZ-AM broadcasts to the Greater Albuquerque area at a frequency of 1510 AM.
AM RADIO STATION

KOBB-AM 39103
Owner: Reier Broadcasting Company Inc.
Editorial: 5445 Johnson Rd, Bozeman, Montana 59718-8333 **Tel:** 1 406 587-9999.
Email: themarketleader@kboz.com
Web site: http://www.kboz.com
Profile: KOBB-AM is a commercial station owned by Reier Broadcasting Company Inc. The format of the station is sports. KOBB-AM broadcasts in the Bozeman, MT area at 1230 AM.
AM RADIO STATION

KOBB-FM 42178
Owner: Reier Broadcasting Company Inc.
Editorial: 5445 Johnson Rd, Bozeman, Montana 59718-8333 **Tel:** 1 406 587-9999.
Email: themarketleader@kboz.com
Web site: http://www.kboz.com
Profile: KOBB-FM is a commercial station owned by Reier Broadcasting Company Inc. The format of the station is oldies music. KOBB-FM broadcasts in the Bozeman, MT area at 93.7 FM.
FM RADIO STATION

KOBE-AM 38908
Owner: Bravo Mic Communications, LLC
Editorial: 101 Perkins Dr, Las Cruces, New Mexico 88005-3295 **Tel:** 1 575 527-1111.
Web site: http://www.b1450.com
Profile: KOBE-AM is a commercial station owned by Bravo Mic Communications, LLC. The format of the station is news, talk and sports. KOBE-AM broadcasts to the Las Cruces, NM area at 1450 AM.
AM RADIO STATION

KOBN-FM 658299
Owner: Oregon Public Broadcasting
Editorial: 7140 SW MacAdam Ave, Portland, Oregon 97219-3013 **Tel:** 1 503 293-1905.
Email: opbnews@opb.org
Web site: http://www.opb.org
Profile: KOBN-FM is a non-commercial station owned by Oregon Public Broadcasting. The format is news and talk. KOBN-FM broadcasts to the Burns, OR area at 90.1 FM.
FM RADIO STATION

KOBO-AM 78282
Owner: Punjabi American Media LLC
Editorial: 3750 McKee Rd Ste B, San Jose, California 95127-2000 **Tel:** 1 408 272-5200.
Email: info@punjabiradiousa.com
Web site: http://punjabiradiousa.com
Profile: KOBO-AM is a commercial station owned by Punjabi American Media LLC. The format of the station is regional Mexican. KOBO-AM broadcasts to the Marysville, CA area at 1450 AM.
AM RADIO STATION

KOCN-FM 41031
Owner: iHeart Media Inc.
Editorial: 903 N Main St, Salinas, California 93906-3912 **Tel:** 1 831 755-8181.
Web site: http://www.koceanradio.com
Profile: KOCN-FM is a commercial station owned by iHeart Media Inc. The format of the station is classic and contemporary R&B. KOCN-FM broadcasts to the Salinas, CA area at a frequency of 105.1 FM.
FM RADIO STATION

KOCP-FM 45922
Owner: Gold Coast Radio, LLC
Editorial: 2284 S Victoria Ave, Ventura, California 93003-6641 **Tel:** 1 805 289-1400.
Web site: http://www.rewind959.com
Profile: KOCP-FM is a commercial station owned by Gold Coast Radio, LLC. The format of the station is classic hits music. KOCP-FM broadcasts to the Ventura, CA area at 95.9 FM.
FM RADIO STATION

KODA-FM 39818
Owner: iHeartMedia Inc.
Editorial: 2000 West Loop S Ste 300, Houston, Texas 77027-3510 **Tel:** 1 713 212-8000.
Web site: http://www.sunny99.com
Profile: KODA-FM is a commercial station owned by iHeartMedia Inc. The format of the station is adult contemporary music. KODA-FM broadcasts to the Houston area at 99.1 FM.
FM RADIO STATION

KODI-AM 39042
Owner: Legend Communications
Editorial: 1949 Mountain View Dr, Cody, Wyoming 82414 **Tel:** 1 307 578-5000.
Email: news@bhrnwy.com
Web site: http://www.mybighornbasin.com
Profile: KODI-AM is a commercial station owned by Legend Communications. The format of the station is sports and talk. KODI-AM broadcasts to the Cody, WY area at 1400 AM.
AM RADIO STATION

KODJ-FM 45969
Owner: iHeartMedia Inc.
Editorial: 2801 Decker Lake Dr, Salt Lake City, Utah 84119-2330 **Tel:** 1 801 908-1300.
Web site: http://941kodj.iheart.com
Profile: KODJ-FM is a commercial station owned by iHeartMedia Inc. The format of the station is oldies. KODJ-FM broadcasts to the Salt Lake City area at 94.1 FM.
FM RADIO STATION

KODL-AM 35027
Owner: Larson-Wynn Inc.
Editorial: 404 E 2nd St, The Dalles, Oregon 97058 **Tel:** 1 541 296-2101.
Email: newsroom@kodl.com
Web site: http://www.kodl.com
Profile: KODL-AM is a commercial station owned by Larson-Wynn Inc. The format of the station is adult standards. KODL-AM broadcasts to The Dalles, OR area at 1440 AM.
AM RADIO STATION

KODM-FM 39819
Owner: Townsquare Media, LLC
Editorial: 11300 State Highway 191 Bldg 2, Midland, Texas 79707-1367 **Tel:** 1 432 561-9809.
Web site: http://mix979fm.com
Profile: KODM-FM is a commercial station owned by Townsquare Media, LLC. The format of the station is adult contemporary music. KODM-FM broadcasts in the Midland, TX area at 97.9 FM.
FM RADIO STATION

KODS-FM 42019
Owner: Americom Broadcasting
Editorial: 961 Matley Ln, Ste 120, Reno, Nevada 89502 **Tel:** 1 775 829-1964.
Web site: http://www.river1037.com
Profile: KODS-FM is a commercial station owned by Americom Broadcasting. The format of the station is

classic hits. KODS-FM broadcasts to the Reno, NV area at 103.7 FM.
FM RADIO STATION

KODY-AM 38353
Owner: Armada Media Corp.
Editorial: 307 E 4th St, North Platte, Nebraska 69101-6903 **Tel:** 1 308 532-3344.
Email: news@huskeradio.com
Web site: http://www.huskeradio.com
Profile: KODY-AM is a commercial station owned by Armada Media Corp. The format of the station is news and talk. KODY-AM broadcasts to the North Platte, NE area at 1240 AM
AM RADIO STATION

KODZ-FM 44827
Owner: Bicoastal Media LLC
Editorial: 1500 Valley River Dr Ste 350, Eugene, Oregon 97401-2163 **Tel:** 1 541 284-3600.
Email: eugenepsa@bicoastalmedia.com
Web site: http://www.kool991.com
Profile: KODZ-FM is a commercial station owned by Bicoastal Media LLC. The format of the station is classic hits. KODZ-FM broadcasts in the Eugene, OR area at 99.1 FM.
FM RADIO STATION

KOEA-FM 46606
Owner: Eagle Bluff Enterprises
Editorial: 116 S Grand Ave, Doniphan, Missouri 63935-1741 **Tel:** 1 573 686-3700.
Email: frn@tcmax.net
Web site: http://foxradionetwork.com
Profile: KOEA-FM is a commercial station owned by Eagle Bluff Enterprises. The format of the station is classic country. KOEA-FM broadcasts to the Doniphan, MO area at 97.5 FM.
FM RADIO STATION

KOEL-AM 37411
Owner: Townsquare Media
Editorial: 2502 S Frederick Ave, Oelwein, Iowa 50662-3116 **Tel:** 1 319 283-1234.
Email: koelam@koel.com
Web site: http://www.koel.com
Profile: KOEL-FM is a commercial station owned by Townsquare Media. The format for the station is agriculture, news, sports and country. KOEL-FM broadcasts to the Cedar Rapids, IA area at 950 AM.
AM RADIO STATION

KOEL-FM 42190
Owner: Townsquare Media
Editorial: 501 Sycamore St Ste 300, Waterloo, Iowa 50703-4651 **Tel:** 1 319 833-4800.
Email: consumerfeedback@townsquaremedia.com
Web site: http://www.k985.com
Profile: KOEL-FM is a commercial station owned by Townsquare Media. The format for the station is classic country. KOEL-FM broadcasts to the Waterloo, IA area at 98.5 FM.
FM RADIO STATION

KOFC-AM 35987
Owner: Bott Broadcasting Co.
Editorial: 2201 S Thompson St, Ste C7, Springdale, Arkansas 72764 **Tel:** 1 479 750-7707.
Web site: http://www.bottradionetwork.com
Profile: KOFC-AM is a commercial station owned by Bott Broadcasting Co. The format of the station is religious talk. KOFC-AM broadcasts to the Springdale, AR area at 1250 AM.
AM RADIO STATION

KOFE-AM 35028
Owner: Plank (Theresa)
Editorial: 201 N 8th St, Saint Maries, Idaho 83861-1869 **Tel:** 1 208 245-1240.
Email: tparrish_kofe@yahoo.com
AM RADIO STATION

KOFI-AM 38464
Owner: KOFI Inc.
Editorial: 317 1st Ave E, Kalispell, Montana 59901 **Tel:** 1 406 755-6690.
Email: kofi@kofiradio.com
Web site: http://www.kofiradio.com
Profile: KOFI-AM is a commercial station owned by KOFI Inc. The format of the station is news and talk. KOFI-AM broadcasts in the Kalispell, MT area at 1180 AM.
AM RADIO STATION

KOFM-FM 46215
Owner: Williams Broadcasting LLC
Editorial: 1710 W Willow Rd Ste 300, Enid, Oklahoma 73703-2432 **Tel:** 1 580 234-4230.
Email: production@kofm.com
Web site: http://www.kofm.com
Profile: KOFM-FM is a commercial station owned by Williams Broadcasting LLC. The format of the station is contemporary country music. KOFM-FM broadcasts to the Oklahoma City area at 103.1 FM.
FM RADIO STATION

KOFO-AM 35029
Owner: Brandy Communications
Editorial: 320 E Radio Road, Ottawa, Kansas 66067-9563 **Tel:** 1 785 242-1220.
Email: kofo@kofo.com
Web site: http://www.kofo.com
Profile: KOFO-AM is a commercial station owned by Brandy Communications. The format of the station is country. KOFO-AM broadcasts to the Ottawa, KS area at 1220 AM.
AM RADIO STATION

KOFX-FM 41043
Owner: Entravision Communications Corp.
Editorial: 5426 N Mesa St, El Paso, Texas 79912-5421 **Tel:** 1 915 581-1126.
Web site: http://www.923thefox.com
Profile: KOFX-FM is a commercial station owned by Entravision Communications Corp. The format of the station is oldies. KOFX-FM broadcasts to the El Paso, TX area at 92.3 FM.
FM RADIO STATION

KOGA-AM 37412
Owner: iHeartMedia Inc.
Editorial: 113 W 4th St, Ogallala, Nebraska 69153-2508 **Tel:** 1 308 284-3633.
Web site: http://930koga.iheart.com
Profile: KOGA-AM is a commercial station owned by iHeartMedia Inc. The format of the station is adult standards. KOGA-AM broadcasts to the Ogallala, NE area at 930 AM.
AM RADIO STATION

KOGA-FM 44800
Owner: iHeartMedia Inc.
Editorial: 113 W 4th St, Ogallala, Nebraska 69153-2508 **Tel:** 1 308 284-3633.
Web site: http://www.997thelake.com
Profile: KOGA-FM is a commercial station owned by iHeartMedia Inc. The format of the station is classic rock. KOGA-FM broadcasts to the Ogallala, NE area at 99.7 FM.
FM RADIO STATION

KOGL-FM 533636
Owner: Oregon Public Broadcasting
Editorial: 7140 SW MacAdam Ave, Portland, Oregon 97219-3013 **Tel:** 1 503 244-3300.
Email: opbnews@opb.org
Web site: http://www.opb.org
Profile: KOGL-FM is a non-commercial station owned by Oregon Public Broadcasting. The format at the station is news and talk. KOGL-FM broadcasts to the Portland, OR area at 89.3 FM.
FM RADIO STATION

KOGM-FM 44801
Owner: Delta Media Corporation
Editorial: 3500 Nw Evangeline Trwy, Carencro, Louisiana 70520-6240 **Tel:** 1 337 896-1600.
Web site: http://www.mustang877.com
Profile: KOGM-FM is a commercial station owned by Delta Media Corporation. The format of the station is classic country. KOGM-FM broadcasts to the Lafayette, LA area at 107.1 FM.
FM RADIO STATION

KOGO-AM 36817
Owner: iHeartMedia Inc.
Editorial: 9660 Granite Ridge Dr Ste 100, San Diego, California 92123-2689 **Tel:** 1 858 292-2000.
Email: kogo@iheartmedia.com
Web site: http://kogo.iheart.com
Profile: KOGO-AM is a commercial station owned by iHeartMedia Inc. The format for the station is news and talk. KOGO-AM broadcasts to the San Diego area at 600 AM.
AM RADIO STATION

KOGT-AM 35030
Owner: G Cap Communications
Tel: 1 409 883-4381.
Email: gstelly@gt.rr.com
Web site: http://www.kogt.com
Profile: KOGT-AM is a commercial station owned by G Cap Communications. The format of the station is classic country. KOGT-AM broadcasts to the Orange, TX area at 1600 AM.
AM RADIO STATION

KOHI-AM 35031
Owner: Mountain Broadcasting Corp.
Editorial: 36200 Pittsburg Rd, Ste C, Saint Helens, Oregon 97051 **Tel:** 1 503 397-1600.
Email: kohi.radio@gmail.com
Web site: http://am1600kohi.com
Profile: KOHI-AM is a commercial station owned by Mountain Broadcasting Corp. The format of the station is news, sports and talk. KOHI-AM broadcasts to the Saint Helens, OR area at 1600 AM.
AM RADIO STATION

KOHL-FM 39820
Owner: Fremont Newark Community College
Editorial: 43600 Mission Blvd, Fremont, California 94539-5847 **Tel:** 1 510 659-6221.
Web site: http://www.kohlradio.com
Profile: KOHL-FM is a non-commercial station owned by Fremont Newark Community College. The format of the station is Top 40/CHR music. KOHL-FM broadcasts in the Fremont, CA area at 89.3 FM.
FM RADIO STATION

KOHN-FM 588452
Owner: Tohono O'Odham Nation
Editorial: Business Loop, 86 Main St South, Sells, Arizona 85634 **Tel:** 1 520 361-5011.
Email: kohn919@hotmail.com
Web site: http://kohnfm.tonation-nsn.gov
Profile: KOHN-FM is a non-commercial station owned by Tohono O'Odham Nation. The format of the station is a ethnic variety format. KOHN-FM broadcasts to the Sells, AZ area at 91.9 FM.
FM RADIO STATION

KOHO-FM 40057
Owner: Icicle Broadcasting, Inc.
Editorial: 7475 Koho Pl, Leavenworth, Washington 98826-9023 **Tel:** 1 509 548-1011.
Email: news@kohoradio.com
Web site: http://www.kohoradio.com
Profile: KOHO-FM is a commercial station owned by Icicle Broadcasting, Inc. The format of the station is adult album alternative. KOHO-FM broadcasts to the Leavenworth, WA area at 101.1 FM.
FM RADIO STATION

KOHT-FM 45803
Owner: iHeartMedia Inc.
Editorial: 3202 N Oracle Rd, Tucson, Arizona 85705-3820 **Tel:** 1 520 618-2100.
Email: hot983comments@yahoo.com
Web site: http://www.hot983.com
Profile: KOHT-FM is a commercial station owned by iHeartMedia Inc. The format of the station is urban contemporary music. KOHTFM broadcasts to the Tucson, AZ area at 98.3 FM.
FM RADIO STATION

KOHU-AM 37413
Owner: West End Radio LLC
Editorial: 80404 Cooney Ln, Hermiston, Oregon 97838-6613 **Tel:** 1 541 567-6500.
Web site: http://www.gohermiston.com
Profile: KOHU-AM is a commercial station owned by West End Radio LLC. The format of the station is classic country. KOHU-AM broadcasts to the Hermiston, OR area at 1360 AM.
AM RADIO STATION

KOIA-FM 855459
Owner: St. Gabriel Communications, LTD
Editorial: 705 Douglas St Ste 238, Sioux City, Iowa 51101-1043 **Tel:** 1 712 224-5342.
Email: fhcradio@fhcradio.com
Web site: http://www.fhcradio.com
Profile: KOAI-FM is a non-commercial station owned by St. Gabriel Communications, LTD. The format of the station is Catholic teaching. KOAI-FM broadcasts to the Sioux City, IA area at a frequency of 88.1 FM.
FM RADIO STATION

KOIL-AM 38967
Owner: NRG Media LLC
Editorial: 5011 Capitol Ave, Omaha, Nebraska 68132-2921 **Tel:** 1 402 342-2000.
Email: omahacares@iheartmedia.com
Web site: http://www.mighty1290koil.com
Profile: KOIL-AM is a commercial station owned by NRG Media LLC. The format of the station is news and talk. KOIL-AM broadcasts to the Omaha, NE, area at 1290 AM.
AM RADIO STATION

KOIR-FM 45813
Owner: Rio Grande Bible Institute Inc.
Editorial: 4300 S Business Highway 281, Edinburg, Texas 78539-9650 **Tel:** 1 956 380-3435.
Email: correo@radioesperanza.com
Web site: http://www.radioesperanza.com
Profile: KOIR-FM is a commercial station owned by Rio Grande Bible Institute Inc. The format of the station is religious Spanish music and news. KOIR-FM broadcasts to the Edinburg, TX area at 88.5 FM.
FM RADIO STATION

KOIT-FM 44802
Owner: Entercom Communications Corp.
Editorial: 201 3rd St Ste 1200, San Francisco, California 94103-3143 **Tel:** 1 415 777-0965.
Email: koit@koit.com
Web site: http://www.koit.com
Profile: KOIT-FM is a commercial station owned by Entercom Communications Corp. The format is adult contemporary music. KOIT-FM broadcasts to the San Francisco area at 96.5 FM.
FM RADIO STATION

KOJM-AM 39024
Owner: New Media Broadcasters
Editorial: 2210 31st St N, Havre, Montana 59501-8003 **Tel:** 1 406 265-7841.
Web site: http://www.kojm.com
Profile: KOJM-AM is a commercial station owned by New Media Broadcasters. The format for the station is classic hits. KOJM-AM broadcasts to the Havre, MT area at 610 AM. KPQX-FM prefers not to receive press materials.
AM RADIO STATION

KOJY-FM 40046
Owner: Mark McVey
Editorial: 22620 195th St, Bloomfield, Iowa 52537-6981 **Tel:** 1 641 664-3721.
Profile: KOJY-FM is a commercial station owned by Mark McVey. The format of the station is southern gospel. KOJY-FM broadcasts to the Bloomfield, IA area at 106.9 FM.
FM RADIO STATION

KOKA-AM 39111
Owner: Alpha Media USA
Editorial: 208 N Thomas St, Shreveport, Louisiana 71137 **Tel:** 1 318 222-3122.
Web site: http://www.koka.am
Profile: KOKA-AM is a commercial station owned by Alpha Media USA (formally owned by Access.1 Communications Corp.) The format of the station is gospel music. KOKA-AM broadcasts to the Shreveport, LA area at 980 AM.
AM RADIO STATION

KOKB-AM 35032
Owner: Team Radio LLC
Editorial: 102 E Grand Ave, Ponca City, Oklahoma 74601-5207 **Tel:** 1 580 762-9930.
Email: tripleplay@eteamradio.com
Web site: http://www.eteamradio.com
Profile: KOKB-AM is a commercial station owned by Team Radio LLC. The format of the station is sports. KOKB-AM broadcasts to the Ponca City, OK area at 1580 AM.
AM RADIO STATION

KOKC-AM 39093
Owner: Tyler Media, LLC.
Editorial: 400 E Britton Rd, Oklahoma City, Oklahoma 73114-7515 **Tel:** 1 405 478-5104.
Email: production@tylermedia.com
Web site: http://www.kokcradio.com
Profile: KOKC-AM is a commercial station owned by Tyler Media, LLC. The format of the station is news and talk. KOKC-AM broadcasts to the Oklahoma City area at 1520 AM.
AM RADIO STATION

KOKE-AM 133729
Owner: Encino Broadcasting, LLC
Editorial: 9434 Parkfield Dr, Austin, Texas 78758-6227 **Tel:** 1 512 453-1491.
Email: spots@austintejas.com
Profile: KOKE-AM is a commercial station owned by Encino Broadcasting, LLC. The format of the station is regional Mexican. KOKE-AM broadcasts to the Austin, TX area at 1600 AM.
AM RADIO STATION

KOKE-FM 501728
Owner: REO Radio Group, LLC
Editorial: 1095 W US Highway 79, Rockdale, Texas 76567-4513 **Tel:** 1 512 416-1100.
Web site: http://kokefm.com
Profile: KOKE-FM is a commercial station owned by REO Radio Group, LLC. The format of the station is Progressive Country, a sub-genre of Texas country music. KOKE-FM broadcasts to the Taylor, TX area at 99.3 FM.
FM RADIO STATION

KOKK-AM 39105
Owner: Performance Radio
Editorial: 1726 Dakota Ave S, Huron, South Dakota 57350 **Tel:** 1 605 352-1933.
Web site: http://www.performance-radio.com
Profile: KOKK-AM is a commercial station owned by Performance Radio. The format of the station is contemporary country. KOKK-AM broadcasts to the Huron, SD area at 1210 AM.
AM RADIO STATION

KOKL-AM 35034
Owner: Third Day Broadcasting, INC.
Editorial: 100 E 7th St, Okmulgee, Oklahoma 74447-4606 **Tel:** 1 918 756-3646.
Email: kokl@sbcglobal.net
Web site: http://www.kokl.net
Profile: KOKL-AM is a commercial station owned by Third Day Broadcasting, INC. The format of the station is country. KOKL-AM broadcasts to the Tulsa, OK area at 1240 AM.
AM RADIO STATION

KOKO-AM 35035
Owner: D&H Media, LLC
Editorial: 800 Pca Rd, Warrensburg, Missouri 64093-9275 **Tel:** 1 660 747-9191.
Email: koko@kwkj.com
Web site: http://www.warrensburgradio.com
Profile: KOKO-AM is a commercial station owned by D&H Media, LLC. The format of the station is oldies music. KOKO-AM broadcasts to the Kansas City, MO, area at 1450 AM.
AM RADIO STATION

KOKO-FM 41174
Owner: Big Broadcasting Inc.
Editorial: 2775 E Shaw Ave, Fresno, California 93710 **Tel:** 1 559 292-9494.
Web site: http://www.koko94.com
Profile: KOKO-FM is a commercial station owned by Big Broadcasting Inc. The format of the station is a variety of hip-hop and rhythmic oldies. KOKO-FM broadcasts to the Fresno, CA area at 94.3 FM.
FM RADIO STATION

KOKP-AM 38532
Owner: Team Radio LLC
Editorial: 122 N 3rd St, Ponca City, Oklahoma 74601-4326 **Tel:** 1 580 762-9930.
Email: tripleplay@eteamradio.com
Web site: http://www.eteamradio.com
Profile: KOKP-AM is a commercial station owned by Team Radio LLC. The format of the station is sports. KOKP-AM broadcasts to the Ponca City, OK area at 1020.
AM RADIO STATION

KOKR-FM 45937
Owner: Sudbury Broadcasting Group
Editorial: 2025 McLarty Dr, Newport, Arkansas 72112-4822 **Tel:** 1 870 523-5891.
Email: legends@rivercountry967.com
Web site: http://www.rivercountry967.com
Profile: KOKR-FM is a commercial station owned by Sudbury Broadcasting Group. The format of the station is contemporary country. KOKR-FM broadcasts to the Newport, AR area at 96.7 FM.
FM RADIO STATION

KOKS-FM 41527
Owner: Calvary Broadcasting
Editorial: 2773 Barron Rd, Poplar Bluff, Missouri 63901-1929 **Tel:** 1 573 686-5080.
Email: koksradio@mycitycable.com
Web site: http://www.koks895fm.org
Profile: KOKS-FM is a non-commercial station owned by Calvary Broadcasting. The format of the station is religious programming. KOKS-FM broadcasts to the Poplar Bluff, MO area at 89.5 FM.
FM RADIO STATION

KOKX-AM 37415
Owner: Withers Broadcasting Co.
Editorial: 108 Washington St, Keokuk, Iowa 52632-2313 **Tel:** 1 319 524-5410.
Profile: KOKX-AM is a commercial station owned by Withers Broadcasting Co. The format of the station is adult standards and talk. The station airs in the Keokuk, IA area at 1310 AM.
AM RADIO STATION

KOKX-FM 44803
Owner: Withers Broadcasting Co.
Editorial: 108 Washington St, Keokuk, Iowa 52632-2313 **Tel:** 1 319 524-5410.
Web site: http://keokukradio.com
Profile: KOKX-FM is a commercial station owned by Withers Broadcasting Co. The format of the station is contemporary christian. KOKX-FM broadcasts to the Koekuk, IA area at 95.3 FM.
FM RADIO STATION

KOKY-FM 42436
Owner: Cumulus Media Inc
Editorial: 700 Wellington Hills Rd, Little Rock, Arkansas 72211 **Tel:** 1 501 401-0200.
Web site: http://www.koky.com
Profile: KOKY-FM is a commercial station owned by Cumulus Media Inc. The format of the station is urban adult contemporary music. KOKY-FM broadcasts in the Little Rock, AR area at 102.1 FM.
FM RADIO STATION

KOKZ-FM 46374
Owner: NRG Media LLC
Editorial: 514 Jefferson St, Waterloo, Iowa 50701-5422 **Tel:** 1 319 234-2200.
Web site: http://www.1057kokz.com
Profile: KOKZ-FM is a commercial station owned by NRG Media LLC. The format for the station is classic hits music. KOKZ-FM broadcasts to the Cedar Rapids, IA area at 105.7 FM.
FM RADIO STATION

KOLA-FM 39822
Owner: Anaheim Broadcasting Corp.
Editorial: 1940 Orange Tree Ln, Ste 200, Redlands, California 92374 **Tel:** 1 909 793-3554.
Web site: http://www.kolafm.com
Profile: KOLA-FM is a commercial station owned by Anaheim Broadcasting Corp. The format of the station is classic hits music. KOLA-FM broadcasts to the Redlands, CA area at 99.9 FM.
FM RADIO STATION

KOLC-FM 42779
Owner: Americom Broadcasting
Editorial: 961 Matley Ln, Reno, Nevada 89502-2188
Tel: 1 775 829-1964.
Email: info@tencountry.com
Web site: http://www.tencountry.com
Profile: KOLC-FM is a commercial station owned by Americom Broadcasting. The format of the station is contemporary country. KOLC-FM broadcasts to the Reno, NV area at 97.3 FM.
FM RADIO STATION

KOLE-AM 39385
Owner: Birach Broadcasting Corp.
Editorial: 303 Katherine St, West Orange, Texas 77630-5324 **Tel:** 1 409 835-2222.
Email: sima@birach.com
Web site: http://www.birach.com/kole.htm
Profile: KOLE-AM is a commercial station owned by Birach Broadcasting Corp. The format of the station is Regional Mexican. KOLE-AM broadcasts to the Beaumont, TX area at 1340 AM.
AM RADIO STATION

KOLI-FM 43644
Owner: Cumulus Media Inc.
Editorial: 4302 Call Field Rd Ste D, Wichita Falls, Texas 76308-2534 **Tel:** 1 940 691-2311.
Web site: http://949theoutlaw.com
Profile: KOLI-FM is a commercial station owned by Cumulus Media Inc. The format of the station is contemporary country music. KOLI-FM broadcasts to the Wichita Falls, TX area at 94.9 FM.
FM RADIO STATION

KOLJ-AM 36628
Owner: White (John L.)
Tel: 1 940 663-5711.
Web site: http://www.radio1150.net
Profile: KOLJ-AM is a commercial station owned by First Broadcasting Co. The format of the station is classic country. KOLJ-AM broadcasts to the Mineral Wells, TX area at 1150 AM.
AM RADIO STATION

KOLL-FM 46852
Owner: Vega Broadcasting
Editorial: 2323D S Old Missouri Rd, Springdale, Arkansas 72764-7468 **Tel:** 1 479 756-8686.
Email: info@ezspanishmedia.com
Profile: KOLL-FM is a commercial station owned by Vega Broadcasting. The format of the station is Regional Mexican. KOLL-FM broadcasts to the Little Rock, AR area at 106.3 FM.
FM RADIO STATION

KOLM-AM 35036
Owner: Townsquare Media
Editorial: 122 4th St SW, Rochester, Minnesota 55902-3320 **Tel:** 1 507 286-1010.
Web site: http://1520theticket.com
Profile: KOLM-AM is a commercial station owned by Townsquare Media. The format of the station is sports. KOLM-AM broadcasts to the Rochester, MN area at 1520 AM.
AM RADIO STATION

KOLT-AM 38731
Owner: Armada Media
Tel: 1 308 632-5667.
Web site: http://www.huskeradio.com
Profile: KOLT-AM is a commercial station owned by Armada Media. The format of the station is news and talk. KOLT-AM broadcasts to the Scottsbluff, NE area at 1320 AM.
AM RADIO STATION

KOLV-FM 39824
Owner: Lakeland Broadcasting
Editorial: 1340 NW 7th St, Willmar, Minnesota 56201
Tel: 1 320 235-1340.
Email: askus@bigcountry100.com
Web site: http://www.bigcountry100.com
Profile: KOLV-FM is a commercial station owned by Lakeland Broadcasting. The format of the station is contemporary country. KOLV-FM broadcasts in the Minneapolis area at 100.1 FM.
FM RADIO STATION

KOLW-FM 44248
Owner: Townsquare Media, LLC
Editorial: 2621 W A St, Pasco, Washington 99301-4702 **Tel:** 1 509 547-9791.
Web site: http://www.hot975online.com
Profile: KOLW-FM is a commercial station owned by Townsquare Media, LLC. The format of the station is Rhythmic/CHR. KOLW-FM broadcasts to the Pasco, WA area at 97.5 FM.
FM RADIO STATION

KOLY-AM 37416
Owner: James River Broadcasting
Editorial: 118 3rd St E, Mobridge, South Dakota 57601-2511 **Tel:** 1 605 845-3654.
Web site: http://www.dakotaradiogroup.com
Profile: KOLY-AM is a commercial station owned by James River Broadcasting. The format of the station is adult standards. KOLY-AM broadcasts to the Mobridge, SD area at 1300 AM.
AM RADIO STATION

KOLY-FM 44804
Owner: James River Broadcasting
Editorial: 118 3rd St E, Mobridge, South Dakota 57601-2511 **Tel:** 1 605 845-3654.
Web site: http://www.drgnews.com/listen/star-99-koly-fm/
Profile: KOLY-FM is a commercial station owned by James River Broadcasting. The format of the station is adult contemporary. KOLY-FM broadcasts to the Mobridge, SD area at 99.5 FM.
FM RADIO STATION

KOLZ-FM 42954
Owner: iHeartMedia Inc.
Editorial: 4270 Byrd Dr, Loveland, Colorado 80538-7074 **Tel:** 1 970 461-2560.
Web site: http://www.koltfm.com
Profile: KOLZ-FM is a commercial station owned by iHeartMedia Inc. The format of the station is contemporary country. KOLZ-FM broadcasts in the Cheyenne, WY area at 100.7 FM.
FM RADIO STATION

KOLZ-FM 42995
Owner: iHeartMedia Inc.
Editorial: 5411 Jefferson St NE Ste 100, Albuquerque, New Mexico 87109-3485 **Tel:** 1 505 830-6400.
Web site: http://www.hotabq.com/main.html
Profile: KOLZ-FM is a commercial station owned by iHeartMedia Inc. The format of the station is rhythmic oldies. KOLZ-FM broadcasts to the Albuquerque, NM area at 95.1 FM.
FM RADIO STATION

KOMA-FM 46439
Owner: Tyler Media, LLC.
Editorial: 400 E Britton Rd, Oklahoma City, Oklahoma 73114-7515 **Tel:** 1 405 478-5104.
Web site: http://www.komaradio.com
Profile: KOMA-FM is a commercial station owned by Tyler Media, LLC. The format of the station is classic hits. KOMA-FM broadcasts to the Oklahoma City area at 92.5 FM
FM RADIO STATION

KOMB-FM 44805
Owner: Fort Scott Broadcasting Co., Inc.
Editorial: 2 N National Ave, Fort Scott, Kansas 66701-1307 **Tel:** 1 620 223-4500.
Web site: http://www.kombfm.com
Profile: KOMB-FM is a commercial station owned by Fort Scott Broadcasting Co., Inc. The format of the station is Adult Hits. KOMB-FM broadcasts to the Fort Scott, KS area at 103.9 FM.
FM RADIO STATION

KOMC-AM 37417
Owner: Earls Broadcasting
Editorial: 202 Courtney St, Branson, Missouri 65616-2434 **Tel:** 1 417 334-6003.
Web site: http://www.mykomc.com
Profile: KOMC-AM is a commercial station owned by Earls Broadcasting. The format of the station is gospel. KOMC-AM broadcasts to the Branson, MO area at 1220 AM.
AM RADIO STATION

KOMC-FM 46826
Owner: Earls Broadcasting
Editorial: 202 Courtney St, Branson, Missouri 65616-2434 **Tel:** 1 417 334-6003.
Email: news@krzk.com
Web site: http://www.hometowndailynews.com
Profile: KOMC-FM is a commercial station owned by Earls Broadcasting. The format of the station is adult contemporary. KOMC-FM broadcasts to the Springfield, MO area at 100.1 FM.
FM RADIO STATION

KOME-FM 857147
Owner: Chisholm Trail Broadcasting
Editorial: 115 W 3rd St, Fort Worth, Texas 76102-7402 **Tel:** 1 817 332-0959.
Web site: http://www.921hankfm.com
Profile: KOME-FM is a commercial station owned by Chisholm Trail Broadcasting. The format of the station is classic and contemporary country music. KOME-FM broadcasts to the Meridian, TX area at 95.3 FM.
FM RADIO STATION

KOMG-FM 43458
Owner: Midwest Family Stations
Editorial: 2453 E Elm St, Springfield, Missouri 65802-2868 **Tel:** 1 417 886-5677.
Web site: http://www.thebull1051.com/
Profile: KOMG-FM is a commercial station owned by Midwest Family Stations. The format of the station is country. KOMG-FM broadcasts to the Springfield, MO area at 105.1 FM.
FM RADIO STATION

KOMJ-AM 37268
Owner: Walnut Radio, LLC
Tel: 1 402 553-1490.
Profile: KOMJ-AM is a commercial station owned by Walnut Radio, LLC. The format of the station is adult standards. KOMJ-AM broadcasts to the Omaha, NE area at AM 1490.
AM RADIO STATION

KOMO-AM 35037
Owner: Sinclair Radio of Seattle, LLC
Editorial: 140 4th Ave N, Seattle, Washington 98109-4940 **Tel:** 1 206 404-4000.
Email: tips@komo4news.com
Web site: http://www.komonews.com
Profile: KOMO-AM is a commercial station owned by Sinclair Radio of Seattle, LLC. The format of the station is news. KOMO-AM broadcasts in the Seattle area at 1000 AM.
AM RADIO STATION

KOMO-FM 43205
Owner: Sinclair Radio of Seattle, LLC
Editorial: 140 4th Ave N, Seattle, Washington 98109-4940 **Tel:** 1 206 404-4000.
Email: tips@komo4news.com
Web site: http://www.komonews.com
Profile: KOMO-FM is a commercial station owned by Sinclair Radio of Seattle, LLC. The format of the station is news and talk. KOMO-FM broadcasts to the Seattle area at 97.7 FM.
FM RADIO STATION

KOMP-FM 44806
Owner: Lotus Communications Corp.
Editorial: 8755 W Flamingo Rd, Las Vegas, Nevada 89147-8667 **Tel:** 1 702 876-1460.
Web site: http://www.komp.com
Profile: KOMP-FM is a commercial station owned by Lotus Communications Corp. The format of the station is rock music. KOMP-FM broadcasts to the Las Vegas area at 92.3 FM.
FM RADIO STATION

KOMR-FM 43707
Owner: Univision Communications Inc.
Editorial: 6006 S 30th St, Phoenix, Arizona 85042-4802 **Tel:** 1 602 308-7900.
Web site: http://www.univision.com/arizona/komr
Profile: KOMR-FM is a commercial station owned by Univision Communications Inc. The format of the station is Spanish Adult Hits. KOMR-FM broadcasts to the Phoenix area at 106.3 FM.
FM RADIO STATION

KOMS-FM 42963
Owner: Cumulus Media Inc.
Editorial: 3811 Rogers Ave, Fort Smith, Arkansas 72903 **Tel:** 1 479 452-0681.
Web site: http://www.bigcountry1073.com
Profile: KOMS-FM is a commercial station owned by Cumulus Media Inc. The format of the station is classic country. KOMS-FM broadcasts to the Fort Smith, AR area at 107.3 FM.
FM RADIO STATION

KOMT-FM 235314
Owner: Dowdy Broadcasting, Inc.
Editorial: 2352 Highway 62 E Business, Mountain Home, Arkansas 72653-6847 **Tel:** 1 870 492-6022.
Web site: http://www.kktz.net
Profile: KOMT-FM is a commercial station owned by Dowdy Broadcasting, Inc. The format of the station is Top 40/CHR. KOMT-FM broadcasts to the Mountain Home, AR area at 93.5 FM.
FM RADIO STATION

KOMW-AM 38977
Owner: North Cascades Broadcasting
Editorial: 320 Emery Dr, Omak, Washington 98841-9237 **Tel:** 1 509 826-0100.
Email: news@komw.net
Web site: http://www.komw.net
Profile: KOMW-AM is a commercial station owned by North Cascades Broadcasting. The format of the station is adult standards music. WOMW-AM broadcasts to the Spokane, WA area at 680 AM.
AM RADIO STATION

KOMX-FM 44807
Owner: Hughes(Jim)
Editorial: 1701 N Banks St, Pampa, Texas 79065
Tel: 1 806 669-6809.
Email: production@kgrokomxradio.com
Web site: http://www.kgrokomxradio.com
Profile: KOMX-FM is a commercial station owned by Jim Hughes. The format of the station is country. KOMX-FM broadcasts to the Pampa, TX area at 100.3 FM.
FM RADIO STATION

KOMY-AM 36590
Owner: Zwerling Broadcasting System Ltd.
Editorial: 2300 Portola Dr, Santa Cruz, California 95062 **Tel:** 1 831 475-1080.
Web site: http://www.1340komy.com
Profile: KOMY-AM is commercial station owned by Zwerling Broadcasting System Ltd. The format of the station is adult standards and easy listening. KOMY-AM broadcasts in the Santa Cruz, CA area at 1340 AM.
AM RADIO STATION

KONA-AM 37418
Owner: Cherry Creek Radio
Editorial: 2823 W Lewis St, Pasco, Washington 99301-6702 **Tel:** 1 509 547-1618.
Email: 610kona@cherrycreekradio.com
Web site: http://www.610kona.com
Profile: KONA-AM is a commercial station owned by Cherry Creek Radio. The format of the station is news and talk. KONA-AM broadcasts to the Pasco, WA area at 610 AM.
AM RADIO STATION

KONA-FM 44808
Owner: Cherry Creek Radio
Editorial: 2823 W Lewis St, Pasco, Washington 99301-6702 **Tel:** 1 509 547-1618.
Web site: http://www.mix1053.com
Profile: KONA-FM is a commercial station owned by Cherry Creek Radio. The format of the station is adult contemporary. KONA-FM broadcasts to the Pasco, WA area at 105.3 FM.
FM RADIO STATION

KOND-FM 45902
Owner: Univision Communications Inc.
Editorial: 601 W Univision Plz, Fresno, California 93704-1092 **Tel:** 1 559 430-8500.
Web site: http://queonda921.univision.com
Profile: KOND-FM is a commercial station owned by Univision Communications Inc. The format of the station is regional Mexican. KOND-FM broadcasts to the Fresno, CA area at 92.1 FM.
FM RADIO STATION

KONE-FM 39946
Owner: Alpha Media
Editorial: 33 Briercroft Office Park, Lubbock, Texas 79412-3020 **Tel:** 1 806 762-3000.
Web site: http://www.rock101.fm
Profile: KONE-FM is a commercial station owned by Alpha Media. The format of the station is classic rock. KONE-FM broadcasts to the Lubbock, TX area at 101.1 FM.
FM RADIO STATION

KONI-FM 42407
Owner: Hochman Hawaii Media
Editorial: 300 Ohukai Rd Ste C318, Kihei, Hawaii 96753-7050 **Tel:** 1 808 875-8866.
Email: koni@hawaii.rr.com
Web site: http://www.koni1047.com
FM RADIO STATION

KONO-AM 37420
Owner: Cox Media Group, Inc.
Editorial: 8122 Datapoint Dr Ste 600, San Antonio, Texas 78229-3446 **Tel:** 1 210 615-5400.
Email: psa@coxinc.com
Web site: http://www.kono1011.com
Profile: KONO-AM is a commercial station owned by Cox Media Group, Inc. The format for the station is Oldies. KONO-AM broadcasts to the San Antonio area at 860 AM.
AM RADIO STATION

KONO-FM 44704
Owner: Cox Media Group, Inc.
Editorial: 8122 Datapoint Dr Ste 600, San Antonio, Texas 78229-3446 **Tel:** 1 210 615-5400.
Email: psa@coxinc.com
Web site: http://www.kono1011.com
Profile: KONO-FM is a commercial station owned by Cox Media Group, Inc. The format for the station is classic hits. KONO-FM broadcasts to the San Antonio area at 101.1 FM.
FM RADIO STATION

KONP-AM 35038
Owner: Radio Pacific Inc.
Editorial: 721 E 1st St, Port Angeles, Washington 98362-3600 **Tel:** 1 360 457-1450.
Email: info@konp.com
Web site: http://www.konp.com
Profile: KONP-AM is a commercial station owned by Radio Pacific Inc. The format of the station is news, talk and sports. KONP-AM broadcasts to the Port Angeles, WA area at 1450 AM.
AM RADIO STATION

KONQ-FM 46666
Owner: Dodge City Community College
Editorial: 3004 N 14th Ave, Dodge City, Kansas 67801 **Tel:** 1 620 225-6783.
Web site: http://www.dc3.edu
Profile: KONQ-FM is a non-commercial station owned by Dodge City Community College. The format of the station is variety. KONQ-FM broadcasts to the Dodge City, KS area at a frequency of 91.9 FM.
FM RADIO STATION

KONY-FM 46661
Owner: Canyon Media Corporation
Editorial: 204 Playa Della Rosita, Washington, Utah 84780 **Tel:** 1 435 628-3643.
Email: kony@infowest.com
Web site: http://www.999konycountry.com
Profile: KONY-FM is a commercial station owned by Canyon Media Corporation. The format of the station is contemporary country. KONY-FM broadcasts to the St. George, UT area at 99.9 FM.
FM RADIO STATION

KOOC-FM 42424
Owner: Townsquare Media, Inc.
Editorial: 608 Moody Ln, Temple, Texas 76504-2952 **Tel:** 1 254 773-5252.
Web site: http://www.myb106.com
Profile: KOOC-FM is a commercial station owned by Townsquare Media, Inc. The format of the station is urban contemporary. KOOC-FM broadcasts to the Temple, TX area at 106.3 FM.
FM RADIO STATION

KOOI-FM 45841
Owner: Access.1 Communications Corp.
Editorial: 210 S Broadway Ave Ste 100, Tyler, Texas 75702-7353 **Tel:** 1 903 581-9966.
Web site: http://www.kooi.com
Profile: KOOI-FM is a commercial station owned by Access.1 Communications Corp. The format of the station is adult contemporary. KOOI-FM broadcasts to the Tyler, TX area at 106.5 FM.
FM RADIO STATION

KOOK-FM 43538
Owner: Revolution Broadcast Co. of The West
Editorial: 2125 Sidney Baker St, Kerrville, Texas 78028-2551 **Tel:** 1 830 896-1230.
Email: production@krvl.com
Profile: KOOK-FM is a commercial station owned by Revolution Broadcast Co. of The West. The format for the station is classic country music. KOOK-FM broadcasts to the Junction, TX area at 93.5 FM.
FM RADIO STATION

KOOL-FM 43153
Owner: CBS Radio
Editorial: 840 N Central Ave, Phoenix, Arizona 85004-2003 **Tel:** 1 602 776-7000.
Web site: http://kool.cbslocal.com
Profile: KOOL-FM is a commercial station owned by CBS Radio. The format of the station is classic hits. KOOL-FM broadcasts to the Phoenix area at 94.5 FM.
FM RADIO STATION

KOOO-FM 46713
Owner: NRG Media LLC
Editorial: 5011 Capitol Ave, Omaha, Nebraska 68132-2921 **Tel:** 1 402 342-2000.
Web site: http://www.1019thekeg.com
Profile: KOOO-FM is a commercial station owned by NRG Media LLC. The format of the station is adult hits. KOOO-FM is licensed to La Vista, NE and broadcasts to the Lincoln and Omaha areas in Nebraska at 101.9 FM.
FM RADIO STATION

KOOQ-AM 37421
Owner: Eagle Radio Inc.
Editorial: 1301 E 4th St, North Platte, Nebraska 69101 **Tel:** 1 308 532-1120.
Web site: http://www.1410amespn.com
Profile: KOOQ-AM is commercial station owned by Eagle Radio Inc. The format of the station is sports. KOOQ-AM broadcasts to North Platte, NE at 1410 AM.
AM RADIO STATION

KOOR-AM 36313
Owner: Bustos Media, LLC
Editorial: 5110 SE Stark St, Portland, Oregon 97215-1751 **Tel:** 1 503 234-5550.
Web site: http://russianradio7.com
Profile: KOOR-AM is a commercial station owned by Bustos Media, LLC. The format of the station is Russian language programming. KOOR-AM broadcasts to the Portland, OR, area at 1010 AM.
AM RADIO STATION

KOOS-FM 46226
Owner: Bicoastal Media LLC
Editorial: 320 Central Ave, Ste 519, Coos Bay, Oregon 97420 **Tel:** 1 541 267-2121.
Email: southcoastpsa@bicoastalmedia.com
Web site: http://www.power1073.com
Profile: KOOS-FM is a commercial station owned by Bicoastal Media LLC. The format of the station is hot adult contemporary music. KOOS-FM broadcasts to the Coos Bay, OR area at 107.3 FM.
FM RADIO STATION

KOOV-FM 46170
Owner: M & M Broadcasters, Ltd
Editorial: 5501 Bagby Ave, Waco, Texas 76711-2300 **Tel:** 1 254 772-0930.
Web site: http://www.929shooterfm.com
Profile: KOOV-FM is a commercial station owned by M & M Broadcasters, Ltd. The format of the station is Texas country music. KOOV-FM broadcasts to the Waco, TX area at 106.9 FM.
FM RADIO STATION

KOOZ-FM 86149
Owner: State of Oregon
Editorial: 1250 Siskiyou Blvd, Ashland, Oregon 97520-5001 **Tel:** 1 541 552-6301.
Email: jprinfo@sou.edu
Web site: http://www.ijpr.org
Profile: KOOZ-FM is a non-commercial station owned by State of Oregon. The format of the station is news and classical music. KOOZ-FM broadcasts in the Myrtle Point, OR area at 94.1 FM.
FM RADIO STATION

KOPB-AM 36195
Owner: Oregon Public Broadcasting
Editorial: 7140 SW MacAdam Ave, Portland, Oregon 97219-3013 **Tel:** 1 503 293-1905.
Email: opbnews@opb.org
Web site: http://www.opb.org
Profile: KOPB-AM is a non-commercial station owned by Oregon Public Broadcasting. The format of the station is news and talk. KOPB-AM broadcasts to the Euguene, OR area at 1600 AM.
AM RADIO STATION

KOPB-FM 42837
Owner: Oregon Public Broadcasting
Editorial: 7140 SW MacAdam Ave, Portland, Oregon 97219-3013 **Tel:** 1 503 293-1905.
Email: opbnews@opb.org
Web site: http://www.opb.org
Profile: KOPB-FM is a non-commercial station owned by Oregon Public Broadcasting. The format of the station is news and talk. KOPB-FM broadcasts to the Portland, OR area at 91.5 FM.
FM RADIO STATION

KOPJ-FM 597160
Owner: Lifetalk Radio Inc.
Editorial: 200 Main Ave S, Park Rapids, Minnesota 56470-1518 **Tel:** 1 800 775-4673.
Web site: http://www.lifetalk.net/
Profile: KOPJ-FM is a non-commercial station owned by Lifetalk Radio Inc. The station's format is Christian music and religous teaching. KOPJ-FM broadcasts to the Sebaka and Park Rapids, MN areas at 89.3 FM.
FM RADIO STATION

KOPN-FM 39826
Owner: New Wave Corporation
Editorial: 915 E Broadway, Columbia, Missouri 65201 **Tel:** 1 573 874-1139.
Email: mail@kopn.org
Web site: http://www.kopn.org
Profile: KOPN-FM is a non-commercial station owned by the New Wave Corporation. The format of the station is variety. KOPN-FM broadcasts to the Columbia, MO area at 89.5 FM.
FM RADIO STATION

KOPR-FM 46383
Owner: Butte Broadcasting Inc.
Editorial: 660 Dewey Blvd, Butte, Montana 59701-3218 **Tel:** 1 406 494-7777.
Email: mail@kbowkopr.com
Web site: http://www.kopr94.net
Profile: KOPR-FM is a commercial station owned by Butte Broadcasting Inc. The format for the station is adult contemporary. KOPR-FM broadcasts to the Butte, MT area at 94.1 FM.
FM RADIO STATION

KOPW-FM 43658
Owner: NRG Media LLC
Editorial: 5011 Capitol Ave, Omaha, Nebraska 68132 **Tel:** 1 402 342-2000.
Web site: http://www.power1069fm.com
Profile: KOPW-FM is a commercial station owned by NRG Media LLC. The format of the station is urban contemporary. KOPW-FM broadcasts to the Omaha, NE area on 106.9 FM.
FM RADIO STATION

KOPY-AM 38827
Owner: Claro Communications Ltd.
Editorial: 2722 N US Highway 281, Alice, Texas 78332 **Tel:** 1 361 664-1884.
Email: claroradio@yahoo.com
Profile: KOPY-AM is a commercial station owned by Claro Communications Ltd. The format of the station is sports. KOPY-AM broadcasts to the Alice, TX at 1070 AM.
AM RADIO STATION

KOPY-FM 46157
Owner: Claro Communications Ltd.
Editorial: 2722 N US Highway 281, Alice, Texas 78332 **Tel:** 1 361 664-1884.
Profile: KOPY-FM is a commercial station owned by Claro Communications Ltd. The format of the station is Hispanic programming. KOPY-FM broadcasts to the Alice, TX area at 92.1 FM.
FM RADIO STATION

KOQL-FM 42965
Owner: Cumulus Media Inc.
Editorial: 503 Old 63 N, Columbia, Missouri 65201-6305 **Tel:** 1 573 449-4141.
Web site: http://www.q1061.com
Profile: KOQL-FM is a commercial station owned by Cumulus Media Inc. The format of the station is rhythmic Top 40/CHR music. KOQL-FM broadcasts to the Columbia, MO area 105.1 FM.
FM RADIO STATION

KOQR-FM 44491
Owner: Doud Media Group LLC
Editorial: 1500 Industrial Blvd Ste 200, Abilene, Texas 79602-8063 **Tel:** 1 325 437-9596.
Web site: http://www.wolfabilene.com/
Profile: KFNA-FM is a commercial station owned by Doud Media Group LLC. The format of the station is top 40/CHR. KFNA-FM broadcasts to Abilene, TX at 96.1 FM.
FM RADIO STATION

KORA-FM 44809
Owner: Brazos Valley Communications LLC
Editorial: 1240 E Villa Maria Rd, Bryan, Texas 77802-2519 **Tel:** 1 979 776-1240.
Web site: http://www.korafm.com
Profile: KORA-FM is a commercial station owned by Brazos Valley Communications LLC. The format of the station is country. KORA-FM broadcasts to the Bryan, TX area at 98.3 FM.
FM RADIO STATION

KORB-FM 814394
Owner: One Ministries, Inc.
Tel: 1 707 526-2765.
Email: korb@broken.fm
Web site: http://www.broken.fm
Profile: KORB-FM is a non-commercial station owned by One Ministries, Inc. The format of the station is Christian rock alternative music. KORB-FM broadcasts to the Hopland, CA area at a frequency of 88.7 FM.
FM RADIO STATION

KORD-FM 45005
Owner: Townsquare Media, LLC
Editorial: 2621 W A St, Pasco, Washington 99301-4702 **Tel:** 1 509 547-9791.
Web site: http://www.1027kord.com
Profile: KORD-FM is a commercial station owned by Townsquare Media, LLC. The format of the station is contemporary country music. KORD-FM broadcasts to the Pasco, WA area at 102.7 FM.
FM RADIO STATION

KORE-AM 35039
Owner: Support Christian Broadcasting Inc.
Editorial: 2080 Laura St, Springfield, Oregon 97477 **Tel:** 1 541 747-5673.
Email: kore@koreradio.com
Web site: http://www.koreradio.com
Profile: KORE-AM is a non-commercial station owned by Support Christian Broadcasting Inc. The format of the station is Christian programming. KORE-AM broadcasts to the Springfield, OR area at 1050 AM.
AM RADIO STATION

KORL-FM 524291
Owner: Hochman-McCann Hawaii, Inc.
Editorial: 900 Fort Street Mall Ste 450, Honolulu, Hawaii 96813-3780 **Tel:** 1 808 538-1180.
Email: korlradio001@hawaii.rr.com
Web site: http://www.hhawaiimedia.com
Profile: KORL-FM is a commercial station owned by Hochman-McCann Hawaii, Inc. The format of the station is oldies. KORL-FM broadcasts to the Honolulu, HI area at 101.1 FM. KORL-FM features multicultural brokered programming.
FM RADIO STATION

KORN-AM 37423
Owner: Riverfront Broadcasting
Editorial: 319 N Main St, Mitchell, South Dakota 57301 **Tel:** 1 605 996-1490.
Email: kornstudio@kornq107.com
Web site: http://www.1490korn.com
Profile: KORN-AM is a commercial station owned by Riverfront Broadcasting. The format of the station is news and talk. KORN-AM broadcasts to the Mitchell, SD area at 1490 AM.
AM RADIO STATION

KORN-FM 46453
Owner: Riverfront Broadcasting, LLC
Editorial: 400 N Rowley St, Mitchell, South Dakota 57301-2617 **Tel:** 1 605 990-5676.
Web site: http://www.korncountry921.com/
Profile: KORN-FM is a commercial station owned by Riverfront Broadcasting, LLC. The format of the station is Country. KORN-FM broadcasts to the Mitchell, SD area at 92.1 FM.
FM RADIO STATION

KORR-FM 42972
Owner: Idaho Wireless Corp.
Editorial: 436 N Main St, Pocatello, Idaho 83204-3018 **Tel:** 1 208 234-1290.
Email: spots@kzbq.com
Web site: http://www.korr104.com
Profile: KORR-FM is a commercial station owned by Idaho Wirelss Corp. The format of the station is hot adult contemporary. KORR-FM broadcasts to the Pocatello, ID, area at 104.1 FM.
FM RADIO STATION

KORT-AM 38978
Owner: 4-K Radio Inc.
Editorial: 612 Pine St, Grangeville, Idaho 83530-1150 **Tel:** 1 208 983-1230.
Web site: http://grangevilleidaho.com/kort
Profile: KORT-AM is a commercial station owned by 4-K Radio Inc. The format of the station is contemporary country music. KORT-AM broadcasts to the Grangeville, ID area at 1230 AM.
AM RADIO STATION

KORT-FM 46413
Owner: 4-K Radio Inc.
Editorial: 612 Pine Street, Grangeville, Idaho 83530-1150 **Tel:** 1 208 983-1230.
Profile: KORT-FM is a commercial station owned by 4-K Radio Inc. The format of the station is contemporary country music. KORT-FM broadcasts to the Grangeville, ID area at 92.7 FM.
FM RADIO STATION

KORV-FM 45763
Owner: Lake County Radio, LLC
Editorial: 69470 S Egan Rd, Burns, Oregon 97720-2537 **Tel:** 1 541 573-2055.
Profile: KORV-FM is a commercial station owned by Lake County Radio, LLC. The format of the station is classic hits. KORV-FM broadcasts to the Lakeview, OR area at a frequency of 93.5 FM.
FM RADIO STATION

KOSB-FM 45894
Owner: Team Radio LLC
Editorial: 114 W 7th Ave, Stillwater, Oklahoma 74074-4049 **Tel:** 1 405 377-5325.
Email: tripleplay@eteamradio.com
Web site: http://tripleplaysportsradio.com
Profile: KOSB-FM is a commercial station owned by Team Radio LLC. The format of the station is sports. KOSB-FM broadcasts to the Stillwater, OK area at 105.1 FM.
FM RADIO STATION

KOSC-FM 39995
Owner: Classical Public Radio Network, LLC
Editorial: 201 3rd St Ste 1200, San Francisco, California 94103-3143 **Tel:** 1 415 546-8710.
Email: feedback@kdfc.com
Web site: http://www.kdfc.com
Profile: KOSC-FM is a non-commercial station owned by Classical Public Radio Network, LLC. The format of the station is classical music. KOSC-FM broadcasts locally to the San Francisco area at 90.3 FM.
FM RADIO STATION

KOSE-AM 39477
Owner: Sudbury Broadcasting Group
Editorial: 125 S 2nd St, Blytheville, Arkansas 72315 **Tel:** 1 870 762-2093.
AM RADIO STATION

KOSF-FM 40941
Owner: iHeart Media Inc.
Editorial: 340 Townsend St Ste 4, San Francisco, California 94107-1698 **Tel:** 1 415 538-1013.
Web site: http://80sradio.iheart.com
Profile: KOSF-FM is a commercial station owned by iHeart Media Inc. The format of the station is 80s music. KOSF-FM broadcasts to the San Francisco area at 103.7 FM.
FM RADIO STATION

KOSG-FM 156165
Owner: South Central Oklahoma Christian Broadcasting
Tel: 1 580 332-0902.
Email: email@thegospelstation.com
Web site: http://www.thegospelstation.com
Profile: KOSG-FM is a commercial station owned by South Central Oklahoma Christian Broadcasting. The format of the station is gospel. KOSG-FM broadcasts to the Bartlesville, OK and Southeast Kansas areas at 103.9 FM.
FM RADIO STATION

KOSI-FM 45748
Owner: Entercom Communications Corp.
Editorial: 4700 S Syracuse St, Ste 1050, Denver, Colorado 80237 **Tel:** 1 303 967-2700.
Web site: http://www.entercomdenver.com
Profile: KOSI-FM is a commercial station owned by Entercom Communications Corp. The format of the station is Lite Rock/Lite AC. KOSI-FM broadcasts to the Denver area at 101.1 FM.
FM RADIO STATION

KOSO-FM 39828
Owner: iHeartMedia Inc.
Editorial: 2121 Lancey Dr, Modesto, California 95355-3036 **Tel:** 1 209 551-1306.
Email: modestopsa@iheartmedia.com
Web site: http://www.b93fm.com/main.html
Profile: KOSO-FM is a commercial station owned by iHeartMedia Inc. The format of the station is Adult

CHR. KOSO-FM broadcasts to the Modesto, CA area at 92.9 FM.
FM RADIO STATION

KOSP-FM 42425
Owner: Midwest Family Stations
Editorial: 2453 E. Elm St., Springfield, Missouri 65802 **Tel:** 1 417 886-5677.
Web site: http://www.929thebeat.com
Profile: KOSP-FM is a commercial station owned by Midwest Family Stations. The format of the station is Top 40/CHR. KOSP-FM broadcasts to the Springfield, MO area at 92.9 FM.
FM RADIO STATION

KOSS-AM 37094
Owner: High Desert Broadcasting LLC
Editorial: 570 East Ave Q9, Palmdale, California 93550 **Tel:** 1 661 947-3107.
Web site: http://www.newstalk1380.com
Profile: KWJL-AM is a commercial station owned by High Desert Broadcasting LLC. The format of the station is news and talk. KWJL-AM broadcasts to the Palmdale, CA area at 1380 AM.
AM RADIO STATION

KOST-FM 46644
Owner: iHeartMedia Inc.
Editorial: 3400 W Olive Ave Ste 550, Burbank, California 91505-5544 **Tel:** 1 818 559-2252.
Web site: http://kost1035.iheart.com
Profile: KOST-FM is a commercial station owned by iHeartMedia Inc. The format of the station is soft rock. KOST-FM broadcasts to the Los Angeles area at 103.5 FM.
FM RADIO STATION

KOSY-AM 37424
Owner: Townsquare Media, LLC
Editorial: 2324 Arkansas Blvd, Texarkana, Arkansas 71854-2016 **Tel:** 1 870 772-3771.
Web site: http://kosy790am.com
Profile: KOSY-AM is a commercial station owned by Townsquare Media, LLC . The format of the station is urban gospel music. KOSY-AM broadcasts to the Shreveport, LA area at 790 AM.
AM RADIO STATION

KOSY-FM 519288
Owner: iHeartMedia Inc.
Editorial: 600 Old Marion Rd NE, Cedar Rapids, Iowa 52402-2159 **Tel:** 1 319 395-0530.
Web site: http://y957fm.iheart.com
Profile: KOSY-FM is a commercial station owned by iHeartMedia Inc. The format of the station is news/talk. KOSY-FM broadcasts to the Cedar Rapids, IA area at 95.7 FM.
FM RADIO STATION

KOTA-AM 35040
Owner: Duhamel Broadcasting
Editorial: 518 Saint Joseph St, Rapid City, South Dakota 57701-2717 **Tel:** 1 605 342-2000.
Email: news@kotaradio.com
Web site: http://www.kotaradio.com
Profile: KOTA-AM is a commercial station owned by Duhamel Broadcasting. The format of the station news, sports and talk. KOTA-AM broadcasts to the Rapid City, SD area at 1380 AM.
AM RADIO STATION

KOTD-FM 544665
Owner: Oregon Public Broadcasting
Editorial: 7140 SW MacAdam Ave, Portland, Oregon 97219-3013 **Tel:** 1 503 293-1905.
Email: opbnews@opb.org
Web site: http://www.opb.org
Profile: KOTD-FM is a non-commercial station owned by Oregon Public Broadcasting. The format of the station is news and talk. KOPB-FM broadcasts to the Portland, OR area at 89.7 FM.
FM RADIO STATION

KOTE-FM 41147
Owner: Niemeyer Communications LLC
Editorial: 1275 P Rd, Eureka, Kansas 67045-4713 **Tel:** 1 620 583-7414.
Web site: http://www.935.kotefm.com
Profile: KOTE-FM is a commercial station owned by Niemeyer Communications LLC. The format of the station is contemporary country and classic rock music. KOTE-FM broadcasts to the Eureka, KS area at 93.5 FM.
FM RADIO STATION

KOTK-AM 376819
Owner: Salem Media Group, Inc.
Editorial: 11717 Burt St Ste 202, Omaha, Nebraska 68154-1500 **Tel:** 1 402 422-1600.
Web site: http://theansweromaha.com/
Profile: KOTK-AM is a commercial station owned by Salem Media Group, Inc. The format of the station is Talk. KOTK-AM broadcasts to the Omaha, NE area at 1420 AM.
AM RADIO STATION

KOTM-FM 44813
Owner: O-Town Communications, Inc.
Editorial: 416 E Main St, Ottumwa, Iowa 52501-3026 **Tel:** 1 641 684-5563.
Email: info@ottumwaradio.com
Web site: http://www.tomfmottumwa.com
Profile: KOTM-FM is a commercial station owned by O-Town Communications, Inc. The format for the station is Top 40/CHR. KOTM-FM broadcasts to the Ottumna, IA area at 97.7 FM.
FM RADIO STATION

KOTN-FM 691236
Owner: Arkansas County Broadcasters Inc.
Editorial: 1818 S Buerkle St, Stuttgart, Arkansas 72160-5804 **Tel:** 1 870 673-1595.
Email: kdew973@yahoo.com
Profile: KAFN-FM is a commercial station owned by Arkansas County Broadcasters Inc. The format of the station is classic country. KAFN-FM broadcasts to the Gould, AR area at 105.5 FM.
FM RADIO STATION

KOTS-AM 37425
Owner: Luna County Broadcasting
Editorial: 1700 S Gold Ave, Deming, New Mexico 88030-5839 **Tel:** 1 575 546-9011.
Email: radio@demingradio.com
Web site: http://www.demingradio.com
Profile: KOTS-AM is a commercial station owned by Luna County Broadcasting. The format of the station is classic country. KOTS-AM broadcasts to the Deming, NM area at 1230 AM.
AM RADIO STATION

KOTZ-AM 35041
Owner: Kotzebue Broadcasting Inc.
Editorial: 396 Lagoon, Kotzebue, Alaska 99752-9999 **Tel:** 1 907 442-3434.
Email: kotzradio@yahoo.com
Web site: http://www.kotz.org
Profile: KOTZ-AM is a non-commercial station owned by Kotzebue Broadcasting, Inc. The format of the station is a variety of music and cultural affairs programming. KOTZ-AM broadcasts in the Kotzebue, AK, area at 720 AM.
AM RADIO STATION

KOUT-FM 42453
Owner: New Rushmore Radio
Editorial: 660 Flormann St, Ste 100, Rapid City, South Dakota 57701 **Tel:** 1 605 343-6161.
Web site: http://www.katradio.com
Profile: KOUT-FM is a commercial station owned by New Rushmore Radio. The format of the station is classic country. KOUT-FM broadcasts to the Rapid City, SD area at 98.7 FM.
FM RADIO STATION

KOUU-AM 37619
Owner: Idaho Wireless Corp.
Editorial: 436 N Main St, Pocatello, Idaho 83204-3018 **Tel:** 1 208 234-1290.
Email: spots@kzbq.com
Profile: KOUU-AM is a commercial station owned by Idaho Wireless Corp. The format of the station is classic country. KOUU-AM broadcasts to Pocatello, ID at 1290 AM.
AM RADIO STATION

KOVC-AM 38426
Owner: Ingstad Family Media
Editorial: 136 Central Ave N, Valley City, North Dakota 58072-2952 **Tel:** 1 701 845-1490.
Web site: http://www.newsdakota.com
Profile: KOVC-AM is a commercial station owned by Ingstad Family Media (dba Sioux Valley Broadcasting). The format of the station is classic country. KOVC-AM broadcasts to the Valley City, ND area at 1490 AM.
AM RADIO STATION

KOVE-AM 39154
Owner: Kenney(Joseph R. and Andrea L.)
Editorial: 1530 Main St, Lander, Wyoming 82520-2658 **Tel:** 1 307 332-5683.
Email: radio1@wyoming.com
Web site: http://www.kdlykove.com
Profile: KOVE-AM is a commercial station owned by Joseph R. Kenney and Andrea L. Kenney. The format of the station is country music. KOVE-AM broadcasts to the Lander, WY area at 1330 AM.
AM RADIO STATION

KOVE-FM 46584
Owner: Univision Communications Inc.
Editorial: 5100 Southwest Fwy, Houston, Texas 77056-7308 **Tel:** 1 713 965-2400.
Web site: http://www.univision.com/houston/kove
Profile: KOVE-FM is a commercial station owned by Univision Communications Inc. The format of the station is Spanish Adult Hits. KOVE-FM broadcasts to the Houston area at 106.5 FM.
FM RADIO STATION

KOVO-AM 36417
Owner: Broadway Media
Editorial: 301 W South Temple, Salt Lake City, Utah 84101-1216 **Tel:** 1 801 537-1414.
Web site: http://www.1280thezone.com
Profile: KOVO-AM is a commercial station owned by Broadway Media. The format of the station is sports talk. KOVO-AM broadcasts to the Salt Lake City, UT area at 960 AM.
AM RADIO STATION

KOWB-AM 39151
Owner: Townsquare Media, LLC
Editorial: 3525 Soldier Springs Rd, Laramie, Wyoming 82070-9017 **Tel:** 1 307 745-4888.
Web site: http://www.kowb1290.com
Profile: KOWB-AM is a commercial station owned by Townsquare Media, LLC. The format of the station is news, sports and talk. KOWB-AM broadcasts to the Laramie, WY area at 1290 AM.
AM RADIO STATION

KOWL-AM 38832
Owner: Cherry Creek Radio
Editorial: 276 Kingsbury Grade Ste 203, Stateline, Nevada 89449-9804 **Tel:** 1 775 580-7130.
Web site: http://www.krltfm.com/kowl-am-radio-lake-tahoe
Profile: KOWL-AM is a commercial station owned by Cherry Creek Radio. The format of the station is news, sports and talk. KOWL-AM broadcasts to the South Lake Tahoe, CA area at 1490 AM.
AM RADIO STATION

KOWY-FM 845868
Owner: Lovcom, Inc.
Tel: 1 307 672-7421.
Email: info@sheridanmedia.com
Web site: http://www.sheridanmedia.com
Profile: KOWY-FM is a commercial station owned by Lovcom, Inc. The format of the station is adult contemporary. KOWY-FM broadcasts to the Sheridan, WY area at a frequency of 102.3 FM.
FM RADIO STATION

KOWZ-AM 37428
Owner: Main Street Broadcasting Inc.
Editorial: 255 Cedardale Dr SE, Owatonna, Minnesota 55060-4425 **Tel:** 1 507 444-9224.
Web site: http://kowzam.com/
Profile: KRUE-AM is a commercial station owned by Main Street Broadcasting Inc. The format of the station is oldies music. KRUE-AM broadcasts to the Owatonna, MN area at 1170 AM.
AM RADIO STATION

KOWZ-FM 43655
Owner: Blooming Prairie Farm Radio Inc.
Editorial: 255 Cedardale Dr SE, Owatonna, Minnesota 55060-4425 **Tel:** 1 507 444-9224.
Email: kowz@kowzonline.com
Web site: http://www.kowzfm.com
Profile: KOWZ-FM is a commercial station owned by Blooming Prairie Farm Radio Inc. The format of the station is adult contemporary music. KOWZ-FM broadcasts to the Owatonna, MN area at 100.9 FM.
FM RADIO STATION

KOXE-FM 44817
Owner: Brown County Broadcasting Co.
Editorial: 300 Carnegie St, Brownwood, Texas 76801-7222 **Tel:** 1 325 646-3505.
Email: upfront@koxe.com
Web site: http://www.koxe.com
Profile: KOXE-FM is a commercial station owned by Brown County Broadcasting Co. The format of the station is country music. KOXE-FM broadcasts in the Brownwood, TX area at 101.3 FM.
FM RADIO STATION

KOXR-AM 35042
Owner: Lazer Broadcasting Corp.
Editorial: 200 S A St Ste 400, Oxnard, California 93030-5723 **Tel:** 1 805 240-2070.
Email: lazerbroadcasting@radiolazer.com
Web site: http://www.radiolazer.com
Profile: KOXR-AM is a commercial station owned by the Lazer Broacasting Corp. The format of the station is Spanish and talk. KOXR-AM broadcasts to the Santa Barbara, CA area at 910 AM.
AM RADIO STATION

KOYA-FM 937274
Owner: Rosebud Sioux Tribe
Tel: 1 605 747-2381.
Email: info@nativepublicmedia.org
Web site: http://www.nativepublicmedia.org
Profile: KOYA-FM is a non-commercial station owned by Rosebud Sioux Tribe. The format of the station features a variety of programming from Native Public Media. The station broadcasts to the Rosebud, SD area at a frequency of 88.1 FM.
FM RADIO STATION

KOY-AM 37429
Owner: iHeartMedia Inc.
Editorial: 4686 E Van Buren St Ste 300, Phoenix, Arizona 85008-6967 **Tel:** 1 602 374-6000.
Web site: http://www.kfyi2.com/main.html
Profile: KOY-AM is a commercial station owned by iHeartMedia Inc. The format of the station is talk. KOY-AM broadcasts to the Phoenix area at 1230 AM.
AM RADIO STATION

KOYE-FM 39739
Owner: Access.1 Communications Corp.
Editorial: 210 S Broadway Ave Ste 100, Tyler, Texas 75702-7353 **Tel:** 1 903 581-9966.
Email: tyr@etradiogroup.com
Web site: http://lainvasora.fm
Profile: KOYE-FM is a commercial station owned by Access.1 Communications Corp. The format of the station is Hispanic and Top 40/CHR. KOYE-FM broadcasts to the Tyler, TX area at 96.7 FM.
FM RADIO STATION

KOYN-FM 41205
Owner: East Texas Broadcasting Inc.
Editorial: 2810 Pine Mill Rd, Paris, Texas 75460-3449 **Tel:** 1 903 785-1068.
Web site: http://www.easttexasradio.com
Profile: KOYN-FM is a commercial station owned by East Texas Broadcasting Inc. The format of the station is contemporary country. KOYN-FM broadcasts to the Paris, TX area at 93.9 FM.
FM RADIO STATION

KOZA-AM 36014
Owner: Stellar Media, Inc.
Editorial: 1319 S Crane Ave, Odessa, Texas 79763-4755 **Tel:** 1 432 333-1227.
Web site: http://www.koza1230.com
Profile: KOZA-AM is a commercial station owned by Stellar Media, Inc. The format of the station is Spanish hits. KOZA-AM broadcasts to the Odessa, TX area at 1230 AM.
AM RADIO STATION

KOZE-AM 37430
Owner: 4-K Radio Inc.
Editorial: 2560 Snake River Ave, Lewiston, Idaho 83501-9717 **Tel:** 1 208 743-2502.
Email: chrisripley@koze.com
Web site: http://www.koze950.com
Profile: KOZE-AM is a commercial station owned by 4-K Radio Inc. The format of the station is news, sports and talk. KOZE-AM broadcasts to the Spokane, WA area at 950 AM.
AM RADIO STATION

KOZE-FM 44819
Owner: 4-K Radio Inc.
Editorial: 2560 Snake River Ave, Lewiston, Idaho 83501 **Tel:** 1 208 743-2502.
Web site: http://www.koze.com
Profile: KOZE-FM is a commercial station owned by 4-K Radio Inc. The format of the station is rock music. KOZE-FM broadcasts to the Lewiston, ID area at 96.5 FM.
FM RADIO STATION

KOZI-AM 37431
Owner: Icicle Broadcasting, Inc.
Editorial: 123 E Johnson Ave, Chelan, Washington 98816 **Tel:** 1 509 682-4033.
Email: air@kozi.com
Web site: http://www.kozi.com
Profile: KOZI-AM is a commercial station owned by Icicle Broadcasting, Inc. The format of the station is adult standards. KOZI-AM broadcasts to the Chelan, WA area at 1230 AM.
AM RADIO STATION

KOZI-FM 44820
Owner: Icicle Broadcasting, Inc.
Editorial: 123 E Johnson Ave, Chelan, Washington 98816 **Tel:** 1 509 682-4033.
Email: kozi@kozi.com
Web site: http://www.kozi.com
Profile: KOZI-FM is a commercial station owned by the Icicle Broadcasting, Inc. The format of the station is adult contemporary. KOZI-FM broadcasts to the Chelan, WA area at 93.5 FM.
FM RADIO STATION

KOZN-AM 37076
Owner: NRG Media LLC
Editorial: 5011 Capitol Ave, Omaha, Nebraska 68132-2921 **Tel:** 1 402 342-2000.
Web site: http://www.1620thezone.com
Profile: KOZN-AM is a commercial station owned by NRG Media LLC. The format of the station is sports. KOZN-AM broadcasts to the Omaha, NE area on 1620 AM.
AM RADIO STATION

KOZQ-FM 37432
Owner: Alpha Media
Editorial: 313 Old Route 66, Saint Robert, Missouri 65584 **Tel:** 1 573 336-4913.
Email: news.kfbd@alphamediausa.com
Web site: http://myozarksonline.com
Profile: KOZQ-FM is a commercial station owned by Alpha Media. The format of the station is Classic Rock. KOZQ-FM broadcasts to the Waynesville, MO area at 102.3 FM. The station targets listeners, ages 18 to 54.
FM RADIO STATION

KOZT-FM 39832
Owner: California Radio Partners Inc.
Editorial: 110 S Franklin St, Fort Bragg, California 95437 **Tel:** 1 707 964-7277.
Email: thecoast@kozt.com
Web site: http://www.kozt.com
Profile: KOZT-FM is a commercial station owned by California Radio Partners Inc. The format of the station is adult album alternative. KOZT-FM broadcasts to the San Francisco area at 95.3 FM.
FM RADIO STATION

KOZY-AM 38809
Owner: Lamke Broadcasting
Editorial: 507 SE 11th St, Grand Rapids, Minnesota 55744 **Tel:** 1 218 999-5699.
Email: info@kozyradio.com
Web site: http://www.kozyradio.com
Profile: KOZY-AM is a commercial station owned by Lamke Broadcasting. The format of the station is oldies music. KOZY-AM broadcasts in the Grand Rapids, MN area at 1320 AM.
AM RADIO STATION

KOZY-FM 493975
Owner: Armada Media
Editorial: 2002 Char Ave, Scottsbluff, Nebraska 69361-2255 **Tel:** 1 308 632-5667.
Profile: KOZY-FM is a commercial station owned by Armada Media. The format of the station is hot AC. KOZY-FM broadcasts to the Scottsbluff, NE area at 101.3 FM.
FM RADIO STATION

KOZZ-FM 44821
Owner: Lotus Communications Corp.
Editorial: 2900 Sutro St, Reno, Nevada 89512-1616
Tel: 1 775 329-9261.
Web site: http://www.kozzradio.com
Profile: KOZZ-FM is a commercial station owned by Lotus Communications Corp. The format of the station is classic rock. KOZZ-FM broadcasts to the Reno, NV area at 105.7 FM.
FM RADIO STATION

KPAC-FM 41045
Owner: Texas Public Radio
Editorial: 8401 Datapoint Dr Ste 800, San Antonio, Texas 78229-5903 **Tel:** 1 210 614-8977.
Email: news@tpr.org
Web site: http://www.tpr.org
Profile: KPAC-FM is a non-commercial station owned by Texas Public Radio. The format of the station is classical. KPAC-FM broadcasts to the San Antonio area at 88.3 FM.
FM RADIO STATION

KPAE-FM 41529
Owner: Port Allen Educ. Broadcasting Found.
Editorial: 13028 Highway 190 W, Port Allen, Louisiana 70767 **Tel:** 1 800 324-1108.
Email: wpaefm@telepak.net
Web site: http://www.soundradio.org
Profile: KPAE-FM is a non-commercial station owned by Port Allen Educ. Broadcasting Found. The format of the station is religious programming. KPAE-FM broadcasts to the Port Allen, LA area at 91.5 FM.
FM RADIO STATION

KPAK-FM 519709
Owner: Flinn Broadcasting Corp.
Editorial: 543 Main St, Kiowa, Kansas 67070
Tel: 1 580 327-1430.
Email: kpakradio@yahoo.com
Web site: http://www.kpak.net
Profile: KPAK-FM is a commercial station owned by Flinn Broadcasting Corp. The format of the station is classic rock. KPAK-FM broadcasts to the Kiowa, KS area at 97.5 FM.
FM RADIO STATION

KPAM-AM 36954
Owner: Pamplin Broadcasting-Oregon, Inc.
Editorial: 6605 SE Lake Rd, Portland, Oregon 97222-2161 **Tel:** 1 503 223-4321.
Email: news@kpam.com
Web site: http://www.kpam.com
Profile: KPAM-AM is a commercial station owned by Pamplin Broadcasting-Oregon, Inc. The format of the station is talk. KPAM-AM broadcasts to the Portland, OR area at 860 AM.
AM RADIO STATION

KPAN-AM 37433
Owner: KPAN Broadcasters
Editorial: 218 E 5th St, Hereford, Texas 79045
Tel: 1 806 364-1860.
Email: kpan@kpanradio.com
Web site: http://www.kpanradio.com
Profile: KPAN-AM is a commercial station owned by KPAN Broadcasters. The format of the station is country and news. KPAN-AM broadcasts to the Hereford, TX area at 860 AM.
AM RADIO STATION

KPAN-FM 44822
Owner: KPAN Broadcasters
Editorial: 218 E 5th St, Hereford, Texas 79045
Tel: 1 806 364-1860.
Email: kpan@kpanradio.com
Web site: http://www.kpanradio.com
Profile: KPAN-FM is a commercial station owned by KPAN Broadcasters. The format of the station is country. KPAN-FM broadcasts to the Hereford, TX area at 106.3 FM.
FM RADIO STATION

KPAS-FM 41530
Owner: Felder(Algie A.)
Tel: 1 915 851-3382.
Profile: KPAS-FM is a commercial station owned by Algie A. Felder. The format of the station is English and Hispanic Christian and gospel music. KPAS-FM broadcasts to the El Paso, TX area at 103.1 FM.
FM RADIO STATION

KPAT-FM 44545
Owner: American General Media
Editorial: 2325 Skyway Dr Ste J, Santa Maria, California 93455-1137 **Tel:** 1 805 922-1041.
Web site: http://www.957thebeatfm.com
Profile: KPAT-FM is a commercial station owned by American General Media. The format of the station is urban contemporary. KPAT-FM broadcasts to the Santa Barbara, CA area at 95.7 FM.
FM RADIO STATION

KPAW-FM 44606
Owner: iHeartMedia Inc.
Editorial: 4270 Byrd Dr, Loveland, Colorado 80538-7074 **Tel:** 1 970 461-2560.
Web site: http://1079thebear.iheart.com
Profile: KPAW-FM is a commercial station owned by iHeartMedia Inc. The format of the station is classic rock. KPAW-FM broadcasts to the Loveland, CO area at 107.9 FM.
FM RADIO STATION

KPAY-AM 38375
Owner: Deer Creek Broadcasting
Editorial: 2654 Cramer Ln, Chico, California 95928
Tel: 1 530 345-0021.
Web site: http://newstalk1290.wordpress.com
Profile: KPAY-AM is a commercial station owned by Deer Creek Broadcasting. The format of the station is news and talk. KPAY-AM broadcasts in the Chico, CA area at 1290 AM.
AM RADIO STATION

KPBR-FM 686975
Owner: Bott Radio Network
Editorial: 10550 Barkley St Ste 108, Overland Park, Kansas 66212-1824 **Tel:** 1 913 642-7770.
Web site: http://www.bottradionetwork.com
Profile: KPBR-FM is a non-commercial station owned by Bott Radio Network. The format of the station is religious. KPBR-FM broadcasts to the Poplar Bluff, MO area at 91.7 FM.
FM RADIO STATION

KPBX-FM 39835
Owner: Spokane Public Radio Inc.
Editorial: 2319 N Monroe St, Spokane, Washington 99205-4548 **Tel:** 1 509 328-5729.
Email: kpbx@kpbx.org
Web site: http://www.kpbx.org
Profile: KPBX-FM is a non-commercial station owned by Spokane Public Radio Inc. The format of the station is news, jazz, folk and classical music. KPBX-FM broadcasts in the Spokane, WA area at 91.1 FM. Do not send any correspondence to the station. The station's public service is exclusively for local arts organizations.
FM RADIO STATION

KPBZ-FM 692438
Owner: Spokane Public Radio Inc.
Editorial: 2319 N Monroe St, Spokane, Washington 99205-4548 **Tel:** 1 509 328-5729.
Email: kpbx@kpbx.org
Web site: http://www.kpbx.org
Profile: KPBZ-FM is a non-commercial station owned by Spokane Public Radio Inc. The format is news and talk. KPBZ-FM broadcasts to the Spokane, WA area at 90.3 FM.
FM RADIO STATION

KPCC-FM 39836
Owner: Pasadena Area Community College District
Editorial: 474 S Raymond Ave, Pasadena, California 91105-2629 **Tel:** 1 626 583-5100.
Email: contact@kpcc.org
Web site: http://www.scpr.org
Profile: KPCC-FM is a non-commercial station owned by Pasadena Area Community College District. The format for the station is news and talk. KPCC-FM broadcasts to the Los Angeles area at 89.3 FM.
FM RADIO STATION

KPCH-FM 39837
Owner: Red Peach LLC
Editorial: 500 N Monroe St, Ruston, Louisiana 71270-3835 **Tel:** 1 318 255-5000.
Email: thepeach993@gmail.com
Web site: http://www.thepeach993.com
Profile: KPCH-FM is a commercial station owned by Red Peach LLC. The format of the station is oldies music. KPCH-FM broadcasts to the Ruston, LA area at 99.3 FM.
FM RADIO STATION

KPCL-FM 40952
Owner: Voice Ministries of Farmington
Editorial: 1103 W Apache St, Farmington, New Mexico 87401-3806 **Tel:** 1 505 327-7202.
Email: kpcl@kpcl.org
Web site: http://www.kpcl.org
Profile: KPCL-FM is a commercial station owned by Voice Ministries of Farmington. The format of the station is contemporary Christian. KPCL-FM broadcasts to the Farmington, NM area at 95.7 FM.
FM RADIO STATION

KPCW-FM 526726
Owner: Community Wireless of Park City
Editorial: 460 Swede Alley, Park City, Utah 84060
Tel: 1 435 649-9004.
Email: letters@kpcw.org
Web site: http://www.kpcw.org
Profile: KPCW-FM is a non-commercial station owned by Community Wireless or Park City. The format for the station is AAA-adult album alternative, news and talk. KPCW-FM broadcasts to the Park City, UT area at 91.9 FM.
FM RADIO STATION

KPDA-FM 544547
Owner: Impact Radio
Editorial: 5660 E Franklin Rd Ste 200, Nampa, Idaho 83687-5133 **Tel:** 1 208 465-9966.
Profile: KPDA-FM is a commercial station owned by Impact Radio. The format of the station is Regional Mexican music. KPDA-FM broadcasts to the Boise, ID area at 100.7 FM.
FM RADIO STATION

KPDQ-AM 37435
Owner: Salem Media Group, Inc.
Editorial: 6400 SE Lake Rd Ste 350, Portland, Oregon 97222-2189 **Tel:** 1 503 786-0600.
Email: contactus@kpdq.com
Web site: http://www.kpdq.com
Profile: KPDQ-AM is a commercial station owned by Salem Media Group, Inc. The format of the station is Christian talk. KPDQ-AM broadcasts in the Portland, OR area at 800 AM.
AM RADIO STATION

KPDQ-FM 44825
Owner: Salem Media Group, Inc.
Editorial: 6400 SE Lake Rd Ste 350, Portland, Oregon 97222-2189 **Tel:** 1 503 786-0600.
Email: contactus@kpdq.com
Web site: http://www.kpdq.fm
Profile: KPDQ-FM is a commercial station owned by Salem Media Group, Inc. The format of the station is religious programming. KPDQ-FM broadcasts to the Portland, OR area at 93.9 FM.
FM RADIO STATION

KPEK-FM 42147
Owner: iHeartMedia Inc.
Editorial: 5411 Jefferson St NE Ste 100, Albuquerque, New Mexico 87109-3485 **Tel:** 1 505 830-6400.
Web site: http://www.1003thepeak.com
Profile: KPEK-FM is a commercial station owned by iHeartMedia Inc. The format of the station is hot adult contemporary music. KPEK-FM broadcasts to the Albuquerque, NM area at 100.3 FM.
FM RADIO STATION

KPEL-AM 37436
Owner: Townsquare Media, LLC
Editorial: 1749 Bertrand Dr, Lafayette, Louisiana 70506 **Tel:** 1 337 233-6000.
Web site: http://www.espn1420.com
Profile: KPEL-AM is a commercial station owned by Townsquare Media, LLC. The format of the station is sports. KPEL-AM broadcasts to the Lafayette, LA area at 1420 AM.
AM RADIO STATION

KPEL-FM 44874
Owner: Townsquare Media, LLC
Editorial: 1749 Bertrand Dr, Lafayette, Louisiana 70506-2054 **Tel:** 1 337 233-6000.
Web site: http://kpel965.com
Profile: KPEL-FM is a local, commercial station owned by Townsquare Media, LLC. The format of the station is news and talk. KPEL-FM broadcasts in the Lafayette, LA area at 96.5 FM.
FM RADIO STATION

KPET-AM 35045
Owner: KPET Inc.
Editorial: 1 Radio Rd, Lamesa, Texas 79331
Tel: 1 806 872-6511.
Email: kpet@pics.net
Profile: KPET-AM is a commercial station owned by KPET Inc. The format of the station is country music. KPET-AM broadcasts in the Lamesa, TX area at 690 AM.
AM RADIO STATION

KPEZ-FM 39840
Owner: iHeartMedia Inc.
Editorial: 3601 S Congress Ave, Austin, Texas 78704-7250 **Tel:** 1 512 684-7300.
Web site: http://www.thebeatatx.com
Profile: KPEZ-FM is a commercial station owned by iHeartMedia Inc. The format of the station is rhythmic Top 40 and urban contemporary. KPEZ-FM broadcasts to the Austin, TX area at 102.3 FM.
FM RADIO STATION

KPFA-FM 39841
Owner: Pacifica Foundation, Inc.
Editorial: 1929 Martin Luther King Jr Way, Berkeley, California 94704-1037 **Tel:** 1 510 848-6767 200.
Email: news@kpfa.org
Web site: http://www.kpfa.org
Profile: KPFA-FM is a non-commercial station owned by the Pacifica Foundation, Inc. The format of the station is variety. KPFA-FM broadcasts to the San Francisco area at 94.1 FM.
FM RADIO STATION

KPFK-FM 39842
Owner: Pacifica Foundation, Inc.
Editorial: 3729 Cahuenga Blvd, North Hollywood, California 91604-3504 **Tel:** 1 818 985-2711.
Web site: http://www.kpfk.org
Profile: KPFK-FM is a non-commercial station owned by the Pacifica Foundation, Inc. The format for the station is variety. KPFK-FM broadcasts to the Los Angeles area at 90.7 FM.
FM RADIO STATION

KPFM-FM 39843
Owner: Dowdy Broadcasting, Inc.
Editorial: 2352 Highway 62 Business, Mountain Home, Arkansas 72653-6847 **Tel:** 1 870 492-6022.
Web site: http://www.kpfm.net
Profile: KPFM-FM is a commercial station owned by Dowdy Broadcasting, Inc. The format of the station is classic country. KPFM-FM broadcasts to the Mountain Home, AR area at 105.5 FM.
FM RADIO STATION

KPFT-FM 39844
Owner: Pacifica Foundation, Inc.
Editorial: 419 Lovett Blvd, Houston, Texas 77006-4018 **Tel:** 1 713 526-4000.
Email: news@kpft.org
Web site: http://www.kpft.org
Profile: KPFT-FM is a non-commercial station owned by Pacifica Foundation, Inc. The format of the station is variety. KPFT broadcasts in the greater Houston area at 90.1 FM.
FM RADIO STATION

KPFX-FM 42113
Owner: Radio FM Media
Editorial: 2720 7th Ave S, Fargo, North Dakota 58103-8710 **Tel:** 1 701 237-4500.
Email: studio@1079thefox.com
Web site: http://www.1079thefox.com
Profile: KPFX-FM is a commercial station owned by Radio FM Media. The format of the station is classic rock music. KPFX-FM broadcasts in the Fargo, ND area at 107.9 FM.
FM RADIO STATION

KPFZ-FM 530515
Owner: Lake County Community Radio
Editorial: 149 N Main St, Lakeport, California 95453-4832 **Tel:** 1 707 263-3640.
Email: kpfz@mchsi.com
Web site: http://kpfz.org/
Profile: KPFZ-FM is a non-commercial station owned by Lake County Community Radio. The format of the station is variety. KPFZ-FM broadcasts to the Lakeport, CA area at 88.1 FM. Before sending a fax, alert the station with a phone call. They occasionally have to turn the fax machine off.
FM RADIO STATION

KPGE-AM 38586
Owner: Lake Powell Communications
Editorial: 91 N 7th Ave, Page, Arizona 86040
Tel: 1 928 645-8181.
Email: news@kxaz.com
Web site: http://www.kxaz.com
Profile: KPGE-AM is a commercial station owned by Lake Powell Communications. The format of the station is classic country. KPGE-AM broadcasts to the Page, AZ area at 1340 AM.
AM RADIO STATION

KPGG-FM 44770
Owner: American Media Investments
Editorial: 1323 College Dr, Texarkana, Texas 75503-3531 **Tel:** 1 903 793-1100.
Profile: KPGG-FM is a commercial station owned by American Media Investments. The format of the station is classic country. KPGG-FM broadcasts to the Texarkana, TX area at 103.9 FM.
FM RADIO STATION

KPGM-AM 36808
Owner: KCD Enterprises Inc.
Editorial: 1200 E. Frank Phillips, Bartlesville, Oklahoma 74005 **Tel:** 1 918 336-1500.
Email: kpgm@bartlesvilleradio.com
Web site: http://www.bartlesvilleradio.com
Profile: KPGM-AM is a commercial station owned by KCD Enterprises Inc. The format of the station is sports talk. KPGM-AM broadcasts to the Pawhuska, OK area at 1500 AM.
AM RADIO STATION

KPGS-FM 525249
Owner: KUTE Inc.
Editorial: 123 Capote Drive, Ignacio, Colorado 81137
Tel: 1 970 563-0255.
Web site: http://www.ksut.org
Profile: KPGS-FM is a non-commerical station owned by KUTE Inc. The format of the station is variety. KPGS-FM broadcasts to the Ignacio, CO area at 88.1 FM.
FM RADIO STATION

KPHI-AM 37450
Owner: Hochman-McCann Hawaii, Inc.
Editorial: 900 Fort Street Mall, Ste 450, Honolulu, Hawaii 96813 **Tel:** 1 808 538-1180.
Email: korlradio001@hawaii.rr.com
Web site: http://www.hhawaiimedia.net
Profile: KPHI-AM is a commercial station owned by Hochman-McCann Hawaii, Inc. The format of the station is a variety of multicultural music. KPHI-AM broadcasts to the Honolulu area at 1130 AM.
AM RADIO STATION

KPHR-FM 46847
Owner: Armada Media Corp.
Editorial: 508 Jenson Ave SE, Watertown, South Dakota 57201-5261 **Tel:** 1 605 884-3548.
Email: power106@iw.net
Web site: http://www.kphrfm.com/
Profile: KPHR-FM is a commercial station owned by Armada Media Corp. The format of the station is classic rock. KPHR-FM broadcasts to the Watertown, SD area at 106.3 FM.
FM RADIO STATION

KPHT-FM 383269
Owner: iHeartMedia Inc.
Editorial: 106 W 24th St, Pueblo, Colorado 81003-2408 **Tel:** 1 719 545-2080.
Web site: http://kpht955.iheart.com
Profile: KPHT-FM is a commercial station owned by iHeartMedia Inc. The format of the station is classic hits. KPHT-FM broadcasts to the Pueblo, CO area at 95.5 FM. The station targets listeners ages 18 to 54, and uses the slogan "Pueblo's Greatest Hits."
FM RADIO STATION

KPHW-FM 43565
Owner: Summit Media Broadcasting LLC
Editorial: 900 Fort Street Mall Ste 700, Honolulu, Hawaii 96813-3701 **Tel:** 1 808 275-1000.
Web site: http://www.power1043.com
Profile: KPHW-FM is a commercial station owned by Summit Media Broadcasting LLC. The format of the station is rhythmic Top 40. KPHW-FM broadcasts to the Honolulu, HI area at 104.3 FM.
FM RADIO STATION

KPHX-AM 35046
Owner: Continental Broadcasting Corp. of Arizona, Inc.
Editorial: 824 E Washington St, Phoenix, Arizona 85034-1004 **Tel:** 1 602 257-1351.
Email: gm@kphx.com
Web site: http://www.1480kphx.com
Profile: KPHX-AM is a commercial station owned by Continental Broadcasting Corp. of Arizona, Inc. The format of the station is liberal talk. KPHX-AM broadcasts to the Phoenix area at 1480 AM.
AM RADIO STATION

KPIG-FM 41141
Owner: Mapleton Communications LLC
Editorial: 1110 Main St, Ste 16, Watsonville, California 95076 **Tel:** 1 831 722-9000.
Email: sales@kpig.com
Web site: http://www.kpig.com
Profile: KPIG-FM is a commercial station owned by Mapleton Communications LLC. The format of the station is adult album alternative music. KPIG-FM broadcasts to Watsonville, CA area at 107.5 FM.
FM RADIO STATION

KPIN-FM 43618
Owner: Rule Communications
Editorial: 219 E Pine St, Ste 112, Pinedale, Wyoming 82941 **Tel:** 1 307 367-2000.
Email: kpin@wyoming.com
Web site: http://www.pinedaleonline.com/kpin
Profile: KPIN-FM is a commercial station owned by Rule Communications. The format of the station is classic country and oldies. KPIN-FM broadcasts to the Pinedale, WY area at 101.1 FM.
FM RADIO STATION

KPIR-AM 35043
Owner: Reynolds (Jerry)
Editorial: 1620 Weatherford Hwy, Granbury, Texas 76048-4830 **Tel:** 1 817 736-0360.
Web site: http://www.kpir.com
Profile: KPIR-AM is a commercial station owned by LR Radio Group. The format of the station is news, talk and sports. KPIR-AM broadcasts to the Granbury, TX area at 1420 AM.
AM RADIO STATION

KPIT-FM 533641
Owner: Jabella Broadcast Network, Inc.
Editorial: 2704 Timberlake Dr, Irving, Texas 75062-8714 **Tel:** 1 903 855-3460.
Email: kpit@kpitradio.com
Web site: http://www.kpitradio.com
Profile: KPIT-FM is a non-commercial station owned by Jabella Broadcast Network, Inc. The format of the station is Christian Hispanic music and programming. KPIT-FM broadcasts to Pittsburg, TX and surrounding areas at 91.7 FM.
FM RADIO STATION

KPJC-AM 34897
Owner: KCCS LLC
Editorial: 3190 Lancaster Dr NE, Salem, Oregon 97305-1350 **Tel:** 1 503 316-1220.
Email: radio@t2tn.com
Web site: http://hebrewnationonline.com/
Profile: KPJC-AM is a commercial station owned by KCCS LLC. The format of the station is Jewish music and talk. KPJC-AM broadcasts to the Salem, OR area at 1220 AM.
AM RADIO STATION

KPKE-AM 36612
Owner: J.H. Rees.
Editorial: 219 N Iowa St, Gunnison, Colorado 81230-2478 **Tel:** 1 970 641-4000.
Email: gunnisonradio@gmail.com
Profile: KPKE-AM is a commercial station owned by J.H. Rees. The format of the station is classic country programming. KPKE-AM broadcasts to the Denver area at 1490 AM.
AM RADIO STATION

KPKJ-FM 559561
Owner: Calvary Chapel of Albuquerque, Inc.
Editorial: 4001 Osuna Rd NE, Albuquerque, New Mexico 87109-4422 **Tel:** 1 505 344-9146.
Email: studio@star88.fm
Profile: KPKJ-FM is a non-commercial station owned by Calvary Chapel of Albuquerque, Inc. The format of the station is Christian contemporary music. KPKJ-FM broadcasts to the Mentmore, NM area at 88.5 FM.
FM RADIO STATION

KPKL-FM 41408
Owner: Spokane Broadcasting Company, LLC
Editorial: 400 South Jef-fer-son St, Suite 304, Spokane, Washington 99204 **Tel:** 1 509 290-6200.
Web site: http://www.kool1071.com
Profile: KPKL-FM is a commercial station owned by Spokane Broadcasting Company, LLC. The format of the station is classic hits. KPKL-FM broadcasts to the Spokane, WA area at 107.1 FM.
FM RADIO STATION

KPKR-FM 527331
Owner: Prescott Valley Broadcasting Co. Inc.
Editorial: 2250 McCulloch Blvd N Ste J, Lake Havasu City, Arizona 86403-5988 **Tel:** 1 928 669-9999.
Web site: http://www.riverratradio.com
Profile: KPKR-FM is a commercial station owned by Prescott Valley Broadcasting Co. Inc. The format of the station is adult hits. KPKR-FM broadcasts to Prescott Valley and Parker, AZ and its surrounding areas at 95.7 FM.
FM RADIO STATION

KPKY-FM 46714
Owner: Rich Broadcasting, LLC
Editorial: 1406 Commerce Way, Idaho Falls, Idaho 83401-1233 **Tel:** 1 208 233-1133.
Web site: http://949therock.com
Profile: KPKY-FM is a commercial station owned by Rich Broadcasting, LLC. The format of the station is classic rock. KPKY-FM broadcasts to the Pocatello, ID area at 94.9 FM.
FM RADIO STATION

KPLA-FM 46486
Owner: Cumulus Media Inc.
Editorial: 503 Old 63 N, Columbia, Missouri 65201-6305
Web site: http://www.kpla.com
Profile: KPLA-FM is a commercial station owned by Cumulus Media Inc. The format of the station is adult contemporary. KPLA-FM broadcasts to the Columbia, MO area at 101.5 FM.
FM RADIO STATION

KPLD-FM 43504
Owner: Canyon Media Corporation
Editorial: 619 S. Bluff Tower 1 Ste. 300, Saint George, Utah 84780 **Tel:** 1 435 628-3643.
Web site: http://www.planet941.com
Profile: KPLD-FM is a commercial station owned by Canyon Media Corporation. The format of the station is hot adult contemporary music. KPLD-FM broadcasts to the St. George, UT area at 105.1 FM.
FM RADIO STATION

KPLM-FM 39845
Owner: Marker Broadcasting
Editorial: 75153 Merle Dr Ste G, Palm Desert, California 92211-5197 **Tel:** 1 760 568-4550.
Email: kplm@markerbroadcasting.com
Web site: http://www.thebig106.com
Profile: KPLM-FM is a commercial station owned by Marker Broadcasting. The format of the station is country music. KPLM-FM broadcasts to the Palm Springs, CA area at 106.1 FM.
FM RADIO STATION

KPLN-FM 429766
Owner: Connoisseur Media LLC
Editorial: 2075 Central Ave, Billings, Montana 59102-4956 **Tel:** 1 406 248-7777.
Web site: http://www.planet1067.com
Profile: KPLN-FM is a commercial station owned by Connoisseur Media LLC. The format of the station is Modern AC. KPLN-FM broadcasts to the Billings, MT area at a frequency of 106.7 FM.
FM RADIO STATION

KPLO-FM 40926
Owner: James River Broadcasting
Editorial: 214 W Pleasant Dr, Pierre, South Dakota 57501 **Tel:** 1 605 224-8686.
Web site: http://www.dakotaradiogroup.com
Profile: KPLO-FM is a commercial station owned by James River Broadcasting. The format of the station is classic country. KPLO-FM broadcasts to the Pierre, SD area at 94.5 FM.
FM RADIO STATION

KPLT-AM 37437
Owner: East Texas Broadcasting Inc.
Editorial: 2810 Pine Mill Rd, Paris, Texas 75460
Tel: 1 903 785-1068.
Email: bud@easttexasradio.com
Web site: http://www.easttexasradio.com
Profile: KPLT-AM is a commercial station owned by East Texas Broadcasting Inc. The format of the station is country. KPLT-AM broadcasts to the Paris, TX area at 1490 AM.
AM RADIO STATION

KPLT-FM 44926
Owner: East Texas Broadcasting Inc.
Editorial: 2810 Pine Mill Rd, Paris, Texas 75460
Tel: 1 903 785-1068.
Web site: http://www.easttexasradio.com
Profile: KPLT-FM is a commercial station owned by East Texas Broadcasting Inc. The format of the station is adult contemporary music. KPLT-FM broadcasts to the Paris, TX area at 107.7 FM.
FM RADIO STATION

KPLV-FM 41039
Owner: iHeart Media Inc.
Editorial: 2880 Meade Ave Ste 250, Las Vegas, Nevada 89102-0713 **Tel:** 1 702 238-7300.
Web site: http://www.my931.com/main.html
Profile: KPLV-FM is a commercial station owned by iHeart Media Inc. The format of the station is adult contemporary. KPLV-FM broadcasts to the Las Vegas area at 93.1 FM.
FM RADIO STATION

KPLW-FM 76083
Owner: Growing Christian Foundation
Editorial: 606 N Western Ave, Wenatchee, Washington 98801-1204 **Tel:** 1 509 665-6641.
Email: kplw@plr.org
Web site: http://www.plr.org
Profile: KPLW-FM is a non-commercial station owned by the Growing Christian Foundation. The format of the station is religious and contemporary Christian music. KPLW-FM broadcasts to the Wenatchee, WA area at 89.9 FM.
FM RADIO STATION

KPLX-FM 46397
Owner: Cumulus Media Inc.
Editorial: West Victory Plaza, 3090 Olive Street, Suite 400, Dallas, Texas 75219 **Tel:** 1 214 526-2400.
Web site: http://www.995thewolf.com
Profile: KPLX-FM is a commercial station owned by Cumulus Media Inc. The format of the station is contemporary country music. KPLX-FM broadcasts to the Dallas area at 99.5 FM.
FM RADIO STATION

KPLY-AM 37419
Owner: Lotus Communications Corp.
Editorial: 2900 Sutro St, Reno, Nevada 89512-1616
Tel: 1 775 329-9261.
Email: kena@kozzradio.com
Profile: KPLY-AM is a commercial station owned by Lotus Communications Corp. The format of the station is sports. KPLY-AM broadcasts to the Reno, NV area at 630 AM.
AM RADIO STATION

KPLZ-FM 44826
Owner: Sinclair Radio of Seattle, LLC
Editorial: 140 4th Ave N, Seattle, Washington 98109-4940 **Tel:** 1 206 404-4000.
Email: starcomment@fisherradio.com
Web site: http://www.star1015.com
Profile: KPLZ-FM is a commercial station owned by Sinclair Radio of Seattle, LLC. The format of the station is hot adult contemporary. KPLZ-FM broadcasts in the Seattle area at 101.5 FM.
FM RADIO STATION

KPMI-AM 824507
Owner: Paskvan Media, Inc.
Editorial: 1410 30Th St Nw Apt 115, Bemidji, Minnesota 56601-4173 **Tel:** 1 218 751-7777.
Profile: KPMI-FM is a commercial station owned by Paskvan Media, Inc. The format of the station is news/talk. WMIS-FM broadcasts locally to the Bemidji, MN area at 1300 AM.
AM RADIO STATION

KPMO-AM 38815
Owner: State of Oregon
Tel: 1 541 552-6301.
Email: jprinfo@sou.edu
Web site: http://www.ijpr.org
Profile: KPMO-AM is a non-commercial station owned by State of Oregon. The format of the station is news programming. KPMO-AM broadcasts to the Mendocino, CA area at 1300 AM.
AM RADIO STATION

KPMW-FM 42974
Owner: Rey-Cel Broadcasting, Inc.
Editorial: 230 Hana Hwy Ste 2, Kahului, Hawaii 96732-2313 **Tel:** 1 808 871-6251.
Profile: KPMW-FM is a commercial station owned by Rey-Cel Broadcasting, Inc. The format of the station is rhythmic Top 40/CHR. The station airs at 105.5 FM from Kahului.
FM RADIO STATION

KPMX-FM 41151
Owner: Northeast Colorado Broadcasting, LLC
Editorial: 117 Main St, Sterling, Colorado 80751
Tel: 1 970 522-4800.
Email: kpmx@necolorado.com
Web site: http://www.kpmx.com
Profile: KPMX-FM is a commercial station owned by Northeast Colorado Broadcasting, LLC. The format of the station is hot adult contemporary. KPMX-FM broadcasts to the Sterling, CO area at 105.7 FM.
FM RADIO STATION

KPNC-FM 39847
Owner: Team Radio LLC
Editorial: 122 N 3rd St, Ponca City, Oklahoma 74601-4326 **Tel:** 1 580 767-1101.
Email: kpnc@eteamradio.com
Web site: http://www.eteamradio.com
Profile: KPNC-FM is a commercial station owned by Team Radio LLC. The format of the station is contemporary country music. KPNC-FM broadcasts to the Ponca City, OK area at 100.7 FM.
FM RADIO STATION

KPND-FM 42763
Owner: Blue Sky Broadcasting Inc.
Editorial: 327 S Marion Ave, Sandpoint, Idaho 83864-1723 **Tel:** 1 208 263-2179.
Profile: KPND-FM is a commercial station owned by Blue Sky Broadcasting Inc. The format of the station is adult album alternative music. KPND-FM broadcasts to the Spokane, WA area at 95.3 FM.
FM RADIO STATION

KPNO-FM 42039
Owner: Praise Network(The)
Editorial: 128 S 4th St, Oneill, Nebraska 68763-1814
Tel: 1 402 336-3886.
Email: email@goodnewsgreatmusic.org
Web site: http://www.goodnewsgreatmusic.org
Profile: KPNO-FM is a non-commercial station owned by The Praise Network. The format of the station is Christian talk and music. KPNO-FM broadcasts to the Norfolk, NE area at 90.9 FM.
FM RADIO STATION

KPNS-AM 37466
Owner: Perry Publishing & Broadcasting Inc.
Editorial: 1701 W Pine Ave, Duncan, Oklahoma 73533-2303 **Tel:** 1 580 255-1350.
Email: kken@cableone.net
Profile: KPNS-AM is a commercial station owned by Perry Publishing & Broadcasting Inc. The format of the station is news and talk. KPNS-AM broadcasts to the Duncan, OK area at 1350 AM.
AM RADIO STATION

KPNT-FM 40971
Owner: Emmis Communications Corp.
Editorial: 800 Saint Louis Union Sta, Saint Louis, Missouri 63103 **Tel:** 1 314 231-1057.
Web site: http://www.1057thepoint.com
Profile: KPNT-FM is a commercial station owned by Emmis Communications Corp. The format of the station is rock alternative. KPNT-FM broadcasts to the St. Louis area at 105.7 FM.
FM RADIO STATION

KPNW-AM 37438
Owner: Bicoastal Media LLC
Editorial: 1500 Valley River Dr Ste 350, Eugene, Oregon 97401-2163 **Tel:** 1 541 485-1120.
Email: 1120kpnw@gmail.com
Web site: http://www.kpnw.com
Profile: KPNW-AM is a commercial station owned by Bicoastal Media LLC. The format of the station is news and talk. KPNW-AM broadcasts to the Eugene, OR area at 1120 AM.
AM RADIO STATION

KPNY-FM 39848
Owner: Mission Nebraska, Inc.
Editorial: 422 Box Butte Ave, Alliance, Nebraska 69301 **Tel:** 1 308 762-3473.
Email: email@mybridgeradio.net
Web site: http://www.mybridgeradio.net
Profile: KPNY-FM is a non-commercial station owned by Mission Nebraska, Inc. The format of the station is religious. KPNY-FM broadcasts to the Alliance, NE area at 102.1 FM.
FM RADIO STATION

KPOA-FM 41678
Owner: Pacific Media Group
Editorial: 311 Ano St, Kahului, Hawaii 96732-1304
Tel: 1 808 877-5566.
Web site: http://www.kpoa.com
Profile: KPOA-FM is a commercial station owned by the Pacific Media Group. The format of the station is adult contemporary music. KPOA-FM broadcasts to the Maui, HI area at 93.5 FM.
FM RADIO STATION

KPOC-AM 37439
Owner: Combined Media Group
Editorial: 1 Radio Dr, Pocahontas, Arkansas 72455
Tel: 1 870 892-5234.
Email: kpoc-krlw@centurytel.net
Profile: KPOC-AM is a commercial station owned by Combined Media Group. The format of the station is adult contemporary. KPOC-AM broadcasts to the Pocahontas, AR area at 1420 AM.
AM RADIO STATION

KPOC-FM 44611
Owner: Combined Media Group
Editorial: 1 Radio Drive, Pocahontas, Arkansas 72455
Tel: 1 870 892-5234.
Email: kpoc-krlw@centurytel.net
Profile: KPOC-FM is a commercial station owned by Combined Media Group. The format of the station is adult contemporary. KPOC-FM broadcasts to the Pocahontas, AR area at 103.9 FM.
FM RADIO STATION

KPOD-AM 38465
Owner: Bicoastal Media LLC
Editorial: 1345 Northcrest Dr, Crescent City, California 95531-2322 **Tel:** 1 707 464-9561.
Email: kpod@bicoastalmedia.com
Web site: http://www.kpod.com
Profile: KPOD-AM is a commercial station owned by Bicoastal Media LLC. The format of the station is talk, news and sports. KPOD-AM broadcasts in the Crescent City, CA area at 1240 AM.
AM RADIO STATION

KPOD-FM 45830
Owner: Bicoastal Media LLC
Editorial: 1345 Northcrest Dr, Crescent City, California 95531-2322 **Tel:** 1 707 464-9561.
Email: kpod@bicoastalmedia.com
Web site: http://www.kpodfm.com
Profile: KPOD-FM is a commercial station owned by Bicoastal Media LLC. The format of the station is contemporary country music. KPOD-FM broadcasts to the Crescent City, CA area at 97.9 AM.
FM RADIO STATION

KPOF-AM 35047
Owner: Pillar of Fire Inc.
Editorial: 3455 W 83rd Ave, Westminster, Colorado 80031-4005 **Tel:** 1 303 428-0910.
Email: info@am91.org
Web site: http://am91.org
Profile: KPOF-AM is a non-commercial station owned by Pillar of Fire Inc. The format of the station is Christian programming. KPOF-AM broadcasts to the Denver area at 910 AM.
AM RADIO STATION

KPOI-FM 77008
Owner: Ohana Broadcast Company LLC
Editorial: 1000 Bishop St Ste 200, Honolulu, Hawaii 96813-4203 **Tel:** 1 808 947-1500.
Email: alt1059@gmail.com
Web site: http://www.alt1059.com
Profile: KPOI-FM is a commercial station owned by Ohana Broadcast Company LLC. The format of the

station is alternative rock. KPOI-FM broadcasts to the Honolulu area at 105.9 FM.
FM RADIO STATION

KPOJ-AM 80362
Owner: iHeartMedia Inc.
Editorial: 13333 SW 68th Pkwy Ste 310, Tigard, Oregon 97223-8304 **Tel:** 1 503 323-6400.
Web site: http://ripcityradio.iheart.com
Profile: KPOJ-AM is a commercial station owned by iHeartMedia Inc. The format of the station is sports talk. KPOJ-AM broadcasts in the Portland, OR area at 620 AM.
AM RADIO STATION

KPOK-AM 35048
Owner: Tri-State Communications, Inc.
Tel: 1 701 523-3883.
Email: kpok@ndsupernet.com
Web site: http://www.kpokradio.com
Profile: KPOK-AM is a commercial station owned by Tri-State Communications, Inc. The format of the station is contemporary country. KPOK-AM broadcasts to the Bowman, ND area at 1340 AM.
AM RADIO STATION

KPOO-FM 39850
Owner: Poor Peoples Radio Inc.
Editorial: 1329 Divisadero St, San Francisco, California 94115 **Tel:** 1 415 346-5373.
Email: news@kpoo.com
Web site: http://www.kpoo.com
Profile: KPOO-FM is a non-commercial station owned by Poor Peoples Radio Inc. The format of the station is variety, featuring jazz, blues, reggae, hip hop, gospel, salsa and samba music. KPOO-FM broadcasts to the San Francisco area at 89.5 FM.
FM RADIO STATION

KPOV-FM 878964
Editorial: 501 NW Bond St, Bend, Oregon 97701-3309 **Tel:** 1 541 322-0863.
Web site: http://www.kpov.org
Profile: KPOV-FM is a non-commercial station owned by the Women's Civic Improvement League. The format of the station is community radio, featuring news, talk and music programming. KPOV-FM broadcasts to the Bend, OR area at a frequency of 88.9 FM.
FM RADIO STATION

KPOW-AM 37440
Owner: MGR Media, LLC
Editorial: 912 Lane 11 1/2, Powell, Wyoming 82435-9222 **Tel:** 1 307 754-5183.
Web site: http://kpow1260.com
Profile: KPOW-AM is a commercial station owned by MGR Media, LLC. The format of the station is news and talk. KPOW-AM broadcasts to the Powell, WY area at 1260 AM.
AM RADIO STATION

KPOW-FM 44541
Owner: Benne Media
Editorial: 301 S Ohio Ave, Sedalia, Missouri 65301
Tel: 1 660 826-5005.
Web site: http://www.power977.com
Profile: KPOW-FM is a commercial station owned by Benne Media. The format of the station is classic hits. KPOW-FM broadcasts to the Kansas City, MO area at 97.7 FM.
FM RADIO STATION

KPPD-FM 598547
Owner: Prairie Public Broadcasting Inc.
Editorial: 1814 N 15th St, Bismarck, North Dakota 58501-2025 **Tel:** 1 701 224-1700.
Email: info@prairiepublic.org
Web site: http://www.prairiepublic.org
Profile: KPPD-FM is a non-commercial station owned by Prairie Public Broadcasting Inc. The format of the station is news, classical and jazz music. KPPD-FM broadcasts to the Devils Lake, ND area at 91.7 FM and is a simulcast of KCND-FM.
FM RADIO STATION

KPPK-FM 389597
Owner: Bicoastal Media LLC
Editorial: 1130 14th Ave, Longview, Washington 98632-3017 **Tel:** 1 360 425-1500.
Email: info@kppk98.3.com
Web site: http://www.kppk98.3.com
Profile: KPPK-FM is a commercial station owned by Bicoastal Media LLC. The format of the station is adult hits music. KPPK-FM broadcasts in the Portland, OR area at 98.3 FM.
FM RADIO STATION

KPPR-FM 41165
Owner: Prairie Public Broadcasting Inc.
Editorial: 207 5th St N, Fargo, North Dakota 58102-4827 **Tel:** 1 701 241-6900.
Email: info@prairiepublic.org
Web site: http://www.prairiepublic.org
Profile: KPPR-FM is a non-commercial station owned by Prairie Public Broadcasting Inc. The primary format of the station is adult album alternative. KPPR-FM broadcasts to the Fargo, ND area at 89.5 FM.
FM RADIO STATION

KPPT-FM 45775
Owner: Agpal Broadcasting Inc.
Editorial: 145 N Coast Hwy, Ste D, Newport, Oregon 97365-3165 **Tel:** 1 541 265-5000.
Email: info@bossradio.net
Web site: http://www.bossradio.net
Profile: KPPT-FM is commercial station owned by Agpal Broadcasting Inc. The format of the station is classic hits music. KPPT-FM broadcasts to the Newport, OR area at 100.7 FM.
FM RADIO STATION

KPPV-FM 46814
Owner: Prescott Valley Broadcasting Co. Inc.
Editorial: 3755 Karicio Ln, Prescott, Arizona 86303-6836 **Tel:** 1 928 445-8289.
Web site: http://www.kppv.com
Profile: KPPV-FM is a commercial station owned by Prescott Valley Broadcasting Co. Inc. The format of the station is adult contemporary. KPPV-FM broadcasts to the Prescott, AZ area at 106.7 FM.
FM RADIO STATION

KPQ-AM 37441
Owner: Cherry Creek Radio
Editorial: 231 N Wenatchee Ave, Wenatchee, Washington 98801-2009 **Tel:** 1 509 665-6565.
Email: newswenatchee@cherrycreekradio.com
Web site: http://www.kpq.com
Profile: KPQ-AM is a commercial station owned by Cherry Creek Radio. The format of the station is news, talk and sports. KPQ-AM broadcasts to the Seattle area at 560 AM.
AM RADIO STATION

KPQ-FM 44828
Owner: Cherry Creek Radio
Editorial: 231 N Wenatchee Ave, Wenatchee, Washington 98801-2009 **Tel:** 1 509 665-6565.
Email: newswenatchee@cherrycreekradio.com
Web site: http://www.thequake1021.com
Profile: KPQ-FM is a commercial station owned by Cherry Creek Radio. The format of the station is classic rock. KPQ-FM broadcasts to the Seattle area at 102.1 FM.
FM RADIO STATION

KPQX-FM 46356
Owner: New Media Broadcasters
Editorial: 2210 31st St N, Havre, Montana 59501-8003 **Tel:** 1 406 265-7841.
Email: news@nmbi.com
Web site: http://www.kpqx.com
Profile: KPQX-FM is a commercial station owned by New Media Broadcasters. The format for the station is contemporary and classic country. KPQX-FM broadcasts to the Havre, MT area at 92.5 FM. KPQX-FM prefers not to receive press materials.
FM RADIO STATION

KPRA-FM 41776
Owner: Family Stations Inc.
Editorial: 290 Hegenberger Rd, Oakland, California 94621-1436 **Tel:** 1 510 568-6200.
Web site: http://www.familyradio.com
Profile: KPRA-FM is a non-commercial radio station owned by Family Stations Inc. The format of the station is religious. KPRA-FM broadcasts to the Sacramento, CA area at 89.5 FM.
FM RADIO STATION

KPRB-FM 44077
Owner: Northeast Colorado Broadcasting, LLC
Editorial: 220 State St, Ste 106, Fort Morgan, Colorado 80701 **Tel:** 1 970 867-7271.
Email: b106@necolorado.com
Web site: http://www.b106.com
Profile: KPRB-FM is a commercial station owned by Northeast Colorado Broadcasting, LLC. The format of the station is adult contemporary. KPRB-FM broadcasts to the Fort Morgan, CO area at 106.3 FM.
FM RADIO STATION

KPRC-AM 35049
Owner: iHeartMedia Inc.
Editorial: 2000 West Loop S Ste 300, Houston, Texas 77027-3510 **Tel:** 1 713 212-8000.
Web site: http://kprcradio.iheart.com
Profile: KPRC-AM is a commercial station owned by iHeartMedia Inc. The format of the station is conservative talk. KPRC-AM broadcasts to the Houston area at 950 AM.
AM RADIO STATION

KPRC-FM 39558
Owner: iHeartMedia Inc.
Editorial: 903 N Main St, Salinas, California 93906-3912 **Tel:** 1 831 755-8181.
Web site: http://salinaslapreciosa.iheart.com
Profile: KPRC-FM is a commercial station owned by iHeartMedia Inc. The format of the station is Hispanic. KPRC-FM broadcasts to the Salinas, CA area on 100.7 FM.
FM RADIO STATION

KPRD-FM 42975
Owner: Praise Network(The)
Editorial: 205 E 7th St Ste 218, Hays, Kansas 67601-4161 **Tel:** 1 785 628-6300.
Email: kprd@kprd.org
Web site: http://www.kprdradio.com
Profile: KPRD-FM is a non-commercial station owned by The Praise Network. The format of the station is contemporary Christian music and talk. KPRD-FM broadcasts to the Hays, KS area at 88.9 FM.
FM RADIO STATION

KPRE-FM 73685
Owner: Public Broadcasting of Colorado Inc.
Editorial: Vail, Colorado **Tel:** 1 303 871-9191.
Email: info@cpr.org
Web site: http://www.cpr.org
Profile: KPRE-FM is a non-commercial station owned by Public Broadcasting of Colorado Inc. The format of the station is classical music and news. KPRE-FM broadcasts to the Vail, CO area at 88.9 FM.
FM RADIO STATION

KPRF-FM 46155
Owner: Townsquare Media, LLC
Editorial: 6214 SW 34th Ave, Amarillo, Texas 79109-4006 **Tel:** 1 806 355-9777.
Web site: http://lonestar987.com
Profile: KPRF-FM is a commercial station owned by Townsquare Media, LLC. The format of the station is classic rock. KPRF-FM broadcasts to the Amarillo, TX area at 98.7 FM.
FM RADIO STATION

KPRH-FM 44219
Owner: Public Broadcasting of Colorado Inc.
Editorial: Montrose, Colorado **Tel:** 1 303 871-9191.
Email: info@cpr.org
Web site: http://www.cpr.org
Profile: KPRH-FM is a non-commercial station owned by Public Broadcasting of Colorado Inc. The format of the station is news and talk. KPRH-FM broadcasts to the Montrose, CO area at 88.3 FM.
FM RADIO STATION

KPRK-AM 35050
Owner: Townsquare Media, LLC
Editorial: 125 W Mendenhall St, Bozeman, Montana 59715-3586 **Tel:** 1 406 586-2352.
Profile: KPRK-AM is a commercial station owned by Townsquare Media, LLC. The format of the station is news/talk. KPRK-AM broadcasts locally to the Bozeman, MT area at a frequency of 1340 AM.
AM RADIO STATION

KPRL-AM 36699
Owner: North County Communications LLC
Editorial: 531 32nd St, Paso Robles, California 93446
Tel: 1 805 238-1230.
Email: reception@kprl.com
Web site: http://www.kprl.com
Profile: KPRL-AM is a commercial station owned by North County Communications LLC. The format of the station is sports, news, and talk. KPRL-AM broadcasts to the Paso Robles, CA area at 1230 AM.
AM RADIO STATION

KPRM-AM 37443
Owner: De La Hunt Broadcasting
Tel: 1 218 732-3306.
Email: kprmkdkk@unitelc.com
Web site: http://www.kkradionetwork.com
Profile: KPRM-AM is a commercial station owned by De La Hunt Broadcasting. The format of the station is classic country music. KPRM-AM broadcasts in the Park Rapids, MN area at 870 AM.
AM RADIO STATION

KPRO-AM 36134
Owner: Impact Radio, Inc.
Editorial: 7351 Lincoln Ave, Riverside, California 92504-4600 **Tel:** 1 951 688-1570.
Email: kproval@aol.com
Web site: http://www.kpro1570.com
Profile: KPRO-AM is a commercial station owned by Impact Radio, Inc. The format of the station is religious programming. KPRO-AM broadcasts to the Riverside, CA area at 1570 AM.
AM RADIO STATION

KPRP-AM 36293
Owner: Summit Media Broadcasting LLC
Editorial: 900 Fort Street Mall Ste 700, Honolulu, Hawaii 96813-3701 **Tel:** 1 808 275-1000.
Web site: http://www.kprpam650.com
Profile: KPRP-AM is a commercial station owned by Summit Media Broadcasting LLC. The format of the station is easy listening. KPRP-AM broadcasts to the Honolulu area at 650 AM.
AM RADIO STATION

KPRR-FM 40940
Owner: iHeart Media Inc.
Editorial: 4045 N Mesa St, El Paso, Texas 79902-1526 **Tel:** 1 915 351-5400.
Web site: http://www.kprr.com
Profile: KPRR-FM is a commercial station owned by iHeart Media Inc. The format of the station is Top 40/CHR music. KPRR-FM broadcasts to the El Paso, TX area at 102.1 FM.
FM RADIO STATION

KPRS-FM 44831
Owner: Carter Broadcast Group
Editorial: 11131 Colorado Ave, Kansas City, Missouri 64137-2546 **Tel:** 1 816 763-2040.
Email: community@kprs.com
Web site: http://www.kprs.com
Profile: KPRS-FM is a commercial station owned by Carter Broadcast Group. The format of the station is urban contemporary and R&B music. KPRS-FM broadcasts to the Kansas City, MO area at 103.3 FM.
FM RADIO STATION

KPRT-AM 37444
Owner: Carter Broadcast Group
Editorial: 11131 Colorado Ave, Kansas City, Missouri 64137-2546 **Tel:** 1 816 763-2040.
Email: community@kprs.com
Web site: http://www.kprs.com/KPRT.aspx
Profile: KPRT-AM is a commercial station owned by Carter Broadcast Group. The format of the station is gospel. KRPT-AM broadcasts to the Kansas City, MO area at 1590 AM.
AM RADIO STATION

KPRV-AM 38409
Owner: Coleman Broadcasting
Editorial: Highway 59 South, Poteau, Oklahoma 74953 **Tel:** 1 918 647-3221.
Email: kprv@windstream.net
Web site: http://www.kprvradio.com
Profile: KPRV-AM is a commercial station owned by Coleman Broadcasting. The format of the station is Adult Standards. KPRV-AM broadcasts to the Poteau, OK area at 1280 AM.
AM RADIO STATION

KPRV-FM 45777
Owner: Coleman Broadcasting
Editorial: 22153 Old US Highway 59, Poteau, Oklahoma 74953 **Tel:** 1 918 647-3221.
Email: kprv@windstream.net
Web site: http://www.kprvradio.com
Profile: KPRV-FM is a commercial station owned by Coleman Broadcasting. The format of the station is lite AC. KPRV-FM broadcasts to the Poteau, OK area at 92.5 FM.
FM RADIO STATION

KPRW-FM 43080
Owner: Results Radio Group
Editorial: 728 Western Ave, Fergus Falls, Minnesota 56537-1095 **Tel:** 1 218 346-4800.
Email: contactus@lakesradio.net
Web site: http://www.lakesradio.net
Profile: KPRW-FM is a commercial station owned by Results Radio Group. The format of the station is adult contemporary. KPRW-FM broadcasts to the Perham, MN area at 99.5.
FM RADIO STATION

KPRZ-AM 35051
Owner: Salem Media Group, Inc.
Editorial: 9255 Towne Centre Dr Ste 535, San Diego, California 92121-3038 **Tel:** 1 858 535-1210.
Web site: http://www.kprz.com
Profile: KPRZ-AM is a commercial station owned by Salem Media Group, Inc. The format of the station is religious talk. KCBQ-AM broadcasts to the San Diego area at 1210 AM.
AM RADIO STATION

KPSA-FM 557337
Owner: SkyWest Media, LLC
Editorial: 1560 N Corbin St, Silver City, New Mexico 88061-6526 **Tel:** 1 575 538-3396.
Email: events@silvercityradio.com
Web site: http://www.977theplanet.com
Profile: KPSA-FM is a commercial station owned by SkyWest Media, LLC. The format of the station is classic rock. KPSA-FM broadcasts to the Silver City, NM area at 97.7 FM.
FM RADIO STATION

KPSF-AM 800216
Owner: CRC Media West, LLC
Editorial: 75-153 Merle Dr., Unit D, Palm Springs, California 92211 **Tel:** 1 760 621-0100.
Web site: http://www.moneyradio1510.com
Profile: KPSF-AM is a commercial station owned by CRC Media West, LLC. The format of the station is business and finance news/talk. KPSF-AM broadcasts to the Palm Springs and Coachella Valley areas of California at a frequency of 1200 AM.
AM RADIO STATION

KPSI-AM 39381
Owner: R & R Radio Corp.
Editorial: 2100 E Tahquitz Canyon Way, Palm Springs, California 92262 **Tel:** 1 760 325-2582.
Web site: http://www.newstalk920.com
Profile: KPSI-AM is a commercial station owned by R & R Radio Corp. The format of the station is news and talk. KPSI-AM broadcasts to the Palm Springs, CA area at 920 AM.
AM RADIO STATION

KPSI-FM 44832
Owner: Alpha Media
Editorial: 1321 N Gene Autry Trl, Palm Springs, California 92262-5473 **Tel:** 1 760 322-7890.
Web site: http://www.mix1005.fm
Profile: KPSI-FM is a commercial station owned by Alpha Media. The format for the station is hot adult contemporary. KPSI-FM broadcasts to the Palm Springs, CA area at 100.5 FM.
FM RADIO STATION

KPSL-FM 42881
Owner: Lotus Communications Corp.
Editorial: 5100 Commerce Dr, Bakersfield, California 93309-0684 **Tel:** 1 661 327-9711.
Web site: http://www.concierto965.com
Profile: KPSL-FM is a commercial station owned by Lotus Communications Corp. The format of the station is Spanish contemporary music. KPSL-FM broadcasts to the Bakersfield, CA area at 96.5 FM.
FM RADIO STATION

KPSM-FM 39851
Owner: Better Living Ministries
Editorial: 910 Main St, Brownwood, Texas 76801
Tel: 1 325 646-5993.
Email: kpsmfm@gmail.com
Web site: http://www.kpsm.net
Profile: KPSM-FM is an commercial station owned by Better Living Ministries. The format of the station is

religious programming. The station broadcasts to the Brownwood, TX area at 99.3 FM.
FM RADIO STATION

KPSO-FM
44503
Owner: Brooks Broadcasting Corp.
Editorial: 304 E Rice St, Falfurrias, Texas 78355-3624 **Tel:** 1 361 325-2112.
Profile: KPSO-FM is a commercial station owned by Brooks Broadcasting Corp. The format of the station is Hispanic and tejano music. KPSO-FM broadcasts to the Corpus Christi, TX area at 106.3 FM.
FM RADIO STATION

KPST-FM
822082
Owner: Entravision Communications Corp.
Editorial: 41601 Corporate Way, Palm Desert, California 92260-1971 **Tel:** 1 760 341-5837.
Profile: KPST-FM is a commercial station owned by Entravision Communications Corp. The format of the station is Regional Mexican. KPST-FM broadcasts to the Coachella Valley, CA region locally at 103.5 FM.
FM RADIO STATION

KPSZ-AM
37332
Owner: Saga Communications
Editorial: 1416 Locust St, Des Moines, Iowa 50309-3014 **Tel:** 1 515 280-1350.
Web site: http://www.praise940.com
Profile: KPSZ-AM is a commercial station owned by Saga Communications. The format of the station is contemporary Christian and religious. KPSZ-AM broadcasts to the Des Moines, IA area at 940 AM.
AM RADIO STATION

KPTJ-FM
854649
Owner: La Unica Broadcasting Company
Editorial: 209 W Beauregard Ave, San Angelo, Texas 76903-5823
Web site: http://www.magia104.com/
Profile: KPTJ-FM is a commercial station owned by La Unica Broadcasting Company. The format of the station is Tejano music. KPTJ-FM broadcasts to the San Angelo, TX area at a frequency of 104.5 FM.
FM RADIO STATION

KPTR-AM
37445
Owner: R & R Radio Corp.
Editorial: 2100 E Tahquitz Canyon Way, Palm Springs, California 92262 **Tel:** 1 760 325-2582.
Web site: http://www.kptram1340.com
Profile: KPTR-AM is commercial station owned by R & R Radio Corp. The format of the station is progressive talk. KPTR-AM broadcasts to the Palm Springs, CA area at 1450 AM.
AM RADIO STATION

KPTT-FM
46030
Owner: iHeartMedia Inc.
Editorial: 4695 S Monaco St, Denver, Colorado 80237-3525 **Tel:** 1 303 713-8000.
Web site: http://www.957theparty.com
Profile: KPTT-FM is a commercial station owned by iHeartMedia Inc. The format of the station is Top 40/CHR. KPTT-FM broadcasts to Denver area at 95.7 FM.
FM RADIO STATION

KPTX-FM
46619
Owner: Parday Inc.
Editorial: 316 S Cedar St, Pecos, Texas 79772
Tel: 1 432 445-2498.
Email: kiun@valornet.com
Web site: http://www.98xfm.com
Profile: KPTX-FM is a commercial station owned by Parday Inc. The format of the station is adult contemporary. KPTX-FM broadcasts to the Pecos, TX area at 98.3 FM.
FM RADIO STATION

KPTZ-FM
751717
Owner: Radio Port Townsend
Tel: 1 360 379-6886.
Email: info@kptz.org
Web site: http://www.kptz.org
Profile: KPTZ-FM is a non-commercial community radio station owned by Radio Port Townsend. The format of the station is variety. KPTZ-FM broadcasts to Port Townsend, WA and surrounding areas at a frequency of 91.9 FM.
FM RADIO STATION

KPUA-AM
37446
Owner: New West Broadcasting
Editorial: 1145 Kilauea Ave, Hilo, Hawaii 96720-4203
Tel: 1 808 935-5461.
Email: news@kpua.net
Web site: http://www.kpua.net
Profile: KPUA-AM is a commercial station owned by New West Broadcasting. The format of the station is news, sports and talk. KPUA-AM broadcasts to the Hilo, HI area at 670 AM.
AM RADIO STATION

KPUG-AM
37447
Owner: Saga Communications
Editorial: 2219 Yew Street Rd, Bellingham, Washington 98229-8855 **Tel:** 1 360 734-9790.
Email: thezone@kpug1170.com
Web site: http://www.kpug1170.com
Profile: KPUG-AM is a commercial station owned by Saga Communications. The format of the station is sports. KPUG-AM broadcasts to the Bellingham, WA area at 1170 AM.
AM RADIO STATION

KPUL-FM
41997
Owner: Positive Impact Media Inc.
Editorial: 33365 335th St, Waukee, Iowa 50263-7033
Tel: 1 515 987-9995.
Web site: http://pulse1017.com
Profile: KPUL-FM is a commercial station owned by Positive Impact Media Inc. The format of the station is contemporary top 40/CHR. KPUL-FM broadcasts to the Des Moines, IA area at 101.7 FM.
FM RADIO STATION

KPUR-AM
38339
Owner: Cumulus Media Inc.
Editorial: 301 S Polk St, Amarillo, Texas 79101-1403
Tel: 1 806 342-5200.
Profile: KPUR-AM is a commercial station owned by Cumulus Media Inc. The format of the station is sports. KPUR-AM broadcasts to the Amarillo, TX area at 1440 AM.
AM RADIO STATION

KPUR-FM
45695
Owner: Cumulus Media Inc.
Editorial: 301 S Polk St Ste 100, Amarillo, Texas 79101-1404 **Tel:** 1 806 342-5200.
Web site: http://www.kpur107.com
Profile: KPUR-FM is a commercial station owned by Cumulus Media Inc. The format of the station is country. KPUR-FM broadcasts to the Amarillo, TX area at 107.1 FM.
FM RADIO STATION

KPUS-FM
44025
Owner: Convergent Broadcasting
Editorial: 615 N Upper Broadway St Ste 105, Corpus Christi, Texas 78401-0703 **Tel:** 1 361 814-3800.
Web site: http://classicrock1045.com
Profile: KPUS-FM is a commercial station owned by Convergent Broadcasting. The format of the station is classic rock. KPUS-FM broadcasts to the Corpus Christi, TX area at a frequency of 104.5 FM.
FM RADIO STATION

KPVR-FM
44824
Owner: Gateway Creative Broadcasting, Inc
Editorial: 30 Tower St, Moscow Mills, Missouri 63362-1139 **Tel:** 1 636 356-9266.
Email: info@joyfmonline.org
Web site: http://boost1019.com
Profile: KPVR-FM is a commercial station owned by Gateway Creative Broadcasting, Inc. The format of the station is Christian CHR. KPVR-FM broadcasts to the St. Louis area at 94.1 FM.
FM RADIO STATION

KPVS-FM
42976
Owner: Pacific Media Group
Editorial: 913 Kanoelehua Ave, Hilo, Hawaii 96720-5116 **Tel:** 1 808 961-0651.
Email: jaz@pmghawaii.com
Web site: http://thebeathawaii.com
Profile: KPVS-FM is a commercial station owned by Pacific Media Group. The format of the station is Rhythmic CHR/Reggae. KPVS-FM broadcasts to the Hilo, HI area at 95.9 FM. The station's slogan is, "The Beat of the Islands."
FM RADIO STATION

KPVW-FM
87192
Owner: Entravision Communications Corp.
Editorial: 20 Sunset Dr Ste 6A, Basalt, Colorado 81621-9387 **Tel:** 1 970 927-7600.
Web site: http://www.tricoloraspen.com
Profile: KPVW-FM is a commercial station owned by Entravision Communications Corp. The format of the station is regional Mexican. KPVW-FM broadcasts to Aspen, Glenwood, CO and the surrounding area at 107.1 FM.
FM RADIO STATION

KPWB-AM
38979
Owner: Dockins Broadcast Group
Editorial: 235 Business Hh, Piedmont, Missouri 63957-9410 **Tel:** 1 573 223-4518.
Web site: http://www.kickincountry105.com
Profile: KPWB-AM is a commercial station owned by Dockins Broadcast Group. The format of the station is country. KPWB-AM broadcasts to the Piedmont, MO area at a frequency of 1140 AM.
AM RADIO STATION

KPWB-FM
46412
Owner: Dockins Broadcast Group
Editorial: 235 Business Hh, Piedmont, Missouri 63957-9410 **Tel:** 1 573 223-4518.
Email: fdj@dockinsbroadcastgroup.com
Web site: http://www.kickincountry105.com
Profile: KPWB-FM is a commercial station owned by Dockins Broadcast Group. The format of the station is country. KPWB-FM broadcasts to the Piedmont, MO area at 104.9 FM.
FM RADIO STATION

KPWK-FM
39975
Owner: iHeartMedia Inc.
Editorial: 351 Elliott Ave W Ste 300, Seattle, Washington 98119-4150 **Tel:** 1 206 494-2000.
Web site: http://power933.iheart.com
Profile: KPWK-FM is a commercial station owned by iHeartMedia Inc. The format of the station is contemporary hits. KPWK-FM broadcasts to the Seattle area at 93.3 FM.
FM RADIO STATION

KPWR-FM
39852
Owner: Meruelo Group
Editorial: 2600 W Olive Ave, Burbank, California 91505-4549 **Tel:** 1 818 953-4200.
Email: power106info@power106.com
Web site: http://www.power106.com
Profile: KPWR-FM is a commercial station owned by Meruelo Group. The format for the station is rhythmic. KPWR-FM broadcasts to the Los Angeles area at 105.9 FM.
FM RADIO STATION

KPWW-FM
39742
Owner: Townsquare Media, LLC
Editorial: 2324 Arkansas Blvd, Texarkana, Arkansas 71854-2016 **Tel:** 1 870 772-3771.
Web site: http://www.power959.com
Profile: KPWW-FM is a commercial station owned by Townsquare Media, LLC. The format of the station is Top 40/CHR. KPWW-FM broadcasts to the Texarkana, AR area at 95.9 FM.
FM RADIO STATION

KPXI-FM
44067
Owner: Hanszen Broadcast Group
Editorial: 1101 Kilgore Dr, Henderson, Texas 75652-5129 **Tel:** 1 903 655-1800.
Web site: http://www.easttexastoday.com
Profile: KPXI-FM is a commercial station owned by Hanszen Broadcast Group. The format of the station is country music. KPXI-FM broadcasts to the Tyler, TX area at 100.7 FM.
FM RADIO STATION

KPXQ-AM
37060
Owner: Salem Media Group, Inc.
Editorial: 2425 E Camelback Rd Ste 570, Phoenix, Arizona 85016-4250 **Tel:** 1 602 955-9600.
Web site: http://www.faithtalk1360.com
Profile: KPXQ-AM is a commercial station owned by Salem Media Group, Inc. The format of the station is religious talk. KPXQ-AM broadcasts to the Phoenix area at 1360 AM.
AM RADIO STATION

KPYG-FM
41148
Owner: Mapleton Radio, LLC
Editorial: 795 Brickly Road, San Luis Obispo, California 93401 **Tel:** 1 831 722-9000.
Web site: http://www.kpig.com
Profile: KPYG-FM is a commercial station owned by Mapleton Radio, LLC. The format of the station is adult album alternative. KPYG-FM broadcasts to the Watsonville, CA area at 94.9 FM.
FM RADIO STATION

KPYK-AM
35089
Owner: Mohnkern Electronics Inc.
Editorial: 1412C W Moore Ave, Terrell, Texas 75160
Tel: 1 972 524-5795.
Web site: http://www.kpyk.com
Profile: KPYK-AM is a commercial station owned by Mohnkern Electronics Inc. The format of the station is oldies. KPYK-AM broadcasts to Terrell, TX, at 1570 AM.
AM RADIO STATION

KPYN-AM
37174
Owner: Freed AM Corp.
Tel: 1 903 796-2817.
Email: info@kpyn.net
Web site: http://www.kpyn.net
Profile: KPYN-AM is a non-commercial station owned by Freed AM Corp. The format of the station is Christian talk. KPYN-AM broadcasts to Atlanta, TX at 900 AM.
AM RADIO STATION

KPYV-AM
430469
Owner: Radio Santismo
Tel: 1 916 442-7389.
Email: kcvv1240am@radiosantisimosacramento.com
Web site: http://radiosantisimosacramento.com
Profile: KPYV-AM is a commercial station owned by Radio Santismo. The format of the station is Spanish Catholic. KPYV-AM broadcasts to the Chico, CA area at 1340 AM.
AM RADIO STATION

KPZA-FM
72540
Owner: Noalmark Broadcasting Corp.
Editorial: 619 N Turner St, Hobbs, New Mexico 88240
Tel: 1 575 397-4969.
Email: kpza@1radiosquare.com
Web site: http://kpzafm.com
Profile: KPZA-FM is a commercial station owned by Noalmark Broadcasting Corp. The format of the station is Hispanic. KPZA-FM broadcasts to the Albuquerque, NM area at 103.7 FM.
FM RADIO STATION

KPZE-FM
413445
Owner: Pecos Valley Broadcasting Company
Editorial: 121 S Canal St Ste C, Carlsbad, New Mexico 88220-5735 **Tel:** 1 575 628-8402.
Web site: http://www.kpze.com
Profile: KPZE-FM is a commercial station owned by Pecos Valley Broadcasting Company. The format of the station is regional Mexican music. KPZE-FM broadcasts to the Albuquerque, NM area at 106.1 FM.
FM RADIO STATION

KPZK-AM
38694
Owner: Cumulus Media Inc
Editorial: 700 Wellington Hills Rd, Little Rock, Arkansas 72211 **Tel:** 1 501 401-0200.
Web site: http://www.power923.com
Profile: KPZK-AM is a commercial station owned by Cumulus Media Inc. The format of the station is urban contemporary. KPZK-AM broadcasts in the Little Rock, AR area at 1250 AM.
AM RADIO STATION

KPZK-FM
4334
Owner: Cumulus Media Inc
Editorial: 700 Wellington Hills Rd, Little Rock, Arkansas 72211 **Tel:** 1 501 401-0200.
Web site: http://www.praisepage.com
Profile: KPZK-FM is a commercial station owned by Cumulus Media Inc. The format of the station is gospel. KPZK-FM broadcasts to the Little Rock, AR at 102.5 FM.
FM RADIO STATION

KQAC-FM
4458
Owner: All Classical Public Media, Inc.
Editorial: 211 SE Caruthers St Ste 200, Portland, Oregon 97214-4502 **Tel:** 1 503 943-5828.
Email: webmaster@allclassical.org
Web site: http://www.allclassical.org
Profile: KQAC-FM is non-commercial station owned by the All Classical Public Media, Inc. The format of the station is classical music. KQAC-FM broadcasts to the Portland, OR area at 89.9 FM.
FM RADIO STATION

KQAD-AM
3744
Owner: Alpha Media
Editorial: 1140 150th Ave, Luverne, Minnesota 56156-4215 **Tel:** 1 507 283-4444.
Web site: http://www.k101fm.net/
Profile: KQAD-AM is a commercial station owned by Alpha Media. The format of the station is Lite Rock/Lite AC. KQAD-AM broadcasts to the Luverne, MN area at 800 AM.
AM RADIO STATION

KQAK-FM
4246
Owner: Horizon Broadcasting Group
Editorial: 854 Ne 4Th St, Bend, Oregon 97701-4711
Tel: 1 541 383-3825.
Email: kqak1057@horizonbroadcastinggroup.com
Web site: http://www.kqak.com
Profile: KQAK-FM is a commercial station owned by the Horizon Broadcasting Group. The format of KQAK-FM is classic hits. The station broadcasts to the Bend, OR area at 105.7 FM.
FM RADIO STATION

KQAM-AM
3703
Owner: Steckline Communications
Editorial: 1632 S Maize Rd, Wichita, Kansas 67209-3912 **Tel:** 1 316 721-8484.
Web site: http://www.kqamradio.com
Profile: KQAM-AM is a commercial station owned by Steckline Communications. The format of the station is news and talk. KQAM-AM broadcasts to the Wichita, KS area at 1480 AM.
AM RADIO STATION

KQAQ-AM
3678
Owner: Hometown Broadcasting Austin, Inc.
Editorial: 109 E Clark St, Albert Lea, Minnesota 56007-2420 **Tel:** 1 507 373-9600.
Email: kqaq@classiccountrylegends.com
Web site: http://www.classiccountrylegends.com
Profile: KQAQ-AM is a commercial station owned by Hometown Broadcasting, Inc. The format of the station is classic country. KNFX-AM broadcasts to the Rochester, MN area on 970 AM.
AM RADIO STATION

KQAV-FM
4443
Owner: High Desert Broadcasting LLC
Editorial: 570 E Avenue Q9, Palmdale, California 93550-4655 **Tel:** 1 661 947-3107.
Web site: http://oldschool935.com
Profile: KQAV-FM is a commercial station owned by High Desert Broadcasting LLC. The format of the station is classic hip hop. KQAV-FM broadcasts in the Palmdale, CA area at 93.5 FM.
FM RADIO STATION

KQAY-FM
4607
Owner: Majestic Communications
Editorial: 902 Date St, Tucumcari, New Mexico 88401-4335 **Tel:** 1 575 461-0522.
Email: ktnmkqay@yahoo.com
Profile: KQAY-FM is a commercial station owned by Majestic Communications. The format of the station is adult contemporary music. KQAY-FM broadcasts to the Tucumcari, NM area at 92.7 FM.
FM RADIO STATION

KQAZ-FM
4594
Owner: Country Mountain Airwaves LLC
Editorial: 391 W Deuce of Clubs Ste C, Show Low, Arizona 85901-5809 **Tel:** 1 928 532-1010.
Email: traffic@majik101.com
Web site: http://www.majik101.com
Profile: KQAZ-FM is a commercial station owned by Country Mountain Airwaves LLC. The format of the station is Lite Rock/Lite AC music. KQAZ-FM broadcasts to the Show Low, AZ and the surrounding areas at 101.7 FM.
FM RADIO STATION

KQBA-FM
6295
Owner: Hutton Broadcasting, LLC
Editorial: 2502 Camino Entrada, Santa Fe, New Mexico 87507-4911 **Tel:** 1 505 471-1067.
Web site: http://www.santafe.com/outlaw
Profile: KQBA-FM is a commercial station owned by Hutton Broadcasting, LLC. The format of the station

is country music. KQBA-FM broadcasts to the Sante Fe, NM area at 107.5 FM.
FM RADIO STATION

KQBB-FM 45975

Owner: Center Broadcasting Company Inc.
Editorial: 307 San Augustine St, Center, Texas 75935-3937 **Tel:** 1 936 598-3304.
Web site: http://www.cbc-radio.com
Profile: KQBB-FM is a commercial station owned by Center Broadcasting Company Inc. The format of the station is country. KQBB-FM broadcasts to the Center, TX area at 100.5 FM.
FM RADIO STATION

KQBK-FM 41126

Owner: Pharis Broadcasting Inc.
Editorial: 321 N Greenwood Ave Ste 201, Fort Smith, Arkansas 72901-3453 **Tel:** 1 479 288-1047.
Web site: http://www.kool1047fm.com
Profile: KQBK-FM is a commercial station owned by Pharis Broadcasting Inc. The format of the station is oldies. KQBK-FM broadcasts to the Fort Smith, AR area at 104.7 FM.
FM RADIO STATION

KQBL-FM 44723

Owner: FM Radio Co LLC
Editorial: 5660 E Franklin Rd Ste 200, Nampa, Idaho 83687-5133 **Tel:** 1 208 465-9966.
Web site: http://www.boisebull.com
Profile: KQBL-FM is a commercial station owned by FM Radio Co LLC. The format of the station is contemporary country music. KDBI-FM broadcasts to the Nampa, ID, area at 101.9 FM.
FM RADIO STATION

KQBO-FM 39597

Owner: Sound Investments Unlimited
Editorial: 102 Kctm Fm 103 Rd, Rio Grande City, Texas 78582-9670 **Tel:** 1 956 487-8224.
Profile: KQBO-FM is a commercial station owned by Sound Investments Unlimited. The format of the station is Hispanic. KQBO-FM broadcasts to the Rio Grande City, TX area at 107.5 FM.
FM RADIO STATION

KQBR-FM 42311

Owner: Townsquare Media, LLC
Editorial: 4413 82nd St Ste 300, Lubbock, Texas 79424-3366 **Tel:** 1 806 798-7078.
Web site: http://lonestar995fm.com
Profile: KQBR-FM is a commercial station owned by Townsquare Media, LLC. The format of the station is contemporary country. KQBR-FM broadcasts to the Lubbock, TX area at 99.5 FM.
FM RADIO STATION

KQBT-FM 39755

Owner: iHeartMedia Inc.
Editorial: 2000 West Loop S Ste 300, Houston, Texas 77027-3510 **Tel:** 1 713 212-8000.
Web site: http://937thebeathouston.iheart.com
Profile: KQBT-FM is a commercial station owned by iHeartMedia Inc. The format of the station is urban contemporary. KQBT-FM broadcasts to the Houston area at 93.7 FM.
FM RADIO STATION

KQBU-AM 37200

Owner: Univision Communications Inc.
Editorial: 2211 E Missouri Ave Ste 300, El Paso, Texas 79903-3837 **Tel:** 1 915 544-9797.
Web site: http://univisionamerica.univision.com
Profile: KQBU-AM is a commercial station owned by Univision Communications Inc. The format of the station is Hispanic news and talk. KQBU-AM broadcasts to the El Paso, TX area at 920 AM.
AM RADIO STATION

KQBU-FM 41590

Owner: Univision Communications Inc.
Editorial: 5100 Southwest Fwy, Houston, Texas 77056-7308 **Tel:** 1 713 965-2400.
Web site: http://www.univision.com/houston/kqbu
Profile: KQBU-FM is a commercial station owned by Univision Communications Inc. The format of the station is regional Mexican. KQBU-FM broadcasts to the Houston area at 93.3 FM.
FM RADIO STATION

KQBZ-FM 45861

Owner: Wendlee Broadcasting
Editorial: 600 Fisk Ave, Brownwood, Texas 76801 **Tel:** 1 325 646-3535.
Email: breeze@wendlee.com
Web site: http://www.kqbz-fm.com
Profile: KQBZ-FM is a commercial station owned by Wendlee Broadcasting. The format of the station is hot adult contemporary. KQBZ-FM broadcasts to the Brownwood, TX area at 96.9 FM.
FM RADIO STATION

KQCB-FM 81145

Owner: Calcomm Stations Oregon LLC
Editorial: 615 Broadway St, Ste 222, Seaside, Oregon 97138 **Tel:** 1 503 738-8668.
Web site: http://www.musicmatters949.com
Profile: KQCB-FM is a commercial station owned by Calcomm Stations Oregon LLC. The format of the station is hot adult contemporary music. KQCB-FM broadcasts to the Seaside, OR area at 94.9 FM.
FM RADIO STATION

KQCH-FM 72923

Owner: E.W. Scripps Co.
Editorial: 10714 Mockingbird Dr, Omaha, Nebraska 68127-1942 **Tel:** 1 402 592-5300.
Email: win@channel941.com
Web site: http://www.channel941.com
Profile: KQCH-FM is a commercial station owned E.W. Scripps Co. The format of the station is Top 40. KQCH-FM broadcasts to the Omaha, NE area at 94.1 FM.
FM RADIO STATION

KQCL-FM 44617

Owner: Townsquare Media, LLC
Editorial: 601 Central Ave N, Faribault, Minnesota 55021-4307 **Tel:** 1 507 334-0061.
Web site: http://www.power96radio.com
Profile: KQCL-FM is a commercial station owned by Townsquare Media, LLC. The format of the station is classic rock. KQCL-FM broadcasts to the Faribault, MN area at 95.9 FM.
FM RADIO STATION

KQCM-FM 44031

Owner: S & H Broadcasting L.L.C.
Editorial: 12370 Hesperia Rd Ste 16, Victorville, California 92395-5808 **Tel:** 1 760 241-1313.
Web site: http://www.kq955.com/main
Profile: KQCM-FM is a commercial station owned by S & H Broadcasting L.L.C. The format of the station is CHR. KQCM-FM broadcasts to the Victorville, CA area at 105.3 FM.
FM RADIO STATION

KQCR-FM 74128

Owner: CD Broadcasting Inc.
Editorial: 1509 4th St NE, Hampton, Iowa 50441-1106 **Tel:** 1 641 456-5656.
Email: klmj@klmj.com
Web site: http://www.radioonthego.com
Profile: KQCR-FM is a commercial station owned by CD Broadcasting Inc. The station's format is adult contemporary music. KQCR-FM broadcasts to the Parkersburg, IA area at 98.9 FM.
FM RADIO STATION

KQCS-FM 46389

Owner: Townsquare Media
Editorial: 1229 Brady St, Davenport, Iowa 52803-4616 **Tel:** 1 563 326-2541.
Web site: http://www.espn935.com
Profile: KQCS-FM is a commercial station owned by Townsquare Media. The target audience of the station is adults, ages 18 to 34. The station is aired locally on 93.5 FM. The format of the station is Classic Hits. KQCS-FM's tagline is "Star 93.5."
FM RADIO STATION

KQCV-AM 39473

Owner: Bott Broadcasting Co.
Editorial: 1919 N Broadway Ave, Oklahoma City, Oklahoma 73103 **Tel:** 1 405 521-0800.
Email: kqcv@bottradionetwork.com
Web site: http://www.bottradionetwork.com
Profile: KQCV-AM is a commercial station owned by Bott Broadcasting Co. The format of the station is Christian and religious programming. KQCV-AM broadcasts to the Oklahoma City area at 800 AM.
AM RADIO STATION

KQCV-FM 46862

Owner: Bott Broadcasting Co.
Editorial: 1919 N Broadway Ave, Oklahoma City, Oklahoma 73103-4407 **Tel:** 1 405 521-0800.
Email: kqcv@bottradionetwork.com
Web site: http://www.bottradionetwork.com
Profile: KQCV-FM is a commercial station owned by Bott Broadcasting Co. The format for the station is religious and Christian programming. KQCV-FM broadcasts to the Oklahoma City area at 95.1 FM.
FM RADIO STATION

KQDI-AM 38432

Owner: Star Radio Corporation
Editorial: 1300 Central Ave W, Great Falls, Montana 59404-3971 **Tel:** 1 406 761-2800.
Email: audiogf@staradio.com
Web site: http://www.newstalk1450.com
Profile: KQDI-AM is a commercial station owned by Fisher Communications, Inc. The format for the station is news and talk. KQDI-AM broadcasts to the Great Falls, MT area at 1450 AM.
AM RADIO STATION

KQDI-FM 45800

Owner: Star Radio Corporation
Editorial: 1300 Central Ave W, Great Falls, Montana 59404-3971 **Tel:** 1 406 761-2800.
Email: audiogf@staradio.com
Web site: http://www.q106rocks.com
Profile: KQDI-FM is a commercial station owned by Fisher Communications, Inc. The format for the station is classic rock. KQDI-FM broadcasts to the Great Falls, MT area at 106.1 FM.
FM RADIO STATION

KQDJ-AM 38756

Owner: Ingstad Family Media
Editorial: 2625 8th Ave SW, Jamestown, North Dakota 58401-6621 **Tel:** 1 701 252-1400.
Email: news@newsdakota.com
Web site: http://www.newsdakota.com
Profile: KQDJ-AM is a commercial station owned by Ingstad Family Media. The format of the station is country. KQDJ-AM broadcasts to the Jamestown, ND area at 1400 AM.
AM RADIO STATION

KQDJ-FM 45794

Owner: Ingstad Family Media
Editorial: 2625 8Th Ave Sw, Jamestown, North Dakota 58401-6621 **Tel:** 1 701 252-1400.
Email: bigdog@daktel.com
Web site: http://www.newsdakota.com
Profile: KQDJ-FM is a commercial station owned by Ingstad Family Media. The format of the station is hot adult contemporary music. KQDJ-FM broadcasts to the Jamestown, ND area at 101.1 FM.
FM RADIO STATION

KQDL-FM 612327

Owner: CSN International
Tel: 1 800 357-4226.
Web site: http://www.csnradio.com
Profile: KQDL-FM is a non-commercial station owned by CSN International. The format of the station is religious. KQDL-FM broadcasts to Portland, OR and surrounding areas at 90.1 FM.
FM RADIO STATION

KQDR-FM 831262

Owner: Prophecy Media Group, LLC (dba Waco Entertainment Group, LLC)
Editorial: 900 Pecan Grove Rd E, Sherman, Texas 75090-1770 **Tel:** 1 254 868-1073.
Web site: http://1073docfm.com
Profile: KQDR-FM is a commercial station owned by Prophecy Media Group, LLC. The format of the station is Top 40/CHR. KQDR-FM broadcasts to the Sherman-Denison, TX area.
FM RADIO STATION

KQDS-AM 38980

Owner: Red Rock Radio Corp.
Editorial: 807 W 37th St, Hibbing, Minnesota 55746-2839 **Tel:** 1 218 722-4321.
Web site: http://95kqds.com
Profile: KQDS-AM is a commercial station owned by Red Rock Radio Corp. The format of the station is sports. KQDS-AM broadcasts to the Duluth, MN area at 1490 AM.
AM RADIO STATION

KQDS-FM 46338

Owner: Midwest Communications Inc.
Editorial: 11 E Superior St Ste 380, Duluth, Minnesota 55802-3016 **Tel:** 1 218 722-4321.
Web site: http://95kqds.com
Profile: KQDS-FM is a commercial station owned by Midwest Communications Inc.. The format of the station is classic rock music. KQDS-FM broadcasts to the Duluth, MN area at 94.9 FM.
FM RADIO STATION

KQDY-FM 44231

Owner: iHeartMedia Inc.
Editorial: 3500 E Rosser Ave, Bismarck, North Dakota 58501-3376 **Tel:** 1 701 255-1234.
Web site: http://kqdy.iheart.com
Profile: KQDY-FM is a commercial station owned by iHeartMedia Inc. The format of the station is contemporary country music. KQDY-FM broadcasts to the Bismarck, ND area at 94.5 FM.
FM RADIO STATION

KQED-FM 39856

Owner: KQED, Inc.
Editorial: 2601 Mariposa St, San Francisco, California 94110-1426 **Tel:** 1 415 553-2129.
Email: assignmentdesk@kqed.org
Web site: http://www.kqed.org
Profile: KQED-FM is a non-commercial station owned by Northern California Public Broadcasting. The format of the station is news and talk. KQED-FM broadcasts to the San Francisco area at 88.5 FM.
FM RADIO STATION

KQEG-FM 41142

Owner: Mississippi Valley Broadcasters LLC
Editorial: 1407 2nd Ave N, Onalaska, Wisconsin 54650 **Tel:** 1 608 782-8335.
Email: news@lacrosseradiogroup.net
Web site: http://www.eagle1027.com
FM RADIO STATION

KQEI-FM 153495

Owner: KQED Inc.
Editorial: 925 L St, Sacramento, California 95814-3702 **Tel:** 1 415 553-2261.
Email: fm@kqed.org
Web site: http://www.kqed.org
FM RADIO STATION

KQEL-FM 395351

Owner: Burt Broadcasting Inc.
Editorial: 501 S Florida Ave, Alamogordo, New Mexico 88310-6018 **Tel:** 1 575 434-1414.
Email: burtbroadcasting@bbiradio.net
Web site: http://www.1079coolfm.net
Profile: KQEL-FM is a commercial station owned by Burt Broadcasting Inc. The format of the station is classic hits music. KQEL-FM broadcasts to the Alamogordo, NM area at 107.9 FM.
FM RADIO STATION

KQEN-AM 38374

Owner: Brooke Communications Inc.
Editorial: 1445 W Harvard Ave, Roseburg, Oregon 97471-2839 **Tel:** 1 541 672-6641.
Web site: http://www.541radio.com
Profile: KQEN-AM is a commercial station owned by Brooke Communications Inc. The format of the station is news, and talk. KQEN-AM broadcasts to the Roseburg, OR area at 1240 AM.
AM RADIO STATION

KQEO-FM 153419

Owner: Sand Hill Media
Editorial: 854 Lindsay Blvd, Idaho Falls, Idaho 83402-1820 **Tel:** 1 208 522-1101.
Email: contactus@arrow107.com
Web site: http://www.arrow107.com
Profile: KQEO-FM is a commercial station owned by Sand Hill Media. The format of the station is classic hits. KQEO-FM broadcasts to the Idaho Falls, ID area at 107.1 FM.
FM RADIO STATION

KQEQ-AM 36188

Owner: Spice Radio
Editorial: 139 W Olive Ave, Fresno, California 93728-3035
Web site: http://www.spiceradioam.com/
Profile: KQEQ-AM is a commercial radio station owned by Spice Radio. The format of the station is southern gospel. KQEQ-AM broadcasts to the Fresno, CA, area at 1210 AM.
AM RADIO STATION

KQEW-FM 46165

Owner: Dallas Properties
Editorial: 303 N Spring St, Fordyce, Arkansas 71742-3317 **Tel:** 1 870 352-7137.
Email: kbjt@windstream.net
Web site: http://www.kbjtkq.com
Profile: KQEW-FM is a commercial station owned by Dallas Properties. The format of the station is news, talk and sports programming. KQEW-FM broadcasts to the Fordyce, AR area at 102.3 FM.
FM RADIO STATION

KQFC-FM 44834

Owner: Cumulus Media Inc
Editorial: 1419 W Bannock St, Boise, Idaho 83702-5234 **Tel:** 1 208 336-3670.
Email: hank@nashfm979.com
Web site: http://www.98kqfc.com
Profile: KQFC-FM is a commercial station owned by Cumulus Media Inc. The format of the station is country. KQFC-FM broadcasts to the Boise, ID area at 97.9 FM.
FM RADIO STATION

KQFM-FM 44835

Owner: West End Radio LLC
Editorial: 80404 Cooney Ln, Hermiston, Oregon 97838-6613 **Tel:** 1 541 567-6500.
Web site: http://www.gohermiston.com
Profile: KQFM-FM is a commercial station owned by West End Radio LLC. The format of the station is Adult Contemporary. KQFM-FM broadcasts to the Hermiston, OR area at 93.7 FM.
FM RADIO STATION

KQFO-FM 43866

Owner: Alexandra Communications
Editorial: 45 S Campbell Rd, Walla Walla, Washington 99362-9597 **Tel:** 1 509 527-1000.
Web site: http://www.theoasis.fm
Profile: KQFO-FM is a commercial station owned by Alexandra Communications. The format of the station is adult hits. KQFO-FM broadcasts to the Tri-Cities, WA area at 100.1 FM.
FM RADIO STATION

KQFX-FM 41990

Owner: My Home Team Media
Editorial: 2505 Lakeview Dr Ste 302B, Amarillo, Texas 79109-1527 **Tel:** 1 806 355-1044.
Web site: http://wild1043fm.com
Profile: KQFX-FM is a commercial station owned by My Home Team Media. The format of the station is Party Hits. KQFX-FM broadcasts to the Amarillo, TX area at 104.3 FM.
FM RADIO STATION

KQFZ-FM 845402

Owner: Templo De Dios, Inc.
Tel: 1 214 643-2569.
Web site: http://www.radiofortaleza.net
Profile: KQFZ-FM is a non-commercial station owned by Templo De Dios, Inc. The format of the station is Hispanic Christian talk and music programming. The station broadcasts to the Greater Dallas, TX area of Sulphur Springs at a frequency of 91.9 FM.
FM RADIO STATION

KQGC-FM 358697

Owner: Nueva Vida
Editorial: 4101 Barbara Loop SE Ste A, Rio Rancho, New Mexico 87124-1011 **Tel:** 1 800 260-5676.
Email: info@nuevavida.com
Web site: http://nuevavida.com
Profile: KQGC-FM is a non-commercial station owned by Nueva Vida Network. The format of the station is Hispanic religious. KQGC-FM broadcasts to the Rio Rancho, NM area at 91.1 FM.
FM RADIO STATION

KQGO-FM 42588

Owner: Go Media
Editorial: 420 N 5th St Ste 150, Minneapolis, Minnesota 55401-2380 **Tel:** 1 612 659-4848.
Email: contact@gomn.com
Web site: http://www.gomn.com/radio
Profile: KQGO is an Alternative Rock-formatted broadcast radio station licensed to Edina, Minnesota, owned and operated by Go Media. It broadcasts to the Twin Cities area at 96.3 FM.
FM RADIO STATION

KQHK-FM 550509
Owner: Armada Media Corp.
Editorial: 1811 W O St, McCook, Nebraska 69001
Tel: 1 308 345-5400.
Email: openline@highplainsradio.net
Web site: http://www.plainsreporter.com
Profile: KQHK-FM is a commercial station owned by Armada Media Corp. The format of the station is classic rock. KQHK-FM broadcasts to the McCook, NE area at 103.9 FM.
FM RADIO STATION

KQHN-FM 73316
Owner: Cumulus Media Inc.
Editorial: 270 Plaza Loop, Cumulus Broadcast Center, Bossier City, Louisiana 71111-4389
Tel: 1 318 549-8500.
Web site: http://i973hits.com
Profile: KQHN-FM is a commercial station owned by Cumulus Media Inc. The format of the station is CHR music. KQHN-FM broadcasts to the Shreveport, LA area at 97.3 FM.
FM RADIO STATION

KQHR-FM 87692
Owner: All Classical Public Media, Inc.
Editorial: 211 SE Caruthers St Ste 200, Portland, Oregon 97214-4502 **Tel:** 1 503 943-5828.
Email: music.info@allclassical.org
Web site: http://www.allclassical.org
Profile: KQHR-FM is a non-commercial station owned by All Classical Public Media, Inc. The format of the station is classical music. KQHR-FM broadcasts to Portland, OR and surrounding areas at 88.1 FM.
FM RADIO STATION

KQHT-FM 41143
Owner: iHeartMedia Inc.
Editorial: 505 University Ave, Grand Forks, North Dakota 58203-3545 **Tel:** 1 701 746-1417.
Web site: http://961thefox.iheart.com
Profile: KQHT-FM is a commercial station owned by iHeartMedia Inc. The station's format is classic hits music. KQHT-FM broadcasts to the Grand Forks, ND area at 96.1 FM.
FM RADIO STATION

KQIB-FM 44245
Owner: JDC Radio Inc.
Editorial: 108 N Broadway St, Broken Bow, Oklahoma 74728-3934 **Tel:** 1 580 584-3388.
Email: kkbi@pine-net.com
Web site: http://www.theq102.com
Profile: KQIB-FM is a commercial station owned by JDC Radio Inc. The format of the station is hot adult contemporary. KQIB-FM broadcasts to the Broken Bow, OK area at 102.9 FM.
FM RADIO STATION

KQIC-FM 44836
Owner: Lakeland Broadcasting
Editorial: 1340 NW 7th St, Willmar, Minnesota 56201
Tel: 1 320 235-1340.
Web site: http://www.yourq102.com
Profile: KQIC-FM is a commercial station owned by Lakeland Broadcasting. The format of the station is hot adult contemporary. KQIC-FM broadcasts in the Willmar, MN area at 102.5 FM.
FM RADIO STATION

KQID-FM 46637
Owner: Cenla Broadcasting Inc.
Editorial: 1115 Texas Ave, Alexandria, Louisiana 71301 **Tel:** 1 318 445-1234.
Web site: http://www.q93fm.com
Profile: KQID-FM is a commercial station owned by Cenla Broadcasting Inc. The format of the station is Top 40/CHR music. KQID-FM broadcasts in the Alexandria, LA area at 93.1 FM.
FM RADIO STATION

KQIE-FM 44969
Owner: LC Media, LP
Editorial: 242 E Airport Dr Ste 106, San Bernardino, California 92408-3408 **Tel:** 1 909 693-4929.
Web site: http://oldschool1047.com
Profile: KQIE-FM is a commercial station owned by LC Media, LP. The format of the station is rhythmic adult contemporary. KQIE-FM broadcasts to the Redlands, CA area at 104.7 FM.
FM RADIO STATION

KQIZ-FM 39858
Owner: Cumulus Media Inc.
Editorial: 301 S Polk St, Ste 100, Amarillo, Texas 79101 **Tel:** 1 806 342-5200.
Web site: http://www.931thebeat.com
Profile: KQIZ-FM is a commercial station owned by Cumulus Media Inc. The format of the station features hip-hop and R&B music programming. KQIZ-FM broadcasts to the Amarillo, TX area at a frequency of 93.1 FM.
FM RADIO STATION

KQJZ-AM 560847
Owner: Anderson Radio Broadcasting Inc.
Editorial: 36581 N Reservoir Rd, Polson, Montana 59860-8471 **Tel:** 1 406 883-5255.
Email: news@andersonbroadcasting.com
Web site: http://www.1340thelounge.com
Profile: KQJZ-AM is a commercial station owned by Anderson Radio Broadcasting Inc. The format of the station is adult standards. KQJZ-FM broadcasts to the Kalispell, MT area at a frequency of 1340 AM.
AM RADIO STATION

KQKI-FM 42937
Owner: Cook(Paul J.)
Editorial: 107 Pluto St, Morgan City, Louisiana 70380-5138 **Tel:** 1 985 395-2853.
Email: news@kqki.com
Web site: http://www.kqki.com
Profile: KQKI-FM is a commercial station owned by Paul J. Cook. The format of the station is country. KQKI-FM broadcasts to the Morgan City, LA area at 95.3 FM.
FM RADIO STATION

KQKK-FM 44443
Owner: De La Hunt Broadcasting
Editorial: Highway 34 West, Walker, Minnesota 56484
Tel: 1 218 547-4000.
Email: kqkkkakk@eot.com
Web site: http://www.kkradionetwork.com
Profile: KQKK-FM is a commercial station owned by De La Hunt Broadcasting. The format of the station is aduly contemporary music. KQKK-FM broadcasts to the Walker, MN area at 101.9 FM.
FM RADIO STATION

KQKQ-FM 46303
Owner: NRG Media LLC
Editorial: 5011 Capitol Ave, Omaha, Nebraska 68132-2921 **Tel:** 1 402 342-2000.
Web site: http://www.q985fm.com
Profile: KQKQ-FM is a commercial station owned by NRG Media LLC. The format of the station is hot adult contemporary music. KQKQ-FM broadcasts to the Omaha, NE area at 98.5 FM.
FM RADIO STATION

KQKS-FM 44883
Owner: Entercom Communications Corp.
Editorial: 4700 S Syracuse St Ste 1050, Denver, Colorado 80237-2713 **Tel:** 1 303 967-2700.
Web site: http://www.ks1075.com
Profile: KQKS-FM is a commercial station owned by Entercom Communications Corp. The format of the station is rhythmic contemporary music. KQKS-FM broadcasts to the Denver area at 107.5 FM.
FM RADIO STATION

KQKX-FM 44643
Owner: WJAG Inc.
Editorial: 309 Braasch Ave, Norfolk, Nebraska 68701-4113 **Tel:** 1 402 371-0780.
Web site: http://www.106kix.com
Profile: KQKX-FM is a commercial station owned by WJAG Inc. The format of the station is country. KQKX-FM broadcasts to the Norfolk, NE area at 106.7 FM.
FM RADIO STATION

KQKY-FM 44837
Owner: NRG Media LLC
Editorial: 2223 Central Ave, Kearney, Nebraska 68847
Tel: 1 308 698-2100.
Email: hits106@gmail.com
Web site: http://www.kqky.com
Profile: KQKY-FM is a commercial station owned by NRG Media LLC. The format of the station is Top 40/CHR music. KQKY-FM broadcasts to the Kearney, NE area at 105.9 FM.
FM RADIO STATION

KQLA-FM 41144
Owner: Eagle Communications, Inc
Editorial: US Highway 77 & W Ash St, Junction City, Kansas 66441 **Tel:** 1 785 762-5525.
Web site: http://www.qcountry1035.com
Profile: KQLA-FM is a commercial station owned by Platinum Broadcasting, Inc. The format of the station is country. KQLA-FM broadcasts to the Junction City, KS area at 103.5 FM.
FM RADIO STATION

KQLB-FM 46592
Owner: VLB Broadcasting Inc.
Editorial: 401 Pacheco Blvd, Los Banos, California 93635 **Tel:** 1 209 827-0123.
Email: pr@kqlb.com
Web site: http://www.kqlb.com
Profile: KQLB-FM is a commercial station owned by VLB Broadcasting Inc. The format of the station is regional Mexican music. KQLB-FM broadcasts in the Los Banos, CA area at 106.9 FM.
FM RADIO STATION

KQLK-FM 43825
Owner: Cumulus Media Inc.
Editorial: 425 Broad St, Lake Charles, Louisiana 70601-4225 **Tel:** 1 337 439-3300.
Web site: http://www.979nashicon.com
Profile: KQLK-FM is a commercial station owned by Cumulus Media Inc. The format of the station is country music. KQLK-FM broadcasts in the Lake Charles, LA area at 97.9 FM.
FM RADIO STATION

KQLL-AM 35056
Owner: Summit Media
Editorial: 150 Spectrum Blvd, Las Vegas, Nevada 89101-4860 **Tel:** 1 702 258-0285.
Web site: http://www.kool1023.com
Profile: KQLL-AM is a commercial station owned by Summit Media (dba S & R Broadcasting, Inc.). The format of the station is Oldies. KQLL-AM broadcasts to the Las Vegas area at 1280 AM.
AM RADIO STATION

KQLM-FM 74173
Owner: Stellar Media, Inc.
Editorial: 1319 S Crane Ave, Odessa, Texas 79763-4755 **Tel:** 1 432 333-1227.
Web site: http://www.q108fm.com
Profile: KQLM-FM is a commercial station owned by Stellar Media, Inc. The format for the station is Spanish language music. The station broadcasts to the Odessa-Midland, Texas at 107.9 FM.
FM RADIO STATION

KQLT-FM 46855
Owner: Mount Rushmore Broadcasting Inc.
Editorial: 218 N Wolcott St, Casper, Wyoming 82601
Tel: 1 307 265-1984.
Profile: KQLT-FM is a commercial station owned by Mount Rushmore Broadcasting Inc. The format for the station is country. KQLT-FM broadcasts to the Casper, WY area at 103.7 FM.
FM RADIO STATION

KQLX-AM 38473
Owner: SMAHH Communications, Inc.
Editorial: 64 Broadway N, Fargo, North Dakota 58102-4934 **Tel:** 1 701 683-5287.
Email: news@gpimonline.com
Web site: http://www.agnews890.com
Profile: KQLX-AM is a commercial station owned by SMAHH Communications, Inc. The format of the station is news. KQLX-AM broadcasts to the Lisbon, ND area at 890 AM.
AM RADIO STATION

KQLX-FM 45838
Owner: SMAHH Communications, Inc.
Editorial: 64 Broadway N, Fargo, North Dakota 58102-4934 **Tel:** 1 701 356-1156.
Email: thunderstudio@thunder1061.com
Web site: http://www.thunder1061.com
Profile: KQLX-FM is a commercial station owned by SMAHH Communications, Inc. The format of the station is classic country. KQLX-FM broadcasts to the Fargo, ND area at 106.1 FM.
FM RADIO STATION

KQMA-FM 44839
Owner: S-Y Communications
Editorial: 205 F St, Phillipsburg, Kansas 67661
Tel: 1 785 543-2151.
Email: radio@kkankqma.com
Web site: http://www.kkankqma.com
Profile: KQMA-FM is a commercial station owned by S-Y Communications. The format of the station is hot adult contemporary music and contemporary country music. KQMA-FM broadcasts to the Phillipsburg, KS area at 92.5 FM.
FM RADIO STATION

KQMG-AM 37426
Owner: KM Communications Inc.
Editorial: 1812 3rd Ave SE, Independence, Iowa 50644-9884 **Tel:** 1 319 332-1812.
Email: kqmgfm@gmail.com
Profile: KQMG-AM is a commercial station owned by KM Communications Inc. The format of the station is classic hits. KQMG-AM broadcasts to the Independence, IA area at 1220 AM.
AM RADIO STATION

KQMG-FM 44814
Owner: KM Communications Inc.
Editorial: 1812 3rd Ave SE, Independence, Iowa 50644-9884 **Tel:** 1 319 332-1812.
Email: kqmgfm@gmail.com
Profile: KQMG-FM is a commercial station owned by KM Communications Inc. The format of the station is classic hits. KQMG-FM broadcasts to the Independence, IA area at 95.3 FM.
FM RADIO STATION

KQMN-FM 42454
Owner: Minnesota Public Radio
Editorial: 901 8th St S, Moorhead, Minnesota 56562
Tel: 1 218 2847-0666.
Email: newsroom@mpr.org
Web site: http://minnesota.publicradio.org/radio/stations/kntnkqmn
Profile: KQMN-FM is a non-commercial station owned by Minnesota Public Radio. The format of the station is classical music. KQMN-FM broadcasts to the Thief River Falls, MN area at 91.5 FM.
FM RADIO STATION

KQMO-FM 151161
Owner: Falcon Broadcasting Inc.
Editorial: 126 S Jefferson Ave, Aurora, Missouri 65605-1635 **Tel:** 1 417 678-0416.
Email: kqmo@radiotalon.com
Web site: http://www.radiotalon.com
Profile: KQMO-FM is a commercial station owned by Falcon Broadcasting Inc. The format of the station is regional Mexican music. KQMO-FM broadcasts to the Springfield, MO area at 97.7 FM.
FM RADIO STATION

KQMQ-FM 44840
Owner: Ohana Broadcast Company LLC
Editorial: 1000 Bishop St Ste 200, Honolulu, Hawaii 96813-4203 **Tel:** 1 808 947-1500.
Web site: http://931dapaina.com
Profile: KQMQ-FM is a commercial station owned by Ohana Broadcast Company LLC. The format of the station is reggae. KQMQ-FM broadcasts to Honolulu at 93.1 FM.
FM RADIO STATION

KQMR-FM 40925
Owner: Univision Communications Inc.
Editorial: 4745 N 7th St, Phoenix, Arizona 85014-3665
Tel: 1 602 308-7900.
Web site: http://1063masvariedad.univision.com
Profile: KQMR-FM is a commercial station owned by Univision Communications Inc. The format of the station is Latin Pop. KQMR-FM broadcasts to the Phoenix area on 100.3 FM.
FM RADIO STATION

KQMS-AM 38468
Owner: Mapleton of Redding, LLC
Editorial: 3360 Alta Mesa Dr, Redding, California 96002-2831 **Tel:** 1 530 226-9500.
Email: steve@kqms.com
Web site: http://www.kqms.com
Profile: KQMS-AM is a commercial station owned by Mapleton of Redding, LLC. The format of the station is news and talk programming. KQMS-AM broadcasts to the Redding, CA area at 1400 AM.
AM RADIO STATION

KQMT-FM 40007
Owner: Entercom Communications Corp.
Editorial: 4700 S Syracuse St, Ste 1050, Denver, Colorado 80237 **Tel:** 1 303 967-2700.
Web site: http://www.995themountain.com
Profile: KQMT-FM is a commercial station that is owned by Entercom Communications Corp. The format of the station is classic rock. KQMT-FM broadcasts to the Denver area at 99.5 FM.
FM RADIO STATION

KQMV-FM 45996
Owner: Hubbard Radio, LLC
Editorial: 3650 131st Ave SE Ste 550, Bellevue, Washington 98006-1334 **Tel:** 1 425 653-9462.
Email: info@movin925.com
Web site: http://www.movin925.com
Profile: KQMV-FM is a commercial station owned by Hubbard Radio, LLC. The format of the station is Top 40. KQMV-FM broadcasts to the Seattle area at 92.5 FM.
FM RADIO STATION

KQNA-AM 39431
Owner: Prescott Valley Broadcasting Co. Inc.
Editorial: 3755 Karicio Ln, Prescott, Arizona 86303-6836 **Tel:** 1 928 445-8289.
Email: kppv@cableone.net
Web site: http://www.kqna.com
Profile: KQNA-AM is a commercial station owned by Prescott Valley Broadcasting Co. Inc. The format of the station is news and talk. KQNA-AM broadcasts to the Prescott, AZ area at 1130 AM.
AM RADIO STATION

KQNG-AM 35100
Owner: Ohana Broadcasting, LLC
Editorial: 4271 Halenani St, Lihue, Hawaii 96766-1312
Tel: 1 808 245-9527.
Email: kong@kongradio.com
Web site: http://www.kuai720am.com
Profile: KQNG-AM is a commercial station owned by Ohana Broadcasting, LLC. The format of the station is contemporary country music. KUAI-AM broadcasts to the Kauai, HI area at 720 AM.
AM RADIO STATION

KQNG-AM 37451
Owner: Ohana Broadcasting, LLC
Editorial: 4271 Halenani St, Lihue, Hawaii 96766
Tel: 1 808 245-9527.
Email: kong@kongradio.com
Web site: http://www.kongradio.com
Profile: KQNG-AM is a commercial radio station that is owned by Ohana Broadcasting, LLC. The format of the station is news, sports and talk. KQNG-AM broadcasts to the Lihue, HI area at 570 AM.
AM RADIO STATION

KQNG-FM 45699
Owner: Ohana Broadcast Company
Editorial: 4271 Halenani St, Lihue, Hawaii 96766-1312
Tel: 1 808 245-9527.
Email: kong@kongradio.com
Web site: http://www.kongradio.com
Profile: KQNG-FM is a commercial station owned by Ohana Broadcast Company. The format of the station is Top 40/CHR. KQNG-FM broadcasts to the Lihue, HI area at 93.5 FM.
FM RADIO STATION

KQNK-AM 39223
Owner: Dierking Communications
Editorial: 17038 Kqnk Rd, Norton, Kansas 67654-5569 **Tel:** 1 785 877-3378.
Email: kqnk@ruraltel.net
Web site: http://www.kqnk.com
Profile: KQNK-AM is a commercial station owned by Dierking Communications. The format of the station is classic rock music. KQNK-AM broadcasts to the Norton, KS area at 1530 AM.
AM RADIO STATION

KQNK-FM 46577
Owner: Dierking Communications
Editorial: 17038 Kqnk Rd, Norton, Kansas 67654-5569 **Tel:** 1 785 877-3378.
Email: kqnk@ruraltel.net
Web site: http://www.kqnk.com
Profile: KQNK-FM is a commercial station owned by Dierking Communications. The format of the station is classic hits music. KQNK-FM broadcasts to the Norton, KS area at 106.7 FM.
FM RADIO STATION

KQNM-AM 594633
Owner: Cibula Radio Company
Editorial: 809 Wellesley Dr NE, Albuquerque, New Mexico 87106-1936 Tel: 1 505 899-5029.
Profile: KQNM-AM is a commerical station owned by Cibula Radio Company. (Whitman, Martha). The format of the station is oldies. KQNM-AM can be heard in the Grants, NM area at 1100 AM.
AM RADIO STATION

KQNM-AM 603282
Owner: Vanguard Media, LLC
Editorial: 1213 San Pedro Dr NE, Albuquerque, New Mexico 87110-6725 Tel: 1 505 899-5029.
Web site: http://koolnm.com
Profile: KQNM-AM is a commercial station owned by Vanguard Media, LLC. The format of the station is classic hits. KQNM-AM broadcasts to the Albuquerque, NM area at 1550 AM.
AM RADIO STATION

KQNT-AM 38323
Owner: iHeartMedia Inc.
Editorial: 808 E Sprague Ave, Spokane, Washington 99202-2126 Tel: 1 509 242-2400.
Web site: http://www.590kqnt.com
Profile: KQNT-AM is a commercial station owned by iHeartMedia Inc. The format of the station is news and talk. KQNT-AM broadcasts to the Spokane, WA area at 590 AM.
AM RADIO STATION

KQOB-FM 86008
Owner: Cumulus Media Inc
Editorial: 4045 NW 64th St Ste 600, Oklahoma City, Oklahoma 73116-2607 Tel: 1 405 460-2623.
Web site: http://www.fun969fm.com/
Profile: KQOB-FM is a commercial station owned by Cumulus Media Inc. The format is classic hits. KQOB-FM broadcasts to the Oklahoma City area at 96.9 FM.
FM RADIO STATION

KQOC-FM 588312
Owner: All Classical Public Media, Inc.
Editorial: 211 SE Caruthers St Ste 200, Portland, Oregon 97214-4502 Tel: 1 503 943-5828.
Email: music.info@allclassical.org
Web site: http://www.allclassical.org
Profile: KQOC-FM is a non-commercial station owned by All Classical Public Media, Inc. The format of the station is classical music. KQOC-FM broadcasts to Lincoln City, OR and surrounding areas.
FM RADIO STATION

KQOD-FM 39649
Owner: iHeartMedia Inc.
Editorial: 2121 Lancey Dr, Modesto, California 95355-3036 Tel: 1 209 551-1306.
Web site: http://mega100fm.iheart.com
Profile: KQOD-FM is a commercial station owned by iHeartMedia Inc. The format of the station is R&B oldies. The station broadcasts to the Modesto, CA area at 100.1 FM.
FM RADIO STATION

KQOH-FM 43509
Owner: Catholic Radio Network
Tel: 1 816 630-1090.
Email: info@thecatholicradionetwork.com
Web site: http://thecatholicradionetwork.com
Profile: KQOH-FM is a non-commercial station owned by Catholic Radio Network. The format of the station is Catholic radio programming. KQOH-FM broadcasts to the Marshfield, MO area at a frequency of 91.9 FM.
FM RADIO STATION

KQOR-FM 444847
Owner: Ouachita Broadcasting Inc.
Editorial: 1600 Reine St S, Mena, Arkansas 71953-3728 Tel: 1 479 394-1450.
Email: menaradio@aol.com
Profile: KQOR-FM is a commercial station owned by Ouachita Broadcasting Inc. The format for the station is oldies. KQOR-FM broadcasts to the Mena, AR area at 105.3 FM.
FM RADIO STATION

KQPM-FM 41159
Owner: Bicoastal Media LLC
Editorial: 140 N Main St, Lakeport, California 95453-4815 Tel: 1 707 263-6113.
Web site: http://www.kqpm.com
Profile: KQPM-FM is a commercial station owned by Bicoastal Media LLC. The format of the station is contemporary country. KQPM-FM broadcasts to the San Francisco area at 105.9 FM.
FM RADIO STATION

KQPN-AM 39514
Owner: Simmons Media Group
Editorial: 203 Beale St Ste 204, Memphis, Tennessee 38103-3727 Tel: 1 901 452-3094.
Web site: http://www.730amyahoosports.com
Profile: KQPN-AM is a commercial station owned by Simmons Media Group. The format of the station is sports. KQPN-AM broadcasts to the Memphis, TN area at 730 AM.
AM RADIO STATION

KQPR-FM 41771
Owner: Hometown Broadcasting, Inc.
Editorial: 109 E Clark St, Albert Lea, Minnesota 56007-2420 Tel: 1 507 373-9600.
Email: kqpr@power96rocker.com
Web site: http://www.power96rocker.com/

Profile: KQPR-FM is a commercial station owned by Hometown Broadcasting, Inc. The format of the station is classic rock. KQPR-FM broadcasts to the Rochester, MN - Mason City, IA area at 96.1 FM.
FM RADIO STATION

KQPT-FM 41176
Owner: Mapleton of Chico, LLC
Editorial: 1459 Humboldt Rd Ste D, Chico, California 95928-9100 Tel: 1 530 899-3600.
Web site: http://www.1075nowfm.com/
Profile: KQPT-FM is a commercial station owned by Mapleton of Chico, LLC. The format of the station is Top 40/CHR. KQPT-FM broadcasts to the Chico, CA area at 107.5 FM.
FM RADIO STATION

KQQF-FM 44841
Owner: SEK Media, Inc
Editorial: 306 W 8th St, Coffeyville, Kansas 67337-5829 Tel: 1 620 251-3800.
Email: news@kggfradio.com
Web site: http://kggfradio.com
Profile: KQQF-FM is a commercial station owned by SEK Media, Inc. The format of the station is Hot AC. KQQF-FM broadcasts to the Tulsa, OK area at 98.9 FM.
FM RADIO STATION

KQQK-FM 42405
Owner: Liberman Broadcasting Inc.
Editorial: 3000 Bering Dr, Houston, Texas 77057-5708 Tel: 1 713 315-3400.
Web site: http://www.elnorteenlinea.com
Profile: KQQK-FM is a commercial station owned by Liberman Broadcasting Inc. The format of the station is regional Mexican. KQQK-FM broadcasts to the Houston area at 107.9 FM.
FM RADIO STATION

KQQL-FM 41032
Owner: iHeartMedia Inc.
Editorial: 1600 Utica Ave S Ste 400, Saint Louis Park, Minnesota 55416-1480 Tel: 1 952 417-3000.
Web site: http://www.kool108.com
Profile: KQQL-FM is a commercial station owned by iHeart Media Inc. The format of the station is classic hits. KQQL-FM broadcasts to the Minneapolis area at 107.9 FM.
FM RADIO STATION

KQQQ-AM 37452
Owner: Radio Palouse Inc.
Editorial: 1101 Old Wawawai Rd, Pullman, Washington 99163-9002 Tel: 1 509 332-6551.
Email: news@pullmanradio.com
Profile: KQQQ-AM is a commercial station owned by Radio Palouse Inc. The format of the station is news, sports and talk. KQQQ-AM broadcasts to the Spokane, WA area at 1150 AM.
AM RADIO STATION

KQQZ-AM 83781
Owner: ShowClubs International, Inc.
Editorial: 6500 W Main St, Belleville, Illinois 62223-3700 Tel: 1 618 394-1430.
Email: info@kqqz1190am.com
Web site: http://www.kqqz1190am.com
Profile: KQQZ-AM is a commercial station owned by Entertainment Media Trust. The format of the station is classic country. KQQZ-AM broadcasts to the St. Louis area at 1190 AM.
AM RADIO STATION

KQRA-FM 86842
Owner: Midwest Family Stations
Editorial: 2453 E Elm St, Springfield, Missouri 65802-2868 Tel: 1 417 886-5677.
Email: info@q1021.fm
Web site: http://www.q1021.fm
Profile: KQRA-FM is a commercial station owned by Midwest Family Stations. The format of the station is rock alternative. KQRA-FM broadcasts in the Springfield, MO area at 102.1 FM.
FM RADIO STATION

KQRC-FM 39601
Owner: Entercom Communications Corp.
Editorial: 7000 Squibb Rd, Mission, Kansas 66202 Tel: 1 913 576-7989.
Email: kqrc@entercom.com
Web site: http://www.989therock.com
Profile: KQRC-FM is a commercial station owned by Entercom Communications Corp. The format for the station is rock music. KQRC-FM broadcasts to the Kansas City, MO area at 98.9 FM.
FM RADIO STATION

KQRK-FM 427159
Owner: Anderson Radio Broadcasting Inc.
Editorial: 36581 N Reservoir Rd, Polson, Montana 59860-8471 Tel: 1 406 883-5255.
Email: news@andersonbroadcasting.com
Web site: http://star92hits.com
Profile: KQRK-FM is a commercial station owned by Anderson Radio Broadcasting Inc. The format of the station is Top 40/CHR. KQRK-FM is licensed to Pablo, MT and broadcasts locally at 99.7 FM.
FM RADIO STATION

KQRN-FM 44844
Owner: Riverfront Broadcasting
Editorial: 319 N Main St, Mitchell, South Dakota 57301 Tel: 1 605 996-1073.
Email: kornnews@kornq107.com
Web site: http://www.q107radio.com
Profile: KQRN-FM is a commercial station owned by Riverfront Broadcasting. The format of the station is

hot adult contemporary music. KQRN-FM broadcasts to the Mitchell, SD, area at 107.3 FM.
FM RADIO STATION

KQRQ-FM 458795
Owner: Duhamel Broadcasting
Editorial: 518 Saint Joseph St, Rapid City, South Dakota 57701-2717 Tel: 1 605 342-2000.
Web site: http://www.q923radio.com
Profile: KQRQ-FM is a commercial station owned by Duhamel Broadcasting. The format of the station is classic hits. KQRQ-FM broadcasts to the Rapid City, SD area at a frequency of 92.3 FM.
FM RADIO STATION

KQRS-FM 44052
Owner: Cumulus Media Inc
Editorial: 2000 Elm St SE, Minneapolis, Minnesota 55414-2531 Tel: 1 612 617-4000.
Web site: http://www.92kqrs.com
Profile: KQRS-FM is a commercial station owned by Cumulus Media Inc. The format of the station is classic rock. KQRS-FM broadcasts to the Minneapolis area at 92.5 FM.
FM RADIO STATION

KQRT-FM 42466
Owner: Entravision Communications Corp.
Editorial: 500 Pilot Rd Ste D, Las Vegas, Nevada 89119-3624 Tel: 1 702 434-0015.
Email: jmonreal@entravision.com
Web site: http://www.tricolor1051.com
Profile: KQRT-FM is a commercial station owned by Entravision Communications Corp. The format of the station is Hispanic programming. KQRT-FM broadcasts to the Las Vegas, NV area at 105.1 FM.
FM RADIO STATION

KQRV-FM 43481
Owner: Toole(Robert Cummings)
Editorial: 302 Missouri Ave, Deer Lodge, Montana 59722-1077 Tel: 1 406 846-1100.
Email: bobsatriver@gmail.com
Profile: KQRV-FM is a commercial station owned by Robert Cummings Toole. The format of the station is news, sports and country. KQRV-FM broadcasts to the Deer Lodge, MT area at 96.9 FM.
FM RADIO STATION

KQRX-FM 42877
Owner: Brazos Communications West, LLC
Editorial: 3303 N Midkiff Rd Ste 115, Midland, Texas 79705-4860 Tel: 1 432 520-9510.
Web site: http://www.rock951online.com
Profile: KQRX-FM is a commercial station owned by Brazos Communications West, LLC. The format of the station is active rock. KQRX-FM broadcasts in the Midland, TX area at 95.1 FM.
FM RADIO STATION

KQSE-FM 471976
Owner: NRC Broadcasting Mountain Group
Tel: 1 970 949-0140.
Web site: http://alwaysmountaintime.com/kqse
Profile: KQSE-FM is a commercial station owned by NRC Broadcasting Mountain Group. The format of the station is Spanish Variety. KQSE-FM broadcasts to the Gypsum, Colorado area at a frequency of 102.5 FM.
FM RADIO STATION

KQSF-FM 217563
Owner: Midwest Communications
Editorial: 500 S Phillips Ave, Sioux Falls, South Dakota 57104-6825 Tel: 1 605 331-5350.
Web site: http://www.q957.com
Profile: KQSF-FM is a commercial station owned by Midwest Communications. The format of the station is oldies. KQSF-FM broadcasts to the Sioux Falls, SD area at 95.7 FM.
FM RADIO STATION

KQSK-FM 39859
Owner: Eagle Communications
Editorial: 331 Main St Ste C, Chadron, Nebraska 69337-2387 Tel: 1 308 432-2060.
Web site: http://www.doubleqcountry.com
Profile: KQSK-FM is a commercial station owned by Eagle Communications. The format of the station is country music. KQSK-FM broadcasts to the Chadron, NE area at 97.5 FM.
FM RADIO STATION

KQSM-FM 39545
Owner: Cumulus Media Inc.
Editorial: 4209 N Frontage Rd, Fayetteville, Arkansas 72703-5002 Tel: 1 479 521-5566.
Web site: http://www.921theticket.com
Profile: KQSM-FM is a commercial station owned by Cumulus Media Inc. The format of the station is sports. KQSM-FM broadcasts in the Fayetteville, AK area 92.1 FM.
FM RADIO STATION

KQSN-FM 41117
Owner: Mur-Thom Broadcasting Inc.
Editorial: 3924 Santa Fe St, Ponca City, Oklahoma 74601-1063 Tel: 1 580 765-5491.
Email: sunny@sunny1047.com
Web site: http://sunny1047.com
Profile: KQSN-FM is a commercial station owned by Mur-Thom Broadcasting Inc. The format of the station is hot adult contemporary music. KQSN-FM broadcasts to the Ponca City, OK area at 100.1 FM.
FM RADIO STATION

KQSP-AM 34986
Owner: Broadcast One, Inc.
Editorial: 919 Lilac Dr N, Minneapolis, Minnesota 55422-4615 Tel: 1 763 230-7602.
Web site: http://www.lapicosa.us
Profile: KQSP-AM is a commercial station owned by Broadcast One, Inc. The format of the station is Tropical. KQSP-AM broadcasts to the Chaska, MN area at 1530 AM.
AM RADIO STATION

KQSR-FM 41268
Owner: El Dorado Broadcasting
Editorial: 755 W 28th St, Yuma, Arizona 85364 Tel: 1 928 344-4980.
Web site: http://www.kqsrfm.com
Profile: KQSR-FM is a commercial station owned by El Dorado Broadcasting. The format of the station is adult contemporary music. KQSR-FM broadcasts to the Yuma, AZ area at 100.9 FM.
FM RADIO STATION

KQSS-FM 41160
Owner: Globecasting, Inc.
Editorial: 5734 S McKinney Ave, Globe, Arizona 85501-4361 Tel: 1 928 425-7186.
Web site: http://www.gila1019.com
Profile: KQSS-FM is a commercial station owned by Globecasting, Inc. The format of the station is contemporary country. KQSS-FM broadcasts to the Globe, AZ area at 98.3 FM.
FM RADIO STATION

KQST-FM 39860
Owner: Yavapai Broadcasting
Editorial: 3405 E State Route 89A Bldg A, Cottonwood, Arizona 86326-5506 Tel: 1 928 634-2286.
Email: q@myradioplace.com
Web site: http://www.myradioplace.com/q.htm
Profile: KQST-FM is a commercial station owned by the Yavapai Broadcasting. The format of the station is Top 40/CHR. KQST-FM broadcasts to the Phoenix, AZ area at 102.9 FM.
FM RADIO STATION

KQSW-FM 44846
Owner: Big Thicket Broadcasting Co.
Editorial: 2717 Yellowstone Rd, Rock Springs, Wyoming 82901-3261 Tel: 1 307 382-5619.
Email: wyoradio@wyoradio.com
Web site: http://www.bestcountryaround.com
Profile: KQSW-FM is a commercial station owned by Big Thicket Broadcasting Co. The format of the station is classic country. KQSW-FM broadcasts to the Salt Lake City area at 96.5 FM.
FM RADIO STATION

KQTH-FM 42234
Owner: E.W. Scripps Co.
Editorial: 7280 E Rosewood St, Tucson, Arizona 85710-1350 Tel: 1 520 722-5486.
Web site: http://www.1041kqth.com
Profile: KQTH-FM is a commercial station owned by E.W. Scripps Co. The format of the station is news and talk. KQTH-FM broadcasts in the Tucson, AZ area at 104.1 FM.
FM RADIO STATION

KQTM-FM 42876
Owner: Team Broadcasting
Editorial: 4131 Barbara Loop SE, Rio Rancho, New Mexico 87124-1362 Tel: 1 505 338-1414.
Web site: http://www.1017theteam.com
Profile: KQTM-FM is a commercial station owned by Team Broadcasting. The format of the station is sports. KQTM-FM broadcasts to the Albuquerque, NM, area at 101.7 FM.
FM RADIO STATION

KQTY-AM 39488
Owner: Zia Broadcasting
Editorial: 113 Union St, Borger, Texas 79007-6019 Tel: 1 806 273-7533.
Email: kqtyradio@yahoo.com
Web site: http://www.kqtyradio.net
Profile: KQTY-AM is a commercial station owned by Zia Broadcasting. The format of the station is news, sports and talk. KQTY-AM broadcasts to the Borger, TX area at 1490 AM.
AM RADIO STATION

KQTY-FM 46878
Owner: Zia Broadcasting
Editorial: 113 Union St, Borger, Texas 79007 Tel: 1 806 273-7533.
Email: kqtyradio@yahoo.com
Web site: http://www.kqtyradio.com
Profile: KQTY-FM is a commercial station owned by Zia Broadcasting. The format of the station is country, Christian, and gospel. KQTY-AM broadcasts to the Borger, TX area at 106.7 FM.
FM RADIO STATION

KQTZ-FM 44061
Owner: Monarch Broadcasting
Editorial: 212 W Cypress St, Altus, Oklahoma 73521 Tel: 1 580 482-1450.
Profile: KQTZ-FM is a commercial station owned by Monarch Broadcasting. The format of the station is adult hits music. KQTZ-FM broadcasts to the Altus, OK area at 105.9 FM.
FM RADIO STATION

United States of America

KQUE-AM 39411
Owner: Aleyua Christian Broadcasting
Editorial: 1600 Pasadena Blvd, Pasadena, Texas 77502-2404 **Tel:** 1 713 965-2400.
Email: info@radioaleluya.org
Web site: http://radioaleluya.org/
Profile: KQUE-AM is a commercial station owned by Aleyua Christian Broadcasting. The format of the station is Hispanic Christian programming. KQUE-AM broadcasts to the Houston area at 980 AM.
AM RADIO STATION

KQUL-FM 42232
Owner: Benne Media
Editorial: 160 Highway 42, Kaiser, Missouri 65047
Tel: 1 573 348-1958.
Web site: http://www.cool1027.com
Profile: KQUL-FM is a commercial station owned by Benne Media. The format of the station is classic hits. KQUL-FM broadcasts in the Kaiser, MO area at 102.7 FM.
FM RADIO STATION

KQUR-FM 44501
Owner: Border Media Partners LLC
Editorial: 107 Calle Del Norte, Ste 212, Laredo, Texas 78041 **Tel:** 1 956 725-1000.
Profile: KQUR-FM is a commercial station owned by Border Media Partners LLC and operated by MBM Radio Laredo, LLC. The format of the station is Spanish Top 40/CHR. KQUR-FM broadcasts to the Laredo, TX area at 94.9 FM.
FM RADIO STATION

KQUS-FM 44847
Owner: US Stations, LLC
Editorial: 125 Corporate Ter, Hot Springs, Arkansas 71913-7248 **Tel:** 1 501 525-9700.
Web site: http://www.us97country.com
Profile: KQUS-FM is a commercial station owned by US Stations, LLC. The format of the station is classic country. KQUS-FM broadcasts to the Hot Springs, AR area at 97.5 FM.
FM RADIO STATION

KQV-AM 35053
Owner: Calvary Inc.
Editorial: 650 Smithfield St Ste 620, Pittsburgh, Pennsylvania 15222-3913 **Tel:** 1 412 562-5900.
Email: kqvnews@kqv.com
Web site: http://www.kqv.com
Profile: KQV-AM is a commercial station owned by Calvary Inc. The format of the station is news. KQV-AM broadcasts to the Pittsburgh area at 1410 AM.
AM RADIO STATION

KQVT-FM 41768
Owner: Townsquare Media, LLC
Editorial: 107 N Star Dr, Victoria, Texas 77904-2082
Tel: 1 361 573-0777.
Web site: http://www.kqvt.com
Profile: KQVT-FM is a commercial station owned by Townsquare Media, LLC. The format for the station is hot adult contemporary. KQVT-FM broadcasts to the Victoria, TX area at 92.3 FM.
FM RADIO STATION

KQWB-AM 37454
Owner: Radio FM Media
Editorial: 2720 7th Ave S, Fargo, North Dakota 58103-8710 **Tel:** 1 701 237-4500.
Profile: KQWB-AM is a commercial station owned by Radio FM Media. The format of the station is classic country. KQWB-AM broadcasts in the Fargo, ND area at 1660 AM.
AM RADIO STATION

KQWB-FM 44849
Owner: Radio FM Media
Editorial: 2720 7th Ave S, Fargo, North Dakota 58103-8710 **Tel:** 1 701 237-4500.
Web site: http://www.q1051rocks.com
Profile: KQWB-FM is a commercial station owned by Radio FM Media. The format of the station is rock music. KQWB-FM broadcasts in the Fargo, ND area at 105.1 FM.
FM RADIO STATION

KQWC-FM 44850
Owner: NRG Media LLC
Editorial: 1020 E 2nd St, Webster City, Iowa 50595-1754 **Tel:** 1 515 832-1570.
Web site: http://www.kqradio.com
Profile: KQWC-FM is a commercial station owned by NRG Media LLC. The format is adult contemporary music. KQWC-FM broadcasts to the Webster City, IA area at 95.7 FM.
FM RADIO STATION

KQXC-FM 42186
Owner: Cumulus Media Inc.
Editorial: 4302 Call Field Rd, Wichita Falls, Texas 76308 **Tel:** 1 940 691-2311.
Web site: http://www.thehot1039.com
Profile: KQXC-FM is a commercial station owned by Cumulus Media Inc. The format of the station is rhythmic Top 40. KQXC-FM broadcasts to the Wichita Falls, TX area at 103.9 FM.
FM RADIO STATION

KQXF-FM 46866
Owner: Sudbury Broadcasting Group
Editorial: 125 S 2nd St, Blytheville, Arkansas 72315
Tel: 1 870 762-2093.
Web site: http://www.todaysbesthits.com
Profile: KQXF-FM is a commercial station owned by Sudbury Services. The format of the station is hot adult contemporary. KQXF-FM broadcasts to the Blytheville, AR area at 107.3 FM.
FM RADIO STATION

KQXI-FM 854655
Owner: Spirit Communications, Inc.
Tel: 1 614 839-7100.
Email: radiou@radiou.com
Web site: http://radiou.com
Profile: KQXI-FM is a non-commercial station owned by Spirit Communications, Inc. The format of the station is Christian CHR/Rock. KQXI-FM broadcasts to the Everett and North Seattle areas in Washington at a frequency of 91.5 FM.
FM RADIO STATION

KQXL-FM 39861
Owner: Cumulus Media Inc
Editorial: 630 Main Street, Baton Rouge, Louisiana 70801 **Tel:** 1 225 926-1106.
Web site: http://www.q106dot5.com
Profile: KQXL-FM is commercial station owned by Cumulus Media Inc. The format of the station is urban adult contemporary music. KQXL-FM broadcasts to the Baton Rouge, LA area at 106.5 FM.
FM RADIO STATION

KQXR-FM 42538
Owner: E.W. Scripps Co.
Editorial: 5257 W Fairview Ave Ste 260, Boise, Idaho 83706-1766 **Tel:** 1 208 344-3511.
Web site: http://www.xrock.com
Profile: KQXR-FM is a commercial station owned by E.W. Scripps Co. The format of the station is rock music. KQXR-FM broadcasts in the Boise, ID area at 100.3 FM.
FM RADIO STATION

KQXT-FM 46694
Owner: iHeartMedia Inc.
Editorial: 6222 W Interstate 10, San Antonio, Texas 78201-2013 **Tel:** 1 210 736-9700.
Web site: http://www.q1019.com
Profile: KQXT-FM is a commercial station owned by iHeartMedia Inc. The format of the station is adult contemporary. KQXT-FM broadcasts to the San Antonio area at 101.9 FM.
FM RADIO STATION

KQXX-FM 46894
Owner: iHeartMedia Inc
Editorial: 901 E Pike Blvd, Weslaco, Texas 78596-4937 **Tel:** 1 956 973-9202.
Web site: http://kissfmrgv.iheart.com/
Profile: KQXX-FM is a commercial station owned by iHeartMedia Inc. The format of the station is Hot AC. KQXX-FM broadcasts to the Weslaco, TX area at 105.5 FM.
FM RADIO STATION

KQXY-FM 44851
Owner: Cumulus Media Inc.
Editorial: 755 S 11th St Ste 102, Beaumont, Texas 77701-3723 **Tel:** 1 409 833-9421.
Web site: http://www.kqxy.com
Profile: KQXY-FM is a commercial station owned by Cumulus Media Inc. The format of the station is Top 40/CHR music. KQXY-FM broadcasts to the Beaumont, TX area at 94.1 FM.
FM RADIO STATION

KQYB-FM 39862
Owner: Midwest Family Stations
Editorial: 201 State St, La Crosse, Wisconsin 54601
Tel: 1 608 782-1230.
Web site: http://www.kq98.com
Profile: KQYB-FM is a commercial station owned by Midwest Family Stations. The format of the station is contemporary country. KQYB-FM broadcasts to the La Crosse, WI area at 98.3 FM.
FM RADIO STATION

KQYX-AM 36343
Owner: American Media Investments
Editorial: 2510 W 20th St, Joplin, Missouri 64804-0216 **Tel:** 1 417 781-1313.
Email: production@ami-joplin.com
Web site: http://1450thedove.com
Profile: KQYX-AM is a commercial station owned by American Media Investments. The format of the station is oldies. KQYX-FM broadcasts to the Joplin, MO area at 1450 AM.
AM RADIO STATION

KQZR-FM 151465
Owner: NRC Broadcasting
Editorial: 2955 Village Dr, Steamboat Springs, Colorado 80487-2143 **Tel:** 1 970 879-5368.
Web site: http://alwaysmountaintime.com/kqzr
Profile: KQZR-FM is a commercial station owned by NRC Broadcasting. The format of the station is classic rock music. KQZR-FM broadcasts to the Steamboat Springs, CO area at 107.3 FM.
FM RADIO STATION

KQZZ-FM 43081
Owner: Double Z Broadcasting Inc.
Editorial: 320 Walnut St W, Devils Lake, North Dakota 58301-3506 **Tel:** 1 701 662-1797.
Web site: http://www.lrradioworks.com
Profile: KQZZ-FM is a commercial station owned by Double Z Broadcasting Inc. The format of the station is hot adult contemporary music. KQZZ-FM broadcasts to the Devils Lake, ND area at 96.7 FM.
FM RADIO STATION

KRAB-FM 41645
Owner: iHeartMedia Inc.
Editorial: 1100 Mohawk St Ste 280, Bakersfield, California 93309-7417 **Tel:** 1 661 322-9929.
Email: krab@iheartmedia.com
Web site: http://krab.iheart.com
Profile: KRAB-FM is a commercial station owned by iheartMedia Inc. The format of the station is rock. KRAB-FM broadcasts to the Bakersfield, CA area at 106.1 FM.
FM RADIO STATION

KRAE-AM 39452
Owner: Proshop Radio Broadcasting LLC
Editorial: 2232 Dell Range Blvd Ste 202, Cheyenne, Wyoming 82009-4942 **Tel:** 1 307 637-0301.
Web site: http://www.1480krae.com
Profile: KRAE-AM is a commercial station owned by Proshop Radio Broadcasting, LLC. The format of the station is 50s, 60s, and sports. KRAE-AM broadcasts to the Cheyenne, WY area at 1480 AM.
AM RADIO STATION

KRAI-FM 44852
Owner: Wild West Radio Inc.
Editorial: 1111 W Victory Way, Craig, Colorado 81625-2950 **Tel:** 1 970 824-6574.
Email: krai@krai.com
Web site: http://www.krai.com
Profile: KRAI-FM is a commercial station owned by Wild West Radio Inc. The format of the station is hot adult contemporary. KRAI-FM broadcasts to the Denver area at 93.7 FM
FM RADIO STATION

KRAJ-FM 41106
Owner: Adelman Broadcasting Inc.
Editorial: 42010 50th St W, Quartz Hill, California 93536-3509 **Tel:** 1 661 718-1552.
Email: contact@adelmanbroadcasting.com
Web site: http://www.theheat1009.com
Profile: KRAJ-FM is a commercial station owned by Adelman Broadcasting Inc. The format of the station is rhythmic contemporary. KRAJ-FM broadcasts to the Ridgecrest, CA area at 100.9 FM.
FM RADIO STATION

KRAK-AM 36705
Owner: CBS Radio
Editorial: 11920 Hesperia Rd, Hesperia, California 92345-1851 **Tel:** 1 760 244-2000.
Web site: http://910cbssports.cbslocal.com
Profile: KRAK-AM is a commercial station owned by CBS Radio. The format of the station is sports. KRAK-AM broadcasts to the Hesperia, CA area at 910 AM.
AM RADIO STATION

KRAO-FM 46854
Owner: Inland Northwest Broadcasting
Editorial: 1114 N Almon St, Moscow, Idaho 83843-8507 **Tel:** 1 208 882-2551.
Email: myradio1025@hotmail.com
Profile: KRAO-FM is a commercial station owned by Inland Northwest Broadcasting. The format of the station is hot AC. KRAO-FM broadcasts to the Moscow, ID area at 102.5 FM.
FM RADIO STATION

KRAV-FM 45749
Owner: Cox Media Group, Inc.
Editorial: 7136 S Yale Ave Ste 500, Tulsa, Oklahoma 74136-6358 **Tel:** 1 918 491-9696.
Web site: http://www.mix965tulsa.com
Profile: KRAV-FM is a commercial station owned by Cox Media Group, Inc. The format of the station is adult contemporary. KRAV-FM broadcasts to the Tulsa, OK area at 96.5 FM.
FM RADIO STATION

KRAY-FM 44854
Owner: Wolfhouse Radio Group Inc.
Editorial: 548 E Alisal St, Salinas, California 93905-2760 **Tel:** 1 831 757-1910.
Web site: http://wolfhouseradio.net
Profile: KRAY-FM is a commercial station owned by Wolfhouse Radio Group Inc. The format of the station is Regional Mexican Hits. KRAY-FM broadcasts to the Salinas, CA area at 103.5 FM.
FM RADIO STATION

KRAZ-FM 217673
Owner: Knight Broadcasting Inc.
Editorial: 1101 S Broadway, Ste C, Santa Maria, California 93454-6660 **Tel:** 1 805 688-5798.
Web site: http://www.krazfm.com
Profile: KRAZ-FM is a commercial station owned by Knight Broadcasting Inc. The format of the station is contemporary country. KRAZ-FM broadcasts to the Santa Barbara, CA area at 105.9 FM.
FM RADIO STATION

KRBA-AM 39069
Owner: Pentagon Communications, LLC
Editorial: 121 S Cotton Sq, Lufkin, Texas 75904-2933
Tel: 1 936 634-6661.
Email: traffic@yatesmedia.com
Web site: http://www.krbaradio.com
Profile: KRBA-AM is a commercial station owned by Yates Media. The format of the station is classic country, gospel music, news and sports. KRBA-AM broadcasts to the Lufkin, TX area at 1340 AM.
AM RADIO STATION

KRBB-FM 39762
Owner: iHeartMedia Inc.
Editorial: 9323 E 37th St N, Wichita, Kansas 67226-2000 **Tel:** 1 316 494-6600.
Web site: http://www.b98fm.com
Profile: KRBB-FM is a commercial station owned by iHeartMedia Inc. The format of the station is Adult Contemporary. KRBB-FM broadcasts to the Wichita, KS area at 97.9 FM. The station's slogan is, "Numer 1 at Work - Wichita's Variety Station."
FM RADIO STATION

KRBD-FM 41867
Owner: Rainbird Community Broadcasting
Editorial: 1101 Copper Ridge Ln, Ketchikan, Alaska 99901-6250 **Tel:** 1 907 225-9655.
Email: news@krbd.org
Web site: http://www.krbd.org
Profile: KRBD-FM is a commercial station owned by Rainbird Community Broadcasting Corp. The format of the station is variety. KRBD-FM's broadcasts in the Ketchikan, AK area.
FM RADIO STATION

KRBE-FM 42788
Owner: Cumulus Media Inc.
Editorial: 9801 Westheimer Rd Ste 700, Houston, Texas 77042-3955 **Tel:** 1 713 266-1000.
Email: feedback@104krbe.com
Web site: http://www.krbe.com
Profile: KRBE-FM is a commercial station owned byCumulus Media Inc. The format of the station is Top 40/CHR. KRBE-FM broadcasts to the Houston area at 104.1 FM.
FM RADIO STATION

KRBI-FM 44855
Owner: Alpha Media
Editorial: 1807 Lee Blvd, North Mankato, Minnesota 56003-2633 **Tel:** 1 507 345-4646.
Web site: http://www.river105.com
Profile: KRBI-FM is a commercial station owned by Alpha Media. The format of the station is classic hits. KRBI-FM broadcasts to the North Mankato, MN area at 105.5 FM.
FM RADIO STATION

KRBL-FM 42978
Owner: Walker Broadcasting and Communications Inc.
Editorial: 1603 13th St, Lubbock, Texas 79401-3817
Tel: 1 806 744-6864.
Profile: KRBL-FM is a commercial station owned by Walker Broadcasting and Communications Inc. The format of the station is classic hits music. KRBL-FM broadcasts to the Lubbock, TX area at 105.7 FM.
FM RADIO STATION

KRBQ-FM 43209
Owner: Entercom Communications Corp.
Editorial: 201 3rd St Ste 1200, San Francisco, California 94103-3143 **Tel:** 1 415 777-0965.
Web site: http://www.q102sf.com
Profile: KRBQ-FM is a commercial station owned by Entercom Communications Corp. The format of the station is Rhythmic Hot AC. KRBQ-FM broadcasts to the San Francisco area at 102.1 FM.
FM RADIO STATION

KRBS-FM 86458
Owner: Bird Street Media Project
Editorial: 2360 Oro Quincy Hwy, Oroville, California 95966-5226 **Tel:** 1 530 534-1200.
Email: krbs@cncnet.com
Web site: http://www.radiobirdstreet.org
FM RADIO STATION

KRBT-AM 38774
Owner: Red Rock Radio Corp.
Editorial: 501 S Lake Ave Ste 200, Duluth, Minnesota 55802-2392 **Tel:** 1 218 728-9500.
Web site: http://radioredzone.com
Profile: KRBT-AM is a commercial station owned by Red Rock Radio Corp.. The format of the station is sports. KRBT-AM broadcasts to the Iron Range areas of Minnesota at 1340 AM.
AM RADIO STATION

KRBW-FM 43248
Owner: American Family Association
Editorial: 107 Park Gate Dr, Tupelo, Mississippi 38801-3010 **Tel:** 1 662 844-8888.
Email: comments@afr.net
Web site: http://www.afr.net
Profile: KRBW-FM is a non-commercial station owned by American Family Association. The format of the station is Adult contemporary Christian music. KRBW-FM broadcasts to the Ottawa, Kansas area at 90.5 FM.
FM RADIO STATION

KRBX-FM 746801
Owner: Boise Community Radio Project, Inc
Editorial: 1020 W Main St Ste 200, Boise, Idaho 83702-5745 **Tel:** 1 208 424-8166.
Email: info@radioboise.org
Web site: http://www.radioboise.org
Profile: KRBX-FM is a non-commercial community radio station owned by Boise Community Radio Project, Inc. The format of the station is variety. KRBX-FM broadcasts to the Boise, ID area at a frequency of 89.9 FM.
FM RADIO STATION

KRBZ-FM 42687
Owner: Entercom Communications Corp.
Editorial: 7000 Squibb Rd, Mission, Kansas 66202-3233 **Tel:** 1 913 576-7965.
Web site: http://www.965thebuzz.com
Profile: KRBZ-FM is a commercial station owned by Entercom Communications Corp. The format of the station is rock alternative music. KRBZ-FM broadcasts to the Kansas City, MO area at 96.5 FM.
FM RADIO STATION

KRCB-FM 43308
Owner: Rural California Broadcasting Corp.
Editorial: 5850 Labath Ave, Rohnert Park, California 94928-2041 **Tel:** 1 707 584-2000.
Email: viewer@krcb.org
Web site: http://radio.krcb.org
Profile: KRCB-FM is a non-commercial station owned by Rural California Broadcasting Corp. The format of the station is variety. KRCB-FM broadcasts to the San Francisco area at 91.1 FM.
FM RADIO STATION

KRCC-FM 39864
Owner: Colorado College
Editorial: 912 N Weber St, Colorado Springs, Colorado 80903-2921 **Tel:** 1 719 473-4801.
Email: info@krcc.org
Web site: http://www.krcc.org
Profile: KRCC-FM is a non-commercial station owned by Colorado College. The format of the station is variety. KRCC-FM broadcasts to the Colorado Springs, CO area at 91.5 FM.
FM RADIO STATION

KRCD-FM 39520
Owner: Univision Communications Inc.
Editorial: 5999 Center Dr, Los Angeles, California 90045-8901 **Tel:** 1 310 846-2800.
Web site: http://www.univision.com/los-angeles/krcd
Profile: KRCD-FM is a commercial station owned by Univision Communications Inc. The format of the station is Spanish Adult Hits. KRCD-FM broadcasts to the Glendale, CA area at 103.9 FM.
FM RADIO STATION

KRCH-FM 44856
Owner: iHeartMedia Inc.
Editorial: 1530 Greenview Dr SW Ste 200, Rochester, Minnesota 55902-4327 **Tel:** 1 507 288-3888.
Web site: http://www.laser1017.com/main.html
Profile: KRCH-FM is a commercial station owned by iHeartMedia Inc. The format of the station is classic rock. KRCH-FM broadcasts to the Rochester, MN area at 101.7 FM.
FM RADIO STATION

KRCK-FM 396826
Owner: Royce International Broadcasting Corporation
Editorial: 73733 Fred Waring Dr Ste 201, Palm Desert, California 92260-2591 **Tel:** 1 760 341-0123.
Web site: http://www.krck.com
Profile: KRCK-FM is a commercial station owned by Royce International Broadcasting Corporation. The format of the station is Top 40/CHR. KRCK-FM broadcasts to the Palm Desert, CA area at 97.7 FM.
FM RADIO STATION

KRCL-FM 41254
Owner: Listeners Community Radio of Utah Inc.
Editorial: 1971 W North Temple, Salt Lake City, Utah 84116-3046 **Tel:** 1 801 363-1818.
Email: fax@krcl.org
Web site: http://www.krcl.org
Profile: KRCL-FM is a non-commercial station owned by Listeners Community Radio of Utah Inc. The format of the station is variety. KRCL-FM broadcasts to the Salt Lake City area at 90.9 FM.
FM RADIO STATION

KRCN-AM 34999
Owner: Pilgrim Communications
Editorial: 614 Kimbark St, Longmont, Colorado 80501-4911 **Tel:** 1 303 776-2323.
Web site: http://www.krcnradio.com
Profile: KRCN-AM is a commercial station owned by Pilgrim Communications. The format of the station is Catholic talk. KRCN-AM broadcasts to the Longmont, CO area at 1060 AM.
AM RADIO STATION

KRCO-AM 39141
Owner: Horizon Broadcasting Group
Editorial: 854 NE 4th St, Bend, Oregon 97701-4711 **Tel:** 1 541 447-6770.
Email: news@horizonbroadcastinggroup.com
Web site: http://www.krcoam.com
Profile: KRCO-AM is a commercial station owned by Horizon Broadcasting Group. The format of the station is classic country. KRCO-AM broadcasts in the Prineville, OR area at 690 AM.
AM RADIO STATION

KRCQ-FM 42423
Owner: Leighton Broadcasting
Editorial: 1119 Jackson Ave, Detroit Lakes, Minnesota 56501-3618 **Tel:** 1 218 847-2001.
Web site: http://www.realcountry102.com
Profile: KRCQ-FM is a commercial station owned by Leighton Broadcasting. The format of the station is country. KRCQ-FM broadcasts to the Detroit Lakes, MN area at 102.3 FM.
FM RADIO STATION

KRCS-FM 44487
Owner: New Rushmore Radio
Editorial: 660 Flormann St, Ste 100, Rapid City, South Dakota 57701 **Tel:** 1 605 343-6161.
Web site: http://www.hot931.com
Profile: KRCS-FM is a commercial station owned by New Rushmore Radio. The format of the station is Top 40/CHR. KRCS-FM broadcasts to the Rapid City, SD area at 93.1 FM.
FM RADIO STATION

KRCU-FM 42457
Owner: Southeast Missouri State Univ.
Editorial: 1 University Plz Ms 300, Cape Girardeau, Missouri 63701-4710 **Tel:** 1 573 651-5070.
Email: comments@krcu.org
Web site: http://www.krcu.org
Profile: KRCU-FM is a non-commercial station owned by Southeast Missouri State Univ. The format of the station is classical and news. KRCU-FM broadcasts to the Cape Giradeau, MO area at 90.9 FM.
FM RADIO STATION

KRCV-FM 42263
Owner: Univision Communications Inc.
Editorial: 5999 Center Dr, Los Angeles, California 90045-8901 **Tel:** 1 310 846-2800.
Web site: http://www.univision.com/los-angeles/krcd
Profile: KRCV-FM is a commercial station owned by Univision Communications Inc. The format of the station is Spanish Adult Hits. KRCV-FM broadcasts to the Los Angeles area at 98.3 FM.
FM RADIO STATION

KRCW-FM 44530
Owner: National Farm Workers Service Center
Editorial: 508 W Lewis St, Pasco, Washington 99301-5536 **Tel:** 1 509 545-0700.
Web site: http://campesina.net/krcw
Profile: KRCW-FM is a commercial station owned by National Farm Workers Service Center. The format of the station is regional Mexican. KRCW-FM broadcasts to the Pasco, WA area at 96.3 FM.
FM RADIO STATION

KRCX-FM 44071
Owner: Entravision Communications Corp.
Editorial: 1436 Auburn Blvd, Sacramento, California 95815-2745 **Tel:** 1 916 646-4000.
Web site: http://www.tricolor999.com
Profile: KRCX-FM is a commercial station owned by Entravision Communications Corp. The format of the station is regional Mexican. KRCX-FM broadcasts to the Sacramento, CA area at 99.9 FM.
FM RADIO STATION

KRCY-FM 42467
Owner: Mad Dog Wireless Inc.
Editorial: 2068 McCulloch Blvd N, Lake Havasu City, Arizona 86403-6663 **Tel:** 1 928 855-1051.
Web site: http://www.maddog.net
Profile: KRCY-FM is a commercial station owned by Mad Dog Wireless Inc. The format of the station is oldies. KRCY-FM broadcasts to the Lake Havasu City, AZ at 96.7 FM.
FM RADIO STATION

KRDA-FM 46902
Owner: Univision Communications Inc.
Editorial: 601 W Univision Plz, Fresno, California 93704-1092 **Tel:** 1 559 430-8500.
Web site: http://www.univision.com/fresno/krda
Profile: KRDA-FM is a commercial station owned by Univision Communications Inc. The format of the station is Spanish adult hits. KRDA-FM broadcasts in the Fresno, CA, area at 107.5 FM.
FM RADIO STATION

KRDD-AM 35055
Owner: Espinoza(Carlos)
Editorial: 170 N Red Bridge Rd, Roswell, New Mexico 88201 **Tel:** 1 575 623-8111.
Email: krddam@yahoo.com
Profile: KRDD-AM is a commercial station owned by Carlos Espinoza. The format of the station is Hispanic adult contemporary music. KRDD-AM broadcasts to the Roswell, NM area at 1320 AM.
AM RADIO STATION

KRDE-FM 43106
Owner: Tri-Media, Inc.
Editorial: 800 N Main St, Globe, Arizona 85501 **Tel:** 1 928 402-9222.
Email: krde@cableone.net
Web site: http://www.krde.com
Profile: KRDE-FM is a commercial station owned by Tri-Media, Inc.. The format of the station is classic and contemporary country. KRDE-FM broadcasts to the Phoenix area at 94.1 FM.
FM RADIO STATION

KRDG-FM 43390
Owner: Mapleton of Redding, LLC
Editorial: 3360 Alta Mesa Dr, Redding, California 96002-2831 **Tel:** 1 530 226-0261.
Web site: http://www.1053classichits.com
Profile: KRDG-FM is a commercial station owned by Mapleton of Redding, LLC. The format of the station is oldies music. KRDG-FM broadcasts to the Redding, CA area at 105.3 FM.
FM RADIO STATION

KRDM-AM 446002
Owner: Red Mountain Broadcasting, LLC
Editorial: 416 SW Black Butte Blvd, Redmond, Oregon 97756-2148 **Tel:** 1 541 548-7621.
Email: sales@radiolabronca.com
Web site: http://www.radiolabronca.com
Profile: KRDM-AM is a commercial station owned by Red Mountain Broadcasting, LLC. The format of the station is Hispanic. KRDM-AM broadcasts to the Redmond, OR area at 1240 AM.
AM RADIO STATION

KRDO-AM 37459
Owner: News-Press & Gazette Co.
Editorial: 399 S 8th St, Colorado Springs, Colorado 80905 **Tel:** 1 719 632-1515.
Email: krdonews@krdo.com
Web site: http://www.krdo.com
Profile: KRDO-AM is a commercial station owned by News-Press & Gazette Co. The format of the station is news and talk. KRDO-AM broadcasts to the Colorado Springs, CO area at 1240 AM.
AM RADIO STATION

KRDO-FM 40039
Owner: News-Press & Gazette Co.
Editorial: 399 S 8th St, Colorado Springs, Colorado 80905-1803 **Tel:** 1 719 632-1515.
Email: radionews@krdo.com
Web site: http://www.krdo.com
Profile: KRDO-FM is a commercial station owned by News-Press & Gazette Co. The format of the station is news and talk. KRDO-FM broadcasts to the Colorado Springs, CO area at 105.5 FM.
FM RADIO STATION

KRDQ-FM 44838
Owner: Rocking M Radio
Editorial: 1065 S Range Ave, Colby, Kansas 67701-3505 **Tel:** 1 785 462-3305.
Email: kxxxkgls@rockingmradio.com
Web site: http://rockingmradio.com
Profile: KRDQ-FM is a commercial radio station owned by Rocking M Radio. The format of the station is hot adult contemporary music. KRDQ-FM broadcasts to Colby, KS at 100.3 FM.
FM RADIO STATION

KRDU-AM 36903
Owner: iHeartMedia Inc.
Editorial: 597 N Alta Ave, Dinuba, California 93618-3202 **Tel:** 1 559 230-4300.
Web site: http://krdu1130.iheart.com
Profile: KRDU-AM is a commercial station owned by IHeart Media and Entertainment. The format of the station is religious programming. KRDU-AM broadcasts to the Dinuba, CA area at 1130 AM.
AM RADIO STATION

KRDX-FM 44298
Owner: Desert West Air Ranchers Corp.
Editorial: 500 E Fry Blvd, Ste L10, Sierra Vista, Arizona 85635 **Tel:** 1 520 459-8201.
Email: info@kkyz.com
Web site: http://www.fox985.com
Profile: KRDX-FM is a commercial station owned by Desert West Air Ranchers Corp. The format of the station is oldies music. KRDX-FM broadcasts to the Tucson, AZ area at 98.5 FM.
FM RADIO STATION

KRDY-AM 34946
Owner: Salem Media Group, Inc.
Editorial: 9601 McAllister Fwy Ste 1200, San Antonio, Texas 78216-4695 **Tel:** 1 210 344-8481.
Email: info@radiosaigonhouston.com
Web site: http://luzsanantonio.com/
Profile: KRDY-AM is a non-commerical station owned by Salem Media Group, Inc. The format of the station is Spanish Contemporary Christian. The station broadcasts to the San Antonio, TX area at a frequency of 1160 AM.
AM RADIO STATION

KRDZ-AM 38303
Owner: Media Logic LLC
Editorial: 32992 US Highway 34, Wray, Colorado 80758-9161 **Tel:** 1 970 332-4171.
Email: krdz@medialogicradio.com
Web site: http://www.krdz.com
Profile: KRDZ-AM is a commercial station owned by Media Logic LLC. The format of the station is sports and classic hits. KRDZ-AM broadcasts to the Wray, CO area at 1440 AM.
AM RADIO STATION

KREB-AM 36889
Owner: Butler Broadcasting
Editorial: 1780 W Holly St, Fayetteville, Arkansas 72703 **Tel:** 1 479 582-3776.
Web site: http://1190thefan.com
Profile: KREB-AM is a commercial station owned by Butler Broadcasting. The format of the station is sports and talk. KREB-AM broadcasts to the Fayetteville, AR area at 1190 AM.
AM RADIO STATION

KREC-FM 41248
Owner: Cherry Creek Radio
Editorial: 750 Ridgeview Dr Ste 204, St George, Utah 84770-2697 **Tel:** 1 435 673-3579.
Email: star98.1fm@gmail.com
Web site: http://www.star98online.com
Profile: KREC-FM is a commercial station owned by Cherry Creek Radio. The format of the station is adult contemporary. KREC-FM broadcasts to the Salt Lake City area at 98.1 FM.
FM RADIO STATION

KRED-FM 44858
Owner: Bicoastal Media LLC
Editorial: 5640 S Broadway St, Eureka, California 95503-6905 **Tel:** 1 707 442-2000.
Email: eurekapsa@bicoastalmedia.com
Web site: http://www.kred923.com
Profile: KRED-FM is a country-format radio station based in Eureka, California. It also provides sports programming.
FM RADIO STATION

KREF-AM 35020
Owner: Metro Radio Group
Editorial: 2020 Alameda St, Norman, Oklahoma 73071-2402 **Tel:** 1 405 321-1400.
Email: production@kref.com
Web site: http://www.sportstalk1400.com
Profile: KREF-AM is a commercial station owned by Metro Radio Group. The format of the station is sports. KREF-AM broadcasts to the Norman, OK area at 1400 AM.
AM RADIO STATION

KREH-AM 36581
Owner: Mass Media Inc.
Editorial: 10613 Bellaire Blvd Ste 900, Houston, Texas 77072-5221 **Tel:** 1 713 917-0050.
Email: info@radiosaigonhouston.com
Web site: http://www.radiosaigonhouston.com
Profile: KREH-AM is a commercial station owned by Mass Media Inc. The format of the station is Vietnamese variety. KREH-AM broadcasts to the Houston area at 900 AM.
AM RADIO STATION

KREI-AM 37461
Owner: Goodradio.TV LLC
Editorial: 1401 Krei Blvd, Farmington, Missouri 63640-1013 **Tel:** 1 573 756-6476.
Web site: http://www.mymoinfo.com
Profile: KREI-AM is a commercial station owned by Goodradio.TV LLC. The format of the station is talk. KREI-AM broadcasts to the St. Louis area at 800 AM.
AM RADIO STATION

KREP-FM 39868
Owner: First Republic Broadcasting Corp.
Editorial: 2307 US Highway 81, Belleville, Kansas 66935 **Tel:** 1 785 527-2266.
Email: kr-92@nckcn.com
Web site: http://www.kr92country.com
Profile: KREP-FM is a commercial station owned by First Republic Broadcasting Corp. The format of the station is country. KREP-FM broadcasts to the Belleville, KS area at 92.1 FM.
FM RADIO STATION

KRES-FM 39869
Owner: Moberly/Macon License Co., LLC
Editorial: 300 W Reed St, Moberly, Missouri 65270-1559 **Tel:** 1 660 263-1500.
Email: kresnews@regionalradio.com
Web site: http://www.centralmoinfo.com
Profile: KRES-FM is a commercial station owned by Moberly/Macon License Co., LLC. The format of the station is country music. KRES-FM broadcasts to the Moberly, MO area at 104.7 FM.
FM RADIO STATION

KREU-FM 519469
Owner: Star 92 Company
Editorial: 5111 Rogers Ave Ste 650, Fort Smith, Arkansas 72903-2096 **Tel:** 1 479 785-2526.
Email: production@kisr.net
Profile: KREU-FM is a commercial station owned by Baker Broadcasting. The format of the station is regional Mexican music. KREU-FM broadcasts to the Fort Smith, AR area at 92.3 FM.
FM RADIO STATION

KREV-FM 39700
Owner: Royce International Broadcasting
Editorial: 400 2Nd St Ste 300, San Francisco, California 94107-1448 **Tel:** 1 415 543-7500.
Web site: http://www.927rev.com
Profile: KREV-FM is a commercial station owned by Royce International Broadcasting. The format of the station is Top 40/CHR. KREV-FM broadcasts to the San Francisco Bay area at 92.7 FM.
FM RADIO STATION

KREW-AM 37558
Owner: Rhattigan Broadcasting
Editorial: 3218 Quincy St, Plainview, Texas 79072-1906 **Tel:** 1 806 296-2771.
Profile: KREW-AM is a commercial station owned by Rhattigan Broadcasting. The format of the station is sports. KREW-AM broadcasts to the Plainview, TX area at 1400 AM.
AM RADIO STATION

KREZ-FM 41913
Owner: Withers Broadcasting Co.
Editorial: 901 S Kingshighway St, Cape Girardeau, Missouri 63703-8003 **Tel:** 1 573 339-7000.
Email: casmus@withersradio.net
Web site: http://www.softrock1047.com
Profile: KREZ-FM is a commercial station owned by Withers Broadcasting Co. The format of the station is adult contemporary. KREZ-FM broadcasts to the Cape Girardeau, MO area at 104.7 FM.
FM RADIO STATION

KRFC-FM 136923
Owner: Public Radio for the Front Range
Editorial: 619 S College Ave Ste 4, Fort Collins, Colorado 80524-3068 **Tel:** 1 970 221-5075.

Web site: http://www.krfcfm.org
Profile: KRFC-FM is a non-commercial station owned by Public Radio for the Front Range. The format of the station is variety. KRFC-FM broadcasts to the Fort Collins, CO area at 88.9 FM.
FM RADIO STATION

KRFE-AM 36230
Owner: Wilkes(Wade)
Editorial: 6602 Martin L King Blvd, Lubbock, Texas 79404-6010 **Tel:** 1 806 745-1197.
Web site: http://wilkesradio.com/
Profile: KRFE-AM is commercial station owned by Wade Wilkes. The format of the station is talk and easy listening. KRFE-AM broadcasts in the Lubbock, TX area at 580 AM.
AM RADIO STATION

KRFM-FM 44861
Owner: Petracom
Editorial: 1838 Commerce Dr Ste A, Lakeside, Arizona 85929-7008 **Tel:** 1 928 368-8100.
Profile: KRFM-FM is a commercial station owned by Petracom. The format of the station is hot adult contemporary music. KRFM-FM broadcasts to the Navajo County, AZ at 96.5 FM.
FM RADIO STATION

KRFN-FM 41164
Owner: The Evans Broadcasting
Editorial: 1755 E Plumb Ln, Reno, Nevada 89502-3647 **Tel:** 1 775 333-0123.
Web site: http://www.renosbestrock.com
Profile: KRFN-FM is a commercial station owned by The Evans Broadcasting Company, Inc. The format of the station is Adult Contemporary. KRFN-FM broadcasts to the Reno, NV area at 100.9 FM.
FM RADIO STATION

KRFO-AM 37463
Owner: Townsquare Media
Editorial: 245 18th St SE, Owatonna, Minnesota 55060-4062 **Tel:** 1 507 451-2250.
Email: krfonews@townsquaremedia.com
Web site: http://www.krforadio.com
Profile: KRFO-AM is a commercial station owned by Townsquare Media. The format of the station is oldies music. KRFO-AM broadcasts to the Owatonna, MN area at 1390 AM.
AM RADIO STATION

KRFO-FM 44862
Owner: Townsquare Media
Editorial: 245 18th St SE, Owatonna, Minnesota 55060-4062 **Tel:** 1 507 451-2250.
Web site: http://www.krforadio.com
Profile: KRFO-FM is a commercial station owned by Townsquare Media. The format of the station is contemporary country music. KRFO-FM broadcasts to the Owatonna, MN area at 104.9 FM.
FM RADIO STATION

KRFS-AM 37464
Owner: CK Broadcasting Inc.
Editorial: 630 W 8th St, Superior, Nebraska 68978-1443 **Tel:** 1 402 879-4741.
Email: krfsfm@yahoo.com
Web site: http://www.krfsfm.com
Profile: KRFS-AM is a commercial station owned by CK Broadcasting Inc. The format of the station is adult contemporary. KRFS-AM broadcasts in the Superior, NE area at 1600 AM.
AM RADIO STATION

KRFS-FM 44863
Owner: CK Broadcasting Inc.
Editorial: 630 W 8th St, Superior, Nebraska 68978-1443 **Tel:** 1 402 879-4741.
Email: krfsfm@yahoo.com
Web site: http://www.krfsfm.com
Profile: KRFS-FM is a commercial station owned by CK Broadcasting Inc. The format of the station is contemporary country music. KRFS broadcasts in the Superior, NE area at 103.9 FM.
FM RADIO STATION

KRFX-FM 46333
Owner: iHeartMedia Inc.
Editorial: 4695 S Monaco St, Denver, Colorado 80237-3525 **Tel:** 1 303 713-8000.
Web site: http://www.thefox.com
Profile: KRFX-FM is a commercial station owned by iHeartMedia Inc. The format of the station is classic rock. KRFX-FM broadcasts to the Denver area at 103.5 FM.
FM RADIO STATION

KRGE-AM 39453
Owner: Christian Ministries of the Valley Inc.
Editorial: 2720 W Business 83, Weslaco, Texas 78596-1225 **Tel:** 1 956 968-7777.
Email: informacion@radiovida.com
Web site: http://www.radiovida.com
Profile: KRGE-AM is a commercial station owned by Christian Ministries of the Valley Inc. The format of the station is Spanish Christian music and talk. KRGE-AM broadcasts to the Weslaco, TX area at 1290 AM.
AM RADIO STATION

KRGI-AM 37465
Owner: Legacy Communications, LLC
Editorial: 3205 W North Front St, Grand Island, Nebraska 68803-4024 **Tel:** 1 308 381-1430.
Email: production@krgi.com
Web site: http://www.newsacrossnebraska.com
Profile: KRGI-AM is a commercial station owned by Legacy Communications, LLC (dba GI Family Radio). The format of the station is news, talk and sports. KRGI-AM broadcasts to the Grand Island, NE area at 1430 AM.
AM RADIO STATION

KRGI-FM 44864
Owner: Legacy Communications, LLC
Editorial: 3205 W North Front St, Grand Island, Nebraska 68803-4024 **Tel:** 1 308 381-1430.
Email: production@krgi.com
Web site: http://www.newsacrossnebraska.com
Profile: KRGI-FM is a commercial station owned by Legacy Communications, LLC (dba GI Family Radio). The format of the station is country. KRGI-FM broadcasts to the Grand Island, NE area at 96.5 FM.
FM RADIO STATION

KRGS-AM 39327
Owner: Western Slope Communications
Editorial: 751 Horizon Ct, Ste 225, Grand Junction, Colorado 81506 **Tel:** 1 970 241-6460.
Email: production@wscradio.net
Profile: KRGS-AM is a commercial station owned by Western Slope Communications. The format of the station is sports. KRGS-AM broadcasts to the Grand Junction, CO area at 960 AM.
AM RADIO STATION

KRGT-FM 130482
Owner: Univision Communications Inc.
Editorial: 6767 W Tropicana Ave Ste 102, Las Vegas, Nevada 89103-4755 **Tel:** 1 702 284-6400.
Web site: http://www.univision.com/content/channel.jhtml?chid=10104&schid=10176
Profile: KRGT-FM is a commercial station owned by Univision Communications Inc. The format of the station is Hispanic urban AC. KRGT-FM broadcasts to the Las Vegas area at 99.3 FM.
FM RADIO STATION

KRGY-FM 46379
Owner: Legacy Communications, LLC
Editorial: 3205 W North Front St, Grand Island, Nebraska 68803-4024 **Tel:** 1 308 381-1430.
Web site: http://newsacrossnebraska.com
Profile: KRGY-FM is a commercial station owned by Legacy Communications, LLC (dba GI Family Radio). The format of the station is classic rock music. KRGY-FM broadcasts to the Grand Island, NE area at 97.3 FM.
FM RADIO STATION

KRHV-FM 44497
Owner: Digerness(Dave & Maryann)
Editorial: 94 Laurel Mountain Rd, Mammoth Lakes, California 93546 **Tel:** 1 760 934-8888.
Email: kmmtradioworks@yahoo.com
Web site: http://www.kmmtradio.com/krhvhome.php
Profile: KRHV-FM is a commercial station owned by Dave and Maryann Digerness. The format of the station is classic rock. KRHV-FM broadcasts to the Mammoth Lakes, CA area at 93.3 FM.
FM RADIO STATION

KRHW-AM 37387
Owner: Withers Broadcasting of Southeast Missouri, LLC
Editorial: 1 Industrial Dr, Sikeston, Missouri 63801
Tel: 1 573 471-2000.
Email: kbxb@withersradio.net
Profile: KRHW-AM is a commercial station owned by Withers Broadcasting of Southeast Missouri, LLC. The format of the station is country music. KRHW-AM broadcasts to the Sikeston, MO, area at 1520 AM.
AM RADIO STATION

KRIB-AM 38960
Owner: Alpha Media
Editorial: 341 S Yorktown Pike, Mason City, Iowa 50401-4533 **Tel:** 1 641 423-1300.
Web site: http://www.discovernorthiowa.com/
Profile: KRIB-AM is a commercial station owned by Alpha Media. The format of the station is oldies. KRIB-AM broadcasts to the Rochester, MN and Mason City, IA areas at 1490 AM.
AM RADIO STATION

KRIG-FM 43774
Owner: KCD Enterprises Inc.
Editorial: 1200 SE Frank Phillips Blvd, Bartlesville, Oklahoma 74003-4332 **Tel:** 1 918 336-1001.
Email: radio@bartlesvilleradio.com
Web site: http://www.bartlesvilleradio.com
Profile: KRIG-FM is a commercial station owned by KCD Enterprises Inc. The format of the station is country. KRIG-FM broadcasts to the Bartlesville, OK area at 104.9 FM.
FM RADIO STATION

KRIK-FM 816198
Owner: Hispanic Target Media, Inc.
Editorial: 406 N Alamo St, Refugio, Texas 78377-2504
Tel: 1 361 526-2497.
Profile: KRIK-FM is a commercial station owned by Hispanic Target Media, Inc. The format of the station is Regional Mexican. KRIK-FM is licensed to Refugio, TX and broadcasts to South Texas including Victoria and Bee counties and surrounding areas.
FM RADIO STATION

KRIL-AM 35057
Owner: Townsquare Media, LLC
Editorial: 11300 State Highway 191 Bldg 2, Midland, Texas 79707-1367 **Tel:** 1 432 563-5499.
Web site: http://1410kril.com
Profile: KRIL-AM is a commercial station owned by Townsquare Media, LLC. The format of the station is classic country. KRIL-AM broadcasts to the Midland, TX area at 1410 AM.
AM RADIO STATION

KRIO-AM 38445
Owner: Rio Grande Bible Institute Inc.
Editorial: 4300 S Business Highway 281, Edinburg, Texas 78539-9650 **Tel:** 1 956 380-3435.
Email: correo@radioesperanza.com
Web site: http://www.radioesperanza.com
Profile: KRIO-AM is a commercial station owned by Rio Grande Bible Institute Inc. The format of the station is Spanish religious music and news. KRIO-AM broadcasts to the Edinburg, TX area at 910 AM.
AM RADIO STATION

KRIO-FM 41772
Owner: Radio Grande Bible Institute Inc.
Editorial: 4300 S Business Highway 281, Edinburg, Texas 78539-9650 **Tel:** 1 956 380-3435.
Email: correo@radioesperanza.com
Web site: http://radioesperanza.com
Profile: KRIO-FM is a non-commerical station owned by Radio Grande Bible Institute Inc. The format of the station is Hispanic music and news. The station broadcasts to the Edinburg, TX area at 97.7 FM.
FM RADIO STATION

KRIV-FM 42616
Owner: Leighton Enterprises Inc.
Editorial: 752 Bluffview Cir, Winona, Minnesota 55987-2515 **Tel:** 1 507 452-4000.
Web site: http://www.winonaradio.com
Profile: KRIV-FM is a commercial station owned by Leighton Enterprises Inc. The format of the station is classic hits. KRIV-FM broadcasts to the Winona, MN area at 101.1 FM.
FM RADIO STATION

KRIZ-AM 36114
Owner: Kris Bennett Broadcasting Co.
Editorial: 2600 S Jackson St, Seattle, Washington 98144-2402 **Tel:** 1 206 323-3070.
Email: ztwins@aol.com
Web site: http://www.ztwins.com
Profile: KRIZ-AM is a commercial station owned by Kris Bennett Broadcasting Co. The format of the station is talk, gospel and urban contemporary. KRIZ-AM broadcasts to the Seattle, WA area at 1420 AM.
AM RADIO STATION

KRJB-FM 39871
Owner: R & J Broadcasting
Editorial: 312 W Main St, Ada, Minnesota 56510-1252
Tel: 1 218 784-2844.
Email: krjbada@loretel.net
Web site: http://www.krjbradio.com
Profile: KRJB-FM is a commercial station owned by R & J Broadcasting. The format of the station is country music. KRJB-FM broadcasts to the Ada, MN area at 106.5 FM.
FM RADIO STATION

KRJC-FM 39872
Owner: Carlson Communications
Editorial: 1250 Lamoille Hwy, Elko, Nevada 89801-4396 **Tel:** 1 775 738-9895.
Web site: http://www.krjc.com
Profile: KRJC-FM is a commercial station owned by Carlson Communications. The format of the station is country. KRJC-FM broadcasts to the Salt Lake City area at 95.3 FM.
FM RADIO STATION

KRJM-FM 238339
Owner: R & J Broadcasting
Editorial: 312 W Main St, Ada, Minnesota 56510-1252
Tel: 1 218 784-2844.
Email: krjm@arvig.net
Web site: http://krjmradio.com
Profile: KRJM-FM is a commercial station owned by R & J Broadcasting. The format of the station is oldies music. KRJM-FM broadcasts to the Ada, MN area at 101.5 FM.
FM RADIO STATION

KRJO-AM 37121
Owner: Holladay Broadcasting Co.
Editorial: 1109 Hudson Ln, Monroe, Louisiana 71201-6003 **Tel:** 1 318 388-2323.
Web site: http://www.krjo.com
Profile: KRJO-AM is a commercial station owned by Holladay Broadcasting Co. The format of the station is classic country. KRJO-AM broadcasts in the Monroe, LA area at 1680 AM.
AM RADIO STATION

KRJT-FM 390878
Owner: Pacific Empire Communications
Editorial: 2510 Cove Ave, La Grande, Oregon 97850-3911
Web site: http://yourboomerradio.com
Profile: KRJT-FM is a commercial station owned by Pacific Empire Communications. The format of the station is oldies music. KRJT-FM broadcasts to the Portland, OR area at 105.9 FM.
FM RADIO STATION

KRJW-AM 902027
Owner: Wynne Broadcasting Co.
Editorial: 1338 Oregon Ave, Klamath Falls, Oregon 97601-6540 **Tel:** 1 541 882-4656.
Email: webmaster@klamathradio.com
Web site: http://www.klamathradio.com/KRJW/Index.html
Profile: KRJW-AM is a commercial station owned by Wynne Broadcasting Co. The format of the station is sports talk. The station airs locally at 1240 AM.
AM RADIO STATION

KRKC-AM 3833
Owner: King City Communications
Editorial: 1134 Broadway St, King City, California 93930-3317 **Tel:** 1 831 385-5421.
Email: krkcdavis@yahoo.com
Web site: http://www.krkc.com
Profile: KRKC-AM is a commercial station owned by King City Communications and operated by Radio Del Rey. The format of the station is country. KRKC-AM broadcasts to the King City, CA area at 1490 AM.
AM RADIO STATION

KRKC-FM 4568
Owner: Radio Del Rey
Editorial: 1134 San Antonio Dr, King City, California 93930 **Tel:** 1 831 385-5421.
Web site: http://www.krkc.com
Profile: KRKC-FM is a commercial station owned by Radio Del Rey. The format of the station is adult contemporary. KRKC-FM broadcasts to the King City, CA area at 102.1 FM.
FM RADIO STATION

KRKH-FM 53356
Owner: Hochman Hawaii Publishing
Editorial: 300 Ohukai Rd, Ste C318, Kihei, Hawaii 96753-7050 **Tel:** 1 808 875-8866.
Web site: http://hhawaiimedia.com
Profile: KRKH-FM is a commercial station owned by Hochman Hawaii Publishing. The format of the station is album-oriented rock. KRKH-FM broadcasts to the Maui area at 97.3 FM.
FM RADIO STATION

KRKI-FM 57776
Owner: Bandlands Broadcasting
Editorial: 1711 W Main St, Rapid City, South Dakota 57702-2564 **Tel:** 1 605 721-9005.
Web site: http://www.995espn.com
Profile: KRKI-FM is a commercial station owned by Bandlands Broadcasting. The format of the station is sports. KRKI-FM broadcasts to the Rapid City, SD area at 99.5 FM.
FM RADIO STATION

KRKK-AM 3746
Owner: Big Thicket Broadcasting Co.
Editorial: 2717 Yellowstone Rd, Rock Springs, Wyoming 82901-3261 **Tel:** 1 307 362-3793.
Web site: http://1360krkk.com
Profile: KRKK-AM is a commercial station owned by Big Thickett Broadcasting Co. The format of the station is sports. KRKK-AM broadcasts to the Rock Springs, WY area at 1360 AM.
AM RADIO STATION

KRKN-FM 4422
Owner: O-Town Communications, Inc.
Editorial: 416 E Main St, Ottumwa, Iowa 52501-3026
Tel: 1 641 684-5563.
Email: info@ottumwaradio.com
Web site: http://www.ottumwaradio.com
Profile: KRKN-FM is a commercial station owned by O-Town Communications, Inc. The format of the station is contemporary country. KRKN-FM broadcasts to the Ottumwa, IA area at 104.3 FM.
FM RADIO STATION

KRKO-AM 3505
Owner: North Sound Media
Editorial: 2707 Colby Ave Ste 1380, Everett, Washington 98201-3568 **Tel:** 1 425 304-1381.
Email: rkonews@krko.com
Web site: http://www.everettpost.com
Profile: KRKO-AM is a commercial station owned by S.R. Broadcasting Company Inc. The format of the station is sports. KRKO-AM broadcasts to the Everett, WA area at 1380 AM.
AM RADIO STATION

KRKR-FM 46514
Owner: Mission Nebraska, Inc.
Tel: 1 888 627-1020.
Email: email@mybridgeradio.net
Web site: http://www.mybridgeradio.net
Profile: KRKR-FM is a non-commercial station owned by Mission Nebraska, Inc. The format of the station is Christian music and religious programming. KRKR-FM broadcasts to the Lincoln, NE area at 95.1 FM.
FM RADIO STATION

KRKS-AM 3923
Owner: Salem Media Group, Inc.
Editorial: 3131 S Vaughn Way Ste 601, Aurora, Colorado 80014-3510 **Tel:** 1 303 750-5687.
Email: krks@krks.com
Web site: http://www.krks.com
Profile: KRKS-AM is a commercial station owned by Salem Media Group, Inc. The format of the station is Christian talk and music. KRKS-AM broadcasts to the Aurora, CO area at 990 AM.
AM RADIO STATION

KRKS-FM 46597
Owner: Salem Media Group, Inc.
Editorial: 3131 S Vaughn Way Ste 601, Aurora, Colorado 80014-3510 **Tel:** 1 303 750-5687.
Web site: http://www.krks.com
Profile: KRKS-FM is a commercial station owned by Salem Media Group, Inc. The format of the station is

Christian talk and music. KRKS-AM broadcasts to the Denver, CO area at 94.7 FM.
FM RADIO STATION

KRKT-FM 46056
Owner: Bicoastal Media LLC
Editorial: 2840 Marion St SE, Albany, Oregon 97322
Tel: 1 541 926-8628.
Web site: http://www.krkt.com
Profile: KRKT-FM is a commercial station owned by Bicoastal Media LLC. The format of the station is country music. KRKT-FM broadcasts to Albany, OR at 99.9 FM.
FM RADIO STATION

KRKX-FM 45908
Owner: Connoisseur Media LLC
Editorial: 2075 Central Ave, Billings, Montana 59102
Tel: 1 406 248-7777.
Web site: http://www.941ksky.com
Profile: KRKX-FM is commercial station owned by Connoisseur Media LLC. The format of the station is contemporary country. KRKX-FM broadcasts in the Billings, MT area at 94.1 FM.
FM RADIO STATION

KRKY-AM 39391
Owner: NRC Broadcasting
Editorial: 130 Ski Hill Rd, Breckenridge, Colorado 80424 **Tel:** 1 970 453-2234.
Profile: KRKY-AM is a commercial station owned by NRC Broadcasting. The format of the station is country. KRKY-AM broadcasts to the Breckenridge, CO area at 930 AM.
AM RADIO STATION

KRKZ-FM 863658
Owner: Alexandra Communications Inc.
Editorial: 170 3rd St, Tillamook, Oregon 97141-9489
Tel: 1 503 842-4422.
Profile: KRKZ-FM is a commercial station owned by Alexandra Communications Inc. The format of the station is Top 40/CHR. KRKZ-FM broadcasts to the Astoria, OR area at 94.3 FM.
FM RADIO STATION

KRLA-AM 34972
Owner: Salem Media Group, Inc.
Editorial: 701 N Brand Blvd, Glendale, California 91203-1295 **Tel:** 1 818 956-5552.
Email: info@krla870.com
Web site: http://www.am870theanswer.com
Profile: KRLA-AM is a commercial station owned by Salem Media Group, Inc. The format of the station is news and talk. KRLA-AM broadcasts to the Los Angeles metro area at 870 AM.
AM RADIO STATION

KRLC-AM 37469
Owner: Ida-Vend Communications Group
Editorial: 805 Stewart Ave, Lewiston, Idaho 83501-4709 **Tel:** 1 208 743-1551.
Profile: KRLC-AM is a commercial station owned by Ida-Vend Communications Group. The format of the station is classic country. KRLC-AM broadcasts to the Spokane, WA area at 1350 AM.
AM RADIO STATION

KRLD-AM 35059
Owner: CBS Radio
Editorial: 4131 N Central Expy, Dallas, Texas 75204-2102 **Tel:** 1 214 525-7000.
Web site: http://www.krld.com
Profile: KRLD-AM is a commercial station owned by CBS Radio. The format of the station is news and talk programming. KRLD-AM broadcasts to the Dallas area at 1080 AM.
AM RADIO STATION

KRLD-FM 39863
Owner: CBS Radio
Editorial: 4131 N Central Expy Ste 1000, Dallas, Texas 75204-2121 **Tel:** 1 214 525-7000.
Web site: http://dfw.cbslocal.com/category/sports
Profile: KRLD-FM is a commercial station owned by CBS Radio. The format of the station is sports. KRLD-FM broadcasts to the Dallas area at 105.3 FM.
FM RADIO STATION

KRLI-FM 132167
Owner: Kanza Inc.
Editorial: 102 N Mason St, Carrollton, Missouri 64633-2159 **Tel:** 1 660 542-0404.
Email: news@kmzu.com
Web site: http://krlicountry.com
Profile: KRLI-FM is a commercial station owned by the Kanza Inc. The format of the station is country music. The station broadcasts to the Kansas City, MO area at 103.9 FM.
FM RADIO STATION

KRLL-AM 36424
Owner: Moniteau Communications Inc.
Editorial: 100 E Buchanan St Ste A, California, Missouri 65018-1979 **Tel:** 1 573 796-3139.
Email: krllnews@embarqmail.com
Profile: KRLL-AM is a commercial station owned by Moniteau Communications Inc. The format of the station is classic country. KRLL-AM broadcasts in the California, MO area at 1420 AM.
AM RADIO STATION

KRLN-AM 37470
Owner: Royal Gorge Broadcasting LLC
Editorial: 1615 Central Ave, Canon City, Colorado 81212-8578 **Tel:** 1 719 275-7488.
Email: krlnnews@gmail.com
Profile: KRLN-AM is a commercial station owned by Royal Gorge Broadcasting LLC. The format of the station is news/talk. KRLN-AM broadcasts to the Canon City, CO area at 1400 AM.
AM RADIO STATION

KRLQ-FM 543920
Owner: Brown (Bill)
Editorial: 1319 N Vienna St, Ruston, Louisiana 71270-2337 **Tel:** 1 318 255-7941.
Email: krlq941fm@bellsouth.net
Web site: http://krlqfm.com
Profile: KRLQ-FM is a commercial station owned by Bill Brown. The format of the station is classic country. KRLQ-FM broadcasts to the Ruston, LA area at 94.1 FM.
FM RADIO STATION

KRLS-FM 44868
Owner: M & H Broadcasting Inc.
Editorial: 1610 N Lincoln St, Knoxville, Iowa 50138
Tel: 1 641 842-3161.
Email: kniakrls@kniakrls.com
Web site: http://www.kniakrls.com
Profile: KRLS-FM is a commercial station owned by M & H Broadcasting Inc. The format of the station is news and music. KRLS-FM broadcasts to the Knoxville, IA area at 92.1 FM.
FM RADIO STATION

KRLT-FM 46154
Owner: Cherry Creek Radio
Editorial: 276 Kingsbury Grade Ste 203, Stateline, Nevada 89449-9804 **Tel:** 1 775 580-7130.
Web site: http://www.krltfm.com
Profile: KRLT-FM is a commercial station owned by Cherry Creek Radio. The format of the station is adult contemporary music. KRLT-FM broadcasts to the South Lake Tahoe, CA area at 93.9 FM.
FM RADIO STATION

KRLV-AM 36504
Owner: Lotus Broadcasting Corp
Editorial: 6655 W Sahara Ave Ste C216, Las Vegas, Nevada 89146-0850
Web site: http://www.lvsportsnetwork.com/fox-sports
Profile: KRLV-AM is a commercial station owned by Lotus Broadcasting Corp. The format of the station is sports. KRLV-AM broadcasts to the Las Vegas area at 1340 AM.
AM RADIO STATION

KRLW-AM 37471
Owner: Combined Media Group
Editorial: 1 Radio Drive, Pocahontas, Arkansas 72455
Tel: 1 870 892-5234.
Email: kpoc-krlw@centurytel.net
Profile: KRLW-AM is a commercial station owned by Combined Media Group. The format of the station is oldies. KRLW-AM broadcasts to the Walnut Ridge, AR area at 1320 AM.
AM RADIO STATION

KRMB-FM 43164
Owner: World Radio Network, Inc.
Editorial: 421 E 9th St, Douglas, Arizona 85607
Tel: 1 520 364-5392.
Email: krmc@lwrn.org
Web site: http://www.worldradionetwork.org/english
Profile: KRMB-FM is a non-commercial radio station that is owned by the World Radio Network, Inc. The format is Hispanic Christian music. The station airs locally on 90.1 FM.
FM RADIO STATION

KRMC-FM 43140
Owner: World Radio Network, Inc.
Editorial: 421 E 9th St, Douglas, Arizona 85607-2123
Tel: 1 520 364-5392.
Email: krmc@lwrn.org
Web site: http://www.worldradionetwork.com
Profile: KRMC-FM is a non-commercial station owned by the World Radio Network, Inc. The format is Hispanic Christian music. KRMC-FM broadcasts to the Douglas, AZ area at 91.7 FM.
FM RADIO STATION

KRMD-AM 37472
Owner: Cumulus Media Inc.
Editorial: 270 Plaza Loop, Bossier City, Louisiana 71111-4389 **Tel:** 1 318 549-8500.
Email: cumulus.shreveport@cumulus.com
Web site: http://www.theticket1007.com/
Profile: KRMD-AM is a commercial station owned by Cumulus Media Inc. The format of the station is sports. KRMD-AM broadcasts to the Shreveport, LA area at 1340 AM.
AM RADIO STATION

KRMD-FM 44869
Owner: Cumulus Media Inc.
Editorial: 270 Plaza Loop, Cumulus Broadcast Center, Bossier City, Louisiana 71111-4389
Tel: 1 318 549-8500.
Email: nashfm1011@gmail.com
Web site: http://www.krmd.com
Profile: KRMD-FM is a commercial station owned by Cumulus Communications. The format of the station is contemporary country music. KRMD-FM broadcasts to the Shreveport, LA area at 101.1 FM.
FM RADIO STATION

KRMG-AM 38710
Owner: Cox Media Group, Inc.
Editorial: 7136 S Yale Ave Ste 500, Tulsa, Oklahoma 74136-6358 **Tel:** 1 918 493-7400.
Email: krmg.news@coxinc.com
Web site: http://www.krmg.com
Profile: KRMG-AM is a commercial station owned by Cox Media Group, Inc. The format of the station is news and talk. KRMG-AM broadcasts to the Tulsa, OK area at 740 AM.
AM RADIO STATION

KRMG-FM 44271
Owner: Cox Media Group, Inc.
Editorial: 7136 S Yale Ave Ste 500, Tulsa, Oklahoma 74136-6358 **Tel:** 1 918 493-7400.
Email: krmg.news@coxinc.com
Web site: http://www.krmg.com
Profile: KRMG-FM is a commercial station owned by Cox Media Group, Inc. The format of the station is news and talk. KRMG-FM broadcasts to the Tulsa, OK area at 102.3 FM.
FM RADIO STATION

KRML-AM 35061
Owner: Wisdom Broadcasting Co. Inc.
Editorial: 27200 Rancho San Carlos Rd, Carmel, California 93923-7911 **Tel:** 1 831 244-0102.
Web site: http://www.krml.com
Profile: KRML-AM is a commercial station owned by Wisdom Broadcasting Co. Inc. The format of the station is adult album alternative. KRML-AM broadcasts to the Carmel, CA area at 1410 AM.
AM RADIO STATION

KRMO-AM 37473
Owner: Eagle Broadcasting Inc.
Editorial: 126 S Jefferson Ave, Aurora, Missouri 65605-1635 **Tel:** 1 417 678-0416.
Email: krmo@radiotalon.com
Web site: http://www.radiotalon.com
Profile: KRMO-AM is a commercial station owned by Eagle Broadcasting Inc. The format of the station is sports, talk and agricultural news. KRMO-AM broadcasts to the Springfield, MO, area at 990 AM.
AM RADIO STATION

KRMP-AM 405744
Owner: Perry Publishing & Broadcasting Inc.
Editorial: 1457 NE 23rd St, Oklahoma City, Oklahoma 73111-3084 **Tel:** 1 405 427-5877.
Web site: http://okcheartandsoul.com
AM RADIO STATION

KRMQ-FM 417667
Owner: Rooney Moon Broadcasting
Editorial: 42437 US 70, Portales, New Mexico 88130-9030 **Tel:** 1 575 359-1759.
Email: ksel@rooneymoon.com
Web site: http://www.big1015.com/
Profile: KRMQ-FM is a commercial station owned by Rooney Moon Broadcasting. The format of the station is classic hits. KRMQ-FM broadcasts to the Portales, NM area at 101.5 FM.
FM RADIO STATION

KRMR-FM 535491
Owner: Rocking M Radio
Editorial: 207 E 7th St Ste 102, Hays, Kansas 67601-4134 **Tel:** 1 785 628-6108.
Email: info@rockingmradio.com
Web site: http://www.1057thepatriot.com
Profile: KRMR-FM is a commercial station owned by Rocking M Radio. The format of the station is talk. KRMR-FM broadcasts to the Hays, KS area at 105.7 FM.
FM RADIO STATION

KRMS-AM 37474
Owner: Viper Communications Inc.
Editorial: 5715 Osage Beach Pkwy, Osage Beach, Missouri 65065-3030 **Tel:** 1 573 348-2772.
Email: info@krmsradio.com
Web site: http://www.krmsradio.com
Profile: KRMS-AM is a commercial station owned by Viper Communications Inc. The format of the station is news and talk. KRMS-AM broadcasts in the Springfield, MO area at 1150 AM.
AM RADIO STATION

KRMW-FM 42577
Owner: Cumulus Media Inc.
Editorial: 4209 N Frontage Rd, Fayetteville, Arkansas 72703-5002 **Tel:** 1 479 521-5566.
Web site: http://www.949nashicon.com
Profile: KRMW-FM is a commercial station owned by Cumulus Media Inc. The format of the station is country music. KRMW-FM broadcasts to the Fayetteville, AR area at 94.9 FM.
FM RADIO STATION

KRMX-FM 46355
Owner: M & M Broadcasters
Editorial: 5501 Bagby Ave, Waco, Texas 76711-2300
Tel: 1 254 772-0930.
Web site: http://www.929shooterfm.com
Profile: KRMX-FM is a commercial station owned by M & M Broadcasters. The format of the station is country music. KRMX-FM airs broadcasts to Waco, TX at 92.9 FM.
FM RADIO STATION

KRMY-AM 36182
Owner: Martin's Broadcasting Inc.
Editorial: 314 N 2nd St, Killeen, Texas 76541-5205
Tel: 1 254 628-7070.
Email: krmy@krmyradio.com
Profile: KRMY-AM is a commercial station owned by Martin's Broadcasting Inc. The format of the station is gospel music. KRMY-AM broadcasts to the Killeen, TX area at 1050 AM.
AM RADIO STATION

KRNA-FM 39874
Owner: Townsquare Media, LLC
Editorial: 425 2nd St SE Ste 450, Cedar Rapids, Iowa 52401-1843 **Tel:** 1 319 365-9431.
Email: krna@krna.com
Web site: http://www.krna.com
Profile: KRNA-FM is a commercial station owned by Townsquare Media, LLC. The format of the station is rock. KRNA-FM broadcasts to the Cedar Rapids, IA area at 94.1 FM.
FM RADIO STATION

KRNB-FM 43150
Owner: Service Broadcasting Corp.
Editorial: 621 NW 6th St, Grand Prairie, Texas 75050-5555 **Tel:** 1 972 263-9911.
Email: community@krnb.com
Web site: http://www.krnb.com
Profile: KRNB-FM is a commercial station owned by Service Broadcasting Corp. The format of the station is urban adult contemporary music. KRNB-FM broadcasts to the Dallas area at 105.7 FM.
FM RADIO STATION

KRNG-FM 43494
Owner: Sierra Nevada Christian Music Assoc.
Editorial: 360 Pyramid St, Wadsworth, Nevada 89442
Tel: 1 775 575-7777.
Email: email@renegaderadio.org
Web site: http://www.renegaderadio.org
FM RADIO STATION

KRNH-FM 41969
Owner: Radio Ranch Ltd.
Editorial: 3505 Fredericksburg Rd, Kerrville, Texas 78028-9272 **Tel:** 1 830 896-4990.
Email: psa@ranchradiogroup.com
Web site: http://923theranch.com
Profile: KRNH-FM is a commercial station owned by Radio Ranch Ltd. The format of the station is country music. KRNH-FM broadcasts to the Kerrville, TX and surrounding communities at 92.3 FM.
FM RADIO STATION

KRNK-FM 46295
Owner: Townsquare Media, LLC
Editorial: 150 Nichols Ave, Casper, Wyoming 82601-1816 **Tel:** 1 307 266-5252.
Web site: http://www.rock967online.com
Profile: KRNK-FM is a commercial station owned by Townsquare Media, LLC. The format for the station is rock alternative. KRNK-FM broadcasts to the Casper-Riverton, WY area at 96.7 FM.
FM RADIO STATION

KRNL-FM 39875
Owner: Cornell College
Editorial: 810 Commons Cir SW, Mount Vernon, Iowa 52314-1000 **Tel:** 1 319 895-4431.
Email: krnl@cornellcollege.edu
Web site: http://cornellcollege.edu/krnl
FM RADIO STATION

KRNN-FM 445522
Owner: Capital Community Broadcasting Inc.
Editorial: 360 Egan Dr, Juneau, Alaska 99801-1769
Tel: 1 907 586-1670.
Email: news@ktoo.org
Web site: http://www.ktoo.org/krnn
Profile: KRNN-FM is a non-commercial station owned by Capital Community Broadcasting Inc. The format of the station is variety. KRNN-FM broadcasts to the Juneau, AK area at 102.7 FM.
FM RADIO STATION

KRNO-FM 44870
Owner: Americom Broadcasting
Editorial: 961 Matley Ln Ste 120, Reno, Nevada 89502-2119 **Tel:** 1 775 829-1964.
Email: info@1069morefm.com
Web site: http://www.sunny1069.com
Profile: KRNO-FM is a commercial station owned by Americom Broadcasting. The format of the station is adult contemporary. KRNO-FM broadcasts to the Reno, NV area at 106.9 FM.
FM RADIO STATION

KRNP-FM 856614
Owner: Armada Media
Editorial: 307 E 4th St, North Platte, Nebraska 69101-6903 **Tel:** 1 308 532-3344.
Web site: http://www.huskeradio.com
Profile: KRNP-FM is a commercial station owned by Armada Media. The format of the station is rock music. The station airs locally to to North Platte, NE area at 100.7 FM.
FM RADIO STATION

KRNQ-FM 44401
Owner: Withers Broadcasting Co.
Editorial: 108 Washington St, Keokuk, Iowa 52632
Tel: 1 319 524-5410.
Email: krnq963@mchsi.com
Web site: http://www.keokukradio.com
Profile: KRNQ-FM is a commercial station owned by Withers Broadcasting Co. The format of the station is classic rock. KRNQ-FM broadcasts to the Northeast Missouri, West Central Illinois, and Southeast Iowa listening areas at a frequency of 96.3 FM.
FM RADIO STATION

KRNT-AM 37475
Owner: Saga Communications
Editorial: 1416 Locust St, Des Moines, Iowa 50309
Tel: 1 515 280-1350.
Web site: http://www.1350krnt.com

Profile: KRNT-AM is a commercial station owned by Saga Communications. The format of the station is adult standards and talk. KRNT-AM broadcasts to the Des Moines, IA area at 1350 AM.
AM RADIO STATION

KRNV-FM 42288
Owner: Entravision Communications Corp.
Editorial: 300 S Wells Ave, Ste 12, Reno, Nevada 89502-1670 **Tel:** 1 775 333-1017.
Web site: http://www.tricolor1021.com
Profile: KRNV-FM is a commercial station owned by Entravision Communications Corp. The format of the station is Hispanic. KRNV-FM broadcasts to the Reno, NV area at 102.1 FM.
FM RADIO STATION

KRNY-FM 40975
Owner: NRG Media LLC
Editorial: 2223 Central Ave, Kearney, Nebraska 68847 **Tel:** 1 308 698-2100.
Web site: http://www.krny.com
Profile: KRNY-FM is a commercial station owned by NRG Media LLC. The format of the station is contemporary country. KRNY-FM broadcasts to the Kearney, NE area at 102.3 FM.
FM RADIO STATION

KROA-FM 39877
Owner: My Bridge Radio
Editorial: 3347 W Capital Ave, Grand Island, Nebraska 68803-1334 **Tel:** 1 888 627-1020.
Email: email@mybridgeradio.net
Web site: http://www.mybridgeradio.net
Profile: KROA-FM is a non-commercial station owned by My Bridge Radio. The format of the station is contemporary Christian and religious talk. KROA-FM broadcasts to the Doniphan, NE area at 95.7 FM.
FM RADIO STATION

KROB-AM 430505
Owner: Claro Communications Ltd.
Editorial: 1734 N Padre Island Dr, Corpus Christi, Texas 78405-4121 **Tel:** 1 361 299-6000.
Web site: http://www.krob1510.com
Profile: KROB-AM is a commercial station owned by Claro Communications Ltd. The format of the station is Hispanic programming. KROB-AM broadcasts to the Corpus Christi, TX area at 1510 AM.
AM RADIO STATION

KROC-AM 37476
Owner: Townsquare Media
Editorial: 122 4th St SW, Rochester, Minnesota 55902-3320 **Tel:** 1 507 286-1010.
Email: news@kroc.com
Web site: http://www.krocam.com
Profile: KROC-AM is a commercial station owned by Townsquare Media. The format of the station is news and talk. KROC-AM broadcasts to the Rochester, MN area at 1340 AM.
AM RADIO STATION

KROC-FM 44872
Owner: Townsquare Media
Editorial: 122 4th St SW, Rochester, Minnesota 55902-3320 **Tel:** 1 507 286-1010.
Email: news@kroc.com
Web site: http://www.kroc.com
Profile: KROC-FM is a commercial station owned by Townsquare Media. The format of the station is Top 40/CHR. KROC-FM broadcasts to the Rochester, MN area at 106.9 FM.
FM RADIO STATION

KROD-AM 39159
Owner: Townsquare Media, LLC
Editorial: 4180 N Mesa St, El Paso, Texas 79902 **Tel:** 1 915 544-9550.
Web site: http://www.krod.com
Profile: KROD-AM is a commercial station owned by Townsquare Media, LLC. The format of the station is sports. KROD-AM broadcasts in the El Paso, TX area at 600 AM.
AM RADIO STATION

KROE-AM 37477
Owner: Lovcom, Inc.
Editorial: 1716 Kroe Ln, Sheridan, Wyoming 82801-9681 **Tel:** 1 307 672-7421.
Web site: http://www.sheridanmedia.com
Profile: KROE-AM is a commercial station owned by Lovcom, Inc. The format of the station is news, sports and talk. KROE-AM broadcasts to the Sheridan, WY area at 930 AM.
AM RADIO STATION

KROF-AM 37478
Owner: Townsquare Media, LLC
Editorial: 1749 Bertrand Dr, Lafayette, Louisiana 70506-2054 **Tel:** 1 337 233-6000.
Web site: http://talkradio960.com
Profile: KROF-AM is a commercial station owned by Townsquare Media, LLC. The format of the station is news and talk. KROF-AM broadcasts to the Lafayette, LA area at 960 AM.
AM RADIO STATION

KROG-FM 46142
Owner: Opus Broadcasting Systems Inc.
Editorial: 511 Rossanley Dr, Medford, Oregon 97501-1771 **Tel:** 1 541 772-0322.
Web site: http://www.969therogue.com
Profile: KROG-FM is a commercial station owned by Opus Broadcasting Systems Inc. The format of the station is rock alternative music. KROG-FM broadcasts to the Medford, OR area at 96.9 FM.
FM RADIO STATION

KROH-FM 775521
Owner: Port Townsend Seventh-Day Adventist Church
Editorial: 1505 Franklin St, Port Townsend, Washington 98368-8121 **Tel:** 1 360 379-8383.
Web site: http://www.radioofhope.org
Profile: KROH-FM is a non-commercial station owned by Port Townsend Seventh-Day Adventist Church. The format of the station features religious programming with a Christian focus. KROH-FM is broadcasts to the Port Townsend, WA area at a frequency of 91.1 FM.
FM RADIO STATION

KROI-FM 42926
Owner: Urban One, Inc.
Editorial: 24 Greenway Plz Ste 900, Houston, Texas 77046-2418 **Tel:** 1 713 623-2108.
Web site: https://radionowhouston.com
Profile: KROI-FM is a commercial station owned by Urban One, Inc. The format of the station is Top 40. KROI-FM broadcasts to the Houston area at 92.1 FM. The station's slogan is, "Houston's LIT Music Station."
FM RADIO STATION

KROK-FM 520100
Owner: Standard Broadcasting Co.
Editorial: 168 Kvvp Dr, Leesville, Louisiana 71446-5817 **Tel:** 1 337 537-9292.
Email: anthony@kvvp.com
Web site: http://www.krok.com
Profile: KROK-FM is a commercial station owned by Standard Broadcasting Co. The format of the station is adult album alternative music. KROK-FM broadcasts to the Leesville, LA area at 95.7 FM.
FM RADIO STATION

KROM-FM 46463
Owner: Univision Communications Inc.
Editorial: 12451 Network Blvd Ste 140, San Antonio, Texas 78249-3336 **Tel:** 1 210 610-4300.
Email: la929estereolahno@univision.com
Web site: http://929sanantonio.univision.com
Profile: KROM-FM is a commercial station owned by Univision Communications Inc. The format of the station is regional Mexican. KROM-FM broadcasts to the San Antonio area at 92.9 FM.
FM RADIO STATION

KROO-AM 39006
Owner: Lake Country Radio LP
Editorial: 114 E Elm St, Breckenridge, Texas 76424-3613 **Tel:** 1 940 549-1330.
Web site: https://www.lakecountrytalkradio.net
Profile: KROO-AM is a commercial station owned by Lake Country Radio LP. The format of the station is News and Talk. KROO-AM broadcasts to Breckenridge, TX at 1430 AM.
AM RADIO STATION

KROP-AM 74344
Owner: Lardog Communications, LLC (Teresa Goodspeed)
Editorial: 120 S Plaza St, Brawley, California 92227-2428 **Tel:** 1 760 344-1300.
Web site: http://www.krop.info/
Profile: KROP-AM is a commercial station owned by Lardog Communications, LLC. The format of the station is conservative talk. The station airs locally at 1300 AM in the El Centro, CA area.
AM RADIO STATION

KROQ-FM 39878
Owner: CBS Radio
Editorial: 5901 Venice Blvd, Los Angeles, California 90034-1708 **Tel:** 1 323 930-1067.
Email: tips@kroq.com
Web site: http://kroq.cbslocal.com
Profile: KROQ-FM is a commercial station owned by CBS Radio. The format of the station is rock alternative. KROQ-FM broadcasts to the Los Angeles area at 106.7 FM.
FM RADIO STATION

KROR-FM 43816
Owner: NRG Media LLC
Editorial: 3532 W Capital Ave, Grand Island, Nebraska 68803 **Tel:** 1 308 381-1077.
Web site: http://www.rock1015.com
FM RADIO STATION

KROS-AM 35063
Owner: KROS Broadcasting Inc.
Editorial: 870 13th Ave N, Clinton, Iowa 52732-5116 **Tel:** 1 563 242-1252.
Email: contactus@krosradio.com
Web site: http://www.krosradio.com
Profile: KROS-AM is a commercial station owned by KROS Broadcasting Inc. The format of the station is full service, featuring a mix of adult contemporary music, news, and sports. KROS-AM broadcasts to the Clinton, IA area at 1340 AM.
AM RADIO STATION

KROX-AM 35064
Owner: Gopher Communications Company
Editorial: 208 S Main St, Crookston, Minnesota 56716-1969 **Tel:** 1 218 281-1140.
Email: krox@rrv.net
Web site: http://www.kroxam.com
Profile: KROX-AM is a commercial station owned by Gopher Communications Company. The format of the station is adult contemporary music, sports and news. KROX-AM broadcasts to the Crookston, MN area at 1260 AM.
AM RADIO STATION

KROX-FM 41634
Owner: Emmis Communications Corp.
Editorial: 8309 N Interstate Hwy 35, Austin, Texas 78753-5720 **Tel:** 1 512 836-5769.
Web site: http://www.101x.com
Profile: KROX-FM is a commercial station owned by Emmis Communications Corp. The format of the station is rock alternative music. KROX-FM broadcasts to the Austin, TX area at 101.5 FM.
FM RADIO STATION

KRPA-AM 62095
Owner: Satnam Media Group, Inc.
Editorial: 404 S 1st St Ste 202, Mount Vernon, Washington 98273-3866 **Tel:** 1 604 590-3510.
Email: ssd@radiopunjab.com
Web site: http://radiopunjab.com/vancouver/
Profile: KRPA-AM is a commercial station owned by Satnam Media Group, Inc. The format of the station features South Asian and Indian focused programming. KRPA-AM broadcasts in the Seattle, WA and Vancouver, BC areas at 1110 AM.
AM RADIO STATION

KRPI-AM 35025
Owner: BBC Broadcasting Inc.
Editorial: 5538 Imhoff Rd, Ferndale, Washington 98248 **Tel:** 1 360 384-5117.
Email: 1550radio@gmail.com
Web site: http://www.krpiradio.com
Profile: KRPI-AM is a commercial station owned by BBC Broadcasting Inc. The format of the station is Indian variety. KRPI-AM broadcasts to the Ferndale, WA area at 1550 AM.
AM RADIO STATION

KRPL-AM 37479
Owner: KRPL Inc.
Editorial: 1114 N Almon St, Moscow, Idaho 83843-8507 **Tel:** 1 208 882-2551.
Email: reception@idavend.com
Profile: KRPL-AM is a commercial station owned by KRPL Inc. The format of the station is sports talk. KRPL-AM broadcasts to the Spokane, WA area at 1400 AM.
AM RADIO STATION

KRPM-FM 154207
Owner: BMG Billings
Editorial: 2425 King Ave W, Billings, Montana 59102-6460 **Tel:** 1 406 238-1000.
Email: psa@twang1051.com
Web site: http://www.twang1075.com
Profile: KRPM-FM is a commercial station owned by BMG Billings. The format of the station is Country. KRPM-FM broadcasts to the Billings, MT area at 107.5 FM.
FM RADIO STATION

KRPR-FM 42512
Owner: Rochester Public Radio
Editorial: 1620 Greenview Dr SW, Rochester, Minnesota 55902-4319 **Tel:** 1 507 288-2376.
Profile: KRPR-FM is a non-commercial station owned by Rochester Public Radio. The format of the station is classic rock music. KRPR-FM broadcasts to the Rochester, MN area at a frequency of 89.9 FM.
FM RADIO STATION

KRPT-FM 41250
Owner: iHeart Media Inc.
Editorial: 6222 W Interstate 10, San Antonio, Texas 78201-2013 **Tel:** 1 210 736-9700.
Web site: http://www.kbuccountry.com/main.html
Profile: KRPT-FM is a commercial station owned by iHeart Media Inc. The format of the station is classic country. KRPT-FM broadcasts to the San Antonio area at 92.5 FM.
FM RADIO STATION

KRPU-AM 38921
Owner: Spice Radio
Editorial: 4135 Northgate Blvd Ste 1, Sacramento, California 95834-1226
Web site: http://radiopunjab.com/sacramento
Profile: KRPU-AM is a commercial station owned by Spice Radio. The format of the station is ethnic East Asian. The station broadcasts to the Sacramento, CA area at 1210 AM.
AM RADIO STATION

KRQB-FM 41639
Owner: Liberman Broadcasting Inc.
Editorial: 1845 Business Center Dr, San Bernardino, California 92408-3467 **Tel:** 1 909 663-1961.
Web site: http://quebuena961.estrellatv.com/
Profile: KRQB-FM is a commercial station owned by Liberman Broadcasting Inc. The format of the station is regional Mexican. KRQB-FM broadcasts to the San Bernardino, CA area at 96.1 FM.
FM RADIO STATION

KRQC-FM 606577
Owner: Davenport Adventist Radio Inc
Editorial: 4444 W Kimberly Rd, Davenport, Iowa 52806-7107 **Tel:** 1 563 391-3016.
Web site: http://www.3abnradio.org
Profile: KRQC-FM is a commercial station owned by Davenport Adventist Radio Inc. The format for the station is Christian music and talk. The target audience of the station is adults, ages 18 to 64. KRQC-FM broadcasts to the Davenport, IA area at 107.9 FM.
FM RADIO STATION

KRQK-FM 44877
Owner: American General Media
Editorial: 2325 Skyway Dr, Santa Maria, California 93455-1137 **Tel:** 1 805 922-1041.
Web site: http://www.1003laley.com
Profile: KRQK-FM is a commercial station owned by American General Media. The format of the station is Regional Mexican. KRQK-FM broadcasts to the Santa Maria, CA area at 100.3 FM.
FM RADIO STATION

KRQN-FM 886136
Owner: Flinn Broadcasting Corp.
Editorial: 425 2nd St SE Fl 4, Cedar Rapids, Iowa 52401-1819 **Tel:** 1 319 892-3574.
Web site: http://i1071.com
Profile: KRQN-FM is a commercial station owned by Flinn Broadcasting Corp. and operated by Townsquare Media, LLC. The format of the station is Top 40/CHR. KRQN-FM broadcasts to the Cedar Rapids, IA area at a frequency of 107.1 FM.
FM RADIO STATION

KRQQ-FM 46206
Owner: iHeartMedia Inc.
Editorial: 3202 N Oracle Rd, Tucson, Arizona 85705-3820 **Tel:** 1 520 618-2100.
Web site: http://www.krq.com
Profile: KRQQ-FM is a commercial station owned by iHeartMedia Inc. The format of the station is Top 40/CHR. KRQQ-FM broadcasts to the Tucson, AZ area on 93.7 FM.
FM RADIO STATION

KRQR-FM 43126
Owner: Results Radio Group
Editorial: 856 Manzanita Ct, Chico, California 95926 **Tel:** 1 530 342-2200.
Web site: http://www.zrockfm.com
Profile: KRQR-FM is a commercial station owned by Results Radio Group. The format of the station is rock alternative. KRQR-FM broadcasts to the Chico, CA area at 106.7 FM.
FM RADIO STATION

KRQT-FM 46682
Owner: Bicoastal Media LLC
Editorial: 1130 14th Ave, Longview, Washington 98632-3017 **Tel:** 1 360 425-1500.
Web site: http://www.rocket107.com
Profile: KRQT-FM is a commercial station owned by Bicoastal Media LLC. The format of the station is classic rock music. KRQT-FM broadcasts to the Portland, OR area at 107.1 FM.
FM RADIO STATION

KRQX-FM 155833
Owner: Redrock Broadcasting
Editorial: 216 W St George Blvd Ste 101, Saint George, Utah 84770-1306 **Tel:** 1 435 6282948.
Email: sunwaveradio@gmail.com
Profile: KRQX-FM is a commercial station owned by Redrock Broadcasting. The format of the station is classic hits. KRQX-FM broadcasts to the St. George, UT area at a frequency of 98.9 FM.
FM RADIO STATION

KRRF-FM 43505
Owner: Cumulus Media Inc.
Editorial: 403 E Montecito St, Santa Barbara, California 93101-1759
Web site: http://www.1063nashicon.com
Profile: KRRF-FM is a commercial station owned by Cumulus Media Inc. The format of the station is country. KRRF-FM broadcasts to the Santa Barbara, CA area at 106.3 FM.
FM RADIO STATION

KRRG-FM 39881
Owner: Guerra Enterprises
Editorial: 6402 N Bartlett Ave, Ste 1, Laredo, Texas 78041-6448 **Tel:** 1 956 724-9800.
Email: livewire@krrg.com
Web site: http://bigbuck98.com
Profile: KRRG-FM is a commercial station owned by Guerra Enterprises. The format of the station is classic country music. KRRG-FM broadcasts to the Laredo, TX, area at 98.1 FM.
FM RADIO STATION

KRRK-FM 44544
Owner: Mad Dog Wireless Inc.
Editorial: 2068 McCulloch Blvd N, Lake Havasu City, Arizona 86403-6712 **Tel:** 1 928 855-1051.
Email: info@maddog.net
Profile: KRRK-FM is a commercial station owned by Mad Dog Wireless Inc. The format of the station is classic rock music. KRRK-FM broadcasts in the Lake Havasu City, AZ area at 100.7 FM.
FM RADIO STATION

KRRL-FM 39690
Owner: iHeartMedia Inc.
Editorial: 3400 W Olive Ave Ste 550, Burbank, California 91505-5544 **Tel:** 1 818 559-2252.
Web site: http://real923la.iheart.com
Profile: KRRL-FM is a commercial station owned by iHeartMedia Inc. The format of the station is urban contemporary and R&B. KRRL-FM broadcasts to the Los Angeles area at 92.3 FM.
FM RADIO STATION

KRRM-FM 519715
Owner: Bell (Shirley M.)
Editorial: 225 Rogue River Hwy, Grants Pass, Oregon 97527-5477 **Tel:** 1 541 479-6497.
Email: krrm@krrm.com

Web site: http://www.krrm.com
Profile: KRRM-FM is a commercial station owned by Shirley M. Bell. The format of the station is country music and talk. KRRM-FM broadcasts to the Grants Pass, OR area at 94.7 FM.
FM RADIO STATION

KRRN-FM 327793
Owner: Entravision Communications Corp.
Editorial: 500 Pilot Rd Ste D, Las Vegas, Nevada 89119-3624 **Tel:** 1 702 434-0015.
Web site: http://www.superestrella927.com
Profile: KRRN-FM is a commercial station owned by Entravision Communications Corp. The format of the station is Hispanic. KRRN-FM broadcasts to the Las Vegas area on 92.7 FM.
FM RADIO STATION

KRRO-FM 45684
Owner: Midwest Communications
Editorial: 500 S Phillips Ave, Sioux Falls, South Dakota 57104-6825 **Tel:** 1 605 331-5350.
Email: krro@krro.com
Web site: http://www.krro.com
Profile: KRRO-FM is a commercial station owned by Midwest Communications. The format of the station is rock/album-oriented rock. KRRO-FM broadcasts to the Sioux Falls, SD area at 103.7 FM.
FM RADIO STATION

KRRP-AM 37057
Owner: Hobbs(Francis V.)
Editorial: 163 Catfish Bend Rd, Coushatta, Louisiana 71019-8828 **Tel:** 1 318 932-7132.
Web site: http://krrpradio.com
AM RADIO STATION

KRRQ-FM 42973
Owner: Cumulus Media Inc
Editorial: 202 Galbert Rd, Lafayette, Louisiana 70506-1806 **Tel:** 1 337 232-1311.
Web site: http://www.krrq.com
Profile: KRRQ-FM is a commercial station owned by Cumulus Media Inc. The format of the station is urban contemporary. KRRQ-FM broadcasts to the Lafayette, LA area at 95.5 FM.
FM RADIO STATION

KRRR-FM 46838
Owner: Appaloosa Broadcasting
Editorial: 1600 Van Lennen Ave, Cheyenne, Wyoming 82001-4636 **Tel:** 1 307 638-8921.
Email: news@radiowyo.com
Web site: http://www.1049krrr.com
Profile: KRRR-FM is a commercial station owned by Appaloosa Broadcasting. The format of the station is oldies. KRRR-FM broadcasts to the Cheyenne, WY area at 104.9 FM.
FM RADIO STATION

KRRS-AM 36213
Owner: California Broadcasting Company, LLC
Editorial: 965 Stony Point Rd, Santa Rosa, California 95407-7129 **Tel:** 1 707 545-1460.
Profile: KRRS-AM is a commercial station owned by California Broadcasting Company, LLC. The format of the station is Regional Mexican music. KRRS-AM broadcasts to the Santa Rosa, CA area at 1460 AM.
AM RADIO STATION

KRRV-FM 44878
Owner: Cenla Broadcasting Inc.
Editorial: 1115 Texas Ave, Alexandria, Louisiana 71301 **Tel:** 1 318 445-1234.
Web site: http://www.krrvonline.com
Profile: KRRV-FM is a commercial station owned by Cenla Broadcasting Inc. The format of the station is country music. KRRV-FM broadcasts to the Alexandria, LA area at 100.3 FM.
FM RADIO STATION

KRRW-FM 43654
Owner: Radio Mankato
Editorial: 59346 Madison Ave, Mankato, Minnesota 56001-8518 **Tel:** 1 507 345-4537.
Email: news@ktoe.com
Web site: http://www.krrw.com
Profile: KRRW-FM is a commercial station owned by Radio Mankato. The format of the station is country. KRRW-FM broadcasts to the Saint James, MN area at 101.5 FM.
FM RADIO STATION

KRRX-FM 44564
Owner: Mapleton of Redding, LLC
Editorial: 3360 Alta Mesa Dr, Redding, California 96002-2831 **Tel:** 1 530 226-9500.
Web site: http://www.106x.com
Profile: KRRX-FM is a commercial station owned by Mapleton of Redding, LLC. The format of the station is rock/album-oriented rock. KRRX-FM broadcasts to the Redding, CA area at 106.1 FM.
FM RADIO STATION

KRRY-FM 39855
Owner: Townsquare Media
Editorial: 408 N 24th St, Quincy, Illinois 62301-3254 **Tel:** 1 217 223-5292.
Web site: http://www.y101radio.com
Profile: KRRY-FM is a commercial station owned by Townsquare Media. The format of the station is hot adult contemporary. KRRY-FM broadcasts to the Quincy, IL; Hannibal, MO; and Keokuk, IA, area at 100.9 FM.
FM RADIO STATION

KRRZ-AM 37484
Owner: iHeartMedia Inc.
Editorial: 1000 20th Ave SW, Minot, North Dakota 58701-6447 **Tel:** 1 701 852-4646.
Web site: http://www.oldies1390.com
Profile: KRRZ-AM is a commercial station owned by iHeartMedia Inc. The format of the station is oldies. KRRZ-AM broadcasts to the Minot-Bismarck, ND area at 1390 AM.
AM RADIO STATION

KRSB-FM 45732
Owner: Brooke Communications Inc.
Editorial: 1445 W Harvard Ave, Roseburg, Oregon 97471 **Tel:** 1 541 672-6641.
Email: country@bciradio.com
Web site: http://www.541radio.com
Profile: KRSB-FM is a commercial station owned by Brooke Communications Inc. The format of the station is contemporary country music. KRSB-FM broadcasts to the Roseburg, OR area at 103.1 FM.
FM RADIO STATION

KRSD-FM 41949
Owner: Minnesota Public Radio
Editorial: 2001 S Summit Ave, Sioux Falls, South Dakota 57197 **Tel:** 1 605 335-6666.
Web site: http://minnesota.publicradio.org/radio/stations/krsd/
Profile: KRSD-FM is a non-commercial station owned by Minnesota Public Radio. The format of the station is classical music. KRSD-FM broadcasts to the Sioux Falls, SD area at 88.1 FM.
FM RADIO STATION

KRSE-FM 44879
Owner: New Northwest Broadcasters LLC
Editorial: 1200 Chesterly Dr Ste 160, Yakima, Washington 98902-7345 **Tel:** 1 509 248-2900.
Web site: http://www.thehawkyakima.com/
FM RADIO STATION

KRSF-FM 799656
Owner: Radio 74 Internationale
Tel: 1 760 375-2355.
Email: contact@radio74.org
Web site: http://krsf.net
Profile: KRSF-FM is a non-commercial station owned by Radio 74 Internationale. The format of the station is Christian teaching and music. KRSF-FM broadcasts to the Ridgecrest, CA area at a frequency of 89.3 FM.
FM RADIO STATION

KRSH-FM 42930
Owner: Wine Country Radio
Editorial: 3565 Standish Ave, Santa Rosa, California 95407 **Tel:** 1 707 588-0707.
Email: studio@krsh.com
Web site: http://www.krsh.com
Profile: KRSH-FM is a commercial station owned by Wine Country Radio. The format of the station is adult album alternative music. KRSH-FM broadcasts to the Santa Rosa, CA area at 95.9 FM.
FM RADIO STATION

KRSJ-FM 44880
Owner: Four Corners Broadcasting LLC
Editorial: 190 Turner Dr, Unit G, Durango, Colorado 81303-8231 **Tel:** 1 970 259-4444.
Email: news@radiodurango.com
Web site: http://www.radiodurango.com/krsj.asp
Profile: KRSJ-FM is a commercial station owned by Four Corners Broadcasting LLC. The format of the station is contemporary country music. KRSJ-FM broadcasts to the Albuquerque, NM area at 100.5 FM.
FM RADIO STATION

KRSK-FM 42815
Owner: Entercom Communications Corp.
Editorial: 0700 SW Bancroft St, Portland, Oregon 97239-4226 **Tel:** 1 503 223-1441.
Web site: http://www.1051thebuzz.com
Profile: KRSK-FM is a commercial station owned by Entercom Communications Corp. The format of the station is hot adult contemporary. KRSK-FM broadcasts in the Portland, OR area at 105.1 FM.
FM RADIO STATION

KRSL-AM 37485
Owner: White Communications
Editorial: 1984 N Main St, Russell, Kansas 67665-1236 **Tel:** 1 785 483-3121.
Email: comments@krsl.com
Web site: http://www.krsl.com
Profile: KRSL-AM is a commercial station owned by White Communications. The format of the station is classic country. KRSL-AM broadcasts to the Russell, KS area at 990 AM.
AM RADIO STATION

KRSL-FM 44593
Owner: White Communications
Editorial: 1984 N Main St, Russell, Kansas 67665-1236 **Tel:** 1 785 483-3121.
Email: comments@krsl.com
Web site: http://www.krsl.com
Profile: KRSL-FM is a commercial station owned by White Communications. The format of the station is adult hits. KRSL-FM broadcasts to the Russell, KS area at 95.9 FM.
FM RADIO STATION

KRSN-AM 36805
Owner: Sutton (David and Gillian)
Editorial: 3801 Arkansas Ave Ste E, Los Alamos, New Mexico 87544-1600 **Tel:** 1 505 663-1490.
Email: INFO@KRSNAM1490.COM
Web site: http://www.krsnam1490.com
Profile: KRSN-AM is a commercial station owned by David and Gillian Sutton. The format of the station is news, talk information and variety. KRSN-AM broadcasts to the Los Alamos, NM area at 1490 AM.
AM RADIO STATION

KRSP-FM 42072
Owner: Bonneville International Corp.
Editorial: 55 N 300 W, Salt Lake City, Utah 84101-3502 **Tel:** 1 801 575-5555.
Web site: http://www.1035thearrow.com
Profile: KRSP-FM is a commercial station owned by Bonneville International Corp. The format of the station is classic rock. KRSP-FM broadcasts to the Salt Lake City area at 103.5 FM.
FM RADIO STATION

KRSQ-FM 42416
Owner: BMG Billings, LLC
Editorial: 222 N 32nd St Fl 10, Billings, Montana 59101-1973 **Tel:** 1 406 238-1000.
Web site: http://www.hot1019.com
Profile: KRSQ-FM is a commercial station owned by BMG Billings, LLC. The format is top 40/CHR. The station airs in the Billings, MT area at 101.9FM.
FM RADIO STATION

KRSR-FM 852442
Owner: Radio 74 Internationale
Tel: 1 760 375-2355.
Email: contact@radio74.org
Web site: http://www.radio74.net
Profile: KRSR-FM is a non-commercial station owned by Radio 74 Internationale. The format of the station is Christian teaching and music. KRSR-FM broadcasts to the Ridgecrest, CA area at a frequency of 90.5 FM.
FM RADIO STATION

KRSS-FM 42999
Owner: Radio Free Ministries
Editorial: 1500 S 14th St, Clarinda, Iowa 51632-3120 **Tel:** 1 712 542-2260.
Web site: http://www.krss.me
Profile: KRSS-FM is a non-commercial station owned by Radio Free Ministries. The format of the station is religious talk and music. KRSS-FM broadcasts to the Omaha, NE area at a frequency of 93.5.
FM RADIO STATION

KRST-FM 42861
Owner: Cumulus Media Inc
Editorial: 500 4th St NW Ste 500, Albuquerque, New Mexico 87102-2172 **Tel:** 1 505 767-6700.
Web site: http://www.nashfm923krst.com
Profile: KRST-FM is a commercial station owned by Cumulus Media Inc. The format for the station is contemporary country. KRST-FM broadcasts to the Albuquerque, NM, area at 92.3 FM.
FM RADIO STATION

KRSV-AM 38475
Owner: SVI Media, LLC
Editorial: 10399 State Highway 238, Afton, Wyoming 83110 **Tel:** 1 307 885-5778.
AM RADIO STATION

KRSV-FM 45859
Owner: SVI Media, LLC
Tel: 1 307 885-5778.
Profile: KRSV-FM is a commercial station owned by SVI Media. The format of the station is Adult Contemporary. It broadcasts to the Afton, Wyoming area at 98.7 FM.
FM RADIO STATION

KRSW-FM 686857
Owner: Minnesota Public Radio
Editorial: 1450 Collegeway, Worthington, Minnesota 56187-3024 **Tel:** 1 507 372-2904.
Web site: http://www.minnesota.publicradio.org/radio/stations/knswkrsw/
Profile: KRSW-FM is a non-commercial station owned by Minnesota Public Radio. The format of the station is classical music. KRSW-FM broadcasts to the Worthington, MN area at 89.3 FM.
FM RADIO STATION

KRSY-AM 38410
Owner: WP Broadcasting LLC
Editorial: 119 N Canyon Rd, Alamogordo, New Mexico 88310-5910 **Tel:** 1 575 437-1505.
Email: krsy@snmradio.com
Web site: http://snmradio.com/krsyam/index.html
Profile: KRSY-AM is a commercial station owned by WP Broadcasting LLC. The format of the station is talk. KRSY-AM broadcasts to the Alamogordo, NM area at 1230 AM.
AM RADIO STATION

KRSY-FM 45776
Owner: WP Broadcasting LLC
Editorial: 119 N Canyon Rd, Alamogordo, New Mexico 88310-5910 **Tel:** 1 575 437-1505.
Email: krsy@snmradio.com
Web site: http://www.snmradio.com
Profile: KRSY-FM is a commercial station owned by WP Broadcasting LLC. The format of the station is country music. KRSY-FM broadcasts to the Albuquerque, NM area at 92.7 FM.
FM RADIO STATION

KRTA-AM 38795
Owner: Opus Broadcasting Systems Inc.
Editorial: 511 Rossanley Dr, Medford, Oregon 97501-1771 **Tel:** 1 541 772-0322.
Email: contact@opusradio.com
Web site: http://opusradio.com/610am/
Profile: KRTA-AM is a commercial station owned by Opus Broadcasting Systems. The format of the station is regional Mexican music. KRTA-AM broadcasts to the Medford, OR area at 610 AM.
AM RADIO STATION

KRTH-FM 41633
Owner: CBS Local Media
Editorial: 5670 Wilshire Blvd Ste 200, Los Angeles, California 90036-5657 **Tel:** 1 323 936-5784.
Web site: http://kearth101.cbslocal.com
Profile: KRTH-FM is a commercial station owned by CBS Radio. The format of the station is classic hits. KRTH-FM broadcasts to the Los Angeles area at 101.1 FM.
FM RADIO STATION

KRTI-FM 42093
Owner: Digity Media, LLC
Editorial: 1801 N 13th Ave E, Newton, Iowa 50208-1308 **Tel:** 1 641 236-5784.
Email: radioinfo@alphamediausa.com
Web site: http://www.myiowainfo.com
Profile: KRTI-FM is a commercial station owned by Digity Media, LLC. The format of the station is hot adult contemporary. KRTI-FM broadcasts to the Newton, IA area at 106.7 FM.
FM RADIO STATION

KRTN-AM 38955
Owner: Enchanted Air Inc.
Editorial: 1128 State St, Raton, New Mexico 87740-2330 **Tel:** 1 575 445-3652.
Email: krtn@bacavalley.com
Profile: KRTN-AM is a commercial station owned by Enchanted Air Inc. The format of the station is adult contemporary music. KRTN-AM broadcasts to the Albuquerque, NM area at 1490 AM.
AM RADIO STATION

KRTN-FM 46293
Owner: Enchanted Air Inc.
Editorial: 1128 State St, Raton, New Mexico 87740-2330 **Tel:** 1 575 445-3652.
Email: krtn@bacavalley.com
Profile: KRTN-FM is a commercial station owned by Enchanted Air Inc. The format of the station is oldies music. KRTN-FM broadcasts to the Albuquerque, NM area at 93.9 FM.
FM RADIO STATION

KRTO-FM 62100
Owner: Emerald Wave Media
Editorial: 718 E Chapel St, Santa Maria, California 93454-4524 **Tel:** 1 805 928-4334.
Profile: KRTO-FM is a commercial station owned by Emerald Wave Media. The format of the station is oldies. KRTO-FM broadcasts to the Santa Maria, CA area at 97.1 FM.
FM RADIO STATION

KRTR-FM 42310
Owner: Summit Media Broadcasting LLC
Editorial: 900 Fort Street Mall Ste. 700, Honolulu, Hawaii 96813-3721 **Tel:** 1 808 275-1000.
Web site: http://www.krater963.com
Profile: KRTR-FM is a commercial station owned by Summit Media Broadcasting LLC. The format of the station is adult contemporary. KRTR-FM broadcasts to the Honolulu area at 96.3 FM.
FM RADIO STATION

KRTS-FM 695340
Owner: Matinee Radio, LLC
Editorial: 111 South Highland Ave., Marfa, Texas 79843 **Tel:** 1 432 729-4578.
Email: info@marfapublicradio.org
Web site: http://www.marfapublicradio.org
Profile: KRTS-FM is a non-commercial station owned by Matinee Radio, LLC. The format of the station is variety. KRTS-FM broadcasts to the Odessa-Midland, TX area at 93.5 FM. The station airs programming on KXWT-FM.
FM RADIO STATION

KRTY-FM 39534
Owner: Empire Broadcasting Systems Corp.
Editorial: 750 Story Rd, San Jose, California 95122-2604 **Tel:** 1 408 293-8030.
Web site: http://www.krty.com
Profile: KRTY-FM is a commercial station owned by Empire Broadcasting Systems Corp. The format of the station is contemporary country. KRTY-FM broadcasts to the San Jose, CA area at 95.3 FM.
FM RADIO STATION

KRTZ-FM 46276
Owner: American General Media
Editorial: 2402 Hawkins St, Cortez, Colorado 81321-9544 **Tel:** 1 970 565-6565.
Email: radio@krtzradio.com
Web site: http://www.krtzradio.com
Profile: KRTZ-FM is a commercial station owned by American General Media. The format of the station is adult contemporary music. KRTZ-FM broadcasts to the Albuquerque, NM area at 98.7 FM.
FM RADIO STATION

KRUF-FM 44957
Owner: Townsquare Media, LLC
Editorial: 6341 Westport Ave, Shreveport, Louisiana 71129-2415 **Tel:** 1 318 688-1130.
Web site: http://k945.com
Profile: KRUF-FM is a commercial station owned by Townsquare Media, LLC. The format of the station is Top 40/CHR. KRUF-FM broadcasts to the Shreveport, LA area at 94.5 FM.
FM RADIO STATION

KRUI-AM 36308
Owner: MTD Inc.
Editorial: 1086 Mechem Dr, Ruidoso, New Mexico 88345-7029 **Tel:** 1 575 258-9922.
Email: mtdradio@mtdradio.com
Profile: KRUI-AM is a commercial station owned by MTD Inc. The format of the station is talk. KRUI-AM broadcasts to the Ruidoso, NM area at 1490 AM.
AM RADIO STATION

KRUI-FM 41677
Owner: Student Broadcasters Inc.
Editorial: 379 IMU, University of Iowa, Iowa City, Iowa 52242 **Tel:** 1 319 335-9525.
Email: krui@uiowa.edu
Web site: http://www.krui.fm
Profile: KRUI-FM is a non-commercial station owned by Student Broadcasters Inc. The format for the station is college variety. KRUI-FM broadcasts to the Iowa City, IA area at 89.7 FM.
FM RADIO STATION

KRUN-AM 37136
Owner: Graham Brothers Communications LLC
Editorial: 1920 Hutchins Ave, Ballinger, Texas 76821-4402 **Tel:** 1 325 365-5500.
Email: krun1400@hotmail.com
Web site: http://www.krunam.com
Profile: KRUN-AM is a commercial station owned by Graham Brothers Communications LLC. The format of the station is contemporary country. KRUN-AM broadcasts to the Ballinger, TX area at 1400 AM.
AM RADIO STATION

KRUP-FM 42968
Owner: McCormick Broadcasting
Editorial: 301 Airport Road, Dillingham, Alaska 99576-9999 **Tel:** 1 907 842-2333.
Profile: KRUP-FM is a commercial station owned by McCormick Broadcasting. The format of the station is talk. KRUP-FM broadcasts to the Anchorage, AK area at a frequency of 99.1 FM.
FM RADIO STATION

KRUS-AM 37486
Owner: Red Peach LLC
Editorial: 500 N Monroe St, Ruston, Louisiana 71270-3835 **Tel:** 1 318 255-5000.
Profile: KRUS-AM is a commercial station owned by Red Peach LLC. The format of the station is gospel music. KRUS-AM broadcasts to the Ruston, LA area at 1490 AM.
AM RADIO STATION

KRUU-FM 798116
Owner: Fairfield Youth Advocacy, Inc.
Editorial: 405 N 2Nd St, Fairfield, Iowa 52556-2467 **Tel:** 1 641 209-1083.
Email: news@kruufm.com
Web site: http://www.kruufm.com
Profile: KRUU-FM is a non-commercial station owned by Fairfield Youth Advocacy, Inc. The format of the station is news and variety. The station airs locally on 100.1 FM.
FM RADIO STATION

KRUZ-AM 37155
Owner: Cumulus Media
Editorial: 434 W Bearcat Dr, Salt Lake City, Utah 84115-2520 **Tel:** 1 801 485-6700.
Web site: http://www.1320kfan.com
Profile: KRUZ-AM is a commercial station owned by Cumulus Media. The format of the station is sports. KRUZ-AM broadcasts to the Salt Lake City area at 1230 AM.
AM RADIO STATION

KRVA-AM 38984
Owner: LRAD Media, LLC
Editorial: 2202 New York Ave Ste 902, Arlington, Texas 76010-0806 **Tel:** 1 214 919-7177.
Email: Info@Saigonradio890am.com
Web site: http://www.saigondallasradio.com/
Profile: KRVA-AM is a commercial station owned by LRAD Media, LLC. The format of the station is Vietnamese language programming. The station broadcasts locally at 1600 AM.
AM RADIO STATION

KRVA-FM 46409
Owner: The Way Radio Group, LLC
Editorial: 616 N Hillcrest Dr, Sulphur Springs, Texas 75482-2335 **Tel:** 1 903 885-7687.
Web site: http://mythundercountry.com
Profile: KRVA-FM is a commercial station owned by The Way Radio Group, LLC. The format of the station is country. KRVA-FM broadcasts to the Sulphur Springs, TX area at 107.1 FM.
FM RADIO STATION

KRVB-FM 43547
Owner: E.W. Scripps Co.
Editorial: 5257 W Fairview Ave Ste 260, Boise, Idaho 83706-1766 **Tel:** 1 208 344-3511.
Web site: http://www.riverinteractive.com
Profile: KRVB-FM is a commercial station owned by E.W. Scripps Co. The format of the station is adult album alternative music. KRVB-FM broadcasts to the Boise, ID area at 94.9 FM.
FM RADIO STATION

KRVC-FM 457284
Owner: Opus Broadcasting Systems Inc.
Editorial: 511 Rossanley Dr, Medford, Oregon 97501-1771 **Tel:** 1 541 772-0322.
Web site: http://opusradio.com/989fm/
Profile: KRVC-FM is a commercial station owned by Opus Broadcasting Systems Inc. The format of the station is Top 40/CHR. KRVC-FM broadcasts to the Medford, OR area at 98.9 FM.
FM RADIO STATION

KRVE-FM 45790
Owner: iHeartMedia Inc.
Editorial: 5555 Hilton Ave Ste 500, Baton Rouge, Louisiana 70808-2564 **Tel:** 1 225 231-1860.
Web site: http://www.961theriver.com
Profile: KRVE-FM is a commercial station owned by Clear iHeartMedia Inc. The format of the station is Lite Rock/Lite AC. KRVE-FM broadcasts to the Baton Rouge, LA area at 96.1 FM.
FM RADIO STATION

KRVF-FM 39950
Owner: LKCM Radio Group LP
Editorial: 214 N Main St, Corsicana, Texas 75110-4620 **Tel:** 1 903 874-8884.
Email: JimNash@TheRanchRadio.com
Web site: http://www.1069theranch.com
Profile: KRVF-FM is a commercial station owned by LKCM Radio Group LP. The format of the station is classic country. KRVF broadcasts to the Corsicana, TX area at 106.9 FM.
FM RADIO STATION

KRVG-FM 83670
Owner: Western Slope Communications
Editorial: 751 Horizon Ct, Ste 225, Grand Junction, Colorado 81506 **Tel:** 1 970 241-6460.
Email: production@wscradio.net
Profile: KRVG-FM is a commercial station owned by Western Slope Communications. The format for the station is classic rock. KRVG-FM broadcasts to the Grand Junction-Montrose, CO area at 95.5 FM.
FM RADIO STATION

KRVI-FM 42658
Owner: E.W. Scripps Co.
Editorial: 2330 W Grand St, Springfield, Missouri 65802-4900 **Tel:** 1 417 865-6614.
Web site: http://www.1067theriver.com
Profile: KRVI-FM is a commercial station owned by E.W. Scripps Co. The format of the station is variety and top 40/CHR. KRVI-FM broadcasts to the Springfield, MO area at 106.7 FM.
FM RADIO STATION

KRVK-FM 44173
Owner: Townsquare Media, LLC
Editorial: 150 Nichols Ave, Casper, Wyoming 82601-1816 **Tel:** 1 307 266-5252.
Web site: http://www.theriver1079.com
Profile: KRVK-FM is a commercial station owned by Townsquare Media, LLC. The format of the station is classic rock music. KRVK-FM broadcasts to the Casper, WY area at 107.9 FM.
FM RADIO STATION

KRVL-FM 46174
Owner: Revolution Broadcasting Co.
Editorial: 2125 Sidney Baker St, Kerrville, Texas 78028-2551 **Tel:** 1 830 896-1230.
Email: contact@revfm.rocks
Web site: http://www.revfmradio.com
Profile: KRVL-FM is a commercial station owned by Revolution Broadcasting Co. The format of the station is classic rock. KRVL-FM broadcasts to the Kerrville, TX area at 94.3 FM.
FM RADIO STATION

KRVN-AM 38981
Owner: Nebraska Rural Radio Association
Editorial: 1007 Plum Creek Pkwy, Lexington, Nebraska 68850 **Tel:** 1 308 324-2371.
Email: krvnam@krvn.com
Web site: http://www.krvn.com
Profile: KRVN-AM is a commercial station owned by Nebraska Rural Radio Association. The format of the station is agricultural programming and classic country. KRVN-AM broadcasts to the Lexington, NE area at 880 AM.
AM RADIO STATION

KRVN-FM 46411
Owner: Nebraska Rural Radio Association
Editorial: 1007 Plum Creek Pkwy, Lexington, Nebraska 68850-2621 **Tel:** 1 308 324-2371.
Email: krvnam@krvn.com
Web site: http://www.krvn.com
Profile: KRVN-FM is a commercial station owned by Nebraska Rural Radio Association. The format of the station is classic country. KRVN-FM broadcasts to the Lexington, NE area at 93.1 FM.
FM RADIO STATION

KRVO-FM 518092
Owner: Rose Communications, Inc.
Editorial: 2432 US Highway 2 E, Kalispell, Montana 59901 **Tel:** 1 406 755-8700.
Email: info@1031theriver.com
Web site: http://www.1031theriver.com
Profile: KRVO-FM is a commercial station owned by Rose Communications, Inc. The format of the station is adult album alternative. KRVO-FM broadcasts to the Kalispell, MT area at 103.1 FM.
FM RADIO STATION

KRVQ-FM 46089
Owner: QAB Media LLC
Editorial: 14 Sierra Drive, Kernville, California 93238 **Tel:** 1 760 376-4500.
Profile: KRVQ-FM is a commercial station owned by QAB Media LLC. The format of the station is classic rock. KRVQ-FM broadcasts to the Kernville, CA area at 104.5 FM.
FM RADIO STATION

KRVR-FM 42969
Owner: Threshold Communications
Editorial: 961 N Emerald Ave, Ste A, Modesto, California 95351 **Tel:** 1 209 544-1055.
Email: theriver@krvr.com
Web site: http://www.krvr.com
Profile: KRVR-FM is a commercial station owned by Threshold Communications. The format of the station is adult hits. KRVR-FM broadcasts to the Modesto, CA area at 105.5 FM.
FM RADIO STATION

KRVV-FM 41620
Owner: Holladay Broadcasting Co.
Editorial: 1109 Hudson Ln, Monroe, Louisiana 71201-6003 **Tel:** 1 318 388-2323.
Email: thebeatmonroe@gmail.com
Web site: http://www.thebeat.net
Profile: KRVV-FM is a commercial station owned by Holladay Broadcasting Co. The format of the station is urban contemporary music. KRVV-FM broadcasts to the Monroe, LA area at 100.1 FM.
FM RADIO STATION

KRVY-FM 235078
Owner: Iowa City Broadcasting Co.
Editorial: 730 Highway 71 NE, Willmar, Minnesota 56201 **Tel:** 1 320 231-1600.
Web site: http://www.k-musicradio.com
Profile: KRVY-FM is a commercial station owned by Iowa City Broadcasting Co. The format of the station is Lite Rock/Lite AC. KRVY-FM broadcasts to the Willmar, MN area at 93.7 FM.
FM RADIO STATION

KRVZ-AM 38596
Owner: Country Mountain Airwaves LLC
Editorial: 391 W Deuce of Clubs, Show Low, Arizona 85901-5809 **Tel:** 1 928 532-1010.
Email: traffic@majik101.com
Profile: KRVZ-AM is a commercial station owned by Country Mountain Airwaves LLC. The format of the station is talk and classic country. KRVZ-AM broadcasts to the Phoenix area at 1400 AM.
AM RADIO STATION

KRWA-FM 493973
Owner: WAY Media Inc.
Editorial: 1707 Main St, Longmont, Colorado 80501-7407 **Tel:** 1 303 702-9293.
Email: impactwichita@wayfm.com
Web site: http://kxwy.wayfm.com
Profile: KRWA-FM is a commercial station owned by WAY Media Inc. The format of the station is contemporary Christian. KRWA-FM broadcasts to the Pueblo, CO area at 90.9 FM.
FM RADIO STATION

KRWB-AM 35066
Owner: Border Broadcasting
Editorial: 113 A Lake St Center, Warroad, Minnesota 56763 **Tel:** 1 218 463-1410.
Email: kq92@mncable.net
Web site: http://www.1410krwb.com
Profile: KRWB-AM is a commercial station owned by Border Broadcasting. The format of the station is classic rock. KRWB-AM broadcasts to the Warroad, MN area at 1410 AM.
AM RADIO STATION

KRWC-AM 35067
Owner: Donnell Inc.
Editorial: 1472 10th St NW, Buffalo, Minnesota 55313-4443 **Tel:** 1 763 682-4444.
Email: info@krwc1360.com
Web site: http://www.krwc1360.com
Profile: KRWC-AM is a commercial station owned by Donnell Inc. The format of the station is news and talk. KRWC-AM's broadcasts to Buffalo, MN at 1360 AM.
AM RADIO STATION

KRWK-FM 44652
Owner: Midwest Communications
Editorial: 1020 25th St S, Fargo, North Dakota 58103-2312 **Tel:** 1 701 237-5346.
Web site: http://mixfargo.com/
Profile: KRWK-FM is a commercial station owned by Midwest Communications. The format of the station is adult contemporary. KRWK-FM broadcasts to the Fargo, ND area at 101.9 FM.
FM RADIO STATION

KRWM-FM 39813
Owner: Hubbard Radio, LLC
Editorial: 3650 131st Ave SE Ste 550, Bellevue, Washington 98006-1334 **Tel:** 1 425 373-5545.
Web site: http://www.warm1069.com
Profile: KRWM-FM is a commercial station owned by Hubbard Radio, LLC. The format of the station is Lite Rock/Lite AC music. KRWM-FM broadcasts to the Bellevue, WA area at 106.9 FM.
FM RADIO STATION

KRWN-FM 42829
Owner: American General Media
Editorial: 212 W Apache St, Farmington, New Mexico 87401-6235 **Tel:** 1 505 327-4449.
Web site: http://www.krwn.com
Profile: KRWN-FM is a commercial station owned by American General Media. The format of the station is Classic Rock. KRWN-FM broadcasts to the Durango, CO area at 92.5 FM.
FM RADIO STATION

KRWP-FM 44287
Owner: Cumulus Media Inc.
Editorial: 1225 S 39 Highway Ste. b, Stockton, Missouri 65785 **Tel:** 1 417 276-5253.
Email: krwp@krwp1077.com
Web site: http://krwp1077.com
Profile: KRWP-FM is a commercial station owned by Cumulus Media Inc. The format of the station is classic country. KRWP-FM broadcasts to the Stockton, MO area at a frequency of 107.7 FM.
FM RADIO STATION

KRWQ-FM 44881
Owner: Bicoastal Media LLC
Editorial: 3624 Avion Dr, Medford, Oregon 97504 **Tel:** 1 541 772-4170.
Web site: http://www.krwq.com
Profile: KRWQ-FM is a commercial station owned by Bicoastal Media LLC. The format of the station is classic and contemporary country music. KRWQ-FM broadcasts to the Medford, OR area at 100.3 FM.
FM RADIO STATION

KRXB-FM 41285
Owner: Texkan Communications
Editorial: 110 E Bowie St, Beeville, Texas 78102-4612 **Tel:** 1 361 358-4941.
Email: krxbfm@sbcglobal.net
Profile: KRXB-FM is a commercial station owned by Texkan Communications. The format of the station is classic rock music. KRXB-FM broadcasts to the Beeville, TX area on 107.1 FM.
FM RADIO STATION

KRXF-FM 436776
Owner: Gross Communications Co.
Editorial: 345 Sw Cyber Dr Ste 101-103, Bend, Oregon 97702-1045 **Tel:** 1 541 388-3300.
Web site: http://www.929online.com/
Profile: KRXF-FM is a commercial station owned by Gross Communications Co. The format of the station is alternative rock music. KRXF-FM broadcasts to the Bend, OR area at 92.9 FM.
FM RADIO STATION

KRXL-FM 44882
Owner: KIRX Inc.
Editorial: 1308 N Baltimore St, Kirksville, Missouri 63501-2509 **Tel:** 1 660 665-9828.
Email: radionws@cableone.net
Web site: http://www.945thex.com
Profile: KRXL-FM is a commercial station owned by KIRX Inc. The format of the station is classic rock music. KRXL-FM broadcasts to the Kirksville, MO area at 94.5 FM.
FM RADIO STATION

KRXO-AM 63241
Owner: Reunion Broadcasting LLC
Editorial: 7777 S Lewis Ave, Tulsa, Oklahoma 74171-0003 **Tel:** 1 918 254-7556.
Web site: http://www.quebuenatulsa.com
Profile: KRXO-AM is a commercial station owned by Reunion Broadcasting LLC. The format is not available. KRXO-AM broadcasts to the Tulsa, OK area at 1270 AM.
AM RADIO STATION

KRXO-FM 39888
Owner: Tyler Media, LLC
Editorial: 400 E Britton Rd, Oklahoma City, Oklahoma 73114-7515 **Tel:** 1 405 478-5104.
Web site: http://www.krxo.com
Profile: KRXO-FM is commercial station owned by Tyler Media, LLC. The format of the station is sports talk. KRXO-FM broadcasts to the Oklahoma City area at 107.7 FM.
FM RADIO STATION

KRXP-FM 44500
Owner: Bahakel Communications
Editorial: 1805 E Cheyenne Rd, Colorado Springs, Colorado 80905-2868 **Tel:** 1 719 634-4896.
Web site: http://www.1039rxp.com
Profile: KRXP-FM is a commercial station owned by Bahakel Communications. The format of the station is rock/album oriented rock. KRXP-FM broadcasts to the Colorado Springs, CO area at 103.9 FM.
FM RADIO STATION

KRXQ-FM 39889
Owner: Entercom Communications Corp.
Editorial: 5345 Madison Ave, Sacramento, California 95841-3141 **Tel:** 1 916 334-7777.
Web site: http://www.krxq.net
Profile: KRXQ-FM is a commercial station owned by Entercom Communications Corp. The format of the station is rock music. KRXQ-FM broadcasts to the Sacramento, CA area at 98.5 FM.
FM RADIO STATION

KRXR-AM 36237
Owner: Juarez(Maria)
Editorial: 501 S Lincoln Ave, Jerome, Idaho 83338 **Tel:** 1 208 324-9267.

Profile: KRXR-AM is a commercial station owned by Maria Juarez. The format of the station is regional Mexican. KXRX-AM broadcasts to the Jerome, ID area at 1480 AM.
AM RADIO STATION

KRXT-FM 40972
Owner: KRXT Inc.
Editorial: 1095 W US Highway 79, Rockdale, Texas 76567 **Tel:** 1 512 446-6985.
Email: krxt@krxt985.com
Web site: http://www.krxt985.com
Profile: KRXT-FM is a commercial station owned by KRXT Inc. The format of the station is classic country. KRXT-FM broadcasts to the Rockdale, TX area at 98.5 FM.
FM RADIO STATION

KRXV-FM 39890
Owner: Highway Radio Inc.
Editorial: 1611 E Main St, Barstow, California 92311-3239 **Tel:** 1 760 256-0326.
Email: highwayradio@highwayradio.com
Web site: http://highwayradio.com
Profile: KRXV-FM is a commercial station owned by Highway Radio Inc. The format for the station is dance music. KRXV-FM broadcasts to the Barstow, CA area at 98.1 FM.
FM RADIO STATION

KRXW-FM 551975
Owner: Minnesota Public Radio
Editorial: 480 Cedar St, Saint Paul, Minnesota 55101-2217 **Tel:** 1 651 290-1500.
Email: newsroom@mpr.org
Web site: http://www.mpr.org/listen/stations/krxw
Profile: KRXW-FM is a non-commercial station owned by Minnesota Public Radio. The format of the station is news and talk. KRXW-FM broadcasts to the Roseau, MN area at 103.5. KRXW-FM is a simulcast of sister station KNOW-FM.
FM RADIO STATION

KRXX-FM 45928
Owner: Kodiak Island Broadcasting Co., Inc.
Editorial: 1315 Mill Bay Rd Ste 1A, Kodiak, Alaska 99615-6411 **Tel:** 1 907 486-5159.
Profile: KRXX-FM is a commercial station owned by Kodiak Island Broadcasting Co., Inc. The format is Hot AC. KRXX-FM broadcasts to the Kodia, AK area at 101.1 FM.
FM RADIO STATION

KRXY-FM 129223
Owner: Olympia Broadcasters, Inc.
Editorial: 2124 Pacific Ave Se, Olympia, Washington 98506-4753 **Tel:** 1 360 236-1010.
Email: krxy@krxy.com
Web site: http://www.945roxy.com
Profile: KRXY-FM is a commercial station owned by Olympia Broadcasters, Inc. The format of the station is hot adult contemporary. KRXY-FM broadcasts in the Olympia, WA area at 94.5 FM.
FM RADIO STATION

KRYD-FM 614804
Owner: Rocky III Investments, Inc.
Editorial: 475 Water Ave, Montrose, Colorado 81401-3401 **Tel:** 1 970 263-4100.
Email: studio@krydradio.com
Web site: http://www.krydfm.com
Profile: KRYD-FM is a commercial station owned by Rocky III Investments, Inc. The format of the station is a variety of rock music. KRYD-FM broadcasts to the Norwood, CO and surrounding areas at 104.9 FM. Translator is 92.7 (Grand Junction).
FM RADIO STATION

KRYK-FM 41599
Owner: New Media Broadcasters
Editorial: 2210 31st St N, Havre, Montana 59501-8003 **Tel:** 1 406 265-7841.
Web site: http://www.kryk.com
Profile: KRYK-FM is a commercial station owned by New Media Broadcasters. The format for the station is hot adult contemporary. KRYK-FM broadcasts to the Havre, MT area at 101.3 FM. KPQX-FM prefers not to receive press materials.
FM RADIO STATION

KRYL-FM 602087
Owner: Hoehman Hawaii Five, Inc.
Editorial: 300 Ohukai Rd Ste C318, Kihei, Hawaii 96753-7050 **Tel:** 1 808 538-1180.
Web site: http://hhawaiimedia.com
Profile: KRYL-FM is a commercial station owned by Hoehman Hawaii Five, Inc. The format of the station is country. KRYL-FM broadcasts to the Haiku, HI area at 106.5.
FM RADIO STATION

KRYP-FM 46307
Owner: Salem Media Group, Inc.
Editorial: 6400 SE Lake Rd Ste 350, Portland, Oregon 97222-2189 **Tel:** 1 503 786-0600.
Web site: http://www.931elrey.com
Profile: KRYP-FM is a commercial station owned by Salem Media Group, Inc. The format of the station is regional Mexican music. KRYP-FM broadcasts to the Portland, OR area on 93.1 FM.
FM RADIO STATION

KRYS-FM 44884
Owner: iHeartMedia Inc.
Editorial: 501 Tupper Lane Radio Plaza, Corpus Christi, Texas 78417-9736 **Tel:** 1 361 289-0111.
Email: k99@clearchannel.com
Web site: http://k99country.iheart.com
Profile: KRYS-FM is a commercial station owned by iHeartMedia Inc. The format of the station is country music. KRYS-FM broadcasts to the Corpus Christi, TX area at 99.1 FM.
FM RADIO STATION

KRZA-FM 41936
Owner: ERMAC Inc.
Editorial: 528 9th St, Alamosa, Colorado 81101-3217 **Tel:** 1 719 589-9057.
Web site: http://www.krza.org
Profile: KRZA-FM is a non-commercial station owned by ERMAC Inc. The format of the station is news and a variety of music and talk programming. KRZA-FM broadcasts in the Denver area at 88.7 FM.
FM RADIO STATION

KRZI-AM 37111
Owner: M & M Broadcasters
Editorial: 5501 Bagby Ave, Waco, Texas 76711-2300 **Tel:** 1 254 772-0930.
Web site: http://www.1660espn.com
Profile: KRZI-AM is a commercial station owned by M & M Broadcasters. The format of the station is sports. KRZI-AM broadcasts to the Waco, TX area at 1660 AM.
AM RADIO STATION

KRZK-FM 43415
Owner: Earls Broadcasting
Editorial: 202 Courtney St, Branson, Missouri 65616-2434 **Tel:** 1 417 334-6063.
Email: news@krzk.com
Web site: http://www.hometowndailynews.com
Profile: KRZK-FM is a commercial station owned by Earls Broadcasting. The format of the station is news/talk. KRZK-FM broadcasts to the Branson, MO area at 106.3 FM.
FM RADIO STATION

KRZN-FM 44096
Owner: Connoisseur Media LLC
Editorial: 2075 Central Ave, Billings, Montana 59102-4956 **Tel:** 1 406 248-7777.
Web site: http://www.963thezone.com
Profile: KRZN-FM is a commercial station owned by Connoisseur Media LLC. The format of the station is rock alternative music. KRZN-FM broadcasts in the Billings, MT area at 96.3 FM.
FM RADIO STATION

KRZR-AM 37551
Owner: iHeartMedia Inc.
Editorial: 83 E Shaw Ave, Fresno, California 93710-7620 **Tel:** 1 559 230-4300.
Web site: http://www.powertalk967.com
Profile: KRZR-AM is a commercial station owned by I Heart Media. The format of the station is news and talk. KRZR-AM broadcasts to the Visalia, CA area at 1400 AM.
AM RADIO STATION

KRZS-AM 38985
Owner: Crain Media Group LLC
Editorial: 111 N Spring St, Searcy, Arkansas 72143-7712 **Tel:** 1 501 268-7123.
Email: production@crainmedia.com
Web site: http://www.crainmedia.com
Profile: KRZS-AM is a commercial station owned by Crain Media Group LLC. The format of the station is news talk. KRZS-AM broadcasts in the Searcy, AR area at 1300 AM.
AM RADIO STATION

KRZY-AM 38385
Owner: Entravision Communications Corp.
Editorial: 2725 Broadbent Pkwy NE, Ste F, Albuquerque, New Mexico 87107 **Tel:** 1 505 342-4141.
Web site: http://www.espndeportes1450.com
Profile: KRZY-AM is a commercial station owned by Entravision Communications Corp. The station is an ESPN Deportes affiliate. The format of the station is Spanish language sports. KRZY-AM broadcasts to the Albuquerque, NM area at 1450 AM.
AM RADIO STATION

KRZY-FM 46735
Owner: Entravision Communications Corp.
Editorial: 2725 Broadbent Pkwy NE, Ste F, Albuquerque, New Mexico 87107 **Tel:** 1 505 342-4141.
Web site: http://www.jose1059.com
Profile: KRZY-FM is a commercial station owned by Entravision Communications Corp. The format of the station is Hispanic adult hits. KRZY-FM broadcasts to the Albuquerque, NM area at 105.9 FM.
FM RADIO STATION

KRZZ-FM 318401
Owner: Spanish Broadcasting System
Editorial: 455 Market St Ste 2300, San Francisco, California 94105-2400 **Tel:** 1 408 546-4000.
Web site: http://www.yosoyraza.com
Profile: KRZZ-FM is a commercial station owned by Spanish Broadcasting System. The format of the station is Regional Mexican music. KRZZ-FM broadcasts to the San Francisco area at 93.3 FM.
FM RADIO STATION

KSAB-FM 46151
Owner: iHeartMedia Inc.
Editorial: 501 Tupper Ln, Corpus Christi, Texas 78417-9736 **Tel:** 1 361 289-0111.
Web site: http://ksabfm.iheart.com
Profile: KSAB-FM is a commercial station owned by iHeartMedia Inc. The format for the station is Hispanic. The station broadcasts to the Corpus Christi, TX area at 99.9 FM.
FM RADIO STATION

KSAC-FM 43247
Owner: Salem Media Group, Inc.
Editorial: 1425 River Park Dr Ste 520, Sacramento, California 95815-4524 **Tel:** 1 916 924-0710.
Web site: http://www.money1055.com
Profile: KSAC-FM is a commercial station owned by Salem Media Group, Inc. The format of the station is business talk. KSAC-FM broadcasts in the Sacramento, CA area at 105.5 FM.
FM RADIO STATION

KSAH-AM 35808
Owner: Alpha Media, Inc.
Editorial: 4050 Eisenhauer Rd, San Antonio, Texas 78218-3409 **Tel:** 1 210 654-5100.
Web site: http://www.nortenosa.com
Profile: KSAH-AM is a commercial station owned by Alpha Media, Inc. The format of the station is Regional Mexican music. KSAH-AM broadcasts to the San Antonio area at 720 AM.
AM RADIO STATION

KSAH-FM 234956
Owner: Alpha Media
Editorial: 4050 Eisenhauer Rd, San Antonio, Texas 78218-3409 **Tel:** 1 210 654-5100.
Web site: http://www.nortenosa.com/
Profile: KSAH-FM is a commercial station owned by Alpha Media. The format of the station is Hispanic Norteno music. KSAH-FM broadcasts to the San Antonio area at 104.1 FM.
FM RADIO STATION

KSAJ-FM 44885
Owner: Morris Communications
Editorial: 200 N Broadway St, Abilene, Kansas 67410-2647 **Tel:** 1 785 272-3456.
Web site: http://www.trueoldies985.com
Profile: KSAJ-FM is a commercial station owned by Morris Communications. The format of the station is oldies music. KSAJ-FM broadcasts to the Salina, KS area at 98.5 FM.
FM RADIO STATION

KSAL-AM 39371
Owner: Morris Communications
Editorial: 131 N Santa Fe Ave Ste 3, Salina, Kansas 67401-2642 **Tel:** 1 785 823-1111.
Web site: http://www.ksal.com
Profile: KSAL-AM is a commercial station owned by Morris Communications. The format of the station is news, talk and sports. KSAL-AM broadcasts to the Wichita, KS area at 1150 AM.
AM RADIO STATION

KSAL-FM 41194
Owner: Morris Communications
Editorial: 131 N Santa Fe Ave Ste 3, Salina, Kansas 67401-2642 **Tel:** 1 785 823-1111.
Web site: http://www.ksal.com
Profile: KSAL-FM is a commercial station owned by Morris Communications. The format of the station is classic hits. KSAL-FM broadcasts in the Salina, KS at 104.9 FM.
FM RADIO STATION

KSAM-AM 382149
Owner: Bee Broadcasting Inc.
Editorial: 2432 US Highway 2 E, Kalispell, Montana 59901 **Tel:** 1 406 755-8700.
Email: sam@sam1240.com
Web site: http://www.beebroadcasting.com
Profile: KSAM-AM is a commercial station owned by Bee Broadcasting Inc. The format of the station is sports. KSAM-AM broadcasts to the Kalispell, MT area at 1240 AM.
AM RADIO STATION

KSAM-FM 46410
Owner: HEH Communications LLC
Editorial: 622 Interstate 45 S, Huntsville, Texas 77340 **Tel:** 1 936 295-2651.
Email: ksamnews@yahoo.com
Web site: http://www.ksam1017.com
Profile: KSAM-FM is a commercial station owned by HEH Communications LLC. The format of the station is country music. KSAM-FM broadcasts to the Huntsville, TX area at 101.7 FM. Newscasts air throughout the day, CT.
FM RADIO STATION

KSAN-FM 43237
Owner: Cumulus Media Inc.
Editorial: 750 Battery St, Third Floor, San Francisco, California 94105-3914 **Tel:** 1 415 995-6800.
Email: thebone@thebone.net
Web site: http://www.1077thebone.com
Profile: KSAN-FM is a commercial station owned by Cumulus Media Inc. The format of the station is classic rock. KSAN-FM broadcasts to the San Francisco area at 107.7 FM.
FM RADIO STATION

KSAS-FM 41269
Owner: Townsquare Media, LLC
Editorial: 827 E Park Blvd Ste 100, Boise, Idaho 83712-7783 **Tel:** 1 208 344-6363.
Web site: http://1035kissfmboise.com/
Profile: KSAS-FM is a commercial station owned by Townsquare Media, LLC. The format of the station is Top 40/CHR music. KSAS-FM broadcasts in the Boise, ID area at 103.5 FM.
FM RADIO STATION

KSAU-FM 39892
Owner: Stephen F. Austin State Univ.
Editorial: 1936 North St Boynton Bldg, Nacogdoches, Texas 75961 **Tel:** 1 936 468-4000.
Email: ksau@sfasu.edu
Web site: http://www.sfasu.edu/ksau
FM RADIO STATION

KSAZ-AM 36260
Owner: Kasa Radio Hogar, Inc
Editorial: 3138 N Freeway Industrial Loop, Tucson, Arizona 85705-5001 **Tel:** 1 520 461-1727.
Email: rk580@live.com
Web site: http://www.radioebenezer580am.com/index.html
Profile: KSAZ-AM is a commercial station owned by Kasa Radio Hogar, Inc. The format of the station is Spanish religious. KSAZ-AM broadcasts to the Tucson, AZ area at 580 AM.
AM RADIO STATION

KSBH-FM 44354
Owner: KSBH, LLC
Editorial: 213 Renee St, Natchitoches, Louisiana 71457-6225 **Tel:** 1 318 354-4000.
Web site: http://www.riverinteractive.com
Profile: KSBH-FM is a commercial station owned by KSBH, LLC. The format of the station is country music. KSBH-FM broadcasts to the Natchitoches, LA area at 94.9 FM.
FM RADIO STATION

KSBK-FM 134079
Owner: First Dallas Media Inc.
Editorial: 400 E Gladstone Ave, Frederick, Oklahoma 73542-4421 **Tel:** 1 866 355-5793.
Email: kcbi@kcbi.org
Web site: http://www.kcbinet.org
Profile: KSBK-FM is a non-commercial station owned by the First Dallas Media Inc. The format of the station is Christian music and talk. KSBK-FM broadcasts to the Frederick, OK area at 91.5 FM.
FM RADIO STATION

KSBL-FM 42754
Owner: Rincon Broadcasting
Editorial: 414 E Cota St, Santa Barbara, California 93101 **Tel:** 1 805 879-8300.
Web site: http://www.klite.com
Profile: KSBL-FM is a commercial station owned by Rincon Broadcasting. The format of the station is adult contemporary music. KSBL-FM broadcasts to the Santa Barbara, CA area at 101.7 FM.
FM RADIO STATION

KSBN-AM 36159
Owner: KSBN Radio Inc.
Editorial: 7 S Howard St Ste 430, Spokane, Washington 99201-3816 **Tel:** 1 509 838-4000.
Email: ksbn@ksbn.net
Web site: http://www.ksbn.net
Profile: KSBN-AM is a commercial station owned by KSBN Radio Inc. The format of the station is business news and talk. KSBN-AM broadcasts to the Spokane, WA area at 1230 AM.
AM RADIO STATION

KSBQ-AM 35070
Owner: Lazer Broadcasting Corp.
Editorial: 200 S A St, Oxnard, California 93030-5717 **Tel:** 1 805 928-9796.
Web site: http://www.radiolazer.com
Profile: KSBQ-AM is a commercial station owned by the Lazer Broadcasting Corp. The format of the station is regional Mexican. KSBQ-AM broadcasts to the Santa Maria, CA area at 1480 AM.
AM RADIO STATION

KSBR-FM 39894
Owner: South Orange County Community College District
Editorial: 28000 Marguerite Pkwy, Mission Viejo, California 92692-3635
Web site: http://www.ksbr.org
Profile: KSBR-FM is a non-commercial station owned by the South Orange County Community College District. The format of the station is smooth AC. KSBR-FM broadcasts to the Mission Viejo, CA area at 88.5 FM.
FM RADIO STATION

KSBV-FM 87894
Owner: Arkansas Valley Broadcasting LLC.
Editorial: 735 Blake St, Salida, Colorado 81201-2919 **Tel:** 1 719 539-9377.
Email: ksbvradio1@gmail.com
Web site: http://www.ksbv.net
Profile: KSBV-FM is a commercial station owned by Arkansas Valley Broadcasting LLC. The format of the station is classic rock. KSBV-FM broadcasts to the Salida, CO area at 93.7 FM.
FM RADIO STATION

KSBZ-FM 46281
Owner: Alaska Broadcast Communications Inc.
Editorial: 611 Lake St, Sitka, Alaska 99835-7402 **Tel:** 1 907 747-5439.
Email: news@abcstations.com
Web site: http://www.sitkaradio.com
Profile: KSBZ-FM is a commercial station owned by Alaska Broadcast Communications Inc. The format of the station is classic rock. KSBZ-FM broadcasts to the Sitka, AK area at 103.1 FM.
FM RADIO STATION

KSCA-FM 43584
Owner: Univision Communications Inc.
Editorial: 655 N Central Ave, Glendale, California 91203-1422 **Tel:** 1 310 846-2800.
Web site: http://www.univision.com/los-angeles/ksca
Profile: KSCA-FM is a commercial station owned by Univision Communications Inc. The format of the station is regional Mexican. KSCA-FM broadcasts to the Glendale, CA area at 101.9 FM.
FM RADIO STATION

KSCB-AM 39116
Owner: Seward County Broadcasting Co.
Editorial: 1410 N Western Ave, Liberal, Kansas 67901-2212 **Tel:** 1 620 624-3891.
Email: news@kscb.net
Web site: http://www.kscb.net
Profile: KSCB-AM is a commercial station owned by Seward County Broadcasting Co. The format of the station is news, sports and talk. KSCB-AM broadcasts to the Wichita, KS area at 1270 AM.
AM RADIO STATION

KSCB-FM 46461
Owner: Seward County Broadcasting Co.
Editorial: 1410 N Western Ave, Liberal, Kansas 67901 **Tel:** 1 620 624-3891.
Email: news@kscb.net
Web site: http://www.kscb.net
Profile: KSCB-FM is a commercial station owned by Seward County Broadcasting Co. The format of the station is adult hits. KSCB-FM broadcasts to the Liberal, KS area at 107.5 FM.
FM RADIO STATION

KSCH-FM 39615
Owner: East Texas Broadcasting Inc.
Editorial: 930 Gilmer St, Sulphur Springs, Texas 75482-4319 **Tel:** 1 903 577-9770.
Web site: http://www.easttexasradio.com
Profile: KSCH-FM is a commercial station owned by East Texas Broadcasting Inc. The format of the station is country music. KSCH-FM broadcasts to the Mount Pleasant, TX area at 95.9 FM.
FM RADIO STATION

KSCJ-AM 39185
Owner: Powell Broadcasting Co.
Editorial: 2000 Indian Hills Dr, Sioux City, Iowa 51104 **Tel:** 1 712 239-2100.
Email: news@kscj.com
Web site: http://www.kscj.com
Profile: KSCJ-AM is a commercial station owned by Powell Broadcasting Co. The format of the station is news, sports and talk. KSCJ-AM broadcasts to the Sioux City, IA area at 1340 AM.
AM RADIO STATION

KSCN-FM 44319
Owner: East Texas Broadcasting Inc.
Editorial: Highway 67 West 1 Mile, Mount Pleasant, Texas 75455 **Tel:** 1 903 577-9770.
Web site: http://www.easttexasradio.com/starcountry
Profile: KSCN-FM is a commercial station owned by East Texas Broadcasting Inc. The format of the station is contemporary country. KSCN-FM's broadcasts in the Mount Pleasant, TX area at 96.9 FM.
FM RADIO STATION

KSCO-AM 36007
Owner: Zwerling Broadcasting System Ltd.
Editorial: 2300 Portola Dr, Santa Cruz, California 95062-4203 **Tel:** 1 831 475-1080.
Web site: http://www.ksco.com
Profile: KSCO-AM is a commercial station owned by Zwerling Broadcasting System Ltd. The format of the station is news and talk. KSCO-AM broadcasts in the Santa Cruz, CA area at 1080 AM.
AM RADIO STATION

KSCQ-FM 41598
Owner: SkyWest Media, LLC
Editorial: 1560 N Corbin St, Silver City, New Mexico 88061-6526 **Tel:** 1 575 538-3396.
Web site: http://www.silvercityradio.com
Profile: KSCQ-FM is a commercial station owned by SkyWest Media, LCC. The format of the station is adult contemporary. KSCQ-FM broadcasts to the Silver City, NM area at 92.9 FM.
FM RADIO STATION

KSCR-AM 37618
Owner: Cumulus Media Inc.
Editorial: 1200 Executive Pkwy Ste 440, Eugene, Oregon 97401-2169 **Tel:** 1 541 284-8500.
Web site: http://www.1320radiounica.com
Profile: KSCR-AM is a commercial station owned by Cumulus Media Inc. The format of the station is Regional Mexican. KSCR-AM broadcasts to the Eugene, OR area at 1320 AM.
AM RADIO STATION

KSCR-FM 44583
Owner: Headwaters Media
Tel: 1 320 235-1194.
Email: info@kkln.com
Profile: KSCR-FM is a commercial station owned by Headwaters Media. The format of the station is adult hits music. KSCR-FM broadcasts to the Benson, MN area at 93.5 FM.
FM RADIO STATION

KSCS-FM 46244
Owner: Cumulus Media Inc
Editorial: 3090 Olive St Ste 400, Dallas, Texas 75219-7640 **Tel:** 1 817 640-1963.
Email: news@wbap.com
Web site: http://www.kscs.com
Profile: KSCS-FM is a commercial station owned by Cumulus Media Inc. The format of the station is contemporary country. KSCS-FM broadcasts to the Dallas-Ft. Worth, TX area at 96.3 FM.
FM RADIO STATION

KSCV-FM 42871
Owner: Bott Broadcasting Co.
Editorial: 1111 S Glenstone Ave Ste 3-102, Springfield, Missouri 65804-0397 **Tel:** 1 417 864-0901.
Web site: http://www.bottradionetwork.com
Profile: KSCV-FM is a non-commercial station owned by Bott Broadcasting Co. The format of the station is religious and Christian programming. KSCV-FM broadcasts to the Springfield, MO area at 90.1 FM.
FM RADIO STATION

KSD-FM 43073
Owner: iHeartMedia Inc.
Editorial: 1001 Highlands Plaza Dr W Ste 200, Saint Louis, Missouri 63110-1337 **Tel:** 1 314 333-8000.
Web site: http://937thebull.iheart.com
Profile: KSD-FM is a commercial station owned by iHeartMedia Inc. The format of the station is contemporary country music. KSD-FM broadcasts to the St. Louis area at 93.7 FM.
FM RADIO STATION

KSDL-FM 44595
Owner: Townsquare Media, LLC
Editorial: 2209 S Limit Ave, Sedalia, Missouri 65301-6950 **Tel:** 1 660 826-1050.
Web site: http://www.923bobfm.com
Profile: KSDL-FM is a commercial station owned by Townsquare Media, LLC. The format of the station is Jack FM-Adult Hits. KSDL-FM broadcasts to the Sedalia, MO area at 92.3 FM.
FM RADIO STATION

KSDM-FM 44887
Owner: Red Rock Radio Corp.
Editorial: 519 3rd St, International Falls, Minnesota 56649 **Tel:** 1 218 283-3481.
Email: production@ksdmradio.com
Web site: http://www.ksdmradio.com
Profile: KSDM-FM is a commercial station owned by Red Rock Radio Corp. The format of the station is country music. KSDM-FM broadcasts in the International Falls, MN area at 104.1 FM.
FM RADIO STATION

KSDN-AM 37489
Owner: Armada Media Corp.
Editorial: 3304 S Highway 281, Aberdeen, South Dakota 57401-8792 **Tel:** 1 605 229-3632.
Email: aberdeenproduction@hubcityradio.com
Web site: http://www.hubcityradio.com
Profile: KSDN-AM is a commercial station owned by Armada Media Corp. The format of the station is news and talk. KSDN-AM broadcasts to the Aberdeen, SD area at 930 AM.
AM RADIO STATION

KSDN-FM 44888
Owner: Armada Media Corp.
Editorial: 3304 S Highway 281, Aberdeen, South Dakota 57401-8792 **Tel:** 1 605 225-5930.
Email: aberdeenproduction@hubcityradio.com
Web site: http://www.hubcityradio.com
Profile: KSDN-FM is a commercial station owned by Armada Media Corp. The format of the station is classic rock music. KSDN-FM broadcasts to the Aberdeen, SC area at 94.1 FM.
FM RADIO STATION

KSDO-AM 36816
Owner: Hi-Favor Broadcasting LLC
Editorial: 344 F St, Ste 200, Chula Vista, California 91910 **Tel:** 1 626 356-4230.
Web site: http://www.nuevavida.com
Profile: KSDO-AM is a commercial station owned by Hi-Favor Broadcasting LLC. The format of the station is Spanish language Christian programming. KSDO-AM broadcasts to the Los Angeles area at 1130 AM.
AM RADIO STATION

KSDQ-FM 762560
Owner: Sunndale Seventh-Day Adventist Church
Editorial: 6818 Audrain Road 9139, Centralia, Missouri 65240-5906 **Tel:** 1 573 682-2164.
Email: ksdqradio@sunnydale.org
Web site: http://ksdqradio.net
Profile: KSDQ-FM is a non-commercial station owned by Sunndale Seventh-Day Adventist Church. The station's format features a variety of programming. KSDQ-FM broadcasts to the Centralia, MO area at a frequency of 88.7 FM.
FM RADIO STATION

KSDR-AM 38920
Owner: Alpha Media
Editorial: 921 9th Ave SE, Watertown, South Dakota 57201-4960 **Tel:** 1 605 886-5747.
Email: kwatprod@digity.me
Web site: http://www.gowatertown.net
Profile: KSDR-AM is a commercial station owned by Alpha Media. The format of the station is news and talk. KSDR-AM broadcasts to the Watertown, SD area at 1480 AM.
AM RADIO STATION

KSDR-FM 46262
Owner: Alpha Media
Editorial: 921 9th Ave SE, Watertown, South Dakota 57201-4960 **Tel:** 1 605 886-5747.
Email: kwatprod@digity.me
Web site: http://www.gowatertown.net
Profile: KSDR-FM is a commercial station owned by Alpha Media. The format of the station is contemporary country. KSDR-FM broadcasts to the Watertown, SD area at 92.9 FM.
FM RADIO STATION

KSDS-FM 39897
Owner: San Diego Community College
Editorial: 1313 Park Blvd, San Diego, California 92101-4712 **Tel:** 1 619 388-3037.
Email: info@jazz88.org
Web site: http://www.jazz88.org
Profile: KSDS-FM is a non-commercial station owned by San Diego Community College. The format of the station is jazz, blues and world music. KSDS-FM broadcasts to the San Diego area at 88.3 FM.
FM RADIO STATION

KSDW-FM 41036
Owner: Calvary Chapel of Costa Mesa
Editorial: 3000 W Macarthur Blvd Ste 500, Santa Ana, California 92704-7947 **Tel:** 1 714 918-6207.
Web site: http://www.ksdwradio.com
Profile: KSDW-FM is a non-commercial station owned by Calvary Chapel of Costa Mesa. The format for the station is religious and Christian programming. KSDW-FM broadcasts to Murrieta, CA area at 88.9 FM.
FM RADIO STATION

KSDZ-FM 39899
Owner: D.J. Broadcasting Corp.
Editorial: 6492 230th Ln, Gordon, Nebraska 69343-5570 **Tel:** 1 308 282-2500.
Email: thetwister@ksdzfm.com
Web site: http://www.ksdzfm.com
Profile: KSDZ-FM is a commercial station owned by D.J. Broadcasting Corp. The format of the station is country. KSDZ-FM broadcasts to the Gordon, NE area at 95.5 FM.
FM RADIO STATION

KSEA-FM 82629
Owner: Campesina Network(La)
Editorial: 608 E Boronda Rd Ste C, Salinas, California 93906-3129 **Tel:** 1 831 754-1469.
Email: paco@campesina.com
Web site: http://www.campesina.com/ksea
Profile: KSEA-FM is a commercial station owned by La Campesina Network. The format of the station is regional Mexican. KSEA-FM broadcasts to the Salinas, CA area at 96.3 FM.
FM RADIO STATION

KSEC-FM 85987
Owner: La Zeta 957 Co.
Editorial: 2323 S Old Missouri Rd, Springdale, Arkansas 72764-7470 **Tel:** 1 479 756-8686.
Email: info@ezspanishmedia.com
Web site: http://www.ezspanishmedia.com
Profile: KSEC-FM is a commercial station owned by La Zeta 957 Co. The format of the station is Hispanic programming. KSEC-FM broadcasts to the Rogers, AR area at 95.7 FM.
FM RADIO STATION

KSED-FM 133959
Owner: Grenax Broadcasting
Editorial: 2409 N 4th St Ste 101, Flagstaff, Arizona 86004-3735 **Tel:** 1 928 779-1177.
Web site: http://www.koltcountry.com
Profile: KSED-FM is a commercial station owned by Grenax Broadcasting. The format of the station is contemporary country. KSED-FM broadcasts to the Flagstaff, AZ area at 107.5 FM.
FM RADIO STATION

KSEF-FM 401693
Owner: Southeast Missouri State Univ.
Editorial: 1 University Plz, MS0300, Cape Girardeau, Missouri 63701-4710 **Tel:** 1 573 651-5070.
Email: comments@krcu.org
Web site: http://www.krcu.org
Profile: KSEF-FM is a non-commerical station owned by Southeast Missouri State Univ. The format of the station is classical and news. KSEF-FM broadcasts to the Farmington, MO area on 88.9 FM.
FM RADIO STATION

KSEG-FM 39879
Owner: Entercom Communications Corp.
Editorial: 5345 Madison Ave, Sacramento, California 95841-3141 **Tel:** 1 916 334-9690.
Web site: http://www.eagle969.com
Profile: KSEG-FM is a commercial station owned by Entercom Communications Corp. The format of the station is classic rock music. KSEG-FM broadcasts to the Sacramento, CA area at 96.9 FM.
FM RADIO STATION

KSEH-FM 43684
Owner: Entravision Communications Corp.
Editorial: 1803 N Imperial Ave, El Centro, California 92243-1333 **Tel:** 1 760 482-7777.
Email: kwst@entravision.com
Web site: http://www.jose945.com
Profile: KSEH-FM is a commercial station owned by Entravision Communications Corp. The format of the station is Hispanic adult hits. KSEH-FM broadcasts to the El Centro, CA area at 94.5 FM.
FM RADIO STATION

KSEI-AM 38467
Owner: Idaho Wireless Corp.
Editorial: 544 N Arthur Ave, Pocatello, Idaho 83204-3002 **Tel:** 1 208 233-2121.
Profile: KSEI-AM is a commercial station owned by Idaho Wireless Corp. The format of the station is sports. KSEI-AM broadcasts to the Pocatello, ID area at 930 AM.
AM RADIO STATION

KSEK-AM 36675
Owner: Southeast Kansas Independent Living (SKIL)
Editorial: 202 E Centennial Dr Ste B2, Pittsburg, Kansas 66762-6572 **Tel:** 1 620 232-9912.
Profile: KSEK-AM is a commercial station owned by the Southeast Kansas Independent Living (SKIL). The format of the station is sports. KSEK-AM broadcasts to the Pittsburg, KS area at 1340 AM.
AM RADIO STATION

KSEK-FM 42161
Owner: Southeast Kansas Independent Living (SKIL)
Editorial: 202 E Centennial Dr Ste B2, Pittsburg, Kansas 66762-6516 **Tel:** 1 620 232-9912.
Web site: http://www.991urock.com
Profile: KSEK-FM is a commercial station owned by Southeast Kansas Independent Living (SKIL). The format of the station is classic rock. KSEK-FM broadcasts to the Pittsburg, KS area at 99.1 FM.
FM RADIO STATION

KSEL-AM 38446
Owner: Rooney Moon Broadcasting
Editorial: 42437 US 70, Portales, New Mexico 88130 **Tel:** 1 575 359-1759.
Email: news@rooneymoon.com
Web site: http://www.kselcountry.com
Profile: KSEL-AM is a commercial station owned by Rooney Moon Broadcasting. The format of the station is country. KSEL-AM broadcasts to the Portales, NM area at 1450 AM.
AM RADIO STATION

KSEL-FM 45812
Owner: Rooney Moon Broadcasting
Editorial: 42437 US 70, Portales, New Mexico 88130 **Tel:** 1 575 359-1759.
Email: news@rooneymoon.com
Web site: http://www.kselcountry.com
Profile: KSEL-FM is a commercial station owned by Rooney Moon Broadcasting. The format of the station is contemporary country music. KSEL-AM broadcasts to the Portales, NM area at 105.9 FM.
FM RADIO STATION

KSEM-FM 44890
Owner: Gaines County Broadcasting
Editorial: 105 NW 11th St, Seminole, Texas 79360-3301 **Tel:** 1 432 758-5878.
Email: kikz-ksem@bajabb.com
Web site: http://www.kikzksem.com/
Profile: KSEM-FM is a commercial station owned by Gaines County Broadcasting. The format of the station is country and Hispanic music. KSEM-FM broadcasts to Seminole, TX at 106.3 FM.
FM RADIO STATION

KSEN-AM 39120
Owner: Townsquare Media, LLC
Editorial: 830 Oilfield Ave, Shelby, Montana 59474-1641 **Tel:** 1 406 434-5241.
Email: ksen@townsquaremedia.com
Web site: http://www.ksenam.com
Profile: KSEN-AM is a commercial station owned by Townsquare Media, LLC. The format of the station is oldies. KSEN-AM broadcasts to the Shelby, MT area at 1150 AM.
AM RADIO STATION

KSEO-AM 37490
Owner: Mid-Continental Broadcasting, LLC
Editorial: 1418 N 1st Ave, Durant, Oklahoma 74701-2812 **Tel:** 1 580 924-3100.
Web site: http://www.klbcfm.com/kseo.html
Profile: KSEO-AM is a commercial station owned by Mid-Continental Broadcasting, LLC. The format of the station is news/talk. KSEO-AM broadcasts to the Durant, OK area at 750 AM.
AM RADIO STATION

KSEQ-FM 40930
Owner: Lotus Communications Corp.
Editorial: 675 Santa Fe Ave, Fresno, California 93721-2724 **Tel:** 1 559 497-1100.
Email: promotions@Q97.com
Web site: http://www.q97.com
Profile: KSEQ-FM is a commercial station owned by Lotus Communications Corp. The format of the station is Top 40/CHR. KSEQ-FM broadcasts to the Visalia, CA area at 97.1 FM.
FM RADIO STATION

KSER-FM 41732
Owner: KSER Foundation
Editorial: 2623 Wetmore Ave, Everett, Washington 98201-2926 **Tel:** 1 425 303-9070.
Email: info@kser.org
Web site: http://www.kser.org
Profile: KSER-FM is a non-commercial station owned by KSER Foundation. The format of the station is a variety of news, talk and world music. KSER-FM broadcasts to the Everett, WA area at 90.7 FM.
FM RADIO STATION

KSES-FM 42236
Owner: Entravision Communications Corp.
Editorial: 67 Garden Ct, Monterey, California 93940-5302 **Tel:** 1 831 373-6767.
Web site: http://www.jose1071.com
Profile: KSES-FM is a commercial station owned by Entravision Communications Corp. The format of the station is Hispanic adult hits. KSES-FM broadcasts to the Salinas, CA area at 107.1 FM.
FM RADIO STATION

KSEV-AM 35910
Owner: Patrick Broadcasting LP
Editorial: 11451 Katy Fwy Ste 215, Houston, Texas 77079-2010 **Tel:** 1 281 588-4800.
Web site: http://www.ksevradio.com
Profile: KSEV-AM is a commercial station owned by Patrick Broadcasting LP. The format of the station is Conservative news and talk. KSEV-AM broadcasts to the Houston area at 700 AM.
AM RADIO STATION

KSEY-AM 39221
Owner: Aulabaugh(Mark)
Editorial: #1 Radio Lane, Seymour, Texas 73680
Tel: 1 940 889-2637.
Profile: KSEY-AM is a commercial station owned by Mark Aulabaugh. The format of the station is sports. KSEY-AM broadcasts to the Seymour, TX area at 1230 AM.
AM RADIO STATION

KSEY-FM 46575
Owner: Aulabaugh(Mark)
Editorial: #1 Radio Lane, Seymour, Texas 76380
Tel: 1 940 889-2637.
Email: fmksey@aol.com
Web site: http://www.kseyfm.com/
Profile: KSEY-FM is a commercial station owned by Mark Aulabaugh. The format of the station is news, talk and country music. KSEY-FM broadcasts to the Wichita Falls, TX area at 94.3 FM.
FM RADIO STATION

KSEZ-FM 46633
Owner: iHeartMedia Inc.
Editorial: 1113 Nebraska St, Sioux City, Iowa 51105-1438 **Tel:** 1 712 258-5595.
Web site: http://www.z98rocks.com
Profile: KSEZ-FM is a commercial station owned by iHeartMedia Inc. The format of the station is classic rock music. KSEZ-FM broadcasts to the Sioux City, IA area at 97.9 FM.
FM RADIO STATION

KSFA-AM 37491
Owner: Townsquare Media, LLC
Editorial: 1216 S 1st St, Lufkin, Texas 75901-4716
Tel: 1 936 639-4455.
Web site: http://www.ksfa860.com
Profile: KSFA-AM is a commercial station owned by Townsquare Media, LLC. The format of the station is news, sports and talk. KSFA-AM broadcasts to the Lufkin, TX area at 860 AM.
AM RADIO STATION

KSFB-AM 37414
Owner: Immaculate Heart Radio
Tel: 1 916 535-0500.
Email: programming@ihradio.org
Web site: http://ihradio.org
Profile: KSFB-AM is a commercial station owned by Immaculate Heart Radio. The format of the station is Catholic religious programming. KSFB-AM broadcasts to the San Francisco, area at 1260 AM.
AM RADIO STATION

KSFC-FM 39900
Owner: Spokane Public Radio Inc.
Editorial: 2319 N Monroe St, Spokane, Washington 99205-4548 **Tel:** 1 509 328-5729.
Email: kpbx@kpbx.org
Web site: http://www.kpbx.org
Profile: KSFC-FM is a non-commercial station owned by Spokane Public Radio Inc. The format of the station is news and talk. KSFC-FM broadcasts to the Spokane, WA area at 91.9 FM.
FM RADIO STATION

KSFI-FM 46447
Owner: Bonneville International Corp.
Editorial: 55 N 300 W, Salt Lake City, Utah 84101-3502 **Tel:** 1 801 595-1003.
Web site: http://www.fm100.com
Profile: KSFI-FM is a commercial station owned by Bonneville International Corp. The format of the station is adult contemporary. KSFI-FM broadcasts to the Salt Lake City area at 100.3 FM.
FM RADIO STATION

KSFM-FM 43383
Owner: CBS Radio
Editorial: 280 Commerce Cir, Sacramento, California 95815-4212 **Tel:** 1 916 923-8000.
Web site: http://ksfm.cbslocal.com
Profile: KSFM-FM is a commercial station owned by CBS Radio. The format of the station is rhythmic Top 40. KSFM-FM broadcasts to the Sacramento, CA area at 102.5 FM.
FM RADIO STATION

KSFO-AM 36234
Owner: Cumulus Media Inc
Editorial: 750 Battery St Fl 3, San Francisco, California 94111 **Tel:** 1 415 995-6800.
Web site: http://www.ksfo.com
Profile: KSFO-AM is a commercial station owned by Cumulus Media Inc. The format of the station is talk. KSFO-AM broadcasts to the San Francisco area at 560 AM.
AM RADIO STATION

KSFR-FM 42970
Owner: Santa Fe Community College
Editorial: 6401 S Richards Ave, Santa Fe, New Mexico 87508-4887 **Tel:** 1 505 428-1259.
Email: news@ksfr.org
Web site: http://www.ksfr.org
Profile: KSFR-FM is a non-commercial station owned by Santa Fe Community College. The format of the station is oldies, talk and news. KSFR-FM broadcasts to the Albuquerque, NM area at 90.7 FM.
FM RADIO STATION

KSFT-FM 489561
Owner: iHeartMedia Inc.
Editorial: 1113 Nebraska St, Sioux City, Iowa 51105-1438 **Tel:** 1 712 258-5595.
Web site: http://www.kiss107siouxcity.com
Profile: KSFT-FM is a commercial station owned by iHeartMedia Inc. The format of the station is hot adult contemporary. KSFT-FM broadcasts to the Sioux City, IA area at 107.1 FM.
FM RADIO STATION

KSFX-FM 42463
Owner: Majestic Communications
Editorial: 5206 W 2nd St, Roswell, New Mexico 88201-8839 **Tel:** 1 575 622-6450.
Web site: http://1005ksfx.com
Profile: KSFX-FM is a commercial station owned by Majestic Communications. The format of the station is classic rock. KSFX-FM broadcasts to the Albuquerque, NM area at 100.5 FM.
FM RADIO STATION

KSGF-AM 37528
Owner: E.W. Scripps Co.
Editorial: 2330 W Grand St, Springfield, Missouri 65802-4900 **Tel:** 1 417 865-6614.
Web site: http://www.ksgf.com
Profile: KSGF-AM is a commercial station owned by E.W. Scripps Co. The format of the station is news and talk. KSGF-AM broadcasts to the Springfield, MO area at 1260 AM.
AM RADIO STATION

KSGF-FM 39623
Owner: E.W. Scripps Co.
Editorial: 2330 W Grand St, Springfield, Missouri 65802-4900 **Tel:** 1 417 865-6614.
Web site: http://www.ksgf.com
Profile: KSGF-FM is a commercial station owned by E.W. Scripps Co. The format of the station is news and talk. KSGF-FM broadcasts to the Springfield, MO area at 104.1 FM.
FM RADIO STATION

KSGG-AM 37216
Owner: Americom Broadcasting
Editorial: 961 Matley Ln, Reno, Nevada 89502-2188
Tel: 1 775 829-1964.
Profile: KSGG-AM is a commercial station owned by Americom Broadcasting. The format of the station is sports. The station airs in the Reno, NV area at 1230 AM.
AM RADIO STATION

KSGL-AM 36673
Owner: Agape Communications
Editorial: 3337 W Central Ave, Wichita, Kansas 67203-4917 **Tel:** 1 316 942-3231.
Email: am900@ksgl.com
Web site: http://www.ksglradio.com/index.html
Profile: KSGL-AM is a commercial station owned by Agape Communications. The format of the station is adult standards. KGSL-AM broadcasts to the Wichita, KS area at 900 AM.
AM RADIO STATION

KSGM-AM 36517
Owner: Donze Communications Inc.
Editorial: 21851 White Sands Rd, Sainte Genevieve, Missouri 63670 **Tel:** 1 573 547-8005.
Email: kbdz@suntimesnews.com
Web site: http://www.suntimesnews.com
Profile: KSGM-AM is a commercial station owned by Donze Communications Inc. the format of the station is classic country. KSGM-AM broadcasts to the Sainte Genevieve, MO area at 980 AM.
AM RADIO STATION

KSGN-FM 39901
Owner: Good News Radio
Editorial: 2048 Orange Tree Ln Ste 200, Redlands, California 92374-4566 **Tel:** 1 909 583-2150.
Email: info@ksgn.com
Web site: http://www.ksgn.com
Profile: KSGN-FM is a non-commercial station owned by Good News Radio. The format of the station is contemporary Christian. KSGN-FM broadcasts to the Redlands, CA area at 89.7 FM.
FM RADIO STATION

KSGT-AM 39218
Owner: Rich Broadcasting, LLC.
Tel: 1 307 733-2120.
Web site: http://590kid.com
Profile: KSGT-AM is a commercial station owned by Rich Broadcasting, LLC. The format of the station is News/Talk. KSGT-AM broadcasts to the Jackson, WY area at 1340 AM.
AM RADIO STATION

KSGU-FM 364032
Owner: Nevada Public Radio
Editorial: 1289 S Torrey Pines Dr, Las Vegas, Nevada 89146-1004 **Tel:** 1 702 258-9895.
Web site: http://www.ksgu.org
Profile: KSGU-FM is a non-commercial station owned by Nevada Public Radio. The format of the station is classical music, news and talk. KSGU-FM broadcasts to the St. George, UT area on 90.3 FM.
FM RADIO STATION

KSHA-FM 45836
Owner: Mapleton of Redding, LLC
Editorial: 3360 Alta Mesa Dr, Redding, California 96002-2831 **Tel:** 1 530 226-9500.
Web site: http://www.kshasta.com
Profile: KSHA-FM is a commercial station owned by Mapleton of Redding, LLC. The format of the station is adult contemporary music. KSHA-FM broadcasts to the Redding, CA area at 104.3 FM.
FM RADIO STATION

KSHE-FM 39902
Owner: Emmis Communications Corp.
Editorial: 800 Saint Louis Union Sta, Saint Louis, Missouri 63103-2296 **Tel:** 1 314 621-0095.
Email: feedback@kshe95.com
Web site: http://www.kshe95.com
Profile: KSHE-FM is a commercial station owned by Emmis Communications Corp. The format of the station is rock music. KSHE-FM broadcasts to the St. Louis area at 94.7 FM.
FM RADIO STATION

KSHJ-AM 34908
Owner: La Promesa Foundation
Editorial: 11511 Katy Fwy Ste 301, Houston, Texas 77079-1921 **Tel:** 1 832 786-4500.
Email: grnonline@grnonline.com
Web site: http://grnonline.com/locations/1430-am-kshj-houston
Profile: KSHJ-AM is a commercial station owned by La Promesa Foundation. The format of the station is Catholic radio programming. KSHJ-AM broadcasts to the Houston area at 1430 AM.
AM RADIO STATION

KSHK-FM 238347
Owner: Ohana Broadcasting Co.
Editorial: 4271 Halenani St, Lihue, Hawaii 96766
Tel: 1 808 245-9527.
Email: kong@kongradio.com
Web site: http://www.kongradio.com
Profile: KSHK-FM is commercial station owned by Ohana Broadcasting Co. The format of the station is classic rock. KSHK-FM broadcasts to the Lihue, HI area at 103.3 FM.
FM RADIO STATION

KSHN-FM 42005
Owner: Trinity River Valley Broadcasting
Editorial: 2099 Sam Houston St, Liberty, Texas 77575-4817 **Tel:** 1 936 336-5793.
Email: news@kshn.com
Web site: http://www.kshn.com
Profile: KSHN-FM is a commercial station owned by Trinity River Valley Broadcasting. The format of the station is adult contemporary, country and oldies music. KSHN-FM broadcasts to the Liberty, TX area at 99.9 FM.
FM RADIO STATION

KSHO-AM 36380
Owner: EADS Broadcasting Corp.
Editorial: 36991 Kgal Dr, Lebanon, Oregon 97355
Tel: 1 541 451-5425.
Email: kgal@kgal.com
Web site: http://www.ksho.net
Profile: KSHO-AM is a station owned by EADS Broadcasting Corp. The format of the station is adult standards music. KSHO-FM broadcasts to Albany, OR area at 920 AM.
AM RADIO STATION

KSHP-AM 36737
Owner: Las Vegas Radio Co. Inc.(The)
Editorial: 2400 S Jones Blvd Ste 3, Las Vegas, Nevada 89146-3130 **Tel:** 1 702 221-1200.
Email: mail@kshp.com
Web site: http://www.kshp.com
Profile: KSHP-AM is a commercial station owned by The Las Vegas Radio Co. Inc. The format of the station is talk. KSHP-AM broadcasts to the Las Vegas area at 1400 AM.
AM RADIO STATION

KSHR-FM 46546
Owner: Bicoastal Media LLC
Editorial: 320 Central Ave, Ste 519, Coos Bay, Oregon 97420 **Tel:** 1 541 267-2121.
Email: southcoastpsa@bicoastalmedia.com
Web site: http://www.kshr.com
Profile: KSHR-FM is a commercial station owned by Bicoastal Media LLC. The format of the station is contemporary country music. KSHR-FM broadcasts to the Coos Bay, OR area at 97.3 FM.
FM RADIO STATION

KSIB-AM 37492
Owner: Dave & Kathy Rieck
Editorial: 1409 Highway 34, Creston, Iowa 50801
Tel: 1 641 782-2155.
Email: news@ksibradio.com
Web site: http://www.ksibradio.com
Profile: KSIB-AM is a commercial station owned by Dave & Kathy Rieck. The format of the station is contemporary country music. KSIB-AM broadcasts to the Creston, IA area at 1520 AM.
AM RADIO STATION

KSIB-FM 44703
Owner: Dave & Kathy Rieck
Editorial: 1409 Highway 34, Creston, Iowa 50801-8304 **Tel:** 1 641 782-2155.
Email: mailbag@ksibradio.com
Web site: http://www.ksibradio.com
Profile: KSIB-FM is a commercial station owned by Dave & Kathy Rieck. The format of the station is contemporary country music. KSIB-FM broadcasts to the Creston, IA area at 101.3 FM.
FM RADIO STATION

KSID-AM 37493
Owner: KSID Radio Inc.
Editorial: 2306 Legion Park Rd, Sidney, Nebraska 69162 **Tel:** 1 308 254-5803.
Web site: http://www.ksidradio.com
Profile: KSID-AM is a commercial station owned by KSID Radio Inc. The format of the station is contemporary country. KSID-AM broadcasts to the Sidney, NE area at 1340 AM.
AM RADIO STATION

KSID-FM 44892
Owner: KSID Radio Inc.
Editorial: PO Box 37, 2306 Legion Park Road, Sidney, Nebraska 69162-0037 **Tel:** 1 308 254-5803.
Email: ksidprod@ksidradio.com
Web site: http://www.ksidradio.com
Profile: KSID-FM is a commercial station owned by KSID Radio Inc. The format of the station is adult contemporary. KSID-FM broadcasts to the Sidney, NE area at 98.7 FM.
FM RADIO STATION

KSIG-AM 39315
Owner: Acadia Broadcast Partners
Editorial: 320 N Parkerson Ave, Crowley, Louisiana 70526-5056 **Tel:** 1 337 783-2520.
Web site: http://www.purecountry1067.com
Profile: KSIG-AM is a commercial station owned by Acadia Broadcast Partners. The format of the station is classic country music. KSIG-AM broadcasts to the Crowley, LA area at 1450 AM.
AM RADIO STATION

KSIG-FM 46671
Owner: Acadia Broadcast Partners
Editorial: 320 N Parkerson Ave, Crowley, Louisiana 70526-5056 **Tel:** 1 337 783-2520.
Web site: http://www.purecountry1067.com
Profile: KSIG-FM is a commercial station owned by Acadia Broadcast Partners. The format of the station is classic country. KSIG-FM broadcasts to the Crowley, LA area at 106.7 FM.
FM RADIO STATION

KSII-FM 42766
Owner: Townsquare Media, LLC
Editorial: 4180 N Mesa St, El Paso, Texas 79902-1420 **Tel:** 1 915 544-9300.
Web site: http://kisselpaso.com
Profile: KSII-FM is a commercial station owned by Townsquare Media, LLC. The format of the station is hot adult contemporary. KSII-FM broadcasts to the El Paso, TX area at 93.1 FM.
FM RADIO STATION

KSIM-AM 35074
Owner: Mississippi River Radio
Editorial: 324 Broadway St, Cape Girardeau, Missouri 63701 **Tel:** 1 573 335-8291.
Email: ksim@riverradio.net
Web site: http://www.1400ksim.com
Profile: KSIM-AM is a commercial station owned by Mississippi River Radio. The format of the station is news and talk. KSIM-AM broadcasts in the Paducah, MO area at 1400 AM.
AM RADIO STATION

KSIR-AM 37112
Owner: Northeast Colorado Broadcasting, LLC
Editorial: 220 State St, Fort Morgan, Colorado 80701-2175 **Tel:** 1 970 867-7271.
Email: farm@necolorado.com
Web site: http://www.ksir.com
Profile: KSIR-AM is a commercial station owned by Northeast Colorado Broadcasting, LLC. The format of the station agriculture news, talk and sports. KSIR-AM broadcasts in the Denver area at 1010 AM.
AM RADIO STATION

KSIS-AM 37494
Owner: Townsquare Media, LLC
Editorial: 2209 S Limit Ave, Sedalia, Missouri 65301-6950 **Tel:** 1 660 826-1050.
Web site: http://www.ksisradio.com
Profile: KSIS-AM is a commercial station owned by Townsquare Media, LLC. The format of the station is talk. KSIS-AM broadcasts to the Sedalia, KS, area at 1050 AM.
AM RADIO STATION

KSIT-FM 39904
Owner: Big Thickett Broadcasting Co.
Editorial: 2717 Yellowstone Rd, Rock Springs, Wyoming 82901-3261 **Tel:** 1 307 362-7034.
Email: wyoradio@wyoradio.com
Web site: http://www.wyoradio.com
Profile: KSIT-FM is a commercial station owned by Big Thickett Broadcasting Co. The format of the station is classic rock. KSIT-FM broadcasts to the Salt Lake City area at 99.7 FM.
FM RADIO STATION

KSIV-AM 35075
Owner: Bott Broadcasting Co.
Editorial: 1750 S Brentwood Blvd Ste 811, Saint Louis, Missouri 63144-1344 **Tel:** 1 314 961-1320.
Email: enelson@bottradionetwork.com
Web site: http://www.bottradionetwork.com
Profile: KSIV-AM is a commercial station owned by Bott Broadcasting Co. The format of the station is religious and Christian programming. KSIV-AM broadcasts to the St. Louis area at 1320 AM.
AM RADIO STATION

KSIV-FM 42387
Owner: Bott Broadcasting Co.
Editorial: 1750 S Brentwood Blvd Ste 811, Saint Louis, Missouri 63144-1344 **Tel:** 1 314 961-1320.
Email: ksiv@bottradionetwork.com
Web site: http://www.bottradionetwork.com
Profile: KSIV-FM is a commercial station owned by Bott Broadcasting Co. The format of the station is religious and Christian programming. KSIV-FM broadcasts to the St. Louis area at 91.5 FM.
FM RADIO STATION

KSIW-AM 36631
Owner: Classic Communications Inc.
Editorial: 1922 22nd St, Woodward, Oklahoma 73801-5307 **Tel:** 1 580 256-0935.
Email: cciradio@sbcglobal.net
Web site: http://www.woodwardradio.com
Profile: KSIW-AM is a commercial station owned by Classic Communications Inc. The format of the station is sports. KSIW-AM broadcasts to the Woodward, OK area at 1450 AM.
AM RADIO STATION

KSIX-AM 35076
Owner: SportsRadioCC, LLC
Editorial: 710 Buffalo St, Ste 605, Corpus Christi, Texas 78401 **Tel:** 1 361 882-5749.
Web site: http://sportsradiocc.com
Profile: KSIX-AM is a commercial station owned by SportsRadioCC, LLC. The format of the station is sports. KSIX-AM broadcasts to the Corpus Christi, TX area at 1230 AM.
AM RADIO STATION

KSIZ-FM 41926
Owner: Buffalo Broadcasting
Editorial: 113 E Alma St, Mount Shasta, California 96067-2203 **Tel:** 1 530 842-4158.
Profile: KSIZ-FM is a commercial station owned by Buffalo Broadcasting. The format of the station is classic rock. KCWH-FM broadcasts to the Weed/ Mount Shasta, CA area at 102.3 FM.
FM RADIO STATION

KSJB-AM 37495
Owner: Chesterman Communications Inc.
Editorial: 2400 8th Ave SW Ste D1, Jamestown, North Dakota 58401-6623 **Tel:** 1 701 252-3570.
Email: news@ksjbam.com
Web site: http://www.ksjbam.com
Profile: KSJB-AM is a commercial station owned by Chesterman Communications Inc. The format of the station is country music and agricultural programming. KSJB-AM broadcasts to the Jamestown, ND area at 600 AM.
AM RADIO STATION

KSJE-FM 41524
Owner: San Juan College
Editorial: 4601 College Blvd, Farmington, New Mexico 87402-4609 **Tel:** 1 505 566-3517.
Email: ksje@sanjuancollege.edu
Web site: http://www.ksje.com
Profile: KSJE-FM is a non-commercial station owned by San Juan College. The format of the station is classical and jazz music. KSJE-FM broadcasts to the Albuquerque, NM area at 90.9 FM.
FM RADIO STATION

KSJI-FM 836978
Owner: Good News Ministries, Inc.
Editorial: 13358 Manchester Rd Ste 100, Des Peres, Missouri 63131-1730 **Tel:** 1 314 909-8569.
Web site: http://joyfmonline.org
Profile: KSJI-FM is a non-commercial station owned by Good News Ministries, Inc. The format of the station is Contemporary Christian music. KSJI-FM broadcasts to the St. Louis, MO area at a frequency of 91.1 FM.
FM RADIO STATION

KSJJ-FM 42287
Owner: Gross Communications Corporation
Editorial: 345 SW Cyber Dr Ste 101-103, Bend, Oregon 97702-1045 **Tel:** 1 541 388-3300.
Web site: http://www.ksjj1029.com
Profile: KSJJ-FM is a commercial station owned by Gross Communications Corporation. The format of the station is contemporary country. KSJJ-FM broadcasts to the Bend, OR area at a frequency of 102.9 FM.
FM RADIO STATION

KSJK-AM 39168
Owner: State of Oregon
Editorial: 1250 Siskiyou Blvd, Ashland, Oregon 97520-5001 **Tel:** 1 541 552-6301.
Email: jprinfo@sou.edu
Web site: http://www.ijpr.org
Profile: KSJK-AM is a non-commercial station owned by State of Oregon. The format of the station is news and talk programming. KSJK-AM broadcasts to the Medford, OR area at 1230 AM.
AM RADIO STATION

KSJL-FM 799662
Owner: Radio 74 Internationale
Tel: 1 760 375-2355.
Email: contact@radio74.org
Web site: http://www.radio74.net
Profile: KSJL-FM is a non-commercial station owned by Radio 74 Internationale. The format of the station is Christian teaching and music. KRSF-FM broadcasts to the Strasburg, CO area at a frequency of 97.7 FM.
FM RADIO STATION

KSJN-FM 41930
Owner: Minnesota Public Radio
Editorial: 480 Cedar St, Saint Paul, Minnesota 55101-2217 **Tel:** 1 651 290-1500.
Email: newsroom@mpr.org
Web site: http://www.mpr.org/listen/stations/knowksjn
Profile: KSJN-FM is a non-commercial station owned by Minnesota Public Radio. The format of the station is classical music. KSJN-FM broadcasts to the St. Paul, MN area at 99.5 FM. KSJN-FM is an NPR/ National Public Radio affiliate.
FM RADIO STATION

KSJO-FM 42793
Owner: Cumulus Media
Editorial: San Francisco, California
Email: contact@bolly923fm.com
Web site: http://bolly923fm.com/
Profile: KSJO-FM is a commercial station owned by Cumulus Media. The format of the station is Ethnic. KSJO-FM broadcasts to the San Francisco Bay area at 92.3 FM.
FM RADIO STATION

KSJP-FM 836991
Owner: Agnus Dei Communications, Inc.
Editorial: 6300 S Old Village Pl Suite 203, Sioux Falls, South Dakota 57108-2102 **Tel:** 1 605 275-4659.
Email: kculhane.agnusdei@midconetwork.com
Profile: KSJP-FM is a commercial station owned by Agnus Dei Communications, Inc. The format of the station is Catholic talk and teaching. KSJP-FM broadcasts to the Aberdeen and Ipswich areas in South Dakota at a frequency of 88.9 FM.
FM RADIO STATION

KSJQ-FM 46478
Owner: Eagle Communications
Editorial: 4104 Country Ln, Saint Joseph, Missouri 64506-4921 **Tel:** 1 816 233-6086.
Web site: http://myqcountry.com
Profile: KSJQ-FM is a commercial station owned by Eagle Communications. The format of the station is contemporary country. KSJQ-FM broadcasts to the Saint Joseph, MO area at 92.7 FM.
FM RADIO STATION

KSJR-FM 39906
Owner: Minnesota Public Radio
Editorial: 300 Wimmer Hall St John's Univ, Collegeville, Minnesota 56321-9999 **Tel:** 1 320 363-7702.
Email: newsroom@mpr.org
Web site: http://minnesota.publicradio.org/radio/stations/knsrksjr
Profile: KSJR-FM is a non-commercial station owned by Minnesota Public Radio. The format of the station is classical music. KSJR-FM broadcasts to the Collegeville, MN area at 90.1 FM.
FM RADIO STATION

KSJT-FM 39908
Owner: Unica Broadcasting Co. (La)
Editorial: 209 W Beauregard Ave, San Angelo, Texas 76903-5823 **Tel:** 1 325 655-1717.
Email: webmaster@lagrande107.com
Web site: http://www.lagrande107.com
Profile: KSJT-FM is a commercial station owned by La Unica Broadcasting Co. The format for the station is Spanish adult contemporary. KSJT-FM broadcasts to the San Angelo, TX area at 107.5 FM.
FM RADIO STATION

KSJV-FM 41681
Owner: Radio Bilingue Inc.
Editorial: 5005 E Belmont Ave, Fresno, California 93727-2441 **Tel:** 1 559 455-5777.
Email: mail@radiobilingue.org
Web site: http://www.radiobilingue.org
Profile: KSJV-FM is a non-commercial station owned by Radio Bilingue Inc. The format of the station is Hispanic music and talk. KSJV-FM broadcasts to the Fresno, CA area at 91.5 FM.
FM RADIO STATION

KSJZ-FM 44893
Owner: Chesterman Communications Inc.
Editorial: 2400 8th Ave SW Ste 1, Jamestown, North Dakota 58401-6631 **Tel:** 1 701 252-3570.
Email: news@ksjbam.com
Web site: http://www.mixjamestown.com
Profile: KSJZ-FM is a commercial station owned by Chesterman Communications Inc. The format of the station is Adult Top 40/CHR music. KSJZ-FM broadcasts to the Jamestown, ND area at 93.3 FM.
FM RADIO STATION

KSKA-FM 39909
Owner: Alaska Public Media
Editorial: 3877 University Dr, Anchorage, Alaska 99508-4676 **Tel:** 1 907 550-8400.
Email: questions@kakm.org
Web site: http://www.kska.org
Profile: KSKA-FM is a non-commercial station owned by Alaska Public Media. The format of the station is news, music and talk. KSKA-FM broadcasts to the Anchorage, AK area at 91.1 FM.
FM RADIO STATION

KSKB-FM 128767
Owner: Florida Public Radio, Inc.
Editorial: 104 E 2nd St, Brooklyn, Iowa 52211-7718
Tel: 1 641 522-7202.
Email: kskb@netins.net
Profile: The station is a non-commercial station owned by Florida Public Radio, Inc. KSKB-FM broadcasts to Des Moines, IA locally at 99.1 FM. The format of the station is religous.
FM RADIO STATION

KSKE-AM 36841
Owner: Rocky Mountain Radio
Editorial: 614 Kimbark St, Longmont, Colorado 80501-4911 **Tel:** 1 303 776-2323.
Web site: http://kvleradio.com
Profile: KSKE-AM is a commercial station owned by Rocky Mountain Radio. The format of the station is news, talk and sports. KSKE-AM broadcasts to the Longmont, CO area at 1450 AM.
AM RADIO STATION

KSKE-FM 40026
Owner: NRC Broadcasting
Editorial: 182 Avon Rd, Ste 240, Avon, Colorado 81620-9999 **Tel:** 1 970 949-0140.
Web site: http://www.kskeradio.com
Profile: KSKE-FM is a commercial station owned by NRC Broadcasting. The format of the station is contemporary country. KSKE-FM broadcasts to the Avon, CO area at 101.7 FM.
FM RADIO STATION

KSKG-FM 46688
Owner: Eagle Radio Inc.
Editorial: 1825 S Ohio St, Salina, Kansas 67401-6601
Tel: 1 785 825-4631.
Profile: KSKG-FM is a commercial station owned by Eagle Radio Inc. The format of the station is contemporary country. KSKG-FM broadcasts to the Salina, KA area at 99.9 FM.
FM RADIO STATION

KSKI-FM 42108
Owner: Rich Broadcasting, LLC.
Editorial: 201 S Main St, Hailey, Idaho 83333-8406
Tel: 1 208 788-7118.
Email: kech95@richbroadcasting.com
Web site: http://www.945kski.com/
Profile: KSKI-FM is a commercial station owned by Rich Broadcasting, LLC. The format of the station is AAA-adult album alternative. KSKI-FM broadcasts to the Ketchum, ID area at 94.5.
FM RADIO STATION

KSKK-FM 42390
Owner: Radio FM Media
Editorial: 11 Bryant Ave SE, Wadena, Minnesota 56482-1543 **Tel:** 1 218 631-3441.
Profile: KSKK-FM is a commercial station owned by Radio FM Media. The format of the station is adult contemporary. KSKK-FM broadcasts to the Minneapolis area at 94.7 FM.
FM RADIO STATION

KSKL-FM 43820
Owner: Armada Media Corp.
Editorial: 1402 E Kansas Ave, Garden City, Kansas 67846-5806 **Tel:** 1 620 276-2366.
Email: production@wksradio.com
Web site: http://westernkansasnews.com
Profile: KSKL-FM is a commercial station owned by Armada Media Corp. The format of the station is oldies. KSKL-FM broadcasts to the Garden City, KS area at 94.5 FM.
FM RADIO STATION

KSKR-AM 35062
Owner: Brooke Communications Inc.
Editorial: 1445 W Harvard Ave, Roseburg, Oregon 97471-2839 **Tel:** 1 541 672-6641.
Web site: http://www.541radio.com
Profile: KSKR-AM is a commercial station owned by Brooke Communications Inc. The format of the station is sports. KSKR-AM broadcasts to the Roseburg, OR area at 1490 AM.
AM RADIO STATION

KSKR-FM 44223
Owner: Brooke Communications Inc.
Editorial: 1445 W Harvard Ave, Roseburg, Oregon 97471-2839 **Tel:** 1 541 672-6641.
Web site: http://www.541radio.com/i101
Profile: KSKR-FM is a commercial station owned by Brooke Communications Inc. The format of the station is Top 40/CHR. KSKR-FM broadcasts to the Roseburg, OR area at 100.9 FM.
FM RADIO STATION

KSKS-FM 46329
Owner: Cumulus Media
Editorial: 1071 W Shaw Ave, Fresno, California 93711-3702 **Tel:** 1 559 490-5800.
Web site: http://www.ksks.com
Profile: KSKS-FM is a commercial station owned by Cumulus Media. The format of the station is country music. KSKS-FM broadcasts to the Fresno, CA area at 93.7 FM.
FM RADIO STATION

KSKU-FM 39910
Owner: Ad Astra Per Aspera Broadcasting, Inc.
Editorial: 10 E 5th Ave, Hutchinson, Kansas 67501-6201 **Tel:** 1 620 665-5758.
Web site: http://www.adastraradio.com/ksku.php
Profile: KSKU-FM is a commercial station owned by Ad Astra Per Aspera Broadcasting, Inc. The format of the station is Top 40/CHR. KSKU-FM broadcasts to the Hutchinson, KS area at 94.7 FM.
FM RADIO STATION

KSKY-AM 35077
Owner: Salem Media Group, Inc.
Editorial: 6400 N Belt Line Rd Ste 110, Irving, Texas 75063-6065 **Tel:** 1 972 870-9949.
Web site: http://www.660amtheanswer.com
Profile: KSKY-AM is a commercial station owned by Salem Media Group, Inc. The format of the station is news and talk programming. KSKY-AM broadcasts to the Irving, TX area at 660 AM.
AM RADIO STATION

KSKZ-FM 43472
Owner: Ingstad Family Media
Editorial: 1402 E Kansas Ave, Garden City, Kansas 67846-5806 **Tel:** 1 620 276-2366.
Email: production@wksradio.com
Web site: http://www.wksradio.com
Profile: KSKZ-FM is a commercial station owned by Ingstad Family Media. The format of the station is hot adult contemporary. KSKZ-FM broadcasts to the Garden City, KS area at 98.1 FM.
FM RADIO STATION

KSL-AM 35078
Owner: KSL Broadcasting
Editorial: 55 N 300 W, Salt Lake City, Utah 84101-3502 **Tel:** 1 801 575-5555.
Email: newstip@ksl.com
Web site: http://www.ksl.com
Profile: KSL-AM is a commercial station owned by KSL Broadcasting. The format of the station is news, sports and talk. KSL-AM broadcasts to the Salt Lake City area at 1160 AM.
AM RADIO STATION

KSLC-FM 39911
Owner: Linfield College
Editorial: 900 SE Baker St, McMinnville, Oregon 97128-6808 **Tel:** 1 503 883-2550.
Email: kslcmusic@gmail.com
Web site: http://www.linfield.edu/kslcfm
Profile: KSLC-FM is a non-commercial college station owned by Linfield College. The format of the station is variety. KSLC-FM broadcasts to the Yamhill County, OR area at 90.3 FM.
FM RADIO STATION

KSLD-AM 134002
Owner: KSRM Radio Inc.
Editorial: 40960 K-Beach Rd, Kenai, Alaska 99611-6445 **Tel:** 1 907 283-8700.
Email: rken18@radiokenai.com
Web site: http://www.radiokenai.com
Profile: KSLD-AM is a commercial station owned by KSRM Radio Inc. The format of the station is sports. KSLD-AM broadcasts to the Kenai, AK, area at 1140 AM.
AM RADIO STATION

KSLE-FM 46844
Owner: One Ten Broadcasting Group Inc.
Editorial: 2 E Main St, Shawnee, Oklahoma 74801-6904 **Tel:** 1 405 878-1803.
Email: kirc1059@aol.com
Web site: http://www.onetenbroadcast.com
Profile: KSLE-FM is a commercial station owned by One Ten Broadcasting Group Inc. The format of the station is oldies music. KSLE-FM broadcasts to the Shawnee, OK area at 104.7 FM.
FM RADIO STATION

KSL-FM 42977
Owner: KSL Broadcasting
Editorial: 55 N 300 W, Salt Lake City, Utah 84101-3502 **Tel:** 1 801 575-5555.
Email: talk@ksl.com
Web site: http://www.ksl.com
Profile: KSL-FM is a commercial station owned by KSL Broadcasting. The format of the station is news, sports and talk. KSL-FM broadcasts to the Salt Lake City area at 1160 AM and simulcasts the programming of KSL-AM.
FM RADIO STATION

KSLG-FM 41860
Owner: Lost Coast Communications
Editorial: 1400 Main St Ste 104, Ferndale, California 95536-9459 **Tel:** 1 707 786-5104.
Email: studio@kslg.com
Web site: http://www.kslg.com
Profile: KSLG-FM is a commercial station owned by Lost Coast Communications. The format of the station is alternative rock. KSLG-FM broadcasts to the Eureka, CA area at 93.1 FM.
FM RADIO STATION

KSLI-AM 36522
Owner: Townsquare Media, LLC
Editorial: 3911 S 1st St, Abilene, Texas 79605
Tel: 1 325 676-7711.
Web site: http://www.1280ksli.com
Profile: KSLI-AM is a commercial station owned by Townsquare Media, LLC. The format of the station is classic country. KSLI-AM broadcasts to the Abilene, TX area at 1280 AM.
AM RADIO STATION

KSLL-AM 37482
Owner: AJB Broadcasting
Editorial: 6 E Main St, Price, Utah 84501-3032
Tel: 1 435 637-1080.
Email: kusabuzz@gmail.com
Web site: http://utahsclassicradio.com
Profile: KSLL-AM is a commercial station owned by AJB Broadcasting. The format of the station is classic rock. KSLL-AM broadcasts to the Price, UT area at 1080 AM.
AM RADIO STATION

KSLO-AM 37496
Owner: Delta Media Corporation
Editorial: 3501 NW Evangeline Trwy, Carencro, Louisiana 70520-6240 **Tel:** 1 337 942-2633.
Web site: http://elsaborradio.com
Profile: KSLO-AM is a commercial station owned by the Delta Media Corporation. The format of the station is regional Mexican. KSLO-AM broadcasts to the Opelousas, LA area at 1230 AM.
AM RADIO STATION

KSLO-FM 800416
Owner: Delta Media Corporation
Editorial: 3501 NW Evangeline Trwy, Carencro, Louisiana 70520-6240 **Tel:** 1 337 896-1600.
Web site: http://elsaborradio.com
Profile: KSLO-FM is a commercial station owned by Delta Media Corporation. The format of the station is regional Mexican. KSLO-FM broadcasts to the Lafayette, LA area at a frequency of 105.3 FM.
FM RADIO STATION

KSLQ-FM 43629
Owner: Brad Hildebrand
Editorial: 511 W 5th St, Washington, Missouri 63090-2205 **Tel:** 1 636 922-6666.
Web site: http://www.kslq.co/
Profile: KSLQ-FM is a commercial station owned by Brad Hildebrand. The format of the station is Hot AC. KSLQ-FM broadcasts to the Washington, MO area at 104.5 FM.
FM RADIO STATION

KSLR-AM 35079
Owner: Salem Media Group, Inc.
Editorial: 9601 McAllister Fwy, San Antonio, Texas 78216-4681 **Tel:** 1 210 344-8481.
Email: contact_us@kslr.com
Web site: http://www.kslr.com
Profile: KSLR-AM is a non-commercial station owned by Salem Media Group, Inc. The format of the station is religious news and talk. KSLR-AM broadcasts to the San Antonio area listeners at 630 AM.
AM RADIO STATION

KSLT-FM 41167
Owner: Bethesda Christian Broadcasting
Editorial: 1853 Fountain Plaza Dr, Rapid City, South Dakota 57702-9315 **Tel:** 1 605 342-6822.
Email: kslt@kslt.com
Web site: http://www.kslt.com
Profile: KSLT-FM is a commercial station owned by Bethesda Christian Broadcasting. The format of the station is Contemporary Christian. KSLT-FM broadcasts to the Rapid City and Black Hills areas in South Dakota at 107.1 FM.
FM RADIO STATION

KSLV-AM 38469
Owner: San Luis Valley Broadcasting
Editorial: 109 Adams St, Monte Vista, Colorado 81144-1421 **Tel:** 1 719 852-3581.
Email: kslv@amigo.net
Web site: http://www.kslvradio.com
Profile: KSLV-AM is a commercial station owned by San Luis Valley Broadcasting. The format of the station is country music. KSLV-AM broadcasts to the Monte Vista, CO area at 1240 AM.
AM RADIO STATION

KSLV-FM 45837
Owner: San Luis Valley Broadcasting
Editorial: 109 Adams St, Monte Vista, Colorado 81144-1421 **Tel:** 1 719 852-3581.
Email: kslv@amigo.net
Web site: http://www.kslvradio.com
Profile: KSLV-FM is a commercial station owned by San Luis Valley Broadcasting. The format of the station is adult contemporary. KSLV-FM broadcasts to the Monte Vista and Alamosa, CO areas at 96.5 FM.
FM RADIO STATION

KSLX-FM 74124
Owner: Hubbard Radio, LLC
Editorial: 4343 E Camelback Rd Ste 200, Phoenix, Arizona 85018-2756 **Tel:** 1 480 941-1007.
Web site: http://www.kslx.com
Profile: KSLX-FM is a commercial station owned by Hubbard Radio, LLC. The format of the station is classic rock. KSLX-FM broadcasts to the Phoenix area at 100.7 FM.
FM RADIO STATION

KSLY-FM 42318
Owner: El Dorado Broadcasting
Editorial: 51 Zaca Ln Ste 100, San Luis Obispo, California 93401-7353 **Tel:** 1 805 545-0101.
Web site: http://www.ksly.com
Profile: KSLY-FM is a commercial station owned by El Dorado Broadcasting. The format of the station is contemporary country. KSLY-FM broadcasts to the San Luis Obispo, CA area at 96.1 FM.
FM RADIO STATION

KSLZ-FM 41099
Owner: iHeartMedia Inc.
Editorial: 1001 Highlands Plaza Dr W Ste 200, Saint Louis, Missouri 63110-1337 **Tel:** 1 314 333-8000.
Web site: http://z1077.iheart.com
Profile: KSLZ-FM is a commercial station owned by iHeartMedia Inc. The format of the station is Top 40/ CHR music. KSLZ-FM broadcasts to the St. Louis area at 107.7 FM.
FM RADIO STATION

KSMA-AM 37497
Owner: American General Media
Editorial: 2215 Skyway Dr, Santa Maria, California 93455-1118 **Tel:** 1 805 925-2582.
Web site: http://www.1240ksma.com
Profile: KSMA-AM is a commercial station owned by American General Media. The format of the station is news and talk. KSMA-AM broadcasts to the Santa Maria, CA area at 1240 AM.
AM RADIO STATION

KSMA-FM 39827
Owner: Coloff Media
Editorial: 201 N Federal Ave, Mason City, Iowa 50401-3209 **Tel:** 1 641 421-7744.
Email: ksma@987kisscountry.com
Web site: http://www.987kisscountry.com
Profile: KSMA-FM is a commercial station owned by Coloff Media. The format of the station is contemporary country. KSMA-FM broadcasts to the Mason City, IA area at 98.7 FM.
FM RADIO STATION

KSMB-FM 46143
Owner: Cumulus Media Inc
Editorial: 202 Galbert Rd, Lafayette, Louisiana 70506-1806 **Tel:** 1 337 232-1311.
Web site: http://www.ksmb.com
Profile: KSMB-FM is a commercial station owned by Cumulus Media Inc. The format of the station is Top 40/CHR. KSMB-FM broadcasts to the Lafayette, LA area at 94.5 FM.
FM RADIO STATION

KSMC-FM 39914
Owner: Saint Mary's College of California
Editorial: 1928 Saint Marys Rd, Moraga, California 94556-2715 **Tel:** 1 925 631-4772.
Email: KSMC@stmarys-ca.edu
Web site: http://www.stmarys-ca.edu/ksmc
Profile: KSMC-FM is a non-commercial station owned by Saint Mary's College of California. The format of the station is variety. KSMC-FM broadcasts to the Moraga, CA area at 89.5 FM.
FM RADIO STATION

KSMD-FM 217655
Owner: Crain Media Group LLC
Editorial: 111 N Spring St, Searcy, Arkansas 72143-7712 **Tel:** 1 501 268-7123.
Email: production@crainmedia.com
Web site: http://www.newstalk991.com
Profile: KSMD-FM is a commercial station owned by Crain Media Group LLC. The format of the station is news, talk and sports. KSMD-FM broadcasts to the Searcy, AR area at 99.1 FM.
FM RADIO STATION

KSME-FM 42008
Owner: iHeartMedia Inc.
Editorial: 4270 Byrd Dr, Loveland, Colorado 80538-7074 **Tel:** 1 970 461-2560.
Web site: http://kissfmcolorado.iheart.com
Profile: KSME-FM is a commercial station owned by iHeartMedia Inc. The format of the station is Top 40/ CHR music. KSME-FM broadcasts to the Fort Collins, CO area at 96.1 FM.
FM RADIO STATION

KSMF-FM 134004
Owner: State of Oregon
Editorial: 1250 Siskiyou Blvd, Ashland, Oregon 97520-5001 **Tel:** 1 541 552-6301.
Email: jprinfo@sou.edu
Web site: http://www.ijpr.org
Profile: KSMF-FM is a non-commercial station owned by the State of Oregon. The format of the station features news and music programming from the Rhythm and News format of Jefferson Public Radio. KSMS-FM broadcasts to the Ashland, OR area at a frequency of 89.1 FM.
FM RADIO STATION

KSMG-FM 39915
Owner: Cox Media Group, Inc.
Editorial: 8122 Datapoint Dr Ste 600, San Antonio, Texas 78229-3446 **Tel:** 1 210 615-5400.
Web site: http://www.magic1053.com
Profile: KSMG-FM is a commercial station owned by Cox Media Group, Inc. The format of the station is hot adult contemporary music. KSMG-FM broadcasts to the San Antonio area at 105.3 FM.
FM RADIO STATION

KSMH-AM 37012
Owner: Immaculate Heart Radio
Tel: 1 530 535-0500.
Email: programming@ihradio.org
Web site: http://ihradio.org
Profile: KSMH-AM is a non-commercial station owned by Immaculate Heart Radio. The format of the station is religious. KSMH-AM broadcasts to the Sacramento, CA area at 1620 AM.
AM RADIO STATION

KSML-AM 36425
Owner: Pentagon Communications, LLC
Editorial: 121 S Cotton Sq, Lufkin, Texas 75904-2933
Tel: 1 936 634-6661.
Email: traffic@yatesmedia.com
Profile: KSML-AM is a commercial station owned by Yates Media. The format of the station is news/talk. KSML-AM broadcasts to the Lufkin, TX area at 1260 AM.
AM RADIO STATION

KSML-FM 44374
Owner: Pentagon Communications, LLC
Editorial: 121 S Cotton Sq, Lufkin, Texas 75904-2933
Tel: 1 936 634-6661.
Email: traffic@yatesmedia.com
Web site: http://www.ksmlradio.com
Profile: KSML-FM is a commercial station owned by Yates Media. The format of the station is Regional and Tejano. KSML-FM broadcasts to the Palm Desert, CA area at 101.9 FM.
FM RADIO STATION

KSMM-AM 37328
Owner: Rocking M Radio
Editorial: 150 Plaza Dr Ste J, Liberal, Kansas 67901-2779 **Tel:** 1 620 624-8156.
Email: ksmmproduction@gmail.com
Web site: http://rockingmradio.com/ksmm-1470
Profile: KSMM-AM is a commercial station owned by Rocking M Radio. The format of the station is oldies. KSMM-AM broadcasts to Liberal, KS area at 1470 AM.
AM RADIO STATION

KSMM-FM 44894
Owner: Rocking M Radio
Editorial: 150 Plaza Dr Ste J, Liberal, Kansas 67901-2779 **Tel:** 1 620 624-8156.
Email: ksmmproduction@gmail.com
Web site: http://rockingmradio.com
Profile: KSMM-FM is a commercial station owned by Rocking M Radio. The format of the station is regional Mexican. KSMM-FM broadcasts to the Liberal, KS area at 101.5 FM.
FM RADIO STATION

KSMO-AM 35080
Owner: KSMO Enterprises
Editorial: 800 S Main St, Salem, Missouri 65560-1637
Tel: 1 573 729-6117.
Email: ksmoski@fidnet.com
Web site: http://www.ksmoradio.com
Profile: KSMO is the Ozark's home of Salem Tiger Sports, Cardinal Baseball, Mizzou Sports, and Blues Hockey! KSMO streams Salem Tiger Sports including Football, Volleyball, Boys and Girls Basketball and Baseball.
AM RADIO STATION

KSMT-FM 39917
Owner: NRC Broadcasting
Editorial: 130 Ski Hill Road, Ste 240, Breckenridge, Colorado 80424 **Tel:** 1 970 453-2234.
Web site: http://www.ksmtradio.com
Profile: KSMT-FM is a commercial station owned by NRC Broadcasting. The format of the station is adult album alternative. KSMT-FM broadcasts to the Breckenridge, CO area at 102.1 FM.
FM RADIO STATION

KSMX-FM 42989
Owner: Rooney Moon Broadcasting
Editorial: 420 N Main St, Clovis, New Mexico 88101-7557 **Tel:** 1 575 763-0338.
Email: news@rooneymoon.com
Web site: http://www.heymix.com
Profile: KSMX-FM is a commercial station owned by Rooney Moon Broadcasting. The format of the station is Hot AC. KSMX-FM broadcasts to the Clovis, NM area at a frequency of 107.5 FM.
FM RADIO STATION

KSMY-FM 81613
Owner: El Dorado Broadcasting
Editorial: 2215 Skyway Dr, Santa Maria, California 93455-1118 **Tel:** 1 805 925-2582.
Web site: http://www.elcompa1067.com
Profile: KSMY-FM is a commercial station owned by El Dorado Broadcasting. The format of the station is Hispanic adult contemporary. KSMY-FM broadcasts to the Santa Maria, CA area at 106.7 FM.
FM RADIO STATION

KSNA-FM 46072
Owner: Sand Hill Media
Editorial: 854 Lindsay Blvd, Idaho Falls, Idaho 83402-1820 **Tel:** 1 208 522-1101.
Web site: http://www.100myfm.com
Profile: KSNA-FM is a commercial station owned by Sand Hill Media. The format of the station is adult contemporary. KSNA-FM broadcasts to the Idaho Falls, ID area at 100.7 FM.
FM RADIO STATION

KSND-FM 42990
Owner: Bustos Media, LLC
Editorial: 285 Liberty St NE Ste 340, Salem, Oregon 97301-3562 **Tel:** 1 503 763-9951.
Profile: KSND-FM is a commercial station owned by Bustos Media, LLC. The format of the station is Regional Mexican. KSND-FM broadcasts to the Salem, OR area at 95.1 FM.
FM RADIO STATION

KSNE-FM 41161
Owner: iHeartMedia Inc.
Editorial: 2880 Meade Ave Ste 250, Las Vegas, Nevada 89102-0713 **Tel:** 1 702 238-7300.
Web site: http://www.ksne.com
Profile: KSNE-FM is a commercial station owned by iHeartMedia Inc. The format of the station is adult contemporary. KSNE-FM broadcasts to the Las Vegas area at 106.5 FM.
FM RADIO STATION

KSNI-FM 44895
Owner: El Dorado Broadcasting
Editorial: 2215 Skyway Dr, Santa Maria, California 93455 **Tel:** 1 805 925-2582.
Web site: http://www.sunnycountry.com
Profile: KSNI-FM is a commercial station owned by El Dorado Broadcasting. The format of the station is classic country. KSNI-FM broadcasts to the Santa Maria, CA area at 102.5 FM.
FM RADIO STATION

KSNM-FM 39919
Owner: Adams Radio Group
Editorial: 1355 California Ave, Las Cruces, New Mexico 88001-4130 **Tel:** 1 575 525-9298.
Web site: http://www.classichits987.com
Profile: KSNM-FM is a commercial station owned by Adams Radio Group. The format of the station is classic hits. KSNM-FM broadcasts to the Las Cruces, NM area at a frequency of 98.7 FM.
FM RADIO STATION

KSNN-FM 334142
Owner: Cherry Creek Radio
Editorial: 106 Rose Ln, Montrose, Colorado 81401-3823 **Tel:** 1 970 249-4546 213.
Email: sunny103@cherrycreekmedia.com
Web site: http://mysunny103.com
Profile: KSNN-FM is a commercial station owned by Cherry Creek Radio. The format of the station is soft AC. KSNN-FM broadcasts to the Grand Junction-Montrose, CO area at 103.7 FM.
FM RADIO STATION

KSNO-FM 42172
Owner: Color Radio Marketing LLC
Editorial: 218 E Valley Rd, El Jebel, Colorado 81623-7735 **Tel:** 1 970 925-4111.
Web site: http://www.ksno.net/
Profile: KSNO-FM is a commercial station owned by Colorado West Broadcasting Inc. The format of the station is adult album alternative music. KSNO-FM broadcasts to the Aspen, CO area at 103.5 FM.
FM RADIO STATION

KSNP-FM 41928
Owner: My Town Media, Inc.
Editorial: 1910 6th St, Burlington, Kansas 66839
Tel: 1 620 364-8807.
Web site: http://www.977thedawg.com
Profile: KSNP-FM is a commercial station owned by My Town Media, Inc. The format of the station is classic rock. KSNP-FM broadcasts to the Burlington, KS area at 97.7 FM.
FM RADIO STATION

KSNQ-FM 518625
Owner: Townsquare Media, LLC
Editorial: 415 Park Ave, Twin Falls, Idaho 83301-7752
Tel: 1 208 733-7512.
Web site: http://983thesnake.com
Profile: KSNQ-FM is a commercial station owned by Townsquare Media, LLC. The format of the station is classic rock music. KSNQ-FM broadcasts to the Idaho Falls, ID area at 98.3 FM.
FM RADIO STATION

KSNR-FM 44514
Owner: iHeartMedia Inc.
Editorial: 505 University Ave, Grand Forks, North Dakota 58203-3545 **Tel:** 1 701 746-1417.
Email: gfprod@iheartmedia.com
Web site: http://thecatfm.iheart.com
Profile: KSNR-FM is a commercial station owned by iHeartMedia Inc. The format of the station is contemporary country. KSNR-FM broadcasts to the Grand Forks, ND area at 92.9 FM.
FM RADIO STATION

KSNS-FM 63698
Owner: Florida Public Radio, Inc.
Editorial: 301 S Main St, Medicine Lodge, Kansas 67104 **Tel:** 1 620 886-3537.
Web site: http://www.krejksns.org
Profile: KSNS-FM is a non-commercial station owned by Florida Public Radio, Inc. The format of the station is contemporary Christian music. KSNS-FM broadcasts to the Medicine Lodge, KS area at 91.5 FM.
FM RADIO STATION

KSNX-FM 44948
Owner: Petracom
Editorial: 27610 N Desierto Dr, Rio Verde, Arizona 85263-6037 **Tel:** 1 928 362-8100.
Profile: KSNX-FM is a commercial station owned by Petracom. The format of the station is classic hits. KSNX-FM broadcasts to the Heber, AZ area at 105.5 FM.
FM RADIO STATION

KSNY-FM 45862
Owner: Snyder Broadcasting Co.
Editorial: 2301 Avenue R, Snyder, Texas 79549-1919
Tel: 1 325 573-9222.
Email: news@ksnyradio.com

Web site: http://bigstarradiogroup.com
Profile: KSNY-FM is a commercial station owned by Snyder Broadcasting Co. The format of the station is classic and contemporary country music. KSNY-FM broadcasts to the Snyder, TX area at 101.5 FM.
FM RADIO STATION

KSOB-FM 235177
Owner: Rocking M Radio
Editorial: 5501 10th St, Great Bend, Kansas 67530-6319 **Tel:** 1 620 792-7108.
Web site: http://centralkansasradio.com/kansascountry96
Profile: KSOB-FM is a commercial station owned by Rocking M Radio. The format of the station is contemporary country. KSOB-FM broadcasts to the Wichita, KS area at 96.7 FM.
FM RADIO STATION

KSOC-FM 39967
Owner: Urban One, Inc.
Editorial: 13760 Noel Rd Ste 1100, Dallas, Texas 75240-1383 **Tel:** 1 972 331-5400.
Web site: http://boom945.com
Profile: KSOC-FM is a commercial station owned by Urban One, Inc. The format of the station is urban AC and oldies R&B. KSOC-FM broadcasts to the Dallas area at 94.5 FM. The station's slogan is, "Classic Hip-Hop and Throwback R&B."
FM RADIO STATION

KSOF-FM 44036
Owner: iHeart Media
Editorial: 83 E Shaw Ave Ste 150, Fresno, California 93710-7622 **Tel:** 1 559 230-4300.
Web site: http://www.softrock989.com
Profile: KSOF-FM is a commercial station owned by IHeart Media and Entertainment. The format of the station is Lite Rock/Lite AC music. KSOF-FM broadcasts in the Fresno, CA area at 98.9 FM.
FM RADIO STATION

KSOH-FM 608179
Owner: Lifetalk Radio Inc.
Tel: 1 615 469-5122.
Email: office@lifetalk.net
Web site: http://www.lifetalk.net
Profile: KSOH-FM is a non-commercial station owned by Lifetalk Radio Inc. The format of the station is Christian programming. KSOH-FM is a transmitter that broadcasts to the Wapato, WA area at 89.5 FM.
FM RADIO STATION

KSOK-AM 76351
Owner: Cowley County Broadcasting
Editorial: 334 E Radio Ln, Arkansas City, Kansas 67005 **Tel:** 1 620 442-5400.
Email: ksok@ksokradio.com
Web site: http://www.ksokradio.com
Profile: KSOK-AM is a commercial station owned by Cowley County Broadcasting. The format of the station is classic country. KSOK-AM broadcasts to the Arkansas City, KS area at 1280 AM.
AM RADIO STATION

KSOK-FM 43596
Owner: Cowley County Broadcasting
Editorial: 334 E Radio Ln, Arkansas City, Kansas 67005 **Tel:** 1 620 442-5400.
Email: ksok@ksokradio.com
Web site: http://www.ksokradio.com
Profile: KSOK-FM is the station owned by Cowley County Broadcasting. The format of the station is contemporary country. KSOK-FM broadcasts to the Arkansas City, KS area at 95.9 FM.
FM RADIO STATION

KSOL-FM 41626
Owner: Univision Communications Inc.
Editorial: 50 Fremont St, San Francisco, California 94105-2278 **Tel:** 1 888 880-5765.
Web site: http://www.univision.com/san-francisco/ksol
Profile: KSOL-FM is a commercial station owned by Univision Communications Inc. The format of the station is regional Mexican music and news. KSOL-FM broadcasts to the San Francisco area at 98.9.
FM RADIO STATION

KSOM-FM 42991
Owner: Meredith Communications LLC
Editorial: 413 Chestnut St, Atlantic, Iowa 50022-1247
Tel: 1 712 243-6885.
Email: ksomnews@mchsi.com
Web site: http://www.965ksom.com
Profile: KSOM-FM is a commercial station owned by Meredith Communications LLC. The format of the station is country. KSOM-FM broadcasts to the Atlantic, IA area at 96.5 FM.
FM RADIO STATION

KSON-FM 44433
Owner: Entercom Communications Corp.
Editorial: 1615 Murray Canyon Rd Ste 710, San Diego, California 92108-4321 **Tel:** 1 619 291-9797.
Email: ksonstudio@kson.com
Web site: http://www.kson.com
Profile: KSON-FM is a commercial station owned by Entercom Communications Corp. The format of the station is country music. KSON-FM broadcasts to the San Diego area at 97.3 FM.
FM RADIO STATION

KSOO-AM 37498
Owner: Townsquare Media, Inc.
Editorial: 5100 S Tennis Ln, Sioux Falls, South Dakota 57108-2212 **Tel:** 1 605 361-0300.
Web site: http://www.ksoo.com
Profile: KSOO-AM is a commercial station owned by Townsquare Media, Inc. The format of the station is sports, news and talk. KSOO-AM broadcasts to the Sioux Falls, SD area at 1140 AM.
AM RADIO STATION

KSOO-FM 541529
Owner: Townsquare Media, Inc.
Editorial: 5100 S Tennis Ln, Sioux Falls, South Dakota 57108-2212 **Tel:** 1 605 361-0300.
Web site: http://www.espn991.com
Profile: KSOO-FM is a commercial station owned by Townsquare Media, Inc. The format of the station is sports. KSOO-FM broadcasts to the Sioux Falls, ID area at 99.1 FM.
FM RADIO STATION

KSOP-AM 37499
Owner: KSOP Inc.
Editorial: 1285 W 2320 S, West Valley City, Utah 84119-1448 **Tel:** 1 801 972-1043.
Web site: http://www.cc1370.com
Profile: KSOP-AM is a commercial station owned by KSOP Inc. The format of the station is classic country. KSOP-AM broadcasts to the West Valley City, UT area at 1370 AM.
AM RADIO STATION

KSOP-FM 44896
Owner: KSOP Inc.
Editorial: 1285 W 2320 S, West Valley City, Utah 84119-1448 **Tel:** 1 801 972-1043.
Web site: http://www.z104country.com
Profile: KSOP-FM is a commercial station owned by KSOP Inc. The format of the station is contemporary country. KSOP-FM broadcasts to the West Valley City, UT area at 104.3 FM.
FM RADIO STATION

KSOQ-FM 44815
Owner: Entercom Communications Corp.
Editorial: 1615 Murray Canyon Rd Ste 710, San Diego, California 92108-4321 **Tel:** 1 619 291-9797.
Web site: http://www.kson.com
Profile: KSOQ-FM is a commercial station owned by Entercom Communications Corp. The format of the station is country music. KSOQ-FM broadcasts to the San Diego area at 92.1 FM.
FM RADIO STATION

KSOR-FM 46518
Owner: State of Oregon
Editorial: 1250 Siskiyou Blvd, Ashland, Oregon 97520-5001 **Tel:** 1 541 552-6301.
Email: jprinfo@sou.edu
Web site: http://www.ijpr.org
Profile: KSOR-FM is a non commercial station owned by State of Oregon. The format of the station features classical music and news programming. KSOR-FM broadcasts to the Medford, OR area at a frequency of 90.5 FM.
FM RADIO STATION

KSOS-FM 39683
Owner: Faith Communications Corp.
Editorial: 2201 S 6th St, Las Vegas, Nevada 89104-2962 **Tel:** 1 702 731-5452.
Email: info@sosradio.net
Web site: http://www.sosradio.net
Profile: KSOS-FM is a non-commerical station owned by Faith Communications Corp. The format of the station contemporary Christian. KSOS-FM broadcasts to the Las Vegas area at 90.5 FM.
FM RADIO STATION

KSOU-AM 37545
Owner: Community First Broadcasting, LLC
Editorial: 128 20th St SE, Sioux Center, Iowa 51250
Tel: 1 712 722-1090.
Email: ksou@siouxcountyradio.com
Web site: http://siouxcountyradio.com
Profile: KSOU-AM is a commercial station owned by Community First Broadcasting, LLC. The format of the station is oldies music concentrating on the 1960s and 1970s. KSOU-AM broadcasts to the Sioux Center, IA area at a frequency of 1090 AM.
AM RADIO STATION

KSOU-FM 44937
Owner: Community First Broadcasting, LLC
Editorial: 128 20th St SE, Sioux Center, Iowa 51250
Tel: 1 712 722-1090.
Email: ksou@siouxcountyradio.com
Web site: http://www.siouxcountyradio.com
Profile: KSOU-FM is a commercial station owned by Community First Broadcasting, LLC. The format of the station is adult contemporary. KSOU-FM broadcasts to the Sioux Center, IA area at 93.9 FM.
FM RADIO STATION

KSOX-AM 37163
Owner: Vision Hispana Incorporated Internacional
Editorial: 1 Paseo Del Prado Ave Bldg 102, Edinburg, Texas 78539-1401 **Tel:** 1 956 383-2777.
Email: visionhispana@sbcglobal.net
Profile: KSOX-AM is a commercial station owned by Vision Hispana Inc. Internacional. The format of the station is Hispanic religious. KSOX-AM broadcasts to the McAllen, TX area at 1240 AM.
AM RADIO STATION

KSPA-AM 35022
Owner: Astor Broadcast Group
Editorial: 12036 Ramona Blvd, El Monte, California 91732-2422 **Tel:** 1 626 444-4442.
Web site: http://www.guadaluperadio.com
Profile: KSPA-AM is a commercial station owned by Astor Broadcast Group. The format of the station is business news and talk. KSPA-AM broadcasts to the North San Diego, CA and Orange County area at 1510 AM.
AM RADIO STATION

KSPC-FM 39923
Owner: Pomona College
Editorial: 340 N College Ave, Claremont, California 91711 **Tel:** 1 909 621-8157.
Email: news@kspc.org
Web site: http://www.kspc.org
Profile: KSPC-FM is a non-commercial station owned by Pomona College. The format of the station is variety. KSPC-FM broadcasts to the Claremont, CA area at 88.7 FM.
FM RADIO STATION

KSPD-AM 39015
Owner: Inspirational Family Radio
Editorial: 1440 S Weideman Ave, Boise, Idaho 83709
Tel: 1 208 377-3790.
Email: info@myfamilyradio.com
Web site: http://www.790kspd.com
Profile: KSPD-AM is a commercial station owned by Inspirational Family Radio. The format of the station is Christian talk programming. KSPD-AM broadcasts to the Boise, ID area at 790 AM.
AM RADIO STATION

KSPE-AM 39372
Owner: Rincon Broadcasting
Editorial: 414 E Cota St, Santa Barbara, California 93101 **Tel:** 1 805 879-8300.
Web site: http://santabarbara.lapreciosa.com
Profile: KSPE-AM is a commercial station owned by Rincon Broadcasting. The format of the station is Spanish oldies. KSPE-AM broadcasts to the Santa Barbara, CA area at 1490 AM.
AM RADIO STATION

KSPI-AM 37500
Owner: Mahaffey Enterprises Inc.
Editorial: 408 E Thomas Ave, Stillwater, Oklahoma 74075-2648 **Tel:** 1 405 372-7800.
Email: stillwaterradio@coxinet.net
Web site: http://www.stillwaterradio.com
Profile: KSPI-AM is a commercial station owned by Mahaffey Enterprises Inc. The format of the station is sports talk. KSPI-AM broadcasts to the Stillwater, OK area at 780 AM.
AM RADIO STATION

KSPI-FM 44897
Owner: Mahaffey Enterprises Inc.
Editorial: 408 E Thomas Ave, Stillwater, Oklahoma 74075-2648 **Tel:** 1 405 372-7800.
Email: stillwaterradio@coxinet.net
Web site: http://www.stillwaterradio.net
Profile: KSPI-FM is a commercial station owned by Mahaffey Enterprises Inc. The format fo the station is hot adult contemporary. KSPI-FM broadcasts to the Stillwater, Ok area at 93.7 FM.
FM RADIO STATION

KSPK-FM 41172
Owner: Mainstreet Broadcasting Company Inc.
Editorial: 516 Main St, Walsenburg, Colorado 81089-2036 **Tel:** 1 719 738-3636.
Email: info@kspk.com
Web site: http://www.kspk.com
Profile: KSPK-FM is a commercial station owned by Mainstreet Broadcasting Company Inc. The format of the station is country. KSPK-FM broadcasts to the Colorado Springs, CO area at 102.3 FM.
FM RADIO STATION

KSPL-FM 134005
Owner: Moody Bible Institute
Editorial: 5408 S Freya St, Spokane, Washington 99223 **Tel:** 1 509 448-2555.
Email: kmbi@moody.edu
Web site: http://www.moodyradionorthwest.fm
Profile: KSPL-FM is a non-commercial station owned by Moody Bible Institute. The format of the station is religious programming. KSPL-FM broadcasts to the Kalispell, MT area at 90.9 FM.
FM RADIO STATION

KSPN-AM 37468
Owner: Walt Disney Co.
Editorial: 800 W Olympic Blvd Ste A200, Los Angeles, California 90015-1375 **Tel:** 1 213 284-7100.
Web site: http://espn.go.com/los-angeles/radio/index
Profile: KSPN-AM is a commercial station owned by Walt Disney Co. The format of the station is sports. KSPN-AM broadcasts to the Los Angeles area at 710 AM.
AM RADIO STATION

KSPN-FM 39924
Owner: NRC Broadcasting
Editorial: 402 Aspen Airport Business Ctr, Ste D, Aspen, Colorado 81611-3542 **Tel:** 1 970 925-5776.
Email: kspnfm@gmail.com
Web site: http://www.kspnradio.com
Profile: KSPN-FM is a commercial station owned by NRC Broadcasting. The format of the station is adult album alternative. KSPN-FM broadcasts to the Aspen, CO area at 100.1 FM.
FM RADIO STATION

KSPO-FM 43013
Owner: Read Broadcasting
Editorial: 6019 S Crestline St, Spokane, Washington 99223-6823 **Tel:** 1 509 443-1000.
Email: acn@acn.cc
Web site: http://www.kpso.com
Profile: KSPO-FM is a commercial station owned by Liberty Broadcasting System, LLC. The format of the station is religious. KSPO-FM broadcasts to the Spokane, WA area at 106.5 FM.
FM RADIO STATION

KSPQ-FM 44962
Owner: Ozark Radio Network Inc.
Editorial: 983 E US Highway 160, West Plains, Missouri 65775-4801 **Tel:** 1 417 256-1025.
Web site: http://www.ozarkareanetwork.com
Profile: KSPQ-FM is a commercial station owned by Ozark Radio Network Inc. The format of the station is classic rock. KSPQ-FM broadcasts to the Springfield, MO area at 93.9 FM.
FM RADIO STATION

KSPW-FM 41883
Owner: E.W. Scripps Co.
Editorial: 2330 W Grand St, Springfield, Missouri 65802-4900 **Tel:** 1 417 865-6614.
Web site: http://www.power965.com
Profile: KSPW-FM is a commercial station owned by the E.W. Scripps Co. The format of the station is Top 40/CHR. KSPW-FM broadcasts to Springfield, MO area at 96.5 FM.
FM RADIO STATION

KSPZ-AM 38718
Owner: Sand Hill Media
Editorial: 854 Lindsay Blvd, Idaho Falls, Idaho 83402-1820 **Tel:** 1 208 522-1101.
Email: contactus@980thezone.com
Web site: http://www.980thezone.com/index.php
Profile: KSPZ-AM is a commercial station owned by Sand Hill Media. KSPZ-AM's format is Sports. KSPZ-AM broadcasts to the Idaho Falls, ID area at 980 AM.
AM RADIO STATION

KSQL-FM 396807
Owner: Univision Communications Inc.
Editorial: 50 Fremont St, San Francisco, California 94105-2278 **Tel:** 1 888 880-5765.
Web site: http://www.univision.com/san-francisco/ksol
Profile: KSQL-FM is a commercial station owned by Univision Communications Inc. The format of the station is regional Mexican. KSQL-FM broadcasts to the San Francisco area at 98.9 FM.
FM RADIO STATION

KSQM-FM 563619
Owner: Sequim Community Broadcasting
Editorial: 577 W Washington St, Ste C, Sequim, Washington 98382-3269 **Tel:** 1 360 681-0000.
Email: news@ksqmfm.com
Web site: http://www.ksqmfm.com
Profile: KSQM-FM is a non-commercial station owned by Sequim Community Broadcasting. The format of the station is oldies, adult standards and jazz. KSQM-FM broadcasts to the Sequim, WA area at 91.5 FM.
FM RADIO STATION

KSQN-FM 80355
Owner: KLO Broadcasting Co.
Editorial: 257 E 200 S Ste 400, Salt Lake City, Utah 84111-2073 **Tel:** 1 801 364-9836.
Web site: http://www.sunny103fm.com
Profile: KSQN-FM is a commercial station owned by KLO Broadcasting Co. The format of the station is adult contemporary. KSQN-FM broadcasts to the Salt Lake City area at 103.1 FM.
FM RADIO STATION

KSQQ-FM 41722
Owner: Morgan Hill Broadcasting
Editorial: 1629 Alum Rock Ave Ste 30, San Jose, California 95116-2418 **Tel:** 1 408 258-9696.
Email: pr@ksqq.com
Web site: http://www.ksqq.com
Profile: KSQQ-FM is a commercial station owned by Morgan Hill Broadcasting. The format of the station is ethnic, featuring Portuguese programming. KSQQ-FM broadcasts to the San Jose, CA area at 96.1 FM.
FM RADIO STATION

KSQY-FM 39925
Owner: Haugo Broadcasting Inc.
Editorial: 3601 Canyon Lake Dr Ste 1, Rapid City, South Dakota 57702-3901 **Tel:** 1 605 343-0888.
Web site: http://www.951ksky.com
Profile: KSQY-FM is a commercial station owned by Haugo Broadcasting Inc. The format of the station is rock. KSQY-FM broadcasts to Rapid City, SD at 95.1 FM.
FM RADIO STATION

KSRA-AM 38470
Owner: Salmon River Communications Inc.
Editorial: 315 Riverfront Dr, Salmon, Idaho 83467-5161 **Tel:** 1 208 756-2218.
Profile: KSRA-AM is a commercial station owned by Salmon River Communications Inc. The format of the station is adult contemporary. KSRA-AM broadcasts to the Salmon, ID area at 960 AM.
AM RADIO STATION

KSRA-FM 45834
Owner: Salmon River Communications Inc.
Editorial: 315 Riverfront Dr, Salmon, Idaho 83467-5161 **Tel:** 1 208 756-2218.
Profile: KSRA-FM is a commercial radio station owned by Salmon River Communications Inc. The format of the station is classic country music. KSRA-FM broadcasts to the Salmon, ID area at 92.7 FM.
FM RADIO STATION

KSRF-FM 235095
Owner: Ohana Broadcasting, LLC
Editorial: 4271 Halenani St, Lihue, Hawaii 96766-1312 **Tel:** 1 808 245-9527.
Email: kong@kongradio.com
Web site: http://www.surf959fm.com
Profile: KSRF-FM is a commercial station owned by Ohana Broadcasting, LLC. The format of the station is Hawaiian music. KSRF-FM broadcasts to the Lihue, HI area at 95.9 FM.
FM RADIO STATION

KSRG-FM 134006
Owner: State of Oregon
Editorial: 1250 Siskiyou Blvd, Ashland, Oregon 97520-5001 **Tel:** 1 541 552-6301.
Email: jprinfo@sou.edu
Web site: http://www.ijpr.org
Profile: KSRG-FM is a commercial station owned by State of Oregon. The format of the station is news, jazz and classical music. KSRG-FM broadcasts to the Ashland, OR area at 88.3. FM.
FM RADIO STATION

KSRM-AM 39032
Owner: KSRM Radio Inc.
Editorial: 40960 Kalifornsky Beach Rd, Kenai, Alaska 99611-6445 **Tel:** 1 907 283-8700.
Email: info@radiokenai.com
Web site: http://www.ksrm.com
Profile: KSRM-AM is a commercial station owned by KSRM Radio Inc. The format of the station is news and talk. KSRM-AM broadcasts to the Kenai, AK area at 920 AM.
AM RADIO STATION

KSRN-FM 42377
Owner: Lazer Broadcasting Corp.
Editorial: 1465 Terminal Way, Reno, Nevada 89502 **Tel:** 1 775 324-4819.
Web site: http://www.radiolazer.com
Profile: KRSN-FM is a commercial station owned by Lazer Broadcasting Corp. The format of the station is regional Mexican. KSRN-FM broadcasts to the Reno, NV area at 107.7 FM.
FM RADIO STATION

KSRO-AM 37501
Owner: Sonoma Media Group
Editorial: 1410 Neotomas Ave, Santa Rosa, California 95405-7533 **Tel:** 1 707 543-0100.
Web site: http://www.ksro.com
Profile: KSRO-AM is a commercial station owned Sonoma Media Group. The format of the station is news and talk. KSRO-AM broadcasts to the San Francisco area at 1350 AM.
AM RADIO STATION

KSRQ-FM 39927
Owner: Northland Community & Technical College
Editorial: 1101 Highway 1 E, Thief River Falls, Minnesota 56701-2528 **Tel:** 1 218 683-8588.
Email: ksrq@northlandcollege.edu
Web site: http://www.radionorthland.org
Profile: KSRQ-FM is a non-commercial station owned by Northland Community & Technical College. The format of the station is adult album alternative music. KSRQ-FM broadcasts to the Thief River Falls, MN area at 90.1 FM.
FM RADIO STATION

KSRR-AM 35082
Owner: Morey Family (Robert)
Editorial: 1454 W Business Park Dr, Orem, Utah 84058-2223 **Tel:** 1 801 224-1400.
Email: richutahradio@gmail.com
Web site: http://kstarradio.wordpress.com
Profile: KSRR-AM is a commercial station owned by Robert Morey Family. The format of the station is variety. KSRR-AM broadcasts to the Orem, UT area at 1400 AM.
AM RADIO STATION

KSRS-FM 41979
Owner: State of Oregon
Editorial: 1250 Siskiyou Blvd, Ashland, Oregon 97520-5001 **Tel:** 1 541 552-6301.
Email: jprinfo@sou.edu
Web site: http://www.ijpr.org
Profile: KSRS-FM is a non-commercial station owned by State of Oregon. The format of the station is news programming and classical music. KSRS-FM broadcasts to the Roseburg, OR area at 91.5 FM.
FM RADIO STATION

KSRT-FM 87185
Owner: Lazer Broadcasting Corp.
Editorial: 5510 Skylane Blvd, Ste 102, Santa Rosa, California 95403 **Tel:** 1 707 284-3069.
Profile: KSRT-FM is a commercial station owned by Lazer Broadcasting Corp. The format of the station is regional Mexican. KSRT-FM broadcasts to the Rohnert Park, CA, area at 107.1 FM.
FM RADIO STATION

KSRV-FM 46330
Owner: Impact Radio
Editorial: 5660 E Franklin Rd, Ste 200, Nampa, Idaho 83687 **Tel:** 1 208 465-9966.
Email: bob@impactradiogroup.com
Web site: http://www.961bobfm.com
Profile: KSRV-FM is a commercial station owned by Impact Radio. The format of the station is adult hits. KSRV-FM broadcasts to the Boise, ID area at 96.1 FM.
FM RADIO STATION

KSRW-FM 43852
Owner: Kessler(Benett)
Editorial: 1280 N Main St Ste J, Bishop, California 93514-2473 **Tel:** 1 760 873-5329.
Web site: http://www.sierrawave.net/ksrw-925-radio-program-guide/
Profile: KSRW-FM is a commercial station owned by Benett Kessler. The format of the station is adult contemporary. KSRW-FM broadcasts to the Bishop, CA area at 92.5 FM.
FM RADIO STATION

KSRX-FM 44334
Owner: Media Logic LLC
Editorial: 803 W Main St, Sterling, Colorado 80751-2813 **Tel:** 1 970 521-2732.
Email: bobfm@medialogicradio.com
Web site: http://www.bobplaysanything.com
Profile: KSRX-FM is a commercial station owned by Media Logic LLC. The format of the station is adult hits. The station broadcasts to the Sterling, CO area at a frequency of 97.5 FM.
FM RADIO STATION

KSRZ-FM 44641
Owner: E.W. Scripps Co.
Editorial: 10714 Mockingbird Dr, Omaha, Nebraska 68127-1942 **Tel:** 1 402 592-5300.
Email: star@104star.com
Web site: http://www.104star.com
Profile: KSRZ-FM is a commercial station owned by E.W. Scripps Co. The format of the station is hot adult contemporary. KSRZ-FM broadcasts to the Omaha, NE area at 104.5 FM.
FM RADIO STATION

KSSA-FM 44412
Owner: KBUF Partnership
Editorial: 1402 E Kansas Ave, Garden City, Kansas 67846-5806 **Tel:** 1 620 276-2366.
Email: lakebuenaks@gmail.com
Profile: KSSA-FM is a commercial station owned by KBUF Partnership. The format of the station is regional Mexican. KSSA-FM broadcasts to the Garden City, KS area at 105.9 FM.
FM RADIO STATION

KSSB-FM 43190
Owner: Lazer Broadcasting Corp.
Editorial: 251 W Main St, Brawley, California 92227-2201 **Tel:** 1 760 344-5858.
Profile: KSSB-FM is a commercial station owned by Lazer Broadcasting Corp. The format of the station is Spanish Classic Hits. KSSB-FM broadcasts to the Calipatria, CA area at a frequency of 100.9 FM.
FM RADIO STATION

KSSE-FM 42682
Owner: Entravision Communications Corp.
Editorial: 5700 Wilshire Blvd Ste 250, Los Angeles, California 90036-3647 **Tel:** 1 323 900-6100.
Web site: http://lasuavecita.entravision.com
Profile: KSSE-FM is a commercial station owned by Entravision Communications Corp. The format of the station is Spanish oldies. KSSE-FM broadcasts to the Los Angeles area at 107.1 FM.
FM RADIO STATION

KSSI-FM 42993
Owner: Sound Enterprises
Editorial: 1621 N Downs St, Ridgecrest, California 93555-2429 **Tel:** 1 760 446-5774.
Email: kssirock@iwvisp.com
Web site: http://www.kssifm.com
Profile: KSSI-FM is a commercial station owned by Sound Enterprises. The format of the station is rock. KSSI-FM broadcasts to the Ridgecrest, CA area at 102.1 FM.
FM RADIO STATION

KSSK-AM 38407
Owner: iHeartMedia Inc.
Editorial: 650 Iwilei Rd Ste 400, Honolulu, Hawaii 96817-5319 **Tel:** 1 808 550-9200.
Web site: http://www.ksskradio.com
Profile: KSSK-AM is a commercial station owned by iHeartMedia Inc. The format of the station is adult contemporary music and news. KSSK-AM broadcasts to the Honolulu area at 590 AM.
AM RADIO STATION

KSSK-FM 45773
Owner: iHeartMedia Inc.
Editorial: 650 Iwilei Rd Ste 400, Honolulu, Hawaii 96817-5319 **Tel:** 1 808 550-9200.
Web site: http://www.ksskradio.com
Profile: KSSK-FM is a commercial station owned by iHeartMedia Inc. The format of the station is adult contemporary music and news. KSSK-FM broadcasts to the Honolulu area at 92.3 FM.
FM RADIO STATION

KSSL-FM 46060
Owner: BWB
Editorial: 735 West Panhandle Avenue, Slaton, Texas 79364 **Tel:** 1 806 828-5775.
Email: ksslradio@gmail.com
Web site: http://www.ksslfm.com
Profile: KSSL-FM is a non-commercial station owned by BWB. The format of the station is classic country. KSSL-FM broadcasts to the Post, TX area at 107.3 FM.
FM RADIO STATION

KSSM-FM 39825
Owner: Townsquare Media, Inc.
Editorial: 608 Moody Ln, Temple, Texas 76504-2952 **Tel:** 1 254 773-5252.
Web site: http://www.mykiss1031.com
Profile: KSSM-FM is a commercial station owned by Townsquare Media, Inc. The format of the station is urban contemporary. KSSN-FM broadcasts to the Temple, TX area at 103.1 FM.
FM RADIO STATION

KSSN-FM 39929
Owner: iHeartMedia Inc.
Editorial: 10800 Colonel Glenn Rd, Little Rock, Arkansas 72204-8017 **Tel:** 1 501 217-5000.
Web site: http://kssn.iheart.com
Profile: KSSN-FM is a commercial station owned by iHeartMedia Inc. The format of the station is country music. KSSN-FM broadcasts to the Little Rock, AR area at 95.7 FM.
FM RADIO STATION

KSSR-AM 36102
Owner: Esquibel LLC
Editorial: 2818 Historic Route 66, Santa Rosa, New Mexico 88435-2751 **Tel:** 1 575 472-5777.
Web site: http://www.kssrradio.com
Profile: KSSR-AM is a commercial station owned by Esquibel LLC. The station's format is variety. KSSR-AM simulcasts the programming of KKJY-FM to the Albuquerque, NM area at 1340.
AM RADIO STATION

KSSR-FM 519211
Owner: Esquibel LLC
Editorial: 2818 Historic Route 66, Santa Rosa, New Mexico 88435-2751 **Tel:** 1 575 472-8000.
Email: kssrradio@yahoo.com
Web site: http://www.kssrradio.com
Profile: KSSR-FM is a commercial station owned by Esquibel LLC. The format is adult hits. KSSR-FM airs to the Santa Rosa, NM area at 95.9 FM.
FM RADIO STATION

KSSS-FM 43788
Owner: iHeartMedia Inc.
Editorial: 3500 E Rosser Ave, Bismarck, North Dakota 58501-3376 **Tel:** 1 701 255-1234.
Web site: http://1015.iheart.com
Profile: KSSS-FM is a commercial station owned by iHeartMedia Inc. The format of the station is rock music. KSSS-FM broadcasts to the Bismarck, ND area at 101.5 FM.
FM RADIO STATION

KSST-AM 35083
Owner: Racy Properties
Editorial: 717 E Shannon Rd, Sulphur Springs, Texas 75482 **Tel:** 1 903 885-3111.
Email: ksst1230@gmail.com
Web site: http://www.ksstradio.com
Profile: KSST-AM is a commercial station owned by Racy Properties. The format of the station is oldies music. KSST-AM broadcasts in the Sulphur Springs, TX area at 1230 AM.
AM RADIO STATION

KSSW-FM 137410
Owner: Jimmy Swaggert Ministries
Editorial: 8919 World Ministries Ave, Baton Rouge, Louisiana **Tel:** 1 225 768-3688.
Email: info@jsm.org
Web site: http://www.jsm.org
Profile: KSSW-FM is a commercial station owned by Jimmy Swaggrt Ministries. The format of the station is Christian programming. KSSW-FM broadcasts to the Nashville, AR area at 96.9 FM.
FM RADIO STATION

KSSX-FM 41647
Owner: iheartMedia Inc.
Editorial: 9660 Granite Ridge Dr Ste 100, San Diego, California 92123-2689 **Tel:** 1 858 292-2000.
Web site: http://www.957kissfm.com
Profile: KSSX-FM is a commercial station owned by iheartMedia Inc. The station's format is rhythmic oldies. KSSX-FM broadcasts to the San Diego area at 95.7 FM.
FM RADIO STATION

KSSZ-FM 43189
Owner: Zimmer Radio Group
Editorial: 3215 Lemone Industrial Blvd Ste 200, Columbia, Missouri 65201-8248 **Tel:** 1 573 875-1099.
Web site: http://www.theeagle939.com
Profile: KSSZ-FM is a commercial station owned by the Zimmer Radio Group. The format of the station is talk. KSSZ-FM broadcasts in the Columbia, MO area at 93.9 FM.
FM RADIO STATION

KSTA-AM 38499
Owner: Wendlee Broadcasting
Editorial: 600 Fisk Ave, Brownwood, Texas 76801 **Tel:** 1 325 625-4188.
Email: ksta1000@gmail.com
Web site: http://www.colemanradio.com
Profile: KSTA-AM is a commercial station owned by Wendlee Broadcasting. The format of the station is classic country. KSTA-AM broadcasts in the Coleman, TX area area at 1000 AM.
AM RADIO STATION

KSTC-AM 38584
Owner: Media Logic LLC
Editorial: 16041 US Highway 34, Fort Morgan, Colorado 80701-4105 **Tel:** 1 970 867-5674.
Web site: http://www.1230kstc.com/index.html
Profile: KSTC-AM is a commercial station owned by Media Logic LLC. The format of the station is classic hits. KSTC-AM broadcasts to the Sterling, CO area at 1230 AM.
AM RADIO STATION

KSTE-AM 36130
Owner: iHeartMedia Inc.
Editorial: 1545 River Park Dr Ste 500, Sacramento, California 95815-4693 **Tel:** 1 916 929-5325.
Web site: http://kste.iheart.com
Profile: KSTE-AM is a commercial station owned by iHeartMedia Inc. The format of the station is talk. KSTE-AM broadcasts to the Sacramento, CA area at 650 AM.
AM RADIO STATION

KSTK-FM 41600
Owner: Wrangell Radio Group Inc.
Editorial: 202 St Michaels Street, Wrangell, Alaska 99929-9999 **Tel:** 1 907 874-2345.
Email: info@kstk.org
Web site: https://www.kstk.org
Profile: KSTK-FM is a non-commercial station owned by the Wrangell Radio Group Inc. The format of the station is public radio programming. KSTK-FM broadcasts in the Wrangell, AK area at 101.7 FM.
FM RADIO STATION

KSTL-AM 36444
Owner: Crawford Broadcasting Co.
Editorial: 10845 Olive Blvd Ste 160, Saint Louis, Missouri 63141-7792 **Tel:** 1 314 878-3600 121.
Email: jubilee690@gmail.com
Web site: http://www.ijubileeradio.com
Profile: KSTL-AM is a commercial station owned by Crawford Broadcasting Co. The format of the station is gospel. KSTL-AM broadcasts to the St. Louis area at 690 AM.
AM RADIO STATION

KSTM-FM 44305
Owner: Simpson College
Editorial: 701 N C St, Indianola, Iowa 50125-1201 **Tel:** 1 515 961-1220.
Email: kstm@simpson.edu
Web site: http://kstmfm.wordpress.com
Profile: KSTM-FM is a non-commercial college station owned by Simpson College. The format of the station is college radio variety. KSTM-FM broadcasts to the Indianola, IA area at a frequency of 88.9 FM.
FM RADIO STATION

KSTN-AM 37502
Owner: Knox, Inc.
Editorial: 2171 Ralph Ave, Stockton, California 95206-3625 **Tel:** 1 209 948-5786.
Profile: KSTN-AM is a commercial station owned by Knox, Inc. The format of the station is contemporary country. KSTN-AM broadcasts to the Stockton, CA area at 1420 AM.
AM RADIO STATION

KSTP-AM 35959
Owner: Hubbard Broadcasting Inc.
Editorial: 3415 University Ave SE, Minneapolis, Minnesota 55414-3327 **Tel:** 1 651 647-1500.
Web site: http://1500espn.com
Profile: KSTP-AM is a commercial station owned by Hubbard Broadcasting Inc. The format of the station is sports talk. KSTP-AM broadcasts to the Minneapolis area at 1500 AM.
AM RADIO STATION

KSTP-FM 41266
Owner: Hubbard Broadcasting Inc.
Editorial: 3415 University Ave SE, Minneapolis, Minnesota 55414-3327 **Tel:** 1 651 642-4141.
Web site: http://www.ks95.com
Profile: KSTP-FM is a commercial station owned by Hubbard Broadcasting Inc. The format of the station is hot adult contemporary music. KSTP-FM broadcasts in the Minneapolis area at 94.5 FM.
FM RADIO STATION

KSTR-FM 45789
Owner: MBC Grand Broadcasting Inc.
Editorial: 1360 E Sherwood Dr, Grand Junction, Colorado 81501-7546 **Tel:** 1 970 254-2100.
Web site: http://961kstr.com
Profile: KSTR-FM is a commercial station owned by MBC Grand Broadcasting Inc. The format of the station is classic rock. KSTR-FM broadcasts to the Grand Junction, CO area at 96.1 FM.
FM RADIO STATION

KSTT-FM 41154
Owner: El Dorado Broadcasting
Editorial: 51 Zaca Ln, Ste 100, San Luis Obispo, California 93401 **Tel:** 1 805 545-0101.
Web site: http://www.kstt.com
Profile: KSTT-FM is a commercial station owned by El Dorado Broadcasting. The format of the station is adult contemporary. KSTT-FM broadcasts to the San Luis Obispo, CA area at 101.3 FM.
FM RADIO STATION

KSTV-AM 37503
Owner: Cherry Creek Radio
Editorial: 3209 W Washington, Stephenville, Texas 76401 **Tel:** 1 254 968-2141.
Email: kstvnews@gmail.com
Web site: http://www.kstvfm.com
Profile: KSTV-AM is a commercial station owned by Cherry Creek Radio, LLC. The format for the station is

regional Mexican music. KSTV-AM broadcasts to the Dallas-Fort Worth, TX, area at 1510 AM.
AM RADIO STATION

KSTV-FM 44901
Owner: Cherry Creek Radio
Editorial: 3209 W Washington, Stephenville, Texas 76401 **Tel:** 1 254 968-2141.
Email: themighty93@gmail.com
Web site: http://www.kstvfm.com
Profile: KSTV-FM is a commercial station owned by Cherry Creek Radio. The format of the station is classic country music. KSTV-FM broadcasts to Stephenville, TX at 93.1 FM.
FM RADIO STATION

KSTX-FM 39932
Owner: Texas Public Radio
Editorial: 8401 Datapoint Dr, Ste 800, San Antonio, Texas 78229-5903 **Tel:** 1 210 614-8977.
Email: news@tpr.org
Web site: http://www.tpr.org
Profile: KSTX-FM is a non-commercial station owned by Texas Public Radio. The format of the station is news and talk. KSTX-FM broadcasts to the San Antonio area at 89.1 FM.
FM RADIO STATION

KSTY-FM 44719
Owner: Royal Gorge Broadcasting LLC
Editorial: 1615 Central Ave, Canon City, Colorado 81212-8578 **Tel:** 1 719 275-7488.
Email: krlnnews@gmail.com
Profile: KSTY-FM is a commercial station owned by Royal Gorge Broadcasting LLC. The format of the station is contemporary country. KSTY-FM broadcasts to the Canon City, CO area at 104.5 FM.
FM RADIO STATION

KSTZ-FM 44871
Owner: Saga Communications
Editorial: 1416 Locust St, Des Moines, Iowa 50309-3014 **Tel:** 1 515 280-1350.
Web site: http://www.star1025.com
Profile: KSTZ-FM is a commercial station owned by Saga Communications. The format of the station is hot adult contemporary music. KSTZ-FM broadcasts to the Des Moines, IA area at 102.5 FM.
FM RADIO STATION

KSUB-AM 37504
Owner: Cherry Creek Radio
Editorial: 5 N Main St, Cedar City, Utah 84720
Tel: 1 435 867-8156.
Web site: http://www.ksub590.com
Profile: KSUB-AM is a commercial station owned by Cherry Creek Radio. The format of the station is talk. KSUB-AM broadcasts in the Cedar City, UT area at 590 AM.
AM RADIO STATION

KSUE-AM 37505
Owner: Sierra Broadcasting Corp.
Editorial: 3015 Johnstonville Rd, Susanville, California 96130-8739 **Tel:** 1 530 257-2121.
Web site: http://www.sierradailynews.com/ksue.html
Profile: KSUE-AM is a commercial station owned by Sierra Broadcasting Corp. The format of the station is news, talk and sports. KSUE-AM broadcasts to the Susanville, CA area at 1240 AM.
AM RADIO STATION

KSUM-AM 37506
Owner: Woodward Broadcasting, Inc.
Editorial: 1371 W Lair Rd, Fairmont, Minnesota 56031-2320 **Tel:** 1 507 235-5595.
Email: info@ksum.com
Web site: http://www.ksum.com
Profile: KSUM-AM is a commercial station owned by Woodward Broadcasting, Inc. The format for the station is country music. KSUM-AM broadcasts to the Fairmont, MN area at 1370 AM.
AM RADIO STATION

KSUN-AM 35868
Owner: Marques(Pedro)
Editorial: 714 N 3rd St, Phoenix, Arizona 85004
Tel: 1 602 252-0030.
Email: ksun@radiofiesta.net
Web site: http://www.radiofiesta.net
Profile: KSUN-AM is a commercial station owned by Pedro Marques. The format of the station is Regional Mexican. KSUN-AM broadcasts to the greater Phoenix, AZ area on 1400 AM.
AM RADIO STATION

KSUP-FM 44904
Owner: Juneau Alaska Communications, LLC
Editorial: 3161 Channel Dr Ste 2, Juneau, Alaska 99801-7866 **Tel:** 1 907 506-3630.
Email: news@abcstations.com
Web site: http://www.mixfmalaska.com
Profile: KSUP-FM is a commercial station owned by Juneau Alaska Communications, LLC. The format of the station is today's top hits. KSUP-FM broadcasts to the Juneau, AK area at 106.3 FM.
FM RADIO STATION

KSUR-AM 42758
Owner: Mount Wilson FM Broadcasters
Tel: 1 310 478-5540.
Email: reception@mountwilsoninc.com
Web site: http://laoldies.com
Profile: KSUR-AM is a commercial station owned by Mount Wilson Broadcasting. The format of the station is Oldies. KSUR-AM broadcasts to the Beverly Hills, CA area at 1260.
AM RADIO STATION

KSUT-FM 42689
Owner: KUTE Inc.
Editorial: 123 Capote Dr, Ignacio, Colorado 81137
Tel: 1 970 563-0255.
Web site: http://www.ksut.org
Profile: KSUT-FM is a commercial station owned by KUTE Inc. The format of the station is a mixed variety of music, news, and talk. KSUT-FM broadcasts to the Ignacio, CO area at 91.3 FM. The station only accepts PSAs through its Web site.
FM RADIO STATION

KSUX-FM 46534
Owner: Powell Broadcasting Co.
Editorial: 2000 Indian Hills Dr, Sioux City, Iowa 51104
Tel: 1 712 239-2100.
Web site: http://www.ksux.com
Profile: KSUX-FM is a commercial station owned by Powell Broadcasting Co. The format of the station is contemporary country music. KSUX-FM broadcasts in the Sioux City, IA area at 101.7 FM.
FM RADIO STATION

KSVA-AM 36951
Owner: Lifetalk Radio Inc.
Editorial: 67 Sandia View Lane, Corrales, New Mexico 87048-8731 **Tel:** 1 505 890-0800.
Email: office@lifetalk.net
Web site: http://www.lifetalk.net
Profile: KSVA-FM is a commercial station owned by Lifetalk Radio Inc. The format of the station is Christian talk and music. KSVA-FM broadcasts to the Albuquerque, NM area at 920 AM.
AM RADIO STATION

KSVC-AM 37507
Owner: Mid-Utah Radio Inc.
Editorial: 390 E Annabella Rd, Richfield, Utah 84701-7084 **Tel:** 1 435 896-4456.
Email: news@midutahradio.com
Web site: http://midutahradio.com/ksvc
Profile: KSVC-AM is a commercial station owned by Mid-Utah Radio Inc. The format of the station is news, talk and sports. KSVC-AM broadcasts to the Salt Lake City area at 980 AM.
AM RADIO STATION

KSVE-AM 39219
Owner: Entravision Communications Corp.
Editorial: 5426 N Mesa St, El Paso, Texas 79912
Tel: 1 915 581-1126.
Profile: KSVE-AM is a commercial station owned by Entravision Communications Corp. The format of the station is Spanish romantica. KSVE-AM broadcasts to the El Paso, TX area at 1650 AM.
AM RADIO STATION

KSVN-AM 35084
Owner: Azteca Broadcasting Corp.
Editorial: 4215 W 4000 S, West Haven, Utah 84401-9631 **Tel:** 1 801 430-7699.
Web site: http://www.aztecautah.com/radio.php
Profile: KSVN-AM is a commercial station owned by Azteca Broadcasting Corp. The format of the station is regional Mexican. KSVN-AM broadcasts to the Salt Lake City area at 730 AM.
AM RADIO STATION

KSVP-AM 39193
Owner: Pecos Valley Broadcasting Company
Editorial: 317 W Quay Ave, Artesia, New Mexico 88210-2158 **Tel:** 1 575 746-2751.
Web site: http://www.pecosvalleybroadcasting.com
Profile: KSVP-AM is a commercial station owned by Pecos Valley Broadcasting Company. The format of the station is news, sports and talk. KSVP-AM broadcasts to the Artesia, NM area at 990 AM.
AM RADIO STATION

KSVR-FM 39933
Owner: Skagit Valley College
Editorial: 2405 E College Way, Mount Vernon, Washington 98273-5821 **Tel:** 1 360 416-7710.
Email: mail@ksvr.org
Web site: http://www.ksvr.org
Profile: KSVR-FM is a non-commercial station owned by Skagit Valley College. The format of the station is Hispanic variety. KSVR-FM broadcasts to the Mount Vernon, WA area at 91.7 FM.
FM RADIO STATION

KSVY-FM 232309
Owner: CommonBond Foundation
Editorial: 164 W Napa St, Sonoma, California 95476-6625 **Tel:** 1 707 933-0808.
Web site: http://ksvy.org/
Profile: KSVY-FM is a non-commercial station owned by the CommonBond Foundation. The format of the station is variety programming. KSVY-FM broadcasts to Sonoma, CA at 91.3 FM.
FM RADIO STATION

KSWB-AM 36443
Owner: KSWB Licensee LLC
Editorial: 615 Broadway St, Ste 222, Seaside, Oregon 97138-6846 **Tel:** 1 503 738-8668.
Web site: http://www.840gold.com
Profile: KSWB-AM is a commercial station owned by KSWB Licensee LLC. The format of the station is oldies music. KSWB-AM broadcasts to Seaside, OR area at 840 AM.
AM RADIO STATION

KSWC-FM 39934
Owner: Southwestern College (The)
Editorial: 100 College St, Winfield, Kansas 67156-2443 **Tel:** 1 620 221-3300.
Email: jinx.radio@sckans.edu
Web site: http://jinxradio.com
Profile: KSWC-FM is a non-commercial college station owned by Southwestern College (The). The format of the station is CHR. KSWC-FM broadcasts to the Winfield, KS area at a frequency of 100.3 FM.
FM RADIO STATION

KSWD-AM 36980
Owner: Seward Media Partners, LLC
Tel: 1 907 224-5793.
Web site: http://www.sewardradio.com
Profile: KSEW-AM is a commercial station owned by Seward Media Partners, LLC. The format of the station is adult contemporary. KSEW-AM broadcasts locally to the Seward, AK area at a frequency of 950 AM.
AM RADIO STATION

KSWD-FM 40969
Owner: Bonneville International Corp.
Editorial: 5900 Wilshire Blvd, Ste 1900, Los Angeles, California 90036 **Tel:** 1 323 634-1800.
Email: station@thesoundla.com
Web site: http://www.thesoundla.com
Profile: KSWD-FM is a commercial station owned by Bonneville International Corp. The format of the station is adult album alternative. KSWD-FM broadcasts to the Los Angeles area at 100.3 FM.
FM RADIO STATION

KSWF-FM 46743
Owner: iHeartMedia Inc.
Editorial: 1856 S Glenstone Ave, Springfield, Missouri 65804-2303 **Tel:** 1 417 890-5555.
Web site: http://www.1005thewolf.com
Profile: KSWF-FM is a commercial station owned by iHeartMedia Inc. The format of the station is country music. KSWF-FM broadcasts to the Springfield, MO area at 100.5 FM.
FM RADIO STATION

KSWG-FM 83870
Owner: Circle S Broadcasting Co. Inc.
Editorial: 801 W Wickenburg Way, Wickenburg, Arizona 85390 **Tel:** 1 602 254-6644.
Web site: http://www.963realcountry.com
Profile: KSWG-FM is a commercial station owned by Circle S Broadcasting Co. Inc. The format of the station is country. KSWG-FM broadcasts to the Wickenburg, AZ area at 96.3 FM.
FM RADIO STATION

KSWI-FM 134077
Owner: Meredith Communications LLC
Editorial: 413 Chestnut St, Atlantic, Iowa 50022-1247
Tel: 1 712 243-6885.
Email: info@iowasuperstation.com
Web site: http://www.ks957.com
Profile: KSWI-FM is a commercial station owned by Meredith Communications LLC. The format of the station is classic hits. KSWI-FM broadcasts to the Atlantic, IA area at 95.7 FM.
FM RADIO STATION

KSWM-AM 35085
Owner: Falcon Broadcasting Inc.
Editorial: 126 S Jefferson Ave, Aurora, Missouri 65605-1635 **Tel:** 1 417 678-0416.
Email: kswm@radiotalon.com
Web site: http://www.radiotalon.com
Profile: KSWM-AM is a commercial station owned by Falcon Broadcasting Inc. The format of the station is news and talk. KSWM-AM broadcasts to the Aurora, CO area at 940 AM.
AM RADIO STATION

KSWN-FM 44018
Owner: GI Family Radio
Editorial: 106 W 8th St, McCook, Nebraska 69001-3508 **Tel:** 1 308 345-1981.
Email: production@krgi.com
Web site: http://newsacrossnebraska.com/?loc=sw
Profile: KSWN-FM is a commercial station owned by GI Family Radio. The format of the station is Top 40/CHR. KSWN-FM broadcasts to the McCook, NE area at 93.9 FM.
FM RADIO STATION

KSWV-AM 36037
Owner: Voz Broadcasting Co. Inc.(La)
Editorial: 102 Taos St, Santa Fe, New Mexico 87505-3832 **Tel:** 1 505 989-7441.
Profile: KSWV-AM is a commercial station owned by Vox Broadcasting Co. Inc. The format of the station is Hispanic variety and regional Mexican. KSWV-AM broadcasts to the Sante Fe, NM area at 810 AM.
AM RADIO STATION

KSWW-FM 43981
Owner: Jodesha Broadcasting Inc.
Editorial: 1520 Simpson Ave, Aberdeen, Washington 98520-4708 **Tel:** 1 360 533-3000.
Email: production@jodesha.com
Web site: http://www.sunny1021.com
Profile: KSWW-FM is a commercial station owned by Jodesha Broadcasting Inc. The format of the station is adult contemporary. KSWW-FM broadcasts to the Seattle area at 102.1 FM.
FM RADIO STATION

KSXY-FM 42878
Owner: Commonwealth Broadcasting LLC
Editorial: 3565 Standish Ave, Santa Rosa, California 95407 **Tel:** 1 707 588-0707.
Web site: http://www.allthehits.fm
Profile: KSXY-FM is a commercial station owned by Commonwealth Broadcasting LLC. The format of the station is Top 40/CHR. KSXY-FM broadcasts to the Sonoma County, CA area at 100.9 FM.
FM RADIO STATION

KSYB-AM 34949
Owner: Amistad Communications
Editorial: 2807 Hilry Huckaby III Avenue, Shreveport, Louisiana 71107 **Tel:** 1 318 222-2744.
Email: ksyb1300@yahoo.com
Web site: http://www.amistadradiogroup.com
Profile: KSYB-AM is a commercial station owned by Amistad Communications. The format of the station is gospel. KSYB-AM broadcasts to the Shreveport, LA area at 1300 AM.
AM RADIO STATION

KSYC-AM 38791
Owner: State of Oregon
Editorial: 1250 Siskiyou Blvd, Ashland, Oregon 97520-5001 **Tel:** 1 541 552-6301.
Email: jprinfo@sou.edu
Web site: http://ijpr.org/
Profile: KSYC-AM is a non-commercial station owned by State of Oregon. The format of the station is news and talk. KSYC-AM broadcasts to the Yreka, CA area at 1490 AM.
AM RADIO STATION

KSYC-FM 46146
Owner: Buffalo Broadcasting
Editorial: 316 Lawrence Ln, Yreka, California 96097-3210 **Tel:** 1 530 842-4158.
Web site: http://www.ksyc1039.com
Profile: KSYC-FM is a commercial station owned and operated by Buffalo Broadcasting. The format of the station is classic and contemporary country. KSYC-FM broadcasts to the Yreka, CA area at 103.9 FM.
FM RADIO STATION

KSYL-AM 39517
Owner: Cenla Broadcasting Inc.
Editorial: 1115 Texas Ave, Alexandria, Louisiana 71301-4836 **Tel:** 1 318 445-1234.
Web site: http://www.ksyl.com
Profile: KSYL-AM is a commercial station owned by Cenla Broadcasting Inc. The format of the station is news and talk. KSYL-AM broadcasts to the Alexandria, LA area at 970 AM.
AM RADIO STATION

KSYM-FM 39935
Owner: San Antonio College
Editorial: 1300 San Pedro Ave, San Antonio, Texas 78212-4201 **Tel:** 1 210 486-5796.
Email: ksym@alamo.edu
Web site: http://www.alamo.edu/sac/ksym
Profile: KSYM-FM is a non-commercial station owned by San Antonio College. The format of the station is adult album alternative and rock alternative. KSYM-FM broadcasts to the San Antonio area at 90.1 FM. Send PSAs to psaksym@hotmail.com.
FM RADIO STATION

KSYN-FM 42768
Owner: Zimmer Radio, Inc.
Editorial: 2702 E 32nd St, Joplin, Missouri 64804
Tel: 1 417 624-1025.
Web site: http://www.ksyn925.com
Profile: KSYN-FM is a commercial station owned by the Zimmer Radio, Inc. The format of the station is Top 40/CHR music. KSYN-FM broadcasts in the Joplin, MO area at 92.5 FM.
FM RADIO STATION

KSYR-FM 43563
Owner: Access.1 Communications Corp.
Editorial: 208 N Thomas Dr, Shreveport, Louisiana 71107-6520 **Tel:** 1 318 222-3122.
Web site: http://www.ksyr.fm
Profile: KSYR-FM is a commercial station owned by Access.1 Communications Corp. The format of the station is regional Mexican music. KSYR-FM broadcasts to the Shreveport, LA area at 92.1 FM.
FM RADIO STATION

KSYV-FM 39936
Owner: Knight Broadcasting Inc.
Editorial: 1101 S Broadway Ste C, Santa Maria, California 93454-6660 **Tel:** 1 805 688-5798.
Web site: http://www.mix96.com
Profile: KSYV-FM is commercial station owned by Knight Broadcasting Inc. The format of the station is adult contemporary. KSYV-FM broadcasts to the Solvang, CA area at 96.7 FM.
FM RADIO STATION

KSYZ-FM 39937
Owner: NRG Media LLC
Editorial: 3532 W Capital Ave, Grand Island, Nebraska 68803 **Tel:** 1 308 381-1077.
Web site: http://www.1077theisland.com
Profile: KSYZ-FM is a commercial station owned by NRG Media LLC. The format of the station is adult hits. KSYZ-FM broadcasts to the Grand Island, NE area at 107.7 FM.
FM RADIO STATION

KSZL-AM 39137
Owner: Dos Costas Communications Corp.
Editorial: 29000 Radio Rd, Barstow, California 92311-1648 **Tel:** 1 760 256-2121.
Email: doscostas@yahoo.com
Profile: KSZL-AM is a commercial station owned by Dos Costas Communications Corp. The format of the station is news and talk. KSZL-AM broadcasts to the Barstow, CA area at 1230 AM.
AM RADIO STATION

KSZR-FM 46424
Owner: Cumulus Media Inc
Editorial: 575 W Roger Rd, Tucson, Arizona 85705
Tel: 1 520 887-1000.
Web site: http://allthehits975.com
Profile: KSZR-FM is a commercial station owned by Cumulus Media Inc. The format of the station is Top 40/CHR. KSZR-FM broadcasts to the Tucson, AZ area at 97.5 FM.
FM RADIO STATION

KTAA-FM 70118
Owner: Bott Broadcasting Co.
Editorial: 1 Academy Blvd, Big Sandy, Texas 75755-5509 **Tel:** 1 913 642-7770 2701.
Web site: http://www.bottradionetwork.com
Profile: KTAA-FM is a commercial owned by Bott Broadcasting Co. The format of the station is Christian talk. KTAA-FM broadcasts to the Tyler, TX area at 90.7 FM.
FM RADIO STATION

KTAC-FM 44027
Owner: Tacoma Broadcasters Inc.
Editorial: 55 Alder St NW, Ste 3, Ephrata, Washington 98823-1696 **Tel:** 1 509 754-2000.
Email: ktac@ktac.com
Web site: http://www.ktac.com
Profile: KTAC-FM is a commercial station owned by Tacoma Broadcasters Inc. The format of the station is religious. KTAC-FM broadcasts to the Ephrata, WA area at 93.9 FM.
FM RADIO STATION

KTAE-AM 37263
Owner: Genuine Austin Radio
Editorial: 112 Allison Cv, Elgin, Texas 78621-3116
Tel: 1 512 416-1100.
Email: info@kokefm.com
Web site: http://www.ktae.net/contact_us.html
Profile: KTAE-AM is a commercial station owned by Genuine Austin Radio. The format of the station is progressive country. KTAE-AM broadcasts to the Austin, TX area at 1490 AM.
AM RADIO STATION

KTAG-FM 46394
Owner: Legend Communications
Editorial: 1949 Mountain View Dr, Cody, Wyoming 82414 **Tel:** 1 307 578-5000.
Email: news@bhrnwy.com
Web site: http://www.mybighornbasin.com
Profile: KTAG-FM is a commercial station owned by Legend Communications. The format of the station is adult contemporary music. KTAG-FM broadcasts to the Cody, WY area at 97.9 FM.
FM RADIO STATION

KTAK-FM 44905
Owner: Edwards Communications LLC
Editorial: 603 E Pershing Ave, Riverton, Wyoming 82501-3605 **Tel:** 1 307 856-2251.
Web site: http://wrrnetwork.com/ktak
Profile: KTAK-FM is a commercial station owned by Edwards Communications LLC. The format for the station is contemporary country. KTAK-FM broadcasts to the Riverton, WY area at 93.9 FM.
FM RADIO STATION

KTAL-FM 39939
Owner: Access.1 Communications Corp.
Editorial: 208 N Thomas Dr, Shreveport, Louisiana 71107-6520 **Tel:** 1 318 222-3122.
Web site: http://www.98rocks.fm
Profile: KTAL-FM is a commercial station owned by Access.1 Communications Corp. The format of the station is classic rock. KTAL-FM broadcasts to the Shreveport, LA area at 98.1 FM.
FM RADIO STATION

KTAM-AM 37509
Owner: Brazos Valley Communications LLC
Editorial: 1240 E Villa Maria Rd, Bryan, Texas 77802-2519 **Tel:** 1 979 776-1240.
Web site: http://radiolegeria1240.com
Profile: KTAM-AM is a commercial station owned by Brazos Valley Communications LLC. The format of the regional Mexican. KTAM-AM broadcasts to the Bryan, TX area at 1240 AM.
AM RADIO STATION

KTAN-AM 37510
Owner: Cherry Creek Radio
Editorial: 2300 E Busby Dr, Sierra Vista, Arizona 85635-3310 **Tel:** 1 520 458-4313.
Email: ktan@cherrycreekradio.com
Web site: http://cherrycreekradio.com
Profile: KTAN-AM is a commercial station owned by Cherry Creek Radio. The format of the station is news and talk. KTAN-AM broadcasts in the Sierra Vista, NV area at 1420 AM.
AM RADIO STATION

KTAO-FM 41173
Owner: Taos Communications Corp.
Tel: 1 575 758-5826.
Email: ktao@newmex.com
Web site: http://www.ktao.com
Profile: KTAO-FM is a commercial station owned by Taos Communications Corp. The format of the station is album adult alternative music. KTAO-FM broadcasts to the Albuquerque, NM area at 101.9 FM.
FM RADIO STATION

KTAP-AM 39278
Owner: Emerald Wave Media
Editorial: 718 E Chapel St, Santa Maria, California 93454-4524 **Tel:** 1 805 928-4334.
Email: traffic@emeraldwavemedia.com
Profile: KTAP-AM is a commercial station owned by Emerald Wave Media. The format of the station is Hispanic programming and Regional Mexican music. KTAP-AM broadcasts to the Santa Maria, CA area at 1600 AM.
AM RADIO STATION

KTAR-AM 38928
Owner: Bonneville International Corp.
Editorial: 7740 N 16th St Ste 200, Phoenix, Arizona 85020-4482 **Tel:** 1 602 274-6200.
Web site: http://arizonasports.com
Profile: KTAR-AM is a commercial station owned by Bonneville International Corp. The format of the station is sports. KTAR-AM broadcasts in the Phoenix area at 620 AM.
AM RADIO STATION

KTAR-FM 424742
Owner: Bonneville International Corp.
Editorial: 7740 N 16th St Ste 200, Phoenix, Arizona 85020-4482 **Tel:** 1 602 274-6200.
Email: news923@ktar.com
Web site: http://www.ktar.com
Profile: KTAR-FM is a commercial station owned by Bonneville International Corp. The format of the station is news and talk. KTAR-FM broadcasts to the Phoenix area at 92.3 FM.
FM RADIO STATION

KTAT-AM 37511
Owner: Morey Broadcasting LLC
Editorial: 207 W Grand Ave, Frederick, Oklahoma 73542-5229 **Tel:** 1 580 335-5923.
Email: kybe959@pldi.net
AM RADIO STATION

KTBA-AM 35809
Owner: Western Indian Ministries
Editorial: Highway 264, 02C Hilltop Drive, HC33 Box 40, Gallup, New Mexico 87301 **Tel:** 1 505 371-5587.
Email: khac@westernindian.org
Web site: http://www.westernindian.net
Profile: KTBA-AM is a non-commercial station owned by Western Indian Ministries. The format of the station is contemporary Christian. KTBA-AM broadcasts to the Tuba City, AZ area on 104.9 FM.
AM RADIO STATION

KTBB-AM 36338
Owner: Gleiser Communications LLC
Editorial: 1001 E Southeast Loop 323 Ste 455, Tyler, Texas 75701-9600 **Tel:** 1 903 593-2519.
Web site: http://www.ktbb.com
Profile: KTBB-AM is a commercial station owned by Gleiser Communications LLC. The format of the station is news, talk and sports. KTBB-AM broadcasts in the Tyler, TX area at 600 AM.
AM RADIO STATION

KTBB-FM 46421
Owner: Gleiser Communications, LLC
Editorial: 140 N Main St, Rusk, Texas 75785-1326
Tel: 1 903 683-2258.
Email: kwrw@mediactr.com
Profile: KTBB-FM is a commercial station owned by Gleiser Communications, LLC. The format of the station is talk. KTBB-FM broadcasts to the Rusk, TX area at 97.5 FM.
FM RADIO STATION

KTBB-FM 46487
Owner: Gleiser Communications LLC
Editorial: 1001 E Southeast Loop 323, Tyler, Texas 75701-9664 **Tel:** 1 903 593-2519.
Web site: http://www.ktbb.com
Profile: KTBB-FM is a commercial station owned by Gleiser Communications LLC. The format of the station is sports. KTBB-FM broadcasts to the Tyler, TX area at 92.1 FM.
FM RADIO STATION

KTBG-FM 39585
Owner: Kansas City Public Television
Editorial: 125 E 31st St, Kansas City, Missouri 64108-3216 **Tel:** 1 816 756-3580.
Web site: http://www.ktbg.fm
Profile: KTBG-FM is a non-commercial station owned by Kansas City Public Television. The format of the station is adult album alternative. KTBG-FM broadcasts to the Kansas City, MO area at 90.9 FM.
FM RADIO STATION

KTBH-FM 525247
Owner: Resonate Hawaii, LLC
Editorial: 688 Kinoole St Ste 112, Hilo, Hawaii 96720-3868 **Tel:** 1 808 837-4104.
Email: kaoi@kaoi.net
Profile: KTBH-FM is a commercial station owned by Resonate Hawaii, LLC. The format of the station is alternative rock. KTBH-FM broadcasts to the Hilo, HI area at 102.1 FM.
FM RADIO STATION

KTBI-AM 36451
Owner: Tacoma Broadcasters Inc.
Editorial: 55 Alder St NW, Ste 3, Ephrata, Washington 98823-1696 **Tel:** 1 509 754-2000.
Email: ktbi@ktbi.com
Web site: http://www.ktbi.com
Profile: KTBI-AM is a commercial station owned by Tacoma Broadcasters Inc. The format of the station is religious. KTBI-AM broadcasts to the Ephrata, WA area at 810 AM.
AM RADIO STATION

KTBJ-FM 43779
Owner: Calvary Chapel Twin Falls
Tel: 1 208 734-6633.
Web site: http://www.csnradio.com
Profile: KTBJ-FM is a non-commercial station owned by Calvary Chapel Twin Falls. The format of the station is Christian and religious programming. KTBJ-FM broadcasts to the Festus, MO area at 89.3 FM.
FM RADIO STATION

KTBL-AM 38911
Owner: Cumulus Media Inc
Editorial: 500 4th St NW, 5th Fl, Albuquerque, New Mexico 87102-5324 **Tel:** 1 505 767-6700.
Web site: http://www.1050talk.com
Profile: KTBL-AM is a commercial station owned by Cumulus Media Inc. The format of the station is news and talk. KTBL-AM broadcasts to the Albuquerque, NM area at 1050 AM.
AM RADIO STATION

KTBQ-FM 44907
Owner: Townsquare Media, LLC
Editorial: 1216 S 1st St, Lufkin, Texas 75901-4716
Tel: 1 936 639-4455.
Web site: http://www.q1077.com
Profile: KTBQ-FM is a commercial station owned by Townsquare Media, LLC. The format of the station is classic rock. KTBQ-FM broadcasts to the Lufkin, TX area at 107.7 FM.
FM RADIO STATION

KTBR-AM 35889
Owner: State of Oregon
Editorial: 1250 Siskiyou Blvd, Ashland, Oregon 97520-5001 **Tel:** 1 541 552-6301.
Email: jprinfo@sou.edu
Web site: http://www.ijpr.org
Profile: KTBR-AM is a non-commercial station owned by State of Oregon. The format of the station is news and talk programming. KTBR-AM broadcasts to the Roseburg, OR area at 950 AM.
AM RADIO STATION

KTBT-FM 39583
Owner: iHeartMedia Inc.
Editorial: 2625 S Memorial Dr, Tulsa, Oklahoma 74129-2601 **Tel:** 1 918 388-5136.
Web site: http://www.921thebeat.com
Profile: KTBT-FM is a commercial station owned by iHeartMedia Inc. The format of the station is Top 40/CHR. KTBT-FM broadcasts to the Tulsa, OK area at 92.1 FM.
FM RADIO STATION

KTBZ-AM 38621
Owner: iHeartMedia Inc.
Editorial: 2625 S Memorial Dr, Tulsa, Oklahoma 74129-2601 **Tel:** 1 918 388-5100.
Web site: http://www.1430thebuzz.com
Profile: KTBZ-AM is a commercial station owned by iHeartMedia Inc. The format of the station is sports. KTBZ-AM broadcasts to the Tulsa, OK area at 1430 AM.
AM RADIO STATION

KTBZ-FM 40067
Owner: iHeartMedia Inc.
Editorial: 2000 West Loop S Ste 300, Houston, Texas 77027-3510 **Tel:** 1 713 212-8000.
Web site: http://www.thebuzz.com
Profile: KTBZ-FM is a commercial station owned by iHeartMedia Inc. The format of the station is rock alternative music. KTBZ-FM broadcasts to the Houston area at 94.5 FM.
FM RADIO STATION

KTCC-FM 39940
Owner: Colby Community College
Editorial: 1255 S Range Ave, Colby, Kansas 67701
Tel: 1 785 462-3984.
FM RADIO STATION

KTCE-FM 238569
Owner: Moenkopi Communications, INC.
Tel: 1 801 370-9999.
Web site: http://www.ktce921.com
Profile: KTCE-FM is a commercial station owned by Moenkopi Communications, INC. The format is hot adult contemporary. The station airs in the Salt Lake City area at 92.1 FM.
FM RADIO STATION

KTCH-FM 44908
Owner: Wayne Radio Works
Editorial: 85592 574th Ave, Wayne, Nebraska 68787-7043 **Tel:** 1 402 375-3700.
Email: ktch@ktch.com
Web site: http://waynedailynews.com
Profile: KTCH-FM is a commercial station owned by Wayne Radio Works. The format of the station is adult hits. KTCH-FM broadcasts to the Wayne, NE area at 104.9 FM.
FM RADIO STATION

KTCK-AM 36322
Owner: Cumulus Media Inc.
Editorial: 3090 Olive St Ste 400, Dallas, Texas 75219-7640 **Tel:** 1 214 526-2400.
Web site: http://www.theticket.com
Profile: KTCK-AM is a commercial station owned by Cumulus Media Inc. The format of the station is sports. KTCK-AM broadcasts to the Dallas area at 1310 AM.
AM RADIO STATION

KTCL-FM 43648
Owner: iHeartMedia Inc.
Editorial: 4695 S Monaco St, Denver, Colorado 80237-3525 **Tel:** 1 303 713-8000.
Web site: http://www.area93.com
Profile: KTCL-FM is a commercial station owned by iHeartMedia Inc. The format of the station is rock alternative music. KTCL-FM broadcasts to the Denver area at 93.3.
FM RADIO STATION

KTCO-FM 46346
Owner: Midwest Communications Inc.
Editorial: 11 E Superior St Ste 380, Duluth, Minnesota 55802-3016 **Tel:** 1 218 722-4321.
Email: kdalnews@mwcradio.com
Web site: http://katcountry989.com/
Profile: KTCO-FM is a commercial station owned by Midwest Communications Inc. The format of the station is country music. KTCO-FM broadcasts in the Duluth, MN area at 98.9 FM.
FM RADIO STATION

KTCR-AM 38812
Owner: Ingstad (James D.)
Editorial: 830 N Columbia Center Blvd, Ste B2, Kennewick, Washington 99336 **Tel:** 1 509 783-0783.
Profile: KTCR-AM is a commercial station owned by Ingstad (James D.). The format of the station is classic country. KTCR-AM broadcasts to the Kennewick, WA area at 1390 AM.
AM RADIO STATION

KTCS-AM 37513
Owner: Big Chief Broadcasting
Editorial: 5304 Highway 45 East, Fort Smith, Arkansas 72916 **Tel:** 1 479 646-6151.
Profile: KTCS-AM is a commercial station owned by Big Chief Broadcasting. The format of the station is southern gospel music. KTCS-AM broadcasts to the Fort Smith, AR area at 1410 AM.
AM RADIO STATION

KTCS-FM 44909
Owner: Big Chief Broadcasting
Editorial: 5304 Highway 45 East, Fort Smith, Arkansas 72916 **Tel:** 1 479 646-6151.
Web site: http://www.ktcs.com
Profile: KTCS-FM is a commercial station owned by Big Chief Broadcasting. The format of the station is classic country. KTCS-FM broadcasts to the Fort Smith, AR area at 99.9 FM.
FM RADIO STATION

KTCT-AM 36013
Owner: Cumulus Media Inc.
Editorial: 750 Battery St Fl 3, San Francisco, California 94111-1523 **Tel:** 1 415 995-6800.
Email: sports@knbr.com
Web site: http://www.knbr.com
Profile: KTCT-AM is a commercial station owned by Cumulus Media Inc. The format of the station is sports. KTCT-AM broadcasts to the San Francisco area at 1050 AM.
AM RADIO STATION

KTCX-FM 43653
Owner: Cumulus Media Inc.
Editorial: 755 S 11th St Ste 102, Beaumont, Texas 77701-3723 **Tel:** 1 409 833-9421.
Web site: http://www.ktcx.com
Profile: KTCX-FM is a commercial station owned by Cumulus Media Inc. The format of the station is urban contemporary music. KTCX-FM broadcasts to the Beaumont, TX area at 102.5 FM.
FM RADIO STATION

KTCZ-FM 44409
Owner: iHeartMedia Inc.
Editorial: 1600 Utica Ave S Ste 400, Minneapolis, Minnesota 55416-1480 **Tel:** 1 952 417-3000.
Web site: http://www.cities97.com
Profile: KTCZ-FM is a commercial station owned by iHeartMedia Inc. The format of the station is adult album alternative music. KTCZ-FM broadcasts in the Minneapolis area at 97.1 FM.
FM RADIO STATION

KTDD-AM 317538
Owner: iHeartMedia Inc.
Editorial: 2030 Iowa Ave, Riverside, California 92507-7415 **Tel:** 1 951 684-1991.
Web site: http://www.foxsportsradio1350.com
Profile: KTDD-AM is a commercial station owned by iHeartMedia Inc. The format of the station is sports. KTDD-AM broadcasts to the Riverside, CA area at 1350 AM.
AM RADIO STATION

KTDE-FM 42101
Owner: Four Rivers Broadcasting Inc.
Editorial: 38958 Cypress Way, Gualala, California 95445-8309 **Tel:** 1 707 884-1000.
Email: thetide@ktde.com
Web site: http://www.ktde.com
Profile: KTDE-FM is a commercial station owned by Four Rivers Broadcasting Inc. The format of the station is classic rock music. KTDE-FM broadcasts to the Gualala, CA area at 100.5 FM.
FM RADIO STATION

KTDH-FM 839709
Owner: Kanza Society Inc.
Editorial: 104 Sw 6Th Ave Suite B-4, Amarillo, Texas 79101-2324 **Tel:** 1 806 367-9088.
Web site: http://www.hppr.org
Profile: KTDH-FM is a non-commercial station owned by Kanza Society Inc. The format of the station is news and classical. The station airs locally at 89.3 FM in the Dalhart, TX area.
FM RADIO STATION

KTDR-FM 43251
Owner: R Communications
Editorial: 307 E 8th St, Del Rio, Texas 78840-3823
Tel: 1 830 775-6291.
Email: info@rcommunications.com
Web site: http://www.rcommunications.com
Profile: KTDR-FM is a commercial station owned by R Communications. The format of the station is adult contemporary. KTDR-FM broadcasts to the Del Rio, TX and surrounding communities at 96.3 FM.
FM RADIO STATION

KTDY-FM 41892
Owner: Townsquare Media, LLC
Editorial: 1749 Bertrand Dr, Lafayette, Louisiana 70506-2054 **Tel:** 1 337 233-6000.
Web site: http://www.999ktdy.com
Profile: KTDY-FM is a commercial station owned by Townsquare Media, LLC. The format of the station is adult contemporary music. KTDY-FM broadcasts to the Lafayette, LA area at 99.9 FM.
FM RADIO STATION

KTDZ-FM 43569
Owner: Last Frontier Mediactive, LLC
Editorial: 819 1st Ave, Fairbanks, Alaska 99701-4449
Tel: 1 907 451-5910.
Web site: http://www.mytedfm.com
Profile: KTDZ-FM is a commercial station owned by Last Frontier Mediactive, LLC. The format of the station is adult hits music. KTDZ-FM broadcasts locally to the Fairbanks, AK area at 98.1 FM.
FM RADIO STATION

KTEA-FM 838717
Owner: Adelman Broadcasting, Inc.
Editorial: 42010 50th St W, Quartz, California 93536
Tel: 1 805 924-0103.
Web site: http://1035ktea.com/
Profile: KTEA-FM is a commercial station owned by Adelman Broadcasting, Inc. The format of the station is classic jazz. KTEA-FM broadcasts to the San Luis Obispo, CA area at a frequency of 103.5 FM.
FM RADIO STATION

KTEC-FM 39943
Owner: Oregon Institute of Technology
Editorial: 3201 Campus Dr, Klamath Falls, Oregon 97601-8801 **Tel:** 1 541 885-1840.
Email: ktec895@gmail.com
Web site: http://www.oit.edu/ktec
Profile: KTEC-FM is a non-commercial college station owned by the Oregon Institute of Technology. The station features a free-form format with a variety of programming. KTEC-FM broadcasts to the Klamath Falls, OR area at a frequency of 89.5 FM.
FM RADIO STATION

KTEE-FM 45940
Owner: Bicoastal Media LLC
Editorial: 320 Central Ave, Ste 519, Coos Bay, Oregon 97420 **Tel:** 1 541 267-2121.
Email: southcoastpsa@bicoastalmedia.com
Web site: http://www.ktee.com
Profile: KTEE-FM is a commercial station owned by Bicoastal Media LLC. The format of the station is adult contemporary music. KTEE-FM broadcasts to the Coos Bay, OR area at 94.9 FM.
FM RADIO STATION

KTEG-FM 46711
Owner: iHeartMedia Inc.
Editorial: 5411 Jefferson St NE Ste 100, Albuquerque, New Mexico 87109-3485 **Tel:** 1 505 830-6400.
Web site: http://www.1041theedge.com
Profile: KTEG-FM is a commercial station owned by iHeartMedia Inc. The format of the station is rock alternative music. KTEG-FM broadcasts to the Albuquerque, NM area at 104.1 FM.
FM RADIO STATION

KTEK-AM 35088
Owner: BUSINESSRADIO HOUSTON LICENSEE LLC
Editorial: 6161 Savoy Dr, Houston, Texas 77036-3308
Tel: 1 713 260-6101.
Email: comments@business1110ktek.com
Web site: http://www.business1110ktek.com
Profile: KTEK-AM is a commercial station owned by BUSINESSRADIO HOUSTON LICENSEE LLC. The format of the station is business talk. KTEK-AM broadcasts to the Houston area at 1110 AM.
AM RADIO STATION

KTEL-AM 36419
Owner: Capps Broadcast Group
Editorial: 13 1/2 E Main St Ste 202, Walla Walla, Washington 99362-1950 **Tel:** 1 509 522-1383.
Web site: http://www.1490ktel.com
Profile: KTEL-AM is a commercial station owned by Capps Broadcast Group. The format of the station is sports. KTEL-AM broadcasts to the Walla Walla, WA area at 1490 AM.
AM RADIO STATION

KTEM-AM 36352
Owner: Townsquare Media, Inc.
Editorial: 608 Moody Ln, Temple, Texas 76504-2952
Tel: 1 254 773-5252.
Web site: http://www.myktem.com
Profile: KTEM-AM is a commercial station owned by Townsquare Media, Inc. The format of the station is news and talk. KTEM-AM broadcasts to the Temple, TX area at 1400 AM.
AM RADIO STATION

KTEX-FM 43568
Owner: iHeartMedia Inc.
Editorial: 901 E Pike Blvd, Weslaco, Texas 78596-4937 **Tel:** 1 956 973-9202.
Web site: http://www.ktex.net
Profile: KTEX-FM is a commercial station owned by iHeartMedia Inc. The format of the station is country music. KTEX-FM broadcasts to the Weslaco, TX area at 100.3 FM.
FM RADIO STATION

KTEZ-FM 86761
Owner: Baldridge-Dumas Communications Inc.
Editorial: 605 San Antonio Ave, Many, Louisiana 71449 **Tel:** 1 318 256-0555.
Email: bdcproduction@bellsouth.net
Web site: http://www.bdcradio.com
Profile: KTEZ-FM is a commercial station owned by Baldridge-Dumas Communications Inc. The format for the station is adult contemporary. KTEZ-FM broadcasts to the Many, LA area at 99.9 FM.
FM RADIO STATION

KTFC-FM 46535
Owner: Bott Radio Network
Editorial: 1534 Buchanan Ave, Sioux City, Iowa 51106-5495 **Tel:** 1 712 252-4621.
Web site: http://www.bottradionetwork.com
Profile: KTFC-FM is a non-commercial station owned by Bott Radio Network. The format of the station is Christian music and talk. KTFC-FM broadcasts to the Sioux City, IA area at 103.3 FM.
FM RADIO STATION

KTFG-FM 42385
Owner: Bott Radio Network
Editorial: 1534 Buchanan Ave, Sioux City, Iowa 51106-5495 **Tel:** 1 712 252-4621.
Profile: KTFG-FM is a non-commercial station owned by Bott Radio Network. The format of the station is Christian and talk. KTFG-FM broadcasts to the Sioux Rapids, IA area at 102.9 FM.
FM RADIO STATION

KTFI-AM 35090
Owner: Salt & Light Radio, Inc.
Editorial: 5601 W Cassia St, Boise, Idaho 83705-1836
Tel: 1 208 344-4774.
Email: info@saltandlightradio.com
Web site: http://www.saltandlightradio.com
Profile: KTFI-AM is a commercial station owned by Salt & Light Radio, Inc. The format of the station is Catholic teaching. KTFI-AM broadcasts to the Twin Falls, ID area at 1270 AM.
AM RADIO STATION

KTFJ-AM 39186
Owner: Swanson(Donald)
Editorial: 1534 Buchanan Ave, Sioux City, Iowa 51106
Tel: 1 712 252-4621.
Profile: KTFJ-AM is a commercial radio station owned by Donald Swanson. The format of the station is religious. KTFJ-AM broadcasts to the Dakota City, IA area at 1250 AM.
AM RADIO STATION

KTFM-FM 41749
Owner: Alpha Media
Editorial: 4050 Eisenhauer Rd, San Antonio, Texas 78218-3409 **Tel:** 1 210 654-5100.
Web site: http://www.ktfm.com
Profile: KTFM-FM is a commercial station owned by Alpha Media. The format of the station is Top 40/ CHR. KTFM-FM broadcasts to the San Antonio area at 94.1.
FM RADIO STATION

KTFS-AM 34905
Owner: Texarkana Radio Center Licenses, LLC
Editorial: 615 Olive St, Texarkana, Texas 75501-5512
Tel: 1 903 793-4671.
Email: faxes@texarkanaradio.com
Web site: http://www.kcmc740.com
Profile: KTFS-AM is a commercial station owned by Texarkana Radio Center Licenses, LLC. The format of the station is sports. KTFS-AM broadcasts to the Texarkana, TX area at 740 AM.
AM RADIO STATION

KTFS-FM 45858
Owner: Texarkana Radio Center Licenses, LLC
Editorial: 615 Olive St, Texarkana, Texas 75501-5512
Tel: 1 903 793-4671.
Email: info@texarkanaradio.com
Web site: http://www.texarkanaradio.com
Profile: KTFS-FM is a commercial station owned by Texarkana Radio Center Licenses, LLC. The format of the station is Talk. KTFS-FM broadcasts to the Texarkana, TX area at 107.1 FM.
FM RADIO STATION

KTFW-FM 43735
Owner: LKCM Radio Group LP
Editorial: 201 Main St, Fort Worth, Texas 76102-3105
Tel: 1 817 332-0959.
Web site: http://www.921hankfm.com
Profile: KTFW-FM is a commercial station owned by LKCM Radio Group LP. The format of the station is classic and contemporary country music. KTFW-FM broadcasts to the Fort Worth, TX area at 92.1 FM.
FM RADIO STATION

KTFX-FM 42967
Owner: Payne Radio Group
Editorial: 501 N Main St, Muskogee, Oklahoma 74401-6348 **Tel:** 1 918 684-1022.
Email: production@okiecountry1017.com
Web site: http://www.okiecountry1017.com
Profile: KTFX-FM is a commercial station owned by Payne Radio Group. The format of the station is contemporary and classic country. KTFX-FM broadcasts to the Tulsa, OK area at 101.7 FM.
FM RADIO STATION

KTGA-FM 518676
Owner: Toga Radio, LLC
Editorial: 106 N. First Street, Saratoga, Wyoming 82331 **Tel:** 1 307 326-8642.
Email: bigfoot@bigfoot99.com
Web site: http://www.bigfoot99.com
Profile: KTGA-FM is a commercial station owned by Toga Radio, LLC. The format of the station is rock and country music. KTGA broadcasts to the Saratoga, WY area at 99.3 FM.
FM RADIO STATION

KTGE-AM 38820
Owner: Wolfhouse Radio Group Inc.
Editorial: 548 E Alisal St, Salinas, California 93905
Tel: 1 831 757-1910.
Profile: KTGE-AM is a commercial station owned by Wolfhouse Radio Group Inc. The format of the station is Hispanic oldies. KTGE-AM broadcasts in the Salinas, CA area at 1570 AM.
AM RADIO STATION

KTGL-FM 40055
Owner: Alpha Media
Editorial: 3800 Cornhusker Hwy, Lincoln, Nebraska 68504-1533 **Tel:** 1 402 466-1234.
Web site: http://www.ktgl.com
Profile: KTGL-FM is a commercial station owned by Alpha Media. The format of the station is classic rock. KTGL-FM broadcasts to the Lincoln, NE area at 92.9 FM.
FM RADIO STATION

KTGO-AM 35091
Owner: Bakken Beacon Media LLC
Editorial: 301 2nd St SE, Tioga, North Dakota 58852-7302 **Tel:** 1 701 664-3322.
Email: news@bakkenbeacon.com
Web site: http://bakkenbeacon.com
Profile: KTGO-AM is a commercial station owned by Bakken Beacon Media LLC. The format of the station is talk. KTGO-AM broadcasts to the Tioga, ND area at 1090 AM.
AM RADIO STATION

KTGR-AM 39409
Owner: Zimmer Radio Group
Editorial: 3215 Lemone Industrial Blvd, Ste 200, Columbia, Missouri 65201 **Tel:** 1 573 875-1099.
Email: cosmoktgr@yahoo.com
Web site: http://www.ktgr.com
Profile: KTGR-AM is a commercial station owned by Zimmer Radio Group. The format of the station is sports. KTGR-AM broadcasts to the Columbia, MO area at 1580 AM.
AM RADIO STATION

KTGR-FM 46384
Owner: Zimmer Radio Group
Editorial: 1805 Westminster Ave, Fulton, Missouri 65251-1067 **Tel:** 1 573 642-3341.
Email: cosmo@zrgmail.com
Web site: http://www.ktgr.com
Profile: KTGR-FM is a commercial station owned by Zimmer Radio Group. The format of the station is sports. KTGR-FM broadcasts to the Jefferson City, MO area at 100.5 FM.
FM RADIO STATION

KTGS-FM 44274
Owner: South Central Oklahoma Christian Broadcasting Inc.
Editorial: 20750 State Hwy 1W, Ada, Oklahoma 74820-5424 **Tel:** 1 580 332-0902.
Email: email@thegospelstation.com
Web site: http://www.thegospelstation.com
Profile: KTGS-FM is a non-commercial station owned by South Central Oklahoma Christian Broadcasting Inc. The format for the station is gospel. KTGS-FM broadcasts to the Ada, OK area at 88.3 FM.
FM RADIO STATION

KTGV-FM 43663
Owner: E.W. Scripps Co.
Editorial: 7280 E Rosewood St, Tucson, Arizona 85710-1350 **Tel:** 1 520 795-1490.
Web site: http://www.1063thegroove.com
Profile: KTGV-FM is a commercial station owned by E.W. Scripps Co. The format of the station is rhythmic oldies. KTGV-FM broadcasts to the Tucson, AZ area at 106.3 FM.
FM RADIO STATION

KTGX-FM 45979
Owner: iHeartMedia Inc.
Editorial: 2625 S Memorial Dr, Tulsa, Oklahoma 74129-2601 **Tel:** 1 918 388-5100.
Web site: http://www.1061thetwister.com
Profile: KTGX-FM is a commercial station owned by iHeartMedia Inc. The format of the station is contemporary country. KTGX-FM broadcasts to the Tulsa, OK area 106.1 FM.
FM RADIO STATION

KTHC-FM 43105
Owner: Cherry Creek Radio
Editorial: 120 E Main St, Sidney, Montana 59270
Tel: 1 406 433-5090.
Email: power95@midrivers.com
Web site: http://www.kthcradio.com
Profile: KTHC-FM is a commercial station owned by Cherry Creek Radio. The format of the station is hot adult contemporary music. KTHC-FM broadcasts to the Sidney, MT area at 95.1 FM.
FM RADIO STATION

KTHE-AM 35092
Owner: Edwards Communications LLC
Editorial: 420 Arapahoe St, Thermopolis, Wyoming 82443-2708 **Tel:** 1 307 864-2119.
Profile: KTHE-AM is a commercial station owned by Edwards Communications. The format of the station is adult standards. KTHE-AM broadcasts to the Thermopolis, WY area at 1240 AM.
AM RADIO STATION

KTHH-AM 38701
Owner: Bicoastal Media LLC
Editorial: 2840 Marion St SE, Albany, Oregon 97322
Tel: 1 541 926-8628.
Web site: http://www.comedy990.com
Profile: KTHH-FM is a commercial station owned by Bicoastal Media LLC. The format of the station is comedy. KTHH-FM broadcasts to the Albany, OR area at 990 AM.
AM RADIO STATION

KTHI-FM 46859
Owner: E.W. Scripps Co.
Editorial: 5257 W Fairview Ave Ste 260, Boise, Idaho 83706-1766 **Tel:** 1 208 344-3511.
Web site: http://www.khits.fm
Profile: KTHI-FM is a commercial station owned by E.W. Scripps Co. The format of the station is classic hits music. KTHI-FM broadcasts to the Boise, ID area at 107.1 FM.
FM RADIO STATION

KTHK-FM 42437
Owner: Riverbend Communications LLC
Editorial: 400 W Sunnyside Rd, Idaho Falls, Idaho 83402-4613 **Tel:** 1 208 523-3722.
Web site: http://www.1055thehawk.com
Profile: KTHK-FM is a commercial station owned by Riverbend Communications LLC. The format of the station is contemporary country. KTHK-FM broadcasts to the Blackfoot, ID area at 105.5 FM.
FM RADIO STATION

KTHN-FM 46636
Owner: Cherry Creek Radio
Editorial: 116 Dalton Ave, La Junta, Colorado 81050
Tel: 1 719 384-5456.
Email: kblj@secom.net
Profile: KTHN-FM is a commercial station owned by Cherry Creek Radio. The format of the station is country. KTHN-FM broadcasts to the La Junta, CO area at 92.1 FM.
FM RADIO STATION

KTHO-AM 36163
Owner: International Aerospace Solutions, Inc.
Editorial: 1001 Heavenly Village Way, South Lake Tahoe, California 96150-7068 **Tel:** 1 530 543-0590.
Email: ktho590@yahoo.com
Web site: http://www.kthoradio.com
Profile: KTHO-AM is a commercial station owned by International Aerospace Solutions, Inc. The format of the station is classic rock and talk. KTHO-AM broadcasts to the Lake Tahoe, CA area at 590 AM.
AM RADIO STATION

KTHP-FM 86760
Owner: Baldridge-Dumas Communications Inc.
Editorial: 605 San Antonio Ave, Many, Louisiana 71449-3018 **Tel:** 1 409 787-3399.
Email: production@bdcradio.com
Web site: http://www.bdcradio.com
Profile: KTHP-FM is a commercial station owned by Baldridge-Dumas Communications Inc. The format for the station is classic country. KTHP-FM broadcasts to the Many, LA area at 103.9 FM.
FM RADIO STATION

KTHQ-FM 42992
Owner: Country Mountain Airwaves LLC
Editorial: 391 E Deuce Of Clubs Ste C, Show Low, Arizona 85901-4807 **Tel:** 1 928 532-1010.
Email: traffic@majik101.com
Web site: http://www.qcountry92.com
Profile: KTHQ-FM is a commercial station owned by Country Mountain Airwaves LLC. The format of the station is contemporary country. KTHQ-FM broadcasts to the Show Low, AZ area at 92.5 FM.
FM RADIO STATION

KTHR-FM 39728
Owner: iHeartMedia Inc.
Editorial: 9323 E 37th St N, Wichita, Kansas 67226-2000 **Tel:** 1 316 494-6600.
Web site: http://alt1073.iheart.com
Profile: KTHR-FM is a commercial station owned by iHeartMedia Inc. The format of the station is alternative rock. KTHR-FM broadcasts in the Wichita, KS area at 107.3 FM. The station's slogan is, "Wichita's Alternative."
FM RADIO STATION

KTHS-AM 37515
Owner: Bunyard Broadcasting
Editorial: #1 Radio Drive, Berryville, Arkansas 72616 **Tel:** 1 870 423-2147.
Email: studio@kthsradio.com
Web site: http://www.kthsradio.com
Profile: KTHS-AM is a commercial station owned by Bunyard Broadcasting. The format of the station i classic hits. KTHS-AM broadcasts to the Berryville, AR at 1480 AM.
AM RADIO STATION

KTHS-FM 44886
Owner: Bunyard Broadcasting
Editorial: #1 Radio Drive, Berryville, Arkansas 72616 **Tel:** 1 870 423-2147.
Email: studio@kthsradio.com
Web site: http://www.kthsradio.com
Profile: KTHS-FM is a commercial station owned by Bunyard Broadcasting. The format of the station is contemporary country. KTHS-FM broadcasts to the Berryville, AR area at 107.1 FM.
FM RADIO STATION

KTHT-FM 43176
Owner: Cox Media Group, Inc.
Editorial: 1990 Post Oak Blvd, Houston, Texas 77056-3818 **Tel:** 1 713 963-1200.
Web site: http://www.countrylegends971.com
Profile: KTHT-FM is a commercial station owned by Cox Media Group, Inc. The format of the station is country music. KTHT-FM broadcasts to the Houston area at 97.1 FM.
FM RADIO STATION

KTHU-FM 43954
Owner: Results Radio Group
Editorial: 856 Manzanita Ct, Chico, California 95926 **Tel:** 1 530 342-2200.
Web site: http://chicothunderheads.com
Profile: KTHU-FM is a commercial station owned by Results Radio Group. The format of the station is classic rock music. KTHU-FM broadcasts to the Chico, CA area at 100.7 FM.
FM RADIO STATION

KTHX-FM 41938
Owner: Lotus Radio Corp.
Editorial: 300 E 2nd St Ste 1400, Reno, Nevada 89501-1566 **Tel:** 1 775 333-0123.
Web site: http://www.myradiox.com
Profile: KTHX-FM is a commercial station owned by Lotus Radio Corp.. The format of the station is adult album alternative. KTHX-FM broadcasts to the Reno, NV area at 100.1 FM.
FM RADIO STATION

KTIA-FM 44653
Owner: Truth Broadcasting
Editorial: 900 8th St, Boone, Iowa 50036-2920 **Tel:** 1 515 432-5014.
Web site: http://www.wtru.com
Profile: KTIA-FM is a non-commercial station owned by the Truth Broadcasting. The format of the station is Christian and religious talk. KTIA-FM broadcasts to the Boone, IA area at 99.3 FM.
FM RADIO STATION

KTIB-AM 36914
Owner: Townsquare Media, LLC
Editorial: 108 Green St, Thibodaux, Louisiana 70301-3048 **Tel:** 1 985 447-6404.
Email: ktib640am@gmail.com
Web site: http://www.ktib640.com
Profile: KTIB-AM is a commercial station owned by Townsquare Media, LLC. The format of the station is talk, sports and oldies music. KTIB-AM broadcasts to the Thibodaux, LA area at 640 AM.
AM RADIO STATION

KTIC-AM 38738
Owner: Nebraska Rural Radio Association
Editorial: 1011 N Lincoln St, West Point, Nebraska 68788-1003 **Tel:** 1 402 372-5423.
Web site: http://www.kticradio.com
Profile: KTIC-AM is a commercial station owned by Nebraska Rural Radio Association. The format of the station is agriculture and classic country music. KTIC-AM broadcasts to the West Point, NE area at 840 AM.
AM RADIO STATION

KTIC-FM 46095
Owner: Nebraska Rural Radio Association
Editorial: 1011 N Lincoln St, West Point, Nebraska 68788 **Tel:** 1 402 372-5423.
Web site: http://www.1079thebull.com
Profile: KTIC-FM is a commercial station owned by Nebraska Rural Radio Association. The format of the station is contemporary country. KTIC-FM broadcasts in the West Point, NE area at 107.9 FM.
FM RADIO STATION

KTIE-AM 36392
Owner: Salem Media Group, Inc.
Editorial: 701 N Brand Blvd Ste 550, Glendale, California 91203-1235 **Tel:** 1 818 956-5552.
Web site: http://www.590ktie.com
Profile: KTIE-AM is a commercial station owned by Salem Media Group, Inc. The format of the station is news and talk. KTIE-AM broadcasts to the San Bernadino, CA area at 590 AM.
AM RADIO STATION

KTIG-FM 41691
Owner: Minnesota Christian Broadcasters Inc.
Editorial: 31287 Brunes St, Pequot Lakes, Minnesota 56472 **Tel:** 1 218 568-4422.
Email: info@mcbiradio.org
Web site: http://theword.mn
Profile: KTIG-FM is a non-commercial station owned by Minnesota Christian Broadcasters Inc. The format of the station is contemporary Christian music. KTIG-FM broadcasts in the Minneapolis area at 102.7 FM.
FM RADIO STATION

KTIJ-FM 44450
Owner: Fuchs Radio Inc.
Editorial: 1515 N Broadway, Hobart, Oklahoma 73651 **Tel:** 1 580 726-5656.
Email: thezone@itlnet.net
Profile: KTIJ-FM is a commercial station owned by Fuchs Radio Inc. The format of the station is Top 40/CHR music. KTIJ-FM broadcasts to the Hobart, OK area at 106.9 FM.
FM RADIO STATION

KTIK-AM 36206
Owner: Cumulus Media Inc
Editorial: 1419 W Bannock St, Boise, Idaho 83702-5234 **Tel:** 1 208 336-3670.
Web site: http://www.ktik.com
Profile: KTIK-AM is a commercial station owned by Cumulus Media Inc. The format of the station is sports. KTIK-AM broadcasts to the Boise, ID area at 1350 AM.
AM RADIO STATION

KTIK-FM 41836
Owner: Cumulus Media Inc
Editorial: 1419 W Bannock St, Boise, Idaho 83702-5234 **Tel:** 1 208 336-3670.
Web site: http://www.ktik.com
Profile: KTIK-FM is a commercial station owned by Cumulus Media Inc. The format of the station is sports. KTIK-FM broadcasts to the Boise, ID area at 93.1 FM.
FM RADIO STATION

KTIL-AM 36985
Owner: Alexandra Communications Inc.
Editorial: 170 3rd St, Tillamook, Oregon 97141-9489 **Tel:** 1 503 842-4422.
Web site: http://www.tillamookradio.com
Profile: KTIL-AM is a commercial station owned byAlexandra Communications Inc. The format of the station is oldies. KTIL-AM broadcasts to Tillamook, OR at 1590 AM.
AM RADIO STATION

KTIL-FM 690803
Owner: Alexandra Communications Inc.
Editorial: 170 3rd St, Tillamook, Oregon 97141-9489 **Tel:** 1 503 842-4422.
Web site: http://www.ktil-radio.com
Profile: KTIL-FM is a commercial station owned by Alexandra Communications Inc. The format of the station is Cumulus Media's "Real Country." KTIL-FM broadcasts to the Tillamook, OR area at 95.9 FM.
FM RADIO STATION

KTIP-AM 36214
Owner: Mayberry Broadcasting Co.
Editorial: 1660 N Newcomb St, Porterville, California 93257-9295 **Tel:** 1 559 784-1450.
Email: live@ktip.com
Web site: http://www.ktip.com
Profile: KTIP-AM is a commercial station owned by Mayberry Broadcasting Co. The format of the station is news and talk. KTIP-AM broadcasts in the Porterville, CA area at 1450 AM.
AM RADIO STATION

KTIQ-AM 231987
Owner: Mapleton Radio, LLC
Editorial: 1020 W Main St, Merced, California 95340-4521 **Tel:** 1 209 723-2192.
Profile: KTIQ-AM is a commercial station owned by Mapleton Radio, LLC. The format of the station is rock. KTIQ-AM broadcasts to the Merced, CA area at a frequency of 1660 AM.
AM RADIO STATION

KTIS-AM 37517
Owner: Northwestern College
Editorial: 3003 Snelling Ave N, Saint Paul, Minnesota 55113-1501 **Tel:** 1 651 631-5000.
Web site: http://myfaithradio.com
Profile: KTIS-AM is a non-commercial station owned by Northwestern College. The format of the station is Christian talk. KTIS-AM broadcasts in the Minneapolis area at 900 AM.
AM RADIO STATION

KTIS-FM 44912
Owner: Northwestern College
Editorial: 3003 Snelling Ave N, Saint Paul, Minnesota 55113-1501 **Tel:** 1 651 631-5000.
Web site: http://myktis.com
Profile: KTIS-FM is a non-commercial station owned by Northwestern College. The format of the station is contemporary Christian music. KTIS-FM broadcasts in the Minneapolis area at 98.5 FM.
FM RADIO STATION

KTIX-AM 37518
Owner: Capps Broadcast Group
Editorial: 2003 NW 56th St, Pendleton, Oregon 97801 **Tel:** 1 541 276-1511.
Email: 1240ktix@cappsbroadcastgroup.com
Web site: http://www.1240ktix.com
Profile: KTIX-AM is a commercial station owned by Capps Broadcast Group. The format of the station is sports. KTIX-AM broadcasts to the Pendleton, OR area at 1240 AM.
AM RADIO STATION

KTJJ-FM 44913
Owner: Goodradio.TV LLC
Editorial: 1401 Krei Blvd, Farmington, Missouri 63640-1013 **Tel:** 1 573 756-6476.
Web site: http://www.mymoinfo.com
Profile: KTJJ-FM is a commercial station owned by Goodradio.TV LLC. The format of the station is country music. KTJJ-FM broadcasts to the Farmington, MO area at 98.5 FM.
FM RADIO STATION

KTJM-FM 41630
Owner: Liberman Broadcasting Inc.
Editorial: 3000 Bering Dr, Houston, Texas 77057-5708 **Tel:** 1 713 315-3400.
Web site: http://larazahouston.estrellatv.com/
Profile: KTJM-FM is a commercial station owned by Liberman Broadcasting. The format of the station is regional Mexican music. KTJM-FM broadcasts to the Beaumont and Port Arthur, TX areas at 98.5 FM.
FM RADIO STATION

KTJS-AM 36944
Owner: Fuchs Radio Inc.
Editorial: 1515 N Broadway, Hobart, Oklahoma 73651 **Tel:** 1 580 726-5656.
Email: thezone@itlnet.net
Web site: http://foxradiook.com
Profile: KTJS-AM is a commercial station owned by Fuchs Radio Inc. The format of the station is classic country. KTJS-AM broadcasts to the Hobart, OK area at 1420 AM.
AM RADIO STATION

KTKC-AM 39217
Owner: Hunt(Leon)
Editorial: 226 N Main St, Springhill, Louisiana 71075-3248 **Tel:** 1 318 539-6000.
Email: spots@ktkcfm.com
Web site: http://www.ktkcfm.com
Profile: KTKC-AM is a commercial station owned by Leon Hunt. The format of the station is news, talk and adult standards music. KTKC-AM broadcasts to the Springhill, LA area at 1460 AM.
AM RADIO STATION

KTKC-FM 46571
Owner: Hunt(Leon)
Editorial: 226 N Main St, Springhill, Louisiana 71075-3248 **Tel:** 1 318 539-6000.
Email: spots@ktkcfm.com
Web site: http://www.ktkcfm.com
Profile: KTKC-FM is a commercial station owned by Leon Hunt. The format of the station is contemporary country. KTKC-FM broadcasts to the Shreveport, LA area at 92.9 FM.
FM RADIO STATION

KTKE-FM 152817
Owner: Truckee Tahoe Radio, LLC
Editorial: 12030 Donner Pass Rd, Truckee, California 96161-0449 **Tel:** 1 530 587-9999.
Email: info@truckeetahoeradio.com
Web site: http://www.truckeetahoeradio.com
Profile: KTKE-FM is a commercial station owned by Truckee Tahoe Radio, LLC. The format of the station is adult album alternative. KTKE-FM broadcasts to the Truckee, CA area at 101.5 FM.
FM RADIO STATION

KTKN-AM 38429
Owner: Alaska Broadcast Communications Inc.
Editorial: 526 Stedman St, Ketchikan, Alaska 99901-6629 **Tel:** 1 907 225-2193.
Email: ktknnews@abcstations.com
Web site: http://ketchikanradio.com
Profile: KTKN-AM is a commercial station owned by Alaska Broadcast Communications Inc. The format of the station is talk programming and hot adult contemporary music. KTKN-AM broadcasts to the Ketchikan, AK area at 930 AM.
AM RADIO STATION

KTKO-FM 86699
Owner: Beeville Investments, LLC
Editorial: 2300 S Washington St, Beeville, Texas 78102 **Tel:** 1 361 358-1490.
Email: kicker106@yahoo.com
Profile: KTKO-FM is a commercial station owned by Beeville Investments, LLC. The format of the station is contemporary country. KTKO-FM broadcasts to the Beeville, TX area at 105.7 FM.
FM RADIO STATION

KTKR-AM 39332
Owner: iHeartMedia Inc.
Editorial: 6222 W Interstate 10, San Antonio, Texas 78201-2013 **Tel:** 1 210 736-9700.
Web site: http://ticket760.iheart.com
Profile: KTKR-AM is a commercial station owned by iHeartMedia Inc. The format of the station is sports. KTKR-AM broadcasts to the San Antonio area at 760 AM.
AM RADIO STATION

KTKS-FM 41110
Owner: Twin Lakes Communications
Editorial: 16875 Highway 52, Barnett, Missouri 65011-3310 **Tel:** 1 573 378-5669.
Email: news@lakeradio.net
Web site: http://www.lakeradio.com
Profile: KTKS-FM is a commercial station owned by Twin Lakes Communications. The format of the station is classic country music. KTKS-FM broadcasts to the Versailles, MO area at 95.1 FM.
FM RADIO STATION

KTKT-AM 38929
Owner: Lotus Communications Corp.
Editorial: 3871 N Commerce Dr, Tucson, Arizona 85705-2983 **Tel:** 1 520 407-4500.
Web site: http://ktkt99.com
Profile: KTKT-AM is a commercial station owned by Lotus Communications. The format of the station is Spanish adult hits. KTKT-AM broadcasts to the Tucson, AZ area on 990 AM.
AM RADIO STATION

KTKU-FM 45909
Owner: Alaska Broadcast Communications Inc.
Editorial: 3161 Channel Dr Ste 2, Juneau, Alaska 99801-7866 **Tel:** 1 907 586-3630.
Email: news@abcstations.com
Web site: http://www.taku105.com
Profile: KTKU-FM is a commercial station owned by Alaska Broadcast Communications Inc. The format for the station is country. KTKU-FM broadcasts to the Juneau, AK area at 105.1 FM.
FM RADIO STATION

KTKX-FM 42006
Owner: Cox Media Group, Inc.
Editorial: 8122 Datapoint Dr Ste 600, San Antonio, Texas 78229-3446 **Tel:** 1 210 615-5400.
Web site: http://eaglesanantonio.com
Profile: KTKX-FM is a commercial station owned by Cox Media Group, Inc. The format for the station is classic rock. KTKX-FM broadcasts to the San Antonio area at 106.7 FM.
FM RADIO STATION

KTKZ-AM 36625
Owner: Salem Media Group, Inc.
Editorial: 1425 River Park Dr Ste 520, Sacramento, California 95815-4524 **Tel:** 1 916 924-0710.
Web site: http://am1380theanswer.com
Profile: KTKZ-AM is a commercial station owned by Salem Media Group, Inc. The format of the station is news and conservative talk. KTKZ-AM broadcasts in the Sacramento, CA area at 1380 AM.
AM RADIO STATION

KTLB-FM 39948
Owner: Alpha Media
Editorial: 200 N 10th St, Fort Dodge, Iowa 50501-3925 **Tel:** 1 515 955-5656.
Web site: http://www.yourfortdodge.com
Profile: KTLB-FM is a commercial station owned by Alpha Media. The format of the station is classic hits. KTLB-FM broadcasts to the Fort Dodge, IA area at 105.9 FM.
FM RADIO STATION

KTLK-AM 37753
Owner: iHeartMedia Inc.
Editorial: 1600 Utica Ave S Ste 400, Minneapolis, Minnesota 55416-1480 **Tel:** 1 952 417-3000.
Web site: http://www.twincitiesnewstalk.com
Profile: KTLK-AM is a commercial station owned by iHeartMedia Inc. The format of the station is news/talk. KTLK-AM broadcasts to the Minneapolis area at 1130 AM.
AM RADIO STATION

KTLO-AM 37519
Owner: Mountain Lakes Broadcasting Inc.
Editorial: 620 Highway 5 N, Mountain Home, Arkansas 72653 **Tel:** 1 870 425-3101.
Email: news@ktlo.com
Web site: http://www.ktlo.com
Profile: KTLO-AM is a commercial station owned by Mountain Lakes Broadcasting Inc. The format is country music. KTLO-AM broadcasts to the Mountain Home, AR area at 1240 AM.
AM RADIO STATION

KTLO-FM 44914
Owner: Mountain Lakes Broadcasting Inc.
Editorial: 620 Highway 5 N, Mountain Home, Arkansas 72653-3012 **Tel:** 1 870 425-3101.
Email: news@ktlo.com
Web site: http://www.ktlo.com
Profile: KTLO-FM is a commercial station owned by Mountain Lakes Broadcasting Inc. The format of the station is adult standards. KTLO-FM broadcasts to the Mountain Home, AR area at 97.9 FM.
FM RADIO STATION

KTLQ-AM 37520
Owner: Payne Radio Group
Editorial: 5686 S Muskogee Ave, Tahlequah, Oklahoma 74464-5487 **Tel:** 1 918 456-2511.
Email: info@lakescountry1021.com
Web site: http://www.lakescountry1021.com/page.php?page_id=171
Profile: KTLQ-AM is a commercial station owned by Payne Radio Group. The format of the station is

classic country. KTLQ-AM broadcasts to the Tahlequah, OK area at 1350 AM.
AM RADIO STATION

KTLR-AM 34892
Owner: WPA Radio LLC
Editorial: 5101 S Shields Blvd Ste A, Oklahoma City, Oklahoma 73129-3217 **Tel:** 1 405 601-6380.
Web site: http://www.ktlr.com
Profile: KTLR-AM is a commercial station owned by WPA Radio LLC. The format of the station is talk. KTLR-AM broadcasts to the Oklahoma City area at 890 AM.
AM RADIO STATION

KTLS-FM 46499
Owner: Chikasaw Nation
Editorial: 1019 N Broadway Ave, Ada, Oklahoma 74820-2036 **Tel:** 1 580 332-2211.
Email: score@cableone.net
Web site: http://www.ktlsradio.com
Profile: KTLS-FM is a commercial station owned by the Chikasaw Nation. The format of the station is classic rock. KTLS-FM broadcasts in the Ada, OK area at 106.5 FM.
FM RADIO STATION

KTLT-FM 42293
Owner: Cumulus Media Inc.
Editorial: 2525 S Danville Dr, Abilene, Texas 79605-6414 **Tel:** 1 325 793-9700.
Web site: http://www.the98x.com
Profile: KTLT-FM is a commercial station owned by Cumulus Media Inc. The format of the station is sports. KTLT-FM broadcasts in the Abilene, TX area at 98.1 FM.
FM RADIO STATION

KTLU-AM 39076
Owner: Whitehead Enterprises, Inc.
Editorial: 618 N Main St, Rusk, Texas 75785
Tel: 1 903 683-5305.
Email: kwrw@mediactr.com
Profile: KTLU-AM is a commercial station owned by Whitehead Enterprises, Inc. The format of the station is classic hits. KTLU-FM broadcasts to the Rusk, TX area at 1580 AM.
AM RADIO STATION

KTLV-AM 35810
Owner: First Choice Broadcasting, Inc.
Editorial: 3336 SE 67th St, Oklahoma City, Oklahoma 73135-1701 **Tel:** 1 405 672-3886.
Email: ktlv1220@aol.com
Web site: http://www.ktlv1220.com
Profile: KTLV-AM is a commercial station owned by First Choice Broadcasting, Inc. The format of the station is gospel music and religious programming. KTLV-AM broadcasts to the Oklahoma City area at 1220 AM.
AM RADIO STATION

KTLW-FM 43720
Owner: Air 1
Editorial: 14820 Sherman Way, Van Nuys, California 91405-2233 **Tel:** 1 818 779-8484.
Web site: http://www.air1.com
Profile: KTLW-FM is a commercial station owned by Air 1. The format is contemporary Christian. KTLW-FM broadcasts to the Los Angeles area at 88.9 FM.
FM RADIO STATION

KTLZ-FM 687602
Owner: Worship Center of Kingsville(The)
Editorial: 929 N Padre Island Dr, Corpus Christi, Texas 78406-1911 **Tel:** 1 361 299-1992.
Web site: http://www.radiolibertad.net/
Profile: KTLZ-FM is a commercial station owned by The Worship Center of Kingsville. The format of the station is Hispanic religious programming. KTLZ-FM broadcasts to the Cuero, TX area at 89.9 FM.
FM RADIO STATION

KTMB-FM 39853
Owner: Ohana Media Group
Editorial: 833 Gambell St, Anchorage, Alaska 99501-3756 **Tel:** 1 907 344-4045.
Web site: http://www.anchorageoldies1021.com
Profile: KTMB-FM is a commercial station owned by Ohana Media Group. The format of the station is oldies. KTMB-FM broadcasts to the Anchorage, AK area at 102.1 FM.
FM RADIO STATION

KTMC-AM 38626
Owner: Southeastern Oklahoma Radio, LLC
Editorial: 1801 E Electric Ave, McAlester, Oklahoma 74501-3824 **Tel:** 1 918 426-1050.
Email: info@mcalesterradio.com
Web site: http://www.mcalesterradio.com
Profile: KTMC-AM is a commercial station owned by Southeastern Oklahoma Radio, LLC. The format of the station is adult standards. KTMC-AM broadcasts to the McAlester, OK area at 1400 AM.
AM RADIO STATION

KTMC-FM 45976
Owner: Southeastern Oklahoma Radio, LLC
Editorial: 1801 E Electric Ave, McAlester, Oklahoma 74501-3824 **Tel:** 1 918 426-1050.
Email: info@mcalesterradio.com
Web site: http://www.mcalesterradio.com
Profile: KTMC-FM is a commercial station owned by Southeastern Oklahoma Radio, LLC. The format of the station is classic rock music. KTMC-FM broadcasts to the McAlester, OK area at 105.1 FM.
FM RADIO STATION

KTMG-FM 44793
Owner: Great Circle Media
Editorial: 116 S Alto St, Prescott, Arizona 86303-3604
Tel: 1 928 445-6880.
Web site: http://www.magic991.com
Profile: KTMG-FM is a commercial station owned by Guyann Corp. The format of the station is Hot AC. KTMG-FM broadcasts to the Prescott, AZ area at 99.1 FM.
FM RADIO STATION

KTMM-AM 36786
Owner: MBC Grand Broadcasting Inc.
Editorial: 1360 E Sherwood Dr, Grand Junction, Colorado 81501-7546 **Tel:** 1 970 254-2100.
Web site: http://www.theteam1340.com/
Profile: KTMM-AM is a commercial station owned by MBC Grand Broadcasting Inc. The format of the station is sports talk. KTMM-AM broadcasts to the Grand Junction, CO area at 1340 AM.
AM RADIO STATION

KTMO-FM 44768
Owner: Pollack Broadcasting Co.
Editorial: 1303 Southwest Drive, Kennett, Missouri 63857 **Tel:** 1 573 888-4616.
Email: monte@semoradio.com
Web site: http://www.ktmoradio.com
Profile: KTMO-FM is a commercial station owned by Pollack Broadcasting Co. The format of the station is contemporary country music. KTMO-FM broadcasts to the Kennett, MO, area at 106.5 FM.
FM RADIO STATION

KTMP-AM 235096
Owner: Creek Broadcasting Corp.
Editorial: 260 N Main St, Heber City, Utah 84032-1650 **Tel:** 1 435 657-1340.
Email: ktmp1340am@gmail.com
Web site: http://www.ktmp1340.com
Profile: KTMP-AM is a commercial station owned by Creek Broadcasting Corp. The format for the station is classic country. KTMP-AM broadcasts to the Heber City, UT, area at 1340 AM.
AM RADIO STATION

KTMQ-FM 317537
Owner: iHeartMedia Inc.
Editorial: 27349 Jefferson Ave Ste 116, Temecula, California 92590-5610 **Tel:** 1 951 296-9050.
Web site: http://www.q1033.com
Profile: KTMQ-FM is a commercial station owned by iHeartMedia Inc. The format of the station is rock. KTMQ-FM broadcasts to the Temecula, CA area at 103.3 FM.
FM RADIO STATION

KTMR-AM 36634
Owner: SIGA Broadcasting Corp.
Tel: 1 713 868-5559.
Email: sigabroadcasting@gmail.com
Profile: KTMR-AM is a commercial station owned by SIGA Broadcasting Corp. The format of the station is business talk. KTMR-AM broadcasts to the Converse, TX area at 1130 AM.
AM RADIO STATION

KTMS-AM 39262
Owner: Rincon Broadcasting
Editorial: 414 E Cota St, Santa Barbara, California 93101-1624 **Tel:** 1 805 879-8300.
Web site: http://ktms.com
Profile: KTMS-AM is a commercial station owned by Rincon Broadcasting. The format of the station is news and talk. KTMS-AM broadcasts to the Santa, Barbara, CA, area at 990 AM.
AM RADIO STATION

KTMT-AM 37381
Owner: Mapleton Radio, LLC
Editorial: 1438 Rossanley Dr, Medford, Oregon 97501-1751 **Tel:** 1 541 779-1550.
Web site: http://www.espn580.com
Profile: KTMT-AM is a commercial station owned by Mapleton Radio, LLC. The format of the station is sports/talk. KTMT-AM broadcasts to the Medford, OR area at 580 AM.
AM RADIO STATION

KTMT-FM 44915
Owner: Mapleton Radio, LLC
Editorial: 1438 Rossanley Dr, Medford, Oregon 97501-1751 **Tel:** 1 541 779-1550.
Email: mikefm@radiomedford.com
Profile: KTMT-FM is a commercial station owned by Mapleton Radio, LLC. The format of the station is Top 40/CHR. KTMT-FM broadcasts to the Medford, OR area at 93.7 FM.
FM RADIO STATION

KTMX-FM 44571
Owner: Nebraska Rural Radio Association
Editorial: 1309 Road 11, York, Nebraska 68467-7513
Tel: 1 402 362-4433.
Email: ktmx@ktmxfm.com
Web site: http://1049maxcountry.com/
Profile: KTMX-FM is a commercial station owned by Nebraska Rural Radio Association. The format of the station is adult contemporary music. KTMX-FM broadcasts to the York, NE area at 104.9 FM.
FM RADIO STATION

KTMY-FM 45243
Owner: Hubbard Broadcasting Inc.
Editorial: 3415 University Ave SE, Minneapolis, Minnesota 55414-3327 **Tel:** 1 651 642-4107.
Web site: http://www.mytalk1071.com
Profile: KTMY-FM is a commercial station owned by Hubbard Broadcasting Inc. The format of the station is talk. KTMY-FM broadcasts in the Minneapolis area at 107.1 FM.
FM RADIO STATION

KTMZ-AM 133733
Owner: Lotus Communications Corp.
Editorial: 3301 Barham Blvd Ste 201, Los Angeles, California 90068-1358 **Tel:** 1 323 851-5959.
Email: kwkw1330@aol.com
Web site: http://www.espn1330.com
Profile: KTMZ-AM is commercial station owned by the Lotus Communications Corp. The format of the station is Hispanic sports. KWKU-AM broadcasts to the Los Angeles area at 1220 AM and simulcasts on KWKW-AM 1330.
AM RADIO STATION

KTNA-FM 42406
Owner: Talkeetna Community Radio Inc.
Editorial: Second Street, Talkeetna, Alaska 99676
Tel: 1 907 733-1700.
Email: info@ktna.org
Web site: http://www.ktna.org
Profile: KTNA-FM is a non-commercial station owned by Talkeetna Community Radio Inc. The format of the station is variety. KTNA-FM broadcasts to the Anchorage, AK area at 88.9 FM.
FM RADIO STATION

KTNC-AM 35094
Owner: KNZA, Inc.
Editorial: 1602 Stone St, Falls City, Nebraska 68355-2663 **Tel:** 1 402 245-2453.
Email: knza@rainbowtel.net
Profile: KTNC-AM is a commercial station owned by KNZA, Inc. The format of the station is oldies. KTNC-AM broadcasts to the Falls City, NE area at 1230 AM.
AM RADIO STATION

KTNF-AM 35637
Owner: Lawson (Chad)
Editorial: 11320 Valley View Rd, Eden Prairie, Minnesota 55344-3613 **Tel:** 1 952 946-8885.
Web site: http://www.am950radio.com
Profile: KTNF-AM is a commercial station owned and operated by Lawson (Chad). The format of the station is talk. KTNF-AM broadcasts to the Eden Prairie, MN area at 950 AM.
AM RADIO STATION

KTNK-AM 36678
Owner: Knight Broadcasting Inc.
Editorial: 111 S I St, Lompoc, California 93436-6700
Tel: 1 805 741-7901.
Web site: http://www.radioktnk.com/
Profile: KTNK-AM is a commercial station owned by Knight Broadcasting Inc. The format of the station is news and talk. KTNK-AM broadcasts to the Santa Maria, CA area at 1410 AM.
AM RADIO STATION

KTNM-AM 38719
Owner: Majestic Communications
Editorial: 902 Date St, Tucumcari, New Mexico 88401-4335 **Tel:** 1 575 461-0522.
Email: ktnmkqay@yahoo.com
Profile: KTNM-AM is a commercial station owned by Majestic Communications. The format of the station is classic country. KTNM-AM broadcasts to the Tucumcari, NM area at 1400 AM.
AM RADIO STATION

KTNN-AM 39464
Owner: Navajo Nation
Editorial: Navajo Shopping Center, Window Rock, Arizona 86515 **Tel:** 1 928 871-2582.
Email: webmaster@ktnnonline.com
Web site: http://www.ktnnonline.com
Profile: KTNN-AM is a commercial station owned by Navajo Nation. The format of the station is country music, and Native American music. KTNN-AM broadcasts to the Albuquerque, NM area at 660 AM.
AM RADIO STATION

KTNO-AM 35850
Owner: Mortenson Broadcasting Co.
Editorial: 5787 S Hampton Rd Ste 205, Dallas, Texas 75232-2255 **Tel:** 1 214 561-9128.
Web site: http://luzdallas.com
Profile: KTNO-AM is a commercial station owned by Mortenson Broadcasting Co. The format of the station is Spanish Contemporary Christian music. KTNO-AM broadcasts to the Dallas area at 1440 AM.
AM RADIO STATION

KTNQ-AM 37522
Owner: Univision Communications Inc.
Editorial: 5999 Center Dr, Los Angeles, California 90045-8901 **Tel:** 1 310 348-3434.
Web site: http://univisionamerica.com
Profile: KTNQ-AM is a commercial station owned by Univision Communications. The format for the station is Spanish news and talk. KTNQ-AM broadcasts to the Los Angeles area at 1020 AM.
AM RADIO STATION

KTNR-FM 43729
Owner: Multimedios Radio Ola
Editorial: 2702 Pine St, Laredo, Texas 78046-6225
Tel: 1 956 726-4738.
Profile: KTNR-FM is a non-commercial station owned by Multimedios Radio Ola. The format for the station is Hispanic Christian programming. KTNR-FM broadcasts to the Kennedy, TX area at 92.1 FM.
FM RADIO STATION

KTNT-FM 39574
Owner: Payne Radio Group
Editorial: Highway 69 & Texanna Rd, Eufaula, Oklahoma 74432 **Tel:** 1 918 689-3663.
Email: kfox_1025@live.com
Web site: http://www.payneradiogroup.com
Profile: KTNT-FM is a commercial station owned by Payne Radio Group. The format of the station is contemporary country. KTNT-FM broadcasts to the Eufaula, OK area at 102.5 FM.
FM RADIO STATION

KTNX-FM 389881
Owner: Dockins Broadcast Group
Editorial: 900 E Karsch Blvd, Farmington, Missouri 63640-3405 **Tel:** 1 573 223-4518.
Profile: KTNX-FM is a commercial station owned by Dockins Broadcast Group. The format of the station is adult contemporary. KTNX-FM broadcasts to the Farmington, MO area at 103.9 FM.
FM RADIO STATION

KTNY-FM 45835
Owner: Lincoln County Broadcasters Inc.
Editorial: 251 W Cedar St, Libby, Montana 59923-2610 **Tel:** 1 406 293-6234.
Email: klcb@frontiernet.net
Web site: http://klcb-ktny.com
Profile: KTNY-FM is a commercial station owned by Lincoln County Broadcasters Inc. The format of the station is Adult hits music. KTNY-FM broadcasts to the Libby, MT area at 101.7 FM.
FM RADIO STATION

KTNZ-AM 36745
Owner: My Home Team Media
Editorial: 2505 Lakeview Dr, 302 B, Amarillo, Texas 79109-1527 **Tel:** 1 806 355-1044.
Web site: http://espn1010.com
Profile: KTNZ-AM is a commercial station owned by My Home Team Media. The format of the station is Sports. KTNZ-AM broadcasts to Amarillo, TX at 1010 AM.
AM RADIO STATION

KTOE-AM 38483
Owner: Radio Mankato
Editorial: 59346 Madison Ave, Mankato, Minnesota 56001-8518 **Tel:** 1 507 345-4537.
Email: news@ktoe.com
Web site: http://www.katoinfo.com
Profile: KTOE-AM is a commercial station owned by Radio Mankato. The format for the station is news talk and sports. KTOE-AM broadcasts to the Mankato, MN area at 1420 AM.
AM RADIO STATION

KTOH-FM 87066
Owner: Hochman Hawaii One, Inc.
Editorial: 4334 Rice St Ste 206, Lihue, Hawaii 96766-1801 **Tel:** 1 808 246-4444.
Email: ktoh@hhawaiimedia.com
Web site: http://roostercountry.com
Profile: KTOH-FM is a commercial station owned by Hochman Hawaii One, Inc. The format of the station is contemporary country. KTOH-FM broadcasts to the Kauai, HI area at 99.9 FM.
FM RADIO STATION

KTOK-AM 39121
Owner: iHeartMedia Inc.
Editorial: 1900 NW Expressway Ste 1000, Oklahoma City, Oklahoma 73118-1854 **Tel:** 1 405 840-5271.
Web site: http://ktok.iheart.com/
Profile: KTOK-AM is a commercial station owned by iHeartMedia Inc. The format of the station is news and talk. KTOK-AM broadcasts to the Oklahoma City area at 1000 AM.
AM RADIO STATION

KTOM-FM 44917
Owner: iHeartMedia Inc.
Editorial: 903 N Main St, Salinas, California 93906-3912 **Tel:** 1 831 755-8181.
Web site: http://www.ktom.com
Profile: KTOM-FM is a commercial station owned by iHeartMedia Inc. The format of the station is contemporary country. KTOM-FM broadcasts to the Salinas, CA area at 92.7 FM.
FM RADIO STATION

KTON-AM 35008
Owner: M & M Broadcasters, Ltd.
Editorial: 901 E 1st St, Cameron, Texas 76520-3404
Tel: 1 281 599-9800.
Web site: http://www.ktaeradio.com
Profile: KTON-AM is a commercial station owned by M & M Broadcasters, Ltd. The format of the station is talk. KTON-AM broadcasts to the Cameron, TX area at 1330 AM.
AM RADIO STATION

KTOO-FM 39953
Owner: Capital Community Broadcasting Inc.
Editorial: 360 Egan Dr, Juneau, Alaska 99801-1769
Tel: 1 907 586-1670.
Email: news@ktoo.org
Web site: http://www.ktoo.org
Profile: KTOO-FM is a non-commercial station owned by Capital Community Broadcasting Inc. The format of the station is news and talk. KTOO-FM broadcasts to the Juneau, AK area at 104.3 FM.
FM RADIO STATION

KTOP-AM 36325
Owner: Cumulus Media Inc.
Editorial: 825 S Kansas Ave, Topeka, Kansas 66612-1233 Tel: 1 785 272-2122.
Web site: http://www.ktop1490.com
Profile: KTOP-AM is a commercial station owned by Cumulus Media Inc. The format of the station is sports. KTOP-AM broadcasts to the Topeka, KS area at 1490 AM.
AM RADIO STATION

KTOP-FM 42503
Owner: Cumulus Media Inc.
Editorial: 825 S Kansas Ave Ste 100, Topeka, Kansas 66612-1233 Tel: 1 785 272-2122.
Web site: http://www.nashfm1029.com/
Profile: KTOP-FM is a commercial station owned by Cumulus Media Inc. The format of the station is country. KTOP-FM broadcasts to the Topeka, KS area at 102.9 FM.
FM RADIO STATION

KTOQ-AM 38947
Owner: Haugo Broadcasting Inc.
Editorial: 3601 Canyon Lake Dr, Rapid City, South Dakota 57702-3900 Tel: 1 605 343-0888.
Web site: http://www.espnrapidcity.com/
Profile: KTOQ-AM is a commercial station owned by Haugo Broadcasting Inc. The format of the station is talk programming. KTOQ-AM broadcasts to the Rapid City, SD area at 1340 AM.
AM RADIO STATION

KTOX-AM 35071
Owner: Creative Broadcasting Services Inc.
Editorial: 100 Balboa St, Needles, California 92363-4113 Tel: 1 760 326-4500.
Email: info@ktox1340.com
Web site: http://www.ktox1340.com
Profile: KTOX-AM is a commercial station owned by Creative Broadcasting Services, Inc. The format for the station is news and talk. KTOX-AM broadcasts to the Needles, CA area at 1340 AM.
AM RADIO STATION

KTOY-FM 42509
Owner: Texarkana Radio Center Licenses, LLC
Editorial: 615 Olive St, Texarkana, Texas 75501-5512 Tel: 1 903 793-4671.
Web site: http://www.ktoy1047.com
Profile: KTOY-FM is a commercial station owned by Texarkana Radio Center Licenses, LLC. The format of the station is urban adult contemporary. KTOY-FM broadcasts to the Texarkana, TX area at 104.5 FM.
FM RADIO STATION

KTOZ-FM 42206
Owner: iHeartMedia Inc.
Editorial: 1856 S Glenstone Ave, Springfield, Missouri 65804-2303 Tel: 1 417 890-5555.
Web site: http://www.alice955.com
Profile: KTOZ-FM is a commercial station owned by iHeartMedia Inc. The format of the station is hot AC. KTOZ-FM broadcasts to the Springfield, MO market at 95.5 FM.
FM RADIO STATION

KTPG-FM 960823
Owner: Flinn Broadcasting Corp.
Editorial: 400 Tower Dr, Paragould, Arkansas 72450-4891 Tel: 1 870 236-7627.
Email: jill@neajillradio.com
Web site: http://www.neajillradio.com
Profile: KTPG-FM is a commercial station owned by Flinn Broadcasting Corp. The format of the station is Hot AC. KTPG-FM broadcasts to the Paragould, AR area at 99.3 FM.
FM RADIO STATION

KTPI-AM 37561
Owner: RZ Radio LLC
Editorial: 570 E Avenue Q9, Palmdale, California 93550-4655 Tel: 1 661 947-3107.
Web site: http://www.magic1340.com
Profile: KTPI-AM is a commercial station owned by RZ Radio LLC. The format of the station is adult standards. KTPI-AM broadcasts to the Lancaster, CA area at 1340 AM.
AM RADIO STATION

KTPI-FM 44918
Owner: iHeartMedia Inc.
Editorial: 352 E Avenue K4, Lancaster, California 93535-4505 Tel: 1 661 942-1121.
Web site: http://ktpi.com
Profile: KTPI-FM is a commercial station owned by iHeartMedia Inc. The format of the station is contemporary country. KTPI-FM broadcasts to the Lancaster, CA area at 97.7 FM.
FM RADIO STATION

KTPK-FM 39955
Owner: JMJ Broadcasting Company Inc.
Editorial: 1210 SW Executive Dr, Topeka, Kansas 66615-3850 Tel: 1 785 273-1069.
Web site: http://www.countrylegends1069.com
Profile: KTPK-FM is a commercial station owned by JMJ Broadcasting Company Inc. The format of the station is classic country. KPTK-FM broadcasts to the Topeka, KS area on 106.9 FM.
FM RADIO STATION

KTPO-FM 816305
Owner: Hellroaring Communications, LLC
Editorial: 327 S Marion Ave, Sandpoint, Idaho 83864-1723 Tel: 1 208 263-2179.
Web site: http://www.953kpnd.com

Profile: KTPO-FM is a commercial station owned by Hellroaring Communications, LLC. The format of the station is adult album alternative. KTPO-FM broadcasts to the Bonner County area in Idaho at a frequency of 106.7 FM.
FM RADIO STATION

KTPT-FM 333583
Owner: Bethesda Christian Broadcasting
Editorial: 1853 Fountain Plaza Dr, Rapid City, South Dakota 57702-9315 Tel: 1 605 342-6822.
Web site: http://www.979thebreeze.com/breeze/
Profile: KTPT-FM is a commercial station owned by Bethesda Christian Broadcasting. The format of the station is contemporary Christian. KTPT-FM broadcasts to the Rapid City, SD area at 97.9 FM.
FM RADIO STATION

KTPZ-FM 524232
Owner: Locally Owned Radio, LLC
Editorial: 21361 Highway 30, Twin Falls, Idaho 83301-0197 Tel: 1 208 735-8300.
Web site: http://www.ktpz927.com
Profile: KTPZ-FM is a commercial station owned by Locally Owned Radio, LLC. The format for the station is hot adult contemporary. KTPZ-FM broadcasts to the Twin Falls, ID area at 92.7 FM.
FM RADIO STATION

KTQM-FM 44919
Owner: Zia Broadcasting Inc.
Editorial: 710 Cr K, Clovis, New Mexico 88101 Tel: 1 575 762-4411.
Email: ktqm@plateautel.net
Profile: KTQM-FM is a commercial station owned by Zia Broadcasting Inc. The format of the station is adult contemporary. KTQM-FM broadcasts to the Clovis, NM area at 99.9 FM.
FM RADIO STATION

KTQX-FM 42506
Owner: Radio Bilingue Inc.
Editorial: 5005 E Belmont Ave, Fresno, California 93727 Tel: 1 559 455-5777.
Web site: http://www.radiobilingue.org
Profile: KTQX-FM is a non-commercial station owned by Radio Bilingue Inc. The format of the station is Hispanic. KTQX-FM broadcasts to the Visalia-Fresno, CA area at 90.1 FM.
FM RADIO STATION

KTRA-FM 41179
Owner: iHeartMedia Inc.
Editorial: 200 E Broadway, Farmington, New Mexico 87401-6418 Tel: 1 505 325-1716.
Web site: http://www.102ktra.com
Profile: KTRA-FM is a commercial station owned by iHeartMedia Inc. The format of the station is country music. KTRA-FM broadcasts to the Farmington, NM area at 102.1 FM.
FM RADIO STATION

KTRB-AM 39509
Owner: Pappas Radio of California, LP
Editorial: 300 Broadway Ste 8, San Francisco, California 94133-4545 Tel: 1 415 713-5526.
Web site: http://espndeportessanfrancisco.com
Profile: KTRB-AM is a commercial station owned by Pappas Radio of California, LP. The format of the station is Spanish language sports. KTRB-AM broadcasts to the San Francisco area at 860 AM.
AM RADIO STATION

KTRC-AM 36530
Owner: Hutton Broadcasting, LLC
Editorial: 2502 Camino Entrada, Santa Fe, New Mexico 87507-4911 Tel: 1 505 471-1067.
Web site: http://www.santafe.com/ktrc
Profile: KTRC-AM is a commercial station owned by Hutton Broadcasting, LLC. The format of the station is progressive talk. KTRC-AM broadcasts to the Santa Fe, NM area at 1260 AM.
AM RADIO STATION

KTRF-AM 37142
Owner: Iowa City Broadcasting Co.
Editorial: 1433 Main Ave N, Thief River Falls, Minnesota 56701 Tel: 1 218 681-1230.
Email: ktrf@mncable.net
Web site: http://www.trfradio.com
Profile: KTRF-AM is a commercial station owned by Iowa City Broadcasting Co. The format of the station is talk. KTRF-AM broadcasts in the Thief River Falls, MN area at 1230 AM.
AM RADIO STATION

KTRG-FM 830852
Owner: Freed AM Corp.
Editorial: 3446 Summerhill Rd #B, Texarkana, Texas 75503-3560 Tel: 1 903 255-7935.
Web site: http://espntexarkana.com
Profile: KTRG-FM is a commercial station owned by Freed AM Corp. The format of the station is sports. KTRG-FM broadcasts to the Texarkana area at a frequency of 94.1 FM.
FM RADIO STATION

KTRH-AM 39097
Owner: iHeartMedia Inc.
Editorial: 2000 West Loop S Ste 300, Houston, Texas 77027-3510 Tel: 1 713 212-8000.
Email: news@ktrh.com
Web site: http://www.ktrh.com
Profile: KTRH-AM is a commercial station owned by iHeartMedia Inc. The format of the station is news and talk programming. KTRH-AM broadcasts to the Houston area at 740 AM.
AM RADIO STATION

KTRI-FM 39958
Owner: Thirteen Forty Productions, Inc.
Editorial: 118 State Dr, Hollister, Missouri 65672-4987 Tel: 1 417 339-1062.
Profile: KTRI-FM is a commercial station owned by Thirteen Forty Productions, Inc. The format of the station is tourist information for the Branson, MO Tri-Lakes area. KTRI-FM broadcasts to the Branson, MO area at 95.9 FM.
FM RADIO STATION

KTRN-FM 235107
Owner: Bluff City Radio, LLC
Editorial: 2215 E Harding Ave Ste 7, Pine Bluff, Arkansas 71601-6880 Tel: 1 870 536-3282.
Email: ktrn1045fm@yahoo.com
Web site: http://ktrn1045.com
Profile: KTRN-FM is a commercial station owned by Bluff City Radio, LLC. The format of the station is adult contemporary. KTRN-FM broadcasts to the Pine Bluff, AR area at 104.5 FM.
FM RADIO STATION

KTRQ-FM 45683
Owner: East Arkansas Broadcasters Inc.
Editorial: 2758 Highway 64, Wynne, Arkansas 72396-4061 Tel: 1 870 238-8141.
Email: radiokwyn@cablelynx.com
Profile: KTRQ-FM is a commercial station owned by East Arkansas Broadcasters Inc. The format of the station is oldies. KTRQ-FM broadcasts to the Wynne, AR area at 102.3 FM.
FM RADIO STATION

KTRR-FM 41186
Owner: Townsquare Media, LLC
Editorial: 600 Main St, Windsor, Colorado 80550 Tel: 1 970 674-2700.
Web site: http://www.tri1025.com
Profile: KTRR-FM is a commercial station owned by Townsquare Media, LLC. The format of the station is adult contemporary. KTRR-FM broadcasts to the Denver area at 102.5 FM.
FM RADIO STATION

KTRS-AM 36481
Owner: CH Holdings LLC
Editorial: 638 W Port Plz, Saint Louis, Missouri 63146-3106 Tel: 1 314 453-5500.
Email: news@ktrs.com
Web site: http://www.ktrs.com
Profile: KTRS-AM is a commercial station owned by CH Holdings LLC. The format of the station is news and talk. KTRS-AM broadcasts to the St. Louis area at 550 AM.
AM RADIO STATION

KTRS-FM 43588
Owner: Townsquare Media, LLC
Editorial: 150 Nichols Ave, Casper, Wyoming 82601-1816 Tel: 1 307 266-5252.
Web site: http://www.kisscasper.com
Profile: KTRS-FM is a commercial station owned by Townsquare Media, LLC. The format for the station is Top 40/CHR. KTRS-FM broadcasts to the Casper-Riverton, WY area at 104.7 FM.
FM RADIO STATION

KTRW-AM 36761
Owner: Read Broadcasting
Editorial: 6019 S Crestline St, Spokane, Washington 99223-6823 Tel: 1 509 443-1000.
Email: ktw@fabulous630.com
Web site: http://www.ktrw.com
Profile: KTRW-AM is a commercial station owned by Read Broadcasting. The format of the station is news and religion. KTRW-AM broadcasts to the Spokane, WA area at 630 AM.
AM RADIO STATION

KTRX-FM 87469
Owner: LKCM Radio Group LP
Editorial: 1205 Northglen St, Ardmore, Oklahoma 73401-1202 Tel: 1 580 226-0421.
Web site: http://www.texomarocks.com
Profile: KTRX-FM is a commercial station owned by LKCM Radio Group LP. The format of the station is classic rock. KTRX-FM broadcasts to the Ardmore, OK area at 92.7 FM. The station's slogan is, "Texacoma's Rock Station."
FM RADIO STATION

KTRY-FM 545939
Owner: Redwood Empire Stereocasters
Editorial: 3392 Mendocino Ave, Santa Rosa, California 95403-2213 Tel: 1 707 528-4434.
Email: holler@ktry.com
Web site: http://www.ktry.com
Profile: KTRY-FM is a commercial station owned by Redwood Empire Stereocasters. The format of the station is country. KTRY-FM broadcasts to the San Francisco area at 106.3 FM.
FM RADIO STATION

KTSA-AM 37525
Owner: Alpha Media, Inc.
Editorial: 4050 Eisenhauer Rd, San Antonio, Texas 78218-3409 Tel: 1 210 654-5100.
Web site: http://www.ktsa.com
Profile: KTSA-AM is a commercial station owned by Alpha Media, Inc.. The format of the station is news and talk. KTSA-AM broadcasts to the San Antonio area at 550 AM.
AM RADIO STATION

KTSE-FM 44054
Owner: Entravision Communications Corp.
Editorial: 6820 Pacific Ave Ste 3A, Stockton, California 95207-2631 Tel: 1 209 474-0154.
Web site: http://www.jose971.com
Profile: KTSE-FM is a commercial station owned by Entravision Communications Corp. The format of the station is Hispanic adult hits. KTSE-FM broadcasts to the Modesto, CA area at 97.1 FM.
FM RADIO STATION

KTSM-AM 37526
Owner: iHeartMedia Inc.
Editorial: 4045 N Mesa St, El Paso, Texas 79902-1526 Tel: 1 915 351-5400.
Web site: http://www.ktsmradio.com
Profile: KTSM-AM is a commercial station owned by iHeartMedia Inc. The format of the station is news and talk. KTSM-AM broadcasts to the El Paso, TX area at 690 AM.
AM RADIO STATION

KTSM-FM 44920
Owner: iHeartMedia Inc.
Editorial: 4045 N Mesa St, El Paso, Texas 79902-1526 Tel: 1 915 351-5400.
Web site: http://www.sunny999fm.com
Profile: KTSM-FM is a commercial station owned by iHeartMedia Inc. The format of the station is Lite Rock/Lite AC music. KTSM-FM broadcasts to the El Paso, TX area at 99.9 FM.
FM RADIO STATION

KTSO-FM 40983
Owner: Stephens Media Group
Editorial: 2448 E 81st St Ste 5500, Tulsa, Oklahoma 74137-4201 Tel: 1 918 492-2660.
Email: studio@941thebreeze.com
Web site: http://941thebreeze.com
Profile: KTSO-FM is a commercial station owned by Stephens Media Group. The format of the station is adult contemporary. KTSO-FM broadcasts to the Tulsa, OK area at a frequency of 94.1 FM. Send all PSAs to kxoj@kxoj.com.
FM RADIO STATION

KTSR-FM 40988
Owner: Townsquare Media, LLC
Editorial: 900 N Lake Shore Dr, Lake Charles, Louisiana 70601-2120 Tel: 1 337 433-1641.
Web site: http://thisstationrocks.com
Profile: KTSR-FM is a commercial station owned by Townsquare Media, LLC. The format of the station is classic rock. KTSR-FM broadcasts to the Lake Charles, LA area at 92.1 FM.
FM RADIO STATION

KTST-FM 39754
Owner: iHeartMedia Inc.
Editorial: 1900 NW Expressway, Oklahoma City, Oklahoma 73118-1802 Tel: 1 405 840-5271.
Web site: http://www.thetwister.com
Profile: KTST-FM is a commercial station owned by iHeartMedia Inc. The format of the station is contemporary country music. KTST-FM broadcasts to the Oklahoma City area at 101.9 FM.
FM RADIO STATION

KTSY-FM 41739
Owner: Idaho Conference of Seven Day Adventists
Editorial: 16115 S Montana Ave, Caldwell, Idaho 83607 Tel: 1 208 459-5879.
Email: family@ktsy.org
Web site: http://www.895ktsy.org
Profile: KTSY-FM is a non-commercial station owned by Idaho Conference of Seventh Day Adventists. The format of the station is contemporary Christian music. KTSY-FM broadcasts to the Boise, ID area at 89.5 FM.
FM RADIO STATION

KTTG-FM 43000
Owner: Pearson Broadcasting
Editorial: 1912 Church St, Barling, Arkansas 72923 Tel: 1 479 484-7285.
Web site: http://www.espnarkansas.com
Profile: KTTG-FM is a commercial station owned by Pearson Broadcasting. The format of the station is sports. KTTG-FM broadcasts to the Fort Smith, AR area at 96.3 FM.
FM RADIO STATION

KTTH-AM 133944
Owner: Bonneville International Corp.
Editorial: 1820 Eastlake Ave E, Seattle, Washington 98102 Tel: 1 206 726-7000.
Email: newsdesk@973kiro.com
Web site: http://www.mynorthwest.com
Profile: KTTH-AM is a commercial station owned by Bonneville International Corp. The format of the station is talk. KTTH-AM broadcasts in the Seattle area at 770 AM.
AM RADIO STATION

KTTI-FM 44921
Owner: El Dorado Broadcasting
Editorial: 755 W 28th St, Yuma, Arizona 85364 Tel: 1 928 344-4980.
Web site: http://www.951ktti.com
Profile: KTTI-FM is a commercial station owned by El Dorado Broadcasting. The format of the station is country music. KTTI-FM broadcasts to the Yuma, AZ area at 95.1 FM.
FM RADIO STATION

United States of America

KTTN-AM 37527
Owner: Par Broadcast Group
Editorial: 804 Main St, Trenton, Missouri 64683-2044
Tel: 1 660 359-2727.
Web site: http://www.kttn.com
Profile: KTTN-AM is a commercial station owned by Par Broadcast Group. The format of the station is Lite Rock/Lite AC. KTTN-AM broadcasts to the Trenton, MO area at 1600 AM.
AM RADIO STATION

KTTN-FM 44922
Owner: Par Broadcast Group
Editorial: 804 Main St, Trenton, Missouri 64683-2044
Tel: 1 660 359-2261.
Web site: http://www.kttn.com/kgozfm
Profile: KTTN-FM is commercial station owned by Par Broadcast Group. The format of the station is classic country. KTTN-FM broadcasts to the Kansas City, MO area at 92.3 FM.
FM RADIO STATION

KTTO-AM 36902
Owner: Sacred Heart Radio
Editorial: 7357 148th Ave NE, Redmond, Washington 98052-4148 **Tel:** 1 425 867-2340.
Email: info@sacredheartradio.org
Web site: http://www.sacredheartradio.org
AM RADIO STATION

KTTR-AM 35097
Owner: Mahaffey Enterprises Inc.
Editorial: 1505 Soest Rd, Rolla, Missouri 65401-3709
Tel: 1 573 364-2525.
Email: kttrkznn@fidmail.com
Web site: http://www.resultsradioonline.com
Profile: KTTR-AM is a commercial station owned by Mahaffey Enterprises Inc. The format of the station is news and talk. KTTR-AM broadcasts to the Rolla, MO area at 1490 AM.
AM RADIO STATION

KTTR-FM 43001
Owner: Mahaffey Enterprises Inc.
Editorial: 1505 Soest Rd, Rolla, Missouri 65401-3709
Tel: 1 573 364-2525.
Email: kznnpsa@yahoo.com
Web site: http://www.resultsradioonline.com
Profile: KTTR-FM is a commercial station owned by Mahaffey Enterprises Inc. The format of the station is news and talk. KTTR-FM broadcasts to the Rolla, MO area at 99.7 FM.
FM RADIO STATION

KTTS-FM 44923
Owner: E.W. Scripps Co.
Editorial: 2330 W Grand St, Springfield, Missouri 65802-4900 **Tel:** 1 417 865-6614.
Email: news@ktts.com
Web site: http://www.ktts.com
Profile: KTTS-FM is a commercial station owned by E.W. Scripps Co. The format of the station is contemporary country music. KTTS-FM broadcasts to the Springfield, MO area at 94.7 FM.
FM RADIO STATION

KTTT-AM 38373
Owner: Alpha Media
Editorial: 1418 25th St, Columbus, Nebraska 68601-2820 **Tel:** 1 402 564-2866.
Web site: http://www.mycentralnebraska.com
Profile: KTTT-AM is a commercial station owned by Alpha Media. The format of the station is classic country. KTTT-AM broadcasts in the Columbus, NE area at 1510 AM.
AM RADIO STATION

KTTU-FM 43314
Owner: Ramar Communications, Inc.
Editorial: 9800 University Ave, Lubbock, Texas 79423-5302 **Tel:** 1 806 745-3434.
Web site: http://www.doublet973.com/
Profile: KTTU-FM is a commercial station owned by Ramar Communications, Inc. The format of the station is sports. KTTU-FM broadcasts to the Lubbock, TX area at a frequency of 97.3 FM.
FM RADIO STATION

KTTX-FM 42852
Owner: Whitehead Inc.(Tom S.)
Editorial: 223 E Main St, Brenham, Texas 77833
Tel: 1 979 776-1061.
Email: news@kwhi.com
Web site: http://www.ktex.com
Profile: KTTX-FM is a commercial station owned by Tom S. Whitehead Inc. The format of the station is country music. KTTX-FM broadcasts to the Houston area at 106.1 FM.
FM RADIO STATION

KTUB-AM 36836
Owner: Adelante Media Group
Editorial: 2722 S Redwood Rd, Salt Lake City, Utah 84119 **Tel:** 1 801 908-8777.
Web site: http://www.adelantemediagroup.com
Profile: KTUB-AM is the ESPN Deportes affiliate in the Salt Lake City, UT market. It is a commercial station owned by Adelante Media Group. The format of the station is Spanish language sports. KTUB-AM broadcasts to the Salt Lake City area at 1600 AM.
AM RADIO STATION

KTUC-AM 39079
Owner: Cumulus Media Inc
Editorial: 575 W Roger Rd, Tucson, Arizona 85705-2616 **Tel:** 1 520 887-1000.
Web site: http://www.ktucam.com
Profile: KTUC-AM is a commercial station owned by Cumulus Media Inc. The format of the station is adult standards music. KTUC-AM broadcasts to the Tucson, AZ area at 1400 AM.
AM RADIO STATION

KTUE-AM 238577
Owner: Bernal(Paulino)
Editorial: 4501 N McColl Rd, McAllen, Texas 78504-2431 **Tel:** 1 956 781-5528.
Web site: http://www.nuevaradiocristiana.com
Profile: KTUE-AM is a non-commercial station owned by Paulino Bernal. The format of the station is Hispanic contemporary Christian. KTUE-AM broadcasts to the McAllen, TX area at 1260 AM.
AM RADIO STATION

KTUF-FM 39964
Owner: KIRX Inc.
Editorial: 1308 N Baltimore St, Kirksville, Missouri 63501-2509 **Tel:** 1 660 665-9828.
Email: radiopark@cableone.net
Web site: http://www.937ktuf.com
Profile: KTUF-FM is a commercial station owned by KIRX Inc. The format of the station is a mix of classic and contemporary country music. KTUF-FM broadcasts to the Kirksville, MO area at 93.7 FM.
FM RADIO STATION

KTUG-FM 966249
Owner: Higher Calling Communications
Editorial: 612 W Main St, Riverton, Wyoming 82501-3311 **Tel:** 1 307 855-4002.
Web site: http://www.1051thepulse.com
Profile: KTUG-FM is a commercial station owned by Higher Calling Communications. The format of the station is Hot AC. The station broadcasts to the Hudson, Wyoming area at a frequency of 105.1 FM.
FM RADIO STATION

KTUI-AM 37529
Owner: Fidelity Broadcasting Inc.
Editorial: 229 Bud St, Sullivan, Missouri 63080-1188
Tel: 1 573 468-5101.
Email: news@ktui.com
Web site: http://www.ktui.com
Profile: KTUI-AM is a commercial station owned by Fidelity Broadcasting Inc. The format of the station is news and talk. KTUI-AM broadcasts to the Sullivan, MO area at 1560 AM.
AM RADIO STATION

KTUI-FM 44924
Owner: Fidelity Broadcasting Inc.
Editorial: 229 Bud St, Sullivan, Missouri 63080-1188
Tel: 1 573 468-5101.
Email: news@ktui.com
Web site: http://www.ktui.com
Profile: KTUI-FM is a commercial station owned by Fidelity Broadcasting Inc. The format of the station is country music and sports. KTUI-FM broadcasts to the Sullivan, MO area at 102.1 FM.
FM RADIO STATION

KTUN-FM 364627
Owner: Wildcat Communications LLC
Editorial: 1201 18Th St Ste 250, Denver, Colorado 80202-1869 **Tel:** 1 970 476-7444.
Profile: KTUN-FM is a commercial station owned by Wildcat Communications LLC. The format for the station is Spanish Hits. KTUN-FM broadcasts to the New Castle, CO area at 94.5 FM.
FM RADIO STATION

KTUT-FM 857227
Owner: Church Planters of America
Tel: 1 877 679-5372.
Email: oldpaths1611@gmail.com
Web site: http://www.oldpathsradio.com
Profile: KTUT-FM is a non-commercial station owned by Church Planters of America. The format of the station is Southern Gospel and Christian teaching. KTUT-FM broadcasts to the Frankfort, SD area at a frequency of 89.5 FM.
FM RADIO STATION

KTUV-AM 36598
Owner: Birach Broadcasting Corp.
Editorial: 8211 Geyer Springs Rd Ste P6, Little Rock, Arkansas 72209-4909 **Tel:** 1 501 562-2661.
Web site: http://ktuvlapantera1440am.com
Profile: KTUV-AM is a commercial station owned by Birach Broadcasting Corp. The format of the station is Hispanic programming. KTUV-AM broadcasts to the Little Rock, AR area at 1440 AM.
AM RADIO STATION

KTUX-FM 39966
Owner: Townsquare Media, LLC
Editorial: 6341 W Port Ave, Shreveport, Louisiana 71129 **Tel:** 1 318 688-1130.
Web site: http://www.therockstation99x.com
Profile: KTUX-FM is a commercial station owned by Townsquare Media, LLC. The format of the station is rock music. KTUX-FM broadcasts to the Shreveport, LA area at 98.9 FM.
FM RADIO STATION

KTUZ-AM 155983
Owner: Tyler Media, LLC
Editorial: 7777 S Lewis Ave, Tulsa, Oklahoma 74171-0003 **Tel:** 1 918 629-1380.
Web site: http://www.ktlr.com
Profile: KTUZ-AM is a commercial station owned by Tyler Media, LLC. The format is religious talk. KTUZ-AM broadcasts to the Tulsa, OK area at 1570 AM.
AM RADIO STATION

KTUZ-FM 43397
Owner: Tyler Media Group Inc.
Editorial: 5101 S Shields Blvd, Oklahoma City, Oklahoma 73129-3217 **Tel:** 1 405 616-5500.
Email: ktuz@tylermedia.com
Web site: http://www.ktuz.com
Profile: KTUZ-FM is a commercial station owned by Tyler Media Group Inc. The format of the station is regional Mexican. KTUZ-FM broadcasts to the Oklahoma City area at 106.7 FM.
FM RADIO STATION

KTWA-FM 44925
Owner: O-Town Communications, Inc.
Editorial: 416 E Main St, Ottumwa, Iowa 52501-3026
Tel: 1 641 684-5563.
Email: info@ottumwaradio.com
Web site: http://www.ottumwaradio.com
Profile: KTWA-FM is a commercial station owned by O-Town Communications, Inc. The format of the station is adult contemporary. KTWA-FM broadcasts to the Ottumwa, IA area at 92.7 FM.
FM RADIO STATION

KTWB-FM 41743
Owner: Backyard Broadcasting
Editorial: 500 S Phillips Ave, Sioux Falls, South Dakota 57104-6825 **Tel:** 1 605 331-5350.
Email: ktwb@ktwb.com
Web site: http://www.ktwb.com
Profile: KTWB-FM is a commercial station owned by Backyard Broadcasting. The format of the station is adult contemporary. KTWB-FM broadcasts in the Sioux Falls, SD area at 101.9 FM.
FM RADIO STATION

KTWO-AM 38959
Owner: Townsquare Media, LLC
Editorial: 150 Nichols Ave, Casper, Wyoming 82601-1816 **Tel:** 1 307 266-5252.
Email: caspernews@gapbroadcasting.com
Web site: http://www.k2radio.com
Profile: KTWO-AM is a commercial station owned by Townsquare Media, LLC. The format of the station is talk. KTWO-AM broadcasts to the Casper, WY area at 1030 AM.
AM RADIO STATION

KTWS-FM 41752
Owner: Combined Communications, Inc.
Editorial: 63088 NE 18th St Ste 200, Bend, Oregon 97701-7102 **Tel:** 1 541 382-5263.
Web site: http://www.thetwins.com
Profile: KTWS-FM is a commercial station owned by Combined Communications, Inc. The format of the station is classic rock. KTWS-FM broadcasts in the Bend, OR area at 98.3 FM.
FM RADIO STATION

KTWV-FM 44051
Owner: CBS Radio
Editorial: 5670 Wilshire Blvd Ste 200, Los Angeles, California 90036-5657 **Tel:** 1 323 937-9283.
Email: wave@ktwv.cbs.com
Web site: http://947thewave.cbslocal.com
Profile: KTWV-FM is a commercial station owned by CBS Radio. The format of the station is smooth AC. KTWV-FM broadcasts to the Los Angeles area at 94.7 FM.
FM RADIO STATION

KTXC-FM 41582
Owner: West Texas Broadcasting, LLC
Editorial: 11320 WCR 127, Midland, Texas 79711
Tel: 1 432 567-9999.
Web site: http://www.laley104fm.com
Profile: KTXC-FM is a commercial station owned by West Texas Broadcasting, LLC. The format for the station is Hispanic programming. KTXC-FM broadcasts to the Midland, TX, area at 104.7 FM.
FM RADIO STATION

KTXG-FM 475982
Owner: American Family Association
Editorial: 2600 State Highway 121, Melissa, Texas 75454 **Tel:** 1 662 844-8888.
Web site: http://www.afr.net
Profile: KTXG-FM is a non-commercial station owned by American Family Association. The format of the station is contemporary Christian. KTXG-FM broadcasts to the Greenville, TX area at 90.5 FM.
FM RADIO STATION

KTXI-FM 44074
Owner: Texas Public Radio
Editorial: 8401 Datapoint Dr, Ste 800, San Antonio, Texas 78229 **Tel:** 1 210 614-8977.
Email: news@tpr.org
Web site: http://www.tpr.org
Profile: KTXI-FM is a non-commercial station owned by Texas Public Radio. The format of the station is classical music, news and talk programming. KTXI-FM broadcasts to the San Antonio area at 90.1 FM.
FM RADIO STATION

KTXJ-FM 44971
Owner: Cross Texas Media Inc.
Editorial: 1408 E Gibson St, Jasper, Texas 75951-6123 **Tel:** 1 409 384-4500.
Email: production@1027ktxj.com
Web site: http://www.1027ktxj.com
Profile: KTXJ-FM is a commercial station owned by Cross Texas Media Inc. The format for the station is southern Gospel. KTXJ-FM broadcasts to the Beaumont-Port Arthur, TX, area at 102.7 FM.
FM RADIO STATION

KTXK-FM 43010
Owner: Texarkana College
Editorial: 2500 N Robison Rd, Texarkana, Texas 75599-0002 **Tel:** 1 903 838-4541 3269.
Web site: http://ktxk.org
Profile: KTXK-FM is a non-commercial station owned by Texarkana College. The format of the station is news/talk and classical. KTXK-FM broadcasts to the Texarkana, TX area at 91.5 FM.
FM RADIO STATION

KTXM-FM 43533
Owner: Kremling Enterprises Inc.
Editorial: 111 Main St, Hallettsville, Texas 77964
Tel: 1 361 798-4333.
Email: texasthunderradio@yahoo.com
Web site: http://www.texasthunderradio.com
Profile: KTXM-FM is a commercial radio station owned by Kremling Enterprises Inc. The format of the station is contemporary country. KTXM-FM broadcasts to the Hallettsville, TX area at 99.9 FM.
FM RADIO STATION

KTXN-FM 43002
Owner: Townsquare Media, LLC
Editorial: 107 N Star Dr, Victoria, Texas 77904-2082
Tel: 1 361 573-0777.
Web site: http://987jack.com
Profile: KTXN-FM is a commercial station owned by Townsquare Media, LLC. The format of the station is adult hits. KTXN-FM broadcasts to the Victoria, TX area at 98.7 FM.
FM RADIO STATION

KTXR-FM 39968
Owner: Meyer Communications
Editorial: 3000 E Chestnut Expy, Springfield, Missouri 65802-2528 **Tel:** 1 417 862-3751.
Web site: http://www.ktxrfm.com
Profile: KTXR-FM is a commercial station owned by Meyer Communications. The format of the station is country. KTXR-FM broadcasts in the Springfield, MO area at 101.3 FM.
FM RADIO STATION

KTXX-FM 79260
Owner: Genuine Austin Radio
Editorial: 912 S Capital of Texas Hwy Ste 400, West Lake Hills, Texas 78746-6176 **Tel:** 1 512 416-1100.
Web site: http://hornfm.com
Profile: KTXX-FM is a commercial station owned by Genuine Austin Radio. The format of the station is sports and classic hits music. KHHL-FM broadcasts to the Austin, TX, area at 104.9 FM.
FM RADIO STATION

KTXY-FM 43669
Owner: Zimmer Radio Group
Editorial: 3215 Lemone Industrial Blvd, Ste 200, Columbia, Missouri 65201 **Tel:** 1 573 875-1099.
Email: y107@zrgmail.com
Web site: http://www.y107.com
Profile: KTXY-FM is a commercial station owned by the Zimmer Radio Group. The format of the station is Top 40/CHR music. KTXY-FM broadcasts to the Jefferson City, MO area at 106.9 FM.
FM RADIO STATION

KTXZ-AM 35098
Owner: Encino Broadcasting, LLC
Editorial: 9434 Parkfield Dr, Austin, Texas 78758-6227 **Tel:** 1 512 453-1491.
Email: spots@austintejas.com
Profile: KTXZ-AM is a commercial station owned by Encino Broadcasting, LLC. The format of the station is Hispanic music. KTXZ-AM broadcasts to the Austin, TX area at 1560 AM.
AM RADIO STATION

KTYD-FM 46617
Owner: Rincon Broadcasting
Editorial: 414 E Cota St, Santa Barbara, California 93101 **Tel:** 1 805 879-8300.
Web site: http://www.ktyd.com
Profile: KTYD-FM is a commercial station owned by Rincon Broadcasting. The format of the station is classic rock. KTYD-FM broadcasts to the Santa Barbara, CA area 99.9 FM.
FM RADIO STATION

KTYL-FM 42742
Owner: Townsquare Media, LLC
Editorial: 3810 Brookside Dr, Tyler, Texas 75701-9420 **Tel:** 1 903 581-0606.
Web site: http://www.mix931fm.com
Profile: KTYL-FM is a commercial station owned by Townsquare Media, LLC. The format of the station is hot adult contemporary. KTYL-FM broadcasts to the Tyler, TX area at 93.1 FM.
FM RADIO STATION

KTYM-AM 35099
Owner: Immaculate Heart Radio
Tel: 1 916 535-0500.
Email: programming@ihradio.com
Web site: http://ihradio.com
Profile: KTYM-AM is a non-commercial station owned by Immaculate Heart Radio. The format of the station is Catholic talk radio. KTYM-AM broadcasts to the Inglewood, CA area at 1460 AM.
AM RADIO STATION

KTZA-FM 46530
Owner: Pecos Valley Broadcasting Company
Editorial: 317 W Quay Ave, Artesia, New Mexico 88210-2158 **Tel:** 1 575 746-2751.
Web site: http://www.pecosvalleybroadcasting.com

Profile: KTZA-FM is a commercial station owned by Pecos Valley Broadcasting Company. The format of the station is country music. KTZA-FM broadcasts to the Albuquerque, NM area at 92.9 FM.
FM RADIO STATION

KTZN-AM 37254
Owner: iHeartMedia Inc.
Editorial: 800 E Dimond Blvd Ste 3-370, Anchorage, Alaska 99515-2058 **Tel:** 1 907 522-1515.
Web site: http://550thezone.iheart.com
Profile: KTZN-AM is a commercial station owned by iHeartMedia Inc. The format of the station is sports. KTZN-AM broadcasts to the Anchorage, AK area at 550 AM.
AM RADIO STATION

KTZR-AM 36076
Owner: iHeartMedia Inc.
Editorial: 3202 N Oracle Rd, Tucson, Arizona 85705-3820 **Tel:** 1 520 618-2100.
Web site: http://foxsports1450.iheart.com
Profile: KTZR-AM is a commercial station owned by iHeartMedia Inc. The format of the station is sports. KTZR-AM broadcasts to the Tucson, AZ area at 1450 AM.
AM RADIO STATION

KTZZ-FM 46827
Owner: Munson Radio Inc.
Editorial: 3313 15th St #F, Black Eagle, Montana 59414-1090 **Tel:** 1 406 761-1310.
Profile: KTZZ-FM is a commercial station owned by Munson Radio Inc. The format of the station is classic rock music. KTZZ-FM broadcasts in the Great Falls, MT area at 93.7 FM.
FM RADIO STATION

KUAD-FM 39972
Owner: Townsquare Media, LLC
Editorial: 600 Main St, Windsor, Colorado 80550
Tel: 1 970 674-2700.
Web site: http://www.k99.com
Profile: KUAD-FM is a commercial station owned by Townsquare Media, LLC. The format of the station is country. KUAD-FM broadcasts to the Windsor, CO area at 99.1 FM.
FM RADIO STATION

KUAL-FM 41953
Owner: Hubbard Broadcasting Inc.
Editorial: 13225 Dogwood Dr, Baxter, Minnesota 56425-8669 **Tel:** 1 218 828-1244.
Email: cooloIdies@cool1035.com
Web site: http://www.cool1035.com
Profile: KUAL-FM is a commercial station owned by Hubbard Broadcasting Inc. The format of the station is oldies. KUAL-FM broadcasts to the Brainerd, MN area at 103.5 FM.
FM RADIO STATION

KUBA-AM 37533
Owner: Results Radio Group
Editorial: 1479 Sanborn Rd, Yuba City, California 95993-6042 **Tel:** 1 530 673-1600.
Email: office@kubaradio.com
Web site: http://www.kubaradio.com
Profile: KUBA-AM is a commercial station owned by Results Radio Group. The format of the station is classic hits and news. KUBA-AM broadcasts to the Sacramento, CA area at 1600 AM.
AM RADIO STATION

KUBB-FM 39974
Owner: Alpha Media
Editorial: 510 W 19th St, Merced, California 95340-4705 **Tel:** 1 209 383-7900.
Email: KUBBemail@aol.com
Web site: http://www.kubb.com
Profile: KUBB-FM is a commercial station owned by Alpha Media. The format of the station is contemporary country. KUBB-FM broadcasts to the Merced, CA area at 96.3 FM.
FM RADIO STATION

KUBC-AM 37534
Owner: Cherry Creek Radio
Editorial: 106 Rose Ln, Montrose, Colorado 81401-3823 **Tel:** 1 970 249-4546.
Email: kubc@cherrycreekmedia.com
Web site: http://580kubc.com
Profile: KUBC-AM is a commercial station owned by Cherry Creek Radio. The format of the station is news and talk. KUBC-AM's broadcasts in the Montrose, CO area at 580 AM. The station's slogan is, "The Voice of the Valley."
AM RADIO STATION

KUBE-FM 43110
Owner: iHeartMedia Inc.
Editorial: 645 Elliott Ave W Ste 400, Seattle, Washington 98119-3911 **Tel:** 1 206 494-2000.
Web site: http://www.kube1049.com
Profile: KUBE-FM is a commercial station owned by iHeartMedia Inc. The format of the station is Rhythmic CHR. KUBE-FM broadcasts to the Seattle area at 104.9 FM.
FM RADIO STATION

KUBL-FM 44235
Owner: Cumulus Media Inc
Editorial: 434 W Bearcat Dr, Salt Lake City, Utah 84115-2520 **Tel:** 1 801 485-6700.
Web site: http://www.kbull93.com
Profile: KUBL-FM is a commercial station owned by Cumulus Media Inc. The format of the station is contemporary country. KUBL-FM broadcasts to the Salt Lake City area at 93.3 FM.
FM RADIO STATION

KUBO-FM 41950
Owner: Radio Bilingue Inc.
Editorial: 531 Main St #2, El Centro, California 92243
Tel: 1 760 331-8874.
Web site: http://www.radiobilingue.org
Profile: KUBO-FM is a non-commercial station owned by Radio Bilingue Inc. The format of the station is Hispanic talk. KUBO-FM broadcasts to the El Centro, CA area at 88.7 FM.
FM RADIO STATION

KUBQ-FM 45729
Owner: Pacific Empire Communications
Editorial: 2510 Cove Ave, La Grande, Oregon 97850
Tel: 1 541 963-4121.
Email: q98@eoni.com
Web site: http://www.987kubq.com
Profile: KUBQ-FM is a commercial station owned by the Pacific Empire Communications. The format of the station is classic rock music. KUBQ-FM broadcasts to La Grande, OR, at 98.7 FM.
FM RADIO STATION

KUBR-AM 38942
Owner: Bernal(Paulino)
Editorial: 4501 N McColl Rd, McAllen, Texas 78504-2431 **Tel:** 1 956 781-5528.
Profile: KUBR-AM is a non-commercial station owned by Paulino Bernal. The format of the station is Hispanic contemporary Christian. KUBR-AM broadcasts to the McAllen, TX area at 1210 AM.
AM RADIO STATION

KUCB-FM 554722
Owner: Unalaska Community Broadcasting
Editorial: 5th & Broadway, Unalaska, Alaska 99685
Tel: 1 907 581-1888.
Email: info@kucb.org
Web site: http://www.kucb.org
Profile: KUCB-FM is a non-commercial station owned by Unalaska Community Broadcasting. The format of the station is variety. KUCB-FM broadcasts to the Unalaska, AK area at 89.7 FM.
FM RADIO STATION

KUCC-FM 762602
Owner: Upper Columbia Media Association
Tel: 1 509 242-0510.
Profile: KUCC-FM is a non-commercial station owned by Upper Columbia Media Association. The format of the station is religious. KUCC-FM airs locally to the Clarkston, WA area at 88.1 FM
FM RADIO STATION

KUCD-FM 42925
Owner: iHeartMedia Inc.
Editorial: 650 Iwilei Rd Ste 400, Honolulu, Hawaii 96817-5319 **Tel:** 1 808 550-9200.
Web site: http://www.star1019.com
Profile: KUCD-FM is a commercial station owned by iHeartMedia Inc. The format of the station is rock alternative. KUCD-FM broadcasts to the Honolulu area at 101.9 FM.
FM RADIO STATION

KUDD-FM 44778
Owner: Broadway Media
Editorial: 50 W Broadway Ste 200, Salt Lake City, Utah 84101-2024 **Tel:** 1 801 524-2600.
Profile: KUDD-FM is a commercial station is owned by Broadway Media. The format of the station is top 40/CHR. KUDD-FM broadcasts to the Salt Lake City area at 105.1 FM.
FM RADIO STATION

KUDL-FM 40031
Owner: Entercom Communications Corp.
Editorial: 5345 Madison Ave, Sacramento, California 95841-3141 **Tel:** 1 916 334-7777.
Web site: http://www.star1065.com
Profile: KUDL-FM is a commercial station owned by Entercom Communications Corp. The format of the station is Hot AC. KUDL-FM broadcasts to the Sacramento, CA area at 106.5 FM.
FM RADIO STATION

KUDU-FM 44301
Owner: Lifetalk Radio Inc.
Editorial: 1318 Ak Hwy,, Tok, Alaska 99780
Tel: 1 907 883-8343.
Web site: http://www.lifetalk.net
FM RADIO STATION

KUEZ-FM 839137
Owner: Bighorn Media
Editorial: 510 E Plumb Ln, Reno, Nevada 89502-3565
Tel: 1 737 737-4350.
Email: jdb.kuez@gmail.com
Web site: http://www.easy1041.com
Profile: KUEZ-FM is a commercial station owned by Bighorn Media. The format of the station is soft oldies music. KUEZ-FM broadcasts locally to the Reno, NV area at a frequency of 104.1 FM.
FM RADIO STATION

KUFO-AM 36649
Owner: Alpha Media
Editorial: 1211 SW 5th Ave Ste 600, Portland, Oregon 97204-3706 **Tel:** 1 503 517-6400.
Email: news@kxl.com
Web site: http://freedom970.com
Profile: KUFO-AM is a commercial station owned by Alpha Media. The format of the station is conservative talk. KUFO-AM broadcasts to the Portland, OR area at 970 AM.
AM RADIO STATION

KUFW-FM 231019
Owner: National Farm Workers Service Center
Editorial: 400 W Caldwell Ave Ste C, Visalia, California 93277-7864 **Tel:** 1 559 622-9401.
Web site: http://www.campesina.net
Profile: KUFW-FM is a commercial station owned by National Farm Workers Service Center. The format of the station is regional Mexican music. KUFW-FM broadcasts to the Visalia, CA area at 90.5 FM.
FM RADIO STATION

KUFX-FM 44008
Owner: Entercom
Editorial: San Jose, California **Tel:** 1 415 777-0965.
Web site: http://www.kfox.com
Profile: KUFX-FM is a commercial station owned by Entercom. The format of the station is classic rock. KUFX-FM broadcasts to the San Jose, CA area at 98.5 FM.
FM RADIO STATION

KUGN-AM 37535
Owner: Cumulus Media Inc.
Editorial: 1200 Executive Pkwy Ste 440, Eugene, Oregon 97401-2169 **Tel:** 1 541 284-8500.
Email: news@kugn.com
Web site: http://www.kugn.com
Profile: KUGN-AM is a commercial station owned by Cumulus Media Inc. The format of the station is news and talk. KUGN-AM broadcasts in the Eugene, OR area at 590 AM.
AM RADIO STATION

KUGR-AM 39033
Owner: Wagonwheel Communications Corp.
Editorial: 40 Shoshone Ave, Green River, Wyoming 82935-5321 **Tel:** 1 307 875-6666.
Email: audio@theradionetwork.net
Web site: http://www.theradionetwork.net
Profile: KUGR-AM is a commercial station owned by Wagonwheel Communications Corp. The format of the station is adult contemporary music. KUGR-AM broadcasts to the Green River, WY area at 1490 AM.
AM RADIO STATION

KUHC-FM 705393
Owner: Kingdom Keys Radio
Editorial: 116 Hillcrest Dr, Seminole, Oklahoma 74868-5810 **Tel:** 1 405 380-3516.
Email: kjrt@kingdomkeys.org
Web site: http://kingdomkeysradio.org
Profile: KUHC-FM is a non-commercial station owned by Kingdom Keys Radio. The format of the station is gospel. KUHC-FM broadcasts to the Clayton, NM area and airs locally at 90.5 FM.
FM RADIO STATION

KUHL-AM 36529
Owner: Knight Broadcasting Inc.
Editorial: 1101 S Broadway Ste C, Santa Maria, California 93454-6660 **Tel:** 1 805 922-7727.
Email: 1440@knightbroadcasting.com
Web site: http://www.am1440.com
Profile: KUHL-AM is a commercial station owned by Knight Broadcasting, Inc. The format of the station is news and talk. KUHL-AM broadcasts to the Santa Maria, CA area at 1410 AM.
AM RADIO STATION

KUIC-FM 43650
Owner: Alpha Media
Editorial: 555 Mason St Ste 245, Vacaville, California 95688-4640 **Tel:** 1 707 446-0200.
Email: news@kuic.com
Web site: http://www.kuic.com
Profile: KUIC-FM is a commercial station owned by Alpha Media. The format of the station is adult contemporary. KUIC-FM broadcasts to the Vacaville, CA area at 95.3 FM.
FM RADIO STATION

KUIK-AM 35101
Owner: Dolphin Communications, Inc.
Editorial: 3355 NE Cornell Rd, Hillsboro, Oregon 97124-5018 **Tel:** 1 503 640-1360.
Email: amradio@kuik.com
Web site: http://www.kuik.com
Profile: KUIK-AM is a commercial station owned by Westside Radio Inc. The format of the station i sTalk. KUIK-AM broadcasts in the Portland, OR area at 1360 AM.
AM RADIO STATION

KUJ-AM 36888
Owner: Alexandra Communications Inc.
Editorial: 45 S Campbell Rd, Walla Walla, Washington 99362-9597 **Tel:** 1 509 527-1000.
Web site: http://www.kujam.com
Profile: KUJ-AM is a commercial station owned by Alexandra Communications Inc. The format of the station is news/talk and sports programming. KUJ-AM broadcasts to the Walla Walla, WA area at 1420 AM.
AM RADIO STATION

KUJ-FM 43989
Owner: Ingstad Radio Washington, LLC
Editorial: 4304 W 24th Ave Ste 200, Kennewick, Washington 99338-2320 **Tel:** 1 509 783-0783.
Web site: http://www.power991fm.com
Profile: KUJ-FM is a commercial station owned by Ingstad Radio Washington, LLC. The format of the station is Top 40/CHR. KUJ-FM broadcasts to the Kennewick, WA area at 99.1 FM.
FM RADIO STATION

KUJZ-FM 44928
Owner: Cumulus Media Inc.
Editorial: 1200 Executive Pkwy Ste 440, Eugene, Oregon 97401-2169 **Tel:** 1 541 284-8500.
Web site: http://www.953thescore.com
Profile: KUJZ-FM is a commercial station owned by Cumulus Media Inc. The format of the station is sports and talk. KUJZ-FM broadcasts to the Eugene, OR area at 95.3 FM.
FM RADIO STATION

KUKA-FM 42519
Owner: Benavides (Jerry)
Editorial: 2722 N Business Highway 281, Alice, Texas 78332 **Tel:** 1 361 668-6666.
Web site: http://www.kukafm.com
Profile: KUKA-FM is a commercial station owned by Jerry Benavides. The format of the station is Hispanic. KUKA-FM broadcasts to the Alice, TX area at 105.9 FM.
FM RADIO STATION

KUKI-AM 37536
Owner: Bicoastal Media LLC
Editorial: 140 N Main St, Lakeport, California 95453-4815 **Tel:** 1 707 263-6113.
Email: kukinews@bicoastalmedia.com
Web site: http://www.lamaquinamusical.net
Profile: KUKI-AM is a commercial station owned by Bicoastal Media LLC. The format of the station is Spanish news and talk. KUKI-AM broadcasts to the Ukiah, CA area at 1400 AM.
AM RADIO STATION

KUKI-FM 45707
Owner: Bicoastal Media LLC
Editorial: 140 N Main St, Lakeport, California 95453-4815 **Tel:** 1 707 263-6113.
Email: kukinews@bicoastalmedia.com
Web site: http://kuki-fm.tritondigitalmedia.com/index.php
Profile: KUKI-FM is a commercial station owned by Bicoastal Media LLC. The format of the station is country music. KUKI-FM broadcasts in the San Francisco area at 103.3 FM.
FM RADIO STATION

KUKN-FM 46296
Owner: Washington Interstate Broadcasting Inc
Editorial: 506 W Cowlitz Way, Kelso, Washington 98626-1177 **Tel:** 1 360 636-0110.
Web site: http://www.kukn.com
Profile: KUKN-FM is a commercial station owned by Washington Interstate Broadcasting Inc. The format of the station is contemporary country. KUKN-FM broadcasts to the Kelso, WA area at 105.5 FM.
FM RADIO STATION

KUKU-FM 46460
Owner: Ozark Radio Network Inc.
Editorial: 983 E US Highway 160, West Plains, Missouri 65775-4801 **Tel:** 1 417 256-1025.
Email: news@ozarkradionetwork.com
Web site: http://www.ozarkareanetwork.com.com
Profile: KUKU-FM is commercial station owned by Ozark Radio Network Inc. The format of the station is classic country. KUKU-FM broadcasts to the Mountain View, MO area at 99.3 FM.
FM RADIO STATION

KULH-FM 44397
Owner: Resources Management Unlimited Inc.
Editorial: 802 Calhoun St, Chillicothe, Missouri 64601-2205 **Tel:** 1 660 646-2255.
Email: 1059thewave@sbcglobal.net
Web site: http://www.1059thewave.com
Profile: KULH-FM is a commercial station owned by Resources Management Unlimited Inc. The format of the station is contemporary Christian. KULH-FM broadcasts to the Chillicothe, MO area at 105.9 FM.
FM RADIO STATION

KULL-FM 43758
Owner: Townsquare Media, LLC
Editorial: 3911 S 1st St, Abilene, Texas 79605-1639
Tel: 1 325 676-7711.
Web site: http://www.trueoldiesabilene.com
Profile: KULL-FM is a commercial station owned by Townsquare Media, LLC. The format of the station is classic hits. KFGL-FM broadcasts to the Abilene, TX area at 100.7 FM.
FM RADIO STATION

KULM-FM 41889
Owner: La Grange Broadcasting
Editorial: 325 Radio Ln, Columbus, Texas 78934
Tel: 1 979 732-5766.
Email: kulmradio@yahoo.com
Web site: http://www.kulmradio.com
Profile: KULM-FM is a commercial station owned by La Grange Broadcasting. The format of the station is contemporary country music. KULM-FM broadcasts to the Columbus, TX area at 98.3 FM.
FM RADIO STATION

KULO-FM 39788
Owner: Hubbard Broadcasting Inc.
Editorial: 604 3rd Ave W, Alexandria, Minnesota 56308-2669 **Tel:** 1 320 762-2154.
Email: email@cool943.com
Web site: http://www.cool943.com
Profile: KULO-FM is a commercial station owned by Hubbard Broadcasting Inc. The format of the station

is oldies. KULO-FM broadcasts to the Alexandria, MN area at 94.3 FM.
FM RADIO STATION

KULP-AM 36009
Owner: Wharton County Radio Inc.
Editorial: 515 E Jackson St, El Campo, Texas 77437-4537 **Tel:** 1 979 543-3303.
Email: news@kulpradio.com
Web site: http://www.kulpradio.com
Profile: KULP-AM is a commercial station owned by Wharton County Radio Inc. The format of the station is classic country. KULP-AM broadcasts to the El Campo, TX area at 1390 AM.
AM RADIO STATION

KULY-AM 38848
Owner: Armada Media Corp.
Editorial: 112 S Main St, Ulysses, Kansas 67880-2518 **Tel:** 1 620 356-1420.
Profile: KULY-AM is a commercial station owned by Armada Media Corp. The format of the station is country music. KULY-AM broadcasts to the Ulysses, KS area at 1420 AM.
AM RADIO STATION

KUMA-AM 37537
Owner: Capps Broadcast Group
Editorial: 2003 NW 56th St, Pendleton, Oregon 97801-4593 **Tel:** 1 541 276-1511.
Email: contact@cappsbroadcastgroup.com
Web site: http://www.mycolumbiabasin.com/
Profile: KUMA-AM is a commercial station owned by Capps Broadcast Group. The format of the station is news and talk. KUMA-AM broadcasts to the Pendleton, OR area at 1290 AM.
AM RADIO STATION

KUMA-FM 492728
Owner: Capps Broadcast Group
Editorial: 2003 NW 56th St, Pendleton, Oregon 97801-4593 **Tel:** 1 541 276-1511.
Web site: http://www.921kuma.com
Profile: KUMA-FM is a commercial station owned by Capps Broadcast Group. The format of the station is adult contemporary. KUMA-FM airs in the Pendleton, OR area at 92.1 FM.
FM RADIO STATION

KUMD-FM 41013
Owner: Regents of the Univ. of MN-Duluth
Editorial: 130 Humanities, 1201 Ordean Ct, Duluth, Minnesota 55812 **Tel:** 1 218 726-7181.
Email: kumd@kumd.org
Web site: http://www.kumd.org
Profile: KUMD-FM is a non-commercial station owned by Regents of the Univ. of MN-Duluth. The format of the station is primarily AAA, but also features a variety of other genres including jazz and blues. KUMD-FM broadcasts to the Duluth, MN area at 103.3 FM.
FM RADIO STATION

KUMR-FM 883761
Owner: Mid Missouri Media, Inc.
Editorial: 1051 Kingshighway St Ste 6, Rolla, Missouri 65401-2981 **Tel:** 1 573 308-1045.
Email: info@mysunny1045.com
Web site: http://www.mysunny1045.com
Profile: KUMR-FM is a commercial station owned by Mid Missouri Media, Inc. The format of the station is Lite AC. KUMR-FM broadcasts to the Rolla, MO area at a frequency of 104.5 FM.
FM RADIO STATION

KUMU-FM 44931
Owner: Ohana Broadcast Company LLC
Editorial: 1000 Bishop St Ste 200, Honolulu, Hawaii 96813-4203 **Tel:** 1 808 947-1500.
Web site: http://www.kumu.com
Profile: KUMU-FM is a commercial station owned by Ohana Broadcast Company LLC. The format of the station is urban adult contemporary. KUMU-FM broadcsts to the Honolulu area at 94.7 FM.
FM RADIO STATION

KUMX-FM 664322
Owner: West Central Broadcasting Co Inc.
Editorial: 168 Kvvp Dr, Leesville, Louisiana 71446-5817 **Tel:** 1 337 537-9000.
Email: reporter@kvvp.com
Web site: http://www.westcentralsbest.com/mix_1067/
Profile: KUMX-FM is a commercial station owned by West Central Broadcasting Co Inc. The format of the station is adult contemporary. KUMX-FM broadcasts to the North Fort Polk, LA area at 106.7 FM.
FM RADIO STATION

KUNA-FM 46166
Owner: Gulf-California Broadcast Co.
Editorial: 42650 Melanie Pl, Palm Desert, California 92211-5170 **Tel:** 1 760 568-6830.
Profile: KUNA-FM is a commercial station owned by Gulf-California Broadcast Co. The format of the station is Regional Mexican. KUNA-FM broadcasts to the Palm Desert, CA area at 96.7 FM.
FM RADIO STATION

KUNC-FM 39984
Owner: Community Radio for Northern Colorado
Editorial: 1901 56th Ave Ste 200, Greeley, Colorado 80634-2950 **Tel:** 1 970 378-2579.
Email: news@kunc.org
Web site: http://www.kunc.org
Profile: KUNC-FM is a non-commercial station owned by Community Radio for Northern Colorado. The format of the station is News/Talk. KUNC-FM broadcasts to the Greeley, CO are at 91.5 FM.
FM RADIO STATION

KUND-FM 44656
Owner: Prairie Public Broadcasting Inc.
Editorial: 1814 N 15th St, Bismarck, North Dakota 58501-2025 **Tel:** 1 701 224-1700.
Email: info@prairiepublic.org
Web site: http://www.prairiepublic.org
Profile: KUND-FM is a non-commercial station owned by Prairie Public Broadcasting Inc. The format of the station is classical and news. KUND-FM broadcasts to the Bismarck, ND area at 89.3 FM.
FM RADIO STATION

KUNK-FM 46168
Owner: Hooten Broadcasting Company, LLC
Editorial: 101 Boatyard Dr Ste E, Fort Bragg, California 95437-5700 **Tel:** 1 707 964-5307.
Email: traffic@theskunkfm.com
Web site: http://www.theskunkfm.com
Profile: KUNK-FM is a commercial station owned by Hooten Broadcasting Company, LLC. The format of the station is adult contemporary. KUNK-FM broadcasts to the Fort Bragg, CA area at 92.7 FM.
FM RADIO STATION

KUNO-AM 38825
Owner: iHeartMedia Inc.
Editorial: 501 Tupper Ln, Corpus Christi, Texas 78417-9736 **Tel:** 1 361 289-0111.
Web site: http://1400kuno.iheart.com
Profile: KUNO-AM is a commercial station owned by iHeartMedia Inc. The format of the station is Hispanic oldies. KUNO-AM broadcasts to the Corpus Christi, TX area at 1400 AM.
AM RADIO STATION

KUNQ-FM 43372
Owner: Media Professionals, Inc.
Editorial: 17647 Highway B, Houston, Missouri 65483-2818 **Tel:** 1 417 967-3353.
Email: traffic@bigcountry99.com
Web site: http://bigcountry99.com
Profile: KUNQ-FM is a commercial station owned by Media Professionals, Inc. The format of the station is new country and classic rock. KUNQ-FM broadcasts to the Houston, MO area at 99.3 FM.
FM RADIO STATION

KUOA-AM 35102
Owner: Hog Radio, Inc.
Editorial: 2250 W Sunset Ave, Springdale, Arkansas 72762-5148 **Tel:** 1 479 303-2034.
Email: thehog@hogsportsradio.com
Web site: http://hogsportsradio.com
Profile: KUOA-AM is a commercial station owned by Hog Radio, Inc. The format of the station is sports. KUOA-AM broadcasts to the Springdale, AR area at 1290 AM.
AM RADIO STATION

KUOL-AM 36506
Owner: Bernal(Paulino)
Editorial: 4501 N McColl Rd, McAllen, Texas 78504-2431 **Tel:** 1 956 781-5528.
Web site: http://www.nuevaradiocristiana.com
Profile: KUOL-AM is a commercial station owned by Paulino Bernal. The format of the station is Hispanic contemporary Christian music. KUOL-AM broadcasts to the McAllen, TX area at 1470 AM.
AM RADIO STATION

KUOO-FM 39989
Owner: Community First Broadcasting
Editorial: Highway 9 West, Spirit Lake, Iowa 51360 **Tel:** 1 712 336-5800.
Email: news@exploreokoboji.com
Web site: http://www.kuooradio.com
Profile: KUOO-FM is a commercial station owned by Community First Broadcasting. The format of the station is adult contemporary music. KUOO-FM broadcasts to the Spirit Lake, IA area at 103.9 FM.
FM RADIO STATION

KUOP-FM 39990
Owner: Capital Public Radio
Editorial: 7055 Folsom Blvd, Sacramento, California 95826-2625 **Tel:** 1 916 278-8900.
Email: news@capradio.org
Web site: http://www.capradio.org
Profile: KUOP-FM is a non-commercial station owned by Capital Public Radio. The format of the station is jazz, news and talk. KUOP-FM broadcasts to the Stockton, CA area at 91.3 FM.
FM RADIO STATION

KUPD-FM 46001
Owner: Hubbard Radio, LLC
Editorial: 1900 W Carmen St, Guadalupe, Arizona 85283-2559 **Tel:** 1 480 838-0400.
Web site: http://www.98kupd.com
Profile: KUPD-FM is a commercial station owned by Hubbard Radio, LLC. The format of the station is rock/album-oriented rock music. KUPD-FM broadcasts to the Phoenix area at 97.9 FM.
FM RADIO STATION

KUPH-FM 43997
Owner: Central Ozark Radio Network Inc.
Editorial: 6962 US Highway 60, Mountain View, Missouri 65548-8198 **Tel:** 1 417 934-0969.
Email: news@ozarkradionetwork.com
Web site: http://www.thefox969radio.com/index.html
Profile: KUPH-FM is a commercial station owned by Central Ozark Radio Network Inc. The format of the station is hot adult contemporary. KUPH-FM broadcasts to the Mountain View, MO area at 96.9 FM.
FM RADIO STATION

KUPI-FM 39522
Owner: Sand Hill Media
Editorial: 854 Lindsay Blvd, Idaho Falls, Idaho 83402 **Tel:** 1 208 522-1101.
Web site: http://www.kupi99.com
Profile: KUPI-FM is a commercial station owned by Sand Hill Media. The format of the station is contemporary country. KUPI-FM broadcasts to the Rexburg, ID area at 99.1 FM.
FM RADIO STATION

KUPL-FM 43416
Owner: Alpha Media
Editorial: 1211 SW 5th Ave Fl 6, Portland, Oregon 97204-3735 **Tel:** 1 503 517-6000.
Web site: http://www.987thebull.com
Profile: KUPL-FM is a commercial station owned by Alpha Media. The format of the station is contemporary country music. KUPL-FM broadcasts in the Portland, OR area at 98.7 FM.
FM RADIO STATION

KUQL-FM 44117
Owner: Saga Communications
Editorial: 501 S Ohlman St, Mitchell, South Dakota 57301-3162 **Tel:** 1 605 996-9667.
Email: kmit@kmit.com
Web site: http://www.kool98.com
Profile: KUQL-FM is a commercial station owned by Saga Communications. The format of the station is oldies. KUQL-FM broadcasts to the Mitchell, SD area at 98.3 FM.
FM RADIO STATION

KUQQ-FM 43061
Owner: Community First Broadcasting
Editorial: Highway 9 West, Spirit Lake, Iowa 51360 **Tel:** 1 712 336-5800.
Email: news@exploreokoboji.com
Web site: http://www.kuqqfm.com
Profile: KUQQ-FM is a commercial station owned by Community First Broadcasting. The format of the station is classic rock music. KUQQ-FM broadcasts to the Spirit Lake, IA area at 102.1 FM.
FM RADIO STATION

KURB-FM 394668
Owner: Cumulus Media Inc
Editorial: 700 Wellington Hills Rd, Little Rock, Arkansas 72211-2026 **Tel:** 1 501 401-0200.
Web site: http://www.b98.com
Profile: KURB-FM is a commercial station owned by Cumulus Media Inc. The format of the station is hot adult contemporary. KURB-FM broadcasts to the Little Rock, AR area at 98.5 FM.
FM RADIO STATION

KURL-FM 35103
Owner: Elenbaas Media Inc.
Editorial: 636 Haugen St, Billings, Montana 59101 **Tel:** 1 406 245-3121.
Email: news@kurlradio.com
Web site: http://www.kurlradio.com
Profile: KURL-FM is a commercial station owned by Elenbaas Media Inc. The format of the station is religious. KURL-FM broadcasts to the Billings, MT area at 93.3 FM.
FM RADIO STATION

KURM-AM 35104
Owner: KERM Inc.
Editorial: 113 E New Hope Rd, Rogers, Arkansas 72758 **Tel:** 1 479 633-0790.
Email: news@kurm.net
Web site: http://www.kurm.net
Profile: KURM-AM is a commercial station owned by KERM Inc. The format of the station is news and talk. KURM-AM broadcasts to the Rogers, AR area at 790 AM.
AM RADIO STATION

KURM-FM 46521
Owner: KERM Inc.
Editorial: 113 E New Hope Rd, Rogers, Arkansas 72758-6058 **Tel:** 1 479 633-0790.
Email: news@kurm.net
Web site: http://www.kurm.net
Profile: KURM-FM is a commercial station owned by KERM Inc. The format of the station is news and talk. KURM-FM broadcasts to the Rogers, AR area at 100.3 FM.
FM RADIO STATION

KURQ-FM 39830
Owner: El Dorado Broadcasting
Editorial: 51 Zaca Ln Ste 100, San Luis Obispo, California 93401-7353
Web site: http://www.newrock1073.com
Profile: KURQ-FM is a commercial station owned by El Dorado Broadcasting. The format of the station is rock/album-oriented rock. KURQ-FM broadcasts to the San Luis Obispo, CA area at 107.3 FM.
FM RADIO STATION

KURR-FM 510666
Owner: Simmons Media Group
Editorial: 216 W St George Blvd Ste 101, Saint George, Utah 84770-1306 **Tel:** 1 435 6282948.
Email: mail@demolink.org
Web site: http://www.mix1031utah.com
Profile: KURR-FM is a commercial station owned by Simmons Media Group. The format of the station is adult hits. KURR-FM broadcasts to the St. George, UT area at 103.1 FM.
FM RADIO STATION

KURS-AM 36267
Owner: Quetzal Bilingual Communications
Editorial: 20720 Marilla St, Chatsworth, California 91311-4407 **Tel:** 1 877 823-0033.
Email: esneradio.com@gmail.com
Web site: http://www.esneradio.com
Profile: KURS-AM is a commercial station owned by Quetzal Bilingual Communications. The format of the station is Spanish language Catholic programming. KURS-AM broadcasts to the San Diego area at 1040 AM.
AM RADIO STATION

KURV-AM 35105
Owner: R Communications
Editorial: 1201 N Jackson Rd Ste 900, McAllen, Texas 78501-5764 **Tel:** 1 956 992-8895.
Email: news@kurv.com
Web site: http://www.kurv.com
Profile: KURV-AM is a commercial station owned by R Communications. The format of the station is news and talk. KURV-AM broadcasts to the Edinburg, TX area at 710 AM.
AM RADIO STATION

KURY-AM 37539
Owner: Eureka Broadcasting Co., Inc.
Editorial: 605 Railroad St, Brookings, Oregon 97415 **Tel:** 1 541 469-2111.
Email: kury@kuryradio.com
Web site: http://kury910.com
Profile: KURY-AM is a commercial station owned by Eureka Broadcasting Co., Inc.The format of the station is adult standards. KURY-AM broadcasts to the Brookings, OR area at 910 AM.
AM RADIO STATION

KURY-FM 44934
Owner: Eureka Broadcasting Inc.
Editorial: 605 Railroad St, Brookings, Oregon 97415 **Tel:** 1 541 469-2111.
Web site: http://kury953.com
Profile: KURY-FM is a commercial station owned by Eureka Broadcasting Co., Inc. The format of the station is classic hits. KURY-FM broadcasts to the Brookings, OR area at a frequency of 95.3 FM.
FM RADIO STATION

KUSA-FM 44830
Owner: AJB Holdings, LLC
Editorial: 6 E Main St, Price, Utah 84501-3032 **Tel:** 1 435 637-1080.
Email: kusabuzz@gmail.com
Web site: http://utahsclassicradio.com
Profile: KUSA-FM is a commercial station owned by AJB Holdings, LLC. The format of the station is modern adult contemporary. KWSA-FM broadcasts to the Price, UT area at 100.1 FM.
FM RADIO STATION

KUSB-FM 434457
Owner: Townsquare Media, Inc.
Editorial: 4303 Memorial Hwy, Mandan, North Dakota 58554-4711 **Tel:** 1 701 250-6602.
Web site: http://1033uscountry.com
Profile: KUSB-FM is a commercial station owned by Townsquare Media, Inc. The format of the station is country music. KUSB-FM broadcasts to the Bismarck, ND area at 103.3 FM.
FM RADIO STATION

KUSH-AM 35106
Owner: Kelly Media, LLC
Editorial: 3818 E Main St, Cushing, Oklahoma 74023 **Tel:** 1 918 225-0922.
Email: kushradio@yahoo.com
Web site: http://www.1600kush.com
Profile: KUSH-AM is a commercial station owned by Kelly Media, LLC. The format for the station is news, sports and talk. KUSH-AM broadcasts to the Cushing, OK area at 1600 AM.
AM RADIO STATION

KUSJ-FM 42315
Owner: Townsquare Media, Inc.
Editorial: 608 Moody Ln, Temple, Texas 76504-2952 **Tel:** 1 254 773-5252.
Web site: http://www.myus105.com
Profile: KUSJ-FM is a commercial station owned by Townsquare Media, Inc.The format of the station is country. KUSJ-FM broadcasts to the Temple, TX area at 105.5 FM.
FM RADIO STATION

KUSO-FM 63611
Owner: Flood Communications
Editorial: 214 N 7th St Ste 1, Norfolk, Nebraska 68701-4086 **Tel:** 1 402 371-0100.
Email: us92@us92.com
Web site: http://www.us92.com
Profile: KUSO-FM is a commercial station owned by Flood Communications LLC. The format of the station is contemporary country. KUSO-FM broadcasts to the Norfolk, NE area at 92.7 FM.
FM RADIO STATION

KUSP-FM 44213
Owner: Pataphysical Broadcasting Foundation
Editorial: 203 8th Ave, Santa Cruz, California 95062-4610 **Tel:** 1 831 476-2800.
Web site: http://www.kusp.org
Profile: KUSP-FM is a non-commercial station owned by Pataphysical Broadcasting Foundation.

The format of the station is variety. KUSP-FM broadcasts to the Santa Cruz, CA area at 88.9 FM.
FM RADIO STATION

KUSQ-FM 44960
Owner: Absolute Communications (dba Radio Werks)
Editorial: 28779 County Highway 35, Worthington, Minnesota 56187 **Tel:** 1 507 372-5962.
Email: info@myradioworks.net
Web site: http://us95.us
Profile: KUSQ-FM is a commercial station owned by Absolute Communications (dba Radio Werks). The format of the station is contemporary country. KUSQ-FM broadcasts to the Worthington, MN area at 95.1 FM.
FM RADIO STATION

KUTE-FM 44200
Owner: KUTE Inc.
Editorial: 123 Capote Drive, Ignacio, Colorado 81137
Tel: 1 970 563-0255.
Web site: http://www.ksut.org
Profile: KUTE-FM is a non-commercial station owned by KUTE Inc. The format of the station is variety. KUTE-FM broadcasts to the Ignacio, CO area at 90.1 FM.
FM RADIO STATION

KUTI-AM 38789
Owner: Townsquare Media, LLC
Editorial: 4010 Summitview Ave, Yakima, Washington 98908-2966 **Tel:** 1 509 972-3461.
Web site: http://1460espnyakima.com
Profile: KUTI-AM is a commercial station owned by Townsquare Media, LLC. The format of the station is sports. KUTI-AM broadcasts in the Yakima, WA at 1460 AM.
AM RADIO STATION

KUTR-AM 338447
Owner: Truth Broadcasting
Editorial: 4405 Providence Ln, Winston Salem, North Carolina 27106-3226 **Tel:** 1 336 759-0363.
Email: info@wtru.com
Web site: http://www.wtru.com
Profile: KUTR-AM is a commercial station owned by Truth Broadcasting. The format of the station is religious talk. KUTR-AM broadcasts to the Salt Lake City area at 820 AM.
AM RADIO STATION

KUTT-FM 46186
Owner: Siebert Communications Inc.
Editorial: 414 4th St, Fairbury, Nebraska 68352-2514
Tel: 1 402 729-3382.
Email: kutt@diodecom.net
Web site: http://www.kutt995.com
Profile: KUTT-FM is a commercial station owned by Siebert Communications Inc. The format of the station is country music. KUTT-FM broadcasts to the Fairbury, NE area at 99.5 FM.
FM RADIO STATION

KUTY-AM 36456
Owner: High Desert Broadcasting LLC
Editorial: 570 E Avenue Q9, Palmdale, California 93550-4655 **Tel:** 1 661 947-3107.
Profile: KUTY-AM is a commercial station owned by High Desert Broadcasting LLC. The format of the station is Mexican oldies. KUTY-AM broadcasts to the Los Angeles area at 1470 AM.
AM RADIO STATION

KUUB-FM 44470
Owner: Lotus Communications Corp.
Editorial: 2900 Sutro St, Reno, Nevada 89512-1616
Tel: 1 775 329-9261.
Web site: http://www.espn945.com
Profile: KUUB-FM is a commercial station owned by Lotus Communications Corp. The format of the station is sports/talk. The station broadcasts to the Reno, NV area at 94.5 FM.
FM RADIO STATION

KUUL-FM 45718
Owner: iHeartMedia Inc.
Editorial: 3535 E Kimberly Rd, Davenport, Iowa 52807-2583 **Tel:** 1 563 344-7000.
Web site: http://www.1013kissfm.com
Profile: KUUL-FM is a commercial station owned by iHeartMedia Inc. The format of the station is Top 40/CHR. KUUL-FM broadcasts to the Davenport, IA area at 101.3 FM.
FM RADIO STATION

KUUU-FM 42397
Owner: Broadway Media
Editorial: 515 S 700 E Ste 1C, Salt Lake City, Utah 84102-2802 **Tel:** 1 801 524 2600.
Web site: http://www.u92online.com
Profile: KUUU-FM is a commercial station owned by Broadway Media. The format of the station is urban contemporary. KUUU-FM broadcasts to the Salt Lake City area at 92.5 FM.
FM RADIO STATION

KUUZ-FM 41689
Owner: Family Worship Center Church, Inc.
Tel: 1 225 768-3288.
Email: info@jsm.org
Web site: http://www.jsm.org
FM RADIO STATION

KUVA-FM 39760
Owner: MBM Radio Uvalde LLC
Editorial: 1400 Batesville Rd, Uvalde, Texas 78801
Tel: 1 830 278-2555.
Email: kuva@rcommunications.com
Profile: KUVA-FM is a commercial station owned by MBM Radio Uvalde LLC. The format of the station is Hispanic music. KUVA-FM broadcasts to the Uvalde, TX area at 102.3 FM.
FM RADIO STATION

KUVR-AM 37540
Owner: Armada Media Corp.
Editorial: 613 4th Ave, Holdrege, Nebraska 68949
Tel: 1 308 995-4020.
Email: kmty@highplainsradio.net
Web site: http://www.kuvr.com
Profile: KUVR-AM is a commercial station owned by Armada Media Corp. The format of the station is oldies music. KUVR-AM broadcasts to the Holdrege, NE area at 1380 AM.
AM RADIO STATION

KUXX-FM 46604
Owner: Community First Broadcasting
Tel: 1 507 847-5400.
Email: info@kkoj.com
Web site: http://www.kkoj.com
Profile: KUXX-FM is a commercial station owned by Community First Broadcasting. The format of the station is country music. KUXX-FM broadcasts to the Jackson, MN area at 105.7 FM.
FM RADIO STATION

KUYI-FM 72768
Owner: Hopi Foundation
Editorial: State Hwy 264, MP 3965, Keams Canyon, Arizona 86034 **Tel:** 1 928 738-5505.
Email: info@kuyi.net
Web site: http://www.kuyi.net
Profile: KUYI-FM is a non-commercial station owned by the Hopi Foundation. The format of the station is Native American-based variety programming. KUYI-FM broadcasts to the Keams Canyon, AZ area at 88.1 FM.
FM RADIO STATION

KUYO-AM 35890
Owner: Wyoming Christian Broadcasting Co.
Editorial: 1423 S Beverly St, Casper, Wyoming 82609-4131 **Tel:** 1 307 577-5896.
Web site: http://www.kuyo.com
Profile: KUYO-AM is a commercial station owned by Wyoming Christian Broadcasting Co. The format of the station is religious and talk. KUYO-AM broadcasts to the Casper-Riverton, WY area at 830 AM.
AM RADIO STATION

KUYY-FM 39626
Owner: Community First Broadcasting
Editorial: 2303 W 18th St, Spencer, Iowa 51301
Tel: 1 712 264-1074.
Web site: http://y100-fm.com
Profile: KUYY-FM is a commercial station owned by Community First Broadcasting, Inc. The format of the station is hot adult contemporary. KUYY-FM broadcasts to the Spencer, IA area at 100.1 FM.
FM RADIO STATION

KUZN-FM 520532
Owner: Aleluya Broadcasting Network
Editorial: 1600 Pasadena Blvd, Pasadena, Texas 77502-2404 **Tel:** 1 713 589-1460.
Profile: KUZN-FM is a commercial station owned by Aleluya Christian Broadcasting. The format of the station is Hispanic contemporary Christian. KUZN-FM broadcasts to the Pasadena, TX area at 88.1 FM.
FM RADIO STATION

KUZZ-AM 37541
Owner: Owens Productions Inc.(Buck)
Editorial: 3223 Sillect Ave, Bakersfield, California 93308 **Tel:** 1 661 326-1011.
Email: kuzznews@buckowens.com
Web site: http://www.kuzzradio.com
Profile: KUZZ-AM is a commercial station owned by Buck Owens Productions Inc. The format of the station is country. KUZZ-AM broadcasts to the Bakersfield, CA area at 550 AM.
AM RADIO STATION

KUZZ-FM 44735
Owner: Owens Productions Inc.(Buck)
Editorial: 3223 Sillect Ave, Bakersfield, California 93308 **Tel:** 1 661 326-1011.
Email: kuzznews@buckowens.com
Web site: http://www.kuzzradio.com
Profile: KUZZ-FM is a commercial station owned by Buck Owens Productions Inc. The format of the station is classic country music. KUZZ-FM broadcasts to the Bakersfield, CA area at 107.9 FM.
FM RADIO STATION

KVAB-FM 43673
Owner: Pacific Empire Radio Corp.
Editorial: 403 Capital St, Lewiston, Idaho 83501-1815
Tel: 1 208 743-6564.
Email: wecare@catfm.com
Web site: http://catfm.com
Profile: KVAB-FM is a commercial station owned by Pacific Empire Radio Corp. The format of the station is classic rock. KVAB-FM broadcasts to the Lewiston, ID at a frequency of 102.9 FM.
FM RADIO STATION

KVAK-AM 39503
Owner: North Wave Communications
Editorial: 501 E Bremner St, Valdez, Alaska 99686
Tel: 1 907 835-5825.
Email: valdeznews@gci.net
Web site: http://www.kvakradio.com
Profile: KVAK-AM is a commercial station owned by North Wave Communications. The format of the station is country and variety. KVAK-AM broadcasts to the Valdez, AK area at 1230 AM.
AM RADIO STATION

KVAK-FM 46898
Owner: North Wave Communications
Editorial: 501 E Bremner St, Valdez, Alaska 99686
Tel: 1 907 835-5825.
Email: valdeznews@gci.net
Web site: http://www.kvakradio.com
Profile: KVAK-FM is a commercial station owned by North Wave Communications. The format of the station is hot adult contemporary and classic rock. KVAK-FM broadcasts to the Valdez, AK area at 93.3 FM.
FM RADIO STATION

KVAS-AM 39472
Owner: Ohana Media Group
Editorial: 285 SW Main Ct, Ste. 200, Warrenton, Oregon 97146-9457 **Tel:** 1 503 861-6620.
Profile: KVAS-AM is a commercial station owned by Ohana Media Group. The format of the station is classic country. KVAS-AM broadcasts to the Astoria, OR area at 1230 AM.
AM RADIO STATION

KVAS-FM 43714
Owner: Ohana Media Group
Editorial: 285 SW Main Ct, Ste 200, Warrenton, Oregon 97146-9457 **Tel:** 1 503 861-6620.
Web site: http://www.kvas1039.com
Profile: KVAS-FM is a commercial station owned by Ohana Media Group. The format of the station is country music. KVAS-FM broadcasts in the Astoria, OR area at 103.9 FM.
FM RADIO STATION

KVAY-FM 42533
Owner: Bob and Lisa DeLancey
Editorial: 224 S Main St, #203, Lamar, Colorado 81052-2867 **Tel:** 1 719 336-8734.
Email: news@kvay.com
Web site: http://www.kvay.com
Profile: KVAY-FM is a commercial station owned by Bob and Lisa DeLancey. The format of the station is contemporary country music. KVAY-FM broadcasts in the Denver and Lamar area, CO at 105.7 FM.
FM RADIO STATION

KVBR-AM 39307
Owner: Hubbard Broadcasting Inc.
Editorial: 13225 Dogwood Dr, Baxter, Minnesota 56425-8669 **Tel:** 1 218 828-1244.
Email: production@brainerdradio.net
Web site: http://www.kvbr.com
Profile: KVBR-AM is a commercial station owned by Hubbard Broadcasting Inc. The format of the station is news and business talk. KVBR-AM broadcasts to the Baxter, MN area at 1340 AM.
AM RADIO STATION

KVCE-AM 36505
Owner: Dallas Broadcasting LLC
Editorial: 6400 N Belt Line Rd Ste 110, Irving, Texas 75063-6065 **Tel:** 1 214 561-9667.
Web site: http://www.kvceradio.com
Profile: KVCE-AM is a commercial station owned by Dallas Broadcasting LLC. The format of the station is talk. KVCE-AM broadcasts to the Dallas area at 1160 AM.
AM RADIO STATION

KVCK-AM 37543
Owner: Wolftrax Broadcasting LLC
Editorial: 324 Main St, Wolf Point, Montana 59201
Tel: 1 406 653-1900.
Email: kvck@nemont.net
Profile: KVCK-AM is a commercial station owned by Wolftrax Broadcasting LLC. The format of the station is classic hits music. KVCK-AM broadcasts to the Wolf Point, MT area at 1450 AM.
AM RADIO STATION

KVCK-FM 44991
Owner: Wolftrax Broadcasting LLC
Editorial: 324 Main St, Wolf Point, Montana 59201
Tel: 1 406 653-1900.
Email: kvck@nemont.net
Profile: KVCK-FM is a commercial station owned by Wolftrax Broadcasting LLC. The format of the station is country. KVCK-FM broadcasts to the Wolf Point, MT area at 92.7 FM.
FM RADIO STATION

KVCL-FM 44936
Owner: Baldridge-Dumas Communications Inc.
Editorial: 304 Kvcl Rd, Winnfield, Louisiana 71483
Tel: 1 318 628-5822.
Email: kvclradio@yahoo.com
Web site: http://kvclradio.com
Profile: KVCL-FM is a commercial station owned by Baldridge-Dumas Communications Inc. The format of the station is country music. KVCL-FM broadcasts to the Winnfield, LA area at 92.1 FM.
FM RADIO STATION

KVCR-FM 39999
Owner: San Bernardino Community College
Editorial: 701 S Mount Vernon Ave, San Bernardino, California 92410 **Tel:** 1 909 384-4444.
Email: info@kvcr.org
Web site: http://www.kvcr.org
Profile: KVCR-FM is a NPR affiliate, non-commercial station owned by San Bernardino Community College. The format of the station is news and talk. KVCR-FM broadcasts to the San Bernardino, CA area at 91.9 FM.
FM RADIO STATION

KVCX-FM 40000
Owner: VCY America Inc.
Editorial: 3434 W Kilbourn Ave, Milwaukee, Wisconsin 53208 **Tel:** 1 414 935-3000.
Email: kvcx@vcyamerica.org
Web site: http://www.vcyamerica.org
Profile: KVCX-FM is a non-commercial station owned by VCY America Inc. The format of the station is religious programming. KVCX-FM broadcasts to the Milwaukee area at 101.5 FM.
FM RADIO STATION

KVCY-FM 41675
Owner: VCY America Inc.
Tel: 1 414 935-3000.
Email: kvcy@vcyamerica.org
Web site: http://www.vcyamerica.org
Profile: KVCY-FM is a non-commercial station owned by VCY America Inc. The format of the station is religious programming. KVCY-FM broadcasts to the Kansas City area at 104.7 FM.
FM RADIO STATION

KVDG-FM 506375
Owner: La Promesa Foundation
Editorial: 1903 S Lamesa Rd, Midland, Texas 79701
Tel: 1 432 682-5476.
Web site: http://www.grnonline.com
Profile: KVDG-FM is a non-commercial station owned by La Promesa Foundation. The format for the station is religious talk programming with a Catholic emphasis. KVDG-FM broadcasts to the Midland, TX area at 90.9 FM.
FM RADIO STATION

KVDU-FM 42822
Owner: iHeartMedia Inc.
Editorial: 929 Howard Ave, New Orleans, Louisiana 70113-1148 **Tel:** 1 504 679-7300.
Web site: http://www.voodoo104.com
Profile: KVDU-FM is a commercial station owned by iHeartMedia Inc. The format of the station is modern AC, with a focus on the 1990s. KVDU-FM broadcasts to the New Orleans area at 104.1 FM.
FM RADIO STATION

KVEC-AM 36010
Owner: El Dorado Broadcasting
Editorial: 51 Zaca Ln Ste 100, San Luis Obispo, California 93401-7353 **Tel:** 1 805 545-0101.
Web site: http://www.920kvec.com
Profile: KVEC-AM is a commercial station owned by El Dorado Broadcasting. The format of the station is news, talk and sports. KVEC-AM broadcasts in the San Luis Obispo, CA area at 920 AM.
AM RADIO STATION

KVEG-FM 77136
Owner: Kemp Broadcasting
Editorial: 3999 Las Vegas Blvd S Ste K, Las Vegas, Nevada 89119-1097 **Tel:** 1 702 736-6161.
Email: programming@kvegas.com
Web site: http://www.kvegas.com
Profile: KVEG-FM is a commercial station owned by Kemp Broadcasting. The format of the station is rhythmic Top 40/CHR. KVEG-FM broadcasts to the Las Vegas area at 97.5 FM.
FM RADIO STATION

KVEL-AM 37546
Owner: Ashley Communications
Editorial: 2425 N Vernal Ave, Vernal, Utah 84078-9587 **Tel:** 1 435 789-0920.
Email: production@kvel.com
Web site: http://920kvel.com
Profile: KVEL-AM is a commercial station owned by Ashley Communications. The format of the station is talk, news and sports. KVEL-AM broadcasts to the Salt Lake City area at 920 AM.
AM RADIO STATION

KVEN-AM 37547
Owner: Cumulus Media Inc.
Editorial: 1376 Walter St, Ventura, California 93003-5658 **Tel:** 1 805 642-8595.
Web site: http://www.1450kven.com
Profile: KVEN-AM is a commercial station owned by Cumulus Media Inc. The format of the station is sports. KVEN-AM broadcasts to the Ventura, CA area at 1450 AM.
AM RADIO STATION

KVER-FM 43145
Owner: World Radio Network, Inc.
Editorial: 11385 James Watt Dr Ste B4, El Paso, Texas 79936-5942 **Tel:** 1 915 544-9190.
Email: kver@inspiracom.org
Web site: http://www.kver.org
Profile: KVER-FM is a non-commercial station owned by World Radio Network, Inc. The format is Hispanic contemporary Christian. KVER-FM broadcasts to the El Paso, TX area at 91.1 FM.
FM RADIO STATION

KVET-AM 39506
Owner: iHeartMedia Inc.
Editorial: 3601 S Congress Ave Bldg F, Austin, Texas 78704-7280 **Tel:** 1 512 684-7300.
Web site: http://am1300thezone.iheart.com
Profile: KVET-AM is a commercial station owned by iHeartMedia Inc. The format of the station is sports. KVET-AM broadcasts to the Austin, TX area at 1300 AM.
AM RADIO STATION

KVET-FM 46900
Owner: iHeartMedia Inc
Editorial: 3601 S Congress Ave, Austin, Texas 78704-7250 **Tel:** 1 512 684-7300.
Web site: http://www.kvet.com
Profile: KVET-FM is a commercial station owned by iHeartMedia Inc. The format of the station is country music. KVET-FM broadcasts to the Austin, TX area at 98.1 FM.
FM RADIO STATION

KVFC-AM 38945
Owner: American General Media
Editorial: 2402 Hawkins, Cortez, Colorado 81321
Tel: 1 970 565-6565.
Web site: http://www.kvfcradio.com
Profile: KVFC-AM is a commercial station owned by American General Media. The format of the station is talk. KVFC-AM broadcasts to the Cortez, CO area at 740 AM.
AM RADIO STATION

KVFD-AM 38406
Owner: Alpha Media
Editorial: 200 N 10th St, Fort Dodge, Iowa 50501-3925 **Tel:** 1 515 955-5656.
Web site: http://www.yourfortdodge.com
Profile: KVFD-AM is a commercial station owned by Alpha Media. The format of the station is talk. KVFD-AM broadcasts to the Fort Dodge, IA area at 1400 AM.
AM RADIO STATION

KVFG-FM 43508
Owner: CBS Radio
Editorial: 11920 Hesperia Rd, Hesperia, California 92345-1851 **Tel:** 1 760 244-2000.
Profile: KVFG-FM is a commercial station owned by CBS Radio. The format of the station is classic hits. KVFG-FM broadcasts to the Hesperia, CA area at 103.1 FM.
FM RADIO STATION

KVFX-FM 45801
Owner: Cache Valley Radio Inc.
Editorial: 810 W 200 N, Logan, Utah 84321-3726
Tel: 1 435 752-1390.
Web site: http://www.utahsvfx.com
Profile: KVFX-FM is a commercial station owned by Cache Valley Radio Inc. The format of the station is Top 40/CHR. KVFX-FM broadcasts to the Salt Lake City area at 94.5 FM.
FM RADIO STATION

KVGB-AM 38476
Owner: Eagle Radio Inc.
Editorial: 1200 Baker Ave, Great Bend, Kansas 67530-4523 **Tel:** 1 620 792-3647.
Web site: http://www.eagleradio.net
Profile: KVGB-AM is a commercial station owned by Eagle Radio Inc. The format of the station is news, talk and sports. KVGB-AM broadcasts to the Great Bend, KS area at 1590 AM.
AM RADIO STATION

KVGB-FM 45833
Owner: Eagle Radio Inc.
Editorial: 1200 Baker Ave, Great Bend, Kansas 67530
Tel: 1 620 792-3647.
Email: comments@theclassicrockstation.com
Web site: http://www.b1043.net
Profile: KVGB-FM is a commercial station owned by Eagle Radio Inc. The format of the station is classic rock. KVGB-FM broadcasts to the Great Bend, KS area at 104.3 FM.
FM RADIO STATION

KVGO-FM 43691
Owner: Cumulus Media Inc.
Editorial: 300 Saint Paul St SW, Preston, Minnesota 55965-1097 **Tel:** 1 507 765-3856.
Web site: http://kvgo1043.com
Profile: KVGO-FM is a commercial station owned by Cumulus Media Inc. The format of the station is oldies. KVGO-FM is licensed to the Spring Valley, MN area and broadcasts locally at a frequency of 104.3 FM.
FM RADIO STATION

KVGQ-FM 616738
Owner: Kemp Broadcasting
Editorial: 3999 Las Vegas Blvd S, Las Vegas, Nevada 89119-1001 **Tel:** 1 702 736-6161.
Web site: http://1069theq.com
Profile: KVGQ-FM is a commercial station owned by Kemp Broadcasting. The format for the station is Hot AC. KVGQ-FM broadcasts to the Overton, NV area at 106.9 FM.
FM RADIO STATION

KVGS-FM 42536
Owner: Beasley Broadcast Group
Editorial: 2920 S Durango Dr, Las Vegas, Nevada 89117-4412 **Tel:** 1 702 730-0300.
Email: email@bbgi.com
Web site: http://1079bob.com
Profile: KVGS-FM is a commercial station owned by Beasley Broadcast Group. The format of the station is adult hits. KVGS-FM broadcasts to the Las Vegas area at 107.9 FM.
FM RADIO STATION

KVHT-FM 45915
Owner: Culhane Communications Inc.
Editorial: 210 W 3rd St, Yankton, South Dakota 57078-4323 **Tel:** 1 605 665-2600.
Email: news@kvht.com
Web site: https://kvhtradio.com
Profile: KVHT-FM is a commercial station owned by Culhane Communications Inc. The format of the station is classic hits. KVHT-FM broadcasts to the Yankton, SD area at 106.3 FM.
FM RADIO STATION

KVI-AM 37548
Owner: Sinclair Radio of Seattle, LLC
Editorial: 140 4th Ave N Ste 340, Seattle, Washington 98109-4940 **Tel:** 1 206 404-8000.
Email: comment@kvi.com
Web site: http://www.kvi.com
Profile: KVI-AM is a commercial station owned by Sinclair Radio of Seattle, LLC. The format of the station is talk. KVI-AM broadcasts in the Seattle area at 570 AM.
AM RADIO STATION

KVIC-FM 42013
Owner: Victoria RadioWorks Inc.
Editorial: 3613 N Main St, Victoria, Texas 77901-2607
Tel: 1 361 573-1047.
Email: kvic@suddenlink.net
Profile: KVIC-FM is a commercial station owned by Victoria RadioWorks Inc. The format of the station is Top 40/CHR. KVIC-FM broadcasts to the Victoria, TX area at a frequency of 104.7.
FM RADIO STATION

KVIK-FM 42515
Owner: Wennes Communications Stations, Inc.
Editorial: 501 W Water St, Decorah, Iowa 52101
Tel: 1 563 382-5863.
Email: kvik@kvikradio.com
Web site: http://www.kvikradio.com
Profile: KVIK-FM is a commercial station owned by Wennes Communications Stations, Inc. The format of the station is classic hits music. KVIK-FM broadcasts to the Decorah, IA area at 104.7 FM.
FM RADIO STATION

KVIL-FM 43168
Owner: CBS Radio
Editorial: 4131 N Central Expy Ste 1000, Dallas, Texas 75204-2121 **Tel:** 1 214 525-7000.
Web site: http://kvil.cbslocal.com
Profile: KVIL-FM is a commercial station owned by CBS Radio. The format of the station is hot adult contemporary. KVIL-FM broadcasts to the Dallas area at 103.7 FM.
FM RADIO STATION

KVIN-AM 36732
Owner: Threshold Communications
Editorial: 961 N Emerald Ave Ste A, Modesto, California 95351-1556 **Tel:** 1 209 544-1055.
Email: thevine@kvin.net
Web site: http://kvin.net
Profile: KVIN-AM is a commercial station owned by Threshold Communications. The format of the station is oldies. KVIN-AM broadcasts to the Modesto, CA area at 920 AM.
AM RADIO STATION

KVIP-AM 37550
Owner: Pacific Cascade Communications Corp.
Editorial: 1139 Hartnell Ave, Redding, California 96002-2113 **Tel:** 1 530 222-4455.
Email: info@kvip.org
Web site: http://www.kvip.org
Profile: KVIP-AM is a non-commercial station owned by Pacific Cascade Communications Corp. The format of the station is talk. KVIP-AM broadcasts to the Redding, CA area at 540 AM.
AM RADIO STATION

KVIP-FM 44939
Owner: Pacific Cascade Communications Corp.
Editorial: 1139 Hartnell Ave, Redding, California 96002-2113 **Tel:** 1 530 222-4455.
Email: info@kvip.org
Web site: http://www.kvip.org
Profile: KVIP-FM is a non-commercial station owned by Pacific Cascade Communications Corp. The format of the station is Christian talk. KVIP-FM broadcasts to the Redding, CA area at 98.1 FM.
FM RADIO STATION

KVIS-AM 38471
Owner: Northeast Oklahoma Broadcasting Network
Editorial: 1 N Main St, Miami, Oklahoma 74354-6322
Tel: 1 918 542-1818.
Email: kglc-kvis@okradiostation.com
Profile: KVIS-AM is a commercial station owned by Northeast Oklahoma Broadcasting Network. The format of the station is southern gospel music. KVIS-AM broadcasts in the Miami, OK area at 910 AM.
AM RADIO STATION

KVIV-AM 35107
Owner: El Paso Y Juarez Companerismo-Cristiano
Editorial: 6060 Surety Dr Ste 100, El Paso, Texas 79905-2033 **Tel:** 1 915 565-2999.
Email: info@kviv1340.com
Web site: http://kviv1340.com
Profile: KVIV-AM is a commercial station owned by El Paso Y Juarez Companerismo-Cristiano. The format of the station is Christian Hispanic religious programming. KVIV-AM broadcasts in the El Paso, TX area at 1340 AM.
AM RADIO STATION

KVJM-FM 43882
Owner: iHeartMedia Inc.
Editorial: 1716 Briarcrest Dr Ste 150, Bryan, Texas 77802-2776 **Tel:** 1 979 268-9696.
Web site: http://www.kissfm1031.com/main.html
Profile: KVJM-FM is a commercial station owned by iHeartMedia Inc. The format of the station is CHR/Top 40. KVJM-FM broadcasts to the Bryan, TX area at 103.1 FM.
FM RADIO STATION

KVJY-AM 36729
Owner: R Communications
Editorial: 1201 N Jackson Rd Ste 900, McAllen, Texas 78501-5764 **Tel:** 1 956 992-8895.
Web site: http://informativord.com
Profile: KVJY-AM is a commercial station owned by R Communications. The format of the station is Spanish News/Talk. KVJY-AM broadcasts to the McAllen, TX area at 840 AM.
AM RADIO STATION

KVKI-FM 42010
Owner: Townsquare Media, LLC
Editorial: 6341 Westport Ave, Shreveport, Louisiana 71129-2415 **Tel:** 1 318 688-1130.
Web site: http://www.965kvki.com
Profile: KVKI-FM is a commercial station owned by Townsquare Media, LLC. The format of the station is adult contemporary music. KVKI-FM broadcasts to the Shreveport, LA area at 96.5 FM.
FM RADIO STATION

KVKK-AM 359602
Owner: De La Hunt Broadcasting
Editorial: 11 Bryant Ave SE, Wadena, Minnesota 56482-1543 **Tel:** 1 218 631-3441.
Email: kskk@eot.com
Web site: http://www.kkradionetwork.com
Profile: KVKK-AM is a commercial station owned by De La Hunt Broadcasting. The format of the station is talk. KVKK-AM broadcasts to the Wadena, MN area at 1070 AM.
AM RADIO STATION

KVLC-FM 43004
Owner: Bravo Mic Communications, LLC
Editorial: 101 Perkins Dr, Las Cruces, New Mexico 88005-3295 **Tel:** 1 575 527-1111.
Web site: http://www.101gold.com
Profile: KVLC-FM is a commercial station owned by Bravo Mic Communications, LLC. The format of the station is oldies. KVLC-FM broadcasts to the Las Cruces, NM area at 101.1 FM.
FM RADIO STATION

KVLD-FM 44381
Owner: East Arkansas Broadcasters Inc.
Editorial: 2705 E Parkway Dr, Russellville, Arkansas 72802-2006 **Tel:** 1 479 968-6816.
Email: news@rivervalleyradio.com
Web site: http://sharpe993.com
Profile: KVLD-FM is a commercial station owned by ast Arkansas Broadcasters Inc. The format of the station is classic rock. KVLD-FM broadcasts to the Russellville, AR area at 99.3 FM.
FM RADIO STATION

KVLF-AM 38497
Owner: Alpine Radio, LLC
Editorial: 500 E Hendryx Ave, Alpine, Texas 79830-2108 **Tel:** 1 432 837-2144.
Email: alpinetxradio@gmail.com
Web site: http://www.bigbenradio.com
Profile: KVLF-AM is a commercial station owned by Alpine Radio, LLC. The format of the station is oldies. KVLF-AM broadcasts to the Alpine, TX area at 92.7 FM.
AM RADIO STATION

KVLG-AM 37552
Owner: KBUK Radio, Inc.
Editorial: 511 FM 155 South, La Grange, Texas 78945
Tel: 1 979 968-3173.
Email: kvlgkbuk@kvlgkbuk.com
Web site: http://www.kvlgkbuk.com
Profile: KVLG-AM is a commercial station owned by KBUK Radio, Inc. The format of the station in classic country. KVLG-AM broadcasts to the La Grange, TX area at 1570 AM.
AM RADIO STATION

KVLI-AM 38747
Owner: QAB Media LLC
Editorial: 14 Sierra Drive, Kernville, California 93238
Tel: 1 760 376-4500.
Profile: KVLI-AM is a commercial station owned by QAB Media LLC. The format of the station is news and talk programming. KVLI-AM broadcasts to the Kernville, CA area at 1140 AM.
AM RADIO STATION

KVLL-FM 493377
Owner: Townsquare Media, LLC
Editorial: 1216 S 1st St, Lufkin, Texas 75901-4716
Tel: 1 936 639-4455.
Web site: http://www.sunny947fm.com
Profile: KVLL-FM is a commercial station owned by Townsquare Media, LLC. The format of the station is adult contemporary. KVLL-FM broadcasts to the Lufkin, TX area at 94.7 FM.
FM RADIO STATION

KVLO-FM 41648
Owner: Arkansas County Broadcasters, Inc.
Editorial: 1818 S Buerkle St, Stuttgart, Arkansas 72160-5804 **Tel:** 1 870 673-1595.
Email: kwakradio@yahoo.com
Profile: KVLO-FM is a commercial station owned by Arkansas County Broadcasters, Inc. The format of the station is adult hits. KVLO-FM broadcasts to the Little Rock, AR area at 101.7 FM.
FM RADIO STATION

KVLV-AM 37553
Owner: Lahontan Valley Broadcasting
Editorial: 1155 Gummow Dr, Fallon, Nevada 89406
Tel: 1 775 423-2243.
Email: kvlv@phonewave.net
Profile: KVLV-AM is a commercial station owned by Lahontan Valley Broadcasting. The format of the station is country. KVLV-AM broadcasts to the Fallon, NV area at 980 AM.
AM RADIO STATION

KVLY-FM 41001
Owner: Entravision Communications Corp.
Editorial: 801 N Jackson Rd, McAllen, Texas 78501-9306 **Tel:** 1 956 661-6000.
Email: kvly@hiline.net
Web site: http://www.mix1079.net
Profile: KVLY-FM is a commercial station owned by Entravision Communications Corp. The format of the station is adult contemporary. KVLY-FM broadcasts to the McAllen, TX area at 107.9 FM.
FM RADIO STATION

KVMA-AM 37055
Owner: Noalmark Broadcasting Corp.
Editorial: 131 S Jackson, Magnolia, Arkansas 71753-3524 **Tel:** 1 870 234-5862.
Email: kvmakvmz@magnoliaradio.com
Web site: http://www.magnoliaradio.com
Profile: KVMA-AM is a commercial station owned by Noalmark Broadcasting Corp. The format of the station is country and news. KVMA-AM broadcasts to the Magnolia, AR area at 630 AM.
AM RADIO STATION

KVMA-FM 44352
Owner: Cumulus Media Inc.
Editorial: 270 Plaza Loop, Cumulus Broadcast Center, Bossier City, Louisiana 71111-4389
Tel: 1 318 549-8500.
Web site: http://www.magic1029fm.com
Profile: KVMA-FM is a commercial station owned by Cumulus Media Inc. The format of the station is urban adult contemporary music. KVMA-FM broadcasts to the Bossier City, LA area at 102.9 FM.
FM RADIO STATION

KVMC-AM 38638
Owner: Baum(James G.)
Editorial: West Highway 80, Colorado City, Texas 79512 **Tel:** 1 325 728-5530.
Email: kvmckaum@sbcglobal.net
Web site: http://www.tsnradio.com
Profile: KVMC-AM is a commercial station owned by James G. Baum. The format of the station is country music. KVMC-AM broadcasts to the Colorado City, TX area at 1320 AM.
AM RADIO STATION

KVMI-AM 38542
Owner: Momentum Broadcasting LP
Editorial: 1401 W Caldwell Ave, Visalia, California 93277-7725 **Tel:** 1 559 553-1500.
Profile: KVMI-AM is a commercial station owned by Momentum Broadcasting LP. The format for the station is Christian/Inspirational. KVMI-AM broadcasts to the Visalia, CA area at 1270 AM.
AM RADIO STATION

KVML-AM 37554
Owner: Clarke Broadcasting Corp.
Editorial: 342 S Washington St, Sonora, California 95370-5020 **Tel:** 1 209 533-1450.
Web site: http://www.kvml.com
Profile: KVML-AM is a commercial station owned by Clarke Broadcasting Corp. The format of the station is news and talk. KVML-AM broadcasts to the Sonora, CA, area at 1450 AM.
AM RADIO STATION

KVMO-FM 958693
Owner: The Montana Radio Company, LLC.
Editorial: 100 W Lyndale Ave Ste B, Helena, Montana 59601-2999 **Tel:** 1 406 442-6645.
Profile: KVMO-FM is a commercial station owned by Montana Radio Company (The). The format of the station is classic country music and broadcasts to the Great Falls, MT area at a frequency of 96.3 FM.
FM RADIO STATION

KVMR-FM 41446
Owner: Nevada City Broadcast Group
Editorial: 401 Spring St, Nevada City, California 95959 **Tel:** 1 530 265-9073.
Email: news@kvmr.org
Web site: http://www.kvmr.org
Profile: KVMR-FM is a non-commercial station owned by Nevada City Broadcast Group. The format of the station is variety. KVMR-FM broadcasts to the Nevada City, CA area at 89.5 FM.
FM RADIO STATION

KVMV-FM 40005
Owner: World Radio Network, Inc.
Editorial: 969 E Thomas Dr, Pharr, Texas 78577-9828
Tel: 1 956 787-9700.
Email: kvmv@kvmv.org
Web site: http://www.kvmv.org
Profile: KVMV-FM is a non-commercial station owned by World Radio Network, Inc. The format is religious and contemporary Christian. KVMV-FM broadcasts to the Pharr, TX area at 96.9 FM.
FM RADIO STATION

KVMX-FM 41033
Owner: Lotus Communications Corp.
Editorial: 5100 Commerce Dr, Bakersfield, California 93309-0684 **Tel:** 1 661 327-9711.
Web site: http://921kix.com
Profile: KVMX-FM is a commercial station owned by Lotus Communications Corp. The format of the station is contemporary country. KVMX-FM broadcasts to the Bakersfield, CA area at 92.1 FM.
FM RADIO STATION

KVMZ-FM 414249
Owner: Noalmark Broadcasting Corp.
Editorial: 131 S Jackson, Magnolia, Arkansas 71753
Tel: 1 870 234-9901.
Email: kvmakvmz@magnoliaradio.com
Web site: http://www.magnoliaradio.com
Profile: KVMZ-FM is a commercial station owned by Noalmark Broadcasting Corp. The format of the station is contemporary country. KVMZ-FM broadcasts to the Magnolia, AR area at 99.1 FM.
FM RADIO STATION

KVNA-AM 38331
Owner: Yavapai Broadcasting
Editorial: 1800 S Milton Rd Ste 105, Flagstaff, Arizona 86001-6323 **Tel:** 1 928 634-2286.
Web site: http://myradioplace.com/kvna
Profile: KVNA-AM is a commercial station owned by Yavapai Broadcasting. The format of the station is news, sports and talk programming. KVNA-AM broadcasts to the Flagstaff, AZ area at 600 AM.
AM RADIO STATION

KVNA-FM 81146
Owner: Yavapai Broadcasting
Editorial: 3405 E State Route 89A Bldg A, Cottonwood, Arizona 86326-5506 **Tel:** 1 928 634-2286.
Email: sunny@myradioplace.com
Web site: http://www.myradioplace.com
Profile: KLOD-FM is a commercial station owned by Yavapai Broadcasting. The format of the station is adult contemporary. KLOD-FM broadcasts to the Flagstaff, AZ area at 100.1 FM.
FM RADIO STATION

KVNF-FM 41455
Owner: North Fork Valley Public Radio Inc.
Editorial: 233 Grand Ave, Paonia, Colorado 81428
Tel: 1 970 527-4866.
Web site: http://www.kvnf.org
Profile: KVNF-FM is a non-commercial station owned by North Fork Valley Public Radio Inc. The format of the station is news, jazz and adult album alternative. KVNF-FM broadcasts to the Paonia, CO area at 90.9 FM.
FM RADIO STATION

KVNI-AM 38958
Owner: Queen B Radio Inc.
Editorial: 500 W Boone Ave, Spokane, Washington 99201-2404 **Tel:** 1 509 324-4000.
Web site: http://kootenaifm.com
Profile: KVNI-AM is a commercial radio station owned by Queen B Radio Inc. The format of the station is adult contemporary. It broadcasts to the Spokane, WA area at 1080 AM.
AM RADIO STATION

KVNN-AM 37549
Owner: Victoria RadioWorks Inc.
Editorial: 3613 N Main St, Victoria, Texas 77901-2607
Tel: 1 361 576-6111.
Profile: KVNN-AM is a commercial station owned by Victoria RadioWorks Inc. The format of the station is news and talk. KVNN-AM broadcasts to the Victoria, TX area at 1340 AM.
AM RADIO STATION

KVNR-AM 36743
Owner: Liberman Broadcasting Inc.
Editorial: 13749 Beach Blvd, Westminster, California 92683-3204 **Tel:** 1 714 918-4444.
Email: radio@littlesaigonradio.com
Web site: http://www.littlesaigonradio.com
Profile: KVNR-AM is a commercial station owned by Liberman Broadcasting Inc. The format of the station is a variety of Asian and Vietnamese programming. KVNR-AM broadcasts to the Santa Ana, CA area at 1480 AM.
AM RADIO STATION

KVNS-AM 39499
Owner: iHeartMedia Inc.
Editorial: 901 E Pike Blvd, Weslaco, Texas 78596-4937 **Tel:** 1 956 973-9202.
Web site: http://www.foxsports1700.com
Profile: KVNS-AM is a commercial station owned by iHeartMedia Inc. The format of the station is sports. KVNS-AM broadcasts to the Weslaco, TX area at 1700 AM.
AM RADIO STATION

KVNT-AM 723080
Owner: Alaska Integrated Media
Editorial: 4700 Business Park Blvd Bldg E, Anchorage, Alaska 99503-7176 **Tel:** 1 907 522-1018.
Email: traffic@alaskaim.com
Web site: http://www.1020kvnt.com
Profile: KVNT-AM is a commercial station owned by Alaska Integrated Media. The format of the station is progressive talk. KVNT-AM broadcasts at a frequency of 1020 AM to the Anchorage, AK area.
AM RADIO STATION

KVNU-AM 38433
Owner: Cache Valley Radio Inc.
Editorial: 810 W 200 N, Logan, Utah 84321-3726
Tel: 1 435 752-5141.
Web site: http://www.610kvnu.com
Profile: KVNU-AM is a commercial station owned by Cache Valley Radio Inc. The format of the station is news and talk programming. KVNU-AM broadcasts to the Logan, UT area at 610 AM.
AM RADIO STATION

KVOB-FM 42140
Owner: Rocking M Radio
Editorial: 641 W Cloud St, Salina, Kansas 67401-5618
Tel: 1 785 827-2100.
Profile: KVOB-FM is a commercial station owned by Rocking M Radio. The format of the station is rock music. KVOB-FM broadcasts to the Salina, KS area at 95.5 FM.
FM RADIO STATION

KVOC-AM 39467
Owner: Mount Rushmore Broadcasting Inc.
Editorial: 218 N Wolcott St, Casper, Wyoming 82601-1923 **Tel:** 1 307 265-1984.
Web site: http://www.kvoc1230am.com/
Profile: KVOC-AM is a commercial station owned by Mount Rushmore Broadcasting Inc. The format of the station is talk. KVOC-AM broadcasts to the Casper, WY area at 1230 AM.
AM RADIO STATION

KVOD-FM 39575
Owner: Public Broadcasting of Colorado Inc.
Editorial: 7409 S Alton Ct, Centennial, Colorado 80112-2301 **Tel:** 1 303 871-9191.
Email: info@cpr.org
Web site: http://www.cpr.org
Profile: KVOD-FM is a non-commercial station owned by Public Broadcasting of Colorado Inc. The format of the station is classical. KVOD-FM broadcasts to the Centennial, CO area at 88.1 FM.
FM RADIO STATION

KVOE-AM 37555
Owner: Emporia Radio Stations Inc.
Editorial: 1420 C Of E Dr, Emporia, Kansas 66801
Tel: 1 620 342-1400.
Email: kvoe@kvoe.com
Web site: http://www.kvoe.com
Profile: KVOE-AM is a commercial station owned by Emporia Radio Stations Inc. The format of the station is adult contemporary, news and talk. KVOE-AM broadcasts to the Emporia, KS area at 1400 AM.
AM RADIO STATION

KVOE-FM 46752
Owner: Emporia Radio Stations Inc.
Editorial: 1420 C Of E Dr, Emporia, Kansas 66801
Tel: 1 620 342-1400.
Email: kvoe@kvoe.com
Web site: http://www.kvoe.com
Profile: KVOE-FM is a commercial station owned by Emporia Radio Stations Inc. The format of the station is country music. KVOE-FM broadcasts to the Emporia, KS area at 101.7 FM.
FM RADIO STATION

KVOI-AM 36277
Owner: Good News Radio Broadcasting Inc.
Editorial: 3222 S Richey Ave, Tucson, Arizona 85713-5498 **Tel:** 1 520 790-2440.
Email: info@kvoi.com
Web site: http://www.kvoi.com
Profile: KVOI-AM is a commercial station owned by Good News Radio Broadcasting Inc. The format of the station is talk. KVOI-AM broadcasts in Tucson, AZ area at 1030 AM.
AM RADIO STATION

KVOK-AM 38567
Owner: Kodiak Island Broadcasting Co., Inc.
Editorial: 1315 Mill Bay Rd Ste 1A, Kodiak, Alaska 99615-6411 **Tel:** 1 907 486-5159.
Email: kvok@ak.net
Web site: http://www.kvok.com
Profile: KVOK-AM is a commercial station owned by Kodiak Island Broadcasting Co., Inc. The station's format is contemporary country. KVOK-AM broadcasts to Kodiak, AK, area at 560 AM. This station also operates on 98.7 FM at 250 wattage.
AM RADIO STATION

KVOM-AM 37556
Owner: East Arkansas Broadcasters Inc.
Editorial: 1835 Highway 113, Morrilton, Arkansas 72110 **Tel:** 1 501 354-2484.
Email: newsroom@kvom.com
Web site: http://www.kvom.com
Profile: KVOM-AM is a commercial station owned by East Arkansas Broadcasters Inc. The format of the station is sports. KVOM-AM's broadcasts to the Morrilton, AR area at 800 AM.
AM RADIO STATION

KVOM-FM 44941
Owner: East Arkansas Broadcasters Inc.
Editorial: 1835 Highway 113, Morrilton, Arkansas 72110-9009 **Tel:** 1 501 354-2485.
Email: newsroom@kvom.com
Web site: http://www.kvom.com
Profile: KVOM-FM is a commercial station owned by East Arkansas Broadcasters Inc. The format of the station is country. KVOM-FM broadcasts to the Morrilton, AR area at 101.7 FM.
FM RADIO STATION

KVON-AM 37557
Owner: Wine Country Broadcasting Co.
Editorial: 1124 Foster Rd, Napa, California 94558-6520 **Tel:** 1 707 252-1440.
Email: psa@kvon.com
Web site: http://www.kvon.com
Profile: KVON-AM is a commercial station owned by Wine Country Broadcasting Co. The format of the station is talk. KVON-AM broadcasts to the San Francisco area at 1440 AM.
AM RADIO STATION

KVOO-FM 45802
Owner: E.W. Scripps Co.
Editorial: 4590 E 29th St, Tulsa, Oklahoma 74114-6208 **Tel:** 1 918 743-7814.
Web site: http://www.kvoo.com
Profile: KVOO-FM is a commercial station owned by the E.W. Scripps Co. The format of the station is contemporary country music. KVOO-FM broadcasts to the Tulsa, OK area at 98.5 FM.
FM RADIO STATION

KVOP-AM 38412
Owner: Rhattigan Broadcasting
Editorial: 3218 Quincy St, Plainview, Texas 79072-1906 **Tel:** 1 806 296-2771.
Web site: http://www.kkyn.net
Profile: KVOP-AM is a commercial station owned by Rhattigan Broadcasting. The format of the station is news, sports and talk. KVOP-AM broadcasts to the Plainview, TX area at 1090 AM.
AM RADIO STATION

KVOQ-AM 36171
Owner: Public Broadcasting of Colorado Inc.
Editorial: 7409 S Alton Ct, Centennial, Colorado 80112-2301 **Tel:** 1 303 871-9191.
Email: info@cpr.org
Web site: http://www.openaircpr.org
Profile: KVOQ-AM is a non-commercial station owned by Public Broadcasting of Colorado Inc. The format of the station is indie rock. KVOQ-AM broadcasts to the Denver area at 1340 AM.
AM RADIO STATION

KVOR-AM 36674
Owner: Cumulus Media Inc
Editorial: 6805 Corporate Dr Ste 130, Colorado Springs, Colorado 80919-1977 **Tel:** 1 719 593-2700.
Email: news@kvor.com
Web site: http://www.kvor.com
Profile: KVOR-AM is a commercial station owned by Cumulus Media Inc. The format of the station is news and talk. KVOR-AM broadcasts to the Colorado Springs, CO area at 740 AM.
AM RADIO STATION

KVOT-AM 409180
Owner: DMC Broadcasting Inc.
Editorial: 125 Camino De La Merced Ste A, Taos, New Mexico 87571-5131 **Tel:** 1 575 758-4491.
Web site: http://www.radiointaos.com
Profile: KVOT-AM is a commercial station owned by DMC Broadcasting Inc. The format of the station is Christian programming. KVOT-AM broadcasts to the Taos, NM area at 1340 AM.
AM RADIO STATION

KVOU-FM 44988
Owner: Rhattigan Broadcasting
Editorial: 1400 Batesville Road, Uvalde, Texas 78801
Tel: 1 830 278-2555.
Email: kvou@rcommunications.com
Profile: KVOU-FM is a commercial station owned by Rhattigan Broadcasting. The format of the station is country music. KVOU-FM broadcasts to the Uvalde, TX residents at 104.9 FM.
FM RADIO STATION

KVOW-AM 37560
Owner: Edwards Communications LLC
Editorial: 603 E Pershing Ave, Riverton, Wyoming 82501-3605 **Tel:** 1 307 856-2251.
Web site: http://wrrnetwork.com/kvow
Profile: KVOW-AM is a commercial station owned by Edwards Communications LLC. The format for the station is news talk. KVOW-AM broadcasts to the Casper-Riverton, WY area at 1450 AM.
AM RADIO STATION

KVOX-AM 37065
Owner: Midwest Communications
Editorial: 1020 25th St S, Fargo, North Dakota 58103-2312 **Tel:** 1 701 237-5346.
Web site: http://www.740thefan.com
Profile: KVOX-AM is a commercial station owned by Midwest Communications. The format of the station is sports. KVOX-AM broadcasts to the Fargo, ND area at 740 AM.
AM RADIO STATION

KVOX-FM 44373
Owner: James Ingstad Broadcast Group
Editorial: 2720 7th Ave S, Fargo, North Dakota 58103-8710 **Tel:** 1 701 237-4500.
Web site: http://www.froggyweb.com
Profile: KVOX-FM is a commercial station owned by James Ingstad Broadcast Group. The format of the station is contemporary country. KVOX-FM broadcasts to the Fargo, ND area at 99.9 FM.
FM RADIO STATION

KVPI-AM 37562
Owner: Ville Platte Broadcasting
Editorial: 809 W Lasalle St, Ville Platte, Louisiana 70586-3129 **Tel:** 1 337 363-2124.
Email: kvpiamfm@gmail.com
Web site: http://kvpionline.com
Profile: KVPI-AM is a commercial station owned by Ville Platte Broadcasting. The format of the station is classic country. KVPI-AM broadcasts to the Ville Platte, LA area at 1050 AM.
AM RADIO STATION

KVPI-FM 44942
Owner: Ville Platte Broadcasting
Editorial: 809 W Lasalle St, Ville Platte, Louisiana 70586-3129 **Tel:** 1 337 363-2124.
Email: kvpiamfm@gmail.com
Web site: http://www.oldies925.com
Profile: KVPI-FM is a commercial station owned by Ville Platte Broadcasting. The format of the station is oldies. KVPI-FM broadcasts to the Ville Platte, LA area at 92.5 FM.
FM RADIO STATION

KVPR-FM 41044
Owner: White Ash Broadcasting
Editorial: 3437 W Shaw Ave Ste 101, Fresno, California 93711-3243 **Tel:** 1 559 275-0764.
Email: kvpr@kvpr.org
Web site: http://www.kvpr.org
Profile: Valley Public Radio is a public radio organization in Fresno, California, broadcasting programming from National Public Radio (NPR) and other public radio producers and distributors, as well as locally produced news, music, talk, and public affairs programs. Valley Public Radio consists of two FM stations–KVPR in Fresno (89.3 MHz) and satellite station KPRX in Bakersfield (89.1 MHz). KPRX signed on in February 1987 as a full satellite of KVPR. The two stations' combined signal covers most of California's San Joaquin Valley, including the cities of Fresno, Bakersfield, Visalia, Madera, Tulare, Clovis, Merced, and Hanford.
FM RADIO STATION

KVRC-AM 37563
Owner: Noalmark Broadcasting Corp.
Editorial: 601 S 7th St, Arkadelphia, Arkansas 71923-6209 **Tel:** 1 870 246-9272.
Profile: KVRC-AM is a commercial station owned by Southwest Arkansas Media, LLC. The format of the station is regional mexican. KVRC-AM broadcasts to the Arkadelphia, AR area at 1240 AM.
AM RADIO STATION

KVRD-FM 46512
Owner: Yavapai Broadcasting
Editorial: 3405 E State Route 89A, Bldg A, Cottonwood, Arizona 86326 **Tel:** 1 928 634-2286.
Email: kvrd@myradioplace.com
Web site: http://www.kvrdfm.com
Profile: KVRD-FM is a commercial station owned by Yavapai Broadcasting. The format of the station is country music. KVRD-FM broadcasts in the Cottonwood, AZ area at 105.7 FM.
FM RADIO STATION

KVRE-FM 42334
Owner: Caddo Broadcasting Co.
Editorial: 122 Desoto Center Dr, Hot Springs Village, Arkansas 71909-3168 **Tel:** 1 501 922-5678.
Email: kvre@kvre.com
Profile: KVRE-FM is a commercial station owned by Caddo Broadcasting Co. The format of the station is adult standards. KVRE-FM broadcasts to the Hot Springs, AR area at 92.9 FM.
FM RADIO STATION

KVRG-FM 446415
Owner: Northeast Broadcasting Co.
Editorial: 3565 Southpark Dr, Jackson, Wyoming 83001 **Tel:** 1 307 732-0384.
Web site: http://www.1037therange.com
Profile: KVRG-FM is a commercial station owned by Northeast Broadcasting Co. The format of the station is classic country. KVRG-FM broadcasts to the Jackson, WY area at 103.7 FM.
FM RADIO STATION

KVRH-AM 37564
Owner: Three Eagles Communications
Editorial: 7600 County Road 120, Salida, Colorado 81201-9423 **Tel:** 1 719 539-0598.
Profile: KVRH-AM is a commercial station owned by Three Eagles Communications. The format of the station is oldies. KVRH-AM broadcasts to the Salida, CO area at 1340 AM.
AM RADIO STATION

KVRH-FM 44943
Owner: Alpha Media
Editorial: 7600 County Road 120, Salida, Colorado 81201-9423 **Tel:** 1 719 539-2575.
Web site: http://thepeak923.com
Profile: KVRH-FM is a commercial station owned by Alpha Media. The format of the station is hot adult

contemporary. KVRH-FM broadcasts to the Denver area at 92.3 FM.
FM RADIO STATION

KVRI-AM 621223
Owner: Multicultural Radio Broadcasting Inc.
Editorial: 4840 Lincoln Rd, Blaine, Washington 98230-9602 **Tel:** 1 360 371-5500.
Email: info@radioindialtd.com
Web site: http://www.radioindialtd.com
Profile: KVRI-AM is a commercial station owned by Multicultural Radio Broadcasting Inc. The format of the station is multicultural featuring Indian programming. KVRI-AM broadcasts to the northwest Washington State and southwest British Columbia area at 1600 AM.
AM RADIO STATION

KVRO-FM 44406
Owner: Mahaffey Enterprises Inc.
Editorial: 408 E Thomas Ave, Stillwater, Oklahoma 74075-2648 **Tel:** 1 405 372-7800.
Web site: http://www.stillwaterradio.net
Profile: KVRO-FM is a commercial station owned by Mahaffey Enterprises Inc. The format of the station is classic rock. KVRO-FM's target audience is adults, ages 18 to 64, in the Stillwater, OK and broadcasts at 101.1 FM.
FM RADIO STATION

KVRP-AM 37565
Owner: Allied Broadcasting
Editorial: 1302 Walnut St, Stamford, Texas 79553-7820 **Tel:** 1 325 773-2771.
Web site: http://www.kvrp.com
Profile: KVRP-AM is a commercial station owned by Allied Broadcasting. The format of the station is contemporary Christian. KVRP-AM broadcasts to the Haskell, TX area at 1400 AM. This station does not accepts press material.
AM RADIO STATION

KVRP-FM 44944
Owner: Allied Broadcasting
Editorial: 1406 N 1st St, Haskell, Texas 79521
Tel: 1 940 864-8505.
Web site: http://www.kvrp.com
Profile: KVRP-FM is a commercial station owned by Allied Broadcasting. The format of the station is contemporary country music. KVRP-FM broadcasts in the Stamford, TX area at 97.1 FM. This station does not accepts press material.
FM RADIO STATION

KVRQ-FM 46051
Owner: Hubbard Radio, LLC
Editorial: 3650 131st Ave SE Ste 550, Bellevue, Washington 98006-1334 **Tel:** 1 425 373-5536.
Web site: http://989rocks.com
Profile: KVRQ-FM is a commercial station owned by Hubbard Radio, LLC. The format of the station is rock. KVRQ-FM broadcasts in the Bellevue, WA area at 98.9 FM.
FM RADIO STATION

KVRS-FM 42505
Owner: American Family Association
Editorial: 107 Park Gate Dr, Tupelo, Mississippi 38801 **Tel:** 1 662 844-8888.
Email: comments@afr.net
Web site: http://www.afr.net
Profile: KVRS-FM is a non-commercial station owned by American Family Association. The format of the station is News Talk KVRS-FM broadcasts to the Lawton, OK area at 90.3 FM.
FM RADIO STATION

KVRT-FM 42701
Owner: South Texas Public Broadcasting
Editorial: 3205 S Staples St, Corpus Christi, Texas 78411-2524 **Tel:** 1 361 855-2213.
Web site: http://www.kedt.org
Profile: KVRT-FM is a non-commercial station owned by South Texas Public Broadcasting. The format of the station is classical, jazz and talk. KVRT-FM broadcasts to the Corpus Christi, TX area at 90.7 FM.
FM RADIO STATION

KVRV-FM 41105
Owner: Sonoma Media Group
Editorial: 1410 Neotomas Ave, Santa Rosa, California 95405-7533 **Tel:** 1 707 543-0100.
Web site: http://www.977theriver.com
Profile: KVRV-FM is a commercial station owned by Sonoma Media Group. The format of the station is classic rock. KVRV-FM broadcasts locally to the San Francisco, CA area at a frequency of 97.7 FM.
FM RADIO STATION

KVRW-FM 42561
Owner: Townsquare Media, LLC
Editorial: 626 SW D Ave, Lawton, Oklahoma 73501-4508 **Tel:** 1 580 581-3600.
Web site: http://1073popcrush.com/
Profile: KVRW-FM is a commercial station owned by Townsquare Media, LLC. The format of the station is CHR. KVRW-FM broadcasts to the Lawton, OK area at 107.3 FM.
FM RADIO STATION

KVSA-AM 35109
Owner: Southeast Arkansas Broadcasters, Inc.
Editorial: 3453 Highway 65 N, Dermott, Arkansas 71638-9562 **Tel:** 1 870 222-4200.
Email: kvsa1220@yahoo.com
AM RADIO STATION

KVSF-AM 800367
Owner: Hutton Broadcasting, LLC
Editorial: 2502 Camino Entrada Ste C, Santa Fe, New Mexico 87507-4911 **Tel:** 1 505 471-1067.
Web site: http://www.santafe.com/espn
Profile: KVSF-AM is a commercial station owned by Hutton Broadcasting, LLC. The format of the station is sports. KVSF-AM broadcasts to the Santa Fe, NM area at a frequency of 1400 AM.
AM RADIO STATION

KVSF-FM 35096
Owner: Hutton Broadcasting, LLC
Editorial: 2502 Camino Entrada Ste C, Santa Fe, New Mexico 87507-4911 **Tel:** 1 505 471-1067.
Web site: http://www.santafe.com/the-voice
Profile: KVSF-FM is a commercial station owned by Hutton Broadcasting, LLC. The format of the station is community radio, primarily news and talk, featuring some music programming. KVSF-FM broadcasts to the Santa Fe, NM area at 101.5 FM
FM RADIO STATION

KVSH-AM 35110
Owner: Heart City Radio Corp.
Editorial: 126 W 3rd St, Valentine, Nebraska 69201
Tel: 1 402 376-2400.
Email: kvsh@sandhillswireless.net
Profile: KVSH-AM is a commercial station owned by Heart City Radio Corp. The format of the station is adult contemporary, country and news. KVSH-AM broadcasts to the Valentine, NE area at 940 AM.
AM RADIO STATION

KVSI-AM 35111
Owner: Tri-State Broadcasting Co.
Editorial: 24681 US Highway Ste 89, Montpelier, Idaho 83254 **Tel:** 1 208 847-1450.
Email: kvsi@dcdi.net
Web site: http://www.kvsi.com
Profile: KVSI-AM is a commercial station owned by Tri-State Broadcasting Co. The format of the station is classic country. KVSI-AM broadcasts to the Montpelier, ID area at 1450 AM.
AM RADIO STATION

KVSL-AM 37566
Owner: New Directions Media, Inc
Tel: 1 928 251-4351.
Email: station@rewind108.com
Web site: http://www.rewind108.com
Profile: KVSL-AM is a commercial station owned by New Directions Media, Inc. The format of the station is adult hits. KVSL-AM broadcasts to the Show Low, AZ area at 1470 AM.
AM RADIO STATION

KVSO-AM 38703
Owner: LKCM Radio Group LP
Editorial: 1205 Northglen St, Ardmore, Oklahoma 73401-1202 **Tel:** 1 580 226-0421.
Web site: http://www.kvso.com
Profile: KVSO-AM is a commercial station owned by LKCM Radio Group LP. The format of the station is sports and is the ESPN Radio affiliate for the Texoma area. KVSO-AM broadcasts in the Ardmore, OK area at 1240 AM. The station's slogan is, "Southern Oklahoma Sports."
AM RADIO STATION

KVSP-FM 36136
Owner: Perry Publishing & Broadcasting Inc.
Editorial: 1528 NE 23rd St, Oklahoma City, Oklahoma 73111-3260 **Tel:** 1 405 427-5877.
Web site: http://www.kvsp.com
Profile: KVSP-AM is a commercial station owned by Perry Publishing & Broadcasting Inc. The format is urban contemporary music. KVSP-AM broadcasts to the Oklahoma City area at 103.5 FM.
FM RADIO STATION

KVSS-FM 44665
Owner: VSS Catholic Communications Inc.
Editorial: 13326 A St, Omaha, Nebraska 68144-3641
Tel: 1 402 571-0200.
Email: kvss@kvss.com
Web site: http://www.spiritcatholicradio.com
Profile: KVSS-FM is a non-commercial station owned by VSS Catholic Communications Inc. The format of the station is Catholic programming. KVSS-FM broadcasts to the Lincoln, NE area at 102.7 FM.
FM RADIO STATION

KVST-FM 44193
Owner: New Wavo Communications Group Inc.
Editorial: 1212 S Frazier St, Conroe, Texas 77301
Tel: 1 936 788-1035.
Email: news@kstarcountry.com
Web site: http://www.kstarcountry.com
Profile: KVST-FM is a commercial station owned by New Wavo Communications Group Inc. The format of the station is country music. KVST-FM broadcasts in the Houston area at 99.7 FM.
FM RADIO STATION

KVSV-AM 37567
Owner: McGrath Publishing Company
Editorial: Highway 24 East, Beloit, Kansas 67420
Tel: 1 785 738-2206.
Email: news@kvsvradio.com
Web site: http://www.kvsvradio.com
Profile: KVSV-AM is a commercial station owned by McGrath Publishing Company. The format of the station is adult contemporary music. KVSV-AM broadcasts to the Beloit, KS area at 1190 AM.
AM RADIO STATION

KVSV-FM 44945
Owner: McGrath Publishing Company
Editorial: 3185 Us 24 Hwy, Beloit, Kansas 67420-1577 **Tel:** 1 785 738-2206.
Email: news@kvsvradio.com
Web site: http://www.kvsvradio.com
Profile: KVSV-FM is a commercial station owned by McGrath Publishing Company. The format of the station is easy listening. KVSV-FM broadcasts to the Beloit, KS area at 105.5 FM.
FM RADIO STATION

KVTA-AM 36569
Owner: Gold Coast Broadcasting, LLC
Editorial: 2284 S Victoria Ave Ste 2G, Ventura, California 93003-6626 **Tel:** 1 805 289-1400.
Email: kvtanews@yahoo.com
Web site: http://kvta.com
Profile: KVTA-AM is a commercial station owned by Gold Coast Broadcasting, LLC. The format of the station is news and talk. KVTA-AM broadcasts to the Ventura, CA area at 1520 AM.
AM RADIO STATION

KVTI-FM 41632
Owner: Clover Park Technical College
Editorial: 4500 Steilacoom Blvd SW, Lakewood, Washington 98499-4004 **Tel:** 1 509 335-6500.
Email: nwpr@wsu.edu
Web site: http://www.nwpr.org
Profile: KVTI-FM is a non-commercial station owned by Clover Park Technical College and operated by Washington State University. The format of the station is news, talk and classical music. KVTI-FM broadcasts to the Tacoma, WA area at 90.9 FM.
FM RADIO STATION

KVTK-AM 38555
Owner: Five Star Communications, Inc.
Editorial: 210 W 3rd St, Yankton, South Dakota 57078-4323 **Tel:** 1 605 665-2600.
Email: sports@kvht.com
Web site: http://www.kvtk.com
Profile: KVTK-AM is a commercial station owned by Five Star Communications, Inc. The format of the station is sports. KVTK-AM broadcasts to the Vermillion, SD area at 1570 AM.
AM RADIO STATION

KVTO-AM 36201
Owner: YMF Media LLC
Editorial: 55 Hawthorne St Ste 900, San Francisco, California 94105-3967 **Tel:** 1 415 566-8808.
Email: info@inlanguageradio.com
Web site: http://www.kvto.net/
Profile: KVTO-AM is a commercial station owned by YMF Media LLC. The format of the station is a variety of Chines language programming. KVTO-AM broadcasts to the San Francisco area at 1400 AM. The station does not have a news department or accept press releases. PSA's are accepted.
AM RADIO STATION

KVTR-AM 38540
Owner: Rudex Broadcasting LTD
Editorial: 15000 7th St Ste 208E, Victorville, California 92395-3853 **Tel:** 1 760 298-3359.
Profile: KVTR-AM is a commercial station owned by Rudex Broadcasting LTD. The format of the station is regional Mexican music. KVTR-AM broadcasts in the Victorville, CA area at 1590 AM.
AM RADIO STATION

KVTY-FM 44120
Owner: Ida-Vend Communications Group
Editorial: 805 Stewart Ave, Lewiston, Idaho 83501-4709 **Tel:** 1 208 746-5056.
Email: idavendbroadcasting@idavend.com
Profile: KVTY-FM is a commercial station owned by Ida-Vend Communications Group. The format of the station is hot adult contemporary. The station broadcasts to the Lewiston, ID area at 105.1 FM.
FM RADIO STATION

KVUU-FM 44220
Owner: iHeartMedia Inc.
Editorial: 2864 S Circle Dr Ste 150, Colorado Springs, Colorado 80906-4128 **Tel:** 1 719 540-9200.
Web site: http://www.my999radio.com
Profile: KVUU-FM is a commercial station owned by iHeartMedia Inc. The format of the station is Top 40/ CHR. KVUU-FM broadcasts to the Colorado Springs, CO area at 99.9 FM.
FM RADIO STATION

KVVA-FM 43777
Owner: Entravision Communications Corp.
Editorial: 501 N 44th St, Ste 425, Phoenix, Arizona 85008 **Tel:** 1 602 776-1400.
Web site: http://www.josephoenix.com
Profile: KVVA-FM is a commercial station owned by Entravision Communications Corp. The format of the station is Hispanic adult hits. KVVA-FM broadcasts to the Phoenix area at 107.1 FM
FM RADIO STATION

KVVF-FM 81515
Owner: Univision Communications Inc.
Editorial: 750 Battery St Ste 200, San Francisco, California 94111-1524 **Tel:** 1 415 733-5765.
Web site: http://hot1057fm.univision.com
Profile: KVVF-FM is a commercial station owned by Univision Communications Inc. The format of the station is hip hop and R&B. KVVF-FM broadcasts to the San Francisco area at 105.7 FM.
FM RADIO STATION

KVVL-FM 44790
Owner: Nodaway Broadcasting Corp
Editorial: 1618 S Main St, Maryville, Missouri 64468-2612 **Tel:** 1 660 582-2151.
Email: traffic@nowadaybroadcasting.com
Web site: http://www.971thevill.com
Profile: KVVL-FM is a commercial station owned by Nodaway Broadcasting Corp. The format of the station is rock music. KVVL-FM broadcasts to the Maryville, MO area at 97.1 FM.
FM RADIO STATION

KVVN-AM 35024
Owner: Pham Radio Communication LLC
Editorial: 55 Hawthorne St Ste 900, San Francisco, California 94105-3967 **Tel:** 1 415 566-8808.
Email: info@inlanguageradio.com
Web site: http://www.kvvn.net/
Profile: KVVN-AM is a commercial station owned by Pham Radio Communication LLC. The format of the station is a variety of Vietnamese music, news and talk. KVVN-AM broadcasts to the San Jose, CA area at 1430 AM.
AM RADIO STATION

KVVP-FM 40013
Owner: Stannard Broadcasting Co.
Editorial: 168 Kvvp Dr, Leesville, Louisiana 71446-5817 **Tel:** 1 337 537-5887.
Web site: http://www.kvvp.com
Profile: KVVP-FM is a commercial station owned by Stannard Broadcasting Co. The format of the station is contemporary country. KVVP-FM broadcasts to the Leesville, LA area at 105.7 FM.
FM RADIO STATION

KVVR-FM 155654
Owner: Cherry Creek Radio
Editorial: 914 13th Ave S, Great Falls, Montana 59405-4406 **Tel:** 1 406 761-7600.
Profile: KVVR-FM is a commercial station owned by Cherry Creek Radio. The format of the station is lite rock. KVVR-FM broadcasts to the Great Falls, MT area at 97.9 FM.
FM RADIO STATION

KVVS-FM 45706
Owner: iHeartMedia Inc.
Editorial: 3400 W Olive Ave Ste 550, Burbank, California 91505-5544 **Tel:** 1 818 559-2252.
Web site: http://www.kiisfm.com
Profile: KVVS-FM is a commercial station owned by iHeartMedia Inc. The format of the station is Top 40/ CHR. KVVS-FM is a simulcast on KIIS-FM. KVVS-FM broadcasts to the Burbank, CA area on 105.5 FM.
FM RADIO STATION

KVVZ-FM 44966
Owner: Univision Communications Inc.
Editorial: 750 Battery St Ste 200, San Francisco, California 94111-1524 **Tel:** 1 415 733-5765.
Web site: http://hot1057fm.univision.com
Profile: KVVZ-FM is a commercial station owned by Univision Communications Inc. The format of the station is hip hop and R&B. The station airs locally on 105.7 FM and is a simulcast of KVVF-FM in San Jose, CA.
FM RADIO STATION

KVWC-AM 37568
Owner: KVWC Inc.
Editorial: 302 Wilbarger St, Vernon, Texas 76384
Tel: 1 940 552-6221.
Email: kvwc@kvwc.com
Web site: http://www.kvwc.com
Profile: KVWC-AM is a commercial station owned by KVWC Inc. The format of the station is a variety of music, including country, oldies, and gospel. KVWC-AM broadcasts to the Vernon, TX area at 1490 AM.
AM RADIO STATION

KVWC-FM 44946
Owner: KVWC Inc.
Editorial: 302 Wilbarger St, Vernon, Texas 76384
Tel: 1 940 552-6221.
Email: kvwc@kvwc.com
Web site: http://www.kvwc.com
Profile: KVWC-FM is a commercial station owned by KVWC Inc. The format of the station is news, country, sports and oldies. KVWC-FM broadcasts to the Vernon, TX area at 93.1 FM.
FM RADIO STATION

KVWF-FM 44233
Owner: Connoisseur Media LLC
Editorial: 1938 N Woodlawn St Ste 150, Wichita, Kansas 67208-1929 **Tel:** 1 316 558-8800.
Web site: http://www.1015hankfm.com/
Profile: KVWF-FM is a commercial station owned by Connoisseur Media LLC. The format of the station is contemporary country. KGGG-FM broadcasts to the Wichita, KS area at 100.5 FM.
FM RADIO STATION

KVWM-AM 37570
Owner: Petracom
Editorial: 1838 Commerce Dr Ste A, Lakeside, Arizona 85929-7008
Profile: KVWM-AM is a commercial station owned by Petracom. The format of the station is news and talk. KVWM-AM broadcasts to the Show Low, AZ area at 970 AM.
AM RADIO STATION

KVXR-AM 578503
Owner: Real Presence Radio
Editorial: 926 50th Ave S, Moorhead, Minnesota 56560-7400 **Tel:** 1 701 795-0122.
Email: businessmanager@realpresenceradio.com
Web site: http://yourcatholicradiostation.com
Profile: KVXR-AM is a non-commercial station owned by Real Presence Radio. The format of the station is religion and talk. KVXR-AM airs in the Moorhead, MN area at 1280 AM.
AM RADIO STATION

KVXX-FM 242146
Owner: Huth Broadcasting Inc.
Editorial: 2654 Cramer Ln, Chico, California 95928-8838 **Tel:** 1 530 592-4299.
Profile: KVXX-FM is a commercial station owned by Huth Broadcasting Inc. The format of the station is alternative rock music. KVXX-FM broadcasts to the Chico, CA area at 101.7 FM.
FM RADIO STATION

KVYB-FM 44030
Owner: Cumulus Media Inc.
Editorial: 1376 Walter St, Ventura, California 93003-5658 **Tel:** 1 805 642-8595.
Web site: http://www.1033thevibe.com
Profile: KVYB-FM is a commercial station owned by Cumulus Media Inc. The format of the station is urban contemporary. KVYB-FM broadcasts to the Ventura, CA area at 103.3 FM.
FM RADIO STATION

KVYN-FM 44949
Owner: Wine Country Broadcasting Co.
Editorial: 1124 Foster Rd, Napa, California 94558-6520 **Tel:** 1 707 258-1111.
Email: psa@kvyn.com
Web site: http://www.993thevine.com
Profile: KVYN-FM is a commercial station owned by Wine Country Broadcasting Co. The format of the station is classic hits. KVYN-FM broadcasts to the Napa, CA area at 99.3 FM.
FM RADIO STATION

KWAC-AM 36684
Owner: Lotus Communications Corp.
Editorial: 5100 Commerce Dr, Bakersfield, California 93309-0684 **Tel:** 1 661 327-9711.
Profile: KWAC-AM is a commercial station owned by Lotus Communications Corp. The format of the station is Hispanic sports. KWAC-FM broadcasts in the Bakersfield, CA area at 1490 AM.
AM RADIO STATION

KWAD-AM 35113
Owner: Hubbard Broadcasting Inc.
Editorial: 201 Jefferson St S, Wadena, Minnesota 56482-1531 **Tel:** 1 218 631-1803.
Web site: http://www.superstationk106.com
Profile: KWAD-AM is a commercial station owned by Hubbard Broadcasting Inc. The format of the station is country music. KWAD-AM broadcasts to the Wadena, MN area at 920 AM.
AM RADIO STATION

KWAI-AM 35972
Owner: Radio Hawaii Inc.
Editorial: 100 N Beretania St Ste 401, Honolulu, Hawaii 96817-4724 **Tel:** 1 808 523-3868.
Email: radiohawaii@inbox.com
Web site: http://kwai1080am.com
Profile: KWAI-AM is a commercial station owned by Radio Hawaii Inc. The format of the station is talk programming. KWAI-AM broadcasts to the Honolulu area at 1080 AM.
AM RADIO STATION

KWAK-AM 39178
Owner: Arkansas County Broadcasters Inc.
Editorial: 1818 S Buerkle St, Stuttgart, Arkansas 72160-5804 **Tel:** 1 870 673-1595.
Email: kwakradio@yahoo.com
Profile: KWAK-AM is a commercial station owned by Arkansas County Broadcasters Inc. The format of the station is sports. KWAK-AM broadcasts to the Stuttgart, AR area at 1240 AM.
AM RADIO STATION

KWAK-FM 46543
Owner: Arkansas County Broadcasters Inc.
Editorial: 1818 S Buerkle St, Stuttgart, Arkansas 72160 **Tel:** 1 870 673-1595.
Email: kdew973@yahoo.com
Profile: KWAK-FM is a commercial station owned by Arkansas County Broadcasters Inc. The format of the station is oldies. KWAK-FM broadcasts to the Stuttgart, AR area at 105.5 FM.
FM RADIO STATION

KWAL-AM 35114
Owner: Metals Broadcasting
Editorial: 120 First St, Osburn, Idaho 83849-9999 **Tel:** 1 208 752-1141.
Email: kwalradio@suddenlinkmail.com
Profile: KWAL-AM is a commercial station owned by Metals Broadcasting. The format of the station is classic country music. KWAL-AM broadcasts to the Spokane, WA area at 620 AM.
AM RADIO STATION

KWAM-AM 38950
Owner: Legacy Media Memphis LLC
Editorial: 5495 Murray Rd, Memphis, Tennessee 38119-3703 **Tel:** 1 901 261-4200.
Email: info@kwam990.com
Web site: http://www.kwam990.com
Profile: KWAM-AM is commercial station owned by Legacy Media Memphis LLC. The format of the station is news and talk. KWAM-AM broadcasts to the Memphis, TN area at 990 AM.
AM RADIO STATION

KWAR-FM 40014
Owner: Wartburg College
Editorial: 100 Wartburg Blvd, Waverly, Iowa 50677-2215 **Tel:** 1 319 352-8209.
Email: yoursound.kwar@gmail.com
Web site: http://wartburgcircuit.org
Profile: KWAR-FM is a non-commercial station owned by Wartburg College. The format of the station is variety. KWAR-FM broadcasts to the Waverly, IA area at a frequency of 89.9 FM.
FM RADIO STATION

KWAT-AM 39046
Owner: Alpha Media
Editorial: 921 9th Ave SE, Watertown, South Dakota 57201-4960 **Tel:** 1 605 886-8444.
Email: kwatnews@digity.me
Web site: http://www.gowatertown.net
Profile: KWAT-AM is a commercial station owned by Alpha Media. The format of the station is news and talk. KWAT-AM broadcasts to the Watertown, SD area at 950 AM.
AM RADIO STATION

KWAV-FM 46747
Owner: Mapleton Communications LLC
Editorial: 5 Harris Ct Bldg C, Monterey, California 93940-5751 **Tel:** 1 831 649-0969.
Email: frontdesk@kwav.com
Web site: http://www.kwav.com
Profile: KWAV-FM is a commercial station owned by Mapleton Communications LLC. The format of the station is adult contemporary. KWAV-FM broadcasts to the Monterey, CA area at 96.9FM.
FM RADIO STATION

KWAY-AM 37571
Owner: Suhr Enterprises(Ael)
Editorial: 110 29th Ave SW, Waverly, Iowa 50677-4301 **Tel:** 1 319 352-3550.
Email: news@kwayradio.com
Web site: http://www.kwayradio.com
Profile: KWAY-AM is a commercial station owned by Ael Suhr Enterprises. The format for the station is classic country. KWAY-AM broadcasts to the Cedar Rapids, IA area at 1470 AM.
AM RADIO STATION

KWAY-FM 44950
Owner: Suhr Enterprises(Ael)
Editorial: 110 29th Ave SW, Waverly, Iowa 50677 **Tel:** 1 319 352-3550.
Email: news@kwayradio.com
Web site: http://www.kwayradio.com
Profile: KWAY-FM is a commercial station owned by Ael Suhr Enterprises. The format for the station is hot adult contemporary. KWAY-FM broadcasts to the Cedar Rapids, IA area at 99.3 FM.
FM RADIO STATION

KWBC-AM 38498
Owner: Bryan Broadcasting
Editorial: 303 E Washington Ave, Ste A, Navasota, Texas 77868-3043 **Tel:** 1 936 825-9007.
Email: news@navasotanews.com
Web site: http://www.navasotanews.com
Profile: KWBC-AM is a commercial station owned by Bryan Broadcasting. The format of the station is news and talk. KWBC-AM broadcasts to the Navasota, TX area at 1550 AM.
AM RADIO STATION

KWBE-AM 35865
Owner: Siebert Communications Inc.
Editorial: 200 Sherman St, Beatrice, Nebraska 68310-3552 **Tel:** 1 402 228-5923.
Web site: http://kwbe.com/
Profile: KWBE-AM is a commercial station owned by Siebert Communications Inc. The format of the station is classic hits and news. KWBE-AM broadcasts to the Beatrice, NE area at 1450 AM
AM RADIO STATION

KWBG-AM 36164
Owner: Riverfront Broadcasting
Editorial: 724 Story St Ste 201, Boone, Iowa 50036-2875 **Tel:** 1 515 432-2046.
Email: kwbgnews@kwbg.com
Web site: http://www.kwbg.com
Profile: KWBG-AM is a commercial station owned by Riverfront Broadcasting. The format of the station is news and talk. KWBG-AM broadcasts to the Boone, IA area at 1590 AM.
AM RADIO STATION

KWBT-FM 43844
Owner: Kennelwood Broadcasting Company, Inc.
Editorial: 4800 W Waco Dr Suite 120, Waco, Texas 76710-7015 **Tel:** 1 254 313-1450.
Web site: http://www.centexbeat.com
Profile: KWBT-FM is a commercial station owned by Kennelwood Broadcasting Company, Inc. The format of the station is rhythmic and urban CHR. KWBT-FM broadcasts to the Waco, TX area at 94.5 FM. The target audience of the station is listeners, ages 18 to 64. KWBT-FM's tagline is "94.5 The Beat." Newscasts air at the top of the hour.
FM RADIO STATION

KWBU-FM 40017
Owner: Brazos Valley Public Broadcasting Foundation
Editorial: 1 Bear Pl, Unit 97296, Waco, Texas 76798-7296 **Tel:** 1 254 710-3426.
Web site: http://www.kwbu.org
Profile: KWBU-FM is a non-commercial station owned by Brazos Valley Public Broadcasting Foundation. The format of the station is classical and news. KWBU-FM broadcasts to the Waco, TX area at 103.3 FM.
FM RADIO STATION

KWBW-AM 37572
Owner: Eagle Communications
Editorial: 825 N Main St, Hutchinson, Kansas 67501-4605 **Tel:** 1 620 662-4486.
Email: bwradio.getsresults@eagleradio.net
Web site: http://www.kwbwradio.com
Profile: KWBW-AM is a commercial station owned by Eagle Radio Inc. The format of the station is news, sports and talk programming. KWBW-AM broadcasts to the Hutchinson, KS area at 1450 AM.
AM RADIO STATION

KWBY-AM 35123
Owner: Distell, Edward
Editorial: 1665 James St, Woodburn, Oregon 97071-3475 **Tel:** 1 503 981-9400.
Web site: http://www.lapantera940.com/contact.php
Profile: KWBY-AM is a commercial station owned by Distell, Edward. The format of the station is regional Mexican music. KWBY-AM broadcasts to Woodburn, OR at 940 AM.
AM RADIO STATION

KWBY-FM 41868
Owner: For The Love of the Game Broadcasting
Editorial: 19623 S US Highway 377 Ste 3, Dublin, Texas 76446-4423 **Tel:** 1 254 968-4776.
Email: kwby@hprnetwork.com
Web site: http://www.kwbyradio.com
Profile: KWBY-FM is a commercial station owned by For The Love of the Game Broadcasting. The format of the station is news and sports. KWBY-FM broadcasts to the Stephenville, TX area and nearby communities at 98.5 FM.
FM RADIO STATION

KWBZ-FM 43851
Owner: Prairie Communications LLP
Editorial: 1645 Highway 104 Ste G, Quincy, Illinois 62305-0081 **Tel:** 1 217 224-4653.
Email: wpwq106@adams.net
Web site: http://www.oldiessuperstation.com
FM RADIO STATION

KWCA-FM 519244
Owner: Absolute Communications, LLC
Editorial: 1784 California St, Redding, California 96001-1905 **Tel:** 1 530 244-1011.
Web site: http://www.mixredding.com
Profile: KUSQ-FM is a commercial station owned by Absolute Communications, LLC. The format of the station is Hot AC. KUSQ-FM broadcasts to the Redding, CA area at a frequency of 101.1 FM.
FM RADIO STATION

KWCD-FM 41843
Owner: Cherry Creek Radio
Editorial: 2300 E Busby Dr, Sierra Vista, Arizona 85635-3310 **Tel:** 1 520 458-4313.
Email: kwcd@cherrycreekradio.com
Web site: http://www.kwcdcountry.com
Profile: KWCD-FM is a commercial station owned by Cherry Creek Radio. The format of the station is contemporary country. KWCD-FM broadcasts to the Sierra Vista, AZ area at 92.3 FM.
FM RADIO STATION

KWCK-FM 46376
Owner: Crain Media Group LLC
Editorial: 111 N Spring St, Searcy, Arkansas 72143-7712 **Tel:** 1 501 268-7123.
Email: production@crainmedia.com
Web site: http://www.crainmedia.com
Profile: KWCK-FM is a commercial station owned by Crain Media Group LLC. The format of the station is classic country. KWCK-FM broadcasts to the Searcy, AR area at 99.9 FM.
FM RADIO STATION

KWCL-FM 41822
Owner: KWCL-FM Broadcasting Company Inc.
Editorial: 230 E Main St, Oak Grove, Louisiana 71263-2557 **Tel:** 1 318 428-9670.
Email: kwcl@bellsouth.net
Web site: http://kwclfm.com
Profile: KWCL-FM is a commercial station owned by KWCL-FM Broadcasting Company Inc. The format of the station is classic hits. KWCL-FM broadcasts in the Oak Grove, LA area at 96.7 FM.
FM RADIO STATION

KWCO-FM 43576
Owner: Mollman Communications, Inc.
Editorial: 627 W Chickasha Ave, Chickasha, Oklahoma 73018 **Tel:** 1 405 224-1560.
Web site: http://www.classichits1055.com
Profile: KWCO-FM is a commercial station owned by Mollman Communications, Inc. The format of the station is classic hits. KWCO-FM broadcasts to the Oklahoma City area at 105.5 FM.
FM RADIO STATION

KWCQ-FM 561311
Owner: Jacobs Radio Programming, LLC
Editorial: 2617 W Falls Ave, Kennewick, Washington 99336-3002 **Tel:** 1 509 302-9874.
Web site: http://www.1073thebeat.com/
Profile: KWCQ-FM is a commercial station owned by Jacobs Radio Programming, LLC. The format of the station is urban contemporary. KWCQ-FM broadcasts to the The Dalles, OR at 106.1 FM.
FM RADIO STATION

KWCX-FM 43007
Owner: KZLZ, LLC
Editorial: 900 W Pattie Rd, Willcox, Arizona 85643 **Tel:** 1 520 384-4626.
Web site: http://www.xwave1049.com
Profile: KWCX-FM is a commercial station owned by Lakeshore Media LLC. The format of the station is variety, with a mix of rock, classic rock, top 40, metal, dance and European music. KWCX-FM broadcasts to the Willcox, AZ area at 104.9 FM.
FM RADIO STATION

KWDD-FM 842413
Owner: Last Frontier Mediactive, LLC
Editorial: 819 1st Ave Ste A, Fairbanks, Alaska 99701-4449 **Tel:** 1 907 451-5910.
Web site: http://www.lfmediactive.com
Profile: KWDD-FM is a commercial station owned by Last Frontier Mediactive, LLC. The format of the station is contemporary country music. KWDD-FM broadcasts to the Fairbanks, AK area at a frequency of 94.3 FM.
FM RADIO STATION

KWDF-AM 35892
Owner: Wilkins Radio Network, Inc.
Editorial: 3735 Rigolette Rd, Pineville, Louisiana 71360-7365 **Tel:** 1 318 640-4373.
Email: kwdf@wilkinsradio.com
Web site: http://wilkinsradio.com/kwdf-840am-alexandria-la
Profile: KWDF-AM is a commercial station owned by Wilkins Radio Network, Inc. The format of the station is religious teaching. KWDF-AM broadcasts to the Alexandria, LA area at 840 AM.
AM RADIO STATION

KWDP-AM 35934
Owner: Yaquina Bay Communications Inc.
Editorial: 906 SW Alder St, Newport, Oregon 97365-4712 **Tel:** 1 541 265-2266.
Email: news@ybcradio.com
Web site: http://www.kbcham.com
Profile: KWDP-AM is a commercial station owned by Yaquina Bay Communications Inc. The format of the station is adult standards music, news and talk. KWDP-AM broadcasts to the Waldport, OR area at 820 AM.
AM RADIO STATION

KWDQ-FM 41178
Owner: Classic Communications Inc.
Editorial: 1922 22nd St, Woodward, Oklahoma 73801-5307 **Tel:** 1 580 254-9102.
Email: cciradio@sbcglobal.net
Web site: http://www.woodwardradio.com
Profile: KWDQ-FM is a commercial station owned by Classic Communications Inc. The format of the station is rock music. KWDQ-FM broadcasts to the Oklahoma City area at 102.3 FM.
FM RADIO STATION

KWDR-FM 928362
Owner: Jacobs Radio Programming, LLC
Editorial: 2617 W Falls Ave, Kennewick, Washington 99336-3002 **Tel:** 1 509 737-8762.
Web site: http://smoothjazz1023.com
Profile: KWDR-FM is a commercial station owned by Jacobs Radio Programming, LLC. The format of the station is smooth jazz. The station broadcasts to the Tri-Cities, WA area at 93.5 FM.
FM RADIO STATION

KWDZ-AM 939265
Owner: Radio Disney Group
Editorial: 2801 Decker Lake Dr Ste 100, Salt Lake City, Utah 84119-2330 **Tel:** 1 801 908-5152.
Profile: KWDZ-AM is a commercial station owned by the Radio Disney Group. The format of the station is children's. The station broadcasts to the Salt Lake City, UT area at a frequency of 910 AM.
AM RADIO STATION

KWED-AM 35115
Owner: Guadalupe Media, Ltd.
Editorial: 609 E Court St, Seguin, Texas 78155-5713 **Tel:** 1 830 379-2234.
Email: cindy@kwed1580.com
Web site: http://www.seguintoday.com
Profile: KWED-AM is a commercial station owned by Guadalupe Media, Ltd. The format of the station is country music. KWED-AM broadcasts to the Seguin, TX area at 1580 AM.
AM RADIO STATION

KWEE-FM 41751
Owner: Alpha Media
Editorial: 3355 NE Cornell Rd, Hillsboro, Oregon 97124-5018 **Tel:** 1 844 640-5959.
Email: contact@we963pdx.com
Web site: http://www.we963pdx.com
Profile: KWEE-FM is a commercial station owned by Alpha Media. The format for the station is rhythmic CHR. KWEE-FM broadcasts to the Portland, OR area at 96.3 FM.
FM RADIO STATION

KWEI-AM 37574
Owner: Treasure Valley Broadcasting
Editorial: 1156 N Orchard St, Boise, Idaho 83706-2234 **Tel:** 1 208 367-1859.
Profile: KWEI-AM is a commercial station owned by the Treasure Valley Broadcasting. The format of the station is Tejano music. KWEI-AM broadcasts to the Boise, ID area at 1260 AM.
AM RADIO STATION

KWEL-AM 36148
Owner: CDA Broadcasting Inc.
Editorial: 310 W Wall St, Midland, Texas 79701-5123
Tel: 1 432 620-9393.
Web site: http://www.kwel.com
Profile: KWEL-AM is a commercial station owned by CDA Broadcasting Inc. The format of the station is talk. KWEL-AM broadcasts to the Midland, TX area at 1070 AM.
AM RADIO STATION

KWEN-FM 46064
Owner: Cox Media Group, Inc.
Editorial: 7136 S Yale Ave Ste 500, Tulsa, Oklahoma 74136-6358 **Tel:** 1 918 494-9500.
Web site: http://www.k95tulsa.com
Profile: KWEN-FM is a commercial station owned by Cox Media Group, Inc. The format of the station is contemporary country. KWEN-FM broadcasts to the Tulsa, OK area at 95.5 FM.
FM RADIO STATION

KWES-AM 570406
Owner: Walton Stations of New Mexico, Inc.
Editorial: 1096 Mechem Dr Ste 230, Ruidoso, New Mexico 88345-7071 **Tel:** 1 575 258-2222.
Email: production@kwes.net
Web site: http://www.kwes.net
Profile: KWES-AM is a commercial station owned by Walton Stations of New Mexico, Inc. The format of the station is sports. KWES-AM broadcasts to the Ruidoso, NM area at 1450 AM.
AM RADIO STATION

KWES-FM 46515
Owner: Walton Stations of New Mexico, Inc.
Editorial: 1096 Mechem Dr Ste 230, Ruidoso, New Mexico 88345-7071 **Tel:** 1 575 258-2222.
Email: production@kwes.net
Web site: http://www.kwes.net
Profile: KWES-FM is a commercial station owned by Walton Stations of New Mexico, Inc. The format of the station is country. KWES-FM broadcasts to the Ruidoso, NM area at 93.5 FM.
FM RADIO STATION

KWEY-AM 38585
Owner: Wright Broadcasting Systems
Editorial: 10040 Highway 54, Weatherford, Oklahoma 73096-3021 **Tel:** 1 580 772-5939.
Email: kwey@wrightwradio.com
Web site: http://www.kwey.com
Profile: KWEY-AM is a commercial station owned by Wright Broadcasting Systems. The format of the station is country music. KWEY-AM broadcasts to the Oklahoma City area at 1590 AM.
AM RADIO STATION

KWEY-FM 45935
Owner: Wright Broadcasting Systems
Editorial: 10040 Highway 54, Weatherford, Oklahoma 73096-3021 **Tel:** 1 580 772-5939.
Email: news@wrightwradio.com
Web site: http://www.kwey.com
Profile: KWEY-FM is a commercial station owned by Wright Broadcasting Systems. The format of the station is country music. KWEY-FM broadcasts to the Oklahoma City area at 95.5 FM.
FM RADIO STATION

KWFB-FM 43391
Owner: KIXC-FM LLC
Editorial: 719 Scott Ave Ste 1009, Wichita Falls, Texas 76301-2632 **Tel:** 1 940 322-1009.
Web site: http://www.bobradio.fm
Profile: KWFB-FM is a commercial station owned by KIXC-FM LLC. The format of the station is Jack FM adult hits. KWFB-FM broadcasts to the Quanah, TX area at 100.9
FM RADIO STATION

KWFC-FM 40021
Owner: Baptist Bible College
Editorial: 2316 N Benton Ave, Springfield, Missouri 65803 **Tel:** 1 417 869-0891.
Email: news@kwfc.org
Web site: http://www.kwfc.org
Profile: KWFC-FM is a non-commercial station owned by Baptist Bible College. The format of the station is southern gospel music. KWFC-FM broadcasts to the Springfield, MO area at 89.1 FM.
FM RADIO STATION

KWFH-FM 41452
Owner: Advance Ministries
Editorial: 510 Acoma Blvd N, Lake Havasu City, Arizona 86403-4838 **Tel:** 1 928 855-9110.
Email: info@kwfh.org
Web site: http://www.kwfh.org
Profile: KWFH-FM is a non-commercial station owned by Advance Ministries. The format of the station is contemporary Christian. KWFH-FM broadcasts to the Parker, AZ area at 90.3 FM.
FM RADIO STATION

KWFJ-FM 43008
Owner: Bible Broadcasting Network
Tel: 1 800 888-7077.
Email: bbn@bbnmedia.org
Web site: http://www.bbnradio.org
Profile: KWFJ-FM is a non-commercial station owned by the Bible Broadcasting Network. The format of the station is Christian music and talk. KWFJ-FM broadcasts to the Roy, WA area at 103.6 FM.
FM RADIO STATION

KWFL-FM 41707
Owner: Family Life Broadcasting System
Editorial: 300 S Lea Ave, Roswell, New Mexico 88203
Tel: 1 505 296-9100.
Web site: http://www.myflr.org
Profile: KWFL-FM is a non-commercial station owned by Family Life Broadcasting System. The format of the station is Christian talk and music. KWFL-FM broadcasts to the Albuquerque, NM area at 99.5 FM. The station does not want to receive any press materials.
FM RADIO STATION

KWFP-FM 135232
Owner: The Evans Broadcasting Company, Inc
Editorial: 300 E 2nd St Ste 1400, Reno, Nevada 89501-1566 **Tel:** 1 775 333-0123.
Web site: http://www.thewolf921.com
Profile: KWFP-FM is a commercial station owned by Wilks Broadcast Group. The format of the station is contemporary country. KWFP-FM broadcasts to the Reno, NV area at 92.1 FM.
FM RADIO STATION

KWFR-FM 42864
Owner: Foster Communications Co. Inc.
Editorial: 2824 Sherwood Way, San Angelo, Texas 76901-3514 **Tel:** 1 325 949-3333.
Web site: http://www.kwfrfm.com
Profile: KWFR-FM is a commercial station owned by Foster Communications Co. Inc. The format of the station is classic rock. KWFR-FM broadcasts to the San Angelo, TX area at 101.9 FM.
FM RADIO STATION

KWFS-AM 39067
Owner: Townsquare Media, LLC
Editorial: 2525 Kell Blvd Ste 200, Wichita Falls, Texas 76308-1008 **Tel:** 1 940 763-1111.
Web site: http://www.newstalk1290.com
Profile: KWFS-AM is a commercial station owned by Townsquare Media, LLC. The format of the station is news and talk. KWFS-AM broadcasts to the Wichita Falls, TX area at 1290 AM.
AM RADIO STATION

KWFS-FM 46403
Owner: Townsquare Media, LLC
Editorial: 2525 Kell Blvd, Wichita Falls, Texas 76308-1064 **Tel:** 1 940 763-1111.
Web site: http://1023blakefm.com
Profile: KWFS-FM is a commercial station owned by Townsquare Media, LLC. The format of the station is contemporary country music. KWFS-FM broadcasts to the Wichita Falls, TX area at 102.3 FM.
FM RADIO STATION

KWFX-FM 43398
Owner: Classic Communications Inc.
Editorial: 1922 22nd St, Woodward, Oklahoma 73801
Tel: 1 580 254-9103.
Email: cciradio@sbcglobal.net
Web site: http://www.woodwardradio.com
Profile: KWFX-FM is a commercial station owned by Classic Communications. The format of the station is classic country music. KWFX-FM broadcasts to the Oklahoma City area at 100.1 FM.
FM RADIO STATION

KWG-AM 36321
Owner: Immaculate Heart Radio
Editorial: 2280 E Weber Ave, Stockton, California 95205-5051 **Tel:** 1 209 462-8307.
Email: programming@ihradio.org
Web site: http://ihradio.org
Profile: KWG-AM is a non-commercial station owned by Immaculate Heart Radio. The format of the station is Catholic programming. KWG-AM broadcasts to the Sacramento, CA area at 1230 AM.
AM RADIO STATION

KWGB-FM 44196
Owner: Rocking M Radio
Editorial: 3023 W 31st St, Goodland, Kansas 67735-9098 **Tel:** 1 785 462-3305.
Email: kxxxkqlf@rockingmradio.com
Web site: http://www.rockingmradio.com
Profile: KWGB-FM is a commercial station owned by Rocking M Radio. The format of the station is contemporary country music. KWGB-FM broadcasts to the Goodland, KS area at 97.9 FM.
FM RADIO STATION

KWGL-FM 83671
Owner: Western Slope Communications
Editorial: 751 Horizon Ct, Ste 225, Grand Junction, Colorado 81506 **Tel:** 1 970 241-6460.
Email: production@wscradio.net
Profile: KWGL-FM is a commercial station owned by Western Slope Communications. The format for the station is classic country. KWGL-FM broadcasts to the Grand Junction-Montrose, CO area at 105.7 FM.
FM RADIO STATION

KWHF-FM 44199
Owner: East Arkansas Broadcasters Inc.
Editorial: 407 W Parker Rd, Jonesboro, Arkansas 72404-8408 **Tel:** 1 870 932-8400.
Web site: http://www.959thewolf.com
Profile: KWHF-FM is a commercial station owned by East Arkansas Broadcasters Inc. The format of the station is classic country. KWHF-FM broadcasts to the Jonesboro, AR area at 95.9 FM.
FM RADIO STATION

KWHI-AM 36467
Owner: Whitehead Inc.(Tom S.)
Editorial: 223 E Main St, Brenham, Texas 77833
Tel: 1 979 836-3655.
Email: news@kwhi.com
Web site: http://www.kwhi.com
Profile: KWHI-AM is a commercial station owned by Tom S. Whitehead Inc. The format of the station is talk and classic country music. KWHI-AM broadcasts to the Brenham, TX area at 1280 AM.
AM RADIO STATION

KWHK-FM 444937
Owner: Ad Astra Per Aspera Broadcasting, Inc.
Editorial: 10 E 5th Ave, Hutchinson, Kansas 67501-6201 **Tel:** 1 620 665-5758.
Profile: KWHK-FM is a commercial station owned by Ad Astra Per Aspera Broadcasting, Inc. The format of the station is oldies music. KWHK-FM broadcasts to Wichita-Hutchinson, KS area at 95.9 FM.
FM RADIO STATION

KWHL-FM 44954
Owner: Alpha Media
Editorial: 301 Arctic Slope Ave Ste 200, Anchorage, Alaska 99518-3035 **Tel:** 1 907 344-9622.
Email: studio@kwhl.com
Web site: http://www.kwhl.com
Profile: KWHL-FM is a commercial station owned by Alpha Media. The format of the station is rock/album-oriented rock. KWHL-FM broadcasts to the Anchorage, AK area at 106.5 FM.
FM RADIO STATION

KWHN-AM 133369
Owner: iHeartMedia Inc.
Editorial: 311 Lexington Ave, Fort Smith, Arkansas 72901-3842 **Tel:** 1 479 782-8888.
Web site: http://kwhn.iheart.com
Profile: KWHN-AM is a commercial station owned by iHeartMedia Inc. The format of the station is news and talk. KWHN-AM broadcasts to the Fort Smith, AR area at 1320 AM.
AM RADIO STATION

KWHQ-FM 46363
Owner: KSRM, Inc.
Editorial: 40960 Kalifornsky Beach Rd, Kenai, Alaska 99611-6445 **Tel:** 1 907 283-8700.
Email: rken18@radiokenai.com
Web site: http://www.radiokenai.com
Profile: KWHQ-FM is a commercial station owned by Blayde Communications Inc. The format of the station is country. KWHQ-FM broadcasts to the Kenai, AK area at 100.1 FM.
FM RADIO STATION

KWHT-FM 44955
Owner: Capps Broadcast Group
Editorial: 2003 NW 56th St, Pendleton, Oregon 97801
Tel: 1 541 276-1511.
Web site: http://www.1035kwheat.com
Profile: KWHT-FM is a commercial station owned by Capps Broadcasting Group. The format of the station is country music. KWHT-FM broadcasts to the Pendleton, OR area at 103.5 FM.
FM RADIO STATION

KWHW-AM 37575
Owner: Monarch Broadcasting
Editorial: 212 W Cypress St, Altus, Oklahoma 73521-3704 **Tel:** 1 580 482-1450.
Web site: http://www.kwhw.com
Profile: KWHW-AM is a commercial station owned by Monarch Broadcasting. The format of the station is country. KWHW-AM broadcasts to the Altus, OK area at 1450 AM.
AM RADIO STATION

KWHW-FM 44866
Owner: Monarch Broadcasting
Editorial: 212 W Cypress St, Altus, Oklahoma 73521
Tel: 1 580 482-1450.
Web site: http://www.kwhw.com
Profile: KWHW-FM is a commercial station owned by Monarch Broadcasting. The format of the station is country music. KRKZ-FM broadcasts to the Altus, OK area at 93.5 FM.
FM RADIO STATION

KWIC-FM 42680
Owner: Cumulus Media Inc.
Editorial: 825 S Kansas Ave, Ste 100, Topeka, Kansas 66612 **Tel:** 1 785 272-2122.
Web site: http://www.eagle993.com
Profile: KWIC-FM is a commercial radio station owned by Cumulus Media. The format of the station is classic hits. KWIC-FM broadcasts to the Topeka, KS area on 99.3 FM.
FM RADIO STATION

KWID-FM 43611
Owner: Lotus Communications Corp.
Editorial: 8755 W Flamingo Rd, Las Vegas, Nevada 89147-8667 **Tel:** 1 702 876-1460.
Web site: http://www.labuenalv.com/
Profile: KWID-FM is a commercial station owned by Lotus Communications Corp. The format of the station is Hispanic oldies. KWID-FM broadcasts to the Las Vegas area at 101.9 FM.
FM RADIO STATION

KWIL-AM 3757
Owner: Extra Mile Media Inc.
Editorial: 34545 Highway 20 SE, Albany, Oregon 97322-9731 **Tel:** 1 541 926-2233.
Web site: http://www.kwil790.com
Profile: KWIL-AM is a commercial station owned by Extra Mile Media Inc. The format of the station is religious and Southern gospel. KWIL-AM broadcasts to the Albany, OR area at 790 AM.
AM RADIO STATION

KWIM-FM 13395
Owner: Western Indian Ministries
Editorial: HC 33 Box 40, Highway 264, 02C Hilltop Drive, Gallup, New Mexico 87301-9701
Tel: 1 505 371-5587.
Email: kwim@westernindian.org
Web site: http://www.westernindian.net
Profile: KWIM-FM is a non-commercial station owned by Western Indian Ministries. The format of the station is contemporary Christian. KWIM-FM broadcasts to the Window Rock, AZ area on 104.9 FM.
FM RADIO STATION

KWIN-FM 4355
Owner: Cumulus Media Inc
Editorial: 3127 Transworld Dr #270, Stockton, California 95206-4988 **Tel:** 1 209 507-8500.
Web site: http://www.kwin.com
Profile: KWIN-FM is a commercial station owned by Cumulus Media Inc. The format of the station is urban contemporary. KWIN-FM broadcasts to the Stockton CA area at 98.3 FM.
FM RADIO STATION

KWIP-AM 3626
Owner: Valley Broadcasting
Editorial: 1405 E Ellendale Ave, Dallas, Oregon 97338-1709 **Tel:** 1 503 623-0245.
Web site: http://www.kwip.com
Profile: KWIP-AM is a commercial station owned by Valley Broadcasting. The format of the station is regional Mexican. KWIP-FM broadcasts to Dallas, OR, at 880 AM.
AM RADIO STATION

KWIQ-AM 3899
Owner: Morris Communications
Editorial: 32 N Mission St Unit B2, Wenatchee, Washington 98801-7210 **Tel:** 1 509 663-5186.
Web site: http://www.kkrt.com
Profile: KWIQ-AM is a commercial station owned by Morris Communications. The format of the station is sports. KWIQ-AM broadcasts to the Moses Lake, WA area at 1020 AM.
AM RADIO STATION

KWIQ-FM 4633
Owner: Morris Communications
Editorial: 11768 Kittleson Rd NE, Moses Lake, Washington 98837-9720 **Tel:** 1 509 765-1761.
Web site: http://www.kwiq.com
Profile: KWIQ-FM is a commercial station owned by Morris Communications. The format of the station is country music. KWIQ-FM broadcasts to the Spokane WA area at 100.5 FM.
FM RADIO STATION

KWIT-FM 4002
Owner: Western Iowa Tech Community College
Editorial: 4647 Stone Ave, Sioux City, Iowa 51106-1918 **Tel:** 1 712 274-6406.
Email: kwitnews@witcc.edu
Web site: http://www.kwit.org
Profile: KWIT-FM is a non-commercial station owned by Western Iowa Tech Community College. The format of the station is news, talk and classical music. KWIT-FM broadcasts to the Sioux City, IA area at 90.3 FM.
FM RADIO STATION

KWIX-AM 3511
Owner: Moberly/Macon License Co., LLC
Editorial: 300 W Reed St, Moberly, Missouri 65270
Tel: 1 660 263-1500.
Email: kresnews@regionalradio.com
Web site: http://www.centralmoinfo.com
Profile: KWIX-AM is a commercial station owned by Moberly/Macon License Co., LLC. The format of the station is news and talk. KWIX-AM broadcasts in the Moberly, MO area at 1230 AM.
AM RADIO STATION

KWJB-AM 3631
Owner: Butler7Media, LLC
Editorial: 5600 W Lovers Ln, Dallas, Texas 75209-4330 **Tel:** 1 214 641-9400.
Web site: http://www.kwjb.com
Profile: KWJB-AM is a commercial station owned by Butler7Media, LLC. The format of the station is News and Talk. KWJB-AM broadcasts to the Canton, TX area at 1510 AM.
AM RADIO STATION

KWJC-FM 4002
Owner: William Jewell College
Editorial: 500 College Hl, Liberty, Missouri 64068
Tel: 1 816 415-5091.
Web site: http://www.jewell.edu
Profile: KWJC-FM is a non-commercial station owned by Willam Jewell College. The format of the

station is contemporary Christian, and airs the programming from K-Love network. KWJC-FM broadcasts to the Liberty, MO area at 91.9 FM.
FM RADIO STATION

KWJJ-FM 44956
Owner: Entercom Communications Corp.
Editorial: 0700 SW Bancroft St, Portland, Oregon 97239-4226 **Tel:** 1 503 223-1441.
Web site: http://www.thewolfonline.com
Profile: KWJJ-FM is a commercial station owned by Entercom Communications Corp. The format of the station is contemporary country music. KWJJ-FM broadcasts to Portland, OR at 99.5 FM.
FM RADIO STATION

KWJK-FM 64048
Owner: Billings Broadcasting LLC
Editorial: 1600 Radio Hill Rd, Boonville, Missouri 65233-1957 **Tel:** 1 660 882-6686.
Email: kwrt@1370kwrt.com
Web site: http://www.1370kwrt.com
Profile: KWJK-FM is a commercial station owned by Billings Broadcasting LLC. The format of the station is adult hits music. KWRT-FM broadcasts to the Boonville, MO area at 93.1 FM.
FM RADIO STATION

KWKA-AM 37578
Owner: Zia Broadcasting Inc.
Editorial: 710 Cr K, Clovis, New Mexico 88101
Tel: 1 575 762-4411.
Email: ktqm@plateautel.net
AM RADIO STATION

KWKC-AM 36804
Owner: Canfin Enterprises Inc.
Editorial: 402 Cypress St, Ste 510, Abilene, Texas 79601 **Tel:** 1 325 672-5442.
Web site: http://www.radioabilene.com
Profile: KWKC-AM is a commercial station owned by Canfin Enterprises Inc. The format of the station is news, talk, and sports. KWKC-AM broadcasts to the Abilene, TX area at 1340 AM.
AM RADIO STATION

KWKH-AM 37579
Owner: Townsquare Media, LLC
Editorial: 6341 W Port Ave, Shreveport, Louisiana 71129 **Tel:** 1 318 688-1130.
Web site: http://1130thetiger.com
Profile: KWKH-AM is a commercial station owned by Townsquare Media, LLC. The format of the station is sports. KWKH-AM broadcasts to the Shreveport, LA area at 1130 AM.
AM RADIO STATION

KWKJ-FM 83738
Owner: D & H Media LLC
Editorial: 800 Pca Rd, Warrensburg, Missouri 64093-9275 **Tel:** 1 660 747-9191.
Web site: http://www.warrensburgradio.com
Profile: KWKJ-FM is a commercial station owned by D & H Media LLC. The format for the station is contemporary country. KWKJ-FM broadcasts to the Warrensbrug, MO area at 98.5 FM.
FM RADIO STATION

KWKK-FM 46665
Owner: East Arkansas Broadcasters Inc.
Editorial: 2705 E Parkway Dr, Russellville, Arkansas 72802-2006 **Tel:** 1 479 968-6816.
Email: news@rivervalleyradio.com
Web site: http://www.riverhitskwkk.com
Profile: KWKK-FM is a commercial station owned by East Arkansas Broadcasters Inc. The format of the station is hot adult contemporary. KWKK-FM broadcasts to the Russellville, AR area at 100.9 FM.
FM RADIO STATION

KWKM-FM 139601
Owner: KM Communications Inc.
Editorial: 1520 E Commerce Ste B, Show Low, Arizona 85901-5277 **Tel:** 1 928 532-2949.
Email: sales@kwkm.com
Web site: http://www.kwkm.com
Profile: KWKM-FM is a commercial station owned by KM Communications Inc. The format is hot adult contemporary music. KWKM-FM broadcasts to the Show Low, AZ area at 95.7 FM.
FM RADIO STATION

KWKR-FM 542826
Owner: Ingstad Family Media
Editorial: 1402 E Kansas Ave, Garden City, Kansas 67846-5806 **Tel:** 1 620 276-2366.
Web site: http://www.westernkansasnews.com/kwkr/
Profile: KWKR-FM is a commercial station owned by Ingstand Family Media. The format of the station is classic rock. KWKR-FM broadcasts to the Garden City, KS area at 99.9 FM.
FM RADIO STATION

KWKW-AM 36019
Owner: Lotus Communications Corp.
Editorial: 3301 Barham Blvd, Los Angeles, California 90068-1480 **Tel:** 1 323 851-5959.
Email: kwkw1330@aol.com
Web site: http://www.radiodeportes.com
Profile: KWKW-AM is a commercial station owned by the Lotus Communications Corp. The format of the station is Spanish sports talk. KWKW-AM broadcasts to the Los Angeles area at 1330 AM and simulcasts on KWKU-AM.
AM RADIO STATION

KWKY-AM 35117
Owner: St. Gabriel Communications, Inc.
Tel: 1 515 223-1150.
Web site: http://www.Iowacatholicradio.com
Profile: KWKY-AM is a commercial station owned by St. Gabriel Communications, Inc. The format of the station is Catholic programming. KWKY-AM broadcasts to the Des Moines, IA area at 1150 AM.
AM RADIO STATION

KWKZ-FM 42504
Owner: Anderson Broadcasting Inc.
Editorial: 753 Enterprise St, Cape Girardeau, Missouri 63703 **Tel:** 1 573 334-7800.
Web site: http://www.kwkz.com
Profile: KWKZ-FM is a commercial station owned by Anderson Broadcasting Inc. The format of the station is classic country. KWKZ-FM broadcasts to the Cape Girardeau, MO area at 106.1 FM.
FM RADIO STATION

KWLA-AM 35118
Owner: Baldridge-Dumas Communications Inc.
Editorial: 605 San Antonio Ave, Many, Louisiana 71449-3018 **Tel:** 1 318 256-5177.
Email: production@bdcradio.com
Web site: http://bdcradio.com
Profile: KWLA-AM is a commercial station owned by Baldridge-Dumas Communications Inc. The format of the station is talk. KWLA-AM broadcasts to the Shreveport, LA area at 1400 AM.
AM RADIO STATION

KWLC-AM 35119
Owner: Luther College
Editorial: 700 College Dr, Decorah, Iowa 52101-1041
Tel: 1 563 387-1240.
Email: kwlcam@luther.edu
Web site: http://luther.edu/kwlc/
Profile: KWLC-AM is a non-commercial station owned by Luther College. The format of the station is variety. KWLC-AM broadcasts to the Decorah, IA area at a frequency of 1240 AM.
AM RADIO STATION

KWLF-FM 45819
Owner: Last Frontier Mediactive, LLC
Editorial: 819 1st Ave Ste A, Fairbanks, Alaska 99701-4449 **Tel:** 1 907 451-5910.
Email: LFM@fbxradio.com
Web site: http://www.kwolf981.com
Profile: KWLF-FM is a commercial station owned by Last Frontier Mediactive, LLC. The format of the station is Top 40/CHR music. KWLF-FM broadcasts to the Fairbanks, AK area at 98.1 FM.
FM RADIO STATION

KWLM-AM 37580
Owner: Lakeland Broadcasting
Editorial: 1340 NW 7th St, Willmar, Minnesota 56201
Tel: 1 320 235-1340.
Email: askus@kwlm.com
Web site: http://www.willmarradio.com/kwlm
Profile: KWLM-AM is a commercial station owned by Lakeland Broadcasting. The format of the station is news and talk. KWLM-AM broadcasts in the Willmar, MN area in the 1340 AM.
AM RADIO STATION

KWLN-FM 43006
Owner: Morris Communications
Editorial: 1124 N Miller St, Wenatchee, Washington 98801-1541 **Tel:** 1 509 663-5186.
Web site: http://www.lanuevaradio.com
Profile: KWLN-FM is a commercial station owned by Morris Communications. The format of the station is Hispanic Top 40/CHR. KWLN-FM broadcasts to the Seattle area at 103.3 FM.
FM RADIO STATION

KWLO-AM 37581
Owner: NRG Media LLC
Editorial: 514 Jefferson St, Waterloo, Iowa 50701-5422 **Tel:** 1 319 234-2200.
Web site: http://www.1330espnradio.com
Profile: KWLO-AM is a commercial station owned by NRG Media LLC. The format for the station is sports. KWLO-AM broadcasts to the Cedar Rapids, IA area at 1330 AM.
AM RADIO STATION

KWLS-FM 46253
Owner: Mid-America AG Network, Inc.
Editorial: 1009 N Rose Hill Rd, Rose Hill, Kansas 67133-9413 **Tel:** 1 620 262-4378.
Web site: http://www.kwlsradio.com
Profile: KWLS-FM is a commercial station owned by Mid-America AG Network, Inc. The format of the station is country. KWLS-FM broadcasts to the Wichita, KS area at 107.9 FM.
FM RADIO STATION

KWLT-FM 133951
Owner: Ashley County Broadcasters
Editorial: 117 E Wellfield Road, Crossett, Arkansas 71635 **Tel:** 1 870 364-2181.
Email: kagh@windstream.net
Web site: http://www.crossettradio.com
Profile: KWLT-FM is a commercial station owned by Ashley County Broadcasters. The format of the station is classic rock. KWLT-FM broadcasts to the Crossett, AR area at 102.7 FM.
FM RADIO STATION

KWLV-FM 40027
Owner: Baldridge-Dumas Communications Inc.
Editorial: 605 San Antonio Ave, Many, Louisiana 71449-3018 **Tel:** 1 318 256-5924.
Email: kwlv@bdcradio.com
Web site: http://www.bdcradio.com
Profile: KWLV-FM is a commercial station owned by Baldridge-Dumas Communications Inc. The format of the station is classic country. KWLV-FM broadcasts to the Shreveport, LA area at 107.1 FM.
FM RADIO STATION

KWLZ-FM 41555
Owner: Mapleton of Redding, LLC
Editorial: 3360 Alta Mesa Dr, Redding, California 96002-2831 **Tel:** 1 530 226-9500.
Web site: http://www.wild993fm.com/
Profile: KWLZ is a commercial station owned by Mapleton of Redding, LLC. The format of the station is Rhythmic Contemporary. KWLZ-FM broadcasts to the Redding, CA area at 99.3 FM.
FM RADIO STATION

KWMC-AM 35120
Owner: Valdez(Minerva Garza)
Editorial: 903 E Cortinas St, Del Rio, Texas 78840-6756 **Tel:** 1 830 775-3544.
Email: kwmc1490@wcsonline.net
Web site: http://kwmc1490.com
Profile: KWMC-AM is a commercial station owned by Minerva Garza Valdez. The format of the station is oldies. KWMC-AM broadcasts to the Del Rio, TX area at 1490 AM.
AM RADIO STATION

KWME-FM 45680
Owner: Johnson Enterprises Inc.
Editorial: 338 S Kley Dr, Wellington, Kansas 67152-8427 **Tel:** 1 620 326-3341.
Email: kley@sutv.com
Web site: http://www.kleyam.com/kwme.html
Profile: KWME-FM is a commercial station owned by Johnson Enterprises Inc. The format of the station is oldies. KWME-FM broadcasts to the Wellington, KS area at 92.7 FM.
FM RADIO STATION

KWMF-AM 62679
Owner: La Promesa Foundation
Tel: 1 888 784-3476.
Profile: KWMF-AM is a commercial station owned by La Promesa Foundation. The format of the station is Hispanic Catholic religious programming. KWMF-AM broadcasts to the Midland, TX area at 1380 AM.
AM RADIO STATION

KWML-AM 37302
Owner: Adams Radio Group
Editorial: 1355 California Ave, Las Cruces, New Mexico 88001-4130 **Tel:** 1 575 525-9298.
Web site: http://kool1045fm.com
Profile: KWML-AM is a commercial station owned by Adams Radio Group. The format of the station is Oldies. KWML-AM broadcasts to the Las Cruces, NM area at 570 AM. The station's slogan is, "The Greatest Hits in Southern New Mexico."
AM RADIO STATION

KWMR-FM 44533
Owner: KWMR
Editorial: 11431 Street Hwy 1 Ste 8, Point Reyes Station, California 94956 **Tel:** 1 415 663-8068.
Web site: http://www.kwmr.org
Profile: KWMR-FM is a non-commercial station owned by KWMR. The format of the station is variety. KWMR-FM broadcasts to the Point Reyes Station, CA area at 90.5 FM.
FM RADIO STATION

KWMT-AM 38885
Owner: Alpha Media
Editorial: 200 N 10th St, Fort Dodge, Iowa 50501-3925 **Tel:** 1 515 576-7333.
Web site: http://www.kwmt.com
Profile: KWMT-AM is a commercial station owned by Alpha Media. The format of the station is classic country. KWMT-AM broadcasts to the Fort Dodge, IA area at 540 AM.
AM RADIO STATION

KWMX-FM 133957
Owner: Grenax Broadcasting
Editorial: 2409 N 4th St Ste 101, Flagstaff, Arizona 86004-3735 **Tel:** 1 928 779-1177.
Web site: http://www.967thewolf.com
Profile: KWMX-FM is a commercial station owned by Grenax Broadcasting. The format of the station is classic rock. KWMX-FM broadcasts to the Phoenix area at 96.7 FM.
FM RADIO STATION

KWMY-FM 429767
Owner: Connoisseur Media LLC
Editorial: 2075 Central Ave, Billings, Montana 59102-4956 **Tel:** 1 406 248-7777.
Web site: http://www.my1059.com
Profile: KWMY-FM is commercial station owned by Connoisseur Media LLC. The format is classic hits. KWMY-FM broadcasts to the Billings, MT area at a frequency of 105.9 FM.
FM RADIO STATION

KWNA-AM 37582
Owner: Buckaroo Broadcasting, LLC
Editorial: 335 W 4th St, Winnemucca, Nevada 89445-3355 **Tel:** 1 702 400-0106.
Web site: http://www.buckarooradio.com/kwna-am-1400-and-104-5
Profile: KWNA-AM is a commercial station owned by Buckaroo Broadcasting, LLC. The format of the station is oldies. KWNA-AM broadcasts to the Winnemucca, NV area on 1400 AM.
AM RADIO STATION

KWNA-FM 44959
Owner: Buckaroo Broadcasting, LLC
Editorial: 335 W 4th St, Winnemucca, Nevada 89445-3355 **Tel:** 1 702 400-0106.
Web site: http://www.buckarooradio.com/knwa-92-7-fm-todays-best-country
Profile: KWNA-FM is a commercial station owned by Buckaroo Broadcasting, LLC. The format of the station is sports. KWNA-FM broadcasts to Winnemucca, NV and the surrounding areas at 92.7 FM.
FM RADIO STATION

KWNC-AM 36967
Owner: Cherry Creek Radio
Editorial: 231 N Wenatchee Ave, Wenatchee, Washington 98801-2009 **Tel:** 1 509 665-6565.
Web site: http://juanradio.co/
Profile: KWNC-AM is a commercial station owned by Cherry Creek Radio. The format of the station is Spanish Adult Hits. KWNC-AM broadcasts to the Wenatchee, WA area at 1370 AM.
AM RADIO STATION

KWND-FM 73411
Owner: Radio Training Network, Inc.
Editorial: 2550 S Campbell Ave Ste 100, Springfield, Missouri 65807-3540 **Tel:** 1 417 889-0883.
Email: onair@kwnd.com
Web site: http://88.3thewind.com
Profile: KWND-FM is a non-commercial station owned by Radio Training Network, Inc. The format of the station is contemporary Christian programming. KWND-FM broadcasts to the Springfield, MO area at 88.3 FM.
FM RADIO STATION

KWNE-FM 40029
Owner: Broadcast Corp. of Mendocino County
Editorial: 1100 Hastings Rd #B, Ukiah, California 95482-7101 **Tel:** 1 707 462-0945.
Email: kwine@kwine.com
Web site: http://www.kwine.com
Profile: KWNE-FM is a commercial radio station owned by Broadcast Corp. of Mendocino County. The format of the station is hot adult contemporary. KWNE-FM broadcasts to the Ukiah, CA area at 94.5 FM.
FM RADIO STATION

KWNG-FM 46348
Owner: Q Media Group, LLC
Editorial: 474 Guernsey Ln, Red Wing, Minnesota 55066-7448 **Tel:** 1 651 388-7151.
Email: news@kwng.com
Web site: http://www.kwng.com
Profile: KWNG-FM is a commercial station owned by Q Media Group, LLC. The format of the station is classic hits. KWNG-FM broadcasts to the Red Wing, MN area at 105.9 FM.
FM RADIO STATION

KWNN-FM 43578
Owner: Cumulus Media Inc
Editorial: 3127 Transworld Dr #270, Stockton, California 95206-4988 **Tel:** 1 209 507-8500.
Web site: http://www.kwin.com
Profile: KWNN-FM is a commercial station owned by Cumulus Media Inc. The format of the station is Top 40/CHR. KWNN-FM broadcasts to the Stockton, CA area at 98.3 FM.
FM RADIO STATION

KWNO-AM 39215
Owner: Leighton Enterprises Inc.
Editorial: 752 Bluffview Cir, Winona, Minnesota 55987-2515 **Tel:** 1 507 452-4000.
Web site: http://www.winonaradio.com
Profile: KWNO-AM is a commercial station owned by Leighton Enterprises Inc. The format of the station is news and talk. KWNO-AM broadcasts to the Winona, MN area at 1380 AM.
AM RADIO STATION

KWNO-FM 46569
Owner: Leighton Enterprises, Inc.
Editorial: 752 Bluffview Cir, Winona, Minnesota 55987-2515 **Tel:** 1 507 452-4000.
Web site: http://www.winonaradio.com
Profile: KWNO-FM is a commercial station owned by Leighton Enterprises Inc. The format of the station is contemporary country. KWNO-FM broadcasts to the Winona, MN area at 99.3 FM.
FM RADIO STATION

KWNR-FM 39751
Owner: iHeartMedia Inc.
Editorial: 2880 Meade Ave, Las Vegas, Nevada 89102-0713 **Tel:** 1 702 238-7300.
Web site: http://www.955thebull.com/main.html
Profile: KWNR-FM is a commercial station owned by iHeartMedia Inc. The format of the station is contemporary country. KWNR-FM broadcasts to the Las Vegas area at 95.5 FM.
FM RADIO STATION

United States of America

KWNS-FM 40030
Owner: Foster(Lottie)
Editorial: 215 Market St, Winnsboro, Texas 75494-2531 **Tel:** 1 903 342-3501.
Email: kwns-fm@peoplescom.net
Profile: KWNS-FM is a commercial station owned by Lottie Foster. The format of the station is southern gospel. KWNS-FM broadcasts to the Winnsboro, TX area at 104.7 FM.
FM RADIO STATION

KWNW-FM 42296
Owner: iHeartMedia Inc.
Editorial: 2650 Thousand Oaks Blvd Ste 4100, Memphis, Tennessee 38118-2451 **Tel:** 1 901 259-1300.
Web site: http://www.1019kissfm.com
Profile: KWNW-FM is a commercial station owned by iHeartMedia Inc. The format of the station is Top 40/CHR music. KWNW-FM broadcasts to the Memphis, TN area at 101.9 FM.
FM RADIO STATION

KWOA-AM 37583
Owner: Absolute Communications (dba Radio Works)
Editorial: 28779 County Highway 35, Worthington, Minnesota 56187-6322 **Tel:** 1 507 372-6165.
Email: info@myradioworks.net
Web site: http://kwoa.com
Profile: KWOA-AM is a commercial station owned by Absolute Communications (dba Radio Works). The format of the station is news/talk. KWOA-AM broadcasts to the Worthington, MN area at 730 AM.
AM RADIO STATION

KWOC-AM 37584
Owner: Max Media
Editorial: 1015 W Pine St, Poplar Bluff, Missouri 63901-4839 **Tel:** 1 573 785-0881.
Email: kwoc@riverradio.net
Web site: http://www.kwoc.com
Profile: KWOC-AM is a commercial station owned by Max Media. The format of the station is news and talk. KWOC-AM broadcasts to the Poplar Bluff, MO area at 930 AM.
AM RADIO STATION

KWOD-AM 36079
Owner: Entercom Communications Corp.
Editorial: 7000 Squibb Rd, Mission, Kansas 66202-3233 **Tel:** 1 913 677-8998.
Web site: http://www.kmbz.com
Profile: KWOD-AM is a commercial station owned by Entercom Communications Corp. The format of the station is business news. KUDL-AM broadcasts to the Kansas City, MO area at 1660 AM.
AM RADIO STATION

KWOF-FM 41563
Owner: Wilks Broadcast Group
Editorial: 720 S Colorado Blvd Ste 1200N, Denver, Colorado 80246-1947 **Tel:** 1 303 832-5665.
Web site: http://www.925thewolf.com
Profile: KWOF-FM is a commercial station owned by Kroenke Sports & Entertainment. The format of the station is contemporary country. KWOF-FM broadcasts to the Denver area at 92.5 FM.
FM RADIO STATION

KWOK-AM 62104
Owner: Alpha Media
Editorial: 1308 Coolidge Rd, Aberdeen, Washington 98520-6317 **Tel:** 1 360 533-1320.
Profile: KWOK-AM is a commercial station owned by Alpha Media. The format of the station is sports. KWOK-AM broadcasts to the Aberdeen, WA area at 1490 AM.
AM RADIO STATION

KWOL-FM 578329
Owner: Rose Communications, Inc.
Editorial: 2432 US Highway 2 E, Kalispell, Montana 59901-2310 **Tel:** 1 406 755-8700.
Email: info@1051cool.com
Web site: http://www.1051cool.com
Profile: KWOL-FM is a commercial station owned by Rose Communications, Inc. The format of the station is oldies music. The station airs locally at 105.1 FM.
FM RADIO STATION

KWON-AM 39130
Owner: KCD Enterprises Inc.
Editorial: 1200 SE Frank Phillips Blvd, Bartlesville, Oklahoma 74003 **Tel:** 1 918 336-1001.
Email: radio@bartlesvilleradio.com
Web site: http://www.bartlesvilleradio.com
Profile: KWON-AM is a commercial station owned by KCD Enterprises Inc. The format of the station is news and talk. KWON-AM broadcasts to the Bartlesville, OK area at 1400 AM.
AM RADIO STATION

KWOR-AM 37585
Owner: Legend Communications
Editorial: 1340 Radio Dr, Worland, Wyoming 82401-8700 **Tel:** 1 307 578-5000.
Email: kwor@bhrnwy.com
Web site: http://www.mybighornbasin.com
Profile: KWOR-AM is a commercial station owned by Legend Communications. The format of the station is news, talk and sports. KWOR-AM broadcasts to the Casper-Riverton, WY area at 1340 AM.
AM RADIO STATION

KWOS-AM 37586
Owner: Zimmer Radio Group
Editorial: 3109 S 10 Mile Dr, Jefferson City, Missouri 65109 **Tel:** 1 573 893-7857.
Email: kwos@zrgmail.com
Web site: http://www.kwos.com
Profile: KWOS-AM is a commercial station owned by Zimmer Radio Group. The format of the station is news and talk programming. KWOS-AM broadcasts to the Jefferson City, MO area at 950 AM.
AM RADIO STATION

KWOW-FM 41244
Owner: Waco Entertainment Group, LLC
Editorial: 6401 Cobbs Dr, Waco, Texas 76710-2536 **Tel:** 1 254 772-6104.
Web site: http://www.1041laley.com
Profile: KWOW-FM is a commercial station owned by Waco Entertainment Group, LLC. The format of the station is regional Mexican music. KWOW-FM broadcasts to the Waco, TX area at 104.1 FM.
FM RADIO STATION

KWOX-FM 40032
Owner: Omni Communications Inc.
Editorial: 101 Centre, 2728 Williams Ave, Woodward, Oklahoma 73801 **Tel:** 1 580 256-4101.
Email: k101@k101online.com
Web site: http://www.k101online.com
Profile: KWOX-FM is a commercial station owned by Omni Communications Inc. The format of the station is country music. KWOX-FM broadcasts to the Oklahoma City area at 101.1 FM.
FM RADIO STATION

KWOZ-FM 40033
Owner: WRD Entertainment Inc.
Editorial: 920 Harrison St Ste C, Batesville, Arkansas 72501-6949 **Tel:** 1 870 793-4196.
Email: kwozfm@yahoo.com
Web site: http://www.ar1033.com
Profile: KWOZ-FM is a commercial station owned by WRD Entertainment Inc. The format of the station is country. KWOZ-FM broadcasts to the Batesville, AR area at 103.3 FM.
FM RADIO STATION

KWPC-AM 39384
Owner: Prairie Communications LLP
Editorial: 3218 Mulberry Ave, Muscatine, Iowa 52761-2319 **Tel:** 1 563 263-2442.
Email: mail@voiceofmuscatine.com
Web site: http://www.voiceofmuscatine.com
Profile: KWPC-AM is a commercial station owned by Prairie Communications LLP. The format of the station is news, talk and classic country music. KWPC-AM broadcasts to the Muscatine, IA area at 860 AM.
AM RADIO STATION

KWPK-FM 87075
Owner: Horizon Broadcasting Group
Editorial: 854 Ne 4Th St, Bend, Oregon 97701-4711 **Tel:** 1 541 383-3825.
Email: news@horizonbroadcastinggroup.com
Web site: http://www.thepeak1041.com
Profile: KWPK-FM is a commercial station owned by Horizon Broadcasting Group. The format of the station is hot adult contemporary. KWPK-FM broadcasts to the Bend, OR area on 104.1 FM.
FM RADIO STATION

KWPM-AM 37587
Owner: Ozark Radio Network Inc.
Editorial: 983 E US Highway 160, West Plains, Missouri 65775-4801 **Tel:** 1 417 256-3131.
Web site: http://www.ozarknewstalk.com
Profile: KWPM-AM is a commercial station owned by Ozark Radio Network Inc. The format of the station is news and talk. KWPM-AM broadcasts to the Springfield, MO area at 1450 AM.
AM RADIO STATION

KWPN-AM 35752
Owner: Cumulus Media Inc
Editorial: 4045 NW 64th St, Oklahoma City, Oklahoma 73116-1684 **Tel:** 1 405 848-0100.
Profile: KWPN-AM is a commercial station owned by Cumulus Media Inc. The format of the station is sports. KWPN-AM broadcasts to the Oklahoma City area at 640 AM.
AM RADIO STATION

KWPT-FM 41987
Owner: Lost Coast Communications
Editorial: 1400 Main St Ste 104, Ferndale, California 95536-9459 **Tel:** 1 707 786-5104.
Web site: http://kwpt.com
Profile: KWPT-FM is a commercial station owned by Lost Coast Communications. The format of the station is classic rock. KWPT-FM broadcasts to the Ferndale, CA area at 100.3 FM.
FM RADIO STATION

KWPW-FM 471881
Owner: Waco Entertainment Group, LLC
Editorial: 6401 Cobbs Dr, Waco, Texas 76710-2536 **Tel:** 1 254 772-6104.
Web site: http://power108fm.com
Profile: KWPW-FM is a commercial station owned by Waco Entertainment Group, LLC. The format is Top 40/CHR. The station broadcasts to the Robinson, TX area at 107.9 FM.
FM RADIO STATION

KWPZ-FM 39761
Owner: Crista Ministries
Editorial: 2211 Rimland Dr Ste 116, Bellingham, Washington 98226-8654 **Tel:** 1 360 922-6222.
Email: comments@praise1065.com
Web site: http://www.praise1065.com
Profile: KWPZ-FM is a non-commercial station owned by Crista Ministries. The format of the station is contemporary Christian music and talk. KWPZ-FM broadcasts to the Lynden, WA area at 106.5 FM.
FM RADIO STATION

KWQW-FM 42155
Owner: Cumulus Media Inc
Editorial: 4143 109th St, Urbandale, Iowa 50322-7925 **Tel:** 1 515 331-9200.
Web site: http://www.983vibe.com/
Profile: KWQW-FM is a commercial station owned by Cumulus Media Inc. The format of the station is classic hip hop. KWQW-FM broadcasts in the Des Moines, IA area at 98.3 FM.
FM RADIO STATION

KWRB-FM 43141
Owner: World Radio Network, Inc.
Editorial: 3320 E Fry Blvd, Sierra Vista, Arizona 85635-2904 **Tel:** 1 520 452-8022.
Email: info@sparkfm.com
Web site: http://www.sparkfm.com
Profile: KWRB-FM is a non-commercial station owned by the World Radio Network, Inc. The format is contemporary Christian music. KWRB-FM broadcasts to the Sierra Vista, AZ area at 90.9 FM.
FM RADIO STATION

KWRD-AM 36779
Owner: Hanszen Broadcast Group
Editorial: 1101 Kilgore Dr, Henderson, Texas 75652-5129 **Tel:** 1 903 655-1800.
Email: info@kwrdonline.com
Web site: http://www.easttexastoday.com
Profile: KWRD-AM is a commercial station owned by Hanszen Broadcast Group. The format of the station is sports. KWRD-AM broadcasts to the Henderson, TX area at 1470 AM.
AM RADIO STATION

KWRD-FM 39676
Owner: Salem Media Group, Inc.
Editorial: 6400 N Belt Line Rd Ste 110, Irving, Texas 75063-6065 **Tel:** 1 214 561-9673.
Web site: http://www.thewordfm.com
Profile: KWRD-FM is a commercial station owned by Salem Media Group, Inc. The format of the station is Christian talk programming. KWRD-FM broadcasts to the Dallas area at 100.7 FM.
FM RADIO STATION

KWRE-AM 36571
Owner: Kaspar Broadcasting Co.
Editorial: 1217 N State Highway 47, Warrenton, Missouri 63383 **Tel:** 1 636 377-2300.
Email: kwrekfav@socket.net
Web site: http://www.kwre.com
Profile: KWRE-AM is a commercial station owned by Kaspar Broadcasting Co. The format of the station is classic country. KWRE-AM broadcasts to the Warrentown, MO area at 730 AM.
AM RADIO STATION

KWRF-AM 37588
Owner: Pines Broadcasting
Editorial: 1255 N Myrtle St, Warren, Arkansas 71671-9701 **Tel:** 1 870 226-2653.
Email: pines.broadcasting@sbcglobal.net
Profile: KWRF-AM is a commercial station owned by Pines Broadcasting. The format of the station is oldies. KWRF-AM broadcasts in the Little Rock, AR area at 860 AM.
AM RADIO STATION

KWRF-FM 44963
Owner: Pines Broadcasting
Editorial: 1255 N Myrtle St, Warren, Arkansas 71671 **Tel:** 1 870 226-2653.
Email: pines.broadcasting@sbcglobal.net
Profile: KWRF-FM is commercial station owned by Pines Broadcasting. The format of the station is contemporary country music. KWRF-FM broadcasts in the Warren, AR area at 105.5 FM.
FM RADIO STATION

KWRK-FM 46851
Owner: Navajo Nation
Editorial: Window Rock Shopping Center, Window Rock, Arizona 86515-9999 **Tel:** 1 928 871-3553.
Email: webmaster@ktnnonline.com
Web site: http://www.ktnnonline.com
Profile: KWRK-FM is a commercial station owned by Navajo Nation. The format of the station is country. KWRK-FM broadcasts to the Albuquerque, NM area at 96.1 FM.
FM RADIO STATION

KWRL-FM 41191
Owner: Elkhorn Media Group
Editorial: 1009 Adams Ave, La Grande, Oregon 97850-2667 **Tel:** 1 541 963-7911.
Web site: http://www.999kwrl.com
Profile: KWRL-FM is a commercial station owned by Elkhorn Media Group. The format of the station is adult contemporary. KWRL-FM broadcasts to the Portland, OR area at 99.9 FM.
FM RADIO STATION

KWRM-AM 36069
Owner: Major Market Stations Inc.
Editorial: 210 Radio Rd, Corona, California 92879-1722 **Tel:** 1 951 737-1370.
Email: bella@kwrn1550am.com
Web site: http://www.kwrm1370am.com
Profile: KWRM-AM is a commercial station owned by Major Market Stations Inc. The format of the station is multilingual variety programming. KWRM-AM broadcasts to the Corona, CA area at 1370 AM.
AM RADIO STATION

KWRN-AM 36038
Owner: Major Market Stations Inc.
Editorial: 15165 7th St Ste D, Victorville, California 92395-3816 **Tel:** 1 760 955-8722.
Email: production@lapoderosa1550am.com
Web site: http://lapoderosa1550am.com
Profile: KWRN-AM is a commercial station owned by Major Market Stations Inc. The format of the station is regional Mexican. KWRN-AM broadcasts to the Victorville, CA area at 1550 AM.
AM RADIO STATION

KWRO-AM 39189
Owner: Bicoastal Media LLC
Editorial: 320 Central Ave, Ste 519, Coos Bay, Oregon 97420 **Tel:** 1 541 267-2121.
Email: southcoastpsa@bicoastalmedia.com
Web site: http://www.kwro.com
Profile: KWRO-AM is a commercial station owned by Bi-Coastal Media LLC. The format of the station is news and talk. KWRO-AM broadcasts to the Eugene, OR area at 630 AM.
AM RADIO STATION

KWRP-AM 35845
Owner: Pueblo Radio Group
Editorial: 3715 Thatcher Ave, Pueblo, Colorado 81005-1255 **Tel:** 1 719 564-0899.
Web site: http://www.oldiesinpueblo.com
Profile: KWRP-AM is a commercial station owned by Pueblo Radio Group. The format of the station is news, talk and sports. KWRP-AM broadcasts to the Pueblo, CO area at 690 AM. Also simulcasts on 100.3 and 93.9 FM.
AM RADIO STATION

KWRQ-FM 42610
Owner: McMurray Communications Inc.
Editorial: 3335 W 8th St, Thatcher, Arizona 85552 **Tel:** 1 928 428-1230.
Email: traffic@mcmurrayradio.com
Web site: http://www.mysouthernaz.com
Profile: KWRQ-FM is a commercial station owned by McMurray Communications Inc. The format of the station is hot adult contemporary music. KWRQ-FM broadcasts to the Safford, AZ area at 102.3 FM.
FM RADIO STATION

KWRT-AM 36512
Owner: Billings Broadcasting LLC
Editorial: 1600 Radio Hill Rd, Boonville, Missouri 65233-1957 **Tel:** 1 660 882-6686.
Email: kwrt@1370kwrt.com
Web site: http://www.1370kwrt.com
Profile: KWRT-AM is a commercial station owned by Billings Broadcasting LLC. The format of the station is country music. KWRT-AM broadcasts in the Boonville, MO area at 1370 AM.
AM RADIO STATION

KWRU-AM 36646
Owner: Multicultural Radio Broadcasting Inc.
Editorial: 2125 N Barton Ave, Fresno, California 93703-2646
Profile: KWRU-AM is a commercial station owned by Multicultural Radio Broadcasting Inc. The format of the station is Hispanic religious. KWRU-AM broadcasts to the Fresno, CA area at 1300 AM.
AM RADIO STATION

KWRV-FM 133962
Owner: Minnesota Public Radio
Editorial: 480 Cedar St, Saint Paul, Minnesota 55101-2217 **Tel:** 1 651 290-1500.
Email: newsroom@mpr.org
Web site: http://www.mpr.org/listen/stations/kwrv
Profile: KWRV-FM is a non-commercial station owned by Minnesota Public Radio. The format of the station is classical. KWVR-FM broadcasts to the Saint Paul, MN area at 91.9 FM.
FM RADIO STATION

KWSC-FM 44323
Owner: Wayne State College
Editorial: 1111 Main St, Humanities 409 A, Wayne, Nebraska 68787 **Tel:** 1 402 375-7424.
Email: thecat@wsc.edu
Web site: http://wildcat.wsc.edu/k92
Profile: KWSC-FM is a non-commercial station owned by Wayne State College. The format of the station is college variety. KWSC-FM broadcasts to the Wayne, NE area at 91.9 FM.
FM RADIO STATION

KWSH-AM 39458
Owner: One Ten Broadcasting Group Inc.
Editorial: 1221 N South 358, Seminole, Oklahoma 74868 **Tel:** 1 405 257-5441.
Email: onetenbroadcast@onetenbroadcast.com
Profile: KWSH-AM is a commercial station owned by One Ten Broadcasting Group Inc. The format of the station is country music. KWSH-AM broadcasts to the Oklahoma City area at 1260 AM.
AM RADIO STATION

KWSL-AM
38807
Owner: iHeartMedia Inc.
Editorial: 1113 Nebraska St, Sioux City, Iowa 51105-1438 **Tel:** 1 712 258-5595.
Web site: http://www.1470kwsl.com/main.html
Profile: KWSL-AM is a commercial station owned by iHeartMedia Inc. The format of the station is Regional Mexican. KWSL-AM broadcasts to the Sioux City, IA area at 1470 AM.
AM RADIO STATION

KWSN-AM
38325
Owner: Midwest Communications
Editorial: 500 S Phillips Ave, Sioux Falls, South Dakota 57104-6825 **Tel:** 1 605 331-5350.
Web site: http://www.kwsn.com
Profile: KWSN-AM is a commercial station owned by Midwest Communications. The format of the station is sports. KWSN-AM broadasts to the Sioux Falls, SD area at 1230 AM.
AM RADIO STATION

KWSO-FM
41456
Owner: Confederated Tribes of Warm Springs
Editorial: 4174 Hwy 3, Warm Springs, Oregon 97761-9999 **Tel:** 1 541 553-1968.
Email: kwsonews@wstribes.org
Web site: http://www.kwso.org
Profile: KWSO-FM is a non-commercial station owned by Confederated Tribes of Warm Springs. The format of the station is variety. KWSO-FM broadcasts to the Warm Springs, OR area at 91.9 FM.
FM RADIO STATION

KWST-AM
36782
Owner: Entravision Communications Corp.
Editorial: 1803 N Imperial Ave, El Centro, California 92243-1333 **Tel:** 1 760 482-7777.
Email: kwst@entravision.com
Profile: KWST-AM is a commercial station owned by Entravision Communications Corp. The format of the station is Spanish adult hits. KWST-AM broadcasts to the El Centro, CA area at 1430 AM.
AM RADIO STATION

KWSW-AM
38790
Owner: Eureka Broadcasting Inc.
Editorial: 1101 Marsh Rd, Eureka, California 95501-1574 **Tel:** 1 707 442-5744.
Web site: http://www.kwsw980.com
Profile: KWSW-AM is a commercial station owned by Eureka Broadcasting Inc. The format of the station is news and talk. KWSW-AM broadcasts to the Eureka, CA area at 980 AM.
AM RADIO STATION

KWSX-AM
36848
Owner: iHeartMedia Inc.
Editorial: 2121 Lancey Dr, Modesto, California 95355-3036 **Tel:** 1 209 551-1306.
Web site: http://powertalk1280.iheart.com
Profile: KWSX-AM is a commercial station owned by iHeartMedia Inc. The format of the station news and talk. KWSX-AM broadcasts to the Sacramento, CA area at 1280 AM.
AM RADIO STATION

KWTF-FM
891228
Owner: KWTF Radio
Editorial: Bodega Bay, California **Tel:** 1 701 681-5983.
Email: info@kwtf.net
Web site: http://kwtf.net
Profile: KWTF-FM is a non-commercial station owned by KWTF Radio. The format of the station is talk and news. KWTF-FM broadcasts to the Bodega Bay area at 88.1 FM.
FM RADIO STATION

KWTG-FM
519480
Owner: Radio Group(The)
Editorial: 917 Ee Wallace Blvd S, Ferriday, Louisiana 71334 **Tel:** 1 318 757-4200.
Email: kfnv@bellsouth.net
Profile: KWTG-FM is a commercial station owned the Radio Group. The format of the station is classic country. KWTG-FM broadcasts to the Ferriday, LA area at 104.7 FM.
FM RADIO STATION

KWTL-AM
578510
Owner: Real Presence Radio
Editorial: 216 Belmont Rd, Grand Forks, North Dakota 58201-4620 **Tel:** 1 701 795-0122.
Email: businessmanager@realpresenceradio.com
Web site: http://yourcatholicradiostation.com
Profile: KWTL-AM is a non-commercial station owned by Real Presence Radio. The format of the station is religion and talk.
AM RADIO STATION

KWTO-AM
37590
Owner: Meyer Communications
Editorial: 3000 E Chestnut Expy, Springfield, Missouri 65802-2528 **Tel:** 1 417 862-5600.
Email: manager@radiospringfield.com
Web site: http://www.newstalk560.com
Profile: KWTO-AM is a commercial station owned by Meyer Communications. The format of the station is news and talk. KWTO-AM broadcasts to the Springfield, MO area at 560 AM.
AM RADIO STATION

KWTO-FM
44964
Owner: Meyer Communications
Editorial: 3000 E Chestnut Expy, Springfield, Missouri 65802-2528 **Tel:** 1 417 862-3751.
Email: messages@radiopriestfield.com
Web site: http://www.jock987.com
Profile: KWTO-FM is a commercial station owned by Meyer Communications. The format of the station is sports/talk. KWTO-FM broadcasts to the Springfield, MO area at 98.7 FM.
FM RADIO STATION

KWTX-AM
37592
Owner: iHeartMedia Inc.
Editorial: 314 W State Highway 6, Waco, Texas 76712-3971 **Tel:** 1 254 776-3900.
Web site: http://newstalk1230.com
Profile: KWTX-AM is a commercial station owned by iHeartMedia Inc. The format of the station is news and talk. KWTX-AM broadcasts to the Waco, TX area at 1230 AM.
AM RADIO STATION

KWTX-FM
44965
Owner: iHeartMedia Inc.
Editorial: 314 W State Highway 6, Waco, Texas 76712-3971 **Tel:** 1 254 776-3900.
Web site: http://www.975online.com
Profile: KWTX-FM is a commercial station owned by iHeartMedia Inc. The format of the station is Top 40/CHR music. KWTX-FM broadcasts to the Waco, TX area at 97.5 FM.
FM RADIO STATION

KWUF-AM
38547
Owner: Wolf Creek Broadcasting LLC
Editorial: 702 S 10th St, Pagosa Springs, Colorado 81147 **Tel:** 1 970 264-5983.
Email: admin@kwuf.com
Web site: http://www.kwuf.com
Profile: KWUF-AM is a commercial station owned by Wolf Creek Broadcasting LLC. The format of the station is a mix of country music, sports and talk programming. KWUF-AM broadcasts to the Pagosa Springs, CO area at 1400 AM.
AM RADIO STATION

KWUF-FM
45907
Owner: Wolf Creek Broadcasting LLC
Editorial: 702 S 10th St, Pagosa Springs, Colorado 81147 **Tel:** 1 970 264-5983.
Email: admin@kwuf.com
Web site: http://www.kwuf.com
Profile: KWUF-FM is a commercial station owned by Wolf Creek Broadcasting LLC. The format of the station is adult hits. KWUF-FM broadcasts to the Pagosa Springs, CO area at 106.1 FM.
FM RADIO STATION

KWUT-FM
44732
Owner: Mid-Utah Radio Inc.
Editorial: 390 E Annabella Rd, Richfield, Utah 84701-7084 **Tel:** 1 435 896-4456.
Email: news@midutahradio.com
Web site: http://midutahradio.com/kwut
Profile: KWUT-FM is a commercial station owned by Mid-Utah Radio Inc. The format of the station is contemporary country music. KWUT-FM broadcasts to the Richfield, UT area at 97.7 FM.
FM RADIO STATION

KWUZ-FM
594252
Owner: Three Eagles Communications
Editorial: 7600 County Road 120, Salida, Colorado 81201-9423 **Tel:** 1 719 539-2575.
Web site: http://www.hippieradio975.com
Profile: KWUZ-FM is a commercial station owned by Three Eagles Communications. The format of the station is classic hits. KWUZ-FM broadcasts to the Salida, CO area at 97.5 FM.
FM RADIO STATION

KWVE-FM
40036
Owner: Calvary Chapel of Costa Mesa, Inc.
Editorial: 3000 W Macarthur Blvd, Ste 500, Santa Ana, California 92704 **Tel:** 1 714 918-6207.
Web site: http://www.kwve.com
Profile: KWVE-FM is a commercial station owned by Calvary Chapel of Costa Mesa, Inc. The format of the station is Christian music and talk. KWVE-FM broadcasts to the Santa Ana, CA area at 107.9 FM.
FM RADIO STATION

KWVN-FM
44930
Owner: Capps Broadcast Group
Editorial: 2003 NW 56th St, Pendleton, Oregon 97801-4593 **Tel:** 1 541 276-1511.
Web site: http://www.mycolumbiabasin.com/
Profile: KWVN-FM is a commercial station owned by Capps Broadcast Group. The format of the station is adult hits. KWVN-FM broadcasts to the Pendleton, OR area at 107.7 FM
FM RADIO STATION

KWVR-AM
38352
Owner: Wallowa Valley Radio LLC
Editorial: 220 W Main St, Enterprise, Oregon 97828 **Tel:** 1 541 426-4577.
Email: kwvramfm@eoni.com
Web site: http://kwvrradio.com
Profile: KWVR-AM is a commercial station owned by Wallowa Valley Radio LLC. The format of the station is news, talk and sports. KWVR-AM broadcasts in the Enterprise, OR area at 1340 AM.
AM RADIO STATION

KWVR-FM
45709
Owner: Wallowa Valley Radio LLC
Editorial: 220 W Main St, Enterprise, Oregon 97828-1373 **Tel:** 1 541 426-4577.
Email: kwvrradio@gmail.com
Web site: http://kwvrradio.com
Profile: KWVR-FM is a commercial station owned by Wallowa Valley Radio LLC. The format of the station is country music. KWVR-FM broadcasts to the Spokane, WA area at 92.1 FM.
FM RADIO STATION

KWWJ-AM
35908
Owner: Salt of the Earth Broadcasting
Editorial: 4638 Decker Dr, Baytown, Texas 77520-1418 **Tel:** 1 281 837-8777.
Email: kwwj1360@yahoo.com
Web site: http://www.kwwj.org
Profile: KWWJ-AM is a commercial station owned by Salt of the Earth Broadcasting. The format of the station is gospel. KWWJ-AM broadcasts to the Baytown, TX area at 1360 AM.
AM RADIO STATION

KWWK-FM
40038
Owner: Townsquare Media
Editorial: 122 4th St SW, Rochester, Minnesota 55902-3320 **Tel:** 1 507 286-1010.
Web site: http://www.quickcountry.com
Profile: KWWK-FM is a commercial station owned by Townsquare Media. The format of the station is country music. KWWK-FM broadcasts to the Rochester, MN area at 96.5 FM.
FM RADIO STATION

KWWN-AM
520017
Owner: Lotus Communications Corp.
Editorial: 8755 W Flamingo Rd, Las Vegas, Nevada 89147-8667 **Tel:** 1 702 876-1460.
Email: espnradio1100@gmail.com
Web site: http://www.espn1100.com
Profile: KWWN-AM is a commercial station owned by Lotus Communications Corp. The format of the station is sports. KWWN-AM broadcasts to the Las Vegas area at 1100 AM.
AM RADIO STATION

KWWR-FM
44967
Owner: Johnson(Anne)
Editorial: 1705 E Liberty St, Mexico, Missouri 65265-3537 **Tel:** 1 573 581-5500.
Email: news@radiogetsresults.net
Web site: http://info.kwwr.com
Profile: KWWR-FM is a commercial station owned by Anne Johnson. The format of the station is country music. KWWR-FM broadcasts to the Mexico, MO area at 91.9 FM.
FM RADIO STATION

KWWV-FM
42255
Owner: Mapleton Communications LLC
Editorial: 795 Buckley Rd, Ste 2, San Luis Obispo, California 93401 **Tel:** 1 805 786-2570.
Web site: http://www.wild1061.com
Profile: KWWV-FM is a commercial station owned by Mapleton Communications LLC. The format of the station is Top 40/CHR. KWWV-FM broadcasts to the San Luis Obispo, CA area at 106.1 FM.
FM RADIO STATION

KWWW-FM
46167
Owner: Cherry Creek Radio
Editorial: 231 N Wenatchee Ave, Wenatchee, Washington 98801-2009 **Tel:** 1 509 665-6565.
Email: newswenatchee@cherrycreekradio.com
Web site: http://www.kw3.com
Profile: KWWW-FM is commercial station owned by Cherry Creek Radio. The format of the station is hot adult contemporary music. KWWW-FM broadcasts to the Wenatchee, WA area at 96.7 FM.
FM RADIO STATION

KWWX-FM
42657
Owner: Cherry Creek Radio
Editorial: 231 N Wenatchee Ave, Wenatchee, Washington 98801-2009 **Tel:** 1 509 665-6565.
Email: newswenatchee@cherrycreekradio.com
Web site: http://juanradio.co
Profile: KWWX-FM is a commercial station owned by Cherry Creek Radio. The format of the station is Spanish Adult Hits. KWWX-FM broadcasts to the Wenatchee, WA area on 106.7 FM.
FM RADIO STATION

KWXD-FM
42207
Owner: My Town Media, Inc.
Editorial: 412 N Locust St, Pittsburg, Kansas 66762-4014 **Tel:** 1 620 232-5993.
Email: sharon@mytown-media.com
Web site: http://www.1035x.net
Profile: KWXD-FM is a commercial station owned by My Town Media, Inc. The format is classic rock. The station airs in the Pittsburg, KS area at 103.5 FM.
FM RADIO STATION

KWXS-FM
809631
Owner: Combined Communications, Inc.
Editorial: 63088 18th St Ste 200, Bend, Oregon 97701-7102 **Tel:** 1 541 382-5263.
Web site: http://wild1077.com
Profile: KWXS-FM is a commercial station owned by Combined Communications, Inc. The format of the station is Top 40 urban contemporary. KXWS-FM broadcasts to the Bend, OR area at a frequency of 107.7 FM.
FM RADIO STATION

KWXT-AM
36196
Owner: Domerese(George)
Editorial: 701 E Main St, Ste 4, Russellville, Arkansas 72801 **Tel:** 1 479 968-1337.
Email: kwxt1490am@yahoo.com
Web site: http://www.kwxt1490am.com
Profile: KWXT-AM is a commercial station owned by George Domerese. The format of the station is Christian programming and Southern gospel music. KWXT-AM broadcasts to the Russellville, AR area at 1490 AM.
AM RADIO STATION

KWXX-FM
44968
Owner: New West Broadcasting
Editorial: 1145 Kilauea Ave, Hilo, Hawaii 96720-4203 **Tel:** 1 808 935-5461.
Web site: http://www.kwxx.com
Profile: KWXX-FM is a commercial station owned by New West Broadcasting. The format of the station is a variety of Hawaiian music. KWXX-FM broadcasts to Hilo, HI at 94.7 FM.
FM RADIO STATION

KWXY-AM
37593
Owner: R & R Radio Corp.
Editorial: 2100 E Tahquitz Canyon Way, Palm Springs, California 92262-7006 **Tel:** 1 760 325-2580.
Email: programs@kwxy.com
Profile: KWXY-AM is a commercial station owned by R & R Radio Corp. The format of the station is talk. KWXY-AM broadcasts to the Palm Springs, CA area at 1340 AM.
AM RADIO STATION

KWYD-FM
41660
Owner: Impact Radio
Editorial: 5660 E Franklin Rd Ste 200, Nampa, Idaho 83687-5133 **Tel:** 1 208 465-9966.
Web site: http://www.wild101fm.com
Profile: KWYD-FM is a commercial station owned by Impact Radio. The format of the station is rhythmic Top 40. KWYD-FM broadcasts to the McCall, ID area at 101.1 FM.
FM RADIO STATION

KWYE-FM
42791
Owner: Cumulus Media
Editorial: 1071 W Shaw Ave, Fresno, California 93711-3702 **Tel:** 1 559 490-1011.
Web site: http://www.y101hits.com
Profile: KWYE-FM is a commercial station owned by Cumulus Media. The format of the station is adult contemporary. KWYE-FM broadcasts in the Fresno, CA area at 101.1 FM.
FM RADIO STATION

KWYK-FM
46163
Owner: Basin Broadcasting Company
Editorial: 1515 W Main St, Farmington, New Mexico 87401-3837 **Tel:** 1 505 325-1996.
Web site: http://www.kwykradio.com
Profile: KWYK-FM is a commercial station owned by Basin Broadcasting Company. The format of the station is adult contemporary music. KWYK-FM broadcasts to the Albuquerque, NM area at 94.9 FM.
FM RADIO STATION

KWYL-FM
44215
Owner: Cumulus Media Inc
Editorial: 595 E Plumb Ln, Reno, Nevada 89502 **Tel:** 1 775 789-6700.
Web site: http://www.wild1029.com
Profile: KWYL-FM is a commercial station owned by Cumulus Media Inc. The format of the station is rhythmic Top 40/CHR. KWYL-FM broadcasts to the Reno, NV are at 102.9 FM.
FM RADIO STATION

KWYN-AM
37594
Owner: East Arkansas Broadcasters Inc.
Editorial: 2758 Highway 64, Wynne, Arkansas 72396-4061 **Tel:** 1 870 238-8141.
Email: eabwynne@cablelynx.com
Web site: http://kwyn.com
Profile: KWYN-AM is an commercial station owned by East Arkansas Broadcasters Inc. The format of the station is country music. KWYN-AM broadcasts to the Wynne, AR area at 1400 AM.
AM RADIO STATION

KWYN-FM
44970
Owner: East Arkansas Broadcasters Inc.
Editorial: 2758 Highway 64, Wynne, Arkansas 72396-4061 **Tel:** 1 870 238-8141.
Email: eabwynne@cablelynx.com
Web site: http://www.kwyn.com
Profile: KWYN-FM is a commercial station owned by East Arkansas Broadcasters Inc. The format of the station is contemporary country. KWYN-FM broadcasts to the Wynne, AR area at 92.5 FM.
FM RADIO STATION

KWYO-AM
36620
Owner: Lovcom, Inc.
Editorial: 1716 Kroe Ln, Sheridan, Wyoming 82801-9681 **Tel:** 1 307 672-7421.
Email: info@sheridanmedia.com
Web site: http://www.sheridanmedia.com
Profile: KWYO-AM is a commercial station owned by Lovcom, Inc. The format of the station is classic country. KWYO-AM broadcasts to the Sheridan, WY area at 1410 AM.
AM RADIO STATION

KWYR-AM
38856
Owner: Midwest Radio Corp.
Editorial: 346 Main St, Winner, South Dakota 57580 **Tel:** 1 605 842-3333.
Email: kwyrnews@gwtc.net
Web site: http://www.kwyr.com
Profile: KWYR-AM is a commercial station owned by the Midwest Radio Corp. The format of the station is

country music. KWYR-AM broadcasts to the Winner, SD area at 1260 AM.
AM RADIO STATION

KWYR-FM 46193
Owner: Midwest Radio Corp.
Editorial: 346 S Main St, Winner, South Dakota 57580-1832 **Tel:** 1 605 842-3333.
Email: kwyrnews@gwtc.net
Web site: http://www.kwyr.com
Profile: KWYR-FM is a commercial station owned by Midwest Radio Corp. The format of the station is adult contemporary. KWYR-FM broadcasts to the Winner, SD area at 93.7 FM.
FM RADIO STATION

KWYW-FM 324134
Owner: Edwards Communications LLC
Editorial: 1002 N 8th St W, Riverton, Wyoming 82501-2427 **Tel:** 1 307 856-2922.
Profile: KWYW-FM is a commercial station owned by Edwards Communications. The format of the station is sports. KWYW-FM broadcasts to the Riverton, WY, area at 99.1 FM.
FM RADIO STATION

KWYY-FM 39959
Owner: Townsquare Media, LLC
Editorial: 150 Nichols Ave, Casper, Wyoming 82601-1816 **Tel:** 1 307 266-5252.
Web site: http://www.mycountry955.com
Profile: KWYY-FM is a commercial station owned by Townsquare Media, LLC. The format for the station is country, featuring contemporary and classic hits. KWYY-FM broadcasts to the Casper-Riverton, WY area at 95.5 FM.
FM RADIO STATION

KXAA-FM 494106
Owner: Wheeler Broadcasting Inc.
Editorial: 115 N Harris Ave, Cle Elum, Washington 98922 **Tel:** 1 509 662-3842.
Email: kxaprod@aol.com
Web site: http://www.kxa937.com
FM RADIO STATION

KXAC-FM 42141
Owner: Radio Mankato
Editorial: 59346 Madison Ave, Mankato, Minnesota 56001-8518 **Tel:** 1 507 345-4537.
Email: news@ktoe.com
Web site: http://www.radiomankato.com
Profile: KXAC-FM is a commercial station owned by Radio Mankato. The format of the station is oldies music. KXAC-FM broadcasts to the Mankato, MN area at 100.5 FM.
FM RADIO STATION

KXAR-AM 37101
Owner: Sudbury Broadcasting Group
Editorial: 1600 S Elm St, Hope, Arkansas 71801-8106 **Tel:** 1 870 777-8868.
Web site: http://www.supercountry105.com
Profile: KXAR-AM is a commercial station owned by Sudbury Broadcasting Group. The format of the station is sports and talk. KXAR-AM broadcasts to the Hope, AR area at 1490 AM.
AM RADIO STATION

KXAZ-FM 45934
Owner: Lake Powell Communications
Editorial: 91 7th Ave, Page, Arizona 86040 **Tel:** 1 928 645-8181.
Email: news@kxaz.com
Web site: http://www.kxaz.com
Profile: KXAZ-FM is a commercial station owned by Lake Powell Communications. The format of the station is classic Hits. KXAZ-FM broadcasts to the Page, AZ area at 93.3 FM.
FM RADIO STATION

KXBA-FM 334189
Owner: Peninsula Communications Inc.
Editorial: 66060 Diamond Ridge Rd, Homer, Alaska 99603-9229 **Tel:** 1 907 235-6000.
Email: kwavefm@xyz.net
FM RADIO STATION

KXBG-FM 46793
Owner: iHeartMedia Inc.
Editorial: 4270 Byrd Dr, Loveland, Colorado 80538-7074 **Tel:** 1 970 461-2560.
Web site: http://www.my979.com
Profile: KXBG-FM is a commercial station owned by iHeartMedia Inc. The format of the station is country music. KXBG-FM broadcasts to the Fort Collins, CO area at 97.9 FM.
FM RADIO STATION

KXBL-FM 41591
Owner: E.W. Scripps Co.
Editorial: 4590 E 29th St, Tulsa, Oklahoma 74114-6208 **Tel:** 1 918 743-7814.
Web site: http://www.bigcountry995.com
Profile: KXBL-FM is a commercial station owned by the E.W. Scripps Co. The format of the station is classic country. KXBL-FM broadcasts to the Tulsa, OK area at 99.5 FM.
FM RADIO STATION

KXBN-FM 44589
Owner: Cherry Creek Radio
Editorial: 750 Ridgeview Dr, Ste 204, St George, Utah 84770 **Tel:** 1 435 673-3579.
Web site: http://www.b92fmonline.com
Profile: KXBN-FM is a commercial station owned by Cherry Creek Radio. The format of the station is Top 40/CHR. KXBN-FM broadcasts to the St. George, UT area at 92.1 FM.
FM RADIO STATION

KXBR-FM 238297
Owner: Heartland Christian Broadcasters Inc.
Editorial: 4090 Highway 11, International Falls, Minnesota 56649 **Tel:** 1 218 285-7398.
Profile: KXBR-FM is a non-commercial station owned by Heartland Christian Broadcasters. The format of the station is Christian rock music. KXBR-FM broadcasts to the International Falls, MN area at 91.9 FM.
FM RADIO STATION

KXBX-AM 37591
Owner: Bicoastal Media LLC
Editorial: 140 N Main St, Lakeport, California 95453-4815 **Tel:** 1 707 263-6113.
Web site: http://www.kxbx.com
Profile: KXBX-AM is a commercial station owned by Bicoastal Media LLC. The format of the station is adult standards and sports. KXBX-AM broadcasts to Lakeport, CA at 1270 AM.
AM RADIO STATION

KXBX-FM 44972
Owner: Bicoastal Media LLC
Editorial: 140 N Main St, Lakeport, California 95453-4815 **Tel:** 1 707 263-6113.
Web site: http://www.kxbxfm.com
Profile: KXBX-FM is a commercial station owned by Bicoastal Media. The format of the station is adult contemporary music. KXBX-FM broadcasts to Lakeport, CA at 98.3 FM.
FM RADIO STATION

KXBZ-FM 42382
Owner: Manhattan Broadcasting
Editorial: 2414 Casement Rd, Manhattan, Kansas 66502 **Tel:** 1 785 776-1350.
Web site: http://www.b1047.com
Profile: KXBZ-FM is a commercial station owned by Manhattan Broadcasting. The format of the station is contemporary country music. KXBZ-FM broadcasts in the Manhattan, KS area at 104.7 FM.
FM RADIO STATION

KXCA-AM 39261
Owner: Perry Publishing & Broadcasting Inc.
Editorial: 1525 SE Flower Mound Rd, Lawton, Oklahoma 73501-6325 **Tel:** 1 580 357 9370.
Web site: http://theticket1380.com
Profile: KXCA-AM is a commercial station owned by Perry Publishing & Broadcasting Inc. The format of the station is R&B oldies. KKRX-AM broadcasts to the Lawton, OK area at 1050 AM.
AM RADIO STATION

KXCI-FM 41181
Owner: Foundation for Creative Broadcasting
Editorial: 220 S 4th Ave, Tucson, Arizona 85701 **Tel:** 1 520 623-1000.
Web site: http://www.kxci.org
Profile: KXCI-FM is a non-commercial station owned by Foundation for Creative Broadcasting. The format of the station is variety. KXCI-FM broadcasts to the Tucson, AZ area at 91.3 FM.
FM RADIO STATION

KXCM-FM 43370
Owner: Copper Mountain Broadcasting
Editorial: 68474 Twentynine Palms Highway, Twentynine Palms, California 92277 **Tel:** 1 760 362-4264.
Email: coppermountainbroadcasting@yahoo.com
Web site: http://www.kxcmradio.com
Profile: KXCM-FM is a commercial station owned by Copper Mountain Broadcasting. The format of the station is contemporary country. KXCM-FM broadcasts to the Los Angeles area at 96.3 FM.
FM RADIO STATION

KXCV-FM 40041
Owner: Board of Regents, NWMSU
Editorial: 800 University Dr, Maryville, Missouri 64468-6015 **Tel:** 1 660 562-1163.
Email: kxcv@nwmissouri.edu
Web site: http://www.kxcv.org
Profile: KXCV-FM is a non-commercial station owned by the Board of Regents, NWMSU. The format for the station is classical, jazz and news. KXCV-FM broadcasts to the Saint Joseph, MO area at 90.5 FM.
FM RADIO STATION

KXDD-FM 44195
Owner: New Northwest Broadcasters LLC
Editorial: 1200 Chesterly Dr Ste 160, Yakima, Washington 98902-7345 **Tel:** 1 509 248-2900.
Web site: http://www.1041kxdd.com
Profile: KXDD-FM is a commercial station owned by New Northwest Broadcasters LLC. The format of the station is country music. KXDD-FM broadcasts in the Yakima, WA area at 104.1 FM.
FM RADIO STATION

KXDG-FM 42733
Owner: Zimmer Radio Inc.
Editorial: 2702 E 32nd St, Joplin, Missouri 64804 **Tel:** 1 417 624-1025.
Web site: http://www.bigdog979.com
Profile: KXDG-FM is a commercial station owned by Zimmer Radio Inc. The format of the station is classic rock music. KXDG-FM broadcasts in the Joplin, MO area at 97.9 FM.
FM RADIO STATION

KXDL-FM 46369
Owner: Prairie Broadcasting Inc.
Editorial: 221 Central Ave, Long Prairie, Minnesota 56347 **Tel:** 1 320 732-2164.
Email: hotrodfm@rea-alp.com
Web site: http://www.kxdlhotrodradio.com
Profile: KXDL-FM is a commercial station owned by Prairie Broadcasting Inc. The format of the station is oldies music. KXDL-FM broadcasts in the Long Prairie, MN area at 99.7 FM.
FM RADIO STATION

KXDR-FM 139988
Owner: Cherry Creek Radio
Editorial: 1600 North Ave W, Ste 101, Missoula, Montana 59801 **Tel:** 1 406 728-5000.
Web site: http://www.1067starfm.com
Profile: KXDR-FM is a commercial station owned by Cherry Creek Radio. The format of the station is Top 40/CHR. KXDR-FM broadcasts to the Missoula, MT area at a frequency of 106.7 FM.
FM RADIO STATION

KXDS-FM 789063
Owner: Dixie State College of Utah
Editorial: 225 S 700 E, Jennings Building, #103, Saint George, Utah 84770-3875 **Tel:** 1 435 879-4319.
Email: 913thestorm@gmail.com
Web site: http://dixie.edu/radio
Profile: KXDS-FM is a non-commercial college station owned by Dixie State College of Utah. The format of the station is Top 40/CHR. KXDS-FM broadcasts to the St. George, UT area at a frequency of 91.3 FM.
FM RADIO STATION

KXDZ-FM 444275
Owner: Mapleton Communications LLC
Editorial: 795 Buckley Rd, Ste 2, San Luis Obispo, California 93401 **Tel:** 1 805 786-2570.
Web site: http://www.953thebeach.com
Profile: KXDZ-FM is a commercial station owned by Mapleton Communications LLC. The format of the station is classic hits. KXDZ-FM broadcasts to the San Luis Obispo, CA area at 100.5 FM.
FM RADIO STATION

KXEG-AM 35124
Owner: Communicom Broadcasting
Editorial: 4020 N 20th St Ste 208, Phoenix, Arizona 85016-6030 **Tel:** 1 602 254-5001.
Web site: http://www.1280kxeg.com/
Profile: KXEG-AM is a commercial station owned by Communicom Broadcasting. The format of the station is Christian music and talk programming. KXEG-AM broadcasts to the Phoenix area at 1280 AM.
AM RADIO STATION

KXEI-FM 42169
Owner: Hi-Line Radio Fellowship
Editorial: 317 1st St, Havre, Montana 59501-3505 **Tel:** 1 406 265-5845.
Email: ynop@ynop.org
Web site: http://www.ynop.org
Profile: KXEI-FM is a non-commercial station owned by Hi-Line Radio Fellowship. The format for the station is contemporary Christian. KXEI-FM broadcasts to the Havre, MT area at 95.1 FM.
FM RADIO STATION

KXEL-AM 39044
Owner: NRG Media LLC
Editorial: 514 Jefferson St, Waterloo, Iowa 50701-5422 **Tel:** 1 319 234-2200.
Web site: http://www.kxel.com
Profile: KXEL-AM is a commercial station owned by NRG Media LLC. The format for the station is news and talk. KXEL-AM broadcasts to the Waterloo and Cedar Rapids, Iowa areas at 1540 AM. The station accepts 30 and 60-second PSAs in CD format. Send them to the station via mail or fax.
AM RADIO STATION

KXEN-AM 35125
Owner: Radio Property Ventures, LLC
Editorial: 5615 Pershing Ave Ste 12, Saint Louis, Missouri 63112-1757 **Tel:** 1 314 454-0400.
Email: kxen@aol.com
Web site: http://www.kxen1010am.com
Profile: KXEN-AM is a commercial station owned by Radio Property Ventures, LLC. The format of the station is Christian talk. KXEN-AM broadcasts to the St. Louis area at 1010 AM.
AM RADIO STATION

KXEO-AM 37595
Owner: Johnson(Anne)
Editorial: 1705 E Liberty St, Mexico, Missouri 65265-3537 **Tel:** 1 573 581-5500.
Email: news@radiogetsresults.net
Web site: http://kxeo.com
Profile: KXEO-AM is a commercial station owned by Anne Johnson. The format of the station is adult contemporary music. KXEO-AM broadcasts in the Mexico, MO area at 1340 AM.
AM RADIO STATION

KXEQ-AM 36110
Owner: Azteca Broadcasting Corp.
Editorial: 225 Linden St, Reno, Nevada 89502-4306 **Tel:** 1 775 827-1111.
Profile: KXEQ-AM is a commercial station owned by Azteca Broadcasting Corp. The format of the station is regional Mexican music. KXEQ-AM broadcasts to the Reno, NV area at 1340 AM.
AM RADIO STATION

KXET-AM 34987
Owner: Bustos Media, LLC
Editorial: 5110 SE Stark St, Portland, Oregon 97215-1751 **Tel:** 1 503 234-5550.
Email: contact@bustosmedia.com
Web site: http://www.pdxrr.com/
Profile: KXET-AM is a commercial station owned by Bustos Media, LLC. The format of the station is Regional Mexican. KXET-AM broadcasts to the Portland, OR area at 1150 AM.
AM RADIO STATION

KXEW-AM 38435
Owner: iHeartMedia Inc.
Editorial: 3202 N Oracle Rd, Tucson, Arizona 85705-3820 **Tel:** 1 520 618-2100.
Web site: http://www.tejano1600.com/main.html
Profile: KXEW-AM is a commercial station owned by iHeartMedia Inc. The format of the station is Tejano music. KXEW-AM broadcasts to the Tucson, AZ, area at 1600 AM.
AM RADIO STATION

KXEX-AM 35126
Owner: RAK Communications Inc.
Editorial: 139 W Olive Ave, Fresno, California 93728 **Tel:** 1 559 233-8803.
Email: rakradio@comcast.net
Profile: KXEX-AM is a commercial station owned by RAK Communications Inc. The format of the station is Hispanic religious programming. KXEX-AM broadcasts to the Fresno, CA area at 1550 AM.
AM RADIO STATION

KXEZ-FM 44024
Owner: Metro Broadcasters-Texas, Inc.
Editorial: 12225 Greenville Ave Ste 359, Dallas, Texas 75243-2089 **Tel:** 1 972 396-1640.
Web site: http://www.kxez.com
Profile: KXEZ-FM is a commercial station owned by Metro Broadcasters-Texas, Inc. The format of the station is country music. KXEZ-FM broadcasts to the Allen, TX area at 92.1 FM.
FM RADIO STATION

KXFC-FM 472985
Owner: Chickasaw Nation
Editorial: 1019 N Broadway, Ada, Oklahoma 74820-6503 **Tel:** 1 580 436-1616.
Email: score@cableone.net
Web site: http://www.kxfcradio.com
Profile: KXFC-FM is a commercial station owned by Chickasaw Nation. The format of the station is Top 40/CHR. KXFC-FM broadcasts to the Ada, OK area at 105.5 FM.
FM RADIO STATION

KXFE-FM 44045
Owner: Arkansas County Broadcasters Inc.
Editorial: 1818 S Buerkle St, Stuttgart, Arkansas 72160-5804 **Tel:** 1 870 673-1595.
Email: kdew973@yahoo.com
Profile: KXFE-FM is a commercial station owned by Arkansas County Broadcasters Inc. The format of the station is contemporary country music. KXFE-FM broadcasts to the Stuttgart, AR area at 106.9 FM.
FM RADIO STATION

KXFF-FM 44898
Owner: Cherry Creek Radio
Editorial: 750 Ridgeview Dr, St George, Utah 84770-2665 **Tel:** 1 435 673-3579.
Web site: http://www.cherrycreekradio.com
Profile: KXFF-FM is a commercial station owned by Cherry Creek Radio. The format of the station is sports. KXFF-FM broadcasts to the Salt Lake City, UT area at a frequency of 106.1 FM.
FM RADIO STATION

KXFG-FM 43166
Owner: CBS Radio
Editorial: 41593 Winchester Rd, Ste 100, Temecula, California 92590 **Tel:** 1 951 693-2206.
Web site: http://www.kfrog929.com
Profile: KXFG-FM is a commercial station owned by CBS Radio. The format of the station is contemporary country. KXFG-FM broadcasts to the Temecula Valley, CA area at 92.9 FM.
FM RADIO STATION

KXFM-FM 43464
Owner: El Dorado Broadcasting
Editorial: 2215 Skyway Dr, Santa Maria, California 93455-1118 **Tel:** 1 805 925-2582.
Web site: http://www.991thefox.com
Profile: KXFM-FM is a commercial station owned by El Dorado Broadcasting. The format of the station is rock. KXFM-FM broadcasts to the Santa Maria, CA area at 99.1 FM.
FM RADIO STATION

KXFT-FM 870194
Owner: Alpha Media
Editorial: 200 N 10th St, Fort Dodge, Iowa 50501-3925 **Tel:** 1 515 955-5656.
Web site: http://www.yourfortdodge.com
Profile: KXFT-FM is a commercial station owned by Alpha Media. The format of the station is adult contemporary. KXFT-FM's target audience is adults, ages 18 to 54, in the Fort Dodge, IA area. The station airs locally at 105.9 FM.
FM RADIO STATION

KXGE-FM 40043
Owner: Townsquare Media
Editorial: 5490 Saratoga Rd, Asbury, Iowa 52002-2593 **Tel:** 1 563 557-1040.

Web site: http://www.eagle102rocks.com
Profile: KXGE-FM is a commercial station owned by Townsquare Media. The format for the station is classic rock music. KXGE-FM broadcasts to the Cedar Rapids, IA area at 102.3 FM.
FM RADIO STATION

KXGF-AM 38481
Owner: Star Radio Corporation
Editorial: 1300 Central Ave W, Great Falls, Montana 59404-3971 **Tel:** 1 406 761-2800.
Email: audiogf@staradio.com
Web site: http://www.1400kxgf.com
Profile: KXGF-AM is a commercial station owned by Fisher Communications, Inc. The format of the station is Fox Sports. KXGF-AM broadcasts to the Great Falls, MT area at 1400 AM.
AM RADIO STATION

KXGL-FM 128038
Owner: JMJ Broadcasting Company Inc.
Editorial: 3505 Olsen Blvd Ste 120, Amarillo, Texas 79109-3035 **Tel:** 1 806 351-2345.
Web site: http://www.1009theeagle.com
Profile: KXGL-FM is a commercial station owned by JMJ Broadcasting Company Inc. The format of the station is classic hits. KXGL-FM broadcasts to the Amarillo, TX area at 100.9 FM.
FM RADIO STATION

KXGN-AM 35127
Owner: Glendive Broadcasting Corp.
Editorial: 210 S Douglas St, Glendive, Montana 59330 **Tel:** 1 406 377-3377.
Email: kxgnkdzn@midrivers.com
Web site: http://www.kxgn.com
Profile: KXGN-AM is a commercial station owned by Glendive Broadcasting Corp. The format for the station is adult contemporary and oldies. KXGN-AM broadcasts to the Glendive, MT area at 1400 AM.
AM RADIO STATION

KXGO-FM 242446
Owner: Lost Coast Communications
Editorial: 1400 Main St Ste 104, Ferndale, California 95536-9459 **Tel:** 1 707 786-5104.
Profile: KXGO-FM is a commercial station owned by Lost Coast Communications. The format is modern rock. KXGO-FMbroadcasts to the Ferndale, CA area at 94.1 FM.
FM RADIO STATION

KXGR-FM 231337
Owner: Calvary Chapel Aurora
Editorial: 18900 E Hampden Ave, Aurora, Colorado 80013-3609 **Tel:** 1 303 628-7200.
Email: studio@897gracefm.com
Web site: http://www.897gracefm.com
Profile: KXGR-FM is a non-commercial station owned by Calvary Chapel Aurora. The format of the station is religious. KXGR-FM broadcasts to the Denver area on 89.7 FM.
FM RADIO STATION

KXGT-FM 46105
Owner: Ingstad Family Media
Editorial: 2625 8th Ave SW, Jamestown, North Dakota 58401-6621 **Tel:** 1 701 252-1400.
Email: news@newsdakota.com
Web site: http://www.newsdakota.com
Profile: KXGT-FM is a commercial station owned by Ingstad Family Media. The format of the station is adult contemporary music. KXGT-FM broadcasts to the Jamestown, ND area at 98.3 FM.
FM RADIO STATION

KXHT-FM 42821
Owner: Flinn Broadcasting Corp.
Editorial: 6080 Mount Moriah Road Ext, Memphis, Tennessee 38115-2645 **Tel:** 1 901 375-9324.
Web site: http://www.hot1071.com
Profile: KXHT-FM is a commercial station owned by Flinn Broadcasting Corp. The format of the station is urban contemporary. KXHT-FM broadcasts to the Memphis, TN area at 107.1 FM.
FM RADIO STATION

KXIA-FM 46538
Owner: Marshalltown Broadcasting Inc.
Editorial: 123 W Main St, Marshalltown, Iowa 50158-5860 **Tel:** 1 641 753-3361.
Email: office@marshalltownbroadcasting.com
Web site: http://www.kixweb.com
Profile: KXIA-FM is a commercial station owned by Marshalltown Broadcasting Inc. The format of the station is contemporary country music. KXIA-FM broadcasts to the Marshalltown, IA area at 101.1 FM.
FM RADIO STATION

KXIC-AM 37596
Owner: iHeartMedia Inc.
Editorial: 1 Stephen Atkins Dr, Iowa City, Iowa 52240-8021 **Tel:** 1 319 354-9500.
Email: news@kxic.com
Web site: http://www.kxic.com
Profile: KXIC-AM is a commercial station owned by iHeartMedia Inc. The format for the station is a news, sports and talk. KXIC-AM broadcasts to the Iowa City, IA area at 800 AM.
AM RADIO STATION

KXIO-FM 42248
Owner: Ozark Mountain Broadcasting, LLC
Editorial: 117 S College Ave, Clarksville, Arkansas 72830-3552
Profile: KXIO-FM is a commercial station owned by Ozark Mountain Broadcasting, LLC. The format of the station is Classic Rock and broadcasts to the Clarksville, Arkansas area at 106.9. The station's slogan is "Today's Best Classic Rock."
FM RADIO STATION

KXIT-AM 37597
Owner: Rogco Family I, LLC
Editorial: 323 Denver Ave, Dalhart, Texas 79022-2711 **Tel:** 1 806 249-4747.
Email: kxitamfm@xit.net
Web site: http://www.kxit.com/
AM RADIO STATION

KXIX-FM 44974
Owner: Bend Radio Group (The)
Editorial: 345 SW Cyber Dr Ste 101-103, Bend, Oregon 97702-1045 **Tel:** 1 541 388-3300.
Web site: http://www.power94.fm
Profile: KXIX-FM is a commercial station owned by Bend Radio Group (The). The format of the station is Top 40/CHR. KXIX-FM broadcasts to the Bend, OR area at a frequency of 94.1 FM. Please contact R.L. Garrigus with all press releases.
FM RADIO STATION

KXJK-AM 37598
Owner: Forrest City Broadcasting Co.
Editorial: 501 E Broadway St, Forrest City, Arkansas 72335-3801 **Tel:** 1 870 633-1252.
Email: radio@arkansas.net
Web site: http://www.arkradio.com
Profile: KXJK-AM is a commercial station owned by Forrest City Broadcasting Co. The format of the station is news, sports and talk. KXJK-AM broadcasts to the Forrest City, AR area at 950 AM.
AM RADIO STATION

KXJM-FM 43066
Owner: iHeartMedia Inc.
Editorial: 13333 SW 68th Pkwy Ste 310, Tigard, Oregon 97223-8304 **Tel:** 1 503 323-6400.
Web site: http://jamn1075.iheart.com
Profile: KXJM-FM is a commercial station owned by iHeartMedia Inc. The format of the station is urban and rhythmic contemporary. KXJM-FM broadcasts to Portland, OR area at 107.5 FM.
FM RADIO STATION

KXKC-FM 45728
Owner: Cumulus Media Inc
Editorial: 202 Galbert Rd, Lafayette, Louisiana 70506 **Tel:** 1 337 232-1311.
Web site: http://www.kxkc.com
Profile: KXKC-FM is a commercial station owned by Cumulus Media Inc. The format of the station is contemporary country music. KXKC-FM broadcasts to the Lafayette, LA area at 99.1 FM.
FM RADIO STATION

KXKL-FM 45792
Owner: Wilks Broadcast Group
Editorial: 720 S Colorado Blvd Ste 1200N, Denver, Colorado 80246-1947 **Tel:** 1 303 832-5665.
Web site: http://www.kool105.com
Profile: KXKL-FM is a commercial station owned by Kroenke Sports & Entertainment. The format of the station is classic hits. KXKL-FM broadcasts to the Denver area at 105.1 FM.
FM RADIO STATION

KXKQ-FM 46279
Owner: McMurray Communications Inc.
Editorial: 3335 W 8th St, Thatcher, Arizona 85552-5414 **Tel:** 1 928 428-1230.
Email: traffic@mcmurrayradio.com
Web site: http://www.mysouthernaz.com
Profile: KXKQ-FM is a commercial station owned by McMurray Communications Inc. The format of the station is contemporary country. KXKQ-FM broadcasts to the Safford, AZ area at 94.5 FM.
FM RADIO STATION

KXKS-AM 39351
Owner: Wilkins Communications Network Inc.
Editorial: 2000 Randolph Rd SE, Ste 103, Albuquerque, New Mexico 87106 **Tel:** 1 505 244-1190.
Email: kxks@wilkinsradio.com
Web site: http://www.wilkinsradio.com
Profile: KXKS-AM is a commercial station owned by Wilkins Communications Inc. The format of the station is religious. KXKS-AM broadcasts to the Albuqueque, NM area at 1190 AM.
AM RADIO STATION

KXKS-FM 46692
Owner: Townsquare Media, LLC
Editorial: 6341 W Port Ave, Shreveport, Louisiana 71129 **Tel:** 1 318 688-1130.
Web site: http://mykisscountry937.com/
Profile: KXKS-FM is a commercial station owned by Townsquare Media, LLC. The format of the station is contemporary country music. KXKS-FM broadcasts to the Shreveport, LA area at 93.7 FM.
FM RADIO STATION

KXKT-FM 42193
Owner: iHeartMedia Inc.
Editorial: 5010 Underwood Ave, Omaha, Nebraska 68132-2236 **Tel:** 1 402 561-2000.
Web site: http://www.thekat.com
Profile: KXKT-FM is a commercial station owned by iHeartMedia Inc. The format of the station is contemporary country. KXKT-FM broadcasts to the Omaha, NE area at 103.3 FM.
FM RADIO STATION

KXKU-FM 44190
Owner: Ad Astra Per Aspera Broadcasting, Inc.
Editorial: 10 E 5th Ave, Hutchinson, Kansas 67501-6201 **Tel:** 1 620 665-5758.
Web site: http://www.adastraradio.com
Profile: KXKU-FM is a commercial station owned by Ad Astra Per Aspera Broadcasting, Inc. The format of the station is classic country. KXKU-FM broadcasts to the Hutchinson, KS area at 106.1 FM.
FM RADIO STATION

KXKX-FM 83737
Owner: Townsquare Media, LLC
Editorial: 2209 S Limit Ave, Sedalia, Missouri 65301-6950 **Tel:** 1 660 826-1050.
Email: kxsiradio@townsquaremedia.com
Web site: http://www.kxkx.com
Profile: KXKX-FM is a commercial station owned by Townsquare Media, LLC. The format of the station is classic country. KXKX-FM broadcasts to the Sedalia, MO, area at 105.7 FM.
FM RADIO STATION

KXKZ-FM 44976
Owner: Red Peach LLC
Editorial: 500 N Monroe St, Ruston, Louisiana 71270-3835 **Tel:** 1 318 255-5000.
Email: z1075fm@bayou.com
Web site: http://www.z1075fm.com
Profile: KXKZ-FM is a commercial station owned by Red Peach LLC. The format of the station is country music. KXKZ-FM broadcasts to the Ruston, LA area at 107.5 FM.
FM RADIO STATION

KXLB-FM 70137
Owner: Townsquare Media, LLC
Editorial: 125 W Mendenhall St, Bozeman, Montana 59715-3586 **Tel:** 1 406 586-2343.
Email: bznproduction@townsquaremedia.com
Web site: http://www.xlcountry.com
Profile: KXLB-FM is a commercial station owned by Townsquare Media, LLC. The format of the station is classic and contemporary country. KXLB-FM broadcasts to the Bozeman, MT area at 100.7 FM.
FM RADIO STATION

KXLE-AM 38389
Owner: KXLE Inc.
Editorial: 1311 Vantage Hwy, Ellensburg, Washington 98926 **Tel:** 1 509 925-1488.
Email: kxle@elltel.net
Profile: KXLE-AM is a commercial station owned by KXLE Inc. The format of the station is news, sports and talk programming. KXLE-AM broadcasts to the Ellensburg, WA area at 1240 AM.
AM RADIO STATION

KXLE-FM 45750
Owner: KXLE Inc.
Editorial: 1311 Vantage Hwy, Ellensburg, Washington 98926 **Tel:** 1 509 925-1488.
Email: kxle@elltel.net
Web site: http://www.kxleradio.com
Profile: KXLE-FM is a commercial station owned by KXLE Inc. The format of the station is classic country. The station airs locally in the Ellensburg, WA area.
FM RADIO STATION

KXL-FM 43063
Owner: Alpha Media
Editorial: 1211 SW 5th Ave Fl 6, Portland, Oregon 97204-3735 **Tel:** 1 503 243-7595.
Email: news@kxl.com
Web site: http://kxl.com
Profile: KXL-FM is a commercial station owned by Alpha Media. The format of the station is news and talk. KXL-FM broadcasts to the Portland, OR area at 101.1 FM.
FM RADIO STATION

KXLG-FM 44933
Owner: Dakota Communications, Ltd.
Editorial: 26 S Broadway, Watertown, South Dakota 57201-3604 **Tel:** 1 605 753-9910.
Web site: http://www.kxlgradio.com
Profile: KXLG-FM is a commercial station owned by Dakota Communications, Ltd and operated under an LMA with TMRG Broadcasting. The format of the station is classic hits. KXLG-FM broadcasts to the Huron, SD area at 99.1 FM.
FM RADIO STATION

KXLI-FM 552404
Owner: Radio Activo Broadcasting
Editorial: 2050 S Eastern Ave, Las Vegas, Nevada 89104-4100 **Tel:** 1 702 444-7777.
Web site: http://www.exafm.com/lasvegas
Profile: KXLI-FM is a commercial station owned by Radio Activo Broadcasting. The format of the station is Spanish CHR. KXLI-FM broadcasts to the Moapa, NV area at 94.5 FM.
FM RADIO STATION

KXLL-FM 445523
Owner: Capital Community Broadcasting Inc.
Editorial: 360 Egan Dr, Juneau, Alaska 99801-1769 **Tel:** 1 907 586-1670.
Email: news@ktoo.org
Web site: http://www.kxll.org
Profile: KXLL-FM is a non-commercial station owned by Capital Community Broadcasting Inc. The format of the station is AAA/modern rock. KXLL-FM broadcasts to the the Juneau, AK area at 100.7 FM.
FM RADIO STATION

KXLM-FM 42379
Owner: Lazer Broadcasting Corp.
Editorial: 200 S 8th St., Ste 400, Oxnard, California 93030 **Tel:** 1 805 240-2070.
Web site: http://www.radiolazer.com/kxlm.php
Profile: KXLM-FM is a commercial station owned by the Lazer Broadcasting Corp. The format of the station is Regional Mexican music and some talk. KXLM-FM broadcasts to the Santa Barbara, CA area at 101.7 FM.
FM RADIO STATION

KXLO-AM 37600
Owner: KXLO Broadcast, Inc.
Editorial: 620 NE Main St, Lewistown, Montana 59457 **Tel:** 1 406 535-3441.
Email: traffic@kxlo-klcm.com
Web site: http://www.kxlo-klcm.com
Profile: KXLO-AM is a commercial station owned by KXLO Broadcast, Inc. The format for the station is contemporary and classic country. KXLO-AM broadcasts to the Lewistown, MT area at 1230 AM.
AM RADIO STATION

KXLP-FM 42722
Owner: Radio Mankato
Editorial: 59346 Madison Ave, Mankato, Minnesota 56001-8518 **Tel:** 1 507 345-4537.
Email: news@ktoe.com
Web site: http://www.kxlp941.com
Profile: KXLP-FM is a commercial station owned by Radio Mankato. The format of the station is classic rock music. KXLP-FM broadcasts in the Minneapolis area at 94.1 FM.
FM RADIO STATION

KXLQ-AM 39362
Owner: Birach Broadcasting
Editorial: 118 W Jefferson St, Osceola, Iowa 50213-1204 **Tel:** 1 248 557-3500.
Web site: http://www.birach.com
Profile: KXLQ-AM is a commercial station owned by Birach Broadcasting. The format of the station is sports. KXLQ-AM broadcasts to the Indianola, IA area at a frequency of 1490 AM.
AM RADIO STATION

KXLR-FM 46388
Owner: Last Frontier Mediactive, LLC
Editorial: 819 1st Ave Ste A, Fairbanks, Alaska 99701-4449 **Tel:** 1 907 451-5910.
Email: LFM@fbxradio.com
Web site: http://www.xrock959.com
Profile: KXLR-FM is a commercial station owned by Last Frontier Mediactive, LLC. The format of the station is classic rock. KXLR-FM broadcasts to the Fairbanks, AK area at 95.9 FM.
FM RADIO STATION

KXLS-FM 69885
Owner: Chisholm Trail Broadcasting
Editorial: 316 E Willow Rd, Enid, Oklahoma 73701-1514 **Tel:** 1 580 237-1390.
Email: info@knid.com
Web site: http://www.knid.com
Profile: KXLS-FM is a commercial station owned by Chisholm Trail Broadcasting. The format of the station is hot adult contemporary music. KXLS-FM broadcasts to Oklahoma City, OK at 95.7 FM.
FM RADIO STATION

KXLT-FM 42266
Owner: Townsquare Media, LLC
Editorial: 827 E Park Blvd Ste 100, Boise, Idaho 83712-7783 **Tel:** 1 208 344-6363.
Web site: http://www.liteonline.com
Profile: KXLT-FM is a commercial station owned by Townsquare Media, LLC. The format of the station is adult contemporary. KXLT-FM broadcasts to the Boise, ID area at 107.9 FM.
FM RADIO STATION

KXLW-FM 63410
Owner: Ohana Media Group
Editorial: 833 Gambell St, Anchorage, Alaska 99501-3756 **Tel:** 1 907 344-4045.
Web site: http://themoose963.com/
Profile: KXLW-FM is a commercial station owned by Ohana Media Group. The format of the station is country. KXLW-FM broadcasts to the Anchorage, AK area at 96.3 FM.
FM RADIO STATION

KXLX-AM 38934
Owner: Queen B Radio Inc.
Editorial: 500 W Boone Ave, Spokane, Washington 99201-2404 **Tel:** 1 509 324-4200.
Email: areyoukiddingme@700espn.com
Web site: http://www.700espn.com
Profile: KXLX-AM is a commercial station owned by Queen B Radio Inc. The format of the station is sports. KXLX-AM broadcasts to the Spokane, WA area at 700 AM.
AM RADIO STATION

KXLY-AM 37601
Owner: Queen B Inc.
Editorial: 500 W Boone Ave, Spokane, Washington 99201-2404 **Tel:** 1 509 329-4000.
Email: news4@kxly.com
Web site: http://www.kxly920.com
Profile: KXLY-AM is a commercial station owned by Queen B Inc. The format of the station is news and talk. KXLY-AM broadcasts to the Spokane, WA area at 920 AM.
AM RADIO STATION

KXLY-FM
44978

Owner: Queen B Inc.
Editorial: 500 W Boone Ave, Spokane, Washington 99201-2404 **Tel:** 1 509 324-4000.
Web site: http://www.thebig999coyotecountry.com
Profile: KXLY-FM is a commercial station owned by Queen B Inc. The format of the station is country music. KXLY-FM broadcasts to the Spokane, WA area at 99.9 FM.
FM RADIO STATION

KXMO-FM
87175

Owner: Mahaffey Enterprises Inc.
Editorial: 1505 Soest Rd, Rolla, Missouri 65401-3709 **Tel:** 1 573 364-2525.
Email: kznnpsa@yahoo.com
Web site: http://www.resultsradioonline.com
Profile: KXMO-FM is a commercial station owned by Mahaffey Enterprises Inc. The format of the station is oldies music. KXMO-FM broadcasts to the Cuba, MO area at 95.3 FM.
FM RADIO STATION

KXMR-AM
36929

Owner: iHeartMedia Inc.
Editorial: 3500 E Rosser Ave, Bismarck, North Dakota 58501-3376 **Tel:** 1 701 255-1234.
Web site: http://www.am710thefan.com/main.html
Profile: KXMR-AM is a commercial station owned by iHeartMedia Inc. The format of the station is sports. KXMR-AM broadcasts to the Bismarck, ND area at 710 AM.
AM RADIO STATION

KXMT-FM
44448

Owner: DMC Broadcasting Inc.
Editorial: 125 Camino De La Merced, A, Taos, New Mexico 87571-5119 **Tel:** 1 575 758-4491.
Web site: http://www.kxmt.com
Profile: KXMT-FM is a commercial station owned by DMC Broadcasting Inc. The format of the station is regional Mexican music. KXMT-FM broadcasts in the Taos, NM area at 99.1 FM.
FM RADIO STATION

KXMX-FM
909671

Owner: G2 Media Group
Editorial: 333 S Kerr Blvd, Sallisaw, Oklahoma 74955-7212 **Tel:** 1 91 790-1051.
Email: themix@kxmx.com
Web site: http://www.kxmx.com
Profile: KXMX-FM is a commercial station owned and operated by G2 Media Group. The format of the station is a variety of music and news programming. The station broadcasts to the Sequoyah County, OK area at a frequency of 105.1 FM.
FM RADIO STATION

KXNA-FM
42278

Owner: Butler Broadcasting
Editorial: 1780 W Holly St, Fayetteville, Arkansas 72703-1307 **Tel:** 1 479 582-3776.
Web site: http://www.newrock1049x.com
Profile: KXNA-FM is a commercial station owned by Butler Broadcasting. The format of the station is rock alternative. KXNA-FM broadcasts to the Fayetteville, AR area at 104.9 FM.
FM RADIO STATION

KXNO-AM
36216

Owner: iHeartMedia Inc.
Editorial: 2141 Grand Ave, Des Moines, Iowa 50312-5303 **Tel:** 1 515 245-8900.
Web site: http://www.kxno.com
Profile: KXNO-AM is a commercial station owned by iHeartMedia Inc. The format of the station is sports. KXNO-AM broadcasts to the Des Moines, IA area at 1460 AM.
AM RADIO STATION

KXNP-FM
45714

Owner: Armada Media Corp.
Editorial: 307 E 4th St, North Platte, Nebraska 69101-6903 **Tel:** 1 308 532-3344.
Web site: http://www.huskeradio.com
Profile: KXNP-FM is a commercial station owned by Armada Media Corp. The format of the station is contemporary country. KXNP-FM broadcasts to the North Platte, NE area at 103.5 FM.
FM RADIO STATION

KXNT-AM
35891

Owner: CBS Radio
Editorial: 7255 S Tenaya Way Ste 100, Las Vegas, Nevada 89113-1900 **Tel:** 1 702 889-7300.
Web site: http://lasvegas.cbslocal.com
Profile: KXNT-AM is a commercial station owned by CBS Radio. The format of the station is news and talk. KXNT-AM broadcasts to the Las Vegas area at 840 AM.
AM RADIO STATION

KXO-AM
37602

Owner: KXO Inc.
Editorial: 420 Main St, El Centro, California 92243 **Tel:** 1 760 352-1230.
Email: kxoamfm@kxoradio.com
Web site: http://www.kxoradio.com
Profile: KXO-AM is a commercial station owned by KXO Inc. The format of the station is oldies. KXO-AM broadcasts to the El Centro, CA area at 1230 AM.
AM RADIO STATION

KXO-FM
44979

Owner: KXO Inc.
Editorial: 420 Main St, El Centro, California 92243 **Tel:** 1 760 352-1230.
Email: kxoamfm@kxoradio.com
Web site: http://www.kxoradio.com
Profile: KXO-FM is a commercial station owned by KXO Inc. The format of the station is adult contemporary music. KXO-FM broadcasts to the El Centro, CA area at 107.5 FM.
FM RADIO STATION

KXOI-AM
36627

Owner: Hispanic Outreach Ministries Inc.
Editorial: 519 N Lauderdale Ave, Odessa, Texas 79763-4167 **Tel:** 1 432 333-5061.
Web site: http://www.radioalabanza.info
Profile: KXOI-AM is a commercial station owned by Hispanic Outreach Ministries Inc. The format of the station is Hispanic contemporary Christian. KXOI-AM broadcasts to the Odessa, TX area at 810 AM.
AM RADIO STATION

KXOJ-FM
46316

Owner: Stephens Media Group
Editorial: 2448 E 81st St Ste 5500, Tulsa, Oklahoma 74137-4201 **Tel:** 1 918 492-2660.
Email: kxoj@kxoj.com
Web site: http://www.kxoj.com
Profile: KXOJ-FM is a commercial station owned by Stephens Media Group. The format of the station is classic hits. KXOJ-FM broadcasts to the Tulsa, OK area at 100.9 FM. Send all PSAs to the main email.
FM RADIO STATION

KXOL-FM
39653

Owner: Spanish Broadcasting System
Editorial: 10281 W Pico Blvd, Los Angeles, California 90064-2674 **Tel:** 1 310 203-0900.
Web site: http://www.mega963.com
Profile: KXOL-FM is a commercial station owned by Spanish Broadcasting System. The format of the station is Spanish CHR/AC. KXOL-FM broadcasts to the Los Angeles area at 96.3 FM.
FM RADIO STATION

KXOO-FM
43120

Owner: Paragon Communications Inc.
Editorial: 220 S Pioneer Rd, Elk City, Oklahoma 73644 **Tel:** 1 580 225-5966.
Email: kxoo@cableone.net
Web site: http://www.kxoofm.com
Profile: KXOO-FM is a commercial station owned by Paragon Communications Inc. The format of the station is contemporary Christian music. KXOO-FM broadcasts in the Elk City, OK, area at 94.3 FM.
FM RADIO STATION

KXOQ-FM
44159

Owner: Eagle Bluff Enterprises
Editorial: 700 North Byp, Kennett, Missouri 63857-1343 **Tel:** 1 573 686-3700.
Email: frn@tcmax.net
Web site: http://foxradionetwork.com
Profile: KXOQ-FM is a commercial station owned by Eagle Bluff Enterprises. The format of the station is classic rock. KXOQ-FM broadcasts to the Kennett, MO area at 104.3 FM.
FM RADIO STATION

KXOR-AM
36955

Owner: Zion Multimedia Oregon Corporation
Editorial: 12145 Woodruff Ave, Downey, California 90241-5605 **Tel:** 1 562 401-4030.
Email: contactenos@zionmultimedia.com
Web site: http://www.radiozion.net
Profile: KXOR-AM is a commercial station owned by Zion Multimedia Oregon Corporation. The format of the station is Spanish-language Christian programming. KXOR-AM Broadcasts to the Eugene, OR area at a frequency of 660 AM.
AM RADIO STATION

KXOS-FM
43485

Owner: 93.9 Holdings, Inc. (Grupo Radio Centro)
Editorial: 2600 W Olive Ave Fl 8, Burbank, California 91505-4553 **Tel:** 1 818 525-5000.
Web site: http://radiocentro939.com
Profile: KXOS-FM is a commercial station owned by 93.9 Holdings, Inc. (Grupo Radio Centro). The format of the station is Top 40/CHR. KXOS-FM broadcasts to the Los Angeles area at 93.9 FM.
FM RADIO STATION

KXOX-AM
37603

Owner: Stein Broadcasting Co., Inc.
Editorial: 1801 Hoyt St, Sweetwater, Texas 79556-2663 **Tel:** 1 325 236-6655.
Email: kxox@att.net
Web site: http://www.kxox.net
Profile: KXOX-AM is a commercial station owned by Stein Broadcasting Co., Inc. The format of the station is country. KXOX-AM broadcasts to the Abilene, TX area at 1240 AM.
AM RADIO STATION

KXOX-FM
44980

Owner: Stein Broadcasting Co., Inc.
Editorial: 1801 Hoyt St, Sweetwater, Texas 79556-2663 **Tel:** 1 325 236-6655.
Email: kxox@att.net
Web site: http://www.kxox.net
Profile: KXOX-FM is a commercial station owned by Stein Broadcasting Co., Inc. The format of the station is country. KXOX-FM broadcasts to the Sweetwater, TX area at 96.7 FM.
FM RADIO STATION

KXPA-AM
36479

Owner: Multicultural Radio Broadcasting Inc.
Editorial: 114 Lakeside Ave, Seattle, Washington 98122-6542 **Tel:** 1 206 292-7800.
Email: kxpacontrolroom@gmail.com
Web site: http://www.kxpa.com
Profile: KXPA-AM is a commercial station owned by Multicultural Radio Broadcasting Inc. The format of the station is Hispanic. KXPA-AM broadcasts to the Seattle area at 1540 AM.
AM RADIO STATION

KXPK-FM
42408

Owner: Entravision Communications Corp.
Editorial: 1907 Mile High Stadium West Cir, Denver, Colorado 80204-1908 **Tel:** 1 303 832-0050.
Web site: http://www.965tricolor.com
Profile: KXPK-FM is a commercial station owned by Entravision Communications Corp. The format of the station is regional Mexican music. KXPK-FM broadcasts to the Denver area at 96.5 FM.
FM RADIO STATION

KXPL-AM
36028

Owner: New Radio System, Inc.
Editorial: 2211 E Missouri Ave #E237, El Paso, Texas 79903-3807 **Tel:** 1 915 587-8822.
Email: kxpl1060am@yahoo.com
Profile: KXPL-AM is a commercial station owned by New Radio System, Inc. The format is ranchero/ regional Mexican. KXPL-AM broadcasts in the El Paso, TX, area at 1060 AM.
AM RADIO STATION

KXPN-AM
217827

Owner: Platte River Radio, Inc.
Editorial: 403 E 25th St, Kearney, Nebraska 68847 **Tel:** 1 308 236-9900.
Email: generalmanager@espnsuperstation.com
Web site: http://www.espnsuperstation.com
Profile: KXPN-AM is a commercial station owned by Platte River Radio, Inc. The format of the station is sports. KXPN-AM broadcasts to the Kearney, NE area at 1460 AM.
AM RADIO STATION

KXPO-AM
38405

Owner: Simmons Broadcasting, Inc.
Editorial: 856 W 12th St, Grafton, North Dakota 58237-2120 **Tel:** 1 701 352-0431.
Email: kxpo@polarcomm.com
Web site: http://www.walshcountydailynews.com
Profile: KXPO-AM is a commercial station owned by Simmons Broadcasting, Inc. The format of the station is classic country. KXPO-AM broadcasts to the Grafton, ND area at 1340 AM.
AM RADIO STATION

KXPS-AM
36105

Owner: CRC Media West, LLC
Editorial: 75-153 Merle Dr Ste D, Palm Desert, California 92211-5197 **Tel:** 1 760 621-0100.
Web site: http://www.1010kxps.com
Profile: KXPS-AM is a commercial station owned by CRC Media West, LLC. The format of the station is sports. KXPS-AM broadcasts to the Palm Springs, CA area at 1010 AM.
AM RADIO STATION

KXPT-FM
46074

Owner: Lotus Communications Corp.
Editorial: 8755 W Flamingo Rd, Las Vegas, Nevada 89147-8667 **Tel:** 1 702 876-1460.
Email: lotussignup@yahoo.com
Web site: http://www.point97.com
Profile: KXPT-FM is a commercial station owned by Lotus Communications Corp. The format of the station is classic rock music. KXPT-FM broadcasts to the Las Vegas area at 97.1 FM.
FM RADIO STATION

KXPZ-FM
43463

Owner: Bravo Mic Communications, LLC
Editorial: 101 Perkins Dr, Las Cruces, New Mexico 88005-3295 **Tel:** 1 575 527-1111.
Web site: http://www.therocketonline.com
Profile: KXPZ-FM is a commercial station owned by Bravo Mic Communications, LLC. The format of the station is adult album alternative. KXPZ-FM broadcasts to the Las Cruces, NM area at 99.5 FM.
FM RADIO STATION

KXQQ-FM
41621

Owner: CBS Radio
Editorial: 7255 S Tenaya Way Ste 100, Las Vegas, Nevada 89113-1900
Web site: http://q100vegas.cbslocal.com
Profile: KXQQ-FM is a commercial station owned by CBS Radio. The format of the station is today's rhythm and Vegas' best throwbacks. KXQQ-FM broadcasts to the Las Vegas area at 100.5 FM.
FM RADIO STATION

KXRA-AM
37604

Owner: Paradis Broadcasting
Editorial: 1312 Broadway St, Alexandria, Minnesota 56308-2534 **Tel:** 1 320 763-3131.
Email: thefolks@kxra.com
Web site: http://www.voiceofalexandria.com
Profile: KXRA-AM is a commercial station owned by Paradis Broadcasting. The format of the station is news and talk. KXRA-AM broadcasts to the Alexandria, MN area at 1490 AM.
AM RADIO STATION

KXRA-FM
44981

Owner: Paradis Broadcasting
Editorial: 1312 Broadway St, Alexandria, Minnesota 56308-2534 **Tel:** 1 320 763-3131.
Email: thefolks@kxra.com
Web site: http://www.voiceofalexandria.com
Profile: KXRA-FM is a commercial station owned by Paradis Broadcasting. The format of the station is classic rock. KXRA-FM broadcasts to the Alexandria, MN area at 92.3 FM.
FM RADIO STATION

KXRB-AM
37605

Owner: Townsquare Media, Inc.
Editorial: 5100 S Tennis Ln, Sioux Falls, South Dakota 57108-2212 **Tel:** 1 605 361-0300.
Web site: http://www.kxrb.com
Profile: KXRB-AM is a commercial station owned by Townsquare Media, Inc. The format of the station is classic country music. KXRB-AM broadcasts to the Sioux Falls, SD area at 1000 AM.
AM RADIO STATION

KXRC-FM
874817

Owner: KRJ Company
Editorial: 1135 Main Ave, Durango, Colorado 81301-5135 **Tel:** 1 970 259-1364.
Email: info@xrock105.com
Web site: http://www.xrock105.com/
Profile: KXRC-FM is a commercial station owned and operated by KRJ Company. The format of the station is classic rock. KXRC-FM broadcasts to the Durango, CO area at a frequency of 105.3 FM.
FM RADIO STATION

KXRE-AM
132662

Owner: Latino Communications
Editorial: 600 S Grant St Ste 600, Denver, Colorado 80209-4146 **Tel:** 1 303 733-5266.
Profile: KXRE-AM is a commercial station owned by Latino Communications. The format of the station is regional Mexican. KXRE-AM broadcasts to the the Denver area at 1490 AM.
AM RADIO STATION

KXRK-FM
41401

Owner: Broadway Media
Editorial: 515 S 700 E Ste 1C, Salt Lake City, Utah 84102-2802 **Tel:** 1 801 524-2600.
Web site: http://www.x96.com
Profile: KXRK-FM is a commercial station owned by Broadway Media. The format of the station is rock alternative. KXRK-FM broadcasts to the Salt Lake City area at 96.3 FM.
FM RADIO STATION

KXRO-AM
38484

Owner: Morris Communications
Editorial: 1308 Coolidge Rd, Aberdeen, Washington 98520-6317 **Tel:** 1 360 533-1320.
Web site: http://www.kxro.com
Profile: KXRO-AM is a commercial station owned by Morris Communications. The format of the station is news and talk. KXRO-AM broadcasts in the Aberdeen, WA area at 1320 AM.
AM RADIO STATION

KXRQ-FM
86749

Owner: Uinta Broadcasting, L.C.
Editorial: 1420 Weatherby Dr Ste 200, Vernal, Utah 84078-8045 **Tel:** 1 435 781-1100.
Profile: KXRQ-FM is a commercial station owned by Uinta Broadcasting, L.C.. The format of the station is Top 40/CHR. KXRQ-FM broadcasts to the Salt Lake City area at 94.3 FM.
FM RADIO STATION

KXRR-FM
42907

Owner: Opus Media Partners
Editorial: 1200 N 18th St, Monroe, Louisiana 71201-5459 **Tel:** 1 318 387-3922.
Web site: http://www.rock106kxrr.com
Profile: KXRR-FM is a commercial station owned by Opus Media Partners. The format of the station is rock music. KXRR-FM broadcasts to the Monroe, LA area at 106.1 FM.
FM RADIO STATION

KXRS-FM
46169

Owner: Lazer Broadcasting Corp.
Editorial: 1950 S Sunwest Ln Ste 302, San Bernardino, California 92408-3227 **Tel:** 1 909 384-9750.
Web site: http://radiolazer1017.com/
Profile: KXRS-FM is a commercial station owned by the Lazer Broadcasting Corp. The format of the station is Regional Mexican. KXRS-FM broadcasts to the Hemet, CA area at 105.7 FM.
FM RADIO STATION

KXRV-FM
736582

Owner: World Radio Link, Inc.
Editorial: 409 N 4Th St, Bismarck, North Dakota 58501-4023 **Tel:** 1 701 751-4757.
Email: mojo@mojo1075.com
Web site: http://www.mojo1075.com
Profile: KXRV-FM is a commercial station owned by World Radio Link, Inc and operated by Radio Bismark-Mandan (Denver, Bob). The format of the station is classic hits. KXRV-FM broadcasts to the Bismark, ND area at a frequency of 107.5.
FM RADIO STATION

KXRX-FM
40987

Owner: Townsquare Media, LLC
Editorial: 2621 W A St, Pasco, Washington 99301-4702 **Tel:** 1 509 547-9791.

Web site: http://97rockonline.com
Profile: KXRX-FM is a commercial station owned by Townsquare Media, LLC. The format of the station is rock. KXRX-FM broadcasts to the Pasco, WA area at 97.1 FM.
FM RADIO STATION

KXRZ-FM 39931
Owner: Paradis Broadcasting
Editorial: 1312 Broadway St, Alexandria, Minnesota 56308-2534 **Tel:** 1 320 763-3131.
Email: thefolks@kxra.com
Web site: http://www.voiceofalexandria.com/z99
Profile: KXRZ-FM is a commercial station owned by Paradis Broadcasting. The format of the station is hot adult contemporary. KXRZ-FM broadcasts to the Alexandria, MN area at 99.3 FM.
FM RADIO STATION

KXSA-FM 44344
Owner: Pines Broadcasting
Editorial: 279 Midway Rte, Monticello, Arkansas 71655-8605 **Tel:** 1 870 367-6854.
Email: pines.radio@sbcglobal.net
Profile: KXSA-FM is a commercial station owned by Pines Broadcasting. The format of the station is classic country. KXSA-FM broadcasts to the Monticello, AR area at 103.1 FM.
FM RADIO STATION

KXSB-FM 43130
Owner: Lazer Broadcasting Corp.
Editorial: 1950 S Sunwest Ln Ste 302, San Bernardino, California 92408-3227 **Tel:** 1 909 384-9750.
Web site: http://radiolazer.com
Profile: KXSB-FM is a commercial station owned by the Lazer Broadcasting Corp. The format for the station is regional Mexican. KXSB-FM broadcasts to the San Bernadino, CA area at 101.7 FM.
FM RADIO STATION

KXSE-FM 42796
Owner: Entravision Communications Corp.
Editorial: 1436 Auburn Blvd, Sacramento, California 95815-2745 **Tel:** 1 916 646-4000.
Web site: http://www.jose1043.com
Profile: KXSE-FM is a commercial station owned by Entravision Communications Corp. The format of the station is Hispanic adult hits. KXSE-FM broadcasts to the Sacramento, CA area on 104.3 FM.
FM RADIO STATION

KXSM-FM 39669
Owner: Lazer Broadcasting Corp.
Editorial: 600 E Market St, Salinas, California 93905-2109 **Tel:** 1 831 422-5019.
Web site: http://www.radiolazer.com
Profile: KXSM-FM is a commercial station owned by Lazer Broadcasting Corp. The format of the station is regional Mexican. KXSM-FM broadcasts to the Monterey, CA area at 93.1 FM.
FM RADIO STATION

KXSN-FM 39679
Owner: Entercom Communications Corp.
Editorial: 1615 Murray Canyon Rd Ste 710, San Diego, California 92108-4321 **Tel:** 1 619 291-9797.
Web site: http://www.sunny981sd.com
Profile: KXSN-FM is a commercial station owned by Entercom Communications Corp. The format of the station is smooth AC. KIFM-FM broadcasts to the San Diego area at 98.1 FM.
FM RADIO STATION

KXSP-AM 38113
Owner: E.W. Scripps Co.
Editorial: 10714 Mockingbird Dr, Omaha, Nebraska 68127-1942 **Tel:** 1 402 592-5300.
Web site: http://www.am590espnradio.com
Profile: KXSP-AM is a commercial station owned by E.W. Scripps Co. The format of the station is sports. KXSP-AM broadcasts to the Omaha, NE area at 590 AM.
AM RADIO STATION

KXSS-AM 38733
Owner: Townsquare Media, LLC
Editorial: 640 Lincoln Ave SE, Saint Cloud, Minnesota 56304-1024 **Tel:** 1 320 251-4422.
Email: thefanman@1390thefan.com
Web site: http://1390thefan.com
Profile: KXSS-AM is a commercial station owned by Townsquare Media, LLC. The format of the station is sports. KXSS-AM broadcasts to the Saint Cloud, MN area at 1390 AM.
AM RADIO STATION

KXSS-FM 42951
Owner: Townsquare Media, LLC
Editorial: 6214 SW 34th Ave, Amarillo, Texas 79109-4006 **Tel:** 1 806 355-9777.
Web site: http://kissfm969.com
Profile: KXSS-FM is a commercial station owned by Townsquare Media, LLC. The format of the station is Top 40/CHR. KXSS-FM broadcasts to the Amarillo, TX area at 96.9 FM.
FM RADIO STATION

KXST-AM 38399
Owner: CBS Radio
Editorial: 7255 S Tenaya Way, Las Vegas, Nevada 89113-1900 **Tel:** 1 702 889-7300.
Web site: http://lasvegas.cbslocal.com/station/cbs-sports-radio-1140/
Profile: KXST-AM is a commercial station owned by CBS Radio. The format of the station is sports programming. KXST-AM broadcasts to the Las Vegas area at 1140 AM.
AM RADIO STATION

KXTC-FM 41905
Owner: iHeartMedia Inc.
Editorial: 1632 S Second St, Gallup, New Mexico 87301-5836 **Tel:** 1 505 863-9391.
Web site: http://www.999xtc.com
Profile: KXTC-FM is a commercial station owned by iHeartMedia Inc. The format of the station is Top 40/CHR music. KXTC-FM broadcasts to the Albuquerque, NM area at 99.9 FM.
FM RADIO STATION

KXTD-AM 153397
Owner: Key Plus Properties LLC
Editorial: 5807 S Garnett Rd Ste K, Tulsa, Oklahoma 74146-6847 **Tel:** 1 918 254-7556.
Email: kxtdr@tulsacoxmail.com
Web site: http://www.quebuenatulsa.com
Profile: KXTD-AM is a commercial station owned by Key Plus Properties LLC. The format of the station is Latin Pop. KXTD-AM broadcasts to the Tulsa, OK area at 1530 AM.
AM RADIO STATION

KXTE-FM 41644
Owner: CBS Radio
Editorial: 7255 S Tenaya Way Ste 100, Las Vegas, Nevada 89113-1900 **Tel:** 1 702 257-1075.
Web site: http://www.x1075lasvegas.com
Profile: KXTE-FM is a commercial station owned by CBS Radio. The format of the station is rock alternative. KXTE-FM broadcasts to the Las Vegas area at 107.5 FM.
FM RADIO STATION

KXTG-AM 37599
Owner: Alpha Media
Editorial: 1211 SW 5th Ave Fl 6, Portland, Oregon 97204-3735 **Tel:** 1 503 243-7595.
Web site: http://www.750thegame.com
Profile: KXTG-AM is a commercial station owned by Alpha Media. The format of the station is sports. KXTG-AM broadcasts to the Portland, OR area at 750 AM.
AM RADIO STATION

KXTK-AM 37049
Owner: Pacific Coast Media, LLC
Editorial: 880 Via Esteban, San Luis Obispo, California 93401-7101 **Tel:** 1 805 547-1280.
Web site: http://www.espnradio1280.com
Profile: KXTK-AM is a commercial station owned by Pacific Coast Media, LLC. The format of the station is sports. KXTK-AM broadcasts to the San Luis Obispo, CA area at 1280 AM.
AM RADIO STATION

KXTL-AM 37606
Owner: Cherry Creek Radio
Editorial: 750 Dewey Blvd, Butte, Montana 59701-3200 **Tel:** 1 406 494-1030.
Email: prodbutte@cherrycreekradio.com
Web site: http://www.kxtl.com
Profile: KXTL-AM is a commercial station owned by Cherry Creek Radio. The format of the station is talk. KXTL-AM broadcasts to the Butte, MT area at 1370 AM.
AM RADIO STATION

KXTN-FM 44217
Owner: Univision Communications Inc.
Editorial: 12451 Network Blvd Ste 140, San Antonio, Texas 78249-3336 **Tel:** 1 210 610-4141.
Web site: http://www.kxtn.com
Profile: KXTN-FM is a commercial station owned by Univision Communications Inc. The format of the station is Hispanic, featuring Tejano music. KXTN-FM broadcasts to the San Antonio area at 107.5 FM.
FM RADIO STATION

KXTO-AM 36245
Owner: Christian Ministries of the Valley, Inc.
Tel: 1 956 968-7777.
Email: informacion@radiovida.com
Web site: http://www.radiovida.com
Profile: KXTO-AM is a commercial station owned by Christian Ministries of the Valley, Inc. The format of the station is Spanish language religious programming. KXTO-AM broadcasts to the Reno, NV area at 1550 AM.
AM RADIO STATION

KXTQ-FM 46485
Owner: Ramar Communications Inc.
Editorial: 9800 University Ave, Lubbock, Texas 79423-5302 **Tel:** 1 806 745-3434.
Web site: http://www.937theeagle.com/
Profile: KXTQ-FM is a commercial station owned by Ramar Communications II Ltd. The format of the station is classic hits. KXTQ-FM broadcasts to the Lubbock, TX area at 93.7 FM.
FM RADIO STATION

KXTQ-FM 798020
Owner: Ramar Communications, Inc.
Editorial: 9800 University Ave, Lubbock, Texas 79423-5302 **Tel:** 1 806 745-3434.
Web site: http://www.1077yesfm.com/
Profile: KXTQ-FM is a commercial station owned by Ramar Communications, Inc. The format of the station is hot adult contemporary. KXTQ-FM broadcasts to the Lubbock, TX area at a frequency of 107.7 FM.
FM RADIO STATION

KXTS-FM 43170
Owner: Sinclair Communications
Editorial: 3565 Standish Ave, Santa Rosa, California 95407 **Tel:** 1 707 588-0707.
Email: exitos@winecountryradio.net
Web site: http://www.exitos987.com
Profile: KXTS-FM is a commercial station owned by Sinclair Communications. The format of the station is regional Mexican. KXTS-FM broadcasts to the Santa Rosa, CA area at 98.7 FM.
FM RADIO STATION

KXTZ-FM 41613
Owner: Mapleton Communications LLC
Editorial: 795 Buckley Rd Ste 2, San Luis Obispo, California 93401-8190 **Tel:** 1 805 786-2570.
Web site: http://953thebeach.com/
Profile: KXTZ-FM is a commercial station owned by Mapleton Communications LLC. The format of the station is classic hits. KXTZ-FM broadcasts to the San Luis Obispo, CA area at 95.3 FM.
FM RADIO STATION

KXUS-FM 41531
Owner: iHeartMedia Inc.
Editorial: 1856 S Glenstone Ave, Springfield, Missouri 65804-2303 **Tel:** 1 417 890-5555.
Email: us97@us97.com
Web site: http://www.us97.com
Profile: KXUS-FM is a commercial station owned by iHeartMedia Inc. The format of the station is classic rock music. KXUS-FM broadcasts to the Springfield, MO area at 97.3 FM.
FM RADIO STATION

KXWA-FM 397767
Owner: WAY Media Inc.
Editorial: 1707 Main St Ste 302, Longmont, Colorado 80501-7403 **Tel:** 1 303 702-9293.
Web site: http://kxwa.wayfm.com
Profile: KXWA-FM is a commercial station owned by WAY Media Inc. The format of the station is contemporary Christian music. KXWA-FM broadcasts to the Centennial, CO and Denver areas at 101.9 FM.
FM RADIO STATION

KXWT-FM 39817
Owner: Matinee Radio, LLC
Editorial: 111 South Highland Ave., Marfa, Texas 79843 **Tel:** 1 432 729-4578.
Web site: http://westtexaspublicradio.org
Profile: KXWT-FM is a non-commercial station owned by Matinee Radio, LLC. The format of the station is variety. KXWT-FM broadcasts in the Odessa-Midland, TX area at 91.3 FM. The station airs KRTS-FM's programming.
FM RADIO STATION

KXXE-FM 43310
Owner: Center Broadcasting Company Inc.
Editorial: 307 San Augustine St, Center, Texas 75935-3937 **Tel:** 1 936 275-3242.
Web site: http://www.cbc-radio.com
Profile: KXXE-FM is a commercial station owned by Center Broadcasting Company Inc. The format of the station is country music. KXXE-FM broadcasts to the Center, TX area at 92.5 FM.
FM RADIO STATION

KXXI-FM 42267
Owner: Millennium Media Inc.
Editorial: 300 W Aztec Ave Ste 200, Gallup, New Mexico 87301-6304 **Tel:** 1 505 863-6851.
Web site: http://www.gallupradio.com
Profile: KXXI-FM is a commercial station owned by Millennium Media Inc. The format of the station is classic rock music. KXXI-FM broadcasts to the Albuquerque, NM area at 93.7 FM.
FM RADIO STATION

KXXJ-AM 768982
Owner: Alaska Broadcast Communications, Inc
Editorial: 3161 Channel Dr Ste 2, Juneau, Alaska 99801-7866 **Tel:** 1 907 586-3630.
Web site: http://www.kinyradio.com
Profile: KXXJ-AM is a commercial station owned by Alaska Broadcast Communications. The format of the station is classic hits. KXXJ-AM broadcasts to the Juneau, AK area at a frequency of 1330 AM.
AM RADIO STATION

KXXK-FM 44669
Owner: Morris Communications
Editorial: 1308 Coolidge Rd, Aberdeen, Washington 98520-6317 **Tel:** 1 360 533-1320.
Web site: http://www.kix953.com
Profile: KXXK-FM is a commercial station owned by Morris Communications. The format of the station is contemporary country music. KXXK-FM broadcasts in the Aberdeen, WA area at 95.3 FM.
FM RADIO STATION

KXXL-FM 537106
Owner: Keyhole Broadcasting LLC
Editorial: 305 S Garner Lake Rd, Gillette, Wyoming 82718-8254 **Tel:** 1 307 687-1003.
Email: koal1061@koal1061.com
Profile: KXXL-FM is a commercial station owned by Keyhole Broadcasting LLC. The format of the station is classic rock. KXXL-FM broadcasts to the Gillette, WY area at 106.1 FM.
FM RADIO STATION

KXXM-FM 42153
Owner: iHeartMedia Inc.
Editorial: 6222 W Interstate 10, San Antonio, Texas 78201-2013 **Tel:** 1 210 736-9700.
Web site: http://961now.iheart.com
Profile: KXXM-FM is a commercial station owned by iHeartMedia Inc. The format of the station is Top 40/CHR music. KXXM-FM broadcasts to the San Antonio area at 96.1 FM. The station's slogan is, "San Antonio's #1 Hit Music Station."
FM RADIO STATION

KXXO-FM 41035
Owner: Three Cities Inc.
Editorial: 119 Washington St NE, Olympia, Washington 98501 **Tel:** 1 360 943-9937.
Email: admin@mixx96.com
Web site: http://www.mixx96.com
Profile: KXXO-FM is a commercial station owned by Three Cities Inc. The format of the station is adult contemporary music. KXXO-FM broadcasts in the Seattle area at 96.1 FM.
FM RADIO STATION

KXXR-FM 43423
Owner: Cumulus Media Inc
Editorial: 2000 Elm St SE, Minneapolis, Minnesota 55414 **Tel:** 1 612 617-4000.
Email: mail@93x.com
Web site: http://www.93x.com
Profile: KXXR-FM is a commercial station owned by Cumulus Media Inc. The format of the station is rock music. KXXR-FM broadcasts to the Minneapolis area at 93.7 FM.
FM RADIO STATION

KXXT-AM 79354
Owner: Communicom Broadcasting
Editorial: 4020 N 20th St Ste 208, Phoenix, Arizona 85016-6030 **Tel:** 1 602 254-5001.
Web site: http://www.1280kxeg.com/
Profile: KXXT-AM is a commercial station owned by Communicom Broadcasting. The format of the station is religious. KXXT-AM broadcasts to the Phoenix area at 1010 AM.
AM RADIO STATION

KXXX-AM 37607
Owner: Rocking M Radio
Editorial: 1065 S Range Ave, Colby, Kansas 67701-3505 **Tel:** 1 785 462-3305.
Email: kxxxkqlsprod@rockingmradio.com
Web site: http://nwksradio.com
Profile: KXXX-AM is a commercial station owned by Rocking M Radio. The format of the station is country. KXXX-AM broadcasts to the Colby, KS area at 790 AM.
AM RADIO STATION

KXXY-FM 44982
Owner: iHeartMedia Inc.
Editorial: 1900 NW Expressway Ste 1000, Oklahoma City, Oklahoma 73118-1854 **Tel:** 1 405 858-1400.
Web site: http://kxy.iheart.com
Profile: KXXY-FM is a commercial station owned by iHeartMedia Inc. The format of the station is country music. KXXY-FM broadcasts to the Oklahoma City area at 96.1 FM.
FM RADIO STATION

KXXZ-FM 338513
Owner: Dos Costas Communications Corp.
Editorial: 29000 Radio Rd, Barstow, California 92311-1648 **Tel:** 1 760 256-2121.
Email: doscostas@yahoo.com
Profile: KXXZ-FM is a commercial station owned by Dos Costas Communications Corp. The format of the station is regional Mexican. KXXZ-FM broadcasts to the Barstow, CA area at 95.9 FM.
FM RADIO STATION

KXYL-AM 38509
Owner: Wendlee Broadcasting
Editorial: 600 Fisk Ave, Brownwood, Texas 76801 **Tel:** 1 325 646-3535.
Email: newstalk@wendlee.com
Web site: http://www.brownwoodradio.com
Profile: KXYL-AM is a commercial station owned by Wendlee Broadcasting. The format of the station is news and talk. KXYL-AM broadcasts to the Brownwood, TX area at 1240 AM.
AM RADIO STATION

KXYL-FM 45870
Owner: Wendlee Broadcasting
Editorial: 600 Fisk Ave, Brownwood, Texas 76801 **Tel:** 1 325 646-3535.
Email: newstalk@wendlee.com
Web site: http://www.wendleebroadcasting.com
Profile: KXYL-FM is a commercial station owned by Wendlee Broadcating. The format of the station is news and talk. KXYL-FM broadcasts in the Brownwood, TX area at 102.3 FM.
FM RADIO STATION

KXYZ-AM 35129
Owner: Multi Cultural Radio Broadcasting, Inc.
Editorial: 1782 W Sam Houston Pkwy N, Houston, Texas 77043-2723 **Tel:** 1 713 490-2538.
Web site: http://kxyzradio.com
Profile: KXYZ-AM is a commercial station owned by Multi Cultural Radio Broadcasting, Inc. The format of the station is ethnic variety; Mandarin & Hindi. KXYZ-AM broadcasts to the Houston area at 1320 AM.
AM RADIO STATION

KXZM-FM 42950
Owner: Lazer Broadcasting Corp.
Editorial: 777 N 1St St Ste 200, San Jose, California 95112-6311 **Tel:** 1 408 899-6331.
Email: contactodirecto@radiolazer.com
Web site: http://www.radiolazer.com

Profile: KXZM-FM is a commercial station owned by Lazer Broadcasting Corp. The format of the station is Regional Mexican. KXZM-FM broadcasts locally to San Jose, CA and the Greater Bay Area at a frequency of 93.7 FM.
FM RADIO STATION

KXZZ-AM 37609
Owner: Cumulus Media Inc.
Editorial: 425 Broad St, Lake Charles, Louisiana 70601-4225 **Tel:** 1 337 436-7277.
Web site: http://www.kxzz1580am.com
Profile: KXZZ-AM is a commercial station owned by Cumulus Media Inc. The format of the station is sports talk. KXZZ-AM broadcasts to the Lake Charles, LA area at 1580 AM.
AM RADIO STATION

KYAA-AM 76412
Owner: People's Radio Inc.
Editorial: 1680 McKee Rd, San Jose, California 95116-1237 **Tel:** 1 831 899-1570.
Email: kyaaradio@yahoo.com
Web site: http://ihradio.com
Profile: KYAA-AM is a commercial station owned by People's Radio Inc. The format of the station is religious. KYAA-AM broadcasts to the Hayward, CA area at 1200 AM.
AM RADIO STATION

KYAH-AM 35013
Tel: 1 561 302-3477.
Email: station@yahradio540.com
Profile: KYAH-AM is a radio station broadcasting a talk format. KYAH 540 AM Talk and Travel Radio, covering all of Utah Delta, Utah.
AM RADIO STATION

KYAK-AM 36986
Owner: Yakima Christian Broadcasting
Editorial: 706 Butterfield Rd, Yakima, Washington 98901 **Tel:** 1 509 452-5925.
Email: kyak@kyak.com
Web site: http://www.kyak.com
Profile: KYAK-AM is a commercial station owned by Yakima Christian Broadcasting. The format of the station is Christian. KYAK-AM broadcasts to the Yakima, WA area at 930 AM.
AM RADIO STATION

KYAL-AM 38951
Owner: Stephens Media Group.
Editorial: 2448 E 81st St Ste 5500, Tulsa, Oklahoma 74137-4201 **Tel:** 1 918 492-2660.
Email: kxoj@kxoj.com
Web site: http://www.sportsanimaltulsa.com
Profile: KYAL-AM is a commercial station owned by Stephens Media Group. The format of the station is sports. KYAL-AM broadcasts to the Tulsa, OK area at 1550 AM. Send all PSAs to the main email.
AM RADIO STATION

KYAL-FM 42517
Owner: Stephens Media Group.
Editorial: 2448 E 81st St Ste 5500, Tulsa, Oklahoma 74137-4201 **Tel:** 1 918 492-2660.
Email: studio@sportsanimalradio.com
Web site: http://www.sportsanimaltulsa.com
Profile: KYAL-FM is a commercial station owned by Stephens Media Group. The format of the station is sports. KYAL-FM broadcasts in the Tulsa, OK area at 97.1 FM. Send all PSAs to kxoj@kxoj.com.
FM RADIO STATION

KYAT-FM 44728
Owner: Millennium Media Inc.
Editorial: 300 W Aztec Ave, Gallup, New Mexico 87301-6304 **Tel:** 1 505 863-6851.
Web site: http://www.gallupradio.com
Profile: KYAT-FM is a commercial station owned by Millennium Media Inc. The format of the station features Navajo-language, Native American programming. KYAT-FM broadcasts to the Gallup, NM area at a frequency of 94.5 FM.
FM RADIO STATION

KYAY-FM 841048
Owner: San Carlos Apache Tribe
Tel: 1 928 475-5929.
Email: info@nativepublicmedia.org
Web site: http://www.nativepublicmedia.org
Profile: KYAY-FM is a non-commercial station owned by the San Carlos Apache Tribe. The format of the station features a variety of programming from Native Public Media. KYAY-FM broadcasts locally at a frequency of 91.1 FM.
FM RADIO STATION

KYBA-FM 42061
Owner: Townsquare Media
Editorial: 122 4th St SW, Rochester, Minnesota 55902-3320 **Tel:** 1 507 286-1010.
Web site: http://www.y105fm.com
Profile: KYBA-FM is a commercial station owned by Townsquare Media. The format of the station is lite rock. KYBA-FM broadcasts to the Rochester, MN, Mason City, IA area at 105.3 FM.
FM RADIO STATION

KYBB-FM 43245
Owner: Townsquare Media, Inc.
Editorial: 5100 S Tennis Ln Ste 200, Sioux Falls, South Dakota 57108-2271 **Tel:** 1 605 339-1140.
Web site: http://www.b1027.com
Profile: KYBB-FM is a commercial station owned by Townsquare Media, Inc. The format of the station is

classic rock. KYBB-FM broadcasts to the Sioux Falls, SD area at 102.7 FM.
FM RADIO STATION

KYBC-AM 39175
Owner: Yavapai Broadcasting
Editorial: 3405 E State Route 89A, Bldg A, Cottonwood, Arizona 86326-5504 **Tel:** 1 928 634-2286.
Email: news@myradioplace.com
Web site: http://www.1600kybc.com
Profile: KYBC-AM is a commercial station owned by Yavapai Broadcasting. The format of the station is adult standards music. KYBC-AM broadcasts to the Cottonwood, AZ area at 1600 AM.
AM RADIO STATION

KYBE-FM 44983
Owner: LKCM Radio Group LP
Editorial: 207 W Grand Ave, Frederick, Oklahoma 73542-5229 **Tel:** 1 580 335-5923.
Email: kybe959@pldi.net
Web site: http://www.coyotenews.com
Profile: KYBE-FM is a commercial station owned by LKCM Radio Group LP. The format of the station is contemporary country. KYBE-FM broadcasts to the Frederick, OK area at 95.7 FM.
FM RADIO STATION

KYBG-FM 41767
Owner: Acadia Broadcast Partners
Editorial: 320 N Parkerson Ave, Crowley, Louisiana 70526-5056 **Tel:** 1 337 783-2520.
Web site: http://www.big1021.com/
Profile: KYBG-FM is a commercial station owned by Acadia Broadcast Partners. The format of the station is adult contemporary music. KYBG-FM broadcasts to the Lafayette, LA area at 102.1 FM.
FM RADIO STATION

KYBI-FM 46401
Owner: Pentagon Communications, LLC
Editorial: 121 Cotton Square, Lufkin, Texas 75901 **Tel:** 1 936 634-6661.
Email: traffic@yatesmedia.com
Web site: http://www.kybiradio.com
Profile: KYBI-FM is a commercial station owned by Yates Media. The format of the station is classic and contemporary country. KYBI-FM broadcasts to the Lufkin, TX area at 100.1 FM.
FM RADIO STATION

KYBR-FM 133724
Owner: Richard El Garcia Broadcasting
Editorial: 403 W Pueblo Dr, Espanola, New Mexico 87532-2530 **Tel:** 1 505 753-2201.
Web site: http://www.radiooso.com
Profile: KYBR-FM is a commercial station owned by Richard El Garcia Broadcasting. The format of the station is classic country. KYBR-FM broadcasts to the Albuquerque, NM area at 92.9 FM.
FM RADIO STATION

KYCA-AM 37611
Owner: Southwest Broadcasting
Editorial: 500 Henry St, Prescott, Arizona 86301-2670 **Tel:** 1 928 445-1700.
Email: prescott@kyca.info
Web site: http://www.kyca.info
Profile: KYCA-AM is a commercial station owned by Southwest Broadcasting. The format of the station is news and talk programming. KYCA-AM broadcasts to the Prescott, AZ, area on 1490 AM.
AM RADIO STATION

KYCC-FM 39580
Owner: Your Christian Companion Network
Editorial: 9019 West Ln, Stockton, California 95210-1401 **Tel:** 1 209 477-3690.
Email: kycc@kycc.org
Web site: http://www.kycc.org
Profile: KYCC-FM is a non-commercial station owned by Your Christian Companion Network. The format of the station is religious. KYCC-FM broadcasts to the Stockton, CA area at 90.1 FM. To submit events or PSA's, it is suggested they are sent into the Community Calendar at this link: https://www.kycc.com/community-calendar.
FM RADIO STATION

KYCH-FM 37577
Owner: Entercom Communications Corp.
Editorial: 0700 SW Bancroft St, Portland, Oregon 97239-4226 **Tel:** 1 503 223-1441.
Web site: http://www.charliefm.com
Profile: KYCH-FM is a commercial station owned by Entercom Communications Corp. The format of the station is adult hits. KYCH-FM broadcasts to the Portland, OR area at 97.1 FM.
FM RADIO STATION

KYCK-FM 40050
Owner: Leighton Enterprises Inc.
Editorial: 1185 9th St NE, Thompson, North Dakota 58278-9343 **Tel:** 1 701 775-4611.
Email: live@97kyck.com
Web site: http://www.97kyck.com
Profile: KYCK-FM is a commercial station owned by Leighton Enterprises Inc. The format of the station is contemporary country music. KYCK-FM broadcasts to the Grand Forks, ND area area at 97.1 FM.
FM RADIO STATION

KYCN-AM 38589
Owner: Smith Broadcasting Inc.
Editorial: 450 E Cole St, Wheatland, Wyoming 82201-8937 **Tel:** 1 307 322-5926.
Email: kzew@wheatlandradio.com

Profile: KYCN-AM is a commercial station owned by Smith Broadcasting Inc. The format of the station is classic country. KYCN-AM broadcasts to the Wheatland, WY area at 1340 AM.
AM RADIO STATION

KYCS-FM 46362
Owner: Wagonwheel Communications Corp.
Editorial: 40 Shoshone Ave, Green River, Wyoming 82935-5321 **Tel:** 1 307 362-6746.
Email: audio@theradionetwork.net
Web site: http://www.theradionetwork.net
Profile: KYCS-FM is a commercial station owned by Wagonwheel Communications Corp. The format of the station is hot AC. KYCS-FM broadcasts to the Green River, WY area at 95.1 FM.
FM RADIO STATION

KYDN-FM 550604
Owner: San Luis Valley Broadcasting
Editorial: 109 Adams St, Monte Vista, Colorado 81144-1421 **Tel:** 1 719 852-3581.
Email: kslv@amigo.net
Web site: http://www.kslvradio.com
Profile: KYDN-FM is a commercial station owned by San Luis Valley Broadcasting. The format of the station is contemporary country. KYDN-FM broadcasts to the Monte Vista, CO area at 95.3 FM.
FM RADIO STATION

KYDT-FM 46846
Owner: Ultimate Caps, Inc.
Editorial: 707 Harding St, Belle Fourche, South Dakota 57717-1402 **Tel:** 1 605 892-2571.
Web site: http://www.kydt.com
Profile: KYDT-FM is a commercial station owned by Ultimate Caps, Inc. The format of the station is country, sports and agricultural programming. KYDT-FM broadcasts to the Belle Fourche, SD area at 103.1 FM.
FM RADIO STATION

KYEE-FM 40051
Owner: Burt Broadcasting Inc.
Editorial: 501 S Florida Ave, Alamogordo, New Mexico 88310-6018 **Tel:** 1 575 434-1414.
Email: burtbroadcasting@bbiradio.net
Web site: http://www.94key.net
Profile: KYEE-FM is a commercial station owned by Burt Broadcasting Inc. The format of the station is adult contemporary music. KYEE-FM broadcasts to the Albuquerque, NM area at 94.3 FM.
FM RADIO STATION

KYEL-FM 135475
Owner: KERM Inc.
Editorial: 201 W 2nd St, Russellville, Arkansas 72801-5003 **Tel:** 1 479 968-1184.
Profile: KYEL-FM is a commercial station owned by KERM Inc. The format of the station is classic country. KYEL-FM broadcasts to the Russellville, Arkansas area at 105.5 FM.
FM RADIO STATION

KYEZ-FM 46737
Owner: Morris Communications
Editorial: 131 N Santa Fe Ave, Ste 3, Salina, Kansas 67401-2642 **Tel:** 1 785 823-1111.
Web site: http://www.y937.com
Profile: KYEZ-FM is a commercial station owned by Morris Communications. The format of the station is contemporary country. KYEZ-FM broadcasts to the Salina, KS area at 93.7 FM.
FM RADIO STATION

KYFB-FM 449031
Owner: Bible Broadcasting Network
Editorial: 4816 S State Highway 91, Denison, Texas 75020 **Tel:** 1 704 523-5555.
Web site: http://www.bbnradio.org
Profile: KYFB-FM is a non-commercial station owned by Bible Broadcasting Network. The format is religious. The station broadcasts to the Denison, TX area at 91.5 FM.
FM RADIO STATION

KYFG-FM 43471
Owner: Bible Broadcasting Network
Editorial: 11530 Carmel Commons Blvd, Charlotte, North Carolina 28226-3976 **Tel:** 1 704 523-5555.
Web site: http://www.bbnradio.org
Profile: KYFG-FM is a non-commercial station owned by Bible Broadcasting Network. The format of the station is religious programming. KYFG-FM broadcasts to the Omaha, NE area at 88.9 FM.
FM RADIO STATION

KYFI-AM 36431
Owner: Bible Broadcasting Network, Inc.
Tel: 1 704 523-5555.
Email: bbn@bbnmedia.org
Web site: http://www.bbnradio.org
Profile: KYFI-AM is a commercial station owned by Bible Broadcasting Network, Inc. The format of the station is Christian and religious talk. KJSL-AM broadcasts to the St. Louis area at 630 AM.
AM RADIO STATION

KYFJ-FM 41903
Owner: Last Bastion Trust
Editorial: 202 Galbert Rd, Lafayette, Louisiana 70506-1806 **Tel:** 1 337 232-1311.
Web site: http://www.rock937fm.com
Profile: KYFJ-FM is a commercial station owned by the Last Bastion Trust. The format of the station is active rock. KRDJ-FM broadcasts to the Lafayette, LA area at 93.7 FM.
FM RADIO STATION

KYFM-FM 46503
Owner: KCD Enterprises Inc.
Editorial: 1200 SE Frank Phillips Blvd, Bartlesville, Oklahoma 74003-4332 **Tel:** 1 918 336-1001.
Email: radio@bartlesvilleradio.com
Web site: http://www.bartlesvilleradio.com
Profile: KYFM-FM is a commercial station owned by KCD Enterprises Inc. The format of the station is adult contemporary. KYFM-FM broadcasts to the Bartlesville, OK area at 100.1 FM.
FM RADIO STATION

KYFR-AM 35912
Owner: Family Stations Inc.
Editorial: 112 N Elm St Suites 2-4, Shenandoah, Iowa 51601-1176 **Tel:** 1 712 246-5151.
Email: kyfrpa@familyradio.org
Web site: http://www.familyradio.org
Profile: KYFR-AM is a non-commercial station owned by Family Stations Inc. The format of the station is religious. KYFR-AM broadcasts to the Shenandoah, IA area at 920 AM.
AM RADIO STATION

KYFS-FM 42410
Owner: Bible Broadcasting Network
Editorial: 228 Scheutz Dr, Schertz, Texas 78154 **Tel:** 1 704 523-5555.
Email: bbn@bbnmedia.org
Web site: http://www.bbnradio.org
Profile: KYFS-FM is a non-commercial station owned by Bible Broadcasting Network. The format of the station is religious. KYFS-FM broadcasts to the San Antonio area at 90.9 FM.
FM RADIO STATION

KYFW-FM 41465
Owner: Bible Broadcasting Network
Editorial: 11530 Carmel Commons Blvd, Charlotte, North Carolina 28226-3976 **Tel:** 1 800 888-7077.
Email: bbn@bbnmedia.org
Web site: http://www.bbnradio.org
Profile: KYFW-FM is a non-commercial station owned by Bible Broadcasting Network. The format of the station is religious programming. KYFW-FM broadcasts to the Derby, KS area at 88.3 FM.
FM RADIO STATION

KYGL-FM 42708
Owner: Townsquare Media, LLC
Editorial: 2324 Arkansas Blvd, Texarkana, Arkansas 71854 **Tel:** 1 870 772-3771.
Email: eagle1063@gmail.com
Web site: http://www.kygl.com
Profile: KYGL-FM is a commercial station owned by Townsquare Media, LLC. The format of the station is classic rock. KYGL-FM broadcasts to the Texarkana, AR area at 106.3 FM.
FM RADIO STATION

KYGO-FM 46057
Owner: Bonneville International Corp.
Editorial: 7800 E Orchard Rd, Greenwood Village, Colorado 80111-2583 **Tel:** 1 303 321-0950.
Web site: http://www.kygo.com
Profile: KYGO-FM is a commercial station owned by Bonneville International Corp. The format of the station is contemporary country music. KYGO-FM broadcasts in the Denver area at 98.5 FM.
FM RADIO STATION

KYIS-FM 40064
Owner: Cumulus Media Inc
Editorial: 4045 NW 64th St Ste 600, Oklahoma City, Oklahoma 73116-2607 **Tel:** 1 405 848-0100.
Web site: http://www.kyis.com
Profile: KYIS-FM is a commercial station owned by Cumulus Media Inc. The format of the station is hot adult contemporary music. KYIS-FM broadcasts to the Oklahoma City area at 98.9 FM.
FM RADIO STATION

KYIX-FM 46872
Owner: Educational Media Foundation
Tel: 1 888 937-2471.
Email: newstip@air1.com
Web site: http://www.air1.com
Profile: KYIX-FM is a non-commercial station owned by Educational Media Foundation. The format of the station is contemporary Christian music at 104.9 FM.
FM RADIO STATION

KYIZ-AM 132282
Owner: Kris Bennett Broadcasting Co.
Editorial: 2600 S Jackson St, Seattle, Washington 98144-2402 **Tel:** 1 206 323-3070.
Email: ztwins@aol.com
Web site: http://www.ztwins.com/
Profile: KYIZ-AM is a commercial station owned by Kris Bennett Broadcasting Co. The format of the station is urban adult contemporary. KYIZ-AM broadcasts to the Seattle area at 1620 AM.
AM RADIO STATION

KYJK-FM 350373
Owner: Spanish Peaks Broadcasting, Inc.
Editorial: 2425 W Central Ave Ste 203, Missoula, Montana 59801-6402 **Tel:** 1 406 721-6800.
Email: jack@missoulabroadcasting.com
Web site: http://www.jackfmmissoula.com
Profile: KYJK-FM is a commercial station owned by Spanish Peaks Broadcasting, Inc., doing business as The Montana Radio Company, LLC. The format of the station is Jack FM. KYJK-FM broadcasts to the Missoula, MT, area at 105.9 FM.
FM RADIO STATION

KYKC-FM 42411
Owner: Chickasaw Nation
Editorial: 1019 N Broadway, Ada, Oklahoma 74820-6503 **Tel:** 1 580 436-1616.
Email: kykc@cableone.net
Web site: http://www.kykc.net
Profile: KYKC-FM is a commercial station owned by the Chickasaw Nation. The format of the station is contemporary country. KYKC-FM broadcasts to the South Central Oklahoma area at a frequency of 100.1 FM.
FM RADIO STATION

KYKD-FM 43050
Owner: Voice for Christ Ministries Inc.
Editorial: 406 Ptarmigan St, Bethel, Alaska 99559-2428 **Tel:** 1 907 543-5953.
Email: kykd@vfcm.org
Web site: http://www.vfcm.org
Profile: KYKD-FM is a commercial station owned by Voice for Christ Ministries Inc. The format of the station is Christian programming. KYKD-FM broadcasts to the Bethel, AK area at 100.1 FM.
FM RADIO STATION

KYKK-FM 43030
Owner: Noalmark Broadcasting Corp.
Editorial: 1423 W Bender Blvd, Hobbs, New Mexico 88240-9252 **Tel:** 1 575 393-1551.
Profile: KYKK-FM is a commercial station owned by the Noalmark Broadcasting Corp. The format of the station is classic hits music. KYKK-FM broadcasts to the Albuquerque, NM area at 95.7 FM.
FM RADIO STATION

KYKM-FM 43532
Owner: Kremling Enterprises Inc.
Editorial: 111 N Main St, Hallettsville, Texas 77964-2727 **Tel:** 1 361 798-4333.
Email: texasthunderradio@yahoo.com
Web site: http://www.texasthunderradio.com
Profile: KYKM-FM is a commercial radio station owned by Kremling Enterprises Inc. The format of the station is contemporary country music. KYKM-FM broadcasts to the Hallettsville, TX area at 94.3 FM.
FM RADIO STATION

KYKN-AM 35130
Owner: Willamette Broadcasting
Editorial: 4205 Cherry Ave NE, Keizer, Oregon 97303 **Tel:** 1 503 390-3014.
Web site: http://www.kykn.com
Profile: KYKN-AM is a commercial station owned by Willamette Broadcasting. The format of the station is news and talk. KYKN-AM broadcasts to the Portland, OR area at 1430 AM.
AM RADIO STATION

KYKR-FM 46107
Owner: iHeartMedia Inc.
Editorial: 2885 Interstate 10 E, Beaumont, Texas 77702-1001 **Tel:** 1 409 896-5555.
Email: kicker951@iheartmedia.com
Web site: http://kykr.iheart.com
Profile: KYKR-FM is a commercial station owned by iHeartMedia Inc. The format of the station is contemporary country music. KYKR-FM broadcasts in the Beaumont, TX area at 95.1 FM.
FM RADIO STATION

KYKS-FM 41910
Owner: Townsquare Media, LLC
Editorial: 1216 S 1st St, Lufkin, Texas 75901-4716 **Tel:** 1 936 639-4455.
Web site: http://www.kicks105.com
Profile: KYKS-FM is a commercial station owned by Townsquare Media, LLC. The format of the station is country music. KYKS-FM broadcasts to the Lufkin, TX area at 105.1 FM.
FM RADIO STATION

KYKX-FM 40052
Owner: Access.1 Communications Corp.
Editorial: 4408 US Highway 259 N, Longview, Texas 75605-7703 **Tel:** 1 903 663-9800.
Email: studio@kykx.com
Web site: http://www.kykx.com
Profile: KYKX-FM is a commercial station owned by Access.1 Communications Corp. The format of the station is contemporary country. KYKX-FM broadcasts to the Longview, TX area at 105.7 FM.
FM RADIO STATION

KYKY-FM 40053
Owner: CBS Radio
Editorial: 1220 Olive St Fl 3, Saint Louis, Missouri 63103-2324 **Tel:** 1 314 621-2345.
Web site: http://y98.radio.com
Profile: KYKY-FM is a commercial station owned by CBS Radio. The format of the station is hot adult contemporary music. KYKY-FM broadcasts to the St. Louis area at 98.1 FM.
FM RADIO STATION

KYKZ-FM 40054
Owner: Cumulus Media Inc.
Editorial: 425 Broad St, Lake Charles, Louisiana 70601-4225 **Tel:** 1 337 439-3300.
Web site: http://www.kykz.com
Profile: KYKZ-FM is a commercial station owned by Cumulus Media Inc. The format is country. The station airs in the Lake Charles, LA area at 96.1 FM.
FM RADIO STATION

KYLC-FM 132298
Owner: American Family Association
Editorial: 107 Parkgate Dr, Tupelo, Mississippi 38801 **Tel:** 1 662 844-8888.
Email: comments@afr.net
Web site: http://www.afr.net
FM RADIO STATION

KYLD-FM 39921
Owner: iHeartMedia Inc.
Editorial: 340 Townsend St, San Francisco, California 94107-1633 **Tel:** 1 415 538-1013.
Web site: http://wild949.iheart.com
Profile: KYLD-FM is a commercial station owned by iHeartMedia Inc. The format of the station is rhythmic Top 40/CHR. KYLD-FM broadcasts to the San Francisco area at 94.9 FM.
FM RADIO STATION

KYLS-AM 39485
Owner: Dockins Broadcast Group
Editorial: 235 Business Hh, Piedmont, Missouri 63957-9410 **Tel:** 1 573 223-4518.
Profile: KYLS-AM is a commercial station owned by Dockins Broadcast Group. The format of the station is classic country. KYLS-AM broadcasts to the Farmington, MO area at 1450 AM.
AM RADIO STATION

KYLS-FM 46875
Owner: Dockins Broadcast Group
Editorial: 900 E Karsch Blvd, Farmington, Missouri 63640-3405 **Tel:** 1 573 701-9590.
Web site: http://froggy96online.com
Profile: KYLS-FM is a commercial station owned by Dockins Broadcast Group. The format of the station is contemporary country music. KYLS-FM broadcasts in the Farmington, MO area at 95.9 FM.
FM RADIO STATION

KYLT-AM 37613
Owner: Cherry Creek Radio
Editorial: 1600 North Ave W, Missoula, Montana 59801 **Tel:** 1 406 728-5000.
Profile: KYLT-AM is a commercial station owned by Cherry Creek Radio. The format for the station is sports. KYLT-AM broadcasts to the Missoula, MT area at 1340 AM.
AM RADIO STATION

KYLW-AM 310821
Owner: Sun Mountain Inc.
Editorial: RR 1, Hardin, Montana 59034 **Tel:** 1 406 665-2828.
Web site: http://www.bigskyradio.net
AM RADIO STATION

KYMG-FM 41291
Owner: iHeart Media Inc.
Editorial: 800 E Dimond Blvd Ste 3-370, Anchorage, Alaska 99515-2058 **Tel:** 1 907 522-1515.
Web site: http://www.magic989fm.com
Profile: KYMG-FM is a commercial station owned by iHeart Media Inc. The format of the station is adult contemporary. KYMG-FM broadcasts to the Anchorage, AK area at 98.9 FM.
FM RADIO STATION

KYMN-AM 35131
Owner: NorthField Media
Editorial: 200 Division St S Ste 260, Northfield, Minnesota 55057-2079 **Tel:** 1 507 645-5695.
Email: contact@kymnradio.net
Web site: http://www.kymnradio.net
Profile: KYMN-AM is a commercial station owned by NorthField Media. The format of the station is adult standards, oldies and classic country. KYMN-AM broadcasts to the Northfield, MN area at 1080 AM.
AM RADIO STATION

KYMS-FM 559093
Owner: Legacy Broadcasting, Inc.
Tel: 1 208 773-4600.
Web site: http://www.kymsradio.com
Profile: KYMS-FM is a non-commerical station owned by Calvary Chapel of Costa Mesa, Inc. The format of the station is Southern Gospel and Religious Teaching. KYMS-FM broadcasts to the Rathdrum, ID area at 89.9 FM.
FM RADIO STATION

KYMV-FM 359518
Owner: Broadway Media
Editorial: 50 W Broadway, Salt Lake City, Utah 84101-2020 **Tel:** 1 801 524-2600.
Web site: http://www.rewind1007.com
Profile: KYMV-FM is a commercial station owned by Broadway Media. The format of the station is adult contemporary. KYMV-FM broadcasts to the Salt Lake City area at 100.7 FM.
FM RADIO STATION

KYMX-FM 43441
Owner: CBS Radio
Editorial: 280 Commerce Cir, Sacramento, California 95815-4212 **Tel:** 1 916 923-6800.
Web site: http://www.kymx.com
Profile: KYMX-FM is a commercial station owned by CBS Radio. The format of the station is adult contemporary. KYMX-FM broadcasts to the Sacramento, CA area on 96.1 FM.
FM RADIO STATION

KYND-AM 36034
Owner: Provenzano(Matt)
Editorial: 16620 Cypress Rosehill Rd, Cypress, Texas 77429 **Tel:** 1 713 271-7888.
Profile: KYND-AM is a commercial station owned by Matt Provenzano. The format of the station is variety programming. KYND-AM broadcasts to the Cypress, TX area at 1520 AM.
AM RADIO STATION

KYNG-AM 36497
Owner: Cumulus Media Inc.
Editorial: 4209 N Frontage Rd, Fayetteville, Arkansas 72703-5002 **Tel:** 1 479 521-5566.
Profile: KYNG-AM is a commercial station owned by Cumulus Media Inc. The format of the station is Sports. KYNG-AM broadcasts to the Fayetteville, AR area at 1590 AM.
AM RADIO STATION

KYNO-AM 36365
Owner: (Ostland) John
Editorial: 336 W Bedford Ave Ste 109, Fresno, California 93711-6189
Web site: http://kynofresno.com
Profile: KYNO-AM is a commercial station owned by John Ostland. The format of the station is oldies. KYNO-AM broadcasts to the Fresno, CA area at 1430 AM.
AM RADIO STATION

KYNR-AM 34936
Owner: Confederated Tribes of the Yakama Nation
Editorial: 711 King Ln, Toppenish, Washington 98948-1170 **Tel:** 1 509 865-5363.
Email: kynr@yakama.com
Profile: KYNR-AM is a non-commercial station owned by Confederated Tribes of the Yakama Nation. The format of the station is variety. KYNR-AM broadcasts to the Yakima, WA area at 1490 AM.
AM RADIO STATION

KYNS-AM 34875
Owner: Mapleton Communications LLC
Editorial: 795 Buckley Rd Ste 2, San Luis Obispo, California 93401-8190 **Tel:** 1 805 786-2570.
Email: sloradiofeedback@gmail.com
Web site: http://www.b937slo.com
Profile: KYNS-AM is a commercial station owned by Mapleton Communications LLC. The format of the station is Soft AC. KYNS-AM broadcasts to the San Luis Obispo, CA area at 1340 AM.
AM RADIO STATION

KYNT-AM 37614
Owner: Riverfront Broadcasting
Editorial: 202 W 2nd St, Yankton, South Dakota 57078 **Tel:** 1 605 665-7892.
Email: news@kynt1450.com
Web site: http://www.kynt1450.com
Profile: KYNT-AM is a commercial station owned by Riverfront Broadcasting. The format of the station is variety. KYNT-AM broadcasts to the Yankton, SD area at 1450 AM.
AM RADIO STATION

KYNU-FM 43093
Owner: Ingstad Family Media
Editorial: 2625 8th Ave SW, Jamestown, North Dakota 58401-6621 **Tel:** 1 701 252-1400.
Email: news@newsdakota.com
Web site: http://www.newsdakota.com
Profile: KYNU-FM is a commercial station owned by Ingstad Family Media. The format of the station is contemporary country music. KYNU-FM broadcasts to the Jamestown, ND area at 95.5 FM.
FM RADIO STATION

KYNZ-FM 41279
Owner: LKCM Radio Group LP
Editorial: 1205 Northglen St, Ardmore, Oklahoma 73401-1202 **Tel:** 1 580 226-0421.
Web site: http://www.kynz.com
Profile: KYNZ-FM is a commercial station owned by LKCM Radio Group LP. The format of the station is oldies music. KYNZ-FM broadcasts to the Ardmore, OK area at 107.1 FM.
FM RADIO STATION

KYOO-AM 39211
Owner: Benne Media
Editorial: 205 N Pike Ave, Bolivar, Missouri 65613-1550 **Tel:** 1 417 326-5257.
Web site: http://www.yourcountry99.com
Profile: KYOO-AM is a commercial station owned by Benne Media. The format of the station is contemporary country. KYOO-AM broadcasts in the Bolivar, MO area at 1200 AM.
AM RADIO STATION

KYOO-FM 46568
Owner: Benne Media
Editorial: 205 N Pike Ave, Bolivar, Missouri 65613-1550 **Tel:** 1 417 326-5257.
Web site: http://kyooradio.com/index.html
Profile: KYOO-FM is a commercial station owned by Benne Media. The format of the station is contemporary country. KYOO-AM broadcasts in the Bolivar, MO area at 99.1 FM.
FM RADIO STATION

KYOS-AM 37615
Owner: Mapleton Radio, LLC
Editorial: 514 West 19th Street, Merced, California 95340 **Tel:** 1 209 723-2192.
Email: kyos@radiomerced.com
Web site: http://www.1480kyos.com
Profile: KYOS-AM is a commercial station owned by Mapleton Radio, LLC. The format of the station is news and talk. KYOS-AM broadcasts to the Merced, CA area at 1480 AM.
AM RADIO STATION

KYOT-FM 44818
Owner: iHeartMedia Inc.
Editorial: 4686 E Van Buren St Ste 300, Phoenix, Arizona 85008-6967 **Tel:** 1 602 374-6000.
Web site: http://955themountain.iheart.com
Profile: KYOT-FM is a commercial station owned by iHeartMedia Inc. The format of the station is adult hits. KYOT-FM broadcasts to the Phoenix area at 95.5 FM.
FM RADIO STATION

KYOX-FM 44224
Owner: Cherry Creek Radio
Editorial: 218 N Austin St, Comanche, Texas 76442-2429 **Tel:** 1 325 356-3090.
Web site: http://www.kyoxfm.com/
Profile: KYOX-FM is a commercial station owned by Cherry Creek Radio. The format of the station is country music. KYOX-FM broadcasts to the Comanche, TX area at 94.3 FM.
FM RADIO STATION

KYOY-FM 73856
Owner: Proshop Radio Broadcasting LLC
Editorial: 2232 Dell Range Blvd Ste 102, Cheyenne, Wyoming 82009-4903 **Tel:** 1 307 637-0301.
Web site: http://www.kyoy.net
Profile: KYOY-FM is a commercial station owned by Proshop Radio Broadcasting LLC. The format for the station is classic hits. KYOY-FM broadcasts to the Kimball, NE area at 92.3 FM.
FM RADIO STATION

KYPA-AM 34957
Owner: Multicultural Radio Broadcasting Inc.
Editorial: 3700 Wilshire Blvd Ste 600, Los Angeles, California 90010-3013 **Tel:** 1 213 487-1300.
Web site: http://www.radiokorea.com/
Profile: KYPA-AM is a commercial station owned by Multicultural Radio Broadcasting Inc. The format of the station is Korean variety. KYPA-AM broadcasts to the Pasadena, CA area at 1540 AM.
AM RADIO STATION

KYPL-FM 44364
Owner: Growing Christian Foundation
Editorial: 606 N Western Ave, Wenatchee, Washington 98801-1204 **Tel:** 1 509 457-0725.
Email: kypl@plr.org
Web site: http://www.plr.org
Profile: KYPL-FM is a non-commercial station owned by Growing Christian Foundation. The format of the station is contemporary Christian. KYPL-FM broadcasts to the Yakima, WA area at 91.1 FM.
FM RADIO STATION

KYQQ-FM 41684
Owner: Kiel Media Group, LLC
Editorial: 4200 N Old Lawrence Rd, Wichita, Kansas 67219-3211 **Tel:** 1 316 838-9141.
Email: news@kfdi.com
Web site: http://www.radiolobo1065.com
Profile: KYQQ-FM is a commercial station owned by Kiel Media Group, LLC. The format of the station is regional Mexican. KYQQ-FM broadcasts to the Wichita, KS area on 106.5 FM.
FM RADIO STATION

KYRA-FM 41982
Owner: Amaturo Group
Editorial: 99 Long Ct Ste 200, Thousand Oaks, California 91360-7400 **Tel:** 1 805 497-8511.
Profile: KYRA-FM is a commercial station owned by Amaturo Group. The format of the station is adult contemporary. KYRA-FM is broadcast to the Thousand Oaks, CA area at 92.7 FM. KYRA-FM simulcasts on KYLA-FM.
FM RADIO STATION

KYRC-FM 42587
Owner: Noalmark Broadcasting Corp.
Editorial: 208 Buena Vista Rd, Hot Springs, Arkansas 71913-8208 **Tel:** 1 501 525-4600.
Web site: http://www.realrock1015.com
Profile: KYRC-FM is a commercial station owned by Noalmark Broadcasting Corp. The format of the station is active rock music. KYRC-FM broadcasts to the Hot Springs, AR area at 93.5 FM.
FM RADIO STATION

KYRM-FM 520095
Owner: World Radio Network, Inc.
Editorial: 2690 S 3rd Ave, Yuma, Arizona 85364-7219 **Tel:** 1 928 341-0919.
Email: manantialyuma@yahoo.com
Web site: http://www.manantialyuma.org
Profile: KYRM-FM is a non-commercial station owned by World Radio Network, Inc. The format is Hispanic religious programming. KYRM-FM broadcasts to the Yuma, AZ area at 91.9 FM.
FM RADIO STATION

KYRN-FM 839379
Owner: Sovereign City Radio Services, LLC
Tel: 1 575 835-2382.
Email: steve@minecountry1021.com
Profile: KYRN-FM is a commercial station owned by Sovereign City Radio Services, LLC. The format of the station is country. KYRN-FM broadcasts to the Socorro, NM area at a frequency of 102.1 FM.
FM RADIO STATION

KYRS-FM 503694
Owner: Thin Air Community Radio
Editorial: 35 W Main Ave Ste 340, Spokane, Washington 99201-0119 **Tel:** 1 509 747-3012.
Web site: http://www.kyrs.org

Profile: KYRS-FM is a non-commercial community station owned by Thin Air Community Radio. The format of the station is variety, with a mix of news, music and locally produced programs. KYRS-FM broadcasts to the Spokane, WA area at a frequency of 88.1 FM.
FM RADIO STATION

KYRV-FM 40061
Owner: iHeartMedia Inc.
Editorial: 1545 River Park Dr Ste 500, Sacramento, California 95815-4693 **Tel:** 1 916 929-5325.
Email: sacramentopsas@iHeartMedia.com
Web site: http://937theriver.iheart.com
Profile: KYRV-FM is a commercial station owned by iHeartMedia Inc. The format of the station is Classic Rock. KYRV-FM broadcasts to the Sacramento, CA area on 93.7 FM.
FM RADIO STATION

KYSC-FM 518673
Owner: Tanana Valley Radio, LLC
Editorial: 3650 Braddock St, Fairbanks, Alaska 99701-7617 **Tel:** 1 907 452-3697.
Web site: http://www.tvtv.com
Profile: KYSC-FM is a commercial station owned by Tanana Valley Radio, LLC. The format of the station is classic hits. KYSC-FM broadcasts to the Fairbanks, AK area at 96.9 FM.
FM RADIO STATION

KYSE-FM 42022
Owner: Entravision Communications Corp.
Editorial: 5426 N Mesa St, El Paso, Texas 79912-5421 **Tel:** 1 915 581-1126.
Web site: http://www.elgato947.com
Profile: KYSE-FM is a commercial station owned by Entravision Communications Corp. The format of the station is regional Mexican. KYSE-FM broadcasts to the El Paso, TX area at 94.7 FM.
FM RADIO STATION

KYSJ-FM 44399
Owner: Hunt Broadcasting, LLC
Editorial: 580 Kingwood Ave, Coos Bay, Oregon 97420-2689 **Tel:** 1 541 266-8531.
Email: rockthewave13@gmail.com
Web site: http://www.thewaveradio1.com/
Profile: KYSJ-FM is a commercial station owned by Hunt Broadcasting, LLC. The format of the station is modern rock. KYSJ-FM broadcasts to the Coos Bay, OR area at 105.9 FM.
FM RADIO STATION

KYSL-FM 41119
Owner: Krystal Broadcasting
Editorial: 701 East Anemone Trail, #203, Dillon, Colorado 80435 **Tel:** 1 970 513-9393.
Email: krystalnews@krystal93.com
Web site: http://www.krystal93.com
Profile: KYSL-FM is a commercial station owned by Krystal Broadcasting. The format of the station is adult album alternative. KYSL-FM broadcasts to the Dillon, CO area at 93.9 FM.
FM RADIO STATION

KYSM-FM 44987
Owner: Alpha Media
Editorial: 1807 Lee Blvd, North Mankato, Minnesota 56003-2633 **Tel:** 1 507 345-4646.
Web site: http://www.country103.com
Profile: KYSM-FM is a commercial station owned by Alpha Media. The format of the station is country. KYSM-FM broadcasts to the North Mankato, MN area at 103.5 FM.
FM RADIO STATION

KYSN-FM 43730
Owner: Cherry Creek Radio
Editorial: 231 N Wenatchee Ave, Wenatchee, Washington 98801-2009 **Tel:** 1 509 665-6565.
Email: newswenatchee@cherrycreekradio.com
Web site: http://www.kysn.com
Profile: KYSN-FM is a commercial station owned by Cherry Creek Radio. The format of the station is country music. KYSN-FM broadcasts in the Seattle area at 97.7 FM.
FM RADIO STATION

KYSR-FM 39711
Owner: iHeartMedia Inc.
Editorial: 3400 W Olive Ave Ste 550, Burbank, California 91505-5544 **Tel:** 1 818 559-2252.
Web site: http://alt987fm.iheart.com
Profile: KYSR-FM is a commercial station owned by iHeartMedia Inc. The format of the station is rock alternative. KYSR-FM broadcasts to the Los Angeles area at 98.7 FM.
FM RADIO STATION

KYSS-FM 46582
Owner: Townsquare Media, LLC
Editorial: 3250 S Reserve St Ste 200, Missoula, Montana 59801-8236 **Tel:** 1 406 728-9300.
Email: realcountry@kyssfm.com
Web site: http://www.kyssfm.com
Profile: KYSS-FM is a commercial station owned by Townsquare Media, LLC. The format of the station is contemporary country. KYSS-FM broadcasts to the Missoula, MT area at 94.9 FM.
FM RADIO STATION

KYST-AM 35134
Owner: Velasquez(Cruz)
Editorial: 7322 Southwest Fwy Ste 500, Houston, Texas 77074-2137 **Tel:** 1 713 779-9292.
Email: contact@la920.com
Web site: http://kyst920am.com/
Profile: KYST-AM is a commercial station owned by Cruz Velasquez. The format of the station is Hispanic talk programming. KYST-AM broadcasts to the Houston area at 920 AM.
AM RADIO STATION

KYSX-FM 44273
Owner: BMG Billings
Editorial: 2425 King Ave W Ste B, Billings, Montana 59102-6460 **Tel:** 1 406 281-8925.
Email: psa@mojo925.com
Profile: KYSX-FM is a commercial station owned by BMG Billings. The format of the station is classic country. KYSX-FM broadcasts to the Billings, MT area at 105.1 FM.
FM RADIO STATION

KYTC-FM 41170
Owner: Alpha Media
Editorial: 341 S Yorktown Pike, Mason City, Iowa 50401-4533 **Tel:** 1 641 423-1300.
Web site: http://www.discovernorthiowa.com
Profile: KYTC-FM is a commercial station owned by Alpha Media. The format of the station is classic hits. KYTC-FM broadcasts to the Mason City, IA area at 102.7 FM.
FM RADIO STATION

KYTE-FM 45664
Owner: Yaquina Bay Communications Inc.
Editorial: 906 SW Alder St, Newport, Oregon 97365-4712 **Tel:** 1 541 265-2266.
Email: news@ybcradio.com
Web site: http://www.kytefm.com
Profile: KYTE-FM is a commercial station owned by Yaquina Bay Communications Inc. The format of the station is hot adult contemporary music. KYTE-FM broadcasts to Newport, OR, at 102.7 FM. The station's slogan is, "Today's Hits and Yesterday's Favorites."
FM RADIO STATION

KYTI-FM 43378
Owner: Lovcom, Inc.
Editorial: 1716 Kroe Ln, Sheridan, Wyoming 82801-9681 **Tel:** 1 307 672-7421.
Email: news@sheridanmedia.com
Web site: http://www.sheridanmedia.com
Profile: KYTI-FM is a commercial station owned by Lovcom, Inc. The format of the station is contemporary country. KYTI-FM broadcasts to the Sheridan, WY area at 93.7 FM.
FM RADIO STATION

KYTN-FM 40092
Owner: Thunderbolt Broadcasting Co.
Editorial: 223 Westgate Dr, Union City, Tennessee 38261-3058 **Tel:** 1 731 885-0051.
Email: newsroom@unioncityradio.com
Web site: http://www.thunderboltradio.com/kytn
Profile: KYTN-FM is a commercial station owned by Thunderbolt Broadcasting Co. The format of the station is country. KYTN-FM broadcasts to the Union City, TN area at 104.9 FM.
FM RADIO STATION

KYTT-FM 40058
Owner: Lighthouse Radio Group
Editorial: 580 Kingwood Ave, Coos Bay, Oregon 97420-2689 **Tel:** 1 541 269-2022.
Web site: http://www.lighthouseradio.com
Profile: KYTT-FM is a commercial station owned by Lighthouse Radio Group. The format of the station is contemporary Christian music. KYTT-FM broadcasts in the Coos Bay, OR at 98.7 FM.
FM RADIO STATION

KYTY-AM 35905
Owner: Maranatha Broadcasting Co. Inc.
Tel: 1 210 545-0810.
Email: staram810@yahoo.com
Web site: http://www.star810.com
Profile: KYTY-AM is a commercial station owned by Maranatha Broadcasting Co. Inc. The format of the station is contemporary Christian music. KYTY-AM broadcasts to the San Antonio area at 810 AM.
AM RADIO STATION

KYTZ-FM 44041
Owner: Simmons Media Group
Editorial: 1403 3Rd St, Langdon, North Dakota 58249-2232 **Tel:** 1 701 256-1080.
Web site: http://www.thevalleysbiggesthits.com
Profile: KYTZ-FM is a commerical station owned by Simmons Media Group. The format of the station is hot adult contemporary. KYTZ-FM broadcasts to the Langdon, ND area at 106.7 FM.
FM RADIO STATION

KYUK-AM 35135
Owner: Bethel Broadcasting Inc.
Editorial: 640 Radio St, Bethel, Alaska 99559-9999
Tel: 1 907 543-3131.
Email: webmaster@kyuk.org
Web site: http://www.kyuk.org
Profile: KYUK-AM is a non-commercial station owned by Bethel Broadcasting Inc. The format of the station is news and talk programming and a variety of music. KYUK-AM broadcasts to the Bethel, AK area at 640 AM.
AM RADIO STATION

KYUN-FM 433128
Owner: Locally Owned Radio, LLC
Editorial: 21361 Highway 30, Twin Falls, Idaho 83301-0197 **Tel:** 1 208 735-8300.
Web site: http://www.bull1021.com
Profile: KYUN-FM is a commercial station owned by Locally Owned Radio, LLC. The format of the station is country music. KYUN-FM broadcasts to the Twin Falls, ID area at 102.1 FM. The station's slogan is, "Idaho's All Star Country."
FM RADIO STATION

KYUS-FM 45688
Owner: Custer County Broadcasting Inc.
Editorial: 508 Main St, Miles City, Montana 59301-3019 **Tel:** 1 406 234-5626.
Email: terry@kyuskmta.com
Web site: http://www.kyuskmta.com
Profile: KYUS-FM is a commercial station owned by Custer County Broadcasting Inc., dba Marks Group Inc. The format of the station is adult hits. KYUS-FM's broadcasts in the Miles City, MT area at 92.3 FM.
FM RADIO STATION

KYVA-AM 37617
Owner: Millennium Media Inc.
Editorial: 300 W Aztec Ave, Gallup, New Mexico 87301-6304 **Tel:** 1 505 863-6851.
Email: administration@gallupradio.com
Web site: http://www.gallupradio.com
Profile: KYVA-AM is a commercial station owned by Millennium Media Inc. The format of the station is oldies. KYVA-AM broadcasts to the Albuquerque, NM area at 1230 AM.
AM RADIO STATION

KYVA-FM 43512
Owner: Millennium Media Inc.
Editorial: 300 W Aztec Ave Ste 200, Gallup, New Mexico 87301-6304 **Tel:** 1 505 863-6851.
Web site: http://www.gallupradio.com
Profile: KYVA-FM is a commercial station owned by Millennium Media Inc. The format of the station is classic hits. KYVA-FM broadcasts to the Gallup, NM area at 103.7 FM.
FM RADIO STATION

KYWA-FM 43159
Owner: WAY Media Inc.
Editorial: 110 S Main St, Wichita, Kansas 67202-3700
Tel: 1 316 831-0907.
Email: impactwichita@wayfm.com
Web site: http://kywa.wayfm.com
Profile: KYWA-FM is a non-commercial station owned by WAY Media Inc. The format of the station is contemporary Christian music. KYWA-FM broadcasts to the Wichita, KS area at 90.7 FM.
FM RADIO STATION

KYW-AM 36508
Owner: CBS Radio
Editorial: 1555 Hamilton St Fl 6, Philadelphia, Pennsylvania 19130-4085 **Tel:** 1 215 238-1060.
Email: newstips@kyw1060info.com
Web site: http://philadelphia.cbslocal.com/station/kyw-newsradio
Profile: KYW-AM is a commercial station owned by CBS Radio. The format of the station is news. KYW-AM broadcasts to the Philadelphia area at 1060 AM.
AM RADIO STATION

KYWD-FM 46895
Owner: iHeartMedia Inc
Editorial: 3202 N Oracle Rd, Tucson, Arizona 85705-3820 **Tel:** 1 520 618-2100.
Web site: http://971thebull.iheart.com
Profile: KYWD-FM is a commercial station owned by iHeartMedia Inc. The format of the station is contemporary country. KYWD-FM broadcasts to the Tucson, AZ area at 97.1 FM.
FM RADIO STATION

KYXK-FM 42475
Owner: Southwest Arkansas Media, LLC
Editorial: 601 S 7th St, Arkadelphia, Arkansas 71923-6209 **Tel:** 1 870 246-9272.
Profile: KYXK-FM is a commercial station owned by Southwest Arkansas Media, LLC. The format of the station is sports. KYXK-FM broadcasts in the Arkadelphia, AR area at 106.9 FM.
FM RADIO STATION

KYXX-FM 42241
Owner: Revolution Broadcast Co.
Editorial: 2125 Sidney Baker St, Kerrville, Texas 78028-2551 **Tel:** 1 830 896-1230.
Email: contact@revfm.rocks
Web site: http://www.revfmradio.com
Profile: KYXX-FM is a commercial station owned by Revolution Broadcast Co. The format for the station is classic country. KYXX-FM broadcasts to the Ozona, TX area at 94.3 AM.
FM RADIO STATION

KYXY-FM 40059
Owner: CBS Radio
Editorial: 8033 Linda Vista Rd, San Diego, California 92111-5108 **Tel:** 1 858 571-7600.
Web site: http://kyxy.cbslocal.com
Profile: KYXY-FM is a commercial station owned by CBS Radio. The format of the station is Lite Rock/Lite AC music. KYXY-FM broadcasts to the San Diego area at 96.5 FM.
FM RADIO STATION

KYYA-AM 40060
Owner: Connoisseur Media, Inc.
Editorial: 2075 Central Ave, Billings, Montana 59102-4956 **Tel:** 1 406 248-7777.
Email: jseymour@connoisseurmedia.com
Web site: http://www.newstalk730.com
Profile: KYYA-AM is a commercial station owned by Connoisseur Media, Inc.. The format of the station is news and talk. KYYA-AM broadcasts in the Billings, MT area at 730 AM.
AM RADIO STATION

KYYI-FM 41112
Owner: Cumulus Media Inc.
Editorial: 4302 Call Field Rd, Wichita Falls, Texas 76308 **Tel:** 1 940 691-2311.
Web site: http://www.bear104.com
Profile: KYYI-FM is a commercial station owned by Cumulus Media Inc. The format of the station is classic rock music. KYYI-FM broadcasts to the Wichita Falls, TX area at 104.7 FM.
FM RADIO STATION

KYYK-FM 44989
Owner: Tomlinson-Leis Communications L.P.
Editorial: 800 W Palestine Ave, Palestine, Texas 75801-7438 **Tel:** 1 903 729-6077.
Email: news@kyyk.com
Web site: http://www.youreasttexas.com
Profile: KYYK-FM is a commercial station owned by Tomlinson-Leis Communications L.P. The format of the station is contemporary country. KYYK-FM broadcasts in the Palestine, TX area at 98.3 FM.
FM RADIO STATION

KYYO-FM 46420
Owner: KGY Inc.
Editorial: 1700 Marine Dr NE, Olympia, Washington 98501-6908 **Tel:** 1 360 943-1240.
Web site: http://www.kayo.fm
Profile: KYYO-FM is a commercial station owned by KGY Inc. The format of the station is country music. KYYO-FM broadcasts to the Seattle area at 96.9 FM.
FM RADIO STATION

KYYS-AM 133738
Owner: Entercom Communications Corp.
Editorial: 1701 S 55th St, Kansas City, Kansas 66106-2241 **Tel:** 1 913 287-1480.
Web site: http://www.x1250.com
Profile: KYYS-AM is a commercial station owned by Entercom Communications Corp and operated by Reyes Media Group. The format of the station is regional Mexican music. KYYS-AM broadcasts to the Kansas City, MO area at 1250 AM.
AM RADIO STATION

KYYT-FM 46648
Owner: Haystack Broadcasting, Inc
Editorial: 620 E 3Rd St, The Dalles, Oregon 97058-2506 **Tel:** 1 541 296-9102.
Web site: http://haystackbroadcasting.com
Profile: KYYT-FM is a commercial station owned by Haystack Broadcasting, Inc. The format of the station is country. KYYT-FM broadcasts to The Dalles, OR area at 102.3 FM.
FM RADIO STATION

KYYW-AM 37246
Owner: Townsquare Media, LLC
Editorial: 3911 S 1st St, Abilene, Texas 79605
Tel: 1 325 676-7711.
Web site: http://1470kyyw.com
Profile: KYYW-AM is a commercial station owned by Townsquare Media, LLC. The format of the station is news/talk. KYYW-AM broadcasts to the Abilene, TX area at a frequency of 1470 AM.
AM RADIO STATION

KYYX-FM 46192
Owner: iHeartMedia Inc.
Editorial: 1000 20th Ave SW, Minot, North Dakota 58701-6447 **Tel:** 1 701 852-4646.
Web site: http://97kicksfm.iheart.com
Profile: KYYX-FM is a commercial station owned by iHeartMedia Inc. The format of the station is contemporary country. KYYX-FM broadcasts to the Minot-Bismarck, ND area at 97.1 FM.
FM RADIO STATION

KYYY-FM 46710
Owner: iHeartMedia Inc.
Editorial: 3500 E Rosser Ave, Bismarck, North Dakota 58501-3376 **Tel:** 1 701 255-1234.
Web site: http://www.y93.fm
Profile: KYYY-FM is a commercial station owned by iHeartMedia Inc. The format of the station is top 40. KYYY-FM broadcasts to the Bismarck, ND area at 92.9 FM.
FM RADIO STATION

KYYZ-FM 44990
Owner: Cherry Creek Radio
Editorial: 410 6th St E, Williston, North Dakota 58801
Tel: 1 701 572-5371.
Web site: http://www.kyyzradio.com
Profile: KYYZ-FM is a commercial station owned by Cherry Creek Radio. The format of the station is contemporary country. KYYZ-FM broadcasts to the Williston, ND area at 96.1 FM.
FM RADIO STATION

KYZK-FM 73809
Owner: Rich Broadcasting, LLC.
Editorial: 201 S Main St, Hailey, Idaho 83333-8406
Tel: 1 208 788-7118.
Email: kech95@richbroadcasting.com
Web site: http://www.star1075.com/
FM RADIO STATION

KYZS-AM 36008
Owner: Gleiser Communications LLC
Editorial: 1001 E Southeast Loop 323, Tyler, Texas 75701-9664 **Tel:** 1 903 593-2519.
Profile: KYZS-AM is a commercial station owned by Gleiser Communications LLC. The format of the station is Spanish sports. KYZS-AM broadcasts to the Tyler, TX area at 1490 AM.
AM RADIO STATION

KZAL-FM 43808
Owner: Icicle Broadcasting, Inc.
Editorial: 32 N Mission St, Wenatchee, Washington 98801-7210 **Tel:** 1 509 667-2400.
Email: znation@zcountry947.com
Web site: http://www.zcountry947.com
Profile: KZAL-FM is a commercial station owned by Icicle Broadcasting, Inc. The format of the station is contemporary country. KZAL-FM broadcasts to the Chelan, WA area at 94.7 FM.
FM RADIO STATION

KZAP-AM 86320
Owner: Mapleton of Chico, LLC
Editorial: 1459 Humboldt Rd Ste A, Chico, California 95928-9100 **Tel:** 1 530 899-3600.
Web site: http://www.kpig.com
Profile: KZAP-AM is a commercial station owned by Mapleton of Chico, LLC. The format of the station is adult album alternative. KZAP-AM broadcasts to the San Francisco area at 1510 AM and simulcasts the programming of KPIG-FM in Watsonville, CA.
AM RADIO STATION

KZAP-FM 39814
Owner: Mapleton Communications LLC
Editorial: 1459 Humboldt Rd Ste D, Chico, California 95928-9100 **Tel:** 1 530 899-3600.
Web site: http://classichits967.com
Profile: KZAP-FM is a commercial station owned by Mapleton Communications LLC. The format of the station is classic hits. KZAP-FM broadcasts to the Chico, CA area at 96.7 FM.
FM RADIO STATION

KZAT-FM 43438
Owner: Camrory Broadcasting
Editorial: 205 W 3rd St, Tama, Iowa 52339-2307
Tel: 1 641 484-5958.
Web site: http://www.radioz955.com
Profile: KZAT-FM is a commercial station owned by Camrory Broadcasting. The format for the station is Spanish AC. KZAT-FM broadcasts to the Cedar Rapids, IA area at 95.5 FM.
FM RADIO STATION

KZBB-FM 40062
Owner: iHeartMedia Inc.
Editorial: 311 Lexington Ave, Fort Smith, Arkansas 72901-3842 **Tel:** 1 479 782-8888.
Email: b98@kzbb.com
Web site: http://www.kzbb.com
Profile: KZBB-FM is a commercial station owned by iHeartMedia Inc. The format of the station is Hot AC. KZBB-FM broadcasts to the Fort Smith, AR area at 97.9 FM.
FM RADIO STATION

KZBD-FM 46731
Owner: Read Broadcasting
Editorial: 1601 E 57th Ave, Spokane, Washington 99223-6623 **Tel:** 1 509 448-1000.
Web site: http://www.now1057fm.com
Profile: KZBD-FM is a commercial station owned by Read Broadcasting. The format of the station is Top 40/CHR. KZBD-FM broadcasts to the Spokane, WA area at 105.7 FM.
FM RADIO STATION

KZBE-FM 44020
Owner: North Cascades Broadcasting
Editorial: 320 Emery Dr, Omak, Washington 98841-9237 **Tel:** 1 509 826-0100.
Email: news@komw.net
Web site: http://www.komw.net
Profile: KZBE-FM is a commercial station owned by North Cascades Broadcasting. The format of the station is adult contemporary. KZBE-FM broadcasts to the Spokane, WA area at 104.3 FM.
FM RADIO STATION

KZBI-FM 556941
Owner: Ruby Radio Corp.
Tel: 1 775 777-1196.
Email: news@rubyradio.fm
Web site: http://kzbi.fm
Profile: KZBI-FM is a commercial station owned by Ruby Radio Corp. The format of the station is news and talk. KZBI-FM broadcasts to the Elko, NV area at 94.5 FM.
FM RADIO STATION

KZBK-FM 44993
Owner: Best Broadcast Group
Editorial: 107 S Main St, Brookfield, Missouri 64628
Tel: 1 660 258-3383.
Email: kzbk@bestbroadcastgroup.com
Web site: http://www.kzbkradio.com
Profile: KZBK-FM is a commercial station owned by Best Broadcast Group. The format of the station is hot adult contemporary music. KZBK-FM broadcasts to the Kansas City, MO area at 96.9 FM.
FM RADIO STATION

KZBL-FM 40063
Owner: Baldridge-Dumas Communications Inc.
Editorial: 400 Jefferson St, Natchitoches, Louisiana 71457 **Tel:** 1 318 352-9696.
Email: production@bdcradio.com
Web site: http://www.bdcradio.com
Profile: KZBL-FM is a commercial station owned by Baldridge-Dumas Communications Inc. The format of the station is oldies music. KZBL-FM broadcasts to the Shreveport, LA area at 100.7 FM.
FM RADIO STATION

KZBQ-FM 44994
Owner: Idaho Wireless Corp.
Editorial: 436 N Main St, Pocatello, Idaho 83204-3018
Tel: 1 208 234-1290.
Email: spots@kzbq.com
Web site: http://www.kzbq.com
Profile: KZBQ-FM is a commercial station owned by Idaho Wireless Corp. The format of the station is country. KZBQ-FM broadcasts to the Pocatello, ID area at 93.9 FM.
FM RADIO STATION

KZBT-FM 42114
Owner: Townsquare Media, LLC
Editorial: 11300 State Highway 191 Bldg 2, Midland, Texas 79707-1367 **Tel:** 1 432 563-9300.
Web site: http://www.b93.net
Profile: KZBT-FM is a commercial station owned by Townsquare Media, LLC. The format of the station is urban contemporary. KZBT-FM broadcasts to the Midland, TX area at 92.3 FM.
FM RADIO STATION

KZCD-FM 41146
Owner: Townsquare Media, LLC
Editorial: 626 SW D Ave, Lawton, Oklahoma 73501
Tel: 1 580 581-3600.
Email: lawtonpsa@townsquaremedia.com
Web site: http://www.z94.com
Profile: KZCD-FM is a commercial station owned by Townsquare Media, LLC. The format of the station is new and classic rock music. KZCD-FM broadcasts to the Lawton, OK area at 94.1 FM.
FM RADIO STATION

KZCH-FM 44317
Owner: iHeartMedia Inc.
Editorial: 9323 E 37th St N, Wichita, Kansas 67226-2000 **Tel:** 1 316 494-6600.
Web site: http://channel963.iheart.com
Profile: KZCH-FM is a commercial station owned by iHeartMedia Inc. The format of the station is Top 40/CHR. KZCH-FM broadcasts to the Wichita, KS area at 96.3 FM. The station's slogan is, "Wichita's #1 Hit Music Station."
FM RADIO STATION

KZCR-FM 44590
Owner: Results Radio Group
Editorial: 728 Western Ave, Fergus Falls, Minnesota 56537-1095 **Tel:** 1 218 736-7596.
Email: contactus@lakesradio.net
Web site: http://www.lakesradio.net
Profile: KZCR-FM is a commercial station owned by Results Radio Group. The format of the station is rock music. KZCR-FM broadcasts to the Fergus Falls, MN area at 103.3 FM.
FM RADIO STATION

KZDC-AM 37062
Owner: Alpha Media
Editorial: 4050 Eisenhauer Rd, San Antonio, Texas 78218-3409 **Tel:** 1 210 654-5100.
Web site: http://www.espnsa.com
Profile: KZDC-AM is a commercial station owned by Alpha Media. The format of the station is sports. KZDC-AM broadcasts to the San Antonio area at 1250 AM.
AM RADIO STATION

KZDG-AM 39480
Owner: CBS Radio
Editorial: 40931 Fremont Blvd, Fremont, California 94538-4307 **Tel:** 1 510 200-4991.
Email: contact@radiozindagi.com
Web site: http://www.radiozindagi.com
Profile: KZDG-AM is a commercial station owned by CBS Radio and managed by CinéMaya Media. The format of the station is South Asian and Indian talk and music programming. KZDG-AM broadcasts to the San Francisco Bay area at 1550 AM.
AM RADIO STATION

KZDV-FM 871338
Owner: Payne Radio Group
Editorial: 1600 W Jackson St, Hugo, Oklahoma 74743-5653 **Tel:** 1 580 326-2555.
Web site: http://payneradiogroup.com/
Profile: KZDV-FM is a commercial station owned by Payne Radio Group. The format for the station is Contemporary Christian. KZDV-FM broadcasts to the Hugo, OK area at 99.5 FM.
FM RADIO STATION

KZDX-FM 46564
Owner: Lee Family Broadcasting
Editorial: 120 S 300 W, Rupert, Idaho 83350-9667
Tel: 1 208 436-4757.
Web site: http://www.hot100now.com
Profile: KZDX-FM is a commercial station owned by Lee Family Broadcasting. The format of the station is Top 40/CHR. KZDX-FM broadcasts to the Rupert, ID area at 99.9 FM.
FM RADIO STATION

KZDY-FM 44113
Owner: Dierking Communications
Editorial: 1937 Highway 24, Glen Elder, Kansas 67446-9461 **Tel:** 1 785 545-3220.
Email: kdnskzdy@nckcn.com
Web site: http://kdcountry94.com
FM RADIO STATION

KZEL-FM 41617
Owner: Cumulus Media Inc.
Editorial: 1200 Executive Pkwy Ste 440, Eugene, Oregon 97401-2169 **Tel:** 1 541 284-8500.
Web site: http://www.96kzel.com
Profile: KZEL-FM is a commercial station owned by Cumulus Media Inc. The format of the station is classic rock music. KZEL-FM broadcasts to the Eugene, OR area at 96.1 FM.
FM RADIO STATION

KZEN-FM 40065
Owner: Alpha Media
Editorial: 1418 25th St, Columbus, Nebraska 68601-2820 **Tel:** 1 402 564-2866.
Web site: http://www.mycentralnebraska.com
Profile: KZEN-FM is a commercial station owned by Alpha Media. The format of the station is contemporary country music. KZEN-FM broadcasts to the Columbus, NE area at 100.3 FM.
FM RADIO STATION

KZEP-FM 44367
Owner: iHeartMedia Inc.
Editorial: 6222 W Interstate 10, San Antonio, Texas 78201-2013 **Tel:** 1 210 736-9700.
Web site: http://www.hot1045.com/main.html
Profile: KZEP-FM is a commercial station owned by iHeartMedia Inc. The format of the station is Rhythmic CHR. KZEP-FM broadcasts to the San Antonio area at 104.5 FM.
FM RADIO STATION

KZER-AM 36901
Owner: Lazer Broadcasting Corp.
Editorial: 1330 Cacique St, Santa Barbara, California 93103-3505 **Tel:** 1 805 240-2070.
Email: lazerbroadcasting@radiolazer.com
Profile: KZER-AM is a commercial station owned by Lazer Broadcasting Corp. The format of the station is regional Mexican. KZER-AM broadcasts to the Santa Barbara, CA area at 1250 AM.
AM RADIO STATION

KZEW-FM 45952
Owner: Smith Broadcasting Inc.
Editorial: 450 E Cole St, Wheatland, Wyoming 82201-8937 **Tel:** 1 307 322-5926.
Email: kzew@wheatlandradio.com
Profile: KZEW-FM is a commercial station owned by Smith Broadcasting Inc. The format of the station is adult contemporary. KZEW-FM broadcasts to the Wheatland, WY area at 101.7 FM.
FM RADIO STATION

KZEY-AM 38964
Owner: RCA Broadcasting LLC.
Editorial: Marshall, Texas
Profile: KZEY-AM is a commercial station owned by RCA Broadcasting LLC. The format of the station is sports. KZEY-AM broadcasts to the Marshall area at 1410 AM.
AM RADIO STATION

KZFM-FM 44996
Owner: Malkan Interactive Communications
Editorial: 2117 Leopard St, Corpus Christi, Texas 78408-3925 **Tel:** 1 361 883-3516.
Email: kzfm@bizstx.rr.com
Web site: http://www.hotz95.com
Profile: KZFM-FM is a commercial station owned by Malkan Interactive Communications. The format of the station is hot adult contemporary. KZFM-FM broadcasts to the Corpus Christi, TX area at 95.5 FM.
FM RADIO STATION

KZFN-FM 44997
Owner: Ida-Vend Communications Group
Editorial: 1114 N Almon St, Moscow, Idaho 83843-8507 **Tel:** 1 208 882-2551.
Profile: KZFN-FM is a commercial station owned by Ida-Vend Communications Group. The format for the station is Top 40/CHR. KZFN-FM broadcasts to the Moscow, ID area at 106.1 FM.
FM RADIO STATION

KZFR-FM 41267
Owner: Golden Valley Comm. Broadcast
Editorial: 341 Broadway St, Chico, California 95928-5342 **Tel:** 1 530 895-0706.
Web site: http://kzfr.org
Profile: KZFR-FM is a non-commercial station owned by Golden Valley Comm. Broadcast. The format of the station is variety. KZFR-FM broadcasts to the Chico, CA area at 90.1 FM.
FM RADIO STATION

KZFS-AM 39035
Owner: iHeartMedia Inc.
Editorial: 808 E Sprague Ave, Spokane, Washington 99202-2126 **Tel:** 1 509 242-2400.
Web site: http://www.up993spokane.com/main.html
Profile: KZFS-AM is a commercial station owned by iHeartMedia Inc. The format of the station is Contemporary Christian. KZFS-AM broadcasts to the Spokane, WA area at 590 AM.
AM RADIO STATION

KZGF-FM 44794
Owner: Leighton Enterprises Inc.
Editorial: 1185 9th St NE, Thompson, North Dakota 58278 **Tel:** 1 701 775-4611.
Email: live@z947.com
Web site: http://z947.com
Profile: KZGF-FM is a commercial station owned by Leighton Enterprises Inc. The format of the station is Top 40/CHR. KZGF-FM broadcasts to the Thompson, ND area at 94.7 FM.
FM RADIO STATION

KZGL-FM 39916
Owner: Great Circle Media
Editorial: 1117 W Route 66, Flagstaff, Arizona 86001-6213 **Tel:** 1 928 774-5231.
Web site: http://eagle.gcmaz.com
Profile: KZGL-FM is a commercial station owned by Great Circle Media. The format of the station is rock. KZGL-FM broadcasts to the Flagstaff, AZ area at 103.7 FM.
FM RADIO STATION

KZGM-FM 556853
Owner: Real Community Radio Network, Inc
Editorial: 1211 Ozark St, Cabool, Missouri 65689-7412 **Tel:** 1 417 200-0522.
Email: radio@kz88.org
Web site: http://www.kz88.org
Profile: KZGM-FM is a non-commercial station owned by Real Community Radio Network, Inc. The format of the station is variety. KZGM-FM broadcasts to the Springfield, MO area at 88.1 FM.
FM RADIO STATION

KZGO-FM 39807
Owner: Go Media
Editorial: 420 N 5th St Ste 150, Ford Center, Minneapolis, Minnesota 55401-2380 **Tel:** 1 612 659-4848.
Web site: http://www.gomn.com
Profile: KZGO (95.3 FM) is a Rhythmic Top 40 radio station licensed to St. Paul, Minnesota, serving the Twin Cities area. The station, known as "Go 95.3", is owned by Go Media, with sister station KQGO.
FM RADIO STATION

KZHE-FM 39786
Owner: A-1 Communications
Editorial: 406 W Union, Magnolia, Arkansas 71753-2747 **Tel:** 1 870 234-7790.
Email: kzhe@kzhe.com
Web site: http://www.kzhe.com
Profile: KZHE-FM is a commercial station owned by A-1 Communications. The format of the station is classic and contemporary country. KZHE-FM broadcasts to the Magnolia, AR area at 100.5 FM.
FM RADIO STATION

KZHK-FM 44519
Owner: Canyon Media Corporation
Editorial: 619 S. Bluff Tower 1 Ste. 300, Saint George, Utah 84780 **Tel:** 1 435 628-3643.
Web site: http://www.959thehawk.com
Profile: KZHK-FM is a commercial station owned by Canyon Media Corporation. The format for the station is classic rock. KZHK-FM broadcasts to the St. George, UT area at 95.9 FM.
FM RADIO STATION

KZHM-FM 939266
Owner: Hispanic Target Media, Inc.
Editorial: 2433 E Palo Verde St, Yuma, Arizona 85365-3619 **Tel:** 1 928 344-3727.
Email: hispanictargetmedia@gmail.com
Web site: http://www.amigo959fm.com
Profile: KZHM-FM is a commercial station owned by Hispanic Target Media, Inc. The format of the station is Regional Mexican. The station broadcasts to the Alamogordo, NM area at a frequency of 95.9 FM.
FM RADIO STATION

KZHN-AM 76328
Owner: Eiffel Tower Broadcasting
Editorial: 402 Munson Place, Ste 111, Rockwall, Texas 75087 **Tel:** 1 903 784-1234.
Email: txn1250@gmail.com
Web site: http://www.txn1250.com
Profile: KZHN-AM is a commercial station owned by Eiffel Tower Broadcasting. The format of the station is classic country music. KZHN-AM broadcasts to the Paris, TX area at 1250 AM.
AM RADIO STATION

KZHR-FM 87889
Owner: Cherry Creek Radio
Editorial: 2823 W Lewis St, Pasco, Washington 99301-6702 **Tel:** 1 509 547-1618.
Web site: http://www.kzhr.com
Profile: KZHR-FM is a commercial station owned by Cherry Creek Radio. The format of the station is Hispanic. KZHR-FM broadcasts to the Pasco, WA area at 92.5 FM.
FM RADIO STATION

KZHS-AM 37338
Owner: Noalmark Broadcasting Corp.
Editorial: 208 Buena Vista Rd, Hot Springs, Arkansas 71913-8208 **Tel:** 1 501 525-4600.
Profile: KZHS-AM is a commercial station owned by Noalmark Broadcasting Corp. The format of the station is news and talk. KZHS-AM broadcasts to the Hot Springs, AR area at 590 AM.
AM RADIO STATION

KZHT-FM 39954
Owner: iHeartMedia Inc.
Editorial: 2801 Decker Lake Dr, Salt Lake City, Utah 84119-2330 **Tel:** 1 801 908-1300.
Web site: http://971zht.iheart.com
Profile: KZHT-FM is a commercial station owned by iHeartMedia Inc. The format of the station is Top 40/CHR. KZHT-FM broadcasts to the Salt Lake City area at 97.1 FM.
FM RADIO STATION

KZIA-FM 41011
Owner: KZIA Inc.
Editorial: 1110 26th Ave SW, Cedar Rapids, Iowa 52404 **Tel:** 1 319 363-2061.
Email: info@kzia.com
Web site: http://www.kzia.com
Profile: KZIA-FM is a commercial station owned by KZIA Inc. The format for the station is Top 40/CHR. KZIA-FM broadcasts to the Cedar Rapids, IA area at 102.9 FM.
FM RADIO STATION

KZII-FM 45804
Owner: Townsquare Media, LLC
Editorial: 4413 82nd St Ste 300, Lubbock, Texas 79424-3366 **Tel:** 1 806 798-7078.
Web site: http://www.1025kiss.com
Profile: KZII-FM is a commercial station owned by Townsquare Media, LLC. The format of the station is Top 40/CHR music. KZII-FM broadcasts to the Lubbock, TX area at 102.5 FM.
FM RADIO STATION

KZIM-AM 39241
Owner: Max Media
Editorial: 324 Broadway St, Cape Girardeau, Missouri 63701-7331 **Tel:** 1 573 335-8291.
Email: kzim@riverradio.net
Web site: http://www.960kzim.com
Profile: KZIM-AM is a commercial station owned by Max Media. The format of the station is news and talk programming. KZIM-AM broadcasts to the Cape Girardeau, MO area at 960 AM.
AM RADIO STATION

KZIN-FM 46469
Owner: Townsquare Media, LLC
Editorial: 830 Oilfield Ave, Shelby, Montana 59474-1641 **Tel:** 1 406 434-5241.
Web site: http://www.k96fm.com
Profile: KZIN-FM is a commercial station owned by Townsquare Media, LLC. The format of the station is contemporary country music. KZIN-FM broadcasts in the Shelby, MT area at 96.7 FM.
FM RADIO STATION

KZIP-AM 35136
Owner: My Home Team Media
Editorial: 3639 Wolflin Ave, Amarillo, Texas 79102-2119 **Tel:** 1 806 355-1044.
Profile: KZIP-AM is a commercial station owned by My Home Team Media. The format of the station is agricultural and farming programming. KZIP-AM broadcasts to the Amarillo, TX area at 1310 AM.
AM RADIO STATION

KZIQ-FM 42812
Owner: Adelman Broadcasting Inc.
Editorial: 731 Balsam St, Ridgecrest, California 93555-3510 **Tel:** 1 760 371-1700.
Email: contact@adelmanbroadcasting.com
Web site: http://www.927qlite.com
Profile: KZIQ-FM is a commercial station owned by Adelman Broadcasting Inc.. The format of the station is AC. KZIQ-FM broadcasts to the Ridgecrest, CA area at 92.7 FM.
FM RADIO STATION

KZIU-FM 43311
Owner: Alexandra Communications
Editorial: 45 S Campbell Rd, Walla Walla, Washington 99362-9597 **Tel:** 1 509 527-1000.
Web site: http://www.crankthehank.com/
Profile: KZIU-FM is a commercial station owned by Alexandra Communications. The format of the station is classic country. KZIU-FM broadcasts to the Walla Walla, WA area at 101.9 FM.
FM RADIO STATION

KZIZ-AM 36062
Owner: Kris Bennett Broadcasting Co.
Editorial: 2600 S Jackson St, Seattle, Washington 98144-2402 **Tel:** 1 206 323-3070.
Email: ztwins@aol.com
Web site: http://www.ztwins.com/
Profile: KZIZ-AM is a commercial station owned by Kris Bennett Broadcasting Co. The format of the station is ethnic. KZIZ-AM broadcasts to the Seattle area at 1560 AM.
AM RADIO STATION

KZJF-FM 44711
Owner: Cumulus Media Inc.
Editorial: 1002 Diamond Rdg Ste 400, Jefferson City, Missouri 65109-7902 **Tel:** 1 573 893-5100.
Web site: http://www.sportsradio1041.com
Profile: KZJF-FM is a commercial station owned by Cumulus Media Inc. The format for the station is sports. KZJF-FM broadcasts to the Jefferson City, MO area at 104.1 FM.
FM RADIO STATION

KZJH-FM 41948
Owner: Rich Broadcasting, LLC.
Editorial: 1140 State Highway 22, Jackson, Wyoming 83001-9401 **Tel:** 1 307 733-2120.
Email: bigmike@richbroadcasting.com
Web site: http://www.kz95rocks.com/
Profile: KZJH-FM is a commercial station owned by Rich Broadcasting, LLC. The format of the station is hot adult contemporary. KZJH-FM is broadcast to the Jackson, WY area at 95.3 FM.
FM RADIO STATION

KZJK-FM 46767
Owner: CBS Radio
Editorial: 625 2nd Ave S, Minneapolis, Minnesota 55402-1912 **Tel:** 1 612 370-0611.
Web site: http://www.1041jackfm.com
Profile: KZJK-FM is a commercial station owned by CBS Radio. The format of the station is adult hits. KZJK-FM broadcasts to the Minneapolis area at 104.1 FM.
FM RADIO STATION

KZKE-FM 43586
Owner: Route 66 Broadcasting LLC
Editorial: 812 E Beale St, Kingman, Arizona 86401-5925 **Tel:** 1 928 753-9100.
Web site: http://www.kgmn.net/KZKE.htm
Profile: KZKE-FM is a commercial station owned by Route 66 Broadcasting LLC. The format of the station is rock music. KZKE-FM broadcasts to the Kingman, AZ area at 103.3 FM.
FM RADIO STATION

KZKR-FM 44446
Owner: First Natchez Radio Group Inc
Editorial: 2 Oferrall St, Natchez, Mississippi 39120-3000 **Tel:** 1 601 442-4895.
Web site: http://www.listenupyall.com
Profile: KZKR-FM is a commercial station owned by First Natchez Radio Group Inc. The format of the station is classic rock. KZKR-FM broadcasts to the Natchez, MS area at a frequency of 105.1 FM. The station does not accept press submissions, requests, and inquiries.
FM RADIO STATION

KZKS-FM 46679
Owner: Western Slope Communications
Editorial: 751 Horizon Ct, Ste 225, Grand Junction, Colorado 81506 **Tel:** 1 970 241-6460.
Email: production@wscradio.net
Web site: http://www.drive105.net
Profile: KZKS-FM is a commercial station owned by Western Slopes Communications. The format for the station is classic hits. KZKS-FM broadcasts to the Grand Junction-Montrose, CO area at 105.3 FM.
FM RADIO STATION

KZKX-FM 40068
Owner: Digity Media
Editorial: 3800 Cornhusker Hwy, Lincoln, Nebraska 68504-1533 **Tel:** 1 402 466-1234.
Web site: http://www.kzkx.com
Profile: KZKX-FM is a commercial station owned by Digity Media. The format of the station is contemporary country. KZKX-FM broadcasts to the Lincoln, NE area at 96.9 FM.
FM RADIO STATION

KZKZ-FM 41658
Owner: Family Communications, Inc.
Editorial: 6420 South Zero St, Fort Smith, Arkansas 72903 **Tel:** 1 479 646-6700.
Email: kzkzfm@kzkzfm.com
Web site: http://www.kzkzfm.com
Profile: KZKZ-FM is a commercial station owned by Family Communications, Inc. The format of the station is Christian teaching and Contemporary Christian music. KZKZ-FM broadcasts to the Fort Smith, AR area at 106.3 FM.
FM RADIO STATION

KZLB-FM 45764
Owner: Alpha Media
Editorial: 200 N 10th St, Fort Dodge, Iowa 50501-3925 **Tel:** 1 515 955-5656.
Web site: http://www.yourfortdodge.com
Profile: KZLB-FM is a commercial station owned by Alpha Media. The format of the station is rock alternative. KZLB-FM broadcasts to the Fort Dodge, IA area at 92.1 FM.
FM RADIO STATION

KZLE-FM 44999
Owner: WRD Entertainment Inc.
Editorial: 920 Harrison St Ste C, Batesville, Arkansas 72501-6949 **Tel:** 1 870 793-4196.
Web site: http://93kzle.com/
Profile: KZLE-FM is a commercial station owned by WRD Entertainment Inc. The format of the station is classic rock. KZLE-FM broadcasts to the Batesville, AR area at 93.1 FM.
FM RADIO STATION

KZLK-FM 310187
Owner: Duhamel Broadcasting
Editorial: 518 Saint Joseph St, Rapid City, South Dakota 57701-2717 **Tel:** 1 605 721-1063.
Email: she1063@dberadio.com
Web site: http://www.she1063.com
Profile: KZLK-FM is a commercial station owned by Duhamel Broadcasting. The format for the station is hot AC. KZLK-FM broadcasts to the Rapid City, SD area at 106.3. The tagline for the station is "She 106.3".
FM RADIO STATION

KZLS-AM 217685
Owner: Champlin Broadcasting
Editorial: 4045 NW 64th St Ste 306, Oklahoma City, Oklahoma 73116-2616 **Tel:** 1 405 633-1099.
Web site: http://radio.securenetsystems.net/v5/KZLS
Profile: KZLS-AM is a commercial station owned by Champlin Broadcasting. The format of the station is talk. KZLS-AM broadcasts to the Oklahoma City, OK area at 1640 AM.
AM RADIO STATION

KZLT-FM 46291
Owner: Leighton Enterprises Inc.
Editorial: 1185 9th St NE, Thompson, North Dakota 58278 **Tel:** 1 701 775-4611.
Web site: http://literock1043.com
Profile: KZLT-FM is a commercial station owned by Leighton Enterprises Inc. The format of the station is adult contemporary. KZLT-FM broadcasts to the Thompson, ND area at 104.3 FM.
FM RADIO STATION

KZLZ-FM 42667
Owner: CSVJ, LLC
Editorial: 2959 E Grant Rd, Tucson, Arizona 85716-2717 **Tel:** 1 520 325-3054.
Web site: http://lapoderosakzlz.com
Profile: KZLZ-FM is a commercial station owned by CSVJ, LLC. The format of the station is Hispanic. KZLZ-FM broadcasts to the Tucson, AZ area at 105.3 FM.
FM RADIO STATION

KZMA-FM 446305
Owner: Stratemeyer Media
Editorial: 203 S Main St, Poplar Bluff, Missouri 63901-5831 **Tel:** 1 573 778-1219.
Web site: http://www.kzmafm.com
Profile: KZMA-FM is a commercial station owned by Stratemeyer Media. The format of the station is adult contemporary. KZMA-FM broadcasts to the Poplar Bluff, MO area at 99.9 FM.
FM RADIO STATION

KZMC-FM 450737
Owner: GI Family Radio
Editorial: 106 W 8th St, McCook, Nebraska 69001-3508 **Tel:** 1 308 345-1981.
Email: production@krgi.com
Web site: http://newsacrossnebraska.com
Profile: KZMC-FM is a commercial station owned by GI Family Radio. The format of the station is rock. KZMC-FM broadcasts to the McCook, NE area at 102.1 FM.
FM RADIO STATION

KZMG-FM 902188
Owner: Impact Radio
Editorial: 5660 E Franklin Rd Ste 200, Nampa, Idaho 83687-5133 **Tel:** 1 208 465-9966.
Profile: KZMG-FM is a commercial station owned by Impact Radio. The format of the station is Hot Ac. The station broadcasts locally at a frequency of 102.7 FM.
FM RADIO STATION

KZMK-FM 44906
Owner: Cherry Creek Radio
Editorial: 2300 E Busby Dr, Sierra Vista, Arizona 85635 **Tel:** 1 520 458-4313.
Email: k101@cherrycreekradio.com
Web site: http://www.allhitskzmk.com
Profile: KZMK-FM is a commercial station owned by Cherry Creek Radio. The format of the station is hot adult contemporary music. KZMK-FM broadcasts to the Sierra Vista, AZ area at 100.9 FM.
FM RADIO STATION

KZML-FM 44349
Owner: Bustos Media, LLC
Editorial: 706 Butterfield Rd, Yakima, Washington 98901-2021 **Tel:** 1 509 457-1000.
Web site: http://www.radiolagrande.com
Profile: KZML-FM is a commercial station owned by Bustos Media, LLC. The format of the station is regional Mexican. KZML-FM broadcasts to the Yakima, WA area at 95.9 FM.
FM RADIO STATION

KZMN-FM 45829
Owner: KOFI Inc.
Editorial: 317 1st Ave E, Kalispell, Montana 59901-9601 **Tel:** 1 406 755-6690.
Email: traffic@monster1039.com
Web site: http://www.monster1039.com
Profile: KZMN-FM is a commercial station owned by KOFI Inc. The format of the station is classic rock. KZMN-FM broadcasts to the Missoula, MT, area at 103.9 FM.
FM RADIO STATION

KZMP-AM 35873
Owner: Liberman Broadcasting
Editorial: 400 Las Colinas Blvd E, Irving, Texas 75039-5579 **Tel:** 1 214 258-2800.
Web site: http://espndeportesdallas.com
Profile: KZMP-AM is a commercial station owned by Liberman Broadcasting and managed by Deportes Media. The format of the station is Hispanic sports. KZMP-AM broadcasts to the Dallas area at 1540 AM.
AM RADIO STATION

KZMP-FM 43382
Owner: Liberman Broadcasting Inc.
Editorial: 1210 E Belt Line Rd, Richardson, Texas 75081-3707 **Tel:** 1 214 675-1754.
Web site: http://www.funasia.net
Profile: KZMP-FM is a commercial station owned by Liberman Broadcasting Inc. and operated by FunAsia. The format of the station is variety, specializing in Indian/Pakistani programming. KZMP-FM broadcasts to the Dallas area at 104.9 FM.
FM RADIO STATION

KZMQ-AM 38804
Owner: Legend Communications
Editorial: 1949 Mountain View Dr, Cody, Wyoming 82414 **Tel:** 1 307 578-5000.
Email: news@bhrnwy.com
Web site: http://www.mybighornbasin.com
Profile: KZMQ-AM is a commercial station owned by Legend Communications. The format of the station is classic country. KZMQ-AM broadcasts in the Greybull, WY area at 1140 AM.
AM RADIO STATION

KZMQ-FM 46182
Owner: Legend Communications
Editorial: 1949 Mountain View Dr, Cody, Wyoming 82414 **Tel:** 1 307 578-5000.
Email: news@bhrnwy.com
Web site: http://www.mybighornbasin.com
Profile: KZMQ-FM is a commercial station owned by Legend Communications. The format of the station is contemporary country music. KZMQ-FM broadcasts to the Cody, WY area at 100.3 FM.
FM RADIO STATION

KZMT-FM 45000
Owner: Cherry Creek Radio
Editorial: 110 E Broadway St, Helena, Montana 59601-4232 **Tel:** 1 406 442-6620.
Email: ebaker@cherrycreekradio.com
Profile: KZMT-FM is a commercial station owned by Cherry Creek Radio. The format of the station is classic rock music. KZMT-FM broadcasts in the Helena, MT area at 101.1 FM.
FM RADIO STATION

KZMU-FM 231027
Owner: Moab Public Radio, Inc.
Editorial: 1734 Rocky Rd, Moab, Utah 84532-3278 **Tel:** 1 435 259-8824.
Email: marty@kzmu.org
Web site: http://www.kzmu.org
Profile: KZMU-FM is a non-commercial station owned by Moab Public Radio, Inc. The format for the station is variety. KZMU-FM broadcasts to the Salt Lake City area at 90.1 FM.
FM RADIO STATION

KZMY-FM 444221
Owner: Townsquare Media, LLC
Editorial: 125 W Mendenhall St Ste 1, Bozeman, Montana 59715-3500 **Tel:** 1 406 586-2343.
Web site: http://my1035.com
Profile: KZMY-FM is a commercial station owned by Townsquare Media, LLC. The format of the station is hot adult contemporary. KZMY-FM broadcasts to the Bozeman, MT area at 103.5 FM.
FM RADIO STATION

KZMZ-FM 42729
Owner: Cenla Broadcasting Inc.
Editorial: 1115 Texas Ave, Alexandria, Louisiana 71301 **Tel:** 1 318 445-1234.
Web site: http://www.969rocks.com
Profile: KZMZ-FM is a commercial station owned by Cenla Broadcasting Inc. The format of the station is classic rock music. KZMZ-FM broadcasts to the Alexandria, LA area at 96.9 FM.
FM RADIO STATION

KZNA-FM 41280
Owner: Kanza Society Inc.
Editorial: 210 N 7th St, Garden City, Kansas 67846 **Tel:** 1 620 275-7444.
Email: hppr@hppr.org
Web site: http://www.hppr.org
Profile: KZNA-FM is a non-commercial station owned by Kanza Society Inc. The format of the station is news and classical. KZNA-FM broadcasts to the Wichita, KS area at 90.5 FM.
FM RADIO STATION

KZNB-AM 36442
Owner: California Broadcasting Company, LLC
Editorial: 965 Stony Point Rd, Santa Rosa, California 95407-7129 **Tel:** 1 707 974-2834.
Profile: KZNB-AM is a commercial station owned by California Broadcasting Company, LLC. The format of the station is Regional Mexican music. KZNB-AM broadcasts to the Petaluma, CA area at 1490 AM.
AM RADIO STATION

KZND-FM 134172
Owner: Alaska Integrated Media
Editorial: 4700 Business Park Blvd, Anchorage, Alaska 99503-7176 **Tel:** 1 907 522-1018.
Email: traffic@alaskaim.com
Web site: http://www.947kznd.com
Profile: KZND-FM is a commercial station owned by Alaska Integrated Media. The format of the station is active rock. KZND-FM broadcasts to the Anchorage, AK area at a frequency of 94.7 FM.
FM RADIO STATION

KZNE-AM 81701
Owner: Bryan Broadcasting
Editorial: 2700 Earl Rudder Fwy S, Ste 5000, College Station, Texas 77845 **Tel:** 1 979 695-9595.
Email: radio@bryanbroadcasting.com
Web site: http://www.kzne.com
Profile: KZNE-AM is a commercial station owned by Bryan Broadcasting. The format of the station is

sports. KZNE-AM broadcasts to the College Station, TX area at 1150 AM.
AM RADIO STATION

KZNG-AM
37620

Owner: US Stations, LLC
Editorial: 125 Corporate Ter, Hot Springs, Arkansas 71913-7248 **Tel:** 1 501 525-9700.
Web site: http://www.myhotsprings.com
Profile: KZNG-AM is a commercial radio station owned by US Stations LLC. The format of the station is news and talk. KZNG-AM broadcasts to the Little Rock, AR area at 1340 AM.
AM RADIO STATION

KZNN-FM
40072

Owner: Mahaffey Enterprises Inc.
Editorial: 1505 Soest Rd, Rolla, Missouri 65401-3709 **Tel:** 1 573 364-2525.
Email: kttrkznn@fidmail.com
Web site: http://www.resultsradioonline.com
Profile: KZNN-FM is a commercial station owned by Mahaffey Enterprises Inc. The format of the station is country. KZNN-FM broadcasts in the Rolla, MO area at 105.3 FM.
FM RADIO STATION

KZNS-AM
39100

Owner: Miller Group (Larry H.)
Editorial: 301 W South Temple, Salt Lake City, Utah 84101-1216 **Tel:** 1 801 537-1414.
Web site: http://www.1280thezone.com
Profile: KZNS-AM is a commercial station owned by Miller Group (Larry H.). The format of the station is sports. KZNS-AM broadcasts to the Salt Lake City area at 1280 AM.
AM RADIO STATION

KZNS-FM
358744

Owner: Miller Broadcasting (Larry H.)
Editorial: 301 W South Temple, Salt Lake City, Utah 84101-1216 **Tel:** 1 801 537-1414.
Web site: http://1280thezone.com
Profile: KZNS-FM is a commercial station owned by Miller Broadcasting (Larry H.). The format of the station is sports. KZNS-FM broadcasts to the Salt Lake City area at 97.5 FM.
FM RADIO STATION

KZNT-AM
37347

Owner: Salem Media Group, Inc.
Editorial: 7150 Campus Dr Ste 150, Colorado Springs, Colorado 80920-3157 **Tel:** 1 719 531-5438.
Web site: http://am1460theanswer.com
Profile: KZNT-AM is a commercial station owned by Salem Media Group, Inc. The format of the station is news and talk. KZNT-AM broadcasts to the Colorado Springs, CO area at 1460 AM.
AM RADIO STATION

KZNU-AM
36700

Owner: Canyon Media Corporation
Editorial: 619 S. Bluff Tower 1 Ste. 300, Saint George, Utah 84780 **Tel:** 1 435 628-3643.
Web site: http://foxnews1450.com
Profile: KZNU-AM is a commercial station owned by Canyon Media Corporation. The format of the station is news and talk. KZNU-AM broadcasts to the St. George, UT area at 1450 AM.
AM RADIO STATION

KZNW-AM
38816

Owner: Cherry Creek Radio
Editorial: 231 N Wenatchee Ave, Wenatchee, Washington 98801 **Tel:** 1 509 665-6565.
Email: newswenatchee@cherrycreekradio.com
Profile: KZNW-AM is a commercial station owned by Cherry Creek Radio. The format of the station is sports. KZNW-AM broadcasts to the Seattle area at 1340 AM.
AM RADIO STATION

KZNX-AM
36686

Owner: American Telecommunications Group, Inc.
Editorial: 912 S Capital of Texas Hwy Ste 400, West Lake Hills, Texas 78746-6176 **Tel:** 1 512 416-1100.
Web site: http://www.radiomujer.com.mx
Profile: KZNX-AM is a commercial station owned by America Telecommunications Group, Inc. The format of the station is Spanish talk. KZNX-AM broadcasts to the Austin, TX area at 1530 AM.
AM RADIO STATION

KZOK-FM
42328

Owner: CBS Radio
Editorial: 1000 Dexter Ave N Ste 100, Seattle, Washington 98109-3577 **Tel:** 1 206 805-1025.
Web site: http://www.kzok.com
Profile: KZOK-FM is a commercial station owned by CBS Radio. The format of the station is classic rock music. KZOK-FM broadcasts to the Seattle area at 102.5 FM.
FM RADIO STATION

KZOO-AM
35137

Owner: Furuya(David)
Editorial: 2454 S Beretania St Ste 203, Honolulu, Hawaii 96826-1524 **Tel:** 1 808 947-5966.
Email: am1210@kzooradio.com
Web site: http://kzoohawaii.com
Profile: KZOO-AM is a commercial station owned by David Furuya. The format of the station is ethnic Japanese, and programming includes music, news, and information. KZOO-AM broadcasts to the Japanese-American community in Honolulu area at 1210 AM.
AM RADIO STATION

KZOQ-FM
45001

Owner: Cherry Creek Radio
Editorial: 1600 North Ave W, Ste 101, Missoula, Montana 59801 **Tel:** 1 406 728-5000.
Web site: http://www.kzoq.com
Profile: KZOQ-FM is a commercial station owned by Cherry Creek Radio. The format is classic rock. KZOQ-FM broadcasts to the Missoula, MT area at 100.1 FM.
FM RADIO STATION

KZOR-FM
45002

Owner: Noalmark Broadcasting Corp.
Editorial: 619 N Turner St, Hobbs, New Mexico 88240-8232 **Tel:** 1 575 397-4969.
Email: kzor@1radiosquare.com
Web site: http://www.kzorfm.com
Profile: KZOR-FM is a commercial station owned by Noalmark Broadcasting Corp. The format of the station is hot adult contemporary. KZOR-FM broadcasts to the Hobbs, NM area at 94.1 FM.
FM RADIO STATION

KZOT-AM
153242

Owner: NRG Media LLC
Editorial: 5011 Capitol Ave, Omaha, Nebraska 68132-2921 **Tel:** 1 402 342-2000.
Web site: http://1620thezone.com
Profile: KZOT-AM is a commercial station owned by NRG Media LLC. The format of the station is sports/talk. KZOT-AM broadcasts to the Omaha, NE area at 1180 AM.
AM RADIO STATION

KZOY-AM
35882

Owner: Cup O Dirt, LLC
Editorial: 401 E 8th St Ste 203, Sioux Falls, South Dakota 57103-7033
Email: sunny@mysunnyradio.com
Web site: http://www.mysunnyradio.com
Profile: KZOY-AM is a commercial station owned by Cup O Dirt, LLC. The format of the station is classic hits of the 80s. KZOY-AM broadcasts to the Brandon and Sioux Falls, SD areas at 1520 AM.
AM RADIO STATION

KZOZ-FM
44329

Owner: American General Media
Editorial: 3620 Sacramento Dr Ste 206, San Luis Obispo, California 93401-7215 **Tel:** 1 805 781-2750.
Email: news@americangeneralmedia.com
Web site: http://www.kzoz.com
Profile: KZOZ-FM is a commercial station owned by American General Media. The format of the station is classic rock. KZOZ-FM broadcasts to the San Luis Obispo, CA area at 93.3 FM.
FM RADIO STATION

KZPA-AM
36295

Owner: Gwandak Public Broadcasting Inc.
Editorial: 1993 E 3rd Ave, Fort Yukon, Alaska 99740 **Tel:** 1 907 662-6356.
Email: kzparadio@hotmail.com
Profile: KZPA-AM is a commercial station owned by Gwandak Public Broadcasting Inc. The format of the station is variety. KZPA-AM broadcasts to the Fort Yukon, AK area at 900 AM.
AM RADIO STATION

KZPK-FM
43158

Owner: Leighton Enterprises Inc.
Editorial: 619 W Saint Germain St, Saint Cloud, Minnesota 56301-3640 **Tel:** 1 320 251-1450.
Web site: http://www.wildcountry99.com
Profile: KZPK-FM is a commercial station owned by Leighton Enterprises Inc. The format of the station is contemporary country music. KZPK-FM broadcasts in the Saint Cloud, MN area at 98.9 FM. Send any press materials to the station's program director.
FM RADIO STATION

KZPO-FM
871611

Owner: Estate of Linda Ware
Editorial: 5119 W Nicholas Ave, Visalia, California 93291-7846 **Tel:** 1 559 733-4211.
Profile: KZPO-FM is a commercial station owned by the Estate of Linda Ware. The format of the station is adult standards. KZPO-FM broadcasts to the Visalia, CA area at a frequency of 103.3 FM.
FM RADIO STATION

KZPR-FM
45003

Owner: iHeartMedia Inc.
Editorial: 1000 20th Ave SW, Minot, North Dakota 58701-6447 **Tel:** 1 701 852-4646.
Web site: http://www.thefox1053.com
Profile: KZPR-FM is a commercial station owned by iHeartMedia Inc. The format of the station is classic rock music. KZPR-FM broadcasts to the Minot, ND area at 105.3 FM.
FM RADIO STATION

KZPS-FM
42196

Owner: iHeartMedia Inc.
Editorial: 14001 Dallas Pkwy Ste 300, Dallas, Texas 75240-7369 **Tel:** 1 214 866-8000.
Web site: http://www.kzps.com
Profile: KZPS-FM is a commercial station owned by iHeartMedia Inc.The format of the station is classic rock. KZPS-FM broadcasts to the Dallas area at 92.5 FM.
FM RADIO STATION

KZPT-FM
46760

Owner: Entercom Communications Corp.
Editorial: 7000 Squibb Rd, Mission, Kansas 66202-3233
Email: 997ThePoint@gmail.com
Web site: http://www.997point.com
Profile: KZPT-FM is a commercial station owned by Entercom Communications Corp. The format of the station is adult contemporary. KZPT-FM broadcasts to the Kansas City, MO area at 99.7 FM.
FM RADIO STATION

KZQD-FM
43552

Owner: Loredo(Mario)
Editorial: 322 S Clay Ave, Liberal, Kansas 67901-3661 **Tel:** 1 620 626-8282.
Email: radiolibertad@sbcglobal.net
Web site: http://kzqdradio.com
Profile: KZQD-FM is a commercial station owned by Mario Loredo. The format of the station is Hispanic religious programming. KZQD-FM broadcasts to the Liberal, KS area at 105.1 FM.
FM RADIO STATION

KZQQ-AM
36802

Owner: Canfin Enterprises Inc.
Editorial: 402 Cypress St, Ste 510, Abilene, Texas 79601 **Tel:** 1 325 672-5442.
Web site: http://www.radioabilene.com
AM RADIO STATION

KZQX-FM
41234

Owner: Chalkhill Communications, LLC
Editorial: 13618 County Road 2127 N, Henderson, Texas 75652-4808 **Tel:** 1 903 643-7711.
Email: kzqxfm@aol.com
Web site: http://www.kzqx.com
Profile: KZQX-FM is a commercial station owned by Chalkhill Communications, LLC. The format of the station is adult standards. KZQX-FM broadcasts to the Longview, TX, area at 100.3 FM.
FM RADIO STATION

KZQZ-AM
37901

Owner: Showclubs International, Inc.
Editorial: 6500 W Main St, Belleville, Illinois 62223-3700 **Tel:** 1 618 394-1430.
Email: info@kzqz1430am.com
Web site: http://www.kzqz1430am.com
Profile: KZQZ-AM is a commercial station owned by Entertainment Media Trust. The format of the station is oldies. KZQZ-AM broadcasts to the St. Louis area at 1430 AM.
AM RADIO STATION

KZRB-FM
41802

Owner: B & H Radio Inc.
Editorial: 710 W Avenue A, Hooks, Texas 75561 **Tel:** 1 903 547-3223.
Email: kzrb@txk.net
Web site: http://www.kzrb103five.com
Profile: KZRB-FM is a commercial station owned by B & H Radio Inc. The format of the station is urban contemporary. KZRB-FM broadcasts to the Texarkana, TX area at 103.5 FM.
FM RADIO STATION

KZRD-FM
44048

Owner: Rocking M Radio
Editorial: 2601 Central Ave, Dodge City, Kansas 67801-6200 **Tel:** 1 620 225-8080.
Web site: http://mykansasradio.com
Profile: KZRD-FM is a commercial station owned Rocking M Radio. The format of the station is rock. KZRD-FM broadcasts to the Dodge City, KS area at 93.9 FM.
FM RADIO STATION

KZRG-AM
39439

Owner: Zimmer Radio Group
Editorial: 2702 E 32Nd St, Joplin, Missouri 64804-4307 **Tel:** 1 417 624-1025.
Email: info@zrgmail.com
Web site: http://www.1310kzrg.com
Profile: KZRG-AM is a commercial station owned by Zimmer Radio Inc. The format of the station is news and talk. KZRG-AM broadcasts to the Joplin, MO area at 1310 AM.
AM RADIO STATION

KZRK-FM
46177

Owner: Cumulus Media Inc.
Editorial: 301 S Polk St Ste 100, Amarillo, Texas 79101-1404 **Tel:** 1 806 342-5200.
Web site: http://www.amarillosrockstation.com
Profile: KZRK-FM is a commercial station owned by Cumulus Media Inc. The format of the station is rock music. KZRK-FM broadcasts in the Amarillo, TX area at 107.9 FM.
FM RADIO STATION

KZRM-FM
44494

Owner: Chama Broadcasting Corporation
Editorial: 2202 HWY 17, Chama, New Mexico 87520-9711 **Tel:** 1 575 756-1617.
Profile: KZRM-FM is a commercial station owned by Chama Broadcasting Corporation. The format of the station is contemporary country. KZRM-FM broadcasts to the Albuquerque, NM area at 96.1 FM.
FM RADIO STATION

KZRO-FM
43095

Owner: Big Tree Communications
Editorial: 113 E Alma St, Mount Shasta, California 96067 **Tel:** 1 530 926-1332.
Email: zmail@zchannelradio.com
Web site: http://www.zchannelradio.com
Profile: KZRO-FM is a commercial station owned by Big Tree Communications. The format of the station is classic hits. KZRO-FM broadcasts to the Mount Shasta, CA area at 100.1 FM.
FM RADIO STATION

KZRR-FM
44080

Owner: iHeartMedia Inc.
Editorial: 5411 Jefferson St NE Ste 100, Albuquerque, New Mexico 87109-3485 **Tel:** 1 505 830-6400.
Email: kzrr@94rock.com
Web site: http://www.94rock.com
Profile: KZRR-FM is a commercial station owned by iHeartMedia Inc. The format of the station is rock music. KZRR-FM broadcasts to the Albuquerque, NM area at 94.1 FM.
FM RADIO STATION

KZRS-FM
41274

Owner: Rocking M Radio
Editorial: 5501 10th St, Great Bend, Kansas 67530-6319 **Tel:** 1 620 792-7108.
Web site: http://centralkansasradio.com/old-school-0179
Profile: KZRS-FM is a commercial station owned by Rocking M Radio. The format of the station is classic hits. KZRS-FM broadcasts to the Great Bend, KS area at 107.9 FM.
FM RADIO STATION

KZRV-FM
41166

Owner: Townsquare Media, LLC.
Editorial: 640 Lincoln Ave SE, Saint Cloud, Minnesota 56304-1024 **Tel:** 1 320 251-4422.
Web site: http://www.rev967.com
Profile: KZRV-FM is a commercial station owned by Townsquare Media, LLC. The format of the station is modern rock music. KZRV-FM broadcasts to the Minneapolis area at 96.7 FM.
FM RADIO STATION

KZRX-FM
43343

Owner: iHeartMedia Inc.
Editorial: 11291 39th St SW, Dickinson, North Dakota 58601-9206 **Tel:** 1 701 227-1876.
Web site: http://www.z92fm.net
Profile: KZRX-FM is a commercial station owned by iHeartMedia Inc. The format of the station is rock/album oriented rock. KZRX-FM broadcasts to the Dickinson, ND area at 92.1 FM.
FM RADIO STATION

KZRZ-FM
40935

Owner: Opus Media Partners
Editorial: 1200 N 18th St Ste D, Monroe, Louisiana 71201-5449 **Tel:** 1 318 387-3922.
Email: sunny983@lagniappebroadcasting.com
Web site: http://www.sunny983.com
Profile: KZRZ-FM is a commercial station owned by Opus Media Partners. The format of the station is adult contemporary music. KZRZ-FM broadcasts in the Monroe, LA area at 98.3 FM.
FM RADIO STATION

KZSB-AM
36354

Owner: Santa Barbara Broadcasting
Editorial: 1317 Santa Barbara St, Santa Barbara, California 93101-2016 **Tel:** 1 805 564-1290.
Email: voices@newspress.com
Web site: http://www.newspress.com
Profile: KZSB-AM is a commercial station owned by Santa Barbara Broadcasting. The format of the station is talk. KZSB-AM broadcasts to the Santa Barbara, CA area at 1290 AM.
AM RADIO STATION

KZSE-FM
41974

Owner: Minnesota Public Radio
Editorial: 206 S Broadway Ste 735, Rochester, Minnesota 55904-6510 **Tel:** 1 507 282-0910.
Web site: http://www.mpr.org/listen/stations/kxlcklse
Profile: KZSE-FM is a non-commercial station owned by Minnesota Public Radio. The format of the station is classical music programming. KZSE-FM broadcasts to the Rochester, MN area at 90.7 FM.
FM RADIO STATION

KZSJ-AM
36750

Editorial: 1630 Oakland Rd Ste A109, San Jose, California 95131-2450 **Tel:** 1 408 223-3130.
Email: qhradio@aol.com
Web site: http://www.quehuongmedia.com
Profile: KZSJ-AM is a commercial station owned by Adelante Media Group. The format of the station is ethnic and multicultural programming, including Vietnamese variety. KZSJ-AM broadcasts to the San Jose, CA area at 1120 AM.
AM RADIO STATION

KZSN-FM
44316

Owner: iHeartMedia Inc.
Editorial: 9323 E 37th St N, Wichita, Kansas 67226-2000 **Tel:** 1 316 494-6600.
Web site: http://1021thebull.iheart.com
Profile: KZSN-FM is a commercial station owned by iHeartMedia Inc. The format of the station is classic country. KZSN-FM broadcasts to the Wichita, KS area at 102.1 FM. The station's slogan is, "Wichita's New Country."
FM RADIO STATION

KZSP-FM
606073

Owner: R Communications
Editorial: 1201 N Jackson Rd Ste 900, McAllen, Texas 78501-5764 **Tel:** 1 956 992-8895.
Web site: http://www.supertejano1021.com
Profile: KZSP-FM is a commercial station owned by R Communications. The format of the station features

Tejano music. KZSP-FM broadcasts to the McAllen, TX area at 95.3.
FM RADIO STATION

KZSQ-FM 45004
Owner: Clarke Broadcasting Corp.
Editorial: 342 S Washington St, Sonora, California 95370 **Tel:** 1 209 533-1450.
Email: star927@clarkebroadcasting.com
Web site: http://www.kzsqfm.com
Profile: KZSQ-FM is a commercial station owned by Clark Broadcasting Corp. The format of the station is adult contemporary. KZSQ-FM broadcasts to the Sonora, CA area at 92.7 FM.
FM RADIO STATION

KZST-FM 40075
Owner: Redwood Empire Stereocasters
Editorial: 3392 Mendocino Ave, Santa Rosa, California 95403-2213 **Tel:** 1 707 528-4434.
Web site: http://www.kzst.com
Profile: KZST-FM is a commercial station owned by Redwood Empire Stereocasters. The format of the station is adult contemporary. KZST-FM broadcasts to the Santa Rosa, CA, area at 100.1 FM.
FM RADIO STATION

KZTA-FM 41387
Owner: Bustos Media, LLC
Editorial: 706 Butterfield Rd, Yakima, Washington 98901-2021 **Tel:** 1 509 457-1000.
Profile: KZTA-FM is a commercial station owned by Bustos Media, LLC. The format of the station is regional Mexican music. KZTA-FM broadcasts to the Yakima, WA area at 96.9 FM.
FM RADIO STATION

KZTB-FM 41886
Owner: Bustos Media, LLC
Editorial: 706 Butterfield Rd, Yakima, Washington 98901-2021 **Tel:** 1 509 457-1000.
Profile: KZTB-FM is a commercial station owned by Bustos Media, LLC. The format of the station is regional Mexican music. KZTB-FM broadcasts to the Yakima, WA area at 97.9 FM.
FM RADIO STATION

KZTD-AM 788813
Owner: Carrera (Emanuel)
Editorial: 2222 Main St, Little Rock, Arkansas 72206-1530 **Tel:** 1 501 308-7225.
Web site: http://www.fiestamexicana1350.com
Profile: KZTD-AM is a commercial station owned by Carrera (Emanuel). The format of the station is Regional Mexican. KZTD-AM broadcasts to the Little Rock, AR area at a frequency of 1350 AM.
AM RADIO STATION

KZTH-FM 526899
Owner: Love Station Inc.(The)
Editorial: 6600 W Highway 60, Ponca City, Oklahoma 74601-7926 **Tel:** 1 580 767-1400.
Email: mail@thehousefm.com
Web site: http://www.thehousefm.com
Profile: KZTH-FM is a non-commercial station owned by The Love Station Inc. The format of the station is contemporary Christian. KZTH-FM broadcasts to the Greater Oklahoma City, OK area (licensed to Piedmont, OK) at 88.5 FM.
FM RADIO STATION

KZTK-FM 691110
Owner: Vision Media Inc.
Editorial: 4 N Langer Ave, Casselton, North Dakota 58012 **Tel:** 1 701 347-5005.
Email: thetruck1039@yahoo.com
Web site: http://www.1039thetruck.com
Profile: KZTK-FM is a commercial station owned by Vision Media Inc. The format of the station is contemporary country. KZTK-FM broadcasts to the Fargo, ND area at 103.9 FM.
FM RADIO STATION

KZTL-FM 856673
Owner: Armada Media
Editorial: 307 E 4th St, North Platte, Nebraska 69101-6903 **Tel:** 1 308 532-3344.
Profile: KZTL-FM is a commercial station owned by Armada Media. The format of the station is adult contemporary. KZTL-FM airs locally at 93.5 FM.
FM RADIO STATION

KZTQ-FM 46673
Owner: Scott Communications LLC
Editorial: 961 Matley Ln, Ste 120, Reno, Nevada 89502-2119 **Tel:** 1 775 829-1964.
Web site: http://www.bob937.com
Profile: KZTQ-FM is a commercial station owned by Scott Communications LLC. The format of the station is adult hits. KZTQ-FM broadcasts to the Reno, NV area at 93.7 FM.
FM RADIO STATION

KZUA-FM 46639
Owner: Petracom
Editorial: 1838 Commerce Dr Ste A, Lakeside, Arizona 85929-7008
Web site: http://921kzua.com
Profile: KZUA-FM is a commercial station owned by Petracom. The format of the station is country music. KZUA-FM broadcasts to the Phoenix area at 92.1 FM.
FM RADIO STATION

KZUE-AM 35138
Owner: Galvan(Nancy)
Editorial: 2715 S Radio Rd, El Reno, Oklahoma 73036 **Tel:** 1 405 262-9184.
Email: kzue@aol.com
Profile: KZUE-AM is a commercial station owned by Nancy Galvan. The format of the station is Hispanic. KZUE-AM broadcasts to the Oklahoma City area at 1460 AM.
AM RADIO STATION

KZUH-FM 42573
Owner: Rocking M Radio
Editorial: 641 W Cloud St, Salina, Kansas 67401-5618 **Tel:** 1 785 827-2100.
Web site: http://www.salina-radio.com
Profile: KZUH-FM is a commercial station owned by Rocking M Radio. The format of the station is Top 40/ CHR. KZUH-FM broadcasts to the Salina, KS area at 92.7 FM.
FM RADIO STATION

KZUL-FM 41277
Owner: Mad Dog Wireless Inc.
Editorial: 2068 McCulloch Blvd N, Lake Havasu City, Arizona 86403 **Tel:** 1 928 855-1051.
Email: maddog@maddog.net
Web site: http://www.maddog.net
FM RADIO STATION

KZUM-FM 41275
Owner: Sunrise Communications, Inc.
Editorial: 3534 S 48th St Ste 6, Lincoln, Nebraska 68506-6425 **Tel:** 1 402 474-5086.
Web site: http://www.kzum.org
Profile: KZUM-FM is a non-commercial station owned by Sunrise Communications, Inc. The format of the station is variety. KZUM-FM broadcasts to the Lincoln, NE area at 89.3 FM.
FM RADIO STATION

KZUS-FM 46158
Owner: Bustos Media, LLC
Editorial: 110 E Broadway Ave Ste 1, Moses Lake, Washington 98837-5931
Web site: http://kzus.lazetaradio.com
Profile: KZUS-FM is a commercial station owned by Bustos Media, LLC. The format of the station is contemporary country music. KULE-FM broadcasts to the Ephrata, WA area at 92.3 FM.
FM RADIO STATION

KZUZ-FM 721621
Owner: Petracom
Editorial: 1838 Commerce Dr Ste A, Lakeside, Arizona 85929-7008 **Tel:** 1 928 368-8100.
Web site: http://www.whitemountainradio.com
Profile: KZUZ-FM is a commercial station owned by Petracom. The format of the station is classic country. KZUZ-FM broadcasts at a frequency of 93.5 to the Show Low, AZ area.
FM RADIO STATION

KZWA-FM 42665
Owner: B & C Broadcasting Inc.
Editorial: 305 Enterprise Blvd, Lake Charles, Louisiana 70601-3240 **Tel:** 1 337 491-9955.
Email: info@kzwafm.com
Web site: http://kzwafm.com
Profile: KZWA-FM is a commercial station owned by B & C Broadcasting Inc. The format of the station is urban contemporary music. KZWA-FM broadcasts to the Lake Charles, LA area at 104.9 FM.
FM RADIO STATION

KZWB-FM 342303
Owner: Wagonwheel Communications Corp.
Editorial: 40 Shoshone Ave, Green River, Wyoming 82935-5321 **Tel:** 1 307 875-6666.
Email: audio@theradionetwork.net
Web site: http://www.theradionetwork.net
Profile: KZWB-FM is a commercial station owned by Wagonwheel Communications Corp. The format of the station is classic hits. KZWB-FM broadcasts to the Green River, WY area at 97.9 FM.
FM RADIO STATION

KZWC-AM 37455
Owner: NRG Media LLC
Editorial: 1020 E 2nd St, Webster City, Iowa 50595-1754 **Tel:** 1 515 832-1570.
Profile: KZWC-AM is a commercial station owned by NRG Media LLC. The format of the station is oldies. KZWC-AM broadcasts to the Des Moines, IA area at 1570 AM.
AM RADIO STATION

KZWV-FM 431797
Owner: Zimmer Radio Group
Editorial: 1081 Osage Beach Rd, Osage Beach, Missouri 65065-2233 **Tel:** 1 573 746-7873.
Email: thewave@1019thewave.com
Web site: http://www.1019thewave.com
Profile: KZWV-FM is a commercial station owned by Zimmer Radio Group. The format of the station is adult contemporary. KZWV-FM broadcasts to the Osage Beach and Jefferson City areas of Missouri at 101.9 FM.
FM RADIO STATION

KZWY-FM 44873
Owner: Lovcom, Inc.
Editorial: 1716 Kroe Ln, Sheridan, Wyoming 82801-9681 **Tel:** 1 307 672-7421.
Email: news@sheridanmedia.com
Web site: http://www.sheridanmedia.com
Profile: KZWY-FM is a commercial station owned by Lovcom, Inc. The format of the station is classic rock. KZWY-FM broadcasts to the Sheridan, WY area at 94.9 FM.
FM RADIO STATION

KZXL-FM 525147
Owner: Pentagon Communications, LLC
Editorial: 121 S Cotton Sq, Lufkin, Texas 75904-2933 **Tel:** 1 936 634-6661.
Email: traffic@yatesmedia.com
Web site: http://www.hot963online.com
Profile: KZXL-FM is a commercial station owned by Pentagon Communications, LLC. The format of the station is urban adult contemporary. KZXL-FM broadcasts to the Lufkin, TX area at 96.3 FM.
FM RADIO STATION

KZXR-AM 36790
Owner: Casa Media Partners, LLC
Editorial: 152101 W County Road 12, Prosser, Washington 99350-7265 **Tel:** 1 509 786-1310.
Profile: KZXR-AM is a commercial station owned by Casa Media Partners, LLC. The format of the station is Hispanic sports. KZXR-AM broadcasts to the Prosser, WA area at 1310 AM. Station's tagline is "La Maquina".
AM RADIO STATION

KZXY-FM 46332
Owner: El Dorado Broadcasting
Editorial: 12370 Hesperia Rd Ste 16, Victorville, California 92395-5808 **Tel:** 1 760 241-1313.
Web site: http://www.y102fm.com
Profile: KZXY-FM is a commercial station owned by El Dorado Broadcasting. The format for the station is adult contemporary. KZXY-FM broadcasts to the Victorville, CA area at 102.3 FM.
FM RADIO STATION

KZYM-AM 36657
Owner: Zimmer Radio Inc.
Editorial: 2702 E 32nd St, Joplin, Missouri 64804 **Tel:** 1 417 624-1025.
Web site: http://www.1230thetalker.com
Profile: KZYM-AM is a commercial station owned by Zimmer Radio Group. The format of the station is talk. KZYM-AM broadcasts to the Joplin, MO area at 1230 AM.
AM RADIO STATION

KZYR-FM 41271
Owner: Cool Radio, LLC
Editorial: 275 Main St, Unit 0201, Edwards, Colorado 81632 **Tel:** 1 970 845-8565.
Web site: http://www.kzyr.com
FM RADIO STATION

KZYX-FM 41283
Owner: Mendocino County Public Broadcasting
Editorial: 9300 Highway 128, Philo, California 95466 **Tel:** 1 707 895-2324.
Email: pd@kzyx.org
Web site: http://www.kzyx.org
Profile: KZYX-FM is a non-commercial station owned by Mendocino County Public Broadcasting. The format of the station is variety. KZYX-FM broadcasts to the San Francisco area at 90.7 FM.
FM RADIO STATION

KZZA-FM 41874
Owner: Liberman Broadcasting Inc.
Editorial: 2410 Gateway Dr, Irving, Texas 75063-2727 **Tel:** 1 972 652-2900.
Web site: http://www.labonita1067.estrellatv.com
Profile: KZZA-FM is a commercial station owned by Liberman Broadcasting Inc. The format of the station is Latin Urban. KZZA-FM broadcasts to the Dallas area at 106.7 FM.
FM RADIO STATION

KZZB-AM 36127
Owner: Martin's Broadcasting Inc.
Editorial: 2531 Calder St, Beaumont, Texas 77702-1915 **Tel:** 1 409 833-0990.
Email: kzzbradio@yahoo.com
Web site: http://kzzbradio.org
Profile: KZZB-AM is a commercial station owned by Martin's Broadcasting Inc. The format of the station is gospel music. KZZB-AM broadcasts to the Beaumont, TX area at 990 AM.
AM RADIO STATION

KZZD-AM 445951
Owner: Entercom Communications Corp.
Editorial: 0700 SW Bancroft St, Portland, Oregon 97239-4226 **Tel:** 1 503 223-1441.
Profile: KZZD-AM is a commercial station owned by Entercom Communications Corp. The format of the station is Spanish language sports. KZZD-AM broadcasts to the Portland, OR area at 1390 FM.
AM RADIO STATION

KZZE-FM 43096
Owner: Bicoastal Media LLC
Editorial: 3624 Avion Dr, Medford, Oregon 97504 **Tel:** 1 541 772-4170.
Web site: http://www.kzze.com
Profile: KZZE-FM is a commercial station owned by Bicoastal Media LLC. The format of the station is rock music. KZZE-FM broadcasts to the Medford, OR area at 106.3 FM.
FM RADIO STATION

KZZI-FM 4349
Owner: Western South Dakota Broadcasting
Editorial: 2827 E Colorado Blvd, Spearfish, South Dakota 57783 **Tel:** 1 605 642-5747.
Email: eagle@dberadio.com
Web site: http://www.myeaglecountry.com
Profile: KZZI-FM is a commercial station owned by Western South Dakota Broadcasting. The format of the station is country. KZZI-FM broadcasts to the Spearfish, SD area at 95.9 FM.
FM RADIO STATION

KZZJ-AM 3514
Owner: Rugby Broadcasters Inc.
Editorial: 230 Highway 2 SE, Rugby, North Dakota 58368 **Tel:** 1 701 776-5254.
Email: kzzj@kzzj.com
Web site: http://www.kzzj.com
Profile: KZZJ-AM is a commercial station owned by Rugby Broadcasters Inc. The format of the station is agricultural and classic country music. KZZJ-AM broadcasts to the Rugby, ND area at 1450 AM.
AM RADIO STATION

KZZK-FM 4303
Owner: Staradio Corp.
Editorial: 329 Maine St, 1st Fl, Quincy, Illinois 62301 **Tel:** 1 217 224-4102.
Email: kzzk@staradio.com
Web site: http://www.kzzk.com
Profile: KZZK-FM is a commercial station owned by Staradio Corp. The format of the station is rock/ album-oriented rock. KZZK-FM broadcasts to the Quincy, IL, Hannibal, MO, Keokuk, IA area at 105.9 FM.
FM RADIO STATION

KZZL-FM 4633
Owner: Inland Northwest Broadcasting
Editorial: 1114 N Almon St, Moscow, Idaho 83843-8507 **Tel:** 1 208 882-2551.
Profile: KZZL-FM is commercial station owned by Inland Northwest Broadcasting. The format of the station is contemporary country. KZZL-FM broadcasts to the Moscow, ID area at 99.5 FM.
FM RADIO STATION

KZZN-AM 3514
Owner: Cody West
Editorial: 2651 County Road 191, Littlefield, Texas 79339-5846 **Tel:** 1 806 385-1490.
Web site: http://www.kzznradio.com
Profile: KZZN-AM is a commercial station owned by Cody West. The format of the station is classic country. KZZN-AM broadcasts to the Littlefield, TX area at 1490 AM.
AM RADIO STATION

KZZO-FM 4092
Owner: CBS Radio
Editorial: 280 Commerce Cir, Sacramento, California 95815-4212 **Tel:** 1 916 923-6800.
Web site: http://now100fm.cbslocal.com
Profile: KZZO-FM is a commercial station owned by CBS Radio. The format of the station is hot adult contemporary. KZZO-FM broadcasts to the Sacramento, CA area at 100.5 FM.
FM RADIO STATION

KZZP-FM 4162
Owner: iHeartMedia Inc.
Editorial: 4686 E Van Buren St Ste 300, Phoenix, Arizona 85008-6967 **Tel:** 1 602 374-6000.
Web site: http://www.1047kissfm.com
Profile: KZZP-FM is a commercial station owned by iHeartMedia Inc. The format of the station is Top 40/ CHR. KZZP-FM broadcasts to the Phoenix area at 104.7 FM.
FM RADIO STATION

KZZQ-FM 837002
Owner: Real Presence Radio
Tel: 1 701 795-0122.
Web site: http://yourcatholicradiostation.com
Profile: KZZQ-FM is a non-commercial station owned by Real Presence Radio. The format of the station is Catholic religion and talk. KZZQ-FM broadcasts locally at 101.9 FM to the Richardton, ND area.
FM RADIO STATION

KZZR-FM 4421
Owner: Bustos Media, LLC
Editorial: 5110 SE Stark St, Portland, Oregon 97215-1751 **Tel:** 1 503 234-5550.
Web site: http://www.bustosmedia.com
Profile: KZZR-FM is a commercial station owned by Bustos Media, LLC. The format of the station is Hispanic. KZZR-FM broadcasts to the Tillamook, OR area at 94.3 FM.
FM RADIO STATION

KZZS-FM 445517
Owner: Legend Communications
Editorial: 1221 Fort St, Buffalo, Wyoming 82834 **Tel:** 1 307 684-5126.
Email: klgt@vcn.com
Profile: KZZS-FM is a commercial station owned by Legend Communications. The format for the station is hot adult contemporary. KZZS-FM broadcasts to the Sheridan, WY area at 98.3 FM.
FM RADIO STATION

KZZT-FM 41276
Owner: Best Broadcast Group
Editorial: 1037County Rd., suite 2326, Moberly, Missouri 65270 **Tel:** 1 660 263-9390.
Email: kzzt@bestbroadcastgroup.com
Web site: http://www.kzztradio.com
Profile: KZZT-FM is a commercial station owned by Best Broadcast Group. The format of the station is classic rock music. KZZT-FM broadcasts to the Brookfield, MO, area at 105.5 FM.
FM RADIO STATION

KZZU-FM 44028
Owner: Queen B Inc.
Editorial: 500 W Boone Ave, Spokane, Washington 99201-2404 **Tel:** 1 509 323-9393.
Email: webmaster@kzzu.com
Web site: http://929zzu.com
Profile: KZZU-FM is a commercial station owned by Queen B Inc. The format of the station is hot adult contemporary. KZZU-FM broadcasts to the Spokane, WA area at 92.9 FM.
FM RADIO STATION

KZZW-FM 857234
Owner: Brooke Williams Trissel
Profile: KZZW-FM is a commercial station owned by Brooke Williams Trissel. The format of the station is classical music. KZZW-FM broadcasts to the Mooreland, OK area at a frequency of 104.5 FM.
FM RADIO STATION

KZZX-FM 45851
Owner: Burt Broadcasting Inc.
Editorial: 501 S Florida Ave, Alamogordo, New Mexico 88310 **Tel:** 1 575 434-1414.
Email: burtbroadcasting@bbiradio.net
Profile: KZZX-FM is a commercial station owned by Burt Broadcasting Inc. The format of the station is contemporary country. KZZX-FM broadcasts to the Alamagordo, NM area at 105.3 FM.
FM RADIO STATION

KZZY-FM 41018
Owner: Double Z Broadcasting Inc.
Editorial: 320 Walnut St W, Devils Lake, North Dakota 58301-3506 **Tel:** 1 701 662-7563.
Web site: http://www.lrradioworks.com/kzzy
Profile: KZZY-FM is a commercial station owned by Double Z Broadcasting Inc. The format of the station is country music. KZZY-FM broadcasts to the Fargo, ND area at 103.5 FM.
FM RADIO STATION

KZZZ-AM 37186
Owner: Cameron Broadcasting Inc.
Editorial: 2350 Miracle Mile Ste 300, Bullhead City, Arizona 86442-7505 **Tel:** 1 928 763-5586.
Web site: http://www.talkatoz.com
Profile: KZZZ-AM is a commercial station owned by Cameron Broadcasting. The format of the station is news and talk programming. KZZZ-AM broadcasts to the Bullhead City, AZ area at 1490 AM.
AM RADIO STATION

Liberty News Radio Network 763229
Editorial: 1259 N 100 W, American Fork, Utah 84003-2703 **Tel:** 1 801 350-3990.
Web site: http://libertynewsradio.com
RADIO NETWORK

Lifestyle Talk Radio Network 46923
Owner: BizTalkRadioNetworks LLC
Editorial: 401 Shippan Ave, Stamford, Connecticut 06902-6075 **Tel:** 1 817 274-1609.
Web site: http://www.biztalkradio.com/LifeStyleTalkRadio
Profile: Radio network distributing talk programming 24 hours a day, five days a week. The network offers a potpourri of live listener call-in programming covering a wide array of issues. Lifestyle Talk Radio, formerly known as Liberty Broadcasting, offers stations a new kind of talk radio that is entertaining, informative and engaging. This approach represents a fresh, compelling alternative to some of the combative styles on the radio today that alienate listeners, or lofty, high-minded rhetoric that lacks any real energy.
RADIO NETWORK

LifeTalk Radio Network 46929
Owner: Adventist Media Center
Editorial: 11291 Pierce St, Riverside, California 92505-2705 **Tel:** 1 800 775-4673.
Email: office@lifetalk.net
Web site: http://www.lifetalk.net
Profile: Radio outlet showcasing Christian and religious-themed programming. Aims to improve listeners lives through interactive talk radio, balanced with quality music and a profound faith-based programming philosophy.
RADIO NETWORK

Linder Farm Network 739351
Editorial: 255 Cedardale Dr Se, Owatonna, Minnesota 55060-4425 **Tel:** 1 507 444-9224.
Web site: http://www.linderfarmnetwork.com
Profile: Produces programming for Minnesota farmers and agriculture.
REGIONAL RADIO NETWORKS

Local News Digital 836432
Owner: Reising Radio Partners Incorporated
Editorial: 825 Washington St, Columbus, Indiana 47201-6265 **Tel:** 1 812 379-1077 2201.
Web site: http://localnewsdigital.com
Profile: Local News Digital provides news stories for Bartholomew, Jackson and Johnson counties in Indiana. Send news in 100 words or less, to their main email address. The news segments can be heard on WTGB-FM, WRZQ-FM, and WXCH-FM.
REGIONAL RADIO NETWORKS

The Louisiana Farm Bureau Agri-news Radio Network 47051
Editorial: 10500 Coursey Blvd Ste 104, Baton Rouge, Louisiana 70816-4045 **Tel:** 1 225 291-2727.
Web site: http://www.lfbarn.com
Profile: Provides state and national agri-news, market information & analysis, current events in the cotton industry, and agri-weather forecasts to 82 stations in Louisiana. Part of the Lousiana Radio Network Inc.
REGIONAL RADIO NETWORKS

Louisiana Radio Network 47052
Editorial: 10500 Coursey Blvd Ste 104, Baton Rouge, Louisiana 70816-4045 **Tel:** 1 225 291-2727.
Email: news@louisianaradionetwork.com
Web site: http://www.louisianaradionetwork.com
Profile: Provides daily market updates and state news, legislative coverage, sports, and weather throughout the day on weekdays to 84 affiliates, as well as hurricane updates and warnings when necessary.
REGIONAL RADIO NETWORKS

Martin Agri Country Network 239145
Editorial: 475 7th Ave, Deer Trail, Colorado 80105 **Tel:** 1 303 769-4432.
Email: aginfo@martinagnetwork.com
Web site: http://martinagnetwork.com
Profile: Colorado's only agriculture radio network serving stations across the state.
REGIONAL RADIO NETWORKS

Metro News Network 815901
Tel: 1 312 878-6420.
Email: newsdesk@mymetronews.org
Web site: http://www.mymetronews.org
Profile: Metro News Network includes news and information for its affiliates.
RADIO NETWORK

Metronews Radio Network 47079
Editorial: 1111 Virginia St E, Charleston, West Virginia 25301-2406 **Tel:** 1 304 346-7055.
Web site: http://www.wvmetronews.com
Profile: The Voice of West Virginia, MetroNews is a network composed of 59 individual radio affiliates throughout West Virginia, reaching every county in the state. News information, story ideas and press releases should be sent to the news director.
REGIONAL RADIO NETWORKS

Mid-America Ag Network 47048
Owner: Steckline Communications
Editorial: 1632 S Maize Rd, Wichita, Kansas 67209-3912 **Tel:** 1 316 721-8484.
Web site: http://www.midamericaagnetwork.com
Profile: Distributes up-to-the-minute agricultural news, weather, cash grain prices, market updates and analysis throughout the day to 44 stations in Kansas and Nebraska. Market information comes from the Kansas City Board of Trade, Chicago Board of Trade and the Chicago Mercantile Exchange. Mid-America Ag Network is part of the Mid-America Network, which also includes the Mid-America News Network and Mid-America Sports Network. They have 28 affiliate station and their CUME is 480,000.
REGIONAL RADIO NETWORKS

Mid-America News Network 231739
Owner: Steckline Communications
Editorial: 1632 S Maize Rd, Wichita, Kansas 67209-3912 **Tel:** 1 316 721-8484.
Web site: http://www.midamericaagnetwork.com
Profile: The Mid-America News Network provides two options for up-to-the-minute news in Kansas and Nebraska. The traditional news network features a two-minute report, with in-depth coverage of news that's important to middle America. The Mid-America NewsMinute hits the highlights and headlines topping the day's news in Kansas. In addition, the Mid-America NewsMinute features two reports daily on Wall Street and its impact on Kansas. Both networks feature the latest sports headlines and stories, specializing in home state teams.
REGIONAL RADIO NETWORKS

Midwest Racing Radio Network 870032
Owner: Midwest Racing Radio Network LLC
Tel: 1 701 219-3273.
Email: midwestracingradio@gmail.com
Profile: Motorsports talk network.
RADIO NETWORK

Minnesota News Network 47056
Owner: Learfield Communications, Inc.
Editorial: 100 N 6th St Ste 476A, Minneapolis, Minnesota 55403-1511 **Tel:** 1 612 321-7200.
Email: newsroom@mnnradio.com
Web site: http://www.minnesotanewsnetwork.com
Profile: Network produces and distributes news, sports and feature programming to commercial stations across Minnesota. MRN is a division of Learfield Communications, Inc.
REGIONAL RADIO NETWORKS

Minnesota Public Radio Network 47094
Owner: American Public Media Group
Editorial: 480 Cedar St, Saint Paul, Minnesota 55101-2217 **Tel:** 1 651 290-1500.
Email: newsroom@mpr.org
Web site: http://www.mpr.org
Profile: Distributes news, public affairs and business programming, as well as jazz and classical music to more than 37 affiliates throughout the state of Minnesota and adjacent states. The mission of Minnesota Public Radio is to enrich the mind and nourish the spirit through radio, related technology and services.
REGIONAL RADIO NETWORKS

Mississippi Agri Network 47057
Editorial: 6311 Ridgewood Rd, Jackson, Mississippi 39211-2035 **Tel:** 1 601 957-1700.
Email: news@telesouth.com
Web site: http://www.msagrinews.com
Profile: Serves 68 stations in Mississippi with farm and agriculture news. From daybreak to sundown the AgriNews Network is a dependable source of information for market prices, new trends and most importantly weather updates.
REGIONAL RADIO NETWORKS

Mississippi News Network 47058
Editorial: 6311 Ridgewood Rd, Jackson, Mississippi 39211-2035 **Tel:** 1 601 957-1700.
Email: news@telesouth.com
Web site: http://www.newsms.fm
Profile: A professional broadcast news network with affiliated stations across Mississippi. Affiliates receive hourly Mississippi newscasts via satellite from 6AM to 6PM Monday through Friday, and 6AM to 9AM on Saturday. The network also airs three sportscasts daily and one on Saturday.
REGIONAL RADIO NETWORKS

Mississippi Public Broadcasting Radio Network 235306
Editorial: 3825 Ridgewood Rd, Jackson, Mississippi 39211-6453 **Tel:** 1 601 432-6565.
Email: programmingquestions@mpbonline.org
Web site: http://www.mpbonline.org
Profile: Mississippi Public Broadcasting is a state agency that encompasses a network of commercial-free radio, television, learning and community outreach services designed to empower and enrich the lives of Mississippians through the creative use of technologies to deliver programs and services that educate, entertain, inspire and inform.
REGIONAL RADIO NETWORKS

Missourinet 47062
Owner: Learfield Communications, Inc.
Editorial: 505 Hobbs Rd, Jefferson City, Missouri 65109-5788 **Tel:** 1 573 893-2829.
Email: info@missourinet.com
Web site: http://www.missourinet.com
Profile: The Missourinet covers the legislature, state government and the top stories from throughout the state. Serves 65 affiliates in Missouri with news, sports, and features throughout the day.
REGIONAL RADIO NETWORKS

Money Matters Financial Network 231266
Editorial: 75 Montebello Rd, Suffern, New York 10901 **Tel:** 1 800 433-0323.
Web site: http://www.mmfn.net
Profile: Money Matters Financial Network is the only true interactive financial network where you ask the questions and choose the topics. The network produces the show Money Matters which is syndicated on seven stations in the tristate NY/NJ/CT area.
RADIO NETWORK

MRN - Motor Racing Network 46933
Owner: International Speedway Corporation
Editorial: 555 Mrn Dr NW, Concord, North Carolina 28027-3620 **Tel:** 1 704 262-6700.
Email: feedback@mrnradio.com
Web site: http://www.mrn.com/?homepage=true
Profile: Network providing live coverage of NASCAR stock car racing plus a weekly telephone talk show and a daily news show. The network also covers over 80 races a year for the NASCAR Winston Cup Series, NASCAR Busch Series, Grand National Division and NASCAR Craftsman Truck Series.
RADIO NETWORK

NBC Sports Radio Network 827322
Editorial: 30 Rockefeller Plz, New York, New York 10112-0015 **Tel:** 1 212 664-4444.
Email: hello@nbcsportsradio.com
Web site: http://www.nbcsportsradio.com
Profile: NBC Sports Radio Network launched in Fall 2012. It is produced by NBC Sports Group and distributed by WestwodOne. The network covers all sports 24/7.
RADIO NETWORK

Nebraska Radio Network 755527
Owner: Learfield Communications, Inc.
Editorial: 4343 O St, Lincoln, Nebraska 68510-1753 **Tel:** 1 402 475-0256.
Web site: http://www.nebraskaradionetwork.com
Profile: The Nebraska Radio Network is a statewide news network providing news and sports programs to more than 35 radio stations. The network covers the legislature and state government from its bureau in Lincoln and also reports on news from throughout the state with the help of affiliate correspondents. Sister networks include: Missourinet, Radio Iowa, Wisconsin Radio Network, SportsTalk Radio Network, South Carolina Radio Network and Brownfield.
REGIONAL RADIO NETWORKS

Network Indiana 47044
Owner: Emmis Communications Corp.
Editorial: 40 Monument Cir Ste 400, Indianapolis, Indiana 46204-3011 **Tel:** 1 317 637-4638.
Email: news@networkindiana.com
Web site: http://www.networkindiana.com
Profile: Indiana's only radio news network provides several state-focused talk shows and the latest updates on news, sports and weather to more than 60 stations across the state.
REGIONAL RADIO NETWORKS

New Jersey Public Radio 47086
Owner: New York Public Radio
Editorial: 160 Varick St, New York, New York 10013-1220 **Tel:** 1 646 829-4400.
Web site: http://www.wnyc.org/section/njpr
Profile: Provides a variety of news, talk, business and public affairs programming to radio stations throughout the state of New Jersey. New Jersey Public Radio covers politics, education, the New Jersey Statehouse, health and medical affairs, environmental issues, youth violence, urban affairs, sports and business in the Garden State. The network is owned by New York Public Radio.
REGIONAL RADIO NETWORKS

NHPR/New Hampshire Public Radio 350162
Owner: New Hampshire Public Radio, Inc.
Editorial: 2 Pillsbury St, Concord, New Hampshire 03301-3523 **Tel:** 1 603 228-8910.
Web site: http://www.nhpr.org
Profile: New Hampshire Public Radio is a non-commercial radio network owned by New Hampshire Public Radio, Inc. New Hampshire Public Radio broadcasts to nine affiliates throughout the state of New Hampshire and surrounding areas. The network offers news and cultural programming, as well as folk music.
REGIONAL RADIO NETWORKS

North Carolina News Network 47067
Owner: Curtis Media Group
Editorial: 3012 Highwoods Blvd Ste 200, Raleigh, North Carolina 27604-1031 **Tel:** 1 919 878-1724.
Web site: http://www.ncnn.com
Profile: Statewide network that produces news stories for over 75 stations from the coast to the mountains. NCNN broadcast newscasts via satellite Monday through Saturday. All capsules include the latest in state news, plus the top sports story.
REGIONAL RADIO NETWORKS

North Dakota News Network 47071
Editorial: 2501 13th Ave S, Fargo, North Dakota 58103-3601 **Tel:** 1 701 237-5000.
Email: americanagnetwork@gmail.com
Web site: http://www.americanagnetwork.com
Profile: The North Dakota News Network delivers news, sports, and traveler's weather & summary to 46 stations in North Dakota, South Dakota, and Western Minnesota.
REGIONAL RADIO NETWORKS

Northern Ag Network 962973
Owner: Northern Broadcasting System, Inc.
Editorial: 600 1st Ave N, Billings, Montana 59101-2654 **Tel:** 1 406 252-6661.
Web site: http://www.northernag.net
Profile: Provides hourly farm news and market reports, weather programs and special features.
REGIONAL RADIO NETWORKS

Northern Broadcasting System 740519
Editorial: 600 1St Ave N, Billings, Montana 59101-2654 **Tel:** 1 406 252-6661.
Email: newsdesk@northernbroadcasting.com
Web site: http://www.northernbroadcasting.com
Profile: Northern Broadcasting System delivers nearly 200 radio programs each week via satellite to listeners in nine states and Canada. It includes the Northern Ag Network which provides farm news and market reports, weather programs and special features, and the Northern News Network, which provides Montana state news programs along with Montana sports, weather and legislative reports.
RADIO NETWORK

Northwest Ag Information Network 47098
Editorial: 173 Baker Ranch Rd, Walla Walla, Washington 99362-6202 **Tel:** 1 509 782-9444.
Web site: http://www.aginfo.net
Profile: Radio programming network producing daily features on agricultural, natural resources and community news topics for affiliates in Oregon, Washington and Idaho.
REGIONAL RADIO NETWORKS

NPR/National Public Radio 46970
Owner: National Public Radio
Editorial: 1111 N Capitol St NE, Washington, District Of Columbia 20002-7502 **Tel:** 1 202 513-2000.
Web site: http://www.npr.org

United States of America

Profile: National Public Radio is an internationally acclaimed producer and distributor of non-commercial news, talk and entertainment programming. A privately supported, not-for-profit membership organization, NPR serves a growing audience of more than 34.6 million Americans each week in partnership with more than 849 independently operated, non-commercial public radio stations. NPR also produces content worldwide for satellite radio, the Internet and podcasting. Press Releases may be sent via the online form located here: http://help.npr.org/customer/portal/emails/new
RADIO NETWORK

NPR/National Public Radio - Austin Bureau 231115
Editorial: 4107 Medical Pkwy, Austin, Texas 78756-3735 **Tel:** 1 512 371-7303.
RADIO NETWORK

NPR/National Public Radio - Chicago Bureau 46992
Editorial: 848 E Grand Ave, Chicago, Illinois 60611-3509 **Tel:** 1 312 948-4600.
RADIO NETWORK

NPR/National Public Radio - Culver City Bureau 128299
Editorial: 9909 Jefferson Blvd, Culver City, California 90232-3505 **Tel:** 1 310 815-4200.
RADIO NETWORK

NPR/National Public Radio - Miami Bureau 821849
Editorial: 172 NE 15th St, Miami, Florida 33132-1348 **Tel:** 1 305 995-1717.
RADIO NETWORK

NPR/National Public Radio - New York Bureau 46991
Editorial: 11 W 42nd St Fl 19, New York, New York 10036-8002 **Tel:** 1 212 880-3500.
Profile: All faxes should be sent to the network headquarters in Washington, DC. Press Releases may be sent via the online form located here: http://help.npr.org/customer/portal/emails/new
RADIO NETWORK

NPR/National Public Radio - San Francisco Bureau 47003
Editorial: 2601 Mariposa St, San Francisco, California 94110-1426
Profile: Press Releases may be sent via the online form located here: http://help.npr.org/customer/portal/emails/new
RADIO NETWORK

Ohio Ag Net 755926
Owner: Agri Communications
Editorial: 1625 Bethel Rd, Columbus, Ohio 43220-2071 **Tel:** 1 614 273-0465.
Email: ocjstaff@ocj.com
Web site: http://www.ocj.com
Profile: Ohio Ag Net provides farm news and information to Ohio producers through traditional local radio stations, a web site, and custom daily reports delivered to farmers' computers through e-mail.
REGIONAL RADIO NETWORKS

The Ohio News Network 47087
Editorial: 605 S Front St Ste 300, Columbus, Ohio 43215-5777 **Tel:** 1 614 460-3850.
Web site: http://www.onnradio.com
Profile: Regional radio news service provides news, sports and weather to affiliate stations.
REGIONAL RADIO NETWORKS

Ohio Public Radio Network 153736
Editorial: 2400 Olentangy River Rd, Columbus, Ohio 43210-1027 **Tel:** 1 614 292-9678.
Web site: http://radio.wosu.org
Profile: Network provides in-depth reports for Ohio's 40-plus public radio stations.
REGIONAL RADIO NETWORKS

Oklahoma News Network 47083
Owner: iHeartMedia Inc.
Editorial: 1900 NW Expressway Ste 1000, Oklahoma City, Oklahoma 73118-1854 **Tel:** 1 405 858-1458.
Profile: Supplies 45 affiliates in Oklahoma with news programming.
REGIONAL RADIO NETWORKS

One Radio Network 830063
Email: email@oneradionetwork.com
Web site: http://www.oneradionetwork.com
Profile: The radio network airs talk show on mostly health, wealth and well being.
RADIO NETWORK

Oregon Public Broadcasting Network 445961
Editorial: 7140 SW Macadam Ave, Portland, Oregon 97219 **Tel:** 1 503 244-9900.
Email: opbnews@opb.org
Web site: http://www.opb.org
Profile: With the goal of developing life-long learning opportunities for people, OPB is continuing to develop new ways to bring information to communities through traditional broadcasting services as well as newer distribution sources available through the Internet, including audio and video streaming, and digital broadcasting. OPB is committed to bringing audiences trusted, well-informed, in-depth coverage of important issues as well as entertaining programming that makes a positive difference in people's lives.
REGIONAL RADIO NETWORKS

Pacifica Radio Network 46967
Owner: Pacifica Foundation, Inc.
Editorial: 1925 Martin Luther King Jr Way, Berkeley, California 94704-1037 **Tel:** 1 510 849-2590.
Email: contact@pacifica.org
Web site: http://pacificanetwork.org
Profile: Producer and distributor of news features and reports for a national radio audience. The goal of the network is to promote the full distribution of public information and to report news and topics not commonly addressed in the mainstream media.
RADIO NETWORK

The Pennsylvania Sports Network 77342
Editorial: 863 Benner Pike, State College, Pennsylvania 16801-7315 **Tel:** 1 814 231-0953.
Web site: http://www.pennlive.com/sportsjamnet
Profile: Network providing sports programs of interest to Central Pennsylvanian listeners. The company boasts the only regionally syndicated radio sports programs in the country targeting one state.
REGIONAL RADIO NETWORKS

Performance Racing Network 790576
Owner: Speedway Motorsports, Inc.
Editorial: 5555 Concord Pkwy S, Concord, North Carolina 28027-4600 **Tel:** 1 704 455-3228.
Web site: http://www.goprn.com
Profile: Performance Racing Network broadcasts all NASCAR-sanctioned Sprint Cup and Nationwide Series events held at Speedway Motorsports-controlled tracks which include Atlanta, Bristol, Infineon, Las Vegas, Charlotte Motor Speedway, New Hampshire, Kentucky Speedway and Texas. It also assists the Indianapolis Motor Speedway Radio Network for the Brickyard 400. Performance Racing Network and Motor Racing Network on most occasions share the same radio affiliates.
RADIO NETWORK

Prairie Public Broadcasting 433428
Editorial: 207 5th St N, Fargo, North Dakota 58102-4827 **Tel:** 1 701 241-6900.
Email: info@prairiepublic.org
Web site: http://www.prairiepublic.org
Profile: Prairie Public is a trusted public service dedicated to building an exciting and productive future for the prairie and its people. It offers a view of the world through national and regional radio programming. It creates a forum for the most important issues facing our region with locally produced, topical documentaries.
REGIONAL RADIO NETWORKS

Premiere Radio Network 46986
Owner: iHeartMedia Inc.
Editorial: 15260 Ventura Blvd Ste 400, Sherman Oaks, California 91403-5300 **Tel:** 1 818 377-5300.
Web site: http://www.premierenetworks.com/default.aspx
Profile: Premiere Radio Networks, a subsidiary of iHeartMedia Inc., was founded in 1987. It syndicates more than 100 radio programs and services to more than 7,800 radio affiliations and reaches over 180 million listeners weekly. Premiere Radio is the number one radio network in the country and has featured such personalities as Rush Limbaugh, Jim Rome, Casey Kasem, Blair Garner and Carson Daly. In addition, Premiere acts as the sales representative for several non-owned radio networks such as the WOR Talk Network and XM Satellite Radio.
RADIO NETWORK

Premiere Radio Network - Grants Pass Bureau 47026
Editorial: 777 NE 7th St, Grants Pass, Oregon 97526-1632 **Tel:** 1 541 955-0100.
RADIO NETWORK

Premiere Radio Network - New York Bureau 231081
Editorial: 1270 Avenue Of The Americas, New York, New York 10020 **Tel:** 1 212 445-3900.
RADIO NETWORK

PRI/Public Radio International 46973
Editorial: 401 2nd Ave N Ste 500, Minneapolis, Minnesota 55401-2097 **Tel:** 1 612 338-5000.
Web site: http://www.pri.org
Profile: Public Radio International, an independent, non-profit corporation, is the nation's leading developer and supplier of non-commercial audio content. PRI's 400 hours of weekly programming falls into four general formats: News and information, comedy and variety, classical music and contemporary music. The programming is broadcast and streamed online by its 400+ affiliate stations throughout the United States and Guam and is available internationally through World Radio Network and nationwide via Sirius Satellite Radio.
RADIO NETWORK

Pulse of Radio 46980
Editorial: 1065 Avenue Of The Americas, Fl 3, New York, New York 10018 **Tel:** 1 212 536-3600.
Web site: http://www.pulseofradio.com
Profile: Network providing a wide range of music and general entertainment programming services. Distributes music formats for adult contemporary, new adult contemporary, alternative rock, classical, urban contemporary, talk and country music genres. Talk shows spotlight the music and entertainment industries. Affiliated with United Stations Radio Networks.
RADIO NETWORK

Pulse of Radio - Nashville Bureau 47010
Editorial: 1108 17th Ave S, Ste B, Nashville, Tennessee 37212-2291 **Tel:** 1 615 340-0077.
Web site: http://www.pulseofradio.com
RADIO NETWORK

Radio America 47991
Owner: American Studies Center(The)
Editorial: 1100 N Glebe, 9th Fl, Arlington, Virginia 22201 **Tel:** 1 703 302-1000.
Email: affiliates@radioamerica.org
Web site: http://www.radioamerica.org
Profile: Radio America is a division of The American Studies Center. The network is driven by its commitment to traditional American values, limited government and the free market. The network features news and talk programs on weekdays and a variety of special programs on weekends.
RADIO NETWORK

Radio Bilingue 657922
Owner: Radio Bilingüe, Inc.
Editorial: 5005 E Belmont Ave, Fresno, California 93727-2441 **Tel:** 1 800 509-4772.
Email: mail@radiobilingue.org
Web site: http://www.radiobilingue.org
Profile: The network is a provider and distributor of Latino public radio programming.
RADIO NETWORK

Radio Disney 46984
Owner: Walt Disney Co.
Editorial: 3800 W Alameda Ave Fl 17, Burbank, California 91505-4300 **Tel:** 1 818 973-4680.
Web site: http://radio.disney.com
Profile: Radio Disney, created by ABC Radio Network, launched in 1996. Radio Disney targets children, ages 2 to 11, with 24-hour interactive daily programming. Music screened for wholesomeness accounts for 90 percent of the programming, including pop, oldies, kids' songs, and television and movie soundtracks.
RADIO NETWORK

Radio Disney - Dallas Bureau 47028
Editorial: 13725 Montfort Dr, Dallas, Texas 75240 **Tel:** 1 972 448-3335.
RADIO NETWORK

Radio Free Asia 76231
Editorial: 2025 M St NW, Ste 300, Washington, District Of Columbia 20036 **Tel:** 1 202 530-4900.
Email: contact@rfa.org
Web site: http://www.rfa.org
Profile: Radio Free Asia (RFA) is a private, non-profit corporation broadcasting news and information in nine languages to listeners in Asia who do not have access to free news media. The purpose of RFA is to deliver accurate and timely news, information and commentary, and to provide a forum for a variety of opinions and voices from within Asian countries.
RADIO NETWORK

Radio Free Europe/Radio Liberty 76233
Editorial: 1201 Connecticut Ave NW, Washington, District Of Columbia 20036-2630 **Tel:** 1 202 457-6900.
Web site: http://www.rferl.org
Profile: The mission of Radio Free Europe/Radio Liberty is to promote democratic values and institutions by disseminating factual information and ideas. From Central Europe to the Pacific, from the Baltic to the Black Sea, from Russia to Central Asia to the Persian Gulf, countries are struggling to overcome autocratic institutions, violations of human rights, centralized economies, ethnic and religious hostilities, regional conflicts, and controlled media. Stability throughout this region, based on democracy and free-market economies, is essential to global peace.
RADIO NETWORK

Radio Iowa 47045
Owner: Learfield Communications, Inc.
Editorial: 2700 Grand Ave, Des Moines, Iowa 50312-5215 **Tel:** 1 515 282-1984.
Email: radioiowa@learfield.com
Web site: http://www.radioiowa.com
Profile: Radio Iowa started in 1987 and now provides news, sports and traffic reports to more than 40 radio stations statewide. Sports coverage includes high school and college sports across the state.
REGIONAL RADIO NETWORKS

Radio Marti 76289
Editorial: 4201 NW 77th Ave, Doral, Florida 33166-6728 **Tel:** 1 305 437-7012.
Email: editor@martinoticias.com
Web site: http://www.martinoticias.com
Profile: Network broadcasting news from the United States to the island of Cuba, with the goal of presenting democratic ideals and information to its citizens. The network airs an all news format.
RADIO NETWORK

Radio Oklahoma Network 429211
Owner: Griffin Communications/QuinStar Radio Networks
Editorial: 7401 N Kelley Ave, Oklahoma City, Oklahoma 73111-8420 **Tel:** 1 405 843-6641.
Web site: http://www.radiooklahoma.net
Profile: Radio Oklahoma Network is a statewide radio network providing news, weather, agriculture reports and sports information to radio stations across Oklahoma. The network is a partnership between Griffin Communications and QuinStar Radio Networks.
REGIONAL RADIO NETWORKS

Radio One 136691
Owner: Urban One, Inc.
Editorial: 8515 Georgia Ave Fl 9, Silver Spring, Maryland 20910-3403 **Tel:** 1 301 306-1111.
Web site: http://urban1.com/vtq-portfolio/radio-one
Profile: Radio One was founded in 1980 and primarily targets African Americans. The network owns and/or operates 69 stations in 22 markets. Many of these stations are in the top 20 African American radio markets. The service also programs one channel on the XM Satellite Radio system. The company's strategy is to expand within existing markets and into new markets that have a significant African American presence.
RADIO NETWORK

Radio Pennsylvania Network 47070
Editorial: 4801 Lindle Rd, Harrisburg, Pennsylvania 17111-2444 **Tel:** 1 800 735-8400.
Web site: http://www.radiopa.com
Profile: Radio Pennsylvania offers a wide array of programming and services to its affiliates, including news, sports, weather, special seasonal programs and live events from the state capital. The network also provides live game coverage, including pre- and post-game analysis, for Penn State, University of Pittsburgh, and all professional sports teams in the state.
REGIONAL RADIO NETWORKS

RAF-STL 908540
Owner: Radio Arts Foundation
Editorial: 7711 Carondelet Ave Ste 302, Saint Louis, Missouri 63105-3313 **Tel:** 1 314 881-3523.
Email: info@rafstl.org
Web site: http://www.rafstl.org
Profile: RAF-STL is the station for the Radio Arts Foundation in St. Louis, broadcasting classical music at 107.3 FM or 96.3-HD2. Radio Arts Foundation is a non-profit organization dedicated to filling the void left when longtime St. Louis classical station KFUO Classic 99 FM went off the air. The station includes broadcasts of live performances, interview with conductors, performers and music personalities, and programming that includes orchestral, chamber, jazz, blues, opera and symphonic music.
FM RADIO STATION

Real Wealth Radio Network 427178
Editorial: 114 Main St, Kewaskum, Wisconsin 53040-8931 **Tel:** 1 877 825-7579.
Email: info@realwealthradio.com
Web site: http://realwealthmedia.com
Profile: The Real Wealth Radio Network produces the Real Wealth Radio program.
REGIONAL RADIO NETWORKS

Reclaiming America For Christ 960191
Owner: Reclaiming America for Christ
Editorial: 1230 N Sooner Rd, Edmond, Oklahoma 73034-7163 **Tel:** 1 405 796-7729.
Web site: http://reclaimamericaforchrist.org
Profile: Christian talk radio network.
RADIO NETWORK

Red River Farm Network 395046
Editorial: 1407 24th Ave S, Grand Forks, North Dakota 58201-6761 **Tel:** 1 701 795-1315.
Email: rrfn@rrfn.com
Web site: http://www.rrfn.com
Profile: Red River Farm Network includes all farming information, including market recaps, livestock, weather forecasts and equipment.
REGIONAL RADIO NETWORKS

The Refuge Media Group 773991
Editorial: 537 Charles Ave, Saint Paul, Minnesota 55103-1910 **Tel:** 1 952 288-2886.
Web site: http://www.refugeradio.com
Profile: The Refuge serves as a network for Christ-centered communities on-air, on-line, and face-to-face throughout the upper Midwest.
REGIONAL RADIO NETWORKS

Republic Broadcasting Network 763208
Editorial: Round Rock, Texas **Tel:** 1 512 246-9549.
Web site: http://republicbroadcasting.org
RADIO NETWORK

RFD Illinois Radio Network 47039
Editorial: 1701 Towanda Ave, Bloomington, Illinois 61701-2057 **Tel:** 1 309 557-3163.
Web site: http://www.farmweeknow.com/radio.aspx
Profile: A service of the Illinois Agricultural Association, RFD Illinois provides agricultural news, markets and weather to farmers statewide.
REGIONAL RADIO NETWORKS

Rumbera Network 963589

Owner: Rumbera Network
Editorial: 5731 NW 74th Ave, Miami, Florida 33166-4215 **Tel:** 1 305 549-8477.
Web site: http://www.rumberanetworkmiami.com
Profile: Rumbera Network fue fundada en Valencia, Estado Carabobo el 30 de septiembre de 1994. Se expandió por varias ciudades de Venezuela. Están en Suramérica, el Caribe, Europa y Norteamérica. Rumbera Network was founded in Valencia, Carabobo in September 1994. It was then expanded to several cities in Venezuela. They are now in South America, the Caribbean, Europe and North America.
RADIO NETWORK

Salem Music Network 46934

Owner: Salem Media Group, Inc.
Editorial: 402 Bna Dr, Nashville, Tennessee 37217-2519 **Tel:** 1 615 367-2210.
Email: info@salemmusicnetwork.com
Web site: http://www.salemmusicnetwork.com
Profile: Salem Music Network provides 24-hour, adult contemporary Christian, praise and southern gospel music and programming vvia digital satellite to more than 250 radio stations throughout the US and Canada. Salem Music Network is just one of the programming options provided by Salem Radio Network.
RADIO NETWORK

Salem Radio Network 46925

Owner: Salem Media Group, Inc.
Editorial: 6400 N Belt Line Rd, Irving, Texas 75063-6093 **Tel:** 1 972 831-1920.
Web site: http://www.srnonline.com
Profile: Broadcast outlet airing a bevy of personality-driven talk shows with viewer call-ins and guests. Also features an hourly news feed spotlighting the latest news and information from around the globe. Salem Radio Network (SRN), created in 1993, serves as a full-service satellite-delivered radio network headquartered in Dallas, TX, serving Christian-formatted and general market news/talk stations, through affiliate partnerships. SRN's central focus is the development and syndication of a broad range of programming specifically targeted to both Christian and general market news and talk radio stations.
RADIO NETWORK

SB Nation Sports Radio 46919

Owner: Gow Broadcasting, LLC
Editorial: 5353 W Alabama St Ste 415, Houston, Texas 77056-5942 **Tel:** 1 800 224-2004.
Web site: http://www.sbnationradio.com
Profile: National network distributing a variety of personality-driven sports talk programming 24 hours a day to over 400 outlets across America. Programming emphasizes listener call-ins, in addition to studio guests, interviews and in-depth analysis of the latest issues in the world of sports.
RADIO NETWORK

Sheridan Gospel Network 46966

Owner: Sheridan Broadcasting Corp.
Editorial: 2424 Old Rex Morrow Rd, Ellenwood, Georgia 30294-3901 **Tel:** 1 404 361-1570.
Web site: http://www.sgnthelight.com
Profile: Producer and distributor of gospel music and talk programs for a national radio audience. The network's primary service is "The Light," a 24 hour, satellite distributed Gospel radio format.
RADIO NETWORK

SIRIUS XM Radio 81024

Owner: SIRIUS XM Radio Inc.
Editorial: 1221 Avenue of the Americas, New York, New York 10020-1001 **Tel:** 1 212 584-5100.
Web site: http://www.siriusxm.com
Profile: SIRIUS XM Radio provides a wide variety of digital entertainment, broadcast live to cars or trucks with crystal clear reception and outstanding digital sound broadcast coast-to-coast. It broadcasts more than 300 channels of programming, including exclusive radio offerings from Howard Stern, Oprah, Opie & Anthony and Martha Stewart, among others.
RADIO NETWORK

SIRIUS XM Radio - Washington Bureau 543100

Owner: SIRIUS XM Radio Inc.
Editorial: 1500 Eckington Pl NE, Washington, District Of Columbia 20002-2128 **Tel:** 1 202 380-4000.
Profile: SIRIUS XM Radio's offices in Washington, D.C.
RADIO NETWORK

Sound of Hope 844996

Editorial: 333 Kearny St Fl 5, San Francisco, California 94108-3268 **Tel:** 1 408 320-5888.
Email: info@sohnetwork.com
Web site: http://sohnetwork.com
Profile: This is a non-profit radio network which provides independent around-the-clock reporting about China and China-related issues. Their programs feature Asian news and culture, traditional Chinese stories, Chinese recipes, lessons on the Chinese language, and more.
RADIO NETWORK

South Carolina Public Radio 47099

Editorial: 1041 George Rogers Blvd, Columbia, South Carolina 29201-4755 **Tel:** 1 803 737-3413.
Email: gasque@scetv.org
Web site: http://www.etvradio.org
Profile: South Carolina Public Radio offers an innovative, multi-media approach with the goal of enhancing educational experiences for educators and students in public schools, colleges, technical colleges and universities. Also offers continuing educational resources to state agencies, hospitals and South Carolina businesses.
REGIONAL RADIO NETWORKS

South Carolina Radio Network 47073

Owner: Learfield Communications, Inc.
Editorial: 1338 Main St Ste 201, Columbia, South Carolina 29201-3276 **Tel:** 1 803 790-4300.
Email: news@southcarolinaradionetwork.com
Web site: http://www.learfield.com
Profile: Supplies 60 stations in South Carolina with news and sports.
REGIONAL RADIO NETWORKS

South Dakota News Network 47072

Editorial: 214 W Pleasant Dr, Pierre, South Dakota 57501-2472 **Tel:** 1 605 224-9911.
Web site: http://americanagnetwork.com/programs/dakota-news-network
Profile: Programming provides news, weather, and sports to 15 stations in South Dakota, North Dakota, and western Minnesota.
REGIONAL RADIO NETWORKS

Southeast AgNet 47036

Owner: AgNet West Media, LLC
Editorial: 5700 SW 34th St Ste 1307A, Gainesville, Florida 32608-5372 **Tel:** 1 352 671-1909.
Email: office@southeastagnet.com
Web site: http://www.southeastagnet.com
Profile: Serves stations in Florida, Georgia and Alabama with news, weather and programming that relates to the region's agricultural industries. Their CUME across FL, GA, and AL is 41.1.
REGIONAL RADIO NETWORKS

Southern Farm Network 47092

Owner: Curtis Media Group
Editorial: 3012 Highwoods Blvd Ste 200, Raleigh, North Carolina 27604-1031 **Tel:** 1 919 876-0674.
Web site: http://www.southernfarmnetwork.com
Profile: Provides farming information and agricultural news to 18 affiliates throughout North and South Carolina. The network features farm news, market prices, agricultural weather, farm calendar and news that anyone in agri-business can use.
REGIONAL RADIO NETWORKS

SRN Broadcasting 235044

Owner: SRN Broadcasting & Marketing Inc.
Tel: 1 847 735-1995.
Email: mail@internetfm.com
Web site: http://www.internetfm.com
Profile: The network focuses on sports programming but also produces and distributes other general interest programming. SRN reporters are at all major sports events, such as the Super Bowl, NBA Finals, World Series, Stanley Cup and NCAA Final Four, providing regular and post-season coverage.
RADIO NETWORK

Starboard Network 155567

Editorial: 1496 Bellevue St, Green Bay, Wisconsin 54311-4205 **Tel:** 1 877 291-0123.
Email: info@relevantradio.com
Web site: http://www.relevantradio.com
Profile: Starboard Network is a leading operator of community Catholic talk radio stations. Starboard Network owns and operates multiple stations and syndicates programming to many affiliated stations throughout the United States. They also provide live streaming audio via the web. Starboard Network has branded its programming as Relevant Radio, a format of Catholic talk radio designed to bridge the gap between faith and everyday life by providing timely programming relevant to today's world. The majority of the programming day consists of live, listener-interactive shows.
RADIO NETWORK

Statehouse News Bureau 391094

Editorial: Ohio Statehouse, Basement Room 015, Columbus, Ohio 43215 **Tel:** 1 614 221-1811.
Web site: http://www.statenews.org
Profile: Founded in 1980, the Statehouse News Bureau was founded to provide educational, comprehensive coverage of election news, legislative issues and other activities surrounding the Statehouse to Ohio's public radio and television stations. Bureau reporters report on the actions of elected officials, government bodies and more.
REGIONAL RADIO NETWORKS

Sun Broadcast Group 594172

Editorial: 101 Plaza Real S Ste 217, Boca Raton, Florida 33432-4856 **Tel:** 1 800 871-6163.
Web site: http://www.sunbgi.com
Profile: A new generation national broadcast network that programs and syndicates its own content, and provides targeted content and advertising solutions across America. The network is committed to offering the highest quality programming that not only delivers ratings success for station affiliates, but also marketing success advertisers.
RADIO NETWORK

Talk Radio Network 46924

Owner: Talk Radio Network
Editorial: 724 E Pine St, Central Point, Oregon 97502-2449 **Tel:** 1 541 664-8827.
Web site: http://www.talkradionetwork.com
Profile: Talk Radio Network distributes a wide variety of talk programming to radio stations nationwide. It spotlights a range of talk-formatted and viewer call-in shows. Topics covered include sports, science and technology, automobiles, politics and general public affairs issues. Hosts are experts and top radio personalities from all walks of life.
RADIO NETWORK

Tennessee Ag-Net 47074

Owner: iHeartMedia Inc.
Editorial: 55 Music Sq W, Nashville, Tennessee 37203-3207 **Tel:** 1 615 664-2400.
Web site: http://www.tennesseeradionetwork.com
Profile: Tennessee Ag-Net provides farm news, market updates and weather to 50 affiliates in Tennessee.
REGIONAL RADIO NETWORKS

Tennessee Radio Network 47075

Owner: iHeartMedia Inc.
Editorial: 55 Music Sq W, Nashville, Tennessee 37203-3207 **Tel:** 1 615 664-2400.
Web site: http://www.tennesseeradionetwork.com
Profile: Distributes news, weather, and sports to 79 stations in Tennessee. The network is owned by Clear Channel Media and Entertainment.
REGIONAL RADIO NETWORKS

Texas Farm Bureau Radio Network 394713

Editorial: 7420 Fish Pond Rd, Waco, Texas 76710-1010 **Tel:** 1 254 772-3030.
Web site: http://www.txfb.org
Profile: Texas Farm Bureau Radio Network is a network created by the Texas Farm Network to educate farmers on agricultural issues, daily market updates, care of farm animals and political aspects as the relate to agriculture.
REGIONAL RADIO NETWORKS

Texas State Network 47077

Owner: CBS Radio
Editorial: 4131 N Central Expy Ste 500, Dallas, Texas 75204-2175 **Tel:** 1 214 525-7000.
Email: tsnnews@cbs.com
Web site: http://www.tsnradio.com
Profile: Texas State Network is the oldest and largest state radio network in America, incorporated by Elliott Roosevelt and others on August 2, 1938. Today, TSN provides news, sports, business, weather, agriculture and talk programming to approximately 130 radio stations.
REGIONAL RADIO NETWORKS

Texas State Network Agri-Business News 47076

Owner: CBS Radio
Editorial: 4131 N Central Expy Ste 1000, Dallas, Texas 75204-2121 **Tel:** 1 214 525-7000.
Email: tsnag@cbs.com
Web site: http://www.tsnradio.com
Profile: The network produces agricultural news programs throughout the day on weekdays, as well as a daily agri-business calendar of events. Hourly three-minute reports keep the listener up to date on factors critical to agriculture from 6:40am to 3:40pm. Topics covered include cotton, livestock, grains, cash and futures market reports, and analysis of why the markets act the way they do.
REGIONAL RADIO NETWORKS

Tiger Financial News Network 155376

Owner: Tiger Financial News Network
Editorial: 601 Cleveland St, Ste 618, Clearwater, Florida 33755 **Tel:** 1 727 467-9190.
Web site: http://www.tfnn.com
Profile: The mission of Tiger Financial News Network is to assist its listeners in achieving their financial objectives, thoughtfully and prudently, through education and ongoing communication. Through its interactive call-in radio talk shows, TFNN is able to teach all levels of investors the technical skills needed for trading in today's marketplace.
RADIO NETWORK

Tiger Radio Network 47063

Editorial: 505 Hobbs Rd, Jefferson City, Missouri 65109-5788 **Tel:** 1 573 893-7200.
Email: sportshelpdesk@learfield.com
Web site: http://www.learfield.com
Profile: Provides more than 50 affiliates in Missouri with sports play-by-play of the University of Missouri at Columbia, Tiger football games, Tiger basketball, Tiger Women's basketball, and other live sporting events from the University.
REGIONAL RADIO NETWORKS

Total Traffic & Weather Network 46982

Owner: iHeartMedia Inc.
Editorial: 1320 Greenway Dr Ste 900, Irving, Texas 75038-7506 **Tel:** 1 214 596-2300.
Web site: http://www.ttwnetwork.com/
Profile: Total Traffic & Weather Network (TTWN) is the largest provider of local content of news, sports, traffic, weather, business and entertainment information. It is a division of Clear Channel Media and Entertainment and has over 2000 affiliated radio and television stations.
RADIO NETWORK

Total Traffic & Weather Network - Midwest Bureau 47014

Owner: iHeartMedia Inc.
Editorial: 161 N Clark St, Chicago, Illinois 60601-3206 **Tel:** 1 312 705-1717.
Email: info@totaltraffic.com
Web site: http://totaltraffic.com
RADIO NETWORK

Total Traffic & Weather Network - Northwest/Mountain Bureau 47021

Owner: iHeartMedia Inc.
Editorial: 221 Main St Ste 900, San Francisco, California 94105-1923
Web site: http://totaltraffic.com
Profile: Total Traffic & Weather Network Northwest/Mountain region.
RADIO NETWORK

Total Traffic & Weather Network - Southeast Bureau 47022

Owner: iHeartMedia Inc.
Editorial: 2970 Clairmont Rd NE, Atlanta, Georgia 30329-1638 **Tel:** 1 770 290-1300.
Web site: http://totaltraffic.com
RADIO NETWORK

Total Traffic & Weather Network - Southwest/Pacific Bureau 47012

Owner: iHeartMedia Inc.
Editorial: 8965 Lindblade St, Culver City, California 90232-2438 **Tel:** 1 714 647-0117.
Email: totaltrafficla@iheartmedia.com
Web site: http://totaltrafficla.com
RADIO NETWORK

United Stations Radio Network 46930

Editorial: 1065 Avenue of the Americas, New York, New York 10018-1878 **Tel:** 1 212 869-1111.
Email: info@unitedstations.com
Web site: http://www.unitedstations.com
Profile: Radio network providing a variety of personality-driven, caller-intensive talk radio programming all delivered to affiliates via satellite. The network provides a variety of music, comedy and information shows and services delivered to affiliates via CD, satellite and the Internet.
RADIO NETWORK

Univision Radio 46964

Owner: Univision Communications Inc.
Editorial: 605 3rd Ave Fl 12, New York, New York 10158-1299 **Tel:** 1 212 455-5200.
Web site: http://www.univision.com
Profile: Network providing a variety of Spanish-language broadcasting to a national Hispanic audience. Univision Radio station formats are composed of a variety of music from throughout the Spanish-speaking world. The network also features a news/talk format that is of particular interest to the audience in the United States.
RADIO NETWORK

USA Radio Networks 46976

Owner: Anthem Broadcasting LLC
Editorial: 819 W Hargett St, Raleigh, North Carolina 27603-1603
Web site: http://usaradionetworks.com
Profile: USA Radio Networks is a nationally distributed radio network, owned by Cross Platform Media, airing programs dealing with a range of general and topical issues. The network provides news and programming to radio stations and radio networks, covering national and international news, business news, sports news and Christian interest news. IRN also provides over 30 long form programs to radio stations and delivers news and programs from a platform of 5 satellite channels for radio stations, 6 XM channels and over 3,000 affiliates. The network became IRN/USA Radio Network when Information Radio Network and USA Radio Network merged on March 3, 2008. Cross Platform Media acquired the network in October 2014. In fall of 2014, the network switch back to its original name, USA Radio Networks.
RADIO NETWORK

USA Radio Networks - Dallas Bureau 523482

Editorial: 2290 Springlake Rd Ste 107, Dallas, Texas 75234-5899
Profile: The Dallas bureau is the original site of the USA Radio Network. This bureau handles IRN/USA Radio Network's business, sports and religion content. All submissions can be directed to the bureau chief via e-mail.
RADIO NETWORK

USDA Radio Network 740411

Editorial: 1400 Independence Ave SW, Rm 1623 C, Washington, District Of Columbia 20783
Tel: 1 202 720-3628.
Profile: Produces agriculture news events and features.
RADIO NETWORK

Vermont Public Radio 433262

Editorial: 365 Troy Ave, Colchester, Vermont 5446
Tel: 1 802 655-9451.
Web site: http://www.vpr.net
Profile: Vermont Public Radio airs programming from National Public Radio (NPR), Public Radio International (PRI), BBC News and American Public Media. The network covers local, national, and international news stories, and also airs jazz, classical and world music.
REGIONAL RADIO NETWORKS

Virginia News Network 47078
Editorial: 3245 Basie Rd, Richmond, Virginia 23228-3404 **Tel:** 1 804 474-0000.
Web site: http://www.virginianewsnetwork.com
Profile: Supplies sports, ski reports, entertainment, weather, agriculture business, political news, national and state headline news, gardening tips, regional sports, and general assembly updates to over 40 stations in Virginia.
REGIONAL RADIO NETWORKS

Voice of America Radio Network 46977
Owner: Government-owned
Editorial: 330 Independence Ave SW, Washington, District Of Columbia 20237-0001 **Tel:** 1 202 203-4959.
Email: coverage-desk@voanews.com
Web site: http://www.voanews.com
Profile: The Voice of America (VOA) is an international news service, supported by the U.S. Government, that serves more than 1,200 affiliate radio and television stations overseas. It provides news about the U.S. and world events in a manner designed to report information accurately.
RADIO NETWORK

Voice of America Radio Network - Los Angeles Bureau 46998
Editorial: 11000 Wilshire Blvd Ste C300, Los Angeles, California 90024-7066 **Tel:** 1 310 235-7227.
Email: la@voanews.com
RADIO NETWORK

Voice of America Radio Network - New York Bureau 46999
Editorial: 26 Federal Plz Ste 30-100, New York, New York 10278-3099 **Tel:** 1 212 264-2345.
RADIO NETWORK

VSA Radio Network 47031
Owner: iHeartMedia Inc.
Editorial: 1900 NW Expressway Ste 1000, Oklahoma City, Oklahoma 73118-1854 **Tel:** 1 405 858-1400.
Web site: http://www.aghub.net/
Profile: The Voice of Southwest Agriculture (VSA) Radio Network provides farm and agricultural news to more than 40 rural stations in Texas. The network also has bureaus in Dallas and San Angelo, Texas.
REGIONAL RADIO NETWORKS

WAAC-FM 45727
Owner: WGOV, Inc
Editorial: 2973 US Highway 84 W, Valdosta, Georgia 31601-0305 **Tel:** 1 229 242-4513.
Web site: http://www.valdostasc93.com
Profile: WAAC-FM is a commercial station owned by WGOV, Inc. The format of the station is contemporary country music. WAAC-FM broadcasts to the Valdosta, GA area at 92.9 FM.
FM RADIO STATION

WAAF-FM 41783
Owner: Entercom Communications Corp.
Editorial: 20 Guest St Fl 3, Boston, Massachusetts 02135-2040 **Tel:** 1 617 779-5400.
Web site: http://www.waaf.com
Profile: WAAF-FM is a commercial station owned by Entercom Communications Corp. The format of the station is rock/album-oriented rock. WAAF-FM broadcasts to the Boston area at 107.3 FM.
FM RADIO STATION

WAAG-FM 46587
Owner: Galesburg Broadcasting Co.
Editorial: 154 E Simmons St, Galesburg, Illinois 61401-4658 **Tel:** 1 309 342-5131.
Email: news@wgil.com
Web site: http://www.fm95online.com
Profile: WAAG-FM is a commercial station owned by Galesburg Broadcasting Co. The format of the station is country. WAAG-FM broadcasts to the Galesburg, IL area at 94.9 FM.
FM RADIO STATION

WAAI-FM 41286
Owner: MTS Broadcasting LLC
Editorial: 2 Bay St, Cambridge, Maryland 21613-1257 **Tel:** 1 410 228-4800.
Email: news@mtslive.com
Web site: http://www.mtslive.com
Profile: WAAI-FM is a commercial station owned by MTS Broadcasting LLC. The format of the station is country music. WAAI-FM broadcasts to the Cambridge, MD area at 100.9 FM.
FM RADIO STATION

WAAJ-FM 43883
Owner: Heartland Ministries, Inc.
Editorial: 219 College St, Hardin, Kentucky 42048 **Tel:** 1 270 437-4369.
Email: studio@elevate.fm
Web site: http://www.elevate.fm
Profile: WAAJ-FM is a non-commercial station owned by Heartland Ministries, Inc. The format of the station is Hot AC and Christian. WAAJ-FM broadcasts to the Hardin, KY, area at 89.7 FM. Send all PSA to the main email address.
FM RADIO STATION

WAAL-FM 44546
Owner: Townsquare Media, Inc.
Editorial: 59 Court St, Binghamton, New York 13901-3270 **Tel:** 1 607 772-8850.
Web site: http://www.991thewhale.com
Profile: WAAL-FM is a commercial station owned by Townsquare Media, Inc. The format of the station is classic rock. WAAL-FM broadcasts to the Binghampton, NY area on 99.1 FM.
FM RADIO STATION

WAAM-AM 35144
Owner: Coolarity A2, LLC
Editorial: 4230 Packard St, Ann Arbor, Michigan 48108-1508 **Tel:** 1 734 971-1600.
Web site: http://www.waamradio.com
Profile: WAAM-AM is a commercial station owned by Coolarity A2, LLC. The format of the station is news and talk. WAAM-AM broadcasts to the Ann Arbor, MI area at 1600 AM.
AM RADIO STATION

WAAO-FM 44413
Owner: Three Notch Communications, LLC
Editorial: 121 E Three Notch St, Andalusia, Alabama 36420-3120 **Tel:** 1 334 222-1166.
Email: waao@waao.com
Web site: http://www.waao.com
Profile: WAAO-FM is a commercial station owned by Three Notch Communications, LLC. The format of the station is contemporary country. The station broadcasts to the Andalusia, Alabama area at a frequency of 93.7 FM.
FM RADIO STATION

WAAV-AM 39455
Owner: Cumulus Media Inc.
Editorial: 3233 Burnt Mill Dr Ste 4, Wilmington, North Carolina 28403-2676 **Tel:** 1 910 763-9977.
Web site: http://www.980waav.com
Profile: WAAV-AM is a commercial station owned by Cumulus Media Inc. The format of the station is news, talk, and sports. WAAV-AM broadcasts in the Wilmington, NC area at 980 AM.
AM RADIO STATION

WAAW-FM 43564
Owner: Neely(Frank)
Editorial: 2166 Park Ave SE, Aiken, South Carolina 29801-6703 **Tel:** 1 803 649-6405.
Web site: http://shout947.com
Profile: WAAW-FM is a commercial station owned by Frank Neely. The format of the station is gospel. WAAW-FM broadcasts to the Aiken, SC area at 94.7 FM.
FM RADIO STATION

WAAX-AM 135299
Owner: iHeartMedia Inc.
Editorial: 6510 Whorton Bend Rd, Gadsden, Alabama 35901-8873 **Tel:** 1 256 543-9229.
Web site: http://www.waax570.com
Profile: WAAX-AM is a commercial station owned by iHeartMedia Inc.The format of the station is news, sports and talk. WAAX-AM broadcasts to the Gadsden, AL area at 570 AM.
AM RADIO STATION

WAAZ-FM 45007
Owner: Whitaker(James T.)
Editorial: 506 W 1st Ave, Crestview, Florida 32536 **Tel:** 1 850 682-3040.
Email: waazwjsb@embarqmail.com
Profile: WAAZ-FM is a commercial station owned by James T. Whitaker. The format for the station is country. WAAZ-FM broadcasts to the Mobile, AL, Pensacola, FL area at 104.7 FM.
FM RADIO STATION

WABC-AM 39290
Owner: Cumulus Media Inc
Editorial: 2 Penn Plz Fl 17, New York, New York 10121-1701 **Tel:** 1 212 613-3800.
Web site: http://www.wabcradio.com
Profile: WABC-AM is a commercial station owned by Cumulus Media Inc. The format of the station is news and talk. WABC-AM broadcasts to the New York City area at 770 AM. The station does not accept press releases as most of their programming is syndicated.
AM RADIO STATION

WABD-FM 45008
Owner: Cumulus Media
Editorial: 2800 Dauphin St Ste 104, Mobile, Alabama 36606-2400 **Tel:** 1 251 652-2000.
Web site: http://www.975wabd.com
Profile: WABD-FM is a commercial station owned by Cumulus Media. The format of the station is Top 40/CHR. WABD-FM airs locally at 97.5 FM in Mobile, AL.
FM RADIO STATION

WABF-AM 35145
Owner: Gulf Coast Broadcasting Company, Inc.
Editorial: 460 S Section St, Fairhope, Alabama 36532-1624 **Tel:** 1 251 928-9228.
Email: wabf1220@bellsouth.net
AM RADIO STATION

WABG-AM 35146
Owner: SPB LLC
Editorial: 68233 County Road 518, Greenwood, Mississippi 38930-7358
Web site: http://www.awesomeam.com
Profile: WABG-AM is a commercial station owned by SPB LLC. The format of the station is blues, classic rock and news. WABG-AM broadcasts to the Greenwood, MS area at 960 AM.
AM RADIO STATION

WABH-AM 38253
Owner: Tower Broadcasting LLC
Editorial: E Washington St Ext, Bath, New York 14810-9801 **Tel:** 1 607 776-3326.
Profile: WABH-AM is a commercial station owned by Tower Broadcasting LLC. The format of the station is Adult Standards. WABH-AM broadcasts to the Bath, NY area at 1380 AM.
AM RADIO STATION

WABJ-AM 37622
Owner: Friends Communications Inc.
Editorial: 121 W Maumee St, Adrian, Michigan 49221-2019 **Tel:** 1 517 265-1500.
Email: traffic@friendsmi.com
Profile: WABJ-AM is a commercial station owned by Friends Communications Inc. The format of the station is news, sports and talk. WABJ-AM broadcasts to the Adrian, MI area at 1490 AM.
AM RADIO STATION

WABK-FM 528240
Owner: Blueberry Broadcasting
Editorial: 125 Community Dr Ste 201, Augusta, Maine 04330-8157 **Tel:** 1 207 623-9000.
Web site: http://www.wabkfm.com
Profile: WABK-FM is a commercial station owned by Blueberry Broadcasting. The format of the station is classic hits. WABK-FM broadcasts to the Bangor, ME market at 104.3 FM.
FM RADIO STATION

WABL-AM 35147
Owner: Spotlight Broadcasting of New Orleans LLC
Editorial: 12515 Bankston Rd, Amite, Louisiana 70422 **Tel:** 1 985 748-8385.
Web site: http://www.wablradio.com
Profile: WABL-AM is a commercial station owned by Spotlight Broadcasting of New Orleans LLC. The format of the station is country music, news and talk. WABL-AM broadcasts to the Amite, LA area at 1570 AM.
AM RADIO STATION

WABN-AM 39019
Owner: Information Communications Corp.
Editorial: 1007A W Main St Ste 100, Abingdon, Virginia 24210-4701 **Tel:** 1 276 623-0030.
Email: wabn1230@gmail.com
Web site: http://www.wabn1230.com
Profile: WABN-AM is a commercial station owned by Information Communications Corp. The format of the station is oldies. WABN-AM broadcasts to the Washington, D.C. area at 1230 AM.
AM RADIO STATION

WABO-AM 37623
Owner: Martin Broadcasting
Editorial: 6746 Highway 184, Waynesboro, Mississippi 39367-9288 **Tel:** 1 601 735-4331.
Web site: http://www.105wabo.com
Profile: WABO-AM is a commercial station owned by Martin Broadcasting. The format of the station is classic hits. WABO-AM broadcasts to the Waynesboro, MS area at 990 AM. Send all press materials and PSAs via fax.
AM RADIO STATION

WABO-FM 45009
Owner: Martin Broadcasting
Editorial: 6746 Highway 184, Waynesboro, Mississippi 39367-9288 **Tel:** 1 601 735-4331.
Web site: http://www.105wabo.com
Profile: WABO-FM is a commercial station owned by Martin Broadcasting. The format of the station is classic hits. WABO-FM broadcasts to the Waynesboro, MS area at 105.5 FM. Send all press materials and PSAs via fax.
FM RADIO STATION

WABR-FM 43317
Owner: Georgia Public Broadcasting
Editorial: 260 14th St NW, Atlanta, Georgia 30318 **Tel:** 1 404 685-2548.
Email: ask@gpb.org
Web site: http://www.gpb.org
Profile: WABR-FM is a non-commercial station owned by Georgia Public Broadcasting. The format of the station is news and classical and jazz music. WABR-FM broadcasts to the Atlanta area at 91.1 FM.
FM RADIO STATION

WABT-FM 45577
Owner: Neversink Radio, LLC
Editorial: 15 Neversink Dr, Port Jervis, New York 12771-3811 **Tel:** 1 845 856-5185.
Web site: http://pocono967.com
Profile: WABT-FM is commercial station owned by Neversink Radio, LLC. The format of the station is classic hits. WABT-FM broadcasts to Port Jervis, NY and its surrounding area at 96.7 FM.
FM RADIO STATION

WABX-FM 43193
Owner: South Central Communications Corp.
Editorial: 1162 Mount Auburn Rd, Evansville, Indiana 47720 **Tel:** 1 812 424-8284.
Web site: http://www.wabx.net
Profile: WABX-FM is a commercial station owned by South Central Communications Corp. The format of the station is classic rock. WBAX-FM broadcasts to the Evansville, IN area at 107.5 FM.
FM RADIO STATION

WACA-AM 36107
Owner: AC Aquisitions LLC
Editorial: 11141 Georgia Ave Ste 310, Wheaton, Maryland 20902-4658 **Tel:** 1 301 942-3500.
Email: cabina@radioamerica.net
Web site: http://www.radioamerica.net
Profile: WACA-AM is a commercial station owned by AC Acquisitions LLC. The format of the station is Spanish talk. WACA-AM broadcasts in the Washington, D.C. area at 1540 AM.
AM RADIO STATION

WACB-AM 35618
Owner: Apple City Broadcasting Co.
Editorial: 133 E Main Ave, Taylorsville, North Carolina 28681-2514 **Tel:** 1 828 632-4621.
Email: news@applecitybroadcasting.com
Profile: WACB-AM is a commercial station owned by Apple City Broadcasting Co. The format of the station is country. WACB-AM broadcasts to the Charlotte, NC area at 860 AM.
AM RADIO STATION

WACC-AM 36000
Owner: Radio Peace Catholic Broadcasting, Inc (Archdiocese of Miami)
Editorial: 1779 NW 28th St, Miami, Florida 33142 **Tel:** 1 305 638-9729.
Email: radiopaz830am@gmail.com
Web site: http://www.paxcc.org/radiopaz
Profile: WACC-AM is a commercial station owned by Radio Peace Catholic Broadcasting, Inc (Archdiocese of Miami). The format of the station is Spanish religious programming. WACC-AM broadcasts to the Miami area at 830 AM.
AM RADIO STATION

WACD-FM 43646
Owner: Results Broadcasting, Inc.
Editorial: N2237 US Highway 45 S, Antigo, Wisconsin 54409 **Tel:** 1 715 623-4124.
Email: wacdwatk@yahoo.com
Web site: http://www.country106.fm
Profile: WACD-FM is a commercial station owned by Results Broadcasting, Inc. The format of the station is contemporary country music. WACD-FM broadcasts to the Antigo, WI area at 106.1 FM.
FM RADIO STATION

WACE-AM 35151
Owner: Carter Broadcasting
Editorial: 50 Braintree Hill Park#308, Braintree, Massachusetts 2184 **Tel:** 1 413 594-6654.
Web site: http://www.waceradio.com
Profile: WACE-AM is a commercial station owned by Carter Broadcasting. The format of the station is religious talk. WACE-AM broadcasts in the greater Springfield, MA area at 730 AM.
AM RADIO STATION

WACG-FM 40081
Owner: Georgia Public Broadcasting
Editorial: 260 14th St NW, Atlanta, Georgia 30318 **Tel:** 1 404 685-2548.
Email: ask@gpb.org
Web site: http://www.gpb.org
Profile: WACG-FM is a non-commercial station owned by Georgia Public Broadcasting. The format of the station is news, jazz and classical music. WACG-FM broadcasts to the Atlanta area at 89.5 FM.
FM RADIO STATION

WACK-AM 38894
Owner: Waynco Radio Inc.
Editorial: 187 Vienna Rd, Newark, New York 14513-9124 **Tel:** 1 315 331-1420.
Email: 1420wacknews@gmail.com
Web site: http://www.1420wack.com
Profile: WACK-AM is a commercial station owned by Waynco Radio Inc. The format of the station is news and talk programming. WACK-AM broadcasts to the Newark, NY area at 1420 AM.
AM RADIO STATION

WACL-FM 40968
Owner: iHeart Media Inc.
Editorial: 207 University Blvd, Harrisonburg, Virginia 22801-3749 **Tel:** 1 540 434-1777.
Web site: http://98rockme.iheart.com
Profile: WACL-FM is a commercial station owned by iHeart Media Inc. The format of the station is rock music. WACL-FM broadcasts to the Harrisonburg, VA area at 98.5 FM.
FM RADIO STATION

WACM-AM 36243
Owner: Red Wolf Broadcasting
Editorial: 34 Sylvan St, West Springfield, Massachusetts 01089-3444 **Tel:** 1 413 781-5200.
Profile: WACM-AM is a commercial station owned by Red Wolf Broadcasting. The format of the station is Hispanic Oldies. WACM-AM broadcasts to the West Springfield, MA area at 1270 AM.
AM RADIO STATION

WACO-FM 44330
Owner: iHeartMedia Inc.
Editorial: 314 W State Highway 6, Waco, Texas 76712-3971 **Tel:** 1 254 776-3900.
Web site: http://www.waco100.com
Profile: WACO-FM is a commercial station owned by iHeartMedia Inc. The format of the station is country music. WACO-FM broadcasts to the Waco, TX area at 99.9 FM.
FM RADIO STATION

WACQ-AM
39423
Owner: Tiger Communications Inc.
Editorial: 320 Barnett Blvd, Tallassee, Alabama 36078-1506 **Tel:** 1 334 283-6888.
Email: wacqradio@elmore.rr.com
Web site: http://www.wacqradio.com
Profile: WBIL-AM is a commercial station owned by Tiger Communications Inc and operated by Fred Hughey. The format is oldies music. The station airs in the Tuskegee, AL area at 580 AM.
AM RADIO STATION

WACR-FM
45010
Owner: URBan Radio Broadcasting, LLC
Editorial: 608 Yellow Jacket Dr, Starkville, Mississippi 39759 **Tel:** 1 662 338-5424.
Web site: http://www.wacr1053.com
Profile: WACR-FM is a commercial station owned by URBan Radio Broadcasting, LLC. The format of the station is Urban Adult Contemporary. WACR-FM broadcasts to the Columbus/Starkville, MS area at a frequency of 105.7 FM.
FM RADIO STATION

WACT-AM
37626
Owner: iHeartMedia Inc.
Editorial: 3900 11th Ave, Tuscaloosa, Alabama 35401-7056 **Tel:** 1 205 344-4589.
Web site: http://969myfm.iheart.com
Profile: WACT-AM is a commercial station owned by iHeartMedia Inc. The format of the station is adult contemporary. WACT-AM broadcasts to the Tuscaloosa, AL area at 1420 AM.
AM RADIO STATION

WACV-FM
829402
Owner: Bluewater Broadcasting, LLC
Editorial: 4101 Wall St Ste A, Montgomery, Alabama 36106-3724 **Tel:** 1 334 244-0961.
Web site: http://bluewaterbroadcasting.com
Profile: WACV-FM is a commercial station owned by Bluewater Broadcasting, LLC. The format of the station is news/talk. WACV-FM broadcasts to the Montgomery, AL area at a frequency of 93.1 FM.
FM RADIO STATION

WADB-AM
37943
Owner: Townsquare Media
Editorial: 8 Robbins St Ste 201, Toms River, New Jersey 08753-7668 **Tel:** 1 848 221-8000.
Web site: http://wobmam.com
Profile: WADB-AM is a commercial station owned by Townsquare Media. The format of the station is news and talk. WADB-AM broadcasts in the Ocean, NJ, area at 1310 AM.
AM RADIO STATION

WADC-AM
38748
Owner: Burbach of WV, LLC
Editorial: 5 Rosemar Cir, Parkersburg, West Virginia 26104-1203 **Tel:** 1 304 485-4565.
Email: jdgreen@resultsradiowv.com
Profile: WADC-AM is a commercial station owned by Burbach of WV, LLC. The format for the station is nostalgia. WADC-AM broadcasts to the Parkersburg, WV area at 1050 AM.
AM RADIO STATION

WADE-AM
36418
Owner: New Life Community Temple of Faith, Inc.
Editorial: 3216 Griffith Rd, Monroe, North Carolina 28112-9521 **Tel:** 1 704 829-9339.
Web site: http://www.newlifectof.org/WDEX_Gospel_1430AM
Profile: WADE-AM is a commercial station owned by New Life Community Temple of Faith, Inc. The format of the station is urban gospel with some religious teaching programming. WADE-AM broadcasts in the Monroe, NC area at 1340 AM.
AM RADIO STATION

WADI-FM
40083
Owner: Power Valley Communications Inc.
Editorial: 121 Front St, Iuka, Mississippi 38852
Tel: 1 662 423-9533.
Email: wadi@bellsouth.net
Profile: WADI-FM is a commercial station owned by Power Valley Communications Inc. The format of the station is contemporary country. WADI-FM broadcasts to the Iuka, MS area at 95.3 FM.
FM RADIO STATION

WADK-AM
36428
Owner: 3G Broadcasting, Inc.
Editorial: 15 Dr. Marcus Wheatland Blvd, Newport, Rhode Island 2818 **Tel:** 1 401 846-1540.
Web site: http://www.wadk.com
Profile: WADK-AM is a commercial station owned by 3G Broadcasting, Inc. The format of the station is news and talk. WADK-AM broadcasts to the Newport, RI area at 1540 AM.
AM RADIO STATION

WADO-AM
35153
Owner: Univision Communications Inc.
Editorial: 485 Madison Ave Fl 3, New York, New York 10022-5869 **Tel:** 1 212 310-6000.
Web site: http://wado1280am.univision.com
Profile: WADO-AM is a commercial station owned by Univision Communications Inc. The format of the station is a variety of Hispanic news and talk. WADO-AM broadcasts to the New York metro area at 1280 AM.
AM RADIO STATION

WADS-AM
36892
Owner: Amor II Inc.
Editorial: 261 Portsea St, New Haven, Connecticut 6519 **Tel:** 1 203 777-7690.
Email: radioamorwads@sbcglobal.net
Profile: WADS-AM is a commercial station owned by Amor II Inc. The format of the station is Hispanic religious programming. WADS-AM broadcasts to the Hartford-New Haven, CT area at 690 AM.
AM RADIO STATION

WADV-AM
35730
Owner: WADV Radio Inc.
Editorial: 720 E Kercher Ave, Lebanon, Pennsylvania 17046-9230 **Tel:** 1 717 273-2611.
Profile: WADV-AM is a commercial station owned by WADV Radio Inc. The format of the station is gospel music. WADV-AM broadcasts in the Lebanon, PA area in the 940 AM.
AM RADIO STATION

WAEB-AM
37627
Owner: iHeartMedia Inc.
Editorial: 1541 Alta Dr Ste 400, Whitehall, Pennsylvania 18052-5632 **Tel:** 1 610 434-1742.
Email: studio@wzzo.com
Web site: http://www.790waeb.com
Profile: WAEB-AM is a commercial station owned by iHeartMedia Inc. The format of the station is news, sports and talk. WAEB-AM broadcasts to the Whitehall, PA area at 790 AM.
AM RADIO STATION

WAEB-FM
45012
Owner: iHeartMedia Inc.
Editorial: 1541 Alta Dr Ste 400, Whitehall, Pennsylvania 18052-5632 **Tel:** 1 610 434-1742.
Web site: http://www.b104.com
Profile: WAEB-FM is a commercial station owned by iHeartMedia Inc. The format of the station is Top 40/CHR. WAEB-FM broadcasts to the Whitehall, PA area at 104.1 FM.
FM RADIO STATION

WAEC-AM
35154
Owner: Beasley Broadcast Group
Editorial: 1465 Northside Dr NW Ste 218, Atlanta, Georgia 30318-4239 **Tel:** 1 404 355-8600.
Web site: http://love860.com
Profile: WAEC-AM is a commercial station owned by Beasley Broadcast Group. The format of the station is Christian. WAEC-AM broadcasts to the Atlanta area at 860 AM.
AM RADIO STATION

WAEF-FM
242124
Owner: American Family Association
Editorial: 107 Park Gate Dr, Tupelo, Mississippi 38801 **Tel:** 1 662 844-8888.
Email: comments@afr.net
Web site: http://www.afr.net
FM RADIO STATION

WAEG-FM
42663
Owner: Perry Broadcasting Company, Inc.
Editorial: 6025 Broadcast Dr, North Augusta, South Carolina 29841-9406 **Tel:** 1 803 279-2330.
Web site: http://923smoothjazz.com
Profile: WAEG-FM is a commercial station owned by Perry Broadcasting Company, Inc. The format of the station is smooth jazz. WAEG-FM broadcasts to the North Augusta, SC area at 92.3 FM.
FM RADIO STATION

WAEI-AM
38317
Owner: Blueberry Broadcasting
Editorial: 184 Target Cir, Bangor, Maine 04401-5718
Tel: 1 207 947-9100.
Profile: WAEI-AM is a commercial station owned by Blueberry Broadcasting. The format of the station is Classic Hits. WAEI-AM broadcasts to the Bangor, ME area at 910 AM.
AM RADIO STATION

WAEV-FM
45013
Owner: iHeartMedia Inc.
Editorial: 245 Alfred St, Savannah, Georgia 31408-3205 **Tel:** 1 912 964-7794.
Email: programming@973kissfm.com
Web site: http://www.973kissfm.com
Profile: WAEV-FM is a commercial station owned by iHeartMedia Inc. The format of the station is Top 40/CHR. WAEV-FM broadcasts to the Savannah, GA area at 97.3 FM.
FM RADIO STATION

WAEW-AM
37629
Owner: Peg Broadcasting Crossville, LLC
Editorial: 961 Miller Ave, Crossville, Tennessee 38555
Tel: 1 931 707-1102.
Email: production.crossville@pegbroadcasting.com
Web site: http://www.1330waew.com
Profile: WAEW-AM is a commercial station owned by Peg Broadcasting Crossville, LLC. The format of the station is talk and oldies. WAEW-AM broadcasts to the Crossville, TN area at 1330 AM.
AM RADIO STATION

WAEY-AM
37630
Owner: L & P Broadcasting Inc.
Editorial: 1 Radio Ln, Princeton, West Virginia 24740-2886 **Tel:** 1 304 425-2151.
Profile: WAEY-AM is a commercial station owned by L & P Broadcasting Inc. The format of the station is gospel. WAEY-AM broadcasts to the Princeton, WV area at 1490 AM.
AM RADIO STATION

WAEZ-FM
41259
Owner: Bristol Broadcasting
Editorial: 901 E Valley Dr, Bristol, Virginia 24201-4913 **Tel:** 1 276 669-8112.
Web site: http://www.electric949.com
Profile: WAEZ-FM is a commercial station owned by Bristol Broadcasting. The format of the station is Top 40/CHR. WAEZ-FM broadcasts to the Bristol, VA area at 94.9 FM.
FM RADIO STATION

WAFC-AM
38607
Owner: Glades Media Co.
Editorial: 530 E Alverdez Ave, Clewiston, Florida 33440-3901 **Tel:** 1 863 983-5900.
Web site: http://gladesmedia.com
Profile: WAFC-AM is a commercial station owned by Glades Media Co. The format of the station is classic hits and oldies. WAFC-AM broadcasts to the Clewiston, FL area at 590 AM.
AM RADIO STATION

WAFC-FM
692732
Owner: BMZ Broadcasting, LLC
Editorial: 530 E Alverdez Ave, Clewiston, Florida 33440-3901 **Tel:** 1 863 983-6106.
Web site: http://www.wafcfm.com
Profile: WAFC-FM is a commercial station owned by BMZ Broadcasting, LLC and operated by Glades Media Co. The format of the station is regional Mexican. WAFC-FM broadcasts to the Okeechobee, FL area at 106.1 FM. The station is a simulcast of sister WAFC-AM 590.
FM RADIO STATION

WAFD-FM
43899
Owner: Summit Media Broadcasting LLC
Editorial: 120 Main St, Sutton, West Virginia 26601-1334 **Tel:** 1 304 765-7373.
Email: production@theboss97fm.com
Web site: http://theboss97fm.com/wafd
Profile: WAFD-FM is a commercial station owned by Summit Media Broadcasting LLC. The format of the station is urban adult contemporary music. WAFD-FM broadcasts to the Sutton, WV area at 100.3 FM.
FM RADIO STATION

WAFJ-FM
42661
Owner: Radio Training Network, Inc.
Editorial: 102 Lecompte Ave, North Augusta, South Carolina 29841 **Tel:** 1 803 819-3125.
Email: info@wafj.com
Web site: http://www.wafj.com
Profile: WAFJ-FM is a non-commercial station owned by Radio Training Network, Inc. The format of the station is Contemporary Christian. WAFJ-AM broadcasts to the North Augusta, SC area at 88.3 FM.
FM RADIO STATION

WAFL-FM
45015
Owner: Delmarva Broadcasting
Editorial: 1666 Blairs Pond Rd, Milford, Delaware 19963-5263 **Tel:** 1 302 422-7575.
Email: staff@eagle977.com
Web site: http://www.eagle977.com
Profile: WAFL-FM is a commercial station owned by Delmarva Broadcasting. The format of the station is hot AC. WAFL-FM broadcasts to the Milford, DE area at 97.7 FM.
FM RADIO STATION

WAFM-FM
46125
Owner: Stanford Communications Inc.
Editorial: 521 Highway 278 W, Amory, Mississippi 38821 **Tel:** 1 662 256-9726.
Email: fm95@fm95radio.com
Web site: http://www.fm95radio.com
Profile: WAFM-FM is a commercial station owned by Stanford Communications Inc. The format of the station is oldies. WAFM-FM broadcasts to the Amory, MS area at 95.3 FM.
FM RADIO STATION

WAFN-FM
40188
Owner: Fun Media Group
Editorial: 981 N Brindlee Mountain Pkwy, Arab, Alabama 35016-1058 **Tel:** 1 256 586-9300.
Email: funradio@otelco.net
Web site: http://www.fun927.com
Profile: WAFN-FM is a commercial station owned by Fun Media Group. The format of the station is oldies. WAFM-FM broadcasts to the Arab, AL area at 92.7 FM.
FM RADIO STATION

WAFR-FM
41861
Owner: American Family Association
Editorial: 107 Parkgate Dr, Tupelo, Mississippi 38801
Tel: 1 662 844-8888.
Email: comments@afr.net
Web site: http://www.afr.net
FM RADIO STATION

WAFS-AM
35967
Owner: Salem Media Group, Inc.
Editorial: 2970 Peachtree Rd NW Ste 700, Atlanta, Georgia 30305-4919 **Tel:** 1 404 995-7300.
Web site: http://biz1190.com
Profile: WAFS-AM is a commercial station owned by Salem Media Group, Inc. The format of the station is business news. WAFS-AM broadcasts to the Atlanta area at 1190 AM.
AM RADIO STATION

WAFT-FM
40085
Owner: Christian Radio Fellowship Inc.
Editorial: 215 Waft Hill Ln, Valdosta, Georgia 31602-6512 **Tel:** 1 229 244-5180.
Email: mail@waft.org
Web site: http://www.waft.org
Profile: WAFT-FM is a non-commercial station owned by the Christian Radio Fellowship Inc. The format of the station is Christian music and talk. WAFT-FM broadcasts to the Valdosta, GA area at 101.1 FM. Their slogan is "Offering Hope When You Need It Most."
FM RADIO STATION

WAFX-FM
40730
Owner: Saga Communications
Editorial: 870 Greenbrier Cir Ste 399, Chesapeake, Virginia 23320-2671 **Tel:** 1 757 366-9900.
Web site: http://www.1069thefox.com
Profile: WAFX-FM is a commercial station owned by Saga Communications. The format of the station is classic hits. WAFX-FM broadcasts to the Norfolk, VA area at 106.9 FM.
FM RADIO STATION

WAFY-FM
41208
Owner: Manning Broadcasting Inc.
Editorial: 5742 Industry Ln, Frederick, Maryland 21704-5191 **Tel:** 1 301 620-7700.
Web site: http://www.key103radio.com
Profile: WAFY-FM is a commercial station owned by Manning Broadcasting Inc. The format of the station is Hot AC. WAFY-FM broadcasts to the Frederick, MD area at 103.1 FM.
FM RADIO STATION

WAFZ-AM
36856
Owner: Glades Media Co.
Editorial: 2105 Immokalee Dr, Immokalee, Florida 34142-3321 **Tel:** 1 239 657-9210.
Email: info@gladesmedia.com
Web site: http://www.radiofiesta.com
Profile: WAFZ-AM is a commercial station owned by the Glades Media Co. The format of the station is regional Mexican music. WAFZ-AM broadcasts to the Immokalee, FL area at 1490 AM.
AM RADIO STATION

WAFZ-FM
43117
Owner: Glades Media Co.
Editorial: 2105 Immokalee Dr, Immokalee, Florida 34142-3321 **Tel:** 1 239 657-9210.
Email: info@gladesmedia.com
Web site: http://www.wafz.com
Profile: WAFZ-FM is a commercial station owned by Glades Media Co. The format of the station is Regional Mexican. WAFZ-FM broadcasts to the Immokalee, FL area at 92.1 FM.
FM RADIO STATION

WAGF-FM
44250
Owner: Wilson Broadcasting, Inc.
Editorial: 4106 Ross Clark Cir, Dothan, Alabama 36303 **Tel:** 1 334 671-1753.
Web site: http://www.wjjn.net
FM RADIO STATION

WAGG-AM
36656
Owner: Summit Media Broadcasting LLC
Editorial: 2700 Corporate Dr Ste 115, Birmingham, Alabama 35242-2735 **Tel:** 1 205 322-2987.
Web site: http://www.610wagg.com
Profile: WAGG-AM is a commercial station owned by Summit Media Broadcasting LLC. The format of the station is gospel. WAGG-AM broadcasts to the Birmingham, AL area at 610 AM.
AM RADIO STATION

WAGH-FM
40086
Owner: iHeartMedia Inc.
Editorial: 1501 13th Ave, Columbus, Georgia 31901-1908 **Tel:** 1 706 576-3000.
Email: info@magic101online.com
Web site: http://www.mymagic101.com
Profile: WAGH-FM is a commercial station owned by iHeartMedia Inc. The format of the station is urban adult contemporary. WAGH-FM broadcasts to the Columbus, GA area at 101.3 FM.
FM RADIO STATION

WAGN-AM
39018
Owner: Radio Plus Bay Cities, LLC
Editorial: 413 10th Ave, Menominee, Michigan 49858-3009 **Tel:** 1 906 863-5551.
Email: email@baycitiesonline.com
Web site: http://www.baycitiesonline.com
Profile: WAGN-AM is a commercial station owned by Radio Plus Bay Cities, LLC. The format of the station is talk. WAGN-AM broadcasts to the Menominee, MI area at 1340 AM.
AM RADIO STATION

WAGO-FM
43843
Owner: Pathway Christian Academy Inc.
Editorial: 205 N Greene St, Snow Hill, North Carolina 28580 **Tel:** 1 252 747-8887.
Email: wago@gomixradio.org
Web site: http://www.gomixradio.org
Profile: WAGO-FM is a non-commercial station owned by Pathway Christian Academy Inc. The format of the station is gospel music and religious programming. WAGO-FM broadcasts to the Snow Hill, NC area at 88.7 FM.
FM RADIO STATION

WAGP-FM 41428
Owner: Community Broadcasting Corp.
Editorial: 638 Terrace Island Gateway, Beaufort, South Carolina 29906 **Tel:** 1 843 525-1859.
Email: info@wagp.net
Web site: http://www.wagp.net
FM RADIO STATION

WAGR-AM 36741
Owner: Service Media Inc.
Editorial: 5102 Durham Chapel Hill Blvd, Durham, North Carolina 27707 **Tel:** 1 910 486-9438.
Profile: WAGR-AM is a commercial station owned by Service Media Inc. The format of the station is gospel. WAGR-AM broadcasts to the Durham, NC area at 1340 AM.
AM RADIO STATION

WAGR-FM 46627
Owner: Sandra U. Cothran, Executrix
Editorial: 100 Radio Road, Lexington, Mississippi 39095 **Tel:** 1 662 834-1025.
Profile: WAGR-FM is a commercial station owned by Sandra U. Cothran, Executrix. The format of the station is R&B Oldies. WAGR-FM broadcasts to the Lexington, MS area at 102.5 FM.
FM RADIO STATION

WAGS-AM 35158
Owner: Beaver Communications
Editorial: 142 Wags Dr, Bishopville, South Carolina 29010-2006 **Tel:** 1 803 484-5415.
Web site: http://www.wagsradio.com
Profile: WAGS-AM is a commercial station owned by Beaver Communications. The format of the station is country. WAGS-AM broadcasts to the Bishopville, SC area at 1380 AM.
AM RADIO STATION

WAGX-FM 42666
Owner: Jewell Schaeffer Broadcasting
Tel: 1 606 564-8474.
Profile: WAGX-FM is a commercial station owned by Jewell Schaeffer Broadcasting. The format of the station is adult contemporary and oldies music. WAGX-FM broadcasts to the Maysville, KY area at 101.3 FM.
FM RADIO STATION

WAGY-AM 35159
Owner: Watson & Dobbins Inc.
Editorial: 129 N Powell St Ste 223, Forest City, North Carolina 28043-3109 **Tel:** 1 828 245-9887.
Email: wagy1320am@yahoo.com
Web site: http://radiostation.org/wagy-1320-am-your-country-1320-in-forest-city-north-carolina/
Profile: WAGY-AM is a commercial station owned by Watson & Dobbins Inc. The format of the station is classic country. WAGY-AM broadcasts to the Forest City, NC area at 1320 AM.
AM RADIO STATION

WAHR-FM 40087
Owner: Black Crow Broadcasting Inc.
Editorial: 1555 the Boardwalk Ste 1, Huntsville, Alabama 35816-1821 **Tel:** 1 256 536-1568.
Email: psa@rocketcitybroadcasting.com
Web site: http://mystar99.com
Profile: WAHR-FM is a commercial station owned by Black Crow Broadcasting Inc. The format of the station is adult contemporary. WAHR-FM broadcasts to the Huntsville, AL area at 99.1 FM.
FM RADIO STATION

WAHT-AM 39254
Owner: Golden Corners Broadcasting
Tel: 1 864 654-4004.
Web site: http://wccpfm.com
Profile: WAHT-AM is a commercial station owned by Golden Corners Broadcasting and under LMA with Byrne Acquisition Group. The format of the station is sports. WAHT-AM broadcasts to the Clemson, SC area at 1560 AM.
AM RADIO STATION

WAIC-FM 40088
Owner: American International College
Editorial: 1000 State St, Springfield, Massachusetts 01109-3151 **Tel:** 1 413 205-3941.
Web site: http://www.cpbn.org
Profile: WAIC-FM is a non-commercial station owned by American International College. The format of the station is news/talk. WAIC-FM broadcasts to the Springfield, MA area at 91.9 FM.
FM RADIO STATION

WAID-FM 40089
Owner: Radio Cleveland Inc.
Editorial: 911 S Davis Ave, Cleveland, Mississippi 38732-3941 **Tel:** 1 662 843-4091.
Profile: WAID-FM is a commercial station owned by Radio Cleveland Inc. The format of the station is urban contemporary music. WAID-FM broadcasts to the Cleveland, MS, area at 106.5 FM. Press releases can be sent via mail.
FM RADIO STATION

WAIF-FM 129019
Owner: Stepchild Radio of Cincinnati
Editorial: 1434 E McMillan St, Cincinnati, Ohio 45206-2225 **Tel:** 1 513 961-8900.
Email: waifcincinnati@gmail.com
Web site: http://www.waif883.org
Profile: WAIF-FM is a non-commercial station owned by Stepchild Radio of Cincinnati. The format of the station is variety. WAIF-FM broadcasts to the Cincinnati area at 88.3 FM.
FM RADIO STATION

WAIK-AM 36785
Owner: Prairie Communications LLP
Editorial: 55 Public Sq, Monmouth, Illinois 61462-1755 **Tel:** 1 309 734-9452.
Email: waiknews@yahoo.com
Web site: http://www.radiomonmouth.com
Profile: WAIK-AM is a commercial station owned by Prairie Communications LLP. The format of the station is news and talk. WAIK-AM broadcasts to the Monmouth, IL area at 1590 AM.
AM RADIO STATION

WAIL-FM 42659
Owner: Florida Keys Media, LLC
Editorial: 93351 Overseas Hwy, Tavernier, Florida 33070-2800 **Tel:** 1 305 852-9085.
Profile: WAIL-FM is a commercial station owned by Florida Keys Media, LLC. The format of the station is classic rock. WAIL-FM broadcasts to the Key West, FL area at 99.5 FM.
FM RADIO STATION

WAIM-AM 36167
Owner: Palmetto Broadcasting Inc.
Editorial: 2203 Old Williamston Rd, Anderson, South Carolina 29621-3036 **Tel:** 1 864 226-1511.
Email: info@waim.us
Web site: http://www.waim.us
Profile: WAIM-AM is a commercial station owned by Palmetto Broadcasting Inc. The format of the station is news and talk. WAIM-AM broadcasts to the Anderson, SC area at 1230 AM.
AM RADIO STATION

WAIN-AM 37631
Owner: Forcht Broadcasting
Editorial: 1521 Liberty Rd, Columbia, Kentucky 42728
Tel: 1 270 384-2135.
Email: wain@forchtbroadcasting.com
Web site: http://www.1270wain.com
Profile: WAIN-AM is a commercial station owned by Forcht Broadcasting. The format of the station is sports. WAIN-AM broadcasts to the Columbia, KY area at 1270 AM.
AM RADIO STATION

WAIN-FM 45017
Owner: Forcht Broadcasting
Editorial: 1521 Liberty Rd, Columbia, Kentucky 42728
Tel: 1 270 384-2135.
Email: wain@forchtbroadcasting.com
Web site: http://www.935wain.com
Profile: WAIN-FM is a commercial station owned by Forcht Broadcasting. The format of the station is contemporary country. WAIN-FM broadcasts to the Columbia, KY area at 95.3 FM.
FM RADIO STATION

WAIO-FM 42880
Owner: iHeartMedia Inc.
Editorial: 100 Chestnut St Ste 1700, Rochester, New York 14604-2418 **Tel:** 1 585 454-4884.
Web site: http://radio951.iheart.com/
Profile: WAIO-FM is a commercial station owned by iHeartMedia Inc. The format of the station is classic rock. WAIO-FM broadcasts to the Rochester, NY area at 95.1 FM.
FM RADIO STATION

WAIS-AM 38550
Owner: Nelsonville TV Cable Inc.
Editorial: 15751 Elm Rock Rd, Nelsonville, Ohio 45764-9304 **Tel:** 1 740 753-4094.
Email: wseo33@nelsonvilletv.com
Profile: WAIS-AM is a commercial station owned by Nelsonville TV Cable Inc. The format of the station is classic country and bluegrass. WAIS-AM broadcasts to the Nelsonville, OH area at 770 AM.
AM RADIO STATION

WAIT-AM 36523
Owner: Newsweb Corp.
Editorial: 5625 N Milwaukee Ave, Chicago, Illinois 60646-6221 **Tel:** 1 773 792-1121.
Web site: http://www.thepromise850.com
Profile: WAIT-AM is a commercial station owned by Newsweb Corp. The format of the station is bilingual Christian. WAIT-AM broadcasts to the Chicago area at 850 AM. The station airs brokered programming.
AM RADIO STATION

WAIV-FM 45787
Owner: Equity Communications LP
Editorial: 8025 Black Horse Pike, Pleasantville, New Jersey 08232-2900 **Tel:** 1 609 484-8444.
Web site: http://sunny1023.com
Profile: WAIV-FM is a commercial station owned by Equity Communications LP. The format of the station is classic hits music. WAIV-FM broadcasts to the West Atlantic City, NJ area at 95.1 FM.
FM RADIO STATION

WAIX-AM 36516
Owner: Empire Broadcasting Corporation
Editorial: 100 Saratoga Village Blvd, Malta, New York 12020-3737 **Tel:** 1 518 899-3000.
Profile: WAIX-AM is a commercial station owned by Empire Broadcasting Corporation. The format of the station is Hot AC. WAIX-AM broadcasts to the Albany, NY area at 1160 AM.
AM RADIO STATION

WAIZ-AM 36638
Owner: Newton-Conover Communications, Inc.
Editorial: 1666 Radio Station Rd, Newton, North Carolina 28658-9488 **Tel:** 1 828 322-9472.
Web site: http://mytotalradio.com/WAIZ
Profile: WAIZ-AM is a commercial station owned by Newton-Conover Communications, Inc. The format of the station is oldies music. WAIZ-AM broadcasts to the Charlotte, NC area at 630 AM.
AM RADIO STATION

WAJC-FM 872930
Owner: Religious Information Network
Editorial: 2993 Snelling Ave N #M160, Saint Paul, Minnesota 55113-1412 **Tel:** 1 651 307-1507.
Web site: http://theremnant.org/
Profile: WAJC-FM is a non-commercial station owned by Religious Information Network. The format of the station is Christian CHR/Rock music. WAJC-FM broadcasts to the Minneapolis-St. Paul, MN area at a frequency of 88.1 FM.
FM RADIO STATION

WAJI-FM 41258
Owner: Sarkes Tarzian Inc.
Editorial: 347 W Berry St Ste 417, Fort Wayne, Indiana 46802-2241 **Tel:** 1 260 423-3676.
Email: CDidier@stfortwayne.com
Web site: http://www.951bestfm.com
Profile: WAJI-FM is a commercial station owned by Sarkes Tarzian Inc. The format of the station is adult contemporary. WAJI-FM broadcasts to the Fort Wayne, IN area at 95.1 FM.
FM RADIO STATION

WAJK-FM 45018
Owner: LaSalle County Broadcasting Corp.
Editorial: 1 Broadcast Ln, Oglesby, Illinois 61348-9539 **Tel:** 1 815 223-3100.
Email: events@993wajk.com
Web site: http://993wajk.com/
Profile: WAJK-FM is a commercial station owned by LaSalle County Broadcasting Corp. The format of the station is hot adult contemporary. WAJK-FM broadcasts to the Chicago area at 99.3 FM.
FM RADIO STATION

WAJL-AM 849121
Owner: Waller-Barton (Linda)
Editorial: 1180 Plywood Trail, South Boston, Virginia 24592 **Tel:** 1 434 572-7608.
Email: wajlradio@live.com
Web site: http://thebeacon1400am.com
AM RADIO STATION

WAJQ-FM 46772
Owner: Blueberry Broadcasting Co.
Editorial: 208 Douglas St, Alma, Georgia 31510
Tel: 1 912 632-1000.
Profile: WAJQ-FM is a commercial station owned by Blueberry Broadcasting Co. The format of the station is country music. WAJQ-FM broadcasts to the Alma, GA area at 104.3 FM.
FM RADIO STATION

WAJR-AM 37633
Owner: West Virginia Radio Corp.
Editorial: 1251 Earl L Core Rd, Morgantown, West Virginia 26505-5881 **Tel:** 1 304 296-0029.
Email: wajr@wvradio.com
Web site: http://www.wajr.com
Profile: WAJR-AM is a commercial station owned by West Virginia Radio Corp. The format of the station is news, talk, and sports. WAJR-AM broadcasts to the Morgantown, WV area at 1440 AM.
AM RADIO STATION

WAJR-FM 46890
Owner: West Virginia Radio Corp.
Editorial: 1065 Radio Park Dr, Mount Clare, West Virginia 26408 **Tel:** 1 304 623-6546.
Email: wajr@wvradio.com
Web site: http://www.wajrfm.com
Profile: WAJR-FM is a commercial station owned by West Virginia Radio Corp. The format of the station is news, sports, and talk. WAJR-FM broadcasts to the Mount Clare, WV area at 103.3 FM.
FM RADIO STATION

WAJV-FM 43903
Owner: URBan Radio Broadcasting, LLC
Editorial: 608 Yellow Jacket Dr, Starkville, Mississippi 39759 **Tel:** 1 662 338-5424.
Web site: http://www.joy989.com
Profile: WAJV-FM is a commercial station owned by URBan Radio Broadcasting, LLC. The format of the station is gospel. WAJV-FM broadcasts to the Starkville, MS area at 98.9 FM.
FM RADIO STATION

WAJZ-FM 41789
Owner: Albany Broadcasting Co.
Editorial: 6 Johnson Rd, Latham, New York 12110
Tel: 1 518 786-6600.
Web site: http://www.jamz963.com
Profile: WAJZ-FM is a commercial station owned by Albany Broadcasting Co. The format of the station is urban contemporary. WAJZ-FM broadcasts to the Latham, NY area at 96.3 FM.
FM RADIO STATION

WAKB-FM 41780
Owner: Perry Broadcasting Company, Inc.
Editorial: 6025 Broadcast Dr, North Augusta, South Carolina 29841-9406 **Tel:** 1 803 279-2330.
Web site: http://www.1009magic.com
Profile: WAKB-FM is a commercial station owned by Perry Broadcasting Company, Inc. The format of the station is urban adult contemporary. WAKB-FM broadcasts to the North Augusta, SC area at 100.9 FM.
FM RADIO STATION

WAKG-FM 45020
Owner: Piedmont Broadcasting Corporation
Editorial: 710 Grove St, Danville, Virginia 24541-1704
Tel: 1 434 793-4411.
Email: wakg@wakg.com
Web site: http://www.wakg.com
Profile: WAKG-FM is a commercial station owned by Piedmont Broadcasting Corporation. The format of the station is contemporary and classic country. WAKG-FM broadcasts to the Danville, VA area at 103.3 FM.
FM RADIO STATION

WAKH-FM 42813
Owner: Southwest Broadcasting
Editorial: 206 N Front St, McComb, Mississippi 39648-3916 **Tel:** 1 601 684-4116.
Email: spots@k106.net
Web site: http://www.k106.net
Profile: WAKH-FM is a commercial station owned by Southwest Broadcasting. The format of the station is country. WAKH-FM broadcasts to the McComb, MS area at 105.7 FM.
FM RADIO STATION

WAKI-AM 39302
Owner: Peg Broadcasting
Editorial: 230 W Colville St, Mc Minnville, Tennessee 37110-3211 **Tel:** 1 931 473-9253.
Email: production.mcminnville@pegbroadcasting.com
Profile: WAKI-AM is a commercial station owned by Peg Broadcasting. The format of the station is sports. WAKI-AM broadcasts to the McMinnville, TN area at 1230 AM.
AM RADIO STATION

WAKK-AM 36464
Owner: Southwest Broadcasting
Editorial: 206 N Front St, McComb, Mississippi 39648-3916 **Tel:** 1 601 684-4116.
Email: spots@k106.net
Web site: https://k106country.wordpress.com
Profile: WKJN-AM is a commercial station owned by Southwest Broadcasting. The format of the station is gospel. WKJN-AM broadcasts in the McComb, MS area at 980 AM.
AM RADIO STATION

WAKM-AM 35164
Owner: Franklin Radio Associates Inc.
Editorial: 222 Mallory Station Rd, Franklin, Tennessee 37067-8201 **Tel:** 1 615 794-1594.
Email: wakm950@comcast.net
Web site: http://wakm950am.tripod.com
Profile: WAKM-AM is a commercial station owned by Franklin Radio Associates Inc. The format of the station is classic country. WAKM-AM broadcasts to the Franklin, TN area at 950 AM.
AM RADIO STATION

WAKO-AM 37634
Owner: Lawrenceville Broadcasting Co. Inc.
Editorial: Business Highway 50 East, Lawrenceville, Illinois 62439 **Tel:** 1 618 943-3354.
Email: wakoradio@yahoo.com
Web site: http://www.wakoradio.com
Profile: WAKO-AM is a commercial station owned by the Lawrenceville Broadcasting Co. Inc. The format of the station is adult contemporary, classic country and oldies music. WAKO-AM broadcasts to the Lawrenceville, IL area at 910 AM.
AM RADIO STATION

WAKO-FM 45021
Owner: Lawrenceville Broadcasting Co. Inc.
Editorial: Business Highway 50 East, Lawrenceville, Illinois 62439 **Tel:** 1 618 943-3354.
Email: wakoradio@yahoo.com
Web site: http://www.wakoradio.com
Profile: WAKO-FM is a commercial station owned by Lawrenceville Broadcasting Co. Inc. The format of the station is adult contemporary, oldies and country music. WAKO-FM broadcasts to the Lawrenceville, IL area at 103.1 FM.
FM RADIO STATION

WAKQ-FM 45022
Owner: WENK of Union City, Inc.
Editorial: 206 N Brewer St, Paris, Tennessee 38242-4028 **Tel:** 1 731 642-7100.
Web site: http://www.kf99kq105.com
Profile: WAKQ-FM is a commercial station owned by WENK of Union City, Inc. The format of the station is Top 40/CHR music. WAKQ-FM broadcasts to the Paris, TN area at 105.5 FM.
FM RADIO STATION

WAKR-AM 37635
Owner: Rubber City Radio Group Inc.
Editorial: 1795 W Market St, Akron, Ohio 44313
Tel: 1 330 869-9800.
Email: news@wakr.net
Web site: http://www.wakr.net
Profile: WAKR-AM is a commercial station owned by Rubber City Radio Group Inc. The format of the station is oldies, sports and talk. WAKR-AM broadcasts to the Akron, OH area at 1590 AM.
AM RADIO STATION

WAKS-FM
44057
Owner: iHeartMedia Inc.
Editorial: 6200 Oak Tree Blvd Ste 400, Independence, Ohio 44131-6934 **Tel:** 1 216 520-2600.
Email: feedback@waks.com
Web site: http://www.kisscleveland.com
Profile: WAKS-FM is a commercial station owned by iHeartMedia Inc. The format of the station is Top 40/ CHR. WAKS-FM broadcasts to the Independence, OH area at 96.5 FM.
FM RADIO STATION

WAKT-FM
41242
Owner: Powell Broadcasting Company, LLC
Editorial: 118 Gwyn Dr, Panama City Beach, Florida 32408-5854 **Tel:** 1 850 234-8858.
Web site: http://www.kickn1035.com/
Profile: WKNK-FM is a commercial station owned by Powell Broadcasting Company, LLC. The format of the station is classic and contemporary country music. WKNK-FM broadcasts in the Panama City, FL area at 103.5 FM.
FM RADIO STATION

WAKU-FM
43701
Owner: Altrua Investments International Corp.
Editorial: 3225 Hartsfield Rd, Tallahassee, Florida 32303-3153 **Tel:** 1 850 926-8000.
Email: info@wave94.com
Web site: http://www.wave94.com
Profile: WAKU-FM is a commercial station owned by Altrua Investments International Corp. The format of the station is contemporary Christian and religious talk. WAKU-FM broadcasts to the Crawfordville, FL area at 94.1 FM.
FM RADIO STATION

WAKV-AM
36813
Owner: Vintage Radio Inc.
Editorial: 213 Gilkey St, Plainwell, Michigan 49080-1220 **Tel:** 1 269 685-2438.
Email: 980am@net-link.net
Web site: http://wakv.blogspot.com
AM RADIO STATION

WAKW-FM
40091
Owner: Pillar of Fire Inc.
Editorial: 6275 Collegevue Pl, Cincinnati, Ohio 45224-1959 **Tel:** 1 513 542-9259.
Web site: http://www.mystar933.com
Profile: WAKW-FM is a commercial station owned by Pillar of Fire Inc. The format of the station is contemporary Christian. WAKW-FM broadcasts to the Cincinnati area at 93.3 FM.
FM RADIO STATION

WAKY-FM
42124
Owner: W & B Broadcasting Inc.
Editorial: 2608 Ring Rd, Elizabethtown, Kentucky 42701-7945 **Tel:** 1 270 766-1035.
Email: waky@wakyradio.com
Web site: http://www.wakyradio.com
Profile: WAKY-FM is a commercial station owned by W & B Broadcasting Inc. The format of the station is classic hits. WAKY-FM broadcasts to the Elizabethtown, KY area at 103.5 FM.
FM RADIO STATION

WAKZ-FM
42508
Owner: iHeartMedia Inc.
Editorial: 7461 South Ave, Youngstown, Ohio 44512-5789 **Tel:** 1 330 965-0057.
Web site: http://www.959kiss.com
Profile: WAKZ-FM is a commercial station owned by iHeartMedia Inc. The format of the station is Top 40/ CHR music. WAKZ-FM broadcasts to the Youngstown, OH area at 95.9 FM.
FM RADIO STATION

WALC-FM
41299
Owner: Radio Training Network, Inc
Tel: 1 864 292-6040.
Web site: http://www.hisradio.com/charleston.php
Profile: WALC-FM is a commercial station owned by Radio Training Network, Inc. The format of the station is Christian adult contemporary. WALC-FM broadcasts to the Greater Charleston, SC area at 100.5 FM.
FM RADIO STATION

WALD-AM
542439
Owner: Glory Communications Inc.
Tel: 1 803 939-9530.
Email: lgrant@wfmv.com
Profile: WALD-AM is a commercial station owned by Glory Communications Inc. The format of the station is Black gospel. WALD-AM broadcasts to the Columbia, SC area at 1080 AM. Its' sister station is WFMV-FM 95.3.
AM RADIO STATION

WALG-AM
39095
Owner: Cumulus Media Inc.
Editorial: 1104 W Broad Ave, Albany, Georgia 31707-4340 **Tel:** 1 229 436-7233.
Web site: http://www.1590walg.com
Profile: WALG-AM is a commercial station owned by Cumulus Media Inc. The format of the station is news and talk. WALG-AM's broadcasts to the Albany, GA area at 1590 AM.
AM RADIO STATION

WALJ-FM
775954
Owner: Apex Broadcasting, Inc.
Editorial: 534 14th St, Tuscaloosa, Alabama 35401-3434 **Tel:** 1 205 523-5770.
Web site: http://www.1051jamz.com
Profile: WALJ-FM is a commercial station owned by Apex Broadcasting, Inc and programmed/ operated by Cox Media Group. The format of the station is urban contemporary. WALJ-FM broadcasts to the Tuscaloosa, AL area at a frequency of 105.1 FM.
FM RADIO STATION

WALK-AM
37636
Owner: Connoisseur Media
Editorial: 66 Colonial Dr, Patchogue, New York 11772-5849 **Tel:** 1 631 475-5200.
Email: walknews@walkradio.com
Web site: http://www.whli.com
Profile: WALK-AM is a commercial station owned by Connoisseur Media. The format of the station is adult standards. WALK-AM broadcasts to the Long Island, NY area at 1370 AM.
AM RADIO STATION

WALK-FM
45023
Owner: Connoisseur Media
Editorial: 66 Colonial Dr, Patchogue, New York 11772-5849 **Tel:** 1 631 475-5200.
Email: walk975@walkradio.com
Web site: http://www.walk975.com
Profile: WALK-FM is a commercial station owned by Connoisseur Media. The format of the station is adult contemporary music. WALK-FM broadcasts throughout the Nassau and Suffolk Counties in New York at 97.5 FM.
FM RADIO STATION

WALL-AM
37637
Owner: Townsquare Media
Editorial: 2 Pendell Rd, Poughkeepsie, New York 12601-1513 **Tel:** 1 845 471-1500.
Web site: http://hudsonvalleytrueoldies.com
Profile: WALL-AM is a commercial station owned by Townsquare Media. The format of the station is classic hits. WALL-FM broadcasts to the Poughkeepsie, NY area at 1340 AM.
AM RADIO STATION

WALR-FM
83626
Owner: Cox Media Group, Inc.
Editorial: 1601 W Peachtree St NE, Atlanta, Georgia 30309-2641 **Tel:** 1 404 897-7500.
Web site: http://www.kiss104fm.com
Profile: WALR-FM is a commercial station owned by Cox Media Group, Inc. The format of the station is urban adult contemporary. WALR-FM broadcasts to the Atlanta area at 104.1 FM.
FM RADIO STATION

WALS-FM
42346
Owner: Studstill Media
Editorial: 3905 Progress Blvd, Peru, Illinois 61354-1121 **Tel:** 1 815 224-2100.
Email: walls102@theradiogroup.net
Web site: http://www.walls102.com
Profile: WALS-FM is a commercial station owned by Studstill Media. The format for the station is contemporary country. WALS-FM broadcasts to the Peru, IL area at 102.1 FM.
FM RADIO STATION

WALT-AM
37638
Owner: New South Communications Inc.
Editorial: 3436 Highway 45 N, Meridian, Mississippi 39301-1509 **Tel:** 1 601 693-3434.
Profile: WALT-AM is a commercial station owned by New South Communications Inc. The format for the station is talk. WALT-AM broadcasts to the Meridian, MS area at 910 AM.
AM RADIO STATION

WALV-FM
46497
Owner: Brewer Broadcasting Inc.
Editorial: 1305 Carter St, Chattanooga, Tennessee 37402 **Tel:** 1 423 265-9494.
Web site: http://www.espnchattanooga.com
Profile: WALV-FM is a commercial station owned by Brewer Broadcasting Inc. The format of the station is sports. WALV-FM broadcasts to the Chattanooga, TN area at 105.1 FM.
FM RADIO STATION

WALX-FM
46635
Owner: Alexander Broadcasting Company, Inc.
Editorial: 273 Persimmon Tree Rd, Valley Grande, Alabama 36701-3131 **Tel:** 1 334 875-9360.
Web site: http://walxradio.com/
Profile: WALX-FM is a commercial station owned by Alexander Broadcasting Company, Inc. The format of the station is classic hits. WALX-FM broadcasts to the Valley Grande, AL area at 100.9 FM.
FM RADIO STATION

WALY-FM
46886
Owner: FM Radio Licenses, LLC
Editorial: 1 Forever Dr, Hollidaysburg, Pennsylvania 16648-3029 **Tel:** 1 814 941-9800.
Web site: http://www.waly1039.com
Profile: WALY-FM is a commercial station owned by FM Radio Licenses, LLC. The format of the station is adult contemporary. WALY-FM broadcasts to the Hollidaysburg, PA area at 103.9 FM.
FM RADIO STATION

WALZ-FM
43188
Owner: Machias Valley Broadcasting
Editorial: 637 Main St, Calais, Maine 4619
Tel: 1 207 454-7545.
Email: wqdy@wqdy.fm
Web site: http://www.wqdy.fm
Profile: WALZ-FM is a commercial station owned by Machias Valley Broadcasting. The format for the station is classic hits. WALZ-FM broadcasts to the Machias, ME area at 95.3 FM.
FM RADIO STATION

WAMC/Northeast Public Radio
47990
Editorial: 318 Central Ave, Albany, New York 12206-2522 **Tel:** 1 518 465-5233.
Email: news@wamc.org
Web site: http://www.wamc.org
Profile: WAMC/Northeast Public Radio is a regional public radio network serving parts of seven northeastern states. These include New York, Massachusetts, Connecticut, Vermont, New Jersey, New Hampshire and Pennsylvania. Stations and translators are in ten locations throughout the region. WAMC/Northeast Public Radio is a member of National Public Radio and an affiliate of Public Radio International.
REGIONAL RADIO NETWORKS

WAMC-FM
41016
Owner: WAMC
Editorial: 318 Central Ave, Albany, New York 12206-2522 **Tel:** 1 518 465-5233.
Email: mail@wamc.org
Web site: http://www.wamc.org
Profile: WAMC-FM is a non-commercial station owned by WAMC. The format of the station is news and talk. WAMC-FM broadcasts to the Albany, NY area at 90.3 FM.
FM RADIO STATION

WAME-AM
35281
Owner: Statesville Family Radio Corporation
Editorial: 113 N Center St, Statesville, North Carolina 28677-5389 **Tel:** 1 704 873-1946.
Web site: http://wameradio.com
Profile: WAME-AM is a commercial station owned by Statesville Family Radio Corporation. The format for the station is classic country. WAME-AM broadcasts to the Charlotte, NC area at 550 AM. The station's slogan is, "Decades of Country Music!"
AM RADIO STATION

WAMI-FM
45024
Owner: Opp Broadcasting Co. Inc.
Editorial: 1807 N Main St, Opp, Alabama 36467
Tel: 1 334 493-3588.
Email: wami@oppcatv.com
Profile: WAMI-FM is a commercial station owned by Opp Broadcasting Co. Inc. The format of the station is classic country. WAMI-FM broadcasts to the Opp, AL area at 102.3 FM.
FM RADIO STATION

WAMJ-FM
43595
Owner: Urban One Inc.
Editorial: 101 Marietta St NW Fl 12, Atlanta, Georgia 30303-2720 **Tel:** 1 404 765-9750.
Web site: http://majicatl.hellobeautiful.com
Profile: WAMJ-FM is a commercial station owned by Urban One Inc. The format of the station is urban AC. WAMJ-FM broadcasts to the Atlanta area at 107.5 FM. The station';s slogan is, "The Real Sound of the ATL."
FM RADIO STATION

WAMK-FM
43907
Owner: WAMC
Editorial: 318 Central Ave, Albany, New York 12206
Tel: 1 518 465-5233.
Email: mail@wamc.org
Web site: http://www.wamc.org
Profile: WAMK-FM is a non-commercial station owned by WAMC. The format of the station is news and talk. WAMK-FM broadcasts to the Kingston, NY area at 90.9 FM.
FM RADIO STATION

WAML-AM
36457
Owner: Walking By Faith Ministries
Editorial: 336 Rodenberg Ave, Biloxi, Mississippi 39531-3444 **Tel:** 1 228 374-9739.
Email: wqfxradio@bellsouth.net
Profile: WAML-AM is a commercial station owned by Walking By Faith Ministries. The format of the station is gospel music. WAML-AM broadcasts in Laurel, MS and its surrounding environs at 1340 AM.
AM RADIO STATION

WAMN-AM
35976
Owner: Two Virginia's Media
Editorial: 4415 Blue Prince Road, Bluefield, West Virginia 24701 **Tel:** 1 304 327-9266.
Web site: http://www.mywillie.com
Profile: WAMN-AM is a commercial station owned by Two Virginia's Media. The format of the station is classic country. WAMN-AM broadcasts to the Bluefield, WV area at 1050 AM.
AM RADIO STATION

WAMO-AM
36934
Owner: Radio Power, Inc.
Editorial: 21 Yost Blvd Ste 505, Pittsburgh, Pennsylvania 15221-5237 **Tel:** 1 412 829-0100.
Web site: http://www.wamo100.com
Profile: WAMO-AM is a commercial station owned by Langer Broadcasting Group, LLC. The format of the station is urban contemporary. WAMO-AM broadcasts to the Pittsburgh area at 660 AM.
AM RADIO STATION

WAMQ-FM
43908
Owner: WAMC
Editorial: 318 Central Ave, Albany, New York 12206-2522 **Tel:** 1 518 465-5233.
Email: mail@wamc.org
Web site: http://www.wamc.org
Profile: WAMQ-FM is a non-commercial station owned by WAMC. The format of the station is news and talk. WAMQ-FM broadcasts to the Albany, NY area at 105.1 FM.
FM RADIO STATION

WAMR-FM
45458
Owner: Univision Communications Inc.
Editorial: 800 S Douglas Rd Ste 111, Coral Gables, Florida 33134-3187 **Tel:** 1 305 447-1140.
Web site: http://www.univision.com/miami/wamr
Profile: WAMR-FM is a commercial station owned by Univision Communications Inc. The format of the station is Spanish Hits. WAMR-FM broadcasts to the Coral Gables, FL area at 107.5 FM.
FM RADIO STATION

WAMT-AM
35161
Owner: Genesis Communications Inc.
Editorial: 1160 S Semoran Blvd, Orlando, Florida 32807-1461 **Tel:** 1 407 380-9255.
Email: wamt@radiogenesis.com
Web site: http://www.newstalkflorida.com
Profile: WAMT-AM is a commercial station owned by Genesis Communications Inc. The format of the station is news talk. WAMT-AM broadcasts to the Orlando, FL area at 1190 AM. The station airs their WWBA-AM's programming during a portion of the day.
AM RADIO STATION

WAMV-AM
35758
Owner: Community First Broadcasters
Editorial: 132 School Road, Amherst, Virginia 24521
Tel: 1 434 946-9000.
Email: wamvradio@aol.com
Web site: http://www.wamvradio1420.com
Profile: WAMV-AM is a commercial station owned by Community First Broadcasters. The format of the station is southern gospel and classic country. WAMV-AM broadcasts to the Amherst, VA area at 1420 AM.
AM RADIO STATION

WAMW-AM
38805
Owner: DLC Media Inc.
Editorial: 800 W National Hwy, Washington, Indiana 47501 **Tel:** 1 812 254-6761.
Web site: http://www.fourstarcountry.com
Profile: WAMW-AM is a commercial station owned by DLC Media Inc. The format of the station is adult standards music. WAMW-AM broadcasts to the Washington, IN area at 1580 AM.
AM RADIO STATION

WAMW-FM
46181
Owner: DLC Media Inc.
Editorial: 800 W National Hwy, Washington, Indiana 47501-3326 **Tel:** 1 812 254-6761.
Web site: http://www.memories1079.com
Profile: WAMW-FM is a commercial station owned by DLC Media Inc. The format of the station is classic hits. WAMW-FM broadcasts to the Washington, IN, area at 107.9 FM.
FM RADIO STATION

WAMX-FM
46609
Owner: iHeartMedia Inc.
Editorial: 134 4th Ave, Huntington, West Virginia 25701-1220 **Tel:** 1 304 525-7788.
Web site: http://www.1063thebrew.com/main.html
Profile: WAMX-FM is a commercial station owned by iHeartMedia Inc. The format of the station is classic rock. WAMX-FM broadcasts to the Huntington, WV area at 106.3 FM.
FM RADIO STATION

WAMY-AM
38785
Owner: Stanford Communications Inc.
Editorial: 521 Highway 278 W, Amory, Mississippi 38821 **Tel:** 1 662 256-9726.
Email: fm95@fm95radio.com
Web site: http://www.fm95radio.com
Profile: WAMY-AM is a commercial station owned by Stanford Communications Inc. The format of the station is news, sports and talk. WAMY-AM broadcasts to the Amory, MS area at 1580 AM.
AM RADIO STATION

WAMZ-FM
46808
Owner: iHeartMedia Inc.
Editorial: 4000 Radio Dr, Louisville, Kentucky 40218-4568 **Tel:** 1 502 479-2222.
Web site: http://wamz.iheart.com/
Profile: WAMZ-FM is a commercial station owned by iHeartMedia Inc. The format of the station is contemporary country music. WAMZ-FM broadcasts in the Louisville, KY area at 97.5 FM.
FM RADIO STATION

WANB-AM
37640
Owner: Broadcast Communications Inc.
Editorial: 369 Tower Rd, Waynesburg, Pennsylvania 15370-3663 **Tel:** 1 724 627-5555.
Email: wanbradio@gmail.com
Web site: http://www.greenecountygold.com/
Profile: WANB-AM is a commercial station owned by Broadcast Communications Inc. The format of the station is country. WANB-AM broadcasts to the Waynesburg, PA area at 1210 AM.
AM RADIO STATION

WANC-FM
42109
Owner: WAMC
Editorial: 318 Central Ave, Albany, New York 12206
Tel: 1 518 465-5233.
Email: mail@wamc.org

Web site: http://www.wamc.org
Profile: WANC-FM is a non-commercial station owned by WAMC. The format of the station is news and talk. WANC-FM broadcasts to the Albany, NY area at 103.9 FM.
FM RADIO STATION

WANG-AM 39273
Owner: Alpha Media
Editorial: 1361 Colony Dr, New Bern, North Carolina 28562-4129 **Tel:** 1 252 639-7900.
Profile: WANG-AM is a commercial station owned by Alpha Media. The format of the station is adult standards and middle of the road format. WANG-AM broadcasts to the New Bern, NC area at 1330 AM.
AM RADIO STATION

WANI-AM 35415
Owner: Auburn Network, Inc.
Editorial: 197 E University Dr, Auburn, Alabama 36832-6725 **Tel:** 1 334 826-2929.
Web site: http://newstalkwani.com
Profile: WANI-AM is a commercial station owned by Auburn Network, Inc. The format of the station is news and talk. WANI-AM broadcasts to the Auburn, AL area at 1400 AM.
AM RADIO STATION

WANK-FM 41439
Owner: Red Hills Broadcasting, LLC
Editorial: 3000 Olson Rd, Tallahassee, Florida 32308-3918 **Tel:** 1 850 386-8004.
Web site: http://www.999hank.fm
Profile: WANK-FM is a commercial station owned by Red Hills Broadcasting, LLC. The format of the station is adult hits. WANK-FM broadcasts to the Tallahassee, FL area at a frequency of 99.9 FM.
FM RADIO STATION

WANO-AM 36932
Owner: Penelope, Inc.
Editorial: 2117 Cumberland Ave, Middlesboro, Kentucky 40965-2876 **Tel:** 1 606 337-9528.
Email: wanocountry@gmail.com
Web site: http://1230wano.com/
Profile: WANO-AM is a commercial station owned by the Penelope, Inc. The format of the station is contemporary and classic country. WANO-AM broadcasts to the Middlesboro, KY area at 1230 AM.
AM RADIO STATION

WANS-AM 36208
Owner: (Bryant) Gary
Editorial: 102 E Shockley Ferry Rd, Anderson, South Carolina 29624-3730 **Tel:** 1 864 224-6733.
Profile: WANS-AM is a commercial station owned by Gary Bryant. The format of the station is sports. WANS-AM broadcasts to the Anderson, SC area at 1280 AM.
AM RADIO STATION

WANT-FM 46599
Owner: Bay-Pointe Broadcasting Inc.
Editorial: 510 Trousdale Ferry Pike, Lebanon, Tennessee 37087-4727 **Tel:** 1 615 449-3699.
Email: info@wantfm.com
Web site: http://www.wantfm.com
Profile: WANT-FM is a commercial station owned by Bay-Pointe Broadcasting Inc. The format of the station is a mix of contemporary and classic country music. WANT-FM broadcasts to the Lebanon, TN area at 98.9 FM.
FM RADIO STATION

WANV-FM 950708
Owner: Forcht Broadcasting
Editorial: 534 Tobacco Rd, London, Kentucky 40741-2200 **Tel:** 1 606 864-2148.
Web site: http://www.967wanv.com
Profile: WANV-FM is a commercial station owned by Forcht Broadcasting. The format of the station is oldies. The station broadcasts to the London, KY area at a frequency of 96.7 FM.
FM RADIO STATION

WAOA-FM 45607
Owner: Cumulus Media Inc.
Editorial: 1800 W Hibiscus Blvd Ste 138, Melbourne, Florida 32901-2624 **Tel:** 1 321 984-1000.
Web site: http://www.wa1a.com
Profile: WAOA-FM is a commercial station owned by Cumulus Media Inc. The format of the station is Top 40/CHR music. WAOA-FM broadcasts to the Melbourne, FL area at 107.1 FM.
FM RADIO STATION

WAOC-AM 39363
Owner: Phillips Broadcasting, LLC
Editorial: 567 Lewis Point Road Ext, Saint Augustine, Florida 32086-5222 **Tel:** 1 904 797-1955.
Web site: http://www.1420sports.com
Profile: WAOC-AM is a commercial station owned by Phillips Broadcasting, LLC. The format of the station is sports. WAOC-AM broadcasts to the Saint Augustine, FL area at 1420 AM.
AM RADIO STATION

WAOK-AM 37642
Owner: CBS Radio
Editorial: 1201 Peachtree St NE, 400 Colony Square, St. 800, Atlanta, Georgia 30361-3503 **Tel:** 1 404 898-8900.
Web site: http://atlanta.cbslocal.com
Profile: WAOK-AM is a commercial station owned by CBS Radio. The format of the station is news and talk. WAOK-AM broadcasts in the Atlanta area at 1380 AM.
AM RADIO STATION

WAOQ-FM 44482
Owner: Alatron Corp. Inc.
Editorial: 1370 N Franklin Rd, Goshen, Alabama 36035-6506 **Tel:** 1 334 335-2877.
Email: office@waoq.com
FM RADIO STATION

WAOR-FM 41916
Owner: St. Joseph Catholic Radio Group
Editorial: 245 W Edison, Mishawaka, Indiana 46545 **Tel:** 1 574 258-5483.
Web site: http://www.waor.com
Profile: WAOR-FM is a commercial station owned by St. Joseph Catholic Radio Group. The format of the station is classic rock. WAOR-FM broadcasts to the Ligonier, Elkhart and Goshen areas in areas at a frequency of 102.7 FM.
FM RADIO STATION

WAOS-AM 36183
Owner: La Favorita Inc.
Editorial: 5815 Westside Rd, Austell, Georgia 30106-3179 **Tel:** 1 770 944-0900.
Email: traffic@lamejorestacion.com
Web site: http://www.lamejorestacion.com
Profile: WAOS-AM is a commercial station owned by La Favorita Inc. The format of the station is regional Mexican. WAOS-AM broadcasts to the Atlanta area at 1600 AM.
AM RADIO STATION

WAOV-AM 36919
Owner: Original Company Inc.(The)
Editorial: 522 Busseron St, Vincennes, Indiana 47591 **Tel:** 1 812 882-6060.
Email: waov@originalcompany.com
Web site: http://www.waovam.com
Profile: WAOV-AM is a commercial station owned by The Original Company Inc. The format of the station is news, sports, and talk. WAOV-AM broadcasts to the Vincennes, IN area at 1450 AM.
AM RADIO STATION

WAOX-FM 518192
Owner: Talley Broadcasting Corp.
Editorial: 6308 Illinois Route 16, Hillsboro, Illinois 62049 **Tel:** 1 618 635-6000.
Email: waox@waoxradio.com
Web site: http://www.waox.com
Profile: WAOX-FM is a commercial station owned by Talley Broadcasting Corp. The format of the station is hot adult contemporary. WAOX-FM broadcasts to the Hillsboro, IL area at 105.3 FM.
FM RADIO STATION

WAOY-FM 43199
Owner: American Family Association
Editorial: 107 Park Gate St., Tupelo, Mississippi 38801 **Tel:** 1 622 844-8888.
Email: comments@afr.net
Web site: http://www.afr.net
FM RADIO STATION

WAPE-FM 41030
Owner: Cox Media Group, Inc.
Editorial: 8000 Belfort Pkwy, Jacksonville, Florida 32256-6934 **Tel:** 1 904 245-8500.
Web site: http://www.wape.com
Profile: WAPE-FM is a commercial station owned by Cox Media Group, Inc. The format of the station is Top 40/CHR. WAPE-FM broadcasts to the Jacksonville, FL area at 95.1 FM.
FM RADIO STATION

WAPF-AM 35172
Owner: Southwest Broadcasting
Editorial: 206 N Front St, McComb, Mississippi 39648 **Tel:** 1 601 684-4116.
Email: spots@k106.net
Profile: WAPF-AM is a commercial station owned by Southwest Broadcasting. The format of the station is gospel. WAPF-AM broadcasts to the McComb, MS area at 1140 AM.
AM RADIO STATION

WAPI-AM 37643
Owner: Cumulus Media Inc
Editorial: 244 Goodwin Crest Dr Ste 300, Birmingham, Alabama 35209-3700 **Tel:** 1 205 945-4646.
Web site: http://www.talk995.com
Profile: WAPI-AM is a commercial station owned by Cumulus Media Inc. The format of the station is news and talk. WAPI-AM broadcasts to the greater Birmingham, AL area at 1070 AM.
AM RADIO STATION

WAPJ-FM 43212
Owner: Torrington Community Radio Foundation, Inc.
Editorial: 40 Water St, Torrington, Connecticut 06790-5318 **Tel:** 1 860 489-9033.
Email: info@wapj.org
Web site: http://wapjfm.com
Profile: WAPJ-FM is a non-commercial station owned by Torrington Community Radio Foundation, Inc. The format of the station is variety. WAPJ-FM broadcasts to the Hartford-New Haven, CT area at 89.9 FM.
FM RADIO STATION

WAPL-FM 45029
Owner: Woodward Communications, Inc.
Editorial: 2800 E College Ave, Appleton, Wisconsin 54915 **Tel:** 1 920 734-9226.
Email: waplstudio@wcinet.com
Web site: http://www.wapl.com
Profile: WAPL-FM is a commercial station owned by Woodward Communications Inc. The format is rock. WAPL-FM broadcasts to the Appleton, WI area at 105.7 FM.
FM RADIO STATION

WAPN-FM 42635
Owner: Public Radio, Inc.
Editorial: 1508 State Ave, Holly Hill, Florida 32117 **Tel:** 1 386 677-4272.
Email: wapn@wapn.net
Web site: http://www.wapn.net
Profile: WAPN-FM is a non-commercial station owned by Public Radio, Inc. The format of the station is religion. WAPN-FM broadcasts to the Holly Hill, FL area at 91.5 FM.
FM RADIO STATION

WAPY-FM 43210
Owner: FM Radio Licenses, LLC
Editorial: 2551 Park Center Blvd, State College, Pennsylvania 16801-3007 **Tel:** 1 814 237-9800.
Web site: http://www.wrscfm.com
Profile: WAPY-FM is a commercial station owned by FM Radio Licenses, LLC. The format of the station is news and talk. WAPY-FM broadcasts to the State College, PA area at 103.1 FM.
FM RADIO STATION

WAQE-AM 37644
Owner: T K C Inc.
Editorial: 1859 21st Ave, Rice Lake, Wisconsin 54868-9502 **Tel:** 1 715 234-9059.
Email: info@waqe.com
Profile: WAQE-AM is a commercial station owned by T K C Inc. The format of the station is sports. WAQE-AM broadcasts to the Minneapolis area at 1090 AM.
AM RADIO STATION

WAQE-FM 45761
Owner: T K C Inc.
Editorial: 1859 21st Ave, Rice Lake, Wisconsin 54868-9502 **Tel:** 1 715 234-9059.
Email: info@waqe.com
Web site: http://www.waqe.com
Profile: WAQE-FM is a commercial station owned by the TKC Inc. The format of the station is hot adult contemporary music. WAQE-FM broadcasts in the Minneapolis area at 97.7 FM.
FM RADIO STATION

WAQG-FM 154868
Owner: American Family Association
Editorial: 107 Parkgate Dr, Tupelo, Mississippi 38801 **Tel:** 1 662 844-8888.
Email: comments@afr.net
Web site: http://www.afr.net
FM RADIO STATION

WAQI-AM 39037
Owner: Univision Communications Inc.
Editorial: 800 S Douglas Rd, Coral Gables, Florida 33134-3125 **Tel:** 1 305 445-4040.
Web site: http://www.univision.com/miami/waqi-am
Profile: WAQI-AM is a commercial station owned by Univision Communications Inc. The format of the station is Hispanic news and talk. WAQI-AM broadcasts to the Coral Gables, FL area at 710 AM.
AM RADIO STATION

WAQL-FM 358986
Owner: American Family Association
Editorial: 107 Park Gate Dr, Tupelo, Mississippi 38801-3010 **Tel:** 1 662 844-8888.
Email: comments@afr.net
Web site: http://www.afr.net
Profile: WAQL-FM is a commercial station owned by the American Family Association. The format of the station is Adult Contemporary Christian programming. WAQL-FM broadcasts to the McComb, MS area on 90.5 FM.
FM RADIO STATION

WAQX-FM 41814
Owner: Cumulus Media Inc
Editorial: 1064 James St, Syracuse, New York 13203-2704 **Tel:** 1 315 472-0200.
Web site: http://www.95x.com
Profile: WAQX-FM is a commercial station owned by Cumulus Media Inc. The format of the station is rock music. WAQX-FM broadcasts to the Syracuse, NY area at 95.7 FM.
FM RADIO STATION

WAQY-FM 45959
Owner: Saga Communications
Editorial: 45 Fisher Ave, East Longmeadow, Massachusetts 1028 **Tel:** 1 413 525-4141.
Web site: http://www.rock102.com
Profile: WAQY-FM is a commercial station owned by Saga Communications. The format of the station is classic rock. WAQY-FM broadcasts to the East Longmeadow, MA area at 102.1 FM.
FM RADIO STATION

WARA-AM 35174
Owner: Attleboro Access Cable Systems Inc.
Editorial: 42 Union St, Attleboro, Massachusetts 02703-2948 **Tel:** 1 508 226-2227.
Web site: http://www.wararadio.com
Profile: WARA-AM is a non-commercial station owned by Attleboro Access Cable Systems, Inc. The format of the station is talk and oldies. WARA-AM broadcasts to the Providence, RI area at 1320 AM.
AM RADIO STATION

WARC-FM 40097
Owner: Allegheny College
Editorial: 520 N Main St #C, Allegheny College, Meadville, Pennsylvania 16335-3903 **Tel:** 1 814 332-3376.
Email: warc@allegheny.edu
Web site: http://www.warcmeadville.org
Profile: WARC-FM is a non-commercial station owned by Allegheny College. The format of the station is variety. WARC-FM broadcasts to the Meadville, PA community at 90.3 FM.
FM RADIO STATION

WARD-AM 63309
Owner: Henderson(Roy)
Editorial: 13999 S West Bay Shore Dr, Traverse City, Michigan 49684 **Tel:** 1 231 947-3220.
Profile: WARD-AM is a commercial station owned by Roy Henderson The format of the station is contemporary country. WARD-AM broadcasts to the Traverse City, MI area at 750 AM.
AM RADIO STATION

WARE-AM 35176
Owner: Success Signal Broadcasting Inc
Editorial: 3 Converse St Ste 101, Palmer, Massachusetts 01069-1538 **Tel:** 1 413 289-2300.
Email: manager@realoldies1250.net
Web site: http://www.realoldies1250.net
Profile: WARE-AM is a commercial station owned by Success Signal Broadcasting Inc. The format of the station is oldies. WARE-AM broadcasts to the Palmer, MA area at 1250 AM.
AM RADIO STATION

WARF-AM 38194
Owner: iHeartMedia Inc.
Editorial: 7755 Freedom Ave NW, North Canton, Ohio 44720-6905 **Tel:** 1 330 836-4700.
Web site: http://sportsradio1350.iheart.com/
Profile: WARF-AM is a commercial station owned by iHeartMedia Inc. The format of the station is sports. WARF-AM broadcasts to the North Canton, OH area at 1350 AM.
AM RADIO STATION

WARH-FM 43161
Owner: Hubbard Broadcasting, Inc.
Editorial: 11647 Olive Blvd, Saint Louis, Missouri 63141-7001 **Tel:** 1 314 983-6000.
Web site: http://www.1065thearch.com
Profile: WARH-FM is a commercial station owned by Hubbard Broadcasting, Inc. The format of the station is adult hits. WARH-FM broadcasts to the St. Louis area at 106.5 FM.
FM RADIO STATION

WARK-AM 37645
Owner: Manning Broadcasting Inc.
Editorial: 880 Commonwealth Ave, Hagerstown, Maryland 21740-6836 **Tel:** 1 301 733-4500.
Profile: WARK-AM is a commercial station owned by Manning Broadcasting Inc. The format of the station is news and talk. WARK-AM broadcasts to the Hagerstown, MD, area at 1490 AM.
AM RADIO STATION

WARM-FM 45525
Owner: Cumulus Media Inc.
Editorial: 5989 Susquehanna Plaza Drive, York, Pennsylvania 17406-8910 **Tel:** 1 717 764-1155.
Web site: http://www.warm1033.com
Profile: WARM-FM is a commercial station owned by Cumulus Media Inc. The format of the station is adult contemporary. WARM-FM broadcasts to the York, PA area at 103.3 FM.
FM RADIO STATION

WARO-FM 42681
Owner: Meridian Broadcasting, Inc.
Editorial: 2824 Palm Beach Blvd, Fort Myers, Florida 33916-1503 **Tel:** 1 239 337-2346.
Web site: http://www.945thearrow.com
Profile: WARO-FM is a commercial station owned by Meridian Broadcasting, Inc. The format of the station is classic rock. WARO-FM broadcasts to the Fort Myers, FL area at 94.5 FM.
FM RADIO STATION

WARQ-FM 42683
Owner: Alpha Media
Editorial: 1900 Pineview Dr, Columbia, South Carolina 29209-5079 **Tel:** 1 803 695-8600.
Web site: http://www.q935.com
Profile: WARQ-FM is a commercial station owned by Alpha Media. The format of the station is hot AC. WARQ-FM broadcasts to the Columbia, SC area at 93.5 FM.
FM RADIO STATION

WARR-AM 36858
Owner: Darensburg Broadcasting
Editorial: 824 US Highway 158 Byp, Warrenton, North Carolina 27589 **Tel:** 1 252 257-5557.
Web site: http://www.warr1520.com
Profile: WARR-AM is a commercial station owned by Darensburg Broadcasting. The format of the station is gospel and R&B oldies. WARR-AM broadcasts to the Warrenton, NC area at 1520 AM.
AM RADIO STATION

WARU-AM 37646
Owner: Hoosier AM/FM LLC
Editorial: 1711 E Wabash Rd, Peru, Indiana 46970-8656 **Tel:** 1 765 473-4448.
Email: waru@mitunes1019.com
Web site: http://www.mitunes1019.com

Profile: WARU-AM is a commercial station owned by Hoosier AM/FM LLC. The format of the station is adult hits. WARU-AM broadcasts to the Peru, IN area at 1600 AM.
AM RADIO STATION

WARU-FM 45030
Owner: Hoosier AM/FM LLC
Editorial: 1711 E Wabash Rd, Peru, Indiana 46970-3656 **Tel:** 1 765 473-4448.
Email: waru@mitunes1019.com
Web site: http://www.mitunes1019.com
Profile: WARU-FM is a commercial station owned by Hoosier AM/FM LLC. The format of the station is adult hits and variety. WARU-FM broadcasts to the Indianapolis area at 101.9 FM.
FM RADIO STATION

WARV-AM 35177
Owner: Blount Communications Group
Editorial: 19 Luther Ave, Warwick, Rhode Island 02886-4615 **Tel:** 1 401 737-0700.
Email: info@warv.net
Web site: http://lifechangingradio.com/warv
Profile: WARV-AM is a commercial station owned by Blount Communications Group. The format of the station is religious music. WARV-AM broadcasts to the Providence, RI-New Bedford, MA area at 1590 AM.
AM RADIO STATION

WARV-FM 44528
Owner: Alpha Media
Editorial: 300 Arboretum Place Suite 590, Richmond, Virginia 23236 **Tel:** 1 804 327-9902.
Web site: http://www.989wolf.com
Profile: WARV-FM is a commercial station owned by Alpha Media. The format of the station is contemporary country. WARV-FM broadcasts to the Richmond, VA area at 100.3 FM.
FM RADIO STATION

WARY-FM 40100
Owner: Westchester Community College
Editorial: 75 Grasslands Rd, Valhalla, New York 10595-1550 **Tel:** 1 914 606-6752.
Email: radprime1@aol.com
Web site: http://881wary.webs.com
Profile: WARY-FM is a non-commercial station owned by Westchester Community College. The format of the station is college variety. WARY-FM broadcasts to the New York City area at 88.1 FM.
FM RADIO STATION

WASC-AM 35178
Owner: New South Broadcasting Corporation
Editorial: 1650 Wofford St, Spartanburg, South Carolina 29301-5748 **Tel:** 1 864 585-1530.
Email: wascradio@bellsouth.net
Profile: WASC-AM is a commercial station owned by New South Broadcasting Corporation. The format of the station is urban adult contemporary. WASC-AM broadcasts to the Spartanburg, SC area at 1530 AM.
AM RADIO STATION

WASG-AM 36928
Owner: Alabama Radio Network
Editorial: 273 Azalea Rd, Two Office Park Rd, Ste. #403, Mobile, Alabama 36609-1970 **Tel:** 1 251 340-0442.
Email: wasg@wilkinsradio.com
Web site: http://www.wilkinsradio.com
Profile: WASG-AM is a commercial station owned by Alabama Radio Network. The format of the station is religious talk with a focus on Christian teaching. WASG-AM broadcasts to the Daphne, AL area at a frequency of 540 AM.
AM RADIO STATION

WASH-FM 43487
Owner: iHeartMedia Inc.
Editorial: 1801 Rockville Pike Fl 5, Rockville, Maryland 20852-1633 **Tel:** 1 240 747-2700.
Web site: http://washfm.iheart.com
Profile: WASH-FM is a commercial station owned by iHeartMedia Inc. The format of the station is adult contemporary music. WASH-FM broadcasts to the Washington, D.C. area at 97.1 FM.
FM RADIO STATION

Washington Radio and Press Service 87881
Editorial: 6702 Pawtucket Rd, Bethesda, Maryland 20817-4836 **Tel:** 1 301 229-2576.
Profile: Radio news service with domestic and Canadian clients. Focuses on coverage of national affairs and politics from a local angle.
RADIO NETWORK

WASJ-FM 42060
Owner: Powell Broadcasting Company, LLC
Editorial: 118 Gwyn Dr, Panama City Beach, Florida 32408-5854 **Tel:** 1 850 234-8858.
Web site: http://bobatthebeach.com
Profile: WASJ-FM is a commercial station owned by Powell Broadcasting Company, LLC. The format of the station is adult hits. WASJ-FM broadcasts to the Panama City, FL area at 105.1 FM.
FM RADIO STATION

WASK-AM 37647
Owner: WASK Inc.
Editorial: 3575 McCarty Ln, Lafayette, Indiana 47905-4985 **Tel:** 1 765 447-2186.
Web site: http://www.espn1450am.com
Profile: WASK-AM is a commercial station owned by WASK Inc. The format of the station is sports. WASK-AM broadcasts to the Lafayette, IN area at 1450 AM.
AM RADIO STATION

WASK-FM 46704
Owner: WASK Inc.
Editorial: 3575 McCarty Ln, Lafayette, Indiana 47905-4985 **Tel:** 1 765 447-2186.
Web site: http://www.wask.com
Profile: WASK-FM is a commercial station owned by Neuhoff Communications. The format for the station is classic hits. WASK-FM broadcasts to the Lafayette, IN area at 98.7 FM.
FM RADIO STATION

WASL-FM 46237
Owner: Burks(W.E.)
Editorial: 2555 Burks Pl, Dyersburg, Tennessee 38024-1724 **Tel:** 1 731 285-1339.
Web site: http://www.100jackfm.com
Profile: WASL-FM is a commercial station owned by W.E. Burks. The format of the station is rock music. WASL-FM broadcasts to the Dyersburg, TN area at 100.1 FM.
FM RADIO STATION

WASR-AM 35179
Owner: Hatch(Grant)
Editorial: 73 Varney Rd, Wolfeboro, New Hampshire 03894-4351 **Tel:** 1 603 569-1420.
Email: mail@wasr.net
Web site: http://www.wasr.net
Profile: WASR-AM is a commercial station owned by Grant Hatch. The format of the station is talk. WASR-AM broadcasts to the Wolfeboro, NH area at 1420 AM.
AM RADIO STATION

WATA-FM 39128
Owner: High Country Adventures, LLC
Editorial: 738 Blowing Rock Rd, Boone, North Carolina 28607-4835 **Tel:** 1 828 264-2411.
Email: highcountryradio@gmail.com
Web site: http://goblueridge.net
Profile: WATA-FM is a commercial station owned by High Country Adventures, LLC, a subsidiary of Curtis Media Group. The format of the station is country. WATA-FM broadcasts to the Boone, NC area at 96.5.
FM RADIO STATION

WATB-AM 36773
Owner: Multicultural Radio Broadcasting Inc.
Editorial: 3589 N Decatur Rd, Scottdale, Georgia 30079-1867 **Tel:** 1 404 508-1420.
Web site: http://www.watb1420.com/
Profile: WATB-AM is a commercial station owned by Multicultural Radio Broadcasting Inc. The format of the station is variety, featuring multicultural programming. WATB-AM broadcasts in the Atlanta area at 1420 AM.
AM RADIO STATION

WATD-FM 42175
Owner: Perry(Edward & Carol)
Editorial: 130 Enterprise Dr, Marshfield, Massachusetts 2050 **Tel:** 1 781 837-1166.
Email: watdnews@gmail.com
Web site: http://www.959watd.com
Profile: WATD-FM is a commercial station owned by Carol & Edward Perry. The format of the station is adult contemporary music. WATD-FM broadcasts to the Boston, MA area 95.9 FM.
FM RADIO STATION

WATG-FM 43909
Owner: TTA Broadcasting Inc.
Editorial: 2 Mount Alto Rd SW, Rome, Georgia 30165-4142 **Tel:** 1 706 378-8040.
Web site: http://www.theridge957.com
Profile: WATG-FM is a commercial station owned by TTA Broadcasting Inc. The format of the station is classic rock. WATG-FM broadcasts to the Chattanooga, TN area at 95.7 FM.
FM RADIO STATION

WATH-AM 37648
Owner: WATH Inc.
Editorial: 300 Columbus Rd, Athens, Ohio 45701 **Tel:** 1 740 593-6651.
Email: news@970wath.com
Web site: http://www.970wath.com
Profile: WATH-AM is a commercial station owned by WATH Inc. The station's format is classic hits. WATH-AM broadcasts to the greater Athens, OH area at 970 AM.
AM RADIO STATION

WATK-AM 37649
Owner: Results Broadcasting, Inc.
Editorial: N2237 US Highway 45 S, Antigo, Wisconsin 54409-8889 **Tel:** 1 715 623-4124.
Email: country106@gmail.com
Web site: http://watkantigo.com
Profile: WATK-AM is a commercial station owned by Results Broadcasting, Inc. The format of the station is adult standards. WATK-AM broadcasts in the Antigo, WI area at 900 AM.
AM RADIO STATION

WATN-AM 37650
Owner: Community Broadcasters, LLC
Editorial: 199 Wealtha Ave, Watertown, New York 13601-1837 **Tel:** 1 315 782-1240.
Web site: http://cbwatertown.com/watn
Profile: WATN-AM is a commercial station owned by Community Broadcasters, LLC. The format of the station is news and talk. WATN-AM broadcasts to the Watertown, NY area at 1240 AM.
AM RADIO STATION

WATQ-FM 43352
Owner: iHeartMedia Inc.
Editorial: 619 Cameron St, Eau Claire, Wisconsin 54703-4708 **Tel:** 1 715 830-4000.
Web site: http://www.moose106.com
Profile: WATQ-FM is a commercial station owned by iHeartMedia Inc. The format of the station is country. WATQ-FM broadcasts to the Eau Claire, WI area at 106.7 FM.
FM RADIO STATION

WATR-AM 36651
Owner: Gilmore(Mark & Steve)
Editorial: 79 Baldwin Ave, Waterbury, Connecticut 06706-1854 **Tel:** 1 203 755-1121.
Email: news@watr.com
Web site: http://www.watr.com
Profile: WATR-AM is a commercial station owned by Mark & Steve Gilmore. The format of the station is news, talk and oldies music. WATR-AM broadcasts to the greater Waterbury, CT area at 1320 AM.
AM RADIO STATION

WATS-AM 37651
Owner: WATS Broadcasting Inc.
Editorial: 193 S Keystone Ave, Sayre, Pennsylvania 18840-1330 **Tel:** 1 570 888-7745.
Email: wats.wavr@cqservices.com
Web site: http://www.choice102.com
Profile: WATS-AM is a commercial station owned by WATS Broadcasting Inc. The format of the station is adult contemporary music. WATS-AM broadcasts to the Sayre, PA area at 960 AM.
AM RADIO STATION

WATT-AM 37652
Owner: MacDonald Garber Broadcasting Inc.
Editorial: 7825 Mackinaw Trl, Cadillac, Michigan 49601-9746 **Tel:** 1 231 775-1263.
Profile: WATT-AM is a commercial station owned by MacDonald Garber Broadcasting Inc. The format of the station is news and talk. WATT-AM broadcasts to the Cadillac, MI area at 1240 AM.
AM RADIO STATION

WATV-AM 35180
Owner: Sheridan Broadcasting Corp.
Editorial: 3025 Ensley Ave, Birmingham, Alabama 35208 **Tel:** 1 205 780-2014.
Email: watv900gold@sheridanbroadcasting.com
Web site: http://www.900goldwatv.com
Profile: WATV-AM is a commercial station owned by Sheridan Broadcasting Corp. The format of the station is a gospel, R&B and talk. WATV-AM broadcasts to the Birmingham, AL area at 900 AM.
AM RADIO STATION

WATW-AM 37653
Owner: Heartland Communications Group, LLC
Editorial: 2320 Ellis Ave, Ashland, Wisconsin 54806-3995 **Tel:** 1 715 682-2727.
Email: productionash@charter.net
Web site: http://www.watwam.com
Profile: WATW-AM is a commercial station owned by Heartland Communications Group, LLC. The format of the station is talk. WATW-AM broadcasts to the Ashland, WI area at 1400 AM.
AM RADIO STATION

WATX-AM 39135
Owner: Stonecom Cookeville LLC
Editorial: 259 S Willow Ave, Cookeville, Tennessee 38501 **Tel:** 1 931 528-6064.
Web site: http://cookevillesnewstalk.com
Profile: WATX-AM is a commercial station owned by Stonecom Cookeville LLC. The format of the station is news/talk. WATX-AM broadcasts to the Cookeville, TN area at 1600 AM.
AM RADIO STATION

WATY-FM 537849
Owner: CP Broadcasting
Editorial: 260 14th St NW, Atlanta, Georgia 30318-5360
Web site: http://www.ilovethetruth.com
Profile: WATY-FM is a non-commercial station owned by Delmarva Educational Association. The format of the station is religious teaching. WATY-FM broadcasts to the Folkston, GA area at 91.3 FM.
FM RADIO STATION

WATZ-FM 45032
Owner: Midwestern Broadcasting Co.
Editorial: 123 Prentiss St, Alpena, Michigan 49707-2831 **Tel:** 1 989 354-8400.
Email: watznews@watz.com
Web site: http://www.watz.com
Profile: WATZ-FM is a commercial station owned by Midwestern Broadcasting Co. The format for the station is contemporary country. WATZ-FM broadcasts to the Alpena, MI area at 99.3 FM.
FM RADIO STATION

WAUB-AM 39408
Owner: Finger Lakes Radio Group
Editorial: 3568 Lenox Rd, Geneva, New York 14456-2058 **Tel:** 1 315 781-7000.
Web site: http://fingerlakesdailynews.com
Profile: WAUB-AM is a commercial station owned by Finger Lakes Radio Group. The format of the station is news, sports and talk programming. WAUB-AM broadcasts to the Geneva, NY area at 1590 AM.
AM RADIO STATION

WAUC-AM 36222
Owner: Marvina Enterprises, Inc.
Editorial: 1310 S Florida Ave, Wauchula, Florida 33873-9479 **Tel:** 1 863 773-9282.
Email: lagrande1310@gmail.com
Profile: WAUC-AM is a commercial station owned by Marvina Enterprises, Inc. The format of the station is Regional Mexican. WAUC-AM broadcasts to the Wauchula, FL area on 1310 AM.
AM RADIO STATION

WAUD-AM 35181
Owner: Tiger Communications Inc.
Editorial: 2514 S College St Ste 104, Auburn, Alabama 36832-6925 **Tel:** 1 334 321-9999.
Web site: http://www.tigercommunications.net
Profile: WAUD-AM is a commercial station owned by Tiger Communications Inc. The format of the station is sports. WAUD-AM broadcasts to the Auburn, AL area at 1230 AM.
AM RADIO STATION

WAUG-AM 36051
Owner: St. Augustine's College
Editorial: 1315 Oakwood Ave, Raleigh, North Carolina 27610-2247 **Tel:** 1 919 516-4750.
Web site: http://www.waug-network.com
Profile: WAUG-AM is a commercial station owned by St. Augustine's College. The format of the station is news, talk and sports. WAUG-AM broadcasts to the Raleigh-Durham, NC area at 750 AM.
AM RADIO STATION

WAUH-FM 83678
Owner: Hometown Broadcasting LLC
Editorial: W7703 Johnson Ct, Wautoma, Wisconsin 54982 **Tel:** 1 920 787-7220.
Email: thebug@wauhradio.com
Web site: http://www.wauhradio.com
Profile: WAUH-FM is a commercial station owned by Hometown Broadcasting LLC. The format is oldies music. WAUH-FM broadcasts to the Wautoma, WI area at 102.3 FM.
FM RADIO STATION

WAUK-AM 35778
Owner: Good Karma Broadcasting
Editorial: 310 W Wisconsin Ave Unit 100, Milwaukee, Wisconsin 53203-2224 **Tel:** 1 414 273-3776.
Web site: http://espn.go.com/milwaukee
Profile: WAUK-AM is a commercial station owned by Good Karma Broadcasting. The format of the station is sports. WAUK-AM broadcasts to the Milwaukee area at 540 AM.
AM RADIO STATION

WAUN-FM 40102
Owner: Magnum Radio Group
Editorial: 1021 N Superior Ave Ste 5, Tomah, Wisconsin 54660-1192 **Tel:** 1 920 388-9286.
Web site: http://www.lamasgrandegb.com
Profile: WAUN-FM is a commercial station owned by Magnum Radio Group. The format of the station is Regional Mexican music. WAUN-FM broadcasts to the Green Bay, WI, area at 92.7 FM.
FM RADIO STATION

WAUO-FM 606289
Owner: American Family Association
Editorial: 107 Park Gate Dr, Tupelo, Mississippi 38801-3010 **Tel:** 1 662 844-8888.
Email: comments@afr.net
Web site: http://www.afr.net
Profile: WAUO-FM is a commerical station owned by American Family Association. The format of the station is News Talk. WAUO-FM is a transmitter that broadcasts to the Hohenwald, TN area at 90.7 FM and simulcasts American Family Radio.
FM RADIO STATION

WAUS-FM 40104
Owner: Andrews Broadcasting Corporation
Editorial: Howard Performing Arts Ctr, Berrien Springs, Michigan 49104 **Tel:** 1 269 471-3400.
Email: waus@andrews.edu
Web site: http://www.waus.org
Profile: WAUS-FM is a non-commercial station owned by Andrews Broadcasting Corporation. The format of the station is classical music. WAUS-FM broadcasts to the Berrien Springs, MI area at 90.7 FM.
FM RADIO STATION

WAVA-AM 35149
Owner: Salem Media Group, Inc.
Editorial: 1901 N Moore St Ste 200, Arlington, Virginia 22209-1706 **Tel:** 1 703 807-2266.
Email: comment@wava.com
Web site: http://www.wava.com
Profile: WAVA-AM is a commercial station owned by Salem Media Group, Inc. The format of the station is Christian talk and music. WAVA-AM broadcasts to the Arlington, VA area at 780 AM.
AM RADIO STATION

WAVA-FM 46842
Owner: Salem Media Group, Inc.
Editorial: 1901 N Moore St Ste 200, Arlington, Virginia 22209-1706 **Tel:** 1 703 807-2266.
Email: comment@wava.com
Web site: http://www.wava.com
Profile: WAVA-FM is a commercial station owned by Salem Media Group, Inc. The format of the station is Christian music and talk. WAVA-FM broadcasts to the Arlington, VA area at 105.1 FM.
FM RADIO STATION

United States of America

WAVC-FM 43231
Owner: Northern Star Broadcasting LLC
Editorial: 1356 Mackinaw Ave, Cheboygan, Michigan
49721-1003 Tel: 1 231 347-4382.
Web site: http://yourdefendingfathers.us/
Profile: WAVC-FM is a commercial station owned by
Northern Star Broadcasting LLC. The format of the
station is Conservative talk. WAVC-FM broadcasts to
the Cheboygan, MI area at 93.9 FM.
FM RADIO STATION

WAVD-FM 42221
Owner: Delmarva Broadcasting
Editorial: 919 Ellegood St, Salisbury, Maryland
21801-8433 Tel: 1 302 422-7575.
Web site: http://www.971thewave.com
Profile: WAVD-FM is a commercial station owned by
Delmarva Broadcasting. The format of the station is
classic hits. WAVD-FM broadcasts to the Salisbury,
MD area at a frequency of 97.1 FM.
FM RADIO STATION

WAVF-FM 40105
Owner: Apex Broadcasting Inc.
Editorial: 2294 Clements Ferry Rd, Charleston, South
Carolina 29492-7729 Tel: 1 843 972-1100.
Email: frontdesk@apexbroadcasting.com
Web site: http://www.1017chuckfm.com
Profile: WAVF-FM is a commercial station owned by
Apex Broadcasting Inc. The format of the station is
adult hits. WAVF-FM broadcasts to the Charleston,
SC area at 101.7 FM.
FM RADIO STATION

WAVH-FM 42675
Owner: Bigler Broadcasting, LLC
Editorial: 900 Western America Cir Ste 506, Mobile,
Alabama 36609-4105 Tel: 1 251 344-1065.
Email: info@fmtalk1065.com
Web site: http://www.fmtalk1065.com
Profile: WAVH-FM is a commercial station owned by
Bigler Broadcasting, LLC. The format for the station is
talk. WAVH-FM broadcasts to the Mobile, AL area at
106.5 FM.
FM RADIO STATION

WAVJ-FM 45448
Owner: Commonwealth Broadcasting Corp.
Editorial: 108 W Main St, Princeton, Kentucky 42445-
1547 Tel: 1 270 365-2072.
Email: wavj@commonwealthbroadcasting.com
Profile: WAVJ-FM is a commercial station owned by
Commonwealth Broadcasting Corp. The format of the
station is oldies music. WAVJ-FM broadcasts to the
Princeton, KY area at 104.9 FM.
FM RADIO STATION

WAVK-FM 41204
Owner: Gamma Broadcasting LLC
Editorial: 11399 Overseas Hwy, Marathon, Florida
33050-3403 Tel: 1 305 872-9100.
Web site: http://977thewave.com
Profile: WAVK-FM is a commercial station owned by
Gamma Broadcasting LLC. The format of the station
is classic and contemporary country. WAVK-FM
broadcasts to the Marathon, FL area at 97.7 FM.
FM RADIO STATION

WAVL-AM 35184
Owner: LHTC Media, Inc.
Editorial: 400 Unity St Ste 200, Latrobe, Pennsylvania
15650-1340 Tel: 1 724 537-3338.
Email: mailbox@lhtcmedia.com
Web site: http://pa-talk.com
Profile: WAVL-AM is a talk station owned by LHTC
Media, Inc. The format of the station is Talk and
News Radio. The station is in Apollo, Pennsylvania
and airs locally on 910 AM.
AM RADIO STATION

WAVN-AM 35897
Owner: Flinn Broadcasting
Editorial: 6080 Mt. Moriah, Memphis, Tennessee
38115 Tel: 1 662 280-9599.
Profile: WAVN-AM is a commercial station owned by
Flinn Broadcasting. The format of the station is
gospel. WAVN-AM broadcasts to the Southaven, MS
area at 1240 AM.
AM RADIO STATION

WAVO-AM 36667
Owner: GHB Broadcasting
Editorial: 5732 N Tryon St, Charlotte, North Carolina
28213 Tel: 1 704 596-4900.
Web site: http://www.1150wavo.com
Profile: WAVO-AM is a commercial station owned by
GHB Broadcasting. The format of the station is adult
standards. WAVO-AM broadcasts to the Charlotte,
NC area at 1150 AM.
AM RADIO STATION

WAVR-FM 45034
Owner: WATS Broadcasting Inc.
Editorial: 193 S Keystone Ave, Sayre, Pennsylvania
18840-1330 Tel: 1 570 888-7745.
Email: wats.wavr@cqservices.com
Web site: http://www.choice102.com
Profile: WAVR-FM is a commercial station owned by
WATS Broadcasting Inc. The format of the station is
adult contemporary music. WAVR-FM broadcasts to
the Sayre, PA area at 102.1 FM.
FM RADIO STATION

WAVS-AM 35185
Owner: Alliance Broadcasting Network
Editorial: 6360 SW 41st Pl, Davie, Florida 33314
Tel: 1 954 584-1170.
Email: info@wavs1170.com
Web site: http://www.wavs1170.com
Profile: WAVS-AM is a commercial station owned by
Alliance Broadcasting Network. The format of the
station is Caribbean music and news programming.
WAVS-AM broadcasts to the Davie, FL area at 1170
AM.
AM RADIO STATION

WAVT-FM 46093
Owner: Pottsville Broadcasting Company Inc.
Editorial: 212 S Centre St, Pottsville, Pennsylvania
17901-3532 Tel: 1 570 622-1360.
Web site: http://www.t102radio.com
Profile: WAVT-FM is a commercial station owned by
Pottsville Broadcasting Company Inc. The format of
the station is hot adult contemporary. WAVT-FM
broadcasts to the Pottsville, PA area at 101.9 FM.
FM RADIO STATION

WAVU-AM 37655
Owner: Sand Mountain Broadcasting Service
Editorial: 3770 US Highway 431, Albertville, Alabama
35950 Tel: 1 256 878-8575.
Email: wqsb@aol.com
Web site: http://www.wavuam.com
Profile: WAVU-AM is a commercial station owned by
Sand Mountain Broadcasting Service. The format of
the station is Southern gospel music. WAVU-AM
broadcasts to the Albertville, AL area at 630 AM.
AM RADIO STATION

WAVV-FM 41206
Owner: Alpine Broadcasting Corp.
Editorial: 11800 Tamiami Tri E, Naples, Florida 34113
Tel: 1 239 793-1011.
Web site: http://www.wavv101.com
Profile: WAVV-FM is a commercial station owned by
Alpine Broadcasting Corp. The format of the station is
easy listening. WAVV-FM broadcasts to the Naples,
FL area at 101.1 FM.
FM RADIO STATION

WAVW-FM 41960
Owner: iHeartMedia Inc.
Editorial: 3771 SE Jennings Rd, Port Saint Lucie,
Florida 34952-7702 Tel: 1 772 335-9300.
Web site: http://wave927.iheart.com
Profile: WAVW-FM is a commercial station owned by
iHeartMedia Inc. The format of the station is country.
WAVW-FM broadcasts to the West Palm Beach, FL
area at 92.7 FM.
FM RADIO STATION

WAVZ-AM 37656
Owner: iHeartMedia Inc.
Editorial: 495 Benham St, Hamden, Connecticut
06514-2009 Tel: 1 203 281-9600.
Web site: http://espnradio1300.iheart.com
Profile: WAVZ-AM is a commercial station owned by
iHeartMedia Inc. The format for the station is sports.
WAVZ-AM broadcasts to the Hartford-New Haven,
CT area at 1300 AM.
AM RADIO STATION

WAWC-FM 42606
Owner: Talking Stick Communications LLC
Editorial: 216 W Market St, Warsaw, Indiana 46580
Tel: 1 574 372-3064.
Web site: http://www.willie1035.com
Profile: WAWC-FM is a commercial station owned by
Talking Stick Communications LLC. The format for
the station is contemporary country music and
sports. WAWC-FM broadcasts to the South Bend, IN
area at 103.5 FM.
FM RADIO STATION

WAWK-AM 35955
Owner: Northeast Indiana Broadcasting Inc.
Editorial: 931 East Ave, Kendallville, Indiana 46755
Tel: 1 260 347-2400.
Web site: http://955fmthehawk.com
Profile: WAWK-AM is a commercial station owned by
Northeast Indiana Broadcasting Inc. The format of the
station is classic hits. WAWK-AM broadcasts to the
Kendallville, IN area at 1140 AM.
AM RADIO STATION

WAWK-FM 685465
Owner: Northeast Indiana Broadcasting Inc.
Editorial: 931 East Ave, Kendallville, Indiana 46755-
1148 Tel: 1 260 347-2400.
Web site: http://955fmthehawk.com
Profile: WAWK-FM is a commercial station owned by
Northeast Indiana Broadcasting Inc. The format of the
station is classic hits. WAWK-FM's broadcasts to the
Kendallville, IN area at 95.5 FM.
FM RADIO STATION

WAWO-AM 39401
Owner: Blueberry Broadcasting Co.
Editorial: 208 Douglas St, Alma, Georgia 31510-1935
Tel: 1 912 632-1000.
Profile: WAWO-AM is a commercial station owned
by Blueberry Broadcasting Co. The format of the
station is gospel. WAWO-AM broadcasts to the Alma,
GA area at 1400 AM.
AM RADIO STATION

WAWZ-FM 40109
Owner: Pillar of Fire Inc.
Tel: 1 732 469-0991.
Email: info@star991.com

Web site: http://www.star991fm.com
Profile: WAWZ-FM is a non-commercial station
owned by Pillar of Fire Inc. The format of the station is
contemporary Christian. WAWZ-FM broadcasts to
the New York area at 99.1 FM.
FM RADIO STATION

WAXB-FM 35622
Owner: Berkshire Broadcasting Corp
Editorial: 98 Mill Plain Rd, Danbury, Connecticut
06811-6101 Tel: 1 203 744-4800.
Email: feedback@b1073fm.com
Web site: http://www.b1073fm.com
Profile: WAXB-FM is a commercial station owned by
Berkshire Broadcasting. The format of the station is
oldies music. WAXB-FM broadcasts to the Danbury,
CT area at 850 AM.
FM RADIO STATION

WAXI-FM 40110
Owner: DLC Media Inc.
Tel: 1 812 254-6761.
Web site: http://www.waxifm.com
Profile: WAXI-FM is a commercial station owned by
DLC Media, Inc. The format of the station is oldies.
WAXI-FM broadcasts to the Rockville, IN area at
104.9 FM.
FM RADIO STATION

WAXL-FM 43092
Owner: DCBroadcasting Inc.
Editorial: 458 3rd Ave, Jasper, Indiana 47546-3533
Tel: 1 812 683-1215.
Email: mailbox@waxl.us
Web site: http://dcbroadcasting.com
Profile: WAXL-FM is a commercial station owned by
DCBroadcasting Inc. The format for the station is
adult contemporary music. WAXL-FM broadcasts to
the Huntingburg, IN, area at 103.3 FM.
FM RADIO STATION

WAXM-FM 42838
Owner: Valley Broadcasting
Editorial: 724 Park Ave NW, Norton, Virginia 24273-
1923 Tel: 1 276 679-1901.
Email: 935@waxm.com
Web site: http://www.waxm.com
Profile: WAXM-FM is a commercial station owned by
Valley Broadcasting. The format of the station is
classic and contemporary country. WAXM-FM
broadcasts to the Norton, VA area at 93.5 FM.
FM RADIO STATION

WAXO-AM 35815
Owner: Marshall County Radio Corp.
Editorial: 217 W Commerce St, Lewisburg,
Tennessee 37091-3337 Tel: 1 931 359-6641.
Web site: http://www.waxo.com
Profile: WAXO-AM is a commercial owned by
Marshall County Radio Corp. The format of the
station is contemporary country. WAXO-AM
broadcasts in the greater Lewisburg, TN area at 1220
AM.
AM RADIO STATION

WAXO-FM 658288
Owner: Marshall County Radio Corp.
Editorial: 217 W Commerce St, Lewisburg,
Tennessee 37091-3337 Tel: 1 931 359-6641.
Web site: http://959waxo.com
Profile: WAXO-FM is a commercial station owned by
Marshall County Radio Corp. The format is
contemporary country. The station airs in the
Lewisburg, TN area at 95.9 FM.
FM RADIO STATION

WAXQ-FM 40554
Owner: iHeartMedia Inc.
Editorial: 32 Avenue of the Americas Fl 3, New York,
New York 10013-2473 Tel: 1 212 377-7900.
Web site: http://q1043.iheart.com
Profile: WAXQ-FM is a commercial station owned by
iHeartMedia Inc. The format of the station is classic
rock. WAXQ-FM broadcasts to the New York City
metro area at 104.3 FM.
FM RADIO STATION

WAXR-FM 81078
Owner: American Family Association
Tel: 1 602 844-8888.
Email: comments@afr.net
Web site: http://www.afr.net
Profile: WAXR-FM is a non-commercial station
owned by American Family Association. The format
of the station is Christian talk. WAXR-FM broadcasts
to the Geneseo, IL area at a frequency of 88.1 FM.
FM RADIO STATION

WAXS-FM 41937
Owner: Southern Communications Corp.
Editorial: 306 S Kanawha St, Beckley, West Virginia
25801 Tel: 1 304 253-7000.
Web site: http://www.groovy94.com
Profile: WAXS-FM is a commercial station owned by
Southern Communications Corp. The format of the
station is classic hits music. WAXS-FM broadcasts to
the Beckley, WV area at 94.1 FM.
FM RADIO STATION

WAXX-FM 45919
Owner: Mid-West Family Broadcasting
Editorial: 944 Harlem St, Altoona, Wisconsin 54720-
1127 Tel: 1 715 832-1530.
Web site: http://www.todayswaxx1045.com
Profile: WAXX-FM is a commercial station owned by
Mid-West Family Broadcasting. The format of the

station is contemporary country. WAXX-FM
broadcasts to the Eau Claire, WI area at 104.5 FM.
FM RADIO STATION

WAXY-AM 38786
Owner: Entercom Communications Corp.
Editorial: 20450 NW 2nd Ave, Miami, Florida 33169-
2505 Tel: 1 305 521-5100.
Web site: http://www.theticketmiami.com
Profile: WAXY-AM is a commercial station owned by
Entercom Communications Corp. The format of the
station is sports. WAXY-AM broadcasts to the Miami
area at 790 AM.
AM RADIO STATION

WAY Media Network Services
856596
Owner: WAY Media Inc.
Tel: 1 719 533-0300.
Web site: http://network.wayfm.com/
Profile: WAY Media Network Services is a division of
WAY Media, Inc. based in Colorado Springs, CO.
Established in 1997, WAY Media Network Services
offers cutting edge, award winning radio
programming to more than 100 radio stations
nationwide. Markets include: Nashville, Denver,
Louisville, Portland, and many more.
RADIO NETWORK

WAYA-FM 44058
Owner: Caswell Capital Partners, LLC
Editorial: 2045 Spaulding Dr, North Charleston, South
Carolina 29406-4960 Tel: 1 843 529-9293.
Email: wayx@wayfm.com
Web site: http://wayx.wayfm.com
Profile: WAYA-FM is a commercial station owned by
Caswell Capital Partners, LLC and operated by WAY-
FM Media Group, Inc. The format of the station is
contemporary Christian. WAYA-FM broadcasts to the
Charleston, SC area at 100.9 FM.
FM RADIO STATION

WAYB-FM 43765
Owner: Family Worship Center Church, Inc.
Editorial: 8919 World Ministries ave, Baton Rouge,
Louisiana 70810-9006 Tel: 1 225 768-3288.
Email: info@jsm.org
Web site: http://www.jsm.org
FM RADIO STATION

WAYC-AM 36327
Owner: Cessna Communications Inc.
Editorial: 134 E Pitt St, 2nd Fl, Bedford, Pennsylvania
15522 Tel: 1 814 623-1000.
Profile: WAYC-AM is a commercial station owned by
Cessna Communications Inc. The format of the
station is adult standards and religious programming.
WAYC-AM broadcasts to the Bedford, PA area at
1600 AM.
AM RADIO STATION

WAYC-FM 42724
Owner: Cessna Communications Inc.
Editorial: 134 E Pitt St Fl 2, Bedford, Pennsylvania
15522-1311 Tel: 1 814 623-1000.
Email: cesscomm@embarqmail.com
Web site: http://www.bedfordcountyradio.com/links/
Star-100-9.html
Profile: WAYC-FM is a commercial station owned by
Cessna Communications Inc. The format of the
station is adult contemporary. WAYC-FM broadcasts
to the Johnstown-Altoona, PA area at 100.9 FM.
FM RADIO STATION

WAYD-FM 363019
Owner: WAY Media Inc.
Editorial: 1945 Scottsville Rd Ste B2 Pmb 363,
Bowling Green, Kentucky 42104-5817
Tel: 1 888 339-2936.
Email: wayd@wayfm.com
Web site: http://www.wayfm.com
Profile: WAYD-FM is a non-commercial station
owned by WAY Media Inc. The format of the station
is contemporary Christian. WAYD-FM broadcasts to
the Bowling Green, KY area on 88.1 FM.
FM RADIO STATION

WAYE-AM 35186
Owner: Rivera Communications
Editorial: 100 Yeager Pkwy, Pelham, Alabama 35124-
1859 Tel: 1 205 358-1100.
Web site: http://www.aquimandalajefa.com/
Profile: WAYE-AM, is the first Regional Mexican
station in the State of Alabama. It is owned by Rivera
Communications. The format of the station is
Hispanic. It features various personalities, promotions
and events geared specifically towards the Latino-
Mexican community in Alabama. The station airs on
1220AM
AM RADIO STATION

WAYF-FM 42611
Owner: WAY Media Inc.
Editorial: 800 Northpoint Pkwy, Ste 881, West Palm
Beach, Florida 33407-1978 Tel: 1 561 881-1929.
Email: wayf@wayfm.com
Web site: http://www.wayfm.com
Profile: WAYF-FM is a non-commercial station
owned by WAY Media Inc. The format of the station
is contemporary Christian. WAYF-FM broadcasts to
the West Palm Beach, FL area at 88.1 FM.
FM RADIO STATION

WAYG-FM 43734
Owner: WAY Media Inc.
Editorial: 3211 Grant Line Rd Ste 1, New Albany,
Indiana 47150-2175 Tel: 1 888 929-1059.
Web site: http://wayi.wayfm.com

Profile: WAYG-FM is a commercial station owned by WAY Media Inc. The format of the station is Contemporary Christian. WLUE-FM broadcasts to the Charlestown, IN area at 104.3 FM.
FM RADIO STATION

WAYH-FM 217283
Owner: WAY Media Inc.
Editorial: 9582 Madison Blvd, Madison, Alabama 35758-9107 **Tel:** 1 256 837-9293.
Email: contact@wayfm.com
Web site: http://www.wayfm.com
Profile: WAYH-FM is a non-commercial station owned by WAY Media Inc. The format of the station is contemporary Christian. WAYH-FM broadcasts to the Madison, AL area at 88.1 FM.
FM RADIO STATION

WAYJ-FM 41356
Owner: Way Media, Inc.
Editorial: 1860 Boy Scout Dr Ste 202, Fort Myers, Florida 33907-2119 **Tel:** 1 239 936-1929.
Web site: http://wayfm.com
Profile: WAYJ-FM is a non-commercial station owned by FWay Media, Inc. The format of the station is contemporary Christian. WAYJ-FM broadcasts to the Southwest Florida area at 89.5 FM.
FM RADIO STATION

WAYK-FM 42879
Owner: WAY Media Inc.
Editorial: 3211 Grant Line Rd Ste 1, New Albany, Indiana 47150-2175 **Tel:** 1 888 929-1059.
Web site: http://wayfm.com
Profile: WAYK-FM is a commercial station owned by WAY Media Inc. The format of the station is Christian AC. WAYK-FM broadcasts to the Louisville, KY area at 105.9 FM.
FM RADIO STATION

WAYM-FM 42614
Owner: WAY Media Inc.
Editorial: 1095 McEwen Dr, Franklin, Tennessee 37067-1611 **Tel:** 1 615 261-9293.
Web site: http://waym.wayfm.com
Profile: WAYM-FM is a non-commercial station owned by WAY Media Inc. The format of the station is contemporary Christian music. WAYM-FM broadcasts to the Franklin, TN area on 90.5 FM.
FM RADIO STATION

WAYN-AM 35187
Owner: WAYN Inc.
Editorial: 1223 Rockingham Rd, Rockingham, North Carolina 28379 **Tel:** 1 910 895-4041.
Profile: WAYN-AM is a commercial station owned by WAYN Inc. The format for the station is adult contemporary. WAYN-AM broadcasts to the Charlotte, NC area at 900 AM.
AM RADIO STATION

WAYP-FM 43962
Owner: WAY Media Inc.
Editorial: 2199 N Monroe St, Tallahassee, Florida 32303-4763 **Tel:** 1 850 422-1929.
Email: wayp@wayfm.com
Web site: http://wayp.wayfm.com
Profile: WAYP-FM is a non-commercial station owned by WAY Media Inc. The format of the station is contemporary Christian music and talk. WAYP-FM broadcasts to Marianna, FL at 88.3 FM.
FM RADIO STATION

WAYQ-FM 217285
Owner: WAY Media Inc.
Editorial: 2277C Wilma Rudolph Blvd, Clarksville, Tennessee 37040-5898 **Tel:** 1 931 647-8883.
Web site: http://www.wayfm.com/?waystation_set_signal=41
Profile: WAYQ-FM is a non-commercial station owned by the WAY Media Inc. The format of the station is contemporary Christian music. WAYQ-FM broadcasts to the Nashville, TN area at 88.3 FM.
FM RADIO STATION

WAYR-AM 35188
Owner: Good Tidings Trust Inc.
Editorial: 2500 Russell Rd, Green Cove Springs, Florida 32043 **Tel:** 1 904 284-1111.
Email: manager@wayradio.org
Web site: http://www.wayradio.org
Profile: WAYR-AM is a non-commercial station owned by Good Tidings Trust Inc. The format of the station is religious. WAYR-AM broadcasts to the greater Orange Park, FL area at 550 AM.
AM RADIO STATION

WAYR-FM 43640
Owner: Good Tidings Trust Inc.
Editorial: 1426 Newcastle St Ste 200, Brunswick, Georgia 31520-7083 **Tel:** 1 912 342-1083.
Email: manager@wayradio.org
Web site: http://www.wayradio.com/
Profile: WAYR-FM is a non-commercial station owned by Good Tidings Trust Inc. The format of the station is contemporary Christian. WAYR-FM broadcasts to the Brunswick, GA area at 90.7 FM.
FM RADIO STATION

WAYS-AM 45037
Owner: Cumulus Media Inc.
Editorial: 544 Mulberry St Ste 500, Macon, Georgia 31201-8258 **Tel:** 1 478 746-6286.
Web site: http://www.waysam.com/station-information
Profile: WAYS-AM is a commercial station owned by Cumulus Media Inc. The format of the station is sports. WAYS-AM broadcasts to the Macon, GA area at 1500 AM.
AM RADIO STATION

WAYT-FM 139451
Owner: WAY Media Inc.
Editorial: 2199 N Monroe St, Tallahassee, Florida 32303-4763 **Tel:** 1 850 422-1929.
Web site: http://www.wayfm.com
Profile: WAYT-FM is a non-commercial station owned by WAY Media Inc. The format is contemporary Christian. The station airs in the Tallahassee, FL area at 88.1FM.
FM RADIO STATION

WAYU-FM 716893
Owner: WAY Media, Inc
Editorial: 3331 Rainbow Dr Ste E, Rainbow City, Alabama 35906-6264 **Tel:** 1 888 239-2936.
Email: supportservices@wayfm.com
Web site: http://www.wayfm.com
Profile: WAYU-FM is a non-commercial station owned by WAY Media, Inc. The format of the station is Christian contemporary music. WAYU-FM broadcasts at a frequency of 91.1 FM to Gadsden, and the northeast Alabama area.
FM RADIO STATION

WAYV-FM 40113
Owner: Equity Communications LP
Editorial: 8025 Black Horse Pike, Pleasantville, New Jersey 08232-2900 **Tel:** 1 609 484-8444.
Email: 951wayv@gmail.com
Web site: http://www.951wayv.com
Profile: WAYV-FM is a commercial station owned by Equity Communications LP. The format of the station is hot adult contemporary. WAYV-FM broadcasts to the West Atlantic City, NJ area at 95.1 FM.
FM RADIO STATION

WAYW-FM 363016
Owner: WAY Media Inc.
Editorial: 1012 W Mcewen Dr, Franklin, Tennessee 37067-1721 **Tel:** 1 615 261-9293.
Email: test@wayfm.com
Web site: http://www.wayfm.com
Profile: WAYW-FM is a non-commercial station owned by WAY Media Inc. The format of the station is contemporary Christian music. WAYW-FM broadcasts to the New Johnsonville, TN area at 89.9 FM.
FM RADIO STATION

WAYX-AM 410498
Owner: Santilla Broadcast Properties, LLC
Editorial: 1766 Memorial Dr Ste 1, Waycross, Georgia 31501-1098 **Tel:** 1 229 426-0083.
Email: myradio@my102.net
Web site: http://www.lovemyfm.com
Profile: WAYX-AM is a commercial station owned by Santilla Broadcast Properties, LLC. The format of the station is Classic Rock. WAYX-AM broadcasts to the Waycross, GA area at 1230 AM.
AM RADIO STATION

WAYY-AM 38561
Owner: Mid-West Family Broadcasting
Editorial: 944 Harlem St, Altoona, Wisconsin 54720-1127 **Tel:** 1 715 832-1530.
Web site: http://www.wayy790.com
Profile: WAYY-AM is a commercial station owned by Mid-West Family Broadcasting. The format of the station is sports and news/talk. WAYY-AM broadcasts to the Altoona, WI area at 790 AM.
AM RADIO STATION

WAYZ-FM 45038
Owner: VerStandig Broadcasting
Editorial: 10960 John Wayne Dr, Greencastle, Pennsylvania 17225-9584 **Tel:** 1 717 597-9200.
Email: info@wayz.com
Web site: http://www.wayz.com
Profile: WAYZ-FM is a commercial station owned by VerStandig Broadcasting. The format of the station is contemporary country music. WAYZ-FM broadcasts to the Greencastle, PA area at 104.7 FM.
FM RADIO STATION

WAZA-FM 439014
Owner: Cumulus Media Networks
Editorial: 6066 Clay Hill Rd, Liberty, Mississippi 39645 **Tel:** 1 601 657-8759.
Profile: WAZA-FM is a commercial station owned by Southwest Broadcasting. The format of the station is R&B. WAZA-FM broadcasts to the McComb, MS area at 107.7 FM.
FM RADIO STATION

WAZK-FM 821156
Owner: Vertical Resources, LLC
Tel: 1 508 228-9770.
Email: info@ackfm.com
Web site: http://www.ackfm.com
Profile: WAZK-FM is a commercial station owned by Vertical Resources, LLC. The format of the station is adult variety. WAZK-FM broadcasts to the Nantucket, M.A. area at a frequency of 97.7 FM.
FM RADIO STATION

WAZL-AM 39191
Owner: Geos Communications
Editorial: 54 Wilmar Dr, Tunkhannock, Pennsylvania 18657-6628 **Tel:** 1 570 836-4200.
Email: comments@gem104.com
Web site: http://www.gem104.com
Profile: WAZL-AM is a commercial station owned by Geos Communications. The format of the station is religous teaching. WAZL-AM broadcasts to the Hazelton, PA area at 1490 AM.
AM RADIO STATION

WAZN-AM 35676
Owner: Multicultural Radio Broadcasting Inc.
Editorial: 500 W Cummings Park, Ste 2600, Woburn, Massachusetts 1801 **Tel:** 1 781 938-0869.
Web site: http://mrbi.net
Profile: WAZN-AM is a commercial station owned by Multicultural Radio Broadcasting Inc. The format of the station is ethnic brokered programming. WAZN-AM broadcasts to the Woburn, MA area at 1470 AM.
AM RADIO STATION

WAZO-FM 70084
Owner: Capitol Broadcasting Company
Editorial: 25 N Kerr Ave Ste C, Wilmington, North Carolina 28405-3403 **Tel:** 1 910 791-3088.
Web site: http://www.z1075.com
Profile: WAZO-FM is a commercial station owned by Capitol Broadcasting Company. The format of the station is Top 40/CHR. WAZO-FM broadcasts to the Wilmington, NC area at 107.5 FM.
FM RADIO STATION

WAZR-FM 41209
Owner: iHeartMedia Inc.
Editorial: 207 University Blvd, Harrisonburg, Virginia 22801-3749 **Tel:** 1 540 434-1777.
Web site: http://937now.iheart.com
Profile: WAZR-FM is a commercial station owned by iHeartMedia Inc. The format for the station is Top 40/CHR. WAZR-FM broadcasts to the Harrisonburg, VA area at 93.7 FM.
FM RADIO STATION

WAZS-AM 36872
Owner: Jabar Communications, Inc.
Editorial: 5081 Rivers Ave, North Charleston, South Carolina 29406-6303 **Tel:** 1 843 554-1063.
Email: traffic@jabarcommunications.com
Web site: http://www.elsol980.com
Profile: WAZS-AM is a commercial station owned by Jabar Communications, Inc. The format of the station is Hispanic and Top 40/CHR music. WAZS-AM broadcasts to the North Charleston, SC area at 980 AM.
AM RADIO STATION

WAZU-FM 705208
Owner: Sirius Synocope, Inc
Editorial: 2122 W Kellogg Ave, West Peoria, Illinois 61604-5587 **Tel:** 1 209 788-9298.
Email: comments@wazufm.org
Web site: http://wazufm.org
Profile: WAZU-FM is a non-commercial station owned by Sirius Synocope, Inc. The station airs at a frequency of 90.7 in Peoria, IL. WAZU-FM is a new concept station with a format of "community radio" where listeners are involved in programming. Listeners will discover music, news reports, opinions and esoterica in an array of styles and languages providing programming to diverse communities and un-served or under-served groups.
FM RADIO STATION

WAZY-FM 40115
Owner: Artistic Media Partners Inc.
Editorial: 3824 S 18th St, Lafayette, Indiana 47909-9102 **Tel:** 1 765 474-1410.
Web site: http://www.wazy.com
Profile: WAZY-FM is a commercial station owned by Artistic Media Partners Inc. The format of the station is Top 40/CHR. WAZY-FM broadcasts to Lafayette, IN at 96.5 FM.
FM RADIO STATION

WAZZ-AM 35327
Owner: Beasley Broadcast Group
Editorial: 508 Person St, Fayetteville, North Carolina 28301-5841 **Tel:** 1 910 486-4114.
Web site: http://sunny943.com
Profile: WAZZ-AM is a commercial station owned by the Beasley Broadcast Group. The format of the station is soft AC. WAZZ-AM broadcasts to the Fayetteville, NC area at 1490 AM.
AM RADIO STATION

WBAB-FM 44521
Owner: Cox Media Group, Inc.
Editorial: 555 Sunrise Hwy, West Babylon, New York 11704-6009 **Tel:** 1 631 587-1023.
Email: wbab@wbab.com
Web site: http://www.wbab.com
Profile: WBAB-FM is a commercial station owned by Cox Media Group, Inc. The format of the station is rock/album-oriented rock. WBAB-FM broadcasts to the New York area at 102.3 FM.
FM RADIO STATION

WBAC-AM 39196
Owner: East Tennessee Radio Group
Editorial: 2640 Commerce Dr NE, Cleveland, Tennessee 37311 **Tel:** 1 423 472-4053.
Profile: WBAC-AM is a commercial station owned by East Tennessee Radio Group. The format of the station is talk, news and sports. WBAC-AM broadcasts to the Cleveland, TN area at 1340 AM.
AM RADIO STATION

WBAD-FM 42804
Owner: Interchange Communications
Editorial: 126 Seven Oaks Road, Greenville, Mississippi 38704-4426 **Tel:** 1 662 335-9265.
Email: wbad.radio@suddenlinkmail.com
Profile: WBAD-FM is a commercial station owned by Interchange Communications . The format for the station is urban contemporary. WBAD-FM broadcasts to the Greenwood-Greenville, MS area at 94.3 FM.
FM RADIO STATION

WBAE-AM 38132
Owner: Saga Communications
Editorial: 420 Western Ave, South Portland, Maine 04106-1704 **Tel:** 1 207 774-4561.
Web site: http://am1490thebay.com
Profile: WBAE-AM is a commercial station owned by Saga Communications. The format of the station is talk. WBAE-AM broadcasts to the South Portland, ME area at 1490 AM.
AM RADIO STATION

WBAF-AM 35189
Owner: Ploener Radio Group
Editorial: 645 Forsyth St, Barnesville, Georgia 30204 **Tel:** 1 770 358-1090.
Profile: WBAF-AM is a commercial station owned by Ploener Radio Group. The format of the station is classic country. WBAF-AM broadcasts to the Barnesville, GA area at 1090 AM.
AM RADIO STATION

WBAG-AM 35190
Owner: Gray Broadcasting Corp.
Editorial: 1745 Burch Bridge Rd, Burlington, North Carolina 27217 **Tel:** 1 336 226-1150.
Email: wbag@bellsouth.net
Web site: http://www.wbag1150.com
Profile: WBAG-AM is a commercial station owned by Gray Broadcasting Corp. The format of the station is news and talk. WBAG-AM broadcasts to the Burlington, NC area at 1150 AM.
AM RADIO STATION

WBAI-FM 40116
Owner: Pacifica Foundation, Inc.
Editorial: 388 Atlantic Ave, Brooklyn, New York 11217-3399
Web site: http://www.wbai.org
Profile: WBAI-FM is a non-commercial station owned by Pacifica Foundation, Inc. The format of the station is variety. WBAI-FM broadcasts to the New York area at 99.5 FM. The station is not interested in product news, gadget news, sports news, celebrity news, entertainment news or any of the other non-news stories.
FM RADIO STATION

WBAK-FM 45677
Owner: Blueberry Broadcasting
Editorial: 184 Target Cir, Bangor, Maine 04401-5718 **Tel:** 1 207 947-9100.
Profile: WBAK-FM is a commercial station owned by Blueberry Broadcasting. The format of the station is Classic Hits. WBAK-FM broadcasts to the Bangor, ME area at 104.7 FM.
FM RADIO STATION

WBAL-AM 37658
Owner: Hearst Television Inc.
Editorial: 3800 Hooper Ave, Baltimore, Maryland 21211-1313 **Tel:** 1 410 467-3000.
Email: news@wbal.com
Web site: http://www.wbal.com
Profile: WBAL-AM is a commercial station owned by Hearst Television Inc. The format of the station is news, sports and talk. WBAL-AM broadcasts to the Baltimore area at 1090 AM.
AM RADIO STATION

WBAM-FM 40117
Owner: Bluewater Broadcasting Co. LLC
Editorial: 4101A Wall St, Ste A, Montgomery, Alabama 36106 **Tel:** 1 334 244-0961.
Web site: http://bamacountry.com
Profile: WBAM-FM is a commercial station owned by Bluewater Broadcasting Co. LLC. The format of the station is contemporary country. WBAM-FM broadcasts to the Montgomery, AL at a frequency of 98.9 FM.
FM RADIO STATION

WBAN-AM 707005
Owner: Port Broadcasting, LLC
Editorial: 379 Riverside Dr, Eddington, Maine 04428-3115
Web site: http://waveradiomaine.com
Profile: WBAN-AM is a commercial station owned by Port Broadcasting, LLC. The format of the station is Soft Adult Contemporary. WBAN-AM broadcasts to the Bangor, ME area at 94.1.
AM RADIO STATION

WBAP-AM 38896
Owner: Cumulus Media Inc
Editorial: 3090 Olive St, Dallas, Texas 75219-7640 **Tel:** 1 214 526-2400.
Email: news@wbap.com
Web site: http://www.wbap.com
Profile: WBAP-AM is a commercial station owned by Cumulus Media Inc. The format of the station is news and talk programming. WBAP-AM broadcasts to the Dallas area at 820 AM.
AM RADIO STATION

WBAP-FM 44078
Owner: Cumulus Media Inc
Editorial: 3090 Olive St Ste 400, Dallas, Texas 75219-7640 **Tel:** 1 817 695-3500.
Web site: http://www.theticket.com/
Profile: WBAP-FM is a commercial station owned by Cumulus Media Inc. The format of the station is

sports. WBAP-FM broadcasts to the Dallas area at 96.7 FM.
FM RADIO STATION

WBAR-FM 42069
Owner: Capital Media Corporation
Editorial: 30 Park Ave, Cohoes, New York 12047-3330 **Tel:** 1 518 237-1330.
Email: events@aliveradio.com
Web site: http://www.aliveradionetwork.com
Profile: WBAR-FM is a commercial station owned by Capital Media Corporation. The format of the station is religious programming. WBAR-FM broadcasts to the Glen Falls, NY area at 94.7 FM.
FM RADIO STATION

WBAT-AM 39182
Owner: Hoosier AM/FM, LLC
Editorial: 820 S Pennsylvania St, Marion, Indiana 46953-2407 **Tel:** 1 765 664-6239.
Email: news@wbat.com
Web site: http://www.wbat.com
Profile: WBAT-AM is a commercial station owned by Hoosier AM/FM, LLC. The format of the station is talk. WBAT-AM broadcasts to the Marion, IN area at 1400 AM.
AM RADIO STATION

WBAV-FM 46681
Owner: Beasley Broadcast Group
Editorial: 1520 South Blvd Ste 300, Charlotte, North Carolina 28203-3701 **Tel:** 1 704 522-1103.
Web site: http://www.v1019.com
Profile: WBAV-FM is a commercial station owned by Beasley Broadcast Group. The format of the station is urban adult contemporary. WBAV-FM broadcasts to the Charlotte, NC area on 101.9 FM.
FM RADIO STATION

WBAX-AM 38494
Owner: Shamrock Communications
Editorial: 149 Penn Ave, Scranton, Pennsylvania 18503-2055 **Tel:** 1 570 346-6555.
Web site: http://www.nepasespnradio.com/
Profile: WBAX-AM is a commercial station owned by Shamrock Communications. The format of the station is sports. WBAX-AM broadcasts to the Scranton, PA area at 1240 AM.
AM RADIO STATION

WBAZ-FM 41426
Owner: Long Island Radio Broadcasting
Editorial: 760 Montauk Hwy, Water Mill, New York 11976-2624 **Tel:** 1 631 267-7800.
Web site: http://www.wbaz.com
Profile: WBAZ-FM is a commercial station owned by Long Island Radio Broadcasting. The format of the station is Lite AC. WBAZ-FM broadcasts to the Bridgehampton, NY area at 102.5 FM. The station only accepts local press releases and PSAs.
FM RADIO STATION

WBBA-FM 45040
Owner: DJ Two Rivers Radio
Editorial: 1260 W Washington St, Pittsfield, Illinois 62363 **Tel:** 1 217 285-5975.
Email: wbba@wbbaradio.com
Web site: http://www.wbbaradio.com
Profile: WBBA-FM is a commercial station owned by DJ Two Rivers Radio. The format of the station is variety. WBBA-FM broadcasts to the Pittsfield, IL area at 97.5 FM.
FM RADIO STATION

WBBB-FM 43041
Owner: Curtis Media Group
Editorial: 3012 Highwoods Blvd, Raleigh, North Carolina 27604-1037 **Tel:** 1 919 876-3831.
Email: wptfnews@curtismedia.com
Web site: http://radio961.com
Profile: WBBB-FM is a commercial station owned by Curtis Media Group. The format of the station is rock/album-oriented rock music. WBBB-FM broadcasts to the Raleigh-Durham, NC area at 96.1 FM.
FM RADIO STATION

WBBC-FM 46509
Owner: Denbar Communications Inc.
Editorial: 950 Kenbridge Rd, Blackstone, Virginia 23824 **Tel:** 1 434 292-4146.
Email: wbbc@bobcatcountryradio.com
Web site: http://www.bobcatcountryradio.com
Profile: WBBC-FM is a commercial station owned by Denbar Communications Inc. The format of the station is contemporary country. WBBC-FM broadcasts to the Blackstone, VA area at 93.5 FM.
FM RADIO STATION

WBBD-AM 38000
Owner: iHeartMedia Inc.
Editorial: 1015 Main St, Wheeling, West Virginia 26003-2709 **Tel:** 1 304 232-1170.
Web site: http://foxsports1400wheeling.iheart.com
Profile: WBBD-AM is a commercial station owned by iHeartMedia Inc. The format of the station is sports. WBBD-AM broadcasts to the Wheeling, WV area at 1400 AM.
AM RADIO STATION

WBBE-FM 358695
Owner: Connoisseur Media LLC
Editorial: 520 N Center St, Bloomington, Illinois 61701-2902 **Tel:** 1 309 834-1100.
Web site: http://www.bob979.com
Profile: WBBE-FM is a commercial station owned by Neuhoff Communications. The format of the station is adult hits. WBBE-FM broadcasts to the Bloomington, IL area at 97.9 FM.
FM RADIO STATION

WBBG-FM 43548
Owner: iHeartMedia Inc.
Editorial: 7461 South Ave, Youngstown, Ohio 44512-5789 **Tel:** 1 330 740-9300.
Web site: http://1061thebullyoungstown.iheart.com/
Profile: WBBG-FM is a commercial station owned by iHeartMedia Inc. The format of the station is Country. WBBG-FM broadcasts to the Youngstown, OH area at 106.1 FM.
FM RADIO STATION

WBBI-FM 62168
Owner: iHeartMedia Inc.
Editorial: 320 N Jensen Rd, Vestal, New York 13850-2111 **Tel:** 1 607 584-5800.
Web site: http://www.b1075country.com/main.html
Profile: WBBI-FM is a commercial station owned by iHeartMedia Inc. The format of the station is contemporary country. WBBI-FM broadcasts to the Binghamton, NY area at 107.5 FM.
FM RADIO STATION

WBBK-FM 46677
Owner: Alabama Media Investments, LLC
Editorial: 285 N Foster St Fl 8, Dothan, Alabama 36303-4541 **Tel:** 1 334 792-0047.
Profile: WBBK-FM is a commercial station owned by Alabama Media Investments, LLC and operated by Low Country Radio, LLC. The format of the station is soul music. WBBK-FM broadcasts to the Dothan, AL area at 93.1 FM.
FM RADIO STATION

WBBL-FM 42157
Owner: Cumulus Media Inc
Editorial: 60 Monroe Center St NW, Grand Rapids, Michigan 49503-2916 **Tel:** 1 616 774-8461.
Web site: http://www.wbbl.com
Profile: WBBL-FM is a commercial station owned by Cumulus Media Inc. The format of the station is sports. WBBL-FM broadcasts to the Grand Rapids, MI area at 107.3 FM.
FM RADIO STATION

WBBM-AM 37662
Owner: CBS Radio
Editorial: 2 Prudential Plaza, Suite 1100, Chicago, Illinois 60601 **Tel:** 1 312 297-7800.
Email: wbbmnewsradiohost@cbsradio.com
Web site: http://chicago.cbslocal.com
Profile: WBBM-AM is a commercial station owned by CBS Radio. The format of the station is news. WBBM-AM broadcasts to the Chicago area at 780 AM.
AM RADIO STATION

WBBM-FM 45041
Owner: CBS Radio
Editorial: 180 N Stetson Ave Ste 963, Chicago, Illinois 60601-6712 **Tel:** 1 312 861-9600.
Web site: http://b96.cbslocal.com
Profile: WBBM-FM is a commercial station owned by CBS Radio. The format of the station is rhythmic Top 40/CHR. WBBM-FM broadcasts to the Chicago area at 96.3 FM.
FM RADIO STATION

WBBN-FM 40119
Owner: Blakeney Communications Inc.
Editorial: 4580 Highway 15 N, Laurel, Mississippi 39440 **Tel:** 1 601 649-0095.
Email: b95@b95country.com
Web site: http://www.b95country.com
Profile: WBBN-FM is a commercial station owned by Blakeney Communications Inc. The format of the station is country. WBBN-FM broadcasts to the Hattiesburg-Laurel, MS area at 95.9 FM.
FM RADIO STATION

WBBO-FM 40732
Owner: Press Communications LLC
Editorial: 2355 W Bangs Ave, Neptune, New Jersey 07753-4111 **Tel:** 1 732 774-4755.
Web site: http://b985radio.com
Profile: WBBO-FM is a commercial station owned by Press Communications LLC. The format of the station is Top 40/CHR. WKMK-FM broadcasts to the Neptune, NJ area at 98.5 FM.
FM RADIO STATION

WBBP-AM 36053
Owner: Bountiful Blessings, Inc.
Editorial: 369 E Ge Patterson Ave, Memphis, Tennessee 38126-3301 **Tel:** 1 901 278-7878.
Email: customerservice@bbless.org
Web site: http://www.bbless.org/wbbp.home.htm
Profile: WBBP-AM is a non-commercial station owned by Bountiful Blessings, Inc. The format of the station is gospel music. WBBP-AM broadcasts to the Memphis, TN area at 1480 AM.
AM RADIO STATION

WBBQ-FM 153669
Owner: iHeartMedia Inc.
Editorial: 2743 Perimeter Pkwy Bldg 100 Ste 100, Augusta, Georgia 30909-6429 **Tel:** 1 706 396-6000.
Web site: http://www.wbbq.com
Profile: WBBQ-FM is a commercial station owned by iHeartMedia Inc. The format of the station is adult contemporary music. WBBQ-FM broadcasts to the Augusta, GA area at 104.3 FM.
FM RADIO STATION

WBBR-AM 36158
Owner: Bloomberg L.P.
Editorial: 731 Lexington Ave, New York, New York 10022-1331 **Tel:** 1 212 617-2000.
Email: release@bloomberg.net
Web site: http://www.bloomberg.com/radio/
Profile: WBBR-AM is a commercial station owned by Bloomberg L.P. The format of the station is news. WBBR-AM broadcasts to the New York City area at 1130 AM. The assignment desk should ONLY be contacted to notify the department of serious business news stories about publicly traded companies. The station airs programming on WXKS-AM.
AM RADIO STATION

WBBS-FM 42131
Owner: iHeartMedia Inc.
Editorial: 500 Plum St Ste 100, Syracuse, New York 13204-1427 **Tel:** 1 315 472-9797.
Web site: http://www.b1047.net
Profile: WBBS-FM is a commercial station owned by iHeartMedia Inc. The format of the station is country. WBBS-FM broadcasts to the Syracuse, NY area at 104.7 FM.
FM RADIO STATION

WBBT-AM 38889
Owner: TCB Broadcasting
Editorial: 473 N Victory Dr, Lyons, Georgia 30436-1947 **Tel:** 1 912 526-8122.
Profile: WBBT-AM is a commercial station owned by TCB Broadcasting. The format of the station is oldies. WBBT-AM broadcasts to the Lyons, GA area at 1340 AM.
AM RADIO STATION

WBBT-FM 44465
Owner: Alpha Media
Editorial: 300 Arboretum Pl, Ste 590, Richmond, Virginia 23236-3481 **Tel:** 1 804 327-9902.
Web site: http://www.bigoldies1073.com
Profile: WBBT-FM is a commercial station owned by Alpha Media. The format of the station is oldies. WBBT-FM broadcasts to the Richmond, VA area at 107.3 FM.
FM RADIO STATION

WBBV-FM 41427
Owner: Debut Broadcasting Inc.
Editorial: 900 Belmont St, Vicksburg, Mississippi 39180-3830 **Tel:** 1 601 636-2340.
Web site: http://www.river101.com
Profile: WBBV-FM is a commercial station owned by Debut Broadcasting Inc. The format of the station is country music. WBBV-FM broadcasts to the Vicksburg, MS area at 101.3 FM.
FM RADIO STATION

WBBW-AM 36721
Owner: Cumulus Media Inc.
Editorial: 4040 Simon Rd, Youngstown, Ohio 44512-1362 **Tel:** 1 330 783-1000.
Email: wbbw@wbbw.com
Web site: http://www.wbbw.com
Profile: WBBW-AM is a commercial station owned by Cumulus Media Inc. The format of the station is sports. WBBW-AM broadcasts to the Youngstown, OH area at 1240 AM.
AM RADIO STATION

WBBX-AM 35193
Owner: Pilgrims Pathway Inc.
Editorial: 705 Greenwood St, Kingston, Tennessee 37763-2522 **Tel:** 1 865 376-6954.
Profile: WBBX-AM is a non-commercial station owned by Pilgrims Pathway Inc. The format of the station is gospel and Christian programming. WBBX-AM broadcasts to the Kingston, TN area at 1410 AM.
AM RADIO STATION

WBBZ-AM 35194
Owner: Muchmore(Tom)
Editorial: 1601 E Oklahoma Ave, Ponca City, Oklahoma 74604-5215 **Tel:** 1 580 765-6607.
Email: wbbz@wbbz.com
Web site: http://www.wbbz.com
Profile: WBBZ-AM is a commercial station owned by Tom Muchmore. The format of the station is classic hits music. WBBZ-AM broadcasts to the Oklahoma City area at 1230 AM.
AM RADIO STATION

WBCB-AM 35195
Owner: Progressive Broadcasting
Editorial: 200 Magnolia Dr, Levittown, Pennsylvania 19054-2007 **Tel:** 1 215 949-1490.
Web site: http://wbcb1490.com
Profile: WBCB-AM is a commercial station owned by Progressive Broadcasting. The format of the station is variety. WBCB-AM broadcasts to the Levittown, PA area at 1490 AM.
AM RADIO STATION

WBCE-AM 35816
Owner: Gray (Wendell)
Editorial: 1136 Barlow Rd, Wickliffe, Kentucky 42087-9288 **Tel:** 1 270 335-5171.
Profile: WBCE-AM is a commercial station owned by Gray (Wendell). The format of the station is religious featuring Christian talk and music programming. WBCE-AM broadcasts locally to the Wickliffe, KY area at a frequency of 1200 AM.
AM RADIO STATION

WBCF-AM 36348
Owner: BCB Incorporated
Editorial: 525 E Tennessee St, Florence, Alabama 35630-5719 **Tel:** 1 256 764-8170.
Email: news@wbcf.com
Web site: http://www.wbcf.com
Profile: WBCF-AM is a commercial station owned by BCB Incorporated. The format of the station is news, sports and talk. WBCF-AM broadcasts to the Florence, AL area at 1240 AM.
AM RADIO STATION

WBCG-FM 86753
Owner: iHeartMedia Inc.
Editorial: 24100 Tiseo Blvd Unit 10, Port Charlotte, Florida 33980-5223 **Tel:** 1 941 206-1188.
Web site: http://www.989myfm.com
Profile: WBCG-FM is a commercial station owned by iHeartMedia Inc. The format of the station is hot AC. WBCG-FM broadcasts to the Port Charlotte, FL area at a frequency of 98.9 FM.
FM RADIO STATION

WBCH-AM 37664
Owner: Barry Broadcasting Co.
Editorial: 119 W State St, Hastings, Michigan 49058 **Tel:** 1 269 945-3414.
Email: wbch@wbch.com
Web site: http://www.wbch.com
Profile: WBCH-AM is a commercial station owned by Barry Broadcasting Co. The format of the station is news and talk radio. WBCH-AM broadcasts to the Grand Rapids area at 1220 AM.
AM RADIO STATION

WBCH-FM 45044
Owner: Barry Broadcasting Co.
Editorial: 119 W State St, Hastings, Michigan 49058-1843 **Tel:** 1 269 945-3414.
Email: wbch@wbch.com
Web site: http://www.wbch.com
Profile: WBCH-FM is a commercial station owned by Barry Broadcasting Co. The format of the station is contemporary country music. WBCH-FM broadcasts in the Hastings, MI area at 100.1 FM.
FM RADIO STATION

WBCI-FM 42785
Owner: Blount Communications Group
Editorial: 122 Main St, Topsham, Maine 04086-1248 **Tel:** 1 207 725-9224.
Email: info@lifechangingradio.com
Web site: http://lifechangingradio.com/wbci
Profile: WBCI-FM is a commercial station owned by Blount Communications Group. The format for the station is Christian talk and music. WBCI-FM broadcasts to the Portland, ME area at 105.9 FM.
FM RADIO STATION

WBCK-FM 500170
Owner: Townsquare Media, LLC
Editorial: 390 Golden Ave, Battle Creek, Michigan 49015-4519 **Tel:** 1 269 963-5555.
Web site: http://wbckfm.com
Profile: WBCK-FM is a commercial station owned by Townsquare Media, LLC . The format of the station is news, sports and talk. WBCK-FM broadcasts to the Battle Creek, MI area at 95.3 FM.
FM RADIO STATION

WBCM-FM 42166
Owner: Midwestern Broadcasting Co.
Editorial: 314 E Front St, Traverse City, Michigan 49684 **Tel:** 1 231 947-7675.
Email: news@wtcmradio.com
Web site: http://www.wtcmi.com
Profile: WBCM-FM is a commercial station owned by Midwestern Broadcasting Co. The format of the contemporary country music. WBCM-FM broadcasts to the Traverse City, MI area at 93.5 FM.
FM RADIO STATION

WBCN-AM 156281
Owner: Beasley Broadcast Group
Editorial: 1520 South Blvd, Charlotte, North Carolina 28203-4786 **Tel:** 1 704 319-9369.
Web site: http://americaspulse1660.com
Profile: WBCN-AM is a commercial station owned by Beasley Broadcast Group. The format of the station is conservative talk. WBCN-AM broadcasts to the Charlotte, NC area at 1660 AM.
AM RADIO STATION

WBCO-AM 38727
Owner: Saga Communications
Editorial: 403 E Rensselaer St, Bucyrus, Ohio 44820-2438 **Tel:** 1 419 562-2222.
Web site: http://www.wbco.com
Profile: WBCO-AM is a commercial station owned by Saga Communications. The format of the station is classic country. WBCO-AM broadcasts to Bucyrus, OH area at 1540 AM.
AM RADIO STATION

WBCP-AM 35885
Owner: Clark and Pirtle Inc.
Editorial: 904 N 4th St, Ste D, Champaign, Illinois 61820 **Tel:** 1 217 359-1580.
Email: wbcpradio@sbcglobal.net
Web site: http://wbcp1580.com
Profile: WBCP-AM is a commercial station owned by Clark and Pirtle Inc. The format of the station is urban AC and gospel music. WBCP-AM broadcasts in the Champaign, IL area at 1580 AM.
AM RADIO STATION

WBCQ-FM 560562
Owner: Weiner (Allan and Barbara)
Editorial: 274 Britton Rd, Monticello, Maine 04760-3110 **Tel:** 1 207 538-9180.
Profile: WBCQ-FM is a commercial station currently owned by Weiner (Allan and Barbara), dba WBCQ Radio. The format of the station is classic country. WBCQ-FM broadcasts to the Aroostook County area in Maine at 94.7 FM.
FM RADIO STATION

WBCR-AM 35519
Owner: Blount County Broadcasting
Tel: 1 865 984-1470.
Email: truthradioam1470@yahoo.com
Web site: http://www.truthradio.tv
Profile: WBCR-AM is a commercial station owned by Blount County Broadcasting. The format of the station is news and talk. WBCR-AM broadcasts to the Alcoa, TN area at 1470 AM.
AM RADIO STATION

WBCR-FM 40122
Owner: Beloit College
Editorial: 700 College St, Box 39, Beloit, Wisconsin 53511-5509 **Tel:** 1 608 363-2402.
Email: wbcrmanager@gmail.com
Web site: http://www.beloit.edu/wbcr
Profile: WBCR-FM is a non-commercial college station owned by Beloit College. The format of the station is variety. WBCR-FM broadcasts to the Beloit, WI area at 90.3 FM.
FM RADIO STATION

WBCT-FM 40399
Owner: iHeartMedia Inc.
Editorial: 77 Monroe Center St NW, Grand Rapids, Michigan 49503-2903 **Tel:** 1 616 459-1919.
Web site: http://b93.iheart.com
Profile: WBCT-FM is a commercial station owned by iHeartMedia Inc. The format of the station is country. WBCT-FM broadcasts to the Grand Rapids, MI area at 93.7 FM.
FM RADIO STATION

WBCU-AM 35196
Owner: Union Carolina Broadcasting Company Inc.
Editorial: 210 E Main St, Union, South Carolina 29379-2327 **Tel:** 1 864 427-2411.
Web site: http://www.wbcuradio.com
Profile: WBCU-AM is a commercial station owned by Union Carolina Broadcasting Company Inc. The format of the station is contemporary country. WBCU-AM broadcasts to the Union, SC area at 1460 AM.
AM RADIO STATION

WBCV-FM 45642
Owner: NRG Media LLC
Editorial: 2301 Plover Rd, Plover, Wisconsin 54467-3910 **Tel:** 1 715 341-8838.
Email: bigcheese@nrgmedia.com
Web site: http://www.bigcheese1079.net
Profile: WBCV-FM is a commercial station owned by NRG Media LLC. The format of the station is rock/album-oriented rock. WBCV-FM broadcasts to the Wausau, WI area at 107.9 FM.
FM RADIO STATION

WBDC-FM 40123
Owner: DCBroadcasting Inc.
Editorial: 511 Newton St, Ste 202, Jasper, Indiana 47546 **Tel:** 1 812 683-4144.
Email: news@wbdc.us
Web site: http://www.wbdc.us
Profile: WBDC-FM is a commercial station owned by DCBroadcasting Inc. The format of the station is classic country music. WBDC-FM broadcasts to the Jasper, IN area at 100.9 FM.
FM RADIO STATION

WBDK-FM 41350
Owner: Nicolet Broadcasting Inc.
Editorial: 30 N 18th Ave Ste 8, Sturgeon Bay, Wisconsin 54235-3207 **Tel:** 1 920 746-9430.
Email: wbdk@doorcountydailynews.com
Web site: http://www.doorcountydailynews.com
Profile: WBDK-FM is a commercial station owned by Nicolet Broadcasting. The format of the station is adult standards of the 60s, 70s and 80s. WBDK-FM broadcasts to the Sturgeon Bay, WI area at 96.7 FM.
FM RADIO STATION

WBDL-FM 43213
Owner: Magnum Radio Group
Editorial: E 5680-A Highway 33 West, Reedsburg, Wisconsin 53959 **Tel:** 1 608 524-1400.
Email: info@magnumbroadcasting.com
Web site: http://www.wbdlfm.com
Profile: WBDL-FM is a commercial station owned by Magnum Radio Group. The format of the station is adult contemporary. WBDL-FM broadcasts to the Reedsburg, WI area at 102.9 FM.
FM RADIO STATION

WBDR-FM 42450
Owner: Community Broadcasters, LLC
Editorial: 199 Wealtha Ave, Watertown, New York 13601-1837 **Tel:** 1 315 782-1240.
Web site: http://cbwatertown.com/theborder/
Profile: WBDR-FM is a commercial station owned by Community Broadcasters, LLC. The format of the station is Top 40/CHR music. WBDR-FM broadcasts to the Watertown, NY area at 106.7 FM.
FM RADIO STATION

WBDT-FM 45981
Owner: Gulf South Communications Inc.
Editorial: 3245 Montgomery Hwy Ste 1, Dothan, Alabama 36303-2150 **Tel:** 1 334 712-9233.
Profile: WDBT-FM is a commercial station owned by Gulf South Communications Inc. The format of the station is news/talk. WDBT-FM broadcasts to the Ozark, AL area at 103.9 FM.
FM RADIO STATION

WBDX-FM 42702
Owner: Partners For Christian Media, Inc.
Editorial: 5512 Ringgold Rd, Ste 214, Chattanooga, Tennessee 37412 **Tel:** 1 423 892-1200.
Email: jocks@j103.com
Web site: http://www.j103.com
Profile: WBDX-FM is a commercial station owned by Partners For Christian Media, Inc. The format of the station is contemporary Christian. WBDX-FM broadcasts to the Chattanooga, TN area at 102.7 FM.
FM RADIO STATION

WBEA-FM 42079
Owner: Long Island Radio Broadcasting
Editorial: 760 Montauk Hwy, Water Mill, New York 11976-2624 **Tel:** 1 631 267-7800.
Web site: http://www.beach1017.com
Profile: WBEA-FM is a commercial station owned by Long Island Radio Broadcasting. The format of the station is Top 40/CHR. WBEA-FM broadcasts in the Long Island, NY area at 101.7 FM.
FM RADIO STATION

WBEB-FM 42322
Owner: Lee(Jerry)
Editorial: 225 E City Ave, Bala Cynwyd, Pennsylvania 19004-1704 **Tel:** 1 610 667-8400.
Email: webmaster@morefmphilly.com
Web site: http://www.morefmphilly.com
Profile: WBEB-FM is a commercial station owned by Jerry Lee. The format is adult contemporary. WBEB-FM broadcasts to the Philadelphia area at 101.1 FM.
FM RADIO STATION

WBEC-AM 37665
Owner: Gamma Broadcasting LLC
Editorial: 211 Jason St, Pittsfield, Massachusetts 01201-5907 **Tel:** 1 413 499-3333.
Email: news@wupe.com
Web site: http://live959.com
Profile: WBEC-AM is a commercial station owned by the Gamma Broadcasting LLC. The format of the station is news, sports and talk. WBEC-AM broadcasts to the Pittsfield, MA area at 1420 AM.
AM RADIO STATION

WBEC-FM 45592
Owner: Gamma Broadcasting LLC
Editorial: 211 Jason St, Pittsfield, Massachusetts 01201-5907 **Tel:** 1 413 499-3333.
Email: news@wupe.com
Web site: http://live959.com
Profile: WBEC-FM is a commercial station owned by Gamma Broadcasting LLC. The format of station is adult contemporary. WBEC-FM broadcasts to the Pittsfield, MA area at 95.9 FM.
FM RADIO STATION

WBEE-FM 45047
Owner: Entercom Communications Corp.
Editorial: 70 Commercial St, Rochester, New York 14614-1010 **Tel:** 1 585 423-2900.
Web site: http://www.wbee.com
Profile: WBEE-FM is a commercial station owned by Entercom Communications Corp. The format of the station is contemporary country. WBEE-FM broadcasts to the Rochester, NY area at 92.5 FM.
FM RADIO STATION

WBEI-FM 43056
Owner: Townsquare Media, Inc.
Editorial: 142 Skyland Blvd, Tuscaloosa, Alabama 35405-4015 **Tel:** 1 205 345-7200.
Web site: http://www.b1017online.com
Profile: WBEI-FM is a commercial station owned by Townsquare Media, Inc. The format of the station is hot adult contemporary. WBEI-FM broadcasts to the Tuscaloosa, AL, area at 101.7 FM.
FM RADIO STATION

WBEJ-AM 35199
Owner: C.B. Radio Inc.
Editorial: 510 Broad St, Elizabethton, Tennessee 37643-2718 **Tel:** 1 423 542-2184.
Email: wbejradio@gmail.com
Web site: http://www.wbej.com
Profile: WBEJ-AM is a commercial station owned by C.B. Radio Inc. The format of the station is country music. WBEJ-AM broadcasts in the Elizabethton, TN area at 1240 AM.
AM RADIO STATION

WBEL-AM 36916
Owner: Big Radio
Editorial: 1 Parker Pl Ste 485, Janesville, Wisconsin 53545-4078 **Tel:** 1 608 758-9025.
Web site: http://www.thebigam1380.com
Profile: WBEL-AM is a commercial station owned by Big Radio. The format of the station is news, talk and sports. WBEL-AM broadcasts to the Janesville, WI area on 1380 AM.
AM RADIO STATION

WBEL-FM 759325
Owner: American Family Association
Tel: 1 270 4623020.
Web site: http://www.afa.net
Profile: WBEL-FM is a non-commercial station owned by the American Family Association. The format of the station is religious. WBEL-FM broadcasts locally to the Cairo, IL area at a frequency of 88.5 FM.
FM RADIO STATION

WBEN-AM 38334
Owner: Entercom Communications Corp.
Editorial: 500 Corporate Pkwy, Ste 200, Buffalo, New York 14226-1263 **Tel:** 1 716 843-0600.
Email: newsroom@wben.com
Web site: http://www.wben.com
Profile: WBEN-AM is a commercial station owned by Entercom Communications Corp. The format of the station is news and talk. WBEN-AM broadcasts to Buffalo, NY at 930 AM.
AM RADIO STATION

WBEN-FM 40279
Owner: Beasley Broadcast Group
Editorial: 1 Bala Plz Ste 424, Bala Cynwyd, Pennsylvania 19004-1421 **Tel:** 1 610 771-0957.
Email: questions@ilikebenfm.com
Web site: http://957benfm.com
Profile: WBEN-FM is a commercial station owned by Beasley Broadcast Group. The format of the station is Jack FM-Adult Hits. WBEN-FM broadcasts to the Philadelphia area at 95.7 FM.
FM RADIO STATION

WBES-AM 39078
Owner: Bristol Broadcasting
Editorial: 817 Suncrest Pl, Charleston, West Virginia 25303-2302 **Tel:** 1 304 744-7020.
Email: news@wqbe.com
Web site: http://95thesportsfox.com
Profile: WBES-AM is a commercial station owned by Bristol Broadcasting. The format of the station is sports. WBES-AM broadcasts to the Charleston, WV area at 1240 AM.
AM RADIO STATION

WBET-AM 38941
Owner: Swick Broadcasting
Editorial: 70808 S Nottawa Rd, Sturgis, Michigan 49091 **Tel:** 1 269 651-2383.
Email: info@wbetfm.com
Web site: http://www.espnradio1230online.com
Profile: WBET-AM is a commercial station owned by Swick Broadcasting. The format of the station is sports. WBET-AM broadcasts to the Sturgis, MI at 1230 AM.
AM RADIO STATION

WBET-FM 46283
Owner: Swick Broadcasting
Editorial: 70808 S Nottawa Rd, Sturgis, Michigan 49091 **Tel:** 1 269 651-2383.
Email: info@wbetfm.com
Web site: http://www.trueoldies993.com
Profile: WBET-FM is a commercial station owned by Swick Broadcasting. The format of the station is oldies music. WBET-FM broadcasts to the Sturgis, MI area at 99.3 FM.
FM RADIO STATION

WBEV-AM 37666
Owner: Good Karma Broadcasting
Editorial: 100 Stoddart St, Beaver Dam, Wisconsin 53916-1306 **Tel:** 1 920 885-4442.
Web site: http://www.wbevradio.com
Profile: WBEV-AM is a commercial station owned by Good Karma Broadcasting. The format of the station is news and talk. WBEV-AM broadcasts to the Beaver Dam, WI area at 1430 AM.
AM RADIO STATION

WBEW-FM 473443
Owner: Chicago Public Media Inc.
Editorial: 848 E Grand Ave, Navy Pier, Chicago, Illinois 60611-3509 **Tel:** 1 312 948-4600.
Email: info@vocalo.org
Web site: http://www.vocalo.org
Profile: WBEW-FM is a non-commercial station owned by Chicago Public Media Inc. The format of the station is variety. WBEW-FM broadcasts to the Chicago area at 89.5 FM. WBEW-FM airs programming on WRTE-FM.
FM RADIO STATION

WBEX-AM 36894
Owner: iHeartMedia Inc.
Editorial: 45 W Main St, Chillicothe, Ohio 45601-3104 **Tel:** 1 740 773-3000.
Email: newsroom@wkkj.com
Web site: http://wbex.iheart.com
Profile: WBEX-AM is a commercial station owned by iHeartMedia Inc. The format of the station is news and talk. WBEX-AM broadcasts to the Chillicothe, OH area at 1490 AM.
AM RADIO STATION

WBEY-FM 334253
Owner: Bay Broadcasting
Editorial: 1637 Dun Swamp Rd, Pocomoke City, Maryland 21851-3300 **Tel:** 1 410 957-1904.
Email: baycountry979@gmail.com
Web site: http://www.easternshoremedia.net
Profile: WBEY-FM is a commercial station owned by Bay Broadcasting. The format of the station is contemporary country. WBEY-FM broadcasts to the Salisbury, MD area at 97.9 FM.
FM RADIO STATION

WBEZ-FM 40124
Owner: Chicago Public Media Inc.
Editorial: 848 E Grand Ave, Chicago, Illinois 60611-3509 **Tel:** 1 312 948-4600.
Email: info@wbez.org
Web site: http://www.wbez.org
Profile: WBEZ-FM is a non-commercial station owned by Chicago Public Media Inc. The format of the station is talk and news. WBEZ-FM broadcasts to the Chicago area at 91.5 FM.
FM RADIO STATION

WBFA-FM 44092
Owner: iHeartMedia Inc.
Editorial: 1501 13th Ave, Columbus, Georgia 31901-1908 **Tel:** 1 706 576-3000.
Web site: http://www.thebeatcolumbus.com
Profile: WBFA-FM is a commercial station owned by iHeartMedia Inc. The format of the station is urban contemporary. WBFA-FM broadcasts to the Columbus, GA area at 98.3 FM.
FM RADIO STATION

WBFB-FM 41289
Owner: Blueberry Broadcasting
Editorial: 184 Target Cir, Bangor, Maine 04401-5718 **Tel:** 1 207 947-9100.
Web site: http://www.971thebear.com
Profile: WBFB-FM is a commercial station owned by Blueberry Broadcasting. The format of the station is contemporary country music. WBFB-FM broadcasts to the Bangor, ME area at 97.1 FM.
FM RADIO STATION

WBFC-AM 36906
Owner: Kentucky Mountain Bible College
Editorial: 2401 Paint Creek Rd, Stanton, Kentucky 40380-9272 **Tel:** 1 606 663-6631.
Web site: http://wp.mountaingospel.org
Profile: WBFC-AM is a commercial radio station owned by Kentucky Mountain Bible College. The format of the station is Southern Gospel. It broadcasts to the Stanton, KY area at 1470 AM.
AM RADIO STATION

WBFD-AM 38603
Owner: Cessna Communications Inc.
Editorial: 134 E Pitt St Fl 2, Bedford, Pennsylvania 15522-1311 **Tel:** 1 814 623-1000.
Email: cesscomm@embarqmail.com
Web site: http://www.bedfordcountyradio.com/links/1310.html
Profile: WBFD-AM is a commercial station owned by Cessna Communications Inc. The format of the station is news and talk. WBFD-AM broadcasts to the Bedford, PA area at 1310 AM.
AM RADIO STATION

WBFE-FM 42551
Owner: Blueberry Broadcasting
Editorial: 184 Target Cir, Bangor, Maine 04401-5718 **Tel:** 1 207 947-9100.
Web site: http://www.971thebear.com
Profile: WBFE-FM is a commercial station owned by Blueberry Broadcasting. The format of the station is contemporary country. WBFE-FM broadcasts to the Ellsworth, ME area at 99.1 FM.
FM RADIO STATION

WBFG-FM 44437
Owner: Crossroads Broadcasting, LLC
Editorial: 584 Smith Ave, Lexington, Tennessee 38351 **Tel:** 1 731 968-3500.
Email: wbfg965@yahoo.com
Profile: WBFG-FM is a commercial station owned by Crossroads Broadcasting, LLC. The format of the station is sports. WBFG-FM broadcasts to the Lexington, TN area at 96.5 FM.
FM RADIO STATION

WBFI-FM 41199
Owner: Bethel Fellowship Church
Editorial: 14457 South Highway 259, Leitchfield, Kentucky 42754 **Tel:** 1 270 257-2689.
Email: wbfiradio@yahoo.com
Web site: http://bethel-fellowship.org
Profile: WBFI-FM is a non-commercial station owned by Bethel Fellowship Church. The format of the station is contemporary Christian and religious programming. WBFI-FM broadcasts to the McDaniels, KY area at 91.5 FM.
FM RADIO STATION

WBFJ-AM 37150
Owner: Triad Family Network
Editorial: 1249 N Trade St, Winston Salem, North Carolina 27101 **Tel:** 1 336 721-1560.
Email: wbfj@wbfj.org
Web site: http://www.stereo1550.com
Profile: WBFJ-AM is a commercial station owned by Triad Family Network. The format of the station is Christian talk. WBFJ-AM broadcasts to the Winston Salem, NC area at the 1550 AM.
AM RADIO STATION

WBFJ-FM 44520
Owner: Triad Family Network
Editorial: 1249 N Trade St, Winston Salem, North Carolina 27101 **Tel:** 1 336 721-1560.
Email: wbfj@wbfj.org
Web site: http://www.wbfj.org
Profile: WBFJ-FM is a non-commercial station owned by the Triad Family Network. The format of the station is contemporary Christian music. WBFJ-FM broadcasts to the Winston Salem, NC area at 89.3 FM.
FM RADIO STATION

WBFM-FM 45614
Owner: Midwest Communications Inc.
Editorial: 2100 Washington Ave, Sheboygan, Wisconsin 53081-7042 **Tel:** 1 920 458-2107.
Web site: http://www.b93radio.com
Profile: WBFM-FM is a commercial station owned by Midwest Communications Inc. The format of the station is contemporary country music. WBFM-FM broadcasts to the Milwaukee area at 93.7 FM.
FM RADIO STATION

WBFN-AM 36533
Owner: Family Life Radio
Editorial: 13799 Donavan Rd, Albion, Michigan 49224-9618 **Tel:** 1 800 776-1070.
Web site: http://www.myflr.org
Profile: WBFN-AM is a commercial station owned by Family Life Radio. The format of the station is gospel and religious music. WBFN-AM broadcasts to the Battle Creek, MI area at 1400 AM.
AM RADIO STATION

WBFO-FM 40126
Owner: State of New York
Editorial: 140 Lower Terrace Horizons Plaza, Buffalo, New York 14202 **Tel:** 1 716 845-7040.
Email: news@wbfo.org
Web site: http://www.wbfo.org
Profile: WBFO-FM is a non-commercial station owned by the State of New York and operated by the University of Buffalo. The format of the station is news and talk, with some jazz music in the evenings. WBFO-FM broadcasts to Buffalo, NY, at 88.7 FM. The station does not accept PSAs.
FM RADIO STATION

WBFR-FM 41425
Owner: Family Stations Inc.
Editorial: 244 Goodwin Crest Dr, Ste 118, Birmingham, Alabama 35209 **Tel:** 1 205 942-3530.
Email: info@familyradio.org
Web site: http://www.familyradio.com
FM RADIO STATION

WBFX-FM 45103
Owner: iHeartMedia Inc.
Editorial: 77 Monroe Center St NW, Grand Rapids, Michigan 49503-2903 **Tel:** 1 616 459-1919.
Web site: http://1013thebrew.iheart.com
Profile: WBFX-FM is a commercial station owned by iHeartMedia Inc. The format of the station is classic hits. WBFX-FM broadcasts to the Grand Rapids, MI area at 101.3 FM.
FM RADIO STATION

WBGA-AM 38963
Owner: iHeartMedia Inc.
Editorial: 3833 US Highway 82, Brunswick, Georgia 31523-7735 **Tel:** 1 912 267-1025.
Profile: WBGA-AM is a commercial station owned by iHeartMedia Inc. The format of the station is urban adult contemporary. WBGA-AM broadcasts to the Brunswick, GA area at 1490 AM.
AM RADIO STATION

WBGE-FM 328069
Owner: Flint Media
Editorial: 521 S Scott St, Bainbridge, Georgia 39819-4101 **Tel:** 1 229 246-7776.
Web site: http://sowegalive.com
Profile: WBGE-FM is a commercial station owned by Flint Media, Inc. The format of the station is Hot AC. WBGE-FM broadcasts to the Bainbridge, GA area at 101.9 FM.
FM RADIO STATION

WBGF-FM 45557
Owner: JVC Media
Editorial: 8895 N Military Trl Ste 206C, West Palm Beach, Florida 33410-6279 **Tel:** 1 561 627-9966.
Web site: http://trueoldiesfla.com
Profile: WBGF-FM is a commercial station owned by JVC Media. The format of the station is Oldies music. WBGF-FM broadcasts to the West Palm Beach, FL area at 93.5 FM.
FM RADIO STATION

WBGG-AM 72998
Owner: iHeartMedia Inc.
Editorial: 200 Fleet St Fl 4, Pittsburgh, Pennsylvania 15220-2908 **Tel:** 1 412 937-1441.
Web site: http://espnpgh.iheart.com
Profile: WBGG-AM is a commercial station owned by iHeartMedia Inc. The format of the station is sports. WBGG-AM broadcasts to the Pittsburgh area at 970 AM.
AM RADIO STATION

WBGG-FM 40111
Owner: iHeartMedia Inc.
Editorial: 7601 Riviera Blvd, Miramar, Florida 33023-6574 **Tel:** 1 954 862-2000.
Web site: http://www.big1059.com
Profile: WBGG-FM is a commercial station owned by iHeartMedia Inc. The format of the station is classic rock music. WBGG-FM broadcasts to the Miramar, FL area at 105.9 FM.
FM RADIO STATION

WBGI-FM 46046
Owner: FM Radio Licenses, LLC
Editorial: 56325 High Ridge Rd, Bellaire, Ohio 43906-9707 **Tel:** 1 740 676-5661.
Web site: http://www.biggiecountry.com
Profile: WBGI-FM is a commercial station owned by FM Radio Licenses, LLC. The format of the station is contemporary country. WYJK-FM broadcasts to the Wheeling, WV Steubenville, OH area at 100.5 FM.
FM RADIO STATION

WBGK-FM 238574
Owner: Roser Communications
Editorial: 185 Genesee St, Ste 1601, Utica, New York 13501 **Tel:** 1 315 734-9245.
Web site: http://www.bugcountry.com
Profile: WBGK-FM is a commercial station owned by Roser Communications. The format of the station is contemporary country music. WBGK-FM broadcasts to the Utica, NY area at 99.7 FM and simulcasts with WBUG-FM.
FM RADIO STATION

WBGL-FM 41198
Owner: Illinois Bible Institute
Editorial: 4101 Fieldstone Rd, Champaign, Illinois 61822-8800 **Tel:** 1 217 359-8232.
Email: wbgl@wbgl.org
Web site: http://www.wbgl.org
Profile: WBGL-FM is a non-commercial station owned by the Illinois Bible Institute. The format of the station is contemporary Christian music and talk. WBGL-FM broadcasts to the Champaign, IL area at 91.7 FM.
FM RADIO STATION

WBGN-AM 38439
Owner: FM Radio Licenses, LLC
Editorial: 1919 Scottsville Rd, Bowling Green, Kentucky 42104-3303 **Tel:** 1 270 843-3333.
Email: production@beaverfm.com
Web site: http://www.1340wbgn.com
Profile: WBGN-AM is a commercial station owned by FM Radio Licenses, LLC. The format of the station is sports. WBGN-AM broadcasts to the Bowling Green, KY area at 1340 AM.
AM RADIO STATION

WBGO-FM 40128
Owner: Newark Public Radio Inc.
Editorial: 54 Park Pl, Newark, New Jersey 07102-4302 **Tel:** 1 973 624-8880.
Web site: http://www.wbgo.org
Profile: WBGO-FM is a non-commercial station owned by Newark Public Radio Inc. The format of the station is jazz, public radio, and other local programming. WBGO-FM broadcasts in the Newark, NJ area at 88.3 FM.
FM RADIO STATION

WBGQ-FM 75551
Owner: Cherokee Broadcasting Co.
Editorial: 448 Highway 25 E, Bean Station, Tennessee 37708-5603 **Tel:** 1 865 993-3639.
Web site: http://www.wbgqfm.com
Profile: WBGQ-FM is a commercial station owned by Cherokee Broadcasting Co. The format of the station is Top 40/CHR. WBGQ-FM broadcasts to the Morristown, TN area at 100.7 FM.
FM RADIO STATION

WBGR-FM 45141
Owner: Big Radio
Editorial: W4765 Radio Ln, Monroe, Wisconsin 53566-9405 **Tel:** 1 608 325-2161.
Email: news@bigradio.fm
Web site: http://www.bigradio.fm
Profile: WBGR-FM is a commercial station owned by Big Radio. The format of the station is oldies. WBGR-FM broadcasts to the Monroe, WI area at 93.7 FM. All staff should be contact via fax.
FM RADIO STATION

WBGV-FM 44444
Owner: Sanilac Broadcasting
Editorial: 19 S Elk St, Sandusky, Michigan 48471-1353 **Tel:** 1 810 648-2700.
Email: renaed@sanilacbroadcasting.com
Web site: http://www.sanilacbroadcasting.com
Profile: WBGV-FM is a commercial station owned by Sanilac Broadcasting. The format of the station is country. WBGV-FM broadcasts to the Sandusky, MI area at 92.5 FM.
FM RADIO STATION

WBGW-FM 41705
Owner: Music Ministries Inc.
Editorial: 4463 E 1200 S, Haubstadt, Indiana 47639 **Tel:** 1 812 386-3342.
Email: mail@thyword.org
Web site: http://www.thyword.org
Profile: WBGW-FM is a non-commercial station owned by Music Ministries Inc. The format of the station is Christian. WBGW-FM broadcasts to the Evansville, IN area at 101.5 FM.
FM RADIO STATION

WBGX-AM 35838
Owner: Great Lakes Radio Inc.
Editorial: 5956 S Michigan Ave, Chicago, Illinois 60637-2108 **Tel:** 1 773 752-1570.
Web site: http://www.gospel1570.com
Profile: WBGX-AM is a commercial station owned by Great Lakes Radio Inc. The format of the station is gospel music and Talk . WBGX-AM broadcasts to the greater Chicago area at 1570 AM.
AM RADIO STATION

WBGZ-AM 35202
Owner: Metroplex Communications, Inc.
Editorial: 227 Market St, Alton, Illinois 62002-6231 **Tel:** 1 618 465-3535.
Email: news@wbgzradio.com
Web site: http://www.wbgzradio.com
Profile: WBGZ-AM is a commercial station owned by Metroplex Communications, Inc. The format of the station is talk. WBGZ-AM broadcasts to Alton, IL and the greater St. Louis area at 1570 AM.
AM RADIO STATION

WBHB-AM 35203
Owner: Broadcast South, LLC
Editorial: 601 W Roanoke Dr, Fitzgerald, Georgia 31750-3633 **Tel:** 1 912 389-0995.
Profile: WBHB-AM is a commercial station owned by Broadcast South, LLC. The format of the station is talk. WBHB-AM broadcasts to the Fitzgerald, GA area at 1240 AM.
AM RADIO STATION

WBHB-FM 45619
Owner: VerStandig Broadcasting
Editorial: 10960 John Wayne Dr, Greencastle, Pennsylvania 17225-9584 **Tel:** 1 717 597-9200.
Email: bigbob@1015bobrocks.com
Web site: http://www.1015bobrocks.com
Profile: WBHB-FM is a commercial station owned by VerStandig Broadcasting. The station's format is rock/album oriented rock. WBHB-AM broadcasts to the Greencastle, PA area at 101.5 FM.
FM RADIO STATION

WBHC-FM 45050
Owner: Bocock Communications
Editorial: 1816 Savannah Hwy, Hampton, South Carolina 29924-6545 **Tel:** 1 803 943-2831.
Web site: http://www.allhits921.blogspot.com
Profile: WBHC-FM is a commercial station owned by Bocock Communications. The format of the station is adult hits. WBHC-FM broadcasts to the Savannah, GA area at 92.1 FM.
FM RADIO STATION

WBHD-FM 46776
Owner: Cumulus Media Inc.
Editorial: 600 Baltimore Drive, 2nd Floor, Wilkes-Barre, Pennsylvania 18702-7901 **Tel:** 1 570 824-9000.
Web site: http://www.97bht.com
Profile: WBHD-FM is a commercial station owned by Cumulus Media Inc. The format of the station is Top 40/CHR. The station broadcasts to the Olyphant/ Scranton, PA area at a frequency of 95.7 FM.
FM RADIO STATION

WBHF-AM 35204
Owner: Rei-Con Management Inc.
Editorial: 7 N Wall St, Cartersville, Georgia 30120-3331 **Tel:** 1 770 386-1450.
Email: news@wbhfradio.org
Web site: http://www.wbhfradio.org
Profile: WBHF-AM is a non-commercial station owned by Rei-Con Management Inc. The format of the station is oldies. WBHF-AM broadcasts to the Cartersville, GA area at 1450 AM.
AM RADIO STATION

WBHJ-FM 43333
Owner: Summit Media Broadcasting LLC
Editorial: 2700 Corporate Dr Ste 115, Birmingham, Alabama 35242-2735 **Tel:** 1 205 322-2987.
Web site: http://www.957jamz.com
Profile: WBHJ-FM is a commercial station owned by Summit Media Broadcasting LLC. The format of the station is urban contemporary. WBHJ-FM broadcasts to the Birmingham, AL area at 95.7 FM.
FM RADIO STATION

WBHK-FM 41917
Owner: Summit Media Broadcasting LLC
Editorial: 2700 Corporate Dr Ste 115, Birmingham, Alabama 35242-2735 **Tel:** 1 205 322-2987.
Web site: http://www.987kiss.com
Profile: WBHK-FM is a commercial station owned by Summit Media Broadcasting LLC. The format of the station is R&B. WBHK-FM broadcasts to the Birmingham, AL area at 98.7 FM.
FM RADIO STATION

WBHM-FM 40986
Owner: UAB at Birmingham
Editorial: 650 11th St S, Birmingham, Alabama 35233-1221 **Tel:** 1 205 934-2606.
Email: info@wbhm.org
Web site: http://www.wbhm.org
Profile: WBHM-FM is a non-commercial station owned by UAB at Birmingham. The format of the station is classical music and news. WBHM-FM broadcasts to Birmingham, AL at 90.3 FM.
FM RADIO STATION

WBHN-AM 35205
Owner: Lighthouse Broadcasting, Inc.
Editorial: 1846 Skyland Dr, Sylva, North Carolina 28779-8008 **Tel:** 1 828 488-2682.
Email: 1590wbhn@gmail.com
Profile: WBHN-AM is a commercial station owned by Lighthouse Broadcasting, Inc. The format of the station is classic country music. WBHN-AM broadcasts in the Bryson City, NC area at 1590 AM.
AM RADIO STATION

WBHP-AM 35206
Owner: iHeartMedia Inc.
Editorial: 26869 Peoples Rd, Madison, Alabama 35756-4632 **Tel:** 1 256 309-2400.
Web site: http://www.wbhpam.com
Profile: WBHP-AM is commercial station owned by iHeartMedia Inc. The format of the station is news, sports and talk. WBHP-AM broadcasts to the Madison, AL area at 1230 AM.
AM RADIO STATION

WBHQ-FM 44294
Owner: Flagler County Broadcasting, LLC
Editorial: 2405 E Moody Blvd, Ste 402, Bunnell, Florida 32110-5994 **Tel:** 1 386 437-1992.
Web site: http://www.beach927.com
Profile: WBHQ-FM is a commercial station owned by Flagler County Broadcasting, LLC. The format of the station is variety hits. WBHQ-FM broadcasts to Bunnell, FL and surrounding areas at 92.7 FM
FM RADIO STATION

WBHR-AM 38251
Owner: Tri-County Broadcasting
Editorial: 1010 2Nd St N, Sauk Rapids, Minnesota 56379-2527 **Tel:** 1 320 252-6200.
Email: mail@660wbhr.com
Web site: http://www.660wbhr.com
Profile: WBHR-AM is a commercial station owned by Tri-County Broadcasting. The format of the station is sports. WBHR-AM broadcasts in the Sauk Rapids, MN area at 660 AM.
AM RADIO STATION

WBHT-FM 41908
Owner: Cumulus Media Inc.
Editorial: 600 Baltimore Drive, 2nd Floor, Wilkes-Barre, Pennsylvania 18702-7901 **Tel:** 1 570 824-9000.
Web site: http://www.97bht.com
Profile: WBHT-FM is a commercial station owned by Cumulus Media Inc. The format of the station is Top 40/CHR music. WBHT-FM broadcasts in the Wilkes Barre, PA area at 97.1 FM.
FM RADIO STATION

WBHV-FM 338739
Owner: Seven Mountains Media, LLC
Editorial: 160 Clearview Ave, State College, Pennsylvania 16803 **Tel:** 1 814 238-5085.
Email: b945@7mountainsmedia.com
Web site: http://b945live.com
Profile: WBHV-FM is a commercial station owned by 2510 Associates. The format of the station is Top 40/ CHR. WBHV-FM broadcasts to the State College, PA, area at 94.5 FM.
FM RADIO STATION

WBHW-FM 43524
Owner: Music Ministries Inc.
Editorial: 4463 E 1200 S, Haubstadt, Indiana 47639 **Tel:** 1 800 264-5550.
Email: mail@thyword.org
Web site: http://www.thyword.org
Profile: WBHW-FM is a non-commercial station owned by Music Ministries Inc. The format of the station is Christian. WBHW-FM broadcasts to the Loogootee, IN area at 88.7 FM and is a simulcast of WBJW-FM.
FM RADIO STATION

WBHY-AM 38672
Owner: Goforth Media Inc.
Editorial: 6530B Spanish Fort Blvd, Ste B, Spanish Fort, Alabama 36527-5000 **Tel:** 1 251 473-8488.
Email: news@goforth.org
Web site: http://www.goforth.org
Profile: WBHY-AM is a commercial station owned by Goforth Media Inc. The format for the station is religious. WBHY-AM broadcasts to the Mobile, AL and Pensacola, FL areas at 840 AM.
AM RADIO STATION

WBHY-FM 46025
Owner: Goforth Media Inc.
Editorial: 6530 Spanish Fort Blvd, Ste B, Spanish Fort, Alabama 36527-5014 **Tel:** 1 251 473-8488.
Email: news@goforth.org
Web site: http://www.goforth.org
Profile: WBHY-FM is a commercial station owned by Goforth Media Inc. The format for the station is contemporary Christian. WBHY-FM broadcasts to the Mobile, AL, Pensacola, FL area at 88.5 FM.
FM RADIO STATION

WBIB-AM 35207
Owner: DeLoach(James)
Editorial: 1075 Dry Hollow Rd, Centreville, Alabama 35042 **Tel:** 1 205 926-6286.
Profile: WBIB-AM is a commercial station owned by James DeLoach. The format of the station is southern gospel. WBIB-AM broadcasts in the Centreville, AL area at 1110 AM.
AM RADIO STATION

WBIE-FM 86900
Owner: American Family Association
Editorial: 107 Parkgate Dr, Tupelo, Mississippi 38801 **Tel:** 1 662 844-8888.
Email: comments@afr.net
Web site: http://www.afr.net
FM RADIO STATION

WBIG-AM 36190
Owner: Big Broadcasting Co.
Editorial: 620 N Eola Rd, Aurora, Illinois 60502 **Tel:** 1 630 851-5200.
Email: wbignews@yahoo.com
Web site: http://www.wbig1280.com
Profile: WBIG-AM is a commercial station owned by Big Broadcasting Co. The format of the station is news and talk. WBIG-AM broadcasts to the greater Chicago area at 1280 AM.
AM RADIO STATION

WBIG-FM 40222
Owner: iHeartMedia Inc.
Editorial: 1801 Rockville Pike Fl 5, Rockville, Maryland 20852-1633 **Tel:** 1 240 747-2700.
Web site: http://wbig.iheart.com
Profile: WBIG-FM is a commercial station owned by iHeartMedia Inc. The format of the station is classic rock. WBIG-FM broadcasts to the Washington, D.C. area at 100.3 FM.
FM RADIO STATION

WBIM-FM 40131
Owner: Bridgewater State College
Editorial: 109 Campus Ctr, Bridgewater, Massachusetts 2325 **Tel:** 1 508 531-1303.
Email: wbim@bridgew.edu
Web site: http://www.bridgew.edu/wbim
Profile: WBIM-FM is a non-commercial station owned by Bridgewater State College. The format of the station is variety. WBIM-FM broadcasts to the Bridgewater, WA area at 91.5 FM.
FM RADIO STATION

WBIN-AM 86440
Owner: Sines(John & Jane)
Editorial: 108 Lifestyle Way, Benton, Tennessee 37307 **Tel:** 1 423 338-2864.
AM RADIO STATION

WBIO-FM 42602
Owner: Cromwell Group Inc.(The)
Editorial: 1115 Tamarack Rd Ste 500, Owensboro, Kentucky 42301-6988 **Tel:** 1 270 683-5200.
Web site: http://www.owensbororadio.com
Profile: WBIO-FM is a commercial station owned by The Cromwell Group Inc. The format for the station is classic country. WBIO-FM broadcasts to the Evansville, IN area at 94.7 FM.
FM RADIO STATION

WBIP-AM 37671
Owner: Community Broadcasting Services Inc.
Editorial: 1100 S Second St, Booneville, Mississippi 38829 **Tel:** 1 662 728-0200.
Email: wbipam@yahoo.com
Profile: WBIP-AM is a commercial station owned by Community Broadcasting Services Inc. The format of the station is classic country. WBIP-AM broadcasts to the Booneville, MO area at 1400 AM.
AM RADIO STATION

WBIW-AM 37672
Owner: Ad-Venture Media Inc.
Editorial: 424 Heltonville Rd W, Bedford, Indiana 47421-9389 **Tel:** 1 812 275-7555.
Email: news@wbiw.com
Web site: http://www.wbiw.com
Profile: WBIW-AM is a commercial radio station owned by Ad-Venture Media Inc. The format of the station is news, talk and sports. WBIW-AM broadcasts to the Bedford, IN area at 1340 AM.
AM RADIO STATION

WBIY-FM 397222
Owner: Oscar Aguero Ministry Inc.
Editorial: 6050 W 20th Ave, Hialeah, Florida 33016-2605 **Tel:** 1 305 826-5555.
Web site: http://www.oscaragueroministry.com
Profile: WBIY-FM is a non-commercial station owned by Oscar Aguero Ministry Inc. The format of the station is Spanish Christian. WBIY-FM broadcasts to the Hialeah, FL area at 88.3 FM.
FM RADIO STATION

WBIZ-AM 37939
Owner: iHeartMedia Inc.
Editorial: 619 Cameron St, Eau Claire, Wisconsin 54703-4708 **Tel:** 1 715 830-4000.
Web site: http://www.sportsradio1400.com
Profile: WBIZ-AM is a commercial station owned by iHeartMedia Inc. The format of the station is sports. WBIZ-AM broadcasts to the Eau Claire, WI area at 1400 AM.
AM RADIO STATION

WBIZ-FM 45052
Owner: iHeartMedia Inc.
Editorial: 619 Cameron St, Eau Claire, Wisconsin 54703-4708 **Tel:** 1 715 830-4000.
Web site: http://www.z100radio.com
Profile: WBIZ-FM is a commercial station owned by iHeartMedia Inc. The format of the station is Top 40/CHR. WBIZ-FM broadcasts to the Eau Claire, WI area at 100.7 FM.
FM RADIO STATION

WBJB-FM 40132
Owner: Brookdale Community College
Editorial: 765 Newman Springs Rd, Lincroft, New Jersey 07738-1543 **Tel:** 1 732 224-2492.
Email: comments@wbjb.org
Web site: http://www.90.5thenight.org
Profile: WBJB-FM is a non-commercial station owned by Brookdale Community College. The format of the station is adult album alternative and news. WBJB-FM broadcasts in the Lincroft, NJ area area at 90.5 FM.
FM RADIO STATION

WBJC-FM 40133
Owner: Baltimore City Community College
Editorial: 6776 Reisterstown Rd Ste 202, Baltimore, Maryland 21215-2362 **Tel:** 1 410 580-5800.
Web site: http://www.wbjc.com
Profile: WBJC-FM is a non-commercial station owned by the Baltimore City Community College. The format of the station is classical music. WBJC-FM broadcasts to the Baltimore area at 91.5 FM.
FM RADIO STATION

WBJI-FM 42335
Owner: R.P. Broadcasting
Editorial: 2115 Washington Ave S, Bemidji, Minnesota 56601-8918 **Tel:** 1 218 751-7777.
Email: news@kkbj.com
Web site: http://www.wbji.com
Profile: WBJI-FM is a commercial station owned by R.P. Broadcasting. The format of the station features a mix of classic and contemporary country music. WBJI-FM broadcasts to the Bemidji, MN area at 98.3 FM.
FM RADIO STATION

WBJW-FM 43732
Owner: Music Ministries Inc.
Editorial: 4463 E 1200 S, Haubstadt, Indiana 47639
Tel: 1 812 386-3342.
Email: mail@thyword.org
Web site: http://www.thyword.org
Profile: WBJW-FM is a non-commercial station owned by Music Ministries Inc. The format of the station is Christian. WBJW-FM broadcasts to the Haubstadt, IN area at 91.7 FM.
FM RADIO STATION

WBJY-FM 242125
Owner: American Family Association
Editorial: 107 Parkgate Dr., Tupelo, Mississippi 38801
Tel: 1 662 844-8888.
Email: comments@afr.net
Web site: http://www.afr.net
FM RADIO STATION

WBJZ-FM 128100
Owner: Caxambas Corp.
Tel: 1 920 230-1047.
Email: psa@b104online.com
Web site: http://www.b104online.com
Profile: WBJZ-FM is a commercial station owned by Caxambas Corp. The format of the station is Top 40/CHR. WBJZ-FM broadcasts to the Ripon, WI area at 104.7 FM.
FM RADIO STATION

WBKA-FM 43135
Owner: Blueberry Broadcasting
Editorial: 184 Target Cir, Bangor, Maine 04401-5718
Tel: 1 877 724-4104.
Email: big104@blueberrybroadcasting.com
Web site: http://big104fm.com
Profile: WBKA-FM is a commercial station owned by Blueberry Broadcasting. The format of the station is classic hits. WBKA-FM broadcasts to the Kennebunk, ME area at 107.7 FM.
FM RADIO STATION

WBKE-FM 40134
Owner: Manchester College
Editorial: 604 E College Ave #19, North Manchester, Indiana 46962-1276 **Tel:** 1 260 982-5272.
Email: 895thebuzz@gmail.com
Web site: http://wbke.manchester.edu
Profile: WBKE-FM is a non-commercial station owned by Manchester College. The format of the station is variety, news, sports and talk. WBKE-FM broadcasts to the Fort Wayne, IN area at 89.5 FM.
FM RADIO STATION

WBKN-FM 44516
Owner: Brookhaven Broadcasting, Inc.
Editorial: 225 S Church St, Brookhaven, Mississippi 39601-3231 **Tel:** 1 601 833-9210.
Email: brookhavenbroadcasting@yahoo.com
Profile: WBKN-FM is a commercial station owned by Brookhaven Broadcasting, Inc. The format of the station is contemporary country music. WBKN-FM broadcasts to the Brookhaven, MS area at 92.1 FM.
FM RADIO STATION

WBKQ-FM 45753
Owner: Backyard Broadcasting
Editorial: 800 E 29th St, Muncie, Indiana 47302-5765
Tel: 1 765 288-4403.
Email: blake@woofboom.com
Web site: http://www.967blakefm.com
Profile: WBKQ-FM is a commercial station owned by Backyard Broadcasting. The format of the station is country music. WBKQ-FM broadcasts to the Muncie, IN area at 96.7 FM.
FM RADIO STATION

WBKR-FM 45735
Owner: Townsquare Media, LLC
Editorial: 3301 Frederica St, Owensboro, Kentucky 42301 **Tel:** 1 270 683-1558.
Email: spots@wbkr.com
Web site: http://www.wbkr.com
Profile: WBKR-FM is a commercial station owned by Townsquare Media, LLC. The format of the station is contemporary country. WBKR-FM broadcasts to the Owensboro, KY at a frequency of 92.5 FM.
FM RADIO STATION

WBKS-FM 151152
Owner: iHeartMedia Inc.
Editorial: 667 W Market St, Lima, Ohio 45801-4603
Tel: 1 419 223-2060.
Web site: http://www.939kisslima.com
Profile: WBKS-FM is a commercial station owned by iHeartMedia Inc.The format of the station is Top 40/CHR music. WBKS-FM broadcasts to the Lima, OH area at 93.9 FM.
FM RADIO STATION

WBKT-FM 43315
Owner: Townsquare Media, LLC
Editorial: 34 Chestnut St, Oneonta, New York 13820-2466 **Tel:** 1 607 432-1030.
Email: cnynews@townsquaremedia.com
Web site: http://www.wbktfm.com
Profile: WBKT-FM is a commercial station owned by Townsquare Media, LLC. The format of the station is contemporary country music. WBKT-FM broadcasts to the Oneonta, NY area at 95.3 FM.
FM RADIO STATION

WBKV-AM 37673
Owner: Bliss Communications Inc.
Editorial: 2410 S Main St, West Bend, Wisconsin 53095-5766 **Tel:** 1 262 334-2344.
Web site: http://www.wibdwestbend.com
Profile: WBKV-AM is a commercial station owned by Bliss Communications Inc. The format of the station is news and talk. WBKV-AM broadcasts to the West Bend, WI area at 1470 AM.
AM RADIO STATION

WBKW-AM 37705
Owner: Southern Communications Corp.
Editorial: 306 S Kanawha St, Beckley, West Virginia 25801-5619 **Tel:** 1 304 252-6452.
Profile: WBKW-AM is a commercial station owned by Southern Communications Corp. The format of the station is religious Catholic. WBKW-AM broadcasts locally in the Beckley, WV area at 1070 AM.
AM RADIO STATION

WBKX-FM 45690
Owner: Chadwick Bay Broadcasting Corporation
Editorial: 4561 Willow Rd, Dunkirk, New York 14048
Tel: 1 716 366-1410.
Web site: http://www.wbkxcountry.com
Profile: WBKX-FM is a commercial station owned by Chadwick Bay Broadcasting Corporation. The format of the station is contemporary country music. WBXX-FM broadcasts to the Dunkirk-Fredonia, NY area at 96.5 FM.
FM RADIO STATION

WBKY-FM 44001
Owner: Magnum Radio Group
Editorial: N2349 Wibu Rd, Poynette, Wisconsin 53955-9556 **Tel:** 1 608 745-0959.
Web site: http://www.buckycountry959.com
Profile: WBKY-FM is a commercial station owned by Magnum Radio Group. The format for the station is contemporary country. WBKY-FM broadcasts to the Portage, WI area at 95.9 FM.
FM RADIO STATION

WBLA-AM 38767
Owner: Baldwin Branch Missionary Baptist Church
Editorial: 4047 Highway 242 South, Elizabethtown, North Carolina 28337 **Tel:** 1 910 645-2396.
Web site: http://www.dabranch1440.com
Profile: WBLA-AM is a commercial station owned by Baldwin Branch Missionary Baptist Church. The format of the station is Christian teaching and Gospel music. WBLA-AM broadcasts to the Elizabethtown, NC area at 1440 AM.
AM RADIO STATION

WBLB-AM 35211
Owner: Nipper(Larry)
Editorial: 3570 Robinson Tract Rd, Pulaski, Virginia 24301 **Tel:** 1 540 980-3411.
Email: wblb1340am@verizon.net
Web site: http://wblb1340am.weebly.com
Profile: WBLB-AM is a commercial station owned by Larry Nipper. The format of the station is Christian. WBLB-AM broadcasts to the Pulaski, VA area at 1340 AM.
AM RADIO STATION

WBLC-AM 35212
Owner: LifeTalk Radio Network
Editorial: 4787 Browder Hollow Rd, Lenoir City, Tennessee 37771 **Tel:** 1 865 986-5332.
Email: wblc3abn@bellsouth.net
AM RADIO STATION

WBLE-FM 40135
Owner: Batesville Broadcasting Co.
Editorial: 1040 Highway 6 W, Batesville, Mississippi 38606-8104 **Tel:** 1 662 563-4664.
Email: country101radio@yahoo.com
Web site: http://www.wble101.com
FM RADIO STATION

WBLF-AM 35213
Owner: Magnum Broadcasting Inc.
Editorial: 315 S Atherton St, State College, Pennsylvania 16801-4045 **Tel:** 1 814 272-1320.
Email: wblfproduction@yahoo.com
Profile: WBLF-AM is a commercial station owned by Magnum Broadcasting Inc. The format of the station is news talk. WBLF-AM broadcasts to the State College, PA area at 970 AM.
AM RADIO STATION

WBLI-FM 40136
Owner: Cox Media Group, Inc.
Editorial: 555 Sunrise Hwy, West Babylon, New York 11704-6009 **Tel:** 1 631 669-9254.
Email: wbli@wbli.com
Web site: http://www.wbli.com
Profile: WBLI-FM is a commercial station owned by Cox Media Group, Inc. The format of the station is Top 40/CHR. WBLI-FM broadcasts to the New York area at 106.1 FM.
FM RADIO STATION

WBLJ-AM 35214
Owner: North Georgia Radio Group
Editorial: 613 Silver Cir, Dalton, Georgia 30721
Tel: 1 706 278-5511.
Email: news@ngaradio.com
Web site: http://wblj1230.com
Profile: WBLJ-AM is a commercial station owned by North Georgia Radio Group. The format of the station is news, sports and talk. WBLJ-AM broadcasts to the Dalton, GA area at 1230 AM.
AM RADIO STATION

WBLJ-FM 46836
Owner: iHeartMedia Inc
Editorial: 1559 W 4th St, Williamsport, Pennsylvania 17701-5650 **Tel:** 1 570 327-1400.
Web site: http://www.billcountry.com
Profile: WBLJ-FM is a commercial station owned by iHeartMedia Inc. The station's format is contemporary country. WBLJ-FM broadcasts to the Williamsport, PA area at 95.3 FM.
FM RADIO STATION

WBLK-FM 40137
Owner: Townsquare Media, LLC
Editorial: 14 Lafayette Sq Ste 1200, Buffalo, New York 14203-1912 **Tel:** 1 716 852-9393.
Web site: http://www.wblk.com
FM RADIO STATION

WBLL-AM 38781
Owner: V-Teck Communications Inc.
Editorial: 1501 Road 235, Bellefontaine, Ohio 43311
Tel: 1 937 592-1045.
Web site: http://www.peakofohio.com
Profile: WBLL-AM is a commercial station owned by V-Teck Communications Inc. The format of the station is news, talk, and sports. WBLL-AM broadcasts in the Bellefontaine, OH area at 1390 AM.
AM RADIO STATION

WBLM-FM 40763
Owner: Townsquare Media, LLC
Editorial: 1 City Ctr, Portland, Maine 04101-6420
Tel: 1 207 774-6364.
Email: wblm@wblm.com
Web site: http://www.wblm.com
Profile: WBLM-FM is a commercial station owned by Townsquare Media, LLC. The format of the station is classic rock. WBLM-FM broadcasts to the Portland, ME area at 102.9 FM.
FM RADIO STATION

WBLO-AM 35705
Owner: GHB Radio, Inc
Editorial: 4801 E Independence Blvd Ste 815, Charlotte, North Carolina 28212-5490 **Tel:** 1 704 405-3172.
Web site: http://www.pepe790.com/
Profile: WBLO-AM is a commercial station owned by GHB Radio, Inc. The format of the station is regional Mexican. WBLO-AM broadcasts to the High Point, NC area at 790 AM.
AM RADIO STATION

WBLQ-AM 37010
Owner: Diponti Communications
Editorial: 16 High St, Westerly, Rhode Island 02891-1985 **Tel:** 1 401 322-9091.
Web site: http://www.wblq.net
Profile: WBLQ-AM is a commercial station owned by Diponti Communications. The format of the station is full service with talk and Lite AC music. WBLQ-AM broadcasts to the Westerly, RI area at 1230 AM.
AM RADIO STATION

WBLR-AM 36548
Owner: Good News Network
Editorial: 2278 Wortham Ln, Grovetown, Georgia 30813-5103 **Tel:** 1 706 309-9610.
Web site: http://www.gnnradio.org
Profile: WBLR-AM is a commercial station owned by Good News Network. The format of the station is Hispanic religious. WBLR-AM broadcasts to the Grovetown, GA area on 1430 AM.
AM RADIO STATION

WBLS-FM 46102
Owner: Emmis Communications Corp.
Editorial: 395 Hudson St Fl 7, New York, New York 10014-7452 **Tel:** 1 212 447-1000.
Email: info@wbls.com
Web site: http://www.wbls.com
Profile: WBLS-FM is a commercial station owned by Emmis Communications Corp. The format of the station is urban adult contemporary. WBLS-FM broadcasts to the New York area at 107.5 FM. ALL correspondence should be forwarded to the station's publicist via e-mail. ALL PSAs should be submitted through the website: wbls.com/psa.
FM RADIO STATION

WBLT-AM 35215
Owner: 3 Daughters Media, Inc.
Editorial: 1035 Avalon Dr, Forest, Virginia 24551-2970
Tel: 1 434 534-6100.
Web site: http://www.espninva.com
Profile: WBLT-AM is a commercial station owned by 3 Daughters Media, Inc. The format of the station is sports. WBLT-AM broadcasts to the Bedford, VA area at 1350 AM.
AM RADIO STATION

WBLU-FM 41483
Owner: Blue Lake Fine Arts Camp
Editorial: 300 E Crystal Lake Rd, Twin Lake, Michigan 49457-9499 **Tel:** 1 231 894-5656.

Web site: http://www.bluelake.org/radio.html
Profile: WBLU-FM is a non-commerical stationed owned by Blue Lake Fine Arts Camp. The format of the station is variety of news and arts programming, jazz, classical and folk music. WBLU-FM broadcasts to the Twin Lake, MI and surrounding areas at 90.3 FM.
FM RADIO STATION

WBLV-FM 41429
Owner: Blue Lake Fine Arts Camp
Editorial: 300 E Crystal Lake Rd, Twin Lake, Michigan 49457-9499 **Tel:** 1 231 894-5656.
Web site: http://www.bluelake.org/radio.html
Profile: WBLV-FM is a non-commerical stationed owned by Blue Lake Fine Arts Camp. The format of the station is variety of news and arts programming, jazz, classical and folk music. WBLV-FM broadcasts to the Twin Lake, MI and surrounding areas at 90.3 FM.
FM RADIO STATION

WBLX-FM 46049
Owner: Cumulus Media Inc.
Editorial: 2800 Dauphin St Ste 104, Mobile, Alabama 36606-2400 **Tel:** 1 251 652-2000.
Web site: http://www.thebigstation93blx.com
Profile: WBLX-FM is a commercial station owned by Cumulus Media Inc. The format for the station is urban contemporary. WBLX-FM broadcasts to the Mobile, AL area at 92.9 FM.
FM RADIO STATION

WBMC-AM 39028
Owner: Peg Broadcasting
Editorial: 230 W Colville St, Mc Minnville, Tennessee 37110-3211 **Tel:** 1 931 473-9253.
Email: production.mcminnville@pegbroadcasting.com
Profile: WBMC-AM is a commercial station owned by Peg Broadcasting. The format of the station is talk. WBMC-AM broadcasts to the McMinnville, TN area at 960 AM. The target audience of the station is adults, ages 18 to 64.
AM RADIO STATION

WBMD-AM 38394
Owner: Family Stations Inc.
Tel: 1 510 821-9000.
Email: info@familyradio.org
Web site: http://www.familyradio.org
Profile: WBMD-AM is a non-commercial station owned by Family Stations Inc. The format of the station is religious programming. WBMD-AM broadcasts to the Baltimore area at 750 AM and simulcasts with WBGR-AM and WFSI-FM.
AM RADIO STATION

WBMH-FM 444969
Owner: Capital Assets, Inc.
Editorial: 4428 N College Ave, Hwy 43, Jackson, Alabama 36545-2017 **Tel:** 1 251 246-4431.
Email: info@bamadixie.com
Web site: http://bamadixie.com/bama106
Profile: WBMH-FM is a commercial station owned by Capital Assets, Inc. The format for the station is classic country. WBMH-FM broadcasts to the Jackson, AL area at 106.1 FM.
FM RADIO STATION

WBMI-FM 42299
Owner: Peggy R. Warner
Editorial: 3275 W M 76, Ste D, West Branch, Michigan 48661-9180 **Tel:** 1 989 345-4269.
Email: wbmi@sbcglobal.net
Profile: WBMI-FM is a commercial station owned by Peggy R. Warner. The format of the station is classic country. WBMI-FM broadcasts to the Flint, MI area at 105.5 FM.
FM RADIO STATION

WBMK-FM 87502
Owner: American Family Association
Editorial: 107 Parkgate Dr, Tupelo, Mississippi 38801
Tel: 1 662 844-8888.
Email: comments@afr.net
Web site: http://www.afr.net
FM RADIO STATION

WBML-AM 36931
Owner: Murray (Christopher L.)
Editorial: 6174 GA Highway 57, Macon, Georgia 31217-3405 **Tel:** 1 404 307-8079.
Profile: WBML-AM is a commercial station owned by Christopher L. Murray, dba WBML-AM RADIO LLC. The format of the station is news and sports. WBML-AM broadcasts to the Macon, GA area at 1350.
AM RADIO STATION

WBMO-FM 42922
Owner: Urban One Inc.
Editorial: 350 E 1st Ave Ste 100, Columbus, Ohio 43201-3792 **Tel:** 1 614 487-1444.
Web site: http://boomcolumbus.com
Profile: WBMO-FM is a commercial station owned by Urban One Inc. The format of the station is Classic Hip Hop. WBMO-FM broadcasts to the Columbus, OH area at 106.3 FM.
FM RADIO STATION

WBMP-FM 42845
Owner: CBS Radio
Editorial: 345 Hudson St Fl 10, New York, New York 10014-7472 **Tel:** 1 212 314-9200.
Web site: http://923amp.cbslocal.com
Profile: WBMP-FM is a commercial station owned by CBS Radio. The format of the station is Top 40/CHR. WBMP-FM broadcasts to the New York area at 92.3 FM.
FM RADIO STATION

WBMQ-AM 38854
Owner: Cumulus Media Inc.
Editorial: 214 Television Cir, Savannah, Georgia 31406-4519 **Tel:** 1 912 961-9000.
Web site: http://www.wbmq.net
Profile: WBMQ-AM is a commercial station owned by Cumulus Media Inc. The format for the station is news and talk. WBMQ-AM broadcasts to the Savannah, GA area at 630 AM.
AM RADIO STATION

WBMV-FM 43572
Owner: Illinois Bible Institute
Editorial: 4101 Fieldstone Rd, Champaign, Illinois 61822-8800 **Tel:** 1 217 359-8232.
Email: wbgl@wbgl.org
Web site: http://www.wbgl.org
Profile: WBMV-FM is a non-commercial station owned by the Illinois Bible Institute. The format of the station is contemporary Christian music. WBMV-FM broadcasts in the Mount Vernon, IL area at 89.7 FM.
FM RADIO STATION

WBMW-FM 41881
Owner: Red Wolf Broadcasting
Editorial: 758 Colonel Ledyard Hwy, Ledyard, Connecticut 06339-1541 **Tel:** 1 860 464-1065.
Email: wbmw@aol.com
Web site: http://www.wbmw.com
Profile: WBMW-FM is a commercial station owned by Red Wolf Broadcasting. The format of the station is Lite Rock/Lite AC music. WBMW-FM broadcasts to the Hartford-New Haven, CT area at 106.5 FM.
FM RADIO STATION

WBMX-FM 44016
Owner: CBS Radio
Editorial: 83 Leo M Birmingham Pkwy, Boston, Massachusetts 02135-1101 **Tel:** 1 617 746-1300.
Web site: http://mix1041.radio.com
Profile: WBMX-FM is a commercial station owned by CBS Radio. The format of the station is hot adult contemporary music. WBMX-FM broadcasts to the Boston area at 104.1 FM.
FM RADIO STATION

WBMZ-FM 45469
Owner: Radio Metter Inc.
Editorial: 1075 E Lillian St, Metter, Georgia 30439-3909 **Tel:** 1 912 685-2136.
Email: wbmz@pineland.net
Profile: WBMZ-FM is a commercial station owned by Radio Metter Inc. The format of the station is classic rock. WBMZ-FM broadcasts to the Metter, GA area at 103.7 FM.
FM RADIO STATION

WBNH-FM 41195
Owner: Central Illinois Radio Fellowship
Editorial: 1919 Mayflower Dr, Pekin, Illinois 61554-9205 **Tel:** 1 309 636-8850.
Email: wbnh@wbnh.org
Web site: http://www.wbnh.org
Profile: WBNH-FM is a non-commercial station owned by Central Illinois Radio Fellowship. The format of the station is religious programming. WBNH-FM broadcasts to the Pekin, IL area at 88.5 FM.
FM RADIO STATION

WBNI-FM 40141
Owner: Indiana Public Broadcasting Systems
Editorial: 3204 Clairmont Ct, Fort Wayne, Indiana 46808-4513 **Tel:** 1 260 452-1189.
Web site: http://www.nipr.fm
Profile: WBNI-FM is a non-commercial station owned by Indiana Public Broadcasting Systems. The format of the station is classical music. WBNI-FM broadcasts to the Fort Wayne, IN area at 94.1 FM.
FM RADIO STATION

WBNJ-FM 704570
Owner: Bill Clanton, Jr.
Tel: 1 609 660-2028.
Web site: http://www.wbnj.org
Profile: WBNJ-FM is a non-commercial radio station owned by Bill Clanton, Jr. The station broadcasts at a frequency of 91.9 out of Barnegat, NJ. The format of the station is adult standards.
FM RADIO STATION

WBNK-FM 583394
Owner: Towers Investment Trust
Editorial: 221 S Front St, New Bern, North Carolina 28560-2135 **Tel:** 1 252 636-3333.
Email: support@bigfishfm.com
Profile: WBNK-FM is a commercial station owned by Towers Investment Trust. The format of the station is contemporary Christian music. WBNK-FM broadcasts to the New Bern, NC area at 92.7 FM.
FM RADIO STATION

WBNL-AM 37674
Owner: Turpen Communications LLC
Editorial: 2177 N State Route 61, Boonville, Indiana 47601-8341 **Tel:** 1 812 897-2080.
Email: rturpen@radio1540.net
Web site: http://www.radio1540.net
Profile: WBNL-AM is a commercial station owned by Turpen Communications LLC. The format for the station is easy listening. WBNL-AM broadcasts to the Evansville, IN area at 1540 AM.
AM RADIO STATION

WBNO-FM 46700
Owner: Impact Radio, LLC
Editorial: 12810 State Route 34, Bryan, Ohio 43506-8809 **Tel:** 1 419 636-3175.
Email: wbno@wbno-wqct.com
Web site: http://www.wbnowqct.com
Profile: WBNO-FM is a commercial station owned by Impact Radio, LLC. The format of the station is classic rock. WBNO-FM broadcasts to the Bryan, OH area at 100.9 FM.
FM RADIO STATION

WBNQ-FM 46471
Owner: Cumulus Media Inc.
Editorial: 236 Greenwood Ave, Bloomington, Illinois 61704-7422 **Tel:** 1 309 829-1221.
Web site: http://www.wbnq.com
Profile: WBNQ-FM is a commercial station owned by Cumulus Media Inc. The format of the station is Top 40/CHR music. WBNQ-FM broadcasts to the Bloomington, IL area at 101.5 FM.
FM RADIO STATION

WBNR-AM 39267
Owner: Pamal Broadcasting, Ltd.
Editorial: 715 Route 52, Beacon, New York 12508-1047 **Tel:** 1 845 838-6000.
Web site: http://www.hvradionet.com
Profile: WBNR-AM is a commercial station owned by Pamal Broadcasting, Ltd. The format of the station is country. WBNR-AM broadcasts to the Beacon, NY area at 1260 AM.
AM RADIO STATION

WBNS-AM 37675
Owner: Radio Ohio Inc.
Editorial: 605 S Front St Fl 300, Columbus, Ohio 43215-5777 **Tel:** 1 614 460-3850.
Web site: http://www.971thefan.com
Profile: WBNS-AM is a commercial station owned by Radio Ohio Inc. The format of the station is sports. WBNS-AM broadcasts to the Columbus, OH area at 1460 AM.
AM RADIO STATION

WBNS-FM 45057
Owner: Radio Ohio Inc.
Editorial: 605 S Front St, Columbus, Ohio 43215
Tel: 1 614 460-3850.
Web site: http://www.971thefan.com
Profile: WBNS-FM is a commercial station owned by Radio Ohio Inc. The format of the station is sports. WBNS-FM broadcasts to the Columbus, OH area at 97.1 FM.
FM RADIO STATION

WBNT-FM 45058
Owner: Oneida Broadcasters Inc.
Editorial: 1126 Buffalo Rd, Oneida, Tennessee 37841
Tel: 1 423 569-8598.
Email: wbnt@highland.net
Web site: http://www.hive105.com
Profile: WBNT-FM is a commercial station owned by Oneida Broadcasters Inc. The format of the station is country and adult contemporary music and news. WBNT-FM broadcasts to the Oneida, TN area at 105.5 FM.
FM RADIO STATION

WBNV-FM 41981
Owner: AVC Communications Inc.
Editorial: 4988 Skyline Dr, Cambridge, Ohio 43725-9729 **Tel:** 1 740 432-5605.
Email: info@yourradioplace.com
Web site: http://www.yourradioplace.com
Profile: WBNV-FM is a commercial station owned by AVC Communications Inc. The format of the station is easy listening. WBNV-FM broadcasts to the Cambridge, OH, area at 93.5 FM.
FM RADIO STATION

WBNW-AM 35898
Owner: Money Matters Radio Inc.
Editorial: 144 Gould St Ste 710, Needham, Massachusetts 02494-2307 **Tel:** 1 781 474-5180.
Web site: http://www.moneymattersboston.com
Profile: WBNW-AM is a commercial station owned by Money Matters Radio Inc. The format of the station is talk. WBNW-AM broadcasts to the Boston, MA area at 1120 AM.
AM RADIO STATION

WBNW-FM 46259
Owner: iHeartMedia Inc.
Editorial: 320 N Jensen Rd, Vestal, New York 13850-2111 **Tel:** 1 607 584-5800.
Web site: http://www.radionow1057.com
Profile: WBNW-FM is a commercial station owned by iHeartMedia Inc. The format of the station is Top 40/CHR. WBNW-FM broadcasts to the Binghamton, NY area at 105.7 FM.
FM RADIO STATION

WBNY-FM 43912
Owner: Buffalo State College
Editorial: 1300 Elmwood Ave, Buffalo, New York 14222-1004 **Tel:** 1 716 878-3080.
Web site: http://www.buffalostate.edu/wbny
Profile: WBNY-FM is a non-commercial station owned by Buffalo State College. The format of the station is rock alternative. WBNY-FM broadcasts to the Buffalo, NY area at 91.3 FM. The station is completely student operated. WBNY-FM's target audience is Buffalo State College students and others interested in a variety of music. The station airs locally on 91.3 FM.
FM RADIO STATION

WBNZ-FM 44408
Owner: Henderson, Roy E.
Editorial: 1532 Forrester Rd, Frankfort, Michigan 49635-9781 **Tel:** 1 231 947-3220.
Profile: Is a local radio station in Frankfort, MI.
FM RADIO STATION

WBOB-AM 36364
Owner: Chesapeake-Portsmouth Broadcasting Corp.
Editorial: 7235 Bonneval Rd, Jacksonville, Florida 32256-7591 **Tel:** 1 904 470-4615.
Email: info@600wbob.com
Web site: http://www.600wbob.com
Profile: WBOB-AM is a commercial station owned by Chesapeake-Portsmouth Broadcasting Corp. The format of the station is news and talk. WBOB-AM broadcasts to the Jacksonville, FL area at 600 AM.
AM RADIO STATION

WBOC-FM 40586
Owner: Draper Holdings
Editorial: 1729 N Salisbury Blvd, Salisbury, Maryland 21801-3330 **Tel:** 1 410 543-1025.
Web site: http://www.delmarvalife.com/radio/
Profile: WBOC-FM is a non-commercial station owned by Draper Holdings. The format of the station is Adult Contemporary. WBOC-FM broadcasts in the Princess Anne, MD area at 102.5 FM.
FM RADIO STATION

WBOG-AM 41877
Owner: Magnum Radio Group
Editorial: 1021 N Superior Ave Ste 5, Tomah, Wisconsin 54660-1192 **Tel:** 1 608 372-9600.
Email: news@magnumbroadcasting.com
Web site: http://www.oldies1460.com
Profile: WBOG-AM is a commercial station owned by Magnum Radio Group. The format of the station is oldies. WBOG-AM broadcasts to the Tomah, WI area at 1460 AM.
AM RADIO STATION

WBOI-FM 79522
Owner: Indiana Public Broadcasting Systems
Editorial: 3204 Clairmont Ct, Fort Wayne, Indiana 46808 **Tel:** 1 260 452-1189.
Web site: http://www.nipr.fm
Profile: WBOI-FM is a non-commercial station owned by Indiana Public Broadcasting Systems. The format of the station is news, talk and jazz. WBOI-FM broadcasts to the Fort Wayne, IN area at 91.3 FM.
FM RADIO STATION

WBOJ-FM 689883
Owner: The Truth, Inc.
Editorial: 1300 Wynnton Rd Ste 110, Columbus, Georgia 31906-5701 **Tel:** 1 706 256-2985.
Email: request@885thetruth.com
FM RADIO STATION

WBOK-AM 35218
Owner: Bakewell Media Co.
Editorial: 1639 Gentilly Blvd, New Orleans, Louisiana 70119-2161 **Tel:** 1 504 943-2146.
Email: wbok1230am@gmail.com
Web site: http://www.wbok1230am.com
Profile: WBOK broadcasts in a Christian radio format. It's current slogan is "Real Talk for Real Times"
AM RADIO STATION

WBOL-AM 39231
Owner: Shaw(John & Opal)
Editorial: 123 W Market St, Bolivar, Tennessee 38008
Tel: 1 731 658-3690.
Web site: http://www.wojg.com
Profile: WBOL-AM is a commercial station owned by John and Opal Shaw. The format of the station is oldies. WBOL-AM broadcasts to the Memphis, TN, market at 1560 AM.
AM RADIO STATION

WBON-FM 80994
Owner: JVC Broadasting Inc.
Editorial: 3075 Veterans Memorial Hwy Ste 201, Ronkonkoma, New York 11779-7600 **Tel:** 1 631 648-2500.
Web site: http://www.lafiestali.com
Profile: WBON-FM is a commercial station owned by JVC Broadasting Inc. The format of the station is Spanish tropical. WBZB-FM broadcasts to the Ronkonkoma, NY area at 98.5 FM.
FM RADIO STATION

WBOP-FM 41824
Owner: Gamma Broadcasting LLC
Editorial: 639 N Main St, Mount Crawford, Virginia 22841-2350 **Tel:** 1 540 432-1063.
Profile: WBOP-FM is a commercial station owned by Gamma Broadcasting LLC. The format for the station is adult contemporary. WBOP-FM broadcasts to the Harrisonburg, VA area at 95.5 FM.
FM RADIO STATION

WBOQ-FM 41265
Owner: Westport Communications
Editorial: 8 Enon St, Beverly, Massachusetts 1915
Tel: 1 978 927-1049.
Web site: http://www.northshore1049.com
Profile: WBOQ-FM is a commercial station owned by Westport Communications. The format of the station is oldies. WBOQ-FM broadcasts to the Beverly, MA area at 104.9 FM.
FM RADIO STATION

WBOS-FM 40144
Owner: Beasley Brodcast Group
Editorial: 55 William T Morrissey Blvd, Dorchester, Massachusetts 02125-3315 **Tel:** 1 617 822-9600.
Web site: http://www.wbos.com
Profile: WBOS-FM is a commercial station owned by Beasley Broadcast Group. The format of the station is rock alternative. WBOS-FM broadcasts to the Boston area at 92.9 FM.
FM RADIO STATION

WBOW-FM 46373
Owner: Midwest Communications Inc.
Editorial: 824 S 3rd St, Terre Haute, Indiana 47807-4609 **Tel:** 1 812 232-4161.
Web site: http://985wbow.com
Profile: WBOW-FM is a commercial station owned by Midwest Communications Inc. The format of the station is adult contemporary. WBOW-FM broadcasts to the Terre Haute, IN area at 98.5 FM.
FM RADIO STATION

WBOX-AM 37677
Owner: Strickland(Ben)
Editorial: 22037 Highway 436, Bogalusa, Louisiana 70427 **Tel:** 1 985 732-4288.
Email: wboxamfm@bellsouth.net
AM RADIO STATION

WBOX-FM 45059
Owner: Strickland(Ben)
Editorial: 22037 Highway 436, Bogalusa, Louisiana 70427 **Tel:** 1 985 732-4288.
Email: wboxamfm@bellsouth.net
Profile: WBOX-FM is a commercial station owned by Ben Strickland. The format of the station is country. WBOX-FM broadcasts to the Bogalusa, LA area at 92.9 FM.
FM RADIO STATION

WBOZ-FM 42332
Owner: Salem Media Group, Inc.
Editorial: 312 S Church St, Murfreesboro, Tennessee 37130-3732 **Tel:** 1 615 890-3233.
Email: info@salemmusicnetwork.com
Web site: http://www.94fmthefish.net
Profile: WBOZ-FM is a commercial station owned by Salem Media Group, Inc. The format of the station is Contemporary Christian music. WBOZ-FM broadcasts to the Murfreesboro, TN area at 104.9 FM.
FM RADIO STATION

WBPC-FM 355365
Owner: Beach Radio, Inc.
Editorial: 3900 Marriott Dr, Panama City Beach, Florida 32408 **Tel:** 1 850 235-2195.
Web site: http://www.beach951.com
Profile: WBPC-FM is a commercial station owned by Beach Radio, Inc. The format of the station is classic hits. WBPC-FM broadcasts to the Panama City, FL area at 95.1 FM.
FM RADIO STATION

WBPE-FM 40433
Owner: Artistic Media Partners Inc.
Editorial: 3824 S 18th St, Lafayette, Indiana 47909-3102 **Tel:** 1 765 474-1410.
Web site: http://www.wbpefm.com
Profile: WBPE-FM is a commercial station owned by Artistic Media Partners Inc. The format for the station is adult hits. WBPE-FM broadcasts to the Lafayette, IN area at 95.3 FM.
FM RADIO STATION

WBPM-FM 44539
Owner: Pamal Broadcasting Ltd.
Editorial: 715 Route 52, Beacon, New York 12508-1047 **Tel:** 1 845 838-6000.
Web site: http://www.wbpmfm.com
Profile: WBPM-FM is a commercial station owned by Pamal Broadcasting Ltd. The format of the station is classic hits. WBPM-FM broadcasts the Poughkeepsie, NY area at 92.9 FM.
FM RADIO STATION

WBPT-FM 41627
Owner: Summit Media Broadcasting LLC
Editorial: 2700 Corporate Dr Ste 115, Birmingham, Alabama 35242-2735 **Tel:** 1 205 916-1100.
Web site: http://www.birminghamseagle.com
Profile: WBPT-FM is a commercial station owned by Summit Media Broadcasting LLC. The format of the station is classic hits. WBPT-FM broadcasts to the Birmingham, AL area at 106.9 FM.
FM RADIO STATION

WBPW-FM 40218
Owner: Townsquare Media, Inc.
Editorial: 551 Main St, Presque Isle, Maine 04769-2450 **Tel:** 1 207 769-6600.
Email: newspi@townsquaremedia.com
Web site: http://bigcountry969.com
Profile: WBPW-FM is a commercial station owned by Townsquare Media, Inc. The format of the station is contemporary country. WBPW-FM broadcasts to the Presque Isle, ME area at 96.9 FM.
FM RADIO STATION

WBPZ-AM 38493
Owner: Schlesinger Communications
Editorial: 21 E Main St, Lock Haven, Pennsylvania 17745-1303 **Tel:** 1 570 748-4038.
Profile: WBPZ-AM is a commercial station owned by Lipez Broadcasting Co. The format of the station is oldies music. WBPZ-AM broadcasts to the Lock Haven, PA area at 1230 AM.
AM RADIO STATION

WBQB-FM 45175
Owner: Centennial Broadcasting II, LLC
Editorial: 1914 Mimosa St, Fredericksburg, Virginia 22405-3213 **Tel:** 1 540 373-7721.
Email: buzzy@wbqb.com
Web site: http://www.b1015.com
Profile: WBQB-FM is a commercial station owned by Centennial Broadcasting II, LLC. The format of the station is hot adult contemporary music. WBQB-FM broadcasts to the Fredericksburg, VA area at 101.5 FM.
FM RADIO STATION

WBQH-AM 153438
Owner: Hubbard Broadcasting
Editorial: 3400 Idaho Ave NW Fl 1, Washington, District Of Columbia 20016-3046 **Tel:** 1 202 450-1693.
Profile: WBQH-AM is a commercial station owned by Hubbard Broadcasting and operated by United Media. The format of the station is regional Mexican. WBQH-AM broadcasts throughout the Washington, D.C. area at 1050 AM.
AM RADIO STATION

WBQK-FM 42736
Owner: Local Voice Media
Editorial: 4732 Longhill Rd Ste 2201, Williamsburg, Virginia 23188-1584 **Tel:** 1 757 565-1079.
Email: music@1079bach.com
Web site: http://www.wbach.net
Profile: WBQK-FM is a commercial station owned by Local Voice Media. The format of the station is classical. WBQK-FM broadcasts to the Williamsburg, VA area at 107.9 FM.
FM RADIO STATION

WBQQ-FM 42634
Owner: WBIN, Inc.
Editorial: 477 Congress St, Portland, Maine 04101-3427 **Tel:** 1 207 797-0780.
Web site: http://www.999thewolf.com
Profile: WBQQ-FM is a commercial station owned by WBIN, Inc. The format of the station is country. WBQQ-FM broadcasts to the Kennebunk, ME area at 99.3 FM.
FM RADIO STATION

WBQT-FM 40403
Owner: Beasley Broadcast Group
Editorial: 55 William T Morrissey Blvd, Dorchester, Massachusetts 02125-3315 **Tel:** 1 617 822-9600.
Web site: http://www.hot969boston.com
Profile: WBQT-FM is a commercial station owned by Beasley Broadcast Group. The format of the station is rhythmic AC. WBQT-FM broadcasts to the Boston area at 96.9 FM.
FM RADIO STATION

WBRB-FM 45708
Owner: West Virginia Radio Corp.
Editorial: 1065 Radio Park Dr, Mount Clare, West Virginia 26408 **Tel:** 1 304 623-6546.
Web site: http://www.1013thebear.com
Profile: WBRB-FM is a commercial station owned by West Virginia Radio Corp. The format of the station is contemporary country music. WBRB-FM broadcasts to the Mt. Clare, WV area at 101.3 FM.
FM RADIO STATION

WBRD-AM 36742
Owner: Birach Broadcasting Corp.
Editorial: 3912 US Highway 301 N, Ellenton, Florida 34222 **Tel:** 1 941 955-1420.
Email: wbrd1420am@yahoo.com
Profile: WBRD-AM is a commercial station owned by Birach Broadcasting Corp. The format of the station is Hispanic. WBRD-AM broadcasts to the Oneco, FL, area at 1420 AM.
AM RADIO STATION

WBRF-FM 42827
Owner: Blue Ridge Radio Inc.
Editorial: 325 Poplar Knob Rd, Galax, Virginia 24333-4106 **Tel:** 1 276 236-9273.
Email: info@blueridgecountry98.com
Web site: http://www.blueridgecountry98.com
Profile: WBRF-FM is a commercial station owned by Blue Ridge Radio Inc. The format of the station is classic country. WBRF-FM broadcasts to the Roanoke-Lynchburg, VA area at 98.1 FM.
FM RADIO STATION

WBRG-AM 35219
Owner: Tri-County Broadcasting
Editorial: 239 Ragland Rd, Madison Heights, Virginia 24572 **Tel:** 1 434 401-0230.
Email: info@wbrgradio.com
Web site: http://www.wbrgradio.com
Profile: WBRG-AM is a commercial station owned by Tri-County Broadcasting. The format of the station is news, talk and sports. WBRG-AM broadcasts to the Madison Heights, VA area at 1050 AM.
AM RADIO STATION

WBRG-FM 573495
Owner: Tri-County Broadcasting
Editorial: 239 Ragland Rd, Madison Heights, Virginia 24572 **Tel:** 1 434 401-0230.
Email: info@wbrgradio.com
Web site: http://www.wbrgradio.com
Profile: WBRG-FM is a commercial station owned by Tri-County Broadcasting . The format of the station is news, talk and sports. WBRG-FM broadcasts to the Madison Heights, VA area at 104.5 and 96.9 FM.
FM RADIO STATION

WBRI-AM 38362
Owner: Wilkins Communication Networks Inc.
Editorial: 4802 E 62Nd St, Indianapolis, Indiana 46220-5236 **Tel:** 1 317 255-5484.
Email: wbri@wilkinsradio.com
Web site: http://www.wilkinsradio.com
Profile: WBRI-AM is a commercial station owned by Wilkins Communication Networks Inc. and licensed by Heritage Christian Radio, Inc. The format of the station is Christian talk and news. WBRI-AM broadcasts to the Indianapolis area at 1500 AM.
AM RADIO STATION

WBRK-AM 37678
Owner: WBRK Inc.
Editorial: 100 North St, Pittsfield, Massachusetts 1201 **Tel:** 1 413 442-1553.
Email: wbrk1340@aol.com
Web site: http://www.wbrk.com
Profile: WBRK-AM is a commercial station owned by WBRK Inc. The format of the station is of news, talk and adult standards. WBRK-AM broadcasts to the Pittsfield, MA area at 1340 AM.
AM RADIO STATION

WBRK-FM 45499
Owner: WBRK Inc.
Editorial: 100 North St, Pittsfield, Massachusetts 1201 **Tel:** 1 413 442-1553.
Email: wbrk1340@aol.com
Web site: http://www.wbrk.com
Profile: WBRK-FM is a commercial station owned by WBRK Inc. The format of the station is hot adult contemporary music. WBRK-FM broadcasts to the Pittsfield, MA area at 101.7 FM.
FM RADIO STATION

WBRM-AM 35220
Owner: WBRM Inc.
Editorial: 147 N Garden St, Marion, North Carolina 28752-3709 **Tel:** 1 828 652-9500.
Email: wbrmnews@gmail.com
Profile: WBRM-AM is a commercial station owned by WBRM Inc. The format of the station is classic country. WBRM-AM broadcasts to the Marion, NC area at 1250 AM.
AM RADIO STATION

WBRN-AM 37679
Owner: Mentor Partners Inc.
Editorial: 18720 16 Mile Rd, Big Rapids, Michigan 49307 **Tel:** 1 231 796-7000.
Email: news@bigrapidsradionetwork.com
Web site: http://www.wbrn.com
Profile: WBRN-AM is a commercial station owned by Mentor Partners Inc.. The format of the station is news, sports and talk. WBRN-AM broadcasts to the Big Rapids, MI area at 1460 AM.
AM RADIO STATION

WBRP-FM 41307
Owner: Guaranty Broadcasting
Editorial: 929 Government St Ste B, Baton Rouge, Louisiana 70802-6034 **Tel:** 1 225 388-9898.
Web site: http://www.talk1073.com
Profile: WBRP-FM is a commercial station owned by Guaranty Broadcasting. The format of the station is news/talk. WBRP-FM broadcasts to the Baton Rouge, LA area at 107.3 FM.
FM RADIO STATION

WBRR-FM 45855
Owner: WESB Inc.
Editorial: 1490 Saint Francis Dr, Bradford, Pennsylvania 16701-3282 **Tel:** 1 814 368-4141.
Email: 1490@wesb.com
Web site: http://www.wbrrfm.com
Profile: WBRR-FM is a commercial station owned by WESB Inc. The format of the station is rock music. WBRR-FM broadcasts to the Buffalo, NY area at 100.1 FM.
FM RADIO STATION

WBRT-AM 37680
Owner: Bardstown Radio Team, LLC
Editorial: 106 S 3rd St, Bardstown, Kentucky 40004 **Tel:** 1 502 348-3943.
Email: wbrt@wbrtradio.com
Web site: http://www.wbrtcountry.com
Profile: WBRT-AM is a commercial station owned by Bardstown Radio Team, LLC. The format of the station is country music. WBRT-AM broadcasts to the Bardstown, KY area at 1320 AM.
AM RADIO STATION

WBRU-FM 40145
Owner: Brown Broadcasting Services
Editorial: 88 Benevolent St, Providence, Rhode Island 02906-2046 **Tel:** 1 401 272-9550.
Web site: http://www.wbru.com
Profile: WBRU-FM is a commercial station owned by Brown Broadcasting Services. The format of the station is rock alternative music. WBRU-FM broadcasts to the Providence, RI area at 95.5 FM.
FM RADIO STATION

WBRV-AM 38631
Owner: Flack Broadcasting Group
Editorial: 7606 N State St, Lowville, New York 13367-1318 **Tel:** 1 315 376-7500.
Email: sales@themoose.net
Web site: http://www.themoose.net
Profile: WBRV-FM is a commercial station owned by Flack Broadcasting Group. The format of the station is oldies. WBRV-FM broadcasts to the Lowville, NY area at 900 AM.
AM RADIO STATION

WBRV-FM 46481
Owner: Flack Broadcasting Group
Editorial: 7606 N State St, Lowville, New York 13367 **Tel:** 1 315 376-7500.
Email: sales@themoose.net
Web site: http://www.themoose.net
Profile: WBRV-FM is a commercial station owned by Flack Broadcasting Group. The format of the station is country music. WBRV-FM broadcasts to the Rome, NY area at 101.3 FM.
FM RADIO STATION

WBRW-FM 44017
Owner: Cumulus Media Inc.
Editorial: 7080 Lee Hwy, Fairlawn, Virginia 24141-8416 **Tel:** 1 540 731-6000.
Web site: http://www.1053thebear.com
Profile: WBRW-FM is a commercial station owned by Cumulus Media Inc. The format for the station is rock music. WBRW-FM broadcasts to the Fairlawn, VA area at 105.3 FM.
FM RADIO STATION

WBRX-FM 43913
Owner: Sherlock Broadcasting
Editorial: 2513 6th Ave, Altoona, Pennsylvania 16602-2129 **Tel:** 1 814 943-6112.
Web site: http://www.mymix947.com
Profile: WBRX-FM is a commercial station owned by Sherlock Broadcasting. The format of the station is adult contemporary music. WBRX-FM broadcasts to the Altoona, PA area at 94.7 FM.
FM RADIO STATION

WBRY-AM 36235
Owner: Volunteer Broadcasting
Editorial: 153 Mile Valley Rd, Woodbury, Tennessee 37190-6133 **Tel:** 1 615 563-2313.
Email: askus@wbry.com
Web site: http://www.wbry.com
Profile: WBRY-AM is a commercial station owned by Volunteer Broadcasting. The format of the station is classic country. WBRY-AM broadcasts to the Woodbury, TN area at 1540 AM.
AM RADIO STATION

WBSA-AM 35222
Owner: Watkins Broadcasting Inc.
Editorial: 1525 Wills Rd, Boaz, Alabama 35957 **Tel:** 1 256 593-4264.
Email: 1300@wbsaam.com
Web site: http://www.wbsaam.com
Profile: WBSA-AM is a commercial station owned by Watkins Broadcasting Inc. The format of the station is Christian programming. WBSA-AM broadcasts to the Boaz, AL area at 1300 AM.
AM RADIO STATION

WBSM-AM 38402
Owner: Townsquare Media, Inc.
Editorial: 22 Sconticut Neck Rd, Fairhaven, Massachusetts 02719-1914 **Tel:** 1 508 993-1767.
Email: news@wbsm.com
Web site: http://www.wbsm.com
Profile: WBSM-AM is a commercial station owned by Townsquare Media, Inc. The format of the station is news, talk, and sports. WBSM-AM broadcasts to the Providence, RI, and New Bedford, MA, area at 1420 AM.
AM RADIO STATION

WBSS-AM 39492
Owner: Longport Media
Editorial: 1601 New Rd, Linwood, New Jersey 08221-1116 **Tel:** 1 609 653-1400.
Web site: http://www.kool983.com
Profile: WBSS-AM is a commercial station owned by Longport Media. The format of the station is classic hits. WBSS-AM broadcasts to the Linwood, NJ area at 1490 AM. the station is a simulcast of WTKU-FM 98.3.
AM RADIO STATION

WBSX-FM 46548
Owner: Cumulus Media Inc.
Editorial: 600 Baltimore Drive, Wilkes-Barre, Pennsylvania 18702-7901 **Tel:** 1 570 824-9000.
Web site: http://www.979x.com
Profile: WBSX-FM is a commercial station owned by Cumulus Media Inc. The format of the station is rock alternative. WBSX-FM broadcasts to the Wilkes Barre, PA area at 97.9 FM.
FM RADIO STATION

WBSZ-FM 42633
Owner: Heartland Communications Group, LLC
Editorial: 2320 Ellis Ave, Ashland, Wisconsin 54806-3995 **Tel:** 1 715 682-2727.
Web site: http://wbszfm.com
FM RADIO STATION

WBTA-AM 37130
Owner: HPL Communications
Editorial: 113 Main St, Batavia, New York 14020 **Tel:** 1 585 344-1490.
Email: news@wbta1490.com
Web site: http://www.wbta1490.com
Profile: WBTA-AM is a commercial station owned by HPL Communications. The format of the station is adult contemporary, news and talk. WBTA-AM broadcasts to the Batavia, NY area at 1490 AM.
AM RADIO STATION

WBT-AM 38676
Owner: Entercom Communications Corp
Editorial: 1 Julian Price Pl, Charlotte, North Carolina 28208-5211 **Tel:** 1 704 570-1110.
Email: wbtnews@wbt.com
Web site: http://www.wbt.com
Profile: WBT-AM is a commercial station owned by Entercom Communications Corp. The format of the station is news and talk. WBT-AM broadcasts to the Charlotte, NC area at 1110 AM.
AM RADIO STATION

WBTC-AM 37080
Owner: Tuscarawas Broadcasting
Editorial: 125 Johnson Dr, Uhrichsville, Ohio 44683-1017 **Tel:** 1 740 922-2700.
Email: wbtc@tusco.net
Web site: http://www.wbtclive.com
Profile: WBTC-AM is a commercial station owned by Tuscarawas Broadcasting. The format of the station is news, talk, and sports. WBTC-AM broadcasts to the Uhrichsville, OH area at 1540 AM.
AM RADIO STATION

WBTF-FM 44087
Owner: L.M. Communications Inc.
Editorial: 401 W Main St, Lexington, Kentucky 40507-1640 **Tel:** 1 859 233-1515.
Web site: http://www.1079thebeat.com
Profile: WBTF-FM is a commercial station owned by L.M. Communications Inc. The format of the station is urban contemporary. WBTF-FM broadcasts locally to the Lexington, KY area at a frequency of 107.9 FM.
FM RADIO STATION

WBT-FM 43022
Owner: Entercom Communications Corp.
Editorial: 1 Julian Price Pl, Charlotte, North Carolina 28208-5211 **Tel:** 1 704 374-3500.
Email: wbtnews@wbt.com
Web site: http://www.wbt.com
Profile: WBT-FM is a commercial station owned by Entercom Communications Corp. The format of the station is news and talk. WBT-FM broadcasts to the Charlotte, NC, area at 99.3 FM.
FM RADIO STATION

WBTG-AM 38390
Owner: Slatton & Associates Broadcasters Inc.
Editorial: 1605 Gospel Rd, Sheffield, Alabama 35660
Tel: 1 256 381-6800.
Email: announcements@wbtgradio.com
Web site: http://www.wbtgradio.com
Profile: WBTG-AM is a commercial station owned by Slatton & Associates Broadcasters Inc. The format of the station is oldies music. WBTG-AM broadcasts to the Sheffield, AL area at 1290 AM.
AM RADIO STATION

WBTG-FM 45747
Owner: Slatton & Associates Broadcasters Inc.
Editorial: 1605 Gospel Rd, Sheffield, Alabama 35660-1823 **Tel:** 1 256 381-6800.
Email: announcements@wbtgradio.com
Web site: http://www.wbtgradio.com
Profile: WBTG-FM is a commercial station owned by Slatton & Associates Broadcasters Inc. The format of the station is gospel. WBTG-FM broadcasts to the Sheffield, AL area at 106.3 FM.
FM RADIO STATION

WBTH-AM 37681
Owner: East Kentucky Radio Network
Editorial: 1240 Radio Dr, Pikeville, Kentucky 41501-4779 **Tel:** 1 304 235-3600.
Email: frontdesk@ekbradio.com
Web site: http://www.900wlsi.com
AM RADIO STATION

WBTI-FM 46385
Owner: Radio First
Editorial: 808 Huron Ave, Port Huron, Michigan 48060-3705 **Tel:** 1 810 982-9000.
Web site: http://www.wbti.com
Profile: WBTI-FM is a commercial station owned by Radio First. The format of the station is hot adult contemporary music. WBTI-FM broadcasts to the Port Huron, MI area at 96.9 FM.
FM RADIO STATION

WBTJ-FM 42767
Owner: iHeartMedia Inc.
Editorial: 3245 Basie Rd, Richmond, Virginia 23228-3404 **Tel:** 1 804 474-0000.
Web site: http://www.1065thebeat.com
Profile: WBTJ-FM is a commercial station owned by iHeartMedia Inc. The format of the station is urban contemporary. WBTJ-FM broadcasts to the Richmond, VA area at 106.5 FM.
FM RADIO STATION

WBTK-AM 38242
Owner: Mount Rich Media LLC
Editorial: 2809 Emerywood Pkwy Ste 540, Richmond, Virginia 23294-3745 **Tel:** 1 804 353-8544.
Web site: http://www.wbtk.com
Profile: WBTK-AM is a commercial station owned by Mount Rich Media LLC. The format of the station is Hispanic religious. WBTK-AM broadcasts to the Richmond, VA area at 1380 AM.
AM RADIO STATION

WBTM-AM 37682
Owner: Piedmont Broadcasting Corporation
Editorial: 710 Grove St, Danville, Virginia 24541-1704
Tel: 1 434 793-4411.
Web site: http://www.wbtm1330.com
Profile: WBTM-AM is a commercial station owned by Piedmont Broadcasting Corporation. The format of the station is classic hits. WBTM-AM broadcasts to the Danville, VA area at 1330 AM.
AM RADIO STATION

WBTN-AM 39074
Owner: Shires Media Partnership
Editorial: 407 Harwood Hill Rd, Bennington, Vermont 05201-8806 **Tel:** 1 802 442-6321.
Email: info@wbtnam.org
Web site: http://www.wbtnam.org
Profile: WBTN-AM is a commercial station owned by Shires Media Partnership. The format of the station is adult contemporary and talk. WBTN-AM broadcasts to the Bennington, VT area at 1370 AM.
AM RADIO STATION

WBTN-FM 46419
Owner: Vermont Public Radio
Editorial: 365 Troy Ave, Colchester, Vermont 05446-3126 **Tel:** 1 802 655-9451.
Email: news@vpr.net
Web site: http://www.vpr.net
FM RADIO STATION

WBTO-FM 41447
Owner: Original Company Inc.(The)
Editorial: 522 Busseron St, Vincennes, Indiana 47591-2030 **Tel:** 1 812 324-2200.
Email: wwblnews@wwbl.com
Web site: http://www.wbtofm.com
Profile: WBTO-FM is a commercial station owned by The Original Company Inc. The format is rock/album oriented rock music. WBTO-FM broadcasts to the Washington, IN area at 102.3 FM.
FM RADIO STATION

WBTP-FM 43557
Owner: iHeartMedia Inc.
Editorial: 4002 W Gandy Blvd, Tampa, Florida 33611-3410 **Tel:** 1 813 832-1000.
Web site: http://www.957thebeat.com
Profile: WBTP-FM is a commercial station owned by iHeartMedia Inc. The format of the station is urban contemporary. WBTP-FM broadcasts to the Tampa, FL area at 95.7 FM.
FM RADIO STATION

WBTQ-FM 41432
Owner: West Virginia Radio Group
Editorial: Washington & Davis Streets, Elkins, West Virginia 26241 **Tel:** 1 304 636-1300.
Profile: WBTQ-FM is a commercial station owned by West Virginia Radio Group. The format of the station is News/Talk. WBTQ-FM broadcasts to the Elkins, WV area at 93.5 FM.
FM RADIO STATION

WBTR-FM 40147
Owner: Gradick Communications LLC
Editorial: 102 Parkwood Cir, Carrollton, Georgia 30117 **Tel:** 1 770 832-9685.
Web site: http://www.b92country.com
Profile: WBTR-FM is a commercial station owned by Gradick Communications. The format of the station is contemporary country. WBTR-FM broadcasts to the Carrollton, GA area at 92.1 FM.
FM RADIO STATION

WBTT-FM 43399
Owner: iHeartMedia Inc.
Editorial: 13320 Metro Pkwy Ste 1, Fort Myers, Florida 33966-4804 **Tel:** 1 239 225-4300.
Web site: http://www.1055thebeat.com
Profile: WBTT-FM is a commercial station owned by iHeartMedia Inc. The format of the station is urban contemporary. WBTT-FM broadcasts to the Fort Myers, FL area at 105.5 FM.
FM RADIO STATION

WBTU-FM 41393
Owner: Adams Radio Group
Editorial: 9604 Coldwater Rd Ste 201, Fort Wayne, Indiana 46825-2096 **Tel:** 1 260 482-9288.
Profile: WBTU-FM is a commercial station owned by Adams Radio Group. The format of the station is contemporary country. WBTU-FM broadcasts to the Fort Wayne, IN area at 93.3 FM.
FM RADIO STATION

WBTX-AM 38504
Owner: Massanutten Broadcasting Co. Inc.
Editorial: 166 Main St, Broadway, Virginia 22815
Tel: 1 540 896-8933.
Email: wbtx@wbtxradio.com
Web site: http://www.wbtxradio.com
Profile: WBTX-AM is a commercial station owned by Massanutten Broadcasting Co. Inc. The format of the station is gospel and religious. WBTX-AM broadcasts to the Broadway, VA area at 1470 AM.
AM RADIO STATION

WBTY-FM 40148
Owner: Strickland (Jim &Nancy)
Editorial: Highway 168 & 37, Homerville, Georgia 31634 **Tel:** 1 912 487-3412.
Web site: http://www.radiobentley.com/
Profile: WBTY-FM is a commercial station owned by Jim & Nancy Strickland. The format of the station is classic hits. WBTY-FM broadcasts to the Homerville, GA area at 98.7 FM.
FM RADIO STATION

WBTZ-FM 43042
Owner: Hall Communications
Editorial: 255 S Champlain St, Burlington, Vermont 5401 **Tel:** 1 802 860-2440.
Email: mailbag@999thebuzz.com
Web site: http://www.999thebuzz.com
Profile: WBTZ-FM is a commercial station owned by Hall Communications. The format of the station is rock alternative. WBTZ-FM broadcasts to the Burlington, VT area at 99.9 FM.
FM RADIO STATION

WBUC-AM 38332
Owner: West Virginia Radio Corp.
Editorial: Washington & Davis Streets, Elkins, West Virginia 26241 **Tel:** 1 304 636-1300.
Profile: WBUC-AM is a commercial station owned by West Virginia Radio Corp. The format of the station is news/talk. WBUC-AM broadcasts to the Buckhannon, WV area at 1460 AM.
AM RADIO STATION

WBUF-FM 40149
Owner: Town Square Media
Editorial: 14 Lafayette Sq, Buffalo, New York 14203-1928 **Tel:** 1 716 852-9292.
Web site: http://929jackfm.com
Profile: WBUF-FM is a commercial station owned by Town Square Media. The format of the station is adult hits. WBUF-FM broadcasts to the Buffalo, NY area at 92.9 FM.
FM RADIO STATION

WBUG-FM 46352
Owner: Roser Communications
Editorial: 185 Genesee St, Ste 1601, Utica, New York 13501 **Tel:** 1 315 734-9245.
Web site: http://www.bugcountry.com
Profile: WBUG-FM is a commercial station owned by Roser Communications. The format of the station is contemporary country music. WBUG-FM broadcasts to the Mohawk Valley, NY region at 101.1 FM and 99.7 FM via a simulcast with WBGK-FM.
FM RADIO STATION

WBUK-FM 87558
Owner: Blanchard River Broadcasting, Co.
Editorial: 551 Lake Cascades Pkwy, Findlay, Ohio 45840-1388 **Tel:** 1 419 422-4545.
Web site: http://www.1063thefox.com
Profile: WBUK-FM is a commercial station owned by Blanchard River Broadcasting, Co. The format of the station is classic rock. WBUK-FM broadcasts to the Lima, OH area at 106.3 FM.
FM RADIO STATION

WBUL-FM 42135
Owner: iHeartMedia Inc.
Editorial: 2601 Nicholasville Rd, Lexington, Kentucky 40503-3307 **Tel:** 1 859 422-1000.
Web site: http://www.wbul.com
Profile: WBUL-FM is a commercial station owned by iHeartMedia Inc. The format of the station is country. WBUL-FM broadcasts to the Lexington, KY area at 98.1 FM.
FM RADIO STATION

WBUS-FM 43697
Owner: FM Radio Licenses, LLC
Editorial: 2551 Park Center Blvd, State College, Pennsylvania 16801-3007 **Tel:** 1 814 237-9800.
Email: businfo@thebus.net
Web site: http://thebus.net
Profile: WBUS-FM is a commercial station owned by FM Radio Licenses, LLC. The format of the station is classic rock. The station broadcasts locally at 93.7 FM.
FM RADIO STATION

WBUT-AM 37683
Owner: Butler County Radio Network
Editorial: 112 Hollywood Dr Ste 203, Butler, Pennsylvania 16001-5697 **Tel:** 1 724 283-1500.
Email: frontdesk@bcrnetwork.com
Web site: http://www.wbut.com
Profile: WBUT-AM is a commercial station owned by Butler County Radio Network. The format of the station is contemporary country. WBUT-AM broadcasts to the Butler, PA area at 1050 AM.
AM RADIO STATION

WBUV-FM 40390
Owner: iHeartMedia Inc.
Editorial: 286 Debuys Rd, Biloxi, Mississippi 39531-2611 **Tel:** 1 228 388-2323.
Web site: http://www.newsradio1049fm.com
Profile: WBUV-FM is a commercial station owned by iHeartMedia Inc. The format of the station is news and talk. WBUV-FM broadcasts to the Biloxi-Gulfport, MS area at 104.9 FM.
FM RADIO STATION

WBUZ-FM 44414
Owner: Cromwell Group Inc.(The)
Editorial: 1824 Murfreesboro Pike, Nashville, Tennessee 37217 **Tel:** 1 615 399-1029.
Web site: http://www.1029thebuzz.com
Profile: WBUZ-FM is a commercial station owned by The Cromwell Group Inc. The format of the station is rock. WBUZ-FM broadcasts in the Nashville, TN area at 102.9 FM.
FM RADIO STATION

WBVB-FM 42286
Owner: iHeartMedia Inc.
Editorial: 134 4th ave, Huntington, West Virginia
Tel: 1 304 525-7788.
Web site: http://b97fm.iheart.com
Profile: WBVB-FM is a commercial station owned by iHeartMedia Inc. The format of the station is classic hits. WBVB-FM broadcasts to the Catlettsburg, KY and Ironton, OH areas at 97.1 FM.
FM RADIO STATION

WBVE-FM 45956
Owner: Cessna Communications Inc.
Editorial: 134 E Pitt St Fl 2, Bedford, Pennsylvania 15522-1311 **Tel:** 1 814 623-1000.
Email: cesscomm@embarqmail.com
Web site: http://www.bedfordcountyradio.com/links/B-Rock.html
Profile: WBVE-FM is a commercial station owned by Cessna Communications Inc., Inc. The format of the station is classic rock. WBVE-FM broadcasts to Bedford, PA at 107.5 FM.
FM RADIO STATION

WBVI-FM 46815
Owner: Tri-County Broadcasting
Editorial: 101 N Main St, Fostoria, Ohio 44830-2215
Tel: 1 419 422-9284.
Email: production@wfob.com
Web site: http://www.wbvi.com
Profile: WBVI-FM is a commercial station owned by Tri-County Broadcasting. The format of the station is adult contemporary music. WBVI-FM broadcasts to the Fostoria, OH area at 96.7 FM.
FM RADIO STATION

WBVM-FM 41048
Owner: Diocese of St. Petersburg
Editorial: 717 S Dale Mabry Hwy Ste 300, Tampa, Florida 33609-4408 **Tel:** 1 813 289-8040.
Email: contact@spiritfm905.com
Web site: http://www.spiritfm905.com
Profile: WBVM-FM is a non-commercial station owned by Diocese of St. Petersburg. The format of the station is contemporary Christian. WBVM-FM broadcasts to the Tampa, FL area at 90.5 FM.
FM RADIO STATION

WBVN-FM 41079
Owner: Anderson(Kenneth)
Editorial: 105 S Market St, Marion, Illinois 62959-2513
Tel: 1 618 997-1500.
Email: wbvn@midwest.net
Web site: http://www.wbvn.org
Profile: WBVN-FM is a non-commercial station owned by Kenneth Anderson. The format of the station is contemporary Christian music. WBVN-FM broadcasts to the Marion, IL area at 104.5 FM.
FM RADIO STATION

WBVP-AM 36369
Owner: Iorio Broadcasting Inc.
Editorial: 1316 7th Ave, Beaver Falls, Pennsylvania 15010-4217 **Tel:** 1 724 846-4100.
Email: 1230@beavercountyradio.com
Web site: http://beavercountyradio.com
Profile: WBVP-AM is a commercial station owned by Iorio Broadcasting Inc. The format of the station is news, talk and sports. WBVP-AM broadcasts to the Beaver Falls, PA area at 1230 AM.
AM RADIO STATION

WBVR-FM 46600
Owner: FM Radio Licenses, LLC
Editorial: 1919 Scottsville Rd, Bowling Green, Kentucky 42104-3303 **Tel:** 1 270 843-3333.
Email: production@beaverfm.com
Web site: http://www.beaverfm.com
Profile: KBVR-FM is a commercial station owned by FM Radio Licenses, LLC. The format of the station is contemporary country. The station broadcasts to the Bowling Green, KY area at a frequency of 96.7 FM.
FM RADIO STATION

WBVV-FM 45051
Owner: iHeartMedia Inc.
Editorial: 5026 Cliff Gookin Blvd, Tupelo, Mississippi 38801-7059 **Tel:** 1 662 842-1067.
Web site: http://big993.iheart.com
Profile: WBVV-FM is a commercial station owned by iHeartMedia Inc. The format of the station is Classic Hits. WBVV-FM broadcasts to the Tupelo, MS area at 99.3 FM.
FM RADIO STATION

WBVX-FM 43647
Owner: L.M. Communications Inc.
Editorial: 401 W Main St, Lexington, Kentucky 40507-1640 **Tel:** 1 859 233-1515.
Web site: http://www.classicrock921.com
Profile: WBVX-FM is a commercial station owned by L.M. Communications Inc. The format of the station is classic hits. WBVX-FM broadcasts locally to the Lexington, KY area at a frequency of 92.1 FM.
FM RADIO STATION

WBWB-FM 40970
Owner: Artistic Media Partners Inc.
Editorial: 304 S State Road 446, Bloomington, Indiana 47401-8837 **Tel:** 1 812 336-8000.
Email: wbwb@wbwb.com
Web site: http://www.wbwb.com
Profile: WBWB-FM is a commercial station owned by Artistic Media Partners Inc. The format of the station is Top 40/CHR music. WBWB-FM broadcasts to the Bloomington, IN area at 96.7 FM.
FM RADIO STATION

WBWC-FM 40153
Owner: Baldwin-Wallace College
Editorial: 275 Eastland Rd, Berea, Ohio 44017
Tel: 1 440 826-2145.
Email: operations@wbwc.com
Web site: http://www.wbwc.com
Profile: WBWC-FM is a non-commercial station owned by Baldwin-Wallace College. The format of the station is rock alternative. WBWC-FM broadcasts to Baldwin-Wallace students and Berea, OH at 88.3 FM.
FM RADIO STATION

WBWL-FM 40291
Owner: iHeartMedia Inc.
Editorial: 10 Cabot Rd Ste 302, Medford, Massachusetts 02155-5173 **Tel:** 1 781 663-2500.
Email: press@thebull1017.com
Web site: http://thebull1017.iheart.com
Profile: WBWL-FM is a commercial station owned by iHeartMedia Inc. The format of the station is contemporary country. WBWL-FM broadcasts to Boston area at 101.7 FM.
FM RADIO STATION

WBWN-FM 41703
Owner: Cumulus Media Inc.
Editorial: 236 Greenwood Ave, Bloomington, Illinois 61704-7422 **Tel:** 1 309 829-1221.
Email: news@wjbc.com
Web site: http://www.wbwn.com
Profile: WBWN-FM is a commercial station owned by Cumulus Media Inc. The format of the station is contemporary country music. WBWN-FM broadcasts to the Bloomington, IL area at 104.1 FM.
FM RADIO STATION

WBWR-FM 41714
Owner: iheartMedia Inc.
Editorial: 2323 W 5th Ave Ste 200, Columbus, Ohio 43204-4988 **Tel:** 1 614 486-6101.
Web site: http://www.thexcolumbus.com/main.html
Profile: WBWR-FM is a commercial station owned by iheartMedia Inc. The format of the station is alternative rock. WBWR-FM broadcasts to the Columbus, OH area at 105.7 FM.
FM RADIO STATION

WBWX-AM 35221
Owner: Bold Gold Media Group
Editorial: 124 E. Main St, Bloomsburg, Pennsylvania
Tel: 1 570 784-1200.
Web site: http://www.whlmam.com
Profile: WBWX-AM is a commercial station owned by Bold Gold Media Group. The format of the station is sports. WBWX-AM broadcasts to the Scranton, PA area at 1280 AM.
AM RADIO STATION

WBWZ-FM 42049
Owner: iHeartMedia Inc.
Editorial: 20 Tucker Dr, Poughkeepsie, New York 12603-1644 **Tel:** 1 845 471-2300.
Web site: http://rock933.iheart.com
Profile: WBWZ-FM is a commercial station owned by iHeartMedia Inc. The format of the station is rock music. WBWZ-FM broadcasts to the Poughkeepsie, NY area at 93.3 FM.
FM RADIO STATION

WBXB-FM 43263
Owner: Willis Broadcasting Co.
Editorial: 1900 Paradise Rd, Edenton, North Carolina 27932 **Tel:** 1 252 482-1903.
Email: wbxbradio@ymail.com
Profile: WBXB-FM is a commercial station owned by Willis Broadcasting Co. The format of the station is gospel music. WBXB-FM broadcasts to the Norfolk, VA area at 100.1 FM.
FM RADIO STATION

WBXE-FM 43943
Owner: Stonecom Cookeville LLC
Editorial: 259 S Willow Ave, Cookeville, Tennessee 38501-3140 **Tel:** 1 931 528-6064.
Web site: http://rock937online.com
Profile: WBXE-FM is a commercial station owned by Stonecom Cookeville LLC. The format of the station is rock music. WBXE-FM broadcasts to the Cookeville, TN area at 93.7 FM.
FM RADIO STATION

WBXQ-FM 41411
Owner: Sounds Good Inc.
Editorial: 2513 6th Ave, Altoona, Pennsylvania 16602-2129 **Tel:** 1 814 224-7501.
Web site: http://www.truecountry943.com
Profile: WBXQ-FM is a commercial station owned by Sounds Good Inc. The format for the station is classic rock. WBXQ-FM broadcasts to the Altoona, PA area at 94.3 FM.
FM RADIO STATION

WBXR-AM 36095
Owner: Wilkins Communication Networks Inc.
Editorial: 2926 Huntsville Hwy, Ste D, Fayetteville, Tennessee 37334-7341 **Tel:** 1 931 433-7017.
Email: wbxr@wilkinsradio.com
Web site: http://www.wilkinsradio.com
AM RADIO STATION

WBXX-FM 45791
Owner: Townsquare Media, LLC
Editorial: 390 Golden Ave, Battle Creek, Michigan 49015-4519 **Tel:** 1 269 660-1049.
Email: vip.support@townsquaremedia.com
Web site: http://1049theedge.com
Profile: WBXX-FM is a commercial station owned by Townsquare Media, LLC. The format of the station is alternative. WBXX-FM broadcasts to the Battle Creek, MI area at 104.9 FM.
FM RADIO STATION

WBYA-FM 44226
Owner: WBIN, Inc.
Editorial: 477 Congress St Ste 3, Portland, Maine 04101-3417 **Tel:** 1 207 797-0780.
Web site: http://www.1055frankfm.com
Profile: WBYA-FM is a commercial station owned by WBIN, Inc. The format of the station is classic hits. WBYA-FM broadcasts to the Portland, ME area at 105.5 FM.
FM RADIO STATION

WBYB-FM 41325
Owner: Colonial Radio Group
Editorial: 1 Bluebird Sq, Olean, New York 14760-2552
Tel: 1 866 454-9564.
Email: news@colonialme.com
Web site: http://www.colonialme.com
Profile: WBYB-FM is a commercial station owned by Colonial Radio Group. The format of the station is contemporary country. WBYB-FM broadcasts to the Kane, PA area at 103.9 FM.
FM RADIO STATION

WBYG-FM 46777
Owner: Big River Radio Inc.
Editorial: 303 8th St, Point Pleasant, West Virginia 25550-1209 **Tel:** 1 304 675-2763.
Email: wbyg@wbyg.com
Web site: http://www.wbyg.com
Profile: WBYG-FM is a commercial station owned by Big River Radio Inc. The format of the station is country music. WBYG-FM broadcasts to Point Pleasant, WV and surrounding communities at 99.5 FM.
FM RADIO STATION

WBYL-FM 46766
Owner: iHeartMedia Inc.
Editorial: 1559 W 4th St, Williamsport, Pennsylvania 17701-5650 **Tel:** 1 570 327-1400.
Web site: http://bill95.iheart.com
Profile: WBYL-FM is a commercial station owned by iHeartMedia Inc. The format of the station is contemporary country music. WBYL-FM broadcasts to the Williamsport, PA area at 95.5 FM.
FM RADIO STATION

WBYN-AM 359426
Owner: Connoisseur Media
Editorial: 107 Paxinosa Rd W, Easton, Pennsylvania 18040-1344 **Tel:** 1 609 829-5500.
Web site: http://www.espnlv.com
Profile: WBYN-AM is a commercial station owned by Connoisseur Media. The format of the station is sports. WBYN-AM broadcasts to the Boyertown, PA area at 1160 AM.
AM RADIO STATION

WBYN-FM 41865
Owner: WDAC Radio Co.
Editorial: 280 Mill St, Boyertown, Pennsylvania 19512-8431 **Tel:** 1 610 369-7777.
Email: info@wbynfm.com
Web site: http://1075alive.com
Profile: WBYN-FM is a commercial station owned by WDAC Radio Co. The format of the station is religious and Christian music. WBYN-FM broadcasts to the Boyertown, PA area at 107.5 FM.
FM RADIO STATION

WBYO-FM 42230
Owner: Four Rivers Community Broadcasting Corp
Editorial: 746 Route 113, Souderton, Pennsylvania 18964-1004 **Tel:** 1 215 721-2141.
Email: wordfm@wordfm.org
Web site: http://www.wordfm.org
Profile: WBYO-FM is a non-commercial station owned by Four Rivers Community Broadcasting Corp. The format of the station is contemporary Christian music and talk. WBYO-FM broadcasts to the Boyertown, PA area at 88.9 FM.
FM RADIO STATION

WBYP-FM 45605
Owner: Zoo-Bel Broadcasting LLC
Editorial: 611 Center Park Ln, Yazoo City, Mississippi 39194-9073 **Tel:** 1 662 746-7676.
Web site: http://www.power107radio.com
Profile: WBYP-FM is a commercial station owned by Zoo-Bel Broadcasting LLC. The format of the station is country and gospel. WBYP-FM broadcasts to the Yazoo City, MS area at 107.1 FM.
FM RADIO STATION

WBYR-FM 40959
Owner: Pathfinder Communications Corp.
Editorial: 1005 Production Rd, Fort Wayne, Indiana 46808-4107 **Tel:** 1 260 471-5100.
Web site: http://www.989thebear.com
Profile: WBYR-FM is a commercial station owned by Pathfinder Communications Corp. The format of the station is rock. WBYR-FM broadcasts to the Fort Wayne, IN area at 98.9 FM.
FM RADIO STATION

WBYS-AM 37684
Owner: Prairie Communications LLP
Editorial: 1000 E Linn St, Canton, Illinois 61520-9401
Tel: 1 309 647-1560.
Email: wbysnews@yahoo.com
Web site: http://www.1560wbys.com
Profile: WBYS-AM is a commercial station owned by Prairie Communications LLP. The format of the station is talk and classic hits music. WBYS-AM broadcasts in the Canton, IL area at 1560 AM.
AM RADIO STATION

WBYT-FM 42848
Owner: Pathfinder Communications Corporation
Editorial: 237 W Edison Rd, Mishawaka, Indiana 46545-3103 **Tel:** 1 574 258-5483.
Web site: http://www.b100.com
Profile: WBYT-FM is a commercial station owned by Pathfinder Communications Corporation, a division of Federated Media. The format for the station is country. WBYT-FM broadcasts to the South Bend, IN area at 100.7 FM.
FM RADIO STATION

WBYY-FM 46687
Owner: Garrison City Broadcasting
Editorial: 101 Back Rd, Dover, New Hampshire 3820
Tel: 1 603 742-0987.
Email: thebay@987thebay.com
Web site: http://www.987thebay.com/
Profile: WBYY-FM is a commercial station owned by Garrison City Broadcasting. The format of the station is Lite Rock/Lite AC music. WBYY-FM broadcasts to the Dover, NH area at 98.7 FM.
FM RADIO STATION

WBYZ-FM 45063
Owner: South Georgia Broadcasters Inc.
Editorial: 4005 Golden Isles Parkway, Baxley, Georgia 31513 **Tel:** 1 912 367-3000.
Email: peggy@wbyz94.com
Web site: http://www.wbyz94.com
Profile: WBYZ-FM is a commercial station owned by South Georgia Broadcasters Inc. The format for the station is country. WBYZ-FM broadcasts to the Baxley, GA area at 94.5 FM.
FM RADIO STATION

WBZA-FM 40438
Owner: Entercom Communications Corp.
Editorial: 70 Commercial St, Rochester, New York 14614-1010 **Tel:** 1 585 423-2900.
Web site: http://www.rochesterbuzz.com
Profile: WBZA-FM is a commercial station owned by Entercom Communications Corp. The format of the station is classic hits. WBZA-FM broadcasts to the Rochester, NY area at 98.9 FM.
FM RADIO STATION

WBZ-AM 35226
Owner: CBS Radio
Editorial: 1170 Soldiers Field Rd, Boston, Massachusetts 02134-1004 **Tel:** 1 617 787-7000.
Email: wbzradionews@wbz.com
Web site: http://boston.cbslocal.com/station/wbz-news-radio
Profile: WBZ-AM is a commercial station owned by CBS Radio. The format of the station is news and talk. WBZ-AM broadcasts to the Boston area at 1030 AM.
AM RADIO STATION

WBZC-FM 43933
Owner: Burlington County College
Editorial: 601 Pemberton Browns Mills Rd, Pemberton, New Jersey 08068-1536 **Tel:** 1 609 894-8900.
Email: z889@rcbc.edu
Web site: http://www.z889.org
Profile: WBZC-FM is a non-commercial college station owned by the Burlington County College. The format of the station is Top 40/CHR. WBZC-FM broadcasts to the Pemberton, NJ area at 88.9 FM. The station is run by students.
FM RADIO STATION

WBZD-FM 41568
Owner: Backyard Broadcasting
Editorial: 1685 Four Mile Dr, Williamsport, Pennsylvania 17701-1975 **Tel:** 1 570 323-8200.
Web site: http://www.wbzd.com
Profile: WBZD-FM is a commercial station owned by Backyard Broadcasting. The format of the station is oldies music. WBZD-FM broadcasts to the Susquehanna Valley, PA area at 93.3 FM.
FM RADIO STATION

WBZE-FM 45049
Owner: Cumulus Media Inc.
Editorial: 3411 W Tharpe St, Tallahassee, Florida 32303-1139 **Tel:** 1 850 201-3000.
Web site: http://www.mystar98.com
FM RADIO STATION

WBZF-FM 46431
Owner: Cumulus Media Inc.
Editorial: 2014 N Irby St, Florence, South Carolina 29501 **Tel:** 1 843 661-5000.
Web site: http://www.glory985.com
Profile: WBZF-FM is a commercial station owned by Cumulus Media Inc. The format of the station is gospel music. WBZF-FM broadcasts to the Florence, SC area at 98.5 FM.
FM RADIO STATION

WBZ-FM 40121
Owner: CBS Radio
Editorial: 83 Leo M Birmingham Pkwy, Boston, Massachusetts 02135-1101 **Tel:** 1 617 746-1300.
Web site: http://boston.cbslocal.com/category/sports
Profile: WBZ-FM is a commercial station owned by CBS Radio. The format of the station is sports. WBZ-FM broadcasts to the Boston area at 98.5 FM.
FM RADIO STATION

WBZG-FM 40487
Owner: Mendota Broadcasting
Editorial: 3905 Progress Blvd, Peru, Illinois 61354
Tel: 1 815 224-2100.
Email: wbzg@theradiogroup.net
Web site: http://www.wbzg.net
Profile: WBZG-FM is a commercial station owned by Mendota Broadcasting. The format for the station is classic rock. WBZG-FM broadcasts to the Peru, IL area at 100.9 FM.
FM RADIO STATION

WBZI-AM 36199
Owner: Town and Country Broadcasting, Inc.
Editorial: 23 E 2nd St, Xenia, Ohio 45385-3415
Tel: 1 866 372-3531.
Email: myclassiccountry@myclassiccountry.com
Web site: http://www.myclassiccountry.com
Profile: WBZI-AM is a commercial station owned by Town and Country Broadcasting, Inc. The format of the station is classic country. WBZI-AM broadcasts to the Xenia, OH area at 1500 AM.
AM RADIO STATION

WBZI-FM 625083
Owner: Town and Country Broadcasting, Inc.
Editorial: 23 E 2nd St, Xenia, Ohio 45385-3415
Tel: 1 937 372-3531.
Email: myclassiccountry@myclassiccountry.com
Web site: http://www.myclassiccountry.com
Profile: WBZI-FM is a commercial station owned by Town and Country Broadcasting, Inc. The format of the station is classic country. WBZI-FM broadcasts to the Xenia, OH area at 100.3 FM.
FM RADIO STATION

WBZJ-FM 45697
Owner: Curtis Media Group
Editorial: 3012 Highwoods Blvd, Raleigh, North Carolina 27604-1037 **Tel:** 1 919 790-9392.
Web site: http://pulse102.com
Profile: WBZJ-FM is a commercial station owned by Curtis Media Group. The format of the station is Top 40/CHR. WYMY-FM broadcasts to the Raleigh, NC area at 96.9 FM.
FM RADIO STATION

WBZN-FM 43365
Owner: Townsquare Media, Inc.
Editorial: 49 Acme Rd, Brewer, Maine 04412-1545
Tel: 1 207 989-5631.
Email: z1073@midmaine.com
Web site: http://www.z1073.com
Profile: WBZN-FM is a commercial station owned by Townsquare Media, Inc. The format of the station is Top 40/CHR. WBZN-FM broadcasts to the Brewer, ME area at 107.3 FM.
FM RADIO STATION

WBZO-FM 42065
Owner: Connoisseur Media
Editorial: 234 Airport Plaza Blvd, Farmingdale, New York 11735-3917 **Tel:** 1 631 770-4200.
Email: webmaster@liradiogroup.com
Web site: http://www.b103.com
Profile: WBZO-FM is a commercial station owned by Connoisseur Media. The format of the station is oldies music. WBZO-FM broadcasts to the Farmingdale, NY area at 103.1 FM.
FM RADIO STATION

WBZR-FM 46857
Owner: Tri-County Broadcasting
Editorial: 301 N Main St, Atmore, Alabama 36502-1715 **Tel:** 1 251 923-0993.
Profile: WBZR-FM is a commercial station owned by Tri-County Broadcasting. The format of the station is classic country. WBZR-FM broadcasts to the Atmore, AL area at 105.9 FM.
FM RADIO STATION

WBZS-FM 554524
Owner: 3 Daughters Media, Inc.
Editorial: 1035 Avalon Dr, Forest, Virginia 24551-2970
Tel: 1 434 534-6100.
Web site: http://www.wiqoradio.com
Profile: WBZS-FM is a commercial station owned by 3 Daughters Media, Inc. The format of the station is news/talk. WBZS-FM broadcasts to the Shawsville, VA area at a frequency of 102.5 FM.
FM RADIO STATION

WBZT-AM 36592
Owner: iHeartMedia Inc.
Editorial: 3071 Continental Dr, West Palm Beach, Florida 33407-3274 **Tel:** 1 561 616-6600.
Web site: http://1230thezone.iheart.com
Profile: WBZT-AM is a commercial station owned by iHeartMedia Inc. The format of the station is sports radio. WBZT-AM broadcasts to the West Palm Beach, FL area at 1230 AM. The station's slogan is, "Palm Beaches Home for the NFL, the Miamia Marlins and the Most Play b Play."
AM RADIO STATION

WBZU-AM 36416
Owner: Entercom Communications Corp.
Editorial: 305 Route 315 Hwy, Pittston, Pennsylvania 18640-3907 **Tel:** 1 570 883-9800.
Web site: http://www.wilknetwork.com
Profile: WBZU-AM is a commercial station owned by Entercom Communications Corp. The format of the

station is news, sports and talk. WBZU-AM broadcasts to the Pittston, PA area at 910 AM.
AM RADIO STATION

WBZV-FM 44103
Owner: Friends Communications Inc.
Editorial: 121 W Maumee St, Adrian, Michigan 49221-2019 **Tel:** 1 517 265-1500.
Email: traffic@friendsmi.com
Profile: WBZV-FM is a commercial station owned by Friends Communications Inc. The format of the station is classic rock. WBZV-FM broadcasts to the Hillsdale, MI area at 102.5 FM.
FM RADIO STATION

WBZW-AM 36771
Owner: Salem Media Group, Inc.
Editorial: 1188 Lake View Dr, Altamonte Springs, Florida 32714-2713 **Tel:** 1 407 682-9494.
Web site: http://www.1520wbzw.com
Profile: WBZW-AM is a commercial station owned by Salem Media Group, Inc. The format of the station is business talk. WBZW-AM broadcasts to the Altamonte Springs, FL area at 1520 AM.
AM RADIO STATION

WBZY-FM 45091
Owner: iHeartMedia Inc.
Editorial: 1819 Peachtree Rd NE Ste 700, Atlanta, Georgia 30309-1849 **Tel:** 1 404 875-8080.
Web site: http://www.1053elpatron.com
Profile: WBZY-FM is a commercial station owned by iHeartMedia Inc. The format of the station is regional Mexican. WBZY-FM broadcasts to the Atlanta area at 105.3 FM.
FM RADIO STATION

WBZZ-FM 40880
Owner: CBS Radio
Editorial: 651 Holiday Dr Ste 2, Pittsburgh, Pennsylvania 15220-2740 **Tel:** 1 412 920-9400.
Web site: http://starpittsburgh.cbslocal.com
Profile: WBZZ-FM is a commercial station owned by CBS Radio. The format of the station is hot adult contemporary. WBZZ-FM broadcasts to the Pittsburgh area at 100.7 FM.
FM RADIO STATION

WCAB-AM 35228
Owner: Bishop (Jim)
Editorial: 191 Whiteside Rd, Rutherfordton, North Carolina 28139 **Tel:** 1 828 287-3356.
Email: wcabam59@nctv.com
Web site: http://www.wcab59.com
Profile: WCAB-AM is a commercial station owned by Jim Bishop. The format of the station is classic country, news and talk. WCAB-AM broadcasts to the Rutherfordton, NC area at 590 AM.
AM RADIO STATION

WCAL-FM 40807
Owner: Student Association Inc.
Editorial: 428 Hickory St, California, Pennsylvania 15419-1341 **Tel:** 1 724 938-5823.
Web site: http://wcal.calu.edu
Profile: WCAL-FM is a non-commercial station owned by Student Association Inc. The format of the station is rock alternative music. WCAL-FM broadcasts to the California, PA at 91.9 FM.
FM RADIO STATION

WCAM-AM 38858
Owner: Kershaw Radio Corp.
Editorial: 5 The Commons, Lugoff, South Carolina 29078 **Tel:** 1 803 438-9002.
Email: wpubradio@bellsouth.net
Web site: http://www.kool1027.com
Profile: WCAM-AM is a commercial station owned by Kershaw Radio Corp. The format of the station is adult standards. WCAM-AM broadcasts to the Lugoff, SC area at 1590 AM.
AM RADIO STATION

WCAN-FM 41692
Owner: WAMC
Editorial: 318 Central Ave, Albany, New York 12206-2522 **Tel:** 1 518 465-5233.
Email: mail@wamc.org
Web site: http://www.wamc.org
Profile: WCAN-FM is a non-commercial station owned by WAMC. The format of the station is news and talk. WCAN-FM broadcasts to the Canajoharie, NY area at 93.3 FM.
FM RADIO STATION

WCAO-AM 36825
Owner: iHeartMedia Inc.
Editorial: 711 W 40th St Ste 350, Baltimore, Maryland 21211-2190 **Tel:** 1 410 366-7600.
Web site: http://heaven600.iheart.com
Profile: WCAO-AM is a commercial station owned by iHeartMedia Inc. The format of the station is gospel music. WCAO-FM broadcasts to the Baltimore area at 600 AM.
AM RADIO STATION

WCAP-AM 35229
Owner: Merrimack Valley Radio LLC
Editorial: 243 Central St, Lowell, Massachusetts 1852 **Tel:** 1 978 454-0404.
Web site: http://www.980wcap.com
Profile: WCAP-AM is a commercial station owned by Merrimack Valley Radio LLC. The format of the station is news, talk, and sports. WCAP-AM broadcasts to Lowell, MA, and its surrounding areas at 980 AM.
AM RADIO STATION

WCAR-AM 35230
Owner: Birach Broadcasting Corp.
Editorial: 32500 Parklane St, Garden City, Michigan 48135-1527 **Tel:** 1 734 525-1111.
Profile: WCAR-AM is a commercial station owned by Birach Broadcasting Corp. The format of the station is sports talk. WCAR-AM is the Yahoo! Sports Radio affiliate for the Greater Detroit area. The station broadcasts locally at 1090 AM.
AM RADIO STATION

WCAT-AM 36147
Owner: Radio Broadcasting Services, Inc.
Editorial: 372 Dorset St, South Burlington, Vermont 05403-6212 **Tel:** 1 802 863-1010.
Profile: WCAT-AM is a commercial station owned by Radio Broadcasting Services, Inc. The format of the station is comedy. WCAT-AM broadcasts to the South Burlington, VT area at 1390 AM.
AM RADIO STATION

WCAT-FM 45217
Owner: Radio Carlisle
Editorial: 728 N Hanover St, Carlisle, Pennsylvania 17013-1534 **Tel:** 1 717 635-7000.
Web site: http://www.red1023.com
Profile: WCAT-FM is a commercial station owned by Radio Carlisle. The format of the station is contemporary country music. WCAT-FM broadcasts to the Camp Hill, PA area at 102.3 FM.
FM RADIO STATION

WCAZ-AM 36358
Owner: Ralla Broadcasting Inc.
Editorial: 86 S Madison St, Carthage, Illinois 62321-1331 **Tel:** 1 217 357-3128.
Email: wcazradio@gmail.com
Web site: http://www.wcazam990.com
Profile: WCAZ-AM is a commercial station owned by Ralla Broadcasting Inc. The format of the station is news and talk programming. WCAZ-AM broadcasts to the Quincy, IL area at 990 AM.
AM RADIO STATION

WCBC-AM 39013
Owner: Cumberland Broadcasting Co.
Editorial: 35 Baltimore St, Cumberland, Maryland 21502-3024 **Tel:** 1 301 724-5000.
Email: newsroom@wcbcradio.com
Web site: http://www.wcbcradio.com
Profile: WCBC-AM is a commercial station owned by Cumberland Broadcasting Co. The format of the station is news and talk. WCBC-AM broadcasts in the Cumberland, MD, area at 1270 AM.
AM RADIO STATION

WCBC-FM 46344
Owner: Cumberland Broadcasting Co.
Editorial: 35 Baltimore St, Cumberland, Maryland 21502-3024 **Tel:** 1 301 724-5000.
Email: newsroom@wcbcradio.com
Web site: http://www.wcbcradio.com
Profile: WCBC-FM is a commercial station owned by Cumberland Broadcasting Co. The format of the station is oldies. WCBC-FM broadcasts to the Cumberland, MD area at 107.1 FM.
FM RADIO STATION

WCBG-AM 37657
Owner: VerStandig Broadcasting
Editorial: 10960 John Wayne Dr, Greencastle, Pennsylvania 17225-9584 **Tel:** 1 717 597-9200.
Email: info@wayz.com
Web site: http://www.1380wcbg.com/
Profile: WCBG-AM is a commercial station owned by VerStandig Broadcasting. The format of the station is sports. WCBG-AM broadcasts to the Greencastle, PA area at 1360 AM.
AM RADIO STATION

WCBH-FM 41081
Owner: Cromwell Group Inc.(The)
Editorial: 209 Lakeland Blvd, Mattoon, Illinois 61938-3904 **Tel:** 1 217 235-5624.
Web site: http://www.radiomattoon.com
Profile: WCBH-FM is a commercial station owned by The Cromwell Group Inc. The format of the station is Top 40/CHR. WCBH-FM broadcasts to the Mattoon, IL area at 104.3 FM.
FM RADIO STATION

WCBJ-FM 44383
Owner: Morgan County Industries Inc.
Editorial: 129 College St, West Liberty, Kentucky 41472-1156 **Tel:** 1 606 668-9225.
Email: radio41472@yahoo.com
Profile: WCBJ-FM is a commercial station owned by Morgan County Industries Inc. The format of the station is adult contemporary WCBJ-FM broadcasts to the West Liberty, KY area at 103.7 FM.
FM RADIO STATION

WCBK-FM 45066
Owner: Mid-America Radio Group
Editorial: 1639 Burton Ln, Martinsville, Indiana 46151-3004 **Tel:** 1 765 342-3394.
Email: wcbk@wcbk.com
Web site: http://www.wcbk.com
Profile: WCBK-FM is a commercial station owned by Mid-America Radio Group. The format of the station is contemporary country music. WCBK-FM broadcasts to the Martinsville, IN area at 102.3 FM.
FM RADIO STATION

WCBL-AM 37688
Owner: Freeland Broadcasting
Editorial: 1039 Egners Ferry Rd, Benton, Kentucky 42025 **Tel:** 1 270 527-3102.
Email: wcbl@freelandbroadcasting.com
Web site: http://thelakecurrent.com
AM RADIO STATION

WCBL-FM 45067
Owner: Freeland Broadcasting
Editorial: 1039 Egners Ferry Rd, Benton, Kentucky 42025 **Tel:** 1 270 527-3102.
Email: wcbl@freelandbroadcasting.com
Web site: http://www.wcblradio.com
FM RADIO STATION

WCBM-AM 36015
Owner: M-10 Broadcasting Inc.
Editorial: 1726 Reisterstown Rd, Ste 117, Pikesville, Maryland 21208 **Tel:** 1 410 580-6800.
Email: am680@wcbm.com
Web site: http://www.wcbm.com
Profile: WCBM-AM is a commercial station owned by M-10 Broadcasting Inc. The format of the station is news and talk. WCBM-AM broadcasts in the greater Baltimore area at 680 AM.
AM RADIO STATION

WCBQ-AM 35231
Owner: Paradise Network
Editorial: 601 Henderson St, Oxford, North Carolina 27565-3450 **Tel:** 1 919 693-3540.
Email: alvin@dralvin.com
Profile: WCBQ-AM is a commercial station owned by Paradise Network. The format of the station is R&B, gospel, and oldies music. WCBQ-AM broadcasts to the Oxford, NC area at 1340 AM.
AM RADIO STATION

WCBR-AM 36680
Owner: WCBR Inc.
Editorial: 154 Moberly Rd., Richmond, Kentucky 40475 **Tel:** 1 859 623-1235.
Email: wcbrradio@gmail.com
Web site: http://www.wcbrradio.com
Profile: WCBR-AM is a commercial station owned by WCBR Inc. The format of the station is religious talk and gospel music. WCBR-AM broadcasts to the Richmond, KY area at 1110 AM.
AM RADIO STATION

WCBS-AM 38681
Owner: CBS Radio
Editorial: 345 Hudson St, New York, New York 10014-4502 **Tel:** 1 212 975-2127.
Email: wcbsamdesk@wcbs880.com
Web site: http://newyork.cbslocal.com/station/wcbs-880
Profile: WCBS-AM is a commercial station owned by CBS Radio. The format of the station is news programming. WCBS-AM broadcasts to the New York area at 880 AM.
AM RADIO STATION

WCBS-FM 46034
Owner: CBS Radio
Editorial: 345 Hudson St, 10th Fl., New York, New York 10014-4502 **Tel:** 1 212 314-9200.
Web site: http://wcbsfm.cbslocal.com
Profile: WCBS-FM is a commercial station owned by CBS Radio. The format of the station is classic hits. WCBS-FM broadcasts throughout the New York area at 101.1 FM.
FM RADIO STATION

WCBT-AM 35232
Owner: Johnson Broadcast Ventures
Editorial: 1406 Saint Andrew St, Tarboro, North Carolina 27886-2532 **Tel:** 1 252 824-7878.
Profile: WCBT-AM is a commercial station owned by Johnson Broadcast Ventures, Ltd. The format of the station is urban inspirational. WCBT-AM broadcasts to the Roanoke Rapids, NC area at 1230 AM.
AM RADIO STATION

WCBX-AM 36595
Owner: Calvary Chapel Twin Falls
Tel: 1 800 357-4226.
Web site: http://www.csnradio.com
Profile: WCBX-AM is a commercial station owned by Calvary Chapel Twin Falls. The format of the station is Christian teaching and Contemporary Christian music. WCBX-AM broadcasts to the South Central Virginia area at 900 AM.
AM RADIO STATION

WCBY-AM 37689
Owner: Northern Star Broadcasting LLC
Editorial: 1356 Mackinaw Ave, Cheboygan, Michigan 49721 **Tel:** 1 231 627-2341.
Profile: WCBY-AM is a commercial station owned by Northern Star Broadcasting LLC. The format of the station is classic country. WCBY-AM broadcasts to the Cheboygan, MI area at 1240 AM.
AM RADIO STATION

WCCD-AM 35233
Owner: New Spirit Revival Center Ministries Inc.
Editorial: 3130 Mayfield Rd, Cleveland Heights, Ohio 44118-1768 **Tel:** 1 216 320-0000.
Web site: http://www.radio1000.org
Profile: WCCD-AM is a commercial station owned by New Spirit Revival Center Ministries Inc. The format of the station is religion. WCCD-AM's broadcasts the Cleveland, OH area at 1000 AM.
AM RADIO STATION

WCCE-FM 496817
Owner: Radio Training Network, Inc.
Editorial: 7610 Falls Of Neuse Rd, Ste 155, Raleigh, North Carolina 27615 **Tel:** 1 919 256-9787.
Email: management@hisradiowrtp.com
Web site: http://www.hisradiowrtp.com
Profile: WCCE-FM is a non-commercial station owned by Radio Training Network, Inc. The format is contemporary Christian. WCCE-FM broadcasts to the Raleigh, NC area at 90.1 FM.
FM RADIO STATION

WCCF-AM 37691
Owner: iHeartMedia Inc.
Editorial: 24100 Tiseo Blvd Unit 10, Port Charlotte, Florida 33980-5223 **Tel:** 1 941 206-1188.
Web site: http://www.wccfam.com
Profile: WCCF-AM is a commerical station owned by iHeartMedia Inc. The format of the station is news and talk programming. WCCF-AM broadcasts to the Port Charlotte, FL area at 1580 AM.
AM RADIO STATION

WCCG-FM 43359
Owner: Carson Communications
Editorial: 115 Gillespie St, Fayetteville, North Carolina 28301-5643 **Tel:** 1 910 484-4932.
Web site: http://www.wccg1045fm.com
Profile: WCCG-FM is a commercial station owned by Carson Communications. The format of the station is urban contemporary. WCCG-FM broadcasts to the Fayetteville, NC area at 104.5 FM.
FM RADIO STATION

WCCH-FM 445516
Owner: Holyoke Community College
Editorial: 303 Homestead Ave, Holyoke, Massachusetts 01040-1091 **Tel:** 1 413 552-2488.
Web site: http://www.hcc.edu/campus-life/student-clubs/interest-clubs/wcch-1035-radio-club
Profile: WCCH-FM is a college station owned by Holyoke Community College. The format for the station is variety. WCCH-FM broadcasts to the Holyoke, MA area at 103.5 FM.
FM RADIO STATION

WCCI-FM 40162
Owner: Carroll County Communications
Editorial: 316 Main St, Savanna, Illinois 61074-1630 **Tel:** 1 815 273-7757.
Email: newssports@wcciradio.com
Web site: http://www.wcciradio.com
Profile: WCCI-FM is a commercial station owned by Carroll County Communications. The format of the station is country. WCCI-FM broadcasts to the Savanna, IL area on 100.3 FM.
FM RADIO STATION

WCCK-FM 42639
Owner: Freeland Broadcasting
Editorial: 7 Aspen St, Calvert City, Kentucky 42029 **Tel:** 1 270 395-5133.
Email: wcck@freelandbroadcasting.com
FM RADIO STATION

WCCL-FM 46209
Owner: FM Radio Licenses, LLC
Editorial: 970 Tripoli St, Johnstown, Pennsylvania 15902-1119 **Tel:** 1 814 534-8975.
Web site: http://cool101online.com
Profile: WCCL-FM is a commercial station owned by FM Radio Licenses, LLC. The format of the station is oldies music. WCCL-FM broadcasts to the Johnstown, PA area at 101.7 FM.
FM RADIO STATION

WCCM-AM 36339
Owner: Costa Eagle Radio Ventures
Editorial: 462 Merrimack St, Methuen, Massachusetts 01844-5804 **Tel:** 1 978 683-7171.
Email: info@1110wccmam.com
Web site: http://www.eagleradio1110.com
Profile: WCCM-AM is a commercial station owned by Costa Eagle Radio Ventures. The format of the station is news/talk. WCCM-AM broadcasts to the Methuen, MA area at 1110 AM.
AM RADIO STATION

WCCN-AM 37692
Owner: Central Wisconsin Broadcasting
Editorial: 1201 E Division St, Neillsville, Wisconsin 54456-2123 **Tel:** 1 715 743-3333.
Email: 1075therock@tds.net
Web site: http://www.cwbradio.com
Profile: WCCN-AM is a commercial station owned by Central Wisconsin Broadcasting. The format of the station is adult standards. WCCN-AM broadcasts to the Clark County, WI area at a frequency of 1370 AM.
AM RADIO STATION

WCCN-FM 45069
Owner: Central Wisconsin Broadcasting
Editorial: 1201 E Division St, Neillsville, Wisconsin 54456-2123 **Tel:** 1 715 743-3333.
Email: 1075therock@tds.net
Web site: http://www.cwbradio.com
Profile: WCCN-FM is a commercial station owned by Central Wisconsin Broadcasting. The format of the station is classic rock. WCCN-FM broadcasts to the Neillsville, WI area at 107.5 FM.
FM RADIO STATION

WCCO-AM 36900
Owner: CBS Radio
Editorial: 625 2nd Ave S Ste 200, Minneapolis, Minnesota 55402-1908 **Tel:** 1 612 370-0698.
Email: newstips@wccoradio.com

Web site: http://minnesota.cbslocal.com
Profile: WCCO-AM is a commercial station owned by CBS Radio. The format of the station is news, talk and sports. WCCO-AM broadcasts to the Minneapolis area at 830 AM.
AM RADIO STATION

WCCP-FM 46614
Owner: Byrne Acquisition Group, LLC
Editorial: 202 Lawrence Rd, Clemson, South Carolina 29631 **Tel:** 1 864 654-4004.
Web site: http://wccpfm.com
Profile: WCCP-FM is a commercial station owned by Golden Corners Broadcasting and under LMA with Byrne Acquisition Group. The format of the station is sports. WCCP-FM broadcasts to the Clemson, SC area at 104.9 FM.
FM RADIO STATION

WCCQ-FM 40163
Owner: Alpha Media LLC
Editorial: 2410 Caton Farm Rd Unit B, Crest Hill, Illinois 60403-1374 **Tel:** 1 815 556-0100.
Web site: http://www.wccq.com
Profile: WCCQ-FM is a commercial station owned by Alpha Media LLC. The format of the station is contemporary country. WCCQ-FM broadcasts to the Crest Hill, IL area at 98.3 FM.
FM RADIO STATION

WCCR-FM 45070
Owner: Clarion County Broadcasting Corp.
Editorial: 1168 Greenville Pike, Clarion, Pennsylvania 16214-6146 **Tel:** 1 814 226-4500.
Email: clarionradio@comcast.net
Profile: WCCR-FM is a commercial station owned by Clarion County Broadcasting Corp. The format of the station is adult contemporary. WCCR-FM broadcasts to the Clarion, PA area at 92.7 FM.
FM RADIO STATION

WCCS-AM 35234
Owner: Renda Broadcasting
Editorial: 840 Philadelphia St Ste 100, Indiana, Pennsylvania 15701-3922 **Tel:** 1 724 465-4700.
Web site: http://www.1160wccs.com
Profile: WCCS-AM is a commercial station owned by Renda Broadcasting. The format of the station is sports. WCCS-AM broadcasts in the Indiana, PA area at 1160 AM.
AM RADIO STATION

WCCV-FM 41680
Owner: Immanuel Broadcasting Network
Editorial: 779 S Erwin St, Cartersville, Georgia 30120
Tel: 1 770 387-0917.
Email: onair@ibn.org
Web site: http://www.ibn.org
Profile: WCCV-FM is a non-commercial station owned by Immanuel Broadcasting Network. The format of the station is religious. WCCV-FM broadcasts to the Cartersville, GA area at 91.7 FM.
FM RADIO STATION

WCCW-AM 37693
Owner: Midwestern Broadcasting Co.
Editorial: 300 E Front St Ste 450, Traverse City, Michigan 49684-5720 **Tel:** 1 231 946-6211.
Profile: WCCW-AM is a commercial station owned by Midwestern Broadcasting Co. The format of the station is sports. WCCW-AM broadcasts to the Traverse City, MI area at 1310 AM. To contact the station or send press materials e-mail Brian Hale at brianh@wccw.fm.
AM RADIO STATION

WCCW-FM 45071
Owner: Midwestern Broadcasting Co.
Editorial: 300 E Front St Ste 450, Traverse City, Michigan 49684-5720 **Tel:** 1 231 946-6211.
Email: prod@wccw.fm
Web site: http://www.wccwi.com
Profile: WCCW-FM is a commerical station owned by Midwestern Broadcasting Co. The format of the station is oldies. The station airs in the Traverse City, MI area at 107.5 FM.
FM RADIO STATION

WCCY-AM 38595
Owner: Houghton Community Broadcasting Corporation
Editorial: 313 E Montezuma Ave, Houghton, Michigan 49931-2112 **Tel:** 1 906 482-7700.
Email: houghtonradio@up.net
Web site: http://www.wccy.com
Profile: WCCY-AM is a commercial station owned by Houghton Community Broadcasting Corporation. The format for the station is adult standards and sports. WCCY-AM broadcasts to the Marquette, MI area at 1400 AM.
AM RADIO STATION

WCDA-FM 44241
Owner: L.M. Communications Inc.
Editorial: 401 W Main St Ste 301, Lexington, Kentucky 40507-1646 **Tel:** 1 859 233-1515.
Web site: http://www.your1063.com
Profile: WCDA-FM is a commercial station owned by L.M. Communications Inc. The format of the station is hot adult contemporary. WCDA-FM broadcasts to the Lexington, KY area at 106.3 FM.
FM RADIO STATION

WCDD-FM 45062
Owner: Prairie Communications LLP
Editorial: 1000 E Linn St, Canton, Illinois 61520
Tel: 1 309 647-1560.
Email: wbysnews@yahoo.com
Web site: http://www.cd1079.net
Profile: WCDD-FM is a commercial station owned by Prairie Communications LLP. The format of the station is country. WCDD-FM broadcasts to the Peoria, IL area at a frequency of 107.9 FM.
FM RADIO STATION

WCDE-FM 43932
Owner: Davis and Elkins College
Editorial: 100 Campus Dr, Elkins, West Virginia 26241-3971 **Tel:** 1 304 637-1352.
Profile: WCDE-FM is a non-commercial station owned by Davis and Elkins College. The format of the station is Contemporary Christian music. WCDE-FM broadcasts to the Elkins, WV area at 90.3 FM.
FM RADIO STATION

WCDK-FM 46510
Owner: Priority Communications
Editorial: 2307 Pennsylvania Ave, Weirton, West Virginia 26062 **Tel:** 1 304 723-1444.
Web site: http://www.1063theriver.com
Profile: WCDK-FM is a commercial station owned by Priority Communications. The format of the station is classic hits. WCDK-FM broadcasts to the Wheeling, WV, Steubenville, WV, area at 106.3 FM.
FM RADIO STATION

WCDL-AM 38821
Owner: Bold Gold Media Group
Editorial: 1049 N Sekol Ave, Scranton, Pennsylvania 18504-1040 **Tel:** 1 570 344-1221.
Email: foxsportsnepa@gmail.com
Web site: http://boldgoldradionepa.com
Profile: WCDL-AM is a commercial station owned by Bold Gold Media Group. The format of the station is sports. WCDL-AM broadcasts to the Carbondale, PA area at 1440 AM.
AM RADIO STATION

WCDO-AM 37694
Owner: CDO Broadcasting, Inc.
Editorial: 75 Main St, Sidney, New York 13838
Tel: 1 607 563-3588.
Email: wcdo@wcdofm.com
Web site: http://www.wcdoradio.com
Profile: WCDO-AM is a commercial station owned by CDO Broadcasting, Inc. The format of the station is adult contemporary. WCDO-AM broadcasts to the Sidney, NY area at 1490 AM.
AM RADIO STATION

WCDO-FM 45072
Owner: CDO Broadcasting, Inc.
Editorial: 75 Main St, Sidney, New York 13838
Tel: 1 607 563-3588.
Email: wcdo@wcdofm.com
Web site: http://www.wcdoradio.com
Profile: WCDO-FM is a commercial station owned by CDO Broadcasting, Inc. The format of the station is adult contemporary music. WCDO-FM broadcasts to the Binghamton, NY area at 100.9 FM. The station simulcasts at WCDO-AM.
FM RADIO STATION

WCDQ-FM 43071
Owner: Forcht Broadcasting
Editorial: 1757 N 175 W, Crawfordsville, Indiana 47933-6107 **Tel:** 1 765 362-8200.
Web site: http://wcdqfm.com
Profile: WCDQ-FM is a commercial station owned by Forcht Broadcasting. The format of the station is a mix of classic and contemporary country music. WCDQ-FM broadcasts to the Crawfordsville, IN area at 106.3 FM.
FM RADIO STATION

WCDS-AM 39407
Owner: Commonwealth Broadcasting Corp.
Editorial: 113 W Public Sq, Ste 400, Glasgow, Kentucky 42141 **Tel:** 1 270 651-6050.
Web site: http://www.espn1450.net
Profile: WCDS-AM is a commercial station owned by Commonwealth Broadcasting Corp. The format of the station is sports. WCDS-AM broadcasts to the Glasgow, KY area at 1230 AM.
AM RADIO STATION

WCDT-AM 35235
Owner: Yarbrough(Tommy)
Editorial: 1201 S College St, Winchester, Tennessee 37398-2413 **Tel:** 1 931 967-2201.
Email: wcdtfeedback@bellsouth.net
Profile: WCDT-AM is a commercial station owned by Tommy Yarbrough. The format of the station is country music. WCDT-AM broadcasts in the Winchester, TN area at 1340 AM.
AM RADIO STATION

WCDX-FM 40167
Owner: Urban One Inc.
Editorial: 2809 Emerywood Pkwy Ste 300, Richmond, Virginia 23294-3743 **Tel:** 1 804 672-9299.
Web site: http://www.ipowerrichmond.com
Profile: WCDX-FM is a commercial station owned by Urban One Inc. The format of the station is urban contemporary. WCDX-FM broadcasts to the Richmond, VA area at 92.1 FM.
FM RADIO STATION

WCDY-FM 906956
Owner: Up North Radio, LLC
Editorial: 9052 E 13th St Unit E, Cadillac, Michigan 49601-8258 **Tel:** 1 231 876-1079.
Email: 1079cdy@gmail.com
Web site: http://www.1079cdy.com
Profile: WCDY-FM is a commercial station owned by Up North Radio, LLC. The format of the station is Hot AC. WCDY-FM broadcasts to the Cadillac, MI area at a frequency of 107.9 FM.
FM RADIO STATION

WCDZ-FM 42642
Owner: Thunderbolt Broadcasting Co.
Editorial: 1410 N Lindell St, Martin, Tennessee 38237-5819 **Tel:** 1 731 364-9595.
Email: newsroom@wcmt.com
Web site: http://www.wcmt.com
Profile: WCDZ-FM is a commercial station owned by Thunderbolt Broadcasting Co. The format of the station is oldies. WCDZ-FM broadcasts to the Martin, TN area at 95.1 FM.
FM RADIO STATION

WCEC-AM 153377
Owner: Costa Eagle Radio Ventures
Editorial: 462 Merrimack St, Methuen, Massachusetts 01844-5804 **Tel:** 1 978 686-9966.
Web site: http://wcec1490am.com
Profile: WCEC-AM is a commercial station owned by Costa Eagle Radio Ventures. The format of the station is sports talk. WCEC-AM broadcasts to the Methuen, MA area at 1490 AM. They do not have any local news content and will not accept pitches. The station does accept PSAs.
AM RADIO STATION

WCED-AM 38723
Owner: Priority Communications
Editorial: 12 W Long Ave, Du Bois, Pennsylvania 15801-2100 **Tel:** 1 814 375-5260.
Email: news@sunny106.fm
Web site: http://www.1420wced.com
Profile: WCED-AM is a commercial station owned by Priority Communications. The format of the station is sports and talk. WCED-AM broadcasts to the Du Bois, PA area at 1420 AM.
AM RADIO STATION

WCEF-FM 40168
Owner: Big River Radio Inc.
Editorial: 98 Cedar Lakes Road, Ripley, West Virginia 25271 **Tel:** 1 304 372-9800.
Web site: http://www.c98.com
Profile: WCEF-FM is a commercial station owned by Big River Radio Inc. The format of the station is comtemporary country music. WCEF-FM broadcasts to the Ripley, WV area at 98.3 FM.
FM RADIO STATION

WCEH-AM 37695
Owner: Georgia Eagle Broadcasting Inc.
Editorial: 218 Eastman Hwy, Hawkinsville, Georgia 31036-5936 **Tel:** 1 478 892-9061.
Email: georgiaeagleproduction@gmail.com
Profile: WCEH-AM is a commercial station owned by Georgia Eagle Broadcasting Inc. The format of the station is Classic Country. WCEH-AM broadcasts to the Hawkinsville, GA area at 610 AM.
AM RADIO STATION

WCEI-FM 45074
Owner: First Media Radio LLC
Editorial: 306 Port St, Easton, Maryland 21601-4101
Tel: 1 410 822-3301.
Email: studio@wceiradio.com
Web site: http://www.wceiradio.com
Profile: WCEI-FM is a commercial station owned by First Media Radio LLC. The format of the station is adult contemporary. WCEI-FM broadcasts to Easton, MD at 96.7 FM.
FM RADIO STATION

WCEL-FM 41713
Owner: WAMC
Editorial: 318 Central Ave, Albany, New York 12206
Tel: 1 518 465-5233.
Email: mail@wamc.org
Web site: http://www.wamc.org
Profile: WCEL-FM is a non-commercial station owned by WAMC. The format of the station is news and talk. WCEL-FM broadcasts to the Albany, NY area at 91.9 FM.
FM RADIO STATION

WCEM-AM 37697
Owner: MTS Broadcasting LLC
Editorial: 2 Bay St, Cambridge, Maryland 21613-1257
Tel: 1 410 228-4800.
Web site: http://www.mtslive.com
Profile: WCEM-AM is a commercial station owned by MTS Broadcasting LLC. The format of the station is adult standards. WCEM-AM broadcasts to the Cambridge, MD area at 1240 AM.
AM RADIO STATION

WCEM-FM 45075
Owner: MTS Broadcasting LLC
Editorial: 2 Bay St, Cambridge, Maryland 21613-1257
Tel: 1 410 228-4800.
Email: news@mtslive.com
Web site: http://www.mtslive.com
Profile: WCEM-FM is a commercial station owned by MTS Broadcasting LLC. The format of the station is hot adult contemporary music. WCEM-FM broadcasts to Cambridge, MD at 106.3 FM.
FM RADIO STATION

WCEN-FM 45076
Owner: Digity LLC
Editorial: 1795 Tittabawassee Rd, Saginaw, Michigan 48604-9431 **Tel:** 1 989 752-3456.
Email: themoose@945themoose.com
Web site: http://www.945themoose.com
Profile: WCEN-FM is a commercial station owned by Digity LLC. The format for the station is contemporary country. WCEN-FM broadcasts to the Flint, MI area at 94.5 FM.
FM RADIO STATION

WCEO-AM 153928
Owner: 21st Century Broadcasting Inc.
Editorial: 108 Columbia Northeast Dr Ste F, Columbia, South Carolina 29223-6433
Tel: 1 803 223-9265.
Web site: http://larazalaraza.com/columbia
Profile: WCEO-AM is a commercial station owned by 21st Century Broadcasting Inc. The format of the station is regional Mexican. WCEO-AM broadcasts to the Columbia, SC area on 840 AM.
AM RADIO STATION

WCEV-AM 35236
Owner: Migala Communications Corp.
Editorial: 5356 W Belmont Ave, Chicago, Illinois 60641 **Tel:** 1 773 282-6700.
Email: wcev@wcev1450.com
Web site: http://www.wcev1450.com
Profile: WCEV-AM is a commercial station owned by Migala Communications Corp. The format of the station is ethnic music and programming. WCEV-AM broadcasts to the Chicago area at 1450 AM.
AM RADIO STATION

WCEZ-FM 155874
Owner: Withers Broadcasting Co.
Editorial: 108 Washington St, Keokuk, Iowa 52632-2313 **Tel:** 1 319 524-5410.
Profile: WCEZ-FM is a commercial station owned by Withers Broadcasting Co. The format of the station is classic hits. WCEZ-FM broadcasts to the Carthage, IL area at a frequency of 93.9 FM.
FM RADIO STATION

WCFB-FM 42740
Owner: Cox Media Group, Inc.
Editorial: 4192 N John Young Pkwy, Orlando, Florida 32804-2620 **Tel:** 1 321 281-2000.
Web site: http://www.star945.com
Profile: WCFB-FM is a commercial station owned by Cox Media Group, Inc. The format of the station is rhythmic oldies. WCFB-FM broadcasts to the Orlando, FL area at 94.5 FM.
FM RADIO STATION

WCFL-FM 42691
Owner: Illinois Bible Institute
Editorial: 4101 Fieldstone Rd, Champaign, Illinois 61822-8800 **Tel:** 1 217 359-8232.
Email: wbgl@wbgl.org
Web site: http://www.wbgl.org
Profile: WCFL-FM is a non-commercial station owned by the Illinois Bible Institute. The format of the station is contemporary Christian. WCFL-FM broadcasts to the Chicago area at 104.7 FM.
FM RADIO STATION

WCFO-AM 36753
Owner: JW Broadcasting
Editorial: 1100 Spring St NW Ste 610, Atlanta, Georgia 30309-2828 **Tel:** 1 404 681-9307.
Web site: http://www.newstalk1160.com
Profile: WCFO-AM is a commercial station owned by JW Broadcasting. The format of the station is talk. WCFO-AM broadcasts to the Atlanta area at 1160 AM.
AM RADIO STATION

WCFR-AM 36977
Owner: Koor Communications
Editorial: 18 Park St, Springfield, Vermont 05156-3023 **Tel:** 1 802 885-1480.
Web site: http://www.wcfram1480.com
Profile: WCFR-AM is a commercial station owned by Koor Communications. The format of the station is adult contemporary. WCFR-AM broadcasts to the Springfield, VT area at 1480 AM.
AM RADIO STATION

WCFS-FM 40171
Owner: CBS Radio
Editorial: 2 Prudential Plaza, Ste 1059, Chicago, Illinois 60601 **Tel:** 1 312 649-0099.
Web site: https://www.facebook.com/cbschicago
Profile: WCFS-FM is a commercial station owned by CBS Radio. The format of the station is news talk. WCFS-FM broadcasts to the Chicago area at 105.9 FM. The station airs WBBM-AM's programming.
FM RADIO STATION

WCFT-FM 45202
Owner: Seven Mountains Media, LLC
Editorial: 12 E Market St, Lewistown, Pennsylvania 17044-2123 **Tel:** 1 717 248-6757.
Web site: http://thisisbigfootcountry.com
Profile: WCFT-FM is a commercial radio station owned by Seven Mountains Media, LLC. The format of the station is country music. It broadcasts to the Wilkes Barre-Scranton, PA area at 106.5 FM.
FM RADIO STATION

WCFW-FM 40169
Owner: Bushland Radio Specialties
Editorial: 318 Well St, Chippewa Falls, Wisconsin 54729-1563 **Tel:** 1 715 723-2257.
Email: wcfwradio@gmail.com
Profile: WCFW-FM is a commercial station owned by Bushland Radio Specialties. The format of the station is adult contemporary. WCFW-FM broadcasts to the Chippewa Falls, WI area at 105.7 FM.
FM RADIO STATION

United States of America

WCFX-FM 41397
Owner: Grenax Broadcasting
Editorial: 5847 Venture Way, Mount Pleasant, Michigan 48858 **Tel:** 1 989 772-4173.
Email: hits@wcfx.com
Web site: http://www.wcfx.com
Profile: WCFX-FM is a commercial station owned by Grenax Broadcasting. The format of the station is Hot AC. WCFX-FM broadcasts in the Mt. Pleasant, WI area at 95.3 FM.
FM RADIO STATION

WCFY-FM 882453
Owner: Christian Fellowship Church Inc
Editorial: 4100 Millersburg Rd, Evansville, Indiana 47725-7361 **Tel:** 1 812 867-6464.
Web site: http://www.99thebridge.org
Profile: WCFY-FM is a low-power commercial station owned by Christian Fellowship Church Inc. The format of the station is Christian music and programming. The station airs in the Evansville, IN area on 99.1 FM.
FM RADIO STATION

WCGC-AM 35239
Owner: GHB Broadcasting
Editorial: 6021 W Wilkinson Blvd, Belmont, North Carolina 28012-2895 **Tel:** 1 704 825-2812.
Web site: http://www.wcgcam.com/
Profile: WCGC-AM is a commercial station owned by GHB Broadcasting. The format of the station is religious and Christian programming. WCGC-AM broadcasts to the Belmont, NC area at 1270 AM.
AM RADIO STATION

WCGL-AM 35240
Owner: JBD Communications
Editorial: 3890 Dunn Ave, Ste 804, Jacksonville, Florida 32218-6429 **Tel:** 1 904 766-9955.
Email: wcgl@aol.com
Web site: http://www.wcgl1360.com
Profile: WCGL-AM is a commercial station owned by JBD Communications. The format of the station is religious and gospel music. WCGL-AM broadcasts to the Jacksonville, FL area at 1360 AM.
AM RADIO STATION

WCGM-FM 573040
Owner: Family Life Ministries, Inc
Editorial: 7634 County Route 14, Bath, New York 14810-7612 **Tel:** 1 607 776-4151.
Email: news@fln.org
Web site: http://www.fln.org
Profile: WCGM-FM is a commercial station owned by Family Life Ministries, Inc. The format of the station is religious programming. WCGM-FM broadcasts to the Wattsburg, PA area at 102.7 FM.
FM RADIO STATION

WCGO-AM 35580
Owner: Pollack Broadcasting Co.
Editorial: 2100 Lee St, Evanston, Illinois 60202-1539 **Tel:** 1 847 475-1590.
Email: info@1590wcgo.com
Web site: http://www.1590wcgo.com
Profile: WCGO-AM is a commercial station owned by Pollack Broadcasting. The format of the station is talk. WCGO-AM broadcasts to the Chicago area at 1590 AM. The station's slogan is, "WCGO is Chicago."
AM RADIO STATION

WCGQ-FM 45685
Owner: PMB Broadcasting, LLC
Editorial: 1820 Wynnton Rd, Columbus, Georgia 31906-2930 **Tel:** 1 706 327-1217.
Web site: http://www.q1073.com
Profile: WCGQ-FM is a commercial station owned by PMB Broadcasting, LLC. The format of the station is Top 40/CHR music. WCGQ-FM broadcasts in the Columbus, GA area at 107.3 FM.
FM RADIO STATION

WCGR-AM 36610
Owner: The Radio Group
Editorial: 3568 Lenox Rd, Geneva, New York 14456-2058 **Tel:** 1 315 781-7000.
Web site: http://www.cuchicago.edu/experience/organizations/student-activity-1111111
Profile: WCGR-AM is a commercial station owned by The Radio Group. The format of the station is Contemporary Country. WCGR-AM broadcasts to the Geneva, NY area at 1550 AM.
AM RADIO STATION

WCGW-AM 38759
Owner: Christian Broadcasting System
Editorial: 3950 Lexington Rd, Versailles, Kentucky 40383-1742 **Tel:** 1 859 873-8844.
Email: 770am@ckcradio.com
Web site: http://www.wcgwam.com
Profile: WCGW-AM is a commercial station owned by Christian Broadcasting System. The format of the station is Southern gospel. WCGW-AM broadcasts to the Lexington, KY area at 770 AM.
AM RADIO STATION

WCGX-AM 36018
Owner: Twin County Broadcasting Corp.
Editorial: 325 Poplar Knob Rd, Galax, Virginia 24333-4106 **Tel:** 1 276 236-2921.
Web site: http://www.wcgx.rocks
Profile: WCGX-AM is a commercial station owned by Twin County Broadcasting Corporation. The format of the station is southern gospel. WCGX-AM broadcasts to the Galax, VA area at 1360 AM.
AM RADIO STATION

WCHA-AM 37699
Owner: Alpha Media
Editorial: 25 Penncraft Ave Fl 4, Chambersburg, Pennsylvania 17201-5600 **Tel:** 1 717 263-0813.
Web site: http://www.thenewfm963.com
Profile: WCHA-AM is a commercial station owned by Alpha Media. The format of the station is oldies. WCHA-AM broadcasts to the Chambersburg, PA area at 800 AM.
AM RADIO STATION

WCHB-AM 36381
Owner: Urban One Inc.
Editorial: 3250 Franklin St, Detroit, Michigan 48207-4219 **Tel:** 1 313 259-2000.
Web site: https://wchbnewsdetroit.com
Profile: WCHB-AM is a commercial station owned by Urban One Inc. The format of the station is talk and gospel. WCHB-AM broadcasts to the Detroit area at 1200 AM.
AM RADIO STATION

WCHC-FM 42652
Owner: College of the Holy Cross
Editorial: 1 College St, Box G, Worcester, Massachusetts 1610 **Tel:** 1 508 793-2475.
Email: wchc@g.holycross.edu
Web site: http://college.holycross.edu/wchc/
Profile: WCHC-FM is a non-commercial college station owned by the College of the Holy Cross. The format of the station is variety. WCHC-FM broadcasts to the Worcester, MA area at 88.1 FM.
FM RADIO STATION

WCHD-FM 40828
Owner: iHeartMedia Inc.
Editorial: 101 Pine St, Dayton, Ohio 45402-2948 **Tel:** 1 937 224-1137.
Web site: http://www.channeldayton.com
Profile: WCHDF-FM is a commercial station owned by iHeartMedia Inc. The format of the station is Top 40/CHR. WCHD-FM broadcasts to the Dayton, OH area at 99.9 FM.
FM RADIO STATION

WCHE-AM 35242
Owner: Chester County Radio Inc.
Editorial: 105 W Gay St, West Chester, Pennsylvania 19380-2923 **Tel:** 1 610 692-3131.
Email: wche@wche1520.com
Web site: http://wche1520.com
Profile: WCHE-AM is a commercial station owned by Chester County Radio Inc. The format of the station is rock music and talk. WCHE-AM broadcasts to the West Chester, PA area on 1520 AM.
AM RADIO STATION

WCHG-FM 44011
Owner: Pocahontas Communications Cooperative Corp.
Editorial: 171 Charger Ln, Hot Springs, Virginia 24445-2809 **Tel:** 1 540 839-5400.
Email: wchgnews@tds.net
Web site: http://www.alleghenymountainradio.org
Profile: WCHG-FM is a non-commercial community station owned by Pocahontas Communications Cooperative Corp. The format of the station is variety. WCHG-FM broadcasts to the Hot Springs, VA area at a frequency of 107.1 FM.
FM RADIO STATION

WCHI-AM 38726
Owner: iHeartMedia Inc.
Editorial: 45 W Main St, Chillicothe, Ohio 45601-3104 **Tel:** 1 740 773-3000.
Web site: http://easy1350.iheart.com/
Profile: WCHI-AM is a commercial station owned by iHeartMedia Inc. The format of the station is soft AC. WCHI-AM broadcasts to the Chillicothe, OH area at 1350 AM.
AM RADIO STATION

WCHJ-AM 37144
Owner: Tillman Broadcasting Network Inc.
Editorial: 983 Sawmill Ln NE, Brookhaven, Mississippi 39601-9501 **Tel:** 1 601 823-9006.
Email: victory1470wchj@birch.net
Profile: WCHJ-AM is a commercial station owned by Tillman Broadcasting Network Inc. The format of the station is gospel. WCHJ-AM broadcasts to the Brookhaven, MS area at 1470 AM.
AM RADIO STATION

WCHL-AM 35243
Owner: Vilcom Communications
Editorial: 88 Vilcom Center Dr Ste 130, Chapel Hill, North Carolina 27514-1660 **Tel:** 1 919 933-4165.
Email: info@chapelboro.com
Web site: http://www.chapelboro.com
Profile: WCHL-AM is a commercial station owned by Vilcom Communications. The format of the station is news, talk and sports. WCHL-AM broadcasts to the Chapel Hill, NC area at 1360 AM.
AM RADIO STATION

WCHM-AM 36070
Owner: Jeffrey T. Batten's WCHM Radio, LLC
Editorial: 683 Grant St Apt U, Clarkesville, Georgia 30523-5432 **Tel:** 1 706 839-1490.
Email: news@wjulradio.com
Web site: http://www.wchmradio.com
Profile: WCHM-AM is a commercial station owned by Jeffrey T. Batten's WCHM Radio, LLC. The format of the station is news and talk. WCHM-AM broadcasts to the Atlanta area at 1490 AM.
AM RADIO STATION

WCHO-AM 38095
Owner: iHeartMedia Inc.
Editorial: 1535 N North St, Washington Court House, Ohio 43160-1111 **Tel:** 1 740 335-0941.
Email: news@buckeyecountry105.com
Web site: http://www.wchoam.com
Profile: WCHO-AM is a commercial station owned by iHeartMedia Inc. The format of the station is classic hits. WCHO-AM broadcasts to the Washington Court House, OH area at 1250 AM.
AM RADIO STATION

WCHO-FM 45078
Owner: iHeartMedia Inc.
Editorial: 1535 N North St, Washington Court House, Ohio 43160-1111 **Tel:** 1 740 335-0941.
Email: news@buckeyecountry105.com
Web site: http://buckeyecountry105.iheart.com
Profile: WCHO-FM is a commercial station owned by iHeartMedia Inc. The format of the station is contemporary country music. WCHO-FM broadcasts to the Washington Courthouse, OH area at 105.5 FM.
FM RADIO STATION

WCHP-AM 35901
Owner: Champlain Radio Inc.
Editorial: 137 Rapids Rd, Champlain, New York 12919 **Tel:** 1 518 298-2800.
Email: wchp@primelink1.net
Web site: http://www.wchp.com
Profile: WCHP-AM is a commercial station owned by Champlain Radio Inc. The format of the station is Christian and religious programming. WCHP-AM broadcasts to the Champlain, NY area at 760 AM.
AM RADIO STATION

WCHR-AM 614022
Owner: NB Broadcasting, LLC
Editorial: 619 Alexander Rd Fl 3, Princeton, New Jersey 08540-6000 **Tel:** 1 609 924-1515.
Web site: http://www.wchram.net
Profile: WCHR-AM is a commercial station owned by Connoisseur Media. The format of the station is Christian programming. WCHR-AM broadcasts to the Flemington, NJ area at 1040 AM.
AM RADIO STATION

WCHR-FM 81150
Owner: Townsquare Media, LLC
Editorial: 8 Robbins St, STE 201, Toms River, New Jersey 08753-7668 **Tel:** 1 848 221-8000.
Web site: http://www.1057thehawk.com
Profile: WCHR-FM is a commercial station owned by Townsquare Media, LLC. The format of the station is classic rock. WCHR-FM broadcasts to the Ocean, NJ area at 105.7 FM.
FM RADIO STATION

WCHS-AM 37701
Owner: West Virginia Radio Corp.
Editorial: 1111 Virginia St E, Charleston, West Virginia 25301-2406 **Tel:** 1 304 342-8131.
Web site: http://58wchs.com
Profile: WCHS-AM is a commercial station owned by West Virginia Radio Corp. The format of the station is news, talk and sports. WCHS-AM broadcasts to the Charleston, WV area at 580 AM.
AM RADIO STATION

WCHT-AM 38365
Owner: Radio Results Network
Editorial: 524 Ludington St, Ste 300, Escanaba, Michigan 49829 **Tel:** 1 906 789-0600.
Email: rrnnews@radioresultsnetwork.com
Web site: http://www.wchtradio.com
Profile: WCHT-AM is a commercial station owned by Radio Results Network. The format of the station is news, sports and talk. WCHT-AM braodcasts to the Escanaba, MI area at 600 AM.
AM RADIO STATION

WCHV-AM 37702
Owner: Monticello Media LLC
Editorial: 1150 Pepsi Pl, Ste 300, Charlottesville, Virginia 22901 **Tel:** 1 434 978-4408.
Web site: http://www.wchv.com
Profile: WCHV-AM is a commercial station owned by Monticello Media LLC. The format of the station is news and talk. WCHV-AM broadcasts in the Charlottesville, VA area at 1200 AM.
AM RADIO STATION

WCHX-FM 41216
Owner: Mifflin County Communications
Editorial: 114 N Logan Blvd, Burnham, Pennsylvania 17009-1810 **Tel:** 1 717 242-1055.
Email: wchx@chx105.com
Web site: http://www.chx105.com
Profile: WCHX-FM is a commercial station owned by Mifflin County Communications. The format of the station is classic rock. WCHX-FM broadcasts to the Burnham, PA area at 105.5 FM.
FM RADIO STATION

WCHY-FM 43203
Owner: Northern Star Broadcasting LLC
Editorial: 1356 Mackinaw Ave, Cheboygan, Michigan 49721-1003 **Tel:** 1 231 922-4981.
Web site: http://www.classicrockthebear.com
Profile: WCHY-FM is a commercial station owned by Northern Star Broadcasting LLC. The format of the station is active rock, a mix of classic and album oriented. WCHY-FM broadcasts to Traverse, MI area at 97.7 FM.
FM RADIO STATION

WCHZ-AM 39468
Owner: Beasley Broadcast Group
Editorial: 4051 Jimmie Dyess Pkwy, Augusta, Georgia 30909 **Tel:** 1 706 396-7000.
Web site: http://95rock.com
Profile: WCHZ-AM is a commercial station owned by Beasley Broadcast Group. The format of the station is active rock. WCHZ-AM broadcasts to the Augusta, GA areat at 1480 AM.
AM RADIO STATION

WCHZ-FM 46856
Owner: Beasley Broadcast Group
Editorial: 4051 Jimmie Dyess Pkwy, Augusta, Georgia 30909-9469 **Tel:** 1 706 396-7000.
Web site: http://hotaugusta.com/
Profile: WCHZ-FM is a commercial station owned by Beasley Broadcast Group. The format of the station is Throwback Hip-Hop and R & B. WCHZ-FM broadcasts to the Augusta, GA area at 93.1 FM.
FM RADIO STATION

WCIB-FM 40170
Owner: iHeartMedia Inc.
Editorial: 154 Barnstable Rd, Hyannis, Massachusetts 02601-2930 **Tel:** 1 508 778-2888.
Email: news@95wxtk.com
Web site: http://cool102.iheart.com
Profile: WCIB-FM is a commercial station owned by iHeartMedia Inc. The format of the station is classic hits. WCIB-FM broadcasts to the Hyannis, MA area at 101.9 FM.
FM RADIO STATION

WCIC-FM 41420
Owner: Illinois Bible Institute
Editorial: 3902 Barring Trce, Peoria, Illinois 61615-2500 **Tel:** 1 309 692-9242.
Email: wcic@wcicfm.org
Web site: http://www.wcicfm.org
Profile: WCIC-FM is a non-commercial station owned by the Illinois Bible Institute. The format of the station is contemporary Christian music and talk. WCIC-FM broadcasts in the Peoria, IL area at 91.5 FM.
FM RADIO STATION

WCID-FM 133862
Owner: Family Life Ministries Inc.
Editorial: 7634 County Route 14, Bath, New York 14810-7612 **Tel:** 1 607 776-4151.
Email: news@fln.org
Web site: http://www.fln.org
Profile: WCID-FM is a non-commercial station owned by Family Life Ministries Inc. The format of the station is contemporary Christian. WCID-FM broadcasts to the Bath, NY area at 89.1 FM.
FM RADIO STATION

WCIE-FM 41375
Owner: Radio Training Network, Inc.
Editorial: 6214 Springer Dr, Port Richey, Florida 34668-5339 **Tel:** 1 727 848-9150.
Email: thejoyfm@thejoyfm.com
Web site: http://florida.thejoyfm.com
Profile: WCIE-FM is a non-commercial station owned by Radio Training Network, Inc. The format of the station is contemporary Christian. WCIE-FM broadcasts to the Port Richey, FL area at 91.5 FM.
FM RADIO STATION

WCIF-FM 41222
Owner: First Baptist Church-Melbourne
Editorial: 3301 Dairy Rd, Melbourne, Florida 32904-7603 **Tel:** 1 321 725-9243.
Email: info@wcif.com
Web site: http://www.wcif.com
Profile: WCIF-FM is a commercial station owned by First Baptist Church-Melbourne. The format of the station is religious. WCIF-FM broadcasts to the Melbourne, FL area at 106.3 FM.
FM RADIO STATION

WCIG-FM 45999
Owner: Family Life Ministries Inc.
Editorial: 7634 County Route 14, Bath, New York 14810-7612 **Tel:** 1 607 776-4151.
Email: news@fln.org
Web site: http://www.fln.org
Profile: WCIG-FM is a non-commercial station owned by Family Life Ministries Inc. The format for the station is contemporary Christian. WCIG-FM broadcasts to the Tunkhannock, PA area at 107.7 FM.
FM RADIO STATION

WCIH-FM 133864
Owner: Family Life Ministries Inc.
Editorial: 7634 County Route 14, Bath, New York 14810-7612 **Tel:** 1 607 776-4151.
Email: news@fln.org
Web site: http://www.fln.org
Profile: WCIH-FM is a non-commercial station owned by Family Life Ministries Inc. The format of the station is contemporary Christian. WCIH-FM broadcasts to the Bath, NY area at 90.3 FM.
FM RADIO STATION

WCII-FM 133868
Owner: Family Life Ministries Inc.
Editorial: 7634 Campbell Road, Bath, New York 14810 **Tel:** 1 607 776-4151.
Email: news@fln.org
Web site: http://www.fln.org
Profile: WCII-FM is a non-commercial station owned by Family Life Ministries Inc. The format of the station

is contemporary Christian. WCII-FM broadcasts to the Bath, NY area at 88.5 FM.
FM RADIO STATION

WCIJ-FM 686944
Owner: Family Life Ministries Inc.
Editorial: 7634 County Route 14, Bath, New York 14810-7612 **Tel:** 1 607 776-4151.
Email: news@fln.org
Web site: http://www.fln.org
Profile: WCIJ-FM is a non-commercial station owned by Family Life Ministries Inc. The format of the station is contemporary Christian. WCIJ-FM broadcasts to the Bath, NY area at 88.9 FM.
FM RADIO STATION

WCIK-FM 41434
Owner: Family Life Ministries Inc.
Editorial: 7634 County Route 14, Bath, New York 14810-7612 **Tel:** 1 607 776-4151.
Email: news@fln.org
Web site: http://www.fln.org
Profile: WCIK-FM is a non-commercial station owned by Family Life Ministries Inc. The format of the station is contemporary Christian. WCIK-FM broadcasts to the Bath, NY area at 103.1 FM.
FM RADIO STATION

WCIL-AM 37704
Owner: Max Media
Editorial: 1431 Country Aire Dr, Carterville, Illinois 62918 **Tel:** 1 618 985-4843.
Web site: http://www.wjpf.com
Profile: WCIL-AM is a commercial station owned by Max Media. The format of the station is news and talk. WCIL-AM broadcasts to the Harrisburg, IL area at 1020 AM.
AM RADIO STATION

WCIL-FM 45080
Owner: Max Media
Editorial: 1431 Country Aire Dr, Carterville, Illinois 62918-5118 **Tel:** 1 618 985-4843.
Email: publicservice@riverradio.net
Web site: http://www.cilfm.com
Profile: WCIL-FM is a commercial station owned by Max Media. The format of the station is Top 40/CHR. WCIL-FM broadcasts to the Carterville, IL area at 101.5 FM. Send PSAs to publicservice@riverradio.net.
FM RADIO STATION

WCIO-FM 43493
Owner: Wolf Radio, Inc.
Editorial: 401 W Kirkpatrick St, Syracuse, New York 13204-1305 **Tel:** 1 315 472-0222.
Web site: http://www.fln.org/
Profile: WCIO-FM is a commercial station owned by Wolf Radio, Inc. The format of the station is Contemporary Christian. WCIO-FM broadcasts to the Syracuse, NY area at 96.7 FM.
FM RADIO STATION

WCIR-FM 45081
Owner: Southern Communications Corp.
Editorial: 306 S Kanawha St, Beckley, West Virginia 25801 **Tel:** 1 304 253-7000.
Web site: http://www.103cir.com
Profile: WCIR-FM is a commercial station owned by Southern Communications Corp. The format of the station is Top 40/CHR. WCIR-FM broadcasts to the Beckley, WV area at 103.7 FM.
FM RADIO STATION

WCIS-AM 35863
Owner: WFM Inc.
Editorial: 2828 NC 126, Morganton, North Carolina 28655-8264 **Tel:** 1 828 584-3176.
Profile: WCIS-AM is a commercial station owned by WFM Inc. The format of the station is gospel and religious programming. WCIS-AM broadcasts to the Morganton, NC area at 760 AM.
AM RADIO STATION

WCIS-FM 45420
Owner: Wolf Radio, Inc.
Editorial: 401 W Kirkpatrick St, Syracuse, New York 13204-1305 **Tel:** 1 315 472-0222.
Web site: http://www.fln.org/
Profile: WCIS-FM is a commercial station owned by Wolf Radio, Inc.. The format is Contemporary Christian. WCIS-FM broadcasts to the Syracuse, NY area at 105.1 FM.
FM RADIO STATION

WCIT-AM 37706
Owner: Childers Media Group, LLC
Editorial: 57 Town Sq, Lima, Ohio 45801-4950
Tel: 1 419 331-1600.
Web site: http://www.940wcit.com
Profile: WCIT-AM is a commercial station owned by Childers Media Group, LLC. The format of the station is sports. WCIT-AM broadcasts to the Lima, OH area at 940 AM.
AM RADIO STATION

WCIY-FM 133870
Owner: Family Life Ministries Inc.
Editorial: 7634 Campbell Creek Rd, Bath, New York 14810 **Tel:** 1 607 776-4151.
Email: news@fln.org
Web site: http://www.fln.org
Profile: WCIY-FM is a non-commercial station owned by Family Life Ministries Inc. The format of the station is contemporary Christian. WCIY-FM broadcasts to the Bath, NY area at 88.9 FM.
FM RADIO STATION

WCIZ-FM 46091
Owner: Stephens Media Group
Editorial: 134 Mullin St, Watertown, New York 13601
Tel: 1 315 788-0790.
Web site: http://www.z93.fm
Profile: WCIZ-FM is a commercial station owned by Stephens Media Group. The format of the station is classic rock music. WCIZ-FM broadcasts to the Watertown, NY area at 93.3 FM.
FM RADIO STATION

WCJC-FM 46537
Owner: Hoosier AM/FM LLC
Editorial: 820 S Pennsylvania St, Marion, Indiana 46953-2407 **Tel:** 1 765 664-6239.
Email: wcjc@comteck.com
Web site: http://www.wcjc.com
Profile: WCJC-FM is a commercial station owned by Hoosier AM/FM LLC. The format of the station is contemporary country music. WCJC-FM broadcasts to the Marion, IN area at 99.3 FM.
FM RADIO STATION

WCJK-FM 40767
Owner: Midwest Communications
Editorial: 504 Rosedale Ave, Nashville, Tennessee 37211-2028 **Tel:** 1 615 259-4567.
Web site: http://www.963jackfm.com
Profile: WCJK-FM is a commercial station owned by Midwest Communications. The format of the station is adult hits. WCJK-FM broadcasts to the Nashville, TN area at 96.3 FM.
FM RADIO STATION

WCJM-FM 43520
Owner: iHeartMedia Inc.
Editorial: 705 4th Ave, West Point, Georgia 31833-1506 **Tel:** 1 706 645-2991.
Web site: http://www.wcjmthebull.com
Profile: WCJM-FM is a commercial station owned by iHeartMedia Inc. The format of the station is contemporary country music. WCJM-FM broadcasts to the West Point, GA area at 100.9 FM.
FM RADIO STATION

WCJO-FM 42260
Owner: Jackson County Broadcasting Inc.
Editorial: 295 E Main St, Jackson, Ohio 45640
Tel: 1 740 286-3023.
Profile: WCJO-FM is a commercial station owned by Jackson County Broadcasting Inc. The format of the station is contemporary country music. WCJO-FM broadcasts to the Jackson, OH area at 97.7 FM.
FM RADIO STATION

WCJU-AM 35245
Owner: Sunbelt Broadcasting Corporation
Editorial: 37 S High School Ave, Columbia, Mississippi 39429-8246 **Tel:** 1 601 736-2616.
Email: wcju@wcjufm.com
Web site: http://www.wcjuam.com
Profile: WCJU-AM is a commercial station owned by Sunbelt Broadcasting Corporation. The format of the station is news and talk. WCJU-AM broadcasts to the Columbia, MS area at 1450 AM.
AM RADIO STATION

WCJU-FM 151274
Owner: Sunbelt Broadcasting Corporation
Editorial: 37 S High School Ave, Columbia, Mississippi 39429-8246 **Tel:** 1 601 736-8889.
Email: wcju@wcjufm.com
Web site: http://www.wcjufm.com
Profile: WCJU-FM is a commercial station owned by Sunbelt Broadcasting Corporation. The format of the station is classic hits. WCJU-FM broadcasts to the Columbia, MS area at 104.9 FM.
FM RADIO STATION

WCJW-AM 35246
Owner: Lloyd Lane Inc.
Editorial: 3258 Merchant Rd, Warsaw, New York 14569-9320 **Tel:** 1 585 786-8131.
Email: news@wcjw.com
Web site: http://www.wcjw.com
Profile: WCJW-AM is a commercial station owned by Lloyd Lane Inc. The format of the station is country. WCJW-AM broadcasts to the Warsaw, NY area at 1140 AM.
AM RADIO STATION

WCJX-FM 43137
Owner: Black Crow Broadcasting Inc.
Editorial: 5348 NW US Highway 41, Lake City, Florida 32055-5550 **Tel:** 1 386 755-9259.
Email: wcjxaudio@gmail.com
Web site: http://wcjx.com
Profile: WCJX-FM is a commercial station owned by Black Crow Broadcasting Inc. The format of the station is classic hits. WCJX-FM broadcasts to the Lake City, FL area at 106.5 FM.
FM RADIO STATION

WCKA-AM 36412
Owner: L.E. Gradick
Editorial: 188 Broadcast Blvd, Jacksonville, Alabama 36265-6659 **Tel:** 1 877 237-0810.
Email: alabama810news@bellsouth.net
Web site: http://www.ala810.com
Profile: WCKA-AM is a commercial station owned by L.E. Gradick. The format of the station is classic country. WCKA-AM broadcasts to the Jacksonville, AL area at 810 AM.
AM RADIO STATION

WCKB-AM 35247
Owner: North Carolina Central Broadcasters
Editorial: 17336 US Highway 421 S, Dunn, North Carolina 28334-5580 **Tel:** 1 910 892-3133.
Email: wckb@wckb780.com
Web site: http://www.wckb780.com
Profile: WCKB-AM is a commercial station owned by North Carolina Central Broadcasters. The format of the station is Southern gospel music. WCKB-AM broadcasts to the Dunn, NC-area at 780 AM.
AM RADIO STATION

WCKC-FM 40904
Owner: Northern Star Broadcasting LLC
Editorial: 1356 Mackinaw Ave, Cheboygan, Michigan 49721-1003 **Tel:** 1 231 627-2341.
Email: thebear@classicrockthebear.com
Web site: http://www.classicrockthebear.com
Profile: WCKC-FM is a commercial station owned by Northern Star Broadcasting LLC. The format of the station is classic rock. WCKC-FM broadcasts to the Cheboygan, MI area at 107.1 FM.
FM RADIO STATION

WCKF-FM 511132
Owner: L.E. Gradick
Editorial: 518 Mountain View Rd, Ashland, Alabama 36251-5060 **Tel:** 1 256 354-1444.
Email: alabama1007@aol.com
Web site: http://wckf100.com
Profile: WCKF-FM is a commercial station owned by L.E. Gradick. The format of the station is country. WCKF-FM broadcasts to the Anniston, AL area at 100.7 FM.
FM RADIO STATION

WCKG-AM 35436
Owner: DuPage Radio, LLC
Editorial: 1314 Kensington Rd, Oak Brook, Illinois 60522-7101 **Tel:** 1 312 380-1530.
Web site: http://www.wckg.com
Profile: WCKG-AM is a commercial station owned by DuPage Radio, LLC. The format of the station is talk radio. WCKG-AM broadcasts in the suburbs of Chicago at AM 760.
AM RADIO STATION

WCKI-AM 35248
Owner: Mediatrix
Editorial: 2 Beeco Rd, Greer, South Carolina 29650
Tel: 1 864 877-8458.
Email: info@catholicradioinsc.com
Web site: http://www.catholicradioinsc.com
Profile: WCKI-AM is a commercial station owned by Mediatrix. The format of the station is Christian talk. WCKI-AM broadcasts to Greer, SC and its surrounding environs at 1300 AM.
AM RADIO STATION

WCKJ-FM 43748
Owner: Christian Ministries Inc.
Editorial: 140 Main St, Essex Junction, Vermont 05452-3208 **Tel:** 1 866 878-8885.
Email: mailroom@thelightradio.net
Web site: http://www.thelightradio.net
Profile: WCKJ-FM is a non-commercial station owned by Christian Ministries Inc. The format of the station is contemporary Christian music and religious programming. WCKJ-FM broadcasts to the Essex Junction, VT area at 90.5 FM.
FM RADIO STATION

WCKM-FM 42843
Owner: Regional Radio Group
Editorial: 238 Bay Rd, Queensbury, New York 12804-2003 **Tel:** 1 518 761-9890.
Web site: http://www.wckm.com
Profile: WCKM-FM is a commercial station owned by Regional Radio Group. The format of the station is classic hits. WCKM-FM broadcasts to the Glens Falls, NY area at 98.5 FM.
FM RADIO STATION

WCKN-FM 45983
Owner: Apex Broadcasting Inc.
Editorial: 2294 Clements Ferry Rd, Charleston, South Carolina 29492-7729 **Tel:** 1 843 972-1100.
Email: frontdesk@apexbroadcasting.com
Web site: http://www.kickin925.com
Profile: WCKN-FM is a commercial station owned by Apex Broadcasting Inc. The format of the station is country. WCKN-FM broadcasts to the Charleston, SC area at 92.5 FM.
FM RADIO STATION

WCKQ-FM 45736
Owner: Forcht Broadcasting
Editorial: 50 Friendship Pike Rd, Campbellsville, Kentucky 42718-2537 **Tel:** 1 270 789-2401.
Web site: http://www.myq104.com
Profile: WCKQ-FM is a commercial station owned by Forcht Broadcasting. The format of the station is hot adult contemporary. WCKQ-FM broadcasts to the Campbellsville, KY area at 104.1 FM.
FM RADIO STATION

WCKR-FM 45082
Owner: Canisteo Valley Broadcasting
Editorial: 5942 County Route 64, Hornell, New York 14843-9730 **Tel:** 1 607 324-1480.
Web site: http://92nashicon.net
Profile: WCKR-FM is a commercial station owned by Canisteo Valley Broadcasting. The format of the station is country music. WCKR-FM broadcasts to the Hornell, NY area at 92.1 FM.
FM RADIO STATION

WCKS-FM 42846
Owner: Gradick Communications LLC
Editorial: 102 Parkwood Cir, Carrollton, Georgia 30117-8353 **Tel:** 1 770 834-5477.
Web site: http://www.gradickcommunications.com
Profile: WCKS-FM is a commercial station owned by Gradick Communications LLC. The format of the station is hot adult contemporary music. WCKS-FM broadcasts to the Carrollton, GA area at 102.7 FM.
FM RADIO STATION

WCKT-FM 41435
Owner: iHeartMedia Inc.
Editorial: 13320 Metro Pkwy Ste 1, Fort Myers, Florida 33966-4804 **Tel:** 1 239 225-4300.
Web site: http://www.catcountry1071.com
Profile: WCKT-FM is a commercial station owned by iHeartMedia Inc. The format of the station is country music. WCKT-FM broadcasts to the Ft. Myers, FL area at 107.1 FM.
FM RADIO STATION

WCKW-AM 37707
Owner: Covenant Network
Editorial: 1908 Short St, Kenner, Louisiana 70062
Tel: 1 314 752-7000.
Web site: http://covenantnet.net
Profile: WCKW-AM is a commercial station owned by Covenant Network. The format of the station is religious talk programming. WCKW-AM broadcasts to the Garyville, LA area at 1010 AM.
AM RADIO STATION

WCKX-FM 40172
Owner: Urban One Inc.
Editorial: 350 E 1st Ave Ste 100, Columbus, Ohio 43201-3792 **Tel:** 1 614 487-1444.
Web site: http://www.mycolumbuspower.com
Profile: WCKX-FM is a commercial station owned by Urban One Inc. The format of the station is urban contemporary music. WCKX-FM broadcasts in the Columbus, OH area at 107.5 FM.
FM RADIO STATION

WCKY-AM 36299
Owner: iHeartMedia Inc.
Editorial: 8044 Montgomery Rd, Cincinnati, Ohio 45236-2919 **Tel:** 1 513 686-8300.
Web site: http://www.espn1530.com
Profile: WCKY-AM is a commercial station owned by iHeartMedia Inc. The format of the station is sports. WCKY-AM broadcasts to the Cincinnati area at 1530 AM.
AM RADIO STATION

WCKY-FM 45579
Owner: iHeartMedia Inc.
Editorial: 125 S Superior St, Toledo, Ohio 43604-8747
Tel: 1 419 244-8321.
Web site: http://www.1037wcky.com
Profile: WCKY-FM is a commercial station owned by iHeartMedia Inc. The format of the station is contemporary country music. WCKY-FM broadcasts to the Findlay, OH area at 103.7 FM.
FM RADIO STATION

WCLA-AM 39422
Owner: W. Danny Swain
Editorial: 316 N River St, Claxton, Georgia 30417
Tel: 1 912 739-9252.
Web site: http://www.wclaradio.net
Profile: WCLA-AM is a commercial station owned by W. Danny Swain. The format for the station is oldies. WCLA-AM broadcasts to the Savannah, GA area at 1470 AM.
AM RADIO STATION

WCLB-AM 39347
Owner: RBH Enterprises Inc.
Editorial: 254 Winnebago Dr, Fond du Lac, Wisconsin 54935-2447 **Tel:** 1 920 921-1071.
Web site: http://www.950thegame.com
Profile: WCLB-AM is a commercial station owned by RBH Enterprises Inc. The format of the station is sports. WCLB-AM broadcasts to the Fond Du Lac, WI area at 950 AM.
AM RADIO STATION

WCLC-AM 38330
Owner: Bible Believers Network
Editorial: 224 W Central Ave, Jamestown, Tennessee 38556-3405 **Tel:** 1 931 879-8188.
Email: news@newlife105.com
Web site: http://www.newlife105.com
Profile: WCLC-AM is a commercial station owned by the Bible Believers Network. The format of the station is southern gospel and religious programming. WCLC-AM broadcasts to the Jamestown, TN area at 1260 AM.
AM RADIO STATION

WCLC-FM 45778
Owner: Bible Believers Network
Editorial: 224 W Central Ave, Jamestown, Tennessee 38556-3405 **Tel:** 1 931 879-8188.
Email: info@newlife105.com
Web site: http://www.newlife105.com
Profile: WCLC-FM is a commercial station owned by the Bible Believers Network. The format of the station is southern gospel and religious programming. WCLC-FM broadcasts to the Jamestown, TN area at 105.1 FM.
FM RADIO STATION

WCLD-FM 45084
Owner: Radio Cleveland Inc.
Editorial: 911 S Davis Ave, Cleveland, Mississippi 38732-3941 **Tel:** 1 662 843-4091.
Profile: WCLD-FM is a commercial station owned by Radio Cleveland, Inc. The format of the station is urban contemporary music. WCLD-FM broadcasts in the Cleveland, MS at 103.9 FM. Send press releases via mail
FM RADIO STATION

WCLE-AM 39107
Owner: Williams Communications Inc.
Editorial: 1860 Executive Park NW Ste E, Cleveland, Tennessee 37312-2743 **Tel:** 1 423 472-6700.
Email: info@mymix1041.com
Web site: http://www.mix104.info
Profile: WCLE-AM is a commercial station owned by Williams Communications Inc. The format for the station is news, sports and talk. WCLE-AM broadcasts to the Cleveland, TN area at 1570 AM.
AM RADIO STATION

WCLE-FM 46455
Owner: Hartline, LLC
Editorial: 1860 Executive Park NW, Cleveland, Tennessee 37312-2752 **Tel:** 1 423 472-6700.
Email: info@mymix1041.com
Web site: http://mix104.info
Profile: WCLE-FM is a commercial station owned by Hartline, LLC. The format for the station is adult contemporary. WCLE-FM broadcasts to the Cleveland, TN area at 104.1 FM.
FM RADIO STATION

WCLG-AM 37710
Owner: Bowers Broadcasting
Editorial: 343 High St, Morgantown, West Virginia 26505-5515 **Tel:** 1 304 292-2222.
Email: psa@wclg.com
Profile: WCLG-AM is a commercial station owned by Bowers Broadcasting. The format of the station is oldies. WCLG-AM broadcasts to the Morgantown, WV area at 1300 AM.
AM RADIO STATION

WCLG-FM 45085
Owner: Bowers Broadcasting
Editorial: 343 High St, Morgantown, West Virginia 26505-5515 **Tel:** 1 304 292-2222.
Email: psa@wclg.com
Web site: http://www.wclg.com
Profile: WCLG-FM is a commercial station owned by Bowers Broadcasting. The format of the station is rock. WCLG-AM broadcasts to the Morgantown, WV area at 100.1 FM.
FM RADIO STATION

WCLI-FM 40454
Owner: Alpha Media
Editorial: 717 E David Rd, Kettering, Ohio 45429-5218 **Tel:** 1 937 294-5858.
Web site: http://www.1015hankfm.com
Profile: WCLI-FM is a commercial station owned by Alpha Media. The format of the station is classjc country. WCLI-FM broadcasts to the Springfield, OH area at 101.5 FM.
FM RADIO STATION

WCLM-AM 36492
Owner: World Media Broadcast
Editorial: 3203 Hull St, Richmond, Virginia 23224-3533 **Tel:** 1 804 231-2186.
Web site: http://www.wclmradioonline.com
Profile: WCLM-AM is a commercial station owned by World Media Broadcast. The format of the station is R&B oldies, talk and gospel. WCLM-AM broadcasts to the Richmond, VA area at 1450 AM.
AM RADIO STATION

WCLN-AM 35249
Owner: Clinton Sampson Radio Company, Inc.
Editorial: 118 E Main St, Clinton, North Carolina 28328-4029 **Tel:** 1 910 592-8949.
Web site: http://www.oldies1170.com
AM RADIO STATION

WCLN-FM 42249
Owner: Christian Listening Network Inc.
Editorial: 996 Helen St, Fayetteville, North Carolina 28303 **Tel:** 1 910 864-5028.
Email: comments@christian107.com
Web site: http://www.christian107.com
Profile: WCLN-FM is a commercial station owned by the Christian Listening Network Inc. The format of the station is religious. WCLN-FM broadcasts to the Charlotte, NC area at 107.3 FM.
FM RADIO STATION

WCLO-AM 37711
Owner: Bliss Communications Inc.
Editorial: 1 S Parker Dr, Janesville, Wisconsin 53545 **Tel:** 1 608 752-7895.
Email: news@wclo.com
Web site: http://www.wclo.com
Profile: WCLO-AM is a commercial station owned by Bliss Communications Inc. The format of the station is news, sports and talk. WCLO-AM broadcasts to the Janesville, WI area at 1230 AM.
AM RADIO STATION

WCLQ-FM 41436
Owner: Christian Life Communications Inc.
Editorial: 4111 Schofield Ave, Ste 10, Schofield, Wisconsin 54476 **Tel:** 1 715 355-5151.
Email: 89q@89q.org
Web site: http://www.89q.org
Profile: WCLQ-FM is a non-commercial station owned by Christian Life Communications Inc. The format of the station is contemporary Christian music and talk. WCLQ-FM broadcasts in Schofield, WI area at 89.5 FM.
FM RADIO STATION

WCLS-FM 40976
Owner: Mid-America Radio Group
Editorial: 2723 N Walnut St, Bloomington, Indiana 47404-2075 **Tel:** 1 812 339-9700.
Email: classichits@wclsfm.com
Web site: http://www.wclsfm.com
Profile: WCLS-FM is a commercial station owned by Mid-America Radio Group. The format for the station is classic hits. WCLS-FM broadcasts to the Indianapolis area at 97.7 FM.
FM RADIO STATION

WCLT-AM 38705
Owner: WCLT Radio Inc.
Editorial: 674 Jacksontown Rd, Heath, Ohio 43056-9376 **Tel:** 1 740 345-4004.
Email: news@wclt.com
Web site: http://www.wclt.com
Profile: WCLT-AM is a commercial station owned by WCLT Radio Inc. The format of the station is sports. WCLT-AM broadcasts to the Newark, OH area at 1430 AM.
AM RADIO STATION

WCLT-FM 46061
Owner: WCLT Radio Inc.
Editorial: 674 Jacksontown Rd, Heath, Ohio 43056 **Tel:** 1 740 345-4004.
Email: news@wclt.com
Web site: http://www.wclt.com
Profile: WCLT-FM is a commercial station owned by WCLT Radio Inc. The format of the station is contemporary country. WCLT-FM broadcasts to the Heath, OH area at 100.3 FM.
FM RADIO STATION

WCLU-AM 39479
Owner: Royse Radio Inc.
Editorial: 229 W Main St, Glasgow, Kentucky 42141-1707 **Tel:** 1 270 651-9149.
Email: wclutraffic@glasgow-ky.com
Web site: http://www.wcluradio.com
Profile: WCLU-FM is a commercial station owned by Royse Radio Inc. The format of the station is variety. WCLU-FM broadcasts to the Glasgow, KY area on 1490 AM.
AM RADIO STATION

WCLU-FM 46868
Owner: Royse Radio Inc.
Editorial: 229 W Main St, Glasgow, Kentucky 42141 **Tel:** 1 270 651-9149.
Email: news@wcluradio.com
Web site: http://www.wcluradio.com
Profile: WCLU-FM is a commercial station owned by Royse Radio Inc. The format of the station is Lite Rock/Lite AC. WCLU-FM broadcasts to the Glasgow, KY area at 102.3 FM.
FM RADIO STATION

WCLV-FM 40175
Owner: WCLV Foundation, Inc.
Editorial: 1375 Euclid Ave, Idea Center, Cleveland, Ohio 44115-1826 **Tel:** 1 216 916-7140.
Email: wclv@ideastream.org
Web site: http://wclv.ideastream.org
Profile: WCLV-FM is a non-commercial station owned by WCLV Foundation, Inc. The format of the station is classical. WCLV-FM broadcasts to the Cleveland area at 104.9 FM.
FM RADIO STATION

WCLW-AM 471998
Owner: Reidsville Baptist Church
Editorial: 116 S Franklin St, Reidsville, North Carolina 27320 **Tel:** 1 336 634-1774.
Profile: WCLW-AM is a non-commercial station owned by Reidsville Baptist Church. The format of the station is Southern gospel. WCLW-AM broadcasts to the Reidsville, NC area at 1130 AM.
AM RADIO STATION

WCLY-AM 35250
Owner: Capitol Broadcasting Company
Editorial: 3100 Highwoods Blvd, Raleigh, North Carolina 27604-1033 **Tel:** 1 919 890-6101.
Web site: http://www.wralsportsfan.com/
Profile: WCLY-AM is a commercial station owned by Capitol Broadcasting Company. The format of the station is Sports. WCLY-AM broadcasts to the greater Raleigh, NC area at 1550 AM.
AM RADIO STATION

WCLZ-FM 44357
Owner: Saga Communications
Editorial: 420 Western Ave, South Portland, Maine 4106 **Tel:** 1 207 774-4561.
Web site: http://www.989wclz.com
Profile: WCLZ-FM is a commercial station owned by Saga Communications. The format of the station is adult album alternative. WCLZ-FM broadcasts to the Portland, ME area at 98.9 FM.
FM RADIO STATION

WCMC-AM 38898
Owner: Equity Communications LP
Editorial: 8025 Black Horse Pike, Pleasantville, New Jersey 08232-2900 **Tel:** 1 609 484-8444.
Web site: http://www.classicoldieswmid.com
Profile: WCMC-AM is a commercial station owned by Equity Communications LP. The format of the station is adult standards. WCMC-AM broadcasts to the Wildwood, NJ area at 1230 AM.
AM RADIO STATION

WCMC-FM 42074
Owner: Capitol Broadcasting Company
Editorial: 3100 Highwoods Blvd Ste 140, Raleigh, North Carolina 27604-1065 **Tel:** 1 919 890-6299.
Web site: http://www.espntriangle.com
Profile: WCMC-FM is a commercial station owned by Capitol Broadcasting Company. The format of the station is sports. WCMC-FM broadcasts to the Raleigh-Durham, NC, area at 99.9 FM.
FM RADIO STATION

WCMD-AM 38851
Owner: West Virgina Radio Corporation of the Alleganies
Editorial: 15 Industrial Blvd E, Cumberland, Maryland 21502-4106 **Tel:** 1 301 759-1005.
Profile: WCMD-AM is a commercial station owned by West Virgina Radio Corporation of the Allegenies. The format of the station is sports. WCMD-AM broadcasts to the Cumberland, MD area at 1230 AM.
AM RADIO STATION

WCME-AM 38001
Owner: Bleikamp (James)
Editorial: 14 Maine St, Brunswick, Maine 04011-2049 **Tel:** 1 207 798-9094.
Web site: http://www.radio9wcme.com
Profile: WCME-AM is a commercial station owned by James Bleikamp. The format of the station is local news, weather and sports. WCME-AM broadcasts to the Midcoast area of Maine at 900 AM.
AM RADIO STATION

WCMF-FM 40177
Owner: Entercom Communications Corp.
Editorial: 70 Commercial St, Rochester, New York 14614-1010 **Tel:** 1 585 423-2900.
Web site: http://www.wcmf.com
Profile: WCMF-FM is a commercial station owned by Entercom Communications Corp. The format of the station is classic rock. WCMF-FM broadcasts to the Rochester, NY area at 96.5 FM.
FM RADIO STATION

WCMG-FM 42199
Owner: Cumulus Media Inc.
Editorial: 2014 N Irby St, Florence, South Carolina 29501-1504 **Tel:** 1 843 661-5000.
Web site: http://www.magic943fm.com
Profile: WCMG-FM is a commercial station owned by Cumulus Media Inc. The format of the station is urban adult contemporary. WCMG-FM broadcasts to the Florence, SC area at 94.3 FM.
FM RADIO STATION

WCMI-AM 36320
Owner: Kindred Communications
Editorial: 401 11th St Ste 200, Huntington, West Virginia 25701-2226 **Tel:** 1 304 523-8401.
Profile: WCMI-AM is a commercial station owned by Kindred Communications. The format of the station is sports. WCMI-AM broadcasts to the Huntington, WV area at 1340 AM.
AM RADIO STATION

WCMI-FM 44515
Owner: Kindred Communications
Editorial: 401 11th St, Huntington, West Virginia 25701-2218 **Tel:** 1 304 523-8401.
Web site: http://www.planet927.com
Profile: WCMI-FM is a commercial station owned by Kindred Communications. The format of the station is rock. WCMI-FM broadcasts to the Huntington, WV area at 92.7 FM.
FM RADIO STATION

WCMJ-FM 45086
Owner: AVC Communications Inc.
Editorial: 4988 Skyline Dr, Cambridge, Ohio 43725-9729 **Tel:** 1 740 432-5605.
Email: avcnews@yourradioplace.com
Web site: http://www.yourradioplace.com
Profile: WCMJ-FM is a commercial station owned by AVC Communications Inc. The format of the station is adult contemporary music. WCMJ-FM broadcasts in the Cambridge, OH area at 96.7 FM.
FM RADIO STATION

WCMM-FM 46462
Owner: Radio Results Network
Editorial: 524 Ludington St, Ste 300, Escanaba, Michigan 49829 **Tel:** 1 906 789-9700.
Email: rrnnews@radioresultsnetwork.com
Web site: http://www.wcmmradio.com
Profile: WCMM-FM is a commercial station owned by Radio Results Network. The format of the station is contemporary country. WCMM-FM broadcasts to the Marquette, MI area at 102.5 FM.
FM RADIO STATION

WCMO-FM 40178
Owner: Marietta College
Editorial: 215 5th St, Marietta, Ohio 45750-4033 **Tel:** 1 740 376-4800.
Web site: http://w3.marietta.edu/~wcmofm/index.htm
Profile: WCMO-FM is a non-commercial college station owned by Marietta College. The format of the station is variety. WCMO-FM broadcasts to the Marietta, OH area at 98.5 FM.
FM RADIO STATION

WCMP-AM 37713
Owner: Red Rock Radio Corp.
Editorial: 15429 Pokegama Lake Rd, Pine City, Minnesota 55063-4592 **Tel:** 1 320 629-7575.
Web site: http://www.radiowcmp.com
Profile: WCMP-AM is a commercial station owned by Red Rock Radio Corp. The format of the station is adult standards music. WCMP-AM broadcasts to the Minneapolis area at 1350 AM.
AM RADIO STATION

WCMP-FM 45087
Owner: Red Rock Radio Corp.
Editorial: 15429 Pokegama Lake Rd, Pine City, Minnesota 55063-4592 **Tel:** 1 320 629-7575.
Web site: http://redrockonair.com
Profile: WCMP-FM is a commercial station owned by Red Rock Radio Corp. The format of the station is contemporary country music. WCMP-FM broadcasts to the Pine City, MN area at 100.9 FM.
FM RADIO STATION

WCMQ-FM 43401
Owner: Spanish Broadcasting System
Editorial: 7007 Nw 77Th Ave, Miami, Florida 33166-2836 **Tel:** 1 305 447-9595.
Web site: http://www.clasica92fm.com
Profile: WCMQ-FM is a commercial radio station owned by Spanish Broadcasting System. The format of the station is Spanish salsa music. WCMQ-FM broadcasts to Coral Gables, FL at 92.3 FM.
FM RADIO STATION

WCMR-AM 37714
Owner: Progressive Broadcasting
Editorial: 25802 County Road 26, Elkhart, Indiana 46517-9132 **Tel:** 1 574 875-5166.
Web site: http://solidgospel1270.com
Profile: WCMR-AM is a commercial station owned by Progressive Broadcasting. The format for the station is gospel and religious teaching. WCMR-AM broadcasts to the South Bend, IN area at 1270 AM.
AM RADIO STATION

WCMS-FM 62206
Owner: Max Radio of the Carolinas
Editorial: 103 W Wood Hill Dr Ste D-E, Nags Head, North Carolina 27959-9395 **Tel:** 1 252 480-4655.
Web site: http://www.wcms.com
Profile: WCMS-FM is a commercial station owned by Max Radio of the Carolinas. The format of the station is contemporary country. WCMS-FM broadcasts to the Nags Head, NC area at 94.5 FM.
FM RADIO STATION

WCMT-AM 37716
Owner: Thunderbolt Broadcasting Co.
Editorial: 1410 N Lindell St, Martin, Tennessee 38237-5819 **Tel:** 1 731 587-9526.
Email: newsroom@wcmt.com
Web site: http://www.wcmt.com
Profile: WCMT-AM is a commercial station owned by the Thunderbolt Broadcasting Co. The format of the station is oldies, news and talk. WCMT-AM broadcasts to the Paducah, KY; Cape Girardeau, MO; Harrisburg, IL areas at 1410 AM.
AM RADIO STATION

WCMT-FM 45089
Owner: Thunderbolt Broadcasting Co.
Editorial: 1410 N Lindell St, Martin, Tennessee 38237-5819 **Tel:** 1 731 587-9526.
Email: newsroom@wcmt.com
Web site: http://www.wcmt.com
Profile: WCMT-FM is a commercial station owned by Thunderbolt Broadcasting Co. The format of the station is adult contemporary. WCMT-FM broadcasts to the Martin, TN area at 101.3 FM.
FM RADIO STATION

WCMX-AM 36740
Owner: Twin City Baptist Temple
Editorial: 194 Electric Ave, Lunenburg, Massachusetts 01462-2214 **Tel:** 1 978 582-4901.
Web site: http://www.hope1000.com
Profile: WCMX-AM is a non-commercial station owned by Twin City Baptist Temple. The format of the station is religious programming and contemporary Christian. WCMX-AM broadcasts to the Lunenburg, MA area at 1000 AM.
AM RADIO STATION

WCMY-AM 37717
Owner: NRG Media LLC
Editorial: 216 W Lafayette St, Ottawa, Illinois 61350 **Tel:** 1 815 434-6050.
Email: info@ottawaradio.net
Web site: http://www.ottawaradio.net
Profile: WCMY-AM is commercial station owned by NRG Media LLC. The format of the station is news and talk. WCMY-AM broadcasts to the Chicago area at 1430 AM.
AM RADIO STATION

WCNA-FM 70457
Owner: Air South Radio Inc.
Editorial: 1241 Cliff Gookin Blvd, Tupelo, Mississippi 38801-6749 **Tel:** 1 662 842-7625.
Profile: WCNA-FM is a commercial station owned by Air South Radio Inc. and operated by SnyderMedia. The format of the station is Smooth AC. WCNA-FM broadcasts to the Tupelo, MS area at a frequency of 95.9 FM.
FM RADIO STATION

WCNC-AM 35253
Owner: East Carolina Radio Group
Editorial: 911 Parsonage St, Elizabeth City, North Carolina 27909 **Tel:** 1 252 335-4379.
Email: psa@ecri.net
Profile: WCNC-AM is a commercial station owned by East Carolina Radio Group. The format of the station is Hispanic. WCNC-AM broadcasts to Elizabeth City, NC at 1240 AM.
AM RADIO STATION

WCNG-FM 41745
Owner: Cherokee Broadcasting Co.
Editorial: 195 Hampton Church Rd, Murphy, North Carolina 28906-8821 **Tel:** 1 828 837-9264.
Email: murphyradio@mail.com
Profile: WCNG-FM is a commercial station owned by Cherokee Broadcasting Co. The format of the station is Lite Rock/Lite AC music. WCNG-FM broadcasts to the Chattanooga, TN area at 102.7 FM.
FM RADIO STATION

WCNI-FM 40180
Owner: Connecticut College Community Radio, Inc.
Editorial: 270 Mohegan Ave, Connecticut College, New London, Connecticut 06320-4125
Tel: 1 860 439-2853.
Email: wcni@conncoll.edu
Web site: http://www.wcniradio.org
Profile: WCNI-FM is a non-commercial station owned by Connecticut College Community Radio, Inc. The format of the station is college variety. WCNI-FM broadcasts to the New London, CT area at 90.9 FM.
FM RADIO STATION

WCNK-FM 41744
Owner: Gamma Broadcasting LLC
Editorial: 30336 Overseas Hwy, Big Pine Key, Florida 33043-3352 **Tel:** 1 305 872-9100.
Web site: http://www.conchcountry.com
Profile: WCNK-FM is a commercial station owned by Gamma Broadcasting LLC. The format of the station is country music. WCNK-FM broadcasts to the Big Pine Key, FL, area at 98.7 FM.
FM RADIO STATION

WCNL-AM 38777
Owner: Koor Communications
Editorial: 11 Main St, Newport, New Hampshire 03773-1504 **Tel:** 1 603 448-0500.
Email: info@country1010.com
Web site: http://www.country1010.com
Profile: WCNL-AM is a commercial station owned by Koor Communications. The format of the station is country. WCNL-AM broadcasts to the Newport, NH, area at 1010 AM.
AM RADIO STATION

WCNN-AM 36382
Owner: Dickey Broadcasting
Editorial: 780 Johnson Ferry Rd NE Ste 500, Atlanta, Georgia 30342-1436 **Tel:** 1 404 688-0068.
Web site: http://www.680thefan.com
Profile: WCNN-AM is a commercial station owned by Dickey Broadcasting. The format of the station is sports. WCNN-AM broadcasts to the Atlanta area at 680 AM.
AM RADIO STATION

WCNO-FM 41133
Owner: National Christian Network
Editorial: 2960 SW Mapp Rd, Palm City, Florida 34990-2737 **Tel:** 1 772 221-1100.
Email: wcno@wcno.com
Web site: http://www.wcno.com
Profile: WCNO-FM is a non-commercial station owned by the National Christian Network. The format of the station is contemporary Christian music and religious programming. WCNO-FM broadcasts to the Palm City, FL area at 89.9 FM.
FM RADIO STATION

WCNR-FM 41720
Owner: Saga Communications
Editorial: 1140 Rose Hill Dr, Charlottesville, Virginia 22903-5128 **Tel:** 1 434 220-2300.
Web site: http://www.1061thecorner.com
Profile: WCNR-FM is a commercial station owned by Saga Communications. The format of the station is adult album alternative music. WCNR-FM broadcasts to the Harrisonburg, VA area at 106.1 FM.
FM RADIO STATION

WCNS-AM 35255
Owner: Laurel Highland Total Communications, Inc. (LHTC)
Editorial: 400 Unity St, Latrobe, Pennsylvania 15650-1341 **Tel:** 1 724 537-3338.
Email: mailbox@wcnsradio.com
Web site: http://www.1480wcns.com
Profile: WCNS-AM is a commercial station owned by Laurel Highland Total Communications, Inc. (LHTC). The format of the station is news-talk. WCNS-AM broadcasts to the Latrobe, PA area at 1480 AM.
AM RADIO STATION

WCNV-FM 472283
Owner: Commonwealth Public Broadcasting
Editorial: 23 Sesame Street, Richmond, Virginia 23235 **Tel:** 1 804 320-1301.
Email: webmaster@ideastations.org
Web site: http://www.ideastations.org/radio
Profile: WCNV-FM is a non-commercial station owned by Commonwealth Public Broadcasting. The format of the station is classical, jazz music and news. WCNV-FM broadcasts to the Richmond, VA area at 89.1 FM. This station does not accept PSAs.
FM RADIO STATION

WCNW-AM 39247
Owner: Vernon R. Baldwin Inc.
Editorial: 8686 Michael Ln, Fairfield, Ohio 45014
Tel: 1 513 829-7700.
Profile: WCNW-AM is a commercial station owned by Vernon R. Baldwin Inc. The format of the station is religious and gospel music. WCNW-AM broadcasts to the Fairfield, OH area at 1560 AM.
AM RADIO STATION

WCNY-FM 40181
Owner: Public Broadcasting Council of Central New York
Editorial: 415 W Fayette St, Syracuse, New York 13204-2941 **Tel:** 1 315 453-2424.
Email: wcny.fm@wcny.org
Web site: http://www.wcny.org
Profile: WCNY-FM is a non-commercial station owned by the Public Broadcasting Council of Central New York. The format of the station is classical and jazz. WCNY-FM broadcasts to the Syracuse, NY area at 91.3 FM.
FM RADIO STATION

WCNZ-AM 37085
Owner: Almodovar Media Corporation
Editorial: 5043 Tamiami Trl E, Naples, Florida 34113-4127 **Tel:** 1 239 558-3058.
Email: info@ardienteradio.com
Web site: http://ardienteradio.com
Profile: WCNZ-AM is a commercial station owned by Almodovar Media Corporation. The format of the station is Spanish Tropical and Hispanic Urban. WCNZ-AM broadcasts to the Marco Island, FL area at 1660 AM.
AM RADIO STATION

WCOA-AM 38875
Owner: Cumulus Media Inc.
Editorial: 6565 N W St Ste 270, Pensacola, Florida 32505-1797 **Tel:** 1 850 478-6011.
Email: wcoa@cumulus.com
Web site: http://www.wcoapensacola.com
Profile: WCOA-AM is a commercial station owned by Cumulus Media Inc. The format of the station is news and talk. WCOA-AM broadcasts to the Pensacola, FL area at 1370 AM.
AM RADIO STATION

WCOD-FM 40182
Owner: iHeartMedia Inc.
Editorial: 154 Barnstable Rd, Hyannis, Massachusetts 02601-2930 **Tel:** 1 508 778-2888.
Web site: http://106wcod.iheart.com
Profile: WCOD-FM is a commercial station owned by iHeartMedia Inc.The format of the station is hot adult contemporary. WCOD-FM broadcasts to the Hyannis, MA area at 106.1 FM.
FM RADIO STATION

WCOE-FM 45090
Owner: La Porte County Broadcasting Co. Inc.
Editorial: 1700 Lincolnway Pl, Ste 8, La Porte, Indiana 46350 **Tel:** 1 219 362-5290.
Web site: http://wcoefm.com
Profile: WCOE-FM is a commercial station owned by La Porte County Broadcasting Co. Inc. The format for the station is country. WCOE-FM broadcasts to the La Porte, IN area at 96.7 FM.
FM RADIO STATION

WCOG-AM 37149
Owner: Curtis Media Group
Editorial: 875 W 5th St, Winston Salem, North Carolina 27101-2505 **Tel:** 1 336 885-2191.
Web site: http://www.triadsports.com
Profile: WCOG-AM is a commercial station owned by Curtis Media Group. The format of the station is sports. WCOG-AM broadcasts to the Winston Salem, NC area at 1320 AM.
AM RADIO STATION

WCOG-FM 133892
Owner: Family Life Ministries Inc.
Editorial: 7634 Campbell Creek Rd, Bath, New York 14810 **Tel:** 1 607 776-4151.
Email: mail@fln.org
Web site: http://www.fln.org
Profile: WCOG-FM is a non-commercial station owned by Family Life Ministries Inc. The format of the station is contemporary Christian. WCOG-FM broadcasts to the Bath, NY area at 100.7 FM.
FM RADIO STATION

WCOH-AM 37718
Owner: iHeartMedia Inc.
Editorial: 154 Boone Dr, Newnan, Georgia 30263-2801 **Tel:** 1 770 683-7234.
Web site: http://www.wcoh.com
Profile: WCOH-AM is a commercial station owned by iHeartMedia Inc. The format of the station is sports. WCOH-AM broadcasts to the Atlanta area at 1400 AM.
AM RADIO STATION

WCOH-FM 40206
Owner: Family Life Ministries Inc.
Editorial: 7634 Campbell Creek Rd, Bath, New York 14810-7612 **Tel:** 1 607 776-4151.
Email: news@fln.org
Web site: http://www.fln.org
Profile: WCOH-FM is a non-commercial station owned by Family Life Ministries Inc. The format of the station is contemporary Christian. WCOH-FM broadcasts to the Du Bois, PA area on 107.3 FM.
FM RADIO STATION

WCOJ-AM 35257
Owner: Holy Spirit Radio Foundation, Inc.
Editorial: 40 Rickert Rd, Doylestown, Pennsylvania 18901-2326 **Tel:** 1 215 345-1570.
Email: 1570am@holyspiritradio.org
Web site: http://www.holyspiritradio.org
Profile: WCOJ-AM is a commercial station owned by Holy Spirit Radio Foundation, Inc. The format of the station is Catholic programming. WCOJ-AM broadcasts to the West Chester, PA area at 1420 AM.
AM RADIO STATION

WCOK-AM 35258
Owner: Gospel Broadcasting
Tel: 1 336 372-5700.
Email: wyzdradio@yahoo.com
Profile: WCOK-AM is a commercial station owned by Gospel Broadcasting. The format of the station is gospel music. WCOK-AM broadcasts to the Sparta, NC area at 1060 AM.
AM RADIO STATION

WCOL-FM 46014
Owner: iHeartMedia Inc.
Editorial: 2323 W 5th Ave, Columbus, Ohio 43204-4899 **Tel:** 1 614 486-6101.
Web site: http://www.wcol.com
Profile: WCOL-FM is a commercial station owned by iHeartMedia Inc. The format of the station is contemporary country music. WCOL-FM broadcasts to the Columbus, OH area at 92.3 FM.
FM RADIO STATION

WCOM-FM 736801
Owner: Public Gallery of Carrboro, Inc.
Editorial: 208 E Main St, Carrboro, North Carolina 27510-2310 **Tel:** 1 919 929-9601.
Email: stationmanager@wcomfm.org
Web site: http://www.wcomfm.org
Profile: WCOM-FM is a non-commercial station owned by Public Gallery of Carrboro, Inc. The format of the station is eclectic talk and news. WCOM-FM broadcasts to the Carrboro, NC area at 103.5 FM.
FM RADIO STATION

WCON-AM 37719
Owner: Habersham Broadcasting Co.
Editorial: 540 N Main St, Cornelia, Georgia 30531-2322 **Tel:** 1 706 778-2241.
Email: wcon@windstream.net
Web site: http://www.wconfm.com
Profile: WCON-AM is a commercial station owned by the Habersham Broadcasting Co. The format of the station is adult standard and gospel music. WCON-AM broadcasts to the Atlanta area at 1450 AM.
AM RADIO STATION

WCON-FM 45092
Owner: Habersham Broadcasting Co.
Editorial: 540 Main St N, Cornelia, Georgia 30531
Tel: 1 706 778-2241.
Email: wcon@windstream.net
Web site: http://www.wconfm.com
Profile: WCON-FM is a commercial station owned by Habersham Broadcasting Co. The format of the station is country music. WCON-FM broadcasts to the Atlanta area at 99.3 FM.
FM RADIO STATION

WCOO-FM 43024
Owner: L.M. Communications Inc.
Editorial: 59 Windermere Blvd, Charleston, South Carolina 29407-7411 **Tel:** 1 843 769-4799.
Email: info@radioofcharleston.com
Web site: http://www.1055thebridge.com
Profile: WCOO-FM is a commercial station owned by L.M. Communications. The format of the station is AAA-adult album alternative. WCOO-FM broadcasts to the Charleston, SC area at 105.5 FM.
FM RADIO STATION

WCOR-AM 39229
Owner: Bay-Pointe Broadcasting Inc.
Editorial: 510 Trousdale Ferry Pike, Lebanon, Tennessee 37087 **Tel:** 1 615 449-3699.
Email: info@wantfm.com
Web site: http://www.wantfm.com
Profile: WCOR-AM is a commercial station owned by Bay-Pointe Broadcasting Inc. The format of the station is a mix of contemporary and classic country music. WCOR-AM broadcasts to the Nashville, TN area at 1490 AM.
AM RADIO STATION

WCOS-AM 37720
Owner: iHeartMedia Inc.
Editorial: 316 Greystone Blvd, Columbia, South Carolina 29210-8007 **Tel:** 1 803 343-1100.
Web site: http://www.foxsportsradio1400.com/main.html
Profile: WCOS-AM is a commercial station owned by iHeartMedia Inc. The format of the station is sports. WCOS-AM broadcasts to the Columbia, SC area at 1400 AM.
AM RADIO STATION

WCOS-FM 76219
Owner: iHeartMedia Inc.
Editorial: 316 Greystone Blvd, Columbia, South Carolina 29210-8007 **Tel:** 1 803 343-1100.
Web site: http://975wcos.iheart.com
Profile: WCOS-FM is a commercial station owned by iHeartMedia Inc. The format of the station is contemporary country. WCOS-FM broadcasts to the Columbia, SC area at 97.5 FM.
FM RADIO STATION

WCOT-FM 133890
Owner: Family Life Ministries Inc.
Editorial: 7634 Campbell Creek Rd, Bath, New York 14810 **Tel:** 1 607 776-4151.
Email: mail@fln.org
Web site: http://www.fln.org
Profile: WCOT-FM is a non-commercial station owned by Family Life Ministries Inc. The format of the station is contemporary Christian. WCOT-FM broadcasts to the Bath, NY area at 90.9 FM.
FM RADIO STATION

WCOU-FM 133891
Owner: Family Life Ministries Inc.
Editorial: 7634 Campbell Creek Rd, Bath, New York 14810-7612 **Tel:** 1 607 776-4151.
Email: mail@fln.org
Web site: http://www.fln.org
Profile: WCOU-FM is a non-commercial station owned by Family Life Ministries Inc. The format of the station is contemporary Christian. WCOU-FM broadcasts to the Bath, NY area at 88.3 FM.
FM RADIO STATION

WCOW-FM 45094
Owner: Sparta-Tomah Broadcasting Co.
Editorial: 113 W Oak St, Sparta, Wisconsin 54656
Tel: 1 608 269-3100.
Email: newsdirector@cow97.com
Web site: http://www.cow97.com
Profile: WCOW-FM is a commercial station owned by Sparta-Tomah Broadcasting Co. The format of the station is contemporary country. WCOW-FM broadcasts in the Sparta, WI area at 97.1 FM.
FM RADIO STATION

WCOX-FM 133896
Owner: Family Life Ministries Inc.
Editorial: 7634 County Route 14, Bath, New York 14810-7612 **Tel:** 1 607 776-4151.
Email: news@fln.org
Web site: http://www.fln.org
Profile: WCOX-FM is a non-commercial station owned by Family Life Ministries Inc. The format of the station is contemporary Christian. WCOX-FM broadcasts to the Bath, NY area at 90.1 FM.
FM RADIO STATION

WCOY-FM 45462
Owner: Staradio Corp.
Editorial: 329 Maine St, 1st Fl, Quincy, Illinois 62301
Tel: 1 217 224-4102.
Email: wcoy@staradio.com
Web site: http://www.wcoy.com
FM RADIO STATION

WCPA-AM 39009
Owner: First Media Radio LLC
Editorial: 801 E Dubois Ave, Du Bois, Pennsylvania 15801-3643 **Tel:** 1 814 371-8300.
Email: q102radio@comcast.net
Profile: WCPA-AM is a commercial station owned by First Media Radio LLC. The format of the station is oldies music. WCPA-AM broadcasts to the Clearfield, PA area at 900 AM.
AM RADIO STATION

WCPC-AM 35864
Owner: Wilkins Communication Networks Inc.
Editorial: 1189 N Jackson St, Houston, Mississippi 38851-8273 **Tel:** 1 662 456-3071.
Email: wcpc@wilkinsradio.com
Web site: http://www.wilkinsradio.com
Profile: WCPC-AM is a commercial station owned by Wilkins Communication Networks Inc. and licensed to Cajun Radio Corporation. The format of the station is religious, gospel and talk. WCPC-AM broadcasts to the Houston, MS area at 940 AM.
AM RADIO STATION

WCPH-AM 36239
Owner: George C. Hudson, III
Editorial: 202 9th St, Etowah, Tennessee 37331-1343
Tel: 1 423 263-5555.
Email: wcphradio@yahoo.com
Profile: WCPH-AM is a commercial station owned by George C. Hudson, III. The format of the station is oldies. WCPH-AM broadcasts to the Chattanooga, TN area at 1220 AM.
AM RADIO STATION

WCPL-FM 937858
Owner: Crawford(David)
Editorial: 140 Magnolia Ave, Merritt Island, Florida 32952-4816
Email: wcplfm@yahoo.com
Web site: http://www.wcplfm.com/
Profile: WCPL-FM is a low-power station owned by David Crawford. The format is Christian Music. WCPL-FM broadcasts in Merrit Island at 95.5 FM.
FM RADIO STATION

WCPM-AM 39491
Owner: Cumberland City Broadcasting, Inc.
Editorial: 101 Keller St, Cumberland, Kentucky 40823
Tel: 1 606 589-4623.
Web site: http://www.wcpmradio.com
Profile: WCPM-AM is a commercial station owned by Cumberland City Broadcasting, Inc. The format of the station is contemporary country music. WCPM-AM broadcasts to the Cumberland, KY area at 1280 AM.
AM RADIO STATION

WCPN-FM 41050
Owner: ideastream
Editorial: 1375 Euclid Ave, Cleveland, Ohio 44115-1844 **Tel:** 1 216 916-6100.
Email: comments@wcpn.org
Web site: http://wcpn.ideastream.org
Profile: WCPN-FM is a non-commercial station owned by ideastream. The format of the station is news, talk and jazz music. WCPN-FM broadcasts to the Cleveland area at 90.3 FM.
FM RADIO STATION

WCPQ-FM 42138
Owner: Newsweb Corp.
Editorial: 6012 S Pulaski Rd, Chicago, Illinois 60629-4538 **Tel:** 1 773 767-1000.
Web site: http://www.chicagoprogressivetalk.com
Profile: WCPQ-FM is a commercial station owned by Newsweb Corp. The format of the station is liberal talk and dance music. WCPQ-FM broadcasts to the southern section of the Chicago metro area at 99.9 FM.
FM RADIO STATION

WCPR-FM 43157
Owner: Alpha Media
Editorial: 1909 E Pass Rd, Gulfport, Mississippi 39507-3779 **Tel:** 1 228 388-2001.
Web site: http://www.979cprrocks.com
Profile: WCPR-FM is a commercial station owned by Alpha Media. The format of the station is rock. WCPR-FM broadcasts to the Biloxi-Gulfport, MS area at 97.9 FM.
FM RADIO STATION

WCPS-AM 36092
Owner: Johnson Broadcast Ventures
Editorial: 1406 Saint Andrew St, Tarboro, North Carolina 27886-2532 **Tel:** 1 252 824-7878.
Profile: WCPS-AM is a commercial station owned by Johnson Broadcast Ventures. The format of the station is gospel and urban oldies music. WCPS-AM broadcasts to the Rocky Mount, NC area at 760 AM.
AM RADIO STATION

WCPT-AM 37632
Owner: Newsweb Corp.
Editorial: 5475 N Milwaukee Ave, Chicago, Illinois 60630-1249 **Tel:** 1 773 792-0400.
Web site: http://www.wcpt820.com
Profile: WCPT-AM is a commercial station owned by Newsweb Corp. The format of the station is talk. WCPT-AM broadcasts during daytime hours only to Crystal Lake, IL and the northern sections of the Chicago metro area at 820 AM.
AM RADIO STATION

WCPT-FM 44327
Owner: Newsweb Corp.
Editorial: 6012 S Pulaski Rd, Chicago, Illinois 60629-4538 **Tel:** 1 773 767-1000.
Web site: http://www.wcpt820.com
Profile: WCPT-FM is a commercial station owned by Newsweb Corp. The format of the station is liberal talk and dance music. WCPT-FM broadcasts to the Chicago area at 92.5 FM.
FM RADIO STATION

WCPV-FM 43431
Owner: Vox Communications
Editorial: 265 Hegeman Ave, Colchester, Vermont 05446-3174 **Tel:** 1 802 655-0093.
Web site: http://www.1013espn.com/
Profile: WCPV-FM is a commercial station owned by Vox Communications. The format is classic rock. The station broadcasts to the Colchester, VT area at 101.3 FM.
FM RADIO STATION

WCPY-FM 40717
Owner: Newsweb Corp.
Editorial: 5475 N Milwaukee Ave, Chicago, Illinois 60630-1249 **Tel:** 1 773 792-0400.
Web site: http://www.chicagoprogressivetalk.com
Profile: WCPY-FM is a commercial station owned by Newsweb Corp. The format of the station is liberal talk and dance music. WCPY-FM broadcasts to the Arlington Heights, IL area and northwest suburbs of Chicago at 106.3 FM.
FM RADIO STATION

WCPZ-FM 45095
Owner: BAS Broadcasting
Editorial: 1640 Cleveland Rd, Sandusky, Ohio 44870-4357 **Tel:** 1 419 625-1010.
Web site: http://www.mix1027.com
Profile: WCPZ-FM is a commercial station owned by BAS Broadcasting. The format of the station is hot adult contemporary music. WCPZ-FM broadcasts to the Cleveland area at 102.7 FM.
FM RADIO STATION

WCQL-FM 45716
Owner: Regional Radio Group
Editorial: 238 Bay Rd, Queensbury, New York 12804-2006 **Tel:** 1 518 761-9890.
Web site: http://www.radiowins.com
Profile: WCQL-FM is a commercial station owned by Regional Radio Group. The format of the station is hot adult contemporary. WCQL-FM broadcasts to the Glens Falls, NY area at 95.9 FM.
FM RADIO STATION

WCQM-FM 46067
Owner: Heartland Communications Group, LLC
Editorial: 1329 4th Ave S, Park Falls, Wisconsin 54552-1926 **Tel:** 1 715 762-3221.
Email: wcqm@pctcnet.net
Web site: http://www.wcqm.com
Profile: WCQM-FM is a commercial station owned by Heartland Communications Group, LLC. The format of the station is contemporary country music. WCQM-FM broadcasts in the Park Falls, WI area at 98.3 FM.
FM RADIO STATION

WCQR-FM 43261
Owner: Positive Alternative Radio
Editorial: 2312 Oak St, Gray, Tennessee 37615
Tel: 1 423 477-5676.
Email: office@wcqr.org
Web site: http://www.wcqr.org
Profile: WCQR-FM is a non-commercial station owned by Positive Alternative Radio. The format of the station is Christian programming. WCQR-FM broadcasts to the Gray, TN area at 88.3 FM
FM RADIO STATION

WCQS-FM 40184
Owner: Western North Carolina Public Radio Inc.
Editorial: 73 Broadway St, Asheville, North Carolina 28801-2919 **Tel:** 1 828 210-4800.
Email: info@wcqs.org
Web site: http://www.wcqs.org
Profile: WCQS-FM is a non-commercial station owned by Western North Carolina Public Radio Inc. The format of the station is talk and classical and jazz music. WCQS-FM broadcasts to the Asheville, NC area at 88.1 FM.
FM RADIO STATION

WCRA-AM 37722
Owner: Cromwell Group Inc.(The)
Editorial: 405 S Banker St, Ste 201, Effingham, Illinois 62401 **Tel:** 1 217 342-4141.
Email: wcrc@wcrc957.com
Web site: http://www.wcra1090.com
Profile: WCRA-AM is a commercial station owned by The Cromwell Group Inc. The format of the station is news and talk. WCRA-AM broadcasts in the Effingham, IL area at 1090 AM.
AM RADIO STATION

WCRC-FM 45096
Owner: Cromwell Group Inc.(The)
Editorial: 405 S Banker St, Ste 201, Effingham, Illinois 62401 **Tel:** 1 217 342-4141.
Email: wcrc@wcrc957.com
Web site: http://www.wcrc957.com
Profile: WCRC-FM is a commercial station owned by The Cromwell Group Inc. The format of the station is country music. WCRC-FM broadcasts to the Effingham, IL area at 95.7 FM.
FM RADIO STATION

WCRE-AM 35259
Owner: Pee Dee Broadcasting LLC
Editorial: 541 Highway 1 S, Cheraw, South Carolina 29520-3811 **Tel:** 1 843 537-7887.
Profile: WCRE-AM is a commercial station owned by Pee Dee Broadcasting LLC. The format for the station is oldies. WCRE-AM broadcasts to the Charlotte, NC area at 1420 AM.
AM RADIO STATION

WCRF-FM 40186
Owner: Moody Bible Institute
Editorial: 9756 Barr Rd, Cleveland, Ohio 44141
Tel: 1 440 526-1111.
Email: wcrf@moody.edu
Web site: http://www.moodyradiocleveland.fm
Profile: WCRF-FM is a commercial station owned by Moody Bible Institute. The format of the station is religious. WCRF-FM broadcasts in the Cleveland area at 103.3 FM.
FM RADIO STATION

WCRI-FM 44063
Editorial: 400 S County Trl Ste A105, Exeter, Rhode Island 02822-3539 **Tel:** 1 401 294-9274.
Email: wcri@classical959.com
Web site: http://classical959.com
Profile: WCRI-FM is a commercial station. The format of the station is oldies. WCRI-FM broadcasts to the Providence, RI area at 95.9 FM.
FM RADIO STATION

WCRJ-FM 44507
Owner: K Love
Editorial: 4190 Belfort Rd Ste 450, Jacksonville, Florida 32216-1405 **Tel:** 1 904 641-9626.
Email: klove@klove.com
Web site: http://www.klove.com
Profile: WCRJ-FM is a non-commercial station owned by Delmarva Educational Association. The format of the station is contemporary Christian music. WCRJ-FM broadcasts to the Jacksonville, FL area at 88.1 FM.
FM RADIO STATION

WCRK-AM 35260
Owner: Radio Acquisition Corp.
Editorial: 510 Economy Road, Morristown, Tennessee 37814 **Tel:** 1 423 586-9101.
Email: wcrk@lcs.net
Web site: http://www.wcrk.com
Profile: WCRK-AM is commercial station owned by the Radio Acquisition Corp. The format of the station is classic hits. WCRK-AM broadcasts to the Morristown, TN area at 1150 AM.
AM RADIO STATION

WCRL-AM 37723
Owner: Blount County Broadcasting
Editorial: 908 2nd Ave E, Oneonta, Alabama 35121-2506
Web site: http://www.classichits953.com
Profile: WCRL-AM is a commercial station owned by Blount County Broadcasting. The format of the station is adult standards music. WCRL-AM broadcasts to the Birmingham, Al area at 1570 AM.
AM RADIO STATION

WCRN-AM 36863
Owner: Carter Broadcasting
Editorial: 276 Turnpike Rd, Westborough, Massachusetts 01581-2857 **Tel:** 1 508 871-7000.
Web site: http://www.wcrnradio.com
Profile: WCRN-AM is a commercial station owned by Carter Broadcasting. The format of the station is talk. WCRN-AM broadcasts to the Boston area at 830 AM.
AM RADIO STATION

WCRQ-FM 43432
Owner: WQDY Inc.
Editorial: 637 Main St, Calais, Maine 4619
Tel: 1 207 454-7545.
Email: wqdy@wqdy.fm
Web site: http://www.wcrqfm.com
Profile: WCRQ-FM is a commercial station owned by WQDY Inc. The format for the station is hot adult contemporary. WCRQ-FM broadcasts to the Calais, ME area at 102.9 FM.
FM RADIO STATION

WCRS-AM 37724
Owner: Anne's Entertainment Vision, Inc.
Editorial: 1220 Bypass 72 NE, Greenwood, South Carolina 29649-2205 **Tel:** 1 864 229-7984.
Web site: http://wlmawcrsradio.com
Profile: WCRS-AM is a commercial station owned by Anne's Entertainment Vision, Inc. The format of the station is variety and talk. WCRS-AM broadcasts to the Greenwood, SC area at 1450 AM.
AM RADIO STATION

WCRT-AM 38837
Owner: Bott Broadcasting Co.
Editorial: 15 Century Blvd Ste 101, Nashville, Tennessee 37214-3692 **Tel:** 1 615 871-1160.
Web site: http://www.bottradionetwork.com
Profile: WCRT-AM is a commercial station owned by Bott Broadcasting Co. The format of the station is Christian talk. WCRT-AM broadcasts to the Nashville, TN, area at 1160 AM.
AM RADIO STATION

WCRU-AM 35143
Owner: Truth Broadcasting
Editorial: 4405 Providence Ln Ste D, Winston Salem, North Carolina 27106-3226 **Tel:** 1 336 759-0363.
Email: info@truthnetwork.com
Web site: http://www.truthnetwork.com/
Profile: WCRU-AM is a commercial station owned by Truth Broadcasting. The format of the station is religion. WCRU-AM broadcasts to Charlotte-Gastonia, NC area at 960 AM.
AM RADIO STATION

WCRV-AM 35262
Owner: Bott Broadcasting Co.
Editorial: 6401 Poplar Ave Ste 640, Memphis, Tennessee 38119-4808 **Tel:** 1 901 763-4640.
Web site: http://www.bottradionetwork.com/stations/tennessee/memphis
Profile: WCRV-AM is a commercial station owned by Bott Broadcasting Co. The format of the station is religious and Christian programming. WCRV-AM broadcasts to the Memphis, TN area at 640 AM.
AM RADIO STATION

WCRX-FM 40189
Owner: Columbia College
Editorial: 33 E Congress Pkwy Ste 700, Chicago, Illinois 60605-1223 **Tel:** 1 312 663-3512.
Email: WCRXDJ@colum.edu
Web site: http://www.wcrx.net
Profile: WCRX-FM is a non-commercial college station owned by Columbia College. The format of the station is variety programming. WCRX-FM broadcasts to the Chicago area at 88.1 FM.
FM RADIO STATION

WCRZ-FM 41396
Owner: Townsquare Media, LLC
Editorial: 3338 E Bristol Rd, Burton, Michigan 48529-1408 **Tel:** 1 810 743-1080.
Web site: http://www.wcrz.com
Profile: WCRZ-FM is a commercial station owned by Townsquare Media, LLC. The format of the station is adult contemporary. WCRZ-FM broadcasts to the Burton, MI area at 107.9 FM.
FM RADIO STATION

WCSF-FM 41474
Owner: College of St. Francis
Editorial: 500 Wilcox St, Joliet, Illinois 60435-6169
Tel: 1 800 735-1500.
Email: wcsf@stfrancis.edu
Web site: http://www.stfrancis.edu/theedge
Profile: WCSF-FM is a non-commercial station college station owned by the College of St. Francis. The format of the station is rock alternative. WCSF-FM broadcasts to the Joliet, IL area at 88.7 FM.
FM RADIO STATION

WCSG-FM 40191
Owner: Cornerstone Communications
Editorial: 1159 E Beltline Ave NE, Grand Rapids, Michigan 49525-5805 **Tel:** 1 616 942-1500.
Web site: http://www.wcsg.org
Profile: WCSG-FM is a non-commercial station owned by Cornerstone Communications. The format of the station is contemporary Christian. WCSG-FM broadcasts to the Grand Rapids, MI area at 91.3 FM.
FM RADIO STATION

WCSI-AM 37725
Owner: White River Broadcasting Co., Inc.
Editorial: 3212 Washington St, Columbus, Indiana 47203-1505 **Tel:** 1 812 372-4448.
Email: news@1010wcsi.com
Web site: http://1010wcsi.com/
Profile: WCSI-AM is a commercial station owned by White River Broadcasting Co., Inc. The format of the station is news, sports and talk. WCSI-AM broadcasts to the Columbus, IN area at 1010 AM.
AM RADIO STATION

WCSJ-AM 217517
Owner: Nelson Multimedia
Editorial: 219 W Washington St, Morris, Illinois 60450-2146 **Tel:** 1 815 941-1000.
Email: wcsj-news@nelsonmultimedia.com
Web site: http://www.wcsjfm.com
Profile: WCSJ-AM is a commercial station owned by Nelson Multimedia. The format of the station is classic hits. WCSJ-AM is a simulcast of WCSJ-FM broadcasts to the Morris, IL area at 1550 AM.
AM RADIO STATION

WCSJ-FM 36643
Owner: Nelson Multimedia
Editorial: 219 W Washington St, Morris, Illinois 60450-2146 **Tel:** 1 815 941-1000.
Email: justin.ritz@nelsonmultimedia.com
Web site: http://www.wcsjfm.com
Profile: WCSJ-FM is a commercial station owned by Nelson Multimedia. The format of the station is classic hits. WCSJ-FM broadcasts in the Morris, IL area at 103.1 FM and is simulcast on 1550 WCSJ-AM.
FM RADIO STATION

WCSL-AM 35263
Owner: KTC Broadcasting
Editorial: 1416 Shelby Hwy, Cherryville, North Carolina 28021-8356 **Tel:** 1 704 435-2844.
Web site: http://ktcbroadcasting.com
Profile: WCSL-AM is a commercial station owned by KTC Broadcasting. The format of the station is classic country. WCSL-AM broadcasts to the Charlotte, NC area at 1590 AM.
AM RADIO STATION

WCSM-AM 37726
Owner: Hayco Broadcasting
Editorial: 6458 Meyer Rd, Celina, Ohio 45822
Tel: 1 419 586-5134.
Email: wcsm@bright.net
Web site: http://www.wcsmradio.com
Profile: WCSM-AM is a commercial station owned by Hayco Broadcasting. The format of the station is news, talk and adult standards. WCSM-AM broadcasts to the Celina, OH area at 1350 AM.
AM RADIO STATION

WCSM-FM 45097
Owner: Hayco Broadcasting
Editorial: 6458 Meyer Rd, Celina, Ohio 45822
Tel: 1 419 586-5134.
Email: wcsm@bright.net
Web site: http://www.wcsmradio.com
Profile: WCSM-FM is a commercial station owned by Hayco Broadcasting. The format of the station is adult contemporary. WCSM-FM broadcasts in the Celina, OH area at 96.7 FM.
FM RADIO STATION

WCSN-FM 4350
Owner: Gulf Coast Broadcasting Company, Inc.
Editorial: 2421 E 2nd St, Gulf Shores, Alabama 36542-3177 **Tel:** 1 251 967-1057.
Email: sunny1057@gulftel.com
Web site: http://www.sunny1057.com
Profile: WCSN-FM is a commercial station owned by Gulf Coast Broadcasting Company, Inc. The format for the station is adult contemporary. WCSN-FM broadcasts to the Mobile, AL area at 105.7 FM.
FM RADIO STATION

WCSP-FM 4021
Owner: C-SPAN
Editorial: 400 N Capitol St NW, Ste 650, Washington, District Of Columbia 20001 **Tel:** 1 202 737-3220.
Email: radio@c-span.org
Web site: http://www.c-span.org
Profile: WCSP-FM is a non-commercial station owned by C-SPAN. The format of the stataion is news and talk. WSCP-FM broadcasts to the Washington area at 90.1 FM.
FM RADIO STATION

WCSR-AM 3772
Owner: WCSR Inc.
Editorial: 170 N West St, Hillsdale, Michigan 49242-1224 **Tel:** 1 517 437-4444.
Email: wcsrinc@gmail.com
Web site: http://www.radiohillsdale.com
Profile: WCSR-AM is a commercial station owned by WCSR Inc. The format of the station is adult contemporary. WCSR-AM broadcasts to the Hillsdale, MI area at 1340 AM.
AM RADIO STATION

WCSR-FM 45098
Owner: WCSR Inc.
Editorial: 170 N West St, Hillsdale, Michigan 49242-1224 Tel: 1 517 437-4444.
Email: wcsrinc@gmail.com
Web site: http://www.radiohillsdale.com
Profile: WCSR-FM is a commercial station owned by WCSR Inc. The format of the station is adult contemporary music. WCSR-FM broadcasts to the Hillsdale, MI area at 92.1 FM
FM RADIO STATION

WCSS-AM 36683
Owner: Cranesville Block
Editorial: 1250 Riverfront Ctr, Amsterdam, New York 12010-4602 Tel: 1 518 684-6000.
Email: wcss@cranesville.com
Web site: http://www.wcss1490.com
Profile: WCSS-AM is a commercial station owned by Cranesville Block. The format of the station is classic hits. WCSS-AM broadcasts to the Amsterdam, NY area at 1490 AM.
AM RADIO STATION

WCST-AM 39297
Owner: Capper Broadcasting Company
Editorial: 440 Radio Station Ln, Berkeley Springs, West Virginia 25411-4273 Tel: 1 304 258-1010.
Email: c929@comcast.net
Profile: WCST-AM is a commercial station owned by Capper Broadcasting Company. The format of the station is news and talk. WCST-AM broadcasts in the Berkeley Springs, WV area at 1010 AM.
AM RADIO STATION

WCSV-AM 235298
Owner: Peg Broadcasting Crossville, LLC
Editorial: 961 Miller Ave, Crossville, Tennessee 38555-4359 Tel: 1 931 707-1102.
Email: production.crossville@pegbroadcasting.com
Web site: http://www.977theticket.com/
Profile: WCSV-AM is a commercial station owned by Peg Broadcasting Crossville, LLC. The format of the station is sports. WCSV-AM broadcasts to the Crossville, TN area at 1490 AM.
AM RADIO STATION

WCSW-AM 37728
Owner: Zoe Communications Inc.
Editorial: 345 Highway 63 S, Shell Lake, Wisconsin 54871 Tel: 1 715 468-9500.
Web site: http://www.wcsw.com
Profile: WCSW-AM is a commercial station owned by Zoe Communications Inc. The format of the station is talk. WCSW-AM broadcasts in the Shell Lake, WI area at 940 AM.
AM RADIO STATION

WCSX-FM 43277
Owner: Beasley Broadcast Group
Editorial: 1 Radio Plaza St, Ferndale, Michigan 48220-2140 Tel: 1 248 398-9470.
Email: feedback@wcsx.com
Web site: http://www.wcsx.com
Profile: WCSX-FM is a commercial station owned by Beasley Broadcast Group. The format of the station is classic rock. WCSX-FM broadcasts to the Detroit area at 94.7 FM.
FM RADIO STATION

WCSY-FM 43896
Owner: Midwest Family Broadcasting
Editorial: 602 Broadway St, South Haven, Michigan 49090-1926 Tel: 1 269 925-1111.
Email: wsjm@wsjm.com
Web site: http://www.wcsy.com
Profile: WCSY-FM is a commercial station owned by Midwest Family Broadcasting. The format of the station is oldies. WCSY-FM broadcasts to the Benton Harbor, MI area at 103.7 FM.
FM RADIO STATION

WCTB-FM 42362
Owner: Mountain Wireless Corp.
Editorial: 208 Middle Rd, Skowhegan, Maine 4976 Tel: 1 207 474-5171.
Email: mix1079@gmail.com
Web site: http://www.935trueoldies.com
Profile: WCTB-FM is a commercial station owned by Mountain Wireless Corp. The format of the station is oldies. WCTB-FM broadcasts to the Skowhegan, ME area at 93.5 FM.
FM RADIO STATION

WCTC-AM 38742
Owner: Beasley Broadcast Group
Editorial: 78 Veronica Ave, Somerset, New Jersey 08873-3417 Tel: 1 732 249-2600.
Web site: http://www.wctcam.com
Profile: WCTC-AM is a commercial station owned by Beasley Broadcast Group. The format of the station is Talk. WCTC-AM broadcasts throughout the central New Jersey area at 1450 AM.
AM RADIO STATION

WCTF-AM 35978
Owner: Family Stations Inc.
Editorial: 45 1/2 East St, Vernon, Connecticut 06066-3847 Tel: 1 860 871-2526.
Web site: http://www.familyradio.com
AM RADIO STATION

WCTG-FM 355511
Owner: Sebago Broadcasting
Editorial: 6455 Maddox Blvd Ste 3, Chincoteague, Virginia 23336-2272 Tel: 1 757 336-1118.
Email: studio@965ctg.com

Web site: http://965ctg.com
Profile: WCTG-FM is a commercial station owned by Sebago Broadcasting. The format for the station is adult hits. WCTG-FM broadcasts to the Norfolk, VA area at 96.5 FM.
FM RADIO STATION

WCTH-FM 40875
Owner: Florida Keys Media, LLC
Editorial: 93351 Overseas Hwy Ste 2, Tavernier, Florida 33070-2800 Tel: 1 305 852-9085.
Web site: http://thundercountry.com/
Profile: WCTH-FM is a commercial station owned by Florida Keys Media, LLC. The format of the station is contemporary country. WCTH-FM broadcasts to the Tavernier, FL area at 100.3 FM.
FM RADIO STATION

WCTK-FM 42795
Owner: Hall Communications
Editorial: 75 Oxford St, Providence, Rhode Island 02905-4722 Tel: 1 401 467-4366.
Email: mail@wctk.com
Web site: http://www.wctk.com
Profile: WCTK-FM is a commercial station owned by Hall Communications. The format of the station is contemporary country music. WCTK-FM broadcasts to the Providence, RI-New Bedford, MA area at 98.1 FM.
FM RADIO STATION

WCTL-FM 40193
Owner: Inspiration Time Inc.
Editorial: 10912 Route 19 N, Waterford, Pennsylvania 16441-5108 Tel: 1 814 796-6000.
Email: wctl@wctl.org
Web site: http://www.wctl.org
Profile: WCTL-FM is a commercial station owned by Inspiration Time Inc. The format of the station is contemporary Christian music. WCTL-FM broadcasts to the Erie, PA area at 106.3 FM.
FM RADIO STATION

WCTO-FM 44257
Owner: Cumulus Media Inc.
Editorial: 2158 Avenue C, Ste 100, Bethlehem, Pennsylvania 18017-2148 Tel: 1 610 266-7600.
Email: cat.studio@cumulus.com
Web site: http://www.catcountry96.fm
Profile: WCTO-FM is a commercial station owned by Cumulus Media Inc. The format of the station is country. WCTO-FM broadcasts to the Bethlehem, PA area at 96.1 FM.
FM RADIO STATION

WCTQ-FM 44549
Owner: iHeartMedia Inc.
Editorial: 1779 Independence Blvd, Sarasota, Florida 34234-2106 Tel: 1 941 552-4800.
Web site: http://www.921thecoast.com
Profile: WCTQ-FM is a commercial station owned by iHeartMedia Inc. The format of the station is country. WCTQ-FM broadcasts to the Sarasota, FL area at 92.1 FM.
FM RADIO STATION

WCTR-AM 35266
Owner: WCTR Broadcasting, LLC
Editorial: 231 Flatland Rd, Chestertown, Maryland 21620-3359 Tel: 1 410 778-1530.
Email: info@wctr.com
Web site: http://www.wctr.com
Profile: WCTR-AM is a commercial station owned by WCTR Broadcasting, LLC. The format of the station is talk. WCTR-AM broadcasts in the Chestertown, MD area at 1530 AM.
AM RADIO STATION

WCTS-AM 35526
Owner: Central Baptist Theological Seminary
Editorial: 900 Forestview Ln N, Minneapolis, Minnesota 55441-5934 Tel: 1 763 417-8270.
Email: wcts@centralseminary.edu
Web site: http://www.wctsradio.com
Profile: WCTS-AM is a non-commercial station owned by Central Baptist Theological Seminary. The format of the station is Christian music and talk. WCTS-AM broadcasts in the Plymouth, MN area at 1030 AM.
AM RADIO STATION

WCTT-AM 37730
Owner: Eubanks Broadcasting Inc.
Editorial: 821 Adams Rd, Corbin, Kentucky 40701-4708 Tel: 1 606 528-4717.
Email: traffic@wctt.com
Web site: http://t1073.com
Profile: WCTT-AM is a commercial station owned by Eubanks Broadcasting Inc. The format of the station is adult standards music and talk programming. WCTT-AM broadcasts to the Lexington, KY area at 680 AM.
AM RADIO STATION

WCTT-FM 45101
Owner: Encore Communications, Inc.
Editorial: 821 Adams Rd, Corbin, Kentucky 40701-4708 Tel: 1 606 528-4717.
Email: traffic@wctt.com
Profile: WCTT-FM is a commercial station owned by Encore Communications, Inc. The format of the station is rock music. WCTT-FM broadcasts to the Corbin, KY area at 107.3 FM.
FM RADIO STATION

WCTW-FM 46218
Owner: iHeartMedia Inc.
Editorial: 5620 State Route 9G, Hudson, New York 12534-4127 Tel: 1 518 828-5006.
Web site: http://www.985thecat.com
Profile: WCTW-FM is a commercial station owned by iHeartMedia Inc. The format of the station is hot AC. WCTW-FM broadcasts to the Hudson, NY area at 98.5 FM.
FM RADIO STATION

WCTY-FM 45102
Owner: Hall Communications
Editorial: 40 Cuprak Rd, Norwich, Connecticut 06360-2008 Tel: 1 860 887-3511.
Email: community@wcty.com
Web site: http://www.wcty.com
Profile: WCTY-FM is a commercial station owned by Hall Communications. The format of the station is country music. WCTY-FM broadcasts to the Hartford-New Haven, CT area at 97.7 FM.
FM RADIO STATION

WCUB-AM 38833
Owner: Cub Radio Inc.
Editorial: 1915 Mirro Dr, Manitowoc, Wisconsin 54220 Tel: 1 920 683-6800.
Web site: http://www.cubradio.com
Profile: WCUB-AM is a commercial station owned by Cub Radio Inc. The format of the station is country music. WCUB-AM broadcasts to the Manitowoc, WI area at 980 AM.
AM RADIO STATION

WCUE-AM 36078
Owner: Family Stations Inc.
Editorial: 4075 Bellaire Ln, Peninsula, Ohio 44264-9786 Tel: 1 510 568-6200.
Web site: http://www.familyradio.com
Profile: WCUE-AM is a non-commercial station owned by Family Stations Inc. The format of the station is religious. WCUE-AM broadcasts to the Cleveland area at 1150 AM.
AM RADIO STATION

WCUM-AM 35977
Owner: Radio Cumbre Broadcasting Inc.
Editorial: 240 Fairfield Ave Floor 2, Bridgeport, Connecticut 06604-4256 Tel: 1 203 335-1450.
Email: info@radiocumbre.am
Web site: http://www.radiocumbre.am
Profile: WCUM-AM is a commercial station owned by Radio Cumbre Broadcasting Inc. The format of the station is Hispanic programming. WCUM-AM broadcasts to the Bridgeport, CT area at 1450 AM.
AM RADIO STATION

WCUP-FM 42734
Owner: Keweenaw Bay Indian Community
Editorial: 805 US41 South, Ste B, Baraga, Michigan 49908 Tel: 1 906 353-9287.
Email: eagleadmin@up.net
Web site: http://www.keepitintheup.com
Profile: WCUP-FM is a commercial station owned and operated by the Keweenaw Bay Indian Community. The format of the station is contemporary country. WCUP-FM broadcasts to the L'Anse, Michigan area at a frequency of 105.7 FM.
FM RADIO STATION

WCUW-FM 40195
Owner: WCUW Inc.
Editorial: 910 Main St, Worcester, Massachusetts 01610-1433 Tel: 1 508 753-1012.
Email: wcuw@wcuw.org
Web site: http://www.wcuw.org
Profile: WCUW-FM is a non-commercial station owned by WCUW Inc. The format of the station is variety. WCUW-FM broadcasts to the Worcester, MA area at 91.3 FM.
FM RADIO STATION

WCVA-AM 38907
Owner: Piedmont Communications Inc.
Editorial: 207 Spicers Mill Rd, Orange, Virginia 22960 Tel: 1 540 825-3900.
Email: traffic@wjmafm.com
Profile: WCVA-AM is a commercial station owned by Piedmont Communications Inc. The format of the station is adult standards music. WCVA-AM broadcasts to the Orange, VA at 1490 AM.
AM RADIO STATION

WCVC-AM 35268
Owner: La Promesa Foundation
Editorial: 117 1/2 Henderson Rd, Tallahassee, Florida 32312-2337 Tel: 1 888 784-3476.
Email: grnonline@grnonline.com
Web site: http://grnonline.com/
Profile: WCVC-AM is a commercial station owned by La Promesa Foundation. The format of the station is Catholic programming. WCVC-AM broadcasts to the Tallahassee, FL area at 1330 AM.
AM RADIO STATION

WCVE-FM 41052
Owner: Commonwealth Public Broadcasting
Editorial: 23 Sesame St, Richmond, Virginia 23235 Tel: 1 804 320-1301.
Email: webmaster@ideastations.org
Web site: http://www.ideastations.org
Profile: WCVE-FM is a non-commercial station owned by Commonwealth Public Broadcasting. The format of the station is classical and jazz music and news. WCVE-FM broadcasts to the Richmond, VA area at 88.9 FM. This station does not accept PSAs.
FM RADIO STATION

WCVG-AM 36121
Owner: Great Lakes Radio LLC
Editorial: 135 W 38th St, Covington, Kentucky 41015-1421 Tel: 1 859 291-2255.
Web site: http://www.gospel1320.com
Profile: WCVG-AM is a commercial station owned by Great Lakes Radio LLC. The format of the station is gospel. WCVG-AM broadcasts to the Covington, KY area at 1320 AM.
AM RADIO STATION

WCVK-FM 41221
Owner: Bowling Green Community Broadcasting
Editorial: 1407 Scottsville Rd, Bowling Green, Kentucky 42104-2433 Tel: 1 270 781-7326.
Email: wcvk@christianfamilyradio.com
Web site: http://www.christianfamilyradio.com
Profile: WCVK-FM is a non-commercial station owned by Bowling Green Community Broadcasting. The format of the station is contemporary Christian. WCVK-FM broadcasts to the Bowling Green, KY area at 90.7 FM.
FM RADIO STATION

WCVL-AM 38364
Owner: Forcht Broadcasting
Editorial: 1757 N 175 W, Crawfordsville, Indiana 47933 Tel: 1 765 362-8200.
Web site: http://www.crawfordsvilleradio.com
Profile: WCVL-AM is a commercial station owned by Forcht Broadcasting. The format of the station is oldies. WCVL-AM broadcasts to the Crawfordsville, IN area at 1550 AM.
AM RADIO STATION

WCVL-FM 42366
Owner: Saga Communications Inc.
Editorial: 1140 Rose Hill Dr, Charlottesville, Virginia 22903-5128 Tel: 1 434 220-2300.
Web site: http://cvillecountry.com
Profile: WCVL-FM is a commercial station owned by Saga Communications Inc. The format of the station is Classic Country. WCVL-FM broadcasts to the Charlottesville, VA area at 92.7 FM.
FM RADIO STATION

WCVO-FM 40196
Owner: One Connection Media Group
Editorial: 881 E Johnstown Rd, Gahanna, Ohio 43230-1851 Tel: 1 614 855-9171.
Email: theriver@1049theriver.com
Web site: http://www.1049theriver.com
Profile: WCVO-FM is a non-commercial station owned by One Connection Media Group. The format of the station is contemporary Christian music. WCVO-FM broadcasts to the Columbus, OH area at 104.9 FM.
FM RADIO STATION

WCVP-AM 37733
Owner: Cherokee Broadcasting Co.
Editorial: 195 Hampton Church Rd, Murphy, North Carolina 28906-8821 Tel: 1 828 837-2151.
Email: murphyradio@mail.com
Profile: WCVP-AM is a commercial station owned by Cherokee Broadcasting Co. The format of the station is talk, gospel and country music. WCVP-AM broadcasts to the Chattanooga, TN area at 600 AM.
AM RADIO STATION

WCVP-FM 45104
Owner: Cherokee Broadcasting Co.
Tel: 1 828 837-2151.
Email: murphyradio@mail.com
Profile: WCVP-FM is a commercial station owned by Cherokee Broadcasting Co. The format of the station is country. WCVP-FM broadcasts to the Robbinsville, NC area at 95.9 FM.
FM RADIO STATION

WCVQ-FM 46888
Owner: Saga Communications
Editorial: 1640 Old Russellville Pike, Clarksville, Tennessee 37043-1709 Tel: 1 931 648-7720.
Web site: http://www.q108.com
Profile: WCVQ-FM is a commercial station owned by Saga Communications (dba 5 Star Radio Group). The format of the station is hot adult contemporary music. WCVQ-FM broadcasts to the Nashville, TN area at 107.9 FM.
FM RADIO STATION

WCVR-AM 39142
Owner: Koor Communications
Editorial: 62 Radio Dr, Randolph, Vermont 5060 Tel: 1 802 728-4411.
Web site: http://www.realcountry1320.com
Profile: WCVR-AM is a commercial station owned by Koor Communications. The format of the station is country. WCVR-AM broadcasts to the Randolph, VT area at 1320 AM.
AM RADIO STATION

WCVS-FM 40702
Owner: Neuhoff Family Limited Partnership
Editorial: 3055 S 4th St, Springfield, Illinois 62703 Tel: 1 217 528-3033.
Web site: http://www.wcvs.com
Profile: WCVS-FM is a commercial station owned by Neuhoff Family Limited Partnership. The format of the station is classic rock. WCVS-FM broadcasts in the Springfield, IL area at 96.7 FM.
FM RADIO STATION

WCVT-FM 40667
Owner: Radio Vermont Group Inc.
Editorial: 9 Stowe St, Waterbury, Vermont 05676-1820 **Tel:** 1 802 244-7321.
Profile: WCVT-FM is a commercial station owned by Radio Vermont Group Inc. The format of the station is adult contemporary. WCVT-FM broadcasts to the Stowe-Burlington, VT area at a frequency of 101.7 FM.
FM RADIO STATION

WCVU-FM 42438
Owner: iHeartMedia Inc.
Editorial: 24100 Tiseo Blvd Unit 10, Port Charlotte, Florida 33980-5223 **Tel:** 1 941 206-1188.
Web site: http://www.wcvu.com
Profile: WCVU-FM is a commercial station owned by iHeartMedia Inc. The format of the station is easy listening music. WCVU-FM broadcasts in the Port Charlotte, FL area at 104.9 FM.
FM RADIO STATION

WCVX-AM 36289
Owner: Christian Broadcasting System, Ltd
Editorial: 635 W 7th St Ste 400, Cincinnati, Ohio 45203-1549 **Tel:** 1 513 533-2500.
Web site: http://christiantalk1160.com
Profile: WCVX-AM is a commercial station owned by Christian Broadcasting System, Ltd. The format of the station is will become Christian Talk on February 1, 2013. WCVX-AM broadcasts to the Cincinnati area at 1160 AM.
AM RADIO STATION

WCWA-AM 37735
Owner: iHeartMedia Inc.
Editorial: 125 S Superior St, Toledo, Ohio 43604-8747 **Tel:** 1 419 244-8321.
Email: wcwa@iheartmedia.com
Web site: http://www.wcwa.com
Profile: WCWA-AM is a commercial station owned by iHeartMedia Inc. The format of the station is sports. WCWA-AM broadcasts to the Toledo, OH area at 1230 AM.
AM RADIO STATION

WCWM-FM 40198
Owner: College of William & Mary
Editorial: WCWM 90.9 FM, College of W&M, Williamsburg, Virginia 23185 **Tel:** 1 757 221-3287.
Email: wcwmxx@wm.edu
Web site: http://www.wm.edu/so/wcwm
Profile: WCWM-FM is a non-commercial station owned by College of William & Mary. The format of the station is college variety. WCWM-FM broadcasts to the Williamsburg, VA area at 90.9 FM.
FM RADIO STATION

WCWS-FM 40200
Owner: College of Wooster(The)
Editorial: 1189 Beall Ave, Lowry Center, Wooster, Ohio 44691-2393 **Tel:** 1 330 263-2240.
Email: wcws@wooster.edu
Web site: http://woo91.spaces.wooster.edu
Profile: WCWS-FM is a non-commercial station owned by The College of Wooster. The format of the station is music and talk. WCWS-FM broadcasts to the students of the College of Wooster and the residents of Wooster, OH area at 90.0 FM.
FM RADIO STATION

WCWV-FM 42858
Owner: Summit Media Broadcasting LLC
Editorial: 120 Main St, Sutton, West Virginia 26601-1334 **Tel:** 1 304 765-7373.
Web site: http://www.nick929.com
Profile: WCWV-FM is a commercial station owned by Summit Media Broadcasting LLC. The format of the station is Top 40/CHR. WCWV-FM broadcasts to the Summersville, WV area at 92.9 FM. Use the main email address for PSAs.
FM RADIO STATION

WCXI-AM 37103
Owner: Birach Broadcasting Corp.
Editorial: 15130 North Rd, Fenton, Michigan 48430-1380 **Tel:** 1 810 750-1911.
Web site: http://www.birach.com/wcxi.html
Profile: WCXI-AM is a commercial station owned by Birach Broadcasting Corp. The format for the station is oldies. WCXI-AM broadcasts to the Fenton, MI area at 1160 AM.
AM RADIO STATION

WCXL-FM 42855
Owner: Max Radio of the Carolinas
Editorial: 103 W Wood Hill Dr Ste D-E, Nags Head, North Carolina 27959-9395 **Tel:** 1 252 480-4655.
Email: info@beach104.com
Web site: http://www.beach104.com
Profile: WCXL-FM is a commercial station owned by Max Radio of the Carolinas. The format of the station is hot adult contemporary. WXCL-FM broadcasts to the Nags Head, NC area at 104.1 FM.
FM RADIO STATION

WCXN-AM 38521
Owner: Birach Broadcasting Corp.
Editorial: 21700 Northwestern Hwy Ste 1190, Southfield, Michigan 48075-4923 **Tel:** 1 248 557-3500.
Web site: http://www.birach.com
Profile: WCXN-AM is a commercial station owned by Birach Broadcasting Corp. The format of the station is Hispanic. WCXN-AM broadcasts to the Hickory, NC area at 1170 AM.
AM RADIO STATION

WCXO-FM 44384
Owner: Clinton County Broadcasting, Inc.
Editorial: 17549 County Farm Rd, Carlyle, Illinois 62231-6303 **Tel:** 1 618 594-2490.
Web site: http://www.wcxo967.com
Profile: WCXO-FM is a commercial station owned by Clinton County Broadcasting, Inc. The format of the station is adult hits music. WCXO-FM broadcasts to the Carlyle, IL area at 96.7 FM.
FM RADIO STATION

WCXR-FM 43489
Owner: Backyard Broadcasting
Editorial: 1685 Four Mile Dr, Williamsport, Pennsylvania 17701 **Tel:** 1 570 323-8200.
Web site: http://www.wzxr.com
Profile: WCXR-FM is a commercial station owned by Backyard Broadcasting. The station's format is classic rock music. WCXR-FM broadcasts to the Susquehanna Valley, PA area at 103.7 FM.
FM RADIO STATION

WCXT-FM 45099
Owner: Midwest Family Stations
Editorial: 580 E Napier Ave, Benton Harbor, Michigan 49022-5816 **Tel:** 1 269 925-1111.
Web site: http://www.983thecoast.com
Profile: WCXT-FM is a commercial station owned by Midwest Family Stations. The format of the station is hot adult contemporary. WCXT-FM broadcasts to the South Haven, MI area at 98.3 FM.
FM RADIO STATION

WCXU-FM 41442
Owner: Canxus Broadcasting Corp.
Editorial: 152 E Green Ridge Rd, Caribou, Maine 04736-3737 **Tel:** 1 207 473-7513.
Email: channelxradio@yahoo.com
Web site: http://www.channelxradio.com
Profile: WCXU-FM is a commercial station owned by Canxus Broadcasting Corp. The format for the station is adult contemporary. WCXU-FM broadcasts to the Caribou, ME area at 97.7 FM.
FM RADIO STATION

WCXX-FM 41441
Owner: Canxus Broadcasting Corp.
Editorial: 152 E Green Ridge Rd, Caribou, Maine 4736 **Tel:** 1 207 473-7513.
Email: channelxradio@yahoo.com
Web site: http://www.channelxradio.com
Profile: WCXX-FM is a commercial station owned by Canxus Broadcasting Corp. The format for the station is adult contemporary. WCXX-FM broadcasts to the Caribou, ME area at 102.3 FM.
FM RADIO STATION

WCYE-FM 42529
Owner: Results Broadcasting, Inc.
Editorial: 38 W Davenport St, Rhinelander, Wisconsin 54501 **Tel:** 1 715 369-9575.
Web site: http://mycoyoteradio.com
Profile: WCYE-FM is a commercial station owned by Results Broadcasting, Inc. The format of the station is features classic and contemporary country music. WCYE-FM broadcasts to the Rhinelander, WI area at a frequency of 93.7 FM.
FM RADIO STATION

WCYK-FM 45702
Owner: Monticello Media LLC
Editorial: 1150 Pepsi Pl Ste 300, Charlottesville, Virginia 22901-2890 **Tel:** 1 434 978-4408.
Web site: http://www.hitkicker997.com
Profile: WCYK-FM is a commercial station owned by Monticello Media LLC. The format of the station is classic country music. WCYK-FM broadcasts in the Charlottesville, VA area at 99.7 FM.
FM RADIO STATION

WCYN-AM 37737
Owner: WCYN Broadcasting Inc.
Editorial: 117 N Main St Ste 3, Cynthiana, Kentucky 41031-2237 **Tel:** 1 859 234-1400.
Web site: http://www.wcyn.com
Profile: WCYN-AM is a commercial station owned by WCYN Broadcasting Inc. The format of the station is country. WCYN-AM broadcasts to the Lexington, KY area at 1400 AM.
AM RADIO STATION

WCYN-FM 45105
Owner: Cumulus Media Inc.
Editorial: 300 W Vine St, Lexington, Kentucky 40507-1621 **Tel:** 1 859 253-5900.
Web site: http://www.wcyn.com/wcynfm
Profile: WCYN-FM is a commercial station owned by Cumulus Media Inc. The format of the station is news/talk. WCYN-FM broadcasts to the Lexington, KY area at 102.3 FM.
FM RADIO STATION

WCYO-FM 46118
Owner: Wallingford Broadcasting LLC
Editorial: 128 Big Hill Ave, Richmond, Kentucky 40475-2008 **Tel:** 1 859 623-1386.
Web site: http://www.wcyofm.com
Profile: WCYO-FM is a commercial station owned by Wallingford Broadcasting LLC. The format for the station features classic and contemporary country music. WCYO-FM broadcasts to the Lexington, KY area at 100.7 FM.
FM RADIO STATION

WCYQ-FM 46833
Owner: E.W. Scripps Co.
Editorial: 1533 Amherst Rd, Knoxville, Tennessee 37909-1204 **Tel:** 1 865 824-1021.
Web site: http://www.q100country.com
Profile: WCYQ-FM is a commercial station owned by E.W. Scripps Co. The format of the station is contemporary country. WCYQ-FM broadcasts to the Knoxville, TN area at 100.3 FM.
FM RADIO STATION

WCYR-AM 410497
Owner: Port Broadcasting, LLC
Editorial: 93 Cottage St Ste 101, Bar Harbor, Maine 04609-1400
Profile: WCYR-AM is a commercial station owned by Port Broadcasting, LLC. The format of the station is Classic Country. WCYR-FM broadcasts to Bangor, ME area 1400 AM. The station's slogan is, "Bangor's Classic Country."
AM RADIO STATION

WCYY-FM 42195
Owner: Townsquare Media, LLC
Editorial: 1 City Ctr, Portland, Maine 04101-6420 **Tel:** 1 207 774-6364.
Web site: http://www.wcyy.com
Profile: WCYY-FM is a commercial station owned by Townsquare Media, LLC. The format of the station is rock alternative. WCYY-FM broadcasts to the Portland, ME area at 94.3 FM.
FM RADIO STATION

WCZE-FM 847195
Owner: Czelada, Jennifer and Edward
Tel: 1 855 411-1037.
Web site: http://c1037.com
Profile: WCZE-FM is a commercial station owned by Jennifer and Edward Czelada. The format of the station is positive country. WCZE-FM broadcasts to the Harbor Beach, MI area at a frequency of 103.7 FM.
FM RADIO STATION

WCZQ-FM 40818
Owner: Neuhoff Communications
Editorial: 250 N Water St, Ste 100, Decatur, Illinois 62523 **Tel:** 1 217 423-9744.
Web site: http://www.hot1055.com
Profile: WCZQ-FM is a commercial station owned by Neuhoff Communications. The format of the station is urban contemporary and R&B. WCZQ-FM broadcasts to the Decatur, IL area at 105.5 FM.
FM RADIO STATION

WCZR-FM 42558
Owner: iHeartMedia Inc.
Editorial: 3771 SE Jennings Rd, Port Saint Lucie, Florida 34952-7702 **Tel:** 1 772 335-9300.
Web site: http://www.wzzr.com
Profile: WCZR-FM is a commercial station owned by iHeartMedia Inc. The format of the station is talk. WCZR-FM broadcasts to the West Palm Beach, FL area at 101.7 FM.
FM RADIO STATION

WCZT-FM 40851
Owner: Coastal Broadcasting Systems, Inc.
Editorial: 1602 Route 47 Floor 2, Rio Grande, New Jersey 08242-1404 **Tel:** 1 609 522-1987.
Web site: http://www.987thecoast.com
Profile: WCZT-FM is a commercial station owned by Coastal Broadcasting Systems, Inc. The format of the station is adult contemporary. WCZT-FM broadcasts to the Wildwood, NJ area at 98.7 FM.
FM RADIO STATION

WCZW-FM 135808
Owner: Good News Media, Inc.
Tel: 1 231 946-1400.
Email: info@goodnewsmediainc.org
Web site: http://www.wljn.com
Profile: WCZW-FM is a commercial station owned by Good News Media, Inc. The format of the station is religious teaching. The station airs in the Traverse City, MI area at 107.9 FM.
FM RADIO STATION

WCZX-FM 40203
Owner: Townsquare Media
Editorial: 2 Pendell Rd, Poughkeepsie, New York 12601-1513 **Tel:** 1 845 471-1500.
Web site: http://www.mix97fm.com
Profile: WCZX-FM is a commercial station owned by Townsquare Media. The format of the station is adult contemporary. WCZX-FM broadcasts throughout Poughkeepsie, New York at 97.7 FM. Do NOT send information not pertaining to the Poughkeepsie local area.
FM RADIO STATION

WCZY-FM 46207
Owner: Central Michigan Communications Inc.
Editorial: 4895 E Wing Rd, Mount Pleasant, Michigan 48858 **Tel:** 1 989 772-9664.
Email: wczy@wczy.net
Web site: http://wczy.net
Profile: WCZY-FM is a commercial station owned by Central Michigan Communications Inc. The format for the station is adult contemporary. WCZY-FM broadcasts to the Flint, MI area at 104.3 FM.
FM RADIO STATION

WCZZ-AM 38351
Owner: Broomfield Broadcasting LLC
Editorial: 210 Montague Ave, Greenwood, South Carolina 29649-1935 **Tel:** 1 864 223-4300.
Email: rejoice1090@gmail.com
Web site: http://rejoice1090.com
Profile: WCZZ-AM is a commercial station owned by Broomfield Broadcasting LLC. The format of the station is Christian talk and music, and gospel. WCZZ-AM broadcasts to the Greenwood, SC area at 1090 AM.
AM RADIO STATION

WDAC-FM 40204
Owner: WDAC Radio Co.
Editorial: 683 Lancaster Pike, New Providence, Pennsylvania 17560-9756 **Tel:** 1 717 284-4123.
Email: postmaster@wdac.com
Web site: http://www.wdac.com
Profile: WDAC-FM is a commercial station owned by WDAC Radio Co. The format of the station is religious. The station broadcasts to the Lancaster, PA area at 94.5 FM.
FM RADIO STATION

WDAD-AM 38615
Owner: Renda Broadcasting
Editorial: 840 Philadelphia St, Indiana, Pennsylvania 15701-3922 **Tel:** 1 724 465-4700.
Web site: http://www.wdadradio.com
Profile: WDAD-AM is a commercial station owned by Renda Broadcasting. The format of the station is oldies music. WDAD-AM broadcasts to the Indiana, PA area at 1450 AM.
AM RADIO STATION

WDAE-AM 38651
Owner: iHeartMedia Inc.
Editorial: 4002 W Gandy Blvd, Tampa, Florida 33611-3410 **Tel:** 1 813 832-1000.
Email: webmaster@620wdae.com
Web site: http://620wdae.iheart.com/
Profile: WDAE-AM is a commercial station owned by iHeartMedia Inc. The format of the station is sports. WDAE-AM broadcasts to the Tampa, FL area at 620 AM.
AM RADIO STATION

WDAF-FM 41897
Owner: Entercom Communications Corp.
Editorial: 7000 Squibb Rd, Mission, Kansas 66202-3233 **Tel:** 1 913 744-3600.
Web site: http://www.1065thewolf.com
Profile: WDAF-FM is a commercial station owned by Entercom Communications Corp. The format of the station is contemporary country. WDAF-FM broadcasts to the Greater Kansas City, MO area at 106.5 FM.
FM RADIO STATION

WDAI-FM 43607
Owner: Cumulus Media Inc.
Editorial: 11640 Highway 17 Byp, Murrells Inlet, South Carolina 29576-9332 **Tel:** 1 843 651-7869.
Web site: http://www.985kissfm.net
Profile: WDAI-FM is a commercial station owned by Cumulus Media Inc. The format of the station is urban contemporary music. WDAI-FM broadcasts to the Murrells Inlet, SC area at 98.5 FM.
FM RADIO STATION

WDAK-AM 38916
Owner: iHeartMedia Inc.
Editorial: 1501 13th Ave, Columbus, Georgia 31901-1908 **Tel:** 1 706 576-3000.
Web site: http://www.newsradio540.com
Profile: WDAK-AM is a commercial station owned by iHeartMedia Inc. The format of the station is news and talk. WDAK-AM broadcasts to the Columbus, GA area at 540 AM.
AM RADIO STATION

WDAL-AM 39427
Owner: North Georgia Radio Group
Editorial: 613 Silver Cir, Dalton, Georgia 30721 **Tel:** 1 706 278-5511.
Profile: WDAL-AM is a commercial station owned by North Georgia Radio Group. The format of the station is Spanish sports. WDAL-AM broadcasts to Dalton, GA at 1430 AM.
AM RADIO STATION

WDAN-AM 37738
Owner: Neuhoff Family Limited Partnership
Editorial: 1501 N Washington Ave, Danville, Illinois 61832-2463 **Tel:** 1 217 442-1700.
Web site: http://www.vermilioncountyfirst.com
Profile: WDAN-AM is commercial station owned by Neuhoff Family Limited Partnership. The format of the station is news, sports and talk. WDAN-AN broadcasts to the Danville, IL area at 1490 AM.
AM RADIO STATION

WDAO-AM 36017
Owner: Johnson Communications
Editorial: 1012 W 3rd St, Dayton, Ohio 45402 **Tel:** 1 937 222-9326.
Email: wdaoam1210@aol.com
Web site: http://www.wdaoradio.com
Profile: WDAO-AM is a commercial station owned by Johnson Communications. The format of the station is urban adult contemporary. WDAO-AM broadcasts to the Dayton, OH area at 1210 AM.
AM RADIO STATION

WDAQ-FM 46698
Owner: Berkshire Broadcasting Corp
Editorial: 98 Mill Plain Rd, Danbury, Connecticut 6811 **Tel:** 1 203 744-4800.
Web site: http://www.98q.com
Profile: WDAQ-FM is a commercial station owned by Berkshire Broadcasting Corp. The format of the station is hot adult contemporary. WDAQ-FM broadcasts to the Danbury, CT area at 98.3 FM.
FM RADIO STATION

WDAR-FM 46821
Owner: iHeartMedia Inc.
Editorial: 181 E Evans St Ste 311, Florence, South Carolina 29506-5505 **Tel:** 1 843 667-4600.
Web site: http://sunny1055online.com
Profile: WDAR-FM is a commercial station owned by iHeartMedia Inc. The format of the station is Contemporary Christian. WDAR-FM broadcasts to the Florence, SC area at 105.5 FM.
FM RADIO STATION

WDAS-AM 38683
Owner: iHeartMedia Inc.
Editorial: 111 Presidential Blvd, Bala Cynwyd, Pennsylvania 19004-1008 **Tel:** 1 610 784-3333.
Web site: http://wjjz.iheart.com
Profile: WDAS-AM is a commercial station owned by iHeartMedia Inc. The format of the station is smooth jazz. WDAS-AM broadcasts to the Philadelphia area at 1480 AM.
AM RADIO STATION

WDAS-FM 46036
Owner: iHeartMedia Inc.
Editorial: 111 Presidential Blvd Ste 100, Bala Cynwyd, Pennsylvania 19004-1009 **Tel:** 1 610 784-3333.
Web site: http://wdasfm.iheart.com
Profile: WDAS-FM is a commercial station owned by iHeartMedia Inc. The format of the station is urban contemporary and R&B. WDAS-FM broadcasts to the Philadelphia area at 105.3 FM.
FM RADIO STATION

WDAV-FM 40205
Owner: Trustees of Davidson College
Editorial: 423 N Main St, Davidson, North Carolina 28036-9405 **Tel:** 1 704 894-8900.
Email: wdav@wdav.org
Web site: http://www.wdav.org
Profile: WDAV-FM is a non-commercial station owned by Trustees of Davidson College. The format of the station is classical music. WDAV-FM broadcasts in the Charlotte, NC area at 89.9 FM.
FM RADIO STATION

WDAY-AM 36803
Owner: Forum Communications Co.
Editorial: 301 8th St S Fl 2, 2nd Fl, Fargo, North Dakota 58103-1826 **Tel:** 1 701 237-6500.
Email: news@wday.com
Web site: http://www.wday.com/radio
Profile: WDAY-AM is a commercial station owned by Forum Communications Co. The format of the station is news, sports and talk. WDAY-AM broadcasts to the Fargo, ND area at 970 AM.
AM RADIO STATION

WDAY-FM 43762
Owner: Midwest Communications
Editorial: 1020 25th St S, Fargo, North Dakota 58103-2312 **Tel:** 1 701 237-5346.
Web site: http://www.y94.com
Profile: WDAY-FM is a commercial station owned by Midwest Communications. The format of the station is Top 40/CHR music. WDAY-FM broadcasts to the Fargo, ND area at 93.7 FM.
FM RADIO STATION

WDBC-AM 38846
Owner: KMB Broadcasting Inc.
Editorial: 604 Ludington St, Escanaba, Michigan 49829 **Tel:** 1 906 786-3800.
Email: wykxinfo@yahoo.com
Web site: http://www.kmbbroadcasting.com/wdbc/index.php
Profile: WDBC-AM is a commercial station owned by KMB Broadcasting Inc. The format of the station is adult standards music, sports and talk programming. WDBC-AM broadcasts to the Marquette, MI, area at 680 AM.
AM RADIO STATION

WDBK-FM 533555
Owner: Camden County College
Editorial: 200 College Dr, Blackwood, New Jersey 08012-3228 **Tel:** 1 856 374-4881.
Email: wdbklive@gmail.com
Web site: http://www.camdencc.edu/studentlife/WDBK-Radio.cfm
Profile: WDBK-FM is a non-commercial college station owned by Camden County College. The format of the station is alternative rock. WDBK-FM broadcasts to the Blackwood, NJ area at 91.5 FM.
FM RADIO STATION

WDBL-AM 317902
Owner: Lightning Broadcasting, LLC
Editorial: 200 Wdbl Rd, Springfield, Tennessee 37172 **Tel:** 1 615 384-9744.
Email: wsgi1100@yahoo.com
Web site: http://wsgi1100.com
Profile: WDBL-AM is a commercial station owned by Lightning Broadcasting, LLC. The format of the station is news and talk. WDBL-AM broadcasts to the Nashville, TN area at 1590 AM.
AM RADIO STATION

WDBN-FM 42364
Owner: Dowdy Broadcasting, Inc.
Editorial: 807 Bellevue Ave, Dublin, Georgia 31021-4847 **Tel:** 1 478 272-4422.
Web site: http://jamz1079.com
Profile: WDBN-FM is a commercial station owned by Dowdy Broadcasting, Inc. The format of the station is urban. WDBN-FM broadcasts to the Dublin, GA area at 107.9 FM.
FM RADIO STATION

WDBO-AM 37741
Owner: Cox Media Group, Inc.
Editorial: 4192 N John Young Pkwy, Orlando, Florida 32804-2620 **Tel:** 1 407 295-5858.
Web site: http://www.espn580orlando.com
Profile: WDBO-AM is a commercial station owned by Cox Media Group, Inc. The format of the station is sports. WDBO-AM broadcasts to the Orlando, FL area at 580 AM. WDBO-AM airs its programming on WHTO-FM.
AM RADIO STATION

WDBO-FM 46375
Owner: Cox Media Group, Inc.
Editorial: 4192 N John Young Pkwy, Orlando, Florida 32804-2620 **Tel:** 1 407 295-5858.
Email: news@news965.com
Web site: http://www.news965.com
Profile: WDBO-FM is a commercial station owned by Cox Media Group, Inc. The format of the station is news and talk. WHTQ-FM broadcasts to the Orlando, FL area at 96.5 FM. WDBO-FM airs WDBO-AM's programming. Send all news tips, press releases and guests requests to news@news965.com.
FM RADIO STATION

WDBQ-AM 37742
Owner: Townsquare Media
Editorial: 5490 Saratoga Rd, Asbury, Iowa 52002-2593 **Tel:** 1 563 557-1040.
Web site: http://www.wdbqam.com
Profile: WDBQ-AM is a commercial station owned byTownsquare Media. The format for the station is news, sports and talk. WDBQ-AM broadcasts to the Cedar Rapids, IA area at 1490 AM.
AM RADIO STATION

WDBQ-FM 42585
Owner: Cumulus Media Inc.
Editorial: 5490 Saratoga Rd, Dubuque, Iowa 52002-2502 **Tel:** 1 563 557-1040.
Web site: http://www.myq1075.com
Profile: WDBQ-FM is a commercial station owned by Cumulus Media Inc. The format of the station is classic hits. WDBQ-FM broadcasts to Dubuque, IA and surrounding communities at 107.5 FM.
FM RADIO STATION

WDBR-FM 45108
Owner: Saga Communications
Editorial: 3501 E Sangamon Ave, Springfield, Illinois 62707-9777 **Tel:** 1 217 753-5400.
Web site: http://www.wdbr.com
Profile: WDBR-FM is a commercial station owned by Saga Communications. The format of the station is Top 40/CHR. WDBR-FM broadcasts to the Springfield, IL area at a frequency of 103.7 FM.
FM RADIO STATION

WDBS-FM 46465
Owner: Summit Media Broadcasting LLC
Editorial: 180 Main St, Sutton, West Virginia 26601-1317 **Tel:** 1 304 765-7373.
Email: info@theboss97fm.com
Web site: http://www.theboss97fm.com
Profile: WDBS-FM is a commercial station owned by Summit Media Broadcasting LLC. The format of the station is country music. WDBS-FM broadcasts to the Sutton, WV area at 97.1 FM.
FM RADIO STATION

WDBX-FM 43300
Owner: Heterodyne Broadcasting
Editorial: 224 N Washington St, Carbondale, Illinois 62901 **Tel:** 1 618 529-5900.
Email: wdbx911@yahoo.com
Web site: http://www.wdbx.org
Profile: WDBX-FM is a non-commercial station owned by Heterodyne Broadcasting. The format of the station is a variety of music and talk. WDBX-FM broadcasts to the Paducah, KY, Cape Girardeau, MO and Harrisburg, IL areas at 91.1 FM.
FM RADIO STATION

WDBY-FM 46449
Owner: Townsquare Media, LLC
Editorial: 1004 Federal Rd, Brookfield, Connecticut 06804-1123 **Tel:** 1 203 775-1212.
Web site: http://kicks1055.com
Profile: WDBY-FM is a commercial station owned by Townsquare Media, LLC. The format of the station is contemporary country. WDBY-FM broadcasts to the Danbury, CT area at 105.5 FM.
FM RADIO STATION

WDBZ-AM 38637
Owner: Urban One Inc.
Editorial: 705 Central Ave Ste 200, 1 Centennial Plaza, Cincinnati, Ohio 45202-1900 **Tel:** 1 513 749-1230.
Web site: https://1015soul.com
Profile: WDBZ-AM is a commercial station owned by Urban One Inc. The format of the station is gospel. WDBZ-AM broadcasts to the Cincinnati area at 1230 AM.
AM RADIO STATION

WDCB-FM 40208
Owner: College of DuPage
Editorial: 425 Fawell Blvd, Glen Ellyn, Illinois 60137-6708 **Tel:** 1 630 942-4200.
Email: info@wdcb.org
Web site: http://www.wdcb.org
Profile: WDCB-FM is a non-commercial station owned by the College of DuPage. The format of the station is news, jazz and blues music. WDCB-FM broadcasts to the Glen Ellyn, IL area at 90.9 FM.
FM RADIO STATION

WDCC-FM 40209
Owner: Central Carolina Community College
Editorial: 1105 Kelly Dr, Sanford, North Carolina 27330 **Tel:** 1 919 718-7382.
Email: wdcc@cccc.edu
Web site: http://www.wdccfm.com
Profile: WDCC-FM is a non-commercial station owned by Central Carolina Community College. The format of the station is top 40/CHR. WDCC-FM broadcasts to the Sanford, NC area at 90.5 FM.
FM RADIO STATION

WDCD-FM 36355
Owner: DJRA Broadcasting
Editorial: 4243 Albany St, Albany, New York 12205-4609 **Tel:** 1 518 862-1540.
Web site: http://www.newlight967.com
Profile: WDCD-FM is a commercial station owned by DJRA Broadcasting. The format of the station features Christian programming. WDCD-FM broadcasts to the Albany, NY area at 96.7 FM.
FM RADIO STATION

WDCF-AM 35270
Owner: Wagenvoord Advertising Group
Editorial: 706 N Myrtle Ave, Clearwater, Florida 33755-4219 **Tel:** 1 727 424-4991.
Email: lola@tantalk1340.com
Web site: http://www.tantalk1340.com
Profile: WDCF-AM is a commercial station owned by Wagenvoord Advertising Group. The format of the station is adult standards music and talk. WDCF-AM broadcasts to the Dade City, FL area on 1350 AM.
AM RADIO STATION

WDCG-FM 42323
Owner: iHeartMedia Inc.
Editorial: 3100 Smoketree Ct Ste 700, Raleigh, North Carolina 27604-1052 **Tel:** 1 919 878-1500.
Web site: http://www.g105.com
Profile: WDCG-FM is a commercial station owned by iHeartMedia Inc. The format of the station is Top 40/CHR. WDCG-FM broadcasts to the Raleigh, NC area at 105.1 FM.
FM RADIO STATION

WDCH-FM 40341
Owner: CBS Radio
Editorial: 1015 Half St SE Ste 200, Washington, District Of Columbia 20003-3320
Web site: http://www.bloomberg.com/radio
Profile: WDCH-FM is a commercial station owned by CBS Radio. Bloomberg Radio took over programming of the station on December 18, 2015. The format of the station is business news and talk. WDCH-FM broadcasts to the Washington, D.C. area at 99.1 FM.
FM RADIO STATION

WDCR-AM 37743
Owner: Dartmouth College
Editorial: 6176 Robinson Hall Fl 3RDDARTMOU, Hanover, New Hampshire 03755-3507
Tel: 1 603 646-3313.
Email: 99Rock@wfrd.com
Web site: http://www.webdcr.com
Profile: WDCR-AM is a non-commercial college station owned by Dartmouth College. The format of the station is college variety, and classic rock during the day. WDCR-AM broadcasts to the Hanover, NH area at 1340 AM.
AM RADIO STATION

WDCR-FM 755689
Owner: St. Mary's Hospital (Decatur)
Editorial: 1800 E Lake Shore Dr, Decatur, Illinois 62521-3810 **Tel:** 1 217 464-2966.
Email: contact@wdcrradio.com
Web site: http://wdcrradio.com
Profile: WDCR-FM is a non-commercial station owned by St. Mary's Hospital (Decatur). The format of the station features Catholic talk radio programming. WDCR-FM broadcasts locally to the Decatur, IL area at a frequency of 88.9 FM.
FM RADIO STATION

WDCT-AM 35271
Owner: Family Radio Ltd.
Editorial: 3251 Old Lee Hwy Ste 506, Fairfax, Virginia 22030-1504 **Tel:** 1 703 273-4000.
Profile: WDCT-AM is a commercial station owned by Family Radio Ltd. The format of the station is religious Korean programming. WDCT-AM broadcasts to the Fairfax, VA area at 1310 AM.
AM RADIO STATION

WDCX-AM 36648
Owner: Crawford Broadcasting Co.
Editorial: 2494 Browncroft Blvd, Rochester, New York 14625-1410 **Tel:** 1 716 883-3010.
Email: info@wdcxradio.com
Web site: http://www.wdcxfm.com
Profile: WDCX-AM is a commercial station owned by Crawford Broadcasting Co. The format of the station is religious talk. WDCX-AM broadcasts to the Rochester, NY area at 990 AM. The station does not accept PSAs.
AM RADIO STATION

WDCX-FM 40212
Owner: Crawford Broadcasting Co.
Editorial: 625 Delaware Ave, Buffalo, New York 14202-1009 **Tel:** 1 716 883-3010.
Email: info@wdcxradio.com
Web site: http://www.wdcxfm.com
Profile: WDCX-FM is a commercial station owned by Crawford Broadcasting Co. The format of the station is contemporary Christian music. WDCX-FM broadcasts to the Buffalo, NY area at 99.5 FM. The station does not accept PSAs.
FM RADIO STATION

WDCY-AM 35674
Owner: Word Christian Broadcasting Inc.
Editorial: 8451 Earl D Lee Blvd Ste B, Douglasville, Georgia 30134-8520 **Tel:** 1 770 920-1520.
Email: wkjohns@comcast.net
Web site: http://www.wordchristianbroadcasting.com
Profile: WDCY-AM is a commercial station owned by Word Christian Broadcasting Inc. The format of the station is religious programming and gospel music. WDCY-AM broadcasts to the Douglasville, GA area at 1520 AM.
AM RADIO STATION

WDCZ-AM 38443
Owner: Kimtron, Inc.
Editorial: 625 Delaware Ave Ste 308, Buffalo, New York 14202-1007 **Tel:** 1 716 883-3010.
Email: info@wdcxradio.com
Web site: http://www.wdcxfm.com
Profile: WDCZ-AM is a commercial station owned by Kimtron, Inc. The format of the station is Christian talk. WDCZ-AM broadcasts to the Buffalo-Niagara Falls, NY area at 970 AM area.
AM RADIO STATION

WDDC-FM 45109
Owner: Zoe Communications Inc.
Editorial: N6912 US Highway 51, Portage, Wisconsin 53901 **Tel:** 1 608 742-1001.
Web site: http://www.thunder100fm.com
Profile: WDDC-FM is a commercial station owned by Zoe Communications Inc. The format for the station is contemporary country. WDDC-FM broadcasts to the Madison, WI area at 100.1 FM.
FM RADIO STATION

WDDD-AM 37744
Owner: Withers Broadcasting Co.
Editorial: 1822 N Court St, Marion, Illinois 62959-4558
Tel: 1 618 997-8123.
Profile: WDDD-AM is a commercial station owned by Withers Broadcasting of Southern Illinois. The format of the station is sports. WDDD-AM broadcasts to the Marion, IL area at 810 AM.
AM RADIO STATION

WDDD-FM 45110
Owner: Withers Broadcasting of Southern Illinois
Editorial: 1822 N Court St, Marion, Illinois 62959-4558
Tel: 1 618 997-8123.
Web site: http://www.mywithersradio.com/wddd
Profile: WDDD-FM is a commercial station owned by Withers Broadcasting of Southern Illinois. The format of the station is contemporary country music. WDDD-FM broadcasts to the Marion, IL areas at 107.3 FM.
FM RADIO STATION

WDDE-FM 829447
Owner: Delaware First Media Corporation
Editorial: 1200 N Dupont Hwy, Dover, Delaware 19901-2202 **Tel:** 1 302 857-7096.
Email: info@delawarefirst.org
Web site: http://delawarepublic.org
Profile: WDDE-FM is a non-commercial station owned by Delaware First Media Corporation. The format of the station is talk and news. WDDE-FM broadcasts to the Dover. DE area at 91.1 FM.
FM RADIO STATION

WDDH-FM 41535
Owner: Laurel Media Inc.
Editorial: 14902 Boot Jack Rd, Ridgway, Pennsylvania 15853-6128 **Tel:** 1 814 772-9700.
Email: spots@houndcountry.com
Web site: http://www.houndcountry.com
Profile: WDDH-FM is a commercial station owned by Laurel Media Inc. The format of the station is classic country. WDDH-FM broadcasts to the Ridgway, PA area at 97.5 FM.
FM RADIO STATION

WDDJ-FM 45719
Owner: Bristol Broadcasting
Editorial: 6000 Bristol Dr, Paducah, Kentucky 42003-9213 **Tel:** 1 270 534-9690.
Email: pd@electric969.com
Web site: http://www.electric969.com
Profile: WDDJ-FM is a commercial station owned by Bristol Broadcasting. The format of the station is Top 40/CHR. WDDJ-FM broadcasts to the Paducah, KY area at 96.9 FM.
FM RADIO STATION

WDDK-FM 40326
Owner: Briar Patch Radio Inc
Editorial: 1271B E Broad St, Greensboro, Georgia 30642-2335 **Tel:** 1 706 453-4140.
Web site: http://www.dock1039.com
Profile: WDDK-FM is a commercial station owned by Briar Patch Radio Inc. The format of the station is

oldies, news and talk. WDDK-FM broadcasts to the Greensboro, GA area at 103.9 FM.
FM RADIO STATION

WDDQ-FM 44542
Owner: Small Town Broadcasting
Editorial: 118 N Patterson St, Valdosta, Georgia 31601-5570 **Tel:** 1 229 259-9301.
Web site: http://www.talk921.com
Profile: WDDQ-FM is a commercial station owned by Small Town Broadcasting. The format of the station is talk. WDDQ-FM broadcasts to the Valdosta, GA area at 92.1 FM.
FM RADIO STATION

WDDV-AM 39132
Owner: iHeartMedia Inc.
Editorial: 1779 Independence Blvd, Sarasota, Florida 34234-2106 **Tel:** 1 941 552-4800.
Web site: http://www.sunnyradioam.com/main.html
Profile: WDDV-AM is a commercial station owned by iHeartMedia Inc. The format of the station is news/talk. WDDV-AM broadcasts to the Sarasota, FL area at 1320 AM.
AM RADIO STATION

WDDW-FM 42096
Owner: Bustos Media, LLC
Editorial: 1138 S 108th St, West Allis, Wisconsin 53214-2433 **Tel:** 1 414 799-1047.
Web site: http://wddw.radiolagrande.com
Profile: WDDW-FM is a commercial station owned by Bustos Media, LLC. The format of the station is regional Mexican. WDDW-FM broadcasts to the Milwaukee area at 104.7 FM.
FM RADIO STATION

WDEA-AM 37746
Owner: Townsquare Media, Inc.
Editorial: 49 Acme Rd, Brewer, Maine 04412-1545 **Tel:** 1 207 989-5631.
Email: cumuluspublicservice@midmaine.com
Web site: http://am1370wdea.com
Profile: WDEA-AM is a commercial station owned by Townsquare Media, Inc. The format of the station is adult standards. WDEA-AM broadcasts to the Brewer, ME area at 1370 AM.
AM RADIO STATION

WDEB-AM 37747
Owner: Westwood One
Editorial: 403 Livingston Ave, Jamestown, Tennessee 38556-3422 **Tel:** 1 931 879-8164.
Email: wdeb@twlakes.net
Profile: WDEB-AM is a commercial station owned by Westwood One. The format of the station is oldies. WDEB-AM broadcasts to the Jamestown, TN area at 1500 AM.
AM RADIO STATION

WDEB-FM 45111
Owner: BAZ Broadcasting Inc.
Editorial: 403 Livingston Ave, Jamestown, Tennessee 38556 **Tel:** 1 931 879-8164.
Email: wdebaudio@twlakes.net
Profile: WDEB-FM is a commercial station owned by BAZ Broadcasting Inc. The format of the station is country. WDEB-FM broadcasts to the Jamestown, TN area at 103.9 FM.
FM RADIO STATION

WDEC-FM 42313
Owner: Sumter Broadcasting
Editorial: 214 Georgia Hwy 30 W., Americus, Georgia 31719 **Tel:** 1 229 924-6500.
Email: wiskwdec@mchsi.com
Web site: http://www.americusradio.com
Profile: WDEC-FM is a commercial station owned by Sumter Broadcasting. The format of the station is adult contemporary. WDEC-FM broadcasts to the Americus, GA area at 94.7 FM.
FM RADIO STATION

WDEF-AM 37748
Owner: Bahakel Communications
Editorial: 2615 Broad St, Chattanooga, Tennessee 37408-3100 **Tel:** 1 423 321-6200.
Web site: http://www.wuuqradio.com/
Profile: WDEF-AM is a commercial station owned by Bahakel Communications. The format of the station is classic country. WDEF-AM broadcasts to the Chattanooga, TN area at 1370 AM.
AM RADIO STATION

WDEF-FM 45112
Owner: Bahakel Communications
Editorial: 2615 Broad St, Chattanooga, Tennessee 37408 **Tel:** 1 423 321-6200.
Web site: http://www.sunny923.com
Profile: WDEF-FM is a commercial station owned by Bahakel Communications. The format of the station is adult contemporary. WDEF-FM broadcasts to the Chattanooga, TN area at 92.3 FM.
FM RADIO STATION

WDEH-AM 37749
Owner: Horne Radio LLC
Tel: 1 865 675-4105.
Profile: WDEH-AM is a commercial station owned by Horne Radio LLC. The format of the station is gospel and religious. WDEH-AM broadcasts to the Sweetwater, TN area at 800 AM.
AM RADIO STATION

WDEL-AM 37750
Owner: Delmarva Broadcasting
Editorial: 2727 Shipley Rd, Wilmington, Delaware 19810-3210 **Tel:** 1 302 478-2700.
Email: wdelnews@wdel.com
Web site: http://www.wdel.com
Profile: WDEL-AM is a commercial station owned by Delmarva Broadcasting. The format of the station is news and talk. WDEL-AM broadcasts to the Philadelphia area at 1150 AM.
AM RADIO STATION

WDEL-FM 46532
Owner: Delmarva Broadcasting Co.
Editorial: 2727 Shipley Rd, Wilmington, Delaware 19810-3210 **Tel:** 1 302 478-2700.
Email: wdelnews@wdel.com
Web site: http://www.wdel.com
Profile: WDEL-FM is a commercial station owned by Delmarva Broadcasting Co. The format of the station is news, talk, and sports. WDEL-FM broadcasts to the Canten and Salem areas of New Jersey at 101.7 FM.
FM RADIO STATION

WDEN-FM 45114
Owner: Cumulus Media Inc.
Editorial: 544 Mulberry St Ste 500, Macon, Georgia 31201-8258 **Tel:** 1 478 746-6286.
Email: wdencrew@yahoo.com
Web site: http://www.wden.com
Profile: WDEN-FM is a commercial station owned by Cumulus Media Inc. The format of the station is contemporary country music. WDEN-FM broadcasts to the Macon, GA area at 99.1 FM.
FM RADIO STATION

WDEO-AM 35743
Owner: Ave Maria Communications
Editorial: 24 Frank Lloyd Wright Dr, Ann Arbor, Michigan 48105-9484 **Tel:** 1 734 930-5200.
Web site: http://www.avemariaradio.net
Profile: WDEO-AM is a non-commercial station owned by Ave Maria Communications. The format of the station is religious talk. WDEO-AM broadcasts to the Ann Arbor, MI area at 990 AM.
AM RADIO STATION

WDER-AM 35904
Owner: Blount Communications Group
Editorial: 8 Lawrence Rd, Derry, New Hampshire 03038-4191 **Tel:** 1 603 437-9337.
Email: info@wder.com
Web site: http://lifechangingradio.com/wder
Profile: WDER-AM is a commercial station owned by Blount Communications Group. The format of the station is religious programming. WDER-AM broadcasts to the Derry, NH area at 1320 AM.
AM RADIO STATION

WDER-FM 71762
Owner: Blount Communications Group
Editorial: 8 Lawrence Rd, Derry, New Hampshire 03038-4191 **Tel:** 1 603 437-9337.
Email: info@wder.com
Web site: http://lifechangingradio.com/wder
Profile: WDER-FM is a commercial station owned by Blount Communications Group. The format of the station is religious programming. WDER-FM broadcasts to the Peterborough, NH area at a frequency of 92.1 FM.
FM RADIO STATION

WDEV-AM 39086
Owner: Radio Vermont Group Inc.
Editorial: 9 Stowe St, Waterbury, Vermont 5676 **Tel:** 1 802 244-7321.
Email: wdev@radiovermont.com
Web site: http://www.wdevradio.com
Profile: WDEV-AM is a commercial station owned by Radio Vermont Group Inc. The format of the station is news, sports, and talk, with an occasional variety of music. WDEV-AM broadcasts to the Waterbury, VT, area at 550 AM.
AM RADIO STATION

WDEV-FM 46433
Owner: Radio Vermont Group Inc.
Editorial: 9 Stowe St, Waterbury, Vermont 05676-1820 **Tel:** 1 802 244-1764.
Email: wdev@radiovermont.com
Web site: http://www.wdevradio.com
Profile: WDEV-FM is a commercial station owned by Radio Vermont Group Inc. The format of the station is news, sports, and talk, with an occasional variety of music. WDEV-FM broadcasts to the Waterbury, VT area at 96.1 FM.
FM RADIO STATION

WDEX-AM 35272
Owner: New Life Broadcasting
Editorial: 3109 Weddington Rd, Monroe, North Carolina 28110-8932 **Tel:** 1 704 289-9339.
Profile: WDEX-AM is a commercial station owned by New Life Broadcasting. The format of the station is gospel music. WDEX-AM broadcasts to the Charlotte, NC area at 1430 AM.
AM RADIO STATION

WDEZ-FM 45116
Owner: Midwest Communications Inc.
Editorial: 557 Scott St, Wausau, Wisconsin 54403-4829 **Tel:** 1 715 842-1672.
Web site: http://www.wdez.com
Profile: WDEZ-FM is a commercial station owned by Midwest Communications. The format of the station is contemporary country music. WDEZ-FM broadcasts to the Wausau, WI area at 101.9 FM.
FM RADIO STATION

WDFB-AM 39339
Owner: Alum Springs Vision & Outreach Corp.
Editorial: 3596 Alum Springs Rd, Danville, Kentucky 40422-9607 **Tel:** 1 859 236-9333.
Email: wdfb@wdfb.org
Web site: http://www.wdfb.com
AM RADIO STATION

WDFB-FM 46697
Owner: Alum Springs Vision & Outreach Corp.
Editorial: 3596 Alum Springs Rd, Danville, Kentucky 40422-9607 **Tel:** 1 859 236-9333.
Email: wdfb@wdfb.org
Web site: http://www.wdfb.com
FM RADIO STATION

WDFM-FM 40215
Owner: iHeartMedia Inc.
Editorial: 2110 Radio Dr, Defiance, Ohio 43512-1977 **Tel:** 1 419 782-9336.
Web site: http://www.981mix.com
Profile: WDFM-FM is a commercial station owned by iHeartMedia Inc. The format of the station is hot adult contemporary. WDFM-FM broadcasts to the Defiance, OH area at 98.1 FM.
FM RADIO STATION

WDFN-AM 37736
Owner: iHeartMedia Inc.
Editorial: 27675 Halsted Rd, Farmington Hills, Michigan 48331-3511 **Tel:** 1 248 324-5800.
Web site: http://wdfn.iheart.com
Profile: WDFN-AM is a commercial station owned by iHeartMedia Inc. The format of the station is sports. WDFN-AM broadcasts to the Detroit area at 1130 AM.
AM RADIO STATION

WDGG-FM 46053
Owner: Kindred Communications
Editorial: 401 11th St Ste 200, Huntington, West Virginia 25701-2226 **Tel:** 1 304 523-8401.
Email: studio@937thedawg.com
Web site: http://www.937thedawg.com
Profile: WDGG-FM is a commercial station owned by Kindred Communications. The format of the station is country music. WDGG-FM broadcasts to the greater Huntington, WV region at 93.7 FM.
FM RADIO STATION

WDGL-FM 40311
Owner: Guaranty Broadcasting
Editorial: 929 Government St, Baton Rouge, Louisiana 70802 **Tel:** 1 225 388-9898.
Web site: http://www.eagle981.com
Profile: WDGL-FM is a commercial station owned by Guaranty Broadcasting. The format of the station is classic rock. WDGL-FM broadcasts to the Baton Rouge, LA area at 98.1 FM.
FM RADIO STATION

WDGM-FM 334151
Owner: Townsquare Media, Inc.
Editorial: 142 Skyland Blvd E, Tuscaloosa, Alabama 35405-4027 **Tel:** 1 205 345-7200.
Web site: http://tide991.com
Profile: WDGM-FM is a commercial station owned by Townsquare Media, Inc. The format of the station is sports. WDGM-FM broadcasts to the Tuscaloosa, AL area at 99.1 FM.
FM RADIO STATION

WDHA-FM 46621
Owner: Beasley Broadcast Group
Editorial: 55 Horsehill Rd, Cedar Knolls, New Jersey 07927-2003 **Tel:** 1 973 538-1250.
Email: rock@wdhafm.com
Web site: http://www.wdhafm.com
Profile: WDHA-FM is a commercial station owned by Beasley Broadcast Group. The format of the station is rock music. WDHA-FM broadcasts in the Cedar Knolls, NJ area at 105.5 FM.
FM RADIO STATION

WDHC-FM 46654
Owner: Capper Broadcasting Company
Editorial: 440 Radio Station Ln, Berkeley Springs, West Virginia 25411 **Tel:** 1 304 258-1010.
Email: c929@comcast.net
Web site: http://www.wdhc.com
Profile: WDHC-FM is a commercial station owned by Capper Broadcasting Company. The format of the station is classic country and contemporary country music. WDHC-FM broadcasts in the Berkeley Springs, WV area at 92.9 FM.
FM RADIO STATION

WDHI-FM 42353
Owner: Townsquare Media, LLC
Editorial: 34 Chestnut St, Oneonta, New York 13820-2466 **Tel:** 1 607 432-1030.
Web site: http://www.wdhifm.com
Profile: WDHI-FM is a commercial station owned by Townsquare Media, LLC. The format of the station is oldies. WDHI-FM broadcasts to the Oneonta, NY area at a frequency of 100.3 FM.
FM RADIO STATION

WDHR-FM 45117
Owner: East Kentucky Radio Network
Editorial: 1240 Radio Dr, Pikeville, Kentucky 41501-4779 **Tel:** 1 606 437-4051.
Email: frontdesk@ekbradio.com
Web site: http://www.wdhr.com
Profile: WDHR-FM is a commercial station owned by East Kentucky Radio Network. The format of the station is contemporary country music. WDHR-FM broadcasts to the Pikeville, KY area at 93.1 FM.
FM RADIO STATION

WDHT-FM 40114
Owner: Alpha Media
Editorial: 717 E David Rd, Dayton, Ohio 45429-5218 **Tel:** 1 937 294-5858.
Web site: http://www.hot1029.com
Profile: WDHT-FM is a commercial station owned by Alpha Media. The format of the station is urban contemporary music. WDHT-FM broadcasts to the Dayton, OH area at 102.9 FM.
FM RADIO STATION

WDIA-AM 39083
Owner: iHeartMedia Inc.
Editorial: 2650 Thousand Oaks Blvd Ste 4100, Memphis, Tennessee 38118-2451 **Tel:** 1 901 259-1300.
Web site: http://www.am1070wdia.com
Profile: WDIA-AM is a commercial station owned by iHeartMedia Inc. The format of the station is R&B music. WDIA-AMbroadcasts to the Memphis, TN area at 1070 AM.
AM RADIO STATION

WDIC-AM 38989
Owner: Virginia Radio Network
Editorial: 2298 Rose Rdg, Clintwood, Virginia 24228 **Tel:** 1 276 835-8626.
Email: wdic@wdicradio.com
Web site: http://www.wdicradio.com
Profile: WDIC-AM is a commercial station owned by Virginia Radio Network. The format of the station is classic country. WDIC-AM broadcasts to the Clintwood, VA area at 1430 AM.
AM RADIO STATION

WDIC-FM 46328
Owner: Dickenson County Broadcasting
Editorial: 2298 Rose Rdg, Clintwood, Virginia 24228-7738 **Tel:** 1 276 835-8626.
Email: wdic@wdicradio.com
Web site: http://www.wdicradio.com
Profile: WDIC-FM is a commercial station owned by Dickenson County Broadcasting. The format of the station is classic hits. WDIC-FM broadcasts to the Clintwood, VA area at 92.1 FM.
FM RADIO STATION

WDIG-AM 35274
Owner: WWC Inc.
Editorial: 4039 Sunset Blvd, Steubenville, Ohio 43952-3577 **Tel:** 1 740 264-1760.
Profile: WDIG-AM is a commercial station owned by WWC Inc.. The format of the station is urban adult contemporary. WDIG-AM broadcasts to the Steubenville, OH area at 950 AM.
AM RADIO STATION

WDIY-FM 42699
Owner: Lehigh Valley Community Broadcasters Association Inc.
Editorial: 301 Broadway, Bethlehem, Pennsylvania 18015 **Tel:** 1 610 694-8100.
Email: news@wdiy.org
Web site: http://www.wdiy.org
Profile: WDIY-FM is a non-commercial station owned by Lehigh Valley Community Broadcasters Association Inc. The format of the station is AAA-adult album alternative, news and classical. WDIY-FM broadcasts to the Bethlehem, PA area at 88.1 FM.
FM RADIO STATION

WDIZ-AM 37844
Owner: iHeartMedia Inc.
Editorial: 1834 Lisenby Ave, Panama City, Florida 32405-3713 **Tel:** 1 850 769-1408.
Web site: http://www.espn590.com
Profile: WDIZ-AM is a commercial station owned by iHeartMedia Inc. The format of the station is sports. WDIZ-AM broadcasts to the Panama City, FL area at 590 AM.
AM RADIO STATION

WDJA-AM 36722
Owner: Radio Christo Mi Redentor Universo 1420AM Inc.
Editorial: 1946 S. Congress Ave., West Palm Beach, Florida 33406 **Tel:** 1 561 278-1420.
Email: info@universo1420.com
Web site: http://www.universo1420.com
Profile: WDJA-AM is a commercial station owned by Radio Christo Mi Redentor Universo 1420AM Inc. The format of the station is Spanish Contemporary Christian. WDJA-AM broadcasts to the Miami area at 1420 AM.
AM RADIO STATION

WDJC-FM 46722
Owner: Crawford Broadcasting Co.
Editorial: 120 Summit Pkwy Ste 200, Birmingham, Alabama 35209-4719 **Tel:** 1 205 879-3324.
Web site: http://www.wdjconline.com
Profile: WDJC-FM is a commercial station owned by Crawford Broadcasting Co. The format of the station is contemporary Christian. WDJC-FM broadcasts to the Birmingham, AL area at 93.7 FM.
FM RADIO STATION

WDJL-AM 36225
Owner: Fifth Avenue Broadcasting
Editorial: 3400 Blue Spring Rd NW Ste A3, Huntsville, Alabama 35810-3446 **Tel:** 1 256 852-1223.
Email: wdjlam@yahoo.com
Web site: http://wdjl1000.net
Profile: WDJL-AM is a commercial station owned by Fifth Avenue Broadcasting. The format of the station is gospel. WDJL-AM broadcasts to the Huntsville, AL area at 1000 AM.
AM RADIO STATION

WDJM-FM 40221
Owner: Framingham State College
Editorial: 100 State St, #516, Framingham, Massachusetts 01702-2499 **Tel:** 1 508 626-4622.
Email: wdjmfm@gmail.com
Web site: http://www.wdjm913.org
Profile: WDJM-FM is a non-commercial college station owned by Framingham State College. The format of the station features a variety of music and talk shows. WDJM-FM broadcasts in the Framingham, MA area at 91.3 FM.
FM RADIO STATION

WDJO-AM 35244
Owner: Alchemy Broadcasting
Editorial: 635 W 7Th St, Cincinnati, Ohio 45203-1513
Tel: 1 513 421-1480.
Web site: http://www.oldies1480.net
Profile: WDJO-AM is a commercial station owned by Alchemy Broadcasting. The format of the station is oldies. WDJO-AM broadcasts to the Cincinnati area at 1480 AM.
AM RADIO STATION

WDJQ-FM 45118
Owner: D.A. Peterson Inc.
Editorial: 393 Smyth Ave, Alliance, Ohio 44601-1562
Tel: 1 330 450-9250.
Web site: http://www.q92radio.com
Profile: WDJQ-FM is a commercial station owned by D.A. Peterson Inc. The format of the station is Top 40/CHR. WZKL-FM broadcasts to the Canton, OH area at 92.5 FM.
FM RADIO STATION

WDJR-FM 40473
Owner: Gulf South Communications Inc.
Editorial: 3245 Montgomery Hwy Ste 1, Dothan, Alabama 36303-2150 **Tel:** 1 334 712-9233.
Web site: http://www.969thelegend.com
Profile: WDJR-FM is a commercial station owned by Gulf South Communications Inc. The format of the station is Adult Contemporary music. WDJR-FM broadcasts to the Dothan, AL area at 96.9 FM.
FM RADIO STATION

WDJS-AM 35275
Owner: Mount Olive Broadcasting Co.
Editorial: 990 N Center St, Mount Olive, North Carolina 28365 **Tel:** 1 919 658-9751.
Profile: WDJS-AM is a commercial station owned by Mount Olive Broadcasting Co. The format of the station is religious. WDJS-AM broadcasts to the Mount Olive, NC area at 1430 AM.
AM RADIO STATION

WDJX-FM 42748
Owner: Alpha Media, LLC
Editorial: 520 S 4th St Ste 200, Louisville, Kentucky 40202-2577 **Tel:** 1 502 625-1220.
Web site: http://www.wdjx.com
Profile: WDJX-FM is a commercial station owned by Alpha Media, LLC. The format of the station is Top 40/CHR music. WDJX-FM broadcasts in the Louisville, KY area at 99.7 FM.
FM RADIO STATION

WDKB-FM 41721
Owner: DeKalb County Radio Ltd.
Editorial: 2201 N 1st St, #95, Dekalb, Illinois 60115
Tel: 1 815 758-0950.
Web site: http://www.b95fm.com
Profile: WDKB-FM is a commercial station owned by DeKalb County Radio Ltd. The format of the station is adult contemporary. WDKB-FM broadcasts to the Dekalb, IL area at 94.9 FM.
FM RADIO STATION

WDKC-FM 235099
Owner: Mid-Atlantic Broadcasting Inc.
Editorial: 8767 Route 414, Liberty, Pennsylvania 16930 **Tel:** 1 570 662-9000.
Email: kc101@frontier.com
Profile: WDKC-FM is a commercial station owned by Mid-Atlantic Broadcasting Inc. The format of the station is contemporary country. WDKC-FM broadcasts to the Mansfield, PA area at 101.5 FM.
FM RADIO STATION

WDKD-AM 37754
Owner: Miller Communications Inc.
Editorial: 593 N Williamsburg County Hwy, Kingstree, South Carolina 29556-6242 **Tel:** 1 803 775-2321.
Web site: http://www.miller.fm
Profile: WDKD-AM is a commercial station owned by Miller Communications Inc. The format of the station is sports. WDKD-AM broadcasts to the Kingstree, SC and surrounding areas at 1310 AM.
AM RADIO STATION

WDKE-FM 43088
Owner: Midwest Communications Inc.
Editorial: 824 S 3rd St, Terre Haute, Indiana 47807-4609 **Tel:** 1 812 232-4161.
Web site: http://959dukefm.com
Profile: WDKE-FM is a commercial station owned by Midwest Communications Inc. The format of the station is country. WDKE-FM broadcasts to the Terre Haute, IN, area at 95.9 FM.
FM RADIO STATION

WDKF-FM 41385
Owner: Midwest Communications Inc.
Editorial: 1420 Bellevue St, Green Bay, Wisconsin 54311-5649 **Tel:** 1 920 435-3771.
Web site: http://935dukefm.com
Profile: WDKF-FM is a commercial station owned by Midwest Communications Inc. The format of the station is classic country. WDKF-FM broadcasts to the Green Bay, WI area at 99.7 FM.
FM RADIO STATION

WDKL-FM 41921
Owner: Educational Media Foundation
Editorial: 5700 W Oaks Blvd, Rocklin, California 95765-3719 **Tel:** 1 916 251-1600.
Web site: http://www.klove.com
Profile: WDKL-FM is a non-commercial station owned by Educational Media Foundation. The format of the station is contemporary Christian and gospel music. WDKL-FM broadcasts to the Morgantown, WV area at 106.9 FM.
FM RADIO STATION

WDKM-FM 42354
Owner: Casper Communications, LLC
Editorial: 1040 W Center St, Adams, Wisconsin 53910-9818 **Tel:** 1 608 339-3221.
Profile: WDKM-FM is a commercial station owned by Casper Communications, LLC. The format of the station is adult contemporary music. WDKM-FM broadcasts to the Adams, WI area at 106.1 FM.
FM RADIO STATION

WDKN-AM 36434
Owner: R & F Communications, Inc.
Editorial: 106 E College St, Dickson, Tennessee 37055-1828 **Tel:** 1 615 446-0752.
Email: wdkn@bellsouth.net
Web site: http://www.wdkn1260am.com/
Profile: WDKN-AM is a commercial station owned by R & F Communications, Inc. The format of the station is country and gospel. WDKN-AM broadcasts to the Dickson, TN area at 1260 AM.
AM RADIO STATION

WDKR-FM 43919
Owner: WDKR, Inc.
Editorial: 120 W Wildwood Dr, Mount Zion, Illinois 62549-1151 **Tel:** 1 217 864-4141.
Email: wxfmwdkr@gmail.com
Profile: WDKR-FM is a commercial station owned by WDKR, Inc. The format of the station is oldies music. WDKR-FM broadcasts in the Decatur, IL area at 107.3 FM.
FM RADIO STATION

WDKS-FM 46390
Owner: Townsquare Media, LLC
Editorial: 117 SE 5th St, Evansville, Indiana 47708-1639 **Tel:** 1 812 425-4226.
Web site: http://1061evansville.com
Profile: WDKS-FM is a commercial station owned by Townsquare Media, LLC. The format for the station is Top 40/CHR. WDKS-FM broadcasts to the Evansville, IN area at 106.1 FM.
FM RADIO STATION

WDKW-FM 130518
Owner: Midwest Communications Inc.
Editorial: 1100 Sharps Ridge Mem Park Dr, Knoxville, Tennessee 37917-3000 **Tel:** 1 865 525-6000.
Web site: http://theduke.fm
Profile: WDKW-FM is a commercial station owned by Midwest Communications Inc. The format of the station is classic country. WDKW-FM broadcasts in the Knoxville, TN area at 95.7 FM.
FM RADIO STATION

WDKX-FM 41261
Owner: Monroe County Broadcasting Co.
Editorial: 683 E Main St, Rochester, New York 14605
Tel: 1 585 262-2050.
Email: wdkx@wdkx.com
Web site: http://www.wdkx.com
Profile: WDKX-FM is a commercial station owned by Monroe County Broadcasting Co. The format of the station is urban contemporary. WDKX-FM broadcasts to the Rochester, NY area at 103.9 FM.
FM RADIO STATION

WDKZ-FM 41742
Owner: iheartMedia Inc.
Editorial: 351 Tilghman Rd, Gateway Crossing, Salisbury, Maryland 21804-1920 **Tel:** 1 410 742-1923.
Email: delmarvapsa@iheartmedia.com
Web site: http://kiss959fm.iheart.com
Profile: WDKZ-FM is a commercial station owned by iheartMedia Inc. The format of the station is Top 40/CHR music. WDKZ-FM broadcasts in the Salisbury, MD area at 105.5 FM.
FM RADIO STATION

WDLA-AM 37755
Owner: Townsquare Media, LLC
Editorial: 34 Chestnut St, Oneonta, New York 13820-2466 **Tel:** 1 607 865-4321.
Web site: http://cnynews.com
Profile: WDLA-AM is a commercial station owned by Townsquare Media, LLC. The format of the station is news, sports and talk. WDLA-AM broadcasts to the Oneonta, NY area at 1270 AM.
AM RADIO STATION

WDLA-FM 45119
Owner: Townsquare Media, LLC
Editorial: 34 Chestnut St, Oneonta, New York 13820-2466 **Tel:** 1 607 865-4321.
Web site: http://www.wdlafm.com
Profile: WDLA-FM is a commercial station owned by Townsquare Media, LLC. The format of the station is contemporary country music. WDLA-FM broadcasts to the Oneonta, NY area at 92.1 FM.
FM RADIO STATION

WDLB-AM 39203
Owner: Seehafer Broadcasting Corp.
Editorial: 1714 N Central Ave, Marshfield, Wisconsin 54449-1514 **Tel:** 1 715 384-2191.
Web site: http://www.wdlbam.com
Profile: WDLB-AM is a commercial station owned by Seehafer Broadcasting Corp. The format of the station is news, talk and oldies music. WDLB-AM broadcasts to the Marshfield, WI area at 1450 AM.
AM RADIO STATION

WDLC-AM 37756
Owner: Neversink Radio, LLC
Tel: 1 845 561-2131.
Email: news@neversinkmediagroup.com
Web site: http://country1077.com
Profile: WDLC-AM is a commercial station owned by Neversink Radio, LLC. The format of the station is contemporary country. WDLC-AM broadcasts to Port Jervis, NY at 1490 AM.
AM RADIO STATION

WDLD-FM 87736
Owner: Alpha Media
Editorial: 25 Penncraft Ave, Chambersburg, Pennsylvania 17201-5600 **Tel:** 1 717 263-0813.
Email: wild@wild967.fm
Web site: http://www.wild967.fm
Profile: WDLD-FM is a commercial station owned by Main Line Broadcasting. The format of the station is urban contemporary. WDLD-FM broadcasts to the Chambersburg, PA area at 96.7 FM.
FM RADIO STATION

WDLJ-FM 140129
Owner: KM Communications Inc.
Editorial: 16808 Old US Highway 50, Carlyle, Illinois 62231-2420 **Tel:** 1 618 594-2620.
Web site: https://wdlj.wordpress.com
Profile: WDLJ-FM is a commercial station owned by KM Communications Inc. The format of the station is classic rock music. WDLJ-FM broadcasts to the Carlyle, IL area at 97.5 FM.
FM RADIO STATION

WDLM-AM 37757
Owner: Moody Bible Institute
Editorial: 18239 E 200th St, Coal Valley, Illinois 61240-9295 **Tel:** 1 309 234-5111.
Email: radiomoody@moody.edu
Web site: https://www.moodyradioqc.fm
Profile: WDLM-AM is a non-commercial station owned by Moody Bible Institute. The format of the station is Spanish religious. WDLM-AM broadcasts in the Moline, IL area at 960 AM.
AM RADIO STATION

WDLM-FM 45120
Owner: Moody Bible Institute
Editorial: 18239 E 200th St, Coal Valley, Illinois 61240-9295 **Tel:** 1 309 234-5111.
Email: wdlm@moody.edu
Web site: http://www.moodyradioqc.fm
Profile: WDLM-FM is a non-commercial station owned by Moody Bible Institute. The format of the station is religion and music. WDLM-FM broadcasts to the Coal Valley, IL area at 89.3 FM.
FM RADIO STATION

WDLR-AM 36764
Owner: ICS Holdings, Inc.
Editorial: 501 Bowtown Rd, Delaware, Ohio 43015-9410 **Tel:** 1 614 754-4922.
Email: admin@1550wdlr.com
Web site: http://1550wdlr.com
Profile: WDLR-AM is a commercial station owned by ICS Holdings, Inc. The format for the station is local news, talk and sports. WDLR-AM broadcasts to the Columbus, OH area at 1550 AM.
AM RADIO STATION

WDLS-AM 38087
Owner: Magnum Radio Group
Editorial: N6912 US Highway 51 #515, Portage, Wisconsin 53901-9678 **Tel:** 1 608 745-0959.
Email: info@magnumbroadcasting.com
Web site: http://www.wdlsam.com
Profile: WDLS-AM a commercial station owned by Magnum Radio Group. The format of the station is classic country. WDLS-AM broadcasts in the Portage, WI area at 900 AM.
AM RADIO STATION

WDLT-FM 41712
Owner: Cumulus Media Inc.
Editorial: 2800 Dauphin St Ste 104, Mobile, Alabama 36606-2400 **Tel:** 1 251 652-2000.
Web site: http://www.1041wdlt.com
Profile: WDLT-FM is a commercial station owned by Cumulus Media Inc. The format of the station is Urban AC. WDLT-FM broadcasts to the Mobile, AL, area at 104.1 FM.
FM RADIO STATION

WDLV-FM 41210
Owner: Educational Media Foundation
Editorial: 330 Himmarshee St Ste 207, Fort Lauderdale, Florida 33312-1712 **Tel:** 1 855 444-5355.
Email: klove@klove.com
Web site: http://www.klove.com
Profile: WDLV-FM is a non-commercial station owned by Educational Media Foundation. The format of the station is contemporary Christian music programming. WDLV-FM broadcasts to the Fort Myers, FL area at 88.7 FM.
FM RADIO STATION

WDLW-AM 36941
Owner: WOBL Radio Inc.
Editorial: 45624 US Highway 20, Oberlin, Ohio 44074
Tel: 1 440 774-1320.
Email: woblwdlw@yahoo.com
Web site: http://www.koolkatwdlw.com
Profile: WDLW-AM is a commercial station owned by WOBL Radio Inc. The format of the station is oldies. WDLW-AM broadcasts to the Oberlin, OH area at 1380 AM.
AM RADIO STATION

WDLX-AM 38169
Owner: Pirate Media Group LLC
Editorial: 525 Evans St, Greenville, North Carolina 27858 **Tel:** 1 252 317-1250.
Web site: http://www.pirateradio930.com
Profile: WDLX-AM is a commercial station owned by Pirate Media Group LLC. The format of the station is talk and sports. WDLX-AM broadcasts to the Greenville, NC area at 930 AM.
AM RADIO STATION

WDLZ-FM 45043
Owner: First Media Radio LLC
Editorial: 1714 W Main St, Murfreesboro, North Carolina 27855-1680 **Tel:** 1 252 398-4111.
Profile: WDLZ-FM is a commercial station owned by First Media Radio LLC. The format of the station is Lite Rock/Lite AC. WDLZ-FM broadcasts to the Murfreesboro, VA area at 98.3 FM.
FM RADIO STATION

WDMC-AM 593449
Owner: Divine Mercy Communications, Inc
Editorial: 2020 W Eau Gallie Blvd Ste 103, Melbourne, Florida 32935-4022 **Tel:** 1 321 757-7717.
Email: info@wdmc920.org
Web site: http://www.divinemercyradio.com/
Profile: WDMC-AM is a non-commercial station owned by Divine Mercy Communications, Inc. The format of the station is Catholic talk. WDMC-AM broadcasts to the Melbourne, FL area at 920 AM.
AM RADIO STATION

WDMG-AM 37759
Owner: Broadcast South, LLC
Editorial: 509 Columbia Ave Ste B, Douglas, Georgia 31533-5021 **Tel:** 1 912 389-0995.
Email: bstraffic@windstream.net
Profile: WDMG-AM is a commercial station owned by Broadcast South, LLC. The format of the station is Spanish Brokered. WDMG-AM broadcasts to the Douglas, GA area at 860 AM.
AM RADIO STATION

WDMG-FM 45122
Owner: Broadcast South, LLC
Editorial: 509 Columbia Ave Ste B, Douglas, Georgia 31533-5021 **Tel:** 1 912 389-0995.
Email: bstraffic@windstream.net
Profile: WDMG-FM is a commercial station owned by Broadcast South, LLC. The format of the station is adult contemporary. WDMG-FM broadcasts to the Albany, GA area at 97.9 FM.
FM RADIO STATION

WDMJ-AM 35279
Owner: Sovereign Communications LLC
Editorial: 1009 W Ridge St, Ste A, Marquette, Michigan 49855 **Tel:** 1 906 225-1313.
Email: wjpd@wjpd.com
Web site: http://www.wjpd.com
Profile: WDMJ-AM is a commercial station owned by Sovereign Communications LLC. The format of the station is news, sports and talk. WDMJ-AM broadcasts to the Marquette, MI area at 1320 AM.
AM RADIO STATION

WDMK-FM 40451
Owner: Urban One, Inc.
Editorial: 3250 Franklin St, Detroit, Michigan 48207-4219 **Tel:** 1 313 259-2000.
Web site: http://www.kissdetroit.com
Profile: WDMK-FM is a commercial station owned by Urban One Inc. The format of the station is urban adult contemporary. WDMK-FM broadcasts to the Detroit area at 105.9 FM.
FM RADIO STATION

WDML-FM 42341
Owner: Volunteer Broadcasting of Illinois, Inc.
Editorial: 3501 Broadway St, Mount Vernon, Illinois 62864 **Tel:** 1 618 242-3333.
Email: wdml@mvn.net
Web site: http://www.wdml.com
Profile: WDML-FM is a commercial station owned by Volunteer Broadcasting of Illinois, Inc. The format of the station is classic rock music. WDML-FM broadcasts to the Mount Vernon, IL area at 106.9 FM.
FM RADIO STATION

WDMO-FM 45500
Owner: Zoe Communications Inc.
Editorial: 125 E 3rd St Ste, New Richmond, Wisconsin 54017-1800 **Tel:** 1 715 246-2254.
Profile: WDMO-FM is a commercial station owned by Zoe Communications Inc. The format of the stations is country. WDMO-FM broadcasts to the Menomonie, WI area at 95.7 FM.
FM RADIO STATION

WDMP-AM 38992
Owner: Dodge Point Broadcasting Co.
Editorial: 2163 State Road 23-151, Dodgeville, Wisconsin 53533 **Tel:** 1 608 935-2302.
Email: wdmp@mhtc.net
Web site: http://www.d99point3.com
Profile: WDMP-AM is a commercial station owned by Dodge Point Broadcasting Co. The format for the station is contemporary country. WDMP-AM broadcasts to the Madison, WI area at 810 AM.
AM RADIO STATION

WDMP-FM 46327
Owner: Dodge Point Broadcasting Co.
Editorial: 2163 State Road 23-151, Dodgeville, Wisconsin 53533-9215 **Tel:** 1 608 935-2302.
Email: wdmp@mhtc.net
Web site: http://www.d99point3.com
Profile: WDMP-FM is a commercial station owned by Dodge Point Broadcasting Co. The format for the station is contemporary country. WDMP-FM broadcasts to the Madison, WI area at 99.3 FM.
FM RADIO STATION

WDMS-FM 45123
Owner: Ark-La-Ms Radio Group, LLC
Editorial: 1383 Pickett St, Greenville, Mississippi 38703-2437 **Tel:** 1 662 334-4559.
Email: wdms@bellsouth.net
Web site: http://www.wdms.fm/
FM RADIO STATION

WDMX-FM 40973
Owner: iHeart Media Inc.
Editorial: 6006 Grand Central Ave, Parkersburg, West Virginia 26105-9125 **Tel:** 1 304 295-6070.
Web site: http://mymix100.iheart.com
Profile: WDMX-FM is a commercial station owned by iHeart Media Inc. The format for the station is classic hits. WDMX-FM broadcasts to the Parkersburg, WV area at 100.1 FM.
FM RADIO STATION

WDNA-FM 41444
Owner: Bascomb Memorial Foundation
Editorial: 2921 Coral Way, Coral Gables, Florida 33145-3205 **Tel:** 1 305 662-8889.
Email: info@wdna.org
Web site: http://www.wdna.org
Profile: WDNA-FM is a non-commercial station owned by Bascomb Memorial Foundation. The format of the station is jazz and news. WDNA-FM broadcasts to the Miami area at 88.9 FM.
FM RADIO STATION

WDNB-FM 64210
Owner: Bold Gold Media Group
Editorial: 1987 State Route 52, Liberty, New York 12754-8316 **Tel:** 1 845 292-7535.
Web site: http://www.thunder102.com
Profile: WDNB-FM is a commercial station owned by Bold Gold Media Group. The format of the station in contemporary country. WDNB-FM broadcasts locally to the Liberty, NY area at 102.1 FM.
FM RADIO STATION

WDNC-AM 36232
Owner: Capitol Broadcasting Company
Editorial: 3100 Highwoods Blvd, Raleigh, North Carolina 27604-1033 **Tel:** 1 919 890-6101.
Web site: http://www.espntriangle.com
Profile: WDNC-AM is a commercial station owned by Capitol Broadcasting Company. The format of the station is sports. WDNC-AM broadcasts to the Raleigh, NC area at 620 AM.
AM RADIO STATION

WDND-AM 36979
Owner: Artistic Media Partners Inc.
Editorial: 3371 Cleveland Road Ext Ste 300, South Bend, Indiana 46628-9780 **Tel:** 1 574 273-9300.
Web site: http://www.u93.com
Profile: WDND-AM is a commercial station owned by Artistic Media Partners Inc. The format of the station is Hot AC. WDND-AM broadcasts to the South Bend, IN area at 1620 AM.
AM RADIO STATION

WDNE-AM 38639
Owner: West Virginia Radio Corp.
Editorial: Washington & Davis Streets, Elkins, West Virginia 26241 **Tel:** 1 304 636-1300.
Email: wdne@wvradio.com
Profile: WDNE-AM is a commercial station owned by West Virginia Radio Corp. The format of the station is adult standards music. WDNE-AM broadcasts in the Elkins, WV area at 1240 AM.
AM RADIO STATION

WDNE-FM 45991
Owner: West Virginia Radio Corp.
Editorial: Washington & Davis Streets, Elkins, West Virginia 26241 **Tel:** 1 304 636-1300.
Email: wdne@wvradio.com
Web site: http://www.wdnefm.com
Profile: WDNE-FM is a commercial station owned by West Virginia Radio Corp. The format of the station is country music. WDNE-FM broadcasts to the Elkins, WV area at 98.9 FM.
FM RADIO STATION

WDNG-AM 35280
Owner: WDNG Inc.
Editorial: 600 Leighton Ave Ste C, Anniston, Alabama 36207-5744 **Tel:** 1 256 236-8291.
Web site: http://www.infignosmedia.com
Profile: WDNG-AM is a commercial station owned by WDNG Inc. The format of the station is news and talk. WDNG-AM broadcasts to the Birmingham, AL area at 1450 AM.
AM RADIO STATION

WDNH-FM 45124
Owner: Bold Gold Media Group
Editorial: 575 Grove St, Honesdale, Pennsylvania 18431-1041 **Tel:** 1 570 253-1616.
Email: jhohman@boldgoldmedia.com
Web site: http://www.boldgoldlakeregion.com
Profile: WDNH-FM is a commercial station owned by Bold Gold Media Group. The format of the station is hot adult contemporary/Top 40. WDNH-FM broadcasts to the Honesdale, PA area at 95.3 FM.
FM RADIO STATION

WDNL-FM 45125
Owner: Neuhoff Family Limited Partnership
Editorial: 1501 N Washington Ave, Danville, Illinois 61832-2463 **Tel:** 1 217 442-1700.
Web site: http://www.vermilioncountryfirst.com
Profile: WDNL-FM is a commercial station owned by Neuhoff Family Limited Partnership. The format of the station is adult contemporary. WDNL-FM broadcasts to the Danville, IL area at 102.1 FM.
FM RADIO STATION

WDNS-FM 45126
Owner: Daily News Broadcasting Co.
Editorial: 804 College St, Bowling Green, Kentucky 42101-2133 **Tel:** 1 270 781-2121.
Web site: http://www.wdnsfm.com
Profile: WDNS-FM is a commercial station owned by Daily News Broadcasting Co. The format for the station is classic rock. WDNS-FM broadcasts to the Bowling Green, KY area at 93.3 FM.
FM RADIO STATION

WDNT-AM 39134
Owner: Beverly Broadcasting Company, LLC
Tel: 1 423 285-6441.
Email: comments@rheacountryradio.com
Web site: http://www.rheacountryradio.com
Profile: WDNT-AM is a commercial station owned by Beverly Broadcasting Company, LLC. The format of the station is classic hits. WDNT-AM broadcasts to the Dayton, TN area at 1280 AM.
AM RADIO STATION

WDNX-FM 40224
Owner: Rural Life Foundation Inc.
Editorial: 11291 Pierce St, Riverside, California 92505-2705 **Tel:** 1 800 775-4673.
Web site: http://www.lifetalk.net
Profile: WDNX-FM is a non-commercial station owned by Rural Life Foundation Inc. The format of the station is religious and Christian programming. WDNX-FM broadcasts to the Savannah, TN area at 89.1 FM.
FM RADIO STATION

WDNY-AM 38535
Owner: Genesee Media Corp.
Editorial: 195 Main St, Dansville, New York 14437-1315 **Tel:** 1 585 335-9369.
Email: wdny@geneseemedia.net
Web site: http://geneseenow.com
Profile: WDNY-AM is a commercial station owned by Genesee Media Corp. The format of the station is classic hits music. WDNY-AM broadcasts to the Dansville, NY at 1400 AM.
AM RADIO STATION

WDOC-AM 39244
Owner: WDOC Inc.
Editorial: 95 Jackson St, Prestonsburg, Kentucky 41653-1010 **Tel:** 1 606 886-8409.
Web site: http://www.wdoc.net
Profile: WDOC-AM is a commercial station owned by WDOC Inc. The format of the station is gospel. WDOC-AM broadcasts to Prestonburg, KY area at 1310 AM.
AM RADIO STATION

WDOD-AM 37761
Owner: Bahakel Communications
Editorial: 2615 Broad St, Chattanooga, Tennessee 37408-3100 **Tel:** 1 423 321-6200.
Web site: http://www.foxsportschattanooga.com
Profile: WDOD-AM is a commercial station owned by Bahakel Communications. The format of the station is sports. WDOD-AM broadcasts to the Chattanooga, TN area on 1310 AM.
AM RADIO STATION

WDOD-FM 45127
Owner: Bahakel Communications
Editorial: 2615 Broad St, Chattanooga, Tennessee 37408-3100 **Tel:** 1 423 321-6200.
Web site: http://www.hits96.com
Profile: WDOD-FM is a commercial station owned by Bahakel Communications. The format of the station is Top 40/CHR. WDOD-FM broadcasts to the Chattanooga, TN area at 96.5 FM.
FM RADIO STATION

WDOE-AM 38336
Owner: Chadwick Bay Broadcasting Corporation
Editorial: 4561 Willow Rd, Dunkirk, New York 14048-9644 **Tel:** 1 716 366-1410.
Email: community@wdoe1410.com
Web site: http://www.chautauquatoday.com
Profile: WDOE-AM is a commercial station owned by Chadwick Bay Broadcasting Corporation. The format of the station is news, sports, and classic hits music. WDOE-AM's broadcasts to the Dunkirk-Fredonia, NY area at 1410 AM.
AM RADIO STATION

WDOG-AM 37762
Owner: Good-Radio Broadcast Co.
Editorial: 2447 Augusta Hwy, Allendale, South Carolina 29810-7007 **Tel:** 1 803 584-3500.
Email: wdog935@aol.com
Web site: http://www.bigdogradio.com
Profile: WDOG-AM is a commercial station owned by Good-Radio Broadcast Co. The format of the station is Pop Oldies from 60-90. WDOG-AM broadcasts to the Allendale, SC area at 1460 AM.
AM RADIO STATION

WDOG-FM 45651
Owner: Good-Radio Broadcast Co.
Editorial: 2447 Augusta Hwy, Allendale, South Carolina 29810-7007 **Tel:** 1 803 584-3500.
Email: wdog935@aol.com
Web site: http://www.bigdogradio.com
Profile: WDOG-FM is a commercial station owned by Good-Radio Broadcast Co. The format of the station is classic country. WDOG-FM broadcasts to the Allendale, SC area at 93.5 FM.
FM RADIO STATION

WDOH-FM 40225
Owner: Childers Media Group, LLC
Editorial: 111 E 2nd St, Delphos, Ohio 45833-1760
Tel: 1 419 331-1600.
Email: literock1071@aol.com
Web site: http://www.literock1071.com
Profile: WDOH-FM is a commercial station owned by Childers Media Group, LLC. The format of the station is Lite Rock/Lite AC. WDOH-FM broadcasts to the Delphos, OH area at 107.1 FM.
FM RADIO STATION

WDOK-FM 46119
Owner: CBS Radio
Editorial: 1041 Huron Rd E, Cleveland, Ohio 44115-1706 **Tel:** 1 216 861-0100.
Web site: http://star102cleveland.cbslocal.com
Profile: WDOK-FM is a commercial station owned by CBS Radio. The format of the station is adult contemporary. WDOK-FM broadcasts to the Cleveland area at 102.1 FM.
FM RADIO STATION

WDOM-FM 40226
Owner: Corporation of Providence College
Editorial: 549 River Ave, Providence, Rhode Island 02918-7000 **Tel:** 1 401 865-2460.
Email: wdomdj@yahoo.com
Profile: WDOM-FM is a non-commercial station owned by the Corporation of Providence College. The format of the station is college variety. WDOM-FM broadcasts to the Providence, RI area at 91.3 FM. The station closes operations during the summer months, beginning in May.
FM RADIO STATION

WDOR-AM 37763
Owner: Door County Broadcasting Co.
Editorial: 800 S 15th Ave, Sturgeon Bay, Wisconsin 54235-1541 **Tel:** 1 920 743-4411.
Email: email@wdor.com
Web site: http://www.wdor.com
Profile: WDOR-AM is a commercial station owned by Door County Broadcasting Co. The format of the station is adult contemporary. WDOR-AM broadcasts to the Door County, WI area at 910 AM.
AM RADIO STATION

WDOR-FM 45128
Owner: Door County Broadcasting Co.
Editorial: 800 S 15th Ave, Sturgeon Bay, Wisconsin 54235 **Tel:** 1 920 743-4411.
Email: email@wdor.com
Web site: http://www.wdor.com
Profile: WDOR-FM is a commercial station owned by Door County Broadcasting Co. The format of the station is adult contemporary music. WDOR-FM broadcasts to the Sturgeon Bay, WI area at 93.9 FM.
FM RADIO STATION

WDOS-AM 39204
Owner: Townsquare Media, LLC
Editorial: 34 Chestnut St, Oneonta, New York 13820-2466 **Tel:** 1 607 432-1030.
Web site: http://cnynews.com
Profile: WDOS-AM is a commercial station owned by Townsquare Media, LLC. The format of the station is news, sports and talk. WDOS-AM broadcasts to the Oneonta, NY area at 730 AM.
AM RADIO STATION

WDOT-FM 43094
Owner: Northeast Broadcasting Co.
Editorial: 169 River St, Montpelier, Vermont 5602
Tel: 1 802 223-2396.
Email: feedback@pointfm.com
Web site: http://www.pointfm.com
Profile: WDOT-FM is a commercial station owned by Northeast Broadcasting Co. The format of the station is adult album alternative music. The station is a simulcast of WNCS-FM. WDOT-FM broadcasts to the Montpelier, VA area at 95.7 FM.
FM RADIO STATION

WDOV-AM 37764
Owner: iHeartMedia Inc.
Editorial: 1575 McKee Rd Ste 206, Dover, Delaware 19904-1382 **Tel:** 1 302 674-1410.
Web site: http://wdov.iheart.com
Profile: WDOV-AM is a commercial station owned by iHeartMedia Inc. The format of the station is news and talk. WDOV-AM broadcasts in the Dover, DE area at 1410 AM.
AM RADIO STATION

WDPC-AM 36860
Owner: Word Christian Broadcasting Inc.
Editorial: 8451 S Cherokee Blvd, Ste B, Douglasville, Georgia 30134 **Tel:** 1 770 920-1520.
Email: wordchr@bellsouth.net
Web site: http://www.wordchristianbroadcasting.com
Profile: WDPC-AM is a commercial station owned by Word Christian Broadcasting Inc. The format of station is Christian and religious programming and gospel music. WDPC-AM broadcasts to the Douglasville, GA area at 1500 AM.
AM RADIO STATION

WDPG-FM 43058
Owner: Dayton Public Radio Inc.
Editorial: 126 N Main St Ste 110, Dayton, Ohio 45402-1766 **Tel:** 1 937 496-3850.
Email: dpr@dpr.org
Web site: http://www.discoverclassical.org
Profile: WDPG-FM is a non-commercial station owned by Dayton Public Radio Inc. The format of the station is classical music. WDPG-FM broadcasts to the Dayton, OH area at 89.9 FM.
FM RADIO STATION

WDPN-AM 37798
Owner: Peterson(Donald A.)
Editorial: 393 Smyth Ave, Alliance, Ohio 44601
Tel: 1 330 821-1111.
Email: news@q92radio.com
Profile: WDPN-AM is a commercial station owned by Donald A. Peterson. The format of the station is easy listening. WDPN-AM broadcasts to the Cleveland-Canton, OH area at 1310 AM.
AM RADIO STATION

WDPR-FM 40227
Owner: Dayton Public Radio Inc.
Editorial: 126 N Main St, Ste 110, Dayton, Ohio 45402
Tel: 1 937 496-3850.
Email: dpr@dpr.org
Web site: http://www.dpr.org
Profile: WDPR-FM is a non-commercial station owned by Dayton Public Radio Inc. The format of the station is classical music. WDPR-FM broadcasts to the Dayton, OH area at 88.1 FM.
FM RADIO STATION

WDRC-AM 38697
Owner: Connoisseur Media
Editorial: 869 Blue Hills Ave, Bloomfield, Connecticut 06002-3710 **Tel:** 1 860 243-1115.
Web site: http://www.talkofconnecticut.com
Profile: WDRC-AM is a commercial station owned by Connoisseur Media. The format of the station is talk. WDRC-AM broadcasts to the Bloomfield, CT area at 1360 AM.
AM RADIO STATION

WDRC-FM 46052
Owner: Connoisseur Media
Editorial: 869 Blue Hills Ave, Bloomfield, Connecticut 06002-3710 **Tel:** 1 860 243-1115.
Web site: http://www.1029thewhale.com/
Profile: WDRC-FM is a commercial station owned by Connoisseur Media. The format of the station is classic rock. WDRC-FM broadcasts in the Bloomfield, CT area at 102.9 FM.
FM RADIO STATION

WDRE-FM 42698
Owner: Equinox Broadcasting Corp.
Editorial: 101 Main St, Johnson City, New York 13790-2426 **Tel:** 1 607 772-1005.
Email: info@equinoxbroadcasting.com
Profile: WDRE-FM is a commercial station owned by Equinox Broadcasting Corp. The format of the station is alternative rock music. WDRE-FM broadcasts to the Johnson City, NY area at 100.5 FM.
FM RADIO STATION

WDRK-FM 133613
Owner: Mid-West Family Broadcasting
Editorial: 944 Harlem St, Altoona, Wisconsin 54720-1127 **Tel:** 1 715 832-1530.
Profile: WDRK-FM is a commercial station owned by Mid-West Family Broadcasting. The format of the station is adult hits. WDRK-FM broadcasts in the Altoona, WI area at 99.9 FM.
FM RADIO STATION

WDRM-FM 46112
Owner: iHeartMedia Inc.
Editorial: 26869 Peoples Rd, Madison, Alabama 35756-4632 **Tel:** 1 256 309-2400.
Web site: http://wdrm.iheart.com
Profile: WDRM-FM is a commercial station owned by iHeartMedia Inc. The format of the station is contemporary country. WDRM-FM broadcasts to the Madison, AL area at 102.1 FM.
FM RADIO STATION

WDRQ-FM 40491
Owner: Cumulus Media Inc.
Editorial: 3011 W Grand Blvd Ste 800, Detroit, Michigan 48202-3086 **Tel:** 1 313 871-9300.
Web site: http://www.nashfm931.com
Profile: WDRQ-FM is a commercial station owned by Cumulus Media Inc. The format of the station is contemporary country. WDRQ-FM broadcasts to the Detroit area at 93.1 FM.
FM RADIO STATION

WDRR-FM 46591
Owner: Beasley Broadcast Group
Editorial: 4051 Jimmie Dyess Pkwy, Augusta, Georgia 30909 **Tel:** 1 706 396-7000.
Web site: http://ilovebobfm.com
Profile: WDRR-FM is a commercial station owned by Beasley Broadcast Group. The format of the station is adult hits. WDRR-FM broadcasts to the Augusta, GA area on 93.9 FM.
FM RADIO STATION

WDRU-AM 35975
Owner: Truth Broadcasting
Editorial: 4405 Providence Ln, Ste D, Winston Salem, North Carolina 27106 **Tel:** 1 336 759-0363.
Email: info@wtru.com
Web site: http://www.wtru.com
Profile: WDRU-AM is a commercial station owned by Truth Broadcasting. The format of the station is Christian talk. WDRU-AM broadcasts to the Winston Salem, NC area at 1030 AM.
AM RADIO STATION

WDRV-FM 40561
Owner: Hubbard Radio, LLC
Editorial: 875 N Michigan Ave Ste 1510, Chicago, Illinois 60611-1874 **Tel:** 1 312 274-9710.
Web site: http://www.wdrv.com
Profile: WDRV-FM is a commercial station owned by Hubbard Radio, LLC. The format of the station is classic rock. WDRV-FM broadcasts to the entire Chicago metro area at 97.1 FM.
FM RADIO STATION

WDSC-AM 37767
Owner: iHeartMedia Inc.
Editorial: 181 E Evans St Ste 311, Florence, South Carolina 29506-5505 **Tel:** 1 843 667-4600.
Profile: WDSC-AM is a commercial station owned by iHeartMedia Inc. The format of the station is gospel. WDSC-AM broadcasts to the Florence, SC area at 800 AM.
AM RADIO STATION

WDSD-FM 42350
Owner: iHeartMedia Inc.
Editorial: 1575 McKee Rd, Dover, Delaware 19904-1382 **Tel:** 1 302 674-1410.
Web site: http://www.wdsd.com
Profile: WDSD-FM is a commercial station owned by iHeartMedia Inc. The format of the station is classic and contemporary country. WDSD-FM broadcasts to the Dover, DE area at 94.7 FM.
FM RADIO STATION

WDSJ-FM 41946
Owner: iheartMedia Inc.
Editorial: 101 Pine St, Dayton, Ohio 45402-2948
Tel: 1 937 224-1137.
Web site: http://www.big1065.com
Profile: WDSJ-FM is a commercial station owned by iheartMedia Inc. The format of the station is classic hits. WDSJ-FM broadcasts in the Dayton, OH area at 106.5 FM.
FM RADIO STATION

WDSL-AM 35282
Owner: Shoaf, Farren
Editorial: 431 Eaton Rd, Mocksville, North Carolina 27028-8653 **Tel:** 1 704 902-9640.
Email: wdsl1520am@yahoo.com
Web site: http://www.wdsl1520.com
Profile: WSDL-AM is a commercial station owned by Farren Soaf. The format of the station is gospel and talk radio. WSDL-AM broadcasts to the Mocksville, NC area at 1520 AM.
AM RADIO STATION

WDSM-AM 37768
Owner: Midwest Communications Inc.
Editorial: 715 E Central Entrance, Duluth, Minnesota 55811-5596 **Tel:** 1 218 722-4321.
Web site: http://www.wdsm710.com
Profile: WDSM-AM is a commercial station owned by Midwest Communications Inc. The format of the station is news and talk. WDSM-AM broadcasts to the Duluth, MN area at 710 AM.
AM RADIO STATION

WDSN-FM 41967
Owner: Priority Communications
Editorial: 12 W Long Ave, Du Bois, Pennsylvania 15801-2100 **Tel:** 1 814 375-5260.
Email: news@sunny1065.fm
Web site: http://www.sunny1065.fm
Profile: WDSN-FM is a commercial station owned by Priority Communications. The format of the station is adult contemporary music. WDSN-FM broadcasts to the Du Bois, PA area at 106.5 FM.
FM RADIO STATION

WDSR-AM 37769
Owner: Newman Media Inc.
Editorial: 2485 S Marion Ave, Lake City, Florida 32025-0051 **Tel:** 1 386 961-9494.
Web site: http://northfloridanow.com
Profile: WDSR-AM is a commercial station owned by Newman Media Inc. The format of the station is country music. WDSR-AM broadcasts to the Lake City, FL area at 1340 AM.
AM RADIO STATION

WDST-FM 41402
Owner: Chet 5 Broadcasting
Editorial: 293 Tinker St, Woodstock, New York 12498-1132 **Tel:** 1 845 679-7600.
Email: live@wdst.com
Web site: http://www.wdst.com
Profile: WDST-FM is a commercial station owned by Chet 5 Broadcasting. The format of the station is adult album alternative music. WDST-FM broadcasts to the Woodstock, NY, area at 100.1 FM.
FM RADIO STATION

WDSY-FM 43138
Owner: CBS Radio
Editorial: 651 Holiday Dr, Pittsburgh, Pennsylvania 15220-2740 **Tel:** 1 412 920-9400.
Web site: http://y108.cbslocal.com
Profile: WDSY-FM is a commercial station owned by CBS Radio. The format of the station is contemporary country. WDSY-FM broadcasts to the Pittsburgh area at 107.9 FM.
FM RADIO STATION

WDTK-AM 35611
Owner: Salem Media Group, Inc.
Editorial: 2 Radio Plaza St, Ferndale, Michigan 48220-2129 **Tel:** 1 248 581-1234.
Web site: http://www.newstalk1400.us
Profile: WDTK-AM is a commercial station owned by Salem Media Group, Inc. The format of the station is news and talk. WDTK-AM broadcasts to the Detroit area at 1400 AM.
AM RADIO STATION

WDTL-FM 45405
Owner: Debut Broadcasting Corporation Inc.
Editorial: 830 Main St, Greenville, Mississippi 38701-4102 **Tel:** 1 601 636-2340.
Web site: http://www.deltacountry.com
Profile: WDTL-FM is a commercial station owned by Debut Broadcasting Corporation Inc.. The format of the station is classic country. WDTL-FM broadcasts locally in the Greenville, MS area at a frequency of 105.7 FM.
FM RADIO STATION

WDTW-FM 45628
Owner: iHeartMedia Inc.
Editorial: 27675 Halsted Rd, Farmington Hills, Michigan 48331-3511 **Tel:** 1 248 324-5800.
Web site: http://www.thedrocks.com/main.html
Profile: WDTW-FM is a commercial station owned by iHeartMedia Inc. The format of the station is classic rock. WDTW-FM broadcasts to the Detroit area at 106.7 FM.
FM RADIO STATION

WDTX-FM 622736
Owner: Sunrise Broadcasting, LLC
Editorial: 1110 E Wausau Ave, Wausau, Wisconsin 54403-3149 **Tel:** 1 715 845-8218.
Web site: http://www.espn1005.com
Profile: WDTX-FM is a commercial station owned by Sunrise Broadcasting, LLC. The format of the station is sports. WDTX-FM broadcasts to Rothschild and Wausau, WI areas at 100.5 FM.
FM RADIO STATION

WDUK-FM 40232
Owner: Stimpson(Edwin)
Editorial: 901 N Promenade St, Havana, Illinois 62644
Tel: 1 309 543-3331.
Profile: WDUK-FM is a commercial station owned by Edwin Stimpson. The format of the station is country music and news. WDUK-FM broadcasts to the Havana, IL area at 99.3.
FM RADIO STATION

WDUL-AM 39011
Owner: Midwest Communications Inc.
Editorial: 715 E Central Entrance, Duluth, Minnesota 55811-5596 **Tel:** 1 218 722-4321.
Web site: http://mwcradio.com/station/71/
Profile: WDUL-AM is a commercial station owned by Midwest Communications Inc. The format of the station is sports. WDUL-AM broadcasts to the Duluth, MN area at 970 AM.
AM RADIO STATION

WDUN-AM 38881
Owner: Jacobs Media Corp.
Editorial: 1102 Thompson Bridge Rd, Gainesville, Georgia 30501 **Tel:** 1 770 532-9921.
Email: info@jacobsmedia.net
Web site: http://www.wdun.com
Profile: WDUN-AM is a commercial station owned by Jacobs Media Corp. The format of the station is news, talk and sports. WDUN-AM broadcasts to the Atlanta area at 550 AM.
AM RADIO STATION

WDUN-FM 45795
Owner: Jacobs Media Corp.
Editorial: 1102 Thompson Bridge Rd, Gainesville, Georgia 30501 **Tel:** 1 770 532-9921.
Email: info@jacobsmedia.net
Web site: http://www.wdun.com
Profile: WDUN-FM is a commercial station owned by Jacobs Media. The format of the station is news/talk. WDUN-FM broadcasts to the Atlanta area at 102.9 FM.
FM RADIO STATION

WDUV-FM 43033
Owner: Cox Media Group, Inc.
Editorial: 11300 4th St N Ste 300, Saint Petersburg, Florida 33716-2941 **Tel:** 1 727 579-2000.
Email: 1055comments@coxtampa.com
Web site: http://www.wduv.com
Profile: WDUV-FM is a commercial station owned by Cox Media Group, Inc. The format of the station is Lite Rock/Lite AC. WDUV-FM broadcasts to the Tampa, FL area at 105.5 FM.
FM RADIO STATION

WDUX-AM 37770
Owner: Laird Broadcasting
Editorial: 200 Tower Rd, Waupaca, Wisconsin 54981
Tel: 1 715 258-5528.
Email: mail@wdux.net
Web site: http://www.wduxradio.com
Profile: WDUX-AM is a commercial station owned by Laird Broadcasting. The format of the station is classic country. WDUX-AM broadcasts to the Waupaca, WI area at 800 AM.
AM RADIO STATION

WDUX-FM 45132
Owner: Laird Broadcasting
Editorial: 200 Tower Rd, Waupaca, Wisconsin 54981
Tel: 1 715 258-5528.
Email: news@wdux.net
Web site: http://www.wduxradio.com
Profile: WDUX-FM is a commercial station owned by Laird Broadcasting. The format of the station is adult contemporary. WDUX-FM broadcasts to the Waupaca, WI area at 92.7 FM.
FM RADIO STATION

WDUZ-AM 42073
Owner: Cumulus Media Inc.
Editorial: 810 Victoria St, Green Bay, Wisconsin 54302-2465 **Tel:** 1 920 468-4100.
Email: thefan@cumulus.com
Web site: http://www.thefan1075.com
Profile: WDUZ-AM is a commercial station owned by Cumulus Media Inc. The format of the station is sports. WDUZ-AM broadcasts to the Green Bay, WI area at 1400 AM.
AM RADIO STATION

WDUZ-FM 37771
Owner: Cumulus Media Inc.
Editorial: 810 Victoria St, Green Bay, Wisconsin 54302-2465 **Tel:** 1 920 468-4100.
Email: thefan@cumulus.com
Web site: http://www.thefan1075.com
Profile: WDUZ-FM is a commercial station owned by Cumulus Media Inc. The format of the station is sports. WDUZ-FM broadcasts to the Green Bay, WI area at 107.5 FM.
FM RADIO STATION

WDVA-AM 35862
Owner: Mitchell Communications
Editorial: 1 Radio Ln, Danville, Virginia 24541-5235
Tel: 1 434 797-1250.
Email: wdvaradio@gmail.com
Web site: http://www.wdvaradio.com
Profile: WDVA-AM is a commercial station that is owned by Mitchell Communications. The format of the station is gospel and Christian. WDVA-AM broadcasts to the Danville, VA area at 1250 AM.
AM RADIO STATION

WDVD-FM 46399
Owner: Cumulus Media Inc.
Editorial: 3011 W Grand Blvd, Ste 800, Detroit, Michigan 48202-3086 **Tel:** 1 313 871-3030.
Web site: http://www.963wdvd.com
Profile: WDVD-FM is a commercial station owned by Cumulus Media Inc. The format of the station is hot adult contemporary music. WDVD-FM broadcasts to the Detroit area at 96.3 FM.
FM RADIO STATION

WDVE-FM 40234
Owner: iHeartMedia Inc.
Editorial: 200 Fleet St Fl 4, Pittsburgh, Pennsylvania 15220-2908 **Tel:** 1 412 937-1441.
Email: feedback@dve.com
Web site: http://www.dve.com
Profile: WDVE-FM is a commercial station owned by iHeartMedia Inc. The format for the station is classic rock. WDVE-FM broadcasts to the Pittsburgh area at 102.5 FM.
FM RADIO STATION

WDVH-AM 35501
Owner: Marc Radio Group, LLC
Editorial: 100 NW 76th Dr Ste 2, Gainesville, Florida 32607-6659 **Tel:** 1 352 313-3150.
Web site: http://www.flafnr.com
Profile: WDVH-AM is a commercial station owned by Marc Radio Group, LLC. The format of the station is news/talk. WDVH-AM broadcasts to the Gainesville, FL area at 980 AM.
AM RADIO STATION

WDVH-FM 41211
Owner: Marc Radio Group, LLC
Editorial: 100 NW 76th Dr Ste 2, Gainesville, Florida 32607-6659 **Tel:** 1 352 463-1345.
Web site: http://www.1017hankfm.com
Profile: WDVH-FM is a commercial station owned by Marc Radio Group, LLC. The format of the station is classic country. WDVH-FM broadcasts to the Gainesville, FL area at 101.7 FM.
FM RADIO STATION

WDVI-FM 45603
Owner: iHeartMedia Inc.
Editorial: 100 Chestnut St Ste 1700, Rochester, New York 14604-2418 **Tel:** 1 585 454-4884.
Web site: http://www.mydrivefm.com
Profile: WDVI-FM is a commercial station owned by iHeartMedia Inc. The format of the station is adult contemporary. WDVI-FM broadcasts to the Rochester, NY area at 100.5 FM.
FM RADIO STATION

WDVM-AM 38913
Owner: Starboard Media Foundation Inc.
Editorial: 1752 Brackett Ave, Eau Claire, Wisconsin 54701 **Tel:** 1 715 855-1439.
Email: info@relevantradio.com
Web site: http://www.relevantradio.com
Profile: WDVM-AM is a commercial station owned by Starboard Media Foundation Inc. The format of the station is religious. WDVM-AM broadcasts to the Eau Claire, WI area at 1050 AM.
AM RADIO STATION

WDVT-FM 42737
Owner: Pamal Broadcasting Ltd.
Editorial: 67 Merchants Row, Rutland, Vermont 5701
Tel: 1 802 775-7500.
Email: thedrive@catamountradio.com
Web site: http://www.945thedrive.com
Profile: WDVT-FM is a commercial station owned by Pamal Broadcasting Ltd. The format of the station is classic hits. WDVT-FM broadcasts to the Rutland, VT area at 94.5 FM.
FM RADIO STATION

WDVX-FM 43936
Owner: Cumberland Communities Communications Corp.
Editorial: 2415 Andersonville Hwy, Clinton, Tennessee 37716 **Tel:** 1 865 494-2020.
Email: studio@wdvx.com
Web site: http://www.wdvx.com
Profile: WDVX-FM is a non-commercial station owned by Cumberland Communities Communications Corp. The format of the station is variety. WDVX-FM broadcasts to the Clinton, TN area at a frequency of 89.9.
FM RADIO STATION

WDWD-AM 37975
Owner: Salem Media Group, Inc.
Editorial: 2970 Peachtree Rd NW Ste 700, Atlanta, Georgia 30305-4919 **Tel:** 1 404 995-7300.
Web site: http://www.faithtalk590.com
Profile: WDWD-AM is a commercial station owned by Salem Media Group, Inc. The format of the station is Christian talk. WDWD-AM broadcasts to the Atlanta area at 590 AM.
AM RADIO STATION

WDWG-FM 46304
Owner: First Media Radio LLC
Editorial: 12714 E State Highway 97, Rocky Mount, North Carolina 27803-4626 **Tel:** 1 252 442-8092.
Email: wecare@firstmedianc.com
Web site: http://www.bigdawg985.com
Profile: WDWG-FM is a commercial station owned by First Media Radio LLC. The format of the station is contemporary country. WDWG-FM broadcasts to the Rocky Mount, NC area at 98.5 FM.
FM RADIO STATION

WDWN-FM 40235
Owner: Cayuga Community College
Editorial: 197 Franklin St, Auburn, New York 13021-3011 **Tel:** 1 315 255-1743 2284.
Email: wdwn@hotmail.com
Web site: http://www.wdwn.fm
Profile: WDWN-FM is a non-commercial station owned by Cayuga Community College. The format of the station is rock alternative. WDWN-FM broadcasts to the Auburn, NY area at 89.1 FM.
FM RADIO STATION

WDWQ-FM 73182
Owner: Midwest Communications Inc.
Editorial: 824 S 3Rd St, Terre Haute, Indiana 47807-4609 **Tel:** 1 812 232-4161.
Web site: http://q1027.com
Profile: WDWQ-FM is a commercial station owned by Midwest Communications Inc.. The format of the station is contemporary country. WDWQ-FM broadcasts to the Terre Haute, IN area at 102.7 FM.
FM RADIO STATION

WDWR-AM 36215
Owner: Divine Word Communications
Editorial: 14 W Gadsden St, Pensacola, Florida 32501-3908 **Tel:** 1 888 784-3476.
Email: grnonline@grnonline.com
Web site: http://grnonline.com/
Profile: WDWR-AM is a non-commercial station owned by La Promesa Foundation. The format of the station is religious. WDWR-AM broadcasts to the Pensacola, FL area at 1230 AM.
AM RADIO STATION

WDWS-AM 37773
Owner: D.W.S. Inc.
Editorial: 2301 S Neil St, Champaign, Illinois 61820-7507 **Tel:** 1 217 351-5300.
Email: newsroom@wdws.com
Web site: http://www.wdws.com
Profile: WDWS-AM is a commercial station owned by D.W.S. Inc. The format of the station is news and talk programming. WDWS-AM broadcasts to the Champaign, IL area at 1400 AM.
AM RADIO STATION

WDXB-FM 42728
Owner: iHeartMedia Inc.
Editorial: 600 Beacon Pkwy W, Birmingham, Alabama 35209-3120 **Tel:** 1 205 439-9600.
Web site: http://www.1025thebull.com
Profile: WDXB-FM is a commercial station owned by iHeartMedia Inc. The format of the station is country music. WDXB-FM broadcasts to the Birmingham, AL area at 102.5 FM.
FM RADIO STATION

WDXC-FM 41957
Owner: Cornett (Jackie&Howard)
Editorial: 12548 Orby Cantrell Hwy, Pound, Virginia 24279-4812 **Tel:** 1 276 796-5411.
Email: wdxc102fm@windstream.net
Web site: http://wdxcfm.com
Profile: WDXC-FM is a commercial station owned by Jackie & Howard Cornett. The format of the station is contemporary country. WDXC-FM broadcasts to the Pound, VA area at 102.3 FM.
FM RADIO STATION

WDXE-AM 37774
Owner: Lakewood Communications LLC
Editorial: 29 Public Sq, Lawrenceburg, Tennessee 38464-3351 **Tel:** 1 931 762-4411.
Email: wdxe@wdxe.com
Web site: http://www.radio7media.com
Profile: WDXE-AM is a commercial station owned by Lakewood Communications LLC. The format of the station is classic country. WDXE-AM broadcasts to the Lawrenceburg, TN area at 1370 AM.
AM RADIO STATION

WDXI-AM 37775
Owner: Hunt(Gerald W.)
Editorial: 1 Radio Park Dr, Jackson, Tennessee 38305-4124 **Tel:** 1 731 427-9611.
Email: kool103fm@yahoo.com
Profile: WDXI-AM is a commercial station owned by Gerald W. Hunt. The format of the station is news and talk. WDXI-AM broadcasts to the Jackson, TN area at 1310 AM.
AM RADIO STATION

WDXQ-AM 38258
Owner: Georgia Eagle Broadcasting Inc.
Editorial: 218 Eastman Hwy, Hawkinsville, Georgia 31036-5936 **Tel:** 1 478 892-9061.
Profile: WDXQ-AM is a commercial station owned by Georgia Eagle Broadcasting Inc. The format of the station is classic hits. WDXQ-AM broadcasts to Cochran, GA at 1440 AM.
AM RADIO STATION

WDXR-AM 38956
Owner: Bristol Broadcasting
Editorial: 6000 Bristol Dr, Paducah, Kentucky 42003-9213 **Tel:** 1 270 554-8255.
Email: news@wkyx.com
Web site: http://www.wkyx.com
Profile: WDXR-AM is a commercial station owned by Bristol Broadcasting. The format of the station is talk. WDXR-AM broadcasts to the Paducah, KY area at 1430 AM.
AM RADIO STATION

WDXX-FM 45583
Owner: Broadsouth Communications
Editorial: 505 Lauderdale St, Selma, Alabama 36701-4528 **Tel:** 1 334 875-3350.
Web site: http://www.dixiecountry.net/home
Profile: WDXX-FM is a commercial station owned by Broadsouth Communications. The format of the station is country. WDXX-FM broadcasts to the Selma, AL area at 100.1 FM. The station airs WINL-FM's programming.
FM RADIO STATION

WDXY-AM 37777
Owner: Miller Communications Inc.
Editorial: 51 Commerce St, Sumter, South Carolina 29150-5014 **Tel:** 1 803 775-2321.
Email: production@miller.fm
Web site: http://www.miller.fm
Profile: WDXY-AM is a commercial station owned by Miller Communications Inc. The format of the station is news, talk and sports. WDXY-AM broadcasts to the Sumter, SC area at 1240 AM.
AM RADIO STATION

WDYG-AM 35754
Owner: WWNT LLC
Editorial: 1733 Columbia Hwy, Dothan, Alabama 36303-5433 **Tel:** 1 334 671-0075.
Email: wwntradio@hotmail.com
Web site: http://www.gem-am.com/
Profile: WDYG-AM is a commercial station owned by WWNT LLC. The format of the station is oldies. WWNT-AM broadcasts to the Dothan, AL area at 1450 AM.
AM RADIO STATION

WDYK-FM 505392
Owner: West Virgina Radio Corporation of the Alleganies
Editorial: 15 Industrial Blvd E, Cumberland, Maryland 21502 **Tel:** 1 301 759-1005.
Web site: http://www.cumberlandsmagic.com
Profile: WDYK-FM is a commercial station owned by West Virgina Radio Corporation of the Alleganies. The format of the station is adult contemporary. WDYK-FM broadcasts to the Cumberland, MD area at 100.5 FM.
FM RADIO STATION

WDYS-FM 155744
Owner: GEOS Communications
Editorial: 54 Wilmar Dr, Tunkhannock, Pennsylvania 18657-6628 **Tel:** 1 570 265-7600.
Email: production@iloveyesfm.com
Web site: http://www.iloveyesfm.com/
Profile: WDYS-FM is a commercial station owned by GEOS Communications. The format for the station is Adult Contemporary. WDYS-FM broadcasts to the Dushore, PA area at 103.9 FM.
FM RADIO STATION

WDZ-AM 37778
Owner: Neuhoff Communications
Editorial: 250 N Water St, Ste 100, Decatur, Illinois 62523-1300 **Tel:** 1 217 423-9744.
Web site: http://www.espndecatur.com
Profile: WDZ-AM is a commercial station owned by Neuhoff Communications. The format of the station is sports. WDZ-AM broadcasts to the Decatur, IL area at 1050 AM.
AM RADIO STATION

WDZH-FM 40480
Owner: CBS Radio
Editorial: 26455 American Dr, Southfield, Michigan 48034-6114 **Tel:** 1 248 327-2900.
Web site: http://987ampradio.cbslocal.com
Profile: WDZH-FM is a commercial station owned by CBS Radio. The format of the station is Top 40/CHR. WDZH-FM broadcasts to the Detroit area at 98.7 FM.
FM RADIO STATION

WDZN-FM 687619
Owner: West Virgina Radio Corporation of the Alleganies
Editorial: 15 Industrial Blvd E, Cumberland, Maryland 21502-4106 **Tel:** 1 301 759-1005.
Web site: http://z100rock.com/
Profile: WVMD-FM is a commercial station owned by West Virgina Radio Corporation of the Allegenies. The format of the station is rock music. WVMD-FM broadcasts to the Cumberland, MD, area at 99.5 FM.
FM RADIO STATION

WDZQ-FM 45136
Owner: Neuhoff Communications
Editorial: 250 N Water St, Ste 100, Decatur, Illinois 62523-1300 **Tel:** 1 217 423-9744.
Web site: http://www.95q.com
Profile: WDZQ-FM is a commercial station owned by Neuhoff Communications. The format of the station is contemporary country music. WDZQ-FM broadcasts to the Decatur, IL at 95.1 FM.
FM RADIO STATION

WDZZ-FM 45137
Owner: Cumulus Media Inc.
Editorial: 6317 Taylor Dr, Flint, Michigan 48507 **Tel:** 1 810 238-7300.
Web site: http://www.wdzz.com
Profile: WDZZ-FM is a commercial station owned by Cumulus Media Inc. The format of the station is urban adult contemporary. WDZZ-FM broadcasts to the Flint, MI area at 92.7 FM.
FM RADIO STATION

WEAI-FM 45957
Owner: Jacksonville Area Radio Broadcasters, Inc.
Editorial: 2161 Old State Rd, Jacksonville, Illinois 62650 **Tel:** 1 217 245-7171.
Web site: http://wlds.com
Profile: WEAI-FM is a commercial station owned by the Jacksonville Area Radio Broadcasters, Inc. The format of the station is hot adult contemporary. WEAI-FM broadcasts in the Jacksonville, IL area at 107.1 FM.
FM RADIO STATION

WEAL-AM 38678
Owner: Entercom Communications Corp.
Editorial: 7819 National Service Rd, Ste 401, Greensboro, North Carolina 27409 **Tel:** 1 336 605-5200.
Web site: http://www.1510weal.com
Profile: WEAL-AM is a commercial station owned by Entercom Communications Corp. The format of the station is gospel music. WEAL-AM broadcasts to the Greensboro-Winston Salem, NC area at 1510 AM.
AM RADIO STATION

WEAM-FM 238671
Owner: Davis Broadcasting
Editorial: 2203 Wynnton Rd, Columbus, Georgia 31906-2531 **Tel:** 1 706 576-3565.
Web site: http://www.praise1007.com
Profile: WEAM-FM is a commercial station owned by Davis Broadcasting. The format of the station is gospel music. WEAM-FM broadcasts to the Columbus, GA area at 100.7 FM.
FM RADIO STATION

WEAN-FM 42897
Owner: Cumulus Media Inc.
Editorial: 1502 Wampanoag Trl, Riverside, Rhode Island 02915-1018 **Tel:** 1 401 433-4200.
Web site: http://www.630wpro.com
Profile: WEAN-FM is a commercial station owned by Cumulus Media Inc. The format of the station is news and talk. WEAN-FM broadcasts to the Riverside, RI area at 99.7 FM.
FM RADIO STATION

WEAS-FM 45138
Owner: Cumulus Media Inc.
Editorial: 214 Television Cir, Savannah, Georgia 31406-4519 **Tel:** 1 912 961-9000.
Web site: http://www.e93fm.com
Profile: WEAS-FM is a commercial station owned by Cumulus Media Inc. The format of the station is urban contemporary. WEAS-FM broadcasts to the Savannah, GA area at 93.1 FM.
FM RADIO STATION

WEAT-FM 42700
Owner: Alpha Media
Editorial: 701 Northpoint Pkwy Ste 500, West Palm Beach, Florida 33407-1960 **Tel:** 1 561 616-4777.
Web site: http://www.sunny1079.com
Profile: WEAT-FM is a commercial station owned by Alpha Media. The format of the station is adult contemporary. WPBZ-FM broadcasts to the West Palm Beach, FL area at 107.9 FM.
FM RADIO STATION

The Weather Channel Radio Network 46956
Editorial: 300 Interstate North Pkwy SE, Atlanta, Georgia 30339 **Tel:** 1 770 226-0000.
Email: twcrn@weather.com
Web site: http://www.weather.com/aboutus/radio
Profile: Network affiliated with The Weather Channel cable television outlet. Provides weather information, forecasts and updates to affiliated stations and satellite radio throughout the United States.
RADIO NETWORK

WEAV-AM 36796
Owner: Vox Communications
Editorial: 265 Hegeman Ave, Colchester, Vermont 05446-3174 **Tel:** 1 802 655-0093.
Web site: http://www.960thezone.com
Profile: WEAV-AM is a commercial station owned by Vox Communications. The format of the station is sports. WEAV-AM broadcasts to the Burlington, VT area at 960 AM.
AM RADIO STATION

WEBB-FM 45584
Owner: Townsquare Media, Inc.
Editorial: 56 Western Ave Ste 13, Augusta, Maine 04330-6348 **Tel:** 1 207 623-4735.
Web site: http://www.b985.fm
Profile: WEBB-FM is a commercial station owned by Townsquare Media, Inc. The format of the station is classic country. WEBB-FM broadcasts to the Augusta, Maine area at 98.5 FM.
FM RADIO STATION

WEBC-AM 37782
Owner: Townsquare Media, LLC
Editorial: 14 E Central Entrance, Duluth, Minnesota 55811-5508 **Tel:** 1 218 727-4500.
Web site: http://squatchrocks.com
Profile: WEBC-AM is a commercial station owned by Townsquare Media, LLC. The format of the station is classic rock. WEBC-AM broadcasts to the Duluth, MN area at 560 AM.
AM RADIO STATION

WEBE-FM 45779
Owner: Cumulus Media Inc.
Editorial: 2 Lafayette St., Bridgeport, Connecticut 06604-6014 **Tel:** 1 203 333-9108.
Web site: http://www.webe108.com
Profile: WEBE-FM is a commercial station owned by Cumulus Media Inc. The format of the station is adult contemporary. WEBE-FM broadcasts to the Bridgeport, CT area at 107.9 FM.
FM RADIO STATION

WEBG-FM 40576
Owner: iHeartMedia Inc.
Editorial: 233 N Michigan Ave, Chicago, Illinois 60601-5519 **Tel:** 1 312 540-2000.
Web site: http://www.big955chicago.com
Profile: WEBG-FM is a commercial station owned by iHeartMedia Inc. The format of the station is contemporary country. WEBG-FM broadcasts in the Chicago area at 95.5 FM.
FM RADIO STATION

WEBJ-AM 35285
Owner: Brewton Broadcasting
Editorial: 301 Downing St, Brewton, Alabama 36426 **Tel:** 1 251 867-5717.
AM RADIO STATION

WEBL-FM 40814
Owner: Mighty Media Group, LP (Memphis First Ventures LP)
Editorial: 230 Goodman Rd E Ste 2, Southaven, Mississippi 38671-8889 **Tel:** 1 901 272.0008.
Web site: http://keninhmb.wix.com/kenandkitty
Profile: WEBL-FM is a commercial station owned by Mighty Media Group, LP (Memphis First Ventures LP). The format of the station is contemporary country. WEBL-FM broadcasts to the Memphis, TN area at 95.3 FM.
FM RADIO STATION

WEBN-FM 42862
Owner: iHeartMedia Inc.
Editorial: 8044 Montgomery Rd Ste 650, Cincinnati, Ohio 45236-2959 **Tel:** 1 513 686-8300.
Web site: http://www.webn.com
Profile: WEBN-FM is a commercial station owned by iHeartMedia Inc. The format of the station is rock. WEBN-FM broadcasts to the Cincinnati area at 102.7 FM.
FM RADIO STATION

WEBO-AM 38524
Owner: Radigan Broadcasting LLC
Editorial: 60 North Ave, Owego, New York 13827-1325 **Tel:** 1 607 687-9933.
Email: news@newsradiowebo.com
Web site: http://www.newsradiowebo.com
Profile: WEBO-AM is a commercial station owned by Radigan Broadcasting LLC. The format of the station is news, sports and adult contemporary. WEBO-AM broadcasts to the Owego, NY area at 1330 AM.
AM RADIO STATION

WEBQ-AM 37783
Owner: Withers Broadcasting Co.
Editorial: 701 S Commercial St, Harrisburg, Illinois 62946-2347 **Tel:** 1 618 252-6307.
Email: webq@mywithersradio.com
Web site: http://webqradio.com
Profile: WEBQ-AM is a commercial station owned by Withers Broadcasting Co. The format of the station is classic country and talk. WEBQ-AM broadcasts to the Paducah, KY; Cape Girardeau, MO; and Harrisburg, IL areas at 1240 AM.
AM RADIO STATION

WEBQ-FM 45139
Owner: Withers Broadcasting Co.
Editorial: 701 S Commercial St, Harrisburg, Illinois 62946-2347 **Tel:** 1 618 252-6307.
Email: webq@mywithersradio.com
Web site: http://www.webqradio.com
Profile: WEBQ-FM is a commercial station owned by Withers Broadcasting Co. The format of the station is adult contemporary. WEBQ-FM broadcasts to the Harrisburg, IL area at 102.3 FM.
FM RADIO STATION

WEBS-AM 35286
Owner: Radio WEBS Inc.
Editorial: 427 S Wall St, Calhoun, Georgia 30701-2431 **Tel:** 1 706 629-1110.
Email: communitynews@webcalhoun.com
Web site: http://www.webscalhoun.com
Profile: WEBS-AM is a commercial station owned by Radio WEBS Inc. The format of the station is oldies music. WEBS-AM broadcasts to the Calhoun, GA area at 1030 AM.
AM RADIO STATION

WEBY-AM 35818
Owner: Spinnaker Communications
Editorial: 7179 Printers Aly, Milton, Florida 32583 **Tel:** 1 850 983-2242.
Email: weby@1330weby.com
Web site: http://www.1330weby.com
Profile: WEBY-AM is a commercial station owned by Spinnaker Communications. The format of the station is news and talk. WEBY-AM broadcasts to the Pensacola, FL area at 1330 AM.
AM RADIO STATION

WEBZ-FM 43121
Owner: iHeartMedia Inc.
Editorial: 1834 Lisenby Ave, Panama City, Florida 32405-3713 **Tel:** 1 850 769-1408.
Web site: http://993thebeat.iheart.com
Profile: WEBZ-FM is a commercial station owned by iHeartMedia Inc. The format of the station is urban contemporary music. WEBZ-FM broadcasts to the Panama City, FL area at 99.3 FM.
FM RADIO STATION

WECB-FM 43580
Owner: Southeast Alabama Broadcasters, LLC
Editorial: 285 N Foster St Fl 8, Dothan, Alabama 36303-4541 **Tel:** 1 334 699-0047.
Web site: http://b1053.com
Profile: WECB-FM is a commercial station owned by Southeast Alabama Broadcasters, LLC and operated by Low Country Radio, LLC. The format of the station is classic country. WECB-FM broadcasts in the Dothan, AL area at 105.3 FM.
FM RADIO STATION

WECC-FM 83612
Owner: Lighthouse Christian Broadcasting
Editorial: 5465 Ga Highway 40 E, Saint Marys, Georgia 31558-4036 **Tel:** 1 912 882-8930.
Email: mail@thelighthousefm.org
Web site: http://www.thelighthousefm.org
Profile: WECC-FM is a non-commercial station owned by Lighthouse Christian Broadcasting. The format of the station is contemporary Christian and religious programming. WECC-FM broadcasts to the Saint Marys, GA area at 89.3 FM.
FM RADIO STATION

WECI-FM 43920
Owner: Earlham College
Editorial: 801 National Rd W #45, Richmond, Indiana 47374-4021 **Tel:** 1 765 983-1246.
Web site: http://www.weciradio.org
Profile: WECI-FM is a non-commercial station owned by Earlham College. The format of the station is variety, including music, news, and talk. WECI-FM broadcasts in the Richmond, IN area at 91.5 FM.
FM RADIO STATION

WECK-AM 39380
Owner: Urban One, Inc.
Editorial: 2900 Genesee St, Cheektowaga, New York 14225-3102 **Tel:** 1716 783 9120.
Web site: http://www.timelessweck.com
Profile: WECK-AM is a commercial station owned by Urban One, Inc.. The format of the station is adult standards. WECK-AM broadcasts to the Buffalo/ Cheektowaga, NY area at 1230 AM.
AM RADIO STATION

WECL-FM　43353
Owner: Mid-West Family Broadcasting
Editorial: 944 Harlem St, Altoona, Wisconsin 54720-1127 Tel: 1 715 832-1530.
Web site: http://www.929thex.com
Profile: WECL-FM is a commercial station owned by Mid-West Family Broadcasting. The format of the station is rock. WECL-FM broadcasts to the Altoona, WI area at 92.9 FM.
FM RADIO STATION

WECO-AM　38343
Owner: Morgan County Broadcasting Co., Inc.
Editorial: 305 N Church St, Wartburg, Tennessee 37887-3164 Tel: 1 423 346-3900.
Email: wecoradio@highland.net
Web site: http://www.wecoradio.com
Profile: WECO-AM is a commercial station owned by Morgan County Broadcasting Co., Inc. The format of the station is gospel. WECO-AM broadcasts to the Wartburg, TN area at 940 AM.
AM RADIO STATION

WECO-FM　45704
Owner: Morgan County Broadcasting Co., Inc.
Editorial: 305 N Church St, Wartburg, Tennessee 37887-3170 Tel: 1 423 346-3900.
Email: wecoradio@highland.net
Web site: http://www.wecoradio.com
Profile: WECO-FM is a commercial station owned by Morgan County Broadcasting Co., Inc. The format of the station is classic and contemporary country. WECO-FM broadcasts to the Wartburg, TN area at 101.3 FM.
FM RADIO STATION

WECQ-FM　40526
Owner: Community Broadcasters LLC.
Editorial: 34 Harbor Blvd Ste 202, Destin, Florida 32541-7365 Tel: 1 850 654-1000.
Web site: http://cbemeraldcoast.com/q92online
Profile: WECQ-FM is a commercial station owned by Community Broadcasters LLC. The format of the station is Top 40/CHR music. WECQ-FM broadcasts to Destin, FL area at 92.1 FM.
FM RADIO STATION

WECR-AM　39397
Owner: High Country Adventures, LLC
Editorial: 1281 Newland Hwy, Newland, North Carolina 28657 Tel: 1 828 733-0188.
Email: wecr@bellsouth.net
Web site: http://www.wecr1130am.com
Profile: WECR-AM is a commercial station owned by High Country Adventures, LLC. The format for the station is Christian and gospel music. WECR-AM broadcasts to the Charlotte, NC area at 1130 AM.
AM RADIO STATION

WECR-FM　46768
Owner: High Country Adventures, LLC
Editorial: 738 Blowing Rock Rd, Boone, North Carolina 28607-4835 Tel: 1 828 264-2411.
Web site: http://www.highway1061fm.com
Profile: WECR-FM is a commercial station owned by High Country Adventures, LLC, a subsidiary of Curtis Media Group. The format of the station is contemporary country. WECR-FM broadcasts to the Boone, NC area at 102.3 FM.
FM RADIO STATION

WECV-FM　46473
Owner: Community Broadcasting, Inc
Tel: 1 615 871-1160.
Email: wcrt@bottradionetwork.com
Web site: http://www.bottradionetwork.com
Profile: WECV-FM is non-commercial station owned by Community Broadcasting, Inc. The format of the station is religious talk. WECV-FM broadcasts to the Nashville, TN area at 89.1 FM.
FM RADIO STATION

WECZ-AM　38136
Owner: Renda Broadcasting
Editorial: 904 N Main St, Punxsutawney, Pennsylvania 15767 Tel: 1 814 938-6000.
Email: rendaprod1@comcast.net
Web site: http://www.weczam1540.com
Profile: WECZ-AM is a commercial station owned by Renda Broadcasting. The format of the station is news and talk. WECZ-AM broadcasts to the Punxsutawney, PA area at 1540 AM.
AM RADIO STATION

WEDB-FM　45183
Owner: RadioJones LLC
Editorial: 211 S Monroe St, Dublin, Georgia 31021-5235 Tel: 1 478 237-1590.
Web site: http://www.magic981fm.com/
Profile: WEDB-FM is a commercial station owned by RadioJones LLC. The format of the station is hot adult contemporary. WEDB-FM broadcasts to the Augusta, GA area at 98.1 FM.
FM RADIO STATION

WEDG-FM　42751
Owner: Cumulus Media Inc.
Editorial: 50 James E Casey Dr, Buffalo, New York 14206-2367 Tel: 1 716 881-4555.
Web site: http://www.wedg.com
Profile: WEDG-FM is a commercial station owned by Cumulus Media Inc. The format of the station is rock alternative music. WEDG-FM broadcasts to the Buffalo, NY area at 103.3 FM.
FM RADIO STATION

WEDI-AM　35264
Owner: Town and Country Broadcasting, Inc.
Editorial: 23 E 2nd St, Xenia, Ohio 45385-3415
Tel: 1 937 372-3531.
Email: myclassiccountry@myclassiccountry.com
Web site: http://www.myclassiccountry.com
Profile: WEDI-AM is a commercial station owned by Town and Country Broadcasting, Inc. The format of the station is classic country. WEDI-AM broadcasts to the Xenia, OH area at 1130 AM.
AM RADIO STATION

WEDJ-FM　46850
Owner: Continental Broadcast Group LLC
Editorial: 1800 N Meridian St, Ste 603, Indianapolis, Indiana 46202-1433 Tel: 1 317 924-1071.
Web site: http://www.wedjfm.com
Profile: WEDJ-FM is a commercial station owned by Continental Broadcast Group LLC. The format of the station is regional Mexican music. WEDJ-FM broadcasts to the greater Indianapolis area at 107.1 FM.
FM RADIO STATION

WEDM-FM　40237
Owner: Metropolitan S.D. of Warren Township
Editorial: 9651 E 21st St, Indianapolis, Indiana 46229-1706 Tel: 1 317 532-6301.
Web site: http://www.wedmfm.com
Profile: WEDM-FM is a non-commercial station owned by Metropolitan S.D. of Warren Township. The format of the station is educational variety. WEDM-FM broadcasts to the Indianapolis area at 91.1 FM.
FM RADIO STATION

WEDO-AM　35287
Owner: 810 Inc.
Editorial: 1985 Lincoln Way, McKeesport, Pennsylvania 15131 Tel: 1 412 664-4431.
Email: wedoradio@comcast.net
Web site: http://www.wedo810.com
Profile: WEDO-AM is a commercial station owned by 810 Inc. The format of the station is variety. WEDO-AM broadcasts to the McKeesport, PA area at 810 AM.
AM RADIO STATION

WEDR-FM　43173
Owner: Cox Media Group, Inc.
Editorial: 2741 N 29th Ave, Hollywood, Florida 33020
Tel: 1 305 444-4404.
Web site: http://www.wedr.com
Profile: WEDR-FM is a commercial station owned by Cox Media Group, Inc. The format of the station is urban contemporary. WEDR-FM broadcasts to the Hollywood, FL area at 99.1 FM.
FM RADIO STATION

WEDW-FM　41670
Owner: Connecticut Public Broadcasting Inc.
Editorial: 1049 Asylum Ave, Hartford, Connecticut 06105-2432 Tel: 1 860 278-5310.
Email: info@wnpr.org
Web site: http://www.wnpr.org
Profile: WEDW-FM is a non-commercial station owned by Connecticut Public Broadcasting Inc. The format of the station is news and talk. WEDW-FM broadcasts to the Hartford, CT area at 88.5 FM.
FM RADIO STATION

WEEB-AM　35288
Owner: Pinehurst Broadcasting
Editorial: 1650 Midland Rd, Southern Pines, North Carolina 28387-2111 Tel: 1 910 692-7440.
Web site: http://www.weeb990.com
Profile: WEEB-AM is a commercial station owned by Pinehurst Broadcasting. The format of the station is news and talk. WEEB-AM broadcasts to the Southern Pines, NC area at 990 AM.
AM RADIO STATION

WEEC-FM　40238
Owner: World Evangelistic Enterprise
Editorial: 1205 Whitefield Cir, Xenia, Ohio 45385-7243 Tel: 1 937 424-1640.
Email: info@weec.org
Web site: http://www.weec.org
Profile: WEEC-FM is a non-commercial station owned by The World Evangelistic Enterprise Corporation (WEEC). The format of the station is gospel music and religious. WEEC-FM broadcasts to the Springfield, OH area at 100.7 FM.
FM RADIO STATION

WEED-AM　38800
Owner: North Star Broadcasting
Editorial: 115 N Church St, Rocky Mount, North Carolina 27804-5402 Tel: 1 252 443-5976.
Profile: WEED-AM is a commercial station owned by North Star Broadcasting. The format of the station is Black Gospel. WEED-AM broadcasts to the Rocky Mount, NC area at 1390 AM.
AM RADIO STATION

WEEF-AM　35289
Owner: Polnet Communications
Editorial: 4320 Dundee Rd, Northbrook, Illinois 60062-1703 Tel: 1 847 498-3350.
Email: polnetradio@gmail.com
Web site: http://www.weefam.com
AM RADIO STATION

WEEI Sports Network　545381
Owner: Entercom Communications Corp.
Editorial: 20 Guest St, Brighton, Massachusetts 02135-2040 Tel: 1 617 779-3500.
Web site: http://www.weei.com
Profile: The WEEI Sports Network provides radio programming from its flagship station, WEEI-AM, to stations in New England and the Northeastern United States. The network has a strong focus on Celtics basketball and Red Sox baseball.
REGIONAL RADIO NETWORKS

WEEI-AM　35290
Owner: Entercom Communications Corp.
Editorial: 20 Guest St Fl 3, Brighton, Massachusetts 02135-2040 Tel: 1 617 779-3500.
Web site: http://www.weei.com
Profile: WEEI-AM is a commercial station owned by Entercom Communications Corp. The format of the station is sports. WEEI-AM broadcasts to the Brighton, MA area at 850 AM.
AM RADIO STATION

WEEI-FM　42128
Owner: Entercom Communications Corp.
Editorial: 20 Guest St Fl 3, Brighton, Massachusetts 02135-2040 Tel: 1 617 779-3500.
Web site: http://www.weei.com
Profile: WEEI-FM is a commercial station owned by Entercom Communications Corp. The format of the station is sports. WEEI-FM broadcasts to the Providence, RI area at 93.7 FM.
FM RADIO STATION

WEEN-AM　39345
Owner: Lafayette Broadcasting Inc.
Editorial: 231 Chaffin Rd, Lafayette, Tennessee 37083 Tel: 1 615 666-2169.
Email: wlct@nctc.com
Web site: http://www.wlct.com
Profile: WEEN-AM is a commercial station owned by Lafayette Broadcasting Inc. The format of the station is gospel music. The station broadcasts to Lafayette, TN at 1460 AM.
AM RADIO STATION

WEEO-AM　36564
Owner: Shippensburg Broadcasting, Inc.
Editorial: 180 York Rd, Carlisle, Pennsylvania 17013
Tel: 1 717 243-1200.
Email: wioo@pa.net
Web site: http://www.wioo.com
Profile: WEEO-AM is a commercial station owned by Shippensburg Broadcasting, Inc. The format of the station is country. WEEO-AM broadcasts to the Carlisle, PA area at 1480 AM.
AM RADIO STATION

WEEO-FM　43462
Owner: Magnum Broadcasting Inc.
Editorial: 37 S Main St, Chambersburg, Pennsylvania 17201-2200 Tel: 1 717 709-0801.
Web site: http://newstalk1037fm.com
Profile: WEEO-FM is a commercial station owned by Magnum Broadcasting Inc. The format of the station is news talk. WEEO-FM broadcasts to the Chambersburg, PA area at 103.7 FM.
FM RADIO STATION

WEEU-AM　35291
Owner: WEEU Broadcasting Co.
Editorial: 34 N 4th St, Reading, Pennsylvania 19601
Tel: 1 610 376-7335.
Email: weeu@weeu.com
Web site: http://www.weeu.com
Profile: WEEU-AM is a commercial station owned by WEEU Broadcasting Co. The format of the station is news and talk. WEEU-AM broadcasts to the Reading, PA area at 830 AM.
AM RADIO STATION

WEEX-AM　39040
Owner: Connoisseur Media
Editorial: 107 Paxinosa Rd W, Easton, Pennsylvania 18040-1344 Tel: 1 610 829-5500.
Web site: http://www.espnlv.com
Profile: WEEX-AM is a commercial station owned by Connoisseur Media. The format of the station is sports. WEEX-AM broadcasts to the Easton, PA area at 1230 AM.
AM RADIO STATION

WEEY-FM　44189
Owner: Great Eastern Radio, LLC
Editorial: 99 Main St Ste B, Keene, New Hampshire 03431-3770 Tel: 1 603 283-1090.
Web site: http://www.weei.com/weei/shows-schedules/weei-935fm-keene-nh
Profile: WEEY-FM is a commercial station owned by Great Eastern Radio, LLC. The format of the station is sports. WEEY-FM is a transmitter of WEEI-FM. WEEY-FM broadcasts to the Lebanon, NH area at 93.5 FM.
FM RADIO STATION

WEFL-AM　88037
Owner: Good Karma Broadcasting
Editorial: 2090 Palm Beach Lakes Blvd Ste 801, West Palm Beach, Florida 33409-6508 Tel: 1 561 697-8353.
Web site: http://www.espnwestpalm.com
Profile: WEFL-AM is a commercial station owned by Good Karma Broadcasting. The format of the station is Spanish sports. WEFL-AM broadcasts to the West Palm Beach, FL area at 760 AM.
AM RADIO STATION

WEFM-FM　40240
Owner: Michigan City FM Broadcasters
Editorial: 1903 Springland Ave, Michigan City, Indiana 46360 Tel: 1 219 879-8201.
Email: wefmr@yahoo.com
Profile: WEFM-FM is a commercial station owned by Michigan City FM Broadcasters. The format of the station is adult contemporary and oldies. WEFM-FM broadcasts to the Michigan City, IN area at 95.9 FM.
FM RADIO STATION

WEFT-FM　41217
Owner: Prairie Air Inc.
Editorial: 113 N Market St, Champaign, Illinois 61820-4004 Tel: 1 217 359-9338.
Email: stationmanager@weft.org
Web site: http://www.weft.org
Profile: WEFT-FM is a non-commercial station owned by Prairie Air Inc. The format of the station is variety. WEFT-FM broadcasts in the Champaign, IL area at 90.1 FM.
FM RADIO STATION

WEFX-FM　42552
Owner: Community Broadcasters, LLC
Editorial: 199 Wealtha Ave, Watertown, New York 13601-1837 Tel: 1 315 786-9552.
Profile: WEFX-FM is a commercial station owned by Community Broadcasters, LLC. The format of the station is contemporary country. WEFX-FM broadcasts to the Watertown, NY area at 100.7 FM.
FM RADIO STATION

WEGB-FM　895225
Owner: Community Bible Church
Editorial: 2837 Noyac Rd, Sag Harbor, New York 11963-1916 Tel: 1 631 725-4155.
Email: faithfm@eastgatebroadcasting.com
Web site: http://eastgatebroadcasting.com
Profile: WEGB-FM is a non-commercial station owned by Community Bible Church. The format of the station is Christian talk and Bible teaching. WEGB-FM broadcasts to the Long Island, NY area at a frequency of 90.7 FM.
FM RADIO STATION

WEGC-FM　44247
Owner: Cumulus Media Inc.
Editorial: 1104 W Broad Ave, Albany, Georgia 31707-4340 Tel: 1 229 888-5000.
Web site: http://www.mix1077albany.com
Profile: WEGC-FM is a commercial station owned by Cumulus Media Inc. The format of the station is adult contemporary music. WEGC-FM broadcasts in the Albany, GA area at 107.7 FM.
FM RADIO STATION

WEGE-FM　45349
Owner: Childers Media Group, LLC
Editorial: 57 Town Sq, Lima, Ohio 45801-4950
Tel: 1 419 331-1600.
Web site: http://www.1049theeagle.com
Profile: WEGE-FM is a commercial station owned by Childers Media Group, LLC. The format of the station is classic rock. WEGE-FM broadcasts to the Lima, OH area at 104.9 FM.
FM RADIO STATION

WEGG-AM　39322
Owner: Conner Media Corp.
Editorial: Highway 117, Rose Hill, North Carolina 28458 Tel: 1 252 633-2143.
Web site: http://yourchristianradio.com/default.aspx
Profile: WEGG-AM is a commercial station owned by Conner Media Corp. The format of the station is gospel music. WEGG-AM broadcasts to the Rose Hill, NC area at 710 AM.
AM RADIO STATION

WEGH-FM　46667
Owner: Sunbury Broadcasting Corp.
Editorial: 1227 County Line Rd, Selinsgrove, Pennsylvania 17870 Tel: 1 570 286-5838.
Email: sales@wqkx.com
Web site: http://www.eagle107.com
Profile: WEGH-FM is a commercial station owned by Sunbury Broadcasting Corp. The format of the station is classic rock music. WEGH-FM broadcasts to the Sunbury, PA area at 107.3 FM.
FM RADIO STATION

WEGR-FM　45974
Owner: iHeartMedia Inc.
Editorial: 2650 Thousand Oaks Blvd Ste 4100, Memphis, Tennessee 38118-2451 Tel: 1 901 259-1300.
Web site: http://www.rock103.com
Profile: WEGR-FM is a commercial station owned by iHeartMedia Inc. The format of the station is classic rock music. WEGR-FM broadcasts to the Memphis, TN area at 102.7 FM.
FM RADIO STATION

WEGS-FM　41218
Owner: Florida Public Radio, Inc.
Editorial: 1836 E Olive Rd, Pensacola, Florida 32514-7555 Tel: 1 321 267-3000.
Email: wpio@gate.net
Web site: http://www.917online.com
FM RADIO STATION

WEGW-FM　43257
Owner: iHeartMedia Inc.
Editorial: 1015 Main St, Wheeling, West Virginia 26003-2709 Tel: 1 304 232-1170.
Web site: http://eagle1075.iheart.com
Profile: WEGW-FM is a commercial station owned by iHeartMedia Inc. The format of the station is rock/album-oriented rock. WEGW-FM broadcasts to the Wheeling, WV area at 107.5 FM.
FM RADIO STATION

WEGX-FM 46790
Owner: iHeartMedia Inc.
Editorial: 181 E Evans St Ste 311, Florence, South Carolina 29506-5505 **Tel:** 1 843 667-4600.
Web site: http://eagle929online.com/#&panel1-1
Profile: WEGX-FM is a commercial station owned by iHeartMedia Inc. The format of the station is contemporary country music. WEGX-FM broadcasts to the Florence, SC area at 92.9 FM.
FM RADIO STATION

WEGZ-FM 40152
Owner: VCY America Inc.
Editorial: 3434 W Kilbourn Ave, Milwaukee, Wisconsin 53208 **Tel:** 1 414 935-3000.
Email: wegz@vcyamerica.org
Web site: http://www.vcyamerica.org
Profile: WEGZ-FM is a non-commercial station owned by VCY America Inc. The format of the station is religious. WEGZ-FM broadcasts to the Milwaukee area at 105.9 FM.
FM RADIO STATION

WEHH-AM 39399
Owner: Tower Broadcasting LLC
Editorial: 1705 Lake St, Elmira, New York 14901-1220 **Tel:** 1 607 733-5626.
Email: towerbroadcasting@hotmail.com
Web site: http://www.wehhelmira.com
Profile: WEHH-AM is a commercial station owned by Tower Broadcasting LLC. The format of the station is adult standards. WEHH-AM broadcasts to the Elmira, NY area at 1600 AM.
AM RADIO STATION

WEHM-FM 42080
Owner: Long Island Radio Broadcasting
Editorial: 760 Montauk Highway, Watermill, New York 11976 **Tel:** 1 631 267-7800.
Email: info@wehm.com
Web site: http://www.wehm.com
Profile: WEHM-FM is a commercial station owned by Long Island Radio Broadcasting. The format of the station is adult album alternative. WEHM-FM broadcasts to the Amagansett, NY area at 92.9 FM.
FM RADIO STATION

WEHN-FM 43182
Owner: Long Island Radio Broadcasting
Editorial: 760 Montauk Hwy, Water Mill, New York 11976-2624 **Tel:** 1 631 267-7800.
Web site: http://www.wehm.com
Profile: WEHN-FM is a commercial station owned by Long Island Radio Broadcasting. The format of the station is adult album alternative. WEHN-FM broadcasts to the East Hampton, NY, region at 96.9 FM.
FM RADIO STATION

WEHP-FM 845138
Editorial: 1229 State St, Erie, Pennsylvania 16501-1913 **Tel:** 1 814 836-1111.
Web site: http://www.happi927.com
Profile: WEHP-FM is a commercial station owned by The Erie Radio Company, LLC. The format of the station is Top 40/CHR. WEHP-FM broadcasts to the Erie, PA area at a frequency of 92.7 FM.
FM RADIO STATION

WEIB-FM 76260
Owner: Cutting Edge Broadcasting Inc.
Editorial: 8 N King St, Northampton, Massachusetts 01060-1150 **Tel:** 1 413 585-1112.
Web site: http://www.weibfm.com
FM RADIO STATION

WEII-FM 40871
Owner: iHeartMedia Inc.
Editorial: 154 Barnstable Rd, Hyannis, Massachusetts 02601-2930 **Tel:** 1 508 778-2888.
Web site: http://www.weei.com/weei/shows-schedules/weei-963fm-cape-cod
Profile: WEII-FM is a commercial station owned by iHeartMedia Inc. The format of the station is sports. WEII-FM broadcasts to the Cape Cod, MA area at 96.3 FM.
FM RADIO STATION

WEIO-FM 41305
Owner: Freeland Broadcasting
Editorial: 215 Baker Rd, Huntingdon, Tennessee 38344-7703 **Tel:** 1 731 986-0242.
Web site: http://www.thefarmradio.com
Profile: WEIO-FM is a commercial station owned by Freeland Broadcasting. The format of the station is contemporary country. WEIO-FM broadcasts to the Huntingdon, TN area at 100.9 FM.
FM RADIO STATION

WEIR-AM 39176
Owner: Priority Communications
Editorial: 2307 Pennsylvania Ave, Weirton, West Virginia 26062 **Tel:** 1 304 723-1444.
Email: news@weir1430.com
Web site: http://www.weir1430.com
Profile: WEIR-AM is a commercial station owned by Priority Communications. The format of the station is sports. WEIR-AM broadcasts to the Wheeling, WV area at 1430 AM.
AM RADIO STATION

WEIS-AM 35294
Owner: Baker Enterprises Inc.
Editorial: 477 S Pratt St, Centre, Alabama 35960-1828 **Tel:** 1 256 927-4232.
Email: weisradio@tds.net
Web site: http://www.weisradio.com
Profile: WEIS-AM is a commercial station owned by Baker Enterprises Inc. The format of the station is country, gospel, news and sports. WEIS-AM broadcasts to the Centre, AL area at 990 AM.
AM RADIO STATION

WEJF-FM 43948
Owner: Florida Public Radio, Inc.
Editorial: 2824B Palm Bay Rd Ne, Palm Bay, Florida 32905-3535 **Tel:** 1 321 722-9998.
Web site: http://www.ggm.info
Profile: WEJF-FM is a non-commercial station owned by Florida Public Radio, Inc. The format of the station is Christian and variety. WEJF-FM broadcasts to the Palm Bay, FL area at 90.3 FM.
FM RADIO STATION

WEJL-AM 38633
Owner: Shamrock Communications
Editorial: 149 Penn Ave, Scranton, Pennsylvania 18503-2055 **Tel:** 1 570 346-6555.
Web site: http://www.nepasespnradio.com/
Profile: WEJL-AM is a commercial station owned by Shamrock Communications. The format of the station is sports. WEJL-AM broadcasts to the Scranton, PA area at 630 AM.
AM RADIO STATION

WEJL-FM 538187
Owner: Shamrock Communications
Editorial: 149 Penn Ave, Scranton, Pennsylvania 18503-2055 **Tel:** 1 570 346-6555.
Web site: http://www.nepasespnradio.com
Profile: WEJL-FM is a commercial station owned by Shamrock Communications. The format of the station is sports. WEJL-FM broadcasts to the Scranton, PA area at 100.1 FM.
FM RADIO STATION

WEJT-FM 43651
Owner: Cromwell Group Inc.(The)
Editorial: 410 N Water St Ste B, Decatur, Illinois 62523-2371 **Tel:** 1 217 428-4487.
Web site: http://www.decaturradio.com
Profile: WEJT-FM is a commercial station owned by the Cromwell Group Inc. The format of the station is adult hits. WEJT-FM broadcasts in the Decatur, IL area at 105.1 FM.
FM RADIO STATION

WEJZ-FM 40243
Owner: Renda Broadcasting
Editorial: 6440 Atlantic Blvd, Jacksonville, Florida 32211 **Tel:** 1 904 727-9696.
Web site: http://www.wejz.com
Profile: WEJZ-FM is a commercial station owned by Renda Broadcasting. The format of the station is adult contemporary music. WEJZ-FM broadcasts to the Jacksonville, FL area at 96.1 FM.
FM RADIO STATION

WEKB-AM 38755
Owner: East Kentucky Radio Network
Editorial: 1240 Radio Dr, Pikeville, Kentucky 41501-4779 **Tel:** 1 606 437-4051.
Email: frontdesk@ekbradio.com
Web site: http://www.myoldiesradio.com
Profile: WEKB-AM is a commercial station owned by East Kentucky Radio Network. The format of the station is adult hits. WEKB-AM broadcasts to the Pikeville, KY area at 1460 AM.
AM RADIO STATION

WEKC-AM 36560
Owner: Parks(Gerald)
Editorial: 402 Main St, Williamsburg, Kentucky 40769-1126 **Tel:** 1 606 549-3000.
Email: wekc@wekcradio.org
Web site: http://www.wekcrad.org
Profile: WEKC-AM is a commercial station owned by Gerald Parks. The format of the station is gospel. WEKC-AM broadcasts to the Williamsburg, KY area at 710 AM.
AM RADIO STATION

WEKL-FM 45190
Owner: iHeartMedia Inc.
Editorial: 2743 Perimeter Pkwy Bldg 100, Suite 300, Augusta, Georgia 30909-6429 **Tel:** 1 706 396-6000.
Web site: http://eagle102.iheart.com
Profile: WEKL-FM is a commercial station owned by iHeartMedia Inc. The format of the station is classic rock. WEKL-FM broadcasts to the Augusta, GA area at 102.3 FM.
FM RADIO STATION

WEKR-AM 35295
Owner: Elk River Broadcasting
Editorial: 7 Old Boonshill Road, Fayetteville, Tennessee 37334 **Tel:** 1 931 433-3545.
Profile: WEKR-AM is a commercial station owned by Elk River Broadcasting. The format of the station is country. WEKR-AM broadcasts to the Fayetteville, TN area at 1240 AM.
AM RADIO STATION

WEKS-FM 43935
Owner: Legacy Media of South Atlanta, LLC.
Editorial: 42 Main St, Senoia, Georgia 30276-1889 **Tel:** 1 770 599-1923.
Email: info@925fmthebear.com
Web site: http://www.925fmthebear.com
Profile: WEKS-FM is a commercial station owned by Legacy Media of South Atlanta, LLC. The format of the station is classic and contemporary country. WEKS-FM broadcasts to the Senoia, GA area at 92.5 FM.
FM RADIO STATION

WEKT-AM 35902
Owner: M & R Broadcasting Inc.
Editorial: 214A Marion St, Elkton, Kentucky 42220 **Tel:** 1 270 265-5636.
Email: wektam1070@yahoo.com
Web site: http://www.wektgospelradio.com
Profile: WEKT-AM is a commercial station owned by M & R Broadcasting Inc. The format of the station is gospel music. WEKT-AM broadcasts to the Nashville, TN area at 1070 AM.
AM RADIO STATION

WEKX-FM 43276
Owner: Whitley Broadcasting
Editorial: 522 Main St, Williamsburg, Kentucky 40769-1127 **Tel:** 1 606 549-2285.
Email: wekx@bellsouth.net
Web site: http://www.werock1027.com
Profile: WEKX-FM is a commercial station owned by Whitley Broadcasting. The format of the station is classic rock. WEKX-FM broadcasts to the Lexington, KY area at 102.7 FM.
FM RADIO STATION

WEKY-AM 35296
Owner: Wallingford Broadcasting LLC
Editorial: 1030 Winchester Rd, Irvine, Kentucky 40336 **Tel:** 1 606 723-5138.
Email: production@wcyofm.com
Web site: http://www.wcyofm.com
Profile: WEKY-AM is a commercial station owned by Wallingford Broadcasting LLC. The format of the station is oldies and talk. WEKY-AM broadcasts to the Lexington, KY area at 1340 AM.
AM RADIO STATION

WEKZ-AM 37785
Owner: Big Radio
Editorial: W4765 Radio Ln, Monroe, Wisconsin 53566-9405 **Tel:** 1 608 325-2161.
Email: news@bigradio.fm
Web site: http://www.bigradio.fm
Profile: WEKZ-AM is a commercial station owned by Big Radio. The format of the station is country music. WEKZ-AM broadcasts to the Monroe, WI area at 1260 AM. All staff should be contact via fax.
AM RADIO STATION

WELB-AM 39251
Owner: Elba Radio Company
Editorial: 20334 Highway 87, Elba, Alabama 36323 **Tel:** 1 334 897-2216.
Email: welbam1350@yahoo.com
Profile: WELB-AM is a commercial station owned by Elba Radio Company. The format of the station is southern gospel. WELB-AM broadcasts to the Elba, AL area at 1350 AM.
AM RADIO STATION

WELC-AM 38612
Owner: West Virginia-Virginia Holding Co, LLC
Editorial: 18385 Coal Heritage Rd, Welch, West Virginia 24801-9773 **Tel:** 1 304 327-9266.
Web site: http://www.mywillie.com/
Profile: WELC-AM is a commercial station owned by the West Virginia-Virginia Holding Co, LLC. The format of the station is Classic Country. WELC-AM broadcasts to the Welch, WV area at 1150 AM.
AM RADIO STATION

WELD-AM 38886
Owner: Thunder Associates LLC
Editorial: 126 Kessel Rd, Fisher, West Virginia 26818-4012 **Tel:** 1 304 538-6062.
Email: weld@hardynet.com
Profile: WELD-AM is a commercial station owned by Thunder Associates LLC. The primary format of the station is talk. WELD-AM broadcasts in the Fisher, WV area at 690 AM.
AM RADIO STATION

WELD-FM 46221
Owner: Thunder Associates LLC
Editorial: 126 Kessel Rd, Fisher, West Virginia 26818-4012 **Tel:** 1 304 538-6062.
Email: weld@hardynet.com
Profile: WELD-FM is a commercial station owned by Thunder Associates LLC. The format of the station is country music. WELD-FM broadcasts to the Fisher, WV area at 101.7 FM.
FM RADIO STATION

WELE-AM 35297
Owner: Wings Communications- LMA Goliath Radio
Editorial: 432 S Nova Rd, Ormond Beach, Florida 32174-6121 **Tel:** 1 386 523-1870.
Profile: WELE-AM is a commercial station owned by Wings Communications. The format of the station is news, talk and sports. WELE-AM broadcasts to the Ormond Beach, FL area at 1380 AM.
AM RADIO STATION

WELI-AM 35298
Owner: iHeartMedia Inc.
Editorial: 495 Benham St, Hamden, Connecticut 06514-2009 **Tel:** 1 203 281-9600.
Web site: http://960weli.iheart.com
Profile: WELI-AM is a commercial station owned by iHeartMedia Inc. The format of the station is news, sports and talk. WELI-AM broadcasts in the greater New Haven, CT area at 960 AM.
AM RADIO STATION

WELJ-FM 40831
Owner: Cumulus Media Inc.
Editorial: 7 Governor Winthrop Blvd, New London, Connecticut 6320 **Tel:** 1 860 443-1980.
Web site: http://www.1047welj.com
Profile: WELJ-FM is a commercial station owned by Cumulus Media Inc. The format for the station is hot adult contemporary. WELJ-FM broadcasts to the New Haven, CT area at 104.7 FM.
FM RADIO STATION

WELK-FM 40245
Owner: West Virginia Radio Corp.
Editorial: Washington & Davis Streets, Elkins, West Virginia 26241 **Tel:** 1 304 636-1300.
Web site: http://947welk.com/
Profile: WELK-FM is a commercial station owned by West Virginia Radio Corp. The format of the station is Hot AC. WELK-FM broadcasts in the Elkins, WV area at 94.7 FM.
FM RADIO STATION

WELL-FM 41298
Owner: Alabama Christian Radio, Inc.
Editorial: 658 Horseshoe Bend Rd, Dadeville, Alabama 36853-2756 **Tel:** 1 334 705-8004.
Email: wellfm@praise887.com
Web site: http://www.praise887.com
Profile: WELL-FM is a non-commercial station owned by Alabama Christian Radio, Inc.. The format of the station is contemporary Christian music. WELL-FM broadcasts to the Dadeville, AL area at 88.7 FM.
FM RADIO STATION

WELM-AM 38735
Owner: Tower Broadcasting LLC
Editorial: 1705 Lake St, Elmira, New York 14901-1220 **Tel:** 1 607 733-5626.
Email: towerbroadcasting@hotmail.com
Profile: WELM-AM is a commercial station owned by Tower Broadcasting LLC. The format of the station is sports. WELM-AM broadcasts to the Elmira, NY area at 1410 AM.
AM RADIO STATION

WELO-AM 39483
Owner: Mississippi Radio Group
Editorial: 2214 S Gloster St, Tupelo, Mississippi 38801 **Tel:** 1 662 842-7658.
Profile: WELO-AM is a commercial station owned by Mississippi Radio Group. The format of the station is classic country. WELO-AM broadcasts to the Tupelo, MS area at 580 AM.
AM RADIO STATION

WELP-AM 35953
Owner: Wilkins Communication Networks Inc.
Editorial: 100 Cross Hill Rd, Easley, South Carolina 29640-8854 **Tel:** 1 864 855-9300.
Email: welp@wilkinsradio.com
Web site: http://www.wilkinsradio.com
Profile: WELP-AM is a commercial station owned by Wilkins Communications Networks Inc. The format of the station is Christian talk. WELP-AM broadcasts to the Easley, SC area at 1360 AM.
AM RADIO STATION

WELR-FM 45143
Owner: Eagle's Nest Inc.
Editorial: 6855 Highway 431, Roanoke, Alabama 36274-4614 **Tel:** 1 334 863-4139.
Email: welr@eagle1023.com
Web site: http://www.eagle1023.com
Profile: WELR-FM is a commercial station owned by Eagle's Nest Inc. The format of the station is country music. WELR-FM broadcasts to the Atlanta area at 102.3 FM.
FM RADIO STATION

WELS-FM 45927
Owner: Eastern Airwaves, LLC
Editorial: 2581 US Highway 70 W, Goldsboro, North Carolina 27530-9553 **Tel:** 1 919 736-1150.
Profile: WELS-FM is a commercial station owned by Eastern Airwaves, LLC (a division of Curtis Media Group). The format of the station is gospel. WELS-FM broadcasts to the Kinston, NC area at 102.9 FM.
FM RADIO STATION

WELY-AM 39209
Owner: Fortune Bay Bois Forte
Editorial: 133 E Chapman St, Ely, Minnesota 55731-1229 **Tel:** 1 218 365-4444.
Email: welydj@wely.com
Web site: http://www.wely.com
Profile: WELY-AM is a commercial station owned by Fortune Bay Bois Forte. The format of the station is news and sports talk. WELY-AM broadcasts in the Ely, MN area at 1450 AM.
AM RADIO STATION

WELY-FM 46565
Owner: Bois Forte Brand
Editorial: 133 E Chapman St, Ely, Minnesota 55731-1229 **Tel:** 1 218 365-4444.
Email: news@wely.com
Web site: http://www.wely.com
Profile: WELY-FM is a commercial station owned by Bois Forte Brand. The format of the station is variety. WELY-FM broadcasts in the Ely, MN area at 94.5 FM.
FM RADIO STATION

WELZ-AM 37788
Owner: Zoo-Bel Broadcasting LLC
Editorial: 204 Church St, Belzoni, Mississippi 39038-3630 **Tel:** 1 662 746-7676.
Web site: http://www.power107radio.com
Profile: WELZ-AM is a commercial station owned by Zoo-Bel Broadcasting LLC. The format of the station

is gospel and blues music. WELZ-AM broadcasts to the Belzoni, MS area at 1460 AM.
AM RADIO STATION

WEMB-AM 37789
Owner: WEMB Inc.
Editorial: 101 Riverview Rd, Erwin, Tennessee 37650-8722 **Tel:** 1 423 743-6123.
Web site: http://www.wemb.com
Profile: WEMB-AM is a commercial station owned by WEMB Inc. The format for the station is country. WEMB-AM broadcasts to the Tri-Cities, TN area at 1420 AM.
AM RADIO STATION

WEMD-AM 37696
Owner: First Media Radio LLC
Editorial: 306 Port St, Easton, Maryland 21601
Tel: 1 410 822-3301.
Email: studio@wceiradio.com
Web site: http://www.wceiradio.com
Profile: WEMD-AM is a commercial station owned by First Media Radio LLC. The format of the station is adult standards. WEMD-AM broadcasts to Easton, MD at 1460 AM.
AM RADIO STATION

WEMG-AM 35679
Owner: Davidson Media Group
Editorial: 1341 N Delaware Ave, Philadelphia, Pennsylvania 19125-4300 **Tel:** 1 215 426-1900.
Web site: http://www.lamega1310am.com
Profile: WEMG-AM is a commercial station owned by Davidson Media Group. The format of the station is Hispanic programming. WEMG-AM broadcasts to the Philadelphia area at 1310 AM.
AM RADIO STATION

WEMI-FM 44276
Owner: Evangel Ministries, Inc.
Editorial: 1909 W 2nd St, Appleton, Wisconsin 54914
Tel: 1 920 749-9456.
Email: wemi@thefamily.net
Web site: http://www.thefamily.net
Profile: WEMI-FM is a non-commercial station owned by Evangel Ministries, Inc. The format of station is contemporary Christian and news. WEMI-FM broadcasts to the Appleton, WI area at 91.9 FM.
FM RADIO STATION

WEMJ-AM 35300
Owner: WBIN, Inc.
Editorial: 2 Capital Plz Ste 105, Concord, New Hampshire 03301-4911 **Tel:** 1 603 224-8486.
Profile: WEMJ-AM is a commercial station owned by WBIN, Inc. The format of the station is news and talk. WEMJ-AM broadcasts to the Laconia, NH area on 1490 AM.
AM RADIO STATION

WEMM-FM 40246
Owner: Mortenson Broadcasting Co.
Editorial: 703 3rd Ave, Huntington, West Virginia 25701 **Tel:** 1 304 525-5141.
Email: audiowemm@hotmail.com
Web site: http://www.wemmfm.com
Profile: WEMM-FM is a commercial station owned by Mortenson Broadcasting Co. The format of the station is religion with a focus on Christian teaching and Southern gospel. WEMM-FM broadcasts to the Huntington, WV area at a frequency of 107.9 FM.
FM RADIO STATION

WEMR-FM 45487
Owner: 2510 Associates
Editorial: 160 Clearview Ave, State College, Pennsylvania 16803 **Tel:** 1 814 238-5085.
Profile: WEMR-FM is a commercial station owned by 2510 Associates. The format of the station is active rock. WEMR-FM broadcasts to the Hollidaysburg, PA area at 98.7 FM.
FM RADIO STATION

WEMX-FM 46660
Owner: Cumulus Media Inc.
Editorial: 631 Main St, Baton Rouge, Louisiana 70801-1911 **Tel:** 1 225 926-1106.
Web site: http://www.max94one.com
Profile: WEMX-FM is a commercial station that is owned by Cumulus Media Inc. The format of the station is urban contemporary music. WEMX-FM broadcasts to the Baton Rouge, LA area at 94.1 FM. Please fax any press material.
FM RADIO STATION

WEMY-FM 43786
Owner: Evangel Ministries, Inc.
Editorial: 1909 W 2nd St, Appleton, Wisconsin 54914
Tel: 1 920 499-9957.
Email: wemy@thefamily.net
Web site: http://www.thefamily.net
Profile: WEMY-FM is a non-commercial station owned by Evangel Ministries, Inc. The format of the station is contemporary Christian. WEMY-FM broadcasts to the Appleton, WI area at 91.5 FM.
FM RADIO STATION

WENC-AM 35301
Owner: Godwin(J.L.)
Editorial: 108 Radio Station Rd, Whiteville, North Carolina 28472-4906 **Tel:** 1 910 642-2133.
Profile: WENC-AM is a commercial station owned by J.L. Godwin. The format of the station is gospel and R&B Oldies. WENC-AM broadcasts to the Whiteville, NC area at 1220 AM.
AM RADIO STATION

WEND-FM 42716
Owner: iHeartMedia Inc.
Editorial: 801 Woodrdg Ctr Dr, Charlotte, North Carolina 28217-1908 **Tel:** 1 704 714-9444.
Web site: http://www.1065.com
Profile: WEND-FM is a commercial station owned by iHeartMedia Inc. The format of the station is rock alternative. WEND-FM broadcasts to the Charlotte, NC area at 106.5 FM.
FM RADIO STATION

WENE-AM 38917
Owner: iHeartMedia Inc.
Editorial: 320 N Jensen Rd, Vestal, New York 13850-2111 **Tel:** 1 607 584-5800.
Web site: http://www.1430theteam.com
Profile: WENE-AM is a commercial station owned by iHeartMedia Inc. The format of the station is sports. WENE-AM broadcasts to the Vestal, NY area at 1430 AM.
AM RADIO STATION

WENG-AM 35302
Owner: Viper Communications Inc.
Editorial: 1355 S River Rd, Englewood, Florida 34223-3913 **Tel:** 1 941 474-3231.
Email: news@wengradio.com
Web site: http://www.wengradio.com
Profile: WENG-AM is a commercial station owned by Viper Communications Inc. The format of the station is news, sports and talk. WENG-AM broadcasts to the Tampa, FL area at 1530 AM.
AM RADIO STATION

WENI-AM 39489
Owner: Sound Communications, LLC
Editorial: 21 E Market St Ste 101, Corning, New York 14830-2650 **Tel:** 1 607 937-8181.
Profile: WENI-AM is a commercial station owned by Sound Communications, LLC. The format of the station is talk. WENI-AM broadcasts to the Corning, NY area at 1450 AM.
AM RADIO STATION

WENI-FM 45744
Owner: Sound Communications, LLC
Editorial: 21 E Market St Ste 101, Corning, New York 14830-2650 **Tel:** 1 607 937-8181.
Web site: http://www.magic927977.com
Profile: WENI-FM is a commercial station owned by Sound Communications, LLC. The format of the station is adult contemporary music. WENI-FM broadcasts to the Corning, NY area at 97.7 FM.
FM RADIO STATION

WENJ-FM 40545
Owner: Townsquare Media, LLC
Editorial: 950 Tilton Rd Ste 200, Northfield, New Jersey 08225-1235 **Tel:** 1 609 645-9797.
Web site: http://www.973espn.com
Profile: WENJ-FM is a commercial station owned by the Townsquare Media, LLC. The format of the station is sports. WENJ-FM broadcasts to the Atlantic City, NJ area at 97.3 FM.
FM RADIO STATION

WENK-AM 37791
Owner: WENK of Union City, Inc.
Editorial: 1729 Nailling Dr, Union City, Tennessee 38261 **Tel:** 1 731 885-1240.
Web site: http://www.wenkwtpr.com
Profile: WENK-AM is a commercial station owned by WENK of Union City, Inc. The format of the station is oldies. WENK-AM broadcasts to the Paducah, KY; Cape Girardeau, MO; Harrisburg, IL areas at 1240 AM.
AM RADIO STATION

WENN-AM 36787
Owner: Summit Media Broadcasting LLC
Editorial: 2700 Corporate Dr Ste 115, Birmingham, Alabama 35242-2735 **Tel:** 1 205 322-2987.
Web site: http://www.easy1021.com/
Profile: WENN-AM is a commercial station owned by Summit Media Broadcasting LLC. The format of the station is Soft AC. WENN-AM is an ESPN Radio affiliate for the Birmingham, AL area and broadcasts at 1320 AM.
AM RADIO STATION

WENO-AM 39131
Owner: Broady Media Group, LLC
Editorial: 2214 Rosa L Parks Blvd Ste 106, Nashville, Tennessee 37228-1341 **Tel:** 1 615 742-6506 22.
Email: info@760thegospel.com
Web site: http://www.760thegospel.com
Profile: WENO-AM is a commercial station owned by Broady Media Group, LLC. The format of the station is gospel. WENO-AM broadcasts in the Nashville, TN area at 760 AM.
AM RADIO STATION

WENR-AM 35304
Owner: George C. Hudson, III
Editorial: 202 9th St, Etowah, Tennessee 37331-1343
Tel: 1 423 263-5555.
Email: wenrradio@yahoo.com
Profile: WENR-AM is a commercial station owned by George C. Hudson, III. The format of the station is gospel. WENR-AM broadcasts to the Chattanooga, TN area at 1090 AM.
AM RADIO STATION

WENT-AM 35305
Owner: Whitney Radio Broadcasting Inc.
Editorial: 138 Harrison St, Gloversville, New York 12078-4804 **Tel:** 1 518 725-7175.
Email: wentnewsroom@hotmail.com
Web site: http://www.am1340went.com
Profile: WENT-AM is a commercial station owned by Whitney Radio Broadcasting Inc. The format of the station is news, talk, sports and adult contemporary music. WENT-AM broadcasts to the Gloversville, NY area at 1340 AM.
AM RADIO STATION

WENU-AM 38527
Owner: Pamal Broadcasting Ltd.
Editorial: 89 Everts Ave, Queensbury, New York 12804-2040 **Tel:** 1 518 793-7733.
Email: production@adirondackbroadcasting.com
Profile: WENU-AM is a commercial station owned by Pamal Broadcasting Ltd. The format of the station is sports. WENU-AM broadcasts locally to Warren County, NY at 1410 AM.
AM RADIO STATION

WENY-AM 38752
Owner: Sound Communications, LLC
Editorial: 21 E Market St Ste 101, Corning, New York 14830-2650 **Tel:** 1 607 937-8181.
Profile: WENY-AM is a commercial station owned by Sound Communications, LLC. The format of the station is talk. WENY-AM broadcasts to the Corning, NY area at 1230 AM.
AM RADIO STATION

WENY-FM 46103
Owner: WS2K Media
Editorial: 21 E Market St Ste 101, Corning, New York 14830-2650 **Tel:** 1 607 937-8181.
Web site: http://www.magic927977.com
Profile: WENY-FM is a commercial station owned by Sound Communications, LLC. The format of the station is adult contemporary. WENY-FM broadcasts to the Corning, NY area at 92.7 FM.
FM RADIO STATION

WENZ-FM 40612
Owner: Urban One, Inc.
Editorial: 6555 Carnegie Ave Ste 100, Cleveland, Ohio 44103-4619 **Tel:** 1 216 579-1111.
Web site: http://www.zhiphopcleveland.com
Profile: WENZ-FM is a commercial station owned by Urban One, Inc. The format of the station is urban contemporary. WENZ-FM broadcasts to the Cleveland area at 107.9 FM.
FM RADIO STATION

WEOA-AM 37900
Owner: BLS Entertainment, Inc.
Editorial: 915 Main St Ste 1, Evansville, Indiana 47708-1857 **Tel:** 1 812 424-8864.
Email: weoa_1@yahoo.com
Profile: WEOA-AM is a commercial station owned by BLS Entertainment, Inc.. The format for the station is urban adult contemporary. WEOA-AM broadcasts to the Evansville, IN area at 1400 AM.
AM RADIO STATION

WEOK-AM 37792
Owner: Townsquare Media
Editorial: 2 Pendell Rd, Poughkeepsie, New York 12601-1513 **Tel:** 1 845 471-1500.
Web site: http://hudsonvalleytrueoldies.com
Profile: WEOK-AM is a commercial station owned by Townsquare Media. The format of the station is Spanish Adult Hits. WEOK-AM broadcasts to the Poughkeepsie, NY area at 1390 AM.
AM RADIO STATION

WEOL-AM 38642
Owner: Elyria-Lorain Broadcasting
Editorial: 538 Broad St Fl 4, Elyria, Ohio 44035-5508
Tel: 1 440 322-3761.
Email: psa@weol.com
Web site: http://weol.northcoastnow.com
Profile: WEOL-AM is a commercial station owned by Elyria-Lorain Broadcasting. The format of the station is news, talk and sports. WEOL-AM broadcasts to the Elyria, OH area at 930 AM.
AM RADIO STATION

WEOS-FM 40249
Owner: Hobart & William Smith Colleges
Editorial: 300 Pulteney St, Geneva, New York 14456-3304 **Tel:** 1 315 781-3456.
Web site: http://weos.publicbroadcasting.net
Profile: WEOS-FM is a non-commercial station owned by Hobart & William Smith Colleges. The format of the station is NPR news and talk. WEOS-FM broadcasts to the Geneva, NY area 89.5 FM.
FM RADIO STATION

WEOW-FM 43341
Owner: Florida Keys Media, LLC
Editorial: 93351 Overseas Hwy, Tavernier, Florida 33070-2800 **Tel:** 1 305 852-9085.
Profile: WEOW-FM is a commercial station owned by Florida Keys Media, LLC. The format of the station is top 40/CHR. WEOW-FM broadcasts to the Key West, FL area at 92.7 FM.
FM RADIO STATION

WEPC-FM 42510
Owner: Toccoa Falls College
Editorial: 292 Old Clarksville Rd, Toccoa, Georgia 30577-6973 **Tel:** 1 800 251-8326.
Email: radio@myfavoritestation.net
Web site: http://www.wrafradio.org
Profile: WEPC-FM is a non-commercial station owned by Toccoa Falls College. The format of the station is religious featuring Christian teaching and gospel music. WEPC-FM airs locally in the Toccoa, GA area 88.5 FM.
FM RADIO STATION

WEPG-AM 35306
Owner: Rodgers(Charles)
Editorial: 105 N Ash Ave, South Pittsburg, Tennessee 37380-1565 **Tel:** 1 423 837-8001.
Email: wepg@att.net
Web site: http://www.wepgradio.com
Profile: WEPG-AM is a commercial station owned by Charles Rodgers. The format of the station is classic country. WEPG-AM broadcasts to the Chattanooga, TN area at 910 AM.
AM RADIO STATION

WEPM-AM 37793
Owner: Prettyman Broadcasting Co.
Editorial: 1606 W King St, Martinsburg, West Virginia 25401-2077 **Tel:** 1 304 263-8868.
Web site: http://www.wepm.com
Profile: WEMP-AM is a commercial station owned by Prettyman Broadcasting Co. The format of the station is news, talk, and sports. WEPM-AM broadcasts in the Martinsburg, WV, area at 1340 AM.
AM RADIO STATION

WEPN-AM 35861
Owner: Walt Disney Co.
Editorial: 125 W End Ave Fl 6, New York, New York 10023-6387 **Tel:** 1 646 699-6800.
Web site: http://espndeportes.espn.go.com/espndeportesradio
Profile: WEPN-AM is a commercial station owned by Walt Disney Co. The format of the station is Spanish sports programming. WEPN-AM broadcasts to the New York area at 1050 AM.
AM RADIO STATION

WEPN-FM 41014
Owner: Emmis Communications Corp.
Editorial: 125 W End Ave Fl 6, New York, New York 10023-6387 **Tel:** 1 646 699-6800.
Web site: http://www.espn.com/newyork/radio
Profile: WEPN-FM is a commercial station owned by Emmis Communications Corp., and managed under LMA with ESPN, Inc. (Walt Disney Co.). The format of the station is sports. WEPN-FM broadcasts to the New York City metro area at 98.7 FM.
FM RADIO STATION

WEQF-FM 72486
Owner: Positive Radio Group
Editorial: 18498 N James Madison Hwy, Dillwyn, Virginia 23936-2906 **Tel:** 1 434 455-0306.
Web site: http://equipfm.org/
Profile: WEQF-FM is a commercial station owned by Positive Radio Group. The format for the station is Religious Teaching. WEQF-FM broadcasts to the Richmond, VA area at 105.3 FM.
FM RADIO STATION

WEQX-FM 40252
Owner: Northshire Communications Inc.
Editorial: 161 Elm St, Manchester Center, Vermont 05255-9641 **Tel:** 1 802 362-4800.
Web site: http://www.weqx.com
Profile: WEQX-FM is a commercial station owned by Northshire Communications Inc. The format of the station is rock alternative music. WEQX-FM broadcasts to the Manchester, VT area at 102.7 FM.
FM RADIO STATION

WERC-AM 38874
Owner: iHeartMedia Inc.
Editorial: 600 Beacon Pkwy W Ste 400, Birmingham, Alabama 35209-3118 **Tel:** 1 205 439-9600.
Web site: http://www.wercfm.com
Profile: WERC-AM is a commercial station owned by iHeartMedia Inc. The format of the station is news/talk. WERC-AM broadcasts to the Birmingham, AL, area at 960 AM.
AM RADIO STATION

WERC-FM 43433
Owner: iHeartMedia Inc.
Editorial: 600 Beacon Pkwy W, Birmingham, Alabama 35209-3120 **Tel:** 1 205 439-9600.
Web site: http://www.talkradio1055.com
Profile: WERC-FM is a commercial station owned by iHeartMedia Inc. The format of the station is news/talk. WERC-FM broadcasts to the Birmingham, AL area at 105.5 FM.
FM RADIO STATION

WERE-AM 37126
Owner: Urban One, Inc.
Editorial: 6555 Carnegie Ave Ste 100, Cleveland, Ohio 44103-4619 **Tel:** 1 216 579-1111.
Web site: http://newstalkcleveland.com
Profile: WERE-AM is a commercial station owned by Urban One, Inc. The format of the station is news and talk. WERE-AM broadcasts in the Cleveland area at 1490 AM.
AM RADIO STATION

WERH-AM 37794
Owner: Fowler(Martha) and Burleson(Susan)
Editorial: 1597 Military St S, Hamilton, Alabama 35570-5026 **Tel:** 1 205 921-3481.
Email: werh@sonet.net
Profile: WERH-AM is a commercial station owned by Martha Fowler and Susan Burleson. The format of the

station is classic country and gospel music. WERH-FM broadcasts to the Hamilton, AL area at 970 AM.
AM RADIO STATION

WERH-FM 45145
Owner: Fowler(Martha) and Burleson(Susan)
Editorial: 1597 Military St S, Hamilton, Alabama 35570 **Tel:** 1 205 921-3481.
Email: werh@sonet.net
Profile: WERH-FM is a commercial station owned by Martha Fowler and Susan Burleson. The format of the station is classic rock music. WERH-FM broadcasts to the Hamilton, AL area at 92.1 FM.
FM RADIO STATION

WERK-FM 44185
Owner: Backyard Broadcasting
Editorial: 800 E 29th St, Muncie, Indiana 47302-5765 **Tel:** 1 765 288-4403.
Email: studio@werkfm.net
Web site: http://www.werkradio.com
Profile: WERK-FM is a commercial station owned by Backyard Broadcasting. The format of the station is oldies music. WERK-FM broadcasts to the Indianapolis area at 104.9 FM.
FM RADIO STATION

WERL-AM 38751
Owner: Heartland Communications Group, LLC
Editorial: 909 N Railroad St, Eagle River, Wisconsin 54521 **Tel:** 1 715 479-4451.
Profile: WERL-AM is a commercial station owned by Heartland Communications Group, LLC. The format of the station is talk. WERL-AM broadcasts to Eagle River, WI area at 950 AM.
AM RADIO STATION

WERO-FM 45121
Owner: Alpha Media
Editorial: 1361 Colony Dr, New Bern, North Carolina 28562-4129 **Tel:** 1 252 639-7900.
Web site: http://www.bob933.com
Profile: WERO-FM is a commercial station owned by Alpha Media. The format of the station is Top 40/CHR music. WERO-FM broadcasts to the Greenville, NC area at 93.3 FM.
FM RADIO STATION

WERQ-FM 45649
Owner: Urban One, Inc.
Editorial: 1705 Whitehead Rd, Baltimore, Maryland 21207-4033 **Tel:** 1 410 332-8200.
Web site: http://www.92q.com
Profile: WERQ-FM is a commercial station owned by Urban One, Inc. The format of the station is urban contemporary music. WERQ-FM broadcasts to the Baltimore area at 92.3 FM.
FM RADIO STATION

WERS-FM 41924
Owner: Emerson College
Editorial: 180 Tremont St, Boston, Massachusetts 02111-1014 **Tel:** 1 617 824-8891.
Email: news@wers.org
Web site: http://www.wers.org
Profile: WERS-FM is a non-commercial station owned by Emerson College. The format of the station is AAA-Adult Album Alternative. WERS-FM broadcasts to the Boston area at 88.9 FM.
FM RADIO STATION

WERT-AM 38616
Owner: First Family Broadcasting Inc.
Editorial: 9070 Mendon Rd, Van Wert, Ohio 45891-9006 **Tel:** 1 419 238-1220.
Email: wert@bright.net
Web site: http://www.wert1220.com
Profile: WERT-AM is a commercial station owned by First Family Broadcasting Inc. The format of the station is adult standards. WERT-AM broadcasts to the Van Wert, OH area at 1220 AM.
AM RADIO STATION

WERU-FM 41215
Owner: Salt Pond Community Broadcasting
Editorial: 1186 Acadia Highway, East Orland, Maine 4431 **Tel:** 1 207 469-6600.
Email: news@weru.org
Web site: http://www.weru.org
Profile: WERU-FM is a non-commercial station owned by Salt Pond Community Broadcasting. The format of the station is variety. WERU-FM broadcasts to the East Orland, ME area at 89.9 FM.
FM RADIO STATION

WERV-FM 86499
Owner: Alpha Media LLC
Editorial: 1884 Plain Ave, Aurora, Illinois 60502-8560 **Tel:** 1 630 898-1580.
Web site: http://www.959theriver.com
Profile: WERV-FM is a commercial station owned by Alpha Media LLC. The format of the station is classic hits music. WERV-FM broadcasts to the Aurora, IL area at 95.9 FM.
FM RADIO STATION

WERX-FM 42814
Owner: East Carolina Radio Group
Editorial: 2422 S Wrightsville Ave, Nags Head, North Carolina 27959-9323 **Tel:** 1 252 441-1024.
Email: psa@ecri.net
Web site: http://www.1025theshark.com
Profile: WERX-FM is a commercial station owned by East Carolina Radio Group. The format of the station is classic hits. WERX-FM broadcasts to Nags Head, NC at 102.5 FM.
FM RADIO STATION

WERZ-FM 43560
Owner: iHeartMedia Inc.
Editorial: 815 Lafayette Rd, Portsmouth, New Hampshire 03801-5406 **Tel:** 1 603 436-7300.
Web site: http://www.z107fm.com
Profile: WERZ-FM is a commercial station owned by iHeartMedia Inc. The format of the station is top 40/ CHR. WERZ-FM broadcasts to the Portsmouth, NH area at 107.1 FM.
FM RADIO STATION

WESA-FM 40233
Owner: Pittsburgh Community Broadcasting Corp.
Editorial: 67 Bedford Sq, Pittsburgh, Pennsylvania 15203-1152 **Tel:** 1 412 381-9131.
Email: news@wesa.fm
Web site: http://wesa.fm
Profile: WESA-FM is a non-commercial station owned by Pittsburgh Community Broadcasting Corp. The format of the station is news talk. WESA-FM broadcasts in the Pittsburgh area at 90.5 FM.
FM RADIO STATION

WESB-AM 38490
Owner: WESB Inc.
Editorial: 1490 Saint Francis Dr, Bradford, Pennsylvania 16701 **Tel:** 1 814 368-4141.
Email: news@wesb.com
Web site: http://www.wesb.com
Profile: WESB-AM is a commercial station owned by WESB Inc. The format of the station is hot adult contemporary, news and talk. WESB-AM broadcasts to the Buffalo, NY area at 1490 AM.
AM RADIO STATION

WESC-FM 45147
Owner: iHeartMedia Inc.
Editorial: 101 N Main St Ste 1000, Greenville, South Carolina 29601-4852 **Tel:** 1 864 242-4660.
Email: raydioguy@aol.com
Web site: http://wescfm.iheart.com
Profile: WESC-FM is a commercial station owned by iHeartMedia Inc. The format of the station is contemporary country. WESC-FM broadcasts to the Greenville, SC area at 92.5 FM.
FM RADIO STATION

WESE-FM 45968
Owner: iHeartMedia, Inc.
Editorial: 5026 Cliff Gookin Blvd, Tupelo, Mississippi 38801-7059 **Tel:** 1 662 842-1067.
Profile: WESE-FM is a commercial station owned by iHeartMedia, Inc. The format of the station is urban contemporary. WESE-FM broadcasts to the Tupelo, MS area at 92.5 FM.
FM RADIO STATION

WESO-AM 36852
Owner: Money Matters Radio Inc.
Editorial: 100 Foster St, Southbridge, Massachusetts 01550-2595 **Tel:** 1 508 909-0970.
Profile: WESO-AM is a commercial station owned by Money Matters Radio Inc. The format of the station is business talk. WESO-AM broadcasts to the Southbridge, MA area at 970 AM.
AM RADIO STATION

WESP-FM 41023
Owner: Southeast Alabama Broadcasters, LLC
Editorial: 3245 Montgomery Hwy Ste 1, Dothan, Alabama 36303-2150 **Tel:** 1 334 712-9233.
Web site: http://1025theq.com/
Profile: WESP-FM is a commercial station owned by Southeast Alabama Broadcasters, LLC and operated by Low Country Radio, LLC. The format of the station is classic hits. WESP-AM broadcasts to the Dothan, AL area at 102.5 FM.
FM RADIO STATION

WESR-AM 38520
Owner: Eastern Shore Radio, Inc.
Editorial: 22479 Front St, Accomac, Virginia 23301-1641 **Tel:** 1 757 787-3200.
Web site: http://www.shoredailynews.com
Profile: WESR-AM is a commercial station owned by Eastern Shore Radio, Inc. The format of the station is classic hits and talk. WESR-AM broadcasts to the Norfolk, VA area at 1330 AM.
AM RADIO STATION

WESR-FM 45874
Owner: Eastern Shore Radio, Inc.
Editorial: 22479 Front St, Accomac, Virginia 23301-1641 **Tel:** 1 757 787-3200.
Web site: http://www.shoredailynews.com
Profile: WESR-FM is a commercial station owned by Eastern Shore Radio, Inc. The format of the station is oldies, adult contemporary, news and talk. WESR-FM broadcasts to the Norfolk, VA area at 103.3 FM.
FM RADIO STATION

West Virginia Public Radio Network 47097
Owner: State of West Virginia
Editorial: 600 Capitol St, Charleston, West Virginia 25301-1223 **Tel:** 1 304 556-4900.
Email: feedback@wvpubcast.org
Web site: http://www.wvpubcast.org
Profile: West Virginia Public Broadcasting has been serving the state for more than 30 years. The network is a widely used educational and cultural institution in the state, with a network of television, radio, Internet and educational resources available to virtually every citizen of every age. The network strives to lead the way in addressing the state's unique needs in education, economic development, and quality-of-life issues through a variety of successful partnerships with individuals, businesses, governments and organizations.
REGIONAL RADIO NETWORKS

WEST-AM 37014
Owner: Grey Matter Broadcasting
Editorial: 1125 Colorado St, Allentown, Pennsylvania 18103-3118 **Tel:** 1 610 434-4801.
Web site: http://laolaradio.com
Profile: WEST-AM is a commercial station owned by Grey Matter Broadcasting. The format of the station is Spanish tropical music. WEST-AM broadcasts to the Allentown, PA area at 1400 AM.
AM RADIO STATION

Westwood One - Los Angeles Bureau 46996
Owner: Cumulus Media
Editorial: 3321 S La Cienega Blvd, Los Angeles, California 90016-3114 **Tel:** 1 310 840-4000.
Web site: http://www.westwoodone.com
RADIO NETWORK

Westwood One News 944111
Owner: Westwood One, Inc.
Editorial: 220 W 42nd St, New York, New York 10036-7200 **Tel:** 1 212 967-2888.
Web site: http://www.westwoodone.com
Profile: Full-service news network produced in partnership with CNN.
RADIO NETWORK

WestwoodOne 46974
Owner: Cumulus Media
Editorial: 220 W 42nd St, New York, New York 10036-7200 **Tel:** 1 212 419-2926.
Web site: http://www.westwoodone.com
Profile: WestwoodOne, previously Dial Global, provides over more than 200 news, sports, music, talk and entertainment programs as well as features, live events and 24/7 formats. Through its subsidiaries, Metro Networks/Shadow Broadcast Services, WestwoodOne provides local content to the radio and TV industries including news, sports, weather, traffic, video news services and other information. SmartRoute Systems, also a subsidiary of WestwoodOne, manages traffic information centers for state and local departments of transportation, and markets traffic and travel content to wireless, Internet, in-vehicle navigation systems and voice portal customers. WestwoodOne serves more than 7,700 radio stations. Its networks reach 225 million people a week.
RADIO NETWORK

WestwoodOne - New York Bureau 684677
Owner: Cumulus Media
Editorial: 220 W 42nd St Fl 4, New York, New York 10036-7200 **Tel:** 1 212 419-2926.
RADIO NETWORK

WestwoodOne - Seattle Bureau 62902
Owner: Cumulus Media
Editorial: 3131 Elliott Ave Ste 770, Seattle, Washington 98121-1044
RADIO NETWORK

WestwoodOne - Seattle Bureau 539296
Owner: Cumulus Media
Editorial: 701 5th Ave, Seattle, Washington 98104-7097 **Tel:** 1 206 386-7770.
RADIO NETWORK

WestwoodOne - Silver Spring Bureau 46994
Owner: Cumulus Media
Editorial: 8403 Colesville Rd, Silver Spring, Maryland 20910-6331 **Tel:** 1 301 628-2300.
RADIO NETWORK

WestwoodOne - Valencia Bureau 47001
Owner: Cumulus Media
Editorial: 25061 Avenue Stanford, Valencia, California 91355-3443
Profile: Entertainment and lifestyle programming.
RADIO NETWORK

WestwoodOne - Washington Bureau 821896
Owner: Cumulus Media
Editorial: 4400 Jenifer St NW, Washington, District Of Columbia 20015-2113 **Tel:** 1 202 840-7900.
RADIO NETWORK

WESX-AM 35308
Owner: Principle Broadcasting
Editorial: 90 Everett Ave, Chelsea, Massachusetts 02150-2311 **Tel:** 1 617 884-4500.
Web site: http://www.wesx1230am.com
Profile: WESX-AM is a commercial station owned by Principle Broadcasting. The format of the station is Hispanic variety. WESX-AM broadcasts to the Marblehead, MA area at 1230 AM.
AM RADIO STATION

WESY-AM 36463
Owner: Interchange Communications
Editorial: 126 Seven Oaks Road, Greenville, Mississippi 38704-4426 **Tel:** 1 662 378-9405.
Profile: WESY-AM is a commercial station owned by Interchange Communications. The format of the station is gospel. WESY-AM broadcasts in the Greenville, MS area at 1580 AM.
AM RADIO STATION

WETB-AM 235100
Owner: Mountain Signals Inc.
Editorial: 231 Brandonwood Dr, Johnson City, Tennessee 37604-2156 **Tel:** 1 423 928-7131.
Email: wetb790am@yahoo.com
Web site: http://wetb790am.wix.com/wetb
Profile: WETB-AM is a non-commercial station owned by Mountain Signals Inc. The format of the station is southern gospel. WETB-AM broadcasts to the Johnson City, TN area at 790 AM.
AM RADIO STATION

WETC-AM 35310
Owner: Sanchez Broadcasting Corporation
Editorial: 2164 Southeast Blvd, Clinton, North Carolina 28328-4758
Profile: WETC-AM is a commercial station owned by Sanchez Broadcasting Corporation. The format of the station is Spanish CHR. WETC-AM broadcasts to the Raleigh, NC area at 540 AM.
AM RADIO STATION

WETN-FM 40258
Owner: Trustees of Wheaton College
Editorial: 501 College Ave, Wheaton, Illinois 60187-5501 **Tel:** 1 630 752-5074.
Email: wetn@wheaton.edu
Web site: http://www.wheaton.edu/wetn
Profile: WETN-FM is a non-commercial station owned by Trustees of Wheaton College. The format of the station is religious, classical and jazz music. WETN-FM broadcasts to the Wheaton, IL area at 88.1 FM.
FM RADIO STATION

WETR-AM 36961
Owner: Moffit Media Inc.
Editorial: 1621 E Magnolia Ave, Knoxville, Tennessee 37917-7825 **Tel:** 1 865 525-0620.
Web site: http://www.talkradio760.com
Profile: WETR-AM is a commercial station owned by Moffit Media Inc. The format of the station is news and talk. WETR-AM broadcasts to the Knoxville, TN area at 760 AM.
AM RADIO STATION

WETT-FM 41225
Owner: Withers Broadcasting Co.
Editorial: 5 Television Dr, Bridgeport, West Virginia 26330-2621 **Tel:** 1 304 848-5000.
Email: news@wdtv.com
Web site: http://www.mix104radio.com
Profile: WETT-FM is a commercial station owned by Withers Broadcasting Co. The format of the station is adult contemporary music. WETT-FM broadcasts to the Bridgeport, WV area at 104.1 FM.
FM RADIO STATION

WETZ-AM 39282
Owner: Dailey Corp.
Editorial: 1130 4Th St, New Martinsville, West Virginia 26155-2110 **Tel:** 1 304 455-1111.
Email: wetz@suddenlinkmail.com
Profile: WETZ-AM is a commercial station owned by Dailey Corp. The format of the station is classic hits. WETZ-AM broadcasts to the New Martinsville, WV area at 1330 AM.
AM RADIO STATION

WEUL-FM 134003
Owner: Gospel Opportunities Inc.
Editorial: 130 Carmen Dr, Marquette, Michigan 49855 **Tel:** 1 906 249-1423.
Email: whwl@whwl.net
Web site: http://www.whwl.net
Profile: WEUL-FM is a non-commercial station owned by Gospel Opportunities Inc. The format for the station is religious programming. WEUL-FM broadcasts to the Marquette, MI area at 98.1 FM.
FM RADIO STATION

WEUP-AM 39237
Owner: Broadcast One
Editorial: 2609 Jordan Ln NW, Huntsville, Alabama 35816-1013 **Tel:** 1 256 837-9387.
Email: promotions@103weup.com
Web site: http://www.weupam.com
Profile: WEUP-AM is a commercial station owned by Broadcast One. The format of the station is gospel and talk. WEUP-AM broadcasts to the Huntsville, AL area at 1700 AM.
AM RADIO STATION

WEUP-FM 46225
Owner: Broadcast One
Editorial: 2609 Jordan Ln NW, Huntsville, Alabama 35816-1030 **Tel:** 1 256 837-9387.
Email: promotions@103weup.com
Web site: http://www.103weup.com
Profile: WEUP-FM is a commercial station owned by Broadcast One. The format of the station is urban contemporary music. WEUP-FM broadcasts in the Huntsville, AL area at 103.1 FM.
FM RADIO STATION

WEUV-AM 69960
Owner: Broadcast One
Editorial: 2609 Jordan Ln NW, Huntsville, Alabama 35816-1013 **Tel:** 1 256 837-9387.
Web site: http://www.103weup.com
Profile: WEUV-AM is a commercial station owned by Broadcast One. The format of the station is urban

contemporary music. WEUV-AM broadcasts to the Huntsville, AL area at 1190 AM.
AM RADIO STATION

WEUZ-FM 46586
Owner: Broadcast One
Editorial: 2609 Jordan Ln NW, Huntsville, Alabama 35816-1013 **Tel:** 1 256 837-9387.
Email: promotions@103weup.com
Web site: http://www.103weup.com
Profile: WEUZ-FM is a commerical station owned by Broadcast One. The format of the station is urban contemporary music. WEUZ-FM broadcasts to the Huntsville, AL area at 92.1 FM.
FM RADIO STATION

WEVA-AM 35311
Owner: Colonial Media Corp.
Editorial: 705 Washington St, Emporia, Virginia 23847-1539 **Tel:** 1 434 634-2133.
Email: info@wevaradio.com
Web site: http://www.wevaradio.com
Profile: WEVA-AM is a commercial station owned by Colonial Media Corp. The format of the station is adult contemporary music. WEVA-AM broadcasts to the Emporia, VA area at 860 AM.
AM RADIO STATION

WEVE-FM 46134
Owner: Red Rock Radio Corp.
Editorial: 906 Old Highway 53, Eveleth, Minnesota 55734-8632 **Tel:** 1 218 741-5922.
Profile: WEVE-FM is a commercial station owned by Red Rock Radio Corp. The format of the station is adult contemporary music. WEVE-FM broadcasts in the Eveleth, MN area at 97.9 FM
FM RADIO STATION

WEVJ-FM 88318
Owner: New Hampshire Public Radio, Inc.
Editorial: 2 Pillsbury Street, Concord, New Hampshire 3301 **Tel:** 1 603 228-8910.
Web site: http://www.nhpr.org
Profile: WEVJ-FM is a non-commercial station owned by New Hampshire Public Radio, Inc. The format of the station is news and talk. WEVJ-FM broadcasts to the Jackson, NH area at 99.5 FM. The station does not accept PSAs.
FM RADIO STATION

WEVL-FM 41053
Owner: Southern Communication Volunteers
Editorial: 518 S Main St, Memphis, Tennessee 38103-4443 **Tel:** 1 901 528-0560.
Email: wevl@wevl.org
Web site: http://www.wevl.org
Profile: WEVL-FM is a non-commercial station owned by Southern Communication Volunteers. The format of the station is variety. WEVL-FM broadcasts to the Memphis area at 89.9 FM.
FM RADIO STATION

WEVN-FM 42520
Owner: New Hampshire Public Radio, Inc.
Editorial: 2 Pillsbury St Fl 6, Concord, New Hampshire 03301-3523 **Tel:** 1 603 228-8910.
Web site: http://www.nhpr.org
Profile: WEVN-FM is a non-commercial station owned by New Hampshire Public Radio, Inc. The station airs in the Concord, NH area at 90.7 FM and plays a talk and news format.
FM RADIO STATION

WEVO-FM 40260
Owner: New Hampshire Public Radio, Inc.
Editorial: 2 Pillsbury St, Concord, New Hampshire 03301-3523 **Tel:** 1 603 228-8910.
Web site: http://www.nhpr.org
Profile: WEVO-FM is a non-commercial station owned by New Hampshire Public Radio, Inc. The format of the station is news and talk. WEVO-FM broadcasts to the Concord, NH area at 89.1 FM.
FM RADIO STATION

WEVR-AM 37797
Owner: Hanten Broadcasting Co. Inc.
Editorial: 178 Radio Rd, River Falls, Wisconsin 54022-8255 **Tel:** 1 715 425-1111.
Email: wevr.am.fm@gmail.com
Profile: WEVR-AM is a commercial station owned by Hanten Broadcasting Co. Inc. The format of the station is Lite Rock/Lite AC. WEVR-AM broadcasts in the River Falls, WI area at 1550 AM.
AM RADIO STATION

WEVR-FM 45148
Owner: Hanten Broadcasting Co. Inc.
Editorial: 178 Radio Rd, River Falls, Wisconsin 54022-8255 **Tel:** 1 715 381-1111.
Email: wevr.am.fm@gmail.com
Profile: WEVR-FM is a commercial station owned by Hanten Broadcasting Co. Inc. The format of the station is Lite Rock/Lite AC music. WEVR-FM broadcasts to the River Falls, WI area at 106.3 FM.
FM RADIO STATION

WEW-AM 35312
Owner: Birach Broadcasting Corp.
Editorial: 2740 Hampton Ave, Saint Louis, Missouri 63139 **Tel:** 1 314 781-9397.
Email: wewradio@aol.com
Web site: http://www.wewradio.com
Profile: WEW-AM is a commercial station owned by Birach Broadcasting Corp. The format of the station is a variety of adult standards music, talk and ethnic programming. WEW-AM broadcasts to the St. Louis area at 770 AM.
AM RADIO STATION

WEWC-AM 36823
Owner: Norsan Broadcasting System
Tel: 1 904 361-3150.
Web site: https://www.1160latinohits.com
Profile: WEWC-AM is a commercial station owned by Norsan Broadcasting System. The format of the station is Hispanic programming and tropical music. WEWC-AM broadcasts to the Coral Springs, FL area at 1160 AM.
AM RADIO STATION

WEWO-AM 36791
Owner: Service Media Inc.
Editorial: 1338 Bragg Blvd, Fayetteville, North Carolina 28301 **Tel:** 1 910 486-9438.
Profile: WEWO-AM is a commercial station owned by Service Media Inc. The format of the station is gospel. WEWO-AM broadcasts to the Fayetteville, NC area at 1460 AM.
AM RADIO STATION

WEXL-AM 36869
Owner: Crawford Broadcasting Co.
Editorial: 12300 Radio Pl, Detroit, Michigan 48228-1029 **Tel:** 1 313 272-3434.
Email: station@wmuz.com
Web site: http://www.wexl1340.com
Profile: WEXL-AM is a commercial station owned by Crawford Broadcasting Co. The format of the station is gospel. WEXL-AM broadcasts to the Detroit area at 1340 AM.
AM RADIO STATION

WEXP-FM 63406
Owner: Woodchuck Radio, LLC
Editorial: 9 Stowe St, Waterbury, Vermont 05676-1820 **Tel:** 1 802 244-7321.
Email: wdev@radiovermont.com
Profile: WEXP-FM is a commercial station owned by Woodchuck Radio, LLC (part of Radio Vermont Group). The format of the station is adult contemporary. WEXP-FM broadcasts to the Rutland, VT area at a frequency of 101.5 FM.
FM RADIO STATION

WEXR-FM 45464
Owner: Meridian Community College Foundation
Editorial: 910 Highway 19 N, Meridian, Mississippi 39307-5801 **Tel:** 1 601 484-8769.
Email: ratkinso@meridiancc.edu
Web site: http://wexr.us
Profile: WEXR-FM is a non-commercial station owned by Meridian Community College Foundation. The format of the station is adult standards. WEXR-FM broadcasts to the Meridian, MS area at 106.9 FM.
FM RADIO STATION

WEXX-FM 79639
Owner: Bristol Broadcasting Company
Editorial: 901 E Valley Dr, Bristol, Virginia 24201-4913 **Tel:** 1 276 669-8112.
Web site: http://www.993thex.com
Profile: WEXX-FM is a commercial station owned by Bristol Broadcasting Company. The format of the station is alternative rock. WEXX-FM broadcasts to the Bristol, VA area at 99.3 FM.
FM RADIO STATION

WEXY-AM 35313
Owner: Multicultural Radio Broadcasting Inc.
Editorial: 412 W Oakland Park Blvd, Wilton Manors, Florida 33311-1712 **Tel:** 1 954 561-1520.
Profile: WEXY-AM is a commercial station owned by Multicultural Radio Broadcasting Inc. The format of the station is gospel. WEXY-AM broadcasts to the Wilton Manors, FL at 1520 AM.
AM RADIO STATION

WEYE-FM 44547
Owner: Positive Alternative Radio
Tel: 1 423 477-5676.
Email: office@wcqr.org
Web site: http://wcqr.org
Profile: WEYE-FM is a non-commercial station owned by Positive Alternative Radio. The format of the station is Christian AC. WEYE-FM broadcasts to the Kingsport, TN area at 104.3 FM.
FM RADIO STATION

WEYY-FM 816307
Owner: Barnes Evangelistic Ministries
Editorial: 7550 W Carroll Rd, Carrollton, Georgia 30116-5900 **Tel:** 1 540 459-7646.
Web site: http://www.barnesministries.com/Radio.htm
Profile: WEYY-FM is a non-commercial station owned by Barnes Evangelistic Ministries. The format of the station is Southern gospel music. WEYY-FM is licensed to Tallapoosa, GA and broadcasts to the West Atlanta Metro and East Alabama areas at a frequency of 88.7 FM.
FM RADIO STATION

WEZB-FM 40262
Owner: Entercom Communications Corp.
Editorial: 400 Poydras St Ste 800, New Orleans, Louisiana 70130-3789 **Tel:** 1 504 593-6376.
Email: wwlnewsroom@yahoo.com
Web site: http://www.b97.com
Profile: WEZB-FM is a commercial station owned by Entercom Communications Corp. The format of the station is Top 40/CHR. WEZB-FM broadcasts to the New Orleans area on 97.1 FM.
FM RADIO STATION

WEZC-FM 45211
Owner: Kaskaskia Broadcasting, Inc.
Editorial: 2980 US Highway 51, Clinton, Illinois 61727-9479 **Tel:** 1 217 935-9590.
Email: whow@randyradio.com
Web site: http://dewittdailynews.com
Profile: WEZC-FM is a commercial station owned by Kaskaskia Broadcasting, Inc. The format of the station is easy listening. WEZC-FM broadcasts to the Clinton, IL area at 95.9 FM.
FM RADIO STATION

WEZE-AM 36290
Owner: Salem Media Group, Inc.
Editorial: 500 Victory Rd Ste 2, North Quincy, Massachusetts 02171-3132 **Tel:** 1 617 328-0880.
Email: contactus@salemradioboston.com
Web site: http://www.wezeradio.com
Profile: WEZE-AM is a commercial station owned by Salem Media Group, Inc. The format of the station is religious news and talk. WEZE-AM broadcasts to the Quincy, MA area at 590 AM.
AM RADIO STATION

WEZF-FM 40264
Owner: Vox Communications
Editorial: 265 Hegeman Ave, Colchester, Vermont 05446-3174 **Tel:** 1 802 655-0093.
Email: star@star929.com
Web site: http://www.star929.com
Profile: WEZF-FM is a commercial station owned by Vox Communications. The format of the station is hot adult contemporary. WEZF-FM broadcasts to the Burlington, VT area at 92.9 FM.
FM RADIO STATION

WEZI-FM 43131
Owner: Cox Media Group, Inc.
Editorial: 8000 Belfort Pkwy, Jacksonville, Florida 32256-6934 **Tel:** 1 904 245-8500.
Web site: http://www.easy1065.com/
Profile: WEZI-FM is a commercial station owned by Cox Media Group, Inc. The format of the station is soft adult contemporary. WEZI-FM broadcasts to the Jacksonville, FL area at 106.5 FM.
FM RADIO STATION

WEZJ-FM 46288
Owner: Whitley Broadcasting
Editorial: 522 Main St, Williamsburg, Kentucky 40769-1127 **Tel:** 1 606 549-2285.
Email: wekx@bellsouth.net
Profile: WEZJ-FM is a commercial station owned by Whitley Broadcasting. The format of the station is country. WEZJ-FM broadcasts to the Lexington, KY area at 104.3 FM.
FM RADIO STATION

WEZL-FM 40265
Owner: iHeartMedia Inc.
Editorial: 950 Houston Northcutt Blvd Ste 201, Mount Pleasant, South Carolina 29464-5645 **Tel:** 1 843 884-2534.
Web site: http://wezl.iheart.com
Profile: WEZL-FM is a commercial station owned by iHeartMedia Inc. The format of the station is contemporary country music. WEZL-FM broadcasts to the Mount Pleasant, SC area at 103.5 FM. The slogan for the station is, "New Country for the Lowcountry."
FM RADIO STATION

WEZN-FM 40934
Owner: Connoisseur Media
Editorial: 440 Wheelers Farms Rd, Milford, Connecticut 06461-9133 **Tel:** 1 203 783-8200.
Web site: http://star999.com
Profile: WEZN-FM is a commercial station owned by Connoisseur Media. The format of the station is adult contemporary. WEZN-FM broadcasts to the Milford, CT area at 99.9 FM.
FM RADIO STATION

WEZO-AM 36274
Owner: Medici Media, Inc.
Editorial: 1802 Killingsworth Rd, Augusta, Georgia 30904-5596 **Tel:** 1 706 364-9361.
Web site: http://www.italkus.com
Profile: WEZO-AM is a commercial station owned by Medici Media, Inc. The format of the station is Conservative talk. WEZO-AM broadcasts to the Augusta, GA area at 1230 AM.
AM RADIO STATION

WEZQ-FM 40603
Owner: Townsquare Media, Inc.
Editorial: 49 Acme Rd, Brewer, Maine 04412-1545 **Tel:** 1 207 989-5631.
Web site: http://929theticket.com
Profile: WEQZ-FM is a commercial station owned by Townsquare Media, Inc. The format of the station is Sports Radop. WEQZ-FM broadcasts to the Brewer, ME area at 92.9 FM.
FM RADIO STATION

WEZR-AM 37137
Owner: Gleason Radio Group
Editorial: 555 Center St, Auburn, Maine 04210-6304 **Tel:** 1 207 784-5868.
Email: news@gleasonmedia.com
Web site: http://www.z1055.com
Profile: WEZR-AM is a commercial station owned by Gleason Radio Group. The format of the station is hot adult contemporary. WEZR-AM broadcasts to the Auburn, ME area at 1240 AM.
AM RADIO STATION

WEZS-AM 36589
Owner: Hammond(Gary W.)
Editorial: 277 Union Ave, Laconia, New Hampshire 03246-3114 **Tel:** 1 603 524-6288.
Web site: http://www.wezs.com
Profile: WEZS-AM is a commercial station owned by Gary W. Hammond. The format of the station is news/talk. WEZS-AM broadcasts to the Boston area at 1350 AM.
AM RADIO STATION

WEZV-FM 45406
Owner: Fidelity Broadcasting Inc.
Editorial: 3926 Wesley St Ste 301, Myrtle Beach, South Carolina 29579-7307 **Tel:** 1 843 903-9962.
Email: staff@wezv.com
Web site: http://www.wezv.com
Profile: WEZV-FM is a commercial station owned by Fidelity Broadcasting Inc. The format of the station is easy listening. WEZV-FM broadcasts to the Myrtle Beach, SC area at 105.9 FM.
FM RADIO STATION

WEZW-FM 43162
Owner: Equity Communications LP
Editorial: 8025 Black Horse Pike, Ste 100, Pleasantville, New Jersey 8232 **Tel:** 1 609 484-8444.
Email: easy931@gmail.com
Web site: http://easy931.com
Profile: WEZW-FM is a commercial station owned by Equity Communications LP. The format of the station is adult hits. WEZW-FM broadcasts to the Atlantic City, NJ area at 93.1 FM.
FM RADIO STATION

WEZX-FM 45990
Owner: Shamrock Communications
Editorial: 149 Penn Ave, Scranton, Pennsylvania 18503-2055 **Tel:** 1 570 346-6555.
Web site: http://www.rock107.com
Profile: WEZX-FM is a commercial station owned by Shamrock Communications. The format of the station is classic rock. WEZX-FM broadcasts to the Scranton, PA area at 107.3 FM.
FM RADIO STATION

WFAD-AM 36623
Owner: Radio Broadcasting Services, Inc.
Editorial: 372 Dorset St, South Burlington, Vermont 05403-6212 **Tel:** 1 802 863-1010.
Profile: WFAD-AM a commercial station owned by Radio Broadcasting Services, Inc. The format of the station is comedy. WFAD-AM broadcasts to the Middlebury, VT area at 1490 AM.
AM RADIO STATION

WFAI-AM 39192
Owner: QC Communications Inc.
Editorial: 704 N King St, Ste 604, Wilmington, Delaware 19801 **Tel:** 1 302 622-8895.
Web site: http://www.faith1510.com
Profile: WFAI-AM is a commercial station owned by QC Communications Inc. The format of the station is gospel music. WFAI-AM broadcasts to the Wilmington, DE area at 1510 AM.
AM RADIO STATION

WFAM-AM 35316
Owner: Wilkins Communications Network Inc.
Editorial: 552 Laney-Walker Ext, Augusta, Georgia 30901 **Tel:** 1 864 585-1885.
Email: wfam@wilkinsradio.com
Web site: http://www.wilkinsradio.com
Profile: WFAM-AM is a commercial station owned by the Wilkins Communications Network Inc. The format of the station is religious talk. WFAM-AM broadcasts to the Augusta, GA area at 1050 AM.
AM RADIO STATION

WFAN-AM 36391
Owner: CBS Radio
Editorial: 345 Hudson St Fl 10, New York, New York 10014-7472 **Tel:** 1 212 315-7000.
Email: pd@wfan.com
Web site: http://newyork.cbslocal.com/station/wfan
Profile: WFAN-AM is a commercial station owned by CBS Radio. The format of the station is sports. WFAN-AM broadcasts to the New York area at 660 AM.
AM RADIO STATION

WFAN-FM 40615
Owner: CBS Radio
Editorial: 345 Hudson St Fl 10, New York, New York 10014-7472 **Tel:** 1 212 315-7000.
Web site: http://www.newyork.cbslocal.com/category/sports
Profile: WFAN-FM is commercial station owned by CBS Radio. The format of the station is sports. WFAN-FM broadcasts to the New York area at 101.9 FM.
FM RADIO STATION

WFAR-FM 41263
Owner: Danbury Community Radio Inc.
Editorial: 25 Chestnut St, Danbury, Connecticut 06810-6816 **Tel:** 1 203 748-0001.
Web site: http://www.radiofamilia.com
Profile: WFAR-FM is a non-commercial station owned by Danbury Community Radio Inc. The format of the station is religious programming and Christian music. WFAR-FM broadcasts to the Danbury, CT area at 93.3 FM.
FM RADIO STATION

United States of America

WFAS-AM
37799
Owner: Cumulus Media Inc.
Editorial: 365 Secor Rd, Hartsdale, New York 10530-1229 **Tel:** 1 914 693-2400.
Web site: http://wfasam.com
Profile: WFAS-AM is a commercial station owned by Cumulus Media Inc. The format of the station is Sports. WFAS-AM broadcasts throughout Westchester County and surrounding areas at 1230 AM.
AM RADIO STATION

WFAT-AM
38611
Owner: County Broadcasting Company, LLC (Northeast Broadcasting Co.)
Editorial: 30 How St, Haverhill, Massachusetts 01830-6131 **Tel:** 1 978 374-4733.
Web site: http://www.amradio700.com
Profile: WFAT-AM is a commercial owned by County Broadcasting Company, LLC (Northeast Broadcasting Co). The format of the station is oldies. WFAT-AM broadcasts to the Orange-Athol, MA areas at 700 AM.
AM RADIO STATION

WFAU-AM
38491
Owner: Blueberry Broadcasting
Editorial: 125 Community Dr Ste 201, Augusta, Maine 04330-8157 **Tel:** 1 207 623-9000.
Email: info@radio9wcme.com
Web site: http://www.900wcme.com
Profile: WFAU-AM is a commercial station owned by Blueberry Broadcasting. The format of the station is sports. WFAU-AM broadcasts to the Augusta, ME area at 1280 AM.
AM RADIO STATION

WFAV-FM
41737
Owner: Milner Broadcasting Co.
Editorial: 292 N Convent St, Bourbonnais, Illinois 60914-2014 **Tel:** 1 815 933-9287.
Email: wvlifm@comcast.net
Web site: http://www.rivervalleyradio.net
Profile: WFAV-FM is a commercial station owned by Milner Broadcasting Co. The format of the station is Top 40/CHR. WFAV-FM broadcasts to the Bourbonnais, IL area at 95.1 FM.
FM RADIO STATION

WFAW-AM
38420
Owner: NRG Media LLC
Editorial: W6355 Eastern Ave, Fort Atkinson, Wisconsin 53538-9335 **Tel:** 1 920 563-9329.
Email: ftareception@nrgmedia.com
Web site: http://www.940wfaw.com
Profile: WFAW-AM is a commercial station owned by NRG Media LLC. The format of the station is news, talk and sports. WFAW-AM broadcasts to the Fort Atkinson, WI area at 940 AM.
AM RADIO STATION

WFAX-AM
35317
Owner: Newcomb Broadcasting Corp.
Editorial: 161 Hillwood Ave Ste B, Falls Church, Virginia 22046-2983 **Tel:** 1 703 532-1220.
Email: wfax@wfax.com
Web site: http://www.wfax.com
Profile: WFAX-AM is a commercial station owned by Newcomb Broadcasting Corp. The format of the station is talk and religious. WFAX-AM broadcasts to the Falls Church, VA, area on 1220 AM.
AM RADIO STATION

WFAY-AM
35315
Owner: CRS Radio Holdings, Inc.
Editorial: 5600 Cliffdale Rd Ste 2801, Fayetteville, North Carolina 28314-2255 **Tel:** 1 910 867-4129.
Web site: http://www.espnfay.com/
Profile: WFAY-AM is a commercial station owned by CRS Radio Holdings, Inc. The format of the station is sports. WFAY-AM broadcasts to the Fayetteville, NC area at 1230 AM.
AM RADIO STATION

WFBC-FM
45152
Owner: Entercom Communications Corp.
Editorial: 25 Garlington Rd, Greenville, South Carolina 29615-4613 **Tel:** 1 864 271-9200.
Web site: http://www.b937online.com
Profile: WFBC-FM is a commercial station owned by Entercom Communications Corp. The format of the station is Top 40/CHR. WFBC-FM broadcasts to the Greenville, SC area at 93.7 FM.
FM RADIO STATION

WFBE-FM
43539
Owner: Cumulus Media Inc.
Editorial: G 4511 Miller Rd, Flint, Michigan 48507-1107 **Tel:** 1 810 720-9510.
Web site: http://www.nashfm951.com
Profile: WFBE-FM is a commercial station owned by Cumulus Media Inc. The format for the station is country. WFBE-FM broadcasts to the Flint, MI area at 95.1 FM.
FM RADIO STATION

WFBG-AM
38322
Owner: FM Radio Licenses, LLC
Editorial: 1 Forever Dr, Hollidaysburg, Pennsylvania 16648-3029 **Tel:** 1 814 941-9800.
Web site: http://www.wfbg.com
Profile: WFBG-AM is a commercial station owned by FM Radio Licenses, LLC. The format of the station is news and talk. WFBG-AM broadcasts to the Hollidaysburg, PA area at 1290 AM.
AM RADIO STATION

WFBL-AM
36161
Owner: Leatherstocking Media Group Inc.
Editorial: 8456 Smokey Hollow Rd, Baldwinsville, New York 13027-8222 **Tel:** 1 315 635-3971.
Email: webmaster@wfbl.com
Web site: http://www.cnytalkradio.com
Profile: WFBL-AM is a commercial station owned by Leatherstocking Media Group Inc. The format of the station is talk. WFBL-AM broadcasts to the Baldwinsville, NY area at 1390 AM.
AM RADIO STATION

WFBQ-FM
45153
Owner: iHeartMedia Inc.
Editorial: 6161 Fall Creek Rd, Indianapolis, Indiana 46220-5032 **Tel:** 1 317 257-7565.
Web site: http://q95.iheart.com
Profile: WFBQ-FM is a commercial station owned by iHeartMedia Inc. The format of the station is rock music. WFBQ-FM broadcasts to the Indianapolis area at 94.7 FM.
FM RADIO STATION

WFBR-AM
35426
Owner: Multicultural Radio Broadcasting Inc.
Editorial: 159 8th Ave NW, Glen Burnie, Maryland 21061 **Tel:** 1 410 761-1590.
Profile: WFBR-AM is commercial station owned by Multicultural Radio Broadcasting Inc. The format of the station is urban oldies music. WFBR-AM broadcasts in the greater Baltimore area at 1590 AM.
AM RADIO STATION

WFBT-FM
44145
Owner: Carolina Christian Radio, Inc.
Editorial: 7211 Ogden Business Ln Ste 201, Wilmington, North Carolina 28411-5301
Tel: 1 910 233-1343.
Profile: WFBT-FM is a commercial station owned by Carolina Christian Radio, Inc.. The format of the station is News and Talk. WFBT-FM broadcasts to the Wilmington, NC, area at 106.7 FM.
FM RADIO STATION

WFBX-AM
79568
Owner: CRS RADIO HOLDINGS INC
Editorial: 126 Hay Street, Fayetteville, North Carolina 28301 **Tel:** 1 910 223-1452.
Profile: WFBX-AM is a commercial station owned by CRS RADIO HOLDINGS INC. The format of the station is sports. WFBX-AM broadcasts to the Fayetteville, NC area on 1450 AM.
AM RADIO STATION

WFBY-FM
40938
Owner: West Virginia Radio Corp.
Editorial: 91 Radio Park Dr, Mount Clare, West Virginia 26408-7240 **Tel:** 1 304 554-3925.
Web site: http://www.wfby.com
Profile: WFBY-FM is a commercial station owned by West Virginia Radio Corp. The format of the station is classic rock. WFBY-FM broadcasts to the Mount Clare, VA area at 102.3 FM.
FM RADIO STATION

WFBZ-FM
45278
Owner: Sparta-Tomah Broadcasting Co.
Editorial: 113 W Oak St, Sparta, Wisconsin 54656
Tel: 1 608 269-3100.
Web site: http://www.espnlacrosse.com
Profile: WFBZ-FM is a commercial station owned by Sparta-Tomah Broadcasting Co. The format of the station is sports. WFBZ-FM broadcasts to the Sparta, WI area at 105.5 FM.
FM RADIO STATION

WFCA-FM
41249
Owner: French Camp Radio Inc.
Editorial: 40 Mecklin Ave, French Camp, Mississippi 39745 **Tel:** 1 662 547-6414.
Email: events@wfcafm108.com
Web site: http://www.wfcafm108.com
FM RADIO STATION

WFCC-FM
40268
Owner: Cape Cod Broadcasting
Editorial: 737 W Main St, Hyannis, Massachusetts 02601-3422 **Tel:** 1 508 771-1224.
Email: wfcc@ccb-media.com
Web site: http://www.wfcc.com
Profile: WFCC-FM is a commercial station owned by Cape Cod Broadcasting. The format of the station is classical. WFCC-FM broadcasts to the Hyannis, MA area at 107.5 FM.
FM RADIO STATION

WFCF-FM
42521
Owner: Flagler College
Editorial: 74 King St, Saint Augustine, Florida 32084-4342 **Tel:** 1 904 819-6313.
Email: wfcf@flagler.edu
Web site: http://www.flagler.edu/campus-life/campus-facilities/wfcf.html
Profile: WFCF-FM is a non-commercial station owned by Flagler College. The format of the station is college variety. WFCF-FM broadcasts to the Saint Augustine, FL area at 88.5 FM.
FM RADIO STATION

WFCI-FM
40269
Owner: Franklin College
Editorial: 101 Branigin Blvd, Franklin, Indiana 46131
Tel: 1 317 738-8205.
Profile: WFCI-FM is a non-commercial station owned by Franklin College. The format of the station is classic rock during the evening, and simulcasts NPR during the day when school is in session. In the summer, WFCI-FM simulcasts NPR all day and night. WFCI-FM broadcasts to the Franklin, IN area at 89.5 FM.
FM RADIO STATION

WFCJ-FM
40270
Owner: Strong Tower Christian Media
Editorial: 1205 Whitefield Cir, Xenia, Ohio 45385-7243
Tel: 1 937 866-2471.
Web site: http://www.wfcj.com
Profile: WFCJ-FM is a non-commercial station owned by Strong Tower Christian Media. The format of the station is religious talk and music. WFCJ-FM broadcasts in the Dayton, OH area at 93.7 FM.
FM RADIO STATION

WFCL-FM
40705
Owner: Vanderbilt Student Communications
Editorial: 630 Mainstream Dr, Nashville, Tennessee 37228-1204 **Tel:** 1 615 760-2903.
Web site: http://www.wpln.org
Profile: WFCL-FM is a non-commercial station owned by Vanderbilt Student Communications. The format of the station is classical music. WFCL-FM broadcasts to the Nashville, TN area at 91.1 FM.
FM RADIO STATION

WFCM-AM
36448
Owner: Moody Bible Institute
Editorial: 1920 E 24th Street Pl, Chattanooga, Tennessee 37404-5810 **Tel:** 1 423 629-8900.
Email: radiomoody@moody.edu
Web site: http://www.radiomoody.org
Profile: WFCM-AM is a non-commercial station owned by Moody Bible Institute. The format of the station is Spanish-language religious. WFCM-AM broadcasts to the Chattanooga, TN area at 710 AM.
AM RADIO STATION

WFCN-AM
46239
Owner: Moody Bible Institute
Editorial: 1617 Lebanon Pike, Nashville, Tennessee 37210-3217 **Tel:** 1 423 629-8900.
Web site: http://www.radiomoody.org
Profile: WFCN-AM is a non-commercial station owned by Moody Bible Institute. The format of the station is Christian Radio. WFCN-AM broadcasts to the Nashville, TN area at 1200 AM.
AM RADIO STATION

WFCV-AM
35318
Owner: Bott Radio Network
Editorial: 3737 Lake Ave, Fort Wayne, Indiana 46805
Tel: 1 260 423-2337.
Email: wfcv@bottradionetwork.com
Web site: http://www.bottradionetwork.com
Profile: WFCV-AM is a commercial station owned by Bott Radio Network. The format of the station is Christian music and talk. WFCV-AM broadcasts to the Fort Wayne, IN area at 1090 AM.
AM RADIO STATION

WFCV-FM
42857
Owner: Bott Radio Network
Editorial: 3737 Lake Ave, Fort Wayne, Indiana 46805-5554 **Tel:** 1 260 423-2337.
Email: wfcv@bottradionetwork.com
Web site: http://www.bottradionetwork.com/stations/indiana/fort-wayne
Profile: WFCV-FM is a commercial station owned by Bott Radio Network. The format of the station is Christian talk. WFCV-FM broadcasts to the Fort Wayne and Greater Northeastern Indiana area at 100.1 FM.
FM RADIO STATION

WFCX-FM
41820
Owner: Northern Broadcast Inc.
Editorial: 1020 Hastings St, Traverse City, Michigan 49686 **Tel:** 1 231 947-0003.
Web site: http://www.943thefoxfm.com
Profile: WFCX-FM is a commercial station owned by Northern Broadcast Inc. The format of the station is classic hits. WFCX-FM broadcasts to the Traverse City, MI area at 94.3 FM.
FM RADIO STATION

WFDF-AM
37800
Owner: The Word Network
Editorial: 20733 W 10 Mile Rd, Southfield, Michigan 48075-1086
Email: info@thewordnetwork.org
Web site: http://www.910amsuperstation.com/
Profile: WFDF-AM is a commercial station owned by The Word Network. The format of the station is Black Gospel and Talk formatted broadcast radio station. WFDF-AM broadcasts locally at 910 AM.
AM RADIO STATION

WFDL-AM
35853
Owner: Radio Plus Inc.
Editorial: 609 Home Ave, Waupun, Wisconsin 53963-1140 **Tel:** 1 920 324-4441.
Email: news@wfdl.com
Web site: http://www.am1170radio.com
Profile: WFDL-AM is a commercial station owned by Radio Plus Inc. The format of the station is adult standards. WFDL-AM broadcasts to the Waupun, WI area at 1170 AM.
AM RADIO STATION

WFDL-FM
42522
Owner: Radio Plus Inc.
Editorial: 210 S Main St, Fond du Lac, Wisconsin 54935 **Tel:** 1 920 924-9697.
Web site: http://www.sunny977.com
Profile: WFDL-FM is a commercial station owned by Radio Plus Inc. The format of the station is adult contemporary. WFDL-FM broadcasts to the Green Bay, WI area at 97.7 FM.
FM RADIO STATION

WFDM-AM
35567
Owner: Omni Broadcasting, LLC
Editorial: 4300 Legendary Dr Ste 280, Destin, Florida 32541-8606 **Tel:** 1 850 244-1400.
Email: omnibroadcastinginc@gmail.com
Web site: http://www.freedom945.com
Profile: WFDM-AM is a commercial station owned by Omni Broadcasting, LLC. The format of the station is news and talk. WFDM-AM broadcasts to the Fort Walton Beach, FL area at 1400 AM.
AM RADIO STATION

WFDM-FM
40627
Owner: Pilgrim Communications Inc.
Editorial: 645 Industrial Dr, Franklin, Indiana 46131-9617 **Tel:** 1 317 736-4040.
Email: production@freedom959.com
Web site: http://www.freedom959.com
Profile: WFDM-FM is a commercial station owned by Pilgrim Communications Inc. The format of the station is talk. WFDM-FM broadcasts to the Franklin, IN area at 95.9 FM.
FM RADIO STATION

WFDR-AM
37063
Owner: Ploener Radio Group
Editorial: 129 W Main St, Manchester, Georgia 31816-1652 **Tel:** 1 706 846-3016.
Profile: WFDR-AM is a commerical station owned by Ploener Radio Group. The format of the station is classic country. WFDR-AM broadcasts to Manchester, GA at 1370 AM.
AM RADIO STATION

WFDX-FM
42192
Owner: Northern Broadcast Inc.
Editorial: 1020 Hastings St, Traverse City, Michigan 49686 **Tel:** 1 231 947-0003.
Web site: http://www.943thefoxfm.com
Profile: WFDX-FM is a commercial station owned by Northern Broadcast Inc. The format of the station is classic hits. WFDX-FM broadcasts to the Traverse City, MI area at 92.5 FM.
FM RADIO STATION

WFEA-AM
38593
Owner: Saga Communications
Editorial: 500 N Commercial St, Manchester, New Hampshire 03101-1151 **Tel:** 1 603 669-5777.
Web site: http://www.wfea1370.com
Profile: WFEA-AM is a commercial station owned by Saga Communications. The format of the station is adult standards. WFEA-AM broadcasts to the Manchester, NH area at 1370 AM.
AM RADIO STATION

WFEB-AM
36949
Owner: Powers Broadcasting Company, LLC
Editorial: 1209 Millerville Highway, Sylacauga, Alabama 35150 **Tel:** 1 256 245-3144.
Email: wfeb1340@mysylacauga.com
Profile: WFEB-AM is a commercial station owned by Powers Broadcasting Company, LLC. The format of the station is news, talk and sports. WFEB-AM broadcasts to the Birmingham, AL area at 1340 AM.
AM RADIO STATION

WFED-AM
395103
Owner: Hubbard Radio, LLC
Editorial: 3400 Idaho Ave NW, Washington, District Of Columbia 20016-3046 **Tel:** 1 202 895-5000.
Web site: http://www.federalnewsradio.com
Profile: WFED-AM, Federal News Radio, is a commercial station owned by Hubbard Radio, LLC. The format of the station is news and talk. WFED-AM broadcasts to the Washington, D.C. area at 1500 AM.
AM RADIO STATION

WFEN-FM
42088
Owner: Faith Center Church
Editorial: 4721 S Main St, Rockford, Illinois 61102-5035 **Tel:** 1 815 964-9336.
Email: info@wfen.org
Web site: http://www.wfen.org
Profile: WFEN-FM is a non-commercial station owned by Faith Center Church. The format of the station is Christian music and talk. WFEN-FM broadcasts to the Rockford, IL area at 88.3 FM.
FM RADIO STATION

WFER-AM
37899
Owner: Heartland Communications Group, LLC
Editorial: 809 W Genesee St, Iron River, Michigan 49935-1226 **Tel:** 1 906 265-5104.
Web site: http://www.wfer.com
Profile: WFER-AM is a commercial station owned by Heartland Communications Group, LLC. The format for the station is classic htis. WFER-AM broadcasts to the Marquette, MI, area at 1230 AM.
AM RADIO STATION

WFEZ-FM
40768
Owner: Cox Media Group, Inc.
Editorial: 2741 N 29th Ave, Hollywood, Florida 33020-1503 **Tel:** 1 305 444-4404.
Web site: http://easy93.com
Profile: WFEZ-FM is a commercial station owned by Cox Media Group, Inc. The format of the station is Soft AC. WFEZ-FM-FM broadcasts to the Hollywood, FL area at 93.1 FM.
FM RADIO STATION

WFFF-AM 37801
Owner: Geiger(Ronald)
Editorial: Gardner Shopping Center, Suite 11, Columbia, Mississippi 39429 **Tel:** 1 601 736-1360.
Email: wfffradio@yahoo.com
Profile: WFFF-AM is a commercial station owned by Ronald Geiger. The format of the station is classic country. WFFF-AM broadcasts to the Columbia, MS area at 1360 AM.
AM RADIO STATION

WFFF-FM 45155
Owner: Geiger(Ronald)
Editorial: Gardner Shopping Center, Suite 11, Columbia, Mississippi 39429 **Tel:** 1 601 736-1360.
Email: wfffradio@yahoo.com
Profile: WFFF-FM is a commercial station owned by Ronald Geiger. The format of the station is adult contemporary. WFFF-FM broadcasts to the Hattiesburg-Laurel, MS area at 96.7 FM.
FM RADIO STATION

WFFG-AM 39034
Owner: Keys Radio Group
Tel: 1 305 743-5563.
Profile: WFFG-AM is a commercial station owned by Keys Radio Group. The format of the station is news and talk programming. WFFG-AM broadcasts to the Marathon, FL area at 1300 AM.
AM RADIO STATION

WFFG-FM 45036
Owner: Pamal Broadcasting Ltd.
Editorial: 89 Everts Ave, Queensbury, New York 12804-2040 **Tel:** 1 518 793-7733.
Profile: WFFG-FM is a commercial station owned by Pamal Broadcasting Ltd. The format of the station is Modern AC. WFFG-FM broadcasts to the Queensbury, NY area at 107.1 FM.
FM RADIO STATION

WFFH-FM 42281
Owner: Salem Media Group, Inc.
Editorial: 402 Bna Dr, Nashville, Tennessee 37217-2519 **Tel:** 1 615 367-2210.
Web site: http://www.94fmthefish.net
Profile: WFFH-FM is a commercial station owned by Salem Media Group, Inc. The format of the station is contemporary Christian music. WFFH-FM broadcasts to the Nashville, TN area at 94.1 FM.
FM RADIO STATION

WFFI-FM 42959
Owner: Salem Media Group, Inc.
Editorial: 402 Bna Dr, Nashville, Tennessee 37217-2519 **Tel:** 1 615 367-2210.
Web site: http://www.94fmthefish.net
Profile: WFFI-FM is a commercial station owned by Salem Media Group, Inc. The format of the station is contemporary Christian music. WFFI-FM broadcasts in the Nashville, TN area at 93.7 FM.
FM RADIO STATION

WFFM-FM 43122
Owner: Plant Broadcasting
Editorial: 601 2nd St W, Tifton, Georgia 31794-4257
Tel: 1 229 382-1340.
Web site: http://www.burnincountryradio.com
Profile: WFFM-FM is a commercial station owned by Three Trees Communications. The format of the station is Country. WFFM-FM broadcasts to the Albany, GA area at 105.7 FM.
FM RADIO STATION

WFFN-FM 45811
Owner: Townsquare Media, Inc.
Editorial: 142 Skyland Blvd E, Tuscaloosa, Alabama 35405-4027 **Tel:** 1 205 345-7200.
Web site: http://www.953thebear.com
Profile: WFFN-FM is a commercial station owned by Townsquare Media, Inc. The format of the station is contemporary country. WFFN-FM broadcasts to the Tuscaloosa, AL area at 95.3 FM.
FM RADIO STATION

WFFX-FM 45194
Owner: iHeartMedia Inc.
Editorial: 6555 U S Highway 98 Ste 8, Hattiesburg, Mississippi 39402-8699 **Tel:** 1 601 296-9800.
Email: contact@thefoxrocks1037.com
Web site: http://www.thefoxrocks1037.com
Profile: WFFX-FM is a commercial station owned by iHeartMedia Inc. The format is rock. The station airs in the Hattiesburg, MS area at 103.7 FM.
FM RADIO STATION

WFGA-FM 86865
Owner: Talking Stick Communications, Inc.
Editorial: 1005 Production Rd, Fort Wayne, Indiana 46808-4107 **Tel:** 1 260 471-5100.
Profile: WFGA-FM is a commercial station owned by Talking Stick Communications, Inc., a division of Federated Media. The format of the station is sports. WFGA-FM broadcasts to the Fort Wayne, IN area at 106.7 FM.
FM RADIO STATION

WFGB-FM 41231
Owner: Sound of Life Inc.
Editorial: 199 Tuytenbridge Rd, Lake Katrine, New York 12449-5417 **Tel:** 1 845 336-6199.
Web site: http://www.soundoflife.org
Profile: WFGB-FM is a non-commercial station owned by Sound of Life Inc. The format of the station is Christian music and talk. WFGB-FM broadcasts to the Lake Katrine, NY area at 89.7 FM.
FM RADIO STATION

WFGE-FM 46611
Owner: FM Radio Licenses, LLC
Editorial: 2551 Park Center Blvd, State College, Pennsylvania 16801-3007 **Tel:** 1 814 237-9800.
Web site: http://www.foreverstatecollege.com/big-froggy-101/
Profile: WFGE-FM is a commercial station owned by FM Radio Licenses, LLC. The format of the station is contemporary country. WFGE-FM broadcasts in the Altoona, PA at 101.1 FM.
FM RADIO STATION

WFGF-FM 42488
Owner: Childers Media Group, LLC
Editorial: 57 Town Sq, Lima, Ohio 45801-4950
Tel: 1 419 331-1600.
Profile: WFGF-FM is a commercial station owned by Childers Media Group, LLC. The format for the station is contemporary country. WFGF-FM broadcasts to the Lima, OH area at 92.1 FM.
FM RADIO STATION

WFGI-AM 37795
Owner: FM Radio Licenses, LLC
Editorial: 123 Blaine Rd, Brownsville, Pennsylvania 15417-9330 **Tel:** 1 724 938-2000.
Web site: http://www.froggyland.com
Profile: WFGI-AM is a commercial station owned by FM Radio Licenses, LLC. The format of the station is contemporary country. WFGI-AM broadcasts to the Brownsville, PA area at 940 AM.
AM RADIO STATION

WFGI-FM 45266
Owner: FM Radio Licenses, LLC
Editorial: 109 Plaza Dr, Johnstown, Pennsylvania 15905-1212 **Tel:** 1 814 255-4186.
Web site: http://www.myfroggy95.com
Profile: WFGI-FM is a commercial station owned by FM Radio Licenses, LLC. The format of the station is contemporary country. WFGI-FM broadcasts to the Johnstown, PA area at 95.5 FM.
FM RADIO STATION

WFGL-AM 36763
Owner: Horizon Christian Fellowship
Editorial: 356 Broad St, Fitchburg, Massachusetts 01420-3030 **Tel:** 1 978 665-9111.
Web site: http://www.horizonfitchburg.org/radio
Profile: WFGL-AM is a commercial station owned by Horizon Christian Fellowship. The format of the station features Christian teaching programs and contemporary Praise and Worship music. WFGL-AM broadcasts to the Fitchburg, MA area at 960 AM.
AM RADIO STATION

WFGM-FM 42771
Owner: AJB Broadcasting Co.
Editorial: 1251 Earl L Core Rd, Morgantown, West Virginia 26505-5881 **Tel:** 1 304 554-3925.
Web site: http://www.931wfgm.com
Profile: WFGM-FM is a commercial station owned by AJG Broadcasting Co. The format of the station is classic hits. WFGM-FM broadcasts to the Buckhannon, WV area at 93.1 FM.
FM RADIO STATION

WFGN-AM 36097
Owner: Hope Broadcasting Inc.
Editorial: 470 Leadmine Rd, Gaffney, South Carolina 29340-4037 **Tel:** 1 864 489-9430.
Profile: WFGN-AM is a commercial station owned by Hope Broadcasting Inc. The format of the station is gospel music. WFGN-AM broadcasts to the Gaffney, SC area at 1180 AM.
AM RADIO STATION

WFGR-FM 42643
Owner: Townsquare Media, LLC
Editorial: 50 Monroe Ave NW, Ste 500, Grand Rapids, Michigan 49503 **Tel:** 1 616 451-4800.
Web site: http://www.wfgr.com
Profile: WFGR-FM is a commercial station owned by Townsquare Media, LLC. The format of the station is classic hits. WFGR-FM broadcasts to the Grand Rapids, MI area at 98.7 FM.
FM RADIO STATION

WFGS-FM 46190
Owner: FM Radio Licenses, LLC
Editorial: 1500 Diuguid Dr, Murray, Kentucky 42071-1669 **Tel:** 1 270 753-2400.
Web site: http://www.froggy103.com
Profile: WFGS-FM is a commercial station owned by FM Radio Licenses, LLC. The format of the station is country. WFGS-FM broadcasts to the Greater Murray, KY area at a frequency of 103.7 FM.
FM RADIO STATION

WFGW-FM 61996
Owner: Blue Ridge Broadcasting Co.
Editorial: 3 Porters Cove Rd, Asheville, North Carolina 28805-2834 **Tel:** 1 828 285-8477.
Web site: http://www.1069thelight.org
Profile: WFGW-FM is a commercial station owned by Blue Ridge Broadcasting Co. The format of the station is Contemporary Christian music.WFGW-FM broadcasts in the Knoxville, TN area at 106.7 FM.
FM RADIO STATION

WFGY-FM 44508
Owner: FM Radio Licenses, LLC
Editorial: 1 Forever Dr, Hollidaysburg, Pennsylvania 16648-3029 **Tel:** 1 814 941-9800.
Web site: http://www.froggyradio.com
Profile: WFGY-FM is a commercial station owned by FM Radio Licenses, LLC. The format of the station is contemporary country. WFGY-FM broadcasts to the Hollidaysburg, PA area at 98.1 FM.
FM RADIO STATION

WFHB-FM 42055
Owner: Bloomington Community Radio Inc.
Editorial: 108 W 4th St, Bloomington, Indiana 47404-5100 **Tel:** 1 812 323-1200.
Email: wfhb@wfhb.org
Web site: http://www.wfhb.org
Profile: WFHB-FM is a non-commercial station owned by Bloomington Community Radio Inc. The format of the station is variety. WFHB-FM broadcasts to the Indianapolis area at 91.3 FM.
FM RADIO STATION

WFHG-AM 38577
Owner: Bristol Broadcasting
Editorial: 901 E Valley Dr, Bristol, Virginia 24201-4913
Tel: 1 276 669-8112.
Profile: WFHG-AM is a commercial station owned by Bristol Broadcasting. The format of the station is sports. WFHG-AM broadcasts to the Bristol, VA area at 980 AM.
AM RADIO STATION

WFHG-FM 46353
Owner: Bristol Broadcasting
Editorial: 901 E Valley Dr, Bristol, Virginia 24201-4913
Tel: 1 276 669-8112.
Web site: http://www.supertalkwfhg.com
Profile: WFHG-FM is a commercial station owned by Bristol Broadcasting. The format of the station is news and talk. WFHG-FM broadcasts to the Bristol, VA area at 92.9 FM.
FM RADIO STATION

WFHK-AM 35320
Owner: Stocks Broadcasting Inc.
Editorial: 22 Cogswell Ave, Pell City, Alabama 35125-2438 **Tel:** 1 205 338-1430.
Web site: http://www.theriver949.com
Profile: WFHK-AM is a commercial station owned by Stocks Broadcasting Inc. The format of the station is classic hits and variety. WFHK-AM broadcasts to the Pell City, AL area at 1430 AM.
AM RADIO STATION

WFHM-FM 86810
Owner: Salem Media Group, Inc.
Editorial: 4 Summit Park Dr Ste 150, Cleveland, Ohio 44131-6921 **Tel:** 1 216 901-0921.
Email: swhite@salemcleveland.com
Web site: http://www.955thefish.com
Profile: WFHM-FM is a commercial station owned by Salem Media Group, Inc. The format of the station is contemporary Christian. WFHM-FM broadcasts to the Cleveland area at 95.5 FM.
FM RADIO STATION

WFHN-FM 45769
Owner: Townsquare Media, Inc.
Editorial: 22 Sconticut Neck Rd, Fairhaven, Massachusetts 02719-1914 **Tel:** 1 508 999-6690.
Web site: http://fun107.com
Profile: WFHN-FM is a commercial station owned by Townsquare Media, Inc. The format of the station is Top 40/CHR. WFHN-FM broadcasts to the Providence, RI and Bedford, MA area at 107.1 FM.
FM RADIO STATION

WFHR-AM 37803
Owner: Seehafer Broadcasting Corp.
Editorial: 645 25th Ave N, Wisconsin Rapids, Wisconsin 54495 **Tel:** 1 715 424-1300.
Email: info@wfhr.com
Web site: http://www.wfhr.com
Profile: WFHR-AM is a commercial station owned by Seehafer Broadcasting Corp. The format for the station is news, sports and talk. WFHR-AM broadcasts to the Wausau, WI, area at 1320 AM.
AM RADIO STATION

WFHT-AM 954912
Owner: Lakeland Broadcasting Company
Editorial: 1017 N Lake Parker Ave, Lakeland, Florida 33805-4723 **Tel:** 1 863 816-5637.
Email: wgbcfmgrover@yahoo.com
Web site: http://wgbcfm.net
Profile: WFHT-AM is a commercial station owned by Lakeland Broadcasting Company, The format of the station is urban adult contemporary and gospel. The station simulcasts at 1390 AM to the Avon Park, Florida area.
AM RADIO STATION

WFIA-AM 37028
Owner: Salem Media Group, Inc.
Editorial: 9960 Corporate Campus Dr Ste 3600, Louisville, Kentucky 40223-4070 **Tel:** 1 502 339-9470.
Web site: http://www.wfia-fm.com
Profile: WFIA-AM is a commercial station owned by Salem Media Group, Inc.The format of the station is Christian music and talk. WFIA-AM broadcasts in the Louisville, KY area at 900 AM.
AM RADIO STATION

WFIA-FM 43727
Owner: Salem Media Group, Inc.
Editorial: 9960 Corporate Campus Dr Ste 3600, Louisville, Kentucky 40223-4070 **Tel:** 1 502 339-9470.
Web site: http://www.wfia-fm.com
Profile: WFIA-FM is a commercial station owned by Salem Media Group, Inc. The format of the station is Christian talk and gospel music. WFIA-FM broadcasts in the Louisville, KY area at 94.7 FM.
FM RADIO STATION

WFIC-AM 35321
Owner: Positive Radio Group
Editorial: 1675 Grandview Rd, Martinsville, Virginia 24112-2319 **Tel:** 1 276 638-5235.
Profile: WFIC-AM is a commercial station owned by Positive Radio Group. The format of the station is Religious teaching. WFIC-AM broadcasts to the Martinsville, VA area at 1530 AM.
AM RADIO STATION

WFIF-AM 35322
Owner: Blount Communications Group
Editorial: 90 Kay Ave, Milford, Connecticut 06460-5421 **Tel:** 1 203 878-5915.
Email: info@wfif.net
Web site: http://lifechangingradio.com
Profile: WFIF-AM is a commercial station owned by Blount Communications Group. The format for the station is religious talk. WFIF-AM broadcasts to the Hartford-New Haven, CT area at 1500 AM.
AM RADIO STATION

WFIL-AM 36231
Owner: Salem Media Group, Inc.
Editorial: 117 Ridge Pike, Lafayette Hill, Pennsylvania 19444-1901 **Tel:** 1 610 828-6965.
Email: wfil@wfil.com
Web site: http://www.wfil.com
Profile: WFIL-AM is a commercial station owned by Salem Media Group, Inc. The format of the station is religious and Christian talk. WFIL-AM broadcasts to the Lafayette Hill, PA area at 560 AM.
AM RADIO STATION

WFIN-AM 37804
Owner: Blanchard River Broadcasting, Co.
Editorial: 551 Lake Cascade Pkwy, Findlay, Ohio 45840 **Tel:** 1 419 422-4545.
Email: wfin@wfin.com
Web site: http://www.wfin.com
Profile: WFIN-AM is a commercial station owned by Blanchard River Broadcasting, Co. The format of the station is news, sports and talk. WFIN-AM broadcasts in the Findlay, OH area at 1330 AM.
AM RADIO STATION

WFIR-AM 36887
Owner: Wheeler Inc.(Mel)
Editorial: 3934 Electric Rd, Roanoke, Virginia 24018-4513 **Tel:** 1 540 387-0234.
Web site: http://www.wfir960.com
Profile: WFIR-AM is a commercial station owned by Mel Wheeler Inc. The format of the station is news and talk. WFIR-AM broadcasts to the Roanoke, VA area at 960 AM.
AM RADIO STATION

WFIT-FM 40276
Owner: Florida Institute of Technology
Editorial: 150 W University Blvd, Melbourne, Florida 32901-6982 **Tel:** 1 321 674-8140.
Email: wfit@fit.edu
Web site: http://www.wfit.org
Profile: WFIT-FM is a non-commercial station owned by Florida Institute of Technology. The format of the station is AAA-Adult album alternative and news. WFIT-FM broadcasts to the Melbourne, FL area at 89.5 FM.
FM RADIO STATION

WFIV-FM 63306
Owner: Horne Radio LLC
Editorial: 517 N Watt Rd, Knoxville, Tennessee 37934-1110 **Tel:** 1 865 675-4105.
Web site: http://www.myi105.com
Profile: WFIV-FM is a commercial station owned by Horne Radio LLC. The format of the station is adult album alternative. WFIV-FM broadcasts to the Knoxville, TN area at 105.3 FM.
FM RADIO STATION

WFIW-AM 37805
Owner: Original Company, Inc. (The)
Tel: 1 618 842-2159.
Email: wfiwwokz@fairfieldwireless.net
Web site: http://www.originalcompany.com
Profile: WFIW-AM is a commercial station owned by Original Company, Inc. (The). The format for the station is news, sports and talk. WFIW-AM broadcasts to the Evansville, IN area at 1390 AM.
AM RADIO STATION

WFIW-FM 45156
Owner: Original Company, Inc. (The)
Tel: 1 618 842-2159.
Email: wfiwwokz@fairfieldwireless.net
Web site: http://www.wfiwradio.com
Profile: WFIW-FM is a commercial station owned by Original Company, Inc. (The). The format for the station is adult hits. WFIW-FM broadcasts to the Evansville, IN area at 104.9 FM.
FM RADIO STATION

WFIX-FM 41201
Owner: Tri-State Inspirational Broadcasting
Editorial: 113 N Seminary St, Florence, Alabama 35630 **Tel:** 1 256 764-9964.
Email: wfix@fixfm.net
Web site: http://www.wfix.net
Profile: WFIX-FM is a non-commercial station owned by Tri-State Inspirational Broadcasting. The format of the station is contemporary Christian music and talk

programming. WFIX-FM broadcasts to the Florence, AL area at 91.3 FM.
FM RADIO STATION

WFIZ-FM 45159
Owner: Cayuga Radio Group
Editorial: 950 Danby Rd Ste 230, Ithaca, New York 14850-5714 **Tel:** 1 607 330-4848.
Web site: http://www.z955.net
Profile: WFIZ-FM is a commercial station owned by Cayuga Radio Group. The format of the station is Top 40/CHR. WFIZ-FM broadcasts to the Dundee, NY area at 95.5 FM.
FM RADIO STATION

WFJA-FM 45157
Owner: WWGP Broadcasting Corporation
Editorial: 2201 Jefferson Davis Hwy, Sanford, North Carolina 27330-8973 **Tel:** 1 919 775-3525.
Email: production@wfjaradio.com
Web site: http://www.classichitsandoldies.com/v2
Profile: WFJA-FM is a commercial station owned by WWGP Broadcasting Corporation. The format of the station is Classic Hits. WFJA-FM broadcasts to the Sanford, NC area at 105.5 FM.
FM RADIO STATION

WFJO-FM 41733
Owner: River City Broadcasting, LLC
Editorial: 9090 Hogan Rd, Jacksonville, Florida 32216-4648 **Tel:** 1 904 641-1011.
Web site: http://www.1010xl.com
Profile: WJXL-FM is a commercial station owned by River City Broadcasting, LLC. The format of the station sports. WJXL-FM broadcasts to the Jacksonville, FL area on 92.5 FM.
FM RADIO STATION

WFJS-AM 38340
Owner: Domestic Church Media Foundation, Inc.
Tel: 1 609 882-9357.
Email: info@domesticchurchmedia.org
Web site: http://www.domesticchurchmedia.org
Profile: WFJS-AM is a commercial station owned by Domestic Church Media Foundation, Inc. The format of the station is Catholic programming. WFJS-AM broadcasts to the Trenton, NJ area at 1260 AM.
AM RADIO STATION

WFJS-FM 755947
Owner: Domestic Church Media Foundation, Inc.
Tel: 1 609 882-9357.
Email: info@domesticchurchmedia.org
Web site: http://www.domesticchurchmedia.org
Profile: WFJS-FM is a non-commercial station owned by Domestic Church Media Foundation, Inc. The format of the station features Catholic programming. WFJS-FM broadcasts locally to the Freehold, NJ area at a frequency of 89.3 FM.
FM RADIO STATION

WFJX-AM 36061
Owner: Perception Media Group, Inc.
Editorial: 1848 Clay St SE, Roanoke, Virginia 24013
Tel: 1 540 343-7109.
Web site: http://www.foxradioroanoke.com
Profile: WFJX-AM is a commercial station owned by Perception Media Group, Inc. The format of the station is news, talk and sports. WFJX-AM broadcasts to the Roanoke, VA area at 910 AM.
AM RADIO STATION

WFKL-FM 43454
Owner: Stephens Media Group
Editorial: 28 E Main Street, 8th Floor, Rochester, New York 14614 **Tel:** 1 585 399-5700.
Web site: http://www.fickle933.com
Profile: WFKL-FM is a commercial station owned by Stephens Media Group. The format of the station is adult hits. WFKL-FM broadcasts to the Rochester, NY area at a frequency of 93.3 FM.
FM RADIO STATION

WFKN-AM 35326
Owner: Paxton Media Group
Editorial: 103 N High St, Franklin, Kentucky 42134-1801 **Tel:** 1 270 586-4481.
Email: wfkn@franklinfavorite.com
Web site: http://www.franklinfavorite.com
Profile: WFKN-AM is a commerial station owned by Paxton Media Group. The format of the station is talk, sports and classic country. WFKN-AM broadcasts to the Franklin, TN area at 1220 AM.
AM RADIO STATION

WFKS-FM 45809
Owner: iHeartMedia Inc.
Editorial: 1388 S Babcock St, One Radio Center, Melbourne, Florida 32901-3009 **Tel:** 1 321 733-1000.
Web site: http://mykiss951.iheart.com
Profile: WFKS-FM is a commercial station owned by iHeartMedia Inc. The format of the station is Top 40/CHR. WFKS-FM broadcasts to the Melbourne, FL, area at 95.1 FM.
FM RADIO STATION

WFKX-FM 40278
Owner: Southern Stone Communications, LLC
Editorial: 111 W Main St, Jackson, Tennessee 38301
Tel: 1 731 427-9616.
Web site: http://www.96kix.fm
Profile: WFKX-FM is a commercial station owned by Southern Stone Communications, LLC. The format of the station is urban contemporary. WFKX-FM broadcasts to the Jackson, TN area at 95.7 FM.
FM RADIO STATION

WFKY-FM 45326
Owner: CapCity Communications LLC
Editorial: 115 W Main St, Frankfort, Kentucky 40601
Tel: 1 502 875-1130.
Web site: http://www.myfroggy1049.com
Profile: WFKY-FM is a commercial station owned by CapCity Communications LLC. The format for the station is country. WFKY-FM broadcasts to the Lexington, KY area at 104.9 FM.
FM RADIO STATION

WFKZ-FM 41233
Owner: Florida Keys Media, LLC
Editorial: 93351 Overseas Hwy Ste 2, Tavernier, Florida 33070-2800 **Tel:** 1 305 852-9085.
Web site: http://sun103.com/
Profile: WFKZ-FM is a commercial station owned by Florida Keys Media, LLC. The format of the station is classic rock. WFKZ-FM broadcasts to the Miami, FL area at 103.1 FM.
FM RADIO STATION

WFLA-AM 38660
Owner: iHeartMedia Inc.
Editorial: 4002A W Gandy Blvd, Tampa, Florida 33611 **Tel:** 1 813 832-1000.
Email: news@970wfla.com
Web site: http://970wfla.iheart.com
Profile: WFLA-AM is a commercial station owned by iHeartMedia Inc. The format of the station is news and talk. WFLA-AM broadcasts to the Tampa, FL area at 970 AM.
AM RADIO STATION

WFLA-FM 43082
Owner: iHeartMedia Inc.
Editorial: 325 John Knox Rd Bldg G, Tallahassee, Florida 32303-4113 **Tel:** 1 850 558-1455.
Web site: http://wflafm.iheart.com
Profile: WBWT-FM is a commercial station owned by iHeartMedia Inc. The format of the station is talk. WBWT-FM broadcasts to the Tallahassee, FL area at 100.7 FM.
FM RADIO STATION

WFLB-FM 43712
Owner: Beasley Broadcast Group
Editorial: 508 Person St, Fayetteville, North Carolina 28301-5841 **Tel:** 1 910 486-4114.
Web site: http://965bobfm.com
Profile: WFLB-FM is a commercial station owned by Beasley Broadcast Group. The format of the station is classic hits music. WFLB-FM broadcasts to the Fayetteville, NC area at 96.5 FM.
FM RADIO STATION

WFLC-FM 43435
Owner: Cox Media Group, Inc.
Editorial: 2741 N 29th Ave, Hollywood, Florida 33020-1503 **Tel:** 1 305 444-4404.
Web site: http://www.hits973.com
Profile: WFLC-FM is a commercial station owned by Cox Media Group, Inc. The format of the station is Top 40. WFLC-FM broadcasts to the Hollywood, FL area at 97.3 FM.
FM RADIO STATION

WFLE-AM 39323
Owner: DreamCatcher Communications Inc.
Editorial: 334 Recreation Park Rd, Flemingsburg, Kentucky 41041 **Tel:** 1 606 849-4433.
Profile: WFLE-AM is a commercial station owned by DreamCatcher Communications Inc. The format for the station is country. WFLE-AM broadcasts to the Lexington, KY area at 1060 AM.
AM RADIO STATION

WFLE-FM 46684
Owner: DreamCatcher Communications Inc.
Editorial: 334 Recreation Park Rd, Flemingsburg, Kentucky 41041-8915 **Tel:** 1 606 849-4433.
Email: wfle48@yahoo.com
Profile: WFLE-FM is a commercial station owned by DreamCatcher Communications Inc. The format of the station is contemporary country music. WFLE-FM broadcasts to the Flemingsburg, KY area at 95.1 FM.
FM RADIO STATION

WFLF-AM 36160
Owner: iHeartMedia Inc.
Editorial: 2500 Maitland Center Pkwy Ste 401, Maitland, Florida 32751-4179 **Tel:** 1 407 916-7800.
Email: news@540wfla.com
Web site: http://1025wfla.iheart.com
Profile: WFLF-AM is a commercial station owned by iHeartMedia Inc. The format of the station is news and talk. WFLF-AM broadcasts to the Maitland, FL area at 540 AM.
AM RADIO STATION

WFLF-FM 42177
Owner: iHeartMedia Inc.
Editorial: 1834 Lisenby Ave, Panama City, Florida 32405-3713 **Tel:** 1 850 769-1408.
Web site: http://945wfla.iheart.com
Profile: WFLF-FM is a commercial station owned by iHeartMedia Inc. The format of the station is news and talk. WFLF-FM broadcasts to the Panama City, FL area at 94.5 FM.
FM RADIO STATION

WFLK-FM 44350
Owner: Finger Lakes Daily News
Editorial: 3568 Lenox Rd, Geneva, New York 14456-2058 **Tel:** 1 315 781-7000.
Web site: http://www.fingerlakesdailynews.com
Profile: WFLK-FM is a commercial station owned Finger Lakes Daily News. The format of the station is contemporary country music. WFLK-FM broadcasts to the Geneva, NY area at 101.7 FM.
FM RADIO STATION

WFLM-FM 42182
Owner: Midway Broadcasting Corp.
Editorial: 6803 S US Highway 1, Port Saint Lucie, Florida 34952-1434 **Tel:** 1 772 460-9356.
Email: management@1047theflame.com
Web site: http://www.wflm.cc
Profile: WFLM-FM is a commercial station owned by Midway Broadcasting Corp. The format of the station is urban adult contemporary. WFLM-FM broadcasts to the Port St. Lucie, FL area at 104.5 FM.
FM RADIO STATION

WFLN-AM 37114
Owner: Integrity Radio of FL LLC
Editorial: 201 Asbury St, Arcadia, Florida 34266-8830
Tel: 1 863 993-1480.
Email: wfln@fiorinibroadcasting.com
Web site: http://wflnradio.com
Profile: WFLN-AM is a commercial station owned by Integrity Radio of FL LLC. The format of the station is news and talk. WFLN-AM broadcasts to the Arcadia, FL area 1480 AM.
AM RADIO STATION

WFLO-AM 37807
Owner: Colonial Broadcasting Co. Inc.
Editorial: 1582 Cumberland Rd, Farmville, Virginia 23901-4034 **Tel:** 1 434 392-4195.
Email: communitycalendar@wflo.net
Web site: http://www.wflo.net
Profile: WFLO-AM is a commercial station owned by Colonial Broadcasting Co. Inc. The format of the station is country music and talk. WFLO-AM broadcasts to the Farmville, VA area at 870 AM.
AM RADIO STATION

WFLO-FM 45158
Owner: Colonial Broadcasting Co. Inc.
Editorial: 1582 Cumberland Rd, Farmville, Virginia 23901-4034 **Tel:** 1 434 392-4195.
Email: communitycalendar@wflo.net
Web site: http://www.wflo.net
Profile: WFLO-FM is a commercial station owned by Colonial Broadcasting Co. Inc. The format of the station is adult contemporary. WFLO-FM broadcasts to the Farmville, VA area at 95.7 FM.
FM RADIO STATION

WFLQ-FM 40280
Owner: Willtronics Broadcasting
Editorial: 2593 N County Road 810 W, West Baden Springs, Indiana 47469-9624 **Tel:** 1 812 936-9100.
Email: wflqfm@smithville.net
Web site: http://www.wflq.com
Profile: WFLQ-FM is a commercial station owned by Willtronics Broadcasting. The format of the station is country music. WFLQ-FM broadcasts in the French Lick, IN area at 100.1 FM.
FM RADIO STATION

WFLR-AM 37808
Owner: Finger Lakes Radio Group
Editorial: 30 Main St, Dundee, New York 14837
Tel: 1 607 243-7158.
Email: wflr@flradiogroup.com
Web site: http://www.fingerlakesdailynews.com
Profile: WFLR-AM is a commercial station owned by Finger Lakes Radio Group. The format of the station is contemporary country. WFLR-AM broadcasts to the Dundee, NY area at 1570 AM.
AM RADIO STATION

WFLR-FM 546629
Owner: Finger Lakes Radio Group
Editorial: 30 Main St, Dundee, New York 14837-1007
Tel: 1 607 243-7158.
Email: wflr@flradiogroup.com
Web site: http://www.fingerlakesdailynews.com
Profile: WFLR-FM is a commercial station owned by Finger Lakes Radio Group. The format of the station is contemporary country. WFLR-FM broadcasts to the Dundee, NY area at 96.9 FM.
FM RADIO STATION

WFLS-FM 45160
Owner: Alpha Media
Editorial: 616 Amelia St, Fredericksburg, Virginia 22401-3887 **Tel:** 1 540 373-1500.
Web site: http://www.wfls.com
Profile: WFLS-FM is a commercial station owned by Alpha Media. The format of the station is classic country. WFLS-FM broadcasts to the Fredericksburg, VA area at 93.3 FM.
FM RADIO STATION

WFLT-AM 35329
Owner: C.E.B.A
Editorial: 317 S Averill Ave, Flint, Michigan 48506-4005 **Tel:** 1 810 239-5733.
Email: wflt1420am@aol.com
Profile: WFLT-AM is a commercial station owned by C.E.B.A. The format of the station is gospel music. WFLT-AM broadcasts in the Flint, MI area at 1420 AM.
AM RADIO STATION

WFLV-FM 40868
Owner: Educational Media Foundation
Tel: 1 954 522-8755.
Email: klove@klove.com
Web site: http://www.klove.com
Profile: WFLV-FM is a non-commercial station owned by Educational Media Foundation. The format of the station is contemporary Christian music. WFLV-FM broadcasts to the West Palm Beach, FL area at 90.7 FM.
FM RADIO STATION

WFLW-AM 37810
Owner: Staples Jr.(Stephen)
Editorial: 150 Worsham Ln, Monticello, Kentucky 42633-1610 **Tel:** 1 606 348-8427.
Web site: http://www.wkym.com
AM RADIO STATION

WFLY-FM 42770
Owner: Albany Broadcasting Co.
Editorial: 6 Johnson Rd, Latham, New York 12110-5641 **Tel:** 1 518 786-6600.
Web site: http://www.fly92.com
Profile: WFLY-FM is a commercial station owned by Albany Broadcasting Co. The format of the station is Top 40/CHR music. WFLY-FM broadcasts to the Albany, NY area at 92.3 FM.
FM RADIO STATION

WFLZ-FM 46013
Owner: iHeartMedia Inc.
Editorial: 4002 W Gandy Blvd, Tampa, Florida 33611-3410 **Tel:** 1 813 832-1000.
Web site: http://933flz.iheart.com
Profile: WFLZ-FM is a commercial station is owned by iHeartMedia Inc. The format of the station is Top 40/CHR music. WFLZ-FM broadcasts to the Tampa Bay, FL area at 93.3 FM.
FM RADIO STATION

WFMB-AM 37734
Owner: Neuhoff Family Limited Partnership
Editorial: 3055 S 4th St, Springfield, Illinois 62703-4009 **Tel:** 1 217 529-3033.
Web site: http://www.sportsradio1450.com
Profile: WFMB-AM is a commercial station owned by Neuhoff Family Limited Partnership. The format of the station is sports and talk. WFMB-AM broadcasts to the Springfield, IL area at 1450 AM. The station targets sports fans of all ages. Newscasts air at various times throughout the day. WFMB-AM's slogan is, "Springfield's sports voice." Podcast is available.
AM RADIO STATION

WFMB-FM 45161
Owner: Neuhoff Family Limited Partnership
Editorial: 3055 S 4th St, Springfield, Illinois 62703-4009 **Tel:** 1 217 528-3033.
Web site: http://www.wfmb.com
Profile: WFMB-FM is a commercial station owned by Neuhoff Family Limited Partnership. The format of the station is country music. WFMB-FM broadcasts to the Springfield, IL area at 104.5 FM. The station's slogan is, "New Country & All Time Favorites."
FM RADIO STATION

WFMC-AM 36124
Owner: Curtis Media Group
Editorial: 2581 US Highway 70 W, Goldsboro, North Carolina 27530-9553 **Tel:** 1 919 734-4211.
Web site: http://curtismedia.com/wfmc
Profile: WFMC-AM is a commercial station owned by Curtis Media Group. The format of the station is gospel music. WFMC-AM broadcasts to the greater Raleigh, NC area at 730 AM.
AM RADIO STATION

WFMD-AM 37811
Owner: iHeartMedia Inc.
Editorial: 5966 Grove Hill Rd, Frederick, Maryland 21703-6012 **Tel:** 1 301 663-4181.
Email: news@wfmd.com
Web site: http://www.wfmd.com
Profile: WFMD-AM is a commercial station owned by iHeartMedia Inc. The format of the station is news, talk and sports. WFMD-AM broadcasts in the Frederick, MD area at 930 AM.
AM RADIO STATION

WFME-FM 42279
Owner: Family Stations Inc.
Editorial: 700 S. Bedford Rd., Mount Kisco, New York 10549 **Tel:** 1 973 736-3600.
Email: websupport@familyradio.org
Web site: http://www.wfme.net
Profile: WFME-FM is a commercial station owned by Family Stations Inc. The format of the station is Christian music and teaching. WDVY-FM broadcasts to the New York City market at 106.3 FM.
FM RADIO STATION

WFMF-FM 45737
Owner: iHeartMedia Inc.
Editorial: 5555 Hilton Ave Ste 500, Baton Rouge, Louisiana 70808-2564 **Tel:** 1 225 231-1860.
Web site: http://www.wfmf.com
Profile: WFMF-FM is a commercial station owned by iHeartMedia Inc. The format of the station is Top 40/CHR. WFMF-FM broadcasts to the Baton Rouge, LA area at 102.5 FM.
FM RADIO STATION

WFMG-FM 45162
Owner: Whitewater Broadcasting
Editorial: 2301 W Main St, Richmond, Indiana 47374-3829 **Tel:** 1 765 962-6533.
Email: news@g1013.com
Web site: http://www.g1013.com
Profile: WFMG-FM is a commercial station owned by Whitewater Broadcasting. The format of the station is

hot adult contemporary music. WFMG-FM broadcasts to the Richmond, IN area at 101.3 FM.
FM RADIO STATION

WFMH-AM
37812
Owner: Jimmy Dale Media, LLC
Editorial: 1707 Warnke Rd NW, Cullman, Alabama 35055-2231 **Tel:** 1 256 734-3271.
Profile: WFMH-AM is a commercial station owned by Jimmy Dale Media, LLC. The format of the station is sports talk. WFMH-AM broadcasts to the Cullman, AL area at 1340 AM.
AM RADIO STATION

WFMH-FM
45163
Owner: TNT Inc.
Editorial: Hwy 12A, Hackleburg, Alabama
Tel: 1 256 810-0613.
Email: hutts955@yahoo.com
Web site: http://big955.com
Profile: WFMH-FM is a commercial station owned by TNT Inc. The format of the station is country music. WFMH-FM broadcasts to the Cullman, AL area at 95.5 FM.
FM RADIO STATION

WFMI-FM
139249
Owner: Communication Systems Inc.
Editorial: 4801 Columbus St Ste 103, Virginia Beach, Virginia 23462-6751 **Tel:** 1 757 490-9364.
Email: rejoice@rejoice1009.com
Web site: http://www.musicalsoulfood.com
Profile: WFMI-FM is a commercial station owned by Communication Systems Inc. The format of the station is gospel. WFMI-FM broadcasts to the Norfolk, VA area at 100.9 FM.
FM RADIO STATION

WFMK-FM
40282
Owner: Townsquare Media, LLC
Editorial: 3420 Pinetree Rd, Lansing, Michigan 48911-4207 **Tel:** 1 517 394-7272.
Web site: http://www.99wfmk.com
Profile: WFMK-FM is a commercial station owned by Townsquare Media, LLC. The format of the station is adult contemporary. WFMK-FM broadcasts to the Lansing, MI area at 99.1 FM.
FM RADIO STATION

WFMM-FM
43662
Owner: TeleSouth Communications Inc.
Editorial: 5266 Old Highway 11 Ste 120, Hattiesburg, Mississippi 39402-7818 **Tel:** 1 601 264-5185.
Web site: http://www.supertalkms.com
Profile: WFMM-FM is a commercial station owned by TeleSouth Communications Inc. The format of the station is talk. WFMM-FM broadcasts to the Hattiesburg, MS area on 97.3 FM.
FM RADIO STATION

WFMN-FM
43950
Owner: TeleSouth Communications Inc.
Editorial: 6311 Ridgewood Rd, Jackson, Mississippi 39211-2035 **Tel:** 1 601 957-1700.
Web site: http://www.supertalk.fm
Profile: WFMN-FM is a commercial station owned by TeleSouth Communications Inc. The format of the station is news, talk and sports. WFMN-FM broadcasts to the Jackson, MS area at 97.3 FM.
FM RADIO STATION

WFMO-AM
37813
Owner: Davidson Media Group
Editorial: 5448 Hwy 41 S, Fairmont, North Carolina 28340 **Tel:** 1 910 628-6781.
Profile: WFMO-AM is a commercial station owned by Davidson Media Group. The format of the station is Hispanic and tropical music. WFMO-AM broadcasts to the Fayetteville, NC area at 860 AM.
AM RADIO STATION

WFMS-FM
40285
Owner: Cumulus Media Inc.
Editorial: 6810 N Shadeland Ave, Indianapolis, Indiana 46220-4236 **Tel:** 1 317 842-9550.
Email: info@wfms.com
Web site: http://www.wfms.com
Profile: WFMS-FM is a commercial station owned by Cumulus Media Inc. The format of the station is country music. WFMS-FM broadcasts to the Indianapolis area at 95.5 FM.
FM RADIO STATION

WFMT-FM
40286
Owner: Window to the World Communications, Inc.
Editorial: 5400 N Saint Louis Ave, Chicago, Illinois 60625-4623 **Tel:** 1 773 279-2000.
Web site: http://www.wfmt.com
Profile: WFMT-FM is a commercial station owned by Window to the World Communications, Inc. The format of the station is classical music. WFMT-FM broadcasts to the Chicago area at 98.7 FM.
FM RADIO STATION

WFMU-FM
40287
Owner: Auricle Communications
Editorial: 43 Montgomery St Fl 4, Jersey City, New Jersey 07302-3856 **Tel:** 1 201 521-1416.
Email: wfmu@wfmu.org
Web site: http://www.wfmu.org
Profile: WFMU-FM is a non-commercial station owned by the Auricle Communications. The format of the station is freeform radio. WFMU-FM broadcasts in the Jersey City, NJ area at 91.1 FM.
FM RADIO STATION

WFMV-FM
42798
Owner: Glory Communications Inc.
Editorial: 2440 Millwood Ave, Columbia, South Carolina 29205-1128 **Tel:** 1 803 939-9530.
Email: lgrant@wfmv.com
Web site: http://www.wfmv.com
Profile: WFMV-FM is a commercial station owned by Glory Communications Inc. The format of the station is gospel. WFMV-FM broadcasts to the Columbia, SC area at 95.3 FM.
FM RADIO STATION

WFMW-AM
37814
Owner: Sound Broadcasters Inc.
Editorial: 2380 N Main St, Madisonville, Kentucky 42431 **Tel:** 1 270 821-4096.
Email: news@wfmw.net
Web site: http://www.wfmw.net
AM RADIO STATION

WFMX-FM
41302
Owner: Mountain Wireless Corp.
Editorial: 208 Middle Rd, Skowhegan, Maine 4976
Tel: 1 207 474-5171.
Email: mix1079@gmail.com
Web site: http://www.mixmaine.com
Profile: WFMX-FM is a commercial station owned by Mountain Wireless Corp. The format of the station is adult contemporary. WFMX-FM broadcasts to the Skowhegan, ME area at 107.9 FM.
FM RADIO STATION

WFMZ-FM
43635
Owner: CapSan Media, LLC
Editorial: 103 W Wood Hill Dr Ste E, Nags Head, North Carolina 27959-9395 **Tel:** 1 252 475-1888.
Web site: http://www.yourclassicrock.com/
Profile: WFMZ-FM is a commercial station owned by CapSan Media, LLC. The format of the station is classic rock. WFMZ-FM broadcasts to the Wanchese, NC area at 104.9 FM.
FM RADIO STATION

WFNC-AM
37815
Owner: Cumulus Media Inc.
Editorial: 1009 Drayton Rd, Fayetteville, North Carolina 28303-3887 **Tel:** 1 910 864-5222.
Web site: http://www.wfnc640am.com
Profile: WFNC-AM is a commercial station owned by Cumulus Media Inc. The format of the station is news and talk. WFNC-AM broadcasts to the Fayetteville, NC area at 640 AM.
AM RADIO STATION

WFNI-AM
36922
Owner: Emmis Communications Corp.
Editorial: 40 Monument Cir, Indianapolis, Indiana 46204-3019 **Tel:** 1 317 266-9422.
Web site: http://1070thefan.com
Profile: WFNI-AM is a commercial station owned by Emmis Communications Corp. The format of the station is sports. WFNI-AM broadcasts to the Indianapolis area at 1070 AM.
AM RADIO STATION

WFNK-FM
45755
Owner: WBIN, Inc.
Editorial: 477 Congress St Ste 3, Portland, Maine 04101-3427 **Tel:** 1 207 797-0780.
Web site: http://www.1075frank.com
Profile: WFNK-FM is a commercial station owned by WBIN, Inc. The format of station is classic hits. WFNK-FM broadcasts to the Portland, ME area at 107.5 FM.
FM RADIO STATION

WFNL-AM
35483
Owner: Curtis Media Group
Editorial: 3012 Highwoods Blvd Ste 201, Raleigh, North Carolina 27604-1031 **Tel:** 1 919 790-9392.
Email: info@curtismedia.com
Web site: http://www.funny570.com
Profile: WFNL-AM is a commercial station owned by Curtis Media Group. The format of the station is comedy. WFNL-AM broadcasts to the Raleigh-Durham, NC area at 570 AM.
AM RADIO STATION

WFNN-AM
36115
Owner: Connoisseur Media LLC
Editorial: 1 Boston Store Pl, Erie, Pennsylvania 16501-2313 **Tel:** 1 814 461-1000.
Web site: http://www.sportsradio1330.com
Profile: WFNN-AM is a commercial station owned by Connoisseur Media LLC. The format of the station is sports. WFNN-AM broadcasts to the Erie, PA area at 1330 AM.
AM RADIO STATION

WFNO-AM
36414
Owner: Crocodile Broadcasting
Editorial: 3850 N Causeway Blvd, Metairie, Louisiana 70002-1752
Profile: WFNO, formerly known as "La Caliente 830am," was acquired from Sunburst Media by Crocodile Broadcasting, owners of KGLA La Tropical, and rebranded it with its original tagline "La Fabulosa 830". It is a Spanish speaking formatted radio station serving the New Orleans, Louisiana area.
AM RADIO STATION

WFNQ-FM
40931
Owner: WBIN, Inc.
Editorial: 20 Industrial Park Dr Ste 1, Nashua, New Hampshire 03062-3178 **Tel:** 1 603 889-1063.
Web site: http://wfnq.nh1media.com/
Profile: WFNQ-FM is a commercial station owned by WBIN, Inc. The format of the station is classic rock. WFNQ-FM broadcasts to the Hooksett, NH area at 106.3 FM.
FM RADIO STATION

WFNR-AM
38952
Owner: Cumulus Media Inc.
Editorial: 7080 Lee Hwy, Fairlawn, Virginia 24141-8416 **Tel:** 1 540 731-6000.
Web site: http://710wfnr.com
Profile: WFNR-AM is a commercial station owned by Cumulus Media Inc. The format of the station is news, talk and sports. WFNR-AM broadcasts to the Fairlawn, VA area at 710 AM.
AM RADIO STATION

WFNS-AM
35342
Owner: MarMac Communications, LLC
Editorial: 436 Mall Blvd, Brunswick, Georgia 31525-1819 **Tel:** 1 912 342-7184.
Email: thefansportsradio@yahoo.com
Web site: http://www.thefansportsradio.com
Profile: WFNS-AM is a commercial station owned by MarMac Communications, LLC. The format of the station is sports. WFNS-AM broadcasts to the Waycross, GA area at 1350 AM.
AM RADIO STATION

WFNT-AM
37077
Owner: Townsquare Media, LLC
Editorial: 3338 E Bristol Rd, Burton, Michigan 48529-1408 **Tel:** 1 810 743-1080.
Web site: http://www.wfnt.com
Profile: WFTN-AM is a commercial station owned by Townsquare Media, LLC. The format of the station is news and talk. WFTN-AM broadcasts to the Burton, MI area at 1470 AM.
AM RADIO STATION

WFNX-FM
45971
Owner: Northeast Broadcasting Co.
Editorial: 362 Green St, Gardner, Massachusetts 01440-1348 **Tel:** 1 978 374-4733.
Profile: WFNX-FM is a commercial station owned by Northeast Broadcasting Co. The format of the station is adult hits. WFNX-FM broadcasts to the Gardner, MA area at 99.9 FM.
FM RADIO STATION

WFNY-AM
139728
Owner: Sleezer(Michael)
Editorial: 101 S Main St, Gloversville, New York 12078-3820 **Tel:** 1 518 725-1108.
Profile: WFNY-AM is a commercial station owned by Michael Sleezer. The format of the station is oldies. WFNY-AM broadcasts to the Gloversville, NY area at 1440 AM.
AM RADIO STATION

WFNZ-AM
37628
Owner: Beasley Broadcast Group
Editorial: 1520 South Blvd Ste 300, Charlotte, North Carolina 28203-3701 **Tel:** 1 704 319-9369.
Web site: http://wfnz.com
Profile: WFNZ-AM is a commercial station owned by Beasley Broadcast Group. The format of the station is sports. WFNZ-AM broadcasts to the Charlotte, NC area at 610 AM.
AM RADIO STATION

WFOB-AM
39432
Owner: Tri-County Broadcasting
Editorial: 101 N Main St, Fostoria, Ohio 44830-2215
Tel: 1 419 435-1430.
Email: production@wfob.com
Web site: http://www.wfob.com
Profile: WFOB-AM is a commercial station owned by Tri-County Broadcasting. The format of the station is sports. WFOB-AM broadcasts to the Fostoria, OH area at 1430 AM.
AM RADIO STATION

WFOF-FM
42644
Owner: Moody Bible Institute
Editorial: 1920 W 53rd St, Anderson, Indiana 46013-1110 **Tel:** 1 888 877-9467.
Web site: http://www.moodyradioindiana.fm/
Profile: WFOF-FM is a non-commercial station owned by Moody Bible Institute. The format of the station is religious. WFOF-FM broadcasts to the Anderson, IN area at 90.3 FM.
FM RADIO STATION

WFOM-AM
77519
Owner: Dickey Broadcasting
Editorial: 780 Johnson Ferry Rd NE Ste 500, Atlanta, Georgia 30342-1436 **Tel:** 1 404 688-0068.
Web site: http://www.1230thefan2.com
Profile: WFOM-AM is a commercial station owned by Dickey Broadcasting. The format of the station is sports. WFOM-AM broadcasts in the Atlanta area at 1230 AM.
AM RADIO STATION

WFON-FM
45914
Owner: RBH Enterprises Inc.
Editorial: 254 Winnebago Dr, Fond du Lac, Wisconsin 54935-2447 **Tel:** 1 920 921-1071.
Email: info@k107.com
Web site: http://www.k107.com
Profile: WFON-FM is a commercial station owned by RBH Enterprises Inc. The format of the station is country music. WFON-FM broadcasts to the Fond du Lac, WI area at 107.1 FM.
FM RADIO STATION

WFOT-FM
690132
Owner: Our Lady of Guadalupe Radio, Inc.
Editorial: 3662 Rugby Dr, Toledo, Ohio 43614-4448
Tel: 1 419 754-1009.
Email: info@annundiationradio.com
Web site: http://www.annunciationradio.com
Profile: WFOT-FM is a non-commercial station owned by Our Lady of Guadalupe Radio, Inc (dba Annunciation Radio). The format of the station is Catholic radio programming. WFOT-FM broadcasts to the mid-Ohio areas of Mansfield, Ashland and Mount Vernon.
FM RADIO STATION

WFOX-FM
45355
Owner: Connoisseur Media
Editorial: 440 Wheelers Farms Rd Ste 302, Milford, Connecticut 06461-9133 **Tel:** 1 203 783-8200.
Web site: http://www.959thefox.com/
Profile: WFOX-FM is a commercial station owned by Connoisseur Media. The format of the station is classic rock. WFOX-FM broadcasts to the Norwalk, CT area at 95.9 FM.
FM RADIO STATION

WFOY-AM
36393
Owner: Phillips Broadcasting, LLC
Editorial: 567 Lewis Point Road Ext, Saint Augustine, Florida 32086-5222 **Tel:** 1 904 797-1955.
Web site: http://www.1240news.com
Profile: WFOY-AM is a commercial station owned by Phillips Broadcasting, LLC. The format of the station is news and talk. WFOY-AM broadcasts to the Jacksonville, FL area at 1240 AM.
AM RADIO STATION

WFPG-FM
45164
Owner: Townsquare Media, LLC
Editorial: 950 Tilton Rd, Ste 200, Northfield, New Jersey 8225 **Tel:** 1 609 645-9797.
Email: lite@literock969.com
Web site: http://www.literock969.com
Profile: WFPG-FM is a commercial station owned by the Townsquare Media, LLC. The format of the station is Lite Rock/Lite AC. WFPG-FM broadcasts to the Northfield, NJ area at 96.9 FM.
FM RADIO STATION

WFPK-FM
40294
Owner: Louisville Public Media
Editorial: 619 S 4th St, Louisville, Kentucky 40202-2403 **Tel:** 1 502 814-6500.
Email: info@louisvillepublicmedia.org
Web site: http://www.wspl.org
Profile: WFPK-FM is a non-commercial station owned by Louisville Public Media. The format of the station is adult album alternative. WFPK-FM broadcasts in the Louisville, KY area at 91.9 FM.
FM RADIO STATION

WFPL-FM
40295
Owner: Louisville Public Media
Editorial: 619 S 4th St, Louisville, Kentucky 40202-2403 **Tel:** 1 502 814-6500.
Email: info@louisvillepublicmedia.org
Web site: http://www.wfpl.org
Profile: WFPL-AM is a non-commercial station owned by Louisville Public Media. The format of the station is news and talk. WFPL-AM broadcasts to the Louisville, KY area at 89.3 FM.
FM RADIO STATION

WFPR-AM
37817
Owner: Northshore Broadcasting Inc.
Editorial: 200 E Thomas St, Hammond, Louisiana 70401 **Tel:** 1 985 345-0060.
Profile: WFPR-AM is a commercial station owned by Northshore Broadcasting Inc. The format of the station is country. WFPR-AM broadcasts to the Hammond, LA area at 1400 AM.
AM RADIO STATION

WFPS-FM
40296
Owner: Big Radio
Editorial: 834 N Tower Rd, Freeport, Illinois 61032
Tel: 1 815 235-7191.
Web site: http://www.bigradio.fm
Profile: WFPS-FM is a commercial station owned by Big Radio. The format of the station is contemporary country music. WFPS-FM broadcasts to the Freeport, IL area at 92.1 FM. All staff should be contact via fax.
FM RADIO STATION

WFQX-FM
46579
Owner: iHeartMedia Inc.
Editorial: 510 Pegasus Ct, Winchester, Virginia 22602-4596 **Tel:** 1 540 662-5101.
Email: winchesterdigital@clearchannel.com
Web site: http://993thefox.iheart.com
Profile: WFQX-FM is a commercial station owned by iHeartMedia Inc. The format of the station is rock alternative. WFQX-FM broadcasts to the Washington, D.C. area at 99.3 FM.
FM RADIO STATION

WFQY-AM
38163
Owner: Titan Broadcasting, LLC
Editorial: 209 Commerce Dr Ste D, Brandon, Mississippi 39042-2756 **Tel:** 1 601 706-4040.
Web site: http://991bday.com
Profile: WFQY-AM is a commercial station owned by Titan Broadcasting, LLC. The format of the station is classic hip hop. The station broadcasts to the Brandon, MS area at 970 AM.
AM RADIO STATION

WFRA-AM 37818
Owner: FM Radio Licenses, LLC
Editorial: 900 Water St, Meadville, Pennsylvania 16335-3428 **Tel:** 1 814 724-1111.
Email: wmgwboss@yahoo.com
Web site: http://www.myantsnetwork.com
Profile: WFRA-AM is a commercial station owned by FM Radio Licenses, LLC. The format of the station is news, talk and sports. WFRA-AM broadcasts to the Franklin, PA area at 1450 AM.
AM RADIO STATION

WFRB-AM 37819
Owner: Dix Communications
Editorial: 242 Finzel Rd, Frostburg, Maryland 21532-4009 **Tel:** 1 301 689-8871.
Web site: http://www.talkradio560.com
Profile: WFRB-AM is a commercial station owned by Dix Communications. The format of the station is talk. WFRB-AM broadcasts in the Frostburg, MD area at 560 AM.
AM RADIO STATION

WFRB-FM 45165
Owner: Forever Media Inc.
Editorial: 242 Finzel Rd, Frostburg, Maryland 21532-4009 **Tel:** 1 301 689-8871.
Web site: http://www.wfrb.com
Profile: WFRB-FM is a commercial station owned by Dix Communications. The format of the station is classic and contemporary country music. WFRB-FM broadcasts to the Frostburg, MD area at 105.3 FM.
FM RADIO STATION

WFRC-FM 41296
Owner: Family Stations Inc.
Editorial: 290 Hegenberger Rd, Oakland, California 94621-1436 **Tel:** 1 510 568-6200.
Email: info@familyradio.org
Web site: http://www.familyradio.com
FM RADIO STATION

WFRD-FM 45166
Owner: Dartmouth College
Tel: 1 603 646-3313.
Email: 99Rock@wfrd.com
Web site: http://www.wfrd.com
Profile: WFRD-FM is a non-commerical station owned by Dartmouth College. The format of the station is rock alternative. WFRD-FM broadcasts to the Hanover, NH area at 99.3 FM.
FM RADIO STATION

WFRE-FM 45167
Owner: iHeartMedia Inc.
Editorial: 5966 Grove Hill Rd, Frederick, Maryland 21703-6012 **Tel:** 1 301 663-4181.
Email: news@wfmd.com
Web site: http://www.wfre.com
Profile: WFRE-FM is a commercial station owned by iHeartMedia Inc. The format of the station is classic and contemporary country music. WFRE-FM broadcasts in the Frederick, MD area at 99.9 FM.
FM RADIO STATION

WFRF-AM 36691
Owner: Faith Radio Network
Editorial: 4015 N Monroe St, Tallahassee, Florida 32303 **Tel:** 1 850 201-1070.
Email: mailbox@faithradio.us
Web site: http://www.faithradio.us
Profile: WFRF-AM is a non-commercial station owned by Faith Radio Network. The format of the station is contemporary Christian, southern gospel, and religious talk. WFRF-AM broadcasts to the Tallahassee, FL area at 1070 AM.
AM RADIO STATION

WFRF-FM 43192
Owner: Faith Radio Network
Editorial: 4015 N Monroe St, Tallahassee, Florida 32303 **Tel:** 1 850 201-1070.
Email: mailbox@faithradio.us
Web site: http://www.faithradio.us
Profile: WFRF-FM is a non-commercial station owned by Faith Radio Network. The format of the station is Christian and religious talk. The station airs locally at 105.7 FM.
FM RADIO STATION

WFRG-FM 46643
Owner: Townsquare Media, LLC
Editorial: 9418 River Rd, Marcy, New York 13403-2071 **Tel:** 1 315 768-9500.
Web site: http://www.bigfrog104.com
Profile: WFRG-FM is a commercial station owned by Townsquare Media, LLC. The format of the station is country music. WFRG-FM broadcasts to the Utica, NY area at 104.3 FM.
FM RADIO STATION

WFRH-FM 42653
Owner: Family Stations Inc.
Editorial: 786 Murray Rd, Kingston, New York 12401-7144 **Tel:** 1 845 336-0234.
Web site: http://www.familyradio.org
Profile: WFRH-FM is a non-commercial station owned by Family Stations Inc. The format of the station is religious. WFRH-FM broadcasts to the West Shokan, NY area at 81.7 FM.
FM RADIO STATION

WFRJ-FM 42654
Owner: Family Stations Inc.
Editorial: 1322 Seanor Rd, Windber, Pennsylvania 15963 **Tel:** 1 814 467-9466.
Email: wfrj44@gmail.com
Web site: http://www.familyradio.com
Profile: WFRJ-FM is a non-commercial station owned by Family Stations Inc. The format of the station is religious. WFRJ-FM broadcasts to the Windber, PA area at 88.9 FM.
FM RADIO STATION

WFRL-AM 36635
Owner: Big Radio
Editorial: 834 N Tower Rd, Freeport, Illinois 61032
Tel: 1 815 235-7191.
Web site: http://www.bigradio.fm
Profile: WFRL-AM is a commercial station owned by Big Radio. The format of the station is oldies. WFRL-AM broadcasts to the Freeport, IL area at 1570 AM. All staff should be contact via fax.
AM RADIO STATION

WFRM-AM 37820
Owner: L-Com Inc.
Editorial: 9 S Main St, Coudersport, Pennsylvania 16915-1301 **Tel:** 1 814 274-8600.
Email: whks@verizon.net
Profile: WFRM-AM is a commercial station owned by L-Com Inc. The format of the station is adult standards. WFRM-AM broadcasts to the Coudersport, PA area at 600 AM.
AM RADIO STATION

WFRN-FM 45169
Owner: Progressive Broadcasting
Editorial: 25802 County Road 26, Elkhart, Indiana 46517-9132 **Tel:** 1 574 875-5166.
Email: events@wfrn.com
Web site: http://wfrn.com
Profile: WFRN-FM is a commercial station owned by Progressive Broadcasting. The format for the station is contemporary Christian. WFRN-FM broadcasts to the South Bend, IN area at 104.7 FM.
FM RADIO STATION

WFRO-FM 45170
Owner: BAS Broadcasting
Editorial: 1281 N River Rd, Fremont, Ohio 43420
Tel: 1 419 332-8218.
Web site: http://www.wfroradio.com
Profile: WFRO-FM is a commercial station owned by BAS Broadcasting. The format of the station is adult contemporary. WFRO-FM broadcasts to the Fremont, OH area at 99.1 FM.
FM RADIO STATION

WFRQ-FM 44168
Owner: Codcomm Inc.
Editorial: 243 South St, Hyannis, Massachusetts 02601-3926 **Tel:** 1 508 775-5678.
Web site: http://capecodradio.com/
Profile: WFRQ-FM is a commercial station owned by Codcomm Inc. The format of the station is Jack FM-Adult Hits. WFRQ-FM broadcasts to the Wast Yarmouth, MA area at 93.5 FM.
FM RADIO STATION

WFRS-FM 43922
Owner: Family Stations Inc.
Editorial: 289 Mount Pleasant Ave, West Orange, New Jersey 07052-4107 **Tel:** 1 973 736-3600.
Email: info@familyradio.org
Web site: http://www.familyradio.org
Profile: WFRS-FM is a non-commercial station owned by Family Stations Inc. The format for the station is religious. WFRS-FM broadcasts to the West Orange, NJ area at 88.9 FM.
FM RADIO STATION

WFRW-FM 961770
Owner: Christian Radio Friends, Inc.
Tel: 1 574 875-5166.
Email: events@wfrn.com
Web site: http://wfrn.com
Profile: WFRW-FM is a non-commercial station owned by Christian Radio Friends, Inc. The format of the station is Contemporary Christian music. The station broadcasts to the Battle Ground, Indiana area at 88.9 FM.
FM RADIO STATION

WFRX-AM 36611
Owner: Withers Broadcasting of Southern Illinois LLC
Editorial: 1822 N Court St, Marion, Illinois 62959-4558
Tel: 1 618 997-8123.
Web site: http://www.mywithersradio.com
Profile: WFRX-AM is a commercial station owned by Withers Broadcasting of Southern Illinois LLC. The format of the station is sports. WFRX-AM broadcasts to the Marion, IL areas at 1300 AM.
AM RADIO STATION

WFRY-FM 44389
Owner: Stephens Media Group
Editorial: 134 Mullin St, Watertown, New York 13601
Tel: 1 315 788-0790.
Web site: http://www.froggy97.com
FM RADIO STATION

WFSC-AM 37822
Owner: Georgia-Carolina Radiocasting Companies LLC
Editorial: 180 Radio Hill Rd, Franklin, North Carolina 28734 **Tel:** 1 828 524-4418.
Email: franklinradio@gacaradio.com
Web site: http://www.1050wfsc.com
Profile: WFSC-AM is a commercial station owned by Georgia-Carolina Radiocasting Companies LLC. The format of the station is oldies. WFSC-AM broadcasts to the Franklin, NC area at 1050 AM.
AM RADIO STATION

WFSH-FM 46765
Owner: Salem Media Group, Inc.
Editorial: 2970 Peachtree Rd NW Ste 700, Atlanta, Georgia 30305-4919 **Tel:** 1 404 995-7300.
Web site: http://www.thefishatlanta.com
Profile: WFSH-FM is a commercial station owned by Salem Media Group, Inc. The format of the station is contemporary Christian. WFSH-FM broadcasts to the Atlanta area at 104.7 FM.
FM RADIO STATION

WFSI-AM 35201
Owner: Family Stations Inc.
Email: info@familyradio.org
Web site: http://www.familyradio.org
Profile: WFSI-AM is a non-commercial station owned by the Family Stations Inc. The format of the station is religious programming. WFSI-AM broadcasts to the Baltimore area at 860 AM.
AM RADIO STATION

WFSO-FM 43923
Owner: Redeemer Broadcasting
Editorial: 60 Butternut Knls, West Shokan, New York 12494-5321 **Tel:** 1 888 724-4427.
Email: ministry@redeemerbroadcasting.org
Web site: http://www.redeemerbroadcasting.org
Profile: WFSO-FM is a non-commercial station owned by Redeemer Broadcasting. The format of the station is Christian programming. WFSO-FM broadcasts to the Olivebridge, NY area at 88.3 FM. The station requested that its e-mail not be listed.
FM RADIO STATION

WFSP-AM 38716
Owner: WFSP Inc.
Editorial: Route 7 West, Kingwood, West Virginia 26537 **Tel:** 1 304 329-1780.
Web site: http://www.prestoncounty.com/wfsp
Profile: WFSP-AM is a commercial station owned by WFSP Inc. The format of the station is talk. WFSP-AM broadcasts to the Kingwood, WV area at 1560 AM.
AM RADIO STATION

WFSP-FM 46070
Owner: WFSP Inc.
Editorial: Route 7 West, Kingwood, West Virginia 26537 **Tel:** 1 304 329-1780.
Email: wfsp@wvdsl.net
Web site: http://www.prestoncounty.com/wfsp
Profile: WFSP-FM is a commercial station owned by WFSP Inc. The format of the station is oldies. WFSP-FM broadcasts to the Kingwood, WV area at 107.7 FM.
FM RADIO STATION

WFSR-AM 38780
Owner: Eastern Broadcasting Co.
Editorial: 125 S Main St, Harlan, Kentucky 40831-2109 **Tel:** 1 606 573-1470.
Email: wtuk-wfsr@harlanonline.net
Profile: WFSR-AM is a commercial station owned by Eastern Broadcasting Co. The format of the station is gospel. WFSR-AM broadcasts to the Harlan, KY area at 970 AM.
AM RADIO STATION

WFST-AM 36294
Owner: Northern Broadcast Ministries Inc.
Editorial: 670 New Sweden Rd, Caribou, Maine 4736
Tel: 1 207 492-6000.
Email: wfst@maine.rr.com
Web site: http://www.familyradiowfst.com
Profile: WFST-AM is a non-commercial station owned by Northern Broadcast Ministries Inc. The format of the station is gospel music. WFST-AM broadcasts to the Caribou, ME area at 600 AM.
AM RADIO STATION

WFSX-FM 43099
Owner: Sun Broadcasting, Inc.
Editorial: 2824 Palm Beach Blvd, Fort Myers, Florida 33916 **Tel:** 1 239 334-1111.
Web site: http://www.925foxnews.com
Profile: WFSX-FM is a commercial station owned by Sun Broadcasting, Inc. The format of the station is news and talk. WFSX-FM broadcasts to the Fort Myers, FL area at 92.5 FM.
FM RADIO STATION

WFSY-FM 45171
Owner: iHeartMedia Inc.
Editorial: 1834 Lisenby Ave, Panama City, Florida 32405-3713 **Tel:** 1 850 769-6161.
Web site: http://www.sunny98.com
Profile: WFSY-FM is a commercial station owned by iHeartMedia Inc. The format of the station is adult contemporary music. WFSY-FM broadcasts to the Panama City, FL area at 98.5 FM.
FM RADIO STATION

WFTA-FM 46508
Owner: Air South Radio Inc.
Editorial: 1241 Cliff Gookin Blvd, Tupelo, Mississippi 38801-6749 **Tel:** 1 662 842-7625.
Web site: http://power101.fm
Profile: Power 101.9 is the adult choice radio station in North Mississippi. Featuring Today's Hits and Yesterday's Favorites.
FM RADIO STATION

WFTD-AM 35932
Owner: Prieto Broadcasting, Inc.
Editorial: 3490 Shallowford Rd NE Ste 302, Atlanta, Georgia 30341-2934 **Tel:** 1 770 825-0990.
Web site: http://laley1080am.com
Profile: WFTD-AM is a commercial station owned by Prieto Broadcasting, Inc. The format of the station is Spanish news and talk. WFTD-AM broadcasts to the Doraville, GA area at 1080 AM.
AM RADIO STATION

WFTF-FM 774632
Owner: Christian Ministries Inc
Editorial: 140 Main St, Essex Junction, Vermont 05452-3208 **Tel:** 1 802 878-8885.
Web site: http://thelightradio.net
Profile: WFTF-FM is a non-commercial station owned by Christian Ministries Inc. The format of the station is contemporary Christian music. WFTF-FM broadcasts to the Rutland, VT area at 90.5 FM.
FM RADIO STATION

WFTG-AM 37823
Owner: Forcht Broadcasting
Editorial: 534 Tobacco Rd, London, Kentucky 40741
Tel: 1 606 864-2148.
Profile: WFTG-AM is a commercial station owned by Forcht Broadcasting. The format for the station is country. WFTG-AM broadcasts to the Lexington, KY area at 1440 AM.
AM RADIO STATION

WFTH-AM 35331
Owner: Tri-City Christian Radio Inc.
Editorial: 227 E Belt Blvd, Richmond, Virginia 23224
Tel: 1 804 233-0765.
Email: faithradio1590am@yahoo.com
Web site: http://faith1590.ning.com
Profile: WFTH-AM is a commercial station owned by Tri-City Christian Radio Inc. The format of the station is black gospel. WFTH-AM broadcasts to the Richmond, VA area at 1590 AM.
AM RADIO STATION

WFTI-FM 41449
Owner: Radio Training Network, Inc.
Editorial: 6469 Parkland Dr, Sarasota, Florida 34243-4091 **Tel:** 1 941 753-2963.
Email: thejoyfm@thejoyfm.com
Web site: http://florida.thejoyfm.com
Profile: WFTI-FM is a non-commercial station owned by Radio Training Network, Inc. The format of the station is Contemporary Christian music. WFTI-FM broadcasts to the Saint Petersburg, FL area at 91.7 FM.
FM RADIO STATION

WFTK-FM 42009
Owner: Cumulus Media Inc.
Editorial: 4805 Montgomery Rd Ste 300, Cincinnati, Ohio 45212-2280 **Tel:** 1 513 241-9898.
Web site: http://www.purerock96.com
Profile: WFTK-FM is a commercial station owned by Cumulus Media Inc. The format of the station is rock. WFTK-FM broadcasts to the Cincinnati area at 96.5 FM.
FM RADIO STATION

WFTL-AM 36798
Owner: JCE Licenses, LLC
Editorial: 701 Northpoint Pkwy Ste 500, West Palm Beach, Florida 33407-1960 **Tel:** 1 561 616-4777.
Web site: http://www.850wftl.com
Profile: WFTL-AM is a commercial station owned by JCE Licenses, LLC. The format of the station is news and talk programming. WFTL-AM broadcasts to South Florida from the North Keys to Fort Pierce at 850 AM.
AM RADIO STATION

WFTM-AM 37824
Owner: Standard Tobacco Co.
Editorial: 626 Forest Ave, Maysville, Kentucky 41056-1412 **Tel:** 1 606 564-3361.
Email: wftmnews@maysvilleky.net
Web site: http://www.wftm.net
Profile: WFTM-AM is a commercial station owned by Standard Tobacco Co. The format of the station is sports. WFTM-AM broadcasts to the Maysville, KY area at 1240 AM.
AM RADIO STATION

WFTM-FM 45172
Owner: Standard Tobacco Co.
Editorial: 626 Forest Ave, Maysville, Kentucky 41056-1412 **Tel:** 1 606 564-3361.
Email: wftmnews@maysvilleky.net
Web site: http://www.wftm.net
Profile: WFTM-FM is a commercial station owned by Standard Tobacco Co. The format of the station is adult contemporary music. WFTM-FM broadcasts to the Cincinnati area at 95.9 FM.
FM RADIO STATION

WFTN-AM 37825
Owner: Northeast Communications Corp.
Editorial: 110 Babbitt Rd, Franklin, New Hampshire 3235 **Tel:** 1 603 934-2500.
Web site: http://www.mix941fm.com
Profile: WFTN-AM is a commercial station owned by Northeast Communications Corp. The format of the station is adult standards. WFTN-AM broadcasts to the Boston area at 1240 AM.
AM RADIO STATION

WFTN-FM 42105
Owner: Northeast Communications Corp.
Editorial: 110 Babbitt Rd, Franklin, New Hampshire 3235 **Tel:** 1 603 253-8080.
Web site: http://www.mix941fm.com
Profile: WFTN-FM is a commercial station owned by Northeast Communications Corp. The format of the

station is hot adult contemporary. WFTN-FM broadcasts to the Boston area at 94.1 FM.
FM RADIO STATION

WFTR-AM 37826
Owner: Royal Broadcasting Inc.
Editorial: 1106 Elm St, Front Royal, Virginia 22630-3736 **Tel:** 1 540 635-4121.
Profile: WFTR-AM is a commercial station owned by Royal Broadcasting Inc. The format of the station is classic country. WFTR-AM broadcasts to the Front Royal, VA area at 1450 AM.
AM RADIO STATION

WFTU-AM 37715
Owner: Five Towns College
Editorial: 305 N Service Rd, Dix Hills, New York 11746-5857
Web site: http://www.ftc.edu/Student%20Life/stu_wftu.html
Profile: WFTU-AM is a non-commercial college station owned by Five Towns College. The format of the station is college variety. WFTU-AM broadcasts to the Long Island, NY area at a frequency of 1570 AM.
AM RADIO STATION

WFTW-AM 37827
Owner: Cumulus Media Inc.
Editorial: 225 Hollywood Blvd NW, Fort Walton Beach, Florida 32548-4725 **Tel:** 1 850 243-2323.
Email: psa@cumulusfwb.com
Web site: http://www.wftw.com
Profile: WFTW-AM is a commercial station owned by Cumulus Media Inc. The format of the station is talk, news and sports. WFTW-AM broadcasts to the Fort Walton Beach, FL area at 1260 AM.
AM RADIO STATION

WFTZ-FM 42694
Owner: Phase Two Communications
Editorial: 1025 Hillsboro Blvd, Manchester, Tennessee 37355-2029 **Tel:** 1 931 728-3458.
Web site: http://www.fantasyradio.com
Profile: WFTZ-FM is a commercial station owned by Phase Two Communications. The format of the station is adult contemporary. WFTZ-FM broadcasts to the Manchester, TN area at 101.5 FM.
FM RADIO STATION

WFUN-AM 37828
Owner: Media One Group
Editorial: 3226 Jefferson Rd, Ashtabula, Ohio 44004-9112 **Tel:** 1 440 993-2126.
Web site: http://www.espn970wfun.com
Profile: WFUN-AM is a commercial station owned by Media One Group. The format of the station is sports. WFUN-AM broadcasts to the Ashtabula, OH area at 970 AM.
AM RADIO STATION

WFUN-FM 128728
Owner: Urban One, Inc.
Editorial: 9666 Olive Blvd, Saint Louis, Missouri 63132-3013 **Tel:** 1 314 989-9550.
Web site: http://oldschool955.com
Profile: WFUN-FM is a commercial station owned by Urban One, Inc. The format of the station is urban adult contemporary music. WFUN-FM broadcasts in the St. Louis area at 95.5 FM.
FM RADIO STATION

WFUR-AM 37829
Owner: Furniture City Broadcasting
Editorial: 399 Garfield Ave SW, Grand Rapids, Michigan 49504 **Tel:** 1 616 451-9387.
Email: wfuramfm@sbcglobal.net
Web site: http://www.wfuramfm.com
Profile: WFUR-AM is a commercial station owned by Furniture City Broadcasting. The format of the station is religious music and talk. WFUR-AM broadcasts to the Grand Rapids, MI area at 1570 AM. The station does not produce their own news.
AM RADIO STATION

WFUR-FM 45174
Owner: Furniture City Broadcasting
Editorial: 399 Garfield Ave SW, Grand Rapids, Michigan 49504-6167 **Tel:** 1 616 451-9387.
Email: wfuramfm@sbcglobal.net
Web site: http://www.wfuramfm.com
Profile: WFUR-FM is a commercial station owned by Furniture City Broadcasting. The format of the station is religious programming. WFUR-FM broadcasts to Grand Rapids, MI at 102.9 FM. The station does not accept press releases as they don't produce their own news.
FM RADIO STATION

WFUS-FM 42745
Owner: iHeartMedia Inc.
Editorial: 4002 W Gandy Blvd, Tampa, Florida 33611-3410 **Tel:** 1 813 832-1000.
Web site: http://us1035.iheart.com
Profile: WFUS-FM is a commercial station owned by iHeartMedia Inc. The format of the station is country. WFUS-FM broadcasts to the Tampa, FL area at 103.5 FM.
FM RADIO STATION

WFUZ-FM 45852
Owner: Shamrock Communications
Editorial: 149 Penn Ave Fl 5, Scranton, Pennsylvania 18503-2055 **Tel:** 1 570 346-6555.
Web site: http://www.radiofm921.com
Profile: WFUZ-FM is a commercial station owned by Shamrock Communications. The format of the station is modern rock. WFUZ-FM broadcasts to the Scranton, PA area at 92.1 FM.
FM RADIO STATION

WFVA-AM 37830
Owner: Centennial Broadcasting
Editorial: 1914 Mimosa St, Fredericksburg, Virginia 22405-3213 **Tel:** 1 540 373-7721.
Web site: http://www.newstalk1230.net
Profile: WFVA-AM is a commercial station owned by the Centennial Broadcasting. The format of the station is news and talk. WFVA-AM broadcasts to the Fredericksburg, VA area at 1230 AM.
AM RADIO STATION

WFVL-FM 43619
Owner: Educational Media Foundation
Editorial: Lumberton, North Carolina **Tel:** 1 916 521-1600.
Web site: http://www.klove.com
Profile: WFVL-FM is a commercial station owned by Educational Media Foundation. The format of the station is Contemporary Christian. WFVL-FM broadcasts to the Fayetteville, NC area at 102.3 FM.
FM RADIO STATION

WFWI-FM 42084
Owner: Federated Media
Editorial: 2915 Maples Rd, Fort Wayne, Indiana 46816-3335 **Tel:** 1 260 447-5511.
Web site: http://www.big923.com/
Profile: WFWI-FM is a commercial station owned by Federated Media. The format of the station is Classic Hits. WFWI-FM broadcasts to the Fort Wayne, IN area at 92.3 FM. Everything is handled out of the sister station WOWO-AM.
FM RADIO STATION

WFWL-AM 38729
Owner: Community Broadcasting Services Inc.
Editorial: 117 Vicksburg Ave, Camden, Tennessee 38320-1613 **Tel:** 1 731 584-7570.
Email: wfwlwrjb@bellsouth.net
Profile: WFWL-AM is a commercial station owned by Community Broadcasting Services Inc. The format of the station is contemporary country. WFWL-AM broadcasts to the Camden, TN area at 1220 AM.
AM RADIO STATION

WFWN-AM 705380
Owner: Sun Broadcasting, Inc.
Editorial: 2824 Palm Beach Blvd, Fort Myers, Florida 33916-1503 **Tel:** 1 239 337-2346.
Profile: WFWN-AM is a commercial station owned by Sun Broadcasting, Inc. The format of the station is sports. The station airs locally at 1240 AM.
AM RADIO STATION

WFXA-FM 44505
Owner: Perry Broadcasting Company, Inc.
Editorial: 6025 Broadcast Dr, North Augusta, South Carolina 29841-9406 **Tel:** 1 803 279-2330.
Web site: http://www.103jamzthefox.com/
Profile: WFXA-FM is a commercial station owned by Perry Broadcasting Company, Inc. The format of the station is urban contemporary. WFXA-FM broadcasts to the North Augusta, SC area at 103.1 FM.
FM RADIO STATION

WFXC-FM 43283
Owner: Urban One, Inc.
Editorial: 8001 Creedmoor Rd Ste 101, Raleigh, North Carolina 27613-4396 **Tel:** 1 919 848-9736.
Web site: http://www.foxyhits.com
Profile: WFXC-FM is a commercial station owned by Urban One, Inc. The format of the station is urban adult contemporary music. WFXC-FM broadcasts to the Raleigh-Durham, NC area at 107.1 FM.
FM RADIO STATION

WFXD-FM 40697
Owner: Great Lakes Radio Inc.
Editorial: 3060 US Highway 41 W, Marquette, Michigan 49855-2293 **Tel:** 1 906 228-6800.
Email: contact@broadcasteverywhere.com
Web site: http://www.wfxd.com
Profile: WFXD-FM is a commercial station owned by Great Lakes Radio Inc. The format for the station is contemporary country music. WFXD-FM broadcasts to the Marquette, MI area at 103.3 FM.
FM RADIO STATION

WFXE-FM 46147
Owner: Davis Broadcasting
Editorial: 2203 Wynnton Rd, Columbus, Georgia 31906-2531 **Tel:** 1 706 576-3565.
Web site: http://www.foxie105fm.com
Profile: WFXE-FM is a commercial station owned by Davis Broadcasting. The format of the station is urban contemporary music. WFXE-FM broadcasts to the Columbus, GA area at 104.9 FM.
FM RADIO STATION

WFXF-FM 40187
Owner: Matrix Broadcasting
Editorial: 8800 US Highway 14, Crystal Lake, Illinois 60012-2740 **Tel:** 1 815 459-7000.
Web site: http://www.rockthefox.com
Profile: WFXF-FM is a commercial station owned by Matrix Broadcasting. The format of the station is classic rock. WFXF-FM broadcasts to the Crystal Lake, IL area at 103.9 FM.
FM RADIO STATION

WFXH-FM 45196
Owner: Alpha Media
Editorial: 401 Mall Blvd, Savannah, Georgia 31406-4878 **Tel:** 1 912 351-9830.
Web site: http://rock1061.com
Profile: WFXH-FM is a commercial station owned by Alpha Media. The format for the station is rock music. WFXH-FM broadcasts to the Savannah, GA area at 106.1 FM.
FM RADIO STATION

WFXJ-AM 39366
Owner: iHeartMedia Inc.
Editorial: 11700 Central Pkwy, Jacksonville, Florida 32224-2600 **Tel:** 1 904 636-0507.
Web site: http://www.sportsradiojax.com
Profile: WFXJ-AM is a commercial station owned by iHeartMedia Inc. The format of the station is sports. WFXJ-AM broadcasts to the Jacksonville, FL area at 930 AM.
AM RADIO STATION

WFXJ-FM 235036
Owner: Media One Group
Editorial: 3226 Jefferson Rd, Ashtabula, Ohio 44004-9112 **Tel:** 1 440 993-2126.
Web site: http://www.thefox1075.com
Profile: WFXJ-FM is a commercial station owned by Media One Group. The format of the station is classic rock music. WFXJ-FM broadcasts in the Cleveland area at 107.5 FM.
FM RADIO STATION

WFXK-FM 41654
Owner: Urban One, Inc.
Editorial: 8001 Creedmoor Rd Ste 101, Raleigh, North Carolina 27613-4396 **Tel:** 1 919 848-9736.
Web site: http://foxync.com
Profile: WFXK-FM is a commercial station owned by Urban One, Inc. The format of the station is adult contemporary and urban contemporary. WFKX-FM broadcasts to the Raleigh, NC area at 104.3 FM.
FM RADIO STATION

WFXM-FM 45489
Owner: Murray Communications
Editorial: 6174 Ga Highway 57, Macon, Georgia 31217-3405 **Tel:** 1 478 745-3301.
Web site: http://www.mypower1071.com
Profile: WFXM-FM is a commercial station owned by Murray Communications. The format of the station is urban contemporary music. WFXM-FM broadcasts to the Macon, GA area at 107.1 FM.
FM RADIO STATION

WFXN-AM 38441
Owner: iHeartMedia Inc.
Editorial: 3535 E Kimberly Rd, Davenport, Iowa 52807-2583 **Tel:** 1 563 344-7000.
Web site: http://www.foxsportsradio1230.com
Profile: WFXN-AM is a commercial station owned by iHeartMedia Inc. The format of the station is sports. WFXN-AM broadcasts to the Davenport, IA area at 1230 AM.
AM RADIO STATION

WFXN-FM 43630
Owner: iHeartMedia Inc.
Editorial: 1400 Radio Ln, Mansfield, Ohio 44906-2525 **Tel:** 1 419 529-2211.
Web site: http://www.foxclassicrock.com
Profile: WFXN-FM is a commercial station owned by iHeartMedia Inc. The format of the station is classic rock music. WFXN-FM broadcasts to the Mansfield, OH area at 102.3 FM.
FM RADIO STATION

WFXO-FM 44070
Owner: Williams Communications Inc.
Editorial: 801 Noble St Ste 30, Anniston, Alabama 36201-0503 **Tel:** 1 256 453-9898.
Email: studio@rock1059.net
Profile: WFXO-FM is a commercial station owned by Williams Communications Inc. The format of the station is urban AC. WFXO-FM broadcasts to the Anniston, AL area at 98.3 FM..
FM RADIO STATION

WFXX-FM 445575
Owner: Haynes Broadcasting
Editorial: 1406 River Falls St, Andalusia, Alabama 36421-2029 **Tel:** 1 334 222-2222.
Email: wfxx@alaweb.com
Web site: http://www.fox107.com
FM RADIO STATION

WFXY-AM 38961
Owner: Penelope, Inc.
Editorial: 2117 Cumberland Ave, Middlesboro, Kentucky 40965-2876 **Tel:** 1 606 248-9399.
Email: wfxyproduction@gmail.com
Web site: http://www.1490wfxy.com
Profile: WFXY-AM is a commercial station owned by Penelope, Inc. The format of the station is classic hits. WFXY-AM broadcasts to the Middlesboro, KY and surrounding communities at 1490 AM.
AM RADIO STATION

WFYB-FM 747112
Owner: Light of Life Ministries, Inc.
Editorial: 160 Riverside Dr, Augusta, Maine 04330-4162 **Tel:** 1 207 622-1340.
Profile: WFYB-FM is a non-commercial station owned by Light of Life Ministries Inc. The format of the station is classical. WFYB-FM broadcasts to the Fryeburg, ME, area at 91.5 FM. This station is simulcasting WWWA-FM 95.3 Winslow/Augusta, ME.
FM RADIO STATION

WFYC-AM 37831
Owner: Jacom Inc.
Editorial: 5310 N State Rd, Alma, Michigan 48801-9713 **Tel:** 1 989 463-3175.
Email: wqbxfm@gmail.com
Profile: WFYC-AM is a commercial station owned by Jacom Inc. The format of the station is sports. WFYC-AM broadcasts to the Alma, MI area at 1280 AM.
AM RADIO STATION

WFYI-FM 40368
Owner: Metropolitan Indianapolis Public Broadcasting
Editorial: 1630 N Meridian St, Indianapolis, Indiana 46202-1429 **Tel:** 1 317 636-2020.
Email: news@wfyi.org
Web site: http://www.wfyi.org
Profile: WFYI-FM is a non-commercial station owned by Indiana Public Broadcasting Systems. The format of the station is news and information. WFYI-FM broadcasts to the Indianapolis area at 90.1 FM.
FM RADIO STATION

WFYR-FM 42648
Owner: Cumulus Media Inc.
Editorial: 120 Eaton St, Peoria, Illinois 61603-4217 **Tel:** 1 309 676-5000.
Web site: http://www.973rivercountry.com
Profile: WFYR-FM is a commercial station owned by Cumulus Media Inc. The format of the station is country music. WFYR-FM broadcasts to the Peoria, IL area at 97.3 FM.
FM RADIO STATION

WFYX-FM 552683
Owner: Great Eastern Radio, LLC
Editorial: 106 N Main St, West Lebanon, New Hampshire 03784-1136 **Tel:** 1 603 298-0332.
Profile: WFYX-FM is a commercial station owned by Great Eastern Radio, LLC. The format of the station is classic hits. WFYX-FM broadcasts to the Walpole, NH area at 96.3 FM.
FM RADIO STATION

WFZX-AM 35169
Owner: Jeff Beak Broadcasting
Editorial: 1913 Barry St Ste B, Oxford, Alabama 36203-2319 **Tel:** 1 256 741-6000.
Email: info@jeffbeakmedia.com
Web site: http://wfzxthefox.com
Profile: WFZX-AM is a commercial station owned by Jeff Beak Broadcasting. The format of the station is classic hits. WFZX-AM broadcasts to the Anniston/Oxford, AL area at 1490 AM.
AM RADIO STATION

WFZX-FM 739674
Owner: Jeff Beck Media
Editorial: 1913 Barry St, Oxford, Alabama 36203-2319 **Tel:** 1 256 741-6000.
Email: info@jeffbeckmedia.com
Web site: http://wtdrthunder.com
Profile: WFZX-FM is a commercial station owned by Jeff Beck Media. The format of the station is classic rock. WFZX-FM broadcasts to the Anniston, AL area airing on WSYA-AM's translator at 104.3 FM.
FM RADIO STATION

WGAA-AM 35333
Owner: Burgess Broadcasting Corp.
Editorial: 413 Lakeview Dr, Cedartown, Georgia 30125-2020 **Tel:** 1 770 748-1340.
Email: wgaaradio@wgaaradio.com
Web site: http://www.wgaaradio.com
Profile: WGAA-AM is a commercial station owned by Burgess Broadcasting Corp. The format is classic hits music. WGAA-AM broadcasts to the Cedartown, GA area at 1340 AM.
AM RADIO STATION

WGAB-AM 39047
Owner: Faith Broadcasting Company
Editorial: 2601 S Boeke Rd, Evansville, Indiana 47714-4933 **Tel:** 1 812 479-5342.
Email: info@faithmusicradio.com
Web site: http://www.faithmusicradio.com
Profile: WGAB-AM is a commercial station owned by Faith Broadcasting Company. The format of the station is gospel music. WGAB-AM broadcasts to the Evansville, IN area at 1180 AM.
AM RADIO STATION

WGAC-AM 39243
Owner: Beasley Broadcast Group
Editorial: 4051 Jimmie Dyess Pkwy, Augusta, Georgia 30909 **Tel:** 1 706 396-7000.
Email: news@wgac.com
Web site: http://www.wgac.com
Profile: WGAC-AM is a commercial station owned by Beasley Broadcast Group. The format of the station is news and talk. WGAC-AM broadcasts to the Augusta, GA area at 580 AM.
AM RADIO STATION

WGAC-FM 42640
Owner: Beasley Broadcast Group
Editorial: 4051 Jimmie Dyess Pkwy, Augusta, Georgia 30909 **Tel:** 1 706 396-7000.
Web site: http://www.wgac.com
Profile: WGAC-FM is a commercial station owned by Beasley Broadcast Group. The format of the station is

rock. WGAC-FM broadcasts to the Augusta, GA area at 95.1 FM.
FM RADIO STATION

WGAD-AM 35410
Owner: Gadsden Radio Media, LLC
Editorial: 301 N 12th St, Gadsden, Alabama 35901-7200 **Tel:** 1 256 570-1350.
Web site: http://wtdrthunder.com
Profile: WGAD-AM is a commercial station owned by Gadsden Radio Media, LLC. The format of the station is Classic Hits. WGAD-AM broadcasts to the Rainbow City, AL at 930 AM.
AM RADIO STATION

WGAI-AM 36397
Owner: Max Media
Editorial: 103 W Wood Hill Dr, Ste D-E, Nags Head, North Carolina 27959 **Tel:** 1 252 480-4655.
Web site: http://www.newsradio560.com
Profile: WGAI-AM is a commercial station owned by Max Media. The format of the station is news and talk. WGAI-AM broadcasts to the Norfolk, VA area at 560 AM.
AM RADIO STATION

WGAM-AM 36270
Owner: Absolute Broadcasting, LLC
Editorial: 149 Main St, Nashua, New Hampshire 03060-2725 **Tel:** 1 603 880-9001.
Email: info@wgamradio.com
Web site: http://espnnhradio.com
Profile: WGAM-AM is a commercial station owned by Absolute Broadcasting, LLC. The format of the station is sports. WGAM-AM broadcasts to the Nashua, NH area at 1250 AM.
AM RADIO STATION

WGAN-AM 38843
Owner: Saga Communications
Editorial: 420 Western Ave, South Portland, Maine 04106-1704 **Tel:** 1 207 774-4561.
Email: news@560wgan.com
Web site: http://www.560wgan.com
Profile: WGAN-AM is a commercial station owned by Saga Communications. The format of the station is news and talk. WGAN-AM broadcasts to the Portland, ME area at 560 AM.
AM RADIO STATION

WGAO-FM 40300
Owner: Dean College
Editorial: 99 Main St, Franklin, Massachusetts 02038-1941 **Tel:** 1 508 541-1623.
Profile: WGAO-FM is a non-commercial station owned by Dean College. The format of the station is rock. WGAO-FM broadcasts to the Franklin, MA area at 88.3 FM.
FM RADIO STATION

WGAP-AM 37007
Owner: Clinton Broadcasters
Editorial: 119 Pine Rd, Clinton, Tennessee 37716-2025 **Tel:** 1 865 675-4105.
Profile: WGAP-AM is a commercial station owned by Clinton Broadcasters. The format of the station is country. WGAP-AM broadcasts to the Knoxville, TN area at 1400 AM.
AM RADIO STATION

WGAR-FM 41602
Owner: iHeartMedia Inc.
Editorial: 6200 Oak Tree Blvd, Cleveland, Ohio 44131-6933 **Tel:** 1 216 520-2600.
Web site: http://www.wgar.com
Profile: WGAR-FM is a commercial station owned by iHeartMedia Inc. The format of the station is country music. WGAR-FM broadcasts to the Cleveland area at 99.5 FM.
FM RADIO STATION

WGAS-AM 75505
Owner: Victory Christian Center
Editorial: 1501 Carrier Dr, Charlotte, North Carolina 28216 **Tel:** 1 704 393-1540.
Email: info@wordnet.org
Web site: http://www.wordnet.org
Profile: WGAS-AM is a non-commercial station owned by Victory Christian Center. The format of the station is black gospel music. WGAS-AM broadcasts to the Charlotte, NC area at 1420 AM.
AM RADIO STATION

WGAT-AM 35335
Owner: Tri-Cities Broadcasting Corporation
Editorial: 173 West Jackson St, Ste 203, Gate City, Virginia 24251 **Tel:** 1 276 386-7025.
Profile: WGAT-AM is a commercial station owned by Tri-Cities Broadcasting Corporation. The format of the station is gospel. WGAT-AM broadcasts to the Gate City, VA area at 1050 AM.
AM RADIO STATION

WGAU-AM 37064
Owner: Cox Media Group, Inc.
Editorial: 850 Bobbin Mill Rd, Athens, Georgia 30606-4208 **Tel:** 1 706 549-1340.
Email: wgau@southernbroadcasting.com
Web site: http://www.1340wgau.com
Profile: WGAU-AM is a commercial station owned by Cox Media Group, Inc. The format of the station is news and talk. WGAU-AM broadcasts to the Athens, GA area at 1340 AM.
AM RADIO STATION

WGAW-AM 217174
Owner: Steven Wendell
Editorial: 362 Green St, Gardner, Massachusetts 01440-1348 **Tel:** 1 978 632-1340.
Email: wgaw1340@wgaw1340.com
Web site: http://www.wgaw1340.com
Profile: WGAW-AM is a commercial station owned by Steven Wendell. The format of the station is news and talk. WGAW-AM broadcasts to the Gardener, MA area at 1340 AM.
AM RADIO STATION

WGBB-AM 37152
Owner: WGBB-AM, Inc
Editorial: 404 Route 109, West Babylon, New York 11704-6214 **Tel:** 1 516 623-1240.
Email: am1240wgbb@yahoo.com
Web site: http://am1240wgbb.com
Profile: WGBB-AM is a commercial station owned by WGBB-AM, Inc. The format of the station is variety. WGBB-AM broadcasts to the West Babylon, NY area at 1240 AM.
AM RADIO STATION

WGBF-AM 39181
Owner: Townsquare Media, LLC
Editorial: 117 SE 5th St, Evansville, Indiana 47708-1639 **Tel:** 1 812 425-4226.
Web site: http://www.newstalk1280.com
Profile: WGBF-AM is a commercial station owned by Townsquare Media, LLC. The format for the station is news, sports and talk. WGBF-AM broadcasts to the Evansville, IN area at 1280 AM.
AM RADIO STATION

WGBF-FM 46536
Owner: Townsquare Media, LLC
Editorial: 117 SE 5th St, Evansville, Indiana 47708-1639 **Tel:** 1 812 425-4226.
Web site: http://www.103gbfrocks.com
Profile: WGBF-FM is a commercial station owned by Townsquare Media, LLC. The format for the station is rock/album-oriented rock. WGBF-FM broadcasts to the Evansville, IN area at 103.1 AM.
FM RADIO STATION

WGBG-FM 45556
Owner: Adams Radio Group
Editorial: 20200 Dupont Blvd, Georgetown, Delaware 19947-3105 **Tel:** 1 302 856-2567.
Email: wgbg@bigclassicrock.com
Web site: http://www.bigclassicrock.com
Profile: WGBG-FM is a commercial station owned by Adams Radio Group. The format of the station is classic rock. WGBG-FM broadcasts to the Georgetown, DE area at 98.5 FM.
FM RADIO STATION

WGBL-FM 62660
Owner: Alpha Media
Editorial: 1909 E Pass Rd, Gulfport, Mississippi 39507-3779 **Tel:** 1 228 388-6000.
Web site: http://www.967thebull.com
Profile: WGBL-FM is a commercial station owned by Alpha Media. The format of the station is rhythmic oldies. WGBL-FM broadcasts to the Gulfport, MS area at a frequency of 96.7 FM.
FM RADIO STATION

WGBQ-FM 857239
Owner: American Family Association
Tel: 1 662 844-8888.
Web site: http://www.afa.net
Profile: WGBQ-FM is a non-commercial station owned by American Family Association. The format of the station is Christian teaching. WGBQ-FM broadcasts to the Lynchburg, TN area at a frequency of 91.9 FM.
FM RADIO STATION

WGBR-AM 37832
Owner: Curtis Media Group
Editorial: 2581 US Highway 70 W, Goldsboro, North Carolina 27530-9553 **Tel:** 1 919 736-1150.
Web site: http://curtismedia.com/wgbr
Profile: WGBR-AM is a commercial station owned by Curtis Media Group. The format of the station is Classic hits. WGBR-AM broadcasts to the greater Raleigh, NC area at 1150 AM.
AM RADIO STATION

WGBW-AM 612358
Owner: WTRW, Inc.
Editorial: 1414 16th St, Two Rivers, Wisconsin 54241-3031 **Tel:** 1 920 863-1234.
Profile: WGBW-AM is a commercial station owned by WTRW, Inc. The format of the station is oldies. WGBW-AM broadcasts to the Green Bay, WI area at 1590 AM.
AM RADIO STATION

WGCA-FM 41272
Owner: Great Commission Broadcasting Corp.
Editorial: 535 Maine St, Ste 10, Quincy, Illinois 62301 **Tel:** 1 217 224-9422.
Email: themix@wgca.org
Web site: http://www.wgca.org
Profile: WGCA-FM is a non-commercial station owned by Great Commission Broadcasting Corp. The format of the station is contemporary Christian. WGCA-FM broadcasts to the Quincy, IL, Hannibal, MO, Keokuk, IA area at 88.5 FM.
FM RADIO STATION

WGCF-FM 43926
Owner: American Family Association
Tel: 1 662 844-8888.
Web site: http://www.afa.net/Radio/
Profile: WGCF-FM is a non-commercial station owned by the American Family Association. The format of the station is religious. WGCF-FM broadcasts locally to the Paducah, KY area at a frequency of 89.3 FM.
FM RADIO STATION

WGCH-AM 35337
Owner: Forte Family Broadcasting
Editorial: 71 Lewis St, Greenwich, Connecticut 06830-5506 **Tel:** 1 203 869-1490.
Web site: http://www.wgch.com
Profile: WGCH-AM is a commercial station owned by Forte Family Broadcasting. The format of the station is business news and talk. WGCH-AM broadcasts to Greenwich, CT, and its surrounding areas at 1490 AM.
AM RADIO STATION

WGCI-FM 45177
Owner: iHeartMedia Inc.
Editorial: 233 N Michigan Ave Ste 2800, Chicago, Illinois 60601-5704 **Tel:** 1 312 540-2000.
Email: chicagolandcommunity@iheartmedia.com
Web site: http://wgci.iheart.com
Profile: WGCI-FM is a commercial station owned by iHeartMedia Inc. The format of the station is urban contemporary. WGCI-FM broadcasts to the Chicago area at 107.5 FM.
FM RADIO STATION

WGCL-AM 37854
Owner: Sarkes Tarzian Inc.
Editorial: 400 One City Ctr, Bloomington, Indiana 47404 **Tel:** 1 812 332-3366.
Email: comments@wgclradio.com
Web site: http://www.wgclradio.com
Profile: WGCL-AM is a commercial station owned by Sarkes Tarzian Inc. The format of the station is news, sports and talk. WGCL-AM broadcasts to the Bloomington, IN area at 1370 AM.
AM RADIO STATION

WGCM-AM 39324
Owner: Dowdy Broadcasting, Inc.
Editorial: 10250 Lorraine Rd, Gulfport, Mississippi 39503-6005 **Tel:** 1 228 896-5500.
Web site: http://www.wgcmam.com/
Profile: WGCM-AM is a commercial station owned by Dowdy Broadcasting, Inc. The format of the station is oldies. WGCM-AM broadcasts to the Gulfport, MS area at 1240 AM.
AM RADIO STATION

WGCM-FM 46685
Owner: Dowdy Broadcasting, Inc.
Editorial: 10250 Lorraine Rd, Gulfport, Mississippi 39503 **Tel:** 1 228 896-5500.
Web site: http://www.coast102.com
Profile: WGCM-FM is a commercial station owned by Dowdy Broadcasting, Inc. The format of the station is classic hits. WGCM-FM broadcasts to the Biloxi-Gulfport, MS area at 102.3 FM.
FM RADIO STATION

WGCO-FM 41082
Owner: Alpha Media
Editorial: 401 Mall Blvd Ste 101D, Savannah, Georgia 31406-4863 **Tel:** 1 912 351-9830.
Web site: http://www.983hank.com/
Profile: WGCO-FM is a commercial station owned by Alpha Media. The format of the station is classic country. WGCO-FM broadcasts to the Savannah, GA area at 98.3 FM.
FM RADIO STATION

WGCR-AM 35981
Owner: Anchor Baptist Church
Editorial: 3232 Hendersonville Hwy, Pisgah Forest, North Carolina 28768-7806 **Tel:** 1 828 884-9427.
Email: admin@wgcr.net
Web site: http://wgcr.net
Profile: WGCR-AM is a non-commercial station owned by Anchor Baptist Church. The format of the station is gospel and religious programming. WGCR-AM broadcasts to the Pisgah Forest, NC area at 720 AM.
AM RADIO STATION

WGCS-FM 40304
Owner: Goshen College Broadcasting
Editorial: 1700 S Main St, Goshen, Indiana 46526-4724 **Tel:** 1 574 535-7488.
Email: globe@goshen.edu
Web site: http://www.globeradio.org
Profile: WGCS-FM is a non-commercial college station owned by Goshen College Broadcasting. The format for the station is adult album alternative. WGCS-FM broadcasts to the South Bend, IN area at 91.1 FM.
FM RADIO STATION

WGCV-AM 35690
Owner: Glory Communications Inc.
Editorial: 2440 Millwood Ave, Columbia, South Carolina 29205-1128 **Tel:** 1 803 796-9533.
Email: traffic@wfmv.com
Web site: http://www.wgcv.net
Profile: WGCV-AM is a commercial station owned by Glory Communications Inc. The format of the station is gospel and talk. WGCV-AM broadcasts to the Columbia, SC area at 620 AM.
AM RADIO STATION

WGCY-FM 41390
Owner: F & G Broadcasting Inc.
Editorial: 607 S Sangamon Ave, Gibson City, Illinois 60936-1720 **Tel:** 1 217 784-8661.
Email: wgcyproduction@hotmail.com
Web site: http://www.wgcyradio.com
Profile: WGCY-FM is a commercial station owned by F&G Broadcasting Inc. The format of the station is easy listening. WGCY-FM broadcasts in the Gibson City, IL area at 106.3 FM.
FM RADIO STATION

WGDJ-AM 38141
Owner: Capital Broadcasting
Editorial: 51 S Pearl St Ste 13, Albany, New York 12207-1500 **Tel:** 1 518 813-4975.
Email: talk@talk1300.com
Web site: http://www.talk1300.com
Profile: WGDJ-AM is a commercial station owned by Capital Broadcasting. The format of the station is talk. WGDJ-AM broadcasts to the Albany, NY area at 1300 AM. All inquiries (press, sales, pitches, PSAs, etc) should be directed to the Operations Manager.
AM RADIO STATION

WGDN-AM 37834
Owner: Apple Broadcasting
Editorial: 3601 West Woods Rd, Gladwin, Michigan 48624 **Tel:** 1 989 426-1031.
Email: win@103country.com
Web site: http://www.103country.com
Profile: WGDN-AM is a commercial station owned by Apple Broadcasting. The format of the station is religious and Christian talk. WGDN-AM broadcasts to the Flint, MI area at 1350 AM.
AM RADIO STATION

WGDN-FM 45178
Owner: Apple Broadcasting
Editorial: 3601 Woods Rd, Gladwin, Michigan 48624-9410 **Tel:** 1 989 426-1031.
Email: win@103country.com
Web site: http://www.103country.com
Profile: WGDN-FM is a commercial station owned by Apple Broadcasting. The format of the station is country. WGDN-FM broadcasts to the Flint, MI area at 103.1 FM.
FM RADIO STATION

WGDR-FM 40217
Owner: Goddard College
Editorial: 123 Pitkin Rd, Plainfield, Vermont 05667-9432 **Tel:** 1 802 454-7367.
Email: wgdr@goddard.edu
Web site: http://www.wgdr.org
Profile: WGDR-FM is a non-commercial station owned by Goddard College. The format of the station is variety. WGDR-FM broadcasts to the Plainfield, VT area at a frequency of 91.5 FM.
FM RADIO STATION

WGEA-AM 37835
Owner: Shelley Broadcasting CO, Inc.
Editorial: 420 E Riverside Ave, Geneva, Alabama 36340-7548 **Tel:** 1 334 239-8987.
Web site: http://www.wgea.us
AM RADIO STATION

WGEE-FM 42142
Owner: Midwest Communications Inc.
Editorial: 1420 Bellevue St, Green Bay, Wisconsin 54311-5649 **Tel:** 1 920 435-3771.
Web site: http://935dukefm.com
Profile: WRQE-FM is a commercial station owned by Midwest Communications Inc. The format of the station is classic country. WRQE-FM broadcasts to the Appleton, WI area at 93.5 FM. It is also a Duke FM format.
FM RADIO STATION

WGEL-FM 40305
Owner: Bond Broadcasting
Editorial: 309 W Main St, Greenville, Illinois 62246
Tel: 1 618 664-3300.
Web site: http://www.wgel.com
Profile: WGEL-FM is a commercial station owned by Bond Broadcasting. The format of the station is country music. WGEL-FM broadcasts to Greenville, IL at 101.7 FM.
FM RADIO STATION

WGEM-AM 37837
Owner: Quincy Broadcasting Inc.
Editorial: 513 Hampshire St, Quincy, Illinois 62301
Tel: 1 217 228-6600.
Email: news@wgem.com
Web site: http://www.wgem.com
Profile: WGEM-AM is a commercial station owned by Quincy Broadcasting Inc. The format of the station is sports. WGEM-AM broadcasts to the Quincy, IL area at 1440 AM.
AM RADIO STATION

WGEM-FM 45179
Owner: Quincy Broadcasting Inc.
Editorial: 513 Hampshire St, Quincy, Illinois 62301
Tel: 1 217 228-6600.
Email: news@wgem.com
Web site: http://www.wgem.com
Profile: WGEM-FM is a commercial station owned by Quincy Broadcasting Inc. The format of the station is news and talk. WGEM-FM broadcasts to the Quincy, IL, Hannibal, MO, Keokuk, IA area at 105.1 FM.
FM RADIO STATION

WGER-FM
40306

Owner: Digity LLC
Editorial: 1795 Tittabawassee Rd, Saginaw, Michigan 48604-9431 **Tel:** 1 989 752-3456.
Web site: http://www.mix1063fm.com
Profile: WGER-FM is a commercial station owned by Digity LLC. The format for the station is hot adult contemporary. WGER-FM broadcasts to the Flint, MI area at 106.3 FM.
FM RADIO STATION

WGES-AM
36108

Owner: ZGS Communications
Editorial: 2005 Pan Am Cir, Ste 250, Tampa, Florida 33607-2359 **Tel:** 1 813 637-8000.
Email: info@genesis680.com
Web site: http://www.genesis680.com
Profile: WGES-AM is a commercial station owned by ZGS Communications. The format of the station is Hispanic contemporary Christian music. WGES-AM broadcasts to the Tampa, FL area at 680 AM.
AM RADIO STATION

WGET-AM
39012

Owner: Forever Media
Editorial: 1560 Fairfield Rd, Gettysburg, Pennsylvania 17325-7252 **Tel:** 1 717 637-3831.
Web site: http://www.foreveryork.com/espn-1320
Profile: WGET-AM is a commercial station owned by Forever Media. The format of the station is sports. WGET-AM broadcasts to the Gettysburg, PA area at 1320 AM.
AM RADIO STATION

WGEX-FM
139769

Owner: iHeartMedia Inc.
Editorial: 809 S Westover Blvd, Albany, Georgia 31707-4953 **Tel:** 1 229 439-9704.
Web site: http://power973.iheart.com
Profile: WGEX-FM is a commercial station owned by iHeartMedia Inc. The format of the station is Top 40/CHR. WGEX-FM broadcasts to the Albany, GA area at 97.3 FM.
FM RADIO STATION

WGEZ-AM
35338

Owner: Big Radio
Editorial: 622 Public Ave, Beloit, Wisconsin 53511-6341 **Tel:** 1 608 365-8865.
Email: wgezam@hotmail.com
Web site: http://www.ironcountry.fm
Profile: WGEZ-AM is a commercial station owned by Big Radio. The format of the station is oldies music. WGEZ-AM broadcasts to the Madison, WI area at 1490 AM.
AM RADIO STATION

WGFA-AM
37838

Owner: Martin(Richard & Margaret)
Editorial: 1973 E 1950 North Rd, Watseka, Illinois 60970-6009 **Tel:** 1 815 432-4955.
Email: info@wgfaradio.com
Web site: http://www.wgfaradio.com
Profile: WGFA-AM is a commercial station owned by Richard & Margaret Martin. The format of the station is news and talk. WGFA-AM broadcasts to the Watseka, IL area at 1360 AM.
AM RADIO STATION

WGFA-FM
45180

Owner: Martin(Richard & Margaret)
Editorial: 1973 E 1950 North Rd, Watseka, Illinois 60970-6009 **Tel:** 1 815 432-4955.
Email: 941fm@wgfaradio.com
Web site: http://www.wgfaradio.com
Profile: WGFA-FM is a commercial station owned by Richard & Margaret Martin. The format of the station is adult contemporary. WGFA-FM broadcasts in the Watseka, IL area at 94.1 FM.
FM RADIO STATION

WGFB-FM
42823

Owner: Mid-West Family Broadcasting
Editorial: 2830 Sandy Hollow Rd, Rockford, Illinois 61109-2369 **Tel:** 1 815 874-7861.
Web site: http://www.b103fm.com
Profile: WGFB-FM is a commercial station owned by Mid-West Family Broadcasting. The format of the station is adult contemporary music. WGFB-FM broadcasts in the Rockford, IL area at 103.1 FM.
FM RADIO STATION

WGFC-AM
35914

Owner: New Life Christian Communication
Editorial: 401 Shooting Creek Road SE, Floyd, Virginia 24091 **Tel:** 1 276 730-0708.
Email: broadcasting@nlcm.net
Web site: http://www.wgfcradio.com
Profile: WGFC-AM is a commercial station owned by New Life Christian Communication. The format of the station is gospel with a focus on Southern, Country, and Bluegrass sub-genres. WGFC-AM broadcasts to the Floyd, VA area at a frequency of 1030 AM.
AM RADIO STATION

WGFG-FM
42655

Owner: Miller Communications Inc.
Editorial: 200 Regional Pkwy Bldg C, Orangeburg, South Carolina 29118-9700 **Tel:** 1 803 536-1710.
Email: production@miller.fm
Web site: http://www.catcountry1053.com
Profile: WGFG-FM is a commercial station owned by Miller Communications Inc. The format of the station is contemporary country. WGFG-FM broadcasts to the Orangeburg, SC area at 105.3 FM.
FM RADIO STATION

WGFJ-FM
45527

Owner: Radio Training Network, Inc.
Editorial: 2420 Wade Hampton Blvd, Greenville, South Carolina 29615-1146 **Tel:** 1 864 292-6040.
Web site: http://www.hisradio.com
Profile: WGFJ-FM is a commercial station owned by Radio Training Network, Inc. The format of the station is contemporary Christian. WGFJ-FM broadcasts to the Greenwood, SC area at 94.1 FM.
FM RADIO STATION

WGFM-FM
45476

Owner: Northern Star Broadcasting LLC
Editorial: 1356 Mackinaw Ave, Cheboygan, Michigan 49721 **Tel:** 1 231 627-2341.
Web site: http://www.realrockradio.fm
Profile: WGFM-FM is a commercial station owned by Northern Star Broadcasting LLC. The format of the station is active rock, a mix of album oriented and classic rock. WGFM-FM broadcasts to Sheboygan, MI and surrounding areas at 105.1 FM.
FM RADIO STATION

WGFN-FM
43202

Owner: Northern Star Broadcasting LLC
Editorial: 1356 Mackinaw Ave, Cheboygan, Michigan 49721-1003 **Tel:** 1 231 627-2341.
Email: thebear@classicrockthebear.com
Web site: http://www.classicrockthebear.com
Profile: WGFN-FM is a commercial station owned by Northern Star Broadcasting LLC. The format of the station is classic rock. WGFN-FM broadcasts to the Cheboygan, MI area at 98.1 FM.
FM RADIO STATION

WGFP-AM
37059

Owner: Just Because Inc.
Editorial: 27 Douglas Rd, Webster, Massachusetts 1570 **Tel:** 1 508 943-9400.
Email: info@coolcountry940.com
Web site: http://www.coolcountry940.com
Profile: WGFP-AM is a commercial station owned by Just Because Inc. The format of the station is classic country. WGFP-AM broadcasts to the Worcester, MA area at 940 AM.
AM RADIO STATION

WGFR-FM
43698

Owner: Adirondack Community College
Editorial: Adirondack Community College, 640 Bay Road, Queensbury, New York 12804 **Tel:** 1 518 743-2311.
Web site: http://www.wgfr.org
Profile: WGFR-FM is a non-commercial college station owned by Adirondack Community College. The format of the station is college variety. WGFR-FM broadcasts to the Queensbury, NY area at 92.7 FM.
FM RADIO STATION

WGFS-AM
35339

Owner: Multicultural Radio Broadcasting Inc.
Editorial: 1151 Hendrick St SW, Covington, Georgia 30014 **Tel:** 1 770 786-1430.
Web site: http://www.mrbi.net
Profile: WGFS-AM is a commercial station owned by Multicultural Radio Broadcasting Inc. The format of the station is variety. WGFS-AM broadcasts in the Atlanta area at 1430 AM.
AM RADIO STATION

WGFT-AM
36820

Owner: Bernard Radio
Editorial: 20 W Federal St Ste T2, Youngstown, Ohio 44503-1420 **Tel:** 1 330 744-5115.
Web site: http://947-star.com/
Profile: WGFT-AM is a commercial station owned by Bernard Radio. The format of the station is talk. WGFT-AM broadcasts to the Youngstown, OH area at 1330 AM.
AM RADIO STATION

WGFX-FM
40307

Owner: Cumulus Media
Editorial: 10 Music Cir E, Nashville, Tennessee 37203-4338 **Tel:** 1 615 321-1067.
Web site: http://www.1045thezone.com
Profile: WGFX-FM is a commercial station owned by Cumulus Media. The format of the station is sports. WGFX-FM broadcasts to the Nashville, TN area at 104.5 FM.
FM RADIO STATION

WGFY-AM
39369

Owner: Charlotte Advent Media Corporation
Editorial: 920 N Sharon Amity Rd, Charlotte, North Carolina 28211-3138 **Tel:** 1 704 364-8973.
Web site: http://charlotteadventistchurch.com
Profile: WGFY-AM is a non-commercial station owned by Charlotte Advent Media Corporation. WGFY-AM broadcasts to the Charlotte, NC area at 1480 AM.
AM RADIO STATION

WGGA-AM
36153

Owner: Jacobs Media Corp.
Editorial: 1102 Thompson Bridge Rd, Gainesville, Georgia 30501-1775 **Tel:** 1 770 532-9921.
Email: news@jacobsmedia.net
Web site: http://www.wdun.com/1240-espn
Profile: WGGA-AM is a commercial station owned by Jacobs Media Corp. The format of the station is sports. WGGA-AM broadcasts to the Gainesville, GA area at 1240 AM.
AM RADIO STATION

WGGC-FM
40308

Owner: Skytower Communications Inc.
Editorial: 1727 US 31W Byp, Bowling Green, Kentucky 42101 **Tel:** 1 270 651-2142.
Web site: http://www.wggc.com
Profile: WGGC-FM is a commercial station owned by Skytower Communications Inc. The format of the station is contemporary country. WGGC-FM broadcasts to the Bowling Green, KY area at 95.1 FM.
FM RADIO STATION

WGGE-FM
46416

Owner: Burbach of WV, LLC
Editorial: 5 Rosemar Cir, Parkersburg, West Virginia 26104 **Tel:** 1 304 485-4565.
Email: requests@froggy99.net
Web site: http://www.froggy99.net
Profile: WGGE-FM is a commercial station owned by Burbach of WV, LLC. The format of the station is classic country. WGGE-FM broadcasts to the Parkersburg, WV area at 99.1 FM.
FM RADIO STATION

WGGG-AM
36749

Owner: Florida Sportstalk Inc.
Editorial: 343 NE 1st Ave, Ocala, Florida 34470
Tel: 1 352 732-2010.
Web site: http://www.espngo1.com
Profile: WGGG-AM is a commercial station owned by Florida Sportstalk Inc. The format of the station is sports. WGGG-AM broadcasts to the Ocala, FL area at 1230 AM.
AM RADIO STATION

WGGH-AM
35340

Owner: Fishback Media Inc.
Editorial: 1801 E Main St, Marion, Illinois 62959
Tel: 1 618 993-8102.
Email: wgghproduction@yahoo.com
Web site: http://www.wggh.net
Profile: WGGH-AM is a commercial station owned by Fishback Media Inc. The format of the station is news and talk. WGGH-AM broadcasts to the Marion, IL area at 1150 AM.
AM RADIO STATION

WGGI-FM
43136

Owner: Entercom Communications Corp.
Editorial: 305 Highway 315, Pittston, Pennsylvania 18640 **Tel:** 1 570 883-1111.
Web site: http://www.froggy101.com
Profile: WGGI-FM is a commercial station owned by Entercom Communications Corp. The format of the station is contemporary county. WGGI-FM broadcasts to the Pittston, PA area at 95.9 FM.
FM RADIO STATION

WGGL-FM
40309

Owner: Minnesota Public Radio
Editorial: 207 W Superior St, Ste 224, Duluth, Minnesota 55802 **Tel:** 1 218 722-9411.
Web site: http://minnesota.publicradio.org/radio/stations/wggl/
Profile: WGGL-FM is a non-commercial station owned by Minnesota Public Radio. The format for the station is classical. WGGL-FM broadcasts to the Marquette, MI area at 91.1 FM.
FM RADIO STATION

WGGN-FM
40310

Owner: Christian Faith Broadcast, Inc.
Editorial: 3809 Maple Ave, Castalia, Ohio 44824
Tel: 1 419 684-5311.
Email: fm97.7@cfbroadcast.net
Web site: http://www.fm977.net
Profile: WGGN-FM is a commercial station owned by Christian Faith Broadcast, Inc. The format of the station is religious and contemporary Christian. WGGN-FM broadcasts to the Castalia, OH area at 97.7 FM.
FM RADIO STATION

WGGO-AM
39169

Owner: Sound Communications, LLC
Editorial: 231 N Union St, Olean, New York 14760-2663 **Tel:** 1 716 945-1590.
Web site: http://wggosports.com
Profile: WGGO-AM is a commercial station owned by Sound Communications, LLC. The format of the station is Sports. WGGO-AM broadcasts to the Salamanca, NY area at 1590 AM.
AM RADIO STATION

WGGY-FM
42651

Owner: Entercom Communications Corp.
Editorial: 305 Highway 315, Pittston, Pennsylvania 18640 **Tel:** 1 570 883-1111.
Web site: http://www.froggy101.com
Profile: WGGY-FM is a commercial station owned by Entercom Communications Corp. The format of the station is contemporary country. WGGY-FM broadcasts to the Pittston, PA area at 101.3 FM.
FM RADIO STATION

WGH-AM
37839

Owner: Max Media
Editorial: 5589 Greenwich Rd Ste 200, Virginia Beach, Virginia 23462-6565 **Tel:** 1 757 671-1000.
Email: theboss@star1310.com
Web site: http://www.star1310.com
Profile: WGH-AM is a commercial station owned by Max Media. The format of WGH-AM is gospel, talk and religious programming. WGH-AM broadcasts to the Virginia Beach, VA area at 1310 AM.
AM RADIO STATION

WGHB-AM
35341

Owner: Pirate Media Group LLC
Editorial: 525 Evans St, Greenville, North Carolina 27858-2311 **Tel:** 1 252 317-1250.
Web site: http://www.pirateradio1250.com
Profile: WGHB-AM is a commercial station owned by Pirate Media Group LLC. The format of the station is talk and sports. WGHB-AM broadcasts to the Greenville, NC area at 1250 AM.
AM RADIO STATION

WGHC-AM
39173

Owner: Georgia-Carolina Radiocasting Companies LLC
Editorial: 18 Radio Lane, Clayton, Georgia 30525
Tel: 1 706 782-4251.
Email: rabunradio@windstream.net
Web site: http://sky104.com
Profile: WGHC-AM is a commercial station owned by Georgia-Carolina Radiocasting Companies LLC. The format of the station is adult standards and news and talk. WGHC-AM broadcasts to the Clayton, GA area at 1400 AM.
AM RADIO STATION

WGH-FM
45181

Owner: Max Media
Editorial: 5589 Greenwich Rd, Ste 200, Virginia Beach, Virginia 23462 **Tel:** 1 757 671-1000.
Web site: http://www.eagle97.com
Profile: WGH-FM is a commercial station owned by Max Media. The format of the station is contemporary country music. WGH-FM broadcasts to the Virginia Beach, VA area at 97.3 FM.
FM RADIO STATION

WGHJ-FM
154941

Owner: Padner Group, LLC
Editorial: 126 Memory Plz, Whiteville, North Carolina 28472-2640 **Tel:** 1 910 642-2005.
Web site: http://www.coolbeach1053.com
Profile: WGHJ-FM is a commercial station owned by Padner Group, LLC. The format of the station is religious teaching. WGHJ-FM broadcasts to the Wilmington, NC area at 105.3 FM.
FM RADIO STATION

WGHL-FM
44540

Owner: Alpha Media
Editorial: 520 S 4th St Fl 2, Louisville, Kentucky 40202-2500 **Tel:** 1 502 625-1220.
Email: easyrock1051@gmail.com
Web site: http://www.oldschool1051.com
Profile: WGHL-FM is a commercial station owned by Alpha Media. The format of the station soft adult contemporary. WGHL-FM broadcasts to the Louisville, KY area at 105.1 FM.
FM RADIO STATION

WGHM-AM
35336

Owner: Absolute Broadcasting, LLC
Editorial: 149 Main St, Ste 210, Nashua, New Hampshire 03060-2725 **Tel:** 1 603 880-9001.
Email: info@wgamradio.com
Web site: http://www.wgamradio.com
Profile: WGHM-AM is a commercial station owned by Absolute Broadcasting, LLC. The format of the station is sports. WGHM-AM broadcasts to the Nashua, NH at 900 AM.
AM RADIO STATION

WGHN-AM
37840

Owner: WGHN Inc.
Editorial: 1 S Harbor Dr, Grand Haven, Michigan 49417 **Tel:** 1 616 842-8110.
Email: news@wghn.com
Web site: http://www.sportsradio1370.com
Profile: WGHN-AM is a commercial station owned by WGHN Inc. The format of the station is sports. WGHN-AM broadcasts to the Grand Rapids, MI area at 1370 AM.
AM RADIO STATION

WGHN-FM
45182

Owner: WGHN Inc.
Editorial: 1 S Harbor Dr, Grand Haven, Michigan 49417 **Tel:** 1 616 842-8110.
Email: news@wghn.com
Web site: http://www.wghn.com
Profile: WGHN-FM is a commercial station owned by WGHN Inc. The format of the station is adult contemporary music. WGHN-FM broadcasts to the Grand Rapids, MI area at 92.1 FM.
FM RADIO STATION

WGHQ-AM
37841

Owner: Pamal Broadcasting Ltd.
Editorial: 715 Route 52, Beacon, New York 12508-1047 **Tel:** 1 845 838-6000.
Email: kcr921@gmail.com
Web site: http://www.hvradionet.com
Profile: WGHQ-AM is a commercial station owned by the Pamal Broadcasting Ltd. The format of the station is classic country. WGHQ-AM broadcasts to the Poughkeepsie, NY area at 920 AM.
AM RADIO STATION

WGHR-FM
46904

Owner: WGUL-FM, Inc.
Editorial: 13825 US Highway 19, Hudson, Florida 34667-1193 **Tel:** 1 727 697-1063.
Email: publicservice@greatesthits106.com
Web site: http://www.greatesthits106.com
Profile: WGHR-FM is non-commercial station owned by WGUL-FM, Inc. The format of the station is oldies. WGHR-FM broadcasts to the Palm Harbor, FL area at 106.3 FM.
FM RADIO STATION

WGHT-AM 35439
Owner: Mariana Broadcasting Inc.
Editorial: 1878 Lincoln Ave, Pompton Lakes, New Jersey 07442-1611 **Tel:** 1 973 839-1500.
Email: news@ghtradio.com
Web site: http://www.wghtradio.com
Profile: WGHT-AM is a commercial radio owned by Mariana Broadcasting Inc. The format of the station is oldies music, news and talk. WGHT-AM broadcasts in the Pompton Lakes, NJ, area at 1500 AM.
AM RADIO STATION

WGIE-FM 45595
Owner: Burbach of WV, LLC
Editorial: 1489 Locust Ave, Fairmont, West Virginia 26554 **Tel:** 1 304 363-8888.
Web site: http://www.froggycountry.net
Profile: WGIE-FM is a commercial station owned by Burbach of WV, LLC. The format of the station is contemporary country. WGIE-FM broadcasts to the Fairmont, WV area at a frequency of 92.7 FM.
FM RADIO STATION

WGIG-AM 39301
Owner: iHeartMedia Inc.
Editorial: 3833 US Highway 82, Brunswick, Georgia 31523-7735 **Tel:** 1 912 267-1025.
Email: scottryfun@gmail.com
Web site: http://1440wgig.net
Profile: WGIG-AM is a commercial station owned by iHeartMedia Inc. The format of the station is news, talk and sports. WGIG-AM broadcasts to the Brunswick, GA region at 1440 AM.
AM RADIO STATION

WGIL-AM 39238
Owner: Galesburg Broadcasting Co.
Editorial: 154 E Simmons St, Galesburg, Illinois 61401-4658 **Tel:** 1 309 342-9194.
Email: news@wgil.com
Web site: http://www.wgil.com
Profile: WGIL-AM is a commercial station owned by Galesburg Broadcasting Co. The format of the station is news, talk and sports. WGIL-AM broadcasts to the Galesburg, IL area at 1400 AM.
AM RADIO STATION

WGIN-AM 36173
Owner: Saga Communications
Editorial: 420 Western Ave, South Portland, Maine 04106-1704 **Tel:** 1 207 774-4561.
Web site: http://www.560wgan.com
Profile: WGIN-AM is a commercial station owned by Saga Communications. The format of the station is news and talk. WGIN-AM broadcasts to South Portland, ME area at 1400 AM.
AM RADIO STATION

WGIR-AM 37842
Owner: iHeartMedia Inc.
Editorial: 70 Foundry St Unit 300, Manchester, New Hampshire 03102-3787 **Tel:** 1 603 625-6915.
Web site: http://nhnewsnetwork610.iheart.com
Profile: WGIR-AM is a commercial station owned by iHeartMedia Inc. The format of the station is news and talk. WGIR-AM broadcasts to the Manchester, NH area at 610 AM.
AM RADIO STATION

WGIR-FM 46853
Owner: iHeartMedia Inc
Editorial: 70 Foundry St Unit 300, Manchester, New Hampshire 03102-3787 **Tel:** 1 603 625-6915.
Web site: http://www.rock101fm.com
Profile: WGIR-FM is a commercial station owned by iHeartMedia Inc. The format of the station is rock music. WGIR-FM broadcasts to the Manchester, NH area at 101.1 FM.
FM RADIO STATION

WGIV-AM 35499
Owner: Neely(Frank)
Editorial: 301 S McDowell St Ste 814, Charlotte, North Carolina 28204-2649 **Tel:** 1 980 236-8611.
Web site: http://www.streetz1033.com
Profile: WGIV-AM is a commercial station owned by Frank Neely. The format of the station is urban contemporary. WGIV-AM broadcasts to the Gastonia, NC area at 1370 AM.
AM RADIO STATION

WGJK-AM 39462
Owner: Woman's World Broadcasting, Inc.
Editorial: 20 John Davenport Dr NW, Rome, Georgia 30165-2536 **Tel:** 1 706 291-9496.
Web site: http://www.995thejock.com
Profile: The Jock is Northwest Georgia's sports authority with coverage of local teams and ESPN Radio programming. Airing on 99.5 FM and 1360 AM. The station is currently owned by Woman's World and is in an LMA through Rome Radio Partners, LLC.
AM RADIO STATION

WGJU-FM 43233
Owner: Baraga Broadcasting, Inc.
Editorial: 7119 M 68, Indian River, Michigan 49749-9472 **Tel:** 1 231 238-0811.
Web site: http://www.baragabroadcasting.com
Profile: WGJU-FM is a non-commercial station owned by Baraga Broadcasting, Inc.. The format of the station is Catholic programming. WGJU-FM broadcasts to the East Tawas and Oscoda areas in Michigan at 91.3 FM.
FM RADIO STATION

WGKA-AM 35343
Owner: Salem Media Group, Inc.
Editorial: 2970 Peachtree Rd NW Ste 700, Atlanta, Georgia 30305-4919 **Tel:** 1 404 995-7300.
Web site: http://am920theanswer.com
Profile: WGKA-AM is a commercial station owned by Salem Media Group, Inc. The format of the station is news and talk. WGKA-AM broadcasts to the Atlanta area at 920 AM.
AM RADIO STATION

WGKC-FM 41710
Owner: S.J. Broadcasting Inc.
Editorial: 2702 Boulder Rd, Urbana, Illinois 61802-6996 **Tel:** 1 217 367-1195.
Web site: http://www.wgkc.net
Profile: WGKC-FM is a commercial station owned by S.J. Broadcasting Inc. The format of the station is contemporary country. WGKC-FM broadcasts to the Champaign, IL, area at 105.9 FM.
FM RADIO STATION

WGKL-FM 44532
Owner: Radio Results Network
Editorial: 524 Ludington St, Ste 300, Escanaba, Michigan 49829 **Tel:** 1 906 789-9700.
Email: rrnnews@radioresultsnetwork.com
Web site: http://www.radioresultsnetwork.com/wgkl/
FM RADIO STATION

WGKS-FM 45815
Owner: L.M. Communications Inc.
Editorial: 401 W Main St Ste 301, Lexington, Kentucky 40507-1640 **Tel:** 1 859 233-1515.
Web site: http://www.969kissfm.com
Profile: WGKS-FM is a commercial station owned by L.M. Communications Inc. The format of the station is adult contemporary. WGKS-FM broadcasts locally to the Lexington, KY area at a frequency of 96.9 FM.
FM RADIO STATION

WGKX-FM 40312
Owner: Cumulus Media Inc.
Editorial: 5629 Murray Rd, Memphis, Tennessee 38119 **Tel:** 1 901 682-1106.
Web site: http://www.kix106.com
Profile: WGKX-FM is a commercial station owned by Cumulus Media Inc. The station's format is contemporary country music. WGKX-FM broadcasts to the Memphis, TN area at 105.9 FM.
FM RADIO STATION

WGKY-FM 41832
Owner: Withers Broadcasting of Paducah, LLC
Editorial: 1700 N 8th St, Paducah, Kentucky 42001-1752 **Tel:** 1 270 335-3696.
Email: paducabtradio@withersradio.net
Web site: http://www.959wgky.com
Profile: WGKY-FM is a commercial station owned by Withers Broadcasting of Paducah, LLC. The format of the station is oldies music. WGKY-FM broadcasts to the Paducah, KY, Cape Girardeau, MO, and Harrisburg, IL communities at 95.9 FM.
FM RADIO STATION

WGL-AM 39087
Owner: Adams Radio Group
Editorial: 2000 Lower Huntington Rd, Fort Wayne, Indiana 46819-1233 **Tel:** 1 260 747-1511.
Web site: http://1250foxsports.com/
Profile: WGL-AM is a commercial station owned by Adams Radio Group. The format of the station is sports. WGL-AM broadcasts to the Fort Wayne, IN area at 1250 AM.
AM RADIO STATION

WGLB-AM 37056
Owner: WGLB LLC
Editorial: 5181 N 35th St, Milwaukee, Wisconsin 53209-5399 **Tel:** 1 414 527-4365.
Email: wglb@wglbam1560.com
Web site: http://www.wglbam1560.com
Profile: WGLB-AM is a commercial station owned by WGLB LLC. The format of the station is gospel music. WGLB-AM broadcasts to the Milwaukee area at 1560 AM.
AM RADIO STATION

WGLC-FM 43790
Owner: Studstill Media
Editorial: 3905 Progress Blvd, Peru, Illinois 61354-1121 **Tel:** 1 815 224-2100.
Email: wglc@theradiogroup.net
Web site: http://www.wglc.net
Profile: WGLC-FM is a commercial station owned by Mendota Broadcasting. The format of the station is country. WGLC-FM broadcasts to the Peru, IL area at 100.1 FM.
FM RADIO STATION

WGLD-AM 37131
Owner: Cumulus Media Inc.
Editorial: 5989 Susquehanna Plaza Drive, York, Pennsylvania 17406 **Tel:** 1 717 764-1155.
Web site: http://www.sportsradio1440.com
Profile: WGLD-AM is a commercial station owned by Cumulus Media Inc. The format of the station is sports. WGLD-AM broadcasts to the York, PA area at 1440 AM.
AM RADIO STATION

WGLF-FM 43490
Owner: Cumulus Media Inc.
Editorial: 3411 W Tharpe St, Tallahassee, Florida 32303-1139 **Tel:** 1 850 201-3000.
Web site: http://www.gulf104.com
Profile: WGLF-FM is a commercial station owned by Cumulus Media Inc. The format of the station is classic hits. WGLF-FM broadcasts to the Tallahassee, FL area at 104.1 FM.
FM RADIO STATION

WGL-FM 152248
Owner: Calvary Radio Network
Tel: 1 219 548-5800.
Email: info@calvaryradionetwork.com
Web site: http://www.calvaryradionetwork.com
Profile: WGL-FM is a commercial station owned by Calvary Radio Network. WGL-FM broadcasts to the Fort Wayne, IN area at 102.9 FM.
FM RADIO STATION

WGLI-FM Radio 137109
Owner: Keweenaw Bay Indian Community
Editorial: 805 US41 South, Ste B, Baraga, Michigan 49908 **Tel:** 1 906 353-9287.
Email: eagleadmin@up.net
Web site: http://www.keepitintheup.com
Profile: WGLI-FM is a commercial station owned by the Keweenaw Bay Indian Community. The format of the station is rock music. WGLI-FM broadcasts to the Hancock, MI area at a frequency of 98.7 FM.
FM RADIO STATION

WGLM-AM 38127
Owner: Packer Radio Greenville, Inc.
Editorial: 9181 SW Greenville Rd, Greenville, Michigan 48838-9404 **Tel:** 1 616 754-1063.
Email: office@m1063.com
Web site: http://www.m1063.com
Profile: WGLM-AM is a commercial station owned by Packer Radio Greenville, Inc. The format of the station is classic country music. WGLM-AM broadcasts to the Greenville, MI area at 1380 AM.
AM RADIO STATION

WGLM-FM 46501
Owner: Packer Radio Greenville, Inc.
Editorial: 9181 S Greenville Rd, Greenville, Michigan 48838-9404 **Tel:** 1 616 754-1063.
Email: office@m1063.com
Web site: http://www.m1063.com
FM RADIO STATION

WGLO-FM 46096
Owner: Cumulus Media Inc.
Editorial: 120 Eaton St, Peoria, Illinois 61603-4217 **Tel:** 1 309 676-5000.
Web site: http://www.955glo.com
Profile: WGLO-FM is a commercial station owned by Cumulus Media Inc. The format of the station is classic rock. WGLO-FM broadcasts to the Peoria, IL area at 95.5 FM.
FM RADIO STATION

WGLQ-FM 45725
Owner: Radio Results Network
Editorial: 524 Ludington St, Ste 300, Escanaba, Michigan 49829 **Tel:** 1 906 789-9700.
Web site: http://www.wglqradio.com/
FM RADIO STATION

WGLR-AM 37843
Owner: Queen B Radio of Wisconsin
Editorial: 51 Means Dr, Platteville, Wisconsin 53818-3829 **Tel:** 1 608 349-2000.
Email: music@queenbradio.com
Web site: http://www.wglr.com
Profile: WGLR-AM is a commercial station owned by Queen B Radio of Wisconsin. The format for the station is sports. WGLR-AM broadcasts to the Platteville, WI area at 1280 AM.
AM RADIO STATION

WGLR-FM 45035
Owner: Queen B Radio of Wisconsin and WISC-TV3
Editorial: 51 Means Dr, Platteville, Wisconsin 53818-3829 **Tel:** 1 608 349-2000.
Email: music@queenbradio.com
Web site: http://www.wglr.com
Profile: WGLR-FM is a commercial station owned by Queen B Radio of Wisconsin. The format for the station is country. WGLR-FM broadcasts to the Madison, WI area at 97.7 FM.
FM RADIO STATION

WGLX-FM 45623
Owner: NRG Media LLC
Editorial: 2301 Plover Rd, Plover, Wisconsin 54467 **Tel:** 1 866 967-9983.
Web site: http://www.wglx.com
Profile: WGLX-FM is a commercial station owned by NRG Media LLC. The format of the station is rock music. WGLX-FM broadcasts to the Wausau, WI, area at 103.3 FM.
FM RADIO STATION

WGLY-FM 43747
Owner: Christian Ministries Inc.
Editorial: 140 Main St, Essex Junction, Vermont 05452-3208 **Tel:** 1 866 878-8885.
Email: mailroom@thelightradio.net
Web site: http://www.thelightradio.net
Profile: WGLY-FM is a non-commercial station owned by Christian Ministries Inc. The format of the station is contemporary Christian music and religious programming. WGLY-FM broadcasts to the Essex Junction, VT area at 91.5 FM.
FM RADIO STATION

WGMD-FM 40320
Owner: Resort Broadcasting
Editorial: 31549 Dutton Ln, Lewes, Delaware 19958-4512 **Tel:** 1 302 945-2050.
Email: news@wgmd.com
Web site: http://www.wgmd.com
Profile: WGMD-FM is a commercial station owned by Resort Broadcasting. The format of the station is news and talk programming. WGMD-AM broadcasts to the Lewes, DE area at 92.7 FM.
FM RADIO STATION

WGMF-AM 38646
Owner: GEOS Communications
Editorial: 54 Wilmar Dr, Tunkhannock, Pennsylvania 18657-6628 **Tel:** 1 570 836-4200.
Email: comments@gem104.com
Web site: http://www.gem104.com
Profile: WGMF-AM is a commercial station owned by GEOS Communications. The format for the station is classic hits. WGMF-AM broadcasts to the Tunkhannock, PA area at 1460 AM.
AM RADIO STATION

WGMG-FM 42645
Owner: Cox Media Group, Inc.
Editorial: 1010 Tower Pl, Watkinsville, Georgia 30677-7752 **Tel:** 1 706 549-6222.
Email: psaathens@coxinc.com
Web site: http://www.magic1021fm.com
Profile: WGMG-FM is a commercial station owned by Cox Media Group, Inc. The format of the station is hot adult contemporary music. WGMG-FM broadcasts to the Crawford, GA area at 102.1 FM.
FM RADIO STATION

WGMI-AM 35665
Owner: Garner Ministries Inc.
Editorial: 613 Tallapoosa St W, Bremen, Georgia 30110-1838 **Tel:** 1 770 537-0840.
Email: wgmifax@yahoo.com
Web site: http://www.1440thetrain.com
Profile: WGMI-AM is a commercial station owned by Garner Ministries Inc. The format of the station is classic hits. WGMI-AM broadcasts to the Bremen, GA area at 1440 AM.
AM RADIO STATION

WGMK-FM 40321
Owner: Flint Media
Editorial: 521 S Scott St, Bainbridge, Georgia 39819-4101 **Tel:** 1 229 246-1960.
Web site: http://sowegalive.com
Profile: WGMK-FM is a commercial station owned by Flint Media. The format of the station is oldies music with a classic rock focus. WGMK-FM broadcasts to the Bainbridge, GA area at 106.3 FM.
FM RADIO STATION

WGML-AM 36175
Owner: Powerhouse Deliverance Church Inc.
Editorial: 308 Rolland St, Hinesville, Georgia 31313-3104 **Tel:** 1 912 368-3399.
Profile: WGML-AM is a non-commercial station owned by Powerhouse Deliverance Church Inc. The format of the station is gospel. WGML-AM broadcasts to the Savannah, GA area at 990 AM.
AM RADIO STATION

WGMM-FM 46880
Owner: Sound Communications, LLC
Editorial: 21 E Market St Ste 101, Corning, New York 14830-2650 **Tel:** 1 607 937-8181.
Email: audioonly@stny.rr.com
Web site: http://www.987gemfm.com
Profile: WGMM-FM is a commercial station owned by Sound Communications, LLC. The format of the station is Classic Hits music. WGMM-FM broadcasts to the Corning, NY area on 98.7 FM.
FM RADIO STATION

WGMN-AM 38699
Owner: 3 Daughters Media, Inc.
Editorial: 1035 Avalon Dr, Forest, Virginia 24551-2970 **Tel:** 1 434 534-6100.
Email: wblt@inbox.com
Web site: http://www.espninva.com
Profile: WGMN-AM is a commercial station owned by 3 Daughters Media, Inc. The format of the station is sports. WGMN-AM broadcasts to the Roanoke, VA area at 1240 AM.
AM RADIO STATION

WGMO-FM 45184
Owner: Zoe Communications Inc.
Editorial: 345 Highway 63 S, Shell Lake, Wisconsin 54871 **Tel:** 1 715 468-9500.
Email: spots@95gmo.com
Web site: http://www.95gmo.com
Profile: WGMO-FM is a commercial station owned by Zoe Communications Inc. The format of the station is classic rock. WGMO-FM broadcasts in the Shell Lake, WI area at 95.3 FM.
FM RADIO STATION

WGMP-AM 39108
Owner: Bluewater Broadcasting Co. LLC
Editorial: 4101 Wall St Ste A, Montgomery, Alabama 36106-3724 **Tel:** 1 334 244-0961.
Email: thegump@bluewaterbroadcasting.com
Web site: http://www.1049thegump.com
Profile: WGMP-AM is a commercial station owned by Bluewater Broadcasting Co. LLC. The format of the station is rock alternative. WGMP-AM broadcasts in the Montgomery, AL area at 1170 AM.
AM RADIO STATION

WGMT-FM 41284
Owner: Vermont Broadcast Associates Inc.
Editorial: 10 Church St, Lyndonville, Vermont 5851
Tel: 1 802 626-9800.
Email: magic977@gmail.com
Web site: http://www.magic977.com
Profile: WGMT-FM is a commercial station owned by Vermont Broadcast Associates Inc. The format of the station is hot adult contemporary music. WGMT-FM broadcasts to the Lyndonville, VT area at 97.7 FM.
FM RADIO STATION

WGMW-FM 43799
Owner: RDA Broadcast Holdings, LLC
Editorial: 1306 E Silver Springs Blvd, Ocala, Florida 34470-6800 **Tel:** 1 352 414-5230.
Email: info@gold99fm.com
Web site: http://www.gold99fm.com
Profile: WGMW-FM is a commercial station owned by RDA Broadcast Holdings, LLC. The format of the station is adult standards. WGMW-FM broadcasts to the Gainesville, FL area at 99.5 FM.
FM RADIO STATION

WGMX-FM 46361
Owner: The Great Marathon Radio Company
Web site: http://www.themixofoldies.com
Profile: WGMX-FM is a commercial station owned by The Great Marathon Radio Company. The format of the station is oldies. WGMX-FM broadcasts to the Marathon, FL area at 94.3 FM.
FM RADIO STATION

WGMY-FM 42036
Owner: iHeartMedia Inc.
Editorial: 325 John Knox Rd Bldg G, Tallahassee, Florida 32303-4113 **Tel:** 1 850 422-3107.
Web site: http://www.1071hitmusicnow.com/main.html
Profile: WGMY-FM is a commercial station owned by iHeartMedia Inc. The format is contemporary hit radio. The station airs in the Tallahassee, FL area at 107.1.
FM RADIO STATION

WGMZ-FM 42122
Owner: iHeartMedia Inc.
Editorial: 304 S 4th St, Gadsden, Alabama 35901-5213 **Tel:** 1 256 549-0931.
Web site: http://www.wgmz.com
Profile: WGMZ-FM is a commercial station owned by iHeartMedia Inc. The format of the station is classic hits. WGMZ-FM broadcasts to the Birmingham, Al area at 93.1 FM.
FM RADIO STATION

WGNA-FM 46059
Owner: Townsquare Media, LLC
Editorial: 1241 Kings Rd, Schenectady, New York 12303-2811 **Tel:** 1 518 881-1515.
Web site: http://www.wgna.com
Profile: WGNA-FM is a commercial station owned by Townsquare Media, LLC. The format of the station is contemporary country. WGNA-FM broadcasts in the Albany, NY area at 107.7 FM.
FM RADIO STATION

WGN-AM 35344
Owner: Tribune Broadcasting Co.
Editorial: 435 N Michigan Ave Ste 720, Chicago, Illinois 60611-4066 **Tel:** 1 312 222-4700.
Email: tips@wgnradio.com
Web site: http://wgnradio.com
Profile: WGN-AM is a commercial station owned by Tribune Broadcasting Co. The format of the station is news and talk. WGN-AM broadcasts to the Chicago area at 720AM.
AM RADIO STATION

WGNB-FM 40953
Owner: Moody Bible Institute
Editorial: 3764 84th Ave, Zeeland, Michigan 49464-9706 **Tel:** 1 616 772-7300.
Email: wgnb@moody.edu
Web site: http://www.moodyradiowestmichigan.fm
Profile: WGNB-FM is a non-commercial station owned by Moody Bible Institute. The format of the station is religious programming and Christian music. WGNB-FM broadcasts to the Zeeland, MI area at 89.3 FM.
FM RADIO STATION

WGNC-AM 35345
Owner: Neisler (Scott)
Editorial: 1366 Startown Rd, Lincolnton, North Carolina 28092-8038 **Tel:** 1 704 868-8222.
Email: 1450am@gmail.com
Web site: http://www.wgnc.net
Profile: WGNC-AM is a commercial station owned by Scott Neisler. The format of the station is news, talk and sports. WGNC-AM broadcasts to the Shelby, NC area at 1450 AM.
AM RADIO STATION

WGNE-FM 40558
Owner: Renda Broadcasting
Editorial: 6440 Atlantic Blvd, Jacksonville, Florida 32211 **Tel:** 1 904 727-9696.
Web site: http://www.999gatorcountry.com
Profile: WGNE-FM is a commercial station owned by Renda Broadcasting. The format of the station is contemporary country. WGNE-FM broadcasts to the Jacksonville, FL area at 99.9 FM.
FM RADIO STATION

WGNG-FM 44552
Owner: Team Broadcasting
Editorial: 503 Ione St, Greenwood, Mississippi 38930-3725 **Tel:** 1 662 453-1646.
Email: wgnlbooth@bellsouth.net
Web site: http://104wgnl.com
Profile: WGNG-FM is a commercial station owned by Team Broadcasting. The format of the station is urban contemporary. WGNG-FM broadcasts to the Greenwood, MS area at 106.3 FM.
FM RADIO STATION

WGNI-FM 42028
Owner: Cumulus Media Inc.
Editorial: 3233 Burnt Mill Dr Ste 4, Wilmington, North Carolina 28403-2676 **Tel:** 1 910 763-9977.
Email: gmail@wgni.com
Web site: http://www.wgni.com
Profile: WGNI-FM is a commercial station owned by Cumulus Media Inc. The format of the station is adult contemporary. WGNI-FM broadcasts to the Wilmington, NC area at 102.7 FM.
FM RADIO STATION

WGNJ-FM 44476
Owner: Great News Radio Inc.
Editorial: 2421 N 1450 East Rd, White Heath, Illinois 61884 **Tel:** 1 217 897-6333.
Email: staff@greatnewsradio.org
Web site: http://www.greatnewsradio.org
Profile: WGNJ-FM is a commercial station owned by Great News Radio Inc. The format of the station is religious programming. WGNJ-FM broadcasts to the White Heath, IL area at 89.3 FM.
FM RADIO STATION

WGNK-FM 44335
Owner: Genesis Broadcasting Network Corp.
Editorial: 19620 Pines Blvd Ste 114, Pembroke Pines, Florida 33029-1303 **Tel:** 1 954 885-7200.
Email: info@lanuevafm.net
Web site: http://lanuevafm.net/cms
Profile: WGNK-FM is a non-commercial station owned by Genesis Broadcasting Network Corp. The format of the station is Spanish Contemporary Christian music programming. WGNK-FM broadcasts to the Miami, FL area at 88.3 FM.
FM RADIO STATION

WGNL-FM 41270
Owner: Team Broadcasting
Editorial: 503 Ione St, Greenwood, Mississippi 38930-3725 **Tel:** 1 662 453-1646.
Email: wgnlbooth@bellsouth.net
Web site: http://104wgnl.com
Profile: WGNL-FM is a commercial station owned by Team Broadcasting. The format of the station is urban adult contemporary music. WGNL-FM broadcasts to the Greenwood, MS area at 104.3 FM.
FM RADIO STATION

WGNR-AM 37886
Owner: Moody Bible Institute
Editorial: 1920 W 53rd St, Anderson, Indiana 46013-1110 **Tel:** 1 765 642-2750.
Email: wgnr@moody.edu
Web site: http://www.moodyradioindiana.fm
Profile: WGNR-AM is a non-commercial station owned by Moody Bible Institute. The format of the station is religious. WGNR-AM broadcasts to the Indianapolis, IN area at 1470 AM.
AM RADIO STATION

WGNR-FM 45340
Owner: Moody Bible Institute
Editorial: 1920 W 53rd St, Anderson, Indiana 46013-1110 **Tel:** 1 765 642-2750.
Email: wgnrnews@moody.edu
Web site: http://www.moodyradioindiana.fm
Profile: WGNR-FM is a commercial radio station owned by Moody Bible Institute. The format of the station is religious. WGNR-FM broadcasts to the Indianapolis area at 97.9 FM.
FM RADIO STATION

WGNS-AM 35347
Owner: Rutherford Group Inc.
Editorial: 306 S Church St, Murfreesboro, Tennessee 37130-3732 **Tel:** 1 615 893-5373.
Web site: http://www.wgnsradio.com
Profile: WGNS-AM is a commercial station owned by Rutherford Group Inc. The format of the station is news, sports and talk. WGNS-AM broadcasts in the Murfreesboro, TN area at 1450 AM.
AM RADIO STATION

WGNU-AM 35348
Owner: Radio Property Ventures, LLC
Editorial: 5615 Pershing Ave Ste 12, Saint Louis, Missouri 63112-1757 **Tel:** 1 314 454-0400.
Web site: http://wgnu920am.com/
Profile: WGNU-AM is a commercial station owned by Radio Property Ventures, LLC. The format of the station is sports and talk. WGNU-AM broadcasts to the St. Louis area at 920 AM.
AM RADIO STATION

WGNV-FM 41294
Owner: Evangel Ministries, Inc.
Editorial: 10945 Country Highway N, Milladore, Wisconsin 54454 **Tel:** 1 715 457-2988.
Email: wgnv@thefamily.net
Web site: http://www.thefamily.net
Profile: WGNV-FM is a non-commercial station owned by Evangel Ministries, Inc. The format of the station is adult contemporary. WGNV-FM broadcasts to the Milladore, WI area at 88.5 FM.
FM RADIO STATION

WGNY-FM 37845
Owner: Sunrise Broadcasting
Editorial: 661 Little Britain Rd, New Windsor, New York 12553-6150 **Tel:** 1 845 561-2131.
Email: foxhelpdesk@foxradio.net
Web site: http://foxradio.us/index.php/on-air/wgny-fm-98-9
Profile: WGNY-FM is a commercial station owned by Sunrise Broadcasting. The format of the station is Oldies Music. WGNY-FM broadcasts to the Poughkeepsie, NY area at 98.9 and simulcasts with WGNY-AM.
FM RADIO STATION

WGNZ-AM 35984
Owner: L & D Broadcasting Inc.
Editorial: 8010 N Main St, Dayton, Ohio 45415
Tel: 1 937 454-9000.
Web site: http://www.wgnz.com
Profile: WGNZ-AM is a commercial station owned by L & D Broadcasting Inc. The format of the station is religious programming and gospel music. WGNZ-AM broadcasts to the Dayton, OH area at 1110 AM.
AM RADIO STATION

WGOC-AM 37977
Owner: Cumulus Media Inc.
Editorial: 162 Free Hill Rd, Gray, Tennessee 37615-3144 **Tel:** 1 423 477-1000.
Profile: WGOC-AM is a commercial station owned by Cumulus Media Inc. The format of the station is business talk. WGOC-AM broadcasts to the Gray, TN area at 1320 AM.
AM RADIO STATION

WGOG-FM 46222
Owner: Georgia-Carolina Radiocasting Companies LLC
Editorial: 2058 Westminster Hwy, Walhalla, South Carolina 29691 **Tel:** 1 864 638-3616.
Web site: http://www.wgog.com
Profile: WGOG-FM is a commercial station owned by Georgia-Carolina Radiocasting Companies LLC. The format of the station is classic country. WGOG-FM broadcasts to the Walhalla, SC area at 96.3 FM.
FM RADIO STATION

WGOH-AM 37846
Owner: Carter County Broadcasting Co.
Editorial: 150 Radio Tower Rd, Grayson, Kentucky 41143 **Tel:** 1 606 474-5144.
Email: mail@wgohwugo.com
Web site: http://www.wgohwugo.com
Profile: WGOH-AM is a commercial station owned by Carter County Broadcasting Co. The format of the station is country music. WGOH-AM broadcasts to the Grayson, KY area at 1370 AM.
AM RADIO STATION

WGOJ-FM 40323
Owner: Bible Broadcasting, Inc.
Editorial: 253 Mill St, Conneaut, Ohio 44030-2537
Tel: 1 440 593-1055.
Email: office@wgojradio.com
Web site: http://www.wgojradio.com
Profile: WGOJ-FM is a non-commercial station owned by Bible Broadcasting, Inc. The format of the station is religious. WGOJ-FM broadcasts to the Conneaut, OH area at 105.5 FM.
FM RADIO STATION

WGOK-AM 35351
Owner: Cumulus Media
Editorial: 2800 Dauphin St Ste 104, Mobile, Alabama 36606-2400 **Tel:** 1 251 652-2000.
Web site: http://www.gospel900.com
Profile: WGOK-AM is a commercial station owned by Cumulus Media. The format of the station is gospel. The station broadcasts to the Mobile, AL area at a frequency of 900 AM.
AM RADIO STATION

WGOL-AM 35824
Owner: Pilati Investments Corporation
Editorial: 113 Washington Ave NW, Russellville, Alabama 35653-2244 **Tel:** 1 256 332-0214.
Email: wgolam@yahoo.com
Web site: http://www.wgolam.com
Profile: WGOL-AM is a commercial station owned by Pilati Investments Corporation. The format of the station is country. WGOL-AM broadcasts to the Russellville, AL area at a frequency of 920 AM.
AM RADIO STATION

WGOP-AM 39400
Owner: Bay Broadcasting
Editorial: 1637 Dun Swamp Rd, Pocomoke City, Maryland 21851-3300 **Tel:** 1 410 957-9797.
Profile: WGOP-AM is a commercial station owned by Bay Broadcasting. The format of the station is oldies music. WGOP-AM broadcasts to the Pocomoke City, MD area at 540 AM.
AM RADIO STATION

WGOS-AM 35352
Owner: Iglesia Nueva Vida of High Point, Inc.
Editorial: 6223 Old Mendenhall Rd, High Point, North Carolina 27261 **Tel:** 1 336 434-5024.
Web site: http://www.cadenaradialnuevavida.com
Profile: WGOS-AM is a non-commercial station owned by Iglesia Nueva Vida of High Point, Inc. The format of the station is Christian talk, and Hispanic programming. WGOS-AM broadcasts to the Greensboro-Winston Salem, NC area at 1070 AM.
AM RADIO STATION

WGOV-FM 41777
Owner: W.G.O.V., Inc.
Editorial: 2973 US Highway 84 W, Valdosta, Georgia 31601-0305 **Tel:** 1 229 242-4513.
Profile: WGOV-FM is a commercial station owned by W.G.O.V., Inc. (dba Magic 95 Entertainment). The format of the station is urban contemporary music. WGOV-FM broadcasts to Valdosta, GA at 96.7 FM.
FM RADIO STATION

WGOW-AM 39099
Owner: Cumulus Media Inc.
Editorial: 821 Pineville Rd, Chattanooga, Tennessee 37405-2601 **Tel:** 1 423 756-6141.
Email: wgow@wgow.com
Web site: http://wgowam.com
Profile: WGOW-AM is a commercial station owned by Cumulus Media Inc. The format of the station is news and talk. WGOW-AM broadcasts to the Chattanooga, TN area at 1150 AM.
AM RADIO STATION

WGOW-FM 43718
Owner: Cumulus Media Inc.
Editorial: 821 Pineville Rd, Chattanooga, Tennessee 37405-2601 **Tel:** 1 423 756-6141.
Email: wgow@wgow.com
Web site: http://www.wgow.com/
Profile: WGOW-FM is a commercial station owned by Cumulus Media Inc. The format for the station is talk. WGOW-FM broadcasts to the Chattanooga, TN area at 102.3 FM.
FM RADIO STATION

WGPA-AM 35833
Owner: CC Broadcasting LLC
Editorial: 429 E Broad St, Bethlehem, Pennsylvania 18018-6337 **Tel:** 1 610 866-8074.
Email: wgpasunny1100@yahoo.com
Web site: http://wgpasunny1100.com
Profile: WGPA-AM is a commercial station owned by Timmer Broadcasting Company. The format of the station is a mix of rockabilly, country, and oldies music; also known as "Ameripolitan." WGPA-AM broadcasts to the Bethlehem, PA area at 1100 AM.
AM RADIO STATION

WGPB-FM 41835
Owner: Georgia Public Broadcasting
Editorial: 260 14th St NW, Atlanta, Georgia 30318
Tel: 1 404 685-2548.
Email: ask@gpb.org
Web site: http://www.gpb.org
Profile: WGPB-FM is a non-commercial station owned by Georgia Public Broadcasting. The format of the station is news and classical music. WGPB-FM broadcasts to the Rome, GA area at 97.7 FM.
FM RADIO STATION

WGPL-AM 38948
Owner: Willis Broadcasting Co.
Editorial: 645 Church St Ste 400, Norfolk, Virginia 23510-1712 **Tel:** 1 757 622-4600.
Email: willisbroadcasting@yahoo.com
Profile: WGPL-AM is a commercial station owned by Willis Broadcasting Co. The format of the station is black gospel. WGPL-AM broadcasts to the Norfolk, VA area at 1350 AM.
AM RADIO STATION

WGPO-FM 608050
Owner: Cook County Community Radio
Editorial: 1712 W Highway 61, Grand Marais, Minnesota 55604-7507 **Tel:** 1 218 387-1070.
Email: wtip@boreal.org
Web site: http://www.wtip.org
Profile: WGPO-FM is a non-commercial station owned by Cook County Community Radio. The format of the station is variety. WGPO-FM broadcasts to the Grand Portage, MN area at 90.1 FM.
FM RADIO STATION

WGPR-FM 40324
Owner: WGPR Inc.
Editorial: 3146 E Jefferson Ave, Detroit, Michigan 48207-5034 **Tel:** 1 313 259-2000.
Web site: http://hothiphopdetroit.com
Profile: WGPR-FM is a commercial station owned by WGPR Inc. The format of the station is urban contemporary. WGPR-FM broadcasts to the Detroit area at 107.5 FM.
FM RADIO STATION

WGQR-FM 46116
Owner: Christian Listening Network Inc.
Editorial: 996 Helen St, Fayetteville, North Carolina 28303 **Tel:** 1 910 864-5028.
Web site: http://www.wgqr1057.com
FM RADIO STATION

WGR-AM 36356
Owner: Entercom Communications Corp.
Editorial: 500 Corporate Pkwy, Ste 200, Buffalo, New York 14226 **Tel:** 1 716 843-0600.
Web site: http://www.wgr550.com
Profile: WGR-AM is a commercial station owned by Entercom Communications Corp. The format of the station is sports. WGR-AM broadcasts to the Buffalo, NY area at 550 AM.
AM RADIO STATION

WGRB-AM 37833
Owner: iHeartMedia Inc.
Editorial: 233 N Michigan Ave Ste 2800, Chicago, Illinois 60601-5704 **Tel:** 1 312 540-2000.
Web site: http://inspiration1390.iheart.com

Profile: WGRB-AM is a commercial station owned by iHeartMedia Inc. The format of the station is gospel. WGRB-AM broadcasts to the Chicago area at 1390 AM.
AM RADIO STATION

WGRC-FM 44150
Owner: Salt & Light Media Ministries
Editorial: 101 Armory Blvd, Lewisburg, Pennsylvania 17837-9504 **Tel:** 1 570 523-1190.
Email: email@wgrc.com
Web site: http://www.wgrc.com
Profile: WGRC-FM is a non-commercial station owned by Salt & Light Media Ministries. The format of the station is contemporary Christian music and news. WGRC-FM broadcasts to the Lewisburg, PA area at 91.3 FM.
FM RADIO STATION

WGRD-FM 43234
Owner: Townsquare Media, LLC
Editorial: 50 Monroe Ave NW, Ste 500, Grand Rapids, Michigan 49503 **Tel:** 1 616 451-4800.
Web site: http://www.wgrd.com
Profile: WGRD-FM is a commercial station owned by Townsquare Media, LLC. The format of the station is rock alternative. WGRD-FM broadcasts to the Grand Rapids, MI area at 97.9 FM.
FM RADIO STATION

WGRF-FM 42750
Owner: Cumulus Media Inc.
Editorial: 50 James E Casey Dr, Buffalo, New York 14206-2367 **Tel:** 1 716 881-4555.
Web site: http://www.97rock.com
Profile: WGRF-FM is a commercial station owned by Cumulus Media Inc. The format of the station is classic rock. WGRF-FM broadcasts to the Buffalo, NY area at 96.9 FM.
FM RADIO STATION

WGRG-FM 396753
Owner: Geneseo Community Radio Group, Inc.
Editorial: 700 N State St, Geneseo, Illinois 61254-1068 **Tel:** 1 309 945-0346.
Profile: WGRG-FM is a commercial station owned by Geneseo Community Radio Group, Inc. The format of the station is adult hits. WGRG-FM broadcasts to the Geneseo, Il area at 100.5 FM.
FM RADIO STATION

WGRI-AM 35710
Owner: Christian Broadcasting System
Editorial: 635 W 7th St, Cincinnati, Ohio 45203-1513 **Tel:** 1 513 533-2500.
Email: calendar@cbslradio.com
Web site: http://inspiration1050.com
Profile: WGRI-AM is a commercial station owned by Christian Broadcasting System.The format of the station is Urban Gospel. WGRI-AM broadcasts to the Cincinnati area at 1050 AM.
AM RADIO STATION

WGRK-AM 37849
Owner: Forcht Broadcasting
Editorial: 50 Friendship Pike Rd, Campbellsville, Kentucky 42718-2537 **Tel:** 1 270 789-1464.
Web site: http://www.kcountry1057.com
Profile: WGRK-AM is a commercial station owned by Forcht Broadcasting. The format of the station is contemporary country. WGRK-AM broadcasts to the Campbellsville, KY area at a frequency of 1540 AM.
AM RADIO STATION

WGRK-FM 45187
Owner: Forcht Broadcasting
Editorial: 50 Friendship Pike Rd, Campbellsville, Kentucky 42718-2537 **Tel:** 1 270 789-1464.
Web site: http://www.kcountry1057.com
Profile: WGRK-FM is a commercial station owned by Forcht Broadcasting. The format of the station is classic and contemporary country. WGRK-FM broadcasts to the Campbellsville, KY area at 105.7 FM.
FM RADIO STATION

WGRM-AM 38349
Owner: Christian Broadcasting of Greenwood, Inc.
Editorial: 1110 Wright St, Greenwood, Mississippi 38930-2237 **Tel:** 1 757 903-4981.
Email: sales@christiannetcast.com
Web site: http://www.christiannetcast.com
Profile: WGRM-AM is a commercial station owned by Christian Broadcasting of Greenwood, Inc. The format of the station is gospel music. WGRM-AM broadcasts to the Greenwood-Greenville, MS area at 1240 AM.
AM RADIO STATION

WGRM-FM 45711
Owner: Christian Broadcasting of Greenwood, Inc.
Editorial: 1110 Wright St, Greenwood, Mississippi 38930-2237 **Tel:** 1 757 903-4981.
Web site: http://www.christiannetcast.com
Profile: WGRM-FM is a commercial station owned by Christian Broadcasting of Greenwood, Inc. The format of the station is gospel music. WGRM-FM broadcasts to the Greenwood, MS area at 93.9 FM.
FM RADIO STATION

WGRN-FM 43925
Owner: Greenville College
Editorial: 315 E College Ave, Greenville, Illinois 62246-1145 **Tel:** 1 618 664-6792.
Email: wgrnbusinessdirector@greenville.edu
Web site: http://www.wgrn.net
Profile: WGRN-FM a non-commercial station owned by Greenville College. The format of the station is contemporary Christian. WGRN-FM broadcasts to Greenville, IL at 89.5 FM.
FM RADIO STATION

WGRO-AM 39149
Owner: Dockins Broadcast Group
Editorial: 9206 W US Highway 90, Lake City, Florida 32055-7502 **Tel:** 1 386 752-0960.
Profile: WGRO-AM is a commercial station owned by Taylor County Broadcasting, Inc. The format of the station is gospel music. WGRO-FM broadcasts to the Lake City, FL area at 960 AM.
AM RADIO STATION

WGRQ-FM 42481
Owner: Telemedia Broadcasting
Editorial: 4414 Lafayette Blvd Ste 100, Fredericksburg, Virginia 22408-4271 **Tel:** 1 540 891-9696.
Web site: http://www.959wgrq.com
Profile: WGRQ-FM is a commercial station owned by Telemedia Broadcasting. The format of the station is classic hits. WGRQ-FM broadcasts to the Fredericksburg, VA area at 95.9.
FM RADIO STATION

WGRR-FM 40139
Owner: Cumulus Media Inc.
Editorial: 4805 Montgomery Rd Ste 300, Cincinnati, Ohio 45212-2280 **Tel:** 1 513 241-9898.
Web site: http://www.wgrr.com
Profile: WGRR-FM is a commercial station owned by Cumulus Media Inc. The format of the station is classic hits. WGRR-FM broadcasts to the Cincinnati area at 103.5 FM.
FM RADIO STATION

WGRT-FM 41872
Owner: Port Huron Family Radio Inc.
Editorial: 624 Grand River Ave, Port Huron, Michigan 48060-3817 **Tel:** 1 810 987-3200.
Email: news@wgrt.com
Web site: http://wgrt.com
Profile: WGRT-FM is a commercial station owned by Port Huron Family Radio Inc. The format for the station is adult contemporary. WGRT-FM broadcasts to the Port Huron, MI area at 102.3 FM.
FM RADIO STATION

WGRV-AM 38757
Owner: Radio Greeneville Inc.
Editorial: 1004 Arnold Rd, Greeneville, Tennessee 37743 **Tel:** 1 423 638-4147.
Email: wgrv@greeneville.com
Web site: http://www.greeneville.com/wgrv
Profile: WGRV-AM is a commercial station owned by Radio Greeneville Inc. The format of the station is classic country music and talk. WGRV-AM broadcasts to the Greeneville, TN area at 1340 AM.
AM RADIO STATION

WGRW-FM 44423
Owner: Word Works Inc.
Editorial: 4265 Hill St, Anniston, Alabama 36206-2107 **Tel:** 1 256 238-9990.
Web site: http://www.graceradio.com
FM RADIO STATION

WGRX-FM 76137
Owner: Telemedia Broadcasting
Editorial: 4414 Lafayette Blvd Ste 100, Fredericksburg, Virginia 22408-4271 **Tel:** 1 540 891-9696.
Web site: http://www.thunder1045.com
Profile: WGRX-FM is a commercial station owned by Telemedia Broadcasting. The format of the station is contemporary country and classic rock music. WGRX-FM's broadcasts to the Fredericksburg, VA area at 104.5 FM.
FM RADIO STATION

WGRY-FM 40644
Owner: Blarney Stone Broadcasting, Inc.
Editorial: 6514 Old Lake Rd, Grayling, Michigan 49738-7348 **Tel:** 1 989 348-6171.
Profile: WGRY-FM is a commercial station owned by Blarney Stone Broadcasting, Inc. The format of the station is sports. WGRY-FM broadcasts to the Grayling, MI area at 101.1 FM.
FM RADIO STATION

WGSF-AM 35948
Owner: Flinn Broadcasting Corp.
Editorial: 3654 Park Ave, Memphis, Tennessee 38111-5626 **Tel:** 1 901 454-9948.
Email: wgsfoffice@bellsouth.net
Web site: http://www.radioambiente1030am.com
Profile: WGSF-AM is a commercial station owned by Flinn Broadcasting Corp. The format of the station is regional Mexican music. WGSF-AM broadcasts to the Memphis, TN area on 1030 AM.
AM RADIO STATION

WGSG-FM 42496
Owner: Son First Broadcasting, Inc.
Editorial: 331 SE Leola Dr., Mayo, Florida 32066-9802 **Tel:** 1 386 294-2525.
Email: wgsg@windstream.net
Profile: WGSG-FM is a commercial station owned by Son First Broadcasting, Inc. The format of the station is gospel and religious talk programming. WGSG-FM broadcasts to the Mayo, FL area at 89.5 FM.
FM RADIO STATION

WGSO-AM 36913
Owner: Northshore Radio, LLC
Editorial: 330 Carondelet St, New Orleans, Louisiana 70130-3144 **Tel:** 1 504 525-3314.
Email: info@wgso.com
Web site: http://www.wgso.com
Profile: WGSO-AM is a commercial station owned by Northshore Radio, LLC. The format of the station is news talk. WGSO-AM broadcasts to the Metairie, LA area at 990 AM.
AM RADIO STATION

WGSP-AM 35354
Owner: Norsan Group
Editorial: 4801 E Independence Blvd, Ste 815, Charlotte, North Carolina 28212-5490 **Tel:** 1 704 442-7277.
Web site: http://pepecharlotte.com
Profile: WGSP-AM is a commercial station owned by Norsan Group. The format of the station is classic hits. WGSP-AM broadcasts to the Charlotte, NC area at 1310 AM.
AM RADIO STATION

WGSP-FM 42132
Owner: Norsan Group
Editorial: 4801 E Independence Blvd Ste 815, Charlotte, North Carolina 28212-5490 **Tel:** 1 704 442-7277.
Web site: http://www.latina1023.com
Profile: WGSP-FM is a commercial station owned by Norsan Group. The format of the station is Hispanic tropical music. WGSP-FM broadcasts to the Charlotte, NC area at 102.3 FM.
FM RADIO STATION

WGSQ-FM 45188
Owner: Cookeville Communications, LLC
Editorial: 698 S Willow Ave, Cookeville, Tennessee 38501-3802 **Tel:** 1 931 526-7144.
Web site: http://www.countrygiant.com
Profile: WGSQ-FM is a commercial station owned by Cookeville Communications, LLC and operated by Great Plains Media. The format of the station is contemporary country. WGSQ-FM broadcasts to the Cookeville, TN area at 94.7 FM.
FM RADIO STATION

WGST-AM 37852
Owner: iHeartMedia Inc.
Editorial: 1819 Peachtree Rd NE Ste 700, Atlanta, Georgia 30309-1849 **Tel:** 1 404 875-8080.
Web site: http://640wgst.iheart.com
Profile: WGST-AM is a commercial station owned by iHeartMedia Inc.The format of the station is news talk. WGST-AM broadcasts to the Atlanta area at 640 AM.
AM RADIO STATION

WGSV-AM 37853
Owner: Guntersville Broadcasting Co.
Editorial: 2301 Thomas Ave, Guntersville, Alabama 35976-2233 **Tel:** 1 256 582-8131.
Email: wgsv@wgsv.com
Web site: http://www.wgsv.com
Profile: WGSV-AM is a commercial station owned by Guntersville Broadcasting Co. The format of the station is talk. WGSV-AM broadcasts to the Guntersville, AL at 1270 AM.
AM RADIO STATION

WGSY-FM 41364
Owner: iHeart Media Inc.
Editorial: 1501 13th Ave, Columbus, Georgia 31901-1908 **Tel:** 1 706 576-3000.
Web site: http://www.sunny100columbus.com
Profile: WGSY-FM is a commercial station owned by iHeart Media Inc. The format of the station is adult contemporary. WGSY-FM broadcasts to the Columbus, GA area at 100.1 FM.
FM RADIO STATION

WGTD-FM 40328
Owner: Gateway Technical College
Editorial: 3520 30th Ave, Kenosha, Wisconsin 53144-1619 **Tel:** 1 262 564-3800.
Web site: http://www.wgtd.org
Profile: WGTD-FM is a non-commercial station owned by Gateway Technical College. The format of the station is news and talk. WGTD-FM broadcasts to the Kenosha, WI, area at 91.1 FM.
FM RADIO STATION

WGTE-FM 40329
Owner: Public Broadcasting Foundation of Northwest Ohio
Editorial: 1270 S Detroit Ave, Toledo, Ohio 43614 **Tel:** 1 419 380-4600.
Email: fm@wgte.org
Web site: http://www.wgte.org
Profile: WGTE-FM is a non-commercial station owned by Public Broadcasting Foundation of Northwest Ohio. The format of the station is classical, jazz and news. WGTE-FM broadcasts to the Toledo, OH area at 91.3 FM.
FM RADIO STATION

WGTF-FM 42664
Owner: Dothan Community Educ. Radio
Editorial: 107 Wanda Ct, Dothan, Alabama 36303-3045 **Tel:** 1 334 794-4770.
Email: wgtf@bbnmedia.org
Profile: WGTF-FM is a non-commercial station owned by Dothan Community Educ. Radio. The format of the station is religious. WGTF-FM broadcasts to the Dothan, AL area at 89.5 FM.
FM RADIO STATION

WGTH-AM 38576
Owner: High Knob Broadcasters, Inc.
Editorial: 394 Edgewater Dr, Cedar Bluff, Virginia 24609-8825 **Tel:** 1 276 964-2502.
Email: wgth@wgth.net
Web site: http://www.wgth.net
Profile: WGTH-AM is a commercial station owned by High Knob Broadcasters, Inc. The format of the station is gospel. WGTH-AM broadcasts to the Cedar Bluff, VA area at 540 AM.
AM RADIO STATION

WGTH-FM 46754
Owner: High Knob Broadcasters, Inc.
Editorial: 394 Edgewater Dr, Cedar Bluff, Virginia 24609 **Tel:** 1 276 964-2502.
Email: wgth@wgth.net
Web site: http://www.wgth.net
Profile: WGTH-FM is a commercial station owned by High Knob Broadcasters, Inc. The format of the station is southern gospel and contemporary christian. WGTH-FM broadcasts to the Cedar Bluff, VA area at 105.5 FM.
FM RADIO STATION

WGTJ-AM 35991
Owner: Vision Communications Inc.
Editorial: 1716 Cleveland Hwy, Gainesville, Georgia 30501-1335 **Tel:** 1 770 297-7485.
Email: news@glory1330.com
Web site: http://www.glory1330.com
Profile: WGTJ-AM is a commercial station owned by Vision Communications Inc. The format of the station is Religious Teaching. WGTJ-AM broadcasts to the Gainesville, GA area at 1330 AM.
AM RADIO STATION

WGTK-AM 36083
Owner: Salem Media Group, Inc.
Editorial: 9960 Corporate Campus Dr Ste 3600, Louisville, Kentucky 40223-4070 **Tel:** 1 502 339-9470.
Web site: http://970amtheanswer.com
Profile: WGTK-AM is a commercial station owned by Salem Media Group, Inc. The format of the station is news and talk. WGTK-AM broadcasts in the Louisville, KY area at 970 AM.
AM RADIO STATION

WGTK-FM 45390
Owner: Salem Media Group, Inc.
Editorial: 920 Wade Hampton Blvd, Greenville, South Carolina 29609-4944 **Tel:** 1 864 242-6240.
Web site: http://www.945theanswer.com
Profile: WGTK-FM is a commercial station owned by the Salem Media Group, Inc.'s Caron Broadcasting, Inc. The format of the station is Conservative Talk. WGTK-FM broadcasts to Greenville, SC at 94.5 FM.
FM RADIO STATION

WGTN-AM 36811
Owner: Stalvey Communications
Editorial: 2508 Highwater street, Georgetown, South Carolina 29440-4555 **Tel:** 1 843 546-1400.
Email: wgtnradio@aol.com
Web site: http://www.wgtnradio.com
Profile: WGTN-AM is a commercial station owned by Stalvey Communications. The format of the station is news, sports and talk. WGTN-AM broadcasts to the Georgetown, SC area at 1400 AM.
AM RADIO STATION

WGTN-FM 43776
Owner: Fidelity Broadcasting Inc.
Editorial: 3926 Wesley St Ste 301, Myrtle Beach, South Carolina 29579-7307 **Tel:** 1 843 903-9962.
Web site: http://www.wezv.com
FM RADIO STATION

WGTO-AM 36861
Owner: Langford Broadcasting
Editorial: 26914 Marcellus Hwy, Dowagiac, Michigan 49047 **Tel:** 1 269 782-5106.
Email: info@wgtoradio.com
Web site: http://www.wgtoradio.com
Profile: WGTO-AM is a commercial station owned by Langford Broadcasting. The format of the station is classic hits. WGTO-AM broadcasts to the Dowagiac, MI area at 910 AM.
AM RADIO STATION

WGTR-FM 42656
Owner: iHeartMedia Inc.
Editorial: 4841 Highway 17 Byp S, Myrtle Beach, South Carolina 29577-6683 **Tel:** 1 843 293-0107.
Web site: http://gator1079.iheart.com
Profile: WGTR-FM is a commercial station owned by iHeartMedia Inc. The format of the station is country. WGTR-FM broadcasts to the Myrtle Beach, SC area at 107.9 FM.
FM RADIO STATION

WGTS-FM 40330
Owner: Columbia Union College Broadcasting Inc.
Editorial: 7600 Flower Ave, Takoma Park, Maryland 20912-7744 **Tel:** 1 301 891-4200.
Email: wgts@wgts919.com
Web site: http://www.wgts919.com
Profile: WGTS-FM is a non-commercial station owned by Columbia Union College Broadcasting Inc. The format of the station is contemporary Christian music. WGTS-FM broadcasts to the Washington, D.C. area at 91.9 FM.
FM RADIO STATION

WGTX-FM 496747

Owner: Dunes 102FM LLC
Editorial: 352 Route 6, Unit 7, Truro, Massachusetts 2652 **Tel:** 1 508 487-1002.
Email: info@dunes102.com
Web site: http://www.dunesradio.com
Profile: WGTX-FM is a commercial station owned by Dunes 102FM LLC. The format of the station is classic hits. WGTX-FM broadcasts to the Provincetown, MA area at 102.3 FM.
FM RADIO STATION

WGTY-FM 46345

Owner: Forever Media Inc.
Editorial: 275 Radio Rd, Hanover, Pennsylvania 17331-1140 **Tel:** 1 717 637-3831.
Email: info@wgty.com
Web site: http://www.foreveryork.com/froggy-107-7
Profile: WGTY-FM is a commercial station owned by Forever Media Inc. The format of the station is country. WGTY-FM broadcasts to the Gettysburg, PA area at 107.7 FM.
FM RADIO STATION

WGTZ-FM 45189

Owner: Alpha Media
Editorial: 717 E David Rd, Dayton, Ohio 45429-5218
Tel: 1 937 294-5858.
Web site: http://softrock929.com
Profile: WGTZ-FM is a commercial station owned by Alpha Media. The format of the station is soft rock. WGTZ-FM broadcasts to the Dayton, OH area at 92.9 FM.
FM RADIO STATION

WGUC-FM 40331

Owner: Cincinnati Public Radio Inc.
Editorial: 1223 Central Pkwy, Cincinnati, Ohio 45214-2812 **Tel:** 1 513 241-8282.
Email: wguc@wguc.org
Web site: http://www.wguc.org
Profile: WGUC-FM is a non-commercial station owned by Cincinnati Public Radio Inc. The format of the station is classical music. WGUC-FM broadcasts to the Cincinnati area at 90.9 FM.
FM RADIO STATION

WGUE-AM 36328

Owner: Mighty Media Group, LP (Memphis First Ventures LP)
Editorial: 230 Goodman Rd E Ste 2, Southaven, Mississippi 38671-8889 **Tel:** 1 662 349-0826.
Web site: http://guessfm.com
Profile: WGUE-AM is a commercial station owned by Mighty Media Group, LP (Memphis First Ventures LP). The format of the station is adult hits. WGUE-AM broadcasts to the Memphis, TN area at 830 AM.
AM RADIO STATION

WGUF-FM 41764

Owner: Renda Broadcasting
Editorial: 10915 K Nine Dr, 2nd Fl, Bonita Springs, Florida 34135 **Tel:** 1 239 495-8383.
Web site: http://www.wguf989.com
Profile: WGUF-FM is a commercial station owned by Renda Broadcasting. The format of the station is talk. WGUF-FM broadcasts to the Naples, FL area at 98.9 FM.
FM RADIO STATION

WGUL-AM 358813

Owner: Salem Media Group, Inc.
Editorial: 5211 W Laurel St Ste A, Tampa, Florida 33607-1736 **Tel:** 1 813 639-1903.
Web site: http://am860theanswer.com
Profile: WGUL-AM is a commercial station owned by Salem Media Group, Inc. The format of the station is news and talk. WGUL-AM broadcasts to the Tampa, FL area at 860 AM.
AM RADIO STATION

WGUN-AM 38379

Owner: W.G.O.V., Inc.
Editorial: 2973 US Highway 84 W, Valdosta, Georgia 31601-0305 **Tel:** 1 229 242-4513.
Profile: WGUN-AM is a commercial station owned by W.G.O.V., Inc.The format of the station is urban adult contemporary. WGOV-AM broadcasts to the Valdosta, GA area at 950 AM.
AM RADIO STATION

WGUO-FM 42902

Owner: Southeast Broadcasting, Inc.
Editorial: 5921 W Main St, Houma, Louisiana 70360-1716 **Tel:** 1 985 274-0117.
Web site: http://www.gumbo949.com
Profile: WGUO-FM is a commercial station owned by Southeast Broadcasting, Inc. The format for the station is Classic Country. The target audience of the station is adults, ages 18 to 64. WGUO-FM broadcasts to the New Orleans area at 94.9 FM. The station's tagline is "Gumbo 94.9."
FM RADIO STATION

WGUS-FM 41945

Owner: Beasley Broadcast Group
Editorial: 4051 Jimmie Dyess Pkwy, Augusta, Georgia 30909-9469 **Tel:** 1 706 396-7000.
Web site: http://www.1027wgus.com
Profile: WGUS-FM is a commercial station owned by Beasley Broadcast Group. The format of the station is Southern gospel music. WGUS-FM broadcasts to the Augusta, GA area at 102.7 FM.
FM RADIO STATION

WGVA-AM 38368

Owner: Finger Lakes Radio Group
Editorial: 3568 Lenox Rd, Geneva, New York 14456
Tel: 1 315 781-7000.
Email: news@flradiogroup.com
Web site: http://flradiogroup.com
Profile: WGVA-AM is a commercial station owned by Finger Lakes Radio Group. The format of the station is news, sports and talk. WGVA-AM broadcasts to the Geneva, NY area at 1240 AM.
AM RADIO STATION

WGVL-AM 38207

Owner: iHeartMedia Inc.
Editorial: 101 N Main St Ste 1000, Greenville, South Carolina 29601-4852 **Tel:** 1 864 991-8203.
Web site: http://foxsports1440.iheart.com
Profile: WGVL-AM is a commercial station owned by iHeartMedia Inc. and in an LMA with Greenville Radio Group, LLC. The format of the station is sports. WGVL-AM broadcasts to the Greenville, SC area at 1440 AM.
AM RADIO STATION

WGVM-AM 37856

Owner: Ark-La-Ms Radio Group, LLC
Editorial: 1383 Pickett St, Greenville, Mississippi 38703-2437 **Tel:** 1 662 334-4550.
Email: wdms@bellsouth.net
Profile: WGVM-AM is a commercial station owned by Ark-La-Ms Radio Group, LLC. The format of the station is classic rock. WGVM-AM broadcasts to the Greenville, MS area at 1260 AM.
AM RADIO STATION

WGVX-FM 43425

Owner: Cumulus Media Inc.
Editorial: 2000 Elm St SE, Minneapolis, Minnesota 55414-2531 **Tel:** 1 612 617-4000.
Email: info@105theticket.com
Web site: http://www.105thevibe.com/
Profile: WGVX-FM is a commercial station owned by Cumulus Media Inc. The format of the station is classic hip hop. WGVX-FM broadcasts to the Greater Minneapolis area at 105.1 FM. WGVX-FM airs programming on WGVY-FM and WVGZ-FM.
FM RADIO STATION

WGVZ-FM 42082

Owner: Cumulus Media Inc.
Editorial: 2000 Elm St SE, Minneapolis, Minnesota 55414-2531 **Tel:** 1 612 617-4000.
Email: info@105theticket.com
Web site: http://www.105thevibe.com/
Profile: WGVZ-FM is a commercial station owned by Cumulus Media Inc. The format of the station is classic hip hop. WGVZ-FM broadcasts to the Minneapolis area at 105.7 FM. The station is a simulcast of WGVX-FM
FM RADIO STATION

WGWD-FM 41330

Owner: Magic Broadcasting, LLC
Editorial: Tallahassee, Florida **Tel:** 1 850 627-7086.
Web site: http://www.talkradio933.com
Profile: WGWD-FM is a commercial station owned by Magic Broadcasting, LLC. The format of the station is talk. WGWD-FM broadcasts in the Quincy, FL area at 93.3 FM.
FM RADIO STATION

WGWM-AM 35506

Owner: WGWM Broadcasting Inc.
Editorial: 948 Moriah Church Rd, London, Kentucky 40741-7635 **Tel:** 1 606 878-0980.
Profile: WGWM-AM is a commercial station owned by WGWM Broadcasting Inc. The format of the station is gospel. WGWM-AM broadcasts to the London, KY area at 980 AM.
AM RADIO STATION

WGXL-FM 46234

Owner: Great Eastern Radio, LLC
Editorial: 31 Hanover St Ste 4, Lebanon, New Hampshire 03766-1357 **Tel:** 1 603 448-1400.
Profile: WGLX-FM is a commercial station owned by Great Eastern Radio, LLC. The format of the station is Hot AC. WGLX-FM broadcasts to the Lebanon, NH area at a frequency of 92.3 FM.
FM RADIO STATION

WGY-AM 38691

Owner: iHeartMedia Inc.
Editorial: 1203 Troy Schenectady Rd, Latham, New York 12110-1046 **Tel:** 1 518 452-4800.
Email: news@wgy.com
Web site: http://wgy.iheart.com
Profile: WGY-AM is a commercial station owned by iHeartMedia Inc. The format of the station is news and talk. WGY-AM broadcasts in the Albany, NY, area at 810 AM. WGY-AM airs programing on WGY-FM.
AM RADIO STATION

WGYE-FM 42183

Owner: Burbach of WV, LLC
Editorial: 1489 Locust Ave, Ste C, Fairmont, West Virginia 26554 **Tel:** 1 304 363-8888.
Web site: http://www.froggycountry.net
Profile: WGYE-FM is a commercial station owned by Burbach of WV, LLC. The format of the station is contemporary country music. WTUS-FM broadcasts to the Fairmont, WV area at 102.7 FM.
FM RADIO STATION

WGY-FM 40354

Owner: iHeartMedia Inc.
Editorial: 1203 Troy Schenectady Rd, Latham, New York 12110-1046 **Tel:** 1 518 452-4800.
Web site: http://wgy.iheart.com/
Profile: WGY-FM is a commercial station owned by iHeartMedia Inc. The format of the station is news talk. WGY-FM airs WGY-AM's programing. WGY-FM broadcasts to the Albany, NY area at 103.1.
FM RADIO STATION

WGYI-FM 46630

Owner: FM Radio Licenses, LLC
Editorial: 900 Water St, Meadville, Pennsylvania 16335-3428 **Tel:** 1 814 724-1111.
Web site: http://www.froggyfun.com
Profile: WGYI-FM is a commercial station owned by FM Radio Licenses, LLC. The format of the station is country music. WGYI-FM broadcasts to the Meadville, PA area at 98.5 FM.
FM RADIO STATION

WGYL-FM 46742

Owner: Treasure & Space Coast Radio
Editorial: 1235 16th St, Vero Beach, Florida 32960-3620 **Tel:** 1 772 567-0937.
Web site: http://thebreeze.fm
Profile: WGYL-FM is a commercial station owned by Treasure & Space Coast Radio. The format of the station is Top 40/CHR. WGYL-FM broadcasts to the Vero Beach, FL area at 93.7 FM.
FM RADIO STATION

WGYM-AM 35714

Owner: Domestic Church Media Foundation
Tel: 1 609 882-9357.
Email: info@domesticchurchmedia.org
Web site: http://www.domesticchurchmedia.org
Profile: WGYM-AM is a non-commercial station owned by Domestic Church Media Foundation. The format of the station is religious. WGYM-AM broadcasts to the Atlantic City, NJ area at 1580 AM.
AM RADIO STATION

WGYV-AM 36303

Owner: Florala Broadcasting Co., Inc.
Editorial: 1604 E Commerce St, Greenville, Alabama 36037-3400 **Tel:** 1 334 382-5444.
Web site: http://wgyv.ezstream.com/
Profile: WGYV-AM is a commercial station owned by Florala Broadcasting Co., Inc. The format of the station is talk. WGYV-AM broadcasts to the Greenville, AL area at 1380 AM.
AM RADIO STATION

WGYY-FM 45657

Owner: FM Radio Licenses, LLC
Editorial: 900 Water St, Meadville, Pennsylvania 16335-3428 **Tel:** 1 814 724-1111.
Email: radio@zoominternet.net
Web site: http://www.froggyfun.com
Profile: WGYY-FM is a commercial station owned by FM Radio Licenses, LLC. The format of the station is country music. WGYY-FM broadcasts to the Meadville, PA area at 100.3 FM.
FM RADIO STATION

WGZB-FM 41642

Owner: Alpha Media
Editorial: 520 S 4th St Ste 200, Louisville, Kentucky 40202-2577 **Tel:** 1 502 625-1220.
Web site: http://www.hiphopb965.com
Profile: WGZB-FM is a commercial station owned by Alpha Media. The format of the station is urban contemporary. WGZB-FM broadcasts to the Louisville, KY area at 96.5 FM.
FM RADIO STATION

WGZZ-FM 43444

Owner: Auburn Network, Inc.
Editorial: 197 E University Dr, Auburn, Alabama 36832-6725 **Tel:** 1 334 826-2929.
Web site: http://www.wingsfm.com
Profile: WGZZ-FM is a commercial station owned by Auburn Network, Inc. The format of the station is classic hits. WGZZ-FM broadcasts to the Tallapoosa, AL area at 100.3 FM.
FM RADIO STATION

WHAG-AM 37857

Owner: Alpha Media
Editorial: 1250 Maryland Ave, Hagerstown, Maryland 21740-7244 **Tel:** 1 301 797-7300.
Web site: http://www.thenewfm963.com
Profile: WHAG-AM is a commercial station owned by Alpha Media. The format of the station is oldies music. WHAG-AM broadcasts to the Hagerstown, MD area at 1410 AM.
AM RADIO STATION

WHAI-FM 45191

Owner: Saga Communications
Editorial: 81 Woodard Rd, Greenfield, Massachusetts 1301 **Tel:** 1 413 774-4301.
Web site: http://www.whai.com
Profile: WHAI-FM is a commercial station owned Saga Communications. The format of the station is adult contemporary music. WHAI-FM broadcasts to the Greenfield, MA area at 98.3 FM.
FM RADIO STATION

WHAJ-FM 45674

Owner: Alpha Media
Editorial: 900 Bluefield Ave, Bluefield, West Virginia 24701-2744 **Tel:** 1 304 327-7114.
Web site: http://www.j1045.com
Profile: WHAJ-FM is a commercial station owned by Alpha Media. The format of the station is hot adult contemporary music. WHAJ-FM broadcasts to the Bluefield, WV area at 104.5 FM.
FM RADIO STATION

WHAK-AM 36384

Owner: Edwards Communications LLC
Editorial: 1491 M 32 W, Alpena, Michigan 49707-8194
Tel: 1 989 354-4611.
Email: news@truenorthradionetwork.com
Web site: http://www.truenorthradionetwork.com
Profile: WHAK-AM is a commercial station owned by Edwards Communications LLC. The format for the station is oldies. WHAK-AM broadcasts to the Alpena, MI area at 960 AM.
AM RADIO STATION

WHAK-FM 42530

Owner: Edwards Communications LLC
Editorial: 1491 M 32 W, Alpena, Michigan 49707-8194
Tel: 1 989 354-4611.
Email: news@truenorthradionetwork.com
Web site: http://www.truenorthradionetwork.com
Profile: WHAK-FM is a commercial station owned by Edwards Communications LLC. The format of the station is oldies. WHAK-FM broadcasts to the Alpena, MI area at 99.9 FM.
FM RADIO STATION

WHAL-AM 38131

Owner: iHeartMedia Inc.
Editorial: 1501 13th Ave, Columbus, Georgia 31901-1908 **Tel:** 1 706 576-3000.
Profile: WHAL-AM is a commercial station owned by iHeartMedia Inc. The format of the station is classic country. WHAL-AM broadcasts to the Columbus, GA area at 1460 AM.
AM RADIO STATION

WHAL-FM 134155

Owner: iHeartMedia Inc.
Editorial: 2650 Thousand Oaks Blvd Ste 4100, Memphis, Tennessee 38118-2451 **Tel:** 1 901 259-1300.
Web site: http://www.hallelujahfm.com
Profile: WHAL-FM is a commercial station owned by iHeartMedia Inc.The format of the station is gospel. WHAL-FM broadcasts to the Memphis, TN area at 95.7 FM.
FM RADIO STATION

WHAM-AM 37859

Owner: iHeartMedia Inc.
Editorial: 100 Chestnut St Ste 1700, 100 Chestnut St, Rochester, New York 14604-2418 **Tel:** 1 585 454-4884.
Email: whamnews@iheartmedia.com
Web site: http://www.wham1180.com
Profile: WHAM-AM is a commercial staion owned by iHeartMedia Inc. The format of the station is news and talk. WHAM-AM broadcasts to the Rochester, NY area at 1180 AM.
AM RADIO STATION

WHAN-AM 35995

Owner: Fifth Estate Broadcasting, LLC
Tel: 1 434 924-0885.
Email: wtju@virginia.edu
Web site: http://www.wtju.net
Profile: WHAN-AM is a commercial station owned by Fifth Estate Broadcasting, LLC and operated by the University of Virginia. The format of the station is a variety of news, talk and music programming. WHAN-AM broadcasts to the Ashland, VA area at 1430 AM.
AM RADIO STATION

WHAP-AM 36873

Owner: Nugent(Steve) and Hios(David)
Editorial: 150 S Mesa Dr, Hopewell, Virginia 23860-2036 **Tel:** 1 804 458-9427.
Profile: WHAP-AM is a commercial station owned by Steve Nugent and David Hios. The format of the station is news, sports and talk. WHAP-AM broadcasts to the Hopewell, VA area at 1340 AM.
AM RADIO STATION

WHAS-AM 37861

Owner: iHeartMedia Inc.
Editorial: 4000 Radio Dr, Louisville, Kentucky 40218-4568 **Tel:** 1 502 479-2222.
Email: whasnews@iheartmedia.com
Web site: http://whas.iheart.com
Profile: WHAS-AM is a commercial station owned by iHeartMedia Inc. The format of the station is news and talk. WHAS-AM broadcasts to the Louisville, KY area at 840 AM.
AM RADIO STATION

WHAT-AM 35358

Owner: Aztec Capital Partners, Inc.
Editorial: 25 Bala Ave Ste 202, Bala Cynwyd, Pennsylvania 19004-3215 **Tel:** 1 484 562-0510.
Email: info@elzolphilly.com
Web site: http://www.elzolphilly.com
Profile: WHAT-AM is a commercial station owned by Aztec Capital Partners, Inc. The format of the station is Hispanic tropical. WHAT-AM broadcasts to the Philadelphia area at 1340 AM.
AM RADIO STATION

WHAT-FM 43078

Owner: Withers Broadcasting of Southern Illinois, LLC
Editorial: 1822 N Court St, Marion, Illinois 62959-4558
Tel: 1 618 997-8123.
Web site: http://www.mywithersradio.com/us

Profile: WHAT-FM is a commercial station owned by Withers Broadcasting of Southern Illinois, LLC. The format of the station is classic country music. WQUL-FM broadcasts to Marion, IL at 97.7 FM.
FM RADIO STATION

WHAW-AM 36876
Owner: DJ Broadcasting
Editorial: 300 Harrison Ave, Weston, West Virginia 26452 **Tel:** 1 304 269-5555.
Email: info@whawradio.com
Web site: http://www.whawradio.com
Profile: WHAW-AM is a commercial station owned by DJ Broadcasting. The format of the station is country. WHAW-AM broadcasts to the Weston, WV area on 980 AM.
AM RADIO STATION

WHAY-FM 41759
Owner: Lavender(Tim)
Editorial: 69 Courthouse Sq, Whitley City, Kentucky 42653-6176 **Tel:** 1 606 376-2218.
Email: radio@hay98.com
Web site: http://www.hay98.com
Profile: WHAY-FM is a commercial station owned by Tim Lavender. The primary format of the station is Americana, but also features classic country, bluegrass, blues, and some rock. WHAY-FM broadcasts to the Whitley City, KY and surrounding communities at 98.3 FM.
FM RADIO STATION

WHAZ-AM 39043
Owner: Capital Media Corporation
Editorial: 30 Park Ave, Cohoes, New York 12047-3330 **Tel:** 1 518 237-1330.
Web site: http://www.aliveradionetwork.com
Profile: WHAZ-AM is a commercial station owned by Capital Media Corporation. The format of the station is religious. WHAZ-AM broadcasts to the Cohoes, NY area at 1330 AM.
AM RADIO STATION

WHAZ-FM 41811
Owner: Capital Media Corporation
Editorial: 30 Park Ave, Cohoes, New York 12047-3330 **Tel:** 1 518 237-1330.
Email: events@aliveradio.com
Web site: http://www.aliveradionetwork.com
Profile: WHAZ-FM is a commercial station owned by Capital Media Corporation. The format of the station is religious programming. WHAZ-FM broadcasts to the Cohoes, NY area at 97.5.
FM RADIO STATION

WHB-AM 36139
Owner: Union Broadcasting Inc.
Editorial: 6721 W 121st St, Overland Park, Kansas 66209-2003 **Tel:** 1 913 344-1500.
Email: info@810whb.com
Web site: http://www.810whb.com
Profile: WHB-AM is a commercial station owned by Union Broadcasting Inc. The format of the station is sports. WHB-AM broadcasts to the Kansas City, MO area at 810 AM.
AM RADIO STATION

WHBB-AM 37862
Owner: Broadsouth Communications
Editorial: 505 Lauderdale St, Selma, Alabama 36701-4528 **Tel:** 1 334 875-3350.
Profile: WHBB-AM is a commercial station owned by Broadsouth Communications. The format of the station is talk. WHBB-AM broadcasts to the Selma, AL area at 1490 AM.
AM RADIO STATION

WHBC-AM 37863
Owner: Digity LLC
Editorial: 550 Market Ave S, Canton, Ohio 44702-2112 **Tel:** 1 330 456-7166.
Email: newstip@whbc.com
Web site: http://www.whbc.com
Profile: WHBC-AM is a commercial station owned by Digity LLC. The format of the station is news, talk and sports. WHBC-AM broadcasts to the Canton, OH area at 1480.
AM RADIO STATION

WHBC-FM 45192
Owner: Digity LLC
Editorial: 550 Market Ave S, Canton, Ohio 44702-2112 **Tel:** 1 330 456-7166.
Web site: http://www.mix941.com
Profile: WHBC-FM is a commercial station owned by Digity LLC. The format of the station is adult contemporary. WHBC-FM broadcasts to the Canton, OH area at 94.1 FM.
FM RADIO STATION

WHBE-AM 36128
Owner: UB Louisville, LLC
Editorial: 11700 Commonwealth Dr, Louisville, Kentucky 40299-6303 **Tel:** 1 502 240-0602.
Web site: http://espnlouisville.com
Profile: WHBE-AM is a commercial station owned by UB Louisville, LLC. The format of the station is sports. WHBE-AM broadcasts to the Louisville, KY area at 680 AM.
AM RADIO STATION

WHBG-AM 39287
Owner: Saga Communications
Editorial: 1820 Heritage Center Way, Harrisonburg, Virginia 22801-8451 **Tel:** 1 540 434-0331.
Web site: http://espnharrisonburg.com
Profile: WHBG-AM is a commercial station owned by Saga Communications. The format for the station is sports. WHBG-AM broadcasts to the Harrisonburg, VA area at 1360 AM. The station does not accept unsolicited faxes. Do NOT e-mail any staff members. Any press information should be sent to WSVA-AM.
AM RADIO STATION

WHBK-AM 35531
Owner: Southern Broadcasting, Inc.
Editorial: 1055 Skyway Dr, Marshall, North Carolina 28753 **Tel:** 1 828 649-3914.
Email: 1460whbk@gmail.com
Web site: http://www.1460whbk.com
Profile: WHBK-AM is a commercial station owned by Southern Broadcasting, Inc. The format of the station is gospel. WHBK-AM broadcasts to the Marshall, NC area at 1460 AM.
AM RADIO STATION

WHBL-AM 37864
Owner: Midwest Communications Inc.
Editorial: 2100 Washington Ave, Sheboygan, Wisconsin 53081-7042 **Tel:** 1 920 458-2107.
Email: whblnews@whbl.com
Web site: http://www.whbl.com
Profile: WHBL-AM is a commercial station owned by Midwest Communications Inc. The format of the station is news, talk and sports. WHBL-AM broadcasts to the Sheboygan, WI area at 1330 AM.
AM RADIO STATION

WHBN-AM 37006
Owner: Hometown Broadcasting, Inc.
Editorial: 2063 Shakertown Rd, Danville, Kentucky 40422-9262 **Tel:** 1 859 236-2711.
Email: hometownradio@bellsouth.net
Web site: http://hometownlive.net
Profile: WHBN-AM is a commercial station owned by Hometown Broadcasting, Inc. The format for the station is country and gospel. WHBN-AM broadcasts to the Lexington, KY area at 1420 AM.
AM RADIO STATION

WHBO-AM 36724
Owner: Genesis Communications Inc.
Editorial: 6080 8th Ave SE, Largo, Florida 33771-2162 **Tel:** 1 813 281-1040.
Web site: http://www.sportstalkflorida.com
Profile: WHBO-AM is a commercial station owned by Genesis Communications Inc. The format of the station is sports. WHBO-AM broadcasts to the Tampa, FL area at 1040 AM.
AM RADIO STATION

WHBQ-AM 35359
Owner: Flinn Broadcasting Corp.
Editorial: 6080 Mount Moriah Road Ext, Memphis, Tennessee 38115-2645 **Tel:** 1 901 375-9324.
Web site: http://www.sports56whbq.com
Profile: WHBQ-AM is a commercial station owned by Flinn Broadcasting Corp. The format of the station is sports. WHBQ-AM broadcasts to the Memphis, TN, market at 560 AM.
AM RADIO STATION

WHBQ-FM 43802
Owner: Flinn Broadcasting Corp.
Editorial: 6080 Mount Moriah Road Ext, Memphis, Tennessee 38115-2645 **Tel:** 1 901 375-9324.
Email: mail@q1075.com
Web site: http://www.q1075.com
Profile: WHBQ-FM is a commercial station owned by Flinn Broadcasting Corp. The format of the station is Top 40/CHR. WHBQ-FM broadcasts to the Memphis, TN area at 107.5 FM.
FM RADIO STATION

WHBR-FM 45930
Owner: Burbach of WV, LLC
Editorial: 5 Rosemar Cir, Parkersburg, West Virginia 26104-1203 **Tel:** 1 304 485-4565.
Web site: http://resultsradiowv.wix.com/the-bear
Profile: WHBR-FM is a commercial station owned by Burbach of WV, LLC. The format of the station is rock alternative. WHBR-FM broadcasts to the Parkersburg, WV area at 103.1 FM.
FM RADIO STATION

WHBT-AM 37668
Owner: Cumulus Media Inc.
Editorial: 3411 W Tharpe St, Tallahassee, Florida 32303-1139 **Tel:** 1 850 201-3000.
Web site: http://www.heaven1410.com
Profile: WHBT-AM is a commercial station owned by Cumulus Media Inc. The format of the station is gospel. WHBT-AM broadcasts to the Tallahassee, FL area at 1410 AM.
AM RADIO STATION

WHBT-FM 43406
Owner: iHeartMedia Inc.
Editorial: 1003 Norfolk Sq, Norfolk, Virginia 23502-3234 **Tel:** 1 757 466-0009.
Web site: http://thebeatva.iheart.com/
Profile: WHBT-FM is a commercial station owned by iHeartMedia Inc. The format of the station is classic hip hop and R&B. WHBT-FM is licensed to Moyock, NC and broadcasts to the Norfolk/Virgina Beach, VA area at 92.1 FM.
FM RADIO STATION

WHBU-AM 38384
Owner: Backyard Broadcasting
Editorial: 800 E 29th St, Muncie, Indiana 47302-5765 **Tel:** 1 765 288-4403.
Web site: http://www.1240whbu.com
Profile: WHBU-AM is a commercial station owned by Backyard Broadcasting. The format of the station is news, talk and sports. WHBU-AM broadcasts to the Muncie, IN area at 1240 AM.
AM RADIO STATION

WHBX-FM 40529
Owner: Cumulus Media Inc.
Editorial: 3411 W Tharpe St, Tallahassee, Florida 32303-1139 **Tel:** 1 850 201-3000.
Web site: http://www.961jamz.com
Profile: WHBX-FM is a commercial station owned by Cumulus Media Inc. The format of the station is urban adult contemporary. WHBX-FM broadcasts to the Tallahassee, FL area at 96.1 FM.
FM RADIO STATION

WHBY-AM 37865
Owner: Woodward Communications, Inc.
Editorial: 2800 E College Ave, Appleton, Wisconsin 54915-3255 **Tel:** 1 920 733-6639.
Web site: http://www.whby.com
Profile: WHBY-AM is a commercial station owned by Woodward Communications, Inc. The format of the station is news, sports and talk programming. WHBY-AM broadcasts to Appleton, WI area at 1150 AM.
AM RADIO STATION

WHBZ-FM 43258
Owner: Midwest Communications Inc.
Editorial: 2100 Washington Ave, Sheboygan, Wisconsin 53081-7042 **Tel:** 1 920 458-2107.
Email: buzz.studio@whbz.fm
Web site: http://www.1065thebuzz.com
Profile: WHBZ-FM is a commercial station owned by Midwest Communications Inc. The format of the station is rock music. WHBZ-FM broadcasts to the Milwaukee area at 106.5 FM.
FM RADIO STATION

WHCC-FM 235108
Owner: Artistic Media Partners Inc.
Editorial: 304 State Road 446, Bloomington, Indiana 47401-8837 **Tel:** 1 812 336-8000.
Email: whcc105@whcc105.com
Web site: http://www.whcc105.com
Profile: WHCC-FM is a commercial station owned by Artistic Media Partners Inc. The format of the station is country music. WHCC-FM broadcasts to the Bloomington, IN area at 105.1 FM.
FM RADIO STATION

WHCF-FM 41487
Owner: Lighthouse Radio Network, Inc.
Editorial: 1476 Broadway, Bangor, Maine 04401-2404 **Tel:** 1 207 947-2751.
Email: contact@whcffm.com
Web site: http://www.whcffm.com
Profile: WHCF-FM is a non-commercial station owned by the Lighthouse Radio Network, Inc. The format of the station is religious talk and contemporary christian music. WHCF-FM broadcasts to the Bangor, ME area at 88.5 FM.
FM RADIO STATION

WHCL-FM 40335
Owner: Hamilton College
Editorial: 198 College Hill Rd, Clinton, New York 13323-1218 **Tel:** 1 315 859-4200.
Email: mngrwhcl@hamilton.edu
Web site: http://www.whcl.org
Profile: WHCL-FM is a non-commercial station owned by Hamilton College. The format of the station is college variety. WHCL-FM broadcasts to the Clinton, NY area at 88.7 FM.
FM RADIO STATION

WHCN-FM 40336
Owner: iHeartMedia Inc.
Editorial: 10 Columbus Blvd, Hartford, Connecticut 06106-1976 **Tel:** 1 860 723-6000.
Web site: http://www.theriver1059.com
Profile: WHCN-FM is a commercial station owned by iHeartMedia Inc. The format of the station is classic hits music. WHCN-FM broadcasts to the Hartford, CT area at 105.9 FM.
FM RADIO STATION

WHCO-AM 35360
Owner: Hirsch Communications
Editorial: 1230 W Broadway St, Sparta, Illinois 62286-1664 **Tel:** 1 618 443-2121.
Email: news@realcountry1230.com
Web site: http://realcountry1230.com
Profile: WHCO-AM is a commercial station owned by Hirsch Communications. The format of the station is classic country. WHCO-AM broadcasts to Sparta, IL at 1230 AM.
AM RADIO STATION

WHCR-FM 43738
Owner: City College of New York
Editorial: City College 138th St & Covenant Ave, Room 11513, New York, New York 10031-9198 **Tel:** 1 212 650-7481.
Email: whcr903fm@whcr.org
Web site: http://www.whcr.org
Profile: WHCR-FM is a non-commercial station owned by the City College of New York. The format of the station is college variety. WHCR-FM broadcasts to the New York City metro area at 90.3 FM.
FM RADIO STATION

WHCU-AM 38764
Owner: Saga Communications
Editorial: 1751 Hanshaw Rd, Ithaca, New York 14850-9105 **Tel:** 1 607 257-6400.
Email: news@cyradiogroup.com
Web site: http://whcuradio.com
Profile: WHCU-AM is a commercial station owned by Saga Communications. The format of the station is news and talk. WHCU-AM broadcasts to the Ithaca, NY area at 870 AM.
AM RADIO STATION

WHCY-FM 40288
Owner: iHeartMedia Inc.
Editorial: 45 Ed Mitchell Ave, Franklin, New Jersey 07416-1588 **Tel:** 1 973 827-2525.
Web site: http://www.max1063.com
Profile: WHCY-FM is a commercial station owned by iHeartMedia Inc. The format of the station is Hot AC music. WHCY-FM broadcasts in the Newton, NJ area at 106.3 FM.
FM RADIO STATION

WHDD-AM 38667
Owner: Tri-State Public Communications, Inc
Editorial: 67 Main St, Sharon, Connecticut 6069 **Tel:** 1 860 364-4640.
Web site: http://www.am1020whdd.com
Profile: WHDD-AM is a commercial station owned by Tri-State Public Communications, Inc. The format of the station is news and talk. WHDD-AM broadcasts to the Sharon, CT area at 1020 AM.
AM RADIO STATION

WHDD-FM 527853
Owner: Tri-State Public Communications, Inc
Editorial: 67 Main St, Sharon, Connecticut 06069-2018 **Tel:** 1 860 364-4640.
Web site: http://www.robinhoodradio.com
Profile: WHDD-FM is a non-commercial station owned by Tri-State Public Communications, Inc. The format of the station is news and talk. WHDD-FM broadcasts to the Sharon, CT area at 91.9 FM.
FM RADIO STATION

WHDG-FM 42500
Owner: NRG Media LLC
Editorial: 3616 Highway 47, Rhinelander, Wisconsin 54501-8819 **Tel:** 1 715 362-1975.
Web site: http://www.whdg.com
Profile: WHDG-FM is a commercial station owned by NRG Media LLC. The format of the station is contemporary country music. WHDG-FM broadcasts to the Rhinelander, WI area at 97.3 FM.
FM RADIO STATION

WHDL-AM 38539
Owner: Community Broadcasters, LLC
Editorial: 3163 Nys Route 417, Olean, New York 14760-1853 **Tel:** 1 716 372-0161.
Profile: WHDL-AM is a commercial station owned by Community Broadcasters, LLC. The format of the station is oldies. WHDL-AM broadcasts to the Olean, NY area at 1450 AM.
AM RADIO STATION

WHDM-AM 36547
Owner: WHDM Broadcasting, Inc.
Editorial: 110 India Rd, Paris, Tennessee 38242-7565 **Tel:** 1 731 644-9455.
Email: news@wmufradio.com
Web site: http://www.whdmradio.com
Profile: WHDM-AM is a commercial station owned by WHDM Broadcasting, Inc. of Tennessee. The format of the station is oldies. WHDM-AM broadcasts to the Paris, TN area at 1440 AM.
AM RADIO STATION

WHDQ-FM 45193
Owner: Great Eastern Radio, LLC
Editorial: 106 N Main St, West Lebanon, New Hampshire 03784-1136 **Tel:** 1 603 298-0332.
Web site: http://www.theqrocks.com
Profile: WHDQ-FM is a commercial station owned by Great Eastern Radio, LLC. The format of the station is classic rock music. WHDQ-FM broadcasts to the West Lebanon, NH area at 106.1 FM.
FM RADIO STATION

WHEB-FM 41727
Owner: iheartMedia Inc.
Editorial: 815 Lafayette Rd, Portsmouth, New Hampshire 03801-5406 **Tel:** 1 603 436-7300.
Web site: http://www.wheb.com
Profile: WHEB-FM is a commercial station owned by iheartMedia Inc. The format of the station is rock. WHEB-FM broadcasts to the Boston area at 100.3 FM.
FM RADIO STATION

WHEE-AM 35361
Owner: Martinsville Media, Inc.
Editorial: 1129 Chatham Rd, Martinsville, Virginia 24112-2149 **Tel:** 1 276 632-9811.
Email: news@martinsvilledaily.com
Web site: http://www.martinsvillemedia.com
Profile: WHEE-AM is a commercial station owned by Martinsville Media, Inc. The format of the station is news and talk. WHEE-AM broadcasts to the Martinsville, VA area at 1370 AM.
AM RADIO STATION

WHEM-FM 43354
Owner: Fourth Dimension Inc.
Editorial: 228 E Lowes Creek Rd, Eau Claire, Wisconsin 54701-7250 **Tel:** 1 715 838-9595.
Email: whem@whem.com
Web site: http://www.whem.com
Profile: WHEM-FM is a non-commercial station owned by Fourth Dimension Inc. The format of the station is contemporary Christian programming. WHEM-FM broadcasts to the Eau Claire, WI area at 91.3 FM.
FM RADIO STATION

WHEN-AM 38792
Owner: iHeartMedia Inc.
Editorial: 500 Plum St Ste 100, Syracuse, New York 13204-1427 **Tel:** 1 315 472-9797.
Web site: http://power620.iheart.com
Profile: WHEN-AM is a commercial station owned by iHeartMedia Inc. The format of the station is Urban AC. WHEN-AM broadcasts to the Syracuse, NY area at 620 AM.
AM RADIO STATION

WHEP-AM 35363
Owner: Stewart Broadcasting Co. Inc.
Editorial: 20109 Hadley rd, Foley, Alabama 36535
Tel: 1 251 943-7131.
Email: whepnews@yahoo.com
Web site: http://www.whep1310.com
Profile: WHEP-AM is a commercial station owned by Stewart Broadcasting Co. Inc. The format for the station is news, talk and adult standards. WHEP-AM broadcasts to the Mobile, AL and Pensacola, FL areas at 1310 AM.
AM RADIO STATION

WHET-FM 738682
Owner: Withers Broadcasting Co.
Editorial: 1822 N Court St, Marion, Illinois 62959-4558
Tel: 1 618 997-8123.
Web site: http://www.mywithersradio.com
Profile: WHET-FM is a commercial station owned by Withers Broadcasting Co. The format of the station is classic country. WHET-FM broadcasts to the Cape Girardeau, MO area at 97.7 FM.
FM RADIO STATION

WHEW-AM 36259
Owner: S.G. Communications
Editorial: 1811 Carters Creek Pike, Franklin, Tennessee 37064-6823
Profile: WHEW-AM is a commercial station owned by S.G. Communications. The format of the station is Hispanic. WHEW-AM broadcasts to the Franklin, TN area at 1380 AM.
AM RADIO STATION

WHEZ-FM 450135
Owner: Lighthouse Gospel Network
Tel: 1 843 332-3182.
Web site: http://www.whezfm.com
FM RADIO STATION

WHFA-AM 35380
Owner: Starboard Media Foundation Inc.
Editorial: 1496 Bellevue St Ste 202, Green Bay, Wisconsin 54311-4205 **Tel:** 1 920 884-1460.
Email: info@relevantradio.com
Web site: http://www.relevantradio.com
Profile: WHFA-AM is a non-commercial station owned by Starboard Media Foundation Inc. The format of the station is religious music. WHFA-FM broadcasts to the Madison, WI area at 1240 AM.
AM RADIO STATION

WHFB-AM 37866
Owner: Gerard Media LLC
Editorial: 2100 Fairplain Ave, Benton Harbor, Michigan 49022-6828 **Tel:** 1 219 879-9810.
Web site: http://whfbradio.com
Profile: WHFB-AM is a commercial station owned by Gerard Media LLC. The format for the station is Conservative talk. WHFB-AM broadcasts to the Benton Harbor, MI area at 1060 AM.
AM RADIO STATION

WHFB-FM 45195
Owner: Mid-West Family Broadcasting
Editorial: 1301 E Douglas Rd, Mishawaka, Indiana 46545-1732 **Tel:** 1 574 233-3141.
Web site: http://www.newcountry999.com
Profile: WHFB-FM is a commercial station owned by Mid-West Family Broadcasting. The format of the station is contemporary country. WHFB-FM broadcasts to the South Bend, IN area at 99.9 FM.
FM RADIO STATION

WHFC-FM 40338
Owner: Harford Community College
Editorial: 401 Thomas Run Rd, Bel Air, Maryland 21015-1627 **Tel:** 1 443 412-2151.
Email: whfc@harford.edu
Web site: http://www.whfc911.org
Profile: WHFC-FM is a non-commercial station owned by Harford Community College. The format of the station is college variety. WHFC-FM broadcasts to the Bel Air, MD area at 91.1 FM.
FM RADIO STATION

WHFM-FM 40709
Owner: Cox Media Group, Inc.
Editorial: 555 Sunrise Hwy, West Babylon, New York 11704-6009 **Tel:** 1 631 587-1023.
Email: wbab@wbab.com
Web site: http://www.wbab.com
Profile: WHFM-FM is a commercial station owned by Cox Media Group, Inc. The format of the station is rock/album-oriented rock. WHFM-FM broadcasts to the West Babylon, NY area at 95.3 FM.
FM RADIO STATION

WHFR-FM 43784
Owner: Henry Ford Community College
Editorial: 5101 Evergreen Road Henry Ford CC, Dearborn, Michigan 48128-1495 **Tel:** 1 313 845-9676.
Email: whfr@hfcc.edu
Web site: http://www.whfr.fm
Profile: WHFR-FM is a non-commercial station owned by Henry Ford Community College. The format of the station is a variety of music including blues, jazz, folk, metal rock, classic rock and urban music. WHFR-FM broadcasts to Dearborn, MI at 89.3 FM.
FM RADIO STATION

WHFS-AM 38650
Owner: Beasley Broadcast Group
Editorial: 9721 Executive Center Dr N Ste 200, Saint Petersburg, Florida 33702-2439 **Tel:** 1 727 579-1925.
Web site: http://moneytalk1010.com
Profile: WHFS-AM is a commercial station owned by Beasley Broadcast Group. The format of the station is business talk. WHFS-AM broadcasts to the Tampa, FL area at 1010 AM.
AM RADIO STATION

WHFX-FM 46318
Owner: iHeartMedia Inc.
Editorial: 3833 US Highway 82, Brunswick, Georgia 31523-7735 **Tel:** 1 912 267-1025.
Email: scottryfun@gmail.com
Web site: http://1077thefox.net
Profile: WHFX-FM is a commercial station owned by iHeartMedia Inc. The format of the station is country. WHFX-FM broadcasts to the Brunswick, GA area at 107.7 FM.
FM RADIO STATION

WHGB-AM 38600
Owner: Cumulus Media Inc.
Editorial: 2300 Vartan Way, Harrisburg, Pennsylvania 17110-9720 **Tel:** 1 717 238-1041.
Web site: http://www.953nashicon.com/
Profile: WHGB-AM is a commercial station owned by Cumulus Media Inc. The format of the station is Country. WHGB-AM broadcasts to the Harrisburg, PA area at 1400 AM.
AM RADIO STATION

WHGG-AM 39414
Owner: Information Communications Corp.
Editorial: 340 Martin Luther King Jr Blvd Ste 100, Bristol, Tennessee 37620-4080 **Tel:** 1 423 878-6279.
Web site: http://loveradio.fm
Profile: WHGG-AM is a commercial station owned by Information Communications Corp. The format of the station is Contemporary Christian. WHGG-AM broadcasts to the Bristol, TN area at 1090 AM.
AM RADIO STATION

WHGH-AM 36165
Owner: Gross(Moses)
Tel: 1 229 228-4124.
Profile: WHGH-AM is a commercial station owned by Moses Gross. The format of the station is urban contemporary music. WHGH-AM broadcasts to the Thomasville, GA area at 840 AM.
AM RADIO STATION

WHGL-FM 45864
Owner: Cantroair Communications Co.
Editorial: 170 Redington Ave, Troy, Pennsylvania 16947 **Tel:** 1 570 297-0100.
Email: whgl100@gmail.com
Web site: http://www.wiggle100.com
Profile: WHGL-FM is a commercial station owned by Cantroair Communications Co. The format is contemporary country music. WHGL-FM broadcasts to the Troy, PA area at 100.3 FM.
FM RADIO STATION

WHGM-AM 35848
Owner: Benjamin-Dane, LLC
Editorial: 1605 Level Rd, Havre de Grace, Maryland 21078-1727
Email: info@smashhits.fm
Web site: http://www.smashhits.fm
Profile: WHGM-AM is a commercial station owned by Benjamin-Dane, LLC. The format of the station is smash hits. WHGM-AM broadcasts to the Baltimore area at 1330 AM.
AM RADIO STATION

WHHD-FM 41212
Owner: Beasley Broadcast Group
Editorial: 4051 Jimmie Dyess Pkwy, Augusta, Georgia 30909-9469 **Tel:** 1 706 396-7000.
Web site: http://www.hd983.com
Profile: WHHD-FM is a commercial station owned by Beasley Broadcast Group. The format of the station is Top 40/CHR. WHHD-FM broadcasts to the Augusta, SC area at 98.3 FM.
FM RADIO STATION

WHHH-FM 43045
Owner: Urban One, Inc.
Editorial: 21 E Saint Joseph St, Indianapolis, Indiana 46204-1025 **Tel:** 1 317 266-9600.
Web site: http://indyhiphop.com
Profile: WHHH-FM is a commercial station owned by Urban One, Inc. The format of the station is rhythmic Top 40/CHR music. WHHH-FM broadcasts to the Indianapolis area at 96.3 FM.
FM RADIO STATION

WHHL-FM 43610
Owner: Urban One, Inc.
Editorial: 9666 Olive Blvd Ste 610, Saint Louis, Missouri 63132-3026 **Tel:** 1 314 989-9550.
Web site: http://www.hot1041stl.com
Profile: WHHL-FM is a commercial station owned by Urban One, Inc. The format of the station is urban contemporary. WHHL-FM broadcasts to the St. Louis area at 104.1 FM.
FM RADIO STATION

WHHM-FM 42146
Owner: Southern Stone Communications, LLC
Editorial: 111 W Main St, Jackson, Tennessee 38301-6147 **Tel:** 1 731 427-9616.
Web site: http://www.star1077.com/
Profile: WHHM-FM is a commercial station owned by Southern Stone Communications, LLC. The format of the station is adult contemporary. WHHM-FM broadcasts to the Jackson, TN area at 107.7 FM.
FM RADIO STATION

WHHQ-AM 35450
Owner: Ave Maria Communications
Tel: 1 734 930-5200.
Web site: http://www.avemariaradio.net
Profile: WHHQ-AM is a commercial station owned by Ave Maria Communications. The format of the station is Catholic radio programming. WHHQ-AM broadcasts to the Saginaw, MI area at 1250 AM.
AM RADIO STATION

WHHT-FM 41135
Owner: Commonwealth Broadcasting Corp.
Editorial: 113 W Public Sq Ste 400, Glasgow, Kentucky 42141-2438 **Tel:** 1 270 651-6050.
Web site: http://www.1037thepoint.net
Profile: WHHT-FM is a commercial station owned by Commonwealth Broadcasting Corp. The format of the station is country. WHHT-FM broadcasts to the Glasgow, KY area at 103.7 FM.
FM RADIO STATION

WHHV-AM 35364
Owner: New Life Christian Communication
Editorial: 343 Virginia St., Hillsville, Virginia 24343
Tel: 1 276 728-9114.
Email: whhv@whhvradio.com
Web site: http://www.whhvradio.com
Profile: WHHV-AM is a commercial station owned by New Life Christian Communication. The format of the station is gospel music. WHHV-AM broadcasts to the Hillsville, VA area at 1400 AM.
AM RADIO STATION

WHHW-AM 37867
Owner: Alpha Media
Editorial: 1 Augustine Place, Hilton Head, South Carolina **Tel:** 1 843 785-9569.
Web site: http://am1130theisland.com
Profile: WHHW-AM is a commercial station owned by Alpha Media. The format of the station is adult standards and smooth jazz. WHHW-AM broadcasts to the Hilton Head, SC area at 1130 AM.
AM RADIO STATION

WHHY-FM 45197
Owner: Cumulus Media Inc.
Editorial: 1 Commerce St, Montgomery, Alabama 36104-3510 **Tel:** 1 334 240-9274.
Web site: http://www.y102montgomery.com
Profile: WHHY-FM is a commercial station owned by Cumulus Media Inc. The format of the station is Top 40/CHR. WHHY-FM broadcasts to the Montgomery, AL area at 101.9 FM.
FM RADIO STATION

WHHZ-FM 44332
Owner: Marc Radio Group, LLC
Editorial: 100 NW 76th Dr Ste 2, Gainesville, Florida 32607-6659 **Tel:** 1 352 313-3150.
Web site: http://www.1005thebuzz.com
Profile: WHHZ-FM is a commercial station owned by Marc Radio Group, LLC. The format of the station is rock alternative. WHHZ-FM broadcasts to the Gainesville, FL area at 100.5 FM.
FM RADIO STATION

WHIC-AM 35757
Owner: Holy Family Communications
Editorial: 1545 East Ave, Rochester, New York 14610-1614 **Tel:** 1 585 271-0530.
Email: info@thestationofthecross.com
Web site: http://www.whicradio.com
Profile: WHIC-AM is a commercial station owned by Holy Family Communications. The format of the station is religious. WHIC-AM broadcasts to the Rochester, NY area at 1460 AM.
AM RADIO STATION

WHIE-AM 35365
Owner: Chappell Communications LLC
Editorial: 1000 Memorial Dr, Griffin, Georgia 30223-4446 **Tel:** 1 770 227-9451.
Email: whieradio@gmail.com
Profile: WHIE-AM is a commercial station owned by Chappell Communictions LLC. The format of the station is country music. WHIE-AM broadcasts to the Griffin, GA area at 1320 AM.
AM RADIO STATION

WHIF-FM 42942
Owner: Putnam Radio Ministries Inc.
Editorial: 201 S Palm Ave, Palatka, Florida 32177-4141 **Tel:** 1 386 325-3334.
Email: info@whif.org
Web site: http://www.whif.org
Profile: WHIF-FM is a non-commercial station owned by Putnam Radio Ministries Inc. The format of the station is contemporary Christian. WHIF-FM broadcasts to the Palatka, FL area at 91.3 FM.
FM RADIO STATION

WHIJ-FM 41332
Owner: Radio Training Network, Inc.
Editorial: 2131 Nw 40Th Ter Ste E, Gainesville, Florida 32605-5800 **Tel:** 1 352 373-9553.
Email: thejoyfm@thejoyfm.com
Web site: http://www.thejoyfm.com
FM RADIO STATION

WHIL-FM 40342
Owner: Spring Hill College
Editorial: 920 Paul W Bryant Dr, Digital Media Center, Tuscaloosa, Alabama 35401-1260 **Tel:** 1 205 348-6644.
Email: comments@apr.org
Web site: http://www.apr.org
Profile: WHIL-FM is a non-commercial station owned by Spring Hill College. The format for the station is classical, news and talk. WHIL-FM broadcasts to the Mobile, AL, Pensacola, FL area at 91.3 FM. They do not accept pre-recorded PSAs.
FM RADIO STATION

WHIM-AM 35726
Owner: Salem Media Group, Inc.
Editorial: 2828 W Flagler St, Miami, Florida 33135-1337 **Tel:** 1 305 644-0800.
Web site: http://www.1080theanswer.com
Profile: WHIM-AM is a commercial station owned by Salem Media Group, Inc. The format of the station is Christian talk and religious. WHIM-AM broadcasts to the Miami area at 1080 AM.
AM RADIO STATION

WHIN-AM 35366
Owner: WHIN Inc.
Editorial: 1625 Highway 109 N, Gallatin, Tennessee 37066 **Tel:** 1 615 451-0450.
Email: whinam@comcast.net
Web site: http://www.whinradio.com
Profile: WHIN-AM is a commercial station owned by WHIN Inc. The format of the station is classic country. WHIN-AM broadcasts in the Gallatin, TN area at 1010 AM.
AM RADIO STATION

WHIO-AM 39356
Owner: Cox Media Group, Inc.
Editorial: 1611 S Main St, Dayton, Ohio 45409-2547
Tel: 1 937 259-2111.
Web site: http://www.newstalkradiowhio.com
Profile: WHIO-AM is a commercial station owned by Cox Media Group, Inc. The format of the station is news and talk. WHIO-AM broadcasts to the Dayton, OH area at 1290 AM.
AM RADIO STATION

WHIO-FM 44214
Owner: Cox Media Group, Inc.
Editorial: 1611 S Main St, Dayton, Ohio 45409-2547
Tel: 1 937 259-2111.
Web site: http://www.whio.com
Profile: WHIO-FM is a commercial station owned by Cox Media Group, Inc. The format of the station is news and talk. WDPT-FM broadcasts to the Dayton, OH area at 95.7 FM.
FM RADIO STATION

WHIP-AM 35367
Owner: Hamrick(Glenn)
Editorial: 2432 Statesville Hwy, Mooresville, North Carolina 28115-7968 **Tel:** 1 704 664-9447.
Web site: http://carolinascene.com/w/whip/index.htm
Profile: WHIP-AM is a commercial station owned by Glenn Hamrick. The format of the station is oldies music. WHIP-AM broadcasts to the Mooresville, NC, at 1350 AM.
AM RADIO STATION

WHIR-AM 37869
Owner: Hometown Broadcasting
Editorial: 2063 Shakertown Rd, Danville, Kentucky 40422-9262 **Tel:** 1 859 236-2711.
Email: hometownradio@hometownlive.net
Web site: http://hometownlive.net
Profile: WHIR-AM is a commercial station owned by Hometown Broadcasting. The format for the station is news, sports and talk. WHIR-AM broadcasts to the Lexington, KY area at 1230 AM.
AM RADIO STATION

WHIS-AM 38314
Owner: Alpha Media
Editorial: 900 Bluefield Ave, Bluefield, West Virginia 24701-2744 **Tel:** 1 304 327-7114.
Web site: http://www.whistalkradio.com
Profile: WHIS-AM is a commercial station owned by Alpha Media. The format of the station is news and talk. WHIS-AM broadcasts to the Bluefield, WV area at 1440 AM.
AM RADIO STATION

WHIT-AM 39246
Owner: Midwest Family Broadcasting
Editorial: 730 Ray O Vac Dr, Madison, Wisconsin 53711 **Tel:** 1 608 273-1000.
Web site: http://www.hitradio1550.com
AM RADIO STATION

WHIZ-AM 37870
Owner: Southeastern Ohio Broadcasting, Inc.
Editorial: 629 Downard Rd, Zanesville, Ohio 43701-5108 **Tel:** 1 740 452-5431.
Email: webmaster@whizamfmtv.com
Web site: http://www.whiznews.com
Profile: WHIZ-AM is a commercial station owned by Southeastern Ohio Broadcasting, Inc. The format of the station is Adult, Contemporary. WHIZ-AM broadcasts locally to the Zanesville, OH area at a frequency of 1240 AM.
AM RADIO STATION

WHIZ-FM 41009
Owner: Southeastern Ohio Broadcastng, Inc.
Editorial: 629 Downard Rd, Zanesville, Ohio 43701-5108 **Tel:** 1 740 452-5431.
Email: webmaster@whizamfmtv.com
Web site: https://www.whiznews.com/radio/z92
Profile: WHIZ-FM is a non-commercial station owned by Southeastern Ohio Broadcastng, Inc. The format of the station is Top 40. WHIZ-FM broadcasts to the Zanesville, OH area at 92.7 FM.
FM RADIO STATION

WHJB-FM 43621
Owner: Renda Broadcasting
Editorial: 2000 Tower Way, Ste 2040, Greensburg, Pennsylvania 15601 **Tel:** 1 724 216-1200.
Web site: http://www.whjbfm.com
Profile: WHJB-FM is a commercial station owned by Renda Broadcasting. The format of the station is classic hits. WHJB-FM broadcasts to the Greensburg area at 107.1 FM.
FM RADIO STATION

WHJD-AM 38260
Owner: Broadcast South, LLC
Editorial: 546 Baxley Hwy, Hazlehurst, Georgia 31539-5917 **Tel:** 1 912 375-4511.
Web site: http://1059thesting.com
Profile: WHJD-AM is a commercial station owned by Broadcast South, LLC. The format for the station is classic country. WHJD-AM broadcasts to the Savannah, GA area at 920 AM.
AM RADIO STATION

WHJJ-AM 38877
Owner: iHeartMedia Inc.
Editorial: 75 Oxford St, Providence, Rhode Island 02905-4722 **Tel:** 1 401 781-9979.
Web site: http://www.920whjj.com
Profile: WHJJ-AM is a commercial station owned by iHeartMedia Inc. The format of the station is news and talk. WHJJ-AM broadcasts to the Providence, RI area at 920 AM.
AM RADIO STATION

WHJT-FM 44404
Owner: Mississippi College
Editorial: 100 S Jefferson, Clinton, Mississippi 39056-4236 **Tel:** 1 601 925-3458.
Email: psas@star93fm.com
Web site: http://www.star93fm.com
Profile: WHJT-FM is a commercial station owned by Mississippi College. The format of the station is contemporary Christian. WHJT-FM broadcasts to the Clinton, MS area at 93.5 FM.
FM RADIO STATION

WHJY-FM 46217
Owner: iHeartMedia Inc.
Editorial: 75 Oxford St, Providence, Rhode Island 02905-4722 **Tel:** 1 401 781-9979.
Email: jocks@whjy.com
Web site: http://www.94hjy.com
Profile: WHJY-FM is a commercial station owned by iHeartMedia Inc. The format of the station is rock music. WHJY-FM broadcasts to the Providence, RI area at 94.1 FM.
FM RADIO STATION

WHK-AM 38772
Owner: Salem Media Group, Inc.
Editorial: 4 Summit Park Dr Ste 150, Independence, Ohio 44131-6921 **Tel:** 1 216 901-0921.
Email: youropinioncounts@whkradio.com
Web site: http://www.whkradio.com
Profile: WHK-AM is a commercial station owned by Salem Media Group, Inc. The format of the station is Conservative talk. WHK-AM broadcasts to the Independence, OH area at 1420 AM.
AM RADIO STATION

WHKB-FM 41965
Owner: Houghton Community Broadcasting Corporation
Editorial: 313 E Montezuma Ave, Houghton, Michigan 49931-2112 **Tel:** 1 906 482-7700.
Email: houghtonradio@up.net
Web site: http://www.kbear102.com
Profile: WHKB-FM is a commercial station owned by Houghton Community Broadcasting Corporation. The format of the station is contemporary country music. WHKB-FM broadcasts to the Houghton, MI area at 102.3 FM.
FM RADIO STATION

WHKF-FM 41060
Owner: iHeartMedia Inc.
Editorial: 600 Corporate Cir, Harrisburg, Pennsylvania 17110-9787 **Tel:** 1 717 540-8800.
Web site: http://www.993kissfm.com
Profile: WHKF-FM is a commercial station owned by iHeartMedia Inc. The format of the station is Top 40/CHR. WHKF-FM broadcasts to the Harrisburg, PA area at 99.3 FM.
FM RADIO STATION

WHKL-FM 43550
Owner: Batesville Broadcasting Co.
Editorial: 1040 Highway 6 W, Batesville, Mississippi 38606-8104 **Tel:** 1 662 563-4664.
Email: country101radio@yahoo.com
Web site: http://www.wble101.com
Profile: WHKL-FM is owned by Batesville Broadcasting Co. The format of the station is oldies music. WHKL-FM's broadcasts to the Memphis, TN area at 106.9 FM.
FM RADIO STATION

WHKN-FM 41020
Owner: Radio Statesboro, Inc.
Editorial: 561 E Olliff St, Statesboro, Georgia 30458-4663 **Tel:** 1 912 764-5446.
Email: wwwnswmcd@yahoo.com
Web site: http://statesboro365.com
Profile: WHKN-FM is a commercial station owned by Radio Statesboro, Inc. The format of the station is classic and contemporary country. WHKN-FM broadcasts to the Statesboro, GA area at 94.9 FM.
FM RADIO STATION

WHKO-FM 46718
Owner: Cox Media Group, Inc.
Editorial: 1611 S Main St, Dayton, Ohio 45409-2547 **Tel:** 1 937 259-2111.
Web site: http://www.k99online.com
Profile: WHKO-FM is a commercial station owned by Cox Media Group, Inc. The format of the station is country. WHKO-FM broadcasts to the Dayton, OH area at 99.1 FM.
FM RADIO STATION

WHKP-AM 35368
Owner: Radio Hendersonville Inc.
Editorial: 1450 7th Ave E, Hendersonville, North Carolina 28792-2860 **Tel:** 1 828 693-9061.
Email: 1450@whkp.com
Web site: http://www.whkp.com
Profile: WHKP-AM is a commercial station owned by Radio Hendersonville Inc. The format of the station is talk and variety programming. WHKP-AM broadcasts to the Hendersonville, NC area at 1450 AM.
AM RADIO STATION

WHKR-FM 41024
Owner: Cumulus Media Inc.
Editorial: 1800 W Hibiscus Blvd Ste 138, Melbourne, Florida 32901-2624 **Tel:** 1 321 984-1000.
Web site: http://www.nashfm1027.com
Profile: WHKR-FM is a commercial station owned by Cumulus Broadcasting. The format of the station is classic and contemporary country music. WHKR-FM broadcasts to the Melbourne, FL area at 102.7 AM.
FM RADIO STATION

WHKS-FM 41975
Owner: L-Com Inc.
Editorial: 42 N Main St, Port Allegany, Pennsylvania 16743 **Tel:** 1 814 642-7004.
Email: whks@verizon.net
Profile: WHKS-FM is a commercial station owned by L-Com Inc. The format of the station is adult contemporary music. WHKS-FM broadcasts to the Port Allegany, NY area at 94.9 FM.
FM RADIO STATION

WHKT-AM 37033
Owner: Chesapeake-Portsmouth Broadcasting Corp.
Editorial: 2202 Jolliff Rd, Chesapeake, Virginia 23321-1416 **Tel:** 1 757 488-1010.
Email: info@1650whkt.com
Web site: http://1650whkt.com
Profile: WHKT-AM is owned by Chesapeake-Portsmouth Broadcasting Corporation. The format is conservative talk. The station broadcasts to the Hampton Roads, VA area at a frequency of 1650 AM.
AM RADIO STATION

WHKW-AM 75002
Owner: Salem Media Group, Inc.
Editorial: 4 Summit Park Dr Ste 150, Cleveland, Ohio 44131-6921 **Tel:** 1 216 901-0921.
Email: kevin.isaacs@salemcleveland.com
Web site: http://www.whkwradio.com
Profile: WHKW-AM is a commercial station owned by Salem Media Group, Inc. The format of the station is religion. WHKW-AM broadcasts to the Cleveland area at 1220 AM.
AM RADIO STATION

WHKX-FM 45045
Owner: Alpha Media
Editorial: 900 Bluefield Ave, Bluefield, West Virginia 24701-2744 **Tel:** 1 304 327-7114.
Web site: http://www.kickscountry.com
Profile: WHKX-FM is a commercial station owned by Alpha Media. The format of the station is classic and contemporary country music. WHKX-FM broadcasts to the Bluefield, WV area at 106.3 FM.
FM RADIO STATION

WHKY-AM 35860
Owner: Long Communications
Editorial: 526 Main Ave SE, Hickory, North Carolina 28602-1103 **Tel:** 1 828 322-1290.
Email: news@whky.com
Web site: http://www.whky.com
Profile: WHKY-AM is a commercial station owned by Long Communications. The format of the station is news, sports and talk. WHKY-AM broadcasts to the Hickory, NC area at 1290 AM.
AM RADIO STATION

WHKZ-AM 39435
Owner: Salem Media Group, Inc.
Editorial: 4 Summit Park Dr Ste 150, Independence, Ohio 44131-6921 **Tel:** 1 216 901-0921.
Email: kevin.isaacs@salemcleveland.com
Web site: http://www.whkwradio.com
Profile: WHKZ-AM is a commercial station owned by Salem Media Group, Inc. The format of the station is religious. WHKZ-AM broadcasts to the Warrenville, OH area at 1220 AM.
AM RADIO STATION

WHLC-FM 42489
Owner: Charisma Radio Corp.
Editorial: 2420 Highway 64 East, Highlands, North Carolina 28741 **Tel:** 1 828 526-1045.
Email: info@whlc.com
Web site: http://www.whlc.com
Profile: WHLC-FM is a commercial station owned by Charisma Radio Corp. The format of the station is easy listening music. WHLC-FM broadcasts locally to the Greenville, SC and Asheville, NC areas at 104.5 FM.
FM RADIO STATION

WHLD-AM 35369
Owner: Cumulus Media Inc.
Editorial: 50 James E Casey Dr, Buffalo, New York 14206-2367 **Tel:** 1 716 881-4555.
Web site: http://www.sportsradio1270.com
Profile: WHLD-AM is a commercial station owned by Cumulus Media Inc. The format of the station is sports. WHLD-AM broadcasts to the Buffalo, NY area at 1270 AM.
AM RADIO STATION

WHLF-FM 44212
Owner: Lakes Media LLC
Editorial: 1210 Porter Ln, South Boston, Virginia 24592-5324 **Tel:** 1 434 572-2988.
Email: news@whlf.com
Web site: http://www.953hlf.com
Profile: WHLF-FM is a commercial station owned by Lakes Media LLC. The format of the station is adult contemporary music. WHLF-FM broadcasts to the Roanoke-Lynchburg, VA area at 95.3 FM.
FM RADIO STATION

WHLG-FM 44118
Editorial: 1670 NW Federal Hwy, Stuart, Florida 34994-9630 **Tel:** 1 772 692-9454.
Email: info@coast1013.com
Web site: http://www.coast1013.com
Profile: WHLG-FM is a commercial station owned by N/A. The format of the station is Hot AC. WHLG-FM broadcasts to the Stuart, FL area at 101.3 FM.
FM RADIO STATION

WHLH-FM 40474
Owner: iHeartMedia Inc.
Editorial: 1375 Beasley Rd, Jackson, Mississippi 39206-2018 **Tel:** 1 601 982-1062.
Web site: http://www.hallelujah955.com
Profile: WHLH-FM is a commercial station owned by iHeartMedia Inc. The format of the station is gospel. WHLH-FM broadcasts to the Jackson, MS area at 95.5 FM.
FM RADIO STATION

WHLI-AM 38601
Owner: Connoisseur Media, Inc.
Editorial: 234 Airport Plaza Blvd Ste 5, Farmingdale, New York 11735-3938 **Tel:** 1 631 770-4200.
Email: webmaster@liradiogroup.com
Web site: http://www.whli.com
Profile: WHLI-AM is a commercial station owned by Connoisseur Media, Inc. The format of the station is adult standards. WHLI-AM broadcasts to the Farmingdale, NY, area at 1100 AM.
AM RADIO STATION

WHLJ-FM 44019
Owner: LaTaurus Productions Inc.
Editorial: 5852 US Highway 84 E, Naylor, Georgia 31641-2954 **Tel:** 1 229 242-9997.
Web site: http://foxy97.com/
Profile: WHLJ-FM is a commercial station owned by LaTaurus Productions Inc. The format of the station is urban adult contemporary and gospel. WHLJ-FM broadcasts to the Valdosta, GA area at 97.5 FM.
FM RADIO STATION

WHLK-FM 46009
Owner: iHeartMedia Inc.
Editorial: 6200 Oak Tree Blvd Ste 400, Independence, Ohio 44131-6934 **Tel:** 1 216 520-2600.
Email: feedback@1065thelake.com
Web site: http://www.1065thelake.com/main.html
Profile: WHLK-FM is a commercial station owned by iHeartMedia Inc. The format of the station is adult hits. WHLK-FM broadcasts in the Cleveland area at 106.5 FM.
FM RADIO STATION

WHLL-AM 38035
Owner: Cumulus Media Inc.
Editorial: 1000 Hall of Fame Ave, Springfield, Massachusetts 01105-2538 **Tel:** 1 413 737-1414.
Web site: http://www.1450thehall.com
Profile: WHLL-AM is a commercial station owned by Cumulus Media Inc. The format of the station is sports. WHLL-AM broadcasts to the Springfield, MA area at 1450 AM.
AM RADIO STATION

WHLM-AM 35254
Owner: Columbia Broadcasting Co.
Editorial: 124 E Main St, Bloomsburg, Pennsylvania 17815 **Tel:** 1 570 784-1200.
Email: whlmam@aol.com
Web site: http://www.whlmam.com
Profile: WHLM-AM is a commercial station owned by Columbia Broadcasting Co. The format of the station is news, talk and sports. WHLM-AM broadcasts to the Bloomsburg, PA area at 930 AM.
AM RADIO STATION

WHLM-FM 41885
Owner: Columbia Broadcasting Co.
Editorial: 124 E Main St, Bloomsburg, Pennsylvania 17815-1807 **Tel:** 1 570 784-1200.
Email: whlmam@aol.com
Web site: http://www.whlmfm.com
Profile: WHLM-FM is a commercial station owned by Columbia Broadcasting Co. The format for the station is classic rock. WHLM-FM broadcasts to the Bloomsburg, Pa. area at 103.5 FM.
FM RADIO STATION

WHLN-AM 35370
Owner: Radio Harlan Inc.
Editorial: 100 Eversole St, Ste 1, Harlan, Kentucky 40831 **Tel:** 1 606 573-2540.
Email: whln@harlanonline.net
Profile: WHLN-AM is a commercial station owned by Radio Harlan Inc. The format of the station is adult contemporary music. WHLN-AM broadcasts to the Harlan, KY area at 1410 AM.
AM RADIO STATION

WHLO-AM 36622
Owner: iHeartMedia Inc.
Editorial: 7755 Freedom Ave NW, North Canton, Ohio 44720-6905 **Tel:** 1 330 836-4700.
Web site: http://640whlo.iheart.com
Profile: WHLO-AM is a commercial station owned by iHeartMedia Inc. The format of the station is news and talk. WHLO-AM broadcasts in the Cleveland area at 640 AM.
AM RADIO STATION

WHLP-FM 518126
Owner: Calvary Radio Network
Editorial: 150 Lincolnway, Ste 2001, Valparaiso, Indiana 46383 **Tel:** 1 219 548-5800.
Email: info@calvaryradionet.com
Web site: http://www.calvaryradionetwork.com
Profile: WHLP-FM is a non-commercial station owned by Calvary Radio Network. The format of the station is Christian music and religious programming. WHLP-FM broadcasts to the Hanna, IN area at 89.9 FM.
FM RADIO STATION

WHLS-AM 39139
Owner: Radio First
Editorial: 808 Huron Ave, Port Huron, Michigan 48060-3705 **Tel:** 1 810 982-9000.
Profile: WHLS-AM is a commercial station owned by Radio First. The format of the station is classic hits. WHLS-AM broadcasts to the Port Huron, MI area at 1450 AM.
AM RADIO STATION

WHLW-FM 43437
Owner: iHeartMedia Inc.
Editorial: 203 Gunn Rd, Montgomery, Alabama 36117-2003 **Tel:** 1 334 274-6464.
Web site: http://www.1043hallelujahfm.com
Profile: WHLW-FM is a commercial station owned by iHeartMedia Inc. The format of the station is urban contemporary gospel. WHLW-FM broadcasts to the Montgomery, AL area at 104.3 FM.
FM RADIO STATION

WHLX-AM 35667
Owner: Radio First
Editorial: 808 Huron Ave, Port Huron, Michigan 48060-3705 **Tel:** 1 810 982-9000.
Profile: WHLX-AM is a commercial station owned by Radio First. The format of the station is classic hits. WHLX-AM broadcasts to the Port Huron, MI area at 1590 AM.
AM RADIO STATION

WHLY-AM 35168
Owner: Times Communications, Inc.
Editorial: 930 E Lincoln Ave, Goshen, Indiana 46528-3504 **Tel:** 1 574 533-3330.
Email: larazaindiana@yahoo.com
Web site: http://www.larazaindiana.com
Profile: WHLY-AM is a commercial station owned by Times Communications, Inc. The format of the station is Regional Mexican. WHLY-AM broadcasts to the South Bend, IL area at a frequency of 1580 AM.
AM RADIO STATION

WHMA-AM 37874
Owner: Williams Communications Inc.
Editorial: 801 Noble St Ste 30, Anniston, Alabama 36201-0503 **Tel:** 1 256 236-1880.
Email: prod983@cableone.net
Web site: http://whmabig95.com
Profile: WHMA-AM is a commercial station owned by Williams Communications Inc. The format of the station is gospel. WHMA-AM broadcasts to the Birmingham, AL area at 1390 AM.
AM RADIO STATION

WHMA-FM 4585
Owner: Williams Communications Inc.
Editorial: 4724 Post Oak Rd, Anniston, Alabama 36206-1783 **Tel:** 1 256 236-1880.
Email: whmabig95@cableone.net
Web site: http://www.whmabig95.com
Profile: WHMA-FM is a commercial station owned by Williams Communications Inc. The format of the station is classic country. WHMA-FM broadcasts to the Anniston, AL area at 95.5FM.
FM RADIO STATION

WHMD-FM 45205
Owner: Northshore Broadcasting Inc.
Editorial: 200 E Thomas St, Hammond, Louisiana 70401-3316 **Tel:** 1 985 345-0060.
Web site: http://kajun107.com/
Profile: WHMD-FM is a commercial station owned by Northshore Broadcasting Inc. The format of the station is country music. WHMD-FM broadcasts to the New Orleans area at 107.1 FM.
FM RADIO STATION

WHME-FM 40344
Owner: LeSEA Broadcasting
Editorial: 61300 Ironwood Rd, South Bend, Indiana 46614 **Tel:** 1 574 291-8200.
Email: whmefm@lesea.com
Web site: http://www.whmefm.com
Profile: WHME-FM is a commercial station owned by LeSEA Broadcasting. The format for the station is contemporary Christian. WHME-FM broadcasts to the South Bend, IN area at 103.1 FM.
FM RADIO STATION

WHMH-FM 45206
Owner: Tri-County Broadcasting
Editorial: 1010 2nd St N, Sauk Rapids, Minnesota 56379 **Tel:** 1 320 252-6200.
Email: mail@rockin101.com
Web site: http://www.rockin101.com
Profile: WHMH-FM is a commercial station owned by Tri-County Broadcasting. The format of the station is rock music. WHMH-FM broadcasts in the Sauk Rapids, MN area at 101.7 FM.
FM RADIO STATION

WHMI-FM 42921
Owner: Krol Communications Inc.
Editorial: 1277 Parkway Dr, Howell, Michigan 48843-7568 **Tel:** 1 517 546-0860.
Email: news@whmi.com
Web site: http://www.whmi.com
Profile: WHMI-FM is a commercial station owned by Krol Communications Inc. The format of the station is classic hits. WHMI-FM broadcasts to the Howell, MI area at 93.5 FM.
FM RADIO STATION

WHMJ-FM 45594
Owner: FM Radio Licenses, LLC
Editorial: 900 Water St, Meadville, Pennsylvania 16335-3428 **Tel:** 1 814 724-1111.
Web site: http://www.mymajicspace.com
Profile: WHMJ-FM is a commercial station owned by FM Radio Licenses, LLC. The format of the station is hot adult contemporary. WHMJ-FM broadcasts to the Meadville, PA area at 99.3 FM.
FM RADIO STATION

WHMP-AM 37875
Owner: Saga Communications
Editorial: 15 Hampton Ave, Northampton, Massachusetts 1060 **Tel:** 1 413 586-7400.
Web site: http://www.whmp.com
Profile: WHMP-AM is a commercial station owned by Saga Communications. The format of the station is news and talk. WHMP-AM broadcasts to the Northampton, MA area at 1400 AM.
AM RADIO STATION

WHMQ-AM 37858
Owner: Saga Communications
Editorial: 81 Woodard Rd, Greenfield, Massachusetts 1301 **Tel:** 1 413 774-4301.
Web site: http://www.whmp.com
Profile: WHMQ-AM is a commercial station owned by Saga Communications. The format of the station is news, sports and talk. WHMQ-AM broadcasts to the Greenfield, MA area at 1240 AM.
AM RADIO STATION

WHMS-FM 74730
Owner: D.W.S. Inc.
Editorial: 2301 S Neil St, Champaign, Illinois 61820-7507 **Tel:** 1 217 351-5300.
Email: 975@whms.com
Web site: http://www.whms.com
Profile: WHMS-FM is a commercial station owned by D.W.S. Inc. The format of the station is Lite Rock/Lite AC music. WHMS-FM broadcasts to the Champaign, IL area at 97.5 FM.
FM RADIO STATION

WHMT-AM 35911
Owner: Coffee County Broadcasting, Inc
Editorial: 1030 Oakdale St, Manchester, Tennessee 37355-5618 **Tel:** 1 931 728-3526.
Email: whmtradio@yahoo.com
Web site: http://tullahomaradio.com
Profile: WHMT-AM is a commercial station owned by Coffee County Broadcasting, Inc. The format of the station is country. WHMT-AM broadcasts to the Tullahoma, TN area at 740 AM.
AM RADIO STATION

WHMX-FM 43220
Owner: Lighthouse Radio Network, Inc.
Editorial: 1476 Broadway, Bangor, Maine 04401-2404 **Tel:** 1 207 262-1057.
Email: contact@solutionfm.com
Web site: http://www.solutionfm.com
Profile: WHMX-FM is a non-commercial station owned by Lighthouse Radio Network, Inc. The format of the station is contemporary Christian music. WHMX-FM broadcasts to the Bangor, ME area at 105.7 FM.
FM RADIO STATION

WHNA-FM 134047
Owner: Seven Mountains Media, LLC
Editorial: 12 E Market St, Lewistown, Pennsylvania 17044-2123 **Tel:** 1 717 248-6757.
Web site: http://hanna923.com
Profile: WHNA-FM is a commercial radio station owned by Seven Mountains Media, LLC. The format of the station is classic hits. WVSL-FM broadcasts to the Selinsgrove, PA area at 92.3 FM.
FM RADIO STATION

WHNC-AM 35371
Owner: Paradise Radio Network
Editorial: 601 Henderson St, Oxford, North Carolina 27565-3450 **Tel:** 1 919 693-3540.
Email: alvin@dralvin.com
Profile: WHNC-AM is a commercial station owned by Paradise Radio Network. The format of the station is R&B, gospel and oldies music. WHNC-AM broadcasts to the Durham, NC area at 1340 AM.
AM RADIO STATION

WHNN-FM 40345
Owner: Cumulus Media Inc.
Editorial: 1740 Champagne Dr N, Saginaw, Michigan 48604-9239 **Tel:** 1 989 776-2100.
Web site: http://www.whnn.com
Profile: WHNN-FM is a commercial station owned by Cumulus Media Inc. The format of the station is adult contemporary. WHNN-FM broadcasts to the Saginaw, MI area at 96.1 FM.
FM RADIO STATION

WHNP-AM 38609
Owner: Saga Communications
Editorial: 15 Hampton Ave, Northampton, Massachusetts 1060 **Tel:** 1 413 586-7400.
Web site: http://www.whmp.com
AM RADIO STATION

WHNR-AM 35784
Owner: GB Enterprises Communications Corp.
Editorial: 1505 Dundee Rd, Winter Haven, Florida 33884-1013 **Tel:** 1 863 299-1141.
Web site: http://www.1170radio.com
Profile: WHNR-AM is a commercial station owned by GB Enterprises Communications Corp. The format of the station is classic country. WHNR-AM broadcasts in the Greater Lakeland, FL area at 1360 AM.
AM RADIO STATION

WHNZ-AM 37027
Owner: iHeartMedia Inc.
Editorial: 4002 W Gandy Blvd, Tampa, Florida 33611-3410 **Tel:** 1 813 839-9393.
Web site: http://whnz.iheart.com/
Profile: WHNZ-AM is a commercial station owned by iHeartMedia Inc. The format of the station is Sports and talk. WHNZ-AM broadcasts to the Tampa, FL area at 1250 AM.
AM RADIO STATION

WHO-AM 37876
Owner: iHeartMedia Inc.
Editorial: 2141 Grand Ave, Des Moines, Iowa 50312-5303 **Tel:** 1 515 245-8900.
Web site: http://www.whoradio.com
Profile: WHO-AM is a commercial station owned by iHeartMedia Inc. The format of the station is news and talk. WHO-AM broadcasts to the Des Moines, IA area at 1040 AM.
AM RADIO STATION

WHOC-AM 39359
Owner: WHOC, Inc.
Editorial: 1016 W Beacon St, Philadelphia, Mississippi 39350-3204 **Tel:** 1 601 656-1490.
Email: wwslfm@bellsouth.net
Web site: http://www.whocmedia.com/
Profile: WHOC-AM is a commercial station owned by WHOC, Inc. The format of the station is talk. WHOC-AM broadcasts to the Philadelphia, MS area at 1490 AM.
AM RADIO STATION

WHOD-FM 45209
Owner: Capital Assets, Inc.
Editorial: 4428 N College Ave, Hwy 43, Jackson, Alabama 36545-2017 **Tel:** 1 251 246-4431.
Email: info@bamadixie.com
Web site: http://bamadixie.com/dixie945
Profile: WHOD-FM is a commercial station owned by Capital Assets, Inc. The format of the station is classic rock. WHOD-FM broadcasts to the Jackson, AL area at 94.5 FM.
FM RADIO STATION

WHOF-FM 446328
Owner: iHeartMedia Inc.
Editorial: 7755 Freedom Ave NW, North Canton, Ohio 44720-6905 **Tel:** 1 330 836-4700.
Web site: http://www.my1017.com
Profile: WHOF-FM is a commercial station owned by iHeartMedia Inc. The format of the station is adult contemporary. WHOF-FM broadcasts to the North Canton, OH area at 107.7 FM.
FM RADIO STATION

WHOG-AM 36044
Owner: Hobson City Broadcasting Co.
Editorial: 1330 Noble St, Ste 25, Anniston, Alabama 36201 **Tel:** 1 256 236-6484.
Email: hog1120@aol.com
Profile: WHOG-AM is a commercial station owned by Hobson City Broadcasting Co. The format of the station is urban contemporary. WHOG-AM broadcasts to the Anniston, AL area on 1120 AM.
AM RADIO STATION

WHOG-FM 46716
Owner: Black Crow Radio, LLC
Editorial: 126 W International Speedway Blvd, Daytona Beach, Florida 32114-4322 **Tel:** 1 386 239-9506.
Web site: http://www.whog957.com
Profile: WHOG-FM is a commercial station owned by Black Crow Radio, LLC. The format of the station is classic rock music. WHOG-FM broadcasts to the Daytona Beach, FL area at 95.7 FM.
FM RADIO STATION

WHOL-AM 35374
Owner: Grey Matter Broadcasting
Editorial: 1125 Colorado St, Allentown, Pennsylvania 18103-3118 **Tel:** 1 610 434-4801.
Web site: http://www.laolaradio.com
Profile: WHOL-AM is a commercial station owned by Grey Matter Broadcasting. The format of the station is Spanish tropical. WHOL-AM broadcasts to the Allentown, PA area at 1600 AM.
AM RADIO STATION

WHOM-FM 40346
Owner: Townsquare Media, LLC
Editorial: 1 City Ctr, Portland, Maine 04101-6420 **Tel:** 1 207 774-6364.
Email: 94.9whom@cumulus.com
Web site: http://www.949whom.com
Profile: WHOM-FM is a commercial station owned by Townsquare Media, LLC. The format of the station is adult contemporary. WHOM-FM broadcasts to the Portland, ME area at 94.9 FM.
FM RADIO STATION

WHON-AM 37878
Owner: Brewer Broadcasting Inc.
Editorial: 2626 Tingler Rd W, Richmond, Indiana 47374 **Tel:** 1 765 962-1595.
Web site: http://www.1017thepoint.com
Profile: WHON-AM is a commercial station owned by Brewer Broadcasting Inc. The format of the station is adult contemporary. WHON-AM broadcasts to the Richmond, IN area at 930 AM.
AM RADIO STATION

WHOO-AM 35324
Owner: Genesis Communications Inc.
Editorial: 1160 S Semoran Blvd Ste A, Orlando, Florida 32807-1461 **Tel:** 1 407 380-9255.
Web site: http://www.sportstalkflorida.com
Profile: WHOO-AM is a commercial station owned by Genesis Communications Inc. The format of the station is sports. WHOO-AM broadcasts to the Orlando, FL area at 1080 AM.
AM RADIO STATION

WHOP-AM 37879
Owner: Forcht Broadcasting Inc.
Editorial: 220 Dink Embrys Buttermilk Rd, Hopkinsville, Kentucky 42240 **Tel:** 1 270 885-5331.
Email: whop@forchtbroadcasting.com
Web site: http://www.lite987whop.com
Profile: WHOP-AM is a commercial station owned by Forcht Broadcasting Inc. The format of the station is news and talk. WHOP-AM broadcasts to the Hopkinsville, KY area at 1230 AM.
AM RADIO STATION

WHOP-FM 45210
Owner: HOP Broadcasting Inc.
Editorial: 220 Dink Embry's Buttermilk Road, Hopkinsville, Kentucky 42241 **Tel:** 1 270 885-5331.
Email: whopamfm@bellsouth.net
Web site: http://www.lite987whop.com
Profile: WHOP-FM is a commercial station owned by HOP Broadcasting Inc. The format of the station is adult contemporary. WHOP-FM broadcasts to the Hopkinsville, KY area at 98.7 FM.
FM RADIO STATION

WHOS-AM 38761
Owner: iHeartMedia Inc.
Editorial: 26869 Peoples Rd, Madison, Alabama 35756-4632 **Tel:** 1 256 353-1750.
Web site: http://www.wbhpam.com
Profile: WHOS-AM is a commercial station owned by iHeartMedia Inc. The format of the station is news, sports and talk. WHOS-AM broadcasts to the Madison, AL area at 800 AM. WHOS-AM is a simulcast of WBHP-AM in Huntsville.
AM RADIO STATION

WHOT-FM 43549
Owner: Cumulus Media Inc.
Editorial: 4040 Simon Rd, Youngstown, Ohio 44512-1362 **Tel:** 1 330 783-1000.
Web site: http://www.hot101.com
Profile: WHOT-FM is a commercial station owned by Cumulus Media Inc. The format of the station is Top 40/CHR. WHOT-FM broadcasts to the Youngstown, OH area at 101.1 FM.
FM RADIO STATION

WHOU-FM 43616
Owner: Northern Maine Media
Editorial: 39 Court St Ste 215, Houlton, Maine 04730-2055 **Tel:** 1 207 532-3600.
Email: production@whoufm.com
Web site: http://www.whoufm.com
Profile: WHOU-FM is a commercial station WBCQ-FM is a commercial station currently owned by County Communications Inc, but operated by Northern Maine Media (Grant, Fred). The format of the station is adult contemporary. WHOU-FM broadcasts to the Houlton, ME area at 100.1 FM.
FM RADIO STATION

WHOW-AM 39518
Owner: Kaskaskia Broadcasting, Inc.
Editorial: 2980 US Highway 51, Clinton, Illinois 61727-9479 **Tel:** 1 217 935-9590.
Email: whownews@randyradio.com
Web site: http://www.dewittdailynews.com/
Profile: WHOW-AM is a commercial station owned by Kaskaskia Broadcasting, Inc. The format of the station is news, talk and agricultural programming. WHOW-AM broadcasts to the Clinton, IL area at 1520 AM.
AM RADIO STATION

WHP-AM 37880
Owner: iHeartMedia Inc.
Editorial: 600 Corporate Cir, Harrisburg, Pennsylvania 17110-9787 **Tel:** 1 717 540-8800.
Email: news@whp580.com
Web site: http://www.whp580.com
Profile: WHP-AM is a commercial station owned by iHeartMedia Inc. The format of the station is news and talk. WHP-AM broadcasts to the greater Harrisburg, PA area at 580 AM.
AM RADIO STATION

WHPC-FM 40348
Owner: Nassau Community College
Editorial: 1 Education Dr, Garden City, New York 11530-6719 **Tel:** 1 516 572-7438.
Email: whpc@ncc.edu
Web site: http://www.ncc.edu/studentlife/whpcradiostation/default.shtml
Profile: WHPC-FM is a non-commercial college station owned by Nassau Community College. The format of the station is variety. WHPC-FM broadcasts to the Garden City, NY area at 90.3 FM.
FM RADIO STATION

WHPD-FM 45129
Owner: LeSEA Broadcasting
Editorial: 61300 Ironwood Rd, South Bend, Indiana 46614-9019 **Tel:** 1 574 291-8200.
Email: pulse@lesea.com
Web site: http://www.pulsefm.com
Profile: WHPD-FM is a commercial station owned by LeSEA Broadcasting. The format for the station is contemporary Christian music. WHPD-FM broadcasts to the Dowagiac, MI area at 92.1 FM and is a simulcast of WHPZ-FM.
FM RADIO STATION

WHPE-FM 40349
Owner: Bible Broadcasting Network
Editorial: 11530 Carmel Commons Blvd, Charlotte, North Carolina 28226-3976 **Tel:** 1 704 523-5555.
Email: bbn@bbnmedia.org
Web site: http://www.bbnradio.org
Profile: WHPE-FM is a non-commercial station owned by Bible Broadcasting Network. The format of the station is religious programming. WHPE-FM broadcasts to the High Point, NC area at 95.5 FM.
FM RADIO STATION

WHPF-FM 781620
Owner: Light of Life Ministries, Inc.
Editorial: 160 Bangor St, Augusta, Maine 04330-4162 **Tel:** 1 207 622-1340.
Email: info@worshipradionetwork.org
Web site: http://www.worshipradionetwork.org
Profile: WHPF-FM is a non-commercial station owned by Light of Life Ministries, Inc. The format of the station features Contemporary Christian music. WHPF-FM broadcasts to the Pittston Farm, ME area at a frequency of 88.1 FM.
FM RADIO STATION

WHPH-FM 45150
Owner: Great South Wireless, LLC
Email: thepeach977@yahoo.com
Web site: http://977thepeach.com/
Profile: WHPH-FM is a commercial station owned by Great South Wireless, LLC. The format of the station is Classic Hits music. WHPH-FM broadcasts to the Clanton, AL area at 97.7 FM.
FM RADIO STATION

WHPI-FM 41226
Owner: Advanced Media Partners LLC
Editorial: 2006 W Altorfer Dr, Peoria, Illinois 61615-1864 **Tel:** 1 309 691-0101.
Web site: http://www.jack1011.com
Profile: WHPI-FM is a commercial station owned by Advanced Media Partners LLC. The format of the station is adult hits. WHPI-FM broadcasts to the Peoria, IL area at 101.1 FM.
FM RADIO STATION

WHPO-FM 40351
Owner: Hooterville Broadcasting Inc.
Editorial: 912 S Dixie Hwy, Hoopeston, Illinois 60942-1965 **Tel:** 1 217 283-7744.
Email: whpo@whporadio.com
Web site: http://www.whporadio.com
Profile: WHPO-FM is a commercial station owned by Hooterville Broadcasting Inc. The format of the station is country. WHPO-FM broadcasts to the Hoopeston, IL area at a frequency of 100.9 FM.
FM RADIO STATION

WHPP-FM 46191
Owner: Grace Broadcasting Services, Inc.
Editorial: 25 Stonebrook Pl Ste G, Jackson, Tennessee 38305-3686 **Tel:** 1 731 663-2327.
Web site: http://www.hippieradio1053.com

Profile: WHPP-FM is a commercial station owned by Grace Broadcasting Services, Inc. The format of the station is classic hits. WHPP-FM broadcasts to the Memphis, TN area at 105.3 FM.
FM RADIO STATION

WHPR-FM 43708
Owner: R. J.'s Late Night Entertainment Corporation
Editorial: 160 Victor St, Highland Park, Michigan 48203-3130 **Tel:** 1 313 868-6612.
Web site: http://fm881whpr.com
Profile: WHPR-FM is a non-commercial station owned by R. J.'s Late Night Entertainment Corporation. The format of the station is oldies and talk. WHPR-FM broadcasts to the Highland Park, MI area at 88.1 FM.
FM RADIO STATION

WHPT-FM 44288
Owner: Cox Media Group, Inc.
Editorial: 11300 4th St N Ste 300, Saint Petersburg, Florida 33716-2941 **Tel:** 1 727 579-2000.
Web site: http://www.theboneonline.com
Profile: WHPT-FM is a commercial station owned by Cox Media Group, Inc. The format of the station is talk. WHPT-FM broadcasts to the Saint Petersburg, FL area at 102.5 FM.
FM RADIO STATION

WHPY-FM 40382
Owner: Kensington Digital Media
Editorial: 49 Music Sq W Fl 3, Nashville, Tennessee 37203-3213 **Tel:** 1 877 393-1555.
Email: info@hippieradio945.com
Web site: http://www.hippieradio945.com
Profile: WHPY-FM is a commercial station owned by Kensington Digital Media. The format of the station is classic hits. WHPY-FM broadcasts to the Greater Nashville, TN area at 94.5 FM.
FM RADIO STATION

WHPZ-FM 42563
Owner: LeSEA Broadcasting
Editorial: 61300 Ironwood Rd, South Bend, Indiana 46614-9019 **Tel:** 1 574 291-8200.
Email: pulse@lesea.com
Web site: http://www.pulsefm.com
Profile: WHPZ-FM is a commercial station owned by LeSEA Broadcasting. The format of the station is contemporary Christian. WHPZ-FM broadcasts to the South Bend, IN area at 96.9 FM.
FM RADIO STATION

WHQA-FM 46247
Owner: The Power Foundation
Tel: 1 877 700-8047.
Web site: http://www.thelifefm.com
Profile: WHQA-FM is a commercial station owned by Power Foundation. The format for the station is Christian music and talk. WHQA-FM broadcasts to the Anderson, SC area at 103.1 FM.
FM RADIO STATION

WHQC-FM 40847
Owner: iHeartMedia Inc.
Editorial: 801 Woodrdg Ctr Dr, Charlotte, North Carolina 28217-1908 **Tel:** 1 704 714-9444.
Web site: http://channel961.iheart.com
Profile: WHQC-FM is a commercial station owned by iHeartMedia Inc. The format of the station is Top 40/CHR. WHQC-FM broadcasts in the Charlotte, NC area at 96.1 FM
FM RADIO STATION

WHQG-FM 45786
Owner: Saga Communications
Editorial: 5407 W McKinley Ave, Milwaukee, Wisconsin 53208 **Tel:** 1 414 978-9000.
Email: headhog@1029thehog.com
Web site: http://www.1029thehog.com
Profile: WHQG-FM is a commercial station owned by Saga Communications. The format of the station is rock music. WHQG-FM broadcasts to the Milwaukee area at 102.9 FM.
FM RADIO STATION

WHQQ-FM 42002
Owner: Cromwell Group Inc.(The)
Editorial: 405 S Banker St Ste 201, Effingham, Illinois 62401-2591 **Tel:** 1 217 342-4141.
Web site: http://www.effinghamradio.com
Profile: WHQQ-FM is a commercial station owned by the Cromwell Group Inc. The format of the station is sports. WHQQ-FM broadcasts in the Mattoon, IL area at 98.9 FM.
FM RADIO STATION

WHQR-FM 41567
Owner: Friends of Public Radio
Editorial: 254 N Front St Ste 300, Wilmington, North Carolina 28401-8600 **Tel:** 1 910 343-1640.
Email: news@whqr.org
Web site: http://www.whqr.org
Profile: WHQR-FM is a non-commercial station owned by Friends of Public Radio. The format of the station is news and classical music. WHQR-FM broadcasts in the Wilmington, NC area at 91.3 FM.
FM RADIO STATION

WHQT-FM 40352
Owner: Cox Media Group, Inc.
Editorial: 2741 N 29th Ave, 3rd Fl, Hollywood, Florida 33020-1503 **Tel:** 1 305 444-4404.
Web site: http://www.hot105fm.com
Profile: WHQT-FM is a commercial station owned by Cox Media Group, Inc. The format of the station is urban adult contemporary. WHQT-FM broadcasts to the Hollywood, FL area at 105.1 FM.
FM RADIO STATION

WHQX-FM 43942
Owner: Alpha Media
Editorial: 900 Bluefield Ave, Bluefield, West Virginia 24701-2744 **Tel:** 1 304 327-7114.
Web site: http://www.kickscountry.com
Profile: WHQX-FM is a commercial station owned by Alpha Media. The format of the station is country music. WHQX-FM broadcasts to the Bluefield, WV area at 107.7 FM.
FM RADIO STATION

WHRB-FM 40353
Owner: Harvard Radio Broadcasting Co. Inc.
Editorial: 389 Harvard St, Cambridge, Massachusetts 2138 **Tel:** 1 617 495-4818.
Email: news@whrb.org
Web site: http://www.whrb.org
Profile: WHRB-FM is a commercial station owned by Harvard Radio Broadcasting Co. Inc. The format of the station is variety. WHRB-FM broadcasts to the Cambridge, MA area at 95.3 FM.
FM RADIO STATION

WHRK-FM 46429
Owner: iHeartMedia Inc.
Editorial: 2650 Thousand Oaks Blvd Ste 4100, Memphis, Tennessee 38118-2451 **Tel:** 1 901 259-1300.
Web site: http://www.k97fm.com
Profile: WHRK-FM is a commercial station owned by iHeartMedia Inc. The format of the station is urban contemporary music. WHRK-FM broadcasts to the Memphis, TN area at 97.1 FM.
FM RADIO STATION

WHRP-FM 43208
Owner: Cumulus Media Inc.
Editorial: 1717 US Highway 72 E, Athens, Alabama 35611-4413 **Tel:** 1 256 830-8300.
Web site: http://www.whrpfm.com
Profile: WHRP-FM is a commercial station owned by Cumulus Media Inc. The format of the station is urban adult contemporary music. WHRP-FM broadcasts to the Huntsville, AL area at 94.1 FM.
FM RADIO STATION

WHRY-AM 39340
Owner: Big G Little O Inc.
Editorial: 209 Harrison St, Ironwood, Michigan 49938-1713 **Tel:** 1 906 932-5234.
Email: wupm@wupm-whry.com
Web site: http://www.wupm-whry.com
Profile: WHRY-AM is a commercial station owned by Big G Little O Inc. The format of the station is Hot AC. WHRY-AM broadcasts in the Ironwood, MI area at 1450 AM.
AM RADIO STATION

WHSB-FM 40357
Owner: Edwards Communications LLC
Editorial: 1491 M 32 W, Alpena, Michigan 49707-8194 **Tel:** 1 989 354-4611.
Email: news@truenorthradionetwork.com
Web site: http://www.truenorthradio.com
Profile: WHSB-FM is a commercial station owned by Edwards Communications LLC. The format for the station is hot adult contemporary. WHSB-FM broadcasts to the Alpena, MI area at 107.7 FM.
FM RADIO STATION

WHSC-AM 38644
Owner: Cumulus Media Inc.
Editorial: 11640 Highway 17 Byp, Murrells Inlet, South Carolina 29576-9332 **Tel:** 1 843 651-7869.
Profile: WHSC-AM is a commercial station owned by Cumulus Media Inc. The format of the station is sports. WHSC-AM broadcasts to the Murrells Inlet, SC area at 1050 AM.
AM RADIO STATION

WHSM-FM 45213
Owner: Red Rock Radio Corp.
Editorial: 16880 W Us Highway 63, Hayward, Wisconsin 54843-7186 **Tel:** 1 715 634-4836.
Email: news@whsm.com
Web site: http://www.whsm.com
Profile: WHSM-FM is a commercial station owned by Red Rock Radio Corp. The format of the station is adult contemporary. WHSM-FM broadcasts in the Hayward, WI area at 101.1 FM.
FM RADIO STATION

WHSR-AM 36994
Owner: Beasley Broadcast Group
Editorial: 6699 N Federal Hwy Ste 200, Boca Raton, Florida 33487-1660 **Tel:** 1 561 997-0074.
Web site: http://www.whsrradio.com
Profile: WHRS-AM is a commercial station owned by Beasley Broadcast Group. The format of the station is ethnic and international talk and entertainment. WHSR-AM broadcasts to the Boca Raton, FL area at 980 AM.
AM RADIO STATION

WHST-FM 42849
Owner: Northern Christian Radio
Editorial: 1511 E M 32, Gaylord, Michigan 49735-9702 **Tel:** 1 989 732-6274.
Email: studio@thepromisefm.com
Web site: http://www.thepromisefm.com
Profile: WHST-FM is a non-commercial station owned by Northern Christian Radio. The format of the station is religious and contemporary Christian programming. WHST-FM broadcasts to the Gaylord, MI area at 106.1 FM.
FM RADIO STATION

WHSX-FM 41825
Owner: Forbis Communications Inc.
Editorial: 1130 S Dixie St, Horse Cave, Kentucky 42749-1462 **Tel:** 1 270 786-1000.
Email: 991@scrtc.com
Web site: http://www.thehoss.com
Profile: WHSX-FM is a commercial station owned by Forbis Communications Inc. The format of the station is contemporary country music. WHSX-FM broadcasts to the Horse Cave, KY area at 99.1 FM.
FM RADIO STATION

WHTA-FM 44083
Owner: Urban One, Inc.
Editorial: 101 Marietta St NW, Atlanta, Georgia 30303-2720 **Tel:** 1 404 765-9750.
Web site: http://hotspotatl.com
Profile: WHTA-FM is a commercial station owned by Urban One, Inc. The format of the station is urban contemporary music. WHTA-FM broadcasts to the Atlanta area at 107.9 FM.
FM RADIO STATION

WHTB-AM 35971
Owner: Karam(Robert & James)
Editorial: 1 Home St, Somerset, Massachusetts 2725 **Tel:** 1 508 678-9727.
Web site: http://www.radiovozdoemigrante.com
Profile: WHTB-AM is a commercial station owned by Robert and James Karam. The format of the station is Portuguese talk programming. WHTB-AM broadcasts to the Somerset, MA area at 1400 AM.
AM RADIO STATION

WHTC-AM 36198
Owner: Midwest Communications Inc.
Editorial: 87 Central Ave, Holland, Michigan 49423-2829 **Tel:** 1 616 392-3121.
Web site: http://www.whtc.com
Profile: WHTC-AM is a commercial station owned by Midwest Communications Inc. The format of the station is and talk. WHTC-AM broadcasts to the Holland, MI area at 1450 AM.
AM RADIO STATION

WHTE-FM 43672
Owner: Monticello Media LLC
Editorial: 1150 Pepsi Pl, Charlottesville, Virginia 22901 **Tel:** 1 434 978-4408.
Web site: http://www.1019hot.com
Profile: WHTE-FM is a commercial station owned by Monticello Media LLC. The format of the station is Top 40/CHR music. WHTE-FM broadcasts to the Charlottesville, VA area at 101.9 FM.
FM RADIO STATION

WHTF-FM 40524
Owner: Red Hills Broadcasting, LLC
Editorial: 3000 Olson Rd, Tallahassee, Florida 32308-3918 **Tel:** 1 850 386-8004.
Web site: http://www.hot1049.com
Profile: WHTF-FM is a commercial station owned by Red Hills Broadcasting, LLC. The format of the station is Top 40/CHR. WHTF-FM broadcasts to the Tallahassee, FL area at 104.9 FM.
FM RADIO STATION

WHTG-AM 37882
Owner: Press Communications LLC
Editorial: 2355 W Bangs Ave, Neptune, New Jersey 07753-4111 **Tel:** 1 732 774-4755.
Web site: http://www.1410amradio.com
Profile: WHTG-AM is a commercial station owned by Press Communications LLC. The format of the station is oldies music. WHTG-AM broadcasts in the Neptune, NJ area at 1410 AM.
AM RADIO STATION

WHTH-AM 37883
Owner: Runnymede Inc.
Editorial: 1000 N 40th St, Newark, Ohio 43055-1467 **Tel:** 1 740 522-8171.
Email: news@wnko.com
Web site: http://www.wnko.com
Profile: WHTH-AM is a commercial station owned by Runnymede Inc. The format of the station is Country. WHTH-AM broadcasts to the Newark, OH area at 790 AM.
AM RADIO STATION

WHTK-AM 36310
Owner: iHeartMedia Inc.
Editorial: 100 Chestnut St Ste 1700, 100 Chestnut St., Rochester, New York 14604-2418 **Tel:** 1 585 454-4884.
Web site: http://www.whtk.com
Profile: WHTK-AM is a commercial station owned by iHeartMedia Inc. The format of the station is sports and talk. WHTK-AM broadcasts to the Rochester, NY area at 1280 AM.
AM RADIO STATION

WHTL-FM 40359
Owner: WHTL Group LLC
Editorial: N35609 Highway 53, Whitehall, Wisconsin 54773-9188 **Tel:** 1 715 538-4341.
Web site: http://whtlradio.com
Profile: WHTL-FM is a commercial station owned by WHTL Group LLC. The format of the station is Classic Hits. WHTL-FM broadcasts to the Whitehall, WI area at 102.3 FM.
FM RADIO STATION

WHTO-FM 139794
Owner: Results Broadcasting
Editorial: 212 W J St, Iron Mountain, Michigan 49801-4646 **Tel:** 1 906 774-5731.
Web site: http://www.1067themountain.com
Profile: WHTO-FM is a commercial station owned by Results Broadcasting. The format of the station is oldies. WHTO-FM broadcasts to the Marquette, MI area at 106.7 FM.
FM RADIO STATION

WHTP-FM 40210
Owner: Mainestream Media
Editorial: 89 Mussey Rd Suite 100, Scarborough, Maine 04074-5900 **Tel:** 1 207 883-0615.
Email: hot1047@mainestreamonline.com
Web site: http://www.hot1047maine.com
Profile: WHTP-FM is a commercial station owned by Mainestream Media. The format of the station is Top 40/CHR. WHTP-FM broadcasts to the Portland, ME area at 104.7 FM.
FM RADIO STATION

WHTQ-FM 40902
Owner: NRG Media LLC
Editorial: 2301 Plover Rd, Plover, Wisconsin 54467 **Tel:** 1 715 341-8838.
Web site: http://www.hot967fm.com
Profile: WHTQ-FM is a commercial station owned by NRG Media LLC. The format of the station is Top 40/CHR. WHTQ-FM broadcasts to the Plover, WI area at 96.7 FM.
FM RADIO STATION

WHTS-FM 40201
Owner: Cumulus Media Inc.
Editorial: 60 Monroe Ctr NW, Grand Rapids, Michigan 49502-0001 **Tel:** 1 616 774-8461.
Web site: http://www.1053hotfm.com
Profile: WHTS-FM is a commercial station owned by Cumulus Media Inc. The format of the station is Top 40/CHR. WHTS-FM broadcasts to the Grand Rapids, MI, area at 105.3 FM.
FM RADIO STATION

WHTT-FM 80343
Owner: Cumulus Media Inc.
Editorial: 50 James E Casey Dr, Buffalo, New York 14206-2367 **Tel:** 1 716 881-4555.
Email: whtt@whtt.com
Web site: http://www.whtt.com
Profile: WHTT-FM is a commercial station owned by Cumulus Media Inc. The format of the station is classic hits. WHTT-FM broadcasts to the Buffalo, NY area at 104.1 FM.
FM RADIO STATION

WHTU-FM 45630
Owner: Mel Wheeler Broadcasting
Editorial: 508 W Oak St, Covington, Virginia 24426-1942 **Tel:** 1 540 962-1133.
Profile: WHTU-FM is a commercial station owned by Mel Wheeler Broadcasting. The format of the station is classic hits music. WHTU-FM broadcasts to the Covington, VA area at 103.9 FM.
FM RADIO STATION

WHTX-AM 35577
Owner: Sagittarius Communications, LLC
Editorial: 5380 Webb Road, Mineral Ridge, Ohio 44515 **Tel:** 1 330 394-7700.
Profile: WHTX-AM is a commercial station owned by Sagittarius Communications, LLC. The format of the station is urban/rhythmic oldies. WHTX-AM broadcasts to the Warren, OH area at 1570 AM.
AM RADIO STATION

WHTY-AM 35601
Owner: Travis Media LLC
Editorial: 2475 Mercer Ave Ste 104, West Palm Beach, Florida 33401-7447 **Tel:** 1 561 242-8155.
Email: infojames@hotmail.com
Web site: http://www.radiovisionnouvelle.com
Profile: WHTY-AM is a commercial station owned by Travis Media LLC. The format of the station is Haitian ethnic programming. WHTY-AM broadcasts to the West Palm Beach area at 1600 AM.
AM RADIO STATION

WHTZ-FM 40360
Owner: iHeartMedia Inc.
Editorial: 32 Avenue of the Americas Fl 3, New York, New York 10013-2473 **Tel:** 1 212 377-7900.
Web site: http://z100.iheart.com
Profile: WHTZ-FM is a commercial station owned by iHeartMedia Inc. The format of the station is Top 40/CHR music. WHTZ-FM broadcasts to the New York City area at 100.3 FM.
FM RADIO STATION

WHUB-AM 38135
Owner: Cookeville Communications, LLC
Editorial: 698 S Willow Ave, Cookeville, Tennessee 38501-3802 **Tel:** 1 931 526-7144.
Web site: http://www.1400thehub.com
Profile: WHUB-AM is a commercial station owned by Cookeville Communications, LLC. The format of the station is news and talk. WHUB-AM broadcasts to the Cookeville, TN area at 1400 AM.
AM RADIO STATION

WHUC-AM 39166
Owner: iHeartMedia Inc.
Editorial: 5620 State Route 9G, Hudson, New York 12534-4127 **Tel:** 1 518 828-5006.
Web site: http://www.1230whuc.com

Profile: WHUC-AM is a commercial station owned by iHeartMedia Inc. The format of the station is adult standards music. WHUC-AM broadcasts to the Hudson, NY area at 1230 AM. Address all mail to Bill Williams, Program Director.
AM RADIO STATION

WHUD-FM 46458
Owner: Pamal Broadcasting Ltd.
Editorial: 715 Route 52, Beacon, New York 12508-1047 **Tel:** 1 845 838-6000.
Web site: http://www.whud.com
Profile: WHUD-FM is a commercial station owned by Pamal Broadcasting Ltd. The format of the station is adult contemporary music. WHUD-FM broadcasts throughout Hudson Valley and Westchester County in New York at 100.7 FM.
FM RADIO STATION

WHUG-FM 46368
Owner: Media One Group, LLC
Editorial: 2 Orchard Rd, Jamestown, New York 14701
Tel: 1 716 487-1151.
Email: news@radiojamestown.com
Web site: http://www.whug.com
Profile: WHUG-FM is a commercial station owned by Media One Group, LLC. The format of the station is country music. WHUG-FM broadcasts in the Jamestown, NY area at 101.9 FM.
FM RADIO STATION

WHUN-AM 36430
Owner: Megahertz LLC
Editorial: 10773 William Penn Hwy, Huntingdon, Pennsylvania 16652-6806 **Tel:** 1 814 643-9620.
Profile: WHUN-AM is a commercial station owned by Forever Communications and operated Megahertz LLC. The format of the station is sports. WLLI-AM broadcasts to the Huntingdon, PA area at 1150.
AM RADIO STATION

WHUN-FM 41988
Owner: FM Radio Licenses, LLC
Editorial: 10773 William Penn Hwy, Huntingdon, Pennsylvania 16652-6806 **Tel:** 1 814 643-1063.
Web site: http://www.hunny103.com/
Profile: WHUN-FM is a commercial station owned by FM Radio Licenses, LLC. The format of the station is oldies. WHUN-FM broadcasts to the Huntingdon, PA area at 103.5.
FM RADIO STATION

WHVE-FM 42188
Owner: Shoreline Communications Inc.
Editorial: 7955 Russell Springs Rd, Russell Springs, Kentucky 42642 **Tel:** 1 270 866-7979.
Email: thewave@ridingthewave.com
Web site: http://www.ridingthewave.com
Profile: WHVE-FM is a commercial station owned by Shoreline Communications Inc. The format of the station is adult contemporary. WHVE-FM broadcasts to the Russell Springs, KY area at 92.7 FM.
FM RADIO STATION

WHVN-AM 35376
Owner: GHB Broadcasting
Editorial: 5732 N Tryon St, Charlotte, North Carolina 28213-6802 **Tel:** 1 704 596-1240.
Web site: http://www.heavenradio.org
Profile: WHVN-AM is a commercial station owned by GHB Broadcasting. The format of the station is religious and Christian programming. WHVN-AM broadcasts to the Charlotte, NC area at 1240 AM.
AM RADIO STATION

WHVO-AM 36531
Owner: Mann, Beth A.
Editorial: 19 Wooldridge Rd, Cadiz, Kentucky 42211-6734 **Tel:** 1 270 886-1480.
Email: wkdz@wkdzradio.com
Web site: http://www.whvoradio.com
Profile: WHVO-AM is a commercial station owned by Beth A. Mann. The format of the station is oldies. WHVO-AM broadcasts to the Cadiz, KY area at 1480 AM.
AM RADIO STATION

WHVR-AM 37887
Owner: Forever Media
Editorial: 275 Radio Rd, Hanover, Pennsylvania 17331-1140 **Tel:** 1 717 637-3831.
Web site: http://www.foreveryork.com
Profile: WHVR-AM is a commercial station owned by Forever Media. The format of the station is classic hits. WHVR-AM broadcasts to the Hanover, PA area at 1280 AM. Press releases/materials and PSA's can be directed to the Promotions Director.
AM RADIO STATION

WHVW-AM 35377
Owner: Ferraro(J.P.)
Editorial: 316 Main St Ste 5, Poughkeepsie, New York 12601-3123 **Tel:** 1 845 471-8180.
Email: whvw@whvw.net
Web site: http://www.whvw.net
Profile: WHVW-FM is a commercial station owned by J.P. Ferraro. The format of the station is oldies. WHVW-FM broadcasts to the Poughkeepsie, NY area at 950 AM.
AM RADIO STATION

WHWG-FM 44418
Owner: Gospel Opportunities Inc.
Editorial: 130 Carmen Dr, Marquette, Michigan 49855
Tel: 1 906 249-1423.
Email: whwl@whwl.net
Web site: http://www.whwl.net
Profile: WHWG-FM is a non-commercial station owned by Gospel Opportunities Inc. The format for the station is religious. WHWG-FM broadcasts to the Marquette, MI area at 89.9 FM.
FM RADIO STATION

WHWH-AM 37888
Owner: Multicultural Radio Broadcasting Inc.
Editorial: 3573 Bristol Pike Rear 102, Bensalem, Pennsylvania 19020-4666 **Tel:** 1 609 333-9432.
Web site: http://www.radiowttm1680.com
Profile: WHWH-AM is a commercial station owned by Multicultural Radio Broadcasting Inc. The format of the station is Hispanic programming. WHWH-AM broadcasts to the Princeton, NJ area at 1350 AM.
AM RADIO STATION

WHWK-FM 46541
Owner: Townsquare Media, Inc.
Editorial: 59 Court St, Binghamton, New York 13901-3270 **Tel:** 1 607 772-8400.
Web site: http://www.981thehawk.com
Profile: WHWK-FM is a commercial station owned by Townsquare Media, Inc. The format of the station is contemporary country. WHWK-FM broadcasts to the Binghamton, NY area at 98.1 FM.
FM RADIO STATION

WHWL-FM 41058
Owner: Gospel Opportunities Inc.
Editorial: 130 Carmen Dr, Marquette, Michigan 49855
Tel: 1 906 249-1423.
Email: whwl@whwl.net
Web site: http://www.whwl.net
Profile: WHWL-FM is a non-commercial station owned by Gospel Opportunities Inc. The format for the station is religious. WHWL-FM broadcasts to the Marquette, MI area at 95.7 FM.
FM RADIO STATION

WHWY-FM 42445
Owner: Community Broadcasters
Editorial: 34 Harbor Blvd Ste 202, Destin, Florida 32541-7365 **Tel:** 1 850 654-1000.
Web site: http://www.highway98country.com
Profile: WHWY-FM is a commercial station ownedy by Community Broadcasters. The format is contemporary country. The station broadcasts at 98.1 FM in Fort Walton Beach, FL and surrounding areas.
FM RADIO STATION

WHXR-FM 43275
Owner: WBIN, Inc.
Editorial: 477 Congress St Ste 3, Portland, Maine 04101-3427 **Tel:** 1 207 797-0780.
Web site: http://www.boneradio.com
Profile: WHXR-FM is a commercial station owned by WBIN, Inc. The format of the station is rock. WHXR-FM broadcasts to the Portland, ME area at 106.3 FM.
FM RADIO STATION

WHXT-FM 44068
Owner: Alpha Media
Editorial: 1900 Pineview Dr, Columbia, South Carolina 29209-5079 **Tel:** 1 803 695-8600.
Web site: http://www.hot1039fm.com
Profile: WHXT-FM is a commercial station owned by Alpha Media. The format of the station is urban contemporary. WHXT-FM broadcasts to the Columbia, SC area at a frequency of 103.9 FM.
FM RADIO STATION

WHYA-FM 42910
Owner: Codcomm Inc.
Editorial: 243 South St, Hyannis, Massachusetts 02601-3926 **Tel:** 1 508 778-6000.
Web site: http://www.y101.cc
Profile: WHYA-FM is a commercial station owned by Codcomm Inc. The format of the station is Top 40/ CHR. WHYA-FM broadcasts to the Cape Cod, MA area at 101.1 FM.
FM RADIO STATION

WHYB-FM 46354
Owner: Radio Plus Bay Cities, LLC
Editorial: 413 10th Ave, Menominee, Michigan 49858-3009 **Tel:** 1 906 863-5551.
Email: reception@baycitiesradio.net
Web site: http://www.baycitiesradio.net
Profile: WHYB-FM is a commercial station owned by Radio Plus Bay Cities, LLC. The format of the station is oldies. WHYB-FM broadcasts to the Menominee, MI area at 103.7 FM.
FM RADIO STATION

WHYF-AM 35918
Owner: Holy Family Radio, Inc
Editorial: 8 W Main St, Shiremanstown, Pennsylvania 17011-6326 **Tel:** 1 717 525-8110.
Email: contact@yourholyfamilyradio.com
Web site: http://www.yourholyfamilyradio.com
Profile: WHYF-AM is a commercial station owned by Holy Family Radio, Inc. The format of the station is Catholic programming. WHYF-AM broadcasts to the Shiremanstown, PA area at 720 AM.
AM RADIO STATION

WHYI-FM 40363
Owner: iHeartMedia Inc.
Editorial: 7601 Riviera Blvd, Miramar, Florida 33023-6574 **Tel:** 1 954 862-2000.
Web site: http://www.y100.com
Profile: WHYI-FM is a commercial station owned by iHeartMedia Inc. The format of the station is Top 40/ CHR music. WHYI-FM broadcasts to the Miami area at 100.7 FM.
FM RADIO STATION

WHYL-AM 37889
Editorial: 728 N Hanover St, Carlisle, Pennsylvania 17013-1534
Profile: WHYL-AM is a commercial station owned by WHYL, Inc. (Harold Z. Swidler). The format of the station is oldies. WHYL-AM broadcasts to the Carlisle, Pennsylvania area at a frequency of 960 AM.
AM RADIO STATION

WHYM-AM 558539
Owner: Miller Communications Inc.
Editorial: 2423 Walker Swinton Rd, Timmonsville, South Carolina 29161-9351 **Tel:** 1 843 678-9393.
Email: production@miller.fm
Web site: http://www.miller.fm
Profile: WHYM-AM is a commercial station owned by Miller Communications Inc. The format of the station is sports. WHYM-AM broadcasts to the Lake City, SC area at 1260 AM.
AM RADIO STATION

WHYN-AM 38425
Owner: iHeartMedia Inc.
Editorial: 1331 Main St Ste 4, Springfield, Massachusetts 01103-1621 **Tel:** 1 413 781-1011.
Web site: http://whyn.iheart.com
Profile: WHYN-AM is a commercial station owned by iHeartMedia Inc. The format of the station is news and talk. WHYN-AM broadcasts in the Springfield, MA area at 560 AM.
AM RADIO STATION

WHYN-FM 45793
Owner: iHeartMedia Inc.
Editorial: 1331 Main St Ste 4, Springfield, Massachusetts 01103-1621 **Tel:** 1 413 781-1011.
Web site: http://www.mix931.com
Profile: WHYN-FM is a commercial station owned by iHeartMedia Inc.The format of the station is hot adult contemporary. WHYN-FM broadcasts to the Springfield, MA area at 93.1 FM.
FM RADIO STATION

WHYY-FM 40365
Owner: WHYY Inc.
Editorial: 150 N 6th St, Independence Mall West, Philadelphia, Pennsylvania 19106-1521
Tel: 1 215 351-1200.
Email: talkback@whyy.org
Web site: http://www.whyy.org
Profile: WHYY-FM is a non-commercial station owned by WHYY Inc. The format of the station is news and talk. WHYY-FM broadcasts to the Philadelphia area at 90.9 FM, and in New Jersey.
FM RADIO STATION

WHZR-FM 41306
Owner: Mid-America Radio Group
Editorial: 425 2nd St, Logansport, Indiana 46947-3410 **Tel:** 1 574 732-1037.
Email: whzr@midamericaradio.net
Web site: http://indianasbestradio.com
Profile: WHZR-FM is a commercial station owned by Mid-America Radio Group. The format of the station is country. WHZR-FM broadcasts to the Logansport, IN, area at 103.7 FM.
FM RADIO STATION

WHZT-FM 42727
Owner: Summit Media Broadcasting LLC
Editorial: 220 N Main St Ste 402, Greenville, South Carolina 29601-2151 **Tel:** 1 864 235-1073.
Web site: http://www.hot981.com
Profile: WHZT-FM is a commercial station owned by Summit Media Broadcasting LLC. The format of the station is rhythmic Top 40/CHR. WHZT-FM broadcasts to the Greenville, SC area at 98.1 FM.
FM RADIO STATION

WHZZ-FM 45231
Owner: MacDonald Broadcasting Co.
Editorial: 600 W Cavanaugh Rd, Lansing, Michigan 48910 **Tel:** 1 517 393-1320.
Email: 1017mikefmweb@gmail.com
Web site: http://www.1017mikefm.com
Profile: WHZZ-FM is a commercial station owned by the MacDonald Broadcasting Co. The format of the station is adult hits music. WHZZ-FM broadcasts to the Lansing, MI area at 101.7 FM.
FM RADIO STATION

WIAA-FM 40366
Owner: Interlochen Center for Arts
Editorial: 4000 M 137, Interlochen, Michigan 49643-8427 **Tel:** 1 231 276-4400.
Email: ipr@interlochen.org
Web site: http://www.interlochen.org/ipr/
FM RADIO STATION

WIAB-FM 355403
Owner: Interlochen Center for Arts
Tel: 1 231 276-4400.
Email: ipr@interlochen.org
Web site: http://interlochenpublicradio.org
FM RADIO STATION

WIAD-FM 40494
Owner: CBS Radio
Editorial: 1015 Half St SE Ste 200, Washington, District Of Columbia 20003-3320 **Tel:** 1 202 479-9227.
Web site: http://www.947freshfm.com
Profile: WIAD-FM is a commercial station owned by CBS Radio. The format of the station is adult contemporary. WIAD-FM broadcasts to the Washington, D.C. area at 94.7 FM.
FM RADIO STATION

WIAL-FM 45218
Owner: Mid-West Family Broadcasting
Editorial: 944 Harlem St, Altoona, Wisconsin 54720-1127 **Tel:** 1 715 832-1530.
Web site: http://www.i94online.com
Profile: WIAL-FM is a commercial station owned by Mid-West Family Broadcasting. The format of the station is Hot AC. WIAL-FM broadcasts to the Altoona, WI area at 94.1 FM.
FM RADIO STATION

WIAM-AM 35379
Owner: Lifeline Ministries, Inc.
Editorial: 1012 East Blvd, Williamston, North Carolina 27892-2804 **Tel:** 1 252 792-4161.
Web site: http://opendoorradio.com
Profile: WIAM-AM is a commercial station owned by Lifeline Ministries, Inc. The format of the station is Classic Country. WIAM-AM broadcasts to the Williamston, NC area at 900 AM.
AM RADIO STATION

WIAN-AM 37952
Owner: Sovereign Communications LLC
Editorial: 1009 W Ridge St Ste A, Marquette, Michigan 49855-3997 **Tel:** 1 906 225-1313.
Email: wjpd@wjpd.com
Web site: http://www.bigcountrygold.com/
AM RADIO STATION

WIBA-AM 37890
Owner: iHeartMedia Inc.
Editorial: 2651 S Fish Hatchery Rd, Fitchburg, Wisconsin 53711-5410 **Tel:** 1 608 274-5450.
Email: wibanews@yahoo.com
Web site: http://wiba.iheart.com
Profile: WIBA-AM is a commercial station owned by iHeartMedia Inc. The format of the station is news and talk. WIBA-AM broadcasts to the Madison, WI area at 1310 AM.
AM RADIO STATION

WIBA-FM 45219
Owner: iHeartMedia Inc.
Editorial: 2651 S Fish Hatchery Rd, Fitchburg, Wisconsin 53711-5410 **Tel:** 1 608 274-5450.
Web site: http://www.wibafm.com
Profile: WIBA-FM is a commercial station owned by iHeartMedia Inc. The format for the station is classic rock. WIBA-FM broadcasts to the Madison, WI, area at 101.5 FM.
FM RADIO STATION

WIBC-FM 512166
Owner: Emmis Communications Corp.
Editorial: 40 Monument Cir Ste 400, Indianapolis, Indiana 46204-3011 **Tel:** 1 317 266-9422.
Email: news@wibc.com
Web site: http://www.wibc.com
Profile: WIBC-FM is a commercial station owned by Emmis Communications Corp. The format is news and talk. WIBC-FM broadcasts to the Indianapolis area at 93.1 FM.
FM RADIO STATION

WIBG-AM 156483
Owner: Brancadora(Enrico S.)
Editorial: 3328 Simpson Ave, Ocean City, New Jersey 08226-2044 **Tel:** 1 609 398-7575.
Web site: http://www.envivoradio.com
Profile: WIBG-AM is a commercial station owned by Enrico S. Brancadora. The format of the station is Spanish CHR. WIBG-AM broadcasts to the Atlantic City, NJ area at 1020 AM.
AM RADIO STATION

WIBG-FM 41888
Owner: WIBG Limited Liability Company
Editorial: 3328 Simpson Ave, Ocean City, New Jersey 08226-2044 **Tel:** 1 609 398-7575.
Web site: http://wibg.com
Profile: WIBG-FM is a commercial station owned by WIBG Limited Liability Company. The format of the station is oldies. WIBG-FM broadcasts to the Philadelphia area at 94.3 FM.
FM RADIO STATION

WIBH-AM 36695
Owner: Ellis(Bass Moury & Ronald)
Editorial: 330 S Main St, Anna, Illinois 62906-1242
Tel: 1 618 833-9424.
Email: wibh@ajinternet.net
Web site: http://www.wibhradio.com
Profile: WIBH-AM is a commercial station owned by Bass Moury and Ronald Ellis. The format of the station is country music. WIBH-AM broadcasts to the Anna, IL, area at 1440 AM.
AM RADIO STATION

WIBI-FM 40369
Owner: Illinois Bible Institute
Editorial: 4101 Fieldstone Rd, Champaign, Illinois 61822-8800 **Tel:** 1 800 475-9245.
Web site: http://www.wbgl.org
Profile: WIBI-FM is a non-commercial station owned by the Illinois Bible Institute. The format of the station is contemporary Christian music. WIBI-FM broadcasts to Carlinville, IL area at 91.1 FM.
FM RADIO STATION

WIBL-FM 69962
Owner: Great Plains Media
Editorial: 108 Boeykens Pl, Normal, Illinois 61761
Tel: 1 309 888-4496.
Web site: http://www.1077thebull.com
Profile: WIBL-FM is a commercial station owned by Great Plains Media. The format of the station is

contemporary country. WIBL-FM broadcasts to the Peoria, IL area at 107.7 FM.
FM RADIO STATION

WIBM-AM 36174
Owner: Jackson Radio Works Inc.
Editorial: 1700 Glenshire Dr, Jackson, Michigan 49201 **Tel:** 1 517 787-9546.
Web site: http://www.espnradio1450.com
Profile: WIBM-AM is a commercial station owned by Jackson Radio Works Inc. The format of the station is sports. WIBM-AM broadcasts to the Jackson, MI area at 1450 AM.
AM RADIO STATION

WIBN-FM 41569
Owner: Brothers Broadcasting Corp.
Editorial: 130 E McConnell St, Oxford, Indiana 47971 **Tel:** 1 765 385-2373.
Email: 98goldproduction@gmail.com
Web site: http://www.981wibn.com
Profile: WIBN-FM is a commercial station owned by Brothers Broadcasting Corp. The format of the station is classic hits. WIBM-FM broadcasts to the Oxford, IN area at 98.1 FM.
FM RADIO STATION

WIBQ-AM 38380
Owner: Midwest Communications Inc.
Tel: 1 812 232-4161.
Web site: http://wibqam.com
Profile: WIBQ-AM is a commercial station owned by Midwest Communications Inc. The format of the station is news/talk. WIBQ-AM broadcasts to the Terre Haute, IN area at 1230 AM
AM RADIO STATION

WIBT-FM 519713
Owner: Mondy-Burke Broadcasting Network
Editorial: 830 Main St, Greenville, Mississippi 38701-4102 **Tel:** 1 662 887-1380.
Email: info@deltaradio.net
Web site: http://www.1047thebeat.com
Profile: WIBT-FM is a commercial station owned by Mondy-Burke Broadcasting Network and operated by Delta Radio Network LLC. The format is urban contemporary. WIBT-FM airs to the Helena, AR area at 104.7 FM.
FM RADIO STATION

WIBV-FM 81142
Owner: Stratemeyer Media
Editorial: 498 Brink Road, Richview, Illinois 62877 **Tel:** 1 618 249-6025.
Email: wibv@wibv102.com
Web site: http://www.wibv102.com
Profile: WIBV-FM is a commercial station owned by Stratemeyer Media. The format of the station is contemporary country. WIBV-FM broadcasts to the Irvington, IL area at 102.1 FM.
FM RADIO STATION

WIBW-AM 37891
Owner: Alpha Media
Editorial: 1210 SW Executive Dr, Topeka, Kansas 66615-3850 **Tel:** 1 785 272-3456.
Email: news@wibw.com
Web site: http://www.wibwnewsnow.com
Profile: WIBW-AM is a commercial station owned by Morris Communications. The format of the station is news, talk and sports. WIBW-AM broadcasts to the Topeka, KS area at 580 AM.
AM RADIO STATION

WIBW-FM 45220
Owner: Morris Communications
Editorial: 1210 SW Executive Dr, Topeka, Kansas 66615-3850 **Tel:** 1 785 272-3456.
Email: news@wibw.com
Web site: http://www.94country.com
Profile: WIBW-FM is a commercial station owned by Morris Communications. The format of the station is contemporary country music. WIBW-FM broadcasts to the Topeka, KS area at 97.3 FM.
FM RADIO STATION

WIBX-AM 38606
Owner: Townsquare Media, LLC
Editorial: 9418 River Rd, Marcy, New York 13403-2071 **Tel:** 1 315 768-9500.
Email: news@wibx950.com
Web site: http://www.wibx950.com
Profile: WIBX-AM is a commercial station owned by Townsquare Media, LLC. The format of the station is news, sports and talk programming. WIBX-AM broadcasts to the Utica, NY area at 950 AM.
AM RADIO STATION

WIBZ-FM 45221
Owner: Miller Communications Inc.
Editorial: 51 Commerce St, Sumter, South Carolina 29150-5014 **Tel:** 1 803 775-2321.
Email: production@miller.fm
Web site: http://www.miller.fm
Profile: WIBZ-FM is a commercial station owned Miller Communications Inc. The format of the station is adult hits. WIBZ-FM broadcasts to the Columbia, SC area at 95.5 FM.
FM RADIO STATION

WICA-FM 238269
Owner: Interlochen Center for Arts
Tel: 1 231 276-4400.
Email: ipr@interlochen.org
Web site: http://ipr.interlochen.org
Profile: WICA-FM is a non-commercial station owned by Interlochen Center for Arts. The format of the station is news and talk. WICA-FM broadcasts to the Interlochen, MI area at 91.5 FM.
FM RADIO STATION

WICB-FM 40370
Owner: Ithaca College
Editorial: 118 Park Hall Ithaca College, Ithaca, New York 14850 **Tel:** 1 607 274-1040.
Email: news@wicb.org
Web site: http://www.wicb.org
Profile: WICB-FM is a non-commercial station owned by Ithaca College. The format of the station is college variety. WICB-FM broadcasts to the Ithaca, NY area at 91.7 FM.
FM RADIO STATION

WICC-AM 38408
Owner: Cumulus Media Inc.
Editorial: 2 Lafayette Sq, Bridgeport, Connecticut 06604-6014 **Tel:** 1 203 366-6000.
Web site: http://www.wicc600.com
Profile: WICC-AM is a commercial station owned by Cumulus Media Inc. The format of the station is news and talk programming. WICC-AM broadcasts in Bridgeport, CT area at 600 AM.
AM RADIO STATION

WICH-AM 37892
Owner: Hall Communications
Editorial: 40 Cuprak Rd, Norwich, Connecticut 6360 **Tel:** 1 860 887-3511.
Email: news@wich.com
Web site: http://www.wich.com
Profile: WICH-AM is a commercial station owned by Hall Communications. The format of the station is adult standards music. WICH-AM broadcasts to the Norwich, CT area at 1310 AM.
AM RADIO STATION

WICK-AM 37893
Owner: Bold Gold Media Group
Editorial: 1049 N Sekol Ave, Scranton, Pennsylvania 18504-1040 **Tel:** 1 570 344-1221.
Web site: http://www.boldgoldradionepa.com/
Profile: WICK-AM is a commercial station owned by Bold Gold Media Group. The format of the station is sports. WICK-AM broadcasts to the Scranton, PA area at 1400 AM.
AM RADIO STATION

WICL-FM 45303
Owner: West Virginia Radio Corporation
Editorial: 1606 W King St, Martinsburg, West Virginia 25401-2077 **Tel:** 1 304 263-8868.
Profile: WICL-FM is a commercial station owned by Prettyman Broadcasting Co. The format of the station is country music. WICL-FM broadcasts to the Martinsburg, MD area at 95.9.
FM RADIO STATION

WICN-FM 40371
Owner: WICN Public Radio Inc.
Editorial: 50 Portland St, Worcester, Massachusetts 01608-2013 **Tel:** 1 508 752-0700.
Email: webmaster@wicn.org
Web site: http://www.wicn.org
Profile: WICN-FM is a non-commercial station owned by WICN Public Radio Inc. The format of the station is jazz. WICN-FM broadcasts to the Worcester, MA area ar 90.5 FM. The station accepts PSAs as long as they are music event related.
FM RADIO STATION

WICO-AM 37894
Owner: Delmarva Broadcasting
Editorial: 919 Ellegood St, Salisbury, Maryland 21801-8433 **Tel:** 1 410 219-3500.
Web site: http://www.wicoam.com
Profile: WICO-AM is a commercial station owned by Delmarva Broadcasting. The format of the station is talk. WICO-AM broadcasts in the Salisbury, MD area at 1320 AM.
AM RADIO STATION

WICO-FM 86881
Owner: Delmarva Broadcasting
Editorial: 919 Ellegood St, Salisbury, Maryland 21801-8433 **Tel:** 1 410 219-3500.
Web site: http://www.wicotalk.com
Profile: WICO-FM is a commercial station owned by Delmarva Broadcasting. The format of the station is adult hits. WICO-FM broadcasts in the Salisbury, MD area at 92.5 FM.
FM RADIO STATION

WICV-FM 41942
Owner: Interlochen Center for Arts
Tel: 1 231 276-4400.
Email: ipr@interlochen.org
Web site: http://www.interlochen.org/ipr
Profile: WICV-FM is a non-commercial station owned by Interlochen Center for Arts. The format of the station is classical. WICV-FM broadcasts to the Interlochen, MI area at 100.9 FM.
FM RADIO STATION

WICY-AM 39002
Owner: Martz Communications
Editorial: 86 Porter Rd, Malone, New York 12953-3701 **Tel:** 1 518 483-1100.
Email: news@country965.com
Web site: http://www.oldiesradioonline.com
Profile: WICY-AM is a commercial station owned by Martz Communications. The format of the station is oldies. WICY-AM broadcasts to the Malone, NY area at 1490 AM.
AM RADIO STATION

WIDG-AM 37895
Owner: Baraga Broadcasting, Inc.
Editorial: 7078 M 68, Indian River, Michigan 49749-9472 **Tel:** 1 231 238-0811.
Web site: http://www.baragabroadcasting.com
Profile: WIDG-AM is a commercial station owned by Baraga Broadcasting, Inc. The format of the station is Catholic programming and music. WIDG-AM broadcasts to the St. Ignace, MI area at 940 AM.
AM RADIO STATION

WIDL-FM 46696
Owner: Edwards Communications LLC
Editorial: 1521 W Caro Rd, Caro, Michigan 48723 **Tel:** 1 989 672-1360.
Email: production@mix921.com
Web site: http://www.tuscolatoday.com
Profile: WIDL-FM is a commercial station owned by Edwards Communications LLC. The format for the station is hot adult contemporary. WDIL-FM broadcasts to the Flint, MI area at 92.1 FM.
FM RADIO STATION

WIDS-AM 36874
Owner: Hammond Broadcasting Inc.
Editorial: 4942 US Highway 27 N, Butler, Kentucky 41006-8653 **Tel:** 1 859 472-1075.
Email: wids@fuse.net
Web site: http://www.wiok.com
Profile: WIDS-AM is a commercial station owned by Hammond Broadcasting Inc. The format of the station is Christian programming and Southern gospel music. WIDS-AM broadcasts in the Butler, KY area at 570 AM.
AM RADIO STATION

WIDU-AM 35382
Owner: WIDU Broadcasting Inc.
Editorial: 1338 Bragg Blvd, Fayetteville, North Carolina 28301-0005 **Tel:** 1 910 486-9438.
Email: widu1600@aol.com
Web site: http://www.widuradio.com/
Profile: WIDU-AM is a commercial station owned by WIDU Broadcasting Inc. The format of the station is gospel, news and talk. WIDU-AM broadcasts to the Fayetteville, NC area at 1600 AM.
AM RADIO STATION

WIEZ-AM 38619
Owner: First Media Radio LLC
Editorial: 12 E Market St, 2nd Fl, Lewistown, Pennsylvania 17044 **Tel:** 1 717 248-6757.
Web site: http://www.wiez.com
Profile: WIEZ-AM is a commercial station owned by First Media Radio LLC. The format of the station is news and talk. WIEZ-AM broadcasts to the Lewistown, PA area at 670 AM.
AM RADIO STATION

WIFA-AM 37907
Owner: Progressive Media, Inc.
Editorial: 818 N Cedar Bluff Rd Ste 102, Knoxville, Tennessee 37923-2201 **Tel:** 1 865 531-2005.
Email: wifa.wijv@gmail.com
Profile: WIFA-FM is a non-commercial station owned by Progressive Media, Inc. The format of the station is contemporary Christian music. WIFA-FM broadcasts to the Knoxville, TN area at 1240 AM.
AM RADIO STATION

WIFC-FM 45223
Owner: Midwest Communications Inc.
Editorial: 557 Scott St, Wausau, Wisconsin 54403 **Tel:** 1 715 842-1672.
Web site: http://www.wifc.com
Profile: WIFC-FM is a commercial station owned by Midwest Communications Inc. The format of the station is Top 40/CHR music. WIFC-FM broadcasts in the Wausau, WI area at 95.5 FM.
FM RADIO STATION

WIFE-FM 40661
Owner: White Water Broadcasting
Editorial: 406 1/2 N Central Ave, Connersville, Indiana 47331-1926 **Tel:** 1 765 825-6411.
Email: news@wifefm.com
Web site: http://www.wifefm.com
Profile: WIFE-FM is a commercial station owned by White Water Broadcasting. The format for the station is contemporary country music. WIFE-FM broadcasts to the Indianapolis area at 94.3 FM.
FM RADIO STATION

WIFI-AM 36016
Owner: Forsyth (John)
Editorial: 123 Egg Harbor Rd, Sewell, New Jersey 08080-9406 **Tel:** 1 609 472-3524.
Email: amradiowifi@gmail.com
Web site: http://wifi1460am.com
Profile: WIFI-AM is a commercial station owned by John Forsyth. The format of the station is block time. WIFI-AM broadcasts to the Burlington, NJ area at 1460 AM. Send PSAs via the USPS.
AM RADIO STATION

WIFM-FM 43392
Owner: Yadkin Valley Broadcasting
Editorial: 813 N Bridge St, Elkin, North Carolina 28621 **Tel:** 1 336 835-2511.
Email: wifm@wifmradio.com
Web site: http://www.wifmradio.com
Profile: WIFM-FM is a commercial station owned by Yadkin Valley Broadcasting. The format of the station is adult contemporary. WIFM-FM broadcasts to the Elkin, NC area at 100.9 FM.
FM RADIO STATION

WIFN-AM 39392
Owner: Dickey Broadcasting
Editorial: 780 Johnson Ferry Rd Ne Ste 500, Atlanta, Georgia 30342-1436 **Tel:** 1 404 688-0068.
Web site: http://1230thefan2.com
Profile: WIFN-AM is a commercial station owned by Dickey Broadcasting. The format of the station is sports. WIFN-AM broadcasts to the Atlanta area at 1340 AM.
AM RADIO STATION

WIFO-FM 45225
Owner: Jesup Broadcasting Corp.
Editorial: 2420 Waycross Hwy, Jesup, Georgia 31545 **Tel:** 1 912 427-3712.
Email: bigdogstaff@bellsouth.net
Profile: WIFO-FM is a commercial station owned by Jesup Broadcasting Corp. The format for the station is country. WIFO-FM broadcasts to the Savannah, GA area at 105.5 FM.
FM RADIO STATION

WIFY-FM 44392
Owner: Radio Broadcasting Services, Inc.
Editorial: 372 Dorset St, South Burlington, Vermont 05403-6212 **Tel:** 1 802 863-1010.
Email: studio@pointfm.com
Web site: http://pointfm.com
Profile: WIFY-FM is a commercial station owned by Radio Broadcasting Services, Inc. The format of the station is AAA. WIFY-FM broadcasts to the South Burlington, VT area at 93.7 FM.
FM RADIO STATION

WIGM-AM 37897
Owner: WIGM Inc.
Editorial: 630 S 8th St, Medford, Wisconsin 54451-2017 **Tel:** 1 715 748-2566.
Profile: WIGM-AM is a commercial station owned by WIGM Inc. The format of the station is sports. WIGM-AM broadcasts to the Medford, WI area at 1490 AM.
AM RADIO STATION

WIGN-AM 35197
Owner: Mountain Music Ministries, LLC
Editorial: 2042 Euclid Ave, Bristol, Virginia 24201-3610 **Tel:** 1 276 591-5800.
Email: manager@wignam.com
Web site: http://www.wignam.com
AM RADIO STATION

WIGO-AM 35677
Owner: MCL/MCM Georgia, LLC
Editorial: 2424 Old Rex Morrow Rd, Ellenwood, Georgia 30294-3901 **Tel:** 1 404 361-8843.
Web site: http://www.wigoam.com
Profile: WIGO-AM is a commercial station owned by MCL/MCM Georgia, LLC. The format of the station is gospel and blues. WIGO-AM broadcasts to the Ellenwood, GA area at 1570 AM.
AM RADIO STATION

WIGO-FM 44004
Owner: Two Rivers Communications Inc.
Editorial: 101 Radio Rd, Kilmarnock, Virginia 22482-3881 **Tel:** 1 804 435-1414.
Web site: http://middlenecknews.com
Profile: WIGO-FM is a commercial station owned by Two Rivers Communications Inc. The format of the station is contemporary country. WIGO-FM broadcasts to the Richmond, VA area at 104.9 FM.
FM RADIO STATION

WIHC-FM 42227
Owner: West Central Michigan Media Ministries
Tel: 1 231 468-2087.
Web site: http://www.strongtowerradio.org
Profile: WIHC-FM is a non-commercial station owned by West Central Michigan Media Ministries. The format of the station is Christian talk. WIHC-FM broadcasts to the Sault Sainte Marie, MI area at 97.9 FM.
FM RADIO STATION

WIHG-FM 46066
Owner: Crossville Radio, Inc.
Editorial: 37 South Dr, Crossville, Tennessee 38555 **Tel:** 1 931 484-1057.
Email: studio@1057thehog.com
Web site: http://www.1057thehog.com
Profile: WIHG-FM is a commercial station owned by Crossville Radio, Inc. The format of the station is classic hits. WIHG-FM broadcasts to the Crossville, TN area at 105.7 FM.
FM RADIO STATION

WIHM-AM 36795
Owner: Covenant Network
Editorial: 4424 Hampton Ave, Saint Louis, Missouri 63109-2232 **Tel:** 1 314 752-7000.
Email: covenantnetwork@juno.com
Web site: http://www.covenantnet.net
Profile: WIHM-AM is a non-commercial station owned by the Covenant Network. The format of the station is religious music and talk. WIHM-AM broadcasts to the St. Louis area at 1410 AM.
AM RADIO STATION

WIHN-FM 40374
Owner: Connoisseur Media LLC
Editorial: 520 N Center St, Bloomington, Illinois 61701-2902 **Tel:** 1 309 834-1100.
Web site: http://www.967irock.com
Profile: WIHN-FM is a commercial station owned by Neuhoff Communications. The format of the station is

rock music. WIHN-FM broadcasts to the Bloomington, IL area at 96.7 FM.
FM RADIO STATION

WIHS-FM 40375
Owner: Connecticut Radio Fellowship
Editorial: 1933 S Main St, Middletown, Connecticut 06457-6150 **Tel:** 1 860 346-1049.
Email: wihs@comcast.net
Web site: http://www.wihsradio.org
Profile: WIHS-FM is a non-commercial station owned by Connecticut Radio Fellowship. The format of the station is religious and contemporary Christian programming. WIHS-FM broadcasts to the Hartford-New Haven, CT area at 104.9 FM.
FM RADIO STATION

WIHT-FM 46012
Owner: iHeartMedia Inc.
Editorial: 1801 Rockville Pike Fl 5, Rockville, Maryland 20852-1633 **Tel:** 1 240 747-2700.
Web site: http://hot995.iheart.com
Profile: WIHT-FM is a commercial station owned by iHeartMedia Inc. The format of the station is Pop Top 40/CHR music. WIHT-FM broadcasts to the Washington, D.C. area at 99.5 FM.
FM RADIO STATION

WIII-FM 45424
Owner: Saga Communications
Editorial: 1751 Hanshaw Rd, Ithaca, New York 14850-9105 **Tel:** 1 607 257-6400.
Web site: http://www.wiii.com
Profile: WIII-FM is a commercial station owned by Saga Communications. The format of the station is classic rock. WIII-FM broadcasts to the Ithaca, NY area at 100.3 FM.
FM RADIO STATION

WIIL-FM 45676
Owner: Alpha Media
Editorial: 8500 Green Bay Rd, Pleasant Prairie, Wisconsin 53158-2721 **Tel:** 1 262 694-7800.
Web site: http://95wiilrock.com
Profile: WIIL-FM is a commercial station owned by Alpha Media. The format of the station is rock music. WIIL-FM broadcasts to the Milwaukee area at 95.1 FM.
FM RADIO STATION

WIIN-AM 38529
Owner: New South Communications Inc.
Editorial: 265 Highpoint Dr, Ridgeland, Mississippi 39157 **Tel:** 1 601 956-0102.
Web site: http://www.us963.com
Profile: WIIN-AM is a commercial station owned by New South Communications Inc. The format of the station is country. WIIN-AM broadcasts to the Ridgeland, MS, area at 780 AM. The station airs WUSJ-AM's programming.
AM RADIO STATION

WIIS-FM 40376
Owner: Keyed Up Communications Co.
Editorial: 1075 Duval St, Ste C17, Key West, Florida 33040-3195 **Tel:** 1 305 292-1133.
Email: mail@island107.com
Web site: http://island107.com
Profile: WIIS-FM is a commercial station owned by Keyed Up Communications Co. The format of the station is rock alternative. WIIS-FM broadcasts to the Key West, FL area at 107.1 FM.
FM RADIO STATION

WIIT-FM 40596
Owner: Illinois Institute of Technology
Editorial: 3201 S State St, Chicago, Illinois 60616-3392 **Tel:** 1 312 567-3087.
Email: wiit@iit.edu
Web site: http://radio.iit.edu
Profile: WIIT-FM is a non-commercial station owned by the Illinois Institute of Technology. The format of the station is variety. WIIT-FM broadcasts to the Chicago area at 88.9 FM.
FM RADIO STATION

WIIZ-FM 43945
Owner: NicWild Communications Inc.
Editorial: 8968 Marlboro Ave, Barnwell, South Carolina 29812 **Tel:** 1 803 259-9797.
Email: thewiz@wiiz979.com
Web site: http://www.wiizfm.com
Profile: WIIZ-FM is a commercial station owned by NicWild Communications Inc. The format of the station is urban contemporary. WIIZ-FM broadcasts to the Barnwell, SC area at 97.9 FM.
FM RADIO STATION

WIJR-AM 37022
Owner: Birach Broadcasting Corp.
Editorial: 13063 Winu Dr, Highland, Illinois 62249-4800 **Tel:** 1 618 654-5615.
Email: info@latremenda880.com
Web site: http://www.birach.com/wijr.htm
Profile: WIJR-AM is a commercial station owned by Birach Broadcasting Corp. The format of the station is regional Mexican. WIJR-AM broadcasts to the Highland, IL area at 880 AM.
AM RADIO STATION

WIJV-FM 41108
Owner: Progressive Media, Inc.
Editorial: 818 N Cedar Bluff Rd Ste 102, Knoxville, Tennessee 37923-2201 **Tel:** 1 865 531-2005.
Email: wifa.wijv@gmail.com
Profile: WIJV-FM is a non-commercial station owned by Progressive Media, Inc. The format of the station is contemporary Christian music. WIJV-FM broadcasts to the Knoxville, TN area at 92.7 FM.
FM RADIO STATION

WIKB-FM 45227
Owner: Heartland Communications Group, LLC
Editorial: 809 W Genesee St, Iron River, Michigan 49935 **Tel:** 1 906 265-5104.
Email: wikb@sbcglobal.net
Web site: http://www.wikb.com
Profile: WIKB-FM is a commercial station owned by Heartland Communications Group, LLC. The format of the station is classic and contemporary country music. WIKB-FM broadcasts to the Marquette, MI, area at 99.1 FM.
FM RADIO STATION

WIKE-AM 39444
Owner: Great Eastern Radio, LLC
Editorial: 3422 Us Route 5, Derby, Vermont 05829-4430 **Tel:** 1 802 766-9236.
Web site: http://1490wike.com
Profile: WIKE-AM is a commercial station owned by Great Eastern Radio, LLC. The format of the station is contemporary country music. WIKE-AM broadcasts to the Derby Center, VT area at 1490 AM.
AM RADIO STATION

WIKI-FM 40377
Owner: Wagon Wheel Broadcasting LLC
Editorial: 2604 Michigan Rd, Madison, Indiana 47250 **Tel:** 1 812 273-2879.
Email: info@953wiki.com
Web site: http://953wiki.com
Profile: WIKI-FM is a commercial station owned by Wagon Wheel Broadcasting LLC. The format of the station is country music. WIKI-FM broadcasts in the Madison, IN area at 95.3 FM.
FM RADIO STATION

WIKK-FM 41985
Owner: Forcht Broadcasting
Editorial: 4667 E Radio Tower Ln, Olney, Illinois 62450-4742 **Tel:** 1 618 393-2156.
Web site: http://www.1035theeagle.com
Profile: WIKK-FM is a commercial station owned by Forcht Broadcasting. The format of the station is Classic Rock. WIKK-FM broadcasts to the Olney, IL area at 103.5 FM.
FM RADIO STATION

WIKQ-FM 46739
Owner: Radio Greeneville Inc.
Editorial: 1004 Arnold Rd, Greeneville, Tennessee 37743-3008 **Tel:** 1 423 639-1831.
Email: wgrv@greeneville.com
Web site: http://greeneville.com/wikq
Profile: WIKQ-FM is a commercial station owned by Radio Greeneville Inc. The format of the station is contemporary country. WIKQ-FM broadcasts to the Greenville, TN area at 103.1 FM.
FM RADIO STATION

WIKS-FM 40378
Owner: Beasley Broadcast Group
Editorial: 207 Glenburnie Dr, New Bern, North Carolina 28560-2815 **Tel:** 1 252 633-1500.
Email: comments@kiss102.com
Web site: http://www.1019online.com
Profile: WIKS-FM is a commercial station owned by the Beasley Broadcast Group. The format of the station is urban adult contemporary music. WIKS-FM broadcasts to the New Bern, NC area at 101.9 FM.
FM RADIO STATION

WIKX-FM 45474
Owner: iHeartMedia Inc.
Editorial: 24100 Tiseo Blvd Unit 10, Port Charlotte, Florida 33980-5223 **Tel:** 1 941 206-1188.
Web site: http://www.kixcountry929.com/main.html
Profile: WIKX-FM is a commercial station owned by iHeartMedia Inc. The format of the station is contemporary country. WIKX-FM broadcasts to the Punta Gorda, FL area at 92.9 FM.
FM RADIO STATION

WIKY-FM 43191
Owner: Midwest Communiations, Inc.
Editorial: 1162 Mount Auburn Rd, Evansville, Indiana 47720-5428 **Tel:** 1 812 424-8284.
Email: news@southcentralmedia.com
Web site: http://www.wiky.com
Profile: WIKY-FM is a commercial station owned by Midwest Communiations, Inc. The format of the station is adult contemporary. WIKY-FM broadcasts to the Evansville, IN area at 104.1 FM.
FM RADIO STATION

WIKZ-FM 45228
Owner: Alpha Media
Editorial: 25 Penncraft Ave, Chambersburg, Pennsylvania 17201-5600 **Tel:** 1 717 263-0813.
Email: mix95.1@mix95.com
Web site: http://www.mix95.com
Profile: WIKZ-FM is a commercial station owned by Alpha Media. The format of the station is hot adult contemporary. WIKZ-FM broadcasts to the Chambersburg, PA area at 95.1 FM.
FM RADIO STATION

WILB-AM 35621
Owner: Living Bread Radio, Inc.
Editorial: 4365 Fulton Dr NW, Canton, Ohio 44718 **Tel:** 1 330 966-2903.
Web site: http://www.livingbreadradio.com
Profile: WILB-AM is a non-commercial station owned by Living Bread Radio, Inc. The format of the station is Catholic news and talk programming. WILB-AM broadcasts to the Canton, OH area at 1060 AM.
AM RADIO STATION

WILB-FM 798383
Owner: Living Bread Radio, Inc.
Editorial: 4365 Fulton Dr Nw, Canton, Ohio 44718-2823 **Tel:** 1 330 966-2903.
Email: info@livingbreadradio.com
Web site: http://www.livingbreadradio.com
Profile: WILB-FM is a non-commercial station owned by Living Bread Radio, Inc. The format of the station is Catholic news and talk programming. The station airs locally at 89.5 FM to the Boardman and Youngstown areas in Ohio.
FM RADIO STATION

WILC-AM 35385
Owner: ZGS Communications
Editorial: 611 Rt 46 W Suite 103, Hasbrouck Heights, New Jersey 7604 **Tel:** 1 201 288-8200.
Email: info@900wilc.com
Web site: http://900wilc.com
Profile: WILC-AM is a commercial station owned by ZGS Communications and operated by Wallis Communications. The format of the station is Conservative Talk. WILC-AM broadcasts to the greater Washington, D.C. metro area at 900 AM.
AM RADIO STATION

WILD-AM 35386
Owner: Urban One, Inc.
Editorial: 500 Victory Rd Ste 2, Quincy, Massachusetts 02171-3132 **Tel:** 1 617 931-1090.
Profile: WILD-AM is commercial station owned by Urban One, Inc. The format of the station is variety featuring China Radio International programming the majority of the day. WILD-AM broadcasts to the greater Boston area at 1090 AM.
AM RADIO STATION

WILE-AM 37902
Owner: AVC Communications Inc.
Editorial: 4988 Skyline Dr, Cambridge, Ohio 43725-9729 **Tel:** 1 740 432-5605.
Email: avcnews@yourradioplace.com
Web site: http://www.yourradioplace.com
Profile: WILE-AM is a commercial station owned by AVC Communications Inc. The format of the station is sports. WILE-AM broadcasts to the Cambridge, OH area at 1270 AM.
AM RADIO STATION

WILE-FM 44015
Owner: AVC Communications Inc.
Editorial: 4988 Skyline Dr, Cambridge, Ohio 43725-9729 **Tel:** 1 740 432-5605.
Email: avcnews@yourradioplace.com
Web site: http://www.yourradioplace.com
Profile: WILE-FM is a commercial station owned by AVC Communications Inc. The format of the station is adult standards. WILE-FM broadcasts to the Wheeling, WV, Steubenville, OH, area at 97.7 FM.
FM RADIO STATION

WILF-FM 733479
Owner: The Power Foundation
Editorial: 185 Commerce Ctr, Greenville, South Carolina 29615-5817 **Tel:** 1 251 809-1915.
Email: info@thelifefm.com
Web site: http://wilffm.com
Profile: WILF-FM is a non-commercial station owned by The Power Foundation. The format of the station is Christian talk. WILF-FM broadcasts to the Brewton, AL area at a frequency of 88.9 FM.
FM RADIO STATION

WIL-FM 45229
Owner: Hubbard Broadcasting, Inc.
Editorial: 11647 Olive Blvd, Saint Louis, Missouri 63141-7001 **Tel:** 1 314 983-6000.
Web site: https://newcountry923.fm
Profile: WIL-FM is a commercial station owned by Hubbard Broadcasting, Inc. The format of the station is contemporary country music. WIL-FM broadcasts to the St. Louis area at 92.3 FM.
FM RADIO STATION

WILI-AM 38523
Owner: Hall Communications
Editorial: 720 Main St, Willimantic, Connecticut 06226-2648 **Tel:** 1 860 456-1111.
Email: wayne@wili.com
Web site: http://www.wili.com/am
Profile: WILI-AM is a commercial station owned by Hall Communications. The format of the station is talk and adult contemporary music. WILI-AM broadcasts to the Hartford-New Haven, CT area at 1400 AM.
AM RADIO STATION

WILI-FM 45886
Owner: Hall Communications
Editorial: 720 Main St, Willimantic, Connecticut 06226-2648 **Tel:** 1 860 456-1111.
Web site: http://www.hitmusici983.com
Profile: WILI-FM is a commercial station owned by Hall Communications. The format of the station is Top 40/CHR music. WILI-FM broadcasts to the Hartford-New Haven, CT area at 98.3 FM.
FM RADIO STATION

WILK-AM 37993
Owner: Entercom Communications Corp.
Editorial: 305 Route 315 Hwy, Pittston, Pennsylvania 18640-3907 **Tel:** 1 570 883-9800.
Web site: http://www.wilknewsradio.com
Profile: WILK-AM is a commercial station owned by Entercom Communications Corp. The format of the station is news, sports and talk. WILK-AM broadcasts to the Pittson, PA area at 980 AM. Tagline: WILK 1300 AM. Slogan: "Northeast PA's Newsradio."
AM RADIO STATION

WILK-FM 45951
Owner: Entercom Communications Corp.
Editorial: 305 Route 315 Hwy, Pittston, Pennsylvania 18640-3907 **Tel:** 1 570 883-9850.
Web site: http://www.wilknetwork.com
Profile: WILK-FM is a commercial station owned by Entercom Communications Corp. The format of the station is news and talk. The station is broadcast to the Pittston, PA area at 103.1 FM.
FM RADIO STATION

WILM-AM 35387
Owner: iHeartMedia Inc.
Editorial: 920 W Basin Rd Ste 400, New Castle, Delaware 19720-1013 **Tel:** 1 302 395-9800.
Email: newsroom@wilm.com
Web site: http://wilm.iheart.com
Profile: WILM-AM is a commercial station owned by iHeartMedia Inc. The format of the station is news and talk. WILM-AM broadcasts to the New Castle, DE, area at 1450 AM.
AM RADIO STATION

WILN-FM 40500
Owner: Magic Broadcasting, LLC
Editorial: 7106 Laird St, Ste 102, Panama City, Florida 32408 **Tel:** 1 850 230-5855.
Web site: http://www.island106.com
Profile: WILN-FM is a commercial station owned by Magic Broadcasting, LLC. The format of the station is Top 40/CHR music. WILN-FM broadcasts to the Panama City, FL area at 105.9 FM.
FM RADIO STATION

WILO-AM 37904
Owner: Kaspar Broadcasting Co.
Editorial: 1401 W Barner St, Frankfort, Indiana 46041 **Tel:** 1 765 659-3339.
Web site: http://www.wilo.us
Profile: WILO-AM is a commercial station owned by the Kaspar Broadcasting Co. The format of the station is oldies. WILO-AM broadcasts to the Frankfort, IN, area at 1570 AM.
AM RADIO STATION

WILQ-FM 43676
Owner: Backyard Broadcasting
Editorial: 1685 Four Mile Dr, Williamsport, Pennsylvania 17701-1975 **Tel:** 1 570 323-8200.
Web site: http://www.wilq.com
Profile: WILQ-FM is a commercial station owned by Backyard Broadcasting. The format of the station is country music. WILQ-FM broadcasts to the Susquehanna Valley, PA area at 105.1 FM.
FM RADIO STATION

WILS-AM 37905
Owner: MacDonald Broadcasting Co.
Editorial: 600 W Cavanaugh Rd, Lansing, Michigan 48910 **Tel:** 1 517 393-1320.
Email: wilsradio@gmail.com
Web site: http://www.1320wils.com
Profile: WILS-AM is a commercial station owned by MacDonald Broadcasting Co. The format of the station is news and talk. WILS-AM broadcasts to the Lansing, MI area at 1320 AM.
AM RADIO STATION

WILT-FM 41369
Owner: Capitol Broadcasting Co., Inc.
Editorial: 122 Cinema Dr, Wilmington, North Carolina 28403-1490 **Tel:** 1 910 791-3088.
Web site: http://sunny1037.com/
Profile: WILT-FM is a commercial station owned by Capitol Broadcasting Co., Inc. The format of the station is Adult Hits. WILT-FM broadcasts to the Wilmington, NC area at 103.7 FM.
FM RADIO STATION

WILY-AM 37906
Owner: Withers Broadcasting Co.
Editorial: 302 S Poplar St, Centralia, Illinois 62801-3922 **Tel:** 1 618 533-5700.
Email: wilynews@mywithersradio.com
Web site: http://www.mywithersradio.com/wily
Profile: WILY-AM is a commercial station owned by Withers Broadcasting Co. The format of the station is oldies. WILY-AM broadcasts to the Centralia, IL area at 1210 AM.
AM RADIO STATION

WILZ-FM 42690
Owner: Cumulus Media Inc.
Editorial: 1740 Champagne Dr N, Saginaw, Michigan 48604 **Tel:** 1 877 943-3591.
Web site: http://www.wheelz.fm
Profile: WILZ-FM is a commercial station owned by Cumulus Media Inc. The format of the station is classic rock. WILZ-FM broadcasts to the Saginaw, MI area at 104.5 FM.
FM RADIO STATION

WIMA-AM 39266
Owner: iHeartMedia Inc.
Editorial: 667 W Market St, Lima, Ohio 45801-4603 **Tel:** 1 419 223-2060.
Web site: http://www.1150wima.com
Profile: WIMA-AM is a commercial station owned by iHeartMedia Inc. The format of the station is news and talk. WIMA-AM broadcasts to the Lima, OH area at 1150 AM.
AM RADIO STATION

WIMC-FM 45739
Owner: Forcht Broadcasting
Editorial: 1757 N 175 W, Crawfordsville, Indiana 47933 **Tel:** 1 765 362-8200.
Web site: http://www.crawfordsvilleradio.com
Profile: WIMC-FM is a commercial station owned by Forcht Broadcasting. The format of the station is classic hits. WIMC-FM broadcasts to the Crawfordsville, IN area at 103.9 FM.
FM RADIO STATION

WIMG-AM 36100
Owner: Morris Broadcasting Co.
Editorial: 1842 S Broad St, Trenton, New Jersey 08610-6002 **Tel:** 1 609 695-1300.
Email: wimg1300@aol.com
Web site: http://www.wimg1300.com
Profile: WIMG-AM is a commercial station owned by Morris Broadcasting Co. The format of the station is urban gospel. WIMG-FM broadcasts to the Trenton, NJ area at 1300 AM.
AM RADIO STATION

WIMI-FM 46531
Owner: J & J Broadcasting
Editorial: 222 S Lawrence St, Ironwood, Michigan 49938-2524 **Tel:** 1 906 932-2411.
Web site: http://www.wimifm.com
Profile: WIMI-FM is commercial station owned by J & J Broadcasting. The format of the station is adult contemporary music. WIMI-FM broadcasts to the Ironwood, MI area at 99.7 FM.
FM RADIO STATION

WIMK-FM 45232
Owner: Northern Star Broadcasting LLC
Editorial: 101 Kent St, Iron Mountain, Michigan 49801-1507 **Tel:** 1 906 774-4321.
Email: prodguy@uplogon.com
Web site: http://www.rockthebear.com
Profile: WIMK-FM is a commercial station owned by Northern Star Broadcasting LLC. The format for the station is rock music. WIMK-FM broadcasts to the Iron Mountain, MI area at 93.1 FM.
FM RADIO STATION

WIMS-AM 35389
Owner: Gerard Media LLC
Editorial: 685 E 1675 N, Michigan City, Indiana 46360-9503 **Tel:** 1 219 879-9810.
Email: news@wimsradio.com
Web site: http://www.wimsradio.com
Profile: WIMS-AM is a commercial station owned by Gerard Media LLC. The format of the station is sports, news and talk. WIMS-AM broadcasts to the southern Chicago area at 1420 AM.
AM RADIO STATION

WIMT-FM 46629
Owner: iHeartMedia Inc.
Editorial: 667 W Market St, Lima, Ohio 45801-4603 **Tel:** 1 419 223-2060.
Web site: http://www.t102.com
Profile: WIMT-FM is a local, commercial station owned by iHeartMedia Inc. The format of the station is country music. WIMT-FM broadcasts in the Lima, OH area at 102.1 FM.
FM RADIO STATION

WIMX-FM 40965
Owner: URBan Radio Broadcasting, LLC
Editorial: 720 Water St, Fl 4, Toledo, Ohio 43604-1883 **Tel:** 1 419 244-6354.
Email: info@urbanradio.fm
Web site: http://www.mix957.net
Profile: WIMX-FM is a commercial station owned by URBan Radio Broadcasting, LLC. The format of the station is urban adult contemporary. WIMX-FM broadcasts to the Toledo, OH area at 97.5 FM.
FM RADIO STATION

WIMZ-FM 42143
Owner: South Central Communications Corp.
Editorial: 1100 Sharps Ridge Road, Knoxville, Tennessee 37917 **Tel:** 1 865 525-6000.
Web site: http://www.wimz.com
FM RADIO STATION

WINA-AM 38337
Owner: Saga Communications
Editorial: 1140 Rose Hill Dr, Charlottesville, Virginia 22903 **Tel:** 1 434 220-2300.
Email: news@wina.com
Web site: http://www.wina.com
Profile: WINA-AM is a commercial station owned by Saga Communications. The format of the station is news and talk. WINA-AM broadcasts to the Charlottesville, VA area at 1070 AM.
AM RADIO STATION

WINC-AM 37908
Owner: Centennial Broadcasting
Editorial: 520 N Pleasant Valley Rd, Winchester, Virginia 22601-5654 **Tel:** 1 540 667-2224.
Email: psa@winc.fm
Web site: http://www.newstalk1400winc.com
Profile: WINC-AM is a commercial station owned by Centennial Broadcasting. The format of the station is news, sports and talk. WINC-AM broadcasts to the Winchester, VA area at 1400 AM.
AM RADIO STATION

WINC-FM 45233
Owner: Centennial Broadcasting
Editorial: 520 N Pleasant Valley Rd, Winchester, Virginia 22601-5654 **Tel:** 1 540 667-2224.
Email: psa@winc.fm
Web site: http://www.winc.fm
Profile: WINC-FM is a commercial station owned by Centennial Broadcasting. The format of the station is hot adult contemporary. WINC-FM broadcasts to the Winchester, VA area at 92.5 FM.
FM RADIO STATION

WIND-AM 39062
Owner: Salem Media Group, Inc.
Editorial: 25 NW Point Blvd, Elk Grove Village, Illinois 60007-1056 **Tel:** 1 847 437-5200.
Web site: http://www.560wind.com
Profile: WIND-AM is a commercial station owned by Salem Media Group, Inc. The format of the station is talk. WIND-AM broadcasts to the Chicago area at 560 AM.
AM RADIO STATION

WINE-AM 36566
Owner: Townsquare Media, LLC
Editorial: 1004 Federal Rd, Brookfield, Connecticut 06804-1123 **Tel:** 1 203 775-1212.
Web site: http://www.940sportsradio.com
Profile: WINE-AM is a commercial station owned by Townsquare Media, LLC. The format of the station is sports. WINE-AM broadcasts to the Brookfield, CT area at 940 AM.
AM RADIO STATION

WING-AM 37909
Owner: Alpha Media
Editorial: 717 E David Rd, Dayton, Ohio 45429-5218 **Tel:** 1 937 294-5858.
Email: daytonsports@yahoo.com
Web site: http://www.wingam.com
Profile: WING-AM is a commercial station owned by Alpha Media. The format of the station is sports. WING-AM broadcasts to the Dayton, OH area at 1410.
AM RADIO STATION

WINI-AM 35390
Owner: Radio Station WINI Partnership
Editorial: 10519 Highway 149 Ste A, Murphysboro, Illinois 62966-3300 **Tel:** 1 618 684-2128.
Email: wini@newstalk1420wini.com
Web site: http://www.newstalk1420wini.com
Profile: WINI-AM is a commercial station owned by Radio Station WINI Partnership. The format of the station is news talk. WINI-AM broadcasts to Murphysboro, IL, and its surrounding areas at 1840 AM.
AM RADIO STATION

WINK-AM 153780
Owner: Fort Myers Broadcasting Company
Editorial: 2824 Palm Beach Blvd, Fort Myers, Florida 33916-1503 **Tel:** 1 239 337-2346.
Web site: http://www.winknewsradio.com
Profile: WINK-AM is a commercial station owned by Fort Myers Broadcasting Company. The format of the station is news and talk. WINK-AM broadcasts to the Fort Myers, FL area at 1200 AM.
AM RADIO STATION

WINK-FM 45235
Owner: Meridian Broadcasting, Inc.
Editorial: 2824 Palm Beach Blvd, Fort Myers, Florida 33916-1503 **Tel:** 1 239 337-2346.
Web site: http://www.winkfm.com
Profile: WINK-FM is a commercial station owned by Meridian Broadcasting, Inc. The format of the station is adult contemporary music. WINK-FM broadcasts to the Fort Myers, FL area at 96.9 FM.
FM RADIO STATION

WINL-FM 41755
Owner: Westburg Broadcasting Alabama, LLC.
Editorial: 1226 Jefferson Rd, Demopolis, Alabama 36732-6205 **Tel:** 1 334 289-9850.
Web site: http://www.dixiecountry.net
Profile: WINL-FM is a commercial station owned by Westburg Broadcasting Alabama, LLC. The format of the station is classic country music. WINL-FM broadcasts to the Demopolis, AL area at 98.5 FM.
FM RADIO STATION

WINN-FM 42805
Owner: White River Broadcasting Co., Inc.
Editorial: 3212 Washington St, Columbus, Indiana 47203-1505 **Tel:** 1 812 372-4448.
Web site: http://www.win1049.com
Profile: WINN-FM is a commercial station owned by White River Broadcasting Co., Inc. The format of the station is Adult CHR. WINN-FM broadcasts to the Columbus, IN area at 104.9 FM.
FM RADIO STATION

WINQ-FM 40380
Owner: Saga Communications
Editorial: 69 Stanhope Ave, Keene, New Hampshire 03431-1577 **Tel:** 1 603 352-9230.
Web site: http://www.wink987.com
Profile: WINQ-FM is a commercial station owned by Saga Communications. The format of the station is country. WINQ-FM broadcasts to the Boston area at 98.7.
FM RADIO STATION

WINR-AM 35391
Owner: iHeartMedia Inc.
Editorial: 320 N Jensen Rd, Vestal, New York 13850-2111 **Tel:** 1 607 584-5800.
Web site: http://www.us969.com/main.html
Profile: WINR-AM is a commercial station owned by iHeartMedia Inc. The format of the station is country. WINR-AM broadcasts to the Binghamton, NY area at 680 AM.
AM RADIO STATION

WINS-AM 39333
Owner: CBS Radio
Editorial: 345 Hudson St Fl 10, New York, New York 10014-7472 **Tel:** 1 212 315-7000.
Email: info@1010winsmail.com
Web site: http://newyork.cbslocal.com/station/1010-wins
Profile: WINS-AM is a commercial station owned by CBS Radio. The format of the station is news. WINS-AM broadcasts to the New York area at 1010 AM.
AM RADIO STATION

WINT-AM 35299
Owner: Spirit Broadcasting Corp.
Editorial: 36913 Stevens Blvd, Willoughby, Ohio 44094-6360 **Tel:** 1 440 946-1330.
Email: email@welw.com
Web site: http://wintradio.com
Profile: WINT-AM is a commercial station owned by Spirit Broadcasting Corp. The format of the station is talk. WINT-AM broadcasts to the Willoughby, OH area at 1330 AM.
AM RADIO STATION

WINX-FM 235105
Owner: First Media Radio LLC
Editorial: 306 Port St, Easton, Maryland 21601-4101 **Tel:** 1 410 822-3301.
Email: production@winxfm.com
Web site: http://www.winxfm.com
Profile: WINX-FM is a commercial station owned by First Media Radio LLC. The format of the station is contemporary country. WINX-FM's tagline is "Shore Country 94.3 FM." The target audience of the station is adults, ages 18 to 54. WINX-FM broadcasts to the Easton, MD area at 94.3 FM.
FM RADIO STATION

WINY-AM 35394
Owner: Osbrey Broadcasting
Editorial: 45 Pomfret St, Putnam, Connecticut 06260-1827 **Tel:** 1 860 928-1350.
Email: news@winyradio.com
Web site: http://www.winyradio.com
Profile: WINY-AM is a commercial station owned by Osbrey Broadcasting. The format of the station is adult contemporary. WINY-AM broadcasts to Putnam, CT at 1350 AM.
AM RADIO STATION

WINZ-AM 38658
Owner: iHeartMedia Inc.
Editorial: 7601 Riviera Blvd, Miramar, Florida 33023-6574 **Tel:** 1 954 862-2000.
Web site: http://940winz.iheart.com
Profile: WINZ-AM is a commercial station owned by iHeartMedia Inc. The format of the station is sports. WINZ-AM broadcasts to the Miami area at 940 AM.
AM RADIO STATION

WIOD-AM 36659
Owner: iHeartMedia Inc.
Editorial: 7601 Riviera Blvd, Miramar, Florida 33023-6574 **Tel:** 1 954 862-2000.
Email: news@wiod.com
Web site: http://wiod.iheart.com
Profile: WIOD-AM is a commercial station owned by iHeartMedia Inc. The format of the station is news and talk. WIOD-AM broadcasts to the Miami area at 610 AM.
AM RADIO STATION

WIOE-FM 42062
Owner: Walsh, Brian R.
Editorial: 722 E Center St, Warsaw, Indiana 46580-3322 **Tel:** 1 574 268-9830.
Email: wioe@kconline.com
Web site: http://wioe.com/site/
Profile: WIOE-FM is a commercial station owned by Walsh, Brian R. The format for the station is oldies. WIOE-FM broadcasts to the Greater Fort Wayne, IN area at 101.1 FM.
FM RADIO STATION

WIOG-FM 45717
Owner: Cumulus Media Inc.
Editorial: 1740 Champagne Dr N, Saginaw, Michigan 48604 **Tel:** 1 989 776-2100.
Web site: http://www.wiog.com
Profile: WIOG-FM is a commercial station owned by Cumulus Media Inc. The format of the station is Top 40/CHR music. WIOG-FM broadcasts to the Saginaw, MI area at 102.5 FM.
FM RADIO STATION

WIOI-AM 36521
Owner: Jones Radio Network
Editorial: 1010 Coles Blvd, Portsmouth, Ohio 45662-2205 **Tel:** 1 606 932-4796.
Email: 1010am@wioiradio.com
Web site: http://www.wioiradio.com
Profile: WIOI-AM is a commercial station owned by Maillet Media Inc. The format of the station is adult standards. WIOI-AM broadcasts to Portsmouth, OH and surrounding communities at 1010 AM.
AM RADIO STATION

WIOK-FM 42847
Owner: Hammond Broadcasting Inc.
Editorial: 4942 US Highway 27 N, Butler, Kentucky 41006-8653 **Tel:** 1 859 472-1075.
Email: wiok@fuse.net
Web site: http://www.wiok.com
Profile: WIOK-FM is a commercial station owned by Hammond Broadcasting Inc. The format of the station is gospel. WIOK-FM broadcasts to Butler, KY area at 107.5 FM.
FM RADIO STATION

WIOL-FM 43187
Owner: Davis Broadcasting
Editorial: 2203 Wynnton Rd, Columbus, Georgia 31906-2531 **Tel:** 1 706 576-3565.
Web site: http://www.1580thezone.com
Profile: WIOL-FM is a commercial station owned by Davis Broadcasting. The format of the station is sports. WIOL-FM broadcasts to the Columbus, GA area at 95.7 FM.
FM RADIO STATION

WION-AM 35395
Owner: Packer Radio WION LLC
Editorial: 1150 Haynor Rd, Ionia, Michigan 48846-8532 **Tel:** 1 616 527-9466.
Email: office@i1430.com
Web site: http://www.i1430.com
Profile: WION-AM is a commercial station owned by Packer Radio WION LLC. The format of the station is full service. WION-AM broadcasts to the Ionia, MI area on 1430 AM.
AM RADIO STATION

WIOO-AM 35396
Owner: WIOO Inc.
Editorial: 180 York Rd, Carlisle, Pennsylvania 17013-3149 **Tel:** 1 717 243-1200.
Email: wioo@pa.net
Web site: http://www.wioo.com
Profile: WIOO-AM is a commercial station owned by WIOO Inc. The format of the station is classic country. WIOO-AM broadcasts to the Carlisle, PA area at 1000 AM.
AM RADIO STATION

WIOQ-FM 40381
Owner: iHeartMedia Inc.
Editorial: 111 Presidential Blvd, Bala Cynwyd, Pennsylvania 19004-1008 **Tel:** 1 610 784-3333.
Web site: http://q102.iheart.com
Profile: WIOQ-FM is a commercial station owned by iHeartMedia Inc. The format of the station is Top 40/CHR. WIOQ-FM broadcasts to the Philadelphia area at 102.1 FM.
FM RADIO STATION

WIOS-AM 37912
Owner: Carroll Broadcasting Co.
Editorial: 523 Meadow Rd, Tawas City, Michigan 48763-9189 **Tel:** 1 989 362-3417.
Email: wkjc@wkjc.com
Web site: http://www.wios.com
Profile: WIOS-AM is a commercial station owned by Carroll Broadcasting Co. The format of the station is talk. WIOS-AM broadcasts to the Tawas City, MI area at 1480 AM.
AM RADIO STATION

WIOT-FM 45236
Owner: iHeartMedia Inc.
Editorial: 125 S Superior St, Toledo, Ohio 43604-8747 **Tel:** 1 419 244-8321.
Web site: http://www.wiot.com
Profile: WIOT-FM is a commercial station owned by iHeartMedia Inc. The format of the station is rock. WIOT-FM broadcasts to the Toledo, OH area at 104.7 FM.
FM RADIO STATION

WIOU-AM 39050
Owner: Hoosier AM/FM LLC
Editorial: 671 E 400 S, Kokomo, Indiana 46902-8101
Web site: http://www.1350amwiou.com
Profile: WIOU-AM is a commercial station owned by Hoosier AM/FM LLC. The format of the station is news, sports and talk. WIOU-AM broadcasts to the Kokomo, IN area at 1350 AM.
AM RADIO STATION

WIOV-AM 38765
Owner: Cumulus Media Inc.
Editorial: 5989 Susquehanna Plaza Drive, York, Pennsylvania 17406 **Tel:** 1 717 738-1191.
Web site: http://www.wiov985.com
Profile: WIOV-AM is a commercial station owned by Cumulus Media Inc. The format of the station is sports. WIOV-AM broadcasts to the Reading, PA area at 1240 AM.
AM RADIO STATION

WIOV-FM 46117
Owner: Cumulus Media Inc.
Editorial: 44 Bethany Rd, Ephrata, Pennsylvania 17522 **Tel:** 1 717 738-1191.
Web site: http://www.wiov.com
Profile: WIOV-FM is a commercial station owned by Cumulus Media Inc. The format of the station is classic country. WIOV-FM broadcasts to the Ephrata, PA area at 105.1 FM.
FM RADIO STATION

WIOZ-AM 37758
Owner: Muirfield Broadcasting
Editorial: 200 Short Rd, Southern Pines, North Carolina 28387 **Tel:** 1 910 692-2107.
Web site: http://www.wioz.com
Profile: WIOZ-AM is a commercial station owned by Muirfield Broadcasting. The format of the station is adult standards. WIOZ-AM broadcasts to the Southern Pines, NC at 550 AM.
AM RADIO STATION

WIOZ-FM 43278
Owner: Muirfield Broadcasting
Editorial: 200 Short Rd, Southern Pines, North Carolina 28387-6289 **Tel:** 1 910 692-2107.
Web site: http://www.star1025fm.com
Profile: WIOZ-FM is a commercial station owned by Muirfield Broadcasting. The format of the station is adult contemporary. WIOZ-FM broadcasts to Southern Pines, NC area at 102.5 FM.
FM RADIO STATION

WIPC-AM 35397
Owner: Super W Media Group Inc.
Editorial: 630A Mountain Lake Cutoff Rd, Lake Wales, Florida 33859-7854 **Tel:** 1 863 679-7178.
Email: wipc1280@yahoo.com
Web site: http://www.radio esperanza1280.com
Profile: WIPC-AM is a commercial station owned by Super W Media Group Inc. The format of the station is Hispanic religious programming. WIPC-AM broadcasts to the Lake Wales, FL area at 1280 AM.
AM RADIO STATION

WIP-FM 40900
Owner: CBS Radio
Editorial: 400 Market St Fl 9, Philadelphia, Pennsylvania 19106-2530 **Tel:** 1 610 949-7800.
Email: web@cbsphilly.com
Web site: http://philadelphia.cbslocal.com/station/94wip
Profile: WIP-FM is a commercial station owned by CBS Radio. The format of the station is sports talk. WIP-FM broadcasts to the Philadelphia area at 94.1 FM. The stations airs WIP-AM's programming.
FM RADIO STATION

WIQO-FM 45239
Owner: 3 Daughters Media, Inc.
Editorial: 1035 Avalon Dr, Forest, Virginia 24551-2970 **Tel:** 1 434 534-6100.
Web site: http://www.wiqoradio.com
Profile: WIQO-FM is a commercial station owned by 3 Daughters Media, Inc. The format of the station is talk. WIQO-FM broadcasts to the Lynchburg, VA area at 100.9 FM.
FM RADIO STATION

WIQQ-FM 45240
Owner: Delta Radio, LLC
Editorial: 830 Main St, Greenville, Mississippi 38701-4102 **Tel:** 1 662 378-2617.
Email: info@deltaradio.net
Web site: http://www.q102.net
Profile: WIQQ-FM is a commercial station owned by Delta Radio, LLC. The format of the station is Top 40/ CHR. WIQQ-FM broadcasts to the Greenville, MS area at 102.3 FM.
FM RADIO STATION

WIQR-AM 36776
Owner: Star Power Communications
Editorial: 800 County Road 4 E, Prattville, Alabama 36067-6610 **Tel:** 1 334 358-0410.
Profile: WIQR-AM is a commercial station owned by Star Power Communications. The format of the station is sports. WIQR-AM broadcasts to the Prattville, AL area at 1410 AM.
AM RADIO STATION

WIRA-AM 36477
Owner: Caribbean Media Group, Inc.
Editorial: 6803 S US Highway 1, Port Saint Lucie, Florida 34952-1434 **Tel:** 1 772 460-9356.
Web site: http://am1400wira.weebly.com
Profile: WIRA-AM is a commercial station owned by Caribbean Media Group, Inc.. The format of the station is Ethnic Haitian. WIRA-AM broadcasts to the Port St. Lucie, FL area at 1400 AM.
AM RADIO STATION

WIRE-FM 892774
Owner: Indiana Community Radio Corporation
Editorial: 107 N Meridian St Ste 2022, Lebanon, Indiana 46052-2384 **Tel:** 1 765 482-4427.
Web site: http://www.radiomom.fm
Profile: WIRE-FM is a non-commercial station owned by Indiana Community Radio Corporation. The format of the station is adult hits. WIRE-FM broadcasts to the Indianapolis, IN area at 91.1 FM.
FM RADIO STATION

WIRK-FM 43331
Owner: Alpha Media
Editorial: 701 Northpoint Pkwy Ste 500, West Palm Beach, Florida 33407-1960 **Tel:** 1 561 868-1100.
Web site: http://www.wirk.com
Profile: WIRK-FM is a commercial station owned by Alpha Media. The format of the station is contemporary country. WIRK-FM broadcasts to the West Palm Beach, FL area at 103.1 FM.
FM RADIO STATION

WIRL-AM 37914
Owner: Alpha Media
Editorial: 331 Fulton St Ste 1200, Peoria, Illinois 61602-1422 **Tel:** 1 309 637-3700.
Email: news@1470wmbd.com
Web site: http://www.1290wirl.com
Profile: WIRL-AM is a commercial station owned by Alpha Media. The format of the station is oldies music. WIRL-AM broadcasts to the Peoria, IL area at 1290 AM.
AM RADIO STATION

WIRN-FM 43239
Owner: Minnesota Public Radio
Editorial: 207 W Superior St, Ste 224, Duluth, Minnesota 55802 **Tel:** 1 218 722-9411.
Email: newsroom@mpr.org
Web site: http://www.mpr.org
Profile: WIRN-FM is a non-commercial station owned by Minnesota Public Radio. The format of the station is news and talk. WIRN-FM broadcasts to the Duluth, MN area at 92.5 FM.
FM RADIO STATION

WIRO-AM 36895
Owner: iHeartMedia Inc.
Editorial: 134 4th Ave, Huntington, West Virginia 25701-1220 **Tel:** 1 304 525-7788.
Web site: http://www.800wvhu.com
Profile: WIRO-AM is a commercial station owned by iHeartMedia Inc. The format of the station is sports. WIRO-AM broadcasts to Huntington, WV at 1230 AM.
AM RADIO STATION

WIRR-FM 41854
Owner: Minnesota Public Radio
Editorial: 207 W Superior St Ste 224, Duluth, Minnesota 55802-4041 **Tel:** 1 218 722-9411.
Email: newsroom@mpr.org
Web site: http://minnesota.publicradio.org/radio/stations/wirnwirr/
Profile: WIRR-FM is a non-commercial station owned by Minnesota Public Radio. The format of the station is classical music. WIRR-FM broadcasts to the Duluth, MN area at 90.9 FM.
FM RADIO STATION

WIRV-AM 38771
Owner: Wallingford Broadcasting LLC
Editorial: 128 Big Hill Ave, Richmond, Kentucky 40475 **Tel:** 1 606 723-5138.
Email: ron@wcyofm.com
Web site: http://wirvam.com
Profile: WIRV-AM is a commercial station owned by Wallingford Broadcasting LLC. The format for the station is oldies and talk. WIRV-AM broadcasts to the Lexington, KY area at 1550 AM.
AM RADIO STATION

WIRX-FM 43285
Owner: Midwest Family Stations
Editorial: 580 E Napier Ave, Benton Harbor, Michigan 49022-5816 **Tel:** 1 269 925-1111.
Email: wirx@wirx.com
Web site: http://www.wirx.com
Profile: WIRX-FM is a commercial station owned by Midwest Family Stations. The format of the station is rock music. WIRX-AM broadcasts in the Benton Harbor, MI area at 107.1 FM.
FM RADIO STATION

WIRY-AM 35398
Owner: Hometown Radio Inc.
Editorial: 4712 State Route 9, Plattsburgh, New York 12901-6035 **Tel:** 1 518 563-1340.
Email: wiry@wiry.com
Web site: http://www.wiry.com
Profile: WIRY-AM is a commercial station owned by Hometown Radio Inc. The format of the station is adult contemporary, oldies and contemporary country music. WIRY-AM broadcasts to the Plattsburgh, NY area at 1340 AM.
AM RADIO STATION

Wisconsin Public Radio 47085
Editorial: 821 University Ave, Madison, Wisconsin 53706-1412 **Tel:** 1 608 263-3970.
Email: listener@wpr.org
Web site: http://www.wpr.org
Profile: Distributes news and informational programming from the Ideas Network and the NPR News and Classical Music Network throughout Wisconsin via a high quality dual service broadcast signal. Provides a wide array of informative and educational public affairs programming from the state capitol of Madison, WI.
REGIONAL RADIO NETWORKS

Wisconsin Radio Network 47081
Owner: Learfield Communications, Inc.
Editorial: 222 State St Ste 403, Madison, Wisconsin 53703-2273 **Tel:** 1 608 251-3900.
Email: info@wrn.com
Web site: http://www.wrn.com
Profile: The Wisconsin Radio Network is a statewide news network providing news and sports programs to more than 55 radio stations. The network covers the legislature and state government from its bureau in Madison and also reports on news from throughout the state with the help of affiliate correspondents.
REGIONAL RADIO NETWORKS

WISE-AM 35399
Owner: Saga Communications
Editorial: 1190 Patton Ave, Asheville, North Carolina 28806-2706 **Tel:** 1 828 259-9695.
Web site: http://espnasheville.com
Profile: WISE-AM is a commercial station owned by Saga Communications. The format of the station is sports. WISE-AM broadcasts to the Asheville, NC area at 1310 AM.
AM RADIO STATION

WISH-FM 235038
Owner: Dana Communications Corp.
Editorial: 303 N Main St, Benton, Illinois 62812-1314 **Tel:** 1 618 435-4392.
Email: wishfm989@gmail.com
Web site: http://www.wish989.com
Profile: WISH-FM is a commercial station owned by Dana Communications Corp. located in McLeansboro, Illinois. The station is a sister station to WMCL-AM and WQRL-FM. WISH-FM is broadcast locally on 98.9 FM. The format of the station is adult contemporary music.
FM RADIO STATION

WISK-AM 37915
Owner: Sumter Broadcasting
Tel: 1 229 924-6500.
Web site: http://www.americusradio.com
Profile: WISK-AM is a commercial station owned by Sumter Broadcasting. The format of the station is regional Mexican. WISK-AM broadcasts in the Atlanta, GA area at 990 AM.
AM RADIO STATION

WISK-FM 45456
Owner: Sumter Broadcasting
Editorial: 215 Georgia Hwy 30 W, Americus, Georgia 31719 **Tel:** 1 229 924-6500.
Email: wiskwdec@mchsi.com
Web site: http://www.americusradio.com
Profile: WISK-FM is a commercial station owned by Sumter Broadcasting. The format of the station is country music. WISK-FM broadcasts to the Americus, GA area at 98.7 FM.
FM RADIO STATION

WISN-AM 37916
Owner: iHeartMedia Inc.
Editorial: 12100 W Howard Ave, Greenfield, Wisconsin 53228-1851 **Tel:** 1 414 545-8900.
Web site: http://www.newstalk1130.com
Profile: WISN-AM is a commercial station owned by iHeartMedia Inc. The format of the station is news and talk. WISN-AM broadcasts to the Greenfield, WI, area at 1130 AM.
AM RADIO STATION

WISP-AM 36502
Owner: Holy Spirit Radio Foundation, Inc.
Editorial: 40 Rickert Rd, Doylestown, Pennsylvania 18901 **Tel:** 1 215 345-1570.
Email: 1570am@holyspiritradio.org
Web site: http://www.holyspiritradio.org
Profile: WISP-AM is a non-commercial station owned by Holy Spirit Radio Foundation, Inc. The format of the station is religious programming. WISP-AM broadcasts to the Doylestown, PA area at 1570 AM.
AM RADIO STATION

WISR-AM 35400
Owner: Butler County Radio Network
Editorial: 112 Hollywood Dr, Butler, Pennsylvania 16001-5691 **Tel:** 1 724 283-1500.
Email: frontdesk@bcrnetwork.com
Web site: http://www.wisr680.com
Profile: WISR-AM is a commercial station owned by the Butler County Radio Network. The format of the station is news and talk. WISR-AM broadcasts to the Butler, PA area at 680 AM.
AM RADIO STATION

WISS-AM 37107
Owner: Hometown Broadcasting LLC
Editorial: 112 N Pearl St, Berlin, Wisconsin 54923-1529 **Tel:** 1 920 361-3551.
Web site: http://www.wissradio.com
Profile: WISS-AM is a commercial station owned by Hometown Broadcasting LLC. The format of the station is classic hits. WISS-AM broadcasts to the Berlin, WI area at 1100 AM.
AM RADIO STATION

WIST-FM 40762
Owner: Norsan Group
Editorial: 4801 E Independence Blvd Ste 815, Charlotte, North Carolina 28212-5490 **Tel:** 1 704 405-3172.
Web site: http://www.larazalaraza.com
Profile: WIST-FM is a commercial station owned by Norsan Group. The format of the station is regional Mexican. WIST-FM broadcasts in the High Point, NC area at 98.3 FM.
FM RADIO STATION

WISW-AM 38395
Owner: Cumulus Media Inc.
Editorial: 1801 Charleston Hwy Ste J, Cayce, South Carolina 29033-2019 **Tel:** 1 803 796-7600.
Web site: http://www.1320thefan.com
Profile: WISW-AM is a commercial station owned by Cumulus Media Inc. The format of the station is sports. WISW-AM broadcasts to the Columbia, SC area at a frequency of 1320 AM.
AM RADIO STATION

WISX-FM 40242
Owner: iHeartMedia Inc.
Editorial: 111 Presidential Blvd Ste 100, Bala Cynwyd, Pennsylvania 19004-1009 **Tel:** 1 610 784-3333.
Web site: http://mixphiladelphia.iheart.com
Profile: WISX-FM is a commercial station owned by iHeartMedia Inc. The format of the station is hot adult contemporary. WISX-FM broadcasts to the Philadelphia area at 106.1 FM.
FM RADIO STATION

WITA-AM 35401
Owner: F.W. Robbert Broadcasting, Inc.
Editorial: 1300 Wwcr Ave, Nashville, Tennessee 37218-3800 **Tel:** 1 865 588-2974.
Web site: http://www.1490wita.com
Profile: WITA-AM is a commercial station owned by F.W. Robbert Broadcasting, Inc. The format of the station is religious and gospel music. WITA-AM broadcasts to the Knoxville, TN area at 1490 AM.
AM RADIO STATION

WITF-FM 40384
Owner: WITF Inc.
Editorial: 4801 Lindle Rd, Harrisburg, Pennsylvania 17111-2444 **Tel:** 1 717 704-3000.
Email: news@witf.org
Web site: http://www.witf.org
Profile: WITF-FM is a non-commercial station owned by WITF Inc. The format of the station is news and talk. WITF-FM broadcasts to the Harrisburg, PA area at 89.5 FM.
FM RADIO STATION

WITL-FM 45241
Owner: Townsquare Media, LLC
Editorial: 3420 Pinetree Rd, Lansing, Michigan 48911-4207 **Tel:** 1 517 394-7272.
Web site: http://www.witl.com
Profile: WITL-FM is a commercial station owned by Townsquare Media, LLC. The format of the station is contemporary country music. WITL-FM broadcasts to the Lansing, MI area at 100.7 FM.
FM RADIO STATION

WITR-FM 40385
Owner: Rochester Institute of Technology
Editorial: 32 Lomb Memorial Dr, Rochester, New York 14623 **Tel:** 1 585 475-2000.
Email: feedback@witr.rit.edu
Web site: http://witr.rit.edu
Profile: WITR-FM is a non-commercial college station owned by Rochester Institute of Technology. The format of the station is college variety. WITR-FM broadcasts to the Rochester, NY area at 89.7 FM.
FM RADIO STATION

WITS-AM 37918
Owner: Cohan Radio Group Inc.
Editorial: 3750 US Highway 27 N Ste 1, Sebring, Florida 33870-1644 **Tel:** 1 863 382-9999.
Web site: http://wits1340am.com
Profile: WITS-AM is a commercial station owned by Cohan Radio Group Inc. The format of the station is adult standards. WITS-AM broadcasts to the Sebring, FL area at 1340 AM.
AM RADIO STATION

WITY-AM 35402
Owner: David Brown
Editorial: 399 Spelter Ave, Tilton, Illinois 61832-8321 **Tel:** 1 217 446-1312.
Email: office@wityradio.com
Web site: http://www.wityradio.com
Profile: WITY-AM is commercial station owned by David Brown. The station's format is adult standards. WITY-AM broadcasts to Vermilion County, IL at 980 AM.
AM RADIO STATION

WITZ-AM 37919
Owner: Jasper on the Air Inc.
Editorial: 1978 S Witz Rd, Jasper, Indiana 47546-2672 **Tel:** 1 812 482-2131.
Email: witz@witzamfm.com
Web site: http://www.witzamfm.com
Profile: WITZ-AM is a commercial station owned by Jasper on the Air Inc. The format of the station is Spanish adult hits and talk. WITZ-FM broadcasts to the Jasper, IN area at 990 AM.
AM RADIO STATION

WITZ-FM 45242
Owner: Jasper on the Air Inc.
Editorial: 1978 S Witz Rd, Jasper, Indiana 47546-2672 **Tel:** 1 812 482-2131.
Email: witz@witzamfm.com
Web site: http://www.witzamfm.com
Profile: WITZ-FM is a commercial station owned by Jasper on the Air Inc. The format of the station is adult contemporary music. WITZ-FM broadcasts to the Jasper, IN area at 104.7 FM.
FM RADIO STATION

WIVG-FM 46811
Owner: Flinn Broadcasting Corp.
Editorial: 6080 Mount Moriah Road Ext, Memphis, Tennessee 38115-2645 **Tel:** 1 901 375-9324.
Web site: http://www.i96memphis.com
Profile: WIVG-FM is a commercial station owned by Flinn Broadcasting Corp. The format of the station is modern rock. WIVG-FM broadcasts to the Memphis, TN area at 96.1 FM.
FM RADIO STATION

WIVK-FM 43483
Owner: Cumulus Media Inc.
Editorial: 4711 Old Kingston Pike, Knoxville, Tennessee 37919-5207 **Tel:** 1 865 588-6511.
Web site: http://www.wivk.com
Profile: WIVK-FM is a commercial station owned by Cumulus Media Inc. The format of the station is contemporary country. WIVK-FM broadcasts to the Knoxville, TN area at 107.7 FM.
FM RADIO STATION

WIVQ-FM 42185
Owner: Mendota Broadcasting
Editorial: 3905 Progress Blvd, Peru, Illinois 61354-1121 **Tel:** 1 815 224-2100.
Email: q@studstillmedia.com
Web site: http://www.qhitmusic.com
Profile: WIVQ-FM is a commercial station owned by Mendota Broadcasting. The format of the station is

Top 40/CHR. WIVQ-FM broadcasts to the Peru, IL area at 103.3 FM.
FM RADIO STATION

WIVR-FM 235132
Owner: Milner Broadcasting Co.
Editorial: 202 E Walnut St, Watseka, Illinois 60970-1356 **Tel:** 1 815 933-9287.
Email: wivrfm@comcast.net
Web site: http://www.rivervalleyradio.net
Profile: WIVR-FM is a commercial station owned by Milner Broadcasting Co. The format of the station is contemporary country music. WIVR-FM broadcasts to the Bourbonnais, IL area at 101.7 FM.
FM RADIO STATION

WIVY-FM 42638
Owner: Gateway Radio Works Inc.
Editorial: 123 E 1st St, Morehead, Kentucky 40351-1701 **Tel:** 1 606 784-9966.
Email: wivy@hotmail.com
Web site: http://wivyradio.com
Profile: WIVY-FM is a commercial station owned by Gateway Radio Works Inc. The format for the station is modern adult contemporary. WIVY-FM broadcasts to the Lexington, KY area at 96.3 FM.
FM RADIO STATION

WIWA-AM 475991
Owner: Church Capital Florida Holdings, LLC.
Editorial: 12538 Village Park Drive, Orlando, Florida 32812-8214 **Tel:** 1 407 506-1270.
Email: 1270am@gmail.com
Web site: http://www.laestaciondelpueblo.com
Profile: WIWA-FM is a commercial station owned by Church Capital Florida Holdings, LLC. The format of the station is Spanish News Talk, with a secondary format of Spanish Contemporary Christian. The station broadcasts to the Orlando, FL area at a frequency of 1160 AM.
AM RADIO STATION

WIWF-FM 46148
Owner: Cumulus Media Inc.
Editorial: 4230 Faber Place Dr Ste 100, North Charleston, South Carolina 29405-8512
Tel: 1 843 277-1200.
Web site: http://www.nashfm969.com
Profile: WIWF-FM is a commercial station owned by Cumulus Media Inc. The format of the station is classic and contemporary country music. WIWF-FM broadcasts to the Charleston, SC area at 96.9 FM.
FM RADIO STATION

WIXC-AM 36288
Owner: Genesis Communications Inc.
Editorial: 6305 State Road 46, Mims, Florida 32754
Tel: 1 813 281-1040.
Email: info@radiogenesis.com
Web site: http://www.newstalkflorida.com
Profile: WIXC-AM is a commercial station owned by Genesis Communications Inc. The format of the station is news and talk. WIXC-AM broadcasts to the Mims, FL area at 1060 AM.
AM RADIO STATION

WIXE-AM 35403
Owner: Monroe Broadcasting
Editorial: 1700 Buena Vista Rd, Monroe, North Carolina 28112-6306 **Tel:** 1 704 289-2525.
Web site: http://www.wixe.com
Profile: WIXE-AM is a commercial station owned by Monroe Broadcasting. The format of the station is classic country and talk. WIXE-AM broadcasts in the Charlotte, NC area at 1190 AM.
AM RADIO STATION

WIXI-AM 35855
Owner: Richardson Broadcasting Corp.
Editorial: 1449 Spaulding Ishade Road, Birmingham, Alabama 35211 **Tel:** 1 205 942-1776.
Web site: http://wixi1360.com
Profile: WIXI-AM is a commercial station owned by Richardson Broadcasting Corp. The format of the station is Regional Mexican. WIXI-AM broadcasts to the Birmingham, AL area at a frequency of 1360 AM.
AM RADIO STATION

WIXK-AM 37921
Owner: Hmong Radio Broadcast
Tel: 1 651 772-3748.
Web site: http://www.wixk1590.com
Profile: WIXK-AM is a commercial station owned by Hmong Radio Broadcast. The format of the station is Hmong music. WIXK-AM broadcasts to the St. Paul, MN area at 1590 AM.
AM RADIO STATION

WIXM-FM 45337
Owner: Northeast Broadcasting Co.
Editorial: 372 Dorset St, South Burlington, Vermont 05403-6212 **Tel:** 1 802 863-1010.
Web site: http://themix1023.com
Profile: WIXM-FM is a commercial station owned by Northeast Broadcasting Co. The format of the station is Hot adult contemporary. WIXM-FM broadcasts to the Saint Albans, VT area at 102.3 FM.
FM RADIO STATION

WIXN-AM 37922
Owner: NRG Media LLC
Editorial: 1460 S College Ave, Dixon, Illinois 61021
Tel: 1 815 288-3341.
Web site: http://www.am1460wixn.com
Profile: WIXN-AM is a commercial station owned by NRG Media LLC. The format of the station is adult standards music. WIXN-AM broadcasts to the Dixon, IL area at 1460 AM.
AM RADIO STATION

WIXO-FM 43598
Owner: Cumulus Media Inc.
Editorial: 120 Eaton St, Peoria, Illinois 61603-4217
Tel: 1 309 676-5000.
Web site: http://www.1057thexrocks.com
Profile: WIXO-FM is a commercial station owned by Cumulus Media Inc. The format of the station is rock/album-oriented rock. WIXO-FM broadcasts to the Peoria, IL area at 105.7 FM.
FM RADIO STATION

WIXT-AM 38630
Owner: Galaxy Communications LP
Editorial: 39 Kellogg Rd, New Hartford, New York 13413-2849 **Tel:** 1 315 797-1330.
Profile: WIXT-AM is a commercial station owned by Galaxy Communications LP. The format of the station is sports. WLFH-AM broadcasts to the Utica, NY area at 1230 AM.
AM RADIO STATION

WIXV-FM 46195
Owner: Cumulus Media Inc.
Editorial: 214 Television Cir, Savannah, Georgia 31406-4519 **Tel:** 1 912 961-9000.
Web site: http://www.rockofsavannah.net
Profile: WIXV-FM is a commercial station owned by Cumulus Media Inc. The format of the station is classic rock. WIXV-FM broadcasts to the Savannah, GA area at 95.5 FM.
FM RADIO STATION

WIXX-FM 45246
Owner: Midwest Communications Inc.
Editorial: 1420 Bellevue St, Green Bay, Wisconsin 54311 **Tel:** 1 920 435-3771.
Web site: http://www.wixx.com
Profile: WIXX-FM is a commercial station owned by Midwest Communications Inc. The format of the station is Top 40/CHR. WIXX-FM broadcasts to the Green Bay, WI area at 101.1 FM.
FM RADIO STATION

WIXY-FM 41989
Owner: Saga Communications
Editorial: 2603 W Bradley Ave, Champaign, Illinois 61821 **Tel:** 1 217 352-4141.
Web site: http://www.wixy.com
Profile: WIXY-FM is a commercial station owned by Saga Communications. The format of the station is contemporary country. WIXY-FM broadcasts to the Champaign, IL area at 100.3 FM.
FM RADIO STATION

WIYD-AM 35405
Owner: Natkim
Editorial: 1428 Saint Johns Ave, Palatka, Florida 32177-4542 **Tel:** 1 386 325-4556.
Email: wiydradio@gmail.com
Web site: http://wiydradio.com
Profile: WIYD-AM is a commercial station owned by Hall Broadcasting Co. The format of station is classic country. WIYD-AM broadcasts to the Palatka, FL area at 1260 AM.
AM RADIO STATION

WIYN-FM 41724
Owner: Double O Radio
Editorial: 34 Chestnut St, Oneonta, New York 13820
Tel: 1 607 432-1030.
Email: wdla@frontiernet.net
Web site: http://wdhifm.com
Profile: WIYN-FM is a commercial station owned by Double O Radio. The format of the station is oldies music. WIYN-FM broadcasts to the Oneonta, NY area at 94.7 FM.
FM RADIO STATION

WIYY-FM 45247
Owner: Hearst Radio, Inc.
Editorial: 3800 Hooper Ave, Baltimore, Maryland 21211-1313 **Tel:** 1 410 338-6596.
Email: studio@98online.com
Web site: http://www.98online.com
Profile: WIYY-FM is a commercial station owned by the Hearst Radio, Inc. The format of the station is rock music. WIYY-FM broadcasts to the Baltimore area at 97.9 FM.
FM RADIO STATION

WIZB-FM 46893
Owner: Radio Training Network, Inc.
Editorial: 2563 Montgomery Hwy Ste 1, Dothan, Alabama 36303-2603 **Tel:** 1 334 699-5672.
Web site: http://alabama.thejoyfm.com
Profile: WIZB-FM is a non-commercial station owned by Radio Training Network, Inc. The format of the station is adult contemporary Christian programming. WIZB-FM broadcasts in the Dothan, AL area at 94.3 FM.
FM RADIO STATION

WIZD-AM 36452
Owner: Letcher County Broadcasting Inc.
Editorial: 486 Lakeside Dr, Jenkins, Kentucky 41537-8917 **Tel:** 1 606 832-2270.
Profile: WIZD-AM is a commercial station owned by Letcher County Broadcasting. The format of the station is oldies. WIZD-AM broadcasts to the Whitesburg, KY area at 1480 AM.
AM RADIO STATION

WIZE-AM 35406
Owner: iHeartMedia Inc.
Editorial: 101 Pine St, Dayton, Ohio 45402-2948
Tel: 1 937 224-1137.
Web site: http://wizeam.com
Profile: WIZE-AM is a commercial station owned by iHeartMedia Inc. The format of the station is classic country. WIZE-AM broadcasts to the Dayton, OH area at 1340 AM.
AM RADIO STATION

WIZF-FM 40391
Owner: Urban One, Inc.
Editorial: 1 Centennial Plz, 705 Central Ave Suite 200, Cincinnati, Ohio 45202 **Tel:** 1 513 679-6000.
Web site: http://www.wiznation.com
Profile: WIZF-FM is a commercial station owned by Urban One, Inc. The format of the station is urban contemporary music. WIZF-FM broadcasts in the Cincinnati area at 101.1 FM.
FM RADIO STATION

WIZM-AM 37923
Owner: Midwest Family Broadcasting
Editorial: 201 State St, La Crosse, Wisconsin 54601-3246 **Tel:** 1 608 782-1230.
Email: news@1410wizm.com
Web site: http://www.1410wizm.com
AM RADIO STATION

WIZM-FM 45248
Owner: Midwest Family Broadcasting
Editorial: 201 State St, La Crosse, Wisconsin 54601-3246 **Tel:** 1 608 782-1213.
Email: zmail@z933.com
Web site: http://www.z933.com
Profile: WIZM-FM is a commercial station owned by Midwest Family Broadcasting. The format of the station is Top 40. WIZM-FM broadcasts to the La Crosse, WI area at 93.3 FM. The station's slogan is, "The #1 Hit Music Station."
FM RADIO STATION

WIZN-FM 40392
Owner: Hall Communications
Editorial: 255 S Champlain St, Burlington, Vermont 05401-4881 **Tel:** 1 802 860-2440.
Email: wizn@wizn.com
Web site: http://www.wizn.com
Profile: WIZN-FM is a commercial station owned by Hall Communications. The format of the station is classic rock. WIZN-FM broadcasts in the Burlington, VT area at 106.7 FM.
FM RADIO STATION

WIZS-AM 35407
Owner: Rose Farm & Rentals Inc.
Editorial: 535 Radio Ln, Henderson, North Carolina 27536-2505 **Tel:** 1 252 492-3001.
Email: wizs@vance.net
Web site: http://www.wizs.com
Profile: WIZS-AM is a commercial station owned by Rose Farm & Rentals Inc. The format of the station is country. WIZS-AM broadcasts to the Henderson, NC area at 1450 AM.
AM RADIO STATION

WIZZ-AM 37146
Owner: P & M Radio LLC
Tel: 1 413 774-5757.
Email: comments@wizzradio.com
Web site: http://www.wizzradio.com
Profile: WIZZ-AM is a commercial station owned by P & M Radio LLC. The format of the station is adult standards. WIZZ-AM broadcasts to the Greenfield, MA area at 1520 AM.
AM RADIO STATION

WJAA-FM 42607
Owner: Midland Media Inc.
Editorial: 1531 W Tipton St, Seymour, Indiana 47274
Tel: 1 812 523-3343.
Email: radio@wjaa.net
Web site: http://www.wjaa.net
Profile: WJAA-FM is a commercial station owned by Midland Media Inc. The format of the station is adult album alternative. WJAA-FM broadcasts to the Seymour, IN area at 93.3 FM.
FM RADIO STATION

WJAD-FM 42513
Owner: Cumulus Media Inc.
Editorial: 1104 W Broad Ave, Albany, Georgia 31707-4340 **Tel:** 1 229 888-5000.
Web site: http://www.rock103albany.com
Profile: WJAD-FM is a commercial station owned by Cumulus Media Inc. The format of the station is rock music. WJAD-FM broadcasts to the Albany, GA area at 103.5 FM.
FM RADIO STATION

WJAG-AM 37926
Owner: WJAG Inc.
Editorial: 309 Braasch Ave, Norfolk, Nebraska 68701-4113 **Tel:** 1 402 371-0780.
Web site: http://www.wjag.com
Profile: WJAG-AM is a commercial station owned by WJAG Inc. The format of the station is news and talk with an emphasis on agricultural news and information. WJAG-AM broadcasts to the Norfolk, NE area at 780 AM.
AM RADIO STATION

WJAG-FM 544492
Owner: WJAG Inc.
Editorial: 309 Braasch Ave, Norfolk, Nebraska 68701-4113 **Tel:** 1 402 371-0780.
Web site: http://www.wjag.com
Profile: WJAG-FM is a commercial station owned by WJAG Inc. The format of the station is news. WJAG-FM broadcasts to the Norfolk, NE area at 105.9 FM.
FM RADIO STATION

WJAK-AM 38883
Owner: Southern Stone Communications, LLC
Editorial: 111 W Main St, Jackson, Tennessee 38301-6147 **Tel:** 1 731 427-9616.
Profile: WJAK-AM is a commercial station owned by Southern Stone Communications, LLC. The format of the station is sports. WJAK-AM broadcasts to the Jackson, TN area at 1460 AM.
AM RADIO STATION

WJAM-AM 39277
Owner: Scott Communications/Alexander Broadcasting
Editorial: 273 Persimmon Tree Rd, Valley Grande, Alabama 36701-3131 **Tel:** 1 334 875-9360.
Profile: WJAM-AM is a commercial station licensed under Scott Communications, Inc, but owned and operated under Bluewater Broadcasting, LLC. The format of the station is urban adult contemporary and gospel. WJAM-AM broadcasts to the Selma, AL area at 1340 AM.
AM RADIO STATION

WJAQ-FM 44309
Owner: MFR Inc.
Editorial: 4376 Lafayette St, Marianna, Florida 32446-3364 **Tel:** 1 850 482-3046.
Email: wjaqfm@gmail.com
Profile: WJAQ-FM is a commercial station owned by MFR Inc. The format of the station is classic country music. WJAQ-FM broadcasts to the Marianna, FL area at 100.9 FM.
FM RADIO STATION

WJAS-AM 37927
Owner: Pittsburgh Radio Partners, LLC
Editorial: 900 Parish St Fl 3, Pittsburgh, Pennsylvania 15220-3425 **Tel:** 1 412 919-8527.
Web site: http://www.1320wjas.com
Profile: WJAS-AM is a commercial station owned by Pittsburgh Radio Partners, LLC. The format of the station is news and talk. WJAS-AM broadcasts to the Pittsburgh area at 1320 AM.
AM RADIO STATION

WJAT-AM 37928
Owner: RadioJones LLC
Editorial: 2 Radio Loop, Swainsboro, Georgia 30401-5673 **Tel:** 1 478 237-1590.
Web site: http://www.am800wjat.com/
Profile: WJAT-AM is a commerical station owned by RadioJones LLC. The format of the station is talk. WJAT-AM broadcasts to the Swainsboro, GA area at 800 AM.
AM RADIO STATION

WJAW-AM 72639
Owner: JAWCO Inc.
Editorial: 925 Lancaster St, Marietta, Ohio 45750-2531 **Tel:** 1 740 373-1490.
Email: news@wmoa1490.com
Web site: http://www.espnwjaw.com
Profile: WJAW-AM is a commercial station owned by JAWCO Inc. The format of the station is sports. WJAW-AM broadcasts to the Marietta, OH area at 630 AM.
AM RADIO STATION

WJAW-FM 44356
Owner: JAWCO Inc.
Editorial: 925 Lancaster St, Marietta, Ohio 45750
Tel: 1 740 373-1490.
Web site: http://www.wmoa1490.com
Profile: WJAW-FM is a commercial station owned by JAWCO Inc. The format for the station is sports. WJAW-FM broadcasts to the Marietta, OH area at 100.9 FM.
FM RADIO STATION

WJAY-AM 36435
Owner: Greater Highway Church of Christ
Editorial: 3004 E Highway 76, Mullins, South Carolina 29574 **Tel:** 1 843 423-1140.
Profile: WJAY-AM is a commercial station owned by Greater Highway Church of Christ. The format of the station is gospel music. WJAY-AM broadcasts to the Marion, SC area at 1280 AM.
AM RADIO STATION

WJBB-AM 35388
Owner: Jeffrey T. Batten's Barrow Radio Broadcasting LLC
Editorial: 850 Arch Tanner Rd, Bethlehem, Georgia 30620-2703 **Tel:** 1 770 867-1300.
Web site: http://www.wjbbradio.com
Profile: WJBB-AM is a commercial station owned by Jeffrey T. Batten's Barrow Radio Broadcasting LLC. The format of the station is classic hits music. WWJBB-AM broadcasts to the Bethlehem, GA area at 1300 AM.
AM RADIO STATION

WJBC-AM 39123
Owner: Cumulus Media Inc.
Editorial: 236 Greenwood Ave, Bloomington, Illinois 61704-7422 **Tel:** 1 309 829-1221.
Email: news@wjbc.com
Web site: http://www.wjbc.com
Profile: WJBC-AM is commercial station owned by Cumulus Media Inc. The format of the station is news

and talk. WJBC-AM broadcasts to the Bloomington, IL area at 1230 AM.
AM RADIO STATION

WJBC-FM 44371
Owner: Cumulus Media Inc.
Editorial: 236 Greenwood Ave, Bloomington, Illinois 61704-7422 **Tel:** 1 309 829-1221.
Email: news@wjbc.com
Web site: http://www.937nashicon.com
Profile: WJBC-FM is a commercial station owned by Cumulus Media Inc. The format of the station is country music. WJBC-FM broadcasts to the Pontiac, IL area at 93.7 FM.
FM RADIO STATION

WJBD-FM 45250
Owner: NRG Media LLC
Editorial: 310 W McMackin St, Salem, Illinois 62881 **Tel:** 1 618 548-2000.
Email: news@wjbdradio.com
Web site: http://www.wjbdradio.com
Profile: WJBD-FM is a commercial station owned by NRG Media LLC. The format of the station is Lite Rock/Lite AC music. WJBD-FM broadcasts to Salem, IL at 100.1 FM.
FM RADIO STATION

WJBE-AM 39038
Owner: Arm & Rage Broadcasting
Editorial: 2340 Martin Luther King Jr Ave, Knoxville, Tennessee 37915-1625 **Tel:** 1 865 247-6928.
Web site: http://www.wjbe.am
Profile: WJBE-AM is a commercial station owned by Arm & Rage Broadcasting. The format of the station is urban contemporary. WJBE-AM broadcasts to the Knoxville, TN area at 1040 AM.
AM RADIO STATION

WJBE-FM 730494
Owner: Big South Community Broadcasting
Editorial: 310 Highway 195 Ste 4, Jasper, Alabama 35503-6513 **Tel:** 1 205 221-2222.
Profile: WJBE-FM is a non-commercial station owned by Big South Community Broadcasting. The format of the station is classic country. WJBE-FM broadcasts to the Jasper, AL area at a frequency of 88.5 FM.
FM RADIO STATION

WJBI-AM 35408
Owner: Batesville Broadcasting Co.
Editorial: 1040 Highway 6 W, Batesville, Mississippi 38606 **Tel:** 1 662 563-4664.
Email: country101radio@yahoo.com
Profile: WJBI-AM is a commercial station owned by Batesville Broadcasting Co. The format of the station is oldies. WJBI-AM broadcasts in the Batesville, MS area at 1290 AM.
AM RADIO STATION

WJBL-FM 45334
Owner: Flambeau Broadcasting Co., Inc.
Tel: 1 715 532-5588.
Profile: WJBL-FM is a commercial station owned by Flambeau Broadcasting Co., Inc. The format of the station is oldies. WJBL-FM broadcasts to the Ladysmith, WI area at 93.1 FM.
FM RADIO STATION

WJBM-AM 35950
Owner: DJ Two Rivers Radio
Editorial: 1010 State Highway 16, Jerseyville, Illinois 62052 **Tel:** 1 618 498-8255.
Email: wjbm@wjbmradio.com
Web site: http://www.wjbmradio.com
Profile: WJBM-AM is a commercial station owned by DJ Two Rivers Radio. The format of the station is news and talk. WJBM-AM broadcasts to Jerseyville, IL at 1480 AM.
AM RADIO STATION

WJBO-AM 38367
Owner: iHeartMedia Inc.
Editorial: 5555 Hilton Ave Ste 500, Baton Rouge, Louisiana 70808-2564 **Tel:** 1 225 231-1860.
Web site: http://www.wjbo.com
Profile: WJBO-AM is a commercial station owned by iHeartMedia Inc. The format of the station is news, talk, and sports. WJBO-AM broadcasts to the Baton Rouge, LA area at 1150 AM.
AM RADIO STATION

WJBP-FM 41667
Owner: Family Life Broadcasting, Inc.
Editorial: 7355 N Oracle Rd, Tucson, Arizona 85704-6325 **Tel** 1 800 776-1070.
Web site: http://myflr.org
Profile: WJBP-FM is a non-commercial station owned by Family Life Broadcasting, Inc. The format of the station is contemporary Christian music programming. WJBP-FM broadcasts to the Tucson, AZ area at 91.5 FM.
FM RADIO STATION

WJBQ-FM 75028
Owner: Townsquare Media, LLC
Editorial: 1 City Ctr Stop 3, Portland, Maine 04101-4009 **Tel:** 1 207 774-6364.
Web site: http://www.wjbq.com
Profile: WJBQ-FM is a commercial station owned by Townsquare Media, LLC. The format of the station is Top 40/CHR. WJBQ-FM broadcasts to the Portland, ME area at 97.9 FM.
FM RADIO STATION

WJBR-FM 45713
Owner: Beasley Broadcast Group
Editorial: 812 Philadelphia Pike, STE C, Wilmington, Delaware 19809-2372 **Tel:** 1 302 765-1160.
Email: info@wjbr.com
Web site: http://www.wjbr.com
Profile: WJBR-FM is a commercial station owned by Beasley Broadcast Group. The format of the station is adult contemporary. WJBR broadcasts to the Wilmington, DE area at 99.5 FM.
FM RADIO STATION

WJBS-AM 35409
Owner: Govan(Harry)
Editorial: 760 Bunch Ford Rd, Holly Hill, South Carolina 29059 **Tel:** 1 803 496-5352.
Email: wjbsam@yahoo.com
Profile: WJBS-AM is a commercial station owned by Harry Govan. The format of the station is gospel. WJBS-AM broadcasts to the Holly Hill, SC area at 1000 AM.
AM RADIO STATION

WJBT-FM 83895
Owner: iHeartMedia Inc.
Editorial: 11700 Central Pkwy, Jacksonville, Florida 32224-2600 **Tel:** 1 904 636-0507.
Web site: http://www.wjbt.com
Profile: WJBT-FM is a commercial station owned by iHeartMedia Inc. The format of the station is urban contemporary music. WJBT-FM broadcasts to the Jacksonville, FL area at 93.3 FM.
FM RADIO STATION

WJBW-AM 36593
Owner: Azure Media, LLC
Tel: 1 772 567-0937.
Web site: http://www.radioazure.com
Profile: WJBW-AM is a commercial station owned by Azure Media, LLC. The format of the station is folk. WJBW-AM broadcasts to the Jupiter and surrounding areas at 1000 AM.
AM RADIO STATION

WJBX-AM 38711
Owner: Beasley Broadcast Group
Editorial: 20125 S Tamiami Trl, Estero, Florida 33928-2117 **Tel:** 1 239 495-2100.
Web site: http://770deportes.com
Profile: WJBX-AM is a commercial station owned by Beasley Broadcast Group. The format of the station is sports and talk. WJBX-AM broadcasts to the Estero, FL area at 770 AM.
AM RADIO STATION

WJBZ-FM 41760
Owner: CD Broadcast LLC
Editorial: 7101 Chapman Hwy, Knoxville, Tennessee 37920-6607 **Tel:** 1 865 577-4885.
Email: info@praise963.com
Web site: http://www.praise963.com
Profile: WJBZ-FM is a commercial station owned by CD Broadcast LLC. The format of the station is gospel. WJBZ-FM broadcasts to the Knoxville, TN area at 96.3 FM.
FM RADIO STATION

WJCF-FM 543439
Owner: Indiana Community Radio Corporation
Editorial: 15 Wood St, Greenfield, Indiana 46140-2162 **Tel:** 1 317 467-1064.
Email: wjcfradio@aol.com
Web site: http://www.wjcfradio.com
Profile: WJCF-FM is a non-commercial station owned by the Indiana Community Radio Corporation. The format of the station is Hot AC and Contemporary Christian music. WJCF-FM broadcasts to the Indianapolis area at a frequency of 88.1.
FM RADIO STATION

WJCH-FM 41338
Owner: Family Stations Inc.
Editorial: 13 Fairlane Dr, Joliet, Illinois 60435-6483 **Tel:** 1 815 725-1331.
Email: familyradio@familyradio.com
Web site: http://www.familyradio.com
Profile: WJCH-FM is a non-commercial station owned by Family Stations Inc. The format of the station is religious. WJCH-FM broadcasts to the Joliet, IL area at 91.9 FM.
FM RADIO STATION

WJCK-FM 42620
Owner: Immanuel Broadcasting Network
Editorial: 9423 Alabama Hwy 21 N, Piedmont, Alabama 36272 **Tel:** 1 800 387-0917.
Email: onair@ibn.org
Web site: http://www.ibn.org
Profile: WJCK-FM is a non-commercial station owned by Immanuel Broadcasting Network. The format of the station is contemporary Christian programming. WJCK-FM broadcasts to the Piedmont, AL area at 88.3 FM.
FM RADIO STATION

WJCL-FM 40393
Owner: Cumulus Media Inc.
Editorial: 214 Television Cir, Savannah, Georgia 31406-4519 **Tel:** 1 912 961-9000.
Web site: http://www.nashfm965.com
Profile: WJCL-FM is a commercial station owned by Cumulus Media Inc. The format of the station is contemporary country. WJCL-FM broadcasts to the Savannah, GA area at 96.5 FM.
FM RADIO STATION

WJCM-AM 36415
Owner: Cohan Radio Group Inc.
Editorial: 3750 US Highway 27 N Ste 1, Sebring, Florida 33870-1644 **Tel:** 1 863 382-9999.
Web site: http://espnhighlands.com
Profile: WJCM-AM is a commercial station owned by Cohan Radio Group Inc. The format of the station is Sports. WJCM-AM broadcasts in the Sebring, FL area at 1050 AM. After 4:00pm EDT the main station line becomes the studio line as well.
AM RADIO STATION

WJCO-FM 558679
Owner: Radio Netowkr
Editorial: 150 Lincolnway Ste 2001, Valparaiso, Indiana 46383-5556 **Tel:** 1 219 548-5800.
Email: info@calvaryradionet.com
Web site: http://www.calvaryradionetwork.com
Profile: WJCO-FM is a non-commercial station owned by Radio Network. The format of the station is Christian music and religious programming. WJCO-FM broadcasts to the Montpelier, IN area at 91.3 FM.
FM RADIO STATION

WJCP-AM 36470
Owner: Taylor (Tom)
Editorial: 2470 N State Highway 7, North Vernon, Indiana 47265-7184 **Tel:** 1 812 346-9527.
Email: wjcp927@yahoo.com
Web site: http://www.wjcpradio.com
Profile: WJCP-AM is a commercial station owned by Tom Taylor. The format of the station is classic hits. WJCP-AM broadcasts to the Indianapolis area at 1460 AM.
AM RADIO STATION

WJCR-FM 41952
Owner: Powell(Don Jr. & Lauree)
Editorial: 13101 Raider Hollow Rd, Upton, Kentucky 42784-9220 **Tel:** 1 270 369-8614.
Email: wjcrfm@yahoo.com
Web site: http://www.wjcr.org
Profile: WJCR-FM is a non-commercial station owned by Don Jr. & Laurie Powell. The format of the station is southern gospel music and religious programming. WJCR-FM broadcasts to the Upton, KY area at 90.1 FM.
FM RADIO STATION

WJCS-FM 44218
Owner: Beacon Broadcasting Corp.
Editorial: 300 E Rock Rd, Allentown, Pennsylvania 18103 **Tel:** 1 610 791-7262.
Email: wjcs@wjcs.org
Web site: http://www.wjcs.org
Profile: WJCS-FM is a non-commercial station owned by Beacon Broadcasting Corp. The format of the station is religious programming. WJCS-FM broadcasts to the Allentown, PA area at 89.3 FM.
FM RADIO STATION

WJCT-FM 40394
Owner: WJCT Inc.
Editorial: 100 Festival Park Ave, Jacksonville, Florida 32202-1309 **Tel:** 1 904 353-7770.
Email: news@wjct.org
Web site: http://www.wjct.org
Profile: WJCT-FM is non-commercial station owned by WJCT Inc. The format of the station is news and talk with easy listening. WJCT-FM broadcasts to the residents of Jacksonville, FL at 89.9 FM.
FM RADIO STATION

WJCV-AM 35823
Owner: Down East Broadcasting Co.
Editorial: 123A Arnold Road Ext, Jacksonville, North Carolina 28546-6541 **Tel:** 1 910 347-6141.
Web site: http://www.wjcv.com
Profile: WJCV-AM is a commercial station owned by Down East Broadcasting Co. The format of the station is religious programming and Southern gospel. WJCV-AM broadcasts to the Jacksonville, NC area at 1290 AM.
AM RADIO STATION

WJCW-AM 39388
Owner: Cumulus Media Inc.
Editorial: 162 Free Hill Rd, Gray, Tennessee 37615-3144 **Tel:** 1 423 477-1000.
Web site: http://www.wjcw.com
Profile: WJCW-AM is a commercial station owned by Cumulus Media Inc. The format of the station is news and talk. WJCW-AM broadcasts to the Gray, TN area at 910 AM.
AM RADIO STATION

WJCX-FM 42243
Owner: Calvary Radio Network, Inc.
Editorial: 150 Lincolnway Ste 2001, Valparaiso, Indiana 46383-5556 **Tel:** 1 219 548-5800.
Web site: http://www.calvaryradionetwork.com
Profile: WJCX-FM is a commercial station owned by Calvary Chapel of Costa Mesa, Inc. The format of the station is Christian music and religious programming. WJCX-FM broadcasts to the Pittsfield, ME area at 99.5 FM.
FM RADIO STATION

WJCY-FM 558690
Owner: Calvary Chapel of Costa Mesa, Inc.
Editorial: 150 Lincolnway, Ste 2001, Valparaiso, Indiana 46383-5556 **Tel:** 1 219 548-5800.
Email: info@calvaryradionet.com
Web site: http://www.calvaryradionetwork.com
Profile: WJCY-FM is a non-commercial station owned by Calvary Chapel of Costa Mesa, Inc. The format of the station is Christian music, religious

programming, and sports. WJCY-FM broadcasts to the Cicero, IN area at 91.5 FM.
FM RADIO STATION

WJCZ-FM 558543
Owner: Calvary Radio Network
Editorial: 150 Lincolnway Ste 2001, Valparaiso, Indiana 46383-5556 **Tel:** 1 219 548-5800.
Email: info@calvaryradionet.com
Web site: http://www.calvaryradionetwork.com
Profile: WJCZ-FM is a non-commerical station owned by Calvary Radio Network. The format of the station is Religious Teaching, religious programming and sports. WJCZ-FM broadcasts to the Milford, IL area at 91.3 FM.
FM RADIO STATION

WJDA-AM 35411
Owner: Principle Broadcasting
Editorial: 90 Everett Ave, Chelsea, Massachusetts 02150-2311 **Tel:** 1 617 884-4500.
Web site: http://www.wjda1300am.com
Profile: WJDA-AM is a commercial station owned by Principle Broadcasting. The format of the station is Hispanic gospel programming. WJDA-AM broadcasts to the Chelsea, MA area at 1300 AM.
AM RADIO STATION

WJDB-FM 45252
Owner: Griffin Broadcasting Corp.
Editorial: 30280 Highway 43, Thomasville, Alabama 36784-5740 **Tel:** 1 334 636-4438.
Email: wjdbradio@yahoo.com
Web site: http://www.wjdb955.com
FM RADIO STATION

WJDF-FM 44116
Owner: Deane Brothers Broadcasting Corp.
Editorial: 9 S Main St Ste 101, Orange, Massachusetts 01364-1226 **Tel:** 1 978 544-5335.
Profile: WJDF-AM is a local, commercial station owned by Deane Brothers Broadcasting Corp. The format of the station is Adult Contemporary. The station airs locally in the Orange, MA area on 97.3 FM.
FM RADIO STATION

WJDK-FM 43411
Owner: Nelson Multimedia
Editorial: 219 W Washington St, Morris, Illinois 60450-2146 **Tel:** 1 815 941-1000.
Email: wcsj-production@nelsonmultimedia.net
Web site: http://wjdkfm.com
Profile: WJDK-FM is a commercial station owned by Nelson Multimedia. The format of the station is hot adult contemporary. WJDK-FM broadcasts to the Morris, IL area at 95.7 FM.
FM RADIO STATION

WJDM-AM 36829
Owner: Multicultural Radio Broadcasting Inc.
Editorial: 449 Broadway Fl 2, New York, New York 10013-2549 **Tel:** 1 212 966-1059.
Web site: http://www.radiocanticonuevo.com/
Profile: WJDM-AM is a commercial station owned by Multicultural Radio Broadcasting Inc. The format is Spanish, talk, and contemporary Christian. WJDM-AM broadcasts to the New York City area at 1530 AM.
AM RADIO STATION

WJDQ-FM 42123
Owner: Mississippi Broadcasters, LLC
Editorial: 3436 Highway 45 N, Meridian, Mississippi 39301-1509 **Tel:** 1 601 693-2661.
Web site: http://www.q101radio.net
Profile: WJDQ-FM is a commercial station owned by Mississippi Broadcasters, LLC. The format of the station is Top 40/CHR. WJDQ-FM broadcasts to the Meridian, MS, area at 101.3 FM.
FM RADIO STATION

WJDR-FM 40395
Owner: Sunbelt Broadcasting Corporation
Editorial: 37 S High School Ave, Columbia, Mississippi 39429-8246 **Tel:** 1 601 731-2298.
Email: wcju@wcjufm.com
Web site: http://www.wcjufm.com/
Profile: WJDR-FM is a commercial station owned by Sunbelt Broadcasting Corporation. The format of the station is country. WJDR-FM broadcasts to the Prentiss, MS area at 98.3 FM.
FM RADIO STATION

WJDS-FM 72044
Owner: Good News Network
Editorial: 2278 Wortham Ln, Grovetown, Georgia 30813-5103 **Tel:** 1 706 309-9610.
Web site: http://www.gnnradio.org
Profile: WJDS-FM is a commercial station owned by Good News Network. The format of the station is Hispanic religious programming. WJDS-FM broadcasts to the Sparta, GA area at 88.7 FM.
FM RADIO STATION

WJDT-FM 41702
Owner: Cherokee Broadcasting Co.
Editorial: 448 Highway 25 E, Bean Station, Tennessee 37708-5603 **Tel:** 1 865 993-3639.
Email: wjdtradio@gmail.com
Web site: http://www.wjdtfm.com
Profile: WJDT-FM is a commercial station owned by Cherokee Broadcasting Co. The format of the station is country. WJDT-FM broadcasts to the Morristown, TN area at 106.5 FM.
FM RADIO STATION

United States of America

WJDX-AM 37933
Owner: iHeartMedia Inc.
Editorial: 1375 Beasley Rd, Jackson, Mississippi 39206-2018 **Tel:** 1 601 982-1062.
Web site: http://www.wjdx.com
Profile: WJDX-AM is a commercial station owned by iHeartMedia Inc. The format of the station is news/talk and sports. WJDX-AM broadcasts to the Jackson, MS area at 620 AM.
AM RADIO STATION

WJDX-FM 43999
Owner: iHeartMedia Inc.
Editorial: 1375 Beasley Rd, Jackson, Mississippi 39206-2018 **Tel:** 1 601 982-1062.
Web site: http://www.1051theriver.com/main.html
Profile: WJDX-FM is a commercial station owned by iHeartMedia Inc. The format of the station is variety. WJDX-FM broadcasts to the Jackson, MS area at 105.1 FM.
FM RADIO STATION

WJDY-AM 37088
Owner: iHeartMedia Inc.
Editorial: 351 Tilghman Rd, Gateway Crossing, Salisbury, Maryland 21804-1920 **Tel:** 1 410 742-1923.
Email: delmarvapsa@iheartmedia.com
Web site: http://newsradio1470.iheart.com
Profile: WJDY-AM is a commercial station owned by iHeartMedia Inc. The format of the station is news and talk. WJDY-AM broadcasts to the Salisbury, MD area at 1470 AM.
AM RADIO STATION

WJEC-FM 46099
Owner: Lamar County Broadcasting
Editorial: 47650 Hwy 17 N, Vernon, Alabama 35592 **Tel:** 1 205 695-9191.
Email: wjec1065@yahoo.com
Web site: http://www.wjec1065.com
Profile: WJEC-FM is a commercial station owned by Lamar County Broadcasting. The format of the station is gospel. WJEC-FM broadcasts locally to the Vernon, AL area at a frequency of 106.5FM.
FM RADIO STATION

WJED-FM 43959
Owner: Bethany Bible College
Editorial: 2573 Hodgesville Rd, Dothan, Alabama 36301 **Tel:** 1 850 547-9405.
Email: wjed911fm@bethanybc.edu
Web site: http://www.bethanybc.edu/radio
Profile: WJED-FM is a non-commercial station owned by Bethany Bible College. The format of the station is Southern gospel music. WJED-FM broadcasts to the Dothan, FL area at 91.1 FM.
FM RADIO STATION

WJEE-FM 788123
Owner: Hazen Ministries, Inc (Denny and Marge)
Editorial: 5716 Louisville St, Louisville, Ohio 44641-9483 **Tel:** 1 330 875-7181.
Email: dennymarge@aol.com
Web site: http://faithministryradio.com
Profile: WJEE-FM is a non-commercial station owned by Hazen Ministries, Inc (Denny and Marge). The format of the station is religion with a focus on Christian teaching. WJEE-FM broadcasts to the Bolivar, OH area at a frequency of 90.1 FM.
FM RADIO STATION

WJEH-AM 39158
Owner: Sunny Broadcasting LLC
Editorial: 117 Portsmouth Rd, Gallipolis, Ohio 45631-1047 **Tel:** 1 740 446-3543.
Web site: http://www.myjoy990.com/
Profile: WJEH-AM is a commercial station owned by Sunny Broadcasting LLC. The format of the station is southern gospel. WJEH-AM broadcasts to the Gallipolis, OH area at 990 AM.
AM RADIO STATION

WJEJ-AM 37934
Owner: Hagerstown Broadcasting Co. Inc.
Editorial: 1135 Haven Rd, Hagerstown, Maryland 21742 **Tel:** 1 301 739-2323.
Email: wjej@myactv.net
Web site: http://www.wjejradio.com
Profile: WJEJ-AM is a commercial station owned by Hagerstown Broadcasting Co. Inc. The format of the station is easy listening music. WJEJ-AM broadcasts to the Hagerstown, MD area at 1240 AM.
AM RADIO STATION

WJEK-FM 62676
Owner: S.J. Broadcasting Inc.
Editorial: 2702 Boulder Rd, Urbana, Illinois 61802-6996 **Tel:** 1 217 365-1195.
Web site: http://sunnycu.com
Profile: WJEK-FM is a commercial station owned by S.J. Broadcasting Inc. The format of the station is adult contemporary. WJEK-FM broadcasts to the Champaign, IL area at 95.3 FM.
FM RADIO STATION

WJEM-AM 35413
Owner: WJEM Inc.
Editorial: 118 N Patterson St, Valdosta, Georgia 31601-5570 **Tel:** 1 229 2599301.
Web site: http://www.thejock1150.com
Profile: WJEM-AM is a commercial station owned by WJEM Inc. The format of the station is sports. WJEM-AM broadcasts to the Valdosta, GA area at 1150 AM.
AM RADIO STATION

WJEN-FM 42514
Owner: Pamal Broadcasting Ltd.
Editorial: 67 Merchants Row, Rutland, Vermont 5701 **Tel:** 1 802 775-7500.
Email: catcountry@catamountradio.com
Web site: http://www.catcountryvermont.com
Profile: WJEN-FM is a commercial station owned by Pamal Broadcasting Ltd. The format of the station is contemporary country. WJEN-FM broadcasts to the Rutland, VT area at 105.3 FM.
FM RADIO STATION

WJEQ-FM 40396
Owner: Prestige Communications
Editorial: 31 E Side Sq, Macomb, Illinois 61455 **Tel:** 1 309 833-2121.
Email: radio@prestigeradio.com
Web site: http://www.prestigeradio.com
Profile: WJEQ-FM is a commercial station owned by Prestige Communications. The format of the station is classic rock. WJEQ-FM broadcasts to the Macomb, IL area at 102.7 FM.
FM RADIO STATION

WJER-AM 37935
Owner: Gary Petricola
Editorial: 646 Boulevard St, Dover, Ohio 44622-2027 **Tel:** 1 330 343-7755.
Email: wjer@wjer.com
Web site: http://www.wjer.com
Profile: WJER-AM is a commercial station owned by Gary Petricola. The format of the station is adult contemporary. WJER-AM broadcasts to the Dover, OH area at 1450 AM.
AM RADIO STATION

WJET-AM 35482
Owner: Connoisseur Media LLC
Editorial: 1 Boston Store Pl, Erie, Pennsylvania 16501-2313 **Tel:** 1 814 461-1000.
Web site: http://www.jetradio1400.com
Profile: WJET-AM is a commercial station owned by Connoisseur Media LLC. The format of the station is news and talk. WJET-AM broadcasts to the Erie, PA area at 1400 AM.
AM RADIO STATION

WJEZ-FM 43350
Owner: Cumulus Media Inc.
Editorial: 315 N Mill St, Pontiac, Illinois 61764-1823 **Tel:** 1 815 844-6101.
Email: news@wjez.com
Web site: http://www.wjez.com
Profile: WJEZ-FM is a commercial station owned by Cumulus Media Inc.. The format of the station is classic hits music. WJEZ-FM broadcasts to the Pontiac, IL area at 98.9 FM.
FM RADIO STATION

WJFC-AM 37154
Owner: Lakeway Broadcasting LLC
Editorial: 1181 N Highway 92, Jefferson City, Tennessee 37760 **Tel:** 1 865 475-3825.
Email: wjfc@radiowjfc.com
Web site: http://wjfcradio.com
Profile: WJFC-AM is a commercial station owned by Lakeway Broadcasting LLC. The format of the station is classic country, gospel and bluegrass. WJFC-AM broadcasts to the Knoxville, TN area at 1480 AM.
AM RADIO STATION

WJFD-FM 40398
Owner: Henry Arruda
Editorial: 651 Orchard St #300, New Bedford, Massachusetts 02744-1008 **Tel:** 1 508 997-2929.
Web site: http://www.wjfd.com
Profile: WJFD-FM is a commercial station owned by Henry Arruda. The format of the station is Portuguese-language Top 40/CHR music. WJFD-FM broadcasts to the New Bedford, MA area at 97.3 FM.
FM RADIO STATION

WJFF-FM 41343
Owner: Radio Catskill
Editorial: 4765 State Route 52, Jeffersonville, New York 12748-6502 **Tel:** 1 845 482-4141.
Web site: http://www.wjffradio.org
Profile: WJFF-FM is a non-commercial station owned by Radio Catskill. The format of the station is a variety. WJFF-FM broadcasts to the Catskill, NY area at 90.5 FM.
FM RADIO STATION

WJFK-AM 38122
Owner: CBS Radio
Editorial: 1015 Half St SE Ste 200, Washington, District Of Columbia 20003-3320 **Tel:** 1 202 479-9227.
Web site: http://washington.cbslocal.com/station/cbs-sports-radio-1580-am/
Profile: WJFK-AM is a commercial station owned by CBS Radio. The format of the station is sports. WJFK-AM broadcasts to the Washington, D.C. area at 1580 AM.
AM RADIO STATION

WJFK-FM 46418
Owner: CBS Radio
Editorial: 1015 Half Street SE, Suite 200, Washington, District Of Columbia 20003-3320
Web site: http://washington.cbslocal.com/station/106-7-the-fan
Profile: WJFK-FM is a commercial station owned by CBS Radio. The format of the station is sports. WJFK-FM broadcasts to the Washington, D.C. area at 106.7 FM.
FM RADIO STATION

WJFL-FM 42203
Owner: Middle Georgia Broadcasting
Editorial: 5440 Tennille Oconee Rd, Tennille, Georgia 31089 **Tel:** 1 478 553-1019.
Email: wjfl@wjfl.com
Web site: http://www.wjfl.com
Profile: WJFL-FM is a commercial station owned by Middle Georgia Broadcasting. The format of the station is adult contemporary music. WJFL-FM broadcasts to the Tennille, GA area at 101.9 FM.
FM RADIO STATION

WJFM-FM 43049
Owner: Family Worship Center Church, Inc.
Editorial: 8919 World Ministries Ave, Baton Rouge, Louisiana 70810-9006 **Tel:** 1 225 768-3288.
Email: info@jsm.org
Web site: http://www.jsm.org
Profile: WJFM-FM is a non-commercial station owned by Family Worship Center Church, Inc. The format of the station is religious music and programming. WJFM-FM broadcasts to the Baton Rouge, LA area at 88.5 FM.
FM RADIO STATION

WJFP-FM 43439
Owner: Black Media Works Inc.
Editorial: 2284 N US Highway 1, Fort Pierce, Florida 34946-8914 **Tel:** 1 321 632-1000.
Email: info@wjfp.com
Web site: http://www.wjfp.com
Profile: WJFP-FM is a non-commercial station owned by Black Media Works Inc. The format is gospel and urban contemporary music. The station airs in the Fort Pierce, FL area at 91.1 FM.
FM RADIO STATION

WJFR-FM 41340
Owner: Family Stations Inc.
Editorial: 290 Hegenberger Rd, Oakland, California 94621-1436 **Tel:** 1 510 568-6200.
Email: info@familyradio.org
Web site: http://www.familyradio.com
Profile: WJFR-FM is a non-commercial station owned by Family Stations Inc. The format of the station is Christian teaching. WJFR-FM broadcasts to the Jacksonville, FL area at a frequency of 88.7 FM.
FM RADIO STATION

WJFX-FM 41034
Owner: Adams Radio Group
Editorial: 9604 Coldwater Rd Ste 201, Fort Wayne, Indiana 46825-2096 **Tel:** 1 260 482-9288.
Web site: http://www.hot1079online.com
Profile: WJFX-FM is a commercial station owned by Adams Radio Group. The format of the station is rhythmic Top 40/CHR music. WJFX-FM broadcasts to the Fort Wayne, IN area at 107.9 FM.
FM RADIO STATION

WJGA-FM 40400
Owner: Earnhart Broadcast Co. Inc.
Editorial: 940 Brownlee Rd, Jackson, Georgia 30233-2418 **Tel:** 1 770 775-3151.
Profile: WJGA-FM is a commercial music station owned by Earnhart Broadcast Co. Inc. The format of the station is adult contemporary music. WJGA-FM broadcasts to the Atlanta area at 92.1 FM.
FM RADIO STATION

WJGK-FM 45185
Owner: Sunrise Broadcasting
Editorial: 661 Little Britain Rd, New Windsor, New York 12553-6150 **Tel:** 1 845 561-2131.
Web site: http://www.foxradio.net/index.php/on-air/fox-103-1-wjgk
Profile: WJGK-FM is a commercial station owned by Sunrise Broadcasting. The format of the station is adult contemporary. WJGK-FM broadcasts to the New York area at 103.1 FM.
FM RADIO STATION

WJGL-FM 46440
Owner: Cox Media Group, Inc.
Editorial: 8000 Belfort Pkwy, Ste 100, Jacksonville, Florida 32256 **Tel:** 1 904 245-8500.
Web site: http://www.969theeagle.com
Profile: WJGL-FM is a commercial station owned by Cox Media Group, Inc. The format of the station is classic hits. WJGL-FM broadcasts to the Jacksonville, FL area at 96.9 FM.
FM RADIO STATION

WJGM-FM 86813
Owner: West Jacksonville Baptist Church, Inc.
Editorial: 5634 Normandy Blvd, Jacksonville, Florida 32205-6249 **Tel:** 1 904 781-4321.
Web site: http://www.westjaxbaptist.org
Profile: WJGM-FM is a commercial station owned by West Jacksonville Baptist Church, Inc. The format of the station is southern gospel music. WJGM-FM broadcasts to the Jacksonville, FL area at 105.7 FM.
FM RADIO STATION

WJGO-FM 44488
Owner: Renda Broadcasting
Editorial: 10915 K Nine Dr, 2nd Fl, Bonita Springs, Florida 34135-6802 **Tel:** 1 239 495-8383.
Web site: http://www.1029bobfm.com
Profile: WJGO-FM is a commercial station owned by Renda Broadcasting. The format of the station is adult hits. WJGO-FM broadcasts to the Fort Myers, FL area at 102.9 FM.
FM RADIO STATION

WJHO-FM 836271
Owner: Alabama Christian Radio Inc.
Editorial: 908 Opelika Rd, Auburn, Alabama 36830-4024 **Tel:** 1 334 705-8004.
Web site: http://wjhofm.com
Profile: WJHO-FM is a non-commercial station owned by Alabama Christian Radio Inc. The format of the station is Contemporary Christian music. WJHO-FM broadcasts to the Alexander City, AL area at a frequency of 89.7 FM.
FM RADIO STATION

WJHT-FM 40317
Owner: FM Radio Licenses, LLC
Editorial: 109 Plaza Dr Ste 2, Johnstown, Pennsylvania 15905-1212 **Tel:** 1 814 255-4186.
Web site: http://www.hot92hits.com/
Profile: WJHT-FM is a commercial station owned by FM Radio Licenses, LLC. The format of the station is Top 40/CHR. WJHT-FM broadcasts to the Johnstown, PA area at 92.1 FM.
FM RADIO STATION

WJHX-AM 608396
Owner: Bar Broadcasting
Editorial: 100 Yeager Pkwy, Pelham, Alabama 35124-1859 **Tel:** 1 205 358-1100.
Profile: WJHX-AM is commercial station owned by Bar Broadcasting. The format of the station is regional Mexican and tropical music. The station airs locally on 620 AM. Newscasts air at the top of the hour.
AM RADIO STATION

WJIB-AM 36312
Owner: Bob Bittner Broadcasting, Inc.
Editorial: 443 Concord Ave, Cambridge, Massachusetts 2138 **Tel:** 1 617 868-7400.
Profile: WJIB-AM is a commercial station owned by Bob Bittner Broadcasting, Inc. The format of the station is adult standards. WJIB-AM broadcasts to the Cambridge, MA area at 740 AM.
AM RADIO STATION

WJIL-AM 37937
Owner: Morgan County Broadcasting Co., Inc.
Editorial: 1251 E Morton Ave, Jacksonville, Illinois 62650-3195 **Tel:** 1 217 245-5119.
Web site: http://www.wjvofm.com/wjilam-talk-1550
Profile: WJIL-AM is a commercial station owned by Morgan County Broadcasting Co., Inc. The format of the station is News/Talk. WJIL-AM broadcasts in the Jacksonville, IL area at 1550 AM.
AM RADIO STATION

WJIM-AM 37938
Owner: Townsquare Media, LLC
Editorial: 3420 Pinetree Rd, Lansing, Michigan 48911-4207 **Tel:** 1 517 394-7272.
Web site: http://www.wjimam.com
Profile: WJIM-AM is a commercial station owned by Townsquare Media, LLC. The format of the station is news and talk. WJIM-AM broadcasts to the Lansing, MI area at 1240 AM.
AM RADIO STATION

WJIM-FM 45256
Owner: Townsquare Media, LLC
Editorial: 3420 Pinetree Rd, Lansing, Michigan 48911-4207 **Tel:** 1 517 394-7272.
Web site: http://975now.com
Profile: WJIM-FM is a commercial station owned by Townsquare Media, LLC. The format of the station is Top 40/CHR. WJIM-FM broadcasts to the Lansing, MI area at 97.5 FM.
FM RADIO STATION

WJIP-AM 37787
Owner: iHeartMedia Inc.
Editorial: 20 Tucker Dr, Poughkeepsie, New York 12603-1644 **Tel:** 1 845 471-2300.
Web site: http://www.247comedy.com
Profile: WJIP-AM is a commercial station owned by iHeartMedia Inc. The format of the station is comedy. WJIP-AM broadcasts to the Ulster County area in New York locally at 1370 AM.
AM RADIO STATION

WJIR-FM 41380
Owner: Glad Tidings Tabernacle Church
Editorial: 1209 United St, Key West, Florida 33040-3409 **Tel:** 1 305 296-4306.
Profile: WJIR-FM is a non-commercial station owned by Glad Tidings Tabernacle Church. The format of the station is Christian music and programming. WJIR-FM broadcasts to the Key West, FL area at 90.9 FM.
FM RADIO STATION

WJIS-FM 41485
Owner: Radio Training Network, Inc.
Editorial: 6469 Parkland Dr, Sarasota, Florida 34243-4091 **Tel:** 1 941 753-0401.
Email: thejoyfm@thejoyfm.com
Web site: http://florida.thejoyfm.com
Profile: WJIS-FM is a non-commercial station owned by Radio Training Network, Inc. The format of the station is contemporary Christian music. WJIS-FM broadcasts to the Tampa, FL area at 88.1 FM.
FM RADIO STATION

WJIV-FM 40404
Owner: Christian Broadcasting System
Editorial: 1668 County Highway 50, Cherry Valley, New York 13320 **Tel:** 1 607 264-3062.
Email: wjiv@hughes.net
Web site: http://www.wjivradio.com

Profile: WJIV-FM is a commercial station owned by Christian Broadcasting System. The format of the station is Christian programming. WJIV-FM broadcasts to the Utica, NY area at 101.9 FM.
FM RADIO STATION

WJIZ-FM 46588
Owner: iHeartMedia Inc.
Editorial: 809 S Westover Blvd, Albany, Georgia 31707-4953 **Tel:** 1 229 439-9704.
Web site: http://www.wjiz.com
Profile: WJIZ-FM is a commercial station owned by iHeartMedia Inc. The format of the station is urban contemporary. WJIZ-FM broadcasts to the Albany, NY area at 96.3 FM.
FM RADIO STATION

WJJB-FM 45912
Owner: Atlantic Coast Radio LLC
Editorial: 779 Warren Ave, Portland, Maine 4103
Tel: 1 207 773-9695.
Web site: http://www.thebigjab.com
Profile: WJJB-FM is a commercial station owned by Atlantic Coast Radio LLC. The format of the station is sports. WJJB-FM broadcasts to the Portland, ME area at 96.3 FM.
FM RADIO STATION

WJJC-AM 35416
Owner: Side Communications Inc.
Editorial: 1801 N Elm St, Commerce, Georgia 30529
Tel: 1 706 335-3155.
Email: wjjc@windstream.net
Web site: http://www.wjjc.net
Profile: WJJC-AM is a commercial station owned by Side Communications Inc. The format of the station is talk. WJJC-AM broadcasts to the Commerce, GA area at 1270 AM.
AM RADIO STATION

WJJF-FM 794869
Owner: Full Power Radio
Editorial: 758 Colonel Ledyard Hwy, Ledyard, Connecticut 06339-1541 **Tel:** 1 860 464-9490.
Web site: http://www.949newsnow.com
Profile: WJJF-FM is a commercial station owned by Full Power Radio. The format of the station is news/talk. WJJF-FM broadcasts to the Connecticut and Eastern Long Island, NY areas at a frequency of 94.9 FM.
FM RADIO STATION

WJJH-FM 45257
Owner: Heartland Communications Group, LLC
Editorial: 2320 Ellis Ave, Ashland, Wisconsin 54806-3995 **Tel:** 1 715 682-2727.
Web site: http://www.wjjhfm.com
Profile: WJJH-FM is a commercial station owned by Heartland Communications Group, LLC. The format of the station is classic rock. WJJH-FM broadcasts to the Ashland, WI area at 96.7 FM.
FM RADIO STATION

WJJK-FM 42063
Owner: Cumulus Media Inc.
Editorial: 6810 N Shadeland Ave, Indianapolis, Indiana 46220-4236 **Tel:** 1 317 842-9550.
Email: info@1045wjjk.com
Web site: http://www.1045wjjk.com
Profile: WJJK-FM is a commercial station owned by Cumulus Media Inc. The format of the station is classic hits. WJJK-FM broadcasts to the Indianapolis area at 104.5 FM.
FM RADIO STATION

WJJL-AM 35417
Owner: Phillips Corp.(M. John)
Editorial: 976 Union Rd #B, West Seneca, New York 14224-3438 **Tel:** 1 716 674-9555.
Email: radio1440@roadrunner.com
AM RADIO STATION

WJJM-AM 37940
Owner: Haislip(Michelle W.)
Editorial: 344 E Church St, Lewisburg, Tennessee 37091-2837 **Tel:** 1 931 359-4511.
Email: wjjm@wjjm.com
Web site: http://www.wjjm.com
Profile: WJJM-AM is a commercial station owned by Michelle W. Haislip. The format of the station is sports and talk. WJJM-AM broadcasts to the Lewisburg, TN area at 1490 AM.
AM RADIO STATION

WJJM-FM 45258
Owner: Haislip(Michelle W.)
Editorial: 344 E Church St, Lewisburg, Tennessee 37091-2837 **Tel:** 1 931 359-4511.
Email: wjjm@wjjm.com
Web site: http://www.wjjm.com
Profile: WJJM-FM is a commercial station owned by Michelle W. Haislip. The format of the station is classic and contemporary country music. WJJM-FM broadcasts to the Lewisburg, TN area at 94.3 FM.
FM RADIO STATION

WJJN-FM 46357
Owner: Wilson Broadcasting, Inc.
Editorial: 4106 Ross Clark Cir, Dothan, Alabama 36303-5741 **Tel:** 1 334 671-1753.
Web site: http://www.wjjn.net
Profile: WJJN-FM is a commercial station owned by Wilson Broadcasting, Inc. The format of the station is urban contemporary music. WJJN-FM broadcasts to the Dothan, AL area at 92.1 FM.
FM RADIO STATION

WJJO-FM 40991
Owner: Midwest Family Stations
Editorial: 730 Rayovac Dr, Madison, Wisconsin 53711-2472 **Tel:** 1 608 273-1000.
Web site: http://www.wjjo.com
Profile: WJJO-FM is a commercial station owned by Midwest Family Stations. The format of the station is rock. WJJO-FM broadcasts to the Madison, WI area at 94.1 FM.
FM RADIO STATION

WJJQ-AM 37941
Owner: Albert Broadcasting Inc.
Editorial: 81 E Mohawk Dr, Tomahawk, Wisconsin 54487 **Tel:** 1 715 453-4482.
Email: wjjq@wjjq.com
Web site: http://www.wjjq.com
Profile: WJJQ-AM is a commercial station owned by Albert Broadcasting Inc. The format of the station is sports talk. WJJQ-AM broadcasts in the Tomahawk, WI area at 810 AM.
AM RADIO STATION

WJJQ-FM 45259
Owner: Albert Broadcasting Inc.
Editorial: 81 E Mohawk Dr, Tomahawk, Wisconsin 54487 **Tel:** 1 715 453-4482.
Email: wjjq@wjjq.com
Web site: http://www.wjjq.com
Profile: WJJQ-FM is a commercial station owned by Albert Broadcasting Inc. The format of the station is oldies, Lite Rock/Lite AC music, news, and talk. WJJQ-FM broadcasts to the Tomahawk, WI area at 92.5 FM.
FM RADIO STATION

WJJR-FM 41383
Owner: Pamal Broadcasting Ltd.
Editorial: 67 Merchants Row, Rutland, Vermont 05701-5910 **Tel:** 1 802 775-7500.
Email: wjjr@catamountradio.com
Web site: http://www.wjjr.net
Profile: WJJR-FM is a commercial station owned by Pamal Broadcasting Ltd. The format of the station is adult contemporary music. WJJR-FM broadcasts to the Rutland, VT area at 98.1 FM.
FM RADIO STATION

WJJS-FM 43991
Owner: iHeartMedia Inc.
Editorial: 3807 Brandon Ave SW Ste 2350, Roanoke, Virginia 24018-1477 **Tel:** 1 540 725-1220.
Web site: http://www.wjjs.com
Profile: WJJS-FM is a commercial station owned by iHeartMedia Inc. The format of the station is Top 40/ CHR music. WJJS-FM broadcasts to the Roanoke, VA area at 104.9 FM.
FM RADIO STATION

WJJX-FM 45721
Owner: iHeartMedia Inc.
Editorial: 3807 Brandon Ave SW Ste 2350, Roanoke, Virginia 24018-1477 **Tel:** 1 540 725-1220.
Web site: http://www.wjjs.com
Profile: WJJX-FM is a commercial station owned by iHeartMedia Inc. The format of the station is Top 40/ CHR music. WJJX-FM broadcasts to the Roanoke, VA area at 102.7 FM.
FM RADIO STATION

WJJY-FM 42301
Owner: Hubbard Broadcasting Inc.
Editorial: 13225 Dogwood Dr, Baxter, Minnesota 56425-8669 **Tel:** 1 218 828-1244.
Email: wjjy@hubbardradio.com
Web site: http://www.1067wjjy.com
Profile: WJJY-FM is a commercial station owned by Hubbard Broadcasting Inc. The format of the station is adult contemporary music. WJJY-FM broadcasts in the St. Paul, MN area at 106.7 FM.
FM RADIO STATION

WJJZ-FM 945189
Owner: Vermont Broadcast Associates Inc.
Editorial: 1303 Concord Ave, Saint Johnsbury, Vermont 5819 **Tel:** 1 802 748-2362.
Profile: WJJZ-FM is a commercial station owned by Vermont Broadcast Associates Inc. The format of the station is contemporary country. The station broadcasts to the Newport, VT area at 94.5 FM.
FM RADIO STATION

WJKB-AM 35514
Owner: Kirkman Broadcasting
Editorial: 60 Markfield Dr Ste 4, Charleston, South Carolina 29407-7907 **Tel:** 1 843 763-6631.
Email: 950@kirkmanbroadcasting.com
Web site: http://www.charlestonsportsradio.com
Profile: WJKB-AM is a commercial station owned by Kirkman Broadcasting. The format of the station is talk. WJKB-AM broadcasts to the Charleston, SC, area at 950 AM.
AM RADIO STATION

WJKD-FM 43169
Owner: Treasure & Space Coast Radio
Editorial: 1235 16th St, Vero Beach, Florida 32960-3620 **Tel:** 1 772 567-0937.
Email: jack@997jackfm.com
Web site: http://www.997jackfm.com
Profile: WJKD-FM is a commercial station owned by Treasure & Space Coast Radio. The format of the station adult hits. WJKD-FM broadcasts to the West Palm Beach, FL area at 99.7 FM.
FM RADIO STATION

WJKE-FM 41357
Owner: Empire Broadcasting Corporation
Editorial: 100 Saratoga Village Blvd Ste 21, Malta, New York 12020-3703 **Tel:** 1 518 899-3000.
Email: 1013thejockey@empirebroadcasting.net
Web site: http://www.1013thejockey.com
Profile: WJKE-FM is a commercial station owned by Empire Broadcasting Corporation. The format of the station is adult contemporary. WJKE-FM broadcasts to the Albany, NY area at 101.3 FM.
FM RADIO STATION

WJKI-FM 43148
Owner: The Voice Radio Network
Editorial: 20200 Dupont Blvd, Georgetown, Delaware 19947-3105 **Tel:** 1 302 856-2567.
Web site: http://thevaultrocks.com
Profile: WJKI-FM is a commercial station owned by The Voice Radio Network. The format of the station is classic rock music. WJKI-FM broadcasts to the Salisbury, MD area at 103.5 FM.
FM RADIO STATION

WJKK-FM 46746
Owner: New South Communications Inc.
Editorial: 265 Highpoint Dr, Ridgeland, Mississippi 39157-6018 **Tel:** 1 601 956-0102.
Web site: http://www.mix987.com
Profile: WJKK-FM is a commercial station owned by New South Communications Inc. The format of the station is adult contemporary music. WJKK-FM broadcasts to the Ridgeland, MS area at 98.7 FM.
FM RADIO STATION

WJKN-AM 35822
Owner: Good Shepherd Radio
Editorial: 704 N East Ave, Jackson, Michigan 49202-3423 **Tel:** 1 517 513-3340.
Email: info@goodshepherdcatholicradio.net
Web site: http://www.goodshepherdcatholicradio.net
Profile: WJKN-AM is a non-commercial station owned by Jackson Lansing Catholic Radio (dba Good Shepherd Catholic Radio). The format of the station is Catholic teaching. The station broadcasts locally at a frequency of 1510 AM.
AM RADIO STATION

WJKW-FM 44123
Owner: Christian Faith Broadcast, Inc.
Editorial: 3809 Maple Ave, Castalia, Ohio 44824-9484
Tel: 1 419 684-5311.
Email: wjkw@cfbroadcast.net
Web site: http://www.wjkw.net
Profile: WJKW-FM is a commercial station owned by Christian Faith Broadcast, Inc. The format of the station is contemporary Christian music. WJKW-FM broadcasts to the Castalia, OH area at 97.7 FM.
FM RADIO STATION

WJKX-FM 349806
Owner: iHeartMedia Inc.
Editorial: 6555 U S Highway 98 Ste 8, Hattiesburg, Mississippi 39402-8699 **Tel:** 1 601 296-9800.
Email: contact@102jkx.com
Web site: http://www.102jkx.com
Profile: WJKX-FM is a commercial station owned by iHeartMedia Inc. The format of the station is urban adult contemporary. WJKX-FM broadcasts to the Hattiesburg, MS, area at 102.5 FM.
FM RADIO STATION

WJKY-AM 35957
Owner: Lake Cumberland Broadcasters
Editorial: 2804 S Highway 127, Russell Springs, Kentucky 42642 **Tel:** 1 270 866-3487.
Email: wjrs1049@duo-county.com
Web site: http://www.lakercountry.com
Profile: WJKY-AM is a commercial station owned by Lake Cumberland Broadcasters. The format of the station is sports. WJKY-AM broadcasts to the Russell Springs, KY area at 1060 AM.
AM RADIO STATION

WJLB-FM 40405
Owner: iHeartMedia Inc.
Editorial: 27675 Halsted Rd, Farmington Hills, Michigan 48331-3511 **Tel:** 1 248 324-5800.
Email: wjlb@fm98wjlb.com
Web site: http://www.fm98wjlb.com
Profile: WJLB-FM is a commercial station owned by iHeartMedia Inc. The format of the station is urban contemporary. WJLB-FM broadcasts to the Detroit area at 97.9 FM.
FM RADIO STATION

WJLD-AM 35420
Owner: Richardson Broadcasting Company
Editorial: 1449 Spaulding Ishkooda Rd, Birmingham, Alabama 35211-5059 **Tel:** 1 205 942-1776.
Email: richardsonbroadcasting@gmail.com
Web site: http://wjldradio.com
Profile: WJLD-AM is a commercial station owned by Richardson Broadcasting Company. The format of the station is talk, blues, R&B music and religious programming. WJLD-AM broadcasts to the Birmingham, AL area at 1400 AM.
AM RADIO STATION

WJLE-AM 37942
Owner: Stribling (Leon)
Editorial: 2606 McMinnville Hwy, Smithville, Tennessee 37166-5071 **Tel:** 1 615 597-4265.
Email: wjle@dtccom.net
Web site: http://www.wjle.com
Profile: WJLE-AM is a commercial station owned by Leon Stribling. The format of the station is country and gospel music. WJLE-AM broadcasts to Smithville, TN area at 1480 AM.
AM RADIO STATION

WJLE-FM 45261
Owner: Stribling(Leon)
Editorial: 2606 McMinnville Hwy, Smithville, Tennessee 37166-5071 **Tel:** 1 615 597-4265.
Email: wjle@dtccom.net
Web site: http://www.wjle.com
Profile: WJLE-FM is a commercial station owned by Leon Stribling. The format of the station is country and gospel music. WJLE-FM broadcasts to the Smithville, TN area at 101.7 FM.
FM RADIO STATION

WJLF-FM 42618
Owner: Radio Training Network, Inc.
Editorial: 2131 Nw 40Th Ter Ste E, Gainesville, Florida 32605-5800 **Tel:** 1 352 373-9553.
Email: thejoyfm@thejoyfm.com
Web site: http://www.thejoyfm.com
Profile: WJLF-FM is a non-commercial station owned by Radio Training Network, Inc. The format of the station is contemporary Christian music. WJLF-FM broadcasts to the Gainesville, FL area at 91.7 FM.
FM RADIO STATION

WJLG-AM 37781
Owner: Cumulus Media Inc.
Editorial: 214 Television Cir, Savannah, Georgia 31406-4519 **Tel:** 1 912 961-9000.
Web site: http://www.900theticket.com
Profile: WJLG-AM is a commercial station owned by Cumulus Media Inc. The format of the station is sports. WJLG-AM broadcasts to the Savannah, GA area at 900 AM.
AM RADIO STATION

WJLH-FM 43132
Owner: Cornerstone Broadcasting Corp.
Editorial: 4295 S Ridgewood Ave, Port Orange, Florida 32127-4512 **Tel:** 1 386 756-9000.
Email: wjlu@wjlu.org
Web site: http://www.wjlu.org
Profile: WJLH-FM is a non-commercial station owned by Cornerstone Broadcasting Corp. The format of the station is Christian educational talk, news and music. WJLH-FM broadcasts to the Port Orange, FL area at 90.3 FM.
FM RADIO STATION

WJLI-FM 46595
Owner: Stratemeyer Media
Editorial: 6120 Waldo Church Rd, Metropolis, Illinois 62960-4903 **Tel:** 1 270 444-0098.
Web site: http://www.radiojelli.com
Profile: WJLI-FM is a commercial station owned by Stratemeyer Media. The format of the station is classic rock. WJLI-FM broadcasts to the Metropolis, IL area at 98.3 FM.
FM RADIO STATION

WJLK-FM 45262
Owner: Townsquare Media, LLC
Editorial: 8 Robbins St Ste 201, Toms River, New Jersey 08753-7668 **Tel:** 1 848 221-8000.
Web site: http://www.943thepoint.com
Profile: WJLK-FM is a commercial station owned by Townsquare Media, LLC. The format of the station is hot adult contemporary music. WJLK-FM broadcasts to the Ocean, NJ area at 94.3 FM.
FM RADIO STATION

WJLS-AM 37944
Owner: West Virginia Radio Corp.
Editorial: 102 N Kanawha St, Beckley, West Virginia 25801-4715 **Tel:** 1 304 253-7311.
Profile: WJLS-AM is a commercial station owned by West Virginia Radio Corp. The format of the station is Southern gospel music. WJLS-AM broadcasts to the Beckley, WV area at 560 AM.
AM RADIO STATION

WJLS-FM 45055
Owner: West Virginia Radio Corp.
Editorial: 102 N Kanawha St, Beckley, West Virginia 25801-4715 **Tel:** 1 304 253-7311.
Web site: http://www.wjls.com
Profile: WJLS-FM is a commercial station owned by West Virginia Radio Corp. The format of the station is country music, featuring contemporary and classic hits. WJLS-FM broadcasts to the Beckley, WV area at 99.5 FM.
FM RADIO STATION

WJLT-FM 43304
Owner: Townsquare Media, LLC
Editorial: 117 SE 5th St, Evansville, Indiana 47708-1639 **Tel:** 1 812 425-4226.
Web site: http://espnevansville.com/
Profile: WJLT-FM is a commercial station owned by Townsquare Media, LLC. The format of the station is sports. WJLT-FM broadcasts to the Evansville, IN area at 105.3 FM.
FM RADIO STATION

WJLU-FM 46087
Owner: Cornerstone Broadcasting Corp.
Editorial: 4295 S Ridgewood Ave, Port Orange, Florida 32127-4512 **Tel:** 1 386 756-9000.
Email: wjlu@wjlu.org
Web site: http://www.wjlu.org
Profile: WJLU-FM is a non-commercial station owned by Cornerstone Broadcasting Corp. The format of the station is Christian educational talk,

news, and music. WJLU-FM broadcasts to the Port Orange, FL area at 89.7 FM.
FM RADIO STATION

WJLX-AM 606002
Owner: Wal Win, LLC
Editorial: 310 Highway 195, Jasper, Alabama 35503-6512 **Tel:** 1 205 221-2222.
Web site: http://oldies1015fm.com
Profile: WJLX-AM is a commercial station owned by Wal Win, LLC. The format of the station is oldies music. WJLX-AM broadcasts to the Jasper, AL area at a frequency of 1240 AM.
AM RADIO STATION

WJLY-FM 44205
Owner: Countryside Broadcasting
Editorial: RR 2 Box 51A, Ramsey, Illinois 62080-9345 **Tel:** 1 618 423-2082.
Email: wjly@frontiernet.net
Web site: http://www.wjly.org
Profile: WJLY-FM is a non-commercial station owned by Countryside Broadcasting. The format of the station is religious programming. WJLY-FM broadcasts to the St. Louis area at 88.3 FM.
FM RADIO STATION

WJMA-FM 46255
Owner: Piedmont Communications Inc.
Editorial: 207 Spicers Mill Rd, Orange, Virginia 22960-1025 **Tel:** 1 540 672-1000.
Email: advertising@wjmafm.com
Web site: http://www.wjmafm.com
Profile: WJMA-FM is a commercial station owned by Piedmont Communications Inc. The format of the station is country music. WJMA-FM broadcasts to the Orange, VA area at 103.1 FM.
FM RADIO STATION

WJMC-AM 37945
Owner: TKC Inc.
Editorial: 1859 21st Ave, Rice Lake, Wisconsin 54868-9502 **Tel:** 1 715 234-2131.
Email: info@wjmcradio.com
Web site: http://www.wjmcradio.com
Profile: WJMC-AM is a commercial station owned by TKC Inc. The format of the station is news, talk and adult standards music. WJMC-AM broadcasts to the Minneapolis area at 1240 AM.
AM RADIO STATION

WJMC-FM 45263
Owner: T K C Inc.
Editorial: 1859 21st Ave, Rice Lake, Wisconsin 54868-9502 **Tel:** 1 715 234-2131.
Email: wjmc@chibardun.net
Web site: http://www.wjmcradio.com
Profile: WJMC-FM is a commercial station owned by T K C Inc. The format of the station is country music. WJMC-FM broadcasts in the Ricelake, WI area at 96.1 FM.
FM RADIO STATION

WJMD-FM 41929
Owner: Hazard Broadcasting Inc.
Editorial: 516 Main St, Hazard, Kentucky 41701-1775 **Tel:** 1 606 439-3358.
Email: wjmd@windstream.net
Web site: http://www.wjmd104.com
Profile: WJMD-FM is a commercial station owned by Hazard Broadcasting Services. The format of the station is gospel. WJMD-FM broadcasts to the Hazard, KY, area at 104.7 FM.
FM RADIO STATION

WJMG-FM 45751
Owner: Circuit Broadcasting of Hattiesburg
Editorial: 1204 Kinnard St, Hattiesburg, Mississippi 39401-1372 **Tel:** 1 601 544-1941.
Profile: WJMG-FM is a commercial station owned by Circuit Broadcasting of Hattiesburg. The format of the station is urban contemporary. WJMG-FM broadcasts to the Hattiesburg, MS area at 92.1 FM.
FM RADIO STATION

WJMH-FM 40130
Owner: Entercom Communications Corp.
Editorial: 7819 National Service Rd, Ste 401, Greensboro, North Carolina 27409 **Tel:** 1 336 605-5200.
Web site: http://www.102jamz.com
Profile: WJMH-FM is a commercial station owned by Entercom Communications Corp. The format of the station urban contemporary. WJMH-FM broadcasts to the Greensboro, NC area at 102.1 FM.
FM RADIO STATION

WJMI-FM 45264
Owner: Alpha Media
Editorial: 731 S Pear Orchard Rd Ste 27, Ridgeland, Mississippi 39157-4839 **Tel:** 1 601 957-1300.
Email: production@wjmi.com
Web site: http://www.wjmi.com
Profile: WJMI-FM is a commercial station owned by Alpha Media. The format of the station is urban contemporary music. WJMI-FM broadcasts to the Jackson, MS area at 99.7 FM.
FM RADIO STATION

WJMJ-FM 41486
Owner: Archdiocese of Hartford
Editorial: 15 Peach Orchard Rd, Prospect, Connecticut 06712-1052 **Tel:** 1 860 242-8800.
Email: wjmj@wjmj.org
Web site: http://www.wjmj.org
Profile: WJMJ-FM is a non-commercial station owned by the Archdiocese of Hartford. The format of the station is religious programming and easy listening music. WJMJ-FM broadcasts to the Bloomfield, CT area at 88.9 FM.
FM RADIO STATION

WJMK-FM 43207
Owner: CBS Radio
Editorial: 180 N Stetson Ave Ste 900, Chicago, Illinois 60601-6728 **Tel:** 1 312 870-6400.
Email: promotions@khitschicago.com
Web site: http://khitschicago.cbslocal.com
Profile: WJMK-FM is a commercial station owned by CBS Radio. The format of the station is classic hits. WJMK-FM broadcasts to the Chicago area at 104.3 FM.
FM RADIO STATION

WJML-AM 36172
Owner: Stone Communications, Inc.
Editorial: 2175 Click Rd, Petoskey, Michigan 49770-8818 **Tel:** 1 231 348-5000.
Email: talk@wjml.com
Web site: http://www.wjml.com
Profile: WJML-AM is a commercial station owned by Stone Communications, Inc. The format of the station is news and talk. WJML-AM broadcasts to the Petoskey, MI area at 1110 AM.
AM RADIO STATION

WJMM-FM 46108
Owner: Christian Broadcasting System
Editorial: 501 Darby Creek Rd, Ste 62, Lexington, Kentucky 40509 **Tel:** 1 859 264-9700.
Email: wjmm@ckcradio.com
Web site: http://www.wjmm.com
Profile: WJMM-FM is a commercial station owned by Christian Broadcasting System. The format of the station is Christian programming. WJMM-FM broadcasts to the Lexington, KY area at 99.1 FM.
FM RADIO STATION

WJMN-FM 40984
Owner: iHeart Media Inc.
Editorial: 10 Cabot Rd Ste 302, Medford, Massachusetts 02155-5173 **Tel:** 1 781 663-2500.
Email: press@jamn945.com
Web site: http://www.jamn945.com
Profile: WJMN-FM is a commercial station owned by iHeart Media Inc. The format of the station is urban contemporary. WJMN-FM broadcasts to the Medford, MA area at 94.5 FM.
FM RADIO STATION

WJMO-AM 37946
Owner: Urban One, Inc.
Editorial: 6555 Carnegie Ave Ste 100, Cleveland, Ohio 44103-4619 **Tel:** 1 216 579-1111.
Web site: http://www.1490wjmo.com
Profile: WJMO-AM is a commercial station owned by Urban One, Inc. The format of the station is gospel music. WJMO-AM broadcasts to the Cleveland area at 1300 AM.
AM RADIO STATION

WJMP-AM 39010
Owner: Media-Com Inc.
Editorial: 2449 State Route 59, Kent, Ohio 44240 **Tel:** 1 330 673-2323.
Email: news@wnir.com
Web site: http://www.wnir.com
Profile: WJMP-AM is a commercial station owned by Media-Com Inc. The format of the station is news and talk. WJMP-AM broadcasts to the Kent, OH area at 1520 AM.
AM RADIO STATION

WJMQ-FM 45882
Owner: Results Broadcasting, Inc.
Editorial: 1456 E Green Bay St, Shawano, Wisconsin 54166-2258 **Tel:** 1 715 524-2194.
Email: resultsbroadcasting@gmail.com
Web site: http://www.frogcountry923.com
Profile: WJMQ-FM is a commercial station owned by Results Broadcasting, Inc. The format of the station is contemporary country. WJMQ-FM broadcasts to the Shawano, WI area at 92.3 FM.
FM RADIO STATION

WJMR-FM 42927
Owner: Saga Communications
Editorial: 5407 W McKinley Ave, Milwaukee, Wisconsin 53208 **Tel:** 1 414 978-9000.
Web site: http://www.jammin983.com
Profile: WJMR-FM is a commercial station owned by Saga Communications. The format of the station is urban adult contemporary music. WJMR-FM broadcasts to the Milwaukee area at 98.3 FM.
FM RADIO STATION

WJMS-AM 39188
Owner: J & J Broadcasting
Editorial: 222 S Lawrence St, Ironwood, Michigan 49938-2524 **Tel:** 1 906 932-2411.
Web site: http://www.wjmsam.com
Profile: WJMS-AM is a commercial station owned by J & J Broadcasting. The format of the station is country music. WJMS-AM broadcasts to the Ironwood, MI area at 590 AM.
AM RADIO STATION

WJMT-AM 37947
Owner: Quicksilver Broadcasting, LLC
Editorial: 120 S Mill St, Merrill, Wisconsin 54452-2534 **Tel:** 1 715 536-6262.
Email: news@z104rocks.com
Web site: http://www.wjmt730.com
Profile: WJMT-AM is a commercial station owned by Quicksilver Broadcasting, LLC. The format of the station is country music. WJMT-AM broadcasts in the Merrill, WI area at 730 AM.
AM RADIO STATION

WJMX-AM 39438
Owner: iHeartMedia Inc.
Editorial: 181 E Evans St Ste 311, Florence, South Carolina 29506-5505 **Tel:** 1 843 667-4600.
Web site: http://newstalk1400online.iheart.com
Profile: WJMX-AM is a commercial station owned by iHeartMedia Inc. The format of the station is news and talk. WJMX-AM broadcasts to the Florence, SC area at 1400 AM.
AM RADIO STATION

WJMX-FM 45265
Owner: iHeartMedia Inc.
Editorial: 181 E Evans St Ste 311, Florence, South Carolina 29506-5505 **Tel:** 1 843 667-4600.
Web site: http://www.103xonline.com
Profile: WJMX-FM is a commercial station owned by iHeartMedia Inc. The format of the station is Hot Adult Contemporary. WJMX-FM broadcasts to the Florence, SC area at 103.3 FM.
FM RADIO STATION

WJMZ-FM 42274
Owner: Summit Media Broadcasting LLC
Editorial: 220 N Main St Ste 402, Greenville, South Carolina 29601-2151 **Tel:** 1 864 235-1073.
Web site: http://www.1073jamz.com
Profile: WJMZ-FM is a commercial station owned by Summit Media Broadcasting LLC. The format of the station is urban adult contemporary. WJMZ-FM broadcasts to the Greenville, SC area at 107.3 FM.
FM RADIO STATION

WJNC-AM 35421
Owner: Atlantic Ridge Telecasters Inc.
Editorial: 4206 Bridges Street Ext. Suit B, Morehead City, North Carolina 28557 **Tel:** 1 252 247-7282.
Email: news@thetalkstation.com
Web site: http://www.wtkf107.com
Profile: WJNC-AM is a commercial station owned by Atlantic Ridge Telecasters Inc. The format of the station is talk, news and sports. WJNC-AM broadcasts to the Newport, NC area at 1240 AM. The station's slogan is, "FM 107 & 1240 The Talk Solution."
AM RADIO STATION

WJNG-FM 43982
Owner: Strattan Broadcasting Inc.
Editorial: 517 1/2 Market St, Johnsonburg, Pennsylvania 15845 **Tel:** 1 814 849-8100.
Email: megarockradio@windstream.net
Web site: http://www.megarock.fm
Profile: WJNG-FM is a commercial station owned by Strattan Broadcasting Inc. The format of the station is classic hits. WJNG-FM broadcasts to the Johnsonburg, PA area at 100.5 FM.
FM RADIO STATION

WJNI-FM 43986
Owner: Kirkman Broadcasting
Editorial: 60 Markfield Dr Ste 4, Charleston, South Carolina 29407-7907 **Tel:** 1 843 763-6631.
Email: wjni@kirkmanbroadcasting.com
Web site: http://wjnifm.com
Profile: WJNI-FM is a commercial station owned by Kirkman Broadcasting. The format of the station is gospel music. WJNI-FM broadcasts to the North Charleston, SC area at 106.3 FM.
FM RADIO STATION

WJNJ-AM 38143
Owner: New Covenant Media
Editorial: 2360 Saint Johns Bluff Rd S #1, Jacksonville, Florida 32246-2310 **Tel:** 1 904 301-9565.
Email: mail@pureradiojax.org
Web site: http://www.pureradiojax.org
Profile: WJNJ-AM is a commercial station owned by New Covenant Media. The format of the station features Gospel programming. WJNJ-AM broadcasts to the Jacksonville, FL area at 1320 AM.
AM RADIO STATION

WJNL-AM 232223
Owner: Stone Communications, Inc.
Editorial: 310 W Front St Ste 411, Traverse City, Michigan 49684-2273 **Tel:** 1 231 947-1210.
Profile: WJNL-AM is a commercial station owned by Stone Communications, Inc. The format of the station is talk. WJNL-AM broadcasts to the Traverse City, MI area at 1210 AM.
AM RADIO STATION

WJNO-AM 36799
Owner: iHeartMedia Inc.
Editorial: 3071 Continental Dr, West Palm Beach, Florida 33407-3274 **Tel:** 1 561 616-6600.
Web site: http://www.wjno.com
Profile: WJNO-AM is commercial station owned by iHeartMedia Inc. The format of the station is news and talk. WJNO-AM broadcasts to the West Palm Beach, FL area at 1290 AM.
AM RADIO STATION

WJNR-FM 40408
Owner: Results Broadcasting
Editorial: 212 W J St, Iron Mountain, Michigan 49801 **Tel:** 1 906 774-5731.
Email: resultsproduction@gmail.com
Web site: http://www.frogcountry.com
Profile: WJNR-FM is a commercial station owned by Results Broadcasting. The format for the station is contemporary country. WJNR-FM broadcasts to the Marquette, MI area at 101.5 FM.
FM RADIO STATION

WJNT-AM 35422
Owner: Alpha Media
Editorial: 731 S Pear Orchard Rd Ste 27, Ridgeland, Mississippi 39157-4839 **Tel:** 1 601 957-1300.
Email: contactus@wjnt.com
Web site: http://www.wjnt.com
Profile: WJNT-AM is a commercial station owned by Alpha Media. The format of the station is news and talk. WJNT-AM broadcasts to the Jackson, MS area at 1180 AM.
AM RADIO STATION

WJNX-AM 35277
Owner: Port St. Lucie Broadcasters
Editorial: 4100 Metzger Rd, Fort Pierce, Florida 34947-1712 **Tel:** 1 772 340-1590.
Email: lagigante@lagigante1330.com
Web site: http://www.lagigante1330.com
Profile: WJNX-AM is a commercial station owned by Port St. Lucie Broadcasters. The format of the station is Spanish language sports and tallk. WJNX-AM broadcasts to West Palm Beach and Fort Pierce, FL area at 1330 AM.
AM RADIO STATION

WJNZ-AM 35770
Owner: Tri City Radio Group, LLC
Editorial: 18647 Fairground Rd, Robertsdale, Alabama **Tel:** 1 251 923-0993.
Profile: WJNZ-AM is a commercial station owned by Tri City Radio Group, LLC. The format of the station is sports. WJNZ-AM broadcasts to the Robertsdale, AL area at 1000 AM.
AM RADIO STATION

WJOB-AM 37105
Owner: Vazquez Development LLC
Editorial: 6405 Olcott Ave., Hammond, Indiana **Tel:** 1 219 844-1230.
Web site: http://www.wjob1230.com
Profile: WJOB-AM is a commercial station owned by Vasquez Development LLC. The format is news and talk. WJOB-AM broadcasts to the Hammond, IN area at 1230 AM.
AM RADIO STATION

WJOC-AM 36276
Owner: Fryar(Sarah Margarett)
Editorial: 805 Chickamauga Ave, Rossville, Georgia 30741-7404 **Tel:** 1 706 861-0800.
Email: wjoc1490@aol.com
Web site: http://www.joy1490.com
Profile: WJOC-AM is a commercial station owned by Sarah Margarett Fryar. The format of the station is Christian talk. WJOC-AM broadcasts to the Rossville, GA area at 1490 AM.
AM RADIO STATION

WJOD-FM 41349
Owner: Townsquare Media
Editorial: 5490 Saratoga Rd, Asbury, Iowa 52002-2593 **Tel:** 1 563 557-1040.
Web site: http://www.103wjod.com
Profile: WJOD-FM is a commercial station owned by Townsquare Media. The format of the station is contemporary country. WJOD-FM broadcasts to the Dubuque, IA area at 103.3 FM.
FM RADIO STATION

WJOI-AM 38089
Owner: Saga Communications
Editorial: 870 Greenbrier Cir Ste 399, Chesapeake, Virginia 23320-2671 **Tel:** 1 757 366-9900.
Web site: http://www.1230wjoi.com
Profile: WJOI-AM is a commercial station owned by Saga Communications. The format of the station is adult standards. WJOI-AM broadcasts to the Chesapeake, VA area at 1230 AM.
AM RADIO STATION

WJOK-AM 37021
Owner: Starboard Media Foundation Inc.
Editorial: 1496 Bellevue St Ste 202, Green Bay, Wisconsin 54311-4205 **Tel:** 1 920 884-1460.
Email: info@relevantradio.com
Web site: http://www.relevantradio.com
Profile: WJOK-AM is a non-commercial station owned by Starboard Media Foundation Inc. The format of the station is religious talk. WJOK-AM broadcasts to the Green Bay, WI area at 1050 AM.
AM RADIO STATION

WJOL-AM 37950
Owner: Alpha Media LLC
Editorial: 2410 Caton Farm Rd Unit B, Crest Hill, Illinois 60403-1374 **Tel:** 1 815 556-0100.
Web site: http://www.wjol.com
Profile: WJOL-AM is a commercial station owned by Alpha Media LLC. The format of the station is talk. WJOL-AM broadcasts to the Joliet, IL area at 1300 AM.
AM RADIO STATION

WJON-AM 37951
Owner: Townsquare Media, LLC
Editorial: 640 Lincoln Ave SE, Saint Cloud, Minnesota 56304-1024 **Tel:** 1 320 251-4422.
Web site: http://www.wjon.com
Profile: WJON-AM is a commercial station owned by Townsquare Media, LLC. The format of the station is news and talk. WJON-AM broadcasts to the Minneapolis area at 1240 AM.
AM RADIO STATION

WJOT-AM 39136
Owner: Hoosier AM/FM LLC
Editorial: 1360 S Wabash St, Wabash, Indiana 46992-4112 **Tel:** 1 260 563-1161.
Web site: http://www.1059thebash.com
Profile: WJOT-AM is a commercial station owned by Hoosier AM/FM LLC. The format of the station is oldies. WJOT-AM broadcasts to the Fort Wayne, IN area at 1510 AM.
AM RADIO STATION

WJOT-FM 46495
Owner: Hoosier AM/FM LLC
Editorial: 1360 S Wabash St, Wabash, Indiana 46992-4112 **Tel:** 1 260 563-1161.
Web site: http://1059thebash.com
Profile: WJOT-FM is a commercial station owned by Hoosier AM/FM LLC. The format of the station is oldies. WJOT-FM broadcasts to the Fort Wayne, IN area at 105.9 FM.
FM RADIO STATION

WJOU-FM 41496
Owner: Oakwood College
Editorial: 7000 Adventist Blvd NW, Huntsville, Alabama 35896-0001 **Tel:** 1 256 726-7420.
Email: wjou@oakwood.edu
Web site: http://www.wjou.org
Profile: WJOU-FM is a non-commercial station owned by Oakwood College. The format of the station is Contemporary Christian/ Inspirational, News and modern AC programming. The station broadcasts to the Huntsville, AL area at 90.1 FM.Its target audience is Oakwood College students and area adult listeners. WJOU-FM's slogan is "The Tennessee Valley's Praise Station." Newscasts air at the top of every hour.
FM RADIO STATION

WJOX-AM 38648
Owner: Cumulus Media Inc.
Editorial: 244 Goodwin Crest Dr, Birmingham, Alabama 35209-3716 **Tel:** 1 205 945-4646.
Web site: http://www.wjoxam.com/
Profile: WJOX-AM is a commercial owned by Cumulus Media Inc. The format of the station is sports. WJOX-AM broadcasts to the Birmingham, AL area at 690 AM.
AM RADIO STATION

WJOX-FM 45028
Owner: Cumulus Media Inc.
Editorial: 244 Goodwin Crest Dr, Birmingham, Alabama 35209-3716 **Tel:** 1 205 945-4646.
Web site: http://www.joxfm.com
Profile: WJOX-FM is a commercial station owned by Cumulus Media Inc. The format of the station is sports. WJOX-FM broadcasts to the Birmingham, AL area at 94.5 FM.
FM RADIO STATION

WJOY-AM 38545
Owner: Hall Communications
Editorial: 70 Joy Dr, South Burlington, Vermont 05403-6118 **Tel:** 1 802 658-1230.
Web site: http://www.wjoy.com
Profile: WJOY-AM is a commercial station owned by Hall Communications. The format of the station is easy listening music. WJOY-AM broadcasts to the South Burlington, VT area at 1230 AM.
AM RADIO STATION

WJPA-AM 38931
Owner: Washington Broadcasting
Editorial: 98 S Main St, Washington, Pennsylvania 15301 **Tel:** 1 724 222-2110.
Email: email@wjpa.com
Web site: http://www.wjpa.com
Profile: WJPA-AM is a commercial station owned by Washington Broadcasting. The format of the station is oldies. WJPA-AM broadcasts to the Washington, PA area at 1450 AM.
AM RADIO STATION

WJPA-FM 46300
Owner: Washington Broadcasting
Editorial: 98 S Main St, Washington, Pennsylvania 15301-6810 **Tel:** 1 724 222-2110.
Email: email@wjpa.com
Web site: http://www.wjpa.com
Profile: WJPA-FM is a commercial station owned by Washington Broadcasting. The format of the station oldies. WJPA-FM broadcasts to the Washington, PA area at 95.3 FM.
FM RADIO STATION

WJPD-FM 45268
Owner: Sovereign Communications LLC
Editorial: 1009 W Ridge St, Ste A, Marquette, Michigan 49855 **Tel:** 1 906 225-1313.
Email: news@wjpd.com
Web site: http://www.wjpd.com
Profile: WJPD-FM is a commercial station owned by Sovereign Communications LLC. The format for the station is country. WJPD-FM broadcasts to the Marquette, MI area at 92.3 FM.
FM RADIO STATION

WJPF-AM 39126
Owner: Max Media
Editorial: 1431 Country Aire Dr, Carterville, Illinois 62918 **Tel:** 1 618 985-4843.
Web site: http://www.wjpf.com
Profile: WJPF-AM is a commercial station owned by Max Media. The format of the station is news and talk. WJPF-AM broadcasts to the Carterville, IL area at 1340 AM.
AM RADIO STATION

WJPH-FM 44252
Owner: Maranatha Ministries
Editorial: 950 Tilton Rd, Ste 101, Northfield, New Jersey 8225 **Tel:** 1 609 646-0057.
Email: letters@praise899.org
Web site: http://www.praise899.org
Profile: WJPH-FM is a non-commercial station owned by Maranatha Ministries. The format of the station is religious. WJPH-FM broadcasts to the Woodbine, NJ area at 89.9 FM.
FM RADIO STATION

WJPT-FM 42216
Owner: Beasley Broadcast Group
Editorial: 20125 S Tamiami Trl, Estero, Florida 33928-2117 **Tel:** 1 239 495-2100.
Web site: http://www.sunny1063.com
Profile: WJPT-FM is a commercial station owned by Beasley Broadcasat Group. The format of the station is adult contemporary. WJPT-FM broadcasts to the Fort Myers, FL area at 106.3 FM.
FM RADIO STATION

WJPZ-FM 41690
Owner: WJPZ Inc.
Editorial: 316 Waverly Ave, Syracuse, New York 13210-2437 **Tel:** 1 315 443-4689.
Email: z89radio@gmail.com
Web site: http://www.z89online.com
Profile: WJPZ-FM is a non-commercial college station owned by WJPZ Inc. The format of the station is Top 40/CHR. WJPZ-FM broadcasts to the Syracuse, NY area at 89.1 FM.
FM RADIO STATION

WJQK-FM 45269
Owner: Lanser Broadcasting Corp.
Editorial: 425 Centerstone Ct, Zeeland, Michigan 49464-2247 **Tel:** 1 616 931-9930.
Email: traffic@jq99.com
Web site: http://www.jq99.com
Profile: WJQK-FM is a commercial station owned by Lanser Broadcasting Corp. The format of the station is contemporary Christian. WJQK-FM broadcasts to the Holland, MI area at 99.3 FM.
FM RADIO STATION

WJQM-FM 153138
Owner: Midwest Family Stations
Editorial: 730 Rayovac Dr, Madison, Wisconsin 53711-2472 **Tel:** 1 608 273-1000.
Email: info@madtownjamz.com
Web site: http://www.madisonjams.com
Profile: WJQM-FM is a commercial station owned by Midwest Family Stations. The format of the station is rhythmic Top 40/CHR. WJQM-FM broadcasts to the Madison, WI area at 93.1 FM.
FM RADIO STATION

WJQQ-FM 45530
Owner: iHeartMedia Inc.
Editorial: 101 1st Radio Ln, Somerset, Kentucky 42503-4639 **Tel:** 1 606 678-5153.
Web site: http://www.q97rock.com/main.html
Profile: WJQQ-FM is a commercial station owned by iHeartMedia Inc. The format for the station is classic rock. WJQQ-FM broadcasts to the Somerset, KY area at 97.1 FM.
FM RADIO STATION

WJQS-AM 39360
Owner: Alpha Media
Editorial: 840 E River Pl Ste 503, Jackson, Mississippi 39202-3487 **Tel:** 1 601 965-2001.
Profile: WJQS-AM is a commercial station owned by Alpha Media. The format of the station is oldies. WJQS-AM broadcasts to the Jackson, MS area at 1400 AM.
AM RADIO STATION

WJQX-FM 42783
Owner: Cumulus Media Inc
Editorial: 244 Goodwin Crest Dr Ste 300, Birmingham, Alabama 35209-3700 **Tel:** 1 205 945-4646.
Web site: http://www.jox2fm.com
Profile: WJQX-FM is a commercial station owned by Cumulus Media Inc. The format of the station is sports. WAPI-FM broadcasts to the Birmingham, AL area at 100.5 FM.
FM RADIO STATION

WJQZ-FM 46701
Owner: DBM Communications
Editorial: 82 Railroad Ave, Wellsville, New York 14895-1143 **Tel:** 1 585 593-6070.
Email: oldiesz103@yahoo.com
Web site: http://www.wjqz18.com
Profile: WJQZ-FM is a commercial station owned by DBM Communications. The format of the station is oldies. WJQZ-FM broadcasts to the Wellsville, NY area at 103.5 FM.
FM RADIO STATION

WJR-AM 39065
Owner: Cumulus Media Inc.
Editorial: 3011 W Grand Blvd Ste 800, Detroit, Michigan 48202-3086 **Tel:** 1 313 875-4440.
Web site: http://www.wjr.com
Profile: WJR-AM is a commercial station owned Cumulus Media Inc. The format of the station is news and talk. WJR-AM broadcasts to the Detroit area at 760 AM.
AM RADIO STATION

WJRB-FM 498297
Owner: WJUL Radio, LLC
Editorial: 1352 Main St Ste 6, Young Harris, Georgia 30582-4314 **Tel:** 1 706 435-7864.
Web site: http://www.wjulradio.com
Profile: WJRB-FM is a commercial station owned by WJUL Radio, LLC (Jeffrey T. Batten). The format of the station is classic country. WJRB-FM broadcasts to the Young Harris, GA area at a frequency of 95.1.
FM RADIO STATION

WJRD-AM 36755
Owner: JRD Inc.
Editorial: 5455 Jug Factory Rd, Tuscaloosa, Alabama 35405-4213 **Tel:** 1 205 345-9573.
Profile: WJRD-AM is a commercial station owned by JRD Inc. The format for the station is oldies. WJRD-AM broadcasts to the Tuscaloosa, AL, area at 1150 AM.
AM RADIO STATION

WJRE-FM 45270
Owner: Virden Broadcasting Corporation
Editorial: 133 E Division St, Kewanee, Illinois 61443 **Tel:** 1 309 853-4471.
Email: regionalradionews@wkei.com
Web site: http://www.1025wjre.com
Profile: WJRE-FM is a commercial station owned by Virden Broadcasting Corporation. The format of the station is country music. WJRE-FM broadcasts to the Kewanee, IL area at 102.5 FM.
FM RADIO STATION

WJRF-FM 41317
Owner: Refuge Media Group
Editorial: 4604 Airpark Blvd, Duluth, Minnesota 55811-5751 **Tel:** 1 218 722-2727.
Web site: http://www.refugeradio.com
Profile: WJRF-FM is a non-commercial station owned by Refuge Media Group. The format of the station is contemporary Christian music. WJRF-FM broadcasts in the Duluth, MN area at 89.5 FM.
FM RADIO STATION

WJRH-FM 40411
Owner: Lafayette College
Editorial: 111 Quad Dr, Easton, Pennsylvania 18042-1707 **Tel:** 1 610 330-5316.
Email: wjrh@lafayette.edu
Web site: http://www.wjrh.org
Profile: WJRH-FM is a commercial station owned by Lafayette College. The format of the station is college variety. WJRH-FM broadcasts to the Philadelphia area at 104.9 FM.
FM RADIO STATION

WJRI-AM 35424
Owner: Foothills Radio Group, LLC
Editorial: 827 Fairview Dr SW, Lenoir, North Carolina 28645-6023 **Tel:** 1 828 758-1033.
Web site: http://www.gofoothills.com/
Profile: WJRI-AM is a commercial station owned by Foothills Radio Group, LLC. The format of the station is news and talk. WJRI-AM broadcasts to the Charlotte, NC area at 1340 AM.
AM RADIO STATION

WJRL-FM 42469
Owner: Alabama Media, LLC
Editorial: 285 N Foster St, Dothan, Alabama 36303-4541 **Tel:** 1 334 792-0047.
Profile: WJRL-FM is a commercial station owned by Alabama Media, LLC. The format of the station is rock. WJRL-FM broadcasts to the Slocomb, AL area at 100.5 FM.
FM RADIO STATION

WJRM-AM 35425
Owner: Family Worship Ministries Inc.
Editorial: 1066 Glenn Rd, Troy, North Carolina 27371 **Tel:** 1 910 576-1390.
Web site: http://www.wjrm.com
Profile: WJRM-AM is a non-commercial station owned by Family Worship Ministries Inc. The format of the station is Southern gospel and contemporary Christian. WJRM-AM broadcasts to the Troy, NC area at 1390 AM.
AM RADIO STATION

WJRR-FM 40745
Owner: iHeartMedia Inc.
Editorial: 2500 Maitland Center Pkwy Ste 401, Maitland, Florida 32751-4179 **Tel:** 1 407 916-7800.
Email: programdirector@wjrr.com
Web site: http://wjrr.iheart.com
Profile: WJRR-FM is a commercial station owned by iHeartMedia Inc. The format of the station is rock alternative music. WJRR-FM broadcasts to the Orlando, FL area at 101.1 FM.
FM RADIO STATION

WJRS-FM 41395
Owner: Lake Cumberland Broadcasters
Editorial: 2804 S Highway 127, Russell Springs, Kentucky 42642 **Tel:** 1 270 343-4444.
Email: wjrs1049@duo-county.com
Web site: http://www.lakercountry.com
Profile: WJRS-FM is a commercial station owned by Lake Cumberland Broadcasters. The format for the station is country. WJRS-FM broadcasts to the Russell Springs, KY area at 104.9 FM.
FM RADIO STATION

WJRV-FM 593822
Owner: Momentum Broadcasting
Editorial: 408 N Cedar Bluff Rd Ste 252, Knoxville, Tennessee 37923-3641 **Tel:** 1 865 246-3848.
Email: spots@river106.com
Web site: http://www.river106.com
Profile: WJRV-FM is a commercial station owned by Momentum Broadcasting. The format of the station is hot adult contemporary. The station airs locally at 106.1 FM. WJRV-FM's tagline is "80s 90s and Now."
FM RADIO STATION

WJRW-AM 38005
Owner: Cumulus Media Inc.
Editorial: 60 Monroe Center St NW Fl 3, Grand Rapids, Michigan 49503-2916 **Tel:** 1 616 456-5461.
Web site: http://www.wjrwam.com
Profile: WJRW-AM is a commercial station owned by Cumulus Media Inc. The format of the station is news and talk. WJRW-AM broadcasts to the Grand Rapids, MI area at 1340 AM.
AM RADIO STATION

WJRZ-FM 42320
Owner: Beasley Broadcast Group
Editorial: 1001 Beach Ave, Manahawkin, New Jersey 08050-3218 **Tel:** 1 609 597-1100.
Web site: http://www.wjrz.com
Profile: WJRZ-FM is a commercial station owned by Beasley Broadcast Group. The format of the station is classic hits. WJRZ-FM broadcasts to the Manahawkin, NJ area at 100.1 FM.
FM RADIO STATION

WJSA-AM 37953
Owner: Covenant Broadcasting Co.
Editorial: 262 Allegheny St, Jersey Shore, Pennsylvania 17740-1442 **Tel:** 1 570 327-1300.
Web site: http://espnwilliamsport.com
Profile: WJSA-AM is a non-commercial station owned by Covenant Broadcasting Co. The format of the station is sports. WJSA-AM broadcasts to the Scranton, PA area at 1600 AM.
AM RADIO STATION

WJSA-FM 45271
Owner: Covenant Broadcasting Co.
Editorial: 262 Allegheny St, Jersey Shore, Pennsylvania 17740-1442 **Tel:** 1 570 398-7200.
Email: news@wjsaradio.com
Web site: http://www.wjsaradio.com
Profile: WJSA-FM is a non-commercial station owned by Covenant Broadcasting Co. The format of the station is Christian music and news. WJSA-FM broadcasts to the Jersey Shore, PA area at 96.3 FM.
FM RADIO STATION

WJSB-AM 37954
Owner: Whitaker(James T.)
Editorial: 506 W 1st Ave, Crestview, Florida 32536 **Tel:** 1 850 682-3040.
Email: waazwjsb@embarqmail.com
Profile: WJSB-AM is a commercial station owned by James T. Whitaker. The format of the station is classic country. WJSB-AM broadcasts to the Mobile, AL and Pensacola, FL areas at 1050 AM.
AM RADIO STATION

WJSC-FM 40412
Owner: Johnson State College
Editorial: 337 College Hl, Johnson, Vermont 5656 **Tel:** 1 802 635-1355.
Web site: http://www.jsc.edu/StudentLife/WJSCFM/default.aspx
Profile: WJSC-FM is a non-commercial station owned by Johnson State College. The format of the station is variety. WJSC-FM broadcasts to the Burlington, VT and Plattsburgh, NY areas at 90.7 FM.
FM RADIO STATION

WJSE-FM 42564
Owner: Coastal Broadcasting Systems, Inc.
Editorial: 1602 Route 47 Floor 2, Rio Grande, New Jersey 08242-1404 **Tel:** 1 609 522-1987.
Web site: http://www.wjserocks.com
Profile: WJSE-FM is a commercial station owned by Coastal Broadcasting Systems, Inc. The format of the station is alternative rock. WJSE-FM broadcasts to the Wildwood, NJ area at 106.7 FM.
FM RADIO STATION

WJSG-FM 41862
Owner: Jackson Broadcasting Co.
Editorial: 180 Airport Rd, Rockingham, North Carolina 28379-4251 **Tel:** 1 910 895-3787.
Email: g104fm@g104fm.com
Web site: http://www.g104fm.com
Profile: WJSG-FM is a commercial station owned by Jackson Broadcasting Co. The format of the station is Christian music. WJSG-FM broadcasts to the Rockingham, NC area at 104.3 FM.
FM RADIO STATION

WJSH-FM 43134
Owner: Northshore Broadcasting Inc.
Editorial: 200 E Thomas St, Hammond, Louisiana 70401-3316 **Tel:** 1 985 345-0060.
Web site: http://www.highway1047.com
Profile: WJSH-FM is a commercial station owned by Northshore Broadcasting Inc. The format of the station is Classic Hit Country. WJSH-FM broadcasts to the New Orleans area on 104.7 FM.
FM RADIO STATION

United States of America

WJSM-FM 45272
Owner: Martinsburg Broadcasting Inc.
Editorial: 724 Rebecca Furnace Road, Martinsburg, Pennsylvania 16662 **Tel:** 1 814 793-2188.
Email: wjsmradio@gmail.com
Web site: http://www.wjsm.com
Profile: WJSM-FM is a commercial station owned by Martinsburg Broadcasting Inc. The format of the station is gospel music and Christian programming. WJSM-FM broadcasts to the Martinsburg, PA area at 92.7 FM.
FM RADIO STATION

WJSN-FM 45273
Owner: Intermountain Broadcasting
Editorial: 1501 Hargis Ln, Jackson, Kentucky 41339-1102 **Tel:** 1 606 666-7531.
Web site: http://wjsn.awardspace.com
Profile: WJSN-FM is a commercial station owned by Intermountain Broadcasting. The format of the station is country music. WJSN-FM broadcasts in the Jackson, KY area at 106.5 FM.
FM RADIO STATION

WJSP-FM 41959
Owner: Georgia Public Broadcasting
Editorial: 260 14th St NW, Atlanta, Georgia 30318 **Tel:** 1 404 685-2548.
Email: ask@gpb.org
Web site: http://www.gpb.org
Profile: WJSP-FM is a non-commercial station owned by Georgia Public Broadcasting. The format of the station is news, classical and jazz music. WJSP-FM broadcasts to the Atlanta area at 88.1 FM.
FM RADIO STATION

WJSQ-FM 46553
Owner: Sliger Enterprises
Editorial: 2110 Oxnard Rd, Athens, Tennessee 37303 **Tel:** 1 423 745-1000.
Email: 1017wlar@bellsouth.net
Profile: WJSQ-FM is a commercial station owned by Sliger Enterprises. The format of the station is contemporary country. WSSQ-FM broadcasts to the Athens, TN area at 101.7 FM.
FM RADIO STATION

WJSR-FM 40413
Owner: Jefferson State Community College
Editorial: 2601 Carson Rd, Birmingham, Alabama 35215 **Tel:** 1 205 856-6095.
Profile: WJSR-FM is a non-commercial station owned by Jefferson State Community College. The format of the station is classic rock. WJSR-FM broadcasts to the Birmingham, AL area at 91.1 FM.
FM RADIO STATION

WJSR-FM 44293
Owner: Summit Media Broadcasting LLC
Editorial: 812 Moorefield Park Drive, Suite 300, Richmond, Virginia 23236 **Tel:** 1 804 330-5700.
Web site: http://www.star1009richmond.com/
Profile: WJSR-FM is a commercial station owned by Summit Media Broadcasting LLC. The format of the station is Classic Hits. WJSR-FM broadcasts to the Richmond, VA area at 100.9 FM.
FM RADIO STATION

WJST-AM 35227
Owner: FM Radio Licenses, LLC
Editorial: 219 Savannah Gardner Rd, New Castle, Pennsylvania 16101-5546 **Tel:** 1 724 346-5070.
Profile: WJST-AM is a commercial station owned by FM Radio Licenses, LLC. The format of the station is sports. WJST-AM broadcasts to the New Castle, PA area at 1280 AM.
AM RADIO STATION

WJSZ-FM 42184
Owner: Krol Communications
Editorial: 103 N Washington St, Owosso, Michigan 48867-2819 **Tel:** 1 989 725-1925.
Email: studio@z925.com
Web site: http://www.z925.com
FM RADIO STATION

WJTA-FM 44134
Owner: Holy Family Communications, Inc
Editorial: 6048 Road 8E, Leipsic, Ohio 45856-9408
Tel: 1 419 943-1511.
Email: wjta88.9@tds.net
Web site: http://www.wjta889.org/
Profile: WJTA-FM is a non-commercial station owned by Holy Family Communications, Inc (Tom and Mary Ann Deitering). The station airs on 88.9FM. It broadcasts out of the Deitering home in Leipsic, OH. The station is currently a simulcast of EWTN/ Ave Maria Catholic Radio. Local programming is planned for the future. The station's first broadcast was in June 2010.
FM RADIO STATION

WJTB-AM 35427
Owner: Taylor Broadcasting
Editorial: 105 Lake Ave, Elyria, Ohio 44035
Tel: 1 440 327-1844.
Profile: WJTB-AM is a commercial station owned by Taylor Broadcasting. The format of the station is gospel. WJTB-AM broadcasts to the Elyria, OH area at 1040 AM.
AM RADIO STATION

WJTF-FM 444965
Owner: Family Life Communications, Inc.
Editorial: 7355 N Oracle Rd, Tucson, Arizona 85704-6325 **Tel:** 1 520 742-6976.

Web site: http://www.myflr.org
FM RADIO STATION

WJTG-FM 41353
Owner: Family Life Communications, Inc.
Editorial: 7355 N Oracle Rd, Tucson, Arizona 85704-6325 **Tel:** 1 520 742-6976.
Web site: http://www.myflr.org
Profile: WJTG-FM is a commercial station owned by Family Life Radio. The format of the station is Contemporary Christian music. WJTG-FM broadcasts to the Fort Valley, GA area at 91.3 FM.
FM RADIO STATION

WJTH-AM 35428
Owner: Cherokee Broadcasting Co.
Editorial: 329 Richardson Rd SE, Calhoun, Georgia 30701 **Tel:** 1 706 629-6397.
Email: am9000@wjth.com
Web site: http://www.wjth.com
Profile: WJTH-AM is a commercial station owned by Cherokee Broadcasting Co. The format of the station is country music. WJTH-AM broadcasts to the Atlanta area at 900 AM.
AM RADIO STATION

WJTI-AM 36423
Owner: El Sol Broadcasting, LLC
Editorial: 611 W National Ave Ste 201, Milwaukee, Wisconsin 53204-1714 **Tel:** 1 414 384-1460.
Email: uniyes@aol.com
Web site: http://www.979radio.com
Profile: WJTI-AM is a commercial station owned by El Sol Broadcasting, LLC. The format of the station is regional Mexican. WJTI-AM broadcasts to the Milwaukee area at 1460 AM.
AM RADIO STATION

WJTK-FM 552143
Owner: Newman Broadcasting Inc.
Editorial: 229 SW Main Blvd, Lake City, Florida 32025-7049 **Tel:** 1 386 758-9696.
Email: news@965wjtk.com
Web site: http://northfloridanow.com/index92.htm
Profile: WJTK-FM is a commercial station owned by Newman Broadcasting Inc. The format of the station is news talk. WJTK-FM broadcasts to the Lake City, FL area at 96.5 FM.
FM RADIO STATION

WJTL-FM 41361
Owner: Creative Ministries Inc.
Editorial: 1875 Junction Rd, Manheim, Pennsylvania 17545-8853 **Tel:** 1 717 392-3690.
Email: contact@wjtl.com
Web site: http://www.wjtl.com
Profile: WJTL-FM is a non-commercial station owned by Creative Ministries Inc. The format of the station is contemporary Christian music. WJTL-FM broadcasts to the Lancaster, PA area at 90.3 FM.
FM RADIO STATION

WJTN-AM 37956
Owner: Media One Group, LLC
Editorial: 2 Orchard Rd, Jamestown, New York 14701
Tel: 1 716 487-1151.
Web site: http://www.wjtn.com
Profile: WJTN-AM is a commercial station owned by Media One Group, LLC. The format of the station is news, talk and sports. WJTN-AM broadcasts to the Jamestown, NY area at 1240 AM.
AM RADIO STATION

WJTO-AM 36362
Owner: Blue Jey Broadcasting
Tel: 1 207 443-6671.
Profile: WJTO-AM is a commercial station owned by Blue Jey Broadcasting. The format of the station is adult standards music. WJTO-AM broadcasts to the Bath, ME area at 730 AM.
AM RADIO STATION

WJTQ-FM 46220
Owner: Cumulus Media Inc.
Editorial: 6565 N W St Ste 270, Pensacola, Florida 32505-1797 **Tel:** 1 850 478-6011.
Web site: http://www.pensacolasjet.com
Profile: WJTQ-FM is a commercial station owned by Cumulus Media Inc. The format of the station is classic hits. WJTQ-FM broadcasts to the Mobile, AL/ Pensacola, FL area at 100.7 FM.
FM RADIO STATION

WJTT-FM 40414
Owner: Brewer Broadcasting Inc.
Editorial: 1305 Carter St, Chattanooga, Tennessee 37402-4412 **Tel:** 1 423 265-9494.
Web site: http://www.power94.com
Profile: WJTT-FM is a commercial station owned by Brewer Broadcasting Inc. The format of the station is urban contemporary. WJTT-FM broadcasts to the Chattanooga, TN area at 94.3 FM.
FM RADIO STATION

WJTY-FM 41360
Owner: Family Life Radio
Editorial: 7355 N Oracle Rd, Tucson, Arizona 85704-6325 **Tel:** 1 800 7761070.
Web site: http://www.myflr.org
Profile: WJTY-FM is a non-commercial station owned by Family Life Radio. The format is contemporary Christian. WJTY-FM broadcasts to Lancaster, WI area at 88.1 FM.
FM RADIO STATION

WJUB-AM 35598
Owner: Jubilation Ministries
Editorial: N5569 State Road 57, Plymouth, Wisconsin 53073-4236 **Tel:** 1 920 893-2661.
Email: 1420thebreeze@mjradio.com
Web site: http://www.1420thebreeze.com
Profile: WJUB-AM is a commercial station owned by Jubilation Ministries. The format of the station is adult standards. WJUB-AM broadcasts to the Milwaukee area at 1420 AM.
AM RADIO STATION

WJUC-FM 43214
Owner: Welch Communications
Editorial: 5902 Southwyck Blvd, Toledo, Ohio 43614
Tel: 1 419 861-9582.
Email: wjuc@aol.com
Web site: http://www.thejuice1073.com
Profile: WJUC-FM is a commercial station owned by Welch Communications. The format of the station is urban contemporary. WJUC-FM broadcasts to the Toledo, OH area at 107.3 FM.
FM RADIO STATION

WJUL-AM 561497
Owner: WJUL Radio, LLC
Editorial: 1352 Main St Ste 6, Young Harris, Georgia 30582-4314 **Tel:** 1 706 379-9770.
Web site: http://www.wjulradio.com
Profile: WJUL-AM is a commercial station owned by WJUL Radio, LLC (Jeffrey Batten). The format of the station is classic hits and oldies. WJUL-AM broadcasts to the Hiawassee, GA area at 1230 AM.
AM RADIO STATION

WJUN-AM 38344
Owner: Starview Media Inc.
Editorial: Old Route 22 East, Mexico, Pennsylvania 17056-9999 **Tel:** 1 717 436-2135.
Profile: WJUN-AM is a commercial station owned by Starview Media Inc. The format of the station is sports. WJUN-AM broadcasts to the Mexico, PA area at station at 1220 AM.
AM RADIO STATION

WJUN-FM 45705
Owner: Seven Mountains Media, LLC
Editorial: 160 W Clearview Ave, State College, Pennsylvania 16803-1617 **Tel:** 1 814 231-0953.
Profile: WJUN-FM is a commercial station owned by Seven Mountains Media, LLC. The format of the station is country music. WJUN-FM broadcasts to the Mexico, PA area at 92.5 FM.
FM RADIO STATION

WJUS-AM 35163
Owner: Grace Baptist Temple Church
Editorial: Highway 14, Marion, Alabama 36756
Tel: 1 334 683-2043.
Email: wjus@bellsouth.net
AM RADIO STATION

WJUV-FM 860488
Owner: La Promesa Foundation
Tel: 1 888 784-3476.
Email: gmonline@grnonline.com
Web site: http://grnonline.com/
Profile: WJUV-FM is a non-commercial station owned by La Promesa Foundation. The format of the station is Catholic teaching programming. The station airs locally at 88.3 FM to the Cullman, AL area.
FM RADIO STATION

WJUX-FM 42081
Owner: Bridgelight Corp.
Editorial: 127 White Oak Ln, Old Bridge, New Jersey 08857-1945 **Tel:** 1 732 901-9953.
Email: info@bridgefm.org
Web site: http://www.bridgefm.org
Profile: WJUX-FM is a non-commercial station owned by Bridgelight Corp. The format for the station is religious talk and music. WJUX-FM broadcasts to the New York area at 99.7 FM.
FM RADIO STATION

WJVC-FM 43180
Owner: JVC MEDIA, LLC
Editorial: 3075 Veterans Memorial Hwy Ste 201, Ronkonkoma, New York 11779-7600 **Tel:** 1 631 648-2500.
Web site: http://licountry.com
Profile: WJVC-FM is a commercial station, owned by JVC MEDIA, LLC. The format of the station is country. WJVC-FM broadcasts in the Medford, NY area at 96.1 FM.
FM RADIO STATION

WJVL-FM 45274
Owner: Bliss Communications Inc.
Editorial: 1 S Parker Dr, Janesville, Wisconsin 53545
Tel: 1 608 752-7895.
Email: news@wclo.com
Web site: http://www.wjvl.com
Profile: WJVL-FM is a commercial station owned by Bliss Communications Inc. The format of the station is country. WJVL-FM broadcasts to the Madison, WI area at 99.9 FM.
FM RADIO STATION

WJVO-FM 45275
Owner: Morgan County Broadcasting Co., Inc.
Editorial: 1251 E Morton Ave, Jacksonville, Illinois 62650-3195 **Tel:** 1 217 245-5119.
Email: wjvofmair@mchsi.com
Web site: http://wjvofm.com/
Profile: WJVO-FM is a commercial station owned by Morgan County Broadcasting Co., Inc. The format of

the station is classic and contemporary country music. WJVO-FM broadcasts in the Jacksonville, IL at 105.5 FM.
FM RADIO STATION

WJVR-FM 837500
Owner: United States CP, LLC
Editorial: 508 W Oak St, Covington, Virginia 24426-1942 **Tel:** 1 540 962-1133.
Web site: http://www.1019theriver.com
Profile: WJVR-FM is a commercial station owned by United States CP, LLC. The format of the station is light adult contemporary. WJVR-FM broadcasts to the Allegheny County, VA area at a frequency of 101.9 FM.
FM RADIO STATION

WJWD-FM 133767
Owner: Calvary Radio Network
Editorial: 150 Lincolnway Ste 2001, Valparaiso, Indiana 46383-5556 **Tel:** 1 219 548-5800.
Email: info@calvaryradionetwork.com
Web site: http://www.calvaryradionetwork.com
Profile: WJWD-FM is a non-commercial station owned by Calvary Chapel of Costa Mesa, Inc. The format of the station is Christian music and religious programming. WJWD-FM broadcasts to the Marshall, WI area at 90.3 FM.
FM RADIO STATION

WJWL-AM 38514
Owner: The Voice Radio Network
Editorial: Georgetown, Delaware **Tel:** 1 302 228-8942.
Profile: WJWL-AM is a commercial station owned by The Voice Radio Network. The format of the station is regional Mexican music. WJWK-AM broadcasts to the Georgetown, DE area at 900 AM.
AM RADIO STATION

WJWT-FM 558730
Owner: Horizon Christian Fellowship
Editorial: 356 Broad St, Fitchburg, Massachusetts 01420-3030 **Tel:** 1 978 665-9111.
Web site: http://renewfm.org
Profile: WJWT-FM is a commercial station owned by Horizon Christian Fellowship. The format of the station is Christian music and religious programming. WJWT-FM broadcasts to the Gardner, MA area at 91.7 FM.
FM RADIO STATION

WJWV-FM 43318
Owner: Georgia Public Broadcasting
Editorial: 260 14th St NW, Atlanta, Georgia 30318
Tel: 1 404 685-2548.
Email: ask@gpb.org
Web site: http://www.gpb.org
Profile: WJWV-FM is a non-commercial station owned by Georgia Public Broadcasting. The format of the station is news, jazz and classical music. WJWV-FM broadcasts to the Atlanta area at 90.9 FM.
FM RADIO STATION

WJWZ-FM 43733
Owner: Bluewater Broadcasting Co. LLC
Editorial: 4101 Wall St Ste A, Montgomery, Alabama 36106-3724 **Tel:** 1 334 244-0961.
Web site: http://www.979jamz.com
Profile: WJWZ-FM is a commercial station owned by Bluewater Broadcasting Co. LLC. The format of the station is urban contemporary. WJWZ-FM broadcasts to the Montgomery, AL area at 97.9 FM.
FM RADIO STATION

WJXA-FM 40909
Owner: Midwest Communications Inc.
Editorial: 504 Rosedale Ave, Nashville, Tennessee 37211-2028 **Tel:** 1 615 259-0929.
Web site: http://www.mix929.com
Profile: WJXA-FM is a commercial station owned by Midwest Communications Inc.. The format of the station is contemporary. WJXA-FM broadcasts in the Nashville, TN area at 92.9 FM.
FM RADIO STATION

WJXB-FM 46472
Owner: Midwest Communications, Inc.
Editorial: 1100 Sharps Ridge Mem Park Dr, Knoxville, Tennessee 37917-3000 **Tel:** 1 865 525-6000.
Web site: http://www.b975.com
Profile: WJXB-FM is a commercial station owned by Midwest Communications, Inc. The format of the station is adult contemporary. WJXB-FM broadcasts to the Knoxville, TN area at 97.5 FM.
FM RADIO STATION

WJXL-AM 35209
Owner: Seven Bridges Radio, LLC
Editorial: 9090 Hogan Rd, Jacksonville, Florida 32216
Tel: 1 904 641-1011.
Web site: http://www.1010xl.com
Profile: WJXL-AM is a commercial station owned by Seven Bridges Radio, LLC. The format of the station is sports. WJXL-AM broadcasts to the Jacksonville, FL area at 1010 AM.
AM RADIO STATION

WJXM-FM 64140
Owner: Mississippi Broadcasters, LLC
Editorial: 3436 Highway 45 N, Meridian, Mississippi 39301-1509 **Tel:** 1 601 693-2661.
Web site: http://www.1057thebeat.com
Profile: WJXM-FM is a commercial station owned by Mississippi Broadcasters, LLC. The format of the station is urban contemporary. WJXM-FM broadcasts to the Meridian, MS area at 107.5 FM.
FM RADIO STATION

WJXN-FM 43526
Owner: Flinn Broadcasting Corporation
Editorial: Jackson, Mississippi **Tel:** 1 901 375-9324.
Web site: http://www.flinn.com
Profile: WJXN-FM is a commercial station owned by Flinn Broadcasting Corporation. The format of the station is classic country. WJXN-FM broadcasts in the Jackson, MS area at 100.9 FM.
FM RADIO STATION

WJXP-FM 786467
Owner: Horizon Christian Fellowship
Editorial: 356 Broad St, Fitchburg, Massachusetts 01420-3030 **Tel:** 1 978 665-9111.
Web site: http://horizonfitchburg.org
Profile: WJXP-FM is a non-commercial station owned by Horizon Christian Fellowship. The format of the station is Contemporary Christian. WJXP-FM broadcasts to the Fitchburg, MA area at a frequency of 90.1 FM.
FM RADIO STATION

WJXQ-FM 40416
Owner: Midwest Communiations, Inc.
Editorial: 2495 Cedar St, Holt, Michigan 48842-7400 **Tel:** 1 517 699-0111.
Web site: http://www.z93hits.com
Profile: WJXQ-FM is a commercial station owned by Midwest Communiations, Inc. The format of the station is rock. WJXQ-FM broadcasts to the Lansing, MI area at 106.1 FM.
FM RADIO STATION

WJXR-FM 40417
Owner: Perich(Greg & Sarah)
Editorial: 28 W Macclenny Ave Ste 9, Macclenny, Florida 32063-2078 **Tel:** 1 904 314-9749.
Web site: http://latina921.com
Profile: WJXR-FM is a commercial station owned by Greg & Sarah Perich. The format of the station is Spanish tropical. WJXR-FM broadcasts to the Jacksonville, FL area at 92.1 FM.
FM RADIO STATION

WJXY-FM 45998
Owner: Colonial Radio Group
Editorial: 4337 Big Barn Dr, Little River, South Carolina 29566-6802
Web site: http://www.colonial.fm
Profile: WJXY-FM is a commercial station owned by Colonial Media & Entertainment. The format of the station is country hits from the 1980s to today. WJXY-FM broadcasts to the Myrtle Beach, SC area at 93.9 FM.
FM RADIO STATION

WJYA-FM 44279
Owner: Positive Alternative Radio
Editorial: 22226 Timberlake Rd., Lynchburg, Virginia 24502 **Tel:** 1 434 237-9798.
Email: office@spiritfm.com
Web site: http://www.spiritfm.com
FM RADIO STATION

WJYD-FM 42163
Owner: Urban One, Inc.
Editorial: 2400 Corporate Exchange Dr Ste 200, Columbus, Ohio 43231-7669 **Tel:** 1 614 487-1444.
Web site: http://joycolumbus.com/
Profile: WJYD-FM is a commercial station owned by Urban One, Inc. The format of the station is urban gospel. WJYD-FM broadcasts to the Columbus, OH area at 107.1 FM.
FM RADIO STATION

WJYI-AM 38418
Owner: Saga Communications
Editorial: 5407 W McKinley Ave, Milwaukee, Wisconsin 53208-2540 **Tel:** 1 414 978-9000.
Web site: http://www.joy1340.com
Profile: WJYI-AM is a commercial station owned by Saga Communications. The format of the station is Christian programming and gospel music. WJYI-AM broadcasts to the Milwaukee area at 1340 AM.
AM RADIO STATION

WJYJ-FM 41571
Owner: Positive Alternative Radio
Editorial: 6546 Lovers Ln, Warrenton, Virginia 20186 **Tel:** 1 540 347-4825.
Email: info@positivehits.org
Web site: http://www.positivehits.org
Profile: WJYJ-FM is a non-commercial station owned by Positive Alternative Radio. The format of the station is contemporary Christian music. WJYJ-FM broadcasts to the Warrenton, VA area at 90.5 FM.
FM RADIO STATION

WJYK-AM 35520
Owner: Battaglia(Stephen and Janis)
Editorial: 1612 Milo Rd, Richmond, Virginia 23225-7416 **Tel:** 1 804 276-2060.
Web site: http://www.joyam980.com
Profile: WJYK-AM is a commercial station owned by Stephen and Janice Battaglia. The format of the station is contemporary Christian music and religious. WJYK-AM broadcasts to the Chase City, VA area at 980 AM.
AM RADIO STATION

WJYO-FM 43960
Owner: Airwaves for Jesus
Editorial: 6211 Briarcliff Rd, Fort Myers, Florida 33912 **Tel:** 1 239 274-9150.
Email: info@kingdom.fm
Web site: http://www.kingdom.fm
Profile: WJYO-FM is a non-commercial station owned by Airwaves for Jesus. The format of the station is gospel. WJYO-FM broadcasts to the Ft. Myers, FL area at 91.5 FM.
FM RADIO STATION

WJYP-AM 37958
Owner: LM Communications, Inc.
Editorial: 100 Kanawha Ter, Saint Albans, West Virginia 25177-2771 **Tel:** 1 304 722-3308.
Email: wjypnet@gmail.com
Web site: http://wjypam.com
Profile: WJYP-AM is a commercial station owned by LM Communications, Inc. The format of the station is sports. WJYP-AM broadcasts to the Saint Albans, WV area at 1300 AM.
AM RADIO STATION

WJYW-FM 44322
Owner: Positive Alternative Radio
Editorial: 505 S Division St, Union City, Ohio 45390 **Tel:** 1 937 968-5633.
Email: office@889joyfm.com
Web site: http://www.889joyfm.com
Profile: WJYW-FM is a commercial station owned by Positive Alternative Radio. The format of the station is contemporary Christian. WJYW-FM broadcasts to the Union City, OH area at 88.9 FM.
FM RADIO STATION

WJYY-FM 41301
Owner: WBIN, Inc.
Editorial: 2 Capital Plz Ste 105, Concord, New Hampshire 03301-4911 **Tel:** 1 603 224-8486.
Web site: http://www.wjyy.com
Profile: WJYY-FM is a commercial station owned by WBIN, Inc. The format of the station is Top 40/CHR music. WJYY-FM broadcasts to the Concord, NH area at 105.5 FM.
FM RADIO STATION

WJYZ-AM 39239
Owner: iHeartMedia Inc.
Editorial: 809 S Westover Blvd, Albany, Georgia 31707-4953 **Tel:** 1 229 439-9704.
Web site: http://www.wjyz.com
Profile: WJYZ-AM is a commercial station owned by iHeartMedia Inc. The format of the station is gospel music. WJYZ-AM broadcasts to the Albany, GA area at 960 AM.
AM RADIO STATION

WJZ-AM 38919
Owner: CBS Radio
Editorial: 1423 Clarkview Rd Ste 1000, Baltimore, Maryland 21209-2134 **Tel:** 1 410 825-1000.
Web site: http://baltimore.cbslocal.com/station/cbs-sports-radio-1300/
Profile: WJZ-AM is a commercial station owned by CBS Radio. The format of the station is sports. WJZ-AM broadcasts to the Baltimore area at 1300 AM.
AM RADIO STATION

WJZD-FM 42209
Owner: WJZD Inc.
Editorial: 10211 Southpark Dr, Gulfport, Mississippi 39503 **Tel:** 1 228 896-5307.
Email: info@wjzd.com
Web site: http://www.wjzd.com
Profile: WJZD-FM is a commercial station owned by WJZD Inc. The format of the station is urban contemporary music. WJZD-FM broadcasts in the Gulfport, MS area at 94.5 FM.
FM RADIO STATION

WJZE-FM 42894
Owner: URBan Radio Broadcasting, LLC
Editorial: 720 Water St, Fl 4, Toledo, Ohio 43604 **Tel:** 1 419 244-6354.
Web site: http://www.hot973.net
Profile: WFZE-FM is a commercial station owned by URBan Radio Broadcasting, LLC. The format of the station is urban contemporary. WFZE-FM broadcasts to the Toledo, OH area at 97.3 FM.
FM RADIO STATION

WJZ-FM 43810
Owner: CBS Radio
Editorial: 1423 Clarkview Rd, Ste 100, Baltimore, Maryland 21209-2190 **Tel:** 1 410 828-7722.
Web site: http://baltimore.cbslocal.com/category/sports/
Profile: WJZ-FM is a commercial station owned by CBS Radio. The format of the station is sports programming. WJZ-FM broadcasts to the Baltimore area at 105.7 FM.
FM RADIO STATION

WJZM-AM 36925
Owner: Cumberland Radio Partners Inc.
Editorial: 925 Martin St, Clarksville, Tennessee 37040-4090 **Tel:** 1 931 645-6414.
Email: 14jzm@wjzm.com
Web site: http://www.wjzm.com
Profile: WJZM-AM is a commercial station owned by Cumberland Radio Partners Inc. The format of the station is sports with some news and talk in the morning. WJZM-AM broadcasts to the Clarksville, TN area at 1400 AM.
AM RADIO STATION

WJZN-AM 38052
Owner: Townsquare Media, Inc.
Editorial: 56 Western Ave Ste 13, Augusta, Maine 04330-6348 **Tel:** 1 207 623-4735.
Web site: http://www.1400and1490.com
Profile: WJZN-AM is a commercial station owned by Townsquare Media, Inc. The format of the station is adult standards. WJZN-AM broadcasts to the Waterville, ME area at 1400 AM.
AM RADIO STATION

WJZQ-FM 45294
Owner: Midwestern Broadcasting Co.
Editorial: 314 E Front St, Traverse City, Michigan 49684 **Tel:** 1 231 947-7675.
Web site: http://www.z93hits.com
Profile: WJZQ-FM is a commercial station owned by Midwestern Broadcasting Co. The format of the station is top 40/CHR. WJZQ-FM broadcasts to the Traverse City, MI area at 92.9 FM.
FM RADIO STATION

WJZR-FM 42077
Owner: North Coast Radio Inc.
Editorial: 1237 E Main St, Rochester, New York 14609-6941 **Tel:** 1 585 288-5020.
Profile: WJZR-FM is a commercial station owned by North Coast Radio Inc. The format of the station is jazz and blues music. WJZR-FM broadcasts to the Rochester, NY area at 105.9 FM.
FM RADIO STATION

WKAA-FM 41679
Owner: Black Crow Broadcasting Inc.
Editorial: 1711 Ellis Dr, Valdosta, Georgia 31601-3573 **Tel:** 1 229 244-8642.
Web site: http://mykixcountry.com/
Profile: WKAA-FM is a commercial station owned by Black Crow Broadcasting Inc. The format of the station is contemporary country . WKAA-FM broadcasts to the Valdosta, GA area at 92.5 FM.
FM RADIO STATION

WKAC-AM 35429
Owner: Limestone Broadcast Company
Editorial: 19245 Al Highway 127, Athens, Alabama 35614-6805 **Tel:** 1 256 232-6827.
Email: wkac@wkac1080.com
Web site: http://www.wkac1080.com
Profile: WKAC-AM is a commercial station owned by Limestone Broadcast Company. The format of the station is oldies. WKAC-AM broadcasts to the Athens, AL area at 1080 AM.
AM RADIO STATION

WKAD-FM 244989
Owner: MacDonald Garber Broadcasting Inc.
Editorial: 7825 Mackinaw Trl, Cadillac, Michigan 49601-9746 **Tel:** 1 231 775-1263.
Web site: http://937fmtheticket.com
Profile: WKAD-FM is a commercial station owned by MacDonald Garber Broadcasting Inc. The format of the station is sports. WKAD-FM broadcasts to the Cadillac, MI area at a frequency of 93.7 FM.
FM RADIO STATION

WKAF-FM 44385
Owner: Entercom Communications Corp.
Editorial: 20 Guest St Fl 3, Boston, Massachusetts 02135-2040 **Tel:** 1 617 779-5400.
Web site: http://www.977rnb.com
Profile: WKAF-FM is a commercial station owned by Entercom Communications Corp. The format of the station is Urban AC and R&B. WKAF-FM broadcasts to the Quincy, MA area at 97.7 FM. The station's slogan is, "Boston's #1 for R&B."
FM RADIO STATION

WKAI-FM 45276
Owner: Prestige Communications
Editorial: 1034 W Jackson St, Macomb, Illinois 61455-1924 **Tel:** 1 309 833-2121.
Email: news@prestigeradio.com
Web site: http://www.macombradio.com
Profile: WKAI-FM is a commercial station owned by Prestige Communications. The format of the station is hot adult contemporary. WKAI-FM broadcasts to the Macomb, IL area at 100.1 FM.
FM RADIO STATION

WKAK-FM 46441
Owner: Cumulus Media Inc.
Editorial: 1104 W Broad Ave, Albany, Georgia 31707-4340 **Tel:** 1 229 888-5000.
Web site: http://www.kcountry104.com
Profile: WKAK-FM is a commercial station owned by Cumulus Media Inc. The format of the station is contemporary country music. WKAK-FM broadcasts to the Albany, GA area at 104.5 FM.
FM RADIO STATION

WKAM-AM 38884
Owner: I.B. Communications
Editorial: 930 E Lincoln Ave, Goshen, Indiana 46528-3504 **Tel:** 1 574 533-3330.
Email: nzepedav13@hotmail.com
Web site: http://lamejor1460am.com
Profile: WKAM-AM is a commercial station owned by I.B. Communications. The format of the station is regional Mexican music. WKAM-AM broadcasts to the South Bend, IN area at 1460 AM.
AM RADIO STATION

WKAN-AM 36797
Owner: Staradio Corp.
Editorial: 70 Meadowview Ctr, Ste 400, Kankakee, Illinois 60901 **Tel:** 1 815 935-9555.
Email: wkannews@staradio.com
Web site: http://www.wkan.com
Profile: WKAN-AM is a commercial station owned by Staradio Corp. The format of the station is news and talk. WKAN-AM broadcasts to the Chicago area at 1320 AM.
AM RADIO STATION

WKAT-AM 35430
Owner: Salem Media Group, Inc.
Editorial: 2828 W Flagler St, Miami, Florida 33135-1337 **Tel:** 1 305 503-1340.
Web site: http://1360wkat.com
Profile: WKAT-AM is a commercial station owned by Salem Media Group, Inc. The format of the station is Spanish Christian/Talk. WKAT-AM broadcasts to the Miami area at 1360 AM.
AM RADIO STATION

WKAV-AM 35431
Owner: Monticello Media LLC
Editorial: 1150 Pepsi Pl Ste 300, Charlottesville, Virginia 22901-2890 **Tel:** 1 434 978-4408.
Profile: WKAV-AM is a commercial station owned by Monticello Media LLC. The format of the station is classic country. WKAV-AM broadcasts to the Charlottesville, VA area at 1400 AM.
AM RADIO STATION

WKAX-AM 35432
Owner: Pilati Investments Corporation
Editorial: 113 Washington Ave NW, Russellville, Alabama 35653-2244 **Tel:** 1 256 332-6103.
Web site: http://www.wkaxam.com/
Profile: WKAX-AM is a commercial station owned by Pilati Investments Corporation. The format of the station is Regional Mexican. WKAX-AM broadcasts to the Russellville, AL area at 1500 AM.
AM RADIO STATION

WKAY-FM 71702
Owner: Galesburg Broadcasting Co.
Editorial: 154 E Simmons St, Galesburg, Illinois 61401 **Tel:** 1 309 342-5131.
Email: kfm@1053kfm.com
Web site: http://www.1053kfm.com
Profile: WKAY-FM is a commercial station owned by Galesburg Broadcasting Co. The format of the station is adult contemporary. WKAY-FM broadcasts to the Galesburg, IL area at 105.3 FM.
FM RADIO STATION

WKAZ-AM 445499
Owner: West Virginia Radio Corp.
Editorial: 1111 Virginia St E, Charleston, West Virginia 25301-2406 **Tel:** 1 304 342-8131.
Profile: WKAZ-AM is a commercial station owned by West Virginia Radio Corp. The format of the station is oldies. The station broadcasts to the Charleston, WV area at 680 AM.
AM RADIO STATION

WKAZ-FM 43250
Owner: West Virginia Radio Corp.
Editorial: 1111 Virginia St E, Charleston, West Virginia 25301-2406 **Tel:** 1 304 342-8131.
Web site: http://www.tailgate1073.com
Profile: WKAZ-FM is a commercial station owned by the West Virginia Radio Corp. The format of the station is variety hits. WKAZ-FM broadcasts to Charleston, WV and surrounding communities at 107.3 FM.
FM RADIO STATION

WKBA-AM 35433
Owner: Moran (David)
Editorial: 2043 10th St NE, Roanoke, Virginia 24012-5309 **Tel:** 1 540 343-5597.
Email: wkba@cox.net
Web site: http://www.theministrystations.com/
Profile: WKBA-AM is a commercial station owned by David Moran. The format of the station is religious and gospel. WKBA-AM broadcasts to the Roanoke, VA area at 1550 AM.
AM RADIO STATION

WKBB-FM 45950
Owner: TeleSouth Communications Inc.
Editorial: 201 Academy Rd Ste 4, Starkville, Mississippi 39759-4161 **Tel:** 1 662 494-1450.
Web site: http://www.supertalkms.com
Profile: WKBB-FM is a commercial station owned by TeleSouth Communications Inc. The format of the station is talk. WKBB-FM broadcasts in the Starkville, MS area at 100.9 FM.
FM RADIO STATION

WKBC-AM 38512
Owner: Wilkes Broadcasting
Editorial: 400 C St, North Wilkesboro, North Carolina 28659-4326 **Tel:** 1 336 667-2221.
Profile: WKBC-AM is a commercial station owned by Wilkes Broadcasting. The format of the station is classic country. WKBC-AM broadcasts to the Greensboro-Winston Salem, NC area at 800 AM.
AM RADIO STATION

WKBC-FM 45880
Owner: Wilkes Broadcasting
Editorial: 400 C St, North Wilkesboro, North Carolina 28659-4326 **Tel:** 1 336 667-2221.
Email: myhitsongs@gmail.com
Profile: WKBC-FM is a commercial station owned by Wilkes Broadcasting. The format of the station is hot adult contemporary. WKBC-FM broadcasts to the North Wilkesboro, NC area at 97.3 FM.
FM RADIO STATION

WKBE-FM 43754
Owner: Pamal Broadcasting Ltd.
Editorial: 89 Everts Ave, Queensbury, New York 12804-2040 **Tel:** 1 518 793-7733.
Web site: http://www.thepointontheweb.com/
Profile: WKBE-FM is a commercial station owned by Pamal Broadcasting Ltd. The format of the station is

CHR. WKBE-FM broadcasts to the Glens Falls, NY area at 107.1 FM.
FM RADIO STATION

WKBH-AM
414124
Owner: Starboard Media Foundation Inc.
Editorial: 1496 Bellevue St Ste 202, Green Bay, Wisconsin 54311-4205 **Tel:** 1 920 884-1460.
Email: info@relevantradio.com
Web site: http://www.relevantradio.com
Profile: WKBH-AM is a non-commercial station owned by Starboard Media Foundation Inc. The format of the station is religious. WKBH-AM broadcasts to the Onalaska, WI area at 1570 AM.
AM RADIO STATION

WKBH-FM
41934
Owner: Mississippi Valley Broadcasters LLC
Editorial: 1407 2nd Ave N, Onalaska, Wisconsin 54650-9166 **Tel:** 1 608 782-8335.
Email: news@lacrosseradiogroup.net
Web site: http://www.classicrock1001.com
Profile: WKBH-FM is a commercial station owned by Mississippi Valley Broadcasters LLC. The format of the station is classic rock. WKBH-FM broadcasts to the Onalaska, WI area at 100.1 FM.
FM RADIO STATION

WKBI-AM
38695
Owner: Allegheny Mountain Network
Editorial: 14902 Boot Jack Rd, Ridgway, Pennsylvania 15853-6128 **Tel:** 1 814 834-2821.
Email: info@wkbiradio.com
Web site: http://www.wkbiradio.com/
Profile: WKBI-AM is a commercial station owned by Allegheny Mountain Network. The format of the station is oldies music. WKBI-AM broadcasts to the Saint Marys, PA area at 93.9 FM.
AM RADIO STATION

WKBI-FM
46048
Owner: Allegheny Mountain Network
Editorial: 137 Melody Rd, Saint Marys, Pennsylvania 15857-2607 **Tel:** 1 814 834-2821.
Email: info@wkbiradio.com
Web site: http://www.wkbiradio.com
Profile: WKBI-FM is a commercial station owned by Allegheny Mountain Network. The format of the station is hot adult contemporary music. WKBI-FM broadcasts to the Saint Marys, PA area at 93.9 FM.
FM RADIO STATION

WKBK-AM
38684
Owner: Saga Communications
Editorial: 69 Stanhope Ave, Keene, New Hampshire 03431-1577 **Tel:** 1 603 352-9230.
Web site: http://wkbkradio.com
Profile: WKBK-AM is a commercial station owned by Saga Communications. The format of the station is news and talk. WKBK-AM broadcasts to the Boston area at 1290 AM.
AM RADIO STATION

WKBL-AM
37004
Owner: Covington Broadcasting Inc.
Editorial: 101 Wkbl Dr, Covington, Tennessee 38019-1581 **Tel:** 1 901 476-7129.
Web site: http://wkbl1250.com/
Profile: WKBL-AM is commercial station owned by Covington Broadcasting Inc. The format of the station is oldies. WKBL-AM broadcasts to the Covington, TN area at 1250 AM.
AM RADIO STATION

WKBM-AM
36574
Owner: Starboard Media Foundation Inc.
Editorial: 145 S Northwest Hwy, Park Ridge, Illinois 60068-4228 **Tel:** 1 224 805-6868.
Email: info@relevantradio.com
Web site: http://www.relevantradio.com
Profile: WKBM-AM is a non-commercial station owned by Starboard Media Foundation Inc. The format of the station is Catholic talk programming. WKBM-AM broadcasts to the Plano, IL area at 930 AM.
AM RADIO STATION

WKBN-AM
37960
Owner: iHeartMedia Inc.
Editorial: 7461 South Ave, Youngstown, Ohio 44512-5789 **Tel:** 1 330 965-0057.
Web site: http://www.570wkbn.com
Profile: WKBN-AM is a commercial station owned by iHeartMedia Inc. The format of the station is news, sports, and talk. WKBN-AM broadcasts to the Youngstown, OH area at 570 AM.
AM RADIO STATION

WKBO-AM
36119
Owner: One Heart Ministries
Editorial: 600 Corporate Cir, Harrisburg, Pennsylvania 17110 **Tel:** 1 717 697-6463.
Email: oneheartministries@verizon.net
Web site: http://www.oneheartministries.com
Profile: WKBO-AM is a commercial station owned by One Heart Ministries. The format of the station is contemporary Christian. WKBO-AM broadcasts to the greater Harrisburg, PA area at 1230 AM.
AM RADIO STATION

WKBQ-FM
44240
Owner: Covington Broadcasting Inc.
Editorial: 101 Wkbl Dr, Covington, Tennessee 38019-1581 **Tel:** 1 901 476-7129.
Web site: http://www.us51country.com
Profile: WKBQ-FM is a commercial station owned by Covington Broadcasting Inc. The format of the station

is contemporary and classic country. WKBQ-FM broadcasts to the Covington, TN area at 93.5 FM.
FM RADIO STATION

WKBU-FM
40653
Owner: Entercom Communications Corp.
Editorial: 400 Poydras St Ste 800, New Orleans, Louisiana 70130-3789 **Tel:** 1 504 593-6376.
Web site: http://www.bayou957.com
Profile: WKBU-FM is a commercial station owned by Entercom Communications Corp. The format of the station is classic rock music. WKBU-FM broadcasts to the New Orleans m area at 95.7 FM.
FM RADIO STATION

WKBV-AM
37961
Owner: Whitewater Broadcasting
Editorial: 2301 W Main St, Richmond, Indiana 47374-3829 **Tel:** 1 765 962-6533.
Email: psa@g1013.com
Web site: http://g1013.com
Profile: WKBV-AM is a commercial station owned by Whitewater Broadcasting. The format of the station is news, talk and sports. WKBV-AM broadcasts to the Richmond, IN area at 1490 AM.
AM RADIO STATION

WKBX-FM
41335
Owner: Neal Ardman
Editorial: 111 N Grove Blvd, Kingsland, Georgia 31548-6347 **Tel:** 1 912 729-6000.
Web site: http://kbay1063.com
Profile: WKBX-FM is a commercial station owned by Neal Ardman. The format of the station is contemporary country music. WKBX-FM broadcasts to the Jacksonville, FL area at 106.3 FM.
FM RADIO STATION

WKBY-AM
35434
Owner: Lawrence G. Campbell Se.
Editorial: 12932 US Highway 29, Chatham, Virginia 24531 **Tel:** 1 434 432-8108.
Email: wkby@gamewood.net
Profile: WKBY-AM is a commercial station owned by Lawrence G. Campbell Se.. The format of the station is gospel. WKBY-AM broadcasts to the Chatham, VA area at 1080 AM.
AM RADIO STATION

WKBZ-AM
38067
Owner: iHeartMedia Inc.
Editorial: 3565 Green St, Norton Shores, Michigan 49444-3875 **Tel:** 1 231 733-2600.
Web site: http://www.newstalk1090.com
Profile: WKBZ-AM is a commercial station owned by iHeartMedia Inc. The format of the station is news and talk. WKBZ-AM broadcasts to the Muskegon, MI area at 1090 AM.
AM RADIO STATION

WKCA-FM
40112
Owner: Gateway Radio Works Inc.
Editorial: 123 E 1St St, Morehead, Kentucky 40351-1701 **Tel:** 1 606 674-2266.
Profile: WKCA-FM is a commercial station owned by Gateway Radio Works Inc. The format of the station is country. WKCA-FM broadcasts to the Georgetown, OH area at 97.7 FM.
FM RADIO STATION

WKCB-AM
37963
Owner: Hindman Broadcasting
Editorial: 1517 Highway 550 W, Hindman, Kentucky 41822 **Tel:** 1 606 785-3129.
Email: killerb@wkcb.com
Web site: http://www.wkcb.com
Profile: WKCB-AM is a commercial station owned by Hindman Broadcasting. The format of the station is Christian talk and music. WKCB-AM broadcasts in the Hindman, KY area at 1340 AM.
AM RADIO STATION

WKCB-FM
45281
Owner: Hindman Broadcasting
Editorial: 1570 Highway 550 W, Hindman, Kentucky 41822-8830 **Tel:** 1 606 785-3129.
Web site: http://www.wkcb.com
Profile: WKCB-FM is a commercial station owned by Hindman Broadcasting. The format of the station is classic rock and adult contemporary music. WKCB-FM broadcasts to the Lexington, KY area at 107.1 FM.
FM RADIO STATION

WKCC-FM
517869
Owner: Chicago Public Media
Editorial: 100 College Dr, Kankakee, Illinois 60901-6505
Email: wkcc@kcc.edu
Web site: http://www.wkccradio.org
Profile: WKCC-FM is a non-commercial station owned by Chicago Public Media . The format of the station is news and talk. WKCC-FM broadcasts to the Kankakee, IL area at 91.1 FM.
FM RADIO STATION

WKCH-FM
43624
Owner: NRG Media LLC
Editorial: W6355 Eastern Ave, Fort Atkinson, Wisconsin 53538-9335 **Tel:** 1 920 563-9329.
Profile: WKCH-FM is a commercial station owned by NRG Media LLC. The format of the station is oldies. WKCH-FM broadcasts to the Milwaukee area at 106.5 FM.
FM RADIO STATION

WKCI-AM
36870
Owner: iHeartMedia Inc.
Editorial: 207 University Blvd, Harrisonburg, Virginia 22801-3749 **Tel:** 1 540 434-1777.
Web site: http://wkcyam.iheart.com
Profile: WKCI-AM is a commercial station owned by iHeartMedia Inc. The format of the station is talk. WKCI-AM broadcasts to the Harrisonburg, VA area at 970 AM.
AM RADIO STATION

WKCI-FM
45282
Owner: iHeartMedia Inc.
Editorial: 495 Benham St, Hamden, Connecticut 06514-2009 **Tel:** 1 203 281-9600.
Web site: http://kc101.iheart.com
Profile: WKCI-FM is a commercial station owned by iHeartMedia Inc. The format of the station is Top 40/CHR music. WCKI-FM broadcasts to the Hartford-New Haven, CT area at 101.3 FM.
FM RADIO STATION

WKCL-FM
41604
Owner: Holy Spirit Bible College Chapel of the Holy Spirit
Editorial: 526 College Park Rd, Ladson, South Carolina 29456-3328 **Tel:** 1 843 553-8740.
Web site: http://www.915wkcl.com
Profile: WKCL-FM is a non-commercial station owned by Holy Spirit Bible College Chapel of the Holy Spirit. The format of the station is religious programming. WKCL-FM broadcasts to the Charleston, SC area at 91.5 FM.
FM RADIO STATION

WKCM-AM
38986
Owner: Cromwell Group Inc.(The)
Editorial: 1115 Tamarack Rd, Owensboro, Kentucky 42301-6984 **Tel:** 1 270 683-5200.
Email: kyproduction@cromwellradio.com
Web site: http://www.owensbororadio.com
Profile: WKCM-AM is a commercial station owned by the Cromwell Group Inc. The format of the station is country music. WKCM-AM broadcasts to the Owensboro, KY area at 1160 AM.
AM RADIO STATION

WKCN-FM
42043
Owner: PMB Broadcasting, LLC
Editorial: 1820 Wynnton Rd, Columbus, Georgia 31906-2930 **Tel:** 1 706 327-1217.
Web site: http://www.ilovekissin.com
Profile: WKCN-FM is a commercial station owned by PMB Broadcasting, LLC. The format of the station is country. WKCN-FM broadcasts to the Columbus, GA area at 99.3 FM.
FM RADIO STATION

WKCO-FM
40421
Owner: Kenyon College
Editorial: Kenyon College, Farr Hall Basement, Gambier, Ohio 43022 **Tel:** 1 740 427-5412.
Email: wkco@kenyon.edu
Web site: http://wkco.kenyon.edu
Profile: WKCO-FM is a non-commercial station owned by Kenyon College. The format of the station is college variety. WKCO-FM broadcasts to the Gambier, OH area at 91.9 FM.
FM RADIO STATION

WKCQ-FM
45283
Owner: MacDonald Broadcasting Co.
Editorial: 2000 Whittier St, Saginaw, Michigan 48601-2271 **Tel:** 1 989 752-8161.
Web site: http://www.98fmkcq.com
Profile: WKCQ-FM is a commercial station owned by MacDonald Broadcasting Co. The format for the station is country. WKCQ-FM broadcasts to the Flint, MI area at 98.1 FM.
FM RADIO STATION

WKCT-AM
37964
Owner: Daily News Broadcasting Co.
Editorial: 804 College St, Bowling Green, Kentucky 42101-2133 **Tel:** 1 270 781-2121.
Web site: http://www.93wkct.com
Profile: WKCT-AM is a commercial station owned by Daily News Broadcasting Co. The format for the station is news and talk. WKCT-AM broadcasts to the Bowling Green, KY area at 930 AM.
AM RADIO STATION

WKCU-AM
37965
Owner: TeleSouth Communications Inc.
Editorial: 1608 S Johns St, Corinth, Mississippi 38834-6547 **Tel:** 1 662 286-8451.
Profile: WKCU-AM is a commercial station owned by TeleSouth Communications Inc. The format of the station is sports. WKCU-AM broadcasts to the Corinth, MS area at a frequency of 1350 AM.
AM RADIO STATION

WKCW-AM
35435
Owner: Metro Radio, Inc
Editorial: 9540 Godwin Dr, Manassas, Virginia 20110-4165 **Tel:** 1 703 330-8224.
Web site: http://www.1420wkcw.com
Profile: WKCW-AM is a commercial station owned by Metro Radio, Inc. The format of the station is adult hits. WKCW-AM broadcasts to the Washington, D.C. area at 1420 AM.
AM RADIO STATION

WKCY-AM
38580
Owner: iHeartMedia Inc.
Editorial: 207 University Blvd, Harrisonburg, Virginia 22801-3749 **Tel:** 1 540 434-1777.

Web site: http://wkcyam.iheart.com
Profile: WKCY-AM is a commercial station owned by iHeartMedia Inc. The format for the station is talk. WACL-FM broadcasts to the Harrisonburg, VA area at 1300 AM.
AM RADIO STATION

WKCY-FM
45939
Owner: iHeartMedia Inc.
Editorial: 207 University Blvd, Harrisonburg, Virginia 22801-3749 **Tel:** 1 540 434-1777.
Web site: http://kcycountry.iheart.com
Profile: WKCY-FM is a commercial station owned by iHeartMedia Inc. The format for the station is country. WKCY-FM broadcasts to the Harrisonburg, VA area at 104.3 FM.
FM RADIO STATION

WKDB-FM
41853
Owner: The Voice Radio Network
Editorial: 20200 Dupont Blvd, Georgetown, Delaware 19947-3105 **Tel:** 1 302 856-2567.
Web site: http://www.max953.com
Profile: WKDB-FM is a commercial station owned by The Voice Radio Network. The format of the station is Spanish Top 40/CHR. WKDB-FM broadcasts to the Salisbury, MD area at 95.3 FM.
FM RADIO STATION

WKDD-FM
45284
Owner: iHeartMedia Inc.
Editorial: 7755 Freedom Ave NW, North Canton, Ohio 44720-6905 **Tel:** 1 330 836-4700.
Web site: http://www.wkdd.com
Profile: WKDD-FM is a commercial station owned by iHeartMedia Inc. The format of the station is hot adult contemporary music. WKKD-FM broadcasts to the North Canton, OH area at 98.1 FM.
FM RADIO STATION

WKDE-AM
37966
Owner: D.J. Broadcasting Corp.
Editorial: 200 Frazier Rd, Altavista, Virginia 24517 **Tel:** 1 434 369-5588.
Email: info@kdcountry.com
Web site: http://www.kdcountry.com
Profile: WKDE-AM is a commercial station owned by D.J. Broadcasting Corp. The format of the station is talk. WKDE-AM broadcasts to the Altavista, VA area at 1000 AM.
AM RADIO STATION

WKDE-FM
45290
Owner: D.J. Broadcasting Corp.
Editorial: 200 Frazier Rd, Altavista, Virginia 24517-1021 **Tel:** 1 434 369-5588.
Email: info@kdcountry.com
Web site: http://www.kdcountry.com
Profile: WKDE-FM is a commercial station owned by D.J. Broadcasting Corp. The format of the station is country. WKDE-FM broadcasts to the Altavista, VA area at 105.5 FM.
FM RADIO STATION

WKDF-FM
42889
Owner: Cumulus Media Inc.
Editorial: 10 Music Cir E, Nashville, Tennessee 37203-4338 **Tel:** 1 615 321-1067.
Web site: http://www.103wkdf.com
Profile: WKDF-FM is a commercial station owned by Cumulus Media Inc. The format of the station is country music. WKDF-FM broadcasts to the Nashville, TN area at 103.3 FM.
FM RADIO STATION

WKDI-AM
35837
Owner: Positive Radio Group
Editorial: 24580 Station Rd, Denton, Maryland 21629-1943 **Tel:** 1 410 479-2288.
Email: wkdi@verizon.net
Web site: http://www.wkdiam840.com
Profile: WKDI-AM is a commercial station owned by Positive Radio Group. The format of the station is Christian news and talk. WKDI-AM is licensed to Denton, MD and broadcasts to the Delmarva Peninsula area at 840 AM.
AM RADIO STATION

WKDJ-FM
41333
Owner: Radio Cleveland Inc.
Editorial: 911 S Davis Ave, Cleveland, Mississippi 38732-3941 **Tel:** 1 662 843-4091.
Profile: WKDJ-FM is a commercial station owned by Radio Cleveland Inc. The format of the station is hot adult contemporary music. WKDJ-FM broadcasts to the Cleveland, MS, area at 96.5 FM. Send press releases via mail.
FM RADIO STATION

WKDK-AM
35437
Owner: Newberry Broadcasting Co.
Editorial: 3000 Hazel St, Newberry, South Carolina 29108-2140 **Tel:** 1 803 276-2957.
Email: contactus@wkdk.com
Web site: http://www.wkdk.com
Profile: WKDK-AM is a commercial station owned by Newberry Broadcasting Co. The format of the station is adult contemporary and country. WKDK-AM broadcasts to the Newberry, SC area at 1240 AM.
AM RADIO STATION

WKDL-AM
519236
Owner: Metro Radio, Inc.
Editorial: 9540 Godwin Dr, Manassas, Virginia 20110 **Tel:** 1 703 330-8244.
Email: metroradioinc@msn.com
Web site: http://www.metroradioinc.com

rofile: WKDL-AM is a commercial station owned by letro Radio, Inc. The format of the station is talk. VKDL-AM broadcasts to the Washington, D.C. area t 1250 AM.
M RADIO STATION

WKDM-AM 35393
wner: Multicultural Radio Broadcasting Inc.
ditorial: 27 William St #11F, New York, New York 0005-2701 Tel: 1 212 431-4300.
Veb site: http://www.wkdm1380am.com/
rofile: WKDM-AM is a commercial station owned by lulticultural Radio Broadcasting Inc. The format of he station is variety. The station's programming is roadcast in Chinese Mandarin Monday through riday and in Spanish on Saturdays and Sundays. VJDM-AM broadcasts to the New York City area at 380 AM.
M RADIO STATION

WKDO-AM 37967
wner: Creal Broadcasting, Inc.
ditorial: 988 Highway 1649, Liberty, Kentucky 42539 el: 1 606 787-7331.
rofile: WKDO-AM is a commercial station owned by real Broadcasting, Inc.. The format of the station is lassic country. WKDO-AM broadcasts in the Liberty, Y area at 1560 AM.
M RADIO STATION

WKDO-FM 45285
wner: Wesley(Carlos)
ditorial: 988 Dry Ridge Rd., Liberty, Kentucky 42539 el: 1 606 787-7331.
rofile: WKDO-FM is a commercial station owned by arlos Wesley. The format for the station is country. VKDO-FM broadcasts to the Lexington, KY area at 8.7 FM.
M RADIO STATION

WKDP-AM 38359
wner: Eubanks Broadcasting Inc.
ditorial: 821 Adams Rd, Corbin, Kentucky 40701-708 Tel: 1 606 528-6617.
mail: news@wkdp.com
Veb site: http://kdcountry99.5.com
rofile: WKDP-AM is a commercial station owned by ubanks Broadcasting Inc. The format of the station s news and talk programming. WKDP-AM roadcasts to the Corbin, KY area at 1330 AM.
M RADIO STATION

WKDP-FM 45720
wner: Eubanks Broadcasting Inc.
ditorial: 821 Adams Rd, Corbin, Kentucky 40701-708 Tel: 1 606 528-6617.
Veb site: http://www.kdcountry995.com
rofile: WKDP-FM is a commercial station owned by ubanks Broadcasting Inc. The format for the station s country. WKDP-FM broadcasts to the Corbin, KY rea at 99.5 FM. Submit PSAs via their website.
M RADIO STATION

WKDQ-FM 40425
wner: Townsquare Media, LLC
ditorial: 117 SE 5th St, Evansville, Indiana 47708-639 Tel: 1 877 437-5995.
Veb site: http://www.wkdq.com
rofile: WKDQ-FM is a commercial station owned by ownsquare Media, LLC. The format of the station is ountry music. WKDQ-FM broadcasts to the vansville, IN area at 99.5 FM.
M RADIO STATION

WKDR-AM 601046
wner: Lunderville(Barry)
ditorial: 195 Main St, Lancaster, New Hampshire 3584-3035 Tel: 1 603 788-3636.
mail: kiss102@together.net
rofile: WKDR-AM is a commercial station owned by arry Lunderville. The format of the station is classic ock. WKDR-AM broadcasts to the Berlin, NH area at 490 AM.
M RADIO STATION

WKDV-AM 36272
wner: Metro Radio, Inc.
ditorial: 9540 Godwin Dr, Manassas, Virginia 20110 el: 1 703 330-8022.
Veb site: http://www.metroradioinc.com
rofile: WKDV-AM is commercial station owned by letro Radio, Inc. The format of the station is egional Mexican. WKDV-AM broadcasts to the lanassas, VA area at 1460 AM.
M RADIO STATION

WKDW-AM 37968
wner: iHeartMedia Inc.
ditorial: 207 University Blvd, Harrisonburg, Virginia 2801-3749 Tel: 1 540 434-1777.
Veb site: http://wkdwam.iheart.com
rofile: WKDW-AM is a commercial station owned y iHeartMedia Inc. The format for the station is lassic country. WKDW-AM broadcasts to the arrisonburg, VA area at 900 AM.
M RADIO STATION

WKDX-AM 62428
wner: McLaurin Group(The)
ditorial: 310 5th St, Hamlet, North Carolina 28345 el: 1 910 582-1997.
mail: wkdxthespirit@yahoo.com
Veb site: http://www.wkdx.net
rofile: WKDX-AM is a commercial station owned by he McLaurin Group. The format of the station is eligious and gospel music. WKDX-AM broadcasts to he Hamlet, NC area at 1250 AM.
M RADIO STATION

WKDZ-AM 37686
Owner: Mann, Beth A.
Editorial: 19 Wooldridge Rd, Cadiz, Kentucky 42211-6734 **Tel:** 1 270 522-3232.
Email: wkdz@wkdzradio.com
Web site: http://www.oldies1480.com
Profile: WKDZ-AM is a commercial station owned by Beth A. Mann. The format of the station is oldies. WKDZ-AM broadcasts to the Cadiz, KY area at 1110 AM.
AM RADIO STATION

WKDZ-FM 45064
Owner: Mann, Beth. A
Editorial: 19 Wooldridge Rd, Cadiz, Kentucky 42211-6734 **Tel:** 1 270 522-3232.
Email: wkdz@wkdzradio.com
Web site: http://www.wkdzradio.com
Profile: WKDZ-FM is a commercial station owned by Beth A. Mann. The format of the station is country music. WKDZ-FM broadcasts to the Cadiz, KY area at 106.5 FM.
FM RADIO STATION

WKEA-FM 44375
Owner: KEA Radio Inc.
Editorial: 19784 John T Reid Pkwy, Scottsboro, Alabama 35768-7909 **Tel:** 1 256 259-2341.
Web site: http://www.wkeafm.com
Profile: WKEA-FM is a commercial station owned by KEA Radio Inc. The format of the station is comtemporary country. WKEA-FM broadcasts to the Scottsboro, AL area at 98.3 FM.
FM RADIO STATION

WKEB-FM 45226
Owner: WIGM Inc.
Editorial: 630 S 8th St, Medford, Wisconsin 54451-2017 **Tel:** 1 715 748-2566.
Email: k99@k99wigm.com
Web site: http://www.k99wigm.com
Profile: WKEB-FM is a commercial station owned by WIGM Inc. The format of the station is classic hits music. WKEB-FM broadcasts to the Medford, WI area at 99.3 FM.
FM RADIO STATION

WKEE-FM 45286
Owner: iHeartMedia Inc.
Editorial: 134 4th Ave, Huntington, West Virginia 25701-1220 **Tel:** 1 304 525-7788.
Email: 100keefm@iheartmedia.com
Web site: http://www.wkee.com
Profile: WKEE-FM is a commercial station owned by iHeartMedia Inc. The format of the station is Top 40/ CHR. WKEE-FM broadcasts to Huntington, WV and surrounding communities at 100.5 FM.
FM RADIO STATION

WKEI-AM 37970
Owner: Virden Broadcasting Corporation
Editorial: 133 E Division St, Kewanee, Illinois 61443-3410 **Tel:** 1 309 853-4471.
Email: news@regionaldailynews.com
Web site: http://regionaldailynews.com
Profile: WKEI-AM is a commercial station owned by Virden Broadcasting Corp. The format of the station is news and talk. WKEI-AM broadcasts to the Kewanee, IL area at 1450 AM.
AM RADIO STATION

WKEK-FM 680983
Owner: Cook County Community Radio
Editorial: 1712 W Highway 61, Grand Marais, Minnesota 55604-7507 **Tel:** 1 218 387-1070.
Web site: http://www.wtip.org
FM RADIO STATION

WKES-FM 42238
Owner: Moody Bible Institute
Editorial: 5800 100th Way N, Saint Petersburg, Florida 33708-3447 **Tel:** 1 727 391-9994.
Web site: https://www.moodyradioflorida.fm
Profile: WKES-FM is a non-commercial station owned by Moody Bible Institute. The format of the station is contemporary Christian music and religious talk. WKES-FM broadcasts to the St. Petersburg, FL area at 91.1 FM. Press releases can be sent by fax.
FM RADIO STATION

WKEU-AM 36956
Owner: WLT & Associates
Editorial: 1000 Memorial Dr, Griffin, Georgia 30223 **Tel:** 1 770 227-5507.
Email: wkeu@aol.com
Web site: http://www.wkeuradio.com
Profile: WKEU-AM is a commercial station owned by WLT & Associates. The format of the station is news, sports and oldies music. WKEU-AM broadcasts to the Griffin, GA area at 1450 AM.
AM RADIO STATION

WKEU-FM 64047
Owner: WLT & Associates
Editorial: 1000 Memorial Dr, Griffin, Georgia 30223-4446 **Tel:** 1 770 227-5507.
Email: info@wkeuradio.com
Web site: http://www.wkeuradio.com
Profile: WKEU-FM is a non-commercial station owned by WLT & Associates. The format of the station is news, talk, and sports. WKEU-FM broadcasts to the Atlanta area at 88.9 FM.
FM RADIO STATION

WKEW-AM 35440
Owner: Truth Broadcasting
Editorial: 4405 Providence Ln, Winston Salem, North Carolina 27106-3226 **Tel:** 1 336 759-0363.
Web site: http://www.1340thelight.com
Profile: WKEW (1400 AM) is a radio station broadcasting a Gospel music format. Licensed to Greensboro, North Carolina, USA, the station is currently owned by Truth Broadcasting Corporation.
AM RADIO STATION

WKEX-AM 35441
Owner: Positive Radio Group
Editorial: 145 Jackson St NE, Blacksburg, Virginia 24060 **Tel:** 1 540 951-9791.
Email: wkexam@yahoo.com
Web site: http://www.espnblacksburg.com
Profile: WKEX-AM is a commercial station owned by Positive Radio Group. The format of the station is sports. WKEX-AM broadcasts to the Blacksburg, VA area at 1430 AM.
AM RADIO STATION

WKEY-AM 37972
Owner: Todd P. Robinson, Inc.
Editorial: 508 W Oak St, Covington, Virginia 24426-1942 **Tel:** 1 540 962-1133.
Email: newssportwvjt@gmail.com
Web site: http://alleghanyhighlandsbigcountry.com
Profile: WKEY-AM is a commercial station owned by Todd P. Robinson, Inc. The format of the station is countryl. WKEY-AM broadcasts to the Covington, VA area at 1340 AM.
AM RADIO STATION

WKEY-FM 41316
Owner: The Great Marathon Radio Company
Tel: 1 305 743-5563.
Email: info@themixofoldies.com
Web site: http://www.themixofoldies.com
Profile: WKEY-FM is a commercial station owned by The Great Marathon Radio Company. The format of the station is oldies. WKEY-FM broadcasts to the Key West, FL area at 93.7 FM.
FM RADIO STATION

WKEZ-AM 38564
Owner: Alpha Media
Editorial: 900 Bluefield Ave, Bluefield, West Virginia 24701-2744 **Tel:** 1 304 327-7114.
Web site: http://www.roosterclassiccountry.com
Profile: WKEZ-AM is a commercial station owned by Alpha Media. The format of the station is classic country. WKEZ-AM broadcasts to the Bluefield, WV area at 1240 AM.
AM RADIO STATION

WKEZ-FM 235041
Owner: The Great Marathon Radio Company
Tel: 1 305 743-5563.
Email: info@themixofoldies.com
Web site: http://www.themixofoldies.com
Profile: WKEZ-FM is a commercial station owned by The Great Marathon Radio Company. The format of the station is oldies. WKEZ-FM broadcasts to the Florida Keys, FL area at 96.9 FM.
FM RADIO STATION

WKFB-AM 35198
Owner: Broadcast Communications Inc.
Editorial: 1918 Lincoln Hwy, North Versailles, Pennsylvania 15137 **Tel:** 1 412 823-7000.
Profile: WKFB-AM is a commercial station owned by Broadcast Communications Inc. The format of the station is classic hits music and talk. WKFB-AM broadcasts to the North Versailles, PA area at 770 AM.
AM RADIO STATION

WKFC-FM 545305
Owner: Choice Radio Corp.
Editorial: 1106 S Main St, London, Kentucky 40741-2108 **Tel:** 1 606 878-9532.
Web site: http://www.wkfcfm.com
Profile: WKFC-FM is a commercial station owned by Choice Radio Corp. The format for the station is variety including classic country, contemporary Christian, classic rock and oldies. WKFC-FM broadcasts to the London, KY area at 101.9 FM.
FM RADIO STATION

WKFI-AM 37973
Owner: Town and Country Broadcasting, Inc.
Editorial: 23 E 2nd St, Xenia, Ohio 45385-3415 **Tel:** 1 937 374-3636.
Email: myclassiccountry@myclassiccountry.com
Web site: http://www.wkfi.com
Profile: WKFI-AM is a commercial station owned by Town and Country Broadcasting, Inc. The format of the station is classic country. WKFI-AM broadcasts to the Wilmington, OH area at 1090 AM.
AM RADIO STATION

WKFM-FM 44125
Owner: Elyria-Lorain Broadcasting
Editorial: 10327 US Highway 250 N, Milan, Ohio 44846 **Tel:** 1 419 609-5961.
Email: k96@wkfm.com
Web site: http://www.wkfm.com
Profile: WKFM-FM is a commercial station owned by Elyria-Lorain Broadcasting. The format of the station is country music. WKFM-FM broadcasts to the Milan, OH area at 96.1 FM.
FM RADIO STATION

WKFN-AM 39497
Owner: Saga Communications
Editorial: 1640 Old Russellville Pike, Clarksville, Tennessee 37043-1709 **Tel:** 1 931 648-7720.
Profile: WKFN-AM is a commercial station owned by Saga Communications (dba 5 Star Radio Group). The format of the station is sports. WKFN-AM broadcasts to the Nashville, TN area at 540 AM.
AM RADIO STATION

WKFR-FM 45287
Owner: Townsquare Media, LLC
Editorial: 4154 Jennings Dr, Kalamazoo, Michigan 49048-1087 **Tel:** 1 269 344-0111.
Email: vip.support@townsquaremedia.com
Web site: http://www.wkfr.com
Profile: WKFR-FM is a commercial station owned by Townsquare Media, LLC. The format of the station is Top 40/CHR. WKFR-FM broadcasts to the Kalamazoo, MI area at 103.3 FM.
FM RADIO STATION

WKFS-FM 41382
Owner: iHeartMedia Inc.
Editorial: 8044 Montgomery Rd Ste 650, Cincinnati, Ohio 45236-2959 **Tel:** 1 513 686-8300.
Web site: http://www.kiss107.com
Profile: WKFS-FM is a commercial station owned by iHeartMedia Inc. The format of the station is Top 40/ CHR. WKFS-FM broadcasts to the Cincinnati area at 107.1 FM.
FM RADIO STATION

WKFX-FM 44538
Owner: T K C Inc.
Editorial: 1859 21st Ave, Rice Lake, Wisconsin 54868-9502 **Tel:** 1 715 736-0991.
Email: news@fox99.com
Web site: http://www.fox99.com
Profile: WKFX-FM is a commercial station owned by T K C Inc. The format of the station is classic hits. The station broadcasts to the Rice Lake, WI area at 99.1 FM.
FM RADIO STATION

WKGA-FM 41918
Owner: Lake Broadcasting, Inc.
Editorial: 1051 Tallapoosa St, Alexander City, Alabama 35010-1552 **Tel:** 1 256 234-6464.
Email: wkgaproduction@gmail.com
Web site: http://www.wkga975.com
Profile: WKGA-FM is a commercial station owned by Lake Broadcasting, Inc. The format of the station is country. WKGA-FM broadcasts to the Alexander City, AL area at 97.5 FM.
FM RADIO STATION

WKGB-FM 40964
Owner: iHeart Media Inc.
Editorial: 320 N Jensen Rd, Vestal, New York 13850-2111 **Tel:** 1 607 584-5800.
Web site: http://www.925kgb.com
Profile: WKGB-FM is a commercial station owned by iHeart Media Inc. The format of the station is rock alternative. WKGB-FM broadcasts to the Binghamton, NY area at 92.5 FM.
FM RADIO STATION

WKGC-AM 38447
Owner: Gulf Coast Community College
Editorial: 5230 W Highway 98, Panama City, Florida 32401 **Tel:** 1 850 873-3500.
Web site: http://www.wkgc.org
Profile: WKGC-AM is a non-commercial station owned by Gulf Coast Community College. The format of the station is classical, news and talk. WKGC-AM broadcasts to the Panama City, FL area at 1480 AM.
AM RADIO STATION

WKGC-FM 45816
Owner: Gulf Coast Community College
Editorial: 5230 W Highway 98, Panama City, Florida 32401-1041 **Tel:** 1 850 873-3500.
Web site: http://www.wkgc.org
Profile: WKGC-FM is a non-commercial station owned by Gulf Coast Community College. The target audience is listeners, ages 18 to 64. The format of the station is music, talk and news. The station broadcasts to the Panama City, FL area at 1480 AM and on 90.7 FM.
FM RADIO STATION

WKGL-FM 44445
Owner: Cumulus Media Inc.
Editorial: 3901 Brendenwood Rd, Rockford, Illinois 61107 **Tel:** 1 815 399-2233.
Web site: http://www.967theeagle.net
Profile: WKGL-FM is a commercial station owned by Cumulus Media Inc. The format for the station is classic rock. WKGL-FM broadcasts to the Rockford, IL area at 96.7 FM.
FM RADIO STATION

WKGM-AM 35442
Owner: Positive Radio Group
Editorial: 13379 Great Spring Rd, Smithfield, Virginia 23430 **Tel:** 1 757 357-9546.
Email: wkgm940@yahoo.com
Profile: WKGM-AM is a commercial station owned by Positive Radio Group. The format of the station is religious. WKGM-AM broadcasts to the Smithfield, VA area at 940 AM.
AM RADIO STATION

United States of America

WKGN-AM 36133
Owner: Norsan Group
Editorial: 1017 Cox St, Knoxville, Tennessee 37919
Tel: 1 865 546-7900.
AM RADIO STATION

WKGR-FM 41787
Owner: iHeartMedia Inc.
Editorial: 3071 Continental Dr, West Palm Beach, Florida 33407-3274 **Tel:** 1 561 616-6600.
Web site: http://www.gater.com
Profile: WKGR-FM is a commercial station owned by iHeartMedia Inc. The format of the station is classic rock music. WKGR-FM broadcasts to the West Palm Beach, FL area at 98.7 FM.
FM RADIO STATION

WKGS-FM 41898
Owner: iHeartMedia Inc.
Editorial: 100 Chestnut St Fl 17, Rochester, New York 14604-2419 **Tel:** 1 585 454-4884.
Web site: http://www.kiss1067.com/main.html
Profile: WKGS-FM is a commercial station owned by iHeartMedia Inc. The format of the station is Top 40. WKGS-FM broadcasts to the Rochester, NY area at a frequency of 106.7 FM.
FM RADIO STATION

WKGX-AM 35443
Owner: Foothills Radio Group, LLC
Editorial: 827 Fairview Dr SW, Lenoir, North Carolina 28645-6023 **Tel:** 1 828 758-1033.
Web site: http://www.gofoothills.com
Profile: WKGX-AM is commercial station owned by Foothills Radio Group, LLC. The format of the station is classic hits. WKGX-AM broadcasts to the Lenoir, NC area at 1080 AM.
AM RADIO STATION

WKHB-AM 36744
Owner: Broadcast Communications Inc.
Editorial: 1918 Lincoln Hwy, North Versailles, Pennsylvania 15137 **Tel:** 1 412 823-7000.
Profile: WKHB-AM is a commercial station owned by Broadcast Communications Inc. The format of the station is oldies music and talk. WKHB-AM broadcasts to the North Versailles, PA area at 620 AM.
AM RADIO STATION

WKHF-FM 739428
Owner: Todd Robinson
Editorial: 828 Main St Ste 1601, Lynchburg, Virginia 24504-1540 **Tel:** 1 434 455-4321.
Email: 937KHF@gmail.com
Web site: http://www.lynchburgradiogroup.com
Profile: WKHF-FM is a commercial station owned by Todd Robinson. The format of the station is Hot AC. WKHF-FM broadcasts to the Lynchburg, VA area at a frequency of 93.7 FM.
FM RADIO STATION

WKHG-FM 46075
Owner: Heritage Media of Kentucky Inc
Editorial: 2160 Brandenburg Rd, Leitchfield, Kentucky 42754-7503 **Tel:** 1 270 259-5692.
Email: info@k105.com
Web site: http://www.k105.com
FM RADIO STATION

WKHI-FM 40993
Owner: Adams Radio Group
Editorial: 20200 Dupont Blvd, Georgetown, Delaware 19947-3105 **Tel:** 1 302 856-2567.
Web site: http://www.bigclassicrock.com
Profile: WKHI-FM is a commercial station owned by Adams Radio Group. The format of the station is classic rock music. WKHI-FM broadcasts to the Georgetown, DE area at 107.7 FM.
FM RADIO STATION

WKHJ-FM 41911
Owner: Radiowerks, Inc.
Editorial: 407 Lothian St, Mountain Lake Park, Maryland 21550-2909 **Tel:** 1 301 334-4272.
Email: office@wkhj.com
Web site: http://www.wkhj.com
Profile: WKHJ-FM is a commercial station owned by Radiowerks, Inc. The format of the station is adult contemporary. WKHJ-FM broadcasts to the Mountain Lake Park, MD area at 104.5 FM.
FM RADIO STATION

WKHK-FM 41618
Owner: Summit Media Broadcasting LLC
Editorial: 812 Moorefield Park Dr, Ste 300, Richmond, Virginia 23236 **Tel:** 1 804 330-5700.
Web site: http://k95country.com
Profile: WKHK-FM is a commercial station owned by Summit Media Broadcasting LLC. The format of the station is country. WKHK-FM broadcasts to the Richmond, VA area at 95.3 FM.
FM RADIO STATION

WKHM-AM 39208
Owner: Jackson Radio Works Inc.
Editorial: 1700 Glenshire Dr, Jackson, Michigan 49201 **Tel:** 1 517 787-9546.
Email: news@wkhm.com
Web site: http://www.wkhm.com
Profile: WKHM-AM is a commercial station owned by Jackson Radio Works Inc. The format of the station is news and talk. WKHM-AM broadcasts to the Jackson, MI area at 970 AM.
AM RADIO STATION

WKHM-FM 46562
Owner: Jackson Radio Works Inc.
Editorial: 1700 Glenshire Dr, Jackson, Michigan 49201-8302 **Tel:** 1 517 787-9546.
Email: news@wkhm.com
Web site: http://www.k1053.com
Profile: WKHM-FM is a commercial station owned by Jackson Radio Works Inc. The format of the station is adult contemporary. WKHM-FM broadcasts to the Jackson, MI area at 105.3 FM.
FM RADIO STATION

WKHQ-FM 45289
Owner: MacDonald Garber Broadcasting Inc.
Editorial: 2095 S US Highway 131, Petoskey, Michigan 49770-9216 **Tel:** 1 231 347-8713.
Email: programming@106khq.com
Web site: http://www.106khq.com
Profile: WKHQ-FM is a commercial station owned by MacDonald Garber Broadcasting Inc. The format of the station is Top 40/CHR. WKHQ-FM broadcasts to the Petoskey, MI area at 105.9 FM.
FM RADIO STATION

WKHT-FM 46370
Owner: E.W. Scripps Co.
Editorial: 1533 Amherst Rd, Knoxville, Tennessee 37909-1204 **Tel:** 1 865 693-1020.
Web site: http://www.hot1045.net
Profile: WKHT-FM is a commercial station owned by E.W. Scripps Co. The format of the station is urban contemporary. WKHT-FM broadcasts to the Knoxville, TN area at 104.5 FM.
FM RADIO STATION

WKHX-FM 45291
Owner: Cumulus Media Inc.
Editorial: 780 Johnson Ferry Rd Fl 5, Atlanta, Georgia 30342-1434 **Tel:** 1 404 497-4701.
Web site: http://www.wkhx.com
Profile: WKHX-FM is a commercial station owned by Cumulus Media Inc. The format of the station is contemporary country. WKHX-FM broadcasts to the Atlanta area at 101.5 FM.
FM RADIO STATION

WKHY-FM 40430
Owner: WASK Inc.
Editorial: 3575 McCarty Ln, Lafayette, Indiana 47905-4985 **Tel:** 1 765 448-1566.
Web site: http://www.wkhy.com
Profile: WKHY-FM is a commercial station owned by Neuhoff Communications. The format of the station is rock music. WKHY-FM broadcasts to the Lafayette, IN area at 93.5 FM. Known as "Lafayette's Rock Station," its target audience is adults, ages 18 to 54.
FM RADIO STATION

WKHZ-AM 36864
Owner: Epcot Broadcasting
Editorial: 306 Port St, Easton, Maryland 21601-4101
Tel: 1 410 723-9100.
Profile: WKHZ-AM is a commercial station owned by Epcot Broadcasting. The format for the station is contemporary playing a variety of music from the 1980s. WKHZ-AM broadcasts to the Ocean City, MD area at 1590 AM.
AM RADIO STATION

WKIB-FM 43570
Owner: W. Russell Withers
Editorial: 901 S Kingshighway St, Cape Girardeau, Missouri 63703 **Tel:** 1 573 339-7000.
Email: news@withersradio.net
Web site: http://www.mix965.net
Profile: WKIB-FM is a commercial station owned by W. Russell Withers. The format of the station is Top 40/CHR. WKIB-FM broadcasts to the Cape Girardeau, MO area at 96.5 FM.
FM RADIO STATION

WKIC-FM 41342
Owner: Leslie County Broadcasting
Editorial: 516 Main St, Hazard, Kentucky 41701-1775
Tel: 1 606 436-9898.
Email: wsgs@windstream.net
Web site: http://www.wsgs.com
Profile: WKIC-FM is a commercial station owned by Leslie County Broadcasting. The format for the station is mix of adult contemporary and adult hits. WKIC-FM broadcasts to the Lexington, KY area at 97.9 FM.
FM RADIO STATION

WKID-FM 41355
Owner: Dial Broadcasting Inc.
Editorial: 315 Ferry St Ste A, Vevay, Indiana 47043-1189 **Tel:** 1 812 427-9590.
Web site: http://froggy959.com
Profile: WKID-FM is a commercial station owned by Dial Broadcasting Inc. The format of the station is country music. WKID-FM broadcasts to the Vevay, IN area at 95.9 FM.
FM RADIO STATION

WKII-AM 39140
Owner: iHeartMedia Inc.
Editorial: 24100 Tiseo Blvd Unit 10, Port Charlotte, Florida 33980-5223 **Tel:** 1 941 206-1188.
Web site: http://www.kixclassics.com
Profile: WKII-AM is a commercial station owned by iHeartMedia Inc. The format of the station is Classic Country. The station airs locally on 1070 AM.
AM RADIO STATION

WKIK-AM 36579
Owner: Somar Communications Inc.
Editorial: 28095 Three Notch Rd, Ste 2B, Mechanicsville, Maryland 20659 **Tel:** 1 301 870-5550.
Email: wkikfm@aol.com
Web site: http://www.country1029wkik.com
Profile: WKIK-AM is a commercial station owned by Somar Communications Inc. The format of the station is country music. WKIK-AM broadcasts to the Mechanicsville, MD area at 1560 AM.
AM RADIO STATION

WKIK-FM 73956
Owner: Somar Communications Inc.
Editorial: 28095 Three Notch Rd, Ste 2B, Mechanicsville, Maryland 20659 **Tel:** 1 301 870-5550.
Email: wkikfm@aol.com
Web site: http://www.country1029wkik.com
Profile: WKIK-FM is a commercial station owned by Somar Communications Inc. The format of the station is contemporary country. WKIK-FM broadcasts to the Mechanicsville, MD area at 102.9 FM.
FM RADIO STATION

WKIM-FM 77112
Owner: Cumulus Media Inc.
Editorial: 5629 Murray Ave, Memphis, Tennessee 38119-3831 **Tel:** 1 901 682-1106.
Web site: http://www.989thevibe.com
Profile: WKIM-FM is a commercial station owned by Cumulus Media Inc. The format of the station is classic hip hop. WKIM-FM broadcasts to the Memphis, TN area at 98.9 FM.
FM RADIO STATION

WKIO-FM 40707
Owner: D.W.S. Inc.
Editorial: 2301 S Neil St, Champaign, Illinois 61820-7507 **Tel:** 1 217 351-5300.
Email: mitm@1079wkio.com
Web site: http://www.1079wkio.com
Profile: WKIO-FM is a commercial station owned by D.W.S. Inc. The format of the station is rock and classic hits. WKIO-FM broadcasts to the Champaign, IL area at 107.9 FM.
FM RADIO STATION

WKIP-AM 38544
Owner: iHeartMedia Inc.
Editorial: 20 Tucker Dr, Poughkeepsie, New York 12603-1644 **Tel:** 1 845 471-2300.
Web site: http://www.newstalkwkip.com
Profile: WKIP-AM is a commercial station owned by iHeartMedia Inc. The format of the station is talk. WKIP-AM broadcasts to the Poughkeepsie, NY area at 1450 AM.
AM RADIO STATION

WKIS-FM 45308
Owner: CBS Radio
Editorial: 194 NW 187th St, Miami, Florida 33169-4050 **Tel:** 1 305 654-1700.
Web site: http://www.wkis.com
Profile: WKIS-FM is a commercial station owned by the CBS Radio. The format of the station is country music. WKIS-FM broadcasts to the Miami area at 99.9 FM.
FM RADIO STATION

WKIT-FM 43043
Owner: Zone Corporation(The)
Editorial: 861 Broadway, Bangor, Maine 04401-2916
Tel: 1 207 990-2800.
Email: wkit@zoneradio.com
Web site: http://www.zoneradio.com/wkit
Profile: WKIT-FM is a commercial station owned by The Zone Corporation. The format of the station is classic rock. WKIT-FM broadcasts to the Bangor, ME area at 100.3 FM.
FM RADIO STATION

WKIX-FM 44260
Owner: Curtis Media Group
Editorial: 4601 Six Forks Rd Ste 520, Raleigh, North Carolina 27609-5210 **Tel:** 1 919 875-9100.
Web site: http://www.kix1029.com
Profile: WKIX-FM is a commercial station owned by Curtis Media Group. The format of the station is classic hits. The station broadcasts locally to the Raleigh-Durham, NC area at a frequency of 102.9 FM.
FM RADIO STATION

WKIZ-AM 36715
Owner: Seattle Streaming Radio LLC
Editorial: 5016 5th Ave, Key West, Florida 33040
Tel: 1 305 947-8979.
Email: gerencia@almavision.tv
Web site: http://www.almavision.tv
Profile: WKIZ-AM is a commercial station owned by Seattle Streaming Radio LLC. The format of the station is Hispanic religious. WKIZ-AM broadcasts to the Miami and Ft. Lauderdale, FL areas at 1500 AM.
AM RADIO STATION

WKJA-FM 834379
Owner: Penfold Communications
Editorial: 5617 Diamond Oaks Dr S Ste 200, Fort Worth, Texas 76117-2804 **Tel:** 1 817 831-9130.
Web site: http://www.kdkr.org
Profile: WKJA-FM is a non-commercial station owned by Penfold Communications, Inc. The format of the station is Christian teaching. WKJA-FM broadcasts to the Brunswick, OH area at a frequency of 89.3 FM.
FM RADIO STATION

WKJC-FM 45293
Owner: Carroll Broadcasting Co.
Editorial: 523 Meadow Rd, Tawas City, Michigan 48763-9189 **Tel:** 1 989 362-3417.
Email: wkjc@wkjc.com
Web site: http://www.wkjc.com
Profile: WKJC-FM is a commercial station owned by Carroll Broadcasting Co. The format of the station is contemporary country music. WKJC-FM broadcasts to the Flint, MI area at 104.7 FM.
FM RADIO STATION

WKJG-AM 38904
Owner: Pathfinder Communications Corporation
Editorial: 2915 Maples Rd, Fort Wayne, Indiana 46816
Tel: 1 260 447-5511.
Email: news@wowo.com
Web site: http://www.espnfortwayne.com
Profile: WKJC-AM is a commercial station owned by Pathfinder Communications Corporation, a division of Federated Media. The format of the station is sports. WKJC-AM broadcasts to the Fort Wayne, IN area at 1380 AM.
AM RADIO STATION

WKJK-AM 36618
Owner: iHeartMedia Inc.
Editorial: 4000 Radio Dr Ste 1, Louisville, Kentucky 40218-4568
Email: psa@cclouisville.com
Web site: http://www.talkradio1080.com
Profile: WKJK-AM is a commercial station owned by iHeartMedia Inc. The format of the station is talk. WKJK-AM broadcasts to the Louisville, KY area at 1080 AM.
AM RADIO STATION

WKJQ-AM 38588
Owner: Clenney Broadcasting Corp.
Editorial: 109 Iron Hill Rd, Parsons, Tennessee 38363
Tel: 1 731 847-3011.
Profile: WKJQ-AM is a commercial station owned by Clenney Broadcasting Corp. The format of the station is gospel. WKJQ-AM broadcasts to the Parsons, TN area at 1550 AM.
AM RADIO STATION

WKJQ-FM 45944
Owner: Clenney Broadcasting Corp.
Editorial: 109 Iron Hill Rd, Parsons, Tennessee 38363-2901 **Tel:** 1 731 847-3011.
Web site: http://www.q973fm.com
Profile: WKJQ-FM is a commercial station owned by Clenney Broadcasting Corp. The format of the station is contemporary country music. WKJQ-FM broadcasts to the Parsons, TN area at 97.3 FM.
FM RADIO STATION

WKJR-AM 37087
Owner: Ruben's Productions, Inc.
Editorial: 129 N Garrard St, Rantoul, Illinois 61866
Tel: 1 217 893-1460.
Email: mrgto@quepasanetwork.com
Web site: http://www.quepasanetwork.com
Profile: WKJR-AM is a commercial station owned by Ruben's Productions, Inc. The format of the station is Hispanic. WKJR-AM broadcasts to the Rantoul, IL area on 1460 AM.
AM RADIO STATION

WKJS-FM 41583
Owner: Urban One, Inc.
Editorial: 2809 Emerywood Pkwy Ste 300, Richmond, Virginia 23294-3743 **Tel:** 1 804 672-9299.
Web site: http://kissrichmond.com/
Profile: WKJS-FM is a commercial station owned by Urban One, Inc. The format of the station is urban adult contemporary. WKJS-FM broadcasts to the Richmond, VA area at 105.7 FM.
FM RADIO STATION

WKJT-FM 43262
Owner: Premier Broadcasting, Inc
Editorial: 206 S Willow St, Effingham, Illinois 62401-3637 **Tel:** 1 217 347-5518.
Email: info@thexradio.com
Web site: http://www.kjcountry.com
Profile: WKJT-FM is a commercial station owned by Premier Broadcasting, Inc. The format of the station is contemporary country music. WKJT-FM broadcasts to the Effingham, IL area at 102.3 FM.
FM RADIO STATION

WKJV-AM 35620
Owner: International Baptist Outreach Mission Inc.
Editorial: 70 Adams Hill Rd, Asheville, North Carolina 28806-3841 **Tel:** 1 828 252-1380.
Email: wkjvradio@cleaninter.net
Web site: http://www.wkjv.com
Profile: WKJV-AM is a commercial station owned by International Baptist Outreach Mission Inc. The format of the station is gospel. WKJV-AM broadcasts to the Asheville, NC area at 1380 AM.
AM RADIO STATION

WKJW-AM 37802
Owner: International Baptist Outreach Mission Inc.
Editorial: 70 Adams Hill Rd, Asheville, North Carolina 28806-3841 **Tel:** 1 828 252-1380.
Email: wkjvradio@cleaninter.net
Web site: http://www.wkjv.com
Profile: WKJW-AM is a commercial station owned by International Baptist Outreach Mission Inc. The format of the station is religious talk. WKJW-AM broadcasts to the Asheville, NC area at 1010 AM.
AM RADIO STATION

WKJX-FM 41309
Owner: East Carolina Radio Group
Editorial: 911 Pasonage St Ext, Elizabeth City, North Carolina 27909 **Tel:** 1 252 335-4379.
Email: psa@ecri.net
Web site: http://www.967theblock.com
Profile: WKJX-FM is a commercial station owned by East Carolina Radio Group. The format of the station is urban contemporary and R & B. WKJX-FM broadcasts to the Elizabeth City, NC area at 96.7 FM.
FM RADIO STATION

WKJY-FM 45955
Owner: Connoisseur Media
Editorial: 234 Airport Plaza Blvd, Farmingdale, New York 11735-3917 **Tel:** 1 631 770-4200.
Email: webmaster@liradiogroup.com
Web site: http://www.kjoy.com
Profile: WKJY-FM is a commercial station owned by Connoisseur Media. The format of the station is adult contemporary. WKJY-FM broadcasts to the Garden City, NY area 98.3 FM.
FM RADIO STATION

WKJZ-FM 42568
Owner: Carroll Broadcasting Co.
Editorial: 523 Meadow Rd, Tawas City, Michigan 48763-9189 **Tel:** 1 989 362-3417.
Email: hitsfm@speednetllc.com
Web site: http://www.hitsfm.net
Profile: WKJZ-FM is a commercial station owned by Carroll Broadcasting Co. The format of the station is classic hits. WKJZ-FM broadcasts to the Flint, MI area at 94.9 FM.
FM RADIO STATION

WKKB-FM 42938
Owner: Red Wolf Broadcasting
Editorial: 75 Oxford St Ste 302, Providence, Rhode Island 02905-4722 **Tel:** 1 401 781-1535.
Email: info@latina1003fm.com
Web site: http://www.latina1003fm.com
Profile: WKKB-FM is a commercial station owned by Red Wolf Broadcasting. The format of the station is Hispanic. WKKB-FM broadcasts to the Providence, RI area at 100.3 FM.
FM RADIO STATION

WKKC-FM 475423
Owner: City Colleges of Chicago
Editorial: 6301 S Halsted St, Chicago, Illinois 60621-2709 **Tel:** 1 773 602-5544.
Email: 893wkkc@gmail.com
Web site: http://www.wkkc.fm
Profile: WKKC-FM is a non-commercial college station owned by The City Colleges of Chicago. The format of the station is urban contemporary. The station airs in the Chicago area at 89.3 FM.
FM RADIO STATION

WKKF-FM 42156
Owner: iHeartMedia Inc.
Editorial: 1203 Troy Schenectady Rd, Latham, New York 12110-1046 **Tel:** 1 518 452-4800.
Web site: http://www.kiss1023.com/main.html
Profile: WKKF-FM is a commercial station owned by iHeartMedia Inc. The format of the station is Top 40. WKKF-FM broadcasts to the Latham, NY area on 102.3 FM.
FM RADIO STATION

WKKG-FM 45296
Owner: White River Broadcasting Co., Inc.
Editorial: 3212 Washington St, Columbus, Indiana 47203-1505 **Tel:** 1 812 372-4448.
Email: studio@wkkg.com
Web site: http://www.wkkg.com
Profile: WKKG-FM is a commercial station owned by White River Broadcasting Co., Inc. The format of the station is country music. WKKG-FM broadcasts to the Columbus, IN area at 101.5 FM.
FM RADIO STATION

WKKI-FM 40434
Owner: Schmitmeyer (Paul)
Editorial: 126 W Fayette St, Celina, Ohio 45822-2108 **Tel:** 1 419 586-7715.
Email: k94@bright.net
Web site: http://www.k943.com
Profile: WKKI-FM is a commercial station owned by Paul Schmitmeyer. The format of the station is rock music. WKKI-FM broadcasts to the Dayton, OH area at 94.3 FM.
FM RADIO STATION

WKKJ-FM 44007
Owner: iHeartMedia Inc.
Editorial: 45 W Main St, Chillicothe, Ohio 45601-3104 **Tel:** 1 740 773-3000.
Email: newsroom@wkkj.com
Web site: http://wkkj.iheart.com/
Profile: WKKJ-FM is a commercial station owned by iHeartMedia Inc. The format of the station is country music. WKKJ-FM broadcasts in the Columbus, OH area at 94.3 FM.
FM RADIO STATION

WKKL-FM 43667
Owner: Cape Cod Community College
Editorial: 2240 Iyannough Rd, West Barnstable, Massachusetts 02668-1532 **Tel:** 1 508 375-4030.
Web site: http://www.capecod.edu/web/wkkl-90.7
Profile: WKKL is a non-commercial station owned by Cape Cod Community College. The format of the station is variety. WKKL-FM broadcasts to Cape Cod, MA area at 90.7 FM.
FM RADIO STATION

WKKN-FM 44181
Owner: Great Eastern Radio, LLC
Editorial: 99 Main St, Keene, New Hampshire 03431-3770 **Tel:** 1 603 283-1090.
Email: thepeak@greateasternradio.com
Web site: http://www.thepeakradio.com
Profile: WKKN-FM is a commercial station owned by Great Eastern Radio, LLC. The format of the station is AAA. WKKN-FM broadcasts to the Lebanon, NH area at 101.7 FM.
FM RADIO STATION

WKKO-FM 46141
Owner: Cumulus Media Inc.
Editorial: 3225 Arlington Ave, Toledo, Ohio 43614-2427 **Tel:** 1 419 725-5700.
Email: k100@k100country.com
Web site: http://www.k100country.com
Profile: WKKO-FM is a commercial station owned by Cumulus Media Inc. The format of the station is contemporary country. WKKO-FM broadcasts to the Toledo, OH area at 99.9 FM.
FM RADIO STATION

WKKP-AM 35786
Owner: Earnhart Broadcast Co. Inc.
Editorial: 940 Brownlee Rd, Jackson, Georgia 30233-2418 **Tel:** 1 770 775-3151.
Profile: WKKP-AM is a commercial station owned by the Earnhart Broadcast Co. Inc. The format of the station is classic country. WKKP-AM broadcasts to the Jackson, GA area at 1410 AM.
AM RADIO STATION

WKKQ-FM 45650
Owner: Barbourville Community Broadcasting
Editorial: 222 Daniel Boone Dr, Barbourville, Kentucky 40906-1104 **Tel:** 1 606 546-4128.
Email: production@wkkqfm.com
Web site: http://www.wkkqfm.com
FM RADIO STATION

WKKR-FM 45297
Owner: iHeartMedia Inc.
Editorial: 915 Veterans Pkwy, Opelika, Alabama 36801-3367 **Tel:** 1 334 745-4656.
Web site: http://kickerfm.iheart.com
Profile: WKKR-FM is a commercial station owned by iHeartMedia Inc. The format of the station is contemporary country music. WKKR-FM broadcasts to the Opelika, AL area at 97.7 FM.
FM RADIO STATION

WKKS-AM 37981
Owner: Brown Communications Inc.
Editorial: 1074 Fairlane Dr, Vanceburg, Kentucky 41179-5403 **Tel:** 1 606 796-3031.
Profile: WKKS-AM is a commercial station owned by Brown Communications Inc. The format of the station is country music. WKKS-AM broadcasts to the Vanceburg, KY area at 1570 AM.
AM RADIO STATION

WKKS-FM 45298
Owner: Brown Communications Inc.
Editorial: 1074 Fairlane Dr, Vanceburg, Kentucky 41179-5403 **Tel:** 1 606 796-3031.
Profile: WKKS-FM is a commercial station owned by Brown Communications Inc. The format of the station is country music and gospel. WKKS-FM broadcasts to the Vanceburg, KY area at 104.9 FM.
FM RADIO STATION

WKKT-FM 40499
Owner: iHeartMedia Inc.
Editorial: 801 Woodrdg Ctr Dr, Charlotte, North Carolina 28217-1908 **Tel:** 1 704 714-9444.
Web site: http://www.969thekat.com/main.html
Profile: WKKT-FM is a commercial station owned by iHeartMedia Inc. The format of the station is country music. WKKT-FM broadcasts to the Charlotte, NC area at 96.9 FM.
FM RADIO STATION

WKKV-FM 42932
Owner: iHeartMedia Inc.
Editorial: 12100 W Howard Ave, Greenfield, Wisconsin 53228-1851 **Tel:** 1 414 545-8900.
Web site: http://www.v100.com
Profile: WKKV-FM is a commercial station owned by iHeartMedia Inc. The format of the station is urban contemporary music. WKKV-FM broadcasts in the greater Milwaukee area at 100.7 FM.
FM RADIO STATION

WKKW-FM 43055
Owner: West Virginia Radio Corp.
Editorial: 1251 Earl L Core Rd, Morgantown, West Virginia 26505-5881 **Tel:** 1 304 296-0029.
Web site: http://www.wkkwfm.com
Profile: WKKW-FM is a commercial station owned by West Virginia Radio Corp. The format of the station is classic country. WKKW-FM broadcasts in the Morgantown, WV area at 97.9 FM.
FM RADIO STATION

WKKX-AM 489663
Owner: RCK 1 Group, LLC
Editorial: 1201 Main St, Wheeling, West Virginia 26003-2850 **Tel:** 1 304 214-1610.
Email: eric@wkkx.com
Web site: http://wkkx.com
Profile: WKKX-AM is a commercial station owned by RCK 1 Group, LLC. The format of the station is news and talk. WKKX-AM broadcasts to the Wheeling, WV area at 1600 AM.
AM RADIO STATION

WKKY-FM 42693
Owner: Music Express Broadcasting
Editorial: 95 W Main St, Geneva, Ohio 44041-1225 **Tel:** 1 440 466-9559.
Email: wkky@wkky.com
Web site: http://www.wkky.com
Profile: WKKY-FM is a commercial station owned by Music Express Broadcasting. The format of the station is contemporary country. WKKY-FM broadcasts to the Geneva, OH are at 104.7 FM.
FM RADIO STATION

WKKZ-FM 40435
Owner: Kirby Broadcasting
Editorial: 1006 Martin Luther King Jr Dr, Dublin, Georgia 31021-5065 **Tel:** 1 478 272-9270.
Email: prod927@bellsouth.net
Web site: http://www.wkkz927.com
Profile: WKKZ-FM is a commercial station owned by Kirby Broadcasting Co. The format of the station is adult contemporary music. WKKZ-FM broadcasts to the Dublin, GA area at 92.7 FM.
FM RADIO STATION

WKLA-AM 37982
Owner: Synergy Media, Inc.
Editorial: 5399 W Wallace Ln, Ludington, Michigan 49431-2439 **Tel:** 1 231 843-0941.
Profile: WKLA-FM is a commercial station owned by Synergy Media, Inc. The format of the station is oldies.The station airs locally at 1450 AM.
AM RADIO STATION

WKLA-FM 45299
Owner: Synergy Media, Inc.
Editorial: 5399 W Wallace Ln, Ludington, Michigan 49431-2439 **Tel:** 1 231 843-0941.
Profile: WKLA-FM is a commercial station owned by Synergy Media, Inc. The format of the station is hot adult contemporary. WKLA-FM broadcasts to the Ludington, MI area at 106.3 FM.
FM RADIO STATION

WKLB-AM 35445
Owner: Sonshine Broadcasting Company, LTD
Tel: 1 225 768-8300.
Email: info@jsm.org
Web site: http://www.sonlifetv.com
Profile: WKLB-AM is a commercial station owned by Sonshine Broadcasting Company, LTD. The format of the station is contemporary Christian. WKLB-AM broadcasts to the Manchester, KY area at 1290 AM.
AM RADIO STATION

WKLB-FM 42089
Owner: Beasley Broadcast Group
Editorial: 55 William T Morrissey Blvd, Dorchester, Massachusetts 02125-3315 **Tel:** 1 617 822-6200.
Web site: http://country1025.com
Profile: WKLB-FM is a commercial station owned by Beasley Broadcast Group. The format of the station is contemporary country music. WKLB-FM broadcasts to the Boston area at 102.5 FM.
FM RADIO STATION

WKLC-FM 45300
Owner: WKLC Inc.
Editorial: 100 Kanawha Ter, Saint Albans, West Virginia 25177-2771 **Tel:** 1 304 722-3308.
Email: traffic@wklc.com
Web site: http://www.wklc.com
Profile: WKLC-FM is a commercial station owned by WKLC Inc. The format of the station is modern rock music. WKLC-FM broadcasts to Saint Albans, WV and surrounding communities at 105.1 FM.
FM RADIO STATION

WKLG-FM 41417
Owner: WKLG Inc.
Editorial: 1460 Jefferson Dr Apt F, Homestead, Florida 33034-2681 **Tel:** 1 305 246-1123.
Email: cs@wklginc.com
Web site: http://www.wklginc.com
Profile: WKLG-FM is a commercial station owned by WKLG Inc. The format of the station is adult alternative. WKLG-FM broadcasts to the Florida City, FL area at 102.1 FM.
FM RADIO STATION

WKLH-FM 41000
Owner: Saga Communications
Editorial: 5407 W McKinley Ave, Milwaukee, Wisconsin 53208-2540 **Tel:** 1 414 978-9000.
Web site: http://wklh.com
Profile: WKLH-FM is a commercial station owned by Saga Communications. The format of the station is classic rock. WKLH-FM broadcasts to the Milwaukee area at 96.5 FM.
FM RADIO STATION

WKLI-FM 45302
Owner: Albany Broadcasting Co.
Editorial: 6 Johnson Rd, Latham, New York 12110-5641 **Tel:** 1 518 786-6600.
Web site: http://www.1009thecat.com
Profile: WKLI-FM is a commercial station owned by Albany Broadcasting Co. The format of the station is contemporary country. WKLI-FM broadcasts to the Latham, NY area at 100.9 FM.
FM RADIO STATION

WKLJ-AM 37721
Owner: Sparta-Tomah Broadcasting Co.
Editorial: 113 W Oak St, Sparta, Wisconsin 54656 **Tel:** 1 608 269-3100.
Web site: http://www.espnlacrosse.com
Profile: WKLJ-AM is a commercial station owned by Sparta-Tomah Broadcasting Co. The format of the station is sports. WKLJ-AM broadcasts to the Sparta, WI area at 1290 AM.
AM RADIO STATION

WKLK-AM 39236
Owner: Quarnstrom Media Group LLC
Editorial: 1104 Cloquet Ave, Cloquet, Minnesota 55720 **Tel:** 1 218 879-4534.
Email: wklk@aol.com
Profile: WKLK-AM is a commercial station owned by Quarnstrom Media Group LLC. The format of the station is adult standards music. WKLK-AM broadcasts to the Cloquet, MN area at 1230 AM.
AM RADIO STATION

WKLK-FM 46603
Owner: Quarnstrom Media Group LLC
Editorial: 1104 Cloquet Ave, Cloquet, Minnesota 55720 **Tel:** 1 218 879-4534.
Email: wklk@aol.com
Profile: WKLK-FM is a commercial station owned by Quarnstrom Media Group LLC. The format of the station is classic rock music. WKLK-FM broadcasts in the Cloquet, MN area at 96.5 FM.
FM RADIO STATION

WKLL-FM 41152
Owner: Galaxy Communications LP
Editorial: 39 Kellogg Rd, New Hartford, New York 13413-2849 **Tel:** 1 315 797-1330.
Web site: http://www.krock.com
Profile: WKLL-FM is a commercial station owned by Galaxy Communications LP. The format of the station is rock music. WKLL-FM broadcasts to the Utica, NY area at 94.9 FM.
FM RADIO STATION

WKLM-FM 41943
Owner: WKLM Radio Inc.
Editorial: 7409 Private Road 341, Millersburg, Ohio 44654-9270 **Tel:** 1 330 674-1953.
Profile: WKLM-FM is a commercial station owned by WKLM Radio Inc. The format of the station is country music. WKLM-FM broadcasts to the Millersburg, OH area at 95.3 FM.
FM RADIO STATION

WKLP-AM 37984
Owner: West Virgina Radio Corporation of the Alleganies
Editorial: 15 Industrial Blvd E, Cumberland, Maryland 21502-4106 **Tel:** 1 301 759-1005.
Profile: WKLP-AM is a commercial station owned by West Virgina Radio Corporation of the Alleganies. The format of the station is sports. WKLP-AM broadcasts to the Cumberland, MD area at 1390 AM.
AM RADIO STATION

WKLQ-AM 38674
Owner: Cumulus Media Inc.
Editorial: 3375 Merriam St Ste 201, Muskegon, Michigan 49444-3173 **Tel:** 1 231 830-0176.
Web site: http://bigtalk1490.com
Profile: WKQL-AM is a commercial station owned by Cumulus Media Inc. The format of the station is news/talk. WKQL-AM broadcasts to the Muskegon, MI area at 1490 AM.
AM RADIO STATION

WKLR-FM 44485
Owner: Summit Media Broadcasting LLC
Editorial: 812 Moorefield Park Dr, Ste 300, Richmond, Virginia 23236 **Tel:** 1 804 330-5700.
Web site: http://www.classicrock965.com
Profile: WKLR-FM is a commercial station owned by Summit Media Broadcasting LLC. The format of the station is classic rock. WKLR-FM broadcasts to the Richmond, VA area at 96.5 FM.
FM RADIO STATION

WKLS-FM 42431
Owner: Williams Communications Inc.
Editorial: 801 Noble St Ste 30, Anniston, Alabama 36201-0503 **Tel:** 1 256 453-9898.
Web site: http://www.rock1059.net
Profile: WKLS-FM is a commercial station owned by Williams Communications Inc. The format of the station is rock. WKLS-FM broadcasts to the Anniston, AL area at 105.9 FM.
FM RADIO STATION

WKLT-FM 41807
Owner: Northern Broadcast Inc.
Editorial: 1020 Hastings St Ste 102, Traverse City, Michigan 49686-3457 **Tel:** 1 231 947-0003.
Web site: http://www.wklt.com
Profile: WKLT-FM is a commercial station owned by Northern Broadcast Inc. The format of the station is classic rock music. WKLT-FM broadcasts to the Traverse City, MI area at a frequency of 97.5 FM.
FM RADIO STATION

WKLV-AM 39157
Owner: Denbar Communications Inc.
Editorial: 950 Kenbridge Rd, Blackstone, Virginia 23824-3105 **Tel:** 1 434 292-4146.
Email: wbbc@bobcatcountryradio.com
Profile: WKLV-AM is a commercial station owned by Denbar Communications Inc. The format of the station is sports. WKLV-AM broadcasts to the Blackstone, VA area at 1400 AM.
AM RADIO STATION

United States of America

WKLW-FM 44522
Owner: B & G Broadcasting Inc.
Editorial: Route 321, Ste 6 Woodland Place, Paintsville, Kentucky 41240-5407 **Tel:** 1 606 789-6664.
Email: news@wklw.com
Web site: http://www.wklw.com
Profile: WKLW-FM is a commercial station owned by B&G Broadcasting Inc. The format of the station is hot adult contemporary music. WKLW-FM broadcasts to the Paintsville, KY area at 94.7 FM.
FM RADIO STATION

WKLX-FM 44424
Owner: Commonwealth Broadcasting Corp.
Editorial: 1823 McIntosh St, Ste 107, Bowling Green, Kentucky 42104 **Tel:** 1 270 846-0222.
Email: bgsamevents@yahoo.com
Web site: http://www.bowlinggreensam.com
Profile: WKLX-FM is a commercial station owned by Commonwealth Broadcasting Corp. The format of the station is adult hits. WKLX-FM broadcasts to the Bowling Green, KY area at 100.7 FM.
FM RADIO STATION

WKLY-AM 35446
Owner: WKLY Broadcasting Company
Editorial: 2235 Bowersville Highway, Hartwell, Georgia 30643 **Tel:** 1 706 376-2233.
Email: wklyradio@hartcom.net
Web site: http://www.wklyradio.com
Profile: WKLY-AM is a commercial station owned by WKLY Broadcasting Corp. The format of the station is country music and gospel. WKLY-AM broadcasts to the Hartwell, GA area at 980 AM.
AM RADIO STATION

WKLZ-FM 42011
Owner: Northern Broadcast Inc.
Editorial: 1020 Hastings St, Traverse City, Michigan 49686-3457 **Tel:** 1 231 947-0003.
Web site: http://www.wklt.com
Profile: WKLZ-FM is a commercial station owned by Northern Broadcast Inc. The format of the station is rock music. The station broadcasts in the Traverse City, MI area at 98.9 FM.
FM RADIO STATION

WKMB-AM 35447
Owner: World Harvest Communications, Inc.
Editorial: 120 W 7th St Ste 215, Plainfield, New Jersey 07060-1629 **Tel:** 1 908 822-1515.
Email: harvestproductions1070@gmail.com
Web site: http://www.enjoyharvest.com
Profile: WKMB-AM is a commercial station owned by World Harvest Communications, Inc. The format of the station is gospel music. WKMB-AM broadcasts to the Plainfield, NJ area at 1070 AM.
AM RADIO STATION

WKMC-AM 36718
Owner: Handsome Brothers Inc.
Editorial: 2513 6th Ave, Altoona, Pennsylvania 16602-2129 **Tel:** 1 814 224-7501.
Web site: http://www.1370wkmc.com
Profile: WKMC-AM is a commercial station owned by Handsome Brothers Inc. The format of the station is oldies music. WKMC-AM broadcasts to the Altoona, PA area at 1370 AM.
AM RADIO STATION

WKMG-AM 36420
Owner: Blakely(Cornell)
Editorial: 1840 Glenn Street Ext, Newberry, South Carolina 29108 **Tel:** 1 803 405-0111.
Profile: WKMG-AM is a commercial station owned by Cornell Blakely. The format of the station is oldies music. WKMG-AM broadcasts to the Newberry, SC area at 1520 AM.
AM RADIO STATION

WKMI-AM 37986
Owner: Townsquare Media, LLC
Editorial: 4154 Jennings Dr, Kalamazoo, Michigan 49048-1087 **Tel:** 1 269 344-0111.
Email: vip.support@townsquaremedia.com
Web site: http://www.wkmi.com
Profile: WKMI-AM is a commercial station owned by Townsquare Media, LLC. The format of the station is news and talk. WKMI-AM broadcasts to the Kalamazoo, MI area at 1360 AM.
AM RADIO STATION

WKMJ-FM 45658
Owner: J&J Broadcasting
Editorial: 326 Quincy St, Hancock, Michigan 49930 **Tel:** 1 906 482-3700.
Email: wmplprod@themix93.com
Web site: http://www.themix93.com
Profile: WKMJ-FM is a commercial station owned by J&J Broadcasting. The format of the station is hot adult contemporary. WKMJ-FM broadcasts to the Hancock, MI area at 93.5 FM.
FM RADIO STATION

WKMK-FM 45214
Owner: Press Communications LLC
Editorial: 2355 W Bangs Ave, Neptune, New Jersey 07753-4111 **Tel:** 1 732 774-4755.
Web site: http://thunder106.com
Profile: WKMK-FM is a commercial station owned by Press Communications LLC. The format of the station is country. WKMK-FM broadcasts to the Neptune, NJ area at 106.3 FM.
FM RADIO STATION

WKML-FM 46794
Owner: Beasley Broadcast Group
Editorial: 508 Person St, Fayetteville, North Carolina 28301-5841 **Tel:** 1 910 483-9565.
Email: country@wkml.com
Web site: http://www.wkml.com
Profile: WKML-FM is a commercial station owned by Beasley Broadcast Group. The format of the station is contemporary country music. WKML-FM broadcasts to the Fayetteville, NC area at 95.7 FM.
FM RADIO STATION

WKMM-FM 40985
Owner: Mar Pat Corporation
Editorial: 106 E Main St, Kingwood, West Virginia 26537 **Tel:** 1 304 329-0967.
Email: wkmmfm@yahoo.com
Web site: http://www.wkmmfm.com
Profile: WKMM-FM is a commercial station owned by Mar Pat Corporation. The format of the station is contemporary country music. WKMM-FM broadcasts in the Kingwood, WV area at 96.7 FM.
FM RADIO STATION

WKMO-FM 45678
Owner: Commonwealth Broadcasting Corp.
Editorial: 611 W Poplar St Ste C2, Elizabethtown, Kentucky 42701-2483 **Tel:** 1 270 763-0800.
Email: news@commonwealthbroadcasting.com
Web site: http://www.kmocountry.com
Profile: WKMO-FM is a commercial station owned by Commonwealth Broadcasting Corp. The format of the station is adult contemporary. WKMO-FM broadcasts to the Louisville, KY area at 99.3 FM.
FM RADIO STATION

WKMQ-AM 38578
Owner: iHeartMedia Inc.
Editorial: 5026 Cliff Gookin Blvd, Tupelo, Mississippi 38801-7059 **Tel:** 1 662 842-1067.
Profile: WKMQ-AM is a commercial station owned by iHeartMedia Inc. The format of the station is news and talk. WKMQ-AM broadcasts to the Tupelo, MS area at 1060 AM.
AM RADIO STATION

WKMX-FM 40440
Owner: Gulf South Communications, Inc.
Editorial: 285 N Foster St Fl 8, Dothan, Alabama 36303-4541 **Tel:** 1 334 792-0047.
Web site: http://www.wkmx.com
Profile: WKMX-FM is a commercial station owned by Gulf South Communications, Inc. The format for the station is Top 40/CHR. WKMX-FM broadcasts to the Dothan, AL area at 106.7 FM.
FM RADIO STATION

WKNA-FM 45339
Owner: Baker Family Stations
Editorial: 1 Radio Ln, Logan, Ohio 43138-8762 **Tel:** 1 740 385-2151.
Web site: http://983samfm.com
Profile: WKNA-FM is a commercial station owned by Baker Family Stations. The format of the station is adult hits. WKNA-FM broadcasts to the Hocking County, OH area at 98.3 FM.
FM RADIO STATION

WKNB-FM 235130
Owner: Radio Partners LLC
Editorial: 310 2nd Ave, Warren, Pennsylvania 16365 **Tel:** 1 814 723-1310.
Email: info@kibcoradio.com
Web site: http://www.kibcoradio.com
Profile: WKNB-FM is a commercial station owned by Radio Partners LLC. The format of the station is country music. WKNB-FM broadcasts to the Warren, PA area at 104.3 FM.
FM RADIO STATION

WKND-AM 35449
Owner: Gois Broadcasting
Editorial: 135 Burnside Ave, East Hartford, Connecticut 06108-3466 **Tel:** 1 860 524-0001.
Profile: WKND-AM is a commercial station owned by Gois Broadcasting. The format of the station is urban adult contemporary music and talk. WKND-AM broadcasts to the Hartford, CT area at 1480 AM.
AM RADIO STATION

WKNE-FM 45304
Owner: Saga Communications
Editorial: 69 Stanhope Ave, Keene, New Hampshire 03431-1584 **Tel:** 1 603 352-9230.
Email: frontdesk@monadnockradiogroup.com
Web site: http://www.wknefm.com
Profile: WKNE-FM is a commercial station owned by Saga Communications. The format of the station is hot adult contemporary. WKNE-FM broadcasts to the Boston area at 103.7 FM.
FM RADIO STATION

WKNG-AM 36389
Owner: Gradick Communications LLC
Editorial: 1546 Golf Course Road, Tallapoosa, Georgia 30176 **Tel:** 1 770 574-1060.
Web site: http://www.gradickcommunications.com
Profile: WKNG-AM is a commercial station owned by Gradick Communications LLC. The format of the station is country music. WKNG-AM broadcasts to the Tallapoosa, GA area at 1000 AM.
AM RADIO STATION

WKNH-FM 408571
Owner: Keene State College
Editorial: 229 Main St, Keene, New Hampshire 03435-0001 **Tel:** 1 603 358-8863.
Web site: http://www.wknh.org
Profile: WKNH-FM is a non-commercial station owned by Keene State College. The format of the station is college variety. WKNH-FM broadcasts to the Keene, NH area at 91.3 FM.
FM RADIO STATION

WKNL-FM 44420
Owner: Hall Communications
Editorial: 40 Cuprak Rd, Norwich, Connecticut 06360-2008 **Tel:** 1 860 887-3511.
Web site: http://www.radioroxy.com
Profile: WKNL-FM is a commercial station owned by Hall Communications. The format for the station is Classic Hits. WKNL-FM broadcasts to the Hartford-New Haven, CT area at 100.9 FM. The station's slogan is, "Big Hits, Big Fun!"
FM RADIO STATION

WKNN-FM 41738
Owner: iHeartMedia Inc.
Editorial: 286 Debuys Rd, Biloxi, Mississippi 39531-2611 **Tel:** 1 228 388-2323.
Web site: http://k99fm.iheart.com
Profile: WKNN-FM is a commercial station owned by iheartMedia Inc. The format is classic country. The station airs in the Biloxi, MS area at 99.1FM.
FM RADIO STATION

WKNO-FM 40443
Owner: Mid-South Public Communications Foundation
Editorial: 7151 Cherry Farms Rd, Cordova, Tennessee 38016-4933 **Tel:** 1 901 325-6544.
Web site: http://www.wknofm.org
Profile: WKNO-FM is a non-commercial station owned by Mid-South Public Communications Foundation. The format of the station is news, talk and classical music. WKNO-FM broadcasts to the Memphis, TN area at 91.1 FM. The station has requested that none of their emails be listed.
FM RADIO STATION

WKNR-AM 36004
Owner: Good Karma Broadcasting
Editorial: 1301 E 9th St, Cleveland, Ohio 44114-1804 **Tel:** 1 216 583-9901.
Web site: http://espn.go.com/cleveland
Profile: WKNR-AM is a commercial station owned by Good Karma Broadcasting. The format of the station is sports. WKNR-AM broadcasts to the Cleveland area at 850 AM.
AM RADIO STATION

WKNS-FM 43252
Owner: Craven Community College
Editorial: 800 College Ct, New Bern, North Carolina 28562 **Tel:** 1 252 638-3434.
Web site: http://www.publicradioeast.org
Profile: WKNS-FM is a non-commercial station owned by Craven Community College. The format of the station is news and talk. WKNS-FM broadcasts to the New Bern, NC area at 90.3 FM.
FM RADIO STATION

WKNU-FM 40444
Owner: WKNU Radio Inc.
Editorial: 2832 Ridge Rd, Brewton, Alabama 36426 **Tel:** 1 251 867-4824.
Email: wknubroadcasting@bellsouth.net
Web site: http://www.wknu.org
Profile: WKNU-FM is a commercial station owned by WKNU Radio Inc. The format of the station is country music. WKNU-FM broadcasts in the Mobile, AL area at 106.3 FM.
FM RADIO STATION

WKNV-AM 36962
Owner: Positive Radio Group
Editorial: 145 Jackson St NE, Blacksburg, Virginia 24060 **Tel:** 1 540 951-9791.
Email: wknv@yahoo.com
Profile: WKNV-AM is a commercial station owned by Positive Radio Group. The format of the station is gospel and religious programming. WKNV-AM broadcasts to the Blacksburg, VA area at 890 AM.
AM RADIO STATION

WKNW-AM 38690
Owner: Sovereign Communications LLC
Editorial: 1402 Ashmun St, Sault Sainte Marie, Michigan 49783-2864 **Tel:** 1 906 635-0995.
Profile: WKNW-AM is a commercial station owned by Sovereign Communications LLC. The format of the station is news and talk. WKNW-AM broadcasts to the Sault Sainte Marie, MI area at 1400 AM.
AM RADIO STATION

WKNY-AM 35963
Owner: Marquee Broadcasting
Editorial: 718 Broadway, Kingston, New York 12401-3450 **Tel:** 1 845 331-1490.
Email: wkny.production@townsquaremedia.com
Web site: http://1490wkny.com
Profile: WKNY-AM is a commercial station owned by Townsquare Media. The format of the station is adult contemporary music. WKNY-AM broadcasts in the Kingston, NY area at 1490 AM.
AM RADIO STATION

WKNZ-FM 535509
Owner: The Bridge of Hope
Editorial: 9078 Appels Rd, Lincoln, Delaware 19960-3417 **Tel:** 1 302 422-6909.
Email: info@887thebridge.com
Web site: http://www.887thebridge.com
Profile: WKNZ-FM is a non-commercial station owned by The Bridge of Hope. The format of the station is contemporary Christian programming. WKNZ-FM broadcasts to the Salisbury, MD market at 88.7 FM.
FM RADIO STATION

WKOA-FM 42705
Owner: Neuhoff Communications
Editorial: 3575 McCarty Ln, Lafayette, Indiana 47905-4985 **Tel:** 1 765 447-2186.
Web site: http://www.wkoa.com
Profile: WKOA-FM is a commercial station owned by Neuhoff Communications. The format of the station is country. WKOA-FM broadcasts to the Lafayette, IN area at 105.3 FM.
FM RADIO STATION

WKOK-AM 39036
Owner: Sunbury Broadcasting Corp.
Editorial: 1227 County Line Rd, Selinsgrove, Pennsylvania 17870-8188 **Tel:** 1 570 286-5838.
Email: newsroom@wkok.com
Web site: http://www.wkok.com
Profile: WKOK-AM is a commercial station owned by Sunbury Broadcasting Corp. The format of the station is news and sports. WKOK-AM broadcasts to the Sunbury, PA area at 1070 AM.
AM RADIO STATION

WKOL-FM 43719
Owner: Hall Communications
Editorial: 70 Joy Dr, South Burlington, Vermont 05403-6118 **Tel:** 1 802 658-1230.
Email: kool105@wkol.com
Web site: http://www.wkol.com
Profile: WKOL-FM is a commercial station owned by Hall Communications. The format of the station is classic hits music. WKOL-FM broadcasts to the Burlington, VT area at 105.1 FM.
FM RADIO STATION

WKOM-FM 46076
Owner: Middle Tennessee Broadcasting Co. Inc.
Editorial: 315 W 7th St, Columbia, Tennessee 38401 **Tel:** 1 931 388-3636.
Email: radio1340@bellsouth.net
Profile: WKOM-FM is a commercial station owned by Middle Tennessee Broadcasting Co. Inc. The format of the station is oldies. WKOM-FM broadcasts to the Columbia, TN area at 101.7 FM.
FM RADIO STATION

WKOR-FM 46909
Owner: Cumulus Media Inc.
Editorial: 200 6th St N Ste 205, Columbus, Mississippi 39701-4552 **Tel:** 1 662 327-1183.
Web site: http://www.k949.net
Profile: WKOR-FM is a commercial station owned by Cumulus Media Inc. The format of the station is country. The station broadcasts to the Columbus, MS area at a frequency of 94.9 FM.
FM RADIO STATION

WKOS-FM 45659
Owner: Cumulus Media Inc.
Editorial: 162 Free Hill Rd, Johnson City, Tennessee 37615-3144 **Tel:** 1 423 477-1000.
Email: greatcountry@greatcountry1049.com
Web site: http://www.greatcountry1049.com
Profile: WKOS-FM is a commercial station owned by Cumulus Media Inc. The format of the station is Country. WKOS-FM broadcasts to the Johnson City, TN area at 104.9 FM.
FM RADIO STATION

WKOV-FM 45305
Owner: Jackson County Broadcasting Inc.
Editorial: 295 E Main St, Jackson, Ohio 45640-1744 **Tel:** 1 740 286-3023.
Profile: WKOV-FM is a commercial station owned by Jackson County Broadcasting Inc. The format of the station is hot adult contemporary. WKOV-FM broadcasts to the Jackson, OH area at 96.7 FM.
FM RADIO STATION

WKOX-AM 36909
Owner: iHeartMedia Inc.
Editorial: 10 Cabot Rd Ste 302, Medford, Massachusetts 02155-5173 **Tel:** 1 781 663-2500.
Web site: http://talk1430.iheart.com
Profile: WKOX-AM is a commercial station owned by iHeartMedia Inc. The format of the station is Spanish hits. WKOX-AM broadcasts to the Medford, MA area at 1430 AM.
AM RADIO STATION

WKOY-FM 45921
Owner: Alpha Media
Editorial: 900 Bluefield Ave, Bluefield, West Virginia 24701-2744 **Tel:** 1 304 327-7114.
Web site: http://www.theeaglefm.com
Profile: WKOY-FM is a commercial station owned by Alpha Media. The format of the station is classic rock music. WKOY-FM broadcasts to the Bluefield, WV area at 100.9 FM.
FM RADIO STATION

WKOZ-AM 39515
Owner: Boswell Media LLC
Editorial: 1 Golf Course Rd, Kosciusko, Mississippi 39090 **Tel:** 1 662 289-1050.
Email: breezy@boswellmedia.net
Web site: http://www.breezynews.com
Profile: WKOZ-AM is a commercial station owned by Boswell Media LLC. The format of the station is R&B oldies and classic soul. WKOZ-AM broadcasts to the Kosciusko, MO area at 1340 AM.
AM RADIO STATION

WKOZ-FM 45550
Owner: Boswell Media LLC
Editorial: Kosciusko, Mississippi **Tel:** 1 601 289-1050.
Email: submit@boswellmedia.net
Web site: http://www.kicks98.com
Profile: WKOZ-FM is a commercial station owned by Boswell Media LLC. The format of the station is oldies. WKOZ-FM broadcasts to the Kosciusko, MO area at 98.3 FM.
FM RADIO STATION

WKPA-AM 36145
Owner: Seven Hills Media, Inc.
Editorial: 2043 10th St NE, Roanoke, Virginia 24012-5309 **Tel:** 1 540 343-5597.
Email: wkba@cox.net
Web site: http://www.theministrystations.com
Profile: WKPA-AM is a commercial station owned by Seven Hills Media, Inc. (David Moran). The format of the station is religious talk. The station airs locally at 1390 AM.
AM RADIO STATION

WKPE-FM 42134
Owner: Cape Cod Broadcasting
Editorial: 737 W Main St, Hyannis, Massachusetts 02601-3422 **Tel:** 1 508 771-1224.
Email: news@ccb-media.com
Web site: http://www.capecountry104.com
Profile: WKPE-FM is a commercial station owned by Cape Cod Broadcasting. The format of the station is country. WKPE-FM broadcasts to the Cape Cod and Hyannis, MA area at 104.7 FM.
FM RADIO STATION

WKPL-FM 45154
Owner: FM Radio Licenses, LLC
Editorial: 131 Pleasant Dr Ste 5U, Aliquippa, Pennsylvania 15001-1300 **Tel:** 1 724 378-1271.
Web site: http://www.picklefm.com
Profile: WKPL-FM is a commercial station owned by FM Radio Licenses, LLC. The format of the station is classic hits and classic rock. WKPL-FM broadcasts to the Aliquippa, PA area at 104.3 FM.
FM RADIO STATION

WKPO-FM 583994
Owner: Robinson Corporation
Editorial: E7601a County Road Ss, Viroqua, Wisconsin 54665-8502 **Tel:** 1 608 637-7200.
Email: wkpo@wkporadio.com
Profile: WKPO-FM is a commercial station owned by Robinson Corporation. The format of the station is variety hits. WKPO-FM broadcasts to the Viroqua, WI area at 105.9 FM.
FM RADIO STATION

WKPQ-FM 46229
Owner: Sound Communications, LLC
Editorial: 1484 Beech St, Hornell, New York 14843 **Tel:** 1 607 324-1596.
Profile: WKPQ-FM is a commercial station owned by Sound Communications, LLC. The format of the station is country. WKPQ-FM broadcasts to the Hornell, NY area at 105.3 FM.
FM RADIO STATION

WKPR-AM 35451
Owner: Kalamazoo Broadcasting Company, Inc.
Editorial: 2244 Ravine Rd, Kalamazoo, Michigan 49004-3506 **Tel:** 1 616 451-9387.
Email: wkprradio@sbcglobal.net
Profile: WKPR-AM is a commercial station owned by Kalamazoo Broadcasting Company, Inc. The format of the station is religious. WKPR-AM broadcasts to the Kalamzoo, MI area at 1440 AM.
AM RADIO STATION

WKPT-AM 37988
Owner: Holston Valley Broadcasting Corp.
Editorial: 222 Commerce St, Kingsport, Tennessee 37660-4319 **Tel:** 1 423 246-9578.
Web site: http://www.espntricities.com
Profile: WKPT-AM is a commercial station owned by Holston Valley Broadcasting Corp. The format of the station is sports. WKPT-AM broadcasts to the Kingsport, TN area at 1400 AM.
AM RADIO STATION

WKPW-FM 43969
Owner: State of Indiana/Eder Vocational Center
Editorial: 8149 W US Highway 40, Knightstown, Indiana 46148-9501 **Tel:** 1 765 345-9070.
Email: wkpw@wkpwfm.com
Web site: http://web01.cabeard.k12.in.us/wkpw/
Profile: WKPW-FM is a non-commercial station owned by State of Indiana/Eder Vocational Center. The format of the station is classic hits. WKPW-FM broadcasts to the Knightstown, IN area at 90.7 FM.
FM RADIO STATION

WKQA-AM 36789
Owner: Booth-Cobb Media LLC
Editorial: 700 Monticello Ave Ste 311, Norfolk, Virginia 23510-2523 **Tel:** 1 757 222-1171.
Email: wkqaradio@hotmail.com
Profile: WKQA-AM is a commericial station owned by Word Broadcasting Network, Inc. The format of the station is Christian talk and religious. WKQA-AM broadcasts to the Norfolk, VA area at 1110 AM.
AM RADIO STATION

WKQB-FM 45970
Owner: West Virginia-Virginia Holding Co, LLC
Editorial: 18385 Coal Heritage Rd, Welch, West Virginia 24801-9773 **Tel:** 1 304 436-2131.
Profile: WKQB-FM is a commercial station owned by West Virginia-Virginia Holding Co, LLC. The format of the station is adult hits. WKQB-FM broadcasts to the Welch, WV area at 102.9 FM.
FM RADIO STATION

WKQC-FM 40263
Owner: Beasley Broadcast Group
Editorial: 1520 South Blvd Ste 300, Charlotte, North Carolina 28203-3701 **Tel:** 1 704 522-1103.
Email: webmaster@k1047.com
Web site: http://www.k1047.com
Profile: WKQC-FM is a commercial station owned by Beasley Broadcast Group. The format of the station is adult contemporary. WKQC-FM broadcasts to the Charlotte, NC area at 104.7 FM.
FM RADIO STATION

WKQH-FM 44100
Owner: Muzzy Broadcasting
Editorial: 500 Division St, Stevens Point, Wisconsin 54481 **Tel:** 1 715 341-9800.
Web site: http://www.b1049.com
Profile: WKQH-FM is a commercial station owned by Muzzy Broadcasting. The format of the station is country music. WKQH-FM broadcasts to the Wausau, WI area at 104.9 FM.
FM RADIO STATION

WKQI-FM 40936
Owner: iHeart Media Inc.
Editorial: 27675 Halsted Rd, Farmington Hills, Michigan 48331-3511 **Tel:** 1 248 324-5800.
Email: email@mojointhemorning.com
Web site: http://channel955.iheart.com
Profile: WKQI-FM is a commercial station owned by iHeart Media Inc. The format of the station is Top 40/CHR. WKQI-FM broadcasts to the Detroit area at 95.5 FM.
FM RADIO STATION

WKQK-AM 36878
Owner: 321 Corporation
Editorial: 2355 Pluckebaum Rd, Cocoa, Florida 32926-5179 **Tel:** 1 321 631-1300.
Web site: http://www.1300wmel.com
Profile: WKQK-AM is a commercial station owned by 321 Corporation. The format of the station is talk. WKQK-AM broadcasts to the Melbourne, FL area at 1300 AM.
AM RADIO STATION

WKQL-FM 518276
Owner: Renda Broadcasting
Editorial: 904 N Main St, Punxsutawney, Pennsylvania 15767 **Tel:** 1 814 938-6000.
Web site: http://www.kool1033fm.com
Profile: WKQL-FM is a commercial station owned by Renda Broadcasting. The format of the station is classic rock. WKQL-FM broadcasts to the Punxsutawney, PA area at 103.3 FM.
FM RADIO STATION

WKQQ-FM 40446
Owner: iHeartMedia Inc.
Editorial: 2601 Nicholasville Rd, Lexington, Kentucky 40503-3307 **Tel:** 1 859 422-1000.
Web site: http://www.wkqq.com/main.html
Profile: WKQQ-FM is a commercial station owned by iHeartMedia Inc. The format of the station is rock. WKQQ-FM broadcasts to the Lexington, KY area at 100.1 FM.
FM RADIO STATION

WKQR-FM 40619
Owner: West Virginia-Virginia Holding Co, LLC
Editorial: 213A Howard Ave, Mullens, West Virginia 25882-1420 **Tel:** 1 304 294-4405.
Web site: http://www.kissplaysthehits.com/
Profile: WKQR-FM is a commercial station owned by West Virginia-Virginia Holding Co, LLC. The format of the station is Top 40/CHR. WKQR-FM broadcasts in the Bluefeld, WV area at 92.7 FM.
FM RADIO STATION

WKQS-FM 43634
Owner: Great Lakes Radio Inc.
Editorial: 3060 US Highway 41 W, Marquette, Michigan 49855-2293 **Tel:** 1 906 228-6800.
Email: contact@broadcasteverywhere.com
Web site: http://www.wkqsfm.com
Profile: WKQS-FM-FM is a commercial station owned by Great Lakes Radio Inc. The format for the station is adult contemporary music. WKQS-FM broadcasts to the Marquette, MI area at 101.9 FM.
FM RADIO STATION

WKQV-FM 496796
Owner: Summit Media Broadcasting LLC
Editorial: 180 Main St, Sutton, West Virginia 26601 **Tel:** 1 304 765-7373.
Email: mail@105kqv.com
Web site: http://www.105kqv.com
Profile: WKQV-FM is a commercial station owned by Summit Media Broadcasting LLC. The format of the station is rock and classic rock. WKQV-FM broadcasts to the Sutton, WV area at 105.5 FM.
FM RADIO STATION

WKQW-AM 39162
Owner: Clarion County Broadcasting Corp.
Editorial: 806C Grandview Road, Oil City, Pennsylvania 16301-1321 **Tel:** 1 814 676-8254.
Email: info@kqw.com
Web site: http://www.venangocountydailynews.com
Profile: WKQW-AM is a commercial station owned by Clarion County Broadcasting Corp. The format of the station is sports. WKQW-AM broadcasts to the Oil City, PA area at 1120 AM.
AM RADIO STATION

WKQW-FM 46522
Owner: Clarion County Broadcasting Corp.
Editorial: 806C Grandview Road, Oil City, Pennsylvania 16301-1337 **Tel:** 1 814 676-8254.
Email: kqwtraffic@usachoice.net
Web site: http://www.venangocountydailynews.com
Profile: WKQW-FM is a commercial station owned by Clarion County Broadcasting Corp. The format of the station is adult contemporary. WKQW-FM broadcasts to the Oil City, PA area at 96.3 FM.
FM RADIO STATION

WKQX-FM 40447
Owner: Cumulus Media
Editorial: 222 Merchandise Mart Plz Ste 230, Chicago, Illinois 60654-1008 **Tel:** 1 312 527-8348.
Web site: http://www.101WKQX.com
Profile: WKQX-FM is a commercial station owned by Cumulus Media. The station airs an alternative rock format. WKQX-FM broadcasts to the Chicago area at 101.1 FM.
FM RADIO STATION

WKQY-FM 45588
Owner: Alpha Media
Editorial: 900 Bluefield Ave, Bluefield, West Virginia 24701-2744 **Tel:** 1 304 327-7114.
Web site: http://www.theeaglefm.com
Profile: WKQY-FM is a commercial station owned by Alpha Media. The format of the station is classic rock music. WKQY-FM broadcasts to the Bluefield, WV area at 100.1 FM.
FM RADIO STATION

WKQZ-FM 40448
Owner: Cumulus Media Inc.
Editorial: 1740 Champagne Dr N, Saginaw, Michigan 48604-9239 **Tel:** 1 989 776-2100.
Web site: http://www.z93kqz.fm
Profile: WKQZ-FM is a commercial station owned by Cumulus Media Inc. The format of the station is rock/album-oriented rock. WKQZ-FM broadcasts to the Saginaw, MI area at 93.3 FM.
FM RADIO STATION

WKRA-AM 37989
Owner: Autry(Billy)
Editorial: 1400 Highway 4 E Ste C, Holly Springs, Mississippi 38635-2140 **Tel:** 1 662 252-1810.
Profile: WKRA-AM is a commercial station owned Independently by Billy Autry. The format of the station is News, Music and Gospel. WKRA-AM broadcasts at a frequency of 1110 AM to the Holly Springs, MS area.
AM RADIO STATION

WKRA-FM 45309
Owner: Autry(Billy)
Editorial: 1400 Highway 4 E, Ste C, Holly Springs, Mississippi 38635 **Tel:** 1 662 252-1810.
Email: power927@gmail.com
FM RADIO STATION

WKRB-FM 43739
Owner: Kingsborough Community College
Editorial: 2001 Oriental Blvd, Brooklyn, New York 11235-2333 **Tel:** 1 718 368-4572.
Email: wkrb@kbcc.cuny.edu
Web site: http://www.wkrb.org
Profile: WKRB-FM is a non-commercial station owned by Kingsborough Community College. The format of the station is Rhythmic CHR. WKRB-FM broadcasts to the Brooklyn, NY area at 90.3 FM.
FM RADIO STATION

WKRC-AM 37708
Owner: iHeartMedia Inc.
Editorial: 8044 Montgomery Rd Ste 650, Cincinnati, Ohio 45236-2959 **Tel:** 1 513 686-8300.
Web site: http://www.55krc.com
Profile: WKRC-AM is a commercial station owned by iHeartMedia Inc. The format of the station is news and talk. WKRC-AM broadcasts to the Cincinnati area at 550 AM.
AM RADIO STATION

WKRD-AM 36644
Owner: iHeartMedia Inc.
Editorial: 4000 Radio Dr, Louisville, Kentucky 40218-4568 **Tel:** 1 502 479-2222.
Web site: http://790krd.iheart.com
Profile: WKRD-AM is a commercial station owned by iHeartMedia Inc. The format of the station is sports. WKRD-AM broadcasts to the Louisville, KY area at 790 AM.
AM RADIO STATION

WKRD-FM 238453
Web site: http://790krd.iheart.com
Profile: WKRD-FM is a commercial station. The format of the station is contemporary country. WKRD-FM broadcasts to the Louisville, KY area on 101.7 FM.
FM RADIO STATION

WKRE-FM 937563
Owner: TBTA Ministries
Editorial: 1900 Crestwood Blvd Ste 111, Irondale, Alabama 35210-2060 **Tel:** 1 205 402-4266.
Web site: http://www.myrevradio.com
Profile: WKRE-FM is a non-commercial station owned by TBTA Ministries. The format of the station features Christian rock and pop music. WKRE-FM broadcasts to the Birmingham, AL area at a frequency of 88.1 FM. The station airs WHUA-FM'a programming.
FM RADIO STATION

WKRF-FM 43238
Owner: Entercom Communications Corp.
Editorial: 305 Highway 315, Pittston, Pennsylvania 18640 **Tel:** 1 570 883-9850.
Web site: http://www.wkrz.com
Profile: WKRF-FM is a commercial station owned by Entercom Communications Corp. The format of the station is Top 40/CHR. WKRF-FM broadcasts to the Pittston, PA area at 107.9 FM.
FM RADIO STATION

WKRH-FM 43075
Owner: Galaxy Communications LP
Editorial: 235 Walton St, Syracuse, New York 13202-1533 **Tel:** 1 315 472-9111.
Web site: http://www.krock.com
Profile: WKRH-AM is a commercial station owned by Galaxy Communications LP. The format of the station is rock music. WKRH-AM broadcasts to the Syracuse, NY area at 106.5 FM.
FM RADIO STATION

WKRK-AM 35453
Owner: Radford Communications, Inc.
Editorial: 427 Hill St, Murphy, North Carolina 28906-3509 **Tel:** 1 828 837-4332.
Web site: http://www.1320am.com
Profile: WKRK-AM is a commercial station owned by Radford Communications, Inc. The format of the station is classic country and gospel. WKRK-AM broadcasts to the Murphy, NC area at 1320 AM.
AM RADIO STATION

WKRK-FM 45512
Owner: CBS Radio
Editorial: 1041 Huron Rd E, Cleveland, Ohio 44115-1706 **Tel:** 1 216 861-0100.
Web site: http://www.923thefan.com
Profile: WKRK-FM is a commercial station owned by CBS Radio. The format of the station is sports news and talk. WKRK-FM broadcasts to the Cleveland area at 92.3 FM. The station does not do interviews since it does not have DJs.
FM RADIO STATION

WKRL-FM 42778
Owner: Galaxy Communications LP
Editorial: 235 Walton St, Syracuse, New York 13202 **Tel:** 1 315 472-9111.
Web site: http://www.krock.com
Profile: WKRL-FM is a commercial station owned by Galaxy Communications LP. The format of the station is rock alternative music. WKRL-FM broadcasts to the Syracuse, NY area at 100.9 FM.
FM RADIO STATION

WKRM-AM 38725
Owner: Middle Tennessee Broadcasting Co. Inc.
Editorial: 315 W 7th St, Columbia, Tennessee 38401 **Tel:** 1 931 388-3636.
Email: radio1340@bellsouth.net
Profile: WKRM-AM is a commercial station owned by Middle Tennessee Broadcasting Co. Inc. The format of the station is adult contemporary music and talk. WKRM-AM broadcasts to the Columbia, TN area at 1340 AM.
AM RADIO STATION

WKRO-FM 42205
Owner: Black Crow Radio, LLC
Editorial: 126 W International Speedway Blvd, Daytona Beach, Florida 32114-4322 **Tel:** 1 386 255-9300.
Web site: http://931coast.com
Profile: WKRO-FM is a commercial station owned by Black Crow Radio, LLC. The format of the station is contemporary country music. WKRO-FM broadcasts to the Daytona Beach, FL area at 93.1 FM.
FM RADIO STATION

WKRQ-FM 42068
Owner: Hubbard Broadcasting, Inc.
Editorial: 2060 Reading Rd, Cincinnati, Ohio 45202 **Tel:** 1 513 699-5102.
Web site: http://www.wkrq.com
Profile: WKRQ-FM is a commercial station owned by Hubbard Broadcasting, Inc. The format of the station is hot adult contemporary. WKRQ-FM broadcasts to the Cincinnati area at 101.9 FM.
FM RADIO STATION

WKRR-FM 40450
Owner: Dick Jr.(James A.)
Editorial: 192 E Lewis St, Greensboro, North Carolina 27406-1459 **Tel:** 1 336 274-8042.
Web site: http://www.rock92.com
Profile: WKRR-FM is a commercial station owned by James A. Dick Jr. The format of the station is classic rock. WKRR-FM broadcasts to the Greensboro, NC area at 92.3 FM.
FM RADIO STATION

WKRS-AM 37991
Owner: Alpha Media
Editorial: 3250 Belvidere Rd, Waukegan, Illinois 60085-6041 **Tel:** 1 847 336-7900.
Web site: http://www.espndeportes1220.com
Profile: WKRS-AM is a commercial station owned by Alpha Media. The format of the station is Spanish sports talk. WKRS-AM is the ESPN Desportes affiliate for the Waukegan and Lake County areas in Illinois and broadcasts locally at 1220 AM.
AM RADIO STATION

United States of America

WKRU-FM 40406
Owner: Cumulus Media Inc.
Editorial: 810 Victoria St, Green Bay, Wisconsin 54302 **Tel:** 1 920 468-4100.
Web site: http://www.wkrufm.com
Profile: WKRU-FM is a commercial station owned by Cumulus Media Inc. The format for the station is adult album alternative. WKRU-FM broadcasts to the Green Bay, WI area at 106.7 FM.
FM RADIO STATION

WKRV-FM 45311
Owner: Cromwell Group Inc.(The)
Editorial: 232 S 4th St, Vandalia, Illinois 62471-2810 **Tel:** 1 618 283-2325.
Email: wkrv@sbcglobal.net
Web site: http://vandaliaradio.com
Profile: WKRV-FM is a commercial station owned by The Cromwell Group Inc. The format of the station is classic hits. WKRV-FM broadcasts to the Vandalia, IL area at 107.1 FM.
FM RADIO STATION

WKRX-FM 45312
Owner: Roxboro Broadcasting Co.
Editorial: 2070 Hurdle Mills Road, Roxboro, North Carolina 27573 **Tel:** 1 336 599-0266.
Email: wkrx@radioroxboro.com
Web site: http://www.radioroxboro.com
Profile: WKRX-FM is a commercial station owned by Roxboro Broadcasting Co. The format of the station is country. WKRX-FM broadcasts to the Roxboro, NC area at 96.7 FM.
FM RADIO STATION

WKRZ-FM 45313
Owner: Entercom Communications Corp.
Editorial: 305 Route 315 Hwy, Pittston, Pennsylvania 18640-3907 **Tel:** 1 570 883-9850.
Web site: http://www.985krz.com
Profile: WKRZ-FM is a commercial station owned by Entercom Communications Corp. The format of the station is Top 40/CHR. WKRZ-FM broadcasts to the Pittston, PA area at 98.5 FM.
FM RADIO STATION

WKSB-FM 46149
Owner: iHeartMedia Inc.
Editorial: 1559 W 4th St, Williamsport, Pennsylvania 17701-5650 **Tel:** 1 570 327-1400.
Web site: http://www.wksb.com
Profile: WKSB-FM is a commercial station owned by iHeartMedia Inc. The format of the station is hot adult contemporary music. WKSB-FM broadcasts to the Williamsport, PA area at 102.7 FM.
FM RADIO STATION

WKSC-FM 40299
Owner: iHeartMedia Inc.
Editorial: 233 N Michigan Ave Ste 2700, Chicago, Illinois 60601-5704 **Tel:** 1 312 540-2000.
Web site: http://1035kissfm.iheart.com
Profile: WKSC-FM is commercial station owned by iHeartMedia Inc. The format of the station is Top 40/ CHR. WKSC-FM broadcasts to the Chicago area at 103.5 FM.
FM RADIO STATION

WKSD-FM 45967
Owner: First Family Broadcasting Inc.
Editorial: 9070 Mendon Rd, Van Wert, Ohio 45891-9006 **Tel:** 1 419 238-1220.
Email: wert@bright.net
Web site: http://www.wert1220.com
Profile: WKSD-FM is a commercial station owned by First Family Broadcasting Inc. The format of the station is sports and oldies. WKSD-FM broadcasts to the Van Wert, OH area at 99.7 FM.
FM RADIO STATION

WKSE-FM 45314
Owner: Entercom Communications Corp.
Editorial: 500 Corporate Pkwy, Ste 200, Buffalo, New York 14226 **Tel:** 1 716 843-0600.
Web site: http://www.kiss985.com
Profile: WKSE-FM is a commercial station owned by Entercom Communications Corp. The format of the station is Top 40/CHR. WKSE-FM broadcasts to the Buffalo, NY area at 98.5 FM.
FM RADIO STATION

WKSF-FM 46187
Owner: iHeartMedia Inc.
Editorial: 13 Summerlin Dr, Asheville, North Carolina 28806-2800 **Tel:** 1 828 257-2700.
Email: ashevillepsa@iheartmedia.com
Web site: http://www.99kisscountry.com
Profile: WKSF-FM is a commercial station owned by iHeartMedia Inc. The format of the station is country. WKSF-FM broadcasts to the Asheville, NC area at 99.9 FM.
FM RADIO STATION

WKSG-FM 44340
Owner: Daystar Public Radio Inc.
Editorial: 7 E Silver Springs Blvd Ste 102, Ocala, Florida 34470-6663 **Tel:** 1 352 369-8950.
Profile: WKSG-FM is a non-commercial station owned by Daystar Public Radio Inc. The format of the station is adult standards. WKSG-FM broadcasts to the Ocala, FL area at 89.5 FM.
FM RADIO STATION

WKSI-FM 45640
Owner: iHeartMedia Inc.
Editorial: 510 Pegasus Ct, Winchester, Virginia 22602-4596 **Tel:** 1 540 662-5101.
Email: winchesterdigital@clearchannel.com
Web site: http://kiss983.iheart.com
Profile: WKSI-FM is a commercial station owned by iHeartMedia Inc. The format of the station is Top 40/ CHR music. WKSI-FM broadcasts to Winchester, VA and surrounding areas at 98.3 FM.
FM RADIO STATION

WKSJ-FM 45316
Owner: iHeartMedia Inc.
Editorial: 555 Broadcast Dr Fl 3, Mobile, Alabama 36606-2936 **Tel:** 1 251 450-0100.
Web site: http://www.95ksj.com
Profile: WKSJ-FM is a commercial station owned by iHeartMedia Inc. The format of the station is country music. WKSJ-AM broadcasts to the Mobile, AL area at 94.9 FM.
FM RADIO STATION

WKSK-AM 35456
Owner: Caddell Broadcasting Inc.
Editorial: 240 Radio Road, West Jefferson, North Carolina 28694 **Tel:** 1 336 246-6001.
Email: wksk@skybest.com
Web site: http://www.580wksk.com
Profile: WKSK-AM is a commercial station owned by Caddell Broadcasting Inc. The format of the station is country. WKSK-AM broadcasts to the West Jefferson, NC area at 580 AM.
AM RADIO STATION

WKSK-FM 46594
Owner: Lakes Media, LLC
Editorial: 16256 Highway 47, South Hill, Virginia 23970 **Tel:** 1 434 447-4007.
Web site: http://www.rewind1019.com
Profile: WKSK-FM is a commercial station owned by Lakes Media, LLC. The format of the station is classic hits with a mixture of oldies and rock. WKSK-FM broadcasts to the South Hill, VA area at a frequency of 101.9 FM.
FM RADIO STATION

WKSL-FM 46721
Owner: iHeartMedia Inc.
Editorial: 11700 Central Pkwy, Jacksonville, Florida 32224-2600 **Tel:** 1 904 636-0507.
Web site: http://979kissfm.iheart.com
Profile: WKSL-FM is a commercial station owned by iHeartMedia Inc. The format of the station is Hot AC. WKSL-FM broadcasts to the Jacksonville, FL area at 97.9 FM.
FM RADIO STATION

WKSM-FM 42860
Owner: Cumulus Media Inc.
Editorial: 225 Hollywood Blvd NW, Fort Walton Beach, Florida 32548-4725 **Tel:** 1 850 243-7676.
Web site: http://www.wksm.com
Profile: WKSM-FM is a commercial station targeting adults ages 18 to 35. Aired locally on 99.9 FM, the format of the station is rock music and features news, weather, and sports updates on the hour throughout the morning.
FM RADIO STATION

WKSN-AM 38587
Owner: Media One Group, LLC
Editorial: 2 Orchard Rd, Jamestown, New York 14701 **Tel:** 1 716 487-1151.
Email: news@radiojamestown.com
Web site: http://www.wksn.com
Profile: WKSN-AM is a commercial station owned by Media One Group, LLC. The format of the station is oldies. WKSN-AM broadcasts to the Jamestown, NY area at 1340 AM.
AM RADIO STATION

WKSO-FM 42343
Owner: First Natchez Corp.
Editorial: 2 Oferrall St, Natchez, Mississippi 39120-3000 **Tel:** 1 601 442-4895.
Web site: http://listenupyall.com/index.php/music/kiss-97
Profile: WKSO-FM is a commercial station owned by First Natchez Corp.. The format of the station is Hot AC. The station broadcasts to the Natchez, Mississippi area at a frequency of 97.3 FM. The station does not accept press submissions, requests, and inquiries.
FM RADIO STATION

WKSP-FM 40706
Owner: iHeartMedia Inc.
Editorial: 2743 Perimeter Pkwy Ste 300, Augusta, Georgia 30909-6429 **Tel:** 1 706 396-6000.
Web site: http://www.963kissfm.com
Profile: WKSP-FM is a commercial station owned by iHeartMedia Inc. The format of the station is urban adult contemporary. WKSP-FM broadcasts to the Augusta, GA area at 96.3 FM.
FM RADIO STATION

WKSQ-FM 40452
Owner: Blueberry Broadcasting
Editorial: 184 Target Cir, Bangor, Maine 04401-5718 **Tel:** 1 207 947-9100.
Web site: http://www.kissfm.net
Profile: WKSQ-FM is a commercial station owned by Blueberry Broadcasting. The format of the station is hot adult contemporary. WKSQ-FM broadcasts to the Bangor, ME area at 94.5 FM.
FM RADIO STATION

WKSR-AM 37910
Owner: Pulaski Broadcasting
Editorial: 104 S 2nd St, Pulaski, Tennessee 38478-3219 **Tel:** 1 931 363-2505.
Email: wksr@igiles.net
Web site: http://www.wksr.com
Profile: WKSR-AM is a commercial station owned by Pulaski Broadcasting. The format of the station is classic country. WKSR-AM broadcasts in the Pulaski, TN area at 1420 AM.
AM RADIO STATION

WKSS-FM 41007
Owner: iHeart Media Inc.
Editorial: 10 Columbus Blvd Ste 1, Hartford, Connecticut 06106-1976 **Tel:** 1 860 723-6000.
Web site: http://kiss957.iheart.com
Profile: WKSS-FM is a commercial station owned by iHeart Media Inc. The format of the station is Top 40/ CHR. WKSS-FM broadcasts to the Hartford, CT area at 95.7 FM.
FM RADIO STATION

WKST-AM 37995
Owner: FM Radio Licenses, LLC
Editorial: 219 Savannah Gardner Rd, New Castle, Pennsylvania 16101-5546 **Tel:** 1 724 346-5070.
Email: wtsutton@yahoo.com
Web site: http://www.wkst.com
Profile: WKST-AM is a commercial station owned by FM Radio Licenses, LLC. The format of the station is news, talk and sports. WKST-AM broadcasts to the New Castle, PA area at 1200 AM.
AM RADIO STATION

WKST-FM 43800
Owner: iHeartMedia Inc.
Editorial: 200 Fleet St Fl 4, Pittsburgh, Pennsylvania 15220-2908 **Tel:** 1 412 937-1441.
Web site: http://www.961kiss.com
Profile: WKST-FM is a commercial station owned by iHeartMedia Inc. The format of the station is Top 40/ CHR. WKST-FM broadcasts to the Pittsburgh area at 96.1 FM.
FM RADIO STATION

WKSW-FM 45216
Owner: Cookeville Communications, LLC
Editorial: 698 S Willow Ave, Cookeville, Tennessee 38501-3802 **Tel:** 1 931 526-7144.
Web site: http://www.kissfm985.com
Profile: WKSW-FM is a commercial station owned by Cookeville Communications, LLC. The format of station is Top 40/CHR. WKSW-FM broadcasts to the Cookeville, TN area at 98.5 FM.
FM RADIO STATION

WKSX-FM 45317
Owner: Edgefield-Saluda Radio Co. Inc.
Editorial: 102 Slide Hill Rd, Johnston, South Carolina 29832-1360 **Tel:** 1 803 275-4444.
Web site: http://www.ksx927.com
Profile: WKSX-FM is a commercial station owned by Edgefield-Saluda Radio Co. Inc. The format of the station is oldies. WKSX-FM broadcasts to the Johnston, SC area at 92.7 FM.
FM RADIO STATION

WKSZ-FM 43467
Owner: Woodward Communications, Inc.
Editorial: 2800 E College Ave, Appleton, Wisconsin 54915 **Tel:** 1 920 734-9226.
Email: kissfm@wcinet.com
Web site: http://www.959kissfm.com
Profile: WKSZ-FM is a commercial station owned by Woodward Communications, Inc. The format is Top 40/CHR music. WKSZ-FM broadcasts to the Green Bay, WI area at 95.9 FM.
FM RADIO STATION

WKTA-AM 35680
Owner: Polnet Communications
Editorial: 4320 Dundee Rd, Northbrook, Illinois 60062-1703 **Tel:** 1 847 498-3350.
Email: polnetradio@gmail.com
Web site: http://www.pclradio.com
Profile: WKTA-AM is a commercial station owned by Polnet Communications. The format of the station is variety ethnic. WKTA-AM broadcasts to the Chicago area at 1330 AM.
AM RADIO STATION

WKTE-AM 35457
Owner: Booth-Newsome Broadcasting
Editorial: 117 WKTE Drive, King, North Carolina 27021 **Tel:** 1 336 983-3111.
Profile: WKTE-AM is a commercial station owned by Booth-Newsome Broadcasting. The format of the station is oldies music. WKTE-AM broadcasts to the King, NC area at 1090 AM.
AM RADIO STATION

WKTG-FM 45318
Owner: Sound Broadcasters Inc.
Editorial: 2380 N Main St, Madisonville, Kentucky 42431 **Tel:** 1 270 821-1156.
Email: wktg@wktg.com
Web site: http://www.wktg.com
Profile: WKTG-FM is a commercial station owned by Sound Broadcasters Inc. The format of the station is rock. WKTG-FM broadcasts to the Madisonville, KY area at 93.9 FM.
FM RADIO STATION

WKTI-FM 42803
Owner: E.W. Scripps Co.
Editorial: 720 E Capitol Dr, Milwaukee, Wisconsin 53212-1308 **Tel:** 1 414 332-9611.
Web site: http://www.wtmj.com/kticountry
Profile: WKTI-FM is a commercial station owned by E.W. Scripps Co. The format of the station is contemporary country. WKTI-FM broadcasts to the Milwaukee area at 94.5 FM.
FM RADIO STATION

WKTJ-FM 42014
Owner: Clearwater Communications LLC
Editorial: 121 Broadway, Farmington, Maine 04938-5821 **Tel:** 1 207 778-3400.
Email: contact@bighitsktj.com
Web site: http://www.wktj.com
Profile: WKTJ-FM is a commercial station owned by Clearwater Communications LLC. The format of the station is variety. WKTJ-FM broadcasts to the Farmington, ME area at 99.3 FM.
FM RADIO STATION

WKTK-FM 40456
Owner: Entercom Communications Corp.
Editorial: 3600 NW 43rd St, Ste B, Gainesville, Florida 32606 **Tel:** 1 352 377-0985.
Web site: http://www.ktk985.com
Profile: WKTK-FM is a commercial station owned by Entercom Communications Corp. The format of the station is adult contemporary. WKTK-FM broadcasts to the Gainesville, FL area at 98.5 FM.
FM RADIO STATION

WKTM-FM 43797
Owner: Good News Network
Editorial: 2278 Wortham Ln, Grovetown, Georgia 30813-5103 **Tel:** 1 706 309-9610.
Web site: http://www.gnnradio.org
Profile: WKTM-FM is a non-commercial station owned by Good News Network. The format of the station is Spanish religious. WKTM-FM broadcasts locally at 106.1 FM to the Soperton, GA area.
FM RADIO STATION

WKTN-FM 40457
Owner: Radio General Ltd.
Editorial: 112 N Detroit St, Kenton, Ohio 43326-1558 **Tel:** 1 419 675-2355.
Email: wktnnews@rrohio.com
Web site: http://www.wktn.com
Profile: WKTN-FM is a commercial station owned by Radio General Ltd. The format of the station is adult contemporary. WKTN-FM broadcasts locally to Columbus, OH at 95.3 FM.
FM RADIO STATION

WKTO-FM 43603
Owner: Mims Community Radio Inc.
Editorial: 900 Old Mission Rd, New Smyrna Beach, Florida 32168-8562 **Tel:** 1 386 427-1095.
Email: info@wkto.net
Web site: http://www.wkto.net
Profile: WKTO-FM is a non-commercial station owned by Mims Community Radio Inc. The format of the station is religous. WKTO-FM broadcasts to New Smyrna Beach, FL area at 88.9 FM.
FM RADIO STATION

WKTP-AM 36784
Owner: Holston Valley Broadcasting Corp.
Editorial: 222 Commerce St, Kingsport, Tennessee 37660-4319 **Tel:** 1 423 246-9578.
Web site: http://www.wkptam.com
Profile: WKTP-AM is a commercial station owned by Holston Valley Broadcasting Corp. The format of the station is sports. WKTP-AM broadcasts to the Johnson City, TN area at 1590 AM.
AM RADIO STATION

WKTQ-AM 39063
Owner: Gleason Radio Group
Editorial: 243 Main St, Norway, Maine 04268-5914 **Tel:** 1 207 743-5911.
Email: info@woxo.com
Web site: http://www.wtme.com
Profile: WKTQ-AM is a commercial station owned by the Gleason Radio Group. The format of the station is news and talk. WKTQ-AM broadcasts to the Norway, ME area at 1450 AM.
AM RADIO STATION

WKTR-AM 36275
Owner: Calvary Chapel of Twin Falls, Inc.
Editorial: 100 Spotswood Bus Pk Cir, Quinque, Virginia 22965 **Tel:** 1 434 985-8585.
Web site: http://www.csnradio.com/
Profile: WKTR-AM is a commercial station owned by Calvary Chapel of Twin Falls, Inc. The format of the station is Religious Teaching. WKTR-AM broadcasts to the Charlottesville, VA area at 840 AM.
AM RADIO STATION

WKTT-FM 45222
Owner: Rojo Broadcasting, LLC
Editorial: 917 Snow Hill Rd Ste A, Salisbury, Maryland 21804-2408 **Tel:** 1 410 219-3500.
Web site: http://live975.com
Profile: WKTT-FM is a commercial station owned by Rojo Broadcasting, LLC. The format of the station is urban contemporary music. WKTT-FM broadcasts to the Salisbury, MD area at 97.5 FM.
FM RADIO STATION

WKTU-FM 43374
Owner: iHeartMedia Inc.
Editorial: 32 Avenue of the Americas Fl 3, New York, New York 10013-2473 **Tel:** 1 212 377-7900.
Web site: http://ktu.iheart.com
Profile: WKTU-FM is a commercial station owned by iHeartMedia Inc. The format of the station is dance music. WKTU-FM broadcasts to the New York area at 103.5 FM.
FM RADIO STATION

WKTX-AM 36122
Owner: Kingstrust, LLC
Editorial: 11906 Madison Ave, Lakewood, Ohio 44107-5027 **Tel:** 1 216 221-0330.
Profile: WKTX-FM is a commercial station owned by Kingstrust, LLC. The format or the station is ethnic. WKTX-FM broadcasts to the Lakewood, OH area at 830 AM.
AM RADIO STATION

WKTY-AM 36679
Owner: Midwest Family Broadcasting
Editorial: 201 State St, La Crosse, Wisconsin 54601
Tel: 1 608 782-1230.
Web site: http://www.580wkty.com
Profile: WKTY-AM is a commercial station owned by Midwest Family Broadcasting. The format of the station is sports. WKTY-AM broadcasts in the La Crosse, WI area at 580 AM.
AM RADIO STATION

WKUA-FM 837501
Owner: TBTA Ministries
Editorial: 1900 Crestwood Blvd Ste 111, Irondale, Alabama 35210-2060 **Tel:** 1 205 402-4266.
Web site: http://www.myrevradio.com
Profile: WKUA-FM is a non-commercial station owned by TBTA Ministries. The format of the station features Christian rock and pop music. WKUA-FM broadcasts to the Birmingham, AL area at a frequency of 88.5 FM.
FM RADIO STATION

WKUB-FM 40459
Owner: Mattox Broadcasting Inc.
Editorial: 2132 US Highway 84, Blackshear, Georgia 31516-1160 **Tel:** 1 912 449-3391.
Email: wkub@almatel.net
Web site: http://waycrossradio.com/1051
Profile: WKUB-FM is a commercial station owned by Mattox Broadcasting Inc. The format of the station is contemporary country. WKUB-FM broadcasts to the Blackshear, GA area at 105.1 FM.
FM RADIO STATION

WKUL-FM 41314
Owner: Jonathan Christian Corp.
Editorial: 214 1st Ave SE, Cullman, Alabama 35055-3402 **Tel:** 1 256 734-0183.
Email: wkulfm@excite.com
Web site: http://www.wkul.com
Profile: WKUL-FM is a commercial station owned by Jonathan Christian Corp. The format of the station is country music, sports and talk. WKUL-FM broadcasts to the Cullman, AL area at 92.1 FM.
FM RADIO STATION

WKUN-AM 35458
Owner: Anderson(B.R.)
Editorial: 1610 Launius Rd, Good Hope, Georgia 30641-2639 **Tel:** 1 770 267-0923.
Web site: http://www.wmoqfm.com
Profile: WKUN-AM is a commercial station owned by B.R. Anderson. The format of the station is gospel music. WKUN-AM broadcasts to the Bostwick, GA area at 1580 AM.
AM RADIO STATION

WKUZ-FM 40460
Owner: Brothers Broadcasting Corp.
Editorial: 1864 S Wabash St, Wabash, Indiana 46992-4120 **Tel:** 1 260 563-4111.
Email: news@wkuz.com
Profile: WKUZ-FM is a commercial station owned by Brothers Broadcasting Corp. The format of the station is adult contemporary. WKUZ-FM broadcasts to the Wabash, IN area at 95.9 FM.
FM RADIO STATION

WKVA-AM 35459
Owner: WVNW Inc.
Editorial: 114 N Logan Blvd, Burnham, Pennsylvania 17009-1810 **Tel:** 1 717 242-1493.
Email: kvatoday@wkva920.com
Web site: http://www.wkva920.com
Profile: WKVA-AM is a commercial station owned by WVNW Inc. The format of the station is oldies. WKVA-AM broadcasts to the Burnham, PA area at 920 AM.
AM RADIO STATION

WKVB-FM 377548
Owner: 2510 Associates
Tel: 1 800 525-5683.
Web site: http://www.klove.com
FM RADIO STATION

WKVE-FM 45025
Owner: Broadcast Communications Inc.
Editorial: 1918 Lincoln Hwy, North Versailles, Pennsylvania 15137-2706 **Tel:** 1 412 823-1301.
Web site: http://kve.fm
Profile: WKVE-FM is a commercial station owned by Broadcast Communications Inc. The format of the station is classic rock. WKVE-FM broadcasts to the Greater Pittsburgh, PA area at 103.1 FM.
FM RADIO STATION

WKVG-AM 36151
Owner: Martin's and Associates Inc.
Editorial: 20 Main St, Jenkins, Kentucky 41537-9614
Tel: 1 606 832-4655.
Email: wkvgradio@windstream.net
Profile: WKVG-AM is a commercial station owned by Martin's and Associates Inc. The format of the station is religious programming and gospel music. WKVG-AM broadcasts to the Jenkins, KY area at 1000 AM.
AM RADIO STATION

WKVI-AM 37998
Owner: Kankakee Valley Broadcasting Inc.
Editorial: 400 W Culver Rd, Knox, Indiana 46534
Tel: 1 574 772-6241.
Email: spots@wkvi.com
Web site: http://www.wkvi.com
Profile: WKVI-AM is a commercial station owned by Kankakee Valley Broadcasting Inc. The format of the station is hot adult contemporary. WKVI-AM broadcasts to the South Bend, IN area at 1520 AM.
AM RADIO STATION

WKVI-FM 45320
Owner: Kankakee Valley Broadcasting Inc.
Editorial: 400 W Culver Rd, Knox, Indiana 46534
Tel: 1 574 772-6241.
Email: spots@wkvi.com
Web site: http://www.wkvi.com
Profile: WKVI-FM is a commercial station owned by Kankakee Valley Broadcasting Inc. The format of the station is hot adult contemporary. WKVI-FM broadcasts to the South Bend, IN area at 99.3 FM.
FM RADIO STATION

WKVL-AM 36830
Owner: Blount Broadcasting Corp.
Editorial: 261 Hannum St, Alcoa, Tennessee 37701-2451 **Tel:** 1 865 984-0729.
Email: info@wkvl.com
Web site: http://wkvl.com
Profile: WKVL-AM is a commercial station owned by Horne Radio LLC. The format of the station is classic country. WKVL-AM broadcasts to the Knoxville, TN area at 850 AM.
AM RADIO STATION

WKVQ-AM 36059
Owner: Baker(Craig)
Editorial: 869 Church St, Eatonton, Georgia 31024-6452 **Tel:** 1 706 485-8792.
Profile: WKVQ-AM is a commercial station owned by Craig Baker. The format of the station is ReligiousTeaching. WKVQ-AM broadcasts to the Eatonton, GA area at 1520 AM.
AM RADIO STATION

WKVS-FM 42553
Owner: Foothills Radio Group, LLC
Editorial: 827 Fairview Dr SW, Lenoir, North Carolina 28645-6023 **Tel:** 1 828 758-1033.
Web site: http://www.foothillsradio.com
Profile: WKVS-FM is a commercial station owned by Foothills Radio Group, LLC. The format of the station is contemporary country music. WKVS-FM broadcasts to the Charlotte, NC area at 103.3 FM.
FM RADIO STATION

WKVT-AM 37999
Owner: Saga Communications
Editorial: 458 Williams St, Brattleboro, Vermont 05301-6235 **Tel:** 1 802 254-2343.
Email: production@wkvt.com
Web site: http://wkvtradio.com
Profile: WKVT-AM is a commercial station owned by Saga Communications. The format of the station is progressive talk and news. WKVT-AM broadcasts to the Brattleboro, VT area at 1490 AM.
AM RADIO STATION

WKVT-FM 45321
Owner: Saga Communications
Editorial: 458 Williams St, Brattleboro, Vermont 05301-6235 **Tel:** 1 802 254-2343.
Email: production@wkvt.com
Web site: http://www.wkvt.com
Profile: WKVT-FM is a commercial station owned by Saga Communications. The format of the station is classic hits. WKVT-FM broadcasts to the Brattleboro, VT area at 92.7 FM.
FM RADIO STATION

WKVX-AM 39187
Owner: Dix Communications
Editorial: 186 S Hillcrest Dr, Wooster, Ohio 44691-3727 **Tel:** 1 330 264-5122.
Email: contact@wqkt.com
Web site: http://wqkt.com/am-960-wkvx/
Profile: WKVX-AM is a commercial station owned by Dix Communications. The format of the station is Classic Hits. WKVX-AM broadcasts to the Cleveland area at 960 AM.
AM RADIO STATION

WKWC-FM 41491
Owner: Kentucky Wesleyan College
Editorial: 3000 Frederica St, Owensboro, Kentucky 42301-6057 **Tel:** 1 270 852-3601.
Email: pantherradio@kwc.edu
Web site: http://kwc.edu/campus-life/campus-clubs-organizations-societies/wkwc-radio-90-3-fm/
FM RADIO STATION

WKWF-AM 36601
Owner: Spottswood & Co.
Editorial: 5450 MacDonald Ave, Key West, Florida 33040-5903 **Tel:** 1 305 296-2523.
Web site: http://www.sportsradio1600.com
Profile: WKWF-AM is a commercial station owned by Spottswood & Co and operated by Clear Channel Media and Entertainment. The format of the station is sports. WKWF-AM broadcasts to the Key West, FL area at 1600 AM.
AM RADIO STATION

WKWI-FM 40461
Owner: Two Rivers Communications Inc.
Editorial: 101 Radio Rd, Kilmarnock, Virginia 22482-3881 **Tel:** 1 804 435-1414.
Email: onair@1017bayfm.com
Profile: WKWI-FM is a commercial station owned by Two Rivers Communications Inc. The format of the station is adult contemporary. WKWI-FM broadcasts to the Kilmarnock, VA area at 101.7 FM.
FM RADIO STATION

WKWK-FM 45140
Owner: iHeartMedia Inc.
Editorial: 1015 Main St, Wheeling, West Virginia 26003-2709 **Tel:** 1 304 232-1170.
Web site: http://mix973wheeling.iheart.com
Profile: WKWK-FM is a commercial station owned by iHeartMedia Inc. The format of the station is adult contemporary. WKWK-FM broadcasts to the Wheeling, WV area at 97.3 FM.
FM RADIO STATION

WKWL-AM 35460
Owner: Williamson Broadcasting
Tel: 1 334 858-6162.
Web site: http://www.wkwl.ezstream.com
Profile: WKWL-AM is a commercial station owned by Williamson Broadcasting. The format of the station is Southern gospel music and religious talk. WKWL-AM broadcasts to the Florala, AL area at 1230 AM.
AM RADIO STATION

WKWN-AM 36315
Owner: Dade County Broadcasting
Editorial: 12544 N Main St, Trenton, Georgia 30752
Tel: 1 706 657-7594.
Web site: http://www.discoverdade.com/newsradio.htm
Profile: WKWN-AM is a commercial station owned by Dade County Broadcasting. The format of the station is news and talk. WKWN-AM broadcasts to the Trenton, GA area at 1420 AM.
AM RADIO STATION

WKWS-FM 45048
Owner: West Virginia Radio Corp.
Editorial: 1111 Virginia St E, Charleston, West Virginia 25301-2406 **Tel:** 1 304 342-8131.
Web site: http://www.961thewolf.com
Profile: WKWS-FM is a commercial station owned by West Virgina Radio Corp. The format of the station is contemporary country music. WKWS-FM broadcasts to the Charleston, WV area at 96.1 FM.
FM RADIO STATION

WKWX-FM 40462
Owner: Melco Inc.
Editorial: 695 Wayne Rd, Box 40, Savannah, Tennessee 38372 **Tel:** 1 731 925-9600.
Email: wkwx@bellsouth.net
Profile: WKWX-FM is a commercial station owned by Melco Inc. The format of the station is contemporary country. WKWX-FM broadcasts to the Savannah, TN area at 93.5 FM.
FM RADIO STATION

WKWY-FM 681012
Owner: Carol Burrow Administratex
Editorial: 341 Radio Station Rd, Tompkinsville, Kentucky 42167-8572 **Tel:** 1 270 487-6119.
Email: kixcountry@windstream.net
FM RADIO STATION

WKXA-FM 45208
Owner: Blanchard River Broadcasting, Co.
Editorial: 551 Lake Cascade Pkwy, Findlay, Ohio 45840 **Tel:** 1 419 422-4545.
Email: wkxa@wkxa.com
Web site: http://www.wkxa.com
Profile: WKXA-FM is a commercial station owned by Blanchard River Broadcasting, Co. The format of the station is country. WKXA-FM broadcasts to the Findlay, OH area at 100.5 FM.
FM RADIO STATION

WKXB-FM 42133
Owner: Capitol Broadcasting Company
Editorial: 25 N Kerr Ave, Ste C, Wilmington, North Carolina 28405 **Tel:** 1 910 791-3088.
Web site: http://www.jammin999fm.com
Profile: WKXB-FM is a commercial station owned by Capitol Broadcasting Company. The format of the station is R&B oldies. WKXB-FM broadcasts to the Wilmington, NC area at 99.9 FM.
FM RADIO STATION

WKXC-FM 41312
Owner: Beasley Broadcast Group
Editorial: 4051 Jimmie Dyess Pkwy, Augusta, Georgia 30909-9469 **Tel:** 1 706 855-9494.
Web site: http://www.kicks99.com
Profile: WKXC-FM is a commercial station owned by the Beasley Broadcast Group. The format of the station is classic country. WKXC-FM broadcasts to the Augusta, GA area at 99.5 FM.
FM RADIO STATION

WKXD-FM 46496
Owner: Stonecom Cookeville LLC
Editorial: 259 S Willow Ave, Cookeville, Tennessee 38501-3140 **Tel:** 1 931 528-6064.
Web site: http://www.1069kickscountry.com
Profile: WKXD-FM is a commercial station owned by Stonecom Cookeville LLC. The format of the station is country. WKXD-FM broadcasts to the Cookeville, TN area at 106.9 FM.
FM RADIO STATION

WKXH-FM 45404
Owner: Vermont Broadcast Associates Inc.
Editorial: 1303 Concord Ave, Saint Johnsbury, Vermont 5819 **Tel:** 1 802 748-2362.
Email: kix1055@gmail.com
Web site: http://www.kix1055.com
Profile: WKXH-FM is a commercial station owned by Vermont Broadcast Associates Inc. The format of the station contemporary country music. WKXH-FM broadcasts to the St. Johnsbury, VT area at 105.5 FM.
FM RADIO STATION

WKXI-FM 46729
Owner: Alpha Media
Editorial: 731 S Pear Orchard Rd Ste 27, Ridgeland, Mississippi 39157-4839 **Tel:** 1 601 957-1300.
Email: production@wjmi.com
Web site: http://www.kixie107.com/
Profile: WKXI-FM is a commercial station owned by Alpha Media. The format of the station is urban contemporary. WKXI-FM broadcasts to the Jackson, MS area at 107.5 FM.
FM RADIO STATION

WKXJ-FM 46656
Owner: iHeartMedia Inc.
Editorial: 7413 Old Lee Hwy, Chattanooga, Tennessee 37421-1142 **Tel:** 1 423 892-3333.
Web site: http://www.kisschattanooga.com
Profile: WKXJ-FM is a commercial station owned by iHeartMedia Inc. The format of the station is Top 40/CHR. WKXJ-FM broadcasts to the Chattanooga, TN area at 103.7 FM.
FM RADIO STATION

WKXL-AM 38002
Owner: New Hampshire Family Radio LLC
Editorial: 37 Redington Rd, Concord, New Hampshire 03301-2440
Email: news@wkxl1450.com
Web site: http://concordnewsradio.com
Profile: WKXL-AM is a commercial station owned by New Hampshire Family Radio LLC. The format of the station is news, talk and sports. WKXL-AM broadcasts to the Concord, NH area at 1450 AM..
AM RADIO STATION

WKXM-FM 46250
Owner: Ad-Media Management Corp
Editorial: 655 Fairview Rd, Winfield, Alabama 35594-4755 **Tel:** 1 205 487-3261.
Profile: WKXM-FM is a commercial station owned by Ad-Media Management Corp. The format of the station is classic hits. WKXM-FM's broadcasts to the Birmingham, AL at 97.7 FM.
FM RADIO STATION

WKXP-FM 45060
Owner: Townsquare Media
Editorial: 2 Pendell Rd, Poughkeepsie, New York 12601-1513 **Tel:** 1 845 471-1500.
Web site: http://hudsonvalleycountry.com
Profile: WKXP-FM is a commercial station owned by Townsquare Media. The format of the station is country. WKPX-FM broadcasts to the Poughkeepsie, NY area on 94.3 FM.
FM RADIO STATION

WKXQ-FM 40463
Owner: LB Sports Production, LLC
Editorial: 108 E Main St, Beardstown, Illinois 62618-1241 **Tel:** 1 217 323-1790.
Email: wrmsfm@gmail.com
Web site: http://www.wkxqfm.com
Profile: WKXQ-FM is a commercial station owned by LB Sports Production, LLC. The format of the station is adult standards. WKXQ-FM broadcasts in the Rushville, IL area at 92.5 FM.
FM RADIO STATION

WKXR-AM 35461
Owner: Oakie Mountain Broadcasting
Editorial: 1119 Eastview Dr, Asheboro, North Carolina 27203-4576 **Tel:** 1 336 625-2187.
Email: wkxr@atomic.net
Web site: http://www.wkxr.com
Profile: WKXR-AM is a commercial station owned by Oakie Mountain Broadcasting. The format of the station is country. WKXR-AM broadcasts to the Asheboro, NC area at 1260 AM.
AM RADIO STATION

WKXS-FM 46841
Owner: Cumulus Media Inc.
Editorial: 3233 Burnt Mill Dr Ste 4, Wilmington, North Carolina 28403-2676 **Tel:** 1 910 763-9977.
Web site: http://www.945thehawkradio.com
Profile: WKXS-FM is a commercial station owned by Cumulus Media Inc. The format of the station is classic hits. WKXS-FM broadcasts to the Wilmington, NC area at 94.5 FM.
FM RADIO STATION

WKXV-AM 35462
Owner: Ra-Tel Broadcasting Company Inc.
Editorial: 5106 Middlebrook Pike, Knoxville, Tennessee 37921-5970 **Tel:** 1 865 558-0900.
Email: wkxv@bellsouth.net
Web site: http://www.wkxvradio.com
Profile: WKXV-AM is a commercial station owned by Ra-Tel Broadcasting Company Inc. The format of the station is religious programming and Southern gospel music. WKXV-AM broadcasts to the Knoxville, TN area at 900 AM.
AM RADIO STATION

WKXW-FM 45698
Owner: Townsquare Media, LLC
Editorial: 109 Walters Ave, Ewing, New Jersey 08638-1829 **Tel:** 1 609 359-5300.
Web site: http://nj1015.com
Profile: WKXW-FM is a commercial station owned by Townsquare Media, LLC. The format of the station is news, talk and classic hits. WKXW-FM broadcasts to the greater Philadelphia, PA area at 101.5 FM.
FM RADIO STATION

WKXX-FM 41852
Owner: Broadcast Media LLC
Editorial: 100 Spurlock St, Rainbow City, Alabama 35906-5864 **Tel:** 1 256 442-3944.
Web site: http://www.wkxx.com
Profile: WKXX-FM is a commercial station owned by Broadcast Media LLC. The format for the station is hot adult contemporary. WKXX-FM broadcasts to the Rainbow City, AL area at 102.9 FM.
FM RADIO STATION

WKXY-FM 35614
Owner: Delta Radio, LLC
Editorial: 3965 Highway 61 N, Cleveland, Mississippi 38732-8738 **Tel:** 1 662 843-3392.
Email: info@deltaradio.net
Web site: http://www.kix921.com
Profile: WKXY-FM is a commercial station owned by Delta Radio, LLC. The format of the station is mainstream country. WKXY-FM broadcasts to the Cleveland, MS area at 92.1 FM.
FM RADIO STATION

WKXZ-FM 45323
Owner: Townsquare Media, LLC
Editorial: 34 Chestnut St, Oneonta, New York 13820-2466 **Tel:** 1 607 432-1030.
Email: cnynews@townsquaremedia.com
Web site: http://www.wkxzfm.com
Profile: WKXZ-FM is a commercial station owned by Townsquare Media, LLC. The format of the station is hot adult contemporary music. WKXZ-FM broadcasts to the Oneonta, NY area at 93.9 FM.
FM RADIO STATION

WKYA-FM 40313
Owner: Starlight Broadcasting Co.
Editorial: 464 State Route 189 S, Greenville, Kentucky 42345 **Tel:** 1 270 338-6655.
FM RADIO STATION

WKY-AM 35464
Owner: Cumulus Media Inc.
Editorial: 4045 NW 64th St Ste 600, Oklahoma City, Oklahoma 73116-2607 **Tel:** 1 405 460-9393.
Web site: http://www.laindomable.com
Profile: WKY-AM is a commercial station owned by Cumulus Media Inc. The format of the station is Regional Mexican. WKY-AM broadcasts to Oklahoma City at 930 AM.
AM RADIO STATION

WKYE-FM 45324
Owner: FM Radio Licenses, LLC
Editorial: 109 Plaza Dr Ste 2, Johnstown, Pennsylvania 15905-1212 **Tel:** 1 814 255-4186.
Web site: http://www.96key.com
Profile: WKYE-FM is a commercial station owned by FM Radio Licenses, LLC. The format of the station is adult contemporary. WKYE-FM broadcasts to the Johnstown, PA area at 96.5 FM.
FM RADIO STATION

WKYH-AM 37153
Owner: Forcht Broadcasting
Tel: 1 606 789-5311.
Email: wsipprod@keybroadcasting.net
Web site: http://www.wkyham.com
Profile: WKYH-AM is a commercial station owned by Forcht Broadcasting. The format of the station is sports. WKYH-AM broadcasts to the Painstville, KY area at 600 AM.
AM RADIO STATION

WKYK-AM 35465
Owner: Mark Media Inc.
Editorial: 749 Saw Mill Hollow Rd, Burnsville, North Carolina 28714 **Tel:** 1 828 682-3510.
Email: 940@wkyk.com
Web site: http://www.ourlocalcommunityonline.com
Profile: WKYK-AM is a commercial station owned by Mark Media Inc. The format of the station is classic country. WKYK-AM broadcasts to the Burnsville, NC area at 940 AM. The station's slogan is, "Super Country K94 Stereo."
AM RADIO STATION

WKYL-FM 42094
Owner: Davenport Broadcasting Inc.
Editorial: 88 C Michael Davenport Blvd, Ste 2, Frankfort, Kentucky 40601-4389 **Tel:** 1 502 839-1021.
Email: classic1021@wkyl.org
Web site: http://www.weku.fm/post/classic-1021-wkyl
Profile: WKYL-FM is a non-commercial station owned by Davenport Broadcasting and programmed by Eastern Kentucky University. The format of the station is primarily classical music programming. WKYL-FM broadcasts to the Greater Lexington and Lawrenceburg area in Kentucky.
FM RADIO STATION

WKYM-FM 45325
Owner: Staples Jr.(Stephen)
Editorial: 150 Worsham Ln, Monticello, Kentucky 42633-1610 **Tel:** 1 606 348-7083.
Web site: http://www.wkym.com
FM RADIO STATION

WKYN-FM 40420
Owner: Gateway Radio Works Inc.
Editorial: 22 West Main Street, Mount Sterling, Kentucky 40353 **Tel:** 1 859 498-1077.
Profile: WKYN-FM is a commercial station owned by Gateway Radio Works Inc. The format for the station is country. WKYN-FM broadcasts to the Lexington, KY area at 107.7 FM.
FM RADIO STATION

WKYO-AM 39337
Owner: Edwards Communications LLC
Editorial: 344 N State St, Caro, Michigan 48723-1538 **Tel:** 1 989 673-3181.
Email: news@mix921.com
Web site: http://www.tuscolatoday.com
Profile: WKYO-AM is a commercial station owned by Edwards Communications LLC. The format of the station is oldies music. WKYO-AM broadcasts to the Caro, MI area at 1360 AM.
AM RADIO STATION

WKYQ-FM 46094
Owner: Bristol Broadcasting
Editorial: 6000 Bristol Dr, Paducah, Kentucky 42003-9213 **Tel:** 1 270 554-0093.
Email: news@wkyq.com
Web site: http://www.wkyq.com
Profile: WKYQ-FM is a commercial station owned by Bristol Broadcasting. The format of the station is contemporary country. WKYQ-FM broadcasts to the Paducah, KY area at 93.3 FM.
FM RADIO STATION

WKYR-FM 46184
Owner: River Country Communications, LLC
Editorial: 1089 S Main St, Burkesville, Kentucky 42717-9402 **Tel:** 1 270 433-7191.
FM RADIO STATION

WKYS-FM 40464
Owner: Urban One, Inc.
Editorial: 8515 Georgia Ave Fl 9, Silver Spring, Maryland 20910-3403 **Tel:** 1 301 306-1111.
Web site: http://kysdc.com
Profile: WKYS-FM is a commercial station owned by Urban One, Inc. The format of the station is urban contemporary music. WKYS-FM broadcasts to the Washington, D.C. area at 93.9 FM.
FM RADIO STATION

WKYW-AM 37806
Owner: Capcity Communications Inc.
Editorial: 115 W Main St, Frankfort, Kentucky 40601-2807 **Tel:** 1 502 875-1130.
Web site: http://passportradio1490.com
Profile: WKYW-AM is a commercial station owned by Forever Communication Inc. The format is smooth AC. The station airs in the Frankfort, KY area at 1490 AM.
AM RADIO STATION

WKYX-AM 38739
Owner: Bristol Broadcasting
Editorial: 6000 Bristol Dr, Paducah, Kentucky 42003-9213 **Tel:** 1 270 554-8255.
Email: news@wkyx.com
Web site: http://www.wkyx.com
Profile: WKYX-AM is a commercial station owned by Bristol Broadcasting. The format of the station is news and talk. WKYX-AM broadcasts in the Paducah, KY area at 570 AM.
AM RADIO STATION

WKYX-FM 46294
Owner: Bristol Broadcasting
Editorial: 6000 Bristol Dr, Paducah, Kentucky 42003-9213 **Tel:** 1 270 554-8255.
Email: news@wkyx.com
Web site: http://www.wkyx.com
Profile: WKYX-FM is a commercial station owned by Bristol Broadcasting. The format of the station is news and talk. WKYX-FM broadcasts to the Paducah, KY area at 94.3 FM.
FM RADIO STATION

WKYZ-FM 44351
Owner: Keys Media Company, Inc
Editorial: 5555 College Rd, Key West, Florida 33040-4307 **Tel:** 1 305 294-1017.
Web site: http://www.pirateradiokeywest.com
Profile: WKYZ-FM is a commercial station owned by Keys Media Company, Inc. The format of the station is adult rock with a mixture of classic and alternative music. WKYZ-FM broadcasts to the Marathon, FL area at 101.7 FM.
FM RADIO STATION

WKZB-FM 46563
Owner: New South Communications, Inc
Tel: 1 601 693-2381.
Web site: http://www.q101radio.net
Profile: WKZB-FM is a commercial station owned by New South Communications, Inc. The format of the station is Top 40/CHR. WKZB-FM broadcasts to the Meridian, MS, area at 101.3 FM.
FM RADIO STATION

WKZC-FM 40465
Owner: Synergy Media, Inc.
Editorial: 5399 W Wallace Ln, Ludington, Michigan 49431-2439 **Tel:** 1 231 843-0941.
Profile: WKZC-FM is a commercial station owned by Synergy Media, Inc. The format of the station is contemporary country music. WKZC-FM broadcasts to the Ludington, MI area at 94.9 FM.
FM RADIO STATION

WKZD-AM 35993
Owner: Abercrombie Broadcasting, Inc.
Editorial: 219 Chestnut St Ne, Hartselle, Alabama 35640-1903 **Tel:** 1 256 773-4114.
Profile: WKZD-AM is a commercial station owned by Abercrombie Broadcasting, Inc. The format of the station is oldies. WKZD-AM broadcasts to the Hartselle, AL area at 1310 AM.
AM RADIO STATION

WKZE-FM 46020
Owner: Willpower Radio LLC
Editorial: 7564 N Broadway, Red Hook, New York 12571-1457 **Tel:** 1 845 758-9810.
Web site: http://981kze.com/
Profile: WKZE-FM is a commercial station owned by Willpower Radio LLC. The format of the station is adult album alternative music. WKZE-FM broadcasts to the Redhook, NY area at 98.1 FM.
FM RADIO STATION

WKZG-FM 43772
Owner: Woodward Communications, Inc.
Editorial: 2800 E College Ave, Appleton, Wisconsin 54915-3255 **Tel:** 1 920 733-6639.
Web site: http://www.kz1043.com
Profile: WKZG-FM is a commercial station owned by Woodward Communications, Inc. The station's format is Hot AC. WKZG-FM broadcasts to the Appleton, WI area at 104.3 FM.
FM RADIO STATION

WKZI-AM 36123
Owner: Word Power Inc.
Editorial: 18889 N 2350th St, Dennison, Illinois 62423 **Tel:** 1 217 826-9673.
Email: wkzi@rr1.net
Web site: http://www.wordpower.us
Profile: WKZI-AM is a commercial station owned by World Power Inc. The format of the station is religious music and talk. WKZI-AM broadcasts to the Dennison, IL area at 800 AM.
AM RADIO STATION

WKZJ-FM 43519
Owner: Davis Broadcasting
Editorial: 2203 Wynnton Rd, Columbus, Georgia 31906-2531 **Tel:** 1 706 576-3565.
Web site: http://www.k927.com
Profile: WKZJ-FM is a commercial station owned by David Broadcasting. The format of the station is adult contemporary. WKZJ-FM broadcasts to the Columbus, GA area at 92.7 FM.
FM RADIO STATION

WKZK-AM 35466
Owner: Gospel Radio Inc.
Editorial: 2 Milledge Rd, Augusta, Georgia 30904-3063 **Tel:** 1 706 738-9191.
Web site: http://www.wkzk.net
Profile: WKZK-AM is a commercial station owned by Gospel Radio Inc. The format of the station is gospel. WKZK-AM broadcasts to the Augusta, GA area at 1600 AM.
AM RADIO STATION

WKZL-FM 40466
Owner: Dick Jr.(James A.)
Editorial: 192 E Lewis St, Greensboro, North Carolina 27406 **Tel:** 1 336 274-8042.
Web site: http://www.1075kzl.com
Profile: WKZL-FM is a commercial station owned by James A. Dick Jr. The format of the station is Top 40/CHR. WKZL-FM broadcasts to the Greensboro-Winston Salem, NC area at 107.5 FM.
FM RADIO STATION

WKZN-AM 38590
Owner: Entercom Communications Corp.
Editorial: 305 Route 315 Hwy, Pittston, Pennsylvania 18640-3907 **Tel:** 1 570 883-9850.
Web site: http://www.wilknetwork.com
Profile: WKZN-AM is a commercial station owned by Entercom Communications Corp. The format of the station is news, sports and talk. WKZN-AM broadcasts to the Wilkes Barre-Scranton, PA area at 1300 AM.
AM RADIO STATION

WKZO-AM 35467
Owner: Midwest Communications Inc.
Editorial: 4200 W Main St, Kalamazoo, Michigan 49006-2749 **Tel:** 1 269 345-7121.
Email: wkzonews@wkzo.com
Web site: http://www.wkzo.com
Profile: WKZO-AM is a commercial station owned by Midwest Communications Inc. The format of the station is news and talk. WKZO-AM broadcasts to the Kalamazoo, MI area at 590 AM.
AM RADIO STATION

WKZO-FM 46529
Owner: Midwest Communications Inc.
Editorial: 4200 W Main St, Kalamazoo, Michigan 49006-2749 **Tel:** 1 269 345-7121.
Email: wkzonews@wkzo.com
Web site: http://www.wkzo.com
Profile: WKZO-FM is a commercial station owned by Midwest Communications Inc. The format of the station is modern rock. WKZO-FM broadcasts to the Grand Rapids, MI area at 96.5 FM.
FM RADIO STATION

WKZP-FM 43152
Owner: iHeartMedia Inc.
Editorial: 351 Tilghman Rd, Gateway Crossing, Salisbury, Maryland 21804-1920 **Tel:** 1 410 742-1923.
Email: delmarvapsa@iheartmedia.com
Web site: http://kiss959fm.iheart.com
Profile: WKZP-FM is a commercial station owned by iHeartMedia Inc. The format of the station is Top 40/CHR. WKZP-FM broadcasts to the Salisbury, MD area. area at 95.9 FM.
FM RADIO STATION

WKZQ-FM 46000
Owner: Alpha Media
Editorial: 1016 Ocala St, Myrtle Beach, South Carolina 29577-8007 **Tel:** 1 843 448-1041.
Web site: http://www.wkzq.net
Profile: WKZQ-FM is a commercial station owned by Alpha Media. The format of the station is rock. WKZQ-FM broadcasts to the Myrtle Beach, SC area at 96.1 FM.
FM RADIO STATION

WKZR-FM 45327
Owner: Beasley(W.R.)
Editorial: 1250 W Charlton St, Milledgeville, Georgia 31061 **Tel:** 1 478 452-0587.
Email: mail@country102fm.com
Web site: http://www.country102fm.com
Profile: WKZR-FM is a commercial station owned by W.R. Beasley. The format of the station is country music. WKZR-FM broadcasts to the Milledgeville, GA area at 102.3 FM.
FM RADIO STATION

WKZS-FM 40166
Owner: Benton-Weatherford Broadcasting Inc. of Tennessee
Editorial: 820 Railroad St, Covington, Indiana 47932-1357 **Tel:** 1 765 793-4823.
Email: info@kisscountryradio.com
Web site: http://www.kisscountryradio.com
Profile: WKZS-FM is a commercial station owned by Benton-Weatherford Broadcasting Inc. of Tennessee. The format of the station is contemporary country. WKZS-FM broadcasts to the Covington, IN area at 103.1 FM.
FM RADIO STATION

WKZU-FM 42940
Owner: Kudzu Communications Inc
Editorial: 107 Spring Street, Ripley, Mississippi 38663 **Tel:** 1 662 837-1023.
Email: classicradiofm@aol.com
Web site: http://www.classicradiofm.com
Profile: WKZU-FM is a commercial station owned by Kudzu Communications Inc. The format of the station is country. WKZU-FM broadcasts to the Ripley, MS area at 104.9 FM.
FM RADIO STATION

WKZW-FM 43573
Owner: Blakeney Communications Inc.
Editorial: 4580 Highway 15 N, Laurel, Mississippi 39440 **Tel:** 1 601 649-0095.
Email: kz943@kz943.com
Web site: http://www.kz94.com
Profile: WKZW-FM is a commercial station owned by Blakeney Communications Inc. The format of the station is adult contemporary music. WKZW-FM broadcasts to the Laurel, MS area at 94.3 FM.
FM RADIO STATION

WKZX-FM 45963
Owner: BP Broadcasters
Editorial: 406 E Broadway St, Lenoir City, Tennessee 37771-3045 **Tel:** 1 865 986-9850.
Email: wkzx@aol.com
Web site: http://laliderwkzx.com
Profile: WKZX-FM is a commercial station owned by BP Broadcasters. The format of the station is regional Mexican programming. WKZX-FM broadcasts to the Lenoir City, TN area at 93.5 FM.
FM RADIO STATION

WKZY-FM 772586
Owner: Woodward Communications, Inc.
Editorial: 2800 E College Ave, Appleton, Wisconsin 54915-3255 **Tel:** 1 920 734-9226.
Web site: http://www.kz1043.com
Profile: WKZY-FM is a commercial station owned by Woodward Communications, Inc. The format of the station is contemporary hits. WKZY-FM broadcasts to the Chilton, WI area at a frequency of 92.9 FM.
FM RADIO STATION

WKZZ-FM 44428
Owner: Broadcast South, LLC
Editorial: 1931 Ga Highway 32 E, Douglas, Georgia 31533 **Tel:** 1 912 389-0995.
Profile: WKZZ-FM is a commercial station owned by Broadcast South, LLC. The format of the station is

adult contemporary. WKZZ-FM broadcasts to the Douglas, GA area at 92.5 FM.
FM RADIO STATION

WLAC-AM
36824
Owner: iHeartMedia Inc.
Editorial: 55 Music Sq W, Nashville, Tennessee 37203-3207 **Tel:** 1 615 664-2400.
Email: programming@wlac.com
Web site: http://wlac.iheart.com
Profile: WLAC-AM is a commercial station owned by iHeartMedia Inc. The format of the station is news and talk. WLAC-AM broadcasts to the Nashville, TN area at 1510 AM.
AM RADIO STATION

WLAD-AM
39338
Owner: Berkshire Broadcasting Corp
Editorial: 98 Mill Plain Rd, Danbury, Connecticut 6811 **Tel:** 1 203 744-4800.
Email: news@wlad.com
Web site: http://www.wlad.com
Profile: WLAD-AM is a commercial station owned by Berkshire Broadcasting Corp. The format of the station is news, talk and sports. WLAD-AM broadcasts to the Danbury, CT area at 800 AM.
AM RADIO STATION

WLAF-AM
35468
Owner: Stair Company
Editorial: 210 N 5th St, La Follette, Tennessee 37766-2301 **Tel:** 1 423 562-3557.
Email: wlaf@bellsouth.net
Web site: http://www.1450wlaf.com
Profile: WLAF-AM is a commercial station owned by Stair Company. The format of the station is Southern gospel. WLAF-AM broadcasts to the La Follette, TN area at 1450 AM.
AM RADIO STATION

WLAG-AM
35469
Owner: Eagle's Nest Inc.
Editorial: 304 Broome St, Lagrange, Georgia 30240 **Tel:** 1 706 845-1023.
Email: welr@eagle1023.com
Web site: http://www.eagle1023.com
Profile: WLAG-AM is a commercial station owned by Eagle's Nest Inc. The format of the station is sports. WLAG-AM broadcasts to the Lagrange, GA area at 1240 AM.
AM RADIO STATION

WLAM-AM
35821
Owner: WBIN, Inc.
Editorial: 477 Congress St Ste 3, Portland, Maine 04101-3417 **Tel:** 1 207 797-0780.
Profile: WLAM-AM is a commercial station owned by WBIN, Inc. The format of the station is oldies. WLAM-AM broadcasts to the Portland, ME area at 1470 AM.
AM RADIO STATION

WLAN-AM
38003
Owner: iHeartMedia Inc.
Editorial: 1685 Crown Ave Ste 100, Lancaster, Pennsylvania 17601-6319 **Tel:** 1 717 295-9700.
Web site: http://www.whp580.com
Profile: WLAN-AM is a commercial station owned by iHeartMedia Inc. The format of the station is Spanish Tropical Music. WLAN-AM broadcasts to the Lancaster, PA area at 1390 AM.
AM RADIO STATION

WLAN-FM
45328
Owner: iHeartMedia Inc.
Editorial: 1685 Crown Ave Ste 100, Lancaster, Pennsylvania 17601-6319 **Tel:** 1 717 295-9700.
Web site: http://fm97.iheart.com
Profile: WLAN-FM is a commercial station owned by iHeartMedia Inc. The format of the station is Top 40/CHR. WLAN-FM broadcasts to the Lancaster, PA area at 96.9 FM.
FM RADIO STATION

WLAP-AM
38004
Owner: iHeartMedia Inc.
Editorial: 2601 Nicholasville Rd, Lexington, Kentucky 40503-3307 **Tel:** 1 859 422-1000.
Email: news@wlap.com
Web site: http://www.wlap.com
Profile: WLAP-AM is a commercial station owned by iHeartMedia Inc. The format of the station is news and talk. WLAP-AM broadcasts to the Lexington, KY area at 630 AM.
AM RADIO STATION

WLAQ-AM
35470
Owner: Cripple Creek Broadcasting
Editorial: 2 Mount Alto Rd SW, Rome, Georgia 30165 **Tel:** 1 706 232-7767.
Email: wlaq@comcast.net
Web site: http://www.wlaq1410.com
Profile: WLAQ-AM is a commercial station owned by Cripple Creek Broadcasting. The format of the station is news, sports and talk. WLAQ-AM broadcasts to the Rome, GA area 1410 AM.
AM RADIO STATION

WLAR-AM
39195
Owner: Sliger Enterprises
Editorial: 2110 Oxnard Rd, Athens, Tennessee 37303 **Tel:** 1 423 745-1000.
Email: 1017wlar@bellsouth.net
Profile: WLAR-AM is a commercial station owned by Sliger Enterprises. The format for the station is contemporary country. WLAR-AM broadcasts to the Chattanooga, TN area at 1450 AM.
AM RADIO STATION

WLAT-AM
36126
Owner: Gois Broadcasting
Editorial: 135 Burnside Ave Fl 2, East Hartford, Connecticut 06108-3421 **Tel:** 1 860 524-0001.
Web site: http://www.goisradio.com
Profile: WLAT-AM is a commercial station owned by Gois Broadcasting. The format for the station is tropical Hispanic music. WLAT-AM broadcasts to the Hartford-New Haven, CT area at 910 AM.
AM RADIO STATION

WLAU-FM
43047
Owner: TeleSouth Communications, Inc.
Editorial: 6311 Ridgewood Rd, Jackson, Mississippi 39211-2035 **Tel:** 1 601 425-2211.
Email: newsms@supertalk.fm
Web site: http://www.supertalk.fm
Profile: WLAU-FM is a commercial station owned by TeleSouth Communications, Inc. The format of the station is talk. WLAU-FM broadcasts to the Hattiesburg, MS area at 99.3 FM.
FM RADIO STATION

WLAV-FM
45330
Owner: Cumulus Media Inc.
Editorial: 60 Monroe Center St NW Fl 3, Grand Rapids, Michigan 49503-2916 **Tel:** 1 616 456-5461.
Web site: http://www.wlav.com
Profile: WLAV-FM is a commercial station owned by Cumulus Media Inc. The format of the station is classic rock. WLAV-FM broadcasts to the Grand Rapids, MI area at 96.9 FM.
FM RADIO STATION

WLAW-FM
397732
Owner: Cumulus Media Inc.
Editorial: 3375 Merriam St Ste 201, Muskegon, Michigan 49444-3173 **Tel:** 1 231 830-0176.
Web site: http://www.muskegonnashicon.com
Profile: WLAW-FM is a commercial station owned by Cumulus Media Inc.. The format of the station is country. WLAW-FM broadcasts to the Muskegon, MI, area at 92.5 FM.
FM RADIO STATION

WLAY-AM
38006
Owner: URBan Radio Broadcasting, LLC
Editorial: 509 N Main St, Tuscumbia, Alabama 35674-2048 **Tel:** 1 256 383-2525.
Web site: http://www.wlaythesound.com
Profile: WLAY-AM is a commercial station owned by Urban Radio Broadcasting, LLC. The format of the station is variety. WLAY-AM broadcasts to the Muscle Shoals, AL area at 1450 AM.
AM RADIO STATION

WLAY-FM
41363
Owner: URBan Radio Broadcasting, LLC
Editorial: 509 N Main St, Tuscumbia, Alabama 35674-2048 **Tel:** 1 256 383-2525.
Email: info@urbanradio.fm
Web site: http://www.wlay1035.com
Profile: WLAY-FM is a commercial station owned by URBan Radio Broadcasting, LLC. The format of the station is classic country music. WLAY-FM broadcasts to the Tuscumbia, AL area at 103.5 FM.
FM RADIO STATION

WLAZ-FM
81001
Owner: Font (Otoniel)
Editorial: 972 E Osceola Pkwy, Kissimmee, Florida 34744-1615 **Tel:** 1 787 625-5858.
Email: info@purapalabra.com
Web site: http://purapalabra.com
Profile: WLAZ-FM is a commercial station owned by Otoniel Font. The format of the station is Christian programming. WLAZ-FM broadcasts to the Kissimmee, FL area at 89.1 FM.
FM RADIO STATION

WLBA-AM
36143
Owner: La Favorita Inc.
Editorial: 5815 Westside Rd, Austell, Georgia 30106-3179 **Tel:** 1 770 944-0900.
Email: traffic@lamejorestacion.com
Web site: http://www.lamejorestacion.com
Profile: WLBA-AM is a commercial station owned by La Favorita Inc. The format of the station is regional Mexican. WLBA-AM broadcasts to the Atlanta area at 1130 AM.
AM RADIO STATION

WLBB-AM
36687
Owner: Gradick Communications LLC
Editorial: 808 Newnan Rd, Carrollton, Georgia 30117-6426 **Tel:** 1 678 601-1330.
Email: news@newstalk1330.com
Web site: http://www.gradickcommunications.com
Profile: WLBB-AM is a commercial station owned by Gradick Communications LLC. The format of the station is news and talk. WLBB-AM broadcasts to the Carrollton, GA area at 1330 AM.
AM RADIO STATION

WLBC-FM
45332
Owner: Backyard Broadcasting
Editorial: 800 E 29th St, Muncie, Indiana 47302-5765 **Tel:** 1 765 288-4403.
Web site: http://www.wlbc.com
Profile: WLBC-FM is a commercial station owned by Backyard Broadcasting. The format of the station is hot adult contemporary music. WLBC-FM broadcasts to the Indianapolis area at 101.4 FM.
FM RADIO STATION

WLBE-AM
35472
Owner: WLBE 790 Inc.
Editorial: 32900 Radio Rd, Leesburg, Florida 34788-3903 **Tel:** 1 352 787-7900.
Web site: http://my790am.com
Profile: WLBE-AM is a commercial station owned by WLBE 790 Inc. The format of the station is oldies and talk. WLBE-AM broadcasts to the Leesburg, FL area at 790 AM.
AM RADIO STATION

WLBF-FM
41313
Owner: Faith Broadcasting
Editorial: 381 Mendel Pkwy E, Montgomery, Alabama 36117 **Tel:** 1 334 271-8900.
Email: mail@faithradio.org
Web site: http://www.faithradio.org
Profile: WLBF-FM is a non-commercial station owned by Faith Broadcasting. The format of the station is Christian religious programming. WLBF-FM broadcasts to the Montgomery, AL area at 89.1 FM.
FM RADIO STATION

WLBG-AM
35473
Owner: Southeastern Broadcast Assocs. Inc.
Editorial: 315 Hillcrest Dr, Laurens, South Carolina 29360-2343 **Tel:** 1 864 984-3544.
Email: mail@wlbg.com
Web site: http://www.wlbg.com
Profile: WLBG-AM is a commercial station owned by Southeastern Broadcast Associates Inc. The format of the station is news, sports, talk and gospel. WLBG-AM broadcasts to the Laurens, SC area at 860 AM.
AM RADIO STATION

WLBK-AM
37109
Owner: Dekalb County Broadcasters, Inc.
Editorial: 2410 Sycamore Rd Ste C, Dekalb, Illinois 60115-2091 **Tel:** 1 815 748-1000.
Email: wlbk@nelsonmultimedia.com
Web site: http://www.1360wlbk.com
Profile: WLBK-AM is a commercial station owned by Dekalb County Broadcasters, Inc. The format of the station is news and talk programming. WLBK-AM broadcasts to the De Kalb, IL area at 1360 AM and is simulcast on WLBK-FM, 98.9 FM.
AM RADIO STATION

WLBN-AM
38009
Owner: Choice Radio Corporation
Editorial: 253 W Main St, Lebanon, Kentucky 40033-1240 **Tel:** 1 270 692-3126.
Web site: http://www.1590wlbn.com
Profile: WLBN-AM is a commercial station owned by Choice Radio Corporation. The format of the station is oldies. WLBN-AM broadcasts in the Lebanon, KY area at 1590 AM.
AM RADIO STATION

WLBQ-AM
35474
Owner: Beech Tree Publishing
Editorial: 107 West Ohio Street, Morgantown, Kentucky 42261 **Tel:** 1 270 526-5393.
Email: info@beechtreenews.com
Web site: http://www.beechtreenews.com
Profile: WLBQ-AM is a commercial station owned by Beech Tree Publishing. The format of the station is news and country. WLBQ-AM broadcasts to the Morgantown, KY area at 1570 AM.
AM RADIO STATION

WLBR-AM
38010
Owner: Lebanon Broadcasting Co.
Editorial: 440 Rebecca Ln, Lebanon, Pennsylvania 17046-1734 **Tel:** 1 717 272-7651.
Profile: WLBR-AM is a commercial station owned by Lebanon Broadcasting Co. The format of the station is variety. WLBR-AM broadcasts to the Lebanon, PA area at 1270 AM.
AM RADIO STATION

WLBW-FM
42559
Owner: Educational Media Foundation
Editorial: 5700 W Oaks Blvd, Rocklin, California 95765-3719 **Tel:** 1 916 251-1600.
Web site: http://www.klove.com
Profile: WLBW-FM is a commercial station owned by Educational Media Foundation. The format of the station is contemporary Christian. WLBW-FM broadcasts to the Ocean City, MD area at 92.1 FM.
FM RADIO STATION

WLBY-AM
38090
Owner: Cumulus Media Inc.
Editorial: 1100 Victors Way, Ann Arbor, Michigan 48108-5220 **Tel:** 1 734 302-8100.
Email: programming@1290wlby.com
Web site: http://www.1290wlby.com
Profile: WLBY-AM is a commercial station owned by Cumulus Media Inc. The format of the station is business talk. WLBY-AM broadcasts to the Ann Arbor, MI area at 1290 AM.
AM RADIO STATION

WLCA-FM
40469
Owner: Lewis & Clark Community College
Editorial: 5800 Godfrey Rd, Godfrey, Illinois 62035-2426 **Tel:** 1 618 466-8936.
Web site: http://www.wlcafm.com
Profile: WLCA-FM is a non-commercial station owned by Lewis & Clark Community College. The format of the station is alternative and new rock music. WLCA-FM broadcasts to the Godfrey, IL area at 89.9 FM.
FM RADIO STATION

WLCC-AM
36194
Owner: Salem Media Group, Inc.
Editorial: 5211 W Laurel St Ste 101, Tampa, Florida 33607-1725 **Tel:** 1 813 639-1903.
Web site: http://760radioluz.com
Profile: WLCC-AM is a commercial station owned by Salem Media Group, Inc. The format of the station is Spanish Christian. WLCC-AM broadcasts to the Tampa Bay, FL area at 760 AM.
AM RADIO STATION

WLCH-FM
41695
Owner: SACA Spanish-American Civic Association
Editorial: 30 N Ann St, Lancaster, Pennsylvania 17602-3063 **Tel:** 1 717 295-7996.
Web site: http://wlchradio.org
Profile: WLCH-FM is a non-commercial station owned by SACA Spanish-American Civic Association. The format of the station is Hispanic talk. WLCH-FM broadcasts in the Lancaster, PA area at 91.3 FM.
FM RADIO STATION

WLCK-AM
38011
Owner: Skytower Communications Inc.
Editorial: 104 1/2 W Public Sq, Scottsville, Kentucky 42164-1175 **Tel:** 1 270 237-3148.
Email: newswatch@wvle.net
AM RADIO STATION

WLCL-FM
45251
Owner: UB Louisville, LLC
Editorial: 11700 Commonwealth Dr, Louisville, Kentucky 40299-6303 **Tel:** 1 502 240-0602.
Profile: WLCL-FM is a commercial station owned by UB Louisville, LLC. The format of the station is sports talk. WLCL-FM broadcasts to the Louisville, KY area at 93.9 FM.
FM RADIO STATION

WLCM-AM
35552
Owner: Christian Broadcasting System
Editorial: 1613 Lawrence Hwy, Charlotte, Michigan 48813 **Tel:** 1 517 543-8200.
Web site: http://www.wlcmradio.com
Profile: WLCM-AM is a commercial station owned by Christian Broadcasting System. The format of the station is religious programming. WLCM-AM broadcasts to the Charlotte, MI area at 1500 AM.
AM RADIO STATION

WLCN-FM
338734
Owner: KM Communications Inc.
Editorial: 1779 2250th St, Atlanta, Illinois 61723-9223 **Tel:** 1 217 648-5510.
Email: lincolncountry@yahoo.com
Web site: http://www.wlcnonline.com
Profile: WLCN-FM is a commercial station owned by KM Communications Inc. The format of the station is contemporary country and classic rock. WLCN-FM broadcasts to the Atlanta, IL area at 96.3 FM.
FM RADIO STATION

WLCO-AM
37752
Owner: Townsquare Media, LLC
Editorial: 3338 E Bristol Rd, Burton, Michigan 48529-1408 **Tel:** 1 810 743-1080.
Profile: WLCO-AM is a commercial station owned by Townsquare Media, LLC. The format for the station is classic country. WLCO-AM broadcasts to the Burton, MI area at 1530 AM.
AM RADIO STATION

WLCQ-FM
536028
Owner: Lighthouse Christian Center
Editorial: 522 Springfield St, Feeding Hills, Massachusetts 01030-2104 **Tel:** 1 413 821-0997.
Email: contact@wlcq.com
Web site: http://www.theq997.com
Profile: WLCQ-FM is a non-commercial station owned by Lighthouse Christian Center. The format of the station is contemporary Christian. WLCQ broadcasts to the Springfield, MA area at 99.7 FM.
FM RADIO STATION

WLCR-AM
37024
Owner: LCR Partners LP
Editorial: 3600 Goldsmith Ln, Louisville, Kentucky 40220-2326 **Tel:** 1 502 451-9527.
Web site: http://www.wlcr.org
Profile: WLCR-AM is a commercial station owned by LCR Partners LP. The format of the station is religious programming. WLCR-AM broadcasts to the Louisville, KY area at 1040 AM.
AM RADIO STATION

WLCS-FM
42555
Owner: Cumulus Media Inc.
Editorial: 3375 Merriam St, Ste 201, Muskegon, Michigan 49444 **Tel:** 1 231 830-0176.
Web site: http://www.983wlcs.com
Profile: WLCS-FM is a commercial station owned by Cumulus Media Inc. The format of the station is classic hits music. WLCS-FM broadcasts to Muskegon, MI at 98.3 FM.
FM RADIO STATION

WLCT-FM
46705
Owner: Lafayette Broadcasting Inc.
Editorial: 231 Chaffin Rd, Lafayette, Tennessee 37083-5004 **Tel:** 1 615 666-2169.
Email: leisureenquiries@wlct.org
Web site: http://www.wlct.org
Profile: WLCT-FM is a commercial station owned by Lafayette Broadcasting Inc. The format of the station

is country. WLCT-FM broadcasts to the Lafayette, TN area at 102.1 FM.
FM RADIO STATION

WLCY-FM 40570
Owner: Renda Broadcasting
Editorial: 840 Philadelphia St, Ste 100, Indiana, Pennsylvania 15701 **Tel:** 1 724 465-4700.
Web site: http://www.catcountry1063.com
Profile: WLCY-FM is a commercial station owned by Renda Broadcasting. The format of the station is contemporary country music. WLCY-FM broadcasts in the Indiana, PA area at 106.3 FM.
FM RADIO STATION

WLDB-FM 40635
Owner: Milwaukee Radio Alliance
Editorial: N72W12922 Good Hope Rd, Menomonee Falls, Wisconsin 53051-4441 **Tel:** 1 414 771-1021.
Email: info@b933fm.com
Web site: http://www.b933fm.com
Profile: WLDB-FM is a commercial station owned by Milwaukee Radio Alliance. The format of the station is adult contemporary. WLDB-FM broadcasts to the Milwaukee area at 93.3 FM.
FM RADIO STATION

WLDE-FM 42158
Owner: Sarkes Tarzian Inc.
Editorial: 347 W Berry St Ste 600, Fort Wayne, Indiana 46802-2241 **Tel:** 1 260 423-3676.
Email: captainchris@wlde.com
Web site: http://www.wlde.com
Profile: WLDE-FM is a commercial station owned by Sarkes Tarzian Inc. The format of the station is classic hits. WLDE-FM broadcasts to the Fort Wayne, IN area at 101.7 FM.
FM RADIO STATION

WLDI-FM 42806
Owner: iHeartMedia Inc.
Editorial: 3071 Continental Dr, West Palm Beach, Florida 33407-3274 **Tel:** 1 561 616-6600.
Web site: http://www.wild955.com
Profile: WLDI-FM is a commercial station owned by iHeartMedia Inc. The format of the station is Top 40/CHR music. WLDI-FM broadcasts to the West Palm Beach, FL area at 95.5 FM.
FM RADIO STATION

WLDR-FM 40470
Owner: Henderson, Roy E.
Editorial: 13999 S West Bay Shore Dr, Traverse City, Michigan 49684-6206 **Tel:** 1 231 947-3220.
Email: wldrnews@gmail.com
Profile: WLDR-FM is a commercial station owned by Roy E. Henderson. The format of the station is adult contemporary. WLDR-FM broadcasts to the Traverse City, MI area at a frequency of 101.9 FM.
FM RADIO STATION

WLDS-AM 38602
Owner: Jacksonville Area Radio Broadcasters, Inc.
Editorial: 2161 Old State Rd, Jacksonville, Illinois 62650 **Tel:** 1 217 245-7171.
Email: wlds@wlds.com
Web site: http://www.weai.com
Profile: WLDS-AM is a commercial station owned by Jacksonville Area Radio Broadcasters, Inc. The format of the station is news, talk and adult contemporary music. WLDS-AM broadcasts in the Jacksonville, IL area at 1180 AM.
AM RADIO STATION

WLDX-AM 35475
Owner: Dean Broadcasting, Inc.
Editorial: 733 Columbus St E, Fayette, Alabama 35555-2623 **Tel:** 1 205 932-9539.
Web site: http://www.wldx.com
Profile: WLDX-AM is a commercial station owned by Thomley Broadcasting Co. The format of the station is country music. WLDX-AM broadcasts to the Fayette, AL area at 990 AM.
AM RADIO STATION

WLDY-AM 38012
Owner: Flambeau Broadcasting Co., Inc.
Editorial: W8746 US Highway 8, Ladysmith, Wisconsin 54848-9565 **Tel:** 1 715 532-5588.
Email: wldywjbl@yahoo.com
Web site: http://wldtwjbl.com
Profile: WLDY-AM is a commercial station owned by Flambeau Broadcasting Co., Inc. The format of the station is sports. WLDY-AM broadcasts to the Ladysmith, WI area at 1340 AM.
AM RADIO STATION

WLEA-AM 38013
Owner: Canisteo Valley Broadcasting
Editorial: 5942 County Route 64, Hornell, New York 14843-9730 **Tel:** 1 607 324-1480.
Email: newsroom@am1480wlea.com
Web site: http://www.am1480wlea.com
Profile: WLEA-AM is a commercial station owned by Canisteo Valley Broadcasting. The format of the station is news. WLEA-AM broadcasts to the Hornell, NY area at 1480 AM.
AM RADIO STATION

WLEC-AM 38014
Owner: BAS Broadcasting
Editorial: 1640 Cleveland Rd, Sandusky, Ohio 44870 **Tel:** 1 419 625-1010.
Web site: http://www.wlec.com
Profile: WLEC-AM is a commercial station owned by BAS Broadcasting. The format of the station is adult standards. WLEC-AM broadcasts to the Sandusky, OH area at 1450 AM.
AM RADIO STATION

WLEL-FM 609460
Owner: Summer Rose Broadcasting
Editorial: 109 E Oglethorpe St, Ellaville, Georgia 31806 **Tel:** 1 229 937-9967.
Web site: http://www.wlelclassichits.com
Profile: WLEL-FM is a commerical station in Americus, GA owned by Summer Rose Broadcasting. The format is classic hits and airs locally on 94.3 FM.
FM RADIO STATION

WLEM-AM 38015
Owner: Salter Communications
Editorial: 241 West 4th St, Emporium, Pennsylvania 15834 **Tel:** 1 814 486-3712.
Email: wlemwqky@yahoo.com
Web site: http://www.theriver989.com
Profile: WLEM-AM is a commercial station owned by Salter Communications. The format of the station is adult hits. WLEM-AM broadcasts to the Emporium, PA area at 1250 AM.
AM RADIO STATION

WLEN-FM 40471
Owner: Lenawee Broadcasting
Editorial: 242 W Maumee St, Adrian, Michigan 49221-2022 **Tel:** 1 517 263-1039.
Email: news@wlen.com
Web site: http://www.wlen.com
Profile: WLEN-FM is a commercial station owned by Lenawee Broadcasting. The format of the station is adult contemporary. WLEN-FM broadcasts to the Adrian, MI area at 103.9 FM.
FM RADIO STATION

WLER-FM 45335
Owner: Butler County Radio Network
Editorial: 112 Hollywood Dr Ste 203, Butler, Pennsylvania 16001-5697 **Tel:** 1 724 283-1500.
Email: frontdesk@bcrnetwork.com
Web site: http://www.977rocks.com
Profile: WLER-FM is a commercial station owned by Butler County Radio Network. The format of the station is active rock music. WLER-FM broadcasts to the Butler, PA area at 97.7 FM.
FM RADIO STATION

WLES-AM 39224
Owner: Truth Broadcasting
Editorial: 2162 Lawrenceville Plank Rd, Lawrenceville, Virginia 23868 **Tel:** 1 336 759-0363.
Email: info@wtru.com
Web site: http://www.wtru.com
Profile: WLES-AM is a commercial station owned by Truth Broadcasting. The format of the station is religious programming. WLES-AM broadcasts to the Lawrenceville, VA area at 590 AM.
AM RADIO STATION

WLEV-FM 40289
Owner: Cumulus Media Inc.
Editorial: 2158 Avenue C, Ste 100, Bethlehem, Pennsylvania 18017 **Tel:** 1 610 266-7600.
Web site: http://www.wlevradio.com
Profile: WLEV-FM is a commercial station owned by Cumulus Media Inc. The format of the station is adult contemporary. WLEV-FM broadcasts to the Bethlehem, PA area at 100.7 FM.
FM RADIO STATION

WLEW-AM 38016
Owner: Thumb Broadcasting Inc.
Editorial: 935 S Van Dyke Rd, Bad Axe, Michigan 48413-9712 **Tel:** 1 989 269-9931.
Email: wlew@avci.net
Web site: http://www.thumbnet.net
Profile: WLEW-AM is a commercial station owned by Thumb Broadcasting Inc. The format of the station is classic country. WLEW-AM broadcasts to the Bad Axe, MI area at 1340 AM.
AM RADIO STATION

WLEW-FM 45336
Owner: Thumb Broadcasting Inc.
Editorial: 935 S Van Dyke Rd, Bad Axe, Michigan 48413-9712 **Tel:** 1 989 269-9931.
Email: wlewradio@gmail.com
Web site: http://www.thumbnet.net
Profile: WLEW-FM is a commercial station owned by Thumb Broadcasting Inc. The format of the station is classic hits. WLEW-FM broadcasts to the Flint, MI area at 102.1 FM.
FM RADIO STATION

WLEY-FM 42126
Owner: Spanish Broadcasting System
Editorial: 150 N Michigan Ave Ste 1040, Chicago, Illinois 60601-7570 **Tel:** 1 312 920-9500.
Web site: http://laley1079.lamusica.com
Profile: WLEY-FM is a commercial station owned by the Spanish Broadcasting System. The format of the station is regional Mexican music. The station offers a digital Podcast. WLEY-FM broadcasts to the Chicago area at 107.9 FM
FM RADIO STATION

WLFA-FM 44144
Owner: Radio Training Network, Inc.
Editorial: 2420 Wade Hampton Blvd, Greenville, South Carolina 29615-1146 **Tel:** 1 864 292-6040.
Email: comments@hisradio.com
Web site: http://www.hisradio.com/asheville.php
Profile: WLFA-FM is a non-commercial station owned by Radio Training Network, Inc. The format of the station is contemporary Christian. WLFA-FM broadcasts to the Greenville, SC area at 91.3 FM.
FM RADIO STATION

WLFF-FM 537636
Owner: Cumulus Media Inc.
Editorial: 11640 Highway 17 Byp, Murrells Inlet, South Carolina 29576-9332 **Tel:** 1 843 651-7869.
Web site: http://www.nashfm1065.com
Profile: WLFF-FM is a commercial station owned by Cumulus Media Inc. The format of the station is contemporary and classic country. WLFF-FM broadcasts to the Charleston, SC area at 106.5 FM.
FM RADIO STATION

WLFJ-AM 37796
Owner: Radio Training Network, Inc.
Editorial: 2420 Wade Hampton Blvd, Greenville, South Carolina 29615-1146 **Tel:** 1 864 292-6040.
Web site: http://www.christiantalk660.com
Profile: WLFJ-AM is a commercial station owned by Radio Training Network, Inc. The format of the station is christian talk. WLFJ-AM broadcasts in the Greenville, SC area at 660 AM.
AM RADIO STATION

WLFJ-FM 41534
Owner: Radio Training Network, Inc.
Editorial: 2420 Wade Hampton Blvd, Greenville, South Carolina 29615-1146 **Tel:** 1 864 292-6040.
Email: comments@hisradio.com
Web site: http://www.hisradio.com
Profile: WLFJ-FM is a non-commercial station owned by Radio Training Network, Inc. The format of the station is contemporary Christian. WLFJ-FM broadcasts to the Greenville, SC area at 89.3 FM.
FM RADIO STATION

WLFK-FM 44415
Owner: Community Broadcasters, LLC
Editorial: 199 Wealtha Ave, Watertown, New York 13601-1837 **Tel:** 1 315 393-1100.
Profile: WLFK-FM is a commercial station owned by Community Broadcasters, LLC. The format of the station is country. WLFK-FM broadcasts to the Ogdensburg, NY area at 95.3 FM.
FM RADIO STATION

WLFN-AM 38030
Owner: Mississippi Valley Broadcasters LLC
Editorial: 1407 2Nd Ave N, Onalaska, Wisconsin 54650-9166 **Tel:** 1 608 782-8335.
Email: news@lacrosseradiogroup.net
Web site: http://www.1490wlfn.com
Profile: WLFN-AM is a commercial station owned by Mississippi Valley Broadcasters LLC. The format of the station is talk. WLFN-AM broadcasts to the Onalaska, WI area at 1490 AM.
AM RADIO STATION

WLFP-FM 42151
Owner: Entercom Communications Corp.
Editorial: 1835 Moriah Woods Blvd Ste 1, Memphis, Tennessee 38117-7122 **Tel:** 1 901 384-5900.
Web site: http://www.941thewolf.com
Profile: WLFP-FM is a commercial station owned by Entercom Communications Corp. The format of the station is contemporary country. WKQK-FM broadcasts to the Memphis, TN area at 94.1 FM.
FM RADIO STATION

WLFR-FM 41522
Owner: Richard Stockton College of New Jersey
Editorial: 101 Vera King Farris Dr, Stockton College of NJ, Galloway, New Jersey 08205-9441
Tel: 1 609 652-4781.
Email: wlfroffice@stockton.edu
Web site: http://wlfr.fm
Profile: WLFR-FM is a non commercial station owned by Richard Stockton College of New Jersey. The format of the station is variety. WLFR-FM boradcasts to the Pomona, NJ area at 91.7 FM.
FM RADIO STATION

WLFS-FM 81119
Owner: RadioTraining Network Inc.
Editorial: 5859 Abercorn St, Ste 3, Savannah, Georgia 31405-5530 **Tel:** 1 912 353-9226.
Web site: http://www.hisradio.com
Profile: WLFS-FM is a non-commercial station owned by RadioTraining Network Inc. The format of the station is contemporary Christian. WLFS-FM broadcasts to the Savannah, GA area at 91.9 FM.
FM RADIO STATION

WLFV-FM 70486
Owner: Alpha Media
Editorial: 300 Arboretum Pl, Ste 590, Richmond, Virginia 23236-3473 **Tel:** 1 804 327-9902.
Web site: http://www.931hankfm.com
Profile: WLFV-FM is a commercial station owned by Alpha Media. The format of the station is classic country. WLFV-FM broadcasts to the Richmond, VA area at 93.1 FM.
FM RADIO STATION

WLFW-FM 46783
Owner: Midwest Communications Inc.
Editorial: 1162 Mount Auburn Rd, Evansville, Indiana 47720-5428 **Tel:** 1 812 424-8284.
Web site: http://935duke.com
Profile: WLFW-FM is a commercial station owned by Midwest Communications Inc. The format of the station is classic country. WJPS-FM broadcasts to the Evansville, IN area at 93.5 FM.
FM RADIO STATION

WLFX-FM 45988
Owner: Wallingford Broadcasting LLC
Editorial: 128 Big Hill Ave, Richmond, Kentucky 40475-2008 **Tel:** 1 606 723-5138.
Web site: http://www.wlfxfm.com
Profile: WLFX-FM is a commercial station owned by Wallingford Broadcasting LLC. The format for the station is Top 40/CHR. WLFX-FM broadcasts to the Lexington, KY area at 106.7 FM.
FM RADIO STATION

WLFZ-AM 35283
Owner: Saga Communications
Editorial: 1640 Old Russellville Pike, Clarksville, Tennessee 37043-1709 **Tel:** 1 931 648-7720.
Web site: http://www.eagle943.com
Profile: WLFZ-AM is a commercial station owned by Saga Communications (dba 5 Star Radio Group). The format is classic hits. WLFZ-AM broadcasts to the Nashville, TN area at 1370 AM.
AM RADIO STATION

WLFZ-FM 40809
Owner: Saga Communications
Editorial: 3501 E Sangamon Ave, Springfield, Illinois 62707-9777 **Tel:** 1 217 753-5400.
Web site: http://capitolwolf.com
Profile: WLFZ-FM is a commercial station owned by Saga Communications. The format of the station is contemporary country. WQQL-FM broadcasts to the Springfield, IL area at a frequency of 101.9 FM.
FM RADIO STATION

WLGC-FM 45338
Owner: Greenup County Broadcasting, Inc.
Editorial: 1524 Winchester Ave, Ashland, Kentucky 41101-7587 **Tel:** 1 606 920-9565.
Email: production@koolhits1057.com
Web site: http://koolhits1057.com/
Profile: WLGC-FM is a commercial station owned by Greenup County Broadcasting, Inc. The format of the station is classic hits. WLGC-FM broadcasts to the Ashland, KY area at 105.7 FM.
FM RADIO STATION

WLGE-FM 529381
Owner: Mesic (Michael J.)
Editorial: 10331 North Water Street, Ephraim, Wisconsin 54211 **Tel:** 1 920 854-3400.
Email: contact@fm1069thelodge.com
Web site: http://www.fm1069thelodge.com
Profile: WLGE-FM is a commercial station owned by Michael J. Mesic. The format of the station is adult album alternative. WLGE-FM broadcasts to the Ephraim, WI area at 106.9 FM.
FM RADIO STATION

WLGH-FM 43371
Owner: Superior Communications
Editorial: 148 E Grand River Ave, Williamston, Michigan 48895 **Tel:** 1 517 381-0573.
Email: 411@smile.fm
Web site: http://www.smile.fm
Profile: WLGH-FM is a non-commercial station owned by Superior Communications. The format of the station is contemporary Christian music and inspirational talk. WLGH-FM broadcasts to the Williamston, MI area at 88.1 FM.
FM RADIO STATION

WLGI-FM 41536
Owner: Regional Baha'i Council of The Southern States
Editorial: 1272 Williams Hill Rd, Hemingway, South Carolina 29554-4039 **Tel:** 1 843 558-9544.
Email: wlgi@usbnc.org
Web site: http://www.wlgi.org
Profile: WLGI-FM is a non-commercial station owned by Regional Baha'i Council of The Southern States. The format of the station is religious music. WLGI-FM broadcasts to the Hemingway, SC area at 90.9 FM.
FM RADIO STATION

WLGN-AM 38018
Owner: WLGN, LLC
Editorial: 1 Radio Ln, Logan, Ohio 43138-8762
Tel: 1 740 385-2151.
Profile: WLGN-AM is a commercial station owned by WLGN, LLC. The format of the station is oldies. WLGN-AM broadcasts to the Hocking County, OH area at 1510 AM.
AM RADIO STATION

WLGP-FM 43965
Owner: Good News Network
Editorial: 2278 Wortham Ln, Grovetown, Georgia 30813-5103 **Tel:** 1 706 309-9610.
Web site: http://www.gnnradio.org
Profile: WLGP-FM is a non-commercial station owned by Good News Network. The format of the station is religious. WLGP-FM broadcasts locally at 100.3 FM to the Harker's Island, NC area.
FM RADIO STATION

WLGT-FM 41440
Owner: Media East, LLC
Editorial: 408 W Arlington Blvd Ste 101C, Greenville, North Carolina 27834-5706 **Tel:** 1 252 446-9262.
Profile: WLGT-FM is a commercial station owned by Media East, LLC. The format of the station is Contemporary Christian. WLGT-FM broadcasts to the New Bern, NC area at 98.3 FM.
FM RADIO STATION

WLGX-FM
44084
Owner: iHeartMedia Inc.
Editorial: 4000 Radio Dr Ste 1, Louisville, Kentucky 40218-4568 **Tel:** 1 502 479-2222.
Web site: http://www.myfmlouisville.com
Profile: WLGX-FM is a commercial station owned by iHeartMedia Inc. The format of the station is adult contemporary and features music from the 1980s and 1990s. WLGX-FM broadcasts to the Louisville, KY area at 100.5 FM.
FM RADIO STATION

WLGZ-FM
42361
Owner: DJRA Broadcasting
Editorial: 2494 Browncroft Blvd, Rochester, New York 14625 **Tel:** 1 585 264-1027.
Email: info@legends1027.com
Web site: http://www.legends1027.com
Profile: WLGZ-FM is a commercial station owned by DJRA Broadcasting. The format of the station is classic hits and oldies. WLGZ-FM broadcasts to the Rochester, NY area at 102.7 FM.
FM RADIO STATION

WLHC-FM
151948
Owner: Woolstone Corporation
Editorial: 102 S Steele St Ste 301, Sanford, North Carolina 27330-4288 **Tel:** 1 919 775-1031.
Email: wlhc@life1031.com
Web site: http://www.life1031.com
Profile: WLHC-FM is a commercial station owned by Woolstone Corporation. The format of the station is oldies and adult standards. WLHC-FM broadcasts to the Sanford, NC area at 103.1 FM.
FM RADIO STATION

WLHH-FM
41304
Owner: Apex Broadcasting Inc.
Editorial: 2 Corpus Christie Pl Ste 100A, Hilton Head Island, South Carolina 29928-1720 **Tel:** 1 843 363-9956.
Web site: http://www.1049thesurf.com
Profile: WLHH-FM is a commercial station owned by Apex Broadcasting Inc.The format for the station is classic hits. WLHH-FM broadcasts to the Hilton Head Island, SC area at 104.9 FM.
FM RADIO STATION

WLHK-FM
40248
Owner: Emmis Communications Corp.
Editorial: 40 Monument Cir, Indianapolis, Indiana 46204-3019 **Tel:** 1 317 266-9700.
Web site: http://www.hankfm.com
Profile: WLHK-FM is a commercial station owned by Emmis Communications Corp. The format of the station is classic and contemporary country. WLHK-FM broadcasts to the Indianapolis area at 97.1 FM.
FM RADIO STATION

WLHM-FM
45523
Owner: Mid-America Radio Group
Editorial: 425 2nd St, Logansport, Indiana 46947-3410 **Tel:** 1 574 722-4000.
Email: mix102wlhm@gmail.com
Web site: http://indianasbestradio.com/index-mix.php
Profile: WLHM-FM is a commercial station owned by Mid-America Radio Group. The format of the station is classic hits. WLHM-FM broadcasts to the Indianapolis area at 102.3 FM.
FM RADIO STATION

WLHR-FM
538534
Owner: Georgia-Carolina Radiocasting Companies LLC
Editorial: 122715 Augusta Rd., Lavonia, Georgia 30553 **Tel:** 1 706 356-0921.
Email: wlhrpro@gmail.com
Web site: http://www.921wlhr.com
Profile: WLHR-FM is a commercial station owned by Georgia-Carolina Radiocasting Companies LLC. The format of the station is a mix of contemporary and classic country. WLHR-FM broadcasts to the Lavonia, GA area at 92.1 FM.
FM RADIO STATION

WLHT-FM
46791
Owner: Townsquare Media, LLC
Editorial: 50 Monroe Ave NW, Ste 500, Grand Rapids, Michigan 49503 **Tel:** 1 616 451-4800.
Web site: http://www.mychannel957.com
Profile: WLHT-FM is a commercial station owned by Townsquare Media, LLC. The format of the station is modern adult contemporary. WLHT-FM broadcasts to the Grand Rapids, MI area at 95.7 FM.
FM RADIO STATION

WLIB-AM
38749
Owner: Emmis Communications Corp.
Editorial: 395 Hudson St Fl 7, New York, New York 10014-7452 **Tel:** 1 212 447-1000.
Email: info@wlib.com
Web site: http://www.wlib.com
Profile: WLIB-AM is a commercial station owned by Emmis Communications Corp.The format of the station is gospel. WLIB-AM broadcasts to the New York area at 1190 AM. ALL correspondence should be forwarded to the station's publicist via e-mail. ALL PSAs should be submitted through the website: wlib.com/psa.
AM RADIO STATION

WLIC-FM
41922
Owner: Calvary Chapel
Editorial: 416 Pennsylvania Ave, Cumberland, Maryland 21502 **Tel:** 1 866 738-3259.
Web site: http://calvarycumberland.org/#/reveal-fm
Profile: WLIC-FM is a non-commercial station owned by Calvary Chapel Cumberland. The format of the station is contemporary Christian and gospel music. WLIC-FM broadcasts to the Cumberland, MD area at 97.1 FM.
FM RADIO STATION

WLIE-AM
35481
Owner: Principle Broadcasting
Editorial: 2395 Ocean Ave, Ronkonkoma, New York 11779-5670 **Tel:** 1 631 580-0540.
Email: wlieproduction@gmail.com
Web site: http://www.wlie540am.com
Profile: WLIE-AM is a commercial station owned by Principle Broadcasting. The format of the station is Hispanic Christian. WLIE-AM broadcasts in the New York City area at 540 AM.
AM RADIO STATION

WLIF-FM
41891
Owner: CBS Radio
Editorial: 1423 Clarkview Rd Ste 100, Baltimore, Maryland 21209-2190 **Tel:** 1 410 296-1019.
Web site: http://todays1019.cbslocal.com
Profile: WLIF-FM is a commercial station owned by CBS Radio. The format of the station is Lite Rock/Lite AC music. WLIF-FM broadcasts to the Baltimore area at 101.9 FM.
FM RADIO STATION

WLIH-FM
41331
Owner: Good Christian Radio Broadcasting Inc.
Editorial: 2352 Charleston Rd, Wellsboro, Pennsylvania 16901 **Tel:** 1 570 724-4272.
Email: info@wlih.com
Web site: http://www.wlih.com
Profile: WLIH-FM is a non-commercial station owned by Good Christian Radio Broadcasting Inc. The format of the station is Christian. WLIH-FM broadcasts to the Wellsboro, PA area at 107.1 FM.
FM RADIO STATION

WLIJ-AM
35477
Owner: Jax Broadcasting, LLC
Editorial: 236 Woodland Dr, Shelbyville, Tennessee 37160-6759 **Tel:** 1 931 684-1514.
Email: wlijradio@gmail.com
Profile: WLIJ-AM is a commercial station owned by Jax Broadcasting, LLC. The format of the station is classic country. WLIJ-AM broadcasts to the Nashville, TN area at 1580 AM.
AM RADIO STATION

WLIK-AM
35478
Owner: WLIK Inc.
Editorial: 640 W Highway 25 70, Newport, Tennessee 37821-8068 **Tel:** 1 423 623-3095.
Web site: http://www.wlik.net
Profile: WLIK-AM is a commercial station owned by WLIK Inc. The format of the station is oldies. WLIK-AM broadcasts to Newport, TN and surrounding areas at 1270 AM.
AM RADIO STATION

WLIL-AM
38605
Owner: Fowler's Holdings Inc.
Editorial: 14542 El Camino Ln, Lenoir City, Tennessee 37771 **Tel:** 1 865 986-7536.
Email: wlilcountry@aol.com
Web site: http://wlilcountry.com
Profile: WLIL-AM is a commercial station owned by Fowler's Holdings Inc. The format of the station is classic country and sports. WLIL-AM broadcasts to the Knoxville, TN area at 730 AM.
AM RADIO STATION

WLIM-AM
35479
Owner: Polnet Communications
Editorial: 41 Pennsylvania Ave, Medford, New York 11763-3717 **Tel:** 1 631 475-1580.
Email: radioadonai1580@gmail.com
Web site: http://www.ministeriodiosestaaqui.com
Profile: WLIM-AM is a commercial station owned by Polnet Communications. The format of the station is Spanish Christian. WLIM-AM broadcasts to the Medford, NY area at 1580 AM.
AM RADIO STATION

WLIN-FM
46800
Owner: Boswell Media LLC
Editorial: 1 Golf Course Rd, Kosciusko, Mississippi 39090 **Tel:** 1 662 289-1050.
Email: breezy@boswellmedia.net
Web site: http://www.breezynews.com
Profile: WLIN-FM is a commercial station owned by Boswell Media LLC. The format of the station is adult contemporary. WLIN-FM broadcasts to the Kosciusko, MO area at 101.1 FM.
FM RADIO STATION

WLIP-AM
38316
Owner: Alpha Media
Editorial: 8500 Green Bay Rd, Pleasant Prairie, Wisconsin 53158-2721 **Tel:** 1 262 694-7800.
Web site: http://www.wlip.com
Profile: WLIP-AM is a commercial station owned by Alpha Media. The format of the station is talk. WLIP-AM broadcasts to the Milwaukee area at 1050 AM.
AM RADIO STATION

WLIQ-AM
37434
Owner: Townsquare Media
Editorial: 408 N 24th St, Quincy, Illinois 62301-3254 **Tel:** 1 573 221-3450.
Web site: http://wliqlite1530.com
Profile: WLIQ-AM is a commercial station owned by Townsquare Media. The format of the station is Lite Rock/Lite AC. WLIQ-AM broadcasts to the Quincy, IL area at 1530 AM.
AM RADIO STATION

WLIR-FM
154814
Owner: Livingstone Broadcasting, Inc.
Tel: 1 631 853-9549.
Profile: WLIR-FM is a commercial station owned by Livingstone Broadcasting, Inc. The format of the station is Christian programming. WLIR-FM broadcasts to the Hampton Bays, NY area at 107.1 FM.
FM RADIO STATION

WLIS-AM
35480
Owner: Crossroads Communications LLC
Editorial: 777 River Rd, Middletown, Connecticut 06457-3922 **Tel:** 1 860 388-1420.
Email: wliswmrd@yahoo.com
Web site: http://www.wliswmrd.net
Profile: WLIS-AM is a commercial station owned by Crossroads Communications LLC. The format for the station is talk. WLIS-AM broadcasts to the Middletown, CT area at 1420 AM.
AM RADIO STATION

WLIT-FM
40468
Owner: iHeartMedia Inc.
Editorial: 233 N Michigan Ave Ste 2700, Chicago, Illinois 60601-5704 **Tel:** 1 312 540-2000.
Web site: http://939myfm.iheart.com
Profile: WLIT-FM is a commercial station owned by iHeartMedia Inc. The format of the station is Hot AC. WLIT-FM broadcasts to the entire Chicago metro area at 93.9 FM.
FM RADIO STATION

WLIV-AM
39447
Owner: Sunny Broadcasting LLC
Editorial: 1130 W Main St, Livingston, Tennessee 38570-2206 **Tel:** 1 931 823-1226.
Web site: http://wlivradio.com
Profile: WLIV-AM is a commercial station owned by Sunny Broadcasting LLC. The format of the station is classic country. WLIV-AM broadcasts to the Nashville, TN area at 920 AM.
AM RADIO STATION

WLIV-FM
46831
Owner: Sunny Broadcasting LLC
Editorial: 1130 W Main St, Livingston, Tennessee 38570-2206 **Tel:** 1 931 823-1226.
Email: wlivprod@twlakes.net
Profile: WLIV-FM is a commercial station owned by Sunny Broadcasting LLC. The format of the station is contemporary country music. WLIV-FM broadcasts to the Livingston, TN area at 104.7 FM.
FM RADIO STATION

WLJA-FM
46570
Owner: Tri-State Communications, Inc.
Editorial: 134 S Main St, Jasper, Georgia 30143-1702 **Tel:** 1 678 454-9350.
Web site: http://wljaradio.com
Profile: WLJA-FM is a commercial station owned by Tri-State Communications, Inc. The format for the station is classic country, southern gospel, and sports. WLJA-FM broadcasts to the Atlanta area at 101.1 FM.
FM RADIO STATION

WLJC-FM
44104
Owner: Hour of Harvest, Inc.
Editorial: 219 WLJC Dr., Beattyville, Kentucky 41311-9043 **Tel:** 1 606 464-3600.
Email: wljc@wljc.com
Web site: http://www.wljc.com
Profile: WLJC-FM is a non-commercial station owned by Hour of Harvest, Inc. The format for the station is religious. WLJC-FM broadcasts to the Beattyville, KY area at 102.1 FM.
FM RADIO STATION

WLJE-FM
45924
Owner: Adams Radio Group
Editorial: 2755 Sager Rd, Valparaiso, Indiana 46383-0721 **Tel:** 1 219 462-6111.
Email: news@argni.com
Web site: http://www.indiana105.com
Profile: WLJE-FM is a commercial station owned by Adams Radio Group. The format of the station is country. WLJE-FM broadcasts to the Valparaiso, IN area at 105.5 FM.
FM RADIO STATION

WLJN-AM
38528
Owner: Good News Media Inc.
Tel: 1 231 946-1400.
Web site: http://www.goodnewsmediainc.org/thesourceam14001370.html
Profile: WLJN-AM is a non-commercial station owned by Good News Media Inc. The format of the station is Christian talk. WLJN-AM broadcasts to the Traverse City, MI area at 1400 AM.
AM RADIO STATION

WLJN-FM
45890
Owner: Good News Media Inc.
Tel: 1 231 946-1400.
Email: info@wljn.com
Web site: http://www.wljn.com
Profile: WLJN-FM is a non-commercial station owned by Good News Media Inc. The format of the station is Christian programming. WLJN-FM broadcasts to the Traverse City, MI area at 89.9 FM.
FM RADIO STATION

WLJR-FM
43652
Owner: Briarwood Presbyterian Church
Editorial: 2200 Briarwood Way, Birmingham, Alabama 35243-2900 **Tel:** 1 205 7765270.
Email: info@briarwood.org
Web site: http://www.briarwood.org/wljr
Profile: WLJR-FM is a non-commercial station owned by the Briarwood Presbyterian Church. The format of the station is gospel music and religious talk. WLJR-FM broadcasts to the Birmingham, AL area at 88.5 FM.
FM RADIO STATION

WLJY-FM
521101
Owner: Seehafer Broadcasting Corp.
Editorial: 645 25th Ave N, Wisconsin Rapids, Wisconsin 54495-2223 **Tel:** 1 715 424-1300.
Email: info@wfhr.com
Web site: http://www.wljyfm.com/
Profile: WLJY-FM is a commercial station owned by Seehafer Broadcasting Corp. The format of the station is adult contemporary. WLJY-FM broadcasts to the Wisconsin Rapids, WI area at 105.5 FM.
FM RADIO STATION

WLKC-FM
44264
Owner: Northeast Broadcasting Co.
Editorial: 30 How St, Haverhill, Massachusetts 01830-6131 **Tel:** 1 978 374-4733.
Web site: http://www.wxrv.com
Profile: WLKC-FM is a commercial station owned by Northeast Broadcasting Co. The format of the station is adult album alternative. WLKC-FM broadcasts to Plymouth, MA at 105.7 FM.
FM RADIO STATION

WLKD-AM
38071
Owner: NRG Media LLC
Editorial: 3616 State Highway 47 N, Rhinelander, Wisconsin 54501-8819 **Tel:** 1 715 362-1975.
Web site: http://www.am1570wlkd.com
Profile: WLKD-AM is a commercial station, owned by NRG Media LLC. The format of the station is soft AC. WLKD-AM broadcasts in the Minocqua, WI area at 1570 AM.
AM RADIO STATION

WLKE-FM
44459
Owner: Radio Partners LLC
Editorial: 104 S Center St, Ebensburg, Pennsylvania 15931-1656 **Tel:** 1 814 472-4060.
Web site: http://www.klove.com
Profile: WLKE-FM is a commercial station owned by Radio Partners LLC. The format of the station is Contemporary Christian. WLKE-FM broadcasts to the Altoona, PA area at 93.5 FM.
FM RADIO STATION

WLKF-AM
36340
Owner: Hall Communications
Editorial: 404 W Lime St, Lakeland, Florida 33815-4651 **Tel:** 1 863 682-8184.
Web site: http://www.wlkf.com
Profile: WLKF-AM is a commercial station owned by Hall Communications. The format of the station is talk. WLKF-AM broadcasts in the Tampa, FL, area at 1430 AM.
AM RADIO STATION

WLKG-FM
42247
Owner: CTJ Communications Ltd.
Editorial: 500 Interchange N, Lake Geneva, Wisconsin 53147-8900 **Tel:** 1 262 249-9600.
Web site: http://www.lake961.com
Profile: WLKG-FM is a commercial station owned by CTJ Communications Ltd. The format of the station is adult contemporary. WLKG-FM broadcasts to the Lake Geneva, WI area at 96.1 FM.
FM RADIO STATION

WLKH-FM
43952
Owner: 2510 Associates
Tel: 1 800 525-5683.
Email: klove@klove.com
Web site: http://www.klove.com
FM RADIO STATION

WLKI-FM
40476
Owner: Swick Broadcasting
Editorial: 2655 N State Road 127, Angola, Indiana 46703 **Tel:** 1 260 665-9554.
Email: wlki@wlki.com
Web site: http://www.wlki.com
Profile: WLKI-FM is a commercial station owned by Swick Broadcasting. The format of the station is Hot AC. WLKI-FM broadcasts to the Angola, IN area at 100.3 FM.
FM RADIO STATION

WLKJ-FM
44346
Owner: 2510 Associates
Tel: 1 800 525-5683.
Web site: http://www.klove.com
Profile: WLKJ-FM is a commercial station owned by 2510 Associates in an LMA agreement with Educational Media Foundation. The format is contemporary Christian. The station airs in the Johnstown, PA area at 105.7 FM.
FM RADIO STATION

WLKK-FM
41641
Owner: Entercom Communications Corp.
Editorial: 500 Corporate Pkwy Ste 200, Buffalo, New York 14226-1263 **Tel:** 1 716 843-0600.
Web site: http://www.alternativebuffalo.com
Profile: WLKK-FM is a commercial station owned by Entercom Communications Corp. The format of the

station is alternative rock. WLKK-FM broadcasts to the Buffalo, NY area at 107.7 FM.
FM RADIO STATION

WLKL-FM 40477
Owner: Lake Land College
Editorial: 5001 Lake Land Blvd, Mattoon, Illinois 61938-9366 **Tel:** 1 217 234-5373.
Email: 899themax@lakelandcollege.edu
Web site: http://www.899themax.com
Profile: WLKL-FM is a non-commercial station owned by Lake Land College. The format of the station is variety. WLKL-FM broadcasts to the Mattoon, IL area at 89.9 FM.
FM RADIO STATION

WLKM-FM 45341
Owner: Impact Radio, LLC
Editorial: 59750 Constantine Rd, Three Rivers, Michigan 49093-9303 **Tel:** 1 269 278-1815.
Email: info@wlkm.com
Web site: http://www.wlkm.com
Profile: WLKM-FM is a commercial station owned by Impact Radio, LLC. The format of the station is adult contemporary. WLKM-FM broadcasts to the Grand Rapids, MI area at 95.9 FM.
FM RADIO STATION

WLKN-FM 40458
Owner: Seehafer Broadcasting Corp.
Editorial: 1050 Linden St, Cleveland, Wisconsin 53015-1469 **Tel:** 1 920 693-3103.
Email: wlkn@wlkn.com
Web site: http://www.wlkn.com
Profile: WLKN-FM is a commercial station owned by Seehafer Broadcasting Corp. The format of the station is adult contemporary. WLKN-FM broadcasts to the Cleveland, WI area at 98.1 FM.
FM RADIO STATION

WLKO-FM 41640
Owner: iHeartMedia Inc.
Editorial: 801 Woodrdg Ctr Dr, Charlotte, North Carolina 28217-1908 **Tel:** 1 704 714-9444.
Web site: http://1029thelake.iheart.com
Profile: WLKO-FM is a commercial station owned by iHeartMedia Inc. The format of the station is adult hits. WLKO-FM broadcasts to the Charlotte, NC area at 102.9 FM.
FM RADIO STATION

WLKQ-FM 41819
Owner: Davis Broadcasting
Editorial: 1176 Satellite Blvd NW Ste 200, Suwanee, Georgia 30024-2881 **Tel:** 1 770 945-9953.
Web site: http://www.laraza1023.com
Profile: WLKQ-FM is a commercial station owned by Davis Broadcasting. The format of the station is Hispanic. WLKQ-FM broadcasts to the Atlanta area at 102.3 FM.
FM RADIO STATION

WLKR-AM 38020
Owner: Elyria-Lorain Broadcasting
Editorial: 10327 US Highway 250 N, Milan, Ohio 44846 **Tel:** 1 419 668-8151.
Email: wlkr@wlkrradio.com
Web site: http://www.wlkrradio.com
Profile: WLKR-AM is a commercial station owned by Elyria-Lorain Broadcasting. The format of the station is classic hits. WLKR-AM broadcasts to the Milan, OH area at 95.3 FM.
AM RADIO STATION

WLKR-FM 45342
Owner: Elyria-Lorain Broadcasting
Editorial: 10327 US Highway 250 N, Milan, Ohio 44846 **Tel:** 1 419 609-5961.
Email: wlkr@wlkrradio.com
Web site: http://www.wlkrradio.com
Profile: WLKR-FM is a commercial station owned by Elyria-Lorain Broadcasting. The format of the station is adult album alternative. WLKR-FM broadcasts to the Milan, OH area at 95.3 FM.
FM RADIO STATION

WLKS-AM 39214
Owner: Morgan County Industries Inc.
Editorial: 129 College St, West Liberty, Kentucky 41472 **Tel:** 1 606 784-4141.
Email: radio41472@yahoo.com
Profile: WLKS-AM is a commercial station owned by Morgan County Industries Inc. The format of the station is oldies. WLKS-AM broadcasts to the West Liberty, KY area at 1450 AM.
AM RADIO STATION

WLKS-FM 46566
Owner: Morgan County Industries Inc.
Editorial: 129 College St, West Liberty, Kentucky 41472-1156 **Tel:** 1 606 743-1029.
Email: radio41472@yahoo.com
Web site: http://www.kick1029wlks.com
Profile: WLKS-FM is a commercial station owned by Morgan County Industries Inc. The format of the station is classic country music. WLKS-FM broadcasts to the West Liberty, KY, area at 102.9 FM.
FM RADIO STATION

WLKT-FM 43149
Owner: iHeartMedia Inc.
Editorial: 2601 Nicholasville Rd, Lexington, Kentucky 40503-3307 **Tel:** 1 859 422-1000.
Web site: http://www.1045thecat.com
Profile: WLKT-FM is a commercial station owned byiHeartMedia Inc. The format of the station is Top 40/CHR. WLKT-FM broadcasts to the Lexington, KY area at 104.5 FM.
FM RADIO STATION

WLKW-AM 35452
Owner: Hall Communications
Editorial: 75 Oxford St, Providence, Rhode Island 02905-4722 **Tel:** 1 401 467-4366.
Web site: http://www.wnbhradio.com/
Profile: WLKW-AM is a commercial station owned by Hall Communications. The format of the station is sports. WLKW-AM broadcasts to the Providence, RI area at 1450 AM.
AM RADIO STATION

WLKX-FM 40478
Owner: Lakes Broadcasting Company, Inc.
Editorial: 14443 Armstrong Blvd NW, Ramsey, Minnesota 55303-7284 **Tel:** 1 763 450-7777.
Web site: http://www.bigqradio.com
Profile: WLKX-FM is a commercial station owned by Lakes Broadcasting Company, Inc. The format of the station is oldies. The station broadcasts to the Forest Lake, MN area at 95.9 FM.
FM RADIO STATION

WLKZ-FM 40479
Owner: Great Eastern Radio, LLC
Editorial: 501 South St Fl 3, Bow, New Hampshire 03304-3416 **Tel:** 1 603 545-0777.
Web site: http://www.thehawkrocks.com
Profile: WLKZ-FM is a commercial station owned by Great Eastern Radio, LLC. The format of the station is classic rock. WLKZ-FM broadcasts to the Gilford, NH area on 104.9 FM.
FM RADIO STATION

WLLD-FM 41884
Owner: Beasley Broadcast Group
Editorial: 9721 Executive Center Dr N Ste 200, Saint Petersburg, Florida 33702-2439 **Tel:** 1 727 579-1925.
Web site: http://www.wild941.com
Profile: WLLD-FM is a commercial station owned by Beasley Broadcast Group. The format of the station is urban contemporary. WLLD-FM broadcasts to the Saint Petersburg, FL area at 94.1 FM.
FM RADIO STATION

WLLE-FM 43511
Owner: Bristol Broadcasting
Editorial: 6000 Bristol Dr, Paducah, Kentucky 42003-9213 **Tel:** 1 270 554-0093.
Email: news@wkyq.com
Web site: http://www.willieradio.com
Profile: WLLE-FM is a commercial station owned by Bristol Broadcasting. The format of the station is country. WLLE-FM broadcasts to the Paducah, KY area at 102.1 FM.
FM RADIO STATION

WLLF-FM 42035
Owner: Cumulus Media Inc.
Editorial: 2030 Pine Hollow Blvd, Hermitage, Pennsylvania 16148-2520 **Tel:** 1 724 346-4113.
Web site: http://www.sportsradio967.com
Profile: WLLF-FM is a commercial station owned by Cumulus Media Inc. The format of the station is sports. WLLF-FM broadcasts to the Youngstown, OH area at 96.7 FM.
FM RADIO STATION

WLLG-FM 42148
Owner: Flack Broadcasting Group
Editorial: 7606 N State St, Lowville, New York 13367
Tel: 1 315 376-7500.
Email: sales@themoose.net
Web site: http://www.themoose.net
FM RADIO STATION

WLLH-AM 35484
Owner: Gois Broadcasting
Editorial: 122 Green St, Worcester, Massachusetts 01604-4138 **Tel:** 1 508 791-2111.
Web site: http://www.goisbroadcasting.com
Profile: WLLH-AM is a commercial station owned by Gois Broadcasting. The format of the station is Spanish variety. WLLH-AM broadcasts to Charlestown, MA at 1400 AM.
AM RADIO STATION

WLLI-AM 38864
Owner: FM Radio Licenses, LLC
Editorial: 109 Plaza Dr, Johnstown, Pennsylvania 15905-1212 **Tel:** 1 814 255-4186.
Web site: http://fanatic.ntjnetwork.com/
Profile: WLLI-AM is a commercial station owned by FM Radio Licenses, LLC. The format of the station is sports, news and talk. WLLI-AM broadcasts to the Johnstown, PA area at 990 AM.
AM RADIO STATION

WLLI-FM 43103
Owner: FM Radio Licenses, LLC
Editorial: 122 Radio Rd, Jackson, Tennessee 38301-3465 **Tel:** 1 731 427-3316.
Web site: http://www.radiowillie.com
Profile: WLLI-FM is a commercial station owned by Forever South Licenses, LLC. The format of the station is classic country. WLLI-FM broadcasts to Dyer, Tennessee at 94.3.
FM RADIO STATION

WLLJ-FM 43681
Owner: Friendship Broadcasting, LLC
Editorial: 5512 Ringgold Rd Ste 214, Chattanooga, Tennessee 37412-3174 **Tel:** 1 423 892-1200.
Email: info@j103.com
Web site: http://www.j103.com
Profile: WLLJ-FM is a commercial station owned by Friendship Broadcasting, LLC. The format of the station is contemporary Christian. WLLJ-FM broadcasts to the Chattanooga, TN area at 103.1 FM.
FM RADIO STATION

WLLK-FM 45253
Owner: iHeartMedia Inc.
Editorial: 101 1st Radio Ln, Somerset, Kentucky 42503-4639 **Tel:** 1 606 678-5151.
Web site: http://www.lake1023.com
Profile: WLLK-FM is a commercial station owned by iHeartMedia Inc. The format for the station is Top 40/CHR. WLLK-FM broadcasts to the Somerset, KY area at 102.3 FM.
FM RADIO STATION

WLLM-AM 36671
Owner: Cornerstone Community Radio Inc.
Editorial: 800 S Postville Dr, Lincoln, Illinois 62656-1287 **Tel:** 1 217 735-9735.
Email: office@wllmradio.com
Web site: http://www.wllmradio.com
Profile: WLLM-AM is a non-commercial station owned by Cornerstone Community Radio Inc. The format of the station is Southern Gospel music and talk. WLLM-AM broadcasts to the Lincoln, IL area at 1370 AM. The station is temporarily off-air due to technical problems resulting from an electrical fire.
AM RADIO STATION

WLLQ-AM 35642
Owner: Davidson Media Group
Editorial: 3025 Waughtown St Ste G, Winston Salem, North Carolina 27107-1679 **Tel:** 1 336 784-9004.
Web site: http://www.quepasamedia.com
Profile: WLLQ-AM is a commercial station owned by Davidson Media Group. The format of the station is Regional Mexican. WLLQ-AM broadcasts to the Raleigh, NC area at 1530 AM.
AM RADIO STATION

WLLR-FM 45810
Owner: iHeartMedia Inc.
Editorial: 3535 E Kimberly Rd, Davenport, Iowa 52807-2583 **Tel:** 1 563 344-7000.
Web site: http://www.1037wllr.com
Profile: WLLR-FM is a commercial station owned by iHeartMedia Inc. The format of the station is contemporary country. WLLR-FM broadcasts to the Davenport, IA area at 103.7 FM.
FM RADIO STATION

WLLT-FM 41025
Owner: Sauk Valley Broadcasting Company
Editorial: 260 Il Route 2, Dixon, Illinois 61021-9111
Tel: 1 815 284-1077.
Email: wllt@comcast.net
Profile: WLLT-FM is a commercial station owned by Sauk Valley Broadcasting Company. The format of the station is oldies music. WLLT-FM broadcasts to the Dixon, IL area at 107.7 FM.
FM RADIO STATION

WLLV-AM 35486
Owner: Golden Door Broadcasting, LLC
Editorial: 2001 W Broadway, Ste 13, Louisville, Kentucky 40203 **Tel:** 1 502 776-1240.
Email: wlouwllv@aol.com
Profile: WLLV-AM is a commercial station owned by Golden Door Broadcasting, LLC. The format of the station is religous programming and teaching. WLLV-AM broadcasts in the Louisville, KY area at 1240 AM.
AM RADIO STATION

WLLW-FM 46781
Owner: Longpoint Media
Editorial: 3568 Lenox Rd, Geneva, New York 14456-2058 **Tel:** 1 315 781-7000.
Email: news@flradiogroup.com
Web site: http://www.fingerlakesdailynews.com
Profile: WLLW-FM is a commercial station owned by Longpoint Media (as of January 1, 2015). The format of the station is classic rock music. WLLW-FM broadcasts to the Geneva, NY area at 99.3 FM.
FM RADIO STATION

WLLX-FM 45345
Owner: Prospect Communications
Editorial: 1212 N Locust Ave, Lawrenceburg, Tennessee 38464 **Tel:** 1 931 363-9997.
Email: wlxnews@bellsouth.net
Web site: http://www.wlxonline.com
Profile: WLLX-FM is a commercial station owned by Prospect Communications. The format of the station is contemporary country music. WLLX-FM broadcasts to the Nashville, TN area at 97.5 FM.
FM RADIO STATION

WLLY-FM 45961
Owner: Glades Media Co.
Editorial: 530 E Alverdez Ave, Clewiston, Florida 33440-3901 **Tel:** 1 863 902-0995.
Web site: http://www.radiofiesta.com
Profile: WLLY-FM is a commercial station owned by Glades Media Co. The format of the station is regional Mexican. WLLY-FM broadcasts to the Clewiston, FL area at 100.5 FM.
FM RADIO STATION

WLMA-AM 36256
Owner: WP Broadcasting, LLC
Editorial: 1 Motes Rd, Sylacauga, Alabama 35150-1731 **Tel:** 1 256 249-4263.
Web site: http://wrfs.fm
Profile: WLMA-AM is a commercial station owned by WP Broadcasting, LLC. The format of the station is smooth adult contemporary. WLMA-AM broadcasts to the Alexander City, AL area at 1050 AM.
AM RADIO STATION

WLMC-AM 36254
Owner: Stalvey Communications
Editorial: 2508 Highwater street, Georgetown, South Carolina 29440-4555 **Tel:** 1 843 546-1400.
Web site: http://www.wlmcradio.com
Profile: WLMC-AM is a commercial station owned by Stalvey Communications. The format of the station is gospel music. WLMC-AM broadcasts to the Georgetown, SC area at 1470 AM.
AM RADIO STATION

WLMD-FM 42038
Owner: Prestige Communications
Editorial: 31 E Side Sq, Macomb, Illinois 61455-2248
Tel: 1 309 833-2121.
Email: news@prestigeradio.com
Web site: http://www.prestigeradio.com
Profile: WLMD-FM is a commercial station owned by Prestige Communications. The format of the station is contemporary country. WLMD-FM broadcasts to the Macomb, IL area at 104.7 FM.
FM RADIO STATION

WLME-FM 46320
Owner: Cromwell Group Inc.(The)
Editorial: 1115 Tamarack Rd, Owensboro, Kentucky 42301-6984 **Tel:** 1 270 683-5200.
Web site: http://www.owensbororadio.com
Profile: WLME-FM is a commercial station owned by The Cromwell Group Inc. The format of the station is sports. WLME-FM broadcasts to the Owensboro, KY area at 102.9 FM.
FM RADIO STATION

WLMG-FM 72744
Owner: Entercom Communications Corp.
Editorial: 400 Poydras St Ste 800, New Orleans, Louisiana 70130-3789 **Tel:** 1 504 593-6376.
Web site: http://www.magic1019.com
Profile: WLMG-FM is a commercial station owned by Entercom Communications Corp. The format of the station is adult contemporary music. WLMG-FM broadcasts to the New Orleans area at 101.9 FM.
FM RADIO STATION

WLMI-FM 42194
Owner: Midwest Communications, Inc.
Editorial: 2495 Cedar St, Holt, Michigan 48842
Tel: 1 517 699-0111.
Web site: http://www.929wlmi.com
Profile: WLMI-FM is a commercial station owned by Midwest Communications, Inc. The format of the station is classic hits. WLMI-FM broadcasts to the Lansing, MI area at 92.7 FM.
FM RADIO STATION

WLML-FM 876108
Owner: Robinson Entertainment, LLC
Editorial: 760 US Highway 1, North Palm Beach, Florida 33408-4419 **Tel:** 1 561 469-6700.
Email: info@legendsradio.com
Web site: http://legendsradio.com
Profile: WLML-FM is a commercial station owned by Robinson Entertainment, LLC. The format of the station is adult standards. WLML-FM broadcasts to the Palm Beach County, FL area at a frequency of 100.3 FM. Station will debut in November 2013.
FM RADIO STATION

WLMR-AM 35532
Owner: Wilkins Communication Networks Inc.
Editorial: 3809 Ringgold Rd, Chattanooga, Tennessee 37412-1639 **Tel:** 1 423 624-4200.
Email: wlmr@wilkinsradio.com
Web site: http://www.wilkinsradio.com
Profile: WLMR-AM is a commercial station owned by Wilkins Communication Networks Inc. The format of the station is religious talk. WLMR-AM broadcasts to the Chattanooga, TN area at 1450 AM.
AM RADIO STATION

WLMV-AM 128433
Owner: Midwest Family Stations
Editorial: 730 Rayovac Dr, Madison, Wisconsin 53711
Tel: 1 608 273-1000.
Web site: http://www.lamovidaradio.com
Profile: WLMV-AM is a commercial station owned by Midwest Family Stations. The format of the station is Hispanic. WLMV-AM broadcasts to the Madison, Wi area at a frequency of 1480 AM.
AM RADIO STATION

WLMX-FM 43196
Owner: Red Rock Radio Corp.
Editorial: 328 100Th St, Amery, Wisconsin 54001-4024 **Tel:** 1 715 268-7185.
Email: info@radio715.com
Web site: http://radio715.com
Profile: WLMX-FM is a commercial station owned by Red Rock Radio Corp. The format of the station is adult variety hits. WLMX-FM broadcasts to the Amery, WI area at 104.9 FM.
FM RADIO STATION

WLMY-FM 41453
Owner: Backyard Broadcasting
Editorial: 1685 Four Mile Dr, Williamsport, Pennsylvania 17701-1975 **Tel:** 1 570 323-8200.
Profile: WLMY-FM is a commercial station owned by Backyard Broadcasting. The format of the station is Lite Rock/Lite AC. WLMY-FM broadcasts to the Williamsport, PA area at 107.9 FM.
FM RADIO STATION

WLNA-AM 39109
Owner: Pamal Broadcasting Ltd.
Editorial: 715 Route 52, Beacon, New York 12508-1047 **Tel:** 1 845 838-6000.
Email: newsroom@pamal.com
Web site: http://www.hvradionet.com
Profile: WLNA-AM is a commercial station owned by Pamal Broadcasting Ltd. The format of the station is classic country. WLNA-AM broadcasts to the Beacon, NY area at 1420 AM.
AM RADIO STATION

WLNC-AM 35488
Owner: Scotland Broadcasting Company, Inc.
Editorial: 1011 Lila Dr, Laurinburg, North Carolina 28352-3221 **Tel:** 1 910 276-1300.
Email: wlnc@wlncradio.com
Web site: http://www.wlncradio.com
Profile: WLNC-AM is a commercial station owned by Scotland Broadcasting Company, Inc. The format of the station is adult contemporary and oldies. WLNC-AM broadcasts to the Laurinburg, NC area at 1300 AM.
AM RADIO STATION

WLND-FM 41649
Owner: iheartMedia Inc.
Editorial: 7413 Old Lee Hwy, Chattanooga, Tennessee 37421-1142 **Tel:** 1 423 892-3333.
Web site: http://www.981thelake.com
Profile: WNLD-FM is a commercial station owned by iheartMedia Inc. The format of the station is adult hits. WLND-FM broadcasts to the Chattanooga, TN area at 98.1 FM.
FM RADIO STATION

WLNG-FM 44148
Owner: Main Street Broadcasting Co., Inc.
Editorial: 23 Redwood Rd, Sag Harbor, New York 11963-2639 **Tel:** 1 631 725-2300.
Email: info@wlng.com
Web site: http://www.wlng.com
Profile: WLNG-FM is a commercial station owned by Main Street Broadcasting Co., Inc. The The format of the station is oldies music. WLNG-FM broadcasts in the Sag Harbor, NY area at 92.1 FM area.
FM RADIO STATION

WLNH-FM 42276
Owner: WBIN, Inc.
Editorial: 2 Capital Plz Ste 105, Concord, New Hampshire 03301-4911 **Tel:** 1 603 224-8486.
Web site: http://www.wlnh.com
Profile: WLNH-FM is a commercial station owned by WBIN, Inc. The format of the station is adult contemporary. WLNH-FM broadcasts to the Gilford, NH area at 98.3 FM.
FM RADIO STATION

WLNI-FM 42449
Owner: Wheeler Inc.(Mel)
Editorial: 3934 Electric Rd, Roanoke, Virginia 24018-4513 **Tel:** 1 434 845-5463.
Web site: http://wlni.com
Profile: WLNI-FM is a commercial station owned by Wheeler Inc.(Mel). The format of the station is news and talk. WLNI-FM broadcasts to the Lynchburg, VA area at 105.9 FM.
FM RADIO STATION

WLNK-FM 46029
Owner: Entercom Communications Corp.
Editorial: 1 Julian Price Pl, Charlotte, North Carolina 28208-5211 **Tel:** 1 704 374-3500.
Web site: http://www.1079thelink.com
Profile: WLNK-FM is a commercial station owned by Entercom Communications Corp. The format of the station is hot adult contemporary music and talk. WLNK-FM broadcasts to the Charlotte, NC area at 107.9 FM.
FM RADIO STATION

WLNL-AM 36821
Owner: Trinity Media Ltd.
Editorial: 3134 Lake Rd, Horseheads, New York 14845-3103 **Tel:** 1 607 330-0223.
Web site: http://www.wlnlradio.org
Profile: WLNL-AM is a commercial station owned by Trinity Media Ltd. The format of the station is contemporary Christian music and religious talk programming. WLNL-AM broadcasts to the Horseheads, NY area at 1000 AM.
AM RADIO STATION

WLNZ-FM 44128
Owner: Lansing Community College
Editorial: 400 N Capitol Ave Ste 1, Lansing, Michigan 48933-1208 **Tel:** 1 517 483-1710.
Email: wlnzradio@gmail.com
Web site: http://www.lcc.edu/radio
Profile: WLNZ-FM is a non-commercial station owned by Lansing Community College. The format of the station is adult album alternative, jazz and blues. WLNZ-FM broadcasts to the Lansing, MI area at 89.7 FM.
FM RADIO STATION

WLOB-AM 35489
Owner: Atlantic Coast Radio LLC
Editorial: 779 Warren Ave, Portland, Maine 04103-1007 **Tel:** 1 207 773-9695.
Email: newstalkwlob@yahoo.com
Web site: http://www.wlobradio.com
Profile: WLOB-AM is a commercial station owned by Atlantic Coast Radio LLC. The format of the station is news talk. WLOB-AM broadcasts to the Portland, ME area at 1310 AM.
AM RADIO STATION

WLOC-AM 36853
Owner: Forbis Communications Inc.
Editorial: 1130 S Dixie St, Horse Cave, Kentucky 42749-1462 **Tel:** 1 270 786-1000.
Email: wloc@scrtc.com
Web site: http://www.wloconline.com
Profile: WLOC-AM is a commercial station owned by Forbis Communications Inc. The format of the station is news, talk, and sports with a focus on Reds Baseball. WLOC-AM broadcasts to the Horse Cave, KY area at 1150 AM.
AM RADIO STATION

WLOE-AM 35490
Owner: Mayo Broadcasting Corporation
Editorial: 1203 Harris St, Eden, North Carolina 27288-6321 **Tel:** 1 336 627-9563.
Web site: http://www.wloewmyn.com
Profile: WLOE-AM is commercial station owned by Mayo Broadcasting Corporation. The format of the station is religious programming, news and talk. WLOE-AM broadcasts to the Greensboro-Winston Salem, NC area at 1490 AM.
AM RADIO STATION

WLOF-FM 44479
Owner: Holy Family Communications
Editorial: 6325 Sheridan Dr, Williamsville, New York 14221-4848 **Tel:** 1 716 839-6117.
Email: info@wlof.net
Web site: http://www.wlof.net
Profile: WLOF-FM is a non-commercial station owned by Holy Family Communications. The format of the station is religious. WLOF-FM broadcasts to the Williamsville, NY area at 101.7 FM.
FM RADIO STATION

WLOH-AM 36563
Owner: Bohach(Mark & Arlene)
Editorial: 2686 N Columbus St Ste 101, Lancaster, Ohio 43130-8404 **Tel:** 1 740 653-4373.
Email: news@wloh.net
Web site: http://www.wloh.net
Profile: WLOH-AM is a commercial station owned by Mark and Arlene Bohach. The format of the station is country. WLOH-AM broadcasts to Lancaster, OH at 1320 AM.
AM RADIO STATION

WLOI-AM 38022
Owner: La Porte County Broadcasting Co. Inc.
Editorial: 1700 Lincolnway Pl, Ste 8, La Porte, Indiana 46350 **Tel:** 1 219 362-6144.
Profile: WLOI-AM is a commercial station owned by the La Porte County Broadcasting Co. Inc. The format of the station is adult standards. WLOI-AM broadcasts to the La Porte, IN area at 1540 AM.
AM RADIO STATION

WLOK-AM 35492
Owner: Gilliam Communications Inc.
Editorial: 363 S 2nd St, Memphis, Tennessee 38103 **Tel:** 1 901 527-9565.
Email: wlokradio@aol.com
Web site: http://www.wlok.com
Profile: WLOK-AM is a commercial station owned by Gilliam Communications Inc. The format of the station is gospel music. WLOK-AM broadcasts to the Memphis, TN area at 1340 AM.
AM RADIO STATION

WLOL-AM 38943
Owner: Starboard Media Foundation Inc.
Editorial: 7575 Golden Valley Rd Ste 310, Golden Valley, Minnesota 55427-4596 **Tel:** 1 612 643-4110.
Email: info@relevantradio.com
Web site: http://www.relevantradio.com
Profile: WLOL-AM is a commercial station owned by Starboard Media Foundation Inc. The format of the station is religious programming. WLOL-AM broadcasts to the Golden Valley, MN area at 1330 AM.
AM RADIO STATION

WLOL-FM 739861
Owner: Light of Life Community, Inc
Editorial: 132 Carubia Dr, Core, West Virginia 26541-7137 **Tel:** 1 304 598-0026.
Email: info@lolradio.org
Web site: http://lolradio.org
Profile: WLOL-FM is a non-commercial station owned by Light of Life Community, Inc. The format of the station is religious featuring a focus on Catholicism. WLOL-FM broadcasts to the Star City, Morgantown, Granville, Westover areas in West Virginia at a frequency of 89.7 FM.
FM RADIO STATION

WLON-AM 35493
Owner: KTC Broadcasting
Editorial: 1416 Shelby Hwy #150, Cherryville, North Carolina 28021-8356 **Tel:** 1 704 735-8071.
Web site: http://www.ktcbroadcasting.com/wlon-1050am.html
Profile: WLON-AM is a commercial station owned by KTC Broadcasting. The format of the station is oldies and sports. WLON-AM broadcasts to the Lincolnton, NC area at 1050 AM.
AM RADIO STATION

WLOP-AM 38023
Owner: Jesup Broadcasting Corp.
Editorial: 2420 Waycross Hwy, Jesup, Georgia 31545-2332 **Tel:** 1 912 427-3711.
Email: bigdogstaff@bellsouth.net
Web site: http://bigdogcountry.com
Profile: WLOP-AM is a commercial station owned by Jesup Broadcasting Corp. The format for the station is sports. WLOP-AM broadcasts to the Savannah, GA area at 1370 AM.
AM RADIO STATION

WLOR-AM 36138
Owner: Black Crow Broadcasting Inc.
Editorial: 1555 the Boardwalk Ste 1, Huntsville, Alabama 35816-1821 **Tel:** 1 256 536-1568.
Web site: http://sunny981.com
Profile: WLOR-AM is a commercial station owned by Black Crow Broadcasting Inc. The format of the station is Classic Hip-Hop and R&B. WLOR-AM broadcasts to the Huntsville, AL area at 1550 AM.
AM RADIO STATION

WLOU-AM 35494
Owner: Golden Door Broadcasting, LLC
Editorial: 2001 W Broadway Ste 13, Louisville, Kentucky 40203-3584 **Tel:** 1 502 776-1240.
Email: wlouwllv@aol.com
Profile: WLOU-AM is a commercial station owned by Golden Door Broadcasting, LLC. The format of the station is gospel music. WLOU-AM broadcasts to the Louisville, KY area at 1350 AM.
AM RADIO STATION

WLOV-FM 800022
Owner: Southern Stone Communications
Editorial: 126 W International Speedway Blvd, Daytona Beach, Florida 32114-4322 **Tel:** 1 386 255-9300.
Web site: http://995wlov.com
Profile: WLOV-FM is a commercial station owned by Susan Hall and operated by Black Crow Radio. The format of the station is soft adult contemporary. WLOV-FM broadcasts to the Daytona Beach, FL area at a frequency of 99.5 FM.
FM RADIO STATION

WLOY-AM 496804
Owner: Three Rivers Media Corp.
Editorial: 110 W Spiller St, Wytheville, Virginia 24382 **Tel:** 1 276 228-3185.
Email: office@threeriversmedia.net
Web site: http://www.wxbx.com
AM RADIO STATION

WLPA-AM 38025
Owner: Hall Communications
Editorial: 1996 Auction Rd, Manheim, Pennsylvania 17545-9159 **Tel:** 1 717 653-0800.
Email: wlpaprogramming@hallradio.net
Web site: http://www.wlpa.com
Profile: WLPA-AM is a commercial station owned by Hall Communications. The format of the station is Sports. WLPA-AM broadcasts to the Manheim, PA area at 1490 AM.
AM RADIO STATION

WLPE-FM 41651
Owner: Good News Network
Editorial: 2278 Wortham Ln, Grovetown, Georgia 30813-5103 **Tel:** 1 706 309-9610.
Web site: http://www.gnnradio.org
Profile: WLPE-FM is a non-commercial station owned by Good News Network. The format of the station is WLPE 91.7 Augusta/Aiken
FM RADIO STATION

WLPK-AM 39138
Owner: Rodgers Broadcasting Corp.
Editorial: 406 1/2 N Central Ave, Connersville, Indiana 47331-1926 **Tel:** 1 765 825-6411.
Web site: http://superoldies1580.com
Profile: WLPK-AM is a commercial station owned by Rodgers Broadcasting Corp. The format of the station is oldies music. WLPK-AM broadcasts to the Connersville, IN area at 1580 AM.
AM RADIO STATION

WLPO-AM 38026
Owner: LaSalle County Broadcasting Corp.
Editorial: 1 Broadcast Ln, Oglesby, Illinois 61348-9539 **Tel:** 1 815 223-3100.
Web site: http://www.wlpoamandfm.com
Profile: WLPO-AM is a commercial station owned by LaSalle County Broadcasting Corp. The format of the station is classic hits. WLPO-AM broadcasts to the Chicago area at 1220 AM.
AM RADIO STATION

WLPR-AM 36211
Owner: Goforth Media Inc.
Editorial: 6530-B Spanish Fort Blvd, Spanish Fort, Alabama 36527-5014 **Tel:** 1 251 473-8488.
Email: news@goforth.org
Web site: http://www.goforth.org
Profile: WLPR-AM is a commercial station owned by Goforth Media Inc. The format of the station is Southern gospel. WLPR-AM broadcasts in the Mobile, AL area at 960 AM.
AM RADIO STATION

WLPR-FM 571622
Owner: Northwest Indiana Public Broadcasting, Inc.
Editorial: 8625 Indiana Pl, Merrillville, Indiana 46410-6369 **Tel:** 1 219 756-5656.
Email: news@lakeshorepublicmedia.org
Web site: http://www.thelakeshorefm.com
Profile: WLPR-FM is a non-commercial station owned by Northwest Indiana Public Broadcasting, Inc. The format of the station is news and talk. WLPR-FM broadcasts to the Merrillville, IN area at 89.1 FM.
FM RADIO STATION

WLPW-FM 45712
Owner: Mountain Communications
Editorial: 159 Santanoni Ave, Saranac Lake, New York 12983-2478 **Tel:** 1 518 891-1544.
Email: news@wnbz.com
Web site: http://wnbz.com
Profile: WLPW-FM is a commercial station owned by Mountain Communications. The format of the station is classic rock. WLPW-FM broadcasts to the Saranac Lake, NY area at 105.5 FM.
FM RADIO STATION

WLQB-FM 44270
Owner: iHeartMedia Inc.
Editorial: 4841 Highway 17 Byp S, Myrtle Beach, South Carolina 29577-6683 **Tel:** 1 843 293-0107.
Web site: http://b935fm.iheart.com
Profile: WLQB-FM is a commercial station owned by iHeartMedia Inc. The format of the station is adult contemporary. WLQB-FM broadcasts to the Ocean Isle, NC area at 93.5 FM.
FM RADIO STATION

WLQH-AM 38834
Owner: Suncoast Radio, Inc.
Editorial: 174 NE 351 Highway, Cross City, Florida **Tel:** 1 727 410-1642.
Web site: http://www.classichits933.com
Profile: WLQH-AM is a commercial station owned by Suncoast Radio, Inc.. The format of the station is classic hits. WLQH-AM broadcasts to the Chiefland, FL area at 940 AM.
AM RADIO STATION

WLQI-FM 45938
Owner: Brothers Broadcasting Corp.
Editorial: 560 W Amsler Rd, Rensselaer, Indiana 47978-8643 **Tel:** 1 219 866-4104.
Email: wrin@ffni.com
Profile: WLQI-FM is a commercial station owned by Brothers Broadcasting Corporation. The format of the station is rock. WLQI-FM broadcasts to the Rensselaer, IN area at 97.7 FM.
FM RADIO STATION

WLQK-FM 43475
Owner: Stonecom Cookeville LLC
Editorial: 259 S Willow Ave, Cookeville, Tennessee 38501 **Tel:** 1 931 528-6064.
Web site: http://www.literock959.com
Profile: WLQK-FM is a commercial station owned by Stonecom Cookeville LLC. The format of the station is Lite Rock/Lite AC. WLQK-FM broadcasts to the Cookeville, TN area at 95.9 FM.
FM RADIO STATION

WLQM-AM 38996
Owner: Franklin Broadcasting Corp.
Editorial: 320 N Franklin St, Franklin, Virginia 23851 **Tel:** 1 757 562-3135.
Email: wlqm@wlqmradio.com
Web site: http://www.wlqmradio.com
Profile: WLQM-AM is a commercial station owned by Franklin Broadcasting Corp. The format of the station is gospel music. WLQM-AM broadcasts to the Franklin, VA area at 1250 AM.
AM RADIO STATION

WLQM-FM 46321
Owner: Franklin Broadcasting Corp.
Editorial: 320 N Franklin St, Franklin, Virginia 23851 **Tel:** 1 757 562-3135.
Email: wlqm@wlqmradio.com
Web site: http://www.wlqmradio.com
Profile: WLQM-FM is a commercial station owned by Franklin Broadcasting Corp. The format of the station is a mix of contemporary and classic country. WLQM-FM broadcasts to the Franklin, VA area at 101.7 FM.
FM RADIO STATION

WLQV-AM 35867
Owner: Salem Media Group, Inc.
Editorial: 2 Radio Plaza St, Ferndale, Michigan 48220-2129 **Tel:** 1 248 581-1234.
Email: contact@salemdetroit.com
Web site: http://www.faithtalk1500.com
Profile: WLQV-AM is a commercial station owned by Salem Media Group, Inc. The format of the station is Christian programming. WLQV-AM broadcasts to the Ferndale, MI area at 1500 AM.
AM RADIO STATION

WLQY-AM 35496
Owner: Entravision Communications Corp.
Editorial: 1055 NE 125th St, North Miami, Florida 33161-5804 **Tel:** 1 305 891-1729.
Email: wlqy@bellsouth.net
Profile: WLQY-AM is a commercial station owned by Entravision Communications Corp. The format of the station is variety programming. WLQY-AM broadcasts to the Miami area at 1320 AM.
AM RADIO STATION

WLRB-AM 38027
Owner: Colchester Radio, Inc.
Editorial: 31 E Side Sq, Macomb, Illinois 61455-2248 **Tel:** 1 309 833-2121.
Email: news@prestigeradio.com
Web site: http://www.prestigeradio.com
Profile: WLRB-AM is a commercial station owned by Colchester Radio, Inc. The format of the station is talk. WLRB-AM broadcasts to the Macomb, IL area at 1510 AM.
AM RADIO STATION

WLRC-AM 35797
Owner: Clayton(B.R. & Martha)
Editorial: Po Box 37, 7760 Highway 72 East, Walnut, Mississippi 38683-0037 **Tel:** 1 662 223-4071.
Web site: http://www.wlrcradio.com
Profile: WLRC-AM is a commercial station owned by B.R. & Martha Clayton. The format of the station is southern gospel and religious. WLRC-AM broadcasts to the Walnut, MS area at 850 AM.
AM RADIO STATION

WLRD-FM 586724
Owner: Christian Faith Broadcast, Inc.
Editorial: 3809 Maple Ave, Castalia, Ohio 44824-9484 **Tel:** 1 419 684-5311.
Email: fm97.7@cfbroadcast.net
Web site: http://www.wlrd.net
Profile: WLRD-FM is a commercial station owned by Christian Faith Broadcast, Inc. The format of the station is Southern gospel. WRLD-FM broadcasts to the Castalia, OH area at 96.9 FM.
FM RADIO STATION

WLRM-AM 36090
Owner: CPT & T RADIO STATION, INC.
Editorial: 6960 Bucknell Rd, Millington, Tennessee 38053-7502 **Tel:** 1 901 872-8861.
Web site: http://www.wlrm1380.com
Profile: WLRM-AM is a non-commercial station owned by CPT & T RADIO STATION, INC. The format of the station is Spanish Contemporary Christian. WLRM-AM broadcasts to the Millington, TN area.
AM RADIO STATION

WLRO-AM 38422
Owner: iHeartMedia Inc.
Editorial: 5555 Hilton Ave Ste 500, Baton Rouge, Louisiana 70808-2564 **Tel:** 1 225 231-1860.
Web site: http://www.1210thescore.com/main.html
Profile: WLRO-AM is a commercial station owned by iHeartMedia Inc. The format of the station is sports and talk. WLRO-AM broadcasts to the Baton Rouge, LA area at 1210 AM.
AM RADIO STATION

WLRQ-FM 44259
Owner: iHeartMedia Inc.
Editorial: 1388 S Babcock St, One Radio Center, Melbourne, Florida 32901-3009 **Tel:** 1 321 733-1000.
Web site: http://literock993.iheart.com
Profile: WLRQ-FM is a commercial station owned by iHeartMedia Inc. The format of the station is easy listening. WLRQ-FM broadcasts to the Melbourne, FL area at 99.3 FM.
FM RADIO STATION

WLRS-AM 573818
Owner: New Albany Broadcasting Co. Inc.
Editorial: 220 Potters Ln, Clarksville, Indiana 47129-1020 **Tel:** 1 812 949-1570.
Web site: http://www.lapoderosaky.com
Profile: WLRS-AM is a commercial station owned by New Albany Broadcasting Co. Inc. The format of the station is Spanish music. WNDA-AM broadcasts to the Clarksville, IN area at 1570 AM.
AM RADIO STATION

WLRT-AM 35982
Owner: Christian Broadcasting System
Editorial: 501 Darby Creek Rd Ste 62, Lexington, Kentucky 40509-2611 **Tel:** 1 859 264-9700.
Email: realtalk@ckcradio.com
Web site: http://www.wlrtradio.com
Profile: WLRT-AM is a commercial station owned by Christian Broadcasting System. The format of the station is news and talk programming. WLRT-AM broadcasts to the Lexington, KY area at 1250 AM.
AM RADIO STATION

WLRW-FM 40486
Owner: Saga Communications
Editorial: 2603 W Bradley Ave, Champaign, Illinois 61821-1823 **Tel:** 1 217 352-4141.
Email: production@mix945.com
Web site: http://www.mix945.com
Profile: WLRW-FM is a commercial station owned by Saga Communications. The format is hot adult contemporary. The station airs at 94.5 FM in the Champaign, IL area.
FM RADIO STATION

WLRX-FM 46806
Owner: iHeartMedia Inc.
Editorial: 134 4th Ave, Huntington, West Virginia 25701-1220 **Tel:** 1 304 525-7788.
Web site: http://www.1071thebear.com/main.html
Profile: WLRX-FM is a commercial station owned by iHeartMedia Inc. The format of the station is classic country. WLRX-FM broadcasts to Huntington, WV and surrounding communities at 107.1 FM.
FM RADIO STATION

WLRY-FM 44178
Owner: Archangel Broadcasting Foundation
Editorial: 4244 Logan Thornville Rd NE, Rushville, Ohio 43150-9751 **Tel:** 1 740 536-0885.
Web site: http://www.wlry.org
Profile: WLRY-FM is a non-commercial station owned by Archangel Broadcasting Foundation. The format of the station is Christian music and talk programming. WLRY-FM broadcasts to the Rushville, OH area at 88.9 FM.
FM RADIO STATION

WLS-AM 38413
Owner: Cumulus Media Inc.
Editorial: 455 N Cityfront Plaza Dr Fl 6, Chicago, Illinois 60611-5579 **Tel:** 1 312 245-1200.
Email: wls.news@wlsam.com
Web site: http://www.wlsam.com
Profile: WLS-AM is a commercial station owned by Cumulus Media Inc. The format of the station is news and talk. WLS-AM broadcasts to the Chicago area at 890 AM. The station offers a digital podcast.
AM RADIO STATION

WLSB-AM 36379
Owner: Joy Christian Communications, Inc.
Tel: 1 931 222-1633.
Email: radio@joychristian.com
Web site: http://joychristianradio.com
Profile: WLSB-AM is a non-commercial station owned by Joy Christian Communications, Inc. The format of the station is Christian teaching. WLSB-AM broadcasts to the Chattanooga, TN area at 1400 AM.
AM RADIO STATION

WLSC-AM 35498
Owner: Banana Jack Productions, LLC
Editorial: 4164 Main St, Loris, South Carolina 29569-3024 **Tel:** 1 843 756-5225.
Email: info@wlscradio.com
Web site: http://www.tigerradio.com
Profile: WLSC-AM is a commercial station owned by Banana Jack Productions, LLC. The format of the station is oldies. WLSC-AM broadcasts to the Loris, SC area at 1240 AM.
AM RADIO STATION

WLSD-AM 36371
Owner: Valley Broadcasting
Editorial: 724 Park Ave NW, Norton, Virginia 24273-1923 **Tel:** 1 276 523-1700.
Web site: http://ww.wlsdradio.com
Profile: WLSD-AM is a commercial station owned by Valley Broadcasting. The format of the station is Southern gospel and religious programming. WLSD-AM broadcasts to the Big Stone Gap, VA area at 1220 AM.
AM RADIO STATION

WLS-FM 45780
Owner: Cumulus Media Inc.
Editorial: 455 N Cityfront Plaza Dr Fl 6, Chicago, Illinois 60611-5579 **Tel:** 1 312 245-1200.
Email: wlsfm.programdirector@947wls.com
Web site: http://www.947wls.com
Profile: WLS-FM is a commercial station owned by Cumulus Media Inc. The format of the station is classic hits. WLS-FM broadcasts to the Chicago area at 94.7 FM.
FM RADIO STATION

WLSG-AM 63461
Owner: B & M Broadcasting, LLC
Editorial: 410 New Bridge St Ste 3B, Jacksonville, North Carolina 28540-4759 **Tel:** 1 910 346-2248.
Email: freedom1120@yahoo.com
Web site: http://www.941thebeach.com
Profile: WLSG-AM is a commercial station owned and operated by B & M Broadcasting, LLC. The format of the station is oldies. WLSG-AM broadcasts to the Wilmington, NC area at 1340 AM.
AM RADIO STATION

WLSH-AM 38962
Owner: J-Systems Franchising Corp.
Editorial: 2147 Market St, Nesquehoning, Pennsylvania 18240-1422 **Tel:** 1 570 645-3123.
Email: wmgh@ptd.net
Web site: http://www.wmgh.com
Profile: WLSH-AM is a commercial station owned by J-Systems Franchising Corp. The format of the station is Easy Listening. WLSH-AM broadcasts to the Lansford, PA area at 1410 AM.
AM RADIO STATION

WLSI-AM 39295
Owner: East Kentucky Radio Network
Editorial: 1240 Radio Dr, Pikeville, Kentucky 41501-4779 **Tel:** 1 304 235-3600.
Email: frontdesk@ekbradio.com
Web site: http://www.900wlsi.com
Profile: WLSI-AM is a commercial station owned by East Kentucky Radio Network. The format of the station is talk. WLSI-AM broadcasts to the Charleston - Huntington, WV area at 900 AM.
AM RADIO STATION

WLSK-FM 45347
Owner: Choice Radio Corporation
Editorial: 253 W Main St, Lebanon, Kentucky 40033-1240 **Tel:** 1 270 692-3126.
Profile: WLSK-FM is a commercial station owned by Choice Radio Corporation. The format of the stations is contemporary country. WLSK-FM broadcasts in the Lebanon, KY area at 100.9 FM.
FM RADIO STATION

WLSM-FM 45348
Owner: Harrison Communications
Editorial: 2142 Highway 14 E, Louisville, Mississippi 39339-7665 **Tel:** 1 662 773-3481.
Email: magic107.1@gmail.com
Profile: WLSM-FM is a commercial station owned by Harrison Communications. The format of the station is adult contemporary music. WLSM-FM broadcasts to the Louisville, MS area at 107.1 FM.
FM RADIO STATION

WLSN-FM 76568
Owner: Minnesota Public Radio
Editorial: 207 W Superior St Ste 224, Duluth, Minnesota 55802-4041 **Tel:** 1 218 722-9411.
Email: newsroom@mpr.org
Web site: http://www.mpr.org/listen/stations/wlsnwmls
Profile: WLSN-FM is a non-commercial station owned by Minnesota Public Radio. The format of the station is news and talk. WLSN-FM broadcasts to the Duluth, MN area at 89.7 FM.
FM RADIO STATION

WLSR-FM 43693
Owner: Galesburg Broadcasting Co.
Editorial: 154 E Simmons St, Galesburg, Illinois 61401 **Tel:** 1 309 342-5131.
Email: news@wgil.com
Web site: http://www.thelaseronline.com
Profile: WLSR-FM is a commercial station owned by Galesburg Broadcasting Co. The format of the station is rock music. WLSR-FM broadcasts to the Galesburg, IL area at 92.7 FM.
FM RADIO STATION

WLSS-AM 35463
Owner: Salem Media Group, Inc.
Editorial: 5211 W Laurel St Ste A, Tampa, Florida 33607-1736 **Tel:** 1 941 363-0930.
Web site: http://am930theanswer.com
Profile: WLSS-AM is a commercial station owned by Salem Media Group, Inc. The format of the station is talk. WLSS-AM broadcasts to the Sarasota, FL, area at 930 AM.
AM RADIO STATION

WLST-FM 45350
Owner: Radio Plus Bay Cities, LLC
Editorial: 413 10th Ave, Menominee, Michigan 49858-3009 **Tel:** 1 906 863-5551.
Email: reception@baycitiesradio.net
Web site: http://catcountry951online.com
Profile: WLST-FM is a commercial station owned by Radio Plus Bay Cities, LLC. The format of the station is contemporary country music. WLST-FM broadcasts to the Menominee, MI area at 95.1 FM.
FM RADIO STATION

WLSV-AM 39342
Owner: DBM Communications
Editorial: 82 Railroad Ave, Wellsville, New York 14895-1143 **Tel:** 1 585 593-6070.
Email: oldiesz103@yahoo.com
Web site: http://www.wlsv.com
Profile: WLSV-AM is a commercial station owned by DBM Communications. The format of the station is country. WLSV-AM broadcasts to the Wellsville, NY area at 790 AM.
AM RADIO STATION

WLSW-FM 40490
Owner: Wall(L. Stanley)
Editorial: 2532 Springfield Pike, Connellsville, Pennsylvania 15425 **Tel:** 1 724 628-2800.
Email: wlswproduction@hotmail.com
Profile: WLSW-FM is a commercial station owned by L. Stanley Wall. The format of the station is classic hits. WLSW-FM broadcasts to the Connellsville, PA area at 103.9 FM.
FM RADIO STATION

WLTA-AM 36491
Owner: Salem Media Group, Inc.
Editorial: 2970 Peachtree Rd NW Ste 700, Atlanta, Georgia 30305-4919 **Tel:** 1 404 995-7300.
Web site: http://www.faithtalk970.com
Profile: WLTA-AM is a commercial station owned by Salem Media Group, Inc. The format of the station is Christian talk. WLTA-AM broadcasts to the Atlanta area at 1400 AM.
AM RADIO STATION

WLTB-FM 45885
Owner: GM Broadcasting
Editorial: 3215 E Main St, Ste 2, Endwell, New York 13760-5905 **Tel:** 1 607 748-9131.
Email: info@magic1017fm.com
Web site: http://www.magic1017fm.com
Profile: WLBT-FM is a commercial station owned by GM Broadcasting. The format of the station is Hot Adult Contemporary and Adult Contemporary. WLBT-FM broadcasts to the Vestal, NY area at 101.7 FM.
FM RADIO STATION

WLTC-FM 617477
Owner: PMB Broadcasting, LLC
Editorial: 1820 Wynnton Rd, Columbus, Georgia 31906-2930 **Tel:** 1 706 327-1217.
Web site: http://www.1037lite.fm
Profile: WLTC-FM is a commercial station owned by PMB Broadcasting, LLC. It features adult contemporary music. The station airs on 103.7 FM in the Columbus, GA area.
FM RADIO STATION

WLTE-FM 961771
Owner: Caron Broadcasting, Inc.
Editorial: 920 Wade Hampton Blvd, Greenville, South Carolina 29609-4944 **Tel:** 1 864 242-6240.
Email: contact@earthfmwrth.com
Web site: http://www.earthfmwrth.com
Profile: WLTE-FM is a commercial station owned by Caron Broadcasting, Inc. The format of the station is classic hits. WLTE-FM broadcasts to the Pendleton, South Carolina area at 103.3 FM.
FM RADIO STATION

WLTF-FM 40891
Owner: Prettyman Broadcasting Co.
Editorial: 1606 W King St, Martinsburg, West Virginia 25401-2077 **Tel:** 1 304 263-8868.
Web site: http://todays975.com
Profile: WLTF-FM is a commercial station owned by Prettyman Broadcasting Co. The format of the station is AC. WLTF-FM broadcasts in the Martinsburg, MD area at 97.5.
FM RADIO STATION

WLTG-AM 36588
Owner: Hour Group Broadcasting Inc.
Editorial: 3100 E 15th St, Panama City, Florida 32405 **Tel:** 1 850 784-9873.
Email: wltg@bellsouth.net
Profile: WLTG-AM is a commercial station owned by Hour Group Broadcasting Inc. The format of the station is news, sports, and talk. WLTG-AM broadcasts to the Panama City, FL area at 1430 AM.
AM RADIO STATION

WLTH-AM 407136
Owner: WLTH Radio Inc.
Editorial: 407 Broadway, Gary, Indiana 46402
Tel: 1 219 885-1370.
Email: wlth1370@yahoo.com
Web site: http://www.wlth1370.com
Profile: WLTH-AM is a commercial station owned by WLTH Radio Inc. The format of the station is talk. WLTH-AM broadcasts to the greater Chicago area at 1370 AM.
AM RADIO STATION

WLTI-AM 37731
Owner: Cumulus Media Inc.
Editorial: 1134 W State Road 38, New Castle, Indiana 47362-9781 **Tel:** 1 765 529-2600.
Profile: WLTI-AM is a commercial station owned by Cumulus Media Inc. The format of the station is classic country. WLTI-AM broadcasts to the Indianapolis area at 1550 AM.
AM RADIO STATION

WLTJ-FM 40492
Owner: Steel City Media
Editorial: 650 Smithfield St, Ste 2200, Pittsburgh, Pennsylvania 15222 **Tel:** 1 412 316-3342.
Web site: http://q929fm.com
Profile: WLTJ-FM is a commercial station owned by Steel City Media. The format of the station is hot AC. WLTJ-FM broadcasts to the Pittsburgh area at 92.9 FM.
FM RADIO STATION

WLTM-FM 40118
Owner: Delta Radio, LLC
Editorial: 830 Main St, Greenville, Mississippi 38701-4102 **Tel:** 1 662 378-2617.
Email: info@deltaradio.net
Web site: http://www.lite979.com
Profile: WLTM-FM is a commercial station owned by Delta Radio, LLC. The format of the station is adult contemporary. WLTM-FM broadcasts to the Greenville, MS area at 97.9 FM.
FM RADIO STATION

WLTN-AM 38903
Owner: Lunderville(Barry)
Editorial: 15 Main St, Littleton, New Hampshire 03561-4037 **Tel:** 1 603 444-3911.
Email: kiss102@together.net
Web site: http://wltnradio.com
Profile: WLTN-AM is a commercial station owned by Barry Lunderville. The format of the station is oldies music. WLTN-AM broadcasts to the Littleton, NH area at 1400 AM.
AM RADIO STATION

WLTN-FM 46240
Owner: Lunderville(Barry)
Editorial: 15 Main St, Littleton, New Hampshire 3561 **Tel:** 1 603 444-3911.
Email: mix967@roadrunner.com
Profile: WLTN-FM is a commercial station owned by Barry Lunderville. The format of the station is adult contemporary music. WLTN-FM broadcasts to the Littleton, NH area at 96.7 FM.
FM RADIO STATION

WLTO-FM 41437
Owner: Cumulus Media Inc.
Editorial: 300 W Vine St Ste 3, Lexington, Kentucky 40507-1806 **Tel:** 1 859 253-5900.
Web site: http://www.hot102.net
Profile: WLTO-FM is a commercial station owned by Cumulus Media Inc. The format of the station is rhythmic Top 40/CHR music. WLTO-FM broadcasts to the Lexington, KY area at 102.5 FM.
FM RADIO STATION

WLTP-AM 39005
Owner: iHeartMedia Inc.
Editorial: 6006 Grand Central Ave, Parkersburg, West Virginia 26105-9125 **Tel:** 1 304 295-6070.
Web site: http://newstalk910wltp.iheart.com
Profile: WLTP-AM is a commercial station owned by iHeartMedia Inc. The format for the station is news and talk. WLTP-AM broadcasts to the Parkersburg, WV area at 910 AM.
AM RADIO STATION

WLTQ-AM 36940
Owner: Mediatrix SC, Inc.
Editorial: 143 Calhoun St, Charleston, South Carolina 29401-3514 **Tel:** 1 866 263-1700.
Web site: http://catholicradioinsc.com

Profile: WLTQ-AM is a non-commercial station owned by Mediatrix SC, Inc. The format of the station is Catholic radio music and teaching programming. WLTQ-AM broadcasts to the Mount Pleasant, SC area at 730 AM.
AM RADIO STATION

WLTT-AM 40719
Owner: Carolina Christian Radio, Inc.
Editorial: 1890 Dawson St, Wilmington, North Carolina 28403-2359 **Tel:** 1 910 343-6005.
Email: comments@1180wltt.com
Web site: http://www.1180wltt.com/
Profile: WLTT-AM is a commercial station owned by Carolina Christian Radio, Inc. The format of the station talk/R&B Oldies. WSFM-AM broadcasts in the Wilmington, NC area at 1180 AM.
AM RADIO STATION

WLTU-FM 46150
Owner: Cub Radio Inc.
Editorial: 1915 Mirro Dr, Manitowoc, Wisconsin 54220-6715 **Tel:** 1 920 683-6800.
Web site: http://www.cubradio.com
Profile: WLTU-FM is a commercial station owned by Cub Radio Inc. The format of the station is country music. WLTU-FM broadcasts to the Manitowoc, WI area at 92.1 FM.
FM RADIO STATION

WLTW-FM 40495
Owner: iHeartMedia Inc.
Editorial: 32 Avenue of the Americas Fl 3, New York, New York 10013-2473 **Tel:** 1 212 377-7900.
Web site: http://litefm.iheart.com
Profile: WLTW-FM is a commercial station owned by iHeartMedia Inc. The format of the station is adult contemporary. WLTW-FM broadcasts to the New York City area at 106.7 FM.
FM RADIO STATION

WLTY-FM 40913
Owner: iHeart Media Inc.
Editorial: 316 Greystone Blvd, Columbia, South Carolina 29210-8007 **Tel:** 1 803 343-1100.
Web site: http://www.967stevefm.com
Profile: WLTY-FM is a commercial station owned by iHeart Media Inc. The format of the station is adult hits. WLTY-FM broadcasts to the Columbia, SC area at 96.7 FM.
FM RADIO STATION

WLUB-FM 40915
Owner: iHeart Media Inc.
Editorial: 2743 Perimeter Pkwy Ste 300, Augusta, Georgia 30909-6429 **Tel:** 1 706 396-6000.
Web site: http://bull1057.iheart.com/
Profile: WLUB-FM is a commercial station owned by iHeart Media Inc. The format of the station is contemporary country. WLUB-FM broadcasts to the Augusta, GA area at 105.7 FM.
FM RADIO STATION

WLUE-AM 36197
Owner: New Albany Broadcasting, Inc.
Editorial: 220 Potters Ln, Clarksville, Indiana 47129-1020 **Tel:** 1 812 949-1570.
Web site: http://www.lapoderosaky.com/
Profile: WLUE-AM is a commercial station owned by New Albany Broadcasting, Inc. The format of the station is Spanish music. WLUE-AM broadcasts to the Eminence, KY and surrounding areas at 1600 AM.
AM RADIO STATION

WLUJ-FM 41327
Owner: Cornerstone Community Radio Inc.
Editorial: 600 W Mason St, Springfield, Illinois 62702-5025 **Tel:** 1 217 528-2300.
Email: comments@wluj.org
Web site: http://www.wluj.org
Profile: WLUJ-FM is a non-commercial station owned by Cornerstone Community Radio Inc. The format of the station is contemporary Christian music and talk. WLUJ-FM broadcasts in Springfield, IL at 89.7 FM and simulcasts in Lincoln, IL at 1370 AM.
FM RADIO STATION

WLUM-FM 42820
Owner: Milwaukee Radio Alliance
Editorial: N72W12922 Good Hope Rd, Menomonee Falls, Wisconsin 53051-4441 **Tel:** 1 414 771-1021.
Email: info@milwaukeeradio.com
Web site: http://www.fm1021milwaukee.com
Profile: WLUM-FM is a commercial station owned by Milwaukee Radio Alliance. The format of the station is alternative music. WLUM-FM broadcasts to the Milwaukee area at 102.1 FM.
FM RADIO STATION

WLUN-FM 42723
Owner: Michigan Radio Communications & Great Lakes Loons(The)
Editorial: 825 E Main St, Midland, Michigan 48640
Tel: 1 989 837-2255.
Web site: http://www.espn1009.com
Profile: WLUN-FM is a commercial station owned by Michigan Radio Communications and Great Lakes Loons(The). The format of the station is sports. WLUN-FM broadcasts to the Saginaw, MI area at 100.9 FM.
FM RADIO STATION

WLUP-FM 43375
Owner: Cumulus Media
Editorial: 190 N State St Fl 8, Chicago, Illinois 60601-3399 **Tel:** 1 312 245-1200.
Web site: http://www.wlup.com
Profile: WLUP-FM is a commercial station owned by Cumulus Media. The format of the station is classic rock music. WLUP-FM broadcasts to the Chicago area at 97.9 FM. The station does not air PSAs.
FM RADIO STATION

WLUS-FM 74862
Owner: Lakes Media LLC
Editorial: 109 Hillsboro St, Oxford, North Carolina 27565 **Tel:** 1 919 693-7900.
Email: studio@us983.com
Web site: http://www.us983.com
Profile: WLUS-FM is a commercial station owned by the Lakes Media LLC. The format of the station is country music. WLUS-FM broadcasts to the Oxford, NC area at 98.3 FM.
FM RADIO STATION

WLUV-AM 37100
Owner: Loves Park Broadcasting Co.
Editorial: 2272 Elmwood Rd, Rockford, Illinois 61103
Tel: 1 815 877-9588.
Profile: WLUV-AM is a commercial station owned by Loves Park Broadcasting Co. The format of the station is country music. WLUV-AM broadcasts in the Rockford, IL area at 1520 AM.
AM RADIO STATION

WLVB-FM 42191
Owner: Radio Vermont Group Inc.
Editorial: Route 15, Morrisville, Vermont 5661
Tel: 1 802 888-4294.
Email: wlvb@radiovermont.com
Profile: WLVB-FM is a commercial station owned by Radio Vermont Group Inc. The format of the station is country. WLVB-FM broadcasts to the Morrisville, VT area at 93.9 FM.
FM RADIO STATION

WLVF-AM 38627
Owner: Landmark Baptist Church Inc.
Editorial: 810 E Hinson Ave, Haines City, Florida 33844-5246 **Tel:** 1 863 422-9583.
Email: info@gospel903.com
Web site: http://www.gospel903.com
Profile: WLVF-AM is a non-commercial station owned by Landmark Baptist Church Inc. The format of the station is southern gospel and religious programming. WLVF-AM broadcasts to the Haines City, FL area at 930 AM.
AM RADIO STATION

WLVF-FM 45984
Owner: Landmark Baptist Church Inc.
Editorial: 810 E Hinson Ave, Haines City, Florida 33844-5246 **Tel:** 1 863 422-9583.
Email: info@gospel903.com
Web site: http://www.gospel903.com
Profile: WLVF-FM is a non-commercial station owned by Landmark Baptist Church Inc. The format is of the station is southern gospel and religious programming. WLVF-FM broadcasts to the Haines City, FL at 90.3 FM.
FM RADIO STATION

WLVH-FM 42040
Owner: iHeartMedia Inc.
Editorial: 245 Alfred St, Savannah, Georgia 31408-3205 **Tel:** 1 912 964-7794.
Email: community@love1011.com
Web site: http://love1011.iheart.com
Profile: WLVH-FM is a commercial station owned by iHeartMedia Inc. The format of the station is urban adult contemporary. WLVH-FM broadcasts to the Savannah, GA area at 101.1 FM.
FM RADIO STATION

WLVJ-AM 35927
Owner: Actualidad 1040 AM, LLC
Editorial: 2555 Ponce De Leon Blvd Ste 225, Coral Gables, Florida 33134-6033 **Tel:** 1 786 388-3855.
Web site: http://actualidadradio.com
Profile: WLVJ-AM is a commercial station owned by Actualidad 1040 AM, LLC. The format of the station is Spanish language news. WLVJ-AM broadcasts to the Miami area at 1040 AM.
AM RADIO STATION

WLVK-FM 902869
Owner: W & B Broadcasting Inc.
Tel: 1 270 766-1035.
Email: wlvk@bigcat1055.com
Web site: http://www.bigcat1055.com
Profile: WLVK-FM is a commercial station owned by W & B Broadcasting Inc. The format of the station is contemporary country. The station airs locally at 105.5 FM in the Elizabethtown, KY area.
FM RADIO STATION

WLVL-AM 35503
Owner: Culver Communications
Editorial: 320 Michigan St, Lockport, New York 14094-1725 **Tel:** 1 716 433-5944.
Email: news@wlvl.com
Web site: http://www.wlvl.com
Profile: WLVL-AM is a commercial station owned by Culver Communications. The format of the station is news, talk, and sports. WLVL-AM broadcasts to the Lockport, NY area at 1340 AM.
AM RADIO STATION

WLVP-AM 74106
Owner: WBIN, Inc.
Editorial: 477 Congress St Ste 3, Portland, Maine 04101-3417 **Tel:** 1 207 797-0780.
Profile: WLVP-AM is a commercial station owned by WBIN, Inc. The format of the station is oldies. WLVP-AM broadcasts to the Portland, ME area at 870 AM.
AM RADIO STATION

WLVQ-FM 43809
Owner: Wilks Broadcast Group
Editorial: 2400 Corporate Exchange Dr Ste 200, Columbus, Ohio 43231-7669 **Tel:** 1 614 451-2191.
Web site: http://www.qfm96.com
Profile: WLVQ-FM is a commercial station owned by Saga Communications Group. The format of the station is rock music. WLVQ-FM broadcasts to the Columbus, OH area on 96.3 FM.
FM RADIO STATION

WLVS-FM 242387
Owner: Gold Coast Broadcasting
Editorial: 624 Sam Phillips St, Florence, Alabama 35630-5859 **Tel:** 1 256 764-8121.
Web site: http://www.wxfl.com
Profile: WLVS-FM is a commercial station owned by Gold Coast Broadcasting. The format of the station is country. WLVS-FM broadcasts to the Florence, AL area at a frequency of 106.5 FM.
FM RADIO STATION

WLVY-FM 46098
Owner: Tower Broadcasting LLC
Editorial: 1705 Lake St, Elmira, New York 14901-1220
Tel: 1 607 733-5626.
Email: towerbroadcasting@hotmail.com
Web site: http://www.94rockfm.com
Profile: WLVY-FM is a commercial station owned by Tower Broadcasting LLC. The format of the station is Top 40/CHR music. WLVY-FM broadcasts to the Elmira, NY area at 94.3 FM.
FM RADIO STATION

WLW-AM 36472
Owner: iHeartMedia Inc.
Editorial: 8044 Montgomery Rd, Cincinnati, Ohio 45236-2919 **Tel:** 1 513 686-8300.
Email: news@700wlw.com
Web site: http://www.700wlw.com
Profile: WLW-AM is a commercial station owned by iHeartMedia Inc. The format of the station is news, sports and talk. WLW-AM broadcasts to the Cincinnati area at 700 AM.
AM RADIO STATION

WLWE-AM 37786
Owner: Eagle's Nest Inc.
Editorial: 6855 Highway 431, Roanoke, Alabama 36274-4614 **Tel:** 1 334 863-6692.
Web site: http://www.eagle1023.com
Profile: WLWE-AM is a commercial station owned by Eagle's Nest Inc. The format of the station is sports. WLWE-AM broadcasts to the Roanoke, AL area at 1360 AM.
AM RADIO STATION

WLWF-FM 41895
Owner: LaSalle County Broadcasting Corp.
Editorial: 1 Broadcast Ln, Oglesby, Illinois 61348-9539 **Tel:** 1 815 223-3100.
Web site: http://20inarowcountry.com
Profile: WLWF-FM is a commercial station owned by Lasalle County Broadcasting Corp. The format of the station is contemporary country. WLWF-FM broadcasts to Ottawa, LaSalle and Peru, IL areas at 96.5 FM.
FM RADIO STATION

WLWI-AM 37868
Owner: Cumulus Media Inc.
Editorial: 1 Commerce St Ste 300, Montgomery, Alabama 36104-3542 **Tel:** 1 334 240-9274.
Web site: http://www.newsradio1440.com
Profile: WLWI-AM is a commercial station owned by Cumulus Media Inc. The format of the station is news and talk. WLWI-AM broadcasts to the Montgomery, AL area at 1440 AM.
AM RADIO STATION

WLWI-FM 45353
Owner: Cumulus Media Inc.
Editorial: 1 Commerce St Ste 300, Montgomery, Alabama 36104-3542 **Tel:** 1 334 240-9274.
Web site: http://www.wlwi.com
Profile: WLWI-FM is a commercial station owned by Cumulus Media Inc. The format of the station is country music. WLWI-FM broadcasts to the Montgomery, AL area at 92.3 FM.
FM RADIO STATION

WLWL-AM 35504
Owner: MarCam Broadcasting
Editorial: 275 River Rd, Rockingham, North Carolina 28379 **Tel:** 1 910 895-9595.
Profile: WLWL-AM is a commercial station owned by MarCam Broadcasting. The format of the station is R&B oldies. WLWL-AM broadcasts to the Rockingham, NC area at 770 AM.
AM RADIO STATION

WLXA-FM 45135
Owner: Lakewood Communications LLC
Editorial: 29 Public Sq, Lawrenceburg, Tennessee 38464-3351 **Tel:** 1 931 762-4411.
Email: wdxe@wdxeradio.com
Web site: http://wdxe.com
Profile: WLXA-FM is a commercial station owned by Lakewood Communications LLC. The format of the station is adult contemporary music. WLXA-FM broadcasts to the Lawrenceburg, TN area at 106.7 FM.
FM RADIO STATION

WLXC-FM 42696
Owner: Cumulus Media Inc.
Editorial: 1801 Charleston Hwy Ste J, Cayce, South Carolina 29033-2019 **Tel:** 1 803 796-9975.
Web site: http://www.kiss-1031.com
Profile: WLXC-FM is a commercial station owned by Cumulus Media Inc. The format of the station is urban adult contemporary. WLXC-FM broadcasts to the Columbia, SC area at 103.1 FM.
FM RADIO STATION

WLXE-AM 36733
Owner: Multicultural Radio Broadcasting Inc.
Editorial: 13321 New Hampshire Ave Ste 207, Silver Spring, Maryland 20904-3450 **Tel:** 1 301 424-9292.
Email: rbcstudios@aol.com
Profile: WLXE-AM is a commercial station owned by Multicultural Radio. The format of the station is Hispanic news and talk. WLXE-AM broadcasts to the Rockville, MD area at 1600 AM.
AM RADIO STATION

WLXG-AM 38448
Owner: L.M. Communications Inc.
Editorial: 401 W Main St, Lexington, Kentucky 40507-1640 **Tel:** 1 859 233-1515.
Web site: http://www.wlxg.com
Profile: WLXG-AM is a commercial station owned by L.M. Communications Inc. The format of the station is sports. WLXG-AM broadcasts in the Lexington, KY area at 1300 AM.
AM RADIO STATION

WLXN-AM 39270
Owner: Davidson County Broadcasting
Editorial: 200 Radio Dr, Lexington, North Carolina 27292-8010 **Tel:** 1 336 248-2716.
Email: info@wlxn.com
Web site: http://www.wlxn.com
Profile: WLXN-AM is a commercial station owned by Davidson County Broadcasting. The format of the station is oldies. WLXN-AM broadcasts to the Lexington, NC area at 1440 AM.
AM RADIO STATION

WLXO-FM 64046
Owner: Clarity Communications Inc
Editorial: 401 W Main St, Lexington, Kentucky 40507-1640 **Tel:** 1 859 233-1515.
Email: comments@hank961.com
Web site: http://www.hank961.com
Profile: WLXO-FM is a commercial station owned by Clarity Communications Inc and managed by LM Communications. The format of the station is classic country. WLXO-FM broadcasts to the Lexington, KY area at 96.1 FM.
FM RADIO STATION

WLXR-FM 45354
Owner: Mississippi Valley Broadcasters LLC
Editorial: 1407 2nd Ave N, Onalaska, Wisconsin 54650-9166 **Tel:** 1 608 782-8335.
Email: news@lacrosseradiogroup.net
Web site: http://www.wlxr.com
Profile: WLXR-FM is a commercial station owned by Mississippi Valley Broadcasters LLC. The format of the station is adult contemporary. WLXR-FM broadcasts to the La Crosse, WI area at 104.9 FM.
FM RADIO STATION

WLXT-FM 45358
Owner: MacDonald-Garber Broadcasting Inc.
Editorial: 2095 S US Highway 131, Petoskey, Michigan 49770 **Tel:** 1 231 347-8713.
Email: mail@lite96.com
Web site: http://www.lite96.com
Profile: WLXT-FM is a commercial station owned by MacDonald-Garber Broadcasting Inc. The format for the station is Lite Rock/Lite AC. WLXT-FM broadcasts to the Petoskey, MI area at 96.3 FM.
FM RADIO STATION

WLXV-FM 45149
Owner: MacDonald Garber Broadcasting Inc.
Editorial: 7825 Mackinaw Trl, Cadillac, Michigan 49601-9746 **Tel:** 1 231 775-1263.
Web site: http://www.hotcountrybull.com/
Profile: WLXV-FM is a commercial station owned by MacDonald Garber Broadcasting Inc. The format of the station is popular country. WLXV-FM broadcasts to the Cadillac, MI area at a frequency of 96.7 FM.
FM RADIO STATION

WLXX-FM 45599
Owner: Cumulus Media Inc.
Editorial: 300 W Vine St Ste 3, Lexington, Kentucky 40507-1806 **Tel:** 1 859 253-5900.
Web site: http://www.929wlxx.com
Profile: WLXX-FM is a commercial station owned by Cumulus Media Inc. The format for the station is contemporary country. WLXX-FM broadcasts to the Lexington, KY area at 92.9 FM.
FM RADIO STATION

WLXZ-FM 87623
Owner: Educational Media Foundation
Tel: 1 800 525-5683.
Web site: http://www.klove.com
Profile: KAXV-FM is a station owned by Educational Media Foundation. This station airs a Religious radio format on 90.3FM. KAXV-FM broadcasts to Pinehurst, North Carolina.
FM RADIO STATION

United States of America

WLYC-AM 36780
Owner: Pioneer Sports Production
Editorial: 460 Market St Ste 310, Williamsport, Pennsylvania 17701-6323 **Tel:** 1 570 327-1300.
Web site: http://www.espnwilliamsport.com
Profile: WLYC-AM is a commercial station owned by Covenant Broadcasting Co. The format of the station is sports. WLYC-AM broadcasts to the Williamsport, PA area at 1050 AM.
AM RADIO STATION

WLYE-FM 43218
Owner: FM Radio Licenses, LLC
Editorial: 227 W Main St, Glasgow, Kentucky 42141-1707 **Tel:** 1 270 651-5290.
Web site: http://www.willie941.com
Profile: WLYE-FM is a commercial station owned by FM Radio Licenses, LLC. The format of the station is classic and contemporary country music. WLYE-FM broadcasts to the Glasgow, KY area at a frequency of 94.1 FM.
FM RADIO STATION

WLYF-FM 46127
Owner: Entercom Communications Corp.
Editorial: 20450 NW 2nd Ave, Miami, Florida 33169-2505 **Tel:** 1 305 521-5100.
Email: litefm@litemiami.com
Web site: http://www.litemiami.com
Profile: WLYF-FM is a commercial station owned by Entercom Communications Corp. The format of the station is Lite Rock/Lite AC music. WLYF-FM broadcasts to the Miami area at 101.5 FM.
FM RADIO STATION

WLYG-AM 38440
Owner: Joy Christian Communications, Inc.
Tel: 1 256 927-9987.
Email: radio@joychristian.com
Web site: http://joychristianradio.com
Profile: WLYG-AM is a commercial station owned by Joy Christian Communications, Inc. The format of the station is Southern gospel. WLYG-AM broadcasts to the Jasper, AL area at 1560 AM.
AM RADIO STATION

WLYI-FM 45507
Owner: Forever Media Inc.
Editorial: 2 Robinson Plz Ste 410, Pittsburgh, Pennsylvania 15205-1048 **Tel:** 1 412 275-3393.
Web site: http://www.foreverpittsburgh.com/willie-103-5
Profile: WOGH-FM is a commercial station owned by Forever Media. The format of the station is 80s and 90s Country music. The station broadcasts to the Pittsburgh, PA, Steubenville-Weirton OH-WV areas at 103.5 FM.
FM RADIO STATION

WLYN-AM 35505
Owner: Multicultural Radio Broadcasting Inc.
Editorial: 500 W Cummings Park, Ste 2600, Woburn, Massachusetts 1801 **Tel:** 1 781 938-0869.
Web site: http://mrbi.net
Profile: WLYN-AM is a commercial station owned by Multicultural Radio Broadcasting Inc. The format of the station is ethnic brokered programming. WLYN-AM broadcasts to the Cambridge, MA area at 1360 AM.
AM RADIO STATION

WLYU-FM 46227
Owner: TCB Broadcasting
Editorial: 473 N Victory Dr, Lyons, Georgia 30436-1947 **Tel:** 1 912 526-8122.
Profile: WLYU-FM is a commercial station owned by TCB Broadcasting. The format for the station is contemporary country. WYLU-FM broadcasts to the Savannah, GA area at 100.9 FM.
FM RADIO STATION

WLYV-AM 36883
Owner: Adams Radio Group
Editorial: 9604 Coldwater Rd Ste 201, Fort Wayne, Indiana 46825-2096 **Tel:** 1 260 747-1511.
Profile: WLYV-AM is a commercial station owned by Adams Radio Group. The format of the station is oldies. WLYV-AM broadcasts to the Fort Wayne, IN area at 1450 AM.
AM RADIO STATION

WLZA-FM 44427
Owner: Metro Radio Inc.
Editorial: 1105A Stark Rd, Starkville, Mississippi 39759-3556 **Tel:** 1 662 324-9601.
Email: wlza@961wlza.com
Web site: http://www.961wlza.com
Profile: WLZA-FM is a commercial station owned by Metro Radio Inc. The format of the station is hot adult contemporary. WLZA-FM broadcasts to the Starkville and East-Central Mississippi area at a frequency of 96.1 FM.
FM RADIO STATION

WLZK-FM 44102
Owner: Benton-Weatherford Broadcasting Inc. of Tennessee
Editorial: 110 India Rd, Paris, Tennessee 38242-7565 **Tel:** 1 731 644-9455.
Email: news@wmufradio.com
Web site: http://www.wmufradio.com/WLZK.html
Profile: WLZK-FM is a commercial station owned by Benton-Weatherford Broadcasting Inc. of Tennessee. The format of the station is hot AC. WLZK-FM broadcasts to the Paris, TN area at 94.1 FM.
FM RADIO STATION

WLZL-FM 40297
Owner: CBS Radio
Editorial: 1015 Half St SE Ste 200, Washington, District Of Columbia 20003-3320 **Tel:** 1 202 479-9227.
Web site: http://elzolradio.radio.com
Profile: WLZL-FM is a non-commercial station owned by CBS Radio. The format of the station is Latin Urban and Pop music. WLZL-FM is licensed to the Annapolis, MD area and broadcasts to the DMV area (Baltimore, MD and Washington, DC) at 107.9 FM.
FM RADIO STATION

WLZN-FM 43324
Owner: Cumulus Media Inc.
Editorial: 544 Mulberry St Ste 500, Macon, Georgia 31201-8258 **Tel:** 1 478 746-6286.
Web site: http://www.blazin923.com
Profile: WLZN-FM is a commercial station owned by Cumulus Media Inc. The format of the station is urban contemporary. WLZN-FM broadcasts to the Macon, GA area on 92.3 FM.
FM RADIO STATION

WLZR-AM 38218
Owner: Cumulus Media Inc.
Editorial: 1800 W Hibiscus Blvd Ste 138, Melbourne, Florida 32901-2624 **Tel:** 1 321 984-1000.
Web site: http://www.sportsradio1560.com
Profile: WLZR-AM is a commercial station owned by Cumulus Media Inc. The format of the station is sports. WLZR-AM broadcasts to the Melbourne, FL area at 1560 AM.
AM RADIO STATION

WLZS-FM 44158
Owner: Seven Mountains Media, LLC
Editorial: 160 W Clearview Ave, State College, Pennsylvania 16803-1617 **Tel:** 1 814 231-0953.
Web site: http://www.wheels1061.com
Profile: WLZS-FM is a commercial station owned by Seven Mountains Media, LLC. The format of the station is oldies music. WLZS-FM broadcasts to the Harrisburg, PA area at 106.1 FM.
FM RADIO STATION

WLZW-FM 45962
Owner: Townsquare Media, LLC
Editorial: 9418 River Rd, Marcy, New York 13403 **Tel:** 1 315 768-9500.
Web site: http://www.lite987.com
Profile: WLZW-FM is a commercial station owned by Townsquare Media, LLC. The format of the station is adult contemporary. WLZW-FM broadcasts to the Utica, NY area at 98.7 FM.
FM RADIO STATION

WLZX-FM 45207
Owner: Saga Communications
Editorial: 45 Fisher Ave, East Longmeadow, Massachusetts 01028-1707 **Tel:** 1 413 525-4141.
Web site: http://www.lazer993.com
Profile: WLZX-FM is a commercial station owned by Saga Communications. The format of the station is rock. WLZX-FM broadcasts to Springfield, MA at 99.3 FM.
FM RADIO STATION

WLZZ-FM 42439
Owner: Swick Broadcasting
Editorial: 05691 State Route 15 Suite B, Bryan, Ohio 43506-8879 **Tel:** 1 419 633-1045.
Email: wlzz@wlzzradio.com
Web site: http://www.wlzzradio.com
Profile: WLZZ-FM is a commercial station owned by Swick Broadcasting. The format of the station is country, news and talk. WLZZ-FM broadcasts to the Montpelier, OH area at 104.5 FM.
FM RADIO STATION

WMAC-AM 38037
Owner: Cumulus Media Inc.
Editorial: 544 Mulberry St Ste 500, Macon, Georgia 31201-8258 **Tel:** 1 478 746-6286.
Web site: http://www.wmac.com
Profile: WMAC-AM is a commercial station owned by Cumulus Media Inc. The format of the station is news, talk and sports. WMAC-AM broadcasts in the Macon, GA area at 940 AM.
AM RADIO STATION

WMAD-FM 43155
Owner: iHeartMedia Inc.
Editorial: 2651 S Fish Hatchery Rd, Fitchburg, Wisconsin 53711-5410 **Tel:** 1 608 274-1070.
Web site: http://www.963starcountry.com
Profile: WMAD-FM is a commercial station owned by iHeartMedia Inc. The format for the station is contemporary country. WMAD-FM broadcasts to the Madison, WI area at 96.3 FM.
FM RADIO STATION

WMAF-AM 36885
Owner: Walker(Geneva)
Editorial: 574 SW Captain Brown Rd, Madison, Florida 32340 **Tel:** 1 850 973-3233.
Email: countrywmaf@embarqmail.com
Web site: http://www.1230wmaf.com/
Profile: WMAF-AM is a commercial station owned by Geneva Walker. The format of the station is classic country. WMAF-AM broadcasts to the Madison, FL area at 1230 AM.
AM RADIO STATION

WMAG-FM 86599
Owner: iHeartMedia Inc.
Editorial: 2B Pai Park Fl 2, Greensboro, North Carolina 27409-9428 **Tel:** 1 336 822-2000.
Web site: http://995wmag.iheart.com
Profile: WMAG-FM is a commercial station owned by iHeartMedia Inc. The format of the station is adult contemporary. WMAG-FM broadcasts to the Greensboro, NC area at 99.5 FM.
FM RADIO STATION

WMAJ-FM 41955
Owner: FM Radio Licenses, LLC
Editorial: 2551 Park Center Blvd, State College, Pennsylvania 16801-3007 **Tel:** 1 814 237-9800.
Email: majic99fm@gmail.com
Web site: http://www.majic99.com
Profile: WMAJ-FM is a commercial station owned by FM Radio Licenses, LLC. The format of the station is adult hits. WMAJ-FM broadcasts to the State College, PA area at 99.5 FM.
FM RADIO STATION

WMAK-AM 37873
Owner: Last Of A Dying Breed Broadcasting
Editorial: 100 E Main St, Linden, Tennessee 37096-3006 **Tel:** 1 724 516-8885.
Web site: http://www.1013hankfm.com
Profile: WMAK-AM is commercial station owned by Last Of A Dying Breed Broadcasting. The format for the station is bluegrass WNKX-AM broadcasts to the Perry County, TN area at 1570 AM.
AM RADIO STATION

WMAL-AM 38033
Owner: Cumulus Media
Editorial: 4400 Jenifer St NW Fl 4, Washington, District Of Columbia 20015-2134 **Tel:** 1 202 686-3100.
Email: news@wmal.com
Web site: http://www.wmal.com
Profile: WMAL-AM is a commercial station owned by Cumulus Media. The format of the station is news and talk. WMAL-AM broadcasts in the Washington area at 630 AM.
AM RADIO STATION

WMAL-FM 43326
Owner: Cumulus Media Inc.
Editorial: 4400 Jenifer St NW Fl 4, Washington, District Of Columbia 20015-2134 **Tel:** 1 202 686-3100.
Web site: http://www.wmal.com
Profile: WMAL-FM is a commercial station owned by Cumulus Media Inc. The format of the station is news/talk. WMAL -FM broadcasts to Washington, D.C. area at 105.9 FM.
FM RADIO STATION

WMAM-AM 38034
Owner: Radio Plus Bay Cities, LLC
Editorial: 413 10th Ave, Menominee, Michigan 49858-3009 **Tel:** 1 906 863-5551.
Email: reception@baycitiesradio.net
Web site: http://www.baycitiesradio.com
Profile: WMAM-AM is a commercial station owned by Radio Plus Bay Cities, LLC. The format of the station is sports. WMAM-AM broadcasts to the Menominee, MI area at 570 AM.
AM RADIO STATION

WMAN-AM 38396
Owner: iHeartMedia Inc.
Editorial: 1400 Radio Ln, Mansfield, Ohio 44906-2525 **Tel:** 1 419 529-2211.
Web site: http://www.wmanfm.com
Profile: WMAN-AM is a commercial station owned by iHeartMedia Inc. The format of the station is news and talk. WMAN-AM broadcasts to the Mansfield, OH area at 1400 AM.
AM RADIO STATION

WMAN-FM 41880
Owner: iHeartMedia Inc.
Editorial: 1400 Radio Ln, Mansfield, Ohio 44906-2525 **Tel:** 1 419 529-2211.
Web site: http://www.wmanfm.com
Profile: WMAN-FM is a commercial station owned by iHeartMedia Inc. The format of the station is news/talk. WMAN-FM broadcasts to the Ashland, OH area at 98.3 FM
FM RADIO STATION

WMAS-FM 45356
Owner: Cumulus Media Inc.
Editorial: 1000 Hall Of Fame Ave, Springfield, Massachusetts 01105-2538 **Tel:** 1 413 737-1414.
Web site: http://www.947wmas.com
Profile: WMAS-FM is a commercial station owned by Cumulus Media Inc. The format of the station is adult contemporary music. WMAS-FM broadcasts to the Springfield, MA area at 94.7 FM.
FM RADIO STATION

WMAX-AM 36064
Owner: Ave Maria Communications
Editorial: 3535 Bay Rd, Saginaw, Michigan 48603-2464 **Tel:** 1 734 930-5200.
Email: amrcomments@avemariaradio.net
Web site: http://www.avemariaradio.net
Profile: WMAX-AM is a commercial station owned by Ave Maria Communications. The format of the station is religious talk. WMAX-AM broadcasts to the Saginaw, MI area at 1440 AM.
AM RADIO STATION

WMAX-FM 42258
Owner: iHeartMedia Inc.
Editorial: 77 Monroe Center St NW, Grand Rapids, Michigan 49503-2903 **Tel:** 1 616 459-1919.
Web site: http://espn961.iheart.com
Profile: WMAX-FM is a commercial station owned by iHeartMedia Inc. The format of the station is sports. WMAX-FM broadcasts to the Grand Rapids, MI area at 96.1 FM.
FM RADIO STATION

WMAY-AM 38030
Owner: Midwest Family Broadcasting
Editorial: 1510 N 3rd Street, Riverton, Illinois 62561 **Tel:** 1 217 629-7077.
Email: wmay@wmay.com
Web site: http://www.wmay.com
Profile: WMAY-AM is a commercial station owned by Midwest Family Broadcasting. The format of the station is news and talk. WMAY-AM broadcasts to the Riverton, IL area at 970 AM.
AM RADIO STATION

WMBA-AM 35508
Owner: Iorio Broadcasting Inc.
Editorial: 1316 7th Ave, Beaver Falls, Pennsylvania 15010-4217 **Tel:** 1 724 846-4100.
Email: 1230@beavercountyradio.com
Web site: http://beavercountyradio.com
Profile: WMBA-AM is a commercial station owned by Iorio Broadcasting Inc. The format of the station is news, sports and talk. WMBA-AM broadcasts to the Beaver Falls, PA area at 1460 AM.
AM RADIO STATION

WMBD-AM 38363
Owner: Alpha Media
Editorial: 331 Fulton St Ste 1200, Peoria, Illinois 61602-1422 **Tel:** 1 309 637-3700.
Email: news@1470wmbd.com
Web site: http://www.1470wmbd.com
Profile: WMBD-AM is a commercial station owned by Alpha Media. The format of the station is news and talk. WMBD-AM broadcasts to the Peoria, IL, area at 1470 AM.
AM RADIO STATION

WMBG-AM 36926
Owner: Williamsburg's Radio Stations Inc.
Editorial: 1005 Richmond Rd, Williamsburg, Virginia 23185 **Tel:** 1 757 229-7400.
Email: info@wmbgradio.com
Web site: http://www.wmbgradio.com
Profile: WMBG-AM is a commercial station owned by Williamsburg's Radio Stations Inc. The format of the station is adult standards. WMBG-AM broadcasts to the Norfolk, VA at 740 AM.
AM RADIO STATION

WMBI-AM 38038
Owner: Moody Bible Institute
Editorial: 820 N La Salle Dr Fl 8, Chicago, Illinois 60610-3214
Email: radiomoody@moody.edu
Web site: http://www.radiomoody.org
Profile: WMBI-AM is a non-commercial station owned by Moody Bible Institute. The format of the station is Spanish-language Christian talk and music. WMBI-AM broadcasts to the Chicago area at 1110 AM.
AM RADIO STATION

WMBI-FM 45357
Owner: Moody Bible Institute
Editorial: 820 N La Salle Blvd, 8th Fl, Chicago, Illinois 60610 **Tel:** 1 312 329-4300.
Email: wmbi@moody.edu
Web site: http://www.moodyradiochicago.fm
Profile: WMBI-FM is a non-commercial station owned by the Moody Bible Institute. The format of the station is religious programming. WMBI-FM broadcasts to the Chicago area at 90.1 FM.
FM RADIO STATION

WMBJ-FM 43806
Owner: Radio Training Network, Inc.
Editorial: 2420 Wade Hampton Blvd, Greenville, South Carolina 29615 **Tel:** 1 864 292-6040.
Email: comments@hisradio.com
Web site: http://www.hisradio.com
Profile: WMBJ-FM is a non-commercial station owned by Radio Training Network, Inc. The format of the station is contemporary Christian. WMBJ-FM broadcasts to the Greenville, SC area at 88.3 FM.
FM RADIO STATION

WMBM-AM 35849
Owner: New Birth Broadcasting
Editorial: 13242 NW 7th Ave, North Miami, Florida 33168 **Tel:** 1 305 769-1100.
Email: wmbm@wmbm.com
Web site: http://www.wmbm.com
Profile: WMBM-AM is a commercial station owned by New Birth Broadcasting. The format of the station is gospel. WMBM-AM broadcasts to the Miami area at 1490 AM.
AM RADIO STATION

WMBN-AM 38280
Owner: MacDonald Garber Broadcasting Inc.
Editorial: 2095 S US Highway 131, Petoskey, Michigan 49770-9216 **Tel:** 1 231 347-8713.
Email: info@1340amtheticket.com
Profile: WMBN-AM is a commercial station owned by MacDonald Garber Broadcasting Inc. The format of the station is sports. WMBN-AM broadcasts to the Petoskey, MI area at 1340 AM.
AM RADIO STATION

WMBR-FM
40501
Owner: Technology Broadcasting Corp.
Editorial: 3 Ames St, Cambridge, Massachusetts 02142-1305 **Tel:** 1 617 253-4000.
Email: psa@wmbr.org
Web site: http://wmbr.mit.edu
Profile: WMBR-FM is a non-commercial station owned by Technology Broadcasting Corp. The format of the station is variety. WMBR-FM broadcasts to the Cambridge, MA area at 88.1 FM.
FM RADIO STATION

WMBS-AM
35510
Owner: Fayette Broadcasting Corporation
Editorial: 44 S Mount Vernon Ave, Uniontown, Pennsylvania 15401 **Tel:** 1 724 438-3900.
Web site: http://www.wmbs590.com
Profile: WMBS-AM is a commercial station owned by Fayette Broadcasting Corporation. The format of the station is adult standards. WMBS-AM broadcasts to the Uniontown, PA area at 590 AM.
AM RADIO STATION

WMBU-FM
43594
Owner: Moody Bible Institute
Editorial: 5189 Lake Norris Rd, Lake, Mississippi 39092-8505 **Tel:** 1 601 775-3100.
Email: wmft@moody.edu
Web site: http://www.moodyradiosouth.fm
Profile: WMBU-FM is a non-commercial radio station owned by the Moody Bible Institute. The format of the station is religious. WMBU-FM broadcasts to the Lake, MS area at 89.1 FM.
FM RADIO STATION

WMBV-FM
41538
Owner: Moody Bible Institute
Editorial: 5710 Watermelon Rd Ste 316, Northport, Alabama 35473-7694 **Tel:** 1 205 758-7900.
Email: wmft@moody.edu
Web site: http://www.moodyradiosouth.fm
Profile: WMBV-FM is a non-commercial station owned by Moody Bible Institute. The format of the station is gospel music and religious talk. WMBV-FM broadcasts to the Dixons Mills, AL area at 91.9 FM.
FM RADIO STATION

WMBW-FM
40502
Owner: Moody Bible Institute
Editorial: 1920 E 24th Street Pl, Chattanooga, Tennessee 37404-5810 **Tel:** 1 423 629-8900.
Email: wmbw@moody.edu
Web site: http://www.moodyradiosoutheast.fm/rdo_home.aspx?id=53029
Profile: WMBW-FM is a non-commercial station owned by Moody Bible Institute. The format is religious music and talk. WMBW-FM broadcasts to the Chattanooga, TN area at 88.9 FM.
FM RADIO STATION

WMBX-FM
43418
Owner: Alpha Media
Editorial: 701 Northpoint Pkwy Ste 500, West Palm Beach, Florida 33407-1960 **Tel:** 1 561 686-9505.
Web site: http://www.x1023.com
Profile: WMBX-FM is a commercial station owned by Alpha Media. The format of the station is urban contemporary. WMBX-FM broadcasts to the West Palm Beach, FL area at 102.3 FM.
FM RADIO STATION

WMBZ-FM
45054
Owner: Magnum Broadcasting
Editorial: 2410 S Main St Ste A, West Bend, Wisconsin 53095-5766 **Tel:** 1 262 334-2344.
Web site: http://www.wbwifm.com
Profile: WMBZ-FM is a commercial station owned by Magnum Broadcasting. The format of the station is country music. WMBZ-FM broadcasts to the Milwaukee area at 92.5 FM.
FM RADIO STATION

WMCA-AM
35512
Owner: Salem Media Group, Inc.
Editorial: 111 Broadway Fl 3, New York, New York 10006-1992 **Tel:** 1 212 372-0097.
Email: contact@nycradio.com
Web site: http://am570themission.com
Profile: WMCA-AM is commercial station owned by Salem Media Group, Inc. The format of the station is religious talk. WMCA-AM broadcasts to the New York City area at 570 AM.
AM RADIO STATION

WMC-AM
38680
Owner: Entercom Communications Corp.
Editorial: 1835 Moriah Woods Blvd, Memphis, Tennessee 38117-7122 **Tel:** 1 901 767-0104.
Profile: WMC-AM is a commercial station owned by Entercom Communications Corp. The format of the station is sports. WMC-AM broadcasts to the Memphis, TN area at 790 AM.
AM RADIO STATION

WMCD-FM
46801
Owner: Radio Statesboro, Inc.
Editorial: 561 E Olliff St, Statesboro, Georgia 30458-4663 **Tel:** 1 912 764-5446.
Web site: http://statesboro365.com
Profile: WMCD-FM is a commercial station owned by Radio Statesboro, Inc. The format of the station is talk. WMCD-FM broadcasts to the Savannah, GA area at 107.3 FM.
FM RADIO STATION

WMCE-AM
36210
Owner: Mercyhurst College
Editorial: 16 W Division St, North East, Pennsylvania 16428-1008 **Tel:** 1 814 725-9963.
Web site: http://www.wmce.fm/
Profile: WMCE-AM is a commercial station owned by Mercyhurst College. The format of the station is oldies music. WMCE-AM broadcasts to the Northeast, PA area at 1530 AM.
AM RADIO STATION

WMC-FM
46033
Owner: Entercom Communications Corp.
Editorial: 1835 Moriah Woods Blvd Ste 1, Memphis, Tennessee 38117-7122 **Tel:** 1 901 767-0104.
Web site: http://www.fm100memphis.com
Profile: WMC-FM is a commercial station owned by Entercom Communications Corp. The format of the station is hot adult contemporary. WMC-FM broadcasts to the Memphis, TN area at 99.7 FM.
FM RADIO STATION

WMCG-FM
40503
Owner: Dowdy Broadcasting, Inc.
Editorial: 807 Bellevue Ave, Dublin, Georgia 31021-4847 **Tel:** 1 478 272-4422.
Profile: WMCG-FM is a commercial station owned by Dowdy Broadcasting, Inc. The format of the station is classic country. WMCG-FM broadcasts to the Dublin, GA area at 104.9 FM.
FM RADIO STATION

WMCH-AM
35513
Owner: Media Link, Inc.
Editorial: 439 Richmond St, Church Hill, Tennessee 37642 **Tel:** 1 423 357-5601.
Email: wmchradio@yahoo.com
Web site: http://www.wmchradio.com
Profile: WMCH-AM is a commercial station owned by Media Link, Inc. The format of the station is religious talk. WMCH-AM broadcasts in the Church Hill, TN area at 1260 AM.
AM RADIO STATION

WMCI-FM
41544
Owner: Cromwell Group Inc.(The)
Editorial: 209 Lake Land Blvd, Mattoon, Illinois 61938-3904 **Tel:** 1 217 235-5624.
Web site: http://www.radiomattoon.com
Profile: WMCI-FM is a commercial station owned by The Cromwell Group Inc. The format of the station features classic and contemporary country music. WMCI-FM broadcasts in the Mattoon, IL area at 101.3 FM.
FM RADIO STATION

WMCJ-AM
541967
Owner: Jimmy Dale Media, LLC
Editorial: 1707 Warnke Rd NW, Cullman, Alabama 35055-2231 **Tel:** 1 256 734-3271.
Profile: WMCJ-AM is a commercial station owned by Jimmy Dale Media, LLC. The format of the station is sports. WMCJ-AM broadcasts to the Cullman, AL area at 1340 AM.
AM RADIO STATION

WMCL-AM
36953
Owner: Dana Communications Corp.
Editorial: 303 N Main St, Benton, Illinois 62812-1314 **Tel:** 1 618 435-4346.
Email: wmcl1060@gmail.com
Web site: http://www.wmclradio.com
Profile: WMCL-AM is a commercial station owned by Dana Communications Corp. The format of the station is classic country. WMCL-AM broadcasts to the McLeansboro, IL area at 1060 AM.
AM RADIO STATION

WMCM-FM
45360
Owner: Blueberry Broadcasting
Tel: 1 207 623-9000.
Web site: http://www.971thebear.com
Profile: WMCM-FM is a commercial station owned by Blueberry Broadcasting. The format of the station is contemporary country music. WMCM-FM broadcasts to the Rockland, ME area at 103.3 FM.
FM RADIO STATION

WMCP-AM
35515
Owner: Maury County Boosters Corp.
Editorial: 886 Mount Olivet Rd, Columbia, Tennessee 38401-8031 **Tel:** 1 931 388-3241.
Profile: WMCP-AM is a commercial station owned by Maury County Boosters Corp. The format of the station is country music. WMCP-AM broadcasts to the Columbia, TN area at 1280 AM.
AM RADIO STATION

WMCT-AM
35516
Owner: Johnson County Broadcasting Co.
Editorial: 1211 N Church St, Mountain City, Tennessee 37683-1115 **Tel:** 1 423 727-6701.
Email: wmct@wmctradio.net
Web site: http://www.wmctradio.net
Profile: WMCT-AM is a commercial station owned by Johnson County Broadcasting Co. The format of the station is country and gospel. WMCT-AM broadcasts to the Mountain City, TN area at 1390 AM.
AM RADIO STATION

WMDB-AM
364260
Owner: TBLC Media, LLC
Editorial: 209 10th Ave S Ste 342, Nashville, Tennessee 37203-0758 **Tel:** 1 615 242-1411.
Email: spanishmc@activa1240.com
Web site: http://laranchera880.com

Profile: WMDB-AM is a commercial station owned by TBLC Media, LLC. The format of the station is Spanish AC. WMDB-AM broadcasts to the Nashville, TN area at 880 AM.
AM RADIO STATION

WMDC-FM
44089
Owner: Radio Plus Inc.
Editorial: 132 N Main St Ste 1, Mayville, Wisconsin 53050-1638 **Tel:** 1 920 387-0000.
Email: bigsky@great98.net
Web site: http://www.great98.net
Profile: WMDC-FM is a commercial station owned by Radio Plus Inc. The format of the station is classic rock. WMDC-FM broadcasts to the Mayville, WI area at 98.7 FM.
FM RADIO STATION

WMDH-FM
45363
Owner: Cumulus Media Inc.
Editorial: 1134 W State Road 38, New Castle, Indiana 47362-9781 **Tel:** 1 765 529-2600.
Web site: http://www.wmdh.com
Profile: WMDH-FM is a commercial station owned by Cumulus Media Inc. The format of the station is contemporary country music. WMDH-FM broadcasts to the Indianapolis area at 102.5 FM.
FM RADIO STATION

WMDJ-FM
42116
Owner: Floyd County Broadcasting Inc.
Editorial: 9030 Ky Route 1428, Allen, Kentucky 41601-9478 **Tel:** 1 606 874-8005.
Email: fm100wmdj@mikrotec.com
Web site: http://www.wmdjfm.com
Profile: WMDJ-FM is a commercial station owned by Floyd County Broadcasting Inc. The format of the station is classic country. WMDJ-FM broadcasts to the Martin, KY area at 100.1 FM.
FM RADIO STATION

WMDM-FM
46867
Owner: Somar Communications Inc.
Editorial: 28095 Three Notch Rd Ste 2B, Mechanicsville, Maryland 20659-3373 **Tel:** 1 301 870-5550.
Web site: http://www.977therocket.com
Profile: WMDM-FM is a commercial station owned by Somar Communications Inc. The format of the station is classic rock. WMDM-FM broadcasts to the Mechanicsville, MD area at 97.7 FM.
FM RADIO STATION

WMDR-AM
382688
Owner: Light of Life Ministries Inc.
Editorial: 160 Riverside Dr, Augusta, Maine 04330-4162 **Tel:** 1 207 622-1340.
Email: wmdr@adelphia.net
Web site: http://www.wmdr.org
Profile: WMDR-AM is a non-commercial station owned by Light of Life Ministries Inc. The format of the station is Christian rock. WMDR-AM broadcasts to the Augusta, ME area at 1340 AM.
AM RADIO STATION

WMDR-FM
363590
Owner: Light of Life Ministries Inc.
Editorial: 160 Riverside Dr, Augusta, Maine 4330 **Tel:** 1 207 622-1340.
Email: info@worshipradionetwork.org
Web site: http://www.godscountry889.com
Profile: WMDR-FM is a non-commercial station owned by Light of Life Ministries Inc. The format of the station is Christian Country and Southern Gospel. WMDR-FM broadcasts to the Augusta, ME area on 88.9 FM.
FM RADIO STATION

WMEA-FM
40507
Owner: Maine Public Broadcasting Network
Editorial: 63 Texas Ave, Bangor, Maine 04401-4324 **Tel:** 1 207 941-1010.
Email: comments@mpbn.net
Web site: http://www.mpbn.net
Profile: WMEA-FM is a non-commercial station owned by Maine Public Broadcasting Network. The format for the station is news and talk. WMEA-FM broadcasts to the Bangor, ME area at 90.1 FM.
FM RADIO STATION

WMED-FM
44106
Owner: Maine Public Broadcasting Network
Editorial: 63 Texas Ave, Bangor, Maine 04401-4324 **Tel:** 1 207 941-1010.
Email: comments@mpbn.net
Web site: http://www.mpbn.net
Profile: WMED-FM is a non-commercial station owned by Maine Public Broadcasting Network. The format of the station is news and talk. WMED-FM broadcasts to the Bangor, ME area at 89.7 FM.
FM RADIO STATION

WMEE-FM
42264
Owner: Federated Media
Editorial: 2915 Maples Rd, Fort Wayne, Indiana 46816 **Tel:** 1 260 447-5511.
Web site: http://www.wmee.com
Profile: WMEE-FM is a commercial station owned by Federated Media. The format of the station is hot adult contemporary. WMEE-FM broadcasts to the Fort Wayne, IN area at 97.3 FM.
FM RADIO STATION

WMEF-FM
44108
Owner: Maine Public Broadcasting Network
Editorial: 63 Texas Ave, Bangor, Maine 04401-4324 **Tel:** 1 207 941-1010.
Email: contactus@mpbn.net

Web site: http://www.mpbn.net
Profile: WMEF-FM is a non-commercial station owned by Maine Public Broadcasting Network. The format of the station is classical, news and talk. WMEF-FM broadcasts to the Bangor, ME area at 106.5 FM.
FM RADIO STATION

WMEH-FM
40509
Owner: Maine Public Broadcasting Network
Editorial: 63 Texas Ave, Bangor, Maine 04401-4324 **Tel:** 1 207 941-1010.
Email: comments@mpbn.net
Web site: http://www.mpbn.net
Profile: WMEH-FM is a non-commercial station owned by Maine Public Broadcasting Network. The format of the station is classical, news and talk. WMEH-FM broadcasts to the Bangor, ME area at 90.9 FM.
FM RADIO STATION

WMEJ-AM
35762
Owner: Hancock Broadcasting
Editorial: 1190 Hollywood Blvd, Bay Saint Louis, Mississippi 39520-1662 **Tel:** 1 228 467-1190.
Profile: WMEJ-AM is a commercial station owned by Hancock Broadcasting. The format of the station is Gospel. WMEJ-AM broadcasts to the Bay Saint Louis, MS area at 1190 AM.
AM RADIO STATION

WMEM-FM
40510
Owner: Maine Public Broadcasting Network
Editorial: 63 Texas Ave, Bangor, Maine 04401-4324 **Tel:** 1 207 941-1010.
Email: comments@mpbn.net
Web site: http://www.mpbn.net
Profile: WMEM-FM is a non-commercial station owned by Maine Public Broadcasting Network. The format of the station is talk and news. WMEME-FM broadcasts to the Bangor, ME area at 106.1 FM.
FM RADIO STATION

WMEN-AM
35775
Owner: JCE Licenses, LLC
Editorial: 2100 Park Central Blvd N Ste 100, Pompano Beach, Florida 33064-2219 **Tel:** 1 954 315-1515.
Web site: http://www.640sports.com
Profile: WMEN-AM is a commercial radio station owned by JCE Licenses, LLC. The format of the station is sports. WMEN-AM broadcasts to the West Palm Beach, FL at 640 AM.
AM RADIO STATION

WMEP-FM
77988
Owner: Maine Public Broadcasting Network
Editorial: 65 Texas Ave, Bangor, Maine 04401-4324 **Tel:** 1 207 941-1010.
Email: contactus@mpbn.net
Web site: http://www.mpbn.net
Profile: WMEP-FM is a commercial station owned by Maine Public Broadcasting Network. The format of the station is classical and news. WMEP-FM broadcasts to the Camden, ME area at 90.5 FM.
FM RADIO STATION

WMEQ-AM
38451
Owner: iHeartMedia Inc.
Editorial: 619 Cameron St, Eau Claire, Wisconsin 54703-4708 **Tel:** 1 715 830-4000.
Web site: http://www.wmeq.com
Profile: WMEQ-AM is a commercial station owned by iHeartMedia Inc. The format of the station is news and talk. WMEQ-AM broadcasts to the Eau Claire, WI area at 880 AM.
AM RADIO STATION

WMEQ-FM
45892
Owner: iHeartMedia Inc.
Editorial: 619 Cameron St, Eau Claire, Wisconsin 54703-4708 **Tel:** 1 715 830-4000.
Web site: http://www.rock921.com
Profile: WMEQ-FM is a commercial station owned by iHeartMedia Inc. The format of the station is classic rock. WMEQ-FM broadcasts to the Eau Claire, WI area at 92.1 FM.
FM RADIO STATION

WMER-AM
35521
Owner: Carter, Jr. (N. Brad)
Editorial: 315 A St, Meridian, Mississippi 39301-4512 **Tel:** 1 601 207-1391.
Email: info@wmerworldwide.com
Web site: http://www.wmerworldwide.com
Profile: WMER-AM is a non-commercial station owned by Carter, Jr. (N. Brad). The format of the station is gospel. WMER-AM broadcasts to the Meridian, MS area at a frequency of 1390 AM.
AM RADIO STATION

WMET-AM
35522
Owner: Guadalupe Radio Network
Editorial: 750 1st St NE Ste 1100, Washington, District Of Columbia 20002-8013 **Tel:** 1 877 636-1160.
Web site: http://grnonline.com/locations/washington-metro
Profile: WMET-AM is a commercial station owned by Guadalupe Radio Network. The format of the station is religious. WMET-AM broadcasts to the Washington, D.C. area at 1160 AM.
AM RADIO STATION

WMEV-AM 38042
Owner: Bristol Broadcasting Company, Inc.
Editorial: 1041 Radio Hill Rd, Marion, Virginia 24354-6597 **Tel:** 1 276 783-3151.
Email: fm94@fm94.com
Web site: http://www.fm94.com
Profile: WMEV-AM is a commercial station owned by Holston Valley Broadcasting Corp. The format of the station is Southern gospel music. WMEV-AM broadcasts to the Marion, VA area at 1010 AM.
AM RADIO STATION

WMEV-FM 45364
Owner: Bristol Broadcasting Company, Inc.
Editorial: 1041 Radio Hill Rd, Marion, Virginia 24354-6597 **Tel:** 1 276 783-3151.
Email: fm94@fm94.com
Web site: http://www.fm94.com
Profile: WMEV-FM is a commercial station owned by Holston Valley Broadcasting Corp. The format of the station is country music. WMEV-FM broadcasts to the Tri-Cities, TN area at 93.9 FM.
FM RADIO STATION

WMEW-FM 44107
Owner: Maine Public Broadcasting Network
Editorial: 65 Texas Ave, Bangor, Maine 04401-4324 **Tel:** 1 207 941-1010.
Email: contactus@mpbn.net
Web site: http://www.mpbn.net
Profile: WMEW-FM is a non-commercial station owned by Maine Public Broadcasting Network. The format of the station is classical, news and talk. WMEW-FM broadcasts to the Waterville, ME area at 91.3 FM.
FM RADIO STATION

WMEZ-FM 43235
Owner: Cumulus Media Inc.
Editorial: 6085 Quintette Rd, Pace, Florida 32571-6759 **Tel:** 1 850 994-5357.
Web site: http://www.softrock941.com
Profile: WMEZ-FM is a commercial station owned by Cumulus Media Inc. The format of the station is Lite Rock/Lite AC. WMEZ-FM broadcasts to the Pensacola, FL area at 94.1 FM.
FM RADIO STATION

WMFA-AM 36191
Owner: W & V Broadcasting Enterprises Inc.
Editorial: 1085 E Central Ave, Raeford, North Carolina 28376 **Tel:** 1 910 875-6225.
Email: wmfa1400@yahoo.com
Profile: WMFA-AM is a commercial station owned by W & V Broadcasting Enterprises Inc. The format of the station is gospel music. WMFA-AM broadcasts to the Raeford, NC area at 1400 AM.
AM RADIO STATION

WMFC-AM 38043
Owner: Monroe Broadcasting Co., Inc.
Editorial: 961 Pineville Rd, Monroeville, Alabama 36460 **Tel:** 1 251 575-3281.
Email: wmfc@frontiernet.net
Profile: WMFC-AM is a commercial station owned by Monroe Broadcasting Co., Inc. The format of the station is oldies. WMFC-AM broadcasts to the Monroeville, AL area at 1360 AM.
AM RADIO STATION

WMFC-FM 45365
Owner: Monroe Broadcasting Co., Inc.
Editorial: 961 Pineville Rd, Monroeville, Alabama 36460-1427 **Tel:** 1 251 575-3281.
Email: wmfc@frontiernet.net
Profile: WMFC-FM is a commercial station owned by Monroe Broadcasting Co., Inc. The format of the station is oldies music. WMFC-FM broadcasts to the Monroeville, AL area at 99.3 FM.
FM RADIO STATION

WMFD-AM 39294
Owner: Capitol Broadcasting Company
Editorial: 25 N Kerr Ave, Ste C, Wilmington, North Carolina 28405 **Tel:** 1 910 791-3088.
Email: am630@live.com
Web site: http://www.am630.net
Profile: WMFD-AM is a commercial station owned by Capitol Broadcasting Company. The format of the station is sports talk. WMFD-AM broadcasts in the Wilmington, NC area at 630 AM.
AM RADIO STATION

WMFE-FM 41055
Owner: Community Communications
Editorial: 11510 E Colonial Dr, Orlando, Florida 32817 **Tel:** 1 407 273-2300.
Email: wmfenews@wmfe.org
Web site: http://www.wmfe.org
Profile: WMFE-FM is a non-commercial station owned by Community Communications. The format of the station is news and talk. WMFE-FM broadcasts to the Orlando, FL area at 90.7 FM. The station does not accept PSAs.
FM RADIO STATION

WMFG-AM 38044
Owner: Midwest Communications Inc.
Editorial: 807 W 37th St, Hibbing, Minnesota 55746-2839 **Tel:** 1 218 263-7531.
Web site: http://mwcradio.com/station/68/
Profile: WMFG-AM is a commercial station owned by Midwest Communications Inc. The format of the station is adult standards. WMFG-AM broadcasts to the Hibbing, MN area at 1240 AM.
AM RADIO STATION

WMFG-FM 45366
Owner: Midwest Communications Inc.
Editorial: 807 W 37th St, Hibbing, Minnesota 55746-2839 **Tel:** 1 218 263-7531.
Web site: http://mwcradio.com/station/69/
Profile: WMFG-FM is a commercial station owned by Midwest Communications Inc. The format of the station is classic hits. WMFG-FM broadcasts to the Hibbing, MN area at 106.3 FM.
FM RADIO STATION

WMFJ-AM 38744
Owner: Cornerstone Broadcasting Corp.
Editorial: 4295 S Ridgewood Ave, Port Orange, Florida 32127-4512 **Tel:** 1 386 756-9094.
Email: wjlu@wjlu.org
Web site: http://www.wjlu.org
Profile: WMFJ-AM is a non-commercial station owned by Cornerstone Broadcasting Corp. The format of the station is religion and contemporary Christian. WMFJ-AM broadcasts to the Port Orange, FL area at 1450 AM.
AM RADIO STATION

WMFM-FM 133778
Owner: South Broadcasting System, Inc.
Editorial: 7007 NW 77th Ave, Miami, Florida 33166-2836 **Tel:** 1 305 447-9595.
Profile: WMFM-FM is a commercial station owned by South Broadcasting System, Inc. The station airs a Spanish tropical format in the Coral Gables, FL are at 107.9 FM. The station is a simulcast of WXDJ-FM.
FM RADIO STATION

WMFN-AM 36179
Owner: Birach Broadcasting Corp.
Editorial: 2422 Burton St SE, Grand Rapids, Michigan 49546-4806 **Tel:** 1 616 451-0551.
Web site: http://www.radioacktiva.com/
Profile: WMFN-AM is a commercial station owned by Birach Broadcasting Corp. The format of the station is Spanish talk. WMFN-AM broadcasts to the Grand Rapids, MI area at 640 AM.
AM RADIO STATION

WMFQ-FM 42741
Owner: JVC Broadcasting Inc.
Editorial: 3357 SW 7th St, Ocala, Florida 34474-1956 **Tel:** 1 352 732-0079.
Web site: http://myq92.com
Profile: WMFQ-FM is a commercial station owned by JVC Broadcasting Inc. The format of the station is hot adult contemporary. WMFQ-FM broadcasts to the Ocala, FL area at 92.9 FM.
FM RADIO STATION

WMFR-AM 38670
Owner: Curtis Media Group
Editorial: 875 W 5th St, Winston Salem, North Carolina 27101 **Tel:** 1 336 885-2191.
Web site: http://www.triadsports.com
Profile: WMFR-AM is a commercial station owned by Curtis Media Group. The format of the station is sports. WMFR-AM broadcasts to the Greensboro, NC area on 1230 AM.
AM RADIO STATION

WMFS-AM 38176
Owner: Entercom Communications Corp.
Editorial: 1835 Moriah Woods Blvd., Building 1, Memphis, Tennessee 38117 **Tel:** 1 901 767-0104.
Web site: http://www.680wsmb.com
Profile: WMFS-AM is a commercial station owned by Entercom Communications Corp. The format of the station is sports. WMFS-AM broadcasts to the Memphis, TN area at 680 AM.
AM RADIO STATION

WMFS-FM 42359
Owner: Entercom Communications Corp.
Editorial: 1835 Moriah Woods Blvd, Building 1, Memphis, Tennessee 38117-7122 **Tel:** 1 901 384-5900.
Web site: http://www.680wsmb.com
Profile: WMFS-FM is a commercial station owned by Entercom Communications Corp. The format of the station sports. WMFS-FM broadcasts to the Memphis, TN area at 92.9 FM.
FM RADIO STATION

WMFU-FM 44039
Owner: Auricle Communications
Editorial: 43 Montgomery St, 4th Fl, Jersey City, New Jersey 7302 **Tel:** 1 201 521-1416.
Email: wfmu@wfmu.org
Web site: http://www.wfmu.org
Profile: WMFU-FM is a non-commercial station owned by Auricle Communications. The format of the station is freeform radio. WMFU-FM broadcasts to the Mount Hope, NY area at 90.1 FM.
FM RADIO STATION

WMFX-FM 40512
Owner: Alpha Media
Editorial: 1900 Pineview Dr, Columbia, South Carolina 29209-5079 **Tel:** 1 803 695-8600.
Web site: http://www.fox1023.com
Profile: WMFX-FM is a commercial station owned by Alpha Media. The format of the station is rock. WMFX-FM broadcasts to the Columbia, SC area at 102.3 FM.
FM RADIO STATION

WMGA-FM 396882
Owner: Kindred Communications
Editorial: 555 5th Ave Ste K, Huntington, West Virginia 25701-1907 **Tel:** 1 304 523-8401.
Email: studio@hits979.com
Web site: http://hits979.com
Profile: WMGA-FM is a commercial station owned by Kindred Communications. The format of the station is Hot AC. WMGA-FM broadcasts to Huntington, WV and surrounding communities at 97.9 FM.
FM RADIO STATION

WMGB-FM 42440
Owner: Cumulus Media Inc.
Editorial: 544 Mulberry St Fl 5, Macon, Georgia 31201-2770 **Tel:** 1 478 746-6286.
Web site: http://www.allthehitsb951.com
Profile: WMGB-FM is a commercial station owned by Cumulus Media Inc. The format of the station is Top 40/CHR music. WMGB-FM broadcasts in the Macon, GA area at 95.1 FM.
FM RADIO STATION

WMGC-AM 35539
Owner: Silva Entertainment
Editorial: 2514 Eugenia Ave, Nashville, Tennessee 37211-2117 **Tel:** 1 615 251-1222.
Email: info@eljefe967fm.com
Web site: http://www.eljefe967fm.com
Profile: WMGC-AM is a commercial station owned by Silva Entertainment. The format of the station is regional Mexican music. WMGC-AM broadcasts to the Nashville, TN area at 810 AM.
AM RADIO STATION

WMGC-FM 40648
Owner: Beasley Broadcast Group
Editorial: 1 Radio Plaza St, Ferndale, Michigan 48220-2140 **Tel:** 1 248 414-5600.
Web site: http://1051thebounce.com
Profile: WMGC-FM is a commercial station owned by Beasley Broadcast Group. The format of the station is Detroit's Throwback Hip Hop and R&B. WMGC-FM broadcasts to the Detroit area at 105.1 FM.
FM RADIO STATION

WMGF-FM 42743
Owner: iHeartMedia Inc.
Editorial: 2500 Maitland Center Pkwy Ste 401, Maitland, Florida 32751-4179 **Tel:** 1 407 916-7800.
Web site: http://magic107.iheart.com
Profile: WMGF-FM is a commercial station owned by iHeartMedia Inc. The format of the station is adult contemporary. WMGF-FM broadcasts to the Maitland, FL area at 107.7 FM.
FM RADIO STATION

WMGG-AM 36468
Owner: Genesis Communications Inc.
Editorial: 800 8th Ave SE, Largo, Florida 33771-2162 **Tel:** 1 813 281-1040.
Profile: WMGG-AM is a commercial station owned by Genesis Communications Inc. The format of the station is Spanish news/talk. WMGG-AM broadcasts to the Tampa, FL area at 1470 AM.
AM RADIO STATION

WMGH-FM 46311
Owner: J-Systems Franchising Corp.
Editorial: 2147 Market St, Nesquehoning, Pennsylvania 18240-1422 **Tel:** 1 570 645-2105.
Email: wmgh@ptd.net
Web site: http://www.wmgh.com
Profile: WMGH-FM is a commercial station owned by owned by J-Systems Franchising Corp. The format of the station is adult contemporary music. WMGH-FM broadcasts to the Lansford, PA area at 105.5 FM.
FM RADIO STATION

WMGI-FM 40513
Owner: Midwest Communications Inc.
Editorial: 824 S 3rd St, Terre Haute, Indiana 47807-4609 **Tel:** 1 812 232-4161.
Email: mixfm@1007mixfm.com
Web site: http://www.mymixfm.com
Profile: WMGI-FM is a commercial station owned by Midwest Communications Inc. The format of the station is Top 40/CHR. WMGI-FM broadcasts to the Terre Haute, IN area at 100.7 FM.
FM RADIO STATION

WMGJ-AM 35799
Owner: Donald(Floyd)
Editorial: 815 Tuscaloosa Ave, Gadsden, Alabama 35901-3162 **Tel:** 1 256 546-4434.
Web site: http://www.wmgjam.com
AM RADIO STATION

WMGK-FM 45369
Owner: Beasley Broadcast Group
Editorial: 1 Bala Plz Ste 339, Bala Cynwyd, Pennsylvania 19004-1424 **Tel:** 1 610 667-8500.
Email: theoffice@wmgk.com
Web site: http://www.wmgk.com
Profile: WMGK-FM is a commercial station owned by Beasley Broadcast Group. The format of the station is classic rock. WMGK-FM broadcasts to the Philadelphia area at 102.9 FM.
FM RADIO STATION

WMGL-FM 42304
Owner: Cumulus Media Inc.
Editorial: 4230 Faber Place Dr, Ste 100, North Charleston, South Carolina 29405 **Tel:** 1 843 277-1200.
Web site: http://www.magic1017.com
Profile: WMGL-FM is a commercial station owned by Cumulus Media Inc. The format of the station is urban adult contemporary music. WMGL-FM broadcasts to the North Charleston, SC area at 107.3 FM.
FM RADIO STATION

WMGM-FM 46724
Owner: Longport Media
Editorial: 1601 New Rd, Linwood, New Jersey 08221-1116 **Tel:** 1 609 653-1400.
Web site: http://1037wmgm.com
Profile: WMGM-FM is a commercial station owned by Longport Media. The format of the station is active rock. WMGM-FM broadcasts to the Atlantic City, NJ area at 103.7 FM.
FM RADIO STATION

WMGN-FM 45370
Owner: Midwest Family Stations
Editorial: 730 Rayovac Dr, Madison, Wisconsin 53711-2472 **Tel:** 1 608 273-1000.
Email: info@magic98.com
Web site: http://www.magic98.com
Profile: WMGN-FM is a commercial station owned by Midwest Family Stations. The format of the station is adult contemporary. WMGN-FM broadcasts to the Madison, WI area at 98.1 FM.
FM RADIO STATION

WMGO-AM 35524
Owner: WMGO Broadcasting Corp.
Editorial: 107 W Peace St, Canton, Mississippi 39046-4535 **Tel:** 1 601 859-2373.
Email: wmgoradio@yahoo.com
Web site: http://www.wmgoradio.com
AM RADIO STATION

WMGP-FM 46377
Owner: iHeartMedia Inc.
Editorial: 154 Boone Dr, Newnan, Georgia 30263-2801 **Tel:** 1 770 683-7234.
Web site: http://www.magic981.com
Profile: WMGP-FM is a commercial station owned by iHeartMedia Inc. The format of the station is classic hits. WMGP-FM broadcasts to the Newnan, GA area at 98.1 FM.
FM RADIO STATION

WMGQ-FM 46086
Owner: Beasley Broadcast Group
Editorial: 78 Veronica Ave, Somerset, New Jersey 08873-3417 **Tel:** 1 732 249-2600.
Web site: http://www.magic983.com
Profile: WMGQ-FM is a commercial station owned by Beasley Broadcast Group. The format of the station is adult contemporary. WMGQ-FM broadcasts in the Somerset, NJ area at 98.3 FM.
FM RADIO STATION

WMGR-AM 37115
Owner: Flint Media
Editorial: 521 S Scott St, Bainbridge, Georgia 39819-4101 **Tel:** 1 229 246-7776.
Profile: WMGR-AM is a commercial station owned by Flint Media, Inc. The format of the station is sports. WMGR-AM broadcasts to the Bainbridge, GA area at 930 AM.
AM RADIO STATION

WMGS-FM 46008
Owner: Cumulus Media Inc.
Editorial: 600 Baltimore Drive, Wilkes-Barre, Pennsylvania 18702-7901 **Tel:** 1 570 824-9000.
Web site: http://www.magic93fm.com
Profile: WMGS-FM is a commercial station owned by Cumulus Media Inc. The format is Lite Rock/Lite AC. WMGS-FM broadcasts to the Wilkes Barre, PA area at 92.9 FM.
FM RADIO STATION

WMGU-FM 45237
Owner: Cumulus Media Inc.
Editorial: 1009 Drayton Rd, Fayetteville, North Carolina 28303-3887 **Tel:** 1 910 864-5222.
Web site: http://www.magic1069.com
Profile: WMGU-FM is a commercial station owned by Cumulus Media Inc. The format of the station is urban adult contemporary. WMGU-FM broadcasts to the Fayetteville, NC area at 106.9 FM.
FM RADIO STATION

WMGV-FM 42029
Owner: Beasley Broadcast Group
Editorial: 207 Glenburnie Dr, New Bern, North Carolina 28560-2815 **Tel:** 1 252 633-1500.
Email: webmaster@v1033.com
Web site: http://www.v1033.com
Profile: WMGV-FM is a commercial station owned by Beasley Broadcast Group. The format of the station is adult contemporary. WMGV-FM broadcasts to the New Bern, NC area at 103.3 FM.
FM RADIO STATION

WMGW-AM 38045
Owner: FM Radio Licenses, LLC
Editorial: 900 Water St, Meadville, Pennsylvania 16335-3428 **Tel:** 1 814 724-1111.
Web site: http://www.myantsnetwork.com/
Profile: WMGW-AM is a commercial station owned by FM Radio Licenses, LLC. The format of the station is news, talk and sports. WMGW-AM broadcasts to the Meadville, PA area at 1490 AM.
AM RADIO STATION

WMGX-FM 46188
Owner: Saga Communications
Editorial: 420 Western Ave, South Portland, Maine 04106-1704 **Tel:** 1 207 774-4561.
Web site: http://www.coast931.com
Profile: WMGX-FM is a commercial station owned by Saga Communications. The format of the station is hot adult contemporary music. WMGX-FM broadcasts to the Portland, ME, area at 93.1 FM.
FM RADIO STATION

WMGY-AM 35525
Owner: Barber, Terry
Editorial: 2305 Upper Wetumpka Rd, Montgomery, Alabama 36107-1345 **Tel:** 1 334 834-3710.
Email: info@wmgyradio.com
Web site: http://www.wmgyradio.com
Profile: WMGY-AM is a commercial station owned by Barber, Terry. The format of the station is southern gospel and religious programming. WMGY-AM broadcasts to the Montgomery, AL area at 800 AM.
AM RADIO STATION

WMGZ-FM 45757
Owner: Southern Stone Broadcasting
Editorial: 156 Lake Laurel Rd NE, Milledgeville, Georgia 31061-9007 **Tel:** 1 478 453-9406.
Email: wmgz.z97@gmail.com
Web site: http://www.z97.fm
Profile: WMGZ-FM is a commercial station owned by Southern Stone Broadcasting. The format of the station is hot adult contemporary. WMGZ-FM broadcasts to the Milledgeville, GA area at 97.7 FM.
FM RADIO STATION

WMHB-FM 44536
Owner: Mayflower Hill Broadcasting Corp.
Editorial: 4000 Mayflower Hill Drive, Waterville, Maine 4901 **Tel:** 1 207 859-5454.
Email: info@wmhb.org
Web site: http://www.wmhb.org
Profile: WMHB-FM is a non-commercial college station owned by Mayflower Hill Broadcasting Corp. The format of the station is variety. WMHB-FM broadcasts in the Waterville, ME area at 89.7 FM.
FM RADIO STATION

WMHQ-FM 156064
Owner: Mars Hill Broadcasting Co Inc.
Editorial: 4044 Makyes Rd, Syracuse, New York 13215-8683 **Tel:** 1 315 469-5051.
Email: mhn@marshillnetwork.org
Web site: http://www.marshillnetwork.org
Profile: WMHQ-FM is a non-commercial station owned by Mars Hill Broadcasting. The format of the station is Christian programming with a focus on teaching and music. The station broadcasts locally to the Malone/Massena, NY and Cornwall, Ontario areas at 90.1 FM.
FM RADIO STATION

WMHR-FM 40516
Owner: Mars Hill Broadcasting Co Inc.
Editorial: 4044 Makyes Rd, Syracuse, New York 13215-9797 **Tel:** 1 315 469-5051.
Email: mhn@marshillnetwork.org
Web site: http://www.marshillnetwork.org
Profile: WMHR-FM is a non-commercial station owned by Mars Hill Broadcasting. The format of the station is Christian programming with a focus on teaching and music. WMHR-FM broadcasts to the Syracuse, NY area at 102.9 FM.
FM RADIO STATION

WMHX-FM 42164
Owner: Entercom Communications Corp.
Editorial: 7601 Ganser Way, Madison, Wisconsin 53719-2074 **Tel:** 1 608 826-0077.
Web site: http://mix1051fm.com
Profile: WMHX-FM is a commercial station owned by Entercom Communications Corp. The format of the station is hot AC. WMHX-FM broadcasts to Madison, WI at 105.1 FM.
FM RADIO STATION

WMIA-FM 43741
Owner: iHeartMedia Inc.
Editorial: 7601 Riviera Blvd, Miramar, Florida 33023-6574 **Tel:** 1 954 862-2000.
Web site: http://www.my939miami.com/
Profile: WMIA-FM is a commercial station owned by iHeartMedia Inc. The format of the station is Rhythmic AC. WMIA-FM broadcasts to the Miami area at 93.9 FM.
FM RADIO STATION

WMIB-FM 43279
Owner: iHeartMedia Inc.
Editorial: 7601 Riviera Blvd, Miramar, Florida 33023-6574 **Tel:** 1 954 862-2000.
Web site: http://1035thebeat.iheart.com
Profile: WMIB-FMis a commercial station owned by iHeartMedia Inc. The format of the station is urban contemporary. WMIB-FM broadcasts to the Miramar, FL area at 103.5 FM.
FM RADIO STATION

WMIC-AM 38505
Owner: Sanilac Broadcasting
Editorial: 19 S Elk St, Sandusky, Michigan 48471-1353 **Tel:** 1 810 648-2700.
Web site: http://www.sanilacbroadcasting.com
Profile: WMIC-AM is a commercial station owned by Sanilac Broadcasting. The format of the station is country, news and talk. WMIC-AM broadcasts to the Sandusky, MI area at 660 AM.
AM RADIO STATION

WMID-AM 38419
Owner: Equity Communications LP
Editorial: 8025 Black Horse Pike Ste 100, Pleasantville, New Jersey 08232-2959
Tel: 1 609 484-8444.
Web site: http://www.classicoldieswmid.com
Profile: WMID-AM is a commercial station owned by Equity Communications LP. The format of the station is oldies music. WMID-AM broadcasts to the West Atlantic City, NJ area at 1340 AM.
AM RADIO STATION

WMIE-FM 46464
Owner: National Christian Network
Editorial: 1150 King St, Cocoa, Florida 32922
Tel: 1 321 632-1000.
Web site: http://www.wmiefm.com
Profile: WMIE-FM is a non-commercial station owned by the National Christian Network. The format of the station is contemporary Christian. WMIE-FM broadcasts to the Cocoa, FL area at 91.5 FM.
FM RADIO STATION

WMIL-FM 45372
Owner: iHeartMedia Inc.
Editorial: 12100 W Howard Ave, Greenfield, Wisconsin 53228-1851 **Tel:** 1 414 545-8900.
Email: eteam@fm106.com
Web site: http://www.fm106.com
Profile: WMIL-FM is a commercial station owned by iHeartMedia Inc. The format of the station is contemporary country. WMIL-FM broadcasts to the greater Milwaukee area at 106.1 FM.
FM RADIO STATION

WMIM-FM 40776
Owner: Cumulus Media Inc.
Editorial: 14 S Monroe St, Monroe, Michigan 48161-2231 **Tel:** 1 734 242-6600.
Web site: http://www.983nashicon.com
Profile: WMIM-FM is a commercial station owned by Cumulus Media Inc. The format of the station is country. WMIM-FM broadcasts to the Monroe, MI area on 98.3 FM.
FM RADIO STATION

WMIN-AM 882498
Owner: Tri-County Broadcasting
Editorial: 1010 2nd St N, Sauk Rapids, Minnesota 56379-2527 **Tel:** 1 320 252-6200.
Email: tcbi.redhouse@gmail.com
Web site: http://www.1010wmin.com
Profile: WMIN-AM is a commercial station owned by Tri-County Broadcasting. The format of the station is adult standards and nostalgia. WMIN-AM broadcasts in the Sauk Rapids, MN area at 1010 AM.
AM RADIO STATION

WMIQ-AM 38047
Owner: Sovereign Communications
Editorial: 101 Kent St, Iron Mountain, Michigan 49801-1507 **Tel:** 1 906 774-4321.
Email: talk1450wmiq@uplogon.com
Web site: http://wmiq.net
Profile: WMIQ-AM is a commercial station owned by Sovereign Communications. The format of the station is news, sports and talk programming. WMIQ-AM broadcasts in the Iron Mountain, MI area at 1450 AM.
AM RADIO STATION

WMIR-AM 37117
Owner: Atlantic Beach Radio
Editorial: 4337 Big Barn Dr, Little River, South Carolina 29566-6802 **Tel:** 1 843 399-2653.
Profile: WMIR-AM is a commercial station owned by Atlantic Beach Radio. The format of the station is gospel. WMIR-AM broadcasts to the Little River, SC area at 1200 AM.
AM RADIO STATION

WMIS-AM 36942
Owner: Natchez Communications
Editorial: 20 E Franklin St, Natchez, Mississippi 39120
Tel: 1 601 442-2522.
Email: wmiswtyj@bellsouth.net
Profile: WMIS-AM is a commercial station owned by Natchez Communications. The format of the station is urban contemporary music. WMIS-AM broadcasts in the Natchez, MS area at 1240 AM.
AM RADIO STATION

WMIS-FM 496728
Owner: Paskvan Media, Inc.
Editorial: 2115 Washington Ave S, Bemidji, Minnesota 56601-8918 **Tel:** 1 218 751-7777.
Web site: http://www.wmisfm.com
Profile: WMIS-FM is a commercial station owned by Paskvan Media, Inc. The format of the station is adult contemporary. WMIS-FM broadcasts locally to the Blackduck, MN area at 92.1 FM.
FM RADIO STATION

WMIT-FM 45373
Owner: Blue Ridge Broadcasting Corp.
Editorial: 3 Porters Cove Rd, Asheville, North Carolina 28805-2834 **Tel:** 1 828 285-8477.
Web site: http://www.1069thelight.org
Profile: WMIT-FM is a non-commercial station owned by Blue Ridge Broadcasting Corp. The format of the station is contemporary Christian. WMIT-FM broadcasts to the Asheville, NC area at 106.9 FM.
FM RADIO STATION

WMIX-AM 38048
Owner: Withers Broadcasting Co.
Editorial: 3501 Broadway St, Mount Vernon, Illinois 62864-2202 **Tel:** 1 618 242-3500.
Email: wmixsite@mywithersradio.com
Web site: http://www.wmix94.com
Profile: WMIX-AM is a commercial station owned by Withers Broadcasting Co. The format of the station is adult standards, and news and talk. WMIX-AM broadcasts to the Mt. Vernon, IL area at 940 AM.
AM RADIO STATION

WMIX-FM 46807
Owner: Withers Broadcasting Co.
Editorial: 3501 Broadway St, Mount Vernon, Illinois 62864-2202 **Tel:** 1 618 242-3500.
Web site: http://www.mywithersradio.com/wmix
Profile: WMIX-FM is a commercial station owned by Withers Broadcasting Co. The format of the station is contemporary country music. WMIX-FM broadcasts to the Mt. Vernon, IL area at 94.1 FM.
FM RADIO STATION

WMIZ-AM 38511
Owner: Clear Communications Inc.
Editorial: 632 Maurice River Pkwy, Vineland, New Jersey 8360 **Tel:** 1 856 692-8888.
Web site: http://www.wmizradio.com
Profile: WMIZ-AM is a commercial station owned by Clear Communications Inc. The format of the station is adult contemporary and Hispanic programming. WMIZ-AM broadcasts to Vineland, NJ area at 1270 AM.
AM RADIO STATION

WMJC-FM 760286
Owner: Horizon Christian Fellowship
Tel: 1 219 548-5800.
Email: info@calvaryradionetwork.com
Web site: http://www.calvaryradionetwork.com
Profile: WMJC-FM, an affiliate of the Calvary Radio Network, is a non-commercial station owned by Horizon Christian Fellowship. The format of the station is religious. WMJC-FM is licensed to the Richland, MI area and broadcasts at a frequency of 91.9 FM.
FM RADIO STATION

WMJD-FM 46101
Owner: Peggy Sue Broadcasting Media Inc.
Editorial: 1011 Radio Dr, Grundy, Virginia 24614-6157
Tel: 1 276 935-7227.
Email: wmjd.fm@gmail.com
Profile: WMJD-FM is a commercial station owned by Peggy Sue Broadcasting Media, Inc. The format of the station is classic country music. WMJD-FM broadcasts to the Grundy, VA area at 100.7 FM.
FM RADIO STATION

WMJH-AM 36080
Owner: Birach Broadcasting
Editorial: 6272 28th St SE, Grand Rapids, Michigan 49546-6902 **Tel:** 1 616 451-0551.
Profile: WMJH-AM is a commercial station owned by Birach Broadcasting. The format of the station is regional Mexican music. WMJH-AM broadcasts to the Grand Rapids, MI area at 810 AM.
AM RADIO STATION

WMJI-FM 40519
Owner: iHeartMedia Inc.
Editorial: 6200 Oak Tree Blvd Ste 400, Independence, Ohio 44131-6934 **Tel:** 1 216 520-2600.
Email: feedback@wmji.com
Web site: http://www.wmji.com
Profile: WMJI-FM is a commercial station owned by iHeartMedia Inc. The format of the station is Oldies, classic hits and talk. WMJI-FM broadcasts to the Independence, OH area at 105.7 FM.
FM RADIO STATION

WMJJ-FM 46219
Owner: iHeartMedia Inc.
Editorial: 600 Beacon Pkwy W Ste 400, Birmingham, Alabama 35209-3118 **Tel:** 1 205 439-9600.
Web site: http://magic96.iheart.com
Profile: WMJJ-FM is a commercial station owned by iHeartMedia Inc. The format of the station is adult contemporary. WMJJ-FM broadcasts to the Birmingham, Al area at 96.5 FM.
FM RADIO STATION

WMJK-FM 44492
Owner: BAS Broadcasting
Editorial: 1640 Cleveland Rd, Sandusky, Ohio 44870-4357 **Tel:** 1 419 625-1010.
Web site: http://www.coast1009.com
Profile: WMJK-FM is a commercial station owned by BAS Broadcasting. The format of the station is a mix of contemporary and classic country. WMJK-FM broadcasts to the Sandusky, OH area at 100.9 FM.
FM RADIO STATION

WMJL-FM 46282
Owner: Joemyers Productions Inc.
Editorial: 251 Club Dr, Marion, Kentucky 42064-1244
Tel: 1 270 965-2271.
Email: wmjlradio@att.net
Web site: http://magic1027.net
Profile: WMJL-FM is a commercial station owned by Joemyers Productions Inc. The format of the station is oldies. WMJL-FM broadcasts to the Marion, KY area at a frequency of 102.7 FM.
FM RADIO STATION

WMJM-FM 42168
Owner: Alpha Media, LLC
Editorial: 520 S 4th St STE 200, Louisville, Kentucky 40202-2500 **Tel:** 1 502 625-1220.
Web site: http://www.1013online.com
Profile: WMJM-FM is a commercial station owned by Alpha Media, LLC. The format of the station is urban adult contemporary, R&B and classical soul. WMJM-FM broadcasts to the Louisville, KY area on 101.3 FM.
FM RADIO STATION

WMJO-FM 41871
Owner: MacDonald Broadcasting Co.
Editorial: 2000 Whittier St, Saginaw, Michigan 48601-2271 **Tel:** 1 989 752-8161.
Web site: http://www.973joefm.com
Profile: WMJO-FM is a commercial station owned by MacDonald Broadcasting Co. The format of the station is hot adult contemporary. WMJO-FM broadcasts to the Saginaw, MI area at 97.3 FM.
FM RADIO STATION

WMJR-AM 36154
Owner: Thy Kingdom Come Network Inc.
Editorial: 110 Dennis Drive, Lexington, Kentucky 40503 **Tel:** 1 859 278-0894.
Email: info@realliferadio.com
Web site: http://www.realliferadio.com
AM RADIO STATION

WMJU-FM 445175
Owner: Brookhaven Broadcasting, Inc.
Editorial: 911 Highway 550, Brookhaven, Mississippi 39601-4447 **Tel:** 1 601 833-9210.
Email: brookhavenbroadcasting@yahoo.com
Profile: WMJU-FM is a commercial station owned by Brookhaven Broadcasting, Inc. The format for the station is hot adult contemporary. WMJU-FM broadcasts to the Bude, MS area at 104.3 FM.
FM RADIO STATION

WMJW-FM 41941
Owner: Radio Cleveland Inc.
Editorial: 911 S Davis Ave, Cleveland, Mississippi 38732-3941 **Tel:** 1 662 843-4091.
Profile: WMJW-FM is a commercial station owned by Radio Cleveland Inc. The format for the station is country. WMJW-FM broadcasts to the Greenwood-Greenville, MS area at 107.5 FM. Send press releases via mail.
FM RADIO STATION

WMJX-FM 43450
Owner: Beasley Broadcast Group
Editorial: 55 William T Morrissey Blvd, Dorchester, Massachusetts 02125-3315 **Tel:** 1 617 822-9600.
Web site: http://www.magic1067.com
Profile: WMJX-FM is a commercial station owned by Beasley Broadcast Group. The format of the station is Soft adult contemporary. WMJX-FM broadcasts to the Dorchester, MA area at 106.7 FM.
FM RADIO STATION

WMJY-FM 42738
Owner: iHeartMedia Inc.
Editorial: 286 Debuys Rd, Biloxi, Mississippi 39531-2611 **Tel:** 1 228 388-2323.
Web site: http://www.magic937.com
Profile: WMJY-FM is a commercial station owned by iHeartMedia Inc. The format of the station is adult contemporary. WMJY-FM broadcasts to the Biloxi, MS at 93.7 FM.
FM RADIO STATION

WMJZ-FM 46132
Owner: Darby Advertising Inc.
Editorial: 3687 Old US Highway 27 S, Gaylord, Michigan 49735 **Tel:** 1 989 732-2341.
Web site: http://www.radioeaglegaylord.com
Profile: WMJZ-FM is a commercial station owned by Darby Advertising Inc. The format of the station is adult hits. WMJZ-FM broadcasts to the Gaylord, MI, area at 101.5 FM.
FM RADIO STATION

WMKC-FM 45374
Owner: Northern Star Broadcasting LLC
Editorial: 1356 Mackinaw Ave, Cheboygan, Michigan 49721 **Tel:** 1 231 627-2341.
Web site: http://www.1029bigcountry.com
Profile: WMKC-FM is a commercial station owned by Northern Star Broadcasting LLC. The format of the station is contemporary country. WMKC-FM broadcasts to the Cheboygan, MI area at 102.9 FM.
FM RADIO STATION

WMKD-FM 364358
Owner: Sovereign Communications LLC
Editorial: 1411 Ashmun St, Sault Sainte Marie, Michigan 49783-2871 **Tel:** 1 906 635-0995.
Profile: WMKD-FM is a commercial station owned by Sovereign Communications LLC. The format for the station is contemporary country. WMKD-FM broadcasts to the Sault Sainte Marie, MI, area at 105.5 FM.
FM RADIO STATION

WMKL-FM 363101
Owner: Call Communications Group, Inc.
Editorial: 8900 SW 168th St, Bldg 4000, Village of Palmetto Bay, Florida 33157-4569 **Tel:** 1 786 429-3606.
Email: md@callfm.com
Web site: http://www.callfm.com
Profile: WMKL-FM is a commercial station owned by Call Communications Group, Inc. The format of the

station is contemporary Christian. WMKL-FM broadcasts to the Miami area at 91.9 FM.
FM RADIO STATION

WMKM-AM 35241
Owner: Communicom Broadcasting
Editorial: 2994 E Grand Blvd, Detroit, Michigan 48202-3134 **Tel:** 1 313 871-1440.
Web site: http://www.1440wdrj.com
Profile: WMKM-AM is a commercial station owned by Communicom Broadcasting. The format of the station is gospel. WMKM-AM broadcasts to the Detroit area at 1440 AM.
AM RADIO STATION

WMKQ-FM 45200
Owner: Magnum Communications
Editorial: 4201 Victory Ave, Racine, Wisconsin 53405-3277 **Tel:** 1 262 634-3311.
Email: racinenews@magnum.media
Web site: http://www.q92country.com
Profile: WMKQ-FM is a commercial station owned by Magnum Communications. The format of the station is contemporary country music. WMKQ-FM broadcasts to the Milwaukee area at 92.1 FM.
FM RADIO STATION

WMKR-FM 43592
Owner: Randy Radio
Editorial: 918 E Park St, Taylorville, Illinois 62568-1916 **Tel:** 1 217 824-3395.
Email: adminasst@randyradio.com
Web site: http://www.taylorvilledailynews.com
Profile: WMKR-FM is a commercial station owned by Randy Radio. The format of the station is country music. WMKR-FM broadcasts in the Taylorville, IL, area at 94.3 FM.
FM RADIO STATION

WMKS-FM 73065
Owner: iHeartMedia Inc.
Editorial: 2B Pai Park, Greensboro, North Carolina 27409-9428 **Tel:** 1 336 822-2000.
Web site: http://www.1003kissfm.com/main.html
Profile: WMKS-FM is a commercial station owned by iHeartMedia Inc. The format of the station is rock. WMKS-FM broadcasts to the Greensboro, NC area at 100.3 FM.
FM RADIO STATION

WMKT-AM 37974
Owner: MacDonald Garber Broadcasting Inc.
Editorial: 2095 S US Highway 131, Petoskey, Michigan 49770-9216 **Tel:** 1 231 347-8713.
Web site: http://www.wmktthetalkstation.com
Profile: WMKT-AM is a commercial station owned by MacDonald Garber Broadcasting Inc. The format of the station is news/talk. WMKT-AM broadcasts to the Traverse City, MI area at a frequency of 1270 AM.
AM RADIO STATION

WMKV-FM 42709
Owner: Maple Knoll Communities
Editorial: 11100 Springfield Pike, Cincinnati, Ohio 45246 **Tel:** 1 513 782-2427.
Email: wmkvfm@mkcommunities.org
Web site: http://www.wmkvfm.org
Profile: WMKV-FM is a non-commercial station owned by Maple Knoll Communities. The format of the station is adult standards. WMKV-FM broadcasts to the Cincinnati area at 89.3 FM.
FM RADIO STATION

WMKW-FM 43226
Owner: Moody Bible Institute
Editorial: 1920 E 24th Street Pl, Chattanooga, Tennessee 37404-5810 **Tel:** 1 423 629-8900.
Email: wmbw@moody.edu
Profile: WMKW-FM is a non-commercial station owned by Moody Bible Institute. The format of the station is religious programming. WSJQ-FM broadcasts to the Chattanooga, TN area at 89.3 FM.
FM RADIO STATION

WMKX-FM 41541
Owner: Strattan Broadcasting Inc.
Editorial: 517 1/2 Market St, Johnsonburg, Pennsylvania 15845 **Tel:** 1 814 849-8100.
Email: megarockstudio@windstream.net
Web site: http://www.megarock.fm
Profile: WMKX-FM is a commercial station owned by Strattan Broadcasting Inc. The format of the station is rock. WMKX-FM broadcasts to the Johnsonburg, PA area at 105.5 FM.
FM RADIO STATION

WMKZ-FM 41636
Owner: Monticello Wayne County Media Inc.
Editorial: 183 Old Hwy 90, Monticello, Kentucky 42633-6801 **Tel:** 1 606 348-3393.
Email: studio@z93country.com
Web site: http://www.wmkz.com
Profile: WMKZ-FM is a commercial station owned by Monticello Wayne County Media Inc. The format for the station is contemporary country. WMKZ-FM broadcasts to the Lexington, KY area at 93.1 FM.
FM RADIO STATION

WMLB-AM 310439
Owner: JW Broadcasting
Editorial: 1100 Spring St NW Ste 610, Atlanta, Georgia 30309-2828 **Tel:** 1 404 681-9307.
Web site: http://www.1690wmlb.com
Profile: WMLB-AM is a commercial station owned by JW Broadcasting. The format of the station is talk and variety. WMLB-AM broadcasts to the Atlanta area at 1690 AM.
AM RADIO STATION

WMLC-AM 35528
Owner: Walking By Faith Ministries
Editorial: 336 Rodenberg Ave, Biloxi, Mississippi 39531-3444 **Tel:** 1 228 374-9739.
Email: wqfxradio@bellsouth.net
Profile: WMLC-AM is a commercial station owned by Walking By Faith Ministries. The format is Urban Gospel/Southern Gospel. WMLC-AM broadcasts to the Biloxi, MS area at 1270 AM.
AM RADIO STATION

WMLJ-FM 42451
Owner: Grace Baptist Church
Tel: 1 304 872-4612.
Email: baptistjoewv@yahoo.com
Web site: http://www.fbnradio.com
Profile: WMLJ-FM is a non-commercial station owned by Grace Baptist Church. The format of the station is religious programming. The station is broadcast to the Summersville, WV area at 90.5 FM.
FM RADIO STATION

WMLL-FM 43469
Owner: Saga Communications
Editorial: 500 North Commercial St, Manchester, New Hampshire 3101 **Tel:** 1 603 669-5777.
Web site: http://www.965themill.com
Profile: WMLL-FM is a commercial station owned by Saga Communications. The format of the station is classic hits. WMLL-FM broadcasts to the Manchester, NH area at 96.5 FM.
FM RADIO STATION

WMLM-AM 35529
Owner: Krol Communications
Editorial: 4170 N State Rd, Alma, Michigan 48801-9316 **Tel:** 1 989 463-4013.
Profile: WMLM-AM is a commercial station owned by Krol Communications. The format of the station is country. WMLM-AM broadcasts to the Alma, MI area at 1520 AM.
AM RADIO STATION

WMLN-FM 40523
Owner: Curry College
Editorial: 1071 Blue Hill Ave, Milton, Massachusetts 2186 **Tel:** 1 617 333-0311.
Web site: http://www.curry.edu/about-curry/news-and-events/curry-radio.html
Profile: WMLN-FM is a non-commercial college station owned by Curry College. The format of the station is variety. WMLN-FM broadcasts to the Milton, MA area at 91.5 FM.
FM RADIO STATION

WMLP-AM 38050
Owner: Sunbury Broadcasting Corp.
Editorial: 1227 County Line Rd, Selinsgrove, Pennsylvania 17870-8188 **Tel:** 1 570 286-5838.
Email: newsroom@wkok.com
Web site: http://www.1380wmlp.com
Profile: WMLP-AM is a commercial station owned by Sunbury Broadcasting Corp. The format of the station is talk. WMLP-AM broadcasts to the Lewisburg, PA area at 1380 AM.
AM RADIO STATION

WMLQ-FM 563826
Owner: Synergy Media, Inc.
Editorial: 5399 W Wallace Ln, Ludington, Michigan 49431-2439 **Tel:** 1 231 843-0941.
Profile: WMLQ-FM is a commercial station owned by Synergy Media, Inc. The format of the station is Talk. WMLQ-FM broadcasts to the Ludington, MI area at 97.7 FM.
FM RADIO STATION

WMLR-AM 35530
Owner: 2 Brothers Broadcasting.
Editorial: 184 Switzerland Rd, Hohenwald, Tennessee 38462-2552 **Tel:** 1 931 796-5966.
Email: wmlr1230am@bellsouth.net
Profile: WMLR-AM is a commercial station owned by 2 Brothers Broadcasting. The format of the station is oldies. WMLR-AM broadcasts to the Hohenwald, TN area at 1230 AM.
AM RADIO STATION

WMLS-FM 76569
Owner: Minnesota Public Radio
Editorial: 207 W Superior St, Ste 224, Duluth, Minnesota 55802 **Tel:** 1 218 722-9411.
Email: newsroom@mpr.org
Web site: http://minnesota.publicradio.org/radio/stations/wlsnwmls/
Profile: WMLS-FM is a non-commercial station owned by Minnesota Public Radio. The format of the station is classical music. WMLS-FM broadcasts to the Duluth, MN area at 88.7 FM.
FM RADIO STATION

WMLT-AM 38051
Owner: Dowdy Broadcasting, Inc.
Editorial: 807 Bellevue Ave, Dublin, Georgia 31021-4847 **Tel:** 1 478 272-4422.
Web site: http://969thebuzz.com/
Profile: WMLT-AM is a commercial station owned by Dowdy Broadcasting, Inc. The format of the station is Sports/Classic Rock. WMLT-AM broadcasts to the Dublin, GA area at 1330 AM.
AM RADIO STATION

WMLU-FM 588399
Owner: Longwood Radio Associates
Editorial: 201 High St, Farmville, Virginia 23909-1800
Tel: 1 434 395-2792.
Email: wmlu@wmlu.org
Web site: http://www.wmlu.org
Profile: WMLU-FM is a non-commercial station owned by Longwood Radio Assoicates. The format of the station is college variety. WMLU-FM broadcasts to the Farmville, VA area at 91.3 FM.
FM RADIO STATION

WMLV-FM 40505
Owner: Educational Media Foundation
Editorial: 330 Himmarshee St Ste 207, Fort Lauderdale, Florida 33312-1712 **Tel:** 1 954 522-8755.
Email: klove@klove.com
Web site: http://www.klove.com
Profile: WMLV-FM is a non-commercial station owned by Educational Media Foundation. The format of the station is contemporary Christian music. WMLV-FM broadcasts to the Pompano Beach, FL area at 89.7 FM.
FM RADIO STATION

WMLX-FM 43819
Owner: iHeartMedia Inc.
Editorial: 667 W Market St, Lima, Ohio 45801-4603
Tel: 1 419 223-2060.
Web site: http://www.mix1033.com
Profile: WMLX-FM is a commercial station owned by iHeartMedia Inc. The format of the station is adult contemporary. WMLX-FM broadcasts to the Lima, OH area at 103.3 FM.
FM RADIO STATION

WMMA-FM 414077
Owner: Starboard Media Foundation Inc.
Editorial: 321 Market St, Wisconsin Rapids, Wisconsin 54494 **Tel:** 1 715 424-5050.
Email: info@relevantradio.com
Web site: http://www.relevantradio.com
Profile: WMMA-FM is a non-commercial station owned by Starboard Media Foundation Inc. The format of the station is religious. WMMA-FM broadcasts to the Wisconsin Rapids, WI area at 93.9 FM.
FM RADIO STATION

WMMB-AM 38442
Owner: iHeartMedia Inc.
Editorial: 1388 S Babcock St, Melbourne, Florida 32901-3009 **Tel:** 1 321 733-1000.
Web site: http://wmmbam.iheart.com
Profile: WMMB-AM is a commercial station owned by iHeartMedia Inc. The format of the station is news and talk. WMMB-AM broadcasts to the Melbourne, FL area at 1240 AM.
AM RADIO STATION

WMMC-FM 43970
Owner: JDL Broadcasting Inc.
Editorial: 627 1/2 Archer Ave, Marshall, Illinois 62441-1267 **Tel:** 1 217 826-8017.
Email: wmmc106@aol.com
Web site: http://www.wmmcradio.com
Profile: WMMC-FM is a commercial station owned by JDL Broadcasting Inc. The format of the station is classic hits music. WMMC-FM broadcasts to the Marshall, IL area at 105.9 FM.
FM RADIO STATION

WMME-FM 45375
Owner: Townsquare Media, Inc.
Editorial: 56 Western Ave Ste 13, Augusta, Maine 04330-6348 **Tel:** 1 207 623-4735.
Web site: http://www.92moose.fm
Profile: WMME-FM is a commercial station owned by Townsquare Media, Inc. The format of the station is Top 40/CHR. WMME-FM broadcasts to the Augusta, ME area at 92.3 FM.
FM RADIO STATION

WMMG-AM 38053
Owner: Meade County Communications Inc.
Editorial: 1715 Bypass Rd, Brandenburg, Kentucky 40108-1623 **Tel:** 1 270 422-3961.
Email: wmmg935@bbtel.com
Web site: http://www.wmmgradio.com
Profile: WMMG-AM is a commercial station owned by Meade County Communications Inc. The format of the station is classic country. WMMG-AM broadcasts to the Brandenburg, KY area at 1140 AM.
AM RADIO STATION

WMMG-FM 45376
Owner: Meade County Communications Inc.
Editorial: 1715 Bypass Rd, Brandenburg, Kentucky 40108 **Tel:** 1 270 422-3961.
Email: wmmg935@bbtel.com
Web site: http://www.wmmgradio.com
Profile: WMMG-FM is a commercial station owned by Meade County Communications Inc. The format of the station is country music. WMMG-FM broadcasts to the Brandenburg, KY area at 93.5 FM.
FM RADIO STATION

WMMI-AM 38867
Owner: Latitude Media, LLC
Editorial: 4895 E Wing Rd, Mount Pleasant, Michigan 48858-7057 **Tel:** 1 989 772-9664.
Email: wczy@wczy.net
Web site: http://wczy.net
Profile: WMMI-AM is a commercial station owned by Latitute Media, LLC. The format for the station is talk. WMMI-AM broadcasts to the Flint, MI area at 830 AM.
AM RADIO STATION

WMMJ-FM 46212
Owner: Urban One, Inc.
Editorial: 8515 Georgia Ave Fl 9, Silver Spring, Maryland 20910-3403 **Tel:** 1 301 306-1111.
Web site: http://mymajicdc.com
Profile: WMMJ-FM is a commercial station owned by Urban One, Inc. The format of the station is urban adult contemporary. WMMJ-FM broadcasts to the Washington, D.C. area at 102.3 FM.
FM RADIO STATION

WMML-AM 37685
Owner: Pamal Broadcasting Ltd.
Editorial: 89 Everts Ave, Queensbury, New York 12804-2040 **Tel:** 1 518 793-7733.
Email: production@adirondackbroadcasting.com
Profile: WMML-AM is a commercial station owned by Pamal Broadcasting Ltd. The format of the station is sports. The station airs locally at 1230 AM.
AM RADIO STATION

WMMM-FM 41795
Owner: Entercom Communications Corp.
Editorial: 7601 Ganser Way, Madison, Wisconsin 53719-2074 **Tel:** 1 608 826-0077.
Email: 1055triplem@entercom.com
Web site: http://www.1055triplem.com
Profile: WMMM-FM is a commercial station owned by Entercom Communications Corp. The format for the station is adult album alternative. WMMM-FM broadcasts to the Madison, WI area at 105.5 FM.
FM RADIO STATION

WMMN-AM 36461
Owner: Spectrum Radio Group, LLC
Tel: 1 301 802-1250.
Web site: http://www.spectrumradiogroup.com
Profile: WMMN-AM is a commercial station owned by Spectrum Radio Group, LLC. The format of the station is sports talk. WMMN-AM broadcasts to the Fairmont, WV area at 920 AM.
AM RADIO STATION

WMMO-FM 41631
Owner: Cox Media Group, Inc.
Editorial: 4192 N John Young Pkwy, Orlando, Florida 32804-2620 **Tel:** 1 321 281-2000.
Web site: http://www.wmmo.com
Profile: WMMO-FM is a commercial station owned by Cox Media Group, Inc. The format of the station is Lite Rock/Lite AC. WMMO-FM broadcasts to the Orlando, FL area at 98.9 FM.
FM RADIO STATION

WMMQ-FM 40527
Owner: Townsquare Media, LLC
Editorial: 3420 Pinetree Rd, Lansing, Michigan 48911-4207 **Tel:** 1 517 394-7272.
Web site: http://www.wmmq.com
Profile: WMMQ-FM is a commercial station owned by Townsquare Media, LLC. The format of the station is classic rock. WMMQ-FM broadcasts to the Lansing, MI area at 94.9 FM.
FM RADIO STATION

WMMR-FM 43178
Owner: Beasley Broadcast Group
Editorial: 1 Bala Plz Ste 424, Bala Cynwyd, Pennsylvania 19004-1421 **Tel:** 1 610 771-0933.
Web site: http://www.wmmr.com
Profile: WMMR-FM is a commercial station owned by Greater Media Inc. The format of the station is rock/album-oriented rock. WMMR-FM broadcasts to the Philadelphia area at 93.3 FM.
FM RADIO STATION

WMMS-FM 43172
Owner: iHeartMedia Inc.
Editorial: 6200 Oak Tree Blvd, Independence, Ohio 44131-6933 **Tel:** 1 216 520-2600.
Web site: http://www.wmms.com
Profile: WMMS-FM is a commercial station owned by iHeartMedia Inc. The format of the station is rock. WMMS-FM broadcasts to the Cleveland area at 100.7 FM.
FM RADIO STATION

WMMT-FM 41322
Owner: Appalshop Inc.
Editorial: 91 Madison Ave, Whitesburg, Kentucky 41858-9317 **Tel:** 1 606 633-0108.
Email: wmmtfm@appalshop.org
Web site: http://www.wmmt.org
Profile: WMMT-FM is a non-commercial station owned by Appalshop Inc. The format of the station is variety. WMMT-FM broadcasts to the Whitesburg, KY, area at 88.7 FM.
FM RADIO STATION

WMMV-AM 36650
Owner: iHeartMedia Inc.
Editorial: 1388 S Babcock St, Melbourne, Florida 32901-3009 **Tel:** 1 321 733-1000.
Web site: http://www.wmmbam.com
Profile: WMMV-AM is a commercial station owned by iHeartMedia Inc. The format of station is news and talk. WMMV-AM broadcasts to the Melbourne, FL area at 1350 AM.
AM RADIO STATION

WMMW-AM 37046
Owner: Connoisseur Media
Editorial: 869 Blue Hills Ave, Bloomfield, Connecticut 06002-3710 **Tel:** 1 860 243-1115.
Web site: http://www.talkofconnecticut.com
Profile: WMMW-AM is a commercial station owned by Connoisseur Media. The format of the station is talk. WMMW-AM broadcasts to the Bloomfield, CT area at 1470 AM.
AM RADIO STATION

WMMX-FM 40856
Owner: iHeartMedia Inc.
Editorial: 101 Pine St, Dayton, Ohio 45402-2948
Tel: 1 937 224-1137.
Web site: http://www.wmmx.com
Profile: WMMX-FM is a commercial station owned by iHeartMedia Inc. The format of the station is hot adult contemporary music. WMMX-FM broadcasts to the Dayton, OH area at 107.7 FM.
FM RADIO STATION

WMMY-FM 830119
Owner: High Country Adventures, LLC
Editorial: 738 Blowing Rock Rd, Boone, North Carolina 28607-4835 **Tel:** 1 828 264-2411.
Profile: WMMY-FM is a commercial station owned by High Country Adventures, LLC, a subsidiary of Curtis Media Group. The format of the station is contemporary country. WMMY-FM broadcasts to the Boone, NC area at 106.1 FM.
FM RADIO STATION

WMNA-FM 45377
Owner: 3 Daughters Media, Inc.
Editorial: 677 Zion Road, Gretna, Virginia 24557-0730
Tel: 1 434 534-6100.
Web site: http://www.wiqoradio.com
Profile: WMNA-FM is a commercial station owned by 3 Daughters Media, Inc. The format of the station is talk. WMNA-FM broadcasts to the Roanoke, VA area at 106.3 FM. Please contact the Program Director with all press releases.
FM RADIO STATION

WMNC-AM 38055
Owner: Cooper Broadcasting Corp.
Editorial: 1103 N Green St, Morganton, North Carolina 28655 **Tel:** 1 828 437-0521.
Email: wmnc@bellsouth.net
Profile: WMNC-AM is a commercial station owned by Cooper Broadcasting Corp. The format of the station is classic country. WMNC-AM broadcasts to the Morganton, NC area at 1430 AM.
AM RADIO STATION

WMNC-FM 45491
Owner: Cooper Broadcasting Corp.
Editorial: 1103 N Green St, Morganton, North Carolina 28655 **Tel:** 1 828 437-0521.
Email: wmnc@bellsouth.net
Web site: http://www.bigdawg92fm.com
Profile: WMNC-FM is a commercial station owned by Cooper Broadcasting Corp. The format of the station is contemporary country. WMNC-FM broadcasts to the Morganton, NC area at 92.1 FM.
FM RADIO STATION

WMNF-FM 41054
Owner: Stubblefield Foundation(Nathan)
Editorial: 1210 E Dr Martin Luther King Jr Blvd, Tampa, Florida 33603-4417 **Tel:** 1 813 238-8001.
Email: newsroom@wmnf.org
Web site: http://www.wmnf.org
Profile: WMNF-FM is a non-commercial station owned by Nathan Stubblefield Foundation. The format of the station is variety. WMNF-FM broadcasts to the Tampa, FL area at 88.5 FM.
FM RADIO STATION

WMNI-AM 38056
Owner: North American Broadcasting
Editorial: 1458 Dublin Rd, Columbus, Ohio 43215-1010
Web site: http://www.wmni.com
Profile: WMNI-AM is a commercial station owned by North American Broadcasting. The format of the station is adult standards. WMNI-AM broadcasts to the Columbus, OH area at 920 AM. Slogan is "Playing America's Best Music."
AM RADIO STATION

WMNI-FM 44043
Owner: North American Broadcasting
Editorial: 1458 Dublin Rd, Columbus, Ohio 43215-1010 **Tel:** 1 614 481-7800.
Web site: http://news.wmni.com/
Profile: WMNI-FM is a commercial station owned by North American Broadcasting. The format of the station is Classic Hits. WMNI-FM broadcasts to the Columbus, OH area at 103.9 FM.
FM RADIO STATION

WMNP-FM 44251
Owner: 3G Broadcasting, Inc.
Editorial: 15 Marcus Wheatland Boulevard, Newport, Rhode Island 2840 **Tel:** 1 401 846-1540.
Web site: http://www.mixx993.com
Profile: WMNP-FM is a commercial station owned by 3G Broadcasting, Inc. The format of the station is Top 40/CHR. WMNP-FM broadcasts to the Newport, RI area at 99.3 FM.
FM RADIO STATION

WMNR-FM 42031
Owner: Town of Monroe, CT
Editorial: 731 Main St, Monroe, Connecticut 06468-2872 **Tel:** 1 203 268-9667.
Email: info@wmnr.org
Web site: http://www.wmnr.org
Profile: WMNR-FM is a non-commercial station owned by the Town of Monroe, CT. The format of the station is classical. WMNR-FM broadcasts to the Monroe, CT area at 88.1 FM.
FM RADIO STATION

WMNV-FM 42020
Owner: Capital Media Corporation
Editorial: 30 Park Ave, Cohoes, New York 12047-3330 **Tel:** 1 518 237-1330.
Email: events@aliveradio.com
Web site: http://www.aliveradionetwork.com
Profile: WMNV-FM is a commercial station owned by Capital Media Corporation. The format of the station is religious programming. WMNV-FM broadcasts to the Cohoes, NY area at 104.1 FM. Address all mail to Paul Lotters.
FM RADIO STATION

WMNX-FM 42139
Owner: Cumulus Media Inc.
Editorial: 3233 Burnt Mill Dr Ste 4, Wilmington, North Carolina 28403-2676 **Tel:** 1 910 763-9977.
Web site: http://www.coast973.com
Profile: WMNX-FM is a commercial station owned by Cumulus Media Inc. The format of the station is urban contemporary. WMNX-FM broadcasts to the Wilmington, NC area at 97.3 FM.
FM RADIO STATION

WMNZ-AM 35983
Owner: Macon County Broadcasting Co.
Editorial: 115 1/2 Cherry St, Montezuma, Georgia 31063 **Tel:** 1 478 472-8386.
Email: wmnz1050am@yahoo.com
Profile: WMNZ-AM is a commercial owned by Macon County Broadcasting Co. The format of the station is contemporary country. WMNZ-AM broadcasts to the Montezuma, GA area at 1050 AM.
AM RADIO STATION

WMOA-AM 37141
Owner: JAWCO Inc.
Editorial: 925 Lancaster St, Marietta, Ohio 45750-2531 **Tel:** 1 740 373-1490.
Email: bsunderman@wmoa1490.com
Web site: http://www.wmoa1490.com
Profile: WMOA-AM is a commercial station owned by JAWCO Inc. The format for the station is Lite Rock/Lite AC. WMOA-AM broadcasts to the Marietta, OH area at 1490 AM.
AM RADIO STATION

WMOB-AM 35875
Owner: Buddy Tucker Association, Inc.
Editorial: 2500 Battleship Pkwy, Mobile, Alabama 36652 **Tel:** 1 251 432-1360.
Email: buddy@buddytuckerassociation.org
Web site: http://buddytuckerassociation.org
AM RADIO STATION

WMOC-FM 663863
Owner: Full Gospel Church of God Written
Editorial: 414 Renwick St, Lumber City, Georgia 31549 **Tel:** 1 912 363-2203.
Email: wmoc887@yahoo.com
Web site: http://www.wmoc887fm.com
Profile: WMOC-FM is a non-commercial station owned by Full Gospel Church of God Written. The format of the station is gospel. WMOC-FM broadcasts to the Lumber City, GA area at a frequency of 88.7 FM.
FM RADIO STATION

WMOD-FM 40639
Owner: WMOD Inc.
Editorial: 200 E Market St, Bolivar, Tennessee 38008-2362 **Tel:** 1 731 658-7328.
Email: wmod@wmodradio.com
Web site: http://wmodradio.com
Profile: WMOD-FM is a commercial station owned by WMOD Inc. The format of the station is primarily classic country music. WMOD-FM broadcasts to the Bolivar, TN area at 96.7 FM.
FM RADIO STATION

WMOG-FM 40999
Owner: iHeart Media Inc.
Editorial: 3833 US Highway 82, Brunswick, Georgia 31523-7735 **Tel:** 1 912 267-1025.
Profile: WMOG-FM is a commercial station owned by iHeart Media Inc. The format of the station is classic hits. WMOG-FM broadcasts to the Brunswick, GA area on 92.7 FM.
FM RADIO STATION

WMOH-AM 35533
Owner: Vernon Baldwin Broadcasting
Editorial: 2081 Fairgrove Ave, Hamilton, Ohio 45011-1967 **Tel:** 1 513 863-1111.
Web site: http://www.wmoh.com
Profile: WMOH-AM is a commercial station owned by Vernon Baldwin Broadcasting. The format of the station is news, talk and sports. WMOH-AM broadcasts to the Hamilton, OH area at 1450 AM.
AM RADIO STATION

WMOI-FM 45378
Owner: Prairie Communications LLP
Editorial: 55 Public Sq, Monmouth, Illinois 61462-1755 **Tel:** 1 309 734-9452.
Email: wakinews@yahoo.com
Web site: http://www.radiomonmouth.com
Profile: WMOI-FM is a commercial station owned by Prairie Communications LLP. The format of the station is adult contemporary. WMOI-FM broadcasts to the Monmouth, IL area at 97.7 FM.
FM RADIO STATION

WMOK-AM 38513
Owner: Withers Broadcasting Co.
Editorial: 339 Fairgrounds Rd, Metropolis, Illinois 62960-2713 **Tel:** 1 618 524-4400.
Email: wmok920@frontier.com
Web site: http://www.920wmok.com
AM RADIO STATION

WMOM-FM 44496
Owner: Bay View Broadcasting
Editorial: 206 E Ludington Ave, Ludington, Michigan 49431 **Tel:** 1 231 845-9666.
Email: news@wmom.fm
Web site: http://www.wmom.fm
Profile: WMOM-FM is a commercial station owned by Bay View Broadcasting. The format of the station is Top 40/CHR. WMOM-FM broadcasts to the Ludington, MI area at 102.7 FM.
FM RADIO STATION

WMON-AM 39419
Owner: LM Communications, Inc.
Editorial: 100 Kanawha Ter, Saint Albans, West Virginia 25177-2771 **Tel:** 1 304 722-3308.
Email: wjypnet@gmail.com
Web site: http://wjypam.com/
Profile: WMON-AM is a commercial station owned by LM Communications, Inc. The format of the station is sports. WMON-AM broadcasts to the Montgomery, WV area at 1340.
AM RADIO STATION

WMOO-FM 46828
Owner: Great Eastern Radio, LLC
Editorial: 3422 US Route 5, Derby, Vermont 05829-4430 **Tel:** 1 802 766-9236.
Email: wmooproduction.vba@gmail.com
Web site: http://www.moo92.com
Profile: WMOO-FM is a commercial station owned by Great Eastern Radio, LLC. The format of the station is hot adult contemporary music. WMOO-FM broadcasts to the Derby, VT area at 92.1 FM.
FM RADIO STATION

WMOP-AM 35534
Owner: Florida Sportstalk Inc.
Editorial: 2320 NE 2nd St, Ocala, Florida 34470-8228
Tel: 1 352 732-2010.
Web site: http://www.floridasportstalk.fm/
Profile: WMOP-AM is a commercial station owned by Florida Sportstalk Inc. The format of the station is sports. WMOP-AM broadcasts to the Ocala, FL area at 900 AM.
AM RADIO STATION

WMOQ-FM 42884
Owner: Bostwick Broadcasting Group
Editorial: 1610 Launius Rd, Good Hope, Georgia 30641-2639 **Tel:** 1 770 267-0923.
Web site: http://www.wmoqfm.com
Profile: WMOQ-FM is a commercial station owned by Bostwick Broadcasting Group. The format of the station is classic country. WMOQ-FM broadcasts to the Good Hope, GA area at 92.3 FM.
FM RADIO STATION

WMOR-FM 45379
Owner: Morgan County Industries Inc.
Editorial: 129 College St, West Liberty, Kentucky 41472-1156 **Tel:** 1 606 784-4141.
Profile: WMOR-FM is a commercial station owned by Morgan County Industries Inc. The format of the station is adult hits. WMOR-FM broadcasts to the West Liberty, KY area at 106.1 FM.
FM RADIO STATION

WMOS-FM 77154
Owner: Cumulus Media Inc.
Editorial: 7 Governor Winthrop Blvd, New London, Connecticut 06320-6428 **Tel:** 1 860 443-1980.
Web site: http://www.1023thewolf.com
Profile: WMOS-FM is a commercial station owned by Cumulus Media Inc. The format of the station is classic rock. WMOS-FM broadcasts to the Hartford-New Haven, CT area at 102.3 FM.
FM RADIO STATION

WMOU-AM 36912
Owner: Lunderville(Barry)
Editorial: 15 Main St, Littleton, New Hampshire 03561-4037 **Tel:** 1 603 752-1230.
Email: kiss102@together.net
Profile: WMOU-AM is a commercial station owned by Barry Lunderville. The format of the station is Hot AC. WMOU-AM broadcasts to the Berlin, NH area at 1230 AM.
AM RADIO STATION

WMOV-AM 39228
Owner: Vandalia Media Partners
Editorial: 527 Gibbs St, Ravenswood, West Virginia 26164-1011 **Tel:** 1 304 273-2544.
Email: contact@wmov1360.com
Web site: http://wmovradio.com
Profile: WMOV-AM is a commercial station owned by Vandalia Media Partners. The format of the station is news and talk. WMOV-AM broadcasts to the Ravenswood, WV area at 1360 AM.
AM RADIO STATION

WMOV-FM 40878
Owner: iHeartMedia Inc.
Editorial: 1003 Norfolk Sq, Norfolk, Virginia 23502-3234 **Tel:** 1 757 466-0009.
Web site: http://www.movin1077fm.com
Profile: WMOV-FM is a commercial station owned by iHeartMedia Inc. The format of the station is rhythmic adult contemporary. WMOV-FM broadcasts to the Norfolk, VA area at 107.7 FM.
FM RADIO STATION

WMOX-AM 35535
Owner: Magnolia State Broadcasting
Editorial: 451 Highway 11/80, Meridian, Mississippi 39301-2779 **Tel:** 1 601 693-1891.
Email: wmox@att.net
Web site: http://www.wmox.net
Profile: WMOX-AM is a commercial station owned by Magnolia State Broadcasting. The format of the station is talk. WMOX-AM broadcasts to the Meridian, MS area at 1010 AM.
AM RADIO STATION

WMOZ-FM 132301
Owner: Quarnstrom Media Group LLC
Editorial: 1104 Cloquet Ave, Cloquet, Minnesota 55720 **Tel:** 1 218 879-4534.
Email: wklk@aol.com
Profile: WMOZ-FM is a commercial station owned by Quarnstrom Media Group LLC. The format of the station is oldies music. WMOZ-FM broadcasts to the Duluth, MN area at 106.9 FM.
FM RADIO STATION

WMPC-AM 35536
Owner: Calvary Bible Church of Lapeer
Editorial: 1800 N Lapeer Rd, Lapeer, Michigan 48446-7794 **Tel:** 1 810 664-6211.
Web site: http://www.wmpc.org
Profile: WMPC-AM is a non-commercial station owned by the Calvary Bible Church of Lapeer. The format of the station is Christian music and talk programming. WMPC-AM broadcasts to the Lapeer, MI, area at 1230 AM.
AM RADIO STATION

WMPI-FM 40532
Owner: Rice Broadcasting Inc.(D.R.)
Editorial: 22 E McClain Ave, Scottsburg, Indiana 47170-1844 **Tel:** 1 812 752-5612.
Web site: http://www.i1053online.com
Profile: WMPI-FM is a commercial station owned by D.R. Rice Broadcasting Inc. The format of the station is contemporary country music. WMPI-FM broadcasts in the Scottsburg, IN area at 105.3 FM.
FM RADIO STATION

WMPL-AM 38059
Owner: J&J Broadcasting
Editorial: 326 Quincy St, Hancock, Michigan 49930-1802 **Tel:** 1 906 482-3700.
Email: wmplprod@themix93.com
Web site: http://www.wmpl920.com
Profile: WMPL-AM is a commercial station owned by J&J Broadcasting. The format of the station is news, sports and talk. WMPL-AM broadcasts to the Hancock, MI area at 920 AM.
AM RADIO STATION

WMPM-AM 35537
Owner: Family Media Group, LLC
Editorial: 1270 Buffalo Rd, Smithfield, North Carolina 27577 **Tel:** 1 919 934-2434.
Email: churchnews@1270wmpm.com
Web site: http://www.1270wmpm.com
Profile: WMPM-AM is a commercial station owned by Family Media Group, LLC. The format of the station is contemporary Christian. WMPM-AM broadcasts to the Smithfield, NC area at 1270 AM.
AM RADIO STATION

WMPO-AM 38060
Owner: Positive Radio Group
Editorial: 39540 Bradbury Rd, Middleport, Ohio 45760-9703 **Tel:** 1 740 992-6485.
Email: office@wyvk.com
Web site: http://www.wyvk.com
Profile: WMPO-AM is a commercial station owned by the Positive Radio Group. The format of the station is sports news and talk. WMPO-AM broadcasts to Middleport, OH and surrounding communities at 1390 AM.
AM RADIO STATION

WMPR-FM 40533
Owner: Maxwell Broadcasting Inc.(J.C.)
Editorial: 1018 Pecan Park Cir, Jackson, Mississippi 39209-6913 **Tel:** 1 601 948-5835.
Email: frontoffice@wmpr901.com
Web site: http://www.wmpr901.com
Profile: WMPR-FM is a commercial station owned by J.C. Maxwell Broadcasting Inc. The format of the station is blues and gospel. WMPR-FM broadcasts to Jackson, MS and its surrounding environs at 90.1 FM.
FM RADIO STATION

WMPS-AM 36976
Owner: Flinn Broadcasting Corp.
Editorial: 6080 Mount Moriah Road Ext, Memphis, Tennessee 38115-2645 **Tel:** 1 901 375-9324.
Email: mail@flinn.com
Web site: http://sunny1210.com
Profile: WMPS-AM is a commercial station owned by Flinn Broadcasting Corp. The format of the station is conservative news/talk. WMPS-AM broadcasts to the Memphis, TN market at AM 1210.
AM RADIO STATION

WMPW-AM 35738
Owner: Lakes Media, LLC
Editorial: 1336 Piney Forest Rd, Danville, Virginia 24540-1606 **Tel:** 1 434 799-1010.
Web site: http://www.morefm1059.com/

Profile: WMPW-AM is a commercial station owned by Lakes Media, LLC. The station airs an adult contemporary format. WMPW-AM broadcasts to the Danville, VA area at a frequency of 105.9 AM.
AM RADIO STATION

WMPX-AM 38061
Owner: Steel Broadcasting
Editorial: 1510 Bayliss St, Midland, Michigan 48640
Tel: 1 989 631-1490.
Email: admin@wmpxwmrx.com
Web site: http://www.wmpxwmrx.com
Profile: WMPX-AM is a commercial station owned by Steel Broadcasting. The format for the station is adult standards. WMPX-AM broadcasts to the Flint, MI area at 1490 AM.
AM RADIO STATION

WMPZ-FM 42676
Owner: Brewer Broadcasting Inc.
Editorial: 1305 Carter St, Chattanooga, Tennessee 37402 **Tel:** 1 423 265-9494.
Web site: http://www.groove93.com
Profile: WMPZ-FM is a commercial station owned by Brewer Broadcasting Inc. The format of the station is urban adult contemporary. WMPZ-FM broadcasts to the Chattanooga, TN area at 93.5 FM.
FM RADIO STATION

WMQA-FM 45620
Owner: NRG Media LLC
Editorial: 3616 State Highway 47 N, Rhinelander, Wisconsin 54501 **Tel:** 1 715 362-1975.
Email: wmqa@nrgnorthwoods.com
Web site: http://www.wmqa.com
Profile: WMQA-FM is a commercial station owned by NRG Media LLC. The format of the station is classic hits. WMQA-FM broadcasts in the Minocqua, WI, area at 95.9 FM.
FM RADIO STATION

WMQM-AM 35956
Owner: Robbert Broadcasting Co.(F.W.)
Editorial: 3704 Whittier Rd, Memphis, Tennessee 38108 **Tel:** 1 901 327-2500.
Web site: http://www.1600wmqm.com
Profile: WMQM-AM is a commercial station owned by F.W. Robbert Broadcasting Co. The format of the station is religious and talk. WMQM-AM broadcasts to the Memphis, TN area at 1600 AM.
AM RADIO STATION

WMQR-FM 43556
Owner: Saga Communications
Editorial: 1820 Heritage Center Way, Harrisonburg, Virginia 22801-8451 **Tel:** 1 540 434-0331.
Web site: http://more961.com
Profile: WMQR-FM is a commercial station owned by Saga Communications. The format of the station is Hot AC. WMQR-FM broadcasts to the Harrisonburg, VA area at 96.1 FM. The station does not accept unsolicited faxes. Do NOT e-mail any staff members. Any press information should be sent to WSVA-AM.
FM RADIO STATION

WMQT-FM 45381
Owner: Taconite Broadcasting
Editorial: 121 N Front St, Ste A, Marquette, Michigan 49855 **Tel:** 1 906 225-9100.
Email: newswmqt@wmqt.com
Web site: http://www.wmqt.com
Profile: WMQT-FM is a commercial station owned by Taconite Broadcasting. The format of the station is hot adult contemporary music. WMQT-FM broadcasts to the Marquette, MI area at 107.7 FM.
FM RADIO STATION

WMQU-AM 38454
Owner: Blarney Stone Broadcasting, Inc.
Editorial: 6514 Old Lake Rd, Grayling, Michigan 49738-7348 **Tel:** 1 989 348-6171.
Web site: http://www.ewtn.com
Profile: WMQU-AM is a commercial station owned by Blarney Stone Broadcasting, Inc. The format of the station is religious teaching. WGRY-AM broadcasts to the Traverse City, MI area at 1230 AM.
AM RADIO STATION

WMQX-FM 40766
Owner: Entercom Communications Corp.
Editorial: 305 Route 315 Hwy, Pittston, Pennsylvania 18640-3907 **Tel:** 1 570 883-9850.
Web site: http://www.max1023.com/
Profile: WHBS-FM is a commercial station owned by Entercom Communications Corp. The format of the station is classic rock. WDMT-FM broadcasts to the Wilkes-Barre, PA area at 102.3 FM. The station's slogan is, "Rock Hits of the 80s and More."
FM RADIO STATION

WMQZ-FM 44295
Owner: Prestige Communications
Editorial: 31 E Side Sq, Macomb, Illinois 61455-2248
Tel: 1 309 833-2121.
Email: news@prestigeradio.com
Web site: http://www.prestigeradio.com
Profile: WMQZ-FM is a commercial station owned by Prestige Communications. The format of the station is oldies. WMQZ-FM broadcasts to the Macomb, IL area at 104.1 FM.
FM RADIO STATION

WMRC-AM 35538
Owner: Tom McAuliffe II
Editorial: 258 Main St, Milford, Massachusetts 01757-2525 **Tel:** 1 508 473-1490.
Email: news@wmrcdailynews.com
Web site: http://www.wmrcradio.com
Profile: WMRC-AM is a commercial station owned by Tom McAuliffe II. The format of the station is adult contemporary. WMRC-AM broadcasts the Milford, MA area at 1490 AM.
AM RADIO STATION

WMRD-AM 35256
Owner: Crossroads Communications LLC
Editorial: 777 River Rd, Middletown, Connecticut 06457-3922 **Tel:** 1 860 347-9673.
Email: wliswmrd@yahoo.com
Web site: http://www.wliswmrd.net
Profile: WMRD-AM is a commercial station owned by Crossroads Communications LLC. The format for the station is talk. WMRD-AM broadcasts to the Middletown, CT area at 1150 AM.
AM RADIO STATION

WMRE-AM 38289
Owner: iHeartMedia Inc.
Editorial: 510 Pegasus Ct, Winchester, Virginia 22602-4596 **Tel:** 1 540 662-5101.
Email: winchesterdigital@clearchannel.com
Web site: http://foxsports1550.iheart.com
Profile: WMRE-AM is a commercial station owned by iHeartMedia Inc. The format of the station is sports. WMRE-AM broadcasts in the Winchester, VA area at 1550 AM.
AM RADIO STATION

WMRF-FM 45964
Owner: First Media Radio LLC
Editorial: 12 E Market St Fl 2, Lewistown, Pennsylvania 17044-2123 **Tel:** 1 717 248-6757.
Email: news@merfradio.com
Web site: http://merfradio.com
Profile: WMRF-FM is a commercial station owned by First Media Radio LLC. The format of the station is hot adult contemporary music. WMRF-FM broadcasts to the Lewistown, PA area at 95.7 FM.
FM RADIO STATION

WMRI-AM 37847
Owner: Hoosier AM/FM LLC
Editorial: 820 S Pennsylvania St, Marion, Indiana 46953-2407 **Tel:** 1 765 664-7396.
Email: production@wmri.com
Web site: http://860espn.com/
Profile: WMRI-AM is a commercial station owned by Hoosier AM/FM LLC. The format of the station is sports. WMRI-AM broadcasts in the Marion, IN area at 860 AM.
AM RADIO STATION

WMRK-FM 42609
Owner: Alexander Broadcasting Company, LLC
Editorial: 4101 Wall St Ste A, Montgomery, Alabama 36106-3724 **Tel:** 1 334 244-0961.
Web site: http://www.klove.com
Profile: WMRK-FM is a commercial station owned by Alexander Broadcasting Company, LLC. The format of the station is Contemporary Christian. WMRK-FM is the K-LOVE affiliate for the Montgomery, AL area and broadcasts at 107.9 FM.
FM RADIO STATION

WMRN-AM 38519
Owner: iHeartMedia Inc.
Editorial: 1330 N Main St, Marion, Ohio 43302-1525
Tel: 1 740 383-1131.
Web site: http://wmrn.iheart.com
Profile: WMRN-AM is a commercial station owned by iHeartMedia Inc. The format of the station is news, sports and talk. WMRN-AM broadcasts to the Marion, OH area at 1490 AM.
AM RADIO STATION

WMRN-FM 40219
Owner: iHeartMedia Inc.
Editorial: 1330 N Main St, Marion, Ohio 43302-1525
Tel: 1 740 383-1131.
Web site: http://www.buckeyecountry943.com
Profile: WMRN-FM is a commercial station owned by iHeartMedia Inc. The format of the station is contemporary country. WMRN-FM broadcasts to the Marion, OH area at 94.3 FM.
FM RADIO STATION

WMRQ2-FM 852018
Owner: Red Wolf Broadcasting
Editorial: 131 New London Tpke Ste 101, Glastonbury, Connecticut 06033-2246
Tel: 1 860 657-1041.
Web site: http://www.bomba971.com
Profile: WMRQ2-FM is owned by Red Wolf Broadcasting. The format for the station is Hispanic music. WMRQ2-FM broadcasts to the Hartford, CT on 97.1 FM. Digital radio technology is used by AM and FM radio stations, via a digital signal embedded in their analog signal, to transmit audio and data.
FM RADIO STATION

WMRQ-FM 46525
Owner: Red Wolf Broadcasting
Editorial: 131 New London Tpke Ste 101, Glastonbury, Connecticut 06033-2246
Tel: 1 860 657-1041.
Email: requests@radio1041.fm
Web site: http://www.radio1041.fm
Profile: WMRQ-FM is a commercial station owned by Red Wolf Broadcasting. The format for the station is rock alternative. WMRQ-FM broadcasts to the Hartford, CT area at 104.1 FM.
FM RADIO STATION

WMRR-FM 42112
Owner: iHeartMedia Inc.
Editorial: 3565 Green St, Norton Shores, Michigan 49444-3875 **Tel:** 1 231 733-2600.
Web site: http://www.wmrr.com
Profile: WMRR-FM is a commercial station owned by iHeartMedia Inc. The format of the station is classic rock music. WMRR-FM broadcasts to the Muskegon, MI and surrounding communities at 101.7 FM.
FM RADIO STATION

WMRS-FM 41320
Owner: Monticello Community Radio
Editorial: 132 N Main St, Monticello, Indiana 47960
Tel: 1 574 583-8933.
Web site: http://www.wmrsradio.com
Profile: WMRS-FM is a commercial station owned by Monticello Community Radio. The format of the station is adult contemporary. WMRS-FM broadcasts to the Indianapolis area at 107.7 FM.
FM RADIO STATION

WMRT-FM 40536
Owner: Marietta College
Editorial: McKinney Media Center, 508 Putnam St, Marietta, Ohio 45750-3032 **Tel:** 1 740 376-4800.
Email: wmrt@marietta.edu
Web site: http://www.wmrtfm.com
Profile: WMRT-FM is a non-commercial station owned by Marietta College. The format for the station is classical and jazz. WMRT-FM broadcasts to the Marietta, OH area at 88.3 FM.
FM RADIO STATION

WMRV-FM 45897
Owner: Genesee Media Corp.
Editorial: 195 Main St, Dansville, New York 14437-1315 **Tel:** 1 585 335-9369.
Web site: http://geneseenow.com
Profile: WMRV-FM is a commercial station owned by Genesee Media Corp. The format of the station is adult contemporary music. WMRV-FM broadcasts to the Dansville, NY area at 93.9 FM.
FM RADIO STATION

WMRX-FM 45383
Owner: Steel Broadcasting
Editorial: 1510 Bayliss St, Midland, Michigan 48640-5507 **Tel:** 1 989 631-1490.
Email: admin@wmpxwmrx.com
Web site: http://www.wmpxwmrx.com
Profile: WMRX-FM is a commercial station owned by Steel Broadcasting. The format for the station is adult standards music. WMRX-FM broadcasts to the Flint, MI area at 97.7 FM.
FM RADIO STATION

WMRZ-FM 377557
Owner: iHeartMedia Inc.
Editorial: 809 S Westover Blvd, Albany, Georgia 31707-4953 **Tel:** 1 229 439-9704.
Web site: http://www.kissalbany.com
Profile: WMRZ-FM is a commercial station owned by iHeartMedia Inc. The format of the station is urban adult contemporary music. WMRZ-FM broadcasts to the Albany, GA area at 98.1 FM.
FM RADIO STATION

WMSA-AM 39502
Owner: Stephens Media Group Massena, LLC
Editorial: 2155 State Highway 420, Massena, New York 13662-3351 **Tel:** 1 315 769-3333.
Email: news@1340wmsa.com
Web site: http://www.1340wmsa.com
Profile: WMSA-AM is a commercial station owned by Stephens Media Group Massena, LLC. The format of the station is news, talk, sports and oldies. WMSA-AM broadcasts to the Massena, NY area at 1340 AM.
AM RADIO STATION

WMSG-AM 37110
Owner: Radiowerks, Inc.
Editorial: 407 Lothian St, Mountain Lake Park, Maryland 21550-2909 **Tel:** 1 301 334-1100.
Email: office@wkhj.com
Web site: http://www.wmsg.com
Profile: WMSG-AM is a commercial station owned by Radiowerks, Inc. The format of the station is oldies. WMSG-AM broadcasts to the Mountain Lake Park, MD area at 1050 AM.
AM RADIO STATION

WMSI-FM 45384
Owner: iHeartMedia Inc.
Editorial: 1375 Beasley Rd, Jackson, Mississippi 39206-2018 **Tel:** 1 601 982-1062.
Web site: http://miss103.iheart.com
Profile: WMSI-FM is a commercial station owned by iHeartMedia Inc. The format of the station is contemporary country. WMSI-FM broadcasts to Jackson, MS area at 102.9 FM.
FM RADIO STATION

WMSJ-FM 79520
Owner: The Positive Radio Network Inc.
Editorial: 1456 US Route 1, Freeport, Maine 4032
Tel: 1 207 865-3448.
Web site: http://www.positive.fm
Profile: WMSJ-FM is a non-commercial station owned by The Positive Radio Network Inc. The format of the station is contemporary Christian. WMSJ-FM broadcasts to the Freeport, ME area at 89.3 FM.
FM RADIO STATION

WMSK-AM 38062
Owner: Henson Media of Union Co. LLC
Editorial: 1339 US Highway 60 W, Morganfield, Kentucky 42437 **Tel:** 1 270 389-1550.
Email: wmsk@bellsouth.net
Web site: http://www.wmskamfm.com
Profile: WMSK-AM is a commercial station owned by Henson Media of Union Co LLC. The format of the station is country. WMSK-AM broadcasts to the Morganfield, KY area at 1550 AM.
AM RADIO STATION

WMSK-FM 63359
Owner: Henson Media, Inc.
Editorial: 1339 US Highway 60 W, Morganfield, Kentucky 42437 **Tel:** 1 270 389-1550.
Email: wmsk@bellsouth.net
Web site: http://www.wmskamfm.com
FM RADIO STATION

WMSP-AM 38029
Owner: Cumulus Media Inc.
Editorial: 1 Commerce St, Montgomery, Alabama 36104-3510 **Tel:** 1 334 240-9274.
Web site: http://www.sportsradio740.com
Profile: WMSP-AM is commercial station owned by Cumulus Media Inc. The format of the station is sports. WMSP-AM broadcasts to the Montgomery, AL area at 740 AM.
AM RADIO STATION

WMSR-AM 36305
Owner: Clutter(Rob)
Editorial: 1030 Oakdale St, Manchester, Tennessee 37355 **Tel:** 1 931 728-3526.
Email: wmsr@thunder1320.com
Web site: http://www.thunder1320.com
Profile: WMSR-AM is a commercial station owned by Rob Clutter. The format of the station is talk. WMSR-AM broadcasts to the Manchester, TN area at 1320 AM.
AM RADIO STATION

WMST-AM 38063
Owner: Gateway Radio Works Inc.
Editorial: 22 W Main St, Mount Sterling, Kentucky 40353-1314 **Tel:** 1 859 498-1150.
Web site: http://www.wmstradio.com
Profile: WMST-AM is a commercial station owned by Gateway Radio Works Inc. The format of the station is adult standards. WMST-AM broadcasts to the Lexington, KY area at 1150 AM.
AM RADIO STATION

WMSU-FM 44040
Owner: URBan Radio Broadcasting, LLC
Editorial: 608 Yellow Jacket Dr, Starkville, Mississippi 39759 **Tel:** 1 662 338-5424.
Web site: http://www.power92jamz.net
Profile: WMSU-FM is a commercial station owned by URBan Radio Broadcasting, LLC. The format of the station is urban contemporary. WMSU-FM broadcasts to the Starkville, MS area at a frequency of 92.1 FM.
FM RADIO STATION

WMSX-FM 46750
Owner: Townsquare Media, LLC
Editorial: 14 Lafayette Sq Ste 1200, Buffalo, New York 14203-1912 **Tel:** 1 716 856-3550.
Web site: http://mix96buffalo.com
Profile: WMSX-FM is a commercial station owned by Townsquare Media, LLC. The format of the station is hot adult contemporary. WMSX-FM broadcasts to the Buffalo, NY area on 96.1 FM.
FM RADIO STATION

WMTA-AM 519733
Owner: Faith Broadcasting Company
Editorial: 1 WMTA Drive, Central City, Kentucky 42330 **Tel:** 1 270 754-1380.
Email: sales@faithmusicmissions.org
Web site: http://www.faith1180.com
Profile: WMTA-AM is a non-commercial station owned by Faith Broadcasting Company. The format of the station is gospel music. WMTA-AM broadcasts to the Central City, KY area at 1380 AM.
AM RADIO STATION

WMT-AM 38064
Owner: iHeartMedia Inc.
Editorial: 600 Old Marion Rd NE, Cedar Rapids, Iowa 52402-2159 **Tel:** 1 319 395-0530.
Email: newsroom@wmtradio.com
Web site: http://www.wmtradio.com
Profile: WMT-AM is a commercial station owned by iHeartMedia Inc. The format of the station is news and talk. WMT-AM broadcasts to the Cedar Rapids, IA area at 600 AM.
AM RADIO STATION

WMTC-AM 38902
Owner: Kentucky Mountain Holiness Assoc.
Editorial: 1036 Highway 541, Jackson, Kentucky 41339-9434 **Tel:** 1 606 666-5006.
Email: studio@mountaingospel.org
Web site: http://www.mountaingospel.org
Profile: WMTC-AM is a commercial station owned by Kentucky Mountain Holiness Assoc. The format of the station is gospel. WMTC-AM broadcasts to the Lexington, KY area at 730 AM.
AM RADIO STATION

WMTC-FM 46241
Owner: Kentucky Mountain Holiness Assoc.
Editorial: 1036 Highway 541, Jackson, Kentucky 41339-9434 **Tel:** 1 606 666-5006.
Email: studio@mountaingospel.org
Web site: http://www.mountaingospel.org
Profile: WMTC-FM is a commercial station owned by Kentucky Mountain Holiness Assoc. The format of the station is gospel music. WMTC-FM broadcasts to the Lexington, KY area at 99.9 FM.
FM RADIO STATION

WMTD-AM 38518
Owner: MountainPlex Media, LLC
Editorial: 211 Ballengee St, Hinton, West Virginia 25951-2318 **Tel:** 1 304 466-1380.
Web site: http://www.radioam1380.com
Profile: WMTD-AM is a commercial station owned by MountainPlex Media, LLC. The format of the station is classic hits music. WMTD-AM broadcasts to the Metro Hinton, WV area at 1380 AM.
AM RADIO STATION

WMTD-FM 45876
Owner: MountainPlex Media II, LLC
Editorial: 415 2nd Ave, Hinton, West Virginia 25951-2427 **Tel:** 1 304 466-1380.
Web site: http://www.theticket102.com
Profile: WMTD-FM is a commercial station owned by MountainPlex Media II, LLC. The format of the station is sports. WMTD-FM broadcasts to the Beckley, WV area at 102.3 FM.
FM RADIO STATION

WMTK-FM 40540
Owner: Vermont Broadcast Associates Inc.
Editorial: 1303 Concord Ave, Saint Johnsbury, Vermont 5819 **Tel:** 1 603 444-5106.
Email: info@notchfm.com
Web site: http://www.notchfm.com
Profile: WMTK-FM is a commercial station owned by Vermont Broadcast Associates Inc. The format of the station is classic hits. WMTK-FM broadcasts to the Burlington, VT area at 106.3 FM.
FM RADIO STATION

WMTL-AM 38721
Owner: Heritage Media of Kentucky Inc
Editorial: 2160 Brandenburg Rd, Leitchfield, Kentucky 42754 **Tel:** 1 270 259-5692.
Email: info@k105.com
Web site: http://www.k105.com
Profile: WMTL-AM is a commercial station owned by Heritage Media of Kentucky Inc. The station broadcasts at a frequency of 870 AM to the Leitchfield, KY area. The format of the station is country.
AM RADIO STATION

WMTM-AM 38065
Owner: Colquitt Broadcasting Co., LLC
Editorial: 100 Wmtm Rd, Moultrie, Georgia 31788-4104 **Tel:** 1 229 985-1300.
Profile: WMTM-AM is a commercial station owned by Colquitt Broadcasting Co., LLC. The format of the station is news and talk. WMTM-AM broadcasts to the Moultrie, GA, area at 1300 AM.
AM RADIO STATION

WMTM-FM 45388
Owner: Colquitt Broadcasting Co., LLC
Editorial: 100 Wmtm Rd, Moultrie, Georgia 31788-4104 **Tel:** 1 229 985-1300.
Web site: http://www.cruisin94.com
Profile: WMTM-FM is a commercial station owned by Colquitt Broadcasting Co., LLC. The format of the station is classic hits. WMTM-FM broadcasts to the Moultrie, GA area at 93.9 FM.
FM RADIO STATION

WMTN-AM 38066
Owner: Radio Acquisition Corp.
Editorial: 510 W Economy Rd, Morristown, Tennessee 37814-3223 **Tel:** 1 423 586-9101.
Web site: http://www.wmtnradio.com
Profile: WMTN-AM is a commercial station owned by Radio Acquisition Corp. The format of the station is classic country music. WMTN-AM broadcasts to the Morristown, TN area at 1300 AM.
AM RADIO STATION

WMTR-AM 39271
Owner: Beasley Broadcast Group
Editorial: 55 Horsehill Rd, Cedar Knolls, New Jersey 07927-2003 **Tel:** 1 973 538-1250.
Web site: http://www.wmtram.com
Profile: WMTR-AM is a commercial station owned by Beasley Broadcast Group. The format of the station is oldies. WMTR-AM broadcasts to the Cedar Knolls, NJ area at 1250 AM.
AM RADIO STATION

WMTR-FM 40339
Owner: Nobco Inc.
Editorial: 303 1/2 N Defiance St, Archbold, Ohio 43502-1193 **Tel:** 1 419 445-9050.
Email: wmtr@rtecexpress.net
Web site: http://www.961wmtr.com
Profile: WMTR-FM is a commercial station owned by Nobco Inc. The format of the station is classic rock. WMTR-FM broadcasts to the Archbold, OH area at 96.1 FM.
FM RADIO STATION

WMTT-FM 41791
Owner: Europa Communications, Inc.
Editorial: 734 Chemung St, Horseheads, New York 14845-2289 **Tel:** 1 607 795-0795.
Email: info@equinoxbroadcasting.com
Web site: http://www.95themet.com/about.html
Profile: WMTT-FM is a commercial station owned by Europa Communications, Inc. The format of the station is classic rock. WMTT-FM broadcasts to the Horseheads, NY area at 94.7 FM.
FM RADIO STATION

WMTX-FM 46004
Owner: iHeartMedia Inc.
Editorial: 4002 W Gandy Blvd, Tampa, Florida 33611-3410 **Tel:** 1 813 832-1000.
Web site: http://www.tampabaysmix.com
Profile: WMTX-FM is a commercial station owned by iHeartMedia Inc. The format of the station is hot adult contemporary. WMTX-FM broadcasts to the Tampa and St. Petersburg, FL areas at 100.7 FM.
FM RADIO STATION

WMTY-FM 45113
Owner: Cumulus Media Inc.
Tel: 1 423 337-5025.
Profile: WLOD-FM is a commercial station owned by Cumulus Media Inc. The format of the station is classic rock. WLOD-FM broadcasts to the Sweetwater, TN area at 98.3 FM.
FM RADIO STATION

WMUB-FM 40542
Owner: Cincinnati Public Radio Inc.
Editorial: 1223 Central Pkwy, Cincinnati, Ohio 45214-2812 **Tel:** 1 513 352-9185.
Email: wmub@cinradio.org
Web site: http://www.wmub.org
Profile: WMUB-FM is a non-commercial station owned by Cincinnati Public Radio Inc. The format of the station is news and talk. WMUB-FM broadcasts to the Cincinnati area at 88.5 FM.
FM RADIO STATION

WMUF-FM 46297
Owner: Benton-Weatherford Broadcasting Inc. of Tennessee
Editorial: 110 India Rd, Paris, Tennessee 38242-7565 **Tel:** 1 731 644-9455.
Email: news@wmufradio.com
Web site: http://www.wmufradio.com/wmuf-fm.html
Profile: WMUF-FM is a commercial station owned by Benton-Weatherford Broadcasting Inc. of Tennessee. The format of the station is classic and contemporary country music. WMUF-FM broadcasts to the Nashville, TN area at 104.7 FM.
FM RADIO STATION

WMUH-FM 85959
Owner: Muhlenberg College
Editorial: 2400 Chew St, Allentown, Pennsylvania 18104-5564 **Tel:** 1 484 664-3239.
Email: wmuh@muhlenberg.edu
Web site: http://www.muhlenberg.edu/wmuh
Profile: WMUH-FM is a non-commercial college station owned by Muhlenberg College. The format of the station is variety. WMUH-FM broadcasts to the Allentown, PA area at 91.7 FM.
FM RADIO STATION

WMUM-FM 43927
Owner: Georgia Public Broadcasting
Editorial: 260 14th St NW, Atlanta, Georgia 30318 **Tel:** 1 404 685-2548.
Email: ask@gpb.org
Web site: http://www.gpb.org
Profile: WMUM-FM is a non-commercial station owned by Georgia Public Broadcasting. The format of the station is news, classical and jazz music. WMUM-FM broadcasts to the Atlanta area at 89.7 FM.
FM RADIO STATION

WMUS-FM 42839
Owner: iHeartMedia Inc.
Editorial: 3565 Green St, Norton Shores, Michigan 49444-3875 **Tel:** 1 231 733-2600.
Web site: http://www.107mus.com
Profile: WMUS-FM is a commercial station owned by iHeartMedia Inc. The format of the station is classic country. WMUS-FM broadcasts to the Muskegon, MI area at 107.9 FM.
FM RADIO STATION

WMUV-FM 42631
Owner: Chesapeake-Portsmouth Broadcasting Corp.
Editorial: The Salem Centre, 7235 Bonneval Rd., Jacksonville, Florida 32256 **Tel:** 1 904 641-9626.
Web site: http://ilovethepromise.com/web
Profile: WMUV-FM is a commercial station owned by Chesapeake-Portsmouth Broadcasting Corp. The format of the station is Christian AC. WMUV-FM broadcasts to the Jacksonville, FL and Southern Georgia areas at 100.7 FM.
FM RADIO STATION

WMUZ-FM 46834
Owner: Crawford Broadcasting Co.
Editorial: 12300 Radio Pl, Detroit, Michigan 48228 **Tel:** 1 313 272-3434.
Email: station@wmuz.com
Web site: http://www.wmuz.com
Profile: WMUZ-FM is a commercial station owned by Crawford Broadcasting Co. The format of the station is religious/Christian talk. WMUZ-FM broadcasts to the Detroit area at 103.5 FM.
FM RADIO STATION

WMVA-AM 35986
Owner: Martinsville Media, Inc.
Editorial: 1129 Chatham Rd, Martinsville, Virginia 24112-2149 **Tel:** 1 276 632-2152.
Email: news@martinsvilledaily.com
Web site: http://martinsvillemedia.com
Profile: WMVA-AM is a commercial station owned by Martinsville Media, Inc. The format of the station is news and talk. WMVA-AM broadcasts to the Martinsville, VA area at 1450 AM.
AM RADIO STATION

WMVB-AM 35624
Owner: Quinn Broadcasting Inc.
Editorial: 4369 S Lincoln Ave, Vineland, New Jersey 08361-7757 **Tel:** 1 609 233-7162.
Email: cartabrava2@aol.com
Web site: http://www.labrav1440.com
Profile: WMVB-AM is a commercial station owned by Quinn Broadcasting Inc.. The format of the station is news talk. WMVB-AM broadcasts to the Millville, NJ area at 1440 AM.
AM RADIO STATION

WMVE-FM 513502
Owner: Commonwealth Public Broadcasting
Editorial: 23 Sesame St, Richmond, Virginia 23235 **Tel:** 1 804 320-1301.
Email: webmaster@ideastations.org
Web site: http://www.ideastations.org/radio
Profile: WMVE-FM is a non-commerical station owned by Commonwealth Public Broadcasting. The format for the station is news, classical and jazz. WMVE-FM broadcasts to the Richmond, VA, area at 90.1 FM. This station does not accept PSAs.
FM RADIO STATION

WMVG-AM 38069
Owner: Beasley(W.R.)
Editorial: 1250 W Charlton St, Milledgeville, Georgia 31061-2600 **Tel:** 1 478 452-0586.
Email: mail@country102fm.com
Web site: http://www.country102fm.com
Profile: WMVG-AM is a commercial station owned by W.R. Beasley. The format of the station is sports. WMVG-AM broadcasts to the Milledgeville, GA area at 1450 AM.
AM RADIO STATION

WMVL-FM 40805
Owner: Vilkie Communications Inc.
Editorial: 16271 Conneaut Lake Rd Ste 102, Meadville, Pennsylvania 16335-3814 **Tel:** 1 814 337-8440.
Email: wmvl@zoominternet.net
Web site: http://www.cool1017online.com
Profile: WMVL-FM is a commercial station owned by Vilkie Communications Inc. The format of the station is oldies. WMVL-FM broadcasts to the Meadville, PA area at 101.7 FM.
FM RADIO STATION

WMVN-FM 79631
Owner: Wolf Radio, Inc.
Editorial: 401 W Kirkpatrick St, Syracuse, New York 13204-1305 **Tel:** 1 315 472-0222.
Email: programming@movin100.com
Web site: http://www.movin100.com
Profile: WMVN-FM is a commercial station owned by Wolf Radio, Inc. The format of the station is rhythmic contemporary/R&B. WMVN-FM broadcasts to the Syracuse, NY area at 100.3 FM.
FM RADIO STATION

WMVO-AM 38895
Owner: BAS Broadcasting
Editorial: 17421 Coshocton Rd, Mount Vernon, Ohio 43050-9256 **Tel:** 1 740 397-1000.
Web site: http://www.wmvo.com
Profile: WMVO-AM is a commercial station owned by BAS Broadcasting. The format of the station is Oldies. WMVO-AM broadcasts to the Mount Vernon, OH, area at 1300 AM.
AM RADIO STATION

WMVP-AM 36619
Owner: Walt Disney Co.
Editorial: 190 N State St Fl 7, Chicago, Illinois 60601-3310 **Tel:** 1 312 980-1000.
Web site: http://www.espn.go.com/chicago/radio
Profile: WMVP-AM is a commercial station owned by Walt Disney Co. The format of the station is sports. WMVP-AM broadcasts to the Chicago area at 1000 AM.
AM RADIO STATION

WMVR-FM 45391
Owner: Dean Miller Broadcasting Corp.
Editorial: 2929 W Russell Rd, Sidney, Ohio 45365 **Tel:** 1 937 492-1270.
Email: onair@hits1055.com
Web site: http://www.hits1055.com
Profile: WMVR-FM is a commercial station owned by Dean Miller Broadcasting Corp. The format of the station is hot adult contemporary music. WMVR-FM broadcasts to the Sidney, OH area at 105.5 FM.
FM RADIO STATION

WMVV-FM 42713
Owner: Life Radio Ministries Inc.
Editorial: 100 S Hill St, Ste 100, Griffin, Georgia 30223 **Tel:** 1 770 229-2020.
Email: contactus@newlife.fm
Web site: http://www.wmvv.com
Profile: WMVV-FM is a non-commercial station owned by Life Radio Ministries Inc. The format of the

station is religious programming. WMVV-FM broadcasts to the Griffin, GA area at 90.7 FM.
FM RADIO STATION

WMVW-FM 687771
Editorial: 100 S Hill St Ste 100, Griffin, Georgia 30223-3400 **Tel:** 1 770 229-2020.
Web site: http://www.wmvv.com
Profile: WMVW-FM is a non-commercial station owned by Life Radio Ministries Inc. The format of the station is religious programming. WMVW-FM broadcasts to the Peachtree City, GA area at 90.7 FM.
FM RADIO STATION

WMWK-FM 44099
Owner: Family Stations Inc.
Editorial: 13 Fairlane Dr, Joliet, Illinois 60435-6483 **Tel:** 1 414 964-9794.
Email: wmwkfm@aol.com
Web site: http://www.familyradio.com
Profile: WMWK-FM is a non-commercial station owned by Family Stations Inc. The format of the station is religious programming. WMWK-FM broadcasts to the Milwaukee area at 88.1 FM.
FM RADIO STATION

WMWM-FM 43175
Owner: Salem State College
Editorial: 352 Lafayette St, Salem, Massachusetts 01970-5348 **Tel:** 1 978 542-8501.
Email: wmwmsalem@gmail.com
Web site: http://www.wmwmsalem.com
Profile: WMWM-FM is a non-commercial station owned by Salem State College. The format of the station is variety. WMWM-FM broadcasts to the Salem, MA area at 91.7 FM.
FM RADIO STATION

WMWV-FM 45900
Owner: Mt. Washington Radio & Gramophone LLC
Editorial: 2 Common Ct Unit A30, North Conway, New Hampshire 03860-5400 **Tel:** 1 603 356-8870.
Email: news@wmwv.com
Web site: http://www.wmwv.com
Profile: WMWV-FM is a commercial station owned by Mt. Washington Radio & Gramophone LLC. The format of the station is adult album alternative. WMWV-FM broadcasts to the North Conway, NH area at 93.5 FM.
FM RADIO STATION

WMWX-FM 429206
Owner: Spryex Communications Inc.
Editorial: 5114 Princeton-Glendale Road, Hamilton, Ohio 45011 **Tel:** 1 513 481-8890.
Email: classx@classxradio.com
Web site: http://classxradio.com
Profile: WMWX-FM is a non-commercial station owned by Spryex Communications Inc. The format of the station is classic rock and adult album alternative. WMWX-FM broadcasts to the Hamilton, OH area on 88.9 FM.
FM RADIO STATION

WMXA-FM 41798
Owner: iHeartMedia Inc.
Editorial: 915 Veterans Pkwy, Opelika, Alabama 36801-3367 **Tel:** 1 334 745-4656.
Web site: http://www.mix967online.com
Profile: WMXA-FM is a commercial station owned by iHeartMedia Inc. The format of the station is hot adult contemporary. WMXA-FM broadcasts to the Opelika, AL area at 96.7 FM.
FM RADIO STATION

WMXB-AM 38999
Owner: Lawson of Tuscaloosa, Inc.
Editorial: 601 Greensboro Ave, Tuscaloosa, Alabama 35401-1749 **Tel:** 1 205 345-4787.
Email: jwlawson@bellsouth.net
Profile: WMXB-AM is a commercial station owned by Lawson of Tuscaloosa, Inc. The format of the station is urban AC. WMXB-AM broadcasts to the Tuscaloosa, AL area at 1280 AM.
AM RADIO STATION

WMXC-FM 45310
Owner: iHeartMedia Inc.
Editorial: 555 Broadcast Dr Fl 3, Mobile, Alabama 36606-2936 **Tel:** 1 251 450-0100.
Email: news@ccmobile.com
Web site: http://www.litemix.com
Profile: WMXC-FM is a commercial station owned by iHeartMedia Inc. The format for the station is adult contemporary. WMXC-FM broadcasts to the Mobile, AL area at 99.9 FM.
FM RADIO STATION

WMXD-FM 42327
Owner: iHeartMedia Inc.
Editorial: 27675 Halsted Rd, Farmington Hills, Michigan 48331-3511 **Tel:** 1 248 324-5800.
Web site: http://www.mix923fm.com
Profile: WMXD-FM is a commercial station owned by iHeartMedia Inc. The format of the station is urban adult contemporary. WMXD-FM broadcasts to the Detroit area at 92.3 FM.
FM RADIO STATION

WMXE-FM 46555
Owner: LM Communications, Inc.
Editorial: 100 Kanawha Ter, Saint Albans, West Virginia 25177 **Tel:** 1 304 722-3308.
Email: mixstudio@wmxe.net
Web site: http://www.wmxe.net
Profile: WMXE-FM is a commercial station owned by LM Communications, Inc. The format of the station is

classic hits. WMXE-FM broadcasts to South Charleston, WV and surrounding communities at 100.9 FM.
FM RADIO STATION

WMXF-AM 39122
Owner: iHeartMedia Inc.
Editorial: 13 Summerlin Dr, Asheville, North Carolina 28806-2800 **Tel:** 1 828 257-2700.
Web site: http://www.am1400thepeak.com
Profile: WMXF-AM is a commercial station owned by iHeartMedia Inc. The format of the station is news and talk. WMXF-AM broadcasts to the Asheville, NC area at 1400 AM.
AM RADIO STATION

WMXH-FM 46153
Owner: Hayden Hamilton Media Strategies
Editorial: 1057 US Highway 211 W, Luray, Virginia 22835-5245 **Tel:** 1 540 743-5167.
Profile: WMXH-FM is a commercial station owned by Hayden Hamilton Media Strategies. The format for the station is adult standards. WMXH-FM broadcasts to the Harrisonburg, VA area at 105.7 FM.
FM RADIO STATION

WMXI-FM 43393
Owner: Rainey Broadcasting Inc.
Editorial: 7501 Highway 49 North, Hattiesburg, Mississippi 39402 **Tel:** 1 601 261-0898.
Email: zoo107@bellsouth.net
Web site: http://www.wmxi.com/
FM RADIO STATION

WMXJ-FM 40946
Owner: Entercom Communications Corp.
Editorial: 20450 NW 2nd Ave, Miami, Florida 33169-2505 **Tel:** 1 305 521-5100.
Web site: http://www.thebeachmiami.com
Profile: WMXJ-FM is a commercial station owned by Entercom Communications Corp. The format of the station is classic hits. WMXJ-FM broadcasts to the Miami area at 102.7 FM.
FM RADIO STATION

WMXL-FM 45329
Owner: iHeartMedia Inc.
Editorial: 2601 Nicholasville Rd, Lexington, Kentucky 40503-3307 **Tel:** 1 859 422-1000.
Web site: http://www.wmxl.com
Profile: WMXL-FM is a commercial station owned by iHeartMedia Inc. The format of the station is hot adult contemporary. WMXL-FM broadcasts to the Lexington, KY area at 94.5 FM.
FM RADIO STATION

WMXM-FM 40549
Owner: Lake Forest College
Editorial: 555 N Sheridan Rd, Lake Forest, Illinois 60045-2338 **Tel:** 1 847 735-5220.
Web site: http://www.wmxm.org
Profile: WMXM-FM is a non-commercial station owned by Lake Forest College. The format of the station is variety. WMXM-FM broadcasts to the Lake Forest, IL area at 88.9 FM.
FM RADIO STATION

WMXN-FM 40824
Owner: KEA Radio Inc.
Editorial: 19784 John T Reid Pkwy, Scottsboro, Alabama 35768-7909 **Tel:** 1 256 259-2341.
Email: production@wkeafm.com
Web site: http://www.1017thestorm.com
Profile: WMXN-FM is a commercial station owned by KEA Radio Inc. The format of the station is classic hits. WMXN-FM broadcasts to the Scottsboro, AL area at 101.7 FM.
FM RADIO STATION

WMXO-FM 45053
Owner: Sound Communications, LLC
Editorial: 231 N Union St, Olean, New York 14760-2663 **Tel:** 1 716 375-1015.
Email: mixtraffic@roadrunner.com
Web site: http://www.themixwmxo.com
Profile: WMXO-FM is a commercial station owned by Sound Communications, LLC. The format of the station is hot adult contemporary music. WMXO-FM broadcasts to the Olean, NY area at 101.5 FM.
FM RADIO STATION

WMXQ-FM 41004
Owner: Backyard Broadcasting
Editorial: 800 E 29th St, Muncie, Indiana 47302-5765 **Tel:** 1 765 378-2080.
Web site: http://www.maxrocks.net
Profile: WMXQ-FM is a commercial station owned by Backyard Broadcasting. The format of the station is classic rock. WMXQ-FM broadcasts to the Muncie, IN area on 93.5 FM.
FM RADIO STATION

WMXS-FM 46301
Owner: Cumulus Media Inc.
Editorial: 1 Commerce St, Montgomery, Alabama 36104-3510 **Tel:** 1 334 240-9274.
Web site: http://www.mix103.com
Profile: WMXS-FM is a commercial station owned by Cumulus Media Inc. The format of the station is Lite Rock/Lite AC. WMXS-FM broadcasts to the Montgomery, AL area at 103.3 FM.
FM RADIO STATION

WMXT-FM 41701
Owner: Cumulus Media Inc.
Editorial: 2014 N Irby St, Florence, South Carolina 29501 **Tel:** 1 843 661-5000.
Web site: http://www.1021thefox.com
Profile: WMXT-FM is a commercial station owned by Cumulus Media Inc. The format of the station is classic rock music. WMXT-FM broadcasts to the Florence, SC area at 102.1 FM.
FM RADIO STATION

WMXU-FM 45543
Owner: Cumulus Media Inc.
Editorial: 200 6th St N Ste 205, Columbus, Mississippi 39701-4552 **Tel:** 1 662 327-1183.
Web site: http://www.mymix1061.com
Profile: WMXU-FM is a commercial station owned by Cumulus Media Inc. The format is adult contemporary and urban contemporary music. The station airs in the Columbus, MS area.
FM RADIO STATION

WMXV-FM 41782
Owner: URBan Radio Broadcasting, LLC
Editorial: 509 N Main St, Tuscumbia, Alabama 35674 **Tel:** 1 256 383-2525.
Email: info@urbanradio.fm
Web site: http://www.wmxv1015.com
Profile: WMXV-FM is a commercial station owned by URBan Radio Broadcasting, LLC. The format of the station is urban contemporary. WMXV-FM broadcasts to the St. Joseph, TN area at 101.5 FM.
FM RADIO STATION

WMXW-FM 40974
Owner: iHeart Media Inc.
Editorial: 320 N Jensen Rd, Vestal, New York 13850-2111 **Tel:** 1 607 584-5800.
Web site: http://mix1033fm.iheart.com
Profile: WMXW-FM is a commercial station owned by iHeart Media Inc. The format of the station is adult contemporary. WMXW-FM broadcasts to the Binghamton, NY area at 103.3 FM.
FM RADIO STATION

WMXX-FM 45392
Owner: Hunt(Gerald W.)
Editorial: 1 Radio Park Dr, Jackson, Tennessee 38305-4124 **Tel:** 1 731 427-9611.
Email: kool103fm@yahoo.com
Web site: http://www.kool103.com
Profile: WMXX-FM is a commercial station owned by Gerald W. Hunt. The format of the station is oldies. WMXX-FM broadcasts to the Jackson, TN area at 103.1 FM.
FM RADIO STATION

WMXY-FM 45279
Owner: iHeartMedia Inc.
Editorial: 7461 South Ave, Youngstown, Ohio 44512-5789 **Tel:** 1 330 965-0057.
Web site: http://www.mix989.com
Profile: WMXY-FM is a commercial station owned by iHeartMedia Inc. The format of the station is hot adult contemporary music. WKBN-FM broadcasts in the Youngstown, OH area at 98.9 FM.
FM RADIO STATION

WMXZ-FM 601515
Owner: Apex Broadcasting Inc.
Editorial: 2294 Clements Ferry Rd, Charleston, South Carolina 29492-7729 **Tel:** 1 843 972-1100.
Web site: http://www.mix96live.com
Profile: WMXZ-FM is a commercial station owned by Apex Broadcasting Inc. The format of the station is Top 40/CHR. WMXZ-FM broadcasts to the Charleston, SC area at 95.9 FM. The station's slogan is, "The Best Music Mix."
FM RADIO STATION

WMYB-FM 70501
Owner: Alpha Media
Editorial: 1016 Ocala St, Myrtle Beach, South Carolina 29577-8007 **Tel:** 1 843 448-1041.
Web site: http://www.star921.net
Profile: WMYB-FM is a commercial station owned by Alpha Media. The format for the station is hot adult contemporary. WMYB-FM broadcasts to the Myrtle Beach, SC area at 92.1 FM.
FM RADIO STATION

WMYF-AM 38866
Owner: iHeartMedia Inc.
Editorial: 815 Lafayette Rd, Portsmouth, New Hampshire 03801-5406 **Tel:** 1 603 436-7300.
Web site: http://www.wmyf.com
Profile: WMYF-AM is a commercial station owned by iHeartMedia Inc. The format of the station is adult standards. WMYF-AM broadcasts to the Portsmouth, NH area at 1380 AM.
AM RADIO STATION

WMYI-FM 40948
Owner: iHeart Media Inc.
Editorial: 101 N Main St Ste 1000, Greenville, South Carolina 29601-4852 **Tel:** 1 864 242-4660.
Web site: http://www.my1025.com/main.html
Profile: WMYI-FM is a commercial station owned by iHeart Media Inc. The format of the station is adult contemporary music. WMYI-FM broadcasts to Greenville, SC at 102.5 FM.
FM RADIO STATION

WMYJ-AM 38039
Owner: Hoosier AM/FM LLC
Editorial: 1639 Burton Ln, Martinsville, Indiana 46151-3004 **Tel:** 1 765 342-3394.
Email: webmaster@wcbk.com
Profile: WMYJ-AM is a commercial station owned by Hoosier AM/FM LLC. The format of the station is solid gospel. WMYJ-AM broadcasts to the Bloomington, IN area at 1540 AM.
AM RADIO STATION

WMYK-FM 232071
Owner: Hoosier AM/FM LLC
Editorial: 671 E 400 S, Kokomo, Indiana 46902 **Tel:** 1 765 455-9850.
Email: kokomoradiotraffic@att.net
Web site: http://www.rock985.com
Profile: WMYK-FM is a commercial station owned by Hoosier AM/FM LLC. The format of the station is rock music. WMYK-FM broadcasts to the Kokomo, IN area at 98.5 FM.
FM RADIO STATION

WMYL-FM 46305
Owner: Clinton Broadcasters
Editorial: 119 Pine Rd, Clinton, Tennessee 37716-2025 **Tel:** 1 865 457-1380.
Email: office@merlefm.com
Web site: http://www.merlefm.com
Profile: WMYL-FM is a commercial station owned by Clinton Broadcasters. The format of the station is classic country. WMYL-FM broadcasts to the Clinton, TN area at 96.7 FM.
FM RADIO STATION

WMYN-AM 35540
Owner: Mayo Broadcasting Corporation
Editorial: 1203 Harris St, Eden, North Carolina 27288-6321 **Tel:** 1 336 427-9696.
Web site: http://www.wloewmyn.com
Profile: WMYN-AM is owned by Mayo Broadcasting Corporation. The format of the station is religious programming, news and talk. WMYN-AM broadcasts to the Greensboro-Winston Salem, NC area at 1420 AM.
AM RADIO STATION

WMYR-AM 36349
Owner: Gulf Breeze Radio License LLC
Editorial: 1061 Collier Center Way Ste 9, Naples, Florida 34110-8403 **Tel:** 1 239 631-2745.
Web site: http://relevantradio.com
Profile: WMYR-AM is a Catholic Faith station titled Relevant Radio owned by iHeartMedia. WMYR-AM broadcasts to the Fort Myers, FL area at 1410 AM.
AM RADIO STATION

WMYX-FM 45393
Owner: Entercom Communications Corp.
Editorial: 11800 W Grange Ave, Hales Corners, Wisconsin 53130 **Tel:** 1 414 529-1250.
Web site: http://www.991wmyx.com
Profile: WMYX-FM is a commercial station owned by Entercom Communications Corp. The format of the station is hot adult contemporary music. WMYX-FM broadcasts to the Milwaukee area at 99.1 FM.
FM RADIO STATION

WMYY-FM 46372
Owner: Capital Media Corporation
Editorial: 30 Park Ave, Cohoes, New York 12047-3330 **Tel:** 1 518 237-1330.
Web site: http://www.aliveradionetwork.com
Profile: WMYY-FM is a commercial station owned by Capital Media Corporation. The format of the station is religious programming. WMYY-FM broadcasts to the Schenectady, NY area at 97.3 FM.
FM RADIO STATION

WMZK-FM 45394
Owner: Quicksilver Broadcasting, LLC
Editorial: 120 S Mill St, Merrill, Wisconsin 54452 **Tel:** 1 715 536-6262.
Email: news@z104rocks.com
Web site: http://www.z104rocks.com
Profile: WMZK-FM is a commercial station owned by Quicksilver Broadcasting, LLC. The format of the station is rock. WMZK-FM broadcasts to the Merrill, WI area at 104.1.
FM RADIO STATION

WMZQ-FM 43044
Owner: iHeartMedia Inc.
Editorial: 1801 Rockville Pike Fl 5, Rockville, Maryland 20852-1633 **Tel:** 1 240 747-2700.
Web site: http://wmzq.iheart.com
Profile: WMZQ-FM is a commercial station owned by iHeartMedia Inc. The format of the station is country. WMZQ-FM broadcasts to the Washington, D.C. area at 98.7 FM.
FM RADIO STATION

WNAE-AM 38072
Owner: Radio Partners LLC
Editorial: 310 2nd Ave, Warren, Pennsylvania 16365 **Tel:** 1 814 723-1310.
Email: newsroom@kibcoradio.com
Web site: http://www.kibcoradio.com
Profile: WNAE-AM is a commercial station owned by Radio Partners LLC. The format of the station is news, talk and sports. WNAE-AM broadcasts to the Warren, PA area at 1310 AM.
AM RADIO STATION

WNAH-AM 35541
Owner: Hermitage Broadcasting Corp.
Editorial: 44 Music Sq E, Nashville, Tennessee 37203-4309 **Tel:** 1 615 254-7611.
Web site: http://www.wnah.com/
Profile: WNAH-AM is a commercial station owned by Hermitage Broadcasting Corp. The format of the station is Christian and religious talk. WNAH-AM broadcasts to the Nashville, TN area at 1360 AM.
AM RADIO STATION

WNAM-AM 38073
Owner: Cumulus Media Inc.
Editorial: 491 S Washburn St Ste 400, Oshkosh, Wisconsin 54904-6733 **Tel:** 1 920 426-3239.
Email: wnamstudio@gmail.com
Web site: http://www.1280wnam.com
Profile: WNAM-AM is a commercial station owned by Cumulus Media Inc. The format of the station is adult standards. WNAM-AM broadcasts to the Oshkosh, WI area at 1280 AM.
AM RADIO STATION

WNAP-AM 35543
Owner: GHB Broadcasting
Editorial: 2311 Old Arch Rd, Norristown, Pennsylvania 19401-2013 **Tel:** 1 610 272-7600.
Email: gospel@wnap1110am.com
Web site: http://www.mygospelhighway11.com
Profile: WNAP-AM is a commercial station owned by GHB Broadcasting. The format of the station is gospel music. WNAP-AM broadcasts to the Norristown, PA area at 1110 AM.
AM RADIO STATION

WNAT-AM 38315
Owner: First Natchez Corp.
Editorial: 2 Oferrall St, Natchez, Mississippi 39120-3000 **Tel:** 1 601 442-4895.
Web site: http://www.listenupyall.com
Profile: WNAT-AM is a commercial station owned by First Natchez Corp. The format of the station is news, talk and sports. WNAT-AM broadcasts to the Natchez, MS area at 1450 AM. The station does not accept press submissions, requests, and inquiries.
AM RADIO STATION

WNAU-AM 35960
Owner: MPM Investment Group
Editorial: 204 Moss Hill Dr, New Albany, Mississippi 38652-3400 **Tel:** 1 662 534-8133.
Email: info@wnau1470.com
Web site: http://wnau1470.com
Profile: WNAU-AM is a commercial station owned by MPM Investment Group. The format of the station is oldies. WNAU-AM broadcasts to the New Albany, MS area at 1470 AM.
AM RADIO STATION

WNAV-AM 35544
Owner: Sajak Broadcasting Corp.
Editorial: 236 Admiral Dr, Annapolis, Maryland 21401-3123 **Tel:** 1 410 263-1430.
Email: news@wnav.com
Web site: http://www.wnav.com
Profile: WNAV-AM is a commercial station owned by Sajak Broadcasting Corp. The format of the station is news, talk and adult contemporary music. WNAV-AM broadcasts to the Annapolis, MD area at 1430 AM.
AM RADIO STATION

WNAW-AM 38860
Owner: Gamma Broadcasting LLC
Editorial: 466 Curran Hwy, North Adams, Massachusetts 01247-3919 **Tel:** 1 413 663-6567.
Email: wnaw@prod.com
Profile: WNAW-AM is a commercial station owned by Gamma Broadcasting LLC. The format of the station is adult contemporary. WNAW-AM broadcasts to the North Adams, MA area at 1230 AM. The station's slogan is, "Your Hometown Station."
AM RADIO STATION

WNAX-AM 38995
Owner: Saga Communications
Editorial: 1609 E Highway 50, Yankton, South Dakota 57078 **Tel:** 1 605 665-7442.
Email: wnax@wnax.com
Web site: http://www.wnax.com
Profile: WNAX-AM is a commercial station owned by Saga Communications. The format of the station is news, talk and sports. WNAX broadcasts in the Sioux Falls, SD area at 570 AM.
AM RADIO STATION

WNAX-FM 46322
Owner: Saga Communications
Editorial: 1609 E Highway 50, Yankton, South Dakota 57078-6406 **Tel:** 1 605 665-7442.
Email: wnax@wnax.com
Web site: http://thewolf1041.com/
Profile: WNAX-FM is a commercial station owned by Saga Communications. The format of the station is contemporary country. WNAX-FM broadcasts to the Sioux Falls, SD area at 104.1 FM.
FM RADIO STATION

WNBB-FM 217548
Owner: Coastal Carolina Radio, LLC
Tel: 1 800 608-9798.
Email: mail@bearpad.com
Profile: WNBB-FM is a commercial station owned by Coastal Carolina Radio, LLC. The format of the station is country. WNBB-FM broadcasts to the New Bern, NC area at 97.9 FM.
FM RADIO STATION

WNBF-AM 39194
Owner: Townsquare Media, Inc.
Editorial: 59 Court St, Binghamton, New York 13901-3270 **Tel:** 1 607 772-8400.
Profile: WNBF-AM is a commercial station owned by Townsquare Media, Inc. The format of the station is news and talk programming. WNBF-AM broadcasts to the Binghamton, NY area at 1290 AM.
AM RADIO STATION

WNBH-AM 36368
Owner: Hall Communications
Editorial: 888 Purchase St Unit 221, New Bedford, Massachusetts 02740-6217 **Tel:** 1 401 467-4366.
Web site: http://www.wnbhradio.com/
Profile: WNBH-AM is a commercial station owned by Hall Communications. The format of the station is sports. WNBH-AM broadcasts to the Boston area at 1340 AM.
AM RADIO STATION

WNBL-FM 40892
Owner: iHeart Media Inc.
Editorial: 100 Chestnut St Fl 17, Rochester, New York 14604-2419 **Tel:** 1 585 454-4884.
Web site: http://www.1073thebull.com/main.html
Profile: WNBL-FM is a commercial station owned by iHeart Media Inc. The format of the station is contemporary country music. WNBL-FM broadcasts to the Rochester, NY area at 107.3 FM.
FM RADIO STATION

WNBM-FM 45151
Owner: Cumulus Media Inc.
Editorial: 2 Penn Plz Fl 17, New York, New York 10121-1701 **Tel:** 1 212 613-8900.
Web site: http://www.radio1039ny.com
Profile: WNBM-FM is a commercial station owned by Cumulus Media Inc. The format of the station is urban adult contemporary music. WNBM-FM broadcasts to the Greater New York area at 103.9 FM.
FM RADIO STATION

WNBP-AM 35546
Owner: Bloomberg L.P.
Editorial: 6 Federal St Fl 2, Newburyport, Massachusetts 01950-2804 **Tel:** 1 978 462-1450.
Web site: http://www.wnbp.com
Profile: WNBP-AM is a commercial station owned by Bloomberg L.P. The format of the station is Business News. WNBP-AM broadcasts to the Newburyport, MA area at 1450 AM.
AM RADIO STATION

WNBS-AM 36473
Owner: FM Radio Licenses, LLC
Editorial: 1500 Diuguid Dr, Murray, Kentucky 42071-1669 **Tel:** 1 270 753-2400.
Email: wnbsnews@gmail.com
Web site: http://www.1340wnbs.com
Profile: WNBS-AM is a commercial station owned by FM Radio Licenses, LLC. The format of the station is news, talk and sports. WNBS-AM broadcasts in the Murray, KY area at 1340 AM.
AM RADIO STATION

WNBT-AM 38074
Owner: Allegheny Mountain Network
Editorial: 12385 Route 6, Wellsboro, Pennsylvania 16901 **Tel:** 1 570 724-1490.
Email: wnbt@ynt.net
Web site: http://www.wnbt.net
Profile: WNBT-AM is a commercial station owned by Allegheny Mountain Network. The format of the station is adult standards. WNBT-AM broadcasts to the Wellsboro, PA area at 1490 AM.
AM RADIO STATION

WNBT-FM 45395
Owner: Allegheny Mountain Network
Tel: 1 570 724-1490.
Email: wnbt@ynt.net
Web site: http://www.wnbt.net
Profile: WNBT-FM is a commercial station owned by Allegheny Mountain Network. The format of the station is adult contemporary. WNBT-FM broadcasts to the Wellsboro, PA area at 104.5 FM.
FM RADIO STATION

WNBU-FM 43027
Owner: Inner Banks Media, LLC
Editorial: 1848 W Arlington Blvd Ste 101B, Greenville, North Carolina 27834-5704 **Tel:** 1 252 672-5900.
Email: prod@ibxmedia.com
Web site: http://www.wnbufm.com
Profile: WNBU-FM is a commercial station owned by Inner Banks Media, LLC. The format of the station is talk. WNBU-FM broadcasts to the New Bern, NC area at 94.1 FM.
FM RADIO STATION

WNBY-AM 38075
Owner: Sovereign Communications LLC
Editorial: Michigan State Hwy 123 South, Newberry, Michigan 49868 **Tel:** 1 906 293-3221.
Web site: http://www.1450wnby.com
Profile: WNBY-AM is a commercial owned by Sovereign Communications LLC. The format of the station is country. WNBY-AM broadcasts to the Newberry, MI area at 1450 AM.
AM RADIO STATION

WNBY-FM 45396
Owner: Sovereign Communications LLC
Editorial: Michigan State Highway 123 South, Newberry, Michigan 49868 **Tel:** 1 906 293-3221.
Email: info@oldies93fm.com
Web site: http://www.oldies93fm.com
Profile: WNBY-FM is a commercial station owned by Sovereign Communications LLC. The format of the station is oldies. WNBY-FM broadcasts to the Newberry, MI area at 93.9 FM.
FM RADIO STATION

WNBZ-AM 38398
Owner: Mountain Communications
Editorial: 159 Santanoni Ave, Saranac Lake, New York 12983-2478 **Tel:** 1 518 891-1544.
Email: news@wnbz.com
Web site: http://www.wnbz.com
Profile: WNBZ-AM is a commercial station owned by Mountain Communications. The format of the station is adult standards music. WNBZ-AM broadcasts to the Saranac Lake, NY area at 1240 AM.
AM RADIO STATION

WNCA-AM 35545
Owner: Chatham Broadcasting Co. Inc.
Editorial: 17890 US Highway 64 W, Siler City, North Carolina 27344-1631 **Tel:** 1 919 742-2135.
Web site: http://www.beachmusic45.com/id19.html
Profile: WNCA-AM is a commercial station owned by Chatham Broadcasting Co. Inc. The format of the station is full service, featuring music, news and talk. WNCA-AM broadcasts to the Siler City, NC area at 1570 AM.
AM RADIO STATION

WNCB-FM 40921
Owner: iHeart Media Inc.
Editorial: 3100 Smoketree Ct Ste 700, Raleigh, North Carolina 27604-1052 **Tel:** 1 919 878-1500.
Web site: http://b939country.iheart.com
Profile: WNCB-FM is a commercial station owned by iHeart Media Inc. The format of the station is contemporary country. WNCB-FM broadcasts to the Raleigh, NC area at 93.9 FM.
FM RADIO STATION

WNCC-FM 45502
Owner: Georgia-Carolina Radiocasting Companies LLC
Editorial: 180 Radio Hill Rd, Franklin, North Carolina 28734 **Tel:** 1 828 524-4418.
Email: franklinradio@gacaradio.com
Web site: http://1050wfsc.com
Profile: WNCC-FM is a commercial station owned by Georgia-Carolina Radiocasting Companies LLC. The format of the station is country. WNCC-FM broadcasts to the Franklin, NC area at 96.7 FM.
FM RADIO STATION

WNCD-FM 45884
Owner: iHeartMedia Inc.
Editorial: 7461 South Ave, Youngstown, Ohio 44512-5789 **Tel:** 1 330 965-0057.
Web site: http://www.933fmthewolf.com/main.html
Profile: WNCD-FM is a commercial station owned by iHeartMedia Inc. The format of the station is rock/album-oriented rock. WNCD-FM broadcasts to the Youngstown, OH area at 93.3 FM.
FM RADIO STATION

WNCH-FM 245066
Owner: Vermont Public Radio
Editorial: 365 Troy Ave, Colchester, Vermont 5446 **Tel:** 1 802 655-9451.
Email: news@vpr.net
Web site: http://www.vpr.net
Profile: WNCH-FM is a non-commercial station owned by Vermont Public Radio. The format is classical music. The station airs at 88.1 FM in the Colcester, VT area.
FM RADIO STATION

WNCI-FM 40553
Owner: iHeartMedia Inc.
Editorial: 2323 W 5th Ave Ste 200, Columbus, Ohio 43204-4988 **Tel:** 1 614 486-6101.
Email: webmaster@wnci.com
Web site: http://www.wnci.com
Profile: WNCI-FM is a commercial station owned by iHeartMedia Inc. The format of the station is Top 40/CHR music. WNCI-FM broadcasts in the Columbus, OH area at 97.9 FM.
FM RADIO STATION

WNCL-FM 41706
Owner: Delmarva Broadcasting
Editorial: 1666 Blairs Pond Rd, Milford, Delaware 19963-5263 **Tel:** 1 302 422-7575.
Web site: http://www.cool1013.com
Profile: WNCL-FM is a commercial station owned by Delmarva Broadcasting. The format of the station is oldies. WNCL-FM broadcasts to the Milford, DE area at 101.3 FM.
FM RADIO STATION

WNCO-AM 38076
Owner: iHeartMedia Inc.
Editorial: 1400 Radio Ln, Mansfield, Ohio 44906-2525 **Tel:** 1 419 529-2211.
Web site: http://www.wncoam.com
Profile: WNCO-AM is a commercial station owned by iHeartMedia Inc. The format of the station is sports. WNCO-AM broadcasts to the Mansfield, OH area at 1340 AM.
AM RADIO STATION

WNCO-FM 45398
Owner: iHeartMedia Inc.
Editorial: 1400 Radio Ln, Mansfield, Ohio 44906-2525 **Tel:** 1 419 529-2211.
Web site: http://www.wncofm.com
Profile: WNCO-FM is a commercial station owned by iHeartMedia Inc. The format of the station is contemporary country. WNCO-FM broadcasts to the Mansfield, OH area at 101.3 FM.
FM RADIO STATION

WNCQ-FM 42090
Owner: Stephens Media Group LLC
Editorial: 1 Bridge Plz, Ste 204, Ogdensburg, New York 13669 **Tel:** 1 315 393-1220.
Web site: http://www.q1029.com
Profile: WNCQ-FM is a commercial station owned by Stephens Media Group LLC. The format of the station is contemporary country music. WNCQ-FM broadcasts to the Ogdensburg, NY area at 102.9 FM.
FM RADIO STATION

WNCS-FM 40555
Owner: Northeast Broadcasting Co.
Editorial: 169 River St, Montpelier, Vermont 5602 **Tel:** 1 802 223-2396.
Email: feedback@pointfm.com
Web site: http://www.pointfm.com
Profile: WNCS-FM is a commercial station owned by Northeast Broadcasting Co. The format of the station is adult album alternative music. WNCS-FM broadcasts to the Montpelier, VT area at 104.7 FM.
FM RADIO STATION

WNCT-AM 523322
Owner: Beasley Broadcast Group
Editorial: 2929 Radio Station Rd, Greenville, North Carolina 27834-0864 **Tel:** 1 252 757-0011.
Email: webmaster@1070wnct.com
Web site: http://beachboogieandblues.com
Profile: WNCT-FM is a commercial station owned by Beasley Broadcast Group. The format of the station is rhythmic oldies and blues. WNCT-FM broadcasts to the Greenville, NC area at 1070 AM.
AM RADIO STATION

WNCT-FM 45399
Owner: Inner Banks Media, LLC
Editorial: 2929 Radio Station Rd, Greenville, North Carolina 27834-0864 **Tel:** 1 252 355-1037.
Web site: https://www.1079wnct.com
Profile: WNCT-FM is a commercial station owned by Inner Banks Media, LLC. The format of the station is classic hits. WNCT-FM broadcasts to the Greenville, NC area at 107.9 FM. The station's slogan is, "Carolina's Greatest Hits."
FM RADIO STATION

WNCV-FM 445943
Owner: Cumulus Media Inc.
Editorial: 225 Hollywood Blvd NW, Fort Walton Beach, Florida 32548-4725 **Tel:** 1 850 243-2323.
Web site: http://www.wncv.com
Profile: WNCV-FM is a commercial station owned by Cumulus Media Inc. The format of the station is adult contemporary. The station broadcasts to the Fort Walton Beach, FL area at 93.3 FM.
FM RADIO STATION

WNCW-FM 41572
Owner: Isothermal Community College
Editorial: 286 ICC Loop Road, Spindale, North Carolina 28160 **Tel:** 1 828 287-8000.
Email: info@wncw.org
Web site: http://www.wncw.org
Profile: WNCW-FM is a non-commercial station owned by Isothermal Community College. The format of the station is adult album alternative. WNCW-FM broadcasts to the Greenville, SC area at 88.7 FM.
FM RADIO STATION

WNCX-FM 44289
Owner: CBS Radio
Editorial: 1041 Huron Rd E, Cleveland, Ohio 44115-1706 **Tel:** 1 216 861-0100.
Web site: http://www.wncx.com
Profile: WNCX-FM is a commercial station owned by CBS Radio. The format of the station is classic rock. WNCX-FM broadcasts to the Cleveland area at 98.5 FM.
FM RADIO STATION

WNCY-FM 43183
Owner: Midwest Communications Inc.
Editorial: 1420 Bellevue St, Green Bay, Wisconsin 54311-5649 **Tel:** 1 920 435-3771.
Web site: http://www.wncy.com
Profile: WNCY-FM is a commercial station owned by Midwest Communications Inc. The format of the station is contemporary country music. WNCY-FM broadcasts to the Green Bay, WI area at 100.3 FM.
FM RADIO STATION

WNDB-AM 38078
Owner: Black Crow Radio, LLC
Editorial: 126 W International Speedway Blvd, Daytona Beach, Florida 32114-4322 **Tel:** 1 386 257-1150.
Web site: http://www.newsdaytonabeach.com
Profile: WNDB-AM is a commercial station owned by Black Crow Radio, LLC. The format of the station is news/talk. WNDB-AM broadcasts to the Daytona Beach, FL area at 1150 AM.
AM RADIO STATION

WNDD-FM 70530
Owner: Ocala Broadcasting Corp. LLC
Editorial: 3602 NE 20th Pl, Ocala, Florida 34470 **Tel:** 1 352 622-9500.
Web site: http://www.windfm.com
Profile: WNDD-FM is a commercial station owned by Ocala Broadcasting Corp. LLC. The format of the station is classic rock. WNDD-FM broadcasts to the Ocala, FL area at 95.5 FM.
FM RADIO STATION

WNDE-AM 38079
Owner: iHeartMedia Inc.
Editorial: 6161 Fall Creek Rd, Indianapolis, Indiana 46220-5032 **Tel:** 1 317 257-7565.
Web site: http://foxsports975.iheart.com/
Profile: WNDE-AM is a commercial station owned by iHeartMedia Inc. The format for the station is sports. WNDE-AM broadcasts to the Indianapolis area at 1260 AM.
AM RADIO STATION

WNDH-FM 41409
Owner: iHeartMedia Inc.
Editorial: 709 N Perry St, Napoleon, Ohio 43545-1520 **Tel:** 1 419 592-8060.
Email: wndh@iheartmedia.com
Web site: http://www.wndh1031.com
Profile: WNDH-FM is a commercial station owned by iHeartMedia Inc. The format of the station is classic hits. WNDH-FM broadcasts to the Napoleon, OH area at 103.1 FM.
FM RADIO STATION

WNDI-AM 38652
Owner: JTM Broadcasting Corp.
Editorial: 556 E State Road 54, Sullivan, Indiana 47882-7701 **Tel:** 1 812 268-6322.
Profile: WNDI-AM is a commercial station owned by JTM Broadcasting Corp. The format of the station is contemporary country music. WNDI-AM broadcasts to the Sullivan, IN area at 1550 AM.
AM RADIO STATION

WNDI-FM 46005
Owner: JTM Broadcasting Corp.
Editorial: 556 E State Road 54, Sullivan, Indiana 47882-7701 **Tel:** 1 812 268-6322.
Profile: WNDI-FM is a commercial station owned by JTM Broadcasting Corp. The format of the station is country music. WNDI-FM broadcasts to the Sullivan, IN area at 95.3 FM.
FM RADIO STATION

WNDN-FM 46152
Owner: Ocala Broadcasting Corp. LLC
Editorial: 3602 NE 20th Pl, Ocala, Florida 34470 **Tel:** 1 352 622-9500.
Web site: http://www.windfm.com
Profile: WNDN-FM is a commercial station owned by Ocala Broadcasting Corp. LLC. The format of the station is classic rock. WNDN-FM broadcasts to the Ocala, FL area at 107.9 FM.
FM RADIO STATION

WNDR-AM 36806
Owner: Wolf Radio, Inc.
Editorial: 401 W Kirkpatrick St, Syracuse, New York 13204-1305 **Tel:** 1 315 472-0222.
Email: wolfdisn@twcny.rr.com
Profile: WNDR-AM is a commercial station owned by Wolf Radio, Inc. The format of the station is Classic Hits. WNDR-AM broadcasts to the Syracuse, NY area at 1340 AM.
AM RADIO STATION

WNDT-FM 43064
Owner: Ocala Broadcasting Corp. LLC
Editorial: 4020 W Newberry Rd, Ste 100, Gainesville, Florida 32607 **Tel:** 1 352 373-6644.
Email: windfm@windfm.com
Web site: http://www.windfm.com
Profile: WNDT-FM is a commercial station owned by Ocala Broadcasting Corp. LLC. The format of the station is classic rock. WNDT-FM broadcasts to the Gainesville, FL area at 92.5 FM.
FM RADIO STATION

WNDV-FM 45400
Owner: Artistic Media Partners Inc.
Editorial: 3371 West Cleveland Road Ext Ste 300, South Bend, Indiana 46628-9404 **Tel:** 1 574 273-9300.
Web site: http://www.u93.com
Profile: WNDV-FM is a commercial station owned by Artistic Media Partners Inc. The format for the station is Hot AC. WNDV-FM broadcasts to the South Bend, IN area at 92.9 FM.
FM RADIO STATION

WNDZ-AM 35879
Owner: Newsweb Corp.
Editorial: 5625 N Milwaukee Ave, Chicago, Illinois 60646-6221 **Tel:** 1 773 792-1121.
Web site: http://www.accessradiochicago.com
Profile: WNDZ-AM is a commercial station owned by Newsweb Corp. The format of the station is a variety of ethnic programming. WNDZ-AM broadcasts to the Chicago area at 750 AM. The station airs brokered programming.
AM RADIO STATION

WNEA-AM 35547
Owner: Word Christian Broadcasting Inc.
Editorial: 8451 Earl D Lee Blvd Ste B, Douglasville, Georgia 30134-8520 **Tel:** 1 770 920-1520.
Email: wkjohns@comcast.net
Web site: http://www.wordchristianbroadcasting.com
Profile: WNEA-AM is a commercial station owned by Word Christian Broadcasting Inc. The format of the station is religious programming and gospel music. WNEA-AM broadcasts to the Douglasville, GA area at 1300 AM.
AM RADIO STATION

WNEB-AM 36478
Owner: Emmanuel Communications, Inc.
Tel: 1 508 767-1230.
Email: info@1230radio.com
Web site: http://1230radio.com
Profile: WNEB-AM is a commercial station owned by Emmanuel Communications, Inc.. The format of the station features Catholic radio programming. WNEB-AM broadcasts to the Worchester, MA area at 1230 AM.
AM RADIO STATION

WNED-FM 45808
Owner: Western New York Public Broadcasting Association
Editorial: 140 Lower Terrace St, Buffalo, New York 14202-4330 **Tel:** 1 716 845-7000.
Email: news@wned.org
Web site: http://www.wned.org
Profile: WNED-FM is a non-commercial station owned by Western New York Public Broadcasting Association. The format of the station is classical. WNED-FM broadcasts to the Buffalo, NY area at 94.5 FM.
FM RADIO STATION

WNEG-AM 35548
Owner: Georgia-Carolina Radiocasting Companies LLC
Editorial: 145 N Alexander St, Toccoa, Georgia 30577-2371 **Tel:** 1 706 886-2191.
Email: wneg@windstream.net
Web site: http://www.wnegradio.com
Profile: WNEG-AM is a commercial station owned by Georgia-Carolina Radiocasting Companies LLC. The format of the station is oldies. WNEG-AM broadcasts to the Toccoa, GA area at 1120 AM.
AM RADIO STATION

WNER-AM 36958
Owner: Stephens Media Group
Editorial: 134 Mullin St, Watertown, New York 13601-3616 **Tel:** 1 315 788-0790.
Web site: http://www.wner1410.com
Profile: WNER-AM is a commercial station owned by Stephens Media Group. The format of the station is sports. WNER-AM broadcasts to the Watertown, NY area at 1410 AM.
AM RADIO STATION

WNES-AM 38319
Owner: Starlight Broadcasting Co.
Editorial: 314 S Main St, Hartford, Kentucky 42347-1129 **Tel:** 1 270 298-3268.
AM RADIO STATION

WNEV-FM 691426
Owner: LT Simes II and Raymond Simes
Editorial: 700 W Martin Luther King Jr Dr Ste 2, West Helena, Arkansas 72390-3526 **Tel:** 1 870 572-9506.
Email: force2@sbcglobal.net
Web site: http://www.force3radio.com
Profile: WNEV-FM is a commercial station owned by Delta Force II Radio. The format of the station is urban contemporary, blues and gospel. WNEV-FM broadcasts to the Friars Point, MS area at 98.7 FM.
FM RADIO STATION

WNEW-FM 46693
Owner: CBS Radio
Editorial: 345 Hudson St Fl 10, New York, New York 10014-7472 **Tel:** 1 212 315-7000.
Web site: http://fresh1027.cbslocal.com
Profile: WNEW-FM is a commercial station owned by CBS Radio. The format of the station is adult contemporary. WNEW-FM broadcasts to the New York area at 102.7 FM.
FM RADIO STATION

WNEX-AM 37026
Owner: Register Communications
Editorial: 1691 Forsyth St, Macon, Georgia 31201
Tel: 1 478 745-5858.
Profile: WNEX-AM is a commercial station owned by Register Communications. The format of the station is gospel music. WNEX-AM broadcasts to the Macon, GA area at 1400 AM.
AM RADIO STATION

WNEZ-AM 36454
Owner: Gois Broadcasting
Editorial: 135 Burnside Ave Floor 2, East Hartford, Connecticut 06108-3466 **Tel:** 1 860 524-0001.
Web site: http://www.latina1230.com
Profile: WNEZ-AM is a commercial station owned by Gois Broadcasting. The format of the station is Hispanic music and romantica. WNEZ-AM broadcasts in the Harford, CT area at 1230 AM.
AM RADIO STATION

WNFA-FM 41311
Owner: Ross Bible Church
Editorial: 2865 Maywood Dr, Port Huron, Michigan 48060 **Tel:** 1 810 985-3260.
Email: info@wnradio.com
Web site: http://www.power883.com
Profile: WNFA-FM is a non-commercial station owned by the Ross Bible Church. The format of the station is contemporary Christian music. WNFA-FM broadcasts to the Port Huron, MI area at 88.3 FM.
FM RADIO STATION

WNFB-FM 45477
Owner: Newman Media Inc.
Editorial: 2485 S Marion Ave, Lake City, Florida 32025-0051 **Tel:** 1 386 961-9494.
Web site: http://www.northfloridanow.com
Profile: WNFB-FM is a commercial station owned by Newman Media Inc. The format of the station is adult contemporary. WNFB-FM broadcasts to the Lake City, FL area at 94.3 FM.
FM RADIO STATION

WNFK-FM 46319
Owner: Taylor County Broadcasting, Inc.
Editorial: 5450 E US 27 Hwy, Perry, Florida 32347-0643 **Tel:** 1 850 584-9210.
Profile: WNFK-FM is a commercial station owned by Taylor County Broadcasting, Inc. The format for the station is contemporary country. WNFK-FM broadcasts to the Perry, FL area at 92.1 FM.
FM RADIO STATION

WNFL-AM 36708
Owner: Midwest Communications Inc.
Editorial: 1420 Bellevue St, Green Bay, Wisconsin 54311 **Tel:** 1 920 435-3771.
Web site: http://www.wnflam.com
Profile: WNFL-AM is a commercial station owned by Midwest Communications Inc. The format of the station is sports. WNFL-AM broadcasts to the Green Bay, WI area at 1440 AM.
AM RADIO STATION

WNFM-FM 45401
Owner: Magnum Broadcasting
Editorial: E 5680-A Highway 33 West, Reedsburg, Wisconsin 53959 **Tel:** 1 608 524-1400.
Email: info@magnumbroadcasting.com
Web site: http://www.wnfmcountry.com
Profile: WNFM-FM is a commercial station owned by Magnum Broadcasting. The format of the station is country. WNFM-FM broadcasts to the Reedsburg, WI, area at 104.9 FM.
FM RADIO STATION

WNFN-FM 43614
Owner: Mid West Communications Inc.
Editorial: 10 Music Cir E, Nashville, Tennessee 37203-4338 **Tel:** 1 615 321-1067.
Web site: http://www.i106hits.com
Profile: WNFN-FM is a commercial station owned by Mid West Communications Inc. The format of the station is Top 40/CHR. WNFN-FM broadcasts to the Nashville, TN area at 106.7 FM.
FM RADIO STATION

WNFR-FM 44121
Owner: Ross Bible Church
Editorial: 2865 Maywood Dr, Port Huron, Michigan 48060 **Tel:** 1 810 985-3260.
Email: info@wnradio.com
Web site: http://www.wnradio.com
Profile: WNFR-FM is a non-commercial station owned by Ross Bible Church. The format of the station is contemporary Christian music and religious programming. WNFR-FM broadcasts to the Port Huron, MI area at 90.7 FM.
FM RADIO STATION

WNFZ-FM 42446
Owner: Oak Ridge FM
Tel: 1 865 525-6000.
Email: wnfz@knoxtalkradio.com
Web site: http://knoxtalkradio.com
Profile: WNFZ-FM is a commercial station owned by Oak Ridge FM. The format of the station is modern rock. WNFZ-FM broadcasts to the Knoxville, TN area at 94.3 FM.
FM RADIO STATION

WNGA-FM 42626
Owner: Educational Media Foundation
Editorial: 705 Brucken Strasse, Helen, Georgia 30545-3606
Web site: http://www.klove.com
Profile: WNGA-FM is a commercial station owned by Educational Media Foundation. The format of the station is a mix of classic country and classic rock. WNGA-FM broadcasts to the Clermont, GA area at 105.1 FM.
FM RADIO STATION

WNGC-FM 42835
Owner: Cox Media Group, Inc.
Editorial: 850 Bobbin Mill Rd, Athens, Georgia 30606-4208 **Tel:** 1 706 549-6222.
Web site: http://www.yourgeorgiacountry.com
Profile: WNGC-FM is a commercial station owned by Cox Media Group, Inc. The format of the station is country music. WNGC-FM broadcasts to the Bogart, GA area at 106.1 FM.
FM RADIO STATION

WNGE-FM 334792
Owner: Sovereign Communications LLC
Editorial: 1009 W Ridge St, Ste A, Marquette, Michigan 49855 **Tel:** 1 906 225-1313.
Email: wjpd@wjpd.com
Profile: WNGE-FM is a commercial station owned by Sovereign Communications LLC. The format of the station is oldies music. WNGE-FM broadcasts to the Marquette, MI area at 99.5 FM.
FM RADIO STATION

WNGH-FM 40642
Owner: Georgia Public Broadcasting
Editorial: 260 14th St NW, Atlanta, Georgia 30318-5360 **Tel:** 1 404 685-2548.
Email: ask@gpb.org
Web site: http://www.gpb.org
Profile: WNGH-FM is a non-commercial station owned by Georgia Public Broadcasting. The format of the station is jazz, classical and news. WNGH-FM broadcasts to the Dalton, GA area at 98.9 FM.
FM RADIO STATION

WNGL-AM 36060
Owner: Archangel Communications, Inc.
Editorial: 370 S Section St, Fairhope, Alabama 36532-1769 **Tel:** 1 251 928-2111.
Email: office@archangelradio.com
Web site: http://www.wngl1410am.com
Profile: WNGL-AM is a commercial station owned by Archangel Communications, Inc. The format for the station is religious. WNGL-AM broadcasts to the Mobile, AL area at 1410 AM.
AM RADIO STATION

WNGN-FM 44256
Owner: Northeast Gospel Broadcasting, Inc.
Editorial: 65 King Rd, Buskirk, New York 12028-2221
Tel: 1 518 686-0975.
Web site: http://www.wvvcutica.com/
Profile: WNGN-FM is a non-commercial station owned by Northeast Gospel Broadcasting, Inc. The format of the station is Religious Teaching. WNGN-FM broadcasts to the Argyle, NY area at 91.9.
FM RADIO STATION

WNGO-AM 87176
Owner: Bristol Broadcasting
Editorial: 6000 Bristol Dr, Paducah, Kentucky 42003-9213 **Tel:** 1 270 554-8255.
Email: news@wkyx.com
Web site: http://www.wkyx.com
Profile: WNGO-AM is a commercial station owned by Bristol Broadcasting. The format of the station is news and talk. WNGO-AM broadcasts to the Paducah, KY area at 1320 AM.
AM RADIO STATION

WNGU-FM 44429
Owner: Georgia Public Broadcasting
Editorial: 260 14th St NW, Atlanta, Georgia 30318
Tel: 1 404 685-2548.
Email: ask@gpb.org
Web site: http://www.gpb.org
Profile: WNGU-FM is a non-commercial station owned by Georgia Public Broadcasting. The format of the station is news, jazz and classical music. WNGU-FM broadcasts to the Atlanta area at 89.5 FM.
FM RADIO STATION

WNGY-FM 40755
Owner: Alpha Media
Editorial: 331 Fulton St, Peoria, Illinois 61602-1486
Tel: 1 309 637-3700.
Web site: http://energy1023.com
Profile: WNGY-FM is a commercial station owned by Alpha Media. The format of the station is Top 40/CHR. WNGY-FM broadcasts to the Peoria, IL, area at 102.3 FM.
FM RADIO STATION

WNGZ-FM 46824
Owner: Community Broadcasters, LLC
Editorial: 2205 College Ave, Elmira, New York 14903-1201 **Tel:** 1 607 732-4400.
Web site: http://www.wngz.com
Profile: WNGZ-FM is a commercial station owned by Community Broadcasters, LLC. The format of the station is classic rock. WNGZ-FM broadcasts to the Elmira, NY area at 104.9 FM.
FM RADIO STATION

WNHW-FM 44111
Owner: WBIN, Inc.
Editorial: 2 Capital Plz Ste 105, Concord, New Hampshire 03301-4911 **Tel:** 1 603 224-8486.
Web site: http://www.933thewolf.com
Profile: WNHW-FM is a commercial station owned by WBIN, Inc. The format of the station is country. WNHW-FM broadcasts to the Hooksett, NH area at 93.3 FM.
FM RADIO STATION

WNIC-FM 46443
Owner: iHeartMedia Inc.
Editorial: 27675 Halsted Rd, Farmington Hills, Michigan 48331-3511 **Tel:** 1 248 324-5800.
Web site: http://www.wnic.com
Profile: WNIC-FM is a commercial station owned by iHeartMedia Inc. The format of the station is adult contemporary. WNIC-FM broadcasts to the Detroit area at 100.3 FM.
FM RADIO STATION

WNIL-AM 38082
Owner: Williams (Marion R.)
Editorial: 237 W Edison Rd Ste 200, Mishawaka, Indiana 46545-3103 **Tel:** 1 574 258-5483.
Web site: http://www.thefanmichiana.com/
Profile: WNIL-AM is a commercial station owned by Williams (Marion R.). The format for the station is sports/talk. WNIL-AM broadcasts to the Niles, MI area at 1290 AM.
AM RADIO STATION

WNIN-FM 40562
Owner: Tri-State Media
Editorial: 405 Carpenter St, Evansville, Indiana 47708
Tel: 1 812 423-2973.
Web site: http://www.wnin.org
Profile: WNIN-FM is a non-commercial radio station owned by Tri-State Media. The format of the station is classical music and news. WNIN-FM broadcasts to the Evansville, IN area at 88.3 FM.
FM RADIO STATION

WNIO-AM 38525
Owner: iHeartMedia Inc.
Editorial: 7461 South Ave, Youngstown, Ohio 44512-5789 **Tel:** 1 330 965-0057.
Web site: http://www.sportsradio1390.com
Profile: WNIO-AM is a commercial station owned by iHeartMedia Inc. The format of the station is sports. WNIO-AM broadcasts to the Youngstown, OH area at 1390 AM.
AM RADIO STATION

WNIR-FM 46342
Owner: Media-Com Inc.
Editorial: 2449 State Route 59, Ravenna, Ohio 44266-1641 **Tel:** 1 330 673-2323.
Email: news@wnir.com
Web site: http://www.wnir.com
Profile: WNIR-FM is a commercial station owned by Media-Com Inc. The format of the station is news and talk. WNIR-FM broadcasts in the Kent, OH area at 100.1 FM.
FM RADIO STATION

WNIS-AM 36453
Owner: Sinclair Telecable Inc.
Editorial: 999 Waterside Dr, Ste 500, Norfolk, Virginia 23510 **Tel:** 1 757 640-8500.
Web site: http://www.wnis.com
Profile: WNIS-AM is a commercial station owned by Sinclair Telecable Inc. The format of the station is news and talk. WNIS-AM broadcasts to the Norfolk, VA area at 790 AM.
AM RADIO STATION

WNIV-AM 35926
Owner: Salem Media Group, Inc.
Editorial: 2970 Peachtree Rd NW Ste 700, Atlanta, Georgia 30305-4919 **Tel:** 1 404 995-7300.
Email: adam.asher@salematlanta.com
Web site: http://www.faithtalk970.com
Profile: WNIV-AM is a commercial station owned by Salem Media Group, Inc. The format of the station is Christian talk. WNIV-AM broadcasts to the Atlanta area at 970 AM.
AM RADIO STATION

WNIX-AM 38083
Owner: Delta Radio, LLC
Editorial: 830 Main St, Greenville, Mississippi 38701-4102 **Tel:** 1 662 378-2617.
Email: info@deltaradio.net
Web site: http://www.wnixradio.com
Profile: WNIX-AM is a commercial station owned by Delta Radio, LLC. The format of the station is news/talk. WNIX-AM broadcasts to the Greenville, MS area at 1330 AM.
AM RADIO STATION

WNJA-FM 42283
Owner: Western New York Public Broadcasting Association
Editorial: 140 Lower Terrace St, Buffalo, New York 14202 **Tel:** 1 716 845-7000.
Email: classical@wned.org
Web site: http://www.wned.org
Profile: WNJA-FM is a non-commercial station owned by the Western New York Public Broadcasting Association. The format of the station is classical music programming. WNJA-FM broadcasts locally to the Jamestown, NY area at 89.7 FM.
FM RADIO STATION

WNJC-AM 36834
Owner: Forsythe Broadcasting Inc.
Editorial: 123 Egg Harbor Rd Ste 302, Sewell, New Jersey 08080-9406 **Tel:** 1 856 227-1360.
Web site: http://www.wnjcradio.com
Profile: WNJC-AM is a commercial station owned by Forsythe Broadcasting Inc. The format of the station is variety. WNJC-AM broadcasts to the Sewell, NJ area at 1360 AM.
AM RADIO STATION

WNJE-AM 36390
Owner: Connoisseur Media LLC
Editorial: 619 Alexander Rd Fl 3, Princeton, New Jersey 08540-6000 **Tel:** 1 609 419-0300.
Web site: http://www.920thejersey.com
Profile: WNJE-AM is a commercial station owned by Connoisseur Media LLC. The format of the station is sports. WNJE-AM broadcasts in the Boyertown, PA area at 920 AM.
AM RADIO STATION

WNJK-FM 947603
Owner: Choice Radio Corp.
Editorial: 116 N Main St #3, Nicholasville, Kentucky 40356-1487 **Tel:** 1 859 885-5377.
Email: news@jessfm.com
Web site: http://www.wnjkfm.com
FM RADIO STATION

WNJM-FM 44473
Owner: WHYY, Inc.
Editorial: 150 N 6th St, Philadelphia, Pennsylvania 19106-1521 **Tel:** 1 215 351-1200.
Email: talkback@whyy.org
Web site: http://www.whyy.org
Profile: WNJM-FM is a non-commercial station owned by WHYY, Inc. and the format of the station is news/talk. WNJM-FM broadcasts to Manahawkin, New Jersey families at 89.9 FM.
FM RADIO STATION

WNJP-FM 961916
Owner: New York Public Radio
Tel: 1 888 928-6577.

Web site: http://www.wnyc.org/section/njpr
Profile: WNJP-FM is a non-commercial station owned by New York Public Radio. The format of the station is news, talk, and jazz. The station broadcasts to the Sussex, New Jersey area at a frequency of 88.5 FM.
FM RADIO STATION

WNJT-FM 43253
Owner: New York Public Radio
Tel: 1 888 928-6577.
Email: publicity@nypublicradio.org
Web site: http://www.wnyc.org/section/njpr
Profile: WNJT-FM is a non-commercial station owned by New York Public Radio.The format of the station is news/talk WNJT-FM broadcasts to the Trenton, NJ area at 88.1 FM.
FM RADIO STATION

WNJY-FM 538541
Owner: New Jersey Public Broadcasting Authority
Editorial: 25 Stockton St, Trenton, New Jersey 08619-1950 **Tel:** 1 609 777-5000.
Email: publicity@nypublicradio.org
Web site: http://www.njpublicradio.org
Profile: WNJY-FM is a non-commercial station owned by New Jersey Public Broadcasting Authority. The format of the station is news/talk. WNJY-FM broadcasts to the Netcong, NJ area at 89.3 FM.
FM RADIO STATION

WNKI-FM 43051
Owner: Community Broadcasters, LLC
Editorial: 2205 College Ave, Elmira, New York 14903-1201 **Tel:** 1 607 732-4400.
Web site: http://www.wink106.com
Profile: WNKI-FM is a commercial station owned by Community Broadcasters, LLC. The format of the station is hot adult contemporary music. WNKI-FM broadcasts to the Elmira, NY area at 106.1 FM.
FM RADIO STATION

WNKJ-FM 41318
Owner: Pennyrile Christian Comm. Inc.
Editorial: 1100 E 18th St, Hopkinsville, Kentucky 42240 **Tel:** 1 270 886-9655.
Email: wnkj@wnkj.org
Web site: http://www.wnkj.org
Profile: WNKJ-FM is a non-commercial station owned by Pennyrile Christian Comm. Inc. The format of the station is religious, and gospel and contemporary Christian music. WNKJ-FM broadcasts to the Hopkinsville, KY area at 89.3 FM.
FM RADIO STATION

WNKO-FM 45402
Owner: Runnymede Inc.
Editorial: 1000 N 40th St, Newark, Ohio 43055-1467 **Tel:** 1 740 522-8171.
Email: studio@wnko.com
Web site: http://www.wnko.com
Profile: WNKO-FM is a commercial station owned by Runnymede Inc. The format of the station is classic hits music. WNKO-FM broadcasts to the Newark, OH, area at 101.7 FM.
FM RADIO STATION

WNKR-FM 42786
Owner: Grant Co. Broadcasters, Inc.
Editorial: 118 S Main St, Dry Ridge, Kentucky 41035-9438 **Tel:** 1 859 824-9106.
Email: wnkrproduction@fuse.net
Web site: http://www.1067wnkr.com
Profile: WNKR-FM is a commercial station owned by Grant Co. Broadcasters, Inc. The format of the station is classic country. WNKR-FM broadcasts to the Dry Ridge, KY area at 106.7 FM.
FM RADIO STATION

WNKS-FM 45510
Owner: Beasley Broadcast Group
Editorial: 1520 South Blvd, Charlotte, North Carolina 28203-4786 **Tel:** 1 704 522-1103.
Web site: http://kiss951.com/
Profile: WNKS-FM is commercial station owned by Beasley Broadcast Group. The format of the station is Top 40/CHR music. WNKS-FM broadcasts to the Charlotte, NC area at 95.1 FM.
FM RADIO STATION

WNKT-FM 43035
Owner: Cumulus Media Inc
Editorial: 1801 Charleston Hwy, Cayce, South Carolina 29033-2019 **Tel:** 1 803 796-7600.
Web site: http://www.1075thegame.com
Profile: WNKT-FM is a commercial station owned by Cumulus Media Inc. The format of the station is sports. WNKT-FM broadcasts to the Columbia, SC area at 107.5 FM.
FM RADIO STATION

WNKX-FM 45203
Owner: Hickman County Broadcasting Co.
Editorial: 150 Highway 50 E, Centerville, Tennessee 37033-5273 **Tel:** 1 931 729-5191.
Email: wnkx@countrykix96.com
Web site: http://www.countrykix96.com
Profile: WNKX-FM is a commercial station owned by the Hickman County Broadcasting Co. The format of the station is country music. WNKX-FM broadcasts to the Nashville, TN area at 96.7.
FM RADIO STATION

WNLA-AM 38084
Owner: Delta Radio
Tel: 1 662 887-1380.
Email: info@deltaradio.net
Web site: http://www.wnlaradio.com
Profile: WNLA-AM is a commercial station owned by Delta Radio. The format of the station is gospel music. WNLA-AM broadcasts in the Indianola, MS area at 1380 AM.
AM RADIO STATION

WNLC-FM 42217
Owner: Hall Communications
Editorial: 40 Cuprak Rd, Norwich, Connecticut 06360-2008 **Tel:** 1 860 887-3511.
Email: feedback@wnlc.com
Web site: http://www.wnlc.com
Profile: WNLC-FM is a commercial station owned by Hall Communications. The format of the station is classic hits. WNLC-FM broadcasts to the Norwich, CT area at 98.7 FM.
FM RADIO STATION

WNLD-FM 43971
Owner: Illinois Bible Institute
Editorial: 4101 Fieldstone Rd, Champaign, Illinois 61822-8800 **Tel:** 1 217 359-8232.
Email: wbgl@wbgl.org
Web site: http://www.wbgl.org
Profile: WNLD-FM is a non-commercial station owned by the Illinois Bible Institute. The format of the station is Christian. WNLD-FM broadcasts to the Decatur, IL area at 88.1 FM.
FM RADIO STATION

WNLF-FM 87523
Owner: Prestige Communications
Editorial: 31 E Side Sq, Macomb, Illinois 61455-2248 **Tel:** 1 309 833-2121.
Email: news@prestigeradio.com
Web site: http://www.prestigeradio.com
Profile: WNLF-FM is a commercial station owned by Prestige Communications. The format of the station is rock alternative. WNLF-FM broadcasts to the Macomb, IL area at 95.9 FM.
FM RADIO STATION

WNLR-AM 35553
Owner: New Life Ministries Inc.
Editorial: 35 Eagle Rock Lane, Churchville, Virginia 24421 **Tel:** 1 540 885-8600.
Email: wnlr@nlministries.org
Web site: http://www.nlministries.org
Profile: WNLR-AM is a commercial station owned by New Life Ministries Inc. The format of the station is contemporary Christian programming. WNLR-AM broadcasts to the Churchville, VA area at 1150 AM.
AM RADIO STATION

WNLT-FM 46589
Owner: Baldwin Broadcasting
Editorial: 8686 Michael Ln, Fairfield, Ohio 45014 **Tel:** 1 513 829-7700.
Web site: http://www.klove.com
Profile: WNLT-FM is a non-commercial station owned by Baldwin Broadcasting but programming is leased by Educational Media Foundation and carries K-Love programming. WNLT-FM broadcasts to the Harrison, OH area at 104.3 FM.
FM RADIO STATION

WNMA-AM 36747
Owner: Multicultural Radio Broadcasting Inc.
Editorial: 2 Alhambra Plz Fl 9, Coral Gables, Florida 33134-5202 **Tel:** 1 305 759-7280.
Web site: http://espndeportesmiami.com
Profile: WNMA-AM is a commercial station owned by Multicultural Radio Broadcasting Inc and under LMA with Deportes Media LLC. The format of the station is Spanish sports. WNMA-AM broadcasts to the Spanish speaking adults in the Miami area at 1210 AM.
AM RADIO STATION

WNMC-FM 44109
Owner: Northwestern Michigan College
Editorial: 1701 E Front St, Traverse City, Michigan 49686 **Tel:** 1 231 995-1090.
Email: wnmc@nmc.edu
Web site: http://www.wnmc.org
Profile: WNMC-FM is a non-commercial station owned by Northwestern Michigan College. The format of the station is a variety. WNMC-FM broadcasts to the Traverse City, MI area at 90.7 FM.
FM RADIO STATION

WNML-AM 37920
Owner: Cumulus Media Inc.
Editorial: 4711 Old Kingston Pike, Knoxville, Tennessee 37919-5207 **Tel:** 1 865 588-6511.
Web site: http://www.sportsanimal99.com
Profile: WNML-AM is a commercial station owned by Cumulus Media Inc. The format of the station is sports. WNML-AM broadcasts to the Knoxville, TN area at 990 AM.
AM RADIO STATION

WNML-FM 338492
Owner: Cumulus Media Inc.
Editorial: 4711 Old Kingston Pike, Knoxville, Tennessee 37919-5207 **Tel:** 1 865 588-6511.
Web site: http://www.sportsanimal99.com
Profile: WNML-FM is a commercial station owned by Cumulus Media Inc. The format of the station is sports. WNML-FM broadcasts to the Knoxville, TN area at 99.1 FM.
FM RADIO STATION

WNMQ-FM 46623
Owner: Cumulus Media Inc.
Editorial: 105 5th St N Ste 400, Columbus, Mississippi 39701-4568 **Tel:** 1 662 327-1183.
Web site: http://www.q1031fm.com
Profile: WNMQ-FM is a commercial station owned by Cumulus Media Inc. The format of the station is Top 40. WNMQ-FM broadcasts to the Columbus, MS area at 103.1 FM. The station's slogan is, "The golden triangle's hit music."
FM RADIO STATION

WNMT-AM 37980
Owner: Midwest Communications Inc.
Editorial: 807 W. 37th St., Hibbing, Minnesota 55746 **Tel:** 1 218 263-7531.
Web site: http://www.wnmtradio.com
Profile: WNMT-AM is commercial station owned by Midwest Communications Inc. The format of the station is news, talk and sports. WNMT-AM broadcasts in the Duluth, MN area at 650 AM.
AM RADIO STATION

WNMX-FM 46317
Owner: Cumulus Media Inc.
Editorial: 7080 Lee Hwy, Fairlawn, Virginia 24141-8416 **Tel:** 1 540 731-6000.
Email: info@cumulus.com
Web site: http://www.mix100fm.com
Profile: WNMX-FM is a commercial station owned by Cumulus Media Inc. The format of the station is hot adult contemporary. WNMX-FM broadcasts to the Fairlawn, VA area at 100.7 FM.
FM RADIO STATION

WNNC-AM 35554
Owner: Newton-Conover Communications, Inc.
Editorial: 1666 Radio Station Rd, Newton, North Carolina 28658-9488 **Tel:** 1 828 464-4041.
Profile: WNNC-AM is a commercial station owned by Newton-Conover Communications, Inc. The format of the station is adult contemporary music and talk. WNNC-AM broadcast to the Newton, NC area at 1230 AM.
AM RADIO STATION

WNND-FM 41546
Owner: Saga Communications
Editorial: 4401 Carriage Hill Ln, Columbus, Ohio 43220-3837 **Tel:** 1 614 451-2191.
Web site: http://www.rewindcolumbus.com
Profile: WNND-FM is a commercial station owned by Saga Communications. The format of the station is classic hits. WNND-FM broadcasts to the Columbus, OH, area at 103.5 FM.
FM RADIO STATION

WNNF-FM 42325
Owner: Cumulus Media Inc.
Editorial: 4805 Montgomery Rd Ste 300, Cincinnati, Ohio 45212-2280 **Tel:** 1 513 241-9898.
Web site: http://www.nashfm941.com
Profile: WNNF-FM is a commercial station owned by Cumulus Media Inc. The station's format is contemporary country. WNNF-FM broadcasts to the Cincinnati area at 94.1 FM.
FM RADIO STATION

WNNG-FM 327593
Owner: Georgia Eagle Broadcasting Inc.
Editorial: 1350 Radio Loop, Warner Robins, Georgia 31088-3626 **Tel:** 1 478 923-3416.
Email: georgiaeagleproduction@gmail.com
Profile: WNNG-FM is a commercial station owned by Georgia Eagle Broadcasting Inc. The format for the station is news/talk. WNNG-FM broadcasts to the Warner Robins, GA area at 99.9 FM.
FM RADIO STATION

WNNH-FM 41019
Owner: WBIN, Inc.
Editorial: 169 Port Rd, Kennebunk, Maine 04043-7737 **Tel:** 1 207 967-0993.
Web site: http://wnnh.nh1media.com
Profile: WNNH-FM is a commercial station owned by WBIN, Inc. The format of the station is classic hits. WNNH-FM broadcasts to the Gilford, NH area at 99.1 FM.
FM RADIO STATION

WNNJ-FM 45244
Owner: iHeartMedia Inc.
Editorial: 45 Ed Mitchell Ave, Franklin, New Jersey 07416-1588 **Tel:** 1 973 827-2525.
Web site: http://www.wnnj.com
Profile: WNNJ-FM is a commercial station owned by iHeartMedia Inc. The format of the station is classic rock. WNNJ-FM broadcasts to the Franklin, NJ area at 103.7 FM.
FM RADIO STATION

WNNK-FM 45953
Owner: Cumulus Media Inc.
Editorial: 2300 Vartan Way, Harrisburg, Pennsylvania 17110-9720 **Tel:** 1 717 238-1041.
Web site: http://www.wink104.com
Profile: WNNK-FM is a commercial station owned by Cumulus Media Inc. The format of the station is hot adult contemporary. WNNK-FM broadcasts to the Harrisburg, PA area at 104.1 FM.
FM RADIO STATION

WNNL-FM 41403
Owner: Urban One, Inc.
Editorial: 8001 Creedmoor Rd Ste 101, Raleigh, North Carolina 27613-4396 **Tel:** 1 919 848-9736.
Web site: http://thelightnc.hellobeautiful.com
Profile: WNNL-FM is a commercial station owned by Urban One, Inc. The format of the station is gospel. WNNL-FM broadcasts to the Raleigh-Durham, NC area at 103.9 FM.
FM RADIO STATION

WNNO-FM 45407
Owner: Magnum Radio Group
Editorial: N2349 Wibu Rd, Poynette, Wisconsin 53955-9556 **Tel:** 1 608 745-0959.
Email: info@magnumbroadcasting.com
Web site: http://www.mix106wnno.com
Profile: WNNO-FM is a commercial station owned by Magnum Radio Group. The format for the station is hot adult contemporary. WNNO-FM broadcasts to the Portage, WI area at 106.9 FM.
FM RADIO STATION

WNNP-FM 42923
Owner: Saga Communications
Editorial: 4401 Carriage Hill Ln, Columbus, Ohio 43220 **Tel:** 1 614 451-2191.
Web site: http://www.rewindcolumbus.com
Profile: WNNP-FM is a commercial station owned by Saga Communications. The format of the station is classic hits. WNNP-FM broadcasts to the Columbus, OH area at 104.3 FM.
FM RADIO STATION

WNNR-AM 36186
Owner: Norsan Broadcasting System
Editorial: 9831 Beach Blvd Ste 7, Jacksonville, Florida 32246-4703 **Tel:** 1 904 683-2198.
Email: admin@norsanmedia.com
Web site: http://larazalaraza.com/jacksonville/
Profile: WNNR-AM is a commercial station owned by Norsan Broadcasting System. The format of the station is regional Mexican. WNNR-AM broadcasts to the Jacksonville, FL area at 970 AM.
AM RADIO STATION

WNNS-FM 45408
Owner: Midwest Family Broadcasting
Editorial: 1510 N Third St, Riverton, Illinois 62561 **Tel:** 1 217 629-7077.
Email: wnns@wnns.com
Web site: http://www.wnns.com
Profile: WNNS-FM is a commercial station owned by Midwest Family Broadcasting. The format of the station is Lite Rock/Lite AC music. WNNS-FM broadcasts to the Springfield, IL area at 98.7 FM.
FM RADIO STATION

WNNT-FM 41406
Owner: Real Media, Inc.
Editorial: 156 Prince street, Tappahannock, Virginia 22560 **Tel:** 1 804 333-4900.
Email: contact@realradio804.com
Web site: http://realradio804.com
Profile: WNNT-FM is a commercial station owned by Real Media, Inc. The format of the station is country. WNNT-FM broadcasts to the Warsaw, VA area at 107.5 FM.
FM RADIO STATION

WNNW-AM 36794
Owner: Costa Eagle Radio Ventures
Editorial: 462 Merrimack St, Methuen, Massachusetts 01844-5804 **Tel:** 1 978 686-9966.
Web site: http://power800am.com
Profile: WNNW-AM is a commercial station owned by Costa Eagle Radio Ventures. The format of the station is Hispanic programming. WNNW-AM broadcasts to the Methuen, MA area at 800 AM.
AM RADIO STATION

WNNW-FM 586441
Owner: Costa Eagle Radio Ventures
Editorial: 462 Merrimack St, Methuen, Massachusetts 01844-5804 **Tel:** 1 978 686-9966.
Web site: http://www.power800am.com
Profile: WNNW-FM is a commercial station owned by Costa Eagle Radio Ventures. The format of the station is Hispanic programming. WNNW-FM broadcasts to the Methuen, MA area at 92.1 FM.
FM RADIO STATION

WNNX-FM 40099
Owner: Cumulus Media Inc.
Editorial: 780 Johnson Ferry Rd Fl 5, Atlanta, Georgia 30342-1434 **Tel:** 1 404 497-4700.
Web site: http://www.atlantasrockstation.com
Profile: WNNX-FM is a commercial station owned by Cumulus Media Inc. The format of the station is classic rock. WNNX-FM broadcasts to the Atlanta area at 100.5 FM.
FM RADIO STATION

WNNZ-AM 35555
Owner: New England Public Radio, Inc.
Editorial: 1525 Main St, Springfield, Massachusetts 01103-1413 **Tel:** 1 413 735-6600.
Email: news@nepr.net
Web site: http://nepr.net
Profile: WNNZ-AM is a commercial station owned by New England Public Radio, Inc. The format of the station is news and talk. WNNZ-AM broadcasts to the Springfield, MA area at 640 AM and 91.7 FM.
AM RADIO STATION

WNOB-FM 217134
Owner: Sinclair Telecable Inc.
Editorial: 999 Waterside Dr, Ste 500, Norfolk, Virginia 23510 **Tel:** 1 757 640-8500.
Web site: http://www.937bobfm.com
Profile: WNOB-FM is a commercial station owned by Sinclair Telecable Inc. The format of the station is adult hits. WNOB-FM broadcasts to the Norfolk, VA area at 93.7 FM.
FM RADIO STATION

United States of America

WNOC-FM 706519
Owner: Our Lady of Guadalupe Radio, Inc.
Editorial: 3662 Rugby Dr, Toledo, Ohio 46314
Tel: 1 419 754-1009.
Email: info@annunciationradio.com
Web site: http://www.annunciationradio.com
Profile: WNOC-FM is a commercial station owned by
Our Lady of Guadalupe Radio, Inc. The format of the
station is Catholic talk programming. WNOC-FM
broadcasts in the Toledo, OH area at 89.7 FM.
FM RADIO STATION

WNOE-FM 42780
Owner: iHeartMedia Inc.
Editorial: 929 Howard Ave, New Orleans, Louisiana
70113-1148 **Tel:** 1 504 679-7300.
Web site: http://wnoe.iheart.com
Profile: WNOE-FM is a commercial station owned by
iHeartMedia Inc. The format of the station is classic
country music. WNOE-FM broadcasts to the New
Orleans area at 101.1 FM. The station's slogan is,
"New Orleans Country Station."
FM RADIO STATION

WNOG-AM 38088
Owner: Sun Broadcasting, Inc.
Editorial: 2824 Palm Beach Blvd, Fort Myers, Florida
33916-1503 **Tel:** 1 239 337-2346.
Web site: http://www.973thefan.com/
Profile: WNOG-AM is a commercial station owned by
Sun Broadcasting, Inc. The format of the station is
sports. WNOG-AM broadcasts to the Ft. Myers, FL
area at 1270 AM.
AM RADIO STATION

WNOH-FM 46289
Owner: iHeartMedia Inc.
Editorial: 1003 Norfolk Sq, Norfolk, Virginia 23502-
3234 **Tel:** 1 757 466-0009.
Web site: http://now105.iheart.com
Profile: WNOH-FM is a commercial station owned by
iHeartMedia Inc. The format of the station is Hot AC.
WNOH-FM broadcasts to the Norfolk, VA area at
105.3 FM.
FM RADIO STATION

WNOI-FM 40569
Owner: H & R Communications
Editorial: 1001 N Olive Rd, Flora, Illinois 62839-2348
Tel: 1 618 662-8331.
Email: info@wnoi.com
Web site: http://www.wnoi.com
Profile: WNOI-FM is a commercial station owned by
H & R Communications. The format of the station is
adult contemporary music. WNOI-FM broadcasts to
the Flora, IL area at 103.9 FM.
FM RADIO STATION

WNOK-FM 43240
Owner: iHeartMedia Inc.
Editorial: 316 Greystone Blvd, Columbia, South
Carolina 29210-8007 **Tel:** 1 803 343-1100.
Web site: http://www.wnok.com
Profile: WNOK-FM is a commercial station owned by
iHeartMedia Inc. The format for the station is Top 40/
CHR. WNOK-FM broadcasts to the Columbia, SC
area at 104.7 FM.
FM RADIO STATION

WNOO-AM 36793
Owner: Clear Media LLC
Editorial: 1108 Hendricks St, Chattanooga,
Tennessee 37406 **Tel:** 1 423 698-8617.
Email: wnoo@epbinternet.com
Web site: http://www.wnooradio.com
Profile: WNOO-AM is a commercial station owned by
Clear Media LLC. The format of the station is gospel
music. WNOO-AM broadcasts to the Chattanooga,
TN area at 1260 AM.
AM RADIO STATION

WNOP-AM 35556
Owner: Sacred Heart Radio
Editorial: 5440 Moeller Ave, Cincinnati, Ohio 45212-
1211 **Tel:** 1 513 731-7740.
Email: info@sacredheartradio.com
Web site: http://www.sacredheartradio.com
Profile: WNOP-AM is a non-commercial station
owned by Sacred Heart Radio. The format of the
station is religious talk programming. WNOP-AM
broadcasts to the Cincinnati area at 740 AM.
AM RADIO STATION

WNOP-FM 681101
Owner: Sacred Heart Radio
Editorial: 5440 Moeller Ave, Cincinnati, Ohio 45212-
1211 **Tel:** 1 513 731-7740.
Email: info@sacredheartradio.com
Web site: http://www.sacredheartradio.com
Profile: WNOP-FM is a non-commercial station
owned by Sacred Heart Radio. The format of the
station is religious talk programming. WNOP-AM
broadcasts to the Versailles, IN area at 89.5 FM.
FM RADIO STATION

WNOR-FM 45409
Owner: Saga Communications
Editorial: 870 Greenbrier Cir Ste 399, Chesapeake,
Virginia 23320-2671 **Tel:** 1 757 366-9900.
Web site: http://www.fm99.com
Profile: WNOR-FM is a commercial station owned by
Saga Communications. The format of the station is
rock. WNOR-FM broadcasts to the Norfolk, VA area
at 98.7 FM.
FM RADIO STATION

WNOS-AM 35557
Owner: CTC Media Group
Editorial: 1202 Pollock St, New Bern, North Carolina
28560-5538 **Tel:** 1 252 638-8888.
Web site: http://www.rfenc.com
Profile: WNOS-AM is a commercial station owned by
the CTC Media Group. The format of the station is
sports and some talk. WNOS-AM broadcasts to New
Bern, NC at 1450 AM.
AM RADIO STATION

WNOW-AM 604013
Owner: TBLC Media LLC
Editorial: 4321 Stuart Andrew Blvd Ste E, Charlotte,
North Carolina 28217-1588 **Tel:** 1 704 6659355.
Web site: http://poderpurasbuenas.com
Profile: WNOW-AM is a commercial station owned
by TBLC Media LLC. The format of the station is
regional Mexican. WNOW-AM broadcasts to the
Charlotte, NC area at 1030 AM.
AM RADIO STATION

WNOW-FM 40120
Owner: Urban One, Inc.
Editorial: 21 E Saint Joseph St, Indianapolis, Indiana
46204-1025 **Tel:** 1 317 266-9600.
Web site: http://www.radionowindy.com
Profile: WNOW-FM is a commercial station owned
by Urban One, Inc.. The format of the station is Top
40/CHR music. WNOW-FM broadcasts to the
Indianapolis area at 100.9 FM.
FM RADIO STATION

WNOX-FM 40551
Owner: E.W. Scripps Co.
Editorial: 1533 Amherst Rd, Knoxville, Tennessee
37909-1204 **Tel:** 1 865 824-1021.
Web site: http://www.931wnox.com
Profile: WNOX-FM is a commercial station owned by
E.W. Scripps Co. The format of the station is classic
hits. WNOX-FM broadcasts to the Knoxville, TN area
at 93.1 FM.
FM RADIO STATION

WNPC-AM 39053
Owner: Bristol Broadcasting
Editorial: 377 Graham St, Newport, Tennessee
37821-2712 **Tel:** 1 423 623-8744.
Profile: WNPC-AM is a commercial station owned by
Bristol Broadcasting. The format of the station is
country. WNPC-AM broadcasts to the Newport, TN
area at 1060 AM.
AM RADIO STATION

WNPC-FM 46396
Owner: Bristol Broadcasting
Editorial: 377 Graham St, Newport, Tennessee
37821-2712 **Tel:** 1 423 623-8744.
Web site: http://www.923wnpc.com
Profile: WNPC-FM is a commercial station owned by
Bristol Broadcasting. The format of the station is
classic country. WNPC-FM broadcasts to the
Newport, TN area at 92.9 FM.
FM RADIO STATION

WNPL-AM 591564
Owner: Fort Myers Broadcasting Co.
Editorial: 2824 Palm Beach Blvd, Fort Myers, Florida
33916-1503 **Tel:** 1 239 337-2346.
Web site: http://www.winknewsradio.com
Profile: WNPL-AM is a commercial station owned by
Fort Myers Broadcasting Co. The format of the
station is news and talk. WNPL-AM broadcasts to the
Fort Myers, FL area at 1460 AM.
AM RADIO STATION

WNPQ-FM 44396
Owner: Tuscarawas Broadcasting
Editorial: 3969 Convenience Cir NW, Ste 205,
Canton, Ohio 44718 **Tel:** 1 330 492-9590.
Email: office@thelight959.com
Web site: http://www.thelight959.com
Profile: WNPQ-FM is a commercial owned by
Tuscarawas Broadcasting. The format of the station
is Christian Contemporary. WNPQ-FM broadcasts to
the Canton, OH area at 95.9 FM.
FM RADIO STATION

WNPR-FM 41068
Owner: Connecticut Public Broadcasting Inc.
Editorial: 1049 Asylum Ave, Hartford, Connecticut
06105-2432 **Tel:** 1 860 278-5310.
Email: info@wnpr.org
Web site: http://www.cpbn.org
Profile: WNPR-FM is a non-commercial station
owned by Connecticut Public Broadcasting Inc. The
format of the station is news and talk. WNPR-FM
broadcasts to the Hartford, CT area at 90.5 FM.
FM RADIO STATION

WNPT-FM 42159
Owner: John Sisty Enterprises Inc.
Editorial: 2110 McFarland Blvd E Ste C, Tuscaloosa,
Alabama 35404-5820
Profile: WNPT-FM is a commercial station owned by
John Sisty Enterprises Inc. The format of the station
is country. WNPT-FM broadcasts to the Linden, AL
and surrounding communities at 102.9 FM.
FM RADIO STATION

WNPV-AM 35559
Owner: WNPV Inc.
Editorial: 1210 Snyder Rd, Lansdale, Pennsylvania
19446-4614 **Tel:** 1 215 855-8211.
Email: info@wnpv1440.com
Web site: http://www.wnpv1440.com

Profile: WNPV-AM is a commercial station owned by
WNPV Inc. The format of the station is news, talk and
sports. WNPV-AM broadcasts to the Lansdale, PA
area at 1440 AM.
AM RADIO STATION

WNPZ-AM 544589
Owner: Metropolitan Management Corporation of
Tennessee
Editorial: 804 N Broadway St, Knoxville, Tennessee
37917-7203 **Tel:** 1 865 525-5756.
Web site: http://www.rejoice1580.com
Profile: WNPZ-AM is a commercial station owned by
Metropolitan Management Corporation of Tennessee.
The format of the station is black gospel. WNPZ-AM
broadcasts to the Knoxville, TN area at a frequency
of 1570 AM.
AM RADIO STATION

WNQM-AM 35560
Owner: Robbert Broadcasting Co.(F.W.)
Editorial: 1300 Wwcr Ave, Nashville, Tennessee
37218 **Tel:** 1 615 255-1300.
Email: askwwcr@wwcr.com
Web site: http://www.1300wnqm.com
Profile: WNQM-AM is a commercial station owned
by F.W. Robbert Broadcasting Co. The format of the
station is religious. WNQM-AM broadcasts to the
Nashville, TN area at 1300 AM.
AM RADIO STATION

WNRG-AM 38743
Owner: Peggy Sue Broadcasting Media Inc.
Editorial: 1011 Radio Dr, Grundy, Virginia 24614-6157
Tel: 1 540 935-2587.
Email: wmjd.fm@gmail.com
Profile: WNRG-AM is a commercial station owned by
Peggy Sue Broadcasting Media Inc. The format of the
station is gospel. WNRG-AM broadcasts to the
Grundy, VA area at 940 AM.
AM RADIO STATION

WNRG-FM 40284
Owner: Saga Communications
Editorial: 5407 W McKinley Ave, Milwaukee,
Wisconsin 53208-2540 **Tel:** 1 414 978-9000.
Web site: http://www.energy1069.com
Profile: WNRG-FM is a commercial station owned by
Saga Communications. The format of the station is
rhythmic contemporary. WNRG-FM broadcasts to
the Milwaukee area at 106.9.
FM RADIO STATION

WNRI-AM 36081
Owner: Bouchard Broadcasting Inc.
Editorial: 786 Diamond Hill Rd, Woonsocket, Rhode
Island 02895-1476 **Tel:** 1 401 769-6925.
Web site: http://www.wnri.com
Profile: WNRI-AM is a commercial station owned by
Bouchard Broadcasting Inc. The format of the station
is news and talk. WRNI-AM broadcasts to the
Woonsocket, RI area at 1380 AM.
AM RADIO STATION

WNRJ-FM 46631
Owner: Dailey Corp.
Editorial: 1601 Grand Central Ave, Vienna, West
Virginia 26105-1082 **Tel:** 1 304 916-1884.
Email: wnrj@suddenlinkmail.com
Profile: WNRJ-FM is a commercial station owned by
Dailey Corp. The format of the station is Hot AC.
WNRJ-FM broadcasts to the New Martinsville, WV
area at 103.9 FM.
FM RADIO STATION

WNRN-FM 43102
Owner: Stu-Comm Inc.
Editorial: 2250 Old Ivy Rd, Ste 2, Charlottesville,
Virginia 22903 **Tel:** 1 434 971-4096.
Email: info@wnrn.org
Web site: http://www.wnrn.org
Profile: WNRN-FM is a commercial station owned by
Stu-Comm Inc. The format of the station is adult
album alternative and rock alternative. WNRN-FM
broadcasts to the Charlottesville, VA area at 91.9 FM.
FM RADIO STATION

WNRP-AM 37089
Owner: ADX Communications
Editorial: 7251 Plantation Rd, Pensacola, Florida
32504-6334 **Tel:** 1 850 437-1620.
Email: news@newsradio1620.com
Web site: http://www.newsradio1620.com
Profile: WNRP-AM is a commercial station owned by
ADX Communications. The format of the station is
news and talk. WNRP-AM broadcasts to the
Pensacola, FL area at 1620 AM.
AM RADIO STATION

WNRQ-FM 43811
Owner: iHeartMedia Inc.
Editorial: 55 Music Sq W, Nashville, Tennessee
37203-3207 **Tel:** 1 615 664-2400.
Web site: http://1059therock.iheart.com
Profile: WNRQ-FM is a commercial station owned by
iHeartMedia Inc. The format of the station is classic
rock music. WNRQ-FM broadcasts to the Nashville,
TN area at 105.9 FM.
FM RADIO STATION

WNRW-FM 42899
Owner: iHeartMedia Inc.
Editorial: 4000 Radio Dr, Louisville, Kentucky 40218-
4568 **Tel:** 1 502 479-2222.
Web site: http://www.989radionow.com/main.html
Profile: WNRW-FM is a commercial station owned by
iHeartMedia Inc. The format of the station is Top 40/

CHR music. WNRW-FM broadcasts to the Louisville,
KY area at 98.9 FM.
FM RADIO STATION

WNRZ-FM 43223
Owner: Community Broadcasting, Inc
Tel: 1 615 871-1160.
Email: wcrt@bottradionetwork.com
Web site: http://www.bottradionetwork.com
Profile: WNRZ-FM is a non-commercial station
owned by Community Broadcasting, Inc. The format
for the station is religious. WNRZ-FM broadcasts to
the Dickson, TN area at 91.5 FM.
FM RADIO STATION

WNSH-FM 40281
Owner: Cumulus Media Inc.
Editorial: 2 Penn Plz Fl 17, New York, New York
10121-1701 **Tel:** 1 212 613-8900.
Web site: http://www.nashfm947.com
Profile: WNSH-FM is a commercial station owned by
Cumulus Media. The format of the station is
contemporary country. WNSH-FM broadcasts to the
Newark, NJ area at 94.7 FM.
FM RADIO STATION

WNSL-FM 45410
Owner: iHeartMedia Inc.
Editorial: 6555 U S Highway 98 Ste 8, Hattiesburg,
Mississippi 39402-8699 **Tel:** 1 601 296-9800.
Email: contact@sl100.com
Web site: http://www.sl100.com
Profile: WNSL-FM is a commercial station owned by
iHeartMedia Inc. The format of the station is top 40
contemporary hit radio.
FM RADIO STATION

WNSN-FM 45411
Owner: Mid-West Family Broadcasting
Editorial: 1301 E Douglas Rd, Mishawaka, Indiana
46545-1732 **Tel:** 1 574 233-3141.
Web site: http://www.sunny1015.com
Profile: WNSN-FM is a commercial station owned by
Mid-West Family Broadcasting. The format of the
station is adult contemporary. WNSN-FM broadcast
to South Bend, IN at 101.5 FM.
FM RADIO STATION

WNSP-FM 42208
Owner: Dot Com Plus, LLC
Editorial: 1100 Dauphin St, Mobile, Alabama 36604-
2571 **Tel:** 1 251 438-5460.
Email: wnsp@wnsp.com
Web site: http://www.wnsp.com
Profile: WNSP-FM is a commercial station owned by
Dot Com Plus, LLC. The format of the station is
sports. WNSP-FM's broadcasts to the Mobile, AL
area on 105.5 FM.
FM RADIO STATION

WNSR-AM 36752
Owner: Southern Wabash Communications Corp.
Editorial: 1815 Division St Ste 110, Nashville,
Tennessee 37203-2753 **Tel:** 1 615 844-1039.
Email: info@wnsr.com
Web site: http://www.wnsr.com
Profile: WNSR-AM is a commercial station owned by
Southern Wabash Communications Corp. The format
of the station is sports. WNSR-AM broadcasts to the
Nashville, TN area at 560 AM.
AM RADIO STATION

WNST-AM 35319
Owner: Nasty 1570 Sports LLC
Editorial: 1550 Hart Rd, Towson, Maryland 21286-
1635 **Tel:** 1 410 821-9678.
Web site: http://www.wnst.net
Profile: WNST-AM is a commercial station owned by
Nasty 1570 Sports LLC. The format of the station is
sports. WNST-AM broadcasts to the Baltimore area
at 1570 AM.
AM RADIO STATION

WNSV-FM 42280
Owner: Dana Communications Corp.
Editorial: 186 E Saint Louis St, Nashville, Illinois
62263-1714 **Tel:** 1 618 327-4444.
Profile: WNSV-FM is a commercial station owned by
Dana Communications Corp. The format of the
station is adult contemporary music. WNSV-FM
broadcasts to the Nashville, IL area at 104.7 FM.
FM RADIO STATION

WNSW-AM 35551
Owner: Starboard Media Foundation Inc.
Tel: 1 920 884-1460.
Email: info@relevantradio.com
Web site: http://www.relevantradio.com
Profile: WNSW-AM is a commercial station owned
by Starboard Media Foundation Inc. The format of
the station is Catholic teaching. WNSW-AM
broadcasts to the New York area at 1430 AM.
AM RADIO STATION

WNSX-FM 44495
Owner: Stony Creek Broadcasting
Editorial: 409 High St, Ellsworth, Maine 04605-2505
Tel: 1 207 667-0002.
Web site: http://wnsxradio.com
Profile: WNSX-FM is a commercial station owned by
Stony Creek Broadcasting. The format of the station
is adult contemporary. WNSX-FM broadcasts to the
Bangor, ME area at 97.7 FM.
FM RADIO STATION

WNSY-FM 46863
Owner: Davis Broadcasting
Editorial: 1176 Satellite Blvd NW Bldg, Suwanee, Georgia 30024-2881 **Tel:** 1 770 623-8772.
Profile: WNSY-FM is a commercial station owned by Davis Broadcasting. The format of the station is Hispanic Top 40/CHR. WNSY-FM broadcasts to the Suwanee, GA area at 100.1 FM.
FM RADIO STATION

WNTA-AM 39375
Owner: Mid-West Family Broadcasting
Editorial: 2830 Sandy Hollow Rd, Rockford, Illinois 61109-2369 **Tel:** 1 815 874-7861.
Web site: http://www.sportsfanradio1330.com
Profile: WNTA-AM is a commercial station owned by Mid-West Family Broadcasting. The format of the station is Sports Talk Radio. WNTA-AM broadcasts to the Rockford, IL area at 1330 AM.
AM RADIO STATION

WNTB-FM 151659
Owner: Hometown Wilmington Media
Editorial: 122 Cinema Dr, Wilmington, North Carolina 28403-1490 **Tel:** 1 910 772-6300.
Email: newsroom@sea-comm.com
Web site: http://gottalovethedude.com/home
Profile: WNTB-FM is a commercial station owned by Hometown Wilmington Media. The format of the station is contemporary country. WNTB-FM broadcasts to the Wilmington, NC area at 106.3 FM.
FM RADIO STATION

WNTC-FM 242202
Owner: Southern Wabash Communications Corp.
Editorial: 1815 Division St Ste 110, Nashville, Tennessee 37203-2753 **Tel:** 1 615 844-1039.
Email: info@wnsr.com
Web site: http://www.wnsr.com
Profile: WNTC-FM is a commercial station owned by Southern Wabash Communications Corp. The format of the station is sports. WNTC-FM broadcasts to the Nashville, TN area at 103.9 FM.
FM RADIO STATION

WNTD-AM 36519
Owner: Starboard Media Foundation Inc.
Tel: 1 312 467-9755.
Email: info@relevantradio.com
Web site: http://www.relevantradio.com
Profile: WNTD-AM is a commercial station owned by Starboard Media Foundation Inc. The format of the station is Catholic talk. WNTD-AM broadcasts to the Chicago area at 950 AM.
AM RADIO STATION

WNTJ-AM 37949
Owner: FM Radio Licenses, LLC
Editorial: 109 Plaza Dr, Johnstown, Pennsylvania 15905-1212 **Tel:** 1 814 255-4186.
Web site: http://www.foreverjohnstown.com
Profile: WNTJ-AM is a commercial station owned by FM Radio Licenses, LLC. The format of the station is sports, news and talk. WNTJ-AM broadcasts in the Johnstown, PA area at 1490 AM.
AM RADIO STATION

WNTK-FM 46133
Owner: Koor Communications
Tel: 1 603 448-0500.
Email: admin@wntk.com
Web site: http://www.wntk.com
Profile: WNTK-FM is a commercial station owned by Koor Communications. The format of the station is news and talk. WNTK-FM broadcasts to the New London, NH area at 99.7 FM.
FM RADIO STATION

WNTM-AM 37990
Owner: iHeartMedia Inc.
Editorial: 555 Broadcast Dr Fl 3, Mobile, Alabama 36606-2936 **Tel:** 1 251 450-0100.
Web site: http://www.newsradio710.com
Profile: WNTM-AM is a commercial station owned by iHeartMedia Inc. The format of the station is news and talk. WNTM-AM broadcasts to the Mobile, AL area at 710 AM.
AM RADIO STATION

WNTN-AM 35563
Owner: Colt Communications LLC
Editorial: 143 Rumford Ave, Auburndale, Massachusetts 02466-1311 **Tel:** 1 617 969-1550.
Email: info@wntn.com
Web site: http://www.wntn.com
Profile: WNTN-AM is a commercial station owned by Colt Communications LLC. The format of the station is variety. WNTN-AM broadcasts to the Auburndale, MA area at 1550 AM.
AM RADIO STATION

WNTO-FM 46615
Owner: Sunny Broadcasting LLC
Editorial: 117 Portsmouth Rd, Gallipolis, Ohio 45631-1047 **Tel:** 1 740 446-3543.
Web site: http://www.sunny93.net
Profile: WNTO-FM is a commercial station owned by Sunny Broadcasting LLC. The format of the station is classic hits. WNTO-FM broadcasts to the Gallipolis, OH, area at 93.1 FM.
FM RADIO STATION

WNTP-AM 232010
Owner: Salem Media Group, Inc.
Editorial: 117 Ridge Pike, Lafayette Hill, Pennsylvania 19444-1901 **Tel:** 1 610 940-0990.
Web site: http://www.newstalk990.com
Profile: WNTP-AM is a commercial station owned by Salem Media Group, Inc. The format of the station is news and talk. WNTP-AM broadcasts to the Lafayette Hill, PA area at 990 AM.
AM RADIO STATION

WNTQ-FM 46011
Owner: Cumulus Media Inc.
Editorial: 1064 James St, Syracuse, New York 13203-2704 **Tel:** 1 315 472-0200.
Web site: http://www.93q.com
Profile: WNTQ-FM is a commercial station owned by Cumulus Media Inc. The format of the station is Top 40/CHR. WNTQ-FM broadcasts to the Syracuse, NY area at 93.1 FM.
FM RADIO STATION

WNTR-FM 46647
Owner: Entercom Communications Corp.
Editorial: 9245 N Meridian St Ste 300, Indianapolis, Indiana 46260-1832 **Tel:** 1 317 816-4000.
Email: indypsa@entercom.com
Web site: http://www.indysmix.com
Profile: WNTR-FM is a commercial station owned by Entercom Communications Corp. The format of the station is Hot AC. WNTR-FM broadcasts to the Indianapolis area at 107.9 FM.
FM RADIO STATION

WNTS-AM 35564
Owner: Davidson Media Group
Editorial: 3745 W Washington St Ste 5, Indianapolis, Indiana 46241-1510 **Tel:** 1 317 924-1071.
Profile: WNTS-AM is a commercial station owned by Davidson Media Group with an LMA from Continental Broadcast Group LLC. The format of the station is regional Mexican. WNTS-AM broadcasts to the Davidson, NC area at 1590 AM.
AM RADIO STATION

WNTT-AM 35565
Owner: Craft(Aileen)
Editorial: 115 Blue Top Rd, Tazewell, Tennessee 37879 **Tel:** 1 423 626-4203.
Web site: http://www.wntt1250am.com
Profile: WNTT-AM is a commercial station owned by Aileen Craft. The format of the station is classic country. WNTT-AM broadcasts to the Tazewell, TN and surrounding areas at 1250 AM.
AM RADIO STATION

WNTX-AM 37809
Owner: Alpha Media
Editorial: 616 Amelia St, Fredericksburg, Virginia 22401-3887 **Tel:** 1 540 374-5500.
Email: lapositiva1350@gmail.com
Web site: http://www.wntxradio.com/
Profile: WNTX-AM is a commercial station owned by Alpha Media The format of the station is regional Mexican and Top 40/CHR. WNTX-AM broadcasts to the Fredericksburg, VA area at 1350 AM.
AM RADIO STATION

WNTY-AM 35566
Owner: Red Wolf Broadcasting
Editorial: Southington, Connecticut **Tel:** 1 860 621-1754.
Web site: http://kool1180.webs.com
Profile: WNTY-AM is a commercial station owned by Red Wolf Broadcasting. The format of the station is oldies. WNTY-AM broadcasts to the Hartford-New Haven, CT area at 990 AM.
AM RADIO STATION

WNUE-FM 41012
Owner: Entravision Communications Corp.
Editorial: 523 Douglas Ave, Altamonte Springs, Florida 32714-2507 **Tel:** 1 407 774-2626.
Web site: http://www.salsa981.com
Profile: WNUE-FM is a commercial station owned by Entravision Communications Corp. The format of the station is Salsa/Caribbean music. WNUE-FM broadcasts to the Greater Orlando, FL area at 98.1 FM.
FM RADIO STATION

WNUQ-FM 45186
Owner: Cumulus Media Inc.
Editorial: 1104 W Broad Ave, Albany, Georgia 31707-4340 **Tel:** 1 229 888-5000.
Web site: http://www.1021nashicon.com
Profile: WNUQ-FM is a commercial station owned by Cumulus Media Inc. The format of the station is country music. WNUQ-FM broadcasts to the Albany, GA area at 102.1 FM.
FM RADIO STATION

WNUS-FM 46339
Owner: iHeartMedia Inc.
Editorial: 6006 Grand Central Ave, Parkersburg, West Virginia 26105-9125 **Tel:** 1 304 295-6070.
Web site: http://107nus.iheart.com
Profile: WNUS-FM is a commercial station owned by iHeartMedia Inc. The format of the station is contemporary country. WNUS-FM broadcasts to the Vienna, WV area at 107.1 FM.
FM RADIO STATION

WNUZ-FM 45965
Owner: VerStandig Broadcasting
Editorial: 10960 John Wayne Dr, Greencastle, Pennsylvania 17225-9584 **Tel:** 1 717 597-9200.
Web site: http://www.921hitsfm.com
Profile: WPPT-FM is a commercial station owned by VerStandig Broadcasting. The format of the station is Top 40/CHR. WPPT-FM broadcasts to the Greencastle, PA area at 92.1 FM.
FM RADIO STATION

WNVA-FM 45412
Owner: Bristol Broadcasting Company
Editorial: 901 E Valley Dr, Bristol, Virginia 24201-4913 **Tel:** 1 276 669-8112.
Web site: http://www.993thex.com
Profile: WNVA-FM is a commercial station owned by Bristol Broadcasting Co., Inc. The format of the station is modern rock. WNVA-FM broadcasts to the Tri-Cities, TN area at 106.3 FM.
FM RADIO STATION

WNVL-AM 36408
Owner: TBLC Media, LLC
Editorial: 209 10th Ave S Ste 342, Nashville, Tennessee 37203-0758 **Tel:** 1 615 242-1411.
Email: spanishmc@activa1240.com
Web site: http://www.activa1240.com
Profile: WNVL-AM is a commercial station owned by TBLC Media, LLC. The format of the station is Regional Mexican music. WNVL-AM broadcasts in the Nashville, TN area at 1240 AM.
AM RADIO STATION

WNVR-AM 35836
Owner: Polnet Communications
Editorial: 3656 W Belmont Ave, Chicago, Illinois 60618-5328 **Tel:** 1 773 588-6300.
Email: polskieradio@polskieradio.com
Web site: http://www.polskieradio.com
Profile: WNVR-AM is a commercial station owned by Polnet Communications. The format of the station is variety. WNVR-AM broadcasts to the Chicago area at 1030 AM.
AM RADIO STATION

WNVY-AM 36778
Owner: Wilkins Communications Network Inc.
Editorial: 2070 N Palafox St, Pensacola, Florida 32501-2145 **Tel:** 1 850 432-3658.
Email: wnvy@wilkinsradio.com
Web site: http://www.wilkinsradio.com
Profile: WNVY-AM is a commercial station owned by the Wilkins Communications Network Inc. The format for the station is gospel. WNVY-AM broadcasts to the Pensacola, FL area at 1070 AM.
AM RADIO STATION

WNVZ-FM 40578
Owner: Entercom Communications Corp.
Editorial: 236 Clearfield Ave Ste 206, Virginia Beach, Virginia 23462-1893 **Tel:** 1 757 497-2000.
Web site: http://www.z104.com
Profile: WNVZ-FM is a commercial station owned by Entercom Communications Corp. The format of the station is rhythmic Top 40/CHR. WNVZ-FM broadcasts to Virginia Beach, VA at 104.5 FM.
FM RADIO STATION

WNWC-AM 39403
Owner: Northwestern College
Editorial: 5606 Medical Cir, Madison, Wisconsin 53719-1204 **Tel:** 1 608 271-1025.
Email: wnwc@unwsp.edu
Web site: http://life1025.com
Profile: WNWC-AM is a non-commercial station owned by Northwestern College. The format for the station is religious. WNWC-AM broadcasts to the Madison, WI area at 1190 AM.
AM RADIO STATION

WNWF-AM 238354
Owner: Andala Enterprises, Inc.
Editorial: 215 Mountain Dr Ste 104, Destin, Florida 32541-2346
Email: 1140thegame@gmail.com
Web site: http://www.1140thegame.com/
Profile: WNWF-AM is a commercial station owned by Andala Enterprises, Inc. The format of the station is sports. WNWF-AM broadcasts to the Destin, FL area at 1140 AM.
AM RADIO STATION

WNWI-AM 36792
Owner: Birach Broadcasting Corp.
Editorial: 934 W 138th St, Riverdale, Illinois 60827 **Tel:** 1 708 201-9600.
Email: sima@birach.com
Web site: http://www.birach.com/wnwi.html
Profile: WNWI-AM is a commercial station owned by Birach Broadcasting Corp. The format of the station is a variety of ethnic programming, mostly Polish. WNWI-AM broadcasts in the greater Chicago area at 1080 AM.
AM RADIO STATION

WNWK-AM 448927
Owner: Ekonomo (Jose Roberto)
Editorial: 1076 S Chapel St, Newark, Delaware 19702-1304 **Tel:** 1 240 481-8242.
Web site: http://www.sabrosaradio.com
Profile: WNWK-AM is a commercial station owned by Jose Roberto Ekonomo. The format of the station is regional Mexican. WNWK-AM broadcasts to the Dover, DE area at 1260 AM.
AM RADIO STATION

WNWN-AM 39030
Owner: Midwest Communications Inc.
Editorial: 4200 W Main St, Kalamazoo, Michigan 49006-2749 **Tel:** 1 269 345-7121.
Email: amy.burrow@mwcradio.com
Web site: http://go955.com
Profile: WNWN-AM is a commercial station owned by the Midwest Communications Inc. The format of the station is urban contemporary. WNWN-AM broadcasts to the Kalamazoo, MI area at 1560 AM.
AM RADIO STATION

WNWN-FM 46712
Owner: Midwest Communications Inc.
Editorial: 25 Michigan Ave W, Battle Creek, Michigan 49017-3610 **Tel:** 1 269 968-1991.
Web site: http://wincountry.com
Profile: WNWN-FM is a commercial station owned by the Midwest Communications Inc. The format of the station is contemporary country music. WNWN-FM broadcasts to the Battle Creek, MI area at 98.5 FM.
FM RADIO STATION

WNWS-FM 87483
Owner: Wireless Group Inc.(The)
Editorial: 207 W Lafayette St, Jackson, Tennessee 38301-6110 **Tel:** 1 731 423-8316.
Web site: http://point5digital.com/tn/
Profile: WNWS-FM is a commercial station owned by The Wireless Group Inc. The format of the station is news and talk. WNWS-FM broadcasts to the Jackson, TN area at 101.5 FM.
FM RADIO STATION

WNWV-FM 45994
Owner: Rubber City Radio Group, Inc.
Editorial: 6133 Rockside Rd, Independence, Ohio 44131-2223 **Tel:** 1 330 869-9800.
Web site: http://1073thewave.net
Profile: WNWV-FM is a commercial station owned by Rubber City Radio Group, Inc. The format of the station is smooth AC. WNWV-FM broadcasts to the Elyria, OH area at 107.3 FM.
FM RADIO STATION

WNWZ-AM 37996
Owner: Townsquare Media, LLC
Editorial: 50 Monroe Ave NW Ste 500, Grand Rapids, Michigan 49503-2656 **Tel:** 1 616 451-4800.
Email: vip.support@townsquaremedia.com
Web site: http://mymagic941.com
Profile: WNWZ-AM is a commercial station owned by Townsquare Media, LLC. The format of the station is Today's R&B and Old School. WNWZ-AM broadcasts to the Grand Rapids, MI area at 1410 AM.
AM RADIO STATION

WNXR-FM 44164
Owner: Heartland Communications Group, LLC
Editorial: 2320 Ellis Ave, Ashland, Wisconsin 54806-3995 **Tel:** 1 715 682-2727.
Web site: http://www.wnxrfm.com
Profile: WNXR-FM is a commercial station owned by Heartland Communications Group, LLC. The format of the station is oldies. WNXR-FM broadcasts to the Ashland, WI area at 107.3 FM.
FM RADIO STATION

WNXT-AM 38526
Owner: Hometown Broadcasting
Editorial: 405 Masonic Bldg, Portsmouth, Ohio 45662 **Tel:** 1 740 353-1161.
Email: wnxtradio@yahoo.com
Web site: http://www.wnxtradio.com
Profile: WNXT-AM is a commercial station owned by Hometown Broadcasting. The format of the station is news, sports and talk. WNXT-AM broadcasts to Portsmouth, OH and surrounding communities at 1260 AM.
AM RADIO STATION

WNXT-FM 45883
Owner: Hometown Broadcasting
Editorial: 405 Masonic Bldg, Portsmouth, Ohio 45662 **Tel:** 1 740 353-1161.
Email: wnxtnews@yahoo.com
Web site: http://www.wnxtradio.com
Profile: WNXT-FM is a commercial station owned by Hometown Broadcasting. The format of the station is adult contemporary. WNXT-FM broadcasts to Portsmouth, OH and surrounding communities at 99.3 FM.
FM RADIO STATION

WNXX-FM 762329
Owner: Guaranty Broadcasting
Editorial: 929 Government St #B, Baton Rouge, Louisiana 70802-6034 **Tel:** 1 225 388-9898.
Web site: http://www.1045espn.com
Profile: WNXX-FM is a commercial station owned by Guaranty Broadcasting. The format of the station is sports. WNXX-FM broadcasts in the Jackson, LA area at 104.5 FM.
FM RADIO STATION

WNYC-AM 38092
Owner: New York Public Radio
Editorial: 160 Varick St, New York, New York 10013-1220 **Tel:** 1 646 829-4400.
Email: newsroom@wnyc.org
Web site: http://www.wnyc.org
Profile: WNYC-AM is a non-commercial station owned by New York Public Radio. The format of the station is news and talk. WNYC-AM broadcasts in the New York City area at 820 AM.
AM RADIO STATION

WNYC-FM 45413
Owner: New York Public Radio
Editorial: 160 Varick St, New York, New York 10013-1220 **Tel:** 1 646 829-4400.
Email: newsroom@wnyc.org
Web site: http://www.wnyc.org
Profile: WNYC-FM is a non-commercial station owned by New York Public Radio. The format of the station is classical music, news and talk. WNYC-FM broadcasts to the New York City area at 93.9 FM.
FM RADIO STATION

WNYE-FM 40579
Owner: NYC Media Group
Editorial: 112 Tillary St, Brooklyn, New York 11201
Tel: 1 212 669-7400.
Web site: http://www.nyc.gov/radio
Profile: WNYE-FM is a non-commercial station owned by NYC Media Group. The format of the station is talk, music, news and educational programming. WNYE-FM broadcasts to New York City at 91.5 FM.
FM RADIO STATION

WNYG-AM 35569
Owner: Radio Cantico Nuevo Inc.
Editorial: 820 Suffolk Ave, Brentwood, New York 11717-4498
Web site: http://www.radiocanticonuevo.com/
Profile: WNYG-AM is a commercial station owned by Radio Cantico Nuevo Inc. The format of the station is Hispanic contemporary Christian. WNYG-AM broadcasts to the Medford, NY area at 1440 AM.
AM RADIO STATION

WNYM-AM 35746
Owner: Salem Media Group, Inc.
Editorial: 111 Broadway Flr 3RD, New York, New York 10006-1901 **Tel:** 1 212 372-0097.
Email: contact@nycradio.com
Web site: http://www.am970theanswer.com
Profile: WNYM-AM is a commercial station owned by Salem Media Group, Inc. The format of the station is news and talk. WNYM-AM broadcasts to the New York City area at 970 AM.
AM RADIO STATION

WNYN-FM 496633
Owner: Devon Broadcasting Company, Inc
Editorial: 288 S River Rd, Bedford, New Hampshire 3110 **Tel:** 1 603 668-6400.
Profile: WNYN-FM is a commercial station owned by Devon Broadcasting Company, Inc. The format is adult contemporary. The station airs in the Bedford, NH area at 99.1 FM.
FM RADIO STATION

WNYQ-FM 45881
Owner: Pamal Broadcasting Ltd.
Editorial: 89 Everts Ave, Queensbury, New York 12804-2040 **Tel:** 1 518 793-7733.
Email: production@adirondackbroadcasting.com
Web site: http://www.classichitswnyq.com
Profile: WNYQ-FM is a commercial station owned by Pamal Broadcasting Ltd. The format of the station is classic hits. WNYQ-FM broadcasts to the Albany-Schenectady-Troy, NY area at 101.7 FM.
FM RADIO STATION

WNYR-FM 46884
Owner: Longpoint Media
Editorial: 3568 Lenox Rd, Geneva, New York 14456-2058 **Tel:** 1 315 781-7000.
Email: news@flradiogroup.com
Web site: http://fingerlakesdailynews.com/webpages/view/WNYR/
Profile: WNYR-FM is a commercial station owned by Longpoint Media (as of January 1, 2015). The format of the station is adult contemporary music. WNYR-FM broadcasts to the Geneva, NY area at 98.5 FM.
FM RADIO STATION

WNYV-FM 46799
Owner: Pine Tree Broadcasting Company
Editorial: 1214 Vermont Route 30 S, Poultney, Vermont 5764 **Tel:** 1 802 287-9031.
Email: wvnrwnyv@yahoo.com
Profile: WNYV-FM is a commercial station owned by Pine Tree Broadcasting Company. The format of the station is adult contemporary. WNYV-FM broadcasts to the Poultney, VT area at 94.1 FM.
FM RADIO STATION

WNYY-AM 39017
Owner: Saga Communications
Editorial: 1751 Hanshaw Rd, Ithaca, New York 14850-9105 **Tel:** 1 607 257-6400.
Web site: http://pureoldies941.com
Profile: WNYY-AM is a commercial station owned by Saga Communications. The format of the station is Oldies music . WNYY-AM broadcasts to the Ithaca, NY area at 1470 AM.
AM RADIO STATION

WNZF-AM 586857
Owner: Flagler County Broadcasting, LLC
Editorial: 2405 E Moody Blvd Ste 402, Bunnell, Florida 32110-5994 **Tel:** 1 386 437-1992.
Email: newsradio@wnzf.com
Web site: http://www.flaglerbroadcasting.com/wnzf/
Profile: WBHQ-FM is a commercial station owned by Flagler County Broadcasting, LLC. The format of the stations is news and talk. WBHQ-FM broadcasts to the Bunnell, FL area at 1550 AM.
AM RADIO STATION

WNZK-AM 35570
Owner: Birach Broadcasting Corp.
Editorial: 21700 Northwestern Hwy Ste 1190, Southfield, Michigan 48075-4923 **Tel:** 1 248 557-3500.
Email: sima@birach.com
Web site: http://www.birach.com
Profile: WNZK-AM is a commercial station owned by Birach Broadcasting Corp. The format of the station is variety. WNZK-AM broadcasts to the Southfield, MI area at 690 AM.
AM RADIO STATION

WNZN-FM 42357
Owner: Pace Foundation
Editorial: 1505 Kansas Ave, Lorain, Ohio 44052-3363
Tel: 1 440 399-3044.
Email: info@wnzn.org
Web site: http://www.wnzn.org/
Profile: WNZN-FM is a commercial station owned by Pace Foundation. The format of the station is religious programming and Christian music. WNZN-FM broadcasts to the Cleveland area at 89.1FM. The target audience of the station is listeners, ages 13 to 100. WNZN-FM's slogan is "Power 89.1."
FM RADIO STATION

WNZZ-AM 38932
Owner: Cumulus Media Inc.
Editorial: 1 Commerce St Ste 300, Montgomery, Alabama 36104-3542 **Tel:** 1 334 240-9274.
Web site: http://www.wnzz950.com
Profile: WNZZ-AM is a commercial station owned by Cumulus Media Inc. The format of the station is adult standards. WNZZ-AM broadcasts to the Montgomery, AL area at 950 AM.
AM RADIO STATION

WOAB-AM 39092
Owner: Saint Joseph Missions
Editorial: 3660 State Route 30 Ste D, Latrobe, Pennsylvania 15650-4309 **Tel:** 1 724 640-0361.
Profile: WAOB-AM is a commercial station owned by Saint Joseph Missions. The format of the station is Catholic programming. WAOB-AM broadcasts to the Pittsburgh area at 860 AM.
AM RADIO STATION

WOAD-AM 38100
Owner: Alpha Media
Editorial: 731 S Pear Orchard Rd Ste 27, Ridgeland, Mississippi 39157-4839 **Tel:** 1 601 957-1300.
Email: production@wjmi.com
Web site: http://www.woad.com
Profile: WOAD-AM is a commercial station owned by Alpha Media. The format of the station is gospel. WOAD-AM broadcasts to the Jackson, MS area at 1300 AM.
AM RADIO STATION

WOAH-FM 45879
Owner: Broadcast Executives Corp.
Editorial: 832 Elma G Miles Pkwy, Hinesville, Georgia 31313-4554 **Tel:** 1 912 408-1063.
Profile: WOAH-FM is a commercial station owned by Broadcast Executives Corp. The format of the station is urban contemporary. WOAH-FM broadcasts to the Hinesville, GA area at 106.3 FM.
FM RADIO STATION

WOAI-AM 38923
Owner: iHeartMedia Inc.
Editorial: 6222 W Interstate 10, San Antonio, Texas 78201-2013 **Tel:** 1 210 736-9700.
Web site: http://woai.iheart.com
Profile: WOAI-AM is a commercial station owned by iHeartMedia Inc. The format of the station is news and talk. WOAI-AM broadcasts to the San Antonio area at 1200 AM.
AM RADIO STATION

WOAP-AM 36561
Owner: Cano's Broadcasting
Editorial: 2301 N M 52, Owosso, Michigan 48867-1142 **Tel:** 1 989 720-9627.
Web site: http://woapradio.com
Profile: WOAP-AM is a commercial station owned by Cano's Broadcasting. The format of the station is oldies. WOAP-AM broadcasts to the Owosso, MI area at 1080 AM.
AM RADIO STATION

WOAY-AM 35859
Owner: Mountaineer Media, Inc.
Editorial: 240 Central Ave, Oak Hill, West Virginia 25901 **Tel:** 1 304 465-0534.
Email: info@woayradio.com
Web site: http://www.woayradio.com
Profile: WOAY-AM is a commercial station owned by Mountaineer Media, Inc. The format of the station is religious and talk. WOAY-AM broadcasts to the Oak Hill, WV area at 860 AM.
AM RADIO STATION

WOBB-FM 42321
Owner: iHeartMedia Inc.
Editorial: 809 S Westover Blvd, Albany, Georgia 31707-4953 **Tel:** 1 229 439-9704.
Web site: http://b100wobb.iheart.com
Profile: WOBB-FM is a commercial station owned by iHeartMedia Inc. The format of the station is country music. WOBB-FM broadcasts to the Albany, GA area at 100.3 FM.
FM RADIO STATION

WOBC-FM 44265
Owner: Oberlin College
Editorial: Wilder 319, 135 W Lorain St, Oberlin, Ohio 44074 **Tel:** 1 440 775-8107.
Email: wobc@oberlin.edu
Web site: http://www.wobc.org
Profile: WOBC-FM is a non-commercial station owned by Oberlin College. The format of the station is variety. WOBC-FM broadcasts to the Cleveland, OH area at 91.5 FM.
FM RADIO STATION

WOBE-FM 87976
Owner: Results Broadcasting
Editorial: 212 W J St, Iron Mountain, Michigan 49801-4646 **Tel:** 1 906 774-5731.
Email: resultsproduction@gmail.com
Web site: http://www.classichitsb100fm.com
Profile: WOBE-FM is a commercial station owned by Results Broadcasting. The format of the station is Top 40/CHR. WOBE-FM broadcasts to the Marquette, MI area at 100.7 FM.
FM RADIO STATION

WOBG-FM 44493
Owner: Burbach of WV, LLC
Editorial: 1489 Locust Ave, Fairmont, West Virginia 26554-1393 **Tel:** 1 304 363-8888.
Web site: http://rock1057.wixsite.com/home
Profile: WOBG-FM is a commercial station owned by Burbach of WV, LLC. The format of the station features rock music programming. WOBG-FM broadcasts to the Fairmont, WV area at 105.7 FM.
FM RADIO STATION

WOBL-AM 35571
Owner: WOBL Radio Inc.
Editorial: 45624 Us Highway 20, Oberlin, Ohio 44074-9486 **Tel:** 1 440 774-1320.
Email: woblwdlw@yahoo.com
Web site: http://www.woblwdlw.com
Profile: WOBL-AM is a commercial station owned by WOBL Radio Inc. The format of the station is country music. WOBL-AM broadcasts in the Oberlin, OH area at 1320 AM.
AM RADIO STATION

WOBM-AM 37058
Owner: Townsquare Media, LLC
Editorial: 8 Robbins St, Toms River, New Jersey 08753-7668 **Tel:** 1 848 221-8000.
Web site: http://mybeachradio.com
Profile: WOBM-AM is a commercial station owned by Townsquare Media, LLC. The format of the station is news and talk. WOBM-AM broadcasts in the New York area at 1160 AM.
AM RADIO STATION

WOBM-FM 44358
Owner: Townsquare Media, LLC
Editorial: 8 Robbins St Ste 201, Toms River, New Jersey 08753-7668 **Tel:** 1 732 269-0927.
Web site: http://www.wobm.com
Profile: WOBM-FM is a commercial station owned by Townsquare Media, LLC. The format of the station is smooth adult contemporary and soft rock. WOBM-FM broadcasts in the Bayville, NJ area at 92.7 FM.
FM RADIO STATION

WOBN-FM 40581
Owner: Otterbein College
Editorial: Otterbein College, Westerville, Ohio 43081-2006 **Tel:** 1 614 823-1557.
Web site: http://www.wobn.net
Profile: WOBN-FM is a non-commercial station owned by Otterbein College. The format of the station is adult album alternative. WOBN-FM broadcasts to the Westerville, OH area at 97.5 FM.
FM RADIO STATION

WOBR-FM 45416
Owner: East Carolina Radio Group
Editorial: 2422 S Wrightsville Ave, Nags Head, North Carolina 27959-9323 **Tel:** 1 252 441-1024.
Email: admin@ecri.net
Web site: http://www.wobr.com
Profile: WOBR-FM is a commercial station owned by East Carolina Radio Group. The format of the station is rock music. WOBR-FM broadcasts to the Nags Head, NC area at 95.3 FM.
FM RADIO STATION

WOBT-AM 38617
Owner: NRG Media LLC
Editorial: 3616 Highway 47, Rhinelander, Wisconsin 54501-8819 **Tel:** 1 715 362-1975.
Profile: WOBT-AM is a commercial station owned by NRG Media LLC. The format of the station is country. WOBT-AM broadcasts to the Rhinelander, WI area at 1240 AM.
AM RADIO STATION

WOBX-AM 38093
Owner: East Carolina Radio Group
Editorial: 3855 Mills Landing Road, Wanchese, North Carolina 27981 **Tel:** 1 252 441-1024.
Profile: WOBX-AM is a commercial station owned by East Carolina Radio Group. The format of the station is Southern Gospel. WOBX-AM broadcasts to Wanchese, NC at 1530 AM.
AM RADIO STATION

WOBX-FM 242213
Owner: East Carolina Radio Group
Editorial: 2422 S Wrightsville Ave, Nags Head, North Carolina 27959-9323 **Tel:** 1 252 441-1024.
Profile: WOBX-FM is a commercial station owned by East Carolina Radio Group. The format of the station is sports. WOBX-FM broadcasts to the Nags Head, NC area at 98.1 FM.
FM RADIO STATION

WOCA-AM 36335
Owner: Westshore Broadcasting Inc.
Editorial: 3100 SW College Rd Ste 199, Ocala, Florida 34474-6223 **Tel:** 1 352 732-8000.
Web site: http://www.thesource1370.com
Profile: WOCA-AM is a commercial station owned by Westshore Broadcasting Inc. The format of the station is news and talk. WOCA-AM broadcasts to the Ocala, FL area at 1370 AM.
AM RADIO STATION

WOC-AM 38358
Owner: iHeartMedia Inc.
Editorial: 3535 E Kimberly Rd, Davenport, Iowa 52807-2583 **Tel:** 1 563 344-7000.
Web site: http://www.woc1420.com
Profile: WOC-AM is a commercial station owned by iHeartMedia Inc. The format of the station is news and talk. WOC-AM broadcasts to the Davenport, IA area at 1420 AM.
AM RADIO STATION

WOCC-AM 36035
Owner: Brabandt(Richard)
Editorial: 211 N Capitol Ave, Corydon, Indiana 47112-1142 **Tel:** 1 812 738-9622.
Web site: http://www.woccradio.com
Profile: WOCC-AM is a commercial station owned by Richard Brabandt. The format of the station is oldies music. WOCC-AM broadcasts to the Corydon, IN area at 1550 AM.
AM RADIO STATION

WOCE-FM 41746
Owner: Whitfield Communications
Editorial: 613 Silver Cir, Dalton, Georgia 30721-4551
Tel: 1 706 278-5511.
Email: quebuena@ngaradio.com
Web site: http://www.quebuena1019.com
Profile: WOCE-FM is a commercial station owned by Whitfield Communications. The format of the station is Hispanic programming. WOCE-FM broadcasts to the Dalton, GA area at 101.9 FM.
FM RADIO STATION

WOCL-FM 513557
Owner: CBS Radio
Editorial: 1800 Pembrook Dr Ste 400, Orlando, Florida 32810-6375 **Tel:** 1 407 919-1000.
Web site: http://1059sunnyfm.cbslocal.com
Profile: WOCL-FM is a commercial station owned by CBS Radio. The format of the station is classic hits. WOCL-FM broadcasts to the Orlando, FL area at 105.9 FM.
FM RADIO STATION

WOCM-FM 42434
Owner: More(Leighton)
Editorial: 117 49th St, Ocean City, Maryland 21842
Tel: 1 410 723-3683.
Web site: http://www.irieradio.com
Profile: WOCM-FM is a commercial station owned by Leighton More. The format of the station is adult album alternative music. WOCM-FM broadcasts to the Ocean City, MD area at 98.1 FM.
FM RADIO STATION

WOCN-AM 35572
Owner: DM FL Licensee, LLC
Editorial: 350 NE 71st St, Miami, Florida 33138
Tel: 1 305 759-7280.
Profile: WOCN-AM is a commercial station owned by DM FL Licensee, LLC. The format of the station is Hispanic talk and tropical music. WOCN-AM broadcasts to the Miami area at 1450 AM.
AM RADIO STATION

WOCN-FM 41850
Owner: Cape Cod Broadcasting
Editorial: 737 W Main St, Hyannis, Massachusetts 02601-3422 **Tel:** 1 508 771-1224.
Email: news@ccb-media.com
Web site: http://www.ocean1047.com
Profile: WOCN-FM is a commercial station owned by Cape Cod Broadcasting. The format of the station is Lite Rock/Lite AC. WOCN-FM broadcasts to the Hyannis, MA area at 104.7 FM.
FM RADIO STATION

WOCO-AM 38094
Owner: Lamardo Inc.
Editorial: 3829 State Highway 22, Oconto, Wisconsin 54153-9426 **Tel:** 1 920 834-3540.
Email: woco@centurytel.net
Web site: http://wocoradio.com
Profile: WOCO-AM is a commercial station owned by Larmardo Inc. The format of the station is classic country. WOCO-AM broadcasts to the Oconto, WI area at 1260 AM.
AM RADIO STATION

WOCO-FM 45417
Owner: Lamardo Inc.
Editorial: 3829 State Highway 22, Oconto, Wisconsin 54153-9426 **Tel:** 1 920 834-3540.
Email: woco@centurytel.net
Profile: WOCO-FM is a commercial station owned by Larmardo Inc. The format of the station is oldies and lite AC. WOCO-FM broadcasts to the Oconto, WI area at 107.1 AM.
FM RADIO STATION

WOCQ-FM 40583
Owner: Adams Radio Group
Editorial: Northgate Office Park Suite 10A, 119 W Naylor Mill Rd, Salisbury, Maryland 21801
Tel: 1 410 202-8102.
Web site: http://www.oc104.com
Profile: WOCQ-FM is a commercial station owned by Adams Radio Group. The format of the station is urban contemporary music. WOCQ-FM broadcasts to the Salisbury, MD area at 103.9 FM.
FM RADIO STATION

WOCV-AM
37676
Owner: Oneida Broadcasters Inc.
Editorial: 1126 Buffalo Rd, Oneida, Tennessee 37841 **Tel:** 1 423 569-8598.
Email: wbnt@highland.net
Web site: http://www.hive105.com
Profile: WOCV-AM is a commercial station owned by Oneida Broadcasters Inc. The format of the station is country and adult contemporary music and news. WOCV-AM broadcasts to the Oneida, TN area at 1310 AM.
AM RADIO STATION

WOCY-FM
44339
Owner: Live Communications
Editorial: 200-B Reid Avenue, Port St. Joe, Florida 32456 **Tel:** 1 850 705-1065.
Profile: WOCY-FM is a commercial station owned by Live Communications. The format of the station is sports. WOCY-FM is licensed to Carrabelle, FL and broadcasts locally at 106.5 FM.
FM RADIO STATION

WODC-FM
46080
Owner: iHeartMedia Inc.
Editorial: 2323 W 5th Ave Ste 200, Columbus, Ohio 43204-4988 **Tel:** 1 614 486-6101.
Email: newsroom@wkkj.com
Web site: http://www.oldies933fm.com
Profile: WODC-FM is a commercial station owned by iHeartMedia Inc. The format for the station is adult hits. WODC-FM broadcasts to the Columbus, OH area at 93.3 FM.
FM RADIO STATION

WODE-FM
46365
Owner: Connoisseur Media
Editorial: 107 Paxinosa Rd W, Easton, Pennsylvania 18040-1344 **Tel:** 1 610 258-6155.
Web site: http://www.999thehawk.com
Profile: WODE-FM is a commercial station owned by Connoisseur Media. The format of the station is classic hits. WODE-FM broadcasts to the Easton, PA area at 99.9 FM.
FM RADIO STATION

WODI-AM
36528
Owner: JKC Media Ventures, LLC
Editorial: 1230 Radio Rd, Brookneal, Virginia 24528-3141 **Tel:** 1 434 376-1230.
Web site: http://www.1230thefan.com
Profile: WODI-AM is a commercial station owned by JKC Media Ventures, LLC and programmed by Dot FM Group, LLC. The format of the station is sports talk. WODI-AM broadcasts to the Brookneal, VA area at 1230 AM.
AM RADIO STATION

WODS-FM
40584
Owner: CBS Radio
Editorial: 83 Leo M Birmingham Pkwy, Boston, Massachusetts 02135-1101 **Tel:** 1 617 787-7500.
Web site: http://1033ampradio.cbslocal.com
Profile: WODS-FM is a commercial station owned by CBS Radio. The format of the station is Top 40. WODS-FM broadcasts to the Boston area at 103.3 FM.
FM RADIO STATION

WODT-AM
38147
Owner: iHeartMedia Inc.
Editorial: 929 Howard Ave, New Orleans, Louisiana 70113-1148 **Tel:** 1 504 679-7300.
Web site: http://www.espndeportes1280.com/main.html
Profile: WODT-AM is a commercial station owned by iHeartMedia Inc. The format of the station is Spanish sports. WODT-AM broadcasts to the New Orleans area at 1280 AM.
AM RADIO STATION

WODY-AM
35573
Owner: Positive Alternative Radio
Editorial: 1675 Grandview Rd, Martinsville, Virginia 24112-2319 **Tel:** 1 276 638-5235.
Web site: http://www.southsidesportsmedia.com
Profile: WODY-AM is a commercial station owned by Positive Alternative Radio. The format of the station is sports. WODY-AM broadcasts to the Martinsville, VA area at 1160 AM.
AM RADIO STATION

WODZ-FM
44254
Owner: Townsquare Media, LLC.
Editorial: 9418 River Rd, Marcy, New York 13403-2071 **Tel:** 1 315 768-9500.
Web site: http://961wodz.com
Profile: WODZ-FM is a commercial station owned by Townsquare Media, LLC. The format of the station is oldies. WODZ-FM broadcasts to the Utica, NY area at 96.1 FM.
FM RADIO STATION

WOEG-AM
38041
Owner: TeleSouth Communications Inc.
Editorial: 110 W Monticello St, Brookhaven, Mississippi 39601-3305 **Tel:** 1 601 587-9363.
Email: feedback@supertalk.fm
Profile: WOEG-AM is a commercial station owned by TeleSouth Communications Inc. The format of the station is gospel. WOEG-AM broadcasts to the Brookhaven, MS area at 1220 AM.
AM RADIO STATION

WOEL-FM
41499
Owner: Maryland Baptist Bible College & Acad.
Editorial: 3141 Old Elk Neck Rd, Elkton, Maryland 21921 **Tel:** 1 410 392-3225.
Web site: http://www.mbcmin.org/woel/
FM RADIO STATION

WOEN-AM
38057
Owner: Sound Communications, LLC
Editorial: 231 N Union St, Olean, New York 14760-2663 **Tel:** 1 716 375-1015.
Email: mixtraffic@roadrunner.com
Profile: WOEN-AM is a commercial station owned by Sound Communications, LLC. The format of the station is classic hits and sports. WOEN-AM broadcasts to the Olean, NY area at 1360 AM.
AM RADIO STATION

WOEZ-FM
863102
Editorial: 1356 Mackinaw Ave, Cheboygan, Michigan 49721-1003 **Tel:** 1 231 627-2341.
Web site: http://www.wqez.fm
Profile: WOEZ-FM is a commercial station owned by Northern Star Broadcasting LLC. The format of the station is soft adult contemporary. WOEZ-FM broadcasts to Cheboygan, MI area at 106.3 FM.
FM RADIO STATION

WOFC-AM
494009
Owner: FM Radio Licenses, LLC
Editorial: 1500 Diuguid Dr, Murray, Kentucky 42071-1669 **Tel:** 1 270 753-2400.
Profile: WOFC-AM is a commercial station owned by FM Radio Licenses, LLC. The format of the station is sports. WOFC-AM broadcasts to the Murray, KY area at 1130 AM.
AM RADIO STATION

WOFX-AM
39310
Owner: iHeartMedia Inc.
Editorial: 1203 Troy Schenectady Rd, Latham, New York 12110-1046 **Tel:** 1 518 452-4800.
Email: wofx@iheartmedia.com
Web site: http://www.foxsports980.com
Profile: WOFX-AM is a commercial station owned by iHeartMedia Inc. The format of the station is sports. WOFX-AM broadcasts to the Latham, NY area at 980 AM.
AM RADIO STATION

WOFX-FM
45612
Owner: Cumulus Media Inc.
Editorial: 4805 Montgomery Rd Ste 300, Cincinnati, Ohio 45212-2280 **Tel:** 1 513 241-9898.
Web site: http://www.foxcincinnati.com
Profile: WOFX-FM is a commercial station owned by Cumulus Media Inc. The format of the station is classic rock music. WOFX-FM broadcasts to the Cincinnati area at 92.5 FM.
FM RADIO STATION

WOGB-FM
43273
Owner: Cumulus Media Inc.
Editorial: 810 Victoria St, Green Bay, Wisconsin 54302 **Tel:** 1 920 468-4100.
Email: wogb@cumulus.com
Web site: http://wogb.fm
Profile: WOGB-FM is a commercial station owned by Cumulus Media. Inc. The format of the station is classic hits. WOGB-FM broadcasts to the Green Bay, WI area at 103.1 FM.
FM RADIO STATION

WOGG-FM
46905
Owner: FM Radio Licenses, LLC
Editorial: 123 Blaine Rd, Brownsville, Pennsylvania 15417-9330 **Tel:** 1 724 938-2000.
Web site: http://www.froggyland.com
Profile: WOGG-FM is a commercial station owned by FM Radio Licenses, LLC. The format of the station is contemporary country. WOGG-FM broadcasts to the Brownsville, PA area at 94.9 FM.
FM RADIO STATION

WOGI-FM
45146
Owner: FM Radio Licenses, LLC
Editorial: 131 Pleasant Dr Ste 5U, Aliquippa, Pennsylvania 15001-1300 **Tel:** 1 724 378-1271.
Web site: http://www.froggyland.com
Profile: WOGI-FM is a commercial station owned by FM Radio Licenses, LLC. The format of the station is contemporary country. WOGI-FM broadcasts to the Pittsburgh area at 104.3 FM.
FM RADIO STATION

WOGK-FM
40528
Owner: Ocala Broadcasting Corp. LLC
Editorial: 3602 NE 20th Pl, Ocala, Florida 34470-4957 **Tel:** 1 352 622-5600.
Email: kcountrynews@aol.com
Web site: http://www.937kcountry.com
Profile: WOGK-FM is a commercial station owned by Ocala Broadcasting Corp. LLC. The format of the station is country. WOGK-FM broadcasts to the Ocala, FL area at 93.7 FM.
FM RADIO STATION

WOGL-FM
45997
Owner: CBS Radio
Editorial: 2 Bala Plz Ste 800, Bala Cynwyd, Pennsylvania 19004-1515 **Tel:** 1 610 668-5900.
Email: questions@wogl.com
Web site: http://wogl.cbslocal.com
Profile: WOGL-FM is commercial station owned by CBS Radio. The format of the station is classic hits music. WOGL-FM broadcasts to the Philadelphia area at 98.1 FM.
FM RADIO STATION

WOGO-AM
39202
Owner: Stewards of Sound Inc.
Editorial: 2396 Hallie Rd, Ste 1, Chippewa Falls, Wisconsin 54729-7519 **Tel:** 1 715 723-1037.
Email: wogo@wogo.com
Web site: http://www.wogo.com
Profile: WOGO-AM is a commercial station owned by Stewards of Sound Inc. The format of the station is news, sports and talk. WOGO-AM broadcasts to the Chippewa Falls, WI area at 680 AM.
AM RADIO STATION

WOGR-AM
37078
Owner: Victory Christian Center
Editorial: 1501 Carrier Dr, Charlotte, North Carolina 28216-3661 **Tel:** 1 704 393-1540.
Email: info@wordnet.org
Web site: http://www.wordnet.org
Profile: WOGR-AM is a non-commercial station owned by the Victory Christian Center. The format of the station is black gospel music. WOGR-AM broadcasts to the Charlotte, NC area at 1540 AM.
AM RADIO STATION

WOGR-FM
407800
Owner: Victory Christian Center
Editorial: 1501 Carrier Dr, Charlotte, North Carolina 28216-3661 **Tel:** 1 704 393-1540.
Email: info@wordnet.org
Web site: http://www.wordnet.org
Profile: WOGR-FM is a non-commercial station owned by Victory Christian Center. The format of the station is black gospel music. WOGR-FM broadcasts to the Charlotte, NC area at 93.3 FM.
FM RADIO STATION

WOGT-FM
41698
Owner: Cumulus Media Inc.
Editorial: 821 Pineville Rd, Chattanooga, Tennessee 37405-2601 **Tel:** 1 423 756-6141.
Web site: http://1079bigfm.com
Profile: WOGT-FM is a commercial station owned by Cumulus Media Inc. The format of the station is oldies. WOGT-FM broadcasts to the Chattanooga, TN area at 107.9 FM.
FM RADIO STATION

WOGY-FM
45292
Owner: FM Radio Licenses, LLC
Editorial: 122 Radio Rd, Jackson, Tennessee 38301-3465 **Tel:** 1 731 427-3316.
Web site: http://www.froggy1041.com
Profile: WOGY-FM is a commercial station owned by FM Radio Licenses, LLC. The format of the station is classic and contemporary country music. WOGY-FM broadcasts to the Jackson, TN area at 104.1 FM.
FM RADIO STATION

WOHF-FM
40571
Owner: BAS Broadcasting
Editorial: 1281 N River Rd, Fremont, Ohio 43420 **Tel:** 1 419 332-8218.
Web site: http://www.wohfradio.com
Profile: WOHF-FM is a commercial station owned by BAS Broadcasting. The format of the station is oldies. WOHF-FM broadcasts to the Toledo, OH area at 92.1 FM.
FM RADIO STATION

WOHI-AM
38096
Owner: FM Radio Licenses, LLC
Editorial: 131 Pleasant Dr Ste 5U, Aliquippa, Pennsylvania 15001-1300 **Tel:** 1 866 586-2338.
Web site: http://www.picklefm.com/
Profile: WOHI-AM is a commercial station owned by FM Radio Licenses, LLC. The format of the station is classic rock. WOHI-AM broadcasts to the Aliquippa, PA area at 1490 AM.
AM RADIO STATION

WOHS-AM
37045
Owner: KTC Broadcasting
Editorial: 1416 Shelby Hwy #150, Cherryville, North Carolina 28021-8356 **Tel:** 1 704 482-1390.
Web site: http://ktcbroadcasting.com
Profile: WOHS-AM is a commercial station owned by KTC Broadcasting. The format of the station is classic and contemporary country. WOHS-AM broadcasts to the Lincolnton, NC area at 1390 AM.
AM RADIO STATION

WOHT-FM
151844
Owner: Century Broadcasting
Editorial: 157 Dowdle Rd, Grenada, Mississippi 38901 **Tel:** 1 662 294-1448.
Email: star92@cableone.net
FM RADIO STATION

WOIC-AM
36542
Owner: Alpha Media
Editorial: 1900 Pineview Dr, Columbia, South Carolina 29209-5079 **Tel:** 1 803 695-8600.
Web site: http://www.espncolumbia.com
Profile: WOIC-AM is a commercial station owned by Alpha Media. The format of the station is sports. WOIC-AM broadcasts to the Columbia, SC area at 1230 AM.
AM RADIO STATION

WOJB-FM
41352
Owner: Lac Courte Oreilles Ojibwe Reservation
Editorial: 13386 W Trepania Rd, Hayward, Wisconsin 54843-2186 **Tel:** 1 715 634-2100.
Email: generalmanager@wojb.org
Web site: http://www.wojb.org
Profile: WOJB-FM is a non-commercial station owned by the Lac Courte Oreilles Ojibwe Community College. The format of the station is variety. WOJB-FM broadcasts in the Hayward, WI area at 88.9 FM.
FM RADIO STATION

WOJC-FM
558687
Owner: Radio Network
Editorial: 150 Lincolnway Ste 2001, Valparaiso, Indiana 46383-5556 **Tel:** 1 219 548-5800.
Email: info@calvaryradionet.com
Web site: http://www.calvaryradionetwork.com
Profile: WOJC-FM is a non-commercial station owned by Radio Network. The format of the station is Christian music and religious programming. WOJC-FM broadcasts to the Crothersville, IN area at 89.7 FM.
FM RADIO STATION

WOJG-FM
46601
Owner: Shaw's Broadcasting
Editorial: 123 W Market St, Bolivar, Tennessee 38008-2325 **Tel:** 1 731 658-3690.
Web site: http://www.wojg.com
Profile: WOJG-FM is a commercial station owned by Shaw's Broadcasting. The format of the station is gospel. WOJG-FM broadcasts to the Bolivar, TN, area at 94.7 FM.
FM RADIO STATION

WOJL-FM
40488
Owner: Piedmont Communications Inc.
Editorial: 207 Spicers Mill Rd, Orange, Virginia 22960 **Tel:** 1 540 967-1142.
Web site: http://1055samfm.com
Profile: WOJL-FM is a commercial station owned by Piedmont Communications Inc. The format of the station is adult hits music. WOJL-FM broadcasts to the Orange, VA area at 105.5 FM.
FM RADIO STATION

WOJO-FM
46393
Owner: Univision Communications Inc.
Editorial: 625 N Michigan Ave Ste 300, Chicago, Illinois 60611-3110 **Tel:** 1 312 981-1800.
Web site: http://www.univision.com/chicago/wojo
Profile: WOJO-FM is a commercial station owned by Univision Communications Inc. The format of the station is regional Mexican music. WOJO-FM broadcasts to the Chicago area at 105.1 FM.
FM RADIO STATION

WOKA-AM
38099
Owner: Coffee County Broadcasters
Editorial: 1310 Walker St W, Douglas, Georgia 31533-7952 **Tel:** 1 912 384-8153.
Email: production1067@gmail.com
Web site: http://www.dixiecountry.com/
AM RADIO STATION

WOKA-FM
45421
Owner: Coffee County Broadcasters
Editorial: 1310 Walker St W, Douglas, Georgia 31533-7952 **Tel:** 1 912 384-8153.
Web site: http://www.1067thebuck.com
Profile: WOKA-FM is a commercial station owned by Coffee County Broadcasters. The format of the station is classic country. WOKA-FM broadcasts to the Douglas, GA area at 106.7 FM.
FM RADIO STATION

WOKB-AM
35575
Owner: Rama Communications Inc.
Editorial: 3765 N John Young Pkwy, Orlando, Florida 32804 **Tel:** 1 407 293-9652.
Email: info@wokbradio.com
Web site: http://www.wokbradio.com
Profile: WOKB-AM is a commercial station owned by Rama Communications Inc. The format of the station is gospel. WOKB-AM broadcasts to the Orlando, FL area at 1600 AM.
AM RADIO STATION

WOKC-AM
36204
Owner: Glades Media Co.
Editorial: 210 W. North Park St, Ste 102, Okeechobee, Florida 34972 **Tel:** 1 863 467-1570.
Email: wokc@gladesmedia.com
Web site: http://www.wokc.com
Profile: WOKC-AM is a commercial station owned by Glades Media Co. The format of the station is classic and contemporary country. WOKC-AM broadcasts to the area of Okeechobee, FL area at 1570 AM.
AM RADIO STATION

WOKD-FM
77142
Owner: Positive Alternative Radio
Editorial: 22226 Timberlake Rd, Lynchburg, Virginia 24502 **Tel:** 1 540 774-9798.
Email: office@spiritfm.com
Web site: http://www.spiritfm.com
FM RADIO STATION

WOKE-FM
44038
Owner: Positive Alternative Radio
Editorial: 3027 Lester Ln, Ashland, Kentucky 41102-9642 **Tel:** 1 877 456-9361.
Email: office@walkfm.org
Web site: http://walkfm.org
Profile: WOKE-FM is a commercial station owned by Positive Alternative Radio, Inc. The format of the

station is Contemporary Christian music. WOKE-FM broadcasts to the Huntington, WV area at a frequency of 98.3 FM.
FM RADIO STATION

WOKH-FM 41321
Owner: Choice Radio Corporation
Editorial: 101 N 3rd St, Bardstown, Kentucky 40004-1525 **Tel:** 1 502 331-7266.
Web site: http://www.wokhfm.com/
Profile: WOKH-FM is a commercial station owned by Choice Radio Corporation. The format of the station is Lite Rock/Lite AC. WOKH-FM broadcasts to the Bardstown, KY area at 102.7 FM.
FM RADIO STATION

WOKI-FM 41029
Owner: Cumulus Media Inc.
Editorial: 4711 Old Kingston Pike, Knoxville, Tennessee 37919 **Tel:** 1 865 588-6511.
Web site: http://987newstalk.com
Profile: WOKI-FM is a commercial station owned by Cumulus Media Inc. The format of the station is news/talk. WOKI-FM broadcasts to the Knoxville, TN area at 98.7 FM.
FM RADIO STATION

WOKK-FM 45423
Owner: Mississippi Broadcasters, LLC
Editorial: 3436 Highway 45 N, Meridian, Mississippi 39301-1509 **Tel:** 1 601 693-2661.
Email: onair@wokk.com
Web site: http://www.wokk.com
Profile: WOKK-FM is a commercial station owned by Mississippi Broadcasters, LLC. The format for the station is contemporary country. WOKK-FM broadcasts to the Meridian, MS area at 97.1 FM.
FM RADIO STATION

WOKN-FM 46771
Owner: Tower Broadcasting LLC
Editorial: 1705 Lake St, Elmira, New York 14901-1220 **Tel:** 1 607 733-5626.
Email: towerbroadcasting@hotmail.com
Web site: http://995woknelmira.com
Profile: WOKN-FM is a commercial station owned by Tower Broadcasting LLC. The format of the station is contemporary country music. WOKN-FM broadcasts to the Elmira, NY area at 99.5 FM.
FM RADIO STATION

WOKO-FM 45906
Owner: Hall Communications
Editorial: 70 Joy Dr, South Burlington, Vermont 05403-6118 **Tel:** 1 802 658-1230.
Email: woko@woko.com
Web site: http://www.woko.com
Profile: WOKO-FM is a commercial station owned by Hall Communications. The format of the station is Contemporary Country music. WOKO-FM broadcasts to the South Burlington, VT area at 98.9 FM.
FM RADIO STATION

WOKQ-FM 40939
Owner: Townsquare Media
Editorial: 292 Middle Rd, Dover, New Hampshire 03820-4901 **Tel:** 1 603 749-9750.
Email: news@wokq.com
Web site: http://www.wokq.com
Profile: WOKQ-FM is a commercial station owned by Townsquare Media. The format of the station is contemporary country music. WOKQ-FM broadcasts to the Dover, NH area at 97.5 FM.
FM RADIO STATION

WOKR-AM 39487
Owner: Genesee Media Corp.
Editorial: 20 Office Park Way, Pittsford, New York 14534-1718 **Tel:** 1 585 335-9369.
Email: sports@theteam.fm
Web site: http://theteam.fm
Profile: WOKR-AM is a commercial station owned by Genesee Media Corp. The format of the station is sports. WOKR-AM broadcasts to the Brockport, NY area at 1590 AM.
AM RADIO STATION

WOKS-AM 38788
Owner: Davis Broadcasting
Editorial: 2203 Wynnton Rd, Columbus, Georgia 31906-2531 **Tel:** 1 706 576-3565.
Web site: http://www.woks1340.com/Homepage/12456878
Profile: WOKS-AM is a commercial station owned by Davis Broadcasting. The format of the station is gospel and oldies. WOKS-AM broadcasts to the Columbus, GA area at 1340 AM.
AM RADIO STATION

WOKV-AM 38101
Owner: Cox Media Group, Inc.
Editorial: 8000 Belfort Pkwy Ste 100, Jacksonville, Florida 32256-6925 **Tel:** 1 904 245-8500.
Web site: http://wokv.com
Profile: WOKV-AM is a commercial station owned by Cox Media Group, Inc. The format of the station is news, sports and talk. WOKV-AM broadcasts to the Jacksonville, FL area at 690 AM.
AM RADIO STATION

WOKV-FM 42129
Owner: Cox Media Group, Inc.
Editorial: 8000 Belfort Pkwy Ste 261, Jacksonville, Florida 32256-6934 **Tel:** 1 904 245-8500.
Web site: http://www.wokv.com
Profile: WOKV-FM-FM is a commercial station owned by Cox Media Group, Inc. The station's format is news/talk/sports. WOKV-FM broadcasts to the Jacksonville, FL area at 104.5 FM.
FM RADIO STATION

WOKW-FM 41303
Owner: Harley(Mark E.)
Editorial: 712 River Rd, Clearfield, Pennsylvania 16830-2958 **Tel:** 1 814 765-4955.
Email: news@wokw.com
Web site: http://www.wokw.com
Profile: WOKW-FM is a commercial station owned by Mark E. Harley. The format of the station is adult contemporary music. WOKW-FM broadcasts to the Clearfield, PA area at 102.9 FM.
FM RADIO STATION

WOKY-AM 38102
Owner: iHeartMedia Inc.
Editorial: 12100 W Howard Ave, Greenfield, Wisconsin 53228-1851 **Tel:** 1 414 545-8900.
Web site: http://www.thebig920.com
Profile: WOKY-AM is a commercial station owned by iHeartMedia Inc. The format of the station is classic country. WOKY-AM broadcasts to the Milwaukee area at 920 AM.
AM RADIO STATION

WOKZ-FM 77650
Owner: Original Company, Inc. (The)
Tel: 1 618 842-2159.
Email: wfiwwokz@fairfieldwireless.net
Web site: http://www.wfiwradio.com
Profile: WOKZ-FM is a commercial station owned by Original Company, Inc. (The). The format of the station is classic country music. WOKZ-FM broadcasts to the Fairfield, IN area at 105.9 FM.
FM RADIO STATION

WOL-AM 38862
Owner: Urban One, Inc.
Editorial: 8515 Georgia Ave Fl 9, Silver Spring, Maryland 20910-3403 **Tel:** 1 301 306-1111.
Web site: http://woldcnews.com/
Profile: WOL-AM is a commercial station owned by Urban One, Inc. The format of the station is African-American news, business, and general interest talk. WOL-AM broadcasts to the Washington D.C. area at 1450 AM.
AM RADIO STATION

WOLB-AM 38296
Owner: Urban One, Inc.
Editorial: 1705 Whitehead Rd, Baltimore, Maryland 21207-4033 **Tel:** 1 410 332-8200.
Web site: http://www.wolb1010.com
Profile: WOLB-AM is a commercial station owned by Urban One, Inc. The format of the station is news and talk. WOLB-AM broadcasts in the Baltimore area at 1010 AM.
AM RADIO STATION

WOLD-FM 45425
Owner: T.E.C.O. Broadcasting, Inc.
Editorial: 405 N Main St, Marion, Virginia 24354-3325 **Tel:** 1 276 783-4042.
Profile: WOLD-FM is a commercial station owned by T.E.C.O. Broadcasting, Inc. The format for the station is classic hits. WOLD-FM broadcasts to the Marion, VA area at 102.5 FM.
FM RADIO STATION

WOLF-FM 45531
Owner: Family Life Ministries Radio
Editorial: 8456 Smokey Hollow Rd, Baldwinsville, New York 13027-8222 **Tel:** 1 315 635-3971.
Web site: http://921fmthewolf.com/
Profile: WOLF-FM is a commercial station owned by Family Life Ministries Radio. The format of the station is country. WOLF-FM broadcasts to the Syracuse, NY area at 92.1 FM.
FM RADIO STATION

WOLG-FM 42841
Owner: Covenant Network
Editorial: 4424 Hampton Ave, Saint Louis, Missouri 63109 **Tel:** 1 314 752-7000.
Email: covenantnetwork@juno.com
Web site: http://www.covenantnet.net
Profile: WOLG-FM is a non-commercial station owned by the Covenant Network. The format of the station is religious music and talk. WOLG-FM broadcasts in the St. Louis area at 95.9 FM.
FM RADIO STATION

WOLH-AM 558547
Owner: Miller Communications Inc.
Editorial: 2423 Walker Swinton Rd, Timmonsville, South Carolina 29161-9351 **Tel:** 1 843 678-9393.
Email: production@miller.fm
Web site: http://www.miller.fm
Profile: WOLH-AM is a commercial station owned by Miller Communications Inc. The format of the station is sports. WOLH-AM broadcasts to the Florence, SC area at 1230 AM.
AM RADIO STATION

WOLI-AM 37097
Owner: TBLC Holdings
Editorial: 225 S Pleasantburg Dr Ste B3, Greenville, South Carolina 29607-2533 **Tel:** 1 864 751-0113.
Profile: WOLI-AM is a commercial station owned by TBLC Holdings. The format for the station is Regional Mexican. WOLI-AM broadcasts to the Greenville/Spartanburg, SC areas at 910 AM.
AM RADIO STATION

WOLL-FM 43396
Owner: iHeartMedia Inc.
Editorial: 3071 Continental Dr, West Palm Beach, Florida 33407-3274 **Tel:** 1 561 616-6600.
Web site: http://www.kool1055.com
Profile: WOLL-FM is a commercial station owned by iHeartMedia Inc. The format of the station is oldies. WOLL-FM broadcasts to the West Palm Beach, FL area at 105.5 FM.
FM RADIO STATION

WOLS-FM 46733
Owner: Norsan Group
Editorial: 4801 E Independence Blvd Ste 815, Charlotte, North Carolina 28212-5490 **Tel:** 1 704 405-3172.
Web site: http://www.larazalaraza.com
Profile: WOLS-FM is a commercial station owned by Norsan Group. The format of the station is regional Mexican WOLS-FM broadcasts to the Charlotte, NC area at 106.1 FM.
FM RADIO STATION

WOLT-FM 42330
Owner: iHeartMedia Inc.
Editorial: 6161 Fall Creek Rd, Indianapolis, Indiana 46220-5032 **Tel:** 1 317 257-7565.
Email: airstaff@alt1033.com
Web site: http://alt1033.iheart.com
Profile: WOLT-FM is a commercial station owned by iHeartMedia Inc. The format for the station is rock alternative music. WOLT-FM broadcasts to the Indianapolis area at 103.3 FM. The station's slogan is, "Indy's alternative."
FM RADIO STATION

WOLV-FM 45946
Owner: Houghton Community Broadcasting Corporation
Editorial: 313 E Montezuma Ave, Houghton, Michigan 49931-2112 **Tel:** 1 906 482-7700.
Email: houghtonradio@up.net
Web site: http://www.thewolf.com
Profile: WOLV-FM is a commercial station owned by Houghton Community Broadcasting Corporation. The format of the station is classic hits. WOLV-FM broadcasts to the Houghton, MI area at 97.7 FM.
FM RADIO STATION

WOLW-FM 41615
Owner: Northern Christian Radio
Editorial: 1511 E M 32, Gaylord, Michigan 49735-9702 **Tel:** 1 989 732-6274.
Email: studio@ncradio.org
Web site: http://www.ncradio.org
Profile: WOLW-FM is a non-commercial station owned by Northern Christian Radio. The format of the station is contemporary Christian and religious programming. WOLW-FM broadcasts to the Gaylord, MI area at 91.1 FM.
FM RADIO STATION

WOLX-FM 40379
Owner: Entercom Communications Corp.
Editorial: 7601 Ganser Way, Madison, Wisconsin 53719-2074 **Tel:** 1 608 826-0077.
Email: wolx@entercom.com
Web site: http://www.wolx.com
Profile: WOLX-FM is a commercial station owned by Entercom Communications Corp. The format of the station is oldies. WOLX-FM broadcasts to the Madison, WI area at 94.9 FM.
FM RADIO STATION

WOLZ-FM 41605
Owner: iHeartMedia Inc.
Editorial: 13320 Metro Pkwy Ste 1, Fort Myers, Florida 33966-4804 **Tel:** 1 239 225-4300.
Email: wolz@iheartmedia.com
Web site: http://www.953theriver.com
Profile: WOLZ-FM is a commercial station owned by iHeartMedia Inc. The format of the station is classic hits. WOLZ-FM broadcasts to the Fort Myers, FL area at 95.3 FM.
FM RADIO STATION

WOMB-FM 770709
Owner: Mary's Children, Inc
Editorial: 8220 W State Road 48, Bloomington, Indiana 47404-9735 **Tel:** 1 812 825-4642.
Email: womb89.9fm@gmail.com
Web site: http://wombradio.com
Profile: WOMB-FM is a non-commercial station ownedy by Mary's Children, Inc. The format of the station features Catholic programming. WOMB-FM broadcasts to the Ellettsville and Bloomington, IN area at a frequency of 89.9 FM.
FM RADIO STATION

WOMC-FM 40587
Owner: CBS Radio
Editorial: 26455 American Dr, Southfield, Michigan 48034-6114 **Tel:** 1 248 327-2900.
Web site: http://womc.cbslocal.com/
Profile: WOMC-FM is a commercial station owned by CBS Radio. The format of the station is classic hits. WOMC-FM broadcasts to the Detroit area at 104.3 FM.
FM RADIO STATION

WOMG-FM 45760
Owner: Cumulus Media Inc.
Editorial: 1801 Charleston Hwy Ste J, Cayce, South Carolina 29033-2019 **Tel:** 1 803 796-9975.
Web site: http://www.nashfm985.com
Profile: WOMG-FM is a commercial station owned by Cumulus Media Inc. The format of the station is country. WOMG-FM broadcasts to the Columbia, SC area at 98.5 FM.
FM RADIO STATION

WOMI-AM 3837
Owner: Townsquare Media, LLC
Editorial: 3301 Frederica St, Owensboro, Kentucky 42301-6082 **Tel:** 1 270 683-1558.
Web site: http://womiowensboro.com
Profile: WOMI-AM is a commercial station owned by Townsquare Media, LLC. The format of the station is news and talk. WOMI-AM broadcasts to the Owensboro, KY area at 1490 AM.
AM RADIO STATION

WOMP-AM 38693
Owner: FM Radio Licenses, LLC
Editorial: 56325 High Ridge Rd, Bellaire, Ohio 43906-9707 **Tel:** 1 740 676-5661.
Profile: WOMP-AM is a commercial station owned by FM Radio Licenses, LLC. The format for the station is classic country. WOMP-AM broadcasts to the Wheeling, WV area at 1290 AM.
AM RADIO STATION

WOMR-FM 41348
Owner: Lower Cape Communications
Editorial: 494 Commercial St Fl 2, Provincetown, Massachusetts 02657-2414 **Tel:** 1 508 487-2619.
Email: info@womr.org
Web site: http://www.womr.org
Profile: WOMR-FM is a non-commercial station owned by Lower Cape Communications. The format of the station is variety. WOMR-FM broadcasts to the Provincetown, MA area at 92.1 FM.
FM RADIO STATION

WOMT-AM 38104
Owner: Seehafer Broadcasting Corp.
Editorial: 3730 Mangin St, Manitowoc, Wisconsin 54220 **Tel:** 1 920 682-0351.
Email: news@womtradio.com
Web site: http://www.womtradio.com
Profile: WOMT-AM is a commercial station owned by Seehafer Broadcasting Corp. The format of the station is adult contemporary music and sports. WOMT-AM broadcasts to the Manitowoc, WI area at 1240 AM.
AM RADIO STATION

WOMX-FM 42684
Owner: CBS Radio
Editorial: 1800 Pembrook Dr, Ste 400, Orlando, Florida 32810-6375 **Tel:** 1 407 919-1000.
Web site: http://www.mix1051.com
Profile: WOMX-FM is a commercial station owned by CBS Radio. The format of the station is hot adult contemporary music. WOMX-FM broadcasts to the Orlando, FL area at 105.1 FM.
FM RADIO STATION

WONA-FM 45426
Owner: Southern Electronics Inc.
Editorial: 1006 S Applegate St, Winona, Mississippi 38967 **Tel:** 1 662 283-1570.
Email: wonafm@gmail.com
Web site: http://www.hawg95.com
Profile: WONA-FM is a commercial station owned by Southern Electronics Inc. The format of the station is country music. WONA-FM broadcasts to the Winona, MS area at 95.1 FM.
FM RADIO STATION

WONC-FM 40588
Owner: North Central College
Editorial: 232 E Chicago Ave, Naperville, Illinois 60540 **Tel:** 1 630 637-8989.
Web site: http://www.wonc.org
Profile: WONC-FM is a non-commercial station owned by North Central College. The format of the station is rock/album oriented rock. WONC-FM broadcasts to the Naperville, IL area at 89.1 FM.
FM RADIO STATION

WOND-AM 39357
Owner: Longport Media
Editorial: 1601 New Rd, Linwood, New Jersey 08221-1116 **Tel:** 1 609 653-1400.
Web site: http://www.wondradio.com
Profile: WOND-AM is a commercial station owned by Longport Media. The format of the station is news and talk. WOND-AM broadcasts to the Linwood, NJ area at 1400 AM.
AM RADIO STATION

WONE-AM 38106
Owner: iHeartMedia Inc.
Editorial: 101 Pine St, Dayton, Ohio 45402-2948 **Tel:** 1 937 224-1137.
Web site: http://wone.iheart.com
Profile: WONE-AM is a commercial station owned by iHeartMedia Inc. The format of the station is sports. WONE-AM broadcasts in the Dayton, OH area at 980 AM.
AM RADIO STATION

WONE-FM 45427
Owner: Rubber City Radio Group Inc.
Editorial: 1795 W Market St, Akron, Ohio 44313-7001 **Tel:** 1 330 869-9800.
Email: news@wakr.net
Web site: http://www.wone.net
Profile: WONE-FM is a commercial station owned by the Rubber City Radio Group Inc. The format of the station is classic rock music. WONE-FM broadcasts to the Akron, OH area at 97.5 FM.
FM RADIO STATION

WONN-AM 38107
Owner: Hall Communications
Editorial: 404 W Lime St, Lakeland, Florida 33815-4651 **Tel:** 1 863 682-8184.
Web site: http://www.wonn.com
Profile: WONN-AM is a commercial station owned by Hall Communications. The format of the station is adult standards music. WONN-AM broadcasts to the Lakeland, FL area at 1230 AM.
AM RADIO STATION

WONN-FM 43046
Owner: Hall Communications
Editorial: 1996 Auction Rd, Manheim, Pennsylvania 17545-9159 **Tel:** 1 717 653-0800.
Web site: http://espnradio927.com
Profile: WONN-FM is a commercial station owned by Hall Communications. The format of the station is sports. WONN-FM broadcasts to the Manheim, PA area at 92.7 FM.
FM RADIO STATION

WONQ-AM 35825
Owner: Florida Broadcasters
Editorial: 1355 E Altamonte Dr, Altamonte Springs, Florida 32701-5011 **Tel:** 1 407 830-0800.
Email: info@1030lagrande.com
Web site: http://www.lagrande1030am.com
Profile: WONQ-AM is a commercial station owned by Florida Broadcasters. The format of the station is Spanish language news talk. WONQ-AM broadcasts to the Altamonte Springs, FL area at 1030 AM.
AM RADIO STATION

WONS-AM 35944
Owner: Expression Production Group
Tel: 1 888 314.3771.
Email: info@wzaqfm.com
Profile: WONS-AM is a commercial station owned by Expression Production Group LLC The format of the station is Southern gospel. WONS-AM broadcasts to the Ashland, KY area at 1080 AM.
AM RADIO STATION

WONW-AM 39272
Owner: iHeartMedia Inc.
Editorial: 2110 Radio Dr, Defiance, Ohio 43512-1977 **Tel:** 1 419 782-8126.
Web site: http://www.wonw1280.com
Profile: WONW-AM is a commercial station owned by iHeartMedia Inc. The format of the station is news, sports and talk. WONW-AM broadcasts to the Defiance, OH area at 1280 AM.
AM RADIO STATION

WOOD-AM 38108
Owner: iHeartMedia Inc.
Editorial: 77 Monroe Center St NW Ste 1000, Grand Rapids, Michigan 49503-2912 **Tel:** 1 616 459-1919.
Email: news@woodradio.com
Web site: http://woodradio.iheart.com
Profile: WOOD-AM is a commercial station owned by iHeartMedia Inc. The format of the station is news, sports and talk. WOOD-AM broadcasts to the Grand Rapids, MI area at 1300 AM.
AM RADIO STATION

WOOD-FM 725641
Owner: iHeartMedia Inc.
Editorial: 77 Monroe Center St NW Ste 1000, Grand Rapids, Michigan 49503-2912 **Tel:** 1 616 459-1919.
Web site: http://www.woodradio.com
Profile: WOOD-FM is a commercial station owned by iHeartMedia Inc. The format of the station is news/talk. WOOD-FM broadcasts to the Grand Rapids, MI at a frequency of 106.9 FM.
FM RADIO STATION

WOOF-AM 38109
Owner: Woof Inc.
Editorial: 2518 Columbia Hwy, Dothan, Alabama 36303 **Tel:** 1 334 792-1149.
Email: woof@ala.net
Web site: http://www.woofradio.com
Profile: WOOF-AM is a commercial station owned by Woof Inc. The format of the station is sports. WOOF-AM broadcasts in the Dothan, AL area at 560 AM.
AM RADIO STATION

WOOF-FM 45429
Owner: Woof Inc.
Editorial: 2518 Columbia Hwy, Dothan, Alabama 36303 **Tel:** 1 334 792-1149.
Email: general@997wooffm.com
Web site: http://www.997wooffm.com
Profile: WOOF-FM is a commercial station owned by Woof Inc. The format of the station is adult contemporary music. WOOF-FM broadcasts in the Dothan, AL area at 99.7 FM.
FM RADIO STATION

WOON-AM 35951
Owner: O-N Radio Inc.
Editorial: 985 Park Ave, Woonsocket, Rhode Island 02895-6332 **Tel:** 1 401 762-1240.
Email: email@onworldwide.com
Web site: http://www.on-radio.com
Profile: WOON-AM is a commercial station owned by O-N Radio Inc. The format of the station is variety. WOON-AM broadcasts to the Woonsocket, RI area at 1240 AM.
AM RADIO STATION

WOOW-AM 35581
Owner: Rouse(James)
Editorial: 405 Evans St, Greenville, North Carolina 27858 **Tel:** 1 252 757-0365.
Email: mvoicenews@yahoo.com
Web site: http://www.jimrousecommunications.com
Profile: WOOW-AM is a commercial station owned by James Rouse. The format of the station is gospel and talk. WOOW-AM broadcasts to the Greenville, NC area at 1340 AM.
AM RADIO STATION

WOOZ-FM 41927
Owner: Max Media
Editorial: 1431 Country Aire Dr, Carterville, Illinois 62918-5118 **Tel:** 1 618 985-4843.
Email: publicservice@riverradio.net
Web site: http://www.z100fm.com
Profile: WOOZ-FM is a commercial station which is owned by Max Media. The format of the station is contemporary country. WOOZ-FM broadcasts to the Carterville, IL area on 99.9 FM. Send PSAs to publicservice@riverradio.net.
FM RADIO STATION

WOPC-FM 903805
Owner: Last Of A Dying Breed Broadcasting
Editorial: 100 E Main St, Linden, Tennessee 37096-3006 **Tel:** 1 724 516-8885.
Web site: http://www.1013hankfm.com
Profile: WOPC-FM is a commercial station owned by Last Of A Dying Breed Broadcasting. The format of the station is classic country. WOPC-FM broadcasts to the Linden, TN area at a frequency of 101.3 FM.
FM RADIO STATION

WOPG-AM 38704
Owner: Pax et Bonum, Inc.
Email: called@pax-et-bonum-radio.org
Web site: http://pax-et-bonum-radio.org
Profile: WOPG-AM is a non-commercial station owned by Pax et Bonum, Inc. The station broadcasts locally at a frequency of 1460 AM.
AM RADIO STATION

WOPI-AM 36783
Owner: Holston Valley Broadcasting Corp.
Tel: 1 423 246-9578.
Web site: http://www.wopi.com
Profile: WOPI-AM is a commercial station owned by Holston Valley Broadcasting Corp. The format of the station is sports. WOPI-AM broadcasts to the Bristol, TN area at 1490 AM.
AM RADIO STATION

WOPP-AM 35582
Owner: E & R Broadcasting Inc.
Editorial: 1101 Cameron Rd, Opp, Alabama 36467-2407 **Tel:** 1 334 493-4545.
Email: wopp@wopp.com
Web site: http://www.wopp.com
Profile: WOPP-AM is a commercial station owned by E & R Broadcasting Inc. The format of the station is classic country and oldies. WOPP-AM broadcasts to the Opp, AL area at 1290 AM.
AM RADIO STATION

WOR-AM 35858
Owner: iHeartMedia Inc.
Editorial: 32 Avenue of the Americas, New York, New York 10013-2473 **Tel:** 1 212 377-7900.
Web site: http://710wor.iheart.com
Profile: WOR-AM is a commercial station owned by iHeartMedia Inc. The format of the station is news and talk. WOR-AM broadcasts to the New York area at 710 AM.
AM RADIO STATION

WORC-AM 35583
Owner: Gois Broadcasting
Editorial: 122 Green St Ste 2R, Worcester, Massachusetts 01604-4138 **Tel:** 1 508 791-2111.
Web site: http://www.megaworcester.com
Profile: WORC-AM is a commercial station owned by Gois Broadcasting. The format of the station is Hispanic programming. WORC-AM broadcasts to the Worcester, MA area at 1310 AM.
AM RADIO STATION

WORC-FM 44362
Owner: Cumulus Media Inc.
Editorial: 250 Commercial St Ste 530, Worcester, Massachusetts 01608-1726 **Tel:** 1 508 752-1045.
Web site: http://www.nashicon989.com
Profile: WORC-FM is a commercial station owned by Cumulus Media Inc. The format of the station is classic country. WORC-FM broadcasts to the Worcester, MA area at 98.9 FM.
FM RADIO STATION

WORD-AM 39370
Owner: Entercom Communications Corp.
Editorial: 25 Garlington Rd, Greenville, South Carolina 29615-4613 **Tel:** 1 864 271-9200.
Web site: http://www.espnupstate.com
Profile: WORD-AM is a commercial station owned by Entercom Communications Corp. The format of the station is sports talk. WORD-AM broadcasts to the Greenville, SC area at 950 AM.
AM RADIO STATION

WORD-FM 46517
Owner: Salem Media Group, Inc.
Editorial: 7 Parkway Ctr Ste 625, Pittsburgh, Pennsylvania 15220-3707 **Tel:** 1 412 937-1500.
Email: word@wordfm.com
Web site: http://www.wordfm.com

Profile: WORD-FM is a commercial station owned by Salem Media Group, Inc. The format of the station is contemporary Christian music and religious talk. WORD-FM broadcasts to the Pittsburgh area at 101.5 FM.
FM RADIO STATION

WORG-FM 44139
Owner: Garris Communications Inc.
Editorial: 1675 Chestnut St, Orangeburg, South Carolina 29115-3327 **Tel:** 1 803 516-8400.
Email: worg@worg.com
Web site: http://www.worg.com
Profile: WORG-FM is a commercial station owned by Garris Communications Inc. The format of the station is adult contemporary. WORG-FM broadcasts to the Orangeburg, SC area at 100.3 FM.
FM RADIO STATION

WORL-AM 75222
Owner: Salem Media Group, Inc.
Editorial: 1188 Lake View Dr, Altamonte Springs, Florida 32714-2713 **Tel:** 1 407 682-9494.
Email: worl@salemorlando.com
Web site: http://www.worl660.com
Profile: WORL-AM is a commercial station owned by Salem Media Group, Inc. The format of the station is news and talk. WORL-AM broadcasts to the Orlando, FL area at 660 AM.
AM RADIO STATION

WORM-AM 38110
Owner: Hunt(Gerald W.)
Editorial: 165 Bowen Dr, Savannah, Tennessee 38372-1490 **Tel:** 1 731 925-7102.
Profile: WORM-AM is a commercial station owned by Gerald W. Hunt. The format of the station is oldies. WORM-AM broadcasts to the Savannah, TN area at 1010 AM.
AM RADIO STATION

WORM-FM 45431
Owner: Hunt(Gerald W.)
Editorial: 165 Bowen Dr, Savannah, Tennessee 38372-1490 **Tel:** 1 731 925-7102.
Email: thewormq105@yahoo.com
Profile: WORM-FM is a commercial station owned by Gerald W. Hunt. The format of the station is country. WORM-FM broadcasts to the Savannah, TN area at 101.7 FM.
FM RADIO STATION

WORQ-FM 42352
Owner: Lakeshore Communications
Editorial: 1253 Schering Rd Unit B, De Pere, Wisconsin 54115-1003 **Tel:** 1 920 494-9010.
Email: mail@q90fm.com
Web site: http://www.q90fm.com
Profile: WORQ-FM is a non-commercial station owned by Lakeshore Communications. The format of the station is contemporary Christian. WORQ-FM broadcasts to the Green Bay, WI area at 90.1 FM.
FM RADIO STATION

WORV-AM 38387
Owner: Circuit Broadcasting of Hattiesburg
Editorial: 1204 Kinnard St, Hattiesburg, Mississippi 39401 **Tel:** 1 601 544-1941.
AM RADIO STATION

WORX-FM 45432
Owner: DCBroadcasting Inc.
Editorial: 1224 E Telegraph Hill Rd, Madison, Indiana 47250-9273 **Tel:** 1 812 265-3322.
Email: thebestmusic@worxradio.com
Web site: http://www.worxradio.com
Profile: WORX-FM is a commercial station owned by DCBroadcasting Inc. The format of the station is adult contemporary music. WORX-FM broadcasts to the Madison, IN area at 96.7 FM.
FM RADIO STATION

WOSA-FM 723363
Owner: WOSU Public Media
Editorial: 2400 Olentangy River Rd, Columbus, Ohio 43210-1027 **Tel:** 1 614 292-9678.
Email: info@wosu.org
Web site: http://www.wosu.org
Profile: WOSA-FM is a non-commercial station owned by WOSU Public Media. The format of the station is classical. The station broadcasts to the Columbus, OH area at a frequency of 101.1 FM.
FM RADIO STATION

WOSF-FM 35946
Owner: Urban One, Inc.
Editorial: 8809 Lenox Pointe Dr Unit A, Charlotte, North Carolina 28273-3377 **Tel:** 1 704 548-7800.
Web site: http://oldschool1053.com
Profile: WOSF-FM is a commercial station owned by Urban One, Inc. The format of the station is R&B oldies featuring hits from the 70s and 80s. WOSF-FM broadcasts to the Charlotte, NC area at 105.3 FM.
FM RADIO STATION

WOSH-AM 39264
Owner: Cumulus Media Inc.
Editorial: 491 S Washburn St, Ste 400, Oshkosh, Wisconsin 54904 **Tel:** 1 920 426-3239.
Email: wosh.news@cumulus.com
Web site: http://www.1490wosh.com
Profile: WOSH-AM is a commercial station owned by Cumulus Media Inc. The format of the station is news, talk and sports. WOSH-AM broadcasts in the Oshkosh, WI area at 1490 AM.
AM RADIO STATION

WOSL-FM 46494
Owner: Urban One, Inc.
Editorial: 705 Central Ave Ste 200, One Centennial Plaza, Cincinnati, Ohio 45202-1900 **Tel:** 1 513 679-6000.
Web site: http://oldschoolcincy.com
Profile: WOSL-FM is a commercial station owned by Urban One, Inc. The format of the station is rhythmic old school music. WOSL-FM broadcasts to the Cincinnati area at 100.3 FM.
FM RADIO STATION

WOSM-FM 40594
Owner: Telesouth Communications Inc.
Editorial: 4720 Radio Rd, Ocean Springs, Mississippi 39564-7509 **Tel:** 1 228 875-9031.
Web site: http://www.supertalkms.com
Profile: WOSM-FM is a commercial station owned by Telesouth Communications Inc. The format of the station is talk. WOSM-FM broadcasts in the Ocean Springs, MS area at 103.1 FM.
FM RADIO STATION

WOSN-FM 43060
Owner: Treasure & Space Coast Radio
Editorial: 1235 16th St, Vero Beach, Florida 32960-3620 **Tel:** 1 772 567-0937.
Web site: http://www.wosnfm.com
FM RADIO STATION

WOSQ-FM 41324
Owner: Seehafer Broadcasting Corp.
Editorial: 1714 N Central Ave, Marshfield, Wisconsin 54449 **Tel:** 1 715 384-2191.
Web site: http://wosqfm.com
Profile: WOSQ-FM is a commercial station owned by Seehafer Broadcasting Corp. The format for the station is sports. WOSQ-FM broadcasts to the Wausau, WI area at 92.3 FM.
FM RADIO STATION

WOSR-FM 42210
Owner: WAMC
Editorial: 318 Central Ave, Albany, New York 12206-2522 **Tel:** 1 518 465-5233.
Email: mail@wamc.org
Web site: http://www.wamc.org
Profile: WOSR-FM is a non-commercial station owned by WAMC. The format of the station is news and talk. WOSR-FM broadcasts to the Albany, NY area at 91.7 FM.
FM RADIO STATION

WOSW-AM 36025
Owner: Cram Communications, LLC
Editorial: 401 W Kirkpatrick St, Syracuse, New York 13204-1305 **Tel:** 1 315 472-0222.
Profile: WOSW-AM is a commercial station owned by Cram Communications, LLC. The format of the station is gospel. WOSW-AM broadcasts to the Fulton, NY area at 1300 AM.
AM RADIO STATION

WOTB-FM 868809
Owner: New Horizon Christian Fellowship
Editorial: 3401 Pontchartrain Dr, Slidell, Louisiana 70458-4849 **Tel:** 1 985 781-3174.
Web site: http://thebridge.fm/
Profile: WOTB-FM is a non-commercial station owned by New Horizon Christian Fellowship. The format of the station is Contemporary Christian music. WOTB-FM broadcasts to the Greater New Orleans area at a frequency of 88.7 FM.
FM RADIO STATION

WOTC-FM 42395
Owner: Valley Baptist Church
Editorial: 146 Parsons Point Ln, Edinburg, Virginia 22824-3635 **Tel:** 1 540 984-8998.
Email: wotcfm@shentel.net
Web site: http://www.valleybaptistchurch.net
Profile: WOTC is a religious formatted station serving Woodstock and Shenandoah, VA. WOTC carries news programming from IRN/USA Radio News.
FM RADIO STATION

WOTE-AM 38530
Owner: Results Broadcasting, Inc.
Editorial: 1456 E Green Bay St, Shawano, Wisconsin 54166-2258 **Tel:** 1 715 524-2194.
Email: wtchwown@yahoo.com
Web site: http://www.1380thelounge.com
Profile: WOTE-AM is a commercial station owned by Results Broadcasting, Inc. The format of the station is adult standards. WOTE-AM broadcasts to the Shawano, WI area at 1380 AM.
AM RADIO STATION

WOTJ-FM 40958
Owner: Grace Missionary Baptist Church
Editorial: 520 Roberts Rd, Newport, North Carolina 28570-8616 **Tel:** 1 252 223-4600.
Email: fbn@fbnradio.com
Web site: http://www.fbnradio.com
Profile: WOTJ-FM is a non-commercial station owned by Grace Missionary Baptist Church. The format of the station is religious programming. WOTJ-FM broadcasts to the Newport, NC area at 90.7 FM.
FM RADIO STATION

WOTL-FM 41438
Owner: Family Stations Inc.
Editorial: 716 N Westwood Ave, A, Toledo, Ohio 43607-3558 **Tel:** 1 815 725-1331.
Email: info@familyradio.org
Web site: http://www.familyradio.com

Profile: WOTL-FM is a commercial station owned by Family Stations Inc. The format of the station is religious programming. WOTL-FM broadcasts to the Toledo, OH area at 90.3 FM.
FM RADIO STATION

WOTR-FM
44180
Owner: Della Jane Woofter
Editorial: 303 Harrison Ave, Weston, West Virginia 26452-2189 **Tel:** 1 304 269-5555.
Email: info@wotrfm.com
Web site: http://www.wotrfm.com
Profile: WOTR-FM is a commercial station owned by Della Jane Woofter. The format of the station is bluegrass and olides music. The station broadcasts locally to the Clarksburg - Weston, WV area at a frequency of 96.3 FM.
FM RADIO STATION

WOTS-AM
36242
Owner: J & V Communications Inc.
Editorial: 222 Hazard St, Orlando, Florida 32804-3030 **Tel:** 1 407 841-8282.
Email: wprd1440@gmail.com
Web site: http://www.wots1220.com
Profile: WOTS-AM is a commercial station owned by J & V Communications Inc. The format of the station is Hispanic religious programming. WOTS-AM broadcasts to the Orlando, FL area at 1220 AM.
AM RADIO STATION

WOTT-FM
577904
Owner: Community Broadcasters, LLC
Editorial: 199 Wealtha Ave, Watertown, New York 13601-1837 **Tel:** 1 315 782-1240.
Profile: WOTT-FM is a commercial station owned by Community Broadcasters, LLC. The format of the station is rock/album-oriented rock. WOTT-FM broadcasts to the Watertown, NY area at 94.1 FM.
FM RADIO STATION

WOTW-FM
40482
Owner: JVC Broadcasting
Editorial: 2301 Lucien Way Ste 180, Maitland, Florida 32751-7034 **Tel:** 1 407 647-5557.
Web site: http://thewolf1031.com
Profile: WOTW-FM is a commercial station owned by JVC Broadcasting. The format of the station is contemporary country. WHKQ-FM broadcasts to the Orlando, FL area at 103.1 FM.
FM RADIO STATION

WOUF-FM
40143
Owner: Henderson, Roy E.
Editorial: 1532 Forrester Rd, Frankfort, Michigan 49635 **Tel:** 1 231 352-6374.
Web site: http://www.wouffm.com
Profile: WOUF-FM is a commercial station owned by Roy E. Henderson. The format of the station is rock/album oriented rock. WOUF-FM broadcasts to the Frankfort, MI area at 99.3 FM.
FM RADIO STATION

WOUR-FM
45434
Owner: Galaxy Communications LP
Editorial: 39 Kellogg Rd, New Hartford, New York 13413 **Tel:** 1 315 797-1330.
Email: askwour@wour.com
Web site: http://www.wour.com
Profile: WOUR-FM is a commercial station owned by Galaxy Communications LP. The format of the station is classic rock. WOUR-FM broadcasts to the Utica, NY area at 96.9 FM.
FM RADIO STATION

WOVK-FM
45671
Owner: iHeartMedia Inc.
Editorial: 1015 Main St, Wheeling, West Virginia 26003-2709 **Tel:** 1 304 232-1170.
Email: wovk987fm@yahoo.com
Web site: http://www.wovk.com
Profile: WOVK-FM is a commercial station owned by iHeartMedia Inc. The format of the station is contemporary country. WOVK-FM broadcasts to the Wheeling, WV area at 98.7 FM.
FM RADIO STATION

WOVM-FM
40472
Owner: Music that Matters, Inc
Editorial: 2300 Riverside Dr, Green Bay, Wisconsin 54301-1900 **Tel:** 1 920 271-2700.
Email: web@theavenue91.com
Web site: http://www.avenueradio.com
Profile: WOVM-FM is a non-commercial station owned by Music that Matters, Inc. The format of the station is jazz. WOVM-FM broadcasts to the Green Bay, WI area at 91.1 FM.
FM RADIO STATION

WOWC-FM
45542
Owner: Peg Broadcasting
Editorial: 230 W Colville St, Mc Minnville, Tennessee 37110-3211 **Tel:** 1 931 473-9253.
Email: production.mcminnville@pegbroadcasting.com
Web site: http://www.1053wowcountry.com
Profile: WOWC-FM is a commercial station owned by Peg Broadcasting. The format of the station is country. WOWC-FM broadcasts to the McMinnnville, TN area at 105.3 FM.
FM RADIO STATION

WOWE-FM
41923
Owner: Praestantia Broadcasting
Editorial: 444 Church St, Flint, Michigan 48502-1324 **Tel:** 1 810 234-4335.
Email: wowe98.9@sbcglobal.net
Profile: WOWE-FM is a commercial station owned by Praestantia Broadcasting. The format of the station is R&B, urban contemporary and oldies. WOWE-FM broadcasts to the Flint, MI area at 98.9 FM.
FM RADIO STATION

WOWF-FM
43704
Owner: Peg Broadcasting Crossville, LLC
Editorial: 961 Miller Ave, Crossville, Tennessee 38555-4359 **Tel:** 1 931 707-1102.
Email: news@pegbroadcasting.com
Web site: http://www.1025wowcountry.com
Profile: WOWF-FM is a commercial station owned by Peg Broadcasting Crossville, LLC. The format of the station is country. WOWF-FM broadcasts to the Crossville, TN area at 102.5 FM.
FM RADIO STATION

WOWI-FM
40597
Owner: iHeartMedia Inc.
Editorial: 1003 Norfolk Sq, Norfolk, Virginia 23502-3234 **Tel:** 1 757 466-0009.
Email: 103jamz@iheartmedia.com
Web site: http://www.103jamz.com
Profile: WOWI-FM is a commercial station owned by iHeartMedia Inc. The format of the station is urban contemporary music. WOWI-FM broadcasts to the Norfolk, VA area at 102.9 FM.
FM RADIO STATION

WOWN-FM
45436
Owner: Results Broadcasting, Inc.
Editorial: 1456 E Green Bay St, Shawano, Wisconsin 54166 **Tel:** 1 715 524-2194.
Email: wtchwown@yahoo.com
Web site: http://www.b993.com
Profile: WOWN-FM is a commercial station owned by Results Broadcasting, Inc. The format of the station is classic hits. WOWN-FM broadcasts to the Shawano, WI area at 99.3 FM.
FM RADIO STATION

WOWO-AM
36353
Owner: Federated Media
Editorial: 2915 Maples Rd, Fort Wayne, Indiana 46816 **Tel:** 1 260 447-5511.
Email: news@wowo.com
Web site: http://www.wowo.com
Profile: WOWO-AM is a commercial station owned by Federated Media. The format of the station is news and talk. WOWO-AM broadcasts to the Fort Wayne, IN area at 1190 AM.
AM RADIO STATION

WOWQ-FM
46081
Owner: First Media Radio LLC
Editorial: 801 E Dubois Ave, Du Bois, Pennsylvania 15801-3643 **Tel:** 1 814 371-6100.
Email: q102radio@comcast.net
Web site: http://www.q102radio.fm
Profile: WOWQ-FM is a commercial station owned by First Media Radio LLC. The format of the station is contemporary country. WOWQ-FM broadcasts to the Du Bois, PA area at 91.1 FM.
FM RADIO STATION

WOWW-AM
39428
Owner: Flinn Broadcasting Corp.
Editorial: 230 Goodman Rd E Ste 202, Southaven, Mississippi 38671-5151 **Tel:** 1 901 272-0008.
Web site: http://rebel953.com/
Profile: WOWW-AM is a commercial station owned by Flinn Broadcasting Corp. and operated by Mighty Media Group LP. The format of the station is country. WOWW-AM broadcasts to the Memphis, TN area at 1430 AM.
AM RADIO STATION

WOWY-FM
43687
Owner: Seven Mountains Media, LLC
Editorial: 160 W Clearview Ave, State College, Pennsylvania 16803-1617 **Tel:** 1 814 238-5085.
Web site: http://www.wowyonline.com
Profile: WOWY-FM is a commercial station owned by 2510 Associates. The format of the station is oldies. WOWY-FM broadcasts to the State College, PA area on 97.1 FM.
FM RADIO STATION

WOXD-FM
41346
Owner: Jason Plunk
Editorial: 302 Highway 7 S, Oxford, Mississippi 38655-8137 **Tel:** 1 662 801-1262.
Email: cmahew955@gmail.com
Web site: http://www.bullseye955.com
Profile: WOXD-FM is a commercial station owned by Jason Plunk. The format of the station is classic rock. WOXD-FM broadcasts in the Oxford, MS area at 95.5 FM.
FM RADIO STATION

WOXF-FM
905393
Owner: Flinn Broadcasting Corp.
Tel: 1 901 375-9324.
Profile: WOXF-FM is a commercial station owned by Flinn Broadcasting Corp. The format of the station is classic hip hop. WOXF-FM broadcasts to the Oxford, MS area at a frequency of 105.1 FM.
FM RADIO STATION

WOXL-FM
43628
Owner: Saga Communications
Editorial: 1190 Patton Ave, Asheville, North Carolina 28806-2706 **Tel:** 1 828 259-9695.
Web site: http://www.965woxl.com
Profile: WOXL-FM is a commercial station owned by Saga Communications. The format of the station is Lite Rock/Lite AC. WOXL-FM broadcasts to the Asheville, NC area at 98.1 FM.
FM RADIO STATION

WOXO-FM
46392
Owner: Gleason Radio Group
Editorial: 243 Main St, Norway, Maine 4268
Tel: 1 207 743-5911.
Email: woxo@woxo.com
Web site: http://www.woxo.com
Profile: WOXO-FM is a commercial station owned by Gleason Radio Group. The format of the station is classic country. WOXO-FM broadcasts to the Norway, ME area at 92.7 FM.
FM RADIO STATION

WOXR-FM
489513
Owner: Vermont Public Radio
Editorial: 365 Troy Ave, Colchester, Vermont 05446-3126 **Tel:** 1 802 655-9451.
Email: news@vpr.net
Web site: http://www.vpr.net
Profile: WOXR-FM is a non-commercial station owned by Vermont Public Radio. The format of the station is classical. WOXR-FM broadcasts to the Burlington, VT area at 90.9 FM. The station does not accept PSAs.
FM RADIO STATION

WOYK-AM
36458
Owner: WOYK Inc.
Editorial: 1051 Dairy Ln, Elizabethtown, Pennsylvania 17022-9547 **Tel:** 1 717 840-0355.
Web site: http://www.woyk1350.com/
Profile: WOYK-AM is a commercial station owned by WOYK Inc. The format of the station is sports. WOYK-AM broadcasts to the Elizabethtown, PA area at 1350 AM. WOYK's slogan is "First in York. First in Sports."
AM RADIO STATION

WOYS-FM
41345
Owner: PD Michael Allen's East Bay Broadcasting
Editorial: 35 Island Dr Ste 16, Eastpoint, Florida 32328-3264 **Tel:** 1 850 670-8450.
Web site: http://www.oysterradio.com
Profile: WOYS-FM is a commercial station owned by PD Michael Allen's East Bay Broadcasting. The format of the station is classic hits music. The station broadcasts in Eastpoint, FL at 100.5 FM.
FM RADIO STATION

WOZI-FM
40600
Owner: Townsquare Media, Inc.
Editorial: 551 Main St, Presque Isle, Maine 04769-2450 **Tel:** 1 207 769-6600.
Email: newspi@townsquaremedia.com
Web site: http://www.1019therock.com
Profile: WOZI-FM is a commercial station owned by Townsquare Media, Inc. The format of the station is classic rock. WOZI-FM broadcasts to the Presque Isle, ME area at 101.9 FM.
FM RADIO STATION

WOZN-AM
38226
Owner: Midwest Family Stations
Editorial: 730 Rayovac Dr., Madison, Wisconsin 53711 **Tel:** 1 608 273-1000.
Web site: http://www.madcitysportszone.com
Profile: WOZN-AM is a commercial station owned by Midwest Family Stations. The station is sports. WOZN-AM broadcasts to the Madison, WI area at 1670 AM.
AM RADIO STATION

WOZN-FM
359747
Owner: Midwest Family Stations
Editorial: 730 Rayovac Dr, Madison, Wisconsin 53711 **Tel:** 1 608 273-1000.
Web site: http://www.madcitysportszone.com
Profile: WOZN-FM is a commercial station owned by Midwest Family Stations. The station is sports. WOZN-FM broadcasts to the Madison, WI area at 106.7 FM.
FM RADIO STATION

WOZQ-FM
44222
Owner: Smith College
Editorial: 100 Elm St, Northampton, Massachusetts 01063-6334 **Tel:** 1 413 585-4956.
Web site: http://wozq919.wix.com/wozq
Profile: WOZQ-FM is a non-commercial station owned by Smith College. The format of the station is college variety. WOZQ-FM broadcasts to the Northampton, MA area at 91.9 FM.
FM RADIO STATION

WOZZ-FM
42215
Owner: Midwest Communications Inc.
Editorial: 557 Scott St, Wausau, Wisconsin 54403-4829 **Tel:** 1 715 842-1672.
Email: the.studio@rock947.com
Web site: http://www.rock947.com
Profile: WOZZ-FM is a commercial station owned by Midwest Communications Inc. The format of the station is classic rock. WOZZ-FM broadcasts to the Wausau, WI area at 94.7 FM.
FM RADIO STATION

WPAD-AM
38357
Owner: Bristol Broadcasting
Editorial: 6000 Bristol Dr, Paducah, Kentucky 42003-9213 **Tel:** 1 270 554-8255.
Email: pd@995thefanpaducah.com
Web site: http://www.995thefanpaducah.com/
Profile: WPAD-AM is a commercial station owned by Bristol Broadcasting. The format of the station is sports. WPAD-AM broadcasts to the Paducah, KY area at 1560 AM.
AM RADIO STATION

WPAE-FM
43348
Owner: Port Allen Educ. Broadcasting Found.
Editorial: 122 E Main St, Centreville, Mississippi 39631 **Tel:** 1 601 645-6515.
Email: wpaefm@telepak.net
Web site: http://www.soundradio.org
Profile: WPAE-FM is a non-commercial station owned by Port Allen Educ. Broadcasting Found. The format of the station is religious. WPAE-FM broadcasts to the Centreville, MS area at 89.7 FM.
FM RADIO STATION

WPAK-AM
35584
Owner: Great Virginia Ventures, Inc
Editorial: 446 Plank Rd, Farmville, Virginia 23901-4015 **Tel:** 1 804 392-8114.
Email: wrmvradio@aol.com
Web site: http://www.crosscountryfm.com
Profile: WPAK-AM is a non-commercial station owned by Great Virginia Ventures, Inc. The format of the station is Christian country music. WPAK-AM broadcasts to the Farmville, VA area at 1490 AM.
AM RADIO STATION

WPAP-FM
40602
Owner: iHeartMedia Inc.
Editorial: 1834 Lisenby Ave, Panama City, Florida 32405-3713 **Tel:** 1 850 769-1408.
Web site: http://925wpap.iheart.com
Profile: WPAP-FM is a commercial station owned by iHeartMedia Inc. The format of the station is country music. WPAP-FM broadcasts to the Panama City, FL area at 92.5 FM.
FM RADIO STATION

WPAQ-AM
36920
Owner: WPAQ Radio, Inc.
Editorial: 2147 Springs Rd, Mount Airy, North Carolina 27030 **Tel:** 1 336 786-6111.
Email: info@wpaq740.com
Web site: http://www.wpaq740.com
Profile: WPAQ-AM is a commercial station owned by WPAQ Radio, Inc. The format of the station is bluegrass and old time music. WPAQ-AM broadcasts to the Mount Airy, NC area at 740 AM.
AM RADIO STATION

WPAR-FM
43789
Owner: Positive Alternative Radio
Editorial: 22226 Timberlake Rd, Lynchburg, Virginia 24502-7305 **Tel:** 1 434 237-9798.
Email: office@spiritfm.com
Web site: http://www.spiritfm.com
Profile: WPAR-FM is a non-commercial station owned by Positive Alternative Radio. The format of the station is contemporary Christian music. WPAR-FM broadcasts to the Lynchburg, VA area at 91.3 FM.
FM RADIO STATION

WPAT-AM
63641
Owner: Multicultural Radio Broadcasting Inc.
Editorial: 27 William St, 11th Fl., New York, New York 10005-2701 **Tel:** 1 212 966-1059.
Web site: http://www.wpat930am.com
Profile: WPAT-AM is a commercial station owned by Multicultural Radio Broadcasting Inc. The format of the station is variety. WPAT-AM broadcasts to the New York area at 930 AM.
AM RADIO STATION

WPAT-FM
43405
Owner: Spanish Broadcasting System
Editorial: 26 W 56th St, New York, New York 10019-3801 **Tel:** 1 212 541-9200.
Email: info@931amor.com
Web site: http://www.931amor.com
Profile: WPAT-FM a commercial station owned by the Spanish Broadcasting System. The format of the station is Hispanic adult hits. WPAT-FM broadcasts to the New York City area at 93.1 FM.
FM RADIO STATION

WPAW-FM
42290
Owner: Entercom Communications Corp.
Editorial: 7819 National Service Rd, Ste 401, Greensboro, North Carolina 27409 **Tel:** 1 336 605-5200.
Web site: http://www.931wolfcountry.com
Profile: WPAW-FM is a commercial station owned by Entercom Communications Corp. The format of the station is contemporary country. WPAW-FM broadcasts to the Greensboro, NC area at 93.1 FM.
FM RADIO STATION

WPAX-AM
38632
Owner: Lenrob Enterprises Inc.
Editorial: 117 Remington Ave, Thomasville, Georgia 31792 **Tel:** 1 229 226-1240.
Web site: http://www.wpaxradio.com
Profile: WPAX-AM is a commercial station owned by Lenrob Enterprises Inc. The format of the station is adult standards and variety. WPAX-AM broadcasts to the Thomasville, GA area at 1240 AM.
AM RADIO STATION

WPBB-FM
58338
Owner: Beasley Broadcast Group
Editorial: 9721 Executive Center Dr N Ste 200, Saint Petersburg, Florida 33702-2439 **Tel:** 1 727 579-1925.
Web site: http://b987fm.com
Profile: WPBB-FM is a commercial station owned by Beasley Broadcast Group. The format of the station is Adult Contemporary. The station broadcasts to the Tampa, Florida area at 98.7 FM. The station's slogan

s, "Today's Hits, Yesterday's Favorites." The station offers a digital podcast.
FM RADIO STATION

WPBC-AM 35764
Owner: Hanmi Broadcasting, Inc (Chang, Kim)
Editorial: 3684 Stewart Rd Ste A3, Atlanta, Georgia 30340-2760 **Tel:** 1 770 986-9500.
Profile: WPBC-AM is a commercial station owned by Hanmi Broadcasting, Inc. The format of the station is gospel. WPBC-AM broadcasts to Decatur, GA and its surrounding areas at 1310 AM.
AM RADIO STATION

WPBG-FM 45740
Owner: Alpha Media
Editorial: 331 Fulton St Ste 1200, Peoria, Illinois 61602-1422 **Tel:** 1 309 637-3700.
Email: news@1470wmbd.com
Web site: http://www.933thedrive.com
Profile: WPGB-FM is a commercial station owned by Alpha Media. The format of the station is classic hits. WPGB-FM broadcasts to the Peoria, IL area at 93.3 FM.
FM RADIO STATION

WPBR-AM 35586
Owner: Palm Beach Radio Group, LLC
Editorial: 2755 S Federal Hwy Ste 15, Boynton Beach, Florida 33435-7743
Web site: http://www.sakpase.fm
Profile: WPBR-AM is a commercial station owned by Omni-Lingual Broadcasting Corp. The format of the station is talk radio targeting the Haitian American Community in Palm Beach County, FL. WPBR-AM broadcasts to the Palm Beach County, FL, area.
AM RADIO STATION

WPBS-AM 35708
Owner: Pacific Star Broadcasting
Editorial: 3230 Steve Reynolds Blvd Ste 219, Duluth, Georgia 30096-8833 **Tel:** 1 770 813-0307.
Email: info@atlantaradiokorea.com
Web site: http://www.atlantaradiokorea.com
Profile: WPBS-AM is an commercial station owned by Pacific Star Broadcasting. The format of the station is Korean talk and music programming. WPBS-AM broadcasts to the Atlanta area at 1040 AM.
AM RADIO STATION

WPBX-FM 45641
Owner: Peg Broadcasting Crossville, LLC
Editorial: 961 Miller Ave, Crossville, Tennessee 38555 **Tel:** 1 931 707-1102.
Web site: http://www.mix993.net
Profile: WPBX-FM is a commercial station owned by Peg Broadcasting Crossville, LLC. The format of the station is adult contemporary. WPBX-FM broadcasts to the Crossville, TN area at 99.3 FM.
FM RADIO STATION

WPCD-FM 41501
Owner: Parkland College
Editorial: 2400 W Bradley Ave, Champaign, Illinois 61821 **Tel:** 1 217 351-2450.
Email: wpcdradio@parkland.edu
Web site: http://www.parkland.edu/wpcd
Profile: WPCD-FM is a non-commercial station owned by Parkland College. The format of the station is urban AC and rock alternative music. WPCD-FM broadcasts in Champaign, IL at 88.7 FM.
FM RADIO STATION

WPCE-AM 36639
Owner: Willis Broadcasting Co.
Editorial: 645 Church St, Norfolk, Virginia 23510-1712 **Tel:** 1 757 622-4600.
Email: willisbroadcasting@yahoo.com
Web site: http://www.wpceradio.com
Profile: WPCE-AM is a commercial station owned by Willis Broadcasting Co. (dba Christian Broadcasting of Portsmouth, LLC.) The format of the station is gospel and religious programming. WPCE-AM broadcasts in the Norfolk, VA area at 1400 AM.
AM RADIO STATION

WPCF-AM 38522
Owner: Evolution Broadcasting, LLC
Editorial: 7106 Laird St Ste 102, Panama City Beach, Florida 32408-7622 **Tel:** 1 850 230-5855.
Web site: http://www.939playfm.com
Profile: WPCF-AM is a commercial station owned by Evolution Broadcasting, LLC. The format of the station is rhythmic dance and electronic dance. WPCF-AM broadcasts to Panama City Beach, FL at 1290 AM.
AM RADIO STATION

WPCH-FM 42441
Owner: iHeartMedia Inc.
Editorial: 7080 Industrial Hwy, Macon, Georgia 31216-7538 **Tel:** 1 478 781-1063.
Web site: http://www.newcountry965.com
Profile: WPCH-FM is a commercial station owned by iHeartMedia Inc. The format of the station is contemporary country. WPCH-FM broadcasts to the Macon, GA area at 96.5 FM.
FM RADIO STATION

WPCK-FM 43515
Owner: Cumulus Media Inc.
Editorial: 810 Victoria St, Green Bay, Wisconsin 54302-2465 **Tel:** 1 920 468-4100.
Web site: http://www.nashfmwisconsin.com
Profile: WPCK-FM is a commercial station owned by Cumulus Media Inc. The format of the station is contemporary country. WPCK-FM broadcasts to the Green Bay, WI area at 104.9 FM.
FM RADIO STATION

WPCL-FM 43227
Owner: Central Pennsylvania Christian Institute, Inc.
Editorial: 2020 Cato Ave, State College, Pennsylvania 16801-2764 **Tel:** 1 800 288-9857.
Email: info@wtlr.org
Web site: http://wtlr.org
Profile: WPCL-FM is a non-commercial station owned by Central Pennsylvania Christian Institute. The format of the station is contemporary Christian and gospel music. WPCL-FM broadcasts to the Johnstown/Ebensburg, MD area at 97.3 FM.
FM RADIO STATION

WPCM-AM 37660
Owner: Curtis Media Group
Editorial: 1109 Tower Dr, Burlington, North Carolina 27215-4425 **Tel:** 1 336 584-0126.
Email: wpcm@curtismedia.com
Profile: WPCM-AM is a commercial station owned by Curtis Media Group. The format of the station is country music. WPCM-AM broadcasts to the Burlington, NC area at 920 AM.
AM RADIO STATION

WPCS-FM 40606
Owner: Pensacola Christian College
Editorial: 250 Brent Ln, Pensacola, Florida 32503-2267 **Tel:** 1 850 479-6570.
Email: rbn@rejoice.org
Web site: http://www.rejoice.org
Profile: WPCS-FM is a non-commercial station owned by Pensacola Christian College. The format of the station is religious programming. WPCS-FM broadcasts to the Pensacola, FL area at 89.5 FM. The station does not do interviews.
FM RADIO STATION

WPCV-FM 45441
Owner: Hall Communications
Editorial: 404 W Lime St, Lakeland, Florida 33815-4651 **Tel:** 1 863 682-8184.
Web site: http://www.wpcv.com
Profile: WPCV-FM is a commercial station owned by Hall Communications. The format of the station is contemporary country music. WPCV-FM broadcasts to the Lakeland, FL area at 97.5 FM.
FM RADIO STATION

WPDA-FM 42058
Owner: Townsquare Media
Editorial: 2 Pendell Rd, Poughkeepsie, New York 12601-1513 **Tel:** 1 845 471-1500.
Web site: http://www.wpdh.com
Profile: WPDA-FM is a commercial station owned by Townsquare Media. The format of the station is rock music. WPDA-FM broadcasts to the Poughkeepsie, NY area at 106.1 FM.
FM RADIO STATION

WPDC-AM 35588
Owner: JVJ Communications
Editorial: 1051 Dairy Ln, Elizabethtown, Pennsylvania 17022-9547 **Tel:** 1 717 367-1600.
Email: espn1600@att.net
Profile: WPDC-AM is a commercial station owned by JVJ Communications. The format of the station is sports. WPDC-AM broadcasts to the Harrisburg, PA area at 1600 AM.
AM RADIO STATION

WPDH-FM 45442
Owner: Townsquare Media
Editorial: 2 Pendell Rd, Poughkeepsie, New York 12601-1513 **Tel:** 1 845 471-1500.
Web site: http://www.wpdh.com
Profile: WPDH-FM is a commercial station owned by Townsquare Media. The format of the station is rock/album-oriented rock music. WPDH-FM broadcasts in the Poughkeepsie, NY area at 101.5 FM.
FM RADIO STATION

WPDM-AM 38116
Owner: Waters Communications Inc.
Editorial: 7064 US Highway 11, Potsdam, New York 13676-3197 **Tel:** 1 315 265-5510.
Web site: http://www.99hits.com
Profile: WPDM-AM is a commercial station owned by Waters Communications Inc. The format of the station is country music. WPDM-AM broadcasts to the Potsdam, NY area on 99.3 FM.
AM RADIO STATION

WPDR-AM 38117
Owner: Magnum Radio Group
Editorial: N6912 US Highway 51, Portage, Wisconsin 53901-9678 **Tel:** 1 608 742-1001.
Email: info@magnumbroadcasting.com
Web site: http://www.wpdr.com
Profile: WPDR-AM is a commercial station owned by Magnum Radio Group. The format for the station is oldies. WPDR-AM broadcasts to the Madison, WI area at 1350 AM.
AM RADIO STATION

WPDT-FM 445996
Owner: Glory Communications Inc.
Editorial: 2440 Millwood Ave, Columbia, South Carolina 29205-1128 **Tel:** 1 843 374-5255.
Email: wpdtpsa@wpdt.net
Web site: http://www.wpdt.net
Profile: WPDT-FM is a commercial station owned by Glory Communications Inc. The format of the station is gospel. WPDT-FM broadcasts to the Columbia, SC area at 105.1 FM.
FM RADIO STATION

WPDX-AM 38673
Owner: Tschudy Broadcasting
Editorial: 59 Mountain Park Dr, Fairmont, West Virginia 26554-8993 **Tel:** 1 304 363-3851.
Web site: http://www.wpdxcountry.com
Profile: WPDX-AM is a commercial station owned by Tschudy Broadcasting. The format of the station is classic country. WPDX-AM broadcasts to the Clarksburg-Weston, WV area at 750 AM.
AM RADIO STATION

WPDX-FM 46026
Owner: Tschudy Broadcasting
Editorial: 59 Mountain Park Dr, Fairmont, West Virginia 26554-8993 **Tel:** 1 304 624-6425.
Email: wpdx@wpdxcountry.com
Web site: http://www.wpdxcountry.com
Profile: WDPX-FM is a commercial station owned by Tschudy Broadcasting. The format of the station is country music. WDPX-FM broadcasts to the Clarksburg-Weston, WV area at 104.9 FM.
FM RADIO STATION

WPEG-FM 42600
Owner: Beasley Broadcast Group
Editorial: 1520 South Blvd Ste 300, Charlotte, North Carolina 28203-3701 **Tel:** 1 704 522-1103.
Web site: http://power98fm.radio.com
Profile: WPEG-FM is a commercial station owned by Beasley Broadcast Group. The format of the station is urban contemporary. WPEG-FM broadcasts to the greater Charlotte, NC area at 97.9 FM.
FM RADIO STATION

WPEH-AM 38118
Owner: Peach Broadcasting
Editorial: 5442 Middleground Road, Louisville, Georgia 30434 **Tel:** 1 478 625-7248.
Profile: WPEH-AM is a commercial station owned by Peach Broadcasting. The format of the station is country and oldies. WPEH-AM broadcasts to the Louisville, GA area at 1420 AM.
AM RADIO STATION

WPEH-FM 45443
Owner: Peach Broadcasting
Editorial: 5442 Middleground Road, Louisville, Georgia 30434 **Tel:** 1 478 625-7248.
Profile: WPEH-FM is a commercial station owned by Peach Broadcasting. The format of the station is country and oldies. WPEH-FM broadcasts to the Louisville, GA area at 92.1 FM.
FM RADIO STATION

WPEI-FM 40364
Owner: Atlantic Coast Radio LLC
Editorial: 779 Warren Ave, Portland, Maine 4103 **Tel:** 1 207 773-9695.
Web site: http://www.weei.com
Profile: WPEI-FM is a commercial station owned by Atlantic Coast Radio LLC. The format of the station is sports. WPEI-FM broadcasts to the Portland, ME area at 95.9 FM.
FM RADIO STATION

WPEK-AM 36607
Owner: iHeartMedia Inc.
Editorial: 13 Summerlin Dr, Asheville, North Carolina 28806-2800 **Tel:** 1 828 257-2700.
Email: ashevillepsa@iheartmedia.com
Web site: http://www.880therevolution.com
Profile: WPEK-AM is a commercial station owned by iHeartMedia Inc. The format of the station is talk. WPEK-AM broadcasts to the Asheville, NC area at 880 AM.
AM RADIO STATION

WPEL-AM 38872
Owner: Montrose Broadcasting Corp.
Editorial: 251 High St, Montrose, Pennsylvania 18801-1444 **Tel:** 1 570 278-2811.
Email: mail@wpel.org
Web site: http://www.wpel.org
Profile: WPEL-AM is a non-commercial station owned by Montrose Broadcasting Corp. The format of the station is Southern gospel. WPEL-AM broadcasts to the Montrose, PA area at 800 AM.
AM RADIO STATION

WPEL-FM 46238
Owner: Montrose Broadcasting Corp.
Editorial: 251 High St, Montrose, Pennsylvania 18801-1444 **Tel:** 1 570 278-2811.
Email: mail@wpel.org
Web site: http://www.wpel.org
Profile: WPEL-FM is a non-commercial station owned by Montrose Broadcasting Corp. The format of the station is religious programming with easy listening and classical music. WPEL-FM broadcasts to the Montrose, PA area at 96.5 FM.
FM RADIO STATION

WPEN-FM 42844
Owner: Beasley Broadcast Group
Editorial: 1 Bala Plz, Bala Cynwyd, Pennsylvania 19004-1409 **Tel:** 1 610 771-9750.
Web site: http://www.975thefanatic.com
Profile: WPEN-FM is a commercial station owned by Beasley Broadcast Group. The format of the station is sports and talk. WPEN-FM broadcasts to the Philadelphia area at 97.5 FM.
FM RADIO STATION

WPEO-AM 35589
Owner: Pinebrook Foundation Inc.
Editorial: 1708 Highview Rd, East Peoria, Illinois 61611-1516 **Tel:** 1 309 698-9736.
Email: wpeo@wpeo.com
Web site: http://www.wpeo.com
Profile: WPEO-AM is a commercial station owned by Pinebrook Foundation Inc. The format of the station is religious talk. WPEO-AM broadcasts to the East Peoria, IL area at 1020 AM.
AM RADIO STATION

WPER-FM 44471
Owner: Positive Alternative Radio
Editorial: 4522 Plank Rd, Fredericksburg, Virginia 22407-0142 **Tel:** 1 540 347-4825.
Email: info@positivehits.org
Web site: http://www.positivehits.org
Profile: WPER-FM is a non-commercial station owned by Positive Alternative Radio. The format of the station is contemporary Christian music. WPER-FM broadcasts in the Warrenton, VA area at 89.9 FM.
FM RADIO STATION

WPET-AM 38120
Owner: Entercom Communications Corp.
Editorial: 7819 National Service Rd, Ste 401, Greensboro, North Carolina 27409 **Tel:** 1 336 275-9738.
Email: tradio@entercom.com
Web site: http://www.wpetam950.com
Profile: WPET-AM is a commercial station owned by Entercom Communications Corp. The format of the station is gospel music. WPET-AM broadcasts to the Greensboro, NC area at 950 AM.
AM RADIO STATION

WPEZ-FM 45444
Owner: Cumulus Media Inc.
Editorial: 544 Mulberry St Ste 500, Macon, Georgia 31201-8258 **Tel:** 1 478 746-6286.
Web site: http://www.z937.com
Profile: WPEZ-FM is a commercial station owned by Cumulus Media Inc. The format of the station is adult contemporary music. WPEZ-FM broadcasts to the Macon, GA area at 93.7 FM.
FM RADIO STATION

WPFC-AM 36493
Owner: Victory & Power Ministries Inc.
Editorial: 6943 Titian Ave, Baton Rouge, Louisiana 70806-2767 **Tel:** 1 225 926-6550.
Email: wpfc1550am@gmail.com
Profile: WPFC-AM is a commercial station owned by Victory & Power Ministries Inc. The format of the station is gospel. WPFC-AM broadcasts to the Baton Rouge, LA area at 1550 AM.
AM RADIO STATION

WPFG-FM 824910
Owner: Cumberland Valley Christian Radio
Editorial: 14 Stover Dr, Carlisle, Pennsylvania 17015-9782 **Tel:** 1 717 241-9734.
Email: wpfgmail@wpfgfm.org
Web site: http://wpfgfm.org
Profile: WPFG-FM is a non-commercial station owned by Cumberland Valley Christian Radio. The format of the station is Christian music and talk programming. WPFG-FM broadcasts to the Carlisle, PA area at a frequency of 91.3 FM.
FM RADIO STATION

WPFJ-AM 35500
Owner: Toccoa Falls College
Editorial: 185 Franklin Plaza Dr, Franklin, North Carolina 28734-3249 **Tel:** 1 800 251-8326.
Email: radio@myfavoritestation.net
Web site: http://www.wrafradio.org
Profile: WPFJ-AM is a non-commercial station owned by Toccoa Falls College. The format of the station is religious featuring Christian teaching and gospel music. WPFJ-AM broadcasts to the Franklin, NC area at 1480 AM.
AM RADIO STATION

WPFL-FM 43400
Owner: Tri-County Broadcasting
Editorial: 20630 Highway 31, Flomaton, Alabama 36441-5210 **Tel:** 1 251 296-1051.
Email: wpflradio@bellsouth.net
Web site: http://wpflradio.com/
Profile: WPFL-FM is a commercial station owned by Tri-County Broadcasting. The format of the station is primarily classic country with some contemporary country hits. WPFL-FM broadcasts to the Flomaton, AL area on 105.1 FM.
FM RADIO STATION

WPFM-FM 40608
Owner: Powell Broadcasting Company, LLC
Editorial: 118 Gwyn Dr, Panama City Beach, Florida 32408-5854 **Tel:** 1 850 234-8858.
Web site: http://hot1079pc.com
Profile: WPFM-FM is a commercial station owned by Powell Broadcasting Company, LLC. The format of the station is Top 40/CHR. WPFM-FM's broadcasts to the Panama City, FL area at 107.9 FM.
FM RADIO STATION

WPFP-AM 38713
Owner: Heartland Communications Group, LLC
Editorial: 1329 4th Ave S, Park Falls, Wisconsin 54552-1926 **Tel:** 1 715 762-3221.
Email: wcqm@pctcnet.net
Web site: http://www.wpfpam.com
AM RADIO STATION

WPFR-AM 38227
Owner: Word Power Inc.
Editorial: 18889 N 2350th St, Dennison, Illinois 62423-2523 **Tel:** 1 217 826-9673.
Email: wpfr@joink.com
Web site: http://www.wordpower.us
Profile: WPFR-AM is a commercial station owned by Word Power Inc. The format of the station is Christian programming. WPFR-AM broadcasts to the Dennison, IL area at 1480 AM.
AM RADIO STATION

WPFR-FM 75691
Owner: Word Power Inc.
Editorial: 18889 N 2350Th St, Dennison, Illinois 62423-2523 **Tel:** 1 217 826-9673.
Email: wpfr@joink.com
Web site: http://www.wordpower.us
Profile: WPFR-FM is a commercial station owned by Word Power Inc. The format of the station is Christian. WPFR-FM broadcasts to the Dennison, IL area at 93.9 FM.
FM RADIO STATION

WPFT-FM 530352
Owner: East Tennessee Radio Group
Editorial: 196 W Dumplin Valley Rd, Kodak, Tennessee 37764-1934 **Tel:** 1 865 932-6002.
Web site: http://mixx1055.com
Profile: WPFT-FM is a commercial station owned by East Tennessee Radio Group. The format of the station is sports. WPFT-FM broadcasts to the Kodak, TN area at 106.3 FM.
FM RADIO STATION

WPFW-FM 40609
Owner: Pacifica Foundation, Inc.
Editorial: 1990 K St NW Ste 14R, Washington, District Of Columbia 20006-1103 **Tel:** 1 202 588-0999.
Email: wpfwradio@gmail.com
Web site: http://www.wpfwfm.org
Profile: WPFW-FM is a non-commercial station owned by Pacifica Foundation, Inc. The format of the station is news/talk and music. WPFW-FM broadcasts to the Washington area at 89.3 FM.
FM RADIO STATION

WPFX-FM 87508
Owner: Toledo Radio LLC
Editorial: 720 Water Street, 4th Floor, Toledo, Ohio 43604 **Tel:** 1 419 255-0107.
Web site: http://1077wolf.com
Profile: WPFX-FM is a commercial station owned by Toledo Radio LLC. The format of the station is contemporary country. WPFX-FM broadcasts to the Toledo, OH area at 107.7 FM.
FM RADIO STATION

WPGA-AM 36562
Owner: Register Communications
Editorial: 1691 Forsyth St, Macon, Georgia 31201 **Tel:** 1 478 745-5858.
Web site: http://www.macon.tv
Profile: WPGA-AM is a commercial station owned by Register Communications. The format of the station is gospel music. WPGA-AM broadcasts to the Macon, GA area at 980 AM.
AM RADIO STATION

WPGA-FM 43282
Owner: Register Communications
Editorial: 1691 Forsyth St, Macon, Georgia 31201 **Tel:** 1 478 745-5858.
Email: mix@macon.tv
Web site: http://www.macon.tv
Profile: WPGA-FM is a commercial station owned by Register Communications. The format of the station is adult contemporary. WPGA-FM broadcasts to the Macon, GA area at 100.9 FM.
FM RADIO STATION

WPGB-FM 42272
Owner: iHeartMedia Inc.
Editorial: 200 Fleet St Fl 4, Pittsburgh, Pennsylvania 15220-2908 **Tel:** 1 412 937-1441.
Web site: http://big1047.iheart.com
Profile: WPGB-FM is a commercial station owned by iHeartMedia Inc. The format of the station is contemporary country. WPGB-FM broadcasts to the Pittsburgh area at 104.7 FM.
FM RADIO STATION

WPGC-FM 45724
Owner: CBS Radio
Editorial: 1015 Half St SE Ste 200, Washington, District Of Columbia 20003-3320 **Tel:** 1 202 479-9227.
Web site: http://www.wpgc.com
Profile: WPGC-FM is a commercial station owned by CBS Radio. The format of the station is urban contemporary. WPGC-FM broadcasts to the Washington, D.C. area at 95.5 FM.
FM RADIO STATION

WPGG-AM 37898
Owner: Townsquare Media, LLC
Editorial: 950 Tilton Rd Ste 200, Northfield, New Jersey 08225-1235 **Tel:** 1 609 645-9797.
Web site: http://wpgg1450.com
Profile: WPGG-AM is a commercial station owned by Townsquare Media, LLC. The format of the station is talk. WENJ-AM broadcasts to the Atlantic City, NJ area at 1450 AM.
AM RADIO STATION

WPGI-FM 45468
Owner: Community Broadcasters, LLC
Editorial: 2205 College Ave, Elmira, New York 14903-1201 **Tel:** 1 607 732-4400.
Web site: http://www.bigpigfm.com
Profile: WPGI-FM is a commercial station owned by Community Broadcasters, LLC. The format of the station is contemporary country music. WPGI-FM broadcasts to the Elmira, NY area at 100.9 FM.
FM RADIO STATION

WPGM-AM 38123
Owner: Montrose Broadcasting Corp.
Editorial: 8 E Market St, Danville, Pennsylvania 17821 **Tel:** 1 570 275-1570.
Web site: http://www.wpgmfm.org
Profile: WPGM-AM is a non-commercial station owned by the Montrose Broadcasting Corp. The format of the station is contemporary Christian music and religious programming. WPGM-AM broadcasts to the Danville, PA area at 1500 AM.
AM RADIO STATION

WPGM-FM 45446
Owner: Montrose Broadcasting Corp.
Editorial: 8 E Market St, Danville, Pennsylvania 17821 **Tel:** 1 570 275-1570.
Web site: http://www.wpgmfm.org
Profile: WPGM-FM is a non-commercial station owned by the Montrose Broadcasting Corp. The format of the station is gospel music and religion. WPGM-FM broadcasts to the Danville, PA area at 96.7 FM.
FM RADIO STATION

WPGP-AM 525771
Owner: Salem Media Group, Inc.
Editorial: 7 Parkway Ctr, Pittsburgh, Pennsylvania 15220-3702 **Tel:** 1 412 937-1500.
Web site: http://www.am1250theanswer.com
Profile: WPGP-AM is a commercial station owned by Salem Media Group, Inc. The format of the station is Conservative Talk. WPGP-AM broadcasts to the Pittsburgh at 1250 AM.
AM RADIO STATION

WPGR-AM 35970
Owner: Saint Joseph Missions
Editorial: 3660 State Route 30 Ste D, Latrobe, Pennsylvania 15650-4309 **Tel:** 1 724 640-0361.
Profile: WPGR-AM is a commercial station owned by Saint Joseph Missions. The format of the station is Catholic programming. WPGR-AM broadcasts to the Pittsburgh area at 1510 AM.
AM RADIO STATION

WPGS-AM 35968
Owner: WPGS Inc.
Editorial: 805 N Dixie Ave, Titusville, Florida 32796-2018 **Tel:** 1 321 383-1000.
Email: WPGS840@aol.com
Web site: http://local840.com
Profile: WPGS-AM is a commercial station owned by WPGS Inc. The format of the station is classic country. WPGS-AM broadcasts to the Titusville, FL area at 840 AM.
AM RADIO STATION

WPGU-FM 40611
Owner: Illini Media Company
Editorial: 512 E Green St Ste 107, Champaign, Illinois 61820-5720 **Tel:** 1 217 337-3100.
Email: wpgu@wpgu.com
Web site: http://www.wpgu.com
Profile: WPGU-FM is a commercial station owned by the Illini Media Co. The format of the station is rock alternative music. WPGU-FM broadcasts in the Champaign, IL area at 107.1 FM.
FM RADIO STATION

WPGW-AM 38124
Owner: WPGW Inc.
Editorial: 1891 W State Road 67, Portland, Indiana 47371 **Tel:** 1 260 726-8729.
Email: wpgw@jayco.net
Web site: http://wpgwradio.com
Profile: WPGW-AM is a commercial station owned by WPGW Inc. The format of the station is adult contemporary music. WPGW-AM broadcasts to the Portland, IN area at 1440 AM.
AM RADIO STATION

WPGW-FM 45447
Owner: WPGW Inc.
Editorial: 1891 W State Road 67, Portland, Indiana 47371 **Tel:** 1 260 726-8729.
Web site: http://wpgwradio.com
Profile: WPGW-FM is a commercial station owned by WPGW Inc. The format of the station is contemporary country music. WPGW-FM broadcasts in the Portland, IN area at 100.9 FM.
FM RADIO STATION

WPGY-AM 39216
Owner: Tri-State Communications, Inc.
Editorial: 134 S Main St, Jasper, Georgia 30143-1702 **Tel:** 1 678 454-9350.
Web site: http://www.wljaradio.com
Profile: WPGY-AM is a commercial station owned by Tri-State Communications, Inc. The format for the station is oldies. WPGY-AM broadcasts to the Atlanta area at 1580 AM.
AM RADIO STATION

WPHB-AM 38762
Owner: Magnum Broadcasting Inc.
Editorial: 1884 Port Matilda Hwy, Philipsburg, Pennsylvania 16866-3128 **Tel:** 1 814 342-2300.
Email: wphb1260@gmail.com
Web site: http://wphbradio.org/
Profile: WPHB-AM is a commercial station owned by Magnum Broadcasting Inc. The format for the station is country and talk. WPHB-AM broadcasts to the State College, PA, area at 1260 AM.
AM RADIO STATION

WPHE-AM 35777
Owner: Radio Salvacion Inc.
Editorial: 321 W Sedgley Ave, Philadelphia, Pennsylvania 19140-4541 **Tel:** 1 215 739-3083.
Web site: http://www.radiosalvacion.com
Profile: WPHE-AM is a commercial station owned by Radio Salvacion Inc. The format of the station is Hispanic religious. WPHE-AM broadcasts to the Philadelphia area at 690 AM.
AM RADIO STATION

WPHI-FM 42790
Owner: Urban One, Inc.
Editorial: 333 E City Ave Ste 700, Bala Cynwyd, Pennsylvania 19004-1521 **Tel:** 1 610 538-1100.
Web site: http://boomphilly.com/
Profile: WPHI-FM is a commercial station owned by Urban One, Inc. The format of the station is Classic Hip Hop. WPHI-FM broadcasts to the Philadelphia area at 107.9 FM.
FM RADIO STATION

WPHK-FM 45901
Owner: La Promesa Foundation
Editorial: 20872 NE Kelley Ave, Blountstown, Florida 32424-1115 **Tel:** 1 850 674-5101.
Web site: http://grnonline.com/
Profile: WPHK-FM is a commercial station owned by La Promesa Foundation. The format of the station is Religious Teaching. WPHK-FM broadcasts in the Blountstown, FL area at 102.7 FM.
FM RADIO STATION

WPHM-AM 39052
Owner: Radio First
Editorial: 808 Huron Ave, Port Huron, Michigan 48060-3705 **Tel:** 1 810 982-9000.
Email: newsroom@bluewaternews.net
Web site: http://www.wphm.net
Profile: WPHM-AM is a commercial station owned by Radio First. The format of the station is news, sports and talk. WPHM-AM broadcasts to the Port Huron, MI area at 1380 AM.
AM RADIO STATION

WPHN-FM 41616
Owner: Northern Christian Radio
Editorial: 1511 E M 32, Gaylord, Michigan 49735-9702 **Tel:** 1 989 732-6274.
Email: studio@ncradio.org
Web site: http://www.ncradio.org
Profile: WPHN-FM is a non-commercial station owned by Northern Christian Radio. The format of the station is religious and contemporary Christian programming. WPHN-FM broadcasts to the Traverse City, MI area at 90.5 FM.
FM RADIO STATION

WPHR-FM 43291
Owner: iHeartMedia Inc.
Editorial: 3071 Continental Dr, West Palm Beach, Florida 33407-3274 **Tel:** 1 561 616-6600.
Web site: http://www.b947freshcountry.com
Profile: WPHR-FM is a commercial station owned by iHeartMedia Inc. The station's format is country. WPHR-FM broadcasts to the greater Fort Pierce, FL area at 94.7 FM and is based out of its West Palm Beach, FL offices.
FM RADIO STATION

WPHT-AM 38643
Owner: CBS Radio
Editorial: 2 Bala Plz, Bala Cynwyd, Pennsylvania 19004-1501 **Tel:** 1 610 668-5800.
Web site: http://philadelphia.cbslocal.com/station/wpht
Profile: WPHT-AM is a commercial station owned by CBS Radio. The format of the station is talk. WPHT-AM broadcasts to the Philadelphia area at 1210 AM.
AM RADIO STATION

WPHZ-FM 42389
Owner: Mitchell Community Broadcasting
Editorial: 424 Heltonville Rd W, Bedford, Indiana 47421-9389 **Tel:** 1 812 275-7555.
Email: comments@wphz.com
Web site: http://www.wphz.com
Profile: WPHZ-FM is a commercial station owned by Mitchell Community Broadcasting. The format of the station is adult contemporary. WPHZ-FM broadcasts to the Bedford, IN area at 102.5 FM.
FM RADIO STATION

WPIA-FM 44451
Owner: Advanced Media Partners LLC
Editorial: 2006 W Altorfer Dr, Peoria, Illinois 61615-1864 **Tel:** 1 309 691-0101.
Web site: http://www.kissfmpeoria.com
Profile: WPIA-FM is a commercial station owned by Advanced Media Partners LLC. The format of the station is Top 40/CHR music. WPIA-FM broadcasts to the Peoria, IL area at 98.5 FM.
FM RADIO STATION

WPIB-FM 44182
Owner: Positive Alternative Radio
Editorial: 22226 Timberlake Rd., Lynchburg, Virginia 24502-7214 **Tel:** 1 434 237-9798.
Email: office@spiritfm.com
Web site: http://www.spiritfm.com
Profile: WPIB-FM is a non-commercial station owned by Positive Alternative Radio. The format of the station is contemporary Christian and religion. WPIB-FM broadcasts to the Blacksburg, VA area at 91.1 FM.
FM RADIO STATION

WPIC-AM 39127
Owner: Cumulus Media Inc.
Editorial: 2030 Pine Hollow Blvd, Hermitage, Pennsylvania 16148-2520 **Tel:** 1 724 346-4113.
Web site: http://www.790wpic.com
Profile: WPIC-AM is a commercial station owned by Cumulus Media Inc. The format of the station is news and talk. WPIC-AM broadcasts to the Hermitage, PA area at 790 AM.
AM RADIO STATION

WPID-AM 35593
Owner: Piedmont Radio Company
Editorial: 412 Cedartown Hwy, Piedmont, Alabama 36272 **Tel:** 1 256 447-9096.
AM RADIO STATION

WPIE-AM 35931
Owner: Taughannock Media, LLC
Editorial: 3100 N Triphammer Rd Ste 100, Lansing, New York 14882-8983 **Tel:** 1 607 533-0057.
Web site: http://www.espnithaca.com
Profile: WPIE-AM is a commercial station owned by Taughannock Media, LLC. The format of the station is sports. WPIE-AM broadcasts to the Elmira, NY area at 1160 AM.
AM RADIO STATION

WPIG-FM 45899
Owner: Community Broadcasters, LLC
Editorial: 3163 Nys Route 417, Olean, New York 14760-1853 **Tel:** 1 716 372-0161.
Web site: http://www.cbolean.com/pig
Profile: WPIG-FM is a commercial station owned by Community Broadcasters, LLC. The format of the station is country, featuring contemporary and classic hits. WPIG-FM broadcasts to the Olean, NY area at 95.7 FM.
FM RADIO STATION

WPIK-FM 41873
Owner: Summerland Media, LLC
Editorial: 22500 Pieces of Eight Rd, Cudjoe Key, Florida 33042-4256 **Tel:** 1 305 745-4162.
Web site: http://www.radioritmolafabulosa.com
Profile: WPIK-FM is a commercial station owned by Summerland Media, LLC. The format of the station is Hispanic. WPIK-FM broadcasts to the Summerland Key, FL area at 102.5 FM.
FM RADIO STATION

WPIL-FM 410772
Owner: Jarrell(Jimmy)
Editorial: 256 Brockford Rd, Heflin, Alabama 36264-1608 **Tel:** 1 256 463-4226.
Email: wpil@wpilfm.com
Web site: http://www.wpilfm.com
Profile: WPIL-FM is a non-commercial station owned by Jimmy Jarrell. The format of the station is variety, featuring a mix of classic country, gospel and bluegrass with a Christian base. WPIL-FM broadcasts to the Heflin, AL area at 91.7 FM.
FM RADIO STATION

WPIM-FM 44183
Owner: Positive Alternative Radio
Editorial: 22226 Timberlake Rd., Lynchburg, Virginia 24502-7214 **Tel:** 1 434 237-9798.
Email: office@spiritfm.com
Web site: http://www.spiritfm.com
FM RADIO STATION

WPIN-AM 36975
Owner: Positive Radio Group
Editorial: 145 Jackson St NE, Blacksburg, Virginia 24060-3931 **Tel:** 1 540 951-9791.
Email: wpin810@yahoo.com
Web site: http://www.espnblacksburg.com/
Profile: WPIN-AM is a commercial station owned by Positive Radio Group. The format of the station is country. WPIN-AM broadcasts to the Blacksburg, VA area at 810 AM.
AM RADIO STATION

WPIN-FM 44184
Owner: Positive Alternative Radio
Editorial: 22226 Timberlake Rd., Lynchburg, Virginia 24502-7214 **Tel:** 1 800 774-9798.
Email: office@spiritfm.com
Web site: http://www.spiritfm.com
Profile: WPIN-FM is a non-commercial station owned by Positive Alternative Radio. The format of the station is contemporary Christian and religion. WPIN-FM broadcasts to the Blacksburg, VA area at 91.5 FM.
FM RADIO STATION

WPIO-FM 40614
Owner: Florida Public Radio, Inc.
Editorial: 505 Josephine St, Titusville, Florida 32796 **Tel:** 1 321 267-3000.
Email: wpio@gate.net
Web site: http://www.noncomradio.net

Profile: WPIO-FM is a non-commercial station owned by Florida Public Radio, Inc. The format of the station is religious. WPOI-FM broadcasts to the Titusville, FL area at 89.3 FM.
FM RADIO STATION

WPIP-AM 36970

Owner: Berean Baptist Church
Editorial: 4135 Thomasville Rd, Winston Salem, North Carolina 27107-4427 **Tel:** 1 336 785-0527.
Email: wpip880am@triad.rr.com
Web site: http://www.wpipbereanradio.org
Profile: WPIP-AM is is a non-commercial station owned by Berean Baptist Church. The format of the station is religious. WPIP-AM broadcasts to the Winston-Salem, NC area at 880 AM.
AM RADIO STATION

WPIR-FM 45887

Owner: Positive Alternative Radio
Editorial: 600 W Clemmonsville Rd, Winston-Salem, North Carolina 27103 **Tel:** 1 336 788-1155.
Email: office@joyfm.org
Web site: http://www.joyfm.org
Profile: WPIR-FM is a non-commercial station owned by Positive Alternative Radio. The format of the station is southern gospel music and religious talk. WPIR-FM broadcasts in the Claremont, NC area at 88.1 FM.
FM RADIO STATION

WPIT-AM 39170

Owner: Salem Media Group, Inc.
Editorial: 7 Parkway Ctr Ste 625, Pittsburgh, Pennsylvania 15220-3707 **Tel:** 1 412 937-1500.
Email: word@wordfm.com
Web site: http://www.wpitam.com
Profile: WPIT-AM is a commercial station owned by Salem Media Group, Inc. The format of the station is religious talk. WPIT-AM broadcasts to the Pittsburgh, PA area at 730 AM.
AM RADIO STATION

WPJL-AM 35595

Owner: WPJL Inc.
Editorial: 515 Bart St, Raleigh, North Carolina 27610 **Tel:** 1 919 834-6401.
Email: wpjl@nc.rr.com
Web site: http://www.wpjlradio.com
Profile: WPJL-AM is a commercial station owned by WPJL Inc. The format of the station is religious programming. WPJL-AM broadcasts in the Raleigh, NC area at 1240 AM.
AM RADIO STATION

WPJM-AM 35596

Owner: Full Gospel WPJM 800 AM Radio Inc.
Editorial: 305 Tryon St, Greer, South Carolina 29651-1822 **Tel:** 1 864 877-1112.
Email: wpjesusmusic@bellsouth.net
Web site: http://800wpjm.com
Profile: WPJM-AM is a commercial station owned by Full Gospel WPJM 800 AM Radio Inc. The format of the station is gospel. WPJM-AM broadcasts to the Greenville, SC and Asheville, NC area at 800 AM.
AM RADIO STATION

WPJS-AM 35876

Owner: WPJS Broadcasting Inc.
Editorial: 1516 4th Ave #B, Conway, South Carolina 29526-5032 **Tel:** 1 843 248-6365.
Profile: WPJS-AM is a commercial station owned by WPJS Broadcasting Inc. The format of the station is gospel music. WPJS-AM broadcasts to the Conway, SC area at 1330 AM.
AM RADIO STATION

WPJX-AM 403904

Owner: Polnet Communications
Editorial: 4320 Dundee Rd, Northbrook, Illinois 60062-1703 **Tel:** 1 847 498-3350.
Email: polnetradio@gmail.com
Web site: http://www.pclradio.com
Profile: WPJX-AM is a commercial station owned by Polnet Communications. The format of the station is Spanish. WPJX-AM broadcasts to the Northbrook, IL area at 1500 AM.
AM RADIO STATION

WPJY-FM 562230

Owner: Positive Alternative Radio
Tel: 1 877 456-9361.
Email: office@walkfm.org
Web site: http://walkfm.org
Profile: WPJY-FM is a non-commercial station owned by Positive Alternative Radio. The format of the station is Contemporary Christian. WPJY-FM broadcasts to the Parkersburg, WV area at 88.7 FM.
FM RADIO STATION

WPKE-AM 38125

Owner: East Kentucky Radio Network
Editorial: 1240 Radio Dr, Pikeville, Kentucky 41501-4779 **Tel:** 1 606 432-8103.
Email: frontdesk@ekbradio.com
Web site: http://www.myoldiesradio.com
Profile: WPKE-AM is a commercial station owned by East Kentucky Radio Network. The format of the station is adult hits. WPKE-AM broadcasts to the Pikeville, KY area at 1240 AM.
AM RADIO STATION

WPKE-FM 46110

Owner: East Kentucky Radio Network
Editorial: 1240 Radio Dr, Pikeville, Kentucky 41501-4779 **Tel:** 1 606 437-4051.
Email: frontdesk@ekbradio.com
Web site: http://www.wpke.com
Profile: WPKE-FM is a commercial station owned by East Kentucky Radio Network. The format of the station is classic rock. WPKE-FM target broadcasts to Pikeville, KY and surrounding communities at 103.1 FM.
FM RADIO STATION

WPKF-FM 43059

Owner: iHeartMedia Inc.
Editorial: 20 Tucker Dr, Poughkeepsie, New York 12603-1644 **Tel:** 1 845 471-2300.
Web site: http://kissfmhv.iheart.com
Profile: WPKF-FM is a commercial station owned by iHeartMedia Inc. The format of the station is rhythmic Top 40/CHR music. WPKF-FM broadcasts to the Poughkeepsie, NY area at 96.1 FM.
FM RADIO STATION

WPKG-FM 217874

Owner: Central Wisconsin Broadcasting
Editorial: 1201 E Division St, Neillsville, Wisconsin 54456-2123 **Tel:** 1 715 743-3333.
Web site: http://www.cwbradio.com
Profile: WPKG-FM is a commercial station owned by Central Wisconsin Broadcasting. The format of the station is Hot AC. WPKG-FM broadcasts to the Clarks County, Wisconsin area at a frequency of 92.7 FM.
FM RADIO STATION

WPKL-FM 45958

Owner: FM Radio Licenses, LLC
Editorial: 123 Blaine Rd, Brownsville, Pennsylvania 15417-9330 **Tel:** 1 724 938-2000.
Web site: http://www.picklefm.com
Profile: WPKL-FM is a commercial station owned by FM Radio Licenses, LLC. The format of the station is classic hits music. WPKL-FM broadcasts in the Brownsville, PA area on 99.3 FM.
FM RADIO STATION

WPKN-FM 40616

Owner: WPKN Inc.
Editorial: 244 Myrtle Ave, Bridgeport, Connecticut 06604-7775 **Tel:** 1 203 331-9756.
Email: press@wpkn.org
Web site: http://www.wpkn.org
Profile: WPKN-FM is a non-commercial station owned by WPKN Inc. The format of the station is variety. WPKN-FM broadcasts in the Bridgeport, CT area at 89.5 FM.
FM RADIO STATION

WPKO-FM 46128

Owner: V-Teck Communications Inc.
Editorial: 1501 Road 235, Bellefontaine, Ohio 43311 **Tel:** 1 937 592-1045.
Email: customerservice@wpko.com
Web site: http://www.peakofohio.com
Profile: WPKO-FM is a commercial station owned by V-Tech Communications Inc. The format of the station is adult contemporary music. WPKO-FM's target audience is adult contemporary music listeners, ages 18 to 64, in the Dayton, OH area. The station's tagline is "Mix 98.3"
FM RADIO STATION

WPKQ-FM 43709

Owner: Townsquare Media
Editorial: 2617 White Mountain Hwy, North Conway, New Hampshire 03860-5120 **Tel:** 1 603 356-7500.
Email: news@wokq.com
Web site: http://www.wokq.com
Profile: WPKQ-FM is a commercial station owned by Townsquare Media. The format of the station is contemporary country. WPKQ-FM broadcasts to the North Conway, NH area at 103.7 FM.
FM RADIO STATION

WPKR-FM 41619

Owner: Cumulus Media Inc.
Editorial: 491 S Washburn St, Oshkosh, Wisconsin 54904-6733 **Tel:** 1 920 426-3239.
Web site: http://www.nashfmwisconsin.com
Profile: WPKR-FM is a commercial station owned by Cumulus Media Inc. The format of the station is contemporary country. WPKR-FM broadcasts to the Green Bay, WI area at 99.5 FM.
FM RADIO STATION

WPKT-FM 41067

Owner: Connecticut Public Broadcasting Inc.
Editorial: 1049 Asylum Ave, Hartford, Connecticut 06105-2432 **Tel:** 1 860 278-5310.
Email: wherewelive@wnpr.org
Web site: http://www.cpbn.org
Profile: WPKT-FM is a non-commercial station owned by Connecticut Public Broadcasting Inc. The format of the station is news and talk. WPKT-FM broadcasts to the Hartford, CT area at 89.1 FM. WPKT-FM airs WNPR-FM's programming.
FM RADIO STATION

WPKV-FM 45142

Owner: FM Radio Licenses, LLC
Tel: 1 916 251-1600.
Profile: WPKV-FM is a commercial station owned by FM Radio Licenses, LLC and operated by Educational Media Foundation. The format is christian music. WPKV-FM broadcasts to the Pittsburgh area at 98.3 FM. This station airs K-Love programming.
FM RADIO STATION

WPKX-AM 36727

Owner: iHeartMedia Inc.
Editorial: 195 McGregor St Ste 810, Manchester, New Hampshire 03102-3755 **Tel:** 1 603 625-6915.
Web site: http://www.foxsports930.com/main.html
Profile: WPKX-AM is a commercial station owned by iHeartMedia Inc. The format of the station is sports talk. WPKX-AM broadcasts to the Manchester, NH area at 930 AM.
AM RADIO STATION

WPKY-AM 38126

Owner: Commonwealth Broadcasting Corp.
Editorial: 108 W Main St, Princeton, Kentucky 42445-1547 **Tel:** 1 270 365-2072.
Email: wavj@commonwealthbroadcasting.com
Profile: WPKY-AM is a commercial station owned by Commonwealth Broadcasting Corp. The format of the station is classic hits. WPKY-AM broadcasts to the Princeton, KY area at 1580 AM.
AM RADIO STATION

WPKZ-AM 35293

Owner: Central Broadcasting Company LLC
Editorial: 762 Water St, Fitchburg, Massachusetts 01420-6497 **Tel:** 1 978 343-3766.
Email: info@wpkz.net
Web site: http://wpkz.net
Profile: WPKZ-AM is a commercial station owned by Central Broadcasting Company LLC. The format of the station is sports and news talk. WPKZ-AM broadcasts to the Fitchburg, MA area at 1280 AM.
AM RADIO STATION

WPLA-AM 37116

Owner: iHeartMedia Inc.
Editorial: 7080 Industrial Hwy, Macon, Georgia 31216-7538 **Tel:** 1 478 781-1063.
Web site: http://www.foxsports1670.com
Profile: WPLA-AM is a commercial station owned by iHeartMedia Inc. The format of the station is sports. WPLA-AM broadcasts to the Macon, GA area at 1670 AM.
AM RADIO STATION

WPLJ-FM 46645

Owner: Cumulus Media Inc
Editorial: 2 Penn Plz, New York, New York 10121-0101 **Tel:** 1 212 613-8900.
Web site: http://www.955plj.nyc
Profile: WPLJ-FM is a commercial station owned by Cumulus Media Inc. The format of the station is hot adult contemporary music. WPLJ-FM broadcasts throughout the New York City area at 95.5 FM.
FM RADIO STATION

WPLK-AM 35682

Owner: Natkin Radio
Editorial: 1428 Saint Johns Ave, Palatka, Florida 32177-4542 **Tel:** 1 386 325-5800.
Email: wplk@wplk.com
Web site: http://www.wplk.com
Profile: WPLK-AM is a commercial station owned by Natkin Radio. The format of the station is adult standards and modern AC. WPLK-AM broadcasts to the Palatka, FL area at 800 AM.
AM RADIO STATION

WPLL-FM 45977

Owner: Marc Radio Group, LLC
Editorial: 100 NW 76th Dr Ste 2, Gainesville, Florida 32607-6659 **Tel:** 1 352 313-3150.
Web site: http://www.1069pulsefm.com
Profile: WPLL-FM is a commercial station owned by Marc Radio Group, LLC. The format of the station is Contemporary Christian. WPLL-FM broadcasts to the Gainesville, FL area at 106.9 FM.
FM RADIO STATION

WPLM-AM 38128

Owner: Plymouth Rock Broadcasting
Editorial: 17 Columbus Rd, Plymouth, Massachusetts 02360-4810 **Tel:** 1 508 746-1390.
Web site: http://www.easy991.com
Profile: WPLM-AM is a commercial station owned by Plymouth Rock Broadcasting. The format of the station is business talk and adult contemporary music programming. WPLM-AM broadcasts to the Plymouth, MA area at 1390 AM.
AM RADIO STATION

WPLM-FM 235055

Owner: Plymouth Rock Broadcasting
Editorial: 17 Columbus Rd, Plymouth, Massachusetts 02360-4810 **Tel:** 1 508 746-1390.
Web site: http://www.easy991.com
Profile: WPLM-FM is a commercial station owned by Plymouth Rock Broadcasting. The format of the station is classic soft hits. WPLM-FM broadcasts to the Plymouth, MA area at 99.1 FM.
FM RADIO STATION

WPLN-AM 88098

Owner: Nashville Public Radio
Editorial: 630 Mainstream Dr, Nashville, Tennessee 37228-1204 **Tel:** 1 615 760-2903.
Email: wpln@wpln.org
Web site: http://www.nashvillepublicradio.org
Profile: WPLN-AM is a non-commercial station owned by Nashville Public Radio. The format of the station is news and talk. WPLN-AM broadcasts to the Nashville, TN area at at 1430 AM.
AM RADIO STATION

WPLN-FM 40617

Owner: Nashville Public Radio
Editorial: 630 Mainstream Dr, Nashville, Tennessee 37228-1204 **Tel:** 1 615 760-2903.
Email: wpln@wpln.org
Web site: http://www.wpln.org
Profile: WPLN-FM is a non-commercial station owned by Nashville Public Radio. The format of the station is news and talk. WPLN-FM broadcasts to the Nashville, TN area at 90.3 FM.
FM RADIO STATION

WPLO-AM 35346

Owner: Prieto Communications
Editorial: 239 Ezzard St, Lawrenceville, Georgia 30046-5936 **Tel:** 1 770 237-9897.
Email: sales@labonita610.com
Web site: http://www.labonita610.com
Profile: WPLO-AM is a commercial station owned by Prieto Communications. The format of the station is Spanish Adult Hits. WPLO-AM broadcasts to the Lawrenceville, GA area at 610 AM.
AM RADIO STATION

WPLR-FM 40618

Owner: Connoisseur Media
Editorial: 440 Wheelers Farms Rd, Milford, Connecticut 06461-9133 **Tel:** 1 203 783-8200.
Web site: http://www.wplr.com
Profile: WPLR-FM is a commercial station owned by Connoisseur Media. The format of the station is classic rock. WPLR-FM broadcasts to the Milford, CT area at 99.1 FM.
FM RADIO STATION

WPLV-AM 36709

Owner: iHeartMedia Inc.
Editorial: 705 4th Ave, West Point, Georgia 31833-1506 **Tel:** 1 706 645-2991.
Web site: http://www.intouch910am.com/default.asp
Profile: WPLV-AM is a commercial station owned by iHeartMedia Inc. The format of the station is urban contemporary and R & B oldies. WPLV-AM broadcasts to the Atlanta area at 1310 AM.
AM RADIO STATION

WPLW-FM 46528

Owner: Curtis Media Group
Editorial: 3012 Highwoods Blvd Ste 201, Raleigh, North Carolina 27604-1031 **Tel:** 1 919 790-9392.
Email: info@curtismedia.com
Web site: http://www.pulse102.com
Profile: WPLW-FM is a commercial station owned by Curtis Media Group. The format of the station is Top 40. WPLW-FM broadcasts to the greater Raleigh, NC area at 102.5 FM.
FM RADIO STATION

WPLY-AM 38192

Owner: Wheeler Inc.(Mel)
Editorial: 3934 Electric Rd, Roanoke, Virginia 24018-4513 **Tel:** 1 540 989-4591.
Web site: http://www.sportsradiova.com
Profile: WPLY-AM is a commercial station owned by Mel Wheeler Inc. The format of the station is Sports. WPLY-AM broadcasts in the Roanoke, VA area at 610 AM.
AM RADIO STATION

WPLZ-FM 46552

Owner: Brewer Broadcasting Inc.
Editorial: 1305 Carter St, Chattanooga, Tennessee 37402 **Tel:** 1 423 265-9494.
Web site: http://www.catcountry953.com
Profile: WPLZ-FM is a commercial station owned by Brewer Broadcasting Inc. The format of the station is contemporary country. WPLZ-FM broadcasts to the Cleveland, TN area at 95.3 FM.
FM RADIO STATION

WPMB-AM 38129

Owner: Cromwell Group Inc.(The)
Editorial: 232 S 4th St, Vandalia, Illinois 62471-2810 **Tel:** 1 618 283-2325.
Email: wkrv@sbcglobal.net
Web site: http://www.vandaliaradio.com
Profile: WPMB-AM is a commercial station owned by the Cromwell Group Inc. The format of the station is adult standards. WPMB-AM broadcasts to Vandalia, IL at 1500 AM.
AM RADIO STATION

WPMH-AM 36501

Owner: Chesapeake-Portsmouth Broadcasting Corp.
Editorial: 2202 Jolliff Rd, Chesapeake, Virginia 23321-1416 **Tel:** 1 757 488-1010.
Email: info@wwip.org
Web site: http://www.wpmh1010.com
Profile: WPMH-AM is a commercial station owned by Chesapeake-Portsmouth Broadcasting Corp. The format of the station is religious talk. WPMH-AM broadcasts to the Chesapeake, VA area at 1010 AM.
AM RADIO STATION

WPMO-AM 36041

Owner: Tri City Radio, LLC
Editorial: 5115 Telephone Rd, Pascagoula, Mississippi 39567-1130 **Tel:** 1 228 762-5683.
Web site: http://www.talkradio1580.com
Profile: WPMO-AM is a commercial station owned by Tri City Radio, LLC. The format of the station is sports. WPMO-AM broadcasts at a frequency of 1580 AM to the Pascagoula, MS area.
AM RADIO STATION

WPMX-FM 43069

Owner: Radio Statesboro, Inc.
Editorial: 561 E Olliff St, Statesboro, Georgia 30458-4663 **Tel:** 1 912 764-5446.
Web site: http://statesboro365.com
Profile: WPMX-FM is a commercial station owned by Radio Statesboro, Inc. The format for the station is adult contemporary. WPMX-FM broadcasts to the Savannah, GA area at 102.9 FM.
FM RADIO STATION

WPMZ-AM 36723
Owner: Video Mundo Broadcasting Co.
Editorial: 1270 Mineral Spring Ave, North Providence, Rhode Island 02904-4637 **Tel:** 1 401 726-8413.
Email: info@poder1110.com
Web site: http://www.poder1110.com
AM RADIO STATION

WPNA-AM 35600
Owner: Alliance Communications, Inc.
Editorial: 408 S Oak Park Ave, Oak Park, Illinois 60302-3876 **Tel:** 1 708 848-8980.
Email: email@wpna1490am.com
Web site: http://radiowpna.com
Profile: WPNA-AM is a commercial station owned by Alliance Communications, Inc. The format of the station is talk programming spoken in the native dialect of Poland. WPNA-AM broadcasts to the Oak Park, IL area at 1490 AM.
AM RADIO STATION

WPNC-FM 44238
Owner: Durlyn Broadcasting Inc.
Editorial: 930 NC Highway 32 S, Plymouth, North Carolina 27962-9354 **Tel:** 1 252 793-9995.
Email: magic96_1963@yahoo.com
Web site: http://magic959online.com
Profile: WPNC-FM is a commercial station owned by Durlyn Broadcasting Inc. The format of the station is adult contemporary. WPNC-FM broadcasts to the Plymouth, NC area at 95.9 FM.
FM RADIO STATION

WPNG-FM 81420
Owner: Broadcast South, LLC
Editorial: 1931Highway 32 E, Douglas, Georgia 31533-9074 **Tel:** 1 912 422-6122.
Profile: WPNG-FM is a commercial station owned by Broadcast South, LLC. The format of the station is Top 40/CHR. WPNG-FM broadcasts to the Pearson, GA area at 101.9 FM.
FM RADIO STATION

WPNH-AM 38130
Owner: Northeast Communications Corp.
Editorial: 110 Babbitt Rd, Franklin, New Hampshire 03235-2105 **Tel:** 1 888 941-1069.
Profile: WPNH-AM is a commercial station owned by Northeast Communications Corp. The format of the station is adult standards music. WPNH-AM broadcasts to the Boston area at 1300 AM.
AM RADIO STATION

WPNH-FM 45450
Owner: Northeast Communications Corp.
Editorial: 110 Babbitt Rd, Franklin, New Hampshire 03235-2105 **Tel:** 1 603 536-2500.
Email: annie@wpnhfm.com
Web site: http://www.wpnhfm.com
Profile: WPNH-FM is a commercial station owned by Northeast Communications Corp. The format of the station is rock alternative music. WPNH-FM broadcasts to the Boston area at 100.1 FM.
FM RADIO STATION

WPNN-AM 35592
Owner: Schroeder(Christopher)
Editorial: 3801 N Pace Blvd, Pensacola, Florida 32505-4344 **Tel:** 1 850 433-1141.
Email: production@talk790.com
Web site: http://www.wpnnradio.com
Profile: WPNN-AM is a commercial station owned by Christopher Schroeder. The format of the station is talk programming. WPNN-AM broadcasts to the Pensacola, FL area at 790 AM.
AM RADIO STATION

WPNW-AM 38275
Owner: Lanser Broadcasting Corp.
Editorial: 425 Centerstone Ct, Zeeland, Michigan 49464-2247 **Tel:** 1 616 931-9930.
Email: news@1260thepledge.com
Web site: http://thepledgeradio.com
Profile: WPNW-AM is a commercial station owned by Lanser Broadcasting Corp. The format of the station is talk. WPNW-AM broadcasts to the Holland, MI area at 1260 AM.
AM RADIO STATION

WPOC-FM 40620
Owner: iHeartMedia Inc.
Editorial: 711 W 40th St Ste 350, Baltimore, Maryland 21211-2190 **Tel:** 1 410 366-7600.
Web site: http://wpoc.iheart.com
Profile: WPOC-FM is a commercial station owned by iHeartMedia Inc.The format of the station is country music. WPOC-FM broadcasts to the Baltimore area at 93.1 FM.
FM RADIO STATION

WPOG-AM 792837
Owner: Grace Baptist Church of Orangeburg
Editorial: 4305 Columbia Rd, Orangeburg, South Carolina 29118-1268 **Tel:** 1 803 536-4300.
Web site: http://wwosradio.net
Profile: WPOG-AM is a commercial station owned by Grace Baptist Church of Orangeburg. The format of the station is religious. WPOG-FM broadcasts to the Saint Matthews, SC area at 710 AM.
AM RADIO STATION

WPOI-FM 40427
Owner: Cox Media Group, Inc.
Editorial: 11300 4th St N Ste 300, Saint Petersburg, Florida 33716-2941 **Tel:** 1 727 579-2000.
Web site: http://www.hot1015tampabay.com
Profile: WPOI-FM is a commercial station owned by Cox Media Group, Inc. The format of the station is Hot AC. WPOI-FM broadcasts to the Saint Petersburg, FL area at 101.5 FM.
FM RADIO STATION

WPOL-AM 36318
Owner: Truth Broadcasting
Editorial: 4405 Providence Ln, Winston Salem, North Carolina 27106-3226 **Tel:** 1 336 759-0363.
Web site: http://www.1340thelight.com
Profile: WPOL-AM is a commercial station owned by Truth Broadcasting. The format of the station is gospel. WPOL-AM broadcasts to the Winston Salem, NC area at 1340 AM.
AM RADIO STATION

WPOP-AM 39160
Owner: iHeartMedia Inc.
Editorial: 10 Columbus Blvd Ste 1, Hartford, Connecticut 06106-1976 **Tel:** 1 860 723-6000.
Email: ctdigital@iheartmedia.com
Web site: http://newsradio1410.iheart.com
Profile: WPOP-AM is a commercial station owned by iHeartMedia Inc. The format of the station is sports. WPOP-AM broadcasts to the Hartford, CT area at 1410 AM.
AM RADIO STATION

WPOR-FM 45451
Owner: Saga Communications
Editorial: 420 Western Ave, South Portland, Maine 04106-1704 **Tel:** 1 207 774-4561.
Email: wpor@wpor.com
Web site: http://www.wpor.com
Profile: WPOR-FM is a commercial station owned by Saga Communications. The format of the station is contemporary country. WPOR-FM broadcasts to the Portland, ME area at 101.9 FM.
FM RADIO STATION

WPOS-FM 40621
Owner: Maumee Valley Broadcasting Association
Editorial: 7112 Angola Rd, Holland, Ohio 43528-9631 **Tel:** 1 419 865-5551.
Email: radio@proclaimfm.com
Web site: http://proclaimfm.com
Profile: WPOS-FM is a non-commercial station owned by Maumee Valley Broadcasting Association. The format of the station is Contemporary Christian. WPOS-FM broadcasts to the Holland, OH area at 102.3 FM.
FM RADIO STATION

WPOW-FM 40622
Owner: CBS Radio
Editorial: 194 NW 187th St, Miami, Florida 33169-4050 **Tel:** 1 305 654-1700.
Web site: http://www.power96.com
Profile: WPOW-FM is a commercial station owned by the CBS Radio The format of the station is rhythmic Top 40/CHR. WPOW-FM broadcasts to the Miami area at 96.5 FM.
FM RADIO STATION

WPPA-AM 38740
Owner: Pottsville Broadcasting Company Inc.
Editorial: 212 S Centre St, Pottsville, Pennsylvania 17901-3532 **Tel:** 1 570 622-1360.
Email: news@pbcradio.com
Web site: http://www.wpparadio.com
Profile: WPPA-AM is a commercial station owned by Pottsville Broadcasting Company Inc. The format of the station is talk. WPPA-AM broadcasts to the Pottsville, PA area at 1360 AM.
AM RADIO STATION

WPPB-FM 40604
Owner: Peconic Public Broadcasting, Inc.
Editorial: 71 Hill St, Southampton, New York 11968-5319 **Tel:** 1 631 591-7000.
Profile: WPPB-FM is a non-commercial station owned by Peconic Public Broadcasting, Inc. The format of the station is variety and news. WPPB-FM broadcasts in the Southhampton, NY, area at 88.3 FM.
FM RADIO STATION

WPPG-FM 231110
Owner: Wolff Broadcasting Corporation.
Editorial: Highway 31 South, Evergreen, Alabama 36401 **Tel:** 1 251 578-3121.
Email: wppg@att.net
Profile: WPPG-FM is a commercial station owned by Wolff Broadcasting Corporation. The format of the station is country music. WPPG-FM broadcasts to the Evergreen, AL area at 101.1 FM.
FM RADIO STATION

WPPI-FM 42308
Owner: Atlantic Coast Radio LLC
Editorial: 779 Warren Ave, Portland, Maine 04103-1007 **Tel:** 1 617 779-3500.
Web site: http://www.weei.com
Profile: WPPI-FM is a commercial station owned by Atlantic Coast Radio LLC. The format of the station is sports. WPPI-FM broadcasts to the Portland, ME area at 95.5 FM. WPPI-FM airs WEEI-AM's programming.
FM RADIO STATION

WPPL-FM 42832
Owner: White(James Timothy)
Editorial: 333 E Highland St, Blue Ridge, Georgia 30513-4544 **Tel:** 1 706 632-9775.
Email: wppl@tds.net
Web site: http://www.mountaincountryradio.com
Profile: WPPL-FM is a commercial station owned by James Timothy White. The format for the station is contemporary country. WPPL-FM broadcasts to the Chattanooga, TN area at 103.9 FM.
FM RADIO STATION

WPPN-FM 40777
Owner: Univision Communications Inc.
Editorial: 625 N Michigan Ave Ste 300, Chicago, Illinois 60611-3110 **Tel:** 1 312 981-1800.
Web site: http://www.univision.com/chicago/wppn
Profile: WPPN-FM is a commercial station owned by Univision Communications Inc. The format of the station is Spanish AC. WPPN-FM broadcasts to the Chicago area at 106.7 FM.
FM RADIO STATION

WPPR-FM 44097
Owner: Georgia Public Broadcasting
Editorial: 260 14th St NW, Atlanta, Georgia 30318 **Tel:** 1 404 685-2548.
Email: news@gpb.org
Web site: http://www.gpb.org
Profile: WPPR-FM is a non-commercial station owned by Georgia Public Broadcasting. The format of the station is news, classical and jazz music. WPPR-FM broadcasts to the Atlanta area at 88.3 FM.
FM RADIO STATION

WPPZ-FM 40455
Owner: Urban One, Inc.
Editorial: 333 E City Ave Ste 700, Bala Cynwyd, Pennsylvania 19004-1521 **Tel:** 1 610 538-1100.
Web site: http://praisephilly.com
Profile: WPPZ-FM is a commercial station owned by Urban One, Inc. The format of the station is gospel. WPPZ-FM broadcasts to the Philadelphia area at 103.9 FM.
FM RADIO STATION

WPRB-FM 40623
Owner: Princeton Broadcasting Service
Editorial: 030 Bloomberg Hall Princeton Uni, Princeton, New Jersey 8544 **Tel:** 1 609 258-3655.
Email: news@wprb.com
Web site: http://www.wprb.com
Profile: WPRB-FM is a commercial station owned by Princeton Broadcasting Service. The format for the station is variety. WPRB-FM broadcasts to the Princeton, NJ area at 103.3 FM.
FM RADIO STATION

WPRD-AM 36334
Owner: J & V Communications Inc.
Editorial: 222 Hazard St, Orlando, Florida 32804-3030 **Tel:** 1 407 841-8282.
Email: wprd1440@gmail.com
Web site: http://www.wprd.com
Profile: WPRD-AM is a commercial station owned by J&V Communications Inc. The format of the station is Hispanic variety. WPRD-AM broadcasts to the Orlando, FL area at 1440 AM.
AM RADIO STATION

WPRE-AM 36730
Owner: Robinson Corporation
Editorial: 640 N Villa Louis Rd, Prairie du Chien, Wisconsin 53821-1338 **Tel:** 1 608 326-2411.
Email: wqpcwpre@mwt.net
Web site: http://www.wpreradio.com
Profile: WPRE-AM is a commercial station owned by Robinson Corporation. The format of the station is classic hits. WPRE-AM broadcasts to the Prairie Du Chien, WI area at 980 AM.
AM RADIO STATION

WPRJ-FM 42398
Owner: Spirit Communications, Inc.
Tel: 1 989 465-9775.
Email: radiou@radiou.com
Web site: http://radiou.com
Profile: WPRJ-FM is a non-commercial station owned by Spirit Communications, Inc. The format of the station is Christian alternative rock music. WPRJ-FM broadcasts to the Coleman, MI area at 101.7 FM.
FM RADIO STATION

WPRK-FM 40624
Owner: Rollins College
Editorial: 1000 Holt Ave, Winter Park, Florida 32789-4499 **Tel:** 1 407 646-2241.
Email: wprkfm@rollins.edu
Web site: http://wprk.org
Profile: WPRK-FM is a non-commercial station owned by Rollins College. The format of the station is Variety. WPRK-FM broadcasts to the Winter Park, FL area at 91.5 FM.
FM RADIO STATION

WPRO-AM 38134
Owner: Cumulus Media Inc.
Editorial: 1502 Wampanoag Trl, Riverside, Rhode Island 02915-1018 **Tel:** 1 401 433-4200.
Email: wpronews@630wpro.com
Web site: http://www.630wpro.com
Profile: WPRO-AM is a commercial station owned by Cumulus Media Inc. The format of the station is news, sports and talk. WPRO-AM broadcasts to the Riverside, RI area at 630 AM.
AM RADIO STATION

WPRO-FM 45452
Owner: Cumulus Media Inc.
Editorial: 1502 Wampanoag Trl, Riverside, Rhode Island 2915 **Tel:** 1 401 433-4200.
Web site: http://www.92profm.com
Profile: WPRO-FM is a commercial station owned by Cumulus Media Inc. The format of the station is Top 40/CHR. WPRO-FM broadcasts to the Riverside, RI area at 92.3 FM.
FM RADIO STATION

WPRR-AM 3697
Owner: WPRR, Inc.
Editorial: 3777 44th St SE, Grand Rapids, Michigan 49512-3945 **Tel:** 1 616 656-2619.
Email: info@publicrealityradio.org
Web site: http://www.publicrealityradio.org
Profile: WPRR-AM is a non-commercial station owned by WPRR, Inc. The format of the station is talk. WPRR-AM broadcasts to the Grand Rapids, MI area at 1680 AM.
AM RADIO STATION

WPRS-AM 39045
Owner: Midwest Communications Inc.
Editorial: 12861 Il Highway 133, Paris, Illinois 61944-6753 **Tel:** 1 812 232-4161.
Web site: http://wibqam.com/
Profile: WPRS-AM is a commercial station owned by Midwest Communications Inc. The format of the station is country. WPRS-AM broadcasts to the Terre Haute, IN area at 1440 AM.
AM RADIO STATION

WPRS-FM 40879
Owner: Urban One, Inc.
Editorial: 8515 Georgia Ave Fl 9, Silver Spring, Maryland 20910-3403 **Tel:** 1 301 306-1111.
Web site: http://praisedc.com
Profile: WPRS-FM is a commercial station owned by Urban One, Inc. The format of the station is gospel. WPRS-FM broadcasts to the Washington, D.C. area at 104.1 FM.
FM RADIO STATION

WPRT-AM 36935
Owner: East Kentucky Radio Network
Editorial: 1240 Radio Dr, Pikeville, Kentucky 41501-4779 **Tel:** 1 304 235-3600.
Email: frontdesk@ekbradio.com
Web site: http://www.900wlsi.com
Profile: WPRT-AM is a commercial station owned by East Kentucky Radio Network. The format of the station is talk. WPRT-AM broadcasts to the Pikeville, KY area at 960 AM.
AM RADIO STATION

WPRT-FM 41857
Owner: Cromwell Group Inc.(The)
Editorial: 1824 Murfreesboro Pike, Nashville, Tennessee 37217-3208 **Tel:** 1 615 399-1029.
Web site: http://www.1025thegame.com
Profile: WPRT-FM is a commercial station owned by The Cromwell Group Inc. The format of the station is sports. WPRT-FM broadcasts to the Nashville, TN area at 102.5 FM.
FM RADIO STATION

WPRV-AM 38267
Owner: Cumulus Media Inc.
Editorial: 1502 Wampanoag Trl, Riverside, Rhode Island 02915-1018 **Tel:** 1 401 433-4200.
Web site: http://www.790business.com
Profile: WPRV-AM is a commercial station owned by Cumulus Media Inc. The format of the station is business talk. WPRV-AM broadcasts to the Riverside RI area at 790 AM.
AM RADIO STATION

WPRW-FM 42228
Owner: iHeartMedia Inc.
Editorial: 2743 Perimeter Pkwy Ste 300, Augusta, Georgia 30909-6429 **Tel:** 1 706 396-6000.
Web site: http://www.power107.net
Profile: WPRW-FM is a commercial station owned by iHeartMedia Inc. The format of the station is urban contemporary. WPRW-FM broadcasts to the Augusta, GA area at 107.7 FM.
FM RADIO STATION

WPRX-AM 35208
Owner: Nievezquez Productions
Editorial: 1253 Berlin Tpke Fl 2, Berlin, Connecticut 06037-3228 **Tel:** 1 860 348-0667.
Email: contact@orielmusic.com
Web site: http://www.wprx1120.net
Profile: WPRX-AM is a commercial station owned by Nievezquez Productions. The format of the station is Hispanic and tropical music. WPRX-AM broadcasts to the New Britain, CT area at 1120 AM.
AM RADIO STATION

WPRY-AM 38988
Owner: Dockins Broadcast Group
Editorial: 872 E Highway 27, Perry, Florida 32347 **Tel:** 1 850 223-1400.
Profile: WPRY-AM is a commercial station owned by Dockins Broadcast Group. The format of the station is oldies. WPRY-AM airs in the Perry, FL area at 1400 AM.
AM RADIO STATION

WPRZ-FM 47630
Owner: Praise Communications, Inc.
Editorial: 219 E Davis St Ste 220, Culpeper, Virginia 22701-3005 **Tel:** 1 540 727-9779.
Email: info@wprz.org
Web site: http://www.wprz.org
Profile: WPRZ-FM is a non-commercial station owned by Praise Communications, Inc. The format of the station is contemporary christian. WPRZ-FM broadcasts to the Washington, DC area at 88.1 FM.
FM RADIO STATION

WPSF-FM 558748
Owner: Call Communications Group, Inc.
Editorial: 8900 SW 168th St, Bldg 4000, Village of Palmetto Bay, Florida 33157-4569 **Tel:** 1 305 662-7736.
Email: md@callfm.com
Web site: http://www.callfm.com
Profile: WPSF-FM is a commercial station owned by Call Communications Group, Inc. The format of the station is contemporary Christian and rock. WPSF-FM broadcasts to the Clewiston, FL area at 91.5 FM.
FM RADIO STATION

WPSK-FM 41323
Owner: Cumulus Media Inc.
Editorial: 7080 Lee Hwy, Fairlawn, Virginia 24141-8416 **Tel:** 1 540 731-6000.
Web site: http://www.nashfm1071.com
Profile: WPSK-FM is a commercial station owned by Cumulus Media Inc. The format of the station is classic and contemporary country music. WPSK-FM broadcasts to the Lynchburg, VA area at 107.1 FM.
FM RADIO STATION

WPSL-AM 35826
Owner: Port St. Lucie Broadcasters
Editorial: 4100 Metzger Rd, Fort Pierce, Florida 34947-1712 **Tel:** 1 772 340-1590.
Email: news@wpsl.com
Web site: http://www.wpsl.com
Profile: WPSL-AM is a commercial station owned by Port St. Lucie Broadcasters. The format of the station is news, sports and talk. WPSL-AM broadcasts to the Port Saint Lucie, FL area at 1590 AM.
AM RADIO STATION

WPSN-AM 37760
Owner: Bold Gold Media Group
Editorial: 575 Grove St, Honesdale, Pennsylvania 18431 **Tel:** 1 570 253-1616.
Web site: http://www.waynepikenews.com
Profile: WPSN-AM is a commercial station owned by Bold Gold Media Group. The format of the station is news talk. WPSN-AM broadcasts to the Honesdale, PA area at 1590 AM.
AM RADIO STATION

WPSO-AM 35604
Owner: ASA Broadcasting Network
Editorial: 109 S Bayview Blvd Ste A, Oldsmar, Florida 34677-3124 **Tel:** 1 813 814-7575.
Email: wzra48@yahoo.com
Web site: http://www.wpso.com
Profile: WPSO-AM is a commercial station owned by ASA Broadcasting Network. The format of the station is variety. WPSO-AM broadcasts to the Oldsmar, FL area at 1500 AM.
AM RADIO STATION

WPSP-AM 36055
Owner: Q Broadcasting
Editorial: 5730 Corporate Way Ste 210, West Palm Beach, Florida 33407-2032 **Tel:** 1 561 9350.
Email: deportes1190@gmail.com
Web site: http://www.wpspradio.com
Profile: WPSP-AM is a commercial radio station owned by Q Broadcasting. The format of the station is Hispanic adult contemporary. WPSP-AM broadcasts to the West Palm Beach, FL area at 1190 AM.
AM RADIO STATION

WPST-FM 45454
Owner: Connoisseur Media
Editorial: 619 Alexander Rd, Princeton, New Jersey 08540-6000 **Tel:** 1 609 419-0300.
Web site: http://www.wpst.com
Profile: WPST-FM is a commercial station owned by Connoisseur Media. The format of the station is Top 40/CHR. WPST-FM broadcasts to the Princeton, NJ area at 94.5 FM.
FM RADIO STATION

WPTB-AM 35605
Owner: Radio Statesboro, Inc.
Editorial: 561 E Olliff St, Statesboro, Georgia 30458-4663 **Tel:** 1 912 764-5446.
Web site: http://statesboro365.com
Profile: WPTB-AM is a commercial station owned by Radio Statesboro, Inc. The format of the station is sports. WPTB-AM broadcasts to the Atlanta area at 850 AM.
AM RADIO STATION

WPTC-FM 44209
Owner: Lycoming Broadcast Foundation
Editorial: 1 College Ave, Williamsport, Pennsylvania 17701-5778 **Tel:** 1 570 320-2400 7548.
Email: wptc@pct.edu
Web site: http://www.pct.edu/wptc
Profile: WPTC-FM is a non-commercial college station owned by Lycoming Broadcast Foundation. The format of the station is modern rock (weekdays) and jazz (weekends). WPTC-FM broadcasts to the Pennsylvania College of Technology community and surrounding areas at a frequency of 88.1 FM.
FM RADIO STATION

WPTE-FM 43521
Owner: Entercom Communications Corp.
Editorial: 236 Clearfield Ave Ste 206, Virginia Beach, Virginia 23462-1893 **Tel:** 1 757 497-2000.
Web site: http://www.pointradio.com
Profile: WPTE-FM is a commercial station owned by Entercom Communications Corp. The format of the station is hot adult contemporary. WPTE-FM broadcasts to the Norfolk, VA area at 94.9 FM.
FM RADIO STATION

WPTF-AM 39066
Owner: Curtis Media Group
Editorial: 3012 Highwoods Blvd Ste 201, Raleigh, North Carolina 27604-1031 **Tel:** 1 919 790-9392.
Email: wptfnews@curtismedia.com
Web site: http://www.wptf.com
Profile: WPTF-AM is a commercial station owned by the Curtis Media Group. The format of the station is news and talk. WPTF-AM broadcasts to the Raleigh-Durham, NC area at 680 AM.
AM RADIO STATION

WPTH-FM 43973
Owner: VCY America, Inc.
Editorial: 3434 W Kilbourn Ave, Milwaukee, Wisconsin 53208-3313 **Tel:** 1 414 935-3000.
Email: wpth@vcyamerica.org
Web site: http://vcyamerica.org
Profile: WPTH-FM is a non-commercial station owned by VCY America, Inc. The format of the station is religious. WPTH-FM broadcasts to the Olney, IL area at 88.1 FM.
FM RADIO STATION

WPTI-FM 42003
Owner: iHeartMedia Inc.
Editorial: 2B Pai Park Fl 2, Greensboro, North Carolina 27409-9428 **Tel:** 1 336 822-2000.
Web site: http://www.945wpti.com/main.html
Profile: WPTI-FM is a commercial station owned by iHeartMedia Inc. The format of the station is news and talk. WPTI-FM broadcasts to the Greensboro, NC area at 94.5 FM.
FM RADIO STATION

WPTJ-FM 546502
Owner: Lay Witness Outreach, Inc.
Editorial: 1811 Millersburg Cynthiana Rd, Paris, Kentucky 40361-9354 **Tel:** 1 859 484-9691.
Web site: http://www.wptj907.com
Profile: WPTJ-FM is a non-commercial station owned by Lay Witness Outreach, Inc. The format of the station is contemporary Christian music. WPTJ-FM broadcasts to the Paris, KY area at 90.7 FM.
FM RADIO STATION

WPTK-AM 36553
Owner: Curtis Media Group
Editorial: 4601 Six Forks Rd Ste 520, Raleigh, North Carolina 27609-5210 **Tel:** 1 919 875-9100.
Web site: http://www.wptf.com
Profile: WPTK-AM is a commercial station owned by Curtis Media Group. The format of the station is news/talk. WPTK-AM broadcasts to the Raleigh-Durham, NC area at 850 AM.
AM RADIO STATION

WPTL-AM 35606
Owner: Skycountry Broadcasting Inc.
Editorial: 133 Pisgah Dr, Canton, North Carolina 28716 **Tel:** 1 828 648-3576.
Email: admin@wptlradio.net
Web site: http://wptlradio.net
Profile: WPTL-AM is a commercial station owned by Skycountry Broadcasting Inc. The format for the station is classic country. WPTL-AM broadcasts to the Canton, NC area at 920 AM.
AM RADIO STATION

WPTM-FM 45455
Owner: First Media Radio LLC
Editorial: 3 E 1st St, Weldon, North Carolina 27890-1560 **Tel:** 1 252 536-3115.
Web site: http://www.1023wptm.com
Profile: WPTM-FM is a commercial station owned by First Media Radio LLC. The format of the station is classic country. WPTM-FM broadcasts to the Roanoke Rapids, NC area at 102.3 FM.
FM RADIO STATION

WPTN-AM 37885
Owner: Cookeville Communications, LLC
Editorial: 698 S Willow Ave, Cookeville, Tennessee 38501-3802 **Tel:** 1 931 526-7144.
Web site: http://www.foxsportsradio1061theeagle.com/
Profile: WPTN-AM is a commercial station owned by Cookeville Communications, LLC. The format of the station is sports. WPTN-AM broadcasts to the Cookeville, TN area at 780 AM.
AM RADIO STATION

WPTQ-FM 46779
Owner: Commonwealth Broadcasting Corp.
Editorial: 113 W Public Sq Ste 400, Glasgow, Kentucky 42141-2438 **Tel:** 1 270 651-6050.
Web site: http://www.1053thepoint.com/
Profile: WPTQ-FM is a commercial station owned by Commonwealth Broadcasting Corp. The format of the station is mainstream rock. WPTQ-FM broadcasts to the Glasgow, KY area on 105.3 FM.
FM RADIO STATION

WPTR-AM 36301
Owner: Empire Broadcasting Corporation
Editorial: 100 Saratoga Village Blvd Ste 21, Malta, New York 12020-3703 **Tel:** 1 518 899-3000.
Web site: http://www.sporty1240.com
Profile: WPTR-AM is a commercial station owned by Empire Broadcasting Corporation. The format of the station is sports. WPTR-AM broadcasts to the Albany, NY area at 1240 AM.
AM RADIO STATION

WPTW-AM 36987
Owner: Muzzy Broadcasting Group
Editorial: 1625 Covington Ave, Piqua, Ohio 45356-2802 **Tel:** 1 937 773-3513.
Web site: http://www.981wptw.com
Profile: WPTW-AM is a commercial station owned by Muzzy Broadcasting Group. The format of the station is classic hits. WPTW-AM broadcasts to the Piqua, OH area at 1570 AM.
AM RADIO STATION

WPTX-AM 39478
Owner: Somar Communications Inc.
Editorial: 28095 Three Notch Rd, Ste 2B, Mechanicsville, Maryland 20659 **Tel:** 1 301 870-5550.
Email: wptxam@aol.com
Profile: WPTX-AM is a commercial station owned by Somar Communications Inc. The format of the station is news, talk and sports. WPTX-AM broadcasts to the Mechanicsville, MD area at 1690 AM.
AM RADIO STATION

WPTY-FM 43737
Owner: JVC Broadcasting Inc.
Editorial: 3075 Veterans Memorial Hwy Ste 201, Ronkonkoma, New York 11779-7600 **Tel:** 1 631 648-2500.
Web site: http://www.party105.com/
Profile: WPTY-FM is a commercial station owned by JVC Broadcasting Inc. The format of the station is Top 40/CHR. WPTY-FM broadcasts to the Long Island, NY area at 105.3 FM.
FM RADIO STATION

WPUB-FM 46196
Owner: Kershaw Radio Corp.
Editorial: 5 The Commons, Lugoff, South Carolina 29078-8949 **Tel:** 1 803 438-9002.
Email: wpubradio@bellsouth.net
Web site: http://www.kool1027.com
Profile: WPUB-FM is a commercial station owned by the Kershaw Radio Corp. The format of the station is oldies. WPUB-FM broadcasts to the Lugoff, SC area at 102.7 FM.
FM RADIO STATION

WPUL-AM 35789
Owner: PSI Communications Inc
Editorial: 427 S Dr Martin Luther King Jr Blvd, Daytona Beach, Florida 32114-4856 **Tel:** 1 386 492-2908.
Web site: http://www.wpul1590.com
Profile: WPUL-AM is a commercial station owned by PSI Communications Inc. The format of the station is news and talk. WPUL-AM broadcasts to the Daytona Beach, FL area on 1590 AM.
AM RADIO STATION

WPUP-FM 45746
Owner: Cox Media Group, Inc.
Editorial: 1010 Tower Pl, Watkinsville, Georgia 30677-7752 **Tel:** 1 706 549-6222.
Web site: http://www.powerathens.com
Profile: WPUP-FM is a commercial station owned by Cox Media Group, Inc. The format of the station is Top 40/CHR. WPUP-FM broadcasts to the Athens, GA area at 100.1 FM.
FM RADIO STATION

WPUR-FM 43803
Owner: Townsquare Media, LLC
Editorial: 950 Tilton Rd, Ste 200, Northfield, New Jersey 8225 **Tel:** 1 609 645-9797.
Web site: http://www.catcountry1073.com
Profile: WPUR-FM is a commercial station owned by the Townsquare Media, LLC. The format for the station is country music. WPUR-FM broadcasts to the Northfield, NJ area at 107.3 FM.
FM RADIO STATION

WPUT-AM 39102
Owner: Townsquare Media, LLC
Editorial: 1004 Federal Rd, Brookfield, Connecticut 06804-1123 **Tel:** 1 203 775-1212.
Profile: WPUT-AM is a commercial station owned by Townsquare Media, LLC. The format of the station is jazz and adult standards. WPUT-AM broadcasts to the Brewster, NY area at 1510 AM.
AM RADIO STATION

WPVA-FM 81607
Owner: Positive Alternative Radio
Editorial: 22226 Timberlake Rd, Lynchburg, Virginia 24502 **Tel:** 1 434 237-9798.
Email: office@spiritfm.com
Web site: http://www.spiritfm.com
Profile: WPVA-FM is a non-commercial station owned by Positive Alternative Radio The format for the station is contemporary Christian. WPVA-FM broadcasts to the Roanoke-Lynchburg, VA area at 90.1 FM.
FM RADIO STATION

WPVL-AM 38629
Owner: Queen B Radio of Wisconsin
Editorial: 51 Means Dr, Platteville, Wisconsin 53818-3829 **Tel:** 1 608 349-2000.
Email: wpvl@queenbradio.com
Web site: http://wpvl.com
Profile: WPVL-AM is a commercial station owned by Queen B Radio of Wisconsin. The format of the station is sports. WPVL-AM broadcasts to the Platteville, WI area at 1590 AM.
AM RADIO STATION

WPVL-FM 45985
Owner: Queen B Radio of Wisconsin
Editorial: 51 Means Dr, Platteville, Wisconsin 53818 **Tel:** 1 608 349-2000.
Email: wpvl@queenbradio.com
Web site: http://www.wpvl.com
Profile: WPVL-FM is a commercial station owned by Queen B Radio of Wisconsin. The format for the station is top 40/CHR. WPVL-FM broadcasts to the Platteville, WI area at 107.1 FM.
FM RADIO STATION

WPVM-FM 155984
Owner: Mountain Area Information Network
Editorial: 34 Wall St Ste 407, Asheville, North Carolina 28801-2705 **Tel:** 1 828 258-0085.
Email: wpvm.103.7@gmail.com
Web site: http://wpvmfm.org
Profile: WPVM-FM is a non-commercial station owned by Mountain Area Information Network. The format of the station is variety. WPVM-FM broadcasts to the Asheville, NC, area at 103.5 FM.
FM RADIO STATION

WPVQ-FM 42393
Owner: Saga Communications
Editorial: 81 Woodard Rd, Greenfield, Massachusetts 1301 **Tel:** 1 413 774-4301.
Web site: http://www.bear953.com
Profile: WPVQ-FM is a commercial station owned by Saga Communications. The format of the station is classic country. WPVQ-FM broadcasts in the Northampton, MA area at 95.3 FM.
FM RADIO STATION

WPWA-AM 36306
Owner: Mount Ocean Media LLC
Editorial: 12 Kent Rd, Aston, Pennsylvania 19014 **Tel:** 1 610 358-1400.
Email: poder1590@wpwa.net
Web site: http://www.wpwa.net
Profile: WPWA-AM is a commercial station owned by Mount Ocean Media LLC. The format of the station is Hispanic religious. WPWA-AM broadcasts to the Aston, PA area at 1590 AM.
AM RADIO STATION

WPWC-AM 35607
Owner: JMK Communications Inc.
Editorial: 1918 Martin Luther King Jr Ave SE, Washington, District Of Columbia 20020-7006 **Tel:** 1 202 413-6160.
Web site: http://www.weactradio.com
Profile: WPWC-AM is a commercial station owned by JMK Communications Inc. The format of the station is progressive talk. WPWC-AM broadcasts to the Woodbridge, VA area at 1480 AM. The station accepts PSA's from members and supporters only.
AM RADIO STATION

WPWQ-FM 42904
Owner: Prairie Communications LLP
Editorial: 1645 Highway 104, Ste G, Quincy, Illinois 62305 **Tel:** 1 217 885-3222.
Email: wpwq106@adams.net
Web site: http://www.oldiessuperstation.com
FM RADIO STATION

WPWX-FM 44326
Owner: Crawford Broadcasting Co.
Editorial: 6336 Calumet Ave, Hammond, Indiana 46324-1243 **Tel:** 1 219 933-4455.
Email: power92feedback@crawfordbroadcasting.com
Web site: http://www.power92chicago.com
Profile: WPWX-FM is a commercial station owned by Crawford Broadcasting Co. The format of the station is urban contemporary music. WPWX-FM broadcasts to the Chicago area at 92.3 FM.
FM RADIO STATION

WPWZ-FM 43497
Owner: First Media Radio LLC
Editorial: 12714 E NC 97, Rocky Mount, North Carolina 27803 **Tel:** 1 252 442-8092.
Email: wecare@firstmedianc.com
Web site: http://www.powerhits95.com
Profile: WPWZ-FM is a commercial station owned by First Media Radio LLC. The format of the station is urban contemporary. WPWZ-FM broadcasts to the Rocky Mount, NC area at 95.5 FM.
FM RADIO STATION

WPXC-FM 41416
Owner: Codcomm Inc.
Editorial: 243 South St, Hyannis, Massachusetts 02601-3926 **Tel:** 1 508 778-6000.
Web site: http://www.pixy103.com
Profile: WPXC-FM is a commercial station owned by Codcomm Inc.. The format of the station is rock/album-oriented rock. WPXC-FM broadcasts to the West Yarmouth, MA area at 102.9 FM.
FM RADIO STATION

WPXN-FM 40626
Owner: Paxton Broadcasting Corp.
Editorial: 361 N Railroad Ave, Paxton, Illinois 60957-1142 **Tel:** 1 217 379-9796.
Email: news@wpxnradio.com
Web site: http://www.wpxnradio.com
Profile: WPXN-FM is a commercial station owned by the Paxton Broadcasting Corp. The format of the station is classic hits. WPXN-FM broadcasts to the Paxton, IL area at 104.9 FM.
FM RADIO STATION

United States of America

WPXY-FM 42324
Owner: Entercom Communications Corp.
Editorial: 70 Commercial St, Rochester, New York 14614-1010 **Tel:** 1 585 423-2900.
Web site: http://www.98pxy.com
Profile: WPXY-FM is a commercial station owned by Entercom Communications Corp. The format of the station is Top 40/CHR. WPXY-FM broadcasts to the Rochester, NY area at 97.9 FM.
FM RADIO STATION

WPXZ-FM 45457
Owner: Renda Broadcasting
Editorial: 904 N Main St, Punxsutawney, Pennsylvania 15767 **Tel:** 1 814 938-6000.
Email: rendaprod1@comcast.net
Web site: http://www.wpxz1041fm.com
Profile: WPXZ-FM is a commercial station owned by Renda Broadcasting. The format of the station is adult contemporary. WPXZ-FM broadcasts to the Punxsutawney, PA area at 104.1 FM.
FM RADIO STATION

WPYA-FM 861247
Owner: Summit Media Broadcasting, LLC
Editorial: 2700 Corporate Dr Ste 115, Birmingham, Alabama 35242-2735 **Tel:** 1 205 322-2987.
Web site: http://www.play973.com/
Profile: WPYA-FM is a commercial station owned by Summit Media Broadcasting LLC. The format of the station is Hot AC. WPYA-FM broadcasts to the Birmingham, AL area at 97.3 FM.
FM RADIO STATION

WPYB-AM 35608
Owner: Benson-Dunn Broadcasting Inc.
Editorial: 2234 Hodges Chapel Road, Benson, North Carolina 27504 **Tel:** 1 919 894-1130.
Web site: http://www.wpyb1130am.com
Profile: WPYB-AM is a commercial station owned by Benson-Dunn Broadcasting Inc. The format of the station is gospel, classic and contemporary country music. WPYB-AM broadcasts to the Benson, NC area at 1130 AM.
AM RADIO STATION

WPYO-FM 43664
Owner: Cox Media Group, Inc.
Editorial: 4192 N John Young Pkwy, Orlando, Florida 32804-2620 **Tel:** 1 407 299-9595.
Web site: http://www.power953.com
Profile: WPYO-FM is a commercial station owned by Cox Media Group, Inc. The format of the station is urban contemporary. WPYO-FM broadcasts to the Orlando, FL area at 95.3 FM.
FM RADIO STATION

WPYR-AM 38294
Owner: Catholic Community Radio, Inc.
Editorial: 8230 Summa Ave Ste A, Baton Rouge, Louisiana 70809-3421 **Tel:** 1 225 448-3754.
Email: info@catholiccommunityradio.org
Web site: http://www.catholiccommunityradio.org
Profile: WPYR-AM is a commercial station owned by Catholic Community Radio, Inc. The format of the station is religious Catholic programming. WPYR-AM broadcasts to the Baton Rouge, LA area at 1380 AM.
AM RADIO STATION

WPYX-FM 43501
Owner: iHeartMedia Inc.
Editorial: 1203 Troy Schenectady Rd, Latham, New York 12110-1046 **Tel:** 1 518 452-4800.
Email: feedback@pyx106.com
Web site: http://www.pyx106.com
Profile: WPYX-FM is a commercial station owned by iHeartMedia Inc. The format of the station is classic rock. WPYX-FM broadcasts to the Albany, NY area at 106.5 FM.
FM RADIO STATION

WPZE-FM 81092
Owner: Urban One, Inc.
Editorial: 101 Marietta St NW, Atlanta, Georgia 30303-2720 **Tel:** 1 404 765-9750.
Web site: http://mypraiseatl.hellobeautiful.com
Profile: WPZE-FM is a commercial station owned by Urban One, Inc. The format of the station is gospel music. WPZE-FM broadcasts to the Atlanta area at 102.5 FM.
FM RADIO STATION

WPZR-FM 42831
Owner: Urban One, Inc.
Editorial: 3250 Franklin St, Detroit, Michigan 48207-4219 **Tel:** 1 313 259-2000.
Web site: http://praise1027detroit.hellobeautiful.com/
Profile: WPZR-FM is a commercial station owned by Urban One, Inc. The format of the station is black gospel. WPZR-FM broadcasts to the Detroit area at 102.7 FM.
FM RADIO STATION

WPZS-FM 43665
Owner: Urban One, Inc.
Editorial: 8809 Lenox Pointe Dr Unit A, Charlotte, North Carolina 28273-3377 **Tel:** 1 704 548-7800.
Web site: http://www.praise1009fm.com
Profile: WPZS-FM is a commercial station owned by Urban One, Inc. The format of the station is gospel. WPZS-FM broadcasts to the Charlotte, NC area at 100.9 FM.
FM RADIO STATION

WPZZ-FM 42799
Owner: Urban One, Inc.
Editorial: 2809 Emerywood Pkwy Ste 300, Richmond, Virginia 23294-3743 **Tel:** 1 804 672-9299.
Web site: http://www.praise1047.com
Profile: WPZZ-FM is a commercial station owned by Urban One, Inc. The format of the station is gospel. WPZZ-FM broadcasts to the Richmond, VA area at 104.7 FM.
FM RADIO STATION

WQAH-FM 445514
Owner: Abercrombie Broadcasting, Inc.
Editorial: 219 Chestnut St, Hartselle, Alabama 35640 **Tel:** 1 256 773-4114.
Email: info@WQAH.com
Web site: http://www.wqah.com
Profile: WQAH-FM is a commercial station owned by Abercrombie Broadcasting, Inc. The format of the station is country. WQAH-FM broadcasts to the Hartselle, AL area at 105.7 FM.
FM RADIO STATION

WQAK-FM 42448
Owner: Thunderbolt Broadcasting Co.
Editorial: 223 Westgate Dr, Union City, Tennessee 38261-3058 **Tel:** 1 731 885-0051.
Email: newsroom@unioncityradio.com
Profile: WQAK-FM is a commercial station owned by Thunderbolt Broadcasting Co. The format of the station is alternative. WQAK-FM broadcasts to the Union City, TN at 105.7 FM.
FM RADIO STATION

WQAL-FM 40628
Owner: CBS Radio
Editorial: 1041 Huron Rd E, Cleveland, Ohio 44115-1706 **Tel:** 1 216 861-0100.
Web site: http://q104.radio.com
Profile: WQAL-FM is a commercial station owned by CBS Radio. The format of the station is hot adult contemporary. WQAL-FM broadcasts to the Cleveland area at 104.1 FM.
FM RADIO STATION

WQAM-AM 38138
Owner: CBS Radio
Editorial: 194 NW 187th St, Miami, Florida 33169-4050 **Tel:** 1 305 654-1700.
Web site: http://miami.cbslocal.com/category/sports
Profile: WQAM-AM is a commercial station owned by CBS Radio. The format of the station is sports. WQAM-AM broadcasts to the Miami area at 560 AM.
AM RADIO STATION

WQBA-AM 38139
Owner: Univision Communications Inc.
Editorial: 800 S Douglas Rd Ste 111, Coral Gables, Florida 33134-3187 **Tel:** 1 305 894-4500.
Web site: http://www.univision.com/miami/wqba-am
Profile: WQBA-AM is a commercial station owned by Univision Communications Inc. The format of the station is Spanish news and talk. WQBA-AM broadcasts to the Miami, FL area at 1140 AM.
AM RADIO STATION

WQBB-FM 43198
Owner: Alpha Media
Editorial: 1909 E Pass Rd, Gulfport, Mississippi 39507-3779 **Tel:** 1 228 388-2001.
Web site: http://www.bob1059.com
Profile: WQBB-FM is a commercial station owned by Alpha Media. The format of the station is adult hits. WHGO-FM broadcasts to the Biloxi-Gulfport, MS area at 105.9 FM.
FM RADIO STATION

WQBE-FM 45459
Owner: Bristol Broadcasting
Editorial: 817 Suncrest Pl, Charleston, West Virginia 25303-2302 **Tel:** 1 304 342-3136.
Email: news@wqbe.com
Web site: http://www.wqbe.com
Profile: WQBE-FM is a commercial station owned by Bristol Broadcasting. The format of the station is contemporary country music. WQBE-FM broadcasts to Charleston, WV and surrounding communities at 97.5 FM.
FM RADIO STATION

WQBJ-FM 42316
Owner: Townsquare Media, LLC
Editorial: 1241 Kings Rd, Schenectady, New York 12303-2811 **Tel:** 1 518 476-1039.
Web site: http://www.q103albany.com
Profile: WQBJ-FM is a commercial station owned by Townsquare Media, LLC. The format of the station is rock music. WQBJ-FM broadcasts to the Albany, NY area 103.5 FM.
FM RADIO STATION

WQBK-FM 45460
Owner: Townsquare Media, LLC
Editorial: 1241 Kings Rd, Schenectady, New York 12303-2811 **Tel:** 1 518 476-1077.
Web site: http://www.q103albany.com
Profile: WQBK-FM is a commercial station owned by Townsquare Media, LLC. The format of the station is rock music. WQBK-FM broadcasts to the Schenectady, NY area at 103.9 FM.
FM RADIO STATION

WQBN-AM 35612
Owner: Radio Tropical, Inc.
Editorial: 5207 E Washington St, Tampa, Florida 33619-3437 **Tel:** 1 813 272-1300.
Email: wqbnradio@gmail.com

Web site: http://www.q1300.com
Profile: WQBN-AM is a commercial station owned by Radio Tropical, Inc. The format of the station is Hispanic. WQBN-AM broadcasts to the Tampa, FL area at 1300 AM.
AM RADIO STATION

WQBQ-AM 35613
Owner: Rama Communications Inc.
Editorial: 1920 County Road 25A, Leesburg, Florida 34748-8266 **Tel:** 1 352 315-1420.
Web site: http://www.1410wqbq.com/
Profile: WQBQ-AM is a commercial station owned by Rama Communications Inc. and under LMA with All-N-One Media Group. The format of the station is black gospel/urban inspirational. WQBQ-AM broadcasts to the Leesburg, FL area at 1410 AM.
AM RADIO STATION

WQBR-FM 42179
Owner: Maximum Impact Comm. Inc.
Editorial: 330 McElhattan Drive, McElhattan, Pennsylvania 17748 **Tel:** 1 570 769-2327.
Email: bear@cub.kcnet.org
Web site: http://www.bear999.com
Profile: WQBR-FM is a commercial station owned by Maximum Impact Comm. Inc. format of the station is contemporary country. WQBR-FM broadcasts to the Avis, PA area at 99.9 FM.
FM RADIO STATION

WQBT-FM 45079
Owner: iHeartMedia Inc.
Editorial: 245 Alfred St, Savannah, Georgia 31408-3205 **Tel:** 1 912 964-7794.
Email: info@941thebeat.com
Web site: http://www.941thebeat.com
Profile: WQBT-FM is a commercial station owned by iHeartMedia Inc. The format for the station is urban contemporary. WQBT-FM broadcasts to the Savannah, GA area at 94.1 FM.
FM RADIO STATION

WQBU-FM 40228
Owner: Univision Communications Inc.
Editorial: 485 Madison Ave Fl 3, New York, New York 10022-5869 **Tel:** 1 212 310-6000.
Web site: http://www.univision.com/nueva-york/wqbu
Profile: WQBU-FM is a commercial station owned by Univision Communications Inc. The format of the station is Spanish news/talk. WQBU-FM broadcasts to the New York area at 92.7 FM.
FM RADIO STATION

WQBX-FM 45176
Owner: Jacom Inc.
Editorial: 5310 N State Rd, Alma, Michigan 48801 **Tel:** 1 989 463-3175.
Email: wqbxfm@gmail.com
Profile: WQBX-FM is a commercial station owned by Jacom Inc. The format of the station is hot adult contemporary music. WQBX-FM broadcasts to the Alma, MI area at 104.9 FM.
FM RADIO STATION

WQBZ-FM 40629
Owner: iHeartMedia Inc.
Editorial: 7080 Industrial Hwy, Macon, Georgia 31216-7538 **Tel:** 1 478 781-1063.
Web site: http://www.q106.fm
Profile: WQBZ-FM is a commercial station owned by iHeartMedia Inc. The format of the station is rock music. WQBZ-FM broadcasts to the Macon, GA area at 106.3 FM.
FM RADIO STATION

WQCB-FM 40630
Owner: Townsquare Media, Inc.
Editorial: 49 Acme Rd, Brewer, Maine 04412-1545 **Tel:** 1 207 989-5631.
Email: cumulusnews@midmaine.com
Web site: http://www.wqcb-fm.com
Profile: WQCB-FM is a commercial station owned by Townsquare Media, Inc. The format of the station is contemporary country. WQCB-FM broadcasts to the Brewer, ME area at 106.5 FM.
FM RADIO STATION

WQCC-FM 42477
Owner: Mississippi Valley Broadcasters LLC
Editorial: 1407 2nd Ave N, Onalaska, Wisconsin 54650-9166 **Tel:** 1 608 782-8335.
Email: news@lacrosseradiogroup.net
Web site: http://www.kicks1063.com/
Profile: WQCC-FM is a commercial station owned by Mississippi Valley Broadcasters LLC. The format of the station is contemporary country. WQCC-FM broadcasts to the Onalaska, WI area at 106.3 FM.
FM RADIO STATION

WQCH-AM 35476
Owner: Radix Broadcasting Inc.
Editorial: 130 Rodeo Dr, La Fayette, Georgia 30728-9201 **Tel:** 1 706 638-3276.
Web site: http://www.wqch.net
Profile: WQCH-AM is a commercial station owned by Radix Broadcasting Inc. The format of the station is contemporary and classic country. WQCH-AM broadcasts to the Chattanooga, TN area at 1590 AM.
AM RADIO STATION

WQCK-FM 46114
Owner: Magnum Broadcasting Inc.
Editorial: 315 S Atherton St, State College, Pennsylvania 16801-4045 **Tel:** 1 814 272-1320.
Web site: http://www.1059qwikrock.com

Profile: WQCK-FM is a commercial station owned by Magnum Broadcasting Inc. The format of the station is rock and classic rock. WQCK-FM broadcasts to the Philipsburg, PA, area at 105.9 FM.
FM RADIO STATION

WQCM-FM 45461
Owner: Alpha Media
Editorial: 25 Penncraft Ave, Chambersburg, Pennsylvania 17201-5600 **Tel:** 1 717 263-0813.
Web site: http://www.wqcmfm.com
Profile: WQCM-FM is a commercial station owned by Alpha Media. The format of the station is classic rock. WQCM-FM broadcasts to the Hagerstown, MD area at 94.3 FM.
FM RADIO STATION

WQCR-AM 35936
Owner: Rivera Communications
Editorial: 100 Yeager Pkwy, Pelham, Alabama 35124-1859 **Tel:** 1 205 358-1100.
Profile: WQCR-AM is commercial station owned by Rivera Communications. The format of the station is regional Mexican and tropical music. The station airs locally on 1500 AM. Newscasts air at the top of the hour.
AM RADIO STATION

WQCS-FM 41498
Owner: Indian River Community College
Editorial: 3209 Virginia Ave, Fort Pierce, Florida 34981-5541 **Tel:** 1 772 465-8989.
Web site: http://www.wqcs.org
Profile: WQCS-FM is a non-commercial station owned by Indian River State College. The format of the station is news, public affairs, and classical music. WQCS-FM broadcasts to the Melbourne, FL area at 88.9 FM.
FM RADIO STATION

WQCT-AM 39341
Owner: Impact Radio, LLC
Editorial: 12810 State Route 34, Bryan, Ohio 43506-8809 **Tel:** 1 419 636-3175.
Email: wbno@wbnowqct.com
Web site: http://www.wbnowqct.com
Profile: WQCT-AM is a commercial station owned by Impact Radio, LLC. The format of the station is oldies. WQCT-AM broadcasts to the Bryan, OH area at 1520 AM.
AM RADIO STATION

WQCY-FM 42905
Owner: Staradio Corp.
Editorial: 329 Maine St, Quincy, Illinois 62301 **Tel:** 1 217 224-4102.
Web site: http://www.1039thefox.com
Profile: WQCY-FM is a commercial station owned by Staradio Corp. The format of the station is classic rock. WQCY-FM broadcasts to the Quincy, IL area at 103.9 FM.
FM RADIO STATION

WQDC-FM 42646
Owner: Door County Radio Group
Editorial: 10331 Water St., Ephraim, Wisconsin 54211 **Tel:** 1 920 743-6677.
Web site: http://doorcountryfm977.com
Profile: WQDC-FM is a commercial station owned by Door County Radio Group. The format of the station is classic hits. WQDC-FM broadcasts to the Sturgeon Bay, WI area at 97.7 FM.
FM RADIO STATION

WQDK-FM 46560
Owner: Max Media
Editorial: 443 Hwy 42 W, Ahoskie, North Carolina 27910-9712 **Tel:** 1 252 332-7993.
Email: wqdk@yahoo.com
Web site: http://www.993thebullfm.com
Profile: WQDK-FM is a commercial station owned by Max Media. The format of the station is country. WQDK-FM broadcasts to the Ahoskie, NC area at 99.3 FM.
FM RADIO STATION

WQDR-FM 46398
Owner: Curtis Media Group
Editorial: 3012 Highwoods Blvd, Raleigh, North Carolina 27604-1037 **Tel:** 1 919 790-9392.
Email: wptfnews@curtismedia.com
Web site: http://www.947qdr.com
Profile: WQDR-FM is a commercial station owned by Curtis Media Group. The format of the station is contemporary country music. WQDR-FM broadcasts to the Raleigh-Durham, NC area at 94.7 FM.
FM RADIO STATION

WQDY-FM 45463
Owner: WQDY Inc.
Editorial: 637 Main St, Calais, Maine 04619-1437 **Tel:** 1 207 454-7545.
Email: news@wqdy.fm
Web site: http://www.wqdy.fm
Profile: WQDY-FM is a commercial station owned by WQDY Inc. The format for the station is classic hits. WQDY-FM broadcasts to the Calais, ME area at 92.7 FM. Send all press submissions/materials to the station's main email.
FM RADIO STATION

WQED-FM 40632
Owner: WQED Multimedia
Editorial: 4802 5th Ave, Pittsburgh, Pennsylvania 15213 **Tel:** 1 412 622-1436.
Email: wqed@wqed.org
Web site: http://www.wqed.org/fm

Profile: WQED-FM is a non-commercial station owned by WQED Multimedia. The format is classical music and news. WQED-FM broadcasts to the Pittsburgh area at 89.3 FM.
FM RADIO STATION

WQEJ-FM 43623
Owner: WQED Multimedia
Editorial: 4802 5th Ave, Pittsburgh, Pennsylvania 15213 **Tel:** 1 412 622-1436.
Email: wqed@wqed.org
Web site: http://www.wqed.org/fm
Profile: WQEJ-FM is a non-commercial station owned by WQED Multimedia. The format is classical music. WQEJ-FM broadcasts to the Pittsburgh area at 89.7 FM.
FM RADIO STATION

WQEL-FM 46079
Owner: Franklin Communications, Inc.
Editorial: 403 E Rensselaer St, Bucyrus, Ohio 44820 **Tel:** 1 419 562-2222.
Web site: http://www.wqel.com
Profile: WQEL-FM is a commercial station owned by Franklin Communications, Inc. The format of the station is classic hits. WQEL-FM broadcasts to the Columbus, OH area at 92.7 FM.
FM RADIO STATION

WQEN-FM 44037
Owner: iHeartMedia Inc.
Editorial: 600 Beacon Pkwy W Ste 400, Birmingham, Alabama 35209-3118 **Tel:** 1 205 439-9600.
Web site: http://www.1037theq.com
Profile: WQEN-FM is a commercial station owned by iHeartMedia Inc. The format of the station is adult contemporary music. WQEN-FM broadcasts to the Birmingham, AL area at 103.7 FM.
FM RADIO STATION

WQEZ-FM 863097
Owner: Northern Star Broadcasting LLC
Editorial: 1356 Mackinaw Ave, Cheboygan, Michigan 49721-1003 **Tel:** 1 231 627-2341.
Web site: http://www.wqez.fm
Profile: WQEZ-FM is a commercial station owned by Northern Star Broadcasting LLC. The format of the station is soft adult contemporary. WJZJ-FM broadcasts to Traverse, MI area at 95.5 FM.
FM RADIO STATION

WQFS-FM 40636
Owner: Guilford College
Editorial: 17714 Founders Hall, Greensboro, North Carolina 27410-4126 **Tel:** 1 336 316-2352.
Email: wqfs@guilford.edu
Web site: http://www.guilford.edu/wqfs
Profile: WQFS-FM is a non-commercial station owned by Guilford College. The format of the station is college variety. WQFS-FM broadcasts to the Greensboro, NC area at 90.9 FM.
FM RADIO STATION

WQFX-AM 36168
Owner: Walking By Faith Ministries
Editorial: 336 Rodenberg Ave, Biloxi, Mississippi 39531-3444 **Tel:** 1 228 374-9739.
Email: wqfxradio@bellsouth.net
Web site: http://www.mypowergospel.com/
Profile: WQFX-AM is a commercial station owned by Walking By Faith Ministries. The format of the station is gospel. WQFX-AM broadcasts to the Biloxi, MS area at 1130 AM.
AM RADIO STATION

WQFX-FM 42386
Owner: Media One Group, LLC
Editorial: 2 Orchard Rd, Jamestown, New York 14701 **Tel:** 1 716 487-1151.
Email: news@radiojamestown.com
Web site: http://www.wqfx1031.com
FM RADIO STATION

WQGA-FM 42774
Owner: iHeartMedia Inc.
Editorial: 3833 US Highway 82, Brunswick, Georgia 31523-7735 **Tel:** 1 912 267-1025.
Web site: http://my103q.com
Profile: WQGA-FM is a commercial station owned by iHeartMedia Inc. The format of the station is Top 40/CHR. WQGA-FM broadcasts to the Brunswick, GA area at 103.3 FM.
FM RADIO STATION

WQGN-FM 45465
Owner: Cumulus Media Inc.
Editorial: 7 Governor Winthrop Blvd, New London, Connecticut 6320 **Tel:** 1 860 443-1980.
Web site: http://www.q105.fm
Profile: WQGN-FM is a commercial station owned by Cumulus Media Inc. The format of the station is Top 40/CHR. WQGN-FM broadcasts to the New London, CT area at 105.5 FM.
FM RADIO STATION

WQGR-FM 881624
Owner: Media One Group
Editorial: 9179 Mentor Ave, Mentor, Ohio 44060-6398 **Tel:** 1 440 974-5900.
Web site: http://www.cougar937.com/
Profile: WQGR-FM is a commercial station owned by Media One Group. The format of the station is Hot AC. The station broadcasts locally at 93.7 FM to Lake County, OH.
FM RADIO STATION

WQHH-FM 46130
Owner: MacDonald Broadcasting Co.
Editorial: 600 W Cavanaugh Rd, Lansing, Michigan 48910 **Tel:** 1 517 393-1320.
Web site: http://www.power965fm.com
Profile: WQHH-FM is a commercial station owned by MacDonald Broadcasting Co. The format of the station is urban contemporary. WQHH-FM broadcasts to the Lansing, MI area at 96.5 FM.
FM RADIO STATION

WQHK-FM 46540
Owner: Federated Media
Editorial: 2915 Maples Rd, Fort Wayne, Indiana 46816-3335 **Tel:** 1 260 447-5511.
Web site: http://www.k105fm.com
Profile: WQHK-FM is a commercial station owned by Federated Media. The format of the station is country music. WQHK-FM broadcasts to the Fort Wayne, IN area at 105.1 FM.
FM RADIO STATION

WQHL-AM 38081
Owner: Black Crow Broadcasting Inc.
Editorial: 1305 Helvenston St SE, Live Oak, Florida 32064 **Tel:** 1 386 362-1250.
Profile: WQHL-AM is a commercial station owned by Black Crow Broadcasting Inc. The format of the station is oldies music. WQHL-AM broadcasts in the Orlando, FL area at 1250 AM.
AM RADIO STATION

WQHL-FM 45466
Owner: Black Crow Broadcasting Inc.
Editorial: 1305 Helvenston St SE, Live Oak, Florida 32064 **Tel:** 1 386 362-1250.
Email: audio@wqhl981.com
Web site: http://www.wqhl981.com
Profile: WQHL-FM is a commercial station owned by Black Crow Broadcasting Inc. The format of the station is contemporary country music. WQHL-FM broadcasts to the Live Oak, FL area at 98.1 FM.
FM RADIO STATION

WQHQ-FM 46016
Owner: iHeartMedia Inc.
Editorial: 351 Tilghman Rd, Gateway Crossing, Salisbury, Maryland 21804-1920 **Tel:** 1 410 742-1923.
Email: delmarvapsa@iheartmedia.com
Web site: http://q105fm.iheart.com
Profile: WQHQ-FM is a commercial station owned by iHeartMedia Inc. The format of the station is adult contemporary music. WQHQ-FM broadcasts to the Salisbury, MD area at 104.7 FM.
FM RADIO STATION

WQHR-FM 42306
Owner: Townsquare Media, Inc.
Editorial: 551 Main St, Presque Isle, Maine 04769-2450 **Tel:** 1 207 769-6600.
Email: newspi@townsquaremedia.com
Web site: http://q961.com
Profile: WQHR-FM is a commercial station owned by Townsquare Media, Inc. The format for the station is hot adult contemporary. WQHR-FM broadcasts to the Presque Isle, ME area at 96.1 FM.
FM RADIO STATION

WQHT-FM 40637
Owner: Emmis Communications Corp.
Editorial: 395 Hudson St Fl 7, New York, New York 10014-7452 **Tel:** 1 212 229-9797.
Email: hot97@hot97.com
Web site: http://www.hot97.com
Profile: WQHT-FM is a commercial station owned by Emmis Communications Corp. The format of the station is urban contemporary. WQHT-FM broadcasts to the New York City metro area at 97.1 FM. ALL correspondence should be forwarded to the station's publicist via e-mail. ALL PSAs should be submitted through the website: hot97.com/psa
FM RADIO STATION

WQHY-FM 46590
Owner: WDOC Inc.
Editorial: 95 Jackson St, Prestonsburg, Kentucky 41653-1010 **Tel:** 1 606 886-8409.
Web site: http://www.q95fm.net
Profile: WQHY-FM is a commercial station owned by WDOC Inc. The format of the station is hot adult contemporary. WQHY-FM broadcasts to the Prestonsburg, KY area at 95.5 FM.
FM RADIO STATION

WQHZ-FM 40397
Owner: Cumulus Media Inc.
Editorial: 471 Robison Rd, Erie, Pennsylvania 16509-5425 **Tel:** 1 814 868-5355.
Web site: http://www.z1023online.com
Profile: WQHZ-FM is a commercial station owned by Cumulus Media Inc. The format of the station is classic rock. WQHZ-FM broadcasts to the Erie, PA area at 102.3 FM.
FM RADIO STATION

WQIC-FM 45590
Owner: Lebanon Broadcasting Co.
Editorial: 440 Rebecca Street, Lebanon, Pennsylvania 17046-1734 **Tel:** 1 717 272-7651.
Profile: WQIC-FM is a commercial station owned by Lebanon Broadcasting Co. The format of the station is adult contemporary music. WQIC-FM broadcasts to the Lebanon, PA area at 100.1 FM.
FM RADIO STATION

WQIK-FM 45467
Owner: iHeartMedia Inc.
Editorial: 11700 Central Pkwy, Jacksonville, Florida 32224-2600 **Tel:** 1 904 636-0507.
Web site: http://www.wqik.com
Profile: WQIK-FM is a commercial station owned by iHeartMedia Inc. The format of the station is classic country. WQIK-FM broadcasts to the Jacksonville, FL area at 99.1 FM.
FM RADIO STATION

WQIL-FM 43955
Owner: GSW, Inc.
Editorial: 807 Bellevue Ave, Dublin, Georgia 31021-4847 **Tel:** 1 478 272-4422.
Web site: http://www.1013wqil.com
Profile: WQIL-FM is a commercial station owned by GSW, Inc. The format of the station is contemporary Christian. WQIL-FM broadcasts to the Dublin, GA area at 101.3 FM.
FM RADIO STATION

WQIO-FM 46414
Owner: BAS Broadcasting
Editorial: 17421 Coshocton Rd, Mount Vernon, Ohio 43050-9256 **Tel:** 1 740 397-1000.
Email: wqio@basbroadcasting.com
Web site: http://www.wqioradio.com
Profile: WQIO-FM is a commercial station owned by BAS Broadcasting. The format of the station is adult contemporary music. WQIO-FM broadcasts in the Mount Vernon, OH, area at 93.7 FM.
FM RADIO STATION

WQJB-FM 518285
Owner: Flinn Broadcasting Corp.
Editorial: 6080 Mont Moriah Rd., Memphis, Tennessee 38115 **Tel:** 1 901 375-9324.
Web site: http://www.klove.com
Profile: WQJB-FM is a commercial station owned by Flinn Broadcasting Corp. and operated by Educational Media Foundation. The format of the station is Contemporary Christian, airing K-LOVE network programming. WQJB-FM broadcasts to the State College, MS area at a frequency of 104.5 FM.
FM RADIO STATION

WQJQ-FM 546293
Owner: Vermont Broadcast Associates Inc.
Editorial: 1303 Concord Ave, Saint Johnsbury, Vermont 05819-8423 **Tel:** 1 802 748-2362.
Email: Magic977@gmail.com
Web site: http://www.magic977.com
Profile: WQJQ-FM is a commercial station owned by Vermont Broadcast Associates Inc. The format of the station is bluegrass. WQJQ-FM is licensed to Barton, VT and broadcasts locally at 100.3 FM.
FM RADIO STATION

WQKI-FM 46211
Owner: Miller Communications Inc.
Editorial: 200 Regional Pkwy Bldg 200, Orangeburg, South Carolina 29118-9700 **Tel:** 1 803 536-1710.
Email: wqki@miller.fm
Web site: http://www.miller.fm
Profile: WQKI-FM is a commercial station owned by Miller Communications Inc. The format of the station is R&B oldies. WQKI-FM broadcasts to the Orangeburg, SC area at 102.9 FM.
FM RADIO STATION

WQKK-FM 43916
Owner: Magnum Broadcasting Inc.
Editorial: 315 S Atherton St, State College, Pennsylvania 16801-4045 **Tel:** 1 814 272-1320.
Web site: http://y106fm.com
Profile: WQKK-FM is a commercial station owned by Magnum Broadcasting Inc. The format of the station is hot AC. WQKK-FM broadcasts to the Wilkes Barre-Scranton, PA area at 106.9 FM.
FM RADIO STATION

WQKL-FM 45438
Owner: Cumulus Media Inc.
Editorial: 1100 Victors Way, Ste 100, Ann Arbor, Michigan 48108 **Tel:** 1 734 302-8100.
Email: programming@annarbors107one.com
Web site: http://www.annarbors107one.com
Profile: WQKL-FM is a commercial station owned by Cumulus Media Inc. The format of the station is adult album alternative. WQKL-FM broadcasts to the Ann Arbor, MI area at 107.1 FM.
FM RADIO STATION

WQKQ-FM 43972
Owner: Pritchard Broadcasting Co.
Editorial: 1610 N. 4th Street, Ste. 300, Burlington, Iowa 52601 **Tel:** 1 319 752-5402.
Email: news@burlingtonradio.com
Web site: http://www.kq92rocks.com
Profile: WQKQ-FM is a commercial station owned by Pritchard Broadcasting Co. The format of the station is classic rock. WQKQ-FM broadcasts to the Burlington, IA area at 92.1 FM.
FM RADIO STATION

WQKR-AM 35375
Owner: Venture Broadcasting
Editorial: 100 Main St Ste 201, Portland, Tennessee 37148-1246 **Tel:** 1 615 325-3250.
Email: wqkr@comcast.net
Web site: http://www.wqkr.com
Profile: WQKR-AM is a commercial station owned by Venture Broadcasting. The format of the station is classic hits music. WQKR-AM broadcasts to the Portland, TN area at 1270 AM. The station also has a simulcast on 95.9 FM.
AM RADIO STATION

WQKS-FM 46454
Owner: Bluewater Broadcasting Co. LLC
Editorial: 4101A Wall St Ste A, Montgomery, Alabama 36106-3656 **Tel:** 1 334 244-0961.
Web site: http://kiss961.com
Profile: WQKS-FM is a commercial station owned by Bluewater Broadcasting Co. LLC. The format of the station is adult contemporary. WQKS-FM broadcasts to the Montgomery, AL area at 96.1 FM.
FM RADIO STATION

WQKT-FM 46545
Owner: Dix Communications
Editorial: 186 S Hillcrest Dr, Wooster, Ohio 44691-3727 **Tel:** 1 330 264-5122.
Email: contact@wqkt.com
Web site: http://www.wqkt.com
Profile: WQKT-FM is a commercial station owned by Dix Communications. The format of the station is classic and contemporary country. WQKT-FM broadcasts to the Cleveland area at 104.5 FM.
FM RADIO STATION

WQKX-FM 42537
Owner: Sunbury Broadcasting Corp.
Editorial: 1227 County Line Rd, Selinsgrove, Pennsylvania 17870-8188 **Tel:** 1 570 286-5838.
Email: equest@wqkx.com
Web site: http://www.wqkx.net
Profile: WQKX-FM is a commercial station owned by Sunbury Broadcasting Corp. The format of the station is hot adult contemporary music. WQKX-FM broadcasts to the Wilkes Barre-Scranton area at 107.3 FM.
FM RADIO STATION

WQKY-FM 45470
Owner: Salter Communications
Editorial: 241 West 4th St, Emporium, Pennsylvania 15834 **Tel:** 1 814 486-3712.
Email: theriver989@yahoo.com
Web site: http://www.theriver989.com
Profile: WQKY-FM is a commercial station owned by Salter Communications. The format of the station is classic hits. WQKY-FM broadcasts to the Emporium, PA area on 98.9 FM.
FM RADIO STATION

WQKZ-FM 235068
Owner: GEM Communications
Editorial: 1978 S Witz Rd, Jasper, Indiana 47546-2672 **Tel:** 1 812 367-1884.
Email: wqkz@psci.net
Web site: http://www.witzamfm.com
Profile: WQKZ-FM is a commercial station owned by GEM Communications. The format of the station is contemporary country music. WQKZ-FM broadcasts to the Jasper, IN, area at 98.5 FM.
FM RADIO STATION

WQLA-AM 38272
Owner: Beverly Broadcasting Company, LLC
Editorial: 912 Forest Ridge Cir, Knoxville, Tennessee 37932-2809 **Tel:** 1 423 566-1000.
Profile: WQLA-AM is a commercial station owned by Beverly Broadcasting Company, LLC. The format of the station is classic country. WQLA-AM broadcasts to the La Follette, TN area at 960 AM.
AM RADIO STATION

WQLB-FM 43394
Owner: Carroll Broadcasting Co.
Editorial: 523 Meadow Rd, Tawas City, Michigan 48763 **Tel:** 1 989 362-3417.
Email: hitsfm@speednetllc.com
Web site: http://www.hitsfm.net
Profile: WQLB-FM is a commercial station owned by Carroll Broadcasting Co. The format of the station is classic rock music. WQLB-FM broadcasts to the Tawas City, MI area at 103.3 FM.
FM RADIO STATION

WQLC-FM 46500
Owner: Dockins Broadcast Group
Editorial: 9206 W US Highway 90, Lake City, Florida 32055-7502 **Tel:** 1 386 755-4102.
Web site: http://www.powercountry102.com
Profile: WQLC-FM is a commercial station owned by Dockins Broadcast Group. The format of the station is contemporary country music. WQLC-FM broadcasts to the Lake City, FL at 102.1 FM.
FM RADIO STATION

WQLF-FM 87473
Owner: Big Radio
Editorial: 834 N Tower Rd, Freeport, Illinois 61032-8650 **Tel:** 1 815 235-7191.
Web site: http://www.wekz.com
Profile: WQLF-FM is a commercial station owned by Big Radio. The format of the station is classic rock. WQLF-FM broadcasts to the Monroe, WI area at 102.1 FM. All staff should be contact via fax.
FM RADIO STATION

WQLH-FM 45133
Owner: Cumulus Media Inc.
Editorial: 810 Victoria St, Green Bay, Wisconsin 54302 **Tel:** 1 920 468-4100.
Web site: http://www.star98.net
Profile: WQLH-FM is a commercial station owned by Cumulus Media Inc. The format of the station is hot adult contemporary. WQLH-FM broadcasts to the Green Bay, WI area at 98.5 FM.
FM RADIO STATION

United States of America

WQLI-FM 518286
Owner: Flint Media
Editorial: 521 S Scott St, Bainbridge, Georgia 39819-4101 **Tel:** 1 229 246-7776.
Web site: http://sowegalive.com
Profile: WQLI-FM is a commercial station owned by Flint Media. The format of the station is AC. WQLI-FM broadcasts to the Pelham, GA area at a frequency of 92.3 FM.
FM RADIO STATION

WQLJ-FM 40436
Owner: TeleSouth Communications Inc.
Editorial: 461 Highway 6 W, Oxford, Mississippi 38655-9073 **Tel:** 1 662 236-0093.
Email: q937@telesouth.com
Web site: http://www.q937.com
Profile: WQLJ-FM is a commercial station owned by TeleSouth Communications Inc. The format of the station is hot adult contemporary music. WQLJ-FM broadcasts to the Oxford, MS area at 93.7 FM.
FM RADIO STATION

WQLK-FM 45473
Owner: Brewer Broadcasting Inc.
Editorial: 2626 Tingler Rd W, Richmond, Indiana 47374-9273 **Tel:** 1 765 962-1595.
Email: news@kicks96.com
Web site: http://www.kicks96.com
Profile: WQLK-FM is a commercial station owned by Brewer Broadcasting Inc. The format of the station is country music. WQLK-FM broadcasts to the Richmond, IN area at 96.1 FM.
FM RADIO STATION

WQLL-AM 36141
Owner: M-10 Broadcasting Inc.
Editorial: 1726 Reisterstown Rd Ste 117, Baltimore, Maryland 21208-2986 **Tel:** 1 410 580-6800.
Web site: http://www.q1370.com
Profile: WQLL-AM is a commercial station owned by M-10 Broadcasting Inc. The format of the station is classic hits. WQLL-AM broadcasts to Baltimore area at 1370 AM.
AM RADIO STATION

WQLN-FM 40640
Owner: Public Broadcasting of Northwest Pennsylvania
Editorial: 8425 Peach St, Erie, Pennsylvania 16509
Tel: 1 814 864-3001.
Email: wqln@wqln.org
Web site: http://www.wqln.org
Profile: WQLN-FM is a non-commercial station owned by Public Broadcasting of Northwest Pennsylvania. The format of the station is news and classical music. WQLN-FM broadcasts to the Erie, PA area at 91.3 FM.
FM RADIO STATION

WQLR-AM 38146
Owner: Midwest Communications Inc.
Editorial: 4200 W Main St, Kalamazoo, Michigan 49006-2749 **Tel:** 1 269 345-7121.
Email: wkzonews@wkzo.com
Web site: http://www.1660thefan.com
Profile: WQLR-AM is a commercial station owned by Midwest Communications Inc. The format of the station is sports. WQLR-AM broadcasts to the Kalamazoo, MI area at 1660 AM.
AM RADIO STATION

WQLT-FM 45701
Owner: Big River Broadcasting Corp.
Editorial: 624 Sam Phillips St, Florence, Alabama 35630-5859 **Tel:** 1 256 764-8121.
Web site: http://www.wqlt.com
Profile: WQLT-FM is a commercial station owned by Big River Broadcasting Corp. The format for the station is adult contemporary. WQLT-FM broadcasts to the Huntsville, AL area at 107.3 FM.
FM RADIO STATION

WQLV-FM 41991
Owner: Cooper(Richard L.)
Editorial: 234 Union St, Millersburg, Pennsylvania 17061-1607 **Tel:** 1 717 362-1099.
Email: info@wqlvfm.com
Web site: http://www.wqlvfm.com
Profile: WQLV-FM is a commercial station owned by Richard L. Cooper. The format of the station is hot adult contemporary music. WQLV-FM broadcasts to the Millersburg, PA area at 98.9 FM.
FM RADIO STATION

WQLX-FM 46325
Owner: iHeartMedia Inc.
Editorial: 45 W Main St, Chillicothe, Ohio 45601-3104
Tel: 1 740 773-3000.
Email: newsroom@wkkj.com
Web site: http://www.wqlx1065.com
Profile: WQLX-FM is a commercial station owned by iHeartMedia Inc. The format of the station is hot adult contemporary. WQLX-FM broadcasts to the Hillsboro, OH area at 106.5 FM.
FM RADIO STATION

WQLZ-FM 42092
Owner: Midwest Family Broadcasting
Editorial: 1510 N 3rd St, Riverton, Illinois 62561-9701
Tel: 1 217 629-7077.
Web site: http://www.wqlz.com
Profile: WQLZ-FM is a commercial station owned by Midwest Family Stations. The format of the station is rock. WQLZ-FM broadcasts to the Springfield, IL area at 97.7 FM. the station's slogan is,
FM RADIO STATION

WQMF-FM 40641
Owner: iHeartMedia Inc.
Editorial: 4000 #1 Radio Dr, Louisville, Kentucky 40218-4568 **Tel:** 1 502 479-2222.
Web site: http://www.wqmf.com
Profile: WQMF-FM is a commercial station owned by iHeartMedia Inc.The format of the station is classic rock music. WQMF-FM broadcasts in the Louisville, KY area at 95.7 FM.
FM RADIO STATION

WQMG-FM 46031
Owner: Entercom Communications Corp.
Editorial: 7819 National Service Rd, Ste 401, Greensboro, North Carolina 27409 **Tel:** 1 336 605-5200.
Web site: http://www.wqmg.com
Profile: WQMG-FM is a commercial station owned by Entercom Communications Corp. The format of the station is urban adult contemporary. WQMG-FM broadcasts to the Greensboro-Winston Salem, NC at 97.1 FM.
FM RADIO STATION

WQMJ-FM 235073
Owner: Roberts Communications
Editorial: 6174 Georgia Highway 57, Macon, Georgia 31217 **Tel:** 1 478 745-3301.
Profile: WQMJ-FM is a commercial station owned by Roberts Communications. The format of the station is R&B oldies. WQMJ-FM broadcasts to the Macon, GA area at 100.1 FM.
FM RADIO STATION

WQMP-FM 40592
Owner: CBS Radio
Editorial: 1800 Pembrook Dr Ste 400, Orlando, Florida 32810-6375 **Tel:** 1 407 919-1000.
Web site: http://1019ampradio.cbslocal.com
Profile: WQMP-FM is a commercial station owned by CBS Radio. The format of the station is CHR. WQMP-FM broadcasts to the Orlando, FL area at 101.9 FM.
FM RADIO STATION

WQMT-FM 41083
Owner: East Tennessee Radio Group
Tel: 1 423 472-4053.
Profile: WQMT-FM is a commercial station owned by East Tennessee Radio Group. The format of the station is Spanish Adult Hits. WQMT-FM broadcasts to the Cleveland, TN area at 93.9 FM.
FM RADIO STATION

WQMU-FM 45972
Owner: Renda Broadcasting
Editorial: 840 Philadelphia St, Ste 100, Indiana, Pennsylvania 15701 **Tel:** 1 724 465-4700.
Web site: http://www.u92radio.com
Profile: WQMU-FM is a commercial station owned by Renda Broadcasting. The format of the station is hot adult contemporary music. WQMU-FM broadcasts in the Indiana, PA area at 92.5 FM.
FM RADIO STATION

WQMX-FM 40207
Owner: Rubber City Radio Group Inc.
Editorial: 1795 W Market St, Akron, Ohio 44313-7001
Tel: 1 330 869-9800.
Email: news@rcrg.net
Web site: http://www.wqmx.com
Profile: WQMX-FM is a commercial station owned by Rubber City Radio Group Inc. The format of the station is country music. WQMX-FM broadcasts to the Akron, OH area at 94.9 FM.
FM RADIO STATION

WQMZ-FM 45692
Owner: Saga Communications
Editorial: 1140 Rose Hill Dr, Charlottesville, Virginia 22903-5128 **Tel:** 1 434 220-2300.
Email: mail@literockz951.com
Web site: http://www.literockz951.com
Profile: WQMZ-FM is a commercial station owned by Saga Communications. The station's format is adult contemporary. WQMZ-FM broadcasts to the Charlottesville, VA area on 95.1 FM.
FM RADIO STATION

WQNA-FM 41683
Owner: Capital Area Career Center
Editorial: 2201 Toronto Rd, Springfield, Illinois 62712-3802 **Tel:** 1 217 529-5431.
Email: info@wqna.org
Web site: http://www.wqna.org
Profile: WQNA-FM is a non-commercial station owned by Capital Area Career Center. The format of the station is college variety. WQNA-FM broadcasts to the Springfield, IL area at 88.3 FM.
FM RADIO STATION

WQNC-FM 42873
Owner: Urban One, Inc.
Editorial: 8809 Lenox Pointe Dr Unit A, Charlotte, North Carolina 28273-3377 **Tel:** 1 704 548-7800.
Web site: http://praisecharlotte.com
Profile: WQNC-FM is a commercial station owned by Urban One, Inc. The format of the station is urban gospel. WQNC-FM broadcasts to the Charlotte, NC area at 92.7 FM. The station airs WPZS-FM's programming.
FM RADIO STATION

WQNO-AM 35696
Owner: Catholic Community Radio, Inc.
Editorial: 8230 Summa Ave Ste A, Baton Rouge, Louisiana 70809-3421 **Tel:** 1 225 448-3754.
Email: info@catholiccommunityradio.org
Web site: http://catholiccommunityradio.org/
Profile: WQNO-AM is a commercial station owned by Catholic Community Radio, Inc.. The format of the station is Catholic radio programming. WQNO-AM broadcasts to the New Orleans area at 690 AM.
AM RADIO STATION

WQNQ-FM 41925
Owner: iHeartMedia Inc.
Editorial: 13 Summerlin Dr, Asheville, North Carolina 28806-2800 **Tel:** 1 828 257-2700.
Email: ashevillepsa@iheartmedia.com
Web site: http://www.star1043.com
Profile: WQNQ-FM is a commercial station owned by iHeartMedia Inc. The format of the station is Top 40. WQNQ-FM broadcasts to the Asheville, NC area at 104.3 FM.
FM RADIO STATION

WQNR-FM 44353
Owner: Tiger Communications Inc.
Editorial: 2514 S College St Ste 104, Auburn, Alabama 36832-6925 **Tel:** 1 334 887-9999.
Web site: http://www.katefm.com
Profile: WQNR-FM is a commercial station owned by Tiger Communications Inc. The format of the station is adult hits. WQNR-FM broadcasts to the Auburn, AL area at 99.9 FM.
FM RADIO STATION

WQNS-FM 46470
Owner: iHeartMedia Inc.
Editorial: 13 Summerlin Dr, Asheville, North Carolina 28806-2800 **Tel:** 1 828 257-2700.
Email: ashevillepsa@iheartmedia.com
Web site: http://1051rocks.iheart.com
Profile: WQNS-FM is a commercial station owned by iHeartMedia Inc. The format for the station is rock. WQNS-FM broadcasts to the Asheville, NC area at 105.1 FM.
FM RADIO STATION

WQNT-AM 36960
Owner: Kirkman Broadcasting
Editorial: 60 Markfield Dr Ste 4, Charleston, South Carolina 29407-7907 **Tel:** 1 843 763-6631.
Web site: http://www.charlestonsportsradio.com
Profile: WQNT-AM is a commercial station owned by Kirkman Broadcasting. The format of the station is sports and talk. WQNT-AM broadcasts to the Charleston, SC area at 1450 AM.
AM RADIO STATION

WQNU-FM 40675
Owner: Summit Media Broadcasting LLC
Editorial: 612 S 4th St, Louisville, Kentucky 40202-2460 **Tel:** 1 502 589-4800.
Web site: http://www.qlouisville.com
Profile: WQNU-FM is a commercial station owned by Summit Media Broadcasting LLC. The format of the station is contemporary country. WQNU-FM broadcasts to the Louisville, KY area at 103.1 FM.
FM RADIO STATION

WQNY-FM 46349
Owner: Saga Communications
Editorial: 1751 Hanshaw Rd, Ithaca, New York 14850-9105 **Tel:** 1 607 257-6400.
Web site: http://www.qcountry1037.com
Profile: WQNY-FM is a commercial station owned by Saga Communications. The format of the station is contemporary country. WQNY-FM broadcasts to the Ithaca, NY area at 103.7 FM.
FM RADIO STATION

WQNZ-FM 45675
Owner: First Natchez Corp.
Editorial: 2 Oferrall St, Natchez, Mississippi 39120-3000 **Tel:** 1 601 442-4895.
Web site: http://www.listenupyall.com
Profile: WQNZ-FM is a commercial station owned by First Natchez Corp. The format of the station is country. WQNZ-FM broadcasts to the Natchez, MS area on 95.1 FM. The station does not accept press submissions, requests, and inquiries.
FM RADIO STATION

WQOK-FM 40643
Owner: Urban One, Inc.
Editorial: 8001 Creedmoor Rd Ste 101, Raleigh, North Carolina 27613-4396 **Tel:** 1 919 848-9736.
Web site: http://hiphopnc.com/
Profile: WQOK-FM is a commercial station owned by Urban One, Inc. The format of the station is urban contemporary music. WQOK-FM broadcasts to the Raleigh-Durham, NC area at 97.5 FM.
FM RADIO STATION

WQOL-FM 40108
Owner: iHeartMedia Inc.
Editorial: 3771 SE Jennings Rd, Port Saint Lucie, Florida 34952-7702 **Tel:** 1 772 335-9300.
Web site: http://www.oldiesradio1037.com
Profile: WQOL-FM is a commercial station owned by iHeartMedia Inc. The station's format is classic hits. WQOL-FM broadcasts to the Fort Pierce, FL area at 103.7 FM.
FM RADIO STATION

WQOM-AM 36514
Owner: Holy Family Communications
Editorial: 100 Mount Wayte Ave Ste 400, Framingham, Massachusetts 01702-5705
Tel: 1 716 839-6117.
Email: info@1060catholic.org
Web site: http://www.1060catholic.org
Profile: WQOM-AM is a non-commercial station owned by Holy Family Communications. The format of the station is religious, specifically Catholic. WQOM-AM broadcasts to the Framingham, MA area at 1060 AM.
AM RADIO STATION

WQON-FM 4582
Owner: Blarney Stone Broadcasting, Inc.
Editorial: 6514 Old Lake Rd, Grayling, Michigan 49738-7348 **Tel:** 1 989 348-6171.
Web site: http://q100-fm.com
Profile: WQON-FM is a commercial station owned by Blarney Stone Broadcasting, Inc. The format of the station is classic rock. WQON-FM broadcasts in the Traverse City, MI area at 100.3 FM.
FM RADIO STATION

WQOP-AM 3703
Owner: Queen of Peace Radio, Inc.
Editorial: 1611 Atlantic Blvd, Atlantic Beach, Florida 32233-2516 **Tel:** 1 904 241-3311.
Email: queenofpeaceradio@yahoo.com
Web site: http://www.qopradio.com
Profile: WQOP-AM is a commercial station owned by Queen of Peace Radio, Inc. The format of the station is religious talk and music. WQOP-AM broadcasts to the Jacksonville, FL area at 1460 AM.
AM RADIO STATION

WQOR-AM 3592
Owner: J.M.J. Radio
Tel: 1 570 287-4670.
Web site: http://www.jmj750.com
Profile: WQOR-AM is a non-commercial station owned by J.M.J. Radio. The format of the station is Catholic programming. WQOR-AM broadcasts to the Williamsville, NY area at 750 AM.
AM RADIO STATION

WQPC-FM 4357
Owner: Robinson Corporation
Editorial: 640 N Villa Louis Rd, Prairie du Chien, Wisconsin 53821-1338 **Tel:** 1 608 326-2411.
Email: wqpcwpre@mwt.net
Web site: http://www.wqpcradio.com
Profile: WQPC-FM is an independent and commercial station owned by Robinson Corporation. The format of the station is country music. WQPC-FM broadcasts to the Prairie du Chien, WI area at 94.3 FM.
FM RADIO STATION

WQPO-FM 4607
Owner: VerStandig Broadcasting
Editorial: 1820 Heritage Center Way, Harrisonburg, Virginia 22801-8451 **Tel:** 1 540 434-0331.
Web site: http://www.q101online.com
Profile: WQPO-FM is a commercial station owned by VerStandig Broadcasting. The format for the station is Top 40/CHR music. WQPO-FM broadcasts to the Harrisonburg, VA area at 100.7 FM. The station does not accept unsolicited faxes. Do NOT e-mail any staff members. Any press information should be sent to WSVA-AM.
FM RADIO STATION

WQPW-FM 4663
Owner: Black Crow Broadcasting Inc.
Editorial: 1711 Ellis Dr, Valdosta, Georgia 31601-3573
Tel: 1 229 244-8642.
Web site: http://mymixvaldosta.com
Profile: WQPW-FM is a commercial station owned by Black Crow Broadcasting Inc. The format of the station is adult contemporary music. WQPW-FM broadcasts to the Valdosta, GA area at 95.7 FM.
FM RADIO STATION

WQQB-FM 4244
Owner: S.J. Broadcasting Inc.
Editorial: 2702 Boulder Rd, Urbana, Illinois 61802-6996 **Tel:** 1 217 367-1195.
Web site: http://www.wqqb.com
Profile: WQQB-FM is a commercial station owned by S.J. Broadcasting Inc. The format of the station is Top 40/CHR music. WQQB-FM broadcasts to the Champaign, IL area at 96.1 FM.
FM RADIO STATION

WQQK-FM 4547
Owner: Cumulus Media Inc.
Editorial: 506 2nd Ave S, Nashville, Tennessee 37210-2002 **Tel:** 1 615 321-1067.
Web site: http://www.92qnashville.com
Profile: WQQK-FM is a commercial station owned by Cumulus Media Inc. The format of the station is urban adult contemporary music. WQQK-FM broadcasts to the Nashville, TN area at 92.1 FM.
FM RADIO STATION

WQQL-FM 4281
Owner: Saga Communications
Editorial: 3501 E Sangamon Ave, Springfield, Illinois 62707-9777 **Tel:** 1 217 753-5400.
Web site: http://www.cool939.com
Profile: WQQL-FM is a commercial radio station owned by the Saga Communications Network. The format of the station is oldies. WQQL-FM broadcasts to Springfield, IL at 93.9 FM and on an FM-translator at 107.5 FM.
FM RADIO STATION

WQQO-FM 4562
Owner: Cumulus Media Inc.
Editorial: 3225 Arlington Ave, Toledo, Ohio 43614-2427 **Tel:** 1 419 725-5700.
Web site: http://www.channel1055.com/
Profile: WQQO-FM is a commercial station owned by Cumulus Media Inc. The format of the station is Top

0. WQQO-FM broadcasts to the Toledo, OH area at 105.5 FM.
FM RADIO STATION

WQQQ-FM 42253
Owner: Ridgefield Broadcasting (Jackson, Dennis)
Editorial: 5151 Park Ave, Fairfield, Connecticut 06825-1090 **Tel:** 1 203 365-6604.
Email: news@wshu.org
Web site: http://www.wshu.org
Profile: WQQQ-FM is a non-commercial public radio station owned by Ridgefield Broadcasting (Jackson, Dennis) and operated by Sacred Heart University. The format of the station is news/talk. WQQQ-FM at 103.3 FM, broadcasting to Noyack, NY and surrounding areas, is a simulcast of WSHU-FM in the Fairfield, CT.
FM RADIO STATION

WQQR-FM 46198
Owner: Bristol Broadcasting
Editorial: 6000 Bristol Dr, Paducah, Kentucky 42003-3213 **Tel:** 1 270 554-8255.
Email: news@wkyx.com
Web site: http://www.947themix.com
Profile: WQQR-FM is a commercial station owned by Bristol Broadcasting. The station's current format is adult contemporary. and broadcasts to the Paducah, KY area on 94.7 FM.
FM RADIO STATION

WQQW-AM 35392
Owner: Entertainment Media Trust
Editorial: 6500 W Main St Ste 315, Belleville, Illinois 62223-3700 **Tel:** 1 618 394-9965.
Profile: WQQW-AM is a commercial station owned by Entertainment Media Trust. The format of the station is Spanish. WQQW-AM broadcasts to the St. Louis area at 1510 AM.
AM RADIO STATION

WQQX-AM 35307
Owner: Entertainment Media Trust
Editorial: 6500 W Main St, Belleville, Illinois 62223-3700 **Tel:** 1 618 394-9965.
Profile: WQQX-AM is a commercial station owned by Entertainment Media Trust. The format of the station is Sports. WQQX-AM broadcasts to the St. Louis area at 1490 AM.
AM RADIO STATION

WQRB-FM 42046
Owner: iHeartMedia Inc.
Editorial: 619 Cameron St, Eau Claire, Wisconsin 54703-4708 **Tel:** 1 715 830-4000.
Web site: http://www.b95radio.com
Profile: WQRB-FM is a commercial station owned by iHeartMedia Inc. The format of the station is contemporary country. WQRB-FM broadcasts to the Eau Claire, WI area at 95.1 FM.
FM RADIO STATION

WQRC-FM 40646
Owner: Cape Cod Broadcasting
Editorial: 737 W Main St, Hyannis, Massachusetts 02601-3422 **Tel:** 1 508 771-1224.
Email: news@ccb-media.com
Web site: http://www.wqrc.com
Profile: WQRC-FM is a commercial station owned by Cape Cod Broadcasting. The format of the station is not adult contemporary. WQRC-FM broadcasts to the Hyannis, MA area at 99.9 FM.
FM RADIO STATION

WQRK-FM 45480
Owner: Ad-Venture Media Inc.
Editorial: 424 Heltonville Rd W, Bedford, Indiana 47421-9389 **Tel:** 1 812 275-7555.
Email: tips@superoldies.net
Web site: http://www.wqrk.com
Profile: WQRK-FM is a commercial station owned by Ad-Venture Media Inc. The format for the station is oldies music. WQRK-AM broadcasts to the Indianapolis area at 105.5 FM.
FM RADIO STATION

WQRL-FM 40647
Owner: Dana Communications Corp.
Editorial: 303 N Main St, Benton, Illinois 62812-1314 **Tel:** 1 618 435-8100.
Email: news@wqrlradio.com
Web site: http://www.wqrlradio.com
Profile: WQRL-FM is a commercial station owned by Dana Communications Corp. The format of the station is oldies music. WRQL-FM broadcasts to the Benton, IL at 106.3 FM.
FM RADIO STATION

WQRN-FM 610631
Owner: VCY America Inc.
Tel: 1 414 935-3000.
Email: wqrn@vcyamerica.org
Web site: http://www.vcyamerica.org
Profile: WQRN-FM is a non-commercial station owned by VCY America. The format of the station is religious programming and Christian music. WQRN-FM broadcasts to the Cook, MN area at 88.9 FM.
FM RADIO STATION

WQRS-FM 46516
Owner: Pembrook Pines Media Group
Editorial: 4104 Killbuck Rd, Salamanca, New York 14779-9612 **Tel:** 1 716 375-1015.
Web site: http://98rockswqrs.com
Profile: WQRS-FM is a commercial station owned by Pembrook Pines Media Group. The format of the station is classic rock. WQRS-FM broadcasts to the Buffalo, NY area at 98.3 FM.
FM RADIO STATION

WQRV-FM 45331
Owner: iHeartMedia Inc.
Editorial: 26869 Peoples Rd, Madison, Alabama 35756-4632 **Tel:** 1 256 353-1750.
Web site: http://1003theriver.iheart.com
Profile: WQRV-FM is a commercial station owned by iHeartMedia Inc. The format of the station is classic hits. WQRV-FM broadcasts to the Huntsville, AL, area at 100.3 FM.
FM RADIO STATION

WQRX-AM 472007
Owner: Good News Network
Editorial: 2278 Wortham Ln, Grovetown, Georgia 30813 **Tel:** 1 706 309-9610 3.
Web site: http://www.gnnradio.org
Profile: WQRX-AM is a commercial station owned by Good News Network. The format of the station is Hispanic religious programming. WQRX-AM broadcsats to the Valley Head, AL area at a frequency of 870 AM.
AM RADIO STATION

WQSB-FM 45481
Owner: Sand Mountain Broadcasting Service
Editorial: 3770 US Highway 431, Albertville, Alabama 35950 **Tel:** 1 256 878-8575.
Email: wqsb@aol.com
Web site: http://www.wqsb.com
Profile: WQSB-FM is a commercial station owned by Sand Mountain Broadcasting Service. The format for the station is country. WQSB-FM broadcasts to the Albertville, AL area at 105.1 FM.
FM RADIO STATION

WQSC-AM 35576
Owner: Kirkman Broadcasting
Editorial: 60 Markfield Dr Ste 4, Charleston, South Carolina 29407-7907 **Tel:** 1 843 763-6631.
Email: info@wqsc1340.com
Web site: http://www.wqsc1340.com
Profile: WQSC-AM is a commercial station owned by Kirkman Broadcasting. The format of the station is news/talk. WQSC-AM broadcasts to the Charleston, SC area at 1340 AM.
AM RADIO STATION

WQSE-AM 36754
Owner: JWL Communications, LLC.
Editorial: 201 Hall Ln, White Bluff, Tennessee 37187-9057 **Tel:** 1 615 797-9785.
Email: wvryfm@gmail.com
Profile: WQSE-AM is a commercial station owned by JWL Communications, LLC. The format of the station is gospel music. WQSE-AM broadcasts in the White Bluff, TN area at 1030 AM.
AM RADIO STATION

WQSH-FM 42057
Owner: Townsquare Media, LLC
Editorial: 1241 Kings Rd, Schenectady, New York 12303-2811 **Tel:** 1 518 476-1039.
Web site: http://www.popcrush1057.com
Profile: WQSH-FM is a commercial station owned by Townsquare Media, LLC. The format of the station is Adult CHR. WQSH-FM broadcasts to the Albany, NY area at 105.7 FM. Please address all mail to Tom Jacobsen, Operations Manager.
FM RADIO STATION

WQSI-FM 395418
Owner: Tiger Communications Inc.
Editorial: 2514 S College St Ste 104, Auburn, Alabama 36832-6925 **Tel:** 1 334 887-9999.
Web site: http://www.fmtalk959.com
Profile: WQSI-FM is a commercial radio station owned by Tiger Communications Inc. The format of the station is talk. The station broadcasts to the Auburn, AL area at 95.9 FM.
FM RADIO STATION

WQSL-FM 42242
Owner: Alpha Media
Editorial: 1361 Colony Dr, New Bern, North Carolina 28562-4129 **Tel:** 1 252 639-7900.
Web site: http://www.mywolfcountry.com
Profile: WQSL-FM is a commercial station owned by Alpha Media. The format of the station is country. WQSL-FM broadcasts to the New Bern, NC area at 92.3 FM.
FM RADIO STATION

WQSM-FM 45482
Owner: Cumulus Media Inc.
Editorial: 1009 Drayton Rd, Fayetteville, North Carolina 28303-3887 **Tel:** 1 910 864-5222.
Web site: http://www.q98fm.com
Profile: WQSM-FM is a commercial station owned by Cumulus Media Inc. The format of the station is hot adult contemporary music. WQSM-FM broadcasts to the Fayetteville, NC area at 98.1 FM.
FM RADIO STATION

WQSO-FM 43561
Owner: iHeartMedia Inc.
Editorial: 815 Lafayette Rd, Portsmouth, New Hampshire 03801-5406 **Tel:** 1 603 436-7300.
Web site: http://www.967thewave.com
Profile: WQSO-FM is a commercial station owned by iHeartMedia Inc. The format of the station is talk. WQSO-FM broadcasts to the Portsmouth, NH area at 96.7 FM.
FM RADIO STATION

WQSR-FM 45759
Owner: iHeartMedia Inc.
Editorial: 711 W 40th St Ste 350, Baltimore, Maryland 21211-2190 **Tel:** 1 410 366-7600.
Web site: http://1027jackfm.iheart.com
Profile: WQSR-FM is a commercial station owned by iHeartMedia Inc. The format of the station is adult hits. WQSR-FM broadcasts to the Baltimore area at 102.7 FM.
FM RADIO STATION

WQSS-FM 41573
Owner: Blueberry Broadcasting
Editorial: 125 Community Dr Ste 201, Augusta, Maine 04330-8157 **Tel:** 1 207 623-9000.
Profile: WQSS-FM is a commercial station owned by Blueberry Broadcasting. The format of the station is adult contemporary. WQSS-FM broadcasts to the Rockland, ME area at 102.5 FM.
FM RADIO STATION

WQST-FM 43775
Owner: American Family Association
Editorial: 107 Park Gate Dr, Tupelo, Mississippi 38801-3010 **Tel:** 1 662 844-8888.
Email: comments@afr.net
Web site: http://www.afr.net
Profile: WQST-FM is a non-commercial station owned by American Family Association. The format of the station is contemporary Christian. WQST-FM broadcasts to the Jackson, MS area at 92.5 FM.
FM RADIO STATION

WQTC-FM 45483
Owner: Seehafer Broadcasting Corp.
Editorial: 3730 Mangin St, Manitowoc, Wisconsin 54220 **Tel:** 1 920 682-0351.
Email: news@womtradio.com
Web site: http://www.womtradio.com
Profile: WQTC-FM is a commercial station owned by Seehafer Broadcasting Corp. The format of the station is classic hits. WQTC-FM broadcasts to the Manitowoc, WI area at 102.3 FM.
FM RADIO STATION

WQTE-FM 45484
Owner: Friends Communications Inc.
Editorial: 121 W Maumee St, Adrian, Michigan 49221-2019 **Tel:** 1 517 265-1500.
Email: traffic@friendsmi.com
Profile: WQTE-FM is a commercial station owned by Friends Communications Inc. The format of the station is contemporary country music. WQTE-FM broadcasts to the Adrian, MI area at 95.3 FM.
FM RADIO STATION

WQTK-FM 45437
Owner: Community Broadcasters, LLC
Editorial: 2315 Knox St, Ogdensburg, New York 13669-1949 **Tel:** 1 315 393-1100.
Email: burgproduction@commbroadcasters.com
Profile: WQTK-FM is a commercial station owned by Community Broadcasters, LLC. The format of the station is news and talk. WQTK-FM broadcasts to the Ogdensburg, NY area at 92.7 FM.
FM RADIO STATION

WQTL-FM 40760
Owner: Red Hills Broadcasting, LLC
Editorial: 3000 Olson Rd, Tallahassee, Florida 32308-3918 **Tel:** 1 850 386-8004.
Web site: http://www.1061thepath.com
Profile: WQTL-FM is a commercial station owned by Red Hills Broadcasting, LLC. The format of the station is a mix of classic rock and adult album alternative. WQTL-FM broadcasts to the Tallahassee, FL area at 106.1 FM.
FM RADIO STATION

WQTT-AM 36248
Owner: ICS Holdings, Inc.
Editorial: 113 S Main St, Marysville, Ohio 43040-1551 **Tel:** 1 614 754-4850.
Email: news@icsohio.com
Web site: http://www.qt1270.com
Profile: WQTT-AM is a commercial station owned by ICS Holdings, Inc. The format of the station is oldies. WQTT-AM broadcasts to the Marysville, OH area at a frequency of 1570 AM.
AM RADIO STATION

WQTU-FM 45485
Owner: Rome Radio Partners
Editorial: 20 John Davenport Dr NW, Rome, Georgia 30165-2536 **Tel:** 1 706 291-9496.
Web site: http://www.q102rome.com
Profile: WQTU-FM is a commercial station owned by Rome Radio Partners. The format of the station is adult contemporary. WQTU-FM broadcasts to the Atlanta area at 102.3 FM.
FM RADIO STATION

WQTW-AM 35615
Owner: Wall(L. Stanley)
Editorial: 2532 Springfield Pike, Connellsville, Pennsylvania 15425-6448 **Tel:** 1 724 532-1778.
Email: wlswproduction@hotmail.com
Profile: WQTW-AM is a commercial station owned by L. Stanley Wall. The format of the station is classic hits. WQTW-AM broadcasts to the Latrobe, PA area at 1570 AM.
AM RADIO STATION

WQTX-FM 41008
Owner: Midwest Communications, Inc.
Editorial: 2495 Cedar St Ste 106, Holt, Michigan 48842-7400 **Tel:** 1 517 699-0111.
Web site: http://team921fm.com
Profile: WQTX-FM is a commercial station owned by Midwest Communications, Inc. The format of the station is sports. WQTX-FM broadcasts to the Holt, MI area at 92.1 FM.
FM RADIO STATION

WQTY-FM 45672
Owner: Original Company Inc.(The)
Editorial: 522 Busseron St, Vincennes, Indiana 47591-2030 **Tel:** 1 812 882-6060.
Web site: http://www.wqtyradio.com
Profile: WQTY-FM is a commercial station owned by The Original Company Inc. The format of the station is classic hits. WQTY-FM broadcasts to the Vincennes, IN area at 93.3 FM.
FM RADIO STATION

WQUA-FM 41533
Owner: Family Worship Center Church, Inc.
Tel: 1 225 768-3288.
Email: info@jsm.org
Web site: http://www.jsm.org
Profile: WQUA-FM is a commercial station owned by Family Worship Center Church, Inc. The format of the station is religious programming. WQUA-FM broadcasts to the Mobile, Al area at 102.1 FM.
FM RADIO STATION

WQUE-FM 45486
Owner: iHeartMedia Inc.
Editorial: 929 Howard Ave, New Orleans, Louisiana 70113-1148 **Tel:** 1 504 679-7300.
Web site: http://www.q93.com
Profile: WQUE-FM is a commercial station owned by iHeartMedia Inc. The format of the station is urban contemporary music. WQUE-FM broadcasts to the New Orleans area at 93.3 FM.
FM RADIO STATION

WQUL-AM 35662
Owner: BJL Broadcasting Inc
Editorial: 360 Sloan Rd, Woodruff, South Carolina 29388-9041 **Tel:** 1 864 476-7184.
Email: wqul959@gmail.com
Web site: http://www.coolq959.com
Profile: WQUL-AM is a commercial station owned by BJL Broadcasting Inc. The format of the station is classic hits. WQUL-AM broadcasts to the Woodruff, SC area at 1510 AM.
AM RADIO STATION

WQUS-FM 45115
Owner: Townsquare Media, LLC
Editorial: 3338 E Bristol Rd, Burton, Michigan 48529 **Tel:** 1 810 742-1470.
Web site: http://us103.com
Profile: WQUS-FM is a commercial station owned by Townsquare Media, LLC. The format of the station is classic rock. WQUS-FM broadcasts to the Burton, MI area at 103.1 FM.
FM RADIO STATION

WQUT-FM 46759
Owner: Cumulus Media Inc.
Editorial: 162 Free Hill Rd, Gray, Tennessee 37615-3144 **Tel:** 1 423 477-1000.
Email: classicrock@wqut.com
Web site: http://www.wqut.com
Profile: WQUT-FM is a commercial station owned by Cumulus Media Inc. The format of the station is classic rock. WQUT-FM broadcasts to the Gray, TN area at 101.5 FM.
FM RADIO STATION

WQVE-FM 40585
Owner: Cumulus Media Inc.
Editorial: 1104 W Broad Ave, Albany, Georgia 31707-4340 **Tel:** 1 229 888-5000.
Web site: http://www.wqvealbany.com
Profile: WQVE-FM is a commercial station owned by Cumulus Media Inc. The format of the station is urban adult contemporary. WQVE-FM broadcasts to the Albany, GA area at 101.7 FM.
FM RADIO STATION

WQWK-AM 38032
Owner: FM Radio Licenses, LLC
Editorial: 2551 Park Center Blvd, State College, Pennsylvania 16801-3007 **Tel:** 1 814 237-9800.
Web site: http://www.foreverstatecollege.com/espn-1450/
Profile: WQWK-AM is a commercial station owned by FM Radio Licenses, LLC. The format of the station is sports. WQWK-AM broadcasts to the State College, PA area at 1450 AM.
AM RADIO STATION

WQWV-FM 43395
Owner: McGuire Broadcasting LLC
Editorial: 2 Alt Ave, Petersburg, West Virginia 26847-1758 **Tel:** 1 304 257-4432.
Email: v103@newcountryv103.com
Web site: http://www.newcountryv103.com
Profile: WQWV-FM is a commercial station owned by McGuire Broadcasting LLC. The format of the station is contemporary country music. WQWV-FM broadcasts to the Petersburg, WV area at 103.7 FM.
FM RADIO STATION

WQXA-FM 46366
Owner: Cumulus Media Inc.
Editorial: 2300 Vartan Way Ste 130, Harrisburg, Pennsylvania 17110-9794 **Tel:** 1 717 238-1041.
Web site: http://www.1057thex.com
Profile: WQXA-FM is a commercial station owned by Cumulus Media Inc. The format of the station is rock

alternative. WQXA-FM broadcasts to Elizabethtown, PA area at 105.7 FM.
FM RADIO STATION

WQXB-FM 46585
Owner: THE RAYANNA CORP
Editorial: 1348 Sunset Dr, Grenada, Mississippi 38901-4000 **Tel:** 1 662 226-1400.
Email: b100@b100country.net
Profile: WQXB-FM airs country music on 100.1 FM and broadcasts to the Grenada, MS area.
FM RADIO STATION

WQXC-FM 43778
Owner: Forum Communications Co.
Editorial: 706 E Allegan St, Otsego, Michigan 49078 **Tel:** 1 269 343-1717.
Email: news@wqxc.com
Web site: http://www.wqxc.com
Profile: WQXC-FM is a commercial station owned by Forum Communications Co. The format of the station is oldies music. WQXC-FM broadcasts to the Ostego, MI area at 100.9 FM.
FM RADIO STATION

WQXE-FM 40652
Owner: Skytower Communications Inc.
Editorial: 233 W Dixie Ave, Elizabethtown, Kentucky 42701-1560 **Tel:** 1 270 736-9830.
Email: quicksie@wqxe.com
Web site: http://www.wqxe.com
Profile: WQXE-FM is a commercial station owned by Skytower Communications Inc. The format is adult contemporary. WQXE-FM broadcasts to the Elizabethtown, KY area at 98.3 FM.
FM RADIO STATION

WQXI-AM 36668
Owner: Big League Broadcasting
Editorial: 210 Interstate North Cir SE, Atlanta, Georgia 30339-2206 **Tel:** 1 404 237-0079.
Email: zonewebmaster@790thezone.com
Web site: http://www.star941atlanta.com
Profile: WQXI-AM is a commercial station owned by Big League Broadcasting. The format of the station is sports. WQXI-AM broadcasts to the Atlanta area at 790 AM.
AM RADIO STATION

WQXK-FM 45488
Owner: Cumulus Media Inc.
Editorial: 4040 Simon Rd, Youngstown, Ohio 44512-1362 **Tel:** 1 330 783-1000.
Web site: http://www.k105country.com
Profile: WQXK-FM is a commercial station owned by Cumulus Media Inc. The format for the station is country music. WQXK-FM broadcasts to the Youngstown, OH area at 105.1 FM.
FM RADIO STATION

WQXL-AM 35617
Owner: Capital City Media, LLC
Editorial: 2440 Millwood Ave, Columbia, South Carolina 29205-1128 **Tel:** 1 803 563-8558.
Email: info@makethepointradio.com
Web site: http://makethepointradio.com
Profile: WQXL-AM is a commercial station owned by Capital City Media, LLC. and operated by Capital City Media, LLC. The format of the station is talk. WQXL-AM broadcasts to the Columbia, SC area at 1470 AM.
AM RADIO STATION

WQXM-AM 35191
Owner: Osvaldo Vega
Editorial: 1355 N Maple Ave, Bartow, Florida 33830-3024 **Tel:** 1 305 345-7177.
Email: programacion@lax1460.com
Web site: http://lax1460.com
Profile: WQXM-AM is a commercial station owned by Osvaldo Vega. The format of the station is Hispanic news talk and entertainment, and regional Mexican music. WQXM-AM broadcasts to the Tampa, FL area at 1460 AM.
AM RADIO STATION

WQXO-AM 38149
Owner: Great Lakes Radio Inc.
Editorial: 3060 Us Highway 41 W, Marquette, Michigan 49855-2293 **Tel:** 1 906 228-6800.
Email: contact@broadcasteverywhere.com
Web site: http://www.greatlakesradio.org
Profile: WQXO-AM is a commercial station owned by Great Lakes Radio Inc. The format for the station is oldies music. WQXO-AM broadcasts to the Marquette, MI area at 1400 AM.
AM RADIO STATION

WQXQ-FM 45679
Owner: Starlight Broadcasting Co.
Editorial: 314 S Main St, Hartford, Kentucky 42347-1129 **Tel:** 1 270 685-1235.
Profile: WQXQ-FM is a commercial station owned by Starlight Broadcasting Co. The format of the station is sports. WQXQ-FM's broadcasts to the Owensboro, KY area.
FM RADIO STATION

WQXR-FM 44315
Owner: New York Public Radio
Editorial: 160 Varick St, New York, New York 10013-1220 **Tel:** 1 646 829-4400.
Web site: http://www.wqxr.org
Profile: WQXR-FM is a non-commercial station owned by the New York Public Radio. The format of the station is classical music. WQXR-FM broadcasts to the New York City area at 105.9 FM.
FM RADIO STATION

WQXZ-FM 45073
Owner: Georgia Eagle Broadcasting Inc.
Editorial: 218 Eastman Highway, Hawkinsville, Georgia 31036 **Tel:** 1 478 892-9061.
Email: gebhawk@gmail.com
Profile: WQXZ-FM is a commercial station owned by Georgia Eagle Broadcasting Inc. The format of the station is oldies. WQXZ-FM broadcasts to the Hawkinsville, GA area at 103.9 FM.
FM RADIO STATION

WQYK-FM 46003
Owner: Beasley Broadcast Group
Editorial: 9721 Executive Center Dr N Ste 200, Saint Petersburg, Florida 33702-2439 **Tel:** 1 727 579-1925.
Web site: http://www.wqyk.com
Profile: WQYK-FM is a commercial station owned by Beasley Broadcast Group. The format of the station is classic country. WQYK-FM broadcasts to the St. Petersburg, FL area at 99.5 FM.
FM RADIO STATION

WQYX-FM 46343
Owner: First Media Radio LLC
Editorial: 801 E Dubois Ave, Du Bois, Pennsylvania 15801-3643 **Tel:** 1 814 371-8300.
Email: fmclearfield@yahoo.com
Web site: http://www.qyxfm.com
Profile: WQYX-FM is a commercial station owned by First Media Radio LLC. The format of the station is Top 40 music. WQYX-FM broadcasts to the Clearfield, PA, area at 93.1 FM.
FM RADIO STATION

WQYZ-FM 42174
Owner: iHeartMedia Inc.
Editorial: 286 Debuys Rd, Biloxi, Mississippi 39531-2611 **Tel:** 1 228 388-2323.
Web site: http://www.925fmthebeat.com/main.html
Profile: WQYZ-FM is a commercial station owned by iHeartMedia Inc. The format of the station is adult contemporary. WQYZ-FM broadcasts to the Biloxi, MS area at 92.5 FM.
FM RADIO STATION

WQZK-FM 45492
Owner: West Virginia Radio Corporation of the Alleganies
Editorial: 15 Industrial Blvd E, Cumberland, Maryland 21502 **Tel:** 1 301 759-1005.
Web site: http://www.941qzk.com
Profile: WQZK-FM is a commercial station owned by West Virginia Radio Corporation of the Alleganies. The format of the station is Top 40/CHR. WQZK-FM broadcasts to Keyser, WV area at 94.1 FM.
FM RADIO STATION

WQZL-FM 40432
Owner: Alpha Media
Editorial: 1361 Colony Dr, New Bern, North Carolina 28562-4129 **Tel:** 1 252 639-7900.
Web site: http://www.mywolfcountry.com/
Profile: WQZL-FM is a commercial station owned by Alpha Media. The format of the station is country. WQZL-FM broadcasts to the New Bern, NC area at 101.1 FM.
FM RADIO STATION

WQZQ-AM 35903
Owner: Cromwell Group Inc.(The)
Editorial: 1824 Murfreesboro Pike, Nashville, Tennessee 37217-3208 **Tel:** 1 615 399-1029.
Web site: http://www.thegamenashville.com
Profile: WQZQ-AM is commercial station owned by The Cromwell Group. The format of the station is classic hits. WQZQ-AM broadcasts in the Nashville, TN area at 830 AM.
AM RADIO STATION

WQZS-FM 235075
Owner: Wahl(Roger)
Editorial: 128 Hunsrick Rd, Meyersdale, Pennsylvania 15552-7247 **Tel:** 1 814 634-9111.
Profile: WQZS-FM is a commercial station owned by Roger Wahl. The station format of the station is oldies music. WQZS-FM broadcasts to the Meyersdale, PA area at 93.3 FM.
FM RADIO STATION

WQZX-FM 41365
Owner: Haynes Broadcasting
Editorial: 205 W Commerce St, Greenville, Alabama 36037 **Tel:** 1 334 382-6633.
Web site: http://www.q94.net
Profile: WQZX-FM is a commercial station owned by Haynes Broadcasting. The format of the station is contemporary country. WQZX-FM broadcasts to the Greenville, AL area at 94.3 FM.
FM RADIO STATION

WQZY-FM 45493
Owner: Dowdy Broadcasting, Inc.
Editorial: 807 Bellevue Ave, Dublin, Georgia 31021-4847 **Tel:** 1 478 272-4422.
Web site: http://www.wqzy.com
Profile: WQZY-FM is a commercial station owned by Dowdy Broadcasting, Inc. The format of the station is country music. WQZY-FM broadcasts to the Dublin, GA area at 95.9 FM.
FM RADIO STATION

WRAA-AM 38831
Owner: Hayden Hamilton Media Strategies
Editorial: 1057 US Highway 211 W, Luray, Virginia 22835-5245 **Tel:** 1 540 743-5167.
Profile: WRAA-AM is a commercial station owned by Hayden Hamilton Media Strategies. The format of the

station is country music. WRAA-AM broadcasts to the Harrisonburg, VA area at 1330 AM.
AM RADIO STATION

WRAB-AM 35619
Owner: Reed Broadcasting LLC
Editorial: 619 S Brindlee Mountain Pkwy, Arab, Alabama 35016-1502 **Tel:** 1 256 586-4123.
Email: wrab@otelco.net
Profile: WRAB-AM is a commercial station owned by Reed Broadcasting LLC. The format for the station is country and gospel. WRAB-AM broadcasts to the Huntsville, AL area at 1380 AM.
AM RADIO STATION

WRAC-FM 40654
Owner: DreamCatcher Communications Inc.
Editorial: 114 S Manchester St, West Union, Ohio 45693-1221 **Tel:** 1 937 544-9722.
Email: c103country@yahoo.com
Web site: http://www.c103.fm
Profile: WRAC-FM is a commercial station owned by DreamCatcher Communications Inc. The format of the station is contemporary country. WRAC-FM broadcasts to the West Union, OH area at 103.1 FM.
FM RADIO STATION

WRAD-AM 39119
Owner: Cumulus Media Inc.
Editorial: 7080 Lee Hwy, Fairlawn, Virginia 24141-8416 **Tel:** 1 540 731-6000.
Profile: WRAD-AM is a commercial station owned by Cumulus Media Inc. The format of the station is oldies. WRAD-AM broadcasts to the Fairlawn, VA area at 1460 AM.
AM RADIO STATION

WRAF-FM 41502
Owner: Toccoa Falls College
Editorial: 292 Old Clarksville Rd, Toccoa, Georgia 30577-6973 **Tel:** 1 800 251-8326.
Web site: http://www.wrafradio.org
Profile: WRAF-FM is a non-commercial station owned by Toccoa Falls College. The format of the station is religious featuring Christian teaching and gospel music. WRAF-FM broadcasts to the Toccoa, GA area at 90.9 FM.
FM RADIO STATION

WRAK-AM 38835
Owner: iHeartMedia Inc.
Editorial: 1559 W 4th St, Williamsport, Pennsylvania 17701-5650 **Tel:** 1 570 327-1400.
Email: wrak@iheartmedia.com
Web site: http://wrak.iheart.com
Profile: WRAK-AM is a commercial station owned by iHeartMedia Inc. The format of the station is news, sports and talk. WRAK-AM broadcasts to the Williamsport, PA area at 1400 AM.
AM RADIO STATION

WRAL-FM 40655
Owner: Capitol Broadcasting Company
Editorial: 3100 Highwoods Blvd, Ste 140, Raleigh, North Carolina 27604-1033 **Tel:** 1 919 890-6101.
Web site: http://www.wralfm.com
Profile: WRAL-FM is a commercial station owned by Capitol Broadcasting Company. The format of the station is adult contemporary. WRAL-FM broadcasts to the Raleigh, NC area at 101.5 FM.
FM RADIO STATION

WRAM-AM 38150
Owner: Prairie Communications LLP
Editorial: 55 Public Sq, Monmouth, Illinois 61462-1755 **Tel:** 1 309 734-9452.
Email: walknews@yahoo.com
Web site: http://www.1330wram.com
Profile: WRAM-AM is a commercial station owned by Prairie Communications LLP. The format of the station is classic country. WRAM-AM broadcasts to the Monmouth, IL area at 1330 AM.
AM RADIO STATION

WRAN-FM 43689
Owner: Randy Radio
Editorial: 918 E Park St, Taylorville, Illinois 62568-1916 **Tel:** 1 217 824-3395.
Email: wran983@randyradio.com
Web site: http://www.wranradio.com
Profile: WRAN-FM is a commercial station owned by Randy Radio. The format of the station is oldies and classic hits music from the 60s, 70s and 80s. WRAN-FM broadcasts to the Taylorville, IL area at a frequency of 98.3 FM.
FM RADIO STATION

WRAR-FM 45494
Owner: Real Media, Inc.
Editorial: 156 Prince St, Tappahannock, Virginia 22560 **Tel:** 1 804 443-4321.
Web site: http://www.wrarfm.com
Profile: WRAR-FM is a commercial station owned by Real Media, Inc. The format of the station is adult contemporary. WRAR-FM broadcasts to the Tappahannock, VA area at 105.5 FM.
FM RADIO STATION

WRAT-FM 40082
Owner: Beasley Broadcast Group
Editorial: 1731 Main St, Belmar, New Jersey 07719-3051 **Tel:** 1 732 681-3800.
Web site: http://www.wrat.com
Profile: WRAT-FM is a commercial station owned by Beasley Broadcast Group. The format of the station is rock music. WRAT-FM broadcasts to the Belmar, NJ area at 95.5 FM.
FM RADIO STATION

WRAW-AM 38152
Owner: iHeartMedia Inc.
Editorial: 1265 Perkiomen Ave, Reading, Pennsylvania 19602-1366 **Tel:** 1 610 376-6671.
Email: webmaster@wrfy.com
Web site: http://www.1340.iheart.com
Profile: WRAW-AM is a commercial station owned by iHeartMedia Inc. The format of the station is oldies. WRAW-AM broadcasts to the Reading, PA area at 1340 AM.
AM RADIO STATION

WRAY-AM 38153
Owner: Princeton Broadcasting Co.
Editorial: 1900 W Broadway St, Princeton, Indiana 47670 **Tel:** 1 812 386-1250.
Email: wray@wrayradio.com
Web site: http://www.wrayradio.com
Profile: WRAY-AM is a commercial station owned by Princeton Broadcasting Co. The format of the station is news, talk, and sports. WRAY-AM broadcasts to the Princeton, IN area at 1250 AM.
AM RADIO STATION

WRAY-FM 45495
Owner: Princeton Broadcasting Co.
Editorial: 1900 W Broadway St, Princeton, Indiana 47670 **Tel:** 1 812 386-1250.
Email: wray@wrayradio.com
Web site: http://www.wrayradio.com
Profile: WRAY-FM is a commercial station owned by Princeton Broadcasting Co. The format of the station is contemporary country music. WRAY-FM broadcasts to the Princeton, IN area at 98.1 FM.
FM RADIO STATION

WRAZ-FM 42218
Owner: Spanish Broadcasting System
Tel: 1 954 885-7200.
Web site: http://lanuevafm.net/cms
Profile: WRAZ-FM is a commercial station owned by Spanish Broadcasting System. The format of the station is Spanish Contemporary Christian music. WRAZ-FM broadcasts to the Key Largo, FL and the Greater Miami area at 106.3 FM.
FM RADIO STATION

WRBA-FM 41389
Owner: Powell Broadcasting Company, LLC
Editorial: 118 Gwyn Dr, Panama City Beach, Florida 32408-5854 **Tel:** 1 850 234-8858.
Web site: http://www.959online.com
Profile: WRBA-FM is a commercial station owned by Powell Broadcasting Company, LLC. The format of the station is classic rock music. The station broadcasts to the Panama City, FL area at 95.9 FM.
FM RADIO STATION

WRBE-FM 46602
Owner: JDL Corporation
Editorial: 3276 Highway 198 W, Lucedale, Mississippi 39452-7914 **Tel:** 1 601 947-8151.
Web site: http://wrbeamfm.com
Profile: WRBE-FM is a commercial station owned by JDL Corporation. The format for the station is gospel and country. WRBE-FM broadcasts to the Lucedale, MS area at 106.9 FM.
FM RADIO STATION

WRBF-FM 745273
Owner: Toole (Howard C.)
Editorial: 20 John Davenport Dr Nw, Rome, Georgia 30165-2536 **Tel:** 1 706 291-9496.
Web site: http://www.1049therebel.com
Profile: WRBF-FM is a commercial station owned by Toole (Howard C.). The format of the station is classic rock. WRBF-FM broadcasts to the Rome, GA area at a frequency of 104.9 FM.
FM RADIO STATION

WRBG-FM 42200
Owner: Seven Mountains Media, LLC
Editorial: 450 Route 204, Selinsgrove, Pennsylvania 17870-7975 **Tel:** 1 570 374-8819.
Email: bigcountryrequest@hotmail.com
Web site: http://b983.com
Profile: WRBG-FM is a commercial station owned by Seven Mountains Media, LLC. The format of the station is contemporary country music. WRBG-FM broadcasts to the Selinsgrove, PA area at 98.3 FM.
FM RADIO STATION

WRBH-FM 41686
Owner: Radio for the Blind and Print Handicapped
Editorial: 3606 Magazine St, New Orleans, Louisiana 70115-2545 **Tel:** 1 504 899-1144.
Web site: http://www.wrbh.org
Profile: WRBH-FM is a non-commercial station owned by Radio for the Blind and Print Handicapped. The format of the station is news and talk. WRBH-FM broadcasts to the New Orleans area at 88.3 FM.
FM RADIO STATION

WRBI-FM 40657
Owner: Lesson Media, LLC
Editorial: 133 S Main St, Batesville, Indiana 47006-1344 **Tel:** 1 812 934-5111.
Email: wrbi@wrbiradio.com
Web site: http://www.wrbiradio.com
Profile: WRBI-FM is a commercial station owned by Lesson Media, LLC. The format of the station is country music. WRBI-FM broadcasts to the Batesville, IN area at 103.9 FM.
FM RADIO STATION

WRBJ-FM 45504
Owner: Roberts Broadcasting Co.
Editorial: 745 N State St, Jackson, Mississippi 39202-3006 **Tel:** 1 601 974-5700.
Web site: http://www.thebeatofthecapital.com
Profile: WRBJ-FM is a commercial station owned by Roberts Broadcasting Co. The format of the station is urban contemporary. WRBJ-FM broadcasts to the Jackson, MS area at 97.7 FM.
FM RADIO STATION

WRBN-FM 46511
Owner: Georgia-Carolina Radiocasting Companies LLC
Editorial: 745 N Main St, Clayton, Georgia 30525-4257 **Tel:** 1 706 782-4251.
Email: sky104wrbn@gmail.com
Web site: http://www.sky104.com
Profile: WRBN-FM is a commercial station owned by Georgia-Carolina Radiocasting Companies LLC. The format of the station is adult contemporary. WRBN-FM broadcasts to the Clayton, GA area at 104.1 FM.
FM RADIO STATION

WRBO-FM 41398
Owner: Cumulus Media Inc.
Editorial: 5629 Murray Ave, Memphis, Tennessee 38119-3831 **Tel:** 1 901 682-1106.
Web site: http://www.1035memphis.com
Profile: WRBO-FM is a commercial station owned by Cumulus Media Inc. The format of the station is R&B oldies. WRBO-FM broadcasts to the Memphis, TN area at 103.5 FM.
FM RADIO STATION

WRBQ-FM 44290
Owner: Beasley Broadcast Group
Editorial: 9721 Executive Center Dr N Ste 200, Saint Petersburg, Florida 33702-2439 **Tel:** 1 727 579-1925.
Web site: http://www.myq105.com
Profile: WRBQ-FM is a commercial station owned by Beasley Broadcast Group. The format of the station is classic hits music. WRBQ-FM broadcasts throughout the Tampa Bay, FL area at 104.7 FM.
FM RADIO STATION

WRBR-FM 40920
Owner: Talking Stick Communications
Editorial: 237 W Edison Rd Ste 200, Mishawaka, Indiana 46545-3103 **Tel:** 1 574 258-5483.
Web site: http://www.wrbr.com
Profile: WRBR-FM is a commercial station owned by Talking Stick Communications. The format for the station is rock. WRBR-FM broadcasts to the South Bend, IN area at 103.9 FM.
FM RADIO STATION

WRBS-AM 39456
Owner: Peter and John Radio Fellowship, Inc.
Editorial: 3500 Commerce Dr, Baltimore, Maryland 21227-1670 **Tel:** 1 410 247-4100.
Email: info@951shinefm.com
Web site: http://www.951shinefm.com
Profile: WRBS-AM is a commercial station owned by Peter and John Radio Fellowship, Inc. The format of the station is religious programming and talk. WRBS-AM broadcasts to the Baltimore area at 1230 AM.
AM RADIO STATION

WRBS-FM 40658
Owner: Peter and John Radio Fellowship, Inc.
Editorial: 3500 Commerce Dr, Baltimore, Maryland 21227-1670 **Tel:** 1 410 247-4100.
Web site: http://www.951shinefm.com
Profile: WRBS-FM is a commercial station owned by Peter and John Radio Fellowship, Inc. The format of the station is contemporary Christian music and religious talk. WRBS-FM broadcasts to Baltimore area at 95.1 FM.
FM RADIO STATION

WRBT-FM 45198
Owner: iHeartMedia Inc.
Editorial: 600 Corporate Cir, Harrisburg, Pennsylvania 17110-9787 **Tel:** 1 717 540-8800.
Web site: http://www.bobradio.com
Profile: WRBT-FM is a commercial station owned by iHeartMedia Inc. The format of the station is contemporary country. WRBT-FM broadcasts to the Harrisburg, PA area at 94.9 FM.
FM RADIO STATION

WRBV-FM 42898
Owner: iHeartMedia Inc.
Editorial: 7080 Industrial Hwy, Macon, Georgia 31216-7538 **Tel:** 1 478 781-1063.
Web site: http://v1017.iheart.com
Profile: WRBV-FM is a commercial station owned by iHeartMedia Inc. The format of the station is urban adult contemporary. WRBV-FM broadcasts to the Macon, GA area at 101.7 FM.
FM RADIO STATION

WRBX-FM 46655
Owner: Register(William Keith)
Editorial: 125 Friar Tuck Circle, Reidsville, Georgia 30453 **Tel:** 1 912 557-4140.
Email: wrbxwtnl@windstream.net
Web site: http://www.wrbx.org
Profile: WRBX-FM is a commercial station owned by William Keith Register. The format for the station is Christian talk and Southern gospel. WRBX-FM broadcasts to the Reidsville, GA area at 104.1 FM.
FM RADIO STATION

WRBZ-AM 35173
Owner: Contemporary Media, Inc.
Editorial: 2305 Upper Wetumpka Rd, Montgomery, Alabama 36107-1345 **Tel:** 1 334 834-3710.
Web site: http://www.wrbzradio.com/
Profile: WRBZ-AM is a commercial station owned by Contemporary Media, Inc. The format of the station is classic hits. WRBZ-AM broadcasts to the Montgomery, AL area at 1250 AM.
AM RADIO STATION

WRCA-AM 35278
Owner: Beasley Broadcast Group
Editorial: 552 Massachusetts Ave, Ste 201, Cambridge, Massachusetts 02139-4088
Tel: 1 617 492-3300.
Email: wrca1330@aol.com
Web site: http://www.1330wrca.com
Profile: WRCA-AM is a commercial station owned by Beasley Broadcast Group. The format of the station is Hispanic variety. WRCA-AM broadcasts to the Cambridge, MA area at 1330 AM.
AM RADIO STATION

WRCD-FM 46896
Owner: Stephens Media Group Massena, LLC
Editorial: 2155 State Highway 420, Massena, New York 13662 **Tel:** 1 315 769-3333.
Web site: http://www.1015thefox.com
Profile: WRCD-FM is a commercial station owned by Stephens Media Group Massena, LLC. The format of the station is classic rock. WRCD-FM broadcasts to the Massena, NY area at 101.5 FM.
FM RADIO STATION

WRCE-AM 39440
Owner: Community Broadcasters, LLC
Editorial: 2205 College Ave, Elmira, New York 14903-1201 **Tel:** 1 607 732-4400.
Web site: http://www.cbelmira.com/classiccountry/
Profile: WRCE-AM is a commercial station owned by Community Broadcasters, LLC. The format of the station is classic country. WRCE-AM broadcasts to the Elmira, NY area at 1490 AM.
AM RADIO STATION

WRCG-AM 38326
Owner: PMB Broadcasting, LLC
Editorial: 1820 Wynnton Rd, Columbus, Georgia 31906-2930 **Tel:** 1 706 327-1217.
Profile: WRCG-AM is a commercial station owned by PMB Broadcasting, LLC. The format of the station is Southern gospel. WRCG-AM broadcasts to the Columbus, GA in the 1420 AM.
AM RADIO STATION

WRCG-FM 760919
Owner: PMB Broadcasting, LLC
Editorial: 1820 Wynnton Rd, Columbus, Georgia 31906-2930 **Tel:** 1 706 327-1217.
Web site: http://www.1069rocks.com
Profile: WRCG-FM (W295AY) is a broadcast translator owned by PMB Broadcasting, LLC. The format of the station is modern rock. WRCG-FM broadcasts to the Columbus, GA area at a frequency of 106.9 FM.
FM RADIO STATION

WRCH-FM 43040
Owner: CBS Radio
Editorial: 10 Executive Dr, Farmington, Connecticut 06032-2841 **Tel:** 1 860 677-6700.
Web site: http://wrch.cbslocal.com
Profile: WRCH-FM is a commercial station owned by CBS Radio. The format of the station is Lite Rock/Lite AC music. WRCH-FM broadcasts to the Hartford-New Haven, CT area at 100.5 FM.
FM RADIO STATION

WRCI-FM 38019
Owner: Impact Radio, LLC
Editorial: 59750 Constantine Rd, Three Rivers, Michigan 49093-9303 **Tel:** 1 269 278-1815.
Email: info@wlkm.com
Web site: http://www.wrciradio.com
Profile: WRCI-FM is a commercial station owned by Impact Radio, LLC. The format of the station is classic country hits. WRCI-FM broadcasts to the Grand Rapids, MI area at 97.1.
FM RADIO STATION

WRCK-AM 39205
Owner: Good Guys Broadcasting
Editorial: 185 Genesee St Ste 1601, Utica, New York 13501-2110 **Tel:** 1 315 734-9245.
Web site: http://www.1550wutq.com
Profile: WRCK-AM is a commercial station owned by Good Guys Broadcasting. The format of the station is sports. WRCK-AM broadcasts to the Utica, NY area at 1480 AM.
AM RADIO STATION

WRCL-FM 81207
Owner: Townsquare Media, LLC
Editorial: 3338 E Bristol Rd, Burton, Michigan 48529
Tel: 1 810 743-1080.
Web site: http://www.club937.com
Profile: WRCL-FM is a commercial station owned by Townsquare Media, LLC. The format of the station is urban contemporary. WRCL-FM broadcasts to the Bristol, MI area at 93.7 FM.
FM RADIO STATION

WRCN-FM 45497
Owner: JVC Broadcasting Inc.
Editorial: 3075 Veterans Memorial Hwy, Ronkonkoma, New York 11779-7667 **Tel:** 1 631 648-2500.
Web site: http://linewsradio.com
Profile: WRCN-FM is a commercial station owned by JVC Broadcasting Inc. The format of the station is news and talk. WRCN-FM broadcasts to the Medford, NY area at 103.9 FM.
FM RADIO STATION

WRCO-AM 38154
Owner: Fruit Broadcasting LLC
Editorial: 1900 Highway 14 E., Richland Center, Wisconsin 53581 **Tel:** 1 608 647-2111.
Email: wrco@wrco.com
Web site: http://www.wrco.com
Profile: WRCO-AM is a commercial station owned by Fruit Broadcasting LLC. The format for the station is adult standards. WRCO-AM broadcasts to the Madison, WI area at 1450 AM.
AM RADIO STATION

WRCO-FM 45498
Owner: Fruit Broadcasting LLC
Editorial: 2111 Bohmann Dr, Richland Center, Wisconsin 53581 **Tel:** 1 608 647-2111.
Email: wrconews@wrco.com
Web site: http://www.wrco.com
Profile: WRCO-FM is a commercial station owned by Fruit Broadcasting LLC. The format for the station is country. WRCO-FM broadcasts to the Madison, WI area at 100.9 FM.
FM RADIO STATION

WRCQ-FM 41213
Owner: Cumulus Media Inc.
Editorial: 1009 Drayton Rd, Fayetteville, North Carolina 28303-3887 **Tel:** 1 910 864-5222.
Web site: http://www.rock103rocks.com
Profile: WRCQ-FM is a commercial station owned by Cumulus Media Inc. The format of the station is rock music. WRCQ-FM broadcasts to the Fayetteville, NC area at 103.5 FM.
FM RADIO STATION

WRCS-AM 39206
Owner: WRCS 970 AM Inc.
Editorial: 443 Nc Highway 42 W, Ahoskie, North Carolina 27910 **Tel:** 1 252 332-3101.
Email: wrcs@embarqmail.com
Profile: WRCS-AM is a commercial station owned by WRCS 970 AM Inc. The format of the station is gospel music. WRCS-AM broadcasts to Ahoskie, NC at 970 AM.
AM RADIO STATION

WRCT-FM 134104
Owner: WRCT Radio, Inc.
Editorial: 5000 Forbes Ave, 1 Wrct Plaza, Pittsburgh, Pennsylvania 15213-3815 **Tel:** 1 412 621-0728.
Email: info@wrct.org
Web site: http://www.wrct.org
Profile: WRCT-FM is a non-commercial station owned by WRCT Radio, Inc. The format of the station is a college variety. WRCT-FM broadcasts to the Pittsburgh area at 88.3 FM.
FM RADIO STATION

WRCV-FM 45245
Owner: NRG Media LLC
Editorial: 1460 S College Ave, Dixon, Illinois 61021
Tel: 1 815 288-3341.
Web site: http://www.rivercountry1017.com
Profile: WRCV-FM is a commercial station owned by NRG Media LLC. The format of the station is country music. WRCV-FM broadcasts to Dixon, IL at 101.7 FM.
FM RADIO STATION

WRDA-FM 62088
Owner: iHeartMedia Inc.
Editorial: 1819 Peachtree Rd NE Ste 700, Atlanta, Georgia 30309-1849 **Tel:** 1 404 607-1336.
Web site: http://www.radio1057.com
Profile: WRDA-FM is a commercial station owned by iHeartMedia Inc. The format of the station is alternative rock. WRDA-FM broadcasts to the greater Atlanta area at 105.7 FM.
FM RADIO STATION

WRDB-AM 38155
Owner: Magnum Radio Group
Editorial: E 5680-A Highway 33 West, Reedsburg, Wisconsin 53959 **Tel:** 1 608 524-1400.
Email: info@magnumbroadcasting.com
Web site: http://www.wrdb.com
Profile: WRDB-AM is a commercial station owned by Magnum Radio Group. The format of the station is adult standards. WRDB-AM broadcasts to the Reedsburg, WI area at 1400 AM.
AM RADIO STATION

WRDF-FM 41696
Owner: Adams Radio Group
Editorial: 9604 Coldwater Rd Ste 201, Fort Wayne, Indiana 46825-2096 **Tel:** 1 260 436-9598.
Email: info@redeemerradio.com
Web site: http://www.redeemerradio.com
Profile: WRDF-FM is a commercial station owned by Adams Radio Group. The format of the station is Catholic radio. WRDF-FM broadcasts to the Fort Wayne, IN area at 106.3 FM.
FM RADIO STATION

WRDL-FM 40663
Owner: Ashland College
Editorial: 401 College Ave, Ashland, Ohio 44805-3702
Tel: 1 419 289-5157.
Email: wrdl@ashland.edu
Web site: http://www.wrdlfm.com
Profile: WRDL-FM is a non-commercial college station owned by Ashland College. The format of the station is Top 40/CHR. WRDL-FM broadcasts to the Ashland, OH area at 88.9 FM.
FM RADIO STATION

WRDO-FM 41855
Owner: Broadcast South, LLC
Editorial: 601 W Roanoke Dr, Fitzgerald, Georgia 31750-3633 **Tel:** 1 229 423-2077.
Web site: http://969wrdo.com/
Profile: WRDO-FM is a commercial station owned by Broadcast South, LLC. The format of the station is Classic Hits. WRDO-FM broadcasts to the Douglas, GA area at 96.9 FM.
FM RADIO STATION

WRDR-FM 155848
Owner: Bridgelight Corp.
Editorial: 127 White Oak Ln, Old Bridge, New Jersey 08857-1945 **Tel:** 1 732 901-9953.
Email: info@bridgefm.org
Web site: http://www.bridgefm.org
Profile: WRDR-FM is a non-commercial station owned by Bridgelight Corp. The format of the station is religious talk and music. WRDR-FM broadcasts to the Howell, NJ area at 89.7 FM.
FM RADIO STATION

WRDT-AM 36559
Owner: Crawford Broadcasting Co.
Editorial: 12300 Radio Pl, Detroit, Michigan 48228-1029 **Tel:** 1 313 272-3434.
Email: station@wmuz.com
Web site: http://www.wrdt560.com
Profile: WRDT-AM is commercial station owned by Crawford Broadcasting Co. The format of the station is Christian programming. WRDT-AM broadcasts to the Detroit area at 560 AM.
AM RADIO STATION

WRDU-FM 40771
Owner: iHeartMedia Inc.
Editorial: 3100 Smoketree Ct, Raleigh, North Carolina 27604-1086 **Tel:** 1 919 878-1500.
Web site: http://wrdu.iheart.com
Profile: WRDU-FM is a commercial station owned by iHeartMedia Inc. The format of the station is classic rock. WRDU-FM broadcasts to the Raleigh, NC area at 100.7 FM.
FM RADIO STATION

WRDW-AM 235076
Owner: Beasley Broadcast Group
Editorial: 4051 Jimmie Dyess Pkwy, Augusta, Georgia 30909 **Tel:** 1 706 396-7000.
Email: ab@wrdwam.com
Web site: http://www.wrdwam.com
Profile: WRDW-AM is a commercial station owned by Beasley Broadcast Group. The format of the station is news, talk, and sports. WRDW-AM broadcasts to the Martinez, GA area at 1630 AM.
AM RADIO STATION

WRDX-FM 45131
Owner: iHeartMedia Inc.
Editorial: 920 W Basin Rd, New Castle, Delaware 19720-1010 **Tel:** 1 302 395-9800.
Web site: http://929tomfm.iheart.com
Profile: WRDX-FM is a commercial station owned by iHeartMedia Inc. The format of the station is adult hits. WRDX-FM broadcasts to the Dover, DE area at 92.9 FM.
FM RADIO STATION

WREB-FM 40409
Owner: Original Company Inc.(The)
Editorial: 2468 W County Road 25 N, Greencastle, Indiana 46135 **Tel:** 1 765 653-9717.
Email: wreb@originalcompany.com
Web site: http://www.wrebfm.com
Profile: WREB-FM is a commercial station owned by The Original Company Inc. The format of the station is adult contemporary. WREB-FM broadcasts to the Indianapolis area at 94.3 FM.
FM RADIO STATION

WREC-AM 38620
Owner: iHeartMedia Inc.
Editorial: 2650 Thousand Oaks Blvd Ste 4100, Memphis, Tennessee 38118-2451 **Tel:** 1 901 259-1300.
Email: news@600wrec.com
Web site: http://www.600wrec.com
Profile: WREC-AM is a commercial station owned by iHeartMedia Inc. The format of the station is news, sports and talk. WREC-AM broadcasts to the Memphis, TN, area at 600 AM.
AM RADIO STATION

WRED-AM 235157
Owner: Atlantic Coast Radio LLC
Editorial: 779 Warren Ave, Portland, Maine 04103-1007 **Tel:** 1 207 773-9695.
Web site: http://www.thebigjab.com
Profile: WRED-AM is a commercial station owned by Atlantic Coast Radio LLC. The format of the station is sports. WRED-AM broadcasts to the Portland, ME area at 1440 AM.
AM RADIO STATION

WREE-FM 40431
Owner: Saga Communications
Editorial: 2603 W Bradley Ave, Champaign, Illinois
61821-1823 Tel: 1 217 352-4141.
Web site: http://rewind925.com
Profile: WREE-FM is a commercial station owned by
Saga Communications (d.b.a. Illini Radio Group). The
format of the station is classic hits. WREE-FM
broadcasts to the Champaign, IL area at 92.5 FM.
FM RADIO STATION

WREJ-AM 37122
Owner: Davidson Media Group
Editorial: 8100 Three Chopt Rd Rm 221, Richmond,
Virginia 23229-4800 Tel: 1 804 377-0990.
Email: rejoice990rva@gmail.com
Web site: http://rejoice990.com/
Profile: WREJ-AM is a commercial station. The
format of the station is gospel. WREJ-AM broadcasts
to the Richmond, VA area at 990 AM.
AM RADIO STATION

WREK-FM 40666
Owner: Georgia Institute of Technology
Editorial: 350 Ferst Dr. NW, Suite 2224, Atlanta,
Georgia 30332-0630 Tel: 1 404 894-2468.
Email: general.manager@wrek.org
Web site: http://www.wrek.org
Profile: WREK-FM is a non-commercial station
owned by the Georgia Institute of Technology. The
format of the station is college variety. WREK-FM
broadcasts in the Atlanta area at 91.1 FM.
FM RADIO STATION

WREL-AM 38157
Owner: First Media Radio LLC
Editorial: 392 E Midland Trl, Lexington, Virginia
24450-5703 Tel: 1 540 463-2161.
Email: 96.7@3wzfm.com
Web site: http://www.wrel.com
Profile: WREL-AM is a commercial station owned by
First Media Radio LLC. The format of the station is
news, sports and talk. WREL-AM broadcasts to the
Lexington, VA area at 1450 AM.
AM RADIO STATION

WREO-FM 45501
Owner: Media One Group
Editorial: 9179 Mentor Ave, Mentor, Ohio 44060-6398
Tel: 1 440 993-2126.
Web site: http://www.mix971fm.com
Profile: WREO-FM is a commercial station owned by
Media One Group. The format of the station is adult
contemporary music. WREO-FM broadcasts to the
Cleveland area at 97. 1 FM.
FM RADIO STATION

WRES-FM 155986
Owner: Empowerment Resource Center of Asheville/
Buncombe County
Editorial: 91 Patton Ave, Asheville, North Carolina
28801-3316 Tel: 1 828 281-3065.
Email: elderhayes.wresfm@gmail.com
Web site: http://www.wresfm.com
Profile: WRES-FM is a non-commercial station
owned by Empowerment Resource Center of
Asheville/Buncombe County. The format of the
station is urban contemporary. WRES-FM broadcasts
to the Asheville, NC area at 100.7 FM.
FM RADIO STATION

WREW-FM 438138
Owner: Hubbard Broadcasting, Inc.
Editorial: 2060 Reading Rd, Cincinnati, Ohio 45202-
1454 Tel: 1 513 699-5959.
Web site: http://www.949cincinnati.com
Profile: WREW-FM is a commercial station owned by
Hubbard Broadcasting, Inc. The format of the station
is adult hits. WREW-FM broadcasts to the Cincinnati
area at 94.9 FM.
FM RADIO STATION

WREY-AM 36498
Owner: Guadalupe Gonzalez
Editorial: 2619 E Lake St, Minneapolis, Minnesota
55406-1925 Tel: 1 612 729-3776.
Web site: http://www.radiorey630am.com
Profile: WREY-AM is a commercial station owned by
Guadalupe Gonzalez. The format of the station is
regional Mexican. WREY-AM broadcasts to the
Minneapolis area at 630 AM.
AM RADIO STATION

WREZ-FM 46816
Owner: Withers Broadcasting of Paducah, LLC
Editorial: 1700 N 8th St, Paducah, Kentucky 42001-
1752 Tel: 1 270 538-5251.
Email: paducantradio@withersradio.net
Web site: http://www.1055thecat.com
Profile: WREZ-FM is a commercial station owned by
Withers Broadcasting of Paducah, LLC. The format of
the station is Top 40/CHR. WREZ-FM broadcasts to
the Paducah, KY area at 105.5 FM.
FM RADIO STATION

WRFA-FM 563337
Owner: Arts Council for Chautauqua County, Inc.
Editorial: 116 E 3rd St, Jamestown, New York 14701-
5402 Tel: 1 716 664-2465.
Email: wrfa@reglenna.com
Web site: http://www.wrfalp.com
Profile: WRFA-FM is a non-commercial station
owned by Arts Council for Chautauqua County, Inc.
The format of the station is variety. WRFA-FM
broadcasts to the Jamestown, NY area at 107.9 FM.
FM RADIO STATION

WRFC-AM 38763
Owner: Cox Media Group, Inc.
Editorial: 1010 Tower Pl, Watkinsville, Georgia 30677-
7752 Tel: 1 706 549-6222.
Email: 960theref@coxradio.com
Web site: http://www.960theref.com
Profile: WRFC-AM is a commercial station owned by
Cox Media Group, Inc. The format of the station is
sports. WRFC-AM broadcasts to the Athens, GA area
at 960 AM.
AM RADIO STATION

WRFD-AM 36422
Owner: Salem Media Group, Inc.
Editorial: 8101 N High St Ste 360, Columbus, Ohio
43235-1442 Tel: 1 614 885-0880.
Email: mail@wrfd.com
Web site: http://thewordcolumbus.com
Profile: WRFD-AM is a commercial station owned by
Salem Media Group, Inc. The format of the station is
religious, talk and agricultural programming. WRFD-
AM broadcasts to the Columbus, OH area at 880 AM.
AM RADIO STATION

WRFF-FM 42032
Owner: iHeartMedia Inc.
Editorial: 111 Presidential Blvd Ste 100, Bala
Cynwyd, Pennsylvania 19004-1009 Tel: 1 610 784-
3333.
Email: radio1045fm@gmail.com
Web site: http://radio1045.iheart.com
Profile: WRFF-FM is a commercial station owned by
iHeartMedia Inc. The format of the station is rock
alternative. WRFF-FM broadcasts to the Philadelphia
area at 104.5 FM.
FM RADIO STATION

WRFG-FM 40668
Owner: Radio Free Georgia Broadcasting Foundation
Editorial: 1083 Austin Ave NE Ste 107, Atlanta,
Georgia 30307-1940 Tel: 1 404 523-3471.
Email: office@wrfg.org
Web site: http://www.wrfg.org
Profile: WRFG-FM is a non-commercial station
owned by the Radio Free Georgia Broadcasting
Foundation. The format of the station is variety.
WRFG-FM broadcasts to the Atlanta area at 89.3 FM.
FM RADIO STATION

WRFK-FM 45430
Owner: Great Eastern Radio, LLC
Editorial: 41 Jacques St, Barre, Vermont 05641-5320
Tel: 1 802 476-4168.
Web site: http://www.1071frankfm.com
Profile: WRFK-FM is a commercial station owned by
Great Eastern Radio, LLC. The format of the station is
adult hits. WRFK-FM broadcasts to the Barre, VT
area at 107.1 FM.
FM RADIO STATION

WRFM-AM 543347
Owner: Indiana Community Radio
Editorial: 15 Wood St, Greenfield, Indiana 46140-
2162 Tel: 1 317 467-1064.
Email: wjcfradio@aol.com
AM RADIO STATION

WRFQ-FM 42149
Owner: iHeartMedia Inc.
Editorial: 950 Houston Northcutt Blvd Ste 201, Mount
Pleasant, South Carolina 29464-5645 Tel: 1 843 884-
2534.
Web site: http://q1045.iheart.com
Profile: WPRFQ-FM is a commercial station owned
by iHeartMedia Inc. The format of the station is
classic rock. WRFQ-FM broadcasts to the
Charleston, SC area at 104.5 FM.
FM RADIO STATION

WRFX-FM 40670
Owner: iHeartMedia Inc.
Editorial: 801 Woodrdg Ctr Dr, Charlotte, North
Carolina 28217-1908 Tel: 1 704 714-9444.
Web site: http://www.wrfx.com
Profile: WRFX-FM is a commercial station owned by
iHeartMedia Inc. The format of the station is classic
rock. WRFX-FM broadcasts to the Charlotte, NC area
at 99.7 FM.
FM RADIO STATION

WRFY-FM 45503
Owner: iHeartMedia Inc.
Editorial: 1265 Perkiomen Ave, Reading,
Pennsylvania 19602-1366 Tel: 1 610 376-6671.
Web site: http://www.y102reading.com
Profile: WRFY-FM is a commercial station owned by
iHeartMedia Inc. The format of the station is adult
hits. WRFY-FM broadcasts to the Reading, PA area
at 102.5 FM.
FM RADIO STATION

WRGA-AM 38158
Owner: Rome Radio Partners
Editorial: 20 John Davenport Dr NW, Rome, Georgia
30165-2536 Tel: 1 706 291-9496.
Email: news@south107.com
Web site: http://wrganews.com
Profile: WRGA-AM is a commercial station owned by
Rome Radio Partners. The format of the station is
news and talk. WRGA-AM broadcasts to the Atlanta
area at 1470 AM.
AM RADIO STATION

WRGC-AM 35625
Owner: Five Forty Broadcasting Company LLC
Editorial: 1846 Skyland Dr, Sylva, North Carolina
28779-8008 Tel: 1 828 586-2221.
Email: info@wrgc.com
Web site: http://wrgc.com
Profile: WRGC-AM is a commercial station owned by
Five Forty Broadcasting Company LLC. The format
for the station is a variety of soft rock, adult
contemporary and country. WRGC-AM broadcasts to
the Sylva, NC area at 540 AM.
AM RADIO STATION

WRGM-AM 35626
Owner: Johnny Appleseed Broadcasting Co. Inc.
Editorial: 2900 Park Ave W, Mansfield, Ohio 44906
Tel: 1 419 529-5900.
Email: newsroom@wmfd.com
Web site: http://www.wrgm.com
Profile: WRGM-AM is a commercial station owned
by Johnny Appleseed Broadcasting Co. Inc. The
format of the station is sports. WRGM-AM
broadcasts to the Cleveland area at 1440 AM.
AM RADIO STATION

WRGN-FM 41384
Owner: Updyke(Burl)
Editorial: 2457 State Route 118, Hunlock Creek,
Pennsylvania 18621 Tel: 1 570 477-3688.
Email: wrgn@epix.net
Web site: http://www.wrgn.com
Profile: WRGN-FM is a non-commercial station
owned by Burl Updyke. The format of the station is
Christian and religious music. WRGN-FM broadcasts
to the Hunlock Creek, PA area at 88.1 FM.
FM RADIO STATION

WRGR-FM 43259
Owner: Mountain Communications
Editorial: 159 Santanoni Ave, Saranac Lake, New
York 12983-2478 Tel: 1 518 891-1544.
Email: news@wnbz.com
Web site: http://wnbz.com
Profile: WRGR-FM is a commercial station owned by
Mountain Communications. The format of the station
is classic rock music. WRGR-FM broadcasts to the
Tupper Lake, NY area at 102.1 FM.
FM RADIO STATION

WRGS-AM 37162
Owner: Debbie Beal
Editorial: 211 Burem Rd, Rogersville, Tennessee
37857-7900 Tel: 1 423 272-2628.
Email: stationmanager@wrgsradio.com
Web site: http://www.wrgsradio.com
Profile: WRGS-AM is a commercial station owned by
Philip Beal. The format of the station is country and
gospel music. WRGS-AM broadcasts to the
Rogersville, TN area at 1370 AM. PSA and
community event submissions should be sent to the
main station's e-mail, or preferably through the online
contact form: http://www.wrgsradio.com/submit-
to.html.
AM RADIO STATION

WRGV-FM 40598
Owner: iHeartMedia Inc.
Editorial: 6485 Pensacola Blvd, Pensacola, Florida
32505-1701 Tel: 1 850 473-0400.
Email: pensacolapromotions@iheartmedia.com
Web site: http://www.1073now.com
Profile: WRGV-FM is a commercial station owned by
iHeartMedia Inc. The format for the station is Top 40/
CHR. WRGV-FM broadcasts to Pensacola, FL area at
103.7 FM.
FM RADIO STATION

WRGZ-FM 40525
Owner: Midwestern Broadcasting Co.
Editorial: 123 Prentiss St, Alpena, Michigan 49707-
2831 Tel: 1 989 354-8400.
Email: watz@watz.com
Web site: http://www.watz.com
Profile: WRGZ-FM is a commercial station owned by
Midwest Broadcasting Co. The format of the station
is contemporary country. WRGZ-FM broadcasts to
the Alpena, MI area at 96.7 FM.
FM RADIO STATION

WRHA-AM 35765
Owner: Beverly Broadcasting Company, LLC
Tel: 1 423 285-6441.
Email: comments@rheacountryradio.com
Web site: http://www.rheacountryradio.com
Profile: WRHA-AM is a commercial station owned by
Beverly Broadcasting Company, LLC. The format of
the station is classic hits. WRHA-AM broadcasts to
the Spring City, TN area at 970 AM.
AM RADIO STATION

WRHC-AM 519738
Owner: Fenix Broadcasting Corp.
Editorial: 330 SW 27th Ave Ste 207, Miami, Florida
33135-2957 Tel: 1 305 541-3300.
Web site: http://cadenaazul.com
Profile: WRHC-AM is a commercial station is owned
by Fenix Broadcasting Corp. The format of the station
is Hispanic. WRHC-AM broadcasts to the Miami area
at 1550 AM.
AM RADIO STATION

WRHD-FM 42085
Owner: Inner Banks Media, LLC
Editorial: 1884 W Arlington Blvd Ste 101C, Greenville,
North Carolina 27834-5704 Tel: 1 252 672-5900.
Web site: http://www.943thegame.com
Profile: WRHD-FM is a commercial station owned by
Inner Banks Media, LLC. The format of the station is
sports. WRHD-FM broadcasts to the Greenville, NC
area at 94.3 FM.
FM RADIO STATION

WRHI-AM 38724
Owner: Our Three Sons Broadcasting
Editorial: 142 N Confederate Ave, Rock Hill, South
Carolina 29730-5314 Tel: 1 803 324-1340.
Email: newsroom@wrhi.com
Web site: http://www.wrhi.com
Profile: WRHI-AM is a commercial station owned by
Our Three Sons Broadcasting. The format for the
station is news and talk. WRHI-AM broadcasts to the
Rock Hill, SC area at 1340 AM.
AM RADIO STATION

WRHK-FM 43812
Owner: Neuhoff Family Limited Partnership
Editorial: 1501 N Washington Ave, Danville, Illinois
61832-2463 Tel: 1 217 442-1700.
Profile: WRHK-FM is a commercial station owned by
Neuhoff Family Limited Partnership. The format of the
station is classic rock. WRHK-FM broadcasts to the
Danville, IL area at 94.9 FM.
FM RADIO STATION

WRHL-AM 38722
Owner: Rochelle Broadcasting Co.
Editorial: 400 May Mart Dr, Rochelle, Illinois 61068-
1720 Tel: 1 815 562-7001.
Web site: http://www.wrhl.net
Profile: WRHL-AM is a commercial station owned by
the Rochelle Broadcasting Company. The format of
the station is news and talk. WRHL-AM broadcasts to
the Rochelle, IL area at 1060 AM.
AM RADIO STATION

WRHL-FM 46082
Owner: Rochelle Broadcasting Co.
Editorial: 400 May Mart Dr, Rochelle, Illinois 61068-
1836 Tel: 1 815 562-7001.
Email: sam@wrhl.net
Web site: http://www.1023thecoyote.com
Profile: WRHL-FM is a commercial station owned by
the Rochelle Broadcasting Co. The format of the
station is adult hits. WRHL-FM broadcasts in the
Rochelle, IL area at 102.3 FM.
FM RADIO STATION

WRHM-FM 46078
Owner: Our Three Sons Broadcasting
Editorial: 142 N Confederate Ave, Rock Hill, South
Carolina 29730-5314 Tel: 1 803 324-1071.
Email: newsroom@wrhi.com
Web site: http://www.fm107.com
Profile: WRHM-FM is a commercial station owned by
Our Three Sons Broadcasting. The format of the
station is contemporary country. WRHM-FM
broadcast to the Rock Hill, SC area at 101.7 FM.
FM RADIO STATION

WRHN-FM 45966
Owner: NRG Media LLC
Editorial: 3616 Highway 47, Rhinelander, Wisconsin
54501-8819 Tel: 1 715 362-1975.
Web site: http://www.wrhn.com
Profile: WRHN-FM is a commercial radio station
owned by NRG Media LLC. The format of the station
is adult hits. WRHN-FM broadcasts to the Wausau,
WI, area at 97.5 FM.
FM RADIO STATION

WRHQ-FM 41796
Owner: Thoroughbred Communications
Editorial: 1102 E 52nd St, Savannah, Georgia 31404-
4216 Tel: 1 912 234-1053.
Email: qualityrock@wrhq.com
Web site: http://www.wrhq.com
Profile: WRHQ-FM is a commercial station owned by
Thoroughbred Communications. The format for the
station is adult contemporary. WRHQ-FM broadcasts
to the Savannah, GA area at 105.3 FM.
FM RADIO STATION

WRHT-FM 41405
Owner: Inner Banks Media, LLC
Editorial: 1884 W Arlington Blvd Ste 101C, Greenville,
North Carolina 27834-5704 Tel: 1 252 355-1037.
Web site: http://www.thundercountryonline.com
Profile: WRHT-FM is a commercial station owned by
Inner Banks Media, LLC. The format of the station is
contemporary country music. WRHT-FM broadcasts
in the Greenville, NC area at 96.3 FM.
FM RADIO STATION

WRIC-FM 42801
Owner: Princeton Broadcasting, Inc.
Editorial: 1 Radio Ln, Princeton, West Virginia 24740-
2886 Tel: 1 304 425-2151.
Web site: http://www.star95.com
Profile: WRIC-FM is a commercial station owned by
Princeton Broadcasting, Inc. The format of the station
is adult contemporary. WRIC-FM broadcasts to the
Richlands, VA area at 97.7 FM.
FM RADIO STATION

WRIE-AM 39252
Owner: Cumulus Media Inc.
Editorial: 471 Robison Rd, Erie, Pennsylvania 16509-
5425 Tel: 1 814 868-5355.
Web site: http://am1260thescore.com
Profile: WRIE-AM is a commercial station owned by
Cumulus Media Inc. The format of the station is
sports. WRIE-AM broadcasts to the Erie, PA area at
1260 AM.
AM RADIO STATION

WRIF-FM 40672
Owner: Beasley Broadcast Group
Editorial: 1 Radio Plaza St, Ferndale, Michigan 48220-2140 **Tel:** 1 248 547-0101.
Web site: http://www.wrif.com
Profile: WRIF-FM is a commercial station owned by Beasley Broadcast Group. The format of the station is rock/album-oriented rock. WRIF-FM broadcasts to the Detroit area at 101.1 FM.
FM RADIO STATION

WRIG-AM 38159
Owner: Midwest Communications Inc.
Editorial: 557 Scott St, Wausau, Wisconsin 54403
Tel: 1 715 842-1672.
Web site: http://foxsports1390.com
Profile: WRIG-AM is a commercial station owned by Midwest Communications Inc. The format of the station is sports. WOFM-FM broadcasts to the Wausau, WI area at 1390 AM.
AM RADIO STATION

WRIK-AM 153439
Owner: Stratemeyer Media
Editorial: 6120 Waldo Church Rd, Metropolis, Illinois 62960-4903 **Tel:** 1 618 564-9836.
Profile: WRIK-AM is a commercial station owned by Stratemeyer Media. The format of the station is contemporary country. WRIK-AM broadcasts to the Metropolis, IL area at 97.5.
AM RADIO STATION

WRIL-FM 40912
Owner: Pine Hills Broadcasting Inc.
Tel: 1 606 248-6565.
Web site: http://www.thebig1063.com
Profile: WRIL-FM is a commercial station owned by Pine Hills Broadcasting Inc. The format of the station is Top 40/CHR. WRIL-FM broadcasts to the Knoxville, TN area at 106.3 FM.
FM RADIO STATION

WRIN-AM 38583
Owner: Brothers Broadcasting Corp.
Editorial: 560 W Amsler Rd, Rensselaer, Indiana 47978-8643 **Tel:** 1 219 866-4104.
Email: wrin@ffni.com
Profile: WRIN-AM is a commercial station owned by Brothers Broadcasting Corp. The format of the station is country. WRIN-AM broadcasts to the Rensselaer, IN area at 1560 AM.
AM RADIO STATION

WRIP-FM 44452
Owner: RIP Radio, LLC (Jackson, Dennis)
Editorial: 134 County Route 12, Windham, New York 12496-5510 **Tel:** 1 518 734-4747.
Web site: http://www.wrip979.com
Profile: WRIP-FM is a commercial station owned by RIP Radio, LLC (Jackson, Dennis). The format of the station is adult contemporary and variety on the weekends. WRIP-FM broadcasts to the Windham, NY area at 97.9 FM.
FM RADIO STATION

WRIR-FM 849137
Owner: Virginia Center For Public Press
Tel: 1 804 622-9747.
Email: info@wrir.org
Web site: http://www.wrir.org
Profile: WRIR-FM is a non-commercial station owned by Virginia Center For Public Press. The format of the station is music, news and views in order to provide a platform for cultural diversity in Richmond. WRIR-FM broadcasts to the Richmond, VA area at 97.3 FM.
FM RADIO STATION

WRIS-AM 36534
Owner: Metromedia Broadcasting LLC
Tel: 1 540 342-1410.
Profile: WRIS-AM is a commercial station owned by Metromedia Broadcasting LLC. The format of the station is religion. WRIS-AM broadcasts to the Roanoke, VA area at a frequency of 1410 AM.
AM RADIO STATION

WRIT-FM 40989
Owner: iHeart Media Inc.
Editorial: 12100 W Howard Ave, Greenfield, Wisconsin 53228-1851 **Tel:** 1 414 545-8900.
Web site: http://www.milwaukeeoldies.com
Profile: WRIT-FM is a commercial station owned by iHeart Media Inc. The format of the station is oldies. WRIT-FM broadcasts to the Milwaukee area at 95.7 FM.
FM RADIO STATION

WRIV-AM 35629
Owner: Crystal Coast Communications
Editorial: 40 W Main St, Riverhead, New York 11901
Tel: 1 631 727-1390.
Email: 1390wriv@gmail.com
Web site: http://www.1390wriv.com
Profile: WRIV-AM is a commercial station owned by Crystal Coast Communications. The format of the station is adult standards music. WRIV-AM broadcasts to the New York City area at 1390 AM.
AM RADIO STATION

WRIX-AM 38900
Owner: The Power Foundation
Editorial: 102 E Shockley Ferry Rd, Anderson, South Carolina 29624-3730
Web site: http://www.thelifefm.com/wrix
Profile: WRIX-AM is a commercial station owned by The Power Foundation. The format of the station is Christian teaching and Southern gospel. WRIX-AM broadcasts to the Anderson, SC area at 1020 AM.
AM RADIO STATION

WRJB-FM 46084
Owner: Magic Valley Publishing Co., Inc
Editorial: 117 Vicksburg Ave, Camden, Tennessee 38320 **Tel:** 1 731 584-4444.
Email: wfwlwrjb@bellsouth.net
Web site: http://www.wrjbradio.com
Profile: WRJB-FM is a commercial station owned by Magic Valley Publishing Co., Inc. The format of the station is hot adult contemporary music. WRJB-FM broadcasts to the Camden, TN area at 95.9 FM.
FM RADIO STATION

WRJC-AM 38965
Owner: WRJC Inc.
Editorial: N5240 Fairway Ln, Mauston, Wisconsin 53948-9357 **Tel:** 1 608 847-6565.
Email: info@wrjc.com
Web site: http://www.wrjc.com
Profile: WRJC-AM is a commercial station owned by WRJC Inc. The format of the station is country. WRJC-AM broadcasts to the Madison, WI area at 1270 AM.
AM RADIO STATION

WRJC-FM 46315
Owner: WRJC Inc.
Editorial: N5240 Fairway Ln, Mauston, Wisconsin 53948-9357 **Tel:** 1 608 847-6565.
Email: info@wrjc.com
Web site: http://www.wrjc.com
Profile: WRJC-FM is a commercial station owned by WRJC Inc. The format for the station is Hot AC/ Modern AC. WRJC-FM broadcasts to the Madison, WI area at 92.1 FM.
FM RADIO STATION

WRJE-AM 359236
Owner: K-5 Communications, LLC
Editorial: 1076 S Chapel St, Newark, Delaware 19702-1304 **Tel:** 1 302 730-4200.
Web site: http://www.sabrosaradio.com
Profile: WRJE-AM is a commercial station owned by K-5 Communications, LLC. The format of the station is Regional Mexican music. WRJE-AM broadcasts to the Dover, DE area at a frequency of 1600 AM.
AM RADIO STATION

WRJL-FM 44331
Owner: Rojo Inc.
Editorial: 5610 Highway 55 E, Eva, Alabama 35621-7927 **Tel:** 1 256 796-8000.
Profile: WRJL-FM is a commercial station owned by Rojo Inc. The format for the station is Southern gospel. WRJL-FM broadcasts to the Huntsville, AL area at 99.9 FM.
FM RADIO STATION

WRJN-AM 38160
Owner: Magnum Communications
Editorial: 4201 Victory Ave, Racine, Wisconsin 53405-3277 **Tel:** 1 262 634-3311.
Email: racinenews@magnum.media
Web site: http://www.wrjn.com
Profile: WRJN-AM is a commercial station owned by Magnum Communications. The format of the station is talk, news and sports. WRJN-AM broadcasts to the Milwaukee area at 1400 AM.
AM RADIO STATION

WRJO-FM 46417
Owner: Heartland Communications Group, LLC
Editorial: 909 N Railroad St, Eagle River, Wisconsin 54521 **Tel:** 1 715 479-4451.
Email: frontdesk@wrjo.com
Web site: http://www.wrjo.com
Profile: WRJO-FM is a commercial station owned by Heartland Communications Group, LLC. The format of the station is oldies music. WRJO-FM broadcasts in the Eagle River, WI area at 94.5 FM.
FM RADIO STATION

WRJR-AM 35599
Owner: Iglesia Nueva Vida of High Point
Tel: 1 336 471-3500.
Profile: WRJR-AM is a commercial station owned by Iglesia Nueva Vida of High Point. The format of the station is Spanish religion. The station broadcasts to the Greater Norfolk, VA area at 670 AM.
AM RADIO STATION

WRJT-FM 44003
Owner: Northeast Broadcasting Co.
Editorial: 169 River St, Montpelier, Vermont 5602
Tel: 1 802 223-2396.
Email: feedback@pointfm.com
Web site: http://www.pointfm.com
Profile: WRJT-FM is a commercial station owned by Northeast Broadcasting Co. The format of the station is adult album alternative music. The station is a simulcast of WNCS-FM. Sister stations include WNCS-FM, WSKI-AM, and WDOT-FM.
FM RADIO STATION

WRJW-AM 36068
Owner: Pearl River Communications Inc.
Editorial: 2438 Highway 43 S, Picayune, Mississippi 39466-8278 **Tel:** 1 601 798-4835.
Email: news@wrjwradio.com
Web site: http://www.wrjwradio.com
Profile: WRJW-AM is a commercial station owned by Pearl River Communications Inc. The format of the station is classic country. WRJW-AM broadcasts to the Picayune, MS area at 1320 AM.
AM RADIO STATION

WRJX-AM 37877
Owner: Capital Assets, Inc.
Editorial: 4428 N College Ave, Hwy 43, Jackson, Alabama 36545-2017 **Tel:** 1 251 246-4431.
Email: info@bamadixie.com
Web site: http://bamadixie.com
Profile: WRJX-AM is a commercial station owned by Capital Assets, Inc. The format of the station is classic country. WRJX-AM broadcasts to the Jackson, AL area at 1230 AM.
AM RADIO STATION

WRJY-FM 42374
Owner: Golden Isles Broadcasting LLC
Editorial: 185 Benedict Rd, Brunswick, Georgia 31520-2938 **Tel:** 1 912 261-1000.
Email: info@goldenislesbroadcasting.com
Web site: http://www.thewave1041.com
Profile: WRJY-FM is a commercial station owned by Golden Isles Broadcasting LLC. The format of the station is country. WRJY-FM broadcasts to the Brunswick, GA area at 104.1 FM.
FM RADIO STATION

WRJZ-AM 36681
Owner: Moffit Media Inc.
Editorial: 1621 E Magnolia Ave, Knoxville, Tennessee 37917-7825 **Tel:** 1 865 525-0620.
Email: joy62@wrjz.com
Web site: http://www.wrjz.com
Profile: WRJZ-AM is a commercial station owned by Moffit Media Inc. The format of the station is religious talk. WRJZ-AM broadcasts to the Knoxville, TN area at 620 AM.
AM RADIO STATION

WRKA-FM 44292
Owner: Summit Media Broadcasting LLC
Editorial: 612 S 4th St, Louisville, Kentucky 40202-2460 **Tel:** 1 502 589-4800.
Web site: http://www.hawklouisville.com
Profile: WRKA-FM is a commercial station owned by Summit Media Broadcasting LLC. The format of the station is classic country. WRKA-FM broadcasts to the Louisville, KY area at 103.9 FM.
FM RADIO STATION

WRKB-AM 36341
Owner: Ford Broadcasting
Editorial: 910 Fairview St, Kannapolis, North Carolina 28083-5206 **Tel:** 1 704 857-1101.
Web site: http://www.fordbroadcasting.com
Profile: WRKB-AM is a commercial station owned by Ford Broadcasting. The format of the station is Southern gospel. WRKB-AM broadcasts to the Kannapolis, NC area at 1460 AM.
AM RADIO STATION

WRKC-FM 40676
Owner: King's College
Editorial: 133 N Franklin St, Wilkes-Barre, Pennsylvania 18701-1401 **Tel:** 1 570 208-5931.
Email: wrkc@kings.edu
Web site: http://departments.kings.edu/wrkc/about.htm
Profile: WRKC-FM is a non-commercial station owned by King's College. The format of the station is college variety. WRKC-FM broadcasts to the Wilkes-Barre, PA area on 88.5 FM.
FM RADIO STATION

WRKD-AM 38161
Owner: Blueberry Broadcasting
Editorial: 15 Payne Ave Route 1 South, Rockland, Maine 04841-2117 **Tel:** 1 207 623-9000.
Profile: WRKD-AM is a commercial station owned by Blueberry Broadcasting. The format of the station is sports. WRKD-AM broadcasts to the Rockland, ME area at 1000 AM.
AM RADIO STATION

WRKF-FM 41080
Owner: Public Radio International
Editorial: 3050 Valley Creek Dr, Baton Rouge, Louisiana 70808-3145 **Tel:** 1 225 926-3050.
Email: news@wrkf.org
Web site: http://www.wrkf.org
Profile: WRKF-FM is a non-commercial station owned by Public Radio International. The format of the station is news. WRKF-FM broadcasts to the Baton Rouge, LA area at 89.3 FM.
FM RADIO STATION

WRKH-FM 40106
Owner: iHeartMedia Inc.
Editorial: 555 Broadcast Dr Fl 3, Mobile, Alabama 36606-2936 **Tel:** 1 251 450-0100.
Web site: http://www.961therocket.com
Profile: WRKH-FM is owned by iHeartMedia Inc. The format of the station is classic rock music. WRKH-FM broadcasts to the Mobile, Alabama area at 96.1 FM.
FM RADIO STATION

WRKI-FM 43286
Owner: Townsquare Media, LLC
Editorial: 1004 Federal Rd, Brookfield, Connecticut 06804-1123 **Tel:** 1 203 775-1212.
Web site: http://www.i95rock.com
Profile: WRKI-FM is a commercial station owned by Townsquare Media, LLC. The format of the station is rock. WRKI-FM broadcasts to the Brookfield, CT area at 95.1 FM.
FM RADIO STATION

WRKK-AM 39394
Owner: iHeartMedia Inc.
Editorial: 1559 W 4th St, Williamsport, Pennsylvania 17701-5650 **Tel:** 1 570 327-1400.
Web site: http://www.wrak.cc
Profile: WRKK-AM is a commercial station owned by iHeartMedia Inc. The format of the station is news and talk. WRKK-AM broadcasts to the Williamsport, PA area at 1200 AM.
AM RADIO STATION

WRKL-AM 36905
Owner: Polnet Communications
Editorial: 449 Broadway Fl 2, New York, New York 10013-2549 **Tel:** 1 908 558-1430.
Web site: http://www.polskieradio.com/
Profile: WRKL-AM is a commercial station owned by Polnet Communications The format of the station is Polish language programming. WRKL-AM broadcasts to the Pomona, NY area at 910 AM.
AM RADIO STATION

WRKM-AM 38162
Owner: Banka (Dennis and Tracy)
Editorial: 109 Z Country Ln, Carthage, Tennessee 37030-1636 **Tel:** 1 615 735-1350.
Email: info@1041theranch.net
Web site: http://www.1041theranch.net
Profile: WRKM-AM is a commercial station owned by Dennis and Tracy Banka. The format of the station is sports. WRKM-AM broadcasts to the Nashville, TN area at 1350 AM.
AM RADIO STATION

WRKN-FM 45083
Owner: Cumulus Media Inc.
Editorial: 201 Saint Charles Ave Ste 201, New Orleans, Louisiana 70170-1017 **Tel:** 1 504 581-7002.
Web site: http://www.nashfm923.com
Profile: WRKN-FM is a commercial station owned by Cumulus Media Inc. The format of the station is country. WRKN-FM broadcasts to the New Orleans area at 92.3 FM.
FM RADIO STATION

WRKO-AM 36897
Owner: Entercom Communications Corp.
Editorial: 20 Guest St Fl 3, Boston, Massachusetts 02135-2040 **Tel:** 1 617 779-3400.
Web site: http://www.wrko.com
Profile: WRKO-AM is a commercial station owned by Entercom Communications Corp. The format of the station is news and talk. WRKO-AM broadcasts to the Boston area at 680 AM.
AM RADIO STATION

WRKQ-AM 36002
Owner: Beverly Broadcasting Company, LLC
Editorial: 880 Englewood Rd, Madisonville, Tennessee 37354-5120 **Tel:** 1 423 442-1446.
Web site: http://www.wrkq.net
Profile: WRKQ-AM is a commercial station owned by Beverly Broadcasting Company, LLC. The format of the station is talk. WRKQ-AM broadcasts to the Madisonville, TN area at 1250 AM.
AM RADIO STATION

WRKR-FM 42391
Owner: Townsquare Media, LLC
Editorial: 4154 Jennings Dr, Kalamazoo, Michigan 49048-1087 **Tel:** 1 269 344-0111.
Email: vip.support@townsquaremedia.com
Web site: http://www.wrkr.com
Profile: WRKR-FM is a commercial station owned by Townsquare Media, LLC. The format of the station is rock. WRKR-FM broadcasts to the Kalamazoo, MI area at 107.7 FM.
FM RADIO STATION

WRKS-FM 43108
Owner: Alpha Media
Editorial: 731 S Pear Orchard Rd Ste 27, Ridgeland, Mississippi 39157-4839 **Tel:** 1 601 957-1300.
Email: info@thezone1059.com
Web site: http://www.thezone1059.com
Profile: WRKS-FM is a commercial station owned by Alpha Media. The format of the station is sports. WRKS-FM broadcasts in the Jackson, MS area at 105.9 FM
FM RADIO STATION

WRKT-FM 42007
Owner: Connoisseur Media LLC
Editorial: 1 Boston Store Pl, Erie, Pennsylvania 16501-2313 **Tel:** 1 814 461-1000.
Email: rocket101@rocket101.com
Web site: http://www.rocket101.com
Profile: WRKT-FM is a commercial station owned by Connoisseur Media LLC. The format of the station is classic rock music. WRKT-FM broadcasts to the Erie, PA area at 100.9 FM.
FM RADIO STATION

WRKU-FM 44474
Owner: Nicolet Broadcasting Inc.
Editorial: 30 N 18th Ave Ste 8, Sturgeon Bay, Wisconsin 54235-3207 **Tel:** 1 920 746-9430.
Email: wbdk@doorcountydailynews.com
Web site: http://www.doorcountydailynews.com
Profile: WRKU-FM is a commercial station owned by Nicolet Broadcasting Inc. The format of the station is adult contemporary. WRKU-FM broadcasts to the Sturgeon Bay, WI area at 102.1 FM.
FM RADIO STATION

WRKW-FM 40389
Owner: FM Radio Licenses, LLC
Editorial: 109 Plaza Dr, Johnstown, Pennsylvania 15905-1212 **Tel:** 1 814 255-4186.
Web site: http://www.rocky99.com
Profile: WRKW-FM is a commercial station owned by FM Radio Licenses, LLC. The format of the station is rock. WRKW-FM broadcasts to the Johnstown, PA area at 99.1 FM.
FM RADIO STATION

WRKX-FM 45506
Owner: NRG Media LLC
Editorial: 216 W Lafayette St, Ottawa, Illinois 61350 **Tel:** 1 815 434-6050.
Web site: http://www.ottawaradio.net
Profile: WRKX-FM is a commercial station owned by NRG Media LLC. The format of the station is adult hits. WRKX-FM broadcasts to the Chicago area at 95.3 FM.
FM RADIO STATION

WRKY-FM 43541
Owner: FM Radio Licenses, LLC
Editorial: 1 Forever Dr, Hollidaysburg, Pennsylvania 16648-3029 **Tel:** 1 814 941-9800.
Web site: http://www.rocky1049.com
Profile: WRKY-FM is a commercial station owned by FM Radio Licenses, LLC. The format of the station is rock. WRKY-FM broadcasts to the Hollidaysburg, PA area at 104.9 FM.
FM RADIO STATION

WRKZ-FM 45368
Owner: North American Broadcasting
Editorial: 1458 Dublin Rd, Columbus, Ohio 43215-1010 **Tel:** 1 614 481-7800.
Web site: http://www.theblitz.com
Profile: WRKZ-FM is a commercial station owned by North American Broadcasting. The format of the station is rock. WRKZ-FM broadcasts to the Columbus, OH area at 99.7 FM.
FM RADIO STATION

WRLA-AM 36875
Owner: Tiger Communications Inc.
Editorial: 503 W 8th St, West Point, Georgia 31833-1570 **Tel:** 1 334 644-1490.
Email: wrla1490@gmail.com
Web site: http://wtrp-wrla.com/
Profile: WRLA-AM is a commercial station owned by Tiger Communications Inc. The format of the station is Contemporary Christian/Religious Teaching. WRLA-AM broadcasts to the Auburn, GA area at 1490 AM.
AM RADIO STATION

WRLB-FM 45514
Owner: Radio Greenbriar, LLC
Editorial: 276 Seneca Trl, Ronceverte, West Virginia 24970-1343 **Tel:** 1 304 645-1400.
Email: radio@wron.net
Web site: http://radiogreenbrier.com
Profile: WRLB-FM is a commercial station owned by Radio Greenbriar, LLC. The format of the station is Hot AC. WRLB-FM broadcasts to the Lewisburg, WV area at 95.3 FM.
FM RADIO STATION

WRLC-FM 238572
Owner: Lycoming College
Editorial: 700 College Pl, Williamsport, Pennsylvania 17701 **Tel:** 1 570 321-4340.
Email: wrlc@lycoming.edu
Web site: http://www.lycoming.edu/orgs/wrlc/
FM RADIO STATION

WRLD-FM 42268
Owner: PMB Broadcasting, LLC
Editorial: 1820 Wynnton Rd, Columbus, Georgia 31906-2930 **Tel:** 1 706 327-1217.
Web site: http://www.boomer953.com/
Profile: WRLD-FM is a commercial station owned by PMB Broadcasting, LLC. The format of the station is classic hits. WRLD-FM broadcasts to the Columbus, GA area at 95.3 FM.
FM RADIO STATION

WRLF-FM 45905
Owner: Spectrum Radio Group, LLC
Tel: 1 301 802-1250.
Profile: WRLF-FM is a commercial station owned by Spectrum Radio Group, LLC. The format of the station is classic rock. WRLF-FM broadcasts to the Fairmont, WV area at 94.3 FM.
FM RADIO STATION

WRLI-FM 44481
Owner: Connecticut Public Broadcasting Inc.
Editorial: 1049 Asylum Ave, Hartford, Connecticut 06105-2432 **Tel:** 1 860 278-5310.
Email: news@wnpr.org
Web site: http://www.wnpr.org
Profile: WRLI-FM is a non-commercial station owned by Connecticut Public Broadcasting Inc. The format of the station is news and talk. WRLI-FM broadcasts to the Hartford, CT area at 91.3 FM.
FM RADIO STATION

WRLL-AM 154899
Owner: Midway Broadcasting Corp.
Editorial: 1000 E 87th St, Chicago, Illinois 60619-6397 **Tel:** 1 773 247-6200.
Web site: http://wrll1450.com/english
Profile: WRLL-AM is a commercial station owned by Midway Broadcasting Corp. The format of the station is Hispanic. WRLL-AM broadcasts to the Chicago area at 1450 AM.
AM RADIO STATION

WRLO-FM 45508
Owner: NRG Media LLC
Editorial: 3616 Highway 47, Rhinelander, Wisconsin 54501-8819 **Tel:** 1 715 362-6140.
Web site: http://www.wrlo.com
Profile: WRLO-FM is a commercial station owned by NRG Media LLC. The format of the station is classic rock. WRLO-FM broadcasts to the Rhinelander, WI, area at 105.3 FM.
FM RADIO STATION

WRLR-FM 359205
Owner: Rondaradio Inc.
Editorial: 629 Pontiac Ct, Round Lake Heights, Illinois 60073-1328 **Tel:** 1 847 546-9757.
Email: studio@wrlr.fm
Web site: http://www.wrlr.fm
Profile: WRLR-FM is a commercial station owned by Rondaradio Inc. The format of the station is variety programming. WRLR-FM broadcasts to the Round Lake Heights, IL area at 98.3 FM.
FM RADIO STATION

WRLS-FM 40678
Owner: Vacationland Broadcasting Inc.
Editorial: 16344 W Radio Hill Rd, Hayward, Wisconsin 54843 **Tel:** 1 715 634-4871.
Email: wrls@cheqnet.net
Web site: http://www.wrlsfm.com
Profile: WRLS-FM is a commercial station owned by Vacationland Broadcasting Inc. The format of the station is adult contemporary. WRLS-FM broadcasts in the Hayward, WI area at 92.3 FM.
FM RADIO STATION

WRLT-FM 42030
Owner: Tuned-In Broadcasting
Editorial: 1310 Clinton St Ste 200, Nashville, Tennessee 37203-2888 **Tel:** 1 615 242-5600.
Email: psa@lightning100.com
Web site: http://www.lightning100.com
Profile: WRLT-FM is a commercial station owned by Tuned-In Broadcasting. The format of the station is adult album alternative. WRLT-FM broadcasts to the Nashville, TN area at 100.1 FM.
FM RADIO STATION

WRLU-FM 44475
Owner: Nicolet Broadcasting Inc.
Editorial: 30 N 18Th Ave Ste 8, Sturgeon Bay, Wisconsin 54235-3207 **Tel:** 1 920 746-9430.
Email: wbdk@doorcountydailynews.com
Web site: http://www.doorcountydailynews.com
Profile: WRLU-FM is a commercial station owned by Nicolet Broadcasting Inc. The format of the station is country. WRLU-FM broadcasts to the Sturgeon Bay, WI area at 104.1 FM.
FM RADIO STATION

WRLX-FM 40559
Owner: iHeartMedia Inc.
Editorial: 3071 Continental Dr, West Palm Beach, Florida 33407-3274 **Tel:** 1 561 616-6600.
Web site: http://www.mia921.com
Profile: WRLX-FM is a commercial station owned by iHeartMedia Inc. The format of the station is Spanish adult contemporary music. WRLX-FM broadcasts to the West Palm Beach, FL area at 92.1 FM.
FM RADIO STATION

WRMA-FM 41805
Owner: Spanish Broadcasting System
Editorial: 7007 NW 77th Ave, Miami, Florida 33166-2836 **Tel:** 1 305 447-9595.
Web site: http://i95fm.lamusica.com
Profile: WRMA-FM is a commercial station owned by the Spanish Broadcasting System. The format of the station features Spanish CHR music. WRMA-FM broadcasts in the greater Miami area at 95.7 FM.
FM RADIO STATION

WRMB-FM 41370
Owner: Moody Bible Institute
Editorial: 1511 W Boynton Beach Blvd, Boynton Beach, Florida 33436-4601 **Tel:** 1 561 737-9762.
Email: wrmb@moody.edu
Web site: http://www.moodyradiosouthflorida.fm
Profile: WRMB-FM is a non-commercial station owned by Moody Bible Institute. The format of the station is religious and christian talk. WRMB-FM broadcasts to the West Palm Beach, FL area at 89.3 FM.
FM RADIO STATION

WRMC-FM 40679
Owner: Middlebury College
Editorial: Campus Activities, Middlebury College, Middlebury, Vermont 05753-0029 **Tel:** 1 802 443-6324.
Email: wrmc911@gmail.com
Web site: http://wrmc.middlebury.edu
Profile: WRMC-FM is a non-commercial station owned by Middlebury College. The format of the station is college variety. WRMC-FM broadcasts to the Middlebury, VT area at 91.1 FM.
FM RADIO STATION

WRMF-FM 43740
Owner: Alpha Media
Editorial: 701 Northpoint Pkwy Ste 500, West Palm Beach, Florida 33407-1960 **Tel:** 1 561 868-1100.
Web site: http://www.wrmf.com
Profile: WRMF-FM is a commercial station owned by Alpha Media. The format of the station is hot adult contemporary music. WRMF-FM broadcasts to the West Palm Beach area at 97.9 FM.
FM RADIO STATION

WRMG-AM 37070
Owner: Ivy Broadcasting
Editorial: 621 4th St., Red Bay, Alabama 35582 **Tel:** 1 256 356-4458.
Web site: http://www.wrmgradio.com
Profile: WRMG-AM is commercial station owned by Ivy Broadcasting. The format of the station is country. WRMG-AM broadcasts to the Red Bay, AL area at 1430 AM.
AM RADIO STATION

WRMJ-FM 40680
Owner: Western Illinois Broadcasting
Editorial: 2104 SE 3rd St, Aledo, Illinois 61231 **Tel:** 1 309 582-5666.
Email: contactus@wrmj.com
Web site: http://www.wrmj.com
Profile: WRMJ-FM is a commercial station owned by Western Illinois Broadcasting. The format of the station is contemporary country music. WRMJ-FM broadcasts to the Aledo, IL area at 102.3 FM.
FM RADIO STATION

WRMK-FM 587631
Owner: Good News Church (The)
Editorial: 400 Warren Rd, Augusta, Georgia 30907-3782 **Tel:** 1 706 739-0022.
Email: wrmk@goodnewsaugusta.com
Web site: http://newstalk1079.com
Profile: WRMK-FM is a low-powered, non-commercial station owned by Good News Church (The). The format of the station is religious programming. WRMK-FM broadcasts in the Montgomery, AL area at 100.3 FM.
FM RADIO STATION

WRMM-FM 43417
Owner: Stephens Media Group
Editorial: 28 E Main St, Fl 8, Rochester, New York 14614-1915 **Tel:** 1 585 399-5700.
Email: info@warm1013.com
Web site: http://www.warm1013.com
Profile: WRMM-FM is a commercial station owned by Stephens Media Group. The format of the station is Lite Rock/Lite AC. WRMM-FM broadcasts to the Rochester, NY area at 101.3 FM. Public service announcements should be faxed.
FM RADIO STATION

WRMN-AM 38164
Owner: Fox Valley Broadcasting.
Editorial: 14 Douglas Ave #B, Elgin, Illinois 60120-5546 **Tel:** 1 847 741-7700.
Web site: http://www.wrmn1410.com
Profile: WRMN-AM is a commercial station owned by Fox Valley Broadcasting Inc. The format of the station is news and talk. WRMN-AM broadcasts to the Elgin, IL area at 1410 AM.
AM RADIO STATION

WRMO-FM 818857
Owner: Pine Tree Broadcasting, LLC
Tel: 1 207 812-3878.
Web site: http://937thewave.com/
Profile: WRMO-FM is a commercial station owned by Pine Tree Broadcasting, LLC. The format of the station is adult contemporary. WRMO-FM broadcasts to the Milbridge, ME area at a frequency of 93.7 FM.
FM RADIO STATION

WRMQ-AM 36221
Owner: Florida Broadcasters
Editorial: 1355 E Altamonte Dr, Altamonte Springs, Florida 32701-5011 **Tel:** 1 407 830-0800.
Web site: http://www.rejoice1140.com
Profile: WRMQ-AM is a commercial station owned by Florida Broadcasters. The format of the station is gospel. WRMQ-AM broadcasts to the Orlando, FL area at 1140 AM.
AM RADIO STATION

WRMR-FM 528962
Owner: Capitol Broadcasting Company
Editorial: 25 N Kerr Ave Ste C, Wilmington, North Carolina 28405-3403 **Tel:** 1 910 791-3088.
Web site: http://www.modernrock987.com
Profile: WRMR-FM is a commercial station owned by Capitol Broadcasting Company. The format of the station is modern rock. WRMR-FM broadcasts to the New Bern, NC area at 98.7 FM.
FM RADIO STATION

WRMS-FM 45891
Owner: LB Sports Productions, LLC
Editorial: 108 E Main St, Beardstown, Illinois 62618 **Tel:** 1 217 323-1790.
Email: wrms943@yahoo.com
Web site: http://www.wrmsfm.com
Profile: WRMS-FM is a commercial station owned by LB Sports Productions, LLC. The format of the station is contemporary country. WRMS-FM broadcasts to the Beardstown, IL area at 94.3 FM.
FM RADIO STATION

WRMT-AM 38968
Owner: First Media Radio LLC
Editorial: 12714 E State Highway 97, Rocky Mount, North Carolina 27803-4626 **Tel:** 1 252 442-8092.
Profile: WRMT-AM is a commercial station owned by First Media Radio LLC. The format of the station is Gospel. WRMT-AM broadcasts to the greater Rocky Mount, NC area at 1490 AM.
AM RADIO STATION

WRNA-AM 35630
Owner: Ford Broadcasting
Editorial: 633 Patterson St, China Grove, North Carolina 28023-2041 **Tel:** 1 704 857-1101.
Web site: http://www.fordbroadcasting.com
Profile: WRNA-AM is a commercial station owned by Ford Broadcasting. The format of the station is southern gospel. WRNA-AM broadcasts to the China Grove, NC area at 1140 AM.
AM RADIO STATION

WRNB-FM 45544
Owner: Urban One, Inc.
Editorial: 333 E City Ave Ste 700, Bala Cynwyd, Pennsylvania 19004-1521 **Tel:** 1 610 538-1100.
Web site: http://www.oldschool1003.com
Profile: WRNB-FM is a commercial station owned by Urban One, Inc. The format of the station is R&B with a focus on the 1970s and 1980s. WRNB-FM broadcasts to the Philadelphia area at 100.3 FM.
FM RADIO STATION

WRND-FM 45107
Owner: Saga Communications
Editorial: 1640 Old Russellville Pike, Clarksville, Tennessee 37043-1709 **Tel:** 1 931 648-7720.
Web site: http://rewind943.com
Profile: WRND-FM is a commercial station owned by Saga Communications (dba 5 Star Radio Group). The format of the station is adult hits. WRND-FM broadcasts to the Nashville, TN area at 94.3 FM.
FM RADIO STATION

WRNE-AM 36632
Owner: Media One Communications
Editorial: 312 E Nine Mile Rd Ste 29D, Pensacola, Florida 32514-1475 **Tel:** 1 850 478-6000.
Email: hill@wrne980.com
Profile: WRNE-AM is a commercial station owned by Media One Communications. The format of the station is a unique blend of R&B, urban, gospel, news and talk. WRNE-AM broadcasts to the Mobile, AL and Pensacola, FL area at 980 AM. Simulcasts on 106.9 FM.
AM RADIO STATION

WRNI-AM 35857
Owner: Rhode Island Public Radio
Editorial: 1 Union Sta, Providence, Rhode Island 02903-1758 **Tel:** 1 401 942-3881.
Email: news@lprri.org
Web site: http://www.lprri.org/inicio/
Profile: WRNI-AM is a non-commercial station owned by Rhode Island Public Radio. The format of the station is Spanish news and talk, carrying Latino Public Radio programming. WRNI-AM broadcasts to the Providence, RI area at 1290 AM.
AM RADIO STATION

WRNI-FM 42840
Owner: Rhode Island Public Radio
Editorial: 1 Union Sta, Providence, Rhode Island 02903-1758 **Tel:** 1 401 351-2800.
Email: news@ripr.org
Web site: http://ripr.org
Profile: WRNI-FM is a non-commercial station owned by Rhode Island Public Radio. The format of the station is news and talk. WRNI-FM broadcasts to the Providence, RI area at 102.7 FM.
FM RADIO STATION

WRNJ-AM 36815
Owner: WRNJ Radio Inc.
Editorial: 100 US Highway 46 E, Hackettstown, New Jersey 07840-2636 **Tel:** 1 908 850-1000.
Email: info@wrnj.com
Web site: http://www.wrnjradio.com
Profile: WRNJ-AM is a commercial station owned by WRNJ Radio Inc. The format of the station is adult contemporary. WRNJ-AM broadcasts to the Hackettstown, NJ area at 1510 AM.
AM RADIO STATION

WRNL-AM 38645
Owner: iHeartMedia Inc.
Editorial: 3245 Basie Rd, Richmond, Virginia 23228-3404 **Tel:** 1 804 474-0000.
Web site: http://www.sportsradio910.com
Profile: WRNL-AM is a commercial station owned by iHeartMedia Inc. The format of the station is sports. WRNL-AM broadcasts to the Richmond, VA area on 910 AM.
AM RADIO STATION

WRNN-AM 38647
Owner: Alpha Media
Editorial: 1016 Ocala St, Myrtle Beach, South Carolina 29577-8007 **Tel:** 1 843 448-1041.
Web site: http://www.wrnn.net
Profile: WRNN-AM is a commercial station owned by Alpha Media. The format of the station is sports. WRNN-AM broadcasts to the Myrtle Beach, SC area at 1450 AM.
AM RADIO STATION

WRNN-FM 42212
Owner: Alpha Media
Editorial: 1016 Ocala St, Myrtle Beach, South Carolina 29577-8007 **Tel:** 1 843 448-1041.
Web site: http://www.wrnn.net
Profile: WRNN-FM is a commercial station owned by Alpha Media. The format of the station is news and talk. WRNN-FM broadcasts to the Myrtle Beach, SC area at 99.5 FM.
FM RADIO STATION

WRNO-FM 40682
Owner: iHeartMedia Inc.
Editorial: 929 Howard Ave, New Orleans, Louisiana 70113-1148 **Tel:** 1 504 679-7300.
Email: programming@wrno.com
Web site: http://wrno.iheart.com
Profile: WRNO-FM is a commercial station owned by iHeartMedia Inc. The format of the station is news and talk. WRNO-FM broadcasts to the New Orleans area at 99.5 FM. The station's slogan is, "The News and Talk of New Orleans."
FM RADIO STATION

WRNQ-FM 46780
Owner: iHeartMedia Inc.
Editorial: 20 Tucker Dr, Poughkeepsie, New York 12603-1644 **Tel:** 1 845 471-2300.
Web site: http://q92hv.iheart.com
Profile: WRNQ-FM is a commercial station owned by iHeartMedia Inc. The format of the station is AC. WRNQ-FM broadcasts to the Poughkeepsie, NY area at 92.1 FM.
FM RADIO STATION

WRNR-AM 35631
Owner: Shenandoah Communications
Editorial: 1762 Eagle School Rd, Martinsburg, West Virginia 25404-0709 **Tel:** 1 304 263-6540.
Email: news@talkradiowrnr.com
Web site: http://www.talkradiowrnr.com
Profile: WRNR-AM is a commercial station owned by Shenandoah Communications. The format of the station is news, talk and sports. WRNR-AM broadcasts to the Martinsburg, WV area at 740 AM.
AM RADIO STATION

WRNR-FM 43249
Owner: Empire Broadcasting
Editorial: 179 Admiral Cochrane Drive, STE 110, Annapolis, Maryland 21401 **Tel:** 1 410 626-0103.
Web site: http://www.wrnr.com
Profile: WRNR-FM is a commercial station owned by Empire Broadcasting. The format of the station is adult album alternative. WRNR-FM broadcasts to the Annapolis area at 103.1 FM.
FM RADIO STATION

WRNS-AM 38369
Owner: Alpha Media
Editorial: 1361 Colony Dr, New Bern, North Carolina 28562-4129 **Tel:** 1 252 639-7900.
Web site: http://www.wrns.com
Profile: WRNS-AM is a commercial station owned by Alpha Media. The format of the station is country music. WRNS-AM broadcasts to the New Bern, NC area at 960 AM.
AM RADIO STATION

WRNS-FM 45742
Owner: Digity LLC
Editorial: 1361 Colony Dr, New Bern, North Carolina 28562-4129 **Tel:** 1 252 639-7900.
Web site: http://www.wrns.com
Profile: WRNS-FM is a commercial station owned by Digity LLC . The format of the station is country music. WRNS-FM broadcasts to the New Bern, NC area at 95.1 FM.
FM RADIO STATION

WRNW-FM 45351
Owner: iHeartMedia Inc.
Editorial: 12100 W Howard Ave, Greenfield, Wisconsin 53228-1851 **Tel:** 1 414 545-8900.
Web site: http://973now.iheart.com
Profile: WRNW-FM is a commercial station owned by iHeartMedia Inc. The format of station is Top 40/CHR. WRNW-FM broadcasts to the Milwaukee area at 97.3 FM.
FM RADIO STATION

WRNX-FM 45978
Owner: iHeartMedia Inc.
Editorial: 1331 Main St Ste 4, Springfield, Massachusetts 01103-1621 **Tel:** 1 413 536-1105.
Email: advertising@kix979.com
Web site: http://www.mykix1009.com
Profile: WRNX-FM is a commercial station owned by iHeartMedia Inc. The format of the station is contemporary country. WRNX-FM broadcasts to the Springfield, MA area at 100.9 FM.
FM RADIO STATION

WRNY-AM 38556
Owner: Galaxy Communications LP
Editorial: 39 Kellogg Rd, New Hartford, New York 13413-2849 **Tel:** 1 315 797-1330.
Profile: WRNY-FM is a commercial station owned by Galaxy Communications LP. The format of the station is sports. WRNY-FM broadcasts to the New Hartford, NY area at 1350 AM.
AM RADIO STATION

WRNZ-FM 41540
Owner: Hometown Broadcasting
Editorial: 2063 Shakertown Rd, Danville, Kentucky 40422-9262 **Tel:** 1 859 236-2711.
Email: hometownradio@bellsouth.net
Web site: http://hometownlive.net
Profile: WRNZ-FM is a commercial station owned by Hometown Broadcasting. The format of the station is hot adult contemporary. WRNZ-FM broadcasts to the Danville, KY area at 105.1 FM.
FM RADIO STATION

WROA-AM 38893
Owner: Dowdy Broadcasting, Inc.
Editorial: 10250 Lorraine Rd, Gulfport, Mississippi 39503 **Tel:** 1 228 896-5500.
AM RADIO STATION

WROC-AM 37661
Owner: Entercom Communications Corp.
Editorial: 70 Commercial St, Rochester, New York 14614-1010 **Tel:** 1 585 423-2900.
Web site: http://www.espnrochester.com
Profile: WROC-AM is a commercial station owned by Entercom Communications Corp. The format of the station is sports. WROC-AM broadcasts to the Rochester, NY area at 950 AM.
AM RADIO STATION

WROD-AM 35632
Owner: Miracle Media Group
Editorial: 100 Marina Point Dr, Daytona Beach, Florida 32114-5059 **Tel:** 1 386 253-0000.
Web site: http://www.therockofdaytona.com
Profile: WROD-AM is a commercial station owned by Miracle Media Group. The format of the station is rock music. WROD-AM broadcasts to the Daytona Beach, FL area at 1340 AM.
AM RADIO STATION

WROI-FM 40683
Owner: Bair Communications Inc.
Editorial: 110 E 8th St, Rochester, Indiana 46975-1560 **Tel:** 1 574 223-6059.
Email: wroi@rtcol.com
Web site: http://www.wroifm.com
Profile: WROI-FM is a commercial station owned by Bair Communications Inc. The format of the station is Classic Hits. WROI-FM broadcasts to the South Bend, IN area at 92.1 FM.
FM RADIO STATION

WROK-AM 38165
Owner: Cumulus Media Inc.
Editorial: 3901 Brendenwood Rd, Rockford, Illinois 61107-2246 **Tel:** 1 815 399-2233.
Email: news@1440wrok.com
Web site: http://www.1440wrok.com
Profile: WROK-AM is a commercial station owned by Cumulus Media Inc. The format of the station is news and talk. WROK-AM broadcasts in the Rockford, IL area at 1440 AM.
AM RADIO STATION

WROK-FM 37751
Owner: Cumulus Media Inc.
Editorial: 544 Mulberry St Ste 500, Macon, Georgia 31201-8258 **Tel:** 1 478 746-6286.
Web site: http://www.rock1055online.com
Profile: WROK-FM is a commercial station owned by Cumulus Media Inc. The format of the station is rock. WROK-FM broadcasts to the Macon, GA area at 105.5 FM.
FM RADIO STATION

WROL-AM 35633
Owner: Salem Media Group, Inc.
Editorial: 500 Victory Rd, North Quincy, Massachusetts 02171-3139 **Tel:** 1 617 328-0880.
Email: contactus@salemradioboston.com
Web site: http://www.wrolradio.com
Profile: WROL-AM is a commercial station owned by Salem Media Group, Inc. The format of the station is contemporary Christian music and talk. WROL-AM broadcasts to the Boston area at 950 AM.
AM RADIO STATION

WROM-AM 36075
Owner: Rome Radio Partners
Editorial: 20 John Davenport Dr NW, Rome, Georgia 30165-2536 **Tel:** 1 706 291-9496.
Web site: http://rrpga.com
Profile: WROM-AM is a commercial station owned by Rome Radio Partners LLC. The format of the station is variety. WROM-AM broadcasts to the Rome, GA area at 710 AM.
AM RADIO STATION

WRON-AM 38166
Owner: Radio Greenbrier, LLC
Editorial: 276 Seneca Trl, Ronceverte, West Virginia 24970 **Tel:** 1 304 645-1400.
Email: radio@wron.net
Web site: http://www.wron.com
Profile: WRON-AM is a commercial station owned by Radio Greenbrier, LLC. The format of the station is news and talk. WRON-AM broadcasts to the Ronceverte, KS area at 1400 AM.
AM RADIO STATION

WRON-FM 45509
Owner: Radio Greenbrier, LCC
Editorial: 276 Seneca Trl, Ronceverte, West Virginia 24970 **Tel:** 1 304 645-1400.
Email: radio@wron.net
Web site: http://www.wron.com
Profile: WRON-FM is a commercial station owned by Radio Greenbrier, LCC. The format of the station is contemporary country music. WRON-FM broadcasts to the Ronceverte, WV area at 103.1 FM.
FM RADIO STATION

WROO-FM 154676
Owner: iHeartMedia Inc.
Editorial: 101 N Main St Ste 1000, Greenville, South Carolina 29601-4852 **Tel:** 1 864 235-1025.
Web site: http://www.1049rocks.com
Profile: WROO-FM is a commercial station owned by iHeartMedia Inc. The format is classic rock music. WROO-FM broadcasts to the Greenville, SC area at 104.9
FM RADIO STATION

WROQ-FM 42176
Owner: Entercom Communications Corp.
Editorial: 25 Garlington Rd, Greenville, South Carolina 29615-4613 **Tel:** 1 864 271-9200.
Web site: http://www.classicrock1011.com
Profile: WROQ-FM is a commercial station owned by Entercom Communications Corp. The format of the station is classic rock music. WROQ-FM broadcasts to the Greenville, SC area at 101.1 FM.
FM RADIO STATION

WROR-FM 42807
Owner: Beasley Broadcast Group
Editorial: 55 William T Morrissey Blvd, Dorchester, Massachusetts 02125-3315 **Tel:** 1 617 822-9600.
Web site: http://www.wror.com
Profile: WROR-FM is a commercial station owned by Beasley Broadcast Group. The format of the station is classic hits music. WROR-FM broadcasts to the Boston area at 105.7 FM. The station's slogan is, "Boston's Greatest Hits."
FM RADIO STATION

WROS-AM 35634
Owner: Hall(Elwyn)
Editorial: 5590 Rio Grande Ave, Jacksonville, Florida 32254-1354 **Tel:** 1 904 353-1050.
Email: wros@wros.net
Web site: http://www.wros.net
Profile: WROS-AM is a commercial station owned by Elwyn Hall. The format of the station is religious. WROS-AM broadcasts to the Jacksonville, FL area at 1050 AM.
AM RADIO STATION

WROU-FM 41856
Owner: Alpha Media
Editorial: 717 E David Rd, Dayton, Ohio 45429-5218 **Tel:** 1 937 294-5858.
Web site: http://www.921wrou.com
Profile: WROU-FM is a commercial station owned by Alpha Media. The format of the station is urban adult contemporary. WROU-FM broadcasts in the Dayton, OH area at 92.1 FM.
FM RADIO STATION

WROV-FM 46054
Owner: iHeartMedia Inc.
Editorial: 3807 Brandon Ave SW Ste 2350, Roanoke, Virginia 24018-1477 **Tel:** 1 540 725-1220.
Web site: http://www.rovrocks.com/main.html
Profile: WROV-FM is a commercial station owned by iHeartMedia Inc. The format of the station is album-oriented rock music. WROV-FM broadcasts to the Roanoke, VA area at 96.3 FM.
FM RADIO STATION

WROW-AM 38167
Owner: Albany Broadcasting Co.
Editorial: 6 Johnson Rd, Latham, New York 12110-5641 **Tel:** 1 518 786-6600.
Web site: http://www.albanymagic.com
Profile: WROW-AM is a commercial station owned by Albany Broadcasting Co. The format of the station is oldies. WROW-AM broadcasts to the Latham, NY area at 590 AM.
AM RADIO STATION

WROX-AM 35635
Owner: LL James Media, LLC
Editorial: 628 Desoto Ave, Clarksdale, Mississippi 38614-5219 **Tel:** 1 662 627-1450.
Web site: http://www.wroxradio.com
Profile: WROX-AM is a commercial station owned by LL James Media, LLC. The format of the station is oldies. WROX-AM broadcasts to the Clarksdale, MS area at 1450 AM.
AM RADIO STATION

WROX-FM 42834
Owner: Sinclair Telecable Inc.
Editorial: 999 Waterside Dr Ste 500, Norfolk, Virginia 23510-3300 **Tel:** 1 757 640-8500.
Web site: http://www.96x.fm
Profile: WROX-FM is a commercial station owned by Sinclair Telecable Inc. The format of the station is rock alternative music. WROX-FM broadcasts in the Norfolk, VA area at 96.1 FM.
FM RADIO STATION

WROY-AM 38168
Owner: Withers Broadcasting Co.
Editorial: 101 N Church St, Carmi, Illinois 62821 **Tel:** 1 618 382-4161.
Web site: http://www.wrul.com
Profile: WROY-AM is a commercial station owned by Withers Broadcasting Co. The format of the station is oldies. WROY-AM broadcasts to the Carmi, IN area at 1460 AM.
AM RADIO STATION

WROZ-FM 45397
Owner: Hall Communications
Editorial: 1996 Auction Rd, Manheim, Pennsylvania 17545-9159 **Tel:** 1 717 653-0800.
Email: wroz@hallradio.net
Web site: http://www.fun1013.com
Profile: WROZ-FM is a commercial station owned by Hall Communications. The format of the station is hot adult contemporary. WROZ-FM broadcasts to the Manheim, PA area at 101.3 FM.
FM RADIO STATION

WRPI-FM 40684
Owner: Rensselaer Polytechnic Institute
Editorial: 1 Wrpi Plz, Troy, New York 12180
Tel: 1 518 276-6248.
Email: wrpi-bm@rpi.edu
Web site: http://www.wrpi.org
Profile: WRPI-FM is a commercial station owned by Rensselaer Polytechnic Institute. The format of the station is college variety. WRPI-FM broadcasts in the Troy, NY area at 91.5 FM. The station does not accept pitching.
FM RADIO STATION

WRPN-AM 39259
Owner: Urban One, Inc.
Editorial: N7502 Radio Rd, Ripon, Wisconsin 54971-9231 **Tel:** 1 920 748-5111.
Web site: http://www.wrpnam.com
Profile: WRPN-AM is a commercial station owned by Urban One, Inc. The format of the station is news, talk and sports. WRPN-AM broadcasts to the Ripon, WI area at 1600 AM.
AM RADIO STATION

WRPN-FM 40685
Owner: Ripon College Board of Trustees
Editorial: 300 W Seward St, Ripon, Wisconsin 54971
Tel: 1 920 748-8717.
Email: wrpn.fm@gmail.com
Web site: http://www.ripon.edu/studentlife/clubs_orgs/media_pubs/wrpn
Profile: WRPN-FM is a non-commercial station owned by Ripon College Board of Trustees. The format of the station is variety. WRPN-FM broadcasts to the Ripon, WI area at 90.1 FM.
FM RADIO STATION

WRPP-FM 139793
Owner: Great Lakes Radio Inc.
Editorial: 3060 US Highway 41 W, Marquette, Michigan 49855-2293 **Tel:** 1 906 228-6800.
Web site: http://wrup.com
Profile: WRPP-FM is a commercial station owned by Great Lakes Radio Inc. The format of the station is classic rock. WRPP-FM broadcasts to the Marquette, MI area at a frequency of 92.7 FM.
FM RADIO STATION

WRPQ-AM 35636
Owner: Baraboo Broadcasting Co.
Editorial: 407 Oak St, Baraboo, Wisconsin 53913-2415 **Tel:** 1 608 356-3974.
Email: wrpqtv43@wrpq.com
Web site: http://www.wrpq.com
Profile: WRPQ-AM is a commercial station owned by Baraboo Broadcasting Co. The format of the station is Lite AC. WRPQ-AM broadcasts to the Madison, WI area at 740 AM.
AM RADIO STATION

WRPR-FM 40686
Owner: Ramapo College
Editorial: 501 Ramapo Valley Rd, Mahwah, New Jersey 07430-1608 **Tel:** 1 201 684-7998.
Web site: http://www.rampaa.edu/wrpf
FM RADIO STATION

WRPW-FM 43679
Owner: Great Plains Media
Editorial: 108 Boeykens Pl, Normal, Illinois 61761-2139 **Tel:** 1 309 888-4496.
Web site: http://www.cities929.com
Profile: WRPW-FM is a commercial station owned by Great Plains Media. The format of the station is talk and news. WRPW-FM broadcasts to the Normal, IL area at 92.9 FM.
FM RADIO STATION

WRQE-FM 45666
Owner: Dix Communications
Editorial: 350 Byrd Ave, Cumberland, Maryland 21502-3219 **Tel:** 1 301 722-6666.
Web site: http://rocky106.com
Profile: WRQE-FM is a commercial station owned by Dix Communications. The format of the station is rock. WRQE-FM broadcasts to the Cumberland, MD area at 106.1 FM.
FM RADIO STATION

WRQK-FM 43344
Owner: iHeartMedia Inc.
Editorial: 7755 Freedom Ave NW, North Canton, Ohio 44720-6905 **Tel:** 1 330 492-4700.
Web site: http://wrqk.iheart.com
Profile: WRQK-FM is a commercial station owned by iHeartMedia Inc. The format of the station is rock. WRQK-FM broadcasts to the Cleveland area at 106.9 FM.
FM RADIO STATION

WRQN-FM 40687
Owner: Cumulus Media Inc.
Editorial: 3225 Arlington Ave, Toledo, Ohio 43614-2427 **Tel:** 1 419 725-5700.
Web site: http://www.935wrqn.com
Profile: WRQN-FM is a commercial station owned by Cumulus Media Inc. The format of the station is oldies. WRQN-FM broadcasts to the Toledo, OH area at 93.5 FM.
FM RADIO STATION

WRQO-FM 42091
Owner: TeleSouth Communications Inc.
Editorial: 110 W Monticello St, Brookhaven, Mississippi 39601 **Tel:** 1 601 835-5005.
Email: supertalk1021@yahoo.com
Web site: http://www.supertalkms.com

Profile: WRQO-FM is a commercial station owned by TeleSouth Communications Inc. The format of the station is talk. WRQO-FM broadcasts to the Jackson, MS, area at 102.1 FM.
FM RADIO STATION

WRQQ-FM 43384
Owner: Cumulus Media Inc.
Editorial: 631 Main St, Baton Rouge, Louisiana 70801-1911 **Tel:** 1 225 926-1106.
Web site: http://www.classichits1033.com
Profile: WRQQ-FM is a commercial station owned by Cumulus Media Inc. The format of the station is classic hits. WCDV-FM broadcasts to the Baton Rouge, LA area at 103.3 FM.
FM RADIO STATION

WRQR-AM 38957
Owner: Benton-Weatherford Broadcasting Inc. of Tennessee
Editorial: 110 India Rd, Paris, Tennessee 38242-7565 **Tel:** 1 731 644-9455.
Email: news@wmufradio.com
Profile: WRQR-AM is a commercial station owned by Benton-Weatherford Broadcasting Inc. of Tennessee. The format of the station is Classic Hits. WRQR-AM broadcasts to the Nashville, TN area at 1000 AM.
AM RADIO STATION

WRQT-FM 43465
Owner: Midwest Family Broadcasting
Editorial: 201 State St, La Crosse, Wisconsin 54601 **Tel:** 1 608 782-1230.
Web site: http://www.957therock.com
Profile: WRQT-FM is a commercial station owned by Midwest Family Broadcasting. The format of the station is rock. WRQT-FM broadcasts to the La Crosse, WI area at 95.7 FM.
FM RADIO STATION

WRQV-FM 775512
Owner: Invisible Allies Ministries
Tel: 1 814 867-3836.
Email: info@revfm.net
Web site: http://www.revfm.net
Profile: WRQV-FM is a non-commercial station owned by Invisible Allies Ministries. The format of the station is Contemporary Christian. WRQV-FM is licensed to Ridgway, PA and can be heard in Jefferson, Elk and northern Clearfield counties in Pennsylvania at 88.1 FM.
FM RADIO STATION

WRQX-FM 45513
Owner: Cumulus Media
Editorial: 4400 Jenifer St NW Fl 4, Washington, District Of Columbia 20015-2134 **Tel:** 1 202 686-3100.
Web site: http://www.mix1073.com
Profile: WRQX-FM is a commercial station owned by Cumulus Media. The format of the station is Top 40/CHR. WRQX-FM broadcasts in the Washington, D.C. area at 107.3. The station does not air news.
FM RADIO STATION

WRQY-FM 42388
Owner: FM Radio Licenses, LLC
Editorial: 56325 High Ridge Rd, Bellaire, Ohio 43906-9707 **Tel:** 1 740 676-5661.
Profile: WRQY-FM is a commercial station owned by FM Radio Licenses, LLC. The format of the station is sports and rock music. WBGI-FM newscasts air on top of the hour throughout the day.
FM RADIO STATION

WRRB-FM 43302
Owner: Townsquare Media
Editorial: 2 Pendell Rd, Poughkeepsie, New York 12601-1513 **Tel:** 1 845 471-1500.
Web site: http://www.wrrv.com
Profile: WRRB-FM is a commercial station owned by Townsquare Media. The format of the station is rock alternative music. WRRB-FM broadcasts to the Poughkeepsie, NY area at 96.9 FM.
FM RADIO STATION

WRRD-AM 35182
Owner: New WRRD LLC
Editorial: 301 W Wisconsin Ave, Milwaukee, Wisconsin 53203-2220 **Tel:** 1 844 967-2789.
Web site: http://newstalk1510am.com/
Profile: WRRD-AM is a commercial station owned by New WRRD LLC. The format of the station is left-wing political talk. WRRD-AM broadcasts to the Milwaukee area at 1510 AM.
AM RADIO STATION

WRR-FM 40689
Owner: City of Dallas Municipality
Editorial: 1516 1st Ave, Dallas, Texas 75210-1008 **Tel:** 1 214 670-8888.
Email: info@wrr101.com
Web site: http://www.wrr101.com
Profile: WRR-FM is a commercial station owned by the City of Dallas Municipality. The format of the station is classical music. WRR-FM broadcasts to the Dallas area at 101.1 FM.
FM RADIO STATION

WRRG-FM 43351
Owner: Triton College
Editorial: 2000 5th Ave, River Grove, Illinois 60171-1907 **Tel:** 1 708 456-0300 3462.
Web site: http://www.wrrg.org
Profile: WRRG-FM is a non-commercial station owned by Triton College. The format of the station is college variety. WRRG-FM broadcasts to the River Grove, IL area at 88.9 FM.
FM RADIO STATION

WRRK-FM 40550
Owner: Steel City Media
Editorial: 650 Smithfield St, Ste 2200, Pittsburgh, Pennsylvania 15222-3925 **Tel:** 1 412 316-3342.
Email: feedback@bobfm969.com
Web site: http://www.bobfm969.com
Profile: WRRK-FM is a commercial station owned by Steel City Media. The format of the station is adult hits. WRRK-FM broadcasts to the Pittsburgh area at 96.9 FM.
FM RADIO STATION

WRRM-FM 41005
Owner: Cumulus Media Inc.
Editorial: 4805 Montgomery Rd Ste 300, Cincinnati, Ohio 45212-2280 **Tel:** 1 513 241-9898.
Web site: http://www.warm98.com
Profile: WRRM-FM is a commercial station owned by Cumulus Media Inc. The format of the station is adult contemporary. WRRM-FM broadcasts to the Cincinnati area at 98.5 FM.
FM RADIO STATION

WRRN-FM 45515
Owner: Radio Partners LLC
Editorial: 310 2nd Ave, Warren, Pennsylvania 16365 **Tel:** 1 814 723-1310.
Email: newsroom@kibcoradio.com
Web site: http://www.kibcoradio.com
Profile: WRRN-FM is a commercial station owned by Radio Partners LLC. The format of the station is oldies music. WRRN-FM broadcasts to the Warren, PA area at 92.3 FM.
FM RADIO STATION

WRRQ-FM 431151
Owner: Equinox Broadcasting Corp.
Editorial: 101 Main St, Johnson City, New York 13790-2426 **Tel:** 1 607 772-1005.
Web site: http://www.cool100.coolesthits.com
Profile: WRRQ-FM is a commercial station owned by Equinox Broadcasting Corp. The format for the station is classic hits. WRRQ-FM broadcasts to the Binghamton, NY area at 106.7 FM.
FM RADIO STATION

WRRR-FM 45516
Owner: Seven Ranges Radio Company Inc.
Editorial: Greens Run Road, Saint Marys, West Virginia 26170 **Tel:** 1 304 684-3400.
Web site: http://www.literock93r.com
Profile: WRRR-FM is a commercial station owned by Seven Ranges Radio Company Inc. The format of the station is adult contemporary. WRRR-FM broadcasts to the Saint Marys, WV area at 93.9 FM.
FM RADIO STATION

WRRV-FM 45288
Owner: Townsquare Media
Editorial: 2 Pendell Rd, Poughkeepsie, New York 12601-1513 **Tel:** 1 845 471-1500.
Web site: http://www.wrrv.com
Profile: WRRV-FM is a commercial station owned byTownsquare Media. The format of the station is rock alternative music. WRRV-FM broadcasts to the Poughkeepsie, NY area at 92.7 FM.
FM RADIO STATION

WRRX-FM 63060
Owner: Cumulus Media Inc.
Editorial: 6565 N W St, Ste 270, Pensacola, Florida 32505 **Tel:** 1 850 478-6011.
Email: wcoa@cumulus.com
Web site: http://www.mymagic106.com
Profile: WRRX-FM is a commercial station owned by Cumulus Media Inc. The format of the station is urban adult contemporary. WRRX-FM broadcasts to the Pensacola, FL area at 106.1 FM.
FM RADIO STATION

WRRZ-AM 35639
Owner: Sanchez Broadcasting Corporation
Editorial: 2164 Southeast Blvd, Clinton, North Carolina 28328-4758
Web site: http://www.radionuevavida880.com
Profile: WRRZ-AM is a commercial station owned by Sanchez Broadcasting Corporation. The format of the station is Spanish Christian music and talk. WRRZ-AM broadcast to the Clinton, NC area at 880 AM.
AM RADIO STATION

WRSA-FM 40690
Owner: NCA Inc.
Editorial: 8402 Memorial Pkwy SW, Huntsville, Alabama 35802-3033 **Tel:** 1 256 885-9797.
Email: wrsa@wrsa.com
Web site: http://www.lite969.com
Profile: WRSA-FM is a commercial station owned by NCA Inc. The format of the station is Lite Rock/Lite AC music. WRSA-FM broadcasts to the Huntsville, AL area at 96.9 FM.
FM RADIO STATION

WRSB-AM 36613
Owner: Genesee Media Corp.
Editorial: 20 Office Park Way, Pittsford, New York 14534-1718 **Tel:** 1 585 919-1482.
Email: sports@theteam.fm
Web site: http://theteam.fm
Profile: WRSB-AM is a commercial station owned by Genesee Media Corp. The format of the station is sports talk. WRSB-AM broadcasts to the Brockport, NY area at 1310 AM.
AM RADIO STATION

WRSC-AM 38171
Owner: FM Radio Licenses, LLC
Editorial: 2551 Park Center Blvd, State College, Pennsylvania 16801-3007 **Tel:** 1 814 237-9800.
Email: wmaj@comcast.net
Profile: WRSC-AM is a commercial station owned by FM Radio Licenses, LLC. The format of the station is sports. WRSC-AM broadcasts to State College, PA at 1390 AM.
AM RADIO STATION

WRSF-FM 40691
Owner: East Carolina Radio Group
Editorial: 2422 S Wrightsville Ave, Nags Head, North Carolina 27959 **Tel:** 1 252 441-1024.
Web site: http://www.dixie1057.com
Profile: WRSF-FM is a commercial station owned by East Carolina Radio Group. The format of the station is contemporary country. WRSF-FM broadcasts to the Nags Head, NC area at 93.3 FM.
FM RADIO STATION

WRSI-FM 44518
Owner: Saga Communications
Editorial: 15 Hampton Ave, Northampton, Massachusetts 1060 **Tel:** 1 413 586-7400.
Web site: http://www.wrsi.com
Profile: WRSI-FM is a commercial station owned by Saga Communications. The format of the station is adult album alternative music. WRSI-FM broadcasts to the Northampton, MA area at 93.9 FM.
FM RADIO STATION

WRSL-AM 545304
Owner: Lincoln-Garrard Broadcasting
Tel: 1 606 365-2126.
Profile: WRSL-AM is a commercial station owned by Lincoln-Garrard Broadcasting. The format for the station is sports. WRSL-AM broadcasts to the Corbin, KY area at 1600 AM.
AM RADIO STATION

WRSO-AM 411496
Owner: Star Over Orlando, Inc.
Editorial: Orlando, Florida **Tel:** 1 407 774-8810.
Profile: WRSO-AM is a commercial station owned and operated by Star Over Orlando, Inc. The format of the station is soft Brazilian. WRSO-AM broadcasts to the Orlando, FL area at 810 AM.
AM RADIO STATION

WRSR-FM 43281
Owner: Krol Communications
Editorial: 103 N Washington St, Owosso, Michigan 48867-2819 **Tel:** 1 989 725-1925.
Web site: http://www.classicfox.com
Profile: WRSR-FM is a commercial station owned by Krol Communications. The format of the station is classic rock. WRSR-FM broadcasts to the Flint, MI area at 103.9 FM.
FM RADIO STATION

WRSV-FM 46137
Owner: North Star Broadcasting
Editorial: 115 N Church St, Rocky Mount, North Carolina 27804-5402 **Tel:** 1 252 937-6111.
Email: soul92_2000@yahoo.com
Web site: http://www.soul92jams.com
Profile: WRSV-FM is a commercial station owned by North Star Broadcasting. The format of the station is urban contemporary and gospel. WRSV-FM broadcasts to the Rocky Mount, NC area at 92.1 FM.
FM RADIO STATION

WRSW-AM 38173
Owner: Talking Stick Communications LLC
Editorial: 216 W Market St, Warsaw, Indiana 46580-2800 **Tel:** 1 574 372-3064.
Profile: WRSW-AM is a commercial station owned by Talking Stick Communications LLC. The format of the station is news/talk. WRSW-AM broadcasts to the Warsaw, IN area at 1480 AM.
AM RADIO STATION

WRSW-FM 45518
Owner: Talking Stick Communications LLC
Editorial: 216 W Market St, Warsaw, Indiana 46580 **Tel:** 1 574 372-3064.
Web site: http://www.wrsw.net
Profile: WRSW-FM is a commercial station owned by Talking Stick Communications LLC. The format for the station is classic rock. WRSW-FM broadcasts to the South Bend, IN area at 107.3 FM.
FM RADIO STATION

WRSY-FM 43084
Owner: Saga Communications
Editorial: 15 Hampton Ave, Northampton, Massachusetts 1060 **Tel:** 1 413 586-7400.
Web site: http://www.wrsi.com
FM RADIO STATION

WRTA-AM 35641
Owner: Handsome Brothers Inc.
Editorial: 2513 6th Ave, Altoona, Pennsylvania 16602 **Tel:** 1 814 943-6112.
Web site: http://www.wrta.com
Profile: WRTA-AM is a commercial station owned by Handsome Brothers Inc. The format of the station is news and talk. WRTA-AM broadcasts to the Altoona, PA area at 1240 AM.
AM RADIO STATION

WRTB-FM 46745
Owner: Mid-West Family Broadcasting
Editorial: 2830 Sandy Hollow Rd, Rockford, Illinois 61109-2369 **Tel:** 1 815 874-7861.
Web site: http://www.953thebull.com
Profile: WRTB-FM is a commercial station owned by Mid-West Family Broadcasting. The format of the station is contemporary country. The station airs locally at 95.3 FM.
FM RADIO STATION

WRTE-FM 40202
Owner: Chicago Public Media Inc.
Editorial: 1401 W 18th St, Chicago, Illinois 60608-3003 **Tel:** 1 312 455-9455.
Web site: http://vocalo.org
Profile: WRTE-FM is a non-commercial station owned by Chicago Public Media Inc. The format of the station is community radio, featuring a variety of news, talk, public affairs and music programming. WRTE-FM broadcasts to the Greater Chicago area at 90.7 FM. WRTE-FM airs WBEW-FM's programming.
FM RADIO STATION

WRTH-FM 42120
Owner: Caron Broadcasting, Inc.
Editorial: 920 Wade Hampton Blvd, Greenville, South Carolina 29609-4944 **Tel:** 1 864 242-6240.
Email: contact@earthfmwrth.com
Web site: http://www.earthfmwrth.com
Profile: WRTH-FM is a commercial station owned by Caron Broadcasting, Inc. The format of the station is classic hits. WRTH-FM broadcasts to the Greenville, SC area at 103.3 FM.
FM RADIO STATION

WRTM-FM 44284
Owner: Commander Communications Corp.
Editorial: 1901 N Frontage Rd, Vicksburg, Mississippi 39180-5184 **Tel:** 1 601 956-1932.
Email: wrtmfm@bellsouth.net
Web site: http://www.smoothsoul1005.com
Profile: WRTM-FM is a commercial station owned by Commander Communications Corp. The formt for the station is R&B. WRTM-FM broadcasts to the Jackson, Miss. area at 1005. FM.
FM RADIO STATION

WRTO-AM 35872
Owner: Univision Communications Inc.
Editorial: 625 N Michigan Ave Ste 300, Chicago, Illinois 60611-3110 **Tel:** 1 312 981-1800.
Web site: http://www.univision.com/chicago/univision-america-1200am
Profile: WRTO-AM is a commercial station owned by Univision Communications Inc. The format of the station is Spanish sports. WRTO-AM broadcasts in the greater Chicago area at 1200 AM.
AM RADIO STATION

WRTO-FM 46367
Owner: Univision Communications Inc.
Editorial: 800 S Douglas Rd Ste 111, Coral Gables, Florida 33134-3187 **Tel:** 1 305 894-4500.
Web site: http://www.univision.com/miami/wrto
Profile: WRTO-FM is a commercial station owned by Unvision Communications Inc. The format of the station is Hispanic Top 40/CHR. WRTO-FM broadcasts to the Coral Gables, FL area at 98.3 FM.
FM RADIO STATION

WRTP-FM 40610
Owner: Radio Training Network, Inc.
Editorial: 7610 Falls Of Neuse Rd, Ste 155, Raleigh, North Carolina 27615 **Tel:** 1 919 256-9787.
Email: management@hisradiowrtp.com
Web site: http://www.hisradiowrtp.com
Profile: WRTP-FM is a non-commercial station owned by Radio Training Network, Inc. The format is contemporary Christian. WRTP-FM broadcasts to the Raleigh, NC area at 88.5 FM.
FM RADIO STATION

WRTR-FM 45011
Owner: iHeartMedia Inc.
Editorial: 3900 11th Ave, Tuscaloosa, Alabama 35401-7056 **Tel:** 1 205 344-4589.
Web site: http://www.news1420.com
Profile: WRTR-FM is a commercial station owned by iHeartMedia Inc. The format of the station is talk. WRTR-FM broadcasts to the Tuscaloosa, AL area at 105.9 FM.
FM RADIO STATION

WRTS-FM 42275
Owner: Connoisseur Media LLC
Editorial: 1 Boston Store Pl, Erie, Pennsylvania 16501-2313 **Tel:** 1 814 461-1000.
Web site: http://www.star104.com
Profile: WRTS-FM is a commercial station owned by Connoisseur Media LLC. The format of the station is Top 40/CHR music. WRTS-FM broadcasts to the Erie, PA area at 103.7 FM.
FM RADIO STATION

WRTT-FM 40556
Owner: Southern Stone Communications, LLC
Editorial: 1555 the Boardwalk Ste 1, Huntsville, Alabama 35816-1821 **Tel:** 1 256 536-1568.
Web site: http://www.rocket951.fm
Profile: WRTT-FM is a commercial station owned by Southern Stone Communications, LLC. The format of the station is rock music. WRTT-FM broadcasts to the Huntsville, AL area at 95.1 FM.
FM RADIO STATION

WRTW-FM 820864
Owner: Hyles-Anderson College
Editorial: 507 State St, Hammond, Indiana 46320-1533 **Tel:** 1 219 228-2995.
Email: info@thekeyfm.com
Web site: http://thekeyfm.com

Profile: WRTW-FM is a non-commercial station owned by Hyles-Anderson College. The format of the station features Christian talk programming. WRTW-FM broadcasts locally to the Crown Point, IN area at a frequency of 90.5 FM.
FM RADIO STATION

WRUB-FM 46480
Owner: iHeartMedia Inc.
Editorial: 1779 Independence Blvd, Sarasota, Florida 34234-2106 **Tel:** 1 941 552-4800.
Web site: http://www.rumbatampabay.com
Profile: WRUB-FM is a commercial station owned by iHeartMedia Inc. The format of the station is Spanish CHR. WRUB-FM broadcasts in the Venice, FL area at 106.5 FM.
FM RADIO STATION

WRUC-FM 40696
Owner: Union College
Editorial: WRUC Union College, Reamar Campus Center, Schenectady, New York 12308
Tel: 1 518 388-6154.
Email: wruc897@gmail.com
Web site: http://wruc.union.edu
FM RADIO STATION

WRUL-FM 45520
Owner: Withers Broadcasting Co.
Editorial: 101 N Church St, Carmi, Illinois 62821-1468
Tel: 1 618 382-4161.
Web site: http://www.wrul.com
Profile: WRUL-FM is a commercial station owned by Withers Broadcasting Co. The format of the station is contemporary country music. WRUL-FM broadcasts to the Carmi, IL area at 97.3 FM.
FM RADIO STATION

WRUM-FM 40220
Owner: iHeartMedia Inc.
Editorial: 2500 Maitland Center Pkwy Ste 401, Maitland, Florida 32751-4179 **Tel:** 1 407 916-7800.
Web site: http://www.rumba1003.com
Profile: WRUM-FM is a commercial station owned by iHeartMedia Inc. The format of the station is Hurban, featuring urban Spanish music and tropical music. WRUM-FM broadcasts to the Orlando, FL, area at 100.3 FM.
FM RADIO STATION

WRUN-FM 563158
Owner: WAMC
Editorial: 318 Central Ave, Albany, New York 12206-2522 **Tel:** 1 518 465-5233.
Email: news@wamc.org
Web site: http://www.wamc.org
Profile: WRUN-FM is a non-commercial station owned by WAMC. The format of the station is news and talk. WRUN-FM broadcasts to the Remsen, NY area at 90.3 FM.
FM RADIO STATION

WRUP-FM 45490
Owner: Great Lakes Radio Inc.
Editorial: 3060 US Highway 41 W, Marquette, Michigan 49855-2293 **Tel:** 1 906 228-6800.
Email: contact@broadcasteverywhere.com
Web site: http://www.wrup.com
Profile: WRUP-FM is a commercial station owned by Great Lakes Radio Inc. The format of the station is classic rock. The station broadcasts to Marquette, MI on 98.3 FM.
FM RADIO STATION

WRUS-AM 38175
Owner: Logan Radio Inc.
Editorial: 1601 Nashville St, Russellville, Kentucky 42276-8853 **Tel:** 1 270 726-2471.
Email: wrus@bellsouth.net
Web site: http://www.wrusam.com
Profile: WRUS-AM is a commercial station owned by Logan Radio Inc. The format of the station is variety. WRUS-AM broadcasts in the Russellville, KY area at 610 AM.
AM RADIO STATION

WRVA-AM 35961
Owner: iHeartMedia Inc.
Editorial: 3245 Basie Rd, Richmond, Virginia 23228-3404 **Tel:** 1 804 474-0000.
Web site: http://www.1140wrva.com
Profile: WRVA-AM is a commercial station owned by iHeartMedia Inc. The format of the station is news and talk. WRVA-AM broadcasts to the Richmond, VA area at 1140 AM.
AM RADIO STATION

WRVB-FM 43710
Owner: iHeartMedia Inc.
Editorial: 6006 Grand Central Ave, Parkersburg, West Virginia 26105-9125 **Tel:** 1 304 295-6070.
Web site: http://102theriver.iheart.com
Profile: WRVB-Fm is a commercial station owned by iHeartMedia Inc. The format of the station is Top 40/ CHR. WRVB-FM broadcasts to the Vienna, WV area at 102.1 FM.
FM RADIO STATION

WRVC-AM 38698
Owner: Kindred Communications
Editorial: 555 5th Ave, Huntington, West Virginia 25701-1907 **Tel:** 1 304 523-8401.
Email: info@supertalk941.com
Web site: http://wrvc.com
Profile: WRVC-AM is a commercial station owned by Kindred Communications. The format of the station is news, talk and sports. WRVC-AM broadcasts to the Huntington, WV area at 930 AM.
AM RADIO STATION

WRVE-FM 46044
Owner: iHeartMedia Inc.
Editorial: 1203 Troy Schenectady Rd, Latham, New York 12110-1046 **Tel:** 1 518 452-4800.
Web site: http://www.995theriver.com
Profile: WRVE-FM is a commercial station owned by iHeartMedia Inc. The format of the station is hot adult contemporary. WRVE-FM broadcasts to the Latham, NY area at 99.5 FM.
FM RADIO STATION

WRVF-FM 45818
Owner: iHeartMedia Inc.
Editorial: 125 S Superior St, Toledo, Ohio 43604-8747
Tel: 1 419 244-8321.
Email: 1015theriver@1015theriver.com
Web site: http://www.1015theriver.com
Profile: WRVF-FM is a commercial station owned by iHeartMedia Inc. The format of the station is Lite Rock/Lite AC music. WRVF-FM broadcasts to the Toledo, OH area at 101.5 FM.
FM RADIO STATION

WRVK-AM 35643
Owner: Saylor Broadcasting Inc.
Editorial: 235 Red Foley Rd, Renfro Valley, Kentucky 40473 **Tel:** 1 606 256-2146.
Email: manager@wrvk1460.com
Web site: http://www.wrvk1460.com
Profile: WRVK-AM is a commercial station owned by Saylor Broadcasting Inc. The format of the station is classic country and news. WRVK-AM broadcasts to the Renfro Valley, KY area at 1460 AM.
AM RADIO STATION

WRVM-FM 40703
Owner: WRVM Inc.
Editorial: 12701 State Highway 32, Suring, Wisconsin 54154 **Tel:** 1 920 842-2900.
Email: wrvm@wrvm.org
Web site: http://wrvmradio.org
Profile: WRVM-FM is a non-commercial station owned by WRVM Inc. The format of the station is religious. WRVM-FM broadcasts to the Green Bay, WI, area at 102.7 FM.
FM RADIO STATION

WRVP-AM 36890
Owner: Radio Vision Christiana Management Corp.
Editorial: 419 Broadway, Paterson, New Jersey 07501-2104 **Tel:** 1 973 881-8700.
Web site: http://www.radiovision.net
Profile: WRVP-AM is a non-commercial station owned by the Radio Vision Christiana Management Corp. The format of the station is Hispanic religious. WRVP-AM broadcasts to the New York metro at 1310 AM.
AM RADIO STATION

WRVQ-FM 41404
Owner: iHeartMedia Inc.
Editorial: 3245 Basie Rd, Richmond, Virginia 23228-3404 **Tel:** 1 804 474-0000.
Web site: http://q94radio.com
Profile: WRVQ-FM is a commercial station owned by iHeartMedia Inc. The format of the station is Top 40/ CHR. WRVQ-FM broadcasts to the Richmond, VA area at 94.5 FM.
FM RADIO STATION

WRVR-FM 45521
Owner: Entercom Communications Corp.
Editorial: 1835 Moriah Woods Blvd, Ste 1, Memphis, Tennessee 38117-7122 **Tel:** 1 901 767-0104.
Email: river104@wrvr.com
Web site: http://www.wrvr.com
Profile: WRVR-FM is a commercial station owned by Entercom Communications Corp. The format of the station is adult contemporary music. WRVR-FM broadcasts to the Memphis, TN, area at 104.5 FM.
FM RADIO STATION

WRVS-FM 41490
Owner: Elizabeth City State Univ.
Editorial: 1704 Weeksville Rd, Elizabeth City, North Carolina 27909-7977 **Tel:** 1 252 335-3517.
Web site: http://www.ecsu.edu/wrvs
Profile: WRVS-FM is a non-commercial station owned by Elizabeth City State Univ. The format of the station is variety. WRVS-FM broadcasts to the Elizabeth City, NC area at 89.9 FM.
FM RADIO STATION

WRVT-FM 75381
Owner: Vermont Public Radio
Editorial: 365 Troy Ave, Colchester, Vermont 05446-3126 **Tel:** 1 802 655-9451.
Email: news@vpr.net
Web site: http://www.vpr.net
Profile: WRVT-FM is a non-commercial station owned by Vermont Public Radio. The format of the station is news and talk. WRVT-FM broadcasts to the Colchester, VT area at 88.7 FM. The station does not accept PSAs.
FM RADIO STATION

WRVV-FM 45212
Owner: iHeartMedia Inc.
Editorial: 600 Corporate Cir, Harrisburg, Pennsylvania 17110-9787 **Tel:** 1 717 540-8800.
Email: wrvv@river973.com
Web site: http://www.river973.com
Profile: WRVV-FM is a commercial station owned by iHeartMedia Inc. The format of the station is classic hits. WRVV-FM broadcasts to the Harrisburg, PA area at 97.3 FM.
FM RADIO STATION

WRVW-FM 40890
Owner: iHeart Media Inc.
Editorial: 55 Music Sq W, Nashville, Tennessee 37203-3207 **Tel:** 1 615 664-2400.
Web site: http://www.1075theriver.com
Profile: WRVW-FM is a commercial station owned by iHeart Media Inc. The format of the station is Top 40/ CHR music. WRVW-FM broadcasts to the Nashville, TN area at 107.5 FM.
FM RADIO STATION

WRVY-FM 43711
Owner: WZOE Inc.
Editorial: 2209 S Main St, Princeton, Illinois 61356-9179 **Tel:** 1 815 875-8014.
Email: newsroom@wzoe.com
Web site: http://www.wzoe.com
Profile: WRVY-FM is a commercial station owned by WZOE Inc. The format of the station is country music. WRVY-FM broadcasts to the Henry, IL area at 100.5 FM.
FM RADIO STATION

WRVZ-FM 43537
Owner: West Virginia Radio Corp.
Editorial: 1111 Virginia St E, Charleston, West Virginia 25301 **Tel:** 1 304 342-8131.
Web site: http://www.987thebeat.com
Profile: WRVZ-FM is a commercial station owned by the West Virginia Radio Corp. The format of the station is urban contemporary. WRVZ-FM broadcasts to Charleston, WV and surrounding communities at 98.7 FM.
FM RADIO STATION

WRWB-FM 612329
Owner: iHeartMedia Inc.
Editorial: 20 Tucker Dr, Poughkeepsie, New York 12603-1644 **Tel:** 1 845 471-2300.
Web site: http://www.wrwdfm.com
Profile: WRWB-FM is a commercial station owned by iHeartMedia Inc. The format of the station is contemporary country. WRWB-FM airs locally on 99.3.
FM RADIO STATION

WRWD-FM 43038
Owner: iHeartMedia Inc.
Editorial: 20 Tucker Dr, Poughkeepsie, New York 12603-1644 **Tel:** 1 845 471-2300.
Web site: http://wrwdcountry.iheart.com
Profile: WRWD-FM is a commercial station owned by iHeartMedia Inc. The format of the station is country. WRWD-FM broadcasts to the Poughkeepsie, NY area at 107.3 FM.
FM RADIO STATION

WRWH-AM 35644
Owner: White County Media LLC
Editorial: 681 Hood St, Cleveland, Georgia 30528-1452 **Tel:** 1 706 865-3181.
Email: info@wrwh.com
Web site: http://www.wrwh.com
Profile: WRWH-AM is a commercial station owned by White County Media LLC. The format of the station is news and talk. WRWH-AM broadcasts to the Atlanta area at 1350 AM.
AM RADIO STATION

WRWM-FM 40090
Owner: Cumulus Media Inc.
Editorial: 6810 N Shadeland Ave, Indianapolis, Indiana 46220-4236 **Tel:** 1 317 842-9550.
Web site: http://www.939thebeat.com
Profile: WRWM-FM is a commercial station owned by Cumulus Media Inc. The format of the station is classic hip hop. WRWM-FM broadcasts to the Indianapolis area at 93.9 FM.
FM RADIO STATION

WRWN-FM 43076
Owner: Alpha Media
Editorial: 1 Saint Augustine Pl, Hilton Head Island, South Carolina 29928-4717 **Tel:** 1 843 785-9569.
Web site: http://www.rewind1079.com
Profile: WRWN-FM is a commercial station owned by Alpha Media. The format of the station is classic hits. WRWN-FM broadcasts to the Savannah, GA, area at 107.9 FM.
FM RADIO STATION

WRXB-AM 35645
Owner: Polnet Communications
Editorial: 3551 42nd Avenue South, Suite B-106, Saint Petersburg, Florida 33711 **Tel:** 1 727 865-1591.
Web site: http://www.wrxb.us
Profile: WRXB-AM is a commercial station owned by Polnet Communications. The station's format is gospel music. WRXB-AM broadcasts to the St. Petersburg, FL area at 1590 AM.
AM RADIO STATION

WRXK-FM 46065
Owner: Beasley Broadcast Group
Editorial: 20125 S Tamiami Trl, Estero, Florida 33928-2117 **Tel:** 1 239 495-2100.
Web site: http://www.96krock.com
Profile: WRXK-FM is a commercial station owned by Beasley Broadcast Group. The format of the station is rock. WRXK-FM broadcasts to the Naples, FL area at 96.1 FM.
FM RADIO STATION

WRXL-FM 46050
Owner: iHeartMedia Inc.
Editorial: 3245 Basie Rd, Richmond, Virginia 23228-3404 **Tel:** 1 804 474-0000.
Web site: http://www.wrxl.com
Profile: WRXL-FM is a commercial station owned by iHeartMedia Inc. The format of the station is rock alternative. WRXL-FM broadcasts to the Richmond, VA area at 102.1 FM.
FM RADIO STATION

WRXO-AM 38177
Owner: Roxboro Broadcasting Co.
Editorial: 2070 Hurdle Mills Road, Roxboro, North Carolina 27573 **Tel:** 1 336 599-0266.
Email: radiod@aol.com
Web site: http://www.radioroxboro.com
Profile: WRXO-AM is a commercial station owned by Roxboro Broadcasting Co. The format of the station is country. WRXO-AM broadcasts to the Roxboro, NC area at 1430 AM.
AM RADIO STATION

WRXP-FM 43424
Owner: Cumulus Media Inc.
Editorial: 2000 Elm St SE, Minneapolis, Minnesota 55414-2531 **Tel:** 1 612 617-4000.
Email: info@105theticket.com
Web site: http://www.105thevibe.com/
Profile: WRXP-FM is a commercial station owned by Cumulus Media Inc. The format of the station is classic hip hop. WRXP-FM's target audience is adults, ages 25 to 44 in the Greater Minneapolis area. The station airs locally on 105.3 FM and is known as "105 The Vibe." The station is a trimulcast with WGVX-FM and WGVZ-FM.
FM RADIO STATION

WRXQ-FM 41423
Owner: Alpha Media LLC
Editorial: 2410 Caton Farm Rd Unit B, Crest Hill, Illinois 60403-1374 **Tel:** 1 815 556-0100.
Web site: http://www.qrockonline.com
Profile: WRXQ-FM is a commercial station owned by Alpha Media LLC . The format of the station is classic rock music. WRXQ-FM broadcasts to the Crest Hill, IL area at 100.7 FM.
FM RADIO STATION

WRXR-FM 46246
Owner: iHeartMedia Inc.
Editorial: 7413 Old Lee Hwy, Chattanooga, Tennessee 37421-1142 **Tel:** 1 423 892-3333.
Web site: http://www.rock105.net
Profile: WRXR-FM is a commercial station owned by iHeartMedia Inc. The format of the station is rock music. WRXR-FM broadcasts to the Chattanooga, TN area at 105.5 FM.
FM RADIO STATION

WRXT-FM 42358
Owner: Positive Alternative Radio
Editorial: 22226 Timberlake Rd, Lynchburg, Virginia 24502-7214 **Tel:** 1 800 774-9798.
Email: office@spiritfm.com
Web site: http://www.spiritfm.com
Profile: WRXT-FM is a non-commercial station owned by Positive Alternative Radio. The format of the station is contemporary Christian. WRXT-FM broadcasts to the Lynchburg, VA area at 90.3 FM.
FM RADIO STATION

WRXV-FM 763600
Owner: Invisible Allies Ministries
Editorial: 925 Houserville Rd, State College, Pennsylvania 16801-7163 **Tel:** 1 814 867-3836.
Email: info@revfm.net
Web site: http://revfm.net
Profile: WRXV-FM is a non-commercial station owned by Invisible Allies Ministries. The format of the station is Contemporary Christian. WRXV-FM broadcasts to the State College, Altoona Philipsburg and Huntingdon areas in Pennsylvania at 89.1 FM.
FM RADIO STATION

WRXX-FM 45522
Owner: Withers Broadcasting Co.
Editorial: 302 S Poplar St, Centralia, Illinois 62801-3922 **Tel:** 1 618 533-5700.
Email: wilynews@mywithersradio.com
Web site: http://www.mywithersradio.com/centralia
Profile: WRXX-FM is a commercial station owned by Withers Broadcasting Co. The format of the station is hot adult contemporary. WRXX-FM broadcasts to the Centralia, IL area at 95.3 FM.
FM RADIO STATION

WRXZ-FM 42960
Owner: iHeartMedia Inc.
Editorial: 4841 Highway 17 Byp S, Myrtle Beach, South Carolina 29577-6683 **Tel:** 1 843 293-0107.
Web site: http://rock107mb.iheart.com
Profile: WRXZ-FM is an commercial station owned by iHeartMedia Inc. The format of the station is rock/ album-oriented rock. WRXZ-FM broadcasts to the Myrtle Beach, SC area at 107.1 FM.
FM RADIO STATION

WRYM-AM 35646
Owner: Eight Forty Broadcasting
Editorial: 1056 Willard Ave, Newington, Connecticut 6111 **Tel:** 1 860 666-5646.
Email: radio@wrym840.com
Web site: http://www.wrymradio.com
Profile: WRYM-AM is a commercial station owned by Eight Forty Broadcasting. The format of the station is

Hispanic music. WRYM-AM broadcasts to the Newington, CT area at 840 AM.
AM RADIO STATION

WRYP-FM 402103
Owner: Horizon Christian Fellowship
Editorial: 356 Broad St, Fitchburg, Massachusetts 01420-3030 **Tel:** 1 888 310-7729.
Email: info@renewfm.org
Web site: http://www.renewfm.org
Profile: WRYP-FM is a non-commercial station owned by Horizon Christian Fellowship. The format of the station is contemporary Christian. WRYP-FM broadcasts to the Fitchburg, MA area at 90.1 FM.
FM RADIO STATION

WRYT-AM 35943
Owner: Covenant Network
Editorial: 4424 Hampton Ave, Saint Louis, Missouri 63109 **Tel:** 1 314 752-7000.
Email: covenantnetwork@juno.com
Web site: http://www.covenantnet.net
Profile: WRYT-AM is a non-commercial station owned by the Covenant Network. The format of the station is contemporary Christian and talk. WRYT-AM broadcasts to the St. Louis area at 1080 AM.
AM RADIO STATION

WRZE-FM 137272
Owner: Qantum Communications Inc.
Editorial: 181 E Evans St Ste 311, Florence, South Carolina 29506-5505 **Tel:** 1 843 667-4600.
Web site: http://swagga941.com/#&panel1-1
Profile: WRZE-FM is a commercial station owned by Qantum Communications Inc. The format of the station is urban contemporary. WRZE-FM broadcasts to the Florence, SC area at 94.1 FM.
FM RADIO STATION

WRZI-FM 42349
Owner: Commonwealth Broadcasting Corp.
Editorial: 611 W Poplar St Ste C2, Elizabethtown, Kentucky 42701-2483 **Tel:** 1 270 763-0800.
Email: lhaggard@commonwealthbroadcasting.com
Web site: http://www.1073thepoint.com
Profile: WRZI-FM is a commercial station owned by Commonwealth Broadcasting Corp. The format of the station is classic rock. WRZI-FM airs at 107.3 FM in the Elizabethtown, KY area.
FM RADIO STATION

WRZK-FM 70437
Owner: Holston Valley Broadcasting Corp.
Editorial: 222 Commerce St, Kingsport, Tennessee 37660-4319 **Tel:** 1 423 246-9578.
Email: news@wtfm.com
Web site: http://www.wrzk.com
Profile: WRZK-FM is a commercial station owned by Holston Valley Broadcasting Corp. The format of the station is rock/album-oriented rock. WRZK-FM broadcasts to the Kingsport, TN area at 95.9 FM.
FM RADIO STATION

WRZN-AM 35997
Owner: Marc Radio Group, LLC
Editorial: 100 NW 76th Dr Ste 2, Gainesville, Florida 32607-6659 **Tel:** 1 352 313-3150.
Email: info@theshepherdradio.com
Web site: http://www.theshepherdradio.com/
Profile: WRZN-AM is a commercial station owned by Marc Radio Group, LLC. The format of the station is religious. WRZN-AM broadcasts to the Hernando, FL area at 720 AM.
AM RADIO STATION

WRZQ-FM 41392
Owner: Reising Radio Partners Inc.
Editorial: 825 Washington St, Columbus, Indiana 47201-6265 **Tel:** 1 812 379-1077.
Email: qmix@qmix.com
Web site: http://www.qmix.com
Profile: WRZQ-FM is a commercial station owned by Reising Radio Partners Inc. The format of the station is adult contemporary music. WRZQ-FM broadcasts to the Indianapolis area at 107.3 FM.
FM RADIO STATION

WRZR-FM 43536
Owner: Hembree Communications Inc.
Editorial: 514 N John F Kennedy Ave, Loogootee, Indiana 47553-1102 **Tel:** 1 812 295-9480.
Email: wrzr@psci.net
Web site: http://wrzr.us/
Profile: WRZR-FM is a commercial station owned by Hembree Communications Inc. The format of the station is classic rock music. WRZR-FM broadcasts to the Loogootee, IN area at 94.5 FM.
FM RADIO STATION

WRZZ-FM 40951
Owner: Burbach of WV, LLC
Editorial: 5 Rosemar Cir, Parkersburg, West Virginia 26104 **Tel:** 1 304 485-4565.
Web site: http://www.z106.net
Profile: WRZZ-FM is a commercial station owned by Burbach of WV, LLC. The format of the station is classic rock. WRZZ-FM broadcasts to the Parkersburg, WV area at 106.1 FM.
FM RADIO STATION

WSAA-FM 544558
Owner: Air 1
Editorial: 601 Hidden Forest Dr, Chattanooga, Tennessee 37421-3442 **Tel:** 1 815 988-3210.
Web site: http://www.air1.com
Profile: WSAA-FM is a commercial station owned by Air 1. The format of the station is Christian rock music programming. WSAA-FM broadcasts to the Cleveland, TN area at 93.1 FM.
FM RADIO STATION

WSAG-FM 445493
Owner: MacDonald Broadcasting Co.
Editorial: 2000 Whittier St, Saginaw, Michigan 48601 **Tel:** 1 989 752-8161.
Web site: http://www.thebay104fm.com
Profile: WSAG-FM is a commercial station owned by MacDonald Broadcasting Co. The format of the station is Lite Rock/Lite AC. WSAG-FM broadcasts to the Saginaw, MI area at 104.1 FM.
FM RADIO STATION

WSAI-AM 36285
Owner: iHeartMedia Inc.
Editorial: 8044 Montgomery Rd Ste 650, Cincinnati, Ohio 45236-2959 **Tel:** 1 513 686-8300.
Web site: http://www.foxsports1360.com
Profile: WSAI-AM is a commercial station owned by iHeartMedia Inc. The format of the station is sports. WSAI-AM broadcasts to the Cincinnati area at 1360 AM.
AM RADIO STATION

WSAK-FM 42047
Owner: Cumulus Media Inc.
Editorial: 292 Middle Rd, Dover, New Hampshire 03820-4901 **Tel:** 1 603 749-9750.
Web site: http://www.shark1053.com
Profile: WSAK-FM is a commercial station owned by Cumulus Media Inc. The format of the station is classic hits. WSAK-FM broadcasts to the Dover, NH area at 102.1 FM.
FM RADIO STATION

WSAL-AM 38178
Owner: Hoosier AM/FM LLC
Editorial: 425 2nd St, Logansport, Indiana 46947-3410 **Tel:** 1 574 722-4000.
Email: 1230wsal@gmail.com
Web site: http://www.indianasbestradio.com
Profile: WSAL-AM is a commercial station owned by Hoosier AM/FM LLC. The format of the station is oldies and talk. WSAL-AM broadcasts to the Indianapolis area at 1230 AM.
AM RADIO STATION

WSAM-AM 38179
Owner: MacDonald Broadcasting Co.
Editorial: 2000 Whittier St, Saginaw, Michigan 48601 **Tel:** 1 989 752-8161.
Web site: http://thebay104fm.com
Profile: WSAM-AM is a commercial station owned by MacDonald Broadcasting Co. The format of the station is Lite Rock/Lite AC music. WSAM-AM broadcasts to the Saginaw, MI area at 1400 AM.
AM RADIO STATION

WSAN-AM 36404
Owner: iHeartMedia Inc.
Editorial: 1541 Alta Dr Ste 400, Whitehall, Pennsylvania 18052-5632 **Tel:** 1 610 434-1742.
Web site: http://1470espndeportes.iheart.com
Profile: WSAN-AM is a commercial station owned by iHeartMedia Inc. The format of the station is sports. WSAN-AM broadcasts to the Whitehall, PA area at 1470 AM.
AM RADIO STATION

WSAQ-FM 46493
Owner: Radio First
Editorial: 808 Huron Ave, Port Huron, Michigan 48060-3705 **Tel:** 1 810 982-9000.
Web site: http://www.wsaq.com
Profile: WSAQ-FM is a commercial station owned by Radio First. The format of the station is country. WSAQ-FM broadcasts to the Port Huron, MI area at 107.1 FM.
FM RADIO STATION

WSAR-AM 35648
Owner: Karam(Robert & James)
Editorial: 1 Home St, Somerset, Massachusetts 02725-1002 **Tel:** 1 508 678-9727.
Email: news@wsar.com
Web site: http://www.wsar.com
Profile: WSAR-AM is a commercial station owned by Robert & James Karam. The format of the station is talk. WSAR-AM broadcasts to the south coast of Massachusetts and the Providence, RI area at 1480 AM.
AM RADIO STATION

WSAT-AM 35649
Owner: 2B Productions, LLC
Editorial: 1525 Jake Alexander Blvd W, Salisbury, North Carolina 28147-1208 **Tel:** 1 704 633-0621.
Web site: http://www.1280wsat.com
Profile: WSAT-AM is a commercial station owned by 2B Productions, LLC. The format of the station is adult standards. WSAT-AM broadcasts to the Charlotte, NC area at 1280 AM.
AM RADIO STATION

WSAU-AM 38180
Owner: Midwest Communications Inc.
Editorial: 557 Scott St, Wausau, Wisconsin 54403-4829 **Tel:** 1 715 842-1672.
Web site: http://www.wsau.com
Profile: WSAU-AM is a commercial station owned by Midwest Communications Inc. The format of the station is news, talk and sports. WSAU-AM broadcasts in the Wausau, WI area at 550 AM.
AM RADIO STATION

WSAU-FM 41606
Owner: Midwest Communications Inc.
Editorial: 557 Scott St, Wausau, Wisconsin 54403-4829 **Tel:** 1 715 842-1672.
Web site: http://www.wsau.com
Profile: WSAU-FM is a commercial station owned by Midwest Communications Inc. The format of the station is news, talk and sports. WSAU-FM broadcasts to the Plover, WI area at 99.9 FM.
FM RADIO STATION

WSBA-AM 38182
Owner: Cumulus Media Inc.
Editorial: 5989 Susquehanna Plaza Dr, York, Pennsylvania 17406-0910 **Tel:** 1 717 764-1155.
Email: info@wsba910.com
Web site: http://www.wsba910.com
Profile: WSBA-AM is a commercial station owned by Cumulus Media Inc. The format of the station is news and talk. WSBA-AM broadcasts to the York, PA area at 910 AM.
AM RADIO STATION

WSB-AM 38181
Owner: Cox Media Group, Inc.
Editorial: 1601 W Peachtree St NE, Atlanta, Georgia 30309-2641 **Tel:** 1 404 897-7500.
Email: newstips@wsbradio.com
Web site: http://www.wsbradio.com
Profile: WSB-AM is a commercial station owned by Cox Media Group, Inc. The format of the station is news and talk. WSB-AM broadcasts to the Atlanta area at 750 AM.
AM RADIO STATION

WSBB-AM 35651
Owner: Diegel Communications LLC
Editorial: 229 Canal St, New Smyrna Beach, Florida 32168-7005 **Tel:** 1 386 428-9091.
Web site: http://www.myam1230.com
Profile: WSBB-AM is a commercial station owned by Diegel Communications LLC. The format of the station is adult contemporary. WSBB-AM broadcasts to the Orlando, FL, area at 1230 AM.
AM RADIO STATION

WSBB-FM 44368
Owner: Cox Media Group, Inc.
Editorial: 1601 W Peachtree St NE, Atlanta, Georgia 30309-2641 **Tel:** 1 404 897-7500.
Email: newstips@wsbradio.com
Web site: http://www.wsbradio.com
Profile: WSBB-FM is a commercial station owned by Cox Media Group, Inc. The format of the station is news and talk. WSBB-FM broadcasts to the Atlanta area at 95.5 FM.
FM RADIO STATION

WSB-FM 45524
Owner: Cox Media Group, Inc.
Editorial: 1601 W Peachtree St NE, Atlanta, Georgia 30309-2641 **Tel:** 1 404 897-7500.
Email: newstips@wsbradio.com
Web site: http://www.b985.com
Profile: WSB-FM is a commercial station owned by Cox Media Group, Inc. The format of the station is adult contemporary. WSB-FM broadcasts to the Atlanta area at 98.5 FM.
FM RADIO STATION

WSBG-FM 45526
Owner: Connoisseur Media
Editorial: 22 S 6th St, Stroudsburg, Pennsylvania 18360-2002 **Tel:** 1 570 421-2100.
Web site: http://www.935sbg.com
Profile: WSBG-FM is a commercial station owned by Connoisseur Media. The format of the station is Hot AC. WSBG-FM broadcasts to the Stroudsburg, PA area at 93.5 FM.
FM RADIO STATION

WSBH-FM 445455
Owner: Horizon Broadcasting Co, LLC
Editorial: 380 N Wickham Rd, Melbourne, Florida 32935-8646 **Tel:** 1 321 752-9850.
Web site: http://www.beach985.com
Profile: WSBH-FM is a commercial station owned by Horizon Broadcasting Co, LLC. The format of the station is classic hits. WSBH-FM broadcasts to the Stuart, FL area at 98.5 FM.
FM RADIO STATION

WSBI-AM 36032
Owner: Casa de Dios
Editorial: 1079 E Trinity Ln, Nashville, Tennessee 37216-3043 **Tel:** 1 615 262-2511.
Profile: WSBI-AM is a commercial station owned by Donnie Cox. The format of the station is classic country music. WSBI-AM broadcasts to the Nashville, TN area at 1210 AM.
AM RADIO STATION

WSBM-AM 38342
Owner: Big River Broadcasting Corp.
Editorial: 624 Sam Phillips St, Florence, Alabama 35630-5859 **Tel:** 1 256 764-8121.
Web site: http://www.wsbm.com
Profile: WSBM-AM is a commercial station owned by Big River Broadcasting Corp. The format of the station is sports. WSBM-AM broadcasts to the Florence, AL area at 1340 AM.
AM RADIO STATION

WSBR-AM 35653
Owner: Beasley Broadcast Group
Editorial: 1650 S Dixie Hwy Floor 5, Boca Raton, Florida 33432-7462 **Tel:** 1 561 997-0074.
Web site: http://www.wsbrradio.com
Profile: WSBR-AM is a commercial station owned by Beasley Broadcast Group. The format of the station is financial business news and talk. WSBR-AM broadcasts to the Boca Raton, FL area at 740 AM.
AM RADIO STATION

WSBS-AM 3616
Owner: Gamma Broadcasting LLC
Editorial: 425 Stockbridge Rd, Great Barrington, Massachusetts 01230-1233 **Tel:** 1 413 528-0860.
Email: fun@wsbs.com
Web site: http://www.wsbs.com
Profile: WSBS-AM is a commercial station owned by Gamma Broadcasting LLC. The format of the station is adult contemporary. WSBS-AM broadcasts to the Great Barrington, MA area at 860 AM.
AM RADIO STATION

WSBT-AM 3818
Owner: Mid-West Family Broadcasting
Editorial: 1301 E Douglas Rd, Mishawaka, Indiana 46545-1732 **Tel:** 1 574 233-3141.
Email: info@wsbtradio.com
Web site: http://www.wsbtradio.com
Profile: WSBT-AM is a commercial station owned by WSBT Inc. The station is owned by Mid-West Family Broadcasting. The format of the station is news, sports, and talk. WSBT-AM broadcasts to South Bend, IN at 960 AM.
AM RADIO STATION

WSBV-AM 3599
Owner: Lamont Alexander Logan
Editorial: 1180 Plywood Trail, South Boston, Virginia 24592 **Tel:** 1 434 572-4418.
Email: llogan@gcronline.com
Web site: http://www.wsbvam.com
Profile: WSBV-AM is a commercial station owned by Lamont Alexander Logan. The format of the station is gospel music. WSBV-AM broadcasts to the South Boston, VA area at 1560 AM.
AM RADIO STATION

WSBW-FM 44642
Owner: Nicolet Broadcasting Inc.
Editorial: 30 N 18Th Ave Ste 8, Sturgeon Bay, Wisconsin 54235-3207 **Tel:** 1 920 746-9430.
Email: wbdk@doorcountydailynews.com
Web site: http://www.doorcountydailynews.com
Profile: WSBW-FM is a commercial station owned by Nicolet Broadcasting Inc. The format of the station is adult standards. WSBW-FM broadcasts to the Sturgeon Bay, WI area at 105.1 FM.
FM RADIO STATION

WSBY-FM 4442
Owner: iHeartMedia Inc.
Editorial: 351 Tilghman Rd, Gateway Crossing, Salisbury, Maryland 21804-1920 **Tel:** 1 410 742-1923.
Email: delmarvapsa@iheartmedia.com
Web site: http://mymagic989.iheart.com
Profile: WSBY-FM is a commercial station owned by iHeartMedia Inc. The format of the station is urban adult contemporary music. WSBY-FM broadcasts to the Salisbury, MD area at 98.9 FM.
FM RADIO STATION

WSBZ-FM 4395
Owner: Carter Broadcasting
Editorial: 1306 Bay Dr, Santa Rosa Beach, Florida 32459-5587 **Tel:** 1 850 267-3279.
Email: office@wsbz.com
Web site: http://www.seabreeze.fm
Profile: WSBZ-FM is a commercial station owned by Carter Broadcasting. The format of the station is smooth jazz. WSBZ-FM broadcasts to the Destin, FL area at 106.3 FM.
FM RADIO STATION

WSCC-FM 4230
Owner: iHeartMedia Inc.
Editorial: 950 Houston Northcutt Blvd Ste 201, Mount Pleasant, South Carolina 29464-5645 **Tel:** 1 843 884-2534.
Web site: http://www.943wsc.com
Profile: WSCC-FM is a commercial station owned by iHeartMedia Inc. The format of the station is news and talk. WSCC-FM broadcasts to the Charleston, SC area at 94.3 FM.
FM RADIO STATION

WSCD-FM 4071
Owner: Minnesota Public Radio
Editorial: 207 W Superior St, Ste 224, Duluth, Minnesota 55802 **Tel:** 1 218 722-9411.
Email: newsroom@mpr.org
Web site: http://access.mpr.org/stations/wscnwscd
Profile: WSCD-FM is a non-commercial station owned by Minnesota Public Radio. The format of the station is classical music. WSCD-FM broadcasts to the Duluth, MN area at 92.9 FM.
FM RADIO STATION

WSCH-FM 4071
Owner: Wagon Wheel Broadcasting LLC
Editorial: 20 E High St, Lawrenceburg, Indiana 47025-1820 **Tel:** 1 812 537-0944.
Email: info@eaglecountryonline.com
Web site: http://www.eaglecountryonline.com
Profile: WSCH-FM is a commercial station owned by Wagon Wheel Broadcasting LLC. The format of the station is contemporary country music. WSCH-FM broadcasts to the Lawrenceburg, IN area at 99.3 FM.
FM RADIO STATION

WSCN-FM 41550
Owner: Minnesota Public Radio
Editorial: 207 W Superior St Ste 224, Duluth, Minnesota 55802-4041 **Tel:** 1 218 722-9411.
Email: newsroom@mpr.org
Web site: http://www.mpr.org/listen/stations/wscnwscd
Profile: WSCN-FM is a non-commercial station owned by Minnesota Public Radio. The format of the station is news and talk. WSCN-FM broadcasts to the Duluth, MN area at 100.5 FM.
FM RADIO STATION

WSCO-AM 36085
Owner: Woodward Communications, Inc.
Editorial: 2800 E College Ave, Appleton, Wisconsin 54915-3255 **Tel:** 1 920 733-6639.
Web site: http://www.953wsco.com
Profile: WSCO-AM is a commercial station owned by Woodward Communications, Inc. The format of the station is sports. WSCO-AM broadcasts to the Appleton, WI area at 1570 AM.
AM RADIO STATION

WSCR-AM 38914
Owner: CBS Radio
Editorial: 180 N Stetson Ave Ste 1250, Chicago, Illinois 60601-6732 **Tel:** 1 312 729-3967.
Web site: http://chicago.cbslocal.com/station/670-the-score
Profile: WSCR-AM is a commercial station owned by CBS Radio. The format of the station is sports. WSCR-AM broadcasts to the Chicago area at 670 AM.
AM RADIO STATION

WSCS-FM 44032
Owner: Colby-Sawyer College
Editorial: 541 Main St, New London, New Hampshire 3257 **Tel:** 1 603 526-3493.
Email: wscs@colby-sawyer.edu
Web site: http://www.colby-sawyer.edu/wscs
Profile: WSCS-FM is a non-commercial station owned by Colby-Sawyer College. The format of the station is college variety. WSCS-FM broadcasts to the New London, NH area at 90.9 FM.
FM RADIO STATION

WSCW-AM 39198
Owner: LM Communications, Inc.
Editorial: 100 Kanawha Ter, Saint Albans, West Virginia 25177-2771 **Tel:** 1 304 722-3308.
Email: wjypnet@gmail.com
Web site: http://www.wscwam.com/
Profile: WSCW-AM is a commercial station owned by LM Communications, Inc. The format of the station is Christian teaching. WSCW-AM broadcasts to the South Charleston, WV area at 1410 AM.
AM RADIO STATION

WSCY-FM 46456
Owner: Northeast Communications Corp.
Editorial: 110 Babbitt Rd, Franklin, New Hampshire 03235-2105 **Tel:** 1 603 934-2500.
Web site: http://www.wscy.com
Profile: WSCY-FM is a commercial station owned by Northeast Communications Corp. The format of the station is classic country. WSCY-FM broadcasts to the Boston area at 106.9 FM.
FM RADIO STATION

WSCZ-FM 41944
Owner: Miller Communications Inc.
Editorial: 200 Regional Pkwy Bldg C, Orangeburg, South Carolina 29118-9700 **Tel:** 1 803 536-1710.
Email: production@miller.fm
Web site: http://www.hot1039fm.com
Profile: WSCZ-FM is a commercial station owned by Miller Communications Inc. The format of the station is urban contemporary. WSCZ-FM broadcasts to the Winnsboro, SC area at 93.9 FM.
FM RADIO STATION

WSDE-AM 36484
Owner: Schoharie County Broadcasting, LLC
Editorial: 813 E Main St Ste 5, Cobleskill, New York 12043-5011 **Tel:** 1 518 234-3400.
Web site: http://www.1190wsde.com
Profile: WSDE-AM is a commercial station owned by Schoharie County Broadcasting, LLC. The format of the station is adult standards. WSDE-AM broadcasts in the Cobleskill, NY area at 1190 AM.
AM RADIO STATION

WSDK-AM 36251
Owner: Blount Communications, Inc
Editorial: 160 Chapel Rd Ste 106, Manchester, Connecticut 06042-8929 **Tel:** 1 860 432-9735.
Email: info@wsdk1550.com
Web site: http://lifechangingradio.com/wsdk
Profile: WSDK-AM is a commercial stationed owned by Blount communications, Inc. The format of the station is Christian talk. WSDK-AM broadcasts to the Hartford, CT area at a frequency of 1550 AM.
AM RADIO STATION

WSDM-FM 552094
Owner: Innovation Center, Inc.
Editorial: 1301 Ohio Street, Terre Haute, Indiana 47807 **Tel:** 1 317 467-1062.
Email: wjcfradio@aol.com
Web site: http://wjcfradio.com
Profile: WSDM-FM is a non-commercial station owned by the Innovation Center, Inc. and operated Indiana Community Radio Corporation. The format of the station is Hot Adult Contemporary music. WSDM-FM broadcasts to the Indianapolis area at a frequency of 90.1 FM.
FM RADIO STATION

WSDO-AM 35718
Owner: J & V Communications Inc.
Editorial: 222 Hazard St, Orlando, Florida 32804
Tel: 1 407 841-8282.
Email: wprd1440@gmail.com
Web site: http://www.wprd.com
Profile: WSDO-AM is commercial station owned by J & V Communications Inc. The format of the station is Hispanic religious talk. WSDO-AM broadcasts to the Orlando, FL area at 1400 AM.
AM RADIO STATION

WSDQ-AM 35941
Owner: Rodgson Inc.
Editorial: 1446 Main St, Dunlap, Tennessee 37327-3704 **Tel:** 1 423 949-5805.
Email: wsdq1190@gmail.com
Web site: http://www.wsdq1190.com
Profile: WJDQ-AM is a commercial station owned by Rodgson Inc. The format of the station is classic country. WSDQ-AM broadcasts to the Dunlap, TN area at 1190 AM.
AM RADIO STATION

WSDR-AM 39180
Owner: Withers Broadcasting Co.
Editorial: 3101 Freeport Rd, Sterling, Illinois 61081-8612 **Tel:** 1 815 625-3400.
Email: wsdr1240@theramp.net
Profile: WSDR-AM is a commercial station owned by Withers Broadcasting Co. The format of the station is news and talk. WSDR-AM broadcasts to the Sterling, IL area at 1240 AM.
AM RADIO STATION

WSDS-AM 35655
Owner: Birach Broadcasting Corp.
Editorial: 580 W Clark Rd, Ypsilanti, Michigan 48198
Tel: 1 734 484-0078.
Email: wsds@explosiva1480.com
Web site: http://www.explosiva1480.com
Profile: WSDS-AM is a commercial station owned by Birach Broadcasting Corp. The format of the station is Hispanic. WSDS-AM broadcasts to the Ypsilanti, MI area at 1480 AM.
AM RADIO STATION

WSDV-AM 36020
Owner: iHeartMedia Inc.
Editorial: 1779 Independence Blvd, Sarasota, Florida 34234-2106 **Tel:** 1 941 552-4800.
Web site: http://sarasotanewsradio.iheart.com
Profile: WSDV-AM is a commercial station owned by iHeartMedia Inc. The format of the station is adult standards. WSDV-AM broadcasts to the Sarasota, FL, area at 1450 AM.
AM RADIO STATION

WSEA-FM 44163
Owner: Cumulus Media Inc.
Editorial: 11640 Highway 17 Byp, Murrells Inlet, South Carolina 29576-9332 **Tel:** 1 843 651-7869.
Web site: http://www.teammyrtlebeach.com
Profile: WSEA-FM is a commercial station owned by Cumulus Media Inc. The format of the station is sports. WSEA-FM broadcasts in the Murrells Inlet, SC area at 100.3 FM.
FM RADIO STATION

WSEG-AM 36850
Owner: MarMac Communications, LLC
Tel: 1 912 920-4441.
Email: wsegradio@yahoo.com
Profile: WSEG-AM is a commercial station owned by MarMac Communications, LLC. The format of the station is sports. WSEG-AM broadcasts to the Savannah, GA/Hilton Head, SC area at 1400 AM.
AM RADIO STATION

WSEI-FM 45529
Owner: Forcht Broadcasting
Editorial: 4667 E Radio Tower Ln, Olney, Illinois 62450 **Tel:** 1 618 393-2156.
Email: freedom929@forchtbroadcasting.com
Web site: http://www.freedom929.com
Profile: WSEI-FM is a commercial station owned by Forcht Broadcasting. The format of the station is contemporary country. WSEI-FM broadcasts to the Olney, IL area at 92.9 FM.
FM RADIO STATION

WSEK-FM 41334
Owner: iHeart Media Inc.
Editorial: 101 1st Radio Ln, Somerset, Kentucky 42503-4639 **Tel:** 1 606 678-5151.
Web site: http://www.k93country.com
Profile: WSEK-FM is a commercial station owned by iHeart Media Inc. The format of the station is contemporary country. WSEK-FM broadcasts to the Lexington, KY area at a frequency of 93.9 FM.
FM RADIO STATION

WSEL-FM 43296
Owner: Collins Jr.(Ollie)
Editorial: Highway 6 East, Pontotoc, Mississippi 38863 **Tel:** 1 662 489-0297.
Email: wselfm96.7@gmail.com
Web site: http://wselradio.com
FM RADIO STATION

WSEM-AM 35656
Owner: Flint Media
Editorial: 521 S Scott St, Bainbridge, Georgia 39819-4101 **Tel:** 1 229 246-1960.
Web site: http://sowegalive.com/
Profile: WSEM-AM is a commercial station owned by Flint Media. The format of the station is news, sports. WSEM-AM broadcasts to the Donalsonville, GA area at 1500 AM.
AM RADIO STATION

WSEN-FM 43313
Owner: Renard Communications Corp.
Editorial: 401 West Kirkpatrick st, East Syracuse, New York 13204 **Tel:** 1 315 472-0222.
Email: info@dinofm.com
Web site: http://dinofm.com
Profile: WSEN-FM is a commercial station owned by Renard Communications Corp. The station is currently stunting formats and broadcasts to the East Syracuse, NY area at 103.9 FM.
FM RADIO STATION

WSEO-FM 45911
Owner: Nelsonville TV Cable Inc.
Editorial: 15751 Elmrock Rd, Nelsonville, Ohio 45764
Tel: 1 740 753-4094.
Email: wseo33@nelsonvilletv.com
Profile: WSEO-FM is a commercial station owned by Nelsonville TV Cable Inc. The format for the station is country. WSEO-FM broadcasts to the Charleston-Huntington, WV area at 107.7 FM.
FM RADIO STATION

WSEV-FM 46906
Owner: East Tennessee Radio Group
Editorial: 196 W Dumplin Valley Rd, Kodak, Tennessee 37764-1934 **Tel:** 1 865 932-6002.
Web site: http://www.mixx1055.com
Profile: WSEV-FM is a commercial station owned by East Tennessee Radio Group. The format of the station is adult contemporary. WSEV-FM broadcasts to Kodak, TN and surrounding areas at 105.5 FM.
FM RADIO STATION

WSEY-FM 43995
Owner: NRG Media LLC
Editorial: 1460 S College Ave, Dixon, Illinois 61021
Tel: 1 815 288-3341.
Web site: http://www.koolfm957.com
Profile: WSEY-FM is a commercial station owned by NRG Media LLC. The format of the station is oldies music. WSEY-FM broadcasts to the Dixon, IL area at 95.7 FM.
FM RADIO STATION

WSEZ-AM 38313
Owner: Diamond Shores Broadcasting LLC
Editorial: 192 S Court St, Paoli, Indiana 47454-1322
Tel: 1 812 723-4484.
Email: wume953@gmail.com
Profile: WSEZ-AM is a commercial station owned by Diamond Shores Broadcasting LLC. The format of the station is oldies music. WSEZ-AM broadcasts to the Paoli, IN area at 1560 AM.
AM RADIO STATION

WSFB-AM 35658
Owner: Small Town Broadcasting
Editorial: 118 N Patterson St, Valdosta, Georgia 31601-5570 **Tel:** 1 229 259-9301.
Profile: WSFB-AM is a commercial station owned by Small Town Broadcasting. The format of the station is Talk. WSFB-AM broadcasts to the Quitman, GA area at 1490 AM.
AM RADIO STATION

WSFC-AM 38185
Owner: iHeartMedia Inc.
Editorial: 101 1st Radio Ln, Somerset, Kentucky 42503-4639 **Tel:** 1 606 678-5151.
Web site: http://www.wsfcam.com
Profile: WSFC-AM is a commercial station owned by iHeartMedia Inc. The format of the station is news, sports and talk. WSFC-AM broadcasts to the Somerset, KY area at 1240 AM.
AM RADIO STATION

WSFE-AM 37971
Owner: iHeartMedia Inc.
Editorial: 101 1st Radio Ln, Somerset, Kentucky 42503-4639 **Tel:** 1 606 678-5151.
Web site: http://www.wsfeam.com
Profile: WSFE-AM is a commercial station owned by iHeartMedia Inc. The format of the station is news and talk. WSFE-AM broadcasts to the Somerset, KY area at 910 AM.
AM RADIO STATION

WSFF-FM 235164
Owner: iHeartMedia Inc.
Editorial: 3807 Brandon Ave SW Ste 2350, Roanoke, Virginia 24018-1477 **Tel:** 1 540 725-1220.
Web site: http://www.1061stevefm.com
Profile: WSFF-FM is a commercial station owned by iHeartMedia Inc. The format of the station is Jack FM-Adult Hits. WSFF-FM broadcasts in the Roanoke, VA area at 106.1 FM.
FM RADIO STATION

WSFL-FM 42025
Owner: Beasley Broadcast Group
Editorial: 207 Glenburnie Dr, New Bern, North Carolina 28560-2815 **Tel:** 1 252 633-1500.
Web site: http://www.wsfl.com
FM RADIO STATION

WSFN-AM 36756
Owner: MarMac Communications, LLC
Editorial: 436 Mall Blvd, Brunswick, Georgia 31525-1819 **Tel:** 1 912 264-6251.
Email: thefansportsradio@yahoo.com
Web site: http://www.thefansportsradio.com
Profile: WSFN-AM is a commercial station owned by MarMac Communications, LLC. The format of the station is sports. WSFN-AM broadcasts to the Brunswick, GA area at 790 AM.
AM RADIO STATION

WSFP-FM 559554
Owner: Superior Communications
Editorial: 148 E Grand River Rd, Williamston, Michigan 48895-8400 **Tel:** 1 517 381-0573.
Email: 411@smile.fm
Web site: http://www.smile.fm
Profile: WSFP-FM is a commercial station owned by Superior Communications. The format of the station is contemporary Christian music and inspirational talk. WSFP-FM broadcasts to the Rust Township, MI area at 88.1 FM.
FM RADIO STATION

WSFQ-FM 43335
Owner: Radio Plus Bay Cities, LLC
Editorial: 413 10th Ave, Menominee, Michigan 49858-3009 **Tel:** 1 906 863-5551.
Email: reception@baycitiesradio.net
Web site: http://www.hits96online.com
Profile: WSFQ-FM is a commercial station owned by Radio Plus Bay Cities, LLC. The format of the station is adult contemporary. WSFQ-FM broadcasts to the Menominee, MI area at 96.3 FM.
FM RADIO STATION

WSFR-FM 43376
Owner: Summit Media Broadcasting LLC
Editorial: 612 S 4th St, Louisville, Kentucky 40202-2460 **Tel:** 1 502 589-4800.
Web site: http://1077theeagle.com
Profile: WSFR-FM is a commercial station owned by Summit Media Broadcasting LLC. The format of the station is classic hits. WSFR-FM broadcasts to the Louisville, KY area at 107.7 FM.
FM RADIO STATION

WSFS-FM 43332
Owner: Entercom
Editorial: 20450 NW 2nd Ave, Miami, Florida 33169-2505 **Tel:** 1 305 521-5100.
Web site: http://www.1043theshark.com
Profile: WSFS-FM is a commercial station owned by Entercom. The format of the station is modern rock. WAXY-FM broadcasts to the Miami, FL area at 104.3 FM.
FM RADIO STATION

WSFW-AM 38186
Owner: CSN International
Editorial: 4002 N 3300 E, Twin Falls, Idaho 83301-0354 **Tel:** 1 208 734-2049.
Email: feedback@csnradio.com
Web site: http://www.csnradio.com
Profile: WSFW-AM is a non-commercial station owned by Calvary Chapel Twin Falls. The format of the station is religious teachings. WSFW-AM broadcasts to the Senecca Falls, NY area at 1110 AM.
AM RADIO STATION

WSFZ-AM 36193
Owner: Sportsrad, Inc.
Editorial: 571 Highway 51, Ste H, Ridgeland, Mississippi 39157-2597 **Tel:** 1 601 675-8255.
Email: info@supersport930.com
Web site: http://www.supersport930.com
Profile: WSFZ-AM is a commercial station owned by Sportsrad, Inc. The format of the station is sports programming. WSFZ-AM broadcasts to the Jackson, MS area at 930 AM.
AM RADIO STATION

WSGA-FM 40138
Owner: WRGO Radio LLC
Editorial: 6605 Abercorn St Ste 213, Savannah, Georgia 31405-5892 **Tel:** 1 912 691-1934.
Web site: http://www.923thundercountry.com
Profile: WSGA-FM is a commercial station owned by WRGO Radio LLC (dba Savannah Radio Group). The format of the station is country. WSGA-FM broadcasts to the Hinesville, GA area at 92.3 FM.
FM RADIO STATION

WSGB-AM 39112
Owner: Summit Media Broadcasting LLC
Editorial: 120 Main St, Sutton, West Virginia 26601-1334 **Tel:** 1 304 765-7373.
Web site: http://theboss97fm.com
Profile: WSGB-AM is a commercial station owned by Summit Media Broadcasting LLC. The format of the station is classic hits. WSGB-AM broadcasts to the Sutton, WV area at 1490 AM.
AM RADIO STATION

WSGC-AM 38187
Owner: Georgia-Carolina Radiocasting Companies LLC
Editorial: 562 Jones St, Elberton, Georgia 30635-1957 **Tel:** 1 706 283-1400.
Email: wsgc@elbertonradio.com
Profile: WSGC-AM is a commercial station owned by Georgia-Carolina Radiocasting Companies LLC. The format of the station is country. WSGC-AM broadcasts to the Elberton, GA area at 1400 AM.
AM RADIO STATION

United States of America

WSGC-FM 45622
Owner: Georgia-Carolina Radiocasting Companies LLC
Editorial: 562 Jones St, Elberton, Georgia 30635-1957
Email: wsgc@elbertonradio.com
Web site: http://www.wsgcradio.com
Profile: WSGC-FM is a commercial station owned by Georgia-Carolina Radiocasting Companies LLC. The format of the station is country music. WSGC-FM broadcasts to the Elberton, GA area at 105.3 FM.
FM RADIO STATION

WSGE-FM 41493
Owner: Board of Trustees, Gaston College
Editorial: 201 Highway 321 S, Dallas, North Carolina 28034-1402 **Tel:** 1 704 922-6552.
Web site: http://www.wsge.org
Profile: WSGE-FM is a non-commercial station owned by Board of Trustees, Gaston College. The format of the station is adult album alternative. WSGE-FM broadcasts to the Charlotte-Gastonia, NC area at 91.7 FM. WSGE-FM is an NPR/National Public Radio affiliate.
FM RADIO STATION

WSGH-AM 35942
Owner: TBLC Media LLC
Editorial: 4015 Brownsboro Rd, Winston Salem, North Carolina 27106-3380 **Tel:** 1 336 768-0050.
Web site: http://www.radiolamovidita.com
AM RADIO STATION

WSGI-AM 35659
Owner: Lightning Broadcasting, LLC
Editorial: 200 Wdbl Rd, Springfield, Tennessee 37172 **Tel:** 1 615 384-9744.
Email: wsgi1100@yahoo.com
Web site: http://www.wsgi1100.com
Profile: WSGI-AM is a commercial station owned by Lightning Broadcasting, LLC. The format of the station is oldies and country. WSGI-AM broadcasts to the Springfield, TN area at 1100 AM.
AM RADIO STATION

WSGL-FM 40721
Owner: Renda Broadcasting
Editorial: 10915 K Nine Dr, 2nd Fl, Bonita Springs, Florida 34135-6802 **Tel:** 1 239 495-8383.
Web site: http://www.1047mixfm.com
FM RADIO STATION

WSGM-FM 42360
Owner: Cumberland Communications Corporations
Editorial: 971 Firetower Road, Tracy City, Tennessee 37387 **Tel:** 1 931 592-7777.
Email: wsgmfm@hotmail.com
FM RADIO STATION

WSGO-AM 37145
Owner: Galaxy Communications LP
Editorial: 235 Walton St, Syracuse, New York 13202-1533 **Tel:** 1 315 472-9111.
Web site: http://galaxycommunications.com
Profile: WSGO-AM is a commercial station owned by Galaxy Communications LP. The format of the station is sports. WSGO-AM broadcasts to the Syracuse, NY area at 1440 AM.
AM RADIO STATION

WSGR-FM 40722
Owner: St. Clair County Comm. College
Editorial: 323 Erie St, Port Huron, Michigan 48060-3812 **Tel:** 1 810 989-5564.
Email: wsgr@sc4.edu
Profile: WSGR-FM is a non-commercial college station owned by St. Clair County Comm. College. The format of the station is alternative rock and free form radio. WSGR-FM broadcasts to the Port Huron, MI area at a frequency of 91.3 FM.
FM RADIO STATION

WSGS-FM 45534
Owner: Mountain Broadcasting Service
Editorial: 516 Main St, Hazard, Kentucky 41701-1775 **Tel:** 1 606 436-2121.
Email: wsgs@windstream.net
Web site: http://www.wsgs.com
FM RADIO STATION

WSGT-FM 823034
Owner: Mattox Broadcasting, Inc.
Editorial: 2132 Us Highway 84, Blackshear, Georgia 31516-1160 **Tel:** 1 912 449-3391.
Profile: WSGT-FM is a commercial station owned by Mattox Broadcasting, Inc. The format of the station is classic hits. WSGT-FM broadcasts locally to the Patterson, GA area at a frequency of 107.1 FM.
FM RADIO STATION

WSGW-AM 38356
Owner: Digity LLC
Editorial: 1795 Tittabawassee Rd, Saginaw, Michigan 48604-9431 **Tel:** 1 989 752-3456.
Email: news@wsgw.com
Web site: http://www.wsgw.com
Profile: WSGW-AM is a commercial station owned by Digity LLC . The format of the station is news, talk and sports. WSGW-AM broadcasts to the Saginaw, MI area at 790 AM.
AM RADIO STATION

WSGW-FM 41725
Owner: Digity LLC
Editorial: 1795 Tittabawassee Rd, Saginaw, Michigan 48604-9431 **Tel:** 1 989 752-3456.
Email: news@wsgw.com
Web site: http://www.fmtalk1005.com
Profile: WSGW-FM is a commercial station owned by Digity LLC . The format of the station is talk and sports. WSGW-FM broadcasts to the Saginaw, MI area at 100.5 FM.
FM RADIO STATION

WSHE-AM 36615
Owner: THE TRUTH, INC.
Editorial: 1501 13th Ave, Columbus, Georgia 31901-1908 **Tel:** 1 706 576-3000.
Web site: http://www.am1270radio.com
Profile: WSHE-AM is a commercial station owned by THE TRUTH, INC,. The format of the station is sports. WSHE-AM broadcasts to the Columbus, GA area at 1270 AM.
AM RADIO STATION

WSHE-FM 41734
Owner: Hubbard Radio, LLC
Editorial: 130 E Randolph St Ste 2780, One Prudential Plaza, Chicago, Illinois 60601-6305 **Tel:** 1 312 297-5100.
Web site: http://wshechicago.com
Profile: WSHE-FM is a commercial station owned by Hubbard Radio, LLC. The format of the station is adult contemporary. WSHE-FM broadcasts to the Chicago area at 100.3 FM.
FM RADIO STATION

WSHH-FM 45535
Owner: Renda Broadcasting
Editorial: 900 Parish St Fl 3, Pittsburgh, Pennsylvania 15220-3425 **Tel:** 1 412 875-9500.
Web site: http://www.wshh.com
Profile: WSHH-FM is a commercial station owned by Renda Broadcasting. The format of the station is Lite Rock/Lite AC. WSHH-FM broadcasts to the Pittsburgh area at 99.7 FM.
FM RADIO STATION

WSHK-FM 42050
Owner: Cumulus Media Inc.
Editorial: 292 Middle Rd, Dover, New Hampshire 03820-4901 **Tel:** 1 603 749-9750.
Web site: http://www.shark1053.com
Profile: WSHK-FM is a commercial station owned by Cumulus Media Inc. The format of the station is classic hits. WSHK-FM broadcasts to the Dover, NH area at 105.3 FM.
FM RADIO STATION

WSHO-AM 35660
Owner: Shadowlands Communications LLC
Editorial: 365 Canal St Ste 1175, New Orleans, Louisiana 70130-1182 **Tel:** 1 504 527-0800.
Email: wsho@compuserve.com
Web site: http://www.wsho.com
Profile: WSHO-AM is a commercial station owned by Shadowlands Communications LLC. The format of the station is religious. WSHO-AM broadcasts to the New Orleans market area at 800 AM.
AM RADIO STATION

WSHV-AM 39242
Owner: Lakes Media LLC
Editorial: 26256 Highway 47 North, South Hill, Virginia 23970 **Tel:** 1 434 447-4007.
Email: wshvam@yahoo.com
Profile: WSHV-AM is a commercial station owned by Lakes Media LLC. The format of the station is urban contemporary music. WSHV-AM broadcasts to the South Hill, VA area at 1370 AM.
AM RADIO STATION

WSHW-FM 45536
Owner: Kaspar Broadcasting Co.
Editorial: 1401 W Barner St, Frankfort, Indiana 46041 **Tel:** 1 765 659-3339.
Email: newsroom@kasparradio.com
Web site: http://www.wshw.com
Profile: WSHW-FM is a commercial station owned by Kaspar Broadcasting Co. The format of the station is Lite Rock/Lite AC music. WSHW-FM broadcasts to the Indianapolis area at 99.7 FM.
FM RADIO STATION

WSHY-AM 35238
Owner: Artistic Media Partners Inc.
Editorial: 3824 S 18th St, Lafayette, Indiana 47909-9102 **Tel:** 1 765 474-1410.
Web site: http://artisticradio.com/stations/lafayette
Profile: WSHY-AM is a commercial station owned by Artistic Media Partners Inc. The format of the station is sports talk. WSHY-AM broadcasts to the Lafayette, IN area at 1410 AM.
AM RADIO STATION

WSIA-FM 43744
Owner: College of Staten Island(The)
Editorial: 2800 Victory Blvd, Staten Island, New York 10314-6609 **Tel:** 1 718 982-3050.
Web site: http://www.wsia.fm
Profile: WSIA-FM is a non-commercial, college station owned by The College of Staten Island. The format of the station is adult alternative. WSIA-FM broadcasts to the Staten Island, NY area at 88.9 FM.
FM RADIO STATION

WSIB-FM 46252
Owner: Grace Broadcasting Services Inc.
Editorial: 25 Stonebrook Pl Ste G322, Jackson, Tennessee 38305-3686 **Tel:** 1 731 855-0098.
Web site: http://www.gracebroadcasting.com
Profile: WSIB-FM is a commercial station owned by Grace Broadcasting Services Inc. The format of the station is adult contemporary. WSIB-FM broadcasts to the Selmer, TN area at 93.9 FM.
FM RADIO STATION

WSIC-AM 38366
Owner: Iredell Broadcasting Inc.
Editorial: 1117 Radio Rd, Statesville, North Carolina 28677-3350 **Tel:** 1 704 872-6345.
Email: news@wsicweb.com
Web site: http://www.wsicweb.com
Profile: WSIC-AM is a commercial station owned by Iredell Broadcasting Inc. The format of the station is news, talk and sports. WSIC-AM broadcasts to the Charlotte, NC, area at 1400 AM.
AM RADIO STATION

WSIG-FM 46202
Owner: Gamma Broadcasting LLC
Editorial: 639 N Main St, Mount Crawford, Virginia 22841-2350
Web site: http://www.969wsig.com
Profile: WSIG-FM is a commercial station owned by Gamma Broadcasting LLC. The format for the station is country. WSIG-FM broadcasts to the Harrisonburg, VA area at 96.9 FM.
FM RADIO STATION

WSIM-FM 44133
Owner: Miller Communications Inc.
Editorial: 2425 Walker Swinton Rd, Timmonsville, South Carolina 29161-9351 **Tel:** 1 843 678-9393.
Email: production@miller.fm
Web site: http://www.miller.fm
Profile: WSIM-FM is a commercial station owned by Miller Communications Inc. The format of the station is Hot AC. WSIM-FM broadcasts to the Florence, SC at 93.7 FM.
FM RADIO STATION

WSIP-AM 38188
Owner: Forcht Broadcasting
Editorial: 127 Main St, Paintsville, Kentucky 41240 **Tel:** 1 606 789-5311.
Email: wsipprod@keybroadcasting.net
Web site: http://www.wsipfm.com
Profile: WSIP-AM is a commercial station owned by Forcht Broadcasting. The format of the station is oldies. WSIP-AM broadcasts to the Paintsville, KY area at 1490 AM
AM RADIO STATION

WSIP-FM 45537
Owner: Forcht Broadcasting
Editorial: 124 Main St, Paintsville, Kentucky 41240 **Tel:** 1 606 789-5311.
Email: wsipprod@keybroadcasting.net
Web site: http://www.wsipfm.com
Profile: WSIP-FM is a commercial station owned by Forcht Broadcasting. The format for the station is country. WSIP-FM broadcasts to the Charleston-Huntington, WV area at 98.9 FM.
FM RADIO STATION

WSIQ-AM 37930
Owner: NRG Media LLC
Editorial: 310 W McMackin St, Salem, Illinois 62881-1721 **Tel:** 1 618 548-2000.
Email: news@wjbdradio.com
Web site: http://www.wjbdradio.com
Profile: WSIQ-AM is commercial station owned by NRG Media LLC. The format of the station is country music. WSIQ-AM broadcasts to the Salem, IL area at 1350 AM.
AM RADIO STATION

WSIR-AM 35661
Owner: Anscombe Broadcasting Group Ltd.
Editorial: 665 Lake Howard Dr SW, Winter Haven, Florida 33880-2577 **Tel:** 1 863 295-9411.
Web site: http://www.familyradio1490.com
Profile: WSIR-AM is a commercial station owned by Anscombe Broadcasting Group Ltd. The format of the station is gospel. WSIR-AM broadcasts to the Tampa Bay, FL area at 1490 AM.
AM RADIO STATION

WSIU-FM 40727
Owner: WSIU Public Broadcasting
Editorial: 1100 Lincoln Dr, Carbondale, Illinois 62901-4306 **Tel:** 1 618 453-4343.
Email: wsiuradio@wsiu.org
Web site: http://www.wsiu.org
Profile: WSIU-FM is a non-commercial station owned by WSIU Public Broadcasting. The format of the station is news and classical music. WSIU-FM broadcasts to the Paducah, KY-Cape Girardeau, MO-Harrisburg, IL areas at 91.9 FM.
FM RADIO STATION

WSIV-AM 38189
Owner: C R A M Communications LLC
Editorial: 7095 Myers Rd, East Syracuse, New York 13057 **Tel:** 1 315 656-2231.
Web site: http://www.wsiv1540.com
Profile: WSIV-AM is a commercial radio station owned by C R AM Communications LLC. The format of the station is gospel music. The station airs to the East Syracuse area at 1540 AM.
AM RADIO STATION

WSIX-FM 41756
Owner: iHeartMedia Inc.
Editorial: 55 Music Sq W, Nashville, Tennessee 37203-3207 **Tel:** 1 615 664-2400.
Web site: http://thebig98.iheart.com
Profile: WSIX-FM is a commercial station owned by iHeartMedia Inc. The format of the station is country music. WSIX-FM broadcasts to the Nashville, TN are at 97.9 FM.
FM RADIO STATION

WSJD-FM 4307
Owner: WSJD Inc.
Editorial: 328 N Market St, Mount Carmel, Illinois 62863-1519 **Tel:** 1 618 263-4300.
Email: wsjd@live.com
Profile: WSJD-FM is a commercial station owned by WSJD Inc. The format of the station is oldies. The station broadcasts locally at a frequency of 100.5 FM
FM RADIO STATION

WSJK-FM 4255
Owner: S.J. Broadcasting Inc.
Editorial: 2702 Boulder Rd, Urbana, Illinois 61802-6996 **Tel:** 1 217 367-1195.
Web site: http://www.espncu.com
Profile: WSJK-FM is a commercial station owned by S.J. Broadcasting Inc. The format of the station is sports/talk. WSJK-FM broadcasts to the Champaign IL area at 93.5 FM.
FM RADIO STATION

WSJL-FM 85528
Owner: Elijah Radio, Inc.
Editorial: 2822 Commerce Blvd, Irondale, Alabama 35210-1216 **Tel:** 1 205 585-6706.
Web site: http://wsjlradio.com
Profile: WSJL-FM is a non-commercial station owned by Elijah Radio, Inc. The format of the station is religious. WSJL-FM broadcasts to the Bessemer, AL area at a frequency of 88.1 FM.
FM RADIO STATION

WSJM-AM 3656
Owner: Midwest Family Stations
Editorial: 580 E Napier Ave, Benton Harbor, Michigan 49022 **Tel:** 1 269 925-1111.
Email: news@wsjm.com
Web site: http://www.wsjm.com
Profile: WSJM-AM is a commercial station owned by Midwest Family Stations. The format of the station is news, talk and sports. WSJM-AM airs locally on 1400 AM to the Benton Harbor, MI area.
AM RADIO STATION

WSJM-FM 4391
Owner: Midwest Family Stations
Editorial: 580 E Napier Ave, Benton Harbor, Michigan 49022 **Tel:** 1 269 925-1111.
Email: news@wsjm.com
Web site: http://www.wsjm.com
Profile: WSJM-FM is a commercial station owned by Midwest Family Stations. The format of the station is news, talk and sports. WSJM-FM broadcasts in the Benton Harbor, MI area at 94.9 FM.
FM RADIO STATION

WSJO-FM 4066
Owner: Townsquare Media, LLC
Editorial: 950 Tilton Rd Ste 200, Northfield, New Jersey 08225-1235 **Tel:** 1 609 645-9797.
Web site: http://www.sojo1049.com
Profile: WSJO-FM is a commercial station owned by the Townsquare Media, LLC. The format is hot adult contemporary. WSJO-FM broadcasts to the Princeton, NJ area at 104.9 FM.
FM RADIO STATION

WSJP-AM 3687
Owner: Starboard Media Foundation Inc.
Tel: 1 920 884-1460.
Email: info@relevantradio.com
Web site: http://www.relevantradio.com
Profile: WJSO-AM is a non-commercial station owned by Starboard Media Foundation. The format of the station is Catholic talk. The station broadcasts locally at 1640 AM to the Greater Milwaukee, WI area
AM RADIO STATION

WSJP-FM 4435
Owner: Starboard Media Foundation Inc.
Tel: 1 262 268-9403.
Email: info@relevantradio.com
Web site: http://www.relevantradio.com
Profile: WSJP-FM is a commercial station owned by Starboard Media Foundation Inc. The format of the station is religious music. WSJP-FM broadcasts to the Port Washington, WI area at 1001 FM.
FM RADIO STATION

WSJR-FM 4433
Owner: Cumulus Media Inc.
Editorial: 600 Baltimore Drive, Wilkes-Barre, Pennsylvania 18702-7901 **Tel:** 1 570 824-9000.
Web site: http://www.greatcountry937.com
Profile: WSJR-FM is a commercial station owned by Cumulus Media Inc. The format of the station is contemporary country. WSJR-FM broadcasts to the Wilkes-Barre, PA area at 93.7 FM.
FM RADIO STATION

WSJS-AM 3819
Owner: Curtis Media Group
Editorial: 875 W 5th St, Winston Salem, North Carolina 27101-2505 **Tel:** 1 336 777-3900.
Web site: http://www.wsjs.com
Profile: WSJS-AM is a commercial station owned by Curtis Media Group. The format of the station is news and talk. WSJS-AM broadcasts to the Greensboro-Winston Salem, NC area at 600 AM.
AM RADIO STATION

WSJW-AM 35820
Owner: Starboard Media Foundation, Inc.
Editorial: 1496 Bellevue Street STE 202, Green Bay, Wisconsin 54311 **Tel:** 1 920 884-1460.
Email: info@relevantradio.com
Web site: http://relevantradio.com
Profile: WSJW-AM is a non-commercial station owned by Starboard Media Foundation, Inc.. The format of the station is Catholic Talk and Teaching. WBSJW-AM broadcasts to the Providence, RI area at a frequency of 550 AM.
AM RADIO STATION

WSJY-FM 45788
Owner: NRG Media LLC
Editorial: W6355 Eastern Ave, Fort Atkinson, Wisconsin 53538-9335 **Tel:** 1 920 563-9329.
Web site: http://www.1073wsjy.com
Profile: WSJY-FM is a commercial station owned by NRG Media LLC. The format of the station is Lite Rock/Lite AC. WSJY-FM broadcasts to the Milwaukee area at 107.3 FM.
FM RADIO STATION

WSJZ-FM 73790
Owner: Cumulus Media Inc.
Editorial: 1800 W Hibiscus Blvd, Melbourne, Florida 32901-2629 **Tel:** 1 321 984-1000.
Web site: http://www.sportsradio959.com
Profile: WSJZ-FM is a commercial station owned by Cumulus Media Inc. The format of the station is sports. WSJZ-FM broadcasts to the Melbourne, FL area at 95.9 FM.
FM RADIO STATION

WSKB-FM 133927
Owner: Westfield State College
Editorial: 577 Western Ave, Ely Hall, Westfield, Massachusetts 01085-2580 **Tel:** 1 413 572-5579.
Web site: http://wsc.ma.edu/wskb
Profile: WSKB-FM is a non-commercial station owned by Westfield State College. The format of the station is college variety. WSKB-FM broadcasts to the Westfield, MA area at 89.5 FM.
FM RADIO STATION

WSKE-FM 45973
Owner: New Millennium Communications Group
Editorial: 151 E 1St Ave, Everett, Pennsylvania 15537-1351 **Tel:** 1 814 652-2600.
Email: wske@penn.com
Profile: WSKE-FM is a commercial station owned by New Millennium Communications Group. The format of the station is country music. WSKE-FM broadcasts to the Everett, PA area at 104.3 FM.
FM RADIO STATION

WSKG-FM 40729
Owner: WSKG Public Telecommunications
Editorial: 601 Gates Rd, Vestal, New York 13850-2288 **Tel:** 1 607 729-0100.
Web site: http://wskg.org/
Profile: WSKG-FM is a non-commercial station owned by WSKG Public Telecommunications. The format of the station is classical, jazz and news. WSKG-FM broadcasts to the Vestal, NY area at 89.3 FM.
FM RADIO STATION

WSKI-AM 35663
Owner: Northeast Broadcasting Co.
Editorial: 169 River St, Montpelier, Vermont 5602
Tel: 1 802 223-2396.
Email: feedback@pointfm.com
Web site: http://www.pointfm.com
Profile: WSKI-AM is a commercial station owned by Northeast Broadcasting Co. The format of the station is sports talk. WSKI-AM broadcasts to the Montpelier, VT area at 1240 AM.
AM RADIO STATION

WSKK-FM 43801
Owner: Kudzu Communications, Inc.
Editorial: 107 E Spring St, Ripley, Mississippi 38663-2043 **Tel:** 1 662 837-1023.
Email: classicradiofm@aol.com
Web site: http://www.classicradiofm.com
Profile: WSKK-FM is a commercial station owned by Kudzu Communications. The format of the station is classic hits. WSKK-FM broadcasts to the Ripley, MS area at 102.3 FM.
FM RADIO STATION

WSKL-FM 349892
Owner: Zona Communications, Inc.
Editorial: 820 Railroad St, Covington, Indiana 47932-1357 **Tel:** 1 765 793-4823.
Email: fmkool929@aol.com
Web site: http://www.kooloIdies.net
Profile: WSKL-FM is a commercial station owned by Zona Communications, Inc. The format of the station is oldies music. WSKL-FM broadcasts to the Covington, IL area at 92.9 FM.
FM RADIO STATION

WSKO-AM 38654
Owner: Cumulus Media Inc.
Editorial: 1064 James St, Syracuse, New York 13203-2704 **Tel:** 1 315 472-0200.
Web site: http://www.thescore1260.com
Profile: WSKO-AM is a commercial station owned by Cumulus Media Inc. The format of the station is sports. WSKO-AM broadcasts to Syracuse, NY at 1260 AM.
AM RADIO STATION

WSKP-AM 36373
Owner: Red Wolf Broadcasting
Editorial: 400 S County Trl Ste A105, Exeter, Rhode Island 02822-3539 **Tel:** 1 401 294-9274.
Web site: http://kool1180.webs.com
Profile: WSKP-AM is a commercial station owned by Red Wolf Broadcasting. The format of the station is oldies. WSKP-AM broadcasts to the Providence, RI area at 1180 AM.
AM RADIO STATION

WSKP-FM 42875
Owner: Red Wolf Broadcasting
Editorial: 758 Colonel Ledyard Hwy, Ledyard, Connecticut 06339-1541 **Tel:** 1 860 464-1065.
Web site: http://www.jammin1077.com
Profile: WSKP-FM is a commercial station owned by Red Wolf Broadcasting. The format of the station is urban contemporary music. WSKP-FM broadcasts to the Hartford-New Haven, CT area at 107.7 FM.
FM RADIO STATION

WSKQ-FM 43498
Owner: Spanish Broadcasting System
Editorial: 26 W 56th St, New York, New York 10019-3801 **Tel:** 1 212 541-9200.
Web site: http://lamega.lamusica.com
Profile: WSKQ-FM is a commercial station owned by Spanish Broadcasting System. The format of the station is tropical Hispanic music. WSKQ-FM broadcasts to the New York City area at 97.9 FM.
FM RADIO STATION

WSKS-FM 43077
Owner: Roser Communications
Editorial: 185 Genesee St, Ste 1601, Utica, New York 13501 **Tel:** 1 315 734-9245.
Email: audio@rosergroup.com
Web site: http://www.cnykiss.com
Profile: WSKS-FM is a commercial station owned by Roser Communications. The format of the station is Top 40/CHR. WSKS-FM broadcasts to the Utica, NY area at 97.9 FM.
FM RADIO STATION

WSKU-FM 45987
Owner: Roser Communications
Editorial: 185 Genesee St Ste 1601, Utica, New York 13501-2110 **Tel:** 1 315 734-9245.
Web site: http://www.cnykiss.com
Profile: WSKU-FM is a commercial station owned by Roser Communications. The format of the station is Top 40/CHR. WSKU-FM broadcasts to the Utica, NY area at 105.5.
FM RADIO STATION

WSKV-FM 44047
Owner: Moore Country 104, LLC
Editorial: 28 W Halls Rd, Stanton, Kentucky 40380-2230 **Tel:** 1 606 663-2811.
Email: wskv@wskvfm.com
Web site: http://www.wskvfm.com
Profile: WSKV-FM is a commercial station owned by Moore Country 104, LLC. The format of the station is country and bluegrass. WSKV-FM broadcasts to the Lexington, KY area at 104.9 FM.
FM RADIO STATION

WSKW-AM 36725
Owner: Mountain Wireless Corp.
Editorial: 208 Middle Rd, Skowhegan, Maine 4976
Tel: 1 207 474-5171.
Email: mix1079@gmail.com
Profile: WSKW-AM is a commercial station owned by Mountain Wireless Corp. The format of the station is sports. WSKW-AM broadcasts to the Skowhegan, ME area at 1160 AM.
AM RADIO STATION

WSKY-AM 35664
Owner: Wilkins Communication Networks Inc.
Editorial: 40 Westgate Pkwy Ste F, Asheville, North Carolina 28806-3886 **Tel:** 1 828 251-2000.
Email: wsky@wilkinsradio.com
Web site: http://www.wilkinsradio.com
Profile: WSKY-AM is a commercial station owned by Wilkins Communication Networks Inc.and licensed by Macon Media, Inc. The format of the station is religious. WSKY-AM broadcasts to the Asheville, NC area at a frequency of 1230 AM.
AM RADIO STATION

WSKY-FM 42326
Owner: Entercom Communications Corp.
Editorial: 3600 NW 43rd St, Ste B, Gainesville, Florida 32606 **Tel:** 1 352 337-9729.
Web site: http://www.thesky973.com
Profile: WSKY-FM is a commercial radio station owned by Entercom Communications Corp. The format of the station is news, talk, and information. The station airs locally on 97.3 FM. The tagline is, "The Sky." Newscasts air at the top and bottom of every hour, ET.
FM RADIO STATION

WSKZ-FM 46445
Owner: Cumulus Media Inc.
Editorial: 821 Pineville Rd, Chattanooga, Tennessee 37405-2601 **Tel:** 1 423 756-6141.
Web site: http://www.kz106.com
Profile: WSKZ-FM is a commercial station owned by Cumulus Media Inc. The format of the station is classic rock. WSKZ-FM broadcasts to the Chattanooga, TN area at 106.5 FM.
FM RADIO STATION

WSLA-AM 35654
Owner: Mapa Broadcasting, L.L.C
Editorial: 38230 Coast Blvd, Slidell, Louisiana 70458-8644 **Tel:** 1 985 643-1560.
Email: wsla1560@bellsouth.net
Web site: http://wslaradio.com
Profile: WSLA-AM is a commercial station owned by Mapa Broadcasting, L.L.C. The format of the station is sports talk. WSLA-AM broadcasts to the Slidell, LA area at 1560 AM.
AM RADIO STATION

WSLB-AM 38191
Owner: Community Broadcasters, LLC
Editorial: 199 Wealtha Ave, Watertown, New York 13601-1837 **Tel:** 1 315 393-1100.
Profile: WSLB-AM is a commercial station owned by Community Broadcasters, LLC. The format of the station sports. WSLB-AM broadcasts to the Ogdensburg, NY area at 1400 AM.
AM RADIO STATION

WSLC-FM 43990
Owner: Wheeler Inc.(Mel)
Editorial: 3934 Electric Rd, Roanoke, Virginia 24018-4513 **Tel:** 1 540 387-0234.
Web site: http://www.949starcountry.com
Profile: WSLC-FM is a commercial station owned by Mel Wheeler, Inc. The format of the station is contemporary country. WSLC-FM broadcasts to the Roanoke, VA area at 94.9 FM.
FM RADIO STATION

WSLD-FM 42054
Owner: Prairie Communications LLP
Editorial: 6534 Highway 89 North, Whitewater, Wisconsin 53190-4190 **Tel:** 1 608 883-6677.
Email: wsld@prariecommunications.net
Web site: http://www.1045wsld.com
Profile: WSLD-FM is a commercial station owned by Prairie Communications LLP. The format of the station is contemporary country. WSLD-FM broadcasts to the Milwaukee area at 104.5 FM.
FM RADIO STATION

WSLK-AM 37018
Owner: Smile Broadcasting LLC
Editorial: 1126 Hendricks Store Rd Ste B, Moneta, Virginia 24121-3337 **Tel:** 1 540 297-7880.
Email: info@wslk880.com
Web site: http://www.wslk880.com
Profile: WSLK-AM is a commercial station owned by Smile Broadcasting LLC. The format of the station is oldies. WSLK-AM broadcasts to Moneta, VA and surrounding areas at 880 AM.
AM RADIO STATION

WSLM-AM 38193
Owner: White (Becky)
Editorial: 1308 E Hackberry St, Salem, Indiana 47167-9604 **Tel:** 1 812 883-3401.
Email: wslmradio@gmail.com
Web site: http://wslmradio.com
AM RADIO STATION

WSLM-FM 45538
Owner: White (Becky)
Editorial: 1308 E Hackberry St, Salem, Indiana 47167-9604 **Tel:** 1 812 883-5750.
Email: wslmradio@gmail.com
Web site: http://wslmradio.com
Profile: WSLM-FM is a commercial station owned by Beck White. The format of the station is classic hits and sports. WSLM-FM broadcasts to the Salem, IN area at 97.9 FM.
FM RADIO STATION

WSLP-FM 521736
Owner: Becker(Jon)
Tel: 1 518 523-4900.
Email: info@wslpfm.com
Web site: http://www.wslpfm.com
Profile: WSLP-FM is a commercial station owned by Jon Becker. The format of the station is adult contemporary. WSLP-FM broadcasts to the Lake Placid, NY area at 93.3 FM.
FM RADIO STATION

WSLQ-FM 45539
Owner: Mel Wheeler Broadcasting Inc.
Editorial: 3934 Electric Rd, Roanoke, Virginia 24018-4513 **Tel:** 1 540 387-0234.
Web site: http://www.q99fm.com
Profile: WSLQ-FM is a commercial station owned by Mel Wheeler Broadcasting Inc. The format of the station is adult contemporary. WSLQ-FM broadcasts to the Roanoke, VA area at 99.1 FM.
FM RADIO STATION

WSLR-FM 692737
Owner: New College Student Alliance
Tel: 1 941 894-6469.
Email: info@wslr.org
Web site: http://www.wslr.org
Profile: WSLR-FM is a non-commercial station owned by New College Student Alliance. The format of the station is variety. WSLR-FM broadcasts to the Sarasota, FL area at 96.5 FM.
FM RADIO STATION

WSLV-AM 35666
Owner: B & E Broadcasting Inc.
Editorial: 25995 State Line Rd, Ardmore, Tennessee 38449-3199 **Tel:** 1 931 427-2178.
Email: wslv@ardmore.net
Web site: http://www.wslvradio.com
Profile: WSLV-AM is a commercial station owned by B & E Broadcasting Inc. The format of the station is adult contemporary. WSLV-AM broadcasts to the Ardmore, TN area at 1110 AM.
AM RADIO STATION

WSLW-AM 38853
Owner: Radio Greenbrier
Editorial: 276 Seneca Trl, Ronceverte, West Virginia 24970 **Tel:** 1 304 645-1327.
Email: radio@wron.net
Web site: http://www.wron.com
Profile: WSLW-AM is a commercial station owned by Radio Greenbrier. The format of the station is sports. WSLW-AM broadcasts to the White Sulphur Springs, WV area at 1310 AM.
AM RADIO STATION

WSLY-FM 46523
Owner: Grantell Broadcasting Co.
Editorial: 11474 Hwy 11, York, Alabama 36925
Tel: 1 205 392-5234.
Profile: WSLY-FM is a commercial station owned by Grantell Broadcasting Co. The format of the station is sports. WSLY-FM broadcasts to the York, AL area at 104.9 FM.
FM RADIO STATION

WSM-AM 38195
Owner: Grand Ole Opry, LLC
Editorial: 2644 McGavock Pike, Nashville, Tennessee 37214-1202 **Tel:** 1 615 458-4650.
Email: email@wsmonline.com
Web site: http://www.wsmonline.com
Profile: WSM-AM is a commercial station owned by Grand Ole Opry, LLC. The format of the station is country music. WSM-AM broadcasts to the Nashville, TN at 650 AM.
AM RADIO STATION

WSMD-FM 43289
Owner: Somar Communications Inc.
Editorial: 28095 Three Notch Rd, Ste 2B, Mechanicsville, Maryland 20659 **Tel:** 1 301 870-5550.
Email: wsmdfm@aol.com
Web site: http://www.star983.com
Profile: WSMD-FM is a commercial station owned by Somar Communications Inc. The format of the station is classic hits music. WSMD-FM broadcasts to the Mechanicsville, MD area at 98.3 FM.
FM RADIO STATION

WSME-AM 36087
Owner: B&M Broadcasting LLC
Editorial: 410 New Bridge St Ste 3B, Jacksonville, North Carolina 28540-4759 **Tel:** 1 910 346-2248.
Email: wsme1120@yahoo.com
Web site: http://www.ctc-media.com
Profile: WSME-AM is a commercial station owned by B&M Broadcasting LLC. The format of the station is oldies. WSME-AM broadcasts to the New Bern, NC area at a frequency of 1120 AM.
AM RADIO STATION

WSMF-FM 769373
Owner: Superior Communications
Editorial: 148 E Grand River Rd, Williamston, Michigan 48895-8400 **Tel:** 1 888 887-7139.
Email: 411@smile.fm
Web site: http://www.smile.fm
Profile: WSMF-FM is a non-commercial station owned by Northland Community Broadcasters. The format of the station is Contemporary Christian. The station broadcasts to the Wayne County and Monroe areas of Michigan at a frequency of 88.1 FM.
FM RADIO STATION

WSM-FM 45540
Owner: Cumulus Media Inc.
Editorial: 506 2nd Ave S, Nashville, Tennessee 37210-2002 **Tel:** 1 615 321-1067.
Web site: http://www.955nashicon.com
Profile: WSM-FM is a commercial station owned by Cumulus Media Inc. The format of the station is contemporary country music. WSM-FM broadcasts to the Nashville, TN area at 95.5 FM.
FM RADIO STATION

WSMG-AM 39373
Owner: Radio Greeneville Inc.
Editorial: 1004 Arnold Rd, Greeneville, Tennessee 37743 **Tel:** 1 423 638-3188.
Email: wsmg@greeneville.com
Web site: http://www.greeneville.com/wsmg
Profile: WSMG-AM is a commercial station owned by Radio Greeneville Inc. The format of the station is oldies music. WSMG-AM broadcasts to the Greenville, TN area at 1450 AM.
AM RADIO STATION

WSMI-AM 38196
Owner: Talley Broadcasting Corp.
Editorial: 6308 Illinois Route 16, Hillsboro, Illinois 62049 **Tel:** 1 217 324-5921.
Email: news@wsmiradio.com
Web site: http://www.wsmiradio.com
Profile: WSMI-AM is a commercial station owned by Talley Broadcasting Corp. The format of the station is classic country and talk. WSMI-AM broadcasts to the Litchfield, IL area at 1540 AM.
AM RADIO STATION

WSMI-FM 45541
Owner: Talley Broadcasting Corp.
Editorial: 6308 Illinois Route 16, Hillsboro, Illinois 62049-3419 **Tel:** 1 217 324-5921.
Email: wsmi@wsmiradio.com
Web site: http://www.wsmiradio.com

Profile: WSMI-FM is a commercial station owned by Talley Broadcasting Corp. The format of the station is contemporary country. WSMI-FM broadcasts in the Litchfield, IL area at 106.1 FM.
FM RADIO STATION

WSMK-FM 42219
Owner: Williams (Marion R.)
Editorial: 925 N 5th St, Niles, Michigan 49120-1601 **Tel:** 1 269 683-4343.
Web site: http://www.wsmkradio.com
Profile: WSMK-FM is a commercial station owned by Marion R. Williams. The format of the station is rhythmic adult contemporary music. WSMK-FM broadcasts to the South Bend, IN area at 99.1 FM.
FM RADIO STATION

WSML-AM 35669
Owner: Curtis Media Group
Editorial: 875 W 5th St, Winston Salem, North Carolina 27101-2505 **Tel:** 1 336 777-3900.
Web site: http://www.triadsports.com
Profile: WSML-AM is a commercial station owned by Curtis Media Group. The format of the station is sports. WSML-AM broadcasts to the Greensboro-Winston Salem, NC area at 600 AM.
AM RADIO STATION

WSMM-FM 46232
Owner: Artistic Media Partners Inc.
Editorial: 3371 W Cleveland Road Ext, Ste 300, South Bend, Indiana 46628 **Tel:** 1 574 273-9300.
Web site: http://www.stream1023.com
Profile: WSMM-FM is a commercial station owned by Artistic Media Partners Inc. The format of the station is oldies. WSMM-FM broadcasts to South Bend, IN area at 102.3 FM.
FM RADIO STATION

WSMN-AM 35670
Owner: Absolute Broadcasting, LLC
Editorial: 149 Main St Ste 210, Nashua, New Hampshire 03060-2725 **Tel:** 1 603 880-9001.
Email: justin@espnnh.com
Web site: http://www.wsmnradio.com
Profile: WSMN-AM is a commercial station owned by Absolute Broadcasting, LLC. The format of the station is talk. WSMN-AM broadcasts to the Nashua, NH area at 1590 AM.
AM RADIO STATION

WSMO-FM 875868
Owner: Smile FM
Editorial: 148 E Grand River Rd, Williamston, Michigan 48895-8400 **Tel:** 1 888 887-7139.
Email: 411@smile.fm
Web site: http://www.smile.fm
Profile: WSMO-FM is a non-commercial station owned by Smile FM. The format of the station is contemporary Christian music. WSMO-FM broadcasts to the Mount Forest, MI area at 91.9 FM.
FM RADIO STATION

WSMS-FM 41366
Owner: Cumulus Media Inc.
Editorial: 200 6th St N Ste 205, Columbus, Mississippi 39701-4552 **Tel:** 1 662 327-1183.
Web site: http://www.999thefoxrocks.com
FM RADIO STATION

WSMT-AM 38197
Owner: Peg Broadcasting, LLC
Editorial: 520 N Spring St, Sparta, Tennessee 38583-1305 **Tel:** 1 931 836-1055.
Web site: http://www.1050wsmt.com
Profile: WSMT-AM is a commercial station owned by Peg Broadcasting, LLC. The format of the station is gospel music. WSMT-AM broadcasts to the Sparta, TN area at 1050 AM.
AM RADIO STATION

WSMW-FM 45315
Owner: Entercom Communications Corp.
Editorial: 7819 National Service Rd, Ste 401, Greensboro, North Carolina 27409 **Tel:** 1 336 605-5200.
Web site: http://www.987simon.com
Profile: WSMW-FM is a commercial station owned by Entercom Communications Corp. The format of the station is adult hits. WSMW-FM broadcasts to the Greensboro-Winston Salem, NC area at 98.7 FM.
FM RADIO STATION

WSMX-AM 35672
Owner: Truth Broadcasting
Editorial: 4405 Providence Ln, Winston Salem, North Carolina 27106-3226 **Tel:** 1 336 768-0050.
Profile: WSMX-AM is a commercial station owned by Truth Broadcasting. The format of the station is Spanish Religious. The station broadcasts locally at 1500 AM in Winston-Salem, NC.
AM RADIO STATION

WSMY-AM 38198
Owner: First Media Radio LLC
Editorial: 3 E 1st St, Weldon, North Carolina 27890-1560 **Tel:** 1 252 536-3115.
Profile: WSMY-AM is a commercial station owned by First Media Radio LLC. The format of the station is sports talk. WSMY-AM broadcasts to the Weldon, NC area at 1400 AM.
AM RADIO STATION

WSNE-FM 40737
Owner: iHeartMedia Inc.
Editorial: 75 Oxford St, Providence, Rhode Island 02905-4722 **Tel:** 1 401 781-9979.
Email: feedback@coast933.com
Web site: http://coast933.iheart.com
Profile: WSNE-FM is a commercial station owned by iHeartMedia Inc. The format of the station is hot adult contemporary. WSNE-FM broadcasts to the Providence, RI area at 93.3 FM.
FM RADIO STATION

WSNG-AM 36486
Owner: Connoisseur Media
Editorial: 869 Blue Hills Ave, Bloomfield, Connecticut 06002-3710 **Tel:** 1 860 243-1115.
Web site: http://www.talkofconnecticut.com
Profile: WSNG-AM is a commercial station owned by Connoisseur Media. The format of the station is talk. WSNG-AM broadcasts to the Bloomfield, CT area at 610 AM.
AM RADIO STATION

WSNI-FM 46041
Owner: Saga Communications
Editorial: 69 Stanhope Ave, Keene, New Hampshire 03431-1577 **Tel:** 1 603 352-9230.
Web site: http://www.sunnykeene.com
Profile: WSNI-FM is a commercial station owned by Saga Communications. The format of the station is adult contemporary. WSNI-FM broadcasts to the Keene, NH area at 97.7 FM.
FM RADIO STATION

WSNJ-AM 38199
Owner: Quinn Communications and Marketing, LLC
Editorial: 4369 S Lincoln Ave, Vineland, New Jersey 08361-7757 **Tel:** 1 856 327-8800.
Email: cartabrava2@aol.com
Web site: http://www.labrava1440.com
Profile: WSNJ-AM is a commercial station owned by Quinn Communications and Marketing, LLC. The format of the station is Hispanic. WSNJ-AM broadcasts to the Bridgeton, NJ area at 1240 AM.
AM RADIO STATION

WSNL-AM 35685
Owner: Christian Broadcasting System
Editorial: 5210 S Saginaw Rd, Flint, Michigan 48507-4468 **Tel:** 1 810 694-4146.
Web site: http://www.cbslradio.com
Profile: WSNL-AM is a commercial station owned by Christian Broadcasting System. The format of the station is contemporary Christian music and religious programming. WSNL-AM broadcasts to the Grand Blanc, MI area at 1500 AM.
AM RADIO STATION

WSNN-FM 45545
Owner: Martz Communications
Editorial: 7064 US Highway 11, Potsdam, New York 13676-3197 **Tel:** 1 315 265-5510.
Email: hits@99hits.com
Web site: http://www.99hits.com
Profile: WSNN-FM is a commercial station owned by Martz Communications. The format of the station is country music. WSNN-FM broadcasts to the Potsdam, NY area at 99.3 FM.
FM RADIO STATION

WSNO-AM 38200
Owner: Great Eastern Radio, LLC
Editorial: 41 Jacques St, Barre, Vermont 05641-5320 **Tel:** 1 802 476-4168.
Profile: WSNO-AM is a commercial station owned by Great Eastern Radio, LLC. The format of the station is news, talk and sports. WSNO-AM broadcasts to the Barre, VT area at 1450 AM.
AM RADIO STATION

WSNQ-FM 40728
Owner: Equity Communications LP
Editorial: 8025 Black Horse Pike, Pleasantville, New Jersey 08232-2900 **Tel:** 1 609 484-8444.
Web site: http://www.951wayv.com/
Profile: WSNQ-FM is a commercial station owned by Equity Communications LP. The format of the station is Top 40/CHR. WSNQ-FM broadcasts to the Ocean City, NJ area at 105.5 FM.
FM RADIO STATION

WSNR-AM 36698
Owner: Davidzon Radio
Editorial: 2508 Coney Island Ave Fl 2, Brooklyn, New York 11223-5026 **Tel:** 1 516 431-6662.
Email: info@DavidzonRadio.com
Web site: http://www.davidzonradio.com
Profile: WSNR-AM is a commercial station owned by Davidson Radio. The format of the station is variety. WSNR-AM broadcasts to the New York City area at 620 AM.
AM RADIO STATION

WSNT-AM 38201
Owner: WSNT Inc.
Editorial: 312 Morningside Dr, Sandersville, Georgia 31082-7626 **Tel:** 1 478 552-5182.
Profile: WSNT-AM in a commercial station owned by WSNT Inc. The format of the station is southern gospel. WSNT-AM broadcasts to the Atlanta area at 1490 AM.
AM RADIO STATION

WSNT-FM 45546
Owner: WSNT Inc.
Editorial: 312 Morningside Dr, Sandersville, Georgia 31082-7626 **Tel:** 1 478 552-5182.
Web site: http://waco100dev.cogentes.com
Profile: WSNT-FM is a commercial station owned by WSNT Inc. The format of the station is country. WNST-FM broadcasts to the Sandersville, GA area at 99.9 FM.
FM RADIO STATION

WSNV-FM 43236
Owner: iHeartMedia Inc.
Editorial: 3807 Brandon Ave SW Ste 2350, Roanoke, Virginia 24018-1477 **Tel:** 1 540 725-1220.
Web site: http://sunny935.com
Profile: WSNV-FM is a commercial station owned by iHeartMedia Inc. The format of the station is classic hits. WSNV-FM broadcasts to the Roanoke, VA area at 93.5 FM.
FM RADIO STATION

WSNW-AM 36330
Owner: Georgia-Carolina Radiocasting Companies LLC
Editorial: 103 Ram Cat Aly, Seneca, South Carolina 29678-3243 **Tel:** 1 864 882-9769.
Web site: http://wsnwradio.com
Profile: WSNW-AM is a commercial station owned by Georgia-Carolina Radiocasting Companies LLC. The format of the station is adult contemporary. WSNW-AM broadcasts to the Seneca, SC area at 1150 AM.
AM RADIO STATION

WSNX-FM 43410
Owner: iHeartMedia Inc.
Editorial: 77 Monroe Center St NW, Grand Rapids, Michigan 49503-2903 **Tel:** 1 616 459-1919.
Web site: http://1045snx.iheart.com
Profile: WSNX-FM is a commercial station owned by iHeartMedia Inc. The format of the station is Top 40/CHR. WSNX-FM broadcasts to the Grand Rapids, MI area at 104.5 FM.
FM RADIO STATION

WSNY-FM 45547
Owner: Saga Communications
Editorial: 4401 Carriage Hill Ln, Columbus, Ohio 43220 **Tel:** 1 614 451-2191.
Web site: http://www.sunny95.com
Profile: WSNY-FM is a commercial station owned by Saga Communications. The format of the station is adult contemporary music. WSNY-FM broadcasts to the Columbus, OH area at 94.7 FM.
FM RADIO STATION

WSNZ-FM 42560
Owner: iHeartMedia Inc.
Editorial: 3807 Brandon Ave SW Ste 2350, Roanoke, Virginia 24018-1477 **Tel:** 1 540 725-1220.
Web site: http://www.1061stevefm.com
Profile: WSNZ-FM is a commercial station owned by iHeartMedia Inc. The format of the station is adult hits. WSNZ-FM broadcasts to the Lynchburg, VA area at 101.7 FM.
FM RADIO STATION

WSOC-FM 41890
Owner: Beasley Broadcast Group
Editorial: 1520 South Blvd, Charlotte, North Carolina 28203-4786 **Tel:** 1 704 522-1103.
Web site: http://thenew1037.cbslocal.com
Profile: WSOC-FM is a commercial station owned by Beasley Broadcast Group. The format of the station is country. WSOC-FM broadcasts to the Charlotte, NC area at 103.7 FM.
FM RADIO STATION

WSOK-AM 38202
Owner: iHeartMedia Inc.
Editorial: 245 Alfred St, Savannah, Georgia 31408-3205 **Tel:** 1 912 964-7794.
Email: community@1230wsok.com
Web site: http://www.1230wsok.com
Profile: WSOK-AM is a commercial station owned by iHeartMedia Inc. The format of the station is gospel. WSOK-AM broadcasts to the Savannah, GA area at 1230 AM.
AM RADIO STATION

WSOL-FM 42023
Owner: iHeartMedia Inc.
Editorial: 11700 Central Pkwy, Jacksonville, Florida 32224-2600 **Tel:** 1 904 636-0507.
Web site: http://www.v1015.com
Profile: WSOL-FM is a commercial station owned by iHeartMedia Inc. The format of the station is urban adult contemporary music. WSOL-FM broadcasts to the Jacksonville, FL area at 101.5 FM.
FM RADIO STATION

WSOM-AM 38203
Owner: Cumulus Media Inc.
Editorial: 4040 Simon Rd, Youngstown, Ohio 44512-1362 **Tel:** 1 330 783-1000.
Web site: http://www.600wsom.com
Profile: WSOM-AM is a commercial station owned by Cumulus Media Inc. The format of the station is news/talk. WSOM-AM broadcasts to the Youngstown, OH area at 600 AM.
AM RADIO STATION

WSON-AM 35673
Owner: Henson Media of Henderson County, LLC
Editorial: 230 2nd St, Henderson, Kentucky 42420-3172 **Tel:** 1 270 826-3923.
AM RADIO STATION

WSOO-AM 38204
Owner: Sovereign Communications LLC
Editorial: 1411 Ashmun St, Sault Sainte Marie, Michigan 49783 **Tel:** 1 906 632-2231.
Email: info@rock101.net
Web site: http://www.1230wsoo.com
AM RADIO STATION

WSOS-AM 35899
Owner: Geddings, Kevin
Editorial: 3000 N Ponce De Leon Blvd, Saint Augustine, Florida 32084-8602 **Tel:** 1 904 495-1370.
Web site: http://staugustineradio.com
Profile: WSOS-AM is a commercial station owned by Geddings, Kevin. The format of the station is oldies. WSOS-AM broadcasts to the St. Augustine, FL area at 1170 AM.
AM RADIO STATION

WSOS-FM 40738
Owner: Chesapeake-Portsmouth Broadcasting Corp.
Editorial: 7235 Bonneval Rd, the Salem Centre, Jacksonville, Florida 32256-7565 **Tel:** 1 904 641-9626.
Web site: http://ilovethepromise.com/web
Profile: WSOS-FM is a commercial station owned by Chesapeake-Portsmouth Broadcasting Corp. The format of the station is news/talk. WSOS-FM broadcasts to the Jacksonville, FL area at 94.1 FM.
FM RADIO STATION

WSOX-FM 44502
Owner: Cumulus Media Inc.
Editorial: 5989 Susquehanna Plaza Drive, York, Pennsylvania 17406-8910 **Tel:** 1 717 764-1155.
Web site: http://www.961wsox.com
Profile: WSOX-FM is a commercial station owned by Cumulus Media Inc. The format of the station is classic hits. WSOX-FM broadcasts to the York, PA area at 96.1 FM.
FM RADIO STATION

WSOY-AM 38205
Owner: Neuhoff Communications
Editorial: 250 N Water St, Ste 100, Decatur, Illinois 62523 **Tel:** 1 217 877-5371.
Email: news@wsoyam.com
Web site: http://www.wsoyam.com
Profile: WSOY-AM a commercial station owned by Neuhoff Communications. The format of the station is news and talk. WSOY-AM broadcasts to the Decatur, IL area at 1340 AM.
AM RADIO STATION

WSOY-FM 45548
Owner: Neuhoff Communications
Editorial: 250 N Water St, Ste 100, Decatur, Illinois 62523 **Tel:** 1 217 877-5371.
Email: news@wsoyam.com
Web site: http://www.y103.com
Profile: WSOY-FM is a commercial station owned by Neuhoff Communications. The format of the station is Top 40/CHR music. WSOY-FM broadcasts to Decatur, IL at 102.9 FM.
FM RADIO STATION

WSPA-FM 44436
Owner: Entercom Communications Corp.
Editorial: 25 Garlington Rd, Greenville, South Carolina 29615-4613 **Tel:** 1 864 271-9200.
Email: wsnwradio@gmail.com
Web site: http://www.magic989online.com
Profile: WSPA-FM is a commercial station owned by Entercom Communications Corp. The format for the station is adult contemporary. WSPA-FM broadcasts to the Greenville, SC area at 98.9 FM.
FM RADIO STATION

WSPC-AM 36768
Owner: Stanly Communications Inc.
Editorial: 1234 Magnolia St, Albemarle, North Carolina 28001 **Tel:** 1 704 983-1580.
Email: wspc@ctc.net
Web site: http://www.1010wspc.com
Profile: WSPC-AM is a commercial station owned by Stanly Communications Inc. The format of the station is news and talk. WSPC-AM broadcasts to the Albemarle, NC area at 1010 AM.
AM RADIO STATION

WSPD-AM 38450
Owner: iHeartMedia Inc.
Editorial: 125 S Superior St, Toledo, Ohio 43604-8747 **Tel:** 1 419 244-8321.
Email: toledonewsroom@iheartmedia.com
Web site: http://www.wspd.com
Profile: WSPD-AM is a commercial station owned by iHeartMedia Inc. The format of the station is news and talk. WSPD-AM broadcasts to the Toledo, OH area at 1370 AM.
AM RADIO STATION

WSPK-FM 46625
Owner: Pamal Broadcasting Ltd.
Editorial: 715 Route 52, Beacon, New York 12508-1047 **Tel:** 1 845 838-6000.
Web site: http://www.k104online.com
Profile: WSPK-FM is a commercial station owned by Pamal Broadcasting Ltd. The format of the station is Top 40/CHR. WSPK-FM broadcasts to the Beacon, NY area on 104.7 FM.
FM RADIO STATION

WSPL-AM
37924
Owner: Mendota Broadcasting
Editorial: Highway 23 North, Streator, Illinois 61364
Tel: 1 815 672-2947.
Email: news@theradiogroup.net
Web site: http://www.am1250wspl.com
Profile: WSPL-AM is a commercial station owned by Mendota Broadcasting. The format of the station is news, talk and sports programming. WSPL-AM broadcasts to the Streator, IL area at 1250 AM.
AM RADIO STATION

WSPM-FM
217709
Owner: Inter Mifica, Inc.
Editorial: 8383 Craig St Ste 280, Indianapolis, Indiana 46250-3596 **Tel:** 1 317 870-8400 21.
Email: info@catholicradioindy.org
Web site: http://www.catholicradioindy.org
Profile: WSPM-FM is a non-commercial station owned by Inter Mifica, Inc. The format of the station is Catholic teaching programming. WSPM-FM broadcasts to the Indianapolis, IN area at 89.1 FM.
FM RADIO STATION

WSPN-FM
40740
Owner: Skidmore College
Editorial: 815 N Broadway, Saratoga Springs, New York 12866 **Tel:** 1 518 580-5787.
Email: wspn@skidmore.edu
Web site: http://www.skidmore.edu/studentorgs/wspn/
FM RADIO STATION

WSPO-AM
38787
Owner: Apex Broadcasting Inc.
Editorial: 2294 Clements Ferry Rd, Charleston, South Carolina 29492-7729 **Tel:** 1 843 972-1100.
Email: cvi@apexbroadcasting.com
Profile: WSPO-AM is a commercial station owned by Apex Broadcasting Inc. The format of the station is gospel. WSPO-AM broadcasts to the Charleston, SC area at 1390 AM.
AM RADIO STATION

WSPQ-AM
35940
Owner: Hawk Communications Ltd.
Editorial: 51 Franklin St, Springville, New York 14141-1340 **Tel:** 1 716 592-1330.
Email: wspq1330@yahoo.com
Web site: http://wspq1330.com
Profile: WSPQ-AM is a commercial station owned by Hawk Communications Ltd. The format of the station is classic hits music. WSPQ-AM broadcasts to the Springville, NY area at 1330 AM.
AM RADIO STATION

WSPR-AM
35152
Owner: Red Wolf Broadcasting
Editorial: 34 Sylvan St, West Springfield, Massachusetts 01089-3444 **Tel:** 1 413 781-5200.
Profile: WSPR-AM is a commercial station owned by Red Wolf Broadcasting. The format of the station is Tropical. WSPR-AM broadcasts in the West Springfield, MA area at 1490 AM.
AM RADIO STATION

WSPT-AM
38290
Owner: Muzzy Broadcasting
Editorial: 500 Division St, Stevens Point, Wisconsin 54481-1838 **Tel:** 1 715 341-9800.
Web site: https://www.979wspt.com/
Profile: WSPT-AM is a commercial station owned by Muzzy Broadcasting. The format of the station is news, talk and oldies. WSPT-AM broadcasts to the Stevens Point, WI area at 1010 AM.
AM RADIO STATION

WSPT-FM
45549
Owner: Muzzy Broadcasting
Editorial: 500 Division St, Stevens Point, Wisconsin 54481 **Tel:** 1 715 341-1300.
Web site: http://www.979wspt.com
Profile: WSPT-FM is a commercial station owned by Muzzy Broadcasting. The format of the station is oldies. WSPT-FM broadcasts in the Stevens Point, WI area at 97.9 FM.
FM RADIO STATION

WSPX-FM
43499
Owner: Glory Communications Inc.
Editorial: 1236 Five Chop Rd, Orangeburg, South Carolina 29115-7047 **Tel:** 1 803 939-9530.
Email: lgrant@wfmv.com
Web site: http://www.columbiainspiration.com
Profile: WSPX-FM is a commercial station owned by Glory Communications Inc. The format of the station is gospel. WSPX-FM broadcasts to the Orangeburg, SC area at 97.5 FM.
FM RADIO STATION

WSPY-AM
80996
Owner: Nelson Enterprises Inc.
Editorial: 1 Broadcast Ctr, Plano, Illinois 60545-2100
Tel: 1 630 552-1000.
Web site: http://www.wspyfm.com/nelson/index.html
Profile: WSPY-AM is a commercial station owned by Nelson Enterprises Inc. The format of the station is classic hits. WSPY-AM broadcasts to the Plano, IL area at 1480 FM.
AM RADIO STATION

WSPY-FM
43295
Owner: Nelson Enterprises Inc.
Editorial: 1 Broadcast Ctr, Plano, Illinois 60545-2100
Tel: 1 630 552-1000.
Web site: http://wspynews.com
Profile: WSPY-FM is a commercial station owned by Nelson Enterprises Inc. The format of the station is Lite Rock/Lite AC. WSPY-FM broadcasts to the Plano, IL area at 107.1 FM.
FM RADIO STATION

WSPZ-AM
38657
Owner: Red Zebra Broadcasting
Editorial: 1801 Rockville Pike Ste 405, Rockville, Maryland 20852-5604 **Tel:** 1 301 230-3500.
Email: management@espn980.com
Web site: http://www.sportstalk570.com
Profile: WSPZ-AM is a commercial station owned by Red Zebra Broadcasting. The format of the station is sports/talk. WSPZ-AM broadcasts to the Silver Spring, MD area at 570 AM. The station is affiliated with ESPN Radio.
AM RADIO STATION

WSQL-AM
36089
Owner: Go Nuts Media
Editorial: 62 W Main St, Brevard, North Carolina 28712 **Tel:** 1 828 877-5252.
Email: info@wsqlradio.com
Web site: http://www.wsqlradio.com
Profile: WSQL-AM is a commercial station owned by Go Nuts Media. The format for the station is variety. WSQL-AM broadcasts to the Brevard, NC area at 1240 AM.
AM RADIO STATION

WSQR-AM
36996
Owner: DeKalb County Broadcasters Inc.
Editorial: 2410 Sycamore Rd Ste C, Dekalb, Illinois 60115-2091 **Tel:** 1 815 748-1000.
Profile: WSQR-AM is a commercial station owned by DeKalb County Broadcasters Inc. The format of the station is classic hits. WSQR-AM broadcasts to the Sycamore, IL area at 1180 AM.
AM RADIO STATION

WSQV-FM
45853
Owner: Schlesinger Communications
Editorial: 21 E Main St, Lock Haven, Pennsylvania 17745-1303 **Tel:** 1 570 748-4038.
Email: info@wsqvradio.com
Web site: http://wsqvradio.com
Profile: WSQV-FM is a commercial station owned by Schlesinger Communications. The format of the station is Classic Hits. WSQV-FMbroadcasts to the Lock Haven, PA area at 92.1 FM.
FM RADIO STATION

WSQX-FM
42887
Owner: WSKG Public Telecommunications
Editorial: 601 Gates Rd, Vestal, New York 13850-2288 **Tel:** 1 607 729-0100.
Web site: http://www.wskg.org/
Profile: WSQX-FM is a non-commercial station owned by WSKG Public Telecommunications. The format of the station is educational and news. WSQX-FM broadcasts to the Binghamton, NY area at 91.5 FM.
FM RADIO STATION

WSRA-AM
35170
Owner: Fulton (Livingston)
Editorial: 2804 N Jefferson St, Albany, Georgia 31701
Tel: 1 229 228-5051.
Web site: http://www.wsraradio.com
Profile: WSRA-AM is a commercial station owned by Livingston Fulton. The format of the station is sports. WSRA-AM broadcasts to the Albany, GA area at 1250 AM.
AM RADIO STATION

WSRB-FM
40884
Owner: Crawford Broadcasting Co.
Editorial: 6336 Calumet Ave, Hammond, Indiana 46324-1243 **Tel:** 1 219 933-4455.
Web site: http://www.1063chicago.com
Profile: WSRB-FM is a commercial station owned by Crawford Broadcasting Co. The format of the station is urban contemporary and R&B. WSRB-FM broadcasts to the Chicago area at 106.3 FM.
FM RADIO STATION

WSRF-AM
36558
Owner: Niche Radio Inc.
Editorial: 1510 NE 162nd St, North Miami Beach, Florida 33162 **Tel:** 1 305 940-1580.
Email: info@wsrf.com
Web site: http://www.wsrf.com
Profile: WSRF-AM is a commercial station owned by Niche Radio Inc. The station follows an ethnic brokered format. WSRF-AM broadcasts to the Miami area at 1580 AM.
AM RADIO STATION

WSRJ-FM
86976
Owner: Northern Broadcast Inc.
Editorial: 1020 Hastings St Ste 102, Traverse City, Michigan 49686-3457 **Tel:** 1 231 947-0003.
Web site: http://www.espnradionorthernmichigan.com
Profile: WSRJ-FM is a commercial station owned by Northern Broadcast Inc. The format of the station is sports. WSRJ-FM broadcasts to the Traverse City, MI area on 105.5 FM.
FM RADIO STATION

WSRK-FM
46558
Owner: Townsquare Media, LLC
Editorial: 34 Chestnut St, Oneonta, New York 13820-2466 **Tel:** 1 607 432-1030.
Email: cnynews@townsquaremedia.com
Web site: http://wsrkfm.com
Profile: WSRK-FM is a commercial station owned by Townsquare Media, LLC. The format of the station is hot adult contemporary music. WSRK-FM broadcasts to the Oneonta, NY area at 103.9 FM.
FM RADIO STATION

WSRM-FM
597395
Owner: Rome Radio Partners
Editorial: 20 John Davenport Dr NW, Rome, Georgia 30165-2536 **Tel:** 1 706 291-9496.
Web site: http://southern935.com
Profile: WSRM-FM is a commercial station owned by Rome Radio Partners. The format of the station is classic country. WSRM-FM broadcasts to the Rome, GA area at 93.5 FM.
FM RADIO STATION

WSRN-FM
40741
Owner: Swarthmore College
Editorial: 500 College Ave, Swarthmore, Pennsylvania 19081-1306 **Tel:** 1 610 328-8335.
Email: wsrnfm@gmail.com
Web site: http://www.wsrnfm.org
Profile: WSRN-FM is a non-commercial station owned by Swarthmore College. The format of the station is college variety. WSRN-FM broadcasts in the Swarthmore, PA area at 91.5 FM.
FM RADIO STATION

WSRO-AM
36513
Owner: Langer Broadcasting Group, LLC
Editorial: 100 Mount Wayte Ave, Framingham, Massachusetts 01702-5705 **Tel:** 1 508 424-2568.
Web site: http://www.wsro.com
Profile: WSRO-AM is a commercial station owned by Langer Broadcasting Group, LLC. The format of the station features community, religious, news, music and entertainment programming all in Portuguese. WSRO-AM broadcasts to the Framingham, MA area at 650 AM.
AM RADIO STATION

WSRQ-AM
154564
Owner: Florida Talk Radio, LLC
Editorial: 3679 Webber St, Sarasota, Florida 34232-4412 **Tel:** 1 941 952-1220.
Email: info@wsrqradio.com
Web site: http://www.sarasotatalkradio.com
Profile: WSRQ-AM is a commercial station owned by Florida Talk Radio, LLC. The format of the station is talk. WSRQ-AM broadcasts to the Sarasota, FL area at 1220 AM.
AM RADIO STATION

WSRS-FM
45687
Owner: iHeartMedia Inc.
Editorial: 96 Stereo Ln, Paxton, Massachusetts 01612-1376 **Tel:** 1 508 757-9696.
Web site: http://961srs.iheart.com
Profile: WSRS-FM is a commercial station owned by iHeartMedia Inc. The format of the station is adult contemporary. WSRS-FM broadcasts to the Paxton, MA area at 96.1 FM.
FM RADIO STATION

WSRT-FM
40933
Owner: Northern Broadcast Inc.
Editorial: 1020 Hastings St Ste 102, Traverse City, Michigan 49686-3457 **Tel:** 1 231 947-0003.
Web site: http://www.espnradionorthernmichigan.com
Profile: WSRT-FM is a commercial station owned by Northern Broadcast Inc. The format of the station is sports. WSRT-FM broadcasts to the Traverse City, MI area at 106.7 FM.
FM RADIO STATION

WSRV-FM
40293
Owner: Cox Media Group, Inc.
Editorial: 1601 W Peachtree St NE, Atlanta, Georgia 30309-2641 **Tel:** 1 404 897-7500.
Web site: http://www.971theriver.com
Profile: WSRV-FM is a commercial station owned by Cox Media Group, Inc. The format of the station is classic hits. WSRV-FM broadcasts to the Atlanta area at 97.1 FM.
FM RADIO STATION

WSRW-AM
38993
Owner: iHeartMedia Inc.
Editorial: 5675 State Route 247, Hillsboro, Ohio 45133-7328 **Tel:** 1 937 393-1590.
Web site: http://www.buckeyecountry105.com/main.html
Profile: WSRW-AM is a commercial station owned by iHeartMedia Inc. The format of the station is classic hits. WSRW-AM broadcasts to the Hillsboro, OH area at 1590 AM.
AM RADIO STATION

WSRW-FM
45428
Owner: iHeartMedia Inc.
Editorial: 77 Monroe Center St NW Ste 1000, Grand Rapids, Michigan 49503-2912 **Tel:** 1 616 459-1919.
Web site: http://westmichiganstar.iheart.com
Profile: WSRW-FM is a commercial station owned by iHeartMedia Inc. The format of the station is adult contemporary. WSRW-FM broadcasts to the Grand Rapids, MI area 105.7 FM.
FM RADIO STATION

WSRY-AM
35657
Owner: Priority Radio, Inc.
Editorial: 179 Stanton Christiana Rd, Newark, Delaware 19702-1619 **Tel:** 1 302 731-0690.
Profile: WSRY-AM is a commercial station owned by World Revivals Inc. The format of the station is sports talk. WSRY-AM broadcasts to the Newark, DE area at 1550 AM.
AM RADIO STATION

WSRZ-FM
41625
Owner: iHeartMedia Inc.
Editorial: 1779 Independence Blvd, Sarasota, Florida 34234-2106 **Tel:** 1 941 552-4800.
Web site: http://www.oldies108.com
Profile: WSRZ-FM is a commercial station owned by iHeartMedia Inc. The format of the station is Classic Hits. WSRZ-FM broadcasts in the Tampa Bay, FL area at 107.9 FM.
FM RADIO STATION

WSSC-AM
35678
Owner: Sumter Baptist Temple Inc.
Editorial: 201 Oswego Road, Sumter, South Carolina 29150-4431 **Tel:** 1 803 469-0288.
Profile: WSSC-AM is a commercial station owned by Sumter Baptist Temple Inc. The format of the station is Christian programming. WSSC-AM broadcasts to the Sumter, SC area at 1340 AM.
AM RADIO STATION

WSSD-FM
41359
Owner: Lakeside Telecommunications
Editorial: 515 W 111th St, Chicago, Illinois 60628
Tel: 1 773 928-8800.
Email: wssdthemusicstation@yahoo.com
Profile: WSSD-FM is a non-commercial station owned by Lakeside Telecommunications. The station's format is variety. WSSD-FM broadcasts to the Chicago area at 88.1 FM.
FM RADIO STATION

WSSG-AM
35974
Owner: Curtis Media Group
Editorial: 2581 US Highway 70 W, Goldsboro, North Carolina 27530-9553 **Tel:** 1 919 736-1150.
Web site: http://goldsborodailynews.com
Profile: WSSG-AM is a commercial station owned by Curtis Media Group, dba Eastern Airwaves LLC. The format of the station is contemporary country. WSSG-AM broadcasts to the Goldsboro, NC area at 1300 AM.
AM RADIO STATION

WSSL-FM
45551
Owner: iHeartMedia Inc.
Editorial: 101 N Main St Ste 1000, Greenville, South Carolina 29601-4852 **Tel:** 1 864 242-1005.
Web site: http://wsslfm.iheart.com
Profile: WSSL-FM is a commercial station owned by iHeartMedia Inc. The format for the station is contemporary country. WSSL-FM broadcasts to the Greenville, SC area at 100.5 FM.
FM RADIO STATION

WSSM-FM
41107
Owner: Artistic Media Partners Inc.
Editorial: 3371 Cleveland Road Ext Ste 300, South Bend, Indiana 46628-9780 **Tel:** 1 574 273-9300.
Web site: http://www.stream1023.com
Profile: WSSM-FM is a commercial station owned by Artistic Media Partners Inc. The format of the station is oldies. WSSM-FM broadcasts to the South Bend, IN area at 97.7 FM.
FM RADIO STATION

WSSO-AM
38208
Owner: Cumulus Media Inc.
Editorial: 200 6th St N Ste 205, Columbus, Mississippi 39701-4552 **Tel:** 1 662 327-1183.
Profile: WSSO-AM is a commercial station owned by Cumulus Media Inc. The format of the station is news, sports and talk. WSSO-AM broadcasts to the Columbus, MS area at 1230 AM.
AM RADIO STATION

WSSP-AM
37790
Owner: Entercom Communications Corp.
Editorial: 11800 W Grange Ave, Hales Corners, Wisconsin 53130-1035 **Tel:** 1 414 529-1250.
Email: live@sportsradio1250.com
Web site: http://www.1057fmthefan.com
Profile: WSSP-AM is a commercial station owned by Entercom Communications Corp. The format of the station is sports. WSSP-AM broadcasts to the Milwaukee area at 1250 AM.
AM RADIO STATION

WSSQ-FM
46539
Owner: Withers Broadcasting Co.
Editorial: 3101 Freeport Rd, Sterling, Illinois 61081-8612 **Tel:** 1 815 625-3400.
Email: wsdr1240@theramp.net
Profile: WSSQ-FM is a commercial station owned by Withers Broadcasting Co. The format of the station is adult contemporary. WSSQ-FM broadcasts to the Sterling, IL area at 94.3 FM.
FM RADIO STATION

WSSR-FM
45343
Owner: Alpha Media
Editorial: 2410 Caton Farm Rd Unit B, Crest Hill, Illinois 60403-1374 **Tel:** 1 815 556-0100.
Web site: http://www.star967.net
Profile: WSSR-FM is a commercial station owned by Alpha Media. The format of the station is adult contemporary music. WSSR-FM broadcasts to the Crest Hill, IL area at 96.7 FM.
FM RADIO STATION

WSSX-FM 41413
Owner: Cumulus Media Inc.
Editorial: 4230 Faber Place Dr Ste 100, North Charleston, South Carolina 29405-8512
Tel: 1 843 277-1200.
Web site: http://www.95sx.com
Profile: WSSX-FM is a commercial station owned by Cumulus Media Inc. The format of the station is top 40/CHR. WSSX-FM broadcasts to the Charleston, SC area at 95.1 FM.
FM RADIO STATION

WSSY-FM 43671
Owner: Georgia Eagle Broadcasting Inc.
Editorial: 218 Eastman Highway, Hawkinsville, Georgia 31036 **Tel:** 1 478 892-9061.
Profile: WSSY-FM is a commercial station owned by Georgia Eagle Broadcasting Inc. The format of the station is adult standards. WSSY-FM broadcasts to the Cordele, GA area at 98.3 FM.
FM RADIO STATION

WSTG-FM 45014
Owner: L & P Broadcasting Inc.
Editorial: 1 Radio Ln, Princeton, West Virginia 24740-2886 **Tel:** 1 304 425-2152.
Web site: http://www.star95.com
Profile: WSTG-FM is a commercial station owned and operated by L & P Broadcasting Inc. The format of the station is adult contemporary music. WSTG-FM broadcasts to the Princeton, WV area at 95.9 FM.
FM RADIO STATION

WSTH-FM 46258
Owner: Premier Radio Networks
Editorial: 1501 13th Ave, Columbus, Georgia 31901
Tel: 1 706 576-3000.
Web site: http://www.mysouth1061.com
Profile: WSTH-FM is a commercial station owned by Premier Radio Networks. The format of the station is country. WSTH-FM broadcasts to the Columbus, GA area at 106.1 FM.
FM RADIO STATION

WSTI-FM 40746
Owner: Black Crow Broadcasting Inc.
Editorial: 1711 Ellis Dr, Valdosta, Georgia 31601-3573
Tel: 1 229 244-8642.
Web site: http://mystar1053.com/
Profile: WSTI-FM is a commercial station owned by Black Crow Broadcasting Inc. The format of the station is urban contemporary music. WSTI-FM broadcasts to Valdosta, GA area at 105.3 FM.
FM RADIO STATION

WSTJ-AM 38209
Owner: Vermont Broadcast Associates Inc.
Editorial: 1303 Concord Ave, Saint Johnsbury, Vermont 5819 **Tel:** 1 802 748-1340.
Email: wstjstudio@gmail.com
Profile: WSTJ-AM is a commercial station owned by Vermont Broadcast Associates Inc. The format of the station is adult standards. WSTJ-AM broadcasts to the St. Johnsbury, VT area at 1340 AM.
AM RADIO STATION

WSTL-AM 429292
Owner: New England Christian Media Inc.
Editorial: 95 Sagamore Rd, Seekonk, Massachusetts 2771 **Tel:** 1 508 336-4233.
Email: info@wstl.us
Web site: http://www.wstl.us
Profile: WSTL-AM is a non-commercial station owned by New England Christian Media Inc. The format of the station is Christian music and talk. WSTL-AM broadcasts to the Seekonk, MA area at 1220 AM.
AM RADIO STATION

WSTM-FM 137103
Owner: Jubilation Ministries
Editorial: N 5569 State Highway 57, Plymouth, Wisconsin 53073-4236 **Tel:** 1 920 893-2661.
Email: wstm@jmiradio.org
Web site: http://www.wstmfm.org
Profile: WSTM-FM is a non-commercial station owned by Jubliation Ministries. The format of the station is contemporary Christian. WSTM-FM broadcasts to the Plymouth, WI area at 91.3 FM.
FM RADIO STATION

WSTO-FM 45552
Owner: South Central Communications Corp.
Editorial: 1162 Mount Auburn Rd, Evansville, Indiana 47720-5428 **Tel:** 1 812 424-8284.
Web site: http://www.hot96.com
Profile: WSTO-FM is a commercial station owned by South Central Communications Corp. The format of the station is Top 40/CHR music. WSTO-FM broadcasts to the Evansville, IN area 96.1 FM.
FM RADIO STATION

WSTQ-FM 45553
Owner: Mendota Broadcasting
Editorial: 3905 Progress Blvd, Peru, Illinois 61354-1121 **Tel:** 1 815 224-2100.
Email: q@studstillmedia.com
Web site: http://www.qhitmusic.com
Profile: WSTQ-FM is a commercial station owned by Mendota Broadcasting. The format of the station is Top 40/CHR. WSTQ-FM broadcasts to the Peru, IL area at 97.7 FM.
FM RADIO STATION

WSTR-FM 43455
Owner: Entercom Communications Corp.
Editorial: 210 Interstate North Cir SE, Atlanta, Georgia 30339-2206 **Tel:** 1 404 261-2970.
Web site: http://www.star941atlanta.com
Profile: WSTR-FM is a commercial station owned by Entercom Communications Corp. The format of the station is Top 40/CHR. WSTR-FM broadcasts to the Atlanta area at 94.1 FM.
FM RADIO STATION

WSTS-FM 45661
Owner: Davidson Media Group
Editorial: 5448 Hwy 41 S, Fairmont, North Carolina 28340 **Tel:** 1 910 628-6781.
Profile: WSTS-FM is a commercial station owned by Davidson Media Group. The format of the station is Southern gospel. WSTS-FM broadcasts to the Fairmont, NC area at 100.9 FM.
FM RADIO STATION

WSTT-AM 36881
Owner: Williams (Marion)
Editorial: 2194 US Highway 319 S, Thomasville, Georgia 31792-1417 **Tel:** 1 229 377-2337.
Web site: http://wstt730.com
Profile: WSTT-AM is a non-commercial station owned by Marion Williams. The format of the station is gospel. WSTT-AM broadcasts to the Thomasville, GA area at 730 AM.
AM RADIO STATION

WSTU-AM 36647
Owner: Treasure Coast Broadcasters
Editorial: 4100 Metzger Rd, Fort Pierce, Florida 34947
Tel: 1 772 340-1590.
Email: wpsl@wpsl.com
Web site: http://www.wstu1450.com
Profile: WSTU-AM is a commercial station owned by Treasure Coast Broadcasters. The format of the station is news, sports and talk. WSTU-AM broadcasts to the Port St. Lucie, FL area at 1450 AM.
AM RADIO STATION

WSTV-FM 46028
Owner: Cap City Communications Inc.
Editorial: 115 W Main St, Frankfort, Kentucky 40601-2807 **Tel:** 1 502 875-1130.
Web site: http://www.star1037.com
Profile: WSTV-FM is a commercial station owned by Cap City Communications Inc. The format for the station is hot adult contemporary. WSTV-FM broadcasts to the Lexington, KY area at 103.7 FM.
FM RADIO STATION

WSTW-FM 45554
Owner: Delmarva Broadcasting Company
Editorial: 2727 Shipley Rd, Wilmington, Delaware 19810-3210 **Tel:** 1 302 478-2700.
Email: wdelnews@wdel.com
Web site: http://www.wstw.com
Profile: WSTW-FM is a commercial station owned by Delmarva Broadcasting Comp. The format of the station is Top 40/CHR. WSTW-FM broadcasts to the Wilmington, DE area at 93.7 FM.
FM RADIO STATION

WSTZ-FM 42136
Owner: iHeartMedia Inc.
Editorial: 1375 Beasley Rd, Jackson, Mississippi 39206-2018 **Tel:** 1 601 982-1062.
Web site: http://www.z106.com
Profile: WSTZ-FM is a commercial station owned by iHeartMedia Inc. The format of the station is classic rock. WSTZ-FM broadcasts to the Jackson, MS area at 106.7 FM.
FM RADIO STATION

WSUA-AM 35681
Owner: Groupo Latino De Ratio (GLR) Networks
Editorial: 2100 Coral Way, Coral Gables, Florida 33145-2635 **Tel:** 1 305 285-1260.
Web site: http://www.caracol1260.com
Profile: WSUA-AM is a commercial station owned by Groupo Latino De Ratio (GLR) Networks. The format of the station is Spanish language news talk. WSUA-AM broadcasts to the Miami area at 1260 AM.
AM RADIO STATION

WSUE-FM 45555
Owner: Sovereign Communications LLC
Editorial: 1411 Ashmun St, Sault Sainte Marie, Michigan 49783 **Tel:** 1 906 632-2231.
Email: webmaster@rock101.net
Web site: http://www.rock101.net
FM RADIO STATION

WSUL-FM 40747
Owner: Watermark Communications
Editorial: 198 Bridgeville Rd, Monticello, New York 12701 **Tel:** 1 845 794-9898.
Web site: http://www.wsul.com
Profile: WSUL-FM is a commercial station owned by Watermark Communications. The format of the station is hot adult contemporary. WSUL-FM broadcasts to the Monticello, NY area at 98.3 FM.
FM RADIO STATION

WSUN-FM 42808
Owner: Cox Media Group, Inc.
Editorial: 11300 4th St N, Saint Petersburg, Florida 33716-2918 **Tel:** 1 727 579-2000.
Email: 97xcomments@97xonline.com
Web site: http://www.97xonline.com
Profile: WSUN-FM is a commercial station owned by Cox Media Group, Inc. The format of the station is user generated rock alternative. WSUN-FM broadcasts to the Tampa, FL area at 97.1 FM.
FM RADIO STATION

WSUS-FM 40749
Owner: iHeartMedia Inc.
Editorial: 45 Ed Mitchell Ave, Franklin, New Jersey 07416-1588 **Tel:** 1 973 827-2525.
Web site: http://www.wsus1023.com
Profile: WSUS-FM is a commercial station owned by iHeartMedia Inc. The format of the station is adult contemporary. WSUS-FM broadcasts to the Franklin, NJ area at 102.3 FM.
FM RADIO STATION

WSUX-AM 38213
Owner: Adams Radio Group
Editorial: 20200 Dupont Blvd, Georgetown, Delaware 19947-3105 **Tel:** 1 302 856-2567.
Profile: WSUX-AM is a commercial station owned by Adams Radio Group The format of the station is adult hits. WSUX-AM broadcasts to the Georgetown, DE area at 1280 AM.
AM RADIO STATION

WSVA-AM 38724
Owner: Saga Communications
Editorial: 1820 Heritage Center Way, Harrisonburg, Virginia 22801-8451 **Tel:** 1 540 434-0331.
Web site: http://www.wsvaonline.com
Profile: WSVA-AM is a commercial station owned by Saga Communications. The format of the station is news and talk. WSVA-AM broadcasts to the Harrisonburg, VA area at 550 AM. The station does not accept unsolicited faxes. WSVA-AM prefers to receive press inquiries via phone. Do NOT e-mail any staff members.
AM RADIO STATION

WSVH-FM 40751
Owner: Georgia Public Broadcasting
Editorial: 260 14th St NW, Atlanta, Georgia 30318-5360 **Tel:** 1 404 685-4788.
Email: ask@gpb.org
Web site: http://www.gpb.org
Profile: WSVH-FM is a non-commercial station owned by Georgia Public Broadcasting. The format of the station is classical, jazz and news. WSVH-FM broadcasts to the Savannah, GA area at 91.1 FM.
FM RADIO STATION

WSVM-AM 35683
Owner: GHB Broadcasting
Editorial: 1117 Praley St SW, Valdese, North Carolina 28690 **Tel:** 1 828 874-0000.
Profile: WSVM-AM is a commercial station owned by GHB Broadcasting. The format of the station is adult standards. WSVM-AM broadcasts to the Valdese, NC area at 1490 AM.
AM RADIO STATION

WSVO-FM 45533
Owner: iHeartMedia Inc.
Editorial: 207 University Blvd, Harrisonburg, Virginia 22801-3749 **Tel:** 1 540 434-1777.
Web site: http://mix931online.iheart.com
Profile: WSVO-FM is a commercial station owned by iHeartMedia Inc. The format for the station is Lite Rock/Lite AC. WSVO-FM broadcasts to the Harrisonburg, VA area at 93.1 FM.
FM RADIO STATION

WSVS-AM 36342
Owner: Gee Communications Inc.
Editorial: 1032 Melody Ln, Crewe, Virginia 23930-4249 **Tel:** 1 434 645-7734.
Web site: http://www.wsvsamfm.com
Profile: WSVS-AM is a commercial station owned by Gee Communications Inc. The format of the station is news, sports and talk. WSVS-AM broadcasts to the Crewe, VA area at 800 AM.
AM RADIO STATION

WSVU-AM 39505
Owner: North Palm Beach Broadcasting Inc.
Editorial: 8895 N Military Trl Ste 206C, West Palm Beach, Florida 33410-6279 **Tel:** 1 561 627-9966.
Web site: http://www.seaviewam960.com
Profile: WSVU-AM is a commercial station owned by North Palm Beach Broadcasting Inc. The format of the station is adult standards. WSVU-AM broadcasts to the West Palm Beach, FL area at 960 AM. Simulcasts on stations 95.9 FM and 106.9 FM.
AM RADIO STATION

WSVX-AM 35840
Owner: 3 Towers Broadcasting LLC
Editorial: 2356 N Morristown Rd, Shelbyville, Indiana 46176-9172 **Tel:** 1 317 398-2200.
Web site: http://www.wsvx.com
Profile: WSVX-AM is a commercial station owned by 3 Towers Broadcasting LLC. The format of the station is Top 40/CHR. WSVX-AM broadcasts to the Indianapolis area at 1520 AM.
AM RADIO STATION

WSWN-AM 38214
Owner: JVC Media
Editorial: 2001 State Road Ste 715, Belle Glade, Florida 33430 **Tel:** 1 561 996-2063.
Web site: http://www.935thebar.com
Profile: WSWN-AM is a commercial station owned by JVC Media. The format of the station is rock music. WSWN-AM broadcasts to the West Palm Beach, FL area at 900 AM.
AM RADIO STATION

WSWR-FM 40752
Owner: iHeartMedia Inc.
Editorial: 1400 Radio Ln, Mansfield, Ohio 44906-2525
Tel: 1 419 529-2211.
Web site: http://www.my1001fm.com
Profile: WSWR-FM is a commercial station owned by iHeartMedia Inc. The format of the station is classic hits. WSWR-FM broadcasts to the Mansfield, OH area at 100.1 FM.
FM RADIO STATION

WSWT-FM 45559
Owner: Alpha Media
Editorial: 331 Fulton St Ste 1200, Peoria, Illinois 61602-1422 **Tel:** 1 309 637-3700.
Email: news@1470wmbd.com
Web site: http://www.mix1069.com
Profile: WSWT-FM is a commercial station owned by Alpha Media. The format of the station is adult contemporary. WSWT-FM broadcasts to the Peoria, IL area at 106.9 FM.
FM RADIO STATION

WSWV-AM 38215
Owner: BC Broadcasting Co. Inc.
Editorial: 282 Westgate Mall Cir, Pennington Gap, Virginia 24277-2879 **Tel:** 1 276 546-2520.
Email: sales@wswv.net
Web site: http://www.wswv.net
Profile: WSWV-AM is a commercial station owned by BC Broadcasting Co. Inc. The format of the station is southern gospel music. WSWV-FM broadcasts to the Pennington Gap, VA area at 1570 AM.
AM RADIO STATION

WSWV-FM 45560
Owner: BC Broadcasting Co. Inc.
Editorial: 282 Westgate Mall Cir, Pennington Gap, Virginia 24277-2879 **Tel:** 1 276 546-2520.
Email: sales@wswv.net
Web site: http://www.wswv.net
Profile: WSWV-FM is a commercial station owned by BC Broadcasting Co. Inc. The format of the station is country music. WSWV-FM broadcasts to the Pennington Gap, VA area at 105.5 FM.
FM RADIO STATION

WSWW-AM 36401
Owner: West Virginia Radio Corp.
Editorial: 1111 Virginia St E, Charleston, West Virginia 25301 **Tel:** 1 304 342-8131.
Web site: http://www.wvradioadvertising.com
Profile: WSWW-AM is a commercial station owned by West Virginia Radio Corp. The format for the station is sports. WSWW-AM broadcasts to the Charleston-Huntington, WV area at 1490 AM.
AM RADIO STATION

WSWW-FM 961744
Owner: West Virginia Radio Corp.
Editorial: 102 N Kanawha St, Beckley, West Virginia 25801-4715
Web site: http://wajr.com/
Profile: WSWW-FM is a commercial station owned by West Virginia Radio Corp. The format of the station is news/talk. The station broadcasts to the Beckley, West Virginia area at 95.7 FM.
FM RADIO STATION

WSYB-AM 38709
Owner: Pamal Broadcasting Ltd.
Editorial: 67 Merchants Row, Rutland, Vermont 05701-5910 **Tel:** 1 802 775-7500.
Web site: http://www.wsyb1380am.com
Profile: WSYB-AM is a commercial station owned by Pamal Broadcasting Ltd. The format of the station is news, talk and sports. WSYB-AM broadcasts to the Rutland, VT area at 1380 AM.
AM RADIO STATION

WSYD-AM 35684
Owner: Granite City Broadcasting Inc.
Editorial: 2147 Springs Rd, Mount Airy, North Carolina 27030-2447 **Tel:** 1 336 786-2147.
Web site: http://www.wsyd1300.com
Profile: WSYD-AM is a commercial station owned by Granite City Broadcasting Inc. The format of the station is country and gospel music. WSYD-AM broadcasts to the Greensboro-Winston Salem, NC area at 1300 AM.
AM RADIO STATION

WSYE-FM 40183
Owner: Mississippi Radio Group
Editorial: 2214 S Gloster St, Tupelo, Mississippi 38801-6814 **Tel:** 1 662 842-7658.
Web site: http://www.sunny933fm.com
FM RADIO STATION

WSYL-AM 38766
Owner: Georgia Eagle Broadcasting Inc.
Editorial: 561 E Olliff St, Statesboro, Georgia 30458-4663 **Tel:** 1 912 764-5446.
Email: wwnswmcd@yahoo.com
Profile: WSYL-AM is a commercial station owned by Georgia Eagle Broadcasting Inc. The format for the station is unavailable. WSYL-AM broadcasts to the Savannah, GA area at 1490 AM.
AM RADIO STATION

WSYN-FM 41006
Owner: Cumulus Media Inc.
Editorial: 11640 Highway 17 Byp, Murrells Inlet, South Carolina 29576-9332 **Tel:** 1 843 651-7869.
Web site: http://sunny1031.com
Profile: WSYN-FM is a commercial station owned by Cumulus Media Inc. The format of the station is

classic hits music. WSYN-FM broadcasts to the Murrells Inlet, SC area at 103.1 FM.
FM RADIO STATION

WSYR-AM 38841
Owner: iHeartMedia Inc.
Editorial: 500 Plum St Ste 400, Syracuse, New York 13204-1401 **Tel:** 1 315 472-9797.
Email: wsyrnews@iheartmedia.com
Web site: http://wsyr.iheart.com
Profile: WSYR-AM is a commercial station owned by iHeartMedia Inc. The format of the station is news and talk. WSYR-AM broadcasts to the Syracuse, NY area at 570 AM. The station airs its programming on WSYR-FM.
AM RADIO STATION

WSYR-FM 43769
Owner: iHeartMedia Inc.
Editorial: 500 Plum St Ste 100, Syracuse, New York 13204-1427 **Tel:** 1 315 472-9797.
Email: wsyrnews@iheartmedia.com
Web site: http://www.wsyr.com/main.html
Profile: WSYR-FM is a commercial station owned by iHeartMedia Inc. The format of the station is news talk. WSYR-FM broadcasts to the Syracuse, NY area at 106.9 FM. The station airs WSYR-AM's programming.
FM RADIO STATION

WSYW-AM 39463
Owner: Continental Broadcast Group LLC
Editorial: 1800 N Meridian St Ste 603, Indianapolis, Indiana 46202-1433 **Tel:** 1 317 924-1071.
Web site: http://www.lajoya810.com
Profile: WSYW-AM is a commercial station owned by Continental Broadcast Group LLC. The format of the station is Regional Mexican. WSYW-AM broadcasts to the Indianapolis area at 810 AM.
AM RADIO STATION

WSYY-AM 38216
Owner: Katahdin Communications
Tel: 1 207 723-9657.
Email: calendar@themountain949.com
Web site: http://www.themountain949.com
Profile: WSYY-AM is a commercial station owned by Katahdin Communications. The format of the station is sports. WSYY-AM broadcasts to the Millinocket, ME area at 1240 AM.
AM RADIO STATION

WSYY-FM 45561
Owner: Katahdin Communications
Tel: 1 207 723-9657.
Email: calendar@themountain949.com
Web site: http://www.themountain949.com
Profile: WSYY-FM is a commercial station owned by Katahdin Communications. The format of the station is Jack FM/adult hits. WSYY-FM broadcasts to the Millinocket, ME area at 94.9 FM.
FM RADIO STATION

WTAB-AM 36429
Owner: WTAB Inc.
Editorial: 210 Avon St, Tabor City, North Carolina 28463 **Tel:** 1 910 653-2131.
Email: wtab@wtabradio.com
Web site: http://www.wtabradio.com
Profile: WTAB-AM is a commercial station owned by WTAB Inc. The format of the station is country and southern gospel music. WTAB-AM broadcasts to the Tabor City, NC area at 1370 AM.
AM RADIO STATION

WTAD-AM 38217
Owner: Staradio Corp.
Editorial: 329 Maine St Fl 1, Quincy, Illinois 62301-3928 **Tel:** 1 217 224-4102.
Email: wtad@staradio.com
Web site: http://www.wtad.com
Profile: WTAD-AM is a commercial station owned by Staradio Corp. The format of the station is news and talk. WTAD-AM broadcasts to the Quincy, IL area at 930 AM.
AM RADIO STATION

WTAG-AM 38328
Owner: iHeartMedia Inc.
Editorial: 58 Stereo Ln, Paxton, Massachusetts 01612-1376 **Tel:** 1 508 795-0580.
Web site: http://wtag.iheart.com
Profile: WTAG-AM is a commercial station owned by iHeartMedia Inc. The format of the station is news, sports and talk. WTAG-AM broadcasts to the Paxton, MA area at 580 AM.
AM RADIO STATION

WTAK-FM 42309
Owner: iHeartMedia Inc.
Editorial: 26869 Peoples Rd, Madison, Alabama 35756-4632 **Tel:** 1 256 309-2400.
Web site: http://www.wtak.com
Profile: WTAK-FM is a commercial station owned by iHeartMedia Inc. The format for the station is classic rock. WTAK-FM broadcasts to the Huntsville, AL area at 106.1 FM.
FM RADIO STATION

WTAL-AM 35686
Owner: Live Communications
Editorial: 1363 E Tennessee St, Tallahassee, Florida 32308-5107 **Tel:** 1 850 877-0105.
Email: wtal@wtal1450.com
Web site: http://www.wtal1450.com
Profile: WTAL-AM is a commercial station owned by Live Communications. The format of the station features Gospel and talk programming. WTAL-AM broadcasts to the Tallahassee, FL area at a frequency of 1450 AM.
AM RADIO STATION

WTAM-AM 38656
Owner: iHeartMedia Inc.
Editorial: 6200 Oak Tree Blvd Fl 4, Independence, Ohio 44131-6933 **Tel:** 1 216 520-2600.
Email: news@wtam.com
Web site: http://www.wtam.com
Profile: WTAM-AM is a commercial station owned by iHeartMedia Inc. The format of the station is news and talk. WTAM-AM broadcasts in the Cleveland area at 1100 AM.
AM RADIO STATION

WTAN-AM 35687
Owner: Wagenvoord Advertising Group
Editorial: 706 N Myrtle Ave, Clearwater, Florida 33755-4219 **Tel:** 1 727 424-4991.
Web site: http://www.tantalk1340.com
Profile: WTAN-AM is a commercial station owned by Wagenvoord Advertising Group. The format of the station is adult standards music and talk. WTAN-AM broadcasts to the Clearwater, FL area at 1340 AM.
AM RADIO STATION

WTAO-FM 40754
Owner: Withers Broadcasting of Southern Illinois LLC
Editorial: 1822 N Court St, Marion, Illinois 62959
Tel: 1 618 997-8123.
Web site: http://www.taorocks.com
Profile: WTAO-FM is a commercial station owned by Withers Broadcasting of Southern Illinois LLC. The format of the station is rock/album oriented rock. WTAO-FM broadcasts to the Carbondale, IL area at 92.7 FM.
FM RADIO STATION

WTAQ-AM 37836
Owner: Midwest Communications Inc.
Editorial: 1420 Bellevue St, Green Bay, Wisconsin 54311-5649 **Tel:** 1 920 435-3771.
Email: wtaq.news@wtaq.com
Web site: http://www.wtaq.com
Profile: WTAQ-AM is a commercial station owned by Midwest Communications Inc. The format of the station is news and talk. WTAQ-AM broadcasts to the Green Bay, WI area at 1360 AM.
AM RADIO STATION

WTAQ-FM 624709
Owner: Midwest Communications Inc.
Editorial: 1420 Bellevue St, Green Bay, Wisconsin 54311-5649 **Tel:** 1 920 435-3771.
Email: wtaq.news@mwcradio.com
Web site: http://www.wtaq.com
Profile: WTAQ-FM is a commercial station owned by Midwest Communications Inc. The format of the station is news and talk. WTAQ-FM broadcasts to the Green Bay, WI area at 97.5 FM.
FM RADIO STATION

WTAR-AM 38219
Owner: Sinclair Telecable Inc.
Editorial: 999 Waterside Dr, Norfolk, Virginia 23510-3300 **Tel:** 1 757 640-8500.
Email: amproduction@wtar.com
Web site: http://www.wtar.com
Profile: WTAR-AM is a commercial station owned by Sinclair Telecable Inc. The format of the station is talk and sports. WTAR-AM broadcasts to Norfolk, VA, at 850 AM.
AM RADIO STATION

WTAW-AM 38562
Owner: Bryan Broadcasting
Editorial: 2700 Earl Rudder Fwy S, College Station, Texas 77845-5010 **Tel:** 1 979 695-9595.
Email: news@bryanbroadcasting.com
Web site: http://www.wtaw.com
Profile: WTAW-AM is a commercial station owned by Bryan Broadcasting. The format of the station is news, talk, and sports. WTAW-AM broadcasts in the College Station, TX area at 1620 AM.
AM RADIO STATION

WTAX-AM 38220
Owner: Saga Communications
Editorial: 3501 E Sangamon Ave, Springfield, Illinois 62707-9777 **Tel:** 1 217 753-5400.
Email: wtaxnews@wtax.com
Web site: http://www.wtax.com
Profile: WTAX-AM is a commercial station owned by Saga Communications. The format of the station is news and talk. WTAX-AM broadcasts to the Springfield, IL area at 1470 AM.
AM RADIO STATION

WTAY-AM 38221
Owner: Original Company, Inc. (The)
Tel: 1 618 544-2191.
Web site: http://www.wfiwradio.com/am-newstalk
Profile: WTAY-AM is a commercial station owned by The Original Company Inc. The format of the station is news/talk. WTAY-AM broadcasts to the Robinson, IL area at 1570 AM.
AM RADIO STATION

WTBC-AM 36594
Owner: John Sisty Enterprises Inc.
Editorial: 2110 McFarland Blvd E Ste C, Tuscaloosa, Alabama 35404-5820 **Tel:** 1 205 758-5523.
Web site: http://www.wtbc1230.com
Profile: WTBC-AM is a commercial station owned by John Sisty Enterprises Inc. The format of the station is classic country music. WTBC-AM broadcasts to the Tuscaloosa, AL, area at 1230 AM.
AM RADIO STATION

WTBF-AM 39441
Owner: Troy Broadcasting Corp.
Editorial: 67 W Court Sq, Troy, Alabama 36081-2611
Tel: 1 334 566-0300.
Email: wtbf947970@gmail.com
Web site: http://wtbf.us
Profile: WTBF-AM is a commercial station owned by Troy Broadcasting Corp. The format of the station is sports and talk. WTBF-AM broadcasts to the Troy, AL area at 970 AM.
AM RADIO STATION

WTBF-FM 46825
Owner: Troy Broadcasting Corp.
Editorial: 67 W Court Sq, Troy, Alabama 36081-2611
Tel: 1 334 566-0300.
Email: wtbf947970@gmail.com
Web site: http://www.wtbf.com
Profile: WTBF-FM is a commercial station owned by Troy Broadcasting Corp. The format of the station is a oldies. WTBF-FM broadcasts to the Troy, AL area at 94.7 FM.
FM RADIO STATION

WTBG-FM 45563
Owner: Wireless Group Inc.(The)
Editorial: 42 S Washington Ave, Brownsville, Tennessee 38012-3032 **Tel:** 1 731 772-3700.
Web site: http://www.brownsvilleradio.com
Profile: WTBG-FM is a commercial station owned by The Wireless Group Inc. The format of the station is country and gospel. WTBG-FM broadcasts to the Brownsville, TN area at 95.3 FM.
FM RADIO STATION

WTBH-FM 41977
Owner: Long Pond Baptist Church
Editorial: 8950 NW 75 Ave, Chiefland, Florida 32626-5139 **Tel:** 1 352 493-2650.
Web site: http://www.wtbhradio.com
Profile: WTBH-FM is a non-commercial station owned by Long Pond Baptist Church. The format of the station is gospel music and religious programming. WTBH-FM broadcasts to the Gainesville, FL area at 91.5 FM.
FM RADIO STATION

WTBI-AM 39255
Owner: Tabernacle Baptist Church
Editorial: 3931 White Horse Rd, Greenville, South Carolina 29611-5546 **Tel:** 1 864 295-2145.
Email: wtbi@tabernacleministries.org
Web site: http://www.tbc.sc
Profile: WTBI-AM is a non-commercial station owned by Tabernacle Baptist Church. The format of the station is religious. WTBI-AM broadcasts to the Greenville, SC area at 1540 AM.
AM RADIO STATION

WTBI-FM 46613
Owner: Tabernacle Baptist Church
Editorial: 3931 White Horse Rd, Greenville, South Carolina 29611-5546 **Tel:** 1 864 295-2145.
Email: wtbi@tabernacleministries.org
Web site: http://www.tbc.sc/wtbi
Profile: WTBI-FM is a non-commercial college station owned by Tabernacle Baptist Church. The format of the station is Christian programming. WTBI-FM broadcasts to the Greenville, SC area at 91.5 FM.
FM RADIO STATION

WTBK-FM 41422
Owner: Choice Radio Corporation
Editorial: 107 Dickenson St, Manchester, Kentucky 40962-1254 **Tel:** 1 606 598-7588.
Email: wtbkradio@yahoo.com
Web site: http://www.wtbkfm.com
Profile: WTBK-FM is a commercial station owned by Choice Radio Corporation. The format of the station is contemporary country. WTBK-FM broadcasts to the Lexington, KY area at 105.7 FM.
FM RADIO STATION

WTBM-FM 44509
Owner: Gleason Radio Group
Editorial: 243 Main St, Norway, Maine 4268
Tel: 1 207 743-5911.
Email: news@gleasonmedia.com
Web site: http://www.woxo.com
Profile: WTBM-FM is a commercial station owned by Gleason Radio Group. The format of the station is classic country. WTBM-FM broadcasts to the Norway, ME area at 100.7 FM.
FM RADIO STATION

WTBN-AM 36945
Owner: Salem Media Group, Inc.
Editorial: 5211 W Laurel St Ste A, Tampa, Florida 33607-1736 **Tel:** 1 813 349-8231.
Email: info@letstalkfaith.com
Web site: http://www.letstalkfaith.com
Profile: WTBN-AM is a commercial station owned by Salem Media Group, Inc. The format of the station is religious talk. WTBN-AM broadcasts in the Tampa, FL area at 570 AM.
AM RADIO STATION

WTBO-AM 38306
Owner: Dix Communications
Editorial: 350 Byrd Ave, Cumberland, Maryland 21502-3219 **Tel:** 1 301 722-6666.
Web site: http://www.cumberlandsriver.com
Profile: WTBO-AM is a commercial station owned by Dix Communications. The format of the station is CHR. WTBO-AM broadcasts in the Cumberland, MD area at 1450 AM.
AM RADIO STATION

WTBQ-AM 36974
Owner: FST Broadcasting Corp.
Editorial: 179 Sanfordville Rd, Warwick, New York 10990-2849 **Tel:** 1 845 651-1110.
Web site: http://www.wtbq.com
Profile: WTBQ-AM is a commercial station owned by the FST Broadcasting Corp. The format of the station is talk and variety. WTBQ-AM broadcasts to Florida, NY area at 1110 AM. Also operates on 93.5 FM
AM RADIO STATION

WTBU-FM 46208
Owner: iHeartMedia Inc.
Editorial: 815 Lafayette Rd, Portsmouth, New Hampshire 03801-5406 **Tel:** 1 603 436-7300.
Web site: http://www.953fmthebull.com/main.html
Profile: WTBU-FM is a commercial station owned by iHeartMedia Inc. The station format of the station is contemporary country. WTBU-FM broadcasts to the Portsmouth, NH area at 95.3 FM.
FM RADIO STATION

WTBX-FM 45564
Owner: Midwest Communications Inc.
Editorial: 807 W 37th St, Hibbing, Minnesota 55746
Tel: 1 218 263-7531.
Web site: http://www.wtbx.com
FM RADIO STATION

WTCA-AM 38223
Owner: Community Service Broadcasters
Editorial: 112 W Washington St, Plymouth, Indiana 46563 **Tel:** 1 574 936-4096.
Email: wtca@am1050.com
Web site: http://www.am1050.com
Profile: WTCA-AM is a commercial station owned by Community Service Broadcasters. The format of the station is classic hits. WTCA-AM broadcasts to the Plymouth, IN area at 1050 AM.
AM RADIO STATION

WTCB-FM 40756
Owner: Cumulus Media Inc.
Editorial: 1301 Gervais St Ste 700, Columbia, South Carolina 29201-3326 **Tel:** 1 803 796-7600.
Web site: http://www.b106fm.com
Profile: WTCB-FM is a commercial station owned by Cumulus Media Inc. The format of the station is hot adult contemporary. WTCB-FM broadcasts to the Columbia, SC area at a frequency of 106.7 FM.
FM RADIO STATION

WTCC-FM 40757
Owner: Springfield Tech Comm. College
Editorial: 1 Armory Sq, Springfield, Massachusetts 01105-1700 **Tel:** 1 413 746-9822.
Web site: http://www.wtccfm.org
Profile: WTCC-FM is a non-commercial station owned by Springfield Technical Community College. The format of the station is college variety. WTCC-FM broadcasts in the Springfield, MA area at 90.7 FM.
FM RADIO STATION

WTCD-FM 44135
Owner: TeleSouth Communications Inc.
Editorial: 3192 Browning Road 520 #520, Greenwood, Mississippi 38930-3830 **Tel:** 1 662 453-2174.
Web site: http://www.supertalkms.com
Profile: WTCD-FM is a commercial radio station owned by TeleSouth Communications Inc. The format of the station is talk. The station broadcasts to the Greenwood, MS area at 96.9 FM.
FM RADIO STATION

WTCH-AM 38224
Owner: Results Broadcasting, Inc.
Editorial: 1456 E Green Bay St, Shawano, Wisconsin 54166-2258 **Tel:** 1 715 524-2194.
Email: resultsbroadcasting@gmail.com
Web site: http://www.wtcham960.com
Profile: WTCH-AM is a commercial station owned by Results Broadcasting, Inc. The format of the station is classic country. WTCH-AM broadcasts to the Shawano, WI area at 960 AM.
AM RADIO STATION

WTCJ-AM 35689
Owner: Cromwell Group Inc.(The)
Editorial: 1115 Tamarack Rd Ste 500, Owensboro, Kentucky 42301-6988 **Tel:** 1 270 683-5200.
Email: kyproduction@cromwellradio.com
Web site: http://www.tellcityradio.com
Profile: WTCJ-AM is a commercial station owned by The Cromwell Group Inc. The format of the station is classic hits. WTCJ-AM broadcasts to the Owensboro, KY area at 1230 AM.
AM RADIO STATION

WTCJ-FM 63803
Owner: Cromwell Group Inc.(The)
Editorial: 1115 Tamarack Rd, Owensboro, Kentucky 42301-6984 **Tel:** 1 270 683-5200.
Web site: http://www.owensbororadio.com
Profile: WTCJ-FM is a commercial station owned by The Cromwell Group Inc. The format of the station is classic rock. WTCJ-FM broadcasts to the Owensboro, KY area at 105.7 FM.
FM RADIO STATION

WTCM-AM
38225

Owner: Midwestern Broadcasting Co.
Editorial: 314 E Front St, Traverse City, Michigan 49684 **Tel:** 1 231 947-7675.
Email: wtcm@wtcmradio.com
Web site: http://www.wtcmradio.com
Profile: WTCM-AM is a commercial station owned by Midwestern Broadcasting Co. The format of the station is news and talk. WTCM-AM broadcasts to the Traverse City, MI area at 580 AM.
AM RADIO STATION

WTCM-FM
45566

Owner: Midwestern Broadcasting Co.
Editorial: 314 E Front St, Traverse City, Michigan 49684 **Tel:** 1 231 947-7675.
Email: wtcm@wtcmradio.com
Web site: http://www.wtcmi.com
Profile: WTCM-FM is a commercial station owned by Midwestern Broadcasting Co. The format of the station is contemporary country music. WTCM-FM broadcasts to the Traverse City, MI area at 103.5 FM.
FM RADIO STATION

WTCO-AM
38370

Owner: Forcht Broadcasting
Editorial: 50 Friendship Pike Rd, Campbellsville, Kentucky 42718-2537 **Tel:** 1 270 789-2401.
Web site: http://www.wtcosports.com
Profile: WTCO-AM is a commercial station owned by Forcht Broadcasting. The format of the station is sports. The station broadcasts to the Campbellsville, Kentucky area at a frequency of 1450 AM.
AM RADIO STATION

WTCQ-FM
45567

Owner: Vidalia Communications Group
Editorial: 1501 Mount Vernon Rd, Vidalia, Georgia 30474-3031 **Tel:** 1 912 537-9202.
Web site: http://www.southeastgeorgiatoday.com
Profile: WTCQ-FM is a commercial station owned by Vidalia Communications Group. The format of the station is adult contemporary. WTCQ-FM broadcasts to the Savannah, GA area at 97.7 FM.
FM RADIO STATION

WTCR-AM
38708

Owner: iHeartMedia Inc.
Editorial: 134 4th Ave, Huntington, West Virginia 25701-1220 **Tel:** 1 304 525-7788.
Web site: http://www.foxsports1420.com
Profile: WTCR-AM is a commercial station owned by iHeartMedia Inc. The format of the station sports. WTCR-AM broadcasts to the Huntington, WV area on 1420 AM.
AM RADIO STATION

WTCR-FM
46062

Owner: iHeartMedia Inc.
Editorial: 134 4th Ave, Huntington, West Virginia 25701-1220 **Tel:** 1 304 525-7788.
Email: wtcr@iheartmedia.com
Web site: http://www.wtcr.com
Profile: WTCR-FM is a commercial station owned by iHeartMedia Inc. The format of the station is classic country. WTCR-FM broadcasts to the Huntington, WV area at 103.3 FM.
FM RADIO STATION

WTCS-AM
38543

Owner: Spectrum Radio Group LLC
Tel: 1 301 802-1250.
Web site: http://www.spectrumradiogroup.com
Profile: WTCS-AM is a commercial station owned by Spectrum Radio Group LLC. The format of the station is news and talk. WTCS-AM broadcasts in the Fairmont, WV area at 1490 AM.
AM RADIO STATION

WTCW-AM
38901

Owner: Forcht Broadcasting
Editorial: 1149 Hwy 1862, Mayking, Kentucky 41837
Tel: 1 606 633-4434.
Email: wxkq@yahoo.com
Web site: http://www.wtcwam.com
Profile: WTCW-AM is a commercial station owned by Forcht Broadcasting. The format of the station is classic country music. WTCW-AM broadcasts to the Mayking, KY area at 920 AM.
AM RADIO STATION

WTCX-FM
46612

Owner: Radio Plus Inc.
Editorial: 210 S Main St, Fond du Lac, Wisconsin 54935-4908 **Tel:** 1 920 924-9697.
Web site: http://www.wtcx.com
Profile: WTCX-FM is a commercial station owned by Radio Plus Inc. The format of the station is classic rock. WTCX-FM broadcasts to the Green Bay, WI area at 96.1 FM.
FM RADIO STATION

WTDK-FM
42444

Owner: MTS Broadcasting LLC
Editorial: 2 Bay St, Cambridge, Maryland 21613-1257
Tel: 1 410 228-4800.
Email: news@mtslive.com
Web site: http://www.mtslive.com
Profile: WTDK-FM is a commercial station owned by MTS Broadcasting LLC. The format of the station is oldies. WTDK-FM broadcasts to the Cambridge, MD area at 107.1 FM.
FM RADIO STATION

WTDR-AM
35334

Owner: Jeff Beak Broadcasting
Editorial: 1913 Barry St Ste 13, Oxford, Alabama 36203-2319 **Tel:** 1 256 546-1611.
Email: info@jeffbeakmedia.com
Web site: http://wtdrthunder.com
Profile: WTDR-AM is a commercial station owned byJeff Beak Broadcasting The format of the station is country. WTDR-AM broadcasts to the Gadsden, AL area at 1350 AM.
AM RADIO STATION

WTDR-FM
40261

Owner: Jeff Beck Broadcasting Group, LLC
Editorial: 1913 Barry St Ste B, Oxford, Alabama 36203-2319 **Tel:** 1 256 741-6000.
Web site: http://www.wtdrthunder.com
Profile: WTDR-FM is a commercial station owned by Jeff Beck Broadcasting Group, LLC. The format of the station is country. WTDR-FM broadcasts to the Oxford, AL area at 92.7 FM.
FM RADIO STATION

WTDY-FM
40837

Owner: CBS Radio
Editorial: 555 E City Ave Ste 330, Bala Cynwyd, Pennsylvania 19004-1137 **Tel:** 1 610 667-9000.
Web site: http://todays965.cbslocal.com
Profile: WTDY-FM is a commercial station owned by CBS Radio. The format of the station is Adult Contemporary. WTDY-FM broadcasts to the Philadelphia area at 96.5 FM. The station's slogan is, "Better Variety, Fewer Commercials."
FM RADIO STATION

WTEB-FM
41520

Owner: Craven Community College
Editorial: 800 College Ct, New Bern, North Carolina 28562-4900 **Tel:** 1 252 638-3434.
Web site: http://publicradioeast.org
Profile: WTEB-FM is a non-commercial station owned by Craven Community College. The format of the station is classical music and news. WTEB-FM broadcasts to the New Bern, NC area at 89.3 FM.
FM RADIO STATION

WTEL-AM
35847

Owner: Beasley Broadcast Group
Editorial: 333 E City Ave Ste 700, Bala Cynwyd, Pennsylvania 19004-1521 **Tel:** 1 610 667-9000.
Web site: http://www.610amwtel.com
Profile: WIP-AM is a commercial station owned by Beasley Broadcast Group. The format of the station is sports. WIP-AM broadcasts to the Philadelphia area at 610 AM.
AM RADIO STATION

WTEM-AM
36690

Owner: Red Zebra Broadcasting
Editorial: 1801 Rockville Pike Ste 405, Rockville, Maryland 20852-5604 **Tel:** 1 301 230-0980.
Web site: http://www.espn980.com
Profile: WTEM-AM is a commercial station owned by Red Zebra Broadcasting. The format of the station is sports. WTEM-AM broadcasts to the Washington, D.C. area at 980 AM.
AM RADIO STATION

WTFM-FM
45306

Owner: Holston Valley Broadcasting Corp.
Editorial: 222 Commerce St, Kingsport, Tennessee 37660-4319 **Tel:** 1 423 246-9578.
Email: news@wtfm.com
Web site: http://www.wtfm.com
Profile: WTFM-FM is owned by Holston Valley Broadcasting Corp. The format of the station is adult contemporary. WTFM-FM broadcasts to the Kingsport, TN area at 98.5 FM.
FM RADIO STATION

WTFX-FM
42339

Owner: iHeartMedia Inc.
Editorial: 4000 Radio Dr, Louisville, Kentucky 40218-4568 **Tel:** 1 502 479-2222.
Web site: http://foxrocks.iheart.com
Profile: WTFX-FM is a commercial station owned by iHeartMedia Inc. The format of the station is rock music. WTFX-FM broadcasts to Louisville, KY at 93.1 FM.
FM RADIO STATION

WTGA-FM
45781

Owner: Radio Georgia Inc.
Editorial: 208 S Center St, Thomaston, Georgia 30286
Tel: 1 706 647-7121.
Email: wtga@fun101fm.com
Web site: http://www.fun101fm.com
Profile: WTGA-FM is commercial station owned by Radio Georgia Inc. The format of the station is adult contemporary. WTGA-FM broadcasts to the Thomaston, GA area at 101.1 FM.
FM RADIO STATION

WTGE-FM
42672

Owner: Guaranty Broadcasting
Editorial: 929 Government St, Ste B, Baton Rouge, Louisiana 70802 **Tel:** 1 225 388-9898.
Web site: http://www.1007thetiger.com
Profile: WTGE-FM is a commercial station owned by Guaranty Broadcasting. The format of the station is contemporary country. WTGE-FM broadcasts to the Baton Rouge, LA area at 100.7 FM.
FM RADIO STATION

WTGF-FM
42853

Owner: Faith Bible College
Editorial: 4670 Highway 90, Milton, Florida 32571-1411 **Tel:** 1 850 994-3747.
Email: wtgf@bellsouth.net
Web site: http://wwwwtgffm.com
Profile: WTGF-FM is a non-commercial station owned by Faith Bible College. The format for the station is religious and Southern gospel. WTGF-FM broadcasts to the Pace, FL area at 90.5 FM.
FM RADIO STATION

WTGG-FM
43206

Owner: Northshore Broadcasting Inc.
Editorial: 200 E Thomas St, Hammond, Louisiana 70401-3316 **Tel:** 1 985 345-0060.
Web site: http://www.tangiradio.net/
Profile: WTGG-FM is commercial station owned by Northshore Broadcasting Inc. The format of the station is oldies. WTGG-FM broadcasts to the Hammond, LA area at 96.5 FM.
FM RADIO STATION

WTGM-AM
38663

Owner: iHeartMedia Inc.
Editorial: 351 Tilghman Rd, Gateway Crossing, Salisbury, Maryland 21804-1920 **Tel:** 1 410 742-1923.
Email: delmarvapsa@iheartmedia.com
Web site: http://foxsports960.iheart.com
Profile: WTGM-AM is a commercial station owned by iHeartMedia Inc. The format of the station is sports. WTGM-AM broadcasts to the Salisbury, MD area at 960 AM.
AM RADIO STATION

WTGN-FM
40758

Owner: Associated Christian Broadcasters
Editorial: 1600 Elida Rd, Lima, Ohio 45805-1510
Tel: 1 419 227-2525.
Email: wtgn@wcoil.com
Web site: http://witnessingthegoodnews.org
Profile: WTGN-FM is a non-commercial station owned by Associated Christin Broadcasters. The format for the station is religious. WTGN-FM broadcasts to the Lima, OH area at 97.7 FM.
FM RADIO STATION

WTGR-FM
44388

Owner: Positive Radio Group
Editorial: 514 Martin St, Greenville, Ohio 45331
Tel: 1 937 548-5085.
Web site: http://www.wtgr.com
Profile: WTGR-FM is a commercial station owned by Positive Radio Group. The format of the station is country music. WTGR-FM broadcasts in the Dayton, OH area at 97.5.
FM RADIO STATION

WTGV-FM
45872

Owner: Sanilac Broadcasting
Editorial: 19 S Elk St, Sandusky, Michigan 48471-1353 **Tel:** 1 810 648-2700.
Email: renaed@sanilacbroadcasting.com
Web site: http://www.sanilacbroadcasting.com
Profile: WTGV-FM is a commercial station owned by Sanilac Broadcasting. The format of the station is Lite Rock/Lite AC. WTGV-FM broadcasts to the Sandusky, MI area at 97.7 FM.
FM RADIO STATION

WTGY-FM
40761

Owner: Family Worship Center Church, Inc.
Tel: 1 225 768-3688.
Email: info@jsm.org
Web site: http://www.jsm.org
FM RADIO STATION

WTGZ-FM
42958

Owner: Tiger Communications Inc.
Editorial: 2514 S College St Ste 104, Auburn, Alabama 36832-6925 **Tel:** 1 334 887-9999.
Web site: http://www.thetiger.fm
Profile: WTGZ-FM is a commercial station owned by Tiger Communications Inc. The format of the station is alternative rock music. WTGZ-FM broadcasts to the Auburn, AL area at 93.9 FM.
FM RADIO STATION

WTHB-AM
37140

Owner: Perry Broadcasting Company, Inc.
Editorial: 6025 Broadcast Dr, North Augusta, South Carolina 29841-9406 **Tel:** 1 803 279-2330.
Web site: http://csrapraise.com/index.html
Profile: WTHB-AM is a commercial station owned by Perry Broadcasting Company, Inc. The format of the station is gospel and talk. WTHB-AM broadcasts to the North Augusta, SC area at 1550 AM.
AM RADIO STATION

WTHB-FM
42662

Owner: Perry Broadcasting Company, Inc.
Editorial: 6025 Broadcast Dr, North Augusta, South Carolina 29841-9406 **Tel:** 1 803 279-2330.
Web site: http://csrapraise.com/index.html
Profile: WTHB-FM is a commercial station owned by Perry Broadcasting Company, Inc. The format of the station is gospel. WTHB-FM broadcasts to the North Augusta, GA area at 96.9 FM.
FM RADIO STATION

WTHD-FM
42338

Owner: Swick Broadcasting
Editorial: 7080 S Nottawa, Sturgis, Michigan
Tel: 1 260 463-8500.
Email: wthd@wthd.net
Web site: http://www.wthd.net
Profile: WTHD-FM is a commercial station owned by Swick Broadcasting. The format for the station is country music. WTHD-FM broadcasts to the South Bend, IN area at 105.5 FM.
FM RADIO STATION

WTHE-AM
3569

Owner: Universal Broadcasting
Editorial: 260 E 2nd St, Mineola, New York 11501
Tel: 1 516 742-1520.
Email: nygospelradio@aol.com
Web site: http://www.wthe1520am.com
Profile: WTHE-AM is a commercial station owned by Universal Broadcasting. The format of the station is gospel music. WTHE-AM broadcasts to the Mineola, NY at 1520 AM.
AM RADIO STATION

WTHG-FM
4220

Owner: Savannah Radio (WRGO Radio, LLC)
Editorial: 63 Ramsgate Rd, Savannah, Georgia 31419-3274 **Tel:** 1 912 369-1047.
Web site: http://www.1047thehawk.com
Profile: WTHG-FM is a commercial station owned by WRGO Radio, LLC dba Savannah Radio. The format of the station is classic hits. WTHG-FM broadcasts to the Savannah, GA area at 104.7 FM.
FM RADIO STATION

WTHI-FM
4556

Owner: Emmis Communications Corp.
Editorial: 918 Ohio St, Terre Haute, Indiana 47807-3733 **Tel:** 1 812 917-3901.
Web site: http://www.hi99.com
Profile: WTHI-FM is a commercial station owned by Emmis Communications Corp. The format of the station is contemporary country music. WTHI-FM broadcasts to the Terre Haute, IN area at 98.7 FM.
FM RADIO STATION

WTHK-FM
4130

Owner: Great Eastern Radio, LLC
Editorial: 106 N Main St, West Lebanon, New Hampshire 03784-1136 **Tel:** 1 603 298-0332.
Email: thepeak@greateasternradio.com
Web site: http://www.thepeakradio.com
Profile: WTHK-FM is a commercial station owned by Great Eastern Radio, LLC. The format of the station is AAA. WTHK-FM broadcasts to the Wilmington, VT area at 100.7 FM.
FM RADIO STATION

WTHN-FM
52446

Owner: Northern Christian Radio
Editorial: 1511 E M 32, Gaylord, Michigan 49735-9702 **Tel:** 1 989 732-6274.
Email: studio@ncradio.org
Web site: http://www.thepromisefm.com
FM RADIO STATION

WTHO-FM
4556

Owner: Camellia City Communications
Editorial: 788 Cedar Rock Rd, Thomson, Georgia 30824-7642 **Tel:** 1 706 595-5122.
Web site: http://www.wtho.com
Profile: WTHO-FM is commercial station owned by Camellia City Communications. The format of the station is country. WTHO-FM broadcasts to the Thomson, GA area at 101.7 FM.
FM RADIO STATION

WTHP-FM
45004

Owner: Good News Network
Editorial: 2278 Wortham Ln, Grovetown, Georgia 30813 **Tel:** 1 706 309-9610.
Web site: http://www.gnnradio.org
Profile: WTHP-FM is a commercial station owned by Good News Network. The format of the station is religious. WTHP-FM broadcasts to the Augusta, GA area at 94.3 FM.
FM RADIO STATION

WTHQ-AM
3940

Owner: Big River Radio Inc.
Editorial: 303 8th St, Point Pleasant, West Virginia 25550-1209 **Tel:** 1 304 675-2763.
Email: wbyg@wbyg.com
Profile: WTHQ-AM is a commercial radio station owned by Big River Radio Inc.. The format of the station is contemporary hits radio. The station broadcasts to the Point Pleasant, WV area at 1030 AM.
AM RADIO STATION

WTHS-FM
4148

Owner: Hope College
Editorial: 257 Columbia Ave, Martha Miller Center 156, Holland, Michigan 49423-3615 **Tel:** 1 616 395-7878.
Email: wthsnews@hope.edu
Web site: http://wths.hope.edu
Profile: WTHS-FM is a non-commercial station owned by Hope College. The format of the station is adult album alternative and variety. WTHS-FM broadcasts to the Holland, MI area at 89.9 FM.
FM RADIO STATION

WTHT-FM
4186

Owner: WBIN, Inc.
Editorial: 477 Congress St Ste 3, Portland, Maine 04101-3427 **Tel:** 1 207 797-0780.
Web site: http://wtht.nh1media.com/
Profile: WTHT-FM is a commercial station owned by WBIN, Inc. The format of the station is classic country. WTHT-FM broadcasts to the Portland, ME area at 99.9 FM.
FM RADIO STATION

WTHU-AM 35920
Owner: Christian Radio Coalition, Inc.
Editorial: 10 Radio Ln, Thurmont, Maryland 21788
Tel: 1 301 637-6736.
Web site: http://wthu.org
Profile: WTHU-AM is a commercial station owned by Christian Radio Coalition, Inc. The format of the station is talk, Sports and news. WTHU-AM broadcasts in the Thurmont, MD area at 1450 AM.
AM RADIO STATION

WTHV-AM 36027
Owner: Eternal Life Ministries Inc.
Editorial: 2352 Jaycee Shack Rd, Valdosta, Georgia 31602-6475 **Tel:** 1 229 245-9848.
Email: wthv810am@yahoo.com
Web site: http://wthvradio.com
Profile: WTHV-AM is a commercial station owned by Eternal Life Ministries Inc. The format of the station is Southern gospel. WTHV-AM broadcasts to the Valdosta, GA area at 810 AM.
AM RADIO STATION

WTIB-FM 38077
Owner: Inner Banks Media, LLC
Editorial: 1884 W Arlington Blvd Ste 101C, Greenville, North Carolina 27834-5704 **Tel:** 1 252 355-1037.
Web site: http://www.wtibfm.com
Profile: WTIB-FM is a commercial station owned by Inner Banks Media, LLC. The format of the station is news, talk and sports. WTIB-FM broadcasts to the Greenville, NC area at 103.7 FM.
FM RADIO STATION

WTIC-AM 38228
Owner: CBS Radio
Editorial: 10 Executive Dr, Farmington, Connecticut 06032-2841 **Tel:** 1 860 677-6700.
Email: wticnews@cbs.com
Web site: http://connecticut.cbslocal.com/station/wtic-news-talk-1080
Profile: WTIC-AM is a commercial station owned by CBS Radio. The format for the station is news and talk. WTIC-AM broadcasts to the Hartford-New Haven, CT area at 1080 AM.
AM RADIO STATION

WTIC-FM 45570
Owner: CBS Radio
Editorial: 10 Executive Dr, Farmington, Connecticut 06032-2841 **Tel:** 1 860 677-6700.
Web site: http://965tic.cbslocal.com
Profile: WTIC-FM is a commercial station owned by CBS Radio. The format of the station is hot adult contemporary. WTIC-FM broadcasts in the Hartford, CT area at 96.5 FM.
FM RADIO STATION

WTIF-AM 38634
Owner: Plant Broadcasting, LLC
Editorial: 114 Kent Rd, Tifton, Georgia 31794-1780
Tel: 1 229 382-1340.
Web site: http://www.99rockfm.com
Profile: WTIF-AM is a commercial radio station owned by Plant Broadcasting, LLC. The format of the station is classic rock. The station broadcasts to the Tifton, GA area at 1340 AM.
AM RADIO STATION

WTIF-FM 46652
Owner: Plant Broadcasting, LLC
Editorial: 114 Kent Rd, Tifton, Georgia 31794-1780
Tel: 1 229 382-1340.
Web site: http://www.wtif1075.com
Profile: WTIF-FM is a commercial station owned by Plant Broadcasting, LLC. The format of the station is contemporary country. WTIF-FM broadcasts to the Tifton, GA, area at 107.5 FM.
FM RADIO STATION

WTIG-AM 35692
Owner: WTIG Inc.
Editorial: 3580 Karen Ave Nw, Massillon, Ohio 44647-9513 **Tel:** 1 330 837-9900.
Email: espn990@gmail.com
Web site: http://www.espn990.com
Profile: WTIG-AM is a commercial station owned by WTIG Inc. The format of the station is sports. WTIG-AM broadcasts to the Massillon, OH area at 990 AM.
AM RADIO STATION

WTIK-AM 35693
Owner: Davidson Media Group
Editorial: 707 Leon St, Durham, North Carolina 27704-4125 **Tel:** 1 919 236-5337.
Web site: http://www.lameganc.com
Profile: WTIK-AM is a commercial station owned by Davidson Media Group and operated by Prieto Broadcasting Inc. The format of the station is Hispanic music. WTIK-AM broadcasts to the Durham, NC area at 1310 AM.
AM RADIO STATION

WTIM-FM 43593
Owner: Randy Radio
Editorial: 918 E Park St, Taylorville, Illinois 62568-1916 **Tel:** 1 217 824-3395.
Email: news@taylorvilledailynews.com
Web site: http://www.taylorvilledailynews.com/pages/index.cfm?id=115
Profile: WTIM-FM is a commercial station owned by the Randy Radio. The format of the station is news, talk, and public affairs programming. WTIM-FM broadcasts in the Taylorville, IL area at 97.3 FM.
FM RADIO STATION

WTIP-FM 43773
Owner: Cook County Community Radio
Editorial: 1712 W Highway 61, Grand Marais, Minnesota 55604-7507 **Tel:** 1 218 387-1070.
Email: wtip@boreal.org
Web site: http://www.wtip.org
Profile: WTIP-FM is a non-commercial station owned by Cook County Community Radio. The format of the station is variety. WTIP-FM broadcasts to the Grand Marais, MN area at 90.7 FM.
FM RADIO STATION

WTIQ-AM 39115
Owner: Radio Results Network
Editorial: 7876 W County Rd, Ste 442, Manistique, Michigan 49854 **Tel:** 1 906 341-8444.
Email: wtiq@radioresultsnetwork.com
Web site: http://www.radioresultsnetwork.com
Profile: WTIQ-AM is a commercial station owned by Radio Results Network. The format of the station is classic country. WTIQ-AM broadcasts to the Escanaba, MI area at 1490 AM.
AM RADIO STATION

WTIV-AM 35695
Owner: FM Radio Licenses, LLC
Editorial: 900 Water St, Meadville, Pennsylvania 16335-3428 **Tel:** 1 814 724-1111.
Email: radio@zoominternet.net
Web site: http://myantsnetwork.com/
Profile: WTIV-AM is a commercial station owned by FM Radio Licenses, LLC. The format of the station is news, sports and talk. WTIV-AM broadcasts to the Titusville, PA area at 1230 AM.
AM RADIO STATION

WTIX-AM 35292
Owner: GHB Broadcasting
Editorial: 212 Signal Hill Dr, Statesville, North Carolina 28625-4327 **Tel:** 1 704 872-0500.
Web site: http://www.mycountrylegends.com/Statesville_Radio_Station.html
Profile: WTIX-AM is a commercial station owned by GHB Broadcasting. The format of the station is adult standards. WTIX-AM is licensed to Concord, NC and broadcasts to the Charlotte, NC area at 1410 AM.
AM RADIO STATION

WTIX-FM 44239
Owner: Fleur de Lis Broadcasting, Inc.
Editorial: 4539 N I 10 Service Rd W Fl 3, Metairie, Louisiana 70006-6575 **Tel:** 1 504 454-9000.
Web site: http://www.wtixfm.com
Profile: WTIX-FM is a commercial station owned by Fleur de Lis Broadcasting, Inc. The format of the station is oldies. WTIX-FM broadcasts to the Metairie, LA area at 94.3 FM.
FM RADIO STATION

WTJS-AM 38229
Owner: FM Radio Licenses, LLC
Editorial: 122 Radio Rd, Jackson, Tennessee 38301-3465 **Tel:** 1 731 427-3316.
Email: studio@wtjs.com
Web site: http://www.wtjs.com
Profile: WTJS-AM is a commercial station owned by FM Radio Licenses, LLC. The format of the station is news, talk and sports programming. WTJS-AM broadcasts to the Jackson, TN area at 1390 AM.
AM RADIO STATION

WTJT-FM 41585
Owner: Thompson(Earl)
Editorial: 957 Highway C 4A, Baker, Florida 32531-8743 **Tel:** 1 850 537-2009.
Email: wtjtradio@yahoo.com
Web site: http://wtjt901fm.com
Profile: WTJT-FM is a non-commercial station owned by Earl Thompson. The format for the station is religious and Southern gospel. WTJT-FM broadcasts to the Mobile, AL, Pensacola, FL area at 90.1 FM.
FM RADIO STATION

WTJV-AM 570396
Owner: J & V Communications Inc.
Editorial: 222 Hazard St, Orlando, Florida 32804-3030
Tel: 1 407 841-8282.
Email: wprd1440@gmail.com
Profile: WTJV-AM is a commercial station owned by J & V Communications Inc. The format of the station is adult standards. WTJV-AM broadcasts to the Orlando, FL market at 1490 AM.
AM RADIO STATION

WTJY-FM 44382
Owner: Positive Alternative Radio
Editorial: 600 W Clemmonsville Rd, Winston Salem, North Carolina 27127-5045 **Tel:** 1 336 788-1155.
Email: office@joyfm.org
Web site: http://www.joyfm.org
Profile: WTJY-FM is a non-commercial station owned by Positive Alternative Radio. The format of the station is Southern Gospel. WTJY-FM broadcasts to the Winston-Salem, NC area at 89.5 FM.
FM RADIO STATION

WTJZ-AM 35698
Owner: Chesapeake-Portsmouth Broadcasting Corp.
Editorial: 553 Michigan Dr, Hampton, Virginia 23669-3832 **Tel:** 1 757 488-1010.
Email: faithbroadcasting@gmail.com
Profile: WTJZ-AM is a commercial station owned by Chesapeake-Portsmouth Broadcasting Corp. The format of the station is Christian and gospel. WTJZ-AM broadcasts to the Hampton, VA area at 1270 AM.
AM RADIO STATION

WTKA-AM 38137
Owner: Cumulus Media Inc.
Editorial: 1100 Victors Way Ste 100, Ann Arbor, Michigan 48108-5220 **Tel:** 1 734 302-8100.
Email: studio@wtka.com
Web site: http://www.wtka.com
Profile: WTKA-AM is a commercial station owned by Cumulus Media Inc. The format of the station is sports. WTKA-AM broadcasts to Ann Arbor, MI, at 1050 AM.
AM RADIO STATION

WTKB-FM 42403
Owner: Solid Rock Broadcasting, LLC
Editorial: 2048 South First St, Ste E, Milan, Tennessee 38358 **Tel:** 1 731 562-9852.
Web site: http://www.victory937.com
Profile: WTKB-FM is a commercial station owned by Solid Rock Broadcasting, LLC. The format of the station is contemporary Christian and news and talk. WTKB-FM broadcasts to the Milan and Jackson, TN areas at 93.7 FM.
FM RADIO STATION

WTKF-FM 42784
Owner: Atlantic Ridge Telecasters Inc.
Editorial: 4206 Bridges Street Ext. Suit B, Morehead City, North Carolina 28557 **Tel:** 1 252 247-7282.
Email: news@thetalkstation.com
Web site: http://www.wtkf107.com
Profile: WTKF-FM is a commercial station owned by Atlantic Ridge Telecaster Inc. The format of the station is news, talk, and sports. WTKF-FM broadcasts in the Newport, NC area at 107.3 FM. The sations slogan is, "FM 107 & AM 1240 The Talk Station."
FM RADIO STATION

WTKG-AM 37732
Owner: iHeartMedia Inc.
Editorial: 77 Monroe Center St NW Ste 1000, Grand Rapids, Michigan 49503-2912 **Tel:** 1 616 459-1919.
Web site: http://wtkg.iheart.com
Profile: WTKG-AM is a commercial station owned by iHeartMedia Inc. The format of the station is news and talk. WTKG-AM broadcasts to the Grand Rapids, MI area at 1230 AM.
AM RADIO STATION

WTKK-FM 40665
Owner: iHeartMedia Inc.
Editorial: 3100 Smoketree Ct, Raleigh, North Carolina 27604-1086 **Tel:** 1 919 878-1500.
Web site: http://www.1061fmtalk.com/main.html
Profile: WTKK-FM is a commercial station owned by iHeartMedia Inc. The format of the station is conservative talk and news. WTKK-FM broadcasts to the Raleigh, NC area at 106.1 FM.
FM RADIO STATION

WTKM-AM 38230
Owner: Kettle Moraine Broadcasting
Editorial: 27 N Main St, Hartford, Wisconsin 53027-1531 **Tel:** 1 262 673-3550.
Email: wtkmradio@gmail.com
Web site: http://www.wtkm.com
Profile: WTKM-AM is a commercial station owned by Kettle Moraine Broadcasting. The format of the station is oldies. WTKM-AM broadcasts to the Hartford, WI area at 1540 AM.
AM RADIO STATION

WTKM-FM 45571
Owner: Kettle Moraine Broadcasting
Editorial: 27 N Main St, Hartford, Wisconsin 53027-1531 **Tel:** 1 262 673-7800.
Email: wtkmradio@gmail.com
Web site: http://www.wtkmradio.com
Profile: WTKM-FM is a commercial station owned by Kettle Moraine Broadcasting. The format of the station is classic country, polka music, and ethnic broadcasting. WTKM-FM broadcasts to the Hartford, WI, area at 104.9 FM.
FM RADIO STATION

WTKP-FM 41741
Owner: Omni Broadcasting Co.
Editorial: 1834 Lisenby Ave, Panama City, Florida 32405-3713 **Tel:** 1 850 244-1400.
Email: omnibroadcastinginc@gmail.com
Web site: http://www.theticketsportsnetwork.com
Profile: WTKP-FM is a commercial station owned by Omni Broadcasting Co. The format of the station is sports talk. WTKP-FM broadcasts to the Panama City, FL area at 93.5 FM. The station is a simulcast of WTKE-FM.
FM RADIO STATION

WTKS-AM 37703
Owner: iHeartMedia Inc.
Editorial: 245 Alfred St, Savannah, Georgia 31408-3205 **Tel:** 1 912 964-7794.
Email: info@newsradio1290wtks.com
Web site: http://www.newsradio1290wtks.com
Profile: WTKS-AM is a commercial station owned by iHeartMedia Inc. The format for the station is news and talk. WTKS-AM broadcasts to the Savannah, GA area at 1290 AM.
AM RADIO STATION

WTKS-FM 42144
Owner: iHeartMedia Inc.
Editorial: 2500 Maitland Center Pkwy Ste 401, Maitland, Florida 32751-4179 **Tel:** 1 407 916-7800.
Web site: http://realradio.iheart.com
Profile: WTKS-FM is a commercial station owned by iHeartMedia Inc. The format of the station is talk. WTKS-FM broadcasts to the Orlando, FL area at 104.1 FM.
FM RADIO STATION

WTKT-AM 37712
Owner: iHeartMedia Inc.
Editorial: 600 Corporate Cir, Harrisburg, Pennsylvania 17110-9787 **Tel:** 1 717 540-8800.
Email: webmaster@1460theticket.com
Web site: http://www.wtkt.com
Profile: WTKT-AM is a commercial station owned by iHeartMedia Inc. The format of the station is sports. WTKT-AM broadcasts to the Harrisburg, PA area at 1460 AM.
AM RADIO STATION

WTKU-FM 46882
Owner: Longport Media
Editorial: 1601 New Rd, Linwood, New Jersey 08221-1116 **Tel:** 1 609 653-1400.
Web site: http://www.kool983.com
Profile: WTKU-FM is a commercial station owned by Longport Media. The format of the station is classic hits. WTKU-FM broadcasts to the Atlantic City, NJ area at 98.3 FM.
FM RADIO STATION

WTKV-FM 44517
Owner: Galaxy Communications LP
Editorial: 235 Walton St, Syracuse, New York 13202
Tel: 1 315 472-9111.
Email: asktk@tk99.net
Web site: http://www.tk99.net
Profile: WTKV-FM is a commercial station owned by Galaxy Communications LP. The format of the station is classic rock. WTKV-FM broadcasts to the Syracuse, NY area at a frequency at 105.5.
FM RADIO STATION

WTKW-FM 42051
Owner: Galaxy Communications LP
Editorial: 235 Walton St, Syracuse, New York 13202
Tel: 1 315 472-9111.
Email: asktk@tk99.net
Web site: http://www.tk99.net
Profile: WTKW-FM is a commercial station owned by Galaxy Communications LP. The format of the station is classic rock. WTKW-FM broadcasts to the Syracuse, NY area at 99.5 FM.
FM RADIO STATION

WTKX-FM 42292
Owner: iHeartMedia Inc.
Editorial: 6485 Pensacola Blvd, Pensacola, Florida 32505-1701 **Tel:** 1 850 473-0400.
Email: radio@tk101.com
Web site: http://www.tk101.com
Profile: WTKX-FM is a commercial station owned by iHeartMedia Inc. The format for the station is rock/album-oriented rock. WTKX-FM broadcasts to the Pensacola, FL area at 101.5 FM.
FM RADIO STATION

WTKY-AM 38231
Owner: Whittimore Enterprises
Editorial: 341 Radio Station Rd, Tompkinsville, Kentucky 42167-8572 **Tel:** 1 270 487-6119.
Email: kixcountry@windstream.net
Profile: WTKY-AM is a commercial station owned by Whittimore Enterprises. The format of the station is classic country. WTKY-AM broadcasts to the Tompkinsville, KY area at 1370 AM.
AM RADIO STATION

WTKY-FM 45572
Owner: Whittimore Enterprises
Editorial: 341 Radio Station Rd, Tompkinsville, Kentucky 42167-8572 **Tel:** 1 270 487-6119.
Email: kixcountry@windstream.net
FM RADIO STATION

WTKZ-AM 36207
Owner: NB Broadcasting, LLC
Editorial: 107 Paxinosa Rd W, Easton, Pennsylvania 18040-1344 **Tel:** 1 610 829-5500.
Email: test@espnlv.com
Web site: http://www.espnlv.com
Profile: WTKZ-AM is a commercial station owned by NB Broadcasting, LLC. The format of the station is sports. WTKZ-AM broadcasts to the Easton, PA area at 1320 AM.
AM RADIO STATION

WTLA-AM 36359
Owner: Galaxy Communications LP
Editorial: 235 Walton St, Syracuse, New York 13202-1533 **Tel:** 1 315 472-9111.
Email: community@galaxycommunications.com
Web site: http://www.espncny.com
Profile: WTLA-AM is a commercial station owned by Galaxy Communications LP. The format of the station is sports. WTLA-AM broadcasts to the Syracuse, NY area at 1200 AM.
AM RADIO STATION

WTLB-AM 38232
Owner: Galaxy Communications LP
Editorial: 39 Kellogg Rd, New Hartford, New York 13413-2849 **Tel:** 1 315 797-1330.
Profile: WTLB-AM is a commercial station owned by Galaxy Communications LP. The format of the station is sports. WLTB-AM broadcasts to the Syracuse, NY area at 1310 AM.
AM RADIO STATION

WTLC-AM 38393
Owner: Urban One, Inc.
Editorial: 21 E Saint Joseph St, Indianapolis, Indiana 46204-1025 **Tel:** 1 317 266-9600.
Web site: http://praiseindy.com
Profile: WTLC-AM is a commercial station owned by Urban One, Inc. The format of the station is gospel music and talk. WTLC-AM broadcasts in the Indianapolis area at 1310 AM.
AM RADIO STATION

WTLC-FM 45754
Owner: Urban One, Inc.
Editorial: 21 E Saint Joseph St, Indianapolis, Indiana 46204-1025 **Tel:** 1 317 266-9600.
Web site: http://www.tlcnaptown.com
Profile: WTLC-FM is a commercial station owned by Urban One, Inc. The format of the station is urban adult contemporary music. WTLC-FM broadcasts to the Indianapolis area at 106.7 FM.
FM RADIO STATION

WTLI-FM 44075
Owner: Superior Communications
Editorial: 148 E Grand River Rd, Williamston, Michigan 48895 **Tel:** 1 517 381-0573.
Email: info@smile.fm
Web site: http://www.smile.fm
FM RADIO STATION

WTLK-AM 35699
Owner: Apple City Broadcasting Co.
Editorial: 133 E Main Ave, Taylorsville, North Carolina 28681-2514 **Tel:** 1 828 632-4621.
Email: wacbwtlk@applecitybroadcasting.com
Profile: WTLK-AM is a commercial station owned by Apple City Broadcasting Co. The format of the station is gospel music. WTLK-AM broadcasts to the greater Taylorsville, NC area at 1570 AM.
AM RADIO STATION

WTLM-AM 38299
Owner: iHeartMedia Inc.
Editorial: 915 Veterans Pkwy, Opelika, Alabama 36801-3367 **Tel:** 1 334 745-4656.
Profile: WTLM-AM is a commercial station owned by iHeartMedia Inc. The format of the station is classic country. WTLM-AM broadcasts to the Opelika, AL area at 1520 AM.
AM RADIO STATION

WTLN-AM 36394
Owner: Salem Media Group, Inc.
Editorial: 1188 Lake View Dr, Altamonte Springs, Florida 32714-2713 **Tel:** 1 407 682-9494.
Email: wtln@wtln.com
Web site: http://www.wtln.com
Profile: WTLN-AM is a commercial station owned by Salem Media Group, Inc. The format of the station is religious music and talk. WTLN-AM broadcasts to the Altamonte Springs, FL area at 950 AM.
AM RADIO STATION

WTLO-AM 35700
Owner: Forcht Broadcasting
Editorial: 290 Wtlo Rd, Somerset, Kentucky 42503
Tel: 1 606 678-8151.
Email: wtlo@usa.com
Web site: http://www.wtloradio.com
Profile: WTLO-AM is a commercial station owned by Forcht Broadcasting. The format of the station is adult standards. WTLO-AM broadcasts to the Somerset, KY area at 1480 AM.
AM RADIO STATION

WTLP-FM 45660
Owner: Hubbard Broadcasting, Inc.
Editorial: 3400 Idaho Ave NW, Washington, District Of Columbia 20016-3046 **Tel:** 1 202 895-5000.
Web site: http://www.wtopnews.com
Profile: WTLP-FM is a commercial station owned by Hubbard Broadcasting, Inc. The format of the station is news and talk. WTLP-FM broadcasts to the Braddock Heights, MD area at 103.9 FM.
FM RADIO STATION

WTLQ-FM 137113
Owner: Fort Myers Broadcasting Co.
Editorial: 2824 Palm Beach Blvd, Fort Myers, Florida 33916-1503 **Tel:** 1 239 337-2346.
Web site: http://www.latino977.com/
Profile: WTLQ-FM is a commercial station owned by Fort Myers Broadcasting Co. The format of the station is Spanish hits. WTLQ-FM broadcasts to the Fort Myers, FL area at 97.7 FM.
FM RADIO STATION

WTLR-FM 41548
Owner: Central Pennsylvania Christian Institute
Editorial: 2020 Cato Ave, State College, Pennsylvania 16801 **Tel:** 1 814 237-9857.
Email: info@cpci.org
Web site: http://cpci.org
Profile: WTLR-FM is a non-commercial station owned by Central Pennsylvania Christian Institute. The format of the station is religious. WTLR-FM broadcasts to the State College, PA area at 89.9 FM.
FM RADIO STATION

WTLS-AM 35701
Owner: Michael Butler Broadcasting, LLC
Editorial: 2045 Alabama Hwy 229, Tallassee, Alabama 36078 **Tel:** 1 334 283-8200.
Web site: http://www.1300wtls.com
Profile: WTLS-AM is a commercial station owned by Michael Butler Broadcasting, LLC. The format of the station is sports and talk. WTLS-AM broadcasts to the Atlanta area at 1300 AM.
AM RADIO STATION

WTLX-FM 41607
Owner: Good Karma Brands
Editorial: 7025 Raymond Rd, Madison, Wisconsin 53719-5053 **Tel:** 1 608 245-9859.
Web site: http://www.espnwisconsin.com
Profile: WTLX-FM is a commercial station owned by Good Karma Brands. The format of the station is sports programming. WTLX-FM broadcasts to the Beaver Dam, WI area at 100.5 FM.
FM RADIO STATION

WTLZ-FM 40862
Owner: Digity LLC
Editorial: 1795 Tittabawassee Rd, Saginaw, Michigan 48604-9431 **Tel:** 1 989 752-3456.
Web site: http://www.kisswtlz.com
Profile: WTLZ-FM is a commercial station owned by Digity LLC. The format of the station is urban contemporary music. WTCF-FM broadcasts to the Saginaw, MI area at 100.5 FM.
FM RADIO STATION

WTMA-AM 35952
Owner: Cumulus Media Inc.
Editorial: 4230 Faber Place Dr Ste 100, Charleston, South Carolina 29405-8512 **Tel:** 1 843 277-1200.
Web site: http://www.wtma.com
Profile: WTMA-AM is a commercial station owned by Cumulus Media Inc. The format of the station is news and talk. WTMA-AM broadcasts to the Charleston, SC area at 1250 AM.
AM RADIO STATION

WTMB-FM 39355
Owner: Magnum Radio Group
Editorial: 1021 N Superior Ave, Ste 5, Tomah, Wisconsin 54660 **Tel:** 1 608 372-9400.
Email: news@magnumbroadcasting.com
Web site: http://www.classicrockwtmb.com
Profile: WTMB-FM is a commercial station owned by Magnum Radio Group. The format of the station is classic rock music. WTMB-FM broadcasts to the Tomah, WI area at 94.5 FM.
FM RADIO STATION

WTME-AM 86724
Owner: Gleason Radio Group
Editorial: 243 Main St, Norway, Maine 4268
Tel: 1 207 743-5911.
Email: news@gleasonmedia.com
Web site: http://www.wtme.com
Profile: WTME-AM is a commercial station owned by Gleason Radio Group. The format of the station is news and religious programming. WTME-AM broadcasts to the Norway, ME area at 780 AM.
AM RADIO STATION

WTMG-FM 42566
Owner: Marc Radio Group, LLC
Editorial: 100 NW 76th Dr Ste 2, Gainesville, Florida 32607-6659 **Tel:** 1 352 313-3150.
Web site: http://www.magic1013.com
Profile: WTMG-FM is a commercial station owned by Marc Radio Group, LLC. The format of the station is urban contemporary. WTMG-FM broadcasts in the Gainesville, FL area at 101.3 FM.
FM RADIO STATION

WTMJ-AM 36465
Owner: E.W. Scripps Co.
Editorial: 720 E Capitol Dr, Milwaukee, Wisconsin 53212-1308 **Tel:** 1 414 332-9611.
Email: wtmjamnewsroom@wtmj.com
Web site: http://www.wtmj.com
Profile: WTMJ-AM is a commercial station owned by E.W. Scripps Co. The format of the station is news, sports and talk. WTMJ-AM broadcasts to the Milwaukee area at 620 AM.
AM RADIO STATION

WTMM-FM 439804
Owner: Townsquare Media, LLC.
Editorial: 1241 Kings Rd, Schenectady, New York 12303-2811 **Tel:** 1 518 881-1515.
Web site: http://1045theteam.com
Profile: WTMM-FM is a commercial station owned by Townsquare Media, LLC. The format of the station is sports. WTMM-FM broadcasts to the Albany, NY area at 104.5 FM
FM RADIO STATION

WTMN-AM 36822
Owner: Marc Radio Group, LLC
Editorial: 100 NW 76th Dr Ste 2, Gainesville, Florida 32607-6659 **Tel:** 1 352 313-3150.
Profile: WTMN-AM is a station owned by Marc Radio Group, LLC and operated by Sunshine Broadcasting. The format of the station is religous teaching. WTMN-AM broadcasts to the Gainsville, FL area at a frequency of 1430 AM.
AM RADIO STATION

WTMP-AM 35702
Owner: West Coast Media Group
Editorial: 407 N Howard Ave Ste 200, Tampa, Florida 33606-1575 **Tel:** 1 813 259-9867.
Web site: http://www.am1150wtmp.com
Profile: WTMP-AM is a commercial station owned by West Coast Media Group. The format of the station is Rhythmic Oldies. WTMP-AM broadcasts to the Tampa area at 1150 AM.
AM RADIO STATION

WTMP-FM 44060
Owner: Davidson Media Group
Editorial: 407 N Howard Ave Ste 200, Tampa, Florida 33606-1575 **Tel:** 1 813 259-9867.
Web site: http://lamexicana961.com
Profile: WTMP-FM is a commercial station owned by Davidson Media Group. The format of the station is regional Mexican. WTMP-FM broadcasts to the Tampa, FL area at 96.1 FM.
FM RADIO STATION

WTMR-AM 35703
Owner: Beasley Broadcast Group
Editorial: 2775 Mount Ephraim Ave, Camden, New Jersey 08104-3211 **Tel:** 1 856 962-8000.
Web site: http://www.wtmrradio.com
Profile: WTMR-AM is a commercial station owned by Beasley Broadcast Group. The format of the station is religious. WTMR-AM broadcasts to the Camden, NJ area at 800 AM.
AM RADIO STATION

WTMT-FM 41086
Owner: Saga Communications
Editorial: 1190 Patton Ave, Asheville, North Carolina 28806-2706 **Tel:** 1 828 259-9695.
Web site: http://www.1059themountain.com
Profile: WTMT-FM is a commercial station owned by Saga Communications. The format of the station is rock. WTMT-FM broadcasts to the Asheville, NC area at 105.9 FM.
FM RADIO STATION

WTMX-FM 40174
Owner: Hubbard Radio, LLC
Editorial: 130 E Randolph St Ste 2700, Chicago, Illinois 60601-6307 **Tel:** 1 312 946-1019.
Web site: http://www.wtmx.com
Profile: WTMX-FM is a commercial station owned by Hubbard Radio, LLC. The format of the station is Hot AC. WTMX-FM broadcasts to the Chicago area at 101.9 FM.
FM RADIO STATION

WTMY-AM 35947
Owner: Polnet Communications
Editorial: 1956 Main St, Sarasota, Florida 34236-5915
Tel: 1 941 955-9387.
Email: traffic.wtmy@gmail.com
Web site: http://www.wtmy.com
Profile: WTMY-AM is a commercial station owned by Polnet Communications. The format of the station is adult standards. WTMY-AM broadcasts to the Sarasota, FL area at 1280 AM.
AM RADIO STATION

WTMZ-AM 36246
Owner: Kirkman Broadcasting
Editorial: 60 Markfield Dr Ste 4, Charleston, South Carolina 29407-7907 **Tel:** 1 843 763-6631.
Email: 950@kirkmanbroadcasting.com
Web site: http://www.charlestonsportsradio.com
Profile: WTMZ-AM is a commercial station owned by Kirkman Broadcasting. The format of the station is sports. WTMZ-AM broadcasts to the Charleston, SC area at 910 AM.
AM RADIO STATION

WTNI-AM 36337
Owner: Alpha Media
Editorial: 1909 E Pass Rd Ste D11, Gulfport, Mississippi 39507-3778 **Tel:** 1 228 388-2001.
Profile: WTNI-AM is a commercial station owned by Alpha Media. The format of the station is sports. WTNI-AM broadcasts to the Biloxi-Gulfport, MS area at 1640 AM.
AM RADIO STATION

WTNJ-FM 40769
Owner: Southern Communications Corp.
Editorial: 306 S Kanawha St, Beckley, West Virginia 25801-5619 **Tel:** 1 304 252-6452.
Web site: http://www.wtnjfm.com
Profile: WTNJ-FM is a commercial station owned by Southern Communications Corp. The format of the station is country music. WTNJ-FM broadcasts to the Beckley, WV area at 105.9 FM.
FM RADIO STATION

WTNK-AM 35419
Owner: Fun Media Group
Editorial: 165 Marlene St, Hartsville, Tennessee 37074-1508 **Tel:** 1 615 374-2111.
Email: funradio@otelco.net
Web site: http://www.funradiotn.com
Profile: WTNK-AM is a commercial station owned by Fun Media Group of Tennessee, LLC. The format of the station is oldies. WTNK-AM broadcasts to the Hartsville, TN area at 1090 AM.
AM RADIO STATION

WTNL-AM 39298
Owner: Register (William Keith)
Editorial: 125 Friar Tuck Circle, Reidsville, Georgia 30453 **Tel:** 1 912 557-4140.
Email: wrbxwtnl@windstream.net
Web site: http://www.wrbx.org
Profile: WTNL-AM is a commercial station owned by Register (William Keith). The format of the station is Christian talk and Southern Gospel. WTNL-AM broadcasts to the Reidsville, GA area at a frequency of 1390 AM.
AM RADIO STATION

WTNM-FM 4413
Owner: TeleSouth Communications Inc.
Editorial: 461 Highway 6 W, Oxford, Mississippi 38655-9073 **Tel:** 1 662 236-0093.
Email: oxford@telesouth.com
Web site: http://www.supertalk.fm
Profile: WTNM-FM is a commercial station owned by TeleSouth Communications Inc. The format of the station is talk. WTNM-FM broadcasts to the Oxford, MS area at 105.5 FM.
FM RADIO STATION

WTNN-FM 45012
Owner: Impact Radio, INC
Editorial: 4049 Williston Rd Ste 7, South Burlington, Vermont 05403-6048 **Tel:** 1 802 864-9750.
Web site: http://eaglecountry975.com
Profile: WTNN-FM is a commercial station owned by Impact Radio, INC. The format of the station is country. WTNN-FM broadcasts to the South Burlington, VT area at a frequency of 97.5 FM.
FM RADIO STATION

WTNQ-FM 4547
Owner: Momentum Broadcasting
Editorial: 305 E Central Ave, La Follette, Tennessee 37766-3618 **Tel:** 1 423 566-1310.
Web site: http://www.goodtime1049.com
Profile: WTNQ-FM is a commercial station owned by Momentum Broadcasting. The format of the station is oldies. WTNQ-FM broadcasts to the La Follette, TN area at 104.9 FM.
FM RADIO STATION

WTNR-FM 4043
Owner: Cumulus Media Inc.
Editorial: 60 Monroe Center St NW, Grand Rapids, Michigan 49503-2916 **Tel:** 1 616 774-8461.
Web site: http://www.nashfm945.com
Profile: WTNR-FM is a commercial station owned by Cumulus Media Inc. The format of the station is country. WTNR-FM broadcasts to the Grand Rapids, MI area at 94.5 FM.
FM RADIO STATION

WTNS-AM 3929
Owner: Coshocton Broadcasting Company
Editorial: 114 N 6th St, Coshocton, Ohio 43812
Tel: 1 740 622-1560.
Web site: http://www.mywtnsradio.com
Profile: WTNS-AM is a commercial station owned by Coshocton Broadcasting Company. The format of the station is classic country. WTNS-AM broadcasts to the Coshocton, OH, area at 1560 AM.
AM RADIO STATION

WTNS-FM 4665
Owner: Coshocton Broadcasting Company
Editorial: 114 N 6th St, Coshocton, Ohio 43812-1601
Tel: 1 740 622-1560.
Email: wtnsnewsroom@sbcglobal.com
Web site: http://www.mywtnsradio.com
Profile: WTNS-FM is a commercial station owned by Coshocton Broadcasting Company. The station's format is adult contemporary. WTNS-FM broadcasts to the Coschocton, OH area at 99.3 FM.
FM RADIO STATION

WTNT-AM 3658
Owner: Metro Radio, Inc
Editorial: Washington, District Of Columbia
Tel: 1 703 659-0406.
Email: info@somoslacapital.com
Web site: http://www.somoslacapital.com
Profile: WTNT-AM is a commercial station owned by Metro Radio, Inc. The format of the station is Spanish AC. WTNT-AM broadcasts to the Washington, DC area at 730 AM.
AM RADIO STATION

WTNV-FM 51921
Owner: Burks(W.E.)
Editorial: 2555 Burks Pl, Dyersburg, Tennessee 38024-1724 **Tel:** 1 731 285-1339.
Web site: http://www.eagle973.net
Profile: WTNV-FM is a commercial station owned by W.E. Burks. The format of the station is contemporary country. WTNV-FM broadcasts to the Dyersburg, TN area at 97.3 FM.
FM RADIO STATION

WTNW-AM 3589
Owner: Shelton Broadcasting
Editorial: 4896 Main St, Jasper, Tennessee 37347-3681 **Tel:** 1 423 942-1700.
Web site: http://www.wtnw820.com
Profile: WTNW-AM is a commercial station owned by Shelton Broadcasting. The format of the station is classic country. WTNW-AM broadcasts to the Jasper, TN area at 820 AM.
AM RADIO STATION

WTNX-FM 4523
Owner: Prospect Communications
Editorial: 104 S 2nd St, Pulaski, Tennessee 38478-3219 **Tel:** 1 931 363-2505.
Email: wksr@wksr.com
Web site: http://www.wksr.com
Profile: WTNX-FM is a commercial station owned by Prospect Communications. The format of the station is adult hits. WTNX-FM broadcasts to the Pulaski, TN area at 106.7 FM.
FM RADIO STATION

WTNY-AM 38732
Owner: Stephens Family LP
Editorial: 134 Mullin St, Watertown, New York 13601-3616 **Tel:** 1 315 788-0790.
Email: smgwatertown@gmail.com
Web site: http://www.790wtny.com
Profile: WTNY-AM is a commercial station owned by Stephens Family LP. The format of the station is news and talk. WTNY-AM broadcasts to the Watertown, NY area at 790 AM.
AM RADIO STATION

WTOB-AM 35706
Owner: TLBC Media
Editorial: 4015 Brownsboro Rd Ste 200, Winston Salem, North Carolina 27106-3380 **Tel:** 1 336 714-2831.
Email: wtobgoodguys@wtob1380.com
Web site: http://wtob1380.com
Profile: WTOB-AM is a commercial station owned and operated by TLBC Media. The format of the station is regional Mexican. WWBG-AM broadcasts to the Winston Salem, NC area at 1380 AM.
AM RADIO STATION

WTOC-AM 38086
Owner: Radio Visión Cristiana Management
Tel: 1 973 881-8700.
Web site: http://www.radiovision.net
Profile: WTOC-AM is a commercial station owned by Radio Visión Cristiana Management. The format of the station is Hispanic religious. WTOC-AM broadcasts to the Newton, NJ area at 1360 AM.
AM RADIO STATION

WTOD-AM 38097
Owner: Cumulus Media Inc.
Editorial: 3225 Arlington Ave, Toledo, Ohio 43614-2427 **Tel:** 1 419 725-5700.
Web site: http://talkradio1470.com
Profile: WTOD-AM is a commercial station owned by Cumulus Media Inc. The format of the station is news/talk. WTOD-AM broadcasts to the Toledo, OH area at 1470 AM.
AM RADIO STATION

WTOE-AM 35707
Owner: Mountain Valley Media Inc.
Editorial: 749 Sawmill Road, Burnsville, North Carolina 28714-6749 **Tel:** 1 828 765-7441.
Email: 1470@wtoe.com
Web site: http://www.wtoe.com
Profile: WTOE-AM is a commercial station owned by Mountain Valley Media Inc. The format of the station is classic hits. WTOE-AM broadcasts to the Burnsville, NC area at 1470 AM.
AM RADIO STATION

WTOF-AM 39510
Owner: Buddy Tucker Association, Inc.
Editorial: 720 S White Ave, Bay Minette, Alabama 36507-7527 **Tel:** 1 251 947-1000.
AM RADIO STATION

WTOH-FM 81709
Owner: Salem Media Group, Inc.
Editorial: 8101 N High St Ste 360, Columbus, Ohio 43235-1442 **Tel:** 1 614 885-0880.
Web site: http://www.989theanswer.com
Profile: WTOH-FM is a commercial station owned by Salem Media Group, Inc. The format of the station is talk. WTOH-FM broadcasts to the Columbus, OH area at 98.9 FM.
FM RADIO STATION

WTOJ-FM 45574
Owner: Community Broadcasters, LLC
Editorial: 199 Wealtha Ave, Watertown, New York 13601 **Tel:** 1 315 782-1240.
Profile: WTOJ-FM is a commercial station owned by Community Broadcasters, LLC. The format of the station is adult contemporary. WTOJ-FM broadcasts to the Watertown, NY area at 103.1 FM.
FM RADIO STATION

WTON-AM 38666
Owner: High Impact Communications Inc.
Editorial: 304 W Beverley St, Staunton, Virginia 24401-4207 **Tel:** 1 540 885-5188.
Email: star94@ntelos.net
Profile: WTON-AM is a commercial station owned by High Impact Communications Inc. The format of the station is sports. WTON-AM broadcasts to Staunton, VA at 1240 AM.
AM RADIO STATION

WTON-FM 46018
Owner: High Impact Communications Inc.
Editorial: 304 W Beverly St, Staunton, Virginia 24401 **Tel:** 1 540 885-5188.
Email: star94@ntelos.net
Profile: WTON-FM is a commercial station owned by High Impact Communications Inc. The format of the station is classic hits music. WTON-FM broadcasts to the Richmond, VA, area at 94.3 FM.
FM RADIO STATION

WTOP-FM 43486
Owner: Hubbard Broadcasting
Editorial: 3400 Idaho Ave NW, Washington, District Of Columbia 20016-3046 **Tel:** 1 202 895-5000.
Web site: http://www.wtop.com
Profile: WTOP-FM is a commercial station owned by Hubbard Broadcasting. The format of the station is news. WTOP-FM broadcasts to the Washington, D.C. area at 103.5 FM.
FM RADIO STATION

WTOS-FM 43555
Owner: Blueberry Broadcasting
Editorial: 125 Community Dr Ste 201, Augusta, Maine 04330-8157 **Tel:** 1 207 623-9000.
Web site: http://www.wtosfm.com
Profile: WTOS-FM is a commercial station owned by Blueberry Broadcasting. The format of the station is rock music. WTOS-FM broadcasts to the Augusta, ME area at 105.1 FM.
FM RADIO STATION

WTOT-AM 631314
Owner: GFR Inc.
Editorial: 4376 Lafayette St Ste A, Marianna, Florida 32446-3300 **Tel:** 1 850 482-3046.
Email: wjaqfm@gmail.com
Profile: WTOT-AM is a commercial station owned by GFR Inc. The format of the station is oldies. WTOT-AM broadcasts to the Marianna, FL area at 980 AM.
AM RADIO STATION

WTOT-FM 43216
Owner: GFR Inc.
Editorial: 4376 Lafayette St Ste A, Marianna, Florida 32446-3300 **Tel:** 1 850 482-3046.
Profile: WTOT-FM is a commercial station owned by GFR Inc. The format of the station is oldies. WTOT-FM broadcasts to the Mariana, FL area at 101.7 FM.
FM RADIO STATION

WTOX-AM 281936
Owner: Davidson Media Group
Editorial: 308 W Broad St, Richmond, Virginia 23220-4240 **Tel:** 1 804 643-0990.
Email: wtox@davidsonmediagroup.com
Web site: http://www.lagrand1480.com
Profile: WTOX-AM is a commercial station owned by Davidson Media Group. The format of the station is Regional Mexican. WTOX-AM broadcasts to the Richmond, VA area at 1480 AM.
AM RADIO STATION

WTOY-AM 35650
Owner: Ward(Irvin)
Editorial: 504 23rd St NW, Roanoke, Virginia 24017 **Tel:** 1 540 344-9869.
Email: wtoyradio@aol.com
Profile: WTOY-AM is a commercial station owned by Irvin Ward. The format of the station is urban contemporary and gospel. WTOY-AM broadcasts to the Roanoke, VA area at 1480 AM.
AM RADIO STATION

WTPA-FM 40770
Owner: Sickafus, Patrick
Editorial: 27 S 34th St, Camp Hill, Pennsylvania 17011-4445 **Tel:** 1 717 695-4976.
Web site: http://www.wtparock.com
Profile: WTPA-FM is a commercial station owned by Patrick Sickafus. The format of the station is classic rock. WTPA-FM broadcasts to the Harrisburg, PA area at 92.1 FM.
FM RADIO STATION

WTPL-FM 41381
Owner: Great Eastern Radio, LLC
Editorial: 501 South St Fl 3, Bow, New Hampshire 03304-3416 **Tel:** 1 603 545-0777.
Email: production@wtplfm.com
Web site: http://www.wtplfm.com
Profile: WTPL-FM is a commercial station owned by Great Eastern Radio, LLC. The format of the station is news, talk and sports. WTPL-FM broadcasts to the Concord, NH area at 107.7 FM.
FM RADIO STATION

WTPR-AM 38234
Owner: WENK of Union City, Inc.
Editorial: 206 N Brewer St, Paris, Tennessee 38242 **Tel:** 1 731 642-7100.
Web site: http://www.wenkwtpr.com
Profile: WTPR-AM is a commercial station owned by WENK of Union City, Inc. The format of the station is oldies. WTPR-AM broadcasts to the Paris, TN area at 710 AM.
AM RADIO STATION

WTPR-FM 43118
Owner: WENK of Union City, Inc.
Editorial: 206 N Brewer St, Paris, Tennessee 38242 **Tel:** 1 731 642-7100.
Web site: http://www.wenkwtpr.com
Profile: WTPR-FM is a commercial station owned by WENK of Union City, Inc. The format of the station is oldies. WTPR-FM broadcasts to the Paris, TN area at 101.7 FM.
FM RADIO STATION

WTPS-AM 36466
Owner: Urban One, Inc.
Editorial: 2809 Emerywood Pkwy Ste 300, Richmond, Virginia 23294-3743 **Tel:** 1 804 672-9299.
Web site: http://www.newstalk1240wtps.com
Profile: WTPS-AM is a commercial station owned by Urban One, Inc. The format for the station is talk and R&B oldies. WTPS-AM broadcasts to the Richmond VA, area at 1240 AM.
AM RADIO STATION

WTPT-FM 42924
Owner: Entercom Communications Corp.
Editorial: 25 Garlington Rd, Greenville, South Carolina 29615-4613 **Tel:** 1 864 271-9200.
Web site: http://www.933theplanetrocks.com
Profile: WTPT-FM is a commercial station owned by Entercom Communications Corp. The format of the station is active rock. WTPT-FM broadcasts to the Greensville, SC area at 93.3 FM.
FM RADIO STATION

WTQR-FM 45575
Owner: iHeartMedia Inc.
Editorial: 2B Pai Park, Greensboro, North Carolina 27409-9428 **Tel:** 1 336 822-2000.
Web site: http://q1041.iheart.com
Profile: WTQR-FM is a commercial station owned by iHeartMedia Inc. The format of the station is contemporary country. WTQR-FM broadcasts to the Greensboro, NC area at 104.1 FM.
FM RADIO STATION

WTQS-AM 545936
Owner: Glory Communications Inc.
Editorial: 1236 Five Chop Rd, Orangeburg, South Carolina 29115-7047 **Tel:** 1 803 585-0499.
Profile: WTQS-AM is a commercial station owned by Glory Communications Inc. The format of the station is Black gospel. WTQS-AM broadcasts to the Orangeburg, SC area at 1490 AM.
AM RADIO STATION

WTQX-FM 40176
Owner: Blueberry Broadcasting
Editorial: 125 Community Dr Ste 201, Augusta, Maine 04330-8157 **Tel:** 1 207 623-9000.
Web site: http://www.wtosfm.com
Profile: WTQX-FM is a commercial station owned by Blueberry Broadcasting. The format of the station is rock music. WTQX-FM broadcasts to the Augusta, ME area at 96.7 FM.
FM RADIO STATION

WTRB-AM 39085
Owner: WTRB, INC.
Editorial: 372 S Jefferson St, Ripley, Tennessee 38063-2052 **Tel:** 1 731 635-1570.
Email: wtrb@newwavecomm.net
Profile: WTRB-AM is a commercial station owned by WTRB, INC. The format of the station is country variety. WTRB-AM broadcasts in the Ripley, TN area at 1570 AM.
AM RADIO STATION

WTRC-AM 36385
Owner: Pathfinder Communications Corporation
Editorial: 237 W Edison Rd, Mishawaka, Indiana 46545-3103 **Tel:** 1 574 258-5483.
Web site: http://www.frank1340.com
Profile: WTRC-AM is a commercial station owned by Pathfinder Communications Corporation, a division of Federated Media. The format of the station is adult standard. WTRC-AM broadcasts to the Elkhart, IN area at 1340 AM.
AM RADIO STATION

WTRC-FM 42447
Owner: Pathfinder Communications Corporation
Editorial: 237 W Edison Rd, Mishawaka, Indiana 46545-3103 **Tel:** 1 574 258-5483.
Web site: http://www.953mnc.com
Profile: WTRC-FM is a commercial station owned by Pathfinder Communications Corporation, a division of Federated Media. The format of the station is news and talk. WTRC-FM broadcasts to the South Bend, IN area at 95.3 FM.
FM RADIO STATION

WTRE-AM 35954
Owner: WTRE, Inc.
Editorial: 1217 W Park Rd, Greensburg, Indiana 47240-7886 **Tel:** 1 812 663-3000.
Email: wtre.wtre@gmail.com
Web site: http://www.1330wtre.com
Profile: WTRE-AM is a commercial station owned by WTRE, Inc. The format for the station is country. WTRE-FM broadcasts to the Indianapolis area at 1330 AM.
AM RADIO STATION

WTRG-FM 41537
Owner: First Media Radio LLC
Editorial: 3 E 1st St, Weldon, North Carolina 27890-1560 **Tel:** 1 252 538-9790.
Web site: http://www.thegreat98fm.com
Profile: WTRG-FM is a commercial station owned by First Media Radio LLC. The format of the station is classic hits. WTRG-FM broadcasts to the Weldon, NC area at 97.9 FM.
FM RADIO STATION

WTRH-FM 41711
Owner: Countryside Broadcasting
Editorial: 2740 N 800 St, Ramsey, Illinois 62080-4005 **Tel:** 1 618 423-2082.
Email: wtrh@frontiernet.net
Web site: http://wtrhradio.com
Profile: WTRH-FM is a commercial station owned by Countryside Broadcasting. The format of the station is oldies, gospel and talk. WTRH-FM broadcasts to the Ramsey, IL area at 93.3 FM.
FM RADIO STATION

WTRM-FM 41308
Owner: American Family Association, Inc.
Editorial: 2045 Valley Ave, Winchester, Virginia 22601-2751 **Tel:** 1 540 723-0123.
Email: office@southernlight.us
Web site: http://www.southernlight.us
Profile: WTRM-FM is a non-commercial station owned by American Family Association, Inc. The format of the station is gospel music and religious talk. WTRM-FM broadcasts in the Winchester, VA area at 91.3 FM.
FM RADIO STATION

WTRN-AM 39253
Owner: Allegheny Mountain Network
Editorial: 5620 E Pleasant Valley Blvd, Tyrone, Pennsylvania 16686-1280 **Tel:** 1 814 684-3200.
Email: wtrnamfm@gmail.com
Profile: WTRN-AM is a commercial station owned by Allegheny Mountain Network. The format of the station is adult contemporary music. WTRN-AM broadcasts to the Altoona, PA area at 1340 AM.
AM RADIO STATION

WTRO-AM 38873
Owner: Burks(W.E.)
Editorial: 2555 Burks Pl, Dyersburg, Tennessee 38024-1724 **Tel:** 1 731 285-1339.
Web site: http://www.wtroradio.net
Profile: WTRO-AM is a commercial station owned by W. E. Burks. The format of the station is oldies. WTRO-AM broadcasts to the Dyersburg, TN area at 1450 AM.
AM RADIO STATION

WTRP-AM 35709
Owner: Tiger Communications Inc.
Editorial: 806 New Franklin Rd, Lagrange, Georgia 30240-1844 **Tel:** 1 706 884-8611.
Email: wtrp@charter.net
Web site: http://wtrp620.com
Profile: WTRP-AM is a commercial station owned by Tiger Communications Inc. The format of the station is oldies. WTRP-AM broadcasts to the Lagrange, GA area at 620 AM.
AM RADIO STATION

WTRS-FM 42291
Owner: JVC Broadcasting Inc.
Editorial: 3357 SW 7th St, Ocala, Florida 34474-1956 **Tel:** 1 352 867-1023.
Web site: http://www.mycountryfla.com
Profile: WTRS-FM is a commercial station owned by JVC Broadcasting Inc. The format is contemporary country music. WTRS-FM broadcasts to the Ocala, FL area at 102.3 FM.
FM RADIO STATION

WTRT-FM 44242
Owner: Heartland Ministries, Inc.
Editorial: 219 College Street, Hardin, Kentucky 42048 **Tel:** 1 270 437-4369.
Email: studio@thrivefm88.com
Web site: http://www.thrivefm88.com
Profile: WTRT-FM is a commercial station owned by Heartland Ministries, Inc. The format of the station is religious teaching. WTRT-FM broadcasts to the Hardin, KY area at 88.1 FM. Send all PSA to the main email address.
FM RADIO STATION

WTRU-AM 36809
Owner: Truth Broadcasting
Editorial: 4405 Providence Ln, Winston Salem, North Carolina 27106-3226 **Tel:** 1 336 759-0363.
Email: info@wtru.com
Web site: http://www.wtru.com
Profile: WTRU-AM is a commercial station owned by Truth Broadcasting. The format of the station is Christian news and talk. WTRU-AM broadcasts to the Winston Salem, NC area at 830 AM.
AM RADIO STATION

WTRV-FM 42100
Owner: Townsquare Media, LLC
Editorial: 50 Monroe Ave NW Ste 500, Grand Rapids, Michigan 49503-2656 **Tel:** 1 616 459-1644.
Email: vip.support@townsquaremedia.com
Web site: http://rivergrandrapids.com
Profile: WTRV-FM is a commercial station owned by Townsquare Media, LLC. The format of the station is Lite Rock/Lite AC. WTRV-FM broadcasts to the Grand Rapids, MI listeners at 100.5 FM.
FM RADIO STATION

WTRW-FM 40982
Owner: Bold Gold Media Group
Editorial: 1049 N Sekol Ave, Scranton, Pennsylvania 18504-1040 **Tel:** 1 570 344-1221.
Web site: http://www.talker943.com
Profile: WTRW-FM is a commercial station owned by Bold Gold Media Group. The format of the station is news and talk. WTRW-FM broadcasts to the Nanticoke, PA area at 94.3 FM.
FM RADIO STATION

WTRX-AM 36759
Owner: Cumulus Media Inc.
Editorial: 6317 Taylor Dr, Flint, Michigan 48507-4683 **Tel:** 1 810 238-7300.
Web site: http://www.wtrxsports.com
Profile: WTRX-AM is a commercial station owned by Cumulus Media Inc. The format of the station is sports and talk. WTRX-AM broadcasts to the Flint, MI area at 1330 AM.
AM RADIO STATION

WTRY-FM 46835
Owner: iHeartMedia Inc.
Editorial: 1203 Troy Schenectady Rd, Latham, New York 12110-1046 **Tel:** 1 518 452-4800.
Web site: http://www.wtry.com
Profile: WTRY-FM is a commercial station owned by CiHeartMedia Inc. The format of the station is oldies. WTRY-FM broadcasts to the Latham, NY area at 98.3 FM.
FM RADIO STATION

United States of America

WTRZ-FM 46358
Owner: Peg Broadcasting
Editorial: 230 W Colville St, Mc Minnville, Tennessee 37110 **Tel:** 1 931 473-9253.
Web site: http://www.star201fm.net
Profile: WTRZ-FM is a commercial station owned by Peg Broadcasting. The format of the station is adult contemporary. WTRZ-FM broadcasts to the McMinnville, TN area at 107.3 FM.
FM RADIO STATION

WTSA-AM 38235
Owner: Four Seasons Media Inc.
Editorial: 464 Putney Rd, Brattleboro, Vermont 05301-9053 **Tel:** 1 802 254-4577.
Email: news@wtsa.net
Web site: http://www.wtsa.net
Profile: WTSA-AM is a commercial station owned by Four Seasons Media Inc. The format of the station is sports. WTSA-AM broadcasts to the Brattleboro, VT, area at 1450 AM.
AM RADIO STATION

WTSA-FM 45576
Owner: Four Seasons Media Inc.
Editorial: 464 Putney Rd, Brattleboro, Vermont 05301-9053 **Tel:** 1 802 254-4577.
Email: news@wtsa.net
Web site: http://www.wtsa.net
Profile: WTSA-FM is a commercial station owned by Four Seasons Media Inc. The format of the station is adult contemporary. WTSA-FM broadcasts to the Brattleboro, VT area at 96.7 FM.
FM RADIO STATION

WTSB-AM 132813
Owner: Lamm Media Group
Editorial: 4001 US Highway 301 S Ste 107, Four Oaks, North Carolina 27524-9249 **Tel:** 1 919 934-6789.
Email: info@wtsbradio.com
Web site: http://www.wtsbradio.com
Profile: WTSB-AM is a commercial station owned by Lamm Media Group. The format of the station is news, country and gospel. WTSB-AM broadcasts to the Four Oaks, NC area at 1090 AM.
AM RADIO STATION

WTSH-FM 46849
Owner: Cox Media Group
Editorial: 850 Bobbin Mill Rd, Athens, Georgia 30606-4208
Email: south107@aol.com
Web site: http://www.yourgeorgiacountry.com
Profile: WTSH-FM is a commercial station owned Cox Media Group. The format of the station is contemporary country.
FM RADIO STATION

WTSK-AM 38240
Owner: Townsquare Media, Inc.
Editorial: 142 Skyland Blvd E, Tuscaloosa, Alabama 35405-4027 **Tel:** 1 205 345-7200.
Web site: http://www.790wtsk.com
Profile: WTSK-AM is a commercial station owned by Townsquare Media, Inc. The format of the station is gospel. WTSK-AM broadcasts to the Tuscaloosa, AL area at 790 AM.
AM RADIO STATION

WTSL-AM 38838
Owner: Great Eastern Radio, LLC
Editorial: 106 N Main St, West Lebanon, New Hampshire 03784-1136 **Tel:** 1 603 448-1400.
Web site: http://www.wtsl.com
Profile: WTSL-AM is a commercial station owned by Great Eastern Radio, LLC. The format of the station is news and talk. WTSL-AM broadcasts to the Connecticut River Valley area at 1400 AM.
AM RADIO STATION

WTSM-FM 154845
Owner: Horizon Broadcasting Company, LLC
Editorial: 435 Saint Francis St, Tallahassee, Florida 32301-2219 **Tel:** 1 850 561-8400.
Email: studio@979espnradio.com
Web site: http://www.979espnradio.com/
Profile: WTSM-FM is a commercial station owned by Horizon Broadcasting Company, LLC. The format of the station is sports. WTSM-FM broadcasts to the Tallahassee, FL area at 97.9 FM.
FM RADIO STATION

WTSN-AM 39329
Owner: Garrison City Broadcasting
Editorial: 101 Back Rd, Dover, New Hampshire 03820-5003 **Tel:** 1 603 742-0987.
Web site: http://www.wtsnam1270.com
Profile: WTSN-AM is a commercial station owned by Garrison City Broadcasting Inc. The format of the station is sports, news and talk. WTSN-AM broadcasts to the Portsmouth, NH area at 1270 AM.
AM RADIO STATION

WTSO-AM 38236
Owner: iHeartMedia Inc.
Editorial: 2651 S Fish Hatchery Rd, Fitchburg, Wisconsin 53711-5410 **Tel:** 1 608 274-5450.
Web site: http://www.thebig1070.com
Profile: WTSO-AM is a commercial station ownded by iHeartMedia Inc. The format of the station is sports. WTSO-AM broadcasts to the Madison WI area at 1070 AM.

WTSR-FM 40772
Owner: The College of New Jersey
Editorial: 2000 Pennington Rd, Ewing, New Jersey 08618-1104 **Tel:** 1 609 771-3200.
Email: wtsr@wtsr.org
Web site: http://wtsr913.wordpress.com
Profile: WTSR-FM is a non-commercial station owned by The College of New Jersey. The format of the station is adult alternative. WTSR-FM broadcasts to the Trenton, NJ area at 91.3 FM.
FM RADIO STATION

WTSS-FM 45722
Owner: Entercom Communications Corp.
Editorial: 500 Corporate Pkwy, Ste 200, Buffalo, New York 14226 **Tel:** 1 716 843-0600.
Web site: http://www.mystar1025.com
Profile: WTSS-FM is a commercial station owned by Entercom Communications Corp. The format of the station is hot adult contemporary music. WTSS-FM broadcasts in the Buffalo, NY area at 102.5 FM.
FM RADIO STATION

WTSV-AM 38237
Owner: Great Eastern Radio, LLC
Editorial: 106 N Main St, West Lebanon, New Hampshire 03784-1136 **Tel:** 1 603 298-0332.
Email: psa@wtsl.com
Web site: http://www.wtsl.com
Profile: WTSV-AM is a commercial station owned by Great Eastern Radio, LLC. The format of the station is news and talk. WTSV-AM broadcasts to the Connecticut River Valley area of New Hampshire and Vermont at 1230 AM.
AM RADIO STATION

WTTB-AM 38782
Owner: Treasure & Space Coast Radio
Editorial: 1235 16th St, Vero Beach, Florida 32960-3620 **Tel:** 1 772 567-0937.
Email: news@wttbam.com
Web site: http://www.wttbam.com
Profile: WTTB-AM is a commercial station owned by Treasure & Space Coast Radio. The format of the station is news and talk programming. WTTB-AM broadcasts to the Vero Beach, FL area at 1490 AM.
AM RADIO STATION

WTTC-AM 38238
Owner: Cantroair Communications Co.
Editorial: 170 Redington Ave, Troy, Pennsylvania 16947 **Tel:** 1 570 297-0100.
Email: whgl100@gmail.com
Web site: http://www.wtzn.com
Profile: WTTC-AM is a commercial station owned by Cantroair Communications Co. The format of the station is Oldies. WTTC-AM broadcasts to the Troy, PA area at 1550 AM.
AM RADIO STATION

WTTC-FM 45578
Owner: Cantroair Communications Co.
Editorial: 170 Redington Ave, Troy, Pennsylvania 16947 **Tel:** 1 570 297-0100.
Email: thebridgefm@frontiernet.net
Web site: http://www.953thebridge.com
Profile: WTTC-FM is a commercial station owned by Cantroair Communications Co. The format of the station is classic hits. WTTC-FM broadcasts ot the Troy, PA area at 95.3 FM.
FM RADIO STATION

WTTF-AM 38239
Owner: BAS Broadcasting
Editorial: 310 E Market St, Tiffin, Ohio 44883-2434 **Tel:** 1 419 447-2212.
Web site: http://www.wttf.com
Profile: WTTF-AM is a commercial station owned by Heidelberg College. The format of the station is oldies, news, and sports. WTTF-AM broadcasts to the Toledo, OH area at 1600 AM.
AM RADIO STATION

WTTH-FM 41851
Owner: Equity Communications LP
Editorial: 8025 Black Horse Pike, Ste 100, Pleasantville, New Jersey 8232 **Tel:** 1 609 484-8444.
Web site: http://www.961wtth.com
Profile: WTTH-FM is a commercial station owned by Equity Communications LP. The format of the station is urban contemporary music. WTTH-FM broadcasts to the West Atlantic City, NJ area at 96.1 FM.
FM RADIO STATION

WTTI-AM 35711
Owner: Hall Broadcasting (Troy)
Editorial: 562 Deck Dr, Rocky Face, Georgia 30740 **Tel:** 1 706 673-2222.
Email: wttiradio1530@yahoo.com
Web site: http://www.wttiradio.com
Profile: WTTI-AM is a commercial station owned by Troy Hall Broadcasting. The format of the station is Contemporary Christian. WTTI-AM broadcasts to the Dalton, GA area at 1530 AM.
AM RADIO STATION

WTTL-AM 39077
Owner: Commonwealth Broadcasting Corp.
Editorial: 265 S Main St, Madisonville, Kentucky 42431 **Tel:** 1 270 821-1310.
Profile: WTTL-AM is a commercial radio station owned by Commonwealth Broadcasting Corp. The format of the station is sports talk. The station airs locally on 1310 AM.
AM RADIO STATION

WTTL-FM 46422
Owner: Commonwealth Broadcasting Corp.
Editorial: 265 S Main St, Madisonville, Kentucky 42431-2557 **Tel:** 1 270 825-1079.
Profile: WYMV-FM is a commercial station owned by Commonwealth Broadcasting Corp. The format of the station is adult contemporary. WYMV-FM broadcasts to the Madisonville, KY area at 106.9 FM.
FM RADIO STATION

WTTM-AM 37009
Owner: Multicultural Radio Broadcasting Inc.
Editorial: 3573 Bristol Pike Rear 102, Bensalem, Pennsylvania 19020-4666 **Tel:** 1 267 527-9886.
Email: wttm1680@yahoo.com
Web site: http://www.radiowttm1680.com
Profile: WTTM-AM is a commercial station owned by Multicultural Radio Broadcasting Inc. The format of the station is Hispanic music and programming. WTTM-AM's broadcasts to the Philadelphia area at 1680 AM.
AM RADIO STATION

WTTN-AM 35841
Owner: Good Karma Broadcasting
Editorial: 100 Stoddart St, Beaver Dam, Wisconsin 53916-1306 **Tel:** 1 920 885-4442.
Web site: http://espndeportes.espn.go.com
Profile: WTTN-AM is a commercial station owned by Good Karma Broadcasting. The format of the station is Spanish sports. WTTN-AM broadcasts to the Watertown, WI area at 1580 AM.
AM RADIO STATION

WTTR-AM 35958
Owner: Sajak Broadcasting Corp.
Editorial: 101 Wttr Ln, Westminster, Maryland 21158-4269 **Tel:** 1 410 848-5511.
Email: news@wttr.com
Web site: http://www.wttr.com
Profile: WTTR-AM is a commercial station owned by Sajak Broadcasting Corp. The format of the station is oldies. WTTR-AM broadcasts to the Westminster, MD area at 1470 AM.
AM RADIO STATION

WTTS-FM 45580
Owner: Sarkes Tarzian Inc.
Editorial: 120 W 7th St Ste 400, Bloomington, Indiana 47404-3869 **Tel:** 1 812 332-3366.
Email: comments@wttsfm.com
Web site: http://www.wttsfm.com
Profile: WTTS-FM is a commercial station owned by Sarkes Tarzian Inc. The format of the station is adult album alternative. WTTS-FM broadcasts to the Indianapolis area at 92.3 FM.
FM RADIO STATION

WTTX-FM 45932
Owner: Positive Alternative Radio
Editorial: 22226 Timberlake Rd, Lynchburg, Virginia 24502-7305 **Tel:** 1 434 352-7607.
Email: office@joyfm.org
Web site: http://www.joyfm.org
Profile: WTTX-FM is a non-commercial station owned by Positive Alternative Radio. The format of the station is Southern gospel. WTTX-FM broadcasts to the Lynchburg, VA area at 107.1 FM.
FM RADIO STATION

WTUA-FM 41968
Owner: Snipe(Alex)
Editorial: 4013 Byrnes Dr, Saint Stephen, South Carolina 29479-3988 **Tel:** 1 843 567-2091.
Email: wtua@tds.net
Web site: http://www.wtuaradio.com
Profile: WTUA-FM is a commercial station owned by Alex Snipe. The format of the station is gospel. WTUA-FM broadcasts to the Saint Stephen, SC area at 106.1 FM.
FM RADIO STATION

WTUE-FM 45581
Owner: iHeartMedia Inc.
Editorial: 101 Pine St, Dayton, Ohio 45402-2948 **Tel:** 1 937 224-1137.
Web site: http://www.wtue.com
Profile: WTUE-FM is a commercial station owned by iHeartMedia Inc. The format of the station is classic rock music. WTUE-FM broadcasts in the Dayton, OH area at 104.7 FM.
FM RADIO STATION

WTUF-FM 45980
Owner: Lenrob Enterprises Inc.
Editorial: 117 Remington Ave, Thomasville, Georgia 31792 **Tel:** 1 229 225-1063.
Web site: http://www.wtufradio.com
Profile: WTUF-FM is a commercial station owned by Lenrob Enterprises Inc. The format of the station is country music. WTUF-FM broadcasts to the Tallahassee, FL Thomasville, GA area at 106.3 FM.
FM RADIO STATION

WTUG-FM 45582
Owner: Townsquare Media, Inc.
Editorial: 142 Skyland Blvd, Tuscaloosa, Alabama 35405-4015 **Tel:** 1 205 345-7200.
Web site: http://www.wtug.com
Profile: WTUG-FM is a commercial station owned by Townsquare Media, Inc. The format of the station is urban adult contemporary music. WTUG-FM broadcasts to the Tuscaloosa, AL area at 92.9 FM.
FM RADIO STATION

WTUK-FM 46129
Owner: Eastern Broadcasting Co.
Editorial: 125 S Main St, Harlan, Kentucky 40831-2109 **Tel:** 1 606 573-1470.
Email: wtuk-wfsr@harlanonline.net
Web site: http://www.wtuk1051.com
Profile: WTUK-FM is a commercial station owned by Eastern Broadcasting Co. The format of the station is country. WTUK-FM broadcasts to the Harlan, KY area at 105.1 FM.
FM RADIO STATION

WTUP-AM 38610
Owner: iHeartMedia, Inc.
Editorial: 5026 Cliff Gookin Blvd, Tupelo, Mississippi 38801-7059 **Tel:** 1 662 842-1067.
Profile: WTUP-AM is a commercial station owned by iHeartMedia, Inc. The format of the station is Oldies. WTUP-AM broadcasts to the Tupelo, Mississippi area at 1490 AM.
AM RADIO STATION

WTUV-AM 35704
Owner: Corona Media Group LLC
Editorial: 1939 Goldsmith Ln Ste 227, Louisville, Kentucky 40218-3178 **Tel:** 1 502 618-4996.
Email: info@coronamediagroup.com
Web site: http://lapoderosaky.com
Profile: WTUV-AM is a commercial station owned by Corona Media Group LLC. The format of the station is regional Mexican. WTUV-AM broadcasts to the Louisville, KY area at 620 AM.
AM RADIO STATION

WTUV-FM 44285
Owner: UB Louisville, LLC
Editorial: 11700 Commonwealth Dr, Louisville, Kentucky 40299-6303 **Tel:** 1 502 240-0602.
Web site: http://www.espnlouisville.com
Profile: WTUV-FM is a commercial station owned by UB Louisville, LLC. The format of the station is sports talk. WTUV-FM broadcasts to the Louisville, KY area at 105.7 FM.
FM RADIO STATION

WTUX-FM 690145
Owner: Blueberry Broadcasting
Editorial: 125 Community Dr Ste 201, Augusta, Maine 04330-8157 **Tel:** 1 207 623-9000.
Web site: http://www.wtosfm.com
Profile: WTUX-FM is a commercial station owned by Blueberry Broadcasting. The format of the station is rock music. WTUX-FM broadcasts to the Gouldsboro, ME area at 101.1 FM.
FM RADIO STATION

WTUZ-FM 41584
Owner: WTUZ Radio Inc.
Editorial: 2424 E High Ave, New Philadelphia, Ohio 44663-3341 **Tel:** 1 330 339-2222.
Email: news@wtuz.com
Web site: http://www.wtuz.com
Profile: WTUZ-FM is a commercial station owned by WTUZ Radio Inc. The format of the station is classic and contemporary country. WTUZ-FM broadcasts to the New Philadelphia, OH area at 99.9 FM.
FM RADIO STATION

WTVB-AM 39352
Owner: Midwest Communications Inc.
Editorial: 182 N Angola Rd, Coldwater, Michigan 49036-9554 **Tel:** 1 517 279-1590.
Email: webmaster.wtvb@wtvbam.com
Web site: http://www.wtvbam.com
Profile: WTVB-AM is a commercial station owned by Midwest Communications Inc. The format of the station is oldies. WTVB-AM broadcasts to the Coldwater, MI area at 1590 AM.
AM RADIO STATION

WTVL-AM 38241
Owner: Townsquare Media, LLC
Editorial: 56 Western Ave Ste 13, Augusta, Maine 04330-6348 **Tel:** 1 207 623-4735.
Web site: http://www.1400and1490.com
Profile: WTVL-AM is a commercial station owned by Townsquare Media, LLC. The format of the station is adult standards music. WTVL-AM broadcasts to the Augusta, ME area at 1490 AM.
AM RADIO STATION

WTVN-AM 36820
Owner: iHeartMedia Inc.
Editorial: 2323 W 5th Ave Ste 200, Columbus, Ohio 43204-4988 **Tel:** 1 614 486-6101.
Email: newsroom@610wtvn.com
Web site: http://610wtvn.iheart.com
Profile: WTVN-AM is a commercial station owned by iHeartMedia Inc. The format of the station is news, sports and talk. WTVN-AM broadcasts to the Columbus, OH area at 610 AM.
AM RADIO STATION

WTVR-FM 45585
Owner: iHeartMedia Inc.
Editorial: 3245 Basie Rd, Richmond, Virginia 23228-3404 **Tel:** 1 804 474-0000.
Web site: http://www.lite98.com
Profile: WTVR-FM is a commercial station owned by iHeartMedia Inc. The format of the station is Lite Rock/Lite AC music. WTVR-FM broadcasts to the Richmond, VA area at 98.1 FM.
FM RADIO STATION

WTVY-FM 40775
Owner: Gulf South Communications, Inc.
Editorial: 285 N Foster St Floor 8, Dothan, Alabama 36303-4541 **Tel:** 1 334 792-0047.
Web site: http://www.955wtvy.com
Profile: WTVY-FM is a commercial station owned by Gulf South Communications, Inc. The format of the station is country music. WTVY-FM broadcasts to the Dothan, AL area at 95.5 FM.
FM RADIO STATION

WTWA-AM 38243
Owner: Camellia City Communications
Editorial: 788 Cedar Rock Rd, Thomson, Georgia 30824-7642 **Tel:** 1 706 595-1561.
Email: wtho@classicsouth.net
Profile: WTWA-AM is a commercial station owned by Camellia City Communications. The format of the station is oldies. WTWA-AM broadcasts to the Thomson, GA area at 1240 AM.
AM RADIO STATION

WTWB-AM 35712
Owner: La Raza Media Group
Editorial: 127 Glenn Rd, Auburndale, Florida 33823-2401 **Tel:** 1 863 968-1100.
Email: laraza1570@gmail.com
Web site: http://www.laraza1570.com
Profile: WTWB-AM is a commercial station owned by La Raza Media Group. The format of the station is regional Mexican. WTWB-AM broadcasts to the Auburndale, FL area at 1570 AM.
AM RADIO STATION

WTWD-AM 36933
Owner: Salem Media Group, Inc.
Editorial: 5211 W Laurel St Ste A, Tampa, Florida 33607-1736 **Tel:** 1 813 349-8231.
Email: info@letstalkfaith.com
Web site: http://www.letstalkfaith.com
Profile: WTWD-AM is a commercial station owned by Salem Media Group, Inc. The format of the station is religious talk. WTWD-AM broadcasts to the Tampa, FL area on 910 AM.
AM RADIO STATION

WTWF-FM 75294
Owner: Connoisseur Media LLC
Editorial: 1 Boston Store Pl, Erie, Pennsylvania 16501-2313 **Tel:** 1 814 461-1000.
Email: production@connoisseurerie.com
Web site: http://www.939thewolf.com
Profile: WTWF-FM is a commercial station owned by Connoisseur Media LLC. The format of the station is country. WTWF-FM broadcasts to the Erie, PA area at 93.9 FM.
FM RADIO STATION

WTWG-AM 37625
Owner: T & W Communications
Editorial: 1910 14th Ave N, Columbus, Mississippi 39701 **Tel:** 1 662 328-1050.
Email: wtwg1050@yahoo.com
AM RADIO STATION

WTWK-AM 37106
Owner: Radio Broadcasting Services, Inc.
Editorial: 372 Dorset St, South Burlington, Vermont 05403-6212 **Tel:** 1 802 863-1010.
Profile: WTWK-AM is a commercial station owned by Radio Broadcasting Services, Inc. The format of the station is business news/talk. WTWK-AM broadcasts to the South Burlington, VT, area at 1070 AM.
AM RADIO STATION

WTWN-AM 38994
Owner: Puffer Broadcasting Inc.
Editorial: Route 302, Wells River, Vermont 05081-9742 **Tel:** 1 802 757-2773.
Email: studio@wykr.com
Web site: http://www.wtwnradio.com
Profile: WTWN-AM is a commercial station owned by Puffer Broadcasting Inc. The format of the station is Christian programming. WTWN-AM broadcasts to the Wells River, VT area at 1100 AM.
AM RADIO STATION

WTWS-FM 468571
Owner: Coltrace Communications, Inc.
Editorial: 125 W Houghton Lake Dr, Prudenville, Michigan 48651 **Tel:** 1 989 366-5364.
Email: wupsfm@yahoo.com
Web site: http://www.ilovethetwister.com
Profile: WTWS-FM is a commercial station owned by Coltrace Communications, Inc. The format of the station is contemporary country. WTWS-FM broadcasts to the Prudenville, MI market at 92.1 FM.
FM RADIO STATION

WTWT-FM 784276
Owner: Calvary Chapel of Russell
Editorial: 8160 Market St, Russell, Pennsylvania 16345-4128 **Tel:** 1 814 757-8744.
Web site: http://www.wtwtfm.org
Profile: WTWT-FM is a non-commercial station owned by Calvary Chapel of Russell. The format of the station features Christian programming, including contemporary Christian music. WTWT-FM broadcasts to the Bradford, PA area at 90.5 FM.
FM RADIO STATION

WTWX-FM 45586
Owner: Guntersville Broadcasting Co.
Editorial: 2301 Thomas Ave, Guntersville, Alabama 35976 **Tel:** 1 256 582-4946.
Email: wtwx@wtwx.com
Web site: http://www.wtwx.com
Profile: WTWX-FM is a commercial station owned by Guntersville Broadcasting Co. The format for the station is country. WTWX-FM broadcasts to the Huntsville, AL area at 95.9 FM.
FM RADIO STATION

WTWZ-AM 35924
Owner: Wood(Terry)
Editorial: 4611 Terry Rd, Ste C, Jackson, Mississippi 39212-5646 **Tel:** 1 601 346-0074.
Email: am1120@wtwzradio.com
Profile: WTWZ-AM is a commercial station owned by Terry Wood. The format of the station is variety with bluegrass music. WTWZ-AM broadcasts to the Jackson, MS area at 1120 AM.
AM RADIO STATION

WTXK-AM 39106
Owner: Frontdoor Broadcasting
Editorial: 1359 Carmichael Way, Montgomery, Alabama 36106-3629 **Tel:** 1 334 239-9750.
Web site: http://www.wtxktheticket.com
Profile: WTXK-AM is a commercial station owned by Frontdoor Broadcasting. The format of the station is sports. WTXK-AM broadcasts to the Ozark, AL area at 1210 AM.
AM RADIO STATION

WTXT-FM 41028
Owner: iHeartMedia Inc.
Editorial: 3900 11th Ave, Tuscaloosa, Alabama 35401-7056 **Tel:** 1 205 344-4589.
Web site: http://www.98txt.com
Profile: WTXT-FM is a commercial station owned by iHeart Media Inc. The station has a music format, airing contemporary country music. WTXT-FM broadcasts to the greater Tuscaloosa, AL area at 98.1 FM.
FM RADIO STATION

WTXY-AM 35713
Owner: WTXY Radio LLC
Editorial: 635 Madison St, Whiteville, North Carolina 28472 **Tel:** 1 910 642-8214.
Web site: http://www.wtxy1540.com
Profile: WTXY-AM is a commercial station owned by Jason Dozier, Robby Kendall & Rod Sheeks. The format of the station is sports. WTXY-AM broadcasts to the Whiteville, NC area at 1540 AM.
AM RADIO STATION

WTYB-FM 43054
Owner: Cumulus Media Inc.
Editorial: 214 Television Cir, Savannah, Georgia 31406-4519 **Tel:** 1 912 961-9000.
Web site: http://www.magic1039fm.com
Profile: WTYB-FM is a commercial station owned by Cumulus Media Inc. The format of the station is urban adult contemporary. WTYB-FM broadcasts to the Savannah, GA area at 103.9 FM.
FM RADIO STATION

WTYD-FM 44267
Owner: Local Voice Media
Editorial: 4732 Longhill Rd Ste 2201, Williamsburg, Virginia 23188-1584 **Tel:** 1 757 565-1079.
Email: music@tideradio.com
Web site: http://www.tideradio.com
Profile: WTYD-FM is a commercial station owned by Local Voice Media. The format of the station is adult album alternative. WTYD-FM broadcasts to the Northern Neck area of Virginia at 92.3 FM.
FM RADIO STATION

WTYE-FM 45562
Owner: Ann Broadcasting Corp.
Editorial: 9016 E 1050th Ave, Robinson, Illinois 62454-7400 **Tel:** 1 618 544-2191.
Email: wtaywtye@yahoo.com
Web site: http://www.wtyefm.com
Profile: WTYE-FM is a commercial station owned by Ann Broadcasting Corp. The format of the station is adult contemporary music. WTYE-FM broadcasts to the Robinson, IL area at 101.7 FM.
FM RADIO STATION

WTYJ-FM 44056
Owner: Natchez Communications
Editorial: 20 E Franklin St, Natchez, Mississippi 39120 **Tel:** 1 601 442-2522.
Email: wmiswtyj@bellsouth.net
FM RADIO STATION

WTYL-AM 38244
Owner: Tylertown Broadcasting Company Inc.
Editorial: 930 Union Rd, Tylertown, Mississippi 39667-2246 **Tel:** 1 601 876-2105.
Email: wtyl@bellsouth.net
Profile: WTYL-AM is a commercial station owned by Tylertown Broadcasting Company Inc. The format of the station is mainstream country. WTYL-AM broadcasts to the Tylertown, MS area at 1290 AM.
AM RADIO STATION

WTYL-FM 45587
Owner: Tylertown Broadcasting Company Inc.
Editorial: 930 Union Rd, Tylertown, Mississippi 39667 **Tel:** 1 601 876-2105.
Profile: WTYL-FM is a commercial station owned by Tylertown Broadcasting Company Inc. The format of the station is mainstream country. WTYL-FM broadcasts to the Tylertown, MS area at 97.7 FM.
FM RADIO STATION

WTYM-AM 35150
Owner: Family-Life Media-Com Inc.
Editorial: 114 S Jefferson St, Kittanning, Pennsylvania 16201-2408 **Tel:** 1 724 543-1380.
Email: admin@wtymradio.com
Web site: http://www.wtymradio.com
Profile: WTYM-AM is a commercial station owned by Family-Life Media-Com Inc. The format of the station is news and talk. WTYM-AM broadcasts to the Kittanning, PA area at 1380 AM.
AM RADIO STATION

WTYS-AM 35715
Owner: Adams(James L., Jr.)
Editorial: 2725 Jefferson St, Marianna, Florida 32448-4557 **Tel:** 1 850 482-2131.
Email: wtysradio@embarqmail.com
Web site: http://www.wtys.cc
Profile: WTYS-AM is a commercial station owned by James L. Adams, Jr. The format of the station is classic country and bluegrass music. WTYS-AM broadcasts to the Marianna, FL area at 1340 AM.
AM RADIO STATION

WTYS-FM 43527
Owner: Adams(James L., Jr.)
Editorial: 2725 Jefferson St, Marianna, Florida 32448 **Tel:** 1 850 482-2131.
Email: wtysradio@embarqmail.com
Web site: http://www.wtys.cc
Profile: WTYS-FM is a commercial station owned by James L. Adams Jr. The format of the station is southern gospel music. WTYS-FM broadcasts to the Marianna, FL area at 94.1 FM.
FM RADIO STATION

WTZA-AM 35357
Owner: K & Z Broadcasting, LLC
Editorial: 3296 Summit Ridge Pkwy Ste 910, Duluth, Georgia 30096-1625 **Tel:** 1 470 375 -8625.
Web site: http://www.vidaatlanta.com/
Profile: WTZA-AM is a commercial station owned by K & Z Broadcasting, LLC. The format of the station is Spanish Contemporary Christian. WTZA-AM broadcasts to the Duluth, GA area at 1010 AM.
AM RADIO STATION

WTZB-FM 43026
Owner: iHeartMedia Inc.
Editorial: 1779 Independence Blvd, Sarasota, Florida 34234-2106 **Tel:** 1 941 552-4800.
Web site: http://www.1059thebuzz.com
Profile: WTZB-FM is a commercial station owned by iHeartMedia Inc. The format of the station is classic rock. WTZB-FM broadcasts to the Tampa Bay, FL area at 105.9.
FM RADIO STATION

WTZE-AM 38245
Owner: Alpha Media
Editorial: 900 Bluefield Ave, Bluefield, West Virginia 24701-2744 **Tel:** 1 304 327-7114.
Web site: http://www.whistalkradio.com
Profile: WTZE-AM is a commercial station owned by Alpha Media. The format of the station is news and talk. WTZE-AM broadcasts to the Bluefield, WV area at 1470 AM.
AM RADIO STATION

WTZN-AM 38503
Owner: Cantroair Communications Co.
Editorial: 170 Redington Ave, Troy, Pennsylvania 16947 **Tel:** 1 570 297-0100.
Web site: http://www.wtzn.com
Profile: WTZN-AM is a commercial station owned by Cantroair Communications Co. The format of the station is Oldies. WTZN-AM broadcasts to the Troy, PA area at 1310 AM.
AM RADIO STATION

WTZQ-AM 35831
Owner: Timeless Media, Inc.
Editorial: 418 Duncan Rd, Flat Rock, North Carolina 28731-4712 **Tel:** 1 828 692-1600.
Email: 1600@wtzq.com
Web site: http://www.wtzq.com
Profile: WTZQ-AM is a commercial station owned by Timeless Media, Inc. The format of the station is adult standards. WTZQ-AM broadcasts to the Hendersonville, NC area at 1600 AM.
AM RADIO STATION

WTZX-AM 35716
Owner: Peg Broadcasting, LLC
Editorial: 520 N Spring St, Sparta, Tennessee 38583-1305 **Tel:** 1 931 836-1055.
Profile: WTZX-AM is a commercial station owned by Peg Broadcasting, LLC. The format of the station is oldie and classic country. WTZX-AM broadcasts to the Nashville, TN area at 860 AM.
AM RADIO STATION

WUAT-AM 35717
Owner: Bownds(Joyce)
Editorial: 101 Main St, Pikeville, Tennessee 37367-4947 **Tel:** 1 423 447-2906.
Web site: http://www.wuatradio.com
Profile: WUAT-AM is a commercial station owned by Joyce Bownds. The format for the station is gospel and country. WUAT-AM broadcasts to the Chattanooga, TN area at 1110 AM.
AM RADIO STATION

WUAW-FM 334432
Owner: Central Carolina Community College
Editorial: 215 Maynard Lake Rd, Erwin, North Carolina 28339-8507 **Tel:** 1 910 897-8070.
Web site: http://www.wuawfm.com
Profile: WUAW-FM is a non-commercial station owned by Central Carolina Community College. The format of the station is rhythmic Top 40. WUAW-FM broadcasts to the Erwin, NC area at 88.3 FM.
FM RADIO STATION

WUBB-FM 43197
Owner: Alpha Media
Editorial: 1 Saint Augustine Pl, Hilton Head Island, South Carolina 29928-4717 **Tel:** 1 843 785-9569.
Email: bob1069shh@gmail.com
Web site: http://www.bob1069.com
Profile: WUBB-FM is a commercial station owned by Alpha Media. The format for the station is country music. WUBB-FM broadcasts to the Hilton Head Island, SC area at 106.9 FM.
FM RADIO STATION

WUBE-FM 45986
Owner: Hubbard Broadcasting, Inc.
Editorial: 2060 Reading Rd, Cincinnati, Ohio 45202-1454 **Tel:** 1 513 699-5105.
Web site: http://www.b105.com
Profile: WUBE-FM is a commercial station owned by Hubbard Broadcasting, Inc. The format of the station is classic country. WUBE-FM broadcasts to the Cincinnati area at 105.1 FM.
FM RADIO STATION

WUBL-FM 42711
Owner: iHeartMedia Inc.
Editorial: 1819 Peachtree Rd NE Ste 700, Atlanta, Georgia 30309-1849 **Tel:** 1 404 875-8080.
Web site: http://www.949thebull.com
Profile: WUBL-FM is a commercial station owned by iHeartMedia Inc. The format of the station is contemporary country. WUBL-FM broadcasts to the Atlanta area at 94.9 FM.
FM RADIO STATION

WUBR-AM 35921
Owner: Red Peach LLC
Tel: 1 318 255-5000.
Email: redpeachllc@gmail.com
Web site: http://www.pelicansportstv.com/
Profile: WUBR-AM is a commercial station owned by Red Peach LLC. The format of the station is sports. WUBR-AM broadcasts to the Baton Rouge, LA area at 910 AM.
AM RADIO STATION

WUBS-FM 42420
Owner: Interfaith Christian Union
Editorial: 702 Lincoln Way W, South Bend, Indiana 46616-1122 **Tel:** 1 574 287-4700.
Email: wubs89.7fm@gmail.com
Web site: http://www.wubs.org
Profile: WUBS-FM is a non-commercial station owned by the Interfaith Christian Union. The format of the station is gospel and religious music. WUBS-FM broadcasts to the South Bend, IN area at 89.7 FM.
FM RADIO STATION

WUBT-FM 42911
Owner: iHeartMedia Inc.
Editorial: 55 Music Sq W, Nashville, Tennessee 37203-3207 **Tel:** 1 615 664-2400.
Web site: http://www.101thebeat.com
Profile: WUBT-FM is a commercial station owned by iHeartMedia Inc. The format of the station is urban contemporary. WUBT-FM broadcasts to the Nashville, TN area at 101.1 FM.
FM RADIO STATION

WUBU-FM 42419
Owner: Partnership Radio
Editorial: 401 E Colfax Ave Ste 300, South Bend, Indiana 46617-2736 **Tel:** 1 574 233-3505.
Email: studio.mix106@outlook.com
Web site: http://www.wubufm.com
Profile: WUBU-FM is a commercial station owned by Partnership Radio. The format for the station is urban adult contemporary music. WUBU-FM broadcasts to the South Bend, IN, area at 106.3 FM.
FM RADIO STATION

WUCL-FM 44379
Owner: New South Communications, Inc
Tel: 1 601 693-3434.
Profile: WUCL-FM is a commercial station owned by New South Communications, Inc. The format of the station is classic country. WUCL-FM broadcasts to the Meridian, MS area at a frequency of 97.9 FM.
FM RADIO STATION

WUCS-FM 42024
Owner: iHeartMedia Inc.
Editorial: 10 Columbus Blvd Ste 1, Hartford, Connecticut 06106-1976 **Tel:** 1 860 723-6000.
Web site: http://www.979espn.com
Profile: WUCS-FM is a commercial station owned by iHeartMedia Inc. The format of the station is sports. WUCS-FM broadcasts to the Hartford, CT area at 97.9 FM.
FM RADIO STATION

WUCZ-FM 45505
Owner: Banka (Dennis and Tracy)
Editorial: 104 Z Country Ln, Carthage, Tennessee 37030 **Tel:** 1 615 735-1350.
Email: info@1041theranch.net
Web site: http://www.1041theranch.net
Profile: WUCZ-FM is a commercial station owned by Dennis and Tracy Banka. The format of the station is contemporary country music. WUCZ-FM broadcasts to the Nashville, TN area at 104.1 FM.
FM RADIO STATION

WUDE-FM 42214
Owner: Hometown Wilmington Media
Editorial: 122 Cinema Dr, Wilmington, North Carolina 28403-1490 **Tel:** 1 910 772-6300.
Email: music@gottalovethedude.com
Web site: http://gottalovethedude.com/home
Profile: WUDE-FM is a commercial station owned by Hometown Wilmington Media. The format of the station is contemporary country. WUDE-FM broadcasts to the Wilmington, NC area at 93.7 FM.
FM RADIO STATION

WUEZ-FM 41699
Owner: Max Media
Editorial: 1431 Country Aire Dr, Carterville, Illinois 62918-5118 **Tel:** 1 618 985-4843.
Email: publicservice@riverradio.net
Web site: http://www.magic951.com
Profile: WUEZ-FM is a commercial station owned by Max Media. The format of the station is classic hits music. WUEZ-FM broadcasts to the Paducah, KY-Cape Girardeau, MO-Harrisburg, IL areas at 95.1 FM. Send PSAs to publicservice@riverradio.net.
FM RADIO STATION

WUFE-AM 38246
Owner: South Georgia Broadcasters Inc.
Editorial: 4005 Golden Isles Parkway, Baxley, Georgia 31513 **Tel:** 1 912 367-3000.
Web site: http://bigwufe.com
Profile: WUFE-AM is a commercial station owned by South Georgia Broadcasters Inc. The format for the station is Adult Contemporary. WUFE-AM broadcasts to the Baxley, GA area at 1260 AM.
AM RADIO STATION

WUFF-FM 45589
Owner: Dodge Broadcasting Inc.
Editorial: 855 College St, Eastman, Georgia 31023-6771 **Tel:** 1 478 374-3437.
Web site: http://www.wolfcountry975.com
Profile: WUFF-FM is a commercial station owned by Dodge Broadcasting Inc. The format of the station is contemporary country music. WUFF-FM broadcasts to the Eastman, GA area at 97.5 FM.
FM RADIO STATION

WUFL-AM 35923
Owner: Family Life Communications, Inc.
Editorial: 7355 N Oracle Rd, Tucson, Arizona 85704-6325 **Tel:** 1 520 742-6976.
Web site: http://www.myflr.org
Profile: WUFL-AM is a non-commercial station owned by Family Life Radio. The format of the station is contemporary Christian programming. WUFL-AM broadcasts to the Clinton Township, MI area at 1030 AM.
AM RADIO STATION

WUFM-FM 43147
Owner: Spirit Communications, Inc.
Editorial: 116 County Line Rd W, Westerville, Ohio 43082 **Tel:** 1 614 839-7100.
Email: radiou@radiou.com
Web site: http://tvulive.com/radiou/
Profile: WUFM-FM is a non-commercial station owned by Spirit Communications, Inc. The format of the station is alternative. WUFM-FM broadcasts to the Westerville, OH area at 88.7 FM.
FM RADIO STATION

WUFN-FM 40782
Owner: Family Life Radio
Editorial: 7355 N Oracle Rd, Tucson, Arizona 85704-6325 **Tel:** 1 800 776-1070.
Web site: http://www.myflr.org
Profile: WUFN-FM is a non-commercial station owned by Family Life Radio. The format of the station is Christian and gospel music. WUFN-FM broadcasts to the Grand Rapids, MI area at 96.7 FM.
FM RADIO STATION

WUFO-AM 35719
Owner: Sheridan Broadcasting Corp.
Editorial: 143 Broadway St, Buffalo, New York 14203-1629 **Tel:** 1 716 834-1080.
Web site: http://www.wufoam.com
Profile: WUFO-AM is a commercial station owned by Sheridan Broadcasting Corp. The format of the station is gospel, R & B and talk. WUFO-AM broadcasts to the Buffalo, NY area at 1080 AM.
AM RADIO STATION

WUGA-FM 41556
Owner: Georgia Public Broadcasting
Editorial: University of Georgia, 1197 S Lumpkin St, Athens, Georgia 30602 **Tel:** 1 706 542-9842.
Email: wuga@uga.edu
Web site: http://www.wuga.org
Profile: WUGA-FM is a non-commercial station owned by the Georgia Public Broadcasting. The format of the station is classical, jazz and news. WUGA-FM broadcasts to the Athens, GA area at 91.7 FM.
FM RADIO STATION

WUGN-FM 40784
Owner: Family Life Communications, Inc.
Editorial: 510 E Isabella Rd, Midland, Michigan 48640-8336 **Tel:** 1 989 631-7060.
Email: 997@997.org
Web site: http://www.myflr.org
Profile: WUGN-FM is a non-commercial station owned by Family Life Communications, Inc.. The format of the station is religious and contemporary Christian programming. WUGN-FM broadcasts to Midland, MI and the surrounding area at 99.7 FM.
FM RADIO STATION

WUGO-FM 45591
Owner: Carter County Broadcasting Co.
Editorial: 150 Radio Tower Rd, Grayson, Kentucky 41143 **Tel:** 1 606 474-5144.
Email: mail@wgohwugo.com
Web site: http://www.wgohwugo.com
Profile: WUGO-FM is a commercial station owned by Carter County Broadcasting Co. The format of the station is adult contemporary music. WUGO-FM broadcasts to the Grayson, KY area at 102.3 FM.
FM RADIO STATION

WUHT-FM 41812
Owner: Cumulus Media Inc.
Editorial: 244 Goodwin Crest Dr, Ste 300, Birmingham, Alabama 35209 **Tel:** 1 205 945-4646.
Web site: http://www.hot1077radio.com
Profile: WUHT-FM is a commercial station owned by Cumulus Media Inc. The format of the station is urban adult contemporary music. WUHT-FM broadcasts to the Birmingham, AL area at 107.7 FM.
FM RADIO STATION

WUHU-FM 45806
Owner: FM Radio Licenses, LLC
Editorial: 1919 Scottsville Rd, Bowling Green, Kentucky 42104-3303 **Tel:** 1 270 843-3333.
Email: production@beaverfm.com
Web site: http://www.allhitwuhu107.com
Profile: WUHU-FM is a commercial station owned by FM Radio Licenses, LLC. The format of the station is hot adult contemporary. WUHU-FM broadcasts to the Bowling Green KY area at 107.1 FM.
FM RADIO STATION

WUIN-FM 35935
Owner: Hometown Wilmington Media
Editorial: 122 Cinema Dr, Wilmington, North Carolina 28403-1490 **Tel:** 1 910 772-6300.
Email: request@983thepenguin.com
Web site: http://983thepenguin.com/home
Profile: WUIN-FM is a commercial station owned by Hometown Wilmington Media. The format of the station is AAA. WUIN-FM broadcasts in the Wilmington, NC area at 98.3 FM.
FM RADIO STATION

WUKL-FM 40343
Owner: FM Radio Licenses, LLC
Editorial: 56325 High Ridge Rd, Bellaire, Ohio 43906-9707 **Tel:** 1 740 676-5661.
Email: kool105@hotmail.com
Web site: http://www.mykool105.com
Profile: WUKL-FM is a commercial station owned by FM Radio Licenses, LLC. The format of the station is oldies. WUKL-FM broadcasts to the Bellaire, OH area at 105.5 FM.
FM RADIO STATION

WUKS-FM 43017
Owner: Beasley Broadcast Group
Editorial: 508 Person St, Fayetteville, North Carolina 28301-5841 **Tel:** 1 910 486-4114.
Web site: http://1077jamz.com/
Profile: WUKS-FM is a commercial station owned by Beasley Broadcast Group. The format of the station is urban adult contemporary music. WUKS-FM broadcasts to the Fayetteville, NC area at 107.7 FM.
FM RADIO STATION

WULF-FM 42936
Owner: Skytower Communications Inc.
Editorial: 233 W Dixie Ave, Elizabethtown, Kentucky 42701 **Tel:** 1 270 765-0943.
Web site: http://www.943wulf.com
Profile: WULF-FM is a commercial station owned by Skytower Communications Inc. The format of the station is contemporary country music. WULF-FM broadcasts to the Elizabethtown, KY area at 94.3 FM.
FM RADIO STATION

WULM-AM 133945
Owner: Radio Maria Inc.
Tel: 1 318 561-6145.
Email: info.usa@radiomaria.org
Web site: http://www.radiomaria.us
Profile: WULM-AM is a commercial station owned by Radio Maria Inc. The format of the station is Catholic and religious. WULM-AM broadcasts to the Springfield, OH area at 1600 AM.
AM RADIO STATION

WULR-AM 36326
Owner: Iglesia Nueva Vida of High Point, Inc.
Editorial: 6223 Old Mendenhall Rd, High Point, North Carolina 27263-3940 **Tel:** 1 336 471-1839.
Email: nuevavida980@yahoo.com
Web site: http://cadenaradialnuevavida.com
Profile: WULR-AM is a commercial station owned by Iglesia Nueva Vida of High Point, Inc.. The format for the station is Spanish Religious. WULR-AM broadcasts to the Charlotte, NC area at 980 AM.
AM RADIO STATION

WULS-FM 42418
Owner: WULS Inc.
Editorial: 702 Madison Ave N, Ste 101, Douglas, Georgia 31533 **Tel:** 1 912 384-9857.
Profile: WULS-FM is a commercial station owned by WULS Inc. The format of the station is Southern gospel. WULS-FM broadcasts to the Douglas, GA area at 103.7 FM.
FM RADIO STATION

WUME-FM 45673
Owner: Diamond Shores Broadcasting LLC
Editorial: 192 S Court St, Paoli, Indiana 47454-1322 **Tel:** 1 812 723-4484.
Email: wume953@gmail.com
Web site: http://wume953.com
Profile: WUME-FM is a commercial station owned by Diamond Shores Broadcasting LLC. The format of the station is adult contemporary music. WUME-FM broadcasts to the Paoli, IN area at 95.3 FM.
FM RADIO STATION

WUMJ-FM 76543
Owner: Urban One, Inc.
Editorial: 101 Marietta St NW Fl 12, Atlanta, Georgia 30303-2720 **Tel:** 1 404 765-9750.
Web site: http://majicatl.hellobeautiful.com
Profile: WUMJ-FM is a commercial station owned by Urban One, Inc. The format of the station is hip-hop. WUMJ-FM broadcasts to the Atlanta area at 97.5 FM.
FM RADIO STATION

WUMP-AM 36287
Owner: Cumulus Media Inc.
Editorial: 1717 US Highway 72 E, Athens, Alabama 35611-4413 **Tel:** 1 256 830-8300.
Web site: http://www.730ump.com
Profile: WUMP-AM is a commercial station owned by Cumulus Media Inc. The format of the station is sports. WUMP-AM broadcasts to the Huntsville, AL area at 730 AM.
AM RADIO STATION

WUMX-FM 46559
Owner: Galaxy Communications LP
Editorial: 39 Kellogg Rd, New Hartford, New York 13413-2849 **Tel:** 1 315 797-1330.
Email: mix@galaxycommunications.com
Web site: http://www.mix1025.com
Profile: WRBY-FM is a commercial station owned by Galaxy Communications LP. The format of the station is hot adult contemporary music. WRBY-FM broadcasts to the Utica, NY area at 102.5 FM.
FM RADIO STATION

WUMY-AM 35996
Owner: Mighty Media Group, LP (Memphis First Ventures LP)
Editorial: 230-2 Goodman Road East Ste 202, Memphis, Tennessee
Web site: http://www.lovebigcountry.com
Profile: WUMY-AM is a commercial station owned by Mighty Media Group, LP (Memphis First Ventures LP). The format of the station is country music. WUMY-AM broadcasts to the Memphis, TN area at a frequency of 1180 AM.
AM RADIO STATION

WUNA-AM 35725
Owner: J & V Communications, Inc.
Editorial: 749 S Bluford Ave, Ocoee, Florida 34761-2942 **Tel:** 1 407 841-8282.
Email: wprd1440@gmail.com
Profile: WUNA-AM is a commercial station owned by J & V Communications, Inc. The format of the station is ethnic. WUNA-AM broadcasts to the Orlando, FL area at 1480 AM.
AM RADIO STATION

WUNN-AM 35720
Owner: Family Life Comunications, Inc.
Editorial: 7355 N Oracle Rd, Tucson, Arizona 85704-6325 **Tel:** 1 520 742-6976.
Web site: http://www.myflr.org
Profile: WUNN-AM is a non-commercial station owned by Family Life Radio. The format of the station is gospel and religious music. WUNN-AM broadcasts to the Grand Rapids, MI area at 1110 AM.
AM RADIO STATION

WUNR-AM 35721
Owner: Champion Broadcasting System
Editorial: 60 Temple Pl, Fl 2, Boston, Massachusetts 02111-1324 **Tel:** 1 617 367-9003.
Email: info@wunr.com
Web site: http://www.wunr.net
Profile: WUNR-AM is a commercial station owned by Champion Broadcasting System. The format of the station is Hispanic programming. WUNR-AM broadcasts in the Boston area at 1600 AM.
AM RADIO STATION

WUNV-FM 43319
Owner: Georgia Public Broadcasting
Editorial: 260 14th St NW, Atlanta, Georgia 30318 **Tel:** 1 404 685-2548.
Email: news@gpb.org
Web site: http://www.gpb.org
Profile: WUNV-FM is a non-commercial station owned by Georgia Public Broadcasting. The format of the station is classical and jazz music, and news talk. WUNV-FM broadcasts to the Atlanta area at 91.7 FM.
FM RADIO STATION

WUOL-FM 40789
Owner: Louisville Public Media
Editorial: 619 S 4th St, Louisville, Kentucky 40202 **Tel:** 1 502 814-6500.
Email: studio@wuol.org
Web site: http://www.wuol.org
Profile: WUOL-FM is a commercial station owned by Louisville Public Media. The format of the station is classical music. WUOL-FM broadcasts to the Louisville, KY area at 90.5 FM.
FM RADIO STATION

WUPE-AM 38248
Owner: Gamma Broadcasting LLC
Editorial: 211 Jason St, Pittsfield, Massachusetts 01201-5907 **Tel:** 1 413 499-3333.
Email: news@wupe.com
Web site: http://www.wupe.com
Profile: WUPE-AM is a commercial station owned by Gamma Broadcasting LLC. The format of the station is oldies. WUPE-AM broadcasts to the Pittsfield, MA area at 1110 AM.
AM RADIO STATION

WUPE-FM 46214
Owner: Gamma Broadcasting LLC
Editorial: 211 Jason St, Pittsfield, Massachusetts 01201-5907 **Tel:** 1 413 499-3333.
Email: news@wupe.com
Web site: http://www.wupe.com
Profile: WUPE-FM is a commercial station owned by Gamma Broadcasting LLC. The format of the station is oldies. WUPE-FM broadcasts to the Pittsfield, MA area at 100.1 FM.
FM RADIO STATION

WUPG-FM 902029
Owner: Radioactive, LLC
Editorial: 308 Cleveland Ave Ste 302, Ishpeming, Michigan 49849-1845 **Tel:** 1 906 485-4313.
Web site: http://www.radioeaglemarquette.com
Profile: WUPG-FM (formerly WUPZ-FM) (96.7 FM) is a radio station licensed to Republic, Michigan. The station is currently owned by Radioactive, LLC and was granted its license on April 17, 2008. The station signed on in July 2008 with a Variety Hits format. On March 4th, 2014, changed formats to Classic Country branded as "Yooper Country 96.7".
FM RADIO STATION

WUPK-FM 42372
Owner: Northern Star Broadcasting LLC
Editorial: 1009 W Ridge St Ste A, Marquette, Michigan 49855-3997 **Tel:** 1 906 225-1313.
Web site: http://www.rockthebear.com
Profile: WUPK-FM is a commercial station owned by Northern Star Broadcasting LLC. The format of the station is classic rock. WUPK-FM broadcasts to the Marquette, MI area at 94.1 FM.
FM RADIO STATION

WUPS-FM 45255
Owner: Coltrace Communications, Inc.
Editorial: 125 W Houghton Lake Dr, Prudenville, Michigan 48651 **Tel:** 1 989 366-5364.
Email: wupsfm@yahoo.com
Web site: http://www.wups.com
FM RADIO STATION

WUPY-FM 41344
Owner: J & J Broadcasting, Inc.
Editorial: 622 River St, Ontonagon, Michigan 49953 **Tel:** 1 906 884-9668.
Email: wupy@jamadots.com
Web site: http://www.wupy101.com
Profile: WUPY-FM is a commercial station owned by J & J Broadcasting, Inc. The format of the station is country music. WUPY-FM broadcasts to Ontonagon, MI and the surrounding area on 101.1 FM.
FM RADIO STATION

WURC-FM 41523
Owner: Rust College Inc.
Editorial: 150 Rust Ave, Holly Springs, Mississippi 38635-2330 **Tel:** 1 662 252-5881.
Web site: http://www.wurc.org
FM RADIO STATION

WURD-AM 35917
Owner: WURD Radio, LLC
Editorial: 1341 N Delaware Ave Ste 300, Philadelphia, Pennsylvania 19125-4309 **Tel:** 1 215 425-7489.
Email: 900amwurd@wurdradio.com
Web site: http://www.900amwurd.com
Profile: WURD-AM is a commercial station owned by WURD Radio, LLC. The format of the station is news and talk. WURD-AM broadcasts to the Philadelphia area at 900 AM. They only accepts PSAs from non-profits.
AM RADIO STATION

WURL-AM 35722
Owner: Bill Davison Evangelistic Association
Editorial: 2999 Radio Park Dr, Moody, Alabama 35004-2242 **Tel:** 1 205 699-9875.
Email: wurlradio@aol.com
Web site: http://www.wurlradio.com
Profile: WURL-AM is a commercial radio station owned by Bill Davison Evangelistic Association. The format of the station is Southern gospel music. WURL-AM broadcasts to the Moody, AL area at 760 AM.
AM RADIO STATION

WURN-AM 889099
Owner: Actualidad 1020 AM, LLC
Editorial: 2555 Ponce De Leon Blvd Ste 225, Coral Gables, Florida 33134-6033 **Tel:** 1 786 388-3868.
Web site: http://actualidadradio.com
Profile: WURN-AM is a commercial station owned by Actualidad 1020 AM, LLC. The format of the station is Spanish language news and talk. WLVJ-AM broadcasts to the Miami area at 1020 AM.
AM RADIO STATION

WURV-FM 41063
Owner: Summit Media Broadcasting LLC
Editorial: 812 Moorefield Park Dr, Ste 300, Richmond, Virginia 23236 **Tel:** 1 804 330-5700.

Web site: http://www.1037play.com
Profile: WURV-FM is a commercial station owned by Summit Media Broadcasting LLC. The format of the station is a hot AC. WURV-FM broadcasts to the Richmond, VA area at 103.7 FM.
FM RADIO STATION

WUSH-FM 42789
Owner: Sinclair Telecable Inc.
Editorial: 999 Waterside Dr, Ste 500, Norfolk, Virginia 23510 **Tel:** 1 757 640-8500.
Web site: http://www.us1061.com
Profile: WUSH-FM is a commercial station owned by Sinclair Telecable Inc. The format of the station is contemporary country. WUSH-FM broadcasts to the Norfolk, VA area at 106.1 FM.
FM RADIO STATION

WUSJ-FM 42071
Owner: New South Communications Inc.
Editorial: 265 Highpoint Dr, Ridgeland, Mississippi 39157-6018 **Tel:** 1 601 956-0102.
Web site: http://www.us963.com
Profile: WUSJ-FM is a commercial station owned by New South Communications Inc. The format of the station is country. WUSJ-FM broadcasts to the Jackson, MS area at 96.3 FM.
FM RADIO STATION

WUSL-FM 40795
Owner: iHeartMedia Inc.
Editorial: 111 Presidential Blvd Ste 100, Bala Cynwyd, Pennsylvania 19004-1009 **Tel:** 1 610 784-3333.
Web site: http://power99.iheart.com
Profile: WUSL-FM is a commercial station owned by iHeartMedia Inc. The format of the station is urban contemporary. WUSL-FM broadcasts to the Philadelphia area at 98.9 FM.
FM RADIO STATION

WUSN-FM 40797
Owner: CBS Radio
Editorial: 180 N Stetson Ave Ste 1000, Chicago, Illinois 60601-6822 **Tel:** 1 312 649-0099.
Web site: http://us995.cbslocal.com
Profile: WUSN-FM is a commercial station owned by CBS Radio. The format of the station is contemporary country. WUSN-FM broadcasts to the Chicago area at 99.5 FM.
FM RADIO STATION

WUSP-AM 38250
Owner: Good Guys Broadcasting
Editorial: 185 Genesee St Ste 1601, Utica, New York 13501-2110 **Tel:** 1 315 734-9245.
Profile: WUSP-AM is a commercial station owned by Good Guys Broadcasting. The format of the station is sports. WUSP-AM broadcasts to the Utica, NY area at 1550 AM.
AM RADIO STATION

WUSQ-FM 41407
Owner: iHeartMedia Inc.
Editorial: 510 Pegasus Ct, Winchester, Virginia 22602-4596 **Tel:** 1 540 662-5101.
Email: yourcommunity@hotmail.com
Web site: http://shenandoahcountryq102.iheart.com
Profile: WUSQ-FM is a commercial station owned by iHeartMedia Inc. The format of the station is contemporary country music. WUSQ-FM broadcasts to the Winchester, VA area at 102.5 FM.
FM RADIO STATION

WUST-AM 35723
Owner: New World Radio
Editorial: 2131 Crimmins Ln, Falls Church, Virginia 22043-1962 **Tel:** 1 703 532-0400.
Email: contactwust@wust1120.com
Web site: http://www.wust1120.com
Profile: WUST-AM is a commercial station owned by New World Radio. The format of the station is a variety of ethnic programming. WUST-AM broadcasts to the Washington D.C. area at 1120 AM.
AM RADIO STATION

WUSY-FM 40798
Owner: iHeartMedia Inc.
Editorial: 7413 Old Lee Hwy, Chattanooga, Tennessee 37421-1142 **Tel:** 1 423 892-3333.
Web site: http://www.us101country.com
Profile: WUSY-FM is a commercial station owned by iHeartMedia Inc. The format of the station is contemporary country. WUSY-FM broadcasts to the Chattanooga, TN area on 100.7 FM.
FM RADIO STATION

WUSZ-FM 45201
Owner: Midwest Communications Inc.
Editorial: 807 W 37th St, Hibbing, Minnesota 55746-2839 **Tel:** 1 218 263-7531.
Web site: http://www.radiousa.com
FM RADIO STATION

WUTQ-FM 42394
Owner: Roser Communications
Editorial: 215 Leland Ave, Utica, New York 13502-2518
Email: talk@wutqfm.com
Web site: http://wutqfm.com
Profile: WUTQ-FM is a commercial station owned by Roser Communications. The format of the station is Soft Talk. WUTQ-FM broadcasts to the Utica, NY area at 100.7 FM.
FM RADIO STATION

WUUB-FM 79392
Owner: Good Karma Broadcasting
Editorial: 2090 Palm Beach Lakes Blvd Ste 801, West Palm Beach, Florida 33409-6508 **Tel:** 1 561 697-8353.
Email: management@gkbsports.com
Web site: http://www.espnwestpalm.com
Profile: WUUB-FM is a commercial station owned by Good Karma Broadcasting. The format of the station is sports. WUUB-FM broadcasts to the West Palm Beach, FL area at 106.3 FM.
FM RADIO STATION

WUUF-FM 46223
Owner: Waynco Radio Inc.
Editorial: 187 Vienna Rd, Newark, New York 14513-9414 **Tel:** 1 315 331-9667.
Email: bigdogfm@rochester.rr.com
Web site: http://www.bigdog1035.com
Profile: WUUF-FM is a commercial station owned by Waynco Radio Inc. The format of the station is classic country. WUUF-FM broadcasts to the Newark, NY area at 103.5 FM.
FM RADIO STATION

WUUQ-FM 45346
Owner: 3 Daughters Media, Inc.
Editorial: 2615 Broad St, Chattanooga, Tennessee 37408-3100 **Tel:** 1 423 643-2212.
Web site: http://www.wuuqradio.com
Profile: WUUQ-FM is a commercial station owned by 3 Daughters Media, Inc. The format of the station is classic country. WUUQ-FM broadcasts to the Chattanooga, TN area at 97.3 FM.
FM RADIO STATION

WUUU-FM 46785
Owner: Pittman Broadcast Services LLC
Editorial: 23369 E Fairgrounds Rd, Franklinton, Louisiana 70438-5135 **Tel:** 1 985 624-9452.
Profile: WUUU-FM is a commercial station owned by Pittman Broadcast Services LLC. The format of the station is comtemporary country. The station broadcasts to the Mandeville, LA area at 98.9 FM.
FM RADIO STATION

WUWG-FM 40841
Owner: Georgia Public Broadcasting
Editorial: 260 14th St NW, Atlanta, Georgia 30318 **Tel:** 1 404 685-2548.
Email: news@gpb.org
Web site: http://www.gpb.org
Profile: WUWG-FM is a non-commercial station owned by Georgia Public Broadcasting. The format of the station is jazz, classical and news. WUWG-FM broadcasts to the Atlanta area at 90.7 FM.
FM RADIO STATION

WUZR-FM 41785
Owner: Original Company Inc.(The)
Editorial: 522 Busseron St, Vincennes, Indiana 47591-2030 **Tel:** 1 812 882-6060.
Email: wuzr@originalcompany.com
Web site: http://www.wuzr.com
Profile: WUZR-FM is a commercial station owned by The Original Company Inc. The format of the station is contemporary country. WUZR-FM broadcasts to the Vincennes, IN area at 105.7 FM.
FM RADIO STATION

WUZZ-FM 42900
Owner: FM Radio Licenses, LLC
Editorial: 900 Water St, Meadville, Pennsylvania 16335-3428 **Tel:** 1 814 724-1111.
Email: radio@zoominternet.net
Web site: http://www.mywuzz.com
Profile: WUZZ-FM is a commercial station owned by FM Radio Licenses, LLC. The format of the station is classic rock music. WUZZ-FM broadcasts to the Meadville, PA area at 94.3 FM.
FM RADIO STATION

WVAF-FM 45667
Owner: West Virginia Radio Corp.
Editorial: 1111 Virginia St E, Charleston, West Virginia 25301-2406 **Tel:** 1 304 342-8131.
Web site: http://www.v100.fm
Profile: WVAF-FM is a commercial station owned by West Virginia Radio Corp. The format of the station is adult contemporary music. WVAF-FM broadcasts to the Charleston, WV area at 99.9 FM.
FM RADIO STATION

WVAL-AM 37053
Owner: Tri-County Broadcasting
Editorial: 1010 2nd St N, Sauk Rapids, Minnesota 56379 **Tel:** 1 320 252-6200.
Web site: http://www.800wval.com
Profile: WVAL-AM is a commercial station owned by Tri-County Broadcasting. The format of the station is classic country. WVAL-AM broadcasts to the Sauk Rapids, MN area at a frequency of 800 AM.
AM RADIO STATION

WVAM-AM 38252
Owner: FM Radio Licenses, LLC
Editorial: 1 Forever Dr, Hollidaysburg, Pennsylvania 16648-3029 **Tel:** 1 814 941-9800.
Web site: http://www.wvamam.com
Profile: WVAM-AM is a commercial station owned by FM Radio Licenses, LLC. The format of the station is sports. WVAM-AM broadcasts to the Hollidaysburg, PA area at 1430 AM.
AM RADIO STATION

WVAQ-FM 44363
Owner: West Virginia Radio Corp.
Editorial: 1251 Earl L Core Rd, Morgantown, West Virginia 26505-5881 **Tel:** 1 304 296-0029.
Web site: http://www.wvaq.com
Profile: WVAQ-FM is a commercial station owned by West Virginia Radio Corp. The format of the station is Top 40/CHR. WVAQ-FM broadcasts to the Morgantown, WV area at 101.9 FM.
FM RADIO STATION

WVAR-AM 36395
Owner: Summit Media Broadcasting LLC
Editorial: 713 Main St, Summersville, West Virginia 26651-1431 **Tel:** 1 304 765-7373.
Email: info@theboss97fm.com
Web site: http://www.summitmediawv.com
Profile: WVAR-AM is a commercial station owned by Summit Media Broadcasting LLC. The format of the station is classic hits. The station is aired in the Sutton, WV area at 600 AM. WVAR-AM is a simulcast of WSGB-AM.
AM RADIO STATION

WVAX-AM 389622
Owner: Saga Communications
Editorial: 1140 Rose Hill Dr, Charlottesville, Virginia 22903-5128 **Tel:** 1 434 220-2300.
Email: news@wina.com
Web site: http://www.wvax.com
Profile: WVAX-AM is a commercial station owned by Saga Communications. The format for the station is sports/talk. WVAX-AM broadcasts to the Charlottesville, VA area at 1450 AM.
AM RADIO STATION

WVAZ-FM 40140
Owner: iHeartMedia Inc.
Editorial: 233 N Michigan Ave Ste 2700, Chicago, Illinois 60601-5704 **Tel:** 1 312 540-2000.
Web site: http://v103.iheart.com
Profile: WVAZ-FM is a commercial station owned by iHeartMedia Inc. The format of the station is urban adult contemporary. WVAZ-FM broadcasts to the Chicago area at 102.7 FM.
FM RADIO STATION

WVBB-FM 46197
Owner: Wheeler, Inc. (Mel)
Editorial: 9196 Seneca Trl S, Ronceverte, West Virginia 24970-8376 **Tel:** 1 304 645-1327.
Email: info@vibe100.com
Web site: http://www.vibe100.com
Profile: WVBB-FM is a commercial station owned by Mel Wheeler, Inc. The format of the station is R&B. WVBB-FM broadcasts to the Ronceverte, WV area at 97.7 FM.
FM RADIO STATION

WVBD-FM 595014
Owner: Summit Media Broadcasting LLC
Editorial: 180 Main St, Sutton, West Virginia 26601-1317 **Tel:** 1 304 765-7373.
Profile: WVBD-FM is a commercial station owned by Summit Media Broadcasting LLC. The format of the station is classic country music.
FM RADIO STATION

WVBE-FM 42044
Owner: Wheeler Inc.(Mel)
Editorial: 3934 Electric Rd, Roanoke, Virginia 24018 **Tel:** 1 540 989-4591.
Email: info@vibe100.com
Web site: http://www.vibe100.com
Profile: WVBE-FM is a commercial station owned by Mel Wheeler Inc. The format of the station is urban adult contemporary. WVBE-FM broadcasts to the Roanoke, VA area at 100.1 FM.
FM RADIO STATION

WVBG-AM 37023
Owner: Owensville Communication
Editorial: 1102 Newitt Vick Dr, Vicksburg, Mississippi 39183-8755 **Tel:** 1 601 883-0848.
Web site: http://www.newstalk1490.net
Profile: WVBG-AM is a commercial station owned by Owensville Communication. The format of the station is talk. WVBG-AM broadcasts to the Vicksburg, MS area at 1490 AM.
AM RADIO STATION

WVBG-FM 469304
Owner: Lendsi Radio
Editorial: 1102 Newitt Vick Dr, Vicksburg, Mississippi 39183 **Tel:** 1 601 883-0848.
Web site: http://www.vicksburgv105.com
Profile: WVBG-FM is a commercial radio station owned by Lendsi Radio. The format of the station is classic hits. WVBG-FM broadcasts to the Vicksburg, MS area at 105.5 FM.
FM RADIO STATION

WVBO-FM 46626
Owner: Cumulus Media Inc.
Editorial: 491 S Washburn St, Ste 400, Oshkosh, Wisconsin 54904 **Tel:** 1 920 426-3239.
Email: wvbo@cumulus.com
Web site: http://www.1039wvbo.com
Profile: WVBO-FM is a commercial station owned by Cumulus Media Inc. The format of the station is oldies. WVBO-FM broadcasts to the Oshkosh, WI area at 103.9 FM.
FM RADIO STATION

WVBR-FM 40803
Owner: Cornell Media Guild
Editorial: 604 E Buffalo St, Ithaca, New York 14850-4297 **Tel:** 1 607 273-4000.
Email: contact@wvbr.com
Web site: http://www.wvbr.com
Profile: WVBR-FM is a commercial station owned by Cornell Media Guild. The format of the station is rock music. WVBR-FM broadcasts to the Ithaca, NY area at 93.5 FM.
FM RADIO STATION

WVBW-FM 40943
Owner: Max Media
Editorial: 5589 Greenwich Rd Ste 200, Virginia Beach, Virginia 23462-6565 **Tel:** 1 757 671-1000.
Web site: http://www.929thewave.com
Profile: WVBW-FM is a commercial station owned by Max Media. The format of the station is classic hits. WVBW-FM broadcasts to the Norfolk, VA area at 92.9 FM.
FM RADIO STATION

WVBX-FM 44198
Owner: Alpha Media
Editorial: 616 Amelia St, Fredericksburg, Virginia 22401-3887 **Tel:** 1 540 374-5500.
Web site: http://www.993thevibe.com
Profile: WVBX-FM is a commercial station owned by Alpha Media. The format of the station is rhythmic Top 40/CHR music. WVBX-FM broadcasts to the Fredericksburg, VA area at 99.3 FM.
FM RADIO STATION

WVBY-FM 41587
Owner: State of West Virginia
Editorial: 600 Capitol St, Charleston, West Virginia 25301-1223 **Tel:** 1 304 556-4900.
Email: feedback@wvpubcast.org
Web site: http://www.wvpubcast.org
Profile: WVBY-FM is a non-commercial station owned by the State of West Virginia. The format of the station is news and talk as well as classical music. WVBY-FM broadcasts to the Charleston, WV area at 88.5 FM.
FM RADIO STATION

WVBZ-FM 433330
Owner: iHeartMedia Inc.
Editorial: 2B Pai Park Fl 2, Greensboro, North Carolina 27409-9428 **Tel:** 1 336 822-2000.
Web site: http://www.1057now.com
Profile: WVBZ-FM is a commercial station owned by iHeartMedia Inc. The format of the station is Top 40/CHR WVBZ-FM broadcasts to the Greensboro, NC area at 105.7 FM.
FM RADIO STATION

WVCC-AM 39027
Owner: iHeartMedia Inc.
Editorial: 154 Boone Dr, Newnan, Georgia 30263-2801 **Tel:** 1 770 683-7234.
Web site: http://720thevoice.iheart.com
Profile: WVCC-AM is a commercial station owned by iHeartMedia Inc. The format of the station is news and talk. WVCC-AM broadcasts to the Newnan, GA area at 720 AM.
AM RADIO STATION

WVCD-AM 36965
Owner: Voorhees College
Tel: 1 803 780-1790.
Email: wvcd@voorhees.edu
Web site: http://teesajohnson.wix.com/wvcd790am
Profile: WVCD-AM is a commercial station owned by Voorhees College. The format of the station is urban contemporary, featuring classic R&B, jazz, oldies, and gospel. WVCD-AM broadcasts to the Denmark, SC area at 790 AM.
AM RADIO STATION

WVCH-AM 35727
Owner: WVCH Communications Inc.
Editorial: 308 E Dutton Mill Rd, Brookhaven, Pennsylvania 19015 **Tel:** 1 610 279-9000.
Web site: http://www.wvch.com
Profile: WVCH-AM is a commercial station owned by WVCH Communications Inc. The format of the station is religious programming and contemporary Christian. WVCH-AM broadcasts to the Brookhaven, PA area at 740 AM.
AM RADIO STATION

WVCO-FM 42365
Owner: CBM Broadcasting Corp.
Editorial: 429 Pine St, North Myrtle Beach, South Carolina 29582 **Tel:** 1 843 445-9491.
Email: surf949@yahoo.com
Web site: http://www.949thesurf.com
Profile: WVCO-FM is a commercial station owned by CBM Broadcasting Corp. The format of the station is classic hits. WVCO-FM broadcasts to the North Myrtle Beach, SC area at 94.9 FM.
FM RADIO STATION

WVCP-FM 42428
Owner: Volunteer State College
Editorial: 1480 Nashville Pike, Ramer Bldg #101, Gallatin, Tennessee 37066-3148 **Tel:** 1 615 230-3618.
Email: wvcp@volstate.edu
Web site: http://www.wvcp.net
Profile: WVCP-FM is a non-commercial station owned by Volunteer State College. The format of the station is oldies. WVCP-FM broadcasts to the Gallatin, TN area at 88.5 FM.
FM RADIO STATION

United States of America

WVCR-FM 40806
Owner: Siena College
Editorial: 515 Loudon Rd, Loudonville, New York 12211-1459 **Tel:** 1 518 782-6750.
Web site: http://www.wvcr.com
Profile: WVCR-FM is a non-commerical station owned by Siena College. The format of the station is adult hits. WVCR-FM broadcasts to the Albany, NY area at 88.3 FM.
FM RADIO STATION

WVCV-AM 38991
Owner: Piedmont Communications Inc.
Editorial: 207 Spicers Mill Rd, Orange, Virginia 22960 **Tel:** 1 540 825-3900.
Email: traffic@wjmafm.com
Profile: WVCV-AM is a commercial station owned by Piedmont Communications. The format of the station is adult standards music. WVCV-AM broadcasts in the Orange, VA area at 1340 AM.
AM RADIO STATION

WVCX-FM 40808
Owner: VCY America Inc.
Editorial: 3434 W Kilbourn Ave, Milwaukee, Wisconsin 53208-3313 **Tel:** 1 414 935-3000.
Email: wvcx@vcyamerica.org
Web site: http://www.vcyamerica.org
Profile: WVCX-FM is a non-commercial station owned by VCY America Inc. The format of the station is religous. WVCX-FM broadcasts to the Milwaukee area at 98.9 FM.
FM RADIO STATION

WVCY-AM 39349
Owner: VCY America Inc.
Editorial: 3434 W Kilbourn Ave, Milwaukee, Wisconsin 53208 **Tel:** 1 414 935-3000.
Email: wvcyam@vcyamerica.org
Web site: http://www.vcyamerica.org
Profile: WVCY-AM is a non-commercial station owned by VCY America Inc. The format of the station is gospel and religious talk. WVCY-AM broadcasts to Milwaukee, WI and surrounding communities at 690 AM.
AM RADIO STATION

WVCY-FM 46709
Owner: VCY America Inc.
Editorial: 3434 W Kilbourn Ave, Milwaukee, Wisconsin 53208-3313 **Tel:** 1 414 935-3000.
Email: wvcyfm@vcyamerica.org
Web site: http://www.vcyamerica.org
Profile: WVCY-FM is a non-commercial station owned by VCY America Inc. The format of the station is gospel music and religious talk. WVCY-FM broadcasts to Milwaukee and the surrounding communities at 107.7 FM.
FM RADIO STATION

WVEE-FM 45593
Owner: CBS Radio
Editorial: 1201 Peachtree St NE, 400 Colony Square, Atlanta, Georgia 30361-3503 **Tel:** 1 404 898-8900.
Web site: http://v103.cbslocal.com
Profile: WVEE-FM is a commercial station owned by CBS Radio. The format of the station is urban contemporary. WVEE-FM broadcasts to the Atlanta area at 103.3 FM.
FM RADIO STATION

WVEI-AM 36426
Owner: Entercom Communications Corp.
Editorial: 181 Moreland St, Worcester, Massachusetts 01609-1049 **Tel:** 1 508 752-5611.
Web site: http://www.weei.com
Profile: WVEI-AM is a commercial station owned by Entercom Communications Corp. The format of the station is sports. WVEI-AM broadcasts to the Worcester, MA area at 1440 AM.
AM RADIO STATION

WVEI-FM 45046
Owner: Entercom Communications Corp.
Editorial: 475 Kilvert St Ste 320, Warwick, Rhode Island 02886-1360 **Tel:** 1 401 244-7260.
Web site: http://www.weei.com
Profile: WVEI-FM is a commercial station owned by Entercom Communications Corp. The format of the station is sports. WVEI-FM broadcasts to the Brighton, MA area at 105.5 FM.
FM RADIO STATION

WVEK-FM 46883
Owner: Holston Valley Broadcasting Corp.
Editorial: 222 Commerce St, Kingsport, Tennessee 37660-4319 **Tel:** 1 423 246-9578.
Email: classichits1027@live.com
Web site: http://www.classichits1027.com
FM RADIO STATION

WVEL-AM 38737
Owner: Cumulus Media Inc.
Editorial: 120 Eaton St, Peoria, Illinois 61603-4217 **Tel:** 1 309 676-5000.
Web site: http://www.wvel.com
Profile: WVEL-AM is a commercial station owned by Cumulus Media Inc. The format of the station is Christian music. WVEL-AM broadcasts to the Peoria, IL area at AM 1140 AM.
AM RADIO STATION

WVES-FM 41708
Owner: Chincoteague Broadcasting Corp.
Editorial: 27214 Mutton Hunk Rd, Parksley, Virginia 23421-3238 **Tel:** 1 757 665-6500.
Email: hotcountry993@yahoo.com
Web site: http://sharecountry.net
Profile: WVES-FM is a commercial station owned by Chincoteague Broadcasting Corp. The format of the station is contemporary country music. WVES-FM broadcasts to the Parksley, VA area at 99.3 FM.
FM RADIO STATION

WVEZ-FM 43421
Owner: Summit Media Broadcasting LLC
Editorial: 612 S 4th St, Louisville, Kentucky 40202-2460 **Tel:** 1 502 589-4800.
Web site: http://www.1069play.com/
Profile: WVEZ-FM is a commercial station owned by Summit Media Broadcasting LLC. The format of the station is adult contemporary. WVEZ-FM broadcasts to the Louisville, KY area at 106.9 FM.
FM RADIO STATION

WVFB-FM 42368
Owner: Whittimore Enterprises
Editorial: 341 Radio Station Rd, Tompkinsville, Kentucky 42167-8572 **Tel:** 1 270 487-6119.
Email: kixcountry@windstream.net
FM RADIO STATION

WVFJ-FM 44370
Owner: Radio Training Network
Editorial: 1175 Senoia Rd, Ste E, Tyrone, Georgia 30290-3608 **Tel:** 1 770 487-4500.
Email: info@wvfj.com
Web site: http://georgia.thejoyfm.com
Profile: WVFJ-FM is a non-commercial station owned by Radio Training Network. The format of the station is adult contemporary Christian music programming. WVFJ-FM broadcasts to the Greater Atlanta, GA area at 93.3 FM.
FM RADIO STATION

WVFM-FM 45475
Owner: Midwest Communications Inc.
Editorial: 4200 W Main St, Kalamazoo, Michigan 49006-2749 **Tel:** 1 269 345-7121.
Email: wkzonews@wkzo.com
Web site: http://www.myfm1065.com
Profile: WVFM-FM is a commercial station owned by Midwest Communications Inc. The format of the station is adult contemporary music. WVFM-FM broadcasts to the Kalamazoo, MI area at 106.5 FM.
FM RADIO STATION

WVFN-AM 36703
Owner: Townsquare Media, LLC
Editorial: 3420 Pinetree Rd, Lansing, Michigan 48911-4207 **Tel:** 1 517 394-7272.
Web site: http://www.thegame730am.com
Profile: WVFN-AM is a commercial station owned by Townsquare Media, LLC. The format of the station is sports programming. WVFN-AM broadcasts to the Lansing, MI area at 730 AM.
AM RADIO STATION

WVGA-FM 44447
Owner: Black Crow Broadcasting Inc.
Editorial: 1711 Ellis Dr, Valdosta, Georgia 31601-3573 **Tel:** 1 229 244-8642.
Web site: http://valdostatoday.com/wvga/
Profile: WVGA-FM is a commercial station owned by Black Crow Broadcasting Inc. The format of the station is news, talk and sports. WVGA-FM broadcasts to the Valdosta, GA area at 105.9 FM.
FM RADIO STATION

WVGB-AM 35728
Owner: Vivian Broadcasting
Editorial: 2121 Boundary St Ste 202, Beaufort, South Carolina 29902-6812 **Tel:** 1 843 466-1122.
Web site: http://945thecoast.com
Profile: WVGB-AM is a commercial station owned by Vivian Broadcasting. The format of the station is gospel. WVGB-AM broadcasts to the Beaufort, SC area at 1490 AM.
AM RADIO STATION

WVGG-AM 39234
Owner: JDL Corporation
Editorial: 3276 Highway 198 W, Lucedale, Mississippi 39452-7914 **Tel:** 1 601 947-8151.
Email: wrbe@wrberadio.com
Web site: http://www.wrberadio.com
Profile: WVGG-AM is a commercial station owned by JDL Corporation. The format of the station is country. WVGG-AM broadcasts to the Lucedale, MS area at 1440 AM.
AM RADIO STATION

WVGM-AM 38360
Owner: 3 Daughters Media, Inc.
Editorial: 1035 Avalon Dr, Forest, Virginia 24551-2970 **Tel:** 1 434 534-6100.
Email: wblt@inbox.com
Web site: http://www.espninva.com
Profile: WVGM-AM is a commercial station owned by 3 Daughters Media, Inc. The format of the station is sports. WVGM-AM broadcasts to the Roanoke, VA area at 1320 AM and is simulcast of WGMN-AM.
AM RADIO STATION

WVHC-FM 42369
Owner: Herkimer County Community College
Editorial: 100 Reservoir Road Technology Ctr, Herkimer, New York 13350-1545 **Tel:** 1 315 866-0300.
Email: wvhc@herkimer.edu
Web site: http://www.herkimer.edu/experience/wvhc-radio
Profile: WVHC-FM is a non-commercial station owned by Herkimer County Community College. The format of the station is jazz. WVHC-FM broadcasts to the Herkimer, NY area at 91.5 FM.
FM RADIO STATION

WVHF-AM 36372
Owner: Holy Family Radio
Editorial: 2504 Ardmore St SE, Grand Rapids, Michigan 49506-4901 **Tel:** 1 616 956-1140.
Email: contact@holyfamilyradio.net
Web site: http://www.holyfamilyradio.net
Profile: WVHF-AM is a non-commercial radio station owned by Amicus Management. The format of the station is religious. WVHF-AM broadcasts to the Grand Rapids, MI and surrounding communities at 1140 AM.
AM RADIO STATION

WVHI-AM 35729
Owner: Word Broadcasting Network, Inc.
Editorial: 2207 E Morgan Ave Ste J, Evansville, Indiana 47711-4355 **Tel:** 1 812 475-9930.
Web site: http://www.wvhi.com
Profile: WVHI-AM is a commercial station owned by Word Broadcasting Network, Inc. The format of the station is religious teaching. WVHI-AM broadcasts in the Evansville, IN area at 1330 AM.
AM RADIO STATION

WVHL-FM 43545
Owner: Farmville Herald Inc.(The)
Editorial: 116 North St, Farmville, Virginia 23901 **Tel:** 1 434 392-9393.
Email: v93@wvhl.net
Web site: http://www.wvhl.net
Profile: WVHL-FM is a commercial station owned by The Farmville Herald Inc. The format of the station is contemporary country. WVHL-FM broadcasts to the Farmville, VA area at 92.9 FM.
FM RADIO STATION

WVHM-FM 42367
Owner: Heartland Ministries, Inc.
Editorial: 219 College St, Hardin, Kentucky 42048 **Tel:** 1 270 437-4095.
Email: studio@wvhm.org
Web site: http://www.wvhm.org
Profile: WVHM-FM provides Southern Gospel Music and local and nationally-syndicated programming in the western Kentucky, southernmost Illinois, and northwest Tennessee regions. The station broadcasts on a translator at 89.1 FM in Madisonville, Kentucky and at 103.5 FM in Central City, Kentucky. Send all PSA to the main email address.
FM RADIO STATION

WVHT-FM 45088
Owner: Max Media
Editorial: 5589 Greenwich Rd, Ste 200, Virginia Beach, Virginia 23462 **Tel:** 1 757 671-1000.
Web site: http://www.hot1005.com
Profile: WVHT-FM is a commercial station owned by Max Media. The format of the station is top 40/CHR. WVHT-FM broadcasts to the Virginia Beach, VA area at 100.5 FM.
FM RADIO STATION

WVHU-AM 72194
Owner: iHeartMedia Inc.
Editorial: 134 4th Ave, Huntington, West Virginia 25701-1220 **Tel:** 1 304 525-7788.
Web site: http://www.800wvhu.com
Profile: WVHU-AM is a commercial station owned by iHeartMedia Inc. The format for the station is news and talk. WVHU-AM broadcasts to the Charleston-Huntington, WV area at 800 AM.
AM RADIO STATION

WVIB-FM 45947
Owner: Cumulus Media Inc
Editorial: 3375 Merriam St, Ste 201, Muskegon, Michigan 49444 **Tel:** 1 231 830-0176.
Web site: http://www.v100fm.com
Profile: WVIB-FM is a commercial station owned by Cumulus Media Inc. The format of the station is urban adult contemporary. WVIB-FM broadcasts to the Muskegon, MI area at 100.1 FM.
FM RADIO STATION

WVIK-FM 40813
Owner: Augustana College
Editorial: 639 38th St, Rock Island, Illinois 61201-2210 **Tel:** 1 309 794-7500.
Email: news@wvik.org
Web site: http://www.wvik.org
Profile: WVIK-FM is a non-commercial station owned by Augustana College. The format of the station is news and classical. WVIK-FM broadcasts to the Rock Island, IL area at 90.3 FM.
FM RADIO STATION

WVIL-FM 44044
Owner: LB Sports Productions LLC
Editorial: 108 E Main St, Beardstown, Illinois 62618-1241 **Tel:** 1 217 3231790.
Web site: http://www.wvilfm.com
Profile: WVIL-FM is a commercial station owned by LB Sports Productions LLC. The format of the station is sports. WVIL-FM broadcasts in the Jacksonville, IL at 101.3 FM.
FM RADIO STATION

WVIN-FM 45596
Owner: Richard Foreman
Editorial: E Washington St Ext, Bath, New York 14810-9801 **Tel:** 1 607 776-3326.
Web site: http://wvinbath.com
Profile: WVIN-FM is a commercial station owned by Richard Foreman. The format of the station is Hot AC. WVIN-FM broadcasts to the Bath, NY area at 98.3 FM.
FM RADIO STATION

WVIP-FM 45768
Owner: Whitney Radio Broadcasting Inc.
Editorial: 411 5th Ave, New Rochelle, New York 10801-2047 **Tel:** 1 914 636-1460.
Email: bob@wvox.com
Web site: http://www.wvipfm.com
Profile: WVIP-FM is a commercial station owned by Whitney Radio Broadcasting Inc. The format of the station is variety. WVIP-FM broadcasts to the New Rochelle, NY area at 93.5 FM.
FM RADIO STATION

WVIV-FM 4083
Owner: Univision Communications Inc.
Editorial: 625 N Michigan Ave Ste 300, Chicago, Illinois 60611-3110 **Tel:** 1 312 981-1800.
Web site: http://maximamusica.univision.com
Profile: WVIV-FM is a commercial station owned by Univision Communications Inc. The format of the station is Hurban featuring Spanish urban contemporary music. WVIV-FM broadcasts to the Chicago area at 103.1 FM.
FM RADIO STATION

WVIX-FM 40937
Owner: Univision Communications Inc.
Editorial: 625 N Michigan Ave Ste 300, Chicago, Illinois 60611-3110 **Tel:** 1 312 981-1800.
Web site: http://maximamusica.univision.com
Profile: WVIX-FM is a commercial station owned by Univision Communications. The format of the station is Hurban featuring Spanish urban contemporary. WVIX-FM broadcasts to the Chicago area at 93.5 FM
FM RADIO STATION

WVJC-FM 40815
Owner: Illinois Eastern Community Colleges
Editorial: 2200 College Dr, Mount Carmel, Illinois 62863-2657 **Tel:** 1 618 262-8641.
Web site: http://myweb.iecc.edu/wvjc
FM RADIO STATION

WVJS-AM 38254
Owner: Cromwell Group Inc.(The)
Editorial: 1115 Tamarack Rd Ste 500, Owensboro, Kentucky 42301-6988 **Tel:** 1 270 683-5200.
Email: kyproduction@cromwellradio.com
Web site: http://www.owensbororadio.com/wvjs/index.html
Profile: WVJS-AM is a commercial station owned by The Cromwell Group Inc. The format of the station is classic hits. WVJS-AM broadcasts to the Evansville, IN area at 1420 AM.
AM RADIO STATION

WVKB-FM 45422
Owner: Commonwealth Broadcasting Corp.
Editorial: 611 W Poplar St Ste C2, Elizabethtown, Kentucky 42701-2483 **Tel:** 1 270 763-0800.
Email: news@commonwealthbroadcasting.com
Web site: http://www.titansradio.com
Profile: WVKB-FM is a commercial station owned by Commonwealth Broadcasting Corp. The format of the station is sports. WVKB-FM broadcasts to the Elizabethtown, KY area at 101.5 FM.
FM RADIO STATION

WVKC-FM 40816
Owner: Knox College
Tel: 1 309 298-1873.
Email: publicradio@wiu.edu
Web site: http://www.tristatesradio.com
Profile: WVKC-FM is a non-commercial station owned by Knox College and managed by Western Illinois University. The format of the station is news, talk and music. WVKC-FM broadcasts to the Galesburg, IL area at 90.7 FM.
FM RADIO STATION

WVKF-FM 41958
Owner: iheartMedia Inc.
Editorial: 1015 Main St, Wheeling, West Virginia 26003-2709 **Tel:** 1 304 232-1170.
Web site: http://kisswheeling.iheart.com
Profile: WVKF-FM is a commercial station owned by iheartMedia Inc. The format of the station is Top 40/CHR. WVKF-FM broadcasts to the Wheeling, WV area at 95.7 FM.
FM RADIO STATION

WVKL-FM 45352
Owner: Entercom Communications Corp.
Editorial: 236 Clearfield Ave Ste 206, Virginia Beach, Virginia 23462-1893 **Tel:** 1 757 497-2000.
Web site: http://www.957rnb.com
Profile: WVKL-FM is a commercial station owned by Entercom Communications Corp. The format of the station is urban adult contemporary and R&B music. WVKL-FM broadcasts to the Virginia Beach, VA area at 95.7 FM.
FM RADIO STATION

WVKO-AM 38255
Owner: Bernard Ohio LLC
Editorial: 3360 E Livingston Ave Ste 2A, Columbus, Ohio 43227-1961 **Tel:** 1 614 824-2550.
Email: info@1580thepraise.com
Web site: http://1580thepraise.com
Profile: WVKO-AM is a commercial station owned by Bernard Ohio LLC. The format of the station is Black Gospel. WVKO-AM broadcasts to the Columbus, OH, area at 1580 AM.
AM RADIO STATION

WVKR-FM
40817
Owner: Vassar College
Editorial: 124 Raymond Ave #726, Poughkeepsie, New York 12604-0001 **Tel:** 1 845 437-5475.
Email: newsdirector@wvkr.org
Web site: http://www.wvkr.org
Profile: WVKR-FM is a non-commercial station owned by Vassar College. The format of the station is college variety. WVKR-FM broadcasts to the Poughkeepsie, NY area at 91.3 FM.
FM RADIO STATION

WVKS-FM
40514
Owner: iHeartMedia Inc.
Editorial: 125 S Superior St, Toledo, Ohio 43604-8747 **Tel:** 1 419 244-8321.
Web site: http://www.925kissfm.com
Profile: WVKS-FM is a commercial station owned by iHeartMedia Inc. The format of the station is Top 40/ CHR music. WVKS-FM broadcasts to the Toledo, OH area at 92.5 FM.
FM RADIO STATION

WVKX-FM
43977
Owner: Wilkins Communications Network Inc.
Editorial: 104 High Hill St, Irwinton, Georgia 31042 **Tel:** 1 478 946-3445.
Profile: WVKX-FM is a commercial station owned by Wilkins Communications Network Inc. The format of the station is urban contemporary music. WVKX-FM broadcasts to the Irwinton, GA area at 103.7 FM.
FM RADIO STATION

WVLC-FM
44098
Owner: Shoreline Communications Inc.
Editorial: 101 E Main St, Campbellsville, Kentucky 42718-2237 **Tel:** 1 270 789-0099.
Email: bigdawg@wvlc.com
Web site: http://www.wvlc.com
Profile: WVLC-FM is a commercial station owned by Shoreline Communications Inc. The format of the station is country. WVLC-FM broadcasts to the Campbellsville, KY area at 99.9 FM.
FM RADIO STATION

WVLD-AM
39280
Owner: Black Crow Broadcasting Inc.
Editorial: 1711 Ellis Dr, Valdosta, Georgia 31601-3573 **Tel:** 1 229 242-4821.
Web site: http://rock1069.com/
Profile: WVLD-AM is a commercial station owned by Black Crow Broadcasting Inc. The format of the station is sports. WVLD-AM broadcasts to the Valdosta, GA area at 1450 AM.
AM RADIO STATION

WVLE-FM
45597
Owner: Skytower Communications Inc.
Editorial: 104 1/2 W Public Sq, Scottsville, Kentucky 42164-1175 **Tel:** 1 270 237-3148.
Email: newswatch@wvle.net
Web site: http://wvle.net
Profile: WVLE-FM is a commercial station owned by Skytower Communications Inc. The format of the station is adult contemporary. WVLE-FM broadcasts to the Nashville, TN area at 99.3 FM.
FM RADIO STATION

WVLF-FM
41293
Owner: Stephens Media Group Massena, LLC
Editorial: 2155 State Highway 420, Massena, New York 13662 **Tel:** 1 315 769-3333.
Email: mikeg@mymix961.com
Web site: http://www.mymix961.com
Profile: WVLF-FM is a commercial station owned by Stephens Media Group Massena, LLC. The format of the station is adult contemporary. WVLF-FM broadcasts to the Massena, NY area at 96.1 FM.
FM RADIO STATION

WVLG-AM
35373
Owner: Senior Broadcasting Corp.
Editorial: 1161 Main St, The Villages, Florida 32159-7721 **Tel:** 1 352 753-1119.
Email: wvlgradio@thevillagesmedia.com
Web site: http://www.thevillagesdailysun.com
Profile: WVLG-AM is a commercial station owned by Senior Broadcasting Corp. The format of the station is adult hits. WVLG-AM broadcasts to The Villages, FL area at 640 AM.
AM RADIO STATION

WVLI-FM
43742
Owner: Milner Broadcasting Enterprises, LLC
Editorial: 292 N Convent St, Bourbonnais, Illinois 60914-2014 **Tel:** 1 815 933-9287.
Web site: http://www.rivervalleyradio.net
Profile: WVLI-FM is a commercial station owned by Newsweb Corp. The format of the station is Top 40/ CHR. WVLI-FM broadcasts to the Kankakee, IL area at 92.7 FM.
FM RADIO STATION

WVLK-AM
38256
Owner: Cumulus Media Inc.
Editorial: 300 W Vine St Ste 3, Lexington, Kentucky 40507-1806 **Tel:** 1 859 253-5900.
Email: news@wvlkam.com
Web site: http://www.wvlkam.com
Profile: WVLK-AM is a commercial station owned by Cumulus Media Inc. The format of the station is news, sports and talk. WVLK-AM broadcasts to the Lexington, KY area at 590 AM.
AM RADIO STATION

WVLK-FM
43466
Owner: Cumulus Media Inc.
Editorial: 300 W Vine St Ste 3, Lexington, Kentucky 40507-1806 **Tel:** 1 859 253-5900.
Web site: http://www.1015nashicon.com
Profile: WVLK-FM is a commercial station owned by Cumulus Media Inc. The format of the station is country. WVLK-FM broadcasts to the Lexington, KY area at 101.5 FM.
FM RADIO STATION

WVLN-AM
38257
Owner: Forcht Broadcasting
Editorial: 4667 E Radio Tower Ln, Olney, Illinois 62450-4742 **Tel:** 1 618 393-2156.
Web site: http://www.wvlnam.com
Profile: WVLN-AM is a commercial station owned by Forcht Broadcasting. The format of the station is sports. WVLN-AM broadcasts to the Olney, IL area at 740 AM.
AM RADIO STATION

WVLS-FM
44010
Owner: Pocahontas Communications Cooperative Corp.
Editorial: 80 Main St, Monterey, Virginia 24465 **Tel:** 1 540 468-1234.
Web site: http://www.alleghenymountainradio.org
Profile: WVLS-FM is a non-commercial community station owned by Pocahontas Communications Cooperative Corp. The format of the station is variety. WVLS-FM broadcasts to the Monterey, VA area at a frequency of 89.7 FM.
FM RADIO STATION

WVLT-FM
45860
Owner: Clear Communications Inc.
Editorial: 632 Maurice River Pkwy, Vineland, New Jersey 08360-2629 **Tel:** 1 856 692-8888.
Web site: http://www.wvlt.com
Profile: WVLT-FM is a commercial station owned by Clear Communications Inc. The format of the station is oldies. WVLT-FM broadcasts to the Vineland, NJ area at 92.1 FM.
FM RADIO STATION

WVLY-AM
36096
Owner: Monroe Communications
Editorial: 1143 Main St, Wheeling, West Virginia 26003-2743 **Tel:** 1 304 233-9859.
Web site: http://www.talkradio1370.com
Profile: WVLY-AM is a commercial station owned by Monroe Communications. The format of the station is talk. WVLY-AM broadcasts to the Wheeling, WV area at 1370 AM.
AM RADIO STATION

WVLY-FM
45418
Owner: Sunbury Broadcasting Corp.
Editorial: 1227 County Line Rd, Selinsgrove, Pennsylvania 17870-8188 **Tel:** 1 570 286-5838.
Web site: http://www.wkok.com/The_Valley/index.html
Profile: WVLY-FM is a commercial station owned by Sunbury Broadcasting Corp. The format of the station is adult contemporary. WVLY-FM broadcasts to the Scranton, PA area at 100.9 FM.
FM RADIO STATION

WVLZ-AM
35834
Owner: Kirkland Wireless Broadcasters Inc.
Editorial: 9040 Executive Park Dr Ste 303, Knoxville, Tennessee 37923-4639 **Tel:** 1 865 243-2877.
Web site: http://www.tnsportsradio.com
Profile: WVLZ-AM is a commercial station owned by Kirkland Wireless Broadcasters Inc. and co-owned by Action Sports Media. The format of the station is sports. WVLZ-AM broadcasts to the Knoxville, TN area at 1180 AM.
AM RADIO STATION

WVMD-FM
40960
Owner: West Virginia Radio Corporation of the Alleghenies
Editorial: 15 Industrial Blvd E, Cumberland, Maryland 21502-4106 **Tel:** 1 301 759-1005.
Web site: http://www.tristateswolf.com
Profile: WVMD-FM is a commercial station owned by West Virginia Radio Corporation of the Allegheneis. The format of the station is contemporary country. WVMD-FM broadcasts to the Romney, WV/ Cumberland, MD area at 100.1 FM.
FM RADIO STATION

WVMJ-FM
44486
Owner: Mt. Washington Radio & Gramophone LLC
Editorial: Settler's Green OVP Route 16, #A30, North Conway, New Hampshire 3860 **Tel:** 1 603 356-8870.
Email: office@conwaymagic.com
Web site: http://www.conwaymagic.com
Profile: WVMJ-FM is a commercial station owned by Mt. Washington Radio & Gramophone LLC. The format of the station is hot adult contemporary. WVMJ-FM broadcasts to the North Conway, NH area at 104.5 FM.
FM RADIO STATION

WVMM-FM
42589
Owner: Messiah College
Editorial: 1 College Ave, Messiah College, Mechanicsburg, Pennsylvania 17055-6805 **Tel:** 1 717 691-6081.
Email: pulsefmmusicmanager@gmail.com
Web site: http://pulse.messiah.edu/wvmm
Profile: WVMM-FM is a non-commercial station owned by Messiah College. The format of the station is contemporary Christian. WVMM-FM broadcasts to Grantham, PA at 90.7 FM.
FM RADIO STATION

WVMP-FM
43917
Owner: City works Community Broadcasting
Editorial: 611 S Jefferson St, Roanoke, Virginia 24011-2419 **Tel:** 1 540 344-2800.
Email: wvmp@1015tvmp.com
Web site: http://www.1015tvmp.com
Profile: WVMP-FM is a commercial station owned by City works Community Broadcasting. The format of the station is AAA-Adult album alternative. The station also works with local cultural and social organizations in order to elevate interest in those areas. WVMP-FM broadcasts to the Vinton, VA area 101.5 FM.
FM RADIO STATION

WVMR-AM
35919
Owner: Pocahontas Communications Cooperative Corp.
Editorial: State Route 28, Dunmore, West Virginia 24934 **Tel:** 1 304 799-6004.
Email: amr@frontiernet.net
Web site: http://www.alleghenymountainradio.org
Profile: WVMR-AM is a non-commercial station owned by the Pocahontas Communications Cooperative Corp. The format of the station is country music and variety. WVMR-AM broadcasts to Pocahontas County, WV at 1370 AM.
AM RADIO STATION

WVMS-FM
44266
Owner: Moody Bible Institute
Editorial: 9756 Barr Rd, Cleveland, Ohio 44141-2806 **Tel:** 1 440 526-1111.
Email: wcrf@moody.edu
Web site: http://www.moodyradiocleveland.fm/
Profile: WVMS-FM is a non-commercial station owned by the Moody Bible Institute. The format of the station is religious. WVMS-FM broadcasts to the Cleveland area at 103.3 FM.
FM RADIO STATION

WVMT-AM
38741
Owner: Sison Broadcasting Inc.
Editorial: 118 Malletts Bay Ave, Colchester, Vermont 5446 **Tel:** 1 802 655-1620.
Email: talk@newstalk620wvmt.com
Web site: http://www.newstalk620wvmt.com
Profile: WVMT-AM is a commercial station owned by Sison Broadcasting Inc. The format of the station is news, sports and talk. WVMT-AM broadcasts to the Colchester, VT area at 620 AM.
AM RADIO STATION

WVMX-FM
42833
Owner: Saga Communications
Editorial: 4401 Carriage Hill Ln, Columbus, Ohio 43220-3837 **Tel:** 1 614 451-2191.
Web site: http://www.mymix1079.com
Profile: WVMX-FM is a commercial station owned by Saga Communications. The format of the station is hot adult contemporary. WVMX-FM broadcasts to the Columbus, OH, area at 107.9 FM.
FM RADIO STATION

WVNA-AM
38259
Owner: URBan Radio Broadcasting, LLC
Editorial: 509 N Main St, Tuscumbia, Alabama 35674-2048 **Tel:** 1 256 383-2525.
Email: info@urbanradio.fm
Web site: http://www.newstalkwvna.com
Profile: WVNA-AM is a commercial station owned by URBan Radio Broadcasting, LLC. The format for the station is news and talk. WVNA-AM broadcasts to the Huntsville, AL area at 1590 AM.
AM RADIO STATION

WVNA-FM
45601
Owner: URBan Radio Broadcasting, LLC
Editorial: 509 N Main St, Tuscumbia, Alabama 35674-2048 **Tel:** 1 256 383-2525.
Email: info@urbanradio.fm
Web site: http://www.bigdog1055.com
Profile: WVNA-FM is a commercial station owned by URBan Radio Broadcasting, LLC. The format of the station is rock. WVNA-FM broadcasts to the Tuscumbia, AL area at 105.5 FM.
FM RADIO STATION

WVNE-AM
36091
Owner: Blount Communications Group
Editorial: 70 James St Ste 201, Worcester, Massachusetts 01603-1045 **Tel:** 1 508 831-9863.
Email: info@wvne.net
Web site: http://lifechangingradio.com/wvne
Profile: WVNE-AM is a commercial station owned by Blount Communications Group. The format of the station is Christian programming. WVNE-AM broadcasts to the Worcester, MA area at 760 AM.
AM RADIO STATION

WVNH-FM
44442
Owner: New Hampshire Gospel Radio Inc.
Editorial: 37 Redington Road, Concord, New Hampshire 3301 **Tel:** 1 603 227-0911.
Email: info@nhgr.org
Web site: http://www.nhgr.org
Profile: WVNH-FM is a non-commercial station owned by New Hampshire Gospel Radio Inc. The format of the station is Christian music and talk. WVNH-FM broadcasts to the Concord, NH area at 91.1 FM.
FM RADIO STATION

WVNI-FM
43546
Owner: Mid-America Radio Group
Editorial: 4317 E 3rd St, Bloomington, Indiana 47401-5551 **Tel:** 1 812 335-9500.
Email: spirit95@spirit95fm.com
Web site: http://www.spirit95fm.com
Profile: WVNI-FM is a commercial station owned by Mid-America Radio Group. The format for the station is contemporary Christian. WVNI-FM broadcasts to the Bloomington, IN area at 95.1 FM.
FM RADIO STATION

WVNJ-AM
36033
Owner: Universal Broadcasting
Editorial: 1086 Teaneck Rd, Ste 4F, Teaneck, New Jersey 7666 **Tel:** 1 201 837-0400.
Email: wvnj1160am@aol.com
Web site: http://www.wvnj.com
Profile: WVNJ-AM is a commercial station owned by Universal Broadcasting. The format of the station is talk. WVNJ-AM broadcasts to the Teaneck, NJ area at 1160 AM. The station does not accept news items as all their news is syndicated.
AM RADIO STATION

WVNL-FM
128724
Owner: Illinois Bible Institute
Editorial: 17280 Lakeside Dr, Carlinville, Illinois 62626-2539 **Tel:** 1 217 359-8232.
Email: wbgl@wbgl.org
Web site: http://www.wbgl.org
Profile: WVNL-FM is a non-commercial station owned by Illinois Bible Institute. The format of the station is contemporary Christian music. WVNL-FM broadcasts to the Vandalia, IL area at 91.7 FM.
FM RADIO STATION

WVNN-AM
39073
Owner: Cumulus Media Inc.
Editorial: 1717 US Highway 72 E, Athens, Alabama 35611-4413 **Tel:** 1 256 830-8300.
Web site: http://www.wvnn.com
Profile: WVNN-FM is a commercial station owned by Cumulus Media Inc. The format of the station is news and talk. WVNN-FM broadcasts to the Huntsville, AL area at 770 AM.
AM RADIO STATION

WVNN-FM
42016
Owner: Cumulus Media Inc.
Editorial: 1717 US Highway 72 E, Athens, Alabama 35611-4413 **Tel:** 1 256 830-8300.
Web site: http://www.wvnn.com
Profile: WVNN-FM is a commercial station owned by Cumulus Media Inc. The format for the station is news and talk simulcasted from WVNN-AM. WVNN-FM broadcasts to the Huntsville, AL area at 92.5 FM.
FM RADIO STATION

WVNO-FM
40821
Owner: Johnny Appleseed Broadcasting Co. Inc.
Editorial: 2900 Park Ave W, Mansfield, Ohio 44906 **Tel:** 1 419 529-5900.
Email: comments@wvno.com
Web site: http://www.wvno.com
Profile: WVNO-FM is a commercial station owned by Johnny Appleseed Broadcasting Co. Inc. The format of the station is adult contemporary music. WVNO-FM broadcasts to the Mansfield, OH area at 106.1 FM.
FM RADIO STATION

WVNR-AM
38599
Owner: Pine Tree Broadcasting Company
Editorial: 1214 Vermont Route 30 S, Poultney, Vermont 5764 **Tel:** 1 802 287-9031.
Email: wvnrwnyv@gmail.com
Profile: WVNR-AM is a commercial station owned by Pine Tree Broadcasting Company. The format of the station is country, oldies and adult contemporary music. WVNR-AM broadcasts to the Poultney, VT area at 1340 AM.
AM RADIO STATION

WVNT-AM
38575
Owner: Burbach of WV, LLC
Editorial: 5 Rosemar Cir, Parkersburg, West Virginia 26104-1203 **Tel:** 1 304 485-4565.
Web site: http://www.wvnt.net
Profile: WVNT-AM is a radio station owned by Burbach of WV, LLC. The format of the station is news and sports. WVNT-AM broadcasts to the Parkersburg, WV area at 1230 AM.
AM RADIO STATION

WVNU-FM
42235
Owner: Southern Ohio Broadcasting Inc.
Editorial: 321 Jefferson St, Greenfield, Ohio 45123 **Tel:** 1 937 981-5050.
Email: news@wvnu.com
Web site: http://www.wvnu.com
Profile: WVNU-FM is a commercial station owned by Southern Ohio Broadcasting Inc. The format of the station is adult contemporary music. WVNU-FM broadcasts to the Greenfield, OH area at 97.5 FM.
FM RADIO STATION

WVNV-FM
46334
Owner: Martz Communications
Editorial: 86 Porter Rd, Malone, New York 12953-3701 **Tel:** 1 518 483-1100.
Email: news@country965.com
Web site: http://www.country965.com
Profile: WVNV-FM is a commercial station owned by Martz Communications. The format of the station is contemporary country music. WVNV-FM broadcasts to the Malone, NY area at 96.5 FM.
FM RADIO STATION

Section 3 World Broadcast

WVNW-FM
42370

Owner: WVNW Inc.
Editorial: 114 N Logan Blvd, Burnham, Pennsylvania 17009-1810 **Tel:** 1 717 242-1493.
Email: wvnw@star967.com
Web site: http://www.star967.com
Profile: WVNW-FM is a commercial station owned by WVNW Inc. The format of the station is contemporary country. WVNW-FM broadcasts to the Burnham, PA area at 96.7 FM.
FM RADIO STATION

WVNZ-AM
36500

Owner: TBLC Media, LLC
Editorial: 308 W Broad St, Richmond, Virginia 23220-4240 **Tel:** 1 804 565-1320.
Email: wvnz@davidsonmediagroup.com
Profile: WVNZ-AM is a commercial station owned by TBLC Media, LLC. The format of the station is Spanish Hits. WVNZ-AM broadcasts to the Richmond, VA area at 1320 AM.
AM RADIO STATION

WVOB-FM
40955

Owner: Bethany Bible College
Editorial: 2573 Hodgesville Rd, Dothan, Alabama 36301-6623 **Tel:** 1 334 671-9862.
Email: wvob913fm@bethanybc.edu
Web site: http://www.gospel91.com
Profile: WVOB-FM is a non-commercial station owned by Bethany Bible College. The format of the station is Southern gospel music. WVOB-FM broadcasts to the Dothan, AL area at 91.3 FM.
FM RADIO STATION

WVOC-AM
36300

Owner: iHeartMedia Inc.
Editorial: 316 Greystone Blvd, Columbia, South Carolina 29210-8007 **Tel:** 1 803 343-1100.
Web site: http://www.wvoc.com/main.html
Profile: WVOC-AM is a commercial station owned by iHeartMedia Inc. The format of the station is news/talk/sports. WVOC-AM broadcasts to the Columbia, SC area at 560 AM.
AM RADIO STATION

WVOC-FM
40715

Owner: iHeartMedia Inc.
Editorial: 316 Greystone Blvd, Columbia, South Carolina 29210-8007 **Tel:** 1 803 343-1100.
Web site: http://www.thebeatcolumbia.com/main.html
Profile: WVOC-FM is a commercial station owned by iHeartMedia Inc. The format of the station is Urban Contemporary. WVOC-FM broadcasts to the Columbia, SC area at 100.1 FM.
FM RADIO STATION

WVOD-FM
41588

Owner: CapSan Media, LLC
Editorial: 637 Harbor Rd, Wanchese, North Carolina 27981 **Tel:** 1 252 475-1888.
Web site: http://www.991thesound.com
Profile: WVOD-FM is a commercial station owned by CapSan Media, LLC. The format of the station is adult album alternative. WVOD-FM broadcasts to the Wanchese, NC area at 99.1 FM.
FM RADIO STATION

WVOE-AM
35732

Owner: Ebony Enterprises Inc.
Editorial: 1528 Old 74 Highway West, Chadbourn, North Carolina 28431 **Tel:** 1 910 654-5621.
Profile: WVOE-AM is a commercial station owned by Ebony Enterprises Inc. The format of the station is gospel, jazz and R&B oldies. WVOE-AM broadcasts to the Chadbourn, NC area at 1590 AM.
AM RADIO STATION

WVOG-AM
35733

Owner: Robbert Broadcasting Co.(F.W.)
Editorial: 2730 Loumor Ave, Metairie, Louisiana 70001-5425 **Tel:** 1 504 831-6941.
Email: wvog@bellsouth.net
Web site: http://www.wwcr.com/wvog.html
Profile: WVOG-AM is a commercial station owned by F.W. Robbert Broadcasting Co. The format of the station is religious talk. WVOG-AM broadcasts to the Metairie, LA area at 600 AM.
AM RADIO STATION

WVOH-FM
45602

Owner: Broadcast South, LLC
Editorial: 546 Baxley Hwy, Hazlehurst, Georgia 31539-5917 **Tel:** 1 912 375-4511.
Web site: http://www.935theeagle.fm/
Profile: WVOH-FM is a commercial station owned by Broadcast South, LLC. The format of the station is classic hits. WVOH-FM broadcasts to the Savannah, GA area at 93.5 FM.
FM RADIO STATION

WVOI-AM
36249

Owner: Almodovar Media Corporation
Editorial: 5043 Tamiami Trl E, Naples, Florida 34113-4127 **Tel:** 1 239 558-3058.
Email: info@ardienteradio.com
Web site: http://ardienteradio.com
Profile: WVOI-AM is a commercial station owned by Almodovar Media Corporation. The format of the station is Spanish Tropical and Hispanic Urban. WVOI-AM broadcasts to the Naples, FL area at 1480 AM.
AM RADIO STATION

WVOJ-AM
231562

Owner: Norsan Broadcasting System
Tel: 1 904 549-2218.
Web site: http://larazalaraza.com
Profile: WVOJ-AM is a commercial station owned by Norsan Broadcasting System. The format of the station is regional Mexican. WVOJ-AM broadcasts to the Jacksonville, FL area at 1570 AM. WJOJ-AM is a simulcast of WNNR-AM.
AM RADIO STATION

WVOK-AM
39129

Owner: Woodard Broadcasting Co.
Editorial: 1215 Church St, Oxford, Alabama 36203-1639 **Tel:** 1 256 835-1580.
Profile: WVOK-AM is a commercial station owned by Woodard Broadcasting Co. The format of the station is oldies. WOXR-AM broadcasts to the Oxford, AL area at 1580 AM.
AM RADIO STATION

WVOK-FM
46474

Owner: Woodard Broadcasting Co.
Editorial: 1215 Church St, Oxford, Alabama 36203-1639 **Tel:** 1 256 835-1580.
Email: email@979wvok.com
Web site: http://www.979wvok.com
Profile: WVOK-FM is a commercial station owned by Woodard Broadcasting Co. The format for the station is Hot AC. WVOK-FM broadcasts to the Oxford, AL area at 97.9 FM.
FM RADIO STATION

WVOL-AM
75280

Owner: Heidelberg Broadcasting LLC
Editorial: 1320 Brick Church Pike, Nashville, Tennessee 37207 **Tel:** 1 615 226-9510.
Email: wvol1470@aol.com
Web site: http://www.wvol1470.com
Profile: WVOL-AM is a commercial station owned by Heidelberg Broadcasting LLC. The format of the station is R&B oldies and urban contemporary music. WVOL-AM broadcasts to the Nashville, TN area at 1470 AM.
AM RADIO STATION

WVOM-FM
42373

Owner: Blueberry Broadcasting
Editorial: 184 Target Cir, Bangor, Maine 04401-5718 **Tel:** 1 207 947-9100.
Web site: http://www.wvomfm.com
Profile: WVOM-FM is a commercial station owned by Blueberry Broadcasting. The format of the station is news, talk and sports. WVOM-AM broadcasts to the Bangor, ME area at 103.9 FM.
FM RADIO STATION

WVON-AM
35736

Owner: Midway Broadcasting Corp.
Editorial: 1000 E 87th St, Chicago, Illinois 60619-6397 **Tel:** 1 773 247-6200.
Email: info@wvon.com
Web site: http://www.wvon.com
Profile: WVON-AM is a commercial station owned by Midway Broadcasting Corp. The format of the station is talk. WVON-AM broadcasts to the Chicago area at 1690 AM.
AM RADIO STATION

WVOP-AM
38262

Owner: Vidalia Communications Group
Editorial: 1501 Mount Vernon Rd, Vidalia, Georgia 30474-3031 **Tel:** 1 912 537-9202.
Web site: http://www.southeastgeorgiatoday.com
Profile: WVOP-AM is a commercial station owned by Vidalia Communications Group. The format of the station is news and talk. WVOP-AM broadcasts to the Vidalia, GA area at 970 AM.
AM RADIO STATION

WVOR-FM
43367

Owner: iHeartMedia Inc.
Editorial: 100 Chestnut St, 1700 Hsbc Plaza, Rochester, New York 14604-2419 **Tel:** 1 585 454-4884.
Web site: http://www.radiosunny.com
Profile: WVOR-FM is a commercial station owned by iHeartMedia Inc. The format of the station is adult contemporary. WVOR-FM broadcasts to the Rochester, NY area at 102.3 FM.
FM RADIO STATION

WVOS-AM
38263

Owner: Watermark Communications
Editorial: 198 Bridgeville Rd, Monticello, New York 12701 **Tel:** 1 845 791-9590.
Web site: http://wvosfm.com
Profile: WVOS-AM is a commercial station owned by Watermark Communications. The format of the station is Spanish sports. WVOS-AM broadcasts to the New York area at 1240 AM.
AM RADIO STATION

WVOS-FM
45604

Owner: Watermark Communications
Editorial: 198 Bridgeville Rd, Monticello, New York 12701 **Tel:** 1 845 794-9898.
Web site: http://www.wvosfm.com
Profile: WVOS-FM is a commercial station owned by Watermark Communications. The format of the station is classic hits. WVOS-FM broadcasts to the New York area at 95.9 FM.
FM RADIO STATION

WVOT-AM
35737

Owner: Kingdon Expansion Corp.
Editorial: 2860 Ward Blvd Ste B, Wilson, North Carolina 27893-1749 **Tel:** 1 252 243-1420.
Profile: WVOT-AM is an commercial station owned by Kingdon Expansion Corp. The format of the station is gospel music. WVOT-AM broadcasts to the Wilson, NC area 1420 AM.
AM RADIO STATION

WVOV-AM
35224

Owner: Bono, Anthony
Editorial: 1237 County Road 295, Higdon, Alabama 35979-6349 **Tel:** 1 877 237-6259.
Email: 1480thefan@gmail.com
Web site: http://www.1480thefan.com
Profile: WVOV-AM is a commercial station owned by Anthony Bono. The format for the station is news, talk, and sports. WVOV-AM broadcasts to the Bridgeport, AL area at 1480 AM.
AM RADIO STATION

WVOW-AM
39250

Owner: Logan Broadcasting
Editorial: 204 Main St Ste 201, Logan, West Virginia 25601-3943 **Tel:** 1 304 752-5080.
Email: newsdepartment@wvowradio.com
Web site: http://wvowradio.com
Profile: WVOW-AM is a commercial station owned by Logan Broadcasting. The format of the station is adult contemporary music and sports. Newscasts air at various times throughout the day.
AM RADIO STATION

WVOW-FM
46608

Owner: Logan Broadcasting
Editorial: 204 Main St Ste 201, Logan, West Virginia 25601-3943 **Tel:** 1 304 752-5080.
Email: newsdepartment@wvowradio.com
Web site: http://wvowradio.com
Profile: WVOW-FM is a commercial station owned by Logan Broadcasting. The format of the station is adult contemporary music and sports. WVOW-FM broadcasts to the Logan, WV area at 101.9 FM and is simulcast on WVOW-AM.
FM RADIO STATION

WVOX-AM
38403

Owner: Whitney Radio Broadcasting Inc.
Editorial: 1 Broadcast Forum, New Rochelle, New York 10801-2094 **Tel:** 1 914 636-1460.
Web site: http://www.wvox.com
Profile: WVOX-AM is a commercial station owned by Whitney Radio Broadcasting Inc. The format of the station is news and talk. WVOX-AM broadcasts to the New Rochelle, NY area at 1460 AM.
AM RADIO STATION

WVPA-FM
75382

Owner: Vermont Public Radio
Editorial: 365 Troy Ave, Colchester, Vermont 05446-3126 **Tel:** 1 802 655-9451.
Email: news@vpr.net
Web site: http://www.vpr.net
Profile: WVPA-FM is a non-commercial station owned by Vermont Public Radio. The format of the station is news and talk. WVPA-FM broadcasts to the St. Johnsbury, VT area at 88.5 FM. The station does not accept PSAs.
FM RADIO STATION

WVPN-FM
41074

Owner: State of West Virginia
Editorial: 600 Capitol St, Charleston, West Virginia 25301-1223 **Tel:** 1 304 556-4900.
Email: feedback@wvpubcast.org
Web site: http://www.wvpubcast.org
Profile: WVPN-FM is a non-commercial station owned by the State of West Virginia. The format of the station is news and talk as well as classical music. WVPN-FM broadcasts to the Charleston, WV area at 88.5 FM. Send or fax one copy only of press releases to West Virginia Public Radio, not its individual stations. No broadcast tape announcements are accepted.
FM RADIO STATION

WVPO-AM
38264

Owner: Connoisseur Media
Editorial: 22 S 6th St, Stroudsburg, Pennsylvania 18360-2002 **Tel:** 1 570 421-2100.
Profile: WVPO-AM is a commercial station owned by Connoisseur Media. The format of the station is talk. WVPO-AM broadcasts to the Stroudsburg, PA area at 840 AM.
AM RADIO STATION

WVPR-FM
40823

Owner: Vermont Public Radio
Editorial: 365 Troy Ave, Colchester, Vermont 05446-3126 **Tel:** 1 802 655-9451.
Web site: http://www.vpr.net
Profile: WVPR-FM is a non-commercial station owned by Vermont Public Radio. The format of the station is news and talk. WVPR-FM broadcasts to the Colchester, VT area at 89.5 FM. The station does not accept PSAs.
FM RADIO STATION

WVPS-FM
41292

Owner: Vermont Public Radio
Editorial: 365 Troy Ave, Colchester, Vermont 5446 **Tel:** 1 802 655-9451.
Email: news@vpr.net
Web site: http://www.vpr.net
Profile: WVPS-FM is a non-commercial station owned by Vermont Public Radio. The format of the station is news and talk. WVPS-FM broadcasts to the Colchester, VT area at 107.9 FM.
FM RADIO STATION

WVQM-FM
4585

Owner: Blueberry Broadcasting
Editorial: 125 Community Dr Ste 201, Augusta, Maine 04330-8157 **Tel:** 1 207 623-9000.
Web site: http://www.wvomfm.com
Profile: WVQM-FM is a commercial station owned by Blueberry Broadcasting. The format of the station is news and talk. WVQM-FM broadcasts to the Augusta, ME area at 101.3 FM.
FM RADIO STATION

WVRA-FM
50183

Owner: Liberty University, Inc.
Editorial: 3700 Candlers Mountain Rd Ste F, Lynchburg, Virginia 24502-2268 **Tel:** 1 454 582-3688
Web site: http://www.myjourneyfm.com
Profile: WVRA-FM is a commercial station owned by Liberty University, Inc. The format of the station is contemporary Christian. WVRA-FM broadcasts to the Rocky Mount, NC area at 107.3 FM.
FM RADIO STATION

WVRB-FM
4414

Owner: Baldwin Broadcasting
Editorial: 8686 Michael Ln, Fairfield, Ohio 45014 **Tel:** 1 513 829-7700.
Web site: http://www.air1.com
Profile: WVRB-FM is a commercial station owned by Baldwin Broadcasting. The format of the station is Christian rock music. WVRB-FM broadcasts to the Wilmore, KY area at 95.3 FM.
FM RADIO STATION

WVRC-AM
3893

Owner: Star Communications, Inc.
Editorial: 106 Radio St, Spencer, West Virginia 25276 **Tel:** 1 304 927-3760.
Email: contact@wvrcfm.com
Web site: http://www.wvrcfm.com
Profile: WVRC-AM is a commercial station owned by Star Communications, Inc. The format for the station is gospel. WVRC-AM broadcasts to the Spencer, WV area at 1400 AM.
AM RADIO STATION

WVRC-FM
4628

Owner: Star Communications, Inc.
Editorial: 106 Radio St, Spencer, West Virginia 25276 **Tel:** 1 304 927-3760.
Email: contact@wvrcfm.com
Web site: http://www.wvrcfm.com
Profile: WVRC-FM is a commercial station owned by Star Communications, Inc. The format of the station is contemporary country music. WVRC-FM broadcasts to the Spencer, WV area at 104.7 FM.
FM RADIO STATION

WVRE-FM
13690

Owner: Radio Dubuque Inc.
Editorial: 1055 University Ave, Dubuque, Iowa 52001-6154 **Tel:** 1 563 690-0800.
Email: theriver@1011theriver.com
Web site: http://www.1011theriver.com
FM RADIO STATION

WVRK-FM
4540

Owner: iHeartMedia Inc.
Editorial: 1501 13th Ave, Columbus, Georgia 31901-1908 **Tel:** 1 706 576-3000.
Web site: http://www.rock103columbus.com
Profile: WVRK-FM is a commercial station owned by iHeartMedia Inc. The format of the station is rock. WVRK-FM broadcasts to the Columbus, GA area at 102.9 FM.
FM RADIO STATION

WVRQ-AM
3826

Owner: Robinson Corporation
Editorial: E7601A County Road SS, Viroqua, Wisconsin 54665 **Tel:** 1 608 637-7200.
Email: wvrq@mwt.net
Web site: http://www.wvrq.com
Profile: WVRQ-AM is a commercial station owned by Robinson Corporation. The format of the station is oldies. WVRQ-AM broadcasts to the Viroqua, WI area at 1360 AM.
AM RADIO STATION

WVRQ-FM
4560

Owner: Robinson Corporation
Editorial: E7601a County Road Ss, Viroqua, Wisconsin 54665-8502 **Tel:** 1 608 637-7200.
Email: wvrq@mwt.net
Web site: http://www.wvrq.com
Profile: WVRQ-FM is a commercial station owned by Robinson Corporation. The format of the station is country music. WVRQ-FM broadcasts to the Viroqua, WI area at 102.3 FM.
FM RADIO STATION

WVRR-FM
13229

Owner: Positive Alternative Radio
Editorial: 3027 Lester Ln, Ashland, Kentucky 41102-9642 **Tel:** 1 877 456-9361.
Email: office@walkfm.org
Web site: http://walkfm.org
Profile: WVRR-FM is a non-commercial station owned by Positive Alternative Radio. The format of the station is contemporary Christian. WVRR-FM broadcast to the Point Pleasant, WV area at 88.1 FM.
FM RADIO STATION

WVRT-FM 44395
Owner: iHeartMedia Inc.
Editorial: 1559 W 4th St, Williamsport, Pennsylvania 17701-5650 **Tel:** 1 570 327-1400.
Web site: http://www.v97fm.com/main.html
Profile: WVRT-FM is a commercial station owned by iHeartMedia Inc. The format of the station is Top 40/CHR music. WVRT-FM broadcasts to the Williamsport, PA area at 97.7 FM.
FM RADIO STATION

WVRV-FM 852403
Owner: Back Door Broadcasting
Editorial: 1359 Carmichael Way, Montgomery, Alabama 36106-3629 **Tel:** 1 334 239-9750.
Web site: http://www.wvrvfmtheriver.com
Profile: WVRV-FM is a commercial station owned by Back Door Broadcasting. The format of the station is Contemporary Christian. WVRV-FM broadcasts to the Montgomery, AL area at a frequency of 97.5 FM.
FM RADIO STATION

WVRW-FM 560686
Owner: Della Jane Woofter
Editorial: 300 Harrison Ave, Weston, West Virginia 26452-2100 **Tel:** 1 304 269-5555.
Email: wvrwtrueoldies@aol.com
Web site: http://www.wvrwfm.com
Profile: WVRW-FM is a commercial station owned by Della Jane Woofter. The format of the station is oldies. The station broadcasts locally to the Glenvill, WV area at a frequency of 107.7 FM.
FM RADIO STATION

WVRY-FM 43287
Owner: JWL Communications, LLC.
Editorial: 201 Hall Ln, White Bluff, Tennessee 37187-1057 **Tel:** 1 615 797-9785.
Email: wvryfm@gmail.com
Profile: WVRY-FM is a commercial station owned by JWL Communications, LLC. The format of the station is gospel music. WVRY-FM broadcasts to the White Bluff, TN area at 105.1 FM.
FM RADIO STATION

WVRZ-FM 42231
Owner: iHeartMedia Inc.
Editorial: 1559 W 4th St, Williamsport, Pennsylvania 17701-5650 **Tel:** 1 570 327-1400.
Web site: http://www.v97fm.com/main.html
Profile: WVRZ-FM is a commercial station owned by iHeartMedia Inc. The format of the station is Top 40/CHR music. WVRZ-FM broadcasts in the Shamokin, PA area at 99.7 FM and is a simulcast of WVRT-FM.
FM RADIO STATION

WVSA-AM 38734
Owner: Lamar County Broadcasting
Editorial: 47650 Hwy 17 N, Vernon, Alabama 35592
Tel: 1 205 695-9191.
Email: wjec1065@yahoo.com
Profile: WVSA-AM is a commercial station owned by Lamar County Broadcasting. The format of the station is sports talk. WVSA-AM broadcasts in the Vernon, AL at 1380 AM.
AM RADIO STATION

WVSC-FM 40303
Owner: Apex Broadcasting
Editorial: 2 Corpus Christie Pl Ste 100A, Hilton Head, South Carolina 29928-1720 **Tel:** 1 888 844-1031.
Web site: http://www.sc103radio.com
Profile: WVSC-FM is a commercial station owned by Apex Broadcasting. The format of the station is adult hits. WVSC-FM broadcasts to the Savannah Georgia-Hilton Head, SC area at 106.1 FM.
FM RADIO STATION

WVSG-AM 38400
Owner: St. Gabriel Radio Inc
Editorial: 4673 Winterset Dr, Columbus, Ohio 43220-3113 **Tel:** 1 614 459-4820.
Email: info@stgabrielradio.com
Web site: http://stgabrielradio.com
Profile: WVSG-AM is a non-commercial station owned by St. Gabriel Radio Inc. The format of the station is Catholic radio programming. WVSG-AM broadcasts to the Columbus, OH area at 820 AM.
AM RADIO STATION

WVSL-AM 38635
Owner: Max Media
Editorial: 450 Route 204, Selinsgrove, Pennsylvania 17870 **Tel:** 1 570 374-8819.
Profile: WVSL-AM is a commercial station owned by Max Media. The format of the station is sports. WVSL-AM broadcasts to the Selinsgrove, PA area at 1240 AM.
AM RADIO STATION

WVSM-AM 35739
Owner: Sand Mountain Advertising Company, Inc.
Editorial: 368 McCurdy Ave N, Rainsville, Alabama 35986-4460 **Tel:** 1 256 638-2137.
Email: wvsm@farmerstel.com
Web site: http://www.wvsm.com
Profile: WVSM-AM is a commercial station owned by Sand Mountain Advertising Company, Inc. The format for the station is gospel. WVSM-AM broadcasts to the Huntsville, AL area at 1500 AM.
AM RADIO STATION

WVSP-FM 40428
Owner: Max Media
Editorial: 5589 Greenwich Rd, Ste 200, Virginia Beach, Virginia 23462 **Tel:** 1 757 671-1000.
Web site: http://www.espnradio941.com
Profile: WVSP-FM is a commercial station owned by Max Media. The format of the station is sports talk. WVSP-FM broadcasts to the Norfolk, VA area at 94.1 FM.
FM RADIO STATION

WVSR-FM 46423
Owner: Bristol Broadcasting
Editorial: 817 Suncrest Pl, Charleston, West Virginia 25303 **Tel:** 1 304 342-3136.
Web site: http://www.electric102.com
Profile: WVSR-FM is a commercial station owned by Bristol Broadcasting. The format of the station is Top 40/CHR. WVSR-FM broadcasts to the Charleston-Huntington, WV area at 102.7 FM.
FM RADIO STATION

WVSZ-FM 44140
Owner: Our Three Sons Broadcasting
Editorial: 142 N Confederate Ave, Rock Hill, South Carolina 29730-5314 **Tel:** 1 803 324-1071.
Email: newsroom@wrhi.com
Web site: http://www.fm107.com
Profile: WVSZ-FM is a commercial station owned by Our Three Sons Broadcasting. The format of the station is country music. WVSZ-FM broadcasts to the Rock Hill, SC area at 94.3 FM
FM RADIO STATION

WVTF-FM 40826
Owner: Virginia Tech Foundation
Editorial: 3520 Kingsbury Cir, Roanoke, Virginia 24014-1356 **Tel:** 1 540 989-8900.
Email: wvtf@vt.edu
Web site: http://www.wvtf.org
Profile: WVTF-FM is a non-commercial station owned by Virginia Tech Foundation. The format of the station is jazz, classical music and news. WVTF-FM broadcasts to the Roanake, VA area at 89.1 FM.
FM RADIO STATION

WVTJ-AM 35378
Owner: Wilkins Communications Network Inc.
Editorial: 2070 N Palafox St, Pensacola, Florida 32501 **Tel:** 1 850 432-3658.
Email: wvtj@wilkinsradio.com
Web site: http://www.wilkinsradio.com
Profile: WVTJ-AM is a commercial station owned by Wilkins Communications Network Inc. The primary format of the station is religious teaching. Its secondary format is gospel. WVTJ-AM broadcasts to the Pensacola, FL area at 610 AM.
AM RADIO STATION

WVTK-FM 43386
Owner: WVTK Radio LLC
Editorial: 63 Maple St Ste 9, Middlebury, Vermont 05753-1603 **Tel:** 1 802 388-2563.
Web site: http://www.921wvtk.com
Profile: WVTK-FM is a commercial station owned by WVTK Radio LLC. The format of the station is adult contemporary. WVTK-FM broadcasts to the Middlebury, VT area at a frequency of 92.1 FM.
FM RADIO STATION

WVTL-AM 39020
Owner: Roser Communications
Editorial: 5816 Route 30, South Amsterdam, New York 12010-8056 **Tel:** 1 518 843-9284.
Web site: http://www.1570wvtl.com
Profile: WVTL-AM is a commercial station owned by Roser Communications. The format of the station is Lite AC. WVTL-AM broadcasts to the Utica, NY area at 1570 AM.
AM RADIO STATION

WVTQ-FM 519219
Owner: Vermont Public Radio
Editorial: 365 Troy Ave, Colchester, Vermont 5446
Tel: 1 802 655-9451.
Email: news@vpr.net
Web site: http://www.vpr.net
Profile: WVTQ-FM is a non-commercial station owned by Vermont Public Radio. The format of the station is talk and classical music. WVTQ-FM broadcasts to the Burlington, VT area at 95.1 FM.
FM RADIO STATION

WVTS-AM 38140
Owner: Bristol Broadcasting
Editorial: 817 Suncrest Pl, Charleston, West Virginia 25303-2302 **Tel:** 1 304 342-3136.
Email: news@wqbe.com
Web site: http://www.wvtsam950.com
Profile: WVTS-AM is a commercial station owned by Bristol Broadcasting. The format of the station is news talk. WVTS-AM broadcasts to the Charleston-Huntington, WV area at 950 AM.
AM RADIO STATION

WVTT-FM 45168
Owner: Colonial Radio Group
Editorial: 1 Bluebird Sq, Olean, New York 14760-2552
Tel: 1 716 372-9564.
Email: news@colonialme.com
Web site: http://www.colonialme.com
Profile: WVTT-FM is a commercial station owned by Colonial Radio Group. The format of the station is news/talk. WVTT-FM broadcasts to the Coudersport, PA at 96.7 FM.
FM RADIO STATION

WVUM-FM 40829
Owner: WVUM Inc.
Editorial: 1306 Stanford Dr, UC 110, Coral Gables, Florida 33124 **Tel:** 1 786 309-8861.
Email: office@wvum.org
Web site: http://www.wvum.org
Profile: WVUM-FM is a non-commercial station owned by WVUM Inc. The format of the station is adult album alternative music. WVUM-FM broadcasts to the Miami area at 90.5 FM.
FM RADIO STATION

WVUS-AM 561234
Owner: Light of Life Community, Inc
Editorial: 132 Carubia Dr, Core, West Virginia 26541-7137 **Tel:** 1 304 598-0026.
Email: info@lolradio.org
Web site: http://www.lolradio.org
Profile: WVUS-AM is a non-commercial station owned by Light of Life Community, Inc. The format of the station is religious, Catholic and music. WVUS-AM broadcasts to the Grafton, WV area at 1190 AM.
AM RADIO STATION

WVVC-FM 759670
Owner: Northeast Gospel Broadcasting, Inc.
Editorial: 65 King Rd, Buskirk, New York 12028-2221
Tel: 1 518 686-0975.
Web site: http://www.northeastgospelbroadcasting.com
Profile: WVVC-FM is a non-commercial station owned by Northeast Gospel Broadcasting, Inc. The format of the station is Christian music and teaching. WVVC-FM broadcasts to the Dolgeville, NY area at 88.1 FM.
FM RADIO STATION

WVVE-FM 45888
Owner: Magic Broadcasting, LLC
Editorial: 7106 Laird St, Panama City, Florida 32408-7653 **Tel:** 1 850 230-5855.
Web site: http://www.getyourgrooveonpc.com
Profile: WVVE-FM is a commercial station owned by Magic Broadcasting, LLC. The format of the station is rhythmic oldies. WVVE-FM broadcasts to the Panama City, FL area at 100.1.
FM RADIO STATION

WVVI-FM 552797
Owner: JKC Communications
Tel: 1 340 773-0995.
Profile: WVVI-FM is a commercial station owned by JKC Communications. The format of the station is country. WVVI-FM broadcasts to Christiansted, U.S. Virgin Islands at 93.5 FM.
FM RADIO STATION

WVVL-FM 46607
Owner: Boll Weevil Communications, LLC
Editorial: 100 N Main St, Enterprise, Alabama 36330
Tel: 1 334 347-5621.
Email: wvvl@weevil101.com
Web site: http://www.weevil101.com
Profile: WVVL-FM is a commercial station owned by Boll Weevil Communications, LLC. The format of the station is classic country. WVVL-FM broadcasts to the Enterprise, AL area at 101.1 FM.
FM RADIO STATION

WVVR-FM 43215
Owner: Saga Communications
Editorial: 1640 Old Russellville Pike, Clarksville, Tennessee 37043-1709 **Tel:** 1 931 648-7720.
Web site: http://beaver1003.com
Profile: WVVR-FM is a commercial station owned by Saga Communications (dba 5 Star Radio Group). The format of the station is contemporary country music. WVVR-FM broadcasts to the Nashville, TN area at 100.3 FM.
FM RADIO STATION

WVVV-FM 78530
Owner: Seven Ranges Radio Company Inc.
Editorial: 1627 Rosemar Rd, Parkersburg, West Virginia 26105-8128 **Tel:** 1 304 295-3100.
Web site: http://www.v969radio.net
Profile: WVVV-FM is a commercial station owned by Seven Ranges Radio Company Inc. The format of the station is adult contemporary music. WVVV-FM broadcasts to the Vienna, WV area at 96.9 FM.
FM RADIO STATION

WVWC-FM 40834
Owner: West Virginia Wesleyan College
Editorial: 59 College Ave #167, Buckhannon, West Virginia 26201-2600 **Tel:** 1 304 473-8292.
Email: c92@wvwc.edu
Web site: http://www.wvwc.edu/academics/schools/social-behavioral-science/communication/c92-fm
Profile: WVWC-FM is a non-commercial college station owned by West Virginia Wesleyan College. It airs an adult alternative format. WVWC-FM broadcasts to the Buckhannon, West Virginia area at 92.1 FM.
FM RADIO STATION

WVXG-FM 42211
Owner: ICS Holdings, Inc.
Editorial: 501 Bowtown Rd, Delaware, Ohio 43015-9410
Web site: http://www.951rocks.com
Profile: WVXG-FM is a commercial radio station that is owned by ICS Holdings, Inc. The format of the station is classic rock. The station airs locally on 95.1 FM.
FM RADIO STATION

WVXM-FM 690141
Owner: Vermont Public Radio
Editorial: 365 Troy Ave, Colchester, Vermont 05446-3126 **Tel:** 1 802 655-9451.
Web site: http://www.vpr.net
Profile: WVXM-FM is a non-commercial station owned by Vermont Public Radio. The format is classical music. WVXM-FM broadcasts to the Middleburg, VT area at 90.1 FM.
FM RADIO STATION

WVXR-FM 46491
Owner: Vermont Public Radio
Editorial: 365 Troy Ave, Colchester, Vermont 05446-3126 **Tel:** 1 802 655-9451.
Web site: http://www.vpr.net
Profile: WVXR-FM is a non-commercial station owned by Vermont Public Radio. The format of the station is classical music. WVXR-FM broadcasts to the Randolph, VT area at 102.1 FM.
FM RADIO STATION

WVXU-FM 40835
Owner: Cincinnati Public Radio Inc.
Editorial: 1223 Central Pkwy, Cincinnati, Ohio 45214-2812 **Tel:** 1 513 352-9170.
Email: wvxu@wvxu.org
Web site: http://www.wvxu.org
Profile: WVXU-FM is a commercial station owned by Cincinnati Public Radio Inc. The format of the station is news and talk. WVXU-FM broadcasts to the Cincinnati area at 91.7 FM.
FM RADIO STATION

WVXX-AM 38391
Owner: Hindlin Broadcasting
Editorial: 740 Duke St Ste 450, Norfolk, Virginia 23510-1544 **Tel:** 1 757 627-9899.
Email: andy@selecta1050.com
Web site: http://www.selecta1050.com
Profile: WVXX-AM is a commercial station owned by Hindlin Broadcasting. The format of the station is Hispanic music. WVXX-AM broadcasts to the Norfolk, VA area on 1050 AM.
AM RADIO STATION

WVYB-FM 43211
Owner: Black Crow Radio, LLC
Editorial: 126 W International Speedway Blvd, Daytona Beach, Florida 32114-4322 **Tel:** 1 386 257-6900.
Web site: http://1033wvyb.com/
Profile: WVYB-FM is a commercial station owned by Black Crow Radio, LLC. The format of the station is Top 40/CHR music. WVYB-FM broadcasts to the Daytona Beach, FL area at 103.3 FM.
FM RADIO STATION

WVYC-FM 44262
Owner: York College of Pennsylvania
Editorial: Student Union Bldg York College, 3rd Floor, York, Pennsylvania 17405 **Tel:** 1 717 815-1932.
Email: gm@wvyc.org
Web site: http://www.wvyc.org
Profile: WVYC-FM is a non-commercial station owned by York College of Pennsylvania. The format of the station is rock alternative music. WVYC-FM broadcasts to the York College of Pennsylvania area at 88.1 FM.
FM RADIO STATION

WVYS-FM 43796
Owner: GEOS Communications
Tel: 1 570 265-7600.
Email: comments@iloveyesfm.com
Web site: http://www.iloveyesfm.com
Profile: WVYS-FM is a commercial station owned by GEOS Communications. The format of the station is adult contemporary. WVYS-FM broadcasts to the Elmira, NY area at 96.9 FM.
FM RADIO STATION

WVZA-FM 43079
Owner: Withers Broadcasting of Southern Illinois LLC
Editorial: 1822 N Court St, Marion, Illinois 62959
Tel: 1 618 997-8123.
Web site: http://www.mywithersradio.com/vza
Profile: WVZA-FM is a commercial station owned by Withers Broadcasting of Southern Illinois LLC. The format of the station is adult contemporary. WVZA-FM broadcasts to the Marion, IL area at 105.1 FM.
FM RADIO STATION

WWAB-AM 35740
Owner: WWAB Inc.
Editorial: 1203 W Chase St, Lakeland, Florida 33815-1349 **Tel:** 1 863 682-2998.
Profile: WWAB-AM is a commercial station owned by WWAB Inc. The format of the station is Urban Contemporary/Urban Gospel. WWAB-AM broadcasts to the Tampa Bay, FL area at 1330 AM.
AM RADIO STATION

WWAC-FM 42870
Owner: Longport Media
Editorial: 1601 New Rd, Linwood, New Jersey 8221
Tel: 1 609 653-1400.
Web site: http://ac1027.com
Profile: WWAC-FM is a commercial station owned by Longport Media. The format of the station is Hot AC. WWAC-FM broadcasts to the Linwood, NJ area at 102.7 FM.
FM RADIO STATION

WWAG-FM 42470
Owner: Brockman(Dan)
Editorial: 1731 Highway 1071, Tyner, Kentucky 40486-8223 **Tel:** 1 606 287-9924.
Web site: http://www.wwagfm.com
FM RADIO STATION

United States of America

WWAV-FM 41594
Owner: Community Broadcasters LLC.
Editorial: 34 Harbor Blvd Ste 202, Destin, Florida 32541-7365 Tel: 1 850 654-1000.
Web site: http://www.1021thewave.com
Profile: WWAV-FM is a commercial station owned by Community Broadcasters LLC. The format for the station is classic hits. WWAV-FM broadcasts to the Destin, FL area at 102.1 FM.
FM RADIO STATION

WWAX-FM 43101
Owner: Red Rock Radio Corp.
Editorial: 501 S Lake Ave Ste 200, Duluth, Minnesota 55802-2392 Tel: 1 218 728-9500.
Email: production@redrockradio.org
Web site: http://nu92.fm
Profile: WWAX-FM is a commercial station owned by Red Rock Radio Corp. The format of the station is Hot AC. WWAX-FM broadcasts to the Duluth, MN area at 92.1 FM.
FM RADIO STATION

WWBA-AM 37029
Owner: Genesis Communications Inc.
Editorial: 800 8th Ave SE, Largo, Florida 33771-2162
Tel: 1 813 281-1040.
Email: contact@newstalkflorida.com
Web site: http://www.newstalkflorida.com/820-news/
Profile: WWBA-AM is a commercial station owned by Genesis Communications Inc. The format of the station is news and talk. WWBA-AM broadcasts to the Tampa, FL area on 820 AM.
AM RADIO STATION

WWBB-FM 40945
Owner: iHeartMedia Inc.
Editorial: 75 Oxford St, Providence, Rhode Island 02905-4722 Tel: 1 401 781-9979.
Email: feedback@b101.com
Web site: http://www.b101.com
Profile: WWBB-FM is a commercial station owned by iHeart Media Inc. The format of the station is classic hits. WWBB-FM broadcasts to the Providence, RI area at 101.5 FM.
FM RADIO STATION

WWBC-AM 39113
Owner: National Christian Network
Editorial: 1150 King St, Cocoa, Florida 32922
Tel: 1 321 632-1510.
Web site: http://www.1510wwbc.com
Profile: WWBC-AM is a non-commercial station owned by National Christian Network. The format of the station is religious programming. WWBC-AM broadcasts to the Cocoa, FL area at 1510 AM.
AM RADIO STATION

WWBD-FM 43993
Owner: Miller Communications Inc.
Editorial: 51 Commerce St, Sumter, South Carolina 29150-5014 Tel: 1 803 775-2321.
Email: production@miller.fm
Profile: WWBD-FM is a commercial station owned by Miller Communications Inc. The format of the station is active rock. WWBD-FM broadcasts to the Sumter, SC area at 94.7 FM.
FM RADIO STATION

WWBF-AM 35741
Owner: Thornburg Communications Inc.
Editorial: 1130 Radio Rd, Bartow, Florida 33830-7600
Tel: 1 863 533-0744.
Web site: http://www.wwbf.com
Profile: WWBF-AM is a commercial station owned by Thornburg Communications Inc. The format for the station is classic hits. WWBF-AM broadcasts to the Bartow, FL area at 1130 AM.
AM RADIO STATION

WWBG-AM 37119
Owner: Davidson Media Group
Editorial: 4015 Brownsboro Rd Ste 200, Winston Salem, North Carolina 27106-3380 Tel: 1 336 714-2831.
Web site: http://www.quepasamedia.com
Profile: WWBG-AM is a commercial station owned by Davidson Media Group and run by Que Pasa Media Network. The format of the station is regional Mexican. WWBG-AM broadcasts to the Greensboro, NC area at a frequency of 1470 AM.
AM RADIO STATION

WWBJ-AM 37955
Owner: Martinsburg Broadcasting Inc.
Editorial: 724 Rebecca Furnace Rd, Martinsburg, Pennsylvania 16662-7302 Tel: 1 814 793-2188.
Email: wjsmradio@gmail.com
Web site: http://www.wjsm.com
Profile: WWBJ-AM is a non-commercial station owned by Martinsburg Broadcasting Inc. The format of the station is Christian programming and music. WWBJ-AM broadcasts to the Martinsburg, PA area at 1110 AM.
AM RADIO STATION

WWBL-FM 42295
Owner: Original Company Inc.(The)
Editorial: 3 E Van Trees St, Washington, Indiana 47501-2942 Tel: 1 812 254-4300.
Email: wwblnews@wwbl.com
Web site: http://www.wwbl.com
Profile: WWBL-FM is a commercial station owned by The Original Company Inc. The format of the station is country music. WWBL-FM broadcasts to the Vincennes, IN area at 106.5 FM.
FM RADIO STATION

WWBN-FM 40322
Owner: Townsquare Media, LLC
Editorial: 3338 E Bristol Rd, Burton, Michigan 48529
Tel: 1 810 743-1080.
Web site: http://www.banana1015.com
Profile: WWBN-FM is a commercial station owned by Townsquare Media, LLC. The format of the station is rock music. WWBN-FM broadcasts to the Flint, MI area at 101.5 FM.
FM RADIO STATION

WWBR-FM 45061
Owner: Mentor Partners Inc.
Editorial: 18720 16 Mile Rd, Big Rapids, Michigan 49307-9303 Tel: 1 231 796-7000.
Email: news@bigrapidsradionetwork.com
Web site: http://www.bigcountry1009.com
Profile: WWBR-FM is a commercial station owned by Mentor Partners Inc. The format of the station is country music. WWBR-FM broadcasts to the Traverse City, MI area at 100.9 FM.
FM RADIO STATION

WWBU-FM 46466
Owner: Cumulus Media Inc.
Editorial: 7080 Lee Hwy, Fairlawn, Virginia 24141-8416 Tel: 1 540 731-6000.
Email: info@cumulus.com
Web site: http://www.supersports1017.com
Profile: WWBU-FM is a commercial station owned by Cumulus Media Inc. The format for the station is sports. WWBU-FM broadcasts to the Fairlawn, VA area at 101.7 FM.
FM RADIO STATION

WWCA-AM 37043
Owner: Starboard Media Foundation Inc.
Editorial: 107 W 78Th Pl, Merrillville, Indiana 46410-5468 Tel: 1 219 736-7524.
Web site: http://www.relevantradio.com
Profile: WWCA-AM is a non-commercial station owned by Starboard Media Foundation Inc. The format of the station is religious. WWCA-AM broadcasts to the Merrillville, IN area at 1270 AM.
AM RADIO STATION

WWCB-AM 35742
Owner: The Mid State Sports Network
Editorial: 122 N Center St, Corry, Pennsylvania 16407-1625 Tel: 1 814 664-8694.
Web site: http://www.wwcbradio.com
Profile: WWCB-AM is a commercial station owned by The Mid State Sports Network. The format of the station is Country. WWCB-AM broadcasts to the Corry, PA area at 1370 AM.
AM RADIO STATION

WWCD-FM 41655
Owner: Fun With Radio Inc.
Editorial: 1036 S Front St, Columbus, Ohio 43206-3402 Tel: 1 614 221-9923.
Email: webmaster@cd1025.com
Web site: http://www.cd1025.com
Profile: WWCD-FM is a commercial station owned by Fun With Radio Inc. The format of the station is rock alternative music. WWCD-FM broadcasts to the Columbus, OH area at 102.5 FM.
FM RADIO STATION

WWCH-AM 38268
Owner: Clarion County Broadcasting Corp.
Editorial: 1168 Greenville Pike, Clarion, Pennsylvania 16214-6146 Tel: 1 814 226-4500.
Email: clarionradio@comcast.net
Profile: WWCH-AM is a commercial station owned by Clarion County Broadcasting Corp. The format of the station is country. WWCH-AM broadcasts to the Clarion, PA area at 1300 AM.
AM RADIO STATION

WWCK-AM 38269
Owner: Cumulus Media Inc.
Editorial: 6317 Taylor Dr, Flint, Michigan 48507-4683
Tel: 1 810 238-7300.
Web site: http://www.supertalk1570.com
Profile: WWCK-AM is a commercial station owned by Cumulus Media Inc. The format of the station is news and talk programming. WWCK-AM broadcasts to the Flint, MI area at 1570 AM.
AM RADIO STATION

WWCK-FM 45608
Owner: Cumulus Media Inc.
Editorial: 6317 Taylor Dr, Flint, Michigan 48507-4683
Tel: 1 810 238-7300.
Web site: http://www.ck1055.fm
Profile: WWCK-FM is a commercial station owned by Cumulus Media Inc. The format of the station is Top 40/CHR. WWCK-FM broadcasts to the Flint, MI area at 105.5 FM.
FM RADIO STATION

WWCL-AM 36012
Owner: Radio Vision Cristiana Management
Tel: 1 973 881-8700.
Web site: http://radiovision.net
Profile: WWCL-AM is a commercial station owned by Radio Vision Cristiana Management. The format of the station is Spanish Christian programming. WWCL-AM broadcasts to the Fort Myers, FL and Naples, FL areas at 1440 AM.
AM RADIO STATION

WWCN-FM 40633
Owner: Beasley Broadcast Group
Editorial: 20125 S Tamiami Trl, Estero, Florida 33928-2117 Tel: 1 239 495-2100.

Web site: http://993espn.com
Profile: WWCN-FM is a commercial station owned by Beasley Broadcast Group. The format of the station is sports talk. WWCN-FM broadcasts to the Ft. Myers, FL area at 99.3 FM.
FM RADIO STATION

WWCO-AM 35744
Owner: Connoisseur Media
Editorial: 869 Blue Hills Ave, Bloomfield, Connecticut 06002-3710 Tel: 1 860 243-1115.
Web site: http://www.talkofconnecticut.com
Profile: WWCO-AM is a commercial station owned by Connoisseur Media. The format of the station is talk. WWCO-AM broadcasts to the Bloomfield, CT area at 1240 AM.
AM RADIO STATION

WWCS-AM 35745
Owner: Birach Broadcasting Corp.
Editorial: 400 Ardmore Blvd, Pittsburgh, Pennsylvania 15221-3019
Profile: WWCS-AM is a commercial station owned by Birach Broadcasting Corp. The format of the station is sports. WWCS-AM broadcasts to Canonsburg, PA at 540 AM.
AM RADIO STATION

WWCT-FM 63227
Owner: Advanced Media Partners LLC
Editorial: 2006 W Altorfer Dr, Peoria, Illinois 61615-1864 Tel: 1 309 691-0101.
Email: info@ampillinois.com
Web site: http://www.wwctfm.com
Profile: WWCT-FM is a commercial station owned by Advanced Media Partners LLC. The format for the station is adult album alternative music. WWCT-FM broadcasts to the Peoria, IL area at 99.9 FM.
FM RADIO STATION

WWDB-AM 37092
Owner: Beasley Broadcast Group
Editorial: 555 E City Ave, Bala Cynwyd, Pennsylvania 19004-1115
Email: webmaster@wwdbam.com
Web site: http://www.wwdbam.com
Profile: WWDB-AM is a commercial station owned by Beasley Broadcast Group. The format of the station is variety featuring music, news and talk multicultural programming. WWDB-AM broadcasts to the Philadelphia area at 860 AM.
AM RADIO STATION

WWDC-FM 45609
Owner: iHeartMedia Inc.
Editorial: 1801 Rockville Pike Fl 5, Rockville, Maryland 20852-1633 Tel: 1 240 747-2700.
Web site: http://dc101.iheart.com
Profile: WWDC-FM is a commercial station owned by iHeartMedia Inc. The format of the station is rock alternative. WWDC-FM broadcasts to the Washington, D.C. area at 101.1 FM.
FM RADIO STATION

WWDE-FM 40838
Owner: Entercom Communications Corp.
Editorial: 236 Clearfield Ave Ste 206, Virginia Beach, Virginia 23462-1893 Tel: 1 757 497-2000.
Web site: http://www.2wd.com
Profile: WWDE-FM is a commercial station owned by Entercom Communications Corp. The format of the station is adult contemporary. WWDE-FM broadcasts to the Virginia Beach, VA area at 101.3 FM.
FM RADIO STATION

WWDJ-AM 156031
Owner: Salem Media Group, Inc.
Editorial: 500 Victory Rd Ste 2, North Quincy, Massachusetts 02171-3132 Tel: 1 617 328-0880.
Email: radioluzboston@gmail.com
Web site: http://radioluzboston.com
Profile: WWDJ-AM is a commercial station owned by Salem Media Group, Inc. The format of the station is Spanish Christian Talk. WWDJ-AM broadcasts to the Boston area at 1150 AM.
AM RADIO STATION

WWDK-FM 75295
Owner: Midwest Communications, Inc.
Editorial: 2495 Cedar St, Holt, Michigan 48842-7400
Tel: 1 517 699-0111.
Web site: http://941theduke.com
Profile: WWDK-FM is a commercial station owned by Midwest Communications, Inc. The format of the station is Classic Country. WWDK-FM broadcasts to the Holt, MI area at 94.1 FM.
FM RADIO STATION

WWDM-FM 40839
Owner: Alpha Media
Editorial: 1900 Pineview Dr, Columbia, South Carolina 29209-5079 Tel: 1 803 695-8600.
Web site: http://www.thebigdm.com
Profile: WWDM-FM is a commercial station owned by Alpha Media. The format of the station is urban adult contemporary. WWDM-FM broadcasts to the Columbia, SC area at 101.3 FM.
FM RADIO STATION

WWDN-AM 35384
Owner: Lakes Media LLC
Editorial: 1336 Piney Forest Rd, Danville, Virginia 24540-1606 Tel: 1 434 799-1010.
Web site: http://www.1045thedan.com
Profile: WWDN-AM is a commercial station owned by Lakes Media LLC. The format of the station is

classic hits and classic rock. WWDN-AM broadcasts to the Danville, VA area at 1580 AM.
AM RADIO STATION

WWDR-AM 3829
Owner: First Media Radio LLC
Editorial: 1714 W Main St, Murfreesboro, North Carolina 27855-1680 Tel: 1 252 398-4111.
Web site: http://bestaround.moonfruit.com
Profile: WWDR-AM is a commercial station owned by First Media Radio LLC. The format of the station is gospel. WWDR-AM broadcasts to the Murfreesboro, NC area at 1080 AM.
AM RADIO STATION

WWDV-FM 4056
Owner: Hubbard Radio, LLC
Editorial: 875 N Michigan Ave Ste 1510, Chicago, Illinois 60611-1874 Tel: 1 312 274-9710.
Web site: http://www.wdrv.com
Profile: WWDV-FM is a commercial station owned by Hubbard Radio, LLC. The format of the station is classic rock. WWDV-FM broadcasts to the Zion, IL area at a frequency of 96.9 FM.
FM RADIO STATION

WWDW-FM 32482
Owner: First Media Radio LLC
Editorial: 3 E 1st St, Weldon, North Carolina 27890-1560 Tel: 1 252 536-3115.
Web site: https://www.3wdfm.com
Profile: WWDW-FM is a commercial station owned by First Media Radio LLC. The format of the station is adult contemporary. WWDW-FM broadcasts to the Weldon, NC area at 107.7 FM.
FM RADIO STATION

WWDX-AM 35423
Owner: Freeland Broadcasting
Editorial: 215 Baker Rd, Huntingdon, Tennessee 38344-7703 Tel: 1 731 986-0242.
Web site: http://www.thefarmradio.com
Profile: WWDX-AM is a commercial station owned by Freeland Broadcasting. The format of the station is classic country. WWDX-AM broadcasts to the Huntingdon, TN area at 1530 AM.
AM RADIO STATION

WWEB-FM 42700
Owner: Choate Rosemary Hall Foundation
Editorial: 333 Christian St, Wallingford, Connecticut 06492-3818 Tel: 1 203 697-2252.
Profile: WWEB-FM is a non-commercial station owned by the Choate Rosemary Hall Foundation. The format of the station is college variety. WWEB-FM broadcasts to the Wallingford, CT area at 89.9 FM.
FM RADIO STATION

WWEC-FM 44263
Owner: Elizabethtown College
Editorial: 1 Alpha Dr, Elizabethtown, Pennsylvania 17022-2298 Tel: 1 717 361-1553.
Email: wwec@etown.edu
Web site: http://wwec.fm
Profile: WWEC-FM is a non-commercial station owned by Elizabethtown College. The format of the station is variety. The station broadcasts to the Elizabethtown, PA area at a frequency of 88.3 FM.
FM RADIO STATION

WWEG-FM 4503
Owner: Manning Broadcasting Inc.
Editorial: 880 Commonwealth Ave, Hagerstown, Maryland 21740-6836 Tel: 1 301 733-4500.
Web site: http://www.1069theeagle.com
Profile: WWEG-FM is a commercial station owned by Manning Broadcasting Inc. The format of the station is classic hits. WWEG-FM broadcasts in the Hagerstown, MD area at 106.9 FM.
FM RADIO STATION

WWEL-FM 4561
Owner: Forcht Broadcasting
Editorial: 534 Tobacco Rd, London, Kentucky 40741
Tel: 1 606 864-2148.
Web site: http://www.sam1039.com
Profile: WWEL-FM is a commercial station owned by Forcht Broadcasting. The format of the station is adult hits. WWEL-FM broadcasts to the London, KY area at 103.9 FM.
FM RADIO STATION

WWET-FM 43316
Owner: Georgia Public Broadcasting
Editorial: 260 14th St NW, Atlanta, Georgia 30318
Tel: 1 404 685-2548.
Email: news@gpb.org
Web site: http://www.gpb.org
Profile: WWET-FM is a commercial station owned by Georgia Public Broadcasting. The format of the station is news, classical and jazz music, and talk. WWET-FM broadcasts to the Hasty, GA area at 91.7 FM.
FM RADIO STATION

WWEV-FM 43668
Owner: War Hill Christian Fellowship, Inc.
Editorial: 1705 Sawnee Dr, Cumming, Georgia 30040-4473 Tel: 1 770 781-9150.
Email: support@victory915.com
Web site: http://victory915.com
Profile: WWEV-FM is a non-commercial station owned by the War Hill Christian Fellowship, Inc. The format of the station is contemporary Christian music. WWEV-FM broadcasts to the Cumming, GA area at 91.5 FM.
FM RADIO STATION

WWFD-AM 543863

Owner: Hubbard Broadcasting, Inc.
Editorial: 3400 Idaho Ave NW, Washington, District Of Columbia 20016-3046 **Tel:** 1 202 895-5000.
Profile: WWFD-AM is a commercial station owned by Hubbard Broadcasting, Inc. The format of the station is AAA. WWFD-AM broadcasts to the Frederick, MD area at 820 AM.
AM RADIO STATION

WWFE-AM 35870

Owner: Fenix Broadcasting Corp.
Editorial: 330 SW 27th Ave Ste 207, Miami, Florida 33135-2957 **Tel:** 1 305 541-3300.
Web site: http://www.lapoderosa.com
Profile: WWFE-AM is a commercial station owned by Fenix Broadcasting Corp. The format of the station is Spanish language news and talk. WWFE-AM broadcasts to the Miami area at 670 AM.
AM RADIO STATION

WWFF-FM 41260

Owner: Cumulus Media Inc.
Editorial: 1717 US Highway 72 E, Athens, Alabama 35611-4413 **Tel:** 1 256 830-8300.
Web site: http://www.933nashicon.com
Profile: WWFF-FM is a commercial station owned by Cumulus Media Inc. The format of the station is country music. WWFF-FM broadcasts to the Huntsville, AL area at 93.3 FM.
FM RADIO STATION

WWFG-FM 40429

Owner: iHeartMedia Inc.
Editorial: 351 Tilghman Rd, Gateway Crossing, Salisbury, Maryland 21804-1920 **Tel:** 1 410 742-1923.
Email: dickraymond@iheartmedia.com
Web site: http://www.froggy999.com
Profile: WWFG-FM is a commercial station owned by iHeartMedia Inc. The format of the station is country music. WWFG-FM broadcasts in the Salisbury, MD area at 99.9 FM.
FM RADIO STATION

WWFM-FM 40840

Owner: Mercer County Community College
Editorial: 1200 Old Trenton Rd, Princeton Junction, New Jersey 08550-3407 **Tel:** 1 609 587-8989.
Email: info@wwfm.org
Web site: http://www.wwfm.org
Profile: WWFM-FM is a non-commercial station owned by Mercer County Community College. The format of the station is classical music. WWFM-FM broadcasts to the Windsor, NJ area at 89.1 FM.
FM RADIO STATION

WWFN-FM 41817

Owner: Cumulus Media Inc.
Editorial: 2014 N Irby St, Florence, South Carolina 29501 **Tel:** 1 843 661-5000.
Web site: http://www.thefanfm.com
Profile: WWFN-FM is a commercial station owned by Cumulus Media Inc. The format of the station is sports. WWFN-FM broadcasts to the Florence, SC area at 100.1 FM.
FM RADIO STATION

WWFW-FM 40872

Owner: Adams Radio Group
Editorial: 9604 Coldwater Rd, Fort Wayne, Indiana 46825-2096 **Tel:** 1 260 747-1511.
Profile: WWFW-FM is a commercial station owned by Adams Radio Group. The format of the station is soft rock. The station broadcasts in Fort Wayne, IN at 103.9 FM.
FM RADIO STATION

WWFX-FM 43891

Owner: Cumulus Media Inc.
Editorial: 250 Commercial St Ste 530, Worcester, Massachusetts 01608-1726 **Tel:** 1 508 752-1045.
Web site: http://www.pikefm.com/
Profile: WWFX-FM is a commercial station owned by Cumulus Media Inc. The format of the station is classic hits. WWFX-FM broadcasts to the Worcester, MA area at 100.1 FM.
FM RADIO STATION

WWFY-FM 41815

Owner: Great Eastern Radio, LLC
Editorial: 41 Jacques St, Barre, Vermont 05641-5320 **Tel:** 1 802 476-4168.
Web site: http://www.froggy1009.com
Profile: WWFY-FM is a commercial station owned by Great Eastern Radio, LLC. The format of the station is country. WWFY-FM broadcasts to the Barre, VT area at a frequency of 100.9 FM.
FM RADIO STATION

WWGB-AM 36716

Owner: Good Body Media
Editorial: 6710 Oxon Hill Rd Ste 100, Oxon Hill, Maryland 20745-1158 **Tel:** 1 301 899-1444.
Email: radio@wwgb.com
Web site: http://www.wwgb.com
Profile: WWGB-AM is a commercial station owned by Good Body Media. The format of the station is Hispanic gospel music and religious programming. WWGB-AM broadcasts to the Suitland, MD area at 1030 AM.
AM RADIO STATION

WWGE-AM 36503

Owner: Pennsylvania Radio Werks LLC
Editorial: 101 W High St Ste 102-A, Ebensburg, Pennsylvania 15931-1538 **Tel:** 1 814 472-0888.
Profile: WWGE-AM is a commercial station owned by Pennsylvania Radio Werks LLC. The format of the station is classic hits music and sports. The station airs at a frequency of 1400 AM to the Johnston, PA area.
AM RADIO STATION

WWGF-FM 43966

Owner: Good News Network
Editorial: 2278 Wortham Ln, Grovetown, Georgia 30813 **Tel:** 1 706 309-9610.
Web site: http://www.gnnradio.org
Profile: WWGF-FM is a commercial station owned by Good News Network. The format of the station is religious. WWGF-FM broadcasts to the Donalsonville area at a frequency of 107.5 FM.
FM RADIO STATION

WWGK-AM 35148

Owner: Good Karma Broadcasting
Editorial: 1301 E 9th St Ste 252, Cleveland, Ohio 44114-1800 **Tel:** 1 216 583-9901.
Web site: http://espn.go.com/cleveland
Profile: WWGK-AM is a commercial station owned by Good Karma Broadcasting. The format of the station is sports. WWGK-AM broadcasts to the Cleveland area at 1540 AM.
AM RADIO STATION

WWGM-FM 43422

Owner: Grace Broadcasting Services Inc.
Editorial: 2263 N Highland Ave, Jackson, Tennessee 38305-4922 **Tel:** 1 731 663-2327.
Web site: http://www.goodnews931.com
Profile: WWGM-FM is a commercial station owned by Grace Broadcasting Services Inc. The format of the station is gospel. WWGM-FM broadcasts to the Jackson, TN area at 93.1 FM.
FM RADIO STATION

WWGO-FM 43068

Owner: Cromwell Group Inc.(The)
Editorial: 209 Lake Land Blvd, Mattoon, Illinois 61938-3904 **Tel:** 1 217 235-5624.
Email: theparty@radiomattoon.com
Web site: http://www.radiolink.com
Profile: WWGO-FM is a commercial station owned by Cromwell Group Inc. The format of the station is classic rock music. WWGO-FM broadcasts to the Mattoon, IL area at 92.1 FM.
FM RADIO STATION

WWGP-AM 38271

Owner: WWGP Broadcasting Corporation
Editorial: 2201 Jefferson Davis Hwy, Sanford, North Carolina 27330 **Tel:** 1 919 775-3525.
Email: production@wfjaradio.com
Web site: http://www.wwgp1050.com/
Profile: WWGP-AM is a commercial station owned by WWGP Broadcasting Corp. The format of the station is country music. WWGP-AM broadcasts in the Sanford, NC area at 1050 AM.
AM RADIO STATION

WWGR-FM 42761

Owner: Renda Broadcasting
Editorial: 10915 K Nine Dr, Bonita Springs, Florida 34135-6802 **Tel:** 1 239 495-8383.
Web site: http://www.gatorcountry1019.com
FM RADIO STATION

WWGY-FM 43402

Owner: FM Radio Licenses, LLC
Editorial: 219 Savannah Gardner Rd, New Castle, Pennsylvania 16101-5546 **Tel:** 1 724 346-5070.
Web site: http://www.froggy95pa.com
Profile: WWGY-FM is a commercial station owned by FM Radio Licenses, LLC. The format of the station is contemporary country music. WWGY-FM broadcasts in the New Castle, PA area at 95.1 FM.
FM RADIO STATION

WWHG-FM 41866

Owner: Big Radio
Editorial: 1 Parker Pl Ste 485, Janesville, Wisconsin 53545-4078 **Tel:** 1 608 758-9025.
Web site: http://www.1059thehog.com
Profile: WWHG-FM is a commercial station owned by Good Karma Broadcasting. The format of the station is classic rock. WWHG-FM broadcasts to the Janesville, WI area at 105.9 FM.
FM RADIO STATION

WWHM-AM 37000

Owner: Miller Communications Inc.
Editorial: 51 Commerce St, Sumter, South Carolina 29150-5014 **Tel:** 1 803 775-2321.
Email: production@miller.fm
Web site: http://www.miller.fm
Profile: WWHM-AM is a commercial station owned by Miller Communications Inc. The format of the station is R&B oldies. WWHM-AM's broadcasts to the Sumter, SC area at 1290 AM.
AM RADIO STATION

WWHN-AM 36177

Owner: Hawkins Broadcasting
Editorial: 10321 S Halsted St, Chicago, Illinois 60628-2321 **Tel:** 1 773 239-3100.
Email: wwhn@sbcglobal.net
Profile: WWHN-AM is a commercial station owned by Hawkins Broadcasting. The format of the station is gospel. WWHN-AM broadcasts to the Joliet, IL and the south suburbs of Chicago at 1510 AM.
AM RADIO STATION

WWHP-FM 40919

Owner: WMS 1 Inc.
Editorial: 407 N Main St, Farmer City, Illinois 61842-1107 **Tel:** 1 309 928-9876.
Email: talk@983talk.com
Web site: http://news.983talk.com/
Profile: WWHP-FM is a commercial station owned by WMS 1 Inc. The format of the station is Talk. WWHP-FM broadcasts in the Farmer City, IL at 98.3 FM.
FM RADIO STATION

WWHQ-FM 44122

Owner: Radiowerks, Inc.
Editorial: 407 Lothian St, Mountain Lake Park, Maryland 21550-2909 **Tel:** 1 301 334-4272.
Email: office@wkhj.com
Web site: http://www.92wwhq.com
Profile: WWHC-FM is a commercial station owned by Radiowerks, Inc. The format of the station is contemporary country. WWHC-FM broadcasts to the Mountain Lake Park, MD area at 92.3 FM.
FM RADIO STATION

WWHT-FM 46145

Owner: iHeartMedia Inc.
Editorial: 500 Plum St Ste 100, Syracuse, New York 13204-1427 **Tel:** 1 315 472-9797.
Web site: http://www.hot1079.com
Profile: WWHT-FM is a commercial station owned by iHeartMedia Inc. The format of the station is hot adult contemporary. WWHT-FM broadcasts to the Syracuse, NY area at 107.9 FM.
FM RADIO STATION

WWHX-FM 354876

Owner: Connoisseur Media LLC
Editorial: 520 N Center St, Bloomington, Illinois 61701-2902 **Tel:** 1 309 834-1100.
Web site: http://www.bloomingtonhits.com
Profile: WWHX-FM is a commercial station owned by Neuhoff Communications. The format of the station is Top 40/CHR. WWHX-FM broadcasts to the Bloomington, IL area at 100.7 FM.
FM RADIO STATION

WWIB-FM 46556

Owner: Stewards of Sound Inc.
Editorial: 2396 Hallie Rd Ste 1, Chippewa Falls, Wisconsin 54729-7519 **Tel:** 1 715 723-1037.
Email: wwib@wwib.com
Web site: http://www.wwib.com
Profile: WWIB-FM is a commercial station owned by Stewards of Sound Inc. The format of the station is contemporary Christian. WWIB-FM broadcasts to the Chippewa Falls, WI area at 103.7 FM.
FM RADIO STATION

WWIC-AM 35747

Owner: Scottsboro Broadcasting Co.
Editorial: 815 W Willow St, Scottsboro, Alabama 35768 **Tel:** 1 256 259-1050.
Email: wwic@scottsboro.org
Web site: http://www.wwicradio.com
Profile: WWIC-AM is a commercial station owned by Scottsboro Broadcasting Co. The format of the station is country music. WIWC-AM broadcasts to the Huntsville, AL area at 1050 AM.
AM RADIO STATION

WWIK-FM 42443

Owner: Kirkman Broadcasting
Editorial: 60 Markfield Dr Ste 4, Charleston, South Carolina 29407-7907 **Tel:** 1 843 763-6631.
Web site: http://www.charlestonsportsradio.com
Profile: WWIK-FM is a commercial station owned by Kirkman Broadcasting. The format of the station is sports. WWIK-FM broadcasts to the North Charleston, SC area at 98.9 FM.
FM RADIO STATION

WWIL-AM 39374

Owner: Carolina Christian Radio, Inc.
Editorial: 3305 Burnt Mill Dr Ste 400, Wilmington, North Carolina 28403-3064 **Tel:** 1 910 763-2452.
Email: rejoice@gospeljoy1490.com
Web site: http://www.gospeljoy1490.net
Profile: WWIL-AM is a non-commercial station owned by Carolina Christian Radio, Inc. The format of the station is gospel. WWIL-AM broadcasts in the Wilmington, NC area at 1490 AM.
AM RADIO STATION

WWIL-FM 46740

Owner: Carolina Christian Radio, Inc.
Editorial: 3305 Burnt Mill Dr, Wilmington, North Carolina 28403-3063 **Tel:** 1 910 763-2452.
Email: church@life905.com
Web site: http://www.life905.com
Profile: WWIL-FM is a commercial station owned by Carolina Christian Radio, Inc. The format of the station is contemporary Christian music and religious programming. WWIL-FM broadcasts to the Wilmington, NC area at 90.5 FM.
FM RADIO STATION

WWIN-AM 38273

Owner: Urban One, Inc.
Editorial: 1705 Whitehead Rd, Baltimore, Maryland 21207-4033 **Tel:** 1 410 332-8200.
Web site: http://www.spirit1400.com
Profile: WWIN-AM is a commercial station owned by Urban One, Inc. The format of the station is gospel music. WWIN-AM broadcasts to the Baltimore area at 1400 AM.
AM RADIO STATION

WWIN-FM 45691

Owner: Urban One, Inc.
Editorial: 1705 Whitehead Rd, Baltimore, Maryland 21207-4033 **Tel:** 1 410 332-8200.
Web site: http://www.magic959baltimore.com
Profile: WWIN-FM is a commercial station owned by Urban One, Inc. The format of the station is urban adult contemporary music. WWIN-FM broadcasts to the Baltimore area at 95.9 FM.
FM RADIO STATION

WWIS-AM 38664

Owner: WWIS Radio Inc.
Editorial: W11573 Town Creek Rd, Black River Falls, Wisconsin 54615 **Tel:** 1 715 284-4391.
Email: wwis@wwisradio.com
Web site: http://www.wwisradio.com
Profile: WWIS-AM is a commercial station owned by WWIS Radio Inc. The format of the station is adult contemporary music. WWIS-AM broadcasts to the Black River Falls, WI area at 1260 AM.
AM RADIO STATION

WWIS-FM 235039

Owner: WWIS Radio Inc.
Editorial: W11573 Town Creek Rd, Black River Falls, Wisconsin 54615 **Tel:** 1 715 284-4391.
Email: wwis@wwisradio.com
Web site: http://www.wwisradio.com
Profile: WWIS-FM is a commercial station owned by WWIS Radio Inc. The format of the station is classic country music. WWIS-FM broadcasts to the Black River Falls, WI area at 99.7 FM.
FM RADIO STATION

WWIZ-FM 40844

Owner: Cumulus Media Inc.
Editorial: 4040 Simon Rd, Youngstown, Ohio 44512-1362 **Tel:** 1 330 783-1000.
Web site: http://www.oldiesz104.com
Profile: WWIZ-FM is a commercial station owned by Cumulus Media Inc. The format of the station is Oldes. WWIZ-FM broadcasts to the Youngstown, OH area at 103.9 FM.
FM RADIO STATION

WWJ-AM 38274

Owner: CBS Radio
Editorial: 26455 American Dr, Southfield, Michigan 48034-6114 **Tel:** 1 248 327-2900.
Email: wwjnewsroom@cbsradio.com
Web site: http://detroit.cbslocal.com
Profile: WWJ-AM is a commercial station owned by CBS Radio. The format of the station is news. WWJ-AM broadcasts to the Detroit area at 950 AM.
AM RADIO STATION

WWJB-AM 37050

Owner: Hernando Broadcasting Co.
Editorial: 55 W Fort Dade Ave, Brooksville, Florida 34601 **Tel:** 1 352 796-7469.
Email: info@wwjb.com
Web site: http://www.wwjb.com
Profile: WWJB-AM is a commercial station owned by Hernando Broadcasting Co. The format of the station is news and talk. WWJB-AM broadcasts in the Brooksville, FL area at 1450 AM.
AM RADIO STATION

WWJC-AM 35750

Owner: VCY America Inc.
Editorial: 3434 W Kilbourn Ave, Milwaukee, Wisconsin 53208-3313 **Tel:** 1 800 729-9829.
Email: vcy@vcyamerica.org
Web site: http://www.vcyamerica.org
Profile: WWJC-AM is a non-commercial station owned by VCY America Inc. The format of the station is Christian talk and teaching. WWJC-AM broadcasts to the Duluth, MN area at 850 AM.
AM RADIO STATION

WWJD-FM 41497

Owner: Alice Lloyd College
Editorial: 100 Purpose Rd, Pippa Passes, Kentucky 41844-9005 **Tel:** 1 606 368-6131.
Email: wwjd@alc.edu
Web site: http://www.alc.edu
Profile: WWJD-FM is a non-commercial station owned by Alice Lloyd College. The format of the station is contemporary Christian. WWJD-FM broadcasts to the Lexington, KY area at 91.7 FM.
FM RADIO STATION

WWJK-FM 41726

Owner: iheartMedia Inc.
Editorial: 11700 Central Pkwy, Jacksonville, Florida 32224-2600 **Tel:** 1 904 636-0507.
Web site: http://www.1073jack.com
Profile: WWJK-FM is a commercial station owned by iheartMedia Inc. The format of the station is adult hits and alternative WWJK-FM broadcasts to Jacksonville, FL at 107.3 FM.
FM RADIO STATION

WWJM-FM 40845

Owner: Perry County Broadcasting
Editorial: 210 S Jackson St, New Lexington, Ohio 43764-1366 **Tel:** 1 740 455-3961.
Email: wwjmp3@aol.com
Web site: http://www.wwjm.com
Profile: WWJM-FM is a commercial station owned by Perry County Broadcasting. The format of the station is adult contemporary music. WWJM-FM broadcasts to the New Lexington, OH area at 105.9 FM.
FM RADIO STATION

United States of America

WWJO-FM 45613
Owner: Townsquare Media, LLC
Editorial: 640 Lincoln Ave SE, Saint Cloud, Minnesota 56304-1024 **Tel:** 1 320 251-4422.
Web site: http://minnesotasnewcountry.com
Profile: WWJO-FM is a commercial station owned by Townsquare Media, LLC. The format of the station is contemporary country music. WWJO-FM broadcasts to the St. Cloud, MN area at 98.1 FM.
FM RADIO STATION

WWKA-FM 45615
Owner: Cox Media Group, Inc.
Editorial: 4192 N John Young Pkwy, Orlando, Florida 32804-2620 **Tel:** 1 321 281-2000.
Email: news@wdbo.com
Web site: http://www.k923orlando.com
Profile: WWKA-FM is a commercial station owned by Cox Media Group, Inc. The format of the station is country. WWKA-FM broadcasts to the Orlando, FL area at 92.3 FM.
FM RADIO STATION

WWKB-AM 38276
Owner: Entercom Communications Corp.
Editorial: 500 Corporate Pkwy, Buffalo, New York 14226-1263 **Tel:** 1 716 843-0600.
Web site: http://www.espn1520.com
Profile: WWKB-AM is a commercial station owned by Entercom Communications Corp. The primary format of the station is sports. WWKB-AM broadcasts to the Buffalo, NY, area at 1520 AM.
AM RADIO STATION

WWKC-FM 41980
Owner: AVC Communications Inc.
Editorial: 4988 Skyline Dr, Cambridge, Ohio 43725 **Tel:** 1 740 732-5777.
Email: avcnews@yourradioplace.com
Web site: http://www.yourradioplace.com
Profile: WWKC-FM is a commercial station owned by AVC Communications Inc. The format of the station is country. WWKC-FM broadcasts to the Cambridge, OH area at 104.9 FM.
FM RADIO STATION

WWKF-FM 45616
Owner: WENK of Union City, Inc.
Editorial: 1729 Nailling Dr, Union City, Tennessee 38261 **Tel:** 1 731 885-1240.
Web site: http://www.kf99kq105.com
Profile: WWKF-FM is a commercial station owned by WENK of Union City, Inc. The format of the station is Top 40/CHR music. WWKF-FM broadcasts to the Union City, TN area at 99.3 FM.
FM RADIO STATION

WWKI-FM 40846
Owner: Cumulus Media Inc.
Editorial: 519 N Main St, Kokomo, Indiana 46901-4619 **Tel:** 1 765 459-4191.
Web site: http://www.wwki.com
Profile: WWKI-FM is a commercial station owned by Cumulus Media Inc. The format of the station is contemporary country music. WWKI-FM broadcasts to the Indianapolis area at 100.5 FM. The station's slogan is, "North Central Indiana's Most Listened-To Country Station."
FM RADIO STATION

WWKL-FM 40194
Owner: Cumulus Media Inc.
Editorial: 2300 Vartan Way, Harrisburg, Pennsylvania 17110-9720 **Tel:** 1 717 238-1041.
Web site: http://www.hot92.com
Profile: WWKL-FM is a commercial station owned by Cumulus Media Inc. The format of the station is Uban music. WWKL-FM broadcasts to the Harrisburg, PA area at 93.5 FM.
FM RADIO STATION

WWKR-FM 43639
Owner: Synergy Media Inc.
Editorial: 5399 W Wallace Ln, Ludington, Michigan 49431 **Tel:** 1 231 843-0941.
Web site: http://www.94k-rock.com
Profile: WWKR-FM is a commercial station owned by Synergy Media Inc. The format of the station is classic rock music. WWKR-FM broadcasts to the Pentwater, MI area at 94.1 FM.
FM RADIO STATION

WWKT-FM 45617
Owner: Miller Communications Inc.
Editorial: 51 Commerce St, Sumter, South Carolina 29150-5014 **Tel:** 1 803 775-2321.
Email: production@miller.fm
Web site: http://www.katcountry993.net
Profile: WWKT-FM is a commercial station owned by Miller Communications Inc. The format of the station is contemporary country. WWKT-FM broadcasts to the Sumter, SC area at 99.3 FM
FM RADIO STATION

WWKU-AM 508980
Owner: Commonwealth Broadcasting Corp.
Editorial: 1823 McIntosh St Ste 107, Bowling Green, Kentucky 42104-1073 **Tel:** 1 270 846-0222.
Email: espnky@yahoo.com
Web site: http://www.espn1450.net
Profile: WWKU-AM is a commercial station owned by Commonwealth Broadcasting Corp. The format of the station is sports. WWKU-AM broadcasts to the Bowling Green, KY area at 1450 AM.
AM RADIO STATION

WWKX-FM 41412
Owner: Cumulus Media Inc.
Editorial: 1502 Wampanoag Trl, Riverside, Rhode Island 02915-1018 **Tel:** 1 401 433-4200.
Web site: http://www.hot1063.com
Profile: WWKX-FM is a commercial station owned by Cumulus Media Inc. The format of the rhythmic Top 40/CHR. WWKX-FM broadcasts to the Riverside, RI area at 106.3 FM.
FM RADIO STATION

WWKY-FM 40356
Owner: Commonwealth Broadcasting Corp.
Editorial: 265 S Main St, Madisonville, Kentucky 42431 **Tel:** 1 270 825-9779.
Profile: WWKY-FM is a commercial station owned by Commonwealth Broadcasting Corp. The format of the station is oldies. WWKY-FM broadcasts to the Madisonville, KY area at 97.7 FM.
FM RADIO STATION

WWKZ-FM 43503
Owner: iHeartMedia, Inc.
Editorial: 5026 Cliff Gookin Blvd, Tupelo, Mississippi 38801-7059 **Tel:** 1 662 842-1067.
Web site: http://kz103.iheart.com/
Profile: WWKZ-FM is a commercial station owned by iHeartMedia, Inc. The format of the station is Top 40/ CHR. WWKZ-FM broadcasts to the Tupelo, MS area at 103.9 FM.
FM RADIO STATION

WWL-AM 38277
Owner: Entercom Communications Corp.
Editorial: 400 Poydras St, Ste 800, New Orleans, Louisiana 70130 **Tel:** 1 504 593-6376.
Email: wwlnewsroom@yahoo.com
Web site: http://www.wwl.com
Profile: WWL-AM is a commercial station owned by Entercom Communications Corp. The format of the station is news, sports and talk. WWL-AM broadcasts to the New Orleans area at 870 AM.
AM RADIO STATION

WWLB-FM 46323
Owner: Alpha Media
Editorial: 300 Arboretum Pl Ste 590, Richmond, Virginia 23236 **Tel:** 1 804 327-9902.
Web site: http://www.989wolf.com
Profile: WWLB-FM is a commercial station owned by Alpha Media. The format of the station is Jack FM-Adult Hits. WWLB-FM broadcasts to the Richmond, VA, area at 98.9 FM.
FM RADIO STATION

WWLD-FM 42348
Owner: Cumulus Media Inc.
Editorial: 3411 W Tharpe St, Tallahassee, Florida 32303 **Tel:** 1 850 201-3000.
Web site: http://www.blazin1023.com
Profile: WWLD-FM is a commercial station owned by Cumulus Media Inc. The format for the station is urban contemporary. WWLD-FM broadcasts to the Tallahassee, FL area at 102.3 FM.
FM RADIO STATION

WWL-FM 43037
Owner: Entercom Communications Corp.
Editorial: 400 Poydras St, Ste 800, New Orleans, Louisiana 70130 **Tel:** 1 504 593-6376.
Email: wwlnewsroom@yahoo.com
Web site: http://www.wwl.com
Profile: WWL-FM is a commercial station owned by Entercom Communications Corp. The format of the station is a news, talk and sports. WWL-FM broadcasts to the New Orleans area at 105.3 FM.
FM RADIO STATION

WWLG-FM 44390
Owner: iHeartMedia Inc.
Editorial: 1819 Peachtree Rd NE Ste. 700, Atlanta, Georgia 30309-1848 **Tel:** 1 404 875-8080.
Web site: http://www.radio1057.com
Profile: WWLG-FM is a commercial station owned by iHeartMedia Inc. The format of the station is alternative rock. WWLG-FM broadcasts to the Atlanta area at 96.7 FM.
FM RADIO STATION

WWLI-FM 45618
Owner: Cumulus Media Inc.
Editorial: 1502 Wampanoag Trl, Riverside, Rhode Island 2915 **Tel:** 1 401 433-4200.
Web site: http://www.lite105.com
Profile: WWLI-FM is a commercial station owned by Cumulus Media Inc. The format of the station is adult contemporary music. WWLI-FM broadcasts to the Riverside, RI area at 105.1 FM.
FM RADIO STATION

WWLL-FM 45065
Owner: Cohan Radio Group Inc.
Editorial: 3750 US Highway 27 N, Sebring, Florida 33870-1690 **Tel:** 1 863 382-9999.
Web site: http://www.cohanradiogroup.com
Profile: WWLL-FM is a commercial station owned by Cohan Radio Group Inc. The format of the station is adult contemporary music. WWLL-FM broadcasts in the Sebring, FL area at 105.7 FM.
FM RADIO STATION

WWLR-FM 41586
Owner: Lyndon State College
Editorial: 1001 College Rd, Lyndonville, Vermont 5851 **Tel:** 1 800 225-1998.
Email: sga@lyndonstate.edu
Web site: http://lyndonstate.edu/offices-services/wwlr-radio-station/
FM RADIO STATION

WWLS-FM 44455
Owner: Cumulus Media Inc
Editorial: 4045 NW 64th St, Oklahoma City, Oklahoma 73116-1684 **Tel:** 1 405 848-0100.
Web site: http://www.thesportsanimal.com
Profile: WWLS-FM is a commercial station owned by Cumulus Media Inc. The format of the station is sports. WWLS-FM broadcasts to the Oklahoma City area at 98.1 FM.
FM RADIO STATION

WWLW-FM 86428
Owner: West Virginia Radio Corp.
Editorial: 1065 Radio Park Dr, Mount Clare, West Virginia 26408 **Tel:** 1 304 623-6546.
Web site: http://www.wvmagic.com
Profile: WWLW-FM is a commercial station owned by West Virginia Radio Corp. The format of the station is adult contemporary. WWLW-FM broadcasts to the Mount Clare, WV area at 106.5 FM.
FM RADIO STATION

WWLX-AM 38278
Owner: Prospect Communications
Editorial: 1212 N Locust Ave, Lawrenceburg, Tennessee 38464-2711 **Tel:** 1 931 762-6200.
Email: wlxnews@bellsouth.net
Web site: http://www.wlxonline.com
Profile: WWLX-AM is a commercial station owned by Prospect Communications. The format of the station is Country. WWLX-AM broadcasts to the Lawrenceburg, TN area at 590 AM.
AM RADIO STATION

WWLZ-AM 37913
Owner: Community Broadcasters, LLC
Editorial: 2205 College Ave, Elmira, New York 14903-1201 **Tel:** 1 607 732-4400.
Web site: http://wwlzam820.com/
Profile: WWLZ-AM is a commercial station owned by Community Broadcasters, LLC. The format of the station is news and talk programming. WWLZ-AM broadcasts to the Elmira, NY area at 820 AM.
AM RADIO STATION

WWMC-AM 38566
Owner: Eastern Airwaves, LLC
Editorial: 2581 US Highway 70 W, Goldsboro, North Carolina 27530-9553 **Tel:** 1 919 736-1150.
Profile: WELS-AM is a commercial station owned by Eastern Airwaves, LLC (a division of Curtis Media Group). The format of the station is black gospel. WELS-AM broadcasts to the Kinston, NC area at 1010 AM.
AM RADIO STATION

WWMG-FM 42102
Owner: iHeartMedia Inc.
Editorial: 203 Gunn Rd, Montgomery, Alabama 36117-2003 **Tel:** 1 334 274-6464.
Web site: http://www.mymagic97.com
Profile: WWMG-FM is a commercial station owned by iHeartMedia Inc. The format of the station is urban adult contemporary. WWMG-FM broadcasts to the Montgomery, AL area at 97.1 FM.
FM RADIO STATION

WWMJ-FM 45621
Owner: Townsquare Media, Inc.
Editorial: 49 Acme Rd, Brewer, Maine 04412-1545 **Tel:** 1 207 989-5631.
Email: i95@midmaine.com
Web site: http://www.wwmj-fm.com
Profile: WWMJ-FM is a commercial station owned by Townsquare Media, Inc. The format of the station is classic hits. WWMJ-FM broadcasts to the Brewer, ME area at 95.7 FM.
FM RADIO STATION

WWMK-AM 36001
Owner: St. Peter the Rock Media, Inc.
Editorial: 145 Ken Mar Industrial Parkway, Broadview Heights, Ohio **Tel:** 1 216 227-1260.
Email: info@am1260therock.com
Web site: http://am1260therock.com
Profile: WWMK-AM is a non-commercial station owned by St. Peter the Rock Media, Inc. The format of the station is Catholic programming. WWMK-AM broadcasts to the Cleveland, OH area at 1260 AM.
AM RADIO STATION

WWMP-FM 44462
Owner: Radio Broadcasting Services, Inc.
Editorial: 372 Dorset St, South Burlington, Vermont 05403-6212 **Tel:** 1 802 863-1010.
Email: joannad@champlainradio.com
Web site: http://www.mp103.com
Profile: WWMP-FM is a commercial station owned by Radio Broadcasting Services, Inc. The format of the station is adult hits. WWMP-FM broadcasts to the South Burlington, VT area at 103.3 FM.
FM RADIO STATION

WWMS-FM 44062
Owner: Mississippi Radio Group
Editorial: 2214 S Gloster St, Tupelo, Mississippi 38801-6814 **Tel:** 1 662 842-7658.
Web site: http://www.miss98.net
Profile: WWMS-FM is a commercial station owned by Mississippi Radio Group. The format of the station is country music. WWMS-FM broadcasts to the Tupelo, MI area at 97.5 FM.
FM RADIO STATION

WWMX-FM 40848
Owner: CBS Radio
Editorial: 1423 Clarkview Rd Ste 100, Baltimore, Maryland 21209-2190 **Tel:** 1 410 825-1065.
Web site: http://mix1065fm.cbslocal.com
Profile: WWMX-FM is a commercial station owned by CBS Radio. The format of the station is hot adult contemporary music. WWMX-FM broadcasts to the Baltimore area at 106.5 FM.
FM RADIO STATION

WWNB-AM 35491
Owner: CTC Media Group
Editorial: 1202 Pollock St, New Bern, North Carolina 28560-5538 **Tel:** 1 252 633-1490.
Web site: http://www.rfenc.com
Profile: WWNB-AM is a commercial owned by the CTC Media Group. The format of the station is sports WWNB-AM broadcasts to the New Bern, NC area at 1490 AM.
AM RADIO STATION

WWNC-AM 38844
Owner: iHeartMedia Inc.
Editorial: 13 Summerlin Dr, Asheville, North Carolina 28806-2800 **Tel:** 1 828 257-2700.
Email: ashevillepsa@iheartmedia.com
Web site: http://www.wwnc.com
Profile: WWNC-AM is a commercial station owned by iHeartMedia Inc. The format for the station is talk. WWNC-AM broadcasts to the Asheville, NC area at 570 AM.
AM RADIO STATION

WWNJ-FM 42021
Owner: Mercer County Community College
Editorial: 1200 Old Trenton Rd, Princeton Junction, New Jersey 08550-3407 **Tel:** 1 609 587-8989.
Email: info@wwfm.org
Web site: http://www.wwfm.org
Profile: WWNJ-FM is a non-commercial station owned by Mercer County Community College. The format of the station is classical music. WWNJ-FM broadcasts to the Princeton Junction, NJ area at 91.1 FM.
FM RADIO STATION

WWNL-AM 36496
Owner: Wilkins Communication Networks Inc.
Editorial: 5316 William Flynn Hwy Ste 3N, Gibsonia, Pennsylvania 15044-9697 **Tel:** 1 724 443-4844.
Email: wwnl@wilkinsradio.com
Web site: http://www.wilkinsradio.com
Profile: WWNL-AM is a commercial station owned by Wilkins Communication Networks Inc. The format for the station is Christian talk. WWNL-AM broadcasts to the Gibsonia, PA area at 1080 AM.
AM RADIO STATION

WWNN-AM 37015
Owner: Beasley Broadcast Group
Editorial: 1650 S Dixie Hwy Fl 5, Boca Raton, Florida 33432-7462 **Tel:** 1 561 997-0074.
Web site: http://www.wwnnradio.com
Profile: WWNN-AM is a commercial station owned by Beasley Broadcast Group. The format of the station is health talk. WWNN-AM broadcasts to the Boca Raton, FL area at 1470 AM.
AM RADIO STATION

WWNQ-FM 324523
Owner: Local Voice Media
Editorial: 1010 Gervais St Ste 100, Columbia, South Carolina 29201-3130 **Tel:** 1 803 753-6800.
Email: country@hometowncolumbia.com
Web site: http://943thedude.com
Profile: WWNQ-FM is a commercial station owned by Local Voice Media. The format of the station is contemporary country. WWNQ-FM broadcasts to the Columbia, SC area at 94.3 FM.
FM RADIO STATION

WWNR-AM 35753
Owner: Southern Communications Corp.
Editorial: 306 S Kanawha St, Beckley, West Virginia 25801-5619 **Tel:** 1 304 253-7000.
Web site: http://wwnrradio.com/
Profile: WWNR-AM is a commercial station owned by Southern Communications Corp. The format of the station is news, sports, and talk. WWNR-AM broadcasts to the Beckley, WV area at 620 AM.
AM RADIO STATION

WWNS-AM 38279
Owner: Radio Statesboro, Inc.
Editorial: 561 E Olliff St, Statesboro, Georgia 30458-4663 **Tel:** 1 912 764-5446.
Profile: WWNS-AM is a commercial station owned by Radio Statesboro, Inc. The format for the station is news. WWNS-AM broadcasts to the Savannah, GA area at 1240 AM.
AM RADIO STATION

WWNW-FM 40850
Owner: Westminster College
Editorial: Westminster College, Box 89, New Wilmington, Pennsylvania 16172 **Tel:** 1 724 946-7242
Email: titanradio@westminster.edu
Web site: http://www.westminster.edu/student/orgs/radio/radio_news.cfm
Profile: WWNW-FM is non-commercial station owned by Westminster College. The format of the station is hot adult contemporary music. WWNW-FM broadcasts in the Westminster, PA area at 88.9 FM.
FM RADIO STATION

WWOD-FM 41315
Owner: Great Eastern Radio, LLC
Editorial: 106 N Main St, West Lebanon, New Hampshire 03784-1136 **Tel:** 1 603 448-1400.
Web site: http://koolnh.com
Profile: WWOD-FM is a commercial station owned by Great Eastern Radio, LLC. The format of the station is classic hits. WWOD-FM broadcasts to the Lebanon, NH area at a frequency of 93.9 FM.
FM RADIO STATION

WWOF-FM 40764
Owner: Red Hills Broadcasting, LLC
Editorial: 3000 Olson Rd, Tallahassee, Florida 32308-3918 **Tel:** 1 850 386-8004.
Web site: http://www.1031thewolf.com
Profile: WWOF-FM is a commercial station owned by Red Hills Broadcasting, LLC. The format of the station is contemporary country music. WWOF-FM broadcasts to the Tallahassee, FL area at 103.1 FM.
FM RADIO STATION

WWOJ-FM 46183
Owner: Cohan Radio Group Inc.
Editorial: 3750 US Highway 27 N Ste 1, Sebring, Florida 33870-1644 **Tel:** 1 863 382-9999.
Web site: http://www.cohanradiogroup.com
Profile: WWOJ-FM is a commercial station owned by Cohan Radio Group Inc. The format of the station is contemporary country. WWOJ-FM broadcasts to the Sebring, FL area at 99.1 FM.
FM RADIO STATION

WWOL-AM 36005
Owner: Holly Springs Baptist Church
Editorial: 1381 W Main St, Forest City, North Carolina 28043-2525 **Tel:** 1 828 245-0078.
Email: wwol@wwol780.com
Web site: http://www.wwol780.com
Profile: WWOL-AM is a commercial station owned by Holly Springs Baptist Church. The format for the station is gospel. WWOL-AM broadcasts to the Greenville, SC; Asheville, NC area at 780 AM.
AM RADIO STATION

WWOS-AM 232068
Owner: Mediatrix SC, Inc.
Editorial: 715 Hampton St, Walterboro, South Carolina 29488-4125 **Tel:** 1 866 263-1700.
Web site: http://catholicradioinsc.com
Profile: WWOS-AM is a non-commercial station owned by Mediatrix SC, Inc.The format of the station is religious with a focus on Catholicism. WWOS-AM broadcasts to the Walterboro, SC area at a frequency of 810 AM.
AM RADIO STATION

WWOT-FM 45453
Owner: FM Radio Licenses, LLC
Editorial: 1 Forever Dr, Hollidaysburg, Pennsylvania 16648-3029 **Tel:** 1 814 941-9800.
Web site: http://www.hot100pa.com/
Profile: WWOT-FM is a commercial station owned by FM Radio Licenses, LLC. The format of the station is Top 40/CHR. WWOT-FM broadcasts to the Hollidaysburg, PA area at 100.1 FM.
FM RADIO STATION

WWOW-AM 35755
Owner: Cause Plus Marketing, LLC
Editorial: 229 Broad St, Conneaut, Ohio 44030-2616 **Tel:** 1 440 593-2233.
Email: wshanleaf@aol.com
Profile: WWOW-AM is a commercial station owned by Cause Plus Marketing, LLC. The format of the station is oldies. WWOW-AM broadcasts to the Conneaut, OH area at 1360 AM.
AM RADIO STATION

WWOZ-FM 40947
Owner: Friends of WWOZ Inc.
Editorial: 1008 N Peters St Fl 2, New Orleans, Louisiana 70116-3317 **Tel:** 1 504 568-1239.
Email: feedback@wwoz.org
Web site: http://www.wwoz.org
Profile: WWOZ-FM is a non-commercial station owned by Friends of WWOZ Inc. The format of the station is jazz and R&B oldies music. WWOZ-FM broadcasts to the New Orleans area at 90.7 FM.
FM RADIO STATION

WWPA-AM 37079
Owner: Backyard Broadcasting
Editorial: 1685 Four Mile Dr, Williamsport, Pennsylvania 17701 **Tel:** 1 570 323-8200.
Profile: WWPA-AM is a commercial station owned by Backyard Broadcasting. The format of the station is news, talk, and sports. WWPA-AM broadcasts to the Williamsport, PA area at 1340 AM.
AM RADIO STATION

WWPC-FM 44176
Owner: Morning Star Academy
Tel: 1 603 859-9170.
Email: wsew@wsew.org
Web site: http://www.wsew.org
Profile: WWPC-FM is a non-commercial station owned by Morning Star Academy. The format for the station is religious programming. WWPC-FM broadcasts to the New Durham, NH area at 91.7 FM.
FM RADIO STATION

WWPG-FM 46502
Owner: Lawson Communications(Jim)
Editorial: 601 Greensboro Ave Ste 507, Tuscaloosa, Alabama 35401-1795 **Tel:** 1 205 345-4787.
Profile: WWPG-FM is a commercial station owned by Lawson Communications. The format of the station is Urban AC. WWPG-FM broadcasts to the Tuscaloosa, AL area at 104.3 FM.
FM RADIO STATION

WWPN-FM 44258
Owner: Santmyire(Ernest F.)
Editorial: 12 N Lavale St, Lavale, Maryland 21502-7201 **Tel:** 1 301 463-5100.
Email: contactus@spirit101.com
Web site: http://www.spirit101.com
Profile: WWPN-FM is a commercial station owned by Ernest F. Santmyire. The format of the station is contemporary Christian. WWPN-FM broadcasts to the Lavale, MD area at 101.1 FM.
FM RADIO STATION

WWPR-AM 36403
Owner: Vidify Media Inc.
Editorial: 5910 Cortez Rd W Ste 130, Bradenton, Florida 34210-2707 **Tel:** 1 941 761-8843.
Web site: http://www.1490wwpr.com
Profile: WWPR-AM is a commercial station owned by Vidify Media Inc. The format of the station is talk. WWPR-AM broadcasts to the Bradenton, FL area at 1490 AM.
AM RADIO STATION

WWPR-FM 40572
Owner: iHeartMedia Inc.
Editorial: 32 Avenue of the Americas Fl 3, New York, New York 10013-2473 **Tel:** 1 212 377-7900.
Web site: http://power1051.iheart.com
Profile: WWPR-FM is a commercial station owned by iHeartMedia Inc. The format of the station is urban contemporary music. WWPR-FM broadcasts to the entire New York City metro area at 105.1 FM.
FM RADIO STATION

WWPW-FM 41643
Owner: iHeartMedia Inc.
Editorial: 1819 Peachtree Rd NE Ste 700, Atlanta, Georgia 30309-1849 **Tel:** 1 404 875-8080.
Web site: http://power961.iheart.com
Profile: WWPW-FM is a commercial station owned by iHeartMedia Inc. The format of the station is top40/CHR music. WWPW-FM broadcasts to the Atlanta area at 96.1 FM.
FM RADIO STATION

WWQM-FM 46593
Owner: Midwest Family Broadcasting
Editorial: 730 Ray O Vac Dr, Madison, Wisconsin 53711 **Tel:** 1 608 273-1000.
Web site: http://www.q106.com
Profile: WWQM-FM is a commercial station owned by Midwest Family Broadcasting. The format of the station is country. WWQM-FM broadcasts to the Madison, WI area at 106.3 FM.
FM RADIO STATION

WWQQ-FM 40855
Owner: Cumulus Media Inc.
Editorial: 3233 Burnt Mill Dr Ste 4, Wilmington, North Carolina 28403-2676 **Tel:** 1 910 763-9977.
Web site: http://www.wwqq101.com
Profile: WWQQ-FM is a commercial station owned by Cumulus Media Inc. The format of the station is country. WWQQ-FM broadcasts to the Wilmington, NC area at 101.3 FM.
FM RADIO STATION

WWRC-AM 38270
Owner: Salem Media Group, Inc.
Editorial: 1901 N Moore St Ste 200, Arlington, Virginia 22209-1706 **Tel:** 1 703 807-2266.
Web site: http://am1260theanswer.com
Profile: WWRC-AM is a commercial station owned by Salem Media Group, Inc. The format of the station is talk. WWRC-AM broadcasts to the Washington, D.C. area at 1260 AM.
AM RADIO STATION

WWRE-FM 46580
Owner: Saga Communications
Editorial: 1820 Heritage Center Way, Harrisonburg, Virginia 22801-8451 **Tel:** 1 540 434-0331.
Web site: http://rewind1051.com
Profile: WWRE-FM is a commercial station owned by Saga Communications. The format of the station is classic hits from the 70s, 80s, and 90s. WWRE-FM broadcasts to the Harrisonburg, VA area at 105.1 FM. The station does not accept unsolicited faxes. Do NOT e-mail any staff members. Any press information should be sent to WSVA-AM.
FM RADIO STATION

WWRF-AM 35949
Owner: Glades Media Radio Group
Editorial: 2326 S Congress Ave Ste 2A, West Palm Beach, Florida 33406-7614 **Tel:** 1 561 721-9950.
Web site: http://www.radiofiesta.com
Profile: WWRF-AM is a commercial station owned by Radio Fiesta, Inc. The format of the station is regional Mexican. WWRF-AM broadcasts to the West Palm Beach, FL area at 1380 AM.
AM RADIO STATION

WWRK-AM 37948
Owner: iHeartMedia Inc.
Editorial: 181 E Evans St Ste 311, Florence, South Carolina 29506-5505 **Tel:** 1 843 665-0970.
Web site: http://swagga941.com/#&panel1-2
Profile: WWRK-AM is a commercial station owned by iHeartMedia Inc. The format of the station is urban contemporary. WWRK-AM broadcasts to the Florence, SC area at 970 AM.
AM RADIO STATION

WWRL-AM 35756
Owner: NJ Broadcasting, LLC.
Editorial: 1802 Oak Tree Rd Ste 201, Edison, New Jersey 08820-2704 **Tel:** 1 732 801-9757.
Email: contact@radiozindagi.com
Web site: http://www.radiozindagi.com
Profile: WWRL-AM is a commercial station owned by Access.1 Communications Corp. The format of the station is Ethnic. WWRL-AM broadcasts to the New York City area at 1600 AM.
AM RADIO STATION

WWRM-FM 41624
Owner: Cox Media Group, Inc.
Editorial: 11300 4th St N Ste 300, Saint Petersburg, Florida 33716-2941 **Tel:** 1 727 579-2000.
Email: 949comments@coxtampa.com
Web site: http://www.mymagic949.com
Profile: WWRM-FM is a commercial station owned by Cox Media Group, Inc. The format of the station is Lite Rock/Lite AC. WWRM-FM broadcasts to the Saint Petersburg, FL area at 94.9 FM.
FM RADIO STATION

WWRQ-FM 41887
Owner: Black Crow Broadcasting Inc.
Editorial: 1711 Ellis Dr, Valdosta, Georgia 31601-3573 **Tel:** 1 229 244-8642.
Web site: http://thebeat1079.com/
Profile: WWRQ-FM is a commercial station owned by Black Crow Broadcasting Inc. The format of the station is rock music. WWRQ-FM broadcasts to the Valdosta, GA area at 107.9 FM.
FM RADIO STATION

WWRR-FM 45610
Owner: Bold Gold Media Group
Editorial: 1049 N Sekol Ave, Scranton, Pennsylvania 18504 **Tel:** 1 570 344-1221.
Web site: http://www.105theriver.net
Profile: WWRR-FM is a commercial station owned by Bold Gold Media Group. The format of the station is classic hits. WWRR-FM broadcasts to the Scranton, PA area at 104.9 FM.
FM RADIO STATION

WWRU-AM 35412
Owner: Multicultural Radio Broadcasting Inc.
Editorial: 449 Broadway, New York, New York 10013-2549 **Tel:** 1 718 358-9300.
Web site: http://mrbi.net
Profile: WWRU-AM is a commercial station owned by Multicultural Radio Broadcasting Inc. The format of the station is variety, featuring brokered Korean-language programming. WWRU-AM broadcasts to the New York City metro area at 1660 AM.
AM RADIO STATION

WWRV-AM 36030
Owner: Radio Vision Christiana Management Corp.
Editorial: 419 Broadway, Paterson, New Jersey 7501 **Tel:** 1 973 881-8700.
Web site: http://www.radiovision.net
Profile: WWRV-AM is a commercial station owned by Radio Vision Christiana Management Corp. The format of the station is Hispanic religious programming. WWRV-AM broadcasts to the Paterson, NJ area at 1330 AM.
AM RADIO STATION

WWRW-FM 45386
Owner: iHeartMedia Inc.
Editorial: 2601 Nicholasville Rd, Lexington, Kentucky 40503-3307 **Tel:** 1 859 422-1000.
Web site: http://www.rewind1055.com
Profile: WWRW-FM is a commercial station owned by iHeartMedia Inc. The format of the station is classic hits. WWRW-FM broadcasts to the Lexington, KY area at 105.5 FM.
FM RADIO STATION

WWRZ-FM 44366
Owner: Hall Communications
Editorial: 404 W Lime St, Lakeland, Florida 33815-4651 **Tel:** 1 863 682-8184.
Web site: http://www.max983fm.com
Profile: WWRZ-FM is a commercial station owned by Hall Communications. The format of the station is adult hits. WWRZ-FM broadcasts in the Lakeland, FL, area at 98.3 FM.
FM RADIO STATION

WWSC-AM 38355
Owner: Regional Radio Group
Editorial: 238 Bay Rd, Queensbury, New York 12804-2003 **Tel:** 1 518 761-9890.
Web site: http://talk1450wwsc.com
Profile: WWSC-AM is a commercial station owned by Regional Radio Group. The format of the station is news and talk. WWSC-AM broadcasts in the Glens Falls, NY area at 1450 AM.
AM RADIO STATION

WWSE-FM 45624
Owner: Media One Group, LLC
Editorial: 2 Orchard Rd, Jamestown, New York 14701 **Tel:** 1 716 487-1151.
Web site: http://www.se933.com
Profile: WWSE-FM is a commercial station owned by Media One Group, LLC. The format of the station is adult contemporary music. WWSE-FM broadcasts to the Jamestown, NY area at 93.3 FM.
FM RADIO STATION

WWSF-AM 35856
Owner: Port Broadcasting, LLC
Editorial: 6 Federal St Fl 2, Newburyport, Massachusetts 01950-2804 **Tel:** 1 978 462-1450.
Web site: http://www.1220thelegends.com
Profile: WWSF-AM is a commercial station owned by Port Broadcasting, LLC. The format of the station is adult standards and modern jazz. WWSF-AM broadcasts to the Sanford, ME area at 1220 AM.
AM RADIO STATION

WWSJ-AM 35930
Owner: Harp(Larry and Helen)
Editorial: 1363 W Parks Rd, Saint Johns, Michigan 48879-9279 **Tel:** 1 989 224-7911.
Email: joy1580@sbcglobal.net
Web site: http://www.joy1580.com
Profile: WWSJ-AM is a commercial station owned by Larry and Helen Harp. The format of the station is urban contemporary gospel. WWSJ-AM broadcasts to the St. Johns, MI area at 1580 AM.
AM RADIO STATION

WWSK-FM 45100
Owner: Connoisseur Media
Editorial: 234 Airport Plaza Blvd Ste 5, Farmingdale, New York 11735-3938 **Tel:** 1 631 770-4200.
Web site: http://www.943theshark.com
Profile: WWSK-FM is a commercial station owned by Connoisseur Media. The format of the station is rock music. WWSK-FM broadcasts in the greater Long Island, NY area at 94.3 FM.
FM RADIO STATION

WWSL-FM 46730
Owner: HGC Inc.
Editorial: 1016 W Beacon St, Philadelphia, Mississippi 39350-3204 **Tel:** 1 601 656-7102.
Email: wwslfm@bellsouth.net
Profile: WWSL-FM is a commercial station owned by HGC Inc. The format of the station is hot adult contemporary music. WWSL-FM broadcasts to the Philadelphia, MS area at 102.3 FM.
FM RADIO STATION

WWSM-AM 36739
Owner: Sickafus, Patrick
Editorial: 621 Cumberland St, Suite 4, Lebanon, Pennsylvania 17042-8500 **Tel:** 1 717 272-1510.
Email: wwsm2@evenlink.com
Web site: http://www.wwsm.us
Profile: WWSM-AM is a commercial station owned by Patrick Sickafus. The format of the station is classic country. WWSM-AM broadcasts to the Harrisburg, PA area at 1510 AM.
AM RADIO STATION

WWSN-FM 46027
Owner: Cumulus Media Inc.
Editorial: 3375 Merriam St Ste 201, Muskegon, Michigan 49444-3173 **Tel:** 1 231 830-0176.
Web site: http://sunny975.com
Profile: WWSN-FM is a commercial station owned by Cumulus Media Inc. The format of the station is adult contemporary. WWSN-FM broadcasts to the Muskegon, MI area at 97.5 FM.
FM RADIO STATION

WWSR-FM 40916
Owner: Childers Media Group, LLC
Editorial: 57 Town Sq, Lima, Ohio 45801-4950 **Tel:** 1 419 331-1600.
Web site: http://931thefan.com
Profile: WWSR-FM is a commercial station owned by Childers Media Group, LLC. The format of the station is sports. WWSR-FM broadcasts to the Lima, OH area at 93.1 FM.
FM RADIO STATION

WWST-FM 40950
Owner: E.W. Scripps Co.
Editorial: 1533 Amherst Rd, Knoxville, Tennessee 37909-1204 **Tel:** 1 865 824-1021.
Web site: http://www.star1021fm.com
Profile: WWST-FM is a commercial station owned by E.W. Scripps Co. The format of the station is Top 40/CHR. WWST-FM broadcasts to the Knoxville, TN area at 102.1 FM.
FM RADIO STATION

WWSW-FM 45625
Owner: iHeartMedia Inc.
Editorial: 200 Fleet St Fl 4, Pittsburgh, Pennsylvania 15220-2908 **Tel:** 1 412 937-1441.
Email: feedback@3wsradio.com
Web site: http://3wsradio.iheart.com
Profile: WWSW-FM is a commercial station owned by iHeartMedia Inc. The format of the station is classic hits. WWSW-FM broadcasts to the Pittsburgh area at 94.5 FM.
FM RADIO STATION

WWTC-AM 35081
Owner: Salem Media Group, Inc.
Editorial: 2110 Cliff Rd, Eagan, Minnesota 55122-3522 **Tel:** 1 651 405-8800.
Email: comments@am1280thepatriot.com
Web site: http://www.am1280thepatriot.com
Profile: WWTC-AM is a commercial station owned by Salem Media Group, Inc. The format of the station is news and talk. WWTC-AM broadcasts to the Minneapolis area at 1280 AM.
AM RADIO STATION

United States of America

WWTF-FM
36541

Owner: iHeartMedia Inc.
Editorial: 2601 Nicholasville Rd, Lexington, Kentucky 40503-3307 **Tel:** 1 859 422-1000.
Web site: http://wtf977rocks.iheart.com
Profile: WWTF-AM is a commercial station owned by iHeartMedia Inc. The format of the station is alternative rock. WWTF-AM broadcasts to the Lexington, KY area at 97.7 FM.
FM RADIO STATION

WWTH-FM
42641

Owner: Edwards Communications LLC
Editorial: 1491 M 32 W, Alpena, Michigan 49707-8194 **Tel:** 1 989 354-4611.
Email: news@truenorthradionetwork.com
Web site: http://www.truenorthradionetwork.com
Profile: WWTH-FM is a commercial station owned by Edwards Communications LLC. The format of the station is classic rock. WWTH-FM broadcasts to Oscoda, MI at 100.7 FM.
FM RADIO STATION

WWTK-AM
38836

Owner: Cohan Radio Group Inc.
Editorial: 3750 US Highway 27 N Ste 1, Sebring, Florida 33870-1644 **Tel:** 1 863 382-9999.
Web site: http://www.cohanradiogroup.com
Profile: WWTK-AM is a commercial station owned by Cohan Radio Group Inc. The format of the station is news and talk. WWTK-AM broadcasts to the Sebring, FL area at 730 AM.
AM RADIO STATION

WWTM-AM
35183

Owner: R & B Communications Inc.
Editorial: 1209 Danville Rd Sw Ste N, Decatur, Alabama 35601-3853 **Tel:** 1 256 353-1400.
Email: feedback@espn1400.info
Web site: http://www.espn1400.info
Profile: WWTM-AM is a commercial station owned by R & B Communications. The format of the station is sports. WWTM-AM broadcasts to the Decatur, AL area at 1400 AM.
AM RADIO STATION

WWTN-FM
41731

Owner: Cumulus Media Inc.
Editorial: 506 2nd Ave S, Nashville, Tennessee 37210-2002 **Tel:** 1 615 321-1067.
Web site: http://www.997wtn.com
Profile: WWTN-FM is a commercial station owned by Cumulus Media Inc. The format of the station is news, talk and sports. WWTN-FM broadcasts in the Nashville, TN area at 99.7 FM.
FM RADIO STATION

WWTR-AM
36518

Owner: EBC Music, Inc.
Editorial: 2088 US Highway 130, Monmouth Junction, New Jersey 08852-3094 **Tel:** 1 732 821-6009.
Email: info@ebcmusic.com
Web site: http://www.ebcmusic.com
Profile: WWTR-AM is a commercial station owned by EBC Music, Inc. The format of the station is variety music, news and talk; primarily ethnic Indian and South Asian programming. WWTR-AM broadcasts to the Cedar Knolls, NJ area at 1170 AM.
AM RADIO STATION

WWTX-AM
38347

Owner: iHeartMedia Inc.
Editorial: 920 W Basin Rd Ste 400, New Castle, Delaware 19720-1013 **Tel:** 1 302 395-9800.
Web site: http://foxsports1290am.iheart.com/
Profile: WWTX-AM is a commercial station owned by iHeartMedia Inc. The format of the station is sports talk. WWTX-AM broadcasts to the Claymont, DE area at 1290 AM.
AM RADIO STATION

WWUF-FM
41288

Owner: Mattox Broadcasting Inc.
Editorial: 2132 US Highway 84, Blackshear, Georgia 31516-1160 **Tel:** 1 912 449-3391.
Email: wkub@almatel.net
Web site: http://waycrossradio.com/977
Profile: WWUF-FM is a commercial station owned by Mattox Broadcasting Inc. The format of the station is hot adult contemporary. WWUF-FM broadcasts to the Blackshear, GA area at 97.7 FM.
FM RADIO STATION

WWUS-FM
40860

Owner: Gamma Broadcasting LLC
Editorial: 30336 Overseas Hwy, Big Pine Key, Florida 33043-3352 **Tel:** 1 305 872-9100.
Web site: http://www.us1radio.com
Profile: WWUS-FM is a commercial station owned by Gamma Broadcasting LLC. The format of the station is classic hits. WWUS-FM broadcasts to the Big Pine Key, FL area at 104.1 FM.
FM RADIO STATION

WWUZ-FM
44161

Owner: Alpha Media
Editorial: 616 Amelia St, Fredericksburg, Virginia 22401-3887
Web site: http://www.969therock.com/
Profile: WWUZ-FM is a commercial station owned by Alpha Media. The format of the station is classic rock music. WWUZ-FM broadcasts to the Fredericksburg, VA area at 96.9 FM.
FM RADIO STATION

WWVA-AM
38311

Owner: iHeartMedia Inc.
Editorial: 1015 Main St, Wheeling, West Virginia 26003-2709 **Tel:** 1 304 232-1170.
Web site: http://newsradio1170.iheart.com
Profile: WWVA-AM is a commercial station owned by iHeartMedia Inc. The format of the station is news, sports and talk. WWVA-AM broadcasts to the Wheeling, WV area at 1170 AM.
AM RADIO STATION

WWVO-FM
825166

Owner: The Power Foundation
Editorial: 2416 Dawson Rd, Albany, Georgia 31707-2344 **Tel:** 1 229 439-1100.
Email: wwvothevoice@gmail.com
Web site: http://www.wwvothevoice.com
Profile: WWVO-FM is a non-commercial station owned by The Power Foundation. The format of the station is Christian music featuring a variety of Southern Gospel, Bluegrass and Modern Praise. WWVO-FM broadcasts to the Albany, GA area at a frequency of 90.7 FM.
FM RADIO STATION

WWVR-FM
40861

Owner: Emmis Communications Corp.
Editorial: 918 Ohio St, Terre Haute, Indiana 47807-3733 **Tel:** 1 812 917-3901.
Web site: http://www.1055theriver.com
Profile: WWVR-FM is a commercial station owned by Emmis Communications Corp. The format of the station is classic rock. WWVR-FM broadcasts to the Terre Haute, IN area at 105.5 FM.
FM RADIO STATION

WWVT-AM
36898

Owner: Virginia Tech Foundation
Editorial: 3520 Kingsbury Lane, Roanoke, Virginia 24014 **Tel:** 1 540 989-8900.
Email: wvtf@vt.edu
Web site: http://www.wvtf.org
Profile: WWVT-AM is a non-commercial station owned by the Virginia Tech Foundation. The format of the station is jazz, classical, news and talk. WWVT-AM broacasts to the Roanoke-Lynchburg, VA area at 1260 AM.
AM RADIO STATION

WWWA-FM
46864

Owner: Light of Life Ministries Inc.
Editorial: 160 Riverside Dr, Augusta, Maine 04330-4162 **Tel:** 1 207 622-1340.
Email: info@worshipradionetwork.org
Web site: http://worshipradionetwork.org
Profile: WWWA-FM is a non-commercial station owned by Light of Life Ministries Inc. The format of the station is contemporary Christian music. WWWA-FM broadcasts to the Augusta, ME, area at 95.3 FM. WFYB-FM is simulcasting from WWWA-FM.
FM RADIO STATION

WWWC-AM
36968

Owner: Foothills Media, Inc.
Editorial: 413 Wilkesboro Blvd, Wilkesboro, North Carolina 28697 **Tel:** 1 336 838-1241.
Email: news@12403wc.com
Web site: http://www.12403wc.com
Profile: WWWC-AM is a commercial station owned by Foothills Media, Inc. The format of the station is gospel and religion. WWWC-AM broadcasts to the Wilkesboro, NC area at 1240 AM.
AM RADIO STATION

WWWE-AM
35471

Owner: Beasley Broadcast Group
Editorial: 1465 Northside Dr Nw Ste 218, Atlanta, Georgia 30318-4239 **Tel:** 1 404 352-9993.
Web site: http://www.1100espndeportes.com
Profile: WWWE-AM is a commercial station owned by Beasley Broadcast Group. The format of the station is sports. The station airs ESPN Deportes from 4pm to 7pm. WWWE-AM broadcasts to the Atlanta area at 1100 AM.
AM RADIO STATION

WWWH-FM
46126

Owner: AMS Radio LLC
Editorial: 1411 Soaring Trl, Marietta, Georgia 30062-3280 **Tel:** 1 404 386-9792.
Profile: WWWH-FM is a commercial station owned by AMS Radio LLC. The format of the station is Hot AC. WWWH-FM broadcasts to the Haleyville, AL area at 92.7 FM.
FM RADIO STATION

WWWI-AM
36218

Owner: Red Rock Radio Corp.
Editorial: 305 W Washington St, Brainerd, Minnesota 56401-2923 **Tel:** 1 218 828-9994.
Email: kkinradio@embarqmail.com
Web site: http://www.redrockradiobrainerd.com/
Profile: WWWI-AM is a commercial station owned by Red Rock Radio Corp. The format of the station is news and talk programming. WWWI-AM broadcasts to the Brainerd, MN area at 1270 AM.
AM RADIO STATION

WWWI-FM
44523

Owner: Red Rock Radio Corp.
Editorial: 305 W Washington St, Brainerd, Minnesota 56401-2923 **Tel:** 1 218 828-9994.
Email: kkinradio@embarqmail.com
Web site: http://www.redrockradiobrainerd.com
Profile: WWWI-FM is a commercial station owned by Red Rock Radio Corp.. The format of the station is classic rock. WWWI-FM broadcasts to the Brainerd, MN area at 95.9 FM.
FM RADIO STATION

WWWK-FM
963929

Owner: Universal Broadcasting Network LLC
Editorial: 5731 NW 74th Ave, Miami, Florida 33166-4215
Web site: http://rumberanetwork105.com/
Profile: WWWK-FM is a commercial station owned by Universal Broadcasting Network LLC, under LMA with Rumbera Network. The format of the station is Hispanic Top 40. The target audience of the station is Hispanics, ages 18 to 54. WWWK-FM's tagline is "Rumbera Network" as it airs the radio network's programming. WWWK-FM broadcasts to the Miami - Fort Lauderdale, FL area area at 105.5 FM.
FM RADIO STATION

WWWL-AM
35668

Owner: Entercom Communications Corp.
Editorial: 400 Poydras St Ste 800, New Orleans, Louisiana 70130-3789 **Tel:** 1 504 593-6376.
Email: wwlnewsroom@yahoo.com
Web site: http://www.3wl1350.com
Profile: WWWL-AM is a commercial station owned by Entercom Communications Corp. The format of the station is news and talk. WWWL-AM broadcasts to the New Orleans area at 1350 AM.
AM RADIO STATION

WWWQ-FM
45204

Owner: Cumulus Media Inc.
Editorial: 780 Johnson Ferry Rd Fl 5, Atlanta, Georgia 30342-1434 **Tel:** 1 404 497-4700.
Web site: http://www.q100atlanta.com
Profile: WWWQ-FM is a commercial station owned by Cumulus Media Inc. The format of the station is Top 40/CHR. WWWQ-FM broadcasts to the Atlanta area at 99.1 FM.
FM RADIO STATION

WWWS-AM
36665

Owner: Entercom Communications Corp.
Editorial: 500 Corporate Pkwy, Ste 200, Buffalo, New York 14226 **Tel:** 1 716 843-0600.
Web site: http://www.am1400solidgoldsoul.com
Profile: WWWS-AM is a commercial station owned by Entercom Communications Corp. The format of the station is R&B oldies. WWWS-AM broadcasts to the Buffalo, NY area at 1400 AM.
AM RADIO STATION

WWWT-FM
46870

Owner: Hubbard Broadcasting, Inc.
Editorial: 3400 Idaho Ave NW, Washington, District Of Columbia 20016-3046 **Tel:** 1 202 895-5000.
Web site: http://www.wtopnews.com
Profile: WWWT-FM is a commercial station owned by Hubbard Broadcasting, Inc. The format of the station is news. WWWT-FM broadcasts to the Washington, D.C. area at 107.7 FM.
FM RADIO STATION

WWWV-FM
45627

Owner: Saga Communications
Editorial: 1140 Rose Hill Dr, Charlottesville, Virginia 22903-5128 **Tel:** 1 434 220-2300.
Web site: http://www.3wv.com
Profile: WWWV-FM is a commercial station owned by the Saga Communications. The format for the station is classic rock. WWWV-FM broadcasts to the Charlottesville, VA area at 97.5 FM.
FM RADIO STATION

WWWW-FM
45238

Owner: Cumulus Media Inc.
Editorial: 1100 Victors Way Ste 100, Ann Arbor, Michigan 48108-5220 **Tel:** 1 734 302-8100.
Web site: http://www.w4country.com
Profile: WWWW-FM is a commercial station owned by Cumulus Media Inc. The format of the station is classic country. WWWW-FM broadcasts to the Ann Arbor, MI area at 102.9 FM.
FM RADIO STATION

WWWX-FM
45784

Owner: Cumulus Media Inc.
Editorial: 491 S Washburn St Ste 400, Oshkosh, Wisconsin 54904-6733 **Tel:** 1 920 426-3239.
Web site: http://www.fox969.com
Profile: WWWX-FM is a commercial station owned by Cumulus Media Inc. The format of the station is modern rock. WWWX-FM broadcasts to the Green Bay, WI area at 96.9 FM.
FM RADIO STATION

WWWY-FM
41609

Owner: White River Broadcasting Co., Inc.
Editorial: 3212 Washington St, Columbus, Indiana 47203-1505 **Tel:** 1 812 372-4448.
Email: riverstudio@1061theriver.com
Web site: http://www.1061theriver.com
Profile: WWWY-FM is a commercial station owned by White River Broadcasting Co., Inc. The format of the station is classic hits. WWWY-FM broadcasts to the Columbus, IN area at 106.1 FM.
FM RADIO STATION

WWWZ-FM
41646

Owner: Cumulus Media Inc.
Editorial: 4230 Faber Place Dr Ste 100, North Charleston, South Carolina 29405-8512
Tel: 1 843 277-1200.
Web site: http://www.z93jamz.com
Profile: WWWZ-FM is a commercial station owned by Cumulus Media Inc. The format of the station is urban contemporary. WWWZ-FM broadcasts to the Charleston, SC area at 93.3 FM.
FM RADIO STATION

WWXL-AM
36943

Owner: Nolan (Juanita H.)
Editorial: 103 3rd St, Manchester, Kentucky 40962-1119 **Tel:** 1 606 598-2319.
Profile: WWXL-AM is a commercial station owned by Juanita H. Nolan. The format of the station is talk, sports and news. WWXL-AM broadcasts to the Manchester, KY area at 1450 AM.
AM RADIO STATION

WWXM-FM
40318

Owner: iHeartMedia Inc.
Editorial: 4841 Highway 17 Byp S, Myrtle Beach, South Carolina 29577-6683 **Tel:** 1 843 293-0107.
Web site: http://mix977.iheart.com
Profile: WWXM-FM is a commercial station owned by iHeartMedia Inc. The format of the station is Top 40/CHR. WWXM-FM broadcasts to the Myrtle Beach, SC area at 97.7 FM.
FM RADIO STATION

WWXT-FM
40521

Owner: Red Zebra Broadcasting
Editorial: 1801 Rockville Pike, Rockville, Maryland 20852-1633 **Tel:** 1 301 230-3500.
Email: redskinsradio@redskins.com
Web site: http://www.espn980.com
Profile: WWXT-FM is a commercial station owned by Red Zebra Broadcasting. The format of the station is sports. WWXT-FM broadcasts to the Washington, D.C. area at 92.7 FM.
FM RADIO STATION

WWXX-FM
217541

Owner: Red Zebra Broadcasting
Editorial: 1801 Rockville Pike Ste 405, Rockville, Maryland 20852-5604 **Tel:** 1 301 230-3500.
Email: management@espn980.com
Web site: http://www.espn980.com
Profile: WWXX-FM is a commercial station owned by Red Zebra Broadcasting. The format of the station is sports. WWXX-FM broadcasts to the Warrenton, VA area at 94.3 FM. Test
FM RADIO STATION

WWYC-AM
38796

Owner: Calvary Chapel Twin Falls
Editorial: Toledo, Ohio **Tel:** 1 208 734-4357.
Email: feedback@csnradio.com
Web site: http://www.csnradio.com/stations/studiowaivered/WWYC.php
Profile: WWYC-AM is a non-commercial station owned by Calvary Chapel Twin Falls. The format of the station is religious. WWYC-AM broadcasts to the Toledo, OH area at 1560 AM.
AM RADIO STATION

WWYL-FM
43163

Owner: Townsquare Media, Inc.
Editorial: 59 Court St, Binghamton, New York 13901-3270 **Tel:** 1 607 772-8400.
Web site: http://www.wild104fm.com
Profile: WWYL-FM is a commercial station owned by Townsquare Media, Inc. The format of the station is Top 40/CHR. WWYL-FM broadcasts to the Binghamton, NY area at a frequency of 104.1 FM.
FM RADIO STATION

WWYN-FM
40863

Owner: Thomas Media
Editorial: 111 W Main St, Jackson, Tennessee 38301-6147 **Tel:** 1 731 427-9616.
Web site: http://wwyn1069.com
Profile: WWYN-FM is a commercial station owned by Thomas Media. The format of the station is classic country. WWYN-FM broadcasts to the Jackson, TN area at 106.9 FM.
FM RADIO STATION

WWYO-AM
35760

Owner: Jennings(Rudolph D.)
Editorial: 608 College Ave, Bluefield, West Virginia 24701 **Tel:** 1 304 327-5651.
Email: wwyo970am@frontier.com
Profile: WWYO-AM is a commercial station owned by Rudolph D. Jennings. The format of the station is full service and variety. WWYO-AM broadcasts in the the Bluefield, WV area at 970 AM.
AM RADIO STATION

WWYY-FM
139467

Owner: Connoisseur Media
Editorial: 22 S 6th St, Stroudsburg, Pennsylvania 18360-2002 **Tel:** 1 570 421-2100.
Web site: http://www.spinradio.fm
Profile: WWYY-FM is a commercial station owned by Connoisseur Media. The format of the station is alternative rock music. WWYY-FM broadcasts to the Stroudsburg, PA area at 107.1 FM.
FM RADIO STATION

WWYZ-FM
43426

Owner: iHeartMedia Inc.
Editorial: 10 Columbus Blvd Ste 1, Hartford, Connecticut 06106-1976 **Tel:** 1 860 723-6000.
Web site: http://country925.iheart.com
Profile: WWYZ-FM is a commercial station owned by iHeartMedia Inc. The format of the station is country music. WWYZ-FM broadcasts to the Hartford, CT area at 92.5 FM.
FM RADIO STATION

WWZD-FM 45941
Owner: iHeartMedia, Inc.
Editorial: 5026 Cliff Gookin Blvd, Tupelo, Mississippi 38801-7059 **Tel:** 1 662 842-1067.
Web site: http://www.wizard106.com
Profile: WWZD-FM is a commercial station owned by iHeartMedia, Inc. The format of the station is country. WWZD-FM broadcasts to the Tupelo, MS area at 106.7 FM.
FM RADIO STATION

WWZQ-AM 36702
Owner: Stanford Communications Inc.
Editorial: 1053 S Meridian St, Aberdeen, Mississippi 39730-3836 **Tel:** 1 662 256-9726.
Email: fm95@fm95radio.com
Web site: http://www.fm95radio.com
Profile: WWZQ-AM is a commercial station owned by Stanford Communications Inc. The format of the station is news, talk and sports. WWZQ-AM broadcasts to the Aberdeen, MS area at 1240 AM.
AM RADIO STATION

WWZW-FM 45598
Owner: First Media Radio LLC
Editorial: 392 E Midland Trl, Lexington, Virginia 24450-5703 **Tel:** 1 540 463-2161.
Email: news@wrel.com
Web site: http://www.3wzfm.com
Profile: WWZW-FM is a commercial station owned by First Media Radio LLC. The format of the station is classic hits. WWZW-FM broadcast to the Lexington, VA area at 96.7 FM.
FM RADIO STATION

WWZY-FM 150678
Owner: Press Communications LLC
Editorial: 2355 W Bangs Ave, Neptune, New Jersey 07753-4111 **Tel:** 1 732 774-4755.
Web site: http://1071theboss.com
Profile: WWZY-FM is a commercial station owned by Press Communications LLC. The format of the station is Classic Rock. WWZY-FM broadcasts to the Neptune, NJ area at 107.1 FM.
FM RADIO STATION

WXAJ-FM 76962
Owner: Neuhoff Family Limited Partnership
Editorial: 3055 S 4th St, Springfield, Illinois 62703-1009 **Tel:** 1 217 528-3033.
Web site: http://www.997themix.com
Profile: WXAJ-FM is a commercial station owned by Neuhoff Family Limited Partnership. The format of the station is Hot Adult Contemporary broadcasts to the Springfield, IL area at 99.7 FM.
FM RADIO STATION

WXAM-AM 35798
Owner: Commonwealth Broadcasting Corp.
Editorial: 611 W Poplar St Ste C2, Elizabethtown, Kentucky 42701-2483 **Tel:** 1 270 358-4707.
Email: news@commonwealthbroadcasting.com
Web site: http://espnradio1430.net
Profile: WXAM-AM is a commercial station owned by Commonwealth Broadcasting Corp. The format for the station is sports. WXAM-AM broadcasts to the Elizabethtown, KY area at 1430 AM.
AM RADIO STATION

WXAN-FM 41377
Owner: Southern Gospetality LLC
Editorial: 9077 Ava Rd, Ava, Illinois 62907-2911
Tel: 1 618 426-3308.
Email: wxangm@yahoo.com
Web site: http://www.mysoutherngospel.net
Profile: WXAN-FM is a commercial station owned by Southern Gospetality LLC. The format of the station is Christian programming. WXAN-FM broadcasts to the Ava, IL area at 103.9 FM.
FM RADIO STATION

WXBB-FM 42523
Owner: Connoisseur Media LLC
Editorial: 1 Boston Store Pl, Erie, Pennsylvania 16501-2313 **Tel:** 1 814 461-1000.
Web site: http://www.947bobfm.com
Profile: WXBB-FM is a commercial station owned by Connoisseur Media LLC. The format of the station is Jack FM - adult hits. WXBB-FM broadcasts to the Erie, PA area at 94.7 FM.
FM RADIO STATION

WXBC-FM 42492
Owner: Breckinridge Broadcasting
Editorial: 110 S Main St, Hardinsburg, Kentucky 40143-2653 **Tel:** 1 270 756-1043.
Email: wxbc@bbtel.com
Web site: http://www.wxbc1043.com
Profile: WXBC-FM is a commercial station owned by Breckinridge Broadcasting, Inc. The format for the station is country. WXBC-FM broadcasts to the Hardinsburg, KY area at 104.3 FM. The target audience of the station is listeners ages 18 to 54.
FM RADIO STATION

WXBD-AM 38571
Owner: Alpha Media
Editorial: 1909 E Pass Rd Ste D11, Gulfport, Mississippi 39507-3778 **Tel:** 1 228 388-2001.
Profile: WXBD-AM is a commercial station owned by Alpha Media. The format for the station is sports. WXBD-AM broadcasts to the Biloxi-Gulfport, MS area at 1490 AM.
AM RADIO STATION

WXBM-FM 40864
Owner: Cumulus Media Inc.
Editorial: 6565 N W St Ste 270, Pensacola, Florida 32505-1797 **Tel:** 1 850 994-5357.
Email: communityannouncement@wxbm.com
Web site: http://www.wxbm.com
Profile: WXBM-FM is a commercial station owned by Cumulus Media Inc. The format for the station is contemporary country. WXBM-FM broadcasts to the Pace, FL area at 102.7 FM.
FM RADIO STATION

WXBN-FM 40852
Owner: Centennial Broadcasting
Editorial: 520 N Pleasant Valley Rd, Winchester, Virginia 22601-5654 **Tel:** 1 540 667-2224.
Web site: http://www.rockthebone.com
Profile: WXBN-FM is a commercial station owned by Centennial Broadcasting. The format of the station is classic country. WXBN-FM broadcasts in the Winchester, VA area at 105.5 FM.
FM RADIO STATION

WXBQ-FM 45942
Owner: Bristol Broadcasting
Editorial: 901 E Valley Dr, Bristol, Virginia 24201-4913
Tel: 1 276 669-8112.
Email: news@wxbq.com
Web site: http://www.wxbq.com
Profile: WXBQ-FM is a commercial station owned by Bristol Broadcasting. The format of the station is classic country. WXBQ-FM broadcasts to the Bristol, VA area at 96.9 FM.
FM RADIO STATION

WXBW-FM 46527
Owner: Kindred Communications
Editorial: 555 5th Ave Ste K, Huntington, West Virginia 25701-1907 **Tel:** 1 304 523-8401.
Email: studio@bigbuck1015.com
Web site: http://www.bigbuck1015.com
Profile: WXBW-FM is a commercial station owned by Kindred Communications . The format of the station is contemporary country. WXBW-FM broadcasts to Huntington, WV and surrounding communities at 101.5 FM.
FM RADIO STATION

WXBX-FM 46901
Owner: Three Rivers Media Corp.
Editorial: 110 W Spiller St, Wytheville, Virginia 24382-1952 **Tel:** 1 276 228-3185.
Email: office@threeriversmedia.net
Web site: http://www.wxbx.com
Profile: WXBX-FM is a commercial station owned by Three Rivers Media Corp. The format of the station is oldies. WXBX-FM broadcasts to the Wytheville, VA area at 95.3 FM.
FM RADIO STATION

WXCC-FM 45629
Owner: East Kentucky Radio Network
Editorial: 1240 Radio Dr, Pikeville, Kentucky 41501-4779 **Tel:** 1 606 437-4051.
Email: frontdesk@ekbradio.com
Web site: http://www.wxccfm.com
Profile: WXCC-FM is a commercial station owned by East Kentucky Radio Network. The format of the station is country. WXCC-FM broadcasts to the Pikeville, KY area at 96.5 FM.
FM RADIO STATION

WXCE-AM 35761
Owner: Red Rock Radio Corp.
Editorial: 328 100Th St, Amery, Wisconsin 54001-4024 **Tel:** 1 715 268-7185.
Email: info@radio715.com
Web site: http://radio715.com
Profile: WXCE-AM is a commercial station owned by Red Rock Radio Corp. The format of the station is adult standards. WXCE-AM broadcasts in the Amery, WI area at 1260 AM.
AM RADIO STATION

WXCH-FM 40979
Owner: Reising Radio Partners Inc.
Editorial: 825 Washington St, Columbus, Indiana 47201-6265 **Tel:** 1 812 379-1077.
Web site: http://www.mojo1029.com
Profile: WXCH-FM is a commercial station owned by Reising Radio Partners Inc. The format of the station is classic hits. WXCH-FM broadcasts to Aurora, IN at 102.9 FM.
FM RADIO STATION

WXCL-FM 86689
Owner: Alpha Media
Editorial: 331 Fulton St Ste 1200, Peoria, Illinois 61602-1422 **Tel:** 1 309 637-3700.
Email: news@1470wmbd.com
Web site: http://www.1049thewolf.com
Profile: WXCL-FM is a commercial station owned by Alpha Media. The format of the station is contemporary country music. WXCL-FM broadcasts in the Peoria, IL, area at 104.9 FM.
FM RADIO STATION

WXCM-FM 62193
Owner: Cromwell Group Inc.(The)
Editorial: 1115 Tamarack Rd, Owensboro, Kentucky 42301-6984 **Tel:** 1 270 683-5200.
Web site: http://www.owensbororadio.com
Profile: WXCM-FM is a commercial station owned by The Cromwell Group Inc. The format of the station is rock music. WXCM-FM broadcasts to the Evansville, IN area at 97.1 FM.
FM RADIO STATION

WXCO-AM 38286
Owner: Sunrise Broadcasting, LLC
Editorial: 1110 E Wausau Ave, Wausau, Wisconsin 54403-3149 **Tel:** 1 715 845-8218.
Web site: http://www.1230wxco.com
Profile: WXCO-AM is a commercial station owned by Sunrise Broadcasting, LLC. The format of the station is oldies. WXCO-AM broadcasts in the Wausau, WI area at 1230 AM.
AM RADIO STATION

WXCR-FM 70231
Owner: Seven Ranges Radio Company Inc.
Editorial: Greens Run Road, Saint Marys, West Virginia 26170 **Tel:** 1 304 684-3400.
Web site: http://www.literock93r.com
Profile: WXCR-FM is a commercial station owned by Seven Ranges Radio Company Inc. The format of the station is classic rock. The station broadcasts to the Saint Mary's, VA area at 92.3 FM.
FM RADIO STATION

WXCV-FM 40867
Owner: WXOF, Inc.
Editorial: 4554 S Suncoast Blvd, Homosassa, Florida 34446-1103 **Tel:** 1 352 628-4444.
Web site: http://www.citrus953.com
Profile: WXCV-FM is a commercial station owned by WXOF, Inc. The format of the station is hot adult contemporary music. WXCV-FM broadcasts in the Homosassa, FL area at 95.3 FM.
FM RADIO STATION

WXCX-FM 62570
Owner: Red Rock Radio Corp.
Editorial: 15429 Pokegama Lake Rd, Pine City, Minnesota 55063-4592 **Tel:** 1 888 629-7575.
Web site: http://www.redrockonair.com
Profile: WXCX-FM is a commercial station owned by Red Rock Radio Corp. The format of the station is adult hits. WXCX-FM broadcasts to the Minneapolis area at 105.7 FM.
FM RADIO STATION

WXCY-FM 41378
Owner: Delmarva Broadcasting
Editorial: 707 Revolution St, Havre de Grace, Maryland 21078-3321 **Tel:** 1 410 939-1100.
Web site: http://www.wxcyfm.com
Profile: WXCY-FM is a commercial station owned by Delmarva Broadcasting. The format of the station is country music. WXCY-FM broadcasts to the Baltimore, MD area at 103.7 FM.
FM RADIO STATION

WXDE-FM 41998
Owner: Delmarva Broadcasting
Editorial: 1666 Blairs Pond Rd, Milford, Delaware 19963-5263 **Tel:** 1 302 422-7575.
Email: news@delaware1059.com
Web site: http://www.delaware1059.com
Profile: WXDE-FM is a commercial station owned by Delmarva Broadcasting. The format of the station is news talk. WXDE-FM broadcasts to the Salisbury, MD area at 105.9 FM.
FM RADIO STATION

WXDJ-FM 40410
Owner: Spanish Broadcasting System
Editorial: 7007 NW 77th Ave, Miami, Florida 33166-2836 **Tel:** 1 305 447-9595.
Web site: http://elzol.com
Profile: WXDJ-FM is a commercial station owned by Spanish Broadcasting System. The format of the station is Spanish tropical. WXDJ-FM broadcasts to the Miami, FL area at 106.7 FM.
FM RADIO STATION

WXDX-FM 42794
Owner: iHeartMedia Inc.
Editorial: 200 Fleet St Fl 4, Pittsburgh, Pennsylvania 15220-2908 **Tel:** 1 412 937-1441.
Web site: http://www.1059thex.com
Profile: WXDX-FM is a commercial station owned by iHeartMedia Inc. The format of the station rock alternative. WXDX-FM broadcasts to the Pittsburgh area at 105.9 FM.
FM RADIO STATION

WXEF-FM 42187
Owner: Premier Broadcasting
Editorial: 206 S Willow St, Effingham, Illinois 62401-3637 **Tel:** 1 217 347-5518.
Email: info@thexradio.com
Web site: http://www.thexradio.com
Profile: WXEF-FM is a commercial station owned by Premier Broadcasting. The format of the station is hot adult contemporary music. WXEF-FM broadcasts in the Effingham, IL area at 97.9 FM.
FM RADIO STATION

WXEM-AM 36063
Owner: La Favorita Inc.
Editorial: 5815 Westside Rd, Austell, Georgia 30106-3179 **Tel:** 1 770 944-0900.
Email: traffic@lamejorestacion.com
Web site: http://www.lamejorestacion.com
Profile: WXEM-AM is a commercial station owned by La Favorita Inc. The format of the station is regional Mexican music. WXEM-AM broadcasts to the Austell, GA area at 1460 AM.
AM RADIO STATION

WXER-FM 46707
Owner: Midwest Communications Inc.
Editorial: 2100 Washington Ave, Sheboygan, Wisconsin 53081 **Tel:** 1 920 458-2107.
Web site: http://www.wxerfm.com
Profile: WXER-FM is a commercial station owned by Midwest Communications Inc. The format of the station is hot adult contemporary music. WXER-FM broadcasts to the Sheboygan, WI area at 104.5 FM.
FM RADIO STATION

WXEX-AM 37037
Owner: Aruba Capital Holdings, LLC
Tel: 1 603 583-4767.
Email: events@wxexradio.com
Web site: http://www.wxexradio.com
Profile: WXEX-AM is a commercial station owned by Aruba Capital Holdings, LLC. The format of the station is oldies. WXEX-AM broadcasts to the Portsmouth, NH area at 1540 AM.
AM RADIO STATION

WXEX-FM 40164
Owner: Aruba Capital Holdings, LLC
Tel: 1 207 324-1183.
Email: events@wxexradio.com
Web site: http://www.wxexradio.com
Profile: WXEX-FM is a commercial station owned by Aruba Capital Holdings, LLC. The format of the station is rock alternative. WXEX-FM broadcasts to the Dover, NH area at 92.1 FM.
FM RADIO STATION

WXFL-FM 42760
Owner: Big River Broadcasting Corp.
Editorial: 624 Sam Phillips St, Florence, Alabama 35630-5859 **Tel:** 1 256 764-8121.
Web site: http://www.kix96country.com/
Profile: WXFL-FM is a commercial station owned by Big River Broadcasting Corp. The format of the station is country. WXFL-FM broadcasts to the Florence, AL area at 96.1 FM.
FM RADIO STATION

WXFM-FM 40869
Owner: Technicom Inc.
Editorial: 120 W Wildwood Dr, Mount Zion, Illinois 62549-1151 **Tel:** 1 217 864-4141.
Email: wxfmwdkr@gmail.com
Profile: WXFM-FM is a commercial station owned by Technicom Inc. The format of the station is country. WXFM-FM broadcasts to the Mt. Zion, IL area at 99.3 FM.
FM RADIO STATION

WXFN-AM 38007
Owner: Backyard Broadcasting
Editorial: 800 E 29th St, Muncie, Indiana 47302
Tel: 1 765 288-4403.
Web site: http://wxfn.com
Profile: WXFN-AM is a commercial station owned by Backyard Broadcasting. The format of the station is sports. WXFN broadcasts in the Muncie, IN area at 1340 AM.
AM RADIO STATION

WXFX-FM 40638
Owner: Cumulus Media Inc.
Editorial: 1 Commerce St Ste 300, Montgomery, Alabama 36104-3542 **Tel:** 1 334 240-9274.
Web site: http://www.wxfx.com
Profile: WXFX-FM is a commercial station owned by Cumulus Media Inc. The format of the station is classic and rock/album-oriented rock. WXFX-FM broadcasts to the Montgomery, AL area at 95.1 FM.
FM RADIO STATION

WXGI-AM 35937
Owner: Urban One, Inc.
Editorial: 2809 Emerywood Pkwy Ste 300, Richmond, Virginia 23294-3743 **Tel:** 1 804 672-9299.
Email: espn950am@redskins.com
Web site: http://www.espn950am.com
Profile: WXGI-AM is a commercial station owned by Urban One, Inc. The format of the station is sports. WXGI-AM broadcasts to the Washington, D.C. area at 950 AM.
AM RADIO STATION

WXGL-FM 44064
Owner: Cox Media Group, Inc.
Editorial: 11300 4th St N Ste 300, Saint Petersburg, Florida 33716-2941 **Tel:** 1 727 577-7131.
Email: 1073comments@coxtampa.com
Web site: http://www.1073theeagle.com
Profile: WXGL-FM is a commercial station owned by Cox Media Group, Inc. The format of the station is classic hits. WXGL-FM broadcasts to the Saint Petersburg, FL area at 107.3 FM.
FM RADIO STATION

WXGM-AM 38897
Owner: WXGM Inc.
Editorial: 6267 Professional Dr, Gloucester, Virginia 23061-4454 **Tel:** 1 804 693-2105.
Email: office@xtra99.com
Profile: WXGM-AM is a commercial station owned by WXGM Inc. The format of the station is oldies. WXGM-AM broadcasts to the Gloucester, VA area at 1420 AM.
AM RADIO STATION

WXGM-FM 46245
Owner: WXGM Inc.
Editorial: 6267 Professional Dr, Gloucester, Virginia 23061-4454 **Tel:** 1 804 693-2105.
Email: news@xtra99.com
Web site: http://www.xtra99.com
Profile: WXGM-FM is a commercial station owned by WXGM Inc. The format of the station is adult

contemporary. WXGM-FM broadcasts to the Gloucester, VA area at 99.1 FM.
FM RADIO STATION

WXGO-AM
38111

Owner: DCBroadcasting Inc.
Editorial: 1224 E Telegraph Hill Rd, Madison, Indiana 47250-9273 **Tel:** 1 812 265-3322.
Email: thebestmusic@worxradio.com
Web site: http://www.worxradio.com
Profile: WXGO-AM is a commercial station owned by DCBroadcasting Inc. The format of the station is oldies. WXGO-AM broadcasts to the Madison, IN area at 1270 AM.
AM RADIO STATION

WXHB-FM
43139

Owner: Blakeney Communications Inc.
Editorial: 4580 Highway 15 N, Laurel, Mississippi 39440 **Tel:** 1 601 544-0095.
Email: wxhb@wxhbfm.com
Web site: http://wxhbfm.com
Profile: WXHB-FM s a commercial station owned by Blakeney Communications Inc. The format is gospel. The station airs in the Laurel, MS area at 96.5FM.
FM RADIO STATION

WXHC-FM
41976

Owner: Eves Broadcasting Inc.
Editorial: 12 S Main St, Homer, New York 13077-1327 **Tel:** 1 607 749-9942.
Email: news@wxhc.com
Web site: http://www.wxhc.com
Profile: WXHC-FM is a commercial station owned by Eves Broadcasting Inc. The format of the station is classic hits. WXHC-FM broadcasts to the Homer, NY area at 101.5 FM.
FM RADIO STATION

WXHL-FM
43994

Owner: Priority Radio, Inc.
Editorial: 2207 Concord Pike, Wilmington, Delaware 19803 **Tel:** 1 302 731-0690.
Email: connect@myreachradio.com
Web site: http://www.myreachradio.com
Profile: WXHL-FM is a non-commercial station owned by Priority Radio, Inc.. The format of the station is religious music. WXHL-FM broadcasts to the greater Philadelphia area at 89.1 FM.
FM RADIO STATION

WXHT-FM
42710

Owner: Black Crow Broadcasting Inc.
Editorial: 1711 Ellis Dr, Valdosta, Georgia 31601-3573 **Tel:** 1 229 249-8200.
Web site: http://myhot1027.com/
Profile: WXHT-FM is a commercial station owned by Black Crow Broadcasting Inc. The format of the station is Top 40/CHR. WXHT-FM broadcasts to the Valdosta, GA area at 102.7 FM.
FM RADIO STATION

WXIL-FM
40870

Owner: Burbach of WV, LLC
Editorial: 5 Rosemar Cir, Parkersburg, West Virginia 26104-1203 **Tel:** 1 304 485-4565.
Email: productionparkersburg@resultsradiowv.com
Web site: http://www.95xil.com/
Profile: WXIL-FM is a commercial station owned by Burbach of WV, LLC. The format for the station is Top 40 hits. WXIL-FM broadcasts at 95.1 FM.
FM RADIO STATION

WXIS-FM
45632

Owner: WEMB Inc.
Editorial: 101 Riverview Rd, Erwin, Tennessee 37650-8722 **Tel:** 1 423 743-6123.
Web site: http://www.jamzfm.com/#new-page
Profile: WXIS-FM is a commercial station owned by WEMB Inc. The format of the station is rhythmic Top 40/CHR. WXIS-FM broadcasts to the Erwin, TN area at 103.9 FM.
FM RADIO STATION

WXIT-AM
36142

Owner: High Country Adventures, LLC
Editorial: 738 Blowing Rock Rd, Boone, North Carolina 28607-4835 **Tel:** 1 828 264-2411.
Web site: http://www.goblueridge.net
Profile: WXIT-AM is a commercial station owned by High Country Adventures, LLC, a subsidiary of Curtis Media Group. The format of the station is top 40/CHR. WXIT-AM broadcasts to the Boone, NC area at 1200 AM.
AM RADIO STATION

WXIZ-FM
45633

Owner: Crystal Communications Corp.
Editorial: 6655 State Route 220, Waverly, Ohio 45690-8987 **Tel:** 1 740 947-7660.
Email: wxiz@roadrunner.com
Web site: http://www.wxiz.com
Profile: WXIZ-FM is a commercial station owned by Crystal Communications Corp. The format of the station is contemporary country music. WXIZ-FM broadcasts to the Waverly, OH, area at 100.9 FM.
FM RADIO STATION

WXJC-AM
36363

Owner: Crawford Broadcasting Co.
Editorial: 120 Summit Pkwy Ste 200, Homewood, Alabama 35209-4719 **Tel:** 1 205 879-3324.
Email: psa@850wxjc.com
Web site: http://850wxjc.com
Profile: WXJC-AM is a commercial station owned by Crawford Broadcasting Co. The format of the station is Christian teaching, talk and Southern gospel

programming. WXJC-AM broadcasts to the Birmingham, AL area at 850 AM.
AM RADIO STATION

WXJC-FM
43495

Owner: Crawford Broadcasting Co.
Editorial: 120 Summit Pkwy Ste 200, Birmingham, Alabama 35209-4719 **Tel:** 1 205 879-3324.
Email: psa@850wxje.com
Web site: http://850wxjc.com
Profile: WXJC-FM is a commercial station owned by Crawford Broadcasting Co. The format of the station is Christian teaching, talk and Southern gospel. WXJC-FM broadcasts to the Birmingham, AL, area at 92.5 FM.
FM RADIO STATION

WXJK-FM
42557

Owner: Layne(David)
Editorial: 31 Edgewood Drive Ext, Farmville, Virginia 23901-4044 **Tel:** 1 434 392-9955.
Web site: http://wxjkfm.com
FM RADIO STATION

WXJO-AM
38148

Owner: Monte Sinai, Inc.
Editorial: 6174 Ga Highway 57, Macon, Georgia 31217-3405 **Tel:** 1 770 920-1520.
Email: wordchr@bellsouth.net
Web site: http://www.wordchristianbroadcasting.com
Profile: WXJO-AM will become a non-commercial station owned by Monte Sinai, Inc. in early 2012. The format of the station is Hispanic religious programming. WXJO-AM broadcasts to the Douglasville, GA area at 1120 AM.
AM RADIO STATION

WXJY-FM
42355

Owner: Cumulus Media Inc.
Editorial: 11640 Highway 17 Byp, Murrells Inlet, South Carolina 29576-9332
Profile: WXJY-FM is a commercial station owned by Cumulus Media Inc. The format of the station is sports. WXJY-FM broadcasts to the Murrells Inlet, SC area at 93.7 FM.
FM RADIO STATION

WXJZ-FM
40889

Owner: JVC Broadcasting Inc.
Editorial: 4424 NW 13th St Ste C5, Gainesville, Florida 32609-1881 **Tel:** 1 352 375-1317.
Web site: http://www.floridasparty.com
Profile: WXJZ-FM is a commercial station owned by JVC Broadcasting Inc. The format of the station is Rhythmic-CHR. WXJZ-FM broadcasts in the Gainesville, FL area at 100.9 FM.
FM RADIO STATION

WXKB-FM
40659

Owner: Beasley Broadcast Group
Editorial: 20125 S Tamiami Trl, Estero, Florida 33928-2117 **Tel:** 1 239 495-2100.
Web site: http://www.b1039.com
Profile: WXKB-FM is a commercial station owned by Beasley Broadcast Group. The format of the station is Top 40/CHR. WXKB-FM broadcasts to the Fort Meyers, FL area at 103.9 FM.
FM RADIO STATION

WXKC-FM
46610

Owner: Cumulus Media Inc.
Editorial: 471 Robison Rd, Erie, Pennsylvania 16509-5425 **Tel:** 1 814 868-5355.
Web site: http://www.classy100.com
Profile: WXKC-FM is a commercial station owned by Cumulus Media Inc. The format of the station is adult contemporary. WXKC-FM broadcasts to the Erie, PA area at 99.9 FM.
FM RADIO STATION

WXKE-FM
86266

Owner: Adams Radio Group
Editorial: 9604 Coldwater Rd Ste 201, Fort Wayne, Indiana 46825-2096 **Tel:** 1 260 747-1511.
Web site: http://963xke.com
Profile: WXKE-FM is a commercial station owned by Adams Radio Group. The format of the station is classic rock music. WXKE-FM broadcasts to the Fort Wayne, IN area at 96.3 FM.
FM RADIO STATION

WXKL-AM
35938

Owner: Macadell & Associates, Inc.
Editorial: 1516 Woodland Ave, Sanford, North Carolina 27330-5652 **Tel:** 1 919 774-1080.
Email: wxkl1290radio@yahoo.com
Profile: WXKL-AM is a commercial station owned by Macadell & Associates, Inc.. The format of the station is urban gospel music. WXKL-AM broadcasts to the Sanford, NC area at 1290 AM.
AM RADIO STATION

WXKO-AM
36226

Owner: Sun Broadcasting, Inc.
Editorial: 1023 Ball St, Perry, Georgia 31069-3307 **Tel:** 1 478 987-1823.
Profile: WXKO-AM is a commercial station owned by Sun Broadcasting, Inc. The format of the station is country. WXKO-AM broadcasts to Fort Valley, GA area at a frequency of 1150 AM.
AM RADIO STATION

WXKQ-FM
46242

Owner: Forcht Broadcasting
Editorial: 1149 Hwy 1862, Mayking, Kentucky 41837 **Tel:** 1 606 633-4434.
Email: wxkq@yahoo.com
Web site: http://www.1039thebulldog.com
Profile: WXKQ-FM is a commercial station owned by Forcht Broadcasting. The format of the station is classic country WXKQ-FM broadcasts to the Mayking, KY area at 103.9 FM.
FM RADIO STATION

WXKR-FM
40593

Owner: Cumulus Media Inc.
Editorial: 3225 Arlington Ave, Toledo, Ohio 43614-2427 **Tel:** 1 419 725-5700.
Web site: http://www.wxkr.com
Profile: WXKR-FM is a commercial station owned by Cumulus Media Inc. The format of the station is classic rock. WXKR-FM broadcasts to the Toledo, OH area at 94.5 FM.
FM RADIO STATION

WXKS-AM
38288

Owner: iHeartMedia Inc.
Editorial: 10 Cabot Rd Ste 303, Medford, Massachusetts 02155-5173 **Tel:** 1 781 396-1430.
Web site: http://www.bloomberg.com/audio
Profile: WXKS-AM is a commercial station owned by iHeartMedia Inc. The format of the station is business news. WXKS-AM broadcasts to the Medford, MA area at 1200 AM. The station airs WBBR-AM's programming.
AM RADIO STATION

WXKS-FM
45634

Owner: iHeartMedia Inc.
Editorial: 10 Cabot Rd Ste 302, Medford, Massachusetts 02155-5173 **Tel:** 1 781 396-1430.
Email: press@kiss108.com
Web site: http://www.kiss108.com
Profile: WXKS-FM is a commercial station owned by iHeartMedia Inc. The format of the station is Top 40/CHR. WXKS-FM broadcasts to the Boston area at 107.9 FM.
FM RADIO STATION

WXKT-FM
43763

Owner: Cox Media Group, Inc.
Editorial: 340 Jesse Jewell Pkwy Se Ste 400, Gainesville, Georgia 30501-7701 **Tel:** 1 706 549-6222.
Web site: http://www.1037chuckfm.com
Profile: WXKT-FM is a commercial station owned by Cox Media Group, Inc. The format of the station is adult hits. WXKT-FM broadcasts to the Washington, GA area at 103.7 FM.
FM RADIO STATION

WXKU-FM
42189

Owner: BK Media, LLC
Editorial: 1534 N Ewing St, Seymour, Indiana 47274-1121 **Tel:** 1 812 522-1390.
Email: info@wxku927.com
Web site: http://www.kix927.com
Profile: WXKU-FM is a commercial station owned by BK Media, LLC. The format of the station is contemporary country music. WXKU-FM broadcasts to the Seymour, IN area at 92.7 FM.
FM RADIO STATION

WXKZ-FM
44033

Owner: Gearheart Broadcasting
Editorial: 98 Church Rd, Harold, Kentucky 41635 **Tel:** 1 606 478-1200.
Profile: WXKZ-FM is a commercial station owned by Gearheart Broadcasting. The format of the station is oldies. WXKZ-FM broadcasts to the Harold, KY area at 105.3 FM.
FM RADIO STATION

WXLA-AM
38770

Owner: MacDonald Broadcasting Co.
Editorial: 600 W Cavanaugh Rd, Lansing, Michigan 48910 **Tel:** 1 517 393-1320.
Profile: WXLA-AM is a commercial station owned by MacDonald Broadcasting Co. The format of the station is adult standards. WXLA-AM broadcasts to the Lansing, MI area at 1180 AM.
AM RADIO STATION

WXLC-FM
45635

Owner: Alpha Media
Editorial: 3250 Belvidere Rd, Waukegan, Illinois 60085-6041 **Tel:** 1 847 336-7900.
Web site: http://www.1023xlc.com
Profile: WXLC-FM is a commercial station owned by Alpha Media. The format of the station is hot adult contemporary. The station broadcasts to the Waukegan, IL area at 102.3 FM.
FM RADIO STATION

WXLF-FM
44511

Owner: WBIN, Inc.
Editorial: 106 N Main St, West Lebanon, New Hampshire 03784-1136 **Tel:** 1 603 298-0123.
Web site: http://www.953thewolf.com
Profile: WXLF-FM is a commercial station owned by WBIN, Inc. The format of the station is country music. WXLF-FM broadcasts to the West Lebanon, NH area at 95.3 FM and simulcasts on WZSH-FM.
FM RADIO STATION

WXLI-AM
35763

Owner: Kirby Broadcasting
Editorial: 1006 Martin Luther King Jr Dr, Dublin, Georgia 31021 **Tel:** 1 478 272-9270.
Email: prod927@bellsouth.net
Profile: WXLI-AM is a commercial station owned by Kirby Broadcasting. The format of the station is classic country and gospel. WXLI-AM broadcasts to the Dublin, GA area at 1230 AM.
AM RADIO STATION

WXLK-FM
40873

Owner: Wheeler Inc.(Mel)
Editorial: 3934 Electric Rd, Roanoke, Virginia 24018-4513 **Tel:** 1 540 774-9200.
Web site: http://www.k92radio.com
Profile: WXLK-FM is a commercial station owned by Mel Wheeler Inc. The format of the station is Top 40/CHR. WXLK-FM broadcasts to the Roanoke, VA area at 92.3 FM.
FM RADIO STATION

WXLM-AM
38211

Owner: Cumulus Media Inc.
Editorial: 7 Governor Winthrop Blvd, New London, Connecticut 06320-6428 **Tel:** 1 860 443-1980.
Web site: http://www.wxlm.fm
Profile: WXLM-AM is a commercial station owned by Cumulus Media Inc.. The format of the station is news/talk/sports. WXLM-AM broadcasts to the New London, CT area at 980 AM.
AM RADIO STATION

WXLN-FM
706512

Owner: Bullock's Christian Broadcasting Corporation
Editorial: 670 Southlawn Dr, Shelbyville, Kentucky 40065-8834 **Tel:** 1 504 321-9447.
Email: wxlnradio@insightbb.com
Web site: http://www.wxlnradio.com
Profile: WXLN-FM is a non-commercial station owned by Bullock's Christian Broadcasting Corporation. The format of the station is Christian Religious talk programming. WXLN-FM broadcasts to the Shelbyville, KY area at 93.3 FM. WXLN's target audience is residents around Shelbyville, KY ages 13 to 100. The tagline is "Power 93.3".
FM RADIO STATION

WXLO-FM
41863

Owner: Cumulus Media Inc.
Editorial: 250 Commercial St Ste 530, Worcester, Massachusetts 01608-1726 **Tel:** 1 508 752-1045.
Web site: http://www.wxlo.com
Profile: WXLO-FM is a commercial station owned by Cumulus Media Inc. The format of the station is hot adult contemporary. WXLO-FM broadcasts to the Worcester, MA area at 104.5 FM.
FM RADIO STATION

WXLP-FM
41127

Owner: Townsquare Media
Editorial: 1229 Brady St, Davenport, Iowa 52803-4616 **Tel:** 1 563 326-2541.
Web site: http://97x.com
Profile: WXLP-FM is a commercial station owned by Townsquare Media. The format of the station is classic rock. WXLP-FM broadcasts to the Davenport, IA area at 96.9 FM.
FM RADIO STATION

WXLR-FM
42204

Owner: Gearheart Broadcasting
Editorial: 99 Church Rd, Harold, Kentucky 41635 **Tel:** 1 606 478-1200.
Web site: http://wxlr.com
FM RADIO STATION

WXLT-FM
46477

Owner: Max Media
Editorial: 1431 Country Aire Dr, Carterville, Illinois 62918-5118 **Tel:** 1 618 985-4843.
Email: publicservice@riverradio.net
Web site: http://www.1035espn.com
Profile: WXLT-FM is a commercial station owned by Max Media. The format of the station is sports. WXLT-FM broadcasts to the Carterville, IL area at 103.5 FM. Send PSAs to publicservice@riverradio.net.
FM RADIO STATION

WXLV-FM
44171

Owner: Lehigh Carbon Community College
Editorial: 4525 Education Park Dr, Schnecksville, Pennsylvania 18078-2502 **Tel:** 1 610 799-1145.
Email: wxvradio@gmail.com
Web site: http://www.wxlvradio.com
Profile: WXLV-FM is a non-commercial station owned by Lehigh Carbon Community College. The format of the station is variety. WXLV-FM broadcasts to the Schnecksville, PA area at 90.3 FM.
FM RADIO STATION

WXLW-AM
36459

Owner: Pilgrim Communications Inc.
Editorial: 645 Industrial Dr, Franklin, Indiana 46131-9617 **Tel:** 1 317 736-4040.
Web site: http://www.freedom95.us
Profile: WXLW-AM is a commercial station owned by Pilgrim Communications Inc. The format of the station is talk. WXLW-AM broadcasts to the Indianapolis area at 950 AM.
AM RADIO STATION

WXLY-FM 40874
Owner: iHeartMedia Inc.
Editorial: 950 Houston Northcutt Blvd Ste 201, Mount Pleasant, South Carolina 29464-5645 **Tel:** 1 843 884-534.
Web site: http://www.y1025.com
Profile: WXLY-FM is a commercial station owned by HeartMedia Inc. The format of the station is adult ontemporary. WXLY-FM broadcasts to the Mount Pleasant, SC area at 102.5 FM.
M RADIO STATION

WXLZ-AM 36576
Owner: Yeary Broadcasting Inc.
Editorial: 265 WXLZ Dr., Lebanon, Virginia 24266 **Tel:** 1 276 889-1073.
Email: wxlz1073@bvu.net
Web site: http://www.wxlz.net
AM RADIO STATION

WXLZ-FM 43294
Owner: Yeary Broadcasting Inc.
Editorial: 265 WXLZ Dr, Lebanon, Virginia 24266 **Tel:** 1 276 889-1073.
Email: wxlz1073@bvu.net
Web site: http://www.wxlz.net
FM RADIO STATION

WXMA-FM 43476
Owner: Alpha Media
Editorial: 520 S 4th St Fl 2, Louisville, Kentucky 0202-2500 **Tel:** 1 502 625-1220.
Email: themaxfm@gmail.com
Web site: http://www.themaxfm.com
Profile: WXMA-FM is a commercial station owned by Alpha Media. The format of the station is hot adult ontemporary music. WXMA-FM broadcasts in the ouisville, KY area at 102.3 FM.
FM RADIO STATION

WXME-AM 36973
Owner: WBCQ Radio
Editorial: 274 Britton Rd, Monticello, Maine 04760-110 **Tel:** 1 207 538-9180.
Profile: WXME-AM is a commercial station owned by WBCQ Radio. The format of the station is talk. WXME-AM broadcasts to the Aroostook County area n Maine at 780 AM.
AM RADIO STATION

WXMG-FM 43280
Owner: Urban One, Inc.
Editorial: 2400 Corporate Exchange Dr Ste 200, Columbus, Ohio 43231-7669 **Tel:** 1 614 487-1444.
Web site: http://mycolumbusmagic.hellobeautiful.om/
Profile: WXMG-FM is a commercial station owned by Urban One, Inc. The format of the station is urban adult contemporary. WXMG-FM broadcasts to the Columbus, OH area at 95.5 FM.
FM RADIO STATION

WXMJ-FM 43357
Owner: FM Radio Licenses, LLC
Editorial: 900 Water St, Meadville, Pennsylvania 6335-3428 **Tel:** 1 814 724-1111.
Web site: http://www.mymajicspace.com
Profile: WXMJ-FM is a commercial station owned by FM Radio Licenses, LLC. The format of the station is ot adult contemporary. WXMJ-FM broadcasts to the Meadville, PA area at 104.5 FM.
FM RADIO STATION

WXMK-FM 41963
Owner: Golden Isles Broadcasting LLC
Editorial: 185 Benedict Rd, Brunswick, Georgia 1520-2938 **Tel:** 1 912 261-1000.
Web site: http://www.magic1059.com
Profile: WXMK-FM is a commercial station owned by Golden Isles Broadcasting LLC. The format of the station is hot adult contemporary. WXMK-FM roadcasts to the Brunswick, GA area at 105.9 FM.
FM RADIO STATION

WXML-FM 42472
Owner: Kayser Broadcast Ministries
Editorial: 1800 E Wyandot Ave, Upper Sandusky, Ohio 43351 **Tel:** 1 419 294-2900.
Email: contactus@newvision.fm
Web site: http://www.newvision.fm
Profile: WXML-FM is a non-commercial station wned by Kayser Broadcast Ministries. The format of he station is religious programming. WXML-FM roadcasts to the Toledo, OH area at 90.1 FM.
FM RADIO STATION

WXMT-FM 41788
Owner: Colonial Radio Group
Editorial: 1 Bluebird Sq, Olean, New York 14760-2552 **Tel:** 1 814 837-9564.
Profile: WXMT-FM is a commercial station owned by Colonial Radio Group. The format of the station is lassic hits. WXMT-FM broadcasts to the Smethport, PA area at 106.3 FM.
FM RADIO STATION

WXMW-FM 746796
Owner: Kayser Broadcast Ministries
Editorial: 1800 E Wyandot Ave, Upper Sandusky, Ohio 43351-9652 **Tel:** 1 419 294-2900.
Email: contactus@newvision.fm
Web site: http://www.newvision.fm
Profile: WXMW-FM is a non-commercial station wned by Kayser Broadcast Ministries. The format of he station is religious programming. WXMW-FM's broadcasts at a frequency of 89.3 FM in the Sycamore, OH area.
FM RADIO STATION

WXMX-FM 41010
Owner: Cumulus Media Inc.
Editorial: 5629 Murray Ave, Memphis, Tennessee 38119-3831 **Tel:** 1 901 682-1106.
Web site: http://www.981themax.com
Profile: WXMX-FM is a commercial station owned by Cumulus Media Inc. The format of the station is rock. WXMX-FM broadcasts to the Memphis, TN area at 98.1 FM.
FM RADIO STATION

WXMZ-FM 45344
Owner: Starlight Broadcasting Co.
Editorial: 314 S Main St, Hartford, Kentucky 42347-1129 **Tel:** 1 270 298-3268.
Profile: WXMZ-FM is a commercial station owned by Starlight Broadcasting Co. The format of the station is gospel. WXMZ-FM broadcasts to the Hartford, KY area at 106.3 FM.
FM RADIO STATION

WXNC-AM 36788
Owner: Norsan Group
Editorial: 4801 E Independence Blvd, Ste 815, Charlotte, North Carolina 28212 **Tel:** 1 770 442-7277.
Profile: WXNC-AM is a commercial station owned by Norsan Group. The format of the station is Hispanic Christian music. WXNC-AM broadcasts to the Charlotte, NC area at 1060 AM.
AM RADIO STATION

WXNR-FM 41589
Owner: Beasley Broadcast Group
Editorial: 207 Glenburnie Dr, New Bern, North Carolina 28560-2815 **Tel:** 1 252 633-1500.
Web site: http://www.995thex.com
Profile: WXNR-FM is a commercial station owned by Beasley Broadcast Group. The format of the station is rock alternative. WXNR-FM broadcasts to the New Bern, NC area at 99.5 FM.
FM RADIO STATION

WXNT-AM 38452
Owner: Entercom Communications Corp.
Editorial: 9245 N Meridian St Ste 300, Indianapolis, Indiana 46260-1832 **Tel:** 1 317 816-4000.
Email: indypsa@entercom.com
Web site: http://www.cbssports1430.com
Profile: WXNT-AM is a CBS Sports Radio affiliate owned by Entercom Communications Corp. The format for the station is sports. WXNT-AM broadcasts to the Indianapolis area at 1430 AM.
AM RADIO STATION

WXNU-FM 401512
Owner: Staradio Corp.
Editorial: 70 Meadowview Ctr, Ste 400, Kankakee, Illinois 60901-2061 **Tel:** 1 815 935-9555.
Email: wxnu@staradio.com
Web site: http://www.xcountry1065.com
Profile: WXNU-FM is a commercial station owned by Staradio Corp. The format of the station is contemporary country music. WXNU-FM broadcasts to the Kankakee, IL, area at 106.5 FM.
FM RADIO STATION

WXNX-FM 46691
Owner: Meridian Broadcasting, Inc.
Editorial: 2824 Palm Beach Blvd, Fort Myers, Florida 33916-1503 **Tel:** 1 239 337-2346.
Web site: http://93x.fm
Profile: WXNX-FM is a commercial station owned by Meridian Broadcasting, Inc. The format of the station is alternative rock. WXNX-FM broadcasts to the Fort Meyers, FL area at a frequency of 93.7 FM.
FM RADIO STATION

WXNY-FM 43583
Owner: Univision Communications Inc.
Editorial: 485 Madison Ave, New York, New York 10022-5803 **Tel:** 1 212 310-6000.
Web site: http://x963fm.univision.com
Profile: WXNY-FM is a commercial station owned by Univision Communications Inc. The format of the station is Spanish CHR Tropical. WXNY-FM broadcasts to the New York area at 96.3 FM.
FM RADIO STATION

WXOF-FM 44228
Owner: WXOF, Inc.
Editorial: 4554 S Suncoast Blvd, Homosassa, Florida 34446-1103 **Tel:** 1 352 746-9596.
Email: staff@thefox967.com
Web site: http://www.thefox967.com/
Profile: WXOF-FM is a commercial station owned by WXOF, Inc. The format of the station is classic hits. WXOF-FM broadcasts to the Homosassa, FL area at 96.7 FM.
FM RADIO STATION

WXOK-AM 39300
Owner: Cumulus Media Inc.
Editorial: 630 Main Street, Baton Rouge, Louisiana 70801 **Tel:** 1 225 926-1106.
Web site: http://www.heaven1460.com
Profile: WXOK-AM is a commercial station owned by Cumulus Media Inc. The format of the station is gospel music. WXOK-AM broadcasts to the Baton Rouge, LA area at 1460 AM.
AM RADIO STATION

WXOQ-FM 41362
Owner: Hunt(Gerald W.)
Editorial: 165 Bowen Dr, Savannah, Tennessee 38372-1490 **Tel:** 1 731 925-7102.
Profile: WXOQ-FM is a commercial station owned by Gerald W. Hunt. The format of the station is country. WXOQ-FM broadcasts to the Savannah, TN area at 105.5 FM.
FM RADIO STATION

WXOS-FM 40537
Owner: Hubbard Broadcasting, Inc.
Editorial: 11647 Olive Blvd, Saint Louis, Missouri 63141-7001 **Tel:** 1 314 983-6000.
Email: webmaster@101sports.com
Web site: http://www.101espn.com
Profile: WXOS-FM is a commercial station owned by Hubbard Broadcasting, Inc. The format of the station is sports. WXOS-FM broadcasts to the St. Louis area at 101.1 FM.
FM RADIO STATION

WXPJ-FM 40575
Owner: WXPN
Editorial: 400 Jefferson St, Hackettstown, New Jersey 07840-2184 **Tel:** 1 908 979-4355.
Profile: WXPJ-FM is a non-commercial station owned by the WXPN. The format of the station is a variety. WXPJ-FM broadcasts in Northeast PA, and Southwest NY area at 91.9 FM.
FM RADIO STATION

WXPK-FM 42818
Owner: Pamal Broadcasting Ltd.
Editorial: 56 Lafayette Ave, Ste 370, White Plains, New York 10603-1684 **Tel:** 1 914 397-0127.
Email: studio@1071thepeak.com
Web site: http://www.1071thepeak.com
Profile: WXPK-FM is a commercial station owned by Pamal Broadcasting Ltd. The format of the station is adult album alternative. WXPK-FM broadcasts to the White Plains, NY area at 107.1 FM.
FM RADIO STATION

WXPR-FM 41075
Owner: White Pine Community Broadcasting Inc.
Editorial: 303 W Prospect St, Rhinelander, Wisconsin 54501-3867 **Tel:** 1 715 362-6000.
Web site: http://www.wxpr.org
Profile: WXPR-FM is a non-commercial station owned by White Pine Community Broadcasting Inc. The format of the station is variety. WXPR-FM broadcasts in the Rhinelander, WI area at 91.7 FM.
FM RADIO STATION

WXPW-FM 44101
Owner: White Pine Community Broadcasting Inc.
Editorial: 303 W Prospect St, Rhinelander, Wisconsin 54501-3867 **Tel:** 1 715 362-6000.
Web site: http://www.wxpr.org
Profile: WXPW-FM is a non-commercial station owned by White Pine Community Broadcasting Inc. The format of the station is variety. WXPW-FM broadcasts in the Rhinelander, WI area at 91.9 FM. WXPW-FM will only accept PSAs in a written format.
FM RADIO STATION

WXQR-FM 40877
Owner: Alpha Media
Editorial: 1361 Colony Dr, New Bern, North Carolina 28562-4129 **Tel:** 1 252 639-7900.
Web site: http://www.myrock105.com
Profile: WXQR-FM is a commercial station owned by Alpha Media. The format of the station is rock. WXQR-FM broadcasts to the New Bern, NC area at 105.5 FM.
FM RADIO STATION

WXQW-AM 38659
Owner: Cumulus Media Inc.
Editorial: 2800 Dauphin St Ste 104, Mobile, Alabama 36606-2400 **Tel:** 1 251 652-2000.
Web site: http://www.660wxqw.com
Profile: WXQW-AM is a commercial station owned by Cumulus Media Inc. The format of the station is talk. WWFF-AM broadcasts to the Mobile, AL area at 660 AM.
AM RADIO STATION

WXRC-FM 43407
Owner: Pacific Broadcasting Group Inc.
Editorial: 1666 Radio Station Rd, Newton, North Carolina 28658-9488 **Tel:** 1 704 527-0957.
Web site: http://www.957theride.com
Profile: WXRC-FM is a commercial station owned by Pacific Broadcasting Group Inc. The format of the station is classic hits. WXRC-FM broadcasts to the Charlotte, NC area at 95.7 FM.
FM RADIO STATION

WXRD-FM 44457
Owner: Adams Radio Group
Editorial: 2755 Sager Rd, Valparaiso, Indiana 46383-0721 **Tel:** 1 219 462-6111.
Email: news@argni.com
Web site: http://www.xrock1039.com
Profile: WXRD-FM is a commercial station owned by Adams Radio Group. The format of the station is classic rock. WXRD-FM broadcasts to the Valparaiso, IN area at 103.9 FM.
FM RADIO STATION

WXRG-FM 45322
Owner: Northeast Broadcasting Co.
Tel: 1 978 374-4733.
Email: info@wxrv.com
Web site: http://theriverboston.com
Profile: WXRG-FM is a commercial station owned by Capital Broadcasting Corporation, Inc. The format of the station is AAA. WXRG-FM broadcasts to the Concord, NH area at 102.3 FM.
FM RADIO STATION

WXRI-FM 43336
Owner: Positive Alternative Radio
Editorial: 600 W Clemmonsville Rd, Winston Salem, North Carolina 27127-5045 **Tel:** 1 336 788-1155.
Email: office@joyfm.org
Web site: http://www.joyfm.org
Profile: WXRI-FM is a non-commercial station owned by Positive Alternative Radio. The format of the station is Southern Gospel. WXRI-FM broadcasts to the Winston Salem, NC area at 91.3 FM.
FM RADIO STATION

WXRL-AM 35766
Owner: Dome Broadcasting Inc.
Editorial: 5426 William St, Lancaster, New York 14086-9320 **Tel:** 1 716 681-1313.
Email: info@wxrl.com
Web site: http://www.wxrl.com
Profile: WXRL-AM is a commercial station owned by Dome Broadcasting Inc. The format of the station is country. WXRL-AM broadcasts to the Lancaster, NY area at 1300 AM.
AM RADIO STATION

WXRO-FM 45637
Owner: Good Karma Broadcasting
Editorial: 100 Stoddart St, Beaver Dam, Wisconsin 53916-1306 **Tel:** 1 920 885-4442.
Web site: http://www.wxroradio.com
Profile: WXRO-FM is a commercial station owned by Good Karma Broadcasting. The format of the station is classic country music. WXRO-FM broadcasts to the Milwaukee area at 95.3 FM.
FM RADIO STATION

WXRQ-AM 35767
Owner: New Life Community Temple of Faith, Inc.
Editorial: 209 Bond St, Mount Pleasant, Tennessee 38474 **Tel:** 1 931 379-3119.
Email: wxrq@yahoo.com
Web site: http://www.1460wxrq.com
Profile: WXRQ-AM is a commercial station owned by New Life Community Temple of Faith, Inc. The format of the station is southern gospel music. WXRQ-AM broadcasts to the Nashville, TN area at 1460 AM.
AM RADIO STATION

WXRR-FM 43107
Owner: Blakeney Communications Inc.
Editorial: 4580 Highway 15 N, Laurel, Mississippi 39440 **Tel:** 1 601 649-0095.
Email: rock104@rock104fm.com
Web site: http://www.rock104fm.com
Profile: WXRR-FM is a commercial station owned by Blakeney Communications Inc. The format of the station is classic rock music. WXRR-FM broadcasts to the Laurel, MS area at 104.5 FM.
FM RADIO STATION

WXRS-AM 38350
Owner: RadioJones LLC
Editorial: 2 Radio Loop, Swainsboro, Georgia 30401-5673 **Tel:** 1 478 237-1590.
Web site: http://www.therocket971.com/
Profile: WXRS-AM is a commercial station owned by RadioJones LLC. The format of the station is oldies. WXRS-AM broadcasts to the Swainsboro, GA area at 1590 AM.
AM RADIO STATION

WXRS-FM 45710
Owner: RadioJones LLC
Editorial: 2 Radio Loop, Swainsboro, Georgia 30401-5673 **Tel:** 1 478 237-1590.
Web site: http://www.wxrs.com/
Profile: WXRS-FM is a commercial station owned by RadioJones LLC. The format of the station is country. WXRS-FM broadcasts to the Swainsboro, GA area at 100.5 FM.
FM RADIO STATION

WXRT-FM 46256
Owner: CBS Radio
Editorial: 180 N Stetson Ave Ste 963, Chicago, Illinois 60601-6712 **Tel:** 1 312 649-0099.
Email: xrtcomments@wxrt.com
Web site: http://wxrt.cbslocal.com
Profile: WXRT-FM is a commercial station owned by CBS Radio. The format of the station is adult album alternative music. WXRT-FM broadcasts to the Chicago area at 93.1 FM.
FM RADIO STATION

WXRV-FM 42800
Owner: Northeast Broadcasting Co.
Editorial: 30 How St, Haverhill, Massachusetts 01830-6131 **Tel:** 1 978 374-4733.
Web site: http://theriverboston.com
Profile: WXRV-FM is a commercial station owned by Northeast Broadcasting Co. The format of the station is AAA - Adult Album Alternative. WXRV-FM broadcasts to Haverhill, MA area at 92.5 FM.
FM RADIO STATION

WXRX-FM 43029
Owner: Mid-West Family Broadcasting
Editorial: 2830 Sandy Hollow Rd, Rockford, Illinois 61109-2369 **Tel:** 1 815 874-7861.
Web site: http://www.wxrx.com
Profile: WXRX-FM is a commercial station owned by Mid-West Family Broadcasting. The format of the

station is rock music. WXRX-FM broadcasts to the Rockford, IL area at 105.9 FM.
FM RADIO STATION

WXRZ-FM 45638
Owner: TeleSouth Communications Inc.
Editorial: 1608 S Johns St, Corinth, Mississippi 38834-6547 **Tel:** 1 662 286-8451.
Web site: http://www.supertalkms.com
Profile: WXRZ-FM is a commercial station owned by TeleSouth Communications Inc. The format of the station is talk. WXRZ-FM broadcasts to the Corinth, MS area at 94.3 FM.
FM RADIO STATION

WXSH-FM 594039
Owner: The Voice Radio Network
Editorial: 20200 Dupont Blvd, Georgetown, Delaware 19947-3105 **Tel:** 1 302 228-8942.
Web site: http://thevaultrocks.com
Profile: WXSH-FM is a commercial station owned by The Voice Radio Network. The format of the station is classic rock. The station airs locally in the Pocomoke City, MD area at 106.1 FM.
FM RADIO STATION

WXSM-AM 35350
Owner: Cumulus Media Inc.
Editorial: 162 Free Hill Rd, Gray, Tennessee 37615-3144 **Tel:** 1 423 477-1064.
Email: sportsmonster@640wxsm.com
Web site: http://www.640wxsm.com
Profile: WXSM-AM is a commercial station owned by Cumulus Media Inc. The format of the station is sports. WXSM-AM broadcasts to the Johnson City, TN area at 640 AM.
AM RADIO STATION

WXSR-FM 42679
Owner: iHeartMedia Inc.
Editorial: 325 John Knox Rd Bldg G, Tallahassee, Florida 32303-4113 **Tel:** 1 850 422-3107.
Web site: http://www.x1015.com
Profile: WXSR-FM is a commercial station owned by iHeartMedia Inc. The format of the station is rock alternative. WXSR-FM broadcasts to the Tallahassee, FL area at 101.5 FM.
FM RADIO STATION

WXSS-FM 40266
Owner: Entercom Communications Corp.
Editorial: 11800 W Grange Ave, Hales Corners, Wisconsin 53130 **Tel:** 1 414 529-1250.
Web site: http://www.1037kissfm.com
Profile: WXSS-FM is a commercial station owned by Entercom Communications Corp. The format of the station is Top 40/CHR music. WXSS-FM broadcasts to the Milwaukee area at 103.7 FM.
FM RADIO STATION

WXST-FM 40961
Owner: Apex Broadcasting Inc.
Editorial: 2294 Clements Ferry Rd, Charleston, South Carolina 29492 **Tel:** 1 843 972-1100.
Email: frontdesk@apexbroadcasting.com
Web site: http://www.star997.com
Profile: WXST-FM is a commercial station owned by Apex Broadcasting Inc. The format of the station is urban adult contemporary. WXST-FM broadcasts to the Charleston, SC area at 99.7 FM.
FM RADIO STATION

WXTA-FM 41697
Owner: Cumulus Media Inc
Editorial: 471 Robison Rd, Erie, Pennsylvania 16509-5425 **Tel:** 1 814 868-5355.
Web site: http://www.979nashfm.com
Profile: WXTA-FM is a commercial station owned by Cumulus Media Inc. The format of the station is contemporary country. WXTA-FM broadcasts to the Erie, PA area at 97.9 FM.
FM RADIO STATION

WXTB-FM 40449
Owner: iHeartMedia Inc.
Editorial: 4002 W Gandy Blvd, Tampa, Florida 33611-3410 **Tel:** 1 813 832-1000.
Web site: http://www.98rock.com
Profile: WXTB-FM is a commercial station owned by iHeartMedia Inc. The format of the station is rock music. WXTB-FM broadcasts to the Tampa, FL area at 97.9 FM.
FM RADIO STATION

WXTG-AM 35591
Owner: Local Voice Media
Editorial: 4732 Longhill Rd Ste 2201, Williamsburg, Virginia 23188-1584 **Tel:** 1 757 565-1079.
Profile: WXTG-AM is a commercial station owned by Local Voice Media. The format of the station is Adult Album Alternative. WXTG-AM broadcasts to the Virginia Beach, VA area at 1490 AM.
AM RADIO STATION

WXTG-FM 80508
Owner: Local Voice Media
Editorial: 232 Business Park Dr Ste 120, Virginia Beach, Virginia 23462-6537 **Tel:** 1 757 565-1079.
Email: music@tideradio.com
Web site: http://tideradio.com
Profile: WXTG-FM is a commercial station owned by Local Voice Media. The format of the station is Adult Album Alternative. WXTG-FM broadcasts to the Virginia Beach, VA area at 102.1 FM.
FM RADIO STATION

WXTK-FM 43666
Owner: iHeartMedia Inc.
Editorial: 154 Barnstable Rd, Hyannis, Massachusetts 02601-2930 **Tel:** 1 508 778-2888.
Email: news@95wxtk.com
Web site: http://95wxtk.iheart.com
Profile: WXTK-FM is a commercial station owned by iHeartMedia Inc. The format of the station is news, talk, and sports. WXTK-FM broadcasts to the Boston area at 95.1 FM.
FM RADIO STATION

WXTL-FM 42933
Owner: Cumulus Media Inc
Editorial: 1064 James St, Syracuse, New York 13203-2704 **Tel:** 1 315 472-0200.
Web site: http://www.1059therebel.com
Profile: WXTL-FM is a commercial station owned by Cumulus Media Inc. The format of the station is classic rock. WXTL-FM broadcasts to the Syracuse, NY area at 105.9 FM.
FM RADIO STATION

WXTN-AM 39260
Owner: Sandra U. Cothran, Executrix
Editorial: 100 Radio Road, Lexington, Mississippi 39095 **Tel:** 1 662 834-1025.
Email: class102@cableone.net
Profile: WXTN-AM is a commercial station owned by Sandra U. Cothran, Executrix. The format of the station is gospel and news. WXTN-AM broadcasts to the Lexington, MS area at 1000 AM.
AM RADIO STATION

WXTQ-FM 45639
Owner: WATH Inc.
Editorial: 300 Columbus Rd, Athens, Ohio 45701-1336 **Tel:** 1 740 593-6651.
Email: psa@wxtq.com
Web site: http://www.wxtq.com
Profile: WXTQ-FM is a commercial station owned by WATH Inc. The format for the station is hot adult contemporary. WXTQ-FM broadcasts to the Athen, OH area at 105.5 FM.
FM RADIO STATION

WXTU-FM 42331
Owner: CBS Radio
Editorial: 555 E City Ave Ste 330, Bala Cynwyd, Pennsylvania 19004-1137 **Tel:** 1 610 667-9000.
Web site: http://925xtu.cbslocal.com
Profile: WXTU-FM is a commercial station owned by CBS Radio. The format of the station is contemporary country. WXTU-FM broadcasts to the Philadelphia area at 92.5 FM.
FM RADIO STATION

WXUR-FM 46663
Owner: Arjuna Broadcasting Corp.
Editorial: 566 Baum Rd, Herkimer, New York 13357 **Tel:** 1 315 266-0250.
Email: wxur@hotmail.com
Web site: http://927thedrive.net
Profile: WXUR-FM is a commercial station owned by Arjuna Broadcasting Corp. The format of the station is adult album alternative. WXUR-FM broadcasts to the Herkimer, NY area at 92.7 FM.
FM RADIO STATION

WXVI-AM 36146
Owner: New Life Ministries Inc.
Editorial: 912 S Perry St, Montgomery, Alabama 36104 **Tel:** 1 334 263-4141.
Profile: WXVI-AM is a commercial station owned by New Life Ministries Inc. The format of the station is gospel. WXVI-AM broadcasts to the Montgomery, AL area at 1600 AM.
AM RADIO STATION

WXVS-FM 42495
Owner: Georgia Public Broadcasting
Editorial: 260 14th St NW, Atlanta, Georgia 30318 **Tel:** 1 404 685-2400.
Email: ask@gpb.org
Web site: http://www.gpb.org
Profile: WXVS-FM is a non-commercial station owned by Georgia Public Broadcasting. The format of the station is classical music, jazz, news and talk. WXVS-FM broadcasts to the Atlanta area at 90.1 FM.
FM RADIO STATION

WXVW-AM 35769
Owner: Dugan (Ryan)
Editorial: 213 Magnolia Ave, Jeffersonville, Indiana 47130-6446 **Tel:** 1 812 725-1457.
Email: contact@1450thesportsbuzz.com
Profile: WXVW-AM is a commercial station owned by Dugan (Ryan). The format of the station is sports/talk. WXVW-AM broadcasts to the Louisville, KY area at 1450 AM.
AM RADIO STATION

WXXB-FM 41319
Owner: WASK Inc.
Editorial: 3575 McCarty Ln, Lafayette, Indiana 47905-4985 **Tel:** 1 765 448-1566.
Web site: http://www.b1029.com
Profile: WXXB-FM is a commercial station owned by Neuhoff Communications. The format of the station is Top 40/CHR. WXXB-FM broadcasts to the Lafayette, IN area at 102.9 FM.
FM RADIO STATION

WXXC-FM 45382
Owner: Hoosier AM/FM LLC
Editorial: 820 S Pennsylvania St, Marion, Indiana 46953-2407 **Tel:** 1 765 664-7396.
Web site: http://www.star1069fm.com
Profile: WXXC-FM is a commercial station owned by Hoosier AM/FM LLC. The format for the station is Hot AC. WXXC-FM broadcasts to the Indianapolis area at 106.9 FM.
FM RADIO STATION

WXXF-FM 43631
Owner: iHeartMedia Inc.
Editorial: 1400 Radio Ln, Mansfield, Ohio 44906-2525 **Tel:** 1 419 529-2211.
Web site: http://www.foxclassicrock.com
Profile: WXXF-FM is a commercial station owned by iHeartMedia Inc. The format of the station is classic rock. WXXF-FM broadcasts to the Mansfield, OH area at 107.7 FM and simulcasts the programming of WFXN-FM in the Mansfield, OH area.
FM RADIO STATION

WXXI-AM 38861
Owner: WXXI Public Broadcast Council
Editorial: 280 State St, Rochester, New York 14614 **Tel:** 1 585 325-7500.
Email: wxxi@wxxi.org
Web site: http://interactive.wxxi.org
Profile: WXXI-AM is a non-commercial station owned by WXXI Public Broadcast Council. The format of the station is news and talk. WXXI-AM broadcasts to the Rochester, NY area at 1370 AM.
AM RADIO STATION

WXXI-FM 46213
Owner: WXXI Public Broadcast Council
Editorial: 280 State St, Rochester, New York 14614-1033 **Tel:** 1 585 325-7500.
Email: radio@wxxi.org
Web site: http://interactive.wxxi.org/classical
Profile: WXXI-FM is a non-commercial station owned by the WXXI Public Broadcasting Council. The format of the station is classical. WXXI-FM broadcasts to the Rochester, NY area at 91.5 FM.
FM RADIO STATION

WXXJ-FM 40388
Owner: Cox Media Group, Inc.
Editorial: 8000 Belfort Pkwy, Ste 100, Jacksonville, Florida 32256 **Tel:** 1 904 245-8500.
Web site: http://www.x1029.com
Profile: WXXJ-FM is a commercial station owned by Cox Media Group, Inc. The format of the station is rock alternative. WXXJ-FM broadcasts to the Jacksonville, FL area at 102.9 FM.
FM RADIO STATION

WXXK-FM 41015
Owner: Great Eastern Radio, LLC
Editorial: 106 N Main St, West Lebanon, New Hampshire 03784-1136 **Tel:** 1 603 448-1400.
Web site: http://www.kixx.com
Profile: WXXK-FM is a commercial station owned by Great Eastern Radio, LLC. The format of the station is contemporary country. WXXK-FM broadcasts to the Lebanon, NH area at 100.5 FM.
FM RADIO STATION

WXXL-FM 40994
Owner: iHeart Media Inc.
Editorial: 2500 Maitland Center Pkwy Ste 401, Maitland, Florida 32751-4179 **Tel:** 1 407 916-7800.
Web site: http://www.xl1067.com
Profile: WXXL-FM is a commercial station owned by iHeart Media Inc. The format of the station is Top 40/CHR. WXXL-FM broadcasts to the Orlando, FL area at 106.7 FM.
FM RADIO STATION

WXXM-FM 40718
Owner: iHeartMedia Inc.
Editorial: 2651 S Fish Hatchery Rd, Fitchburg, Wisconsin 53711-5410 **Tel:** 1 608 274-1070.
Web site: http://www.themic921.com
Profile: WXXM-FM is a commercial station owned by iHeartMedia Inc. The format of the station is progressive talk. WXXM-FM broadcasts to the Madison, WI area at 92.1 FM.
FM RADIO STATION

WXXQ-FM 43403
Owner: Cumulus Media Inc.
Editorial: 3901 Brendenwood Rd, Rockford, Illinois 61107 **Tel:** 1 815 399-2233.
Web site: http://www.q985online.com
Profile: WXXQ-FM is a commercial station owned by Cumulus Media Inc. The format of the station is country music. WXXQ-FM broadcasts to the Rockford, IL area at 98.5 FM.
FM RADIO STATION

WXXS-FM 43771
Owner: Lunderville(Barry)
Editorial: 195 Main St, Lancaster, New Hampshire 3584 **Tel:** 1 603 788-3636.
Email: kiss102@together.net
Profile: WXXS-FM is a commercial station owned by Barry Lunderville. The format of the station is Hot AC. WXXS-FM broadcasts to the Portland, ME area at 102.3 FM.
FM RADIO STATION

WXXX-FM 46092
Owner: Sison Broadcasting Inc.
Editorial: 118 Malletts Bay Ave, Colchester, Vermont 5446 **Tel:** 1 802 655-1620.
Email: 95triplex@95triplex.com
Web site: http://www.95triplex.com
Profile: WXXX-FM is a commercial station owned by Sison Broadcasting Inc. The format of the station is Top 40/CHR music. WXXX-FM broadcasts to the Colchester, VT market at 95.5 FM.
FM RADIO STATION

WXXY-FM 41521
Owner: WXXI Public Broadcast Council
Editorial: 280 State St, Rochester, New York 14601 **Tel:** 1 585 325-7500.
Email: wxxi@wxxi.org
Web site: http://www.wxxi.org
Profile: WXXY-FM is a non-commercial station owned by WXXI Public Broadcast Council. The format of the station is classical, news, talk and public radio. WXXY-FM broadcasts to the Houghton, NY area at 90.3 FM.
FM RADIO STATION

WXYB-AM 36181
Owner: ASA Broadcasting Network
Editorial: 109 S Bayview Blvd Ste A, Oldsmar, Florida 34677-3124 **Tel:** 1 727 725-5555.
Email: wzra48@yahoo.com
Web site: http://www.wpso.com
Profile: WXYB-AM is a commercial station owned by ASA Broadcasting Network. The format of the station is ethnic programming. WXYB-AM broadcasts to the Oldsmar, FL area at 1520 AM.
AM RADIO STATION

WXYG-AM 882500
Owner: Tri-County Broadcasting
Editorial: 1010 2nd St N, Sauk Rapids, Minnesota 56379-2527 **Tel:** 1 320 252-6200.
Email: tcbi.redhouse@gmail.com
Web site: http://www.540wxyg.com
Profile: WXYG-AM is a commercial station owned by Tri-County Broadcasting. The format of the station is classic rock. WXYG-AM broadcasts in the Sauk Rapids, MN area at 540 AM.
AM RADIO STATION

WXYK-FM 46784
Owner: Alpha Media
Editorial: 1909 E Pass Rd, Gulfport, Mississippi 39507-3779 **Tel:** 1 228 388-2001.
Web site: http://www.1071themonkey.net
Profile: WXYK-FM is a commercial station owned by Alpha Media. The format of the station is Top 40/CHR music. WXYK-FM broadcasts to the Gulfport, MS area at 107.1 FM.
FM RADIO STATION

WXYM-FM 46717
Owner: Magnum Radio Group
Editorial: 1021 N Superior Ave, Ste 5, Tomah, Wisconsin 54660 **Tel:** 1 608 372-9400.
Email: news@magnumbroadcasting.com
Web site: http://www.mix96wxym.com
Profile: WXYM-FM is a commercial station owned by the Magnum Radio Group. The format of the station is hot adult contemporary. WXYM-FM broadcasts to the Tomah, WI area at 96.1 FM.
FM RADIO STATION

WXYT-AM 36233
Owner: CBS Radio
Editorial: 26455 American Dr, Southfield, Michigan 48034-6114 **Tel:** 1 248 372-2900.
Web site: http://detroit.cbslocal.com/station/talk-radio-1270-am-wxyt/
Profile: WXYT-AM is a commercial station owned by CBS Radio. The format of the station is sports. WXYT-AM broadcasts to the Detroit area at 1270 AM.
AM RADIO STATION

WXYT-FM 45267
Owner: CBS Radio
Editorial: 26455 American Dr, Southfield, Michigan 48034-6114 **Tel:** 1 248 327-2900.
Web site: http://detroit.cbslocal.com/category/sports
Profile: WXYT-FM is a commercial station owned by CBS Radio. The format of the station is sports. WXYT-FM broadcasts to the Detroit area at 97.1 FM.
FM RADIO STATION

WXYY-FM 45359
Owner: Alpha Media
Editorial: 401 Mall Blvd Ste 101D, Savannah, Georgia 31406-4863 **Tel:** 1 912 351-9830.
Web site: http://y100savannah.com
Profile: WXYY-FM is a commercial station owned by Alpha Media. The format of the station is Hot AC. WXYY-FM airs locally in the Hinesville, GA area at 100.1 FM.
FM RADIO STATION

WXZO-FM 43743
Owner: Vox Communications
Editorial: 265 Hegeman Ave, Colchester, Vermont 5446 **Tel:** 1 802 655-0093.
Web site: http://www.theplanet967.com
Profile: WXZO-FM is a commercial station owned by Vox Communications. The format of the station is Top 40 CHR. WXZO-FM broadcasts to the Burlington, VT area at 96.7 FM.
FM RADIO STATION

WXZQ-FM 43613
Owner: Piketon Communication Corp.
Editorial: 6655 State Route 220, Waverly, Ohio 45690-8987 **Tel:** 1 740 947-0059.
Email: wxiz@roadrunner.com
Web site: http://wxzqfm.com
Profile: WXZQ-FM is a commercial station owned by Piketon Communication Corp. The format of the station is Top 40/CHR. WXZQ-FM broadcasts to the Waverly, OH area at 100.1 FM.
FM RADIO STATION

WXZZ-FM 43241
Owner: Cumulus Media Inc.
Editorial: 300 W Vine St Ste 3, Lexington, Kentucky 40507-1806 **Tel:** 1 859 253-5900.
Web site: http://www.zrock103.com
Profile: WXZZ-FM is a commercial station owned by Cumulus Media Inc. The format of the station is rock. WXZZ-FM broadcasts to the Lexington, KY at 103.3 FM.
FM RADIO STATION

WYAB-FM 43551
Owner: SSR Communications Inc.
Editorial: 740 Highway 49, Ste R, Flora, Mississippi 39071-9653 **Tel:** 1 601 879-0093.
Email: info@wyab.com
Web site: http://www.wyab.com
Profile: WYAB-FM is a commercial station owned by SSR Communications Inc. The format of the station is talk. WYAB-FM broadcasts to the Flora, MS area at 103.9 FM.
FM RADIO STATION

WYAM-AM 37052
Owner: Decatur Communication Properties, LLC
Editorial: 1301 Central Pkwy Sw, Decatur, Alabama 35601-4817 **Tel:** 1 256 355-4567.
Profile: WYAM-AM is a commercial station owned by Decatur Communications Properties, LLC. The format of the station is Hispanic music. WYAM-AM broadcasts in the Decatur, AL area at 890 AM.
AM RADIO STATION

WYAV-FM 40881
Owner: Alpha Media
Editorial: 1016 Ocala St, Myrtle Beach, South Carolina 29577-8007 **Tel:** 1 843 448-1041.
Web site: http://www.wave104.net
Profile: WYAV-FM is a commercial station owned by Alpha Media. The format of the station is classic rock music. WYAV-FM broadcasts to the Myrtle Beach, SC area at 104.1 FM.
FM RADIO STATION

WYAY-FM 40882
Owner: Cumulus Media Inc
Editorial: 780 Johnson Ferry Rd, Atlanta, Georgia 30342-1434 **Tel:** 1 404 843-6000.
Email: newsroom@newsradio1067.com
Web site: http://www.newsradio1067.com
Profile: WYAY-FM is a commercial station owned by Cumulus Media Inc. The format of the station is news/talk. WYAY-FM broadcasts to the Atlanta area at 106.7 FM.
FM RADIO STATION

WYBA-FM 539368
Owner: Bible Broadcasting Network
Editorial: 385 Airport Rd, Coldwater, Michigan 49036-9313 **Tel:** 1 704 523-5555.
Email: bbn@bbnmedia.org
Web site: http://www.bbnradio.org
Profile: WYBA-FM is a non-commercial station owned by Bible Broadcasting Networ . The format of the station is religious music and programming. WYBA-FM broadcasts to the Coldwater, MI area at 90.1 FM.
FM RADIO STATION

WYBB-FM 41379
Owner: L.M. Communications Inc.
Editorial: 59 Windermere Blvd, Charleston, South Carolina 29407-7411 **Tel:** 1 843 769-4799.
Web site: http://www.my98rock.com/
Profile: WYBB-FM is a commercial station owned by L.M. Communications Inc. The format of the station is rock/album-oriented rock. WYBB-FM broadcasts to the Charleston, SC area at 98.1 FM.
FM RADIO STATION

WYBC-AM 35550
Owner: Yale Broadcasting Co.
Editorial: 142 Temple St, Ste 203, New Haven, Connecticut 6510 **Tel:** 1 203 776-4118.
Email: news@wshu.org
Web site: http://www.wshu.org
Profile: WYBC-AM is a commercial station owned by Yale Broadcasting Co. The station is being managed by Sacred Heart University. The format of the station is news/talk and classical music. WYBC-AM broadcasts to the Hartford-New Haven, CT area at 1340 AM.
AM RADIO STATION

WYBC-FM 40883
Owner: Yale Broadcasting Co.
Editorial: 142 Temple St Ste 203, New Haven, Connecticut 06510-2600 **Tel:** 1 203 776-4118.
Email: 943wybc@gmail.com
Web site: http://www.943wybc.com
Profile: WYBC-FM is a commercial station owned by Yale Broadcasting Co. and operated by Connoisseur Media. The format of the station is R&B Oldies music. WYBC-FM broadcasts to the Hartford-New Haven, CT area at 94.3 FM.
FM RADIO STATION

WYBF-FM 42484
Owner: Cabrini College
Editorial: 610 King of Prussia Rd, Radnor, Pennsylvania 19087-3623 **Tel:** 1 610 902-8453.
Email: wybf891@gmail.com
Web site: http://www.wybf.com
Profile: WYBF-FM is a commercial station owned by Cabrini College. The format of the station is college variety. WYBF-FM broadcasts to the Wayne, PA area at 89.1 FM.
FM RADIO STATION

WYBK-FM 40236
Owner: Bible Broadcasting Network, Inc
Editorial: 1815 Union Ave, Chattanooga, Tennessee 37404-3530 **Tel:** 1 800 888-7077.
Email: bbn@bbnmedia.org
Web site: http://bbnradio.org
Profile: WYBK-FM is a non-commercial station owned by Bible Broadcasting Network, Inc. The format for the station is religious. WYBK-FM broadcasts to the Chattanooga, TN area at 89.7 FM.
FM RADIO STATION

WYBL-FM 354623
Owner: Media One Group
Editorial: 3226 Jefferson Rd, Ashtabula, Ohio 44004 **Tel:** 1 440 993-2126.
Web site: http://www.983thebull.com
Profile: WYBL-FM is a commercial station owned by Media One Group. The format of the station is classic country. WYBL-FM broadcasts to the Ashtabula, OH area at 98.3 FM.
FM RADIO STATION

WYBR-FM 40079
Owner: Mentor Partners Inc.
Editorial: 18720 16 Mile Rd, Big Rapids, Michigan 49307 **Tel:** 1 231 796-7000.
Email: news@bigrapidsradionetwork.com
Web site: http://www.wybr.com
Profile: WYBR-FM is a commercial station owned by Mentor Partners Inc. The format of the station is hot adult contemporary. WYBR-FM broadcasts to the Big Rapids, MI area at 102.3 FM.
FM RADIO STATION

WYBT-AM 38538
Owner: Blountstown Communications
Editorial: 20872 NE Kelley Ave, Blountstown, Florida 32424 **Tel:** 1 850 674-5101.
Profile: WYBT-AM is a commercial station owned by Blountstown Communications. The format of the station is oldies. WYBT-AM broadcasts to the Blountstown, FL area at 1000 AM.
AM RADIO STATION

WYBX-FM 689260
Owner: Bible Broadcasting Network, Inc.
Tel: 1 800 888-7077.
Email: bbn@bbnmedia.org
Web site: http://www.bbnradio.org
Profile: WYBX-FM is a non-commercial station owned by Bible Broadcasting Network, Inc.. The format of the station is religious talk and teaching. The station is aired locally on 88.3 FM in the Lower Florida Keys area.
FM RADIO STATION

WYBY-AM 37992
Owner: Bible Broadcasting Network
Tel: 1 704 523-5555.
Email: bbn@bbnmedia.org
Web site: http://www.bbnradio.org
Profile: WYBY-AM is a non-commercial station owned by Bible Broadcasting Network. The format of the station is Christian religious programming. WYBY-AM broadcasts to the Cortland, NY area at 920 AM.
AM RADIO STATION

WYBZ-FM 42486
Owner: Y-Bridge Broadcasting
Editorial: 2895 Maysville Pike Unit A, Zanesville, Ohio 43701-7439 **Tel:** 1 740 453-6004.
Email: news@wybz.com
Web site: http://www.wybz.com
Profile: WYBZ-FM is a commercial station owned by Y-Bridge Broadcasting. The format of the station is Classic Hits. WYBZ-FM broadcasts to the Zanesville, OH area at 107.3 FM.
FM RADIO STATION

WYCA-FM 43200
Owner: Crawford Broadcasting Co.
Editorial: 6336 Calumet Ave, Hammond, Indiana 46324-1243 **Tel:** 1 219 933-4455.
Web site: http://www.rejoice102.com
Profile: WYCA-FM is a commercial station owned by Crawford Broadcasting Co. The format of the station is gospel music. WYCA-FM broadcasts to the Chicago area at 102.3 FM.
FM RADIO STATION

WYCB-AM 35773
Owner: Urban One, Inc.
Editorial: 8515 Georgia Ave Fl 9, Silver Spring, Maryland 20910-3403 **Tel:** 1 301 306-1111.
Web site: https://myspiritdc.com
Profile: WYCB-AM is a commercial station owned by Urban One, Inc. The format of the station is gospel music. WYCB-AM broadcasts to the Lanham, MD area at 1340 AM.
AM RADIO STATION

WYCD-FM 40230
Owner: CBS Local Media
Editorial: 26455 American Dr, Southfield, Michigan 48034-6114 **Tel:** 1 248 327-2900.
Web site: http://wycd.cbslocal.com
Profile: WYCD-FM is a commercial station owned by CBS Radio. The format of the station is contemporary country. WYCD-FM broadcasts to the Detroit area at 99.5 FM.
FM RADIO STATION

WYCE-FM 41508
Owner: Grand Rapids Cable Access Center Inc.
Editorial: 711 Bridge St NW, Grand Rapids, Michigan 49504-5560 **Tel:** 1 616 459-4788.
Email: comment@wyce.org
Web site: http://www.grcmc.org
Profile: WYCE-FM is a non-commercial station owned by Grand Rapids Cable Access Center Inc. The format of the station is variety. WYCE-FM broadcasts to the Grand Rapids, MI area at 88.1 FM.
FM RADIO STATION

WYCK-AM 36546
Owner: Bold Gold Media Group
Editorial: 1049 N Sekol Ave, Scranton, Pennsylvania 18504-1040 **Tel:** 1 570 344-1221.
Email: foxsportsnepa@gmail.com
Web site: http://www.boldgoldradionepa.com
Profile: WYCK-AM is a commercial station owned by Bold Gold Media Group. The format of the station is Classic Hits. WYCK-AM broadcasts to the Scranton, PA area at 1340 AM.
AM RADIO STATION

WYCM-FM 41203
Owner: Artistic Media Partners Inc.
Editorial: 3824 S 18th St, Lafayette, Indiana 47909-9102 **Tel:** 1 765 474-1410.
Profile: WYCM-FM is a commercial owned by Artistic Media Partners Inc. The format of the station is contemporary country music. WYCM-FM broadcasts in the Lafayette, IN area at 95.7 FM.
FM RADIO STATION

WYCR-FM 45643
Owner: Forever Media
Editorial: 275 Radio Rd, Hanover, Pennsylvania 17331-1140 **Tel:** 1 717 792-0098.
Web site: http://www.foreveryork.com/rocky-98-5
Profile: WYCR-FM is a commercial station owned by Forever Media. The format of the station is Classic Rock. WYCR-FM broadcasts to the Hanover, PA area at 98.5 FM.
FM RADIO STATION

WYCT-FM 235112
Owner: ADX Communications
Editorial: 7251 Plantation Rd, Pensacola, Florida 32504-6334 **Tel:** 1 850 262-6000.
Email: comments@CatCountry987.com
Web site: http://www.catcountry987.com
Profile: WYCT-FM is a commercial station owned by ADX Communications. The format of the station is country. WYCT-FM broadcasts to the Pensacola, FL area at 98.7 FM.
FM RADIO STATION

WYCV-AM 35774
Owner: Freedom Broadcasting Corp.
Editorial: 398 S Main St Highway 321-A, Granite Falls, North Carolina 28630 **Tel:** 1 828 396-3361.
Web site: http://www.gospel9.com
Profile: WYCV-AM is a commercial station owned by Freedom Broadcasting Corp. The format of the station is Southern gospel music. WYCV-AM broadcasts to the Granite Falls, NC area at 900 AM.
AM RADIO STATION

WYCY-FM 42485
Owner: Bold Gold Media Group
Editorial: 575 Grove St, Honesdale, Pennsylvania 18431-1041 **Tel:** 1 570 253-1616.
Web site: http://www.boldgoldlakeregion.com
Profile: WYCY-FM is commercial station owned by Bold Gold Media Group. The format of the station is classic hits. WYCY-FM broadcasts to the Honesdale, PA, area at 105.3 FM.
FM RADIO STATION

WYDB-FM 42340
Owner: iHeartMedia Inc.
Editorial: 101 Pine St, Dayton, Ohio 45402-2948
Tel: 1 937 224-1137.
Web site: http://www.945litefm.com
Profile: WYDB-FM is a commercial station owned byiHeartMedia Inc. The format of the station is Top 40 Chart. WYDB-FM broadcasts to the Dayton, OH area at 94.5 FM.
FM RADIO STATION

WYDE-AM 39367
Owner: Crawford Broadcasting Co.
Editorial: 120 Summit Pkwy, Birmingham, Alabama 35209-4741 **Tel:** 1 205 879-3324.
Email: psa@wdjconline.com
Web site: http://www.101wyde.com
Profile: WYDE-AM is a commercial station owned by Crawford Broadcasting Co. The format of the station is talk. WYDE-AM broadcasts to the Birmingham, AL area at 1260 AM.
AM RADIO STATION

WYDE-FM 44119
Owner: Crawford Broadcasting Co.
Editorial: 120 Summit Pkwy, Birmingham, Alabama 35209-4741 **Tel:** 1 205 879-3324.
Email: manager@101wyde.com
Web site: http://www.101wyde.com
Profile: WYDE-FM is a commercial station owned by Crawford Broadcasting Co. The format of the station is talk. WYDE-FM broadcasts to Birmingham, AL area at 101.1 FM.
FM RADIO STATION

WYDK-FM 41983
Owner: Big Fish Broadcasting LLC
Editorial: 1347 S Eufaula Ave Ste H, Eufaula, Alabama 36027-3000 **Tel:** 1 334 232-4532.
Email: info@dock979.com
Web site: http://www.dock979.com
Profile: WYDK-FM is a commercial station owned by Big Fish Broadcasting LLC. The format of the station is classic hits music. The station airs locally at 97.9 FM.
FM RADIO STATION

WYDL-FM 394597
Owner: Flinn Broadcasting Corp.
Editorial: 102 N Cass St, Corinth, Mississippi 38834-5726 **Tel:** 1 662 284-4611.
Profile: WYDL-FM is a commercial station owned by Flinn Broadcasting Corp. The format of the station is classic rock. WYDL-FM is licensed to the Middleton, TN area and broadcasts at a frequency of 100.7 FM.
FM RADIO STATION

WYDR-FM 42677
Owner: Midwest Communications Inc.
Editorial: 1420 Bellevue St, Green Bay, Wisconsin 54311-5649 **Tel:** 1 920 435-3771.
Web site: http://943jackfm.com/
Profile: WYDR-FM is a commercial station owned by Midwest Communications Inc. The format of the station is adult hits. WYDR-FM broadcasts to the Green Bay, WI area at 94.3 FM.
FM RADIO STATION

WYDS-FM 42455
Owner: Cromwell Group Inc.(The)
Editorial: 410 N Water St STE B, Decatur, Illinois 62523-2369 **Tel:** 1 217 428-4487.
Email: wydscontests@cromwellradio.com
Web site: http://www.decaturradio.com
Profile: WYDS-FM is a commercial station owned by The Cromwell Group Inc. The format of the station is Top 40/CHR. WYDS-FM broadcasts to the Decatur, IL area at 93.1 FM.
FM RADIO STATION

WYDU-AM 35780
Owner: Service Media, Inc.
Tel: 1 910 483-6111.
Email: widu1600@aol.com
Web site: http://www.widuradio.com/
Profile: WYDU-AM is a commercial station owned by Service Media, Inc. The format of the station is gospel music and religious talk. WYDU-AM broadcasts to the Red Springs, NC area at 1160 AM.
AM RADIO STATION

WYEA-AM 36302
Owner: Marble City Media, LLC
Editorial: 1 Motes Rd, Sylacauga, Alabama 35150-1731 **Tel:** 1 256 249-4263.
Email: info@wyea.net
Web site: http://www.wyea.net
Profile: WYEA-AM is a commercial radio station owned by Marble City Media, LLC. The format of the station is classic hits. WYEA-AM broadcasts to the South Central Alabama area locally at 1290 AM.
AM RADIO STATION

WYEC-FM 139877
Owner: Virden Broadcasting Corporation
Editorial: 133 E Division St, Kewanee, Illinois 61443-3410 **Tel:** 1 309 853-4471.
Email: wyec@wyec.com
Web site: http://www.wyec.com
Profile: WYEC-FM is a commercial station owned by Virden Broadcasting Corporation. The format of the station is Adult Hits. WYEC-FM broadcasts to the Kewanee, IL area at 93.9 FM.
FM RADIO STATION

WYEP-FM 40885
Owner: Pittsburgh Community Broadcasting Corp.
Editorial: 67 Bedford Sq, Pittsburgh, Pennsylvania 15203-1152 **Tel:** 1 412 381-9131.
Email: info@wyep.org
Web site: http://www.wyep.org
Profile: WYEP-FM is a non-commercial station owned by Pittsburgh Community Broadcasting Corp. The format of the station is adult album alternative. WYEP-FM broadcasts to the Pittsburgh area at 91.3 FM.
FM RADIO STATION

WYEZ-FM 43221
Owner: Fidelity Broadcasting Inc.
Editorial: 3926 Wesley St Ste 301, Myrtle Beach, South Carolina 29579-7307 **Tel:** 1 843 903-9962.
Email: staff@wezv.com
Web site: http://www.wezv.com
Profile: WYEZ-FM is a commercial station owned by Fidelity Broadcasting Inc. The format of the station is Rhythmic Contemporary/R&B. WYEZ-FM broadcasts to the Myrtle Beach, SC area at 94.5 FM.
FM RADIO STATION

WYFA-FM 40886
Owner: Bible Broadcasting Network
Editorial: 1388 Old Waynesboro Rd, Waynesboro, Georgia 30830 **Tel:** 1 706 523-5555.
Web site: http://www.bbnradio.org
Profile: WYFA-FM is a non-commercial station owned by Bible Broadcasting Network. The format of the station is religious. WYFA-FM broadcasts to the Waynesboro, GA area at 107.1 FM.
FM RADIO STATION

United States of America

WYFB-FM 41367
Owner: Bible Broadcasting Network
Editorial: 11530 Carmel Commons Blvd, Charlotte, North Carolina 28226-3976 **Tel:** 1 704 523-5555.
Email: bbn@bbnmedia.org
Web site: http://www.bbnradio.org
Profile: WYFB-FM is a non-commercial station owned by Bible Broadcasting Network. The format of the station is religious. WYFB-FM broadcasts to the Keystone Heights, FL area at 90.5 FM.
FM RADIO STATION

WYFE-FM 41445
Owner: Bible Broadcasting Network
Tel: 1 704 523-5555.
Email: bbn@bbnmedia.org
Web site: http://www.bbnradio.org
Profile: WYFE-FM is a non-commercial station owned by Bible Broadcasting Network. The format of the station is religious. WYFE-FM broadcasts to the Tampa, FL area at 88.9 FM.
FM RADIO STATION

WYFG-FM 41368
Owner: Bible Broadcasting Network
Tel: 1 704 523-5555.
Web site: http://www.bbnradio.org
Profile: WYFG-AFM is a non-commercial station owned by Bible Broadcasting Network. The format for the station is religious. WYFG-FM broadcasts to the Greenville, SC; Asheville, NC area at 91.1 FM.
FM RADIO STATION

WYFH-FM 41593
Owner: Bible Broadcasting Network
Editorial: 6150 Cannons Campground Rd, Cowpens, South Carolina 29330-9605 **Tel:** 1 800 888-7077.
Email: bbn@bbnmedia.org
Web site: http://www.bbnradio.org
Profile: WYFH-FM is a non-commercial station owned by Bible Broadcasting Network. The format of the station is religious talk. WYFH-FM broadcasts to the Cowpens, SC, area at 90.7 FM.
FM RADIO STATION

WYFI-FM 40887
Owner: Bible Broadcasting Network
Tel: 1 800 888-7077.
Email: bbn@bbnmedia.org
Web site: http://www.bbnradio.org
Profile: WYFI-FM is a non-commercial station owned by Bible Broadcasting Network. The format of the station is Christian programming. WYFI-FM broadcasts to the Norfolk, VA area at 99.7 FM. This station DOES NOT want any PR contact.
FM RADIO STATION

WYFJ-FM 41341
Owner: Bible Broadcasting Network
Editorial: 407 S Washington Hwy, Ashland, Virginia 23005 **Tel:** 1 800 888-7077.
Web site: http://www.bbnradio.org
Profile: WYFI-FM is a non-commercial station owned by Bible Broadcasting Network. The format of the station is Christian programming. WYFI-FM broadcasts to the Ashland, VA area at 99.9 FM. This station DOES NOT want any PR contact.
FM RADIO STATION

WYFK-FM 41372
Owner: Bible Broadcasting Network
Tel: 1 704 523-5555.
Email: bbn@bbnmedia.org
Web site: http://www.bbnradio.org
Profile: WYFK-FM is a non-commercial station owned by Bible Broadcasting Network. The format of the station is religious. WYFK-FM broadcasts to the Columbus, GA area at 89.5 FM.
FM RADIO STATION

WYFL-FM 40888
Owner: Bible Broadcasting Network
Editorial: 11530 Carmel Commons Blvd, Charlotte, North Carolina 28226-3976 **Tel:** 1 704 523-5555.
Email: bbn@bbnmedia.org
Web site: http://www.bbnradio.org
Profile: WYFL-FM is a non-commercial station owned by Bible Broadcasting Network. The format of the station is religious programming. WYFL-FM broadcasts to the Wake Forest, NC area at 92.5 FM.
FM RADIO STATION

WYFM-FM 46476
Owner: Cumulus Media Inc.
Editorial: 4040 Simon Rd, Youngstown, Ohio 44512-1362 **Tel:** 1 330 783-1000.
Web site: http://www.y-103.com
Profile: WYFM-FM is a commercial station owned by Cumulus Media Inc. The format of the station is classic rock. WYFM-FM broadcasts to the Youngstown, OH area at 102.9 FM.
FM RADIO STATION

WYFN-AM 36104
Owner: Bible Broadcasting Network
Tel: 1 704 523-5555.
Email: bbn@bbnmedia.org
Web site: http://www.bbnradio.org
Profile: WYFN-AM is a non-commercial station owned by Bible Broadcasting Network. The format of the station is religious programming. WYFN-AM broadcasts to the Nashville, TN area at 980 AM.
AM RADIO STATION

WYFO-FM 41592
Owner: Bible Broadcasting Network
Tel: 1 704 523-5555.
Email: bbn@bbnmedia.org
Web site: http://www.bbnradio.org
Profile: WYFO-FM is a non-commercial station owned by Bible Broadcasting Network. The format of the station is religious and Christian programming. WYFO-FM broadcasts to the Lakeland, FL area at 91.9 FM.
FM RADIO STATION

WYFQ-AM 36257
Owner: Bible Broadcasting Network
Editorial: 11530 Carmel Commons Blvd, Charlotte, North Carolina 28226-3976 **Tel:** 1 704 523-5555.
Email: bbn@bbnmedia.org
Profile: WYFQ-AM is a non-commercial station owned by Bible Broadcasting Network. The format of the station is religious. WYFQ-AM broadcasts to the Charlotte, NC area at 930 AM.
AM RADIO STATION

WYFQ-FM 42916
Owner: Bible Broadcasting Network
Editorial: 11530 Carmel Commons Blvd, Charlotte, North Carolina 28226-3976 **Tel:** 1 704 523-5555.
Email: bbn@bbnmedia.org
Profile: WYFQ-FM is a non-commercial station owned by Bible Broadcasting Network. The format of the station is religious. WYFQ-FM broadcasts to the Charlotte, NC area at 93.5 FM.
FM RADIO STATION

WYFW-FM 41430
Owner: Bible Broadcasting Network
Tel: 1 704 523-5555.
Web site: http://www.bbnradio.org
Profile: WYFW-FM is a non-commercial station owned by Bible Broadcasting Network. The format of the station is religious programming. WYFW-FM broadcasts to the Waynesboro, GA area at 89.5 FM.
FM RADIO STATION

WYFX-FM 46371
Owner: Original Company Inc.(The)
Editorial: 7109 Upton Rd, Mount Vernon, Indiana 47620-9418 **Tel:** 1 812 838-4484.
Web site: http://www.originalcompany.com/pages/7817272.php
Profile: WYFX-FM is a commercial station owned by The Original Company Inc. The format of the station is news/talk. The station broadcasts locally at a frequency of 106.7 FM.
FM RADIO STATION

WYGB-FM 73877
Owner: Reising Radio Partners Inc.
Editorial: 825 Washington St, Columbus, Indiana 47201-6265 **Tel:** 1 812 379-1077.
Web site: http://www.korncountry.com
Profile: WYGB-FM is a commercial station owned by Reising Radio Partners Inc. The format of the station is contemporary country music. WYGB-FM broadcasts to the Indianapolis area at 102.9 FM.
FM RADIO STATION

WYGC-FM 40419
Owner: JVC Broadcasting Inc.
Tel: 1 352 867-1023.
Web site: http://1049wowfm.com
Profile: WYGC-FM is a commercial station owned by JVC Broadcasting Inc. The format is classic hits music. WYGC-FM broadcasts to the Gainesville, FL area at 104.9 FM.
FM RADIO STATION

WYGE-FM 44115
Owner: Ethel Huff Broadcasting
Editorial: 201 E 2nd St, London, Kentucky 40741-1403 **Tel:** 1 606 877-1326.
Email: wygeradio@yahoo.com
Web site: http://www.wygeradio.com
Profile: WYGE-FM is a commercial station owned by Ethel Huff Broadcasting. The format for the station is Christian. WYGE-FM broadcasts to the Lexington, KY area at 92.3 FM.
FM RADIO STATION

WYGH-AM 36388
Owner: Hammond Broadcasting Inc.
Editorial: 4942 US Highway 27 N, Butler, Kentucky 41006-8653 **Tel:** 1 859 472-1075.
Email: wygh@fuse.net
Web site: http://www.wiok.com
Profile: WYGH-AM is a commercial station owned by Hammond Broadcasting Inc. The format of the station is Southern gospel music and Hispanic religious programming. WYGH-AM broadcasts to the Paris, KY, area at 1440 AM.
AM RADIO STATION

WYGL-FM 45989
Owner: Max Media
Editorial: 450 Route 204, Selinsgrove, Pennsylvania 17870-7975 **Tel:** 1 570 374-1155.
Web site: http://radiobigfoot.com
Profile: WYGL-FM is a commercial station owned by Max Media. The format of the station is contemporary country music. WYGL-FM broadcasts to the Central Pennsylvania area at 100.5 FM.
FM RADIO STATION

WYGM-AM 36409
Owner: iHeartMedia Inc.
Editorial: 2500 Maitland Center Pkwy, Maitland, Florida 32751-7224 **Tel:** 1 407 916-7800.
Web site: http://969thegame.iheart.com
Profile: WYGM-AM is a commercial station owned by iHeartMedia Inc. The format is sports. WYGM-AM broadcasts to the Orlando, FL area at 740 AM.
AM RADIO STATION

WYGO-FM 42482
Owner: Sliger Enterprises
Editorial: 2110 Oxnard Rd, Athens, Tennessee 37303-1956 **Tel:** 1 423 745-1000.
Email: wygo@bellsouth.net
Web site: http://www.wygofm.com
Profile: WYGO-FM is a commercial station owned by Sliger Enterprises. The format of the station is hot adult contemporary. WYGO-FM broadcasts to the Athens, TN area at 99.5 FM.
FM RADIO STATION

WYGR-AM 35776
Owner: WYGR Broadcasting
Editorial: 1303 Chicago Dr SW, Wyoming, Michigan 49509 **Tel:** 1 616 452-8589.
Email: wygr1530@yahoo.com
Web site: http://www.wygr.net
Profile: WYGR-AM is a commercial station owned by WYGR Broadcasting. The format of the station is urban contemporary. WYGR-AM broadcasts to the Wyoming, MI area at 1530 AM.
AM RADIO STATION

WYGS-FM 44035
Owner: Good Shepherd Radio
Editorial: 825 Washington St, Columbus, Indiana 47201-6265 **Tel:** 1 812 373-9947.
Web site: http://www.wygs.org
Profile: WYGS-FM is a non-commercial station owned by Good Shepherd Radio. The format of the station is gospel music. WYGS-FM broadcasts to the Columbus, IN area at 91.1 FM.
FM RADIO STATION

WYGY-FM 40151
Owner: Hubbard Broadcasting, Inc.
Editorial: 2060 Reading Rd, Cincinnati, Ohio 45202-1454 **Tel:** 1 513 699-5103.
Web site: http://www.theworldwidewolf.com
Profile: WYGY-FM is a commercial station owned by Hubbard Broadcasting, Inc. The format of the station is classic country. WYGY-FM broadcasts to the Cincinnati area at 97.3 FM.
FM RADIO STATION

WYHL-AM 39210
Owner: URBan Radio Broadcasting, LLC
Editorial: 3436 Highway 45 N, Meridian, Mississippi 39301-1509 **Tel:** 1 601 693-2661.
Profile: WYHL-AM is a commercial station owned by URBan Radio Broadcasting, LLC. The format of the station is gospel. WYHL-AM broadcasts to the Meridian, MS area at 1450 AM.
AM RADIO STATION

WYHM-AM 38712
Owner: The Holler, Inc.
Editorial: 319 W Rockwood St, Rockwood, Tennessee 37854-2245 **Tel:** 1 865 250-6718.
Profile: WYHM-AM is a commercial station owned by Southern Media Group, Inc. The format of the station is a mix of classic country and classic rock. WYHM-AM broadcasts to the Knoxville, TN area at 580 AM.
AM RADIO STATION

WYHT-FM 45762
Owner: iHeartMedia Inc.
Editorial: 1400 Radio Ln, Mansfield, Ohio 44906-2525 **Tel:** 1 419 529-2211.
Web site: http://www.wyht.com
Profile: WYHT-FM is a commercial station owned by iHeartMedia Inc. The format of the station is hot adult contemporary. WYHT-FM broadcasts to the Mansfield, OH area at 105.3 FM.
FM RADIO STATION

WYJB-FM 45511
Owner: Albany Broadcasting Co.
Editorial: 6 Johnson Rd, Latham, New York 12110-5641 **Tel:** 1 518 786-6600.
Web site: http://www.b95.com
Profile: WYJB-FM is a commercial station owned by Albany Broadcasting Co. The format of the station is Lite Rock/Lite AC music. WYJB-FM broadcasts in the Albany, NY area at 95.5 FM.
FM RADIO STATION

WYJJ-FM 46874
Owner: FM Radio Licenses, LLC
Editorial: 122 Radio Rd, Jackson, Tennessee 38301-3465 **Tel:** 1 731 427-3316.
Web site: http://www.jamminjackson.com
Profile: WYJJ-FM is a commercial station owned by FM Radio Licenses, LLC. The format is urban contemporary. WYJJ-FM broadcasts to the Trenton, TN area at 97.7 FM.
FM RADIO STATION

WYKE-FM 44065
Owner: Baynet Management, Inc.
Editorial: 5399 W Gulf To Lake Hwy, Lecanto, Florida 34461-8531 **Tel:** 1 352 527-2341.
Web site: http://www.keysports1043.com
Profile: WYKE-FM is a commercial station owned by Baynet Management, Inc. The format of the station is sports. WYKE-FM broadcasts to the Lecanto, FL area at 104.3 FM.
FM RADIO STATION

WYKM-AM 35828
Owner: Mountain States Radio Inc.
Editorial: 714 Nicholas St, Rupert, West Virginia 25984 **Tel:** 1 304 392-6003.
Email: wykm@frontiernet.net
Profile: WYKM-AM is a commercial station owned by Mountain States Radio Inc. The format of the station is classic country. WYKM-FM broadcasts to the Rupert, WV area at 1250 AM.
AM RADIO STATION

WYKR-FM 46324
Owner: Puffer Broadcasting Inc.
Editorial: 1047 Route 302, Wells River, Vermont 5081
Tel: 1 802 757-2773.
Email: studio@wykr.com
Web site: http://www.wykr.com
Profile: WYKR-FM is a commercial station owned by Puffer Broadcasting Inc. The format of the station is country. WYKR-FM broadcasts to the Wells River, VT area at 101.3 FM.
FM RADIO STATION

WYKS-FM 45645
Owner: Gillen Broadcasting Corp.
Editorial: 7120 SW 24th Ave, Gainesville, Florida 32607-3705 **Tel:** 1 352 331-2200.
Email: kiss1053@aol.com
Web site: http://www.kiss1053.com
Profile: WYKS-FM is a commercial station owned by Gillen Broadcasting Corp. The format of the station is Top 40/CHR music. WYKS-FM broadcasts to the Gainesville, FL area at 105.3 FM.
FM RADIO STATION

WYKT-FM 41252
Owner: Staradio Corp.
Editorial: 70 Meadowview Ctr Ste 400, Kankakee, Illinois 60901-2061 **Tel:** 1 815 935-9555.
Web site: http://www.1055theticket.com
Profile: WYKT-FM is a commercial station owned by Staradio Corp. The format of the station is Sports. WYKT-FM broadcasts to the Kankakee, IL area at 105.5 FM.
FM RADIO STATION

WYKX-FM 46185
Owner: KMB Broadcasting Inc.
Editorial: 604 Ludington St, Escanaba, Michigan 49829 **Tel:** 1 906 786-3800.
Email: wykxinfo@yahoo.com
Web site: http://kmbbroadcasting.com/wykx
Profile: WYKX-FM is a commercial station owned by KMB Broadcasting Inc. The format for the station is country. WYKX-FM broadcasts to the Escanaba, MI area at 104.7 FM.
FM RADIO STATION

WYKY-FM 553523
Owner: Forcht Broadcasting
Editorial: 290 Wtlo Rd, Somerset, Kentucky 42503-3728 **Tel:** 1 606 678-8151.
Email: wtlo@usa.com
Web site: http://www.somerset106.com
Profile: WYKY-FM is a commercial station owned by Forcht Broadcasting. The format of the station is adult hits. WYKY-FM broadcasts to the Somerset, KY area at 106.1 FM.
FM RADIO STATION

WYKZ-FM 42941
Owner: iHeartMedia Inc.
Editorial: 245 Alfred St, Savannah, Georgia 31408-3205 **Tel:** 1 912 964-7794.
Email: river@987theriver.com
Web site: http://www.987theriver.com
Profile: WYKZ-FM is a commercial station owned by iHeartMedia Inc. The format of the station is adult contemporary. WYKZ-FM broadcasts to the Savannah, GA area at 98.7 FM.
FM RADIO STATION

WYLD-AM 38292
Owner: iHeartMedia Inc.
Editorial: 929 Howard Ave, New Orleans, Louisiana 70113-1148 **Tel:** 1 504 679-7300.
Web site: http://www.am940.com
Profile: WYLD-AM is a commercial station owned by iHeartMedia Inc. The format of the station is gospel music. WYLD-AM broadcasts to the New Orleans area at 940 AM.
AM RADIO STATION

WYLD-FM 45646
Owner: iHeartMedia Inc.
Editorial: 929 Howard Ave, New Orleans, Louisiana 70113-1148 **Tel:** 1 504 679-7300.
Web site: http://wyldfm.iheart.com
Profile: WYLD-FM is a commercial station owned by iHeartMedia Inc. The format of the station is urban adult contemporary music. WYLD-FM broadcasts to the New Orleans area at 98.5 FM.
FM RADIO STATION

WYLF-AM 3582
Owner: M.B. Communications
Editorial: 100 Main St, Penn Yan, New York 14527-1233 **Tel:** 1 315 536-0850.
Email: admin@wylf.com
Web site: http://www.wylf.com
Profile: WYLF-AM is a commercial station owned by M.B. Communications. The format of the station is adult standards music. WYLF-AM broadcasts to the Penn Yan, NY area at 850 AM.
AM RADIO STATION

WYLK-FM 43133
Owner: Northshore Broadcasting Inc.
Editorial: 324 E Lockwood St, Covington, Louisiana 70433-2914 **Tel:** 1 985 867-5990.
Web site: http://lake947sports.wordpress.com
Profile: WYLK-FM is a commercial station owned by Northshore Broadcasting Inc. The format for the station is adult contemporary music. WYLK-FM broadcasts to the Hammond, LA area at 94.7 FM. Their tagline is "The Lake" and their slogan is "The Northshore's Radio Station."
FM RADIO STATION

WYLL-AM 35507
Owner: Salem Media Group, Inc.
Editorial: 25 NW Point Blvd Ste 400, Elk Grove Village, Illinois 60007-1030 **Tel:** 1 847 956-5030.
Web site: http://www.1160hope.com
Profile: WYLL-AM is a commercial station owned by Salem Media Group, Inc. The format of the station is Christian talk. WYLL-AM broadcasts to the entire Chicago metro area at 1160 AM.
AM RADIO STATION

WYLS-AM 39161
Owner: Grantell Broadcasting Co.
Editorial: 11474 U S Highway 11, York, Alabama 36925 **Tel:** 1 205 392-5234.
Profile: WYLS-AM is a commercial station owned by Grantell Broadcasting Co. The format for the station is blues. WYLS-AM broadcasts to the York, AL area at 670 AM.
AM RADIO STATION

WYMB-AM 38293
Owner: Cumulus Media Inc.
Editorial: 2014 N Irby St, Florence, South Carolina 29501-1504 **Tel:** 1 843 661-5000.
Profile: WYMB-AM is a commercial station owned by Cumulus Media Inc. The format of the station is sports. WYMB-AM broadcasts to the Florence, SC area at 920 AM.
AM RADIO STATION

WYMC-AM 36074
Owner: JDM Communications Inc.
Editorial: 197 Wymc Dr, Mayfield, Kentucky 42066-6832 **Tel:** 1 270 247-1430.
Email: radio@wymcradio.com
Web site: http://www.mywymc.com
Profile: WYMC-AM is a commercial station owned by JDM Communications Inc. The format of the station is oldies music. WYMC-AM broadcasts to the Paducah, KY and Cape Girardeau, MO areas at 1430 AM.
AM RADIO STATION

WYMC-FM 610646
Owner: JDM Communications Inc.
Editorial: 197 Wymc Dr, Mayfield, Kentucky 42066-6832 **Tel:** 1 270 247-1430.
Email: radio@wymcradio.com
Web site: http://www.mywymc.com
Profile: WYMC-FM is a commercial station owned by JDM Communications Inc. The format of the station is oldies. WYMC-FM broadcasts to the Paducah, KY and Cape Girardeau, MO area at 93.9 FM.
FM RADIO STATION

WYMG-FM 40992
Owner: Saga Communications
Editorial: 3501 E Sangamon Ave, Springfield, Illinois 62707-9777 **Tel:** 1 217 753-5400.
Email: wymg@wymg.com
Web site: http://www.wymg.com
Profile: WYMG-FM is a commercial station owned by Saga Communications. The format of the station is classic rock. WYMG-FM broadcasts to the Springfield, IL area at 100.5 FM.
FM RADIO STATION

WYMJ-FM 518611
Owner: Dailey Corp.
Editorial: 1130 4th St, New Martinsville, West Virginia 26155 **Tel:** 1 304 455-1111.
Email: wetz@suddenlinkmail.com
Profile: WYMJ-FM is a commercial station owned by Dailey Corp. The format of the station is country. WYMJ-FM broadcasts to the New Martinsville, WV area at 99.5 FM.
FM RADIO STATION

WYMM-AM 35735
Owner: Radio Puissance International
Editorial: 5900 Pickettville Rd, Jacksonville, Florida 32254-1172 **Tel:** 1 904 786-2400.
Email: info@radiopuissanceinter.com
Web site: http://www.radiopuissanceinter.com
Profile: WYMM-AM is a commercial station owned by Radio Puissance International. The format of the station is a variety of French-Creole language programming. WYMM-AM broadcasts to the Jacksonville, FL area at 1530 AM.
AM RADIO STATION

WYMX-FM 45875
Owner: TeleSouth Communications Inc.
Editorial: 3192 Browning Road 520 #520, Greenwood, Mississippi 38930-3830 **Tel:** 1 662 453-2174.
Profile: WYMX-FM is a commercial station owned by TeleSouth Communications Inc. The format of the station is oldies music. The station airs in the Greenwood, MS area at 99.1 FM.
FM RADIO STATION

WYMY-FM 45440
Owner: Curtis Media Group
Editorial: 1109 Tower Dr, Burlington, North Carolina 27215-4425 **Tel:** 1 336 584-0126.
Email: wpcm@curtismedia.com
Web site: http://www.laleync.com
Profile: WYMY-FM is a commercial station owned by Curtis Media Group. The station is regional Mexican. WZTK-FM broadcasts to the Burlington, NC, area at 96.9 FM.
FM RADIO STATION

WYNA-FM 44320
Owner: iHeartMedia Inc.
Editorial: 4841 Highway 17 Byp S, Myrtle Beach, South Carolina 29577-6683 **Tel:** 1 843 293-0107.
Web site: http://1049bobfm.iheart.com
Profile: WYNA-FM is a commercial station owned by iHeartMedia Inc. The format of the station is adult hits music. WYNA-FM broadcasts to the Myrtle Beach, SC area at 104.9 FM.
FM RADIO STATION

WYNC-AM 36258
Owner: Semora Broadcasting
Editorial: 545 Fire Tower Road, Yanceyville, North Carolina 27379 **Tel:** 1 336 694-7343.
Email: wync@embarqmail.com
Profile: WYNC-AM is a commercial station owned by Semora Broadcasting, Inc. The format of the station is gospel music. WYNC-AM broadcasts in the Greensboro, NC area at 1540 AM.
AM RADIO STATION

WYND-AM 35878
Owner: Buddy Tucker Association, Inc.
Editorial: 316 Taylor Rd E, Deland, Florida 32724-7817 **Tel:** 1 904 734-1310.
Email: wynd@buddytuckerassociation.org
Web site: http://www.buddytuckerassociation.org
Profile: WYND-AM is a commercial station owned by Buddy Tucker Association, Inc. The format of the station is religious. WYND-AM broadcasts to the Deland, FL area at 1310 AM.
AM RADIO STATION

WYNF-AM 242486
Owner: iHeartMedia Inc.
Editorial: 2743 Perimeter Pkwy Ste 100-300, Augusta, Georgia 30909-6415 **Tel:** 1 706 396-6000.
Email: augustapsa@iheartmedia.com
Web site: http://www.foxsportsaugusta.com/main.html
Profile: WYNF-AM is a commercial station owned by iHeartMedia Inc. The format of the station is sports. WYNF-AM broadcasts to the Augusta, GA area at 1340 AM.
AM RADIO STATION

WYNK-FM 45647
Owner: iHeartMedia Inc.
Editorial: 5555 Hilton Ave Ste 500, Baton Rouge, Louisiana 70808-2564 **Tel:** 1 225 231-1860.
Web site: http://www.wynkcountry.com
Profile: WYNK-FM is a commercial station owned by iHeartMedia Inc. The format of the station is country music. WYNK-FM broadcasts to the Baton Rouge, LA area at 101.5 FM.
FM RADIO STATION

WYNL-FM 41940
Owner: Bristol Broadcasting Company
Editorial: 817 Suncrest Pl, Charleston, West Virginia 25303-2302 **Tel:** 1 304 342-3136.
Web site: http://newlife945.com
Profile: WYNL-FM is a commercial station owned by Bristol Broadcasting. The format of the station is Contemporary Christian. WYNL-FM broadcasts to the Charleston, WV area at 94.5 FM.
FM RADIO STATION

WYNN-AM 38345
Owner: Cumulus Media Inc.
Editorial: 2014 N Irby St, Florence, South Carolina 29501-1504 **Tel:** 1 843 661-5000.
Web site: http://www.glory985.com
Profile: WYNN-AM is a commercial station owned by Cumulus Media Inc. The format of the station is gospel music. WYNN-AM broadcasts to the Florence, SC area at 540 AM.
AM RADIO STATION

WYNN-FM 45703
Owner: Cumulus Media Inc.
Editorial: 2014 N Irby St, Florence, South Carolina 29501 **Tel:** 1 843 661-5000.
Web site: http://www.wynn1063.com
Profile: WYNN-FM is a commercial station owned by Cumulus Media Inc. The format of the station is urban contemporary music. WYNN-FM broadcasts to the Florence, SC area at 106.3 FM.
FM RADIO STATION

WYNR-FM 46659
Owner: iHeartMedia Inc.
Editorial: 3833 US Highway 82, Brunswick, Georgia 31523-7735 **Tel:** 1 912 267-1025.
Web site: http://1025wynr.net
Profile: WYNR-FM is a commercial station owned by iHeartMedia Inc. The format of the station is contemporary country. WYNR-FM broadcasts to the Brunswick, GA area at 102.5 FM.
FM RADIO STATION

WYNT-FM 40895
Owner: iHeart Media Inc.
Editorial: 1330 N Main St, Marion, Ohio 43302-1525 **Tel:** 1 740 383-1131.
Web site: http://www.majic959.com
Profile: WYNT-FM is a commercial station owned by iHeart Media Inc. The format of the station is Hot AC. WYNT-FM broadcasts to the Marion, OH area at 95.9 FM.
FM RADIO STATION

WYNU-FM 41415
Owner: FM Radio Licenses, LLC
Editorial: 122 Radio Rd, Jackson, Tennessee 38301-3465 **Tel:** 1 731 427-3316.
Email: jkproduction@forevercom.com
Web site: http://fmu92.com
Profile: WYNU-FM is a commercial station owned by FM Radio Licenses, LLC. The format of the station is classic hits. WYNU-FM broadcasts to the Jackson, TN area at 92.3 FM.
FM RADIO STATION

WYNW-FM 414079
Owner: Starboard Media Foundation Inc.
Editorial: 645 25Th Ave N, Wisconsin Rapids, Wisconsin 54495-2223 **Tel:** 1 715 424-1300.
Email: info@relevantradio.com
Web site: http://www.relevantradio.com
Profile: WYNW-FM is a non-commercial station owned by Starboard Media Foundation Inc. The format of the station is religious and talk. WYNW-FM broadcasts to the Wisconsin Rapids, WI area at 92.9 FM.
FM RADIO STATION

WYNZ-FM 45648
Owner: Saga Communications
Editorial: 420 Western Ave, South Portland, Maine 04106-1704 **Tel:** 1 207 774-4561.
Web site: http://rewind1009.com
Profile: WYNZ-FM is a commercial station owned by Saga Communications. The format of the station is classic hits. WYNZ-FM broadcasts to the South Portland, ME area at 100.9 FM.
FM RADIO STATION

WYOO-FM 43323
Owner: Magic Broadcasting, LLC
Editorial: 7106 Laird St Ste 102, Panama City, Florida 32408-7622 **Tel:** 1 850 230-5855.
Email: talk@magicfl.com
Web site: http://www.talkradio101.com
Profile: WYOO-FM is a commercial station owned by Magic Broadcasting, LLC. The format for the station is talk. WYOO-FM broadcasts to the Panama City, FL area at 101.1 FM.
FM RADIO STATION

WYOS-AM 37161
Owner: Townsquare Media, Inc.
Editorial: 59 Court St, Binghamton, New York 13901-3270 **Tel:** 1 607 772-8400.
Web site: http://espnbinghamton.com/
Profile: WYOS-AM is a commercial station owned by Townsquare Media, Inc. The format of the station is sports. WYOS-AM broadcasts to the Binghampton, NY area at 1360 AM.
AM RADIO STATION

WYOY-FM 42885
Owner: New South Communications Inc.
Editorial: 265 Highpoint Dr, Ridgeland, Mississippi 39157 **Tel:** 1 601 956-0102.
Web site: http://www.y101.com
Profile: WYOY-FM is a commercial station owned by New South Communications Inc. The format of the station is Top 40/CHR music. WYOY-FM broadcasts to the Jackson, MS area at 101.7 FM.
FM RADIO STATION

WYPC-AM 37987
Owner: Jackson County Broadcasting Inc.
Editorial: 295 E Main St, Jackson, Ohio 45640-1744 **Tel:** 1 740 286-3023.
Profile: WYPC-AM is a commercial station owned by Jackson County Broadcasting Inc. The format of the station is sports. WYPC-AM broadcasts to the Jackson, OH area at 1330 AM.
AM RADIO STATION

WYPF-FM 42548
Owner: WYPR License Holding LLC
Editorial: 2216 N Charles St, Baltimore, Maryland 21218 **Tel:** 1 410 235-1660.
Email: frontdesk@wypr.org
Web site: http://www.wypr.org
Profile: WYPF-FM is a non-commercial station owned by WYPR License Holding LLC. The format is news, talk and jazz. WYPF-FM broadcasts to the Baltimore area at 88.1 FM.
FM RADIO STATION

WYPL-FM 41978
Owner: Cossitt Library
Editorial: 3030 Poplar Ave, Memphis, Tennessee 38111-3527 **Tel:** 1 901 415-2752.
Web site: http://www.memphislibrary.org/wypl/index.html
Profile: WYPL-FM is a variety news, talk, music, children's programming station, which serves the Memphis area. The station is privately owned by the Memphis/Shelby County Public Library and Information Center. Send any information to the station via fax.
FM RADIO STATION

WYPM-FM 46199
Owner: WITF Inc.
Editorial: 4801 Lindle Rd, Harrisburg, Pennsylvania 17111-2444 **Tel:** 1 717 704-3000.
Email: news@witf.org
Web site: http://www.witf.org
Profile: WYPM-FM is a commercial station owned by WITF Inc. The format of the station is news and talk. WYPM-FM broadcasts to the Chambersburg, MD area at 93.3 FM.
FM RADIO STATION

WYPR-FM 40402
Owner: WYPR License Holding LLC
Editorial: 2216 N Charles St, Baltimore, Maryland 21218 **Tel:** 1 410 235-1660.
Email: frontdesk@wypr.org
Web site: http://www.wypr.org
Profile: WYPR-FM is a non-commercial station owned by WYPR License Holding LLC. The format of the station is talk, news and jazz. WYPR-FM broadcasts to Baltimore area at 88.1 FM.
FM RADIO STATION

WYPV-FM 42867
Owner: Northern Star Broadcasting LLC
Editorial: 1356 Mackinaw Ave, Cheboygan, Michigan 49721-1003 **Tel:** 1 231 627-2341.
Web site: http://yourdefendingfathers.us
Profile: WYPV-FM is a commercial station owned by Northern Star Broadcasting LLC. The format of the station is Conservative talk. WYPV-FM broadcasts to the Mackinaw City, MI area at 94.5.
FM RADIO STATION

WYPZ-FM 45600
Owner: Murray (Christopher L.)
Editorial: 6174 Hwy 57, Macon, Georgia 31217 **Tel:** 1 404 307-8079.
Profile: WYPZ-FM is a commercial station owned by Christopher L. Murray, dba Praise 107.5 FM Radio LLC. The format of the station is black gospel. WYPZ-FM broadcasts to the Macon, GA area at 107.5 FM.
FM RADIO STATION

WYQQ-FM 789352
Owner: Epic Light Network, Inc.
Editorial: 29 Trolley Crossing Rd #A, Charlton, Massachusetts 01507-1351 **Tel:** 1 508 216-0901.
Email: contact@theq901.com
Web site: http://www.theq901.com
Profile: WYQQ-FM is a non-commercial station owned by Epic Light Network, Inc. The format of the station is Christian CHR music. WYQQ-FM broadcasts to the Greater Worcester, MA area at a frequency of 90.1 FM.
FM RADIO STATION

WYQS-FM 40819
Owner: Western North Carolina Public Radio Inc.
Editorial: 73 Broadway St, Asheville, North Carolina 28801-2919 **Tel:** 1 828 210-4800.
Email: info@wcqs.org
Web site: http://www.wcqs.org
Profile: WYQS-FM is a non-commercial station owned by Western North Carolina Public Radio Inc. The format of the station is news and talk. WYQS-FM broadcasts to the Madison, NC area at 90.5 FM.
FM RADIO STATION

WYRB-FM 445547
Owner: Crawford Broadcasting Co.
Tel: 1 219 933-4455.
Web site: http://www.soul1063radio.com
Profile: WYRB-FM is a commercial station by Crawford Broadcasting Co. The format of the station is urban contemporary. WYRB-FM broadcasts to the Rockford, IL area at 106.3 FM.
FM RADIO STATION

WYRD-AM 36405
Owner: Entercom Communications Corp.
Editorial: 25 Garlington Rd, Greenville, South Carolina 29615-4613 **Tel:** 1 864 271-9200.
Web site: http://www.espnupstate.com
Profile: WYRD-AM is a commercial station owned by Entercom Communications Corp. The format of the station is sports talk. WYRD-AM broadcasts to the Greenville, SC area at 1330 AM.
AM RADIO STATION

WYRD-FM 128424
Owner: Entercom Communications Corp.
Editorial: 25 Garlington Rd, Greenville, South Carolina 29615-4613 **Tel:** 1 864 271-9200.
Web site: http://www.1063word.com
Profile: WYRD-FM is a commercial station owned by Entercom Communications Corp. The format of the station is news and talk and sports. WYRD-FM broadcasts to the Greenville, SC area at 106.3 FM.
FM RADIO STATION

WYRE-FM 46726
Owner: Cortona Media, LLC
Editorial: 253 Zygmont Ct, Saint Augustine, Florida 32084-5846 **Tel:** 1 904 824-5500.
Email: production@wyrefm.com
Web site: http://www.wyrefm.com
Profile: WYRE-FM is a commercial station owned by Cortona Media, LLC. The format of the station is Hot AC. WYRE-FM broadcasts to the Jacksonville, FL area at 105.5 FM.
FM RADIO STATION

WYRK-FM 40896
Owner: Townsquare Media, LLC
Editorial: 14 Lafayette Sq, Buffalo, New York 14203-1928 **Tel:** 1 716 852-7444.
Web site: http://www.wyrk.com
Profile: WYRK-FM is a commercial station owned by Townsquare Media, LLC. The format of the station is contemporary country. WYRK-FM broadcasts to the Buffalo, NY area at 106.5 FM.
FM RADIO STATION

WYRN-AM 39165
Owner: A and D Broadcasting, Inc.
Editorial: 495 Building, Highway 561 East, Louisburg, North Carolina 27549 **Tel:** 1 919 496-4071.
Profile: WYRN-AM is a commercial station owned by A and D Broadcasting, Inc. The format of the station is gospel, R&B and oldies. WYRN-AM broadcasts to the greater Raleigh, NC area at 1480 AM.
AM RADIO STATION

WYRO-FM 43430
Owner: Davis Broadcasting Media
Editorial: 295 E Main St, Jackson, Ohio 45640-1744
Tel: 1 740 286-3023.
FM RADIO STATION

WYRQ-FM 40897
Owner: Little Falls Radio Corp.
Editorial: 16405 Haven Rd, Little Falls, Minnesota 56345 **Tel:** 1 320 632-2992.
Web site: http://www.fallsradio.com
Profile: WYRQ-FM is a commercial station owned by Little Falls Radio Corp. The format of the station is contemporary country music. WYRQ-FM broadcasts to the Little Falls, MN area at 92.1 FM.
FM RADIO STATION

WYRS-FM 42863
Owner: WYRS Broadcasting
Tel: 1 609 978-1678.
Email: info@wyrs.org
Web site: http://www.wyrs.org
Profile: WYRS-FM is a non-commercial station owned by WYRS Broadcasting. The format of the station is Christian. WYRS-FM broadcasts to the Manahawkin, NJ area at 90.7 FM.
FM RADIO STATION

WYRY-FM 40898
Owner: Tri-Valley Broadcasting
Editorial: 30 Warwick Rd Ste 10, Winchester, New Hampshire 03470-2819 **Tel:** 1 603 239-8200.
Email: wyry@wyry.com
Web site: http://1049nashiconradio.com
Profile: WYRY-FM is a commercial station owned by Tri-Valley Broadcasting. The format of the station is contemporary country. WYRY-FM broadcasts to the Winchester, NH area at 104.9 FM.
FM RADIO STATION

WYSA-FM 44126
Owner: Side By Side Inc.
Editorial: 5105 Glendale Ave Ste C, Toledo, Ohio 43614-1842 **Tel:** 1 419 389-0893.
Email: yesfm@yeshome.com
Web site: http://www.yeshome.com
FM RADIO STATION

WYSC-FM 45106
Owner: Cinecom Broadcasting Systems Inc.
Editorial: Highway 341 South, McRae, Georgia 31055
Tel: 1 229 868-5611.
Profile: WYSC-FM is a commercial station owned by Cinecom Broadcasting Systems Inc. The format of the station is urban adult contemporary. WYSC-FM broadcasts to the Macon, GA area at 102.7 FM.
FM RADIO STATION

WYSE-AM 35748
Owner: Saga Communications
Editorial: 1190 Patton Ave, Asheville, North Carolina 28806-2706 **Tel:** 1 828 259-9695.
Web site: http://www.1310bigwise.com
Profile: WYSE-AM is a commercial station owned by Saga Communications. The format of the station is sports. WYSE-AM broadcasts to the Asheville, NC area at 970 AM.
AM RADIO STATION

WYSH-AM 35854
Owner: Clinton Broadcasters
Editorial: 111 Hillcrest Dr, Clinton, Tennessee 37716-2024 **Tel:** 1 865 457-1380.
Email: wysh@wyshradio.com
Web site: http://www.wyshradio.com
AM RADIO STATION

WYSL-AM 36669
Owner: Radio Livingston Ltd.
Editorial: 5620 S Lima Rd, Avon, New York 14414-9791 **Tel:** 1 585 346-3000.
Email: news@wysl1040.com
Web site: http://www.wysl1040.com
Profile: WYSL-AM is a commercial station owned by Radio Livingston Ltd. The format of the station is news, talk and sports. WYSL-AM broadcasts to the Avon, NY area at 1040 AM.
AM RADIO STATION

WYSM-FM 937906
Owner: Side By Side Inc.
Editorial: 5105 Glendale Ave Ste C, Toledo, Ohio 43614-1842 **Tel:** 1 419 389-0893.
Email: yesfm@yeshome.com
Web site: http://www.yeshome.com
Profile: WYSM-FM is a non-commercial station owned by Side By Side Inc. The format of the station is contemporary Christian. WYSZ-FM broadcasts to the Lima, OH area at 89.3 FM.
FM RADIO STATION

WYSS-FM 46043
Owner: Sovereign Communications LLC
Editorial: 1402 Ashmun St, Sault Sainte Marie, Michigan 49783 **Tel:** 1 906 635-0995.
Web site: http://www.yesfm.net
Profile: WYSS-FM is a commercial station owned by Sovereign Communications LLC. The format of the station is Top 40/CHR music. WYSS-FM broadcasts to the Sault Sainte Marie, MI area at 99.5 FM.
FM RADIO STATION

WYSX-FM 43839
Owner: Stephens Media Group LLC
Editorial: 1 Bridge Plz, Ste 204, Ogdensburg, New York 13669 **Tel:** 1 315 393-1220.
Web site: http://www.yesfm.com
Profile: WYSX-FM is a commercial station owned by Stephens Media Group LLC. The format of the station is Top 40/CHR. WYSX-FM broadcasts to the Ogdensburg, NY area at 96.7 FM.
FM RADIO STATION

WYSZ-FM 42487
Owner: Side By Side Inc.
Editorial: 5105 Glendale Ave STE C, Toledo, Ohio 43614-1850 **Tel:** 1 419 389-0893.
Email: yesfm@yeshome.com
Web site: http://www.yeshome.com
Profile: WYSZ-FM is a non-commercial station owned by Side By Side Inc. The format of the station is contemporary Christian. WYSZ-FM broadcasts to the Toledo, OH area at 89.3 FM.
FM RADIO STATION

WYTE-FM 46557
Owner: NRG Media LLC
Editorial: 2301 Plover Rd, Plover, Wisconsin 54467
Tel: 1 715 341-8838.
Web site: http://www.wyte.com
Profile: WYTE-FM is a commercial station owned by NRG Media LLC. The format of the station is contemporary country. WYTE-FM broadcasts in the Plover, WI, area at 106.5 FM.
FM RADIO STATION

WYTI-AM 35781
Owner: Jefferson(William E.)
Editorial: 275 Glennwood Dr, Rocky Mount, Virginia 24151-2136 **Tel:** 1 540 483-9955.
Email: wyti@wytiradio.com
Web site: http://www.wytiradio.com
Profile: WYTI-AM is a commercial station owned by William E. Jefferson. The format of the station is classic country, bluegrass and gospel music. WYTI-AM broadcasts to the Rocky Mount, VA area at 1570 AM.
AM RADIO STATION

WYTK-FM 43113
Owner: Valley Broadcasting
Editorial: 113 N Seminary St, Florence, Alabama 35630-4701 **Tel:** 1 256 764-9390.
Email: thescore@bellsouth.net
Web site: http://www.939thescore.com
Profile: WYTK-FM is a commercial station owned by Valley Broadcasting. The format of the station is sports. WYTK-FM broadcasts to the Florence, AL area at 93.9 FM.
FM RADIO STATION

WYTM-FM 40903
Owner: Time Broadcasting Inc.
Editorial: 76 Molino Rd, Fayetteville, Tennessee 37334-3813 **Tel:** 1 931 433-1531.
Profile: WYTM-FM is a commercial station owned by Time Broadcasting Inc. The format of the station is country. WYTM-FM broadcasts to the Huntsville, AL area at 105.5 FM.
FM RADIO STATION

WYTN-FM 41354
Owner: Family Stations Inc.
Editorial: 3930 Sunset Blvd, Youngstown, Ohio 44512
Tel: 1 815 725-1331.
Email: info@familyradio.org
Web site: http://www.familyradio.com
Profile: WYTN-FM is a commercial station owned by Family Stations Inc. The format of the station is religious programming. WYTN-FM broadcasts to the Youngstown, OH area at 91.7 FM.
FM RADIO STATION

WYTS-AM 154292
Owner: iHeartMedia Inc.
Editorial: 2323 W 5th Ave Ste 200, Columbus, Ohio 43204-4988 **Tel:** 1 614 486-6101.
Web site: http://www.am1230wyts.com
Profile: WYTS-AM is a commercial station owned by iHeartMedia Inc.The format of the station is urban AC. WYTS-AM broadcasts to the Columbus, OH area at 1230 AM.
AM RADIO STATION

WYTZ-FM 43895
Owner: Midwest Family Stations
Editorial: 580 E Napier Ave, Benton Harbor, Michigan 49022 **Tel:** 1 269 925-1111.
Email: wildbill@wytz.com
Web site: http://975ycountry.com
Profile: WYTZ-FM is a commercial station owned by Midwest Family Stations. The format of the station is country music. WYTZ-FM broadcasts to the Benton Harbor, MI area at 97.5 FM.
FM RADIO STATION

WYUL-FM 43360
Owner: Martz Communications
Editorial: 86 Porter Rd, Malone, New York 12953
Tel: 1 518 483-1100.
Email: news@country965.com
Web site: http://www.947hits.com
Profile: WYUL-FM is a commercial station owned by Martz Communications. The format of the station is Top 40/CHR music. WYUL-FM broadcasts to the Malone, NY and Pointe-Claire, QC area at 94.7 FM.
FM RADIO STATION

WYUM-FM 44091
Owner: Vidalia Communications Group
Editorial: 1501 Mount Vernon Rd, Vidalia, Georgia 30474-3031 **Tel:** 1 912 538-1017.
Web site: http://www.southeastgeorgiatoday.com
Profile: WYUM-FM is a commercial station owned by Vidalia Communications Group. The format for the station is classic country. WYUM-FM broadcasts to the Savannah, GA area at 101.7 FM.
FM RADIO STATION

WYUR-FM 578738
Owner: Milner Broadcasting Co.
Editorial: 202 E Walnut St, Watseka, Illinois 60970-1356 **Tel:** 1 815 933-9287.
Email: wvlifm@comcast.net
Web site: http://www.rivervalleyradio.net
Profile: WYUR-FM is a commercial station owned by Milner Broadcasting Co. The format of the station is contemporary country. WYUR-FM broadcasts to the Gilman, IL area at 103.7 FM.
FM RADIO STATION

WYUS-AM 38297
Owner: Delmarva Broadcasting
Editorial: 1666 Blairs Pond Rd, Milford, Delaware 19963-5263 **Tel:** 1 302 422-7575.
Web site: http://www.espn930.com/
Profile: WYUS-AM is a commercial station owned by Delmarva Broadcasting. The format of the station is Sports. WYUS-AM broadcasts in the Milford, DE area at 930 AM.
AM RADIO STATION

WYUU-FM 40866
Owner: Beasley Broadcast Group
Editorial: 9721 Executive Center Dr N Ste 200, Saint Petersburg, Florida 33702-2439 **Tel:** 1 727 579-1925.
Web site: http://www.925maxima.com
Profile: WYUU-FM is a commercial station owned by Beasley Broadcast Group. The format of the station is Hispanic music. WYUU-FM broadcasts to the Tampa, FL, area at 92.5 FM.
FM RADIO STATION

WYVE-AM 39507
Owner: Three Rivers Media Corp.
Editorial: 110 W Spiller St, Wytheville, Virginia 24382-1952 **Tel:** 1 276 228-3185.
Email: office@threeriversmedia.net
Web site: http://www.wyve.com
AM RADIO STATION

WYVK-FM 45380
Owner: Positive Radio Group
Editorial: 39520 Bradbury Rd, Middleport, Ohio 45760-9703 **Tel:** 1 740 992-6485.
Email: k92thefrog@yahoo.com
Web site: http://www.wyvk.com
Profile: WYVK-FM is a commercial station owned by Positive Radio Group. The format for the station is classic rock. WYVK-FM broadcasts to the Charleston-Huntington, WV area at 92.1 FM.
FM RADIO STATION

WYVN-FM 41262
Owner: Midwest Communications Inc.
Editorial: 87 Central Ave, Holland, Michigan 49423-2829 **Tel:** 1 616 392-3121.
Email: info@927thevan.com
Web site: http://www.927thevan.com
Profile: WYVN-FM is a commercial station owned by Midwest Communications Inc. The format of the station is classic hits. WYVN-FM broadcasts to the Holland, MI area at 92.7 FM.
FM RADIO STATION

WYWY-AM 38298
Owner: Barbourville Community Broadcasting
Editorial: 222 Daniel Boone Dr, Barbourville, Kentucky 40906-1104 **Tel:** 1 606 546-4128.
Email: production@wkkqfm.com
Web site: http://www.wywyradio.com
Profile: WYWY-AM is a commercial station owned by Barbourville Community Broadcasting. The format of the station is gospel. WYWY-AM broadcasts to the Barbourville, KY area at 950 AM.
AM RADIO STATION

WYXB-FM 73362
Owner: Emmis Communications Corp.
Editorial: 40 Monument Cir, Ste 600, Indianapolis, Indiana 46204 **Tel:** 1 317 684-1057.
Web site: http://www.b1057.com
Profile: WYXB-FM is a commercial station owned by Emmis Communications Corp. The format for the station is Lite Rock/Lite AC. WYXB-FM broadcasts to the Indianapolis area at 105.7 FM.
FM RADIO STATION

WYXC-AM 35782
Owner: Clarion Communication, Inc.
Editorial: 1410 Highway 411 Ne, Cartersville, Georgia 30121-5115 **Tel:** 1 770 334-8302.
Email: news@newstalk1270.com
Web site: http://www.newstalk1270.com
Profile: WYXC-AM is a commercial station owned by Clarion Communication, Inc. The format of the station is news/talk. WYXC-AM broadcasts to the Cartersville, GA area at a frequency of 1270 AM.
AM RADIO STATION

WYXE-AM 36475
Owner: Iglesia de Dios Hispana Pentecostal
Editorial: 1079 E Trinity Ln, Nashville, Tennessee 37216-3043 **Tel:** 1 615 227-1130.
Email: contacto@radiovida1130.com
Web site: http://www.radiovida1130.com
Profile: WYXE-AM is a commercial station owned by Iglesia de Dios Hispana Pentecostal. The format of the station is Hispanic religious programming. WYXE-AM broadcasts to the Tacoma, WA area at 1130 AM.
AM RADIO STATION

WYXI-AM 35783
Owner: Cornerstone Broadcasting Inc.
Editorial: 104 Cherry St, Athens, Tennessee 37303-7401 **Tel:** 1 423 745-1390.
Email: wyxi@bellsouth.net
Web site: http://www.wyxi.com
Profile: WYXI-AM is a commercial station owned by Cornerstone Broadcasting Inc. The format for the station is oldies and talk. WYXI-AM broadcasts to the Chattanooga, TN area at 1390 AM.
AM RADIO STATION

WYXL-FM 46111
Owner: Saga Communications
Editorial: 1751 Hanshaw Rd, Ithaca, New York 14850-9105 **Tel:** 1 607 257-6400.
Web site: http://www.lite97fm.com
Profile: WYXL-FM is a commercial station owned by Saga Communications. The format of the station is adult contemporary. WYXL-FM broadcasts to the Ithaca, NY area at 97.3 FM.
FM RADIO STATION

WYXY-FM 40367
Owner: Saga Communications
Editorial: 2603 W Bradley Ave, Champaign, Illinois 61821-1823 **Tel:** 1 217 352-4141.
Web site: http://www.wixy.com
Profile: WYXY-FM is a commercial station owned by Saga Communications. The format of the station is country. WYXY-FM broadcasts to the Champaign, IL area at 99.1 FM.
FM RADIO STATION

WYYC-AM 39041
Owner: Wilkins Communications Network Inc.
Editorial: 1545 N Queen St, York, Pennsylvania 17404-2129 **Tel:** 1 717 848-4418.
Email: wyyc@wilkinsradio.com
Web site: http://www.wilkinsradio.com
Profile: WYYC-AM is a commercial station owned by Wilkins Communications Network Inc. The format of the station is Christian programming. WYYC-AM broadcasts to the York, PA area at 1250 AM.
AM RADIO STATION

WYYD-FM 40905
Owner: iHeart Media Inc.
Editorial: 3807 Brandon Ave SW, SW Suite 2350, Roanoke, Virginia 24018-1490 **Tel:** 1 540 725-1220.
Web site: http://newcountry1079.iheart.com
Profile: WYYD-FM is a commercial station owned by iHeart Media Inc. The format of the station is country. WYYD-FM broadcasts to the Roanoke, VA area at 107.9 FM.
FM RADIO STATION

WYYS-FM 73779
Owner: Mendota Broadcasting
Editorial: 3905 Progress Blvd, Peru, Illinois 61354
Tel: 1 815 224-2100.
Email: wyys@theradiogroup.net
Web site: http://www.classichits106.com
Profile: WYYS-FM is a commercial station owned by Mendota Broadcasating. The format of the station is classic hits. WYYS-FM broadcasts to the Peru, IL area at 106.1 FM.
FM RADIO STATION

WYYU-FM 46810
Owner: North Georgia Radio Group
Editorial: 613 Silver Cir, Dalton, Georgia 30721-4551
Tel: 1 706 278-5511.
Email: mix1045@ngaradio.com
Web site: http://mixx1045.com
Profile: WYYU-FM is a commercial station owned by North Georgia Radio Group. The format of the station is adult contemporary. WYYU-FM broadcasts to the Dalton, GA area at 104.5 FM.
FM RADIO STATION

WYYX-FM 43502
Owner: Magic Broadcasting, LLC
Editorial: 7106 Laird St, Ste 102, Panama City, Florida 32408 **Tel:** 1 850 230-5855.
Web site: http://www.wyyx.com
Profile: WYYX-FM is a commercial station owned by Magic Broadcasting, LLC. The format of the station is rock alternative music. WYYX-FM broadcasts to the Panama City, FL area at 97.7 FM.
FM RADIO STATION

WYYY-FM 46180
Owner: iHeartMedia Inc.
Editorial: 500 Plum St Ste 100, Syracuse, New York 13204-1427 **Tel:** 1 315 472-9797.
Web site: http://www.y94fm.com
Profile: WYYY-FM is a commercial station owned by iHeartMedia Inc. The format of the station is adult contemporary. WYYY-FM broadcasts to the Syracuse, NY area at 94.5 FM.
FM RADIO STATION

WYYZ-AM 36616
Owner: Enlightment LLC
Editorial: 268 Hood Rd, Jasper, Georgia 30143-1124 **Tel:** 1 706 692-4100.
Email: wyyz_1490am@yahoo.com
Web site: http://www.wyyzradio.com
Profile: WYYZ-AM is a commercial station owned by Enlightment LLC. The format of the station is classic country, gospel and talk. WYYZ-AM broadcasts in the Jasper, GA area at 1490 AM.
AM RADIO STATION

WYZB-FM 46734
Owner: Cumulus Media Inc.
Editorial: 225 Hollywood Blvd NW, Fort Walton Beach, Florida 32548-4725 **Tel:** 1 850 243-2323.
Web site: http://www.nashfm1055.com
Profile: WYZB-FM is a commercial station owned by Cumulus Media Inc. The format for the station is contemporary country. WYZB-FM broadcasts to the Fort Walton Beach, FL area at 105.5 FM.
FM RADIO STATION

WYZD-AM 35785
Owner: Gospel Broadcasting Inc.
Editorial: 121 Atkins St, Dobson, North Carolina 27017 **Tel:** 1 336 356-1560.
Email: wyzdradio@yahoo.com
Web site: http://www.wyzdradio.org
Profile: WYZD-AM is a non-commercial station owned by Gospel Broadcasting Inc. The format of the station is gospel and religious programming. WYZD-AM broadcasts to the Dobson, NC area at 1560 AM.
AM RADIO STATION

WYZE-AM 36036
Owner: GHB Broadcasting
Editorial: 1111 Boulevard SE, Atlanta, Georgia 30312-3810 **Tel:** 1 404 622-7802.
Email: wyzepressmail@bellsouth.net
Web site: http://www.wyzeradio.com
Profile: WYZE-AM is a non-commercial station owned by GHB Broadcasting. The format of the station is gospel. WYZE-AM broadcasts to the Atlanta area at 1480 AM.
AM RADIO STATION

WYZI-AM 36495
Owner: Oconee River Broadcasting
Editorial: 259 Turner St, Royston, Georgia 30662-3920 **Tel:** 1 706 246-0059.
Web site: http://farmradio810.com
Profile: WYZI-AM is a commercial station owned by Oconee River Broadcasting. The format of the station is talk programming focused on agriculture and farming. WYZI-AM broadcasts to the Royston, GA area at 810 AM.
AM RADIO STATION

WZAB-AM 552095
Owner: Salem Media Group, Inc.
Editorial: 2828 W Flagler St, Miami, Florida 33135-1337 **Tel:** 1 305 644-0800.
Web site: http://www.880thebiz.com
Profile: WZAB-AM is a commercial station owned by Salem Media Group, Inc.The format of the station is business news and talk. WZAB-AM broadcasts to the Miami area at 880 AM.
AM RADIO STATION

WZAC-FM 44337
Owner: Price Broadcasting
Editorial: 351 Hopkins Ave, Danville, West Virginia 25053 **Tel:** 1 304 369-5201.
Email: wzac@frontier.com
Profile: WZAC-FM is a commercial station owned by Price Broadcasting. The format of the station is country music. WZAC-FM broadcasts to the Danville, WV area at 92.5 FM.
FM RADIO STATION

WZAD-FM 41790
Owner: Townsquare Media
Editorial: 2 Pendell Rd, Poughkeepsie, New York 12601-1513 **Tel:** 1 845 471-1500.
Web site: http://www.hudsonvalleycountry.com
Profile: WZAD-FM is a commercial station owned by Townsquare Media. The format of the station is contemporary country. WZAD-FM broadcasts to the Poughkeepsie, NY area at 97.3 FM.
FM RADIO STATION

WZAE-FM 696413
Owner: Radio Training Network, Inc.
Editorial: 102 Lecompte Ave, North Augusta, South Carolina 29841-3032 **Tel:** 1 803 819-3125.
Email: info@wafj.com
Web site: http://www.wafj.com
Profile: WZAE-FM is a non-commercial station owned by Radio Training Network, Inc. The format of the station is Contemporary Christian. WZAE-FM broadcasts to the Wadley, SC area at 93.3 FM.
FM RADIO STATION

WZAK-FM 40906
Owner: Urban One Inc.
Editorial: 6555 Carnegie Ave Ste 100, Cleveland, Ohio 44103-4619 **Tel:** 1 216 579-1111.
Web site: https://wzakcleveland.com
Profile: WZAK-FM is a commercial station owned by Urban One Inc. The format of the station is urban adult contemporary. WZAK-FM broadcasts to the Cleveland area at 93.1 FM.
FM RADIO STATION

WZAM-AM 38249
Owner: Taconite Broadcasting
Editorial: 121 N Front St, Ste A, Marquette, Michigan 49855 **Tel:** 1 906 225-9100.
Web site: http://www.espn970.com
Profile: WZAM-AM is a commercial station owned by Taconite Broadcasting. The format of the station is sports. WZAM-AM broadcasts to the Marquette, MI area at 970 AM.
AM RADIO STATION

WZAN-AM 38295
Owner: Saga Communications
Editorial: 420 Western Ave, South Portland, Maine 04106-1704 **Tel:** 1 207 774-4561.
Web site: http://www.970wzan.com
Profile: WZAN-AM is a commercial station owned by Saga Communications. The format of the station is Sports. WZAN-AM broadcasts to the Portland, ME area at 970 AM.
AM RADIO STATION

WZAP-AM 35787
Owner: RAM Communications Inc.
Editorial: 11373 Wallace Pike, Bristol, Virginia 24202-2743 **Tel:** 1 276 669-6950.
Email: wzapradio@aol.com
Web site: http://www.wzapradio.com
Profile: WZAP-AM is a commercial station owned by RAM Communications Inc. The format of the station is religious programming. WZAP-AM broadcasts to the Bristol, VA area at 690 AM.
AM RADIO STATION

WZAQ-FM 42906
Owner: Expression Production Group
Editorial: 113 E Madison St, Louisa, Kentucky 41230-1324 **Tel:** 1 606 638-9203.
Email: info@wzaqfm.com
Web site: http://www.ignitefm.com
Profile: WZAQ-FM is a commercial station owned by Expression Production Group. The format for the station is contemporary Christian. WZAQ-FM broadcasts to the Charleston-Huntington, WV area at 92.3 FM.
FM RADIO STATION

WZAT-FM 43889
Owner: Cumulus Media Inc.
Editorial: 214 Television Cir, Savannah, Georgia 31406-4519 **Tel:** 1 912 961-9000.
Web site: http://www.1021thesound.com/station-information
Profile: WZAT-FM is a commercial station owned by Cumulus Media Inc. The format of the station is Hot AC. WZAT-FM broadcasts to the Savannah, GA area at 102.1 FM.
FM RADIO STATION

WZAX-FM 43174
Owner: First Media Radio LLC
Editorial: 12714 Hwy 97 E, Rocky Mount, North Carolina 27803 **Tel:** 1 252 442-8092.
Email: wecare@firstmedianc.com
Web site: http://www.993rockcity.com
Profile: WZAX-FM is a commercial station owned by First Media Radio LLC. The format of the station is classic rock. WZAX-FM broadcasts to the Rocky Mount, NC area at 99.3 FM.
FM RADIO STATION

WZAZ-AM 38679
Owner: Titus Harvest Dome Spectrum Church Inc
Editorial: 4190 Belfort Rd, Ste 450, Jacksonville, Florida 32216 **Tel:** 1 904 470-4707.
Email: programming@wzaz.com
Web site: http://www.wzaz.com
Profile: WZAZ-AM is a commercial station owned by Titus Harvest Dome Spectrum Church Inc. The format of the station is gospel. WZAZ-AM broadcasts in the Jacksonville, FL area at 1400 AM.
AM RADIO STATION

WZBA-FM 41786
Owner: Shamrock Communications
Editorial: 11350 McCormick Rd, Exec Plaza 3 #701, Hunt Valley, Maryland 21031-1002 **Tel:** 1 410 771-8484.
Web site: http://www.thebayonline.com
Profile: WZBA-FM is a commercial station owned by Shamrock Communications Inc. The format of the station is classic rock music. WZBA-FM broadcasts to Baltimore area at 100.7 FM.
FM RADIO STATION

WZBB-FM 42816
Owner: Brook(Donny)
Editorial: 10899 Virginia Ave, Bassett, Virginia 24055-2790 **Tel:** 1 276 629-7999.
Email: traffic@wzbbfm.com
Web site: http://www.supercountryonline.com
Profile: WZBB-FM is a commercial station owned by Donny Brook. The format of the station is country. WZBB-FM broadcasts to the Rocky Mount, VA area at 99.9 FM.
FM RADIO STATION

WZBC-FM 40907
Owner: Boston College
Editorial: 107 McElroy Commons, Boston College, Chestnut Hill, Massachusetts 2167 **Tel:** 1 617 552-3511.
Email: wzbcfm@gmail.com
Web site: http://www.wzbc.org
Profile: WZBC-FM is non-commercial station owned by Boston College. The format of the station is rock alternative. WZBC-FM broadcasts to the Boston area at 90.3 FM.
FM RADIO STATION

WZBD-FM 42345
Owner: Adams County Radio Inc.
Editorial: 955 US Highway 27 N, Berne, Indiana 46711-1023 **Tel:** 1 260 726-8729.
Email: wzbd@onlyinternet.net
Web site: http://www.wzbd.com
Profile: WZBD-FM is a commercial station owned by Adams County Radio Inc. The format of the station is adult contemporary music. WZBD-FM broadcasts to the Berne, IN area at 92.7 FM.
FM RADIO STATION

WZBG-FM 41995
Owner: Local Boys and Girls Broadcasting
Editorial: 49 Commons Dr, Litchfield, Connecticut 6759 **Tel:** 1 860 567-3697.
Email: info@wzbg.com
Web site: http://www.973wzbg.com
Profile: WZBG-FM is a commercial station owned by Local Boys and Girls Broadcasting. The format for the station is adult contemporary. WZBG-FM broadcasts to the Hartford-New Haven, CT area at 97.3 FM.
FM RADIO STATION

WZBH-FM 45877
Owner: Adams Radio Group
Editorial: 20200 Dupont Blvd, Georgetown, Delaware 19947-3105 **Tel:** 1 302 856-2567.
Web site: http://www.wzbhrocks.com
Profile: WZBH-FM is a commercial station owned by Adams Radio Group. The format of the station is rock/album oriented rock music. WZBH-FM broadcasts in the Salisbury, MD area at 93.5 FM.
FM RADIO STATION

WZBK-AM 37985
Owner: Saga Communications
Editorial: 69 Stanhope Ave, Keene, New Hampshire 03431-1577 **Tel:** 1 603 352-9230.
Web site: http://espnkeene.com/
Profile: WZBK-AM is a commercial station owned by Saga Communications and is the ESPN Radio affliate for the Keene, NH area. The format of the station is sports. WZBK-AM broadcasts at 1220 AM.
AM RADIO STATION

WZBN-FM 79650
Owner: Greater 2nd Mt. Olive Missionary Baptist Church
Editorial: 235 W Roosevelt Ave Ste 203, Albany, Georgia 31701-5110 **Tel:** 1 229 888-3778.
Email: power1055albany@gmail.com
Web site: http://www.power105theking.com
Profile: WZBN-FM is a commercial station owned by Light Media. The format of the station is contemporary gospel music. WZBN-FM broadcasts to the Albany, GA area at 105.5 FM.
FM RADIO STATION

WZBO-AM 342579
Owner: East Carolina Radio Group
Editorial: 911 Parsonage St, Elizabeth City, North Carolina 27909 **Tel:** 1 252 335-4379.
Profile: WZBO-AM is a commercial station owned by East Carolina Radio Group. The format of the station is Hispanic. WZBO-AM broadcasts to the Elizabeth City, NC area at 1260 AM.
AM RADIO STATION

WZBQ-FM 43638
Owner: iHeartMedia Inc.
Editorial: 3900 11th Ave, Tuscaloosa, Alabama 35401-7056 **Tel:** 1 205 344-4589.
Web site: http://www.941zbq.com
Profile: WZBQ-FM is a commercial station owned by iHeartMedia Inc. The format of the station is Top 40/ CHR music. WZBQ-FM broadcasts to the Tuscaloosa, AL area at 94.1 FM.
FM RADIO STATION

WZBX-FM 46265
Owner: Radio Statesboro, Inc.
Editorial: 561 E Olliff St, Statesboro, Georgia 30458-4663 **Tel:** 1 912 764-5446.
Web site: http://statesboro365.com
Profile: WZBX-FM is a commercial station owned Radio Statesboro, Inc. The format of the station is classic rock. WZBX-FM broadcasts to the Savannah, GA area at 106.5 FM.
FM RADIO STATION

WZBZ-FM 40142
Owner: Equity Communications LP
Editorial: 8025 Black Horse Pike, Pleasantville, New Jersey 08232-2900 **Tel:** 1 609 484-8444.
Web site: http://993thebuzz.com
Profile: WZBZ-FM is a commercial station owned by Equity Communications LP. The format of the station is urban contemporary. WZBZ-FM broadcasts to the Atlantic City, NJ area at 99.3 FM.
FM RADIO STATION

WZCB-FM 45889
Owner: iHeartMedia Inc.
Editorial: 2323 W 5th Ave Ste 200, Columbus, Ohio 43204-4988 **Tel:** 1 614 486-6101.
Web site: http://www.thebeat1067.com/main.html
Profile: WZCB-FM a commercial station owned by iHeartMedia Inc. The format of the station is urban contemporary. WCGX-FM broadcasts to the Dublin, OH area at 106.7 FM.
FM RADIO STATION

WZCC-AM 231404
Owner: Suncoast Radio, Inc.
Editorial: 174 Ne 351 Hwy, Cross City, Florida 32628-3120 **Tel:** 1 352 498-0304.
Web site: http://www.classichits933.com
Profile: WZCC-AM is a commercial station owned by Suncoast Radio, Inc. The format of the station is classic hits music. The station airs locally at 1240 AM.
AM RADIO STATION

WZCH-FM 42474
Owner: iHeartMedia Inc.
Editorial: 7080 Industrial Hwy, Macon, Georgia 31216-7538 **Tel:** 1 478 781-1063.
Web site: http://www.newcountry1025.com
Profile: WZCH-FM is a commercial station owned by iHeartMedia Inc. and licensed to the Aloha Station Trust, LLC. The format of the station is contemporary country. WZCH-FM broadcasts to the Macon, GA area at 102.5 FM.
FM RADIO STATION

WZCP-FM 43412
Owner: One Connection Media Group
Editorial: 881 E Johnstown Rd, Gahanna, Ohio 43230-1851 **Tel:** 1 614 855-9171.
Email: theriver@1049theriver.com
Web site: http://www.riverradio.com
Profile: WZCP-FM is a non-commercial station owned by One Connection Media Group. The format of the station is contemporary Christian. WZCP-FM broadcasts to the Chillicothe, OH area at 89.3 FM.
FM RADIO STATION

WZCR-FM 46524
Owner: iHeartMedia Inc.
Editorial: 5620 State Route 9G, Hudson, New York 12534-4127 **Tel:** 1 518 828-5006.
Web site: http://www.cruisin935.com
Profile: WZCR-FM is a commercial station owned by iHeartMedia Inc. The format of the station is oldies. WZCR-FM broadcasts to the Hudson, NY area at 93.5 FM.
FM RADIO STATION

WZCT-AM 36072
Owner: Bonner/Carlile Enterprises Inc.
Editorial: 1111 E Willow St, Scottsboro, Alabama 35768-2210 **Tel:** 1 256 574-1330.
Email: wzct5000watts@scottsboro.org
Web site: http://www.southerngospelam1330.com
AM RADIO STATION

WZCY-FM 40677
Owner: Cumulus Media Inc.
Editorial: 2300 Vartan Way Ste 130, Harrisburg, Pennsylvania 17110-9794 **Tel:** 1 717 238-1041.
Web site: http://www.nashfm1067.com
Profile: WZCY-FM is a commercial station owned by Cumulus Media Inc. The format of the station is contemporary country. WZCY-FM broadcasts to the Harrisburg, PA area at 106.7 FM.
FM RADIO STATION

WZDA-FM 40893
Owner: iHeart Media Inc.
Editorial: 101 Pine St, Dayton, Ohio 45402-2948 **Tel:** 1 937 224-1137.
Profile: WZDA-FM is a commercial station owned by iHeart Media Inc. The format of the station is rock alternative music. WZDA-FM broadcasts to the Dayton, OH area at 103.9 FM.
FM RADIO STATION

WZDB-FM 588310
Owner: First Media Radio LLC
Editorial: 801 E Dubois Ave, Du Bois, Pennsylvania 15801-3643 **Tel:** 1 814 371-8300.
Email: q102radio@comcast.net
Web site: http://www.959zdb.com
Profile: WZDB-FM is a commercial station owned by First Media Radio LLC. The format of the station is classic rock. WZDB-FM broadcasts to the Du Bois, PA area at 95.9 FM.
FM RADIO STATION

WZDM-FM 42826
Owner: Original Company Inc.(The)
Editorial: 522 Busseron St, Vincennes, Indiana 47591 **Tel:** 1 812 882-6060.
Email: wzdm@wzdm.com
Web site: http://www.wzdm.com
Profile: WZDM-FM is a commercial station owned The Original Company Inc. The format of the station is adult contemporary. WZDM-FM broadcasts to the Vincennes, IN area at 92.1 FM.
FM RADIO STATION

WZDQ-FM 86521
Owner: Southern Stone Communications, LLC
Editorial: 111 W Main St, Jackson, Tennessee 38301-6147 **Tel:** 1 731 427-9616.
Email: 1023therocket@thomasmedia.fm
Web site: http://jacksonnewsnow.com
Profile: WZDQ-FM is a commercial station owned by Southern Stone Communications, LLC. The format of

the station is rock/album-oriented rock. WZDQ-FM broadcasts to the Jackson, TN area at 102.3 FM.
FM RADIO STATION

WZEB-FM 41543
Owner: The Voice Radio Network
Editorial: 20200 Dupont Blvd, Georgetown, Delaware 19947-3105 **Tel:** 1 302 856-2567.
Web site: http://power1017.com
Profile: WZEB-FM is a commercial station owned by The Voice Radio Network. The format of the station is urban contemporary music. WZEB-FM broadcasts in the Salisbury, MD area at 101.7 FM.
FM RADIO STATION

WZEE-FM 45652
Owner: iHeartMedia Inc.
Editorial: 2651 S Fish Hatchery Rd, Fitchburg, Wisconsin 53711-5410 **Tel:** 1 608 274-1070.
Web site: http://www.z104fm.com
Profile: WZEE-FM is a commercial station owned by iHeartMedia Inc. The format of the station is Top 40/CHR. WZEE-FM broadcasts to the Madison, WI area at 104.1 FM.
FM RADIO STATION

WZEP-AM 35788
Owner: Walton County Broadcasting Inc.
Editorial: 449 N 12th St, Defuniak Springs, Florida 32433-0411 **Tel:** 1 850 892-3158.
Email: wzep@wzep1460.com
Web site: http://www.wzep1460.com
Profile: WZEP-AM is a commercial station owned by Walton County Broadcasting Inc. The format of the station is variety, including country and oldies. WZEP-AM broadcasts to the DeFuniak Springs, FL area at 1460 AM.
AM RADIO STATION

WZEW-FM 40908
Owner: Dot Com Plus, LLC
Editorial: 1100 Dauphin St, Ste E, Mobile, Alabama 36604 **Tel:** 1 251 438-5460.
Email: 92zew@92zew.net
Web site: http://www.92zew.net
Profile: WZEW-FM is a commercial station owned by Dot Com Plus, LLC . The format for the station is adult album alternative. WZEW-FM broadcasts to the Mobile, AL area at 92.1 FM.
FM RADIO STATION

WZEZ-FM 73869
Owner: Urban One, Inc.
Editorial: 2809 Emerywood Pkwy Ste 300, Richmond, Virginia 23294-3743 **Tel:** 1 804 672-9299.
Web site: https://espnrichmond.com
Profile: WZEZ-FM is a commercial station owned by Urban One, Inc. The format of the station is sports. WZEZ-FM broadcasts to the Richmond, VA area at 100.5 FM.
FM RADIO STATION

WZFC-FM 41245
Owner: Centennial Broadcasting
Editorial: 520 N Pleasant Valley Rd, Winchester, Virginia 22601-5654 **Tel:** 1 540 667-2224.
Profile: WZFC-FM is a commercial station owned by Centennial Broadcasting. The format of the station is classic country. WZFC-FM broadcasts to the Winchester, VA area at 104.9 FM.
FM RADIO STATION

WZFG-AM 538314
Owner: Bakken Beacon Media LLC
Editorial: 3301 University Dr S, Fargo, North Dakota 58104-6289 **Tel:** 1 701 271-1100.
Email: news@flagfamily.com
Web site: http://am1100theflag.com
Profile: WZFG-AM is a commercial station owned by Bakken Beacon Media LLC. The format of the station is news and talk. WZFG-AM broadcasts to the Fargo, ND area at 1100 AM.
AM RADIO STATION

WZFM-FM 518251
Owner: Positive Radio Group
Editorial: 145 Jackson St NE, Blacksburg, Virginia 24060 **Tel:** 1 540 951-9791.
Profile: WZFM-FM is a commercial station owned by Positive Radio Group. The format of the station is classic hits. WZFM-FM broadcasts to the Blacksburg, VA area at 101.3 FM.
FM RADIO STATION

WZFR-FM 658744
Owner: Faith Radio Network, Inc.
Editorial: 35 Island Dr Ste 16, Eastpoint, Florida 32328-3264 **Tel:** 1 850 201-1070.
Web site: http://www.faithradio.us
Profile: WZFR-FM is a commercial station owned by Faith Radio Network, Inc. The format of the station is Christian and religious talk. WZFR-FM broadcasts to the Eastpoint, FL area at 104.5 FM.
FM RADIO STATION

WZFT-FM 40146
Owner: iHeartMedia Inc.
Editorial: 711 W 40th St Ste 350, Baltimore, Maryland 21211-2190 **Tel:** 1 410 366-7600.
Web site: http://z1043.iheart.com
Profile: WZFT-FM is a commercial station owned by iHeartMedia Inc.The format of the station is Top 40/CHR. WZFT-FM broadcasts to Baltimore area at 104.3 FM.
FM RADIO STATION

WZFX-FM 40910
Owner: Beasley Broadcast Group
Editorial: 508 Person St, Fayetteville, North Carolina 28301 **Tel:** 1 910 486-4114.
Email: wzfx@foxy99.com
Web site: http://www.foxy99.com
Profile: WZFX-FM is a commercial station owned by Beasley Broadcasting Group. The format of the station is urban contemporary music. WZFX-FM broadcasts to the Fayetteville, NC area at 99.1 FM.
FM RADIO STATION

WZGC-FM 40911
Owner: CBS Radio
Editorial: 1201 Peachtree St NE Ste 800, Atlanta, Georgia 30361-3510 **Tel:** 1 404 898-8900.
Web site: http://atlanta.cbslocal.com/station/92-9-the-game/
Profile: WZGC-FM is a commercial station owned by the CBS Radio. The format of the station is sports. WZGC-FM broadcasts to the Atlanta area at 92.9 FM.
FM RADIO STATION

WZGL-FM 521241
Owner: Illinois Bible Institute
Editorial: 4101 Fieldstone Rd, Champaign, Illinois 61822-8800 **Tel:** 1 217 359-8232.
Email: wbgl@wbgl.org
Web site: http://www.wbgl.org
Profile: WZGL-FM is a non-commercial station owned by the Illinois Bible Institute. The format of the station is contemporary Christian music and talk. WZGL-FM broadcasts to the Champaign, IL area at 88.1 FM.
FM RADIO STATION

WZGM-AM 35579
Owner: HRN Broadcasting Inc.
Editorial: 101 West St, Black Mountain, North Carolina 28711-3166 **Tel:** 1 828 669-6224.
Web site: https://1350wzgm.wordpress.com
Profile: WZGM-AM is a commercial station owned by HRN Broadcasting Inc and operated by News Talk 50, Inc. The format of the station is talk. WZGM-AM broadcasts to the Asheville, NC area at 1350 AM.
AM RADIO STATION

WZGN-FM 42752
Owner: Monticello Media LLC
Editorial: 1150 Pepsi Pl, Ste 300, Charlottesville, Virginia 22901 **Tel:** 1 434 978-4408.
Web site: http://www.generations1023.com
Profile: WZGN-FM is a commercial station owned by Monticello Media LLC. The format of the station is classic hits. WZGN-FM broadcasts in the Charlottesville, VA area at 102.3 FM.
FM RADIO STATION

WZGO-FM 469262
Owner: Pathway Christian Academy Inc.
Editorial: 205 N Greene St, Snow Hill, North Carolina 28580 **Tel:** 1 252 747-8887.
Email: wago@gomixradio.org
Web site: http://www.gomixradio.org
Profile: WZGO-FM is a non-commercial station owned by Pathway Christian Academy Inc. The format of the station is Christian programming. WZGO-FM broadcasts to the Snow Hill, NC area at 91.1 FM.
FM RADIO STATION

WZGV-AM 35574
Owner: HRN Broadcasting Inc.
Editorial: 201 W Morehead St Ste 200, Charlotte, North Carolina 28202-1508 **Tel:** 1 704 332-0646.
Email: sports@espn730.com
Web site: http://www.espn730.com
Profile: WZGV-AM is a commercial station owned by HRN Broadcasting Inc. The format of the station is sports. The station is affiliated with ESPN Radio. WZGV-AM broadcasts to the Charlotte, NC area at 730 AM.
AM RADIO STATION

WZGX-AM 35671
Owner: BAR Broadcasting, Inc.
Editorial: 100 Yeager Pkwy, Pelham, Alabama 35124-1859 **Tel:** 1 205 358-1100.
Profile: WZGX-AM is a commercial station owned by BAR Broadcasting, Inc.. The format of the station is regional Mexican. WZGX-AM broadcasts to the Bessemer, AL area at 1450 AM.
AM RADIO STATION

WZHD-FM 687604
Owner: Equinox Broadcasting Corporation
Tel: 1 607 772-1005.
Profile: WZHD-FM is a commercial station owned by Equinox Broadcasting Corporation. The format of the station is classic hits. The station broadcasts locally at 97.1 FM to the Canaseraga, NY area.
FM RADIO STATION

WZHF-AM 36910
Owner: Multicultural Radio Broadcasting Inc.
Editorial: 13321 New Hampshire Ave Ste 207, Silver Spring, Maryland 20904-3450 **Tel:** 1 301 879-9077.
Web site: http://www.wzhfradio.com
Profile: WZHF-AM is a commercial station owned by Multicultural Radio Broadcasting Inc. WZHF-AM broadcasts to Silver Spring, MD at 1390 AM.
AM RADIO STATION

WZHR-AM 36859
Owner: Radio World
Editorial: 706 N Myrtle Ave, Clearwater, Florida 33755-4219 **Tel:** 1 727 441-3311.
Web site: http://wzhr.tantalk1340.com/
Profile: WZHR-AM is a commercial station owned by Radio World. The format of the station is contemporary Christian. WZHR-AM broadcasts to the Tampa area at 1400 AM.
AM RADIO STATION

WZHT-FM 42107
Owner: iHeartMedia Inc.
Editorial: 203 Gunn Rd, Montgomery, Alabama 36117-2003 **Tel:** 1 334 274-6464.
Web site: http://www.myhot105.com
Profile: WZHT-FM is a commercial station owned by iHeartMedia Inc. The format of the station is urban contemporary. WZHT-FM broadcasts to the Montgomery, AL area at 105.7 FM.
FM RADIO STATION

WZID-FM 45948
Owner: Saga Communications
Editorial: 500 N Commercial St, Manchester, New Hampshire 03101-1151 **Tel:** 1 603 669-5777.
Web site: http://www.wzid.com
Profile: WZID-FM is a commercial station owned by Saga Communications. The format of the station is adult contemporary music. WZID-FM broadcasts to the Manchester, NH area at 95.7 FM.
FM RADIO STATION

WZIM-FM 75461
Owner: Great Plains Media
Editorial: 108 Boeykens Pl, Normal, Illinois 61761-2139 **Tel:** 1 309 888-4496.
Web site: http://www.magic995fm.com
Profile: WZIM-FM is a commercial station owned by Great Plains Media. The format of the station is adult contemporary. WZIM-FM broadcasts to the Normal, IL area at 99.5 FM.
FM RADIO STATION

WZJS-FM 46475
Owner: High Country Adventures, LLC
Editorial: 738 Blowing Rock Rd, Boone, North Carolina 28607-4835 **Tel:** 1 828 264-2411.
Email: info@wataradio.com
Web site: http://goblueridge.net
Profile: WZJS-FM is a commercial station owned by High Country Adventures, LLC, a subsidiary of Curtis Media Group. The format of the station is classic hits. WZJS-FM broadcasts to the Boone, NC area at 100.7 FM.
FM RADIO STATION

WZJY-AM 35790
Owner: Jabar Communications, Inc.
Editorial: 5081 Rivers Ave, North Charleston, South Carolina 29406-6303 **Tel:** 1 843 554-1063.
Web site: http://www.elsol980.com
Profile: WZJY-AM is a commercial station owned by Jabar Communications, Inc. The format of the station is Hispanic Top 40/CHR. WZJY-AM broadcasts to the North Charleston, SC area at 1480 AM.
AM RADIO STATION

WZJZ-FM 46492
Owner: iHeartMedia Inc.
Editorial: 13320 Metro Pkwy Ste 1, Fort Myers, Florida 33966-4804 **Tel:** 1 239 225-4300.
Web site: http://y100florida.iheart.com/
Profile: WZJZ-FM is a commercial station owned by iHeartMedia Inc. The format of the station is Hot AC. WZJZ-FM broadcasts to the Fort Myers, FL area at 100.1 FM.
FM RADIO STATION

WZKB-FM 44372
Owner: Carolina's Christian Broadcasting Inc.
Editorial: 409 Warsaw Rd, Clinton, North Carolina 28328-3550 **Tel:** 1 910 592-7601.
Profile: WZKB-FM is a commercial station owned by Carolina's Christian Broadcasting Inc. The format of the station is Hispanic CHR. WZKB-FM broadcasts to the Wallace, NC area at 94.3 FM.
FM RADIO STATION

WZKR-FM 584697
Owner: Morning Star Media, LLC
Editorial: 613 22nd Ave, Meridian, Mississippi 39301-5022 **Tel:** 1 601 693-1103.
Email: wharrison@telesouth.com
Web site: http://www.supertalk.fm/
Profile: WZKR-FM is a commercial station owned by Morning Star Media, LLC. The format of the station is talk. WZKR-FM broadcasts to the Meridian, MS area at 103.3 FM.
FM RADIO STATION

WZKS-FM 43915
Owner: Mississippi Broadcasters, LLC
Editorial: 3436 Highway 45 N, Meridian, Mississippi 39301-1509 **Tel:** 1 601 483-5477.
Email: meridianproduction@urbanradio.fm
Web site: http://www.104kissfm.com/
Profile: WZKS-FM is a commercial station owned by Mississippi Broadcasters, LLC. The format for the station is urban adult contemporary music. WZKS-FM broadcasts to the Meridian, MS area at 104.1 FM.
FM RADIO STATION

WZKT-FM 41935
Owner: Curtis Media Group
Editorial: 2581 US Highway 70 W, Goldsboro, North Carolina 27530-9553 **Tel:** 1 919 587-0977.
Web site: http://goldsborodailynews.com
Profile: WZKT-FM is a commercial station owned by Curtis Media Group. The format of the station is contemporary country. WZKT-FM broadcasts to the Raleigh, NC area at 97.7 FM.
FM RADIO STATION

WZKX-FM 45472
Owner: Dowdy Broadcasting, Inc.
Editorial: 10250 Lorraine Rd, Gulfport, Mississippi 39503 **Tel:** 1 228 896-5500.
Web site: http://www.kicker108.com
Profile: WZKX-FM is a commercial station owned by Dowdy Broadcasting, Inc. The format of the station is contemporary country music. WZKX-FM broadcasts to the Gulfport, MS area at 107.9 FM.
FM RADIO STATION

WZKY-AM 36770
Owner: Stanly Communications Inc.
Editorial: 1234 Magnolia St, Albemarle, North Carolina 28001 **Tel:** 1 704 983-1580.
Email: wspc@ctc.net
Web site: http://www.1010wspc.com
Profile: WZKY-AM is a commercial station owned by Stanly Communications Inc. The format of the station is oldies. WZKY-AM broadcasts to the Albemarle, NC area at 1580 AM.
AM RADIO STATION

WZKZ-FM 43111
Owner: Sound Communications
Editorial: 3012 Eastside Ave, Wellsville, New York 14895-9527 **Tel:** 1 585 593-9553.
Email: wzkz@wny.twcbc.com
Profile: WZKZ-FM is a commercial station owned by Sound Communications. The format of the station is contemporary country. WZKZ-FM broadcasts to the Wellsville, NY area at 101.9 FM.
FM RADIO STATION

WZLA-FM 41347
Owner: Rocket 88 Broadcasting, LLP.
Editorial: 112 N Main St, Abbeville, South Carolina 29620-1727 **Tel:** 1 864 366-5785.
Email: z93@wctel.net
Web site: http://www.wzlaradio.com
Profile: WZLA-FM is a commercial station owned by Rocket 88 Broadcasting, LLP. The format of the station is country classics. WZLA-FM broadcasts to the Abbeville, SC area at 92.9 FM.
FM RADIO STATION

WZLB-FM 40651
Owner: Community Broadcasters LLC.
Editorial: 34 Harbor Blvd Ste 202, Destin, Florida 32541-7365 **Tel:** 1 850 654-1000.
Profile: WZLB-FM is a commercial station owned by Community Broadcasters LLC. The station's format is active rock. WZLB-FM broadcasts to the Mobile, AL, Pensacola, FL area at 103.1 FM.
FM RADIO STATION

WZLD-FM 41388
Owner: iHeartMedia Inc.
Editorial: 6555 U S Highway 98 Ste 8, Hattiesburg, Mississippi 39402-8699 **Tel:** 1 601 296-9800.
Email: contact@wzldfm.com
Web site: http://www.wzldfm.com
Profile: WZLD-FM is a commercial station owned by iHeartMedia Inc. The format of the station is urban contemporary. WZLD-FM broadcasts to the Hattiesburg, MS area at 106.3 FM.
FM RADIO STATION

WZLF-FM 40125
Owner: WBIN, Inc.
Editorial: 8 Glen Road, West Lebanon, New Hampshire 03784-1136 **Tel:** 1 603 298-0332.
Web site: http://www.953thewolf.com
Profile: WZLF-FM is a commercial station owned by WBIN, Inc. The format of the station is country. WZLF-FM broadcasts to the West Lebanon, NH area at 107.1 FM.
FM RADIO STATION

WZLK-FM 46650
Owner: East Kentucky Radio Network
Editorial: 1240 Radio Dr, Pikeville, Kentucky 41501-4779 **Tel:** 1 606 437-4051.
Email: frontdesk@ekbradio.com
Web site: http://www.1075zrock.com
Profile: WZLK-FM is a commercial station owned by East Kentucky Radio Network. The format for the station is Top 40/CHR. WZLK-FM broadcasts to the Pikeville, KY area at 107.5 FM.
FM RADIO STATION

WZLO-FM 41816
Owner: Zone Corporation(The)
Editorial: 14 E Main St, Dover Foxcroft, Maine 04426-1414 **Tel:** 1 207 564-2642.
Email: wzlo@zoneradio.com
Web site: http://www.wzlofm.com
Profile: WZLO-FM is a commercial station owned by The Zone Corporation. WZLO-FM broadcasts to the Dover Foxcroft, ME area at 103.1 FM. The station's format is Adult Alternative music.
FM RADIO STATION

WZLQ-FM 46873
Owner: Mississippi Radio Group
Editorial: 2214 S Gloster St, Tupelo, Mississippi 38801-6814 **Tel:** 1 662 842-7658.
Web site: http://www.z985.net
Profile: WZLQ-FM is a commercial station owned by Mississippi Radio Group. The format of the station is rock. WZLQ-FM broadcasts to the Columbus, MS area at 98.5.
FM RADIO STATION

WZLR-FM 42262
Owner: Cox Media Group, Inc.
Editorial: 1611 S Main St, Dayton, Ohio 45409-2547
Tel: 1 937 259-2111.
Web site: http://www.953theeagle.com
Profile: WZLR-FM is a commercial station owned by Cox Media Group, Inc. The format of the station is classic rock. WZLR-FM broadcasts to the Dayton, OH area at 95.3 FM.
FM RADIO STATION

WZLT-FM 45653
Owner: Lexington Broadcasting Service, Inc.
Editorial: 584 Smith Ave, Lexington, Tennessee 38351 **Tel:** 1 731 968-9990.
Email: wzlt993@yahoo.com
Web site: http://www.wzlt993.com
Profile: WZLT-FM is a commercial station owned by Lexington Broadcasting Service, Inc. The format of the station is adult contemporary. WZLT-FM broadcasts to the Lexington, TN area at 99.3 FM.
FM RADIO STATION

WZLX-FM 40914
Owner: CBS Radio
Editorial: 83 Leo M Birmingham Pkwy, Boston, Massachusetts 2135 **Tel:** 1 617 746-5100.
Web site: http://www.wzlx.com
Profile: WZLX-FM is a commercial station owned by CBS Radio. The format of the station is classic rock. WZLX-FM broadcasts to the Boston area at 100.7 FM.
FM RADIO STATION

WZLY-FM 134023
Owner: Wellesley College
Editorial: 106 Central St, Wellesley, Massachusetts 02481-8203 **Tel:** 1 781 283-2690.
Email: wzly@wellesley.edu
Web site: http://www.wzly.net
Profile: WZLY-FM is a non-commercial college station owned by Wellesley College. The primary format of the station is AAA. WZLY-FM broadcasts to Wellesley, MA at 91.5 FM.
FM RADIO STATION

WZMG-AM 36891
Owner: iHeartMedia Inc.
Editorial: 915 Veterans Pkwy, Opelika, Alabama 36801-3367 **Tel:** 1 334 745-4656.
Web site: http://hallelujah910am.iheart.com
Profile: WZMG-AM is a commercial station owned by iHeartMedia Inc. The format of the station is gospel music. WZMG-AM broadcasts to the Opelika, AL area at 910 AM.
AM RADIO STATION

WZMJ-FM 44069
Owner: Lake Murray Communications, LLC
Editorial: 109 Old Chapin Rd Ste R, Lexington, South Carolina 29072-2065 **Tel:** 1 803 785-9596.
Web site: http://www.lakemurrayradio.com
Profile: WZMJ-FM is a commercial station owned by Lake Murray Communications, LLC. The format of the station is adult hits. WZMJ-FM broadcasts to Columbia, SC at 93.1 FM.
FM RADIO STATION

WZMR-FM 46097
Owner: Albany Broadcasting Co.
Editorial: 6 Johnson Rd, Latham, New York 12110-5641 **Tel:** 1 518 786-6600.
Web site: http://www.1049thepeak.com/
Profile: WZMR-FM is a commercial station owned by Albany Broadcasting Co. The format of the station is Triple A. WZMR-FM broadcasts in the Albany, NY area at 104.9 FM.
FM RADIO STATION

WZMX-FM 40498
Owner: CBS Radio
Editorial: 10 Executive Dr, Farmington, Connecticut 6032 **Tel:** 1 860 677-6700.
Web site: http://www.hot937.com
Profile: WZMX-FM is a commercial station owned by CBS Radio. The format of the station is urban contemporary. WZMX-FM broadcasts to the Farmington, CT area at 93.7 FM.
FM RADIO STATION

WZNE-FM 43146
Owner: Stephens Media Group
Editorial: 28 E Main St Fl 8, Rochester, New York 14614-1915 **Tel:** 1 585 399-5700.
Email: info@thezone941.com
Web site: http://www.thezone941.com
Profile: WZNE-FM is a commercial station owned by Stephens Media Group. The format of the station is rock alternative. WZNE-FM broadcasts to the Rochester, NY area at 94.1 FM.
FM RADIO STATION

WZNF-FM 76551
Owner: Dowdy Broadcasting, Inc.
Editorial: 10250 Lorraine Rd, Gulfport, Mississippi 39503-6005 **Tel:** 1 228 896-5500.
Web site: http://www.953gorilla.com
Profile: WZNF-FM is a commercial station owned by Dowdy Broadcasting, Inc. The format of the station is Top 40/CHR. WZNF-FM broadcasts to the Biloxi and Gulfport, MS area at 95.3 FM.
FM RADIO STATION

WZNG-AM 37123
Owner: Jax Broadcasting, LLC
Editorial: 236 Woodland Dr, Shelbyville, Tennessee 37160-6759 **Tel:** 1 931 680-1214.
Email: wlijradio@gmail.com
Web site: http://www.thisisjaxradio.com
Profile: WZNG-AM is a commercial station owned by Jax Broadcasting, LLC. The format of the station is news, sports, and talk. WZNG-AM broadcasts to the Shelbyville, TN area at 1400 AM.
AM RADIO STATION

WZNJ-FM 45654
Owner: Westburg Broadcasting Alabama, LLC.
Editorial: 1226 Jefferson Rd, Demopolis, Alabama 36732-6205 **Tel:** 1 334 289-1106.
Profile: WZNJ-FM is a commercial station owned by Westburg Broadcasting Alabama, LLC. The format of the station is Urban AC. WZNJ-FM broadcasts to the Demopolis, AL area at 106.5 FM.
FM RADIO STATION

WZNL-FM 42404
Owner: Sovereign Communications, LLC
Editorial: 101 Kent St, Iron Mountain, Michigan 49801
Tel: 1 906 774-4321.
Profile: WZNL-FM is a commercial station owned by Sovereign Communications, LLC. The format of the station is adult contemporary. WZNL-FM broadcasts to the Norway, MI area at a frequency of 94.3 FM.
FM RADIO STATION

WZNP-FM 552093
Owner: One Connection Media Group
Editorial: 881 E Johnstown Rd, Gahanna, Ohio 43230-1851 **Tel:** 1 614 855-9171.
Email: theriver@1049theriver.com
Web site: http://www.riverradio.com
Profile: WZNP-FM is a non-commercial station owned by One Connection Media Group. The format of the station is adult contemporary Christian. WZNP-FM broadcasts to the Newark, OH area at 89.3 FM.
FM RADIO STATION

WZNS-FM 43479
Owner: Cumulus Media Inc.
Editorial: 225 Hollywood Blvd NW, Fort Walton Beach, Florida 32548-4725 **Tel:** 1 850 243-7676.
Web site: http://www.z96.com
Profile: WZNS-FM is a commercial station owned by Cumulus Media Inc. The format of the station is Top 40 music, consisting of contemporary pop and rock. WZNS-FM's tagline is "Z-96."
FM RADIO STATION

WZNX-FM 41894
Owner: Cromwell Group Inc.(The)
Editorial: 410 N Water St, Ste B, Decatur, Illinois 62523-2371 **Tel:** 1 217 428-4487.
Web site: http://www.1067thefox.com
Profile: WZNX-FM is a commercial station owned by The Cromwell Group Inc. The format of the station is classic rock. WZNX-FM broadcasts to the Decatur, IL area at 106.7 FM.
FM RADIO STATION

WZNZ-AM 37138
Owner: Queen of Peace Radio, Inc.
Editorial: 7235 Bonneval Rd, Jacksonville, Florida 32256-7591 **Tel:** 1 904 470-4615.
Email: feedback@1600thebeach.com
Web site: http://www.1600thebeach.com
Profile: WZNZ-AM is a commercial station owned by Queen of Peace Radio, Inc. WZNZ-AM broadcasts to the Jacksonville Beach, FL area at 1600 AM.
AM RADIO STATION

WZOB-AM 35791
Owner: Central Broadcasting Inc.
Editorial: 1605 Roland Walls Dr., Fort Payne, Alabama 35967-0748 **Tel:** 1 256 845-2810.
Email: 1250wzobam@gmail.com
Profile: WZOB-AM is a commercial station owned by Central Broadcasting Inc. The format of the station is classic country. WZOB-AM broadcasts to the Fort Payne, AL area at 1250 AM.
AM RADIO STATION

WZOC-FM 45414
Owner: Mid-West Family Broadcasting
Editorial: 1301 E Douglas Rd, Mishawaka, Indiana 46545-1732 **Tel:** 1 574 233-3141.
Web site: http://www.z943radio.com
Profile: WZOC-FM is a commercial station owned by Mid-West Family Broadcasting. The format of the station is oldies. WZOC-FM broadcasts to the Plymouth, IN area at 94.3 FM.
FM RADIO STATION

WZOE-AM 38300
Owner: WZOE Inc.
Editorial: 2209 S Main St, Princeton, Illinois 61356-9179 **Tel:** 1 815 875-8014.
Email: newsroom@wzoe.com
Web site: http://www.wzoe.com
Profile: WZOE-AM is a commercial station owned by WZOE Inc. The format of the station is news and talk. WZOE-AM broadcasts to the Princeton, IL area at 1490 AM.
AM RADIO STATION

WZOE-FM 45655
Owner: WZOE Inc.
Editorial: 2209 S Main St, Princeton, Illinois 61356-9179 **Tel:** 1 815 875-8014.
Email: newsroom@wzoe.com
Web site: http://www.wzoe.com
Profile: WZOE-FM is a commercial station owned by WZOE Inc. The format of the station is classic hits. WZOE-FM broadcasts to the Princeton, IL area at 98.1 FM.
FM RADIO STATION

WZOK-FM 45656
Owner: Cumulus Media Inc.
Editorial: 3901 Brendenwood Rd, Rockford, Illinois 61107 **Tel:** 1 815 399-2233.
Web site: http://www.97zokonline.com
Profile: WZOK-FM is a commercial station owned by Cumulus Media Inc. The format of the station is Top 40/CHR music. WZOK-FM broadcasts in the Rockford, IL area at 97.5 FM.
FM RADIO STATION

WZOM-FM 46620
Owner: iHeartMedia Inc.
Editorial: 2110 Radio Dr, Defiance, Ohio 43512-1977
Tel: 1 419 782-8126.
Web site: http://www.1057thebull.com
Profile: WZOM-FM is a commercial station owned by iHeartMedia Inc. The format of the station is contemporary country. WZOM-FM broadcasts to the Defiance, OH area at 105.7 FM.
FM RADIO STATION

WZON-AM 35792
Owner: Zone Corporation(The)
Editorial: 861 Broadway, Bangor, Maine 04401-2916
Tel: 1 207 990-2800.
Web site: http://www.zoneradio.com
Profile: WZON-AM is a commercial station owned by The Zone Corporation. The format of the station is news/talk. WZON-AM broadcasts to the Bangor, ME area at 620 AM.
AM RADIO STATION

WZOO-AM 35793
Owner: Faith Enterprises, Inc.
Editorial: 2641 Lazy Pine Rd, Randleman, North Carolina 27317-7542 **Tel:** 1 336 672-0944.
Email: info@wzooradio.com
Web site: http://www.wzooradio.com
Profile: WZOO-AM is a commercial station owned by Faith Enterprises, Inc. The format of the station is classic hits. WZOO-AM broadcasts to the Randleman, NC area at 710 AM.
AM RADIO STATION

WZOO-FM 40957
Owner: Media One Group
Editorial: 3226 Jefferson Rd, Ashtabula, Ohio 44004
Tel: 1 440 993-2126.
Web site: http://www.magicoldies1025.com
Profile: WZOO-FM is a commercial station owned by Media One Group. The format of the station is oldies. WZOO-FM broadcasts in the Ashtabula, OH area at 102.5 FM.
FM RADIO STATION

WZOR-FM 43706
Owner: Woodward Communications, Inc.
Editorial: 2800 E College Ave, Appleton, Wisconsin 54915 **Tel:** 1 920 734-9226.
Email: razor@wcinet.com
Web site: http://www.razor947.com
Profile: WZOR-FM is a commercial station owned by Woodward Communications, Inc. The format is rock alternative. WZOR-FM broadcasts to the Appleton, WI area at 94.7 FM.
FM RADIO STATION

WZOT-AM 36427
Editorial: 602 W Elm St, Rockmart, Georgia 30153-1734 **Tel:** 1 770 684-7849.
Email: info@wzotradio.com
Web site: http://wzotradio.com
Profile: WZOT-AM is a commercial station. The format of the station is classic country. WZOT-AM broadcasts to the Rockmart, GA area at 1220 AM.
AM RADIO STATION

WZOZ-FM 40917
Owner: Townsquare Media, LLC
Editorial: 34 Chestnut St, Oneonta, New York 13820-2466 **Tel:** 1 607 432-1030.
Email: cnynews@townsquaremedia.com
Web site: http://www.wzozfm.com
Profile: WZOZ-FM is a commercial station owned by Townsquare Media, LLC. The format of the station is classic hits. WZOZ-FM broadcasts to the Oneonta, NY area at 103.1 FM.
FM RADIO STATION

WZPL-FM 40918
Owner: Entercom Communications Corp.
Editorial: 9245 N Meridian St Ste 300, Indianapolis, Indiana 46260-1832 **Tel:** 1 317 816-4000.
Email: indypsa@entercom.com
Web site: http://www.wzpl.com
Profile: WZPL-FM is a commercial station owned by Entercom Communications Corp. The format for the station is hot adult contemporary music. WZPL-FM broadcasts to the Indianapolis area at 99.5 FM.
FM RADIO STATION

WZPN-FM 40836
Owner: Advanced Media Partners LLC
Editorial: 2006 W Altorfer Dr, Peoria, Illinois 61615-1864 **Tel:** 1 309 691-0101.
Web site: http://espnpeoria.com
Profile: WZPN-FM is a commercial station owned by Advanced Media Partners LLC. The format of the station is sports. WZPN-FM broadcasts to the Peoria, IL area at 96.5 FM.
FM RADIO STATION

WZPR-FM 139150
Owner: Max Radio of the Carolinas
Editorial: 103 W. Woodhull Dr., Ste E, Nags Head, North Carolina 27959 **Tel:** 1 252 480-4465.
Web site: http://www.yourclassicrock.com
Profile: WZPR-FM is a commercial station owned by Max Radio of the Carolinas. The format of the station is classic rock. WZPR-FM broadcasts to the Wanchese, NC area at 92.3 FM.
FM RADIO STATION

WZPS-AM 39426
Owner: Mortenson Broadcasting Co.
Editorial: 703 3rd Ave, Huntington, West Virginia 25701-1421 **Tel:** 1 304 525-5141.
Web site: http://www.spirit1200.com/Listen.html
Profile: WZPS-AM is a commercial station owned by Mortenson Broadcasting Co. The format of the station is Gospel Music. WZPS-AM broadcasts to the Huntington, WV area at 1200 AM. Its sister station is WEMM-FM 107.9. Direct all PSAs to the Program Director.
AM RADIO STATION

WZPW-FM 42601
Owner: Cumulus Media Inc.
Editorial: 120 Eaton St, Peoria, Illinois 61603-4217
Tel: 1 309 676-5000.
Web site: http://www.powerpeoria.com
Profile: WZPW-FM is a commercial station owned by Cumulus Media Inc. The format of the station is rhythmic Top 40/CHR. WZPW-FM broadcasts to the Peoria, IL area at 92.3 FM.
FM RADIO STATION

WZQQ-AM 37976
Owner: Mountain Broadcasting Service
Editorial: 516 Main St, Hazard, Kentucky 41701-1775
Tel: 1 606 436-2121.
Email: wsgsfm@windstream.net
Web site: http://wsgs.com
Profile: WZQQ-AM is a commercial station owned by Mountain Broadcasting Service. The format of the station is classic rock. WZQQ-AM broadcasts to the Hazard, KY area at 1390 AM.
AM RADIO STATION

WZQZ-AM 36845
Owner: HS Production Inc.
Editorial: 10143 Commerce St, Summerville, Georgia 30747-1356 **Tel:** 1 706 859-1180.
Email: chattooga1180am@hotmail.com
Web site: http://www.chattoogainfo.com
Profile: WZQZ-AM is a commercial station owned by HS Production Inc. The format of the station is classic country. WZQZ-AM broadcasts to the Summerville, GA area at 1180 AM.
AM RADIO STATION

WZRC-AM 36200
Owner: Multicultural Radio Broadcasting Inc.
Editorial: 27 William St #11F, New York, New York 10005-2701 **Tel:** 1 212 431-4300.
Email: am1480program@mrbi.com
Web site: http://www.nyam1480.com
Profile: WZRC-AM is a commercial station owned by Multicultural Radio Broadcasting Inc. The format of the station is Cantonese news and talk. WZRC-AM broadcasts to the New York area at 1480 AM.
AM RADIO STATION

WZRH-FM 41830
Owner: Cumulus Media Inc.
Editorial: 201 Saint Charles Ave Ste 201, New Orleans, Louisiana 70170-1017 **Tel:** 1 504 581-7002.
Web site: http://www.1061theunderground.com
Profile: WZRH-FM is a commercial station owned by Cumulus Media Inc. The format of the station is Modern Rock. WZRH-FM broadcasts to the New Orleans area at 106.1 FM.
FM RADIO STATION

WZRN-FM 526942
Owner: Pathway Christian Academy, Inc.
Editorial: 232 Roanoke Ave Ste A, Roanoke Rapids, North Carolina 27870-1916 **Tel:** 1 252 308-0885.
Email: info@gomixradio.org
Web site: http://www.gomixradio.org/contact-us/
Profile: WZRN-FM is a non-commercial station owned by Pathway Christian Academy, Inc. The format of the station is contemporary christian. WZRN-FM broadcasts to the Roanoke and Norlina, NC areas at 90.5 FM. Send PSA's to the main email address.
FM RADIO STATION

WZRR-FM 46002
Owner: Cumulus Media Inc
Editorial: 244 Goodwin Crest Dr Ste 300, Birmingham, Alabama 35209-3700 **Tel:** 1 205 945-4646.
Web site: http://www.995nashicon.com
Profile: WZRR-FM is a commercial station owned by Cumulus Media Inc. The format of the station is Country. WZRR-FM broadcasts to the Birmingham, AL area at 99.5 FM.
FM RADIO STATION

WZRT-FM 46063
Owner: Pamal Broadcasting Ltd.
Editorial: 67 Merchants Row, Rutland, Vermont 05701-5910 **Tel:** 1 802 775-5597.
Web site: http://www.z971.com
Profile: WZRT-FM is a commercial station owned by Pamal Broadcasting Ltd. The format of the station is Top 40/CHR. WZRT-FM broadcasts to the Rutland, VT area at 97.1 FM.
FM RADIO STATION

United States of America

WZRU-FM 43299
Owner: Roanoke Valley Communications Inc.
Editorial: 232 Roanoke Ave Ste A, Roanoke Rapids, North Carolina 27870-1916 **Tel:** 1 252 308-0885.
Email: wago@gomixradio.org
Web site: http://www.gomixradio.org
Profile: WZRU-FM is a non-commercial station owned by Roanoke Valley Communications Inc. The format of the station is contemporary Christian. WZRU-FM broadcasts to the Roanoke, NC area at 90.1 FM. Send PSA's to the main email address.
FM RADIO STATION

WZRV-FM 45173
Owner: Royal Broadcasting Inc.
Editorial: 1106 Elm St, Front Royal, Virginia 22630 **Tel:** 1 540 635-4121.
Web site: http://www.theriver953online.com
Profile: WZRV-FM is a commercial station owned by Royal Broadcasting Inc. The format of the station is classic hits. WZRV-FM broadcasts in the Front Royal, VA area at 95.3 FM.
FM RADIO STATION

WZRX-FM 42636
Owner: iHeartMedia Inc.
Editorial: 667 W Market St, Lima, Ohio 45801-4603 **Tel:** 1 419 223-2060.
Web site: http://www.wzrxfm.com
Profile: WZRX-FM is a commercial station owned by iHeartMedia Inc. The format of the station is rock music. WZRX-FM broadcasts to the Lima, OH area at a frequency of 107.5 FM.
FM RADIO STATION

WZSK-AM 38614
Owner: New Millennium Communications Group
Editorial: 151 E 1st Ave, Everett, Pennsylvania 15537-1351 **Tel:** 1 814 652-2600.
Email: wzsk@penn.com
Profile: WZSK-AM is a commercial station owned by the New Millennium Communications Group. The format of the station is news and talk. WZSK-AM broadcasts to the Everett, PA area at 1040 AM.
AM RADIO STATION

WZSN-FM 45723
Owner: Broomfield Broadcasting LLC
Editorial: 210 Montague Ave, Greenwood, South Carolina 29649 **Tel:** 1 864 223-4300.
Email: sunny@sunny103-5.com
Web site: http://www.sunny103-5.com
Profile: WZSN-FM is a commercial station owned by Broomfield Broadcasting LLC. The format for the station is soft adult contemporary. WZSN-FM broadcasts to the Greenwood, SC area at 103.5 FM.
FM RADIO STATION

WZSP-FM 44073
Owner: Solmart Media, LLC
Editorial: 7891 US Highway 17 S, Zolfo Springs, Florida 33890-4728 **Tel:** 1 863 494-4111.
Email: info@lazeta.fm
Web site: http://www.lazeta.fm
Profile: WZSP-FM is a commercial station owned by Solmart Media, LLC. The station's format is Hispanic. WZSP-FM broadcasts to the Zolfo Springs, FL area at 105.3 FM.
FM RADIO STATION

WZSR-FM 45631
Owner: Matrix Broadcasting
Editorial: 8800 US Highway 14, Crystal Lake, Illinois 60012-2740 **Tel:** 1 815 459-7000.
Web site: http://www.star105.com
Profile: WZSR-FM is a commerical station owned by Matrix Broadcasting. The format of the station is adult contemporary music. WZSR-FM broadcasts to Crystal Lake, IL and the far northwest suburbs of Chicago at 105.5 FM.
FM RADIO STATION

WZST-FM 40534
Owner: Spectrum Radio Group, LLC
Tel: 1 301 802-1250.
Web site: http://www.spectrumradiogroup.com
Profile: WZST-FM is a commercial station owned by Spectrum Radio Group, LLC. The format of the station is hot adult contemporary. WZST-FM broadcasts to the Fairmont, WV area at 100.9 FM
FM RADIO STATION

WZTA-AM 36577
Owner: iHeartMedia Inc.
Editorial: 3771 SE Jennings Rd, Port Saint Lucie, Florida 34952-7702 **Tel:** 1 772 335-9300.
Web site: http://www.waxe1370.com/main.html
Profile: WZTA-AM is a commercial station owned by iHeartMedia Inc. The format of the station is talk. WZTA-AM broadcasts to the Fort Pierce, FL area at 1370 AM.
AM RADIO STATION

WZTF-FM 42371
Owner: iHeartMedia Inc.
Editorial: 181 E Evans St Ste 311, Florence, South Carolina 29506-5505 **Tel:** 1 843 667-4600.
Web site: http://theflo1029.com/#&panel1-1
Profile: WZTF-FM is a commercial station owned by iHeartMedia Inc. The format of the station is urban adult contemporary. WWRK-FM broadcasts to the Florence, SC, area at 102.9 FM.
FM RADIO STATION

WZTI-AM 36629
Owner: Milwaukee Radio Alliance
Editorial: N72W12922 Good Hope Rd, Menomonee Falls, Wisconsin 53051-4441 **Tel:** 1 414 778-1933.
Web site: http://www.milwaukeesparty.com
Profile: WZTI-AM is a commercial station owned by Milwaukee Radio Alliance. The format of the station is oldies. WZTI-AM broadcasts to the Milwaukee area at 1290 AM.
AM RADIO STATION

WZTK-FM 924734
Owner: Midwestern Broadcasting Co.
Editorial: 123 Prentiss St, Alpena, Michigan 49707-2831 **Tel:** 1 989 354-8400.
Email: watz@watz.com
Web site: http://www.watz.com/WZTK.php
Profile: WZTK-FM is a commercial station owned by the Midwestern Broadcasting Co. The format of the station is news, talk, and sports. The station broadcasts locally to the Alpena, MI area at 105.7 FM.
FM RADIO STATION

WZTR-FM 43123
Owner: Ridgeline Communications, LLC
Editorial: 1376 Ben Higgins Rd, Dahlonega, Georgia 30533-5262 **Tel:** 1 706 867-1043.
Email: info@thunder1043fm.com
Web site: http://www.thunder1043fm.com
Profile: WZTR-FM is a commercial station owned by Ridgeline Communications, LLC. The format of the station is country and classic rock, with a focus on Americana. WZTR-FM broadcasts to the Dahlonega, GA area at 104.3 FM.
FM RADIO STATION

WZTU-FM 46010
Owner: iHeartMedia Inc.
Editorial: 7601 Riviera Blvd, Miramar, Florida 33023-6574 **Tel:** 1 305 503-0069.
Web site: http://tu949fm.iheart.com
Profile: WZTU-FM is a commercial station owned by iHeartMedia Inc. The format of the station is Hispanic Top 40/CHR music. WZTU-FM broadcasts to the Miramar, FL area at 94.9 FM.
FM RADIO STATION

WZUM-AM 35269
Owner: Pittsburgh Public Media
Editorial: 4736 Penn Ave, Pittsburgh, Pennsylvania 15224-1341 **Tel:** 1 203 323-7300.
Web site: http://www.wyzr.org/
Profile: WZUM-AM is a commercial station owned by Pittsburgh Public Media. The format of the station is jazz. WZUM-AM broadcasts to the Greater Pittsburgh area at 1550 AM.
AM RADIO STATION

WZUM-FM 40802
Owner: Pittsburgh Public Media
Tel: 1 202 370-6627.
Email: info@pittsburghpublicmedia.org
Web site: http://www.pghjazzchannel.org
Profile: WZUM-FM is a non-commercial station owned by Pittsburgh Public Media. The format of the station is jazz. WZUM-FM broadcasts locally at 88.1 FM.
FM RADIO STATION

WZUN-FM 42895
Owner: Galaxy Communications LP
Editorial: 235 Walton St, Syracuse, New York 13202-1226 **Tel:** 1 315 472-9111.
Email: asksunny@thesunnyspot.com
Web site: http://www.thesunnyspot.com
Profile: WZUN-FM is a commercial station owned by Galaxy Communications LP. The format of the station is classic hits. WZUN-FM broadcasts to the Syracuse, NY area at 102.1 FM.
FM RADIO STATION

WZUS-FM 41920
Owner: Cromwell Group Inc.(The)
Editorial: 410 N Water St Ste C, Decatur, Illinois 62523-2372 **Tel:** 1 217 450-8255.
Web site: http://www.decaturradio.com
Profile: WZUS-FM is a commercial radio station owned by Comwell Group Inc. The format of the station is talk. WZUS-FM broadcasts to the Decatur, IL area at 100.9 FM.
FM RADIO STATION

WZUU-FM 41758
Owner: Forum Communications Co.
Editorial: 706 E Allegan St, Otsego, Michigan 49078-1306 **Tel:** 1 269 343-1717.
Email: NEWS@WQXC.COM
Web site: http://www.wzuu.com
Profile: WZUU-FM is a commercial station owned by Forum Communications Co. The format of the station is rock music. WZUU-FM broadcasts to the Otsego, MI area at 92.5 FM.
FM RADIO STATION

WZVA-FM 43514
Owner: Mountain Empire Media, LLC
Editorial: 405 N Main St, Marion, Virginia 24354-3325 **Tel:** 1 276 783-4042.
Web site: http://www.1035thundercountry.com
Profile: WZVA-FM is a commercial station owned by Mountain Empire Media, LLC. The format of the station is contemporary hit radio. WZVA-FM broadcasts to the Marion, VA area at 103.5 FM.
FM RADIO STATION

WZVL-FM 45199
Owner: Southeastern Ohio Broadcasting, Inc.
Editorial: 629 Downard Rd, Zanesville, Ohio 43701-5108 **Tel:** 1 740 452-5431.
Email: webmaster@whizamfmtv.com
Web site: http://www.whiznews.com
Profile: WZVL-FM is a commercial station owned by Southeastern Ohio Broadcasting. The format of the station is contemporary country. WZVL-FM broadcasts to the Baltimore, OH and surrounding areas at 103.7 FM.
FM RADIO STATION

WZVN-FM 41394
Owner: Adams Radio Group
Editorial: 2755 Sager Rd, Valparaiso, Indiana 46383-0721 **Tel:** 1 219 462-6111.
Email: news@argni.com
Web site: http://www.z1071.com
Profile: WZVN-FM is a commercial station owned by Adams Radio Group. The format of the station is adult contemporary. WZVN-FM broadcasts to the Valparaiso, IN area at 107.1 FM.
FM RADIO STATION

WZWP-FM 624515
Owner: One Connection Media Group
Editorial: 881 E Johnstown Rd, Gahanna, Ohio 43230-1852 **Tel:** 1 614 855-9171.
Email: theriver@1049theriver.com
Web site: http://www.riverradio.com
Profile: WZWP-FM is a non-commercial station owned by One Connection Media Group. The format of the station is adult contemporary Christian. WZWP-FM broadcasts to the West Union, OH area at 89.3 FM.
FM RADIO STATION

WZWW-FM 41668
Owner: First Media Radio LLC
Editorial: 160 W Clearview Ave, State College, Pennsylvania 16803-1617 **Tel:** 1 814 231-0953.
Web site: http://www.3wz.com
Profile: WZWW-FM is a commercial station owned by First Media Radio LLC. The format for the station is hot adult contemporary. WZWW-FM broadcasts to the Johnstown-Altoona, PA area at 95.3 FM.
FM RADIO STATION

WZWZ-FM 46378
Owner: Hoosier AM/FM LLC
Editorial: 671 E 400 S, Kokomo, Indiana 46902 **Tel:** 1 765 453-1212.
Email: kokomoradiotraffic@att.net
Web site: http://www.z925fm.com
Profile: WZWZ-FM is a commercial station owned by Hoosier AM/FM LLC. The format of the station is adult contemporary. WZWZ-FM broadcasts to the Kokomo, IN area at 92.5 FM.
FM RADIO STATION

WZXL-FM 46243
Owner: Equity Communications LP
Editorial: 8025 Black Horse Pike, Ste 100, Pleasantville, New Jersey 8232 **Tel:** 1 609 484-8444.
Web site: http://www.wzxl.com
Profile: WZXL-FM is a commercial station owned by Equity Communications LP. The format of the station is classic rock. WZXL-FM broadcasts to the Pleasantville, NJ area at 100.7 FM.
FM RADIO STATION

WZXM-FM 489907
Owner: Four Rivers Community Broadcasting Corp.
Editorial: 746 Route 113, Souderton, Pennsylvania 18964-1004 **Tel:** 1 215 721-2141.
Email: wordfm@wordfm.org
Web site: http://www.wordfm.org
Profile: WZXM-FM is a non-commercial station owned by Four Rivers Community Broadcasting Corp. The format of the station is Christian Contemporary. WZXM-FM broadcasts to the Harrisburg, PA area at 88.1 FM.
FM RADIO STATION

WZXR-FM 43293
Owner: Backyard Broadcasting
Editorial: 1685 Four Mile Dr, Williamsport, Pennsylvania 17701-1975 **Tel:** 1 570 323-8200.
Web site: http://www.wzxr.com
Profile: WZXR-FM is a commercial station owned by Backyard Broadcasting. The station's format is classic rock music. WZXR-FM broadcasts to the Susquehanna Valley at 99.3 FM.
FM RADIO STATION

WZXV-FM 42095
Owner: Calvery Chapel of the Finger Lakes
Editorial: 1777 Rochester Rd, Farmington, New York 14425-9619 **Tel:** 1 585 398-3569.
Email: manager@wzxv.org
Web site: http://www.wzxv.org
Profile: WZXV-FM is a non-commercial station owned by Calvery Chapel of the Finger Lakes. The format of the station is religion. WZXV-FM broadcasts to the Rochester, NY area at 99.7 FM.
FM RADIO STATION

WZYP-FM 46406
Owner: Cumulus Media Inc.
Editorial: 1717 US Highway 72 E, Athens, Alabama 35611 **Tel:** 1 256 830-8300.
Web site: http://www.wzyp.com
Profile: WZYP-FM is a commercial station owned by Cumulus Media Inc. The format of the station is Top 40/CHR. WZYP-FM broadcasts to the Huntsville, AL area at 104.3 FM.
FM RADIO STATION

WZYX-AM 35794
Owner: Wiseman Media
Editorial: 540 Cumberland St W, Cowan, Tennessee 37318-3115 **Tel:** 1 931 967-7471.
Web site: http://www.wzyxradio.net
Profile: WZYX-AM is a commercial station owned by Wiseman Media. The format of the station is adult hits. WZYX-AM broadcasts to the Cowan, TN area at 1440 AM.
AM RADIO STATION

WZZA-AM 35795
Owner: Muscle Shoals Broadcasting
Editorial: 1570 Woodmont Dr, Tuscumbia, Alabama 35674-3850 **Tel:** 1 256 381-1862.
Web site: http://www.wzzaradio.com
Profile: WZZA-AM is a commercial station owned by Muscle Shoals Broadcasting. The format for the station is gospel and R&B. WZZA-AM broadcasts to the Huntsville, AL area at 1410 AM.
AM RADIO STATION

WZZB-AM 37931
Owner: Midnight Hour Broadcasting, LLC
Editorial: 1534 N Ewing St, Seymour, Indiana 47274-1121 **Tel:** 1 812 522-1390.
Web site: http://wzzb1390.com
Profile: WZZB-AM is a commercial station owned by Midnight Hour Broadcasting, LLC. The format of the station is adult contemporary. WZZB-AM broadcasts to the Seymour, IN area at 1390 AM.
AM RADIO STATION

WZZH-FM 537768
Owner: Four Rivers Community Broadcasting Corp
Editorial: 746 Route 113, Souderton, Pennsylvania 18964-1004 **Tel:** 1 215 721-2141.
Email: wordfm@wordfm.org
Web site: http://www.wordfm.org
Profile: WZZH-FM is a non-commercial station owned by Four Rivers Community Broadcasting Corp. The format of the station is contemporary Christian music and talk. WZZH-FM broadcasts to the Scranton, PA and surrounding areas at 90.9 FM.
FM RADIO STATION

WZZI-FM 44269
Owner: Todd P. Robinson, Inc.
Editorial: 19 Wadsworth St Ste C, Lynchburg, Virginia 24501-2633 **Tel:** 1 434 845-3698.
Web site: http://www.lynchburgradiogroup.com
Profile: WZZI-FM is a commercial station owned by Todd P. Robinson, Inc. The format of the station is hot adult contemporary. WZZI-FM broadcasts to the Lynchburg, VA area at 106.9 FM.
FM RADIO STATION

WZZK-FM 43696
Owner: Summit Media Broadcasting LLC
Editorial: 2700 Corporate Dr Ste 115, Birmingham, Alabama 35242-2735 **Tel:** 1 205 916-1100.
Web site: http://www.wzzk.com
Profile: WZZK-FM is a commercial station owned by Summit Media Broadcasting LLC. The format of the station is classic country. WZZK-FM broadcasts to the Birmingham, AL area at 104.7 FM.
FM RADIO STATION

WZZL-FM 42375
Owner: Withers Broadcasting of Paducah, LLC
Editorial: 1700 N 8th St, Paducah, Kentucky 42001-1752 **Tel:** 1 270 538-5272.
Email: prod@withersradio.net
Web site: http://www.wzzl.com
Profile: WZZL-FM is a commercial station owned by Withers Broadcasting of Paducah, LLC. The format of the station is rock. WZZL-FM broadcasts to the Paducah, KY area at 106.7 FM.
FM RADIO STATION

WZZN-FM 43780
Owner: Great South Wireless, LLC
Editorial: 108 Woodson St NW, Huntsville, Alabama 35801-5521 **Tel:** 1 256 382-0724.
Email: radio7933@aol.com
Web site: http://www.977thezone.com
Profile: WZZN-FM is a commercial station owned by Great South Wireless, LLC. The format of the station is sports talk. WZZN-FM broadcasts to the Huntsville, AL area at a frequency of 97.7 FM.
FM RADIO STATION

WZZO-FM 42273
Owner: iHeartMedia Inc.
Editorial: 1541 Alta Dr Ste 400, Whitehall, Pennsylvania 18052-5632 **Tel:** 1 610 434-1742.
Email: studio@wzzo.com
Web site: http://www.951zzo.com/
Profile: WZZO-FM is a commercial station owned by iHeartMedia Inc. The format of the station is rock. WZZO-FM broadcasts to the Whitehall, PA area at 95.1 FM.
FM RADIO STATION

WZZP-FM 81032
Owner: Saga Communications
Editorial: 1640 Old Russellville Pike, Clarksville, Tennessee 37043-1709 **Tel:** 1 931 648-7720.
Web site: http://www.z975.com
Profile: WZZP-FM is a commercial station owned by Saga Communications (dba 5 Star Radio Group). The format of the station is rock music. WZZP-FM broadcasts to the Nashville, TN area at 97.5 FM.
FM RADIO STATION

WZZQ-AM 37779
Owner: Fowler Broadcast Communications, Inc
Editorial: 340 Providence Rd, Gaffney, South Carolina
29341-2006 Tel: 1 864 489-9066.
Web site: http://wzzqradio.com
Profile: WZZQ-AM is a commercial station owned by
Fowler Broadcast Communications, Inc. The format
of the station is contemporary country. WZZQ-AM
broadcasts to the Gaffney, SC area at 1500 AM.
AM RADIO STATION

WZZR-FM 40566
Owner: iHeartMedia Inc.
Editorial: 3071 Continental Dr, West Palm Beach,
Florida 33407-3274 Tel: 1 561 616-6600.
Web site: http://www.wzzr.com
Profile: WZZR-FM is a commercial station owned by
iHeartMedia Inc. The format of the station is talk.
WZZR-FM broadcasts to the West Palm Beach, FL,
area at 94.3 FM.
FM RADIO STATION

WZZS-FM 42305
Owner: Solmart Media, LLC
Editorial: 7891 US Highway 17 S, Zolfo Springs,
Florida 33890-4728 Tel: 1 863 494-4111.
Web site: http://lanumero1.fm
Profile: WZZS-FM is a commercial station owned by
Solmart Media, LLC. The format of the station is
Mexican Regional Dance. WZZS-FM broadcasts to
the Zolfo Springs, FL area at 106.9 FM.
FM RADIO STATION

WZZT-FM 42714
Owner: Withers Broadcasting Co.
Editorial: 3101 Freeport Rd, Sterling, Illinois 61081-
9612 Tel: 1 815 625-3400.
Email: wsdr1240@theramp.net
Profile: WZZT-FM is a commercial station owned by
Withers Broadcasting Co. The format of the station is
classic country. WZZT-FM broadcasts to the Sterling,
IL area at 102.7 FM.
FM RADIO STATION

WZZU-FM 42730
Owner: Mel Wheeler Broadcasting, Inc.
Editorial: 19 Wadsworth St Ste C, Lynchburg, Virginia
24501-2633 Tel: 1 434 845-3698.
Web site: http://www.rocktheplanet.fm
FM RADIO STATION

WZZW-AM 39249
Owner: iHeartMedia Inc.
Editorial: 134 4th Ave, Huntington, West Virginia
25701-1220 Tel: 1 304 525-7788.
Web site: http://www.800wvhu.com
Profile: WZZW-AM is a commercial station owned by
iHeartMedia Inc. The format for the station is news
and talk. WZZW-AM broadcasts to the Charleston-
Huntington, WV area at 1600 AM.
AM RADIO STATION

WZZY-FM 40922
Owner: Whitewater Broadcasting
Editorial: 2301 W Main St, Richmond, Indiana 47374
Tel: 1 765 962-6533.
Email: news@todaysmusicmix.com
Web site: http://www.todaysmusicmix.com
Profile: WZZY-FM is a commercial station owned by
Whitewater Broadcasting. The format of the station is
adult contemporary music. WZZY-FM broadcasts in
the Richmond, IN area at 98.3.
FM RADIO STATION

WZZZ-FM 969043
Owner: Hometown Broadcasting, Inc.
Editorial: 110 S Main St, Royal Oak, Michigan 48067-
3630
Profile: WZZZ-FM is a commercial station owned by
Hometown Broadcasting, Inc.. The format for the
station is Classic Rock. WZZZ-FM broadcasts to the
Portsmouth, OH area at 107.5 FM.
FM RADIO STATION

XEMO-AM 38745
Owner: Uniradio Corp.
Editorial: 5030 Camino De La Siesta, Ste 403, San
Diego, California 92108-3120 Tel: 1 619 497-0600.
Web site: http://www.uniradio.com
Profile: XEMO-AM is a commercial station owned by
Grupo Uniradio Corp. The format of the station is
regional Mexican. XEMO-AM broadcasts to the San
Diego area at 860 AM.
AM RADIO STATION

XEPE-AM 358652
Owner: Broadcast Company of the Americas
Editorial: 6160 Cornerstone Ct E Ste 100, San Diego,
California 92121-3724 Tel: 1 858 535-2500.
Web site: http://www.espn1700.com
Profile: XEPE-AM is a commercial station owned by
Broadcast Company of the Americas. The format of
the station is sports. XEPE-AM broadcasts in the San
Diego area at 1700 AM.
AM RADIO STATION

XERCN-AM 404261
Owner: Grupo Uniradio Corp.
Editorial: 5030 Camino De La Siesta Ste 403, San
Diego, California 92108-3120 Tel: 1 664 683-5288
40.
Web site: http://www.uniradioinforma.com/
uniradio1470/main.php
Profile: XERCN-AM is a commercial station owned
by Grupo Uniradio Corp. The format of the station is
Hispanic news, talk, sports, and entertainment

programming. XERCN-AM broadcasts to the San
Diego-Tijuana area at 1470 AM.
AM RADIO STATION

XEWW-AM 36689
Owner: GLR Southern California Inc.
Editorial: 3500 W Olive Ave Ste 250, Burbank,
California 91505-5526 Tel: 1 818 972-4200.
Web site: http://www.wradio690.com
Profile: XEWW-AM is a commercial station owned by
GLR Southern California Inc. The format of the station
is Hispanic talk. XEWW-AM broadcasts to the Los
Angeles area at 690 AM.
AM RADIO STATION

XEXX-AM 36040
Owner: Radiorama, S.A. de C.V.
Editorial: 353 3rd Ave, Ste 201, Chula Vista, California
91910 Tel: 1 619 427-1420.
Profile: XEXX-AM is a commercial station owned by
Radiorama, S.A. de C.V. The format of the station is
Hispanic news, talk and sports. XEXX-AM broadcasts
to the San Diego area at 1420 AM.
AM RADIO STATION

XHFG-FM 46090
Owner: Grupo Uniradio Corp.
Editorial: 5030 Camino De La Siesta, Ste 403, San
Diego, California 92108 Tel: 1 619 497-0600.
Web site: http://www.pulsarfm.com
Profile: XHFG-FM is a commercial station owned by
Grupo Uniradio Corp. The format of the station is
Spanish and English Top 40/CHR. XHFG-FM
broadcasts to the San Diego area at 107.3 FM.
FM RADIO STATION

XHNK-FM 139726
Owner: Grupo Radiorama
Editorial: 1510 Calle Del Norte Ste 2, Laredo, Texas
78041-6048 Tel: 1 956 727-3670.
Email: grupo@radiorama.com.mx
Web site: http://www.radiorama.com
Profile: XHNK-FM is a commercial station owned by
Grupo Radiorama. The format of the station is
Spanish and English Top 40/CHR. XHNK-FM
broadcasts to the Laredo, TX and Nuevo Laredo,
Tamaulipas, Mexico areas at a frequency of 99.3 FM.
FM RADIO STATION

XHPX-FM 595079
Owner: Mvs Radio
Editorial: 5862 Cromo Dr Ste 151, El Paso, Texas
79912-5510 Tel: 1 915 231-5500.
Web site: http://www.exafm.com/elpaso
Profile: XHPX-FM is a commercial station owned by
Mvs Radio. The format is Hispanic adult
contemporary. The station airs to the El Paso, TX
area at 98.3 FM.
FM RADIO STATION

XHRM-FM 44081
Owner: Local Media San Diego
Editorial: 6160 Cornerstone Ct E Ste 100, San Diego,
California 92121-3724 Tel: 1 858 888-7000.
Web site: http://lmasandiego.com
Profile: XHRM-FM is a commercial station owned by
Local Media San Diego. The format of the station is
R&B oldies music. XHRM-FM broadcasts to the San
Diego area at 92.5 FM.
FM RADIO STATION

XHTY-FM 404256
Owner: Uniradio Corp.
Editorial: 5030 Camino De La Siesta, Ste 403, San
Diego, California 92108 Tel: 1 619 497-0600.
Web site: http://invasora997.com
Profile: XHTY-FM is a commercial station owned by
Uniradio Corp. The format of the station is regional
Mexican music. XHTY-FM broadcasts to the San
Diego area at 99.7 FM.
FM RADIO STATION

XHTZ-FM 41845
Owner: Local Media San Diego
Editorial: 6160 Cornerstone Ct E Ste 100, San Diego,
California 92121-3724 Tel: 1 858 535-2500.
Web site: http://www.z90.com
Profile: XHTZ-FM is a commercial station owned by
Local Media San Diego. The format of the station is
rhythmic Top 40/CHR music. XHTZ-FM broadcasts
to the San Diego area at 90.3 FM.
FM RADIO STATION

XLNC-FM 62587
Owner: XLNC1 Inc.
Editorial: 1690 Frontage Rd, Chula Vista, California
91911 Tel: 1 619 575-9090.
Email: info@xlnc1.org
Web site: http://www.hitsforever.org
Profile: XLNC-FM is a non-commercial station
owned by XLNC1 Inc. The format of the station is
classical music. XLNC-FM broadcasts at a frequency
of 104.9 FM to the San Diego / Baja California region.
FM RADIO STATION

XLTN-FM 137374
Owner: Grupo Imagen
Editorial: 2403 Hoover Ave, National City, California
91950-6619 Tel: 1 619 336-7800.
Email: envio@1045radiolatina.com
Web site: http://www.1045radiolatina.com
Profile: XLTN-FM is a commercial station owned by
Grupo Imagen. The format of the station is Hispanic
adult contemporary music. XLTN-FM broadcasts to
the National City, CA area at 104.5 FM.
FM RADIO STATION

XOCL-FM 39652
Owner: MVS Radio
Editorial: 1690 Frontage Rd, Chula Vista, California
91911-3936 Tel: 1 619 429-8702.
Web site: http://www.diego993.com
Profile: XOCL-FM is a commercial station owned by
MVS Radio. The format for the station is Spanish
oldies. XOCL-FM broadcasts to the San Diego and
Baja California areas at 99.3 FM.
FM RADIO STATION

XPRS-AM 36099
Owner: Broadcast Company of the Americas
Editorial: 6160 Cornerstone Ct E, San Diego,
California 92121-3720 Tel: 1 858 535-2500.
Web site: http://www.themighty1090.com
Profile: XPRS-AM is a commercial station owned by
Broadcast Company of the Americas. The format for
the station is sports. XPRS-AM broadcasts to the San
Diego area at 1090 AM.
AM RADIO STATION

XPRS-FM 592485
Owner: Broadcast Company of the Americas
Editorial: 6160 Cornerstone Ct E Ste 100, San Diego,
California 92121-3724 Tel: 1 858 535-2500.
Email: dmason@bcaradio.com
Web site: http://www.1057maxfm.com
Profile: XPRS-FM is a commercial station owned by
Broadcast Company of the Americas. The format of
the station is classic hits. XPRS-FM broadcasts to the
San Diego area at 105.7.
FM RADIO STATION

XSUR-AM 238625
Owner: Mount Wilson FM Broadcasters
Editorial: 1500 Cotner Ave, Los Angeles, California
90025-3303 Tel: 1 310 478-5540.
Web site: http://www.jazzandblues.org/
Profile: XSUR-AM is a commercial station owned by
Mount Wilson FM Broadcasters. The format of the
station is news and talk. XSUR-AM broadcasts to the
Los Angeles area at 540 AM.
AM RADIO STATION

XTRA-FM 45662
Owner: Local Media San Diego
Editorial: 6160 Cornerstone Ct E, Ste 100, San Diego,
California 92121-3724 Tel: 1 858 888-7000.
Web site: http://www.91x.com
Profile: XTRA-FM is a commercial station owned by
Local Media San Diego. The format of the station is
rock alternative. XTRA-FM broadcasts to the San
Diego area at 91.1 FM.
FM RADIO STATION

Yancey Agri Network 47059
Editorial: 1900 NW Expressway Ste 1000, Oklahoma
City, Oklahoma 73118-1854 Tel: 1 405 840-5271.
Profile: The network distributes agriculture, farm
news and market reports to stations in the southern
area of the United States.
REGIONAL RADIO NETWORKS

Television

¡HOLA! TV 941654
Editorial: 7291 NW 74th St, Medley, Florida 33166-
2407 Tel: 1 305 777-1900.
Web site: http://hola.tv
Profile: Covers topics covered by the magazine
¡HOLA!. Includes exclusive information from the world
of royalty and celebrities, society, designers, fashion
and more. All communications should be through
their marketing department.
TELEVISION NETWORK

ABC Television Network 33051
Owner: Walt Disney Co.
Editorial: 77 W 66th St, New York, New York 10023-
6201 Tel: 1 212 456-7777.
Email: abcnews@abcnews.com
Web site: http://abc.go.com
Profile: ABC Television Network is a national
broadcast television network providing a range of
general entertainment fare. The network airs
numerous original drama and comedy series, daytime
dramas, children's shows, theatrical film airings,
news broadcasts, public affairs forums and exclusive
sports events programming. It also provides
programming to affiliated stations nationwide.
TELEVISION NETWORK

**ABC Television Network -
Atlanta Bureau** 33107
Editorial: 3845 Pleasantdale Rd, Atlanta, Georgia
30340-4205 Tel: 1 678 245-7570.
Profile: The newsroom at ABC News in Atlanta
prefers to have items faxed to the main fax number.
TELEVISION NETWORK

**ABC Television Network -
Beijing Bureau** 721330
Editorial: 4-1-71Jianguomenwai Diplomatic Cmpd,
Chaoyang Dist, Beijing 100600 Tel: 86 10 65322671.
TELEVISION NETWORK

**ABC Television Network -
Burbank Bureau** 156209
Editorial: 500 S Buena Vista St, Burbank, California
91521-0001 Tel: 1 818 560-1000.
TELEVISION NETWORK

**ABC Television Network -
Chicago Bureau** 33091
Editorial: 190 N State St Fl 3, Chicago, Illinois 60601-
3303 Tel: 1 312 899-4015.
TELEVISION NETWORK

**ABC Television Network - Coral
Gables Bureau** 33111
Editorial: 2 Alhambra Plz Ph 1C, Coral Gables, Florida
33134-5237 Tel: 1 305 448-9036.
Email: abctv.miami.bureau@abc.com
TELEVISION NETWORK

**ABC Television Network -
Glendale Bureau** 33092
Editorial: 500 Circle Seven Dr, Glendale, California
91201-2331 Tel: 1 818 553-5500.
Email: deskabcla@gmail.com
TELEVISION NETWORK

**ABC Television Network -
Seattle Bureau** 79605
Editorial: 140 4th Ave N, Seattle, Washington 98109-
4940 Tel: 1 206 404-9112.
TELEVISION NETWORK

**ABC Television Network -
Washington Bureau** 33093
Editorial: 1717 Desales St NW, Washington, District
Of Columbia 20036-4401 Tel: 1 202 222-7700.
TELEVISION NETWORK

Azteca 135595
Editorial: 1139 Grand Central Ave, Glendale,
California 91201-2423 Tel: 1 310 432-7650.
Email: info@aztecaamerica.com
Web site: http://us.azteca.com
Profile: Azteca is TV Azteca's wholly-owned Spanish
language broadcasting network for the U.S. Hispanic
market. The network supplies TV Azteca's content,
including telenovelas, news, sports, and other
entertainment.
TELEVISION NETWORK

Azteca - New York Bureau 529412
Editorial: 1430 Broadway Fl 10, New York, New York
10018-3308 Tel: 1 646 360-1788.
Web site: http://us.azteca.com
TELEVISION NETWORK

Bounce TV 768972
Owner: Bounce Media, LLC
Editorial: 600 Galleria Pkwy SE Ste 1900, Atlanta,
Georgia 30339-5990
Email: info@bouncetv.com
Web site: http://bouncetv.com
Profile: Bounce TV is a television network that
features a programming mix of theatrical motion
pictures, live sporting events, documentaries,
specials, inspirational faith-based programs, off-net
series, original programming and more. The network
is geared towards African-American audiences. The
network launched in fall 2011.
TELEVISION NETWORK

Buckeye TV 870543
Editorial: 1849 Cannon Dr, Columbus, Ohio 43210-
1208 Tel: 1 614 247-7320.
Web site: http://buckeyetv.osu.edu
Profile: Buckeye TV is Ohio State's on-campus
television station producing OSU news and sports
content for campus channel 19 and on the Web. A
member of The Lantern Media Group.
TELEVISION STATION

CBS Television Network 33053
Owner: CBS Corporation
Editorial: 524 W 57th St, New York, New York 10019-
2930 Tel: 1 212 975-4321.
Web site: http://www.cbs.com
Profile: Nationally-distributed broadcast television
network providing a variety of news, information and
entertainment programming to over 200 local
affiliates. Assets include an extensive news reporting
and public affairs division, exclusive coverage of
major sporting events around the globe via CBS
Sports, and original first-run comedy and drama
series via CBS Entertainment.
TELEVISION NETWORK

**CBS Television Network -
Atlanta Bureau** 33109
Editorial: 817 W Peachtree St NE Ste 305, Atlanta,
Georgia 30308-1168
TELEVISION NETWORK

**CBS Television Network -
Chicago Bureau** 33120
Editorial: 22 W Washington St, Chicago, Illinois
60602-1605 Tel: 1 312 899-2121.
TELEVISION NETWORK

**CBS Television Network - China
Bureau** 953608
Editorial: Chaoyang District, Beijing
TELEVISION NETWORK

CBS Television Network - Dallas Bureau
33102
Editorial: 5001 Spring Valley Rd Ste 1060E, Dallas, Texas 75244-3960
TELEVISION NETWORK

CBS Television Network - Los Angeles Bureau
33096
Editorial: 7800 Beverly Blvd, Los Angeles, California 90036-2112 **Tel:** 1 323 575-2345.
Email: cbsla@cbsnews.com
TELEVISION NETWORK

CBS Television Network - Miami Bureau
33105
Editorial: 8900 NW 18th Ter, Doral, Florida 33172-2623 **Tel:** 1 305 571-4400.
TELEVISION NETWORK

CBS Television Network - San Francisco Bureau
33101
Editorial: 855 Battery St, San Francisco, California 94111-1503 **Tel:** 1 415 362-8177.
TELEVISION NETWORK

CBS Television Network - Washington Bureau
33095
Editorial: 2020 M St NW, Washington, District Of Columbia 20036-3304 **Tel:** 1 202 457-4321.
TELEVISION NETWORK

CGTN America
828128
Owner: China Central Television
Editorial: 1099 New York Ave NW Ste 200, Washington, District Of Columbia 20001-4889 **Tel:** 1 202 639-4747.
Web site: https://america.cgtn.com
Profile: CGTN America is a national news network affiliated with China Central Television News. The network aims to inform, engage, and provide debate on a range of issues of relevance to American and global viewers with a particular interest in China and Asia.
TELEVISION NETWORK

Cox Broadcasting Corporation
77622
Owner: Cox Media Group, Inc.
Editorial: 400 N Capitol St NW Ste 750, Washington, District Of Columbia 20001-1536 **Tel:** 1 202 777-7000.
Web site: http://www.coxenterprises.com
Profile: Cox entered the television industry in 1948 and now owns or operates 15 TV stations in 11 markets reaching 30 million viewers.
TELEVISION NETWORK

Cozi TV
860169
Owner: NBC Universal
Editorial: 30 Rockefeller Plz, New York, New York 10112-0015 **Tel:** 1 212 664-4444.
Web site: http://www.cozitv.com
Profile: Cozi TV is a digital multicast television network bringing viewers America's most beloved and iconic television series, hit movies and original programming brought to you by the NBC Owned Television Stations. Well-known shows like Magnum, P.I., The Bionic Woman, Highway to Heaven, The Lone Ranger and The Six Million Dollar Man are featured on the network. Cozi TV also airs a wide range of movies, showcasing iconic actors spanning generations, including legends Rock Hudson and Doris Day and modern day actors George Clooney and Drew Barrymore. The flagship station is WNBC-TV in New York.
TELEVISION NETWORK

CW Television Network
424735
Owner: CW Network, LLC
Editorial: 3300 W Olive Ave, Burbank, California 91505-4640 **Tel:** 1 818 977-2500.
Email: feedback@cwtv.com
Web site: http://www.cwtv.com
Profile: The CW Television Network is a joint venture of CBS Corp. and Warner Bros. The network officially launched in September 2006. The CW Network consists of a six night, 13 hour programming lineup, Sunday through Friday, with a Saturday morning animation block. Altogether the network airs 30 hours of programming over seven days.
TELEVISION NETWORK

Daystar Television Network
86391
Editorial: 3901 Highway 121, Bedford, Texas 76021-3009 **Tel:** 1 817 571-1229.
Email: contactus@daystar.com
Web site: http://www.daystar.com
Profile: The Daystar Television Network is headquartered in the greater Dallas/Fort Worth Metroplex and is a division of Word Of God Fellowship, Inc., a Georgia-based 501(c)3 non-profit organization. The Network owns and/or operates broadcast television stations in: Philadelphia, PA; San Francisco, CA; Boston, MA; Dallas, TX; Atlanta, GA; Houston, TX; Seattle, WA; Tampa, FL; Phoenix, AZ; Denver, CO; Sacramento, CA; Stockton, CA; Modesto, CA; Raleigh, NC; Nashville, TN; San Antonio, TX; Memphis, TN; Buffalo, NY; Las Vegas, NV; Little Rock, AR; Knoxville, TN; Honolulu, HI; Maui, HI; Jackson, MS; Macon, GA; Gainesville, GA; and Apex, NC. Daystar is seen nationwide on DirecTV and Dish Network (in six major metro areas).
TELEVISION NETWORK

Escape
937296
Owner: Katz Broadcasting
Email: escape-info@katzbroadcasting.com
Web site: http://www.escapetv.com
Profile: Escape is a digital broadcast network offering feature film programming targeted at women.
TELEVISION NETWORK

Estrella TV
604117
Owner: Liberman Broadcasting Inc.
Editorial: 1845 W Empire Ave, Burbank, California 91504-3402 **Tel:** 1 818 563-5722.
Web site: http://www.estrellatv.com
Profile: Estrella TV is a Spanish-language television network owned by Liberman Broadcasting Inc. The network launched on September 14, 2009. KRCA-TV is the flagship affiliate for Estrella TV.
TELEVISION NETWORK

ETTV America
690070
Owner: Eastern Broadcasting Co.
Editorial: 18430 San Jose Ave Ste A, City of Industry, California 91748-1263 **Tel:** 1 626 581-8899.
Web site: http://www.ettvamerica.com
Profile: ETTV America is a Chinese language news and business network.
TELEVISION NETWORK

Focus TV
878395
Editorial: 229 N Vermont St, Covington, Louisiana 70433-3239 **Tel:** 1 985 635-0333.
Web site: http://www.focustvonline.com
Profile: A religious network that features programming consisting of religious, entertaining, informative news and cultural shows to every Catholic.
TELEVISION NETWORK

FOX Broadcasting Company
33054
Owner: News Corporation Ltd.
Editorial: 10201 W Pico Blvd, Los Angeles, California 90064-2606 **Tel:** 1 310 369-3553.
Email: askfox@fox.com
Web site: http://www.fox.com
Profile: National broadcast network providing entertainment and feature programming to 185 primary affiliates throughout the United States. Programming fare includes original dramatic and comedy series, theatrical and made-for-tv films, and exclusive broadcast rights to NFL football, Major League baseball, and NASCAR.
TELEVISION NETWORK

FOX Broadcasting Company - Chicago Bureau
33097
Editorial: 55 W Wacker Dr, Chicago, Illinois 60601-1610 **Tel:** 1 312 494-0428.
Email: askfox@fox.com
TELEVISION NETWORK

Fox Broadcasting Company - New York Bureau
33099
Editorial: 1211 Avenue of the Americas, New York, New York 10036-8701 **Tel:** 1 212 556-2400.
Email: askfox@fox.com
TELEVISION NETWORK

Grit
937295
Owner: Katz Broadcasting
Email: grit-info@katzbroadcasting.com
Web site: http://www.grittv.com
Profile: Grit is a digital broadcast network offering feature film programming targeted at men.
TELEVISION NETWORK

here!
604935
Owner: Here Media, Inc.
Editorial: 242 W 17th St, Ste 1200, New York, New York 10011-5302 **Tel:** 1 212 242-8100.
Email: editor@advocate.com
Web site: http://www.heretv.com
Profile: Founded in 2002, here! airs on all major U.S. cable systems as a 24-hour subscription service. here! appears in 96 of the top 100 U.S. markets, including every top 10 market. here! was also the first gay network originating in the U.S. to launch internationally.
TELEVISION NETWORK

ION Media Networks
33050
Owner: ION Media Networks
Editorial: 601 Clearwater Park Rd, West Palm Beach, Florida 33401-6233 **Tel:** 1 561 659-4122.
Web site: http://www.iontelevision.com
Profile: ION Television airs programming seven days a week, 24 hours a day and reaches over 260 million Americas in 100 million homes in the U.S. via nationwide broadcast television, cable and satellite distribution systems. The ION Television entertainment line-up features a combination of classic and more recent TV hits, popular movies, sports and special events.
TELEVISION NETWORK

ION Media Networks - New York Bureau
154655
Editorial: 1330 Avenue Of The Americas, New York, New York 10019 **Tel:** 1 212 757-3100.
TELEVISION NETWORK

The Jewish Life Television Network
526096
Owner: Phil Blazer Communications
Editorial: 16501 Ventura Blvd, Ste 504, Encino, California 91436 **Tel:** 1 818 786-4000.
Email: info@blazermediagroup.com
Web site: http://www.jltv.tv
Profile: The Jewish Life Television Network (JLTV) is the first television network featuring Jewish-themed programming for all Americans, both Jewish and non-Jewish. JLTV features news and sports, movies, music videos, documentaries, magazine programs, shows for children and young adults, comedy and more.
TELEVISION NETWORK

K42DJ
483585
Owner: Una Vez Mas LP
Editorial: 1701 N Market St Ste 500, Dallas, Texas 75202-2001 **Tel:** 1 214 754-7008.
Email: contacto@aztecaamerica.com
Web site: http://www.aztecaamerica.com
Profile: K42DJ is the Azteca America affiliate for the El Paso, TX market. The station is owned by Una Vez Mas LP. K42DJ broadcasts locally on channel 42.
TELEVISION STATION

KAAH-TV
62886
Owner: Trinity Broadcasting Network
Editorial: 1152 Smith St, Honolulu, Hawaii 96817-5101 **Tel:** 1 808 521-5826.
Web site: http://tbn.org
Profile: KAAH-TV is the Trinity Broadcast Network affiliate for the Honolulu market. The station is owned by Trinity Broadcasting Network. KAAH-TV broadcasts locally on channel 26.
TELEVISION STATION

KAAL-TV
31369
Owner: Hubbard Broadcasting Inc.
Editorial: 1701 10th Pl NE, Austin, Minnesota 55912-4003 **Tel:** 1 507 437-6666.
Email: news@kaaltv.com
Web site: http://www.kaaltv.com
Profile: KAAL-TV is the ABC network affiliate for the Rochester, MN - Mason City, IA market. The station is owned by Hubbard Broadcasting Inc. KAAL-TV broadcasts locally on channel 6.
TELEVISION STATION

KABB-TV
31370
Owner: Sinclair Broadcast Group, Inc.
Editorial: 4335 NW Loop 410, San Antonio, Texas 78229-5136 **Tel:** 1 210 366-1129.
Email: news@kabb.com
Web site: http://www.foxsanantonio.com
Profile: KABB-TV is the FOX affiliate for the San Antonio market. The station is owned by the Sinclair Broadcast Group, Inc. KABB-TV broadcasts locally on channel 29.
TELEVISION STATION

KABC2-TV
606262
Owner: Walt Disney Co.
Editorial: 500 Circle Seven Dr, Glendale, California 91201-2331 **Tel:** 1 818 863-7500.
Email: pr@myabc7.com
Web site: http://abc7.com
Profile: KABC2-TV is a multicast channel of KABC-TV. A multicast channel is a separate channel that shares the bandwith of the main station but can air unique programming. KABC2-TV is the Live Well HD Network affiliate for the Los Angeles market. The station is owned by Walt Disney Co. KABC2-TV broadcasts locally on channel 7.2.
TELEVISION STATION

KABC3-TV
606265
Owner: Walt Disney Co.
Editorial: 500 Circle Seven Dr, Glendale, California 91201-2331 **Tel:** 1 818 863-7500.
Email: pr@myabc7.com
Web site: http://abc7.com
Profile: KABC3-TV is a multicast channel of KABC-TV. A multicast channel is a separate channel that shares the bandwith of the main station but can air unique programming. KABC3-TV airs programming for the local weather now channel for the Los Angeles market. The station is owned by Walt Disney Co. KABC3-TV broadcasts locally on channel 7.3.
TELEVISION STATION

KABC-TV
31371
Owner: Walt Disney Co.
Editorial: 500 Circle Seven Dr, Glendale, California 91201-2331 **Tel:** 1 818 863-7777.
Email: eyewitnessnews@myabc7.com
Web site: http://abc7.com
Profile: KABC-TV is the ABC affiliate for the Los Angeles market. The station is owned by Walt Disney Co. KABC-TV broadcasts locally on channel 7. The station prefers that all news correspondence be sent to the news department email or fax number.
TELEVISION STATION

KABE-TV
133831
Owner: Univision Communications Inc.
Editorial: 5801 Truxtun Ave, Bakersfield, California 93309 **Tel:** 1 661 324-0031.
Profile: KABE-TV is the Univision network affiliate for the Bakersfield, CA market. The station is owned by Univision Communications Inc. KABE-TV broadcasts locally on channel 39.
TELEVISION STATION

KACV-TV
32287
Owner: Amarillo College
Editorial: 2408 S Jackson St, Amarillo, Texas 79109-2312 **Tel:** 1 806 371-5222.
Email: panhandlepbs@actx.edu
Web site: http://panhandlepbs.org
Profile: KACV-TV is the PBS affiliate for the Amarillo, TX market. The station is owned by Amarillo College. KACV-TV broadcasts locally on channel 2.
TELEVISION STATION

KADF-TV
390767
Owner: Azteca America
Editorial: 911 W Anderson Ln Ste 200, Austin, Texas 78757-1562 **Tel:** 1 512 329-0514.
Email: contacto@aztecaamerica.com
Web site: http://www.aztecaamerica.com
Profile: KADF-TV is the Azteca America affiliate for the Austin, TX market. The station is owned by Azteca America Television Group. KADF-TV broadcasts locally on channel 20. Public service announcements must be sent to the mailing address, which is the corporate headquarters in Dallas.
TELEVISION STATION

KADN2-TV
708102
Owner: Bayou City Broadcasting Lafayette Inc.
Editorial: 123 N Easy St, Lafayette, Louisiana 70506-1914 **Tel:** 1 337 237-1500.
Email: news@kadn.com
Web site: http://www.cajunfirst.com
Profile: KADN2-TV is a multicast channel of KADN-TV. A multicast is a separate channel that shares the bandwidth of the main station but can air unique programming KADN2-TV is the local MyNetworkTV affiliate on channel15.2 for the Lafayette, LA market. KADN2-TV is owned by Bayou City Broadcasting Lafayette Inc.
TELEVISION STATION

KADN-TV
31372
Owner: Bayou City Broadcasting Lafayette Inc.
Editorial: 123 N Easy St, Lafayette, Louisiana 70506-1914 **Tel:** 1 337 237-1500.
Email: news@kadn.com
Web site: http://www.cajunfirst.com
Profile: KADN-TV is the FOX affiliate for the Lafayette, LA. The station is owned by Bayou City Broadcasting Lafayette Inc. KADN-TV broadcasts locally on channel 15.
TELEVISION STATION

KAEF-TV
32841
Owner: Bonten Media Group, LLC
Editorial: 333 6th St Ste C, Eureka, California 95501-1035 **Tel:** 1 707 444-2323.
Email: news@northcoastnewstv.com
Web site: http://www.krcrtv.com/kaef/index.html
Profile: KAEF-TV is an ABC affiliate for the Eureka, CA market. The station is owned Bonten Media Group, LLC. KAEF-TV broadcasts locally on channel 23.
TELEVISION STATION

KAET2-TV
611663
Owner: Arizona Board of Regents
Editorial: 555 N Central Ave Ste 500, Phoenix, Arizona 85004-1252 **Tel:** 1 602 496-8888.
Email: eight@asu.edu
Web site: http://www.azpbs.org
Profile: KAET2-TV is a multicast of KAET-TV. A multicast channel is a separate channel that shares the bandwidth of the main station but can air unique programming. KAET2-TV airs programming from Create in the Phoenix market. The Station broadcasts from Arizona State University and is part of ASU's Walter Cronkite School of Journalism and Mass Communication. It is licensed and owned by Arizona Board of Regents on behalf of ASU. KAET2-TV broadcasts locally on channel 8.2.
TELEVISION STATION

KAET3-TV
611669
Owner: Arizona Board of Regents
Editorial: 555 N Central Ave, Phoenix, Arizona 85004-1247 **Tel:** 1 602 496-8888.
Email: eight@asu.edu
Web site: http://www.azpbs.org
Profile: KAET3-TV is a multicast of KAET-TV. A multicast channel is a separate channel that shares the bandwidth of the main station but can air unique programming. KAET3-TV airs programming from PBS World in the Phoenix market. The Station broadcasts from Arizona State University and is part of ASU's Walter Cronkite School of Journalism and Mass Communication. It is licensed and owned by Arizona Board of Regents on behalf of ASU. KAET3-TV broadcasts "Eight World" locally on channel 8.3.
TELEVISION STATION

KAET4-TV
611675
Owner: Arizona Board of Regents
Editorial: 555 N Central Ave Ste 500, Phoenix, Arizona 85004-1252 **Tel:** 1 602 496-8888.
Email: eight@asu.edu
Web site: http://www.azpbs.org
Profile: KAET4-TV is a multicast of KAET-TV. A multicast channel is a separate channel that shares the bandwidth of the main station but can air unique programming. KAET4-TV airs programming from KBAQ-FM in the Phoenix market. The Station broadcasts from Arizona State University and is part of ASU's Walter Cronkite School of Journalism and Mass Communication. It is licensed and owned by Arizona Board of Regents on behalf of ASU. KAET2-TV broadcasts locally on channel 8.4.
TELEVISION STATION

KAET-TV 31373
Owner: Arizona Board of Regents
Editorial: 555 N Central Ave, Phoenix, Arizona 85004-1247 **Tel:** 1 602 496-8888.
Email: eight@asu.edu
Web site: http://www.azpbs.org
Profile: KAET-TV is the PBS affiliate for the Phoenix market. The Station broadcasts from Arizona State University and is part of ASU's Walter Cronkite School of Journalism and Mass Communication. It is licensed and owned by Arizona Board of Regents on behalf of ASU. KAET-TV broadcasts locally on channel 8.
TELEVISION STATION

KAGS-TV 792695
Owner: London Broadcasting
Editorial: 2800 S Texas Ave Ste 101, Bryan, Texas 77802-5361 **Tel:** 1 979 703-8404.
Email: news@kagstv.com
Web site: http://kagstv.com
Profile: KAGS-TV is the NBC affiliate for the Waco, TX market. The station is owned by London Broadcasting. KAGS-TV broadcasts locally on channel 23.
TELEVISION STATION

KAIL-TV 31375
Owner: Trans America Broadcasting
Editorial: 1590 Alluvial Ave, Clovis, California 93611-9567 **Tel:** 1 559 299-9753.
Web site: http://www.kail.tv
Profile: KAIL-TV is the local MyNetworkTV affiliate for the Fresno-Visalia, CA market. The station is owned by Trans America Broadcasting. KAIL-TV is broadcast locally on channel 53.
TELEVISION STATION

KAIT-TV 31376
Owner: Raycom Media Inc.
Editorial: 472 County Road 766, Jonesboro, Arkansas 72401-9748 **Tel:** 1 870 931-8888.
Email: news@kait8.com
Web site: http://www.kait8.com
Profile: KAIT-TV is the ABC affiliate for the Jonesboro, AR market. The station is owned by Raycom Media Inc. KAIT-TV broadcasts locally on channel 8.
TELEVISION STATION

KAJA-TV 32569
Owner: Evening Post Publishing Co.
Editorial: 301 Artesian St, Corpus Christi, Texas 78401-2701 **Tel:** 1 361 886-6100.
Web site: http://www.kristv.com
Profile: KAJA-TV is a Telemundo affiliate for the Corpus Christi, TX market. The station is owned by Evening Post Publishing Company. KAJA-TV broadcasts locally on channel 68. To contact the station please use the "Contact us" form on the website.
TELEVISION STATION

KAJB2-TV 829861
Owner: Entravision Communications Corp.
Editorial: 1803 N Imperial Ave, El Centro, California 92243-1333 **Tel:** 1 760 482-7777.
Profile: KAJB2-TV is a multicast channel of KAJB-TV. A multicast channel is a separate channel that shares the bandwidth of the main station but can air unique programming. KAJB2-TV is the MundoFOX affiliate for the Yuma, AZ- El Centro, CA market. The station is owned by Entravision Communications Corp. KAJB2-TV broadcasts locally on channel 54.2.
TELEVISION STATION

KAJB-TV 153301
Owner: Entravision Communications Corp.
Editorial: 1803 N Imperial Ave, El Centro, California 92243-1333 **Tel:** 1 760 482-7777.
Web site: http://noticias.entravision.com/el-centro
Profile: KAJB-TV is an independent affiliate for the Yuma, AZ, El Centro, CA market. The station is owned by Entravision Communications Corp. KAJB-TV broadcasts locally on channel 54.
TELEVISION STATION

KAJ-TV 525000
Owner: Cordillera Communications Inc.
Editorial: 301 1st Ave E, Kalispell, Montana 59901-4935 **Tel:** 1 406 756-5888.
Email: kajnews@kpax.com
Web site: http://www.kpax.com
Profile: KAJ-TV is the CBS affiliate for the Kalispell, MT Market. The station is owned by Cordillera Communications Inc. KAJ-TV broadcasts locally on channel 18.
TELEVISION STATION

KAKE-TV 32698
Owner: Lockwood Broadcasting Group
Editorial: 1500 N West St, Wichita, Kansas 67203-1323 **Tel:** 1 316 943-4221.
Email: news@kake.com
Web site: http://www.kake.com
Profile: KAKE-TV is the ABC network affiliate for the Wichita-Hutchinson, KS market. The station is owned by Gray Television, Inc. KAKE-TV broadcasts locally on channel 10.
TELEVISION STATION

KAKM-TV 31377
Owner: Alaska Public Telecommunications Inc.
Editorial: 3877 University Dr, Anchorage, Alaska 99508-4676 **Tel:** 1 907 550-8400.
Web site: http://www.alaskapublic.org/television
Profile: KAKM-TV is the PBS network affiliate for the Anchorage, AK market. The station is owned by Alaska Public Telecommunications Inc. KAKM-TV broadcasts locally on channel 7.
TELEVISION STATION

KAKW-TV 32525
Owner: Univision Communications Inc.
Editorial: 2233 W North Loop Blvd, Austin, Texas 78756-2324 **Tel:** 1 512 453-8899.
Email: Noticias62@univision.net
Web site: http://univisionaustin.univision.com
Profile: KAKW-TV is the Univision affiliate for the Austin, TX market. The station is owned by Univision Communications Inc. KAKW-TV broadcasts locally on channel 62.
TELEVISION STATION

KALB2-TV 834846
Owner: Gray Television, Inc.
Editorial: 605 Washington St, Alexandria, Louisiana 71301-8028 **Tel:** 1 318 445-2456.
Email: news@kalb.com
Web site: http://www.kalb.com
Profile: KALB2-TV is a multicast channel of KALB-TV. A multicast channel is a separate channel that shares the bandwidth of the main station but can air unique programming. KALB2-TV is the CBS Network for the Alexandria, LA market. The station is owned by Gray Television, Inc. KALB2-TV broadcasts locally on channel 5.2.
TELEVISION STATION

KALB-TV 31378
Owner: Gray Television, Inc.
Editorial: 605 Washington St, Alexandria, Louisiana 71301-8028 **Tel:** 1 318 445-2456.
Email: news@kalb.com
Web site: http://www.kalb.com
Profile: KALB-TV is the NBC affiliate for the Alexandria, LA, market. The station is owned by Hoak Media LLC. KALB-TV broadcasts locally on channel 5.
TELEVISION STATION

KAMC-TV 31379
Owner: VHR Broadcasting of Lubbock
Editorial: 7403 University Ave, Lubbock, Texas 79423-1424 **Tel:** 1 806 745-2828.
Web site: http://everythinglubbock.com
Profile: KAMC-TV is the ABC network affiliate for the Lubbock, TX market. The station is owned by VHR Broadcasting of Lubbock. KAMC-TV broadcasts locally on channel 28.
TELEVISION STATION

KAME-TV 31380
Owner: Sinclair Broadcast Group, Inc.
Editorial: 4920 Brookside Ct, Reno, Nevada 89502-4102 **Tel:** 1 775 856-2121.
Web site: http://www.foxreno.com
Profile: KAME-TV is the MyNetworkTV affiliate for the Reno, NV market. The station is owned by Sinclair Broadcast Group, Inc. KAME-TV broadcasts locally on channel 20.
TELEVISION STATION

KAMR-TV 31381
Owner: Nexstar Broadcasting Group
Editorial: 1015 S Fillmore St, Amarillo, Texas 79101 **Tel:** 1 806 383-3321.
Email: news@kamr.com
Web site: http://myhighplains.com
Profile: KAMR-TV is the NBC network affiliate for the Amarillo, TX market. The station is owned by Nexstar Broadcasting Group. KAMR-TV broadcasts locally on channel 4.
TELEVISION STATION

KANG-TV 389654
Owner: Entravision Communications Corp.
Editorial: 10313 Younger Rd, Midland, Texas 79706-2622 **Tel:** 1 325 482-9277.
Profile: KANG-TV is the UniMas affiliate for the Midland, TX market. The station is owned by Entravision Communications Corp. KANG-TV broadcast locally on channel 41.
TELEVISION STATION

KAPP2-TV 809181
Owner: Apple Valley Broadcasting, Inc.
Tel: 1 509 453-0351.
Web site: http://metvnetwork.com
Profile: KAPP2-TV is a multicast channel of KAPP-TV. A multicast channel is a separate channel that shares the bandwidth of the main station but can air unique programming. KAPP2-TV is the Me-TV Network affiliate for the Spokane, WA market. The station is owned by Apple Valley Broadcasting, Inc. KAPP2-TV broadcasts locally on channel 35.2.
TELEVISION STATION

KAPP-TV 32633
Owner: Apple Valley Broadcasting, Inc.
Tel: 1 509 453-0351.
Web site: http://www.kapptv.com
Profile: KAPP-TV is the ABC affiliate for the Yakima, WA market. The station is owned by Apple Valley Broadcasting, Inc. KAPP-TV broadcasts locally on channel 35.
TELEVISION STATION

KARD-TV 31383
Owner: Nexstar Broadcasting Group
Editorial: 200 Pavilion Rd, West Monroe, Louisiana 71292 **Tel:** 1 318 323-1972.
Email: news@nbc10news.net
Web site: http://myarklamiss.com
Profile: KARD-TV is the FOX network affiliate for the Monroe, LA, El Dorado, AR market. The station is owned by Quorum Broadcasting Co. KARD-TV broadcasts locally on channel 14.
TELEVISION STATION

KARE2-TV 789676
Owner: TEGNA Inc.
Editorial: 8811 Highway 55, Golden Valley, Minnesota 55427-4762 **Tel:** 1 763 546-1111.
Email: news@kare11.com
Web site: http://static.karell.com
Profile: KARE2-TV is a multicast channel of KARE-TV. A multicast channel is a separate channel that shares the bandwith of the main station but can air unique programming. KARE2-TV is the WeatherNation TV affiliate for the Minneapolis market. The station is owned by TEGNA Inc. KARE2-TV broadcasts locally on channel 11.2.
TELEVISION STATION

KARE-TV 31384
Owner: TEGNA Inc.
Editorial: 8811 Highway 55, Golden Valley, Minnesota 55427-4762 **Tel:** 1 763 546-1111.
Email: news@kare11.com
Web site: http://www.kare11.com
Profile: KARE-TV is the NBC affiliate serving the Minneapolis-Saint Paul market. The station is owned by TEGNA Inc. KARE-TV broadcasts locally on channel 11.
TELEVISION STATION

KARK-TV 31385
Owner: Nexstar Broadcasting Group
Editorial: 1401 W Capitol Ave Ste 104, Little Rock, Arkansas 72201-2940 **Tel:** 1 501 340-4444.
Email: news4@kark.com
Web site: http://www.arkansasmatters.com
Profile: KARK-TV is the NBC affiliate for the Little Rock, AR market. The station is owned by Nextstar Broadcasting Group. KARK-TV broadcasts locally on channel 4.
TELEVISION STATION

KARZ-TV 32595
Owner: Nexstar Broadcasting Group
Editorial: 1401 W Capitol Ave, Ste 104, Little Rock, Arkansas 72201-2940 **Tel:** 1 501 340-4444.
Web site: http://www.arkansasmatters.com
Profile: KARZ-TV is the local MyNetworkTV affiliate for the Little Rock, AR market. The station is owned by Nexstar Broadcasting Group. KARZ-TV broadcasts locally on channel 42.
TELEVISION STATION

KASA-TV 31468
Owner: Ramar Communications
Editorial: 2400 Monroe St NE, Albuquerque, New Mexico 87110-4063 **Tel:** 1 505 884-5353.
Web site: http://www.kasa.com
Profile: KASA-TV is the Telemundo affiliate for the Albuquerque, NM market. The station is owned by Ramar Communications. KASA-TV broadcasts locally on channel 2.
TELEVISION STATION

KASN-TV 32248
Owner: Mission Broadcasting
Editorial: 1401 W Capitol Ave Ste 104, Little Rock, Arkansas 72201-2940 **Tel:** 1 501 340-4444.
Email: news@fox16.com
Web site: http://www.fox16.com/the-cwarkansas
Profile: KASN-TV is the CW affiliate for the Little Rock, AR market. The station is owned by Mission Broadcasting Group. KASN-TV broadcasts locally on channel 38.
TELEVISION STATION

KASW-TV 32472
Owner: Nexstar Broadcasting Group
Editorial: 5555 N 7th Ave, Phoenix, Arizona 85013-1701 **Tel:** 1 480 661-6161.
Web site: http://www.cw6phoenix.com
Profile: KASW-TV is a CW affiliate for the Phoenix market. The station is owned by Nexstar Broadcasting Group. KASW-TV broadcasts locally on channel 61.
TELEVISION STATION

KASY-TV 32532
Owner: Tamer Media
Editorial: 13 Broadcast Plz SW, Albuquerque, New Mexico 87104-1056 **Tel:** 1 505 797-1919.
Web site: http://kwbq.com
Profile: KASY-TV is the MyNetworkTV affiliate for the Albuquerque, NM market. KASY-TV is owned by Tamer Media. KASY-TV broadcasts locally on channel 50.
TELEVISION STATION

KATC-TV 31386
Owner: Evening Post Publishing Co.
Editorial: 1103 Eraste Landry Rd, Lafayette, Louisiana 70506-3043 **Tel:** 1 337 235-3333.
Email: news@katctv.com
Web site: http://www.katc.com
Profile: KATC-TV is the ABC network affiliate for the Lafayette, LA market. The station is owned by Evening Post Publishing Co. KATC-TV broadcasts locally on channel 3.
TELEVISION STATION

KATU2-TV 613858
Owner: Sinclair Broadcast Group
Editorial: 2153 NE Sandy Blvd, Portland, Oregon 97232-2819 **Tel:** 1 503 231-4222.
Email: thedesk@katu.com
Web site: http://www.katu.com
Profile: KATU2-TV is a multicast of KATU-TV. A multicast channel is a separate channel that shares the bandwith of the main station but can air unique programming. KATU2-TV airs programming from This TV Network in the Portland, OR market. The station is owned by Sinclair Broadcast Group. KATU2-TV broadcasts locally on channel 2.2.
TELEVISION STATION

KATU-TV 31388
Owner: Sinclair Broadcast Group, Inc.
Editorial: 2153 NE Sandy Blvd, Portland, Oregon 97232-2819 **Tel:** 1 503 231-4222.
Email: newstips@katu.com
Web site: http://www.katu.com
Profile: KATU-TV is the ABC affiliate for the Portland, OR market. The station is owned by Sinclair Broadcast Group, Inc. KATU-TV broadcasts locally on channel 2.
TELEVISION STATION

KATV-TV 31389
Owner: Sinclair Broadcast Group, Inc.
Editorial: 401 Main St, Little Rock, Arkansas 72201-3801 **Tel:** 1 501 324-7777.
Email: newsroom@katv.com
Web site: http://www.katv.com
Profile: KATV-TV is the ABC affiliate for the Little Rock, AR market. The station is owned by Sinclair Broadcast Group, Inc. KATV-TV broadcasts locally on channel 7.
TELEVISION STATION

KAUT-TV 32404
Owner: Tribune Broadcasting Co.
Editorial: 444 E Britton Rd, Oklahoma City, Oklahoma 73114-7515 **Tel:** 1 405 478-4300.
Web site: http://kfor.com/category/freedom-43
Profile: KAUT-TV is the MyNetworkTV affiliate for the Oklahoma City market. The station is owned by Tribune Broadcasting Co. KAUT-TV broadcasts locally on channel 43.
TELEVISION STATION

KAUZ-TV 31390
Owner: Raycom Media Inc.
Editorial: 3601 Seymour Hwy, Wichita Falls, Texas 76309-1605 **Tel:** 1 940 322-6957.
Email: news@kauz.com
Web site: http://www.newschannel6now.com
Profile: KAUZ-TV is the CBS affiliate for the Wichita Falls, TX-Lawton, OK market. The station is owned by Raycom Media Inc. KAUZ-TV broadcasts locally on channel 6.
TELEVISION STATION

KAVU-TV 31391
Owner: Saga Communications
Editorial: 3808 N Navarro St, Victoria, Texas 77901-2621 **Tel:** 1 361 575-2500.
Email: staff@newscenter25.com
Web site: http://www.crossroadstoday.com
Profile: KAVU-TV is the ABC affiliate for the Victoria, TX market. The station is owned by the Saga Communications. KAVU-TV broadcasts locally on channel 25.
TELEVISION STATION

KAWB-TV 32817
Owner: Lakeland Public Television
Editorial: 422 NW 3rd St, Brainerd, Minnesota 56401-2917 **Tel:** 1 218 855-0022.
Email: news@lptv.org
Web site: https://lptv.org
Profile: KAWB-TV is a PBS network affiliate for the Minneapolis-St. Paul market. The station is owned by Lakeland Public Television. KAWB-TV broadcasts locally on channel 22.
TELEVISION STATION

KAWE3-TV 612570
Owner: Lakeland Public Television
Editorial: 1500 Birchmont Dr NE, Bemidji, Minnesota 56601-2600 **Tel:** 1 218 751-3407.
Email: news@lptv.org
Web site: http://www.lptv.org
Profile: KAWE3-TV is a multicast of KAWE-TV. A multicast channel is a separate channel that shares the bandwidth of the main station but can air unique programming. KAWE3-TV airs Lakeland Kids in the Minneapolis market. The station is owned by Lakeland Public Television. KAWE3-TV broadcasts locally on channel 9.3.
TELEVISION STATION

KAWE4-TV 612574
Owner: Lakeland Public Television
Editorial: 1500 Birchmont Dr NE, Bemidji, Minnesota 56601-2600 **Tel:** 1 218 751-3407.
Email: news@lptv.org
Web site: http://www.lptv.org
Profile: KAWE4-TV is a multicast of KAWE-TV. A multicast channel is a separate channel that shares the bandwidth of the main station but can air unique programming. KAWE4-TV airs programming from Lakeland Create in the Minneapolis market. The station is owned by Lakeland Public Television. KAWE4-TV broadcasts locally on channel 9.4.
TELEVISION STATION

KAWE5-TV 612580
Owner: Lakeland Public Television
Editorial: 1500 Birchmont Dr NE, Bemidji, Minnesota 56601-2600 **Tel:** 1 218 751-3407.
Email: news@lptv.org
Web site: http://www.lptv.org
Profile: KAWE5-TV is a multicast of KAWE-TV. A multicast channel is a separate channel that shares the bandwith of the main station but can air unique

programming. KAWE5-TV airs programming from Lakeland Plus in the Minneapolis market. The station is owned by Lakeland Public Television. KAWE5-TV broadcasts locally on channel 9.5.
TELEVISION STATION

KAWE6-TV 612584
Owner: Lakeland Public Television
Editorial: 1500 Birchmont Dr NE, Bemidji, Minnesota 56601-2600 **Tel:** 1 218 751-3407.
Email: news@lptv.org
Web site: http://www.lptv.org
Profile: KAWE6-TV is a multicast of KAWE-TV. A multicast channel is a separate channel that shares the bandwith of the main station but can air unique programming. KAWE6-TV airs programming from Lakeland MN in the Minneapolis market. The station is owned by Lakeland Public Television. KAWE6-TV broadcasts locally on channel 9.6.
TELEVISION STATION

KAYU-TV 32365
Owner: Northwest Broadcasting
Editorial: 4600 S Regal St, Spokane, Washington 99223-7960 **Tel:** 1 509 448-2828.
Email: fox28@kayutv.com
Web site: http://www.myfoxspokane.com
Profile: KAYU-TV is the FOX affiliate for the Spokane market. The station is owned by Northern Broadcasting. KAYU-TV broadcasts locally on channel 28. News is produced by KHQ-TV.
TELEVISION STATION

KAZA-TV 79035
Owner: Pappas Telecasting Companies
Editorial: 1139 Grand Central Ave, Glendale, California 91201-2423 **Tel:** 1 818 247-0400.
Web site: http://us.azteca.com/azteca54
Profile: KAZA-TV is the Azteca America affiliate for the Los Angeles market. The station is owned by Pappas Telecasting Companies. KAZA-TV broadcasts locally on channel 54.
TELEVISION STATION

KAZD-TV 32360
Owner: Una Vez Mas LP
Editorial: 703 Mckinney Ave Ste 240, Dallas, Texas 75202-1039 **Tel:** 1 214 754-7008.
Profile: KAZD-TV is an Azteca America station for the Dallas market. The station is owned by Una Vez Mas LP. KAZD-TV broadcasts locally on channel 55.
TELEVISION STATION

KAZQ2-TV 617296
Owner: Alpha-Omega Broadcasting of New Mexico
Editorial: 4501 Montgomery Blvd NE, Albuquerque, New Mexico 87109-1286 **Tel:** 1 505 884-8355.
Email: info@kazq32.org
Web site: http://www.kazq32.org
Profile: KAZQ2-TV is a multicast of KAZQ-TV. A multicast channel is a separate channel that shares the bandwith of the main station but can air unique programming. KAZQ2-TV airs programming from GOD TV in the Albuquerque, NM market. The station is owned by Alpha-Omega Broadcasting of New Mexico. KAZQ2-TV broadcasts locally on channel 32.2.
TELEVISION STATION

KAZQ3-TV 617302
Owner: Alpha-Omega Broadcasting of New Mexico
Editorial: 4501 Montgomery Blvd NE, Albuquerque, New Mexico 87109-1286 **Tel:** 1 505 884-8355.
Email: info@kazq32.org
Web site: http://www.kazq32.org
Profile: KAZQ3-TV is a multicast of KAZQ-TV. A multicast channel is a separate channel that shares the bandwith of the main station but can air unique programming. KAZQ3-TV airs programming from KTVS-TV in the Albuquerque, NM market. The station is owned by Alpha-Omega Broadcasting of New Mexico. KAZQ3-TV broadcasts locally on channel 32.3.
TELEVISION STATION

KAZQ-TV 32306
Owner: Alpha-Omega Broadcasting of New Mexico
Editorial: 4501 Montgomery Blvd NE, Albuquerque, New Mexico 87109-1286 **Tel:** 1 505 884-8355.
Email: info@kazq32.org
Web site: http://www.kazq32.org
Profile: KAZQ-TV is an independent station for the Albuquerque, NM market. The station is owned by Alpha-Omega Broadcasting of New Mexico. KAZQ-TV broadcasts locally on channel 32.
TELEVISION STATION

KAZT2-TV 612337
Owner: KAZT LLC
Editorial: 4343 E Camelback Rd, Ste 130, Phoenix, Arizona 85018-8305 **Tel:** 1 602 977-7700.
Web site: http://www.arizonasown.com
Profile: KAZT2-TV is a multicast of KAZT-TV. A multicast channel is a separate channel that shares the bandwith of the main station but can air unique programming. KAZT2-TV airs programming from Retro Television Network in the Phoenix market. The station is owned by KAZT LLC. KAZT2-TV broadcasts locally on channel 7.2.
TELEVISION STATION

KAZT-TV 31679
Owner: KAZT LLC
Editorial: 4343 E Camelback Rd Ste 130, Phoenix, Arizona 85018-8305 **Tel:** 1 602 977-7700.
Email: programming@aztv.com
Web site: http://www.aztv.com
Profile: KAZT-TV is an independent network station for the Phoenix market. The station is owned by KAZT LLC. KAZT-TV broadcasts locally on channel 7.
TELEVISION STATION

KBAK-TV 31392
Owner: Fisher Communications, Inc.
Editorial: 1901 Westwind Dr, Bakersfield, California 93301-3016 **Tel:** 1 661 327-7955.
Email: news@bakersfieldnow.com
Web site: http://www.bakersfieldnow.com
Profile: KBAK-TV is the CBS affiliate for the Bakersfield, CA market. The station is owned by Fisher Communications, Inc. KBAK-TV broadcasts locally on channel 29.
TELEVISION STATION

KBCA-TV 390769
Owner: Wilderness Communications, LLC
Editorial: 3501 NW Evangeline Trwy, Carencro, Louisiana 70520-6240 **Tel:** 1 337 896-1600.
Web site: http://www.yourcwtv.com/partners/alexandria
Profile: KBCA-TV is the CW affiliate for the Lafayette, LA market. The station is owned by Wilderness Communications, LLC and operated by Delta Media Corporation. KBCA-TV broadcasts locally on channel 41.
TELEVISION STATION

KBCB2-TV 771580
Owner: World Television Washington LLC.
Editorial: 4164 Meridian St Ste 102, Bellingham, Washington 98226-5583 **Tel:** 1 360 647-8842.
Web site: http://www.kbcbtv.com
Profile: KBCB2-TV is a multicast channel of KBCB-TV. A multicast channel is a separate channel that shares the bandwidth of the main station but can air unique programming. KBCB2-TV is the local Estrella TV affiliate on Channel 24.2 for the Seattle- Tacoma, WA market. KBCB2-TV is owned by World Television of Washington LLC.
TELEVISION STATION

KBCB-TV 32597
Owner: World Television of Washington LLC
Editorial: 4164 Meridian St Ste 102, Bellingham, Washington 98226-5583 **Tel:** 1 360 647-8842.
Web site: http://www.kbcbtv.com
Profile: KBCB-TV is an independent commercial station for the Seattle market. The station is owned by World Television of Washington LLC. KBCB-TV broadcasts locally on channel 24.
TELEVISION STATION

KBCW-TV 31395
Owner: CBS Television Stations
Editorial: 855 Battery St, San Francisco, California 94111-1503 **Tel:** 1 415 765-8144.
Web site: http://cwsanfrancisco.cbslocal.com
Profile: KBCW-TV is the CW affiliate for the San Francisco market. The station is owned by CBS Television Stations. KBCW-TV broadcasts locally on channel 44. KBCW-TV does not accept news press releases since they do not air any local newscasts.
TELEVISION STATION

KBDI2-TV 609807
Owner: Colorado Public Television
Editorial: 2900 Welton St Fl 1, Denver, Colorado 80205-3007 **Tel:** 1 303 293-1212.
Email: info@cpt12.org
Web site: http://www.cpt12.org
Profile: KBDI2-TV is a multicast of KBDI-TV. A multicast channel is a separate channel that shares the bandwith of the main station but can air unique programming. KBDI2-TV airs programming from the Documentary Channel in the Denver market. The station is owned by Colorado Public Television. KBDI2-TV broadcasts locally on channel 12.2. All PSA's must go to the main email address, which will then be sent to the appropriate contact.
TELEVISION STATION

KBDI3-TV 609814
Owner: Colorado Public Television
Editorial: 2900 Welton St Fl 1, Denver, Colorado 80205-3007 **Tel:** 1 303 296-1212.
Email: info@cpt12.org
Web site: http://www.cpt12.org
Profile: KBDI3-TV is a multicast of KBDI-TV. A multicast channel is a separate channel that shares the bandwith of the main station but can air unique programming. KBDI3-TV airs programming from the MHz Worldview in the Denver market. The station is owned by Colorado Public Television. KBDI3-TV broadcasts locally on channel 12.3. All PSA's must go to the main email address, which will then be sent to the appropriate contact.
TELEVISION STATION

KBDI-TV 31394
Owner: Colorado Public Television
Editorial: 2900 Welton St Fl 1, Denver, Colorado 80205-3007 **Tel:** 1 303 296-1212.
Email: info@cpt12.org
Web site: http://www.cpt12.org
Profile: KBDI-TV is the PBS network affiliate for the Denver, CO market. The station is owned by Colorado Public Television. KBDI-TV broadcasts locally on channel 12. KBDI-TV is known as CPT 12. All PSA's must go to the main email address, which will then be sent to the appropriate contact.
TELEVISION STATION

KBEH-TV 31629
Owner: Hero Broadcasting, LLC
Editorial: 5757 W Century Blvd Ste 490, Los Angeles, California 90045-6409 **Tel:** 1 310 216-0063.
Web site: http://www.canal63.com
Profile: KBEH-TV is a Tr3s affiliate station for the Los Angeles market. The station is owned by Hero Broadcasting, LLC. KBEH-TV broadcasts locally on channel 63. The station airs an eight-hour block of CNN Latino, from 3pm to 11 pm.
TELEVISION STATION

KBFD-TV 32285
Owner: Allen Broadcasting
Editorial: 1188 Bishop St Ph 1, Honolulu, Hawaii 96813-3300 **Tel:** 1 808 521-8066.
Email: news@kbfd.com
Web site: http://www.kbfd.com
Profile: KBFD-TV is an independent station for the Honolulu market. The station is owned by Allen Broadcasting. KBFD-TV broadcasts locally on channel 32.
TELEVISION STATION

KBFX-TV 154087
Owner: Fisher Communications, Inc.
Editorial: 1901 Westwind Dr, Bakersfield, California 93301-3016 **Tel:** 1 661 327-7955.
Email: news@bakersfieldnow.com
Web site: http://www.bakersfieldnow.com
Profile: KBFX-TV is the FOX affiliate for Bakersfield, CA. The station is owned by Fisher Communications, Inc. KBFX-TV broadcasts locally on channel 58.
TELEVISION STATION

KBIM-TV 31396
Owner: Media Genral
Editorial: 214 N Main St, Roswell, New Mexico 88201-4723 **Tel:** 1 575 622-2120.
Email: newsdesk@krqe.com
Web site: http://www.kbimtv.com
Profile: KBIM-TV is the CBS affiliate for the Albuquerque, NM market. The station is owned by Media General. KBIM-TV broadcasts locally on channel 10.
TELEVISION STATION

KBJR-TV 31397
Owner: Quincy Newspapers
Editorial: 246 S Lake Ave, Duluth, Minnesota 55802-2304 **Tel:** 1 218 720-9600.
Email: news@kbjr.com
Web site: http://www.northlandsnewscenter.com
Profile: KBJR-TV is the NBC affiliate for the Duluth, MN/Superior, WI market. The station is owned by Quincy Newspapers. KBJR-TV broadcasts locally on channel 6.
TELEVISION STATION

KBLR-TV 32522
Owner: NBC Universal
Editorial: 450 Fremont St Ste 310, Las Vegas, Nevada 89101-5627 **Tel:** 1 702 258-0039.
Web site: http://www.telemundolasvegas.com
Profile: KBLR-TV is the Telemundo affiliate for Las Vegas market. The station is owned by NBC Universal. KBLR-TV broadcasts locally on channel 39.
TELEVISION STATION

KBMT2-TV 698902
Owner: TEGNA Inc.
Editorial: 525 Interstate 10 S, Beaumont, Texas 77701-3708 **Tel:** 1 409 833-7512.
Email: 12news@kbmt12.com
Profile: KBMT2-TV is a multicast channel of KBMT-TV. A multicast channel is a separate channel that shares the bandwidth of the main station but can air unique programming. KBMT2-TV is the NBC affiliate for the Beaumont, TX market. The station is owned by TEGNA Inc.
TELEVISION STATION

KBMT4-TV 698904
Owner: TEGNA Inc.
Editorial: 525 Interstate 10 S, Beaumont, Texas 77701-3708 **Tel:** 1 409 833-7512.
Web site: http://www.12newsnow.com
Profile: KBMT4-TV is a multicast channel of KBMT-TV. A multicast channel is a separate channel that shares the bandwidth of the main station but can air unique programming. KBMT4-TV is the Azteca America affiliate for the Beaumont, TX market. The station is owned by TEGNA Inc. KBMT4-TV broadcasts locally on channel 12.4.
TELEVISION STATION

KBMT-TV 31398
Owner: TEGNA Inc.
Editorial: 525 Interstate 10 S, Beaumont, Texas 77701-3708 **Tel:** 1 409 833-7512.
Email: 12News@kbmt12.com
Web site: http://www.12newsnow.com
Profile: KBMT-TV is the local ABC television affiliate for the Beaumont-Port Arthur, TX market. The station is owned by TEGNA Inc. KBMT-TV broadcasts locally on channel 12
TELEVISION STATION

KBMY-TV 32634
Owner: Forum Communications Co.
Editorial: 1811 N 15th St #701, Bismarck, North Dakota 58501-2026 **Tel:** 1 701 223-1700.
Email: traffic@fox26.tv
Web site: http://www.wday.com
Profile: KBMY-TV is the ABC affiliate for the Minot-Bismarck, ND market. The station is owned by Forum Communications Co. KBMY-TV broadcasts locally on channel 17.
TELEVISION STATION

KBNT-TV 74185
Owner: Entravision Communications Corp.
Editorial: 5770 Ruffin Rd, San Diego, California 92123-1013 **Tel:** 1 858 576-1919.
Email: kbntnews@entravision.com
Web site: http://www.univisionsandiego.com
Profile: KBNT-TV is the Univision network affiliate for the San Diego market. The station is owned by Entravision Communications Corp. KBNT-TV broadcasts locally on channel 17.
TELEVISION STATION

KBNZ-TV 702893
Owner: Zolo Media
Editorial: 63090 Sherman Rd, Bend, Oregon 97701-5750 **Tel:** 1 541 749-5151.
Email: info@zolomedia.com
Web site: http://zolomedia.com/networks/KBNZ
Profile: KBNZ-TV is the CBS affiliate for the Bend, OR market. The station is owned by Zolo Media. KBNZ-TV broadcasts locally on channel 7.
TELEVISION STATION

KBOI-TV 31393
Owner: Fisher Communications, Inc.
Editorial: 140 N 16th St, Boise, Idaho 83702-5132 **Tel:** 1 208 472-2222.
Email: news@kboi2.com
Web site: http://www.kboi2.com
Profile: KBOI-TV is a CBS affiliate in the Boise, ID market. The station is owned by Fisher Communications, Inc. KBOI-TV broadcasts locally on channel 2.
TELEVISION STATION

KBSI-TV 31399
Owner: Sinclair Broadcast Group, Inc.
Editorial: 806 Enterprise St, Cape Girardeau, Missouri 63703 **Tel:** 1 573 334-1223.
Web site: http://www.kbsi23.com
Profile: KBSI-TV is the FOX network affiliate for the Paducah, KY; Cape Girardeau, MO and Harrisburg, IL market. The station is owned by Sinclair Broadcast Group, Inc. KBSI-TV broadcasts locally on channel 23.
TELEVISION STATION

KBTC2-TV 611678
Owner: Bates Technical College
Editorial: 2320 S 19th St, Tacoma, Washington 98405-2946 **Tel:** 1 253 680-7700.
Email: programming@kbtc.org
Web site: http://www.kbtc.org
Profile: KBTC2-TV is a multicast of KBTC-TV. A multicast channel is a separate channel that shares the bandwith of the main station but can air unique programming. KBTC2-TV airs programming from Create in the Seattle market. The station is owned by Bates Technical College. KBTC2-TV broadcasts locally on channel 28.2.
TELEVISION STATION

KBTC-TV 32722
Owner: Bates Technical College
Editorial: 2320 S 19th St, Tacoma, Washington 98405 **Tel:** 1 253 680-7700.
Email: programming@kbtc.org
Web site: http://www.kbtc.org
Profile: KBTC-TV is the PBS affiliate for the Seattle-Tacoma market. The station is owned by Bates Technical College. KXLN-TV broadcasts locally on channel 28.
TELEVISION STATION

KBTF-TV 390685
Owner: Univision Communications Inc.
Editorial: 5801 Truxtun Ave, Bakersfield, California 93309-0609 **Tel:** 1 661 324-0031.
TELEVISION STATION

KBTR-TV 32451
Owner: Louisiana Television Broadcasting LLC
Editorial: 1650 Highland Rd, Baton Rouge, Louisiana 70802-7018 **Tel:** 1 225 387-2222.
Profile: KBTR-TV is an independent station for the Baton Rouge, LA market. The station is owned by Louisiana Television Broadcasting LLC. The station broadcasts on channel 41.
TELEVISION STATION

KBTU-TV 591891
Owner: Adelante Media Group
Editorial: 2722 S Redwood Rd Ste 1, Salt Lake City, Utah 84119-8410 **Tel:** 1 801 908-8777.
Profile: KBTU-TV is the MundoFOX affiliate for the Salt Lake City market.. The station is owned by Adelante Media Group and broadcasts on channel 23. All programming is aired in Spanish.
TELEVISION STATION

KBTV-TV 31498
Owner: Sinclair Broadcast Group
Editorial: 6155 Eastex Fwy Ste 300, Beaumont, Texas 77706-6707 **Tel:** 1 409 892-6622.
Email: news@kfdm.com
Web site: http://www.fox4beaumont.com
Profile: KBTV-TV is the FOX affiliate for the Beaumont-Port Arthur, TX market. The station is owned by Nexstar Broadcasting Group. KBTV-TV broadcasts locally on channel 4.
TELEVISION STATION

KBTX-TV 32446
Owner: Gray Television
Editorial: 4141 E 29th St, Bryan, Texas 77802-4305 **Tel:** 1 979 846-7778.
Email: news@kbtx.com

Web site: http://www.kbtx.com
Profile: KBTX-TV is the CBS affiliate for the Waco, TX market. The station is owned by Gray Television KBTX-TV broadcasts locally on channel 3.
TELEVISION STATION

KBVO-TV 390602
Owner: Nexstar Media Group, Inc.
Editorial: 908 W Martin Luther King Jr Blvd, Austin, Texas 78701-1018 **Tel:** 1 512 476-3636.
Web site: http://myaustintv.clientmediaserver.com
Profile: KBVO-TV is the local MyNetworkTV affiliate on channel 51 for the greater Austin, TX area. KBVO-TV is owned by Nexstar Media Group, Inc. and is a sister station to KXAN-TV.
TELEVISION STATION

KBVU-TV 32519
Owner: Esteem Broadcasting, LLC
Editorial: 333 6th St, Eureka, California 95501-1035 **Tel:** 1 707 442-2999.
Web site: http://www.krcrtv.com/station/about-our-stations/20902556
Profile: KBVU-TV is a FOX affiliate for the Eureka, CA market. The station is owned by Esteem Broadcasting, LLC. KBVU-TV broadcasts locally on channel 28.
TELEVISION STATION

KBZK-TV 87709
Owner: Cordillera Communications Inc.
Editorial: 90 Television Way, Bozeman, Montana 59718-7749 **Tel:** 1 406 922-2400.
Email: newstips@kbzk.com
Web site: http://www.kbzk.com
Profile: KBZK-TV is the CBS affiliate located in Bozeman, MT. The station is owned by Cordillera Communications Inc. KBZK-TV broadcasts locally on channel 7.
TELEVISION STATION

KBZO-TV 133736
Owner: Entravision Communications Corp.
Editorial: 6502 Caprock Dr, Lubbock, Texas 79412-3712 **Tel:** 1 806 763-6051.
Web site: http://noticias.entravision.com/lubbock
Profile: KBZO-TV is the Univision network affiliate for the Lubbock, TX market. The station is owned by Entravision Communications Corp. KBZO-TV broadcasts locally on channel 51.
TELEVISION STATION

KCAL-TV 31475
Owner: CBS Television Stations
Editorial: 4200 Radford Ave, Studio City, California 91604-2189 **Tel:** 1 818 655-2000.
Email: kcbstvassignmentdesk@cbs.com
Web site: http://losangeles.cbslocal.com
Profile: KCAL-TV is an independent affiliate for the Los Angeles market. The station is owned by CBS Television Stations. KCAL-TV broadcasts locally on channel 9.
TELEVISION STATION

KCAU-TV 32635
Owner: Nexstar Broadcasting Group, Inc.
Editorial: 625 Douglas St, Sioux City, Iowa 51101-1215 **Tel:** 1 712 277-2345.
Email: news@kcautv.com
Web site: http://www.siouxlandmatters.com
Profile: KCAU-TV is the ABC network affiliate for the Sioux City, IA market. The station is owned by Nexstar Broadcasting Group, Inc.. KCAU-TV broadcasts locally on channel 9.
TELEVISION STATION

KCBA-TV 31402
Owner: Seal Rock Broadcasters, LLC
Editorial: 1550 Moffett St, Salinas, California 93905-3342 **Tel:** 1 831 642-4400.
Web site: http://www.kcba.com
Profile: KCBA-TV is the FOX affiliate for the Salinas-Monterey, CA market. The station is owned by Seal Rock Broadcasters, LLC. KCBA-TV broadcasts locally on channel 35.
TELEVISION STATION

KCBB-TV 476757
Owner: Cocola Broadcasting Companies
Editorial: 706 W Herndon Ave, Fresno, California 93650-1033 **Tel:** 1 559 435-7000.
Email: info@cocolatv.com
Web site: http://www.cocolatv.com
Profile: KCBB-TV is the Azteca America affiliate for the Fresno-Visalia, CA market. The station is owned by Cocola Broadcasting Companies. KCBB-TV broadcasts locally on channel 51.
TELEVISION STATION

KCBD-TV 31403
Owner: Raycom Media Inc.
Editorial: 5600 Avenue A, Lubbock, Texas 79404-4598 **Tel:** 1 806 744-1414.
Email: 11listens@kcbd.com
Web site: http://www.kcbd.com
Profile: KCBD-TV is the NBC affiliate for the Lubbock, TX market. The station is owned by Raycom Media Inc. KCBD-TV broadcasts locally on channel 11.
TELEVISION STATION

KCBS-TV 31404
Owner: CBS Television Stations
Editorial: 4200 Radford Ave, Studio City, California 91604-2189 **Tel:** 1 818 655-2000.
Email: kcbstvassignmentdesk@cbs.com
Web site: http://losangeles.cbslocal.com
Profile: KCBS-TV is the CBS affiliate for the Los Angeles market. The station is owned by CBS Television Stations. KCBS-TV broadcasts locally on channel 2.
TELEVISION STATION

KCCI-TV 31405
Owner: Hearst Television Inc.
Editorial: 888 9th St, Des Moines, Iowa 50309-1202 **Tel:** 1 515 247-8888.
Email: news@kcci.com
Web site: http://www.kcci.com
Profile: KCCI-TV is the CBS affiliate for the Des Moines, IA market. The station is owned by Heast Television Inc. KCCI-TV broadcasts locally on channel 8.
TELEVISION STATION

KCDO-TV 608108
Owner: Newsweb Corporation
Editorial: 3001 S Jamaica Ct Ste 210, Aurora, Colorado 80014-2668 **Tel:** 1 303 925-0303.
Email: info@k3colorado.com
Web site: http://www.k3colorado.com
TELEVISION STATION

KCEC-TV 32376
Owner: Entravision Communications Corp.
Editorial: 1907 Mile High Stadium West Cir, Denver, Colorado 80204-1908 **Tel:** 1 303 832-0050.
Web site: http://www.somosnoticiascolorado.com
Profile: KCEC-TV is a Univision affiliate for the Denver market. The station is owned by Entravision Communications Corp. KCEC-TV broadcasts locally on channel 50.
TELEVISION STATION

KCEN2-TV 829864
Owner: TEGNA Inc.
Editorial: 314 S I H 35, Eddy, Texas 76524-2463 **Tel:** 1 254 859-5481.
Email: news@kcentv.com
Profile: KCEN2-TV is a multicast channel of KCEN-TV. A multicast channel is a separate channel that shares the bandwidth of the main station but can air unique programming. KCEN2-TV is the MundoFOX affiliate for the Waco, TX market. The station is owned by TEGNA Inc. KCEN2-TV broadcasts locally on channel 6.2.
TELEVISION STATION

KCEN-TV 31406
Owner: TEGNA Inc.
Editorial: 314 S I H 35, Eddy, Texas 76524-2463 **Tel:** 1 254 859-5481.
Email: news@kcentv.com
Web site: http://www.kcentv.com
Profile: KCEN-TV is the NBC affiliate for the Waco, TX market. The station is owned by TEGNA Inc. KCEN-TV broadcasts locally on channel 6.
TELEVISION STATION

KCET2-TV 607036
Owner: Community TV of Southern California
Editorial: 2900 W Alameda Ave Unit 600, Burbank, California 91505-4267 **Tel:** 1 747 201-5000.
Email: contact@kcet.org
Web site: http://www.kcet.org
Profile: KCET2-TV is a multicast channel of KCET-TV. A multicast channel is a separate channel that shares the bandwith of the main station but can air unique programming. KCET-TV2 is the KCET Kids & Family Channel affiliate for the Los Angeles market. The station is owned by Community TV of Southern California. KCET2-TV broadcasts locally on channel 28.2. The station prefers to be contacted by e-mail.
TELEVISION STATION

KCET3-TV 607041
Owner: Community TV of Southern California
Editorial: 2900 W Alameda Ave Unit 600, Burbank, California 91505-4267 **Tel:** 1 747 201-5000.
Email: contact@kcet.org
Web site: http://www.kcet.org
Profile: KCET3-TV is a multicast channel of KCET-TV. A multicast channel is a separate channel that shares the bandwidth of the main station but can air unique programming. KCET3-TV is the V-me affiliate for the Los Angeles market. The station is owned by Community TV of Southern California. KCET3-TV broadcasts locally on channel 28.3. The station prefers to be contacted by e-mail.
TELEVISION STATION

KCET4-TV 607044
Owner: Community TV of Southern California
Editorial: 2900 W Alameda Ave Unit 600, Burbank, California 91505-4267 **Tel:** 1 747 201-5000.
Email: contact@kcet.org
Web site: http://www.kcet.org
Profile: KCET4-TV is a multicast channel of KCET-TV. A multicast channel is a separate channel that shares the bandwith of the main station but can air unique programming. KCET-TV4 is the MHz Worldview affiliate for the Los Angeles market. The station is owned by Community TV of Southern California. KCET3-TV broadcasts locally on channel 28.4. The station prefers to be contacted by e-mail.
TELEVISION STATION

KCET-TV 31407
Owner: KCETLink
Editorial: 2900 W Alameda Ave, Burbank, California 91505-4220 **Tel:** 1 747 201-5000.
Email: contact@kcet.org
Web site: http://www.kcet.org
Profile: KCET-TV is the an independent affiliate for the Los Angeles market. The station is owned by KCETLink. KCET-TV broadcasts locally on channel 28. The station prefers to be contacted by e-mail.
TELEVISION STATION

KCFW-TV 32757
Owner: Bonten Media Group, LLC
Editorial: 401 1st Ave E, Kalispell, Montana 59901-4937 **Tel:** 1 406 755-5239.
Email: news@kcfw.com
Web site: http://www.nbcmontana.com
Profile: KCFW-TV is the NBC affiliate for the Missoula, MT market. The station is owned by Bonten Media Group, LLC. KCFW-TV broadcasts locally on channel 9.
TELEVISION STATION

KCHF-TV 32305
Owner: Son Broadcasting
Editorial: 27556 I 25 East Frontage Rd, Santa Fe, New Mexico 87508-0269 **Tel:** 1 505 473-1111.
Email: info@sonbroadcasting.org
Web site: http://www.sonbroadcasting.org
Profile: KCHF-TV is an independent station for the Albuquerque, NM market. The station is owned by Son Broadcasting. KCHF-TV broadcasts locally on channel 11.
TELEVISION STATION

KCIT-TV 31409
Owner: Mission Broadcasting
Editorial: 1015 S Fillmore St, Amarillo, Texas 79101-3517 **Tel:** 1 806 374-1414.
Email: foxtalk@fox14.tv
Web site: http://myhighplains.com
Profile: KCIT-TV is the FOX network affiliate for the Amarillo, TX market. The station is owned by Mission Broadcasting. KCIT-TV broadcasts locally on channel 14.
TELEVISION STATION

KCNC-TV 31410
Owner: CBS Television Stations
Editorial: 1044 Lincoln St, Denver, Colorado 80203-2714 **Tel:** 1 303 861-4444.
Email: kcncnews@cbs.com
Web site: http://denver.cbslocal.com
Profile: KCNC-TV is the CBS affiliate for the Denver market. The station is owned by CBS Television Stations. KCNC-TV broadcasts locally on channel 4.
TELEVISION STATION

KCNS-TV 32272
Owner: NRJ TV, LLC
Editorial: 1700 Montgomery St Ste 400, San Francisco, California 94111-1025 **Tel:** 1 415 954-7149.
Profile: KCNS-TV is the MundoFOX affiliate for the San Francisco market. The station is owned by NRJ TV, LLC. The format of the station is Hispanic programming. KCNS-TV broadcasts locally on channel 38.
TELEVISION STATION

KCOP2-TV 798011
Owner: Fox Broadcasting Company
Editorial: 1999 S Bundy Dr, Los Angeles, California 90025-5203 **Tel:** 1 310 584-2000.
Web site: http://www.bouncetv.com
Profile: KCOP2-TV is a multicast channel of KCOP-TV. A multicast channel is a separate channel that shares the bandwidth of the main station but can air unique programming. KCOP2-TV is the local Bounce TV affiliate on channel 13.2 for the Los Angeles market. KCOP2-TV is owned by Fox Broadcasting Company.
TELEVISION STATION

KCOP-TV 31411
Owner: FOX Broadcasting Company
Editorial: 1999 S Bundy Dr, Los Angeles, California 90025-5203 **Tel:** 1 310 584-2000.
Web site: http://www.foxla.com/my13
Profile: KCOP-TV is the MyNetworkTV affiliate for the Los Angeles market. The station is owned by FOX Broadcasting Company. KCOP-TV broadcasts locally on channel 13.
TELEVISION STATION

KCOS-TV 31412
Owner: El Paso Public TV Foundation
Editorial: 9050 Viscount Blvd Ste A440, El Paso, Texas 79925-6511 **Tel:** 1 915 590-1313.
Web site: http://www.kcostv.org
Profile: KCOS-TV is the PBS affiliate for the El Paso, TX market. The station is owned by El Paso Public TV Foundation. KCOS-TV broadcasts locally on channel 13.
TELEVISION STATION

KCOY-TV 31413
Owner: Cowles Publishing Company
Editorial: 1211 W McCoy Ln, Santa Maria, California 93455-1036 **Tel:** 1 805 925-1200.
Email: assignmentdesk@keyt.com
Web site: http://www.keyt.com
Profile: KCOY-TV is the CBS network affiliate for the Santa Barbara, CA market. The station is owned by Cowles Publishing Company. KCOY-TV broadcasts locally on channel 12. The station has a shared-services agreement with KEYT-TV.
TELEVISION STATION

KCPM-TV 390765
Owner: GIG Inc.
Tel: 1 701 364-9900.
Web site: http://www.kcpm.tv
Profile: KCPM-TV is the MyNetworkTV affiliate for the Fargo, ND market. The station is owned by GIG Inc. KCPM-TV broadcasts locally on channel 27.
TELEVISION STATION

KCPO-TV 389779
Owner: GIG Inc.
Editorial: 2229 W 50th St, Sioux Falls, South Dakota 57105-6525 **Tel:** 1 605 334-0026.
Email: mail@kcpo.tv
Web site: http://www.kcpo.tv
Profile: KCPO-TV is an independent station for the Sioux Falls, SD market. The station is owned by GIG Inc. KCPO-TV broadcasts locally on channel 26.
TELEVISION STATION

KCPQ2-TV 612595
Owner: Tribune Broadcasting Co.
Editorial: 1813 Westlake Ave N, Seattle, Washington 98109-2706 **Tel:** 1 206 674-1313.
Email: tips@q13fox.com
Web site: http://www.q13fox.com
Profile: KCPQ2-TV is a multicast of KCPQ-TV. A multicast channel is a separate channel that shares the bandwith of the main station but can air unique programming. KCPQ2-TV airs programming from The Local Accuweather Channel in the Seattle market. The station is owned by Tribune Broadcasting Co. KCPQ2-TV broadcasts locally on channel 13.2.
TELEVISION STATION

KCPQ-TV 31415
Owner: Tribune Broadcasting Co.
Editorial: 1813 Westlake Ave N, Seattle, Washington 98109-2706 **Tel:** 1 206 674-1313.
Email: tips@q13fox.com
Web site: http://www.q13fox.com
Profile: KCPQ-TV is the FOX affiliate for the Seattle-Tacoma market. The station is owned by Tribune Broadcasting Co. KCPQ-TV broadcasts locally on channel 13.
TELEVISION STATION

KCPT3-TV 621855
Owner: Kansas City Public Television
Editorial: 125 E 31st St, Kansas City, Missouri 64108-3299 **Tel:** 1 816 756-3580.
Web site: http://www.kcpt.org
Profile: KCPT3-TV is a multicast channel of KCPT-TV. A multicast is a separate channel that shares the bandwith of the main station but can air unique programming. KCPT3-TV airs how to, DIY and instructional programming from Create in the Kansas City, MO market. The station is owned by Kansas City Public Television. KCPT3-TV broadcasts locally on channel 19.3.
TELEVISION STATION

KCPT-TV 31416
Owner: Kansas City Public Television
Editorial: 125 E 31st St, Kansas City, Missouri 64108-3216 **Tel:** 1 816 756-3580.
Email: customer_service@kcpt.org
Web site: https://www.kcpt.org
Profile: KCPT-TV is the PBS affiliate for the Kansas City, MO market. The station is owned by Kansas City Public Television. KCPT-TV broadcasts locally on channel 19.
TELEVISION STATION

KCRA2-TV 612907
Owner: Hearst Television Inc.
Editorial: 3 Television Cir, Sacramento, California 95814-0750 **Tel:** 1 916 446-3333.
Web site: http://metvnetwork.com
Profile: KCRA2-TV is the MeTV Network affiliate for the Sacramento, CA market. The station is owned by Hearst Television Inc. KCRA2-TV broadcasts locally on channel 3.2. KCRA2-TV is a multicast channel of KCRA-TV. A multicast channel is a separate channel that shares the bandwidth of the main station but can air unique programming. The station specializes in syndicated reruns of classic TV programs of the 1950s through the 1980s.
TELEVISION STATION

KCRA-TV 31417
Owner: Hearst Television Inc.
Editorial: 3 Television Cir, Sacramento, California 95814-0750 **Tel:** 1 916 446-3333.
Email: newstips@kcra.com
Web site: http://www.kcra.com/
Profile: KCRA-TV is the NBC network affiliate for the Sacramento, CA market. The station is owned by Hearst Television Inc. KCRA-TV broadcasts locally on channel 3.
TELEVISION STATION

KCRG-TV 31418
Owner: Gazette Company (The)
Editorial: 501 2nd Ave SE, Cedar Rapids, Iowa 52401-1303 **Tel:** 1 319 399-5900.
Email: newsreleases@kcrg.com
Web site: http://www.kcrg.com
Profile: KCRG-TV is the ABC affiliate for the Cedar Rapids, IA market. The station is owned by The Gazette Company. KCRG-TV broadcasts locally on channel 9.
TELEVISION STATION

KCRP-TV 135814
Owner: Entravision Communications Corp.
Editorial: 102 N Mesquite St, Corpus Christi, Texas 78401-2823 **Tel:** 1 361 883-2823.
Profile: KCRP-TV is the Telefutura affiliate for the Corpus Christi, TX market. The station is owned by Entravision Communications Corp. KCRP-TV broadcasts locally on channel 41.
TELEVISION STATION

KCSG-TV 32555
Owner: Southwest Media LLC
Editorial: 158 W 1600 S Ste 200, Saint George, Utah 84770-7272 **Tel:** 1 435 634-1400.
Email: programming@kcsg.com
Web site: http://www.kcsg.com
Profile: KCSG-TV is an independent station for the Saint George, UT market. The station is owned by Southwest Media LLC. The station does not have a newsroom. KCSG-TV broadcasts locally on channel 14.
TELEVISION STATION

KCSI-TV 76864
Owner: Cable Services, Inc.
Editorial: 308 2nd St SW, Jamestown, North Dakota 58401-4117 **Tel:** 1 701 252-2400.
Email: news@kcsitv.com
Web site: http://www.kcsitv.com
Profile: KCSI-TV is an independent station in the Fargo, ND market. The station is owned by Cable Services, Inc. KCSI-TV broadcasts locally on channel 32.
TELEVISION STATION

KCSO-TV 128436
Owner: Serestar Communications Corporation
Editorial: 500 Media Pl, Sacramento, California 95815-3733 **Tel:** 1 916 567-3300.
Email: telemundo33@serestar.com
Web site: http://telemundo33sacramento.com
Profile: KCSO-TV is the Telemundo affiliate for the Sacramento, CA market. The station is owned by Serestar Communications Corporation. KCSO-TV broadcasts locally on channel 33.
TELEVISION STATION

KCTS2-TV 612340
Owner: KCTS Television
Editorial: 401 Mercer St, Seattle, Washington 98109-4699 **Tel:** 1 206 728-6463.
Email: start@kcts9.org
Web site: http://www.kcts.org
Profile: KCTS2-TV is a multicast of KCTS-TV. A multicast channel is a separate channel that shares the bandwith of the main station but can air unique programming. KCTS2-TV airs programming from V-me in the Seattle market. The station is owned by KCTS Television. KCTS2-TV broadcasts locally on channel 9.2.
TELEVISION STATION

KCTS3-TV 612343
Owner: KCTS Television
Editorial: 401 Mercer St, Seattle, Washington 98109-4699 **Tel:** 1 206 728-6463.
Email: start@kcts9.org
Web site: http://www.kcts.org
Profile: KCTS3-TV is a multicast of KCTS-TV. A multicast channel is a separate channel that shares the bandwith of the main station but can air unique programming. KCTS3-TV airs programming from Create in the Seattle market. The station is owned by KCTS Television. KCTS3-TV broadcasts locally on channel 9.3.
TELEVISION STATION

KCTS-TV 31422
Owner: KCTS Television
Editorial: 401 Mercer St, Seattle, Washington 98109-4699 **Tel:** 1 206 728-6463.
Email: start@kcts9.org
Web site: http://www.kcts9.org
Profile: KCTS-TV is the PBS affiliate for the Seattle market. The station is owned by KCTS Television. KCTS-TV broadcasts locally on channel 9.
TELEVISION STATION

KCTU2-TV 702063
Owner: River City Broadcasting, Inc.
Editorial: 2100 E Douglas Ave, Wichita, Kansas 67214-4336 **Tel:** 1 316 267-8855.
Email: kctu@kctu.com
Web site: http://www.kctu.com
Profile: KCTU2-TV is a multicast channel of KCTU-TV. A multicast channel is a separate channel that shares the bandwith of the main station but can air unique programming. KCTU2-TV is in the Wichita, KS market. The station is owned by River City Broadcasting, Inc. KCTU2-TV broadcasts locally on channel 43.2.
TELEVISION STATION

KCTU-TV 87978
Owner: River City Broadcasting Inc.
Editorial: 2100 E Douglas Ave, Wichita, Kansas 67214-4336 **Tel:** 1 316 267-8855.
Email: kctu@kctu.com
Web site: http://www.kctu.com
Profile: KCTU-TV is an independent affiliate for the Wichita-Hutchinson, KS market. The station is owned by River City Broadcasting Inc. KCTU-TV broadcasts locally on channel 5.
TELEVISION STATION

KCTV-TV 31423
Owner: Meredith Broadcasting Group
Editorial: 4500 Shawnee Mission Pkwy, Fairway, Kansas 66205-2509 **Tel:** 1 913 677-5555.
Email: newsdesk@kctv5.com
Web site: http://www.kctv5.com
Profile: KCTV-TV is the CBS affiliate for the Kansas City, MO market. The station is owned by Meredith Broadcasting Group. KCTV-TV broadcasts locally on channel 5.
TELEVISION STATION

KCVB-TV 736562
Owner: Cache Valley Television
Tel: 1 435 752-7537.
Web site: http://thevalleychannel.com
Profile: KCVB-TV is an independent channel for the Salt Lake City market. The station is owned by Cache Valley Television. KCVB- TV broadcasts locally on channel 26.
TELEVISION STATION

KCVU-TV 32419
Owner: Esteem Broadcasting, LLC
Editorial: 300 Main St, Chico, California 95928-5438 **Tel:** 1 530 893-1234.
Web site: http://www.krcrtv.com/kcvufox20/19008234
Profile: KCVU-TV is a FOX affiliate for the Chico, CA market. The station is owned by Esteem Broadcasting, LLC. KCVU-TV broadcasts locally on channel 20.
TELEVISION STATION

KCWC-TV 32372
Owner: Central Wyoming College
Editorial: 2660 Peck Ave, Riverton, Wyoming 82501-2215 **Tel:** 1 307 856-6944.
Email: tdugas@cwc.edu
Web site: http://www.wyomingpbs.org
Profile: KCWC-TV is the PBS affiliate for the Riverton, WY market. The station is owned by Central Wyoming College. KCWC-TV broadcasts locally on channel 4.
TELEVISION STATION

KCWE2-TV 620995
Owner: Hearst Television Inc.
Editorial: 6455 Winchester Ave, Kansas City, Missouri 64133-4609 **Tel:** 1 816 221-2900.
Web site: http://www.kmbc.com/kcwetv
Profile: KCWE2-TV is a multicast of KCWE-TV. A multicast channel is a separate channel that shares the bandwith of the main station but can air unique programming. KCWE2-TV airs programming from This TV Network in the Kansas City, MO market. The station is owned by Hearst Television Inc. KCWE2-TV broadcasts locally on channel 29.2.
TELEVISION STATION

KCWE-TV 63264
Owner: Hearst Television Inc.
Editorial: 6455 Winchester Ave, Kansas City, Missouri 64133-4609 **Tel:** 1 816 221-9999.
Email: news@kmbc.com
Web site: http://www.kmbc.com/kcwetv
Profile: KCWE-TV is the CW affiliate for the Kansas City, MO market. The station is owned by Hearst Television Inc. KCWE-TV broadcasts locally on channel 29.
TELEVISION STATION

KCWI-TV 139620
Editorial: 500 SW 7th St Ste 300, Des Moines, Iowa 50309-4506 **Tel:** 1 515 457-9645.
Email: news@weareiowa.com
Web site: http://www.weareiowa.com/kcwi2
Profile: KCWI-TV is the CW affiliate for the Des Moines, IA market. KCWI-TV broadcasts locally on channel 23.
TELEVISION STATION

KCWX2-TV 615018
Owner: Corridor Television LLP
Tel: 1 512 391-0641.
Web site: http://www.kcwx.com
Profile: KCWX2-TV is a multicast of KCWX-TV. A multicast channel is a separate channel that shares the bandwith of the main station but can air unique programming. KCWX2-TV airs programming from the This TV Network in the San Antonio market. The station is owned by Corridor Television LLP. KCWX2-TV broadcasts locally on channel 2.2.
TELEVISION STATION

KCWX-TV 72047
Owner: Corridor Television LLP
Editorial: 1402 West Ave, Austin, Texas 78701-1528 **Tel:** 1 512 391-0641.
Web site: http://www.kcwx.com
Profile: KCWX-TV is the My Television affiliate for the San Antonio market. The station is owned by Corridor Television LLP. KCWX-TV broadcasts locally on channel 2.
TELEVISION STATION

KCWY-TV 154088
Owner: Gray Television
Editorial: 141 Progress Cir, Mills, Wyoming 82644-7701 **Tel:** 1 307 577-0013.
Email: comments@kcwy13.com
Web site: http://www.kcwy13.com
Profile: KCWY-TV is the NBC affiliate for the Casper and Riverton, WY market. The station is owned by Bozeman Trail Communications Company. KCWY-TV broadcasts locally on channel 13.
TELEVISION STATION

KCYU-TV 32558
Owner: Northwest Broadcasting
Editorial: 1205 W Lincoln Ave, Yakima, Washington 98902-2535 **Tel:** 1 509 574-4141.
Web site: http://www.myfoxyakima.com
Profile: KCYU-TV is the FOX affiliate for Yakima, WA market. The station is owned by Northwest Broadcasting. KCYU-TV broadcasts locally on channel 41.
TELEVISION STATION

KDAF-TV 31424
Owner: Tribune Broadcasting Co.
Editorial: 8001 John W Carpenter Fwy, Dallas, Texas 75247-4718 **Tel:** 1 214 252-9233.
Email: newstips@cw33.com
Web site: http://cw33.com
Profile: KDAF-TV is the CW affiliate for the Dallas market. The station is owned by Tribune Broadcasting Co. KDAF-TV broadcasts locally on channel 33.
TELEVISION STATION

KDBC-TV 31425
Owner: Sinclair Broadcast Group
Editorial: 200 S Alto Mesa Dr, El Paso, Texas 79912-4426 **Tel:** 1 915 833-8585.
Web site: http://www.cbs4local.com
Profile: KDBC-TV is the CBS affiliate for the El Paso, TX market. The station is owned by Sinclair Broadcast Group. KDBC-TV broadcasts locally on channel 4.
TELEVISION STATION

KDCU-TV 603173
Owner: Entravision Communications Corp.
Editorial: 2815 E 37th St N, Wichita, Kansas 67219 **Tel:** 1 316 838-1212.
Email: programming@univisionkansas.com
Web site: http://www.univisionkansas.com
Profile: KDCU-TV is the Univision affiliate for the Wichita, KS market. The station is owned by Entravision Communications Corp. KDCU-TV broadcasts locally on channel 31.
TELEVISION STATION

KDEN-TV 32423
Owner: NBC Universal
Editorial: 2851 S Parker Rd Ste 1130, Aurora, Colorado 80014-2732 **Tel:** 1 303 338-2390.
Web site: http://www.telemundodenver.com
Profile: KDEN-TV is the Telemundo network affiliate for the Denver market. The station is owned by NBC Universal. KDEN-TV broadcasts locally on channel 25.
TELEVISION STATION

KDFI2-TV 800864
Owner: Fox Broadcasting Company
Editorial: 400 N Griffin St, Dallas, Texas 75202-1905 **Tel:** 1 214 720-4444.
Profile: KDFI2-TV is a multicast channel of KDFI-TV. A multicast channel is a separate channel that shares the bandwith of the main station but can air unique programming. KDFI2-TV is the Bounce TV affiliate for the Dallas market. The station is owned by Fox Broadcasting Company. KDVI-TV broadcasts locally on channel 27.2.
TELEVISION STATION

KDFI-TV 31427
Owner: Fox Broadcasting Company
Editorial: 400 N Griffin St, Dallas, Texas 75202-1905 **Tel:** 1 214 720-4444.
Web site: http://www.fox4news.com/kdfi-my27
Profile: KDFI-TV is a MyNetworkTV affiliate for the Dallas-Fort Worth market. The station is owned by Fox Broadcasting Company. KDFI-TV broadcasts locally on channel 27.
TELEVISION STATION

KDF-TV 32570
Owner: Evening Post Publishing Co.
Editorial: 409 S Staples St, Corpus Christi, Texas 78401-3330 **Tel:** 1 361 886-6100.
Web site: http://www.kristv.com
Profile: KDF-TV is the FOX network affiliate for the Corpus Christi, TX market. The station is owned by the Evening Post Publishing Co. KDF-TV broadcasts locally on channel 47. To contact the station please use the online contact form.
TELEVISION STATION

KDFW-TV 31428
Owner: Fox Broadcasting Company
Editorial: 400 N Griffin St, Dallas, Texas 75202-1905 **Tel:** 1 214 720-4444.
Email: kdfw@kdfwfox4.com
Web site: http://www.fox4news.com
Profile: KDFW-TV is the FOX affiliate for the Dallas-Fort Worth market. The station is owned by Fox Broadcasting Company. KDFW broadcasts locally on channel 4.
TELEVISION STATION

KDFX-TV 154098
Owner: News-Press & Gazette Co.
Editorial: 42650 Melanie Pl, Palm Desert, California 92211 **Tel:** 1 760 779-1507.
Web site: http://kesq.com
Profile: KDFX-TV is the FOX affiliate for the Palm Desert, CA market. The station is owned by News-Press & Gazette Co. KDFX-TV broadcasts locally on channel 33.
TELEVISION STATION

KDIN-TV 32702
Owner: Iowa Public Television
Editorial: 6450 Corporate Dr, Johnston, Iowa 50131-7700 **Tel:** 1 515 725-9700.
Email: publicinformation@iptv.org
Web site: http://www.iptv.org
Profile: KDIN-TV is the PBS affiliate for the Des Moines, IA market. The station is owned by Iowa Public Television. KDIN-TV broadcasts locally on channel 11.
TELEVISION STATION

KDJT-TV 432429
Owner: Entravision Communications Corp.
Editorial: 67 Garden Ct, Monterey, California 93940 **Tel:** 1 831 373-6767.
Web site: http://www.ksmstv.com
TELEVISION STATION

KDKA-TV 31429
Owner: CBS Television Stations
Editorial: 420 Fort Duquesne Blvd Ste 100, Pittsburgh, Pennsylvania 15222-1416 **Tel:** 1 412 575-2200.
Email: newsdesk@kdka.com
Web site: http://pittsburgh.cbslocal.com
Profile: KDKA-TV is the CBS affiliate for the Pittsburgh market. The station is owned by CBS Television Stations. KDKA-TV broadcasts locally on channel 2.
TELEVISION STATION

KDKF-TV 32348
Owner: Chambers Communications Corp.
Editorial: 1090 Knutson Ave, Medford, Oregon 97504-4164 **Tel:** 1 541 883-3131.
Web site: http://www.kdrv.com
Profile: KDKF-TV is an ABC affiliate for the Klamath Falls, OR market. The station is owned by Chambers Communications Corp. KDKF-TV broadcasts locally on channel 31.
TELEVISION STATION

KDLH-TV 31430
Owner: Sagamore Hill Broadcasting
Editorial: 246 S Lake Ave, Duluth, Minnesota 55802-2304 **Tel:** 1 218 720-9600.
Web site: http://www.northlandsnewscenter.com
Profile: KDLH-TV is the CBS affiliate for Duluth, MN, Superior, WI market. The station is owned by Sagamore Hill Broadcasting. KDLH-TV broadcasts locally on channel 3.
TELEVISION STATION

KDLT-TV 31431
Owner: Red River Broadcasting
Editorial: 3600 S Westport Ave, Sioux Falls, South Dakota 57106-6342 **Tel:** 1 605 361-5555.
Email: news@kdlt.com
Web site: http://www.kdlt.com
Profile: KDLT-TV is the NBC affiliate for the Sioux Falls, SD market. The station is owned by Red River Broadcasting. KDLT-TV broadcasts locally on channel 46.
TELEVISION STATION

KDMD-TV 32392
Owner: Ketchikan TV, LLC
Editorial: 1310 E 66th Ave, Anchorage, Alaska 99518-1915 **Tel:** 1 907 562-5363.
Web site: http://kdmd.tv
Profile: KDMD-TV is the ION Television affiliate for the Anchorage, AK market. The station is owned by Ketchikan TV, LLC. KDMD-TV broadcasts locally on channel 33.
TELEVISION STATION

KDNL-TV 31432
Owner: Sinclair Broadcast Group, Inc.
Editorial: 1215 Cole St, Saint Louis, Missouri 63106-3818 **Tel:** 1 314 436-3030.
Email: info@abcstlouis.com
Web site: http://www.abcstlouis.com
Profile: KDNL-TV is the ABC affiliate in St. Louis. The station is owned by Sinclair Broadcast Group, Inc. KDNL-TV broadcasts locally on channel 30. The station does not have a news department, newscasts are produced by St. Louis NBC affiliate KSDK-TV. News related items must be sent to KSDK-TV.
TELEVISION STATION

KDOC-TV 31433
Owner: Ellis Communications
Editorial: 625 N Grand Ave, Santa Ana, California 92701-4347 **Tel:** 1 949 442-9800.
Email: feedback@kdoc.tv
Web site: http://www.kdoctv.net
Profile: KDOC-TV is an independent, commercial station for the Los Angeles market. The station is owned by Ellis Communications. KDOC-TV broadcasts locally on channel 56.
TELEVISION STATION

KDOV-TV 938104
Owner: UCB USA Inc.
Editorial: 2070 Milligan Way, Medford, Oregon 97504-5894 **Tel:** 1 541 776-5368.
Email: thedove@thedove.us
Web site: http://thedove.us/tv
Profile: KDOV-TV is a non-commercial station owned by UCB USA Inc. for the Medford, OR market. KDOV-TV broadcasts locally on channel 43. The station carries religious Christian programming from the Christian Broadcasting Network.
TELEVISION STATION

KDRV-TV 32263
Owner: Heartland Media
Editorial: 1090 Knutson Ave, Medford, Oregon 97504-4164 **Tel:** 1 541 773-1212.
Email: newsdesk@kdrv.com
Web site: http://www.kdrv.com
Profile: KDRV-TV is the ABC affiliate for the Medford, OR market. The station is owned by Heartland Media. KDRV-TV broadcasts locally on channel 12.
TELEVISION STATION

KDSM-TV 31434
Owner: Sinclair Broadcast Group, Inc.
Editorial: 4023 Fleur Dr, Des Moines, Iowa 50321
Tel: 1 515 287-1717.
Email: comments@kdsm17.com
Web site: http://www.kdsm17.com
Profile: KDSM-TV is the FOX network affiliate for the Des Moines, IA market. The station is owned by Sinclair Broadcast Group, Inc. KDSM-TV broadcasts locally on channel 17.
TELEVISION STATION

KDTN-TV 32331
Owner: Word of God Fellowship, Inc.
Editorial: 3901 Highway 121, Bedford, Texas 76021-3009 **Tel:** 1 817 571-1229.
Email: contactus@daystar.com
Web site: http://www.daystar.com
Profile: KDTN-TV is the Daystar Television Network affiliate for the Dallas-Fort Worth market. The station is owned by Word of God Fellowship, Inc. KDTN-TV broadcasts locally on channel 43.
TELEVISION STATION

KDTP-TV 153317
Owner: Daystar Television Network
Editorial: 222 Navajo Blvd, Holbrook, Arizona 86025
Tel: 1 928 524-1652.
Profile: KDTP-TV is a Daystar Network affiliate for the Phoenix market. The station is owned by Daystar Television Network. KDTP-TV broadcasts locally on channel 11.
TELEVISION STATION

KDTV2-TV 607791
Owner: Univision Communications Inc.
Editorial: 50 Fremont St, Fl 41, San Francisco, California 94105-2240 **Tel:** 1 415 538-8000.
Email: noticias14@tv.univision.com
Profile: KDTV2-TV is a multicast channel of KDTV-TV. A multicast channel is a separate channel that shares the bandwith of the main station but can air unique programming. KDTV2-TV airs programming from KFSF-TV for the San Francisco market. It is owned by Univision Communications Inc. KDTV2-TV broadcasts locally on channel 14.2.
TELEVISION STATION

KDTV-TV 31436
Owner: Univision Communications Inc.
Editorial: 1530 Oakland Rd Ste 150, San Jose, California 95112-1250 **Tel:** 1 415 538-8000.
Email: noticias14@univision.net
Web site: http://univision14.univision.com
Profile: KDTV-TV is the Univision affiliate for the San Francisco market. The station is owned by Univision Communications Inc. KDTV broadcasts locally on channel 14.
TELEVISION STATION

KDTX2-TV 610882
Owner: Trinity Broadcasting Network
Editorial: 2900 W Airport Fwy, Irving, Texas 75062-6017 **Tel:** 1 972 313-1333.
Web site: http://www.tbn.org
Profile: KDTX2-TV is a multicast of KDTX-TV. A multicast channel is a separate channel that shares the bandwith of the main station but can air unique programming. KDTX2-TV airs programming from The Church Channel in the Dallas market. The station is owned by Trinity Broadcasting Network. KDTX2-TV broadcasts locally on channel 58.2.
TELEVISION STATION

KDTX3-TV 610886
Owner: Trinity Broadcasting Network
Editorial: 2900 W Airport Fwy, Irving, Texas 75062-6017 **Tel:** 1 972 313-1333.
Web site: http://www.tbn.org
Profile: KDTX3-TV is a multicast of KDTX-TV. A multicast channel is a separate channel that shares the bandwith of the main station but can air unique programming. KDTX3-TV airs programming from JUICE TV and Smile of a Child TV in the Dallas market. The station is owned by Trinity Broadcasting Network. KDTX3-TV broadcasts locally on channel 58.3.
TELEVISION STATION

KDTX4-TV 610888
Owner: Trinity Broadcasting Network
Editorial: 2900 W Airport Fwy, Irving, Texas 75062-6017 **Tel:** 1 972 313-1333.
Web site: http://www.tbn.org
Profile: KDTX4-TV is a multicast of KDTX-TV. A multicast channel is a separate channel that shares the bandwith of the main station but can air unique programming. KDTX4-TV airs programming from Enlace USA in the Dallas market. The station is owned by Trinity Broadcasting Network. KDTX4-TV broadcasts locally on channel 58.4.
TELEVISION STATION

KDTX5-TV 610890
Owner: Trinity Broadcasting Network
Editorial: 2900 W Airport Fwy, Irving, Texas 75062-6017 **Tel:** 1 972 313-1333.
Web site: http://www.tbn.org
Profile: KDTX5-TV is a multicast of KDTX-TV. A multicast channel is a separate channel that shares the bandwith of the main station but can air unique programming. KDTX5-TV airs programming from TBN Salsa in the Dallas market. The station is owned by Trinity Broadcasting Network. KDTX5-TV broadcasts locally on channel 58.5.
TELEVISION STATION

KDTX-TV 32316
Owner: Trinity Broadcasting Network
Editorial: 2900 W Airport Fwy, Irving, Texas 75062-6017 **Tel:** 1 972 313-1333.
Web site: http://www.tbn.org
Profile: KDTX-TV is a Trinity Broadcast Network affiliate for the Dallas-Fort Worth market. The station is owned by Trinity Broadcast Network. KDTX broadcasts locally on channel 58.
TELEVISION STATION

KDVR-TV 32737
Owner: Tribune Broadcasting Co.
Editorial: 100 E Speer Blvd, Denver, Colorado 80203-3437 **Tel:** 1 303 595-3131.
Email: tips@kdvr.com
Web site: http://www.kdvr.com
Profile: KDVR-TV is the FOX affiliate for the Denver market. The station is owned by Tribune Broadcasting Co. KDVR-TV broadcasts locally on channel 31.
TELEVISION STATION

KEBQ-TV 350209
Owner: Minority Broadcasting, LLC.
Editorial: 1280 Bowie St, Beaumont, Texas 77701-2732 **Tel:** 1 409 813-1000.
Web site: http://www.mytv9.com/
Profile: KEBQ-TV is a MyNetwork TV affiliate for the Beaumont, TX market. The station is owned by Minority Broadcasting LLC. KEBQ-TV broadcasts locally on channel 9.
TELEVISION STATION

KECI-TV 32636
Owner: Bonten Media Group, LLC
Editorial: 340 W Main St, Missoula, Montana 59802-4149 **Tel:** 1 406 721-2063.
Email: news@keci.com
Web site: http://www.nbcmontana.com/keci/news
Profile: KECI-TV is the NBC affiliate for Missoula, MT market. The station is owned by Bonten Media Group, LLC. KECI-TV broadcasts locally on channel 13. All press materials can go to the main email address.
TELEVISION STATION

KECY2-TV 809328
Owner: Gulf California Broadcasting
Editorial: 1965 S 4th Ave Ste B, Yuma, Arizona 85364-5666 **Tel:** 1 928 539-9990.
Web site: http://www.yourtvfamily.com
Profile: KECY2-TV is a multicast channel of KECY-TV. A multicast channel is a separate channel that shares the bandwith of the main station but can air unique programming. KECY2-TV is the ABC Television network for the Yuma, AZ market. The station is owned by Gulf California Broadcasting. KECY2-TV broadcasts locally on channel 9.2.
TELEVISION STATION

KECY-TV 31438
Owner: News-Press & Gazette Company
Editorial: 1965 S 4th Ave, Yuma, Arizona 85364-5666
Tel: 1 928 539-9990.
Email: news@kecytv.com
Web site: http://kecytv.com
Profile: KECY-TV is the FOX affiliate for the Yuma, AZ market. The station is owned by News-Press and Gazette Company. KECY-TV broadcasts locally on channel 9.
TELEVISION STATION

KEDT-TV 31439
Owner: South Texas Public Broadcasting
Editorial: 4455 S Padre Island Dr Ste 38, Corpus Christi, Texas 78411-5122 **Tel:** 1 361 855-2213.
Web site: http://www.kedt.org
Profile: KEDT-TV is a PBS affiliate for the Corpus Christi, TX market. The station is owned by South Texas Public Broadcasting. KEDT-TV broadcasts locally on channel 16.
TELEVISION STATION

KEET-TV 31440
Owner: Redwood Empire Public TV
Editorial: 7246 Humboldt Hill Rd, Eureka, California 95503-7119 **Tel:** 1 707 445-0813.
Email: letters@keet-tv.org
Web site: http://www.keet.org
Profile: KEET-TV channel 13, or KEET Redwood Empire Public Television, is a PBS affiliate that broadcasts out of Eureka, California. The station broadcasts mostly PBS syndicated programming.
TELEVISION STATION

KEJT-TV 342500
Owner: NBC Telemundo
Editorial: 5180 Commerce Dr, Ste I, Murray, Utah 84107-8190 **Tel:** 1 801 313-9500.
Web site: http://www.telemundoutah.net
Profile: KEJT-TV is a Telemundo affiliate for the Salt Lake City market. The station is owned by NBC Telemundo. KEJT-TV broadcasts locally on channel 50.
TELEVISION STATION

KELO-TV 32637
Owner: New Young Broadcasting
Editorial: 501 S Phillips Ave, Sioux Falls, South Dakota 57104 **Tel:** 1 605 336-1100.
Email: news@keloland.com
Web site: http://www.keloland.com
Profile: KELO-TV is the CBS affiliate for the Sioux Falls, SD market. The station is owned by New Young Broadcasting. KELO-TV broadcasts locally on channel 11.
TELEVISION STATION

KELV-TV 133914
Owner: Entravision Communications Corp.
Editorial: 500 Pilot Rd, Las Vegas, Nevada 89119-3625 **Tel:** 1 702 947-2727.
Profile: KELV-TV is the UniMas affiliate for the Las Vegas market. The station is owned by Entravision Communications Corp. KELV-TV broadcasts locally on channel 27.
TELEVISION STATION

KEMO-TV 31459
Owner: Una Vez Mas Holdings LLC
Editorial: 533 Mendocino Ave, Santa Rosa, California 95401-5241 **Tel:** 1 707 526-5050.
Profile: KEMO-TV is an Azteca America affiliate for the San Francisco market. The station is owned by Una Vez Mas Holdings LLC. KEMO-TV broadcasts locally on channel 50.
TELEVISION STATION

KENS2-TV 615020
Owner: TEGNA Inc.
Editorial: 5400 Fredericksburg Rd, San Antonio, Texas 78229-3504 **Tel:** 1 210 366-5000.
Web site: http://www.kens5.com
Profile: KENS2-TV is a multicast of KENS-TV. A multicast channel is a separate channel that shares the bandwith of the main station but can air unique programming. KENS2-TV airs programming from Estrella TV in the San Antonio market. The station is owned by TEGNA Inc. KENS2-TV broadcasts locally on channel 5.2.
TELEVISION STATION

KENS-TV 31441
Owner: TEGNA Inc.
Editorial: 5400 Fredericksburg Rd, San Antonio, Texas 78229-3504 **Tel:** 1 210 366-5000.
Email: news@kens5.com
Web site: http://www.kens5.com
Profile: KENS-TV is the CBS affiliate for the San Antonio, TX market. The station is owned by TEGNA Inc. KENS-TV broadcasts locally on channel 5.
TELEVISION STATION

KENV2-TV 618672
Owner: Sunbelt Broadcasting Co.
Editorial: 1025 Chilton Cir, Elko, Nevada 89801-2599
Tel: 1 775 777-8500.
Email: news@kenvtv.com
Web site: http://www.kenvtv.com
Profile: KENV2-TV is a multicast of KENV-TV. A multicast channel is a separate channel that shares the bandwith of the main station but can air unique programming. KENV2-TV airs programming from ThisTV Network in the Salt Lake City market. The station is owned by Sunbelt Broadcasting Co. KENV2-TV broadcasts locally on channel 4.2.
TELEVISION STATION

KENV-TV 32552
Owner: Sunbelt Broadcasting Co.
Editorial: 1025 Chilton Cir, Elko, Nevada 89801-2599
Tel: 1 775 777-8500.
Email: news@kenvtv.com
Web site: http://www.kenvtv.com
Profile: KENV-TV is a NBC affiliate for the Salt Lake City market. The station is owned by Sunbelt Broadcasting Co. KENV-TV broadcasts locally on channel 10.
TELEVISION STATION

KEPR-TV 32760
Owner: Fisher Communications, Inc.
Editorial: 2807 W Lewis St, Pasco, Washington 99301-6708 **Tel:** 1 509 547-0547.
Email: newsroom@keprtv.com
Web site: http://www.keprtv.com
Profile: KEPR-TV is the CBS affiliate for the Yakima, WA market. The station is owned by Fisher Communications, Inc. KEPR-TV broadcasts locally on channel 19.
TELEVISION STATION

KERA2-TV 610515
Owner: North Texas Public Broadcasting
Editorial: 3000 Harry Hines Blvd, Dallas, Texas 75201-1098 **Tel:** 1 214 871-1390.
Web site: http://www.kera.org
Profile: KERA2-TV is a multicast of KERA-TV. A multicast channel is a separate channel that shares the bandwith of the main station but can air unique programming. KERA2-TV airs programming from World network in the Dallas market. The station is owned by North Texas Public Broadcasting. KERA2-TV broadcasts locally on channel 13.2. Programs from PBS.
TELEVISION STATION

KERA-TV 31443
Owner: North Texas Public Broadcasting
Editorial: 3000 Harry Hines Blvd, Dallas, Texas 75201
Tel: 1 214 871-1390.
Web site: http://www.kera.org
Profile: KERA-TV is the PBS affiliate for the Dallas-Fort Worth market. The station is owned by North Texas Public Broadcasting. KERA-TV broadcasts locally on channel 13.
TELEVISION STATION

KERO-TV 31444
Owner: E.W. Scipps Co.
Editorial: 321 21st St, Bakersfield, California 93301-4120 **Tel:** 1 661 637-2323.
Email: news@kero.com
Web site: http://www.turnto23.com
Profile: KERO-TV is the ABC television affiliate for Bakersfield, CA. The station is owned by E.W. Scipps Co. KERO-TV broadcasts locally on channel 23.
TELEVISION STATION

KESE-TV 331229
Owner: News-Press & Gazette Company
Editorial: 1965 S 4th Ave Ste B, Yuma, Arizona 85364-5666 **Tel:** 1 928 539-9990.
TELEVISION STATION

KESQ-TV 31445
Owner: News-Press & Gazette Co.
Editorial: 31276 Dunham Way, Thousand Palms, California 92276-3310 **Tel:** 1 760 773-0342.
Email: newsline3@kesq.com
Web site: http://www.kesq.com
Profile: KESQ-TV is the ABC affiliate for the Palm Springs, CA market. The station is owned by News-Press & Gazette Co. KESQ-TV broadcasts locally on channel 42. In February 2012, the station merged operations with KPSP-TV.
TELEVISION STATION

KETC2-TV 613401
Owner: St. Louis Regional Public Media Inc.
Editorial: 3655 Olive St, Dana Brown Comm Center, Saint Louis, Missouri 63108-3601 **Tel:** 1 314 512-9000.
Email: letters@ketc.org
Web site: http://ninenet.org
Profile: KETC2-TV is a multicast of KETC-TV. A multicast channel is a separate channel that shares the bandwith of the main station but can air unique programming. KETC2-TV airs programming from KETC Kids in the St. Louis market. The station is owned by St. Louis Regional Public Media Inc. KETC2-TV broadcasts locally on channel 9.2.
TELEVISION STATION

KETC3-TV 613402
Owner: St. Louis Regional Public Media Inc.
Editorial: 3655 Olive St, Dana Brown Comm Center, Saint Louis, Missouri 63108-3601 **Tel:** 1 314 512-9000.
Email: letters@ketc.org
Web site: http://ninenet.org
Profile: KETC3-TV is a multicast of KETC-TV. A multicast channel is a separate channel that shares the bandwith of the main station but can air unique programming. KETC3-TV airs programming from PBS World in the St. Louis market. The station is owned by St. Louis Regional Public Media Inc. KETC3-TV broadcasts locally on channel 9.3.
TELEVISION STATION

KETC4-TV 613404
Owner: St. Louis Regional Public Media Inc.
Editorial: 3655 Olive St, Dana Brown Comm Center, Saint Louis, Missouri 63108-3601 **Tel:** 1 314 512-9000.
Email: letters@ketc.org
Web site: http://ninenet.org
Profile: KETC4-TV is a multicast of KETC-TV. A multicast channel is a separate channel that shares the bandwith of the main station but can air unique programming. KETC4-TV airs programming from Create in the St. Louis market. The station is owned by St. Louis Regional Public Media Inc. KETC4-TV broadcasts locally on channel 9.4.
TELEVISION STATION

KETC-TV 31446
Owner: St. Louis Regional Public Media Inc.
Editorial: 3655 Olive St, Saint Louis, Missouri 63108-3601 **Tel:** 1 314 512-9000.
Web site: http://ninenet.org
Profile: KETC-TV is the PBS network affiliate for the St. Louis market. The station is owned by St. Louis Regional Public Media Inc. KETC-TV broadcasts locally on channel 9.
TELEVISION STATION

KETD-TV 32422
Owner: Liberman Broadcasting Inc.
Editorial: 1117 Cherokee St Ste 200, Denver, Colorado 80204-3638 **Tel:** 1 303 749-3800.
Profile: KETD-TV is an independent station for the Denver market. The station is owned by Liberman Broadcasting, Inc. KETD-TV broadcasts locally on channel 53.
TELEVISION STATION

KETK-TV 32266
Owner: Communications Corp. of America
Editorial: 4300 Richmond Rd, Tyler, Texas 75703-1201 **Tel:** 1 903 581-5656.
Web site: http://www.ketknbc.com
Profile: KETK-TV is the NBC affiliate for the Longview, TX market. The station is owned by Communications Corp. of America. KETK-TV broadcasts locally on channel 56.
TELEVISION STATION

KETV-TV 31447
Owner: Hearst Television Inc.
Editorial: 2665 Douglas St, Omaha, Nebraska 68131-2626 **Tel:** 1 402 345-7777.
Email: news@ketv.com
Web site: http://www.ketv.com
Profile: KETV-TV is the ABC network affiliate for the Omaha, NE market. The station is owned by Hearst Television Inc. KETV-TV broadcasts locally on channel 7.
TELEVISION STATION

KEUS-TV 389765
Owner: Entravision Communications Corp.
Tel: 1 325 482-9277.
Profile: KEUS-LP is a low-powered Entravision television affiliate for the San Angelo, TX market. The station owned by Entravision Communications Corp. KEUS-LP is broadcast locally on channel 31.
TELEVISION STATION

KEVC-TV 390683
Owner: Entravision Communications Corp.
Editorial: 41601 Corporate Way, Palm Desert, California 92260-1971 **Tel:** 1 760 341-5837.
Web site: http://noticias.entravision.com/palm-springs
Profile: KEVC-TV is the Telefutura affiliate for the Los Angeles market. The station is owned by Entravision Communications Corp. KEVC-TV broadcasts locally on channel 5.
TELEVISION STATION

KEVN-TV 32638
Owner: Gray Television, Inc.
Editorial: 2001 Skyline Dr, Rapid City, South Dakota 57701-4492 **Tel:** 1 605 394-7777.
Email: news@blackhillsfox.com
Web site: http://www.blackhillsfox.com
Profile: KEVN-TV is the FOX affiliate for the Rapid City, SD market. The station is owned by Gray Television. KEVN-TV broadcasts locally on channel 7.
TELEVISION STATION

KEVU-TV 32436
Owner: California-Oregon Broadcasting
Editorial: 2940 Chad Dr, Eugene, Oregon 97408-7343
Tel: 1 541 683-3434.
Web site: http://www.oregonsfox.com
Profile: KEVU-TV is the MyNetworkTV affiliate for the Eugene, OR market. The station is owned by California-Oregon Broadcasting. KEVU-TV broadcasts locally on channel 23.
TELEVISION STATION

KEYC2-TV 557885
Owner: United Communications Corp.
Editorial: 1570 Lookout Dr, North Mankato, Minnesota 56003-2502 **Tel:** 1 507 625-7905.
Email: keycnews@keyc.com
Web site: http://www.keyc.com
Profile: KEYC2-TV is a multicast channel of KEYC-TV. A multicast channel is a separate channel that shares the bandwith of the main station but can air unique programming. KEYC-TV is the local FOX affiliate on channel 12.2 for the Minneapolis-St.Paul area. It is owned by United Communications Corp.
TELEVISION STATION

KEYC-TV 31448
Owner: United Communications Corp.
Tel: 1 507 625-7905.
Email: keycnews@keyc.com
Web site: http://www.keyc.com
Profile: KEYC-TV is a CBS affiliate in the Mankato, MN market. The station is owned by United Communications Corp. KEYC-TV broadcasts locally on channel 12.
TELEVISION STATION

KEYE2-TV 605327
Owner: Sinclair Broadcast Group, Inc.
Editorial: 10700 Metric Blvd, Austin, Texas 78758-4523 **Tel:** 1 512 835-0042.
Web site: http://www.telemundoaustin.com
Profile: KEYE2-TV is a multicast channel of KEYE-TV. A multicast channel is a separate channel that shares the bandwidth of the main station but can air unique programming. KEYE2-TV is the local Telemundo affiliate on channel 42.2 for the Austin, TX market. KEYE2-TV is owned by Sinclair Broadcast Group, Inc.
TELEVISION STATION

KEYE-TV 31400
Owner: Sinclair Broadcast Group, Inc.
Editorial: 10700 Metric Blvd, Austin, Texas 78758-4523 **Tel:** 1 512 835-0042.
Email: news@cbsaustin.com
Web site: http://www.keyetv.com
Profile: KEYE-TV is the CBS affiliate for the Austin, TX market. The station is owned by Sinclair Broadcast Group, Inc. KEYE-TV broadcasts locally on channel 42.
TELEVISION STATION

KEYT-TV 31449
Owner: News-Press & Gazette Co.
Editorial: 730 Miramonte Dr, Santa Barbara, California 93109-1417 **Tel:** 1 805 882-3933.
Email: assignmentdesk@keyt.com
Web site: http://www.keyt.com
Profile: KEYT-TV is the ABC network affiliate for the Santa Barbara, CA market. The station is owned by News-Press & Gazette Co. KEYT-TV broadcasts locally on channel 3.
TELEVISION STATION

KEYU-TV 342883
Owner: Raycom Media Inc.
Editorial: 7900 Broadway Dr, Amarillo, Texas 79108-2409 **Tel:** 1 806 383-1010.
Email: noticias@telemundoamarillo.com
Web site: http://www.newschannel10.com/category/221444/telemundo
Profile: KEYU-TV is the Telemundo affiliate for the Amarillo, TX market. The station is owned by Raycom Media Inc.. KEYU-TV broadcasts locally on channel 31. Send all press materials to the newsroom email address.
TELEVISION STATION

KEZI-TV 31450
Owner: Heartland Media
Editorial: 2975 Chad Dr, Eugene, Oregon 97408-7344
Tel: 1 541 485-5611.
Web site: http://www.kezi.com
Profile: KEZI-TV is the ABC news affiliate for the Eugene, OR market. The station is owned by Heartland Media. KEZI-TV broadcasts locally on channel 9.
TELEVISION STATION

KFBB2-TV 972174
Owner: Cowles Publishing Co.
Editorial: 3200 Old Havre Hwy, Black Eagle, Montana 59414-1078 **Tel:** 1 406 453-4377.
Web site: http://www.kfbb.com
Profile: KFBB2-TV is a multicast channel of KFBB-TV. A multicast channel is a separate channel that shares the bandwidth of the main station but can air unique programming. KFBB-TV is the a FOX and MyNetworkTV affiliate for the Great Falls, MT market. The station is owned by Cowles Publishing Co. KFBB2-TV broadcasts locally on channel 5.2.
TELEVISION STATION

KFBB-TV 31451
Owner: Cowles Publishing Co.
Editorial: 3200 Old Havre Hwy, Black Eagle, Montana 59414-1078 **Tel:** 1 406 453-4377.
Email: newsroom@kfbb.com
Web site: http://www.kfbb.com
Profile: KFBB-TV is the ABC affiliate for the Great Falls, MT market. The station is owned by Cowles Publishing Co. KFBB-TV broadcasts locally on channel 5.
TELEVISION STATION

KFDA-TV 31452
Owner: Raycom Media Inc.
Editorial: 7900 Broadway Dr, Amarillo, Texas 79108-2409 **Tel:** 1 806 383-1010.
Email: newsroom@newschannel10.com
Web site: http://www.newschannel10.com
Profile: KFDA-TV is the CBS network affiliate for the Amarillo, TX market. The station is owned by Raycom Media Inc. KFDA-TV broadcasts locally on channel 10.
TELEVISION STATION

KFDF-TV 32614
Owner: Pinnacle Media, LLC
Editorial: 510 N Greenwood Ave, Fort Smith, Arkansas 72901-3510 **Tel:** 1 479 785-4600.
Email: info@duo-media.com
Web site: http://www.duo-media.com
Profile: KFDF-TV is the Me TV affiliate for the Fort Smith, AR market. The station is owned by Pinnacle Media, LLC. KFDF-TV broadcasts locally on channel 31.2.
TELEVISION STATION

KFDM-TV 31453
Owner: Sinclair Broadcast Group, Inc.
Editorial: 2955 I-10 East, Beaumont, Texas 77702
Tel: 1 409 892-6622.
Email: news@kfdm.com
Web site: http://www.kfdm.com
Profile: KFDM-TV is the CBS network affiliate for the Beaumont- Port Arthur, TX market. The station is owned by Sinclair Broadcast Group, Inc. KFDM-TV broadcasts locally on channel 6.
TELEVISION STATION

KFDX-TV 31454
Owner: Nexstar Broadcasting Group
Editorial: 4500 Seymour Hwy, Wichita Falls, Texas 76309 **Tel:** 1 940 691-0003.
Email: kfdx@kfdx.com
Web site: http://texomashomepage.com
Profile: KFDX-TV is an NBC affiliate for the Wichita Falls, TX-Lawton, OK market. The station is owned by Nexstar Broadcasting Group. KFDX-TV broadcasts locally on channel 3.
TELEVISION STATION

KFFV2-TV 611619
Owner: OTA Broadcasting, LLC
Editorial: 3223 3rd Ave S Ste 200, Seattle, Washington 98134-1943 **Tel:** 1 206 624-2222.
Email: info@aztecaamerica.com
Web site: http://us.azteca.com
Profile: KFFV2-TV is a multicast of KFFV-TV. A multicast channel is a separate channel that shares the bandwith of the main station but can air unique programming. KFFV2-TV airs programming from Azteca in the Seattle market. The station is owned by OTA Broadcasting, LLC. KFFV2-TV broadcasts locally on channel 44.2.
TELEVISION STATION

KFFV3-TV 611627
Owner: OTA Broadcasting, LLC
Editorial: 3223 3rd Ave S, Seattle, Washington 98134-1943 **Tel:** 1 206 624-2222.
Email: info@aattv.com
Web site: http://aattv.com
Profile: KFFV3-TV is a multicast of KFFV-TV. A multicast channel is a separate channel that shares the bandwith of the main station but can air unique programming. KFFV3-TV airs programming from AAT Television in the Seattle market. The station is owned by OTA Broadcasting, LLC. KFFV3-TV broadcasts locally on channel 44.3.
TELEVISION STATION

KFFV4-TV 611636
Owner: OTA Broadcasting, LLC
Editorial: 3223 3Rd Ave S Ste 200, Seattle, Washington 98134-1943 **Tel:** 1 206 624-2222.
Profile: KFFV4-TV is a multicast of KFFV-TV. A multicast channel is a separate channel that shares the bandwith of the main station but can air unique programming. KFFV4-TV airs programming from the Untamed Sports channel. The station is owned by OTA Broadcasting, LLC. KFFV4-TV broadcasts locally on channel 44.4.
TELEVISION STATION

KFFV-TV 72049
Owner: OTA Broadcasting, LLC
Editorial: 1715 E Madison St, Seattle, Washington 98122-2732 **Tel:** 1 206 624-2222.
Email: info@otabroadcasting.com
Web site: http://otabroadcasting.com/?p=46
Profile: KFFV-TV is a commercial station owned by OTA Broadcasting, LLC in the Seattle market. The KFFV-TV broadcasts locally on channel 44 and airs infomercials.
TELEVISION STATION

KFFX-TV 32557
Owner: Northwest Broadcasting
Editorial: 2509 W Falls Ave, Kennewick, Washington 99336-3041 **Tel:** 1 509 735-1700.
Email: fox11@kffxtv.com
Web site: http://www.myfoxtricities.com
Profile: KFFX-TV is the FOX affiliate for the Yakima, WA market. The station is owned by Northwest Broadcasting. KFFX-TV broadcasts locally on channel 11.
TELEVISION STATION

KFJX-TV 376778
Owner: Surtsey Media, LLC
Editorial: 2950 NE Hwy 69, Pittsburg, Kansas 66762
Tel: 1 417 782-1414.
Email: news@fox14tv.com
Web site: http://www.fox14tv.com
Profile: KFJX-TV is a FOX affiliate for the Pittsburg, KS market. The station is owned by Surtsey Media, LLC. KFJX-TV is broadcast locally on channel 14.
TELEVISION STATION

KFLA-TV 622726
Owner: Mayhugh (Roy)
Editorial: 701 Perdew Ave, Ridgecrest, California 93555-2422
Web site: http://www.kfla.tv
Profile: KFLA-TV is an independent station for the Bakersfield, CA market. The station is owned by Roy Mayhugh. KFLA-TV broadcasts locally on channel 8.
TELEVISION STATION

KFMB3-TV 773220
Owner: Midwest Television Inc.
Editorial: 7677 Engineer Rd, San Diego, California 92111-1515 **Tel:** 1 858 571-8888.
Profile: KFMB3-TV is a multicast channel of KFMB-TV. A multicast channel is a separate channel that shares the bandwith of the main station but can air unique programming. KFMB3-TV is the Me-TV Network for the San Diego market. The station is owned by Midwest Television Inc. KFMB3-TV broadcasts locally on channel 8.3.
TELEVISION STATION

KFMB-TV 31455
Owner: Midwest Television Inc.
Editorial: 7677 Engineer Rd, San Diego, California 92111-1515 **Tel:** 1 858 571-8888.
Email: desk@kfmb.com
Web site: http://www.cbs8.com
Profile: KFMB-TV is the CBS Television Network affiliate for the San Diego market. The station is owned by Midwest Television Inc. and broadcasts locally on channel 8.
TELEVISION STATION

KFME-TV 32681
Owner: Prairie Public Broadcasting Inc.
Editorial: 207 5th St N, Fargo, North Dakota 58102
Tel: 1 701 241-6900.
Email: info@prairiepublic.org
Web site: http://www.prairiepublic.org
Profile: KFME-TV is the PBS affiliate for the Fargo, ND market. The station is owned by Prairie Public Broadcasting Inc. KFME-TV broadcasts locally on channel 13.
TELEVISION STATION

KFNB-TV 32639
Owner: Wyomedia Corporation
Editorial: 1856 Skyview Dr, Casper, Wyoming 82601-9638 **Tel:** 1 307 577-5923.
Email: tvtraffic@kfnbtv.com
Profile: KFNB-TV is a FOX affiliate for the Casper, WY market. The station is owned by Wyomedia Corporation. KFNB-TV broadcasts locally on channel 20.
TELEVISION STATION

KFOL-TV 861288
Owner: Folse Communications LLC
Editorial: 1202 Saint Charles St, Houma, Louisiana 70360-2774 **Tel:** 1 985 876-3456.
Email: news10@htv10.tv
Web site: http://bayoutimelive.com
Profile: KFOL-TV is the in independent station in the New Orelans market. The station is owned by Folse Communications LLC. KFOL-TV broadcasts locally on channel 7.
TELEVISION STATION

KFOR2-TV 619953
Owner: Tribune Broadcasting Co.
Editorial: 444 E Britton Rd, Oklahoma City, Oklahoma 73114-7515 **Tel:** 1 405 424-4444.
Email: news4@kfor.com
Web site: http://www.kfor.com
Profile: KFOR2-TV is a multicast of KFOR-TV. A multicast channel is a separate channel that shares the bandwith of the main station but can air unique programming. KFOR2-TV airs 24 hour weather programming from NBC in the Oklahoma City market. The station is owned by Tribune Broadcasting Co. KFOR2-TV broadcasts locally on channel 4.2.
TELEVISION STATION

KFOR-TV 31662
Owner: Tribune Broadcasting Co.
Editorial: 444 E Britton Rd, Oklahoma City, Oklahoma 73114-7515 **Tel:** 1 405 424-4444.
Email: news4@kfor.com
Web site: http://www.kfor.com
Profile: KFOR-TV is the NBC affiliate for Oklahoma City market. KFOR-TV is owned by Tribune Broadcasting Co. KFOR-TV broadcasts on channel 4.
TELEVISION STATION

KFOX-TV 31408
Owner: Sinclair Broadcast Group, Inc.
Editorial: 200 S Alto Mesa Dr, El Paso, Texas 79912-4426 **Tel:** 1 915 833-8585.
Email: webmaster@kfoxtv.com
Web site: http://www.kfoxtv.com
Profile: KFOX-TV is the FOX affiliate for the El Paso, TX market. The station is owned by Sinclair Broadcast Group, Inc.. KFOX-TV broadcasts locally on channel 14.
TELEVISION STATION

KFPH-TV 32418
Owner: Univision Communications Inc.
Editorial: 2158 N 4th St, Flagstaff, Arizona 86004-4235 **Tel:** 1 928 527-1300.
Profile: KFPH-TV is the Telefutura affiliate on channel 13 for the Phoenix, AZ market. The station is owned by Univision Communications Inc. KFPH-TV broadcasts locally on channel 13.
TELEVISION STATION

KFPX-TV 32582
Owner: ION Media Networks
Editorial: 4570 114th St, Urbandale, Iowa 50322
Tel: 1 515 331-3939.
Profile: KFPX-TV is the ION Television affiliate for the Des Moines, IA market. KFPX-TV is owned by ION Media Networks. KFPX-TV broadcasts locally on channel 39.
TELEVISION STATION

KFQX-TV 87707
Owner: Mission Broadcasting
Editorial: 345 Hillcrest Dr, Grand Junction, Colorado 81501-7446 **Tel:** 1 970 242-5000.
Email: news@krextv.com
Web site: http://www.westernslopenow.com/
Profile: KFQX-TV is the FOX affiliate for the Grand Junction-Montrose, CO market. The station is owned by Mission Broadcasting. KFQX-TV broadcasts locally on channel 4.
TELEVISION STATION

KFRE-TV 32377
Owner: Sinclair Broadcast Group
Editorial: 5111 E McKinley Ave, Fresno, California 93727-2033 **Tel:** 1 559 255-2600.
Email: newsdesk@kmph.com
Web site: http://kmph-kfre.com
Profile: KFRE-TV is the CW affiliate for the Fresno-Visalia, CA market. The station is owned bySinclair Broadcast Group. KFRE-TV broadcasts locally on channel 59.
TELEVISION STATION

KFSF2-TV 607793
Owner: Univision Communications Inc.
Editorial: 50 Fremont St, Fl 41, San Francisco, California 94105-2240 **Tel:** 1 415 538-8000.
Email: noticias14@tv.univision.com
Profile: KFSF2-TV is a multicast channel of KFSF-TV. A multicast channel is a separate channel that shares the bandwith of the main station but can air unique programming. KFSF2-TV airs programming from KDTV-TV for the San Francisco market. It is owned by Univision Communications Inc. KFSF2-TV broadcasts locally on channel 66.2.
TELEVISION STATION

KFSF-TV 32453
Owner: Univision Communications Inc.
Editorial: 50 Fremont St, San Francisco, California 94105-2278 **Tel:** 1 415 538-8000.
Profile: KFSF-TV is an UniMas affiliate for the San Francisco area. The station is owned by Univision Communications Inc. KFSF-TV broadcasts locally on channel 66.
TELEVISION STATION

KFSM-TV 31456
Owner: Tribune Broadcasting Co.
Editorial: 318 N 13th St, Fort Smith, Arkansas 72901-2835 **Tel:** 1 479 783-3131.
Email: news@kfsm.com
Web site: http://5newsonline.com
Profile: KFSM-TV is the CBS affiliate for the Fort Smith, AR market. The station is owned by Tribune Broadcasting Co. KFSM-TV broadcasts locally on channel 5.
TELEVISION STATION

KFSN-TV 31457

Owner: Walt Disney Co.
Editorial: 1777 G St, Fresno, California 93706-1616
Tel: 1 559 442-1170.
Email: kfsndesk@abc.com
Web site: http://abc30.com
Profile: KFSN-TV is the ABC affiliate for the Fresno-Visalia, CA market. The station is owned by the Walt Disney Co. KFSN-TV broadcasts locally on channel 30.
TELEVISION STATION

KFTA-TV 442173

Owner: Nexstar Broadcasting Group
Editorial: 15 S Block Ave Ste 101, Fayetteville, Arkansas 72701-6099 **Tel:** 1 479 571-5100.
Email: news@knwa.com
Web site: http://www.nwahomepage.com
Profile: KFTA-TV is the FOX affiliate for the Fayetteville, AR area. The station is owned by Nexstar Broadcasting Group. KFTA-TV broadcasts locally on channel 24.
TELEVISION STATION

KFTH-TV 31480

Owner: Univision Communications Inc.
Editorial: 5100 Southwest Fwy, Houston, Texas 77056-7308 **Tel:** 1 713 965-2400.
Web site: http://tv.univision.com/unimas
Profile: KFTH-TV is the UniMás affiliate for the Houston market. The station is owned by Univision Communications Inc. KFTH-TV broadcasts locally on channel 67. Station does not have a news department. This station also does not have a local program director. All programming is handled by corporate.
TELEVISION STATION

KFTL-TV 32362

Owner: LocusPoint Network
Editorial: 1965 Adams Ave, San Leandro, California 94577-1005 **Tel:** 1 510 632-5385.
Email: mail@kftl.com
Web site: http://www.kftl.com
Profile: KFTL-TV is an independent station for the San Francisco market. The station is owned by LocusPoint Network. KFTL-TV broadcasts locally on channel 28.
TELEVISION STATION

KFTR-TV 32507

Owner: Univision Communications Inc.
Editorial: 5999 Center Dr, Los Angeles, California 90045-8901 **Tel:** 1 310 216-3434.
Profile: KFTR-TV is an UniMas affiliate for Los Angeles market. The station is owned by Univision Communications Inc. KFTR-TV broadcasts locally on channel 46.
TELEVISION STATION

KFTU-TV 87241

Owner: Univision Communications Inc.
Editorial: 1111 N G Ave, Douglas, Arizona 85607-1926 **Tel:** 1 520 805-1773.
Profile: KFTU-TV is an UniMas affiliate for the Tucson, AZ market. The station is owned by Univision Communications Inc. KFTU-TV broadcasts locally on channel 3.
TELEVISION STATION

KFTV-TV 31458

Owner: Univision Communications Inc.
Editorial: 601 W Univision Plz, Fresno, California 93704-1092 **Tel:** 1 559 222-2121.
Email: kftvnews@univision.net
Web site: http://univisionfresno.univision.com
Profile: KFTV-TV is the Univision affiliate for the Fresno-Visalia, CA market. The station is owned by Univision Communications Inc. KFTV-TV broadcasts locally on channel 21.
TELEVISION STATION

KFVE-TV 32352

Owner: MCG Capital / Hawaii Five Subsidiary LLC
Editorial: 420 Waiakamilo Rd Ste 205, Honolulu, Hawaii 96817-4950 **Tel:** 1 808 847-3246.
Email: info@kfve.com
Web site: http://www.k5thehometeam.com
Profile: KFVE-TV is the MyNetworkTV affiliate for the Honolulu market. The station is owned by MCG Capital / Hawaii Five Subsidiary LLC. KFVE-TV broadcasts locally on channel 5. In October 2009 KFVE-TV, KGMB-TV and KHNL-TV formed an independently run local news service(LNS) sharing newsgathering resources to provide pool coverage of non-exclusvie events. The local news service is run by an independent managing editor who will determine the stories to be covered each day by the news service.
TELEVISION STATION

KFVS-TV 31460

Owner: Raycom Media Inc.
Editorial: 310 Broadway St, Cape Girardeau, Missouri 63701-7331 **Tel:** 1 573 335-1212.
Email: news@kfvs12.com
Web site: http://www.kfvs12.com
Profile: KFVS-TV is the CBS network affiliate for the Paducah, KY; Cape Girardeau, MO and Harrisburg, IL market. The station is owned by Raycom Media Inc. KFVS-TV broadcasts locally on channel 12.
TELEVISION STATION

KFWD-TV 32315

Owner: H I C Broadcasting
Editorial: 606 Young St, Dallas, Texas 75202-4810
Tel: 1 214 977-6780.
Web site: http://www.mundomax.com
Profile: KFWD-TV is the MundoFOX affiliate for the Dallas market. The station is owned by HIC Broadcasting. KFWD-TV broadcasts locally on channel 52.
TELEVISION STATION

KFXA-TV 32488

Owner: Sinclair Broadcasting Company
Editorial: 600 Old Marion Rd NE, Cedar Rapids, Iowa 52402-2159 **Tel:** 1 319 395-9060.
Email: news@fox28iowa.com
Web site: http://www.fox28iowa.com
Profile: KFXA-TV is the FOX affiliate for the Cedar Rapids, IA market. The station is owned by Sinclair Broadcasting Company. KFXA-TV broadcasts locally on channel 28.
TELEVISION STATION

KFXB-TV 31437

Owner: Christian Television Network
Editorial: 744 Main St, Dubuque, Iowa 52001
Tel: 1 563 690-1704.
Email: ctnofiowa@mchsi.com
Web site: http://www.kfxb.net
Profile: KFXB-TV is an independent station for the Dubuque, IA market. The station is owned by Christian Television Network. KFXB-TV broadcasts locally on channel 40.
TELEVISION STATION

KFXF-TV 32487

Owner: Gray Television, Inc.
Editorial: 3650 Braddock St, Fairbanks, Alaska 99701-7617 **Tel:** 1 907 452-3697.
Web site: http://tvtv.com/
Profile: KFXF-TV is the FOX affiliate for the Fairbanks, AK market. The station is owned by TGray Television, Inc. KFXF-TV broadcasts locally on channel 7.
TELEVISION STATION

KFXK2-TV 708353

Owner: White Knight Broadcasting
Editorial: 701 N Access Rd, Longview, Texas 75602-4205 **Tel:** 1 903 236-0051.
Profile: KFXK2-TV is a multicast channel of KFXK-TV. A multicast channel is a separate channel that shares the bandwidth of the main station but can air unique programming. KFXK2-TV is the local MyNetworkTV affiliate on channel 51.2 for the Longview, TV market. KFXK2-TV is owned by White Knight Broadcasting.
TELEVISION STATION

KFXK-TV 31512

Owner: White Knight Broadcasting
Editorial: 4300 Richmond Rd, Tyler, Texas 75703-1201 **Tel:** 1 903 581-5656.
Web site: http://www.myeasttex.com/
Profile: KFXK-TV is the FOX affiliate for the Longview, TX market. The station is owned by White Knight Broadcasting. KFXK-TV broadcasts locally on channel 51.
TELEVISION STATION

KFXL-TV 431552

Owner: Omaha World-Herald Co.
Editorial: 707 N 48th St, Ste B, Lincoln, Nebraska 68504 **Tel:** 1 308 743-2494.
Web site: http://www.foxnebraska.com
Profile: KFXL-TV is the FOX affiliate for the Lincoln, NE market. The station is owned by Omaha World-Herald Co. KCWL-TV broadcasts locally on channel 51.
TELEVISION STATION

KFXO-TV 33009

Owner: News-Press & Gazette Co.
Editorial: 62990 O B Riley Rd, Bend, Oregon 97703-9001 **Tel:** 1 541 383-2121.
Email: ktvz@ktvz.com
Profile: KFXO-TV is the FOX affiliate for the Bend, OR market. The station is owned by News-Press & Gazette Co. KFXO-TV broadcasts locally on channel 39. Send all mail to the station's post office box address and not to the street address.
TELEVISION STATION

KFXP-TV 63268

Owner: Compass Communications of Idaho
Editorial: 902 E Sherman St, Pocatello, Idaho 83201-5762 **Tel:** 1 208 232-3141.
Web site: http://www.kfxp.com
Profile: KFXP-TV is the This TV affiliate for the Pocatello, ID market. The station is owned by Compass Communications of Idaho. KFXP-TV broadcasts locally on channel 31.
TELEVISION STATION

KFXV-TV 886683

Owner: Entravision Communications Corp.
Editorial: 801 N Jackson Rd, McAllen, Texas 78501-9306 **Tel:** 1 956 687-4848.
Email: news@foxrio2.com
Web site: http://www.foxrio2.com
Profile: KFXV-TV is the FOX affiliate for the Brownsville - Mc Allen, TX market. The station is owned by Entravision Communications Corp. KFXV-TV broadcasts locally on channel 67.
TELEVISION STATION

KFYR-TV 32640

Owner: Gray Television, Inc.
Editorial: 200 N 4th St, Bismarck, North Dakota 58501-4004 **Tel:** 1 701 255-5757.
Email: news@kfyrtv.com
Web site: http://www.kfyrtv.com
Profile: KFYR-TV is the NBC affiliate for the Bismarck, ND market. The station is owned by Gray Television, Inc. KFYR-TV broadcasts locally on channel 5.
TELEVISION STATION

KGAN-TV 31461

Owner: Sinclair Broadcast Group, Inc.
Editorial: 600 Old Marion Rd NE, Cedar Rapids, Iowa 52402-2159 **Tel:** 1 319 395-9060.
Email: newsreleases@kfxa.tv
Web site: http://www.cbs2iowa.com
Profile: KGAN-TV is the CBS affiliate for the Cedar Rapids, IA market. The station is owned by Sinclair Broadcast Group, Inc. KGAN-TV broadcasts locally on channel 2.
TELEVISION STATION

KGBT-TV 31462

Owner: Sinclair Broadcast Group, Inc.
Editorial: 9201 W Expressway 83, Harlingen, Texas 78552-6624 **Tel:** 1 956 366-4444.
Email: producers@valleycentral.com
Web site: http://www.valleycentral.com
Profile: KGBT-TV is the CBS affiliate for the Brownsville-McAllen, TX market. The station is owned by Sinclair Broadcast Group, Inc. KGBT-TV broadcasts locally on channel 4.
TELEVISION STATION

KGCW2-TV 617507

Owner: Grant Communications Inc.
Editorial: 937 E 53rd St, Davenport, Iowa 52807-2614
Tel: 1 563 386-1818.
Email: fox18news@kljb.com
Web site: http://www.kgcwtv.com
Profile: KGCW2-TV is a multicast of KGCW-TV. A multicast channel is a separate channel that shares the bandwith of the main station but can air unique programming. KGCW2-TV airs programming from This TV Network in the Davenport, IA market. The station is owned by Grant Communications Inc. KGCW2-TV broadcasts locally on channel 26.2.
TELEVISION STATION

KGCW3-TV 800884

Owner: Grant Communications Inc.
Editorial: 937 E 53rd St, Davenport, Iowa 52807-2614
Tel: 1 563 386-1818.
Email: fox18news@kljb.com
Web site: http://www.kgcwtv.com
Profile: KGCW3-TV is a multicast channel of KGCW-TV. A multicast channel is a separate channel that shares the bandwith of the main station but can air unique programming. KGCW3-TV is the Me-TV Network for the Davenport, IA market. The station is owned by Grant Communications Inc. KGCW3-TV broadcasts locally on channel 26.3. The station will launch April 17, 2012.
TELEVISION STATION

KGCW-TV 32990

Owner: Grant Communications Inc.
Editorial: 937 E 53rd St, Davenport, Iowa 52807-2614
Tel: 1 563 386-1818.
Email: fox18news@kljb.com
Web site: http://www.kgcwtv.com
Profile: KGCW-TV is the CW affiliate for the Davenport, IA, Rock Island, IL-Moline, IL market. The station is owned by Grant Communications Inc. KGCW-TV broadcasts locally on channel 26.
TELEVISION STATION

KGET-TV 31463

Owner: Nexstar Broadcasting Group
Editorial: 2120 L St, Bakersfield, California 93301-2331 **Tel:** 1 661 283-1700.
Email: 17news@kget.com
Web site: http://www.kerngoldenempire.com
Profile: KGET-TV is the NBC affiliate for the Bakersfield, CA market. The station is owned by Nexstar Broadcasting Group. KGET-TV broadcasts locally on channel 17.
TELEVISION STATION

KGJT-TV 418043

Owner: Nexstar Media Group
Editorial: 345 Hillcrest Dr, Grand Junction, Colorado 81501-7446 **Tel:** 1 970 242-5000.
Web site: http://www.westernslopenow.com/
Profile: KGTV-TV is My Network affiliate for the Grand Junction, CO market. The station is owned by Nexstar Media Group. KGTV-TV broadcasts locally on channel 27.
TELEVISION STATION

KGMB-TV 32641

Owner: Raycom Media Inc.
Editorial: 420 Waiakamilo Rd Ste 205, Honolulu, Hawaii 96817-4950 **Tel:** 1 808 847-3246.
Email: news@hawaiinewsnow.com
Web site: http://www.hawaiinewsnow.com
Profile: KGMB-TV is the CBS affiliate for the Honolulu market. The station is owned by Raycom Media Inc. KGMB-TV broadcasts locally on channel 9. In October 2009 KGMB-TV, KHNL-TV and KFVE-TV formed an independently run local news service(LNS) sharing newsgathering resources to provide pool coverage of non-exclusvie events. The local news service is run by an independent managing editor who will determine the stories to be covered each day by the news service.
TELEVISION STATION

KGMC6-TV 809929

Owner: Cocola Broadcasting Companies
Editorial: 706 W Herndon Ave, Fresno, California 93650-1033 **Tel:** 1 559 435-7000.
Email: info@cocolatv.com
Web site: http://www.metvfresno.net
Profile: KGMC6-TV is a multicast channel of KGMC-TV. A multicast channel is a separate channel that shares the bandwith of the main station but can air unique programming. KGMC6-TV is the Me-TV Network for the Fresno, CA market. The station is owned by Cocola Broadcasting Companies. KGMC6-TV broadcasts locally on channel 43.6.
TELEVISION STATION

KGMC-TV 32486

Owner: Cocola Broadcasting Companies
Editorial: 706 W Herndon Ave, Fresno, California 93650-1033 **Tel:** 1 559 435-7000.
Email: info@cocolatv.com
Web site: http://www.cocolatv.com
Profile: KGMC-TV is the MundoFOX affiliate for the Fresno-Visalia, CA market. The station is owned by Cocola Broadcasting Companies. KGMC-TV broadcasts locally on channel 43.
TELEVISION STATION

KGMM-TV 235317

Owner: Caballero Acquisition LLC
Editorial: 3310 Keller Springs Rd, Carrollton, Texas 75006-4940 **Tel:** 1 972 788-0533.
Web site: http://www.mtvtr3s.com
Profile: KGMM-TV is the MTV Tr3s affilliate for the San Antonio, TX market. The station is owned by Caballero Acquisition LLC. KGMM-TV broadcasts locally on channel 44.
TELEVISION STATION

KGNS2-TV 691206

Owner: Gray Television, Inc.
Editorial: 120 W Del Mar Blvd, Laredo, Texas 78041-2203 **Tel:** 1 956 727-8888.
Email: newsteam@kgns.tv
Web site: http://www.kgns.tv
Profile: KGNS2-TV is a multicast channel of KGNS-TV. A multicast channel is a separate channel that shares the bandwith of the main station but can air unique programming. KGNS2-TV is the ABC affiliate for the Laredo, TX. The station is owned by Gray Television, Inc. KGNS2-TV broadcasts locally on channel 8.2.
TELEVISION STATION

KGNS-TV 31466

Owner: Gray Television, Inc.
Editorial: 120 W Del Mar Blvd, Laredo, Texas 78041-2203 **Tel:** 1 956 727-8888.
Email: newsteam@kgns.tv
Web site: http://www.kgns.tv
Profile: KGNS-TV is the NBC affiliate for the Laredo, TX, market. The station is owned by Gray Television, Inc. KGNS-TV broadcasts locally on channel 8.
TELEVISION STATION

KGO2-TV 610901

Owner: Walt Disney Co.
Editorial: 900 Front St, San Francisco, California 94111-1427 **Tel:** 1 415 954-7777.
Email: abc7listens@kgo-tv.com
Web site: http://abclocal.go.com/kgo
Profile: KGO2-TV is a multicast of KGO-TV. A multicast channel is a separate channel that shares the bandwith of the main station but can air unique programming. KGO2-TV airs programming from ABC News and Live Well in the San Francisco market. The station is owned by Walt Disney Co. KGO2-TV broadcasts locally on channel 7.2.
TELEVISION STATION

KGO3-TV 610905

Owner: Walt Disney Co.
Editorial: 900 Front St, San Francisco, California 94111-1427 **Tel:** 1 415 954-7777.
Email: abc7listens@kgo-tv.com
Web site: http://abclocal.go.com/kgo
Profile: KGO3-TV is a multicast of KGO-TV. A multicast channel is a separate channel that shares the bandwith of the main station but can air unique programming. KGO3-TV airs programming from ABC7 AccuWeather Now in the San Francisco market. The station is owned by Walt Disney Co. KGO3-TV broadcasts locally on channel 7.3.
TELEVISION STATION

KGO-TV 31467

Owner: Walt Disney Co.
Editorial: 900 Front St, San Francisco, California 94111-1427 **Tel:** 1 415 954-7777.
Email: kgotv.desk@abc.com
Web site: http://abc7news.com
Profile: KGO-TV is the ABC affiliate for the San Francisco market. The station is owned by Walt Disney Co. KGO-TV broadcasts locally on channel 7.
TELEVISION STATION

KGPE-TV 31500

Owner: Nexstar Broadcasting Group
Editorial: 5035 E McKinley Ave, Fresno, California 93727-1964 **Tel:** 1 559 222-2411.
Email: newsdesk@cbs47.tv
Web site: http://www.cbs47.tv
Profile: KGPE-TV is the CBS affiliate for the Fresno-Visalia, CA market. The station is owned by Nexstar Broadcasting Group. KGPE-TV broadcasts locally on channel 47.
TELEVISION STATION

KGPT-TV 350323

Owner: Great Plains Television Network, LLC
Editorial: 110 S Main St, Wichita, Kansas 67202-3700
Tel: 1 316 201-4800.
Email: info@wichitachannels.com
Web site: http://www.wichitachannels.com
Profile: KGPT-TV is a low-powered television station for the Wichita, KS market. The station is owned by

Great Plains Television Network, LLC. KGPT-TV broadcasts locally on channel 49.
TELEVISION STATION

KGPX-TV 72054
Owner: ION Media Networks
Editorial: 1201 W Sprague Ave, Spokane, Washington 99201-4102 **Tel:** 1 509 340-3400.
Profile: KGPX-TV is the ION Television affiliate for the Spokane, WA market. The station is owned by ION Media Networks. KGPX-TV broadcasts locally on channel 34.
TELEVISION STATION

KGTV-TV 31469
Owner: E.W. Scripps Co.
Editorial: 4600 Air Way, San Diego, California 92102-2528 **Tel:** 1 619 237-1010.
Email: kgtv_assignmentdesk@kgtv.com
Web site: http://www.10news.com
Profile: KGTV-TV is the ABC network affiliate in the San Diego market. The station is owned by E.W. Scripps Co. KGTV-TV broadcasts locally on channel 10.
TELEVISION STATION

KGUN2-TV 775302
Owner: E.W. Scripps Co.
Editorial: 7280 E Rosewood St, Tucson, Arizona 85710-1350 **Tel:** 1 520 722-5486.
Profile: KGUN2-TV is a multicast channel of KGUN-TV. A multicast channel is a separate channel that shares the bandwith of the main station but can air unique programming. KGUN2-TV is the Live Well Network for the Tucson market. The station is owned by E.W. Scripps Co. KGUN2-TV broadcasts locally on channel 9.2. KGUN2-TV launched October 1, 2011.
TELEVISION STATION

KGUN-TV 31470
Owner: E.W. Scripps Co.
Editorial: 7280 E Rosewood St, Tucson, Arizona 85710-1350 **Tel:** 1 520 722-5486.
Email: news@kgun9.com
Web site: http://www.kgun9.com
Profile: KGUN-TV is the ABC network affiliate for the Tucson, AZ, market. The station is owned by E.W. Scripps Co. KGUN-TV broadcasts locally on channel 9.
TELEVISION STATION

KGW2-TV 613986
Owner: Sander Media, LLC.
Editorial: 1501 SW Jefferson St, Portland, Oregon 97201-2549 **Tel:** 1 503 226-5000.
Email: newsdesk@kgw.com
Web site: http://www.kgw.com
Profile: KGW2-TV is a multicast of KGW-TV. A multicast channel is a separate channel that shares the bandwith of the main station but can air unique programming. KGW2-TV airs programming from the Estrella Network in the Portland, OR market. The station is owned by Sander Media, LLC. KGW2-TV broadcasts locally on channel 8.2.
TELEVISION STATION

KGWC-TV 32642
Owner: Mark III Media Inc.
Editorial: 1856 Skyview Dr, Casper, Wyoming 82601-9638 **Tel:** 1 307 577-5923.
Web site: http://k2radio.com/tags/kgwc-tv/
Profile: KGWC-TV is the CBS affiliate for Casper-Riverton, WY market. The station is owned by Mark III Media Inc. KGWC-TV broadcasts locally on channel 14.
TELEVISION STATION

KGWN-TV 32643
Owner: Yellowstone Holdings
Editorial: 2923 E Lincolnway, Cheyenne, Wyoming 82001-6149 **Tel:** 1 307 634-7755.
Email: news@kgwn.tv
Web site: http://www.kgwn.tv
Profile: KGWN-TV is the CBS affiliate for the Cheyenne, WY/Scottsbluff, NE market. The station is owned by Yellowstone Holdings. KGWN-TV broadcasts locally on channel 5.
TELEVISION STATION

KGW-TV 31471
Owner: TEGNA Inc.
Editorial: 1501 SW Jefferson St, Portland, Oregon 97201-2549 **Tel:** 1 503 226-5000.
Email: newsdesk@kgw.com
Web site: http://www.kgw.com
Profile: KGW-TV is the NBC affiliate for the Portland, Oregon market. The station is owned by TEGNA Inc. KGW-TV broadcasts locally on channel 8.
TELEVISION STATION

KHBS2-TV 829587
Owner: Hearst Television Inc.
Editorial: 2415 N Albert Pike Ave, Fort Smith, Arkansas 72904-5617 **Tel:** 1 479 783-4040.
Web site: http://www.4029tv.com/
Profile: KHBS2-TV is a multicast channel of KHBS-TV. A multicast channel is a separate channel that shares the bandwith of the main station but can air unique programming. The station is owned by Hearst Television Inc. KHBS2-TV broadcasts locally on channel 40.2.
TELEVISION STATION

KHBS-TV 31474
Owner: Hearst Television Inc.
Editorial: 2415 N Albert Pike Ave, Fort Smith, Arkansas 72904-5617 **Tel:** 1 479 783-4040.
Email: comments@thehometownchannel.com
Web site: http://www.4029tv.com
Profile: KHBS-TV is the ABC affiliate for the Fort Smith, AR market. The station is owned by Hearst Television Inc. KHBS-TV broadcasts locally on channel 40.
TELEVISION STATION

KHDF-TV 390681
Owner: Una Vez Mas Television Group
Editorial: 600 Whitney Ranch Dr, Ste C12, Henderson, Nevada 89014 **Tel:** 1 702 387-1963.
Web site: http://www.aztecaamerica.com
Profile: KHDF-TV is the Azteca America affiliate for the Las Vegas market. The station is owned by Una Vez Mas Television Group. KHDF-TV broadcasts locally on channel 19. All public service announcements should be directed to the mailing address, which is the corporate headquarters in Dallas.
TELEVISION STATION

KHET-TV 32701
Owner: Hawaii Public Television Foundation
Editorial: 2350 Dole St, Honolulu, Hawaii 96822-2410 **Tel:** 1 808 973-1000.
Email: email@pbshawaii.org
Web site: http://www.pbshawaii.org
Profile: KHET-TV is the PBS network affiliate for the Honolulu, HI market. The station is owned by Hawaii Public Television Foundation. KHET-TV broadcasts locally on channel 11.
TELEVISION STATION

KHGI-TV 32644
Owner: Pappas Telecasting Companies
Editorial: 1078 25th Rd, Axtell, Nebraska 68924 **Tel:** 1 308 743-2494.
Email: news@nebraska.tv
Web site: http://www.nebraska.tv
Profile: KHGI-TV is the ABC affiliate for the Kearney, NE market. The station is owned by Pappas Telecasting Companies. KHGI-TV broadcasts locally on channel 13.
TELEVISION STATION

KHLM2-TV 607613
Owner: Lotus Communications Corp.
Editorial: 6200 Tarnef Dr, Houston, Texas 77074-3706 **Tel:** 1 832 615-4343.
Profile: KHLM2-TV is a multicast channel of KHLM-TV. A multicast channel is a separate channel that shares the bandwith of the main station but can air unique programming. KHLM2-TV airs programming from mbc network for the Houston market. It is owned by Lotus Communications Corp. KHLM2-TV broadcasts locally on channel 43.2.
TELEVISION STATION

KHLM3-TV 607621
Owner: Lotus Communications Corp.
Editorial: 6200 Tarnef Dr, Houston, Texas 77074-3706 **Tel:** 1 832 615-4343.
Profile: KHLM3-TV is a multicast channel of KHLM-TV. A multicast channel is a separate channel that shares the bandwith of the main station but can air unique programming. KHLM3-TV airs infomercial programming. It is owned by Lotus Communications Corp. KHLM3-TV broadcasts locally on channel 43.3.
TELEVISION STATION

KHLM4-TV 607622
Owner: Lotus Communications Corp.
Editorial: 6200 Tarnef Dr, Houston, Texas 77074-3706 **Tel:** 1 832 615-4343.
Profile: KHLM4-TV is a multicast channel of KHLM-TV. A multicast channel is a separate channel that shares the bandwith of the main station but can air unique programming. KHLM4-TV airs programming from Para Oracion network. It is owned by Lotus Communications Corp. KHLM4-TV broadcasts locally on channel 43.4.
TELEVISION STATION

KHLM-TV 457320
Owner: Lotus Communications Corp.
Editorial: 6200 Tarnef Dr, Houston, Texas 77074-3706 **Tel:** 1 832 615-4343.
Web site: http://channel43houston.com
Profile: KHLM-TV is an independent station in the Houston market. The station is owned by Lotus Communications Corp. KHLM-TV brodcasts locally on channel 43.
TELEVISION STATION

KHMT-TV 32484
Owner: Nexstar Broadcasting Group
Editorial: 445 S 24th St W, Billings, Montana 59102-6201 **Tel:** 1 406 652-4743.
Web site: http://yourbigsky.com
Profile: KHMT-TV is the FOX affiliate for the Billings, MT, market. The station is owned by Nexstar Broadcasting Group. KHMT-TV broadcasts locally on channel 4. KHMT-TV shares a staff with sister station KSVI-TV.
TELEVISION STATION

KHNL-TV 32729
Owner: Raycom Media Inc.
Editorial: 420 Waiakamilo Rd Ste 205, Honolulu, Hawaii 96817-4950 **Tel:** 1 808 847-3246.
Email: news@hawaiinewsnow.com
Web site: http://www.hawaiinewsnow.com
Profile: KHNL-TV is the NBC affiliate for the Honolulu market. The station is owned by Raycom Media Inc. KHNL-TV broadcasts locally on channel 8. In October 2009 KHNL-TV, KGMB-TV and KFVE-TV formed an independently run local news service(LNS) sharing newsgathering resources to provide pool coverage of non-exclusvie events. The local news service is run by an independent managing editor who will determine the stories to be covered each day by the news service.
TELEVISION STATION

KHOG-TV 31476
Owner: Hearst Television Inc.
Editorial: 2809 W Ajax Ave Ste 200, Rogers, Arkansas 72758-6245 **Tel:** 1 479 783-4029.
Email: news@4029tv.com
Web site: http://www.4029tv.com
Profile: KHOG-TV is the ABC affiliate for the Fayetteville, AR market. The station is owned by Hearst Television Inc. KHOG-TV broadcasts locally on channel 29.
TELEVISION STATION

KHON-TV 32645
Owner: Nexstar Media Group, Inc.
Editorial: 88 Piikoi St, Honolulu, Hawaii 96814-4245 **Tel:** 1 808 591-2222.
Email: news@khon2.com
Web site: http://www.khon2.com
Profile: KHON-TV is the FOX affiliate for the Honolulu market. The station is owned by Nexstar Media Group, Inc. KHON-TV broadcasts locally on channel 2.
TELEVISION STATION

KHOU2-TV 608183
Owner: TEGNA Inc.
Editorial: 1945 Allen Pkwy, Houston, Texas 77019-2506 **Tel:** 1 713 526-1111.
Web site: http://www.khou.com
Profile: KHOU2-TV is an independent affiliate for the Houston market. The station is owned by TEGNA Inc. KHOU2-TV broadcasts locally on channel 11.2 and airs Bounce TV programming. KHOU2-TV is a multicast channel of KHOU-TV. A multicast channel is a separate channel that shares the bandwith of the main station but can air unique programming.
TELEVISION STATION

KHOU-TV 31477
Owner: TEGNA Inc.
Editorial: 1945 Allen Pkwy, Houston, Texas 77019-2506 **Tel:** 1 713 526-1111.
Email: assignments@khou.com
Web site: http://www.khou.com
Profile: KHOU-TV is the CBS affiliate for the Houston market. The station is owned by TEGNA Inc. KHOU-TV broadcasts locally on channel 11.
TELEVISION STATION

KHPK-TV 376721
Owner: Mako Communications, LLC
Editorial: 518 Peoples St, Corpus Christi, Texas 78401-2320 **Tel:** 1 361 883-1763.
Profile: KHPK-TV is an independent station for the Corpus Christi, TX area. The station is owned by Mako Communications, LLC. KHPK-TV broadcasts locally on channel 28.
TELEVISION STATION

KHQ2-TV 573870
Owner: Cowles Publishing Co.
Editorial: 1201 W Sprague Ave, Spokane, Washington 99201 **Tel:** 1 509 448-6000.
Email: khqnewsdesk@khq.com
Web site: http://www.khq.com
Profile: KHQ2-TV is a multicast channel of KHQ-TV A multicast channel is a separate channel that shares the bandwith of the main station but can air unique programming. KHQ2-TV is the local NBC affiliate on Channel 6.2 for the Spokane, WA market. KHQ2-TV is owned by Cowles Publishing Co.
TELEVISION STATION

KHQA2-TV 728008
Owner: Sinclair Broadcast Group, Inc.
Editorial: 301 S 36Th St, Quincy, Illinois 62301-5833 **Tel:** 1 217 222-6200.
Email: khqa@khqa.com
Web site: http://www.connecttristates.com
Profile: KHQA2-TV is a multicast channel of KHQA-TV. A multicast channel is a separate channel that shares the bandwith of the main station but can air unique programming. KHQA2-TV is the local ABC affiliate on channel 7.2 for the Quincy, IL/Hannibal, MO/ Keokuk, IA market. KHQA2-TV is owned by Sinclair Broadcast Group, Inc.
TELEVISION STATION

KHQA-TV 31479
Owner: Sinclair Broadcast Group, Inc.
Editorial: 301 S 36th St, Quincy, Illinois 62301-5833 **Tel:** 1 217 222-6200.
Email: news7@khqa.com
Web site: http://www.connecttristates.com
Profile: KHQA-TV is the CBS affiliate for the Quincy, IL/Hannibal, MO/Keokuk, IA market. The station is owned by Sinclair Broadcast Group, Inc. KHQA-TV broadcasts locally on channel 7.
TELEVISION STATION

KHQ-TV 31478
Owner: Cowles Publishing Company
Editorial: 1201 W Sprague Ave, Spokane, Washington 99201-4102 **Tel:** 1 509 448-6000.
Email: khqnewsdesk@khq.com
Web site: http://www.khq.com
Profile: KHQ-TV is the NBC affiliate for the Spokane, WA market. The station is owned by Cowles Publishing Company. KHQ-TV broadcasts locally on channel 6.
TELEVISION STATION

KHRR-TV 32413
Owner: NBC Universal
Editorial: 5151 E Broadway Blvd Ste 600, Tucson, Arizona 85711-3783 **Tel:** 1 520 396-2600.
Email: telemundoarizona@nbuni.com
Profile: KHRR-TV is the Telemundo network affiliate for the Tucson, AZ market. The station is owned by NBC Universal. KHRR-TV broadcasts locally on channel 40.
TELEVISION STATION

KHSL-TV 31481
Owner: GOCOM Media of Northern California, L.L.C.
Editorial: 3460 Silverbell Rd, Chico, California 95973-0388 **Tel:** 1 530 342-0141.
Email: news@actionnewsnow.com
Web site: http://www.actionnewsnow.com
Profile: KHSL-TV is the local CBS television affiliate for the Chico, CA market. The station is owned by GOCOM Media of Northern California, L.L.C. KHSL-TV broadcasts locally on channel 12.
TELEVISION STATION

KIAH2-TV 610705
Owner: Tribune Broadcasting Co.
Editorial: 7700 Westpark Dr, Houston, Texas 77063-6414 **Tel:** 1 713 781-3939.
Email: news@39online.com
Web site: http://www.39online.com
Profile: KIAH2-TV is a multicast of KIAH-TV. A multicast channel is a separate channel that shares the bandwith of the main station but can air unique programming. KIAH2-TV airs programming from Universal Sports in the Houston market. The station is owned by Tribune Broadcasting Co. KIAH2-TV broadcasts locally on channel 39.2.
TELEVISION STATION

KIAH-TV 31482
Owner: Tribune Broadcasting Co.
Editorial: 7700 Westpark Dr, Houston, Texas 77063-6414 **Tel:** 1 713 781-3939.
Email: news@newsfixnow.com
Web site: http://cw39.com
Profile: KIAH-TV is the CW affiliate for the Houston market. The station is owned by Tribune Broadcasting Co. KIAH-TV broadcasts locally on channel 39.
TELEVISION STATION

KICU-TV 31483
Owner: Cox Media Group, Inc.
Editorial: 2102 Commerce Dr, San Jose, California 95131-1804 **Tel:** 1 408 953-3636.
Web site: http://www.ktvu.com/news/ktvuplus
Profile: KICU-TV is an independent station for the San Jose, CA market. The station is owned by Cox Media Group, Inc. KICU-TV broadcasts locally on channel 36.
TELEVISION STATION

KIDK-TV 31484
Owner: Fisher Communications, Inc.
Editorial: 1915 N Yellowstone Hwy, Idaho Falls, Idaho 83401-1605 **Tel:** 1 208 525-8888.
Email: newsdesk@localnews8.com
Web site: http://www.localnews8.com/kidk/index.html
Profile: KIDK-TV is the CBS affiliate for the Idaho Falls, ID market. The station is owned by Fisher Communications, Inc. KIDK-TV broadcasts locally on channel 3.
TELEVISION STATION

KIDY-TV 31485
Owner: TEGNA Inc.
Tel: 1 325 655-6006.
Web site: http://www.myfoxzone.com
Profile: KIDY-TV is the FOX affiliate for the San Angelo, Texas market. The station is owned by TEGNA Inc. KIDY-TV broadcasts locally on channel 6
TELEVISION STATION

KIDZ-TV 376332
Owner: TEGNA Inc.
Editorial: 5 S Chadbourne St, San Angelo, Texas 76903-5805 **Tel:** 1 325 655-6006.
Profile: KIDZ-TV is the MyNetwork TV affiliate for the Abilene-Sweetwater, TX market. The station is owned by TEGNA Inc. KIDZ-TV broadcasts locally on channel 42.
TELEVISION STATION

KIEM-TV 31486
Owner: Pollack Broadcasting Co.
Editorial: 5650 S Broadway St, Eureka, California 95503-6905 **Tel:** 1 707 443-3123.
Email: kiemnews@hotmail.com
Web site: http://kiem-tv.com
Profile: KIEM-TV is the NBC affiliate for the Eureka, CA, market. The station is owned by Pollack Broadcasting Co. KIEM-TV broadcasts locally on channel 3.
TELEVISION STATION

KIFI-TV 31487
Owner: News-Press & Gazette Co.
Editorial: 1915 N Yellowstone Hwy, Idaho Falls, Idaho 83401-1605 **Tel:** 1 208 525-8888.
Email: newsdesk@localnews8.com
Web site: http://www.localnews8.com

Profile: KIFI-TV is the ABC affiliate for the Idaho Falls, ID market. The station is owned by the News-Press & Gazette Co. KIFI-TV broadcasts locally on channel 8.
TELEVISION STATION

KIII2-TV 859008
Owner: TEGNA Inc.
Editorial: 5002 S Padre Island Dr, Corpus Christi, Texas 78411-4206 **Tel:** 1 361 986-8300.
Email: news@kiiitv.com
Profile: KIII2-TV is a multicast channel of KIII-TV. A multicast channel is a separate channel that shares the bandwidth of the main station but can air unique programming. KIII2-TV is the Me TV Network for the Corpus Christi, TX market. The station is owned by TEGNA Inc. KIII2-TV broadcasts locally on channel 3.2.
TELEVISION STATION

KIII3-TV 882020
Owner: TEGNA Inc.
Editorial: 5002 S Padre Island Dr, Corpus Christi, Texas 78411-4206 **Tel:** 1 361 986-8300.
Profile: KIII3-TV is a multicast channel of KIII-TV. A multicast channel is a separate channel that shares the bandwidth of the main station but can air unique programming. KIII3-TV is the MundoFOX affiliate for the Corpus Christi, TX market. The station is owned by TEGNA Inc. KIII3-TV broadcasts locally on channel 3.3. The station does not have a news department.
TELEVISION STATION

KIII-TV 31488
Owner: TEGNA Inc.
Editorial: 5002 S Padre Island Dr, Corpus Christi, Texas 78411-4206 **Tel:** 1 361 986-8300.
Email: news@kiiitv.com
Web site: http://www.kiiitv.com
Profile: KIII-TV is the ABC affiliate for the Corpus Christi, TX market. The station is owned by TEGNA Inc. KIII-TV broadcasts locally on channel 3.
TELEVISION STATION

KIIO-TV 837793
Owner: Chang Media Group
Editorial: Los Angeles, California **Tel:** 1 877 365-2824.
Email: info@kiio.tv
Profile: KIIO-TV is a local station in the San Francisco market. The station is owned by Chang Media group. KIIO-TV broadcasts locally on channel 10.
TELEVISION STATION

KIIT-TV 418219
Owner: Gray Television, Inc.
Editorial: 8020 N Highway 83, North Platte, Nebraska 69101-8080 **Tel:** 1 308 532-2222.
Web site: http://www.knopnews2.com
Profile: KIIT-TV is a FOX affiliate for the North Platte, NE market. The station is owned by Gray Television, Inc. KIIT-TV broadcasts locally on channel 11.
TELEVISION STATION

KIKU-TV 31472
Owner: NRJ TV, LLC
Editorial: 737 Bishop St Ste 1430, Honolulu, Hawaii 96813-3204 **Tel:** 1 808 847-2021.
Email: info@kikutv.com
Web site: http://www.kikutv.com
Profile: KIKU-TV is an independent station for the Honolulu market. The station is owned by NRJ TV, LLC. KIKU-TV broadcasts locally on channel 20.
TELEVISION STATION

KILM-TV 32336
Owner: Sunbelt Broadcasting Co.
Editorial: 747 E Green St Ste 200, Pasadena, California 91101-2147 **Tel:** 1 760 241-6464.
Profile: KILM-TV is an independent station for the Los Angeles market. The station is owned by Sunbelt Broadcasting Co. KILM-TV broadcasts locally on channel 64.
TELEVISION STATION

KIMA-TV 32646
Owner: Fisher Communications, Inc.
Editorial: 2801 Terrace Heights Dr, Yakima, Washington 98901-1455 **Tel:** 1 509 575-0029.
Email: tips@kimatv.com
Web site: http://www.kimatv.com
Profile: KIMA-TV is the CBS affiliate for the Yakima, WA market. The station is owned by Fisher Communications, Inc. KIMA-TV broadcasts locally on channel 29.
TELEVISION STATION

KIMT-TV 31490
Owner: MidAmerica Holdings, LLC
Editorial: 112 N Pennsylvania Ave, Mason City, Iowa 50401-3404 **Tel:** 1 641 423-2540.
Email: news@kimt.com
Web site: http://www.kimt.com
Profile: KIMT-TV is the CBS affiliate for the Rochester, MN, Mason City, IA market. The station is owned by MidAmerica Holdings, LLC. KIMT-TV broadcasts locally on channel 3.
TELEVISION STATION

KINC-TV 32550
Owner: Entravision Communications Corp.
Editorial: 500 Pilot Rd, Las Vegas, Nevada 89119-3625 **Tel:** 1 702 434-0015.
Web site: http://noticias.entravision.com/las-vegas
Profile: KINC-TV is the Univision affiliate for the Las Vegas market. The station is owned by Entravision Communications Corp. KINC-TV broadcasts locally on channel 15.
TELEVISION STATION

KING2-TV 611996
Owner: TEGNA Inc.
Editorial: 333 Dexter Ave N, Seattle, Washington 98109-5107 **Tel:** 1 206 448-5555.
Email: newstips@king5.com
Web site: http://www.king5.com
Profile: KING2-TV is a multicast of KING-TV. A multicast channel is a separate channel that shares the bandwith of the main station but can air unique programming. KING2-TV airs programming from Universal Sports in the Seattle. The station is owned by TEGNA Inc. KING2-TV broadcasts locally on channel 5.2.
TELEVISION STATION

KING-TV 31491
Owner: TEGNA Inc.
Editorial: 1501 1st Ave S Ste 300, Seattle, Washington 98134-1464 **Tel:** 1 206 448-5555.
Email: newstips@king5.com
Web site: http://www.king5.com
Profile: KING-TV is the NBC affiliate for the Seattle-Tacoma market. The station is owned by TEGNA Inc. KING-TV broadcasts locally on channel 5.
TELEVISION STATION

KINT-TV 31492
Owner: Entravision Communications Corp.
Editorial: 5426 N Mesa St, El Paso, Texas 79912-5421 **Tel:** 1 915 581-1126.
Email: noticias26@entravision.com
Web site: http://www.kint.com
Profile: KINT-TV is the Univision affiliate for the El Paso, TX market. The station is owned by Entravision Communications Corp. KINT-TV broadcasts locally on channel 26.
TELEVISION STATION

KION-TV 31536
Owner: News-Press & Gazette Co.
Editorial: 1550 Moffett St, Salinas, California 93905-3342 **Tel:** 1 831 784-6300.
Email: newstips@kionrightnow.com
Web site: http://www.kion546.com
Profile: KION-TV is the CBS affiliate for the Salinas, CA market. The station is owned by News-Press & Gazette Co. KION-TV broadcasts locally on channel 46.
TELEVISION STATION

KIRO2-TV 586591
Owner: Cox Media Group, Inc.
Editorial: 2807 3rd Ave, Seattle, Washington 98121-1260 **Tel:** 1 206 728-7777.
Email: newstips@kirotv.com
Web site: http://www.kirotv.com
Profile: KIRO2-TV is a multicast of KIRO-TV. A multicast channel is a separate channel that shares the bandwith of the main station but can air unique programming. KIRO2-TV airs programming from the Retro Television Network in the Seattle market. The station is owned by Cox Media Group, Inc. KIRO2-TV broadcasts locally on channel 7.2.
TELEVISION STATION

KIRO-TV 31493
Owner: Cox Media Group, Inc.
Editorial: 2807 3rd Ave, Seattle, Washington 98121-1242 **Tel:** 1 206 728-7777.
Email: newstips@kirotv.com
Web site: http://www.kiro7.com/live-stream
Profile: KIRO-TV is the CBS affiliate for the Seattle-Tacoma market. The station is owned by Cox Media Group, Inc. KIRO-TV broadcasts locally on channel 7.
TELEVISION STATION

KITV-TV 32647
Owner: SJL Broadcasting
Editorial: 801 S King St, Honolulu, Hawaii 96813-3008 **Tel:** 1 808 535-0400.
Email: info@kitv.com
Web site: http://www.kitv.com
Profile: KITV-TV is the ABC network affiliate for the Honolulu market. The station is owned by SJL Broadcasting. KITV-TV broadcasts locally on channel 4.
TELEVISION STATION

KIVI2-TV 775482
Owner: Kiel Media Group, LLC
Editorial: 1866 E Chisholm Dr, Nampa, Idaho 83687-6805 **Tel:** 1 208 336-6682.
Profile: KIVI2-TV is a multicast channel of KIVI-TV. A multicast channel is a separate channel that shares the bandwith of the main station but can air unique programming. KIVI2-TV is the Live Well HD Network for the Boise market. The station is owned by Kiel Media Group, LLC. KIVI2-TV broadcasts locally on channel 9.2.
TELEVISION STATION

KIVI3-TV 857693
Owner: Kiel Media Group, LLC
Editorial: 1866 E Chisholm Dr, Nampa, Idaho 83687-6805 **Tel:** 1 208 336-6682.
Profile: KIVI3-TV is a multicast channel of KIVI-TV. A multicast channel is a separate channel that shares the bandwith of the main station but can air unique programming. KIVI3-TV is The Nashville Network for the Boise market. The station is owned by Kiel Media Group, LLC. KIVI3-TV broadcasts locally on channel 6.3.
TELEVISION STATION

KIVI-TV 31496
Owner: Kiel Media Group, LLC
Editorial: 1866 E Chisholm Dr, Nampa, Idaho 83687-6805 **Tel:** 1 208 336-0500.
Email: news@idahoonyourside.com
Web site: http://www.kivitv.com
Profile: KIVI-TV is the ABC network affiliate for the Boise, ID market. The station is owned by Kiel Media Group, LLC. KIVI-TV broadcasts locally on channel 6.
TELEVISION STATION

KJBO-TV 418044
Owner: Mission Broadcasting
Editorial: 4500 Seymour Hwy, Wichita Falls, Texas 76309-2602 **Tel:** 1 940 691-1808.
Web site: http://www.nexstar.tv/stations-kjbo
TELEVISION STATION

KJCT-TV 31499
Owner: News-Press & Gazette Co.
Editorial: 2531 Blichman Ave, Grand Junction, Colorado 81505-1021 **Tel:** 1 970 245-8880.
Email: newsroom@kjct8.com
Web site: http://www.kjct8.com
Profile: KJCT-TV is the ABC affiliate for the Grand Junction-Montrose, CO, market. The station is owned by News-Press & Gazette Co. KJCT-TV broadcasts locally on channel 8.
TELEVISION STATION

KJLA2-TV 606864
Owner: Costa de'Oro Media, LLC
Editorial: 2323 Corinth Ave, Los Angeles, California 90064-1701 **Tel:** 1 310 943-5288.
Web site: http://www.kjla.com
Profile: KJLA2-TV is a multicast channel of KJLA-TV. A multicast channel is a separate channel that shares the bandwith of the main station but can air unique programming. KJLA2-TV is the LATV affiliate for the Los Angeles market. The station is owned by Costa de'Oro Media, LLC. KJLA2-TV broadcasts locally on channel 57.2.
TELEVISION STATION

KJLA3-TV 606866
Owner: Costa de'Oro Media, LLC
Editorial: 2323 Corinth Ave, Los Angeles, California 90064-1701 **Tel:** 1 310 943-5288.
Web site: http://www.kjla.com
Profile: KJLA3-TV is a multicast channel of KJLA-TV. A multicast channel is a separate channel that shares the bandwith of the main station but can air unique programming. KJLA3-TV airs programming from Korean International Broadcasting for the Los Angeles market. The station is owned by Costa de'Oro Media, LLC. KJLA3-TV broadcasts locally on channel 57.3.
TELEVISION STATION

KJLA4-TV 606868
Owner: Costa de'Oro Media, LLC
Editorial: 2323 Corinth Ave, Los Angeles, California 90064-1701 **Tel:** 1 310 943-5288.
Web site: http://www.kjla.com
Profile: KJLA4-TV is a multicast channel of KJLA-TV. A multicast channel is a separate channel that shares the bandwith of the main station but can air unique programming. KJLA4-TV airs Vietnamese programming from Saigon Entertainment Television for the Los Angeles market. The station is owned by Costa de'Oro Media, LLC. KJLA4-TV broadcasts locally on channel 57.4.
TELEVISION STATION

KJLA5-TV 606871
Owner: Costa de'Oro Media, LLC
Editorial: 2323 Corinth Ave, Los Angeles, California 90064-1701 **Tel:** 1 310 943-5288.
Web site: http://www.kjla.com
Profile: KJLA5-TV is a multicast channel of KJLA-TV. A multicast channel is a separate channel that shares the bandwith of the main station but can air unique programming. KJLA5-TV airs Vietnamese programming from Saigon TV for the Los Angeles market. The station is owned by Costa de'Oro Media, LLC. KJLA5-TV broadcasts locally on channel 57.5.
TELEVISION STATION

KJLA6-TV 606874
Owner: Costa de'Oro Media, LLC
Editorial: 2323 Corinth Ave, Los Angeles, California 90064-1701 **Tel:** 1 310 943-5288.
Web site: http://www.kjla.com
Profile: KJLA6-TV is a multicast channel of KJLA-TV. A multicast channel is a separate channel that shares the bandwith of the main station but can air unique programming. KJLA6-TV airs programming from Vietnamese Broadcasting Services for the Los Angeles market. The station is owned by Costa de'Oro Media, LLC. KJLA6-TV broadcasts locally on channel 57.6.
TELEVISION STATION

KJLA7-TV 606875
Owner: Costa de'Oro Media, LLC
Editorial: 2323 Corinth Ave, Los Angeles, California 90064-1701 **Tel:** 1 310 943-5288.
Web site: http://www.kjla.com
Profile: KJLA7-TV is a multicast channel of KJLA-TV. A multicast channel is a separate channel that shares the bandwith of the main station but can air unique programming. KJLA7-TV airs programming from the Voz y Vision network for the Los Angeles market. The station is owned by Costa de'Oro Media, LLC. KJLA7-TV broadcasts locally on channel 57.7.
TELEVISION STATION

KJLA8-TV 606876
Owner: Costa de'Oro Media, LLC
Editorial: 2323 Corinth Ave, Los Angeles, California 90064-1701 **Tel:** 1 310 943-5288.
Web site: http://www.kjla.com
Profile: KJLA8-TV is a multicast channel of KJLA-TV. A multicast channel is a separate channel that shares the bandwith of the main station but can air unique programming. KJLA8-TV airs programming from KVMD-TV and the Armenian-Russian Television Network for the Los Angeles market. The station is owned by Costa de'Oro Media, LLC. KJLA8-TV broadcasts locally on channel 57.8.
TELEVISION STATION

KJLA9-TV 606880
Owner: Costa de'Oro Media, LLC
Editorial: 2323 Corinth Ave, Los Angeles, California 90064-1701 **Tel:** 1 310 943-5288.
Web site: http://www.kjla.com
Profile: KJLA9-TV is a multicast channel of KJLA-TV. A multicast channel is a separate channel that shares the bandwith of the main station but can air unique programming. KJLA9-TV airs programming from Jewelry Television network for the Los Angeles market. The station is owned by Costa de'Oro Media, LLC. KJLA9-TV broadcasts locally on channel 57.9.
TELEVISION STATION

KJLA-TV 32375
Owner: Costa de'Oro Media, LLC
Editorial: 2323 Corinth Ave, Los Angeles, California 90064-1701 **Tel:** 1 310 943-5288.
Email: lcardenas@latv.com
Web site: http://www.kjla.com
Profile: KJLA-TV is an independent station for the Los Angeles market. The station is owned by Costa de'Oro Media, LLC. KJLA-TV broadcasts locally on channel 57.
TELEVISION STATION

KJNP-TV 31501
Owner: Evangelistic Alaska Missionary Fellowship
Editorial: 2501 Mission Rd, North Pole, Alaska 99705-6361 **Tel:** 1 907 488-2216.
Email: kjnp@mosquitonet.com
Web site: http://www.mosquitonet.com/~kjnp
Profile: KJNP-TV is an affiliate of the Trinity Broadcasting Network for the Fairbanks, AK market. The station is owned by Evangelistic Alaska Missionary Fellowship. KJNP-TV broadcasts locally on channel 4.
TELEVISION STATION

KJPX-TV 350210
Owner: Kenny (Gary M. & Deborah R.)
Editorial: 5397 E 7th St, Joplin, Missouri 64801
Tel: 1 417 623-4646.
Email: kjpxtv@gmail.com
Profile: KJPX-TV is the Retro TV affiliate for the Joplin, MO market. The station is owned by Gary M. Kenny and Deborah R. Kenny. KJPX-TV broadcasts locally on channel 35.
TELEVISION STATION

KJRH-TV 31502
Owner: E.W. Scripps Co.
Editorial: 3701 S Peoria Ave, Tulsa, Oklahoma 74105-3263 **Tel:** 1 918 743-2222.
Email: news@kjrh.com
Web site: http://www.kjrh.com
Profile: KJRH-TV is the NBC affiliate for the Tulsa, OK market. The station is owned by E.W. Scripps Co. KJRH-TV broadcasts locally on channel 2.
TELEVISION STATION

KJTL-TV 32284
Owner: Mission Broadcasting
Editorial: 4500 Seymour Hwy, Wichita Falls, Texas 76309-2602 **Tel:** 1 940 691-0003.
Email: staff-kjtl@nexstar.tv
Web site: http://www.texomashomepage.com
Profile: KJTL-TV is the local FOX affiliate for the Wichita Falls, TX market. The station is owned by Mission Broadcasting. KJTL-TV broadcasts locally on Channel 18.
TELEVISION STATION

KJTV-TV 31503
Owner: Ramar Communications II Ltd.
Editorial: 9800 University Ave, Lubbock, Texas 79423-5302 **Tel:** 1 806 745-3434.
Email: news@fox34.com
Web site: http://www.myfoxlubbock.com
Profile: KJTV-TV is the FOX affiliate for the Lubbock, TX market. The station is owned by Ramar Communications II Ltd. KJTV-TV broadcasts locally on channel 34.
TELEVISION STATION

KJWP-TV 32546
Owner: PMCM TV, LLC
Editorial: 2 Paragon Way Ste 800, Freehold, New Jersey 07728-9573 **Tel:** 1 732 462-2015.
Web site: http://kjwp2.com
Profile: KJWP-TV is the Me-TV affiliate for the Philadelphia market. The station is owned by PMCM TV, LLC. KJWP-TV broadcasts locally on channel 2. The station does not have a news department, but airs public affairs programming.
TELEVISION STATION

KJZZ-TV 32283
Owner: Sinclair Broadcast Group, Inc.
Editorial: 301 W South Temple, Salt Lake City, Utah 84101-1216 **Tel:** 1 801 839-1234.
Web site: http://www.kjzz.com

Profile: KJZZ-TV is an independent station for the Salt Lake City market. The station is owned by Sinclair Broadcast Group, Inc.. KJZZ-TV broadcasts locally on channel 14.
TELEVISION STATION

KKCO-TV 32547
Owner: Gray Television, Inc.
Editorial: 2531 Blichman Ave, Grand Junction, Colorado 81505-1021 **Tel:** 1 970 243-1111.
Email: tips@kkco11news.com
Web site: http://www.nbc11news.com
Profile: KKCO-TV is the NBC affiliate for the Grand Junction-Montrose, CO, market. The station is owned by Gray Television, Inc. KKCO-TV broadcasts locally on channel 11.
TELEVISION STATION

KKEY-TV 318168
Owner: Nexstar Media Group, Inc.
Editorial: 2120 L St, Bakersfield, California 93301-2331 **Tel:** 1 661 283-1700.
Email: 17News@kget.com
Web site: http://www.telemundobakersfield.com
Profile: KKEY-TV is a Telemundo affiliate for the Bakersfield, CA market. The station is owned by Nexstar Broadcasting Group. KKEY-TV broadcasts locally on channel 11.
TELEVISION STATION

KKFX-TV 32528
Owner: News-Press & Gazette Co.
Editorial: 1211 W McCoy Ln, Santa Maria, California 93455-1036 **Tel:** 1 805 925-1200.
Web site: http://www.kcoy.com
Profile: KKFX-TV is a FOX affiliate for the Santa Maria, CA market. The station is owned by News-Press & Gazette Co. KKFX-TV broadcasts locally on channel 24. KKFX-TV also airs on channel 11 for area cable systems.
TELEVISION STATION

KKPX2-TV 609317
Owner: ION Media Networks
Editorial: 600 Price Ave, Ste B, Redwood City, California 94063-1413 **Tel:** 1 650 261-1370.
Web site: http://www.qubo.com
Profile: KKPX2-TV is independent affiliate for the San Francisco market. The station is owned by ION Media Networks. KKPX2-TV broadcasts locally on channel 65.2. KKPX2-TV broadcasts children's programming from the qubo network. KKPX2-TV is a multicast channel of KKPX-TV. A multicast channel is a separate channel that shares the bandwidth of the main station but can air unique programming.
TELEVISION STATION

KKPX3-TV 609482
Owner: ION Media Networks
Editorial: 600 Price Ave, Ste B, Redwood City, California 94063-1413 **Tel:** 1 650 261-1370.
Web site: http://www.ionlife.com
Profile: KKPX3-TV is independent affiliate for the San Francisco market. The station is owned by ION Media Networks. KKPX3-TV broadcasts locally on channel 65.3. KKPX2-TV broadcasts ION Life, a network dedicated to lifestyle programming. KKPX3-TV is a multicast channel of KKPX-TV. A multicast channel is a separate channel that shares the bandwidth of the main station but can air unique programming.
TELEVISION STATION

KKPX4-TV 609484
Owner: ION Media Networks
Editorial: 600 Price Ave Ste B, Redwood City, California 94063-1413 **Tel:** 1 650 261-1370.
Web site: http://www.worship.net
Profile: KKPX4-TV is independent affiliate for the San Francisco market. The station is owned by ION Media Networks. KKPX4-TV broadcasts locally on channel 65.4. KKPX4-TV airs programming from The Worship Network. KKPX4-TV is a multicast channel of KKPX-TV. A multicast channel is a separate channel that shares the bandwidth of the main station but can air unique programming.
TELEVISION STATION

KKPX-TV 32400
Owner: ION Media Networks
Editorial: 660 Price Ave Ste B, Redwood City, California 94063-1431 **Tel:** 1 650 261-1370.
Profile: KKPX-TV is the ION Television affiliate for the San Francisco market. The station is owned by ION Media Networks. KKPX-TV broadcasts locally on channel 65.
TELEVISION STATION

KKRA-TV 350211
Owner: Rapid Broadcasting
Editorial: 2424 S Plaza Dr, Rapid City, South Dakota 57702-9379 **Tel:** 1 605 355-0024.
Web site: http://www.newscenter1.tv/
Profile: KKRA-TV is the MyNetworkTV affiliate for the Rapid City, SD market. The station is owned by Rapid Broadcasting. KKRA-TV broadcasts locally on channel 24.
TELEVISION STATION

KKTV2-TV 728617
Owner: Grey Television, Inc.
Editorial: 520 E Colorado Ave, Colorado Springs, Colorado 80903-3604 **Tel:** 1 719 578-0000.
Web site: http://www.kktv.com/mntv
Profile: KKTV2-TV is a multicast channel of KKTV-TV. A multicast channel is a separate channel that shares the bandwidth of the main station but can air unique programming. KKTV2-TV is the My Network TV for the Colorado Springs, CO market. The station is owned by Grey Television, Inc. KKTV2-TV broadcasts locally on channel 11.2.
TELEVISION STATION

KKTV-TV 31505
Owner: Gray Television, Inc.
Editorial: 520 E Colorado Ave, Colorado Springs, Colorado 80903-3604 **Tel:** 1 719 634-2844.
Email: news@kktv.com
Web site: http://www.kktv.com
Profile: KKTV-TV is the CBS affiliate for the Colorado Springs, CO market. The station is owned by Gray Television, Inc. KKTV-TV broadcasts locally on channel 11.
TELEVISION STATION

KLAF-TV 75514
Owner: Nexstar Broadcasting Group
Editorial: 123 N Easy St, Lafayette, Louisiana 70506-1914 **Tel:** 1 337 237-1500.
Email: news@kadn.com
Web site: http://www.cajunfirst.com
Profile: KLAF-TV is the local MyNetworkTV affiliate for the Lafayette, LA market. The station is owned by Nexstar Broadcasting Group. KLAF-TV broadcasts locally on channel 17.
TELEVISION STATION

KLAS2-TV 619948
Owner: Landmark Communications Inc.
Editorial: 3228 Channel 8 Dr, Las Vegas, Nevada 89109-9000 **Tel:** 1 702 792-8888.
Email: newsdesk@klastv.com
Web site: http://www.lasvegasnow.com
Profile: KLAS2-TV is a multicast of KLAS-TV. A multicast channel is a separate channel that shares the bandwith of the main station but can air unique programming. KLAS2-TV is the Me-TV network in the Las Vegas market. The station is owned by Landmark Communications Inc. KLAS2-TV broadcasts locally on channel 8.2.
TELEVISION STATION

KLAS-TV 31506
Owner: Nexstar Broadcasting Group
Editorial: 3228 Channel 8 Dr, Las Vegas, Nevada 89109-9000 **Tel:** 1 702 792-8888.
Email: newsdesk@8newsnow.com
Web site: http://www.lasvegasnow.com
Profile: KLAS-TV is the CBS affiliate for the Las Vegas market. The station is owned by Nexstar Broadcasting Group. KLAS-TV broadcasts locally on channel 8.
TELEVISION STATION

KLAX-TV 31507
Owner: Pollack Broadcasting Co.
Editorial: 1811 England Dr, Alexandria, Louisiana 71303-4115 **Tel:** 1 318 473-0031.
Email: bzimmerman@klax-tv.com
Web site: http://www.klax-tv.com
Profile: KLAX-TV is the ABC affiliate for the Alexandria, LA, market. The station is owned by Pollack Broadcasting Co. KLAX-TV broadcasts locally on channel 31.
TELEVISION STATION

KLBK-TV 31508
Owner: Nexstar Broadcasting Group
Editorial: 7403 University Ave, Lubbock, Texas 79423-1424 **Tel:** 1 806 745-2345.
Web site: http://www.everythinglubbock.com
Profile: KLBK-TV is the CBS network affiliate for the Lubbock, TX market. The station is owned by Nexstar Broadcasting Group. KLBK-TV broadcasts locally on channel 13.
TELEVISION STATION

KLCW-TV 390694
Owner: Ramar Communications II Ltd.
Editorial: 9800 University Ave, Lubbock, Texas 79423-5302 **Tel:** 1 806 745-3434.
Web site: http://www.lubbockcw.com
Profile: KLCW-TV is the CW affiliate for the Lubbock, TX market. The station is owned by Ramar Communications II Ltd. KLCW-TV broadcasts locally on channel 22.
TELEVISION STATION

KLDO-TV 31510
Owner: Entravision Communications Corp.
Editorial: 222 Bob Bullock Loop, Laredo, Texas 78043-4206 **Tel:** 1 956 727-0027.
Email: noticias27@entravision.com
Web site: http://noticias.entravision.com/laredo
Profile: KLDO-TV is the FOX affiliate for the Laredo, TX, market. The station is owned by Entravision Communications Corp. KLDO-TV broadcasts locally on channel 27.
TELEVISION STATION

KLEG-TV 133923
Owner: Viswanath (Dilip)
Editorial: 703 McKinney Ave, Ste 240, Dallas, Texas 75202-1039 **Tel:** 1 214 754-7008.
Web site: http://www.aztecaamerica.com
Profile: KLEG-TV is an affiliate of Azteca America for the Dallas-Fort Worth market. The station is owned by Dilip Viswanath. KLEG-TV broadcasts locally on channel 44.
TELEVISION STATION

KLEW-TV 32766
Owner: Sinclair Broadcast Group, Inc.
Editorial: 2626 17th St, Lewiston, Idaho 83501-6312 **Tel:** 1 208 746-2636.
Email: klewnews@klewtv.com
Web site: http://www.klewtv.com
Profile: KLEW-TV is the CBS affiliate for the Spokane market. The station is owned by Sinclair Broadcast Group, Inc. KLEW-TV broadcasts locally on channel 3.
TELEVISION STATION

KLFY2-TV 791883
Owner: New Young Broadcasting
Editorial: 1808 Eraste Landry Rd, Lafayette, Louisiana 70506-1911 **Tel:** 1 337 981-4823.
Web site: http://www.klfy.com
Profile: KLFY2-TV is a multicast channel of KLFY-TV. A multicast channel is a separate channel that shares the bandwith of the main station but can air unique programming. KLFY2-TV is the Live Well Network for the Lafayette, LA market. The station is owned by New Young Broadcasting. KLFY2-TV broadcasts locally on channel 10.2.
TELEVISION STATION

KLFY-TV 31511
Owner: New Young Broadcasting
Editorial: 1808 Eraste Landry Rd, Lafayette, Louisiana 70506-1911 **Tel:** 1 337 981-4823.
Email: news@klfy.com
Web site: http://www.klfy.com
Profile: KLFY-TV is the CBS network affiliate for the Lafayette, LA market. The station is owned by New Young Broadcasting. KLFY-TV broadcasts locally on channel 10.
TELEVISION STATION

KLHO-TV 390932
Owner: Aracelis Ortiz Corporation.
Editorial: 4501 W Expressway 83, Harlingen, Texas 78552-3604 **Tel:** 1 956 421-2635.
Profile: KLHO-TV is an independent station for the Brownsville - Mc Allen, TX market. The station is owned by Aracelis Ortiz Corporation. KLHO-TV broadcasts locally on channel 17.
TELEVISION STATION

KLJB-TV 32738
Owner: Marshall Broadcasting Group
Editorial: 937 E 53rd St, Davenport, Iowa 52807-2614 **Tel:** 1 563 386-1818.
Email: newsroom@whbf.com
Web site: http://www.ourquadcities.com
Profile: KLJB-TV is a FOX affiliate for the Davenport, IA/Rock Island, IL/Moline, IL market. The station is owned by Marshall Broadcasting Group. KLJB-TV broadcasts locally on channel 18.
TELEVISION STATION

KLKN2-TV 788624
Owner: Citadel Communications
Editorial: 3240 S 10Th St, Lincoln, Nebraska 68502-4401 **Tel:** 1 402 434-8000.
Email: 8@klkntv.com
Web site: http://www.klkntv.com
Profile: KLKN2-TV is a multicast channel of KLKN-TV. A multicast channel is a separate channel that shares the bandwith of the main station but can air unique programming. KLKN2-TV is the Live Well HD Network for the Lincoln, NE market. The station is owned by Citadel Communications. KLKN2-TV broadcasts locally on channel 8.2.
TELEVISION STATION

KLKN-TV 32748
Owner: Cumulus Media Inc
Editorial: 3240 S 10th St, Lincoln, Nebraska 68502-4401 **Tel:** 1 402 436-2252.
Email: 8@klkntv.com
Web site: http://www.klkntv.com
Profile: KLKN-TV is the ABC affiliate for the Lincoln, NE market. The station is owned by Cumulus Media Inc. KLKN-TV broadcasts locally on channel 8.
TELEVISION STATION

KLPN-TV 417935
Owner: White Knight Broadcasting
Editorial: 4300 Richmond Rd, Tyler, Texas 75703-1201 **Tel:** 1 903 581-5656.
TELEVISION STATION

KLRA-TV 328238
Owner: Pinnacle Media, LLC
Editorial: 1 Shackleford Dr Ste 400, Little Rock, Arkansas 72211-2859
Profile: KLRA-TV is the Univision affiliate for the Little Rock, AR market. The station is owned by Pinnacle Media, LLC. KLRA-TV broadcasts locally on channel 58.
TELEVISION STATION

KLRN2-TV 614890
Owner: Alamo Public Telecommunications Council
Editorial: 501 Broadway St, San Antonio, Texas 78215-1820 **Tel:** 1 210 270-9000.
Email: info@klrn.org
Web site: http://www.klrn.org
Profile: KLRN2-TV is a multicast of KLRN-TV. A multicast channel is a separate channel that shares the bandwith of the main station but can air unique programming. KLRN2-TV airs programming from KLRN Encore in the San Antonio market. The station is owned by Alamo Public Telecommunications Council. KLRN2-TV broadcasts locally on channel 9.2.
TELEVISION STATION

KLRN3-TV 614893
Owner: Alamo Public Telecommunications Council
Editorial: 501 Broadway St, San Antonio, Texas 78215-1820 **Tel:** 1 210 270-9000.
Email: info@klrn.org
Web site: http://www.klrn.org
Profile: KLRN3-TV is a multicast of KLRN-TV. A multicast channel is a separate channel that shares the bandwith of the main station but can air unique programming. KLRN3-TV airs programming from V-me in the San Antonio market. The station is owned by Alamo Public Telecommunications Council. KLRN3-TV broadcasts locally on channel 9.3.
TELEVISION STATION

KLRN4-TV 61490
Owner: Alamo Public Telecommunications Council
Editorial: 501 Broadway St, San Antonio, Texas 78215-1820 **Tel:** 1 210 270-9000.
Email: info@klrn.org
Web site: http://www.klrn.org
Profile: KLRN4-TV is a multicast of KLRN-TV. A multicast channel is a separate channel that shares the bandwith of the main station but can air unique programming. KLRN4-TV airs programming from Create in the San Antonio market. The station is owned by Alamo Public Telecommunications Counci KLRN4-TV broadcasts locally on channel 9.4.
TELEVISION STATION

KLRN-TV 3151
Owner: Alamo Public Telecommunications Council
Editorial: 501 Broadway St, San Antonio, Texas 78215-1820 **Tel:** 1 210 270-9000.
Email: info@klrn.org
Web site: http://www.klrn.org
Profile: KLRN-TV is a PBS affiliate for the San Antonio market. The station is owned by Alamo Public Telecommunications Council. KLRN-TV broadcasts locally on channel 9.
TELEVISION STATION

KLRT-TV 3151
Owner: Nexstar Broadcasting Group
Editorial: 1401 W Capitol Ave Ste 104, Little Rock, Arkansas 72201-2940 **Tel:** 1 501 340-4444.
Email: news@fox16.com
Web site: http://www.fox16.com
Profile: KLRT-TV is the FOX affiliate for the Little Rock, AR market. The station is owned by Nexstar Broadcasting Group. KLRT-TV broadcasts locally on channel 16.
TELEVISION STATION

KLRU2-TV 61730
Owner: Capital of Texas Public Telecommunications
Editorial: 2504-B Whitis ave, StopA0701, Austin, Texas 78712-1617 **Tel:** 1 512 471-4811.
Email: info@klru.org
Web site: http://www.klru.org
Profile: KLRU2-TV is a multicast of KLRU-TV. A multicast channel is a separate channel that shares the bandwith of the main station but can air unique programming. KLRU2-TV airs programming from the Create Network in the Austin, TX market. The station is owned by Capital of Texas Public Telecommunications. KLRU-G broadcasts locally on channel 18.2.
TELEVISION STATION

KLRU3-TV 61730
Owner: Capital of Texas Public Telecommunications
Editorial: 250-B4 Whitis Ave StopA0701, Austin, Texas 78712-1617 **Tel:** 1 512 471-4811.
Email: info@klru.org
Web site: http://www.klru.org
Profile: KLRU3-TV is a multicast of KLRU-TV. A multicast channel is a separate channel that shares the bandwith of the main station but can air unique programming. KLRU3-TV airs programming from the Q Network in the Austin, TX market. The station is owned by Capital of Texas Public Telecommunications. KLRU3-TV broadcasts locally on channel 18.3.
TELEVISION STATION

KLRU-TV 3151
Owner: Capital of Texas Public Telecommunications
Editorial: 2504 Whitis Ave #B, Austin, Texas 78712-1538 **Tel:** 1 512 475-9029.
Email: info@klru.org
Web site: http://www.klru.org
Profile: KLRU-TV is a PBS affiliate for the Austin, TX market. The station is owned by Capital of Texas Public Telecommunications. KLRU-TV broadcasts locally on channel 18.
TELEVISION STATION

KLSR-TV 3236
Owner: California-Oregon Broadcasting
Editorial: 2940 Chad Dr, Eugene, Oregon 97408-7343 **Tel:** 1 541 683-3434.
Email: info@oregonsfox.com
Web site: http://www.oregonsfox.com
Profile: KLSR-TV is the FOX affiliate for the Eugene, OR market. The station is owned by California-Oregon Broadcasting. KLSR-TV broadcasts locally on channel 34.
TELEVISION STATION

KLST-TV 3151
Owner: Nexstar Broadcasting Group
Editorial: 2800 Armstrong St, San Angelo, Texas 76903 **Tel:** 1 325 949-8800.
Email: klstnews@klst.net
Web site: http://conchovalleyhomepage.com
Profile: KLST-TV is the CBS affiliate for the San Angelo, TX, market. The station is owned by Nexstar Broadcasting Group. KLST-TV broadcasts locally on channel 8.
TELEVISION STATION

KLTJ-TV 32269

Owner: Word of God Fellowship, Inc.
Editorial: 1050 Gemini St, Houston, Texas 77058-1706 **Tel:** 1 281 212-1022.
Email: contactus@daystar.com
Web site: http://www.daystar.com
Profile: KLTJ-TV is the Daystar affiliate for the Houston maket. The station is owned by Word of God Fellowship, Inc. KLTJ-TV broadcasts locally on channel 23.
TELEVISION STATION

KLTV-TV 32648

Owner: Raycom Media Inc.
Editorial: 105 W Ferguson St, Tyler, Texas 75702-7203 **Tel:** 1 903 597-5588.
Email: newsproducers@kltv.com
Web site: http://www.kltv.com
Profile: KLTV-TV is the ABC affiliate for the Tyler, TX market. The station is owned by Raycom Media Inc. KLTV-TV broadcasts locally on channel 7.
TELEVISION STATION

KLUZ-TV 31517

Owner: Entravision Communications Corp.
Editorial: 2725 Broadbent Pkwy NE Ste F, Albuquerque, New Mexico 87107-1635
Tel: 1 505 342-4141.
Email: univisionnm@entravision.com
Web site: http://www.kluz.tv
Profile: KLUZ-TV is the Univision affiliate in the Albuquerque, NM market. The station is owned by Entravision Communications Corp. KLUZ-TV broadcasts locally on channel 41. The outlet does not accept faxes. Email is the preferred method of contact.
TELEVISION STATION

KLWB-TV 418068

Owner: Wilderness Communications, LLC
Editorial: 3501 NW Evangeline Trwy, Carencro, Louisiana 70520-6240 **Tel:** 1 337 896-1600.
Web site: http://lafayette.thistv.com
Profile: KLWB-TV is the This TV affiliate for the Lafayette, LA market. The station is owned by Wilderness Communications, LLC and is operated by Delta Media Corporation. KLWB-TV broadcasts locally on channel 50.
TELEVISION STATION

KMAX-TV 31584

Owner: CBS Television Stations
Editorial: 2713 Kovr Dr, West Sacramento, California 95605-1600 **Tel:** 1 916 374-1300.
Email: newsroom@kmaxtv.com
Web site: http://sacramento.cbslocal.com
Profile: KMAX-TV is the CW network affiliate for the Sacramento, CA, market. The station is owned by CBS Television Stations. KMAX-TV broadcasts locally on channel 31.
TELEVISION STATION

KMBC2-TV 621001

Owner: Hearst Television Inc.
Editorial: 6455 Winchester Ave, Kansas City, Missouri 64133-4609 **Tel:** 1 816 221-9999.
Email: kmbcnewstips@thekansascitychannel.com
Web site: http://www.kmbc.com
Profile: KMBC2-TV is a multicast of KMBC-TV. A multicast channel is a separate channel that shares the bandwith of the main station but can air unique programming. KMBC2-TV airs 24 local weather programming from KMBC Digital Weather Channel in the Kansas City, MO market. The station is owned by Hearst Television Inc. KMBC2-TV broadcasts locally on channel 9.2.
TELEVISION STATION

KMBC-TV 31519

Owner: Hearst Television Inc.
Editorial: 6455 Winchester Ave, Kansas City, Missouri 64133-4609 **Tel:** 1 816 221-9999.
Email: news@kmbc.com
Web site: http://www.kmbc.com
Profile: KMBC-TV is the ABC affiliate for the Kansas City, MO area. The station is owned by Hearst Television Inc. KMBC-TV broadcasts locally on channel 9.
TELEVISION STATION

KMBY2-TV 721278

Owner: Cocola Broadcasting Companies
Editorial: 706 W Herndon Ave, Fresno, California 93650-1033 **Tel:** 1 559 435-7000.
Web site: http://www.cocolatv.com
Profile: KMBY2-TV is a multicast channel of KMBY-TV. A multicast channel is a separate channel that shares the bandwith of the main station but can air unique programming. KMBY2-TV is the Estrella TV for the Monterey-Salinas, CA market. The station is owned by Cocola Broadcasting Companies. WLS2-TV broadcasts locally on channel 19.2.
TELEVISION STATION

KMBY-TV 721262

Owner: Cocola Broadcasting Companies
Editorial: 706 W Herndon Ave, Fresno, California 93650-1033 **Tel:** 1 559 435-7000.
Email: info@cocolatv.com
Web site: http://www.cocolatv.com
Profile: KMBY-TV is the MundoFOX affiliate for the Monterey, CA market. The station is owned by Cocola Broadcasting Companies. KMBY-TV broadcasts locally on channel 19.
TELEVISION STATION

KMCE-TV 390599

Owner: KMCE Inc.
Editorial: 1961 Main St, Ste 224, Watsonville, California 95076-3027 **Tel:** 1 831 724-0143.
Email: info@kmce.tv
Web site: http://www.azteca43.tv
Profile: KMCE-LP is an Azteca América affiliate serving the vicinity of Monterey, Salinas, and Santa Cruz- Channel 29, California. The station is licensed to Monterey and broadcasts from Fremont Peak, however, KMCE's studeios are located in Watsonville.
TELEVISION STATION

KMCI-TV 32347

Owner: E.W. Scripps Co.
Editorial: 4720 Oak St, Kansas City, Missouri 64112-2236 **Tel:** 1 816 753-4141.
Email: desk@kshb.com
Web site: http://www.kshb.com/38-the-spot
Profile: KMCI-TV is an independent affiliate for the Kansas City, MO market. The station is owned by E.W. Scripps Co. KMCI-TV broadcasts locally on channel 38.
TELEVISION STATION

KMCT-TV 31520

Owner: Lamb Broadcasting Inc.
Editorial: 701 Parkwood Dr, West Monroe, Louisiana 71291-5435 **Tel:** 1 318 322-1399.
Email: events@thevoicenetwork.tv
Web site: http://thevoicenetwork.tv
Profile: KMCT-TV is an independent station for the Monroe, LA/El Dorado, AR market. The station is owned by Lamb Broadcasting Inc. KMCT-TV broadcasts locally on channel 39.
TELEVISION STATION

KMEG-TV 31521

Owner: Titan Broadcasting LLC
Editorial: 100 Gold Cir, Dakota Dunes, South Dakota 57049-5316 **Tel:** 1 712 277-3554.
Email: news@siouxlandnews.com
Web site: http://www.siouxlandnews.com
Profile: KMEG-TV is the CBS network affiliate for the Sioux City, IA market. The station is owned by Titan Broadcasting LLC. KMEG-TV broadcasts locally on channel 14.
TELEVISION STATION

KMEX-TV 31522

Owner: Univision Communications Inc.
Editorial: 5999 Center Dr, Los Angeles, California 90045-8901 **Tel:** 1 310 216-3434.
Email: noticiasunivision34@univision.net
Web site: http://www.univision.com/los-angeles
Profile: KMEX-TV is the Univision affiliate for the Los Angeles market. The station is owned by Univision Communications Inc. KMEX-TV broadcasts locally on channel 34.
TELEVISION STATION

KMGH2-TV 613343

Owner: E.W. Scipps Co.
Editorial: 123 E Speer Blvd, Denver, Colorado 80203-3417 **Tel:** 1 303 832-7777.
Web site: http://www.thedenverchannel.com
Profile: KMGH2-TV is an Azteca America affiliate for the Denver market. The station is owned by E.W. Scipps Co. KMGH2-TV broadcasts locally on channel 7.2. The station is a simulcast of low power sister station KZCO-TV. KMGH2-TV is a multicast channel of KMGH-TV. A multicast channel is a separate channel that shares the bandwidth of the main station but can air unique programming.
TELEVISION STATION

KMGH3-TV 613344

Owner: E.W. Scipps Co.
Editorial: 123 E Speer Blvd, Denver, Colorado 80203-3417 **Tel:** 1 303 832-7777.
Web site: http://www.thedenverchannel.com/
Profile: KMGH3-TV is an independent affiliate for the Denver market. The station is owned by E.W. Scipps Co. KMGH3-TV broadcasts locally on channel 7.3. The station airs programming from music-oriented television Fuse TV. KMGH3-TV is a multicast channel of KMGH-TV. A multicast channel is a separate channel that shares the bandwidth of the main station but can air unique programming.
TELEVISION STATION

KMGH-TV 31523

Owner: E.W. Scipps Co.
Editorial: 123 E Speer Blvd, Denver, Colorado 80203-3417 **Tel:** 1 303 832-0200.
Email: newstips@thedenverchannel.com
Web site: http://www.thedenverchannel.com
Profile: KMGH-TV is the ABC network affiliate for the Denver market. The station is owned by E.W. Scipps Co. KMGH-TV broadcasts locally on channel 7.
TELEVISION STATION

KMID-TV 31525

Owner: Nexstar Broadcasting Group
Editorial: 3200 Laforce Blvd, Midland, Texas 79706-4696 **Tel:** 1 432 563-2222.
Email: news@kmid.tv
Web site: http://www.yourbasin.com
Profile: KMID-TV is the ABC affiliate for the Midland, TX market. The station is owned by Nexstar Broadcasting Group. KMID-TV broadcasts locally on channel 2.
TELEVISION STATION

KMIR-TV 31526

Owner: OTA Broadcasting
Editorial: 72920 Parkview Dr, Palm Desert, California 92260-9357 **Tel:** 1 760 568-3636.
Email: news@kmir.com
Web site: http://www.kmir.com
Profile: KMIR-TV is the NBC affiliate in Palm Desert, CA, serving Palm Springs and the Coachella Valley. The station is owned by OTA Broadcasting. KMIR-TV broadcasts locally on channel 6.
TELEVISION STATION

KMIZ2-TV 787471

Owner: JW Broadcasting
Editorial: 501 Business Loop 70 E, Columbia, Missouri 65201-3909 **Tel:** 1 573 449-0917.
Email: news@kmiz.com
Web site: http://www.kmiz.com
Profile: KMIZ2-TV is a multicast channel of KMIZ-TV. A multicast channel is a separate channel that shares the bandwith of the main station but can air unique programming. KMIZ2-TV is the Me-TV affiliate for the Columbia-Jefferson City, MO market. The station is owned by JW Broadcasting. KMIZ2-TV broadcasts locally on channel 17.2.
TELEVISION STATION

KMIZ-TV 31527

Owner: News-Press & Gazette Co.
Editorial: 501 Business Loop 70 E, Columbia, Missouri 65201-3909 **Tel:** 1 573 449-0917.
Email: news@kmiz.com
Web site: http://www.abc17news.com
Profile: KMIZ-TV is the ABC network affiliate for the Columbia-Jefferson City, MO market. The station is owned by News-Press & Gazette Co. KMIZ-TV broadcasts locally on channel 17.
TELEVISION STATION

KMLM-TV 32388

Owner: Prime Time Christian Broadcasting Inc.
Editorial: 12706 W Highway 80 E, Odessa, Texas 79765-9611 **Tel:** 1 432 563-0420.
Email: info@glc.us.com
Web site: http://www.glc.us.com
Profile: KMLM-TV is the independent affiliate for the Odessa, TX market. The station is owned by Prime Time Christian Broadcasting Inc. KMLM-TV broadcasts locally on channel 42.
TELEVISION STATION

KMOH-TV 81140

Owner: Hero Broadcasting, LLC
Tel: 1 928 753-2724.
Web site: http://www.mundomaxphoenix.com
Profile: KMOH-TV is the MundoFOX affiliate for the Phoenix market (but is contacted at Miami Lakes, FL). The station is owned by Hero Broadcasting, LLC. KMOH-TV broadcasts locally on channel 6.
TELEVISION STATION

KMOL-TV 472309

Owner: Saga Communications
Editorial: 3808 N Navarro St, Victoria, Texas 77901-2621 **Tel:** 1 361 575-2500.
Web site: http://www.crossroadstoday.com
Profile: KMOL-TV is the NBC affiliate for the Victoria, TX market. The station is owned by Saga Communications. KMOL-TV broadcasts locally on channel 17.
TELEVISION STATION

KMOT-TV 32768

Owner: Gray Television
Editorial: 1800 16th St SW, Minot, North Dakota 58701-6400 **Tel:** 1 701 852-4101.
Email: kmot@kmot.com
Web site: http://www.kmot.com
Profile: KMOT-TV is a television station in the Minot, ND area that simulcasts the programming of KFYR-TV, the NBC affiliate in Bismarck, ND. It is owned by Gray Television. KMOT-TV broadcasts locally on channel 10. The station shares some staff with sister station KFYR-TV.
TELEVISION STATION

KMOV2-TV 613862

Owner: Meredith Corp.
Editorial: 1 S Memorial Dr, Saint Louis, Missouri 63102-2425 **Tel:** 1 314 621-4444.
Email: news@kmov.com
Web site: http://www.kmov.com
Profile: KMOV2-TV is a multicast of KMOV-TV. A multicast channel is a separate channel that shares the bandwith of the main station but can air unique programming. KMOV2-TV airs programming from 4 Warn Skytracker Doppler in the St. Louis market. The station is owned by Meredith Corp. KMOV2-TV broadcasts locally on channel 4.2.
TELEVISION STATION

KMOV-TV 31530

Owner: Meredith Corporation
Editorial: 1 S Memorial Dr, Saint Louis, Missouri 63102-2425 **Tel:** 1 314 621-4444.
Email: news@kmov.com
Web site: http://www.kmov.com
Profile: KMOV-TV is the CBS affiliate for the St. Louis market. The station is owned by Meredith Corporation. KMOV-TV broadcasts locally on channel 4.
TELEVISION STATION

KMPH-TV 31531

Owner: Sinclair Broadcast Group
Editorial: 5111 E McKinley Ave, Fresno, California 93727-2033 **Tel:** 1 559 255-2600.
Email: newsdesk@kmph.com
Web site: http://www.kmph.com
Profile: KMPH-TV is the FOX affiliate for the Fresno-Visalia, CA market. The station is owned by Sinclair Broadcast Group. KMPH-TV broadcasts locally on channel 26.
TELEVISION STATION

KMPX-TV 390600

Owner: Liberman Broadcasting Inc.
Editorial: 2410 Gateway Dr, Irving, Texas 75063-2727
Tel: 1 972 652-2900.
Profile: KMPX-TV is an independent station for the Dallas-Fort Worth market. The station is owned by Liberman Broadcasting Inc. KMPX-TV broadcasts locally on channel 29.
TELEVISION STATION

KMSB-TV 31532

Owner: TEGNA Inc.
Editorial: 7831 N Business Park Dr, Tucson, Arizona 85743-9622 **Tel:** 1 520 770-1123.
Email: desk@tucsonnewsnow.com
Web site: http://www.tucsonnewsnow.com
Profile: KMSB-TV is the FOX network affiliate for the Tucson, AZ market. The station is owned by TEGNA Inc. KMSB-TV broadcasts locally on channel 11.
TELEVISION STATION

KMSP-TV 31534

Owner: Fox Broadcasting Company
Editorial: 11358 Viking Dr, Eden Prairie, Minnesota 55344-7238 **Tel:** 1 952 944-9999.
Email: fox9news@foxtv.com
Web site: http://www.fox9.com
Profile: KMSP-TV is a FOX affiliate for the Minneapolis-St. Paul market. The station is owned by Fox Broadcasting Company. KMSP-TV broadcasts locally on channel 9.
TELEVISION STATION

KMSS-TV 31535

Owner: Marshall Broadcasting Group
Editorial: 3519 Jewella Ave, Shreveport, Louisiana 71109-4419 **Tel:** 1 318 631-5677.
Web site: http://www.kmsstv.com
Profile: KMSS-TV is the FOX affiliate for the Shreveport, LA market. The station is owned by Marshall Broadcasting Group. KMSS-TV broadcasts locally on channel 33.
TELEVISION STATION

KMTF-TV 32598

Owner: Gray Television
Editorial: 100 W Lyndale Ave Ste B, Helena, Montana 59601-2999 **Tel:** 1 406 457-1010.
Email: news@ktvh.com
Web site: http://www.cwhelena.com
Profile: KMTF-TV is the CW affiliate for the Helena, MT market. The station is owned by Rocky Mountain Broadcasting. KMTF-TV broadcasts locally on channel 10.
TELEVISION STATION

KMTP2-TV 610124

Owner: Minority Television Project
Editorial: 31 Airport Blvd Ste E, South San Francisco, California 94080-6519 **Tel:** 1 415 777-3232.
Web site: http://www.kmtp.tv
TELEVISION STATION

KMTP4-TV 610126

Owner: Minority Television Project
Editorial: 31 Airport Blvd Ste E, South San Francisco, California 94080-6519 **Tel:** 1 415 777-3232.
Web site: http://www.kmtp.tv
TELEVISION STATION

KMTP5-TV 610128

Owner: Minority Television Project
Editorial: 31 Airport Blvd Ste E, South San Francisco, California 94080-6519 **Tel:** 1 415 777-3232.
Web site: http://www.kmtp.tv
Profile: KMTP5-TV is a multicast of KMTP-TV. A multicast channel is a separate channel that shares the bandwith of the main station but can air unique programming. KMTP5-TV airs programming from the NDT TV in the San Francisco market. The station is owned by Minority Television Project. KMTP5-TV broadcasts locally on channel 32.5.
TELEVISION STATION

KMTP-TV 32378

Owner: Minority Television Project
Editorial: 31 Airport Blvd Ste E, South San Francisco, California 94080-6519 **Tel:** 1 415 777-3232.
Web site: http://www.kmtp.tv
Profile: KMTP-TV is an independent station in the San Francisco market. The station is owned by the Minority Television Project. KMTP-TV broadcasts locally on channel 32.
TELEVISION STATION

KMTR-TV 32741

Owner: Roberts Media, LLC
Editorial: 3825 International Ct, Springfield, Oregon 97477-1086 **Tel:** 1 541 746-1600.
Email: newsdesk@kmtr.com
Web site: http://nbc16.com
Profile: KMTR-TV is the NBC affiliate for the Eugene, OR market. The station is owned by Roberts Media, LLC. KMTR-TV broadcasts locally on channel 16.
TELEVISION STATION

KMTV2-TV 778500

Owner: E.W. Scripps Co.
Editorial: 10714 Mockingbird Dr, Omaha, Nebraska 68127-1942 **Tel:** 1 402 592-3333.

Web site: http://www.action3news.com
Profile: KMTV2-TV is a multicast channel of KMTV-TV. A multicast channel is a separate channel that shares the bandwidth of the main station but can air unique programming. KMTV2-TV is the Live Well Network for the Omaha market. The station is owned by E.W. Scripps Co. KMTV2-TV broadcasts locally on channel 3.2.
TELEVISION STATION

KMTV-TV   31537
Owner: E.W. Scripps Co.
Editorial: 10714 Mockingbird Dr, Omaha, Nebraska 68127-1942 **Tel:** 1 402 592-3333.
Email: news@3newsnow.com
Web site: http://www.3newsnow.com
Profile: KMTV-TV is the CBS affiliate for the Omaha, NE, market. The station is owned by E.W. Scripps Co. KMTV-TV broadcasts locally on channel 3.
TELEVISION STATION

KMTW-TV   72418
Owner: Newport Television, LLC
Editorial: 316 N West St, Wichita, Kansas 67203-1205 **Tel:** 1 316 942-2424.
Web site: http://www.mytvwichita.com
Profile: KMTW-TV is the MyNetworkTV network affiliate for the Wichita-Hutchinson, KS market. The station is owned by Newport Television, LLC. KMTW-TV broadcasts locally on channel 36.
TELEVISION STATION

KMUV-TV   418225
Owner: News-Press & Gazette Co.
Editorial: 1550 Moffett St, Salinas, California 93905-3342 **Tel:** 1 831 757-2323.
Web site: http://www.kionrightnow.com/t23
Profile: KMUV-TV is a Telemundo affiliate for the Salinas, CA market. The station is owned by News-Press & Gazette Co. KMUV-TV broadcasts locally on channel 23.
TELEVISION STATION

KMVT-TV   31538
Owner: Gray Television
Editorial: 1100 Blue Lakes Blvd N, Twin Falls, Idaho 83301-3305 **Tel:** 1 208 733-1100.
Email: newstips@kmvt.com
Web site: http://www.kmvt.com
Profile: KMVT-TV is the CBS affiliate for the Twin Falls, ID, market. The station is owned by Gray Television. KMVT-TV broadcasts locally on channel 11.
TELEVISION STATION

KMYS-TV   31594
Owner: Sinclair Broadcast Group, Inc.
Editorial: 4335 NW Loop 410, San Antonio, Texas 78229 **Tel:** 1 210 366-1129.
Email: kmys@kmys.tv
Web site: http://www.kmys.tv
Profile: KMYS-TV is the CW affiliate for the greater San Antonio and Kerrville, TX areas. The station is owned by Sinclair Broadcast Group, Inc. KMYS-TV broadcasts locally on channel 35.
TELEVISION STATION

KMYT-TV   32374
Owner: Cox Media Group, Inc.
Editorial: 2625 S Memorial Dr, Tulsa, Oklahoma 74129-2601 **Tel:** 1 918 491-0023.
Web site: http://www.fox23.com/content/my41tulsa/my41tulsaNEW/default.aspx
Profile: KMYT-TV is the MyNetworkTV affiliate for the greater Tulsa, OK area. The station is owned by Cox Media Group, Inc. KMYT-TV broadcasts locally on channel 41.
TELEVISION STATION

KMYU-TV   63263
Owner: Sinclair Broadcast Group, Inc. Group
Editorial: 299 S Main St, Salt Lake City, Utah 84111-1919 **Tel:** 1 801 839-1234.
Web site: http://www.kmyu.tv
Profile: KMYU-TV is an This TV Network affiliate for the greater St. George, UT-area. The station is owned by Sinclair Broadcast Group, Inc. KMYU-TV broadcasts to the area on channel 12.
TELEVISION STATION

KNAT2-TV   618694
Owner: Trinity Broadcasting Network
Editorial: 1510 Coors Blvd NW, Albuquerque, New Mexico 87121-1152 **Tel:** 1 505 836-6585.
Profile: KNAT2-TV is a multicast of KNAT-TV. A multicast channel is a separate channel that shares the bandwidth of the main station but can air unique programming. KNAT2-TV airs religious programming from The Church Channel in the Albuquerque, NM market. The station is owned by Trinity Broadcasting Network. KNAT2-TV broadcasts locally on channel 23.2.
TELEVISION STATION

KNAT3-TV   618696
Owner: Trinity Broadcasting Network
Editorial: 1510 Coors Blvd NW, Albuquerque, New Mexico 87121-1152 **Tel:** 1 505 836-6585.
Profile: KNAT3-TV is a multicast of KNAT-TV. A multicast channel is a separate channel that shares the bandwidth of the main station but can air unique programming. KNAT3-TV airs Christian music videos from JCTV in the Albuquerque, NM market. The station is owned by Trinity Broadcasting Network. KNAT3-TV broadcasts locally on channel 23.3.
TELEVISION STATION

KNAT4-TV   618698
Owner: Trinity Broadcasting Network
Editorial: 1510 Coors Blvd NW, Albuquerque, New Mexico 87121-1152 **Tel:** 1 505 836-6585.
Profile: KNAT4-TV is a multicast of KNAT-TV. A multicast channel is a separate channel that shares the bandwidth of the main station but can air unique programming. KNAT4-TV airs Hispanic Christian programming from Enlace USA in the Albuquerque, NM market. The station is owned by Trinity Broadcasting Network. KNAT4-TV broadcasts locally on channel 23.4.
TELEVISION STATION

KNAT5-TV   618699
Owner: Trinity Broadcasting Network
Editorial: 1510 Coors Blvd NW, Albuquerque, New Mexico 87121-1152 **Tel:** 1 505 836-6585.
Profile: KNAT5-TV is a multicast of KNAT-TV. A multicast channel is a separate channel that shares the bandwidth of the main station but can air unique programming. KNAT5-TV airs children's Christian programming from Smile of a Child in the Albuquerque, NM market. The station is owned by Trinity Broadcasting Network. KNAT5-TV broadcasts locally on channel 23.5.
TELEVISION STATION

KNAT-TV   32304
Owner: Trinity Broadcasting Network
Editorial: 1510 Coors Blvd NW, Albuquerque, New Mexico 87121 **Tel:** 1 505 836-6585.
Profile: KNAT-TV is the Trinity Broadcasting Network affiliate for the Albuquerque, NM market. The station is owned by Trinity Broadcasting Network. KNAT-TV broadcasts locally on channel 23.
TELEVISION STATION

KNBC2-TV   606252
Owner: NBC Universal
Editorial: 100 Universal City Plz Bldg 2120, Universal City, California 91608-1002 **Tel:** 1 818 684-4444.
Email: knbc.news@nbc.com
Web site: http://www.cozitv.com
Profile: KNBC2-TV is a multicast channel of KNBC-TV. A multicast channel is a separate channel that shares the bandwidth of the main station but can air unique programming. KNBC2-TV is the NBC Nonstop affiliate for the Los Angeles market. The station is owned by NBC Universal. KNBC2-TV broadcasts locally on channel 4.2. The channel airs a mix of classic television series from the 1950s through the 1980s, movies and lifestyle programming.
TELEVISION STATION

KNBC4-TV   556533
Owner: NBC Universal
Editorial: 100 Universal City Plz Bldg 2120, Universal City, California 91608-1002 **Tel:** 1 818 684-4444.
Email: knbc.news@nbc.com
Web site: http://www.nbclosangeles.com
Profile: KNBC4-TV is a multicast channel of KNBC-TV. A multicast channel is a separate channel that shares the bandwidth of the main station but can air unique programming. KNBC4-TV is the NBC affiliate for the Los Angeles market. The station is owned by NBC Universal. KNBC4-TV broadcasts locally on channel 4.4.
TELEVISION STATION

KNBC-TV   31540
Owner: NBCUniversal Media, LLC
Editorial: 100 Universal City Plz Bldg 2120, Universal City, California 91608-1002 **Tel:** 1 818 684-4444.
Email: tips@nbcla.com
Web site: http://www.nbclosangeles.com
Profile: KNBC-TV is the NBC affiliate for the Los Angeles market. The station is owned by NBC Universal. KNBC-TV broadcasts locally on channel 4.
TELEVISION STATION

KNBN-TV   71569
Owner: Rapid Broadcasting
Editorial: 2424 S Plaza Dr, Rapid City, South Dakota 57702-9379 **Tel:** 1 605 355-0024.
Web site: http://www.newscenter1.tv/
Profile: KNBN-TV is the NBC affiliate of Rapid City, SD. The station owned by Rapid Broadcasting. It broadcasts on channel 21.
TELEVISION STATION

KNCT-TV   31541
Owner: Central Texas College
Editorial: 6200 W. Centex Expressway, Killeen, Texas 76549 **Tel:** 1 254 526-1176.
Email: knct@knct.org
Web site: http://www.knct.org
Profile: KNCT-TV is the PBS affiliate for Waco, TX market. The station is owned by Central Texas College. KNCT-TV broadcasts on channel 46.
TELEVISION STATION

KNDO-TV   32649
Owner: Cowles Publishing Co.
Editorial: 216 W Yakima Ave, Yakima, Washington 98902-3406 **Tel:** 1 509 225-2308.
Email: news@kndo.com
Web site: http://www.kndo.com
Profile: KNDO-TV is the NBC network affiliate for the Yakima, WA market. The station is owned by Cowles Publishing Co. KNDO-TV broadcasts locally on channel 23.
TELEVISION STATION

KNEP-TV   32759
Owner: Gray Television, Inc.
Editorial: 1523 1st Ave, Scottsbluff, Nebraska 69361-3106 **Tel:** 1 308 632-3071.
Email: scottsbluffdesk@nbcneb.com
Web site: http://www.nbcneb.com/scottsbluff/home/
Profile: KNEP-TV is a transmitter located in Scottsbluff, NE, that simulcasts the programming of KOTA-TV, the ABC affiliate for Scottsbluff. It is owned by Gray Television, Inc. KNEP-TV broadcasts locally on channel 4.
TELEVISION STATION SATELLITE

KNEX-TV   588373
Owner: Azteca America
Editorial: 1701 N Market St Ste 500A, Dallas, Texas 75202-1807 **Tel:** 1 214 754-7008.
Web site: http://www.aztecaamerica.com
Profile: KNEX-TV is the Azteca America affiliate for the Laredo, TX market. The station broadcasts locally on channel 4. All PSAs should be sent in BETA format.
TELEVISION STATION

KNIC-TV   78895
Owner: Univision Communications Inc.
Editorial: 12451 Network Blvd Ste 140, San Antonio, Texas 78249-3336 **Tel:** 1 210 610-4141.
Web site: http://univisionaustin.univision.com
Profile: KNIC-TV is the UniMas affiliate for the San Antonio market. The station is owned by Univision Communications Inc. KNIC-TV broadcasts locally on channel 17.
TELEVISION STATION

KNIN-TV   32485
Owner: Raycom Media Inc.
Editorial: 1866 E Chisholm Dr, Nampa, Idaho 83687-6805 **Tel:** 1 208 336-0500.
Web site: http://www.knin.com
Profile: KNIN-TV is the FOX affiliate for the Boise, ID market. The station is owned by Raycom Media Inc. KNIN-TV broadcasts locally on channel 9.
TELEVISION STATION

KNLC2-TV   613170
Owner: New Life Evangelistic Center
Editorial: 1411 Locust St, Saint Louis, Missouri 63103-2332 **Tel:** 1 314 436-2424.
Web site: http://www.knlc.tv
Profile: KNLC2-TV is a multicast of KNLC-TV. A multicast channel is a separate channel that shares the bandwidth of the main station but can air unique programming. KNLC2-TV airs programming from RES in the St. Louis market. The station is owned by New Life Evangelistic Center. KNLC2-TV broadcasts locally on channel 24.2.
TELEVISION STATION

KNLC-TV   31542
Owner: New Life Evangelistic Center
Editorial: 1411 Locust St, Saint Louis, Missouri 63103-2332 **Tel:** 1 314 436-2424.
Web site: http://knlc.tv
Profile: KNLC-TV is an independent station for the Saint Louis, MO market. The station is owned by New Life Evangelistic Center. KNLC-TV broadcasts locally on channel 24.
TELEVISION STATION

KNLJ-TV   32299
Owner: Christian Television Network
Tel: 1 573 896-5105.
Email: knljtv@yahoo.com
Web site: http://www.knlj.tv
Profile: KNLJ-TV is an independent station for the Columbia-Jefferson, MO market. The station is owned by Christian Television Network. KNLJ-TV broadcasts locally on channel 20.
TELEVISION STATION

KNMT2-TV   612954
Owner: National Minority Television, Inc.
Editorial: 432 NE 74th Ave, Portland, Oregon 97213-6312 **Tel:** 1 503 252-0792.
Web site: http://tbn.org
Profile: KNMT2-TV is a multicast of KNMT-TV. A multicast channel is a separate channel that shares the bandwidth of the main station but can air unique programming. KNMT2-TV airs programming from The Church Channel in the Portland, OR market. The station is owned by National Minority Television, Inc. KNMT2-TV broadcasts locally on channel 24.2.
TELEVISION STATION

KNMT3-TV   612956
Owner: National Minority Television, Inc.
Editorial: 432 NE 74th Ave, Portland, Oregon 97213-6312 **Tel:** 1 503 252-0792.
Web site: http://tbn.org
Profile: KNMT3-TV is a multicast of KNMT-TV. A multicast channel is a separate channel that shares the bandwidth of the main station but can air unique programming. KNMT3-TV airs programming from JCTV in the Portland, OR market. The station is owned by National Minority Television, Inc. KNMT3-TV broadcasts locally on channel 24.3.
TELEVISION STATION

KNMT4-TV   612959
Owner: National Minority Television, Inc.
Editorial: 432 NE 74th Ave, Portland, Oregon 97213-6312 **Tel:** 1 503 252-0792.
Web site: http://tbn.org
Profile: KNMT4-TV is a multicast of KNMT-TV. A multicast channel is a separate channel that shares the bandwidth of the main station but can air unique programming. KNMT4-TV airs programming from

Enlace USA in the Portland, OR market. The station is owned by National Minority Television, Inc. KNMT4-TV broadcasts locally on channel 24.4.
TELEVISION STATION

KNMT5-TV   612961
Owner: National Minority Television, Inc.
Editorial: 432 NE 74th Ave, Portland, Oregon 97213-6312 **Tel:** 1 503 252-0792.
Web site: http://tbn.org
Profile: KNMT5-TV is a multicast of KNMT-TV. A multicast channel is a separate channel that shares the bandwidth of the main station but can air unique programming. KNMT5-TV airs programming from Smile of a Child in the Portland, OR market. The station is owned by National Minority Television, Inc. KNMT5-TV broadcasts locally on channel 24.5.
TELEVISION STATION

KNMT-TV   32350
Owner: National Minority Television, Inc.
Editorial: 432 NE 74th Ave, Portland, Oregon 97213-6312 **Tel:** 1 503 252-0792.
Web site: http://tbn.org
Profile: KNMT-TV is the Trinity Broadcasting Network affiliate for the Portland, OR market. The station is owned by National Minority Television, Inc. KNMT-TV broadcasts locally on channel 24.
TELEVISION STATION

KNOE-TV   31544
Owner: Gray Television, Inc.
Editorial: 1400 Oliver Rd, Monroe, Louisiana 71201-5020 **Tel:** 1 318 388-8888.
Email: news@knoe.com
Web site: http://www.knoe.com
Profile: KNOE-TV is the CBS network affiliate for the Monroe, LA, El Dorado, AR market. The station is owned by Gray Television, Inc. KNOE-TV broadcasts locally on channel 8.
TELEVISION STATION

KNOP-TV   31545
Owner: Gray Television, Inc
Editorial: 8020 N Highway 83, North Platte, Nebraska 69101-8080 **Tel:** 1 308 532-2222.
Web site: http://www.knopnews2.com
Profile: KNOP-TV is the NBC affiliate for the North Platte, NE, market. The station is owned by Gray Television, Inc. KNOP-TV broadcasts locally on channel 2.
TELEVISION STATION

KNPB-TV   32277
Owner: Ch. 5 Public Broadcasting Inc.
Editorial: 1670 N Virginia St, Reno, Nevada 89503-0703 **Tel:** 1 775 784-4555.
Email: info@knpb.org
Web site: http://www.knpb.org
Profile: KNPB-TV is the PBS affiliate for the Reno, NV market. The station is owned by Channel 5 Public Broadcasting Inc. KNPB-TV broadcasts locally on channel 5.
TELEVISION STATION

KNSD2-TV   613149
Owner: NBC Universal
Editorial: 9680 Granite Ridge Dr, San Diego, California 92123-2673 **Tel:** 1 619 231-3939.
Web site: http://www.nbcsandiego.com
Profile: KNSD2-TV is a multicast channel of KNSD-TV. A multicast channel is a separate channel that shares the bandwidth of the main station but can air unique programming. KNSD2-TV is the Cozi TV affiliate for the San Diego market. The station is owned by NBC Universal. KNSD2-TV broadcasts locally on channel 39.2.
TELEVISION STATION

KNSD-TV   31421
Owner: NBC Universal
Editorial: 9680 Granite Ridge Dr, San Diego, California 92123-2673 **Tel:** 1 619 231-3939.
Email: nbcsandiegodesk@nbcuni.com
Web site: http://www.nbcsandiego.com
Profile: KNSD-TV is the NBC affiliate for the San Diego market. The station is owned by NBC Universal. KNSD-TV broadcasts locally on channel 7.
TELEVISION STATION

KNSO-TV   128431
Owner: NBC Universal
Editorial: 30 E River Park Pl W Ste 200, Fresno, California 93720-1546 **Tel:** 1 559 252-5101.
Email: publicidad@holaciudad.com
Profile: KNSO-TV is the Telemundo affiliate for the Fresno-Visalia, CA market. The station is owned by NBC Universal. KNSO-TV broadcasts locally on channel 51. KNSO-TV does not has a news department.
TELEVISION STATION

KNTV2-TV   610132
Owner: NBC Universal
Editorial: 2450 N 1st St, San Jose, California 95131-1002 **Tel:** 1 408 432-6221.
Web site: http://www.cozitv.com
Profile: KNTV2-TV is a multicast channel of KNTV-TV. A multicast channel is a separate channel that shares the bandwidth of the main station but can air unique programming. KNTV2-TV is the Cozi TV affiliate for the San Francisco and Bay Area market. The station is owned by NBC Universal. KNTV2-TV broadcasts locally on channel 12.2.
TELEVISION STATION

KNTV3-TV 610136
Owner: NBC Universal
Editorial: 2450 N 1st St, San Jose, California 95131-1002 **Tel:** 1 408 432-6221.
Email: newstips@nbcbayarea.com
Web site: http://www.nbcbayarea.com
Profile: KNTV3-TV is a multicast of KNTV-TV. A multicast channel is a separate channel that shares the bandwith of the main station but can air unique programming. KNTV3-TV airs programming from Universal Sports in the San Francisco market. The station is owned by NBC Universal. KNTV3-TV broadcasts locally on channel 12.3.
TELEVISION STATION

KNTV-TV 31546
Owner: NBC Universal
Editorial: 2450 N 1st St, San Jose, California 95131-1002 **Tel:** 1 408 432-6221.
Email: newstips@nbcbayarea.com
Web site: http://www.nbcbayarea.com
Profile: KNTV-TV is the NBC affiliate for the San Francisco market. The station is owned by NBC Universal. KNTV-TV broadcasts locally on channel 11.
TELEVISION STATION

KNVA-TV 32454
Owner: 54 Broadcasting
Editorial: 908 W Martin Luther King Jr Blvd, Austin, Texas 78701-1018 **Tel:** 1 512 478-5400.
Email: news@kxan.com
Web site: http://www.thecwaustin.com
Profile: KNVA-TV is the CW affiliate for the Austin, TX market. The station is owned by 54 Broadcasting. KNVA-TV broadcasts locally on channel 54.
TELEVISION STATION

KNVN-TV 31414
Owner: GOCOM Media of Northern California, L.L.C.
Editorial: 3460 Silverbell Rd, Chico, California 95973-0388 **Tel:** 1 530 893-2424.
Email: news@actionnewsnow.com
Web site: http://www.actionnewsnow.com/home
Profile: KNVN-TV is the NBC network affiliate for the Chico- Redding, CA market. The station is owned by GOCOM Media of Northern California, L.L.C. KNVN-TV broadcasts locally on channel 24.
TELEVISION STATION

KNVO-TV 32441
Owner: Entravision Communications Corp.
Editorial: 801 N Jackson Rd, McAllen, Texas 78501-9306 **Tel:** 1 956 687-4848.
Email: noticias48@entravision.com
Web site: http://www.knvotv48.com
Profile: KNVO-TV is the Univision network affiliate for the McAllen, TX market. The station is owned by Entravision Communications Corp. KNVO-TV airs locally on channel 48.
TELEVISION STATION

KNVV-TV 133920
Owner: Entravision Communications Corp.
Editorial: 300 S Wells Ave, Ste 12, Reno, Nevada 89502-1670 **Tel:** 1 775 333-1017.
Web site: http://www.univisionreno.com
Profile: KNVV-TV is the Telefutura affiliate in the Reno, NV. The station is owned by Entravision Communications Corp. KNVV-TV broadcasts locally on channel 41.
TELEVISION STATION

KNWA-TV 32726
Owner: Nexstar Broadcasting Group
Editorial: 609 W Dickson St Fl 3, Fayetteville, Arkansas 72701-5017 **Tel:** 1 479 571-5100.
Email: news@knwa.com
Web site: http://nwahomepage.com
Profile: KNWA-TV is the NBC affiliate for the Fort Smith, AR market. The station is owned by Nexstar Broadcasting Group. KNWA-TV broadcasts locally on channel 51
TELEVISION STATION

KNWS-TV 390768
Owner: Una Vez Mas, LP
Editorial: 1216 E Jasmine Ave, McAllen, Texas 78501-5726 **Tel:** 1 956 631-0289.
Web site: http://www.aztecaamerica.com
Profile: KNWS-TV is the Azteca America affiliate for the McAllen, TX market. The station is owned by Una Vez Mas, LP. KNWS-TV broadcasts locally on channels 57. All public service announcements should be sent to the mailing address, which is the corporate headquarters in Dallas.
TELEVISION STATION

KNXT-TV 32259
Owner: Roman Catholic Diocese/Fresno
Editorial: 1550 N Fresno St, Fresno, California 93703-3711 **Tel:** 1 559 488-7440.
Email: knxt@dioceseoffresno.org
Web site: http://www.knxt.tv
Profile: KNXT-TV is a non-commercial, independent station in Fresno, California. It airs locally on channel 49. KNXT-TV is owned by the Roman Catholic Diocese of Fresno, California. The station accepts 15-second PSAs in Beta format.
TELEVISION STATION

KNXV2-TV 612001
Owner: E.W. Scripps Co.
Editorial: 515 N 44th St, Phoenix, Arizona 85008-6537 **Tel:** 1 602 273-1500.
Email: assignmentdesk@abc15.com
Web site: http://www.abc15.com
Profile: KNXV2-TV is a multicast of KNXV-TV. A multicast channel is a separate channel that shares the bandwith of the main station but can air unique programming. KNXV2-TV airs programming from GoAZ.TV Traffic and AccuWeather in the Phoenix market. The station is owned by E.W. Scripss Co. KNXV2-TV broadcasts locally on channel 15.2.
TELEVISION STATION

KNXV-TV 31547
Owner: E.W. Scripps Co.
Editorial: 515 N 44th St, Phoenix, Arizona 85008-6511 **Tel:** 1 602 273-1500.
Email: assignmentdesk@abc15.com
Web site: http://www.abc15.com
Profile: KNXV-TV is the ABC affiliate in Phoenix. It is owned by E.W. Scripps Co. KNXV-TV broadcasts locally on channel 15. Local news airs in the morning and evenings daily. desk@abc15.com is the station's typical distribution list for news releases, it is goes to everyone.
TELEVISION STATION

KOAA-TV 31548
Owner: Evening Post Publishing Co.
Editorial: 5520 Tech Center Dr, Colorado Springs, Colorado 80905-1740 **Tel:** 1 719 632-5030.
Email: news@koaa.com
Web site: http://www.koaa.com
Profile: KOAA-TV is the NBC affiliate for the Colorado Springs, CO market. The station is owned by Evening Post Publishing Co. KOAA-TV broadcasts locally on channel 5.
TELEVISION STATION

KOAM-TV 31549
Owner: Saga Communications
Editorial: 2950 NE Highway 69, Pittsburg, Kansas 66762 **Tel:** 1 417 624-0233.
Email: news@koamtv.com
Web site: http://www.koamtv.com
Profile: KOAM-TV is the CBS affiliate in the Joplin, MO-Pittsburg, KS market. The station is owned by Saga Communications. KOAM-TV broadcasts locally on channel 7.
TELEVISION STATION

KOAT2-TV 618974
Owner: Hearst Television Inc.
Editorial: 3801 Carlisle Blvd NE, Albuquerque, New Mexico 87107-4530 **Tel:** 1 505 884-7777.
Email: koatdesk@hearst.com
Web site: http://www.koat.com
Profile: KOAT2-TV is a multicast of KOAT-TV. A multicast channel is a separate channel that shares the bandwith of the main station but can air unique programming. KOAT2-TV airs Hispanic programming from Estrella TV in the Albuquerque, NM market. The station is owned by Hearst Television Inc. KOAT2-TV broadcasts locally on channel 7.2.
TELEVISION STATION

KOAT-TV 32723
Owner: Hearst Television Inc.
Editorial: 3801 Carlisle Blvd NE, Albuquerque, New Mexico 87107-4501 **Tel:** 1 505 884-7777.
Email: koatdesk@hearst.com
Web site: http://www.koat.com
Profile: KOAT-TV is the ABC affiliate for the Albuquerque, NM market. The station is owned by Hearst Television Inc. KOAT-TV broadcasts locally on channel 7.
TELEVISION STATION

KOB2-TV 730804
Owner: Hubbard Broadcasting Inc.
Editorial: 4 Broadcast Plz SW, Albuquerque, New Mexico 87104-1000 **Tel:** 1 505 243-4411.
Web site: http://www.kob.com
Profile: KOB2-TV is a multicast channel of KOB-TV. A multicast channel is a separate channel that shares the band with of the main station but can air unique programming. KOB2-TV is the This TV for the Albuquerque, MN market. The station is owned by Hubbard Broadcasting. KOB2-TV broadcasts locally on channel 4.2.
TELEVISION STATION

KOBI-TV 32651
Owner: California-Oregon Broadcasting
Editorial: 125 S Fir St, Medford, Oregon 97501-3115 **Tel:** 1 541 779-5555.
Email: newsrelease@kobi5.com
Web site: http://kobi5.com
Profile: KOBI-TV is the NBC affiliate for the Medford, OR market. The station is owned by California-Oregon Broadcasting. KOBI-TV broadcasts locally on channel 5.
TELEVISION STATION

KOB-TV 32650
Owner: Hubbard Broadcasting Inc.
Editorial: 4 Broadcast Plz SW, Albuquerque, New Mexico 87104-1000 **Tel:** 1 505 243-4411.
Email: news@kob.com
Web site: http://www.kob.com
Profile: KOB-TV is the NBC affiliate for the Albuquerque, NM market. The station is owned by Hubbard Broadcasting Inc. KOB-TV broadcasts locally on channel 4.
TELEVISION STATION

KOCB-TV 31465
Owner: Sinclair Broadcast Group, Inc.
Editorial: 1228 E Wilshire Blvd, Oklahoma City, Oklahoma 73111-8402 **Tel:** 1 405 843-2525.
Web site: http://www.cwokc.com
Profile: KOCB-TV is a CW affiliate for the Oklahoma City market. The station is owned by Sinclair Broadcast Group, Inc. KOCB-TV is broadcast on channel 34.
TELEVISION STATION

KOCE2-TV 606152
Owner: KOCE-TV Foundation
Editorial: 3080 Bristol St Ste 100, Costa Mesa, California 92626-3060 **Tel:** 1 714 241-4100.
Web site: http://www.pbssocal.org
Profile: KOCE2-TV is a multicast channel of KOCE-TV. A multicast channel is a separate channel that shares the bandwidth of the main station but can air unique programming. KOCE2-TV is PBS affiliate on Channel 50.2 for the Los Angeles market. KOCE2-TV is owned by KOCE-TV Foundation.
TELEVISION STATION

KOCE3-TV 606135
Owner: KOCE-TV Foundation
Editorial: 3080 Bristol St Ste 100, Costa Mesa, California 92626-3060
Email: questions@pbssocal.org
Web site: http://www.pbssocal.org
Profile: KOCE3-TV is a multicast channel of KOCE-TV. A multicast channel is a separate channel that shares the bandwidth of the main station but can air unique programming. KOCE3-TV is PBS affiliate on Channel 50.3 for the Los Angeles market. KOCE3-TV is owned by KOCE-TV Foundation.
TELEVISION STATION

KOCE4-TV 606144
Owner: KOCE-TV Foundation
Editorial: 3080 Bristol St Ste 100, Costa Mesa, California 92626-3060 **Tel:** 1 714 861-4300.
Web site: http://www.pbssocal.org
Profile: KOCE4-TV is a multicast channel of KOCE-TV. A multicast channel is a separate channel that shares the bandwidth of the main station but can air unique programming. KOCE4-TV is PBS affiliate on Channel 50.4 for the Los Angeles market and is a direct simulcast of KOCE-TV. KOCE3-TV is owned by KOCE-TV Foundation.
TELEVISION STATION

KOCE-TV 31550
Owner: PBS Socal
Editorial: 3080 Bristol St Ste 100, Costa Mesa, California 92626-3060 **Tel:** 1 714 241-4100.
Email: questions@pbssocal.org
Web site: http://www.pbssocal.org
Profile: KOCE-TV is the PBS affiliate for the Los Angeles market. The station is owned by the PBS Socal. KOCE-TV broadcasts locally on channel 50. KOCE-TV is also known as PBS SoCal.
TELEVISION STATION

KOCO2-TV 826962
Owner: Hearst Television Inc.
Editorial: 1300 E Britton Rd, Oklahoma City, Oklahoma 73131-2007
Web site: http://metvnetwork.com
Profile: KOCO2-TV is a multicast channel of KOCO-TV. A multicast channel is a separate channel that shares the bandwith of the main station but can air unique programming. KOCO2-TV is the MeTV Network for the Oklahoma City market. The station is owned by Hearst Television Inc. KOCO2-TV broadcasts locally on channel 5.2. The station specializes in syndicated reruns of classic TV programs of the 1950s through the 1980s.
TELEVISION STATION

KOCO-TV 31551
Owner: Hearst Television Inc.
Editorial: 1300 E Britton Rd, Oklahoma City, Oklahoma 73131-2007 **Tel:** 1 405 478-3000.
Email: desk@koco.com
Web site: http://www.koco.com
Profile: KOCO-TV is the ABC affiliate for the Oklahoma City market. The station is owned by Hearst Television Inc. KOCO-TV broadcasts locally on channel 5.
TELEVISION STATION

KODE-TV 31552
Owner: Mission Broadcasting
Editorial: 1502 S Cleveland Ave, Joplin, Missouri 64801-3569 **Tel:** 1 417 623-7260.
Web site: http://fourstateshomepage.com
Profile: KODE-TV is the ABC affiliate for the Joplin, MO market. The station is owned by Mission Broadcasting. KODE-TV broadcasts locally on channel 12.
TELEVISION STATION

KODF-TV 390692
Owner: Right Hook Media Group, Inc.
Editorial: 7007 NW 77th Ave, Miami, Florida 33166-2836 **Tel:** 1 304 644-4800.
Web site: http://www.mega.tv
Profile: KODF-TV is a Mega TV affiliate for the Dallas / Fort Worth Metroplex, licensed in Britton, Texas. The station is owned by Right Hook Media Group, Inc. KODF-TV broadcasts locally on channel 26.
TELEVISION STATION

KOET2-TV 618797
Owner: OETA (Oklahoma Public Television Network)
Editorial: 7403 N Kelley Ave, Oklahoma City, Oklahoma 73111-8420 **Tel:** 1 405 848-8501.
Email: info@oeta.tv
Web site: http://www.oeta.tv
Profile: KOET2-TV is a multicast of KOET-TV. A multicast channel is a separate channel that shares the bandwith of the main station but can air unique programming. KOET2-TV airs programming from the OETA OKLA in the Oklahoma City market. The station is owned by OETA. KOET2-TV broadcasts locally on channel 31.2.
TELEVISION STATION

KOFY4-TV 608548
Owner: Granite Broadcasting Corp.
Editorial: 2500 Marin St, San Francisco, California 94124-1015 **Tel:** 1 415 821-2020.
Web site: http://www.kofytv.com
Profile: KOFY4-TV is an independent station for the San Francisco market. The station is owned by Granite Broadcasting Corp. KOFY4-TV broadcasts locally on channel 20.4. KOFY4-TV broadcasts programming from Azteca America. KOFY4-TV is a multicast channel of KOFY-TV. A multicast channel is a separate channel that shares the bandwidth of the main station but can air unique programming.
TELEVISION STATION

KOFY-TV 31553
Owner: Granite Broadcasting Corp.
Editorial: 2500 Marin St, San Francisco, California 94124-1015 **Tel:** 1 415 821-2020.
Web site: http://www.kofytv.com
Profile: KOFY-TV is an independent station for the San Francisco market. The station is owned by Granite Broadcasting Corp. KOFY-TV broadcasts locally on channel 20.
TELEVISION STATION

KOHD-TV 504663
Owner: Zolo Media
Editorial: 63090 Sherman Rd, Bend, Oregon 97701-5750 **Tel:** 1 541 749-5151.
Web site: http://zolomedia.com/networks/kohd
Profile: KOHD-TV is the ABC affiliate for the Bend, OR market. The station is owned by Zolo Media. The station airs no local newscasts. KOHD-TV broadcasts locally on channel 51.
TELEVISION STATION

KOIN-TV 31555
Owner: Nexstar Media Group, Inc.
Editorial: 222 SW Columbia St, Portland, Oregon 97201-6600 **Tel:** 1 503 464-0600.
Email: news@koin.com
Web site: http://www.koin.com
Profile: KOIN-TV is the CBS network affiliate for the Portland, OR market. The station is owned by Nexstar Media Group, Inc. KOIN-TV broadcasts locally on channel 6.
TELEVISION STATION

KOKH-TV 31556
Owner: Sinclair Broadcast Group, Inc.
Editorial: 1228 E Wilshire Blvd, Oklahoma City, Oklahoma 73111-8402 **Tel:** 1 405 843-2525.
Email: kokhnews@sbgnet.com
Web site: http://www.okcfox.com
Profile: KOKH-TV is the FOX affiliate for the Oklahoma City market. The station is owned by Sinclair Broadcast Group, Inc. KOKH-TV broadcasts locally on channels 25 and 34.
TELEVISION STATION

KOKI-TV 31557
Owner: Cox Media Group, Inc.
Editorial: 2625 S Memorial Dr, Tulsa, Oklahoma 74129-2601 **Tel:** 1 918 491-0023.
Email: news@fox23.com
Web site: http://www.fox23.com
Profile: KOKI-TV is the FOX affiliate for the Tulsa, OK market. The station is owned by Cox Media Group, Inc. KOKI-TV broadcasts locally on channel 23.
TELEVISION STATION

KOLD-TV 31558
Owner: Raycom Media Inc.
Editorial: 7831 N Business Park Dr, Tucson, Arizona 85743-9622 **Tel:** 1 520 744-1313.
Email: desk@kold.com
Web site: http://www.tucsonnewsnow.com
Profile: KOLD-TV is the CBS network affiliate for the Tucson, AZ market. The station is owned by Raycom Media Inc. KOLD-TV broadcasts locally on channel 13.
TELEVISION STATION

KOLN-TV 32652
Owner: Gray Television, Inc.
Editorial: 840 N 40th St, Lincoln, Nebraska 68503-2800 **Tel:** 1 402 467-4321.
Email: desk@1011now.com
Web site: http://www.1011now.com
Profile: KOLN-TV is the CBS affiliate for the Lincoln, NE market. The station is owned by Gray Television, Inc. KOLN-TV broadcasts locally on channel 10.
TELEVISION STATION

KOLO-TV 31559
Owner: Gray Television, Inc.
Editorial: 4850 Ampere Dr, Reno, Nevada 89502-2302 **Tel:** 1 775 858-8888.
Email: news@kolotv.com
Web site: http://www.kolotv.com
Profile: KOLO-TV is the ABC affiliate for the Reno, NV market. The station is owned by Gray Television, Inc. KOLO-TV broadcasts locally on channel 8.
TELEVISION STATION

KOLR-TV 31560
Owner: Mission Broadcasting
Editorial: 2650 E Division St, Springfield, Missouri 65803-5228 **Tel:** 1 417 862-1010.
Web site: http://www.ozarksfirst.com
Profile: KOLR-TV is the CBS network affiliate for the Springfield, MO market. The station is owned by

Mission Broadcasting. KOLR-TV broadcasts locally on channel 10.
TELEVISION STATION

KOMO2-TV 611612
Owner: Fisher Communications, Inc.
Editorial: 140 4th Ave N Ste 370, Seattle, Washington 98109-4940 **Tel:** 1 206 404-4000.
Email: tips@komo4news.com
Web site: http://www.komonews.com
Profile: KOMO2-TV is a multicast of KOMO-TV. A multicast channel is a separate channel that shares the bandwith of the main station but can air unique programming. KOMO2-TV airs programming from the This TV network in the Seattle market. The station is owned by Fisher Communications Inc. KOMO2-TV broadcasts locally on channel 4.2.
TELEVISION STATION

KOMO-TV 31561
Owner: Sinclair Broadcast Group
Editorial: 140 4th Ave N, Seattle, Washington 98109-4940 **Tel:** 1 206 404-4000.
Email: tips@komo4news.com
Web site: http://www.komonews.com
Profile: KOMO-TV is the ABC affiliate for the Seattle market. The station is owned by Sinclair Broadcast Group. KOMO-TV broadcasts locally on channel 4.
TELEVISION STATION

KONG-TV 32562
Owner: TEGNA Inc.
Editorial: 333 Dexter Ave N, Seattle, Washington 98109-5107 **Tel:** 1 206 448-5555.
Email: newstips@king5.com
Web site: http://www.king5.com
Profile: KONG-TV is an independent station for the Seattle-Tacoma market. The station is owned by TEGNA Inc. KONG-TV broadcasts locally on channel 6.
TELEVISION STATION

KOOD-TV 32713
Owner: Smoky Hills Public Television
Editorial: 604 Elm St, Bunker Hill, Kansas 67626 **Tel:** 1 785 483-6990.
Email: shptv@shptv.org
Web site: http://www.smokhillstv.org
Profile: KOOD-TV is the PBS affiliate for Wichita-Hutchinson, KS market. The station is owned by Smoky Hills Public Television. KOOD-TV broadcasts locally on channel 16.
TELEVISION STATION

KOPB-TV 32707
Owner: Oregon Public Broadcasting
Editorial: 7140 SW MacAdam Ave, Portland, Oregon 97219-3013 **Tel:** 1 503 244-9900.
Email: opbnews@opb.org
Web site: http://www.opb.org
Profile: KOPB-TV is the PBS network affiliate for the Portland, OR market. The station is owned by Oregon Public Broadcasting (OPB). KOPB-TV broadcasts locally on channel 10 and is the flagship station of OPB.
TELEVISION STATION

KOPX2-TV 619759
Owner: ION Media Networks
Editorial: 13424 Railway Dr, Oklahoma City, Oklahoma 73114-2272 **Tel:** 1 405 751-6800.
Profile: KOPX2-TV is a multicast of KOPX-TV. A multicast channel is a separate channel that shares the bandwith of the main station but can air unique programming. KOPX2-TV airs children's programming from the qubo network in the Oklahoma City market. The station is owned by ION Media Networks. KOPX2-TV broadcasts locally on channel 62.2.
TELEVISION STATION

KOPX3-TV 619761
Owner: ION Media Networks
Editorial: 13424 Railway Dr, Oklahoma City, Oklahoma 73114-2272 **Tel:** 1 405 751-6800.
Profile: KOPX3-TV is a multicast of KOPX-TV. A multicast channel is a separate channel that shares the bandwith of the main station but can air unique programming. KOPX3-TV airs lifestyle programming from the ION Life network in the Oklahoma City market. The station is owned by ION Media Networks. KOPX3-TV broadcasts locally on channel 62.3.
TELEVISION STATION

KOPX4-TV 619763
Owner: ION Media Networks
Editorial: 13424 Railway Dr, Oklahoma City, Oklahoma 73114-2272 **Tel:** 1 405 751-6800.
Profile: KOPX4-TV is a multicast of KOPX-TV. A multicast channel is a separate channel that shares the bandwith of the main station but can air unique programming. KOPX4-TV airs Christian programming from the Worship network in the Oklahoma City market. The station is owned by ION Media Networks. KOPX4-TV broadcasts locally on channel 62.4.
TELEVISION STATION

KOPX-TV 32727
Owner: ION Media Networks
Editorial: 13424 Railway Dr, Oklahoma City, Oklahoma 73114-2272 **Tel:** 1 405 751-6800.
Profile: KOPX-TV is the local ION Television affiliate in Oklahoma City, Oklahoma. KOPX-TV airs locally on channel 62. The station does not air any local news programs.
TELEVISION STATION

KORK-TV 390933
Owner: WATCHTV Inc.
Editorial: 1628 NW Everett St, Portland, Oregon 97209 **Tel:** 1 503 241-2411.
TELEVISION STATION

KORO-TV 31564
Owner: Entravision Communications Corp.
Editorial: 102 N Mesquite St, Corpus Christi, Texas 78401-2823 **Tel:** 1 361 883-2823.
Email: noticias28@entravision.com
Web site: http://noticias.entravision.com/corpus-christi
Profile: KORO-TV is the Telefutura network affiliate for the Corpus Christi, TX market. The station is owned by Entravision Communications Corp. KORO-TV broadcasts locally on channel 28.
TELEVISION STATION

KOSA-TV 31565
Owner: ICA Broadcasting I LLC
Editorial: 4101 E 42nd St Ste J7, Odessa, Texas 79762-7245 **Tel:** 1 432 580-5672.
Email: news@cbs7.com
Web site: http://www.cbs7.com
Profile: KOSA-TV is the CBS affiliate for the Odessa-Midland TX market. The station is owned by ICA Broadcasting I LLC. KOSA-TV broadcasts locally on channel 7.
TELEVISION STATION

KOTA-TV 32653
Owner: Gray Television, Inc.
Editorial: 518 Saint Joseph St, Rapid City, South Dakota 57701-2717 **Tel:** 1 605 342-2000.
Email: kotanews@kotatv.com
Web site: http://www.kotatv.com
Profile: KOTA-TV is the ABC affiliate for the Rapid City, SD market. The station is owned by Gray Television, Inc. KOTA-TV broadcasts locally on channel 3.
TELEVISION STATION

KOTR-TV 837088
Owner: Mirage Media 2, LLC
Editorial: 2511 Garden Rd Ste C150, Monterey, California 93940-5386 **Tel:** 1 831 655-5687.
Web site: http://www.mytvmonterey.com
Profile: KOTR-TV is the local MyNetworkTV affiliate for the Salinas-Monterey, CA market. The station is owned by Mirage Media 2, LLC. It airs on channel 11. his station does not air any local newscasts.
TELEVISION STATION

KOTV-TV 31566
Owner: Griffin Communications, LLC
Editorial: 303 N Boston Ave, Tulsa, Oklahoma 74103-1602 **Tel:** 1 918 732-6000.
Email: newsdesk@newson6.net
Web site: http://www.newson6.com
Profile: KOTV-TV is the CBS affiliate for the Tulsa, OK market. The station is owned by Griffin Communications, LLC. KOTV-TV broadcasts locally on channel 6.
TELEVISION STATION

KOVR-TV 31567
Owner: CBS Television Stations
Editorial: 2713 Kovr Dr, West Sacramento, California 95605-1600 **Tel:** 1 916 374-1313.
Email: news@kovr.com
Web site: http://sacramento.cbslocal.com
Profile: KOVR-TV is the CBS affiliate for the Sacramento, CA market. The station is owned by CBS Television Stations. KOVR-TV broadcasts locally on channel 13.
TELEVISION STATION

KOZL-TV 31426
Owner: Nexstar Broadcasting Group
Editorial: 2650 E Division St, Springfield, Missouri 65803-5228 **Tel:** 1 417 862-2727.
Web site: http://www.ozarksfirst.com
Profile: KOZL-TV is an independent station for the Springfield, MO market. The station is owned by Nexstar Broadcasting Group. KOZL-TV broadcasts locally on channel 27.
TELEVISION STATION

KPAX-TV 31569
Owner: Cordillera Communications Inc.
Editorial: 1049 W Central Ave, Missoula, Montana 59801 **Tel:** 1 406 542-4400.
Email: news@kpax.com
Web site: http://www.kpax.com
Profile: KPAX-TV is the CBS affiliate for the Missoula, MT, market. The station is owned by Cordillera Communications Inc. KPAX-TV broadcasts locally on channel 8.
TELEVISION STATION

KPAZ2-TV 612597
Owner: Trinity Broadcasting Network
Editorial: 3551 E McDowell Rd, Phoenix, Arizona 85008-3847 **Tel:** 1 602 273-1477.
Email: kpaz@tbn.org
Web site: http://tbn.org
Profile: KPAZ2-TV is a multicast of KPAZ-TV. A multicast channel is a separate channel that shares the bandwith of the main station but can air unique programming. KPAZ2-TV airs programming from The Church Channel in the Phoenix market. The station is owned by Trinity Broadcasting Network. KPAZ2-TV broadcasts locally on channel 21.2.
TELEVISION STATION

KPAZ3-TV 612598
Owner: Trinity Broadcasting Network
Editorial: 3551 E McDowell Rd, Phoenix, Arizona 85008-3847 **Tel:** 1 602 273-1477.
Email: kpaz@tbn.org
Web site: http://tbn.org
Profile: KPAZ3-TV is a multicast of KPAZ-TV. A multicast channel is a separate channel that shares the bandwith of the main station but can air unique programming. KPAZ3-TV airs programming from JCTV in the Phoenix market. The station is owned by Trinity Broadcasting Network. KPAZ3-TV broadcasts locally on channel 21.3.
TELEVISION STATION

KPAZ4-TV 612600
Owner: Trinity Broadcasting Network
Editorial: 3551 E McDowell Rd, Phoenix, Arizona 85008-3847 **Tel:** 1 602 273-1477.
Email: kpaz@tbn.org
Web site: http://tbn.org
Profile: KPAZ4-TV is a multicast of KPAZ-TV. A multicast channel is a separate channel that shares the bandwith of the main station but can air unique programming. KPAZ4-TV airs programming from Enlace USA in the Phoenix market. The station is owned by Trinity Broadcasting Network. KPAZ4-TV broadcasts locally on channel 21.4.
TELEVISION STATION

KPAZ5-TV 612601
Owner: Trinity Broadcasting Network
Editorial: 3551 E McDowell Rd, Phoenix, Arizona 85008-3847 **Tel:** 1 602 273-1477.
Email: kpaz@tbn.org
Web site: http://tbn.org
Profile: KPAZ5-TV is a multicast of KPAZ-TV. A multicast channel is a separate channel that shares the bandwith of the main station but can air unique programming. KPAZ5-TV airs programming from Smile of a Child TV in the Phoenix market. The station is owned by Trinity Broadcasting Network. KPAZ5-TV broadcasts locally on channel 21.5.
TELEVISION STATION

KPAZ-TV 31570
Owner: Trinity Broadcasting Network
Editorial: 3551 E McDowell Rd, Phoenix, Arizona 85008-3847 **Tel:** 1 602 273-1477.
Email: kpaz@tbn.org
Web site: http://tbn.org
Profile: KPAZ-TV is the Phoenix affiliate for the Trinity Broadcast Network. The station is owned by Trinity Broadcasting Network. KPAZ-TV broadcasts locally on channel 21.
TELEVISION STATION

KPBT-TV 32267
Owner: Permian Basin Public Telecommunications
Tel: 1 432 563-5728.
Email: basinpbs@basinpbs.org
Web site: http://basinpbs.org
Profile: KPBT-TV is a PBS affiliate for the Odessa-Midland, TX market. The station is owned by Permian Basin Public Telecommunications. KPBT-TV broadcasts locally on channel 36.
TELEVISION STATION

KPCB-TV 63273
Owner: Prime Time Christian Broadcasting Inc.
Editorial: 12706 W Highway 80 E, Odessa, Texas 79765-9611 **Tel:** 1 432 563-0420.
Email: info@glc.us.com
Web site: http://www.godslearningchannel.com
Profile: KPCB-TV is an independent channel for the Snyder, TX market. The station is owned by Prime Time Christian Broadcasting Inc. KPCB-TV broadcasts locally on channel 17.
TELEVISION STATION

KPDF-TV 417937
Owner: Una Vez Mas LP
Editorial: 4001 E Broadway Rd, Ste B17, Phoenix, Arizona 85040-8821 **Tel:** 1 602 437-0181.
Web site: http://www.aztecaamerica.com
Profile: KPDF-TV is the Azteca America affiliate for the Phoenix market. The station is owned by Una Vez Mas LP. KPDF-TV broadcasts locally on channel 41.
TELEVISION STATION

KPDX-TV 32750
Owner: Meredith Broadcasting Group
Editorial: 14975 NW Greenbrier Pkwy, Beaverton, Oregon 97006-5731 **Tel:** 1 503 906-1249.
Email: fox12comments@kptv.com
Web site: http://www.kptv.com
Profile: KPDX-TV is the MyNetworkTV affiliate for the Beaverton, OR market. The station is owned by Meredith Broadcasting Group. KPDX-TV broadcasts locally on channel 49.
TELEVISION STATION

KPEJ2-TV 687590
Owner: Marshall Broadcasting Group
Editorial: 3200 Laforce Blvd, Midland, Texas 79706-4696 **Tel:** 1 432 563-2222.
Email: news@kmid.tv
Web site: http://www.yourbasin.com
Profile: KPEJ2-TV is a multicast channel of KPEJ-TV. A multicast channel is a separate channel that shares the bandwith of the main station but can air unique programming. KPEJ2-TV is the Estrella TV affiliate for the Odessa TX market. The station is owned by Marshall Broadcasting Group. KPEJ2-TV broadcasts locally on channel 24.2.
TELEVISION STATION

KPEJ-TV 31572
Owner: Marshall Broadcasting Group
Editorial: 3200 Laforce Blvd, Midland, Texas 79706-4696 **Tel:** 1 432 563-2222.
Web site: http://www.yourbasin.com
Profile: KPEJ-TV is the FOX affiliate for the Odessa-Midland, TX market. The station is owned by Marshall Broadcasting Group. KPEJ-TV broadcasts locally on channel 24.
TELEVISION STATION

KPHE-TV 620133
Owner: Lotus Communications Corp.
Editorial: 2412 E University Dr, Phoenix, Arizona 85034-6911 **Tel:** 1 602 220-9944.
Email: info@kphetv.com
Web site: http://www.kphetv.com
Profile: KPHE-TV is an independent station for the Phoenix area. The station is owned by Lotus Communications Corp. KPHE-TV broadcasts locally on channel 44. The station broadcasts CNN Latino programming from 3pm until 11pm.
TELEVISION STATION

KPHO2-TV 612347
Owner: Meredith Corporation
Editorial: 4016 N Black Canyon Hwy, Phoenix, Arizona 85017-4730 **Tel:** 1 602 264-1000.
Email: phxnewsdesk@meredith.com
Web site: http://www.kpho.com
Profile: KPHO2-TV is a multicast of KPHO-TV. A multicast channel is a separate channel that shares the bandwith of the main station but can air unique programming. KPHO2-TV airs programming from Weather Now in the Phoenix market. The station is owned by Meredith Corporation. KPHO2-TV broadcasts locally on channel 5.2.
TELEVISION STATION

KPHO-TV 31573
Owner: Meredith Corporation
Editorial: 5555 N 7th Ave, Phoenix, Arizona 85013-1701 **Tel:** 1 602 264-1000.
Email: phxnewsdesk@meredith.com
Web site: http://www.cbs5az.com
Profile: KPHO-TV is the CBS affiliate for the Phoenix market. The station is owned by Meredith Corporation. KPHO-TV broadcasts locally on channel 5.
TELEVISION STATION

KPIC-TV 32773
Owner: Sinclair Broadcast Group, Inc.
Editorial: 655 W Umpqua St, Roseburg, Oregon 97471-2955 **Tel:** 1 541 672-4481.
Email: kpic4news@kpic.com
Web site: http://www.kpic.com
Profile: KPIC-TV is the CBS affiliate for the Roseburg, OR area. The station is owned by Sinclair Broadcast Group, Inc. KPIC-TV broadcasts locally on channel 4.
TELEVISION STATION

KPIX-TV 31574
Owner: CBS Television Stations
Editorial: 855 Battery St, San Francisco, California 94111-1503 **Tel:** 1 415 362-5550.
Email: newsdesk@kpix.com
Web site: http://sanfrancisco.cbslocal.com
Profile: KPIX-TV is the CBS affiliate for the San Francisco market. The station is owned by CBS Television Stations. KPIX-TV broadcasts locally on channel 5.
TELEVISION STATION

KPLC-TV 31575
Owner: Raycom Media Inc.
Editorial: 320 Division St, Lake Charles, Louisiana 70601-4228 **Tel:** 1 337 439-9071.
Email: news@kplctv.com
Web site: http://www.kplctv.com
Profile: KPLC-TV is the NBC affiliate for the Lake Charles, LA, market. The station is owned by Raycom Media Inc. KPLC-TV broadcasts locally on channel 7.
TELEVISION STATION

KPLE-TV 83343
Owner: Killeen Christian Broadcasting Corp.
Editorial: 502 E Elms Rd Ste D, Killeen, Texas 76542-6413 **Tel:** 1 254 554-3683.
Web site: http://www.kpletv.org
Profile: KPLE-TV is Christian broadcasting for Central Texas. It is a 501 (c)3 non-profit.
TELEVISION STATION

KPLR-TV 31576
Owner: Tribune Broadcasting Co.
Editorial: 2250 Ball Dr, Saint Louis, Missouri 63146-8602 **Tel:** 1 314 213-2222.
Email: ktvinews@tvstl.com
Web site: http://www.kplr11.com
Profile: KPLR-TV is the CW affiliate for the St. Louis market. The station is owned byTribune Broadcasting Co. KPLR-TV broadcasts locally on channel 11.
TELEVISION STATION

KPMR-TV 134151
Owner: Entravision Communications Corp.
Editorial: 1467 Fairway Dr, Santa Maria, California 93455-1404 **Tel:** 1 805 685-3800.
Email: kpmrtv@entravision.com
Web site: http://www.kpmrtv.com
Profile: KPMR-TV is the Univision affiliate for the Goleta, CA market. The station is owned by Entravision Communications Corp. KPMR-TV airs locally on channel 38. All programming issues are handled by their parent company. The station

accepts PSAs in CD and DVC Pro formats only in Spanish.
TELEVISION STATION

KPNX2-TV 612164
Owner: TEGNA Inc.
Editorial: 200 E Van Buren St, Phoenix, Arizona 85004-2238 **Tel:** 1 602 257-1212.
Web site: http://www.12news.com
Profile: KPNX2-TV is a multicast of KPNX-TV. A multicast channel is a separate channel that shares the bandwith of the main station but can air unique programming. KPNX2-TV airs programming from 12 News Weather Plus in the Phoenix market. The station is owned by TEGNA Inc. KNTV2-TV broadcasts locally on channel 12.2.
TELEVISION STATION

KPNX-TV 31577
Owner: TEGNA Inc.
Editorial: 200 E Van Buren St, Phoenix, Arizona 85004-2238 **Tel:** 1 602 257-1212.
Email: desk@12news.com
Web site: http://www.12news.com
Profile: KPNX-TV is the NBC network affiliate for the Phoenix market. The station is owned by TEGNA Inc. KPNX-TV broadcasts locally on channel 12.
TELEVISION STATION

KPNZ-TV 242467
Owner: Liberman Broadcasting Inc.
Editorial: 150 N Wright Brothers Dr Ste 520, Salt Lake City, Utah 84116-3189 **Tel:** 1 801 744-2000.
Web site: http://www.lbimedia.com
Profile: KPNZ-TV is an independent station for the Salt Lake City market. The station is owned by Liberman Broadcasting Inc. KPNZ-TV broadcasts locally on channel 24.
TELEVISION STATION

KPOB-TV 32884
Owner: Wheeler Inc.(Mel)
Editorial: 3690 Highway 67 N, Poplar Bluff, Missouri 63901-8139 **Tel:** 1 573 785-0404.
Web site: http://www.wsiltv.com
Profile: KPOB-TV is the ABC affiliate for the Paducah, KY; Cape Girardeau, MO and Harrisburg, IL market. The station is owned by Mel Wheeler Inc. KPOB-TV broadcasts locally on channel 15.
TELEVISION STATION

KPPX2-TV 612170
Owner: ION Media Networks
Editorial: 2777 E Camelback Rd, 101, Phoenix, Arizona 85016-4352 **Tel:** 1 602 340-1466.
Profile: KPPX2-TV is a multicast of KPPX-TV. A multicast channel is a separate channel that shares the bandwith of the main station but can air unique programming. KPPX2-TV airs programming from qubo in the Phoenix market. The station is owned by ION Media Networks. KPPX2-TV broadcasts locally on channel 51.2.
TELEVISION STATION

KPPX3-TV 612171
Owner: ION Media Networks
Editorial: 2777 E Camelback Rd, Ste 101, Phoenix, Arizona 85016-4352 **Tel:** 1 602 340-1466.
Profile: KPPX3-TV is a multicast of KPPX-TV. A multicast channel is a separate channel that shares the bandwith of the main station but can air unique programming. KPPX3-TV airs programming from ION Life in the Phoenix market. The station is owned by ION Media Networks. KPPX3-TV broadcasts locally on channel 51.3.
TELEVISION STATION

KPPX-TV 63274
Owner: ION Media Networks
Editorial: 2777 E Camelback Rd Ste 101, Phoenix, Arizona 85016-4348 **Tel:** 1 602 340-1466.
Web site: http://ionmedianetwork.com
Profile: KPPX-TV is the ION Television affiliate for the Phoenix market. The station is owned by ION Media Networks. KPPX-TV broadcasts locally on channel 51.
TELEVISION STATION

KPRC2-TV 610548
Owner: Graham Media Group
Editorial: 8181 Southwest Fwy, Houston, Texas 77074-1705 **Tel:** 1 713 222-2222.
Email: desk@kprc.com
Web site: http://www.click2houston.com
Profile: KPRC2-TV is a multicast of KPRC-TV. A multicast channel is a separate channel that shares the bandwith of the main station but can air unique programming. KPRC2-TV airs programming from This TV in the Houston market. The station is owned by Post-Newsweek Stations Inc. KPRC2-TV broadcasts locally on channel 2.2.
TELEVISION STATION

KPRC-TV 31578
Owner: Graham Media Group
Editorial: 8181 Southwest Fwy, Houston, Texas 77074-1705 **Tel:** 1 713 222-2222.
Email: desk@kprc.com
Web site: http://www.click2houston.com
Profile: KPRC-TV is the NBC affiliate for the Houston market. The station is owned by Graham Media Group. KPRC-TV broadcasts locally on channel 2.
TELEVISION STATION

KPSE-TV 418045
Owner: OTA Broadcasting
Editorial: 72920 Parkview Dr, Palm Desert, California 92260-9357 **Tel:** 1 760 568-3636.
Profile: KPSE-TV is the MyNetworkTV affiliate for the Palm Desert, CA market. The station is owned by OTA Broadcasting. KPSE-TV broadcasts locally on channel 50.
TELEVISION STATION

KPTB-TV 63272
Owner: Prime Time Christian Broadcasting Inc.
Editorial: 12706 W Highway 80 E, Odessa, Texas 79765-9611 **Tel:** 1 432 563-0420.
Email: info@glc.us.com
Web site: http://www.glc.us.com
Profile: KPTB-TV is an independent station serving the Lubbock, TX market. The station is owned by Prime Time Christian Broadcasting Inc. KPTB-TV broadcasts locally on channel 16.
TELEVISION STATION

KPTH-TV 63275
Owner: Sinclair Broadcast Group
Editorial: 100 Gold Cir, Dakota Dunes, South Dakota 57049-5316 **Tel:** 1 712 277-3554.
Email: news@siouxlandnews.com
Web site: http://www.siouxlandnews.com
Profile: KPTH-TV is the local FOX affiliate for the Sioux City, IA market. The station is owned by Sinclair Broadcast Group. KPTH-TV broadcasts locally on channel 44.
TELEVISION STATION

KPTM3-TV 687588
Owner: Pappas Telecasting Companies
Editorial: 4625 Farnam St, Omaha, Nebraska 68132-3222 **Tel:** 1 402 558-4200.
Email: contact42@kptm.com
Web site: http://www.fox42kptm.com
Profile: KPTM3-TV-TV is a multicast channel of KPTM-TV-TV. A multicast channel is a separate channel that shares the bandwith of the main station but can air unique programming. KPTM3-TV-TV is the Estrella TV affiliate for the Omaha NE market. The station is owned by Pappas Telecasting Companies. KPTM3-TV-TV broadcasts locally on channel 42.3.
TELEVISION STATION

KPTM-TV 31579
Owner: Sinclair Broadcast Group
Editorial: 4625 Farnam St, Omaha, Nebraska 68132-3222 **Tel:** 1 402 558-4200.
Email: frontdesk@kptm.com
Web site: http://fox42kptm.com
Profile: KPTM-TV is the FOX and i Network affiliate for the Omaha, NE market. The station is owned by Sinclair Broadcast Group. KPTM-TV broadcasts locally on channel 42.
TELEVISION STATION

KPTS-TV 31580
Owner: Kansas Public Telecommunications Service Inc.
Editorial: 320 W 21st St N, Wichita, Kansas 67203 **Tel:** 1 316 838-3090.
Email: news@kpts.org
Web site: http://www.kpts.org
Profile: KPTS-TV is the PBS network affiliate for the Wichita-Hutchinson, KS market. The Station is owned by Kansas Public Telecommunications Service Inc. KPTS-TV broadcasts locally on channel 8.
TELEVISION STATION

KPTV-TV 31581
Owner: Meredith Broadcasting Group
Editorial: 14975 NW Greenbrier Pkwy, Beaverton, Oregon 97006-5731 **Tel:** 1 503 906-1249.
Email: fox12news@kptv.com
Web site: http://www.kptv.com
Profile: KPTV-TV is the FOX affiliate for the Portland market. The station is owned by Meredith Broadcasting Group. KPTV-TV broadcasts locally on channel 12.
TELEVISION STATION

KPVI-TV 32724
Owner: Idaho Broadcast Partners
Editorial: 902 E Sherman St, Pocatello, Idaho 83201-5762 **Tel:** 1 208 232-6666.
Email: newsroom@kpvi.com
Web site: http://www.kpvi.com
Profile: KPVI-TV is the NBC affiliate for the Idaho Falls, ID market. The station is owned by Idaho Broadcast Partners. KPVI-TV broadcasts locally on channel 6.
TELEVISION STATION

KPVM-TV 350354
Owner: Van Winkle (Vernon)
Editorial: 890 Higley Rd, Pahrump, Nevada 89048 **Tel:** 1 775 727-9400.
Web site: http://www.kpvm.tv
Profile: KPVM-TV is the ION Television affiliate for the Las Vegas market. The station is owned by Vernon Van Winkle. KPVM-TV broadcasts locally on channel 41 and digital channel 46.
TELEVISION STATION

KPXB-TV 32344
Owner: ION Media Networks
Editorial: 4124 McHard Rd, Missouri City, Texas 77489-5413 **Tel:** 1 281 820-4900.
Web site: http://www.iontelevision.com
Profile: KPXB-TV is the ION Television affiliate for the Houston market. The station is owned by ION Media Networks. KPXB-TV broadcasts locally on channel 49.
TELEVISION STATION

KPXC2-TV 613339
Owner: ION Media Networks
Editorial: 3001 S Jamaica Ct, Aurora, Colorado 80014-2656 **Tel:** 1 303 751-5959.
Web site: http://www.qubo.com
Profile: KPXC2-TV is independent affiliate for the Denver, CO market. The station is owned by ION Media Networks. KPXC2-TV broadcasts locally on channel 59.2. The station airs children's programming from the qubo network. KPXC2-TV is a multicast channel of KPXC-TV. A multicast channel is a separate channel that shares the bandwidth of the main station but can air unique programming.
TELEVISION STATION

KPXC3-TV 613341
Owner: ION Media Networks
Editorial: 3001 S Jamaica Ct, Aurora, Colorado 80014-2656 **Tel:** 1 303 751-5959.
Web site: http://www.ionlife.com
Profile: KPXC3-TV is an ION Television affiliate for the Denver, CO market. The station is owned by ION Media Networks. KPXC 3-TV broadcasts locally on channel 59.3. The station airs lifestyle programming. KPXC 3-TV is a multicast channel of KPXC-TV. A multicast channel is a separate channel that shares the bandwidth of the main station but can air unique programming.
TELEVISION STATION

KPXC4-TV 613342
Owner: ION Media Networks
Editorial: 3001 S Jamaica Ct, Aurora, Colorado 80014-2656 **Tel:** 1 303 751-5959.
Web site: http://www.worship.net
Profile: KPXC4-TV is an independent affiliate for the Denver, CO market. The station is owned by ION Media Networks. KPXC4-TV broadcasts locally on channel 59.4. The station airs alternative Christian worship-themed programming. KPXC4-TV is a multicast channel of KPXC -TV. A multicast channel is a separate channel that shares the bandwidth of the main station but can air unique programming.
TELEVISION STATION

KPXC-TV 31673
Owner: ION Media Networks
Editorial: 3001 S Jamaica Ct, Aurora, Colorado 80014-2656 **Tel:** 1 303 751-5959.
Profile: KPXC-TV is the ION Television affiliate for the Denver, CO market. The station is owned by ION Media Networks. KPXC-TV broadcasts locally on channel 59.
TELEVISION STATION

KPXD2-TV 609958
Owner: ION Media Networks
Editorial: 600 Six Flags Dr, Ste 652, Arlington, Texas 76011-6353 **Tel:** 1 817 633-6843.
Profile: KPXD2-TV is a multicast of KXPD-TV. A multicast channel is a separate channel that shares the bandwith of the main station but can air unique programming. KPXD2-TV airs programming from the qubo network in the Dallas market. The station is owned by ION Media Networks. KPXD2-TV broadcasts locally on channel 68.2.
TELEVISION STATION

KPXD3-TV 609968
Owner: ION Media Networks
Editorial: 600 Six Flags Dr, Ste 652, Arlington, Texas 76011-6353 **Tel:** 1 817 633-6843.
Profile: KPXD3-TV is a multicast of KXPD-TV. A multicast channel is a separate channel that shares the bandwith of the main station but can air unique programming. KPXD2-TV airs programming from the ION Life network in the Dallas market. The station is owned by ION Media Networks. KPXD3-TV broadcasts locally on channel 68.3.
TELEVISION STATION

KPXD4-TV 609969
Owner: ION Media Networks
Editorial: 600 Six Flags Dr, Ste 652, Arlington, Texas 76011-6353 **Tel:** 1 817 633-6843.
Profile: KPXD4-TV is a multicast of KXPD-TV. A multicast channel is a separate channel that shares the bandwith of the main station but can air unique programming. KPXD4-TV airs programming from the Worship Network in the Dallas market. The station is owned by ION Media Networks. KPXD4-TV broadcasts locally on channel 68.4.
TELEVISION STATION

KPXD-TV 32559
Owner: ION Media Networks
Editorial: 600 Six Flags Dr, Ste 652, Arlington, Texas 76011-6353 **Tel:** 1 817 633-6843.
Profile: KPXD-TV is the ION Television affiliate for the Dallas-Fort Worth, TX market. The station is owned by ION Media Networks. KPXD-TV broadcasts locally on channel 68.
TELEVISION STATION

KPXE2-TV 621692
Owner: ION Media Networks
Editorial: 4220 Shawnee Mission Pkwy, Fairway, Kansas 66205-2532 **Tel:** 1 913 722-0798.
Email: viewermail@ionmedia.com
Web site: http://iontelevision.com
Profile: KPXE2-TV is a multicast of KPXE-TV. A multicast channel is a separate channel that shares the bandwith of the main station but can air unique programming. KPXE2-TV airs children's programming from qubo in the Kansas City, MO market. The station is owned by ION Media Networks. KPXE2-TV broadcasts locally on channel 50.2.
TELEVISION STATION

KPXE3-TV 621694
Owner: ION Media Networks
Editorial: 4220 Shawnee Mission Pkwy, Fairway, Kansas 66205-2532 **Tel:** 1 913 722-0798.
Email: viewermail@ionmedia.com
Web site: http://iontelevision.com
Profile: KPXE3-TV is a multicast of KPXE-TV. A multicast channel is a separate channel that shares the bandwith of the main station but can air unique programming. KPXE3-TV airs lifestyle programming from ION Life in the Kansas City, MO market. The station is owned by ION Media Networks. KPXE3-TV broadcasts locally on channel 50.3.
TELEVISION STATION

KPXE-TV 31713
Owner: ION Media Networks
Editorial: 4220 Shawnee Mission Pkwy, Fairway, Kansas 66205-2532 **Tel:** 1 913 722-0798.
Email: viewermail@ionmedia.com
Web site: http://iontelevision.com
Profile: KPXE-TV is the ION Television affiliate for the Kansas City, MO market. The station is owned by ION Media Networks. KPXE-TV broadcasts locally on channel 50.
TELEVISION STATION

KPXG2-TV 614741
Owner: ION Media Networks
Editorial: 811 SW Naito Pkwy, Portland, Oregon 97204-3330 **Tel:** 1 503 222-2221.
Web site: http://www.qubo.com
Profile: KPXG2-TV is a multicast of KPXG-TV. A multicast channel is a separate channel that shares the bandwith of the main station but can air unique programming. KPXG2-TV airs programming from the qubo Network in the Portland, OR market. The station is owned by ION Media Networks. KPXG2-TV broadcasts locally on channel 22.2.
TELEVISION STATION

KPXG3-TV 614743
Owner: ION Media Networks
Editorial: 811 SW Naito Pkwy, Portland, Oregon 97204-3330 **Tel:** 1 503 222-2221.
Web site: http://www.ionlife.com
Profile: KPXG3-TV is a multicast of KPXG-TV. A multicast channel is a separate channel that shares the bandwith of the main station but can air unique programming. KPXG3-TV airs programming from the ION Life Network in the Portland, OR market. The station is owned by ION Media Networks. KPXG3-TV broadcasts locally on channel 22.3.
TELEVISION STATION

KPXG4-TV 614746
Owner: ION Media Networks
Editorial: 811 SW Naito Pkwy, Portland, Oregon 97204-3330 **Tel:** 1 503 222-2221.
Web site: http://ionline.tv
Profile: KPXG4-TV is a multicast of KPXG-TV. A multicast channel is a separate channel that shares the bandwith of the main station but can air unique programming. KPXG4-TV airs programming from ION Media Networks in the Portland, OR market. The station is owned by ION Media Networks. KPXG4-TV broadcasts locally on channel 22.4.
TELEVISION STATION

KPXG-TV 31700
Owner: ION Media Networks
Editorial: 811 SW Naito Pkwy, Portland, Oregon 97204-3330 **Tel:** 1 503 222-2221.
Web site: http://ionline.tv
Profile: KPXG-TV is the ION Television affiliate for the Portland, OR market. The station is owned by ION Media Networks. KPXG-TV broadcasts locally on channel 22. The station has no news or ad sales department. PSA's are not accepted.
TELEVISION STATION

KPXJ-TV 63276
Owner: Minden Television Company
Editorial: 312 E Kings Hwy, Shreveport, Louisiana 71104-3504 **Tel:** 1 318 861-5811.
Web site: http://www.ktbs.com
Profile: KPXJ-TV is the CW affiliate for the Shreveport, LA, market. The station is owned by Minden Television Company. KPXJ-TV broadcasts locally on channel 21. KPXJ-TV has no news department, newscasts are produced by KTBS-TV.
TELEVISION STATION

KPXL-TV 32628
Owner: ION Media Networks
Editorial: 6100 Bandera Rd, San Antonio, Texas 78238-1652 **Tel:** 1 210 682-2626.
Web site: http://www.iontelevision.com
Profile: KPXL-TV is the ION Television affiliate for the San Antonio market. The station is owned by ION Media Networks. KPXL-TV broadcasts locally on channel 26.
TELEVISION STATION

KPXM2-TV 612323
Owner: ION Media Networks
Editorial: 22601 176th St NW, Big Lake, Minnesota 55309-5102 **Tel:** 1 763 263-8666.
Profile: KPXM2-TV is a multicast of KPXM-TV. A multicast channel is a separate channel that shares the bandwith of the main station but can air unique programming. KPXM2-TV airs programming from the qubo in the Minneapolis market. The station is owned by ION Media Networks. KPXM2-TV broadcasts locally on channel 41.2.
TELEVISION STATION

KPXM3-TV 612325
Owner: ION Media Networks
Editorial: 22601 176th St NW, Big Lake, Minnesota 55309-5102 **Tel:** 1 763 263-8666.
Profile: KPXM3-TV is a multicast of KPXM-TV. A multicast channel is a separate channel that shares the bandwith of the main station but can air unique programming. KPXM3-TV airs programming from the ION Life in the Minneapolis market. The station is owned by ION Media Networks. KPXM3-TV broadcasts locally on channel 41.3.
TELEVISION STATION

KPXM-TV 32327
Owner: ION Media Networks
Editorial: 22601 176th St NW, Big Lake, Minnesota 55309-5102 **Tel:** 1 763 263-8666.
Web site: http://iontelevision.com
Profile: KPXM-TV is the ION Television affiliate for the Minneapolis - St. Paul, MN market. The station is owned by ION Media Networks. KPXM-TV broadcasts locally on channel 41.
TELEVISION STATION

KPXN2-TV 607301
Owner: ION Media Networks
Editorial: 2600 W Olive Ave, Ste 900, Burbank, California 91505-4568 **Tel:** 1 818 563-1005.
Profile: KPXN2-TV is a multicast channel of KPXN-TV. A multicast channel is a separate channel that shares the bandwith of the main station but can air unique programming. KPXN2-TV airs programming from qubo for the Los Angeles market. The station is owned by ION Media Networks. KPXN2-TV broadcasts locally on channel 30.2.
TELEVISION STATION

KPXN3-TV 607306
Owner: ION Media Networks
Editorial: 2600 W Olive Ave, Ste 900, Burbank, California 91505-4568 **Tel:** 1 818 563-1005.
Profile: KPXN3-TV is a multicast channel of KPXN-TV. A multicast channel is a separate channel that shares the bandwith of the main station but can air unique programming. KPXN3-TV airs programming from ION Life for the Los Angeles market. The station is owned by ION Media Networks. KPXN3-TV broadcasts locally on channel 30.3.
TELEVISION STATION

KPXN4-TV 607307
Owner: ION Media Networks
Editorial: 2600 W Olive Ave, Ste 900, Burbank, California 91505-4568 **Tel:** 1 818 563-1005.
Profile: KPXN4-TV is a multicast channel of KPXN-TV. A multicast channel is a separate channel that shares the bandwith of the main station but can air unique programming. KPXN4-TV airs programming from the Worship Network for the Los Angeles market. The station is owned by ION Media Networks. KPXN4-TV broadcasts locally on channel 30.4.
TELEVISION STATION

KPXN-TV 32461
Owner: ION Media Networks
Editorial: 2600 W Olive Ave Ste 900, Burbank, California 91505-4568 **Tel:** 1 818 563-1005.
Web site: http://iontelevison.com
Profile: KPXN-TV is the ION Television affiliate for the Los Angeles, CA market. The station is owned by ION Media Networks. KPXN-TV broadcasts locally on channel 30.
TELEVISION STATION

KPXO-TV 32581
Owner: ION Media Networks
Editorial: 875 Waimanu St, Ste 630, Honolulu, Hawaii 96813-5265 **Tel:** 1 808 591-1275.
Profile: KPXO-TV is the ION Television affiliate for the Honolulu market. The station is owned by ION Media Networks. KPXO-TV broadcasts locally on channel 66.
TELEVISION STATION

KPXR-TV 63102
Owner: ION Media Networks
Editorial: 1957 Blairs Ferry Rd NE, Cedar Rapids, Iowa 52402-5891 **Tel:** 1 319 378-1260.
Profile: KPXR-TV is the ION Television affiliate for the Cedar Rapids, IA market. The station is owned by ION Media Networks. KPXR-TV broadcasts locally on channel 48.
TELEVISION STATION

KQCA2-TV 613095
Owner: Hearst Television Inc.
Editorial: 58 Television Cir, Sacramento, California 95814-0750 **Tel:** 1 916 447-5858.
Web site: http://www.thistv.com
Profile: KQCA2-TV is an independent affiliate for the Sacramento, CA market. The station is owned by Hearst Television Inc. KQCA2-TV broadcasts locally on channel 58.2. The station broadcasts general entertainment programming from This TV Network. KQCA2-TV is a multicast channel of KQCA-TV. A multicast channel is a separate channel that shares the bandwidth of the main station but can air unique programming.
TELEVISION STATION

KQCA-TV 31600
Owner: Hearst Television Inc.
Editorial: 3 Television Cir, Sacramento, California 95814-0750 **Tel:** 1 916 447-3333.
Email: newstips@kcra.com
Web site: http://www.kcra.com/my58
Profile: KQCA-TV is the MyNetworkTV affiliate for the Sacramento, CA market. The station is owned by Hearst Television Inc. KQCA-TV broadcasts locally on channel 58.
TELEVISION STATION

KQCK-TV 355466
Owner: Casa Media Partners
Editorial: 2923 E Lincolnway, Cheyenne, Wyoming 82001-6149 **Tel:** 1 307 634-9890.
Email: kqck@tv.com
Profile: KQCK-TV is the MundoFOX affiliate for the Cheyenne, WY-Scottsbluff, NE and Denver market. The station is owned by Casa Media Partners. KQCK-TV broadcasts locally on channel 33. The station does not have a news department.
TELEVISION STATION

KQCW-TV 31524
Owner: Griffin Communications, LLC
Editorial: 303 N Boston Ave, Tulsa, Oklahoma 74103-1602 **Tel:** 1 918 732-6000.
Email: newsdesk@newson6.net
Web site: http://www.tulsacw.com
Profile: KQCW-TV is the CW affiliate for the Tulsa, OK market. The station is owned by Griffin Communications, LLC. KQCW-TV broadcasts locally on channel 19 and Cox Cable channel 12.
TELEVISION STATION

KQDF-TV 417938
Owner: Una Vez Mas LP
Editorial: 1701 N Market St Ste 500, Dallas, Texas 75202-2001 **Tel:** 1 214 754-7008.
Web site: http://www.aztecaamerica.com
Profile: KQDF-TV is the Azteca America affiliate for the Albuquerque, NM market. The station is owned by Una Vez Mas LP. KQDF-TV broadcasts locally on channel 25.
TELEVISION STATION

KQDS-TV 32590
Owner: Curtis Squire Inc.
Editorial: 2001 London Rd, Duluth, Minnesota 55812-2126 **Tel:** 1 218 728-1622.
Email: fox21news@kqdsfox21.tv
Web site: http://www.fox21online.com
Profile: KQDS-TV is the FOX affiliate for the Duluth, MN market. The station is owned by Curtis Squire Inc. KQDS-TV broadcasts locally on channel 21.
TELEVISION STATION

KQED2-TV 610525
Owner: KQED, Inc.
Editorial: 50 W San Fernando St Ste 110, San Jose, California 95113-2415 **Tel:** 1 408 795-5400.
Email: tv@kqed.org
Web site: http://www.kqed.org/tv
Profile: KQED2-TV is a multicast of KQED-TV. A multicast channel is a separate channel that shares the bandwith of the main station but can air unique programming. The station is known as KQED Plus.The station is owned by KQED, Inc. KQED2-TV broadcasts locally to the San Francisco area on channel 9.2.
TELEVISION STATION

KQED3-TV 610519
Owner: KQED, Inc.
Editorial: 2601 Mariposa St, San Francisco, California 94110-1426 **Tel:** 1 415 864-2000.
Email: tv@kqed.org
Web site: http://www.kqed.org/tv
Profile: KQED3-TV is a multicast of KQED-TV. A multicast channel is a separate channel that shares the bandwith of the main station but can air unique programming. KQED3-TV airs programming from World network in the San Francisco market. The station is owned by Northern California Public Broadcasting. KQED3-TV broadcasts locally on channel 9.3.
TELEVISION STATION

KQED-TV 31582
Owner: KQED, Inc.
Editorial: 2601 Mariposa St, San Francisco, California 94110-1426 **Tel:** 1 415 864-2000.
Email: assignmentdesk@kqed.org
Web site: http://www.kqed.org/tv
Profile: KQED-TV is the PBS affiliate for the San Francisco market. The station is owned by Northern California Public Broadcasting. KQED-TV broadcasts locally on channel 9.
TELEVISION STATION

KQEG-TV 235304
Owner: Magnum Broadcasting
Editorial: 505 King St, La Crosse, Wisconsin 54601-9204 **Tel:** 1 608 784-0876.
Web site: http://www.kqegtv.com
Profile: KQEG-TV is an independent affiliate for the La Crosse, WI market. The station is owned by Magnum Broadcasting. KQEG-TV broadcasts locally on channel 23.
TELEVISION STATION

KQFX-TV 151888
Owner: News-Press & Gazette Company
Editorial: 501 Business Loop 70 E, Columbia, Missouri 65201-3909 **Tel:** 1 573 449-0917.
Email: news@kmiz.com
Web site: http://www.abc17news.com/
Profile: KQFX-TV is the FOX affiliate for the Columbia, MO market. The station is owned by News-Press & Gazette Company. KQFX-TV broadcasts locally on channel 22.
TELEVISION STATION

KQSL-TV 837786
Owner: Chang Media Group
Editorial: Fort Bragg, California **Tel:** 1 877 365-2824.
Email: changmedia@aol.com
Profile: KQSL-TV is the TheCoolTV affiliate for the San Francisco market. The station is owned by Chang Media group. KQSL-TV broadcasts locally on channel 8. The station airs music videos around the clock.
TELEVISION STATION

KQTV-TV 31583
Owner: MidAmerica Holdings, LLC
Editorial: 4000 Faraon St, Saint Joseph, Missouri 64506-3185 **Tel:** 1 816 364-2222.
Email: news@kq2.com
Web site: http://stjoechannel.com
Profile: KQTV-TV is the ABC affiliate for the St. Joseph, MO, market. The station is owned by MidAmerica Holdings, LLC. KQTV-TV broadcasts locally on channel 2.
TELEVISION STATION

KRBC-TV 32654
Owner: Nexstar Broadcasting Group
Editorial: 4510 S 14th St, Abilene, Texas 79605-4797 **Tel:** 1 325 692-4242.
Email: news@krbc.tv
Web site: http://www.bigcountryhomepage.com
Profile: KRBC-TV is the NBC affiliate for the Abilene-Sweetwater, TX market. The station is owned by Nexstar Broadcasting Group. KRBC-TV broadcasts locally on channel 9.
TELEVISION STATION

KRBK-TV 708366
Owner: Koplar Communications
Editorial: 170 S Enterprise Ste 103, Springfield, Missouri 65804-1851 **Tel:** 1 417 522-0020.
Web site: http://www.fox5krbk.com
Profile: KRBK-TV is the MyNetworkTV and FOX Network affiliate for Springfield and Southwest Missouri. The station is owned by Koplar Communications. KRBK-TV broadcasts locally on channel 49.
TELEVISION STATION

KRCA2-TV 607275
Owner: Liberman Broadcasting Inc.
Editorial: 1845 W Empire Ave, Burbank, California 91504-3402 **Tel:** 1 828 563-5722.
Profile: KRCA2-TV is a multicast channel of KRCA-TV. A multicast channel is a separate channel that shares the bandwith of the main station but can air unique programming. KRCA2-TV is the HTTV USA network for the Los Angeles market. The station is owned by Liberman Broadcasting Inc. KRCA2-TV broadcasts locally on channel 62.2.
TELEVISION STATION

KRCA-TV 32397
Owner: Liberman Broadcasting Inc.
Editorial: 1845 W Empire Ave, Burbank, California 91504-3402 **Tel:** 1 818 563-5722.
Email: info@lbimedia.com
Web site: http://www.estrellatv.com
Profile: KRCA-TV is the Estrella TV affiliate for the Los Angeles market. The station is owned by Liberman Broadcasting Inc. KRCA-TV broadcasts locally on channel 62.
TELEVISION STATION

KRCB2-TV 610687
Owner: Rural California Broadcasting Corp.
Editorial: 5850 Labath Ave, Rohnert Park, California 94928-2041 **Tel:** 1 707 584-2000.
Email: viewer@krcb.org
Web site: http://www.krcb.org
Profile: KRCB2-TV is a multicast of KRCB-TV. A multicast channel is a separate channel that shares the bandwith of the main station but can air unique programming. KRCB2-TV airs programming from the Create network in the San Francisco market. The station is owned by Rural California Broadcasting Corp. KRCB2-TV broadcasts locally on channel 22.2.
TELEVISION STATION

KRCB3-TV 610689
Owner: Rural California Broadcasting Corp.
Editorial: 5850 Labath Ave, Rohnert Park, California 94928-2041 **Tel:** 1 707 584-2000.
Email: viewer@krcb.org
Web site: http://www.krcb.org
Profile: KRCB3-TV is a multicast of KRCB-TV. A multicast channel is a separate channel that shares the bandwith of the main station but can air unique programming. KRCB3-TV is a simulcast of KRCB-FM in the San Francisco market. The station is owned by Rural California Broadcasting Corp. KRCB3-TV broadcasts locally on channel 22.3.
TELEVISION STATION

KRCB-TV 32255
Owner: Rural California Broadcasting Corp.
Editorial: 5850 Labath Ave, Rohnert Park, California 94928-2041 **Tel:** 1 707 584-2000.
Email: viewer@krcb.org
Web site: http://www.krcb.org
Profile: KRCB-TV is the PBS affiliate for the San Francisco market. The station is owned by the Rural California Broadcasting Corp. KRCB-TV broadcasts locally on channel 22.
TELEVISION STATION

KRCG-TV 3158
Owner: Sinclair Broadcast Group, Inc.
Editorial: 10188 Old US Highway 54, New Bloomfield Missouri 65063 **Tel:** 1 573 896-5144.
Email: news@krcg.com
Web site: http://www.connectmidmissouri.com
Profile: KRCG-TV is the CBS affiliate for the Columbia-Jefferson City, MO market. The station is owned by Sinclair Broadcast Group, Inc. KRCG-TV broadcasts locally on channel 13.
TELEVISION STATION

KRCR-TV 3268
Owner: Bonten Media Group, LLC
Editorial: 755 Auditorium Dr, Redding, California 96001-0920 **Tel:** 1 530 243-7777.
Email: news@krcrtv.com
Web site: http://www.krcrtv.com
Profile: KRCR-TV is the ABC affiliate for Chico, CA. The station is owned byBonten Media Group, LLC. KRCR-TV broadcasts locally on channel 7.
TELEVISION STATION

KRCW2-TV 613408
Owner: Tribune Broadcasting Co.
Editorial: 10255 SW Arctic Dr, Beaverton, Oregon 97005-4167 **Tel:** 1 503 644-3232.
Web site: http://portlandscw32.com
Profile: KRCW2-TV is a multicast of KRCW-TV. A multicast channel is a separate channel that shares the bandwith of the main station but can air unique programming. KRCW2-TV airs programming from Universal Sports in the Portland, OR market. The station is owned by Tribune Broadcasting Co. KRCW2-TV broadcasts locally on channel 32.2.
TELEVISION STATION

KRCW-TV 32455
Owner: Tribune Broadcasting Co.
Editorial: 10255 SW Arctic Dr, Beaverton, Oregon 97005-4167 **Tel:** 1 503 644-3232.
Web site: http://portlandscw.com
Profile: KRCW-TV is the CW affiliate for the Beaverton, OR market. The station is owned by Tribune Broadcasting Co. KRCW-TV broadcasts locally on channel 32.
TELEVISION STATION

KRDK-TV 31705
Owner: Major Market Broadcasting
Profile: KRDK-TV is an independent station in the Fargo, ND market. The station is owned by Major Market Broadcasting. KRDK-TV broadcasts locally on channel 4.
TELEVISION STATION

KRDO-TV 31586
Owner: News-Press & Gazette Co.
Editorial: 399 S 8th St, Colorado Springs, Colorado 80905-1803 **Tel:** 1 719 632-1515.
Email: krdonews@krdo.com
Web site: http://www.krdotv.com
Profile: KRDO-TV is the ABC affiliate for the Colorado Springs, CO market. The station is owned by News-Press & Gazette Co. KRDO-TV broadcasts locally on channel 13.
TELEVISION STATION

KREM-TV 31587
Owner: TEGNA Inc.
Editorial: 4103 S Regal St, Spokane, Washington 99223-7737 **Tel:** 1 509 448-2000.
Email: newstips@krem.com
Web site: http://www.krem.com
Profile: KREM-TV is the CBS affiliate for the Spokane, Washington market. The station is owned by TEGNA Inc. KREM-TV broadcasts locally on channel 2.
TELEVISION STATION

KREN-TV 32464
Owner: Entravision Communications Corp.
Editorial: 300 S Wells Ave, Ste 12, Reno, Nevada 89502-1670 **Tel:** 1 775 333-1017.
Web site: http://www.entravision.com
Profile: KREN-TV is the Univision affiliate for the Reno, NV, area. The station is owned by Entravision Communications Corp. KREN-TV broadcasts locally on channel 27.
TELEVISION STATION

KRET-TV 350208
Owner: Camino Real Communications LLC
Editorial: 41625 Eclectic St Ste J1, Palm Desert, California 92260-1908 **Tel:** 1 760 674-8550.
Email: kret-tv@hotmail.com
Web site: http://www.krettv.com
Profile: KRET-TV is the MeTV affiliate broadcasting to the Palm Desert, CA area. KRET-TV is owned by Camino Real Communications LLC. KRET-TV broadcasts locally on channel 45.
TELEVISION STATION

KREX-TV 32655
Owner: Gray Television, Inc.
Editorial: 345 Hillcrest Dr, Grand Junction, Colorado 81501-7446 **Tel:** 1 970 242-5000.
Email: news@krextv.com
Web site: http://www.westernslopenow.com
Profile: KREX-TV is the CBS affiliate for the Grand Junction-Montrose, CO market. The station is owned by Gray Television, Inc. KREX-TV broadcasts locally on channel 5.
TELEVISION STATION

KRGV-TV 31588

Owner: Manship Family(The)
Editorial: 900 E Expressway 83, Weslaco, Texas 78596-4500 **Tel:** 1 956 968-5555.
Email: news@krgv.com
Web site: http://www.krgv.com
Profile: KRGV-TV is the ABC affiliate for the Brownsville-Mc Allen, TX market. The station is owned by The Manship Family. KRGV-TV broadcasts locally on channel 5.
TELEVISION STATION

KRHD-TV 79350

Owner: Centex LP
Editorial: 1716 Briarcrest Dr Ste 220, Bryan, Texas 77802-2753 **Tel:** 1 254 754-2525.
Email: newsroom@kxxv.com
Web site: http://www.abc40.com
Profile: KRHD-TV is the ABC affiliate for the Waco, TX market. The station is owned by Centex LP. KRHD-TV broadcasts locally on channel 40.
TELEVISION STATION

KRIS-TV 31589

Owner: Evening Post Publishing Co.
Editorial: 301 Artesian St, Corpus Christi, Texas 78401-2701 **Tel:** 1 361 883-7070.
Email: newsroom@kristv.com
Web site: http://www.kristv.com
Profile: KRIS-TV is the NBC network affiliate for the Corpus Christi, TX market. The station is owned by Evening Post Publishing Co. KRIS-TV broadcasts locally on channel 6. To contact the station please use the online contact form.
TELEVISION STATION

KRIV-TV 31590

Owner: Fox Broadcasting Company
Editorial: 4261 Southwest Fwy, Houston, Texas 77027-7201 **Tel:** 1 713 479-2600.
Email: newsdesk@fox26.com
Web site: http://www.fox26houston.com
Profile: KRIV-TV is the FOX affiliate for the Houston market. The station is owned by Fox Broadcasting Company. KRIV-TV broadcasts locally on channel 26.
TELEVISION STATION

KRMA-TV 31592

Owner: Rocky Mountain PBS
Editorial: 1089 Bannock St, Denver, Colorado 80204-4036 **Tel:** 1 303 892-6666.
Email: news@rmpbs.org
Web site: http://www.rmpbs.org
Profile: KRMA-TV is the PBS affiliate for the Denver, CO market. The station is owned by Rocky Mountain PBS. KRMA-TV broadcasts locally on channel 6.
TELEVISION STATION

KRMJ-TV 32629

Owner: Rocky Mountain PBS
Editorial: 2520 Blichman Ave, Grand Junction, Colorado 81505-1010 **Tel:** 1 970 245-1818.
Web site: http://www.rmpbs.org
Profile: KRMJ-TV is a PBS affiliate for the Grand Junction-Montrose, CO market. The station is owned by Rocky Mountain PBS. KRMJ-TV airs on channel 18.
TELEVISION STATION

KRMT-TV 32482

Owner: Daystar Television Network
Editorial: 12014 W 64th Ave, Arvada, Colorado 80004-4010 **Tel:** 1 303 423-4141.
Email: daystar.denver@daystar.com
Profile: KRMT-TV is the Daystar network affiliate for the Denver market. The station is owned by Daystar Television Network. KRMT-TV broadcasts locally on channel 41.
TELEVISION STATION

KRNS-TV 417931

Owner: Entravision Communications Corp.
Editorial: 300 S Wells Ave Ste 12, Reno, Nevada 89502-1670 **Tel:** 1 775 333-1017.
Web site: http://www.cwreno.com
Profile: KRNS-TV is an Entravision Communications Corp. station for the Reno, NV area. KRNS-TV broadcasts locally on channel 46.
TELEVISION STATION

KRNV-TV 31419

Owner: Sinclair Broadcast Group, Inc.
Editorial: 1790 Vassar St, Reno, Nevada 89502-2721 **Tel:** 1 775 322-4444.
Email: assignmenteditors@krnv.com
Web site: http://www.mynews4.com
Profile: KRNV-TV is the NBC affiliate for the Reno, NV market. The station is owned by Sinclair Broadcast Group, Inc. KRNV-TV broadcasts locally on channel 4.
TELEVISION STATION

KRON3-TV 610937

Owner: New Young Broadcasting
Editorial: 900 Front St Fl 3, San Francisco, California 94111-1427 **Tel:** 1 415 441-4444.
Web site: http://www.kron4.com
Profile: KRON3-TV is a multicast of KRON-TV. A multicast channel is a separate channel that shares the bandwith of the main station but can air unique programming. KRON3-TV airs traffic maps and cameras to the San Francisco market. The station is owned by New Young Broadcasting. KRON3-TV broadcasts locally on channel 4.3.
TELEVISION STATION

KRON-TV 31593

Owner: Standard General Fund, L.P.
Editorial: 900 Front St Fl 3, San Francisco, California 94111-1427 **Tel:** 1 415 441-4444.
Email: assignmentdesk@kron.com
Web site: http://kron4.com
Profile: KRON-TV is a MyNetworkTV affiliate for the San Francisco market. The station is owned by Standard General Fund, L.P. KRON-TV broadcasts locally on channel 4.
TELEVISION STATION

KRQE-TV 31464

Owner: Nexstar Media Group, Inc.
Editorial: 13 Broadcast Plz SW, Albuquerque, New Mexico 87104-1056 **Tel:** 1 505 243-2285.
Email: newsdesk@krqe.com
Web site: http://www.krqe.com
Profile: KRQE-TV is the CBS affiliate for the Albuquerque, NM market. The station is owned by Nexstar Media Group, Inc. KRQE-TV broadcasts locally on channel 13.
TELEVISION STATION

KRTN2-TV 681847

Owner: Ramar Communications II Ltd.
Editorial: 2400 Monroe St NE, Albuquerque, New Mexico 87110-4063 **Tel:** 1 505 884-5353.
Web site: http://www.metvnetwork.com
Profile: KRTN2-TV is a multicast channel of KRTN-TV. A multicast channel is a separate channel that shares the bandwith of the main station but can air unique programming. KRTN2-TV is owned by Ramar Communications II Ltd. The station broadcasts on Channel 33.2 for the Albuquerque, NM market. KRTN2-TV airs KTEL-TV's programming. KTEL-TV is the local Telemundo affiliate in the Albuquerque, NM market.
TELEVISION STATION

KRTN-TV 681841

Owner: Ramar Communications II Ltd.
Editorial: 2400 Monroe St NE, Albuquerque, New Mexico 87110-4063 **Tel:** 1 505 884-5353.
Web site: http://www.metvnetwork.com
Profile: KRTN-TV is the Retro Television affiliate for the Albuquerque, NM market. The station is owned by Ramar Communications II Ltd. KRTN-TV broadcasts locally on channel 33.
TELEVISION STATION

KRTV-TV 31595

Owner: Cordillera Communications Inc.
Editorial: 3300 Old Havre Hwy, Black Eagle, Montana 59414-1079 **Tel:** 1 406 791-5400.
Email: krtvnews@krtv.com
Web site: http://www.krtv.com
Profile: KRTV-TV is the CBS affiliate for the Great Falls, MT market. The station is owned by Cordillera Communications Inc. KRTV-TV broadcasts locally on channel 3.
TELEVISION STATION

KRVU-TV 350067

Owner: Sainte Partners II, LP
Editorial: 300 Main St, Chico, California 95928-5438 **Tel:** 1 530 893-1234.
Email: info@fox30.com
Web site: http://www.krcrtv.com/station/about-our-stations/-/20902556/-/8rm377/-/
Profile: KRVU-TV is the MyNetwork TV affiliate for the Chico, CA - Redding, CA market. The station is owned by Sainte Partners II, LP. KRVU-TV broadcasts locally on channel 21.
TELEVISION STATION

KRWB-TV 539313

Owner: Tamer Media
Editorial: 13 Broadcast Plz SW, Albuquerque, New Mexico 87104-1056 **Tel:** 1 505 797-1919.
Web site: http://www.newmexicoscw.tv
TELEVISION STATION

KRXI-TV 32471

Owner: Sinclair Broadcast Group, Inc.
Editorial: 4920 Brookside Ct, Reno, Nevada 89502-4102 **Tel:** 1 775 856-1100.
Web site: http://www.foxreno.com
Profile: KRXI-TV is the FOX affiliate for the Reno, NV market. The station is owned by Sinclair Broadcast Group, Inc. KRXI-TV broadcasts locally on channel 11.
TELEVISION STATION

KSAA-TV 376453

Owner: Mako Communications, LLC
Editorial: 518 Peoples St, Corpus Christi, Texas 78401 **Tel:** 1 361 883-1763.
Profile: KSAA-TV is an independent station for the Corpus Christi, TX area. The station is owned by Mako Communications, LLC. KSAA-TV broadcasts locally on channel 28.
TELEVISION STATION

KSAN-TV 32753

Owner: Mission Broadcasting
Editorial: 2800 Armstrong St, San Angelo, Texas 76903-2755 **Tel:** 1 325 949-8800.
Email: klstnews@klst.net
Web site: http://conchovalleyhomepage.com
Profile: KSAN-TV is the NBC affiliate for the San Angelo, TX market. The station is owned by Mission Broadcasting. KSAN-TV broadcasts locally on channel 16.
TELEVISION STATION

KSAS-TV 32736

Owner: Sinclair Broadcast Group, Inc.
Editorial: 316 N West St, Wichita, Kansas 67203-1205 **Tel:** 1 316 942-2424.
Web site: http://www.foxkansas.com
Profile: KSAS-TV is the FOX affiliate for the Wichita-Hutchinson, KS market. The station is owned by Sinclair Broadcast Group, Inc. KSAS-TV broadcasts locally on channel 24. The station has no news department; news are produced by KSNW-TV.
TELEVISION STATION

KSAT2-TV 618374

Owner: Graham Media Group
Editorial: 1408 N Saint Marys St, San Antonio, Texas 78215-1739 **Tel:** 1 210 351-1200.
Email: news@ksat.com
Web site: http://www.ksat.com
Profile: KSAT2-TV is a multicast of KSAT-TV. A multicast channel is a separate channel that shares the bandwith of the main station but can air unique programming. KSAT2-TV airs programming from Me-TV in the San Antonio, TX market. The station is owned by Graham Media Group. KSAT2-TV broadcasts locally on channel 12.2.
TELEVISION STATION

KSAT3-TV 618377

Owner: Graham Media Group
Editorial: 1408 N Saint Marys St, San Antonio, Texas 78215-1739 **Tel:** 1 210 351-1200.
Email: news@ksat.com
Web site: http://www.ksat.com
Profile: KSAT3-TV is a multicast of KSAT-TV. A multicast channel is a separate channel that shares the bandwith of the main station but can air unique programming. KSAT3-TV airs programming from .2 Net in the San Antonio, TX market. The station is owned by Graham Media Group. KSAT3-TV broadcasts locally on channel 12.3.
TELEVISION STATION

KSAT-TV 31597

Owner: Graham Media Group
Editorial: 1408 N Saint Marys St, San Antonio, Texas 78215-1739 **Tel:** 1 210 351-1200.
Email: news@ksat.com
Web site: http://www.ksat.com
Profile: KSAT-TV is the ABC affiliate for the San Antonio, TX market. The station is owned byGraham Media Group. KSAT-TV broadcasts locally on channel 12.
TELEVISION STATION

KSAW-TV 376659

Owner: E.W. Scripps Co.
Editorial: 834 Falls Ave Ste 1180, Twin Falls, Idaho 83301-3364 **Tel:** 1 208 734-6022.
Email: news@todays6.com
Web site: http://www.kivitv.com/twin-falls
Profile: KSAW-TV is the ABC affiliate for the Twin Falls, ID market. The station is owned by E.W. Scripps Co. KSAW-TV broadcasts locally on channel 6.
TELEVISION STATION

KSAX-TV 32725

Owner: Hubbard Broadcasting Inc.
Editorial: 3415 University Ave W, Saint Paul, Minnesota 55114-1019 **Tel:** 1 651 646-5555.
Email: ksax@ksax.com
Web site: http://kstp.com
Profile: KSAX-TV is an ABC affiliate for the Alexandria market. The station is owned by Hubbard Broadcasting Inc. KSAX-TV broadcasts locally on channel 43 and features the programming of KSTP-TV.
TELEVISION STATION

KSAZ-TV 31641

Owner: Fox Broadcasting Company
Editorial: 511 W Adams St, Phoenix, Arizona 85003-1608 **Tel:** 1 602 257-1234.
Email: fox10.desk@foxtv.com
Web site: http://www.fox10phoenix.com
Profile: KSAZ-TV is the FOX affiliate for Phoenix market. The station is owned by Fox Broadcasting Company. KSAZ-TV broadcasts locally on channel 10. Station prefers PR professionals to pitch reporters directly by e-mail rather than using the news department e-mail.
TELEVISION STATION

KSBI2-TV 617313

Owner: Family Broadcasting Group, INC.
Editorial: 9802 N Morgan Rd, Yukon, Oklahoma 73099-1900 **Tel:** 1 405 470-0993.
Email: info@ksbitv.com
Web site: http://www.ksbitv.com
Profile: KSBI2-TV is a multicast of KSBI-TV. A multicast channel is a separate channel that shares the bandwith of the main station but can air unique programming. KSBI2-TV airs programming from KXOC-TV in the Oklahoma City market. The station is owned by Family Broadcasting Group, Inc. KSBI2-TV broadcasts locally on channel 52.2.
TELEVISION STATION

KSBI-TV 32318

Owner: Family Broadcasting Group, Inc.
Editorial: 9802 N Morgan Rd, Yukon, Oklahoma 73099-1900 **Tel:** 1 405 470-0993.
Web site: http://www.news9.com/category/290703/ksbi-tv
Profile: KSBI-TV is an independent station for the Oklahoma City market. The station is owned by Family Broadcasting Group, Inc. KSBI-TV broadcasts locally on channel 52. The station has no news department.
TELEVISION STATION

KSBW2-TV 748306

Owner: Hearst Television Inc.
Editorial: 238 John St, Salinas, California 93901-3339 **Tel:** 1 831 758-8888.
Web site: http://www.ksbw.com
Profile: KSBW2-TV, also called Central Coast ABC is a multicast channel of KSBW-TV. A multicast channel is a separate channel that shares the bandwidth of the main station but can air unique programming. KSBW2-TV is the ABC affiliate for the Monterey-Salinas, CA market. The station is owned by Hearst Television Inc. KSBW2-TV broadcasts locally on channel 8.2. The channel airs coverage of various live events and news.
TELEVISION STATION

KSBW-TV 31598

Owner: Hearst Television Inc.
Editorial: 238 John St, Salinas, California 93901-3339 **Tel:** 1 831 758-8888.
Email: news@ksbw.com
Web site: http://www.ksbw.com
Profile: KSBW-TV is an NBC affiliate for the Salinas, CA market. The station is owned by Hearst Television Inc. KSBW-TV broadcasts locally on channel 8.
TELEVISION STATION

KSBY-TV 31599

Owner: Cordillera Communications Inc.
Editorial: 1772 Calle Joaquin, San Luis Obispo, California 93405-7210 **Tel:** 1 805 541-6666.
Email: news@ksby.com
Web site: http://www.ksby.com
Profile: KSBY-TV is the NBC affiliate for the San Luis Obispo, CA market. The station is owned by Cordillera Communications Inc. KSBY-TV broadcasts locally on channel 6.
TELEVISION STATION

KSCE-TV 32389

Owner: Ch. 38 Christian Television
Tel: 1 915 532-8588.
Email: ksce@aol.com
Web site: http://www.kscetv.com
Profile: KSCE-TV is an independent station for the El Paso, TX market. The station is owned by Channel 38 Christian Television. KSCE-TV broadcasts locally on channel 38.
TELEVISION STATION

KSCI2-TV 607047

Owner: NRJ TV, LLC
Editorial: 1990 S Bundy Dr Ste 850, Los Angeles, California 90025-5253 **Tel:** 1 310 478-1818.
Email: news@kscitv.com
Web site: http://www.la18.tv
Profile: KSCI2-TV is a multicast channel of KSCI-TV. A multicast channel is a separate channel that shares the bandwith of the main station but can air unique programming. KSCI2-TV airs programming from the United Television Broadcasting for the Los Angeles market. The station is owned by NRJ TV, LLC. KSCI2-TV broadcasts locally on channel 18.2.
TELEVISION STATION

KSCI3-TV 607049

Owner: NRJ TV, LLC
Editorial: 1990 S Bundy Dr Ste 850, Los Angeles, California 90025-5253 **Tel:** 1 310 478-1818.
Email: info@1918.tv
Web site: http://www.la18.tv
Profile: KSCI3-TV is a multicast channel of KSCI-TV. A multicast channel is a separate channel that shares the bandwith of the main station but can air unique programming. KSCI3-TV airs Korean programming from MBC-D for the Los Angeles market. The station is owned by NRJ TV, LLC. KSCI3-TV broadcasts locally on channel 18.3.
TELEVISION STATION

KSCI4-TV 607054

Owner: NRJ TV, LLC
Editorial: 1990 S Bundy Dr Ste 850, Los Angeles, California 90025-5253 **Tel:** 1 310 478-1818.
Email: info@la18.tv
Web site: http://www.la18.tv
Profile: KSCI4-TV is a multicast channel of KSCI-TV. A multicast channel is a separate channel that shares the bandwith of the main station but can air unique programming. KSCI4-TV airs Korean programming from the Christian Global Network TV for the Los Angeles market. The station is owned by NRJ TV, LLC. KSCI4-TV broadcasts locally on channel 18.4.
TELEVISION STATION

KSCI5-TV 607057

Owner: NRJ TV, LLC
Editorial: 1990 S Bundy Dr Ste 850, Los Angeles, California 90025-5253 **Tel:** 1 310 478-1818.
Email: news@kscitv.com
Web site: http://www.la18.tv
Profile: KSCI5-TV is a multicast channel of KSCI-TV. A multicast channel is a separate channel that shares the bandwith of the main station but can air unique programming. KSCI5-TV airs Armenian programming from the USArmenian Network for the Los Angeles market. The station is owned by NRJ TV, LLC. KSCI5-TV broadcasts locally on channel 18.5.
TELEVISION STATION

KSCI7-TV 607058

Owner: NRJ TV, LLC
Editorial: 1990 S Bundy Dr Ste 850, Los Angeles, California 90025-5253 **Tel:** 1 310 478-1818.
Email: news@kscitv.com

Web site: http://www.la18.tv
Profile: KSCI7-TV is a multicast channel of KSCI-TV. A multicast channel is a separate channel that shares the bandwith of the main station but can air unique programming. KSCI7-TV airs Vietnamese programming from the Vietnamese American Network for the Los Angeles market. The station is owned by NRJ TV, LLC. KSCI7-TV broadcasts locally on channel 18.7.
TELEVISION STATION

KSCI8-TV 607060
Owner: NRJ TV, LLC
Editorial: 1990 S Bundy Dr Ste 850, Los Angeles, California 90025-5253 **Tel:** 1 310 478-1818.
Email: news@kscitv.com
Web site: http://www.la18.tv
Profile: KSCI8-TV is a multicast channel of KSCI-TV. A multicast channel is a separate channel that shares the bandwith of the main station but can air unique programming. KSCI8-TV airs Chinese programming from the main station for the Los Angeles market. The station is owned byNRJ TV, LLC. KSCI8-TV broadcasts locally on channel 18.8.
TELEVISION STATION

KSCI-TV 31601
Owner: NRJ TV, LLC
Editorial: 1990 S Bundy Dr Ste 850, Los Angeles, California 90025-5253 **Tel:** 1 310 478-1818.
Email: info@la18.tv
Web site: http://www.la18.tv
Profile: KSCI-TV is an independent station for the Los Angeles market. The station is owned by NRJ TV, LLC. KSCI-TV broadcasts locally on channel 18. News is featured in the following languages: Cantonese, Japanese, Korean, Mandarin, and Vietnamese.
TELEVISION STATION

KSCW-TV 63092
Owner: Schurz Communications Inc.
Editorial: 2815 E 37th St N, Wichita, Kansas 67219 **Tel:** 1 316 838-1212.
Web site: http://www.kansascw.com
Profile: KSCW-TV is the CW affiliate for the Wichita, KS market. The station is owned by Schurz Communications Inc. KSCW-TV broadcasts locally on channel 33.
TELEVISION STATION

KSDK2-TV 614575
Owner: TEGNA Inc.
Editorial: 1000 Market St, Saint Louis, Missouri 63101-2011 **Tel:** 1 314 421-5055.
Email: newstips@ksdk.com
Web site: http://www.bouncetv.com
Profile: KSDK2-TV is a multicast of KSDK-TV. A multicast channel is a separate channel that shares the bandwith of the main station but can air unique programming. KSDK2-TV airs programming from Bounce TV in the St. Louis market. The station is owned by TEGNA Inc. KSDK2-TV broadcasts locally on channel 5.2.
TELEVISION STATION

KSDK-TV 31602
Owner: TEGNA Inc.
Editorial: 1000 Market St, Saint Louis, Missouri 63101-2011 **Tel:** 1 314 421-5055.
Email: comments@ksdk.com
Web site: http://www.ksdk.com
Profile: KSDK-TV is the NBC network affiliate for the St. Louis market. The station is owned by TEGNA Inc. KSDK-TV broadcasts locally on channel 5.
TELEVISION STATION

KSDX-TV 438145
Owner: Liberman Broadcasting Inc.
Editorial: 1845 W Empire Ave, Burbank, California 91504-3402 **Tel:** 1 818 563-5722.
Email: info@lbimedia.com
Web site: http://www.estrella.tv
Profile: KSDX-TV is a satellite tower that simulcasts the programming of KCRA-TV, an independent station in Burbank, CA, specifically for the San Diego market. The station is owned by Liberman Broadcasting Inc. KSDX-TV broadcasts locally on channel 29.
TELEVISION STATION

KSDY3-TV 886699
Owner: Bereavision
Editorial: 12124 Ramona Blvd, El Monte, California 91732-2430
Web site: http://bereavision.tv
Profile: KSDY3-TV is a satellite station located in El Monte, California. It is owned by Bereavision. KSDY3-TV broadcasts locally on channel 50.3.
TELEVISION STATION

KSEE-TV 31603
Owner: Nexstar Broadcasting Group
Editorial: 5035 E McKinley Ave, Fresno, California 93727-1964 **Tel:** 1 559 222-2411.
Email: newsdesk@ksee.com
Web site: http://www.yourcentralvalley.com
Profile: KSEE-TV is the NBC affiliate for the Fresno-Visalia, CA market. The station is owned by Nexstar Broadcasting Group. KSEE-TV broadcasts locally on channel 24.
TELEVISION STATION

KSFY2-TV 822019
Owner: Hoak Media LLC
Tel: 1 605 336-7936.
Web site: http://www.ksfy.com
Profile: KSFY2-TV is a multicast channel of KSFY-TV. A multicast channel is a separate channel that shares the bandwith of the main station but can air unique programming. KSFY2-TV is the CW Network for the Sioux Falls, SD market. The station is owned by Hoak Media LLC. KSFY2-TV broadcasts locally on channel 13.2. This station will being to air September 12, 2012.
TELEVISION STATION

KSFY-TV 32656
Owner: Gray Television, Inc.
Editorial: 325 S 1st Ave Ste 100, Sioux Falls, South Dakota 57104-6494 **Tel:** 1 605 336-1300.
Email: news@ksfy.com
Web site: http://www.ksfy.com
Profile: KSFY-TV is the ABC affiliate for the Sioux Falls, SD market. The station is owned by Gray Television, Inc. KSFY-TV broadcasts locally on channel 13.
TELEVISION STATION

KSHB2-TV 620852
Owner: E.W. Scripps Co.
Editorial: 4720 Oak St, Kansas City, Missouri 64112-2236 **Tel:** 1 816 753-4141.
Email: news@nbcactionnews.com
Web site: http://www.actionnews.com
Profile: KSHB2-TV is a multicast of KSHB-TV. A multicast channel is a separate channel that shares the bandwith of the main station but can air unique programming. KSHB2-TV airs 24 hour weather programming from Action Weather Plus in the Kansas, MO market. The station is owned by E.W. Scripps Co. KSHB2-TV broadcasts locally on channel 41.2.
TELEVISION STATION

KSHB-TV 31604
Owner: Scripps Media, Inc.
Editorial: 4720 Oak St, Kansas City, Missouri 64112-2236 **Tel:** 1 816 753-4141.
Email: desk@kshb.com
Web site: http://www.kshb.com
Profile: KSHB-TV is the NBC affiliate for the Kansas City, MO market. The station is owned by Scripps Media, Inc. KSHB-TV broadcasts locally on channel 41.
TELEVISION STATION

KSHV-TV 32416
Owner: Nexstar Broadcasting Group
Editorial: 3519 Jewella Ave, Shreveport, Louisiana 71109-4419 **Tel:** 1 318 631-5677.
Email: info@kmsstv.com
Web site: http://www.kshv.com
Profile: KSHV-TV is the MyNetworkTV affiliate for the Shreveport, LA market. The station is owned by Nexstar Broadcasting Group. KSHV-TV broadcasts locally on channel 45.
TELEVISION STATION

KSKN-TV 32544
Owner: TEGNA Inc.
Editorial: 4103 S Regal St, Spokane, Washington 99223-7737 **Tel:** 1 509 448-2000.
Email: newsdesk@krem.com
Web site: http://www.krem.com/cwtv/
Profile: KSKN-TV is the CW affiliate for the Spokane market. The station is owned by TEGNA Inc. KSKN-TV broadcasts locally on channel 22.
TELEVISION STATION

KSL2-TV 621860
Owner: KSL Broadcasting
Editorial: Broadcast House, 55 North 300 West, Salt Lake City, Utah 84180 **Tel:** 1 801 575-5555.
Email: assignment.desk@ksl.com
Web site: http://www.ksl.com
Profile: KSL2-TV is a multicast channel of KSL-TV. A multicast is a separate channel that shares the bandwith of the main station but can air unique programming. KSL2-TV airs sports programming from Universal Sports in the Salt Lake City market. The station is owned by KSL Broadcasting. KSL2-TV broadcasts locally on channel 5.2.
TELEVISION STATION

KSL3-TV 621863
Owner: KSL Broadcasting
Editorial: Broadcast House, 55 North 300 West, Salt Lake City, Utah 84180 **Tel:** 1 801 575-5555.
Email: assignment.desk@ksl.com
Web site: http://www.ksl.com
Profile: KSL3-TV is a multicast channel of KSL-TV. A multicast is a separate channel that shares the bandwith of the main station but can air unique programming. KSL3-TV airs 24 hour weather programming from NBC Plus in the Salt Lake City market. The station is owned by KSL Broadcasting. KSL3-TV broadcasts locally on channel 5.3.
TELEVISION STATION

KSLA-TV 31606
Owner: Raycom Media Inc.
Editorial: 1812 Fairfield Ave, Shreveport, Louisiana 71101-4431 **Tel:** 1 318 222-1212.
Email: comments@ksla.com
Web site: http://www.ksla.com
Profile: KSLA-TV is the CBS affiliate for the Shreveport, LA, market. The station is owned by Raycom Media Inc. KSLA-TV broadcasts locally on channel 12.
TELEVISION STATION

KSL-TV 31605
Owner: KSL Broadcasting
Editorial: 55 N 300 W, Broadcast House, Salt Lake City, Utah 84101-3502 **Tel:** 1 801 575-5555.
Email: assignment.desk@ksl.com
Web site: http://www.ksl.com
Profile: KSL-TV is the NBC affiliate for the Salt Lake City market. The station is owned by KSL Broadcasting. KSL-TV broadcasts locally on channel 5.
TELEVISION STATION

KSMN2-TV 612591
Owner: Pioneer Public Television
Editorial: 120 W Schlieman Ave, Appleton, Minnesota 56208-1341 **Tel:** 1 800 726-3178.
Email: yourtv@pioneer.org
Web site: http://www.pioneer.org
Profile: KSMN2-TV is a multicast of KSMN-TV. A multicast channel is a separate channel that shares the bandwith of the main station but can air unique programming. KSMN2-TV airs programming from Create in the Appleton, MN market. The station is owned by Pioneer Public Television. KSMN2-TV broadcasts locally on channel 20.2.
TELEVISION STATION

KSMN3-TV 612592
Owner: Pioneer Public Television
Editorial: 120 W Schlieman Ave, Appleton, Minnesota 56208-1341 **Tel:** 1 800 726-3178.
Email: yourtv@pioneer.org
Web site: http://www.pioneer.org
Profile: KSMN3-TV is a multicast of KSMN-TV. A multicast channel is a separate channel that shares the bandwith of the main station but can air unique programming. KSMN3-TV airs programming from Pioneer MN in the Appleton, MN market. The station is owned by Pioneer Public Television. KSMN3-TV broadcasts locally on channel 20.3.
TELEVISION STATION

KSMN4-TV 612593
Owner: Pioneer Public Television
Editorial: 120 W Schlieman Ave, Appleton, Minnesota 56208-1341 **Tel:** 1 800 726-3178.
Email: yourtv@pioneer.org
Web site: http://www.pioneer.org
Profile: KSMN4-TV is a multicast of KSMN-TV. A multicast channel is a separate channel that shares the bandwith of the main station but can air unique programming. KSMN4-TV airs programming from Pioneer PTV in the Appleton, MN market. The station is owned by Pioneer Public Television. KSMN4-TV broadcasts locally on channel 20.4.
TELEVISION STATION

KSMN-TV 72048
Owner: Pioneer Public Television
Editorial: 120 W Schlieman Ave, Appleton, Minnesota 56208-1341 **Tel:** 1 320 289-2622.
Email: yourtv@pioneer.org
Web site: http://www.pioneer.org
Profile: KSMN-TV is the PBS affiliate for the Appleton, MN market. The station is owned by Pioneer Public Television. KSMN-TV broadcasts locally on channel 20.
TELEVISION STATION

KSMO2-TV 771491
Owner: Meredith Broadcasting Group
Editorial: 4500 Shawnee Mission Pkwy, Fairway, Kansas 66205-2509 **Tel:** 1 913 677-5555.
Web site: http://kctv5.com
Profile: KSMO2-TV is a multicast channel of KSMO-TV. A multicast channel is a separate channel that shares the bandwidth of the main station but can air unique programming. KSMO2-TV is the local Bounce TV affiliate on channel 62.2 for the Kansas City, MO market. KSMO2-TV is owned by Meredith Broadcasting Group.
TELEVISION STATION

KSMO-TV 31718
Owner: Meredith Broadcasting Group
Editorial: 4500 Shawnee Mission Pkwy, Fairway, Kansas 66205-2509 **Tel:** 1 913 677-5555.
Web site: http://www.kctv5.com
Profile: KSMO-TV is the local MyNetworkTV affiliate for the Kansas City, MO market. The station is owned by Meredith Broadcasting Group. KSMO-TV broadcasts locally on channel 62.
TELEVISION STATION

KSMQ-TV 31607
Owner: KSMQ Public Service Media, Inc.
Editorial: 2000 8th Ave NW, Austin, Minnesota 55912-1177 **Tel:** 1 507 481-2095.
Email: ksmq@ksmq.org
Web site: http://www.ksmq.org
Profile: KSMQ-TV is the PBS affiliate for the Rochester, MN-Mason City, IA area. The station is owned by KSMQ Public Service Media, Inc. KSMQ-TV broadcasts locally on channel 15.
TELEVISION STATION

KSMS-TV 32273
Owner: Entravision Communications Corp.
Editorial: 67 Garden Ct, Monterey, California 93940-5302 **Tel:** 1 831 373-6767.
Web site: http://www.ksmstv.com
Profile: KSMS-TV is the Univision affiliate for the Salinas, CA market. The station is owned by Entravision Communications Corporation. KSMS-TV broadcasts locally on channel 67.
TELEVISION STATION

KSNF-TV 31608
Owner: Nexstar Broadcasting Group
Editorial: 1502 S Cleveland Ave, Joplin, Missouri 64801-3569 **Tel:** 1 417 781-2345.
Web site: http://www.fourstateshomepage.com
Profile: KSNF-TV is the NBC affiliate for the Joplin, MO-Pittsburg, KS market. The station is owned by Nexstar Broadcasting Group. KSNF-TV broadcasts locally on channel 16.
TELEVISION STATION

KSNT-TV 31609
Owner: Nexstar Media Group, Inc.
Editorial: 6835 NW US Highway 24, Topeka, Kansas 66618-5507 **Tel:** 1 785 582-4000.
Email: news@ksnt.com
Web site: http://ksnt.com
Profile: KSNT-TV is the NBC network affiliate for the Topeka, KS market. The station is owned by Nexstar Media Group, Inc. KSNT-TV broadcasts locally on channel 27.
TELEVISION STATION

KSNV2-TV 620057
Owner: Sinclair Broadcast Group, Inc.
Editorial: 1500 Foremaster Ln, Las Vegas, Nevada 89101-1103 **Tel:** 1 702 642-3333.
Email: news@news3lv.com
Web site: http://www.news3lv.com
Profile: KSNV2-TV is a multicast of KSNV-TV. A multicast channel is a separate channel that shares the bandwith of the main station but can air unique programming. KSNV2-TV airs outdoor sports programming from the Untamed Sports Network to the Las Vegas market. The station is owned by Sinclair Broadcast Group, Inc. KSNV2-TV broadcasts locally on channel 3.2.
TELEVISION STATION

KSNV3-TV 620058
Owner: Sinclair Broadcast Group, Inc.
Editorial: 1500 Foremaster Ln, Las Vegas, Nevada 89101-1103 **Tel:** 1 702 642-3333.
Email: news@news3lv.com
Web site: http://www.news3lv.com
Profile: KSNV3-TV is a multicast of KSNV-TV. A multicast channel is a separate channel that shares the bandwith of the main station but can air unique programming. KSNV3-TV airs all AntennaTV to the Las Vegas market. The station is owned by Sinclair Broadcast Group, Inc. KSNV-TV broadcasts locally on channel 3.3.
TELEVISION STATION

KSNV-TV 31682
Owner: Sinclair Broadcast Group, Inc.
Editorial: 1500 Foremaster Ln, Las Vegas, Nevada 89101-1103 **Tel:** 1 702 657-3150.
Email: news@news3lv.com
Web site: http://www.news3lv.com
Profile: KSNV-TV is the NBC affiliate for the Las Vegas market. The station is owned by Sinclair Broadcast Group, Inc. KSNV-TV broadcasts locally on channel 3.
TELEVISION STATION

KSNW-TV 32697
Owner: Nexstar Media Group, Inc.
Editorial: 833 N Main St, Wichita, Kansas 67203-3606 **Tel:** 1 316 265-3333.
Email: news@ksn.com
Web site: http://www.ksn.com
Profile: KSNW-TV is the NBC network affiliate for the Wichita-Hutchinson, KS market. The station is owned by Nexstar Media Group, Inc. KSWN-TV broadcasts locally on channel 3.
TELEVISION STATION

KSPK-TV 331203
Owner: Mainstreet Broadcasting Company Inc.
Editorial: 516 Main St, Walsenburg, Colorado 81089-2036 **Tel:** 1 719 738-3636.
Email: info@kspk.com
Web site: http://www.kspk.com
Profile: KSPK-TV is an independent station for the Colorado Springs, CO market. It is owned by Mainstreet Broadcasting Company Inc. KSPK-TV broadcasts locally on channel 28.
TELEVISION STATION

KSPR-TV 31610
Owner: Piedmont Television Holdings, LLC
Editorial: 999 W Sunshine St, Springfield, Missouri 65807-2443 **Tel:** 1 417 831-1333.
Email: news@kspr.com
Web site: http://www.kspr.com
Profile: KSPR-TV is the ABC network affiliate for the Springfield, MO market. The station is owned by Piedmont Television Holdings, LLC. KSPR-TV broadcasts locally on channel 33.
TELEVISION STATION

KSPS-TV 31611
Owner: Friends of KSPS
Editorial: 3911 S Regal St, Spokane, Washington 99223-7721 **Tel:** 1 509 354-7800.
Email: ksps@ksps.org
Web site: http://www.ksps.org
Profile: KSPS-TV is the PBS affiliate for the Spokane, WA market. The station is owned by Friends of KSPS. KSPS-TV broadcasts locally on channel 7.
TELEVISION STATION

KSPX2-TV 613314
Owner: ION Media Networks
Editorial: 3352 Mather Field Rd, Rancho Cordova, California 95670-5966 **Tel:** 1 916 368-2929.
Web site: http://www.qubo.com
Profile: KSPX2-TV is independent affiliate for the Sacramento, CA market. The station is owned by ION Media Networks. KSPX2-TV broadcasts locally on channel 29.2. The station airs children's programming from the qubo network. KSPX2-TV is a multicast channel of KSPX-TV. A multicast channel is a

separate channel that shares the bandwidth of the main station but can air unique programming.
TELEVISION STATION

KSPX3-TV 613324
Owner: ION Media Networks
Editorial: 3352 Mather Field Rd, Rancho Cordova, California 95670-5966 **Tel:** 1 916 368-2929.
Web site: http://www.ionlife.com
Profile: KSPX3-TV is an ION Television affiliate for the Sacramento, CA market. The station is owned by ION Media Networks. KSPX3-TV broadcasts locally on channel 29.3. The station airs lifestyle programming. KSPX3-TV is a multicast channel of KSPX-TV. A multicast channel is a separate channel that shares the bandwidth of the main station but can air unique programming.
TELEVISION STATION

KSPX-TV 32421
Owner: ION Media Networks
Editorial: 3352 Mather Field Rd, Rancho Cordova, California 95670-5966 **Tel:** 1 916 368-2929.
Profile: KSPX-TV is the ION Television affiliate for the Sacramento, CA market. The station is owned by ION Media Networks. KSPX-TV broadcasts locally on channel 29.
TELEVISION STATION

KSRW-TV 73302
Owner: Kessler(Benett)
Editorial: 1280 N Main St, Bishop, California 93514-2473 **Tel:** 1 760 873-5329.
Web site: http://www.sierrawave.net
Profile: KSRW-TV is an independent station for the Los Angeles market. The station is owned by Benett Kessler. KSRW-TV broadcasts locally on channel 33.
TELEVISION STATION

KSST-TV 135304
Owner: Hopkins County Broadcasting
Editorial: 717 E Shannon Rd, Sulphur Springs, Texas 75482 **Tel:** 1 903 885-3111.
Web site: http://www.ksstradio.com
Profile: KSST-TV is an independent station for the Dallas-Fort Worth, TX market. The station is owned by Hopkins County Broadcasting. KSST-TV broadcasts locally on channel 18.
TELEVISION STATION

KSTC-TV 32515
Owner: Hubbard Broadcasting Inc.
Editorial: 3415 University Ave W, Saint Paul, Minnesota 55114-2099 **Tel:** 1 651 645-4500.
Email: newstips@kstp.com
Web site: http://www.kstc45.com
Profile: KSTC-TV is an independent station for the Minneapolis-St. Paul market. The station is owned by Hubbard Broadcasting Inc. KSTC-TV broadcasts locally on channel 45.
TELEVISION STATION

KSTP2-TV 612169
Owner: Hubbard Broadcasting Inc.
Editorial: 3415 University Ave W, Saint Paul, Minnesota 55114-1019 **Tel:** 1 651 646-5555.
Email: newsreply@kstp.com
Web site: http://www.kstp.com
Profile: KSTP2-TV is a multicast of KSTP-TV. A multicast channel is a separate channel that shares the bandwith of the main station but can air unique programming. KSTP2-TV is the Live Well Network in the Minneapolis market. The station is owned by Hubbard Broadcasting Inc. KSTP2-TV broadcasts locally on channel 5.2.
TELEVISION STATION

KSTP3-TV 772903
Owner: Hubbard Broadcasting Inc.
Editorial: 3415 University Ave W, Saint Paul, Minnesota 55114-1019 **Tel:** 1 651 646-5555.
Email: newsreply@kstp.com
Web site: http://www.kstp.com
Profile: KSTP3-TV is a multicast channel of KSTP-TV. A multicast channel is a separate channel that shares the bandwith of the main station but can air unique programming. KSTP3-TV is the Me-TV Network for the Saint Paul, Minneapolis market. The station is owned by Hubbard Broadcasting Inc. KSTP3-TV broadcasts locally on channel 5.3.
TELEVISION STATION

KSTP-TV 31612
Owner: Hubbard Broadcasting Inc.
Editorial: 3415 University Ave W, Saint Paul, Minnesota 55114-1019 **Tel:** 1 651 646-5555.
Email: tips@kstp.com
Web site: http://www.kstp.com
Profile: KSTP-TV is the ABC affiliate for the Minneapolis-St. Paul market. It is owned by Hubbard Broadcasting Inc. KSTP-TV broadcasts locally on channel 5.
TELEVISION STATION

KSTR-TV 32387
Owner: Univision Communications Inc.
Editorial: 2323 Bryan St Ste 1900, Dallas, Texas 75201-2646 **Tel:** 1 214 758-2300.
Web site: http://www.univision.com/dallas/kuvn
Profile: KSTR-TV is the Telefutura affiliate for the Dallas-Fort Worth market. The station is owned by Univision Communications Inc. KSTR-TV broadcasts locally on channel 48.
TELEVISION STATION

KSTS-TV 31613
Owner: NBC Universal
Editorial: 2450 N 1st St, San Jose, California 95131-1002 **Tel:** 1 408 944-4848.
Web site: http://www.telemundoareadelabahia.com
Profile: KSTS-TV is the Telemundo affiliate for the California Bay Area market. The station is owned by NBC Universal. KSTS broadcasts locally on channel 48.
TELEVISION STATION

KSTU-TV 31614
Owner: Tribune Broadcasting Co.
Editorial: 5020 W Amelia Earhart Dr, Salt Lake City, Utah 84116-2853 **Tel:** 1 801 532-1300.
Email: news@fox13now.com
Web site: http://www.fox13now.com
Profile: KSTU-TV is the FOX affiliate for the Salt Lake City market. The station is owned by Tribune Broadcasting Co. KSTU-TV broadcasts locally on channel 13.
TELEVISION STATION

KSTW-TV 31615
Owner: CBS Television Stations
Editorial: 1000 Dexter Ave N, STE 205, Seattle, Washington 98109-3582 **Tel:** 1 206 441-1111.
Email: cw11@kstwtv.com
Web site: http://cwseattle.cbslocal.com
Profile: KSTW-TV is the CW affiliate for the Seattle-Tacoma, WA market. The station is owned by CBS Television Stations. KSTW-TV broadcasts locally on channel 11. The station does not accept press releases, and it has no news department.
TELEVISION STATION

KSVI-TV 32693
Owner: Nexstar Broadcasting Group
Editorial: 445 S 24th St W, Billings, Montana 59102-6201 **Tel:** 1 406 652-4743.
Web site: http://www.yourbigsky.com
Profile: KSVI-TV is the ABC affiliate station for the Billings, MT, market. The station is owned by Nexstar Broadcasting Group. KSVI-TV broadcasts locally on channel 6. KSVI-TV shares a staff with sister station KHMT-TV.
TELEVISION STATION

KSVN-TV 476734
Owner: Azteca Broadcasting Corp.
Web site: http://ksvn.tv/
Profile: KSVN-TV is the Azteca America affiliate for the Ogden, UT market. The station is owned by Azteca Broadcasting Corp. KSVN-TV broadcasts locally on channel 49.
TELEVISION STATION

KSWB-TV 31644
Owner: Tribune Broadcasting Co.
Editorial: 7191 Engineer Rd, San Diego, California 92111-1406 **Tel:** 1 858 492-9269.
Email: news@fox5sandiego.com
Web site: http://www.fox5sandiego.com
Profile: KSWB-TV is the FOX affiliate in the San Diego market. The station is owned by Tribune Broadcasting Co. KSWB-TV broadcasts locally on channel 69.
TELEVISION STATION

KSWO-TV 31616
Owner: Raycom Media Inc.
Editorial: 1401 SE 60th St, Lawton, Oklahoma 73501-5076 **Tel:** 1 580 355-7000.
Email: news@kswo.com
Web site: http://www.kswo.com
Profile: KSWO-TV is the ABC network affiliate for the Wichita Falls, TX-Lawton, OK market. The station is owned by Raycom Media Inc. KSWO-TV broadcasts locally on channel 7.
TELEVISION STATION

KSWT2-TV 716777
Owner: Pappas Telecasting Companies
Editorial: 1301 S 3rd Ave, Yuma, Arizona 85364-3663 **Tel:** 1 928 782-5113.
Email: news@kecytv.com
Web site: http://www.kswt.com
Profile: KSWT2-TV is multichannel channel of KSWT-TV. A multicast channel is a separate channel that shares the bandwidth of the main station but can air unique programming.
TELEVISION STATION

KSWT-TV 31712
Owner: Pappas Telecasting Companies
Editorial: 1965 S 4th Ave, Yuma, Arizona 85364-5666 **Tel:** 1 928 782-5113.
Email: news@kecytv.com
Web site: http://www.kswt.com
Profile: KSWT-TV is the CBS affiliate for the Yuma, AZ/El Centro, CA market. The station is owned by Pappas Telecasting Companies. KSWT-TV broadcasts locally on channel 13.
TELEVISION STATION

KSYS-TV 32706
Owner: Southern Oregon Public TV Inc.
Editorial: 28 S Fir St Ste 200, Medford, Oregon 97501-2698 **Tel:** 1 541 779-0808.
Email: info@soptv.org
Web site: http://www.soptv.org
Profile: KSYS-TV is the PBS station for the Medford, OR market. The station is owned by Southern Oregon Public TV Inc. KSYS-TV broadcasts locally on channel 8. The station does not accept Public Service Announcements or Community Event Submissions.
TELEVISION STATION

KTAB-TV 31617
Owner: Nexstar Broadcasting Group
Editorial: 4510 S 14th St, Abilene, Texas 79605-4737 **Tel:** 1 325 695-2777.
Email: news@ktab.tv
Web site: http://bigcountryhomepage.com
Profile: KTAB-TV is the CBS network affiliate for the Abilene-Sweetwater, TX market. The station is owned by Nexstar Broadcasting Group. KTAB-TV broadcasts locally on channel 32.
TELEVISION STATION

KTAJ-TV 32278
Owner: Trinity Broadcasting Network
Editorial: 9670 N Seymour Ave, Kansas City, Missouri 64153-1869 **Tel:** 1 286 4640.
Email: ktaj@tbn.org
Web site: https://www.tbn.org/content/ktaj-tv-kansascity-mo
Profile: KTAJ-TV is a Trinity Broadcasting Network affiliate for the Saint Joseph, MO market. The station is owned by Trinity Broadcasting Network. KTAJ-TV broadcasts locally on channel 16.
TELEVISION STATION

KTAL-TV 31618
Owner: Nexstar Broadcasting Group
Editorial: 3150 N Market St, Shreveport, Louisiana 71107-4005 **Tel:** 1 318 629-6000.
Email: ktal@ktalnews.tv
Web site: http://arklatexhomepage.com
Profile: KTAL-TV is the NBC affiliate for the Shreveport, LA, market. The station is owned by Nexstar Broadcasting Group. KTAL-TV broadcasts locally on channel 6.
TELEVISION STATION

KTAN-TV 426638
Owner: KTN Media
Editorial: 4525 Wilshire Blvd, Los Angeles, California 90010-3837 **Tel:** 1 323 964-0101.
Profile: KTAN-TV is an independent station for the Los Angeles market. The station is owned by KTN Media. KTAN-TV broadcasts locally on channel 57.3.
TELEVISION STATION

KTAS-TV 32414
Owner: R & C Enterprises
Editorial: 330 Carmen Ln, Santa Maria, California 93458-7702 **Tel:** 1 805 928-7700.
Email: ktastv@fix.net
Profile: KTAS-TV is the Telemundo affiliate for the Santa Barbara, CA market. The station is owned by R & C Enterprises. KTAS-TV broadcasts locally on channel 33.
TELEVISION STATION

KTAZ-TV 32412
Owner: NBC Universal
Editorial: 4625 S 33rd Pl, Phoenix, Arizona 85040-2861 **Tel:** 1 602 648-3901.
Email: telemundoarizona@nbcuni.com
Web site: http://www.telemundoarizona.com
Profile: KTAZ-TV is the Telemundo affiliate for the Phoenix market. The station is owned by NBC Universal. KTAZ-TV broadcasts locally on channel 39.
TELEVISION STATION

KTBC-TV 31619
Owner: Fox Broadcasting Company
Editorial: 119 E 10th St, Austin, Texas 78701-2419 **Tel:** 1 512 476-7777.
Email: news@fox7.com
Web site: http://www.fox7austin.com
Profile: KTBC-TV is the FOX affiliate for the Austin, TX market. The station is owned by Fox Broadcasting Company. KTBC-TV broadcasts locally on channel 7.
TELEVISION STATION

KTBN2-TV 606478
Owner: Trinity Broadcasting Network
Editorial: 2442 Michelle Dr, Tustin, California 92780-7015 **Tel:** 1 714 832-2950.
Web site: http://www.thechurchchannel.org
Profile: KTBN2-TV is an affiliate of The Church Channel Network in the Los Angeles market. The station is owned by the Trinity Broadcasting Network. KTBN-TV broadcasts locally on channel 40.2. The channel broadcasts church service programs 24 hours per day, seven days a week from several of America's leading churches. KTBN2-TV is a multicast channel of KTBN-TV. A multicast channel is a separate channel that shares the bandwidth of the main station but can air unique programming.
TELEVISION STATION

KTBN3-TV 606481
Owner: Trinity Broadcasting Network
Editorial: 2442 Michelle Dr, Tustin, California 92780-7015 **Tel:** 1 714 832-2950.
Web site: http://www.jctv.org
Profile: KTBN3-TV is the local affiliate of JCTV Network in the Los Angeles market. The station is owned by the Trinity Broadcasting Network. KTBN-TV broadcasts locally on channel 40.3. KTBN3-TV airs a variety of religious and Christian music related programming and videos geared towards young adults. KTBN3-TV is a multicast channel of KTBN-TV. A multicast channel is a separate channel that shares the bandwidth of the main station but can air unique programming.
TELEVISION STATION

KTBN4-TV 606485
Owner: Trinity Broadcasting Network
Editorial: 2442 Michelle Dr, Tustin, California 92780-7015 **Tel:** 1 714 832-2950.
Web site: http://www.tbnenlaceusa.com/espanol/
Profile: KTBN4-TV is local affiliate of Enlace USA Network on Channel 40.4 for the Los Angeles, CA market. The channel airs programming from the United States version of the Spanish-language cable television network, providing Christian programming to the Hispanic community. No news is produced by the station. KTBN4-TV is owned by Trinity Broadcasting Network. KTBN4-TV is a multicast channel of KTBN-TV. A multicast channel is a separate channel that shares the bandwidth of the main station but can air unique programming.
TELEVISION STATION

KTBN5-TV 606495
Owner: Trinity Broadcasting Network
Editorial: 2442 Michelle Dr, Tustin, California 92780-7015 **Tel:** 1 714 832-2950.
Web site: http://www.smileofachildtv.org
Profile: KTBN5-TV is local affiliate of Smile of a Child TV on Channel 40.5 for the Los Angeles, CA market. The channel airs children's Christian programming. No news is produced by the station. KTBN5-TV is owned by Trinity Broadcasting Network. KTBN5-TV is a multicast channel of KTBN-TV. A multicast channel is a separate channel that shares the bandwidth of the main station but can air unique programming.
TELEVISION STATION

KTBN-TV 31620
Owner: Trinity Broadcasting Network
Editorial: 2442 Michelle Dr, Tustin, California 92780 **Tel:** 1 714 832-2950.
Email: comments@tbn.org
Web site: http://www.tbn.org
Profile: KTBN-TV is an affiliate of Trinity Broadcast Network in the Los Angeles market. The station is owned by the Trinity Broadcasting Network. KTBN-TV broadcasts locally on channel 40.
TELEVISION STATION

KTBO2-TV 620269
Owner: Trinity Broadcasting Network
Editorial: 1600 E Hefner Rd, Oklahoma City, Oklahoma 73131-1610 **Tel:** 1 405 848-1414.
Email: ktbo@tbn.org
Web site: http://www.tbn.org
Profile: KTBO2-TV is a multicast of KTBO-TV. A multicast channel is a separate channel that shares the bandwith of the main station but can air unique programming. KTBO2-TV airs Christian programming from The Church Channel in the Oklahoma City market. The station is owned by Trinity Broadcasting Network. KTBO2-TV broadcasts locally on channel 14.2.
TELEVISION STATION

KTBO3-TV 620272
Owner: Trinity Broadcasting Network
Editorial: 1600 E Hefner Rd, Oklahoma City, Oklahoma 73131-1610 **Tel:** 1 405 848-1414.
Email: ktbo@tbn.org
Profile: KTBO3-TV is a multicast of KTBO-TV. A multicast channel is a separate channel that shares the bandwith of the main station but can air unique programming. KTBO3-TV airs Christian music videos from JCTV in the Oklahoma City market. The station is owned by Trinity Broadcasting Network. KTBO3-TV broadcasts locally on channel 14.3.
TELEVISION STATION

KTBO4-TV 620275
Owner: Trinity Broadcasting Network
Editorial: 1600 E Hefner Rd, Oklahoma City, Oklahoma 73131-1610 **Tel:** 1 405 848-1414.
Email: ktbo@tbn.org
Profile: KTBO4-TV is a multicast of KTBO-TV. A multicast channel is a separate channel that shares the bandwith of the main station but can air unique programming. KTBO4-TV airs Hispanic Christian programming from Enlace USA in the Oklahoma City market. The station is owned by Trinity Broadcasting Network. KTBO4-TV broadcasts locally on channel 14.4.
TELEVISION STATION

KTBO5-TV 620278
Owner: Trinity Broadcasting Network
Editorial: 1600 E Hefner Rd, Oklahoma City, Oklahoma 73131-1610 **Tel:** 1 405 848-1414.
Email: ktbo@tbn.org
Profile: KTBO5-TV is a multicast of KTBO-TV. A multicast channel is a separate channel that shares the bandwith of the main station but can air unique programming. KTBO5-TV airs children's Christian programming from Smile of a Child in the Oklahoma City market. The station is owned by Trinity Broadcasting Network. KTBO5-TV broadcasts locally on channel 14.5.
TELEVISION STATION

KTBO-TV 31621
Owner: Trinity Broadcasting Network
Editorial: 1600 E Hefner Rd, Oklahoma City, Oklahoma 73131-1610 **Tel:** 1 405 848-1414.
Email: ktbo@tbn.org
Web site: http://www.tbn.org
Profile: KTBO-TV is the local TBN affiliate for Oklahoma City. Broadcast locally on Channel 14, the station airs various TBN programs, as well as two original shows: "Joy in Our Town," a public affairs program and "Praise the Lord," a ministry program. Contact can be made by phone or mail.
TELEVISION STATION

KTBS-TV 31622
Owner: KTBS Inc.
Editorial: 312 E Kings Hwy, Shreveport, Louisiana 71104-3504 **Tel:** 1 318 861-5880.
Email: pressreleases@ktbs.com
Web site: http://www.ktbs.com

Profile: KTBS-TV is the ABC affiliate for the Shreveport, LA, market. The station is owned by KTBS Inc. KTBS-TV broadcasts locally on channel 3.
TELEVISION STATION

KTBU-TV 32563
Owner: Spanish Broadcasting System
Editorial: 7026 Old Katy Rd Ste 254, Houston, Texas 77024-2186 **Tel:** 1 713 351-0755.
Profile: KTBU-TV is an independent station for the Houston market. The station is owned by Spanish Broadcasting System. KTBU-TV broadcasts locally on channel 55.
TELEVISION STATION

KTBW2-TV 612765
Owner: Trinity Broadcasting Network
Editorial: 1909 S 341st Pl, Federal Way, Washington 98003-6006 **Tel:** 1 253 927-7720.
Email: ktbw@tbn.org
Web site: http://www.tbn.org/publicfile/ktbw
Profile: KTBW2-TV is a multicast of KTBW-TV. A multicast channel is a separate channel that shares the bandwith of the main station but can air unique programming. KTBW2-TV airs programming from The Church Channel in the Tacoma, WA market. The station is owned by Trinity Broadcasting Network. KTBW2-TV broadcasts locally on channel 20.2.
TELEVISION STATION

KTBW3-TV 612767
Owner: Trinity Broadcasting Network
Editorial: 1909 S 341st Pl, Federal Way, Washington 98003-6006 **Tel:** 1 253 927-7720.
Email: ktbw@tbn.org
Web site: http://www.tbn.org/publicfile/ktbw
Profile: KTBW3-TV is a multicast of KTBW-TV. A multicast channel is a separate channel that shares the bandwith of the main station but can air unique programming. KTBW3-TV airs programming from JCTV in the Tacoma, WA market. The station is owned by Trinity Broadcasting Network. KTBW3-TV broadcasts locally on channel 20.3.
TELEVISION STATION

KTBW4-TV 612770
Owner: Trinity Broadcasting Network
Editorial: 1909 S 341st Pl, Federal Way, Washington 98003-6006 **Tel:** 1 253 927-7720.
Email: ktbw@tbn.org
Web site: http://www.tbn.org/publicfile/ktbw
Profile: KTBW4-TV is a multicast of KTBW-TV. A multicast channel is a separate channel that shares the bandwith of the main station but can air unique programming. KTBW4-TV airs programming from Enlace USA in the Tacoma, WA market. The station is owned by Trinity Broadcasting Network. KTBW4-TV broadcasts locally on channel 20.4.
TELEVISION STATION

KTBW5-TV 612773
Owner: Trinity Broadcasting Network
Editorial: 1909 S 341st Pl, Federal Way, Washington 98003-6006 **Tel:** 1 253 927-7720.
Email: ktbw@tbn.org
Web site: http://www.tbn.org/publicfile/ktbw
Profile: KTBW5-TV is a multicast of KTBW-TV. A multicast channel is a separate channel that shares the bandwith of the main station but can air unique programming. KTBW5-TV airs programming from Smile of a Child in the Tacoma, WA market. The station is owned by Trinity Broadcasting Network. KTBW5-TV broadcasts locally on channel 20.5.
TELEVISION STATION

KTBW-TV 32281
Owner: Trinity Broadcasting Network
Editorial: 1909 S 341st Pl, Federal Way, Washington 98003-6006 **Tel:** 1 253 927-7720.
Email: ktbw@tbn.org
Web site: http://tbn.org
Profile: KTBW-TV is the Trinity Broadcasting Network affiliate for the Tacoma, WA market. The station is owned by Trinity Broadcasting Network. KTBW-TV broadcasts locally on channel 20.
TELEVISION STATION

KTBY-TV 31623
Owner: Coastal Television Broadcasting Company, LLC
Editorial: 2700 E Tudor Rd, Anchorage, Alaska 99507-1136 **Tel:** 1 907 274-0404.
Web site: http://www.youralaskalink.com
Profile: KTBY-TV is the FOX affiliate for the Anchorage, AK market. The station is owned by Coastal Television Broadcasting Company, LLC. KTBY-TV broadcasts locally on channel 4.
TELEVISION STATION

KTCA2-TV 612775
Owner: Twin Cities Public Television
Editorial: 172 4th St E, Saint Paul, Minnesota 55101-1447 **Tel:** 1 651 222-1717.
Email: viewerservices@tpt.org
Web site: http://www.tpt.org
Profile: KTCA2-TV is a multicast of KTCA-TV. A multicast channel is a separate channel that shares the bandwith of the main station but can air unique programming. KTCA2-TV airs programming from tptMN in the Minneapolis market. The station is owned by Twin Cities Public Television. KTCA2-TV broadcasts locally on channel 2.2.
TELEVISION STATION

KTCA3-TV 612777
Owner: Twin Cities Public Television
Editorial: 172 4th St E, Saint Paul, Minnesota 55101-1492 **Tel:** 1 651 222-1717.
Email: viewerservices@tpt.org
Web site: http://www.tpt.org
Profile: KTCA3-TV is a multicast of KTCA-TV. A multicast channel is a separate channel that shares the bandwith of the main station but can air unique programming. KTCA3-TV airs programming from tptLife in the Minneapolis market. The station is owned by Twin Cities Public Television. KTCA3-TV broadcasts locally on channel 2.3.
TELEVISION STATION

KTCA4-TV 612780
Owner: Twin Cities Public Television
Editorial: 172 4th St E, Saint Paul, Minnesota 55101-1447 **Tel:** 1 651 222-1717.
Email: viewerservices@tpt.org
Web site: http://www.tpt.org
Profile: KTCA4-TV is a multicast of KTCA-TV. A multicast channel is a separate channel that shares the bandwith of the main station but can air unique programming. KTCA4-TV airs programming from tptWX in the Minneapolis market. The station is owned by Twin Cities Public Television. KTCA4-TV broadcasts locally on channel 2.4.
TELEVISION STATION

KTCA-TV 31624
Owner: Twin Cities Public Television
Editorial: 172 4th St E, Saint Paul, Minnesota 55101
Tel: 1 651 222-1717.
Email: viewerservices@tpt.org
Web site: http://www.tpt.org
Profile: KTCA-TV is the PBS affiliate for the Saint Paul, MN market. The station is owned by Twin Cities Public Television. KTCA-TV broadcasts locally on channel 2.
TELEVISION STATION

KTDO-TV 235151
Owner: ZGS Communications
Editorial: 10033 Carnegie Ave, El Paso, Texas 79925-1505 **Tel:** 1 915 591-9595.
Email: telenoticiaselpaso@holaciudad.com
Web site: http://www.holaciudad.com/el_paso/telemundo/
Profile: KTDO-TV is the Telemundo affiliate for the El Paso, TX market. The station is owned by ZGS Communications. KTDO-TV broadcasts locally on channel 48.
TELEVISION STATION

KTEL-TV 153572
Owner: Ramar Broadcasting
Editorial: 2400 Monroe St NE, Albuquerque, New Mexico 87110-4063 **Tel:** 1 806 745-3434.
Web site: http://www.telemundonewmexico.com
Profile: KTEL-TV is the Telemundo affiliate for the Albuquerque, NM market. The station is owned by Ramar Broadcasting. KTEL-TV broadcasts locally on channel 47.
TELEVISION STATION

KTEN2-TV 682502
Owner: Channel 49 Acquisition Corporation
Editorial: 10 High Point Cir, Denison, Texas 75020-1258 **Tel:** 1 903 337-4000.
Email: newsteam@kten.com
Web site: http://www.kten.com
Profile: KTEN2-TV is a multicast channel of KTEN-TV. A multicast channel is a separate channel that shares the bandwidth of the main station but can air unique programming. KTEN2-TV is the local CW affiliate on Channel 10.2 for the Sherman, TX market. KTEN2-TV is owned by Channel 49 Acquisition Corporation.
TELEVISION STATION

KTEN3-TV 682510
Owner: Channel 49 Acquisition Corporation
Editorial: 10 High Point Cir, Denison, Texas 75020-1258 **Tel:** 1 903 337-4000.
Email: newsteam@kten.com
Web site: http://www.kten.com
Profile: KTEN3-TV is a multicast channel of KTEN-TV. A multicast channel is a separate channel that shares the bandwidth of the main station but can air unique programming. KTEN3-TV is the local ABC affiliate on Channel 10.3 for the Sherman, TX market. KTEN3-TV is owned by Channel 49 Acquisition Corporation.
TELEVISION STATION

KTEN-TV 31626
Owner: Lockwood Broadcasting Group
Editorial: 10 High Point Cir, Denison, Texas 75020-1258 **Tel:** 1 903 337-4000.
Email: newsteam@kten.com
Web site: http://www.kten.com
Profile: KTEN-TV is the NBC network affiliate for the Sherman, TX, Ada, OK market. The station is owned by Channel 49 Acquisition Corporation. KTEN-TV broadcasts locally on channel 10.
TELEVISION STATION

KTFD-TV 133887
Owner: Entravision Communications Corp.
Editorial: 1907 Mile High Stadium West Cir, Denver, Colorado 80204-1908 **Tel:** 1 303 832-0050.
Profile: KTFD-TV is the Telefutura and Univision affiliate for the Denver, CO market. The station is owned by Entravision Communications Corp. KTFD-TV broadcasts locally on channel 10.
TELEVISION STATION

KTFF-TV 135301
Owner: Univision Communications Inc.
Editorial: 601 W Univision Plz, Fresno, California 93704-1092 **Tel:** 1 559 222-2121.
Email: kftvnews@univision.net
Web site: http://www.univision.net
Profile: KTFF-TV is a Telefutura affiliate for the Fresno, CA market. The station is owned by Univision Communications. KTFF-TV broadcasts locally on channel 61.
TELEVISION STATION

KTFK-TV 418230
Owner: Univision Communications Inc.
Editorial: 1710 Arden Way, Sacramento, California 95815-5008 **Tel:** 1 916 927-1900.
Web site: http://www.tv.univision.com/unimas
Profile: KTFK-TV is the UniMas affiliate for the Sacramento, CA market. The station is owned by Univision Communications Inc. KTFK-TV broadcasts locally on channel 64.
TELEVISION STATION

KTFN2-TV 829855
Owner: Entravision Communications Corp.
Editorial: 5426 N Mesa St, El Paso, Texas 79912-5421 **Tel:** 1 915 581-1126.
Profile: KTFN2-TV is a multicast channel of KTFN-TV. A multicast channel is a separate channel that shares the bandwidth of the main station but can air unique programming. KTFN2-TV is the MundoFOX affiliate for the El Paso, TX market. The station is owned by Entravision Communications Corp. KTFN2-TV broadcasts locally on channel 65.2. The station does not have a news department.
TELEVISION STATION

KTFN-TV 32567
Owner: Entravision Communications Corp.
Editorial: 5426 N Mesa St, El Paso, Texas 79912-5421 **Tel:** 1 915 581-1126.
Profile: KTFN-TV is the Telefutura affiliate for the El Paso, TX market. The station is owned by Entravision Communications Corp. KTFN-TV broadcasts locally on channel 65.
TELEVISION STATION

KTFQ-TV 63081
Owner: Univision Communications Inc.
Editorial: 2725 Broadbent Pkwy NE Ste F, Albuquerque, New Mexico 87107-1635
Tel: 1 505 342-4141.
Profile: KTFQ-TV is the UniMas affiliate for the Albuquerque, NM market. The station is owned by Univision Communications Inc. KTFQ-TV broadcasts locally on channel 14.
TELEVISION STATION

KTHV-TV 31628
Owner: TEGNA Inc.
Editorial: 720 S Izard St, Little Rock, Arkansas 72201-4026 **Tel:** 1 501 376-1111.
Email: sales@thv11.com
Web site: http://www.thv11.com
Profile: KTHV-TV is the CBS affiliate for the Little Rock, AR market. The station is owned by TEGNA Inc. KTHV-TV broadcasts locally on channel 11.
TELEVISION STATION

KTIV-TV 31630
Owner: Quincy Newspapers Inc.
Editorial: 2929 Signal Hill Dr, Sioux City, Iowa 51108-1409 **Tel:** 1 712 239-4100.
Email: ktivnews@ktiv.com
Web site: http://www.ktiv.com
Profile: KTIV-TV is the NBC affiliate for the Sioux City, IA market. The station is owned by Quincy Newspapers Inc. KTIV-TV broadcasts locally on channel 4.
TELEVISION STATION

KTKA-TV 31631
Owner: PBC Broadcasting
Editorial: 6835 NW US Highway 24, Topeka, Kansas 66618-5507 **Tel:** 1 785 582-4000.
Email: 27news@kansasfirstnews.com
Web site: http://www.kansasfirstnews.com
Profile: KTKA-TV is the ABC network affiliate for the Topeka, KS market. The station is owned by PBC Broacasting. KTKA-TV broadcasts locally on channel 49.
TELEVISION STATION

KTKO-TV 410441
Owner: TKO, Inc.
Editorial: 500 N Main St, Harrison, Arkansas 72601-3536 **Tel:** 1 870 741-2566.
Email: tko8@windstream.net
Web site: http://www.tko8.com
Profile: KTKO-TV is the MeTV network affiliate for the Springfield, MO market. The station is owned by TKO, Inc. WTKO-TV broadcasts locally on channel 8.
TELEVISION STATION

KTLA2-TV 606258
Owner: Tribune Broadcasting Co.
Editorial: 5800 W Sunset Blvd, Los Angeles, California 90028-6607 **Tel:** 1 323 560-5500.
Email: ktlastoryideas@tribune.com
Web site: http://www.ktla.com
Profile: KTLA2-TV is a multicast channel of KTLA-TV. A multicast channel is a separate channel that shares the bandwidth of the main station but can air unique programming. KTLA2-TV is the This TV for the Los Angeles market. The station is owned by Tribune Broadcasting Co. KTLA2-TV broadcasts locally on channel 5.2.
TELEVISION STATION

KTLA-TV 31632
Owner: Tribune Broadcasting Co.
Editorial: 5800 W Sunset Blvd, Los Angeles, California 90028-6607 **Tel:** 1 323 460-5500.
Email: ktla@ktla.com
Web site: http://www.ktla.com
Profile: KTLA-TV is the CW affiliate for the Los Angeles market. The station is owned by Tribune Broadcasting Co. KTLA-TV broadcasts locally on channel 5. KTLA Morning News has about 225,000 viewers per quarter hour.
TELEVISION STATION

KTLM-TV 63097
Owner: NBC Universal
Editorial: 3900 N 10th St, McAllen, Texas 78501-1735
Tel: 1 956 686-0040.
Email: ktlmnews@telemundo.com
Web site: http://www.telemundo40.com
Profile: KTLM-TV is the Telemundo affiliate for the McAllen-Brownsville, TX area. The station is owned by NBC Universal. KTLM-TV broadcasts locally on channel 40.
TELEVISION STATION

KTLN-TV 32580
Owner: OTA Broadcasting
Editorial: 100 Pelican Way, San Rafael, California 94901-5592 **Tel:** 1 415 485-5856.
Email: ktln@tln.com
Web site: http://www.ktln.tv
Profile: KTLN-TV is an independent station for the San Francisco market. The station is owned by OTA Broadcasting. KTLN-TV broadcasts locally on channel 68.
TELEVISION STATION

KTMD-TV 31633
Owner: NBC Universal
Editorial: 1235 North Loop W, Houston, Texas 77008-1758 **Tel:** 1 713 974-4848.
Email: ktmd_newsdesk@telemundo.com
Web site: http://www.telemundohouston.com
Profile: KTMD-TV is the Telemundo affiliate for the Houston market. The station is owned by NBC Universal. KTMD-TV broadcasts locally on channel 47.
TELEVISION STATION

KTMF-TV 32430
Owner: Cowles Publishing Co.
Editorial: 2200 Stephens Ave, Missoula, Montana 59801-7904 **Tel:** 1 406 542-8900.
Email: abcfoxmt@abcfoxmontana.com
Web site: http://www.abcfoxmontana.com
Profile: KTMF-TV is the ABC affiliate for the Missoula, MT market. The station is owned by Cowles Publishing Co. KTMF-TV broadcasts locally on channel 23.
TELEVISION STATION

KTMJ-TV 31533
Owner: Nexstar Media Group, Inc.
Editorial: 6835 NW US Highway 24, Topeka, Kansas 66618-5507 **Tel:** 1 785 582-4000.
Email: news@ksnt.com
Web site: http://kansasfirstnews.com
Profile: KTMJ-TV is the FOX affiliate for the Topeka, KS area. The station is owned by Nexstar Media Group, Inc. KTMJ-TV broadcasts locally on channel 43.
TELEVISION STATION

KTMO-TV 390594
Owner: Raycom Media Inc.
Editorial: 7900 Broadway Dr, Amarillo, Texas 79108-2409 **Tel:** 1 806 383-1010.
Email: newsroom@newschannel10.com
Web site: http://www.newschannel10.com/category/221444/telemundo
Profile: KTMO-TV is a Telemundo affiliate for the Amarillo, TX market. The station is owned by Raycom Media Inc. KTMO-TV broadcasts locally on channel 36. The station is a satellite station of KEYU-TV, and simulcasts their programming. Send all press materials to KEYU-TV.
TELEVISION STATION

KTMV-TV 32624
Owner: Lopez Broadcasting
Editorial: 2209 N Padre Island Dr, Corpus Christi, Texas 78408-2432 **Tel:** 1 361 289-7788.
Profile: KTMV-TV is an independent station for the Corpus Christi, TX market. The station is owned by Humberto Lopex. KTMV-TV broadcasts locally on channel 8.
TELEVISION STATION

KTNC-TV 32998
Owner: TITAN-TV Broadcasting Group
Editorial: 1700 Montgomery St Ste 400, San Francisco, California 94111-1025 **Tel:** 1 415 398-4242.
Web site: http://www.estrellatvsf.com
Profile: KTNC-TV is an independent station for the San Francisco market. The station is owned by TITAN-TV Broadcasting Group. KTNC-TV broadcasts locally on channel 42.
TELEVISION STATION

KTNL-TV 31634
Owner: Denali Media Juneau, Corp.
Editorial: 208 Lake St, Sitka, Alaska 99835-7582
Tel: 1 907 929-9700.
Email: stationmail@cbssoutheastak.com
Web site: http://www.cbssoutheastak.com
Profile: KTNL-TV is the CBS affiliate for the Sitka, AK market. The station is owned by Denali Media Juneau, Corp. KTNL-TV broadcasts locally on channel 13.
TELEVISION STATION

KTNV2-TV 619939
Owner: E.W. Scripps Co.
Editorial: 3355 S Valley View Blvd, Las Vegas, Nevada 89102-8216 **Tel:** 1 702 876-1313.
Email: desk@ktnv.com
Web site: http://www.ktnv.com
Profile: KTNV2-TV is a multicast of KTNV-TV. A multicast channel is a separate channel that shares the bandwith of the main station but can air unique programming. KTNV2-TV airs Hispanic programming from the Mexicanal network in the Las Vegas market. The station is owned by E.W. Scripps Co. KTNV2-TV broadcasts locally on channel 13.2.
TELEVISION STATION

KTNV3-TV 777058
Owner: E.W. Scripps Co.
Editorial: 3355 S Valley View Blvd, Las Vegas, Nevada 89102-8216 **Tel:** 1 702 876-1313.
Web site: http://www.ktnv.com
Profile: KTNV3-TV is a multicast of KTNV-TV. A multicast channel is a separate channel that shares the bandwith of the main station but can air unique programming. KTNV3-TV airs programming from the Live Well Network in the Las Vegas market. The station is owned by E.W. Scripps Co. KTNV3-TV broadcasts locally on channel 13.3.
TELEVISION STATION

KTNV-TV 31635
Owner: E.W. Scripps Co.
Editorial: 3355 S Valley View Blvd, Las Vegas, Nevada 89102-8216 **Tel:** 1 702 876-1313.
Email: desk@ktnv.com
Web site: http://www.ktnv.com
Profile: KTNV-TV is the ABC affiliate for the Las Vegas market. The station is owned by the E.W. Scripps Co. KTNV-TV broadcasts locally on channel 13.
TELEVISION STATION

KTOO-TV 31636
Owner: Capital Community Broadcasting Inc.
Editorial: 360 Egan Dr, Juneau, Alaska 99801-1769 **Tel:** 1 907 586-1670.
Email: news@ktoo.org
Web site: http://www.ktoo.org
Profile: KTOO-TV is the PBS affiliate for the Juneau, AK, market. The station is owned by the Capital Community Broadcasting Inc. KTOO-TV broadcasts locally on channel 3.
TELEVISION STATION

KTOV-TV 376647
Owner: GH Broadcasting
Editorial: 600 Leopard St Ste 1924, Corpus Christi, Texas 78401-0461 **Tel:** 1 361 600-3800.
Web site: http://www.ktov.com
Profile: KTOV-TV is a MyNetworkTV affiliate for the Corpus Christi, TX market. The station is owned by GH Broadcasting. KTOV-TV broadcasts locally on channel 21.
TELEVISION STATION

KTPN-TV 708384
Owner: White Knight Broadcasting
Editorial: 4300 Richmond Rd, Tyler, Texas 75703-1201 **Tel:** 1 903 236-0051.
TELEVISION STATION

KTPX-TV 32577
Owner: ION Media Networks
Editorial: 5800 E Skelly Dr Ste 101, Tulsa, Oklahoma 74135-6419 **Tel:** 1 918 664-1044.
Profile: KTPX-TV is the ION Television affiliate for the Tulsa, OK, market. The station is owned by ION Media Networks. KTPX-TV broadcasts locally on channel 28.
TELEVISION STATION

KTRE-TV 32782
Owner: Raycom Media Inc.
Editorial: 358 Tv Rd, Pollok, Texas 75969-4644 **Tel:** 1 936 853-5873.
Email: ktrenews@ktre.com
Web site: http://www.ktre.com
Profile: KTRE-TV is the ABC affiliate for the Tyler, TX market. The station is owned by Raycom Media Inc. KTRE-TV broadcasts locally on channel 9.
TELEVISION STATION

KTRK2-TV 610913
Owner: Walt Disney Co.
Editorial: 3310 Bissonnet St, Houston, Texas 77005-2195 **Tel:** 1 713 666-0713.
Email: ktrk.news.releases@abc.com
Web site: http://abclocal.go.com/ktrk
Profile: KTRK2-TV is a multicast of KTRK-TV. A multicast channel is a separate channel that shares the bandwith of the main station but can air unique programming. KTRK2-TV airs programming from Live Well in the Houston market. The station is owned by Walt Disney Co. KTRK2-TV broadcasts locally on channel 13.3.
TELEVISION STATION

KTRK3-TV 610919
Owner: Walt Disney Co.
Editorial: 3310 Bissonnet St, Houston, Texas 77005-2195 **Tel:** 1 713 666-0713.
Email: ktrk.news.releases@abc.com
Web site: http://abclocal.go.com/ktrk
Profile: KTRK3-TV is a multicast of KTRK-TV. A multicast channel is a separate channel that shares the bandwith of the main station but can air unique programming. KTRK3-TV airs programming from ABC 13 Weather Now in the Houston market. The station is owned by Walt Disney Co. KTRK3-TV broadcasts locally on channel 13.3.
TELEVISION STATION

KTRK-TV 31637
Owner: Walt Disney Co.
Editorial: 3310 Bissonnet St, Houston, Texas 77005-2114 **Tel:** 1 713 666-0713.
Email: ktrk.news.releases@abc.com
Web site: http://abc13.com
Profile: KTRK-TV is the ABC affiliate for the Houston market. The station is owned by the Walt Disney Co. KTRK-TV broadcasts locally on channel 13.
TELEVISION STATION

KTRV-TV 31638
Owner: Block Communications Inc.
Editorial: 1 6th St N, Nampa, Idaho 83687-3485 **Tel:** 1 208 466-1200.
Web site: http://www.iontelevision.com
Profile: KTRV-TV is the independent station for the Boise, ID market. The station is owned by Block Communications Inc. KTRV-TV broadcasts locally on channel 12.
TELEVISION STATION

KTSB-TV 133886
Owner: Entravision Communications Corp.
Editorial: 3700 State St Ste 300, Santa Barbara, California 93105-3128 **Tel:** 1 805 685-3800.
Profile: KTSB-TV is the Telefutura affiliate for the Santa Monica, CA market. The station is owned by Entravision Communications Corp. KTSB-TV broadcasts locally on channel 43.
TELEVISION STATION

KTSC-TV 32310
Owner: Rocky Mountain PBS
Editorial: 2200 Bonforte Blvd, Pueblo, Colorado 81001-4901 **Tel:** 1 719 543-8800.
Web site: http://www.rmpbs.org
Profile: KTSC-TV is the PBS affiliate for the Pueblo, CO market. The station is owned by Rocky Mountain PBS. KTSC-TV broadcasts locally on channel 8.
TELEVISION STATION

KTSF2-TV 609996
Owner: Lincoln Broadcasting Co.
Editorial: 100 Valley Dr, Brisbane, California 94005-1350 **Tel:** 1 415 468-2626.
Email: ktsfassignmentdesk@ktsftv.com
Web site: http://www.kstf.com
Profile: KTSF2-TV is a multicast of KTSF-TV. A multicast channel is a separate channel that shares the bandwith of the main station but can air unique programming. KTSF2-TV airs programming from the MBC America network in the San Francisco market. The station is owned by Lincoln Broadcasting Co. KTSF2-TV broadcasts locally on channel 26.2.
TELEVISION STATION

KTSF3-TV 610003
Owner: Lincoln Broadcasting Co.
Editorial: 100 Valley Dr, Brisbane, California 94005-1350 **Tel:** 1 415 468-2626.
Web site: http://www.ktsf.com
Profile: KTSF3-TV is a multicast of KTSF-TV. A multicast channel is a separate channel that shares the bandwith of the main station but can air unique programming. KTSF3-TV airs programming from the KBS World network in the San Francisco market. The station is owned by Lincoln Broadcasting Co. KTSF3-TV broadcasts locally on channel 26.3.
TELEVISION STATION

KTSF-TV 31639
Owner: Lincoln Broadcasting Co.
Editorial: 100 Valley Dr, Brisbane, California 94005-1318 **Tel:** 1 415 468-2626.
Web site: http://www.ktsf.com
Profile: KTSF-TV is an independent station for the San Francisco market. The station is owned by Lincoln Broadcasting Co. KTSF-TV broadcasts locally on channel 26.
TELEVISION STATION

KTSM-TV 31640
Owner: Communications Corp. of America
Editorial: 801 N Oregon St, El Paso, Texas 79902-4001 **Tel:** 1 915 532-5421.
Web site: http://www.elpasoproud.com
Profile: KTSM-TV is the NBC affiliate for the El Paso, TX market. The station is owned by Communications Corp. of America. KTSM-TV broadcasts locally on channel 9. KTSM-TV is responsible for KDBC-TV's news operations.
TELEVISION STATION

KTTC-TV 31642
Owner: Quincy Media Inc.
Editorial: 6301 Bandel Rd NW, Rochester, Minnesota 55901-8798 **Tel:** 1 507 288-4444.
Email: news@kttc.com
Web site: http://www.kttc.com
Profile: KTTC-TV is the NBC affiliate for the Rochester, MN, Mason City, IA market. The station is owned by Quincy Media Inc. KTTC-TV broadcasts locally on channel 10.
TELEVISION STATION

KTTU-TV 31435
Owner: TEGNA Inc.
Editorial: 7831 N Business Park Dr, Tucson, Arizona 85743-9622 **Tel:** 1 520 624-0180.
Email: desk@tucsonnewsnow.com
Web site: http://www.tucsonnewsnow.com
Profile: KTTU-TV is the MyNetworkTV network affiliate for the Tucson, AZ market. The station is owned by TEGNA Inc. KTTU-TV broadcasts locally on channel 18.
TELEVISION STATION

KTTV-TV 31643
Owner: FOX Broadcasting Company
Editorial: 1999 S Bundy Dr, Los Angeles, California 90025-5203 **Tel:** 1 310 584-2000.
Email: news@fox11.com
Web site: http://www.foxla.com
Profile: KTTV-TV is the FOX affiliate for the Los Angeles market. The station is owned by FOX Broadcasting Company. KTTV-TV broadcasts to the Los Angeles area on channel 11.
TELEVISION STATION

KTTW-TV 32735
Owner: Independent Communications
Editorial: 2817 W 11Th St, Sioux Falls, South Dakota 57104-2540 **Tel:** 1 605 338-0017.
Email: fox7@kttw.com
Web site: http://www.kttw.com
Profile: KTTW-TV is the Fox affiliate for the Sioux Falls, SD market. The station is owned by Independent Communications. KTTW-TV broadcasts locally on channel 7.
TELEVISION STATION

KTUL-TV 31645
Owner: Sinclair Broadcast Group, Inc.
Editorial: 3333 S 29th West Ave, Tulsa, Oklahoma 74107-4213 **Tel:** 1 918 445-8888.
Email: news@ktul.com
Web site: http://www.ktul.com
Profile: KTUL-TV is the ABC affiliate for the Tulsa, OK, market. The station is owned bySinclair Broadcast Group, Inc. KTUL-TV broadcasts locally on channel 8.
TELEVISION STATION

KTUU-TV 31646
Owner: Schurz Communications Inc.
Editorial: 501 E 40th Ave, Anchorage, Alaska 99503-6009 **Tel:** 1 907 762-9202.
Email: news_desk@ktuu.com
Web site: http://www.ktuu.com
Profile: KTUU-TV is the NBC affiliate for the Anchorage, AK market. The station is owned by Schurz Communications Inc. KTUU-TV broadcasts locally on channel 2. PR professionals are advised to contact the newsroom with any press releases/story ideas.
TELEVISION STATION

KTUZ-TV 327967
Owner: Tyler Media Group Inc.
Editorial: 5101 S Shields Blvd, Oklahoma City, Oklahoma 73129-3217 **Tel:** 1 405 616-5500.
Web site: http://www.ktuztv.com
Profile: KTUZ-TV is a Telemundo affiliate for the Oklahoma City area. The station is owned by Tyler Media Group Inc. KTUZ-TV broadcasts locally on channel 30.
TELEVISION STATION

KTVA-TV 31647
Owner: Denali Media Holdings
Editorial: 1001 Northway Dr Ste 202, Anchorage, Alaska 99508-2015 **Tel:** 1 907 273-3192.
Email: 11news@ktva.com
Web site: http://www.ktva.com
Profile: KTVA-TV is the CBS network affiliate for the Anchorage, AK market. The station is owned by Denali Media Holdings. KTVA-TV broadcasts locally on channel 11. Please direct all press releases/ materials and story ideas to the News Director.
TELEVISION STATION

KTVB-TV 31648
Owner: TEGNA Inc.
Editorial: 5407 W Fairview Ave, Boise, Idaho 83706-1162 **Tel:** 1 208 375-7277.
Email: ktvbnews@ktvb.com
Web site: http://www.ktvb.com
Profile: KTVB-TV is the NBC affiliated for the Boise, ID market. The station is owned by TEGNA Inc. KTVB-TV broadcasts locally on channel 7.
TELEVISION STATION

KTVC-TV 32473
Owner: Better Life Television, Inc.
Tel: 1 541 474-3089.
Web site: http://www.betterlifetv.tv
Profile: KTVC-TV is a non commerical independent station in the Eugene, OR market. The station is owned by Better Life Television, Inc. KTVC-TV broadcasts locally on channel 18. The station airs Christian programming.
TELEVISION STATION

KTVD2-TV 785993
Owner: TEGNA Inc.
Editorial: 500 E Speer Blvd, Denver, Colorado 80203-4187 **Tel:** 1 303 871-9999.
Profile: KTVD2-TV is a multicast channel of KTVD-TV. A multicast channel is a separate channel that shares the bandwith of the main station but can air unique programming. KTVD2-TV is the ME-TV affiliate for the Denver market. The station is owned by TEGNA Inc. KTVD2-TV broadcasts locally on channel 20.2.
TELEVISION STATION

KTVD-TV 32247
Owner: TEGNA Inc.
Editorial: 500 E Speer Blvd, Denver, Colorado 80203-4187 **Tel:** 1 303 871-9999.
Email: newstips@9news.com
Web site: http://www.mytvdenver.com
Profile: KTVD-TV is the MyNetworkTV affiliate for the Denver market. The station is owned by TEGNA Inc. KTVD-TV broadcasts locally on channel 20.
TELEVISION STATION

KTVE-TV 31649
Owner: Nexstar Broadcasting Group
Editorial: 200 Pavilion Rd, West Monroe, Louisiana 71292-9481 **Tel:** 1 318 323-1972.
Email: news@nbc10news.net
Web site: http://myarklamiss.com
Profile: KTVE-TV is the NBC affiliate for the Monroe, LA and El Dorado, AR market. The station is owned by Nexstar Broadcasting Group. KTVE-TV broadcasts locally on channel 10.
TELEVISION STATION

KTVF-TV 31650
Owner: Gray Television, Inc.
Editorial: 3650 Braddock St, Fairbanks, Alaska 99701-7617 **Tel:** 1 907 458-1800.
Email: montebowen@ktvf11.com
Web site: http://www.webcenter11.com
Profile: KTVF-TV is the NBC affiliate for the Fairbanks, AK market. The station is owned by Gray Television, Inc. KTVF-TV broadcasts locally on channel 11.
TELEVISION STATION

KTVH-TV 31651
Owner: Gray Television
Editorial: 100 W Lyndale Ave Ste A, Helena, Montana 59601-2999 **Tel:** 1 406 457-1212.
Email: news@ktvh.com
Web site: http://www.ktvh.com
Profile: KTVH-TV is the NBC affiliate for the Helena, MT market. The station is owned by Beartooth Communications. KTVH-TV broadcasts locally on channel 12.
TELEVISION STATION

KTVI-TV 31652
Owner: Tribune Broadcasting Co.
Editorial: 2250 Ball Dr, Saint Louis, Missouri 63146-8602 **Tel:** 1 314 213-2222.
Email: ktvinews@tvstl.com
Web site: http://fox2now.com
Profile: KTVI-TV is the FOX affiliate for the St. Louis market. The station is owned by Tribune Broadcasting Co. KTVI-TV broadcasts locally on channel 2.
TELEVISION STATION

KTVK2-TV 611989
Owner: Meredith Corporation
Editorial: 5555 N 7th Ave, Phoenix, Arizona 85013-1701 **Tel:** 1 602 207-3333.
Email: 3tvnews@azfamily.com
Web site: http://www.azfamily.com
Profile: KTVK2-TV is a multicast of KTVK-TV. A multicast channel is a separate channel that shares the bandwith of the main station but can air unique programming. KTVK2-TV airs programming from This TV in the Phoenix market. The station is owned by Meredith Corporation. KTVK2-TV broadcasts locally on channel 3.2.
TELEVISION STATION

KTVK-TV 31653
Owner: Meredith Corporation
Editorial: 5555 N 7th Ave, Phoenix, Arizona 85013-1701 **Tel:** 1 602 207-3333.
Email: 3tvnews@azfamily.com
Web site: http://www.azfamily.com
Profile: KTVK-TV is an independent station for the Phoenix market. The station is owned by Meredith Corporation. KTVK-TV broadcasts locally on channel 3.
TELEVISION STATION

KTVL-TV 31654
Owner: Sinclair Broadcast Group, Inc.
Editorial: 1440 Rossanley Dr, Medford, Oregon 97501 **Tel:** 1 541 773-7373.
Email: ktvl@ktvl.com
Web site: http://www.ktvl.com
Profile: KTVL-TV is the CBS affiliate for the Medford, OR market. The station is owned by Sinclair Broadcast Group, Inc. KTVL-TV broadcasts locally on channel 10.
TELEVISION STATION

KTVM-TV 32783
Owner: Bonten Media Group, LLC
Editorial: 201 S Wallace Ave Ste A5, Bozeman, Montana 59715-4888 **Tel:** 1 406 586-0296.
Email: news@ktvm.com
Web site: http://www.nbcmontana.com/ktvm/news
Profile: KTVM-TV is the NBC affiliate for the Bozeman, MT market. The station is owned by Bonten Media Group, LLC. KTVM-TV broadcasts locally on channel 6.
TELEVISION STATION

KTVN-TV 31655
Owner: Sarkes Tarzian Inc.
Editorial: 4925 Energy Way, Reno, Nevada 89502-4105 **Tel:** 1 775 858-2222.
Email: producers@ktvn.com
Web site: http://www.ktvn.com
Profile: KTVN-TV is the CBS affiliate for the Reno, NV market. The station is owned by Sarkes Tarzian Inc. KTVN-TV broadcasts locally on channel 2.
TELEVISION STATION

KTVO2-TV 685529
Owner: Sinclair Broadcast Group, Inc.
Editorial: 15518 Us Highway 63, Kirksville, Missouri 63501-6905 **Tel:** 1 660 627-3333.
Profile: KTVO2-TV is a multicast channel of KTVO-TV. A multicast channel is a separate channel that shares the bandwith of the main station but can air unique programming. KTVO2-TV is the CBS affiliate for the Kirksville, MO market. The station is owned by Sinclair Broadcast Group, Inc. KTVO2-TV broadcasts locally on channel 3.2.
TELEVISION STATION

KTVO-TV 31656
Owner: Sinclair Broadcast Group, Inc.
Editorial: 15518 US Highway 63, Kirksville, Missouri 63501-6905 **Tel:** 1 660 627-3333.
Email: news@ktvo.com
Web site: http://www.heartlandconnection.com
Profile: KTVO-TV is the ABC affiliate for the Ottumwa, IA/Kirksville, MO, market. The station is owned by Sinclair Broadcast Group, Inc. KTWO-TV broadcasts locally on channel 33.
TELEVISION STATION

KTVQ-TV 31657
Owner: Cordillera Communications Inc.
Editorial: 3203 3rd Ave N, Billings, Montana 59101-1945 **Tel:** 1 406 252-5611.
Email: news@ktvq.com
Web site: http://www.ktvq.com
Profile: KTVQ-TV is CBS affiliate for the Billings, MT market. The station is owned by Cordillera Communications Inc. KTVQ-TV broadcasts locally on channel 2.
TELEVISION STATION

KTVS-TV 155324
Owner: Alpha-Omega Broadcasting of New Mexico
Editorial: 4501 Montgomery Blvd NE, Albuquerque, New Mexico 87109-1286 **Tel:** 1 505 884-8355.
Email: info@kazq32.org
Web site: http://ktvs36.com/
Profile: KTVS-TV is an independent station for the Albuquerque, NM market. The station is owned by Alpha-Omega Broadcasting of New Mexico. KTVS-TV is broadcast locally on channel 36.
TELEVISION STATION

KTVT-TV 31658
Owner: CBS Television Stations
Editorial: 12001 N Central Expy, Dallas, Texas 75243-3700 **Tel:** 1 817 451-1111.
Email: news@ktvt.com
Web site: http://dfw.cbslocal.com
Profile: KTVT-TV is the CBS affiliate for the Dallas-Fort Worth market. The station is owned by CBS Television Stations. KTVT-TV broadcasts locally on channel 11.
TELEVISION STATION

KTVU2-TV 608219
Owner: Cox Media Group, Inc.
Editorial: 2 Jack London Sq, Oakland, California 94607-3727 **Tel:** 1 510 834-1212.
Web site: http://www.latv.com
Profile: KTVU2-TV is an independent affiliate for the San Francisco market. The station is owned by Fox Broadcasting Company. KTVU-TV broadcasts locally on channel 2.2. KTVU2-TV broadcasts programming from LATV, a bilingual music and entertainment network. KTVU2-TV TV is a multicast channel of KTVU-TV. A multicast channel is a separate channel that shares the bandwidth of the main station but can air unique programming.
TELEVISION STATION

KTVU-TV 31659
Owner: Cox Media Group, Inc.
Editorial: 2 Jack London Sq, Oakland, California 94607-3727 **Tel:** 1 510 834-1212.
Email: newstips@foxtv.com
Web site: http://www.ktvu.com
Profile: KTVU-TV is a FOX affiliate for the San Francisco market. The station is owned by Cox Media Group, Inc.. KTVU-TV broadcasts locally on channel 2.
TELEVISION STATION

KTVW2-TV 611644
Owner: Univision Communications Inc.
Editorial: 6006 S 30th St, Phoenix, Arizona 85042-4802 **Tel:** 1 602 243-3333.
Email: ktvwassignment@univision.net
Web site: http://univisionarizona.univision.com
Profile: KTVW2-TV is a multicast of KTVW-TV. A multicast channel is a separate channel that shares the bandwidth of the main station but can air unique programming. KTVW-TV airs programming from KFPH-TV in the Phoenix market. The station is owned by Univision Communications Inc. KTVW2-TV broadcasts locally on channel 33.2.
TELEVISION STATION

KTVW-TV 31660
Owner: Univision Communications Inc.
Editorial: 6006 S 30th St, Phoenix, Arizona 85042-4802 **Tel:** 1 602 243-3333.
Email: ktvwassignment@univision.net
Web site: http://univisionarizona.univision.com
Profile: KTVW-TV is the Univision network affiliate for the Phoenix, AZ market. The station is owned by Univision Communications Inc. KTVW-TV broadcasts locally on channel 33.
TELEVISION STATION

KTVX2-TV 618358
Owner: Nexstar Broadcasting Group
Editorial: 2175 W 1700 S, Salt Lake City, Utah 84104-4200 **Tel:** 1 801 975-4444.
Email: news@abc4.com
Web site: http://www.abc4.com
Profile: KTVX2-TV is a multicast of KTVX-TV. A multicast channel is a separate channel that shares the bandwith of the main station but can air unique programming. KTVX-TV airs programming from Untamed Sports TV in the Salt Lake City market. The station is owned by Newport Television, LLC. KTVX2-TV broadcasts locally on channel 4.2.
TELEVISION STATION

KTVX-TV 31661
Owner: Nexstar Broadcasting Group
Editorial: 2175 W 1700 S, Salt Lake City, Utah 84104-4200 **Tel:** 1 801 975-4444.
Email: news@abc4.com
Web site: http://www.good4utah.com
Profile: KTVX-TV is the ABC affiliate for the Salt Lake City market. The station is owned by Nexstar Broadcasting Group. KTVX-TV broadcasts locally on channel 4.
TELEVISION STATION

KTVZ-TV 31663
Owner: News-Press & Gazette Co.
Editorial: 62990 O B Riley Rd, Bend, Oregon 97703-9001 **Tel:** 1 541 383-2121.
Email: stories@ktvz.com
Web site: http://www.ktvz.com
Profile: KTVZ-TV is the NBC affiliate for the Bend, OR market. The station is owned by the News-Press & Gazette Co. KTVZ-TV broadcasts locally on channel 21. Send all mail to the station's post office box address and not to the street address.
TELEVISION STATION

KTWO-TV 31664
Owner: Silvertone Broadcasting
Editorial: 1896 Skyview Dr, Casper, Wyoming 82601-9638 **Tel:** 1 307 237-3711.
Email: info@k2tv.com
Web site: http://www.k2tv.com
Profile: KTWO-TV is the ABC affiliate for the Casper-Riverton market. The station is owned by Silvertone Broadcasting. KTWO-TV broadcasts locally on channel 2.
TELEVISION STATION

KTWT-TV 390929
Owner: Neuhoff Family Limited Partnership
Editorial: 1100 Blue Lakes Blvd N, Twin Falls, Idaho 83301-3305 **Tel:** 1 208 733-1100.
Email: newstips@kmvt.com
Web site: http://www.kmvt.com/news/
Profile: KTWT-TV is the CW Television Network affiliate for the Twin Falls, ND markets. The station is owned by Neuhoff Family Limited Partnership. KTWT-TV broadcasts locally on channel 43. KTWT-TV will become a Fox affiliate on July 1, 2012, and will also debut three daily newscasts.
TELEVISION STATION

KTXA-TV 31666
Owner: CBS Television Stations
Editorial: 12001 N Central Expy, Dallas, Texas 75243-3700 **Tel:** 1 817 451-1111.
Web site: http://dfw.cbslocal.com/station/txa-21
Profile: KTXA-TV is an independent television station serving the Dallas–Fort Worth area. The station is owned by the CBS Television Stations. KTXA-TV airs locally on channel 21.
TELEVISION STATION

KTXD-TV 483582
Owner: London Broadcasting
Editorial: 15455 Dallas Pkwy Ste 100, Addison, Texas 75001-6739 **Tel:** 1 214 628-9900.
Email: info@ktxdtv.com
Web site: http://texas47.com
Profile: KTXD-TV is an independent affiliate for the Amarillo, TX market. The station is owned by London Broadcasting. KTXD-TV broadcasts locally on channel 43. Station has no news department and no original programming.
TELEVISION STATION

KTXH-TV 31667
Owner: Fox Broadcasting Company
Editorial: 4261 Southwest Fwy, Houston, Texas 77027-7201 **Tel:** 1 713 479-2600.
Web site: http://www.my20houston.com
Profile: KTXH-TV is the MyNetworkTV and FOX affiliate for the Houston market. The station is owned by Fox Broadcasting Company. KTXH-TV broadcasts locally on channel 20. The station does not have a public service director.
TELEVISION STATION

KTXL2-TV 614830
Owner: Tribune Broadcasting Co.
Editorial: 4655 Fruitridge Rd, Sacramento, California 95820-5201 **Tel:** 1 916 454-4422.
Email: fox40programming@fox40.com
Web site: http://www.latv.com
Profile: KTXL2-TV is the FOX affiliate for the Sacramento, CA market. The station is owned by Tribune Broadcasting Co. KTXL2-TV broadcasts locally on channel 40.2. The station airs programming from LATV, a bilingual music and entertainment network. KTXL2-TV is a multicast channel of KTXL-TV. A multicast channel is a separate channel that shares the bandwidth of the main station but can air unique programming.
TELEVISION STATION

KTXL-TV 31668
Owner: Tribune Broadcasting Co.
Editorial: 4655 Fruitridge Rd, Sacramento, California 95820 **Tel:** 1 916 454-4422.
Email: news@fox40.com
Web site: http://www.fox40.com
Profile: KTXL-TV is the FOX affiliate for the Sacramento, CA market. The station is owned by Tribune Broadcasting Co. KTXL-TV broadcasts locally on channel 40.
TELEVISION STATION

KTXS-TV 31669
Owner: Bonten Media Group, Inc.
Editorial: 4420 N Clack St, Abilene, Texas 79601-9257 **Tel:** 1 325 677-2281.
Web site: http://www.ktxs.com
Profile: KTXS-TV is the ABC affiliate for the Abilene, TX, market. The station is owned by Bonten Bonten Media Group, Inc. KTXS-TV broadcasts locally on channel 12.
TELEVISION STATION

KUAT-TV 32720
Owner: Arizona Board of Regents
Editorial: 1423 E University Blvd, Tucson, Arizona 85721 **Tel:** 1 520 621-5828.
Email: newsroom@azpm.org
Web site: http://tv.azpm.org/whatson
Profile: KUAT-TV is the PBS network affiliate for the Tucson, AZ market. The station is owned by Arizona Board of Regents. KUAT-TV broadcasts locally on channel 6.
TELEVISION STATION

KUBD-TV 491532
Owner: Denali Media Juneau, Corp.
Editorial: 2417 Tongass Ave, Ketchikan, Alaska 99901-5900 **Tel:** 1 907 929-9700.
Web site: http://www.cbssoutheastak.com
Profile: KUBD-TV is the CBS Television affiliate for the Juneau, AK market. The station is owned by Denali Media Juneau, Corp. KUBD-TV broadcasts locally on channel 4.
TELEVISION STATION

KUBE-TV 32603
Owner: Titan Broadcasting
Editorial: 2401 Fountain View Dr, Houston, Texas 77057-4827 **Tel:** 1 713 467-5757.
Web site: http://www.kube57.com
Profile: KUBE-TV is an independent station for the Houston market. The station is owned by Titan Broadcasting. KUBE-TV broadcasts locally on channel 57 and channel 53 on Comcast.
TELEVISION STATION

KUCW-TV 32566
Owner: Nexstar Broadcasting Corp
Editorial: 2175 W 1700 S, Salt Lake City, Utah 84104-4200 **Tel:** 1 801 975-4444.
Email: news@abc4.com
Web site: http://www.4utah.com/home
Profile: KUCW-TV is a CW affiliate for the Salt Lake City market. The station is owned by Newport Television, LLC. KUCW-TV broadcasts locally on channel 30.
TELEVISION STATION

KUDF-TV 588384
Owner: Una Vez Mas Television Group
Editorial: 1701 N Market St Ste 500, Dallas, Texas 75202-2001 **Tel:** 1 214 754-7008.
Web site: http://www.aztecaamerica.com
Profile: KUDF-TV is the Azteca America affiliate for the Tucson, AZ market. The station is owned by Una Vez Mas Television Group. KUDF-TV broadcasts locally on channel 14.
TELEVISION STATION

KUEN2-TV 615036
Owner: Board of Regents-State of Utah
Editorial: 101 Wasatch Dr, Salt Lake City, Utah 84112-1799 **Tel:** 1 801 581-2999.
Web site: http://www.uen.org/tv
Profile: KUEN2-TV is a multicast of KUEN-TV. A multicast channel is a separate channel that shares the bandwith of the main station but can air unique programming. KUEN2-TV airs programming from MHz WorldView in the Salt Lake City market. The station is owned by Board of Regents-State of Utah. KUEN2-TV broadcasts locally on channel 9.2.
TELEVISION STATION

KUEN-TV 32403
Owner: Board of Regents-State of Utah
Editorial: 101 Wasatch Dr, Salt Lake City, Utah 84112-1799 **Tel:** 1 801 581-2999.
Web site: http://www.uen.org/tv
Profile: KUEN-TV is an independent station in the Salt Lake City market. The station is owned by Board of Regents-State of Utah. KUEN-TV broadcasts locally on channel 9.
TELEVISION STATION

KUIL-TV 128167
Owner: TEGNA Inc.
Editorial: 525 Interstate 10 S, Beaumont, Texas 77701-3708 **Tel:** 1 409 833-7512.
Email: 12news@kbmttv.com
Web site: http://www.12newsnow.com
Profile: KUIL-TV is the MundoFOX affiliate for the Beaumont-Port Arthur, TX market. The station is owned by TEGNA Inc. KUIL-TV broadcasts locally on channel 12.
TELEVISION STATION

KUKC-TV 34282
Owner: Media Vista Group
Editorial: 5405 Taylor Rd Ste 10, Naples, Florida 34109-1899 **Tel:** 1 239 254-9995.
Web site: http://www.kukc48.com
Profile: KUKC-TV is the Univision affiliate for the Kansas City, MO market. The station is owned by Media Vista Group. KUKC-TV broadcasts locally on channel 48.
TELEVISION STATION

KULR-TV 3167
Owner: Cowles Publishing Co.
Editorial: 2045 Overland Ave, Billings, Montana 59102-6454 **Tel:** 1 406 656-8000.
Email: news@kulr.com
Web site: http://www.kulr8.com
Profile: KULR-TV is the NBC affiliate for the Billings, MT, market. The station is owned by Cowles Publishing Co. KULR-TV broadcasts locally on channel 8.
TELEVISION STATION

KUNA-TV 23533
Owner: News-Press & Gazette Co.
Editorial: 42650 Melanie Pl, Palm Desert, California 92211-5170 **Tel:** 1 760 568-6830.
Web site: http://www.kesq.com/kunamundo
Profile: KUNA-TV is a Telemundo affiliate for the Los Angeles market. The station is owned by News-Press & Gazette Co. KUNA-TV broadcasts locally on channel 15.
TELEVISION STATION

KUNP2-TV 82985
Owner: Sinclair Broadcast Group
Editorial: 2153 NE Sandy Blvd, Portland, Oregon 97232-2819 **Tel:** 1 503 231-4222.
Profile: KUNP2-TV is a multicast channel of KUPN-TV. A multicast channel is a separate channel that shares the bandwidth of the main station but can air unique programming. KUNP2-TV is the MundoFOX affiliate for the Portland, OR market. The station is owned by Sinclair Broadcast Group. KUNP2-TV broadcasts locally on channel 47.2.
TELEVISION STATION

KUNP-TV 32819
Owner: Sinclair Broadcast Group
Editorial: 2153 NE Sandy Blvd, Portland, Oregon 97232-2819 **Tel:** 1 503 231-4222.
Web site: http://www.kunptv.com
Profile: KUNP-TV is the Univision affiliate for the Portland, OR market. The station is owned by Sinclair Broadcast Group. KUNP-TV broadcasts locally on channel 47.
TELEVISION STATION

KUNS2-TV 82986
Owner: Sinclair Broadcast Group
Editorial: 140 4th Ave N, Seattle, Washington 98109-4940 **Tel:** 1 206 404-5867.
Web site: http://kunstv.com
Profile: KUNS2-TV is a multicast channel of KUNS-TV. A multicast channel is a separate channel that shares the bandwidth of the main station but can air unique programming. The station is owned by Sinclair Broadcast Group. KUNS2-TV broadcasts locally on channel 51.2.
TELEVISION STATION

KUNS-TV 44116
Owner: Sinclair Broadcast Group
Editorial: 140 4th Ave N, Seattle, Washington 98109-4940 **Tel:** 1 206 404-6684.
Email: noticias@kunstv.com
Web site: http://www.kunstv.com
Profile: KUNS-TV is the Univision affiliate for the Seattle market. The station is owned by Sinclair Broadcast Group. KUNS-TV broadcasts locally on channel 51.
TELEVISION STATION

KUNU-TV 33123
Owner: Saga Communications
Editorial: 3808 N Navarro St, Victoria, Texas 77901-2621 **Tel:** 1 361 575-2500.
Web site: http://www.crossroadstoday.com
Profile: KUNU-TV is the Univision affiliate for the Victoria, TX market. The station is owned by Saga Communications. KUNU-TV broadcasts locally on channel 31.
TELEVISION STATION

KUNW-TV 41822
Owner: Fisher Communications, Inc.
Editorial: 2801 Terrace Heights Dr, Yakima, Washington 98901-1455 **Tel:** 1 509 575-0029.
Web site: http://www.kunwtv.com
Profile: KUNW-TV is owned by Fisher Communications. It is a Univision affiliate airing on channel 2.
TELEVISION STATION

KUOT-TV 35038
Owner: EICB-TV LLC
Editorial: 9801 S Bryant Ave, Moore, Oklahoma 73160-9551 **Tel:** 1 972 293-2256.
Web site: http://www.crosstalk.org
Profile: KUOT-TV is an Global Christian Network affiliate for the Oklahoma City area. The station is owned by EICB-TV LLC. KUOT-TV broadcasts locally on channel 19.
TELEVISION STATION

KUPB-TV 63234
Owner: Entravision Communications Corp.
Editorial: 10313 Younger Rd, Midland, Texas 79706-2622 **Tel:** 1 432 563-1826.
Email: noticias18@entravision.com
Web site: http://noticias.entravision.com/midland-odessa
Profile: KUPB-TV is the Univision affiliate for the Midland, TX market. The station is owned by Entravision Communications Corp. KUPB-TV broadcasts locally on channel 18.
TELEVISION STATION

KUPT-TV 32625
Owner: Ramar Communications II Ltd.
Editorial: 9800 University Ave, Lubbock, Texas 79423-5302 **Tel:** 1 806 745-3434.
Profile: KUPT-TV is the local MyNetworkTV affiliate for the Lubbock, TX market. The station is owned by Ramar Communications II Ltd. KUPT-TV broadcasts locally on channel 29.
TELEVISION STATION

KUPX2-TV 621703
Owner: ION Media Networks
Editorial: 466 Lawndale Dr, Ste C, Salt Lake City, Utah 84115-2975 **Tel:** 1 801 474-0016.
Profile: KUPX2-TV is a multicast of KUPX-TV. A multicast channel is a separate channel that shares the bandwidth of the main station but can air unique programming. KUPX2-TV airs children's programming from qubo in the Salt Lake City market. The station is owned by ION Media Networks. KUPX2-TV broadcasts locally on channel 16.2.
TELEVISION STATION

KUPX3-TV 621709
Owner: ION Media Networks
Editorial: 466 Lawndale Dr, Ste C, Salt Lake City, Utah 84115-2975 **Tel:** 1 801 474-0016.
Profile: KUPX3-TV is a multicast of KUPX-TV. A multicast channel is a separate channel that shares the bandwidth of the main station but can air unique programming. KUPX3-TV airs lifestyle programming from ION Life in the Salt Lake City market. The station is owned by ION Media Networks. KUPX3-TV broadcasts locally on channel 16.3.
TELEVISION STATION

KUPX4-TV 621711
Owner: ION Media Networks
Editorial: 466 Lawndale Dr, Salt Lake City, Utah 84115-2935 **Tel:** 1 801 474-0016.
Profile: KUPX4-TV is a multicast of KUPX-TV. A multicast channel is a separate channel that shares the bandwidth of the main station but can air unique programming. KUPX4-TV airs Christian programming from The Worship Network in the Salt Lake City market. The station is owned by ION Media Networks. KUPX4-TV broadcasts locally on channel 16.4.
TELEVISION STATION

KUPX-TV 31563
Owner: ION Media Networks
Editorial: 466 Lawndale Dr, Ste C, Salt Lake City, Utah 84115-2975 **Tel:** 1 801 474-0016.
Profile: KUPX-TV is the ION Television affiliate for Salt Lake City, UT market. The station is owned by ION Media Networks. KUPX-TV broadcasts locally on channel 16.
TELEVISION STATION

KUQI-TV 687695
Owner: National Communications
Editorial: 600 Leopard St Ste 1924, Corpus Christi, Texas 78401-0461 **Tel:** 1 361 600-3800.
Email: contact@kuqitv.com
Web site: http://www.kuqitv.com
Profile: KUQI-TV is the FOX network affiliate for the Corpus Christi, TX market. The station is owned by National Communications. KQUI-TV broadcasts locally on channel 38.
TELEVISION STATION

KUSA2-TV 612513
Owner: TEGNA Inc.
Editorial: 500 E Speer Blvd, Denver, Colorado 80203-4187 **Tel:** 1 303 871-9999.
Profile: KUSA2-TV is an independent affiliate for the Denver market. The station is owned by TEGNA Inc. KUSA2-TV broadcasts locally on channel 9.2. KUSA2-TV broadcasts strictly local weather related programming, by WeatherNation. KUSA2-TV is a multicast channel of KUSA-TV. A multicast channel is a separate channel that shares the bandwidth of the main station but can air unique programming.
TELEVISION STATION

KUSA3-TV 612517
Owner: TEGNA Inc.
Editorial: 500 E Speer Blvd, Denver, Colorado 80203-4187 **Tel:** 1 303 871-9999.
Profile: KUSA3-TV is an independent affiliate for the Denver market. The station is owned by TEGNA Inc. KUSA3-TV broadcasts locally on channel 9.3. KUSA3-TV broadcasts strictly Universal Sports programming. KUSA3-TV is a multicast channel of KUSA-TV. A multicast channel is a separate channel that shares the bandwidth of the main station but can air unique programming.
TELEVISION STATION

KUSA-TV 31677
Owner: TEGNA Inc.
Editorial: 500 E Speer Blvd, Denver, Colorado 80203-4187 **Tel:** 1 303 871-9999.
Email: newstips@9news.com
Web site: http://www.9news.com
Profile: KUSA-TV is the NBC network affiliate for the Denver market. The station is owned by TEGNA Inc. KUSA-TV broadcasts locally on channel 9.
TELEVISION STATION

KUSD-TV 32711
Owner: South Dakota Public Broadcasting
Editorial: 555 N Dakota St, Vermillion, South Dakota 57069 **Tel:** 1 605 677-5861.
Web site: http://www.sdpb.org
Profile: KUSD-TV is the PBS affiliate for the Sioux Falls, SD market. The station is owned by South Dakota Public Broadcasting. KUSD-TV broadcasts locally on channel 2.
TELEVISION STATION

KUSI-TV 31678
Owner: McKinnon Broadcasting Co.
Editorial: 4575 Viewridge Ave, San Diego, California 92123-1623 **Tel:** 1 858 571-5151.
Email: news@kusi.com
Web site: http://www.kusi.com
Profile: KUSI-TV is an independent station in San Diego. The station is owned by McKinnon Broadcasting Co. It airs locally on channel 9. Contact the assignment desk by fax or phone.
TELEVISION STATION

KUTH-TV 153387
Owner: Univision Television Group
Editorial: 5140 W Amelia Earhart Dr Ste C-D, Salt Lake City, Utah 84116-2985 **Tel:** 1 801 715-3240.
Email: noticiasunivision32@univision.net
Profile: KUTH-TV is the Univision affiliate for the Salt Lake City market. The station is owned by Univision Television Group. KUTH-TV is broadcast locally on channel 32.
TELEVISION STATION

KUTP-TV 31680
Owner: Fox Broadcasting Company
Editorial: 511 W Adams St, Phoenix, Arizona 85003-1608 **Tel:** 1 602 257-1234.
Web site: http://www.kutp.com
Profile: KUTP-TV is the MyNetworkTV affiliate for the Phoenix market. The station is owned by Fox Broadcasting Company. KUTP-TV broadcasts locally on channel 45.
TELEVISION STATION

KUTU-TV 349918
Owner: Tyler Media Group
Editorial: 5101 S Shields Blvd, Oklahoma City, Oklahoma 73129-3217 **Tel:** 1 918 234-0125.
Profile: KUTU-TV is the Univision affiliate for the Tulsa, OK market. The station is owned by Equity Media Holdings Corporation. KUTU-TV broadcasts locally on channel 25.
TELEVISION STATION

KUTV-TV 31681
Owner: Sinclair Broadcast Group, Inc.
Editorial: 299 S Main St Ste 150, Salt Lake City, Utah 84111-2209 **Tel:** 1 801 839-1234.
Email: newsdesk@kutv2.com
Web site: http://www.kutv.com
Profile: KUTV-TV is the CBS affiliate for the Salt Lake City market. The station is owned by Sinclair Broadcast Group, Inc. KUTV-TV broadcasts locally on channel 2.
TELEVISION STATION

KUVI-TV 32335
Owner: Univision Communications Inc.
Editorial: 5801 Truxtun Ave, Bakersfield, California 93309-0609 **Tel:** 1 661 324-0045.
Web site: http://www.45kuvi.com
Profile: KUVI-TV is the MyNetworkTV affiliate in the Bakersfield, CA market. The station is owned by Univision Communications Inc. KUVI-TV broadcasts locally on channel 45.
TELEVISION STATION

KUVM-TV 588372
Owner: Mako Communications
Editorial: 7322 Southwest Fwy Ste 1500, Houston, Texas 77074-2020 **Tel:** 1 713 773-2721.
Profile: KUVM-TV is the MundoFOX affiliate for the Houston market. The station is owned by Mako Communications. KUVM-TV broadcasts locally on channel 34.
TELEVISION STATION

KUVN-TV 32322
Owner: Univision Communications Inc.
Editorial: 2323 Bryan St Ste 1900, Dallas, Texas 75201-2646 **Tel:** 1 214 758-2300.
Email: 23@univision.net
Web site: http://www.univision.com/dallas/kuvn
Profile: KUVN-TV is the Univision affiliate for the Dallas market. The station is owned by Univision Communications Inc. KUVN-TV broadcasts locally on channel 23.
TELEVISION STATION

KUVS-TV 32463
Owner: Univision Communications Inc.
Editorial: 1710 Arden Way, Sacramento, California 95815-5008 **Tel:** 1 916 927-1900.
Email: kuvsnews@univision.net
Web site: http://www.univision.com/sacramento/kuvs
Profile: KUVS-TV is the Univision network affiliate for the Sacramento, CA market. The station is owned by Univision Communications Inc. KUVS-TV broadcasts locally on channel 19.
TELEVISION STATION

KUVU-TV 382467
Owner: Sainte Partners II, LP
Editorial: 730 7th St, Ste 100, Eureka, California 95501-1178 **Tel:** 1 707 422-2999.
Web site: http://www.eurekatelevision.tv
Profile: KUVU-TV is the CW affiliate for the Eureka, CA market. The station is owned by Sainte Partners II, LP. KUVU-TV broadcasts locally on channel 9.
TELEVISION STATION

KVAL-TV 32658
Owner: Sinclair Broadcast Group, Inc.
Editorial: 4575 Blanton Rd, Eugene, Oregon 97405-4902 **Tel:** 1 541 342-4961.
Email: kvalnews@kval.com
Web site: http://www.kval.com
Profile: KVAL-TV is the CBS network affiliate for the Eugene, OR market. The station is owned by Sinclair Broadcast Group, Inc. KVAL-TV broadcasts locally on channel 13.
TELEVISION STATION

KVBC-TV 32535
Owner: Ventura Broadcasting
Editorial: 706 W Herndon Ave, Fresno, California 93650-1033 **Tel:** 1 559 783-2524.
Email: info@cocolatv.com
Web site: http://tvidavision.com
Profile: KVBC-TV is the Tvida Vision affiliate for the Fresno, CA market. The station is owned by Cocola Broadcasting Companies, LLC, leased to Ventura Tv. KVBC-TV airs locally on channel 13.
TELEVISION STATION

KVCR2-TV 606257
Owner: San Bernardino Community College
Editorial: 701 S Mount Vernon Ave, San Bernardino, California 92410-2705 **Tel:** 1 909 384-4443.
Email: info@kvcr.org
Web site: http://www.kvcr.org
Profile: KVCR2-TV is a multicast channel of KVCR-TV. A multicast channel is a separate channel that shares the bandwidth of the main station but can air unique programming. KVCR2-TV is the local PBS affiliate, broadcast on channel 24.2 for the viewers in San Bernardino, CA, and surrounding areas. The station is owned and operated by the San Bernardino Community College District. KVCR2-TV is a direct simulcast of KVCR-TV Channel 24.
TELEVISION STATION

KVCR3-TV 606261
Owner: San Bernardino Community College
Editorial: 701 S Mount Vernon Ave, San Bernardino, California 92410-2705 **Tel:** 1 909 384-4443.
Web site: http://www.kvcr.org
Profile: KVCR3-TV is an independent affiliate, it broadcasts on channel 24.3 for the viewers in San Bernardino, CA, and surrounding areas. The station is owned and operated by the San Bernardino Community College District. KVCR3-TV is a multicast channel of KVCR-TV. A multicast channel is a separate channel that shares the bandwidth of the main station but can air unique programming.
TELEVISION STATION

KVCR4-TV 606263
Owner: San Bernardino Community College
Editorial: 701 S Mount Vernon Ave, San Bernardino, California 92410-2705 **Tel:** 1 909 384-4443.
Web site: http://www.kvcr.org
Profile: KVCR4-TV is a local PBS Network affliate, it broadcasts on channel 24.4 for the viewers in San Bernardino, CA, and surrounding areas. The station is owned and operated by the San Bernardino Community College District. KVCR4-TV is a multicast channel of KVCR-TV. A multicast channel is a separate channel that shares the bandwidth of the main station but can air unique programming.
TELEVISION STATION

KVCR-TV 31683
Owner: San Bernardino Community College
Editorial: 701 S Mount Vernon Ave, San Bernardino, California 92410-2705 **Tel:** 1 909 384-4350.
Email: memberservices@kvcr.org
Web site: http://www.kvcr.org
Profile: KVCR-TV is a PBS affiliate for the Los Angeles market. The station is owned by the San Bernardino Community College District. KVCR-TV is broadcast locally on channel 24.
TELEVISION STATION

KVCT-TV 32568
Owner: Surtsey Productions, Inc.
Editorial: 3808 N Navarro St, Victoria, Texas 77901-2621 **Tel:** 1 361 575-2500.
Email: staff@newscenter25.com
Web site: http://www.crossroadstoday.com
Profile: KVCT-TV is the FOX affiliate for the Victoria, TX market. The station is owned by Surtsey Productions, Inc. KVCT-TV broadcasts locally on channel 19.
TELEVISION STATION

KVCW-TV 32340
Owner: Sinclair Broadcast Group, Inc.
Editorial: 3830 S Jones Blvd, Las Vegas, Nevada 89103 **Tel:** 1 702 382-2121.
Web site: http://www.thecwlasvegas.tv
Profile: KVCW-TV is a CW Television Network affiliate for the Las Vegas market. The station is owned by Sinclair Broadcast Group, Inc. KVCW-TV broadcasts locally on channel 33.
TELEVISION STATION

KVDA-TV 32345
Owner: NBC Universal
Editorial: 6234 San Pedro Ave, San Antonio, Texas 78216-7208 **Tel:** 1 210 340-8860.
Email: noticias_60_telemundo@nbcuni.com
Web site: http://www.telemundosanantonio.com
Profile: KVDA-TV is the Telemundo affiliate for the San Antonio market. The station is owned by NBC Universal. KVDA-TV broadcasts locally on channel 60.
TELEVISION STATION

KVDF-TV 417939
Owner: Station Group, LLC
Editorial: 816 Camaron St Ste 244, San Antonio, Texas 78212-5106 **Tel:** 1 210 277-5800.
Web site: http://www.aztecaamerica.com
Profile: KVDF-TV is the Azteca America affiliate for San Antonio. The station is owned by Stations Group, LLC. KVDF-TV broadcasts locally on channels 18 and 31. All public service announcements should be directed to the mailing address, which is the corporate headquarters in Dallas.
TELEVISION STATION

KVEA-TV 31684
Owner: NBC Universal
Editorial: 100 Universal City Plz Bldg 2120, Universal City, California 91608-1002 **Tel:** 1 818 684-5711.
Email: noticierotelemundo52@nbcuni.com
Web site: http://www.telemundo52.com
Profile: KVEA-TV is a Telemundo affiliate for the Los Angeles market. The station is owned by NBC Universal. KVEA-TV broadcasts locally on channel 52.
TELEVISION STATION

KVEO-TV 31685
Owner: Communications Corp. of America
Editorial: 394 N Expressway, Brownsville, Texas 78521-2259 **Tel:** 1 956 544-2323.
Email: news@kveo.com
Web site: http://www.rgvproud.com
Profile: KVEO-TV is the NBC affiliate for the Brownsville-Mc Allen, TX market. The station is owned by Communications Corp. of America. KVEO-TV broadcasts locally on channel 23.
TELEVISION STATION

KVER-TV 119788
Owner: Entravision Communications Corp.
Editorial: 41601 Corporate Way, Palm Desert, California 92260-1971 **Tel:** 1 760 341-5837.
Web site: http://noticias.entravision.com/palm-springs
Profile: KVER-TV is the Univision affiliate for the Los Angeles market. The station is owned by Entravision Communications Corp. KVER-TV broadcasts locally on channel 4.
TELEVISION STATION

KVEW-TV 32786
Owner: Apple Valley Broadcasting, Inc.
Editorial: 601 N Edison St, Kennewick, Washington 99336-1968 **Tel:** 1 509 735-8369.
Email: kvewnews@kvewtv.com
Web site: http://www.kvewtv.com
Profile: KVEW-TV is the ABC affiliate for the Yakima, WA market. The station is owned by Apple Valley Broadcasting, Inc. KVEW-TV broadcasts locally on channel 42.
TELEVISION STATION

KVHP-TV 31686
Owner: National Communications Inc.
Editorial: 129 W Prien Lake Rd, Lake Charles, Louisiana 70601-8570 **Tel:** 1 337 474-1316.
Email: news@watchfox.com
Web site: http://www.watchfox29.com/
Profile: KVHP-TV is the FOX affiliate for the Lake Charles, LA, market. The station is owned by National Communications Inc. KVHP-TV broadcasts locally on channel 29.
TELEVISION STATION

KVIA2-TV 714830
Owner: News-Press & Gazette Co.
Editorial: 4140 Rio Bravo St, El Paso, Texas 79902-1002 **Tel:** 1 915 496-7777.
Email: kvia@kvia.com
Profile: KVIA2-TV is a multicast channel of KVIA-TV. A multicast channel is a separate channel that shares the bandwidth of the main station but can air unique programming. KVIA2-TV is the local CW affiliate on channel 7.2 for the El Paso, TX market. KVIA2-TV is owned by News-Press & Gazette Co.
TELEVISION STATION

KVIA3-TV 714844
Owner: News-Press & Gazette Co.
Editorial: 4140 Rio Bravo St, El Paso, Texas 79902-1002 **Tel:** 1 915 496-7777.
Email: kvia@kvia.com
Web site: http://www.kvia.com
Profile: KIVA3-TV is a multicast channel of KVIA-TV. A multicast channel is a separate channel that shares the bandwidth of the main station but can air unique programming. KVIA3-TV is the local StormTRACK Weather affiliate on channel 7.3 for the El Paso, TX market. KVIA3-TV is owned by News-Press & Gazette Co.
TELEVISION STATION

KVIA-TV 32659
Owner: News-Press & Gazette Co.
Editorial: 4140 Rio Bravo St, El Paso, Texas 79902
Tel: 1 915 496-7777.
Email: kvia@kvia.com
Web site: http://www.kvia.com

Profile: KVIA-TV is the ABC affiliate for the El Paso, TX market. The station is owned by News-Press & Gazette Co. KVIA-TV broadcasts locally on channel 7.
TELEVISION STATION

KVIE2-TV 614638
Owner: KVIE-TV Inc.
Editorial: 2030 W El Camino Ave, Sacramento, California 95833-1866 **Tel:** 1 916 929-5843.
Web site: http://www.kvie.org
Profile: KVIE2-TV is the PBS affiliate for the Sacramento, CA market. The station is owned by KVIE-TV Inc. KVIE2-TV broadcasts locally on channel 6.2. The station airs alternative PBS programming different from its channel 6.1. KVIE2-TV is a multicast channel of KVIE-TV. A multicast channel is a separate channel that shares the bandwidth of the main station but can air unique programming.
TELEVISION STATION

KVIE3-TV 614641
Owner: KVIE-TV Inc.
Editorial: 2030 W El Camino Ave, Sacramento, California 95833-1866 **Tel:** 1 916 929-5843.
Web site: http://www.vmetv.com
Profile: KVIE3-TV is and independent affiliate for the Sacramento, CA market. The station is owned by KVIE-TV Inc. KVIE3-TV broadcasts locally on channel 6.3. The station airs Spanish language programming from V-me network. KVIE3-TV is a multicast channel of KVIE-TV. A multicast channel is a separate channel that shares the bandwidth of the main station but can air unique programming.
TELEVISION STATION

KVIE-TV 31687
Owner: KVIE Inc.
Editorial: 2030 W El Camino Ave, Sacramento, California 95833-1866 **Tel:** 1 916 929-5843.
Web site: http://www.kvie.org
Profile: KVIE-TV is the PBS member for the Sacramento, Stockton, Modesto, CA market. The station is owned by KVIE-TV Inc. KVIE-TV broadcasts locally on channel 6.
TELEVISION STATION

KVII-TV 32660
Owner: Sinclair Broadcast Group, Inc.
Editorial: 1 Broadcast Ctr, Amarillo, Texas 79101-4328 **Tel:** 1 806 373-1787.
Email: pronews7@kvii.com
Web site: http://abc7amarillo.com
Profile: KVII-TV is the local ABC affiliate for the Amarillo, TX. The station is owned by Sinclair Broadcast Group, Inc. KVII-TV broadcasts locally on channel 7.
TELEVISION STATION

KVIQ-TV 31688
Owner: Redwood Television Partners LLC
Editorial: 730 7th St, Eureka, California 95501-1166 **Tel:** 1 707 443-6666.
Web site: http://www.kviqcbs17.com
Profile: KVIQ-TV is the CBS affiliate in the Eureka, CA market. The station is owned by Redwood Television Partners LLC. KVIQ-TV broadcasts locally on channel 6.
TELEVISION STATION

KVLY-TV 31627
Owner: Gray Television
Editorial: 1350 21st Ave S, Fargo, North Dakota 58103-5237 **Tel:** 1 701 237-5211.
Email: mail@valleynewslive.com
Web site: http://www.valleynewslive.com
Profile: KVLY-TV is the NBC affiliate for the Fargo, ND market. The station is owned by Gray Television. KVLY-TV broadcasts locally on channel 11.
TELEVISION STATION

KVMD-TV 32601
Owner: KVMD Licensee LLC
Editorial: 28202 Cabot Rd., Suite 300, Laguna Niguel, California 92677 **Tel:** 1 760 366-9881.
Web site: http://www.kvmdtv.com
Profile: KVMD-TV is an independent station for the Los Angeles market. The station is owned by KVMD Licensee LLC. KVMD-TV broadcasts locally on channel 31.
TELEVISION STATION

KVOA-TV 31689
Owner: Evening Post Publishing Co.
Editorial: 209 W Elm St, Tucson, Arizona 85705-6539 **Tel:** 1 520 792-2270.
Email: newstips@kvoa.com
Web site: http://www.kvoa.com
Profile: KVOA-TV is the NBC network affiliate for the Tucson, AZ market. The station is owned by Evening Post Publishing Co. KVOA-TV broadcasts locally on channel 4.
TELEVISION STATION

KVOS-TV 31690
Owner: OTA Broadcasting, LLC
Editorial: 3111 Newmarket St, STE 108, Bellingham, Washington 98226 **Tel:** 1 360 671-1212.
Email: media@kvos.com
Web site: http://www.kvos.com
Profile: KVOS-TV is a MeTV affiliate for the Seattle-Tacoma market. The station is owned by OTA Broadcasting, LLC. KVOS-TV broadcasts locally on channel 12.
TELEVISION STATION

KVPT2-TV 616478
Owner: Valley Public Television Inc.
Editorial: 1544 Van Ness Ave, Fresno, California 93721-1213 **Tel:** 1 559 266-1800.
Email: web@valleypbs.org
Web site: http://www.valleypbs.org
Profile: KVPT2-TV is a multicast of KVPT-TV. A multicast channel is a separate channel that shares the bandwith of the main station but can air unique programming. KVPT2-TV airs programming from Create TV in the Fresno, CA market. The station is owned by Valley Public Television Inc. KVPT2-TV broadcasts locally on channel 18.2.
TELEVISION STATION

KVPT3-TV 616479
Owner: Valley Public Television Inc.
Editorial: 1544 Van Ness Ave, Fresno, California 93721-1213 **Tel:** 1 559 266-1800.
Email: web@valleypbs.org
Web site: http://www.valleypbs.org
Profile: KVPT3-TV is a multicast of KVPT-TV. A multicast channel is a separate channel that shares the bandwith of the main station but can air unique programming. KVPT3-TV airs programming from V-me in the Fresno, CA market. The station is owned by Valley Public Television Inc. KVPT3-TV broadcasts locally on channel 18.3.
TELEVISION STATION

KVPT-TV 32258
Owner: Valley Public Television Inc.
Editorial: 1544 Van Ness Ave, Fresno, California 93721 **Tel:** 1 559 266-1800.
Email: web@valleypbs.org
Web site: http://www.valleypbs.org
Profile: KVPT-TV is the PBS affiliate for the Fresno, CA market. The station is owned by Valley Public Television Inc. KVPT-TV broadcasts locally on channel 18.
TELEVISION STATION

KVRR-TV 32661
Owner: Red River Broadcasting
Editorial: 4015 9th Ave S, Fargo, North Dakota 58103-2105 **Tel:** 1 701 277-1515.
Web site: http://www.kvrr.com
Profile: KVRR-TV is the FOX affiliate for the Fargo, ND market. The station is owned by Red River Broadcasting. KVRR-TV broadcasts locally on channel 15.
TELEVISION STATION

KVTF-TV 390680
Owner: Entravision Communications Corp.
Editorial: 801 N Jackson Rd, McAllen, Texas 78501-9306 **Tel:** 1 956 687-4848.
Profile: KVTF-TV is the Telefutura Television Network for the Brownsville-McAllen, TX market. The station is owned by Entravision Communications Corp. KVTF-TV broadcasts locally on channel 20.
TELEVISION STATION

KVTH-TV 32480
Owner: Agape Church Inc.
Editorial: 701 Napa Valley Dr, Little Rock, Arkansas 72211-2303 **Tel:** 1 501 223-2525.
Email: viewers@vtntv.com
Web site: http://www.vtntv.com
Profile: KVTH-TV is an independent station for the Hot Springs, AR market. The station is owned by Agape Church Inc. KVTH-TV broadcasts locally on channel 26.
TELEVISION STATION

KVTJ-TV 32600
Owner: Agape Church Inc.
Editorial: 701 Napa Valley Dr, Little Rock, Arkansas 72211-2303 **Tel:** 1 501 223-2525.
Web site: http://www.vtntv.com
Profile: KVTJ-TV is a Victory Television Network affiliate for the Jonesboro, AR market. The station is owned by Agape Church Inc. KVTJ-TV broadcasts locally on channel 48. The station features religious programming and produces several original shows.
TELEVISION STATION

KVTN-TV 32351
Owner: Agape Church Inc.
Editorial: 701 Napa Valley Dr, Little Rock, Arkansas 72211-2303 **Tel:** 1 501 223-2525.
Email: viewers@vtntv.com
Web site: http://www.vtntv.com
Profile: KVTN-TV is an independent station for the Little Rock, AR market. The station is owned by Agape Church Inc. KVTN-TV broadcasts locally on channel 25.
TELEVISION STATION

KVTX-TV 331235
Owner: Saga Communications
Editorial: 3808 N Navarro St, Victoria, Texas 77901-2621 **Tel:** 1 361 575-2500.
Web site: http://www.crossroadstoday.com
Profile: KVTX-TV is the Telemundo affiliate for the Victoria, TX market. The station is owned by Saga Communications. KVTX-TV broadcasts locally on channel 45.
TELEVISION STATION

KVUE2-TV 609872
Owner: TEGNA Inc.
Editorial: 3201 Steck Ave, Austin, Texas 78757-8062 **Tel:** 1 512 459-6521.
Email: news@kvue.com
Web site: http://www.kvue.com
Profile: KVUE2-TV is a multicast channel of KVUE-TV. A multicast channel is a separate channel that shares the bandwidth of the main station but can air unique programming. KVUE2-TV airs programming from the Estrella TV network on channel 24.2 for the Austin, TX market. KVUE2-TV is owned by TEGNA Inc.
TELEVISION STATION

KVUE-TV 31692
Owner: TEGNA Inc.
Editorial: 3201 Steck Ave, Austin, Texas 78757-8062 **Tel:** 1 512 459-6521.
Email: news@kvue.com
Web site: http://www.kvue.com
Profile: KVUE-TV is the ABC affiliate for the Austin, TX market. The station is owned by TEGNA Inc. KVUE-TV broadcasts locally on channel 24.
TELEVISION STATION

KVVU-TV 31693
Owner: Meredith Broadcasting Group
Editorial: 25 Tv 5 Dr, Henderson, Nevada 89014-2332 **Tel:** 1 702 435-5555.
Email: 5newsdesk@kvvu.com
Web site: http://www.fox5vegas.com
Profile: KVVU-TV is the FOX affiliate for the Las Vegas market. The station is owned by Meredith Broadcasting Group. KVVU-TV broadcasts locally on channel 5.
TELEVISION STATION

KVYE-TV 32538
Owner: Entravision Communications Corp.
Editorial: 1803 N Imperial Ave, El Centro, California 92243-1333 **Tel:** 1 760 482-7777.
Web site: http://www.kvyetv.com
Profile: KVYE-TV is the Univision affiliate for the Yuma, AZ-El Centro, CA market. The station is owned by Entravision Communications Corp. KVYE-TV broadcasts locally on channel 7.
TELEVISION STATION

KWBA-TV 32585
Owner: E.W. Scripps Co.
Editorial: 7280 E Rosewood St, Tucson, Arizona 85710-1350 **Tel:** 1 520 722-5486.
Email: info@thecwtucson.com
Web site: http://www.thecwtucson.com
Profile: KWBA-TV is the CW network affiliate for the Tucson, AZ market. The station is owned by E.W. Scripps Co. KWBA-TV broadcasts locally on channel 58. News programs are produced by sister station KGUN-TV.
TELEVISION STATION

KWBH-TV 418078
Owner: Rapid Broadcasting
Editorial: 2424 S Plaza Dr, Rapid City, South Dakota 57702-9379 **Tel:** 1 605 355-0024.
Web site: http://yourcwtv.com/partners/rapidcity
Profile: KWBH-TV is a CW affiliate in Rapid City, SD. The station is owned by Rapid Broadcasting and airs on channel 27.
TELEVISION STATION

KWBJ-TV 32611
Owner: Price Media
Editorial: 608 Michigan St, Morgan City, Louisiana 70380-3239 **Tel:** 1 985 384-6960.
Email: info@kwbj.net
Profile: KWBJ-TV is an Independent station broadcasting to the Morgan City, LA market. The station is owned by Price Media. KWBJ-TV broadcasts locally on channel 39.
TELEVISION STATION

KWBQ-TV 63101
Owner: Tamer Media
Editorial: 13 Broadcast Plz SW, Albuquerque, New Mexico 87104-1056 **Tel:** 1 505 797-1919.
Web site: http://kwbq.com
Profile: KWBQ-TV is the CW affiliate for the Albuquerque, NM market. The station is owned by Tamer Media. KWBQ-TV broadcasts locally on channel 19.
TELEVISION STATION

KWCE-TV 79810
Owner: Pollack Broadcasting Co.
Editorial: 1811 England Dr, Alexandria, Louisiana 71303-4115 **Tel:** 1 318 473-0031.
Email: info@luken.tv
Web site: http://myretrotv.com
Profile: KWCE-TV is the Go Retro! affiliate for the Alexandria, LA, market. The station is owned by Pollack Broadcasting Co. KWCE-TV broadcasts locally on channel 27. The station has no news department.
TELEVISION STATION

KWCH-TV 32696
Owner: Sunflower Broadcasting
Editorial: 2815 E 37th St N, Wichita, Kansas 67219-3545 **Tel:** 1 316 838-1212.
Email: news@kwch.com
Web site: http://www.kwch.com
Profile: KWCH-TV is the CBS network affiliate for the Wichita-Hutchinson, KS market. The station is owned by Sunflower Broadcasting. KWCH-TV broadcasts locally on channel 12.
TELEVISION STATION

KWES-TV 32657
Owner: Raycom Media Inc.
Editorial: 11320 W County Road 127, Odessa, Texas 79765 **Tel:** 1 432 567-9991.
Web site: http://www.newswest9.com
Profile: KWES-TV is the NBC affiliate for the Odessa-Midland, TX. The station is owned by Raycom Media Inc. KWES-TV broadcasts locally on channel 9.
TELEVISION STATION

KWET2-TV 61879
Owner: OETA (Oklahoma Public Television Network)
Editorial: 7403 N Kelley Ave, Oklahoma City, Oklahoma 73111-8420 **Tel:** 1 405 848-8501.
Email: info@oeta.tv
Web site: http://www.oeta.tv
Profile: KWET2-TV is a multicast of KWET-TV. A multicast channel is a separate channel that shares the bandwith of the main station but can air unique programming. KWET2-TV airs programming from the OETA OKLA in the Oklahoma City market. The station is owned by OETA. KWET2-TV broadcasts locally on channel 8.2.
TELEVISION STATION

KWEX-TV 31695
Owner: Univision Communications Inc.
Editorial: 12451 Network Blvd Ste 140, San Antonio, Texas 78249-3336 **Tel:** 1 210 610-4141.
Web site: http://www.univision.com/san-antonio/kwex
Profile: KWEX-TV is the Univision affiliate for the San Antonio market. The station is owned by Univision Communications Inc. KWEX-TV broadcasts locally on channel 41.
TELEVISION STATION

KWGN-TV 31696
Owner: Tribune Broadcasting Co.
Editorial: 100 E Speer Blvd, Denver, Colorado 80203-3437 **Tel:** 1 303 595-3131.
Email: news@denvernewshd.com
Web site: http://kdvr.com/category/on-air/on-channel-2
Profile: KWGN-TV is the CW affiliate for the Denver market. The station is owned by Tribune Broadcasting Co. KWGN-TV broadcasts locally on channel 2.
TELEVISION STATION

KWHB-TV 32261
Owner: LeSEA Broadcasting
Editorial: 8835 S Memorial Dr, Tulsa, Oklahoma 74133-4315 **Tel:** 1 918 254-4701.
Web site: http://www.kwhb.com
Profile: KWHB-TV is an independent station for the Tulsa, OK market. The station is owned by LeSEA Broadcasting. KWHB-TV broadcasts locally on channel 47.
TELEVISION STATION

KWHE-TV 32740
Owner: LeSEA Broadcasting
Editorial: 1188 Bishop St Ste 502, Honolulu, Hawaii 96813-3302 **Tel:** 1 808 538-1414.
Email: kwhe@lesea.com
Web site: http://www.kwhe.com
Profile: KWHE-TV is independent station for the Honolulu market. The station is owned by LeSEA Broadcasting. KWHE-TV broadcasts locally on channel 14.
TELEVISION STATION

KWHS-TV 80620
Owner: LeSEA Broadcasting
Editorial: 1710 Briargate Blvd Ste 423, Colorado Springs, Colorado 80920-3488 **Tel:** 1 719 228-0651.
Web site: http://www.kwhs.COM
Profile: KWHS-TV is an independent station for the Denver, CO market. The station is owned by LeSEA Broadcasting. KWHS-TV broadcasts locally on channel 51.
TELEVISION STATION

KWHY-TV 31697
Owner: Meruelo Group
Editorial: 4975 W Pico Blvd, Los Angeles, California 90019-4231 **Tel:** 1 213 344-3724.
Profile: KWHY-TV is an independent station in the Los Angeles market. The station is owned by Meruelo Group. KWHY-TV broadcasts locally on Channel 22.
TELEVISION STATION

KWKB-TV 32632
Owner: KM Communications Inc.
Editorial: 1547 Baker Ave, West Branch, Iowa 52358-8639 **Tel:** 1 319 643-5952.
Email: kwkbtransfer@gmail.com
Web site: http://www.kwkb.tv
Profile: KWKB-TV is the CW and MyNetwork TV affiliate for the Cedar Rapids, IA market. The station is owned by KM Communications Inc. KWKB-TV broadcasts locally on channel 20.
TELEVISION STATION

KWKT-TV 32286
Owner: Communications Corp. of America
Editorial: 8803 Woodway Dr, Waco, Texas 76712-3634 **Tel:** 1 254 776-3844.
Email: info@kwkt.com
Web site: http://www.kwkt.com
Profile: KWKT-TV is the FOX affiliate for the Waco, TX market. The station is owned by Communications Corp. of America. KWKT-TV broadcasts locally on channel 44.
TELEVISION STATION

KWNB-TV 32789
Owner: Pappas Telecasting Companies
Tel: 1 308 743-2494.
Web site: http://www.nebraska.tv
Profile: KWNB-TV is a transmitter located in Kearney, NE that simulcasts the programming of KHGI-TV, the

ABC affiliate in Axtell, NE. It is owned by Pappas Telecasting Companies. KWNB-TV broadcasts locally on channel 6.
TELEVISION STATION

KWPX2-TV 612330
Owner: ION Media Networks
Editorial: 8112-C 304th Avenue SE, Preston, Washington 98050 **Tel:** 1 452 222-6010.
Profile: KWPX2-TV is a multicast of KWPX-TV. A multicast channel is a separate channel that shares the bandwith of the main station but can air unique programming. KWPX2-TV airs programming from qubo in the Seattle market. The station is owned by ION Media Networks. KWPX2-TV broadcasts locally on channel 33.2.
TELEVISION STATION

KWPX3-TV 612333
Owner: ION Media Networks
Editorial: 8112-C 304th Avenue SE, Preston, Washington 98050 **Tel:** 1 425 222-6010.
Profile: KWPX3-TV is a multicast of KWPX-TV. A multicast channel is a separate channel that shares the bandwith of the main station but can air unique programming. KWPX3-TV airs programming from ION Life in the Seattle market. The station is owned by ION Media Networks. KWPX3-TV broadcasts locally on channel 33.3.
TELEVISION STATION

KWPX4-TV 612335
Owner: ION Media Networks
Editorial: 8112-C 304th Avenue SE, Preston, Washington 98050 **Tel:** 1 425 222-6010.
Profile: KWPX4-TV is a multicast of KWPX-TV. A multicast channel is a separate channel that shares the bandwith of the main station but can air unique programming. KWPX4-TV airs programming from The Worship Network in the Seattle market. The station is owned by ION Media Networks. KWPX4-TV broadcasts locally on channel 33.4.
TELEVISION STATION

KWPX-TV 32489
Owner: ION Media Networks
Editorial: 8112-C 304th Aveune SE, Preston, Washington 98050 **Tel:** 1 425 222-6010.
Web site: http://ionmedianetworks.com
Profile: KWPX-TV is the ION Television affiliate for the Seattle-Tacoma market. The station is owned by ION Media Networks. KWPX-TV broadcasts locally on channel 33.
TELEVISION STATION

KWQC-TV 31698
Owner: Gray Television, Inc.
Editorial: 805 Brady St, Davenport, Iowa 52803-5211 **Tel:** 1 563 383-7000.
Email: news@kwqc.com
Web site: http://www.kwqc.com
Profile: KWQC-TV is the NBC affiliate for Davenport, IA market. The station is owned by New Young Broadcasting. KWQC-TV broadcasts locally on channel 6.
TELEVISION STATION

KWSD-TV 331265
Owner: J.F. Broadcasting, LLC
Tel: 1 605 341-3135.
Email: oct13ber@msn.com
Profile: KWSD-TV is the Me-TV affiliate for the Sioux Falls, SD market. The station is owned by J.F. Broadcasting, LLC. KWSD-TV airs locally on channel 36.
TELEVISION STATION

KWTV-TV 31699
Owner: Griffin Communications, LLC
Editorial: 7401 N Kelley Ave, Oklahoma City, Oklahoma 73111 **Tel:** 1 405 843-6641.
Email: newsdesk@news9.net
Web site: http://www.news9.com
Profile: KWTV-TV is the CBS affiliate for the Oklahoma City market. KWTV-TV is owned by Griffin Communications, LLC. KWTV-TV broadcasts locally on channel 9.
TELEVISION STATION

KWTX-TV 32445
Owner: Gray Television, Inc.
Editorial: 6700 American Plz, Waco, Texas 76712-3976 **Tel:** 1 254 776-1330.
Email: news@kwtx.com
Web site: http://www.kwtx.com
Profile: KWTX-TV is the CBS affiliate for the Waco, TX market. The station is owned by Gray Television Incorporated. KWTX-TV broadcasts locally on channel 10.
TELEVISION STATION

KWWL3-TV 586688
Owner: Quincy Newspapers Inc.
Editorial: 500 E 4th St, Waterloo, Iowa 50703-5798 **Tel:** 1 319 291-1200.
Email: comments@kwwl.com
Web site: http://www.kwwl.com/
Profile: KWWL3-TV is a multicast channel of KWWL-TV. A multicast channel is a separate channel that shares the bandwith of the main station but can air unique programming. KWWL3-TV is the Me-TV network for the Cedar Rapids, Iowa market. The station is owned by Quincy Newspapers Inc. KWWL3-TV broadcasts locally on channel 7.3.
TELEVISION STATION

KWWL-TV 31701
Owner: Quincy Newspapers Inc.
Editorial: 500 E 4th St, Waterloo, Iowa 50703-5798 **Tel:** 1 319 291-1200.
Email: kwwlnews@kwwl.com
Web site: http://www.kwwl.com
Profile: KWWL-TV is the NBC affiliate for the Cedar Rapids, IA market. The station is owned by Quincy Newspapers Inc. KWWL-TV broadcasts locally on channel 7.
TELEVISION STATION

KWWT-TV 350312
Owner: Camino Real Communications LLC
Editorial: 1901 E 37th St Ste 207, Odessa, Texas 79762-6210 **Tel:** 1 432 272-7514.
Email: kwwt@grandecom.com
Web site: http://yourcwtv.com/partners/odessa/index.php
Profile: KWWT-TV is a Me-TV affiliate for the Odessa-Midland, TX market. The staion is owned by Camino Real Communications LLC. KWWT-TV broadcasts locally on channel 30.
TELEVISION STATION

KWYB2-TV 964564
Owner: Cowles Publishing Co.
Editorial: 3825 Harrison Ave #B, Butte, Montana 59701-6810 **Tel:** 1 406 782-7185.
Web site: http://www.abcfoxmontana.com
Profile: KWYB2-TV is a multicast channel of KWYB-TV. A multicast channel is a separate channel that shares the bandwidth of the main station but can air unique programming. KWYB2-TV is the FOX affiliate for the Butte, MT market. The station is owned by Cowles Publishing Co. KWYB2-TV broadcasts locally on channel 18.2.
TELEVISION STATION

KWYB-TV 32549
Owner: Cowles Publishing Co.
Editorial: 3825 Harrison Ave #B, Butte, Montana 59701-6810 **Tel:** 1 406 782-7185.
Email: abcfoxmt@abcfoxmontana.com
Web site: http://www.abcfoxmontana.com
Profile: KWYB-TV is the ABC affiliate for the Butte, MT market. The station is owned by Cowles Publishing Co. KWYB-TV broadcasts locally on channel 18.
TELEVISION STATION

KWYF-TV 232158
Owner: Wyomedia Corporation
Editorial: 1856 Skyview Dr, Casper, Wyoming 82601-9638 **Tel:** 1 307 577-5923.
Profile: KWYF-TV is the CW affiliate for the Casper-Riverton, WY market. The station is owned by Wyomedia Corporation. KWYF-TV broadcasts locally on channel 26.
TELEVISION STATION

KXAN-TV 32574
Owner: Nexstar Media Group, Inc.
Editorial: 908 W Martin Luther King Jr Blvd, Austin, Texas 78701-1018 **Tel:** 1 512 476-3636.
Email: desk@kxan.com
Web site: http://www.kxan.com
Profile: KXAN-TV is the NBC affiliate for the Austin, TX market. The station is owned by Nexstar Media Group, Inc. KXAN-TV broadcasts locally on channel 36.
TELEVISION STATION

KXAS2-TV 607631
Owner: NBC Universal
Editorial: 4805 Amon Carter Blvd, Fort Worth, Texas 76155-2211 **Tel:** 1 817 429-5555.
Web site: http://www.cozitv.com
Profile: KXAS2-TV, also called DFW Nonstop, is a multicast channel of KXAS-TV. A multicast channel is a separate channel that shares the bandwidth of the main station but can air unique programming. KXAS2-TV is the Cozi TV affiliate for the Dallas – Ft. Worth market. The station is owned by NBC Universal. KXAS2-TV broadcasts locally on channel 5.2. The channel airs movies, classic television shows and lifestyle programming.
TELEVISION STATION

KXAS-TV 31702
Owner: NBC Universal
Editorial: 4805 Amon Carter Blvd, Fort Worth, Texas 76155-2211 **Tel:** 1 800 232-5927.
Email: newstips@nbcdfw.com
Web site: http://www.nbcdfw.com
Profile: KXAS-TV is the NBC affiliate for the Dallas-Fort Worth market. The station is owned by a joint venture of NBC Universal (76%) and LIN Television (24%) - its only other sister station under this co-ownership is KNSD in San Diego. However, because NBC has majority control of the station, KXAS is run as an NBC owned and operated station. KXAS-TV broadcasts locally on channel 5.
TELEVISION STATION

KXDF-TV 154106
Owner: Tanana Valley Television Co.
Editorial: 3650 Braddock St, Fairbanks, Alaska 99701-7617 **Tel:** 1 907 452-3697.
Email: news@tvtv.com
Web site: http://www.tvtv.com
Profile: KXD-TV is the CBS affiliate for the Fairbanks, AK market. The station is owned by Tanana Valley Television Co. KXD-TV broadcasts locally on channel 13.
TELEVISION STATION

KXGN-TV 31703
Owner: Glendive Broadcasting Corp.
Editorial: 210 S Douglas St, Glendive, Montana 59330-1623 **Tel:** 1 406 377-3377.
Web site: http://www.kxgn.com
Profile: KXGN-TV is the CBS affiliate for the Glendive, MT market. The station is owned by Glendive Broadcasting Corp. KXGN-TV broadcasts locally on channel 5.
TELEVISION STATION

KXII-TV 31704
Owner: Gray Television, Inc.
Editorial: 4201 Texoma Pkwy, Sherman, Texas 75090-1935 **Tel:** 1 903 892-8123.
Email: news12@kxii.com
Web site: http://www.kxii.com
Profile: KXII-TV is the CBS, FOX, and MyNetworkTV affiliate for Sherman, TX market. The station is owned by Gray Television. KXII-TV broadcasts locally on channel 12.
TELEVISION STATION

KXLA2-TV 606586
Owner: Ulloa(Ron)
Editorial: 2323 Corinth Ave, Los Angeles, California 90064-1701 **Tel:** 1 310 478-0055.
Web site: http://www.kxlatv.com
Profile: KXLA2-TV is a local TELE FE affilate for the Los Angles market. The station is owned by Ron Ulloa. KXLA-TV broadcasts locally on channel 44.2. The majority of the station's programming is Spanish language religious programming. KXLA2-TV is a multicast channel of KXLA-TV. A multicast channel is a separate channel that shares the bandwidth of the main station but can air unique programming.
TELEVISION STATION

KXLA3-TV 606592
Owner: Ulloa(Ron)
Editorial: 2323 Corinth Ave, Los Angeles, California 90064-1701 **Tel:** 1 310 478-0055.
Web site: http://www.kxlatv.com
Profile: KXLA3-TV is a local independent SK Health network affilate for the Los Angeles market. The station is owned by Ron Ulloa. KXLA-TV broadcasts locally on channel 44.3. The majority of the station's programming is Korean health related programming. KXLA3-TV is a multicast channel of KXLA-TV. A multicast channel is a separate channel that shares the bandwidth of the main station but can air unique programming.
TELEVISION STATION

KXLA4-TV 606598
Owner: Ulloa(Ron)
Editorial: 2323 Corinth Ave, Los Angeles, California 90064-1701 **Tel:** 1 310 478-0055.
Web site: http://www.kxlatv.com
Profile: KXLA4-TV is a local independent network broadcasting Little SaigonTV for the Los Angles market. The station is owned by Ron Ulloa. KXLA-TV broadcasts locally on channel 44.4. The majority of the station's programming is Vietnamese programming. KXLA4-TV is a multicast channel of KXLA-TV. A multicast channel is a separate channel that shares the bandwidth of the main station but can air unique programming.
TELEVISION STATION

KXLA5-TV 606964
Owner: Ulloa(Ron)
Editorial: 2323 Corinth Ave, Los Angeles, California 90064-1701 **Tel:** 1 310 478-0055.
Profile: KXLA5-TV is a local independent network broadcasting TV Korea for the Los Angeles market. The station is owned by Ron Ulloa. KXLA-TV broadcasts locally on channel 44.5. The majority of the station's programming is Korean programming. KXLA5-TV is a multicast channel of KXLA-TV. A multicast channel is a separate channel that shares the bandwidth of the main station but can air unique programming.
TELEVISION STATION

KXLA6-TV 606966
Owner: Ulloa(Ron)
Editorial: 2323 Corinth Ave, Los Angeles, California 90064-1701 **Tel:** 1 310 478-0055.
Profile: KXLA6-TV is a local independent network broadcasting IAVC Mandarin TV for the Los Angeles market. The station is owned by Ron Ulloa. KXLA-TV broadcasts locally on channel 44.6. The majority of the station's programming is Mandarin programming. KXLA5-TV is a multicast channel of KXLA-TV. A multicast channel is a separate channel that shares the bandwidth of the main station but can air unique programming.
TELEVISION STATION

KXLA-TV 417941
Owner: Ulloa(Ron)
Editorial: 2323 Corinth Ave, Los Angeles, California 90064-1701 **Tel:** 1 310 478-0055.
Web site: http://www.kxlatv.com
Profile: KXLA-TV is an independent station for the Los Angles market. The station is owned by Ron Ulloa. KXLA-TV broadcasts locally on channel 44.
TELEVISION STATION

KXLF-TV 31706
Owner: Cordillera Communications Inc.
Editorial: 1003 S Montana St, Butte, Montana 59701-2839 **Tel:** 1 406 496-8400.
Email: newstips@kxlf.com
Web site: http://www.kxlf.com
Profile: KXLF-TV is the CBS affiliate for the Butte, MT market. The station is owned by Cordillera Communications Inc. KXLF-TV broadcasts locally on channel 4.
TELEVISION STATION

KXLH-TV 418217
Owner: Cordillera Communications Inc.
Editorial: 100 W Lyndale Ave, Helena, Montana 59601-2999 **Tel:** 1 406 422-1018.
Email: krtvnews@krtv.com
Web site: http://www.kxlh.com
Profile: KXLH-TV is a CBS affiliate for the Helena, MT market. The station is owned by Cordillera Communications Inc. KXLH-TV broadcasts locally on channel 9.
TELEVISION STATION

KXLN-TV 32343
Owner: Univision Communications Inc.
Editorial: 5100 Southwest Fwy, Houston, Texas 77056-7308 **Tel:** 1 713 662-4545.
Email: univision45@univision.net
Web site: http://houston.univision.com
Profile: KXLN-TV is the Univision affiliate for the Houston market. The station is owned by Univision Communications Inc. KXLN-TV broadcasts locally on channel 45. This station does not have a local program director. All programming is handled by corporate.
TELEVISION STATION

KXLT-TV 32328
Owner: SagamoreHill Broadcasting
Editorial: 6301 Bandel Rd NW, Rochester, Minnesota 55901-8798 **Tel:** 1 507 252-4747.
Email: news@myfox47.com
Web site: http://www.myfox47.com
Profile: KXLT-TV is the FOX affiliate for the Rochester, MN market. The station is owned by SagamoreHill Broadcasting. KXLT-TV is broadcast locally on channel 47.
TELEVISION STATION

KXLY2-TV 809174
Owner: Spokane Television
Editorial: 500 W Boone Ave, Spokane, Washington 99201-2404 **Tel:** 1 509 324-4004.
Web site: http://metvnetwork.com
Profile: KXLY2-TV is a multicast channel of KXLY-TV. A multicast channel is a separate channel that shares the bandwith of the main station but can air unique programming. KXLY2-TV is the Me-TV Network affiliate for the Spokane, WA market. The station is owned by Spokane Television. KXLY2-TV broadcasts locally on channel 4.2.
TELEVISION STATION

KXLY-TV 31707
Owner: Spokane Television
Editorial: 500 W Boone Ave, Spokane, Washington 99201-2404 **Tel:** 1 509 324-4004.
Email: news4@kxly.com
Web site: http://www.kxly.com
Profile: KXLY-TV is the ABC affiliate for the Spokane, WA market. The station is owned by Spokane Television. KXLY-TV broadcasts locally on channel 4.
TELEVISION STATION

KXMB-TV 32791
Owner: Nexstar Broadcasting Group
Editorial: 1811 N 15th St, Bismarck, North Dakota 58501-2026 **Tel:** 1 701 223-9197.
Web site: http://www.myndnow.com
Profile: KXMB-TV is the CBS network affiliate for the Minot-Bismarck, ND market. The station is owned by Nexstar Broadcasting Group. KXMB-TV broadcasts locally on channel 12.
TELEVISION STATION

KXMC-TV 32663
Owner: Nexstar Broadcasting Group
Editorial: 2121 2nd St SE, Minot, North Dakota 58701-6559 **Tel:** 1 701 852-2104.
Email: krohrich@kxnet.com
Web site: http://www.kxnet.com/category/225352/news-kxmc-cbs13
Profile: KXMC-TV is the CBS affiliate for the Minot-Bismarck, ND market. The station is owned by Nexstar Broadcasting Group. KXMC-TV broadcasts locally on channel 13.
TELEVISION STATION

KXNW-TV 32334
Owner: Tribune Broadcasting Co.
Editorial: 4201 N Shiloh Dr Ste 169, Fayetteville, Arkansas 72703-5180 **Tel:** 1 479 783-1191.
Web site: http://5newsonline.com
Profile: KXNW-TV is the RTN/Retro Television Network affiliate for the Fort Smith, AR market. The station is owned by Tribune Broadcasting Co. KXNW-TV broadcasts locally on channel 34.
TELEVISION STATION

KXOF2-TV 829860
Owner: Entravision Communications
Editorial: 222 Bob Bullock Loop, Laredo, Texas 78043-4206 **Tel:** 1 956 727-0027.
Profile: KXOF2-TV is a multicast channel of KXOF-TV. A multicast channel is a separate channel that shares the bandwidth of the main station but can air unique programming. KXOF2-TV is the MundoFOX affiliate for the Laredo, TX market. The station is owned by Entravision Communications Corp. KXOF2-TV broadcasts locally on channel 39.2.
TELEVISION STATION

United States of America

KXOF-TV 829811
Owner: Entravision Communications
Editorial: 222 Bob Bullock Loop, Laredo, Texas
78043-4206 **Tel:** 1 956 727-0027.
Email: noticias27@entravision.com
Web site: http://www.mylaredofox.com
Profile: KXOF-TV is the FOX affiliate for the Laredo,
TX, market. The station is owned by Entravision
Communications Corp. KXOF-TV broadcasts locally
on channel 39.
TELEVISION STATION

KXRM-TV 31708
Owner: Sinclair Broadcast Group, Inc.
Editorial: 560 Wooten Rd, Colorado Springs,
Colorado 80915-3524 **Tel:** 1 719 596-2100.
Email: news@kxrm.com
Web site: http://www.fox21news.com
Profile: KXRM-TV is the FOX affiliate in Colorado
Springs, CO. The station is owned by Sinclair
Broadcast Group, Inc. KXRM-TV broadcasts locally
on channel 21.
TELEVISION STATION

KXTQ-TV 133740
Owner: Ramar Communications II Ltd.
Editorial: 9800 University Ave, Lubbock, Texas
79423-5302 **Tel:** 1 806 745-3434.
Email: news@ramarcom.com
Web site: http://www.telemundolubbock.com
Profile: KXTQ-TV is the Telemundo network affiliate
for the Lubbock, TX market. The station is owned by
Ramar Communications II Ltd. KXTQ-TV broadcasts
locally on channel 46.
TELEVISION STATION

KXTS-TV 376585
Owner: Saga Communications
Editorial: 3808 N Navarro St, Victoria, Texas 77901-
2621 **Tel:** 1 361 575-2500.
Web site: http://www.crossroadstoday.com
Profile: KXTS-TV is the Univision affiliate for the
Victoria, TX market. The station is owned by Saga
Communications. KXTS-TV broadcasts locally on
channel 41.
TELEVISION STATION

KXTU-TV 152463
Owner: Sinclair Broadcast Group, Inc.
Editorial: 560 Wooten Rd, Colorado Springs,
Colorado 80915-3524 **Tel:** 1 719 596-2100.
Email: info@kxrm.com
Web site: http://www.sococw.com
Profile: KXTU-TV is the CW affiliate for the Colorado
Springs, CO, area. The station is owned by Sinclair
Broadcast Group, Inc. KXTU-TV broadcasts locally
on channel 57.
TELEVISION STATION

KXTV-TV 31709
Owner: TEGNA Inc.
Editorial: 400 Broadway, Sacramento, California
95818-2041 **Tel:** 1 916 321-3300.
Email: desk@abc10.com
Web site: http://www.abc10.com
Profile: KXTV-TV is the ABC network affiliate for the
Sacramento, CA market. The station is owned by
TEGNA Inc. KXTV-TV broadcasts locally on channel
10.
TELEVISION STATION

KXTX-TV 31710
Owner: NBC Universal
Editorial: 4805 Amon Carter Blvd, Fort Worth, Texas
76155-2211 **Tel:** 1 817 429-5555.
Email: noticierodallas@telemundo.com
Web site: http://www.telemundodallas.com
Profile: KXTX-TV is the Telemundo affiliate for the
Dallas-Fort Worth market. The station is owned by
NBC Universal. KXTX-TV broadcasts locally on
channel 39.
TELEVISION STATION

KXUN-TV 328235
Owner: Pinnacle Media, LLC
Editorial: 510 N Greenwood Ave, Fort Smith,
Arkansas 72901-3510 **Tel:** 1 479 785-4600.
Web site: http://espanoltvarkansas.com/home.php
Profile: KXUN-TV is the Univision affiliate for the Ft.
Smith, AR market. The station is owned by Pinnacle
Media, LLC. KXUN-TV broadcasts locally on channel
43.
TELEVISION STATION

KXVA-TV 139417
Owner: TEGNA Inc.
Editorial: 4127 S Danville Dr, Abilene, Texas 79605-
7230 **Tel:** 1 325 655-6006.
Email: kidy-communitycalendar@foxsanangelo.com
Web site: http://www.myfoxzone.com
Profile: KXVA-TV is the FOX affiliate for the Abilene,
TX market. The station is owned by TEGNA Inc.
KXVA-TV broadcasts locally on channel 15.
TELEVISION STATION

KXVO-TV 32456
Owner: Sinclair Broadcast Group
Editorial: 4625 Farnam St, Omaha, Nebraska 68132-
3222 **Tel:** 1 402 554-1500.
Email: frontdesk@kptm.com
Web site: http://www.cw15kxvo.com
Profile: KXVO-TV is the CW affiliate for the Omaha,
NE market. The station is owned by Sinclair
Broadcast Group. KXVO-TV broadcasts locally on
channel 15.
TELEVISION STATION

KXVU-TV 623776
Owner: Sainte Partners II, LP
Editorial: 300 Main St, Chico, California 95928
Tel: 1 530 893-1234.
Web site: http://www.telemundo17.com
Profile: KXVU-TV is the Telemundo affiliate on for
Spanish speaking viewers in Chico, CA area. The
station is owned by Sainte Partners II, LP. KCSO-TV
broadcasts locally on channel 17.
TELEVISION STATION

KXXV-TV 31711
Owner: Raycom Media Inc.
Editorial: 1909 S New Rd, Waco, Texas 76711-1829
Tel: 1 254 754-2525.
Email: news25@kxxv.com
Web site: http://www.kxxv.com
Profile: KXXV-TV is the ABC affiliate for the Waco, TX
market. The station is owned by Raycom Media Inc.
KXXV-TV broadcasts locally on channel 25.
TELEVISION STATION

KYAV-TV 151458
Owner: Desert Television
Editorial: 1139 Grand Central Ave, Glendale,
California 91201-2423 **Tel:** 1 760 343-5700.
Email: contacto@aztecaamerica.com
Web site: http://us.azteca.com
Profile: KYAV-TV is the Azteca America affiliate for
the Los Angeles market. The station is owned by
Desert Television. KYAV-TV broadcasts locally on
channel 19.
TELEVISION STATION

KYAZ-TV 32439
Owner: Una Vez Mas LP
Editorial: 7322 Southwest Fwy Ste 1500, Houston,
Texas 77074-2077 **Tel:** 1 281 661-7338.
Web site: http://uvmtv.com
Profile: KYAZ-TV is a digital Spanish station for the
Houston market. The station is owned by Una Vez
Mas LP. KYAZ-TV broadcasts locally on channel
51.1.
TELEVISION STATION

KYDF-TV 476476
Owner: Una Vez Mas LP
Editorial: 1701 N Market St Ste 500, Dallas, Texas
75202-2001 **Tel:** 1 214 754-7008.
Web site: http://www.aztecaamerica.com
Profile: KDYF-TV is the Azteca America affiliate for
the Corpus Christi, TX market. The station is owned
by Una Vez Mas LP. KDYF-TV broadcasts locally on
channel 64. All public service announcements should
be directed to the mailing address, the corporate
headquarters in Dallas, in BETA format.
TELEVISION STATION

KYES-TV 32366
Owner: Fireweed Communications LLC.
Editorial: 3700 Woodland Dr, Ste 800, Anchorage,
Alaska 99517-2588 **Tel:** 1 907 248-5937.
Web site: http://www.kyes.com
Profile: KYES-TV is the local MyNetworkTV affiliate
for the Anchorage, AK market. The station is owned
by Fireweed Communications LLC. The station
broadcasts locally on channel 5.
TELEVISION STATION

KYIN-TV 32479
Owner: Iowa Public Television
Editorial: 6450 Corporate Dr, Johnston, Iowa 50131-
7700 **Tel:** 1 515 242-3100.
Email: publicinformation@iptv.org
Web site: http://www.iptv.org
Profile: KYIN-TV is the PBS affiliate for the Johnston,
IA market. The station is owned by the State of Iowa.
KYIN-TV broadcasts locally on channel 24.
TELEVISION STATION

KYLE-TV 32458
Owner: Communications Corp. of America
Editorial: 2402 Broadmoor Dr Ste B101, Bryan, Texas
77802-2800 **Tel:** 1 979 774-1800.
Email: info@kwkt.com
Web site: http://www.kyle28.com
Profile: KYLE-TV is the FOX affiliate for the Waco, TX
market. The station is owned by Communications
Corp. of America. KYLE-TV broadcasts locally on
channel 28.
TELEVISION STATION

KYMA-TV 32240
Owner: Blackhawk Broadcasting
Editorial: 1385 S Pacific Ave, Yuma, Arizona 85365-
1725 **Tel:** 1 928 782-1111.
Email: news@kyma.com
Web site: http://www.kyma.com
Profile: KYMA-TV is the NBC affiliate for the Yuma,
AZ/El Centro, CA market. The station is owned by
Blackhawk Broadcasting. KYMA-TV broadcasts
locally on channel 11.
TELEVISION STATION

KYOU-TV 31554
Owner: Ottumwa Media Holding LLC
Editorial: 820 W 2nd St, Ottumwa, Iowa 52501-2212
Tel: 1 641 684-5415.
Web site: http://www.kyoutv.com
Profile: KYOU-TV is the Fox affiliate for the Ottumwa,
IA market. The station is owned by Ottumwa Media
Holding LLC. KYOU-TV broadcasts locally on
channel 15.
TELEVISION STATION

KYTV-TV 31714
Owner: Schurz Communications Inc.
Editorial: 999 W Sunshine St, Springfield, Missouri
65807-2443 **Tel:** 1 417 268-3000.
Email: newsproducers@ky3.com
Web site: http://www.ky3.com
Profile: KYTV-TV is the NBC affiliate for the
Springfield, MO market. The station is owned by
Schurz Communications Inc. KYTV-TV broadcasts
locally on channel 3.
TELEVISION STATION

KYTX2-TV 829865
Owner: TEGNA Inc.
Editorial: 2211 E Southeast Loop 323, Tyler, Texas
75701-8321 **Tel:** 1 903 581-2211.
Email: news@cbs19.com
Web site: http://www.cbs19.tv/
Profile: KYTX2-TV is a multicast channel of KYTX-TV.
A multicast channel is a separate channel that shares
the bandwidth of the main station but can air unique
programming. KYTX2-TV is the MundoFOX affiliate
for the Tyler-Longview, TX market. The station is
owned by TEGNA Inc. KYTX2-TV broadcasts locally
on channel 19.2.
TELEVISION STATION

KYTX-TV 232348
Owner: TEGNA Inc.
Editorial: 2211 E Southeast Loop 323, Tyler, Texas
75701-8321 **Tel:** 1 903 581-2211.
Web site: http://www.cbs19.tv
Profile: KYTX-TV is the CBS affiliate for the Tyler-
Longview, TX market. The station is owned by
TEGNA Inc. KYTX-TV broadcasts locally on channel
19.
TELEVISION STATION

KYUK-TV 31715
Owner: Bethel Broadcasting Inc.
Editorial: 640 Radio St, Bethel, Alaska 99559
Tel: 1 907 543-3131.
Email: shane@kyuk.org
Web site: http://www.kyuk.org
Profile: KYUK-TV is the PBS affiliate for the Bethel,
AK market. The station is owned by Bethel
Broadcasting, Inc. KYUK-TV broadcasts locally on
channel 4.
TELEVISION STATION

KYUR-TV 31489
Owner: Coastal Television Broadcasting Company
LLC
Editorial: 2700 E Tudor Rd, Anchorage, Alaska
99507-1136 **Tel:** 1 907 561-1313.
Web site: http://www.youralaskalink.com
Profile: KYUR-TV is the ABC network affiliate for the
Anchorage, AK market. The station is owned by
Coastal Television Broadcasting Company LLC.
KYUR-TV broadcasts locally on channel 13.
TELEVISION STATION

KYVE-TV 31716
Owner: KCTS Television
Editorial: 12 S 2nd St, Yakima, Washington 98901-
2618 **Tel:** 1 509 452-4700.
Email: viewer@KCTS9.org
Web site: http://www.kyve.org
Profile: KYVE-TV is the PBS affiliate for the Yakima,
WA market. The station is owned by KCTS Television.
KYVE-TV broadcasts locally on channel 47.
TELEVISION STATION

KYVV-TV 830049
Owner: SATV 10, LLC
Editorial: 80 Las Palmas Dr, Del Rio, Texas 78840
Tel: 1 830 775-5988.
Email: info@mundofox10.com
Web site: http://www.mundofox10sanantonio.com
Profile: KYVV-TV is the MundoFOX affiliate for the
San Antonio market. The station is owned by SATV
10, LLC. KYVV-TV broadcasts locally on channel 28.
The station does not have a news department.
TELEVISION STATION

KYW-TV 31717
Owner: CBS Television Stations
Editorial: 1555 Hamilton St, Philadelphia,
Pennsylvania 19130-4085 **Tel:** 1 215 977-5300.
Email: 3onyourside@cbs3.com
Web site: http://philadelphia.cbslocal.com
Profile: KYW-TV is the local CBS affiliate for the
Philadelphia market.The station is owned by the CBS
Television Stations subsidiary of CBS Corporation,
and is the sister station to CW station WPSG. The
two stations share studios and office facilities located
just north of Center City Philadelphia, KYW's
transmitter is located in the Roxborough section of
Philadelphia. The station broadcasts locally on
channel 3.
TELEVISION STATION

KZCO-TV 476478
Owner: McGraw-Hill Broadcasting
Editorial: 123 E Speer Blvd, Denver, Colorado 80203
Tel: 1 303 832-0200.
Email: 7newsdesk@kmgh.com
Web site: http://www.thedenverchannel.com
Profile: KZCO-TV is the Azteca America affiliate for
the Denver market. The station is owned by McGraw-
Hill Broadcasting. KZCO-TV broadcasts locally on
channel 27.
TELEVISION STATION

KZCS-TV 476482
Owner: McGraw-Hill Broadcasting
Editorial: 123 E Speer Blvd, Denver, Colorado 80203
Tel: 1 303 832-0200.
Email: 7newsdesk@kmgh.com
Web site: http://www.thedenverchannel.com/azteca/
index.html
Profile: KZCS-TV is the Azteca America affiliate for
the Denver, CO market. The station is owned by
McGraw-Hill Broadcasting Company. KZCS-TV
broadcasts locally on channel 23.
TELEVISION STATION

KZDF-TV 588380
Owner: Una Vez Mas LP
Editorial: 1701 N Market St Ste 500, Dallas, Texas
75202-2001 **Tel:** 1 214 754-7008.
Web site: http://www.aztecaamerica.com
Profile: KZDF-TV is the Azteca America affiliate for
the Santa Barbara, CA market. The station is owned
by Una Vez Mas LP. KZDF-TV broadcasts locally on
channel 8.
TELEVISION STATION

KZJL-TV 63091
Owner: Liberman Broadcasting Inc.
Editorial: 3000 Bering Dr, Houston, Texas 77057-
5708 **Tel:** 1 713 315-3400.
Web site: http://www.lbimedia.com
Profile: KZJL-TV is an independent station in the
Houston market. The station is owned by Liberman
Broadcasting Inc. KZJL-TV broadcasts locally on
channel 61.
TELEVISION STATION

KZJO-TV 31671
Owner: Tribune Broadcasting Co.
Editorial: 1813 Westlake Ave N, Seattle, Washington
98109-2706 **Tel:** 1 206 674-1313.
Email: tips@q13fox.com
Web site: http://q13fox.com/joetv
Profile: KZJO-TV is the MyNetworkTV affiliate for the
Seattle-Tacoma market. The station is owned by
Tribune Broadcasting Co. KMYQ-TV broadcasts
locally on channel 22.
TELEVISION STATION

KZKC-TV 476766
Owner: E.W. Scipps Co.
Editorial: 321 21st St, Bakersfield, California 93301-
4120 **Tel:** 1 661 637-2323.
Web site: http://www.turnto23.com/azteca42
Profile: KZKC-TV is the Azteca America affiliate for
the Bakersfield, CA market. The station is owned by
E.W. Scipps Co. KZKC-TV broadcasts locally on
channel 42.
TELEVISION STATION

KZSD-TV 377560
Owner: E.W. Scipps Co.
Editorial: 4600 Air Way, San Diego, California 92102-
2528 **Tel:** 1 619 237-1010.
Email: 10news@kgtv.com
Web site: http://www.10news.com/azteca
Profile: KZSD-TV is the Azteca America affiliate for
the San Diego market. The station is owned by E.W.
Scipps Co. KZSD-TV broadcasts locally on channel
41.
TELEVISION STATION

KZTV-TV 31719
Owner: Eagle Creek Broadcasting
Editorial: 301 Artesian St, Corpus Christi, Texas
78401-2701 **Tel:** 1 361 884-6666.
Web site: http://www.kztv10.com
Profile: KZTV-TV is the CBS affiliate for the Corpus
Christi, TX market. The station is owned by Eagle
Creek Broadcasting. KZTV-TV broadcasts locally on
channel 10.
TELEVISION STATION

Latinoamerica Televisión 842269
Email: info@latele.tv
Web site: http://www.ltv.la
Profile: Latinoamerica Television is a channel with
exclusive content from Latin America to the U.S.
Hispanic audience. Programming fare includes
movies, sporting events, news and information,
current affairs, children's programs, comedy, variety
and talk shows and dramatic series.
TELEVISION NETWORK

Link TV 592920
Editorial: 901 Battery St Ste 308, San Francisco,
California 94111-1350 **Tel:** 1 415 248-3950.
Email: contact@linktv.org
Web site: http://www.linktv.org
Profile: Nationwide television channel dedicated to
providing Americans with global perspectives on
news, events and culture. The channel was launched
in December 1999 on DIRECTV and was later added
to EchoStar's DISH Network. The channel is available
as a basic service in more than 31 million U.S. homes
that receive direct broadcast satellite television. Link
TV broadcasts programs that engage, educate and
activate viewers to become involved in the world.
These programs provide a unique perspective on
international news, current events, and diverse
cultures, presenting issues not often covered in the
U.S. media.
TELEVISION NETWORK

MeTV 719876
Owner: Weigel Broadcasting Co.
Editorial: 26 N Halsted St, Chicago, Illinois 60661-
2107 **Tel:** 1 312 705-2600.
Web site: http://www.metvnetwork.com

Profile: ME TV is a national television network consisting of classic television programs.
TELEVISION NETWORK

MyNetworkTV 424715
Owner: News Corporation
Editorial: 1211 Avenue of the Americas, New York, New York 10036-8701 **Tel:** 1 212 301-5400.
Web site: http://www.mynetworktv.com
Profile: MyNetworkTV launched on September 5, 2006. It offers a wide array of entertainment programming. Most of its affiliates are former affiliates of The WB and UPN that did not join the CW Network. MyNetworkTV is a sister network of the FOX Broadcasting Network.
TELEVISION NETWORK

NBC Television Network 33052
Owner: NBC Universal
Editorial: 30 Rockefeller Plz, New York, New York 10112-0015 **Tel:** 1 212 664-4444.
Email: nbcnewsmediarelations@nbcuni.com
Web site: http://www.nbc.com
Profile: The NBC Television Network's strength derives from combining NBC's strong national identity and programming with the local identity and programming of its affiliates in communities across America. The sale of advertising time enables the NBC Television Network to provide programming to the public free of charge. Affiliated television stations are an integral part of NBC's overall broadcast service. The NBC Television Network broadcasts approximately 5,000 hours of TV programming each year, transmitting to more than 200 affiliated stations across the United States. These independently owned affiliates then broadcast the NBC signal to an estimated 99 percent of all homes in the United States with television sets. In addition to airing NBC's national programming, affiliates serve their communities by producing news, sports, and public affairs programming that addresses local needs.
TELEVISION NETWORK

NBC Television Network - Atlanta Bureau 33108
Owner: NBC Universal
Editorial: 1 Monroe Pl NE, Atlanta, Georgia 30324-4836 **Tel:** 1 404 881-0154.
Web site: http://www.nbc.com
Profile: Atlanta Bureau of NBC Television Network.
TELEVISION NETWORK

NBC Television Network - Charlotte Bureau 776615
Owner: NBC Universal
Editorial: 925 Woodrdg Ctr Dr, Charlotte, North Carolina 28217-1986 **Tel:** 1 704 329-8700.
Web site: http://www.nbc.com
Profile: NBC Television Network bureau in Charlotte, North Carolina.
TELEVISION NETWORK

NBC Television Network - Chicago Bureau 33094
Owner: NBC Universal
Editorial: 454 N Columbus Dr, Chicago, Illinois 60611-5807 **Tel:** 1 312 836-5566.
Web site: http://www.nbc.com
Profile: The Chicago Bureau of NBC Television Network.
TELEVISION NETWORK

NBC Television Network - Fort Worth Bureau 33122
Owner: NBC Universal
Editorial: 3900 Barnett St, Fort Worth, Texas 76103-1400 **Tel:** 1 214 871-7373.
Web site: http://www.nbc.com
Profile: Fort Worth Bureau of NBC Television Network.
TELEVISION NETWORK

NBC Television Network - London Bureau 696406
Owner: NBC Universal
Tel: 44 207 843-8700.
Email: london.newsdesk@nbc.com
Web site: http://www.nbc.com
Profile: London Bureau of NBC Television Network.
TELEVISION NETWORK

NBC Television Network - New Orleans Bureau 358876
Editorial: 846 Howard Ave, New Orleans, Louisiana 70113-1134 **Tel:** 1 504 528-8744.
TELEVISION NETWORK

NBC Television Network - Universal City Bureau 33100
Owner: NBC Universal
Editorial: 100 Universal City Plz, Universal City, California 91608-1002 **Tel:** 1 818 777-1000.
Web site: http://www.nbc.com
Profile: Universal City Bureau of NBC Television Network.
TELEVISION NETWORK

NBC Television Network - Washington Bureau 33090
Owner: NBC Universal
Editorial: 4001 Nebraska Ave NW, Washington, District Of Columbia 20016-2733 **Tel:** 1 202 885-4200.
Email: nbcdcpressadvisories@nbc.com
Profile: Washington Bureau of NBC Television Network.
TELEVISION NETWORK

Pan Desi 585460
Editorial: 1 Ethel Rd, Edison, New Jersey 08817-2838
Tel: 1 732 287-2500.
Email: team@pandesi.com
Web site: http://www.pandesi.com
Profile: Pan Desi (Day-see) is an English language television network for South Asians in America. The network, which launched in 2008, uniquely targets the audience of Americanized people of Indian, Pakistani and similar South Asian descent. Pan Desi's audience of South-Asian Americans represents one of the most affluent and fastest-growing ethnic groups in the United States. The network offers programming for Desi families, women, men, teens and children. The networks programming slate includes entertainment, movies, sports, magazine shows, late night comedy blocks and issues-based, interactive audience participation programs that make use of in-person, telephone and computer technologies. Programming from the Pan Desi Network is available nationwide to more than seventeen million households through an agreement with CoLours TV.
TELEVISION NETWORK

PBS/Public Broadcasting Service 33055
Editorial: 2100 Crystal Dr, Arlington, Virginia 22202-3784 **Tel:** 1 703 739-5000.
Email: pressroom@pbs.org
Web site: http://www.pbs.org
Profile: PBS is a media enterprise that serves 355 public non-commercial television stations and reaches nearly 73 million people each week through on-air and online content. Bringing diverse viewpoints to television and the Internet, PBS provides high-quality documentary and dramatic entertainment. PBS is a leading provider of digital learning content for pre-K-12 educators, and offers a broad array of other educational services. The national broadcast entity, founded in 1969, provides quality TV programming and related services to 355 non-commercial stations serving all 50 states, Puerto Rico, the U.S. Virgin Islands, Guam and American Samoa.
TELEVISION NETWORK

Premium Sports Inc. 620043
Editorial: 170 Columbus Ave Ste 201, San Francisco, California 94133-5160 **Tel:** 1 415 400-4869.
Web site: http://www.premiumsportsinc.com
Profile: Premium Sports Inc. features live broadcasts of popular international soccer, rugby, Gaelic sports and boxing. Past featured sporting events include, the Euro Cup, IRB Rugby World Cup, Barclays Premier League, the UEFA Champions League. Premium Sports is available via a closed-circuit satellite feed.
TELEVISION NETWORK

Qubo Channel 555162
Owner: Ion Media Networks, NBC Universal, Corus Nelvana, Scholastic Media
Editorial: 810 7Th Ave, New York, New York 10019-5818 **Tel:** 1 212 603-8488.
Email: pr@qubo.com
Web site: http://www.qubo.com
Profile: Qubo is a groundbreaking bilingual, multi-platform entertainment destination for children that focuses on literacy, values and healthy lifestyles while celebrating the unlimited possibilities of a child's imagination. Most of Qubo's shows are associated with popular children's books, and the network's interstitial programming continues to reinforce messages about early literacy and healthy living.
TELEVISION NETWORK

RTN/Retro Television 430054
Owner: Luken Communications
Editorial: 225 E 8th St, Chattanooga, Tennessee 37402-2200 **Tel:** 1 423 468-5100.
Web site: http://www.myretrotv.com
Profile: RTV/Retro Televison is a broadcast television network that provides retro programming to its affiliates across the country. Most of its programming includes re-runs of classic television shows such as Hogan's Heroes, Family Ties and The Brady Bunch.
TELEVISION NETWORK

Swiss TV - Washington Bureau 541539
Editorial: 2000 M St NW, #370, Washington, District Of Columbia 20036 **Tel:** 1 202 429-9668.
Web site: http://www.sf.tv
Profile: The Washington, D.C. bureau of Swiss TV. Swiss TV's Web site is not available in English. The bureau prefers that press materials be submitted via fax.
TELEVISION NETWORK

Telemundo 33070
Owner: NBC Universal
Editorial: 2290 W 8th Ave, Hialeah, Florida 33010-2017 **Tel:** 1 305 884-8200.
Email: tmassignmentdesk@nbcuni.com
Web site: http://www.telemundo.com
Profile: Spanish-language broadcast network targeting the Hispanic audience in the United States and around the world. Lineup includes motion pictures, comedies, game shows, news and information programming, sporting events, concerts, theater and novelas.
TELEVISION NETWORK

Telemundo - Los Angeles Bureau 471893
Editorial: 10 Universal City Plz, Universal City, California 91608-1002 **Tel:** 1 818 777-1000.
TELEVISION NETWORK

Telemundo - New York Bureau 564677
Editorial: 30 Rockefeller Plz Rm 764E-3, New York, New York 10112-0015 **Tel:** 1 201 969-4247.
TELEVISION NETWORK

Telemundo - Washington Bureau 231018
Editorial: 400 N Capitol St NW Ste 850, Washington, District Of Columbia 20001-1555 **Tel:** 1 202 737-7830.
TELEVISION NETWORK

ThisTV 689372
Owner: Weigel Broadcasting Co.
Editorial: 26 N Halsted St, Chicago, Illinois 60661-2107 **Tel:** 1 312 705-2600.
Web site: http://www.thistv.com
Profile: ThisTV offers movies and mini series. ThisTV is owned by Weigel Broadcasting Co.
TELEVISION NETWORK

TV Marti 76290
Editorial: 2200 NW 72nd Ave, Miami, Florida 33152-9001 **Tel:** 1 305 437-7000.
Email: editor@martinoticias.com
Web site: http://www.martinoticias.com
Profile: Television network broadcasting news from the United States to the island of Cuba, with the goal of presenting democratic ideals and information to its citizens.
TELEVISION NETWORK

UniMas 75529
Editorial: 9405 NW 41st St, Doral, Florida 33178-2301
Tel: 1 305 421-2900.
Web site: http://tv.univision.com/unimas
Profile: Spanish-language network reaching 86% of all Hispanic homes throughout the United States. Broadcasting 24 hours a day, the network includes news, novelas, talk shows, variety shows, movies and sports programming. The network does not accept unsolicited faxes. The network launched in January 2002. On January 7, 2013, the network rebranded from TeleFutura Television Network to UniMas.
TELEVISION NETWORK

Univision Television Network 33058
Owner: Univision Communications Inc.
Editorial: 8551 NW 30th Ter, Doral, Florida 33122-1908 **Tel:** 1 305 471-3900.
Web site: http://www.univision.com
Profile: Univision Television provides an extensive lineup of Spanish language programming produced in the United States and throughout the Hispanic world. Programming fare includes movies, sporting events, news and information, current affairs, children's programs, comedy, variety and talk shows and dramatic series.
TELEVISION NETWORK

Univision Television Network - New York Bureau 33112
Editorial: 605 3rd Ave, Fl 12, New York, New York 10158 **Tel:** 1 212 455-5200.
Web site: http://www.univision.com
TELEVISION NETWORK

Univision Television Network - Washington Bureau 33113
Editorial: 101 Constitution Ave NW, Ste 810E, Washington, District Of Columbia 20001
Tel: 1 202 682-6160.
TELEVISION NETWORK

V-me 458813
Owner: V-me Media Inc.
Editorial: 450 W 33rd St Fl 11, New York, New York 10001-2650 **Tel:** 1 212 273-4800.
Web site: http://www.vmetv.com
Profile: Spanish-language network featuring programming adapted specifically for American Latinos. Features a diverse range of regular programming and specials focusing on kids, lifestyle, history, public affairs, science, the arts and entertainment.
TELEVISION NETWORK

W21AU-TV 608390
Owner: Central Florida Broadcast Company
Editorial: 4307 Vineland Rd Ste H1/H2, Orlando, Florida 32811-7178 **Tel:** 1 407 982-2268.
Web site: http://www.mundomaxorlando.com
Profile: W21AU-TV is the MundoFox network affiliate for the Orlando, FL market. The station is owned by Central Florida Broadcast Company. W21AU-TV broadcasts locally on channel 21. The station does not have a news department.
TELEVISION STATION

WAAY-TV 31720
Owner: Raycom Media Inc.
Editorial: 1000 Monte Sano Blvd SE, Huntsville, Alabama 35801-6137 **Tel:** 1 256 533-3131.
Email: newsroom@waaytv.com
Web site: http://www.waaytv.com
Profile: WAAY-TV is the ABC affiliate for the Huntsville, AL market. The station is owned by Huntsville Broadcast Corporation. WAAY-TV broadcasts locally on channel 31.
TELEVISION STATION

WABC2-TV 606242
Owner: Walt Disney Co.
Editorial: 7 Lincoln Sq, New York, New York 10023-7219 **Tel:** 1 212 456-7000.
Email: wabctv-newsdesk@abc.com
Web site: http://abc7ny.com
Profile: WABC2-TV is a multicast channel of WABC-TV. A multicast channel is a separate channel that shares the bandwidth of the main station but can air unique programming. WABC2-TV is the local Live Well HD Network affiliate on channel 7.2 for the greater Metropolitan New York, New Jersey, and Connecticut areas (including 29 counties). It is owned by Walt Disney Co.
TELEVISION STATION

WABC3-TV 556015
Owner: Walt Disney Co.
Editorial: 7 Lincoln Sq, New York, New York 10023-7219 **Tel:** 1 212 456-7000.
Email: wabctv-newsdesk@abc.com
Web site: http://abc7ny.com
Profile: WABC3-TV is a multicast channel of WABC-TV. A multicast channel is a separate channel that shares the bandwidth of the main station but can air unique programming. WABC3-TV is the local ABC affiliate on channel 7.3 for the greater Metropolitan New York, New Jersey, and Connecticut areas (including 29 counties). It is owned by Walt Disney Co.
TELEVISION STATION

WABC-TV 31721
Owner: Walt Disney Co.
Editorial: 7 Lincoln Sq, New York, New York 10023-7219 **Tel:** 1 212 456-7000.
Email: abc7ny@abc.com
Web site: http://abc7ny.com
Profile: WABC-TV is the ABC affiliate for the New York market. The station is owned by Walt Disney Co. WABC-TV broadcasts locally on channel 7. PR professionals should send submissions to the assignment desk by fax and clearly number the pages in the top right hand corner and include the subject on each page. The station prefers not to have press releases e-mailed. The station accepts 10-second PSAs in Beta format. The station's news content also appears on Taxi TV. Contact the New Media Account Executive for advertising opportunities.
TELEVISION STATION

WABG-TV 31722
Owner: Commonwealth Communications
Editorial: 849 Washington Ave, Greenville, Mississippi 38701-3727 **Tel:** 1 662 332-0949.
Email: newsroom@wabg.com
Web site: http://www.wabg.com
Profile: WABG-TV is the ABC affiliate for the Greenwood-Greenville, MS market. The station is owned by Commonwealth Communications. WABG-TV broadcasts locally on channel 6.
TELEVISION STATION

WABI-TV 31723
Owner: Community Broadcasting Service
Editorial: 35 Hildreth St, Bangor, Maine 04401-5740
Tel: 1 207 947-8321.
Email: 5news@wabi.tv
Web site: http://www.wabi.tv
Profile: WABI-TV is the CBS network affiliate for the Bangor, ME market. The station is owned by Community Broadcasting Service. WABI-TV broadcasts locally on channel 5.
TELEVISION STATION

WABM-TV 32381
Owner: Sinclair Broadcast Group, Inc.
Editorial: 651 Beacon Pkwy W Ste 105, Birmingham, Alabama 35209-3128 **Tel:** 1 205 403-3340.
Web site: http://www.wabm68.com
Profile: WABM-TV is the MyNetworkTV affiliate for the Birmingham, AL market. The station is owned by Sinclair Broadcasting Group, Inc. WABM-TV broadcasts locally on channel 68.
TELEVISION STATION

WACH-TV 31775
Owner: Sinclair Broadcast Group, Inc.
Editorial: 1400 Pickens St Ste 600, Columbia, South Carolina 29201-3465 **Tel:** 1 803 252-5757.
Email: news@wach.com
Web site: http://www.wach.com
Profile: WACH-TV is the FOX affiliate for the Columbia, SC, market. The station is owned by Sinclair Broadcast Group, Inc.. WACH-TV broadcasts locally on channel 57.
TELEVISION STATION

WACX3-TV 612375
Owner: Associated Christian TV System
Editorial: 123 E Central Pkwy, Altamonte Springs, Florida 32701-3464 **Tel:** 1 407 263-4040.
Web site: http://www.insp.com
Profile: WACX3-TV is an INSP network affiliate for the Orlando, FL market. The station is owned by Associated Christian TV System. WACX3-TV broadcasts locally on channel 40.3. The station broadcasts inspirational programming. WACX3-TV is a multicast channel of WACX-TV. A multicast channel is a separate channel that shares the bandwidth of the main station but can air unique programming.
TELEVISION STATION

WACX-TV 342180
Owner: Associated Christian TV System
Editorial: 123 E Central Pkwy, Altamonte Springs, Florida 32701-3464 **Tel:** 1 407 263-4040.
Email: superchannel555@superchannel.com
Web site: http://www.wacxtv.com
Profile: WACX-TV is an independent station for the Orlando, FL market. The station is owned by Associated Christian TV System. WACX-TV broadcasts locally on channel 40.
TELEVISION STATION

WACY-TV 32443
Owner: E.W. Scripps Co.
Editorial: 1391 North Rd, Green Bay, Wisconsin 54313-5723 **Tel:** 1 920 490-2626.
Web site: http://www.wacy.com
Profile: WACY-TV is the MyNetworkTV network affiliate for the Greenbay-Appleton, WI market. The station is owned by E.W. Scripps Co. WACY-TV broadcasts locally on channel 32.
TELEVISION STATION

WADL2-TV 611653
Owner: Adell Broadcasting
Editorial: 35000 Adell Dr., Clinton Township, Michigan 48035 **Tel:** 1 586 790-3838.
Web site: http://www.wadldetroit.com
Profile: WADL2-TV is a multicast of WADL2-TV. A multicast channel is a separate channel that shares the bandwith of the main station but can air unique programming. WADL2-TV airs programming from Universal Sports in the Detroit market. The station is owned by Adell Broadcasting. WADL2-TV broadcasts locally on channel 38.2.
TELEVISION STATION

WADL-TV 32325
Owner: Adell Broadcasting
Editorial: 35000 Adell Dr, Clinton Township, Michigan 48035-6026 **Tel:** 1 586 790-3838.
Web site: http://www.wadldetroit.com
Profile: WADL-TV is a commercial station for the Detroit market. The station is owned by Adell Broadcasting. WADL-TV broadcasts locally on channel 38.
TELEVISION STATION

WAFB-TV 31724
Owner: Raycom Media Inc.
Editorial: 844 Government St, Baton Rouge, Louisiana 70802-6030 **Tel:** 1 225 383-9999.
Email: news@wafb.com
Web site: http://www.wafb.com
Profile: WAFB-TV is the CBS affiliate for the Baton Rouge, LA market. The station is owned by Raycom Media Inc. WAFB-TV broadcasts locally on channel 9.
TELEVISION STATION

WAFF-TV 31725
Owner: Raycom Media Inc.
Editorial: 1414 Memorial Pkwy NW, Huntsville, Alabama 35801-5933 **Tel:** 1 256 533-4848.
Email: news@waff.com
Web site: http://www.waff.com
Profile: WAFF-TV is the NBC affiliate for the Huntsville, AL, market area. The station is owned by Raycom Media Inc. WAFF-TV broadcasts locally on channel 48.
TELEVISION STATION

WAGA-TV 31726
Owner: Fox Broadcasting Company
Editorial: 1551 Briarcliff Rd NE, Atlanta, Georgia 30306-2217 **Tel:** 1 404 875-5555.
Email: newstipsatlanta@foxtv.com
Web site: http://www.fox5atlanta.com
Profile: WAGA-TV is the FOX affiliate for the Atlanta market. The station is owned by Fox Broadcasting Company. WAGA-TV broadcasts locally on channel 5.
TELEVISION STATION

WAGM2-TV 800123
Owner: NEPSK Inc.
Editorial: 12 Brewer Rd, Presque Isle, Maine 04769-5077 **Tel:** 1 207 764-4461.
Email: news@wagmtv.com
Web site: http://wagmtv.com
Profile: WAGM2-TV is a multicast channel of WAGM-TV. A multicast channel is a separate channel that shares the bandwith of the main station but can air unique programming. WAGM2-TV is the CBS affiliate for the Presque Isle, ME market. The station is owned by NEPSK Inc. WAGM2-TV broadcasts locally on channel 8.2.
TELEVISION STATION

WAGM-TV 31727
Owner: Gray Media Inc.
Editorial: 12 Brewer Rd, Presque Isle, Maine 04769-5077 **Tel:** 1 207 764-4461.
Email: news@wagmtv.com
Web site: http://www.wagmtv.com
Profile: WAGM-TV is the FOX affiliate for the Presque Isle, ME, market. The station is owned by NEPSK Inc. WAGM-TV broadcasts locally on channel 8.
TELEVISION STATION

WAGT-TV 31728
Owner: Gray Television, Inc.
Editorial: 1336 Augusta West Pkwy, Augusta, Georgia 30909-6427 **Tel:** 1 706 826-0026.
Web site: http://www.26nbc.com
Profile: WAGT-TV is the NBC affiliate for the Augusta, GA market. The station is owned by Gray Television, Inc. WAGT-TV broadcasts locally on channel 26.
TELEVISION STATION

WAGV-TV 153529
Owner: Living Faith Broadcasting Inc.
Editorial: 8594 Hidden Valley Rd, Abingdon, Virginia 24210-4858 **Tel:** 1 276 676-3806.
Email: info@livingfaithtv.com
Web site: http://www.lftvnetwork.com
TELEVISION STATION

WAHU-TV 390678
Owner: Gray Television, Inc.
Editorial: 999 2nd St SE, Charlottesville, Virginia 22902-6172 **Tel:** 1 434 242-1919.
Email: news@newsplex.com
Web site: http://www.newsplex.com
TELEVISION STATION

WAKA-TV 31729
Owner: Bahakel Communications
Editorial: 3251 Harrison Rd, Montgomery, Alabama 36109-4321 **Tel:** 1 334 271-8888.
Email: news@waka.com
Web site: http://www.alabamanews.net
Profile: WAKA-TV is the CBS affiliate in Montgomery, AL market. The station is owned by Bahakel Communications. WAKA-TV broadcasts locally on channel 8. WAKA-TV, WNCF-TV, and WBMM-TV are known as Alabama News Network.
TELEVISION STATION

WALA-TV 31731
Owner: Meredith Corporation
Editorial: 1501 Satchel Paige Dr, Mobile, Alabama 36606-2532 **Tel:** 1 251 434-1010.
Email: fox10desk@fox10tv.com
Web site: http://www.fox10tv.com
Profile: WALA-TV is the FOX affiliate for the Mobile, AL market. The station is owned by Meredith Corporation. WALA-TV broadcasts locally on channel 10.
TELEVISION STATION

WALB2-TV 721760
Owner: Raycom Media Inc.
Editorial: 1709 Stuart Ave, Albany, Georgia 31707-1701 **Tel:** 1 229 446-1010.
Email: news@walb.com
Web site: http://www.walb.com
Profile: WALB2-TV is a multicast channel of WALB-TV. A multicast channel is a separate channel that shares the bandwith of the main station but can air unique programming. WALB2-TV is the ABC Network for the Albany, GA market. The station is owned by Raycom Media Inc. WALB2-TV broadcasts locally on channel 10.2.
TELEVISION STATION

WALB-TV 31732
Owner: Raycom Media Inc.
Editorial: 1709 Stuart Ave, Albany, Georgia 31707-1701 **Tel:** 1 229 446-1010.
Email: news@walb.com
Web site: http://www.walb.com
Profile: WALB-TV is the NBC network affiliate for the Albany, GA market. The station is owned by Raycom Media Inc. WALB-TV broadcasts locally on channel 10.
TELEVISION STATION

WAMI-TV 32508
Owner: Univision Communications Inc.
Editorial: 9405 NW 41st St, Doral, Florida 33178-2301 **Tel:** 1 305 471-3946.
Profile: WAMI-TV is the UniMas affiliate for the Miami market. The station is owned by Univision Communications Inc. WAMI-TV broadcasts locally on channel 69.
TELEVISION STATION

WAMY-TV 793010
Owner: Grant Broadcasting System II
Editorial: 1309 Memorial Pkwy NW, Huntsville, Alabama 35801-5932 **Tel:** 1 256 533-5454.
Web site: http://www.fox54.com/category/215571/my8
Profile: WAMY-TV is the MyNetworkTV affiliate for Huntsville, AL. The station is owned and operated by Grant Communication Inc. All programs are syndicated MyNetworkTV shows.
TELEVISION STATION

WAND-TV 31733
Owner: Block Communications Inc.
Editorial: 904 W South Side Dr, Decatur, Illinois 62521-4022 **Tel:** 1 217 424-2500.
Email: news@wandtv.com
Web site: http://www.wandtv.com
Profile: WAND-TV is the NBC affiliate for the Decatur, IL market. The station is owned by Block Communications Inc. WAND-TV broadcasts locally on channel 17.
TELEVISION STATION

WANE-TV 31734
Owner: Nexstar Media Group, Inc.
Editorial: 2915 W State Blvd, Fort Wayne, Indiana 46808-1803 **Tel:** 1 260 481-1515.
Email: newsrelease@wane.com
Web site: http://www.wane.com
Profile: WANE-TV is the CBS affiliate for the Fort Wayne, IN market. The station is owned by Nexstar Media Group, Inc. WANE-TV broadcasts locally on channel 15.
TELEVISION STATION

WAOE-TV 63093
Owner: Four Seasons Broadcasting
Editorial: 2907 Springfield Rd, East Peoria, Illinois 61611-4878 **Tel:** 1 309 674-5900.
Web site: http://www.my59.tv
Profile: WAOE-TV is the MyNetworkTV affiliate for the Peoria and Bloomington, IL area. The station is owned by Four Seasons Broadcasting. WAOE-TV broadcasts locally on channel 59.
TELEVISION STATION

WAOH-TV 376446
Owner: Media-Com Inc.
Editorial: 2449 State Route 59, Kent, Ohio 44240
Tel: 1 216 521-3529.
Email: staff@wnir.com
Profile: WAOH-TV is an independent station for the Cleveland area. The station is owned by Media-Com Inc. The station broadcasts locally on channel 29.
TELEVISION STATION

WAOW-TV 31735
Owner: Quincy Newspapers Inc.
Editorial: 1908 Grand Ave, Wausau, Wisconsin 54403-6870 **Tel:** 1 715 842-2251.
Email: news@waow.com
Web site: http://www.waow.com
Profile: WAOW-TV is the ABC network affiliate for the Wausau, WI market. The station is owned by Quincy Newspapers Inc. WAOW-TV broadcasts locally on channel 9.
TELEVISION STATION

WAPK-TV 32579
Owner: Holston Valley Broadcasting Corp.
Editorial: 222 Commerce St, Kingsport, Tennessee 37660-4319
Email: newstips@wkpttv.com
Web site: http://wapk.tv
Profile: WAPK-TV is the MyNetworkTV affiliate for the Tri-Cities, TN market. The station is owned by Holston Valley Broadcasting Corp. WAPK-TV broadcasts locally on channel 36.
TELEVISION STATION

WAPT-TV 31736
Owner: Hearst Television Inc.
Editorial: 7616 Channel 16 Way, Jackson, Mississippi 39209-9634 **Tel:** 1 601 922-1607.
Email: news@wapt.com
Web site: http://www.wapt.com
Profile: WAPT-TV is the ABC affiliate for the Jackson, MS market. The station is owned by Hearst Television Inc. WAPT-TV broadcasts locally on channel 16.
TELEVISION STATION

WAQP-TV 32301
Owner: TCT of Michigan Inc.
Editorial: 11717 Rt. 37, Marion, Illinois 62959
Tel: 1 989 249-1220.
Email: waqp@tct.tv
Web site: http://www.tct.tv
Profile: WAQP-TV is an independent station for the Flint, MI market. The station is owned by TCT of Michigan Inc. WAQP-TV broadcasts locally on channel 49.
TELEVISION STATION

WATC2-TV 747433
Owner: Community Television Inc.
Editorial: 1862 Enterprise Dr, Norcross, Georgia 30093-1107 **Tel:** 1 770 300-9828.
Web site: http://www.watc.tv
Profile: WATC2-TV is a multicast channel of WATC-TV. A multicast channel is a separate channel that shares the bandwidth of the main station but can air unique programming. WATC2-TV is an independent network affiliate on Channel 57.2 for the Atlanta, GA market. WATC2-TV is owned by Community Television Inc.
TELEVISION STATION

WATC-TV 32541
Owner: Community Television Inc.
Editorial: 1862 Enterprise Dr, Norcross, Georgia 30093-1107 **Tel:** 1 770 300-9828.
Web site: http://www.watc.tv
Profile: WATC-TV is an independent station for the Atlanta market. The station is owned by Community Television Inc. WATC-TV broadcasts locally on channel 57.
TELEVISION STATION

WATE2-TV 791879
Owner: New Young Broadcasting
Editorial: 1306 N Broadway St, Knoxville, Tennessee 37917-6501 **Tel:** 1 865 637-6666.
Web site: http://www.wate.com
Profile: WATE2-TV is a multicast channel of WATE-TV. A multicast channel is a separate channel that shares the bandwith of the main station but can air unique programming. WATE2-TV is the Live Well Network for the Knoxville, TN market. The station is owned by New Young Broadcasting. WATE2-TV broadcasts locally on channel 6.2.
TELEVISION STATION

WATE-TV 31737
Owner: New Young Broadcasting
Editorial: 1306 N Broadway St, Knoxville, Tennessee 37917-6501 **Tel:** 1 865 637-6666.
Email: newsroom@wate.com
Web site: http://www.wate.com
Profile: WATE-TV is the ABC affiliate for the Knoxville, TN market. The station is owned by New Young Broadcasting. WATE-TV broadcasts locally on channel 6.
TELEVISION STATION

WATL-TV 31738
Owner: TEGNA Inc.
Editorial: 1 Monroe Pl NE, Atlanta, Georgia 30324-4836 **Tel:** 1 404 892-1611.
Email: news@11alive.com
Web site: http://www.myatltv.com
Profile: WATL-TV is the MyNetworkTV affiliate for the Atlanta market. The station is owned by TEGNA Inc. WATL-TV broadcasts locally on channel 36.
TELEVISION STATION

WATM-TV 32815
Owner: Palm Television LP
Editorial: 1450 Scalp Ave, Johnstown, Pennsylvania 15904-3321 **Tel:** 1 814 266-8088.
Web site: http://www.abc23.com
Profile: WATM-TV is the ABC affiliate for the Johnstown-Altoona, PA market. The station is owned by Palm Television LP. WATM-TV broadcasts locally on channel 23. The station does not have a news department.
TELEVISION STATION

WATN-TV 32059
Owner: Nexstar Broadcasting Group
Editorial: 1725 N Shelby Oaks Dr, Memphis, Tennessee 38134-7444 **Tel:** 1 901 323-2430.
Email: newsdesk@localmemphis.com
Web site: http://www.localmemphis.com
Profile: WATN-TV is the ABC affiliate for the Memphis, TN market. The station is owned by Nexstar Broadcasting Group. WATN-TV is broadcast on channel 24.
TELEVISION STATION

WAVE2-TV 620042
Owner: Raycom Media Inc.
Editorial: 725 S Floyd St, Louisville, Kentucky 40203-2391 **Tel:** 1 502 585-2201.
Email: newsrelease@wave3.com
Web site: http://www.wave3.com
Profile: WAVE2-TV is a multicast of WAVE-TV. A multicast channel is a separate channel that shares the bandwith of the main station but can air unique programming. WAVE2-TV airs programming from This TV Network to the Louisville, KY market. The station is owned by Raycom Media Inc. WAVE2-TV broadcasts locally on channel 3.2.
TELEVISION STATION

WAVE3-TV 620046
Owner: Raycom Media Inc.
Editorial: 725 S Floyd St, Louisville, Kentucky 40203-2337 **Tel:** 1 502 585-2201.
Email: newsrelease@wave3.com
Web site: http://www.wave3.com
Profile: WAVE3-TV is a multicast of WAVE-TV. A multicast channel is a separate channel that shares the bandwith of the main station but can air unique programming. WAVE3-TV airs 24 hour weather programming from WAVE 3 Weather Network to the Louisville, KY market. The station is owned by Raycom Media Inc. WAVE3-TV broadcasts locally on channel 3.3.
TELEVISION STATION

WAVE-TV 31739
Owner: Raycom Media Inc.
Editorial: 725 S Floyd St, Louisville, Kentucky 40203-2391 **Tel:** 1 502 585-2201.
Email: newsrelease@wave3.com
Web site: http://www.wave3.com
Profile: WAVE-TV is the NBC affiliate for the Louisville, KY market. The station is owned by Raycom Media Inc. WAVE-TV broadcasts locally on channel 3.
TELEVISION STATION

WAVY-TV 31740
Owner: Nexstar Media Group, Inc.
Editorial: 300 Wavy St, Portsmouth, Virginia 23704-5200 **Tel:** 1 757 393-1010.
Email: newsdesk@wavy.com
Web site: http://www.wavy.com
Profile: WAVY-TV is the NBC affiliate for the Norfolk, VA market. The station is owned by Nexstar Media Group, Inc. WAVY-TV broadcasts locally on channel 10.
TELEVISION STATION

WAWV-TV 31743
Owner: Mission Broadcasting
Editorial: 10849 N US Highway 41, Farmersburg, Indiana 47850-8099 **Tel:** 1 812 696-2121.
Web site: http://www.mywabashvalley.com
Profile: WAWV-TV is the ABC affiliate for the Terre Haute, IN market. The station is owned by Mission Broadcasting. WAWV-TV broadcasts locally on channel 38.
TELEVISION STATION

WAXC-TV 376458
Owner: LAKE BROADCASTING, INC.
Editorial: 1051 Tallapoosa St, Alexander City, Alabama 35010-1552 **Tel:** 1 256 234-6464.
Web site: http://www.sportzblitzlive.com
Profile: WAXC-TV is an independent station for the Montgomery, AL area. The station is owned by Venture Television, LLC. WAXC-TV broadcasts locally at channel 31.
TELEVISION STATION

WAXN-TV 32502
Owner: Cox Media Group, Inc.
Editorial: 1901 N Tryon St, Charlotte, North Carolina 28206-2733 **Tel:** 1 704 338-9999.
Web site: http://www.wsoctv.com/live-stream

Profile: WAXN-TV is an independent station for the Charlotte, NC market. The station is owned by Cox Media Group, Inc. WAXN-TV broadcasts locally on channel 64.
TELEVISION STATION

WAX-TV 376450
Owner: Media-Com Inc.
Editorial: 2449 State Route 59, Kent, Ohio 44240
Tel: 1 216 521-3529.
Email: staff@wnir.com
Profile: WAX-TV is an independent station for the Cleveland area. The station is owned by Media-Com Inc. The station broadcasts locally on channel 35.
TELEVISION STATION

WAZS-TV 476521
Owner: Jabar Communications, Inc.
Editorial: 5081 Rivers Ave, North Charleston, South Carolina 29406-6303 **Tel:** 1 843 554-1063.
Email: traffic@jabarcommunications.com
Web site: http://jabarcommunications.com
Profile: WAZS-TV is the Azteca America affiliate for the Charleston, SC market. The station is owned by Jabar Communications, Inc. WAZS-TV broadcasts locally on channel 22.
TELEVISION STATION

WAZT-TV 32319
Owner: Jones Broadcasting
Editorial: 158 Front Royal Pike Ste 307, Winchester, Virginia 22602-4324 **Tel:** 1 540 431-4504.
Email: email@wazt.com
Web site: http://www.wazt.com
Profile: WAZT-TV is an independent station for the Woodstock, VA market. The station is owned by Jones Broadcasting. WAZT-TV broadcasts locally on channel 10.
TELEVISION STATION

WBAL2-TV 614576
Owner: Hearst Television Inc.
Editorial: 3800 Hooper Ave, Baltimore, Maryland 21211-1313 **Tel:** 1 410 467-3000.
Email: newstips@wbaltv.com
Web site: http://wbaltv.com
Profile: WBAL2-TV is a multicast of WBAL-TV. A multicast channel is a separate channel that shares the bandwith of the main station but can air unique programming. WBAL2-TV airs programming from the MeTV Network. The station is owned by Hearst Television Inc. WBAL2-TV broadcasts locally on channel 11.2. The station specializes in syndicated reruns of classic TV programs of the 1950s through the 1980s.
TELEVISION STATION

WBAL-TV 31744
Owner: Hearst Television Inc.
Editorial: 3800 Hooper Ave, Baltimore, Maryland 21211-1313 **Tel:** 1 410 467-3000.
Email: newstips@wbaltv.com
Web site: http://www.wbaltv.com
Profile: WBAL-TV is the NBC affiliate for the Baltimore market. The station is owned by Hearst Television Inc. WBAL-TV broadcasts locally on channel 11.
TELEVISION STATION

WBAY3-TV 791602
Owner: Gray Television, Inc.
Editorial: 115 S Jefferson St, Green Bay, Wisconsin 54301-4534 **Tel:** 1 920 432-3331.
Email: wbay@wbay.com
Web site: http://wbay.com
Profile: WBAY3-TV is a multicast channel of WBAY-TV. A multicast channel is a separate channel that shares the bandwith of the main station but can air unique programming. WBAY3-TV is the Live Well Network for the Green Bay, WI market. The station is owned by Gray Television, Inc. WBAY3-TV broadcasts locally on channel 2.3.
TELEVISION STATION

WBAY-TV 31745
Owner: Gray Television, Inc.
Editorial: 115 S Jefferson St, Green Bay, Wisconsin 54301-4534 **Tel:** 1 920 432-3331.
Email: news@wbay.com
Web site: http://www.wbay.com
Profile: WBAY-TV is the ABC network affiliate for the Green Bay-Appleton, WI market. The station is owned by Gray Television, Inc. WBAY-TV broadcasts locally on channel 2.
TELEVISION STATION

WBBH-TV 31746
Owner: Waterman Broadcasting
Editorial: 3719 Central Ave, Fort Myers, Florida 33901-8220 **Tel:** 1 239 939-2020.
Email: newstips@nbc-2.com
Web site: http://www.nbc-2.com
Profile: WBBH-TV is the NBC affiliate for the Fort Myers - Naples, FL market. The station is owned by Waterman Broadcasting. WBBH-TV broadcasts locally on channel 2.
TELEVISION STATION

WBBJ3-TV 781375
Owner: Bahakel Communication
Editorial: 346 Muse St, Jackson, Tennessee 38301-3620 **Tel:** 1 731 424-4515.
Web site: http://www.wbbjtv.com/
Profile: WBBJ3-TV is a multicast channel of WBBJ-TV. A multicast channel is a separate channel that shares the bandwith of the main station but can air unique programming. WBB3-TV is the CBS Network for the Jackson, TN market. The station is owned by Bahakel Communications. WBBJ3-TV broadcasts locally on channel 7.3.
TELEVISION STATION

WBBJ-TV 31747
Owner: Bahakel Communications
Editorial: 346 Muse St, Jackson, Tennessee 38301-3620 **Tel:** 1 731 424-4515.
Email: 7news@wbbjtv.com
Web site: http://www.wbbjtv.com
Profile: WBBJ-TV is the ABC affiliate for the Jackson, TN, market. The station is owned by Bahakel Communications. WBBJ-TV broadcasts locally on channel 7. Press Releases should be sent to the newsroom email as they then reach the assignment editor, news director, and newscast producers.
TELEVISION STATION

WBBM-TV 31748
Owner: CBS Television Stations
Editorial: 22 W Washington St, Chicago, Illinois 60602-1605 **Tel:** 1 312 899-2222.
Email: wbbmtvdesk@cbs.com
Web site: http://chicago.cbslocal.com
Profile: WBBM-TV is the CBS affiliate for the Chicago market. The station is owned by CBS Television Stations. WBBM-TV broadcasts locally on channel 2.
TELEVISION STATION

WBCC2-TV 609790
Owner: Eastern Florida State College
Editorial: 1519 Clearlake Rd Bldg 13, Cocoa, Florida 32922-6598
Email: wefstv@easternflorida.edu
Web site: http://wefstv.org
Profile: WEFS2-TV is a multicast of WEFS-TV. A multicast channel is a separate channel that shares the bandwith of the main station but can air unique programming. WEFS2-TV airs programming from the University of Central Florida in the Orlando-Daytona Beach, FL market. The station is owned by Eastern Florida State College. WEFS2-TV broadcasts locally on channel 68.2.
TELEVISION STATION

WBCC3-TV 609792
Owner: Eastern Florida State College
Editorial: 1519 Clearlake Rd Bldg 13, Cocoa, Florida 32922-6598 **Tel:** 1 321 433-7111.
Email: wefstv@easternflorida.edu
Web site: http://wefstv.org
Profile: WEFS3-TV is a multicast of WEFS-TV. A multicast channel is a separate channel that shares the bandwith of the main station but can air unique programming. WEFS3-TV airs programming from Brevard Public Schools in the Orlando-Daytona Beach, FL market. The station is owned by Eastern Florida State College. WEFS3-TV broadcasts locally on channel 68.3.
TELEVISION STATION

WBCC4-TV 609797
Owner: Eastern Florida State College
Editorial: 1519 Clearlake Rd Bldg 13, Cocoa, Florida 32922-6598 **Tel:** 1 321 433-7111.
Email: wefstv@easternflorida.edu
Web site: http://www.wefstv.org
Profile: WEFS4-TV is a multicast of WEFS-TV. A multicast channel is a separate channel that shares the bandwith of the main station but can air unique programming. WEFS4-TV airs programming from the Florida Knowledge Network and the Florida Channel in the Orlando-Daytona Beach, FL market. The station is owned by Eastern Florida State College. WEFS4-TV broadcasts locally on channel 68.4.
TELEVISION STATION

WBCC-TV 32296
Owner: Brevard Community College
Editorial: 1519 Clearlake Rd Bldg 13, Cocoa, Florida 32922-6598 **Tel:** 1 321 433-7111.
Email: wefstv@easternflorida.edu
Web site: http://www.wefstv.org
Profile: WEFS-TV is the PBS network affiliate for the Orlando-Daytona Beach, FL market. The station is owned by Eastern Florida State College. WEFS-TV broadcasts locally on channel 68.
TELEVISION STATION

WBCF-TV 238273
Owner: BCB Incorporated
Editorial: 525 E Tennessee St, Florence, Alabama 35630 **Tel:** 1 256 764-8170.
Web site: http://www.wbcf.com
Profile: WBCF-TV is an independent station for the Florence, AL market. The station is owned by BCB Incorporated. WBCF-TV broadcasts locally on channel 3.
TELEVISION STATION

WBDT-TV 32469
Owner: ACME Television, LLC
Editorial: 4595 S Dixie Dr, Moraine, Ohio 45439-2111 **Tel:** 1 937 293-2101.
Web site: http://www.daytonscw.com
Profile: WBDT-TV is the CW affiliate for the Dayton, OH market. The station is owned by ACME Television, LLC. WBDT-TV broadcasts locally on channel 26.
TELEVISION STATION

WBFF2-TV 613181
Owner: Sinclair Broadcast Group, Inc.
Editorial: 2000 W 41st St, Baltimore, Maryland 21211-1420 **Tel:** 1 410 467-4545.
Email: news@foxbaltimore.com
Web site: http://www.foxbaltimore.com
Profile: WBFF2-TV is a multicast of WBFF-TV. A multicast channel is a separate channel that shares the bandwith of the main station but can air unique programming. WBFF2-TV airs programming from This TV in the Baltimore market. The station is owned by Sinclair Broadcast Group, Inc. WBFF2-TV broadcasts locally on channel 45.2.
TELEVISION STATION

WBFF-TV 31749
Owner: Sinclair Broadcast Group, Inc.
Editorial: 2000 W 41st St, Baltimore, Maryland 21211-1420 **Tel:** 1 410 467-4545.
Email: sales@foxbaltimore.com
Web site: http://www.foxbaltimore.com
Profile: WBFF-TV is the FOX network affiliate for the Baltimore, MD market. The station is owned by Sinclair Broadcast Group, Inc. WBFF-TV broadcasts locally on channel 45.
TELEVISION STATION

WBFS-TV 31750
Owner: CBS Television Stations
Editorial: 8900 NW 18th Ter, Doral, Florida 33172-2623 **Tel:** 1 305 621-3333.
Email: wfornews@cbs.com
Web site: http://miami.cbslocal.com
Profile: WBFS-TV is the MyNetworkTV affiliate for the Miami market. The station is owned by CBS Television Stations. WBFS-TV broadcasts locally on channel 33.
TELEVISION STATION

WBGH-TV 86790
Owner: Nexstar Broadcasting Group
Editorial: 203 Ingraham Hill Rd, Binghamton, New York 13903-5504 **Tel:** 1 607 771-3434.
Email: news@nc34.com
Web site: http://www.binghamtonhomepage.com/home
Profile: WBGH-TV is the NBC network affiliate for the Binghamton, NY market. The station is owned by Nexstar Broadcasting Group. WBGH-TV broadcasts locally on channel 20.
TELEVISION STATION

WBGN-TV 76121
Owner: OTA Broadcasting, LLC
Editorial: 975 Greentree Rd, Pittsburgh, Pennsylvania 15220-3315 **Tel:** 1 412 922-9576.
Email: wbgn@wbgn.com
Web site: http://www.wbgn.com
Profile: WBGN-TV is an independent station for the Pittsburgh market. The station is owned by Bruno-Goodworth Network, Inc. WBGN-TV broadcasts locally on channel 21.
TELEVISION STATION

WBGT-TV 32620
Owner: WBGT LLC
Editorial: 1320 Buffalo Rd, Ste 111, Rochester, New York 14624-1841 **Tel:** 1 585 235-1870.
Email: info@wbgttv.com
Web site: http://www.wbgttv.com
Profile: WBGT-TV is the MyNetworkTV affiliate for the Rochester, NY market. The station is owned by WBGT LLC. WBGT-TV broadcasts locally on channel 18.
TELEVISION STATION

WBIH-TV 154619
Owner: Flinn Broadcasting Corp.
Editorial: 225 N Memorial Dr, Prattville, Alabama 36067-3344 **Tel:** 1 334 491-2900.
Email: wbihdt@gmail.com
Profile: WBIH-TV is an independent station for the Montgomery, AL market. The station is owned by Flinn Broadcasting Corporation. WBIH-TV broadcasts locally on channel 29.
TELEVISION STATION

WBII-TV 350310
Owner: Mid-South Broadcasting Inc.
Editorial: 36 Court St, Ashland, Mississippi 38603-6210 **Tel:** 1 662 224-3220.
Email: wbiitv@yahoo.com
Web site: http://www.wbiitv.8m.com
Profile: WBII-TV is an independent station for the Ashland, MS market. The station is owned by Mid-South Broadcasting Inc. WBII-TV broadcasts locally on channel 20.
TELEVISION STATION

WBIN3-TV 778482
Owner: WBIN, Inc.
Editorial: 11 A St, Derry, New Hampshire 03038-1721 **Tel:** 1 603 845-1000.
Profile: WBIN3-TV is a multicast channel of WBIN-TV. A multicast channel is a separate channel that shares the bandwith of the main station but can air unique programming. WBIN3-TV is the CoolTV affiliate for the Boston market. The station is owned by WBIN, Inc. WBIN3-TV broadcasts locally on channel 50.3.
TELEVISION STATION

WBIN-TV 32003
Owner: WBIN, Inc.
Editorial: 11 A St, Derry, New Hampshire 03038-1721 **Tel:** 1 603 845-1000.
Email: info@wbintv.com
Web site: http://www.wbintv.com
Profile: WBIN-TV is an Independent affiliate for the Boston market. The station is owned by WBIN, Inc. WBIN-TV broadcasts locally on channel 50.
TELEVISION STATION

WBIR-TV 31752
Owner: TEGNA Inc.
Editorial: 1513 Bill Williams Ave, Knoxville, Tennessee 37917-3861 **Tel:** 1 865 637-1010.
Email: news@wbir.com
Web site: http://www.wbir.com
Profile: WBIR-TV is the NBC affiliate for the Knoxville, TN market. The station is owned by TEGNA Inc. WBIR-TV broadcasts locally on channel 10.
TELEVISION STATION

WBKB3-TV 844670
Owner: Thunder Bay Broadcasting Corp.
Editorial: 1390 N Bagley St, Alpena, Michigan 49707-8101 **Tel:** 1 989 356-3434.
Web site: http://www.wbkb11.com
Profile: WBKB3-TV is a multicast channel of WBKB-TV. A multicast channel is a separate channel that shares the bandwidth of the main station but can air unique programming. WBKB3-TV is the ABC Television Network for the Alpena, Michigan market. The station is owned by Thunder Bay Broadcasting Corp. WBKB3-TV broadcasts locally on channel 11.3.
TELEVISION STATION

WBKB-TV 31753
Owner: Thunder Bay Broadcasting Corp.
Editorial: 1390 N Bagley St, Alpena, Michigan 49707-8101 **Tel:** 1 989 356-3434.
Email: news@wbkb11.com
Web site: http://www.wbkb11.com
Profile: WBKB-TV is the local CBS affiliate for Alpena, MI. The station is owned by Thunder Bay Broadcasting Corp. WBKB-TV broadcasts locally on channel 11.
TELEVISION STATION

WBKI-TV 32274
Owner: Block Communication
Editorial: 624 W Mohamed A1 Blvd, Louisville, Kentucky 40203 **Tel:** 1 502 809-3400.
Web site: http://www.wbki.tv
Profile: WBKI-TV is the CW affiliate for the Louisville, KY market. The station is owned by Block Communication. WBKI-TV broadcasts locally on channel 28 and 34.
TELEVISION STATION

WBKO-TV 31754
Owner: Gray Television, Inc.
Editorial: 2727 Russellville Rd, Bowling Green, Kentucky 42101-3976 **Tel:** 1 270 781-1313.
Email: news@wbko.com
Web site: http://www.wbko.com
Profile: WBKO-TV is the ABC affiliate for the Bowling Green, KY, market. The station is owned by Gray Television, Inc. WBKO-TV broadcasts locally on channel 13.
TELEVISION STATION

WBMA2-TV 614906
Owner: Sinclair Broadcast Group, Inc.
Editorial: 800 Concourse Pkwy Ste 200, Hoover, Alabama 35244-1874 **Tel:** 1 205 403-3340.
Email: newstips@abc3340.com
Web site: http://www.abc3340.com
Profile: WBMA2-TV is a multicast of WBMA-TV. A multicast channel is a separate channel that shares the bandwith of the main station but can air unique programming. WBMA2-TV airs weather programming in the Birmingham, AL market. The station is owned by Sinclair Broadcast Group, Inc. WBMA2-TV broadcasts locally on channel 40.2.
TELEVISION STATION

WBMA-TV 31780
Owner: Sinclair Broadcast Group, Inc.
Editorial: 800 Concourse Pkwy Ste 200, Hoover, Alabama 35244-1874 **Tel:** 1 205 403-3340.
Email: newstip@abc3340.com
Web site: http://www.abc3340.com
Profile: WBMA-TV is the ABC affiliate for the Birmingham, AL market. The station is owned by Sinclair Broadcast Group, Inc. WBMA-TV broadcasts locally on channel 40.
TELEVISION STATION

WBME4-TV 614859
Owner: Weigel Broadcasting Co.
Editorial: 809 S 60th St, Milwaukee, Wisconsin 53214-3363 **Tel:** 1 414 777-5800.
Profile: WBME4-TV is a multicast of WBME-TV. A multicast channel is a separate channel that shares the bandwith of the main station but can air unique programming. WBME4-TV airs programming from the Telemundo affiliate in the Milwaukee market. The station is owned by Weigel Broadcasting Co. WBME4-TV broadcasts locally on channel 49.4.
TELEVISION STATION

WBME-TV 32363
Owner: Weigel Broadcasting Co.
Editorial: 809 S 60Th St Floor 1, Milwaukee, Wisconsin 53214-3363 **Tel:** 1 414 777-5800.
Profile: WBME-TV is an independent station for the Milwaukee market. The station is owned by Weigel Broadcasting Co. WBME-TV broadcasts locally on channel 49.
TELEVISION STATION

WBMM-TV 342789
Owner: Bahakel Communications
Editorial: 3251 Harrison Rd, Montgomery, Alabama 36109-4321 **Tel:** 1 334 271-8888.
Web site: http://www.cwmontgomery.com
Profile: WBMM-TV is the CW network affiliate for the Montgomery, AL market. The station is owned by Bahakel Communications. WBMM-TV broadcasts

locally on channel 22. WAKA-TV, WNCF-TV, and WBMM-TV are known as Alabama News Network.
TELEVISION STATION

WBNA2-TV
620669
Owner: Word Broadcasting Network, Inc.
Editorial: 3701 Fern Valley Rd, Louisville, Kentucky 40219-1918 **Tel:** 1 502 964-2121.
Web site: http://www.wbna21.com
Profile: WBNA2-TV is a multicast of WBNA-TV. A multicast channel is a separate channel that shares the bandwith of the main station but can air unique programming. WBNA2-TV airs children's programming from qubo in the Louisville, KY market. The station is owned by Word Broadcasting Network, Inc. WBNA2-TV broadcasts locally on channel 21.2.
TELEVISION STATION

WBNA3-TV
620681
Owner: Word Broadcasting Network, Inc.
Editorial: 3701 Fern Valley Rd, Louisville, Kentucky 40219-1918 **Tel:** 1 502 964-2121.
Web site: http://www.wbna21.com
Profile: WBNA3-TV is a multicast of WBNA-TV. A multicast channel is a separate channel that shares the bandwith of the main station but can air unique programming. WBNA3-TV airs lifestyle programming from international Christian programming from GOD TV/The Light in the Louisville, KY market. The station is owned by Word Broadcasting Network, Inc. WBNA3-TV broadcasts locally on channel 21.3.
TELEVISION STATION

WBNA4-TV
620688
Owner: Word Broadcasting Network, Inc.
Editorial: 3701 Fern Valley Rd, Louisville, Kentucky 40219-1918 **Tel:** 1 502 964-2121.
Web site: http://www.wbna21.com
Profile: WBNA4-TV is a multicast of WBNA-TV. A multicast channel is a separate channel that shares the bandwith of the main station but can air unique programming. WBNA4-TV airs programming from the Retro Television Network in the Louisville, KY market. The station is owned by Word Broadcasting Network, Inc. WBNA4-TV broadcasts locally on channel 21.4.
TELEVISION STATION

WBNA-TV
32241
Owner: Word Broadcasting Network, Inc.
Editorial: 3701 Fern Valley Rd, Louisville, Kentucky 40219 **Tel:** 1 502 964-2121.
Web site: http://www.wbna21.com
Profile: WBNA-TV is the ION Television affiliate for the Louisville, KY, market. The station is owned by Word Broadcasting Network, Inc. WBNA-TV broadcasts locally on channel 21.
TELEVISION STATION

WBND-TV
32470
Owner: Weigel Broadcasting Co.
Editorial: 53550 Generations Dr, South Bend, Indiana 46635-1570 **Tel:** 1 574 344-5500.
Email: news57@abc57.com
Web site: http://www.abc57.com
Profile: WBND-TV is the ABC affiliate for the South Bend, IN, market. It is owned by Weigel Broadcasting Co. WTVC-TV broadcasts locally on channel 57.
TELEVISION STATION

WBNG-TV
31756
Owner: Quincy Newspapers
Editorial: 560 Columbia Dr, Johnson City, New York 13790-3300 **Tel:** 1 607 729-8812.
Email: wbng-newsroom@wbngtv.com
Web site: http://www.wbng.com
Profile: WBNG-TV is the CBS affiliate for the Binghamton, NY market. The station is owned by Quincy Newspapers. WBNG-TV broadcasts locally on channel 12.
TELEVISION STATION

WBNS2-TV
615059
Owner: Dispatch Broadcast Group
Editorial: 770 Twin Rivers Dr, Columbus, Ohio 43215-1159 **Tel:** 1 614 460-3700.
Web site: http://www.10tv.com
Profile: WBNS2-TV is a multicast of WBNS-TV. A multicast channel is a separate channel that shares the bandwith of the main station but can air unique programming. WBNS2-TV airs programming from AccuWeather in the Columbus, OH market. The station is owned by Dispatch Broadcast Group. WBNS2-TV broadcasts locally on channel 10.2.
TELEVISION STATION

WBNS-TV
31757
Owner: Dispatch Broadcast Group
Editorial: 770 Twin Rivers Dr, Columbus, Ohio 43215-1127 **Tel:** 1 614 460-3950.
Email: wbnsdesk@10tv.com
Web site: http://www.10tv.com
Profile: WBNS-TV is the CBS affiliate for the Columbus, OH market. The station is owned by Dispatch Broadcast Group. WBNS-TV broadcasts locally on channel 10.
TELEVISION STATION

WBNX3-TV
842113
Owner: Winston Broadcasting Network
Editorial: 2690 State Rd, Cuyahoga Falls, Ohio 44223-1644 **Tel:** 1 440 843-5555.
Web site: http://www.wbnx.com
Profile: WBNX3-TV is a multicast of WBNX-TV that airs programming from the ThisTV network for the Cleveland market. The station is owned by Winston Broadcasting Network. WBNX3-TV broadcasts locally on channel 55.3.
TELEVISION STATION

WBNX-TV
31758
Owner: Winston Broadcasting Network
Editorial: 2690 State Rd, Cuyahoga Falls, Ohio 44223-1644 **Tel:** 1 440 843-5555.
Email: vwrfdbk@wbnx.com
Web site: http://www.wbnx.com
Profile: WBNX-TV is a CW affiliate for the Cleveland market. The station is owned by Winston Broadcasting Network. WBNX-TV broadcasts locally on channel 55.
TELEVISION STATION

WBOC2-TV
557532
Owner: Draper Communications, Inc.
Editorial: 1729 N Salisbury Blvd, Salisbury, Maryland 21801-3330 **Tel:** 1 410 749-1111.
Email: news@wboc.com
Web site: http://www.fox21delmarva.com
Profile: WBOC2-TV is a multicast channel of WBOC-TV. A multicast channel is a separate channel that shares the bandwidth of the main station but can air unique programming. WBOC2-TV is the local FOX affiliate on Channel 21.2 for the Salisbury, MD market. WBOC2-TV is owned by Draper Communications, Inc.
TELEVISION STATION

WBOC-TV
31759
Owner: Draper Communications, Inc.
Editorial: 1729 N Salisbury Blvd, Salisbury, Maryland 21801-3330 **Tel:** 1 410 749-1111.
Email: news@wboc.com
Web site: http://www.wboc.com
Profile: WBOC-TV is the CBS network affiliate for the Salisbury, MD market. The station is owned by Draper Communications, Inc. WBOC-TV broadcasts locally on channel 16.
TELEVISION STATION

WBOY-TV
31760
Owner: Nexstar Broadcasting Group Inc.
Editorial: 904 W Pike St, Clarksburg, West Virginia 26301-2555 **Tel:** 1 304 623-3311.
Email: news@wboy.com
Web site: http://www.wvalways.com
Profile: WBOY-TV is the NBC affiliate for the Clarksburg-Weston, VA market. WBOY-TV broadcasts locally on channel 12. The station was previously owned by West Virginia Media Holdings LLC but has been acquired by Nexstar Broadcasting Group.
TELEVISION STATION

WBPH-TV
32364
Owner: Sunshine Family Television Corp.
Editorial: 813 N Fenwick St, Allentown, Pennsylvania 18109-1808 **Tel:** 1 610 433-4400.
Email: info@wbph.org
Web site: http://www.wbph.org
Profile: WBPH-TV, is an independent station for the Philadelphia market. The station is owned by Sunshine Family Television Corp. WBPH-TV broadcasts locally on channel 60.
TELEVISION STATION

WBPI-TV
389883
Owner: Watchmen Broadcasting
Editorial: 1750 Knox Ave, Beech Island, South Carolina 29841-2963 **Tel:** 1 803 278-3618.
Email: info@wbpi.org
Web site: http://www.wbpi.org
Profile: WBPI-TV is an independent station serving the Augusta, Georgia market. The station is owned by Watchmen Broadcasting Productions International. WBPI-TV broadcasts locally on channel 49.
TELEVISION STATION

WBPX2-TV
609592
Owner: ION Media Networks
Editorial: 1120 Soldiers Field Rd, Boston, Massachusetts 02134-1004 **Tel:** 1 617 787-4114.
Web site: http://www.qubo.com
Profile: WBPX2-TV is an independent affiliate for the Boston market. The station is owned by ION Media Networks. WBPX2-TV broadcasts locally on channel 68.2. WBPX2-TV broadcasts children's programming from the qubo network. WBPX2-TV is a multicast channel of WBPX-TV. A multicast channel is a separate channel that shares the bandwidth of the main station but can air unique programming.
TELEVISION STATION

WBPX3-TV
609593
Owner: ION Media Networks
Editorial: 1120 Soldiers Field Rd, Boston, Massachusetts 02134-1004 **Tel:** 1 617 787-6868.
Web site: http://www.ionlife.com
Profile: WBPX3-TV is an ION Television affiliate for the Boston market. The station is owned by ION Media Networks. WBPX3-TV broadcasts locally on channel 68.3. WBPX3-TV broadcasts lifestyle programming from the ION Life Network. WBPX3-TV is a multicast channel of WBPX-TV. A multicast channel is a separate channel that shares the bandwidth of the main station but can air unique programming.
TELEVISION STATION

WBPX4-TV
609731
Owner: ION Media Networks
Editorial: 1120 Soldiers Field Rd, Boston, Massachusetts 02134-1004 **Tel:** 1 617 787-6868.
Web site: http://www.worship.net
Profile: WBPX4-TV is an independent affiliate for the Boston market. The station is owned by ION Media Networks. WBPX4-TV broadcasts locally on channel 68.4. WBPX4-TV broadcasts religious and worship programming from the Worship Network. WBPX4-TV is a multicast channel of WBPX-TV. A multicast channel is a separate channel that shares the bandwidth of the main station but can air unique programming.
TELEVISION STATION

WBPX-TV
32751
Owner: ION Media Networks
Editorial: 1120 Soldiers Field Rd, Boston, Massachusetts 02134-1004 **Tel:** 1 617 787-6868.
Profile: WBPX-TV is the ION Television affiliate for the Boston market. The station is owned by ION Media Networks. WBPX-TV broadcasts locally on channel 68.
TELEVISION STATION

WBQC-TV
32621
Owner: Block Broadcasting, Inc.
Tel: 1 513 631-8825.
Email: info@wkrp.tv
Web site: http://www.wkrp.tv
Profile: WBQC-TV is an independent station for the Cincinnati market. The station is owned by Block Broadcasting, Inc. WBQC-TV broadcasts locally on channel 38.
TELEVISION STATION

WBQM-TV
872103
Owner: Buenavision TV Network NY, LLC
Editorial: 904 23rd St, Union City, New Jersey 07087-2117 **Tel:** 1 646 558-6270.
Email: contact@buenavisiontv.com
Web site: http://buenavisiontv.com
Profile: WBQM-TV is the an independent affiliate for the New York City market. The station is owned by Buenavision TV Network NY, LLC. WBQM-TV broadcasts locally on channel 3.
TELEVISION STATION

WBQP-TV
235375
Owner: Watson(Vernon)
Editorial: 312 E Nine Mile Rd Ste 29D, Pensacola, Florida 32514-1475 **Tel:** 1 850 478-6000.
Email: wbqp@wbqp.com
Web site: http://www.wbqp.com
Profile: WBQP-TV is an independent station for the Mobile, AL-Pensacola, FL, market. It is owned by Vernon Watson. WBQP-TV broadcasts locally on channel 12.
TELEVISION STATION

WBRA-TV
32685
Owner: Blue Ridge Public Television
Editorial: 1215 McNeil Dr SW, Roanoke, Virginia 24015-4706 **Tel:** 1 540 344-0991.
Email: info@blueridgepbs.org
Web site: http://www.blueridgepbs.org
Profile: WBRA-TV is the PBS network affiliate for the Roanoke-Lynchburg, VA market. The station is owned by Blue Ridge Public Television. WBRA-TV broadcasts locally on channel 15.
TELEVISION STATION

WBRC-TV
31761
Owner: Raycom Media Inc.
Editorial: 1720 Valley View Dr, Birmingham, Alabama 35209-1251 **Tel:** 1 205 322-6666.
Email: newstip@wbrc.com
Web site: http://www.wbrc.com
Profile: WBRC-TV is the FOX affiliate for the Birmingham, AL market. The station is owned by Raycom Media Inc. WBRC-TV broadcasts locally on channel 6.
TELEVISION STATION

WBRE-TV
31762
Owner: Nexstar Broadcasting Group
Editorial: 62 S Franklin St, Wilkes-Barre, Pennsylvania 18701-1201 **Tel:** 1 570 823-2828.
Email: newsdesk@pahomepage.com
Web site: http://www.pahomepage.com
Profile: WBRE-TV is the NBC affiliate for the Wilkes-Barre and Scranton, PA market. The station is owned by Nexstar Broadcasting Group. WBRE-TV broadcasts locally on Channel 28.
TELEVISION STATION

WBRL-TV
238272
Owner: Communications Corp. of America
Editorial: 10000 Perkins Rd, Baton Rouge, Louisiana 70810-1527 **Tel:** 1 225 819-0010.
Email: info@tvbatonrouge.com
Web site: http://www.cw21br.com
Profile: WBRL-TV is the CW affiliate for the Baton Rouge, LA market. The station is owned by Communications Corp. of America. WBRL-TV broadcasts locally on channel 21.
TELEVISION STATION

WBRW-TV
749479
Editorial: 8100 Wicker, Washington, Michigan 48094-2921 **Tel:** 1 586 697-5344.
Email: contact@micommunitymedia.org
Web site: http://wbrwtv.com
Profile: WBRW-TV is an independent community television station based in Washington, MI. It serves Bruce Township, the Village of Romeo and Washington Township. WBRW-TV is part of the non-profit Michigan Community Media. The studio provides training, facilities and equipment to community residents, students and organizations for production of local television.
TELEVISION STATION

WBRZ-TV
31763
Owner: Louisiana Television Broadcasting LLC
Editorial: 1650 Highland Rd, Baton Rouge, Louisiana 70802-7018 **Tel:** 1 225 387-2222.
Email: news@wbrz.com
Web site: http://www.wbrz.com
Profile: WBRZ-TV is the ABC affiliate for the Baton Rouge, LA market. The station is owned by Louisiana Television Broadcasting LLC. WBRZ-TV broadcasts locally on channel 2.
TELEVISION STATION

WBSF-TV
417743
Owner: Sinclair Broadcast Group, Inc.
Editorial: 3463 W Pierson Rd, Flint, Michigan 48504-6905 **Tel:** 1 810 687-1000.
Email: news@nbc25.net
Web site: http://www.minbcnews.com
Profile: WBSF-TV is the CW affiliate for the Bay City, MI area. The station is owned by Sinclair Broadcast Group, Inc.. WBSF-TV broadcasts locally on channel 46.
TELEVISION STATION

WBTS-TV
72050
Owner: NBC Universal
Editorial: 160 Wells Ave, Newton, Massachusetts 02459-3302 **Tel:** 1 617 630-5000.
Email: tips@nbcboston.com
Web site: http://www.nbcboston.com
Profile: WBTS-TV is the NBC affiliate for the Boston market, focusing on news across Greater Boston, Southern New Hampshire, and Cape Cod. The station is owned by NBC Universal. WBTS-TV broadcasts locally on channel 8.
TELEVISION STATION

WBTV2-TV
891013
Owner: Raycom Media Inc.
Editorial: 1 Julian Price Pl, Charlotte, North Carolina 28208-5211 **Tel:** 1 704 374-3500.
Web site: http://www.wbtv.com
Profile: WBTV2-TV is a multicast channel of WBTV-TV. A multicast channel is a separate channel that shares the bandwidth of the main station but can air unique programming. WBTV2-TV is the Bounce Network for the Charlotte market. The station is owned by Raycom Media Inc. WBTV2-TV broadcasts locally on channel 3.2.
TELEVISION STATION

WBTV-TV
31764
Owner: Raycom Media Inc.
Editorial: 1 Julian Price Pl, Charlotte, North Carolina 28208 **Tel:** 1 704 374-3500.
Email: assignmentdesk@wbtv.com
Web site: http://www.wbtv.com
Profile: WBTV-TV is the CBS network affiliate for the Charlotte, NC market. The station is owned by Raycom Media Inc. WBTV-TV broadcasts locally on channel 3.
TELEVISION STATION

WBTW-TV
31765
Owner: Nexstar Media Group, Inc.
Editorial: 101 McDonald Ct, Myrtle Beach, South Carolina 29588-6134 **Tel:** 1 843 317-1313.
Email: news@wbtw.com
Web site: http://www.wbtw.com
Profile: WBTW-TV is the CBS affiliate for the Florence-Myrtle Beach, SC market. The station is owned by Nexstar Media Group, Inc. WBTW-TV broadcasts locally on channel 13.
TELEVISION STATION

WBUI2-TV
607644
Owner: Sinclair Broadcast Group
Editorial: 2680 E Cook St, Springfield, Illinois 62703-1902 **Tel:** 1 217 523-8855.
Web site: http://www.centralillinoiscw.com
Profile: WBUI2-TV is a multicast channel of WBUI-TV. A multicast channel is a separate channel that shares the bandwidth of the main station but can air unique programming. WBUI2-TV airs programming from This TV network for the Springfield-Decatur, IL market. It is owned by Sinclair Broadcast Group. WBUI2-TV broadcasts locally on channel 23.2.
TELEVISION STATION

WBUI-TV
31836
Owner: Sinclair Broadcast Group
Editorial: 2680 E Cook St, Springfield, Illinois 62703-1902 **Tel:** 1 217 523-8855.
Web site: http://www.centralillinoiscw.com
Profile: WBUI-TV is the CW affiliate for the Springfield-Decatur, IL market. The station is owned by Sinclair Broadcast Group. WBUI-TV broadcasts locally on channel 23.
TELEVISION STATION

WBUP-TV
80787
Owner: Thunder Bay Broadcasting Corp.
Editorial: 1705 Ash St, Ishpeming, Michigan 49849-1076 **Tel:** 1 906 204-2436.
Email: news@abc10up.com
Web site: http://www.abc10up.com
TELEVISION STATION

WBUY2-TV
620280
Owner: Trinity Broadcasting Network
Editorial: 3447 Cazassa Rd, Memphis, Tennessee 38116-3609 **Tel:** 1 901 396-9541.
Email: wbuy@tbn.org
Profile: WBUY2-TV is a multicast of WBUY-TV. A multicast channel is a separate channel that shares the bandwith of the main station but can air unique programming. WBUY2-TV airs Christian programming from The Church Channel in the Memphis, TN market. The station is owned by Trinity Broadcasting Network. WBUY2-TV broadcasts locally on channel 40.2.
TELEVISION STATION

WBUY3-TV 620283
Owner: Trinity Broadcasting Network
Editorial: 3447 Cazassa Rd, Memphis, Tennessee 38116-3609 **Tel:** 1 901 396-9541.
Email: wbuy@tbn.org
Profile: WBUY3-TV is a multicast of WBUY-TV. A multicast channel is a separate channel that shares the bandwith of the main station but can air unique programming. WBUY3-TV airs Christian music videos from JCTV in the Memphis, TN market. The station is owned by Trinity Broadcasting Network. WBUY3-TV broadcasts locally on channel 40.3.
TELEVISION STATION

WBUY4-TV 620285
Owner: Trinity Broadcasting Network
Editorial: 3447 Cazassa Rd, Memphis, Tennessee 38116-3609 **Tel:** 1 901 396-9541.
Email: wbuy@tbn.org
Profile: WBUY4-TV is a multicast of WBUY-TV. A multicast channel is a separate channel that shares the bandwith of the main station but can air unique programming. WBUY4-TV airs Hispanic Christian programming from Enlace USA in the Memphis, TN market. The station is owned by Trinity Broadcasting Network. WBUY4-TV broadcasts locally on channel 40.4.
TELEVISION STATION

WBUY5-TV 620291
Owner: Trinity Broadcasting Network
Editorial: 3447 Cazassa Rd, Memphis, Tennessee 38116-3609 **Tel:** 1 901 396-9541.
Email: wbuy@tbn.org
Profile: WBUY5-TV is a multicast of WBUY-TV. A multicast channel is a separate channel that shares the bandwith of the main station but can air unique programming. WBUY5-TV airs children's Christian programming from Smile of a Child in the Memphis, TN market. The station is owned by Trinity Broadcasting Network. WBUY5-TV broadcasts locally on channel 40.5.
TELEVISION STATION

WBUY-TV 32391
Owner: Trinity Broadcasting Network
Editorial: 3447 Cazassa Rd, Memphis, Tennessee 38116-3609 **Tel:** 1 901 396-9541.
Email: wbuy@tbn.org
Web site: http://tbn.org
Profile: WBUY-TV is a TBN affiliate for the Memphis, TN market. The station is owned by Trinity Broadcasting Network. WBUY-TV broadcasts locally on channel 40.
TELEVISION STATION

WBWP-TV 151946
Owner: H & R Productions
Editorial: 7354 Central Industrial Dr, Riviera Beach, Florida 33404-3413 **Tel:** 1 561 863-0417.
Web site: http://www.mundofox57.com
Profile: WBWP-TV is the MundoFOX affiliate for the West Palm Beach, FL market. The station is owned by H & R Productions. WBWP-TV broadcasts locally on channel 57.
TELEVISION STATION

WBXH-TV 376983
Owner: Raycom Media Inc.
Editorial: 844 Government St, Baton Rouge, Louisiana 70802-6030 **Tel:** 1 225 383-9999.
Email: news@wafb.com
Web site: http://www.wafb.com/category/4769/wbxh-tv
Profile: WBXH-TV is the MyNetworkTV affiliate for the Baton Rouge, LA market. The station is owned by Raycom Media Inc. WBXH-TV broadcassts locally on channel 16.
TELEVISION STATION

WBXI-TV 390679
Owner: Quincy Newspapers
Editorial: 560 Columbia Dr, Johnson City, New York 13790-3300 **Tel:** 1 607 729-8812.
Email: wbng@wbngtv.com
Web site: http://www.binghamtonscw.com
Profile: WBXI-TV is the CW affiliate for the Johnson City, NY market. The station is owned by Quincy Newspapers. WBXI-TV broadcasts locally on channel 47.
TELEVISION STATION

WBXX-TV 63123
Owner: Lockwood Broadcasting Group
Editorial: 10427 Cogdill Rd, Ste 100, Knoxville, Tennessee 37932 **Tel:** 1 865 777-9220.
Web site: http://www.easttennesseescw.com
Profile: WBXX-TV is the CW affiliate for the greater Knoxville, TN area. The station is owned by Lockwood Broadcasting Group. WBXX-TV broadcasts locally on channel 20.
TELEVISION STATION

WBZ-TV 31766
Owner: CBS Television Stations
Editorial: 1170 Soldiers Field Rd, Boston, Massachusetts 02134-1004 **Tel:** 1 617 787-7000.
Email: newstips@wbztv.com
Web site: http://boston.cbslocal.com
Profile: WBZ-TV is the CBS affiliate for the Boston market. The station is owned by CBS Television Stations. WBZ-TV broadcasts locally on channel 4.
TELEVISION STATION

WCAU2-TV 610508
Owner: NBC Universal
Editorial: 10 Monument Rd, Bala Cynwyd, Pennsylvania 19004-1712 **Tel:** 1 610 668-5510.
Email: tips@nbcphiladelphia.com
Web site: http://www.nbcphiladelphia.com
Profile: WCAU2-TV, also called NBC Philadelphia NonStop channel, is a multicast of WCAU-TV. A multicast channel is a separate channel that shares the bandwith of the main station but can air unique programming. WCAU2-TV airs programming from NBC NonStop in the Philadelphia market. The station is owned by NBC Universal. WCAU2-TV broadcasts locally on channel 10.2.
TELEVISION STATION

WCAU3-TV 610509
Owner: NBC Universal
Editorial: 10 Monument Rd, Bala Cynwyd, Pennsylvania 19004-1712 **Tel:** 1 610 668-5510.
Email: tips@nbcphiladelphia.com
Web site: http://www.nbcphiladelphia.com
Profile: WCAU3-TV is a multicast of WCAU-TV. A multicast channel is a separate channel that shares the bandwith of the main station but can air unique programming. WCAU3-TV airs programming from Universal Sports in the Philadelphia market. The station is owned by NBC Universal. WCAU3-TV broadcasts locally on channel 10.3.
TELEVISION STATION

WCAU-TV 31767
Owner: NBC Universal
Editorial: 10 Monument Rd, Bala Cynwyd, Pennsylvania 19004-1712 **Tel:** 1 610 668-5510.
Email: tips@nbcphiladelphia.com
Web site: http://www.nbcphiladelphia.com
Profile: WCAU-TV is the NBC affiliate for the Philadelphia area. The station is owned by NBC Universal. WCAU-TV broadcasts locally on channel 10.
TELEVISION STATION

WCAV-TV 353155
Owner: Gray Television, Inc.
Editorial: 999 2nd St SE, Charlottesville, Virginia 22902-6172 **Tel:** 1 434 242-1919.
Email: news@newsplex.com
Web site: http://www.newsplex.com
Profile: WCAV-TV is the CBS affiliate for the Charlottesville, VA market. The station is owned by Gray Television, Inc. WCAV-TV broadcasts locally on channel 19.
TELEVISION STATION

WCAX-TV 31768
Owner: Mount Mansfield Television
Editorial: 30 Joy Dr, South Burlington, Vermont 05403-6118 **Tel:** 1 802 652-6300.
Email: channel3@wcax.com
Web site: http://www.wcax.com
Profile: WCAX-TV is the CBS affiliate for the Burlington, VT/Plattsburgh, NY market. The station is owned by Mount Mansfield Television. WCAX-TV broadcasts locally on channel 3.
TELEVISION STATION

WCBD-TV 31770
Owner: Nexstar Media Group, Inc.
Editorial: 210 W Coleman Blvd, Mount Pleasant, South Carolina 29464-3426 **Tel:** 1 843 884-2222.
Email: newstip@wcbd.com
Web site: http://www.counton2.com
Profile: WCBD-TV is the NBC affiliate for the Charleston, SC market. The station is owned by Nexstar Media Group, Inc. WCBD-TV broadcasts locally on channel 2.
TELEVISION STATION

WCBI-TV 31771
Owner: Morris Multimedia, Inc.
Editorial: 201 5th St S, Columbus, Mississippi 39701-5729 **Tel:** 1 662 327-4444.
Email: news@wcbi.com
Web site: http://www.wcbi.com
Profile: WCBI-TV is the CBS network affiliate for the Columbus, MS market. The station is owned by Morris Multimedia Inc. WCBI-TV broadcasts locally on channel 4.
TELEVISION STATION

WCBS2-TV 779227
Owner: CBS Television Station
Editorial: 524 W 57Th St #8, New York, New York 10019-2930 **Tel:** 1 212 975-4321.
Web site: http://newyork.cbslocal.com
Profile: WCBS2-TV is a multicast channel of WCBS-TV. A multicast channel is a separate channel that shares the bandwith of the main station but can air unique programming. WCBS2-TV is also known as CBS New York Plus and combines news and information from WCBS-TV, WCBS-AM, WINS-AM and WFAN-AM. The station is owned by CBS Television Stations. WCBS2-TV broadcasts locally on channel 2.2. The station will debut in late 2011.
TELEVISION STATION

WCBS-TV 31772
Owner: CBS Television Stations
Editorial: 524 W 57Th St #8, New York, New York 10019-2930 **Tel:** 1 212 975-4321.
Email: desk@cbs2ny.com
Web site: http://newyork.cbslocal.com
Profile: WCBS-TV is the CBS affiliate for the New York City market. The station is owned by CBS Television Stations. WCBS-TV broadcasts locally on channel 2. In the few areas of the eastern United States where viewers cannot receive CBS programs over-the-air, WCBS-TV is available on satellite to subscribers of DirecTV, which also provides coverage of the station to Latin America and major U.S. air carriers via the LiveTV inflight entertainment system. As of March 4, 2009, WCBS-TV is once again available to Dish Network customers as part of All American Direct's distant network package.
TELEVISION STATION

WCCB3-TV 613861
Owner: Bahakel Communications
Editorial: 1 Television Pl, Charlotte, North Carolina 28205-7038 **Tel:** 1 704 372-1800.
Web site: http://www.wccbcharlotte.com
Profile: WCCB3-TV is a multicast of WCCB-TV. A multicast channel is a separate channel that shares the bandwith of the main station but can air unique programming. WCCB3-TV airs programming from MeTV in the Charlotte, NC market. The station is owned by Bahakel Communications. WCCB3-TV broadcasts locally on channel 18.3.
TELEVISION STATION

WCCB-TV 31773
Owner: Bahakel Communications
Editorial: 1 Television Pl, Charlotte, North Carolina 28205-7038 **Tel:** 1 704 372-1800.
Email: newsdesk@wccbcharlotte.com
Web site: http://www.wccbcharlotte.com
Profile: WCCB-TV is the CW affiliate for the Charlotte, NC market. The station is owned by Bahakel Communications. WCCB-TV broadcasts locally on channel 18.
TELEVISION STATION

WCCO-TV 31774
Owner: CBS Television Stations
Editorial: 90 S 11th St, Minneapolis, Minnesota 55403-2414 **Tel:** 1 612 339-4444.
Email: wcconewstips@wcco.com
Web site: http://minnesota.cbslocal.com
Profile: WCCO-TV is the CBS affiliate for the Minneapolis market. The station is owned by CBS Television Stations. WCCO-TV broadcasts locally on channel 4.
TELEVISION STATION

WCCT2-TV 613406
Owner: Tribune Broadcasting Co.
Editorial: 285 Broad St, Hartford, Connecticut 06105-3785 **Tel:** 1 860 527-6161.
Email: wccttv@gmail.com
Web site: http://www.ct.com
Profile: WCCT2-TV is a multicast of WCCT-TV. A multicast channel is a separate channel that shares the bandwith of the main station but can air unique programming. WCCT2-TV airs programming from This TV in the Hartford, CT market. The station is owned by Tribune Broadcasting Co. WCCT2-TV broadcasts locally on channel 20.2.
TELEVISION STATION

WCCT-TV 32177
Owner: Tribune Broadcasting Co.
Editorial: 285 Broad St, Hartford, Connecticut 06105-3785 **Tel:** 1 860 527-6161.
Email: wccttv@gmail.com
Web site: http://www.ct.com
Profile: WCCT-TV is the CW network affiliate in the Hartford-New Haven, CT market. The station is owned by Tribune Broadcasting Co. WCCT-TV broadcasts locally on channel 20.
TELEVISION STATION

WCCU-TV 32390
Owner: Sinclair Broadcast Group
Editorial: 2680 E Cook St, Springfield, Illinois 62703-1902 **Tel:** 1 217 523-8855.
Web site: http://www.foxillinois.com
Profile: WCCU-TV is the FOX affiliate for the Springfield-Decatur, IL market. The station is owned by Sinclair Broadcast Group. WCCU-TV broadcasts locally on channel 27.
TELEVISION STATION

WCET2-TV 620975
Owner: Gr. Cincinnati TV Educ. Found.
Editorial: 1223 Central Pkwy, Cincinnati, Ohio 45214-2890 **Tel:** 1 513 381-4033.
Email: comments@cetconnect.org
Web site: http://www.wcet.org
Profile: WCET2-TV is a multicast of WCET-TV. A multicast channel is a separate channel that shares the bandwith of the main station but can air unique programming. WCET2-TV airs how-to, DIY and instructional programming from Create in the Cincinnati market. The station is owned by Gr. Cincinnati TV Educ. Found. WCET2-TV broadcasts locally on channel 48.2.
TELEVISION STATION

WCET3-TV 620978
Owner: Gr. Cincinnati TV Educ. Found.
Editorial: 1223 Central Pkwy, Cincinnati, Ohio 45214-2890 **Tel:** 1 513 381-4033.
Email: comments@cetconnect.org
Web site: http://www.wcet.org
Profile: WCET3-TV is a multicast of WCET-TV. A multicast channel is a separate channel that shares the bandwith of the main station but can air unique programming. WCET3-TV airs programming from CET World in the Cincinnati market. The station is owned by Gr. Cincinnati TV Educ. Found. WCET3-TV broadcasts locally on channel 48.3.
TELEVISION STATION

WCET-TV 31777
Owner: Gr. Cincinnati TV Educ. Found.
Editorial: 1223 Central Pkwy, Cincinnati, Ohio 45214-2812 **Tel:** 1 513 381-4033.
Email: comments@cetconnect.org
Web site: http://www.cetconnect.org
Profile: WCET-TV is the PBS affiliate for the Cincinnati market. The station is owned by the Greater Cincinnati TV Education Foundation. WCET-TV broadcasts locally on channel 48.
TELEVISION STATION

WCFE-TV 31779
Owner: Mountain Lake Public Telecommunications Council
Editorial: 1 Sesame St, Mountain Lake Pbs, Plattsburgh, New York 12901-6411 **Tel:** 1 518 563-9770.
Email: mlpbs@mountainlake.org
Web site: http://www.mountainlake.org
Profile: WCFE-TV is the PBS affiliate for the Plattsburgh, NY market. The station is owned by the Mountain Lake Public Telecommunications Council. WCFE-TV broadcasts locally on channel 57.
TELEVISION STATION

WCGV-TV 31781
Owner: Sinclair Broadcast Group, Inc.
Editorial: 11520 W Calumet Rd, Milwaukee, Wisconsin 53224-3156 **Tel:** 1 414 815-4100.
Email: info@my24milwaukee.com
Web site: http://www.my24milwaukee.com
Profile: WCGV-TV is the local MyNetworkTV affiliate for the Milwaukee market. The station is owned by Sinclair Broadcast Group, Inc. WCGV-TV broadcasts locally on channel 24.
TELEVISION STATION

WCHS-TV 31782
Owner: Sinclair Broadcast Group, Inc.
Editorial: 1301 Piedmont Rd, Charleston, West Virginia 25301-1426 **Tel:** 1 304 346-5358.
Email: news@wchstv.com
Web site: http://www.wchstv.com
Profile: WCHS-TV is the ABC affiliate for the Charleston-Huntington WV, market. The station is owned by Sinclair Broadcast Group, Inc. WCHS-TV broadcasts locally on channel 8.
TELEVISION STATION

WCHU-TV 586663
Owner: Venture Technologies Group LLC
Tel: 1 312 814-7395.
Profile: WCHU-TV is an Azteca América affiliate station in Hartford, Connecticut, USA. The station is owned by Venture Technologies Group and broadcasts on UHF channel 38 from the WCCC-FM tower on Avon Mountain in West Hartford, CT.
TELEVISION STATION

WCIA-TV 32732
Owner: Nexstar Broadcasting Group
Editorial: 509 S Neil St, Champaign, Illinois 61820-5219 **Tel:** 1 217 356-8333.
Email: news@wcia.com
Web site: http://www.illinoishomepage.net
Profile: WCIA-TV is the CBS affiliate for the Springfield, IL/Decatur, IL market. The station is owned by Nexstar Broadcasting Group. WCIA-TV broadcasts locally on channel 3.
TELEVISION STATION

WCIU2-TV 607608
Owner: Weigel Broadcasting Co.
Editorial: 26 N Halsted St, Chicago, Illinois 60661-2107 **Tel:** 1 312 705-2600.
Email: news@wciu.com
Web site: http://www.metvchicago.com
Profile: WCIU2-TV is an independent station for the Chicago market. The station is owned by Weigel Broadcasting Co. WCIU2-TV broadcasts locally on channel 26.2. The station is a simulcast of low power station WWME-TV, airing MeTV classic entertainment programming. WCIU2-TV is a multicast channel of WCIU-TV. A multicast channel is a separate channel that shares the bandwidth of the main station but can air unique programming.
TELEVISION STATION

WCIU3-TV 607618
Owner: Weigel Broadcasting Co.
Editorial: 26 N Halsted St, Chicago, Illinois 60661-2107 **Tel:** 1 312 705-2600.
Email: news@wciu.com
Web site: http://www.metvchicago.com
Profile: WCIU3-TV is an independent station for the Chicago market. The station is owned by Weigel Broadcasting Co. WCIU3-TV broadcasts locally on channel 26.3. The station is a simulcast of low power station WMEU-TV, airing MeTV classic entertainment programming. WCIU3-TV is a multicast channel of WCIU-TV. A multicast channel is a separate channel that shares the bandwidth of the main station but can air unique programming.
TELEVISION STATION

WCIU4-TV 607623
Owner: Weigel Broadcasting Co.
Editorial: 26 N Halsted St, Chicago, Illinois 60661-2107 **Tel:** 1 312 705-2600.
Email: news@wciu.com
Web site: http://www.this.tv
Profile: WCIU4-TV is an independent station for the Chicago market. The station is owned by Weigel Broadcasting Co. WCIU4-TV broadcasts locally on channel 26.4. The station airs programming from This TV, featuring general and classic entertainment. WCIU4-TV is a multicast channel of WCIU-TV. A multicast channel is a separate channel that shares

the bandwidth of the main station but can air unique programming.
TELEVISION STATION

WCIU-TV 31783
Owner: Weigel Broadcasting Co.
Editorial: 26 N Halsted St, Chicago, Illinois 60661-2107 **Tel:** 1 312 705-2600.
Email: news@wciu.com
Web site: http://www.wciu.com
Profile: WCIU-TV is an independent station for the Chicago market. The station is owned by Weigel Broadcasting Co. WCIU-TV broadcasts locally on channel 26.
TELEVISION STATION

WCIV-TV 31784
Owner: Sinclair Broadcast Group, Inc.
Editorial: 888 Allbritton Blvd, Mount Pleasant, South Carolina 29464-3033 **Tel:** 1 843 881-4444.
Web site: http://mytvcharleston.com
Profile: WCIV-TV is the MyNetworkTV affiliate for the Charleston, South Carolina market. The station is owned by Sinclair Broadcast Group, Inc. WCIV-TV broadcasts locally on channel 4.
TELEVISION STATION

WCIX-TV 32977
Owner: Nexstar Broadcasting Group
Editorial: 509 S Neil St, Champaign, Illinois 61820-5219 **Tel:** 1 217 356-8333.
Email: news@wcfn.tv
Web site: http://illinoishomepage.net
Profile: WCIX-TV is the MyNetworkTV affiliate for the Springfield-Decatur IL market. The station is owned by Nexstar Broadcasting Group. WCIX-TV broadcasts locally on channel 49.
TELEVISION STATION

WCJB-TV 31786
Owner: Diversified Communications
Editorial: 6220 NW 43rd St, Gainesville, Florida 32653-3334 **Tel:** 1 352 377-2020.
Email: tv20news@wcjb.com
Web site: http://www.wcjb.com
Profile: WCJB-TV is the ABC affiliate for the Gainesville, FL market. The station is owned by Diversified Communications. WCJB-TV broadcasts locally on channel 20.
TELEVISION STATION

WCLF-TV 31787
Owner: Christian Television Network
Editorial: 6922 142nd Ave, Largo, Florida 33771
Tel: 1 727 535-5622.
Web site: http://www.ctnonline.com
Profile: WCLF-TV is an independent station for the Tampa-St. Petersburg, FL market. The station is owned by Christian Television Network. WCLF-TV broadcasts locally on channel 22.
TELEVISION STATION

WCLJ2-TV 613410
Owner: Trinity Broadcasting Network
Editorial: 2528 US Highway 31 S, Greenwood, Indiana 46143-9773 **Tel:** 1 317 535-5542.
Email: wcljpa@tbn.org
Web site: http://tbn.org
Profile: WCLJ2-TV is a multicast of WCLJ-TV. A multicast channel is a separate channel that shares the bandwidth of the main station but can air unique programming. WCLJ2-TV airs programming from The Church Channel in the Indianapolis market. The station is owned by Trinity Broadcasting Network. WCLJ2-TV broadcasts locally on channel 42.2. The station does not accept press releases.
TELEVISION STATION

WCLJ3-TV 613413
Owner: Trinity Broadcasting Network
Editorial: 2528 US Highway 31 S, Greenwood, Indiana 46143-9773 **Tel:** 1 317 535-5542.
Email: wcljpa@tbn.org
Web site: http://tbn.org
Profile: WCLJ3-TV is a multicast of WCLJ-TV. A multicast channel is a separate channel that shares the bandwidth of the main station but can air unique programming. WCLJ3-TV airs programming from JCTV in the Indianapolis market. The station is owned by Trinity Broadcasting Network. WCLJ3-TV broadcasts locally on channel 42.3. The station does not accept press releases.
TELEVISION STATION

WCLJ4-TV 613416
Owner: Trinity Broadcasting Network
Editorial: 2528 US Highway 31 S, Greenwood, Indiana 46143-9773 **Tel:** 1 317 535-5542.
Email: wcljpa@tbn.org
Profile: WCLJ4-TV is a multicast of WCLJ-TV. A multicast channel is a separate channel that shares the bandwidth of the main station but can air unique programming. WCLJ4-TV airs programming from Enlace USA in the Indianapolis market. The station is owned by Trinity Broadcasting Network. WCLJ4-TV broadcasts locally on channel 42.4. The station does not accept press releases.
TELEVISION STATION

WCLJ5-TV 613420
Owner: Trinity Broadcasting Network
Editorial: 2528 US Highway 31 S, Greenwood, Indiana 46143-9773 **Tel:** 1 317 535-5542.
Email: wcljpa@tbn.org
Profile: WCLJ5-TV is a multicast of WCLJ-TV. A multicast channel is a separate channel that shares the bandwidth of the main station but can air unique programming. WCLJ5-TV airs programming from Smile of a Child in the Indianapolis market. The station is owned by Trinity Broadcasting Network. WCLJ5-TV broadcasts locally on channel 42.5. The station does not accept press releases.
TELEVISION STATION

WCLJ-TV 32308
Owner: Trinity Broadcasting Network
Editorial: 2528 US Highway 31 S, Greenwood, Indiana 46143-9773 **Tel:** 1 317 535-5542.
Email: wcljpa@tbn.org
Profile: WCLJ-TV is the Trinity Broadcasting Network affiliate for the Indianapolis market. The station is owned by Trinity Broadcasting Network. WCLJ-TV broadcasts locally on channel 42.
TELEVISION STATION

WCMH2-TV 621870
Owner: Nexstar Media Group, Inc.
Editorial: 3165 Olentangy River Rd, Columbus, Ohio 43202-1518 **Tel:** 1 614 263-4444.
Email: newsdesk@nbc4i.com
Web site: http://www.nbc4i.com
Profile: WCMH2-TV is a multicast channel of WCMH-TV. A multicast is a separate channel that shares the bandwidth of the main station but can air unique programming. WCMH2-TV airs entertainment programming from MeTV in the Columbus, OH market. The station is owned by Nexstar Media Group, Inc. WCMH2-TV broadcasts locally on channel 4.2.
TELEVISION STATION

WCMH-TV 31788
Owner: Nexstar Media Group, Inc.
Editorial: 3165 Olentangy River Rd, Columbus, Ohio 43202-1518 **Tel:** 1 614 263-4444.
Email: newsdesk@nbc4i.com
Web site: http://www.nbc4i.com
Profile: WCMH-TV is the NBC affiliate for the Columbus, OH market. The station is owned by Nexstar Media Group, Inc. WCMH-TV broadcasts locally on channel 4.
TELEVISION STATION

WCMO-TV 231392
Owner: Marietta College
Editorial: 215 5th St, Marietta, Ohio 45750-4033
Tel: 1 740 376-4802.
TELEVISION STATION

WCNC2-TV 613984
Owner: TEGNA Inc.
Editorial: 1001 Woodrdg Ctr Dr, Charlotte, North Carolina 28217-1902 **Tel:** 1 704 329-3636.
Email: news@wcnc.com
Web site: http://www.wcnc.com
Profile: WCNC2-TV is a multicast of WCNC-TV. A multicast channel is a separate channel that shares the bandwith of the main station but can air unique programming. WCNC2-TV airs programming from the WCNC-WX in the Charlotte, NC market. The station is owned by TEGNA Inc. WCNC2-TV broadcasts locally on channel 36.2.
TELEVISION STATION

WCNC-TV 32042
Owner: TEGNA Inc.
Editorial: 1001 Woodrdg Ctr Dr, Charlotte, North Carolina 28217-1902 **Tel:** 1 704 329-3636.
Email: desk@wcnc.com
Web site: http://www.wcnc.com
Profile: WCNC-TV is the NBC affiliate for the Charlotte, NC market. The station is owned by TEGNA Inc. WCNC-TV broadcasts locally on channel 36. Alternate emails for the station are news@wcnc.com and assignmentdesk@wcnc.com.
TELEVISION STATION

WCNY2-TV 617521
Owner: Public Broadcasting Council of Central New York
Editorial: 415 W. Fayette St., Syracuse, New York 13204 **Tel:** 1 315 453-2424.
Email: wcny_online@wcny.org
Web site: http://www.wcny.org
Profile: WCNY2-TV is a multicast of WCNY-TV. A multicast channel is a separate channel that shares the bandwith of the main station but can air unique programming. WCNY2-TV airs programming from Create/Think Bright Network in the Syracuse, NY market. The station is owned by Public Broadcasting Council of Central New York. WCNY2-TV broadcasts locally on channel 24.2.
TELEVISION STATION

WCNY3-TV 617523
Owner: Public Broadcasting Council of Central New York
Editorial: 415 W. Fayette St., Syracuse, New York 13204 **Tel:** 1 315 453-2424.
Email: wcny_online@wcny.org
Web site: http://www.wcny.org
Profile: WCNY3-TV is a multicast of WCNY-TV. A multicast channel is a separate channel that shares the bandwith of the main station but can air unique programming. WCNY3-TV airs programming from Cinema 24 in the Syracuse, NY market. The station is owned by Public Broadcasting Council of Central New York. WCNY3-TV broadcasts locally on channel 24.3. Contact the station by phone or fax.
TELEVISION STATION

WCNY-TV 31789
Owner: Public Broadcasting Council of Central New York
Editorial: 415 W. Fayette St., Syracuse, New York 13204 **Tel:** 1 315 453-2424.
Email: wcny_online@wcny.org
Web site: http://www.wcny.org
Profile: WCNY-TV is the PBS network affiliate for the Syracuse, NY market. The station is owned by Public Broadcasting Council of Central New York. WCNY-TV broadcasts locally on channel 24.
TELEVISION STATION

WCOV-TV 31790
Owner: Woods Communications
Editorial: 1 Wcov Ave, Montgomery, Alabama 36111-2099 **Tel:** 1 334 288-7020.
Web site: http://www.wcov.com
Profile: WCOV-TV is the FOX affiliate for the Montgomery, AL market. The station is owned by Woods Communications. WCOV-TV broadcasts locally on channel 20.
TELEVISION STATION

WCPO2-TV 620861
Owner: E.W. Scripps Co.
Editorial: 1720 Gilbert Ave, Cincinnati, Ohio 45202-1401 **Tel:** 1 513 721-9900.
Email: newsite@wcpo.com
Web site: http://www.wcpo.com
Profile: WCPO2-TV is a multicast of WCPO-TV. A multicast channel is a separate channel that shares the bandwith of the main station but can air unique programming. WCPO2-TV airs 24 hour local weather programming from Weather Tracker in the Cincinnati market. The station is owned by E.W. Scripps Co. WCPO2-TV broadcasts locally on channel 9.2.
TELEVISION STATION

WCPO-TV 31791
Owner: E.W. Scripps Co.
Editorial: 1720 Gilbert Ave, Cincinnati, Ohio 45202-1401 **Tel:** 1 513 721-9900.
Email: newsdesk@wcpo.com
Web site: http://www.wcpo.com
Profile: WCPO-TV is the ABC affiliate for the serving the Cincinnati area. The station is owned by E.W. Scripps Co. WCPO-TV broadcasts locally on channel 9.
TELEVISION STATION

WCPX2-TV 607098
Owner: ION Media Networks
Editorial: 333 S Desplaines St, Ste 101, Chicago, Illinois 60661-5514 **Tel:** 1 312 376-8520.
Web site: http://www.qubo.com/
Profile: WCPX2-TV is the qubo network affliate for the Chicago market. The station is owned by ION Media Networks. WCPX-TV broadcasts locally on channel 38.2. WXPX2-TV airs children's programming from the qubo network. WCPX2-TV is a multicast channel of WCPX-TV. A multicast channel is a separate channel that shares the bandwidth of the main station but can air unique programming.
TELEVISION STATION

WCPX3-TV 607105
Owner: ION Media Networks
Editorial: 333 S Desplaines St, Ste 101, Chicago, Illinois 60661-5514 **Tel:** 1 312 376-8520.
Web site: http://www.iontelevision.com
Profile: WCPX3-TV is the Ion Life network affliate for the Chicago market. The station is owned by ION Media Networks. WCPX-TV broadcasts locally on channel 38.3. WCPX3-TV airs programming from Ion Health Channel. WCPX3-TV is a multicast channel of WCPX-TV. A multicast channel is a separate channel that shares the bandwidth of the main station but can air unique programming.
TELEVISION STATION

WCPX4-TV 607358
Owner: ION Media Networks
Editorial: 333 S Desplaines St, Ste 101, Chicago, Illinois 60661-5514 **Tel:** 1 312 376-8520.
Profile: WCPX4-TV is the Worship TV Channel affliate for the Chicago market. The station is owned by ION Media Networks. WCPX-TV broadcasts locally on channel 38.4. WCPX4-TV airs religious programming from the Worship TV Channel. WCPX4-TV is a multicast channel of WCPX-TV. A multicast channel is a separate channel that shares the bandwidth of the main station but can air unique programming.
TELEVISION STATION

WCPX-TV 31778
Owner: ION Media Networks
Editorial: 333 S Desplaines St, Chicago, Illinois 60661-5514 **Tel:** 1 312 376-8520.
Web site: http://www.iontelevision.com
Profile: WCPX-TV is the ION Television affiliate for the Chicago market. The station is owned by ION Media Networks. WCPX-TV broadcasts locally on channel 38.
TELEVISION STATION

WCSC-TV 31793
Owner: Raycom Media Inc.
Editorial: 2126 Charlie Hall Blvd, Charleston, South Carolina 29414 **Tel:** 1 843 402-5555.
Email: wcscdesk@live5news.com
Web site: http://www.live5news.com
Profile: WCSC-TV is the CBS affiliate for the Charleston, SC market. The station is owned by Raycom Media Inc. WCSC-TV broadcasts locally on channel 5.
TELEVISION STATION

WCSH-TV 31794
Owner: TEGNA Inc.
Editorial: 1 Congress Sq, Portland, Maine 04101-3801 **Tel:** 1 207 828-6666.
Email: newscenter@wcsh6.com
Web site: http://www.wcsh6.com
Profile: WCSH-TV is the NBC affiliate for the Portland, Maine market. The station is owned by TEGNA Inc. WCSH-TV broadcasts locally on channel 6.
TELEVISION STATION

WCTE-TV 3179
Owner: Upper Cumberland Broadcasting Council
Editorial: 1151 Stadium Drive, Suite 104, Cookeville, Tennessee 38501 **Tel:** 1 931 528-2222.
Web site: http://www.wcte.org
Profile: WCTE-TV is the PBS affiliate for the Cookeville, TN market. The station is owned by Upper Cumberland Broadcasting Council. WCTE-TV broadcasts locally on channel 22.
TELEVISION STATION

WCTI-TV 3179
Owner: Bonten Media Group, LLC
Editorial: 225 Glenburnie Dr, New Bern, North Carolina 28560-2815 **Tel:** 1 252 638-1212.
Email: news@wcti12.com
Web site: http://www.wcti12.com
Profile: WCTI-TV is the ABC affiliate for the Greenville, NC market. The station is owned by Bonten Media Group, LLC. WCTI-TV broadcasts locally on channel 12.
TELEVISION STATION

WCTV-TV 3179
Owner: Gray Television, Inc.
Editorial: 1801 Halstead Blvd, Tallahassee, Florida 32309-3431 **Tel:** 1 850 893-6666.
Email: news@wctv.tv
Web site: http://www.wctv.tv
Profile: WCTV-TV is the CBS affiliate for the Tallahassee, FL-Thomasville, GA market. The station is owned by Gray Television, Inc. WCTV-TV broadcast locally on channel 6.
TELEVISION STATION

WCTX2-TV 61279
Owner: Nexstar Media Group, Inc.
Editorial: 8 Elm St, New Haven, Connecticut 06510-2006 **Tel:** 1 203 782-5900.
Email: feedback@wctx.com
Web site: http://www.wtnh.com
Profile: WCTX2-TV is a multicast of WCTX-TV. A multicast channel is a separate channel that shares the bandwith of the main station but can air unique programming. WCTX2-TV airs local weather programming from SkyMax 8 24 Hour Weather in the Hartford-New Haven, CT market. The station is owned by Nexstar Media Group, Inc. WCTX2-TV broadcasts locally on channel 59.2.
TELEVISION STATION

WCTX-TV 3246
Owner: Nexstar Media Group, Inc.
Editorial: 8 Elm St, New Haven, Connecticut 06510-2006 **Tel:** 1 203 782-5900.
Email: wtnh@wtnh.com
Web site: http://www.wtnh.com
Profile: WCTX-TV is the MyNetworkTV network affiliate in the Hartford-New Haven, CT market. The station is owned by Nexstar Media Group, Inc. WCTX-TV broadcasts locally on channel 59.
TELEVISION STATION

WCUU-TV 32475
Owner: Weigel Broadcasting Co.
Editorial: 26 N Halsted St, Chicago, Illinois 60661
Tel: 1 312 705-2600.
Profile: WCUU-TV is an independent station for the Chicago market. The station is owned by Weigel Broadcasting Co. WCUU-TV broadcasts locally on channel 48.
TELEVISION STATION

WCVB2-TV 82695
Owner: Hearst Television Inc.
Editorial: 5 Tv Pl, Needham Heights, Massachusetts 02494-2302 **Tel:** 1 781 433-4490.
Web site: http://metvnetwork.com
Profile: WCVB2-TV is a multicast channel of WCVB-TV. A multicast channel is a separate channel that shares the bandwith of the main station but can air unique programming. WCVB2-TV is the MeTV Network for the Boston market. The station is owned by Hearst Television Inc. WCVB2-TV broadcasts locally on channel 5.2. The station specializes in syndicated reruns of classic TV programs of the 1950s through the 1980s.
TELEVISION STATION

WCVB-TV 3179
Owner: Hearst Television Inc.
Editorial: 5 Tv Pl, Needham Heights, Massachusetts 02494-2302 **Tel:** 1 781 449-0400.
Email: wcvbnews@hearst.com
Web site: http://www.wcvb.com
Profile: WCVB-TV is the ABC affiliate for the Boston market. The station is owned by Hearst Television Inc. WCVB broadcasts locally on channel 5.
TELEVISION STATION

WCVE-TV 3266
Owner: Public Television
Editorial: 23 Sesame St, Richmond, Virginia 23235-3713 **Tel:** 1 804 320-1301.
Web site: http://ideastations.org
Profile: WCVE-TV is the PBS affiliate for the Richmond, VA market. The station is owned by Commonwealth Public Broadcasting. WCVE-TV broadcasts locally on channel 23.
TELEVISION STATION

WCWF-TV 32093
Owner: Nexstar Media Group, Inc.
Editorial: 787 Lombardi Ave, Green Bay, Wisconsin 54304-3925 **Tel:** 1 920 787-8781.
Email: fox11sales@wluk.com
Web site: http://www.cw14online.com
Profile: WCWF-TV is the CW network affiliate for the Green Bay-Appleton, WI market. The station is owned by Nexstar Media Group, Inc. WCWF-TV broadcasts locally on channel 14.
TELEVISION STATION

WCWG-TV 31823
Owner: Lockwood Broadcasting, Inc.
Editorial: 2A Pai Park, Greensboro, North Carolina 27409-9428 **Tel:** 1 336 307-4900.
Email: info@wcwg.com
Web site: http://triad20.com
Profile: WCWG-TV is the CW network affiliate for the Greensboro-Winston Salem, NC market. The station is owned by Lockwood Broadcasting, Inc. WCWG-TV broadcasts locally on channel 20.
TELEVISION STATION

WCWJ-TV 31924
Owner: Nextar Broadcasting
Editorial: 9117 Hogan Rd, Jacksonville, Florida 32216-4647 **Tel:** 1 904 641-1700.
Web site: http://www.yourjax.com
Profile: WCWJ-TV is the CW affiliate for the Jacksonville, FL market. The station is owned by Nextar Broadcasting. WCWJ-TV broadcasts locally on channel 17.
TELEVISION STATION

WCWN-TV 32571
Owner: Sinclair Broadcast Group, Inc.
Editorial: 1400 Balltown Rd, Schenectady, New York 12309-4301 **Tel:** 1 518 381-4900.
Web site: http://www.cwalbany.com
Profile: WCWN-TV is the CW affiliate for the Schenectady, Albany and Troy, NY markets. The station is owned by Sinclair Broadcast Group, Inc. WCWN-TV broadcasts locally on channel 45.
TELEVISION STATION

WCWW-TV 128192
Owner: Weigel Broadcasting Co.
Editorial: 53550 Generations Dr, South Bend, Indiana 46635-1570 **Tel:** 1 574 344-5500.
Web site: http://www.thecw25.com
Profile: WCWW-TV is the CW affiliate for the South Bend, IN, market. It is owned by Weigel Broadcasting Co. WCWW-TV broadcasts locally on channel 25.
TELEVISION STATION

WCYB-TV 31799
Owner: Bonten Media Group, LLC
Editorial: 101 Lee St, Bristol, Virginia 24201-4363 **Tel:** 1 276 645-1555.
Email: news@wcyb.com
Web site: http://www.wcyb.com
Profile: WCYB-TV is the NBC affiliate for the Bristol, TN market. The station is owned by Bonten Media Group, LLC. WCYB-TV broadcasts locally on channel 5.
TELEVISION STATION

WDAF-TV 31800
Owner: Tribune Broadcasting Co.
Editorial: 3030 Summit St, Kansas City, Missouri 64108-3312 **Tel:** 1 816 753-4567.
Email: news@wdaftv4.com
Web site: http://www.fox4kc.com
Profile: WDAF-TV is the FOX affiliate for the Kansas City, MO market. The station is owned byTribune Broadcasting Co. WDAF-TV broadcasts locally on channel 4.
TELEVISION STATION

WDAM-TV 31801
Owner: Raycom Media Inc.
Editorial: 2362 Highway 11 Moselle, Moselle, Mississippi 39459-8925 **Tel:** 1 601 544-4730.
Email: info@wdam.com
Web site: http://www.wdam.com
Profile: WDAM-TV is the NBC affiliate for the Hattiesburg, MS market. The station is owned by Raycom Media Inc. WDAM-TV broadcasts locally on channel 7.
TELEVISION STATION

WDAY-TV 32666
Owner: Forum Communications Co.
Editorial: 301 8th St S, Fargo, North Dakota 58103-1826 **Tel:** 1 701 237-6500.
Email: news@wday.com
Web site: http://www.wday.com
Profile: WDAY-TV is the ABC affiliate for the Fargo, ND market. The station is owned by Forum Communications Co. WDAY-TV broadcasts locally on channel 6.
TELEVISION STATION

WDAZ-TV 32796
Owner: Forum Communications Co.
Editorial: 2220 S Washington St, Grand Forks, North Dakota 58201-6346 **Tel:** 1 701 775-2511.
Email: news@wdaz.com
Web site: http://www.wdaz.com
Profile: WDAZ-TV is the ABC affiliate for the Fargo, ND market. The station is owned by Forum Communications Company. WDAZ-TV broadcasts locally on channel 8.
TELEVISION STATION

WDBD-TV 31802
Owner: American Spirit Media, LLC
Editorial: 715 S Jefferson St, Jackson, Mississippi 39201-5622 **Tel:** 1 601 948-3333.
Web site: http://www.msnewsnow.com
Profile: WDBD-TV is the FOX affiliate for the Jackson, MS market. The station is owned by American Spirit Media, LLC and operated by Raycom Media. WDBD-TV broadcasts locally on channel 40.
TELEVISION STATION

WDBJ2-TV 524562
Owner: Schurz Communications Inc.
Editorial: 2807 Hershberger Rd NW, Roanoke, Virginia 24017-1941 **Tel:** 1 540 344-7000.
Web site: http://www.wdbj7.com
Profile: WDBJ2-TV is a multicast channel of WDBJ-TV. A multicast channel is a separate channel that shares the bandwidth of the main station but can air unique programming. WDBJ2-TV is the local MyNetworkTV affiliate on Channel 7.2 for the Roanoke-Lynchburg, VA market. WDBJ2-TV is owned by Schurz Communications Inc.
TELEVISION STATION

WDBJ-TV 31803
Owner: Gray TV
Editorial: 2807 Hershberger Rd NW, Roanoke, Virginia 24017-1941 **Tel:** 1 540 344-7000.
Email: news@wdbj7.com
Web site: http://www.wdbj7.com
Profile: WDBJ-TV is the CBS network affiliate for the Roanoke-Lynchburg, VA markets. The station is owned by Schurz Communications Inc. WDBJ-TV broadcasts locally on channel 7.
TELEVISION STATION

WDCA-TV 31804
Owner: Fox Broadcasting Company
Editorial: 5151 Wisconsin Ave NW, Washington, District Of Columbia 20016-4124 **Tel:** 1 202 244-5151.
Email: wttg.desk@foxtv.com
Web site: http://www.fox5dc.com/my20dc
Profile: WDCA-TV is the MyNetworkTV affiliate for the Washington, D.C. market. The station is owned by Fox Broadcasting Company. WDCA-TV broadcasts locally on channel 20.
TELEVISION STATION

WDCQ-TV 32714
Owner: Delta College
Editorial: 1961 Delta Rd, University Center, Michigan 48710-1001 **Tel:** 1 989 686-9362.
Email: wdcq@delta.edu
Web site: http://www.deltabroadcasting.org
Profile: WDCQ-TV is a PBS affiliate for the Saginaw, Bay City and Midland, MI markets. The station is owned by Delta College. WDCQ-TV broadcasts locally on channel 19.
TELEVISION STATION

WDCW2-TV 610693
Owner: Tribune Broadcasting Co.
Editorial: 2121 Wisconsin Ave NW Ste 350, Washington, District Of Columbia 20007-2270 **Tel:** 1 202 965-5050.
Web site: http://www.antennatv.tv
Profile: WDCW2-TV is a multicast of WDCW-TV. A multicast channel is a separate channel that shares the bandwith of the main station but can air unique programming. WDCW2-TV airs programming from Antenna TV in the Washington, D.C. market. The station is owned by Tribune Broadcasting Co. WDCW2-TV broadcasts locally on channel 50.2.
TELEVISION STATION

WDCW-TV 31848
Owner: Tribune Broadcasting Co.
Editorial: 2121 Wisconsin Ave NW Ste 350, Washington, District Of Columbia 20007-2270 **Tel:** 1 202 965-5050.
Web site: http://www.dcq50.com
Profile: WDCW-TV is the CW affiliate for the Washington, D.C. market. The station is owned by Tribune Broadcasting Co. WDCW-TV broadcasts locally on channel 50.
TELEVISION STATION

WDEF-TV 31806
Owner: Morris Multimedia, Inc.
Editorial: 3300 Broad St, Chattanooga, Tennessee 37408-3061 **Tel:** 1 423 785-1227.
Email: news@wdef.com
Web site: http://www.wdef.com
Profile: WDEF-TV is the CBS affiliate for the Chattanooga, TN market. The station is owned by Morris Multimedia, Inc. WDEF-TV broadcasts locally on channel 12.
TELEVISION STATION

WDFX-TV 32384
Owner: Raycom Media Inc.
Editorial: 2221 Ross Clark Cir, Dothan, Alabama 36301-5059 **Tel:** 1 334 794-3434.
Web site: http://www.wdfxfox34.com
Profile: WDFX-TV is the FOX affiliate for the Dothan, AL, market. The station is owned by Raycom Media Inc. WDFX-TV broadcasts locally on channel 34.
TELEVISION STATION

WDGA-TV 476761
Owner: North Georgia Television
Editorial: 101 S Spencer St, Dalton, Georgia 30721-3122 **Tel:** 1 706 278-9713.
Email: info@wdnntv.com
Web site: http://www.wdgatv.com
Profile: WDGA-TV is the Heartland TV affiliate for the Chattanooga, TN market. The station is owned by North Georgia Television. WDGA-TV broadcasts locally on channel 43.
TELEVISION STATION

WDHN-TV 31807
Owner: Nexstar Broadcasting Group
Editorial: 5274 E State Highway 52, Webb, Alabama 36376-5512 **Tel:** 1 334 793-1818.
Email: screws@wdhn.com
Web site: http://dothanfirst.com
Profile: WDHN-TV is the ABC affiliate for the Dothan, AL market. The station is owned by Nexstar Broadcasting Group. WDHN-TV broadcasts locally on channel 18.
TELEVISION STATION

WDIG-TV 707473
Owner: WDIG, LLC
Editorial: 101 Lona St, Dublin, Georgia 31021-3372 **Tel:** 1 478 275-4444.
Email: tv35@tv35.tv
Web site: http://www.tv35.tv
Profile: WDIG-TV is an independent, low-powered station for the Dublin, GA area. The station is owned by WDIG, LLC. WDIG-TV broadcasts locally at channel 35.
TELEVISION STATION

WDIO2-TV 781322
Owner: Hubbard Broadcasting Inc.
Editorial: 10 Observation Rd, Duluth, Minnesota 55811-3506 **Tel:** 1 218 727-6864.
Email: news@wdio.com
Web site: http://www.wdio.com
Profile: WDIO2-TV is a multicast channel of WDIO-TV. A multicast channel is a separate channel that Me-TV Network for the Duluth, MN market. The station is owned by Hubbard Broadcasting Inc. WDIO2-TV broadcasts locally on channel 10.2.
TELEVISION STATION

WDIO-TV 32667
Owner: Hubbard Broadcasting Inc.
Editorial: 10 Observation Rd, Duluth, Minnesota 55811 **Tel:** 1 218 727-6864.
Email: news@wdio.com
Web site: http://www.wdio.com
Profile: WDIO-TV is the ABC network affiliate for the Duluth, MN-Superior, WI market. The station is owned by Hubbard Broadcasting Inc. WDIO-TV broadcasts locally on channel 10.
TELEVISION STATION

WDIV2-TV 612594
Owner: Graham Media Group
Editorial: 550 W Lafayette Blvd, Detroit, Michigan 48226-3123 **Tel:** 1 313 222-0444.
Email: news@wdiv.com
Web site: http://www.clickondetroit.com
Profile: WDIV2-TV is a multicast of WDIV-TV. A multicast channel is a separate channel that shares the bandwith of the main station but can air unique programming. WDIV2-TV airs programming from This TV in the Detroit market. The station is owned by Graham Media Group. WDIV2-TV broadcasts locally on channel 4.2.
TELEVISION STATION

WDIV-TV 31808
Owner: Graham Media Group
Editorial: 550 W Lafayette Blvd, Detroit, Michigan 48226-3123 **Tel:** 1 313 222-0444.
Email: news@wdiv.com
Web site: http://www.clickondetroit.com
Profile: WDIV-TV is the NBC affiliate for the Detroit market. The station is owned byGraham Media Group. WDIV-TV broadcasts locally on channel 4.
TELEVISION STATION

WDJT2-TV 614864
Owner: Weigel Broadcasting Co.
Editorial: 809 S 60th St, Milwaukee, Wisconsin 53214-3363 **Tel:** 1 414 777-5800.
Email: newsdesk@cbs58.com
Profile: WDJT2-TV is a multicast of WDJT-TV. A multicast channel is a separate channel that shares the bandwith of the main station but can air unique programming. WDJT2-TV airs programming from WMLW-TV in the Milwaukee market. The station is owned by Weigel Broadcasting Co. WDJT2-TV broadcasts locally on channel 58.2.
TELEVISION STATION

WDJT3-TV 614870
Owner: Weigel Broadcasting Co.
Editorial: 809 S 60th St, Milwaukee, Wisconsin 53214-3363 **Tel:** 1 414 777-5800.
Email: newsdesk@cbs58.com
Profile: WDJT3-TV is a multicast of WDJT-TV. A multicast channel is a separate channel that shares the bandwith of the main station but can air unique programming. WDJT3-TV airs programming from Heroes & Icons in the Milwaukee market. The station is owned by Weigel Broadcasting Co. WDJT3-TV broadcasts locally on channel 58.3.
TELEVISION STATION

WDJT4-TV 614874
Owner: Weigel Broadcasting Co.
Editorial: 809 S 60th St, Milwaukee, Wisconsin 53214-3363 **Tel:** 1 414 777-5800.
Email: newsdesk@cbs58.com
Profile: WDJT4-TV is a multicast of WDJT-TV. A multicast channel is a separate channel that shares the bandwith of the main station but can air unique programming. WDJT4-TV airs programming from the Shorewest TV in the Milwaukee market. The station is owned by Weigel Broadcasting Co. WDJT4-TV broadcasts locally on channel 58.4.
TELEVISION STATION

WDJT-TV 32332
Owner: Weigel Broadcasting Co.
Editorial: 809 S 60th St Fl 1, Milwaukee, Wisconsin 53214-3363 **Tel:** 1 414 777-5800.
Email: newsdesk@cbs58.com
Web site: http://www.cbs58.com
Profile: WDJT-TV is the CBS affiliate for the Milwaukee market. The station is owned by Weigel Broadcasting Co. The station broadcasts locally on channel 58.
TELEVISION STATION

WDKA-TV 32537
Owner: WDKA Aquisitions Corp.
Editorial: 806 Enterprise St, Cape Girardeau, Missouri 63703 **Tel:** 1 573 334-1223.
Web site: http://www.mywdka.com
Profile: WDKA-TV is the MyNetworkTV network affiliate for the Paducah, KY; Cape Girardeau, MO and Harrisburg, IL market. The station is owned by WDKA Aquisitions Corp. WDKA-TV broadcasts locally on channel 49.
TELEVISION STATION

WDKY-TV 31809
Owner: Sinclair Broadcast Group, Inc.
Editorial: 836 Euclid Ave Ste 201, Lexington, Kentucky 40502-1972 **Tel:** 1 859 269-5656.
Email: news@foxlexington.com
Web site: http://www.foxlexington.com
Profile: WDKY-TV is the FOX affiliate for the Lexington, KY, market. It is owned by Sinclair Broadcast Group, Inc. WDKY-TV broadcasts locally on channel 56. WDKY-TV's newscast is produced by their sister station WKYT-TV.
TELEVISION STATION

WDLI-TV 31810
Owner: Trinity Broadcasting Network
Editorial: 1764 Wadsworth Rd, Akron, Ohio 44320-3142 **Tel:** 1 330 753-5542.
Email: wdli@tbn.org
Profile: WDLI-TV is the local TBN affiliate for Canton, Ohio. Broadcast locally on Channel 17, the station airs various TBN programs.
TELEVISION STATION

WDNI-TV 32517
Owner: Urban One, Inc.
Editorial: 21 E Saint Joseph St, Indianapolis, Indiana 46204-1025 **Tel:** 1 317 266-9600.
Web site: http://www.imc.tv
Profile: WDNI-TV is a Telemundo station for the Indianapolis market. The station is owned by Urban One, Inc. WDNI-TV broadcasts locally on channel 65.
TELEVISION STATION

WDNN-TV 506164
Owner: North Georgia Television
Editorial: 101 S Spencer St, Dalton, Georgia 30721-3122 **Tel:** 1 706 278-9713.
Email: info@wdnntv.com
Web site: http://www.wdnntv.com
TELEVISION STATION

WDPX-TV 491533
Owner: ION Media Networks
Editorial: 1120 Soldiers Field Rd, Boston, Massachusetts 2134 **Tel:** 1 617 787-6868.
Profile: WDPX-TV is the ION Media Networks affiliate for the Boston market. The station is owned by ION Media Networks. WDPX-TV broadcasts locally on channel 68.
TELEVISION STATION

WDRB-TV 32742
Owner: Block Communications Inc.
Editorial: 624 W Muhammad Ali Blvd, Louisville, Kentucky 40203-1915 **Tel:** 1 502 585-0811.
Email: news@wdrb.com
Web site: http://www.wdrb.com
Profile: WDRB-TV is the FOX affiliate for the Louisville, KY market. The station is owned by Block Communications Inc. WDRB-TV broadcasts locally on channel 41.
TELEVISION STATION

WDSC2-TV 612891
Owner: Daytona State College
Editorial: 1200 W International Speedway Blvd, Daytona Beach, Florida 32114-2817 **Tel:** 1 386 506-4415.
Profile: WDSC2-TV is independent affiliate for the Orlando-Daytona Beach, FL market. The station is owned by Daytona State College. WDSC2-TV broadcasts locally on channel 15.2. The station broadcasts various news, entertainment and educational programming. WDSC2-TV is a multicast channel of WDSC-TV. A multicast channel is a separate channel that shares the bandwidth of the main station but can air unique programming.
TELEVISION STATION

WDSC3-TV 612896
Owner: Daytona State College
Editorial: 1200 W International Speedway Blvd, Daytona Beach, Florida 32114-2817 **Tel:** 1 386 506-4415.
Profile: WDSC3-TV is independent affiliate for the Orlando-Daytona Beach, FL market. The station is owned by Daytona State College. WDSC3-TV broadcasts locally on channel 15.3. The station broadcasts various news, entertainment and ethnic programming. WDSC3-TV is a multicast channel of

WDSC-TV. A multicast channel is a separate channel that shares the bandwidth of the main station but can air unique programming.
TELEVISION STATION

WDSC-TV 32370
Owner: Daytona State College
Editorial: 1200 W International Speedway Blvd, Daytona Beach, Florida 32114-2817 **Tel:** 1 386 506-4415.
Email: wdsc@daytonastate.edu
Web site: http://www.wdsctv.org
Profile: WDSC-TV is the PBS network affiliate for the Orlando-Daytona Beach, FL market. The station is owned by Daytona State College. WDSC-TV broadcasts locally on channel 15.
TELEVISION STATION

WDSI-TV 31812
Owner: Sinclair Broadcast Group, Inc.
Editorial: 1101 E Main St, Chattanooga, Tennessee 37408-1611 **Tel:** 1 423 265-0061.
Web site: http://www.myfoxchattanooga.com/category/307012/wdsi
Profile: WDSI-TV is the this TV affiliate and Comet TV affiliate for the Chattanooga, TN, market. The station is owned by New Age Media, LLC. WDSI-TV broadcasts locally on channel 61.
TELEVISION STATION

WDSU2-TV 800578
Owner: Hearst Television
Editorial: 846 Howard Ave, New Orleans, Louisiana 70113-1134 **Tel:** 1 504 679-0600.
Email: newsdesk@wdsu.com
Web site: http://www.wdsu.com
Profile: WDSU2-TV is a multicast channel of WDUS-TV. A multicast channel is a separate channel that shares the bandwith of the main station but can air unique programming. WDSU2-TV is the Me-TV Network for the New Orleans, LA market. The station is owned by Hearst Television. WDSU2-TV broadcasts locally on channel 6.2.
TELEVISION STATION

WDSU-TV 31813
Owner: Hearst Television Inc.
Editorial: 846 Howard Ave, New Orleans, Louisiana 70113-1134 **Tel:** 1 504 679-0600.
Email: newsdesk@wdsu.com
Web site: http://www.wdsu.com
Profile: WDSU-TV is the NBC affiliate for the New Orleans market. The station is owned by Hearst Television Inc. WDSU-TV broadcasts locally on channel 6.
TELEVISION STATION

WDTN-TV 31814
Owner: Nexstar Media Group, Inc.
Editorial: 4595 S Dixie Dr, Moraine, Ohio 45439-2111 **Tel:** 1 937 293-2101.
Email: newstips@wdtn.com
Web site: http://www.wdtn.com
Profile: WDTN-TV is the NBC affiliate the Dayton, OH market. The station is owned by Nexstar Media Group, Inc. WDTN-TV broadcasts locally on channel 2.
TELEVISION STATION

WDTV-TV 31815
Owner: Gray Television, Inc.
Editorial: 5 Television Dr, Bridgeport, West Virginia 26330-2621 **Tel:** 1 304 848-5000.
Email: news@wdtv.com
Web site: http://www.wdtv.com
Profile: WDTV-TV is the CBS affiliate for the Clarksburg-Weston, WV market. The station is owned by Gray Television, Inc. WDTV-TV broadcasts locally on channel 5.
TELEVISION STATION

WDVM-TV 31870
Owner: Nexstar Broadcasting Group
Editorial: 13 E Washington St, Hagerstown, Maryland 21740-5605 **Tel:** 1 301 797-4400.
Email: news@localdvm.com
Web site: http://www.localdvm.com
Profile: WDVM-TV and localDVM.com is a source for local news, weather and sports in Maryland, South Central Pennsylvania, Northern Virginia and the Northern Shenandoah Valley, and the Eastern Panhandle of West Virginia. WDVM is located in Hagerstown, Maryland with additional offices and News Bureaus in Chantilly, Virginia, Germantown, Maryland and Winchester, Virginia. The station is owned by Nexstar Broadcasting Group. WDVM-TV broadcasts locally on channel 25. Send all Press Releases to the newsroom at news@localdvm.com.
TELEVISION STATION

WEAC-TV 153808
Owner: Alabama Heritage Communications
Editorial: 700 Pelham Rd N, Jacksonville, Alabama 36265-1602 **Tel:** 1 256 831-4624.
Web site: http://www.tv24.tv
Profile: WEAC-TV is an independent station for the Jacksonville, AL market. The station is owned by Alabama Heritage Communications. WEAC-TV broadcasts locally on channel 24.
TELEVISION STATION

WEAR-TV 31817
Owner: Sinclair Broadcast Group, Inc.
Editorial: 4990 Mobile Hwy, Pensacola, Florida 32506-3230 **Tel:** 1 850 456-3333.
Email: news@weartv.com
Web site: http://www.weartv.com
Profile: WEAR-TV is the ABC affiliate for the Mobile, AL-Pensacola, FL market. It is owned by Sinclair Broadcast Group, Inc. WEAR-TV broadcasts locally on channel 3.
TELEVISION STATION

WEAU-TV 31818
Owner: Gray Television, Inc.
Editorial: 1907 S Hastings Way, Eau Claire, Wisconsin 54701 **Tel:** 1 715 835-1313.
Email: news@weau.com
Web site: http://www.weau.com
Profile: WEAU-TV is the NBC affiliate for the Eau Claire, WI market. The station is owned by Gray Television, Inc. WEAU-TV broadcasts locally on channel 13.
TELEVISION STATION

WEBR-TV 444286
Owner: OTA Broadcasting, LLC
Editorial: 3201 Jermantown Rd Ste 380, Fairfax, Virginia 22030-2881 **Tel:** 1 703 364-5300.
Email: info@otabroadcasting.com
Web site: http://www.otabroadcasting.com
TELEVISION STATION

WECP-TV 833229
Editorial: 8195 Front Beach Rd, Panama City, Florida 32407-4820 **Tel:** 1 850 234-7777.
Profile: WECP-TV is the CBS affiliate for the Panama City, FL market. The station is owned by Gray Television, Inc. WECP-TV broadcasts locally on Channel 18.
TELEVISION STATION

WECT-TV 31819
Owner: Raycom Media Inc.
Editorial: 322 Shipyard Blvd, Wilmington, North Carolina 28412-1835 **Tel:** 1 910 791-8070.
Email: newsroom@wect.com
Web site: http://www.wect.com
Profile: WECT-TV is the NBC network affiliate for the Wilmington, NC market. The station is owned by Raycom Media Inc. WECT-TV broadcasts locally on channel 6.
TELEVISION STATION

WEDH-TV 32668
Owner: Connecticut Public Broadcasting Inc.
Editorial: 1049 Asylum Ave, Hartford, Connecticut 06105-2432 **Tel:** 1 860 278-5310.
Email: audiencecare@cptv.org
Web site: http://www.cpbn.org
Profile: WEDH-TV is a PBS affiliate for the Hartford, CT market. The station is owned by Connecticut Public Broadcasting Inc. WEDH-TV broadcasts locally on channel 24.
TELEVISION STATION

WEDU2-TV 612016
Owner: Florida West Coast Public Broadcasting Inc.
Editorial: 1300 N Boulevard, Tampa, Florida 33607-5645 **Tel:** 1 813 254-9338.
Web site: http://www.wedu.org
Profile: WEDU2-TV is a multicast of WEDU-TV. A multicast channel is a separate channel that shares the bandwith of the main station but can air unique programming. WEDU2-TV airs programming from V-me in the Tampa, FL market. The station is owned by Florida West Coast Public Broadcasting Inc. WEDU2-TV broadcasts locally on channel 3.2.
TELEVISION STATION

WEDU3-TV 612019
Owner: Florida West Coast Public Broadcasting Inc.
Editorial: 1300 N Boulevard, Tampa, Florida 33607-5645 **Tel:** 1 813 254-9338.
Web site: http://www.wedu.org
Profile: WEDU3-TV is a multicast of WEDU-TV. A multicast channel is a separate channel that shares the bandwith of the main station but can air unique programming. WEDU3-TV airs programming from the Florida Knowledge Network and The Florida Channel in the Tampa, FL market. The station is owned by Florida West Coast Public Broadcasting Inc. WEDU3-TV broadcasts locally on channel 3.3.
TELEVISION STATION

WEDU4-TV 612022
Owner: Florida West Coast Public Broadcasting Inc.
Editorial: 1300 N Boulevard, Tampa, Florida 33607-5645 **Tel:** 1 813 254-9338.
Web site: http://www.wedu.org
Profile: WEDU4-TV is a multicast of WEDU-TV. A multicast channel is a separate channel that shares the bandwith of the main station but can air unique programming. WEDU4-TV airs programming from WEDU World in the Tampa, FL market. The station is owned by Florida West Coast Public Broadcasting Inc. WEDU4-TV broadcasts locally on channel 3.4.
TELEVISION STATION

WEDU-TV 31820
Owner: Florida West Coast Public Broadcasting Inc.
Editorial: 1300 N Boulevard, Tampa, Florida 33607-5645 **Tel:** 1 813 254-9338.
Web site: http://www.wedu.org
Profile: WEDU-TV is the PBS affiliate for the Tampa-St. Petersburg, FL market. The station is owned by Florida West Coast Public Broadcasting Inc. WEDU-TV broadcasts locally on channel 3.
TELEVISION STATION

WEEK-TV 31821
Owner: Quincy Newspapers
Editorial: 2907 Springfield Rd, East Peoria, Illinois 61611-4878 **Tel:** 1 309 698-2525.
Email: news25@week.com
Web site: http://www.week.com
Profile: WEEK-TV is the NBC, ABC, and CW affiliate for the Peoria-Bloomington, IL market. The station is owned by Quincy Newspapers. WEEK-TV broadcasts locally on channel 25.
TELEVISION STATION

WEHT-TV 31822
Owner: Nexstar Broadcasting Group
Editorial: 800 Marywood Dr, Henderson, Kentucky 42420-2431 **Tel:** 1 812 424-7777.
Email: eyewitnessnews@tristatehomepage.com
Web site: http://tristatehomepage.com
Profile: WEHT-TV is the ABC affiliate for the Evansville, IN market. The station is owned by Nexstar Broadcasting Group. WEHT-TV broadcasts locally on channel 25.
TELEVISION STATION

WELF-TV 32495
Owner: Trinity Broadcasting Network
Editorial: 384 S Campus Rd, Lookout Mountain, Georgia 30750-4508 **Tel:** 1 706 820-1663.
Email: welf@tbn.org
Profile: WELF-TV is the Trinity Broadcasting affiliate for the Chattanooga, TN market. The station is owned by Trinity Broadcasting Network. WELF-TV broadcasts locally on channel 23.
TELEVISION STATION

WEMT-TV 31828
Owner: Bonten Media Group, LLC
Editorial: 101 Lee St, Bristol, Virginia 24201-4363 **Tel:** 1 276 821-9296.
Email: foxtrivc@foxtricities.com
Web site: http://www.wcyb.com/foxtricities
Profile: WEMT-TV is the FOX affiliate for the Johnson City, TN market. The station is owned by Bonten Media Group, LLC. WEMT-TV broadcasts locally on channel 39.
TELEVISION STATION

WENH-TV 32708
Owner: New Hampshire Public Broadcasting
Editorial: 268 Mast Rd, Durham, New Hampshire 03824-4601 **Tel:** 1 603 868-1100.
Email: themailbox@nhptv.org
Web site: http://www.nhptv.org
Profile: WENH-TV is the PBS affiliate for the Boston market. The station is owned by New Hampshire Public Broadcasting. WENH-TV is broadcast locally on channel 11.
TELEVISION STATION

WENY2-TV 867919
Owner: Lilly Broadcasting
Editorial: 474 Old Ithaca Rd, Horseheads, New York 14845-7212 **Tel:** 1 607 739-3636.
Web site: http://www.weny.com
Profile: WENY2-TV is a multicast channel of WENY-TV. A multicast channel is a separate channel that shares the bandwith of the main station but can air unique programming. WENY2-TV is the CBS Network for the Elmira, NY market. The station is owned by Lilly Broadcasting. WENY2-TV broadcasts locally on channel 36.2.
TELEVISION STATION

WENY-TV 31824
Owner: Lilly Broadcasting
Editorial: 474 Old Ithaca Rd, Horseheads, New York 14845-7212 **Tel:** 1 607 739-3636.
Web site: http://www.weny.com
Profile: WENY-TV is the ABC affiliate for the Elmira, NY market. The station is owned by Lilly Broadcasting. WENY-TV broadcasts locally on channel 36.
TELEVISION STATION

WEPX-TV 153393
Owner: ION Media Networks
Editorial: 1301 S Glenburnie Rd, New Bern, North Carolina 28562 **Tel:** 1 252 636-2550.
Profile: WEPX-TV is the MyNetworkTV affiliate for the Greenville, NC market. The station is owned by ION Media Networks. WEPX-TV broadcasts locally on channel 38.
TELEVISION STATION

WESH-TV 31825
Owner: Hearst Television Inc.
Editorial: 1021 N Wymore Rd, Winter Park, Florida 32789-1717 **Tel:** 1 407 645-2222.
Email: wesh2news@gmail.com
Web site: http://www.wesh.com
Profile: WESH-TV is the NBC affiliate for the Orlando-Daytona Beach, FL market. The station is owned by Hearst Television Inc. WESH-TV broadcasts locally on channel 2.
TELEVISION STATION

WETK-TV 32709
Owner: Vermont ETV Inc.
Editorial: 204 Ethan Allen Ave, Colchester, Vermont 05446-3308 **Tel:** 1 802 655-4800.
Email: view@vpt.org
Web site: http://www.vpt.org
Profile: WETK-TV is the PBS affiliate for the Colchester, VT market. The station is owned by Vermont ETV Inc. WETK-TV broadcasts locally on channel 33.
TELEVISION STATION

WETM2-TV 586189
Owner: Newport Television, LLC
Editorial: 101 E Water St, Elmira, New York 14901-3000 **Tel:** 1 607 733-5518.
Web site: http://www.wetmtv.com
Profile: WETM2-TV is a multicast channel of WETM-TV. A multicast channel is a separate channel tha shares bandwidth of the main station but can air unique programming. WETM2-TV is an independent station on channel 18.2 for the Elmira, NY market. WETM2-TV is owned by Newport Television, LLC.
TELEVISION STATION

WETM-TV 3182
Owner: Nexstar Broadcasting Group
Editorial: 101 E Water St, Elmira, New York 14901-3000 **Tel:** 1 607 733-5518.
Email: news@wetmtv.com
Web site: http://www.mytwintiers.com
Profile: WETM-TV is the NBC affiliate for the Elmira, NY, market. The station is owned by Nexstar Broadcasting Group. WETM-TV broadcasts locally or channel 18.
TELEVISION STATION

WEUX2-TV 80080
Owner: Grant Communication
Editorial: 3403 State St Ste 3, Eau Claire, Wisconsin 54701-7155 **Tel:** 1 715 831-2548.
Web site: http://www.fox2548.com
Profile: WEUX2-TV is a multicast channel of WEUX-TV. A multicast channel is a separate channel that shares the bandwith of the main station but can air unique programming. WEUX2-TV is the Me-TV Network for the La Crosse- Eau Claire, WI market. The station is owned by Grant Communications. WEUX2-TV broadcasts locally on channel 48.2.The station launched April 17, 2012.
TELEVISION STATION

WEVV-TV 3183
Owner: Bayou City Broadcasting
Editorial: 477 Carpenter St, Evansville, Indiana 47708-1027 **Tel:** 1 812 464-4444.
Email: news@wevv.com
Web site: http://www.wevv.com
Profile: WEVV-TV is the CBS affiliate for the Evansville, IN market. The station is owned by Bayou City Broadcasting. WEVV-TV broadcasts locally on channel 44.
TELEVISION STATION

WEWS-TV 3183
Owner: E.W. Scripps Co.
Editorial: 3001 Euclid Ave, Cleveland, Ohio 44115-2516 **Tel:** 1 216 431-5555.
Email: newsdesk@wews.com
Web site: http://www.newsnet5.com
Profile: WEWS-TV is the ABC network affiliate for the Cleveland, OH market. The station is owned by E.W. Scripps Co. WEWS-TV broadcasts locally on channel 5.
TELEVISION STATION

WEYI3-TV 811831
Owner: Sinclair Broadcast Group, Inc.
Editorial: 3463 W Pierson Rd, Flint, Michigan 48504-6905 **Tel:** 1 989 755-0525.
Email: news@nbc25.net
Web site: http://www.minbcnews.com
Profile: WEYI3-TV is a multicast of WEYI-TV. A multicast channel is a separate channel that shares the bandwith of the main station but can air unique programming. WEYI3-TV airs programming from Bounce TV in the Flint, MI, market. The station is owned by Sinclair Broadcast Group, Inc. WEYI3-TV broadcasts locally on channel 25.3.
TELEVISION STATION

WEYI-TV 31832
Owner: Sinclair Broadcast Group, Inc.
Editorial: 3463 W Pierson Rd, Flint, Michigan 48504-6905 **Tel:** 1 810 687-1000.
Email: news@nbc25.net
Web site: http://nbc25news.com
Profile: WEYI-TV is the NBC affiliate for the Flint, MI, market. It is owned by Sinclair Broadcast Group, Inc.. WEYI-TV broadcasts locally on channel 25.
TELEVISION STATION

WFAA2-TV 607940
Owner: WFAA TV, Inc.
Editorial: 606 Young St, Dallas, Texas 75202-4810 **Tel:** 1 214 748-9631.
Web site: http://www.wfaa.com
Profile: WFAA2-TV is the independent affiliate for the Dallas-Fort Worth market. The station is owned by WFAA TV, Inc. WFAA2-TV broadcasts locally on channel 8.2 and airs news and weather from WFAA-TV. WFAA2-TV is a multicast channel of WFAA-TV. A multicast channel is a separate channel that shares the bandwidth of the main station but can air unique programming.
TELEVISION STATION

WFAA3-TV 607941
Owner: WFAA TV, Inc.
Editorial: 606 Young St, Dallas, Texas 75202-4810 **Tel:** 1 214 748-9631.
Profile: WFAA3-TV is the independent affiliate for the Dallas-Fort Worth market. The station is owned by WFAA TV, Inc. WFAA3-TV broadcasts locally on channel 8.3 and airs 24/7 traffic. WFAA3-TV is a multicast channel of WFAA-TV. A multicast channel is a separate channel that shares the bandwidth of the main station but can air unique programming.
TELEVISION STATION

WFAA-TV 31833
Owner: TEGNA Inc.
Editorial: 606 Young St, Dallas, Texas 75202-4810 **Tel:** 1 214 748-9631.
Email: news8@wfaa.com
Web site: http://www.wfaa.com

Profile: WFAA-TV is the ABC affiliate for the Dallas-Fort Worth market. The station is owned by TEGNA Inc. WFAA-TV broadcasts locally on channel 8.
TELEVISION STATION

WFDC-TV
32477
Owner: Univision Communications Corp.
Editorial: 101 Constitution Ave NW, Washington, District Of Columbia 20001-2133 **Tel:** 1 202 522-8640.
Email: wfdc.noticias@entravision.com
Web site: http://noticias.entravision.com/washington-dc
Profile: WFDC-TV is the Univision affiliate for the Washington, D.C. market. The station is owned by Univision Communications Corp. WFDC-TV broadcasts locally on channel 14.
TELEVISION STATION

WFEM-TV
376641
Owner: Marlar (H. Earl)
Tel: 1 865 938-1185.
Web site: http://www.wfem-tv12.com
Profile: WFEM-TV is an independent station for the Knoxville, TN market. The station is owned by H. Earl Marlar. WFEM-TV broadcasts locally on channel 12.
TELEVISION STATION

WFFF-TV
32556
Owner: Nexstar Broadcasting Group
Editorial: 298 Mountain View Dr, Colchester, Vermont 05446-5955 **Tel:** 1 802 660-9333.
Email: news@fox44.net
Web site: http://www.mychamplainvalley.com
Profile: WFFF-TV is the FOX affiliate for the Burlington, VT market. The station is owned by Nexstar Broadcasting Group. WFFF-TV broadcasts locally on channel 44.
TELEVISION STATION

WFFT-TV
31835
Owner: MidAmerica Holdings, LLC
Editorial: 3707 Hillegas Rd, Fort Wayne, Indiana 46808-1351 **Tel:** 1 260 471-5555.
Email: fox55@wfft.com
Web site: http://www.fortwaynehomepage.net
Profile: WFFT-TV is the FOX affiliate for the Fort Wayne, IN market. The station is owned by MidAmerica Holdings, LLC. WFFT-TV broadcasts locally on channel 55.
TELEVISION STATION

WFGC-TV
32425
Owner: Christian Television Network
Editorial: 1900 S Congress Ave Ste A, Palm Springs, Florida 33406-6689 **Tel:** 1 561 642-3361.
Email: gm@wfgc.com
Web site: http://www.wfgctelevision.com
Profile: WFGC-TV is the Christian Television Network affiliate for Palm Beach, FL market. The station is owned by Christian Television Network. WFGC-TV broadcasts locally on channel 61.
TELEVISION STATION

WFGX-TV
32386
Owner: Sinclair Broadcast Group, Inc.
Editorial: 4990 Mobile Hwy, Pensacola, Florida 32506-3230 **Tel:** 1 850 456-3333.
Email: news@weartv.com
Web site: http://www.wfgxtv.com
Profile: WFGX-TV is a MyNetworkTV affiliate for the Mobile, AL-Pensacola, FL, market. The station is owned by Sinclair Broadcast Group, Inc. WFGX-TV broadcasts locally on channel 35.
TELEVISION STATION

WFIE2-TV
616069
Owner: Raycom Media Inc.
Editorial: 1115 Mount Auburn Rd, Evansville, Indiana 47720-5427 **Tel:** 1 812 426-1414.
Email: wfie@14news.com
Web site: http://www.14news.com
Profile: WFIE2-TV is a multicast of WFIE-TV. A multicast channel is a separate channel that shares the bandwith of the main station but can air unique programming. WFIE2-TV airs 24/7 Weather Now to the Evansville, IN market. The station is owned by Raycom Media Inc. WFIE2-TV broadcasts locally on channel 14.2.
TELEVISION STATION

WFIE3-TV
616073
Owner: Raycom Media Inc.
Editorial: 1115 Mount Auburn Rd, Evansville, Indiana 47720-5427 **Tel:** 1 812 426-1414.
Email: wfie@14news.com
Web site: http://www.14news.com
Profile: WFIE3-TV is a multicast of WFIE-TV. A multicast channel is a separate channel that shares the bandwith of the main station but can air unique programming. WFIE3-TV airs programming from This TV Network to the Evansville, IN market. The station is owned by Raycom Media Inc. WFIE3-TV broadcasts locally on channel 14.3.
TELEVISION STATION

WFIE-TV
31837
Owner: Raycom Media Inc.
Editorial: 1115 Mount Auburn Rd, Evansville, Indiana 47720-5427 **Tel:** 1 812 426-1414.
Email: newsdesk@14news.com
Web site: http://www.14news.com
Profile: WFIE-TV is the NBC news affiliate for the Evansville, IN market. The station is owned by Raycom Media Inc. WFIE-TV broadcasts locally on channel 14.
TELEVISION STATION

WFLA2-TV
612346
Owner: Nexstar Media Group, Inc.
Editorial: 200 S Parker St, Tampa, Florida 33606-2308 **Tel:** 1 813 228-8888.
Email: news@wfla.com
Web site: http://www.wfla.com
Profile: WFLA2-TV is a multicast of WFLA-TV. A multicast channel is a separate channel that shares the bandwith of the main station but can air unique programming. WFLA2-TV airs programming from Retro Television Network in the Tampa, FL market. The station is owned by Nexstar Media Group, Inc. WFLA2-TV broadcasts locally on channel 8.2.
TELEVISION STATION

WFLA-TV
32213
Owner: Nexstar Media Group, Inc.
Editorial: 200 S Parker St, Tampa, Florida 33606-2308 **Tel:** 1 813 228-8888.
Email: news@wfla.com
Web site: http://www.wfla.com
Profile: WFLA-TV is the NBC affiliate for the Tampa-St. Petersburg market. The station is owned by Nexstar Media Group, Inc.WFLA-TV broadcasts locally on channel 8.
TELEVISION STATION

WFLD-TV
31838
Owner: Fox Broadcasting Company
Editorial: 205 N Michigan Ave, Chicago, Illinois 60601-5927 **Tel:** 1 312 565-5532.
Email: news@foxchicago.com
Web site: http://www.fox32chicago.com
Profile: WFLD-TV is the FOX affiliate for the Chicago market. The station is owned by the Fox Broadcasting Company. WFLD-TV broadcasts locally on channel 32. WFLD airs over forty hours of news every week, along with airing syndicated first run talk/court/reality shows, off-network sitcoms, Fox's primetime network programming and sports.
TELEVISION STATION

WFLI-TV
31839
Owner: Sinclair Broadcast Group, Inc.
Tel: 1 423 265-0061.
Web site: http://chattanoogacw.com
Profile: WFLI-TV is the CW affiliate for the Chattanooga, TN market. The station is owned by Sinclair Broadcast Group, Inc. WFLI-TV broadcasts locally on channel 53.
TELEVISION STATION

WFLX-TV
31840
Owner: Raycom Media Inc.
Editorial: 1100 Banyan Blvd, West Palm Beach, Florida 33401-5000 **Tel:** 1 561 845-2929.
Email: fox29news@wflx.com
Web site: http://www.wflx.com
Profile: WFLX-TV is the Fox affiliate for the West Palm Beach, FL market. The station is owned by Raycom Media Inc. WFLX-TV broadcasts locally on channel 29.
TELEVISION STATION

WFMJ2-TV
760342
Owner: WFMJ Television Inc.
Editorial: 101 W Boardman St, Youngstown, Ohio 44503-1305 **Tel:** 1 303 744-8611.
Web site: http://www.wbcb.tv
Profile: WFMJ2-TV is a multicast of WFMJ-TV. A multicast is a separate channel that shares the bandwidth of the main station but can air unique programming. WFMJ2-TV is the local CW affiliate on channel 21.2 for the Youngstown, OH market. WFMJ2-TV is owned by WFMJ Television Inc. The station is also known as The CW, WBCB.
TELEVISION STATION

WFMJ-TV
31841
Owner: WFMJ Television Inc.
Editorial: 101 W Boardman St, Youngstown, Ohio 44503-1305 **Tel:** 1 330 744-8611.
Email: news@wfmj.com
Web site: http://www.wfmj.com
Profile: WFMJ-TV is the NBC affiliate for the Youngstown, OH market. The station is owned by WFMJ Television Inc. WFMJ-TV broadcasts locally on channel 21.
TELEVISION STATION

WFMY-TV
31842
Owner: TEGNA Inc.
Editorial: 1615 Phillips Ave, Greensboro, North Carolina 27405-5127 **Tel:** 1 336 379-9369.
Email: news@wfmy.com
Web site: http://www.wfmynews2.com
Profile: WFMY-TV is the CBS affiliate for the Greensboro-Winston Salem, NC market. The station is owned by TEGNA Inc. WFMY-TV broadcasts locally on channel 2.
TELEVISION STATION

WFMZ2-TV
607625
Owner: Maranatha Broadcasting Co. Inc.
Editorial: 300 E Rock Rd, Allentown, Pennsylvania 18103-7599 **Tel:** 1 610 797-4530.
Email: news@wfmz.com
Web site: http://www.wfmz.com
Profile: WFMZ2-TV is a multicast channel of WFMZ-TV. A multicast channel is a separate channel that shares the bandwith of the main station but can air unique programming. WFMZ2-TV airs programming from The AccuWeather Channel for the Philadelphia area. It is owned by Maranatha Broadcasting Co. Inc. WFMZ2-TV broadcasts locally on channel 69.2.
TELEVISION STATION

WFMZ3-TV
607628
Owner: Maranatha Broadcasting Co. Inc.
Editorial: 300 E Rock Rd, Allentown, Pennsylvania 18103-7599 **Tel:** 1 610 797-4530.
Email: news@wfmz.com
Web site: http://www.wfmz.com
Profile: WFMZ3-TV is a multicast channel of WFMZ-TV. A multicast channel is a separate channel that shares the bandwith of the main station but can air unique programming. WFMZ3-TV airs programming from The Me-TV Television Network for the Philadelphia area. It is owned by Maranatha Broadcasting Co. Inc. WFMZ3-TV broadcasts locally on channel 69.3.
TELEVISION STATION

WFMZ-TV
31843
Owner: Maranatha Broadcasting Co. Inc.
Editorial: 300 E Rock Rd, Allentown, Pennsylvania 18103-7599 **Tel:** 1 610 797-4530.
Email: news@wfmz.com
Web site: http://www.wfmz.com
Profile: WFMZ-TV is an independent affiliate for the Philadelphia area. The station is owned by Maranatha Broadcasting Co. Inc. WFMZ-TV broadcasts locally on channel 69.
TELEVISION STATION

WFNA-TV
135711
Owner: Nexstar Media Group, Inc.
Editorial: 1501 Satchel Paige Dr, Mobile, Alabama 36606-2532 **Tel:** 1 251 434-1010.
Web site: http://www.thegulfcoastcw.com
Profile: WFNA-TV is the CW affiliate for the greater Mobile, AL and Pensacola, FL market. The station is owned by Nexstar Media Group, Inc. WFNA-TV broadcasts locally on channel 55.
TELEVISION STATION

WFOR-TV
31785
Owner: CBS Television Stations
Editorial: 8900 NW 18th Ter, Doral, Florida 33172-2623 **Tel:** 1 305 591-4444.
Email: wfornews@wfor.cbs.com
Web site: http://miami.cbslocal.com/
Profile: WFOR-TV is the CBS affiliate for the Miami-Fort Lauderdale, FL market. The station is owned by CBS Television Stations. WFOR-TV broadcasts locally on channel 4.
TELEVISION STATION

WFOX2-TV
618793
Owner: Cox Media Group, Inc.
Editorial: 11700 Central Pkwy Unit 2, Jacksonville, Florida 32224-2600 **Tel:** 1 904 642-3030.
Email: news@actionnewsjax.com
Web site: http://www.fox30jax.com
Profile: WFOX2-TV is a multicast of WFOX-TV. A multicast channel is a separate channel that shares the bandwith of the main station but can air unique programming. WFOX2-TV airs programming from the My Network TV and Retro Network Television in the Jacksonville, FL market. The station is owned by Cox Media Group, Inc. WFOX2-TV broadcasts locally on channel 30.2.
TELEVISION STATION

WFOX-TV
31741
Owner: Cox Media Group, Inc.
Editorial: 11700 Central Pkwy Unit 2, Jacksonville, Florida 32224-2600 **Tel:** 1 904 642-3030.
Email: news@actionnewsjax.com
Web site: http://www.fox30jax.com
Profile: WFOX-TV is the FOX affiliate for the Jacksonville, FL market. The station is owned by Cox Media Group, Inc. WFOX-TV broadcasts locally on channel 30.
TELEVISION STATION

WFQX-TV
32734
Owner: Cadillac Telecasting Co.
Editorial: 7669 S 45 Rd, Cadillac, Michigan 49601-8034 **Tel:** 1 231 775-9813.
Email: news@fox33.com
Web site: http://www.mifox32.com
Profile: WFQX-TV is the local FOX affiliate for Cadillac, MI. The station is owned by Cadillac Telecasting Co. WFQX-TV broadcasts locally on channel 32.
TELEVISION STATION

WFRV-TV
32669
Owner: Nexstar Broadcasting Group
Editorial: 1181 E Mason St, Green Bay, Wisconsin 54301-3427 **Tel:** 1 920 437-5411.
Email: tips@wearegreenbay.com
Web site: http://wearegreenbay.com
Profile: WFRV-TV is the CBS affiliate for the Green Bay-Appleton, WI market. The station is owned by Nexstar Broadcasting Group, Inc. WFRV-TV broadcasts locally on channel 5.
TELEVISION STATION

WFSB2-TV
612935
Owner: Meredith Broadcasting Group
Editorial: 333 Capital Blvd, Rocky Hill, Connecticut 06067-3578 **Tel:** 1 860 728-3333.
Email: newsdesk3@wfsb.com
Web site: http://www.wfsb.com
Profile: WFSB2-TV is a multicast of WFSB-TV. A multicast channel is a separate channel that shares the bandwith of the main station but can air unique programming. WFSB2-TV airs programming from CBS 3 Springfield in the Hartford-New Haven, CT market. The station is owned by Meredith Broadcasting Group. WFSB2-TV broadcasts locally on channel 3.2.
TELEVISION STATION

WFSB3-TV
612939
Owner: Meredith Broadcasting Group
Editorial: 333 Capital Blvd, Rocky Hill, Connecticut 06067-3578 **Tel:** 1 860 728-3333.
Email: newsdesk3@wfsb.com
Web site: http://www.wfsb.com
Profile: WFSB3-TV is a multicast of WFSB-TV. A multicast channel is a separate channel that shares the bandwith of the main station but can air unique programming. WFSB3-TV airs programming from Eyewitness News Now in the Hartford-New Haven, CT market. The station is owned by Meredith Broadcasting Group. WFSB3-TV broadcasts locally on channel 3.3.
TELEVISION STATION

WFSB4-TV
612942
Owner: Meredith Broadcasting Group
Editorial: 333 Capital Blvd, Rocky Hill, Connecticut 06067-3578 **Tel:** 1 860 728-3333.
Email: newsdesk3@wfsb.com
Web site: http://www.wfsb.com
Profile: WFSB4-TV is a multicast of WFSB-TV. A multicast channel is a separate channel that shares the bandwith of the main station but can air unique programming. WFSB4-TV airs programming from in the Hartford-New Haven, CT market. The station is owned by Meredith Broadcasting Group. WFSB4-TV broadcasts locally on channel 3.4.
TELEVISION STATION

WFSB-TV
31844
Owner: Meredith Broadcasting Group
Editorial: 333 Capital Blvd, Rocky Hill, Connecticut 06067-3578 **Tel:** 1 860 728-3333.
Email: newsdesk3@wfsb.com
Web site: http://www.wfsb.com
Profile: WFSB-TV is the CBS network affiliate in the Hartford-New Haven, CT market. The station is owned by Meredith Broadcasting Group. WFSB-TV broadcasts locally on channel 3.
TELEVISION STATION

WFTC-TV
31495
Owner: FOX/UTV Holdings, Inc.
Editorial: 11358 Viking Dr, Eden Prairie, Minnesota 55344-7238 **Tel:** 1 952 944-9999.
Email: fox9news@foxtv.com
Web site: http://www.fox9.com/my29
Profile: WFTC-TV is the MyNetworkTV affiliate for the Minneapolis-St. Paul, MN market. The station is owned by FOX/UTV Holdings, Inc. WFTC-TV broadcasts locally on channel 29.
TELEVISION STATION

WFTS2-TV
612003
Owner: E.W. Scripps Co.
Editorial: 4045 N Himes Ave, Tampa, Florida 33607-6651 **Tel:** 1 813 354-2828.
Email: newstips@wfts.com
Web site: http://www.abcactionnews.com
Profile: WFTS2-TV is a multicast of WFTS-TV. A multicast channel is a separate channel that shares the bandwith of the main station but can air unique programming. WFTS2-TV airs programming from AccuWeather Channel in the Tampa, FL market. The station is owned by E.W. Scripps Co. WFTS2-TV broadcasts locally on channel 28.2.
TELEVISION STATION

WFTS-TV
31845
Owner: E.W. Scripps Co.
Editorial: 4045 N Himes Ave, Tampa, Florida 33607-6651 **Tel:** 1 813 354-2828.
Email: newstips@wfts.com
Web site: http://www.abcactionnews.com
Profile: WFTS-TV is the ABC affiliate for the Tampa-St. Petersburg market. The station is owned by E.W. Scripps Co. WFTS-TV broadcasts locally on channel 28.
TELEVISION STATION

WFTT-TV
32385
Owner: Entravision Communications Corp.
Editorial: 2610 W Hillsborough Ave, Tampa, Florida 33614-6132 **Tel:** 1 813 872-6262.
Email: noticiastampa@entravision.com
Web site: http://www.wveatv.com
Profile: WFTT-TV is the Telefutura affiliate for the Tampa-St. Petersburg, FL market. The station is owned by Entravision Communications Corp. WFTT-TV broadcasts locally on channel 50.
TELEVISION STATION

WFTV2-TV
612497
Owner: Cox Media Group, Inc.
Editorial: 490 E South St, Orlando, Florida 32801-2816 **Tel:** 1 407 841-9000.
Email: news@wftv.com
Web site: http://www.wftv.com
Profile: WFTV2-TV is the Mega TV affiliate for the Orlando-Daytona Beach, FL market. The station is owned by Cox Media Group, Inc. WFTV-TV broadcasts locally on channel 9.2. WFTV2-TV broadcasts Spanish-language content and programming. WFTV2-TV is a multicast channel of WFTV-TV. A multicast channel is a separate channel that shares the bandwith of the main station but can air unique programming.
TELEVISION STATION

WFTV-TV
31846
Owner: Cox Media Group, Inc.
Editorial: 490 E South St, Orlando, Florida 32801-2816 **Tel:** 1 407 841-9000.
Email: news@wftv.com
Web site: http://www.wftv.com
Profile: WFTV-TV is the ABC affiliate for the Orlando-Daytona Beach, FL market. The station is owned by

Cox Media Group, Inc. WFTV-TV broadcasts locally on channel 9.
TELEVISION STATION

WFTX-TV 31847
Owner: E.W. Scripps Co.
Editorial: 621 SW Pine Island Rd, Cape Coral, Florida 33991-1950 **Tel:** 1 239 574-3636.
Email: news@fox4now.com
Web site: http://www.fox4now.com
Profile: WFTX-TV is the FOX affiliate for the Fort Myers-Naples, FL market. The station is owned by E.W. Scripps Co. WFTX-TV broadcasts locally on channel 4.
TELEVISION STATION

WFUN-TV 920956
Owner: America CV Network, LLC
Editorial: 13001 NW 107th Ave, Hialeah Gardens, Florida 33018-1104 **Tel:** 1 305 592-4141.
Email: noticias41@americateve.com
Web site: http://www.americateve.com
Profile: WFUN-TV is the América Tevé network affiliate for the North Miami-Dade and Broward counties in Florida. The station is owned by America CV Network, LLC, and is a simulcast of WJAN-TV. WFUN-TV broadcasts locally on channel 48.2.
TELEVISION STATION

WFUT2-TV 607027
Owner: Univision Communications Inc.
Editorial: 500 Frank W Burr Blvd Ste 6, Teaneck, New Jersey 07666-6802 **Tel:** 1 201 287-4141.
Web site: http://tv.univision.com/unimas
Profile: WFUT2-TV is a multicast channel of WFUT-TV. A multicast channel is a separate channel that shares the bandwith of the main station but can air unique programming. WFUT2-TV airs programming from WXTV-TV for the greater New York market. The station is owned by Univision Communications Inc. WFUT2-TV broadcasts locally on channel 68.2.
TELEVISION STATION

WFUT-TV 133741
Owner: Univision Communications Inc.
Editorial: 500 Frank W Burr Blvd, Teaneck, New Jersey 07666-6804 **Tel:** 1 201 287-4141.
Web site: http://tv.univision.com/unimas
Profile: WFUT-TV is the UniMas affiliate for the New York market. The station is owned by Univision Communications Inc. WFUT-TV airs locally on channel 68.
TELEVISION STATION

WFWA-TV 32885
Owner: Fort Wayne Public Television
Editorial: 2501 E Coliseum Blvd, Fort Wayne, Indiana 46805 **Tel:** 1 260 484-8839.
Email: info@wfwa.org
Web site: http://www.wfwa.org
Profile: WFWA-TV is a PBS affiliate for the Fort Wayne, IN market. The station is owned by Fort Wayne Public Television. WFWA-TV broadcasts locally on channel 39.
TELEVISION STATION

WFXB-TV 31868
Owner: Bahakel Communications
Editorial: 3364 Huger St, Myrtle Beach, South Carolina 29577 **Tel:** 1 843 828-4300.
Web site: http://www.wfxb.com
Profile: WFXB-TV is the FOX affiliate for the Florence-Myrtle Beach, SC market. The station is owned by Bahakel Communications. WFXB-TV broadcasts locally on channel 43.
TELEVISION STATION

WFXG-TV 32367
Owner: Southeastern Media Holdings, LLC
Editorial: 3933 Washington Rd, Augusta, Georgia 30907-2350 **Tel:** 1 706 650-5400.
Email: foxit2us@wfxg.com
Web site: http://www.wfxg.com
Profile: WFXG-TV is the Fox affiliate for the Augusta, GA market. The station is owned by Southeastern Media Holdings, LLC. WFXG-TV broadcasts locally on channel 54.
TELEVISION STATION

WFXI-TV 32254
Owner: Bonten Media Group, LLC
Editorial: 225 Glenburnie Dr, New Bern, North Carolina 28560-2815 **Tel:** 1 252 638-1212.
Web site: http://www.wcti12.com/foxeasterncarolina
Profile: WFXI-TV is the FOX affiliate for the Greenville, NC market. The station is owned by Bonten Media Group, LLC. WFXI-TV broadcasts locally on channel 8.
TELEVISION STATION

WFXL-TV 32148
Owner: Sinclair Broadcast Group, Inc.
Editorial: 1201 Stuart Ave, Albany, Georgia 31707-1803 **Tel:** 1 229 435-3100.
Email: newsdesk@wfxl.com
Web site: http://wfxl.com/
Profile: WFXL-TV is the FOX affiliate for the Albany, GA market. The station is owned by Sinclair Broadcast Group, Inc. WFXL-TV broadcasts locally on channel 31.
TELEVISION STATION

WFXP-TV 32264
Owner: Mission Broadcasting
Editorial: 8455 Peach St, Erie, Pennsylvania 16509 **Tel:** 1 814 864-2400.
Web site: http://www.yourerie.com
Profile: WFXP-TV is the FOX affiliate for the Erie, PA market. The station is owned by Mission Broadcasting. WFXP-TV broadcasts locally on channel 66.
TELEVISION STATION

WFXR-TV 32379
Owner: Nexstar Broadcasting Group, Inc.
Editorial: 5305 Valleypark Dr Ste 1, Roanoke, Virginia 24019-3082 **Tel:** 1 540 344-2127.
Web site: http://www.virginiafirst.com
Profile: WFXR-TV is the FOX network affiliate for the Roanoke-Lynchburg, VA market. The Station is owned by Nexstar Broadcasting Group. WFXR-TV broadcasts locally on channel 27.
TELEVISION STATION

WFXT-TV 31849
Owner: Cox Media Group, Inc.
Editorial: 25 Fox Dr, Dedham, Massachusetts 02026-4595 **Tel:** 1 781 467-2525.
Email: desk@fox25.com
Web site: http://www.fox25boston.com
Profile: WFXT-TV is the FOX affiliate for the Boston market. WFXT-TV is owned by Cox Media Group, Inc. WFXT broadcasts locally on channel 25.
TELEVISION STATION

WFXV-TV 32279
Owner: Mission Broadcasting
Editorial: 5956 Smith Hill Rd, Utica, New York 13502 **Tel:** 1 315 797-5220.
Web site: http://www.cnyhomepage.com
Profile: WFXV-TV is the FOX affiliate for the Rome, NY market. The station is owned by Mission Broadcasting. WFXV-TV broadcasts locally on channel 33.
TELEVISION STATION

WFXZ-TV 476266
Owner: Boston Broadcasting Corp.
Editorial: 1165 Chestnut St, Newton, Massachusetts 02464-1308 **Tel:** 1 781 569-5399.
Email: dtv@usa.com
Web site: http://www.mundomaxboston.com
Profile: WFXZ-TV is the MundoFOX affiliate for the Boston market. The station is owned by Boston Broadcasting Corp. WFXZ-TV broadcasts locally on channel 24.
TELEVISION STATION

WFYI2-TV 614579
Owner: Indiana Public Broadcasting Systems
Editorial: 1630 N Meridian St, Indianapolis, Indiana 46202-1429 **Tel:** 1 317 636-2020.
Email: viewerswfyi@wfyi.org
Web site: http://www.wfyi.org
Profile: WFYI2-TV is a multicast of WFYI-TV. A multicast channel is a separate channel that shares the bandwith of the main station but can air unique programming. WFYI2-TV airs programming from the V-me Network in the Indianapolis market. The station is owned by Indiana Public Broadcasting Systems. WFYI2-TV broadcasts locally on channel 20.2.
TELEVISION STATION

WFYI3-TV 614580
Owner: Indiana Public Broadcasting Systems
Editorial: 1630 N Meridian St, Indianapolis, Indiana 46202-1429 **Tel:** 1 317 636-2020.
Email: viewerswfyi@wfyi.org
Web site: http://www.wfyi.org
Profile: WFYI3-TV is a multicast of WFYI-TV. A multicast channel is a separate channel that shares the bandwith of the main station but can air unique programming. WFYI3-TV airs programming from the Create Network in the Indianapolis market. The station is owned by Indiana Public Broadcasting Systems. WFYI3-TV broadcasts locally on channel 20.3.
TELEVISION STATION

WFYI-TV 32699
Owner: Metropolitan Indianapolis Public Broadcasting Co.
Editorial: 1630 N Meridian St, Indianapolis, Indiana 46202-1429 **Tel:** 1 317 636-2020.
Email: news@wfyi.org
Web site: http://www.wfyi.org
Profile: WFYI-TV is the PBS/NPR affiliate for the Indianapolis, IN market. The station is owned by Metropolitan Indianapolis Public Broadcasting Co . WFYI-TV broadcasts locally on channel 20.
TELEVISION STATION

WGAL2-TV 621018
Owner: Hearst Television Inc.
Editorial: 1300 Columbia Ave, Lancaster, Pennsylvania 17603-4751 **Tel:** 1 717 393-5851.
Email: news8@wgal.com
Web site: http://www.wgal.com
Profile: WGAL2-TV is a multicast of WGAL-TV. A multicast channel is a separate channel that shares the bandwith of the main station but can air unique programming. WGAL2-TV airs programming from This TV in the Lancaster, PA market. The station is owned by Hearst Television Inc. WGAL2-TV broadcasts locally on channel 8.2.
TELEVISION STATION

WGAL-TV 31850
Owner: Hearst Television Inc.
Editorial: 1300 Columbia Ave, Lancaster, Pennsylvania 17603-4765 **Tel:** 1 717 393-5851.
Email: news8@wgal.com
Web site: http://www.wgal.com
Profile: WGAL-TV is the NBC affiliate for the Harrisburg, PA market. The station is owned by Hearst Television Inc. WGAL-TV broadcasts locally on channel 8.
TELEVISION STATION

WGBA3-TV 772961
Owner: E.W. Scripps Co.
Editorial: 1391 North Rd, Green Bay, Wisconsin 54313-5723
Email: comments@nbc26.com
Web site: http://jrn.com/nbc26
Profile: WGBA3-TV is a multicast channel of WGBA-TV. A multicast channel is a separate channel that shares the bandwith of the main station but can air unique programming. WGBA3-TV is the Me-TV Network for the Green Bay, WI market. The station is owned by E.W. Scripps Co. WGBA3-TV broadcasts locally on channel 26.3.
TELEVISION STATION

WGBA-TV 31851
Owner: E.W. Scripps Co.
Editorial: 1391 North Rd, Green Bay, Wisconsin 54313-5723 **Tel:** 1 920 494-2626.
Email: comments@nbc26.com
Web site: http://jrn.com/nbc26
Profile: WGBA-TV is the NBC network affiliate for the Greenbay-Appleton, WI market. The station is owned by E.W. Scripps Co. WGBA-TV broadcasts locally on channel 26.
TELEVISION STATION

WGBC-TV 32380
Owner: Waypoint Media
Editorial: 1151 Crestview Cir, Meridian, Mississippi 39301-8669 **Tel:** 1 601 485-3030.
Web site: http://www.wgbctv.com
Profile: WGBC-TV is the FOX affiliate for the Meridan, MS market. The station is owned by Waypoint Media. WGBC-TV broadcasts locally on channel 30.
TELEVISION STATION

WGBO-TV 31852
Owner: Univision Communications Inc.
Editorial: 541 N Fairbanks Ct Ste 1100, Chicago, Illinois 60611-3388 **Tel:** 1 312 670-1000.
Email: univisionchicago@tv.univision.com
Web site: http://chicago.univision.com
Profile: WGBO-TV is the Univision affiliate for the Chicago market. The station is owned by Univision Communications Inc. WGBO-TV broadcasts locally on channel 66.
TELEVISION STATION

WGCB2-TV 618385
Owner: Red Lion Television Inc.
Editorial: 2900 Windsor Rd, Red Lion, Pennsylvania 17356-8534 **Tel:** 1 717 246-1681.
Email: info@family49.com
Web site: http://www.family49.com
Profile: WGCB2-TV is a multicast of WGCB-TV. A multicast channel is a separate channel that shares the bandwith of the main station but can air unique programming. WGCB2-TV airs programming from My Family TV in the Red Lion, PA market. The station is owned by Red Lion Television Inc. WGCB2-TV broadcasts locally on channel 49.2.
TELEVISION STATION

WGCB-TV 31855
Owner: NRJ TV, LLC
Editorial: 2900 Windsor Rd, Red Lion, Pennsylvania 17356-8534 **Tel:** 1 717 246-1681.
Email: info@family49.com
Web site: http://www.family49.com
Profile: WGCB-TV is an independent station for the Harrisburg, PA market. The station is owned by NRJ TV, LLC. WGCB-TV broadcasts locally on channel 49.
TELEVISION STATION

WGCL-TV 31865
Owner: Meredith Broadcasting Group
Editorial: 425 14th St NW, Atlanta, Georgia 30318-7965 **Tel:** 1 404 327-3200.
Email: news@cbs46.com
Web site: http://www.cbs46.com
Profile: WGCL-TV is the CBS affiliate for the Atlanta market. The station is owned by Meredith Broadcasting Group. WGCL-TV broadcasts locally on channel 46.
TELEVISION STATION

WGEM-TV 31856
Owner: Quincy Media Inc.
Editorial: 513 Hampshire St, Quincy, Illinois 62301-2930 **Tel:** 1 217 228-6600.
Email: news@wgem.com
Web site: http://www.wgem.com
Profile: WGEM-TV is the NBC affiliate for the Quincy, IL/Hannibal, MO/Keokuk, IA market. The station is owned by Quincy Media Inc. WGEM-TV broadcasts locally on channel 10.
TELEVISION STATION

WGEN-TV 32505
Owner: Mapale LLC
Editorial: 1800 NW 94th Ave, Doral, Florida 33172-2329 **Tel:** 1 305 860-2544.
Profile: WGEN-TV is an Azteca America affiliate for the Miami-Fort Lauderdale market. The station is owned by Mapale LLC. WGEN-TV broadcasts locally on channel 8.
TELEVISION STATION

WGFL-TV 32606
Owner: New Age Media, LLC
Editorial: 1703 NW 80th Blvd, Gainesville, Florida 32606-9178 **Tel:** 1 352 332-1128.
Web site: http://mycbs4.com
Profile: WGFL-TV is the CBS affiliate for the Gainesville, FL market. The station is owned by New Age Media of Gainesville License, LLC. WGFL-TV broadcasts locally on channel 28.
TELEVISION STATION

WGGB2-TV 68161(
Owner: Meredith Corporation
Editorial: 1300 Liberty St, Springfield, Massachusetts 01104-1153 **Tel:** 1 413 733-4040.
Email: tips@westernmassnews.com
Web site: http://www.westernmassnews.com
Profile: WGGB2-TV is a multicast channel of WGGB-TV. A multicast is a separate channel that shares the bandwidth of the main station but can air unique programming. WGGB2-TV is the local FOX affiliate on channel 40.2 for the Springfield, MA market. WGGB2-TV is owned by Meredith Corporation.
TELEVISION STATION

WGGB-TV 31857
Owner: Meredith Corporation
Editorial: 1300 Liberty St, Springfield, Massachusetts 01104-1153 **Tel:** 1 413 733-4040.
Email: tips@westernmassnews.com
Web site: http://www.westernmassnews.com
Profile: WGGB-TV is the ABC affiliate for the Springfield, MA market. The station is owned by Meredith Corporation. WGGB-TV broadcasts locally on channel 40.
TELEVISION STATION

WGGN-TV 31858
Owner: Christian Faith Broadcast, Inc.
Editorial: 3809 Maple Ave, Castalia, Ohio 44824-9484 **Tel:** 1 419 684-5311.
Web site: http://www.wggn.tv
Profile: WGGN-TV is an independent affiliate in Cleveland, OH market. The station is owned by Christian Faith Broadcast, Inc. WGGN-TV broadcasts locally on channel 52.
TELEVISION STATION

WGGS-TV 31859
Owner: Carolina Christian Broadcasting, Inc.
Editorial: 3409 Rutherford Road Ext, Taylors, South Carolina 29687-2133 **Tel:** 1 864 244-1616.
Email: programming@wggs16.com
Web site: http://wggs16.com
Profile: WGGS-TV is an independent station for the Greenville/Spartanburg/Anderson, SC market. Also, the Asheville, NC market. The station is owned by Carolina Christian Broadcasting, Inc. WGGS-TV broadcasts locally on channel 16.
TELEVISION STATION

WGHP-TV 31861
Owner: Tribune Broadcasting Co.
Editorial: 2005 Francis St, High Point, North Carolina 27263-1865 **Tel:** 1 336 841-8888.
Email: news@wghp.com
Web site: http://www.myfox8.com
Profile: WGHP-TV is the FOX affiliate for the Greensboro-Winston Salem, NC market. The station is owned by Tribune Broadcasting Co. WGHP-TV broadcasts locally on channel 8.
TELEVISION STATION

WGMB-TV 32383
Owner: Nexstar Broadcasting Group
Editorial: 10000 Perkins Rd, Baton Rouge, Louisiana 70810-1527 **Tel:** 1 225 769-0044.
Web site: http://www.brproud.com
Profile: WGMB-TV is the Fox affiliate for the Baton Rouge, LA market. The station is owned by Nexstar Broadcasting Group. WGMB-TV broadcasts locally on channel 44.
TELEVISION STATION

WGME-TV 31862
Owner: Sinclair Broadcast Group, Inc.
Editorial: 81 Northport Dr, Portland, Maine 04103-3668 **Tel:** 1 207 797-1313.
Email: tvmail@wgme.com
Web site: http://www.wgme.com
Profile: WGME-TV is the CBS network affiliate for the Portland, ME market. The station is owned by Sinclair Broadcast Group, Inc. WGME-TV broadcasts locally on channel 13.
TELEVISION STATION

WGN2-TV 606403
Owner: Tribune Broadcasting Co.
Editorial: 2501 W Bradley Pl, Chicago, Illinois 60618-4701 **Tel:** 1 773 528-2311.
Email: wgntvinfo@tribunemedia.com
Web site: http://www.wgntv.com
Profile: WGN2-TV is a multicast channel of WGN-TV. A multicast channel is a separate channel that shares the bandwith of the main station but can air unique programming. WGN2-TV is the Antenna TV affiliate for the Chicago market. The station is owned by Tribune Broadcasting Co. WGN2-TV broadcasts locally on channel 9.2.
TELEVISION STATION

WGN3-TV 883866
Owner: Tribune Broadcasting Co.
Editorial: 2501 W Bradley Pl, Chicago, Illinois 60618-4701 **Tel:** 1 773 528-2311.
Web site: http://www.wgntv.com
Profile: WGN3-TV is a multicast channel of WGN-TV. A multicast channel is a separate channel that shares the bandwith of the main station but can air unique programming. WGN3-TV is the This TV affiliate for the Chicago market. The station is owned by Tribune

Broadcasting Co. WGN3-TV broadcasts locally on channel 9.3. The station airs classic movies.
TELEVISION STATION

WGNM-TV 32399
Owner: Christian Television Network
Editorial: 178 Steven Dr, Macon, Georgia 31210-5852
Tel: 1 478 474-8400.
Email: production@wgnm.com
Web site: http://www.wgnm.com
Profile: WGNM-TV is an affiliate of the Christian Television Network for the Macon, GA, area. The station airs locally on channel 64. It provides minimal public affairs programming, so there are few PR opportunities available. Contact the programming director with any further inquiries. The station accepts PSAs in DVC Pro format.
TELEVISION STATION

WGNO-TV 31864
Owner: Tribune Broadcasting Co.
Editorial: 1 Galleria Blvd Ste 850, Metairie, Louisiana 70001-7542 **Tel:** 1 504 525-3838.
Email: news@wgno.com
Web site: http://wgno.com
Profile: WGNO-TV is the ABC affiliate for the New Orleans market. The station is owned by Tribune Broadcasting Co. WGNO-TV broadcasts locally on channel 26.
TELEVISION STATION

WGNT-TV 32226
Owner: Tribune Broadcasting Co.
Editorial: 720 Boush St, Norfolk, Virginia 23510-1502
Tel: 1 757 446-1000.
Web site: http://wgnt.com
Profile: WGNT-TV is the CW affiliate for the Norfolk, VA market. The station is owned by Tribune Broadcasting Co. WGNT-TV broadcasts locally on channel 27.
TELEVISION STATION

WGN-TV 31863
Owner: Tribune Broadcasting Co.
Editorial: 2501 W Bradley Pl, Chicago, Illinois 60618-4701 **Tel:** 1 773 528-2311.
Email: wgntvinfo@tribunemedia.com
Web site: http://www.wgntv.com
Profile: WGN-TV is an independent station in the Chicago market. The station is owned by Tribune Broadcasting Co. WGN-TV broadcasts locally on channel 9. The station dropped the CW affiliation on September 1, 2016.
TELEVISION STATION

WGPX-TV 32339
Owner: ION Media Networks
Editorial: 1114 N Ohenry Blvd, Greensboro, North Carolina 27405-7120 **Tel:** 1 336 272-9227.
Web site: http://www.iontelevision.com
Profile: WGPX-TV is the ION Television affiliate for the Greensboro-Winston Salem, NC market. The station is owned by ION Media Networks. WGPX-TV broadcasts locally on channel 16.
TELEVISION STATION

WGRZ-TV 31867
Owner: TEGNA Inc.
Editorial: 259 Delaware Ave, Buffalo, New York 14202-2008 **Tel:** 1 716 849-2222.
Email: newsdesk@wgrz.com
Web site: http://www.wgrz.com
Profile: WGRZ-TV is the NBC affiliate for the Buffalo, NY market. The station is owned by TEGNA Inc. WGRZ-TV broadcasts locally on channel 2.
TELEVISION STATION

WGSA-TV 32627
Owner: Southern TV Corporation
Editorial: 401 Mall Blvd Ste 201B, Savannah, Georgia 31406-4867 **Tel:** 1 912 692-8000.
Web site: http://www.wgsa.tv
Profile: WGSA-TV is the CW affiliate for Savannah, GA. The station is owned by Southern TV Corporation. WGSA-TV broadcasts locally on channel 34.
TELEVISION STATION

WGTE-TV 32260
Owner: Public Broadcasting Foundation of Northwest Ohio
Editorial: 1270 S Detroit Ave, Toledo, Ohio 43614
Tel: 1 419 380-4600.
Email: public_relations@wgte.org
Web site: http://www.wgte.org
Profile: WGTE-TV is the PBS affiliate for the Toledo, OH area. The station is owned by Public Broadcasting Foundation of Northwest Ohio. WGTE-TV broadcasts locally on channel 30.
TELEVISION STATION

WGTU-TV 32670
Owner: Sinclair Broadcast Group, Inc.
Editorial: 8513 East Traverse HWY, Traverse City, Michigan 49684 **Tel:** 1 231 946-2900.
Email: newsroom@upnorthlive.com
Web site: http://www.upnorthlive.com
Profile: WGTU-TV is the ABC affiliate for the Traverse City-Cadillac, MI market. The station is owned by Sinclair Broadcast Group, Inc.. WGTU-TV broadcasts locally on channel 29.
TELEVISION STATION

WGTV2-TV 608541
Owner: Georgia Public Broadcasting
Editorial: 260 14th St NW, Atlanta, Georgia 30318-5360 **Tel:** 1 404 685-2400.
Web site: http://pbskids.org
Profile: WGTV2-TV is the PBS affiliate for the Atlanta market. The station is owned by Georgia Public Broadcasting. WGTV2-TV broadcasts locally on channel 8.2. WGTV2-TV broadcasts children's programming from PBS Kids. WGTV2-TV is a multicast channel of WGTV-TV. A multicast channel is a separate channel that shares the bandwidth of the main station but can air unique programming.
TELEVISION STATION

WGTV3-TV 608544
Owner: Georgia Public Broadcasting
Editorial: 260 14th St NW, Atlanta, Georgia 30318-5360 **Tel:** 1 404 685-2400.
Web site: http://www.pbs.org
Profile: WGTV3-TV is the PBS affiliate for the Atlanta market. The station is owned by Georgia Public Broadcasting. WGTV3-TV broadcasts locally on channel 8.3. WGTV3-TV broadcasts various entertainment, documentaries, science and current affairs programming from PBS World. WGTV3-TV is a multicast channel of WGTV-TV. A multicast channel is a separate channel that shares the bandwidth of the main station but can air unique programming.
TELEVISION STATION

WGTV-TV 32671
Owner: Georgia Public Broadcasting
Editorial: 260 14th St NW, Atlanta, Georgia 30318-5360 **Tel:** 1 404 685-2400.
Email: ask@gpb.org
Web site: http://www.gpb.org
Profile: WGTV-TV is the PBS affiliate for the Atlanta market. The station is owned by Georgia Public Broadcasting. WGTV-TV broadcasts locally on channel 8.
TELEVISION STATION

WGTW-TV 32401
Owner: Trinity Broadcasting Network
Editorial: 1810 Columbia Ave, Folcroft, Pennsylvania 19032-1904 **Tel:** 1 610 583-1370.
Web site: http://tbn.org
Profile: WGTW-TV is the TBN affiliate for the Philadelphia market. The station is owned by Trinity Broadcasting Network. WGTW-TV broadcasts locally on channel 27.
TELEVISION STATION

WGWG-TV 32504
Owner: Howard Stirk Holdings
Web site: http://www.hsh.media
Profile: WGWG-TV is an independent station in the Charleston, SC, market. The station is owned by Howard Stirk Holdings. The station airs programming from Heroes & Icons. WGWG-TV broadcasts locally on channel 34.
TELEVISION STATION

WGXA2-TV 657799
Owner: Sinclair Broadcast Group, Inc.
Editorial: 599 Martin Luther King Jr Blvd, Macon, Georgia 31201-3364 **Tel:** 1 478 745-2424.
Web site: http://wgxa.tv/
Profile: WGXA2-TV is a multicast of WGXA-TV. A multicast channel is a separate channel that shares the bandwith of the main station but can air unique programming. WGXA2-TV airs programming from PBS World in the Salt Lake City market. The station is owned by Sinclair Broadcast Group, Inc. WGXA2-TV is the local ABC affiliate and it broadcasts locally on channel 24.2. Contact can be made by phone, fax or e-mail.
TELEVISION STATION

WGXA-TV 31869
Owner: Sinclair Broadcast Group, Inc.
Editorial: 599 Martin Luther King Jr Blvd, Macon, Georgia 31201-3364 **Tel:** 1 478 745-2424.
Email: news@wgxa-tv.com
Web site: http://www.wgxa.tv
Profile: WGXA-TV is the FOX affiliate for the Macon, GA market. The station is owned by Sinclair Broadcast Group, Inc. WGXA-TV broadcasts locally on channel 24.
TELEVISION STATION

WHAM2-TV 706268
Owner: Sinclair Broadcasting Group
Editorial: 4225 W Henrietta Rd, Rochester, New York 14623-5225 **Tel:** 1 585 334-8700.
Email: news@13wham.com
Web site: http://cwrochester.com
Profile: WHAM2-TV is a multicast channel of WHAM-TV. A multicast channel is a separate channel that shares the bandwith of the main station but can air unique programming. WHAM2-TV is the CW Television Network affiliate for the Rochester, NY market. The station is owned by Sinclair Broadcasting Group. WHAM2-TV broadcasts locally on channel 13.2.
TELEVISION STATION

WHAM-TV 32033
Owner: Sinclair Broadcast Group, Inc.
Editorial: 4225 W Henrietta Rd, Rochester, New York 14623-5225 **Tel:** 1 585 334-8700.
Email: news@13wham.com
Web site: http://www.13wham.com
Profile: WHAM-TV is the ABC network affiliate for the Rochester, NY market. The station is owned by Sinclair Broadcast Group, Inc. WHAM-TV broadcasts locally on channel 13.
TELEVISION STATION

WHAS2-TV 617304
Owner: TEGNA Inc.
Editorial: 520 W Chestnut St, Louisville, Kentucky 40202-2235 **Tel:** 1 502 582-7840.
Email: assign@whas11.com
Web site: http://www.whas11.com
Profile: WHAS2-TV is a multicast of WHAS-TV. A multicast channel is a separate channel that shares the bandwith of the main station but can air unique programming. WHAS2-TV airs programming from WHAS Stormteam Weather/The Local AccuWeather Channel in the Louisville, KY market. The station is owned by TEGNA Inc. WHAS2-TV broadcasts locally on channel 11.2.
TELEVISION STATION

WHAS-TV 31871
Owner: TEGNA Inc.
Editorial: 520 W Chestnut St, Louisville, Kentucky 40202-2235 **Tel:** 1 502 582-7711.
Email: assign@whas11.com
Web site: http://www.whas11.com
Profile: WHAS-TV is the ABC affiliate for the Louisville, KY market. WHAS-TV is owned by TEGNA Inc. WHAS-TV broadcasts locally on channel 11.
TELEVISION STATION

WHBF-TV 31872
Owner: Nextar Broadcasting Inc.
Editorial: 231 18th St, Rock Island, Illinois 61201-8706 **Tel:** 1 309 786-5441.
Web site: http://www.whbf.com
Profile: WHBF-TV is the CBS affiliate for the Davenport, IA and Rock Island-Moline, IL market. The station is owned by Nextar Broadcasting Inc. WHBF-TV broadcasts locally on channel 4.
TELEVISION STATION

WHBQ-TV 31873
Owner: Cox Media Group, Inc.
Editorial: 485 S Highland St, Memphis, Tennessee 38111-4398 **Tel:** 1 901 320-1313.
Email: news@myfoxmemphis.com
Web site: http://www.fox13memphis.com
Profile: WHBQ-TV is the FOX affiliate for the Memphis, TN market. The station is owned by Cox Media Group, Inc. WHBQ-TV broadcasts locally on channel 13.
TELEVISION STATION

WHBR-TV 32320
Owner: Christian Television Network
Editorial: 6500 Pensacola Blvd, Pensacola, Florida 32505 **Tel:** 1 850 473-8633.
Web site: http://www.whbr.org
Profile: WHBR-TV is an independent network for the Mobile, AL, Pensacola, FL market. The station is owned by Christian Television Network. WHBR-TV broadcasts locally on channel 33.
TELEVISION STATION

WHCT-TV 476512
Owner: Venture Technologies Group LLC
Editorial: 5757 Wilshire Blvd Ste 470, Los Angeles, California 90036-3658 **Tel:** 1 323 469-5638.
Web site: http://www.wuvntv.com
Profile: WHCT-TV is the Azteca America affiliate for the Los Angeles, CA market. The station is owned by Venture Technologies Group LLC. WHCT-TV broadcasts locally on channel 38.
TELEVISION STATION

WHDF-TV 32037
Owner: Huntsville TV, LLC
Editorial: 840 Cypress Mill Rd, Florence, Alabama 35630-2013 **Tel:** 1 256 767-1515.
Web site: http://www.thevalleyscw.tv
Profile: WHDF-TV is the CW affiliate for the Florence, AL market. The station is owned by Huntsville TV, LLC. WHDF-TV broadcasts locally on channel 15.
TELEVISION STATION

WHDH2-TV 610690
Owner: Sunbeam Broadcasting Corp.
Editorial: 7 Bulfinch Pl, Boston, Massachusetts 02114-2904 **Tel:** 1 617 725-0777.
Email: news@whdh.com
Web site: http://www1.whdh.com
Profile: WHDH2-TV is a multicast of WHDH-TV. A multicast channel is a separate channel that shares the bandwith of the main station but can air unique programming. WHDH2-TV airs programming from This TV in the Boston market. The station is owned by Sunbeam Broadcasting Corp. WHDH2-TV broadcasts locally on channel 7.2.
TELEVISION STATION

WHDH-TV 32010
Owner: Sunbeam Broadcasting Corp.
Editorial: 7 Bulfinch Pl, Boston, Massachusetts 02114-2904 **Tel:** 1 617 725-0777.
Email: news@whdh.com
Web site: http://www.whdh.com
Profile: WHDH-TV is an independent station in the Boston market. The station is owned by Sunbeam Broadcasting Corp. WHDH-TV broadcasts locally on channel 7.
TELEVISION STATION

WHDT-TV 86373
Owner: Marksteiner(Guenter)
Editorial: 5244 SW Orchid Bay Dr, Palm City, Florida 34990-8519 **Tel:** 1 561 983-6300.
Web site: http://www.whdt.net
Profile: WHDT-TV is a commercial station owned by Guenter Marksteiner. WHDT broadcasts on channel 9. WHDT-TV serves West Palm Beach, FL and its environs.
TELEVISION STATION

WHEC-TV 31874
Owner: Hubbard Broadcasting Inc.
Editorial: 191 East Ave, Rochester, New York 14604-2605 **Tel:** 1 585 546-5670.
Email: news10@whec.com
Web site: http://www.whec.com
Profile: WHEC-TV is the NBC network affiliate for the Rochester, NY market. The station is owned by Hubbard Broadcasting Inc. WHEC-TV broadcasts locally on channel 10.
TELEVISION STATION

WHFT2-TV 615006
Owner: Trinity Broadcasting Network
Editorial: 3324 Pembroke Rd, Pembroke Park, Florida 33021-8320 **Tel:** 1 954 962-1700.
Email: hillsong@hillsong.com
Web site: http://www.thechurchchannel.org
Profile: WHFT2-TV is an independent affiliate for the Miami-Fort Lauderdale, FL market. The station is owned by Trinity Broadcasting Network. WHFT2-TV broadcasts locally on channel 45.2. The station airs religious programming from The Church Channel network. WHFT2-TV is a multicast channel of WHFT-TV. A multicast channel is a separate channel that shares the bandwidth of the main station but can air unique programming.
TELEVISION STATION

WHFT3-TV 615007
Owner: Trinity Broadcasting Network
Editorial: 3324 Pembroke Rd, Pembroke Park, Florida 33021-8320 **Tel:** 1 954 962-1700.
Email: whft@tbn.org
Web site: http://www.thechurchchannel.com
Profile: WHFT3-TV is an independent affiliate for the Miami-Fort Lauderdale, FL market. The station is owned by Trinity Broadcasting Network. WHFT3-TV broadcasts locally on channel 45.3. The station airs Christian music videos and programming from JCTV network, targeting young adults. WHFT3-TV is a multicast channel of WHFT-TV. A multicast channel is a separate channel that shares the bandwidth of the main station but can air unique programming.
TELEVISION STATION

WHFT4-TV 615008
Owner: Trinity Broadcasting Network
Editorial: 3324 Pembroke Rd, Pembroke Park, Florida 33021-8320 **Tel:** 1 954 962-1700.
Email: whft@tbn.org
Web site: http://www.tbnenlaceusa.org
Profile: WHFT4-TV is Trinity Broadcasting Network affiliate for the Miami-Fort Lauderdale, FL market. The station is owned by Trinity Broadcasting Network. WHFT4-TV broadcasts locally on channel 45.4. The station airs Christian Hispanic programming from Enlace USA network. WHFT 4-TV is a multicast channel of WHFT-TV. A multicast channel is a separate channel that shares the bandwidth of the main station but can air unique programming.
TELEVISION STATION

WHFT5-TV 615009
Owner: Trinity Broadcasting Network
Editorial: 3324 Pembroke Rd, Pembroke Park, Florida 33021-8320 **Tel:** 1 954 962-1700.
Email: whft@tbn.org
Web site: http://www.smileofachildtv.org
Profile: WHFT5-TV is an independent affiliate for the Miami-Fort Lauderdale, FL market. The station is owned by Trinity Broadcasting Network. WHFT5-TV broadcasts locally on channel 45.5. The station airs children's Christian programming from the Smile of a Child network. WHFT 5-TV is a multicast channel of WHFT -TV. A multicast channel is a separate channel that shares the bandwidth of the main station but can air unique programming.
TELEVISION STATION

WHFT-TV 32294
Owner: Trinity Broadcasting Network
Editorial: 3324 Pembroke Rd, Pembroke Park, Florida 33021-8320 **Tel:** 1 954 962-1700.
Email: hello@hillsong.com
Web site: https://hillsong.com/channel
Profile: WHFT-TV is the Trinity Broadcasting Network affiliate for the Miami-Fort Lauderdale, FL market. The station is owned by Trinity Broadcasting Network. WHFT-TV broadcasts locally on channel 45.
TELEVISION STATION

WHHI-TV 78781
Owner: Burn(John)
Editorial: 32 Office Park Rd Ste 103, Hilton Head Island, South Carolina 29928-4659 **Tel:** 1 843 785-4545.
Email: news@whhitv.com
Web site: http://www.whhitv.com
Profile: WHHI-TV is an independent affiliate for the Hilton Head Island, SC market. The station is owned by John Burn. WHHI-TV broadcasts locally on channel 30.
TELEVISION STATION

WHIO-TV 31875
Owner: Cox Media Group, Inc.
Editorial: 1611 S Main St, Dayton, Ohio 45409-2547
Email: 7online@whiotv.com
Web site: http://www.whio.com
Profile: WHIO-TV is the CBS affiliate for the Dayton, OH market. The station is owned by Cox Media Group, Inc. WHIO-TV broadcasts locally on channel 7.
TELEVISION STATION

WHIZ-TV
31876

Owner: Southeastern Ohio Broadcasting, Inc.
Editorial: 629 Downard Rd, Zanesville, Ohio 43701-5108 **Tel:** 1 740 452-5431.
Email: newsroom@whizmediagroup.com
Web site: http://www.whiznews.com
Profile: WHIZ-TV is the NBC affiliate for the Zanesville, OH, market. The station is owned by Southeastern Ohio Broadcasting, Inc. WHIZ-TV broadcasts locally on channel 18.
TELEVISION STATION

WHKY-TV
31877

Owner: Long Communications
Editorial: 526 Main Ave SE, Hickory, North Carolina 28602 **Tel:** 1 828 322-5115.
Email: whky@whky.com
Web site: http://www.whky.com
Profile: WHKY-TV is an independent station for the Charlotte, NC market. The station is owned by Long Communications. WHKY-TV broadcasts locally on channel 14.
TELEVISION STATION

WHLT-TV
32356

Owner: Nexstar Media Group, Inc.
Editorial: 5912 U S Highway 49 Ste A, Hattiesburg, Mississippi 39401-7569 **Tel:** 1 601 545-2077.
Email: cfarrish@whlt.com
Web site: http://www.whlt.com
Profile: WHLT-TV is the CBS affiliate for the Hattiesburg-Laurel, MS market. The station is owned by Nexstar Media Group, Inc. WHLT-TV broadcasts locally on channel 22 with local newscast at 10 p.m. weeknights.
TELEVISION STATION

WHLV2-TV
615005

Owner: Trinity Broadcasting Network
Editorial: 4525 Vineland Rd Ste 210, Orlando, Florida 32811-7231 **Tel:** 1 407 841-9458.
Web site: http://www.thechurchchannel.org
Profile: WHLV2-TV is an independent affiliate for the Orlando-Daytona Beach, FL market. The station is owned by Trinity Broadcasting Network. WHLV2-TV broadcasts locally on channel 52.2. The station airs religious programming from The Church Channel network. WHLV2-TV is a multicast channel of WHLV-TV. A multicast channel is a separate channel that shares the bandwidth of the main station but can air unique programming.
TELEVISION STATION

WHLV-TV
32126

Owner: Trinity Broadcasting Network
Editorial: 4525 Vineland Rd Ste 210, Orlando, Florida 32811-7231 **Tel:** 1 407 423-5200.
Web site: http://www.thechurchchannel.com
Profile: WHLV-TV is a Trinity Broadcasting Network affiliate for the Orlando-Daytona Beach, FL market. The station is owned by Trinity Broadcasting Network. WHLV-TV broadcasts locally on channel 52.
TELEVISION STATION

WHMB2-TV
614762

Owner: LeSEA Broadcasting
Editorial: 10511 Greenfield Ave, Noblesville, Indiana 46060-4198 **Tel:** 1 317 773-5050.
Web site: http://www.whmbtv.com
Profile: WHMB2-TV is a multicast of WHMB-TV. A multicast channel is a separate channel that shares the bandwith of the main station but can air unique programming. WHMB2-TV airs programming from World Harvest Television in the Indianapolis market. The station is owned by LeSEA Broadcasating. WHMB2-TV broadcasts locally on channel 40.2.
TELEVISION STATION

WHMB-TV
31879

Owner: LeSEA Broadcasting
Editorial: 10511 Greenfield Ave, Noblesville, Indiana 46060-4198 **Tel:** 1 317 773-5050.
Email: whmb@lesea.com
Web site: http://www.whmbtv.com
Profile: WHMB-TV is an independent station for the Indianapolis market. The station is owned by LeSEA Broadcasting. WHMB-TV broadcasts locally on channel 40.
TELEVISION STATION

WHME-TV
31880

Owner: LeSEA Broadcasting
Editorial: 61300 S. Ironwood Rd, South Bend, Indiana 46614-9738 **Tel:** 1 574 291-8200.
Email: broadcasting@lesea.com
Web site: http://www.whme.com
Profile: WHME-TV is an independent station for the South Bend, IN, market. It is owned by LeSEA Broadcasting. WHME-TV broadcasts locally on channel 46.
TELEVISION STATION

WHNO-TV
32499

Owner: LeSEA Broadcasting
Editorial: 839 Saint Charles Ave Ste 307, New Orleans, Louisiana 70130-3733 **Tel:** 1 504 681-0120.
Web site: http://www.whno.com
Profile: WHNO-TV is an independent affiliate for the New Orleans, LA market. The station is owned by LeSea Broadcasting. WHNO-TV broadcasts locally on channel 20.
TELEVISION STATION

WHNS2-TV
618332

Owner: Meredith Broadcasting Group
Editorial: 21 Interstate Ct, Greenville, South Carolina 29615-5098 **Tel:** 1 864 288-2100.
Email: foxcarolinanews@foxcarolina.com
Web site: http://www.foxcarolina.com
Profile: WHNS2-TV is a multicast of WHNS-TV. A multicast channel is a separate channel that shares the bandwith of the main station but can air unique programming. WHNS2-TV airs all weather programming in the Greenville, SC and Asheville, NC market. The station is owned by Meredith Broadcast Group. WHNS2-TV broadcasts locally on channel 21.2.
TELEVISION STATION

WHNS-TV
31882

Owner: Meredith Broadcasting Group
Editorial: 21 Interstate Ct, Greenville, South Carolina 29615-5014 **Tel:** 1 864 288-2100.
Email: foxcarolinanews@foxcarolina.com
Web site: http://www.foxcarolina.com
Profile: WHNS-TV is the FOX affiliate for the Greenville, SC and Asheville, NC market. The station is owned by Meredith Broadcasting Group. WHNS-TV broadcasts locally on channel 21.
TELEVISION STATION

WHNT2-TV
621864

Owner: Tribune Broadcasting Co.
Editorial: 200 Holmes Ave NW, Huntsville, Alabama 35801-4903 **Tel:** 1 256 533-1919.
Email: news.department@whnt.com
Web site: http://www.whnt.com
TELEVISION STATION

WHNT-TV
31883

Owner: Tribune Broadcasting Co.
Editorial: 200 Holmes Ave NW, Huntsville, Alabama 35801-4903 **Tel:** 1 256 533-1919.
Email: news.department@whnt.com
Web site: http://www.whnt.com
Profile: WHNT-TV is the CBS affiliate for the Huntsville, AL, market. The station is owned by Tribune Broadcasting Co. WHNT-TV broadcasts locally on channel 19.
TELEVISION STATION

WHOI-TV
31885

Owner: Sinclair Broadcast Group, Inc.
Editorial: 2907 Springfield Rd, East Peoria, Illinois 61611-4878
Web site: http://yourcwtv.com/partners/peoria
Profile: WHOI-TV is the Comet affiliate for the Peoria-Bloomington, IL market. The station is owned by Sinclair Broadcast Group, Inc. WHOI-TV broadcasts locally on channel 19.
TELEVISION STATION

WHO-TV
31884

Owner: Tribune Broadcasting Co.
Editorial: 1801 Grand Ave, Des Moines, Iowa 50309-3309 **Tel:** 1 515 242-3500.
Email: releases@whotv.com
Web site: http://www.whotv.com
Profile: WHO-TV is the NBC affiliate for the Des Moines, IA market. The station is owned by Tribune Broadcasting Co. WHO-TV broadcasts locally on channel 13.
TELEVISION STATION

WHP2-TV
618356

Owner: Sinclair Broadcast Group, Inc.
Editorial: 3300 N 6Th St, Harrisburg, Pennsylvania 17110-1400 **Tel:** 1 717 238-2100.
Email: news@cbs21.com
Web site: http://www.whptv.com
Profile: WHP2-TV is a multicast of WHP-TV. A multicast channel is a separate channel that shares the bandwith of the main station but can air unique programming. WHP2-TV airs programming from My 21.2 in the Harrisburg, PA market. The station is owned by Sinclair Broadcast Group, Inc. WHP2-TV broadcasts locally on channel 21.2.
TELEVISION STATION

WHPM-TV
779449

Owner: Waypoint Media
Editorial: 140 Mayfair Rd Ste 1200, Hattiesburg, Mississippi 39402-1746 **Tel:** 1 601 602-3174.
Email: info@whpmtv.com
Web site: http://www.myfox23.com
Profile: WHPM-TV is the FOX affiliate for the Hattiesburg, MS market. The station is owned by Waypoint Media. WHPM-TV broadcasts locally on channel 23.
TELEVISION STATION

WHP-TV
31886

Owner: Sinclair Broadcast Group, Inc.
Editorial: 3300 N 6th St, Harrisburg, Pennsylvania 17110-1421 **Tel:** 1 717 238-2100.
Email: news@cbs21.com
Web site: http://www.local21news.com
Profile: WHP-TV is the CBS affiliate for the Harrisburg, PA area. The station is owned by Sinclair Broadcast Group, Inc. WHP-TV broadcasts locally on channel 21.
TELEVISION STATION

WHPX-TV
32175

Owner: ION Media Networks
Editorial: 3 Shaws Cv Ste 226, New London, Connecticut 06320-4948 **Tel:** 1 860 444-2626.
Profile: WHPX-TV is the ION Television affiliate in the Hartford-New Haven, CT market. The station is owned by ION Media Networks. WHPX-TV broadcasts locally on channel 26.
TELEVISION STATION

WHSG2-TV
610708

Owner: Trinity Broadcasting Network
Editorial: 1550 Agape Way, Decatur, Georgia 30035-1341 **Tel:** 1 404 288-1156.
Email: whsg@tbn.org
Profile: WHSG2-TV is a multicast of WHSG-TV. A multicast channel is a separate channel that shares the bandwith of the main station but can air unique programming. WHSG2-TV airs programming from The Church Channel in the Atlanta market. The station is owned by Trinity Broadcasting Network. WHSG2-TV broadcasts locally on channel 63.2.
TELEVISION STATION

WHSG3-TV
610714

Owner: Trinity Broadcasting Network
Editorial: 1550 Agape Way, Decatur, Georgia 30035-1341 **Tel:** 1 404 288-1156.
Email: whsg@tbn.org
Profile: WHSG3-TV is a multicast of WHSG-TV. A multicast channel is a separate channel that shares the bandwith of the main station but can air unique programming. WHSG3-TV airs programming from JUICE TV and Smile of a Child TV in the Atlanta market. The station is owned by Trinity Broadcasting Network. WHSG3-TV broadcasts locally on channel 63.3. The station does not produce a newscast and is non-commercial.
TELEVISION STATION

WHSG4-TV
610719

Owner: Trinity Broadcasting Network
Editorial: 1550 Agape Way, Decatur, Georgia 30035-1341 **Tel:** 1 404 288-1156.
Email: whsg@tbn.org
Profile: WHSG4-TV is a multicast of WHSG-TV. A multicast channel is a separate channel that shares the bandwith of the main station but can air unique programming. WHSG4-TV airs programming from Enlace USA in the Atlanta market. The station is owned by Trinity Broadcasting Network. WHSG4-TV broadcasts locally on channel 63.4. The station does not produce a newscast and is non-commercial.
TELEVISION STATION

WHSG5-TV
610724

Owner: Trinity Broadcasting Network
Editorial: 1550 Agape Way, Decatur, Georgia 30035-1341 **Tel:** 1 404 288-1156.
Email: whsg@tbn.org
Profile: WHSG5-TV is a multicast of WHSG-TV. A multicast channel is a separate channel that shares the bandwith of the main station but can air unique programming. WHSG5-TV airs programming from TBN Salsa in the Atlanta market. The station is owned by Trinity Broadcasting Network. WHSG5-TV broadcasts locally on channel 63.5. The station does not produce a newscast and is non-commercial.
TELEVISION STATION

WHSG-TV
32396

Owner: Trinity Broadcasting Network
Editorial: 1550 Agape Way, Decatur, Georgia 30035-1341 **Tel:** 1 404 288-1156.
Email: whsg@tbn.org
Profile: WHSG-TV is a Trinity Broadcasting Network affiliate for the Atlanta market. The station is owned by Trinity Broadcasting Network. WHSG-TV broadcasts locally on channel 63.
TELEVISION STATION

WHSV2-TV
797048

Owner: Gray Television Inc.
Editorial: 50 N Main St, Harrisonburg, Virginia 22802-3719 **Tel:** 1 540 433-9191.
Web site: http://www.whsv.com/thevalleysfox/home
Profile: WHSV-TV is a multicast channel of WHSV-TV. A multicast channel is a separate channel that shares the bandwith of the main station but can air unique programming. WHSV2-TV is the Fox Network for the Harrisonburg, VA market. The station is owned by Gray Television Inc. WHSV2-TV broadcasts locally on channel 3.2.
TELEVISION STATION

WHSV-TV
31889

Owner: Gray Television, Inc.
Editorial: 50 N Main St, Harrisonburg, Virginia 22802-3719 **Tel:** 1 540 433-9191.
Email: newsroom@whsv.com
Web site: http://www.whsv.com
Profile: WHSV-TV is the ABC affiliate for the Harrisonburg, VA market. The station is owned by Gray Television Inc. WHSV-TV broadcasts locally on channel 3.
TELEVISION STATION

WHTM2-TV
620984

Owner: Sinclair Broadcast Group, Inc.
Editorial: 3235 Hoffman St, Harrisburg, Pennsylvania 17110-2226 **Tel:** 1 717 236-2727.
Web site: http://www.whtm.com
Profile: WHTM2-TV is a multicast of WHTM-TV. A multicast channel is a separate channel that shares the bandwith of the main station but can air unique programming. WHTM2-TV airs programming from Retro Television Network in the Harrisburg, PA market. The station is owned by Sinclair Broadcast Group, Inc. WHTM2-TV broadcasts locally on channel 27.2.
TELEVISION STATION

WHTM3-TV
620986

Owner: Sinclair Broadcast Group, Inc.
Editorial: 3235 Hoffman St, Harrisburg, Pennsylvania 17110-2226 **Tel:** 1 717 236-1444.
Web site: http://www.whtm.com
Profile: WHTM3-TV is a multicast of WHTM-TV. A multicast channel is a separate channel that shares the bandwith of the main station but can air unique programming. WHTM3-TV airs local weather programming from The AccuWeather Channel in the Harrisburg, PA market. The station is owned by Sinclair Broadcast Group, Inc. WHTM3-TV broadcasts locally on channel 27.3.
TELEVISION STATION

WHTM-TV
31890

Owner: Sinclair Broadcast Group, Inc.
Editorial: 3235 Hoffman St, Harrisburg, Pennsylvania 17110-2226 **Tel:** 1 717 236-2727.
Email: news@abc27.com
Web site: http://www.abc27.com
Profile: WHTM-TV is the ABC affiliate for the Harrisburg, PA market. The station is owned by Sinclair Broadcast Group, Inc. WHTM-TV broadcasts locally on channel 27.
TELEVISION STATION

WHTN-TV
31891

Owner: Christian Television Network
Editorial: 9582 Lebanon Rd, Mount Juliet, Tennessee 37122 **Tel:** 1 615 754-0039.
Web site: http://www.ctntv.org
Profile: WHTN-TV is an independent affiliate for the Nashville, TN market. The station is owned by Christian Television Network. WHTN-TV broadcasts locally on channel 38.
TELEVISION STATION

WHYY2-TV
610928

Owner: WHYY Inc.
Editorial: Independence Mall West, 150 N 6th St, Philadelphia, Pennsylvania 19106 **Tel:** 1 215 351-1200.
Email: newsroom@whyy.org
Web site: http://www.whyy.org
Profile: WHYY2-TV is a multicast of WHYY-TV. A multicast channel is a separate channel that shares the bandwith of the main station but can air unique programming. WHYY2-TV airs programming from Y Arts to the Philadelphia market. The station is owned by WHYY Inc. WHYYT2-TV broadcasts locally on channel 12.2.
TELEVISION STATION

WHYY3-TV
610934

Owner: WHYY Inc.
Editorial: Independence Mall West, 150 N 6th St, Philadelphia, Pennsylvania 19106 **Tel:** 1 215 351-1200.
Email: newsroom@whyy.org
Web site: http://www.whyy.org
Profile: WHYY3-TV is a multicast of WHYY-TV. A multicast channel is a separate channel that shares the bandwith of the main station but can air unique programming. WHYY3-TV airs programming from Y Info to the Philadelphia market. The station is owned by WHYY Inc. WHYY3-TV broadcasts locally on channel 12.3.
TELEVISION STATION

WHYY-TV
32728

Owner: WHYY Inc.
Editorial: 150 N 6th St, Independence Mall West, Philadelphia, Pennsylvania 19106-1521
Tel: 1 215 351-1200.
Email: talkback@whyy.org
Web site: http://www.whyy.org
Profile: WHYY-TV is the local PBS affiliate for the Philadelphia market. The station is owned by WHYY Inc. WHYY broadcasts locally on channel 12.
TELEVISION STATION

WIAT2-TV
618338

Owner: Nexstar Media Group, Inc.
Editorial: 2075 Golden Crest Dr, Birmingham, Alabama 35209-1143 **Tel:** 1 205 322-4200.
Email: newsrelease@cbs42.com
Web site: http://www.cbs42.com
Profile: WIAT2-TV is a multicast of WIAT-TV. A multicast channel is a separate channel that shares the bandwith of the main station but can air unique programming. WIAT2-TV airs programming from Untamed Sports TV in the Birmingham, AL market. The station is owned by Nexstar Media Group, Inc. WIAT2-TV broadcasts locally on channel 42.2.
TELEVISION STATION

WIAT3-TV
618347

Owner: Nexstar Media Group, Inc.
Editorial: 2075 Golden Crest Dr, Birmingham, Alabama 35209-1143 **Tel:** 1 205 322-4200.
Email: newsrelease@cbs42.com
Web site: http://www.cbs42.com
Profile: WIAT3-TV is a multicast of WIAT-TV. A multicast channel is a separate channel that shares the bandwith of the main station but can air unique programming. WIAT3-TV airs programming from CBS 42 Weather in the Birmingham, AL market. The station is owned by Nexstar Media Group, Inc. WIAT3-TV broadcasts locally on channel 42.3.
TELEVISION STATION

WIAT-TV
31755

Owner: Nexstar Media Group, Inc.
Editorial: 2075 Golden Crest Dr, Birmingham, Alabama 35209-1143 **Tel:** 1 205 322-4200.
Email: newstip@wiat.com
Web site: http://wiat.com
Profile: WIAT-TV is the CBS affiliate for the Birmingham, AL market. The station is owned by Nexstar Media Group, Inc. WIAT-TV broadcasts locally on channel 42.
TELEVISION STATION

WIBW-TV 31892
Owner: Gray Television, Inc.
Editorial: 631 SW Commerce Pl, Topeka, Kansas 66615-1234 **Tel:** 1 785 272-6397.
Email: 13news@wibw.com
Web site: http://www.wibw.com
Profile: WIBW-TV is the CBS affiliate for the Topeka, KS market. The station is owned by Gray Television Inc. WIBW-TV broadcasts locally on channel 13.
TELEVISION STATION

WICD-TV 31893
Owner: Sinclair Broadcast Group, Inc.
Editorial: 250 S Country Fair Dr, Champaign, Illinois 61821-2920 **Tel:** 1 217 351-8500.
Email: comments@wicd15.com
Web site: http://www.wicd15.com
Profile: WICD-TV is the ABC affiliate for the Springfield-Decatur market. The station is owned by Sinclair Broadcast Group, Inc. WICD-TV broadcasts locally on channel 15. This station does not produce any newscasts.
TELEVISION STATION

WICS-TV 31894
Owner: Sinclair Broadcast Group, Inc.
Editorial: 2680 E Cook St, Springfield, Illinois 62703-1902 **Tel:** 1 217 753-5620.
Email: news@wics.com
Web site: http://www.wics.com
Profile: WICS-TV is the ABC affiliate for the Springfield-Decatur, IL market. The station is owned by Sinclair Broadcast Group, Inc. WICS-TV broadcasts locally on channel 20.
TELEVISION STATION

WICU-TV 31895
Owner: SJL Communications
Editorial: 3514 State St, Erie, Pennsylvania 16508-2834 **Tel:** 1 814 454-5201.
Email: news@wicu12.com
Web site: http://www.erietvnews.com
Profile: WICU-TV is the NBC affiliate for the Erie, PA viewing area. The station is owned by SJL Communications. WICU-TV broadcasts locally on channel 12.
TELEVISION STATION

WICZ-TV 31896
Owner: Northwest Broadcasting
Editorial: 4600 Vestal Pkwy E, Vestal, New York 13850-3687 **Tel:** 1 607 770-4040.
Email: fox40news@wicz.com
Web site: http://www.wicz.com
Profile: WICZ-TV is the FOX network affiliate for the Binghamton, NY market. The station is owned by Northwest Broadcasting. WICZ-TV broadcasts locally on channel 40.
TELEVISION STATION

WIFR-TV 31897
Owner: Gray Television, Inc.
Editorial: 2523 N Meridian Rd, Rockford, Illinois 61101-2237 **Tel:** 1 815 987-5300.
Email: news@wifr.com
Web site: http://www.wifr.com
Profile: WIFR-TV is the CBS network affiliate for the Rockford, IL market. The station is owned by Grey Television, Inc. WIFR-TV broadcasts locally on channel 23.
TELEVISION STATION

WIFS-TV 32631
Owner: Byrne Acquisition Group
Editorial: 2814 Syene Rd, Madison, Wisconsin 53713-3204 **Tel:** 1 608 270-5700.
Web site: http://wi57.tv
Profile: WIFS-TV is an independent station for the Madison, WI market. The station is owned by Byrne Acquisition Group. WIFS-TV broadcasts locally on channel 57. PSA's on data DVD or flash drive are accepted, send via mail.
TELEVISION STATION

WILM2-TV 876041
Owner: Capitol Broadcasting Company
Editorial: 333 Wrightsville Ave, Ste C, Wilmington, North Carolina 28403 **Tel:** 1 910 332-7002.
Profile: WILM2-TV is a multicast channel of WILM-TV. A multicast channel is a separate channel that shares the bandwidth of the main station but can air unique programming. WLIM2-TV is the MeTv Network for the Wilmington, NC market. The station is owned by Capitol Broadcasting Company. WILM2-TV broadcasts locally on channel 10.2.
TELEVISION STATION

WILM-TV 63115
Owner: Capitol Broadcasting Company
Editorial: 3333 Wrightsville Ave Ste G, Wilmington, North Carolina 28403-4115 **Tel:** 1 910 332-7002.
Web site: http://www.videoonline.com
Profile: WILM-TV is the CBS affiliate for the Wilmington, NC market. The station is owned by Capitol Broadcasting Company. WILM-TV broadcasts locally on channel 10. The station will end it's CBS affiliation on January 1, 2017.
TELEVISION STATION

WILX-TV 31901
Owner: Gray Television, Inc.
Editorial: 500 American Rd, Lansing, Michigan 48911-6968 **Tel:** 1 517 393-0110.
Email: news@wilx.com
Web site: http://www.wilx.com
Profile: WILX-TV is the NBC affiliate for the Lansing, MI market. The station is owned by Gray Television, Inc. WILX-TV broadcasts locally on channel 10.
TELEVISION STATION

WINK-TV 31902
Owner: Fort Myers Broadcasting Co.
Editorial: 2824 Palm Beach Blvd, Fort Myers, Florida 33916-1503 **Tel:** 1 239 334-1111.
Email: desk@winknews.com
Web site: http://www.winknews.com
Profile: WINK-TV is the CBS network affiliate for the Fort Myers-Naples, FL market. The station is owned by Fort Myers Broadcasting Co. WINK-TV broadcasts locally on channel 11.
TELEVISION STATION

WINM-TV 32426
Owner: Tri-State Christian TV
Editorial: 3632 Butler Rd, Fort Wayne, Indiana 46808-3815 **Tel:** 1 260 483-9809.
Email: winm@tct.tv
Web site: http://www.tct.tv/index.php
Profile: WINM-TV is an independent station for the Fort Wayne, IN market. The station is owned by Tri-State Christian TV. WINM-TV broadcasts locally on channel 63.
TELEVISION STATION

WINP-TV 32067
Owner: ION Media Networks
Editorial: 4802 5th Ave, Pittsburgh, Pennsylvania 15213-2942 **Tel:** 1 412 622-6426.
Web site: http://www.ionmedianetworks.com
Profile: WINP-TV is the ION affiliate in the Pittsburgh, PA market. The station is owned by ION Media Networks. WQEX-TV broadcasts to the Pittsburgh aread on channel 16.
TELEVISION STATION

WIPX-TV 32527
Owner: ION Media Networks
Editorial: 2441 Production Dr, Ste 104, Indianapolis, Indiana 46241-4929 **Tel:** 1 317 486-0633.
Profile: WIPX-TV is the ION Television affiliate for the Indianapolis market. The station is owned by ION Media Networks. WIPX-TV broadcasts locally on channel 63.
TELEVISION STATION

WIS2-TV 688526
Owner: Raycom Media Inc.
Editorial: 1111 Bull St, Columbia, South Carolina 29201-3722 **Tel:** 1 803 799-1010.
Email: countonwis@wistv.com
Web site: http://wistv.com
Profile: WIS2-TV is a multicast channel of WIS-TV. A multicast channel is a separate channel that shares the bandwith of the main station but can air unique programming. WIS2-TV is the ThisTV for the Columbia, SC market. The station is owned by Raycom Media Inc. WIS2-TV broadcasts locally on channel 10.2.
TELEVISION STATION

WISC-TV 31904
Owner: Television Wisconsin Inc.
Editorial: 7025 Raymond Rd, Madison, Wisconsin 53719-5053 **Tel:** 1 608 271-4321.
Email: tips@channel3000.com
Web site: http://www.channel3000.com
Profile: WISC-TV is the CBS affiliate for the Madison, WI market. The station is owned by Television Wisconsin Inc. WISC-TV broadcasts locally on channel 3.
TELEVISION STATION

WISE-TV 31943
Owner: SagamoreHill Broadcasting
Editorial: 3401 Butler Rd, Fort Wayne, Indiana 46808-3811 **Tel:** 1 260 471-9087.
Email: info@fortwaynecw.com
Web site: http://yourcwtv.com/partners/fortwayne
Profile: WISE-TV is the CW affiliate for the Fort Wayne, IN market. The station is owned by SagamoreHill Broadcasting. WISE-TV broadcasts locally on channel 33.
TELEVISION STATION

WISH2-TV 612793
Owner: Nexstar Media Group, Inc.
Editorial: 1950 N Meridian St, Indianapolis, Indiana 46202-1304 **Tel:** 1 317 923-8888.
Email: newsdesk@wishtv.com
Web site: http://www.wishtv.com
Profile: WISH2-TV is a multicast of WISH-TV. A multicast channel is a separate channel that shares the bandwith of the main station but can air unique programming. WISH2-TV airs programming from Local Weather Station in the Indianapolis market. The station is owned by Nexstar Media Group, Inc. WISH2-TV broadcasts locally on channel 8.2.
TELEVISION STATION

WISH3-TV 612796
Owner: Nexstar Media Group, Inc.
Editorial: 1950 N Meridian St, Indianapolis, Indiana 46202-1304 **Tel:** 1 317 923-8888.
Email: newsdesk@wishtv.com
Web site: http://www.wishtv.com
Profile: WISH3-TV is a multicast of WISH-TV. A multicast channel is a separate channel that shares the bandwith of the main station but can air unique programming. WISH3-TV airs programming from the Justice Network. The station is owned by Nexstar Media Group, Inc. WISH3-TV broadcasts locally on channel 8.3.
TELEVISION STATION

WISH-TV 31905
Owner: Nexstar Media Group, Inc.
Editorial: 1950 N Meridian St, Indianapolis, Indiana 46202-1304 **Tel:** 1 317 923-8888.
Email: newsdesk@wishtv.com
Web site: http://www.wishtv.com
Profile: WISH-TV is the CW affiliate station for the Indianapolis market. The station is owned by Nexstar Media Group, Inc. WISH-TV broadcasts locally on channel 8.
TELEVISION STATION

WISN-TV 31906
Owner: Hearst Television Inc.
Editorial: 759 N 19th St, Milwaukee, Wisconsin 53233-2126 **Tel:** 1 414 937-1212.
Email: wisntvnews@hearst.com
Web site: http://www.wisn.com
Profile: WISN-TV is a ABC affiliate for the Milwaukee, WI market. The station is owned by Hearst Television Inc. WISN-TV broadcasts locally on channel 12.
TELEVISION STATION

WIS-TV 31903
Owner: Raycom Media Inc.
Editorial: 1111 Bull St, Columbia, South Carolina 29201-3722 **Tel:** 1 803 799-1010.
Email: countonwis@wistv.com
Web site: http://www.wistv.com
Profile: WIS-TV is the NBC affiliate for the Columbia, SC, market. It is owned by Raycom Media Inc. WIS-TV broadcasts locally on channel 10.
TELEVISION STATION

WITF-TV 31907
Owner: WITF Inc.
Editorial: 4801 Lindle Rd, Harrisburg, Pennsylvania 17111-2444 **Tel:** 1 717 704-3000.
Email: news@witf.org
Web site: http://www.witf.org
Profile: WITF-TV is the PBS affiliate for the Harrisburg, PA area. The station is owned by WITF Inc. WITF-TV broadcasts locally on channel 33.
TELEVISION STATION

WITI2-TV 621865
Owner: Tribune Broadcasting Co.
Editorial: 9001 N Green Bay Rd, Milwaukee, Wisconsin 53209-1204 **Tel:** 1 414 355-6666.
Email: fox6news@fox6now.com
Web site: http://www.fox6now.com
Profile: WITI2-TV is a multicast channel of WITI-TV. A multicast is a separate channel that shares the bandwith of the main station but can air unique programming. WITI2-TV airs entertainment programming from Retro Television Network in the Milwaukee market. The station is owned by Tribune Broadcasting Co. WITI2-TV broadcasts locally on channel 6.2.
TELEVISION STATION

WITI-TV 31908
Owner: Tribune Broadcasting Co.
Editorial: 9001 N Green Bay Rd, Milwaukee, Wisconsin 53209-1204 **Tel:** 1 414 355-6666.
Email: fox6news@fox6now.com
Web site: http://fox6now.com
Profile: WITI-TV is the FOX affiliate for the Milwaukee market. The station is owned by Tribune Broadcasting Co. WITI-TV broadcasts locally on channel 6.
TELEVISION STATION

WITN-TV 31909
Owner: Gray Television, Inc.
Editorial: 275 E Arlington Blvd, Greenville, North Carolina 27858-5015 **Tel:** 1 252 946-3131.
Web site: http://www.witn.com
Profile: WITN-TV is the NBC affiliate for the Greenville, NC market. The station is owned by Gray Television, Inc. WITN-TV broadcasts locally on channel 7.
TELEVISION STATION

WIVB-TV 31910
Owner: Nexstar Media Group, Inc.
Editorial: 2077 Elmwood Ave, Buffalo, New York 14207-1903 **Tel:** 1 716 876-7333.
Email: newsroom@wivb.com
Web site: http://www.wivb.com
Profile: WIVB-TV is the CBS affiliate for the Buffalo, NY market. The station is owned by Nexstar Media Group, Inc. WIVB-TV broadcasts locally on channel 4.
TELEVISION STATION

WIVM-TV 354523
Owner: Lucinda DeVaul-Tonges
Editorial: 6755 Freedom Ave NW, North Canton, Ohio 44720 **Tel:** 1 330 494-9303.
Email: info@wivmtv.com
Web site: http://www.wivmtv.com
Profile: WIVM-TV is an Independent affiliate for the Cleveland market. The station is owned by Lucinda DeVaul-Tonges. WIVM-TV broadcasts locally on channel 52.
TELEVISION STATION

WIVT-TV 31992
Owner: Nexstar Broadcasting Group
Editorial: 203 Ingraham Hill Rd, Binghamton, New York 13903-5504 **Tel:** 1 607 771-3434.
Email: news@nc34.com
Web site: http://www.binghamtonhomepage.com
Profile: WIVT-TV is the ABC affiliate for the Binghamton, NY market. The station is owned by Nexstar Broadcasting Group. WIVT-TV broadcasts locally on channel 34.
TELEVISION STATION

WJAC-TV 31913
Owner: Sinclair Broadcast Group, Inc.
Editorial: 49 Old Hickory Ln, Johnstown, Pennsylvania 15905-3367 **Tel:** 1 814 255-7600.
Email: news@wjactv.com
Web site: http://www.wjactv.com
Profile: WJAC-TV is the NBC affiliate for the Johnstown-Altoona, PA. The station is owned by Sinclair Broadcast Group, Inc. WJAC-TV broadcasts locally on channel 6.
TELEVISION STATION

WJAL-TV 32239
Owner: Entravision Communications Corp.
Editorial: 262 Swamp Fox Rd, Chambersburg, Pennsylvania 17202-8882 **Tel:** 1 717 375-4000.
Web site: http://www.wjal.com
Profile: WJAL-TV is an independent station for the Chambersburg, PA area. The station is owned by Entravision Communications Corp. WJAL-TV broadcasts locally on channel 68.
TELEVISION STATION

WJAN-TV 132093
Owner: America CV Network, LLC
Editorial: 13001 NW 107th Ave, Hialeah Gardens, Florida 33018-1104 **Tel:** 1 305 592-4141.
Email: noticias41@americateve.com
Web site: http://www.americateve.com
Profile: WJAN-TV is the América Tevé network affiliate for the Miami-Fort Lauderdale, FL market. The station is owned by America CV Network, LLC. WJAN-TV broadcasts locally on channel 41.
TELEVISION STATION

WJAR-TV 31914
Owner: Nexstar Media Group, Inc.
Editorial: 23 Kenney Dr, Cranston, Rhode Island 02920-4403 **Tel:** 1 401 455-9100.
Email: news@wjar.com
Web site: http://www.turnto10.com
Profile: WJAR-TV is the NBC affiliate for the Providence, RI-New Bedford, MA market. The station is owned by Nexstar Media Group, Inc. WJAR-TV broadcasts locally on channel 10.
TELEVISION STATION

WJAX-TV 32011
Owner: Cox Media Group, Inc.
Editorial: 11700 Central Pkwy Unit 2, Jacksonville, Florida 32224-2600 **Tel:** 1 904 642-3030.
Email: news@actionnewsjax.com
Web site: http://www.actionnewsjax.com
Profile: WJAX-TV is the CBS affiliate for the Jacksonville, FL market. The station is owned by Cox Media Group, Inc. WJAX-TV broadcasts locally on channel 47.
TELEVISION STATION

WJBF-TV 31915
Owner: Nexstar Media Group, Inc.
Editorial: 1336 Augusta West Pkwy, Augusta, Georgia 30909-6427 **Tel:** 1 706 722-6664.
Email: producers@wjbf.com
Web site: http://www.wjbf.com
Profile: WJBF-TV is the ABC affiliate for the Augusta, GA market. The station is owned by Nexstar Media Group, Inc. WJBF-TV broadcasts locally on channel 6.
TELEVISION STATION

WJBK-TV 31916
Owner: Fox Broadcasting Company
Editorial: 16550 W 9 Mile Rd, Southfield, Michigan 48075-4705 **Tel:** 1 248 557-2000.
Email: fox2newsdesk@foxtv.com
Web site: http://www.fox2detroit.com
Profile: WJBK-TV is the FOX affiliate for the Detroit market. The station is owned by Fox Broadcasting Company. WJBK-TV broadcasts locally on channel 2.
TELEVISION STATION

WJCL-TV 31917
Owner: Hearst Television Inc.
Editorial: 1375 Chatham Pkwy Fl 3, Savannah, Georgia 31405-0301 **Tel:** 1 912 925-0022.
Email: breakingnews@wjcl.com
Web site: http://www.wjcl.com
Profile: WJCL-TV is the ABC affiliate for the Savannah, GA market. The station is owned by Hearst Television Inc. WJCL-TV broadcasts locally on channel 22.
TELEVISION STATION

WJCT2-TV 620654
Owner: WJCT Inc.
Editorial: 100 Festival Park Ave, Jacksonville, Florida 32202-1309 **Tel:** 1 904 353-7770.
Email: news@wjct.org
Web site: http://www.wjct.org
Profile: WJCT2-TV is a multicast of WJCT-TV. A multicast channel is a separate channel that shares the bandwith of the main station but can air unique programming. WJCT2-TV airs how-to, DIY, and other instructional programming from Create in the Jacksonville, FL market. The station is owned by WJCT Inc. WJCT2-TV broadcasts locally on channel 7.2.
TELEVISION STATION

WJCT3-TV 620658
Owner: WJCT Inc.
Editorial: 100 Festival Park Ave, Jacksonville, Florida 32202-1309 **Tel:** 1 904 353-7770.
Email: news@wjct.org
Web site: http://www.wjct.org
Profile: WJCT3-TV is a multicast of WJCT-TV. A multicast channel is a separate channel that shares

United States of America

the bandwith of the main station but can air unique programming. WJCT3-TV airs programming from PBS World in the Jacksonville, FL market. The station is owned by WJCT Inc. WJCT3-TV broadcasts locally on channel 7.3.
TELEVISION STATION

WJCT4-TV 620660
Owner: WJCT Inc.
Editorial: 100 Festival Park Ave, Jacksonville, Florida 32202-1309 **Tel:** 1 904 353-7770.
Email: news@wjct.org
Web site: http://www.wjct.org
Profile: WJCT4-TV is a multicast of WJCT-TV. A multicast channel is a separate channel that shares the bandwith of the main station but can air unique programming. WJCT4-TV airs programming from WJCT More! and The Florida Channel in the Jacksonville, FL market. The station is owned by WJCT Inc. WJCT4-TV broadcasts locally on channel 7.4.
TELEVISION STATION

WJCT5-TV 620664
Owner: WJCT Inc.
Editorial: 100 Festival Park Ave, Jacksonville, Florida 32202-1309 **Tel:** 1 904 353-7770.
Email: news@wjct.org
Web site: http://www.wjct.org
Profile: WJCT5-TV is a multicast of WJCT-TV. A multicast channel is a separate channel that shares the bandwith of the main station but can air unique programming. WJCT5-TV airs programming from The Florida Knowledge Network and WJCT Informational in the Jacksonville, FL market. The station is owned by WJCT Inc. WJCT5-TV broadcasts locally on channel 7.5.
TELEVISION STATION

WJCT-TV 31918
Owner: WJCT Inc.
Editorial: 100 Festival Park Ave, Jacksonville, Florida 32202-1309 **Tel:** 1 904 353-7770.
Email: news@wjct.org
Web site: http://www.wjct.org
Profile: WJCT-TV is the PBS affiliate for Jacksonville, FL market. The station is owned by WJCT Inc. WJCT-TV broadcasts locally on channel 7.
TELEVISION STATION

WJEB2-TV 619773
Owner: Jacksonville Broadcasting, Inc.
Editorial: 3101 Emerson Expy, Jacksonville, Florida 32207-4965 **Tel:** 1 904 399-8413.
Email: prayer@wjeb.org
Web site: http://www.wjeb.org
Profile: WJEB2-TV is a multicast of WJEB-TV. A multicast channel is a separate channel that shares the bandwith of the main station but can air unique programming. WJEB2-TV airs religious programming from The Church Channel in the Jacksonville, FL market. The station is owned by Jacksonville Broadcasting, Inc. WJEB2-TV broadcasts locally on channel 59.2.
TELEVISION STATION

WJEB3-TV 619776
Owner: Jacksonville Broadcasting, Inc.
Editorial: 3101 Emerson Expy, Jacksonville, Florida 32207-4965 **Tel:** 1 904 399-8413.
Email: prayer@wjeb.org
Web site: http://www.wjeb.org
Profile: WJEB3-TV is a multicast of WJEB-TV. A multicast channel is a separate channel that shares the bandwith of the main station but can air unique programming. WJEB3-TV airs Christian music videos from JCTV in the Jacksonville, FL market. The station is owned by Jacksonville Broadcasting, Inc. WJEB3-TV broadcasts locally on channel 59.3.
TELEVISION STATION

WJEB4-TV 619778
Owner: Jacksonville Broadcasting, Inc.
Editorial: 3101 Emerson Expy, Jacksonville, Florida 32207-4965 **Tel:** 1 904 399-8413.
Email: prayer@wjeb.org
Web site: http://www.wjeb.org
Profile: WJEB4-TV is a multicast of WJEB-TV. A multicast channel is a separate channel that shares the bandwith of the main station but can air unique programming. WJEB4-TV airs Hispanic Christian programming from Enlace USA in the Jacksonville, FL market. The station is owned by Jacksonville Broadcasting, Inc. WJEB4-TV broadcasts locally on channel 59.4.
TELEVISION STATION

WJEB5-TV 619779
Owner: Jacksonville Broadcasting, Inc.
Editorial: 3101 Emerson Expy, Jacksonville, Florida 32207-4965 **Tel:** 1 904 399-8413.
Email: prayer@wjeb.org
Web site: http://www.wjeb.org
Profile: WJEB5-TV is a multicast of WJEB-TV. A multicast channel is a separate channel that shares the bandwith of the main station but can air unique programming. WJEB5-TV airs children's Christian programming from Smile of a Child in the Jacksonville, FL market. The station is owned by Jacksonville Broadcasting, Inc. WJEB5-TV broadcasts locally on channel 59.5.
TELEVISION STATION

WJEB-TV 32369
Owner: Jacksonville Broadcasting, Inc.
Editorial: 3101 Emerson Expy, Jacksonville, Florida 32207-4965 **Tel:** 1 904 399-8413.
Email: prayer@wjeb.org
Web site: http://www.wjeb.org

Profile: WJEB-TV is the Trinity Broadcasting Network affiliate for the Jacksonville, FL market. The station is owned by Jacksonville Broadcasting, Inc. WJEB-TV broadcasts locally on channel 59.
TELEVISION STATION

WJET-TV 31919
Owner: Nexstar Broadcasting Group
Editorial: 8455 Peach St, Erie, Pennsylvania 16509-4791 **Tel:** 1 814 864-2400.
Email: actionnews24@wjettv.com
Web site: http://www.yourerie.com
Profile: WJET-TV is the ABC network affiliate for the Erie, PA market. The station is owned by Nexstar Broadcasting Group. WJET-TV broadcasts locally on channel 24.
TELEVISION STATION

WJFB-TV 32500
Owner: Bryant Broadcasting Inc.
Editorial: 200 E Spring St, Lebanon, Tennessee 37087-3633 **Tel:** 1 615 444-8206.
Profile: WJFB-TV is the independent affiliate for the Nashville, TN market. The station is owned by Bryant Broadcasting Inc. WJFB-TV broadcasts locally on channel 66.
TELEVISION STATION

WJFW-TV 31920
Owner: Rockfleet Broadcasting Inc.
Editorial: 3217 County G, Rhinelander, Wisconsin 54501-3900 **Tel:** 1 715 365-8812.
Email: email@wjfw.com
Web site: http://www.wjfw.com
Profile: WJFW-TV is the NBC affiliate for the Wausau, Wisconsin market. The station is owned by Rockfleet Broadcasting Inc. WJFW-TV broadcasts locally on channel 12.
TELEVISION STATION

WJGV-TV 32526
Owner: Pentecostal Revival Assoc. Inc
Editorial: 115 Harrell Ln, Palatka, Florida 32177-7781 **Tel:** 1 386 325-6323.
Email: gospelvisiontv48@yahoo.com
Web site: http://www.gospelvisiontv.com
Profile: WJGV-TV is an independent station for the Jacksonville, FL market. The station is owned by Pentecostal Revival Assoc. Inc. WJGV-TV broadcasts locally on channel 48.
TELEVISION STATION

WJHG-TV 31921
Owner: Gray Television, Inc.
Editorial: 8195 Front Beach Rd, Panama City, Florida 32407-4820 **Tel:** 1 850 234-7777.
Email: news@wjhg.com
Web site: http://www.wjhg.com
Profile: WJHG-TV is the NBC affiliate for Panama City, FL market. The station is owned by Gray Television, Inc. WJHG-TV broadcasts locally on channel 7.
TELEVISION STATION

WJHL-TV 31922
Owner: Nexstar Media Group, Inc.
Editorial: 338 E Main St, Johnson City, Tennessee 37601-5730 **Tel:** 1 423 926-2151.
Email: news@wjhl.com
Web site: http://www.wjhl.com
Profile: WJHL-TV is the CBS affiliate for the Tri-Cities market in Tennessee. The station is owned by Nexstar Media Group, Inc. WJHL-TV broadcasts locally on channel 11.
TELEVISION STATION

WJKT-TV 32897
Owner: Nexstar Broadcasting Group
Editorial: 231 Oill Well Rd Apt A1, Jackson, Tennessee 38305-8038 **Tel:** 1 731 736-2172.
Email: newsdesk@localmemphis.com
Web site: http://www.localmemphis.com
Profile: WJKT-TV is the FOX affiliate for the Jackson, TN market. The station is owned by Nexstar Broadcasting Group. WJKT-TV broadcasts locally on channel 16.
TELEVISION STATION

WJLA2-TV 607929
Owner: Sinclair Broadcast Group, Inc.
Editorial: 1100 Wilson Blvd Fl 6, Arlington, Virginia 22209-2249 **Tel:** 1 703 236-9552.
Email: newsdesk@wjla.com
Web site: http://www.accuweather.com
Profile: WJLA2-TV is an independent affiliate for the Washington, D.C. market. The station is owned by Sinclair Broadcast Group, Inc. WJLA2-TV broadcasts locally on channel 7.2. The station airs programming from the Live Well Network. WJLA2-TV is a multicast channel of WJLA-TV. A multicast channel is a separate channel that shares the bandwidth of the main station but can air unique programming.
TELEVISION STATION

WJLA3-TV 607933
Owner: Sinclair Broadcast Group, Inc.
Editorial: 1100 Wilson Blvd Fl 6, Arlington, Virginia 22209-2249 **Tel:** 1 703 236-9552.
Email: newsdesk@wjla.com
Web site: http://www.myretrotv.com
Profile: WJLA3-TV is an independent affiliate for the Washington, D.C. market. The station is owned by Sinclair Broadcast Group, Inc. WJLA3-TV broadcasts locally on channel 7.3. The station airs programming from the Live Well Network. On July 1, WJLA3-TV will launch programming from the Live Well Network. WJLA3-TV is a multicast channel of WJLA-TV. A multicast channel is a separate channel that shares

the bandwidth of the main station but can air unique programming.
TELEVISION STATION

WJLA-TV 31926
Owner: Sinclair Broadcast Group, Inc.
Editorial: 1100 Wilson Blvd Fl 6, Arlington, Virginia 22209-2249 **Tel:** 1 703 236-9552.
Email: newsdesk@wjla.com
Web site: http://www.wjla.com
Profile: WJLA-TV is the ABC affiliate for the Washington, D.C. market. The station is owned by Sinclair Broadcast Group, Inc. WJLA-TV broadcasts locally on channel 7. Press releases can be sent via the main email at newsdesk@wjla.com or at tips@wjla.com.
TELEVISION STATION

WJRT-TV 31928
Owner: Gray Television
Editorial: 2302 Lapeer Rd, Flint, Michigan 48503-4221 **Tel:** 1 810 233-3130.
Email: abc12news@abc12.com
Web site: http://www.abc12.com
Profile: WJRT-TV is the ABC affiliate for the Flint, MI market. The station is owned by Gray Television. WJRT-TV broadcasts locally on channel 12.
TELEVISION STATION

WJTC-TV 31930
Owner: Sinclair Broadcast Group, Inc.
Editorial: 661 Azalea Rd, Mobile, Alabama 36609-1515 **Tel:** 1 251 602-1513.
Web site: http://www.utv44.com
Profile: WJTC-TV is an independent station for the Mobile, AL market. The station is owned by Sinclair Broadcast Group, Inc. WJTC-TV broadcasts locally on channel 44.
TELEVISION STATION

WJTS-TV 32408
Owner: DCBroadcasting Inc.
Editorial: 458 3rd Ave, Jasper, Indiana 47546-3533 **Tel:** 1 812 482-2727.
Email: news@wjts.tv
Web site: http://www.wjts.tv
Profile: WJTS-TV is an independent station for the Evansville, IN market. The station is owned by DCBroadcasting Inc. WJTS-TV broadcasts locally on channel 18.
TELEVISION STATION

WJTV-TV 31931
Owner: Nexstar Media Group, Inc.
Editorial: 1820 Tv Rd, Jackson, Mississippi 39204-4148 **Tel:** 1 601 372-6311.
Web site: http://www.wjtv.com
Profile: WJTV-TV is the CBS affiliate for the Jackson, MS market. The station is owned by Nexstar Media Group, Inc. WJTV-TV broadcasts locally on channel 12.
TELEVISION STATION

WJW-TV 31925
Owner: Tribune Broadcasting Co.
Editorial: 5800 S Marginal Rd, Cleveland, Ohio 44103-1040 **Tel:** 1 216 432-4240.
Email: tips@fox8.com
Web site: http://www.fox8.com
Profile: WJW-TV is the FOX affiliate for the Cleveland market. The station is owned by Tribune Broadcasting Co. WJW-TV broadcasts locally on channel 8.
TELEVISION STATION

WJXT3-TV 620035
Owner: Graham Media Group
Editorial: 4 Broadcast Pl, Jacksonville, Florida 32207-8613 **Tel:** 1 904 399-4000.
Web site: http://www.news4jax.com
Profile: WJXT3-TV is a multicast of WJXT-TV. A multicast channel is a separate channel that shares the bandwith of the main station but can air unique programming. WJXT3-TV airs Hispanic programming from LATV to the Jacksonville, FL market. The station is owned by Graham Media Group. WJXT3-TV broadcasts locally on channel 4.3.
TELEVISION STATION

WJXT-TV 31933
Owner: Graham Media Group
Editorial: 4 Broadcast Pl, Jacksonville, Florida 32207-8613 **Tel:** 1 904 399-4000.
Email: producer@wjxt.com
Web site: http://www.news4jax.com
Profile: WJXT-TV is an independent affiliate for the Jacksonville, FL market. The station is owned by Graham Media Group. WJXT-TV broadcasts locally on channel 4.
TELEVISION STATION

WJXX2-TV 618966
Owner: TEGNA Inc.
Editorial: 1070 E Adams St, Jacksonville, Florida 32202-1902 **Tel:** 1 904 354-1212.
Email: news@firstcoastnews.com
Web site: http://www.firstcoastnews.com
Profile: WJXX2-TV is a multicast of WJXX-TV. A multicast channel is a separate channel that shares the bandwith of the main station but can air unique programming. WJXX2-TV airs 24 hours weather programming from First Coast News Weather in the Jacksonville, FL market. The station is owned by TEGNA Inc. WJXX2-TV broadcasts locally on channel 25.2.
TELEVISION STATION

WJXX-TV 32542
Owner: TEGNA Inc.
Editorial: 1070 E Adams St, Jacksonville, Florida 32202-1902 **Tel:** 1 904 354-1212.
Email: newstips@firstcoastnews.com
Web site: http://www.firstcoastnews.com
Profile: WJXX-TV is the ABC network affiliate for the Jacksonville, FL market. The station is owned by TEGNA Inc. WJXX-TV broadcasts locally on channel 25.
TELEVISION STATION

WJYL-TV 354817
Owner: Celebration Ministries Inc.
Tel: 1 812 949-9595.
Email: prayer@wjyl.org
Web site: http://www.wjyl.org
Profile: WJYL-TV is a Trinity Broadcasting Network affiliate for the Louisville, KY market. The station is owned by Celebration Ministries Inc. WJYL-TV broadcasts locally on channel 45.
TELEVISION STATION

WJYS-TV 32447
Owner: Jovon Broadcasting
Editorial: 18600 Oak Park Ave, Tinley Park, Illinois 60477-3980 **Tel:** 1 708 633-0001.
Web site: http://www.wjys.tv
Profile: WJYS-TV is an independent station for the Chicago market. The station is owned by Jovon Broadcasting. WJYS-TV airs locally on channel 62.
TELEVISION STATION

WJZ-TV 31934
Owner: CBS Television Stations
Editorial: 3725 Malden Ave, Baltimore, Maryland 21211-1322 **Tel:** 1 410 466-0013.
Email: newsroom@wjz.com
Web site: http://baltimore.cbslocal.com
Profile: WJZ-TV is the CBS network affiliate for the Baltimore market. The station is owned by CBS Television Stations. WJZ-TV broadcasts locally on channel 13.
TELEVISION STATION

WJZY2-TV 763548
Owner: Fox Television Stations
Editorial: 3501 Performance Rd, Charlotte, North Carolina 28214-9056
Profile: WJZY2-TV is a multicast channel of WJZY-TV. A multicast channel is a separate channel that shares the bandwidth of the main station but can air unique programming. WJZY2-TV is the local Antenna TV affiliate for the Charlotte, NC market. The station is owned by Fox Television Stations.
TELEVISION STATION

WJZY-TV 32245
Owner: Fox Television Stations
Editorial: 3501 Performance Rd, Charlotte, North Carolina 28214-9056 **Tel:** 1 704 398-0046.
Email: newstips@myfoxcarolinas.com
Web site: http://www.fox46charlotte.com
Profile: WJZY-TV is the FOX affiliate for the Charlotte, NC area. The station is owned by Fox Television Stations. WJZY-TV broadcasts locally on channel 46.
TELEVISION STATION

WKBD-TV 31937
Owner: CBS Television Stations
Editorial: 26905 W 11 Mile Rd, Southfield, Michigan 48033 **Tel:** 1 248 355-7000.
Web site: http://cwdetroit.cbslocal.com
Profile: WKBD-TV is the CW affiliate for the Detroit market. The station is owned by CBS Television Stations. WKBD-TV broadcasts locally on channel 50.
TELEVISION STATION

WKBN-TV 31938
Owner: Nexstar Media Group, Inc.
Editorial: 3930 Sunset Blvd, Youngstown, Ohio 44512-1307 **Tel:** 1 330 782-1144.
Email: assignment@wkbn.com
Web site: http://www.wkbn.com
Profile: WKBN-TV is the CBS affiliate for the Youngstown, OH market. The station is owned by Nexstar Media Group, Inc. WKBN-TV broadcasts locally on channel 27.
TELEVISION STATION

WKBT-TV 31939
Owner: QueenB Television LLC
Editorial: 141 6Th St S, La Crosse, Wisconsin 54601-4153 **Tel:** 1 608 782-4678.
Email: news8@wkbt.com
Web site: http://www.news8000.com
Profile: WKBT-TV is the CBS affiliate for the La Crosse, WI market. The station is owned by QueenB Television LLC. WKBT-TV broadcasts locally on channel 8.
TELEVISION STATION

WKBW-TV 31940
Owner: E.W. Scripps Co.
Editorial: 7 Broadcast Plz, Buffalo, New York 14202-2611 **Tel:** 1 716 845-6100.
Email: news@wkbw.com
Web site: http://www.wkbw.com
Profile: WKBW-TV is the ABC affiliate for the Buffalo, NY market. The station is owned by E.W. Scripps Co. WKBW-TV broadcasts locally on channel 7.
TELEVISION STATION

WKCF2-TV 612903
Owner: Hearst Television Inc.
Editorial: 1021 N Wymore Rd, Winter Park, Florida 32789-1717 **Tel:** 1 407 645-1818.
Web site: http://www.wesh.com/cw18
Profile: WKCF2-TV is independent affiliate for the Orlando-Daytona Beach, FL market. The station is owned by Hearst Television Inc. WKCF2-TV broadcasts locally on channel 18.2. WKCF2-TV air various general entertainment programming from This TV Network. WKCF2-TV is a multicast channel of WKCF-TV. A multicast channel is a separate channel that shares the bandwidth of the main station but can air unique programming.
TELEVISION STATION

WKCF3-TV 612905
Owner: Hearst Television Inc.
Editorial: 1021 N Wymore Rd, Winter Park, Florida 32789-1717 **Tel:** 1 407 645-1818.
Web site: http://www.wesh.com/cw18
Profile: WKCF3-TV is independent affiliate for the Orlando-Daytona Beach, FL market. The station is owned by Hearst Television Inc. WKCF3-TV broadcasts locally on channel 18.3. WKCF3-TV airs Spanish programming from Estrella TV. WKCF3-TV is a multicast channel of WKCF-TV. A multicast channel is a separate channel that shares the bandwidth of the main station but can air unique programming.
TELEVISION STATION

WKCF-TV 32244
Owner: Hearst Television Inc.
Editorial: 1021 N Wymore Rd, Winter Park, Florida 32789 **Tel:** 1 407 645-1818.
Email: wesh2news@gmail.com
Web site: http://www.wesh.com/cw18
Profile: WKCF-TV is the CW network affiliate for the Orlando-Daytona Beach, FL market. The station is owned by Hearst Television Inc. WKCF-TV broadcasts locally on channel 18.
TELEVISION STATION

WKEF-TV 32250
Owner: Sinclair Broadcast Group, Inc.
Editorial: 2245 Corporate Pl, Miamisburg, Ohio 45342-1164 **Tel:** 1 937 263-4500.
Email: comments@abc22now.com
Web site: http://www.abc22now.com
Profile: WKEF-TV is the ABC affiliate for the Dayton, OH market. The station is owned by Sinclair Broadcast Group, Inc. WKEF-TV broadcasts locally on channel 22.
TELEVISION STATION

WKMG2-TV 614646
Owner: Graham Media Group
Editorial: 4466 N John Young Pkwy, Orlando, Florida 32804-1939 **Tel:** 1 407 521-1200.
Web site: http://www.clickorlando.com
Profile: WKMG2-TV is an independent affiliate for the Orlando-Daytona Beach, FL market. The station is owned by Graham Media Group. WKMG2-TV broadcasts locally on channel 6.2. The station airs programming from LATV, a Spanish bilingual music and entertainment network. WKMG2-TV is a multicast channel of WKMG-TV. A multicast channel is a separate channel that shares the bandwidth of the main station but can air unique programming.
TELEVISION STATION

WKMG-TV 31792
Owner: Graham Media Group
Editorial: 4466 N John Young Pkwy, Orlando, Florida 32804-1939 **Tel:** 1 407 521-1200.
Email: desk@wkmg.com
Web site: http://www.clickorlando.com
Profile: WKMG-TV is the CBS affiliate for the Orlando-Daytona Beach, FL market. The station is owned by Graham Media Group. WKMG-TV broadcasts locally on channel 6.
TELEVISION STATION

WKOI-TV 32307
Owner: Trinity Broadcasting Network
Editorial: 1702 S 9th St, Richmond, Indiana 47374-7203 **Tel:** 1 765 935-2390.
Profile: WKOI-TV is the Trinity Broadcasting Network (TBN) affiliate for the Richmond, IN area. The station is owned by Trinity Broadcasting Network. WKOI-TV broadcasts locally on channel 43.
TELEVISION STATION

WKOP-TV 32321
Owner: East Tennessee PBS
Editorial: 1611 E Magnolia Ave, Knoxville, Tennessee 37917-7825 **Tel:** 1 865 595-0220.
Web site: http://www.easttennesseepbs.org
Profile: WKOP-TV is the PBS affiliate for the Knoxville, TN market. The station is owned by East Tennessee PBS. WKOP-TV broadcasts locally on channel 15.
TELEVISION STATION

WKOW-TV 31945
Owner: Quincy Newspapers Inc.
Editorial: 5727 Tokay Blvd, Madison, Wisconsin 53719-1219 **Tel:** 1 608 274-1234.
Email: news@wkow.com
Web site: http://www.wkow.com
Profile: WKOW-TV is the ABC affiliate for the Madison, WI market. The station is owned by Quincy Newspapers Inc. WKOW-TV broadcasts locally on channel 27.
TELEVISION STATION

WKPT-TV 31946
Owner: Holston Valley Broadcasting Corp.
Editorial: 222 Commerce St, Kingsport, Tennessee 37660-4319 **Tel:** 1 423 246-9578.
Email: info@wkpttv.com
Web site: http://www.wkpttv.com
Profile: WKPT-TV is the ABC affiliate for the Kingsport, TN market. The station is owned by Holston Valley Broadcasting Corp. WKPT-TV broadcasts locally on channel 19.
TELEVISION STATION

WKRC2-TV 578327
Owner: Sinclair Broadcast Group, Inc.
Editorial: 1906 Highland Ave, Cincinnati, Ohio 45219-3104 **Tel:** 1 513 763-5500.
Email: local12@local12.com
Web site: http://www.cwcincinnati.com
Profile: WKRC2-TV is a multicast channel of WKRC-TV. A multicast channel is a separate channel that shares the bandwidth of the main station but can air unique programming. WKRC2-TV is the local CW affiliate on Channel 12.2 for the Cincinnati, OH market. WKRC2-TV is owned by Sinclair Broadcast Group, Inc.
TELEVISION STATION

WKRC-TV 31947
Owner: Sinclair Broadcast Group, Inc.
Editorial: 1906 Highland Ave, Cincinnati, Ohio 45219-3104 **Tel:** 1 513 763-5500.
Email: local12@local12.com
Web site: http://www.local12.com
Profile: WKRC-TV is the CBS affiliate for the Cincinnati market. The station is owned by Sinclair Broadcast Group, Inc. WKRC-TV broadcasts locally on channel 12.
TELEVISION STATION

WKRG-TV 31948
Owner: Nexstar Media Group, LLC
Editorial: 555 Broadcast Dr, Mobile, Alabama 36606-2936 **Tel:** 1 251 479-5555.
Email: news5@wkrg.com
Web site: http://www.wkrg.com
Profile: WKRG-TV is the CBS affiliate for the Mobile, AL-Pensacola, FL, market. It is owned by Nexstar Media Group, LLC. WKRG-TV broadcasts locally on channel 5.
TELEVISION STATION

WKRN2-TV 613849
Owner: Media General
Editorial: 441 Murfreesboro Pike, Nashville, Tennessee 37210-2842 **Tel:** 1 615 369-7222.
Email: programming@wkrn.com
Web site: http://www.wkrn.com
Profile: WKRN2-TV is a multicast of WKRN-TV. A multicast channel is a separate channel that shares the bandwith of the main station but can air unique programming. WKRN2-TV airs programming from the Nashville WX Channel in the Nashville, TN market. The station is owned by Media General. WHSG2-TV broadcasts locally on channel 2.2.
TELEVISION STATION

WKRN3-TV 825348
Owner: Nexstar Media Group, LLC
Editorial: 441 Murfreesboro Pike, Nashville, Tennessee 37210-2842 **Tel:** 1 615 369-7222.
Email: programming@wkrn.com
Web site: http://www.wkrn.com
Profile: WKRN3-TV is a multicast of WKRN-TV. A multicast channel is a separate channel that shares the bandwith of the main station but can air unique programming. WKRN3-TV airs programming from the Live Well Network in the Nashville, TN market. The station is owned by Nexstar Media Group, LLC.WKRN3-TV broadcasts locally on channel 2.3.
TELEVISION STATION

WKRN-TV 31949
Owner: Nexstar Media Group, LLC
Editorial: 441 Murfreesboro Pike, Nashville, Tennessee 37210-2842 **Tel:** 1 615 369-7222.
Email: news@wkrn.com
Web site: http://www.wkrn.com
Profile: WKRN-TV is the ABC affiliate for the Nashville, TN market. The station is owned by Nexstar Media Group, LLC. WKRN-TV broadcasts locally on channel 2.
TELEVISION STATION

WKTB-TV 694914
Owner: Capitol Group
Editorial: 4675 River Green Pkwy, Duluth, Georgia 30096-2583 **Tel:** 1 770 497-0076.
Email: info@telemundoatlanta.com
Web site: http://www.telemundoatlanta.com
Profile: WKTB-TV is the Telemundo affiliate serving the Duluth, GA area. The station is owned by Capitol Group. WKTB-TV airs locally on channel 47.
TELEVISION STATION

WKTC-TV 32592
Owner: Columbia Broadcasting Inc.
Editorial: 120 Pontiac Business Center Dr, Elgin, South Carolina 29045-9171 **Tel:** 1 803 419-6363.
Web site: http://www.wktctv.com
Profile: WKTC-TV is the MyNetworkTV affiliate for the Elgin, SC market. The station is owned by Columbia Broadcasting Inc. WKTC-TV broadcasts locally on channel 63
TELEVISION STATION

WKTV-TV 31950
Owner: Heartland Media
Editorial: 5936 Smith Hill Rd, Utica, New York 13502-6520 **Tel:** 1 315 733-0404.
Email: news@wktv.com
Web site: http://www.wktv.com
Profile: WKTV-TV is the NBC affiliate for the Utica, NY, market. The station is owned by Heartland Media. WKTV-TV broadcasts locally on channel 2.
TELEVISION STATION

WKYC2-TV 612906
Owner: TEGNA Inc.
Editorial: 1333 Lakeside Ave E, Cleveland, Ohio 44114-1134 **Tel:** 1 216 344-3333.
Profile: WKYC2-TV is independent affiliate for the Cleveland market. The station is owned by TEGNA Inc. WKYC-TV broadcasts locally on channel 3.2. The station broadcasts local weather information only. WKYC2-TV is a multicast channel of WKYC-TV. A multicast channel is a separate channel that shares the bandwith of the main station but can air unique programming.
TELEVISION STATION

WKYC-TV 31951
Owner: TEGNA Inc.
Editorial: 1333 Lakeside Ave E, Cleveland, Ohio 44114-1134 **Tel:** 1 216 344-3333.
Email: newsdesk@wkyc.com
Web site: http://www.wkyc.com
Profile: WKYC-TV is the NBC network affiliate for the Cleveland market. The station is owned by TEGNA Inc. WKYC-TV broadcasts locally on channel 3.
TELEVISION STATION

WKYI-TV 354665
Owner: New Albany Broadcasting Co. Inc.
Editorial: 220 Potters Ln, Clarksville, Indiana 47129-1020 **Tel:** 1 812 949-9843.
Web site: http://www.wkyitv.com
Profile: WKYI-TV is an independent station for the Louisville, KY market. The station is owned by New Albany Broadcasting Co. Inc. WKYI-TV broadcasts locally on channel 24.
TELEVISION STATION

WKYT-TV 31952
Owner: Gray Television, Inc.
Editorial: 2851 Winchester Rd, Lexington, Kentucky 40509-9581 **Tel:** 1 859 299-0411.
Email: newstip@wkyt.com
Web site: http://www.wkyt.com
Profile: WKYT-TV is the CBS affiliate for the Lexington, KY, market. The station is owned by Gray Television Inc. WKYT-TV broadcasts locally on channel 27.
TELEVISION STATION

WLAJ-TV 32330
Owner: Young Broadcasting
Editorial: 5815 S Pennsylvania Ave, Lansing, Michigan 48911-5230 **Tel:** 1 517 394-5300.
Web site: http://www.wlaj.com
Profile: WLAJ-TV is the ABC affiliate for the Lansing, MI market. The station is owned by Young Broadcasting. WLAJ-TV broadcasts locally on channel 3. Station has no news department.
TELEVISION STATION

WLAX2-TV 800804
Owner: Grant Communications
Editorial: 1305 Interchange Pl, La Crosse, Wisconsin 54603-1673 **Tel:** 1 608 781-0025.
Email: news@fox25fox48.com
Web site: http://www.fox2548.com
Profile: WLAX2-TV is a multicast channel of WLAX-TV. A multicast channel is a separate channel that shares the bandwith of the main station but can air unique programming. WLAX2-TV is the Me-TV Network for the La Crosse- Eau Claire, WI market. The station is owned by Grant Communications. WLAX2-TV broadcasts locally on channel 25.2.The station launched April 17, 2012.
TELEVISION STATION

WLAX-TV 31954
Owner: Nexstar Broadcasting Group, Inc.
Editorial: 1305 Interchange Pl, La Crosse, Wisconsin 54603-1673 **Tel:** 1 608 781-0025.
Email: news@fox25fox48.com
Web site: http://www.fox2548.com
Profile: WLAX-TV is the FOX affiliate for the La Crosse, WI market. The station is owned by Nexstar Broadcasting Group. WLAX-TV broadcasts locally on channel 25.
TELEVISION STATION

WLBT-TV 31955
Owner: Raycom Media Inc.
Editorial: 715 S Jefferson St, Jackson, Mississippi 39201-5622 **Tel:** 1 601 948-3333.
Email: news@wlbt.com
Web site: http://www.msnewsnow.com
Profile: WLBT-TV is the NBC affiliate for the Jackson, MS market. The station is owned by Raycom Media Inc. WLBT-TV broadcasts locally on channel 3.
TELEVISION STATION

WLBZ-TV 31956
Owner: TEGNA Inc.
Editorial: 329 Mount Hope Ave, Bangor, Maine 04401-4238 **Tel:** 1 207 942-4821.
Email: newscenter@wlbz2.com
Web site: http://www.wlbz2.com
Profile: WLBZ-TV is the NBC affiliate for the Bangor, ME market. The station is owned by TEGNA Inc. WLBZ-TV broadcasts locally on channel 2.
TELEVISION STATION

WLEX-TV 31957
Owner: WLEX Communications LLC
Editorial: 1065 Russell Cave Rd, Lexington, Kentucky 40505-3409 **Tel:** 1 859 259-1818.
Email: news@lex18.com
Web site: http://www.lex18.com
Profile: WLEX-TV is the NBC affiliate for the Lexington, KY, market. It is owned by WLEX Communications LLC. WLEX-TV broadcasts locally on channel 18.
TELEVISION STATION

WLFG-TV 32462
Owner: Living Faith Broadcasting Inc.
Editorial: 8594 Hidden Valley Rd, Abingdon, Virginia 24210-4858 **Tel:** 1 276 676-3806.
Email: info@livingfaithtv.com
Web site: http://www.lftvnetwork.com
Profile: WLFG-TV is a commercial station for the Tri-Cities, TN market. The station is owned by Living Fatih Broadcasting Inc. WLFG-TV broadcasts locally on channel 68.
TELEVISION STATION

WLFI-TV 31958
Owner: MidAmerica Holdings, LLC
Editorial: 2605 Yeager Rd, West Lafayette, Indiana 47906-1337 **Tel:** 1 765 463-1800.
Email: newsroom@wlfi.com
Web site: http://www.wlfi.com
Profile: WLFI-TV is the CBS affiliate in West Lafayette, IN. The station is owned by MidAmerica Holdings, LLC. It airs locally on channel 18.
TELEVISION STATION

WLFL-TV 31959
Owner: Sinclair Broadcast Group, Inc.
Editorial: 3012 Highwoods Blvd Ste 101, Raleigh, North Carolina 27604-1030 **Tel:** 1 919 872-2854.
Web site: http://www.raleighcw.com
Profile: WLFL-TV is the CW affiliate for the Raleigh, NC market. The station is owned by Sinclair Broadcasting Group, Inc. WLFL-TV broadcasts locally on channel 22.
TELEVISION STATION

WLFT-TV 389887
Owner: Touch Family Broadcasting
Editorial: 13567 Plank Rd, Baker, Louisiana 70714-4922 **Tel:** 1 225 774-7780.
Web site: http://www.wlft.com
Profile: WLFT-TV is an independent affiliate for the Baton Rouge, LA market. The station is owned by Touch Family Broadcasting. WLFT-TV broadcasts locally on channel 30.
TELEVISION STATION

WLIO2-TV 968747
Owner: Lima Communications Corp.
Editorial: 1424 Rice Ave, Lima, Ohio 45805-1949 **Tel:** 1 419 228-8835.
Web site: http://www.hometownstations.com
Profile: WLIO2-TV is a multicast channel of WLIO-TV. A multicast channel is a separate channel that shares the bandwidth of the main station but can air unique programming. WLIO2-TV is the FOX Network for the Lima, OH market. The station is owned by Lima Communications Corp. WLIO2-TV broadcasts locally on channel 8.2.
TELEVISION STATION

WLIO-TV 31961
Owner: Lima Communications Corp.
Editorial: 1424 Rice Ave, Lima, Ohio 45805-1949 **Tel:** 1 419 228-8835.
Email: newsrelease@wlio.com
Web site: http://www.hometownstations.com
Profile: WLIO-TV is the NBC affiliate for the Lima, OH, market. The station is owned by Lima Communications Corp. WLIO-TV broadcasts locally on channel 8.
TELEVISION STATION

WLIW2-TV 606642
Owner: WNET.org
Editorial: 450 W 33rd St Fl 7, New York, New York 10001-2603 **Tel:** 1 516 367-2100.
Email: programming@wliw.org
Web site: http://www.wliw.org
Profile: WLIW2-TV is a multicast channel of WLIW-TV. A multicast channel is a separate channel that shares the bandwith of the main station but can air unique programming. WLIW-TV is the local PBS Create Network affiliate on channel 21.2 for the greater Metropolitan New York area. It is owned by WNET.org.
TELEVISION STATION

WLIW3-TV 606643
Owner: WNET.org
Editorial: 450 W 33rd St Fl 7, New York, New York 10001-2603 **Tel:** 1 516 367-2100.
Email: programming@wliw.org
Web site: http://www.wliw.org
Profile: WLIW3-TV is a multicast channel of WLIW-TV. A multicast channel is a separate channel that shares the bandwith of the main station but can air unique programming. WLIW-TV3 is the local PBS World affiliate on channel 21.3 for the greater Metropolitan New York area. It is owned by WNET.org.
TELEVISION STATION

WLIW-TV 31962

Owner: WNET.org
Editorial: 450 W 33rd St Fl 7, New York, New York 10001-2603 **Tel:** 1 516 367-2100.
Email: programming@wliw.org
Web site: http://www.wliw.org
Profile: WLIW-TV is the PBS affiliate for the New York market. The station is owned by WNET.org. WLIW-TV broadcasts locally on channel 21.
TELEVISION STATION

WLJC-TV 32276

Owner: Hour of Harvest, Inc.
Editorial: 219 WLJC Drive, Beattyville, Kentucky 41311 **Tel:** 1 606 464-3600.
Email: wljc@wljc.com
Web site: http://www.wljc.com
Profile: WLJC-TV is an independent station for the Beattyville, KY market. The station is owned by Hour of Harvest, Inc. WLJC-TV broadcasts locally on channel 65.
TELEVISION STATION

WLJT-TV 31963

Owner: West Tennessee Public Television
Editorial: 210 Hurt St, Room 152, Martin, Tennessee 38238 **Tel:** 1 731 881-7561.
Web site: http://www.wljt.org
Profile: WLJT-TV is the PBS affiliate for the Paducah, KY/Cape Girardeau, MO/Harrisburg, IL market. The station is owned by West Tennessee Public Television. WLJT-TV broadcasts locally on channel 11.
TELEVISION STATION

WLKY-TV 31964

Owner: Hearst Television Inc.
Editorial: 1918 Mellwood Ave, Louisville, Kentucky 40206-1035 **Tel:** 1 502 893-3671.
Email: newstips@wlky.com
Web site: http://www.wlky.com
Profile: WLKY-TV is the CBS affiliate for the Louisville, KY market. The station is owned by Hearst Televison Inc. WLKY-TV broadcasts locally on channel 32.
TELEVISION STATION

WLLA2-TV 617307

Owner: Christian Faith Broadcast, Inc.
Editorial: 7048 E N Ave, Kalamazoo, Michigan 49048-9784 **Tel:** 1 269 345-6421.
Email: wlla@cfbroadcast.net
Web site: http://www.metvkalamazoo.com
Profile: WLLA2-TV is a multicast of WLLA-TV. A multicast channel is a separate channel that shares the bandwith of the main station but can air unique programming. WLLA2-TV airs programming from the Family Christian Network of Costa Rica in the Kalamazoo, MI market. The station is owned by Christian Faith Broadcast, Inc. WLLA2-TV broadcasts locally on channel 64.2.
TELEVISION STATION

WLLA-TV 32312

Owner: Christian Faith Broadcast, Inc.
Editorial: 7048 E N Ave, Kalamazoo, Michigan 49048-9784 **Tel:** 1 269 345-6421.
Email: wlla@cfbroadcast.net
Web site: http://www.wlla.tv
Profile: WLLA-TV is the independent affiliate for the Kalamazoo, MI market. The station is owned by Christian Faith Broadcast, Inc. WLLA-TV broadcasts locally on channel 64.
TELEVISION STATION

WLMB-TV 32578

Owner: Dominion Broadcasting Inc.
Editorial: 825 Capital Commons Dr, Toledo, Ohio 43615-6375 **Tel:** 1 419 720-9562.
Email: info@wlmb.com
Web site: http://www.wlmb.com
Profile: WLMB-TV is a Christian Family Network affiliate for the Toledo, OH market. The station is owned by Dominion Broadcasting Inc. WLMB-TV broadcasts locally on channel 40.
TELEVISION STATION

WLMO-TV 87426

Owner: West Central Broadcasting, Inc.
Editorial: 1424 Rice Ave, Lima, Ohio 45805-1949 **Tel:** 1 419 228-8835.
Email: newsrelease@wlio.com
Web site: http://www.hometownstations.com
Profile: WLMO-TV is the CBS affiliate for the Lima, OH market. The station is owned by West Central Broadcasting, Inc. WLMO-TV broadcasts locally on channel 38.
TELEVISION STATION

WLMT2-TV 618796

Owner: Newport Television, LLC
Editorial: 2701 Union Avenue Ext, Memphis, Tennessee 38112-4400 **Tel:** 1 901 323-2430.
Email: newsdesk@myeyewitnessnews.com
Web site: http://www.myeyewitnessnews.com
Profile: WLMT2-TV is a multicast of WLMT-TV. A multicast channel is a separate channel that shares the bandwith of the main station but can air unique programming. WLMT2-TV airs programming from the Retro Network Television in the Memphis, TN market. The station is owned by Newport Television, LLC. WLMT2-TV broadcasts locally on channel 30.2.
TELEVISION STATION

WLMT-TV 32690

Owner: Nexstar Broadcasting Group
Editorial: 1725 N Shelby Oaks Dr, Memphis, Tennessee 38134-7444 **Tel:** 1 901 323-2430.
Web site: http://www.localmemphis.com
Profile: WLMT-TV is the CW affiliate for the Memphis, TN market. The station is owned by Nexstar Broadcasting Group. WLMT-TV broadcasts locally on channel 30.
TELEVISION STATION

WLNE2-TV 788000

Owner: Citadel Communications, LLC
Editorial: 10 Orms St, Providence, Rhode Island 02904-2228 **Tel:** 1 401 453-8000.
Email: news@abc6.com
Web site: http://www.abc6.com
Profile: WLNE2-TV is a multicast channel of WLNE-TV. A multicast channel is a separate channel that shares the bandwith of the main station but can air unique programming. WLNE2-TV is the ABC Live Well Network for the Providence, RI New Bedford, MA market. The station is owned by Citadel Communications, LLC. WLEN2-TV broadcasts locally on channel 6.2.
TELEVISION STATION

WLNE-TV 31965

Owner: Citadel Communications, LLC
Editorial: 10 Orms St, Providence, Rhode Island 02904-2228 **Tel:** 1 401 453-8000.
Email: news@abc6.com
Web site: http://www.abc6.com
Profile: WLNE-TV is the local ABC affiliate for the Providence, RI and New Bedford, MA area. The station is owned by Citadel Communications, LLC. WLNE-TV broadcasts locally on channel 6.
TELEVISION STATION

WLNS2-TV 791746

Owner: New Young Broadcasting
Editorial: 2820 E Saginaw St, Lansing, Michigan 48912-4240 **Tel:** 1 517 372-8282.
Web site: http://www.wlns.com
Profile: WLNS2-TV is a multicast channel of WLNS-TV. A multicast channel is a separate channel that shares the bandwith of the main station but can air unique programming. WLNS2-TV is the Live Well Network for the Lansing, MI market. The station is owned by New Young Broadcasting. WLNS2-TV broadcasts locally on channel 6.2.
TELEVISION STATION

WLNS-TV 31966

Owner: New Young Broadcasting
Editorial: 2820 E Saginaw St, Lansing, Michigan 48912-4296 **Tel:** 1 517 372-8282.
Email: newstips@wlns.com
Web site: http://www.wlns.com
Profile: WLNS-TV is the CBS affiliate for the Lansing, MI market. The station is owned by New Young Broadcasting. WLNS-TV broadcasts locally on channel 6.
TELEVISION STATION

WLNY-TV 31960

Owner: CBS Television Stations
Editorial: 524 W 57th St, New York, New York 10019-2930 **Tel:** 1 631 777-8855.
Email: desk@cbs2ny.com
Web site: http://newyork.cbslocal.com/station/wlny
Profile: WLNY-TV is an independent station for the New York market. The station is owned by CBS Television Stations. WLNY-TV broadcasts locally on channel 55. The station merged with WCBS-TV in June 2012.
TELEVISION STATION

WLOO-TV 324716

Owner: Tougaloo College
Editorial: 1 Great Pl, Jackson, Mississippi 39209-9300 **Tel:** 1 601 977-7732.
Profile: WLOO-TV is the MyNetworkTV affiliate for the Jackson, MS market. The station is owned by Tougaloo College. WLOO-TV broadcasts locally on channel 41.
TELEVISION STATION

WLOS2-TV 618391

Owner: Sinclair Broadcast Group, Inc.
Editorial: 110 Technology Dr, Asheville, North Carolina 28803-3477 **Tel:** 1 828 684-1340.
Email: news@wlos.com
Web site: http://www.wlos.com
Profile: WLOS2-TV is a multicast of WLOS-TV. A multicast channel is a separate channel that shares the bandwith of the main station but can air unique programming. WLOS2-TV airs programming from My Network TV in the Greenville, SC-Asheville, NC market. The station is owned by Sinclair Broadcast Group, Inc. WLOS2-TV broadcasts locally on channel 13.2.
TELEVISION STATION

WLOS-TV 31967

Owner: Sinclair Broadcast Group, Inc.
Editorial: 110 Technology Dr, Asheville, North Carolina 28803-3477 **Tel:** 1 828 684-1340.
Email: news@wlos.com
Web site: http://www.wlos.com
Profile: WLOS-TV is the ABC affiliate for the Greenville, SC-Asheville, NC area. The station is owned by Sinclair Broadcast Group, Inc. WLOS-TV broadcasts locally on channel 13.
TELEVISION STATION

WLOV-TV 32198

Owner: Lingard Broadcasting Company
Editorial: 1359 Beech Springs Rd, Saltillo, Mississippi 38866-5714 **Tel:** 1 662 842-2227.
Email: news@wtva.com
Web site: http://www.wlov.com
Profile: WLOV-TV is a FOX affiliate for the Tupelo, MS market. The station is owned by Lingard Broadcasting Company. WLOV-TV broadcasts locally on channel 27.
TELEVISION STATION

WLOX2-TV 800535

Owner: Raycom Media Inc.
Editorial: 208 Debuys Rd, Biloxi, Mississippi 39531-3501 **Tel:** 1 228 896-1313.
Email: news@wlox.com
Web site: http://www.wlox.com
Profile: WLOX2-TV is a multicast of WLOX-TV. A multicast channel is a separate channel that shares the bandwidth of the main station but can air unique programming. WLOX2-TV is the local CBS affiliate on Channel 13.2 for the Biloxi market. WLOX2-TV is owned by Raycom Media Inc.
TELEVISION STATION

WLOX-TV 31968

Owner: Raycom Media Inc.
Editorial: 208 Debuys Rd, Biloxi, Mississippi 39531-3501 **Tel:** 1 228 896-1313.
Email: producers@wlox.com
Web site: http://www.wlox.com
Profile: WLOX-TV is the ABC network affiliate for the Biloxi-Gulfport, MS market. The station is owned by Raycom Media Inc. WLOX-TV broadcasts locally on channel 13.
TELEVISION STATION

WLPX-TV 32612

Owner: ION Media Networks
Editorial: 600C Prestige Park Dr, Hurricane, West Virginia 25526-8422 **Tel:** 1 304 760-1029.
Profile: WLPX-TV is the ION Television affiliate for the Charleston-Huntington WV, market. The station is owned by ION Media Networks. WLPX-TV broadcasts locally on channel 29.
TELEVISION STATION

WLQP-TV 70153

Owner: West Central Ohio Broadcasting, Inc.
Editorial: 1424 Rice Ave, Lima, Ohio 45805-1949 **Tel:** 1 419 228-8835.
Web site: http://hometownstations.com
Profile: WLQP-TV is the ABC affiliate for the Lima, OH market. The station is owned by West Central Ohio Broadcasting, Inc. . WLQP-TV broadcasts locally on channel 18.
TELEVISION STATION

WLS2-TV 606405

Owner: Walt Disney Co.
Editorial: 190 N State St Ste, Chicago, Illinois 60601-3379 **Tel:** 1 312 750-7777.
Web site: http://livewellnetwork.com
Profile: WLS2-TV is a multicast channel of WLS-TV. A multicast channel is a separate channel that shares the bandwidth of the main station but can air unique programming. WLS2-TV is the Live Well HD Network for the Chicago market. The station is owned by Walt Disney. WLS2-TV broadcasts locally on channel 7.2.
TELEVISION STATION

WLS3-TV 606407

Owner: Walt Disney Co.
Editorial: 190 N State St, Chicago, Illinois 60601-3379 **Tel:** 1 312 750-7777.
Email: wls-tv.website@abc.com
Web site: http://abclocal.go.com/wls
Profile: WLS3-TV is a multicast channel of WLS-TV. A multicast channel is a separate channel that shares the bandwidth of the main station but can air unique programming. WLS3-TV is the Live Well HD Network for the Chicago market. The station is owned by Walt Disney. WLS3-TV broadcasts locally on channel 7.3.
TELEVISION STATION

WLS-TV 31970

Owner: Walt Disney Co.
Editorial: 190 N State St, Chicago, Illinois 60601-3302 **Tel:** 1 312 750-7777.
Email: wls.desk@abc.com
Web site: http://abc7chicago.com
Profile: WLS-TV is the ABC affiliate for the Chicago market. The station is owned by Walt Disney Co. WLS-TV broadcasts locally on channel 7. The news department does NOT accept any unsolicited story ideas or submissions via e-mail; send them via fax.
TELEVISION STATION

WLTV-TV 31971

Owner: Univision Communications Inc.
Editorial: 9405 NW 41st St, Doral, Florida 33178-2301 **Tel:** 1 305 471-3900.
Email: noticias23@univision.net
Web site: http://www.univision.com/miami/wltv
Profile: WLTV-TV is the Univision affiliate for the Miami-Fort Lauderdale market. The station is owned by Univision Communications Inc. WLTV-TV broadcasts locally on channel 23.
TELEVISION STATION

WLTX-TV 31972

Owner: TEGNA Inc.
Editorial: 6027 Garners Ferry Rd, Columbia, South Carolina 29209-1304 **Tel:** 1 803 776-3600.
Email: news19@wltx.com
Web site: http://www.wltx.com
Profile: WLTX-TV is the CBS affiliate for the Columbia, SC, market. It is owned by TEGNA Inc. WLTX-TV broadcasts locally on channel 19.
TELEVISION STATION

WLTZ-TV 31973

Owner: SagamoreHill Broadcasting
Editorial: 6140 Buena Vista Rd, Columbus, Georgia 31907-5209 **Tel:** 1 706 561-3838.
Email: wltz@wltz.com
Web site: http://www.wltz.com
Profile: WLTZ-TV is the NBC affiliate for the Columbus, GA market. The station is owned by SagamoreHill Broadcasting. WLTZ-TV broadcasts locally on channel 38.
TELEVISION STATION

WLUC-TV 31974

Owner: Gray Television, Inc.
Editorial: 177 US Highway 41 E, Negaunee, Michigan 49866-9662 **Tel:** 1 906 475-4161.
Email: wlucnews@wluctv6.com
Web site: http://www.uppermichiganssource.com
Profile: WLUC-TV is the NBC and FOX affiliate for the Marquette, MI, market. The station is owned byGray Television, Inc. WLUC-TV broadcasts locally on channel 6.
TELEVISION STATION

WLUK-TV 31975

Owner: Sinclair Broadcast Group, Inc.
Editorial: 787 Lombardi Ave, Green Bay, Wisconsin 54304-3925 **Tel:** 1 920 494-8711.
Email: fox11news@wluk.com
Web site: http://www.fox11online.com
Profile: WLUK-TV is the FOX affiliate for the Greenbay-Appleton, WI market. The station is owned by Sinclair Broadcast Group, Inc. WLUK-TV broadcasts locally on channel 11.
TELEVISION STATION

WLVI-TV 31976

Owner: Sunbeam Broadcasting Corp.
Editorial: 7 Bulfinch Pl, Boston, Massachusetts 02114-2904 **Tel:** 1 617 725-0777.
Web site: http://whdh.com/cw56
Profile: WLVI-TV is the CW affiliate for the Boston market. The station is owned by Sunbeam Broadcasting Corp. WLVI-TV broadcasts locally on channel 56.
TELEVISION STATION

WLVT2-TV 609987

Owner: Lehigh Valley Public Telecommunications Corporation
Editorial: 123 Sesame St, Bethlehem, Pennsylvania 18015-4799 **Tel:** 1 610 867-4677.
Web site: http://www.wlvt.org
Profile: WLVT2-TV is a multicast of WLVT-TV. A multicast channel is a separate channel that shares the bandwith of the main station but can air unique programming. WLVT2-TV airs programming from the V-me network to the Philadelphia market. The station is owned by Lehigh Valley Public Telecommunications Corporation. WLVT2-TV broadcasts locally on channel 39.2.
TELEVISION STATION

WLVT3-TV 609994

Owner: Lehigh Valley Public Telecommunications Corporation
Editorial: 123 Sesame St, Bethlehem, Pennsylvania 18015-4799 **Tel:** 1 610 867-4677.
Web site: http://www.wlvt.org
Profile: WLVT3-TV is a multicast of WLVT-TV. A multicast channel is a separate channel that shares the bandwith of the main station but can air unique programming. WLVT3-TV airs programming from the Create network to the Philadelphia market. The station is owned by Lehigh Valley Public Telecommunications Corporation. WLVT3-TV broadcasts locally on channel 39.3. The station does not offer advertising, but does acknowledgement of underwriters.
TELEVISION STATION

WLVT-TV 31977

Owner: Lehigh Valley Public Telecommunications Corporation
Editorial: 839 Sesame St, Bethlehem, Pennsylvania 18015-1391 **Tel:** 1 610 867-4677.
Web site: http://www.wlvt.org
Profile: WLVT-TV is a PBS affiliate for the Philadelphia market. The station is owned by Lehigh Valley Public Telecommunications Corporation. WLVT-TV is broadcast locally on channel 39.
TELEVISION STATION

WLWC2-TV 696851

Owner: OTA Broadcasting
Editorial: 275 Westminster St Ste 100, Providence, Rhode Island 02903-3434 **Tel:** 1 401 351-8828.
Web site: http://www.thecwprov.com
Profile: WLWC2-TV is a Hispanic digital subchannel of WLWC-TV for the Providence, RI-New Bedford, MA market. The station is owned by OTA Broadcasting. WLWC2-TV broadcasts locally on channel 28.2.
TELEVISION STATION

WLWC-TV 32536

Owner: OTA Broadcasting
Editorial: 275 Westminster St, Providence, Rhode Island 02903-3434 **Tel:** 1 401 351-8828.
Web site: http://www.thecwprov.com/
Profile: WLWC-TV is the CW affiliate for the Providence, RI-New Bedford, MA market. The station is owned by OTA Broadcasting. WLWC-TV broadcasts locally on channel 28.
TELEVISION STATION

WLWT2-TV 621010
Owner: Hearst Television Inc.
Editorial: 1700 Young St, Cincinnati, Ohio 45202-6821 **Tel:** 1 513 412-5000.
Email: newsdesk@wlwt.com
Web site: http://www.wlwt.com
Profile: WLWT2-TV is a multicast of WLWT-TV. A multicast channel is a separate channel that shares the bandwith of the main station but can air unique programming. WLWT2-TV airs 24 local weather programming from NBC 5 Weather Plus in the Cincinnati market. The station is owned by Hearst Television Inc. WLWT2-TV broadcasts locally on channel 5.2.
TELEVISION STATION

WLWT-TV 31978
Owner: Hearst Television Inc.
Editorial: 1700 Young St, Cincinnati, Ohio 45202-6821 **Tel:** 1 513 412-5000.
Email: newsdesk@wlwt.com
Web site: http://www.wlwt.com
Profile: WLWT-TV is the NBC affiliate for the Cincinnati, OH market. the station is owned by Hearst Television Inc. WLWT-TV is broadcast locally on channel 5.
TELEVISION STATION

WLXI-TV 31979
Owner: Radiant Life Ministries, Inc.
Editorial: 2109 Patterson St, Greensboro, North Carolina 27407-2531 **Tel:** 1 336 855-5610.
Email: wlxi@tct.tv
Web site: http://www.tct.tv
Profile: WLXI-TV is the Tri-State Christian Television (TCT) network affiliate for the Greensboro-Winston Salem, NC market. The station is owned by Radiant Life Ministries, Inc. WLXI-TV broadcasts locally on channel 61.
TELEVISION STATION

WLYH-TV 31980
Owner: Newport Television, LLC
Editorial: 3300 N 6th St, Harrisburg, Pennsylvania 17110-1421 **Tel:** 1 717 238-2100.
Email: news@cbs21.com
Web site: http://cwcentralpa.com
Profile: WLYH-TV is the CW affiliate for the Harrisburg, PA market. The station is owned by Newport Television, LLC. WLYH-TV broadcasts locally on channel 15.
TELEVISION STATION

WLZE-TV 342804
Owner: Media Vista Group
Editorial: 5405 Taylor Rd Ste 10, Naples, Florida 34109-1899 **Tel:** 1 239 254-9995.
Web site: http://dlatinos.tv/mediavista/
Profile: WLZE-TV is a Univision affiliate for the Fort Myers-Naples, FL market. The station is owned by Media Vista Group. WLZE-TV broadcasts locally on channel 51.
TELEVISION STATION

WMAK-TV 389888
Owner: Daystar Television Network
Editorial: 3901 Highway 121, Bedford, Texas 76021-3009 **Tel:** 1 817 571-1229.
Web site: http://www.daystar.com
Profile: WMAK is a Daystar Network affiliate for the Knoxville market.
TELEVISION STATION

WMAQ2-TV 606400
Owner: NBC Universal
Editorial: 454 N Columbus Dr, Chicago, Illinois 60611-5807 **Tel:** 1 312 836-5555.
Web site: http://www.cozitv.com
Profile: WMAQ2-TV is a multicast channel of WMAQ-TV. A multicast channel is a separate channel that shares the bandwith of the main station but can air unique programming. WMAQ2-TV is the Cozi TV affiliate for the Chicago market. The station is owned by NBC Universal. WMAQ2-TV broadcasts locally on channel 5.2.
TELEVISION STATION

WMAQ3-TV 606401
Owner: NBC Universal
Editorial: 454 N Columbus Dr, Chicago, Illinois 60611-5555 **Tel:** 1 312 836-5555.
Email: assignmentdesk@nbcuni.com
Web site: http://www.nbcchicago.com
Profile: WMAQ3-TV is a multicast channel of WMAQ-TV. A multicast channel is a separate channel that shares the bandwith of the main station but can air unique programming. WMAQ3-TV is the Universal Sports affiliate for the Chicago market. The station is owned by NBC Universal. WMAQ3-TV broadcasts locally on channel 5.3.
TELEVISION STATION

WMAQ-TV 31982
Owner: NBC Universal
Editorial: 454 N Columbus Dr, Chicago, Illinois 60611-5807 **Tel:** 1 312 836-5555.
Email: tips@nbcchicago.com
Web site: http://www.nbcchicago.com
Profile: WMAQ-TV is the NBC affiliate for the Chicago market. The station is owned by NBC Universal. WMAQ-TV broadcasts locally on channel 5.
TELEVISION STATION

WMAR3-TV 614574
Owner: E.W. Scipps Co.
Editorial: 6400 York Rd, Baltimore, Maryland 21212-2117 **Tel:** 1 410 377-2222.
Web site: http://www.abc2news.com
Profile: WMAR3-TV is a multicast of WMAR-TV. A multicast channel is a separate channel that shares the bandwith of the main station but can air unique programming. WMAR3-TV airs programming from local weather radar in the Baltimore market. The station is owned by E.W. Scripps Co. WMAR3-TV broadcasts locally on channel 2.3.
TELEVISION STATION

WMAR-TV 31983
Owner: E.W. Scripps Co.
Editorial: 6400 York Rd, Baltimore, Maryland 21212-2117 **Tel:** 1 410 377-2222.
Email: newsroom@wmar.com
Web site: http://www.abc2news.com
Profile: WMAR-TV is the ABC affiliate for the Baltimore market. The station is owned by E.W. Scripps Co. WMAR-TV broadcasts locally on channel 2.
TELEVISION STATION

WMAZ-TV 31984
Owner: TEGNA Inc.
Editorial: 1314 Gray Hwy, Macon, Georgia 31211-1904 **Tel:** 1 478 752-1313.
Email: eyewitnessnews@13wmaz.com
Web site: http://www.13wmaz.com
Profile: WMAZ-TV is the CBS affiliate for the Macon, GA market. The station is owned by TEGNA Inc. WMAZ-TV broadcasts locally on channel 13.
TELEVISION STATION

WMBB-TV 31985
Owner: Nexstar Broadcasting, Inc.
Editorial: 613 Harrison Ave, Panama City, Florida 32401-2623 **Tel:** 1 850 769-2313.
Email: news@wmbb.com
Web site: http://www.mypanhandle.com
Profile: WMBB-TV is the ABC affiliate for Panama City, FL market. The station is owned by Nexstar Broadcasting. WMBB-TV broadcasts locally on channel 13.
TELEVISION STATION

WMBC2-TV 606653
Owner: Mountain Broadcasting Corp.
Editorial: 99 Clinton Rd, West Caldwell, New Jersey 07006-6601 **Tel:** 1 973 852-0300.
Email: news@wmbctv.com
Web site: http://us.cgntv.net/18.4
Profile: WMBC2-TV is a multicast channel of WMBC-TV. A multicast channel is a separate channel that shares the bandwith of the main station but can air unique programming. WMBC2-TV airs Christian Global Network TV (CGN TV) programming on channel 63.2 for the greater Metropolitan New York area. It is owned by Mountain Broadcasting Corp.
TELEVISION STATION

WMBC3-TV 606658
Owner: Mountain Broadcasting Corp.
Editorial: 99 Clinton Rd, West Caldwell, New Jersey 07006-6601 **Tel:** 1 973 852-0300.
Email: news@wmbctv.com
Web site: http://www.wmbctv.com
Profile: WMBC3-TV is a multicast channel of WMBC-TV. A multicast channel is a separate channel that shares the bandwith of the main station but can air unique programming. WMBC3-TV is the Sinovision television affiliate that airs on channel 63.3 for the greater Metropolitan New York area. It is owned by Mountain Broadcasting Corp.
TELEVISION STATION

WMBC4-TV 606659
Owner: Mountain Broadcasting Corp.
Editorial: 99 Clinton Rd, West Caldwell, New Jersey 07006-6601 **Tel:** 1 973 850-0300.
Email: news@wmbctv.com
Web site: http://www.wmbctv.com
Profile: WMBC4-TV is a multicast channel of WMBC-TV. A multicast channel is a separate channel that shares the bandwith of the main station but can air unique programming. WMBC3-TV is the Sinovision affiliate for the greater Metropolitan New York area that airs on channel 63.4 It is owned by Mountain Broadcasting Corp.
TELEVISION STATION

WMBC-TV 32501
Owner: Mountain Broadcasting Corp.
Editorial: 99 Clinton Rd, West Caldwell, New Jersey 07006-6601 **Tel:** 1 973 852-0300.
Email: news@wmbctv.com
Web site: http://www.wmbctv.com
Profile: WMBC-TV is an independent station for the New York market. The station is owned by Mountain Broadcasting Corp. WMBC-TV broadcasts locally on channel 18.
TELEVISION STATION

WMBD-TV 31986
Owner: Nexstar Broadcasting Group
Editorial: 3131 N University St, Peoria, Illinois 61604-1316 **Tel:** 1 309 688-3131.
Email: news@wmbd.com
Web site: http://centralillinoisproud.com
Profile: WMBD-TV is the CBS affiliate for the Peoria-Bloomington, IL market. The station is owned by Nexstar Broadcasting Group. WMBD-TV broadcasts locally on channel 31.
TELEVISION STATION

WMBF-TV 536671
Owner: Raycom Media Inc.
Editorial: 918 Frontage Rd E, Myrtle Beach, South Carolina 29577-6700 **Tel:** 1 843 839-9623.
Email: news@wmbfnews.com
Web site: http://www.wmbfnews.com
Profile: WMBF-TV is the NBC affiliate for the Myrtle Beach, SC market. The station is owned by Raycom Media Inc. WMBF-TV broadcasts locally on channel 32.
TELEVISION STATION

WMC2-TV 620052
Owner: Raycom Media Inc.
Editorial: 1960 Union Ave, Memphis, Tennessee 38104-4031 **Tel:** 1 901 726-0555.
Email: desk@wmctv.com
Web site: http://www.wmctv.com
Profile: WMC2-TV is a multicast of WMC-TV. A multicast channel is a separate channel that shares the bandwith of the main station but can air unique programming. WMC2-TV airs programming from This TV Network to the Memphis, TN market. The station is owned by Raycom Media Inc. WMC2-TV broadcasts locally on channel 5.2.
TELEVISION STATION

WMC3-TV 620054
Owner: Raycom Media Inc.
Editorial: 1960 Union Ave, Memphis, Tennessee 38104-4031 **Tel:** 1 901 726-0555.
Email: desk@wmctv.com
Web site: http://www.wmctv.com
Profile: WMC3-TV is a multicast of WMC-TV. A multicast channel is a separate channel that shares the bandwith of the main station but can air unique programming. WMC3-TV airs 24 hour weather programming from Action News Weather Plus to the Memphis, TN market. The station is owned by Raycom Media Inc. WMC3-TV broadcasts locally on channel 5.3.
TELEVISION STATION

WMCF-TV 31989
Owner: Trinity Broadcasting Network
Editorial: 300 Mendel Pkwy W, Montgomery, Alabama 36117-5406 **Tel:** 1 334 272-0045.
Email: wmcf@tbn.org
Profile: WMCF-TV is the Trinity Broadcasting Network affiliate for the Montgomery, AL market. The station is owned by Trinity Broadcasting Network. WMCF-TV broadcasts locally on channel 45.
TELEVISION STATION

WMCN2-TV 771490
Owner: Lenfest Broadcasting LLC
Editorial: 100 Dobbs Ln Ste 112, Cherry Hill, New Jersey 08034-1436 **Tel:** 1 609 569-7280.
Email: contact@wmcn.tv
Web site: http://www.thenewwmcn.com
Profile: WMCN2-TV is a multicast channel of WMCN-TV. A multicast channel is a separate channel that shares the bandwidth of the main station but can air unique programming. WMCN2-TV is the local Bounce TV affiliate on channel 44.2 for the Philadelphia market. WMCN2-TV is owned by Lenfest Broadcasting LLC.
TELEVISION STATION

WMCN-TV 32433
Owner: Lenfest Broadcasting LLC
Editorial: 100 Dobbs Ln Ste 112, Cherry Hill, New Jersey 08034-1436 **Tel:** 1 609 569-7280.
Email: contact@wmcn.tv
Web site: http://www.thenewwmcn.com
Profile: WMCN-TV is an independent station for the Atlantic City, NJ market. The station is owned by Lenfest Broadcasting LLC. WMCN-TV broadcasts locally on channel 53.
TELEVISION STATION

WMC-TV 31987
Owner: Raycom Media Inc.
Editorial: 1960 Union Ave, Memphis, Tennessee 38104-4031 **Tel:** 1 901 726-0555.
Email: desk@wmctv.com
Web site: http://www.wmcactionnews5.com
Profile: WMC-TV is the local NBC affiliate for the Memphis, TN market. The station is owned by Raycom Media Inc. WMC-TV is broadcast on channel 5.
TELEVISION STATION

WMDN-TV 32503
Owner: Waypoint Media
Editorial: 1151 Crestview Cir, Meridian, Mississippi 39301-8669 **Tel:** 1 601 693-2424.
Web site: http://www.wgbctv.com
Profile: WMDN-TV is the CBS affiliate for the Meridian, MS, market. The station is owned by Waypoint Media. WMDN-TV broadcasts locally on channel 24.
TELEVISION STATION

WMDO-TV 79762
Owner: Entravision Communications Corp.
Editorial: 101 Constitution Ave NW, Washington, District Of Columbia 20001-2133 **Tel:** 1 202 522-8640.
Web site: http://noticias.entravision.com/washington-dc
Profile: WMDO-TV is the UniMas affiliate for the Silver Spring, MD market. The station is owned by Entravision Communications Corp. WMDO-TV broadcasts locally on channel 47.
TELEVISION STATION

WMDT-TV 50101
Owner: Marquee Broadcasting
Editorial: 202 W Main St, Salisbury, Maryland 21801-4907 **Tel:** 1 410 742-4747.
Email: news@wmdt.com
Web site: http://www.wmdt.com
Profile: WMDT-TV is an ABC affiliate for the Salisbury, MD market. The station is owned by Delmarva Broadcast Services. WMDT-TV broadcasts locally on channel 47.
TELEVISION STATION

WMEB-TV 32743
Owner: Maine Public Broadcasting Network
Editorial: 63 Texas Ave, Bangor, Maine 04401-4324
Tel: 1 207 941-1010.
Email: radionews@mpbn.net
Web site: http://www.mpbn.net
Profile: WMEB-TV is the PBS network affiliate for the Bangor, ME market. The station is owned by Maine Public Broadcasting Network. WMEB-TV broadcasts locally on channel 12.
TELEVISION STATION

WMFD-TV 32435
Owner: Mid-State Television Inc.
Editorial: 2900 Park Ave W, Mansfield, Ohio 44906-1062 **Tel:** 1 419 529-5900.
Email: newsroom@wmfd.com
Web site: http://www.wmfd.com
Profile: WMFD-TV is an independent station for the Cleveland market. The station is owned by Mid-State Television Inc. WMFD-TV broadcasts locally on channel 68.
TELEVISION STATION

WMFE2-TV 612504
Owner: Community Communications
Editorial: 11510 E Colonial Dr, Orlando, Florida 32817-4699 **Tel:** 1 407 273-2300.
Web site: http://www.vmetv.com
Profile: WMFE2-TV is an independent affiliate for the Orlando, FL market. The station is owned by Community Communications. WMFE2-TV broadcasts locally on channel 24.2. WMFE2-TV broadcasts only programming from V-me, a Hispanic television network in the US. WMFE2-TV is a multicast channel of WMFE-TV. A multicast channel is a separate channel that shares the bandwidth of the main station but can air unique programming.
TELEVISION STATION

WMFE3-TV 612507
Owner: Community Communications
Editorial: 11510 E Colonial Dr, Orlando, Florida 32817-4699 **Tel:** 1 407 273-2300.
Email: wmfe@wmfe.org
Web site: http://www.wmfe.org
Profile: WMFE3-TV is a PBS affiliate for the Orlando, FL market. The station is owned by Community Communications. WMFE3-TV broadcasts locally on channel 24.3. WMFE3-TV broadcasts popular PBS and local programming. WMFE3-TV is a multicast channel of WMFE-TV. A multicast channel is a separate channel that shares the bandwidth of the main station but can air unique programming.
TELEVISION STATION

WMFE4-TV 612510
Owner: Community Communications
Editorial: 11510 E Colonial Dr, Orlando, Florida 32817-4699 **Tel:** 1 407 273-2300.
Email: wmfe@wmfe.org
Web site: http://www.wmfe.org
Profile: WMFE4-TV is a PBS affiliate for the Orlando, FL market. The station is owned by Community Communications. WMFE4-TV broadcasts locally on channel 24.4. WMFE4-TV broadcasts educational programming from the Florida Knowledge Network. WMFE4-TV is a multicast channel of WMFE-TV. A multicast channel is a separate channel that shares the bandwidth of the main station but can air unique programming.
TELEVISION STATION

WMFP-TV 32407
Owner: NRJ TV, LLC
Editorial: 11 Lakeland Park Dr, Peabody, Massachusetts 01960-3835 **Tel:** 1 978 717-5633.
Profile: WMFP-TV is the Me TV affiliate for the Boston market. The station is owned by NRJ TV, LLC. WMFP-TV broadcasts locally on channel 62.
TELEVISION STATION

WMGT-TV 31994
Owner: Morris Multimedia, Inc.
Editorial: 301 Poplar St, Macon, Georgia 31201
Tel: 1 478 745-4141.
Web site: http://www.41nbc.com
Profile: WMGT-TV is the NBC affiliate for the Macon, GA market. The station is owned by Morris Multimedia, Inc. WMGT-TV broadcasts locally on channel 41.
TELEVISION STATION

WMLW-TV 87563
Owner: Weigel Broadcasting Co.
Editorial: 809 S 60th St, Milwaukee, Wisconsin 53214-3363 **Tel:** 1 414 777-5800.
Email: newsdesk@cbs58.com
Profile: WMLW-TV is an independent station in the Milwaukee market. The station is owned by Weigel Broadcasting Co. WMLW-TV broadcasts locally on channel 49.1.
TELEVISION STATION

WMOR2-TV 612166
Owner: Hearst Television Inc.
Editorial: 7201 E Hillsborough Ave, Tampa, Florida 33610-4126 **Tel:** 1 813 626-3232.
Web site: http://www.mor-tv.com
Profile: WMOR2-TV is a multicast of WMOR-TV. A multicast channel is a separate channel that shares the bandwith of the main station but can air unique programming. WMOR2-TV airs programming from

This TV in the Tampa, FL market. The station is owned by Hearst Television Inc. WMOR2-TV broadcasts locally on channel 32.2.
TELEVISION STATION

WMOR3-TV 612167
Owner: Hearst Television Inc.
Editorial: 7201 E Hillsborough Ave, Tampa, Florida 33610-4126 **Tel:** 1 813 626-3232.
Web site: http://www.mor-tv.com/estrellatv/index.html
Profile: WMOR3-TV is a multicast of WMOR-TV. A multicast channel is a separate channel that shares the bandwith of the main station but can air unique programming. WMOR3-TV airs programming from Estrella TV in the Tampa, FL market. The station is owned by Hearst Television Inc. WMOR3-TV broadcasts locally on channel 32.3.
TELEVISION STATION

WMOR-TV 32138
Owner: Hearst Television Inc.
Editorial: 7201 E Hillsborough Ave, Tampa, Florida 33610-4126 **Tel:** 1 813 626-3232.
Web site: http://www.mor-tv.com
Profile: WMOR-TV is an independent affiliate in Tampa Bay, Florida area. The station is owned by Hearst Television Inc.
TELEVISION STATION

WMPB2-TV 612921
Owner: Maryland Public Television
Editorial: 11767 Owings Mills Blvd, Owings Mills, Maryland 21117-2892 **Tel:** 1 410 356-5600.
Email: comments@mpt.org
Web site: http://www.mpt.org
Profile: WMPB2-TV is a multicast of WMPB-TV. A multicast channel is a separate channel that shares the bandwith of the main station but can air unique programming. WMPB2-TV airs programming from MPT 2 in the Baltimore market. The station is owned by Maryland Public Television. WMPB2-TV broadcasts locally on channel 29.2.
TELEVISION STATION

WMPB3-TV 612926
Owner: Maryland Public Television
Editorial: 11767 Owings Mills Blvd, Owings Mills, Maryland 21117-2892 **Tel:** 1 410 356-5600.
Email: comments@mpt.org
Web site: http://www.mpt.org
Profile: WMPB3-TV is a multicast of WMPB-TV. A multicast channel is a separate channel that shares the bandwith of the main station but can air unique programming. WMPB2-TV airs programming from V-me in the Baltimore market. The station is owned by Maryland Public Television. WMPB3-TV broadcasts locally on channel 29.3.
TELEVISION STATION

WMPB-TV 32712
Owner: Maryland Public Television
Editorial: 11767 Owings Mills Blvd, Owings Mills, Maryland 21117 **Tel:** 1 410 356-5600.
Email: comments@mpt.org
Web site: http://www.mpt.org
Profile: WMPB-TV is the PBS affiliate for the Baltimore market. The station is owned by Maryland Public Television. WMPB-TV broadcasts locally on channel 67.
TELEVISION STATION

WMPV-TV 32249
Owner: Trinity Broadcasting Network
Editorial: 1668 W I65 Service Rd S, Mobile, Alabama 36693-5102 **Tel:** 1 251 661-2101.
Email: wmpv@tbn.org
Web site: http://www.tbn.org
Profile: WMPV-TV is the Trinity Broadcasting Network affiliate for the Mobile, AL market. The station is owned by Trinity Broadcasting Network. WMPV-TV broadcasts locally on channel 21.
TELEVISION STATION

WMSN-TV 31996
Owner: Sinclair Broadcast Group, Inc.
Editorial: 7847 Big Sky Dr, Madison, Wisconsin 53719-4957 **Tel:** 1 608 833-0047.
Email: tips@channel3000.com
Web site: http://www.fox47.com
Profile: WMSN-TV is a FOX affiliate for the Madison, WI market. The station is owned by Sinclair Broadcast Group, Inc. WMSN-TV broadcasts locally on channel 47.
TELEVISION STATION

WMTV-TV 31997
Owner: Gray Television, Inc.
Editorial: 615 Forward Dr, Madison, Wisconsin 53711-2441 **Tel:** 1 608 274-1515.
Email: news@nbc15.com
Web site: http://www.nbc15.com
Profile: WMTV-TV is the NBC affiliate for Madison, WI market. The station is owned by Gray Television, Inc. WMTV-TV airs locally on channel 15.
TELEVISION STATION

WMTW-TV 31998
Owner: Hearst Television Inc.
Editorial: 4 Ledgeview Dr, Westbrook, Maine 04092-3939 **Tel:** 1 207 782-1800.
Email: wmtw@wmtw.com
Web site: http://www.wmtw.com
Profile: WMTW-TV is the ABC affiliate for the Portland, ME market. The station is owned by Hearst Television Inc. WMTW-TV broadcasts locally on channel 8.
TELEVISION STATION

WMUR2-TV 782300
Editorial: 100 S Commercial St, Manchester, New Hampshire 03101-2605 **Tel:** 1 603 669-9999.
Web site: http://www.wmur.com
Profile: WMUR2-TV is a Me-TV affiliate for the Boston, MA market. The station is owned by Hearst Television Inc. WMUR2-TV broadcasts locally on channel 9.2. WMUR2-TV broadcasts programming from Me-TV and news. The station is a multicast channel of WMUR-TV. A multicast channel is a separate channel that shares the bandwidth of the main station but can air unique programming.
TELEVISION STATION

WMUR-TV 31999
Owner: Hearst Television Inc.
Editorial: 100 S Commercial St, Manchester, New Hampshire 03101-2605 **Tel:** 1 603 669-9999.
Email: storyideas@wmur.com
Web site: http://www.wmur.com/index.html
Profile: WMUR-TV is the ABC affiliate for the Boston market. The station is owned by Hearst Television, Inc. WMUR-TV broadcasts locally on channel 9.
TELEVISION STATION

WMVS-TV 32672
Owner: Milwaukee Area Technical College
Editorial: 1036 N 8th St, Milwaukee, Wisconsin 53233-1409 **Tel:** 1 414 271-1036.
Email: friends@matc.edu
Web site: http://www.mptv.org
Profile: WMVS-TV is the PBS affiliate for the Milwaukee area. The station is owned by Milwaukee Area Technical College. WMVS-TV airs on channel 10.
TELEVISION STATION

WMYA2-TV 618664
Owner: Sinclair Broadcast Group, Inc.
Editorial: 33 Villa Rd Suite 105, Greenville, South Carolina 29615-3037 **Tel:** 1 864 297-1313.
Email: news@wlos.com
Web site: http://www.my40.tv
Profile: WMYA2-TV is a multicast of WMYA-TV. A multicast channel is a separate channel that shares the bandwith of the main station but can air unique programming. WMYA2-TV airs programming from the ABC Network in the Greenville, SC-Asheville, NC market. The station is owned by Sinclair Broadcast Group, Inc. WMYA2-TV broadcasts locally on channel 40.2.
TELEVISION STATION

WMYA-TV 32521
Owner: Sinclair Broadcast Group, Inc.
Editorial: 33 Villa Rd Ste 105, Greenville, South Carolina 29615-3037 **Tel:** 1 864 297-1313.
Email: comments@wlos.com
Web site: http://www.my40.tv
Profile: WMYA-TV is the MyNetworkTV affiliate for the Greenville, SC-Asheville, NC market. The station is owned by Sinclair Broadcast Group, Inc. WMYA-TV broadcasts locally on channel 40.
TELEVISION STATION

WMYD2-TV 774859
Owner: E.W. Scripps Co.
Editorial: 27777 Franklin Rd Ste 1220, Southfield, Michigan 48034-8262 **Tel:** 1 248 355-2020.
Profile: WMYD2-TV is a multicast of WMYD-TV. A multicast channel is a separate channel that shares the bandwidth of the main station but can air unique programming. WMYD2-TV is the local TheCoolTV affiliate on Channel 20.2 for the Detroit market. WMYD2-TV is owned by E.W. Scripps Co.
TELEVISION STATION

WMYD-TV 32219
Owner: E.W. Scripps Co.
Editorial: 20777 W 10 Mile Rd, Southfield, Michigan 48075-1086 **Tel:** 1 248 827-7777.
Email: wxyzdesk@wxyz.com
Web site: http://www.wxyz.com/tv20detroit
Profile: WMYD-TV is the MyNetworkTV affiliate for the Detroit market. The station is owned by Granite Broadcasting Corp. WMYD-TV broadcasts locally on channel 20. The station DOES NOT do any satellite interviews and is only looking for materials relevant to the Detroit area.
TELEVISION STATION

WMYG-TV 390588
Owner: New Age Media, LLC
Editorial: 1703 NW 80th Blvd, Gainesville, Florida 32606-9178 **Tel:** 1 352 332-1128.
Web site: http://www.mygtn.tv
Profile: WMYG-TV is the MyNetwork affiliate for the Gainesville, FL market. The station is owned by New Age Media, LLC. WMYG-TV broadcasts locally on channel 45.
TELEVISION STATION

WMYO-TV 32996
Owner: Block Communications Inc.
Editorial: 624 W Muhammad Ali Blvd, Louisville, Kentucky 40203-1915 **Tel:** 1 502 584-6441.
Web site: http://www.fox41.com
Profile: WMYO-TV is the MyNetworkTV affiliate for the Louisville, KY market. The station is owned by Block Communications Inc. WMYO-TV broadcasts locally on channel 58.
TELEVISION STATION

WMYT3-TV 614000
Owner: Capitol Broadcasting Company
Editorial: 3501 Performance Rd, Charlotte, North Carolina 28214-9056 **Tel:** 1 704 944-3300.
Web site: http://www.wmyt12.com
Profile: WMYT3-TV is a multicast of WMYT-TV. A multicast channel is a separate channel that shares the bandwith of the main station but can air unique programming. WMYT3-TV airs programming from WGBT-TV/WordNet in the Charlotte, NC market. The station is owned by Capitol Broadcasting Company. WMYT3-TV broadcasts locally on channel 55.3.
TELEVISION STATION

WMYT-TV 32497
Owner: Capitol Broadcasting Company
Editorial: 3501 Performance Rd, Charlotte, North Carolina 28214-9056 **Tel:** 1 704 944-3300.
Email: newstips@myfoxcarolinas.com
Web site: http://www.wmyt12.com
Profile: WMYT-TV is the MyNetworkTV network affiliate for the Charlotte, NC market. The station is owned by Capitol Broadcasting Company. WMYT-TV broadcasts locally on channel 55.
TELEVISION STATION

WMYV-TV 31860
Owner: Sinclair Broadcast Group, Inc.
Editorial: 3500 Myer Lee Dr, Winston Salem, North Carolina 27101 **Tel:** 1 336 274-4848.
Web site: http://www.my48.tv
Profile: WMYV-TV is the MyNetworkTV affiliate for the Greensboro-Winston Salem, NC market. The station is owned by Sinclair Broadcast Group, Inc. WMYV-TV broadcasts locally on channel 48.
TELEVISION STATION

WNAB-TV 32474
Owner: Lambert Communications
Editorial: 631 Mainstream Dr, Nashville, Tennessee 37228 **Tel:** 1 615 259-5617.
Web site: http://www.cw58.tv
Profile: WNAB-TV is the CW affiliate for the Nashville, TN market. The station is owned by Lambert Communications. WNAB-TV broadcasts locally on channel 58.
TELEVISION STATION

WNAC2-TV 729570
Owner: Nexstar Media Group, LLC
Editorial: 25 Catamore Blvd, East Providence, Rhode Island 02914-1203 **Tel:** 1 401 438-7200.
Web site: http://www.myritv.com
Profile: WNAC2-TV is a multicast channel of WNAC-TV. A multicast channel is a separate channel that shares the bandwidth of the main station but can air unique programming. WNAC2-TV is the local MyNetworkTV affiliate on channel 64.2 for the East Providence, RI market. WNAC2-TV is owned by Nexstar Media Group, LLC.
TELEVISION STATION

WNAC-TV 32000
Owner: Nexstar Media Group, LLC
Editorial: 25 Catamore Blvd, East Providence, Rhode Island 02914-1203 **Tel:** 1 401 438-7200.
Email: desk@wpri.com
Web site: http://www.foxprovidence.com
Profile: WNAC-TV is the FOX affiliate for the Providence, RI-New Bedford, MA market. The station is owned by Nexstar Media Group, LLC. WNAC-TV broadcasts locally on channel 64.
TELEVISION STATION

WNBC2-TV 583523
Owner: NBC Universal
Editorial: 30 Rockefeller Plz, New York, New York 10112-0015 **Tel:** 1 212 664-4444.
Email: wnbc.newsdesk@nbcuni.com
Web site: http://www.cozitv.com
Profile: WNBC2-TV is a multicast of WNBC-TV. A multicast channel is a separate channel that shares the bandwidth of the main station but can air unique programming. WNBC2-TV is the local Cozi TV affiliate on Channel 4.2 for the New York City market. WNBC2-TV is owned by NBC Universal.
TELEVISION STATION

WNBC4-TV 606085
Owner: NBC Universal
Editorial: 30 Rockefeller Plz Fl 7, New York, New York 10112-0015 **Tel:** 1 212 664-4444.
Email: wnbc.newsdesk@nbcuni.com
Web site: http://www.nbcnewyork.com/
Profile: WNBC4-TV is a multicast of WNBC-TV. A multicast channel is a separate channel that shares the bandwidth of the main station but can air unique programming. WNBC4-TV is the local Universal Sports affiliate on Channel 4.4 for the New York City market. WNBC4-TV is owned by NBC Universal.
TELEVISION STATION

WNBC-TV 32001
Owner: NBC Universal
Editorial: 30 Rockefeller Plz Fl 7, New York, New York 10112-0015 **Tel:** 1 212 664-4444.
Email: desk@nbcnewyork.com
Web site: http://www.nbcnewyork.com
Profile: WNBC-TV is the NBC affiliate for the New York market. The station is owned by NBC Universal. WNBC-TV broadcasts locally on channel 4.
TELEVISION STATION

WNBW-TV 573810
Owner: MPS Media, LLC
Editorial: 1703 NW 80th Blvd, Gainesville, Florida 32606-9178 **Tel:** 1 352 332-1128.
Web site: http://mycbs4.com
Profile: WNBW-TV is the NBC affiliate for the Gainesville, FL market. The station is owned by MPS Media, LLC. WNBW-TV broadcasts locally on channel 9.
TELEVISION STATION

WNCE-TV 151194
Owner: (Jackson)Jesse, (Carusone) Peter & (Cass) Steven
Editorial: 126 Glen St, Glens Falls, New York 12801-4432 **Tel:** 1 518 798-8000.
Web site: http://www.looktvonline.com
TELEVISION STATION

WNCF-TV 31935
Owner: Bahakel Communications
Editorial: 3251 Harrison Rd, Montgomery, Alabama 36109-4321 **Tel:** 1 334 270-8888.
Email: news@waka.com
Web site: http://www.alabamanews.net
Profile: WNCF-TV is the ABC affiliate for the Montgomery, AL market. The station is owned by Bahakel Communications. WNCF-TV broadcasts locally on channel 32. WAKA-TV, WNCF-TV, and WBMM-TV are known as Alabama News Network.
TELEVISION STATION

WNCN2-TV 612928
Owner: Nexstar Media Group, LLC
Editorial: 1205 Front St, Raleigh, North Carolina 27609-7526 **Tel:** 1 919 836-1717.
Email: newstips@wncn.com
Web site: http://www.wncn.com
Profile: WNCN2-TV is a multicast of WNCN-TV. A multicast channel is a separate channel that shares the bandwith of the main station but can air unique programming. WNCN2-TV airs programming from Antenna TV in the Raleigh-Durham, NC market. The station is owned by Nexstar Media Group, LLC. WNCN2-TV broadcasts locally on channel 17.2.
TELEVISION STATION

WNCN3-TV 612930
Owner: Nexstar Media Group, LLC
Editorial: 1205 Front St, Raleigh, North Carolina 27609-7526 **Tel:** 1 919 836-1717.
Web site: http://www.wncn.com
Profile: WNCN3-TV is a multicast of WNCN-TV. A multicast channel is a separate channel that shares the bandwith of the main station but can air unique programming. WNCN3-TV airs programming from Justice Network in the Raleigh-Durham, NC market. The station is owned by Nexstar Media Group, LLC. WNCN3-TV broadcasts locally on channel 17.3.
TELEVISION STATION

WNCN-TV 32271
Owner: Nexstar Media Group, LLC
Editorial: 1205 Front St, Raleigh, North Carolina 27609-7526 **Tel:** 1 919 836-1717.
Email: newstips@wncn.com
Web site: http://www.wncn.com
Profile: WNCN-TV is the CBS network affiliate for the Raleigh-Durham, NC market. The station is owned by Nexstar Media Group, LLC. WNCN-TV broadcasts locally on channel 17.
TELEVISION STATION

WNCR-TV 457700
Owner: On The Map, Inc.
Editorial: 1280 S Wesleyan Blvd, Rocky Mount, North Carolina 27803-4503 **Tel:** 1 252 407-8365.
Email: news@wncrtv41.com
Web site: http://www.wncrtv41.com
Profile: WNCR-TV is an independent, non-profit station in the Raleigh - Durham, NC market. The station is owned by On The Map, Inc. WNCR-TV broadcasts locally on channel 41.
TELEVISION STATION

WNCT-TV 32002
Owner: Nexstar Media Group, LLC
Editorial: 3221 Evans St, Greenville, North Carolina 27834-6928 **Tel:** 1 252 355-8500.
Email: newsdesk@wnct.com
Web site: http://www.wnct.com
Profile: WNCT-TV is the CBS affiliate for the Greenville, NC market. The station is owned by Nexstar Media Group, LLC. WNCT-TV broadcasts locally on channel 9.
TELEVISION STATION

WNDA-TV 235262
Owner: Dominion Media Inc.
Editorial: 220 Potters Ln, Clarksville, Indiana 47129-1020 **Tel:** 1 812 949-9843.
Web site: http://www.indiana9.com
Profile: WNDA-TV is an independent station for the Louisville, KY market. The station is owned by Dominion Media Inc. WNDA-TV broadcasts locally on channel 9.
TELEVISION STATION

WNDU-TV 32004
Owner: Gray Television, Inc.
Editorial: 54516 Indiana State Route 933, South Bend, Indiana 46637-3357 **Tel:** 1 574 284-3000.
Email: newscenter16@wndu.com
Web site: http://www.wndu.com
Profile: WNDU-TV is a local NBC affiliate for the South Bend, IN market. The station is owned by Gray Television, Inc. WNDU-TV broadcasts locally on channel 16.
TELEVISION STATION

WNDY-TV 31988
Owner: Nexstar Media Group, LLC
Editorial: 1950 N Meridian St, Indianapolis, Indiana 46202-1304 **Tel:** 1 317 923-8888.
Web site: http://wishtv.com/myindy-tv
Profile: WNDY-TV is the MyNetworkTV affiliate for the Indianapolis market. The station is owned by

Nexstar Media Group, LLC. WNDY-TV broadcasts locally on channel 23.
TELEVISION STATION

WNED-TV 32005
Owner: Western New York Public Broadcasting Association
Editorial: 140 Lower Terrace St, Buffalo, New York 14202-4330 **Tel:** 1 716 845-7000.
Email: viewerservices@wned.org
Web site: http://www.wned.org
Profile: WNED-TV is a PBS affiliate for the Buffalo, NY area. The station is owned by Western New York Public Broadcasting Association. WNED-TV broadcasts locally on channel 17.
TELEVISION STATION

WNEM-TV 32007
Owner: Meredith Broadcasting Group
Editorial: 107 N Franklin St, Saginaw, Michigan 48607-1263 **Tel:** 1 989 755-8191.
Email: wnem@wnem.com
Web site: http://www.wnem.com
Profile: WNEM-TV is the CBS affiliate for the Bay City, Saginaw, Midland, Flint, MI, market. It is owned by Meredith Broadcasting Group. WNEM-TV broadcasts locally on channel 5.
TELEVISION STATION

WNEO2-TV 614999
Owner: Western Reserve Public Media
Editorial: 1750 Campus Center Dr, Kent, Ohio 44240 **Tel:** 1 330 677-4549.
Email: programming@westernreservepublicmedia.org
Profile: WNEO2-TV is the PBS affiliate for the Youngstown, OH market. The station is owned by Western Reserve Public Media. WNEO2-TV broadcasts locally on channel 45.2. The station airs programming from PBS Fusion as well as locally produced programming, Ohio Channel and Classic Arts Showcase. WNEO2-TV is a multicast channel of WNEO-TV. A multicast channel is a separate channel that shares the bandwidth of the main station but can air unique programming.
TELEVISION STATION

WNEO3-TV 615001
Owner: Western Reserve Public Media
Editorial: 1750 Campus Center Drive, Kent, Ohio 44240 **Tel:** 1 330 677-4549.
Email: programming@westernreservepublicmedia.org
Web site: http://www.mhznetworks.org/mhzworldview
Profile: WNEO3-TV is a non-commercial, educational station for the Youngstown, OH market. The station is owned by Western Reserve Public Media. WNEO3-TV broadcasts locally on channel 45.3. The station airs MHz Worldview programming. WNEO3-TV is a multicast channel of WNEO-TV. A multicast channel is a separate channel that shares the bandwidth of the main station but can air unique programming.
TELEVISION STATION

WNEO4-TV 615002
Owner: Western Reserve Public Media
Editorial: 1750 Campus Center Drive, Kent, Ohio 44240 **Tel:** 1 330 677-4549.
Email: programming@westernreservepublicmedia.org
Web site: http://www.vmetv.com
Profile: WNEO4-TV is a non-commercial, educational station for the Youngstown, OH market. The station is owned by Western Reserve Public Media. WNEO4-TV broadcasts locally on channel 45.4. The station airs programming from V-me, a Hispanic television network. WNEO4-TV is a multicast channel of WNEO-TV. A multicast channel is a separate channel that shares the bandwidth of the main station but can air unique programming.
TELEVISION STATION

WNEO-TV 32691
Owner: Western Reserve Public Media
Editorial: 1750 Campus Center Drive, Kent, Ohio 44240 **Tel:** 1 330 677-4549.
Email: programs@westernreservepublicmedia.org
Web site: http://www.westernreservepublicmedia.org
Profile: WNEO-TV is the PBS affiliate for the Youngstown, OH market. The station is owned by Western Reserve Public Media. WNEO-TV broadcasts locally on channel 45.
TELEVISION STATION

WNEP2-TV 583245
Owner: Tribune Broadcasting Co.
Editorial: 16 Montage Mountain Rd, Moosic, Pennsylvania 18507-1753 **Tel:** 1 570 346-7474.
Email: newstip@wnep.com
Web site: http://www.wnep.com
Profile: WNEP2-TV is a multicast channel of WNEP2-TV. A multicast channel is a separate channel that shares the bandwidth of the main station but can air unique programming. WNEP2-TV is the local ABC affiliate on Channel 16.2 for the Wilkes-Barre and Scranton, PA market. WNEP2-TV is owned by Tribune Broadcasting Co.
TELEVISION STATION

WNEP-TV 32008
Owner: Tribune Broadcasting Co.
Editorial: 16 Montage Mountain Rd, Moosic, Pennsylvania 18507-1753 **Tel:** 1 570 346-7474.
Email: newstip@wnep.com
Web site: http://www.wnep.com
Profile: WNEP-TV is the ABC affiliate for the Wilkes-Barre and Scranton, PA market. The station is owned by Tribune Broadcasting Co. WNEP-TV broadcasts locally on channel 16.
TELEVISION STATION

WNET2-TV 606646
Owner: WNET.org
Editorial: 825 8th Ave Fl 14, New York, New York 10019-7416 **Tel:** 1 212 560-1313.
Email: programming@thirteen.org
Web site: http://www.thirteen.org
Profile: WNET2-TV is a multicast channel of WNET-TV. A multicast channel is a separate channel that shares the bandwith of the main station but can air unique programming. WNET2-TV is the local Kids Thirteen affiliate on channel 13.2 for the greater Metropolitan New York area. It is owned by WNET.org.
TELEVISION STATION

WNET3-TV 606649
Owner: WNET.org
Editorial: 825 8th Ave Fl 14, New York, New York 10019-7416 **Tel:** 1 212 560-1313.
Email: programming@thirteen.org
Web site: http://www.thirteen.org
Profile: WNET3-TV is a multicast channel of WNET-TV. A multicast channel is a separate channel that shares the bandwith of the main station but can air unique programming. WNET3-TV is the local V-Me affiliate on channel 13.3 for the greater Metropolitan New York area. It is owned by WNET.org.
TELEVISION STATION

WNET-TV 32009
Owner: WNET.org
Editorial: 825 8th Ave Fl 14, New York, New York 10019-7416 **Tel:** 1 212 560-1313.
Email: programming@thirteen.org
Web site: http://www.thirteen.org
Profile: WNET-TV is the PBS affiliate for the New York market. The station is owned by WNET.org. WNET-TV broadcasts locally on channel 13.
TELEVISION STATION

WNEU-TV 32311
Owner: NBC Universal
Editorial: 160 Wells Ave, Newton, Massachusetts 02459-3302 **Tel:** 1 617 630-5000.
Web site: http://www.telemundoboston.com
Profile: WNEU-TV is the Telemundo affiliate for the Boston market. The station is owned by NBC Universal. WNEU-TV broadcasts locally on channel 60.
TELEVISION STATION

WNIN-TV 32012
Owner: WNIN Tri-State Public Media, Inc.
Editorial: 405 Carpenter St, Evansville, Indiana 47708 **Tel:** 1 812 423-2973.
Email: membership@wnin.org
Web site: http://www.wnin.org
Profile: WNIN-TV is the PBS affiliate for the Evansville, IN market. The station is owned by Indiana Public Broadcasting Systems. WNIN-TV broadcasts locally on channel 9.
TELEVISION STATION

WNIT-TV 32013
Owner: Indiana Public Stations
Editorial: 300 W Jefferson Blvd, South Bend, Indiana 46601-1513 **Tel:** 1 574 675-9648.
Email: wnit@wnit.org
Web site: http://www.wnit.org
Profile: WNIT-TV is the PBS affiliate for the South Bend, IN market. It is owned by Indiana Public Broadcasting Stations. WNIT-TV broadcasts locally on channel 34.
TELEVISION STATION

WNJT-TV 32710
Owner: New Jersey Public Broadcasting Authority
Editorial: 125 W State St, Trenton, New Jersey 08608-1101 **Tel:** 1 609 777-0031.
Email: NJTVprogramming@njtvonline.org
Web site: http://njtvonline.org
Profile: WNJT-TV is a PBS affiliate for the Trenton, NJ market. The station is owned by New Jersey Public Broadcasting Authority and operated by Public Media of New Jersey. WNJT-TV broadcasts locally on channel 52. The station does not have a news department.
TELEVISION STATION

WNJU-TV 32014
Owner: NBC Universal
Editorial: 2200 Fletcher Ave, Fort Lee, New Jersey 07024-5005 **Tel:** 1 201 969-4247.
Email: wnju47@nbcuni.com
Web site: http://www.telemundo47.com
Profile: WNJU-TV is the Telemundo affiliate for the New York City market. The station is owned by NBC Universal. WNJU-TV broadcasts locally on channel 47. Do not contact assignment editors directly. The station strongly suggests using the news department's e-mail to send all press releases.
TELEVISION STATION

WNKY2-TV 966567
Owner: Marquee Broadcasting
Editorial: 325 Emmett Ave Ste N, Bowling Green, Kentucky 42101-3975 **Tel:** 1 270 781-2140.
Web site: http://www.wnky.net
Profile: WNKY2-TV is a multicast channel of WNKY-TV. A multicast channel is a separate channel that shares the bandwidth of the main station but can air unique programming. WNKY2-TV airs CBs programming. The station is owned by Max Media. WNKY2-TV broadcasts locally on channel 16.2.
TELEVISION STATION

WNKY-TV 32428
Owner: Marquee Broadcasting
Editorial: 325 Emmett Ave Ste N, Bowling Green, Kentucky 42101-3975 **Tel:** 1 270 781-2140.
Email: wnky@wnky.com
Web site: http://www.wnky.com
Profile: WNKY-TV is the NBC affiliate for Bowling Green, KY. The station is owned by Max Media. WNKY-TV broadcasts locally on channel 40.
TELEVISION STATION

WNLO-TV 32256
Owner: Nexstar Media Group, LLC
Editorial: 2077 Elmwood Ave, Buffalo, New York 14207-1903 **Tel:** 1 716 874-4410.
Email: wivbweb@wivb.com
Web site: http://www.cw23.com
Profile: WNLO-TV is the CW affiliate for the Buffalo, NY market. The station is owned by Nexstar Media Group, LLC. WNLO-TV broadcasts locally on channel 23.
TELEVISION STATION

WNNE-TV 32016
Owner: Hearst Television Inc.
Editorial: 203 Dewitt Dr, White River Junction, Vermont 05001-2027 **Tel:** 1 802 295-3100.
Email: feedback@wptz.com
Web site: http://www.wptz.com/news/vermont-new-york/upper-valley-wnne
Profile: WNNE-TV is the NBC affiliate for the Burlington, VT market. The station is owned by Hearst Television Inc. WNNE-TV broadcasts locally on channel 31.
TELEVISION STATION

WNOL-TV 32017
Owner: Tribune Broadcasting Co.
Editorial: 1 Galleria Blvd, Ste 850, Metairie, Louisiana 70001 **Tel:** 1 504 525-3838.
Email: nola38@tribune.com
Web site: http://www.nola38.com/
Profile: WNOL-TV is the CW affiliate for the New Orleans market. The station is owned by the Tribune Broadcasting Co. WNOL-TV broadcasts locally on channel 38.
TELEVISION STATION

WNPT2-TV 612953
Owner: Nashville Public Television Inc.
Editorial: 161 Rains Ave, Nashville, Tennessee 37203-5330 **Tel:** 1 615 259-9325.
Email: tv8@wnpt.org
Web site: http://www.wnpt.org
TELEVISION STATION

WNPT-TV 31805
Owner: Nashville Public Television Inc.
Editorial: 161 Rains Ave, Nashville, Tennessee 37203-5330 **Tel:** 1 615 259-9325.
Email: tv8@wnpt.org
Web site: http://www.wnpt.org
Profile: WNPT-TV is the PBS affiliate for the Nashville, TN market. The station is owned by Nashville Public Television Inc. WNPT-TV broadcasts locally on channel 8.
TELEVISION STATION

WNPX-TV 32437
Owner: ION Media Networks
Editorial: 1281 N Mount Juliet Rd Ste L, Mount Juliet, Tennessee 37122-3314 **Tel:** 1 615 773-6100.
Web site: http://www.iontelevision.com
Profile: WNPX-TV is the ION Television affiliate for the Nashville, TN market. The station is owned by ION Media Networks. WNPX-TV broadcasts locally on channel 28.
TELEVISION STATION

WNTZ-TV 32429
Owner: White Knight Broadcasting
Editorial: 4615 Parliament Dr, Alexandria, Louisiana 71303-2759 **Tel:** 1 318 443-4700.
Email: community@fox48tv.com
Web site: http://www.fox48tv.com
Profile: WNTZ-TV is the FOX and MyNetworkTV affiliate for the Alexandria, LA market. The station is owned by White Knight Broadcasting. WNTZ-TV broadcasts locally on channel 48.
TELEVISION STATION

WNUV-TV 32021
Owner: Cunningham Broadcasting Corp.
Editorial: 2000 W 41st St, Baltimore, Maryland 21211-1420 **Tel:** 1 410 467-4545.
Email: webmaster@foxbaltimore.com
Web site: http://www.cwbaltimore.com
Profile: WNUV-TV is the FOX and CW network affiliate for the Baltimore market. The station is owned by Cunningham Broadcasting Corp. WNUV-TV broadcasts locally on channel 54.
TELEVISION STATION

WNVT-TV 32679
Owner: MHz Networks Corporation
Editorial: 8101A Lee Hwy, Falls Church, Virginia 22042-1195 **Tel:** 1 703 770-7100.
Email: viewerservices@mhznetworks.org
Web site: http://www.mhznetworks.org
Profile: WNVT-TV is the MHz Network affiliate in the Washington, DC market. The station is owned by Commonwealth Public Broadcasting. WNVT-TV broadcasts locally on channel 30.
TELEVISION STATION

WNWO-TV 32022
Owner: Sinclair Broadcast Group
Editorial: 300 S Byrne Rd, Toledo, Ohio 43615-6217 **Tel:** 1 419 535-0024.
Email: news@wnwo.com
Web site: http://nbc24.com
Profile: WNWO-TV is the NBC network affiliate for the Toledo, OH market. The station is owned by Sinclair Broadcast Group. WNWO-TV broadcasts locally on channel 24.
TELEVISION STATION

WNYB-TV 32434
Owner: Faith Broadcasting
Editorial: 5775 Big Tree Rd, Orchard Park, New York 14127-2208 **Tel:** 1 716 662-2659 1300.
Email: wnyb@tct.tv
Web site: http://www.tct.tv
Profile: WNYB-TV is the Tri-State Christian Television (TCT) affiliate for the Buffalo, NY market. The station is owned by Faith Broadcasting WNYB-TV broadcasts locally on channel 26.
TELEVISION STATION

WNYE2-TV 606885
Owner: NYC Media Group
Editorial: 112 Tillary St, Brooklyn, New York 11201-2926 **Tel:** 1 212 669-7400.
Email: submissions@media.nyc.gov
Web site: http://www.nyc.gov/media
Profile: WNYE2-TV is a multicast channel of WNYE-TV. A multicast channel is a separate channel that shares the bandwith of the main station but can air unique programming. WNYE2-TV airs City Drive Live programming for the greater New York market. The station is owned by NYC Media Group. WNYE2-TV broadcasts locally on channel 25.2.
TELEVISION STATION

WNYE-TV 32024
Owner: NYC Media Group
Editorial: 1 Centre St, New York, New York 10007-1602 **Tel:** 1 212 669-7400.
Email: submissions@media.nyc.gov
Web site: http://www.nyc.gov/media
Profile: WNYE-TV is a PBS affiliate for the New York market. The station is owned by NYC Media Group. WNYE-TV broadcasts locally on channel 25
TELEVISION STATION

WNYF-TV 76597
Owner: United Communications Corp.
Editorial: 120 Arcade St, Watertown, New York 13601-3279 **Tel:** 1 315 788-3800.
Email: news@wwnytv.net
Web site: http://www.wwnytv.com
Profile: WYNF-TV is the FOX affiliate in the Watertown, NY market. The station is owned by United Communications Corp. WYNF-TV broadcasts locally on channel 28.
TELEVISION STATION

WNYN-TV 476516
Owner: TVC NY License LLC
Editorial: 1443 Park Ave Fl 6, New York, New York 10029-4623 **Tel:** 1 305 994-1700.
Email: info@wnyntv.com
Web site: http://www.furiamusicaltv.com
Profile: WNYN-TV is the Azteca America affiliate for the New York market. The station is owned by TVC NY License LLC. WNYN-TV broadcasts locally on channel 39. They do not accept PSA's.
TELEVISION STATION

WNYO-TV 32257
Owner: Sinclair Broadcast Group, Inc.
Editorial: 699 Hertel Ave, Ste 100, Buffalo, New York 14207 **Tel:** 1 716 447-3200.
Email: programming@mytvbuffalo.com
Web site: http://www.mytvbuffalo.com
Profile: WNYO-TV is the MyNetworkTV affiliate for the Buffalo, NY area. The station is owned by Sinclair Broadcasting Group, Inc. WNYO-TV broadcasts locally on channel 49.
TELEVISION STATION

WNYS-TV 32533
Owner: RKMedia Inc
Editorial: 1000 James St, Syracuse, New York 13203-2704 **Tel:** 1 315 472-6800.
Web site: http://foxsyracuse.com
Profile: WNYS-TV is the local MyNetworkTV affiliate station for the Syracuse, NY market. The station is owned by RKMedia Inc., but is under a LMA with Sinclair Broadcast Group. WNYS-TV broadcasts locally on channel 43.
TELEVISION STATION

WNYT-TV 32025
Owner: Hubbard Broadcasting Inc.
Editorial: 715 N Pearl St, Menands, New York 12204-1826 **Tel:** 1 518 436-4791.
Email: newstips@wnyt.com
Web site: http://www.wnyt.com
Profile: WNYT-TV is the NBC affiliate for the Albany, Troy, and Schenectady, NY markets. The station is owned by Hubbard Broadcasting Inc. WNYT-TV broadcasts locally on channel 13.
TELEVISION STATION

WNYW2-TV 606080
Owner: Fox Broadcasting Company
Editorial: 205 E 67th St, New York, New York 10065-6050 **Tel:** 1 201 452-3800.
Web site: http://www.myfoxny.com
Profile: WNYW2-TV is a multicast channel of WNYW-TV. A multicast channel is a separate channel that shares the bandwidth of the main station but can air

unique programming. WNYW-TV is the local MyNetwork TV affiliate on Channel 5.2 for the New York market. WNYW2-TV is owned by Fox Broadcasting Company.
TELEVISION STATION

WNYW-TV 32026
Owner: Fox Broadcasting Company
Editorial: 205 E 67th St, New York, New York 10065-6050 **Tel:** 1 212 452-3808.
Web site: http://www.fox5ny.com
Profile: WNYW-TV is the FOX affiliate for the New York market. The station is owned by Fox Broadcasting Company. WNYW-TV broadcasts locally on channel 5. News tips should be sent on station's Facebook page.
TELEVISION STATION

WOAI2-TV 621685
Owner: Sinclair Broadcast Group, Inc.
Editorial: 1031 Navarro St, San Antonio, Texas 78205-1321 **Tel:** 1 210 226-4444.
Email: webteam@news4sanantonio.com
Web site: http://www.woai.com
Profile: WOAI2-TV is a multicast of WOAI-TV. A multicast channel is a separate channel that shares the bandwith of the main station but can air unique programming. WOAI2-TV airs Hispanic programming from Mexicanal in the San Antonio market. The station is owned by Sinclair Broadcast Group, Inc. WOAI2-TV broadcasts locally on channel 4.2.
TELEVISION STATION

WOAI-TV 31528
Owner: Sinclair Broadcast Group, Inc.
Editorial: 4335 NW Loop 410, San Antonio, Texas 78229-5136 **Tel:** 1 210 226-4444.
Email: news@kabb.com
Web site: http://www.news4sanantonio.com
Profile: WOAI-TV is the NBC affiliate for the San Antonio market. The station is owned by High Sinclair Broadcast Group, Inc. WOAI-TV is broadcast locally on channel 4.
TELEVISION STATION

WOAY-TV 32028
Owner: Thomas Broadcasting
Editorial: 7113 Legends Highway, Oak Hill, West Virginia 25901 **Tel:** 1 304 469-3361.
Email: news@woay.com
Web site: http://woay.com
Profile: WOAY-TV is the ABC network affiliate for the Bluefield-Beckely, WV market. The station is owned by Thomas Broadcasting. WOAY-TV broadcasts locally on channel 50.
TELEVISION STATION

WOBZ-TV 376454
Owner: Kesler (Andrea Joy)
Editorial: 1337 Old Hare Rd, East Bernstadt, Kentucky 40729 **Tel:** 1 606 843-9999.
Email: wobztv9@yahoo.com
Web site: http://www.wobz9.com
Profile: WOBZ-TV is an independent station for the Lexington, KY market. The station is owned by Andrea Joy Kesler. WOBZ-TV broadcasts locally on channel 9.
TELEVISION STATION

WOCK-TV 338133
Owner: KM Communications Inc.
Editorial: 5235 N Kedzie Ave, Chicago, Illinois 60625-4726 **Tel:** 1 773 588-0070.
Web site: http://mundofox13.com
Profile: WOCK-TV is the MundoFOX affiliate for the Chicago market. The station is owned by KM Communications Inc. WOCK-TV broadcasts locally on channel 13. The station does not have a news department.
TELEVISION STATION

WOFL-TV 32029
Owner: Fox Broadcasting Company
Editorial: 35 Skyline Dr, Lake Mary, Florida 32746-6202 **Tel:** 1 407 644-3535.
Email: news@foxwofl.com
Web site: http://www.fox35orlando.com
Profile: WOFL-TV is the FOX network affiliate for the Orlando-Daytona Beach, FL market. The station is owned by Fox Broadcasting Company. WOFL-TV broadcasts locally on channel 35.
TELEVISION STATION

WOGX-TV 32030
Owner: Fox Broadcasting Company
Editorial: 4727 NW 53rd Ave Ste A, Gainesville, Florida 32653-4899 **Tel:** 1 352 371-0051.
Web site: http://www.wogx.com
Profile: WOGX-TV is the FOX affiliate for the Gainsville, FL market. The station is owned by Fox Broadcasting Company. WOGX-TV broadcasts locally on Channel 51.
TELEVISION STATION

WOHL2-TV 856602
Owner: West CentrBroadcasting, Inc.
Editorial: 1424 Rice Ave, Lima, Ohio 45805-1949
Tel: 1 419 228-8835.
Profile: WOHL2-TV is a multicast channel of WOHL-TV. A multicast channel is a separate channel that shares the bandwidth of the main station but can air unique programming. WHOL2-TV is the simulcast of WLMO-TV for the Lima, OH area. The station is owned by West Central Broadcasting, Inc. WOHL2-TV broadcasts locally on channel 35.2.
TELEVISION STATION

WOHL-TV 32524
Owner: West Central Broadcasting, Inc.
Editorial: 1424 Rice Ave, Lima, Ohio 45805-1949
Tel: 1 419 228-8835.
Email: newsrelease@wlio.com
Web site: http://www.hometownstations.com
Profile: WOHL-TV is the FOX affiliate for the Lima, OH market. The station is owned by West Central Broadcasting, Inc. WOHL-TV broadcasts locally on channel 18.
TELEVISION STATION

WOIO-TV 32032
Owner: Raycom Media Inc.
Editorial: 1717 E 12th St, Cleveland, Ohio 44114-3246
Tel: 1 216 771-1943.
Email: 19tips@woio.com
Web site: http://www.cleveland19.com
Profile: WOIO-TV is the CBS affiliate for the Cleveland, OH market. The station is owned by Raycom Media Inc. WOIO-TV broadcasts locally on channel 19.
TELEVISION STATION

WOI-TV 32031
Owner: Nextar Broadcasting Group
Editorial: 3903 Westown Pkwy, West Des Moines, Iowa 50266-1009 **Tel:** 1 515 457-9645.
Email: news@weareiowa.com
Web site: http://www.weareiowa.com
Profile: WOI-TV is the ABC affiliate for the West Des Moines, IA market. The station is owned by Nextar Broadcasting Group. WOI-TV broadcasts locally on channel 5.
TELEVISION STATION

WOLF-TV 32584
Owner: New Age Media of Pennsylvania License, LLC
Editorial: 1181 Highway 315 Blvd, Plains, Pennsylvania 18702-6928 **Tel:** 1 570 970-5600.
Email: myfoxnepa@fox56.com
Web site: http://www.myfoxnepa.com
Profile: WOLF-TV is the local FOX affiliate for the Scranton, Wilkes-Barre, PA market. The station is owned by New Age Media of Gainesville License, LLC. WOLF-TV broadcasts locally on channel 56.
TELEVISION STATION

WOLO-TV 32034
Owner: Bahakel Communications
Editorial: 5807 Shakespeare Rd, Columbia, South Carolina 29223-7209 **Tel:** 1 803 754-7525.
Email: eyewitnessnews@wolo.com
Web site: http://www.abccolumbia.com
Profile: WOLO-TV is the ABC affiliate in the Columbia, SC, market. The station is owned by Bahakel Communications. WOLO-TV broadcasts locally on channel 25.
TELEVISION STATION

WOOD2-TV 619949
Owner: Nexstar Media Group, LLC
Editorial: 120 College Ave SE, Grand Rapids, Michigan 49503-4404 **Tel:** 1 616 456-8888.
Email: news@woodtv.com
Web site: http://www.woodtv.com
Profile: WOOD2-TV is a multicast of WOOD-TV. A multicast channel is a separate channel that shares the bandwith of the main station but can air unique programming. WOOD2-TV airs programming from My Network TV in the Grand Rapids, MI market. The station is owned by Nexstar Media Group, LLC. WOOD2-TV broadcasts locally on channel 8.2.
TELEVISION STATION

WOOD3-TV 619951
Owner: Nexstar Media Group, LLC
Editorial: 120 College Ave SE, Grand Rapids, Michigan 49503-4404 **Tel:** 1 616 456-8888.
Email: news@woodtv.com
Web site: http://www.woodtv.com
Profile: WOOD3-TV is a multicast of WOOD-TV. A multicast channel is a separate channel that shares the bandwith of the main station but can air unique programming. WOOD3-TV airs weather programming from Storm Team 8 Live Doppler Network in the Grand Rapids, MI market. The station is owned by Nexstar Media Group, LLC. WOOD3-TV broadcasts locally on channel 8.3.
TELEVISION STATION

WOOD-TV 32035
Owner: Nexstar Media Group, LLC
Editorial: 120 College Ave SE, Grand Rapids, Michigan 49503-4404 **Tel:** 1 616 456-8888.
Email: newsroom@woodtv.com
Web site: http://www.woodtv.com
Profile: WOOD-TV is the NBC affiliate for the Grand Rapids, MI market. The station is owned by Nexstar Media Group, LLC. WOOD-TV broadcasts locally on channel 8.
TELEVISION STATION

WOPX2-TV 614182
Owner: ION Media Networks
Editorial: 7091 Grand National Dr, Ste 100, Orlando, Florida 32819-8382 **Tel:** 1 407 370-5600.
Web site: http://www.qubo.com
Profile: WOPX2-TV is independent affiliate for the Orlando, FL market. The station is owned by ION Media Networks. WOPX2-TV broadcasts locally on channel 56.2. The station airs children's programming from the qubo network. WOPX2-TV is a multicast channel of WOPX-TV. A multicast channel is a separate channel that shares the bandwidth of the main station but can air unique programming.
TELEVISION STATION

WOPX3-TV 614185
Owner: ION Media Networks
Editorial: 7091 Grand National Dr, Ste 100, Orlando, Florida 32819-8382 **Tel:** 1 407 370-5600.
Web site: http://www.ionlife.com
Profile: WOPX3-TV is an ION Life affiliate for the Orlando, FL market. The station is owned by ION Media Networks. WOPX3-TV broadcasts locally on channel 56.3. The station airs lifestyle programming. WOPX3-TV is a multicast channel of WOPX-TV. A multicast channel is a separate channel that shares the bandwidth of the main station but can air unique programming.
TELEVISION STATION

WOPX4-TV 614186
Owner: ION Media Networks
Editorial: 7091 Grand National Dr, Ste 100, Orlando, Florida 32819-8382 **Tel:** 1 407 370-5600.
Web site: http://www.worship.net
Profile: WOPX4-TV is independent affiliate for the Orlando, FL market. The station is owned by ION Media Networks. WOPX4-TV broadcasts locally on channel 56.4. The station airs Christian worship-themed programming. WOPX4-TV is a multicast channel of WOPX-TV. A multicast channel is a separate channel that shares the bandwidth of the main station but can air unique programming.
TELEVISION STATION

WOPX-TV 31742
Owner: ION Media Networks
Editorial: 7091 Grand National Dr, Ste 100, Orlando, Florida 32819-8382 **Tel:** 1 407 370-5600.
Profile: WOPX-TV is the ION Television affiliate for the Orlando, FL market. The station is owned by ION Media Networks. WOPX-TV broadcasts locally on channel 56.
TELEVISION STATION

WOTF-TV 31995
Owner: Univision Communications Inc.
Editorial: 523 Douglas Ave, Altamonte Springs, Florida 32714-2507 **Tel:** 1 321 254-4343.
Profile: WOTF-TV is the Telefutura affiliate for the Orlando-Daytona Beach, FL market. The station is owned by Univision Communications Inc. WOTF-TV broadcasts locally on channel 43.
TELEVISION STATION

WOTH2-TV 615028
Owner: Block Broadcasting, Inc.
Editorial: 7737 Reinhold Dr, Cincinnati, Ohio 45237-2805 **Tel:** 1 513 631-3800.
Email: info@wkrp.tv
Web site: http://www.wkrptv.tv
Profile: WOTH2-TV is a multicast of WOTH-TV. A multicast channel is a separate channel that shares the bandwith of the main station but can air unique programming. WOTH2-TV airs programming from WBQC-TV in the Cincinnati market. The station is owned by Block Broadcasting, Inc. WOTH2-TV broadcasts locally on channel 25.2.
TELEVISION STATION

WOTH3-TV 615031
Owner: Block Broadcasting, Inc.
Editorial: 7737 Reinhold Dr, Cincinnati, Ohio 45237-2805 **Tel:** 1 513 631-8825 1.
Email: info@wbqc.com
Web site: http://www.wothtv.com
Profile: WOTH3-TV is a multicast of WOTH-TV. A multicast channel is a separate channel that shares the bandwith of the main station but can air unique programming. WOTH3-TV airs programming from The Retro TV Network in the Cincinnati market. The station is owned by Block Broadcasting, Inc. WOTH3-TV broadcasts locally on channel 25.3.
TELEVISION STATION

WOTH4-TV 615032
Owner: Block Broadcasting, Inc.
Editorial: 7737 Reinhold Dr, Cincinnati, Ohio 45237-2805 **Tel:** 1 513 631-8825 1.
Email: info@wbqc.com
Web site: http://www.wothtv.com
Profile: WOTH4-TV is a multicast of WOTH-TV. A multicast channel is a separate channel that shares the bandwith of the main station but can air unique programming. WOTH4-TV airs programming from Jewelry Television in the Cincinnati market. The station is owned by Block Broadcasting, Inc. WOTH4-TV broadcasts locally on channel 25.4.
TELEVISION STATION

WOTH-TV 350380
Owner: Block Broadcasting, Inc.
Editorial: 7737 Reinhold Dr, Cincinnati, Ohio 45237-2805 **Tel:** 1 513 631-8825 1.
Email: info@wkrp.tv
Web site: http://www.wothtv.com
Profile: WOTH-TV is an independent station for the Cincinnati market. The station is owned by Block Broadcasting, Inc. WOTH-TV broadcasts locally on channel 25.
TELEVISION STATION

WOTV2-TV 619952
Owner: Nexstar Media Group, LLC
Editorial: 120 College Ave SE, Grand Rapids, Michigan 49503-4404 **Tel:** 1 616 456-8888.
Email: news@woodtv.com
Web site: http://www.wotv.com
Profile: WOTV2-TV is a multicast of WOTV-TV. A multicast channel is a separate channel that shares the bandwith of the main station but can air unique programming. WOTV2-TV airs programming from My TV Network in the Grand Rapids, MI market. The station is owned by Nexstar Media Group, LLC. WOTV2-TV broadcasts locally on channel 4.2.
TELEVISION STATION

WOTV-TV 3218
Owner: Nexstar Media Group, LLC
Editorial: 120 College Ave SE, Grand Rapids, Michigan 49503-4404 **Tel:** 1 616 456-8888.
Email: info@wotv4women.com
Web site: http://www.wotv4women.com
Profile: WOTV-TV is the ABC affiliate for the Battle Creek, MI market. The station is owned by Nexstar Media Group, LLC. WOTV-TV broadcasts locally on channel 4.
TELEVISION STATION

WOWK-TV 3203
Owner: Nexstar Broadcasting Group Inc.
Editorial: 555 5th Ave, Huntington, West Virginia 25701-1907 **Tel:** 1 304 720-6550.
Email: news@wowktv.com
Web site: http://www.tristateupdate.com
Profile: WOWK-TV is the CBS affiliate for CBS for the Huntington, WV market. WOWK-TV broadcasts locally on channel 13. The station was previously owned by West Virginia Media Holdings LLC but has been acquired by Nexstar Broadcasting Group.
TELEVISION STATION

WOWT-TV 3203
Owner: Gray Television, Inc.
Editorial: 3501 Farnam St, Omaha, Nebraska 68131-3301 **Tel:** 1 402 346-6666.
Email: sixonline@wowt.com
Web site: http://www.wowt.com
Profile: WOWT-TV is the NBC network affiliate for the Omaha, NE market. The station is owned by Gray Television, Inc. WOWT-TV broadcasts locally on channel 6.
TELEVISION STATION

WPBF2-TV 62099
Owner: Hearst Television Inc.
Editorial: 3970 RCA Blvd, Ste 7007, Palm Beach Gardens, Florida 33410-4295 **Tel:** 1 561 694-2525.
Email: news@wpbf.com
Web site: http://www.wpbf.com
Profile: WPBF2-TV is a multicast of WPBF-TV. A multicast channel is a separate channel that shares the bandwidth of the main station but can air unique programming. WPBF2-TV airs Hispanic programming from Estrella TV in the West Palm Beach, FL market. The station is owned by Hearst Television Inc. WPBF2-TV broadcasts locally on channel 25.2.
TELEVISION STATION

WPBF-TV 3224
Owner: Hearst Television Inc.
Editorial: 3970 Rca Blvd Ste 7007, Palm Beach Gardens, Florida 33410-4295 **Tel:** 1 561 694-2525.
Email: news@wpbf.com
Web site: http://www.wpbf.com
Profile: WPBF-TV is the ABC affiliate for the West Palm Beach, FL market. The station is owned by Hearst Television Inc. WPBF-TV broadcasts locally on channel 25.
TELEVISION STATION

WPBN-TV 3268
Owner: Sinclair Broadcast Group, Inc.
Editorial: 8513 E Traverse Hwy, Traverse City, Michigan 49684-5562 **Tel:** 1 231 947-7770.
Email: newsroom@upnorthlive.com
Web site: http://www.upnorthlive.com
Profile: WPBN-TV is the NBC affiliate for the Traverse City-Cadillac, MI market. The station is owned by Sinclair Broadcast Group, Inc. WPBN-TV broadcasts locally on channel 7.
TELEVISION STATION

WPBS-TV 3269
Owner: St. Lawrence Valley ETV Council Inc.
Editorial: 1056 Arsenal St, Watertown, New York 13601-2210 **Tel:** 1 315 782-3142.
Web site: http://www.wpbstv.org
Profile: WPBS-TV is a PBS affiliate for the Watertown, NY market. The station is owned by St. Lawrence Valley ETV Council Inc. WPBS-TV broadcasts locally on channel 16.
TELEVISION STATION

WPBT2-TV 612387
Owner: Community TV Foundation of South Florida Inc
Editorial: 14901 NE 20th Ave, North Miami, Florida 33181-1121 **Tel:** 1 305 949-8321.
Web site: http://www.wpbt2.org
Profile: WPBT2-TV is the PBS affiliate for the Miami-Ft. Lauderdale market. The station is owned by Community TV Foundation of South Florida Inc. WPBT2-TV broadcasts locally on channel 2.2. The station airs only lifestyle and human interest programming from the libraries of PBS and American Public Television. WPBT2-TV is a multicast channel of WPBT-TV. A multicast channel is a separate channel that shares the bandwidth of the main station but can air unique programming.
TELEVISION STATION

WPBT3-TV 612390
Owner: Community TV Foundation of South Florida Inc
Editorial: 14901 NE 20th Ave, North Miami, Florida 33181-1121 **Tel:** 1 305 949-8321.
Email: channel2@channel2.org
Web site: http://www.channel2.org
Profile: WPBT3-TV is an independent affiliate for the Miami-Ft. Lauderdale market. The station is owned by Community TV Foundation of South Florida Inc.

WPBT3-TV broadcasts locally on channel 2.3. The station airs programming from V-me, a Hispanic television network in the US. WPBT3-TV is a multicast channel of WPBT-TV. A multicast channel is a separate channel that shares the bandwidth of the main station but can air unique programming.
TELEVISION STATION

WPBT-TV 32040
Owner: Community TV Foundation of South Florida Inc
Editorial: 14901 NE 20th Ave, North Miami, Florida 33181-1121 **Tel:** 1 305 949-8321.
Email: channel2@channel2.org
Web site: http://www.channel2.org
Profile: WPBT-TV is the PBS affiliate for the Miami-Ft. Lauderdale market. The station is owned by Community TV Foundation of South Florida Inc. WPBT-TV broadcasts locally on channel 2. The station airs only business and financial news.
TELEVISION STATION

WPCB-TV 32673
Owner: Cornerstone TeleVision
Editorial: 1 Signal Hill Dr, Wall, Pennsylvania 15148-1436 **Tel:** 1 412 824-3930.
Email: info@ctvn.org
Web site: http://www.ctvn.org
Profile: WPCB-TV is the Cornerstone TeleVision affiliate for the Pittsburgh market. The station is owned by Cornerstone TeleVision. WPCB-TV broadcasts locally on channel 40.
TELEVISION STATION

WPCH-TV 32270
Owner: Meredith Broadcasting Group
Editorial: 425 14th St NW, Atlanta, Georgia 30318-7965 **Tel:** 1 404 325-4646.
Email: peachtreetv@meredith.com
Web site: http://www.peachtreetv.com
Profile: WPCH-TV is an independent station for the Atlanta market. The station is owned by Meredith Broadcasting Group. WPCH-TV broadcasts locally on channel 17.
TELEVISION STATION

WPCT-TV 63211
Owner: Beach TV Properties, Inc.
Editorial: 8317 Front Beach Rd Ste 23, Panama City Beach, Florida 32407-4893 **Tel:** 1 850 234-2773.
Email: localnews@tripsmarter.com
Web site: http://www.tripsmarter.com
Profile: WPCT-DT is an independent station for the Panama City, FL market. The station is owned by Beach TV Properties, Inc. WPCT-DT broadcasts locally on channel 47.
TELEVISION STATION

WPCW-TV 475974
Owner: CBS Television Stations
Editorial: 420 Fort Duaesne Blvd STE 100, Pittsburgh, Pennsylvania 15222 **Tel:** 1 412 575-2245.
Email: feedback@wpcwtv.com
Web site: http://cwpittsburgh.cbslocal.com
Profile: WPCW-TV is a CW affiliate for the Pittsburgh market. The station is owned by CBS Television Stations. WPCW-TV broadcasts locally on channel 19.
TELEVISION STATION

WPDE-TV 32043
Owner: Sinclair Broadcast Group, Inc.
Editorial: 10 University Blvd, Conway, South Carolina 29526-8682 **Tel:** 1 843 234-9733.
Email: abc15news@wpde.com
Web site: http://wpde.com
Profile: WPDE-TV is the ABC affiliate for the Florence-Myrtle Beach, SC market. The station is owned by Sinclair Broadcast Group, Inc. WPDE-TV broadcasts locally on channel 15.
TELEVISION STATION

WPEC2-TV 620894
Owner: Sinclair Broadcast Group, Inc.
Editorial: 1100 Fairfield Dr, West Palm Beach, Florida 33407-2391 **Tel:** 1 561 844-1212.
Web site: http://cbs12.com
Profile: WPEC2-TV is a multicast of WPEC-TV. A multicast channel is a separate channel that shares the bandwidth of the main station but can air unique programming. WPEC2-TV airs Hispanic programming from 232 Mi Pueblo TV in the West Palm Beach, FL market. The station is owned by Sinclair Broadcast Group, Inc. WPEC2-TV broadcasts locally on channel 12.2.
TELEVISION STATION

WPEC3-TV 620900
Owner: Sinclair Broadcast Group, Inc.
Editorial: 1100 Fairfield Dr, West Palm Beach, Florida 33407-2391 **Tel:** 1 561 844-1212.
Web site: http://cbs12.com
Profile: WPEC3-TV is a multicast of WPEC-TV. A multicast channel is a separate channel that shares the bandwidth of the main station but can air unique programming. WPEC3-TV airs weather programming from CBS 12 Now in the West Palm Beach, FL market. The station is owned by Sinclair Broadcast Group, Inc. WPEC3-TV broadcasts locally on channel 12.3.
TELEVISION STATION

WPEC-TV 32044
Owner: Sinclair Broadcast Group, Inc.
Editorial: 1100 Fairfield Dr, West Palm Beach, Florida 33407-2391 **Tel:** 1 561 844-1212.
Email: newstips@cbs12.com
Web site: http://www.cbs12.com
Profile: WPEC-TV is the CBS affiliate for the West Palm Beach, FL market. The station is owned by Sinclair Broadcast Group, Inc. WPEC-TV broadcasts locally on channel 12. The station has requested that personnel or main email addresses not be listed.
TELEVISION STATION

WPFO-TV 156065
Owner: Sinclair Broadcast Group
Editorial: 233 Oxford St Ste 35, Portland, Maine 04101-3032 **Tel:** 1 207 828-0023.
Email: tvmail@wgme.com
Web site: http://fox23maine.com
Profile: WPFO-TV is a Fox affiliate for the Waterville/Portland, ME, area. The station is owned by Sinclair Broadcast Group. WPFO-TV broadcasts locally on channel 23.
TELEVISION STATION

WPGA-TV 32475
Owner: Register Communications
Editorial: 1691 Forsyth St, Macon, Georgia 31201-1407 **Tel:** 1 478 745-5858.
Web site: http://www.macon.tv
Profile: WPGA-TV is an independent channel for the Macon, GA market. The station is owned by Register Communications. WPGA-TV broadcasts locally on channel 58.
TELEVISION STATION

WPGD2-TV 613422
Owner: Trinity Broadcasting Network
Editorial: 36 Music Village Blvd, Hendersonville, Tennessee 37075-2752 **Tel:** 1 615 822-1243.
Email: wpgdtraffic@tbn.org
Web site: http://tbn.org
Profile: WPGD2-TV is a multicast of WPGD-TV. A multicast channel is a separate channel that shares the bandwidth of the main station but can air unique programming. WPGD2-TV airs programming from The Church Channel in the Nashville, TN market. The station is owned by Trinity Broadcasting Network. WPGD2-TV broadcasts locally on channel 50.2.
TELEVISION STATION

WPGD3-TV 613423
Owner: Trinity Broadcasting Network
Editorial: 36 Music Village Blvd, Hendersonville, Tennessee 37075-2752 **Tel:** 1 615 822-1243.
Email: wpgd@tbn.org
Profile: WPGD3-TV is a multicast of WPGD-TV. A multicast channel is a separate channel that shares the bandwidth of the main station but can air unique programming. WPGD3-TV airs programming from JCTV in the Nashville, TN market. The station is owned by Trinity Broadcasting Network. WPGD3-TV broadcasts locally on channel 50.3.
TELEVISION STATION

WPGD4-TV 613442
Owner: Trinity Broadcasting Network
Editorial: 36 Music Village Blvd, Hendersonville, Tennessee 37075-2752 **Tel:** 1 615 822-1243.
Email: wpgd@tbn.org
Web site: http://tbn.org
Profile: WPGD4-TV is a multicast of WPGD-TV. A multicast channel is a separate channel that shares the bandwidth of the main station but can air unique programming. WPGD4-TV airs programming from Enlace USA in the Nashville, TN market. The station is owned by Trinity Broadcasting Network. WPGD4-TV broadcasts locally on channel 50.4.
TELEVISION STATION

WPGD5-TV 613445
Owner: Trinity Broadcasting Network
Editorial: 36 Music Village Blvd, Hendersonville, Tennessee 37075-2752 **Tel:** 1 615 822-1243.
Email: wpgd@tbn.org
Web site: http://tbn.org
Profile: WPGD5-TV is a multicast of WPGD-TV. A multicast channel is a separate channel that shares the bandwidth of the main station but can air unique programming. WPGD5-TV airs programming from Smile of a Child in the Nashville, TN market. The station is owned by Trinity Broadcasting Network. WPGD5-TV broadcasts locally on channel 50.5.
TELEVISION STATION

WPGD-TV 32493
Owner: Trinity Broadcasting Network
Editorial: 36 Music Village Blvd, Hendersonville, Tennessee 37075-2752 **Tel:** 1 615 822-1243.
Web site: http://tbn.org
Profile: WPGD-TV is the Trinity Broadcasting Network (TBN) affiliate for the Nashville, TN market. The station is owned by Trinity Broadcasting Network. WPGD-TV broadcasts locally on channel 50.
TELEVISION STATION

WPGH-TV 32045
Owner: Sinclair Broadcast Group, Inc.
Editorial: 750 Ivory Ave, Pittsburgh, Pennsylvania 15214-1606 **Tel:** 1 412 931-5300.
Web site: http://www.wpgh53.com
Profile: WPGH-TV is the FOX affiliate for the Pittsburgh market. The station is owned by Sinclair Broadcast Group, Inc. WPGH-TV broadcasts locally on channel 53.
TELEVISION STATION

WPGX-TV 32046
Owner: Raycom Media Inc.
Editorial: 700 W 23rd St Ste C, Panama City, Florida 32405-3936 **Tel:** 1 850 784-0028.
Web site: http://www.myfox28.com
Profile: WPGX-TV is the FOX affiliate in Panama City, FL. The station is owned by Raycom Media Inc. WPGX-TV broadcasts locally on channel 28.
TELEVISION STATION

WPHL2-TV 610695
Owner: Tribune Broadcasting Co.
Editorial: 5001 Wynnefield Ave, Philadelphia, Pennsylvania 19131-2500 **Tel:** 1 215 878-1700.
Email: feedback@phl17.com
Web site: http://www.phl17.com
Profile: WPHL2-TV is a multicast of WPHL-TV. A multicast channel is a separate channel that shares the bandwith of the main station but can air unique programming. WPHL2-TV airs programming from This TV in the Philadelphia market. The station is owned by Tribune Broadcasting Co. WPHL2-TV broadcasts locally on channel 17.2.
TELEVISION STATION

WPHL-TV 32047
Owner: Tribune Broadcasting Co.
Editorial: 5001 Wynnefield Ave, Philadelphia, Pennsylvania 19131-2500 **Tel:** 1 215 878-1700.
Email: feedback@phl17.com
Web site: http://phl17.com
Profile: WPHL-TV is the MyNetworkTV affiliate for the Philadelphia market. The station is owned by Tribune Broadcasting Co. WPHL-TV broadcasts locally on channel 17.
TELEVISION STATION

WPIX2-TV 606088
Owner: Tribune Broadcasting Co.
Editorial: 220 E 42nd St, New York, New York 10017-5806 **Tel:** 1 212 949-1100.
Web site: http://www.wpix.com
Profile: WPIX2-TV is a multicast channel of WPIX-TV. A multicast channel is a separate channel that shares the bandwidth of the main station but can air unique programming. WPIX2-TV is the local AntennaTV affiliate on Channel 11.2 for the New York market. WPIX2-TV is owned by Tribune Broadcasting Co.
TELEVISION STATION

WPIX3-TV 606090
Owner: Tribune Broadcasting Co.
Editorial: 220 E 42nd St, New York, New York 10017-5806 **Tel:** 1 212 949-1100.
Web site: http://www.wpix.com
Profile: WPIX3-TV is a multicast channel of WPIX-TV. A multicast channel is a separate channel that shares the bandwidth of the main station but can air unique programming. WPIX3-TV is the local ThisTV affiliate on Channel 11.3 for the New York market. WPIX3-TV is owned by Tribune Broadcasting Co.
TELEVISION STATION

WPIX-TV 32048
Owner: Tribune Broadcasting Co.
Editorial: 220 E 42nd St Fl, New York, New York 10017-5806 **Tel:** 1 212 949-1100.
Email: news@pix11.com
Web site: http://www.pix11.com
Profile: WPIX-TV is the CW network affiliate for the New York market. The station is owned by the Tribune Broadcasting Co. WPIX-TV broadcasts locally on channel 11.
TELEVISION STATION

WPLG2-TV 614824
Owner: BH Media
Editorial: 3401 Hallandale Beach Blvd, Pembroke Park, Florida 33023-5728 **Tel:** 1 954 364-2500.
Web site: http://local10.com
Profile: WPLG2-TV is the ME TV affiliate for the Miami-Fort Lauderdale, FL market. The station is owned by BH Media. WPLG2-TV broadcasts locally on channel 10.2. WPLG2-TV is the Me-TV affiliate for the Miami market. A multicast channel is a separate channel that shares the bandwidth of the main station but can air unique programming.
TELEVISION STATION

WPLG-TV 32049
Owner: BH Media
Editorial: 3401 Hallandale Beach Blvd, Pembroke Park, Florida 33023-5728 **Tel:** 1 954 364-2500.
Email: newsdesk@wplg.com
Web site: http://www.local10.com
Profile: WPLG-TV is the ABC affiliate for the Miami-Fort Lauderdale, FL market. The station is owned by BH Media. WPLG-TV broadcasts locally on channel 10.
TELEVISION STATION

WPME-TV 32594
Owner: Cottonwood Communications
Editorial: 4 Ledgeview Dr, Westbrook, Maine 04092-3939 **Tel:** 1 207 772-3535.
Email: wpxt@ourmaine.com
Web site: http://www.ourmaine.com
Profile: WPME-TV is the CW Television Network affiliate for the Portland, ME market. The station is owned by Cottonwood Communications. WPME-TV broadcasts locally on channel 35.
TELEVISION STATION

WPMF-TV 390766
Owner: Chladek (James)
Editorial: 1221 Brickell Ave Ste 2520, Miami, Florida 33131-3231 **Tel:** 1 818 241-5400.
Profile: WPMF-TV is the My Family TV affiliate for the Miami market. The station is owned by James Chladek. WPMF-TV broadcasts locally on channel 38.
TELEVISION STATION

WPMI-TV 32050
Owner: Sinclair Broadcast Group, Inc.
Editorial: 661 Azalea Rd, Mobile, Alabama 36609-1515 **Tel:** 1 251 602-1500.
Email: local15@local15tv.com
Web site: http://www.local15tv.com
Profile: WPMI-TV is the NBC affiliate for the Mobile, AL-Pensacola, FL, market. It is owned by Sinclair Broadcast Group, Inc. WPMI-TV broadcasts locally on channel 15.
TELEVISION STATION

WPMT2-TV 618674
Owner: Tribune Broadcasting Co.
Editorial: 2005 S Queen St, York, Pennsylvania 17403-4806 **Tel:** 1 717 843-0043.
Web site: http://www.fox43.com
Profile: WPMT2-TV is a multicast of WPMT-TV. A multicast channel is a separate channel that shares the bandwith of the main station but can air unique programming. WPMT2-TV airs all news programming from Fox 43 in the Harrisburg, PA market. The station is owned by Tribune Broadcasting Co. WPMT2-TV broadcasts locally on channel 43.2.
TELEVISION STATION

WPMT-TV 32051
Owner: Tribune Broadcasting Co.
Editorial: 2005 S Queen St, York, Pennsylvania 17403-4806 **Tel:** 1 717 843-0043.
Email: news@fox43.com
Web site: http://www.fox43.com
Profile: WPMT-TV is the FOX affiliate for the Harrisburg, PA market. The station is owned by Tribune Broadcasting Co. WPMT-TV broadcasts locally on channel 43.
TELEVISION STATION

WPNT-TV 32596
Owner: Sinclair Broadcast Group, Inc.
Editorial: 750 Ivory Ave, Pittsburgh, Pennsylvania 15214-1606 **Tel:** 1 412 931-5300.
Web site: http://www.22thepoint.com
Profile: WPNT-TV is the MyNetworkTV affiliate station for the Pittsburgh, PA area. The station is owned by Sinclair Broadcast Group, Inc. WPNT-TV airs locally on channel 22.
TELEVISION STATION

WPNY-TV 32576
Owner: Mission Broadcasting
Editorial: 5956 Smith Hill Rd, Utica, New York 13502-6522 **Tel:** 1 315 797-5220.
Web site: http://www.cnyhomepage.com
Profile: WPNY-TV is the MyNetworkTV baffiliate for the Utica, NY market. The station is owned by Mission Broadcasting. WPNY-TV broadcasts locally on channel 53.
TELEVISION STATION

WPPX-TV 32125
Owner: ION Media Networks
Editorial: 3901B Main St Ste 301, Philadelphia, Pennsylvania 19127-2191 **Tel:** 1 215 482-4770.
Web site: http://iontelevision.com
Profile: WPPX-TV is the local ION Television affiliate for the Philadelphia market. The station is owned by ION Media Networks. WPPX-TV broadcasts locally on channel 61.
TELEVISION STATION

WPRI-TV 32052
Owner: Nexstar Media Group, LLC
Editorial: 25 Catamore Blvd, East Providence, Rhode Island 02914-1203 **Tel:** 1 401 438-7200.
Email: desk@wpri.com
Web site: http://www.wpri.com
Profile: WPRI-TV is the CBS affiliate for the Providence, RI-New Bedford, MA market. The station is owned by Nexstar Media Group, LLC. WPRI-TV broadcasts locally on channel 12.
TELEVISION STATION

WPSD-TV 32053
Owner: Paxton Media Group
Editorial: 100 Television Ln, Paducah, Kentucky 42003-7905 **Tel:** 1 270 415-1900.
Web site: http://www.wpsdlocal6.com
Profile: WPSD-TV is the NBC network affiliate for the Paducah, KY; Cape Girardeau, MO and Harrisburg, IL market. The station is owned by Paxton Media Group. WPSD-TV broadcasts locally on channel 6.
TELEVISION STATION

WPSG-TV 31853
Owner: CBS Television Stations
Editorial: 1555 Hamilton St, Philadelphia, Pennsylvania 19130-4085 **Tel:** 1 215 977-5700.
Email: tips@cbs3.com
Web site: http://cwphilly.cbslocal.com
Profile: WPSG-TV is the CW affiliate for the Philadelphia market. The station is owned by CBS Television Stations. WPSG-TV broadcasts locally on channel 57.
TELEVISION STATION

WPTA-TV 32055
Owner: Quincy Media
Editorial: 3401 Butler Rd, Fort Wayne, Indiana 46808-3811 **Tel:** 1 260 483-0584.
Email: newsroom@incnow.tv
Web site: http://www.wpta21.com
Profile: WPTA-TV is the ABC affiliate for the Fort Wayne, IN market. The station is owned by Quincy Media. WPTA-TV broadcasts locally on channel 21.
TELEVISION STATION

WPTD-TV 32680
Owner: Greater Dayton Public TV Inc.
Editorial: 110 S Jefferson St, Dayton, Ohio 45402-2402 **Tel:** 1 937 220-1600.
Web site: http://www.thinktv.org
Profile: WPTD-TV is the PBS affiliate for the Dayton, OH, market. The station is owned by Greater Dayton Public TV Inc. WPTD-TV broadcasts locally on channel 16.
TELEVISION STATION

WPTO-TV 32827
Owner: Think TV Network
Editorial: 110 S Jefferson St, Dayton, Ohio 45402 **Tel:** 1 937 220-1600.
Web site: http://www.thinktv.org
Profile: WPTO-TV is the PBS affiliate for the Dayton, OH market. The station is owned by the Think TV Network. WPTO-TV broadcasts locally on channel 14.
TELEVISION STATION

WPTV2-TV 620845
Owner: E.W. Scripps Co.
Editorial: 1100 Banyan Blvd, West Palm Beach, Florida 33401-5000 **Tel:** 1 561 655-5455.
Email: newstips@wptv.com
Web site: http://www.wptv.com
Profile: WPTV2-TV is a multicast of WPTV-TV. A multicast channel is a separate channel that shares the bandwith of the main station but can air unique programming. WPTV2-TV airs Me-TV programming in the West Palm Beach, FL market. The station is owned by E.W. Scripps Co. WPTV2-TV broadcasts locally on channel 5.2.
TELEVISION STATION

WPTV-TV 32058
Owner: E.W. Scripps Co.
Editorial: 1100 Banyan Blvd, West Palm Beach, Florida 33401-5000 **Tel:** 1 561 655-5455.
Email: newstips@wptv.com
Web site: http://www.wptv.com
Profile: WPTV-TV is the local NBC affiliate on Channel 5 for the West Palm Beach, FL market. The station is owned by E.W. Scripps Co. WPTV-TV broadcasts locally on channel 5.
TELEVISION STATION

WPTZ2-TV 852396
Owner: Hearst Television Inc.
Editorial: 5 Television Dr, Plattsburgh, New York 12901-7252 **Tel:** 1 518 561-5555.
Web site: http://www.wptz.com
Profile: WPTZ2-TV is a multicast channel of WPTZ-TV. A multicast channel is a separate channel that shares the bandwidth of the main station but can air unique programming. WPTZ2-TV is the CW and Me-TV Network for the Burlington, VT and Pittsburgh, NY market. The station is owned by Hearst Television Inc. WPTZ2-TV broadcasts locally on channel 5.2.
TELEVISION STATION

WPTZ-TV 32060
Owner: Hearst Television Inc.
Editorial: 5 Television Dr, Plattsburgh, New York 12901-7252 **Tel:** 1 518 561-5555.
Email: newstips@wptz.com
Web site: http://www.wptz.com
Profile: WPTZ-TV is the NBC affiliate for the Burlington, VT/Plattsburgh, NY market. The station is owned by Hearst Television Inc. WPTZ-TV broadcasts locally on channel 5.
TELEVISION STATION

WPVI2-TV 610908
Owner: Walt Disney Co.
Editorial: 4100 City Ave, Philadelphia, Pennsylvania 19131-1691 **Tel:** 1 215 878-9700.
Web site: http://abclocal.go.com/wpvi
Profile: WPVI2-TV is a multicast of WPVI-TV. A multicast channel is a separate channel that shares the bandwith of the main station but can air unique programming. WPVI2-TV airs programming from Live Well in the Philadelphia market. The station is owned by Walt Disney Co. WPVI2-TV broadcasts locally on channel 13.2.
TELEVISION STATION

WPVI3-TV 610911
Owner: Walt Disney Co.
Editorial: 4100 City Ave, Philadelphia, Pennsylvania 19131-1610 **Tel:** 1 215 878-9700.
Web site: http://abclocal.go.com/wpvi
Profile: WPVI3-TV is a multicast of WPVI-TV. A multicast channel is a separate channel that shares the bandwith of the main station but can air unique programming. WPVI3-TV airs programming from the Live Well Network in the Philadelphia market. The station is owned by Walt Disney Co. WPVI3-TV broadcasts locally on channel 13.3.
TELEVISION STATION

WPVI-TV 32061
Owner: Walt Disney Co.
Editorial: 4100 City Ave, Philadelphia, Pennsylvania 19131-1610 **Tel:** 1 215 878-9700.
Email: wpvi-tv.newsdesk@abc.com
Web site: http://6abc.com
Profile: WPVI-TV is the ABC affiliate for the Philadelphia market. The station is owned by the Walt Disney Co. WPVI-TV broadcasts locally on channel 6. Press materials must be sent via fax or via the station's web site.
TELEVISION STATION

WPVN4-TV 879580
Owner: Polnet Communications
Editorial: 3656 W Belmont Ave, Chicago, Illinois 60618-5328 **Tel:** 1 773 588-6300.
Email: info@polvision.com
Web site: http://www.polvision.com
Profile: WPVN4-TV is a multicast channel of WPVN-TV. A multicast channel is a separate channel that shares the bandwidth of the main station but can air unique programming. WPVN4-TV is the Polvision network affiliate for the Chicago market. The station covers news from Poland. The station is owned by Polnet Communications. WPVN4-TV broadcasts locally on channel 24.4.
TELEVISION STATION

WPWR-TV 32062
Owner: Fox Broadcasting Company
Editorial: 205 N Michigan Ave, Chicago, Illinois 60601-5927 **Tel:** 1 312 565-5532.
Profile: WPWR-TV is the CW affiliate for the Chicago market. The station is owned by the Fox Broadcasting Company. WPWR-TV broadcasts locally on channel 50.
TELEVISION STATION

WPXA2-TV 609586
Owner: ION Media Networks
Editorial: 200 Cobb Pkwy N, Ste 114, Marietta, Georgia 30062-3538 **Tel:** 1 770 919-0575.
Web site: http://www.qubo.com
Profile: WPXA2-TV is an independent affiliate for the Atlanta market. The station is owned by ION Media Networks. WPXA2-TV broadcasts locally on channel 14.2. WPXA2-TV broadcasts children's programming from the qubo network. WPXA2-TV is a multicast channel of WPXA-TV. A multicast channel is a separate channel that shares the bandwidth of the main station but can air unique programming.
TELEVISION STATION

WPXA3-TV 609587
Owner: ION Media Networks
Editorial: 200 Cobb Pkwy N, Ste 114, Marietta, Georgia 30062-3538 **Tel:** 1 770 919-0575.
Web site: http://www.ionlife.com
Profile: WPXA3-TV is ION Television affiliate for the Atlanta market. The station is owned by ION Media Networks. WPXA3-TV broadcasts locally on channel 14.3. WPXA3-TV broadcasts lifestyle programming from the ION Life network. WPXA2-TV is a multicast channel of WPXA-TV. A multicast channel is a separate channel that shares the bandwidth of the main station but can air unique programming.
TELEVISION STATION

WPXA4-TV 609591
Owner: ION Media Networks
Editorial: 200 Cobb Pkwy N, Ste 114, Marietta, Georgia 30062-3538 **Tel:** 1 770 919-0575.
Web site: http://www.worship.net
Profile: WPXA4-TV is an independent affiliate for the Atlanta market. The station is owned by ION Media Networks. WPXA4-TV broadcasts locally on channel 14.4. WPXA4-TV broadcasts worship and religious programming from The Worship Network. WPXA4-TV is a multicast channel of WPXA-TV. A multicast channel is a separate channel that shares the bandwidth of the main station but can air unique programming.
TELEVISION STATION

WPXA-TV 134852
Owner: ION Media Networks
Editorial: 200 Cobb Pkwy N, Ste 114, Marietta, Georgia 30062-3538 **Tel:** 1 770 919-0575.
Web site: http://www.iontelevision.com
Profile: WPXA-TV is the ION Television affiliate for the Atlanta market. The station is owned by ION Media Networks. WPXA-TV broadcasts locally on channel 14.
TELEVISION STATION

WPXC2-TV 618975
Owner: ION Media Networks
Editorial: 7434 Blythe Island Hwy, Brunswick, Georgia 31523-6257 **Tel:** 1 912 267-0021.
Profile: WPXC2-TV is a multicast of WPXC-TV. A multicast channel is a separate channel that shares the bandwith of the main station but can air unique programming. WPXC2-TV airs children's programming from qubo in the Jacksonville, FL market. The station is owned by ION Media Networks. WPXC2-TV broadcasts locally on channel 21.2 and is made up of children's programming.
TELEVISION STATION

WPXC3-TV 618976
Owner: ION Media Networks
Editorial: 7434 Blythe Island Hwy, Brunswick, Georgia 31523-6257 **Tel:** 1 912 267-0021.
Web site: http://iontelevision.com
Profile: WPXC3-TV is a multicast of WPXC-TV. A multicast channel is a separate channel that shares the bandwidth of the main station but can air unique programming. WPXC3-TV airs lifestyle programming from ION Life in the Jacksonville, FL market. The station is owned by ION Media Networks. WPXC3-TV broadcasts locally on channel 21.3.
TELEVISION STATION

WPXC4-TV 618977
Owner: ION Media Networks
Editorial: 7434 Blythe Island Hwy, Brunswick, Georgia 31523-6257 **Tel:** 1 912 267-0021.
Web site: http://iontelevision.com
Profile: WPXC4-TV is a multicast of WPXC-TV. A multicast channel is a separate channel that shares the bandwith of the main station but can air unique programming. WPXC4-TV airs Christian programming from The Worship Network in the Jacksonville, FL market. The station is owned by ION Media Networks. WPXC4-TV broadcasts locally on channel 21.4.
TELEVISION STATION

WPXC-TV 32394
Owner: ION Media Networks
Editorial: 7434 Blythe Island Hwy, Brunswick, Georgia 31523-6257 **Tel:** 1 912 267-0021.
Profile: WPXC-TV is the ION Television affiliate for the Jacksonville, FL market. The station is owned by ION Media Networks. WPXC-TV broadcasts locally on channel 21.
TELEVISION STATION

WPXE2-TV 621715
Owner: ION Media Networks
Editorial: 6161 N Flint Rd, Ste F, Glendale, Wisconsin 53209-3749 **Tel:** 1 414 247-0117.
Web site: http://www.ionmedia.com
TELEVISION STATION

WPXE3-TV 621716
Owner: ION Media Networks
Editorial: 6161 N Flint Rd, Ste F, Glendale, Wisconsin 53209-3749 **Tel:** 1 414 247-0117.
Web site: http://www.iontelevision.com
Profile: WPXE3-TV is a multicast of WPXE-TV. A multicast channel is a separate channel that shares the bandwith of the main station but can air unique programming. WPXE3-TV airs lifestyle programming from ION Life in the Milwaukee market. The station is owned by ION Media Networks. WPXE3-TV broadcasts locally on channel 55.3.
TELEVISION STATION

WPXE-TV 32289
Owner: ION Media Networks
Editorial: 6161 N Flint Rd, Ste F, Glendale, Wisconsin 53209 **Tel:** 1 414 247-0117.
Web site: http://www.iontelevision.com
Profile: WPXE-TV is the ION Television affiliate for the Milwaukee market. The station is owned by ION Media Networks. WPXE-TV broadcasts locally on channel 55.
TELEVISION STATION

WPXH-TV 32309
Owner: ION Media Networks
Editorial: 2085 Golden Crest Dr, Birmingham, Alabama 35209-1143 **Tel:** 1 205 870-4404.
Web site: http://ionmedia.com
Profile: WPXH-TV is the ION Television affiliate for the Birmingham, AL market. The station is owned by ION Media Networks. WPXH-TV broadcasts locally on channel 44.
TELEVISION STATION

WPXI2-TV 614023
Owner: Cox Media Group, Inc.
Editorial: 4145 Evergreen Rd, Pittsburgh, Pennsylvania 15214-4145 **Tel:** 1 412 237-1100.
Web site: http://www.wpxi.com
Profile: WPXI2-TV is a multicast of WPXI-TV. A multicast channel is a separate channel that shares the bandwith of the main station but can air unique programming. WPXI2-TV airs programming from the Retro Television Network in the Pittsburgh market. The station is owned by Cox Media Group, Inc. WPXI2-TV broadcasts locally on channel 11.2.
TELEVISION STATION

WPXI-TV 32063
Owner: Cox Media Group, Inc.
Editorial: 4145 Evergreen Rd, Pittsburgh, Pennsylvania 15214-1636 **Tel:** 1 412 237-1100.
Web site: http://www.wpxi.com
Profile: WPXI-TV is the NBC affiliate for the Pittsburgh market. The station is owned by Cox Media Group, Inc. WPXI-TV broadcasts locally on channel 11.
TELEVISION STATION

WPXJ-TV 72052
Owner: ION Media Networks
Editorial: 726 Exchange St Ste 819, Buffalo, New York 14210-1463 **Tel:** 1 716 852-1818.
Web site: http://www.iontelevision.com
Profile: WPXJ-TV is the ION Television affiliate for the Buffalo, NY market. The station is owned by ION Media Networks. WPXJ-TV broadcasts locally on channel 51.
TELEVISION STATION

WPXK-TV 32438
Owner: ION Media Networks
Editorial: 9000 Executive Park Dr Bldg D, Knoxville, Tennessee 37923-4685 **Tel:** 1 865 531-4037.
Web site: http://www.iontelevision.com
Profile: WPXK-TV is the ION Television affiliate for the Jellico, TN market. The station is owned by ION Media Networks. WPXK-TV broadcasts locally on channel 54.
TELEVISION STATION

WPXL-TV 32540
Owner: ION Media Networks
Editorial: 3900 Veterans Blvd, suite 202, Metairie, Louisiana 70002 **Tel:** 1 504 887-9795.
Profile: WPXL-TV is the ION Television affiliate for the New Orleans market. The station is owned by ION Media Networks. It broadcasts locally on channel 49.
TELEVISION STATION

WPXM2-TV 613506
Owner: ION Media Networks
Editorial: 14901 NE 20th Ave, North Miami, Florida 33181-1121 **Tel:** 1 305 424-4058.
Web site: http://www.qubo.com
Profile: WPXM2-TV is independent affiliate for the Miami-Fort Lauderdale, FL market. The station is owned by ION Media Networks. WPXM2-TV broadcasts locally on channel 35.2. The station airs children's programming from the qubo network. WPXM2-TV is a multicast channel of WPXM-TV. A multicast channel is a separate channel that shares the bandwidth of the main station but can air unique programming.
TELEVISION STATION

WPXM3-TV 613507
Owner: ION Media Networks
Editorial: 14901 NE 20th Ave, North Miami, Florida 33181-1121 **Tel:** 1 305 424-4058.
Web site: http://www.qubo.com
Profile: WPXM3-TV is a Ion Life affiliate for the Miami-Fort Lauderdale, FL market. The station is owned by ION Media Networks. WPXM3-TV broadcasts locally on channel 35.3. The station airs lifestyle programming. WPXM3-TV is a multicast channel of WPXM-TV. A multicast channel is a separate channel that shares the bandwidth of the main station but can air unique programming.
TELEVISION STATION

WPXM-TV 32424
Owner: ION Media Networks
Editorial: 14901 NE 20th Ave, North Miami, Florida 33181-1121 **Tel:** 1 305 424-4058.
Web site: http://www.qubo.com
Profile: WPXM-TV is the ION Television affiliate for the Miami-Fort Lauderdale, FL market. The station is owned by ION Media Networks. WPXM-TV broadcasts locally on channel 35.
TELEVISION STATION

WPXN2-TV 606081
Owner: ION Media Networks
Editorial: 810 7th Ave Fl 31, New York, New York 10019-5870 **Tel:** 1 212 757-3100.
Web site: http://iontelevision.com
Profile: WPXN2-TV is a multicast channel of WPXN-TV. A multicast channel is a separate channel that shares the bandwidth of the main station but can air unique programming. WPXN2-TV is the local qubo affiliate on Channel 31.2 for the New York market. WPXN2-TV is owned by ION Media Networks.
TELEVISION STATION

WPXN3-TV 606082
Owner: ION Media Networks
Editorial: 810 7th Ave Fl 31, New York, New York 10019-5870 **Tel:** 1 212 757-3100.
Web site: http://iontelevision.com
Profile: WPXN3-TV is a multicast channel of WPXN-TV. A multicast channel is a separate channel that shares the bandwidth of the main station but can air unique programming. WPXN3-TV is the local ION Life affiliate on Channel 31.3 for the New York market. WPXN3-TV is owned by ION Media Networks.
TELEVISION STATION

WPXN4-TV 606083
Owner: ION Media Networks
Editorial: 810 7th Ave Fl 31, New York, New York 10019-5870 **Tel:** 1 212 757-3100.
Web site: http://iontelevision.com
Profile: WPXN4-TV is a multicast channel of WPXN-TV. A multicast channel is a separate channel that shares the bandwidth of the main station but can air unique programming. WPXN4-TV is the local Worship affiliate on Channel 31.4 for the New York market. WPXN4-TV is owned by ION Media Networks.
TELEVISION STATION

WPXN-TV 32023
Owner: ION Media Networks
Editorial: 810 7th Ave Fl 32, New York, New York 10019-5868 **Tel:** 1 212 757-3100.
Web site: http://iontelevision.com
Profile: WPXN-TV is the ION Television affiliate for the New York market. The station is owned by ION Media Networks. WPXN-TV broadcasts locally on channel 31.
TELEVISION STATION

WPXP2-TV 613499
Owner: ION Media Networks
Editorial: 14901 NE 20th Ave, North Miami, Florida 33181-1121 **Tel:** 1 954 703-1920.
Web site: http://www.qubo.com
Profile: WPXP2-TV is independent affiliate for the West Palm Beach, FL market. The station is owned by ION Media Networks. WPXP2-TV broadcasts locally on channel 67.2. The station airs children's programming from the qubo network. WPXP2-TV is a multicast channel of WPXP-TV. A multicast channel is a separate channel that shares the bandwidth of the main station but can air unique programming.
TELEVISION STATION

WPXP3-TV 613500
Owner: ION Media Networks
Editorial: 14901 NE 20th Ave, North Miami, Florida 33181-1121 **Tel:** 1 305 424-4058.
Web site: http://www.qubo.com
Profile: WPXP3-TV is a Ion Life affiliate for the West Palm Beach, FL market. The station is owned by ION Media Networks. WPXP3-TV broadcasts locally on channel 67.3. The station airs lifestyle programming. WPXP3-TV is a multicast channel of WPXP-TV. A multicast channel is a separate channel that shares

the bandwidth of the main station but can air unique programming.
TELEVISION STATION

WPXP-TV 32561
Owner: ION Media Networks
Editorial: 14901 NE 20th Ave, North Miami, Florida 33181-1121 **Tel:** 1 305 424-4189.
Web site: http://www.qubo.com
Profile: WPXP-TV is the ION Television affiliate for the West Palm Beach, FL market. The station is owned by ION Media Networks. WPXP-TV broadcasts locally on channel 67.
TELEVISION STATION

WPXQ2-TV 614735
Owner: ION Media Networks
Editorial: 3 Shaws Cv Ste 226, New London, Connecticut 06320-4948 **Tel:** 1 800 444-2626.
Profile: WPXQ2-TV is a multicast of WPXQ-TV. A multicast channel is a separate channel that shares the bandwith of the main station but can air unique programming. WPXQ2-TV airs programming from the qubo Network in the Providence, RI; New Bedford, MA market. The station is owned by ION Media Networks. WPXQ2-TV broadcasts locally on channel 17.
TELEVISION STATION

WPXQ3-TV 614738
Owner: ION Media Networks
Editorial: 3 Shaws Cv Ste 226, New London, Connecticut 06320-4948 **Tel:** 1 800 444-2626.
Profile: WPXQ3-TV is a multicast of WPXQ-TV. A multicast channel is a separate channel that shares the bandwith of the main station but can air unique programming. WPXQ3-TV airs programming from the ION Life Network in the Providence, RI; New Bedford, MA market. The station is owned by ION Media Networks. WPXQ3-TV broadcasts locally on channel 17.
TELEVISION STATION

WPXQ4-TV 614740
Owner: ION Media Networks
Editorial: 3 Shaws Cv Ste 226, New London, Connecticut 06320-4948 **Tel:** 1 800 444-2626.
Profile: WPXQ4-TV is a multicast of WPXQ-TV. A multicast channel is a separate channel that shares the bandwith of the main station but can air unique programming. WPXQ4-TV airs programming from The Worship Network in the Providence, RI; New Bedford, MA market. The station is owned by ION Media Networks. WPXQ4-TV broadcasts locally on channel 17.
TELEVISION STATION

WPXQ-TV 32520
Owner: ION Media Networks
Editorial: 3 Shaws Cv Ste 226, New London, Connecticut 06320-4948 **Tel:** 1 860 444-2626.
Profile: WPXQ-TV is the ION Television affiliate for the Providence, RI; New Bedford, MA market. The station is owned by ION Media Networks. WPXQ-TV broadcasts locally on channel 17.
TELEVISION STATION

WPXR-TV 32290
Owner: ION Media Networks
Editorial: 401 3rd St SW, Roanoke, Virginia 24011-1507 **Tel:** 1 540 857-0038.
Web site: http://iononline.tv
Profile: WPXR-TV is the ION Television affiliate for the Roanoke, VA market. The station is owned by ION Media Networks. WPXR-TV broadcasts locally on channel 38.
TELEVISION STATION

WPXS-TV 31776
Owner: Day Star
Editorial: 4751 Cartter Rd, Kell, Illinois 62853 **Tel:** 1 618 822-6900.
Profile: WPXS-TV is the RTN/Retro Television Network affiliate for the St. Louis, MO market. The station is owned by Day Star. WPXS-TV is broadcast locally on channel 13.
TELEVISION STATION

WPXT-TV 32064
Owner: Cottonwood Communications
Editorial: 4 Ledgeview Dr, Westbrook, Maine 04092-3939 **Tel:** 1 207 774-0051.
Email: wpxt@ourmaine.com
Web site: http://www.ourmaine.com
Profile: WPXT-TV is the CW affiliate in Portland, ME. The station is owned by Cottonwood Communications, LLC. WPXT-TV broadcasts locally on channel 51.
TELEVISION STATION

WPXV-TV 32346
Owner: ION Media Networks
Editorial: 3702 Nansemond Pkwy #C, Suffolk, Virginia 23435-1218 **Tel:** 1 757 538-3906.
Profile: WPXV-TV is the local ION Television affiliate for the Norfolk, VA market. The station is owned by ION Media Networks. WPXV-TV broadcasts locally on channel 49.
TELEVISION STATION

WPXW2-TV 609970
Owner: ION Media Networks
Editorial: 6199 Old Arrington Ln, Fairfax Station, Virginia 22039-1350 **Tel:** 1 703 503-7966.
Web site: http://iononline.tv
Profile: WPXW2-TV is a multicast of WPXW-TV. A multicast channel is a separate channel that shares the bandwith of the main station but can air unique programming. WPXW2-TV airs programming from the qubo network in the Washington, D.C. market. The station is owned by ION Media Networks. WPXW2-TV broadcasts locally on channel 66.2.
TELEVISION STATION

WPXW3-TV 609973
Owner: ION Media Networks
Editorial: 6199 Old Arrington Ln, Fairfax Station, Virginia 22039-1350 **Tel:** 1 703 503-7966.
Web site: http://iononline.tv
Profile: WPXW3-TV is a multicast of WPXW-TV. A multicast channel is a separate channel that shares the bandwith of the main station but can air unique programming. WPXW3-TV airs programming from the ION Life network in the Washington, D.C. market. The station is owned by ION Media Networks. WPXW3-TV broadcasts locally on channel 66.3.
TELEVISION STATION

WPXW-TV 32133
Owner: ION Media Networks
Editorial: 6199 Old Arrington Ln, Fairfax Station, Virginia 22039-1350 **Tel:** 1 703 503-7966.
Web site: http://iononline.tv
Profile: WPXW-TV is the ION Television affiliate for the Washington, D.C. market. The station is owned by ION Media Networks. WPXW-TV broadcasts locally on channel 66.
TELEVISION STATION

WPXX2-TV 619769
Owner: ION Media Networks
Editorial: 3145 Brother Blvd, Bartlett, Tennessee 38133 **Tel:** 1 901 384-9324.
Web site: http://ionmedianetworks.com
Profile: WPXX2-TV is a multicast of WPXX-TV. A multicast channel is a separate channel that shares the bandwidth of the main station but can air unique programming. WPXX2-TV airs children's programming from the qubo network in the Memphis, TN market. The station is owned by ION Media Networks. WPXX2-TV broadcasts locally on channel 50.2.
TELEVISION STATION

WPXX3-TV 619771
Owner: ION Media Networks
Editorial: 3145 Brother Blvd, Bartlett, Tennessee 38133 **Tel:** 1 901 384-9324.
Web site: http://ionmedianetworks.com
Profile: WPXX3-TV is a multicast of WPXX-TV. A multicast channel is a separate channel that shares the bandwidth of the main station but can air unique programming. WPXX3-TV airs lifestyle programming from the ION Life network in the Memphis, TN market. The station is owned by ION Media Networks. WPXX3-TV broadcasts locally on channel 50.3.
TELEVISION STATION

WPXX-TV 32516
Owner: ION Media Networks
Editorial: 3145 Brother Blvd, Bartlett, Tennessee 38133 **Tel:** 1 901 384-9324.
Web site: http://ionmedianetworks.com
Profile: WPXX-TV is the ION Television affiliate for the Memphis, TN market. The station is owned by ION Media Networks. WXX-TV broadcasts locally on channel 50.
TELEVISION STATION

WQAD2-TV 610010
Owner: Tribune Broadcasting Co.
Editorial: 3003 Park 16th St, Moline, Illinois 61265-6060 **Tel:** 1 309 736-3300.
Email: news@wqad.com
Web site: http://www.wqad.com
Profile: WQAD2-TV is a multicast of WQAD-TV. A multicast channel is a separate channel that shares the bandwidth of the main station but can air unique programming. WQAD2-TV airs programming from the Quad Cities Weather Channel in the Davenport, IA market. The station is owned by Tribune Broadcasting Co. WQAD2-TV broadcasts locally on channel 8.2.
TELEVISION STATION

WQAD3-TV 610013
Owner: Tribune Broadcasting Co.
Editorial: 3003 Park 16th St, Moline, Illinois 61265-6060 **Tel:** 1 309 764-8888.
Email: news@wqad.com
Web site: http://www.wqad.com
Profile: WQAD3-TV is a multicast of WQAD-TV. A multicast channel is a separate channel that shares the bandwidth of the main station but can air unique programming. WQAD3-TV airs programming from My TV 16 network in the Davenport, IA market. The station is owned by Tribune Broadcasting Co. WQAD3-TV broadcasts locally on channel 8.3.
TELEVISION STATION

WQAD-TV 32065
Owner: Tribune Broadcasting Co.
Editorial: 3003 Park 16th St, Moline, Illinois 61265-6060 **Tel:** 1 309 764-8888.
Email: news@wqad.com
Web site: http://www.wqad.com
Profile: WQAD-TV is the ABC affiliate for the Davenport, IA market. The station is owned by Tribune Broadcasting Co. WQAD-TV broadcasts locally on channel 8.
TELEVISION STATION

WQAW-TV 483586
Owner: Una Vez Mas LP
Editorial: 1701 N Market St Ste 500, Dallas, Texas 75202-2001 **Tel:** 1 214 754-7008.
Web site: http://www.aztecaamerica.com
Profile: WQAW-TV is the Azteca America affiliate for the Washington, D.C. market. The station is owned by Una Vez Mas LP. WQAW-TV broadcasts locally on channel 20. All PSAs should be sent in BETA format.
TELEVISION STATION

WQCW-TV 32605
Owner: Gray Television
Editorial: 800 Gallia St Ste 430, Portsmouth, Ohio 45662-4074 **Tel:** 1 304 697-4780.
Web site: http://www.wqcw.com
Profile: WQCW-TV is the local CW affiliate for the Charleston-Huntington, WV market. The station is owned by Gray Television. WQCW-TV broadcasts locally on channel 23.
TELEVISION STATION

WQED2-TV 613847
Owner: WQED Multimedia
Editorial: 4802 5th Ave, Pittsburgh, Pennsylvania 15213-2942 **Tel:** 1 412 622-1300.
Web site: http://www.wqed.org/tv/
Profile: WQED2-TV is a multicast of WQED-TV. A multicast channel is a separate channel that shares the bandwith of the main station but can air unique programming. WQED2-TV airs programming from The WQED Create Channel in the Pittsburgh market. The station is owned by WQED Multimedia. WQED2-TV broadcasts locally on channel 13.2.
TELEVISION STATION

WQED3-TV 613848
Owner: WQED Multimedia
Editorial: 4802 5th Ave, Pittsburgh, Pennsylvania 15213-2942 **Tel:** 1 412 622-1300.
Web site: http://www.wqed.org
Profile: WQED3-TV is a multicast of WQED-TV. A multicast channel is a separate channel that shares the bandwith of the main station but can air unique programming. WQED3-TV airs programming from The WQED Neighborhood Channel in the Pittsburgh market. The station is owned by WQED Multimedia. WQED3-TV broadcasts locally on channel 13.3.
TELEVISION STATION

WQED-TV 32066
Owner: WQED Multimedia
Editorial: 4802 5th Ave, Pittsburgh, Pennsylvania 15213 **Tel:** 1 412 622-1300.
Email: wqed@wqed.org
Web site: http://www.wqed.org
Profile: WQED-TV is the PBS network affiliate for the Pittsburgh market. The station is owned by WQED Multimedia. WQED-TV broadcasts locally on channel 13.
TELEVISION STATION

WQHS-TV 32513
Owner: Univision Communications Inc.
Editorial: 2861 W Ridgewood Dr, Parma, Ohio 44134-4336 **Tel:** 1 440 888-0061.
Profile: WQHS-TV is an Univision network affiliate for the Cleveland market. The station is owned by Univision Communications Inc. WQHS-TV broadcasts locally on channel 34.
TELEVISION STATION

WQLN-TV 32068
Owner: Public Broadcasting of Northwest Pennsylvania
Editorial: 8425 Peach St, Erie, Pennsylvania 16509 **Tel:** 1 814 864-3001.
Email: wqln@wqln.org
Web site: http://www.wqln.org
Profile: WQLN-TV is the PBS network affiliate for the Erie, PA market. The station is owned by Public Broadcasting of Northwest Pennsylvania. WQLN-TV broadcasts locally on channel 54.
TELEVISION STATION

WQOW-TV 32813
Owner: Quincy Newspapers Inc.
Editorial: 5545 State Road 93, Eau Claire, Wisconsin 54701-9618 **Tel:** 1 715 835-1881.
Email: news@wqow.com
Web site: http://www.wqow.com
Profile: WQOW-TV is the ABC network affiliate for the La Crosse-Eau Claire, WI market. The station is owned by Quincy Newspapers Inc. WQOW-TV broadcasts locally on channel 18.
TELEVISION STATION

WQPX-TV 72055
Owner: ION Media Networks
Editorial: 409 Lackawanna Ave Ste 700, Scranton, Pennsylvania 18503-2061 **Tel:** 1 570 344-6400.
Email: psa@ionmedia.com
Web site: http://www.ionmedia.com
Profile: WQPX-TV is the ION Television affiliate for the Scranton and Wilkes Barre, PA market. The station is owned by ION Media Networks. WQPX-TV broadcasts locally on channel 32.
TELEVISION STATION

WQRF-TV 32069
Owner: Nexstar Broadcasting Group
Editorial: 1917 N Meridian Rd, Rockford, Illinois 61101-9215 **Tel:** 1 815 963-5413.
Email: newsdesk@wtvo.com
Web site: http://mystateline.com
Profile: WQRF-TV is the FOX network affiliate for the Rockford, IL market. The station is owned by Nexstar Broadcasting Group. WQRF-TV broadcasts locally on channel 39.
TELEVISION STATION

WQTV-TV 63128
Owner: Raycom Media Inc.
Editorial: 310 Broadway St, Cape Girardeau, Missouri 63701 **Tel:** 1 573 335-1212.
Profile: WQTV-TV is the CW affiliate for the Cape Girardeau, MO market. The station is owned by Raycom Media Inc. WQTV-TV broadcasts locally on channel 24.
TELEVISION STATION

WQXT-TV 354517
Owner: A1A TV Inc.
Editorial: 127 Hercules Rd, Saint Augustine, Florida 32086-6717 **Tel:** 1 904 794-6774.
Web site: http://www.drudgereport.com
Profile: WQXT-TV is an independent station for the Jacksonville, FL market. The station is owned by A1A TV Inc. WQXT-TV broadcasts locally on channel 22.
TELEVISION STATION

WRAL2-TV 614010
Owner: Capitol Broadcasting Company
Editorial: 2619 Western Blvd, Raleigh, North Carolina 27606-2125 **Tel:** 1 919 821-8555.
Email: assignmentdesk@wral.com
Web site: http://www.wral.com
Profile: WRAL2-TV is a multicast of WRAL-TV. A multicast channel is a separate channel that shares the bandwith of the main station but can air unique programming. WRAL2-TV airs programming from the This TV Network in the Raleigh-Durham, NC market. The station is owned by Capitol Broadcasting Company. WRAL2-TV broadcasts locally on channel 5.2.
TELEVISION STATION

WRAL-TV 32070
Owner: Capitol Broadcasting Company
Editorial: 2619 Western Blvd, Raleigh, North Carolina 27606-2125 **Tel:** 1 919 821-8555.
Email: assignmentdesk@wral.com
Web site: http://www.wral.com
Profile: WRAL-TV is the NBC network affiliate for the Raleigh-Durham, NC market. The station is owned by Capitol Broadcasting Company. WRAL-TV broadcasts locally on channel 5.
TELEVISION STATION

WRAY-TV 32492
Owner: Tri-State Christian Television
Editorial: 4909 Expressway Dr Ste E, Wilson, North Carolina 27893-8135 **Tel:** 1 252 243-0584.
Web site: http://www.tct.tv
Profile: WRAY-TV is an independent station for the Raleigh/Durham, NC market. The station is owned by Tri-State Christian Television. WRAY-TV broadcasts locally on channel 30.
TELEVISION STATION

WRAZ2-TV 586598
Owner: Capitol Broadcasting Company
Editorial: 2619 Western Blvd, Raleigh, North Carolina 27606-2125 **Tel:** 1 919 595-5050.
Email: assignmentdesk@wral.com
Web site: http://www.fox50.com
Profile: WRAZ2-TV is a multicast of WRAZ-TV. A multicast channel is a separate channel that shares the bandwith of the main station but can air unique programming. WRAZ2-TV airs programming from the RTV Raleigh-Durham in the Raleigh-Durham, NC market. The station is owned by Capitol Broadcasting Company. WRAZ2-TV broadcasts locally on channel 50.2.
TELEVISION STATION

WRAZ-TV 32476
Owner: Capitol Broadcasting Company
Editorial: 2619 Western Blvd, Raleigh, North Carolina 27606-2125 **Tel:** 1 919 595-5050.
Email: assignmentdesk@wral.com
Web site: http://www.fox50.com
Profile: WRAZ-TV is the FOX network affiliate for the Raleigh-Durham, NC market. The Station is owned by Capitol Broadcasting Company. WRAZ-TV broadcasts locally on channel 50.
TELEVISION STATION

WRBJ-TV 408491
Owner: Trinity Broadcasting Network
Editorial: 745 N State St, Jackson, Mississippi 39202-3006 **Tel:** 1 601 974-5700.
Web site: http://www.tbn.org
Profile: WRBJ-TV is the CW affiliate for the Jackson, MS market. The station is owned by Trinity Broadcasting Network. WRBJ-TV broadcasts locally on channel 34.
TELEVISION STATION

WRBL-TV 32071
Owner: Nexstar Media Group, LLC
Editorial: 1350 13th Ave, Columbus, Georgia 31901-2303 **Tel:** 1 706 323-3333.
Email: news@wrbl.com
Web site: http://www.wrbl.com
Profile: WRBL-TV is the CBS network affiliate for the Columbus, GA market. The station is owned by Nexstar Media Group, LLC. WRBL-TV broadcasts locally on channel 3.
TELEVISION STATION

WRBU2-TV 773229
Owner: Ion Media Networks
Editorial: 1408 N Kingshighway Blvd Ste 300, Saint Louis, Missouri 63113-1420 **Tel:** 1 314 367-4600.
Profile: WRBU2-TV is a multicast channel of WEBU-TV. A multicast channel is a separate channel that shares the bandwidth of the main station but can air unique programming. WRBU2-TV is the Me-TV

Network for the St. Louis, MO market. The station is owned by Ion Media Networks. WRBU2-TV broadcasts locally on channel 46.2.
TELEVISION STATION

WRBU-TV 32518
Owner: ION Media Networks
Editorial: 1408 N Kingshighway Blvd Ste 300, Saint Louis, Missouri 63113-1420 **Tel:** 1 314 367-4600.
Web site: http://www.my46stl.com
Profile: WRBU-TV is the MyNetworkTV affiliate for the St. Louis market. The station is owned by ION Media Networks. WRBU-TV broadcasts locally on channel 46.
TELEVISION STATION

WRBW-TV 32449
Owner: Fox Broadcasting Company
Editorial: 35 Skyline Dr, Lake Mary, Florida 32746-6202 **Tel:** 1 407 644-3535.
Web site: http://www.my65orlando.com
Profile: WRBW-TV is a local MyNetworkTV affiliate in Orlando, FL. The station is owned by Fox Broadcasting Company. WRBW-TV broadcasts locally on channel 65.
TELEVISION STATION

WRC2-TV 610140
Owner: NBC Universal
Editorial: 4001 Nebraska Ave NW, Washington, District Of Columbia 20016-2733 **Tel:** 1 202 885-4000.
Web site: http://www.nbcwashington.com
Profile: WRC2-TV is a multicast of WRC-TV. A multicast channel is a separate channel that shares the bandwith of the main station but can air unique programming. WRC2-TV airs programming from Cozi TV in the Washington, D.C. market. The station is owned by NBC Universal. WRC2-TV broadcasts locally on channel 48.2.
TELEVISION STATION

WRC3-TV 610143
Owner: NBC Universal
Editorial: 4001 Nebraska Ave NW, Washington, District Of Columbia 20016-2733 **Tel:** 1 202 885-4000.
Email: news4pr@nbcuni.com
Web site: http://www.nbcwashington.com
Profile: WRC2-TV is a multicast of WRC-TV. A multicast channel is a separate channel that shares the bandwith of the main station but can air unique programming. WRC2-TV airs programming from Universal Sports in the Washington, D.C. market. The station is owned by NBC Universal. WRC2-TV broadcasts locally on channel 48.3.
TELEVISION STATION

WRCB-TV 32074
Owner: Sarkes Tarzian Inc.
Editorial: 900 Whitehall Rd, Chattanooga, Tennessee 37405-3249 **Tel:** 1 423 267-5412.
Email: news@wrcbtv.com
Web site: http://www.wrcbtv.com
Profile: WRCB-TV is the NBC affiliate in the Chattanooga, TN market. The station is owned by Sarkes Tarzian Inc. WRCB-TV broadcasts locally on channel 3.
TELEVISION STATION

WRCF-TV 602074
Owner: LocusPoint Networks LLC
Editorial: 414 Lake Howell Rd, Maitland, Florida 32751-5900 **Tel:** 1 407 681-6052.
Web site: http://www.wrcftv.com/
Profile: WRCF-TV is the Retro Television affiliate for the Orlando, FL area. The station is owned by LocusPoint Networks LLC. The station airs on channel 29.
TELEVISION STATION

WRC-TV 32073
Owner: NBC Universal
Editorial: 4001 Nebraska Ave NW, Washington, District Of Columbia 20016-2733 **Tel:** 1 202 885-4000.
Email: news4desk@nbcuni.com
Web site: http://www.nbcwashington.com
Profile: WRC-TV is the NBC affiliate for the Washington, D.C. market. The station is owned by NBC Universal. WRC-TV broadcasts locally on channel 4.
TELEVISION STATION

WRCX-TV 128603
Owner: Ross Communications
Editorial: 708 W Hillcrest Ave, Dayton, Ohio 45406-1944 **Tel:** 1 937 275-7677.
Email: wrcxtv@gmail.com
Web site: http://www.wrcxtv40.com
Profile: WRCX-TV is an independent station for the Dayton, OH market. The station is owned by Ross Communications. WRCX-TV broadcasts locally on channel 40.
TELEVISION STATION

WRDC-TV 32056
Owner: Sinclair Broadcast Group, Inc.
Editorial: 3012 Highwoods Blvd, Ste 101, Raleigh, North Carolina 27604 **Tel:** 1 919 872-2854.
Web site: http://www.myrdctv.com
Profile: WRDC-TV is the MyNetworkTV affiliate for the greater Raleigh, NC market. The station is owned by Sinclair Broadcast Group, Inc. WRDC-TV broadcasts locally on channel 28
TELEVISION STATION

WRDE-TV 613919
Owner: NBC Universal
Editorial: 17585 Nassau Commons Blvd Ste 3, Lewes, Delaware 19958-6286 **Tel:** 1 302 703-6104.
Email: news@wrde.com
Web site: http://www.wrdetv.com
Profile: WRDE-TV is the NBC affiliate for the Salisbury, MD market. The station covers the areas of Sussex County and the Eastern Shore of Maryland. WRDE-TV is owned by NBC Universal and broadcasts locally on channel 31.
TELEVISION STATION

WRDM-TV 132268
Owner: ZGS Communications
Editorial: 886 Maple Ave, Hartford, Connecticut 06114-2331 **Tel:** 1 860 956-1303.
Email: info@zgsgroup.com
Web site: http://www.holaciudad.com/nuevainglaterra/telemundo-hartford.html
Profile: WRDM-TV is the Telemundo affiliate for the Hartford-New Haven, CT market. The station is owned by ZGS Communications. WRDM-TV broadcasts locally on channel 50.
TELEVISION STATION

WRDQ2-TV 586596
Owner: Cox Media Group, Inc.
Editorial: 490 E South St, Orlando, Florida 32801-2816 **Tel:** 1 407 841-9000.
Email: news@wftv.com
Web site: http://www.myretrotv.com
Profile: WRDQ2-TV is an independent station for the Orlando, FL market. The station is owned by Cox Media Group, Inc. WRDQ2-TV broadcasts locally on channel 27.2. WRDQ2-TV broadcasts programming from the Retro Television Network only. WRDQ2-TV is a multicast channel of WRDQ-TV. A multicast channel is a separate channel that shares the bandwidth of the main station but can air unique programming.
TELEVISION STATION

WRDQ-TV 72831
Owner: Cox Media Group, Inc.
Editorial: 490 E South St, Orlando, Florida 32801-2816 **Tel:** 1 407 841-9000.
Email: news@wftv.com
Web site: http://www.wftv.com
Profile: WRDQ-TV is an independent station for the Orlando, FL market. The station is owned by Cox Media Group, Inc. WRDQ-TV broadcasts locally on channel 27.
TELEVISION STATION

WRDW-TV 32075
Owner: Gray Television, Inc.
Editorial: 1301 Georgia Ave, North Augusta, South Carolina 29841-3019 **Tel:** 1 803 278-1212.
Email: newsroom@wrdw.com
Web site: http://www.wrdw.com
Profile: WRDW-TV is the CBS affiliate for the Augusta, GA market. The station is owned by Gray Television, Inc. WRDW-TV broadcasts locally on channel 12.
TELEVISION STATION

WREG2-TV 619955
Owner: Tribune Broadcasting Co.
Editorial: 803 Channel 3 Dr, Memphis, Tennessee 38103-4603 **Tel:** 1 901 543-2333.
Email: news@wreg.com
Web site: http://www.wreg.com
Profile: WREG2-TV is a multicast of WREG-TV. A multicast channel is a separate channel that shares the bandwith of the main station but can air unique programming. WREG2-TV airs 24 hour weather programming in the Memphis, TN market. The station is owned by Tribune Broadcasting Co. KREG2-TV broadcasts locally on channel 3.2.
TELEVISION STATION

WREG-TV 32076
Owner: Tribune Broadcasting Co.
Editorial: 803 Channel 3 Dr, Memphis, Tennessee 38103-4603 **Tel:** 1 901 543-2333.
Email: news@wreg.com
Web site: http://www.wreg.com
Profile: WREG-TV is the CBS affiliate for the Memphis, TN market. The station is owned by Tribune Broadcasting Co. WREG-TV broadcasts locally on channel 3.
TELEVISION STATION

WREX-TV 32078
Owner: Quincy Newspapers Inc.
Editorial: 10322 Auburn Rd, Rockford, Illinois 61101-9130 **Tel:** 1 815 335-2213.
Email: news@wrex.com
Web site: http://www.wrex.com
Profile: WREX-TV is the NBC network affiliate for the Rockford, IL market. The station is owned by Quincy Newspapers Inc. WREX-TV broadcasts locally on channel 13.
TELEVISION STATION

WRGB-TV 32079
Owner: Sinclair Broadcast Group, Inc.
Editorial: 1400 Balltown Rd, Schenectady, New York 12309 **Tel:** 1 518 346-6666.
Email: news@cbs6albany.com
Web site: http://www.cbs6albany.com
Profile: WRGB-TV is the CBS affiliate for the Schenectady, Albany, and Troy, NY markets. The station is owned by Sinclair Broadcast Group, Inc. WRGB-TV broadcasts locally on channel 6.
TELEVISION STATION

WRGT-TV 32080
Owner: Sinclair Broadcast Group, Inc.
Editorial: 2245 Corporate Pl, Miamisburg, Ohio 45342-1164 **Tel:** 1 937 263-4500.
Web site: http://www.fox45now.com
Profile: WRGT-TV is the FOX affiliate for the Dayton, OH market. The station is owned by Sinclair Broadcast Group, Inc. WRGT-TV broadcasts locally on channel 45.
TELEVISION STATION

WRIC3-TV 825358
Owner: New Young Broadcasting
Editorial: 301 Arboretum Pl, Richmond, Virginia 23236-3490 **Tel:** 1 804 330-8888.
Web site: http://www.wric.com
Profile: WRIC3-TV is a multicast channel of WRIC-TV. A multicast channel is a separate channel that shares the band with of the main station but can air unique programming. WRIC3-TV is the Live Well Network for the Nashville market. The station is owned by New Young Broadcasting. WRIC3-TV broadcasts locally on channel 8.2.
TELEVISION STATION

WRIC-TV 32212
Owner: New Young Broadcasting
Editorial: 301 Arboretum Pl, Richmond, Virginia 23236 **Tel:** 1 804 330-8888.
Email: news@wric.com
Web site: http://www.wric.com
Profile: WRIC-TV is the ABC affiliate for the Richmond, VA, market. The station is owned by New Young Broadcasting. WRIC-TV broadcasts locally on channel 8.
TELEVISION STATION

WRIW-TV 418227
Owner: ZGS Communications
Editorial: 23 Kenney Dr, Cranston, Rhode Island 02920-4403 **Tel:** 1 401 463-5575.
Web site: http://www.holaciudad.com
Profile: WRIW-TV is the Telemundo affiliate for the Cranston, RI market. The station is owned by ZGS Communications. WRIW-TV broadcasts locally on channel 50.
TELEVISION STATION

WRLH-TV 32082
Owner: Sinclair Broadcast Group, Inc.
Editorial: 1925 Westmoreland St, Richmond, Virginia 23230-3225 **Tel:** 1 804 358-3535.
Email: newsroom@nbc12.com
Web site: http://www.foxrichmond.com
Profile: WRLH-TV is the FOX and MyNetworkTV affiliate for the Richmond, VA market. The station is owned by Sinclair Broadcast Group, Inc. WRLH-TV broadcasts locally on channel 35.
TELEVISION STATION

WRLM-TV 32027
Owner: Radiant Life Ministries, Inc.
Editorial: 4385 Sherman Rd, Kent, Ohio 44240
Tel: 1 330 677-6760.
Profile: WRLM-TV is an independent station for the Cleveland market. The station is owned by Radiant Life Ministries, Inc. WRLM-TV broadcasts locally on channel 47.
TELEVISION STATION

WRMD-TV 133909
Owner: ZGS Communications
Editorial: 4107 W Spruce St Ste 250, Tampa, Florida 33607-2347 **Tel:** 1 813 319-4949.
Web site: http://www.holaciudad.com/estados_unidos/
Profile: WRMD-TV is the Telemundo affiliate for the Tampa-St. Petersburg, FL market. The station is owned by ZGS Communications. WRMD-TV broadcasts locally on channel 49.
TELEVISION STATION

WRNN2-TV 606665
Owner: WRNN License Company, LLC
Editorial: 800 Westchester Ave Ste S640, Rye Brook, New York 10573-1356 **Tel:** 1 914 417-2700.
Email: comments@rnntv.com
Web site: http://www.rnntv.com
Profile: WRNN2-TV is a multicast channel of WRNN-TV. A multicast channel is a separate channel that shares the bandwith of the main station but can air unique programming. WRNN2-TV airs CCTV-9 CCTV International English Service programming on channel 48.2 for the greater Metropolitan New York area. It is owned by WRNN License Company, LLC.
TELEVISION STATION

WRNN-TV 32178
Owner: WRNN License Company, LLC
Editorial: 800 Westchester Ave STE S-640, Rye Brook, New York 10573-1354 **Tel:** 1 914 417-2700.
Email: newsdesk@fios1news.com
Web site: http://www.rnntv.com
Profile: WRNN-TV is an independent station for the New York market. The station is owned by WRNN License Company, LLC. WRNN-TV broadcasts locally on channel 48.
TELEVISION STATION

WROC-TV 32083
Owner: Nexstar Broadcasting Group
Editorial: 201 Humboldt St, Rochester, New York 14610-1041 **Tel:** 1 585 224-8888.
Email: newsroom@rochesterhomepage.net
Web site: http://www.rochesterfirst.com
Profile: WROC-TV is the CBS affiliate for the Rochester, NY market. The station is owned by Nexstar Broadcasting Group. WROC-TV airs locally on channel 8.
TELEVISION STATION

WRPQ-TV 519699
Owner: Baraboo Broadcasting Co.
Editorial: 407 Oak St, Baraboo, Wisconsin 53913
Tel: 1 608 356-3974.
Email: wrpqtv43@wrpq.com
Web site: http://www.wrpq.com
TELEVISION STATION

WRPX2-TV 614758
Owner: ION Media Networks
Editorial: 3209 Gresham Lake Rd, Ste 151, Raleigh, North Carolina 27615-3759 **Tel:** 1 919 827-4800.
Profile: WRPX2-TV is a multicast of WRPX-TV. A multicast channel is a separate channel that shares the bandwith of the main station but can air unique programming. WRPX2-TV airs programming from qubo in the Raleigh-Durham, NC market. The station is owned by ION Media Networks. WRPX2-TV broadcasts locally on channel 47.2.
TELEVISION STATION

WRPX3-TV 614760
Owner: ION Media Networks
Editorial: 3209 Gresham Lake Rd, Ste 151, Raleigh, North Carolina 27615-3759 **Tel:** 1 919 827-4800.
Profile: WRPX3-TV is a multicast of WRPX-TV. A multicast channel is a separate channel that shares the bandwith of the main station but can air unique programming. WRPX3-TV airs programming from ION Life in the Raleigh-Durham, NC market. The station is owned by ION Media Networks. WRPX3-TV broadcasts locally on channel 47.3.
TELEVISION STATION

WRPX4-TV 614761
Owner: ION Media Networks
Editorial: 3209 Gresham Lake Rd, Ste 151, Raleigh, North Carolina 27615-3759 **Tel:** 1 919 827-4800.
Profile: WRPX4-TV is a multicast of WRPX-TV. A multicast channel is a separate channel that shares the bandwith of the main station but can air unique programming. WRPX4-TV airs programming from The Worship Network in the Raleigh-Durham, NC market. The station is owned by ION Media Networks. WRPX4-TV broadcasts locally on channel 47.4.
TELEVISION STATION

WRPX-TV 32253
Owner: ION Media Networks
Editorial: 3209 Gresham Lake Rd, Ste 151, Raleigh, North Carolina 27615-3759 **Tel:** 1 919 827-4800.
Profile: WRPX-TV is the ION Television affiliate for the Raleigh, NC market. The station is owned by ION Media Networks. WRPX-TV broadcasts locally on channel 47.
TELEVISION STATION

WRSP-TV 32084
Owner: Sinclair Broadcast Group
Editorial: 2680 E Cook St, Springfield, Illinois 62703-1902 **Tel:** 1 217 523-8855.
Web site: http://www.foxillinois.com
Profile: WRSP-TV is the FOX affiliate for the Springfield-Decatur, IL market. The station is owned by Sinclair Broadcast Group. WRSP-TV broadcasts locally on channel 55.
TELEVISION STATION

WRTV2-TV 612934
Owner: E.W. Scipps Co.
Editorial: 1330 N Meridian St, Indianapolis, Indiana 46202-2303 **Tel:** 1 317 635-9788.
Email: newstips@theindychannel.com
Web site: http://www.theindychannel.com
Profile: WRTV2-TV is a multicast of WRTV-TV. A multicast channel is a separate channel that shares the bandwith of the main station but can air unique programming. WRTV2-TV airs programming from the 6 News 24/7 in the Indianapolis market. The station is owned by E.W. Scipps Co. WRTV2-TV broadcasts locally on channel 6.2.
TELEVISION STATION

WRTV-TV 32085
Owner: E.W. Scripps Co.
Editorial: 1330 N Meridian St, Indianapolis, Indiana 46202-2303 **Tel:** 1 317 635-9788.
Email: news@wrtv.com
Web site: http://www.theindychannel.com
Profile: WRTV-TV is the ABC affiliate for the Indianapolis market. The station is owned by E.W. Scipps Co. WRTV-TV broadcasts locally on channel 6.
TELEVISION STATION

WRXY-TV 32491
Owner: Christian Television Network
Editorial: 40000 Horseshoe Rd, Punta Gorda, Florida 33982-7739 **Tel:** 1 239 543-7200.
Email: office@wrxytv.com
Web site: http://www.ctn10.com
Profile: WRXY-TV is the Christian Television Network affiliate for the Fort Myers, FL market. The station is owned by Christian Television Network. WRXY-TV broadcasts locally on channel 49.
TELEVISION STATION

WSAV-TV 32086
Owner: Nexstar Media Group, LLC
Editorial: 1430 E Victory Dr, Savannah, Georgia 31404-4108 **Tel:** 1 912 651-0300.
Email: newsemailalert@wsav.com
Web site: http://www.wsav.com

Profile: WSAV-TV is the NBC affiliate for the Savannah, GA market. The station is owned by Nexstar Media Group, LLC. WSAV-TV broadcasts locally on channel 3.
TELEVISION STATION

WSAW2-TV 708412
Owner: Gray Television, Inc.
Editorial: 1114 Grand Ave, Wausau, Wisconsin 54403-6688 **Tel:** 1 715 845-4211.
Web site: http://www.wsaw.com/station/mntv
Profile: WSAW2-TV is a multicast of WSAW-TV. A multicast is channel is a separate channel that shares bandwidth of the main station but can air unique programming. WSAW2-TV is the local MyNetworkTV affiliate on Channel 7.2 for the Wausau, WI market. WSAW2-TV is owned by Gray Television, Inc.
TELEVISION STATION

WSAW-TV 32087
Owner: Gray Television, Inc.
Editorial: 1114 Grand Ave, Wausau, Wisconsin 54403-6688 **Tel:** 1 715 845-4211.
Email: news@wsaw.com
Web site: http://www.wsaw.com
Profile: WSAW-TV is the CBS network affiliate for the Wausau, WI market. The station is owned by Gray Television, Inc. WSAW-TV broadcasts locally on channel 7.
TELEVISION STATION

WSAZ-TV 32088
Owner: Gray Television, Inc.
Editorial: 111 Columbia Ave, Charleston, West Virginia 25302-2303 **Tel:** 1 304 690-3069.
Email: news@wsaz.com
Web site: http://www.wsaz.com
Profile: WSAZ-TV is the NBC affiliate for the Charleston-Huntington, WV, market. It is owned by Gray Television, Inc. WSAZ-TV broadcasts locally on channel 3.
TELEVISION STATION

WSBE-TV 32090
Owner: Rhode Island Public Telecommunications Authority
Editorial: 50 Park Ln, Providence, Rhode Island 02907-3124 **Tel:** 1 401 222-3636.
Web site: http://www.ripbs.org
Profile: WSBE-TV is the PBS affiliate for the Providence, RI-New Bedford, MA market. The station is owned by the Rhode Island Public Telecommunications Authority. WSBE-TV broadcasts locally on channel 36.
TELEVISION STATION

WSBK-TV 32091
Owner: CBS Television Stations
Editorial: 1170 Soldiers Field Rd, Boston, Massachusetts 02134-1004 **Tel:** 1 617 787-7000.
Email: newstips@wbztv.com
Web site: http://boston.cbslocal.com/station/tv38
Profile: WSBK-TV is the MyNetworkTV affiliate station for the Boston market. The station is owned by CBS Television Stations. WSBK broadcasts locally on channel 38.
TELEVISION STATION

WSBS-TV 390879
Owner: Spanish Broadcasting System
Editorial: 7007 Nw 77Th Ave, Miami, Florida 33166-2836 **Tel:** 1 305 644-4800.
Web site: http://www.mega.tv
Profile: WSBS-TV is an independent station for the Miami market. The station is owned by Spanish Broadcasting System. WSBS-TV broadcasts locally on channel 22.
TELEVISION STATION

WSBT-TV 32092
Owner: Sinclair Broadcast Group, Inc.
Editorial: 1301 E Douglas Rd, Mishawaka, Indiana 46545-1732 **Tel:** 1 574 233-3141.
Email: wsbtnews@wsbt.com
Web site: http://www.wsbt.com
Profile: WSBT-TV is the CBS affiliate for the South Bend, IN, market. It is owned by Sinclair Broadcast Group, Inc. WSBT-TV broadcasts locally on channel 22. Send all press releases to the main email wsbtnews@wsbt.com.
TELEVISION STATION

WSB-TV 32089
Owner: Cox Media Group, Inc.
Editorial: 1601 W Peachtree St NE, Atlanta, Georgia 30309-2641 **Tel:** 1 404 897-7000.
Email: newstip@wsbtv.com
Web site: http://www.wsbtv.com
Profile: WSB-TV is the ABC affiliate for the Atlanta market. The station is owned by Cox Media Group, Inc. WSB-TV broadcasts locally on channel 2.
TELEVISION STATION

WSCV-TV 32094
Owner: NBC Universal
Editorial: 15000 SW 27th St, Miramar, Florida 33027-4147 **Tel:** 1 305 888-5151.
Email: reporte@telemundo51.com
Web site: http://www.telemundo51.com
Profile: WSCV-TV is a Telemundo affiliate for the Miramar, FL market. The station is owned by NBC Universal. WSCV-TV broadcasts locally on channel 51.
TELEVISION STATION

WSEE-TV 32095
Owner: Lilly Broadcasting of Pennsylvania
Editorial: 3514 State St, Erie, Pennsylvania 16508-2834 **Tel:** 1 814 454-5201.
Email: news@wsee.tv
Web site: http://www.erietvnews.com
Profile: WSEE-TV is the CBS network affiliate for the Erie, PA market. The station is owned by Lilly Broadcasting of Pennsylvania. WSEE-TV broadcasts locally on channel 35.
TELEVISION STATION

WSET-TV 32096
Owner: Sinclair Broadcast Group, Inc.
Editorial: 2320 Langhorne Rd, Lynchburg, Virginia 24501-1547 **Tel:** 1 434 528-1313.
Email: newsdesk@wset.com
Web site: http://www.wset.com
Profile: WSET-TV is the ABC affiliate for the Roanoke-Lynchburg, VA market. The station is owned by Sinclair Broadcast Group, Inc. WSET-TV broadcasts locally on channel 13.
TELEVISION STATION

WSFA2-TV 723398
Owner: Raycom Media Inc.
Editorial: 12 E Delano Ave, Montgomery, Alabama 36105-2214 **Tel:** 1 334 288-1212.
Web site: http://www.wsfa.com
Profile: WSFA2-TV is a multicast channel of WAFA-TV. A multicast channel is a separate channel that shares the bandwith of the main station but can air unique programming. WSFA2-TV is the Retro Television Network for the Montgomery, AL market. The station is owned by Raycom Media Inc. WSFA2-TV broadcasts locally on channel 12.2.
TELEVISION STATION

WSFA-TV 32097
Owner: Raycom Media Inc.
Editorial: 12 E Delano Ave, Montgomery, Alabama 36105-2214 **Tel:** 1 334 288-1212.
Email: news@wsfa.com
Web site: http://www.wsfa.com
Profile: WSFA-TV is the NBC affiliate for the Montgomery, AL market. The station is owned by Raycom Media Inc. WSFA-TV broadcasts locally on channel 12.
TELEVISION STATION

WSFJ-TV 32098
Owner: Trinity Broadcasting Network
Editorial: 7790 N. Central Drive, Columbus, Ohio
Tel: 1 740 548-3800.
Web site: http://www.tbn.org
Profile: WSFJ-TV is an independent television station for Columbus, OH. The station is owned by Trinity Broadcasting Network. WSFJ-TV broadcasts locally on channel 51.
TELEVISION STATION

WSFL2-TV 614837
Owner: Tribune Broadcasting Co.
Editorial: 500 E Broward Blvd Ste 800, Fort Lauderdale, Florida 33394-3018 **Tel:** 1 954 627-7300.
Web site: http://www.justicenetworktv.com
Profile: WSFL2-TV is a Justice Network affiliate for the Miami-Fort Lauderdale, FL market. The station is owned by Tribune Broadcasting Co. WSFL2-TV broadcasts locally on channel 39.2. The station airs programming from the Justice Network. WSFL2-TV is a multicast channel of WSFL-TV. A multicast channel is a separate channel that shares the bandwidth of the main station but can air unique programming.
TELEVISION STATION

WSFL-TV 31816
Owner: Tribune Broadcasting Co.
Editorial: 500 E Broward Blvd Ste 800, Fort Lauderdale, Florida 33394-3018 **Tel:** 1 954 627-7300.
Email: feedback_wsfl@tribunemedia.com
Web site: http://sflcw.com
Profile: WSFL-TV is the CW affiliate for the Miami-Fort Lauderdale, FL market. The station is owned by Tribune Broadcasting Co. WSFL-TV broadcasts locally on channel 39.
TELEVISION STATION

WSFX-TV 31923
Owner: Southeastern Media Acquisitions, LLC
Editorial: 322 Shipyard Blvd, Wilmington, North Carolina 28412-1835 **Tel:** 1 910 791-8070.
Email: newsroom@wect.com
Web site: http://www.wsfx.com
Profile: WSFX-TV is the FOX affiliate for the Wilmington, NC market. The station is owned by Southeastern Media Acquisitions, LLC. WSFX-TV broadcasts locally on channel 26.
TELEVISION STATION

WSHM-TV 382094
Owner: Meredith Corporation
Editorial: 1300 Liberty St, Springfield, Massachusetts 01104-1153 **Tel:** 1 413 733-4040.
Email: tips@westernmassnews.com
Web site: http://www.westernmassnews.com
Profile: WSHM-TV is the CBS affiliate for the Springfield, MA market. The station is owned by Meredith Corporation. WSHM-TV broadcasts locally on channel 3.
TELEVISION STATION

WSIL-TV 32700
Owner: Wheeler Inc.(Mel)
Editorial: 1416 Country Aire Dr, Carterville, Illinois 62918-5122 **Tel:** 1 618 985-2333.
Email: news@wsiltv.com
Web site: http://www.wsiltv.com
Profile: WSIL-TV is the ABC network affiliate for the Paducah, KY; Cape Girardeau, MO and Harrisburg, IL market. The station is owned by Mel Wheeler Inc. WSIL-TV broadcasts locally on channel 3.
TELEVISION STATION

WSIU-TV 32100
Owner: WSIU Public Broadcasting
Editorial: 1100 Lincoln Dr. Ste 1003, SIU Code 6602, Carbondale, Illinois 62901 **Tel:** 1 618 453-4343.
Email: tvnews@siu.edu
Web site: http://www.wsiu.org
Profile: WSIU-TV is the PBS network affiliate for the Paducah, KY; Cape Girardeau, MO and Harrisburg, IL market. The station is owned by WSIU Public Broadcasting. WSIU-TV broadcasts locally on channel 8.
TELEVISION STATION

WSJV-TV 32102
Owner: Sinclair Broadcast Group
Editorial: 58096 County Road 7, Elkhart, Indiana 46517-9223 **Tel:** 1 574 233-3141.
Email: wsbtnews@wsbt.com
Web site: http://www.wsbt.com
Profile: WSJV-TV is a Heroes and Icons Network affiliate for the South Bend, IN, market. It is owned by Sinclair Broadcast Group. WSJV-TV broadcasts locally on channel 28.
TELEVISION STATION

WSKG-TV 32103
Owner: WSKG Public Telecommunications
Editorial: 601 Gates Rd, Vestal, New York 13850
Tel: 1 607 729-0100.
Email: wskgcomment@wskg.org
Web site: http://www.wskg.org
Profile: WSKG-TV is the PBS affiliate for the Binghamton, NY market. The station is owned by WSKG Public Telecommunications. WSKG-TV broadcasts locally on channel 46.
TELEVISION STATION

WSKY2-TV 620055
Owner: Sky Television LLC
Editorial: 218 Salters Creek Rd, Hampton, Virginia 23661-1909 **Tel:** 1 757 382-0004.
Email: programming@wsky4.com
Web site: http://www.sky4tv.com
Profile: WSKY2-TV is a multicast of WSKY-TV. A multicast channel is a separate channel that shares the bandwidth of the main station but can air unique programming. WSKY2-TV airs sports programming from Universal Sports to the Norfolk, VA market. The station is owned by Sky Television LLC. WSKY2-TV broadcasts locally on channel 4.2.
TELEVISION STATION

WSKY-TV 139568
Owner: Sky Television LLC
Editorial: 218 Salters Creek Rd, Hampton, Virginia 23661-1909 **Tel:** 1 757 382-0004.
Email: programming@wsky4.com
Web site: http://wwwsky4tv.com
Profile: WSKY-TV is an independent station in the Norfolk, VA area. The station is owned by Sky Television LLC. WSKY-TV broadcasts locally on channel 4.
TELEVISION STATION

WSLS-TV 32104
Owner: MidAmerica Holdings, LLC
Editorial: 401 3rd St SW, Roanoke, Virginia 24011-1507 **Tel:** 1 540 981-9126.
Email: news@wsls.com
Web site: http://www.wsls.com
Profile: WSLS-TV is the NBC network affiliate for the Roanoke-Lynchburg, VA market. The station is owned by MidAmerica Holdings, LLC. WSLS-TV broadcasts locally on channel 10.
TELEVISION STATION

WSMH-TV 32105
Owner: Sinclair Broadcast Group, Inc.
Editorial: 3463 W Pierson Rd, Flint, Michigan 48504-6905 **Tel:** 1 810 785-8866.
Web site: http://www.wsmh.com
Profile: WSMH-TV is the FOX affiliate for the Flint, MI market. The staion is owned by Sinclair Broadcast Group, Inc. WSMH-TV broadcasts locally on channel 66.
TELEVISION STATION

WSMV2-TV 612945
Owner: Meredith Broadcasting Group
Editorial: 5700 Knob Rd, Nashville, Tennessee 37209-4596 **Tel:** 1 615 353-4444.
Web site: http://watchtnn.com
Profile: WSMV2-TV is a multicast of WSMV-TV. A multicast channel is a separate channel that shares the bandwith of the main station but can air unique programming. WSMV2-TV airs programming from The Nashville Network in the Nashville, TN market. The station is owned by Meredith Broadcasting Group. WSMV2-TV broadcasts locally on channel 4.2.
TELEVISION STATION

WSMV-TV 32106
Owner: Meredith Broadcasting Group
Editorial: 5700 Knob Rd, Nashville, Tennessee 37209-4523 **Tel:** 1 615 353-4444.
Email: news@wsmv.com
Web site: http://www.wsmv.com
Profile: WSMV-TV is the NBC affiliate for the Nashville, TN market. The station is owned by Meredith Broadcasting Group. WSMV-TV is broadcast locally on channel 4.
TELEVISION STATION

WSNS-TV 32107
Owner: NBC Universal
Editorial: 454 N Columbus Dr, Chicago, Illinois 60611-5807 **Tel:** 1 312 836-3000.
Email: assignmentdeskwsns@nbcuni.com
Web site: http://www.telemundochicago.com
Profile: WSNS-TV is the Telemundo affiliate for the Chicago market. The station is owned by NBC Universal. WSNS-TV broadcasts locally on channel 44.
TELEVISION STATION

WSOC2-TV 614015
Owner: Cox Media Group, Inc.
Editorial: 1901 N Tryon St, Charlotte, North Carolina 28206-2733 **Tel:** 1 704 338-9999.
Email: assignment@wsoc-tv.com
Web site: http://www.wsoctv.com
Profile: WSOC2-TV is a multicast of WSOC-TV. A multicast channel is a separate channel that shares the bandwith of the main station but can air unique programming. WSOC2-TV is the Telemundo affiliate for the Charlotte, NC market. The station is owned by Cox Media Group, Inc. WSOC2-TV broadcasts locally on channel 9.2.
TELEVISION STATION

WSOC-TV 32108
Owner: Cox Media Group, Inc.
Editorial: 1901 N Tryon St, Charlotte, North Carolina 28206-2733 **Tel:** 1 704 338-9999.
Email: assignment@wsoc-tv.com
Web site: http://www.wsoctv.com
Profile: WSOC-TV is the Telemundo network affiliate for the Charlotte, NC market. The station is owned by Cox Media Group, Inc. WSOC-TV broadcasts locally on channel 9.
TELEVISION STATION

WSOT-TV 355477
Owner: Sunnycrest Baptist Church
Editorial: 2172 W Chapel Pike, Marion, Indiana 46952-1567 **Tel:** 1 765 664-3047.
Email: traffic@wsot-tv.com
Web site: http://www.wsot-tv.com
Profile: WSOT-TV is an independent station for the Indianapolis market. The station is owned by Sunnycrest Baptist Church. WSOT-TV broadcasts locally on channel 57.
TELEVISION STATION

WSPA2-TV 621871
Owner: Nexstar Media Group, LLC
Editorial: 250 International Dr, Spartanburg, South Carolina 29303-6637 **Tel:** 1 864 576-7777.
Email: assignmentdesk@wspa.com
Web site: http://www.wspa.com
Profile: WSPA2-TV is a multicast channel of WSPA-TV. A multicast is a separate channel that shares the bandwith of the main station but can air unique programming. WSPA2-TV airs entertainment and weather programming from Retro Television Network in the Spartanburg, SC market. The station is owned by Nexstar Media Group, LLC. WSPA2-TV broadcasts locally on channel 7.2.
TELEVISION STATION

WSPA-TV 32109
Owner: Nexstar Media Group, LLC
Editorial: 250 International Dr, Spartanburg, South Carolina 29303-6637 **Tel:** 1 864 576-7777.
Email: assignmentdesk@wspa.com
Web site: http://www.wspa.com
Profile: WSPA-TV is the local CBS affiliate for the Greenville, SC/Asheville, NC market. The station is owned by Nexstar Media Group, LLC. WSPA-TV is broadcast locally on channel 7.
TELEVISION STATION

WSPX-TV 32630
Owner: ION Media Networks
Editorial: 6508 Basile Rowe, Ste B, East Syracuse, New York 13057 **Tel:** 1 315 414-0178.
Web site: http://www.ionline.tv
Profile: WSPX-TV is the ION Television affiliate for the Syracuse, NY market. The station is owned by ION Media Networks. WSPX-TV broadcasts locally on channel 56.
TELEVISION STATION

WSRE-TV 32110
Owner: Pensacola Junior College
Editorial: 1000 College Blvd, Pensacola, Florida 32504 **Tel:** 1 850 484-1200.
Web site: http://www.wsre.org
Profile: WSRE-TV is the PBS affiliate for the Pensacola, FL market. The station is owned by the Pensacola Junior College. WSRE-TV broadcasts locally on channel 23.
TELEVISION STATION

WSST-TV 32333
Owner: Sunbelt-South Telecommunications Ltd.
Editorial: 112 S 7th St, Cordele, Georgia 31015-4209
Tel: 1 229 273-0001.
Web site: http://www.wsst51.com
Profile: WSST-TV is an independent station for the Albany, GA market. The station is owned by Sunbelt-South Telecommunications Ltd. WSST-TV broadcasts locally on channel 51.
TELEVISION STATION

WSTM-TV 32111
Owner: Sinclair Broadcast Group, Inc.
Editorial: 1030 James St, Syracuse, New York 13203-2704 **Tel:** 1 315 477-9400.
Email: news@cnycentral.com
Web site: http://www.cnycentral.com

Profile: WSTM-TV is the NBC network affiliate for the Syracuse, NY market. The station is owned by Sinclair Broadcast Group, Inc. WSTM-TV broadcasts locally on channel 3.
TELEVISION STATION

WSTQ-TV
156522
Owner: Sinclair Broadcast Group, Inc.
Editorial: 1030 James St, Syracuse, New York 13203-2704 **Tel:** 1 315 477-9400.
Email: news@cnycentral.com
Web site: http://www.cnycentral.com
Profile: WSTQ-TV is the CW affiliate for the Syracuse, NY market. The station is owned by Sinclair Broadcast Group, Inc. WSTQ-TV broadcasts locally on channel 14.
TELEVISION STATION

WSTR-TV
31899
Owner: Sinclair Broadcast Group, Inc.
Editorial: 1906 Highland Ave, Cincinnati, Ohio 45219-3104 **Tel:** 1 513 641-4400.
Web site: http://www.star64.tv
Profile: WSTR-TV is the MyNetworkTV affiliate for the Cincinnati, OH market. The station is owned by Sinclair Broadcast Group, Inc. WSTR-TV broadcasts locally on channel 64.
TELEVISION STATION

WSTY-TV
350379
Owner: Great Oaks Broadcasting
Editorial: 740 S Morrison Blvd, Hammond, Louisiana 70403-5402 **Tel:** 1 985 902-8888.
Email: news@wstytv.com
Web site: http://wsty.com
Profile: WSTY-TV is an independent affiliate for the Hammond, LA market. The station is owned by Great Oaks Broadcasting. WSTY-TV broadcasts to the Hammond, LA area on channel 23.
TELEVISION STATION

WSVN2-TV
614836
Owner: Sunbeam Broadcasting Corp.
Editorial: 1401 79th Street Cswy, North Bay Village, Florida 33141-4181 **Tel:** 1 305 751-6692.
Email: newsdesk@wsvn.com
Web site: http://www.wsvn.com
Profile: WSVN2-TV is an independent affiliate for the greater Miami area. The station is owned by Sunbeam Broadcasting Corp. WSVN2-TV broadcasts locally on channel 7.2. The station airs Spanish programming from the Estrella TV network. WSVN2-TV is a multicast channel of WSVN-TV. A multicast channel is a separate channel that shares the bandwidth of the main station but can air unique programming.
TELEVISION STATION

WSVN-TV
32112
Owner: Sunbeam Broadcasting Corp.
Editorial: 1401 79th Street Cswy, North Bay Village, Florida 33141-4104 **Tel:** 1 305 751-6692.
Email: newsdesk@wsvn.com
Web site: http://www.wsvn.com
Profile: WSVN-TV is the local FOX affiliate for the greater Miami area. The station is owned by Sunbeam Broadcasting Corp. WSVN-TV broadcasts locally on channel 7.
TELEVISION STATION

WSWB-TV
32583
Owner: MPS Media
Editorial: 1181 Highway 315 Blvd, Plains, Pennsylvania 18702-6928 **Tel:** 1 570 970-5600.
Email: myfoxnepa@fox56.com
Web site: http://www.myfoxnepa.com
Profile: WSWB-TV is the CW affiliate for the greater Scranton, Wilkes-Barre, and Hazleton, PA market. The station is owned by MPS Media. WSWB-TV broadcasts locally on channel 38.
TELEVISION STATION

WSWF-TV
602077
Owner: LocusPoint Networks LLC
Editorial: 414 Lake Howell Rd, Maitland, Florida 32751-5900 **Tel:** 1 407 383-4566.
Web site: http://wswf.tv/
TELEVISION STATION

WSWG-TV
153497
Owner: Gray Television, Inc.
Editorial: 415 Pine Ave Ste 100, Albany, Georgia 31701-2536 **Tel:** 1 229 985-1340.
Web site: http://www.wswg.tv
Profile: WSWG-TV is the CBS affiliate for the Albany, GA market. The station is owned by Gray Television. WSWG-TV broadcasts locally on channel 44.
TELEVISION STATION

WSYM3-TV
772954
Owner: E.W. Scripps Co.
Editorial: 600 W Saint Joseph St Ste 47, Lansing, Michigan 48933-2265 **Tel:** 1 517 484-1147.
Email: fox47news@fox47news.com
Web site: http://www.fox47news.com
Profile: WSYM3-TV is a multicast channel of WSYM-TV. A multicast channel is a separate channel that shares the bandwidth of the main station but can air unique programming. WSYM3-TV is the Me-TV Network for the Lansing, MI market. The station is owned by E.W. Scripps Co. WAYM3-TV broadcasts locally on channel 47.3.
TELEVISION STATION

WSYM-TV
32115
Owner: E.W. Scripps Co.
Editorial: 600 W Saint Joseph St Ste 47, Lansing, Michigan 48933-2265 **Tel:** 1 517 484-7747.
Email: fox47news@fox47news.com
Web site: http://www.fox47news.com
Profile: WSYM-TV is the Fox affiliate for the Lansing, MI, market. The station is owned by E.W. Scripps Co. WSYM-TV broadcasts locally on channel 47.
TELEVISION STATION

WSYR-TV
31911
Owner: Nextar Television
Editorial: 5904 Bridge St, East Syracuse, New York 13057-2941 **Tel:** 1 315 446-9999.
Email: assignmentdesk@localsyr.com
Web site: http://www.localsyr.com
Profile: WSYR-TV is the ABC affiliate for the Syracuse, NY market. The station is owned by Newport Television, LLC. WSYR-TV broadcasts locally on channel 9.
TELEVISION STATION

WSYT-TV
32116
Owner: Bristol Cohen
Editorial: 1000 James St, Syracuse, New York 13203-2704 **Tel:** 1 315 472-6800.
Web site: http://www.foxsyracuse.com
Profile: WSYT-TV is the Fox affiliate for the Syracuse, NY market. The station is owned by Bristol Cohen. WSYT-TV broadcasts locally on channel 68.
TELEVISION STATION

WSYX2-TV
618661
Owner: Sinclair Broadcast Group, Inc.
Editorial: 1261 Dublin Rd, Columbus, Ohio 43215-7000 **Tel:** 1 614 481-6666.
Web site: http://www.abc6onyourside.com
Profile: WSYX2-TV is a multicast of WSYX-TV. A multicast channel is a separate channel that shares the bandwith of the main station but can air unique programming. WSYX2-TV airs programming from MyTV Columbus/FUNimation Channel/This TV in the Columbus, OH market. The station is owned by Sinclair Broadcast Group, Inc. WSYX2-TV broadcasts locally on channel 6.2.
TELEVISION STATION

WSYX-TV
32117
Owner: Sinclair Broadcast Group, Inc.
Editorial: 1261 Dublin Rd, Columbus, Ohio 43215-7000 **Tel:** 1 614 481-6666.
Email: webmaster@wsyx6.com
Web site: http://www.abc6onyourside.com
Profile: WSYX-TV is the ABC affiliate in the Columbus, OH market. The station is owned by Sinclair Broadcast Group, Inc. WSYX-TV broadcasts locally on channel 6.
TELEVISION STATION

WTAE2-TV
614577
Owner: Hearst Television Inc.
Editorial: 400 Ardmore Blvd, Pittsburgh, Pennsylvania 15221-3019 **Tel:** 1 412 242-4300.
Web site: http://www.wtae.com
Profile: WTAE2-TV is a multicast of WTAE-TV. A multicast channel is a separate channel that shares the bandwith of the main station but can air unique programming. WTAE2-TV airs programming from the This TV Network in the Pittsburgh market. The station is owned by Hearst Television Inc. WTAE2-TV broadcasts locally on channel 4.2.
TELEVISION STATION

WTAE-TV
32118
Owner: Hearst Television Inc.
Editorial: 400 Ardmore Blvd, Pittsburgh, Pennsylvania 15221-3019 **Tel:** 1 412 242-4300.
Email: news@wtae.com
Web site: http://www.wtae.com
Profile: WTAE-TV is the ABC affiliate for the Pittsburgh market. The station is owned by Hearst Television Inc. WTAE-TV broadcasts locally on channel 4.
TELEVISION STATION

WTAJ-TV
32119
Owner: Nexstar Broadcasting Group
Editorial: 5000 6th Ave, Altoona, Pennsylvania 16602
Tel: 1 814 942-1010.
Web site: http://wearecentralpa.com/
Profile: WTAJ-TV, is the CBS affiliate for the Johnstown - Altoona, PA market. The station is owned by Nexstar Broadcasting Group. WTAJ-TV broadcasts locally on channel 10.
TELEVISION STATION

WTAM-TV
553632
Owner: SIMA Communications
Editorial: 1805 N Franklin St, Tampa, Florida 33602-2233 **Tel:** 1 813 221-3100.
Web site: http://miratv.tv
Profile: WTAM-TV is an independent station for the Tampa, FL market. The station is owned by SIMA Communications. WTAM-TV broadcasts locally on channel 30.
TELEVISION STATION

WTAP-TV
32120
Owner: Gray Television, Inc.
Editorial: 1 Television Plz, Parkersburg, West Virginia 26101-7501 **Tel:** 1 304 485-4588.
Email: news@thenewscenter.tv
Web site: http://www.wtap.com
Profile: WTAP-TV is the NBC affiliate for the Parkersburg, WV market. The station is owned by Gray Television, Inc. WTAP-TV broadcasts locally on channel 15.
TELEVISION STATION

WTAT-TV
32121
Owner: Sinclair Broadcast Group, Inc.
Editorial: 4301 Arco Ln, North Charleston, South Carolina 29418-6009 **Tel:** 1 843 744-2424.
Email: comments@wtat24.com
Web site: http://www.foxcharleston.com
Profile: WTAT-TV is a Fox affiliate for the Charleston, SC, area. The station is owned by Sinclair Broadcast Group, Inc. The station does not have an original news program, so there are no opportunities for PR professionals at this time. Contact the programming manager with any further inquiries.
TELEVISION STATION

WTCI-TV
32123
Owner: Greater Chattanooga PTV Corp.
Editorial: 7540 Bonnyshire Dr, Chattanooga, Tennessee 37416-6001 **Tel:** 1 423 702-7800.
Web site: http://www.wtcitv.org
Profile: WTCI-TV is a PBS affiliate for the Chattanooga, TN market. The station is owned by the Greater Chattanooga Public Television Corporation. WTCI-TV broadcasts locally on channel 45.
TELEVISION STATION

WTCN-TV
72023
Owner: Sinclair Broadcast Group, Inc.
Editorial: 1700 Palm Beach Lakes Blvd Ste 150, West Palm Beach, Florida 33401-2007 **Tel:** 1 561 681-3434.
Web site: http://www.my15wtcn.com
Profile: WTCN-TV is the MyNetworkTV affiliate for the West Palm Beach, FL market. The station is owned by Sinclair Broadcast Group, Inc. WTCN-TV broadcasts locally on channel 15.
TELEVISION STATION

WTCT-TV
32124
Owner: Tri-State Christian TV
Editorial: 11717 Route 37, Marion, Illinois 62959-8356
Tel: 1 618 997-4700.
Email: media@tct.tv
Web site: http://www.tct.tv
Profile: WTCT-TV is an independent affiliate for the Marion, IL market. The station is owned by Tri-State Christian TV. WTCT-TV broadcasts locally on channel 27.
TELEVISION STATION

WTEN3-TV
586677
Owner: Young Broadcasting
Editorial: 341 Northern Blvd, Albany, New York 12204-1001 **Tel:** 1 518 436-4822.
Email: news@wten.com
Web site: http://www.news10.com
Profile: WTEN3-TV is a multicast channel of WTEN-TV. A multicast channel is a separate channel that shares the bandwith of the main station but can air unique programming. WTEN3-TV is the Live Well Network for the Albany market. The station is owned by Young Broadcasting. WTEN3-TV broadcasts locally on channel 10.3.
TELEVISION STATION

WTEN-TV
32674
Owner: Young Broadcasting
Editorial: 341 Northern Blvd, Albany, New York 12204-1001 **Tel:** 1 518 436-4822.
Email: news@news10.com
Web site: http://www.news10.com
Profile: WTEN-TV is the ABC affiliate for the Albany, Schenectady - and Troy, NY broadcasts. The station is owned by Young Broadcasting. WTEN-TV broadcasts locally on channel 10.
TELEVISION STATION

WTGL-TV
153630
Owner: Good Life Broadcasting
Editorial: 31 Skyline Dr, Lake Mary, Florida 32746
Tel: 1 407 215-6745.
Email: info@tv45.org
Web site: http://www.tv45.org
Profile: WTGL-TV is an independent station for the Orlando-Daytona Beach, FL market. The station is owned by Good Life Broadcasting. WTGL-TV broadcasts locally on channel 45.
TELEVISION STATION

WTGS-TV
32127
Owner: Sinclair Broadcast Group, Inc.
Editorial: 1375 Chatham Pkwy Fl 3, Savannah, Georgia 31405-0301 **Tel:** 1 912 925-2287.
Web site: http://fox28media.com
Profile: WTGS-TV is the FOX affiliate for the Savannah, GA market. The station is owned by Sinclair Broadcast Group, Inc. WTGS-TV broadcasts locally on channel 28.
TELEVISION STATION

WTHI2-TV
771950
Owner: MidAmerica Holdings, LLC
Editorial: 800 Ohio St, Terre Haute, Indiana 47807-3720 **Tel:** 1 812 232-9481.
Email: news10@wthitv.com
Web site: http://www.wthitv.com
Profile: WTHI2-TV is a multicast channel of WTHI-TV. A multicast channel is a separate channel that shares the bandwidth of the main station but can air unique programming. WTHI2-TV is the Fox Broadcasting Network for the Terre Haute, IN market. The station is owned by MidAmerica Holdings, LLC WTHI2-TV broadcasts locally on channel 10.2. This Channel launched September 1, 2011.
TELEVISION STATION

WTHI-TV
32128
Owner: MidAmerica Holdings, LLC
Editorial: 800 Ohio St, Terre Haute, Indiana 47807-3720 **Tel:** 1 812 232-9481.
Email: news10@wthitv.com
Web site: http://www.wthitv.com
Profile: WTHI-TV is the CBS network affiliate for the Terre Haute, IN market. The station is owned by MidAmerica Holdings, LLC. WTHI-TV broadcasts locally on channel 10.
TELEVISION STATION

WTHR2-TV
614572
Owner: Dispatch Broadcast Group
Editorial: 1000 N Meridian St, Indianapolis, Indiana 46204-1015 **Tel:** 1 317 636-1313.
Email: 13news@wthr.com
Web site: http://www.wthr.com
Profile: WTHR2-TV is a multicast of WTHR-TV. A multicast channel is a separate channel that shares the bandwidth of the main station but can air unique programming. WTHR2-TV airs programming from SkyTrack Weather Network in the Indianapolis market. The station is owned by Dispatch Broadcast Group. WTHR2-TV broadcasts locally on channel 13.2.
TELEVISION STATION

WTHR3-TV
614573
Owner: Dispatch Broadcast Group
Editorial: 1000 N Meridian St, Indianapolis, Indiana 46204-1015 **Tel:** 1 317 636-1313.
Email: 13news@wthr.com
Web site: http://www.whtr.com
TELEVISION STATION

WTHR-TV
32129
Owner: Dispatch Broadcast Group
Editorial: 1000 N Meridian St, Indianapolis, Indiana 46204-1015 **Tel:** 1 317 636-1313.
Email: newsdesk@wthr.com
Web site: http://www.wthr.com
Profile: WTHR-TV is the NBC affiliate for the Indianapolis market. The station is owned by Dispatch Broadcast Group. WTHR-TV broadcasts locally on channel 13.
TELEVISION STATION

WTIC-TV
32130
Owner: Tribune Broadcasting Co.
Editorial: 285 Broad St, Hartford, Connecticut 06105-3785 **Tel:** 1 860 527-6161.
Email: newsteam@fox61.com
Web site: http://fox61.com
Profile: WTIC-TV is the FOX network affiliate in the Hartford-New Haven, CT market. The station is owned by Tribune Broadcasting Co. WTIC-TV broadcasts locally on channel 61. WTIC-TV shares news operations with the Record-Journal of Meriden, Connecticut.
TELEVISION STATION

WTJP2-TV
618678
Owner: Trinity Broadcasting Network
Editorial: 313 Rosedale St, Gadsden, Alabama 35901-5361 **Tel:** 1 256 546-8860.
Profile: WTJP2-TV is a multicast of WTJP-TV. A multicast channel is a separate channel that shares the bandwith of the main station but can air unique programming. WTJP2-TV airs religious programming from The Church Channel in the Birmingham, AL market. The station is owned by Trinity Broadcasting Network. WTJP2-TV broadcasts locally on channel 60.2.
TELEVISION STATION

WTJP3-TV
618679
Owner: Trinity Broadcasting Network
Editorial: 313 Rosedale St, Gadsden, Alabama 35901-5361 **Tel:** 1 256 546-8860.
Profile: WTJP3-TV is a multicast of WTJP-TV. A multicast channel is a separate channel that shares the bandwith of the main station but can air unique programming. WTJP3-TV airs Christian music videos from JCTV in the Birmingham, AL market. The station is owned by Trinity Broadcasting Network. WTJP3-TV broadcasts locally on channel 60.3.
TELEVISION STATION

WTJP4-TV
618680
Owner: Trinity Broadcasting Network
Editorial: 313 Rosedale St, Gadsden, Alabama 35901-5361 **Tel:** 1 256 546-8860.
Profile: WTJP4-TV is a multicast of WTJP-TV. A multicast channel is a separate channel that shares the bandwith of the main station but can air unique programming. WTJP4-TV airs Hispanic Christian programming from Enlace USA in the Birmingham, AL market. The station is owned by Trinity Broadcasting Network. WTJP4-TV broadcasts locally on channel 60.4.
TELEVISION STATION

WTJP5-TV
618683
Owner: Trinity Broadcasting Network
Editorial: 313 Rosedale St, Gadsden, Alabama 35901-5361 **Tel:** 1 256 546-8860.
Profile: WTJP5-TV is a multicast of WTJP-TV. A multicast channel is a separate channel that shares the bandwith of the main station but can air unique programming. WTJP5-TV airs Christian children's programming from Smile of a Child in the Birmingham, AL market. The station is owned by Trinity Broadcasting Network. WTJP5-TV broadcasts locally on channel 60.5.
TELEVISION STATION

WTJP-TV 32132
Owner: Trinity Broadcasting Network
Editorial: 313 Rosedale St, Gadsden, Alabama 35901-5361 **Tel:** 1 256 546-8860.
Web site: http://wtjp.com
Profile: WTJP-TV is the Trinity Broadcasting Network affiliate for the Birmingham, AL market. The station is owned by Trinity Broadcasting Network. WTJP-TV broadcasts locally on channel 60.
TELEVISION STATION

WTJR-TV 32359
Owner: Christian Television Network
Editorial: 222 N 6th St, Quincy, Illinois 62301-2906
Tel: 1 217 228-1616.
Email: tv16@wtjr.org
Web site: http://www.wtjr.org
Profile: WTJR-TV is a Trinity Broadcast Network affiliate for the Quincy, IL/Hannibal, MO/ Keokuk, IA market. The station is owned by Christian Television Network. WTJR-TV is broadcast locally on channel 16.
TELEVISION STATION

WTKR-TV 32134
Owner: Tribune Broadcasting Co.
Editorial: 720 Boush St, Norfolk, Virginia 23510-1502
Tel: 1 757 446-1000.
Email: desk@wtkr.com
Web site: http://www.wtkr.com
Profile: WTKR-TV is the CBS affiliate for the Norfolk, VA market. The station is owned by Tribune Broadcasting Co. WTKR-TV broadcasts locally on channel 3.
TELEVISION STATION

WTLH-TV 32252
Owner: Sinclair Broadcast Group, Inc.
Editorial: 950 Commerce Blvd, Midway, Florida 32343-6617 **Tel:** 1 850 576-4990.
Web site: http://www.metv.com
Profile: WTLH-TV is the MeTV affiliate for the Tallahassee, FL-Thomasville, GA market. The station is owned by Sinclair Broadcast Group, Inc. WTLH-TV broadcasts locally on channel 49.
TELEVISION STATION

WTLJ2-TV 620059
Owner: TCT of Michigan Inc.
Editorial: 10290 48th Ave, Allendale, Michigan 49401-9379 **Tel:** 1 616 895-4154.
Email: wtlj@tct.tv
Web site: http://www.tct.tv
Profile: WTLJ2-TV is a multicast of WTLJ-TV. A multicast channel is a separate channel that shares the bandwith of the main station but can air unique programming. WTLJ2-TV airs Christian programming in HD from the TCT Network to the Grand Rapids, MI market. The station is owned by TCT of Michigan Inc. WTLJ2-TV broadcasts locally on channel 54.2.
TELEVISION STATION

WTLJ-TV 32302
Owner: TCT of Michigan Inc.
Editorial: 10290 48th Ave, Allendale, Michigan 49401-9379 **Tel:** 1 616 895-4154.
Email: wtlj@tct.tv
Web site: http://www.tct.tv
Profile: WTLJ-TV is a non-commercial affiliate of the TCT network for the Allendale, MI area. The station is owned by Tri-State Christian Television of Michigan Inc. WTLJ-TV broadcasts locally on channel 54.
TELEVISION STATION

WTLV2-TV 618967
Owner: TEGNA Inc.
Editorial: 1070 E Adams St, Jacksonville, Florida 32202-1902 **Tel:** 1 904 354-1212.
Email: news@firstcoastnews.com
Web site: http://www.firstcoastnews.com
Profile: WTLV2-TV is a multicast of WTLV-TV. A multicast channel is a separate channel that shares the bandwith of the main station but can air unique programming. WTLV2-TV airs sports programming from Universal Sports in the Jacksonville, FL market. The station is owned by TEGNA Inc. WTLV2-TV broadcasts locally on channel 12.2.
TELEVISION STATION

WTLV-TV 32135
Owner: TEGNA Inc.
Editorial: 1070 E Adams St, Jacksonville, Florida 32202-1902 **Tel:** 1 904 354-1212.
Email: newstips@firstcoastnews.com
Web site: http://www.firstcoastnews.com
Profile: WTLV-TV is the NBC affiliate for the Jacksonville, FL market. The station is owned by TEGNA Inc. WTLV-TV broadcasts locally on channel 12.
TELEVISION STATION

WTLW-TV 32136
Owner: American Christian TV Services
Editorial: 1844 Baty Rd, Lima, Ohio 45807-1938
Tel: 1 419 339-4444.
Email: traffic@wtlw.com
Web site: http://www.wtlw.com
Profile: WTLW-TV is an independent station for the Lima, OH market. The station is owned by American Christian TV Services. WTLW-TV broadcasts locally on channel 44.
TELEVISION STATION

WTMJ2-TV 621850
Owner: E.W. Scripps Co.
Editorial: 720 E Capitol Dr, Milwaukee, Wisconsin 53212-1308 **Tel:** 1 414 332-9611.
Email: news@tmj4.com
Web site: http://www.tmj4.com
Profile: WTMJ2-TV is a multicast channel of WTMJ-TV. A multicast is a separate channel that shares the bandwith of the main station but can air unique programming. WTMJ2-TV airs 24 hour weather programming from Storm Team 4 TV. The station is owned by E.W. Scripps Co. WTMJ2-TV broadcasts locally on channel 4.2.
TELEVISION STATION

WTMJ3-TV 609579
Owner: E.W. Scripps Co.
Editorial: 720 E Capitol Dr, Milwaukee, Wisconsin 53212-1308 **Tel:** 1 414 332-9611.
Email: news@tmj4.com
Web site: http://www.tmj4.com
Profile: WTMJ3-TV is a multicast channel of WTMJ-TV. A multicast is a separate channel that shares the bandwith of the main station but can air unique programming. WTMJ3-TV airs programming from Live Well Network. The station is owned by E.W. Scripps Co. WTMJ3-TV broadcasts locally on channel 4.3.
TELEVISION STATION

WTMJ-TV 32137
Owner: E.W. Scripps Co.
Editorial: 720 E Capitol Dr, Milwaukee, Wisconsin 53212-1308 **Tel:** 1 414 332-9611.
Email: news@tmj4.com
Web site: http://www.tmj4.com
Profile: WTMJ-TV is the NBC affiliate for the Milwaukee market. The station is owned by E.W. Scripps Co. WTMJ-TV broadcasts locally on channel 4.
TELEVISION STATION

WTMO-TV 133906
Owner: ZGS Communications
Editorial: 1650 Sand Lake Rd Ste 340, Orlando, Florida 32809-9119 **Tel:** 1 407 888-2288.
Web site: http://www.holaciudad.com/orlando/home.html
Profile: WTMO-TV is the Telemundo affiliate for the Orlando-Daytona Beach, FL market. The station is owned by ZGS Communications. WTMO-TV broadcasts locally on channel 31.
TELEVISION STATION

WTNH-TV 32139
Owner: Nexstar Media Group, LLC
Editorial: 8 Elm St, New Haven, Connecticut 06510-2006 **Tel:** 1 203 784-8888.
Email: news8@wtnh.com
Web site: http://www.wtnh.com
Profile: WTNH-TV is the ABC network affiliate in the Hartford-New Haven, CT market. The station is owned by Nexstar Media Group, LLC WTNH-TV broadcasts locally on channel 8.
TELEVISION STATION

WTNZ-TV 31941
Owner: Raycom Media Inc.
Editorial: 9000 Executive Park Dr Bldg 300, Knoxville, Tennessee 37923-4685 **Tel:** 1 865 693-4343.
Web site: http://foxville43.revrocket.us
Profile: WTNZ-TV is the FOX affiliate for the Knoxville, TN market. The station is owned by Raycom Media Inc. WTNZ-TV broadcasts locally on channel 43.
TELEVISION STATION

WTOC-TV 32140
Owner: Raycom Media Inc.
Editorial: 11 The News Place Chatham Center, Savannah, Georgia 31405-1398 **Tel:** 1 912 234-1111.
Email: newsrelease@wtoc.com
Web site: http://www.wtoctv.com
Profile: WTOC-TV is the CBS affiliate for the Savannah, GA area. The station is owned by Raycom Media Inc. WTOC-TV broadcasts locally on channel 11.
TELEVISION STATION

WTOG-TV 32141
Owner: CBS Television Stations
Editorial: 365 105th Ter NE, Saint Petersburg, Florida 33716-3330 **Tel:** 1 727 576-4444.
Web site: http://cwtampa.cbslocal.com/
Profile: WTOG-TV is the CW affiliate for the Tampa/St.Petersburg, FL market. The station is owned by CBS Television Stations. It broadcasts locally on channel 44.
TELEVISION STATION

WTOK2-TV 708415
Owner: Gray Television, Inc.
Editorial: 815 23rd Ave, Meridian, Mississippi 39301-5016
Profile: WTOK2-TV is a multicast channel of WTOK-TV. A multicast channel is a separate channel that shares bandwidth of the main station but can air unique programming. WTOK2-TV is the local MyNetworkTV affiliate on channel 11.2 for the Meridian, MS market. WTOK2-TV is owned by Gray Television, Inc.
TELEVISION STATION

WTOK-TV 32142
Owner: Gray Television, Inc.
Editorial: 815 23rd Ave, Meridian, Mississippi 39301-5016 **Tel:** 1 601 693-1441.
Email: newsall@wtok.com
Web site: http://www.wtok.com
Profile: WTOK-TV is the ABC affiliate for the Meridian, MS, market. The station is owned by Gray Television Inc. WTOK-TV broadcasts locally on channel 11.
TELEVISION STATION

WTOL-TV 32143
Owner: Raycom Media Inc.
Editorial: 730 N Summit St, Toledo, Ohio 43604-1808
Tel: 1 419 248-1111.
Email: news@toledonewsnow.com
Web site: http://www.wtol.com
Profile: WTOL-TV is the CBS network affiliate for the Toledo, OH market. The station is owned by Raycom Media Inc. WTOL-TV broadcasts locally on channel 11.
TELEVISION STATION

WTOV-TV 32144
Owner: Sinclair Broadcast Group, Inc.
Editorial: 9 Red Donley Plaza, Mingo Junction, Ohio 43938 **Tel:** 1 740 282-9999.
Email: newsdesk@wtov.com
Web site: http://www.wtov9.com
Profile: WTOV-TV is the NBC network affiliate for the Wheeling, WV, Steubenville, OH market. The station is owned by Sinclair Broadcast Group, Inc. WTOV-TV broadcasts locally on channel 9.
TELEVISION STATION

WTRF-TV 32145
Owner: Nexstar Broadcasting Group Inc.
Editorial: 96 16th St, Wheeling, West Virginia 26003-3660 **Tel:** 1 304 232-7777.
Email: news@wtrf.com
Web site: http://www.yourohiovalley.com
Profile: WTRF-TV is the CBS network affiliate for the Wheeling, WV, Stuebenville, OH market. The station was previously owned by West Virginia Media Holdings LLC but has been acquired by Nexstar Broadcasting Group. WTFR-TV broadcasts locally on channel 7.
TELEVISION STATION

WTSP2-TV 612165
Owner: TEGNA Inc.
Editorial: 11450 Gandy Blvd N, Saint Petersburg, Florida 33702-1908 **Tel:** 1 727 577-1010.
Email: desk@wtsp.com
Web site: http://www.wtsp.com
Profile: WTSP2-TV is a multicast of WTSP-TV. A multicast channel is a separate channel that shares the bandwith of the main station but can air unique programming. WTSP2-TV airs programming from 10 Connects Weather Now in the Tampa, FL market. The station is owned by TEGNA Inc. WTSP2-TV broadcasts locally on channel 10.2.
TELEVISION STATION

WTSP-TV 32149
Owner: TEGNA Inc.
Editorial: 11450 Gandy Blvd N, Saint Petersburg, Florida 33702-1908 **Tel:** 1 727 577-1010.
Email: desk@wtsp.com
Web site: http://www.wtsp.com
Profile: WTSP-TV is the CBS affiliate for the Tampa-St. Petersburg, Florida market. The station is owned by TEGNA Inc. WTSP-TV broadcasts locally on channel 10.
TELEVISION STATION

WTTA-TV 32368
Owner: Sinclair Media II, Inc.
Editorial: 7622 Bald Cypress Pl, Tampa, Florida 33614-2417 **Tel:** 1 813 886-9882.
Web site: http://www.great38.com
Profile: WTTA-TV is the MyNetworkTV affiliate for the Tampa-St. Petersburg, FL market. The station is owned by Sinclair Media II, Inc. WTTA-TV broadcasts locally on channel 38.
TELEVISION STATION

WTTE-TV 32150
Owner: Sinclair Broadcast Group, Inc.
Editorial: 1261 Dublin Rd, Columbus, Ohio 43215-7000 **Tel:** 1 614 481-6666.
Web site: http://www.myfox28columbus.com
Profile: WTTE-TV is the FOX affiliate for the Columbus, OH market. The station is owned by Sinclair Broadcast Group, Inc. WTTE-TV broadcasts locally on channel 28.
TELEVISION STATION

WTTG-TV 32151
Owner: Fox Broadcasting Company
Editorial: 5151 Wisconsin Ave NW, Washington, District Of Columbia 20016-4124 **Tel:** 1 202 244-5151.
Email: wttg.desk@foxtv.com
Web site: http://www.fox5dc.com
Profile: WTTG-TV is a FOX affiliate for the Washington, D.C. market. The station is owned by FOX Broadcasting Company. WTTG-TV broadcasts locally on channel 5.
TELEVISION STATION

WTTO-TV 32749
Owner: Sinclair Broadcast Group, Inc.
Editorial: 651 Beacon Pkwy W Ste 105, Birmingham, Alabama 35209-3128 **Tel:** 1 205 403-3340.
Web site: http://www.wtto21.com
Profile: WTTO-TV is the CW affiliate for the Birmingham, AL market. The station is owned by Sinclair Broadcast Group, Inc. WTTO-TV broadcasts locally on channel 21.
TELEVISION STATION

WTTV-TV 32152
Owner: Tribune Broadcasting Co.
Editorial: 6910 Network Pl, Indianapolis, Indiana 46278-1929 **Tel:** 1 317 632-5900.
Email: news4@cbs4indy.com
Web site: http://cbs4indy.com
Profile: WTTV-TV is the CBS network affiliate for the Indianapolis, IN market. The station is owned by Tribune Broadcasting Co. WTTV-TV broadcasts locally on channel 4.
TELEVISION STATION

WTTW2-TV 607361
Owner: Window To The World Communications, Inc.
Editorial: 5400 N Saint Louis Ave, Chicago, Illinois 60625-4623 **Tel:** 1 773 583-5000.
Web site: http://www.wttw.com
Profile: WTTW2-TV is a PBS affiliate for the Chicago market. The station is owned by Window To The World Communications, Inc. WTTW-TV broadcasts locally on channel 11.2. WTTW2-TV is known as Prime and airs a variety of news and entertainment programming. WTTW2-TV is a multicast channel of WTTW-TV. A multicast channel is a separate channel that shares the bandwidth of the main station but can air unique programming.
TELEVISION STATION

WTTW3-TV 607366
Owner: Window To The World Communications, Inc.
Editorial: 5400 N Saint Louis Ave, Chicago, Illinois 60625-4623 **Tel:** 1 773 583-5000.
Web site: http://www.wttw.com
Profile: WTTW3-TV is a PBS affiliate for the Chicago market. The station is owned by Window To The World Communications, Inc. WTTW-TV broadcasts locally on channel 11.3. WTTW3-TV airs a variety of news and entertainment programming. WTTW3-TV is a multicast channel of WTTW-TV. A multicast channel is a separate channel that shares the bandwidth of the main station but can air unique programming.
TELEVISION STATION

WTTW4-TV 607368
Owner: Window To The World Communications, Inc.
Editorial: 5400 N Saint Louis Ave, Chicago, Illinois 60625-4623 **Tel:** 1 773 583-5000.
Web site: http://www.vmetv.com
Profile: WTTW4-TV is a independent affiliate for the Chicago market. The station is owned by Window To The World Communications, Inc. WTTW-TV broadcasts locally on channel 11.4. WTTW4-TV airs programming from V-me the Spanish TV Network with a variety of news, sports and entertainment. WTTW4-TV is a multicast channel of WTTW-TV. A multicast channel is a separate channel that shares the bandwidth of the main station but can air unique programming.
TELEVISION STATION

WTTW-TV 32153
Owner: Window to the World Communications, Inc.
Editorial: 5400 N Saint Louis Ave, Chicago, Illinois 60625-4623 **Tel:** 1 773 583-5000.
Web site: http://www.wttw.com
Profile: WTTW is a PBS affiliate for the Chicago market. The station is owned by Window To The World Communications, Inc. WTTW-TV broadcasts locally on channel 11. Contact the station via the online form.
TELEVISION STATION

WTVA2-TV 830282
Editorial: 1359 Beech Springs Road, Tupelo, Mississippi 38866
Email: psullivan@wtva.com
Web site: http://www.wtva.com
TELEVISION STATION

WTVA-TV 32154
Owner: Heartland Media
Editorial: 1359 Road 681 Beech Spring Rd, Tupelo, Mississippi 38801 **Tel:** 1 662 842-7620.
Email: news@wtva.com
Web site: http://www.wtva.com
Profile: WTVA-TV is the NBC network affiliate for the Columbus, MS market. The station is owned by WTVA Inc. WTVA-TV broadcasts locally on channel 9.
TELEVISION STATION

WTVC-TV 32155
Owner: Sinclair Broadcast Group, Inc.
Editorial: 4279 Benton Dr, Chattanooga, Tennessee 37406-1284 **Tel:** 1 423 756-5500.
Email: producers@newschannel9.com
Web site: http://newschannel9.com
Profile: WTVC-TV is the ABC affiliate for the Chattanooga, TN, market. It is owned by Sinclair Broadcast Group, Inc. WTVC-TV broadcasts locally on channel 9.
TELEVISION STATION

WTVD2-TV 613842
Owner: Walt Disney Co.
Editorial: 411 Liberty St, Durham, North Carolina 27701-3407 **Tel:** 1 919 683-1111.
Email: wtvdassignmentdesk@abc.com
Web site: http://abclocal.go.com/wtvd
Profile: WTVD2-TV is a multicast of WTVD-TV. A multicast channel is a separate channel that shares the bandwith of the main station but can air unique programming. WTVD2-TV airs programming from Live Well HD in the Raleigh-Durham, NC market. The station is owned by Walt Disney Co. WTVD2-TV broadcasts locally on channel 11.2.
TELEVISION STATION

WTVD3-TV 613844
Owner: Walt Disney Co.
Editorial: 411 Liberty St, Durham, North Carolina 27701-3407 **Tel:** 1 919 683-1111.
Web site: http://abclocal.go.com/wtvd
Profile: WTVD3-TV is a multicast of WTVD-TV. A multicast channel is a separate channel that shares the bandwith of the main station but can air unique

programming. WTVD3-TV airs programming from Eyewitness News Now in the Raleigh-Durham, NC market. The station is owned by Walt Disney Co. WTVD3-TV broadcasts locally on channel 11.3.
TELEVISION STATION

WTVD-TV 32156
Owner: Walt Disney Co.
Editorial: 411 Liberty St, Durham, North Carolina 27701-3407 **Tel:** 1 919 683-1111.
Email: wtvdassignmentdesk@abc.com
Web site: http://abc11.com
Profile: WTVD-TV is the ABC affiliate for the greater Durham, Raleigh, and Fayetteville, NC market. The station is owned by the Walt Disney Co. WTVD-TV broadcasts locally on channel 11.
TELEVISION STATION

WTVE-TV 32157
Owner: Reading Broadcasting Inc.
Editorial: 1729 N 11th St, Reading, Pennsylvania 19604 **Tel:** 1 610 921-9181.
Web site: http://www.wtve.com
Profile: WTVE-TV is an independent station for the Reading, PA market. The station is owned by Reading Broadcasting Inc. WTVE-TV broadcasts locally on channel 51.
TELEVISION STATION

WTVF2-TV 613173
Owner: E.W. Scripps Co.
Editorial: 474 James Robertson Pkwy, Nashville, Tennessee 37219-1212 **Tel:** 1 615 244-5000.
Email: newsroom@newschannel5.com
Web site: http://www.newschannel5.com
Profile: WTVF-TV is a multicast of WTVF2-TV. A multicast channel is a separate channel that shares the bandwith of the main station but can air unique programming. WTVF2-TV airs programming from NewsChannel 5+ in the Nashville, TN market. The station is owned by E.W. Scripps Co. WTVF2-TV broadcasts locally on channel 5.2.
TELEVISION STATION

WTVF3-TV 613176
Owner: Kiel Media Group, LLC
Editorial: 474 James Robertson Pkwy, Nashville, Tennessee 37219-1212 **Tel:** 1 615 244-5000.
Email: newsroom@newschannel5.com
Web site: http://www.newschannel5.com
Profile: WTVF-TV is a multicast of WTVF3-TV. A multicast channel is a separate channel that shares the bandwidth of the main station but can air unique programming. WTVF3-TV airs programming from This TV in the Nashville, TN market. The station is owned by Kiel Media Group, LLC. WTVF3-TV broadcasts locally on channel 5.3.
TELEVISION STATION

WTVF-TV 32158
Owner: E.W. Scripps Co.
Editorial: 474 James Robertson Pkwy, Nashville, Tennessee 37219-1212 **Tel:** 1 615 244-5000.
Email: newsroom@newschannel5.com
Web site: http://www.newschannel5.com
Profile: WTVF-TV is the CBS affiliate for the Nashville, TN market. The station is owned by E.W. Scripps Co. WTVF-TV broadcasts locally on channel 5.
TELEVISION STATION

WTVG-TV 32159
Owner: Gray Television
Editorial: 4247 Dorr St, Toledo, Ohio 43607-2134 **Tel:** 1 419 531-1313.
Email: wtvg.news@13abc.com
Web site: http://www.13abc.com
Profile: WTVG-TV is the ABC network affiliate for the Toledo, OH market. The station is owned by Gray Television. WTVG-TV broadcasts locally on channel 13.
TELEVISION STATION

WTVH-TV 32160
Owner: Granite Broadcasting Corp.
Editorial: 1030 James St, Syracuse, New York 13203-2704 **Tel:** 1 315 477-9400.
Email: news@cnycentral.com
Web site: http://www.cnycentral.com
Profile: WTVH-TV is the CBS affiliate station for the Syracuse, NY market. The station is owned by Granite Broadcasting. WTVH-TV broadcasts locally on channel 5.
TELEVISION STATION

WTVI2-TV 614012
Owner: Charlotte-Mecklenburg Public Broadcasting Authority
Editorial: 3242 Commonwealth Ave, Charlotte, North Carolina 28205-6225 **Tel:** 1 704 330-5942.
Web site: http://www.wtvi.org
Profile: WTVI2-TV is a multicast of WTVI-TV. A multicast channel is a separate channel that shares the bandwith of the main station but can air unique programming. WTVI2-TV airs programming from the WTVI-CV, the Civic Channel in the Charlotte, NC market. The station is owned by Charlotte-Mecklenburg Public Broadcasting Authority. WTVI2-TV broadcasts locally on channel 42.2.
TELEVISION STATION

WTVI3-TV 614013
Owner: Charlotte-Mecklenburg Public Broadcasting Authority
Editorial: 3242 Commonwealth Ave, Charlotte, North Carolina 28205-6225 **Tel:** 1 704 330-5942.
Web site: http://www.wtvi.org
Profile: WTVI3-TV is a multicast of WTVI-TV. A multicast channel is a separate channel that shares the bandwith of the main station but can air unique programming. WTVI3-TV airs programming from the WTVI Create in the Charlotte, NC market. The station is owned by Charlotte-Mecklenburg Public Broadcasting Authority. WTVI3-TV broadcasts locally on channel 42.3.
TELEVISION STATION

WTVI-TV 32161
Owner: Charlotte-Mecklenburg Public Broadcasting Authority
Editorial: 3242 Commonwealth Ave, Charlotte, North Carolina 28205-6225 **Tel:** 1 704 372-2442.
Web site: http://www.wtvi.org
Profile: WTVI-TV is the PBS affiliate for the Charlotte, NC market. The station is owned by the Charlotte-Mecklenburg Public Broadcasting Authority. WTVI-TV broadcasts locally on channel 42.
TELEVISION STATION

WTVJ2-TV 614642
Owner: NBC Universal
Editorial: 15000 SW 27th St, Miramar, Florida 33027-4147 **Tel:** 1 954 622-6000.
Web site: http://www.nbcmiami.com
Profile: WTVJ2-TV, also called Miami Nonstop is a multicast channel of WTVJ-TV. A multicast channel is a separate channel that shares the bandwidth of the main station but can air unique programming. WTVJ2-TV is the NBC Nonstop affiliate for the Miami market. The station is owned by NBC Universal. WTVJ2-TV broadcasts locally on channel 6.2. The channel airs coverage of various live events and news.
TELEVISION STATION

WTVJ3-TV 614644
Owner: NBC Universal
Editorial: 15000 SW 27th St, Miramar, Florida 33027-4147 **Tel:** 1 954 622-6000.
Web site: http://www.nbcmiami.com
Profile: WTVJ3-TV is the NBC network affiliate for the Miami- Fort Lauderdale, FL market. The station is owned by NBC Universal. The station airs NBC Universal Sports programming. WTVJ3-TV is a multicast channel of WTVJ-TV. A multicast channel is a separate channel that shares the bandwidth of the main station but can air unique programming.
TELEVISION STATION

WTVJ-TV 32162
Owner: NBC Universal
Editorial: 15000 SW 27th St, Miramar, Florida 33027-4147 **Tel:** 1 954 622-6000.
Email: wtvjdesk@nbc.com
Web site: http://www.nbcmiami.com
Profile: WTVJ-TV is the NBC network affiliate for the Miami- Fort Lauderdale, FL market. The station is owned by NBC Universal. WTVJ-TV broadcasts locally on channel 6.
TELEVISION STATION

WTVM-TV 32163
Owner: Raycom Media Inc.
Editorial: 1909 Wynnton Rd, Columbus, Georgia 31906-2931 **Tel:** 1 706 494-5400.
Email: newsrelease@wtvm.com
Web site: http://www.wtvm.com
Profile: WTVM-TV is the ABC network affiliate for the Columbus, GA market. The station is owned by Raycom Media Inc. WTVM-TV broadcasts locally on channel 9.
TELEVISION STATION

WTVO-TV 32164
Owner: Nexstar Broadcasting Group
Editorial: 1917 N Meridian Rd, Rockford, Illinois 61101-9215 **Tel:** 1 815 963-5413.
Email: newsdesk@wtvo.com
Web site: http://mystateline.com
Profile: WTVO-TV is the ABC network affiliate for the Rockford, IL market. The station is owned by Nexstar Broadcasting Group. WTVO-TV broadcasts locally on channel 17.
TELEVISION STATION

WTVP-TV 32165
Owner: Illinois Valley Public Telecommunications Corp.
Editorial: 101 State St, Peoria, Illinois 61602-1547 **Tel:** 1 309 677-4747.
Email: wtvpmail@wtvp.org
Web site: http://www.wtvp.org
Profile: WTVP-TV is the PBS affiliate for the Peoria-Bloomington, IL market. The station is owned by Illinois Valley Public Telecommunications Corp. WTVP-TV broadcasts locally on channel 47.
TELEVISION STATION

WTVQ-TV 32166
Owner: Morris Multimedia Inc.
Editorial: 6940 Man O War Blvd, Lexington, Kentucky 40509-8412 **Tel:** 1 859 294-3636.
Email: news@wtvq.com
Web site: http://www.wtvq.com
Profile: WTVQ-TV is the ABC affiliate for the Lexington, KY, market. It is owned by Morris Multimedia Inc. WTVQ-TV broadcasts locally on channel 36.
TELEVISION STATION

WTVR-TV 32167
Owner: Tribune Broadcasting Co.
Editorial: 3301 W Broad St, Richmond, Virginia 23230-5007 **Tel:** 1 804 254-3600.
Email: newstips@wtvr.com
Web site: http://www.wtvr.com
Profile: WTVR-TV is the CBS affiliate for the Richmond, VA, market. The station is owned by Tribune Broadcasting Co. WTVR-TV broadcasts locally on channel 6.
TELEVISION STATION

WTVT-TV 32169
Owner: Fox Broadcasting Company
Editorial: 3213 W Kennedy Blvd, Tampa, Florida 33609-3006 **Tel:** 1 813 876-1313.
Email: news@wtvt.com
Web site: http://www.fox13news.com
Profile: WTVT-TV is the FOX affiliate for the Tampa-St. Petersburg, FL, market. The station is owned by Fox Broadcasting Company. WTVT-TV broadcasts locally on channel 13.
TELEVISION STATION

WTVW-TV 32170
Owner: Nexstar Broadcasting Group
Editorial: 800 Marywood Dr, Henderson, Kentucky 42420-2431 **Tel:** 1 812 424-7777.
Email: eyewitnessnews@tristatehomepage.com
Web site: http://www.tristatehomepage.com/
Profile: WTVW-TV is the CW Television Network affiliate for the Evansville, IN area. The station is owned by Nexstar Broadcasting Group. WTVW-TV broadcasts locally on channel 7.
TELEVISION STATION

WTVX2-TV 614766
Owner: Sinclair Broadcast Group, Inc.
Editorial: 1700 Palm Beach Lakes Blvd Ste 150, West Palm Beach, Florida 33401-2007 **Tel:** 1 561 681-3434.
Web site: http://www.cw34.com
Profile: WTVX2-TV is a multicast of WTVX-TV. A multicast channel is a separate channel that shares the bandwith of the main station but can air unique programming. WTVX2-TV airs programming from Azteca America in the West Palm Beach, FL. The station is owned by Sinclair Broadcast Group, Inc. WTVX2-TV broadcasts locally on channel 34.2.
TELEVISION STATION

WTVX3-TV 614767
Owner: Sinclair Broadcast Group, Inc.
Editorial: 1700 Palm Beach Lakes Blvd Ste 150, West Palm Beach, Florida 33401-2007 **Tel:** 1 561 681-3434.
Web site: http://www.cw34.com
Profile: WTVX3-TV is a multicast of WTVX-TV. A multicast channel is a separate channel that shares the bandwith of the main station but can air unique programming. WTVX3-TV airs programming from MyNetwork TV in the West Palm Beach, FL. The station is owned by Sinclair Broadcast Group, Inc. WTVX3-TV broadcasts locally on channel 34.3.
TELEVISION STATION

WTVX4-TV 614769
Owner: Sinclair Broadcast Group, Inc.
Editorial: 1700 Palm Beach Lakes Blvd Ste 150, West Palm Beach, Florida 33401-2007 **Tel:** 1 561 681-3434.
Web site: http://www.cw34.com
Profile: WTVX4-TV is a multicast of WTVX-TV. A multicast channel is a separate channel that shares the bandwith of the main station but can air unique programming. WTVX4-TV airs programming from The Retro Television Network in the West Palm Beach, FL. The station is owned by Sinclair Broadcast Group, Inc. WTVX4-TV broadcasts locally on channel 34.4.
TELEVISION STATION

WTVX5-TV 692082
Owner: Sinclair Broadcast Group, Inc.
Editorial: 1700 Palm Beach Lakes Blvd Ste 150, West Palm Beach, Florida 33401-2007 **Tel:** 1 561 681-3434.
Web site: http://cw34.com
Profile: WTVX5-TV is a multicast of WTVX-TV. A multicast channel is a separate channel that shares the bandwith of the main station but can air unique programming. WTVX5-TV airs programming from LA TV in the West Palm Beach, FL. The station is owned by Sinclair Broadcast Group, Inc. WTVX5-TV broadcasts locally on channel 34.5.
TELEVISION STATION

WTVX-TV 32295
Owner: Sinclair Broadcast Group, Inc.
Editorial: 1700 Palm Beach Lakes Blvd Ste 150, West Palm Beach, Florida 33401-2007 **Tel:** 1 561 681-3434.
Web site: http://www.cw34.com
Profile: WTVX-TV is the CW affiliate for the West Palm Beach, FL market. The station is owned by Sinclair Broadcast Group, Inc. WTVX-TV broadcasts locally on channel 34.
TELEVISION STATION

WTVY2-TV 863781
Owner: Gray Television, Inc.
Editorial: 285 N Foster St, Dothan, Alabama 36303-4541 **Tel:** 1 334 792-3195.
Web site: http://www.wtvy.com
Profile: WTVY2-TV is a multicast channel of WTVY-TV. A multicast channel is a separate channel that shares the bandwidth of the main station but can air unique programming. WTVY2-TV is the MyNetoworkTV and Me-TV Network for the Dothan, AL market. The station is owned by Gray Television, Inc. WTVY2-TV broadcasts locally on channel 4.2.
TELEVISION STATION

WTVY-TV 32171
Owner: Gray Television, Inc.
Editorial: 285 N Foster St, Dothan, Alabama 36303-4541 **Tel:** 1 334 792-3195.
Email: news@wtvy.com
Web site: http://www.wtvy.com
Profile: WTVY-TV is the CBS affiliate for the Dothan, AL market. The station is owned by Gray Television, Inc. WTVY-TV broadcasts locally on Channel 4.
TELEVISION STATION

WTVZ-TV 32172
Owner: Sinclair Broadcast Group, Inc.
Editorial: 900 Granby St, Norfolk, Virginia 23510 **Tel:** 1 757 622-3333.
Web site: http://www.mytvz.com
Profile: WTVZ-TV is the MyNetworkTV affiliate for the Norfolk, VA market. The station is owned by Sinclair Broadcast Group, Inc. WTVZ-TV broadcasts locally on channel 33.
TELEVISION STATION

WTWC-TV 32173
Owner: Sinclair Broadcast Group, Inc.
Editorial: 8440 Deer Lk S, Tallahassee, Florida 32312 **Tel:** 1 850 893-4140.
Web site: http://www.wtwc40.com
Profile: WTWC-TV is the NBC affiliate in Tallahassee, FL. The station is owned by Sinclair Broadcast Group, Inc. WTWC-TV airs locally on channel 40.
TELEVISION STATION

WTWO-TV 32174
Owner: Nexstar Broadcasting Group
Editorial: 10849 N US Highway 41, Farmersburg, Indiana 47850-8099 **Tel:** 1 812 696-2121.
Email: news@wtwo.com
Web site: http://www.mywabashvalley.com
Profile: WTWO-TV is the NBC network affiliate for the Terre Haute, IN market. The station is owned by Nexstar Broadcasting Group. WTWO-TV broadcasts locally on channel 2.
TELEVISION STATION

WTXF-TV 32251
Owner: Fox Broadcasting Company
Editorial: 330 Market St, Philadelphia, Pennsylvania 19106-2706 **Tel:** 1 215 925-2929.
Email: fox29.newsdesk@foxtv.com
Web site: http://www.fox29.com
Profile: WTXF-TV is the FOX affiliate for the Philadelphia market. The station is owned by the Fox Broadcasting Company. WTXF-TV broadcasts locally on channel 29.
TELEVISION STATION

WTXL-TV 32176
Owner: Raycom Media Inc.
Editorial: 1620 Commerce Blvd, Midway, Florida 32343-6611 **Tel:** 1 850 893-3127.
Email: abc27news@wtxl.tv
Web site: http://www.wtxl.com
Profile: WTXL-TV is the ABC affiliate for Tallahassee, FL. The station is owned by Southern Broadcasting Corp. of Sarasota. WTXL-TV broadcasts locally on channel 27.
TELEVISION STATION

WUAB-TV 32179
Owner: Raycom Media Inc.
Editorial: 1717 E 12th St, Cleveland, Ohio 44114-3246 **Tel:** 1 216 771-1943.
Email: 19tips@woio.com
Web site: http://www.my43.net
Profile: WUAB-TV is the MyNetworkTV affiliate for the Cleveland market. The station is owned by Raycom Media Inc. WUAB-TV broadcasts locally on channel 43.
TELEVISION STATION

WUCW-TV 32326
Owner: Sinclair Broadcast Group, Inc.
Editorial: 1640 Como Ave, Saint Paul, Minnesota 55108-2710 **Tel:** 1 651 646-2300.
Web site: http://www.thecw23.com
Profile: WUCW-TV is the CW affiliate in the Minneapolis-St. Paul market. The station is owned by Sinclair Broadcast Group, Inc. WUCW-TV broadcasts locally on channel 23.
TELEVISION STATION

WUGA-TV 32006
Owner: Marquee Broadcasting
Editorial: 120 Hooper St, Athens, Georgia 30602-5042
Web site: http://www.wugatv.org
Profile: WUGA-TV is the PBS affiliate for the Athens, GA market. It is owned by Marquee Broadcasting. WUGA-TV broadcasts locally on channel 32.
TELEVISION STATION

WUHF-TV 32181
Owner: Sinclair Broadcast Group, Inc.
Editorial: 4225 W Henrietta Rd, Rochester, New York 14623-5225 **Tel:** 1 585 334-8700.
Email: news@13wham.com
Web site: http://foxrochester.com
Profile: WUHF-TV is the FOX affiliate for the Rochester, NY market. The station is owned by Sinclair Broadcast Group, Inc. The station broadcasts locally on channel 31.
TELEVISION STATION

WUMN-TV 414227
Owner: Media Vista Group
Editorial: 527 Marquette Ave Ste 150, Minneapolis, Minnesota 55402-1207 **Tel:** 1 612 455-3960.

Web site: http://www.wumn13.com
Profile: WUMN-TV is the Univision affiliate for the Minneapolis market. The station is owned by Media Vista Group. WUMN-TV broadcasts locally on channel 13.
TELEVISION STATION

WUNI-TV 31878
Owner: Entravision Communications Corp.
Editorial: 33 4th Ave, Needham, Massachusetts 02494-2704 **Tel:** 1 781 433-2727.
Web site: http://noticias.entravision.com/nueva-inglaterra
Profile: WUNI-TV is the Univision affiliate for the Boston market. The station is owned by Entravision Communications Corp. WUNI-TV broadcasts locally on channel 27.
TELEVISION STATION

WUPA-TV 32191
Owner: CBS Television Stations
Editorial: 2700 Northeast Expy NE Bldg A, Atlanta, Georgia 30345-1845 **Tel:** 1 404 325-6969.
Web site: http://cwatlanta.cbslocal.com
Profile: WUPA-TV is the CW affiliate for the Atlanta market. The station is owned by CBS Television Stations. WUPA-TV broadcasts locally on channel 69.
TELEVISION STATION

WUPL-TV 32490
Owner: TEGNA Inc.
Editorial: 1024 N Rampart St, New Orleans, Louisiana 70116-2406 **Tel:** 1 504 529-4444.
Email: pressrelease@wwltv.com
Web site: http://wupltv.com
Profile: WUPL-TV is the MyNetworkTV affiliate for the New Orleans, LA market. The station is owned by TEGNA Inc. WUPL-TV broadcasts locally on channel 54.
TELEVISION STATION

WUPV-TV 32282
Owner: Southeast Media
Editorial: 5710 Midlothian Tpke, Richmond, Virginia 23225-6116 **Tel:** 1 804 230-1212.
Web site: http://www.cwrichmond.tv
Profile: WUPV-TV is the CW affiliate for the Richmond, VA market. The station is owned by Southeast Media. WUPV-TV broadcasts locally on channel 65.
TELEVISION STATION

WUPW-TV 32183
Owner: American Spirit Media
Editorial: 730 N Summit St, Toledo, Ohio 43604-1808 **Tel:** 1 419 244-3600.
Email: news@toledonewsnow.com
Web site: http://www.toledonewsnow.com
Profile: WUPW-TV is the FOX affiliate on Channel 36 for the Toledo, OH market. The station is owned by American Spirit Media. WUPW-TV is broadcast locally on channel 36.
TELEVISION STATION

WUPX-TV 235408
Owner: ION Media Networks
Editorial: 2166 McCausey Rdg, Frenchburg, Kentucky 40322-8349 **Tel:** 1 606 768-9282.
Web site: http://iontelevision.com
Profile: WUPX-TV is an ION Television affiliate for the Lexington, KY market. The station is owned by ION Media Networks. WUPX-TV broadcasts locally on channel 67.
TELEVISION STATION

WUSA2-TV 608414
Owner: TEGNA Inc.
Editorial: 4100 Wisconsin Ave NW, Washington, District Of Columbia 20016-2810 **Tel:** 1 202 895-5999.
Email: 9news@wusa9.com
Web site: http://wusa9.com
Profile: WUSA2-TV is an independent affiliate for the Washington, D.C. market. The station is owned by TEGNA Inc. WUSA-TV broadcasts locally on channel 9.2. WUSA2-TV broadcasts weather news and radar. WUSA2-TV is a multicast channel of WUSA-TV. A multicast channel is a separate channel that shares the bandwidth of the main station but can air unique programming.
TELEVISION STATION

WUSA-TV 32184
Owner: TEGNA Inc.
Editorial: 4100 Wisconsin Ave NW, Washington, District Of Columbia 20016-2810 **Tel:** 1 202 895-5999.
Email: wusa-assignmentdesk@wusa9.com
Web site: http://www.wusa9.com
Profile: WUSA-TV is the CBS affiliate for the Washington, D.C. market. The station is owned by TEGNA Inc. WUSA-TV broadcasts locally on channel 9.
TELEVISION STATION

WUTB2-TV 796295
Owner: Sinclair Broadcast Group
Editorial: 2000 W 41st St, Baltimore, Maryland 21211-1420 **Tel:** 1 410 467-4545.
Web site: http://mytvbaltimore.com
Profile: WUTB2-TV is a multicast channel of WUTB-TV. A multicast channel is a separate channel that shares the bandwidth of the main station but can air unique programming. WUTB2-TV is the Bounce TV Network for the Baltimore, MD market. The station is owned by Sinclair Broadcast Group. WUTB2-TV broadcasts locally on channel 24.2.
TELEVISION STATION

WUTB-TV 32510
Owner: Sinclair Broadcast Group
Editorial: 2000 W 41st St, Baltimore, Maryland 21211-1420 **Tel:** 1 410 467-4545.
Web site: http://mytvbaltimore.com
Profile: WUTB-TV is the MyNetworkTV affiliate for the Baltimore market. The station is owned by Sinclair Broadcast Group. WUTB-TV broadcasts locally on channel 24.
TELEVISION STATION

WUTF-TV 32511
Owner: Entravision Communications Corp.
Editorial: 33 4th Ave, Needham, Massachusetts 02494-2704 **Tel:** 1 781 433-2727.
Profile: WUTF-TV is the UniMas affiliate for the Boston market. The station is owned by Entravision Communications Corp. WUTF-TV broadcasts locally on channel 66.
TELEVISION STATION

WUTH-TV 139495
Owner: Entravision Communications Corp.
Editorial: 1 Constitution Plz Fl 7, Hartford, Connecticut 06103-1816 **Tel:** 1 860 278-1818.
Web site: http://www.wuvn.com
Profile: WUTH-TV is the Telefutura affiliate serving Hartford, CT. The station is owned by Entravision Communications Corp. WUTH-TV broadcasts locally on channel 47.
TELEVISION STATION

WUTR-TV 32187
Owner: Mission Broadcasting
Editorial: 5956 Smith Hill Rd, Utica, New York 13502-6522 **Tel:** 1 315 797-5220.
Web site: http://www.cnyhomepage.com
Profile: WUTR-TV is the ABC affiliate for the Utica, NY market. The station is owned by Mission Broadcasting. WUTR-TV broadcasts locally on channel 20.
TELEVISION STATION

WUTV-TV 32188
Owner: Sinclair Broadcast Group, Inc.
Editorial: 699 Hertel Ave Ste 100, Buffalo, New York 14207-2341 **Tel:** 1 716 447-3200.
Email: comments@sbgi.net
Web site: http://www.wutv.com
Profile: WUTV-TV is the local FOX affiliate for the Buffalo, NY area. The station is owned by Sinclair Broadcast Group, Inc. WUTV-TV broadcasts locally on channel 29.
TELEVISION STATION

WUVC-TV 31942
Owner: Univision Communications Inc.
Editorial: 4505 Falls of Neuse Rd Ste 660, Raleigh, North Carolina 27609-2505 **Tel:** 1 919 872-7440.
Email: noticias40@univision.net
Profile: WUVC-TV is the Univision affiliate for the Fayetteville, NC market. The station is owned by Univision Communications Inc. WUVC-TV airs locally on channel 40.
TELEVISION STATION

WUVF-TV 342803
Owner: Media Vista Group
Editorial: 5405 Taylor Rd Ste 10, Naples, Florida 34109-1899 **Tel:** 1 239 254-9995.
Web site: http://www.dlatinos.com/univision
Profile: WUVF-TV is a Univision affiliate for the Fort Myers-Naples, FL market. The station is owned by Media Vista Group. WUVF-TV broadcasts locally on channel 2.
TELEVISION STATION

WUVG2-TV 607799
Owner: Univision Communications Inc.
Editorial: 3350 Peachtree Rd NE, Atlanta, Georgia 30326-1039 **Tel:** 1 404 926-2300.
Profile: WUVG2-TV is a multicast channel of WUVG-TV. A multicast channel is a separate channel that shares the bandwidth of the main station but can air unique programming. WUVG2-TV is the local UniMas network for the Atlanta market. It is owned by Univision Communications Inc. WUVG2-TV broadcasts locally on channel 34.2.
TELEVISION STATION

WUVG-TV 32314
Owner: Univision Communications Inc.
Editorial: 3350 Peachtree Rd NE Ste 1250, Atlanta, Georgia 30326-1424 **Tel:** 1 404 926-2300.
Web site: http://www.univisionatlanta.com
Profile: WUVG-TV is the Univision affiliate for the Atlanta market. The station is owned by Univision Communications Inc. WUVG-TV broadcasts locally on channel 34.
TELEVISION STATION

WUVM-TV 476759
Owner: Una Vez Mas Atlanta License, LLC
Editorial: 2700 Northeast Expy NE Ste C600, Atlanta, Georgia 30345-1898 **Tel:** 1 404 315-7102.
Web site: http://us.azteca.com
Profile: WUVM-TV is the Azteca America affiliate for the Atlanta market. The station is owned by and operated by Una Vez Mas Atlanta License, LLC. WUVM-TV broadcasts locally on channel 4. Public service announcements should be sent to the mailing address, which is the corporate headquarters in Dallas.
TELEVISION STATION

WUVN-TV 32604
Owner: Entravision Communications Corp.
Editorial: 1 Constitution Plz, Hartford, Connecticut 06103-1803 **Tel:** 1 781 433-2727.
Web site: http://noticias.entravision.com/mercado/hartford-springfield
Profile: WUVN is the Connecticut affiliate for the Univision network. It is licensed to Hartford, CT and the tower is located in Avon, CT. Owned by Entravision Communications Corp., the station broadcasts on channel 18.
TELEVISION STATION

WUVP-TV 31888
Owner: Univision Communications Inc.
Editorial: 4449 Delsea Dr, Newfield, New Jersey 08344-9609 **Tel:** 1 856 690-3738.
Email: noticias65@univision.net
Web site: http://www.univision.com/philadelphia/wuvp
Profile: WUVP-TV is the Univision affiliate for the Philadelphia market. The station is owned by Univision Communications Inc. WUVP-TV broadcasts locally on channel 65.
TELEVISION STATION

WUXP-TV 31769
Owner: Sinclair Broadcast Group, Inc.
Editorial: 631 Mainstream Dr, Nashville, Tennessee 37228 **Tel:** 1 615 259-5617.
Web site: http://www.mytv30web.com
Profile: WUXP-TV is the MyNetworkTV affiliate for the Nashville, TN market. The station is owned by Sinclair Broadcast Group, Inc. WUXP-TV broadcasts locally on channel 30.
TELEVISION STATION

WVAH-TV 32189
Owner: Sinclair Broadcast Group, Inc.
Editorial: 1301 Piedmont Rd, Charleston, West Virginia 25301-1426 **Tel:** 1 304 346-5358.
Email: news@wvah.com
Web site: http://www.wvah.com
Profile: WVAH-TV is the FOX affiliate for the Charleston-Huntington, WV market. It is owned by Sinclair Broadcast Group, Inc. WVAH-TV broadcasts locally on channel 11.
TELEVISION STATION

WVAW-TV 324377
Owner: Gray Television, Inc.
Editorial: 999 2nd St SE, Charlottesville, Virginia 22902-6172 **Tel:** 1 434 242-1919.
Email: news@newsplex.com
Web site: http://www.newsplex.com
Profile: WVAW-TV is the ABC affiliate for the Charlottesville, VA market. The station is owned by Gray Television, Inc. WVAW-TV broadcasts locally on channel 16.
TELEVISION STATION

WVBT-TV 32531
Owner: Nexstar Media Group, LLC
Editorial: 300 Wavy St, Portsmouth, Virginia 23704-5200 **Tel:** 1 757 393-4343.
Email: newsdesk@wavy.com
Web site: http://www.fox43tv.com
Profile: WVBT-TV is the FOX affiliate for the Norfolk, VA market. The station is owned by Nexstar Media Group, LLC. WVBT-TV broadcasts locally on channel 43.
TELEVISION STATION

WVCY-TV 32288
Owner: VCY America Inc.
Editorial: 3434 W Kilbourn Ave, Milwaukee, Wisconsin 53208 **Tel:** 1 414 935-3000.
Email: wvcy-tv@vcyamerica.org
Web site: http://www.vcyamerica.org
Profile: WVCY-TV is an independent station for the Milwaukee market. The station is owned by VCY America Inc. WVCY-TV broadcasts locally on channel 30.
TELEVISION STATION

WVEA2-TV 611606
Owner: Entravision Communications Corp.
Editorial: 2610 W Hillsborough Ave, Tampa, Florida 33614-6132 **Tel:** 1 813 872-6262.
Email: noticiastampa@entravision.com
Web site: http://www.wveatv.com
Profile: WVEA2-TV is a multicast of WVEA-TV. A multicast channel is a separate channel that shares the bandwith of the main station but can air unique programming. WVEA-TV airs programming from the LATV network to the Tampa, FL market. The station is owned by Entravision Communications Corp. WVEA2-TV broadcasts locally on channel 62.2.
TELEVISION STATION

WVEA-TV 75602
Owner: Entravision Communications Corp.
Editorial: 2610 W Hillsborough Ave, Tampa, Florida 33614-6132 **Tel:** 1 813 872-6262.
Email: noticiastampa@entravision.com
Web site: http://www.wveatv.com
Profile: WVEA-TV is the Univision affiliate for the Tampa, FL market. The station is owned by Entravision Communications Corp. WVEA-TV broadcasts locally on channel 62.
TELEVISION STATION

WVEC-TV 32190
Owner: TEGNA Inc.
Editorial: 613 Woodis Ave, Norfolk, Virginia 23510-1017 **Tel:** 1 757 625-1313.
Email: news@wvec.com
Web site: http://13newsnow.com
Profile: WVEC-TV is the ABC affiliate for the Norfolk, VA market. The station is owned by TEGNA Inc. WVEC-TV broadcasts locally on channel 13.
TELEVISION STATION

WVEN-TV 32593
Owner: Entravision Communications Corp.
Editorial: 523 Douglas Ave, Altamonte Springs, Florida 32714-2507 **Tel:** 1 407 774-2626.
Email: wvendesk@entravision.com
Web site: http://www.wventv.com
Profile: WVEN-TV is the local Univision affiliate for the Orlando-Daytona Beach, FL market. The station is owned by Entravision Communications Corp. WVEN-TV broadcasts locally on channel 26.
TELEVISION STATION

WVFX-TV 31981
Owner: Gray Television, Inc.
Editorial: 5 Television Dr, Bridgeport, West Virginia 26330-2621 **Tel:** 1 304 848-5000.
Email: news@wdtv.com
Web site: http://www.wdtv.com/fox10.cfm
Profile: WVFX-TV is the FOX and CW affiliate for the Clarksburg-Weston, WV market. The station is owned by Gray Television, Inc. WVFX-TV broadcasts locally on channel 10.
TELEVISION STATION

WVII-TV 32193
Owner: Rockfleet Broadcasting Inc.
Editorial: 371 Target Cir, Bangor, Maine 04401-5721 **Tel:** 1 207 945-6457.
Email: tv7news@wvii.com
Web site: http://www.foxbangor.com
Profile: WVII-TV is the ABC network affiliate for the Bangor, ME market. The station is owned by Rockfleet Broadcasting Inc. WVII-TV broadcasts locally on channel 7.
TELEVISION STATION

WVIR3-TV 671051
Owner: Virginia Broadcasting Corp.
Editorial: 503 E Market St, Charlottesville, Virginia 22902-5301 **Tel:** 1 434 220-2900.
Email: newsdesk@nbc29.com
Web site: http://www.nbc29.com
Profile: WVIR3-TV is a multicast channel of WVIR-TV A multicast channel is a separate channel that shares the bandwidth of the main station but can air unique programming. WVIR3-TV is the local CW Television Network affiliate on Channel 29.3 for the Charlottesville, Va. market. WVIR3-TV is owned by the Virginia Broadcasting Corp.
TELEVISION STATION

WVIR-TV 32194
Owner: Virginia Broadcasting Corp.
Editorial: 503 E Market St, Charlottesville, Virginia 22902-5301 **Tel:** 1 434 220-2900.
Email: newsdesk@nbc29.com
Web site: http://www.nbc29.com
Profile: WVIR-TV is the NBC news affiliate for the Charlottesville, VA market. The station is owned by Virginia Broadcasting Corp. WVIR-TV broadcasts locally on channel 29.
TELEVISION STATION

WVIT2-TV 613167
Owner: NBC Universal
Editorial: 1422 New Britain Ave, West Hartford, Connecticut 06110-1632 **Tel:** 1 860 521-3030.
Email: news@nbcconnecticut.com
Web site: http://www.nbcconnecticut.com
Profile: WVIT-TV is a multicast of WVIT2-TV. A multicast channel is a separate channel that shares the bandwith of the main station but can air unique programming. WVIT2-TV airs programming from NBC Plus in the Hartford-New Haven, CT market. The station is owned by NBC Universal. WVIT2-TV broadcasts locally on channel 30.2.
TELEVISION STATION

WVIT3-TV 613168
Owner: NBC Universal
Editorial: 1422 New Britain Ave, West Hartford, Connecticut 06110-1632 **Tel:** 1 860 521-3030.
Email: news@nbcconnecticut.com
Web site: http://www.nbcconnecticut.com
Profile: WVIT-TV is a multicast of WVIT3-TV. A multicast channel is a separate channel that shares the bandwith of the main station but can air unique programming. WVIT3-TV airs programming from Universal Sports in the Hartford-New Haven, CT market. The station is owned by NBC Universal. WVIT3-TV broadcasts locally on channel 30.3.
TELEVISION STATION

WVIT-TV 32195
Owner: NBC Universal
Editorial: 1422 New Britain Ave, West Hartford, Connecticut 06110-1632 **Tel:** 1 860 521-3030.
Email: news@nbcconnecticut.com
Web site: http://www.nbcconnecticut.com
Profile: WVIT-TV is the NBC network affiliate in the Hartford-New Haven, CT market. The Station is owned by NBC Universal. WVIT-TV broadcasts locally on channel 30.
TELEVISION STATION

WVIZ2-TV 613096
Owner: ideastream
Editorial: 1375 Euclid Ave, Cleveland, Ohio 44115-1826 **Tel:** 1 216 916-6100.
Profile: WVIZ2-TV is an independent affiliate for the Cleveland market. The station is owned by ideastream. WVIZ2-TV broadcasts locally on channel 25.2. The station airs programming from the Ohio Channel, which consists of live and delayed coverage

of the Ohio House of Representatives, Ohio Senate and the Ohio Supreme Court, proceedings of some state commissions, as well as public affairs. WVIZ2-TV is a multicast channel of WVIZ-TV. A multicast channel is a separate channel that shares the bandwidth of the main station but can air unique programming.
TELEVISION STATION

WVIZ3-TV 613097
Owner: ideastream
Editorial: 1375 Euclid Ave, Cleveland, Ohio 44115-1826 **Tel:** 1 216 916-6100.
Web site: http://www.pbs.org
Profile: WVIZ3-TV is a PBS affiliate for the Cleveland market. The station is owned by ideastream. WVIZ3-TV broadcasts locally on channel 25.3. The station airs PBS documentaries, science, current affairs, and history programming. WVIZ3-TV is a multicast channel of WVIZ-TV. A multicast channel is a separate channel that shares the bandwidth of the main station but can air unique programming.
TELEVISION STATION

WVIZ4-TV 613098
Owner: ideastream
Editorial: 1375 Euclid Ave, Cleveland, Ohio 44115-1844 **Tel:** 1 216 916-6100.
Web site: http://www.createtv.com
Profile: WVIZ4-TV is a PBS affiliate for the Cleveland market. The station is owned by ideastream. WVIZ4-TV broadcasts locally on channel 25.4. WVIZ4-TV broadcasts lifestyle and human interest programming from the libraries of PBS and American Public Television. WVIZ4-TV is a multicast channel of WVIZ-TV. A multicast channel is a separate channel that shares the bandwidth of the main station but can air unique programming.
TELEVISION STATION

WVIZ-TV 32196
Owner: ideastream
Editorial: 1375 Euclid Ave, Cleveland, Ohio 44115-1844 **Tel:** 1 216 916-6100.
Email: comments@wviz.org
Web site: http://wviz.ideastream.org
Profile: WVIZ-TV is the PBS affiliate for the Cleveland market. The station is owned by ideastream. WVIZ-TV broadcasts locally on channel 25.
TELEVISION STATION

WVLA-TV 32072
Owner: Nexstar Broadcasting Group
Editorial: 10000 Perkins Rd, Baton Rouge, Louisiana 70810-1527 **Tel:** 1 225 766-3233.
Email: news-wvla@nexstar.tv
Web site: http://www.brproud.com
Profile: WVLA-TV is the NBC affiliate for the Baton Rouge, LA market. The station is owned by Nexstar Broadcasting Group. WVLA-TV broadcasts locally on channel 33.
TELEVISION STATION

WVLR-TV 152956
Owner: D'Andrea(Bob), founder of Christian Television Network
Editorial: 306 Kyker Ferry Rd, Kodak, Tennessee 37764-1843 **Tel:** 1 865 932-4803.
Web site: http://www.dt48.org
Profile: WVLR-TV is an independent station for the Kodak, TN market. The station is owned by Bob D'Andrea. WVLR-TV broadcasts locally on channel 48.
TELEVISION STATION

WVLT-TV 32242
Owner: Gray Television, Inc.
Editorial: 6450 Papermill Dr, Knoxville, Tennessee 37919-4812 **Tel:** 1 865 450-8888.
Email: wvlt.news@wvlt-tv.com
Web site: http://www.local8now.com
Profile: WVLT-TV is the CBS and MyNetworkTV affiliate for the Knoxville, TN market. The station is owned by Gray Television, Inc. WVLT-TV broadcasts locally on channel 8.
TELEVISION STATION

WVNS-TV 32529
Owner: Nexstar Broadcasting Group Inc.
Editorial: 141 Old Cline Rd, Ghent, West Virginia 25843-9343 **Tel:** 1 304 929-6420.
Email: news@wvnstv.com
Web site: http://www.wearewvproud.com
Profile: WVNS-TV is the CBS network affiliate for the Bluefield-Beckely, WV market. The station is owned by Nexstar Broadcasting Group. WVNS-TV broadcasts locally on channel 59.
TELEVISION STATION

WVNY-TV 32197
Owner: Nexstar Broadcasting
Editorial: 298 Mountain View Dr, Colchester, Vermont 05446-5955 **Tel:** 1 802 660-9333.
Web site: http://www.mychamplainvalley.com
Profile: WVNY-TV is the ABC affiliate for the Burlington, VT market. The station is owned by Nexstar Boadcasting. WVNY-TV broadcasts locally on channel 22.
TELEVISION STATION

WVPX2-TV 613483
Owner: ION Media Networks
Editorial: 1333 Lakeside Ave E, Cleveland, Ohio 44114-1134 **Tel:** 1 216 344-7465.
Web site: http://www.qubo.com
Profile: WVPX2-TV is independent affiliate for the Cleveland, OH market. The station is owned by ION Media Networks. WVPX2-TV broadcasts locally on channel 23.2. The station airs children's programming from the qubo network. WVPX2-TV is a multicast channel of WVPX-TV. A multicast channel is a separate channel that shares the bandwidth of the main station but can air unique programming.
TELEVISION STATION

WVPX3-TV 613492
Owner: ION Media Networks
Editorial: 1333 Lakeside Ave E, Cleveland, Ohio 44114-1134 **Tel:** 1 216 344-7465.
Web site: http://www.ionlife.com
Profile: WVPX3-TV is a Ion Telelvision affiliate for the Cleveland, OH market. The station is owned by ION Media Networks. WVPX3-TV broadcasts locally on channel 23.3. The station airs lifestyle programming. WVPX3-TV is a multicast channel of WVPX-TV. A multicast channel is a separate channel that shares the bandwidth of the main station but can air unique programming.
TELEVISION STATION

WVPX-TV 31730
Owner: ION Media Networks
Editorial: 1333 Lakeside Ave E, Cleveland, Ohio 44114-1134 **Tel:** 1 216 344-7465.
Profile: WVPX-TV is the ION Television affiliate for the Cleveland, OH market. The station is owned by ION Media Networks. WVPX-TV broadcasts locally on channel 23.
TELEVISION STATION

WVTM2-TV 621868
Owner: Hearst Television Inc.
Editorial: 1732 Valley View Dr, Birmingham, Alabama 35209-1251 **Tel:** 1 205 933-1313.
Email: wvtm13@wvtm.com
Web site: http://www.wvtm13.com
Profile: WVTM2-TV is a multicast channel of WVTM-TV. A multicast is a separate channel that shares the bandwith of the main station but can air unique programming. WVTM2-TV airs entertainment programming from Retro Television Network in the Birmingham, AL market. The station is owned by Hearst Television Inc. WVTM2-TV broadcasts locally on channel 13.2.
TELEVISION STATION

WVTM-TV 32199
Owner: Hearst Television Inc.
Editorial: 1732 Valley View Dr, Birmingham, Alabama 35209-1251 **Tel:** 1 205 933-1313.
Email: wvtm13@wvtm.com
Web site: http://www.wvtm13.com
Profile: WVTM-TV is the NBC affiliate for the Birmingham, Alabama market. The station is owned by Hearst Television Inc. WVTM-TV broadcasts locally on channel 13.
TELEVISION STATION

WVTV-TV 32200
Owner: Sinclair Broadcast Group, Inc.
Editorial: 11520 W Calumet Rd, Milwaukee, Wisconsin 53224-3156 **Tel:** 1 414 815-4100.
Web site: http://www.cw18milwaukee.com
Profile: WVTV-TV is the CW affiliate for the Milwaukee market. The station is owned by Sinclair Broadcast Group, Inc. WVTV-TV broadcasts locally on channel 18.
TELEVISION STATION

WVTX-TV 382489
Owner: Bruno-Goodworth Network, Inc.
Editorial: 92 16th St, Wheeling, West Virginia 26003-3660 **Tel:** 1 412 922-9576.
Web site: http://www.wbgn.com
Profile: WVTX-TV is a transmitter located in Wheeling, WV that simulcasts the programming of WBGN-TV, in Pittsburgh. It is owned by Bruno-Goodworth Network, Inc. WVTX-TV broadcasts locally on channel 28.
TELEVISION STATION

WVUE2-TV 707764
Owner: Raycom Media Inc.
Editorial: 1025 S Jefferson Davis Pkwy, New Orleans, Louisiana 70125-1218 **Tel:** 1 504 486-6161.
Email: fox8news@fox8tv.net
Web site: http://www.bouncetv.com
Profile: WVUE2-TV is a multicast channel of WVUE-TV. A multicast channel is a separate channel that shares the bandwith of the main station but can air unique programming. WVUE2-TV is the Bounce TV affiliate for the New Orleans, LA market. The station is owned by Raycom Media Inc. WVUE2-TV broadcasts locally on channel 8.2.
TELEVISION STATION

WVUE-TV 32201
Owner: Raycom Media Inc.
Editorial: 1025 S Jefferson Davis Pkwy, New Orleans, Louisiana 70125-1218 **Tel:** 1 504 486-6161.
Email: fox8news@fox8live.com
Web site: http://www.fox8live.com
Profile: WVUE-TV is the FOX affiliate for the New Orleans market. The station is owned by Raycom Media Inc. WVUE-TV broadcasts locally on channel 8.
TELEVISION STATION

WVVA-TV 32203
Owner: Quincy Media
Editorial: 3052 Big Laurel Hwy, Bluefield, West Virginia 24701-4969 **Tel:** 1 304 325-5487.
Email: news@wvva.com
Web site: http://www.wvva.com
Profile: WVVA-TV is the NBC affiliate in Bluefield, WV. The station is owned by Quincy Newspapers Inc. WVVA-TV broadcasts locally on channel 6.
TELEVISION STATION

WVVH-TV 457686
Owner: Video Voice, Inc.
Tel: 1 631 537-0273.
Email: info@wvvh.com
Web site: http://www.wvvh.com
Profile: WVVH-TV is an independent affiliate for the New York City market. The station is owned by Video Voice, Inc. WVVH-TV broadcasts locally on channel 50.
TELEVISION STATION

WWAY-TV 32204
Owner: Morris Multimedia, Inc.
Editorial: 615 N Front St, Wilmington, North Carolina 28401-3325 **Tel:** 1 910 762-8581.
Email: newsroom@wwaytv3.com
Web site: http://www.wwaytv3.com
Profile: WWAY-TV is the ABC and CBS affiliate for the Wilmington, NC market. The station is owned by Morris Multimedia, Inc. WWAY-TV broadcasts locally on channel 3.
TELEVISION STATION

WWBT-TV 32205
Owner: Raycom Media Inc.
Editorial: 5710 Midlothian Tpke, Richmond, Virginia 23225-6116 **Tel:** 1 804 230-1212.
Email: newsroom@nbc12.com
Web site: http://www.nbc12.com
Profile: WWBT-TV is the NBC affiliate for the Richmond, VA market. The station is owned by Raycom Media Inc. WWBT-TV broadcasts locally on channel 12. Do NOT pitch the station satellite interviews.
TELEVISION STATION

WWCI-TV 519060
Owner: V-1 Productions Inc.
Editorial: 1082 12th St, Vero Beach, Florida 32960-6707 **Tel:** 1 772 978-0023.
Email: wwcitv10@bellsouth.net
Web site: http://www.wwcitv.com
Profile: WWCI-TV is an independent station for the West Palm Beach, FL market. The station is owned by V-1 Productions Inc. WWCI-TV broadcasts locally on channel 10. Accepts PSAs only if pertaining to Vero Beach activities.
TELEVISION STATION

WWCP-TV 32675
Owner: Peak Media LLC
Editorial: 1450 Scalp Ave, Johnstown, Pennsylvania 15904-3374 **Tel:** 1 814 266-8088.
Web site: http://www.fox8tv.com
Profile: WWCP-TV is the Fox affiliate for the Johnstown-Altoona, PA market. The station is owned by Peak Media LLC. WWCP-TV broadcasts locally on channel 8. WWCP-TV has no news department. Newscast are produced by WJAC-TV.
TELEVISION STATION

WWCW-TV 31927
Owner: Grant Broadcast Inc.
Editorial: 5305 Valleypark Drive, Suite 1, Roanoke, Virginia 24019 **Tel:** 1 540 344-2127.
Web site: http://www.virginiafirst.com
Profile: WWCW-TV is the CW network affiliate for the Roanoke-Lynchburg, VA market. The Station is owned by Grant Communications Inc. WWCW-TV broadcasts locally on channel 21.
TELEVISION STATION

WWDP-TV 32565
Owner: Value Vision Inc.
Editorial: 2 Bert Dr Ste 4, West Bridgewater, Massachusetts 02379-1033 **Tel:** 1 508 586-4677.
Profile: WWDP-TV is an independent affiliate for the West Bridgewater, MA market. The station is owned by Value Vision Inc. WWDP-TV broadcasts locally on channel 46.
TELEVISION STATION

WWHB-TV 128164
Owner: Sinclair Broadcast Group, Inc.
Editorial: 1700 Palm Beach Lakes Blvd Ste 150, West Palm Beach, Florida 33401-2007 **Tel:** 1 561 681-3434.
Web site: http://azteca48.com
Profile: WWHB-TV is an independent station for the West Palm Beach, FL market. The station is owned by Sinclair Broadcast Group, Inc. WWHB broadcasts locally on channel 48.
TELEVISION STATION

WWHO-TV 32342
Owner: Sinclair Broadcast Group
Editorial: 1261 Dublin Rd, Columbus, Ohio 43215-7000 **Tel:** 1 614 485-5300.
Email: feedback@cwcolumbus.com
Web site: http://www.cwcolumbus.com
Profile: WWHO-TV is the CW affiliate for the Columbus, OH market. The station is owned by Sinclair Broadcast Group. WWHO-TV broadcasts locally on channel 53.
TELEVISION STATION

WWJ-TV 31866
Owner: CBS Television Stations
Editorial: 26905 W 11 Mile Rd, Southfield, Michigan 48033-2292 **Tel:** 1 248 355-7000.
Web site: http://detroit.cbslocal.com
Profile: WWJ-TV is the CBS affiliate for the Detroit market. The station is owned by CBS Television Stations. WWJ-TV broadcasts locally on channel 62.
TELEVISION STATION

WWLP-TV 32207
Owner: Nexstar Media Group, LLC
Editorial: 1 Broadcast Ctr, Chicopee, Massachusetts 01013-1829 **Tel:** 1 413 377-2200.
Email: news@wwlp.com
Web site: http://www.wwlp.com
Profile: WWLP-TV is the NBC affiliate for the Springfield, MA market. The station is owned by Nexstar Media Group, LLC. WWLP-TV broadcasts locally on channel 22.
TELEVISION STATION

WWL-TV 32206
Owner: TEGNA Inc.
Editorial: 1024 N Rampart St, New Orleans, Louisiana 70116-2406 **Tel:** 1 504 529-4444.
Email: pressrelease@wwltv.com
Web site: http://www.wwltv.com
Profile: WWL-TV is the CBS affiliate for the New Orleans market. The station is owned by TEGNA Inc. WWL-TV broadcasts locally on channel 4.
TELEVISION STATION

WWMB-TV 32543
Owner: Sinclair Broadcast Group, Inc.
Editorial: 1194 Atlantic Ave, Conway, South Carolina 29526-8222 **Tel:** 1 843 234-9733.
Profile: WWMB-TV is the CW affiliate for the Florence-Myrtle Beach, SC market. The station is owned by Sinclair Broadcast Group, Inc. WWMB-TV broadcasts locally on channel 21.
TELEVISION STATION

WWME2-TV 768980
Owner: Weigel Broadcasting Co.
Editorial: 26 N Halsted St, Chicago, Illinois 60661-2107 **Tel:** 1 312 705-2600.
Profile: WWME2-TV is a multicast channel of WWME-TV. A multicast channel is a separate channel that shares the bandwidth of the main station but can air unique programming. WWME2-TV is the local Bounce TV affiliate on channel 23.2 for the Chicago market. WWME2-TV is owned by Weigel Broadcasting Co.
TELEVISION STATION

WWME-TV 133856
Owner: Weigel Broadcasting Co.
Editorial: 26 N Halsted St, Chicago, Illinois 60661
Tel: 1 312 705-2600.
Web site: http://www.metvchicago.com
Profile: WWME-TV is an independent station for the Chicago market. The station is owned by Weigel Broadcasting Co. WWME-TV broadcasts locally on channel 23.
TELEVISION STATION

WWMT2-TV 561445
Owner: Sinclair Broadcast Group, Inc.
Editorial: 590 W Maple St, Kalamazoo, Michigan 49008-1990 **Tel:** 1 269 388-3333.
Email: desk@wwmt.com
Web site: http://www.wwmt.com
Profile: WWMT2-TV is a multicast channel of WWMT-TV. The station is owned by Sinclair Broadcast Group, Inc. A multicast channel is a separate channel that shares the bandwidth of the main station but can air unique programming.
TELEVISION STATION

WWMT-TV 32208
Owner: Sinclair Broadcast Group, Inc.
Editorial: 590 W Maple St, Kalamazoo, Michigan 49008-1926 **Tel:** 1 269 388-3333.
Email: desk@wwmt.com
Web site: http://www.wwmt.com
Profile: WWMT-TV is the local CBS affiliate for the greater Kalamazoo, MI area. The station is owned by Sinclair Broadcast Group, Inc. WWMT-TV broadcasts locally on channel 3.
TELEVISION STATION

WWNY-TV 32209
Owner: United Communications Corp.
Editorial: 120 Arcade St, Watertown, New York 13601-3279 **Tel:** 1 315 788-3800.
Email: news@wwnytv.com
Web site: http://www.wwnytv.net
Profile: WWNY-TV is the CBS affiliate for Watertown, NY. The station is owned by United Communications Corp. WWNY-TV broadcasts locally on channel 7.
TELEVISION STATION

WWOR3-TV 795159
Owner: Fox Broadcasting Company
Editorial: 9 Broadcast Plz, Secaucus, New Jersey 07094-2913 **Tel:** 1 201 348-0009.
Web site: http://www.bouncetv.com
Profile: WWOR3-TV is a multicast channel of WWOR-TV. A multicast channel is a separate channel that shares the bandwith of the main station but can air unique programming. WWOR3-TV is the Bounce TV Network for the New York market. The station is owned by FOX Broadcasting Company. WWOR3-TV broadcasts locally on channel 9.3.
TELEVISION STATION

WWOR-TV 32210
Owner: Fox Broadcasting Company
Editorial: 9 Broadcast Plz, Secaucus, New Jersey 07094-2913 **Tel:** 1 201 348-0009.
Email: 9newsdesk@foxtv.com
Web site: http://www.my9nj.com
Profile: WWOR-TV is the MyNetworkTV affiliate for the New York market. The station is owned by Fox Broadcasting Company. WWOR-TV broadcasts locally on channel 9.
TELEVISION STATION

WWRS2-TV 618778
Owner: Trinity Broadcasting Network
Editorial: 1275 N Barker Rd, Brookfield, Wisconsin 53045-5201 **Tel:** 1 920 387-9052.
Web site: http://tbn.org
Profile: WWRS2-TV is a multicast of WWRS-TV. A multicast channel is a separate channel that shares the bandwith of the main station but can air unique programming. WWRS2-TV airs religious programming from The Church Channel in the Milwaukee market. The station is owned by Trinity Broadcasting Network. WWRS2-TV broadcasts locally on channel 52.2.
TELEVISION STATION

WWRS3-TV 618782
Owner: Trinity Broadcasting Network
Editorial: 1275 N Barker Rd, Brookfield, Wisconsin 53045-5201 **Tel:** 1 920 387-9052.
Web site: http://tbn.org
Profile: WWRS3-TV is a multicast of WWRS-TV. A multicast channel is a separate channel that shares the bandwith of the main station but can air unique programming. WWRS3-TV airs Christian music videos programming from JCTV in the Milwaukee market. The station is owned by Trinity Broadcasting Network. WWRS3-TV broadcasts locally on channel 52.3.
TELEVISION STATION

WWRS4-TV 618785
Owner: Trinity Broadcasting Network
Editorial: 1275 N Barker Rd, Brookfield, Wisconsin 53045-5201 **Tel:** 1 920 387-9052.
Web site: http://tbn.org
Profile: WWRS4-TV is a multicast of WWRS-TV. A multicast channel is a separate channel that shares the bandwith of the main station but can air unique programming. WWRS4-TV airs Hispanic Christian programming from Enlace USA in the Milwaukee market. The station is owned by Trinity Broadcasting Network. WWRS4-TV broadcasts locally on channel 52.4.
TELEVISION STATION

WWRS5-TV 618788
Owner: Trinity Broadcasting Network
Editorial: 1275 N Barker Rd, Brookfield, Wisconsin 53045-5201 **Tel:** 1 920 387-9052.
Web site: http://tbn.org
Profile: WWRS5-TV is a multicast of WWRS-TV. A multicast channel is a separate channel that shares the bandwith of the main station but can air unique programming. WWRS5-TV airs children's Christian programming from Smile of a Child in the Milwaukee market. The station is owned by Trinity Broadcasting Network. WWRS5-TV broadcasts locally on channel 52.5.
TELEVISION STATION

WWRS-TV 390586
Owner: Trinity Broadcasting Network
Editorial: 1275 N Barker Rd, Brookfield, Wisconsin 53045-5201 **Tel:** 1 920 387-9052.
Web site: http://tbn.org
Profile: WWRS-TV is a Trinity Broadcasting Network affiliate for the Milwaukee market. The station is owned by Trinity Broadcasting Network. WWRS-TV broadcasts locally on channel 52.
TELEVISION STATION

WWSB-TV 32211
Owner: Raycom Media Inc.
Editorial: 1477 10th St, Sarasota, Florida 34236-4048 **Tel:** 1 941 923-8840.
Email: news@mysuncoast.com
Web site: http://www.mysuncoast.com
Profile: WWSB-TV is the ABC affiliate for the Tampa-St. Petersburg, FL market. The station is owned by Southern Broadcasting Corp. of Sarasota. WWSB-TV broadcasts locally on channel 40.
TELEVISION STATION

WWSI-TV 79759
Owner: NBC Universal
Editorial: 1341 N Delaware Ave, Philadelphia, Pennsylvania 19125-4300 **Tel:** 1 215 634-8862.
Email: wwsinews@nbcuni.com
Web site: http://www.telemundo62.com
Profile: WWSI-TV is a Telemundo affiliate for the Philadelphia market. The station is owned by NBC Universal. WWSI-TV broadcasts locally on channel 49.
TELEVISION STATION

WWTI-TV 32291
Owner: Nexstar Broadcasting Group
Editorial: 1222 Arsenal St, Watertown, New York 13601-2297 **Tel:** 1 315 785-8850.
Email: news@myabc50.com
Web site: http://www.informnny.com
Profile: WWTI-TV is the ABC affiliate for the Watertown, NY market. The station is owned by Nexstar Broadcasting Group. WWTI-TV broadcasts locally on channel 50.
TELEVISION STATION

WWTO2-TV 607375
Owner: Trinity Broadcasting Network
Editorial: 420 E Stevenson Rd, Ottawa, Illinois 61350-9530 **Tel:** 1 815 434-2700.
Web site: http://www.thechurchchannel.org
Profile: WWTO2-TV is an affiliate of The Church Channel Network for the Chicago market. The station is owned by the Trinity Broadcasting Network. WWTO-TV broadcasts locally on channel 35.2. The channel broadcasts church service programs 24 hours per day, seven days a week from several of America's leading churches. WWTO2-TV is a multicast channel of WWTO-TV. A multicast channel is a separate channel that shares the bandwidth of the main station but can air unique programming.
TELEVISION STATION

WWTO3-TV 607552
Owner: Trinity Broadcasting Network
Editorial: 420 E Stevenson Rd, Ottawa, Illinois 61350-9530 **Tel:** 1 815 434-2700.
Profile: WWTO3-TV is an affiliate of JCTV Network for the Chicago market. The station is owned by the Trinity Broadcasting Network. WWTO-TV broadcasts locally on channel 35.3. The channel broadcasts programming from JUICE TV, a young adult television network devoted to Christian music videos, and and Smile of a Child TV, a network dedicated to providing family-oriented and children's religious programming. WWTO3-TV is a multicast channel of WWTO-TV. A multicast channel is a separate channel that shares the bandwidth of the main station but can air unique programming.
TELEVISION STATION

WWTO4-TV 607562
Owner: Trinity Broadcasting Network
Editorial: 420 E Stevenson Rd, Ottawa, Illinois 61350-9530 **Tel:** 1 815 434-2700.
Web site: http://www.tbnenlaceusa.com/espanol/
Profile: WWTO4-TV is an affiliate of Enlace USA Network for the Chicago market. The station is owned by the Trinity Broadcasting Network. WWTO-TV broadcasts locally on channel 35.4. The channel broadcasts Enlace USA the United States version of the Spanish-language cable television network providing Christian programming to the Hispanic community. WWTO4-TV is a multicast channel of WWTO-TV. A multicast channel is a separate channel that shares the bandwidth of the main station but can air unique programming.
TELEVISION STATION

WWTO5-TV 607563
Owner: Trinity Broadcasting Network
Editorial: 420 E Stevenson Rd, Ottawa, Illinois 61350-9530 **Tel:** 1 815 434-2700.
Web site: http://www.tbn-salsa.org
Profile: WWTO5-TV is an affiliate of TBN Salsa for the Chicago market. The station is owned by the Trinity Broadcasting Network. WWTO-TV broadcasts locally on channel 35.5. The channel broadcasts Spanish Christian programming. WWTO5-TV is a multicast channel of WWTO-TV. A multicast channel is a separate channel that shares the bandwidth of the main station but can air unique programming.
TELEVISION STATION

WWTO-TV 32292
Owner: Trinity Broadcasting Network
Editorial: 420 E Stevenson Rd, Ottawa, Illinois 61350-9530 **Tel:** 1 815 434-2700.
Web site: http://www.tbn.org
Profile: WWTO-TV is the Trinity Broadcasting Network affiliate for the Chicago market. The station is owned by the Trinity Broadcasting Network. WWTO-TV broadcasts locally on channel 35.
TELEVISION STATION

WWTV-TV 32676
Owner: Heritage Broadcasting Company of Michigan
Tel: 1 231 775-3478.
Email: info@9and10news.com
Web site: http://www.9and10news.com
Profile: WWTV-TV is the CBS affiliate for the Traverse City-Cadillac, MI market. The station is owned by Heritage Broadcasting Company of Michigan. WWTV-TV broadcasts locally on channel 9.
TELEVISION STATION

WXAX-TV 483587
Owner: Una Vez Mas LP
Editorial: 1701 N Market St Ste 500, Dallas, Texas 75202-2001 **Tel:** 1 214 754-7008.
Web site: http://www.aztecaamerica.com
Profile: WXAX-TV is the Azteca America affiliate for the Tampa, FL market. The station is owned by Una Vez Mas LP. WXAX-TV broadcasts locally on channel 26. Send all PSAs to the corporate headquarters in Dallas, TX via BETA format.
TELEVISION STATION

WXCW2-TV 829863
Owner: Sun Broadcasting
Editorial: 2824 Palm Beach Blvd, Fort Myers, Florida 33916-1503 **Tel:** 1 239 479-5500.
Web site: http://wxcw.com
Profile: WXCW2-TV is a multicast channel of WXCW-TV. A multicast channel is a separate channel that shares the bandwidth of the main station but can air unique programming. WXCW2-TV is the MundoFOX affiliate for the Fort Myers-Naples, FL TX market. The station is owned by Sun Broadcasting. WXCW2-TV broadcasts locally on channel 46.2.
TELEVISION STATION

WXCW-TV 32337
Owner: Sun Broadcasting
Editorial: 2824 Palm Beach Blvd, Fort Myers, Florida 33916-1503 **Tel:** 1 239 479-5500.
Web site: http://wxcw.com
Profile: WXCW-TV is the CW affiliate for the Fort Myers-Naples, FL market. The station is owned by Sun Broadcasting. WXCW-TV broadcasts locally on channel 46.
TELEVISION STATION

WXEL2-TV 620873
Owner: Barry Telecommunications, Inc.
Editorial: 3401 S Congress Ave, Boynton Beach, Florida 33426-8499 **Tel:** 1 561 737-8000.
Email: info@wxel.org
Web site: http://www.wxel.org
Profile: WXEL2-TV is a multicast of WXEL-TV. A multicast channel is a separate channel that shares the bandwith of the main station but can air unique programming. WXEL2-TV airs how to, DIY and instructional programming from PBS Create in the West Palm Beach, FL market. The station is owned by Barry Telecommunications, Inc. WXEL2-TV broadcasts locally on channel 42.2.
TELEVISION STATION

WXEL3-TV 620880
Owner: Barry Telecommunications, Inc.
Editorial: 3401 S Congress Ave, Boynton Beach, Florida 33426-8499 **Tel:** 1 561 737-8000.
Email: info@wxel.org
Web site: http://www.wxel.org
Profile: WXEL3-TV is a multicast of WXEL-TV. A multicast channel is a separate channel that shares the bandwith of the main station but can air unique programming. WXEL3-TV airs Hispanic programming from V-me in the West Palm Beach, FL market. The station is owned by Barry Telecommunications, Inc. WXEL3-TV broadcasts locally on channel 42.3.
TELEVISION STATION

WXEL4-TV 620887
Owner: Barry Telecommunications, Inc.
Editorial: 3401 S Congress Ave, Boynton Beach, Florida 33426-8499 **Tel:** 1 561 737-8000.
Email: info@wxel.org
Web site: http://www.wxel.org
Profile: WXEL4-TV is a multicast of WXEL-TV. A multicast channel is a separate channel that shares the bandwith of the main station but can air unique programming. WXEL4-TV airs regional programming from The Florida Knowledge Network and The Florida Channel in the West Palm Beach, FL market. The station is owned by Barry Telecommunications, Inc. WXEL4-TV broadcasts locally on channel 42.4.
TELEVISION STATION

WXEL-TV 32293
Owner: Barry Telecommunications, Inc.
Editorial: 3401 S Congress Ave, Boynton Beach, Florida 33426 **Tel:** 1 561 737-8000.
Email: info@wxel.org
Web site: http://www.wxel.org
Profile: WXEL-TV is a PBS affiliate for the West Palm Beach, FL area. The station is owned by the Barry Telecommunications, Inc. WXEL-TV broadcasts locally on channel 42.
TELEVISION STATION

WXFT-TV 32509
Owner: Univision Communications Inc.
Editorial: 541 N Fairbanks Ct, Chicago, Illinois 60611-3306 **Tel:** 1 312 670-1000.
Profile: WXFT-TV is the UniMas affiliate for the Chicago market. The station is owned by Univision Communications Inc. WXFT-TV broadcasts locally on channel 60.
TELEVISION STATION

WXIA2-TV 608419
Owner: TEGNA Inc.
Editorial: 1 Monroe Pl NE, Atlanta, Georgia 30324-4836 **Tel:** 1 404 892-1611.
Profile: WXIA2-TV is an independent affiliate for the Atlanta market. The station is owned by TEGNA Inc. WXIA2-TV broadcasts locally on channel 11.2. WIXA2-TV broadcasts programming from WeatherNation. WXIA2-TV is a multicast channel of WXIA-TV. A multicast channel is a separate channel that shares the bandwidth of the main station but can air unique programming.
TELEVISION STATION

WXIA3-TV 608420
Owner: TEGNA Inc.
Editorial: 1 Monroe Pl NE, Atlanta, Georgia 30324-4836 **Tel:** 1 404 892-1611.
Profile: WXIA3-TV is an independent affiliate for the Atlanta market. The station is owned by TEGNA Inc. WXIA3-TV broadcasts locally on channel 11.3. WIXA2-TV broadcasts Universal Sports. WXIA3-TV is a multicast channel of WXIA-TV. A multicast channel is a separate channel that shares the bandwidth of the main station but can air unique programming.
TELEVISION STATION

WXIA-TV 32214
Owner: TEGNA Inc.
Editorial: 1 Monroe Pl NE, Atlanta, Georgia 30324-4836 **Tel:** 1 404 892-1611.
Email: news@11alive.com
Web site: http://www.11alive.com
Profile: WXIA-TV is the NBC affiliate for the Atlanta market. The station is owned by TEGNA Inc. WXIA-TV broadcasts locally on channel 11.
TELEVISION STATION

WXII-TV 32215
Owner: Hearst Television Inc.
Editorial: 700 Coliseum Dr, Winston Salem, North Carolina 27106-5313 **Tel:** 1 336 721-9944.
Email: newstips@wxii12.com
Web site: http://www.wxii12.com
Profile: WXII-TV is the NBC affiliate for the Greensboro-Winston Salem, NC market. The station is owned by Hearst Television Inc. WXII-TV broadcasts locally on channel 12.
TELEVISION STATION

WXIN-TV 32216
Owner: Tribune Broadcasting Co.
Editorial: 6910 Network Pl, Indianapolis, Indiana 46278-1929 **Tel:** 1 317 632-5900.
Email: fox59news@fox59.com
Web site: http://www.fox59.com
Profile: WXIN-TV is the FOX network affiliate for the Indianapolis market. The station is owned by Tribune Broadcasting Co. WXIN-TV broadcasts locally on channel 59.
TELEVISION STATION

WXIX2-TV 612201
Owner: Raycom Media Inc.
Editorial: 19 Broadcast Plaza, 635 West 7th Street, Cincinnati, Ohio 45203 **Tel:** 1 513 421-1919.
Email: desk@fox19now.com
Web site: http://www.fox19.com
Profile: WXIX2-TV is a multicast of WXIX-TV. A multicast channel is a separate channel that shares the bandwith of the main station but can air unique programming. WXIX2-TV airs programming from the This TV and local sports in the Cincinnati market. The station is owned by Raycom Media Inc. WXIX2-TV broadcasts locally on channel 19.2.
TELEVISION STATION

WXIX-TV 32217
Owner: Raycom Media Inc.
Editorial: 635 W 7th St, 19 Broadcast Plaza, Cincinnati, Ohio 45203-1513 **Tel:** 1 513 421-1919.
Email: desk@fox19now.com
Web site: http://www.fox19.com
Profile: WXIX-TV is the FOX affiliate for the Cincinnati market. The station is owned by Raycom Media Inc. WXIX-TV broadcasts locally on channel 19.
TELEVISION STATION

WXLV-TV 32019
Owner: Sinclair Broadcast Group, Inc.
Editorial: 3500 Myer Lee Dr, Winston Salem, North Carolina 27101-6223 **Tel:** 1 336 722-4545.
Web site: http://www.abc45.com
Profile: WXLV-TV is the ABC affiliate for the Greensboro-Winston Salem, NC market. The station is owned by Sinclair Broadcast Group, Inc. WXLV-TV is broadcasted locally on channel 45.
TELEVISION STATION

WXMI-TV 32218
Owner: Tribune Broadcasting Co.
Editorial: 3117 Plaza Dr NE, Grand Rapids, Michigan 49525-2901 **Tel:** 1 616 364-8722.
Email: news@fox17online.com
Web site: http://www.fox17online.com
Profile: WXMI-TV is the FOX network affiliate for the Grand Rapids, MI market. The station is owned by Tribune Broadcasting Co. WXMI-TV broadcasts locally on channel 17.
TELEVISION STATION

WXMS-TV 81703
Owner: American Spirit Media, LLC
Editorial: 715 S Jefferson St, Jackson, Mississippi 39201-5622 **Tel:** 1 601 948-3333.
Web site: http://www.msnewsnow.com
Profile: WXMS-TV is the ME-TV station affiliate for the Jackson, MS market. The station is owned by American Spirit Media, LLC and operated by Raycom Media. WXMS-TV broadcasts locally on channel 27.
TELEVISION STATION

WXOW-TV 32677
Owner: Quincy Newspapers Inc.
Editorial: 3705 County 25, La Crescent, Minnesota 55947-9779 **Tel:** 1 507 895-9969.
Email: wxowaedesk@wxow.com
Web site: http://www.wxow.com
Profile: WXOW-TV is the ABC television affiliate for the La Crosse, Wisconsin, market. The station is owned by Quincy Newspapers Inc. WXOW-TV broadcasts locally on channel 19.
TELEVISION STATION

WXPX-TV 32448
Owner: ION Media Networks
Editorial: 14444 66th St N, Clearwater, Florida 33764-7204 **Tel:** 1 727 479-1054.
Profile: WXPX-TV is the ION Television affiliate for the Tampa-St. Petersburg, FL market. The station is owned by ION Media Networks. WXPX-TV broadcasts locally on channel 66.
TELEVISION STATION

WXSP-TV 88196
Owner: Nexstar Media Group, LLC
Editorial: 120 College Ave SE, Grand Rapids, Michigan 49503-4404 **Tel:** 1 616 456-1818.
Email: newsroom@woodtv.com
Web site: http://www.wxsp.com
Profile: WXSP-TV is the MyNetworkTV affiliate on Channel 18 for the greater western Michigan area. WXSP-TV is owned and operated by Nexstar Media Group, LLC and does not produce local newscasts or programming. WXSP-TV rebroadcasts news from sister station WOOD-TV Channel 8, Monday through Friday at 7pm, ET.
TELEVISION STATION

WXTV2-TV 606895
Owner: Univision Communications Inc.
Editorial: 500 Frank W Burr Blvd Ste 6, Teaneck, New Jersey 07666-6802 **Tel:** 1 201 287-4141.
Email: noticias41ny@univision.net
Web site: http://nuevayork.univision.com
Profile: WXTV2-TV is a multicast channel of WXTV-TV. A multicast channel is a separate channel that shares the bandwidth of the main station but can air

United States of America

unique programming. WXTV2-TV airs programming from WFUT-TV for the greater New York market. The station is owned by Univision Communications Inc. WXTV2-TV broadcasts locally on channel 41.2.
TELEVISION STATION

WXTV-TV 32220
Owner: Univision Communications Inc.
Editorial: 500 Frank W Burr Blvd Ste 6, Teaneck, New Jersey 07666-6802 **Tel:** 1 201 287-4141.
Email: noticias41ny@univision.net
Web site: http://nuevayork.univision.com
Profile: WXTV-TV is the Univision affiliate for the New York market. The station is owned by Univision Communications Inc. WXTV-TV broadcasts locally on channel 41.
TELEVISION STATION

WXTX-TV 32221
Owner: Southeastern Media Holdings, LLC
Editorial: 6524 Buena Vista Rd, Columbus, Georgia 31907-5399 **Tel:** 1 706 561-5400.
Email: newsleader@wtvm.com
Web site: http://www.wxtx.com
Profile: WXTX-TV is the FOX affiliate for the Columbus, GA market. The station is owned by Southeastern Media Holdings, LLC. WXTX-TV broadcasts locally on channel 54. The station does not have a news department or any original programming. Subsequently, there are no opportunities for publicity.
TELEVISION STATION

WXVO-TV 354529
Owner: Weathervision
Editorial: 2911 Shortcut Rd, Pascagoula, Mississippi 39567-1809 **Tel:** 1 228 762-0464.
Web site: http://www.wkfk.com
Profile: WXVO-TV is the ION Television affiliate for the Biloxi-Gulfport, MS area. The station is owned by Weathervision. WXVO-TV broadcasts locally on channel 7.
TELEVISION STATION

WXXA-TV 32223
Owner: Newport Television, LLC
Editorial: 341 Northern Blvd, Albany, New York 12204-1001 **Tel:** 1 518 433-4286.
Email: news@fox23news.com
Web site: http://www.fox23news.com
Profile: WXXA-TV is the FOX affiliate for the Albany, NY market. The station is owned by Newport Television, LLC. WXXA-TV broadcasts locally on channel 23.
TELEVISION STATION

WXXI-TV 32224
Owner: WXXI Public Broadcast Council
Editorial: 280 State St, Rochester, New York 14614-1033 **Tel:** 1 585 325-7500.
Email: newsroom@wxxi.org
Web site: http://interactive.wxxi.org
Profile: WXXI-TV is the PBS affiliate for the Rochester, NY market. The station is owned by WXXI Public Broadcast Council. WXXI-TV broadcasts locally on channel 21.
TELEVISION STATION

WXXV2-TV 799881
Owner: Morris Medie
Editorial: 14351 Highway 49, Gulfport, Mississippi 39503-8648 **Tel:** 1 228 832-2525.
Email: promotions@wxxv25.com
Web site: http://www.wxxv25.com
Profile: WXXV2-TV is a multicast channel of WXXV-TV. A multicast channel is a separate channel that shares the bandwith of the main station but can air unique programming. WXXV2-TV is the NBC Network for the Biloxi-Golfport, MS market. The station is owned by Morris Medie. WXXV2-TV broadcasts locally on channel 25.2. This channel launched July 1, 2012.
TELEVISION STATION

WXXV-TV 32300
Owner: Morris Multimedia Inc.
Editorial: 14351 Highway 49, Gulfport, Mississippi 39503-8648 **Tel:** 1 228 832-2525.
Email: newsrelease@wxxv25.com
Web site: http://www.wxxv25.com
Profile: WXXV-TV is the FOX affiliate for the Gulfport, MS area. The station is owned by Morris Multimedia Inc. WXXV-TV broadcasts locally on channel 25. The station does not have a news department, but they air PSAs. Send PSAs by postal mail in DVD or by email in JPEG format.
TELEVISION STATION

WXYZ2-TV 586589
Owner: E.W. Scripps Co.
Editorial: 20777 W 10 Mile Rd, Southfield, Michigan 48075-1086 **Tel:** 1 248 827-7777.
Email: wxyzdesk@wxyz.com
Web site: http://www.wxyz.com
Profile: WXYZ2-TV is a multicast of WXYZ-TV. A multicast channel is a separate channel that shares the bandwith of the main station but can air unique programming. WXYZ2-TV airs programming from the Retro Televison Network in the Detroit market. The station is owned by E.W. Scripps Co. WXYZ2-TV broadcasts locally on channel 7.2.
TELEVISION STATION

WXYZ3-TV 612005
Owner: E.W. Scripps Co.
Editorial: 20777 W 10 Mile Rd, Southfield, Michigan 48075-1086 **Tel:** 1 248 827-7777.
Web site: http://www.bouncetv.com

Profile: WXYZ3-TV is a multicast of WXYZ-TV. A multicast channel is a separate channel that shares the bandwith of the main station but can air unique programming. WXYZ3-TV airs programming from the Bounce network in the Detroit market. The station is owned by E.W. Scripps Co. WXYZ3-TV broadcasts locally on channel 7.3.
TELEVISION STATION

WXYZ-TV 32225
Owner: E.W. Scripps Co.
Editorial: 20777 W 10 Mile Rd, Southfield, Michigan 48075-1086 **Tel:** 1 248 827-7777.
Email: wxyzdesk@wxyz.com
Web site: http://www.wxyz.com
Profile: WXYZ-TV is the ABC affiliate for the Detroit market. The station is owned by E.W. Scripps Co. WXYZ-TV broadcasts locally on channel 7.
TELEVISION STATION

WYAM-TV 32523
Owner: Decatur Communication Properties, LLC
Editorial: 1301 Central Pkwy Sw, Decatur, Alabama 35601-4817 **Tel:** 1 256 355-4567.
Email: valleytalktv51@yahoo.com
Profile: WYAM-TV is an independent station for the Huntsville, AL market. The station is owned by Decatur Communication Properties, LLC. WYAM-TV broadcasts locally on channel 51.
TELEVISION STATION

WYBE2-TV 608558
Owner: Independence Public Media
Editorial: 8200 Ridge Ave, Philadelphia, Pennsylvania 19128-2903 **Tel:** 1 215 483-3900.
Web site: http://www.mindtv.org
Profile: WYBE2-TV is an independent affiliate for the Philadelphia market. The station is owned by Independence Public Media. WYBE2-TV broadcasts locally on channel 35.2. WYBE2-TV airs international programming from Global MiND TV. WYBE2-TV is a multicast channel of WYBE-TV. A multicast channel is a separate channel that shares the bandwidth of the main station but can air unique programming.
TELEVISION STATION

WYBE3-TV 608560
Owner: Independence Public Media
Editorial: 8200 Ridge Ave, Philadelphia, Pennsylvania 19128-2903 **Tel:** 1 215 483-3900.
Web site: http://mindtv.org
Profile: WYBE3-TV is an independent affiliate for the Philadelphia market. The station is owned by Independence Public Media. WYBE3-TV broadcasts locally on channel 35.3. WYBE3-TV airs MHz Worldview programming. WYBE3-TV is a multicast channel of WYBE-TV. A multicast channel is a separate channel that shares the bandwidth of the main station but can air unique programming.
TELEVISION STATION

WYBE-TV 32371
Owner: Independence Public Media
Editorial: 441 N 5th St STE 200, Philadelphia, Pennsylvania 19128-2903 **Tel:** 1 215 483-3900.
Email: feedback@mindtv.org
Web site: http://www.independencemedia.org
Profile: WYBE-TV is the Mind Media Independence affiliate for the Philadelphia market. The station is owned by Independence Public Media. WYBE-TV broadcasts locally on channel 35.
TELEVISION STATION

WYBU-TV 32615
Owner: Christian Television Network
Editorial: 705 4th Pl, Phenix City, Alabama 36869-6913 **Tel:** 1 334 298-5916.
Web site: http://www.wybutv.com
Profile: WYBU-TV is an independent station for the Columbus, GA market. The station is owned by Christian Television Network. WYBU-TV broadcasts locally on channel 16.
TELEVISION STATION

WYCC2-TV 607078
Owner: City Colleges of Chicago
Editorial: 6258 S Union Ave, Chicago, Illinois 60621-2041 **Tel:** 1 773 838-7878.
Web site: http://www.wycc.org
Profile: WYCC2-TV is a PBS affiliate for the Chicago market. The station is owned by City Colleges of Chicago. WYCC-TV broadcasts locally on channel 20.2. It debuted in February 1983. The station broadcasts how-to programs, adult educational courses, college telecourses, children's programs, travel programs, drama, music, and PBS programming. WYCC2-TV is a multicast channel of WYCC-TV. A multicast channel is a separate channel that shares the bandwidth of the main station but can air unique programming.
TELEVISION STATION

WYCC-TV 32227
Owner: City Colleges of Chicago
Editorial: 6258 S Union Ave, Chicago, Illinois 60621-2041 **Tel:** 1 773 487-1327.
Web site: http://www.wycc.org
Profile: WYCC-TV is a PBS affiliate for the Chicago market. The station is owned by City Colleges of Chicago. WYCC-TV broadcasts locally on channel 20.
TELEVISION STATION

WYCW2-TV 621872
Owner: Nexstar Media Group, LLC
Editorial: 250 International Dr, Spartanburg, South Carolina 29303-6637 **Tel:** 1 864 576-7777.
Email: assignmentdesk@wspa.com
Web site: http://www.wspa.com

Profile: WYCW2-TV is a multicast channel of WYCW-TV. A multicast is a separate channel that shares the bandwith of the main station but can air unique programming. WYCW2-TV airs programming from WSPA-TV in the Spartanburg, SC market. The station is owned by Nexstar Media Group, LLC. WYCW2-TV broadcasts locally on channel 62.2.
TELEVISION STATION

WYCW-TV 32317
Owner: Nexstar Media Group, LLC
Editorial: 250 International Dr, Spartanburg, South Carolina 29303-6637 **Tel:** 1 864 576-7777.
Email: assignmentdesk@wspa.com
Web site: http://www.carolinascw.com
Profile: WYCW-TV is the CW affiliate for the Spartanburg, SC market. The station is owned by Nexstar Media Group, LLC. WYCW-TV broadcasts locally on channel 62.
TELEVISION STATION

WYDC-TV 32466
Owner: Vision Communications LLC
Editorial: 33 E Market St, Corning, New York 14830-2614 **Tel:** 1 607 937-5000.
Email: news@wydctv.com
Web site: http://wydc-tv.com/
Profile: WYDC-TV is the FOX affiliate for the Elmira, NY market. The station is owned by Vision Communications LLC. WYDC-TV broadcasts locally on channel 48.
TELEVISION STATION

WYES-TV 32228
Owner: Greater N.O. ETV Foundation
Editorial: 916 Navarre Ave, New Orleans, Louisiana 70124 **Tel:** 1 504 486-5511.
Email: info@wyes.org
Web site: http://www.wyes.org
Profile: WYES-TV is a PBS affiliate for the New Orleans market. The station is owned by the Greater N.O. ETV Foundation. WYES-TV broadcasts locally on channel 12.
TELEVISION STATION

WYFF-TV 32229
Owner: Hearst Television Inc.
Editorial: 505 Rutherford St, Greenville, South Carolina 29609-5313 **Tel:** 1 864 242-4404.
Email: newstips@wyff4.com
Web site: http://www.wyff4.com
Profile: WYFF-TV is the NBC affiliate for the Greenville, SC market. The station is owned by Hearst Television Inc. WYFF-TV broadcasts locally on channel 4.
TELEVISION STATION

WYFX-TV 72605
Owner: Nexstar Media Group, LLC
Editorial: 3930 Sunset Blvd, Youngstown, Ohio 44512-1307 **Tel:** 1 330 782-1144.
Email: assignment@wkbn.com
Web site: http://wkbn.com/
Profile: WYFX-TV is the FOX affiliate for Youngstown, OH market. The station is owned by Nexstar Media Group, LLC. WYFX-TV broadcasts locally on channel 17.
TELEVISION STATION

WYHB-TV 235410
Owner: Benns(Ying)
Editorial: 4278B Bonny Oaks Dr, Chattanooga, Tennessee 37406-1666 **Tel:** 1 423 698-8839.
Email: wyhbtv44@gmail.com
Web site: http://www.wyhbtv44.com
Profile: WYHB-TV is an independent station for the Chattanooga, TN market. The station is owned by Ying Benns. WYHB-TV broadcasts locally on channel 44. The best way to send information is by fax.
TELEVISION STATION

WYIN-TV 32230
Owner: Northwest Indiana Public Broadcasting, Inc.
Editorial: 8625 Indiana Pl, Merrillville, Indiana 46410-6369 **Tel:** 1 219 756-5656.
Email: news@lakeshorepublicmedia.org
Web site: http://lakeshorepublicmedia.org
Profile: WYIN-TV is the PBS affiliate for the Chicago market. The station is owned by Northwest Indiana Public Broadcasting, Inc. WYIN-TV broadcasts locally on channel 56.
TELEVISION STATION

WYMT-TV 32231
Owner: Gray Television, Inc.
Editorial: 199 Black Gold Blvd, Hazard, Kentucky 41701-2602 **Tel:** 1 606 436-5757.
Email: newstip@wymtnews.com
Web site: http://www.wymt.com/
Profile: WYMT-TV is the CBS affiliate for the Lexington, KY, market. It is owned by Gray Television Inc. WYMT-TV broadcasts locally on channel 57.
TELEVISION STATION

WYOU-TV 32232
Owner: Mission Broadcasting
Editorial: 409 Lackawanna Ave, Scranton, Pennsylvania 18503-2062 **Tel:** 1 570 823-2828.
Email: newsdesk@pahomepage.com
Web site: http://www.pahomepage.com
Profile: WYOU-TV is the CBS affiliate for the Wilkes-Barre and Scranton, PA market. The station is owned by Mission Broadcasting. WYOU-TV airs locally on channel 22.
TELEVISION STATION

WYPX-TV 32324
Owner: ION Media Networks
Editorial: 1 Charles Blvd Ste 5, Guilderland, New York 12084-9568 **Tel:** 1 518 464-0143.
Web site: http://iontelevision.com
Profile: WYPX-TV is the ION Television affiliate for the Albany-Schenectady-Troy, NY market. The station is owned by ION Media Networks. WYPX-TV broadcasts locally on channel 50.
TELEVISION STATION

WYTU-TV 390590
Owner: Weigel Broadcasting Co.
Editorial: 809 S 60th St, Milwaukee, Wisconsin 53214-3363 **Tel:** 1 414 777-5800.
Profile: WYTU-TV is the Telemundo affiliate for the Milwaukee market. The station is owned by Weigel Broadcasting Co. WYTU-TV broadcasts locally on channel 63.
TELEVISION STATION

WYTV-TV 32233
Owner: Nexstar Media Group, LLC
Editorial: 3930 Sunset Blvd, Youngstown, Ohio 44512-1307 **Tel:** 1 330 782-1144.
Email: assignment@wytv.com
Web site: http://www.wytv.com
Profile: WYTV-TV is the ABC affiliate for the Youngstown, OH market. The station is owned by Nexstar Media Group, LLC. WYTV-TV broadcasts locally on channel 33.
TELEVISION STATION

WYYW-TV 882414
Owner: Evansville Low Power Partnership
Editorial: 300 SE Riverside Dr Ste 100, Evansville, Indiana 47713-1036
Email: info@wtsntv.com
Web site: http://www.wtsntv.com
Profile: WYYW-TV is the MyNetworkTV affiliate for the Evansville, IN market. The station is owned by Evansville Low Power Partnership. WYYW-TV broadcasts locally on channel 15. The station broadcasts community programming and local events in the Evansville, Indiana area.
TELEVISION STATION

WYZZ-TV 32234
Owner: Nexstar Broadcasting Group
Editorial: 3131 N University St, Peoria, Illinois 61604-1316 **Tel:** 1 309 688-3131.
Email: news@wmbd.com
Web site: http://www.centralillinoisproud.com
Profile: WYZZ-TV is the FOX affiliate for the Peoria, IL/Bloomington IL market. The station is owned by Nexstar Broadcasting Group. WYZZ-TV broadcasts locally on channel 43.
TELEVISION STATION

WZDC-TV 133905
Owner: ZGS Communications
Editorial: 3939 Campbell Ave Ste 100, Arlington, Virginia 22206-3441 **Tel:** 1 703 820-8333.
Email: info@holaciudad.com
Web site: http://washington.holaciudad.com
Profile: WZDC-TV is the Telemundo affiliate for the Washington D.C. Metro Area market. The station is owned by ZGS Communications. WZDC-TV broadcasts locally on channel 25.
TELEVISION STATION

WZDX3-TV 800814
Owner: Grant Communications
Editorial: 1309 Memorial Pkwy NW, Huntsville, Alabama 35801-5932 **Tel:** 1 256 533-5454.
Web site: http://www.fox54.com
Profile: WZDX3-TV is a multicast channel of WZDX-TV. A multicast channel is a separate channel that shares the bandwith of the main station but can air unique programming. WZDX3-TV is the Me-TV Network for the Huntsville, AL market. The station is owned by Grant Communications. WZDX3-TV broadcasts locally on channel 54.3. The station launched April 17, 2012.
TELEVISION STATION

WZDX-TV 32235
Owner: Nexstar Broadcasting Group, Inc.
Editorial: 1309 Memorial Pkwy NW, Huntsville, Alabama 35801-5932 **Tel:** 1 256 533-5454.
Email: news@rocketcitynow.com
Web site: http://www.rocketcitynow.com
Profile: WZDX-TV is the Fox affiliate for the Huntsville, AL market. The station is owned by Nexstar Broadcasting Group. WZDX-TV broadcasts locally on channel 54.
TELEVISION STATION

WZME2-TV 612950
Owner: NRJ TV, LLC
Editorial: 7 Wakeley St, Seymour, Connecticut 06483-2819 **Tel:** 1 203 881-1153.
Web site: http://www.wzmetv.com
Profile: WZME2-TV is a multicast of WZME-TV. A multicast channel is a separate channel that shares the bandwith of the main station but can air unique programming. WZME2-TV airs Retro Television Network programming in the New York City market. The station is owned by NRJ TV, LLC. WZME2-TV broadcasts locally on channel 43.2.
TELEVISION STATION

WZME-TV 32506
Owner: NRJ TV, LLC
Editorial: 7 Wakeley St, Seymour, Connecticut 06483-2819 **Tel:** 1 203 881-1153.
Web site: http://www.wzmetv.com

Profile: WZME-TV is the Me-TV affiliate for the New York City market. The station is owned by NRJ TV, LLC. WZME-TV broadcasts locally on channel 43.
TELEVISION STATION

WZPA-TV 588374
Owner: Una Vez Mas Television Group
Editorial: 1701 N Market St Ste 500, Dallas, Texas 75202-2001 **Tel:** 1 214 754-7008.
Web site: http://www.aztecaamerica.com
Profile: WZPA-TV is the Azteca America affiliate for the Philadelphia market. The station is owned by Una Vez Mas Television Group. WZPA-TV broadcasts locally on channel 33. All PSAs should be sent in BETA format.
TELEVISION STATION

WZPX-TV 32548
Owner: ION Media Networks
Editorial: 2610 Horizon Dr SE, Ste 135, Grand Rapids, Michigan 49546 **Tel:** 1 616 222-4343.
Web site: http://www.wzpxtv.com
Profile: WZPX-TV is the local ION Television affiliate for the Grand Rapids, MI market. The station is owned by ION Media Networks. WZPX-TV broadcasts locally on channel 43.
TELEVISION STATION

WZRB-TV 324787
Owner: ION Media Networks
Editorial: 1747 Cushman Dr, Columbia, South Carolina 29204-1656 **Tel:** 1 803 714-2347.
Web site: http://ionmedianetworks.com
Profile: WZRB-TV is a CW affiliate for the Columbia, SC market. The station is owned by ION Media Networks. WZRB-TV broadcasts locally on channel 47.
TELEVISION STATION

WZTD-TV 618074
Owner: ZGS Communications
Editorial: 23 Sesame St, Richmond, Virginia 23235-3713 **Tel:** 1 804 330-3155.
Web site: http://www.holaciudad.com
Profile: WZDT-TV is a Telemundo network affiliate located in Richmond, VA. The station airs locally on channel 45 and broadcasts to the greater Richmond, VA area. The station is owned by ZGS Communications.
TELEVISION STATION

WZTV-TV 32236
Owner: Sinclair Broadcast Group, Inc.
Editorial: 631 Mainstream Dr, Nashville, Tennessee 37228-1203 **Tel:** 1 615 259-5617.
Email: news@fox17.com
Web site: http://www.fox17.com
Profile: WZTV-TV is the FOX affiliate for the Nashville, TN market. The station is owned by Sinclair Broadcast Group, Inc. WZTV-TV broadcasts locally on channel 17.
TELEVISION STATION

WZVN-TV 31829
Owner: Montclair Communications
Editorial: 3719 Central Ave, Fort Myers, Florida 33901-8220 **Tel:** 1 239 939-2020.
Email: newstips@abc-7.com
Web site: http://www.abc-7.com
Profile: WZVN-TV is the ABC network affiliate for the Fort Myers-Naples, FL market. The station is owned by Montclair Communications. WZVN-TV broadcasts locally on channel 26.
TELEVISION STATION

WZZM2-TV 618970
Owner: TEGNA Inc.
Editorial: 645 3 Mile Rd NW, Grand Rapids, Michigan 49544-1601 **Tel:** 1 616 785-1313.
Email: news@wzzm13.com
Web site: http://www.wzzm13.com
Profile: WZZM2-TV is a multicast of WZZM-TV. A multicast channel is a separate channel that shares the bandwith of the main station but can air unique programming. WZZM2-TV airs weather programming from 13 On Target Weather Network in the Grand Rapids, MI market. The station is owned by TEGNA Inc. WZZM2-TV broadcasts locally on channel 13.2.
TELEVISION STATION

WZZM-TV 32237
Owner: TEGNA Inc.
Editorial: 645 3 Mile Rd NW, Grand Rapids, Michigan 49544-1601 **Tel:** 1 616 785-1313.
Email: news@wzzm13.com
Web site: http://www.wzzm13.com
Profile: WZZM-TV is the ABC affiliate for the Grand Rapids, MI market. The station is owned by TEGNA Inc. WZZM-TV broadcasts locally on channel 13.
TELEVISION STATION

XDTV-TV 75806
Owner: Entravision Communications Corp.
Editorial: 5770 Ruffin Rd, San Diego, California 92123-1013 **Tel:** 1 858 576-1919.
Web site: http://www.mytv13.com
Profile: XDTV-TV is the MyNetworkTV for the San Diego market. The station is owned by Entravision Communications Corp. XDTV-TV broadcasts locally on channel 13.
TELEVISION STATION

XEWT-TV 32313
Owner: Televisa/Energy Communications Corp.
Editorial: 637 3rd Ave, Chula Vista, California 91910-5707 **Tel:** 1 619 585-9398.
Web site: http://www.xewt12.com
Profile: XEWT-TV is an independent network affiliate in the San Diego market. The station is owned by Televisa/Energy Communications Corp. XEWT-TV broadcasts locally on channel 12.
TELEVISION STATION

XHAS-TV 32329
Owner: Entravision Communications Corp.
Editorial: 5770 Ruffin Rd, San Diego, California 92123-1013 **Tel:** 1 858 856-1919.
Web site: https://noticiasya.com/san-diego
Profile: XHAS-TV is the Azteca América network affiliate in the San Diego and Tijuana markets. The station is owned by Entravision Communications Corp. XHAS-TV broadcasts locally on channel 33.
TELEVISION STATION

XHDTV-TV 882013
Owner: Entravision Communications Corp.
Editorial: 5770 Ruffin Rd, San Diego, California 92123-1013 **Tel:** 1 858 576-1919.
Web site: http://www.mytv13.com/
Profile: XHDTV-TV is the MundoFOX affiliate for the San Diego market. The station is owned by Entravision Communications Corp. XHDTV-TV broadcasts to the Tijuana–San Diego area on channel 49. The station does not have a news department.
TELEVISION STATION

XHRIO-TV 881792
Owner: Entravision Communications Corp.
Editorial: 801 N Jackson Rd, McAllen, Texas 78501-9306 **Tel:** 1 956 687-4848.
Email: newsroom@foxrio2.com
Web site: https://www.foxrio2.com/
Profile: XHRIO-TV is the MundoFOX affiliate for the Brownsville - McAllen, TX market. The station is owned by Entravision Communications Corp. XHRIO-TV broadcasts to the Rio Grande Valley area on channel 2. The station is known as MundoFox Valle. The station does not have a news department.
TELEVISION STATION

Cable

10 News 34675
Owner: McGraw-Hill Companies
Editorial: 4600 Air Way, San Diego, California 92102-2528 **Tel:** 1 619 237-1010.
Email: kgtv_web@10news.com
Web site: http://www.10news.com
Profile: 10 News provides round-the-clock news, weather and sports distributed to cable systems throughout metropolitan San Diego and Southern California. News produced and provided by KGTV-TV San Diego.
REGIONAL CABLE NETWORK

A&E 34580
Owner: A+E Networks
Editorial: 235 E 45th St, New York, New York 10017-3305 **Tel:** 1 212 210-1400.
Web site: http://www.aetv.com
Profile: National arts and entertainment network, producing a wide array of original programming from mysteries to award-winning biographies of famous individuals. Features documentaries and series covering everything from crime and justice to transportation and flight.
CABLE NETWORK

ABC NewsOne 34777
Owner: Walt Disney Co.
Editorial: 47 W 66th St, New York, New York 10023-6201 **Tel:** 1 212 456-4110.
Web site: http://www.abcnews.com
Profile: ABC NewsOne is a 24-hour syndicated news feed service of the ABC Television Network. Provides repackaged audio and video feeds of developing news, sports and weather events to over 200 affiliates throughout the country, along with foreign news agencies and other ABC News programs.
CABLE NETWORK

ABC NewsOne - Washington Bureau 34854
Editorial: 1717 Desales St NW, Washington, District Of Columbia 20036-4407 **Tel:** 1 202 222-7525.
CABLE NETWORK

AccentHealth 34711
Owner: AccentHealth, Inc.
Editorial: 7844 Woodland Center Blvd, Tampa, Florida 33614-2409 **Tel:** 1 813 349-7127.
Web site: http://www.accenthealth.com
Profile: AccentHealth provides national coverage in 10,500 waiting rooms of healthcare offices across the United States. Owned by CNN and AccentHealth, the network aims to provide informative programming for patients at the point of care. PR professionals are advised to contact the network's staff by e-mail.
CABLE NETWORK

AccentHealth - New York Bureau 80298
Editorial: 747 3rd Ave Fl 14, New York, New York 10017-2803 **Tel:** 1 212 763-5100.
CABLE NETWORK

The Africa Channel 355267
Editorial: 11135 Magnolia Blvd Ste 110, North Hollywood, California 91601-3819 **Tel:** 1 818 655-9977.
Email: info@theafricachannel.com
Web site: http://www.theafricachannel.com
Profile: The Africa Channel is an all-English, high-quality "all Africa" television network. All of the network's programming is filmed, produced, and originally aired in Africa, reformatted for American audiences. Programming is produced in conjunction with Weller/Grossman Productions.
CABLE NETWORK

AIB/Atlanta Interfaith Broadcasters 524401
Owner: Atlanta Interfaith Broadcasters, Inc.
Editorial: 1075 Spring St NW, Atlanta, Georgia 30309-3817 **Tel:** 1 404 892-0454.
Email: production@aibtv.com
Web site: https://aibtv.com
Profile: Atlanta Interfaith Broadcasters, Inc. (AIB) seeks to enhance the spiritual, intellectual and social well-being of its viewers by delivering exceptional faith-based, educational and public service programming to the greater metropolitan Atlanta community. Viewers find liberal and conservative viewpoints, as well as Christian, Muslim, Jewish, Buddhists, Hindus and others presenting their views. AIB's programming addresses social concerns, promotes community awareness and fosters discussion about issues that impact us all.
REGIONAL CABLE NETWORK

Alabama Cable Network 740859
Editorial: 7619 Highway 78, Dora, Alabama 35062-2121 **Tel:** 1 888 242-8517.
Web site: http://alabamacablenetwork.com
Profile: The Alabama Cable Network produces programming for Alabama college and high school football.
REGIONAL CABLE NETWORK

Al-Arabiya TV - New York Bureau 619653
Owner: MBC Group
Editorial: 405 E 42nd St, New York, New York 10017-3507 **Tel:** 1 212 355-5845.
Web site: http://www.alarabiya.net
Profile: Arabic language provider of news and current affairs worldwide.
CABLE NETWORK

Alhurra 354616
Owner: Middle East Broadcasting Networks
Editorial: 7600 Boston Blvd, Springfield, Virginia 22153-3136 **Tel:** 1 703 852-9000.
Email: comments@alhurra.com
Web site: http://www.alhurra.com
Profile: This commercial-free channel is devoted to broadcasting news, talk shows and information programms on health, entertainment, sports, fashion, science and technology. The channel is part of the Middle East Broadcasting Networks and financed by the US government.
CABLE NETWORK

Alhurra-Iraq 354621
Owner: Middle East Broadcasting Networks
Editorial: 7600 Boston Blvd, Springfield, Virginia 22153-3136 **Tel:** 1 703 852-9000.
Email: comments@alhurra.com
Web site: http://www.alhurra.com
Profile: Satellite channel broadcasts news from Alhurra, as well as news, talk shows and informational programming specifically dealing with Iraq. The channel is part of the Middle East Broadcasting Networks, Inc. and financed by the US government.
CABLE NETWORK

Altitude Sports and Entertainment 350120
Editorial: 1000 Chopper Cir, Denver, Colorado 80204-5805 **Tel:** 1 303 405-1100.
Web site: http://www.altitude.tv
Profile: Seen in more than 3.1 million homes in a 10-state territory, Altitude is the television home of the Colorado Avalanche, Denver Nuggets, Colorado Rapids, Colorado Mammoth, Colorado Eagles, the Big Sky Conference, the Rocky Mountain Athletic Conference, ESPN Syndication (including Big 12 Conference and Western Athletic Conference events) as well as local and regional sports, entertainment and public service programming. A full list of Altitude programming and other information is available on the website.
REGIONAL CABLE NETWORK

AMC 34603
Owner: AMC Networks Inc.
Editorial: 11 Penn Plz, New York, New York 10001-2006 **Tel:** 1 516 803-4300.
Email: info-amc@amc.com
Web site: http://www.amc.com
Profile: Launched in 1984, AMC is a 24-hour, movie-based network, dedicated to the American movie fan. The network, which reaches over 90 million homes, offers a comprehensive library of popular movies and a critically-acclaimed slate of original programming.
CABLE NETWORK

American Forces Network Broadcast Center 557485
Editorial: 23755 Z St, Riverside, California 92518-2077 **Tel:** 1 951 413-2351.
Email: dmajointdesk@dma.mil
Web site: http://myafn.dodmedia.osd.mil
Profile: American Forces Network Broadcast Center (AFN-BC) operates and provides multi-channel broadcast quality radio and television services and expanded internal information products to all Department of Defense members and their families stationed overseas, on contingency operations, and onboard Navy ships around the world. All entertainment, news, sports and information programming is acquired and distributed by AFN based on the popularity of programs within the specific Department of Defense audience demographics, the unique interests of military audiences and AFN scheduling needs.
CABLE NETWORK

American Heroes Channel 34723
Owner: Discovery Communications, Inc.
Editorial: 1 Discovery Pl, Silver Spring, Maryland 20910-3354 **Tel:** 1 240 662-3709.
Web site: http://www.ahctv.com
Profile: Formerly known as Discovery Wings Channel and the Military Channel, American Heroes Channel focuses on all aspects of the armed forces, military strategies and personnel throughout the ages. The channel has formed partnerships with the USO, the National D-Day Museum and the Congressional Medal of Honor Foundation to develop programming for the channel as well as educational campaigns and public service announcements. ** A vast majority of programming aired on Discovery is developed by producers outside the network. As a result, it is suggested that most shows should be contacted via network headquarters in Silver Spring. **
CABLE NETWORK

Animal Planet 34645
Owner: Discovery Communications, Inc.
Editorial: 1 Discovery Pl, Silver Spring, Maryland 20910-3354 **Tel:** 1 240 662-2000.
Web site: http://www.animalplanet.com
Profile: Launched in October 1996, Animal Planet is the only television network dedicated exclusively to the connection between humans and animals. Animal Planet gives men and women, parents and children a co-viewing experience that inspires them with the wow, whoa and wonders of the animal kingdom. The network's original programming brings together people of all ages by tapping into a fundamental fascination with animals and providing a diverse mix of programming including original movies, adventure series, sports, drama and sitcoms. The network has more than 88 million subscribers.
CABLE NETWORK

Animal Planet - New York Bureau 652389
Editorial: 850 3Rd Ave Ste 1004, New York, New York 10022-7256 **Tel:** 1 212 548-5555.
CABLE NETWORK

Antena 3 Television - New York Bureau 619966
Editorial: 450 W 33rd St, Fl 14, New York, New York 10001-2626 **Tel:** 1 212 506-6187.
Web site: http://www.antena3tv.es
CABLE NETWORK

Arizona NewsChannel 34687
Owner: Cox Communications, Inc.
Editorial: 5555 N 7th Ave, Phoenix, Arizona 85013-1701 **Tel:** 1 602 207-3333.
Email: 3tvnews@azfamily.com
Web site: http://www.azfamily.com
Profile: 24-hour cable news channel serving the Phoenix metropolitan area and providing extensive coverage of local news, weather and sports. News programming is produced by KTVK-TV in Phoenix.
REGIONAL CABLE NETWORK

ASPiRE 816582
Owner: Magic Johnson Enterprises
Editorial: 2077 Convention Center Concourse Ste 300, Atlanta, Georgia 30337-4210
Email: info@magicjent.com
Web site: http://aspiretv.tv
Profile: ASPiRE is a cable network delivering entertainment and programming catered to African-Americans families. The network will feature a diverse slate of original and acquired programming in the categories of movies, documentaries, short films, music, comedy, visual and performing arts, faith and inspirational programs. The network launched in late June 2012.
CABLE NETWORK

Associated Press Television News 33089
Editorial: 1100 13th St NW, Washington, District Of Columbia 20005-4051 **Tel:** 1 202 641-9000.
Email: info@ap.org
Web site: http://www.aptn.com
Profile: The Associated Press Television News serves as television news agency with bureaus in over 80 cities around the globe. Covers not just hard news - there are also thousands of features, plus stories on entertainment, people, culture, city scenes, lifestyles etc. More than 1,000 U.S. media Web sites and 4,300 television and radio stations depend on the Associated Press for text stories, audio, video, graphics, and photo services for building their on-air and online products and services. Founded in 1848, AP is the world's oldest and largest newsgathering organization, serving more than one billion people worldwide. Their broadcast division based in Washington, D.C.
CABLE NETWORK

Associated Press Television News - Albany Bureau 781372
Editorial: 645 Albany Shaker Rd, Albany, New York 12211-1158 **Tel:** 1 518 458-7821.
Email: apalbany@ap.org
CABLE NETWORK

The Associated Press Television News - Atlanta Bureau 788040
Editorial: 101 Marietta St NW Ste 2450, Atlanta, Georgia 30303-2772 **Tel:** 1 404 522-8971.
CABLE NETWORK

Associated Press Television News - Chicago Bureau 617280
Editorial: 10 S Wacker Dr Ste 2500, Chicago, Illinois 60606-7491 **Tel:** 1 312 781-0500.
Email: chifax@ap.org
CABLE NETWORK

Associated Press Television News - Dallas Bureau 832420
Editorial: 4851 Lyndon B Johnson Fwy Ste 300, Dallas, Texas 75244-6047 **Tel:** 1 972 991-2100.
Email: aptexas@ap.org
CABLE NETWORK

Associated Press Television News - Los Angeles Bureau 33129
Editorial: 221 S Figueroa St Ste 300, Los Angeles, California 90012-2552 **Tel:** 1 213 626-1200.
Email: losangeles@ap.org
CABLE NETWORK

Associated Press Television News - New York Bureau 33128
Editorial: 450 W 33rd St Fl 14, New York, New York 10001-2626 **Tel:** 1 212 621-1670.
CABLE NETWORK

Associated Press Television News - San Francisco Bureau 386844
Editorial: 303 2nd St Ste N680, San Francisco, California 94107-3643 **Tel:** 1 415 495-1708.
Email: sanfrancisco@ap.org
CABLE NETWORK

AWE 358704
Owner: Herring Broadcasting, Inc.
Editorial: 4575 Morena Blvd, San Diego, California 92117-3649 **Tel:** 1 858 270-6900.
Email: info@herringbroadcasting.com
Web site: http://www.awetv.com
Profile: AWE is a 24/7 high definition cable television network devoted to taking viewers on a journey of how wealth is achieved, used and enjoyed. AWE defines wealth as an abundance of good, not just money.
CABLE NETWORK

AXS TV 523047
Owner: AXS TV
Editorial: 320 S Walton St, Dallas, Texas 75226-1972 **Tel:** 1 214 698-3800.
Web site: http://www.axs.tv
Profile: AXS TV (formerly HDNet) launched September 2001 by co-founders Mark Cuban, (owner of the Dallas Mavericks), and Philip Garvin of Colorado Studios. The network produces and televises pop culture, music, fashion and more. In July 2012, HDNet rebranded to AXS TV.
CABLE NETWORK

AXS TV - Denver Bureau 523057
Editorial: 8269 E 23Rd Ave, Denver, Colorado 80238-3556 **Tel:** 1 303 542-5600.
Profile: AXS TV Denver bureau.
CABLE NETWORK

BabyFirstTV 475980
Owner: BabyFirstTV, LLC
Editorial: 10390 Santa Monica Blvd, Los Angeles, California 90025-5058 **Tel:** 1 888 251-2229.
Web site: http://www.babyfirsttv.com
Profile: BabyFirstTV is the first cable and satellite channel in the United States dedicated to providing innovative programming designed to inspire baby's learning in a delightful and engaging way. Programming is developed by child development experts and specifically tailored to meet the needs of babies and toddlers up to three years of age in a safe, positive, commercial-free learning environment. In addition to original children's series, BabyFirstTV offers programming from popular children's DVDs, a series for parents offering tips and advice on various parenting topics and interactive tools to help parents better understand the developmental benefits each program offers their babies.
CABLE NETWORK

Bay News 9 34714
Owner: Charter Communications
Editorial: 700 Carillon Pkwy Ste 9, Saint Petersburg, Florida 33716-1123 **Tel:** 1 727 329-2400.
Email: desk@charter.com
Web site: http://www.baynews9.com
Profile: Regional cable news network providing 24 hours of reports for the Tampa and St. Petersburg, Florida area. Format is an around-the-clock, repeating news wheel with frequent updates on local and national news, weather, sports, health, technology, and information.
REGIONAL CABLE NETWORK

BBC America 34718
Owner: British Broadcasting Corp.
Editorial: 1120 Avenue of the Americas Fl 5, New York, New York 10036-6700 **Tel:** 1 212 705-9300.
Web site: http://www.bbcamerica.com
Profile: BBC America delivers U.S. audiences high-quality, innovative and intelligent programming. Established in 1998, it has been the launch pad for talent embraced by American mainstream pop culture, including Ricky Gervais, Gordon Ramsay, Graham Norton, and successful programming formats including ground-breaking non-scripted television like Top Gear and top-rated science-fiction like Doctor Who. Owned by BBC Worldwide, the commercial arm of the BBC, BBC America has attracted both critical acclaim and major awards including an Emmy, four Golden Globes and ten Peabody Awards. The channel attracts one of cable's most affluent and educated audiences and is available on digital cable and satellite TV in more than 68 million homes. There is no original news programming on BBC America; news is produced by BBC in London.
CABLE NETWORK

BBC/British Broadcasting Corporation 86893
Owner: British Broadcasting Corp.
Editorial: 1120 Avenue of the Americas Fl 5, New York, New York 10036-6700
Email: bbcnews24@bbc.co.uk
Web site: http://www.bbc.com
Profile: A worldwide leader in program and news production since the 1920s. It provides a wide range of distinctive programs and services for everyone, free of commercial interests and political bias. They include television, radio, national, local, children's, educational, language and other services for key interest groups.
CABLE NETWORK

BBC/British Broadcasting Corporation - Los Angeles Bureau 684684
Editorial: 10351 Santa Monica Blvd Ste 250, Los Angeles, California 90025-6952 **Tel:** 1 310 228-1001.
CABLE NETWORK

BBC/British Broadcasting Corporation - Miami Bureau 457620
Editorial: 255 Alhambra Cir Fl 10, Coral Gables, Florida 33134-7411 **Tel:** 1 305 461-6999.
CABLE NETWORK

BBC/British Broadcasting Corporation - New York Bureau 86895
Editorial: United Nations Room C-309, New York, New York 10017 **Tel:** 1 212 688-6266.
CABLE NETWORK

BBC/British Broadcasting Corporation - Washington Bureau 86898
Editorial: 2000 M St NW Ste 800, Washington, District Of Columbia 20036-3386 **Tel:** 1 202 223-2050.
CABLE NETWORK

The Berns Bureau 79017
Editorial: 50 Constitution Ave NE, Washington, District Of Columbia 20002 **Tel:** 1 202 314-5165.
Profile: Independent news service that reports on Washington news and news makers for radio stations and networks. The bureau primarily focuses on stories regarding agricultural news and issues.
CABLE NETWORK

BET/Black Entertainment Television 34572
Owner: Viacom Inc.
Editorial: 1540 Broadway, New York, New York 10036-4039 **Tel:** 1 212 205-3000.
Web site: http://www.bet.com
Profile: BET/Black Entertainment Television is a 24-hour entertainment and news network geared toward African Americans ages 18 to 34. It features a variety of family-oriented programming. The network does not have any daily or weekly shows that accept guests. All inquiries can go to the Public Relations Manager. BET moved its headquarters to New York City in July 2017.
CABLE NETWORK

Big Ten Network 491858
Owner: Big Ten Conference
Editorial: 600 W Chicago Ave Ste 875, Chicago, Illinois 60654-2531 **Tel:** 1 312 665-0700.
Web site: http://btn.com
Profile: The Big Ten Network, launched August 30, 2007, is dedicated to covering the Big Ten Conference and its 11 member institutions. It provides unprecedented access to an extensive schedule of conference sports events and shows; original programs in academics, the arts and sciences; campus activities and associated personalities.
CABLE NETWORK

Biz Television 609547
Editorial: 810 E Abram St, Arlington, Texas 76010-1277 **Tel:** 1 817 274-1609.
Email: info@biztelevision.com
Web site: http://www.biztelevision.com
Profile: Biz Television is a national television network that focuses on managing money in all phases of life. The programming is distinctive, educational and entertaining and addresses the broad range of personal planning, finance, money and investment needs of individuals, families, investors and entrepreneurs.
CABLE NETWORK

Bloomberg Television 33078
Owner: Bloomberg L.P.
Editorial: 731 Lexington Ave, New York, New York 10022-1331 **Tel:** 1 212 318-2000.
Email: release@bloomberg.net
Web site: http://www.bloomberg.com/live
Profile: A 24-hour business and financial news channel delivering tools and information for businesses and investors. Shown via 10 networks in seven languages, Bloomberg Television reaches more than 310 million homes around the world. The network utilizes world-class resources to present up-to-the-minute market coverage, and features anchors and journalists who deliver news with added perspectives and analyses.
CABLE NETWORK

Bloomberg Television - Beijing Bureau 775649
Owner: Bloomberg L.P.
Editorial: Winland IFC, Beijing 100033
Profile: A 24-hour business and financial news channel delivering tools and information for businesses and investors. Shown via 10 networks in seven languages, Bloomberg Television reaches more than 200 million homes around the world. The network utilizes world-class resources to present up-to-the-minute market coverage, and features anchors and journalists who deliver news with added perspectives and analyses.
CABLE NETWORK

Bloomberg Television - Hong Kong Bureau 721314
Editorial: Fl 25 Cheung Kong Centre, 2 Queen's Rd, Central, Hong Kong **Tel:** 852 29 776600.
CABLE NETWORK

Bloomberg Television - London Bureau 483925
Editorial: 39-45 Finsbury Square, London, England EC2A 1PQ **Tel:** 44 20 73307460.
Email: newsalert@bloomberg.net
Profile: Bloomberg Television London bureau.
CABLE NETWORK

Bloomberg Television - Los Angeles Bureau 231617
Editorial: 6500 Wilshire Blvd Ste 2360, Los Angeles, California 90048-4916 **Tel:** 1 310 201-3400.
Profile: Bloomberg Television Los Angeles bureau.
CABLE NETWORK

Bloomberg Television - San Francisco Bureau 778746
Editorial: 3 Pier Ste 101, San Francisco, California 94111-2036 **Tel:** 1 415 617-7100.
Profile: This is the San Francisco bureau for Bloomberg Television Network. To reach the staff, call the newsroom and ask for them by name to be transferred.
CABLE NETWORK

Bloomberg Television - Singapore Bureau 829388
Editorial: 12th Floor Capital Square, 23 Church Street, Singapore 49481 **Tel:** 65 62121200.
CABLE NETWORK

Bloomberg Television - Tokyo Bureau 231125
Editorial: 2-3-2 Marunouchi Chiyoda-ku, Tokyo 1000005 **Tel:** 81 332018900.
CABLE NETWORK

Bloomberg Television - Washington Bureau 33126
Editorial: 1399 New York Ave NW Fl 11, Washington, District Of Columbia 20005-4749 **Tel:** 1 202 624-1800.
CABLE NETWORK

Bravo 34604
Owner: NBC Universal
Editorial: 30 Rockefeller Plz Fl 46, New York, New York 10112-0015 **Tel:** 1 212 664-4444.
Email: bravofeedback@nbc.com
Web site: http://www.bravotv.com
Profile: Bravo is an arts and culture network featuring a variety of programs presented in an original and engaging way. Currently seen in more than 76 million homes, Bravo is the television destination for viewers who want creativity, experimentation and innovation. The network offers programming with a unique point of view, featuring original series and specials, feature films (both independent and mainstream) and performance specials and compelling documentary series.
CABLE NETWORK

Bravo - Los Angeles Bureau 736675
Owner: NBC Universal
Editorial: 10 Universal City Plz, Universal City, California 91608-1002
CABLE NETWORK

Bright House Local on Demand 560587
Owner: Charter Communications
Editorial: 700 Carillon Pkwy Ste 9, Saint Petersburg, Florida 33716-1123 **Tel:** 1 727 329-2300.
Web site: http://www.baynews9.com/localondemand.html
Profile: Local On Demand offers news features, sports, travel, entertainment and food programming. Viewers can explore destinations for local daytrips, take a virtual tour of a local museum, discover a new restaurant, or watch a long-form interview with one of their favorite stars.
REGIONAL CABLE NETWORK

The California Channel 34685
Owner: California Channel(The)
Editorial: 1121 L St, Ste 110, Sacramento, California 95814 **Tel:** 1 916 444-9792.
Email: contact_us@calchannel.com
Web site: http://www.calchannel.com
Profile: Nonprofit public affairs cable network for the state of California. Transmits live and taped coverage of state government and legislative proceedings to serve homes, schools and businesses throughout the entire state.
REGIONAL CABLE NETWORK

Capitol News Service 722027
Editorial: 310 N Monroe St, Tallahassee, Florida 32301-7622 **Tel:** 1 850 224-5546.
Web site: http://www.flanews.com
Profile: Capitol News Service provides coverage of Florida's Capitol to state and national news outlets.
CABLE NETWORK

The Cartoon Network 34602
Owner: Time Warner Inc.
Editorial: 1050 Techwood Dr NW, Atlanta, Georgia 30318-5604 **Tel:** 1 404 827-1700.
Email: cartooncomments@turner.com
Web site: http://www.cartoonnetwork.com
Profile: The 24-hour network is devoted to providing cartoon and animation programming. Drawing from the world's largest cartoon library, Cartoon Network showcases unique original cartoon ventures. The network is currently seen in more than 97 million U.S. homes and 166 countries around the world, offering cable service in original, acquired and classic entertainment for youth and families.
CABLE NETWORK

Cartoon Network - Burbank Bureau 759077
Owner: Time Warner Inc.
Editorial: 300 N 3Rd St, Burbank, California 91502-1107
Email: cartooncomments@turner.com
Web site: http://www.cartoonnetwork.com
CABLE NETWORK

Cartoon Network - New York Bureau 759220
Owner: Time Warner Inc.
Editorial: 1 Time Warner Ctr Fl 19, New York, New York 10019-8017 **Tel:** 1 212 2750000.
Email: cartooncomments@turner.com
Web site: http://www.cartoonnetwork.com
CABLE NETWORK

Catholic TV 877532
Owner: iCatholic Media, Inc.
Editorial: 34 Chestnut St, Watertown, Massachusetts 02472-2339 **Tel:** 1 617 923-0220.
Email: info@catholictv.com
Web site: http://www.catholictv.com
Profile: CatholicTV is the largest diocesan Catholic television station in the world and presents a blend of spiritual, educational, and entertaining programming.
CABLE NETWORK

CBN/Christian Broadcasting Network 34784
Owner: Christian Broadcasting Network(The)
Editorial: 977 Centerville Tpke, Virginia Beach, Virginia 23463-1001 **Tel:** 1 757 226-7000.
Web site: http://www.cbn.com
Profile: CBN's mission is to prepare the United States of America and the nations of the world for the coming of Jesus Christ and the establishment of the kingdom of God on Earth. The network is headquartered in Virginia Beach, VA with bureaus in Washington, D.C. and Jerusalem.
CABLE NETWORK

CBN/Christian Broadcasting Network - Washington Bureau 526049
Editorial: 1919 M St NW, Ste 100, Washington, District Of Columbia 20036 **Tel:** 1 202 833-2707.
CABLE NETWORK

CBS Newspath 34789
Owner: CBS Corporation
Editorial: 524 W 57th St, New York, New York 10019-2930 **Tel:** 1 212 975-2881.
Email: newspath@cbs.com
Web site: http://www.cbs.com
Profile: CBS Newspath is the unit of CBS News that provides a full spectrum of services for local affiliates to use in producing their news broadcasts. CBS Newspath is part of each station's daily editorial process, assisting in the coordination, exchange and distribution of news. It ensures the timely movement

f material from CBS News to affiliates and among ffiliates nationwide.
CABLE NETWORK

CBS Newspath - Irving Bureau 231182
ditorial: 300 E Royal Ln Ste 125, Irving, Texas 5039-3514 **Tel:** 1 972 869-2000.
mail: newspathsouthwestregion@cbs.com
CABLE NETWORK

CBS Newspath - Studio City Bureau 231179
ditorial: 4200 Radford Ave, Studio City, California 1604 **Tel:** 1 818 655-2500.
CABLE NETWORK

CBS Newspath - Washington Bureau 34853
ditorial: 2020 M St NW, Washington, District Of Columbia 20036-3304 **Tel:** 1 202 457-4321.
Profile: The bureau mostly covers the White House, Capitol Hill and Federal Government.
CABLE NETWORK

CBS Sports Network 132315
Owner: CBS Corporation
Editorial: 28 E 28th St Fl 15, New York, New York 10016-7939 **Tel:** 1 212 975-5100.
Web site: http://www.cbssportsnetwork.com
Profile: CBS Sports Network is the original 24-hour cable network dedicated to capturing the passion of college sports. Available to up to 95 million homes nationwide, we cover 25 men's and women's sports. The network televises more than 250 live events each year, including 50 football games and over 140 basketball games, in HD. In addition, CBS Sports Network is the Home of Armed Forces Football, with exclusive rights to home Army, Navy and Air Force games. Throughout the year, the network also airs a full slate of original programming such as behind-the-scenes series, documentaries and studio coverage featuring expert analysis, predictions, in-depth interviews and more. CBS Sports Network was rebranded from CBS College Sports Network in April 2011. The network was founded in 1999 as CSTV and launched in April 2003 from the network's New York City-based Chelsea Piers Studio, the Field House. In January 2006, CSTV was purchased by CBS Corporation.
CABLE NETWORK

Central Oregon Television 334763
Editorial: 63049 Lower Meadow Dr, Bend, Oregon 97701-5818 **Tel:** 1 541 312-6548.
Web site: http://zolomedia.com/cotv
Profile: COTV (Central Oregon Television) is classified as a local origination cable channel and is a member of the BendBroadband family. Located on Channel 11 in the channel line-up, COTV is proud to bring viewers one-of-a-kind local programming.
REGIONAL CABLE NETWORK

Centric 602665
Owner: Viacom Inc.
Editorial: 1235 W St NE, Washington, District Of Columbia 20018-1101 **Tel:** 1 202 608-2000.
Email: contactus@bet.com
Web site: http://www.centrictv.com
Profile: Centric is a network that mirrors the network BET, but targeted towards a more mature audience. Centric's programming includes a mix of music, lifestyle programming and retro viewing including regular scheduled episodes of Soul Train.
CABLE NETWORK

CET: Comcast Entertainment Television 785583
Owner: Comcast Cable Communications Inc.
Editorial: 1601 Mile High Stadium Cir, Denver, Colorado 80204-1953 **Tel:** 1 303 603-2025.
Email: denver_cet@cable.comcast.com
Web site: http://www.comcastentertainmenttv.com
Profile: Showcases local programming in the Denver area.
REGIONAL CABLE NETWORK

Channel 12 - Northwest Community Television 324161
Editorial: 6900 Winnetka Ave N, Brooklyn Park, Minnesota 55428-1669 **Tel:** 1 763 533-8196.
Email: news@twelve.tv
Web site: http://www.twelve.tv
Profile: Channel 12 Northwest Community Television provides professionally-produced local news, sports and special events coverage for cable subscribers in the northwest suburbs of Minneapolis.
REGIONAL CABLE NETWORK

Channel One News 34781
Owner: Houghton Mifflin Harcourt
Editorial: 345 7th Ave Fl 6, New York, New York 10001-5053 **Tel:** 1 212 329-8377.
Email: contactus@channelone.com
Web site: http://www.channelone.com
Profile: Peabody and Telly Award-winning Channel One News is a television news network for teens, reaching nearly six million young people in middle schools and high schools nationwide - broadcast each day to close to 1 in 4 of all teenagers in the U.S. The dynamic, daily broadcast and supplementary educational resources inform, educate, and inspire teens, connecting them with important current events and the world around them. Channel One News has covered fast-breaking global events from regions such as Haiti, Chile, Mexico, Sierra Leone, North Korea, Afghanistan, Sri Lanka, Germany and Qatar.
CABLE NETWORK

Chiller Network 583409
Owner: NBC Universal
Editorial: 900 Sylvan Avenue, 1 CNBC Plaza, Englewood Cliffs, New Jersey 7632 **Tel:** 1 818 777-1300.
Email: feedback@chillertv.com
Web site: http://www.chillertv.com
Profile: Network is dedicated to the popular horror genre. It features exclusive horror and thriller programming from favorite mainstream series.
CABLE NETWORK

Chung T'ien Television - Monterey Park Bureau 882887
Owner: Want Want China Holdings
Editorial: 1255 Corporate Center Dr Ste 212, Monterey Park, California 91754-7616 **Tel:** 1 323 415-0068.
Email: ctiusa@ctitv.com.tw
Web site: http://www.ctitv.com.tw
Profile: Chung T'ien Television (CTi TV), owned by Want Want China Holdings is a Taiwan-based television network featuring Mandarin-language news, lifestyle, entertainment and talk programming. The US office is based in Los Angeles and distributed by Comcast.
CABLE NETWORK

Cinemax 733901
Owner: Time Warner Inc.
Editorial: 1100 Avenue of the Americas, New York, New York 10036-6712 **Tel:** 1 212 512-1000.
Web site: http://www.cinemax.com
Profile: Cinemax offers collection of premium television networks that broadcasts feature films, documentaries and special behind-the-scenes features. It was launched in August 1980 and is sister networks with HBO/Home Box Office.
CABLE NETWORK

Citybuzz 619637
Owner: Vidicom
Editorial: 1775 Broadway, New York, New York 10019-1903 **Tel:** 1 212 895-8300.
Web site: http://vidicom.com
Profile: Citybuzz selects the best in upscale restaurants, nightlife, shopping, entertainment, hotels, and exploration activities in every major city in the United States. Citybuzz's content is seen on television, hotel broadcasts, cruise lines, and in-flight programs.
CABLE NETWORK

Classic Arts Showcase 34638
Tel: 1 323 878-0283.
Email: casmail@sbcglobal.net
Web site: http://www.classicartsshowcase.org
Profile: Classic Arts Showcase is a non-commercial operation that presents clips of 16 different arts disciplines such as opera, ballet and classical music 24 hours a day, free and unscrambled. Available to all non-commercial broadcasters or individuals in North and South America. The network is a monumental audience development project provided as a public service to stimulate interest and support for the arts. There is no other programming produced at the network.
CABLE NETWORK

CLTV/Chicagoland Television 34599
Owner: Tribune Broadcasting Co.
Editorial: 2501 W Bradley Pl, Chicago, Illinois 60618-4701 **Tel:** 1 773 528-2311.
Email: info@wgntv.com
Web site: http://www.cltv.com
Profile: Chicagoland TV (CLTV) is a 24-hour news and information channel serving the five-county Chicago metropolitan area and Northwest Indiana. The network does not accept VNRs or Satellite Media Tours (SMTs). CLTV is owned and operated by Tribune Broadcasting Co. CLTV is in the process of being sold to Sinclair Broadcast Group, and is expected to close at the end of 2017.
REGIONAL CABLE NETWORK

CMT/Country Music Television 34588
Owner: Viacom Inc.
Editorial: 330 Commerce St, Nashville, Tennessee 37201-1821 **Tel:** 1 615 335-8400.
Email: viewerservices@cmt.com
Web site: http://www.cmt.com
Profile: Country Music Television (CMT), a unit of Viacom's MTV Networks (NYSE: VIA and VIA.B), is the leading television and digital authority on country music and entertainment, reaching more than 90 million homes in the U.S. CMT offers a mix of music, news, live concerts and series and is the top resource for country music on demand. The network's digital platforms include the 24-hour music channel CMT Pure Country, CMT Mobile and CMT VOD. CMT was launched in 1983.
CABLE NETWORK

CN100 The Comcast Network 691789
Editorial: 688 N Industrial Dr, Elmhurst, Illinois 60126-1520
Web site: http://www.cn100.tv
REGIONAL CABLE NETWORK

CNBC Cable Network 34757
Owner: NBC Universal
Editorial: 900 Sylvan Ave, Englewood Cliffs, New Jersey 07632-3312 **Tel:** 1 201 735-2622.
Email: planning@nbcuni.com
Web site: http://www.cnbc.com
Profile: CNBC offers in-depth and breaking news coverage, focusing on politics, business, finance and entertainment. Programming includes live ongoing coverage of daily stock market activity, breaking business news, and in-depth interviews with top business analysts and executives. PR professionals should be aware that CNBC typically covers only publicly-traded companies worth over 500 million dollars, the exception being a smaller company that is somehow directly related to a major national or international news story. Send press releases to the CNBC assignment desk or to the producer of the appropriate CNBC program. The network has 9,500,000 monthly viewers in US and Canada.
CABLE NETWORK

CNBC Cable Network - Chicago Bureau 34797
Editorial: 1 S Wacker Dr, Chicago, Illinois 60606-4614
Tel: 1 312 750-4080.
CABLE NETWORK

CNBC Cable Network - Hong Kong Bureau 963367
Editorial: CNBC Asia - Hong Kong Bureau, Room 5409, 54th Floor, Central Plaza, Hong Kong
Tel: 852 25095163.
Email: editor@cnbcasia.com
Web site: http://www.cnbcasia.com
Profile: The CNBC Hong Kong Bureau covers business news in Asia, and is branded as CNBC Asia.
CABLE NETWORK

CNBC Cable Network - San Francisco Bureau 872886
Editorial: 1 Market St, San Francisco, California 94105-1420 **Tel:** 1 415 792-5000.
CABLE NETWORK

CNBC Cable Network - Singapore Bureau 238463
Editorial: 10 Anson Rd, #06-01 International Plaza, Singapore 79903 **Tel:** 65 116563230488.
Email: editor@cnbcasia.com
Web site: http://www.cnbcasia.com
Profile: The CNBC Singapore Bureau covers business news in Asia, and is branded as CNBC Asia. CNBC Asia reaches 400 million homes in China.
CABLE NETWORK

CNBC Cable Network - Sydney Bureau 963377
Editorial: 1/7 Bridge St, Sydney NSW 2000
Tel: 61 2 8023-6613.
Email: editor@cnbcasia.com
Web site: http://www.cnbcasia.com
Profile: The CNBC Sydney Bureau covers business news in Asia, and is branded as CNBC Asia.
CABLE NETWORK

CNBC Cable Network - Universal City Bureau 34799
Editorial: 100 Universal City Plz Ste 260, Universal City, California 91608-1002 **Tel:** 1 818 622-2622.
CABLE NETWORK

CNBC Cable Network - Washington Bureau 34798
Editorial: 1025 Connecticut Ave NW, Washington, District Of Columbia 20036-5405 **Tel:** 1 202 776-7418.
Email: cnbcdcproducers@nbcuni.com
CABLE NETWORK

CNN Airport 34712
Owner: Time Warner Inc.
Editorial: 1 Cnn Ctr NW, Atlanta, Georgia 30303-2762
Tel: 1 404 827-5131.
Email: airportnetwork2@cnn.com
Web site: http://www.cnn.com/cnn/programs/airport.network/
Profile: CNN Airport features programming that is specific to airports and relevant to air travelers. Programming consists of 35% news and weather, 25% live sports, 15% lifestyle, 15% travel, and 10% local and regional content. The network has sponsorships with national sport organizations which allows them to provide live broadcasts of sporting events. Entertainment content from Time Warner brands are also featured. Each hour local airports feature a one-minute spot of local and public service programming. CNN Airport is offered in 48 airports, covering more than 2,100 gates and other viewing areas and represents more than 250 million viewers annually. The network launched in 1992 as CNN Airport Network.
CABLE NETWORK

CNN en Español 34680
Owner: Time Warner Inc.
Editorial: 1 Cnn Ctr NW, Atlanta, Georgia 30303-2762
Tel: 1 404 878-1555.
Email: cnnespanol@cnn.com
Web site: http://cnnespanol.cnn.com
Profile: CNN en Espanol is a 24-hour, Spanish-language news network currently available throughout Latin America and the United States. It is the first 24-hour network in a language other than English produced independently by CNN. CNN en Espanol provides continuous news reports on major world events, live breaking news coverage supported by in-depth analysis, worldwide business and financial news, global weather updates, sports and features.
CABLE NETWORK

CNN en Español - Miami Bureau 923752
Owner: Time Warner Inc.
Editorial: 601 Brickell Key Dr Ste 403, Miami, Florida 33131-2652 **Tel:** 1 305 400-6801.
Web site: http://cnnespanol.cnn.com
Profile: Miami Bureau of CNN en Español covering the latest news.
CABLE NETWORK

CNN en Español - New York Bureau 235007
Owner: Time Warner Inc.
Editorial: 1 Time Warner Ctr, New York, New York 10019-6038
Profile: CNN en Español based at the New York Bureau covers the latest news for Hispanic viewers.
CABLE NETWORK

CNN en Español - Washington Bureau 86838
Owner: Time Warner Inc.
Editorial: 820 1st St NE, Washington, District Of Columbia 20229-1114 **Tel:** 1 202 515-2990.
Profile: CNN en Español based at the Washington Bureau covering the latest news for Hispanic viewers.
CABLE NETWORK

CNN International 34640
Editorial: 1 Cnn Ctr NW, Atlanta, Georgia 30303-2762
Tel: 1 404 827-1500.
Email: pitch@cnn.com
Web site: http://edition.cnn.com
Profile: CNN International, worldwide cable and satellite distribution arm of the vast Cable News Network, was launched in 1985. It provides round-the-clock breaking news coverage and public affairs programming designed to appeal to audiences around the globe.
CABLE NETWORK

CNN International - South Asia Bureau 720096
Editorial: S-2 Level Block F Intl Trade Tower, Nehru Place, New Delhi 110019 **Tel:** 91 11 41699117.
Web site: http://edition.cnn.com/middle-east
CABLE NETWORK

CNN International - Tokyo Bureau 720068
Editorial: Landic Toranomon Bg 3-7-10 #9, Toranomon, Minato-ku, Tokyo 105-0001
Tel: 81 35 776-2255.
Web site: http://edition.cnn.com/ASIA
CABLE NETWORK

CNN Newsource 34770
Owner: Time Warner Inc.
Editorial: 1 Cnn Ctr NW, Atlanta, Georgia 30303-2762
Tel: 1 404 827-2659.
Web site: http://newsource.cnn.com/Login.aspx?ReturnUrl=%2f
Profile: CNN Newsource is the world's most extensive syndicated news service, comprised of over 700 local news-producing affiliates, including TV stations and cable news channels throughout North America. CNN Newsource is the affiliate wire service division of CNN. The service re-distributes CNN's news and information, and on occasion covers stories of its own. CNN Newsource partners receive everything needed to efficiently produce local newscasts including: multiple daily feeds targeted to key news dayparts, providing regional, national and international news, weather, sports, medical, business, lifestyle and entertainment stories, along with graphics and exclusive Newsource-produced franchise pieces; dependable live opportunities via correspondents on the scene of breaking news and select feature stories; and localized CNN Marketsource reports live from the floor of the NYSE.
CABLE NETWORK

CNN Newsource - Washington Bureau 34816
Editorial: 1620 I St NW Ste 1000, Washington, District Of Columbia 20006-4026 **Tel:** 1 202 777-7266.
Web site: http://newsource.cnn.com
CABLE NETWORK

CNN/Cable News Network 34756
Owner: Time Warner Inc.
Editorial: 1 Cnn Ctr NW, Atlanta, Georgia 30303-2762
Tel: 1 404 827-1500.
Email: nationaldesk@cnn.com
Web site: http://us.cnn.com
Profile: Worldwide cable news network providing live, ongoing coverage of news around the globe 24 hours a day. Regular programs spotlight public affairs, news, politics, science, technology, business, food, medicine, fashion, sports and entertainment. Also emphasizes topical and in-depth interviews and discussions with newsmakers, politicians, celebrities and people in the news.
CABLE NETWORK

CNN/Cable News Network - Abu Dhabi Bureau 610114
Tel: 1 971 240-1245.
Web site: http://arabic.cnn.com

Profile: CNN bureau based in Abu Dhabi.
CABLE NETWORK

CNN/Cable News Network - Beijing Bureau 472982
Editorial: 12-163 Jianwai Diplomatic Compound, Beijing 100600 **Tel:** 86 10 65326013.
Web site: http://edition.cnn.com/asia
CABLE NETWORK

CNN/Cable News Network - Berlin Bureau 558515
Editorial: Johannisstrasse 20, Berlin 10117
Tel: 49 30 726193838.
CABLE NETWORK

CNN/Cable News Network - Brookline Bureau 34844
Editorial: 637 Washington St Ste 208, Brookline, Massachusetts 02446-4579 **Tel:** 1 617 264-9905.
CABLE NETWORK

CNN/Cable News Network - Chicago Bureau 34793
Editorial: 435 N Michigan Ave Ste 715, Chicago, Illinois 60611-4027 **Tel:** 1 312 645-8555.
Email: chibiz@turner.com
CABLE NETWORK

CNN/Cable News Network - Dallas Bureau 34795
Editorial: 1201 Main St Ste 1525, Dallas, Texas 75202-3969 **Tel:** 1 214 747-1440.
Email: cnndallas@turner.com
Profile: CNN/Cable News Network bureau in Dallas.
CABLE NETWORK

CNN/Cable News Network - Los Angeles Bureau 34794
Editorial: 6430 W Sunset Blvd, Los Angeles, California 90028-7901 **Tel:** 1 323 993-5000.
CABLE NETWORK

CNN/Cable News Network - Moscow Bureau 232259
Editorial: Kutuzovsky Prospekt 7/4, Kv 256, Moscow 121248 **Tel:** 7 0952434056.
CABLE NETWORK

CNN/Cable News Network - New York Bureau 34792
Editorial: 1 Time Warner Ctr Fl 5, New York, New York 10019-6038 **Tel:** 1 212 275-7800.
Profile: New York bureau of CNN.
CABLE NETWORK

CNN/Cable News Network - North Miami Bureau 34801
Editorial: 12000 Biscayne Blvd Ste 101, North Miami, Florida 33181-2742 **Tel:** 1 305 400-7640.
CABLE NETWORK

CNN/Cable News Network - San Francisco Bureau 34796
Editorial: 50 California St Ste 950, San Francisco, California 94111-4606 **Tel:** 1 415 438-5000.
CABLE NETWORK

CNN/Cable News Network - Washington Bureau 34791
Editorial: 820 1st St NE, Washington, District Of Columbia 20229-1114 **Tel:** 1 202 898-7900.
CABLE NETWORK

Comcast Hometown Network 972782
Editorial: 3055 Comcast Pl, Livermore, California 94551-7594 **Tel:** 1 415 252-6300.
Email: info@comcasthometown.com
Web site: http://www.comcasthometown.com
Profile: The network covers Northern and Central California. It features regional programming, and unique local content.
REGIONAL CABLE NETWORK

The Comcast Network 71627
Editorial: 1351 S Columbus Blvd, Philadelphia, Pennsylvania 19147-5505 **Tel:** 1 215 468-2222.
Email: cn8_tv@cable.comcast.com
Web site: http://www.csnphilly.com
Profile: The Comcast Network provides more than nine million Comcast cable viewers with a unique brand of live, interactive television delivered over its own fiber-optic network to 12 states and 20 television markets stretching from Maine to Virginia and Washington, D.C. It was created by Comcast Cable Communications in 1996 to provide its customers with an information resource that would address local, regional and national issues while allowing community members to voice their opinions. Headquartered in Philadelphia, The Comcast Network offers consistent programming throughout the Northeast with the aid of its six studios in Baltimore, Boston, Delaware, New York, Philadelphia and Washington, D.C. It has quickly grown to become the nation's leading regional cable network, airing more than 90 hours a week of original programming.
REGIONAL CABLE NETWORK

Comcast SportsNet Chicago 309902
Owner: Comcast Corporation
Editorial: 350 N Orleans St, Chicago, Illinois 60654-1975 **Tel:** 1 312 222-6000.
Email: csnchicagowebsite@comcastsportsnet.com
Web site: http://www.csnchicago.com
Profile: Comcast SportsNet Chicago is home to all Chicago's favorite teams: Cubs, White Sox, Bulls and Blackhawks. Comcast SportsNet boasts over 260 live, professional games plus all the news and analysis that goes with them. From SportsRise to SportsNite, no play is left unturned. Pre-game and post-game shows break down each game to the last detail. With the only complete look at the day's events, teams and players, Comcast SportsNet is the destination for Chicago's real sports fans.
CABLE NETWORK

Comcast SportsNet Mid-Atlantic 34613
Owner: Comcast Corporation
Editorial: 7700 Wisconsin Ave Ste 200, Bethesda, Maryland 20814-3515 **Tel:** 1 301 718-3200.
Web site: http://www.csnmidatlantic.com
Profile: Comcast SportsNet Mid-Atlantic is a 24-hour regional cable television network dedicated solely to providing sports coverage and news to viewers in Maryland, Virginia, Delaware and the District of Columbia, as well as parts of Pennsylvania and West Virginia. Game coverage and sports news includes local and national, professional and amateur sports, including the Washington Capitols (NHL), Washington Wizards (NBA), D.C. United (MLS), Washington Redskins (NFL), Atlantic Coast Conference and Colonial Athletic Association.
REGIONAL CABLE NETWORK

Comcast SportsNet New England 34635
Owner: Comcast Corporation
Editorial: 42 3rd Ave, Burlington, Massachusetts 01803-4414 **Tel:** 1 781 270-7200.
Web site: http://www.csnne.com
Profile: The network provides a variety of sports-related programming throughout New England. Programming includes live Boston Celtics NBA basketball games and news, as well as nightly New England sports news and extensive coverage of regional collegiate sports.
REGIONAL CABLE NETWORK

Comcast SportsNet Northwest 538251
Editorial: 300 N Winning Way, Portland, Oregon 97227-2108 **Tel:** 1 503 736-5142.
Email: CSNNW@csnnw.com
Web site: http://www.csnnw.com
Profile: Comcast SportsNet Northwest brings Portland Trail Blazers fans more games, more HD and more news than any other network. Viewers get the scoop with pre- and post-game shows, Trail Blazers specials and weekly original shows. College fans can catch football and basketball featuring University of Oregon and Portland State University. Programming includes games, coaches shows, news shows and highlights, and tracking of all the NCAA favorites including Oregon State University, University of Portland, University of Washington and Washington State University. The network has also introduced high-quality NHL match-ups, featuring the Vancouver Canucks and best of NHL match-ups from rinks across the country. In addition, there's outdoor and adventure programming as well as unprecedented local sports news coverage.
REGIONAL CABLE NETWORK

Comcast SportsNet Philadelphia 34710
Owner: Comcast Corporation
Editorial: 3601 S Broad St, Philadelphia, Pennsylvania 19148-5250 **Tel:** 1 215 952-2200.
Email: askcsn@comcastsportsnet.com
Web site: http://www.csnphilly.com
Profile: 24-hour regional sports cable network serving eastern and central Pennsylvania, southern New Jersey and northern Delaware. Features live broadcasts of Philadelphia Phillies baseball, Philadelphia 76ers basketball and Philadelphia Flyers NHL hockey.
REGIONAL CABLE NETWORK

Comedy Central 34585
Owner: Viacom Inc.
Editorial: 345 Hudson St, New York, New York 10014-4502 **Tel:** 1 212 767-8600.
Web site: http://www.cc.com
Profile: Comedy Central is a round-the-clock national comedy network featuring 60 percent original programming. Comedy Central presents comedy stars from the past and present along with today's newcomers. Comedy Central's schedule is an eclectic mix of original programming, stand-up comedy, sketch comedy, classic television shows and movies. Comedy Central is a division of Viacom Inc.
CABLE NETWORK

Comedy Central - Los Angeles Bureau 358960
Editorial: 1575 N Gower St, Los Angeles, California 90028-6487 **Tel:** 1 310 752-8000.
CABLE NETWORK

Connecticut Network 306210
Owner: Connecticut Public Affairs Network Inc.
Editorial: 21 Oak St Ste 605, Hartford, Connecticut 06106-8016 **Tel:** 1 860 246-1553.
Email: ctn@cga.ct.gov
Web site: http://www.ctn.state.ct.us
Profile: The Connecticut Network's (CT-N) purpose is to provide the citizens of Connecticut with unbiased coverage of state government deliberations and public policy events. The network is owned by the non-profit organization Connecticut Public Affairs Network Inc. CT-N is aired on the Internet and on cable or public "access" channels throughout Connecticut.
REGIONAL CABLE NETWORK

Cooking Channel 79615
Owner: Scripps Networks, Inc.
Editorial: 9721 Sherrill Blvd, Knoxville, Tennessee 37932-3330 **Tel:** 1 865 694-2700.
Web site: http://www.cookingchanneltv.com
Profile: Cooking Channel is a 24-hour network that caters to avid food lovers by focusing on food information and instructional cooking programming. The network launched on May 31, 2010.
CABLE NETWORK

Cornerstone TV 519232
Owner: Cornerstone Television, Inc.
Editorial: 1 Signal Hill Dr, Wall, Pennsylvania 15148-1436 **Tel:** 1 412 824-3930.
Email: info@ctvn.org
Web site: http://www.ctvn.org
Profile: Cornerstone TV is a viewer-supported ministry absolutely committed to using television as a force for good. The network aims to impact our culture by broadcasting the Gospel and bringing a fresh, positive, Christ-centered outlook.
CABLE NETWORK

Cowboy Channel 34571
Owner: Rural Media Group
Editorial: 921 Village Sq, Gretna, Nebraska 68028-7853 **Tel:** 1 402 289-2085.
Web site: http://www.thecowboychannel.com
Profile: The Cowboy Channel is a 24-hour television network airing more than 50 hours of original, values-based programs weekly providing a reliable, safe viewing destination for today's family. The network is available to more than 30 million TV households nationwide via cable systems and broadcast stations nationwide. It targets families looking for a wholesome alternative to standard television fare. Appealing family programs include kids' series, original concerts, comedy, crafts, health, and live talk along with movies and inspirational shows.
CABLE NETWORK

Cox Sports Television 390772
Owner: Cox Enterprises
Editorial: 2121 Airline Dr Fl 2, Metairie, Louisiana 70001-5945 **Tel:** 1 504 358-6113.
Email: coxsportstv@cox.com
Web site: http://www.coxsportstv.com
Profile: Launched in October of 2002, Cox Sports Television features regional sports programming in the entire Gulf South. The network delivers top professional, collegiate and high school events and shows with strong regional interests from Texas to Florida.
REGIONAL CABLE NETWORK

Crown City Media 552526
Owner: Tami DeVine
Editorial: 1015 N Lake Ave, Pasadena, California 91104-4573 **Tel:** 1 626 344-8314.
Email: info@crowncitynews.com
Web site: http://www.crowncitynews.com
Profile: Crown City Media creates video content for television and the Internet. It produces CCN - Crown City News on a weekly basis, as well as commercials and promotional videos for businesses and organizations.
REGIONAL CABLE NETWORK

C-SPAN 34573
Owner: National Cable Satellite Corporation
Editorial: 400 N Capitol St Nw Ste 650, Washington, District Of Columbia 20001-1550 **Tel:** 1 202 737-3220.
Email: DCeditor@c-span.org
Web site: http://www.c-span.org
Profile: Cable network broadcasting live gavel-to-gavel coverage of the United States House of Representatives. Also airs public affairs programs, speeches, seminars and government committee meetings of interest to viewers around the nation. Due to the kind of programming the network airs, very few editors are pitchable.
CABLE NETWORK

C-SPAN2 34663
Owner: National Cable Satellite Corporation
Editorial: 400 N Capitol St NW, Ste 650, Washington, District Of Columbia 20001 **Tel:** 1 202 737-3220.
Email: events@c-span.org
Web site: http://www.c-span.org
Profile: Network providing live gavel-to-gavel coverage of the United States Senate in session. Also features Senate committee hearings and public affairs programming.
CABLE NETWORK

C-SPAN3 76274
Owner: National Cable Satellite Corporation
Editorial: 400 N Capitol St NW, Ste 650, Washington, District Of Columbia 20001 **Tel:** 1 202 737-3220.
Email: events@c-span.org
Web site: http://www.c-span.org
Profile: C-SPAN3 televises key national events from Washington, D.C., including congressional hearings, press conferences, the best in political seminars and conferences and National Press Club speeches in the unique long-form style that's classic C-SPAN. Late nights and weekends, C-SPAN3 spotlights American history with award-winning original history series such as: The Lincoln-Douglas Debates, Traveling Tocqueville's America, and American Presidents: Life Portraits.
CABLE NETWORK

DCTV/DeKalb County Television Network 553150
Owner: Dekalb County
Editorial: 1300 Commerce Dr Fl 6, Decatur, Georgia 30030-3222 **Tel:** 1 404 371-2989.
Email: dctv@dekalbcountyga.gov
Web site: http://www.co.dekalb.ga.us/dctv/index.html
Profile: DCTV reports on the news, services and events uniquely focused on DeKalb County. It is available to all Comcast Cable subscribers in DeKalb County on channel 23.
REGIONAL CABLE NETWORK

Department of Defense (DoD) 761893
Owner: Defense Media Activity
Editorial: 601 N Fairfax St, Alexandria, Virginia 22314-2054 **Tel:** 1 301 222-6780.
Web site: http://www.defense.gov
Profile: Department of Defense (DoD) formerly "The Pentagon Channel" broadcasts military news and information for the 2.6 million members of the U.S. Armed Forces through programming including, Department of Defense news briefings, military news, interviews with top Defense officials, short stories about the work of our military.
CABLE NETWORK

Destination America 496643
Owner: Discovery Communications, Inc.
Editorial: 1 Discovery Pl, Silver Spring, Maryland 20910-3354 **Tel:** 1 240 662-2000.
Web site: http://america.discovery.com
Profile: Destination America is a network that celebrates the people, places and stories of the U.S. Original series cover such diverse subjects as American food from Tex Mex to barbecue; American mysteries from Jesse James' lost fortune to Area 51; America's heroes from those who embody the values of our past to those who invent the technology of our future; as well as never before seen footage of America's iconic landmarks, including Yellowstone National Park to the Everglade swamps. On May 26, 2012, Planet Green rebranded to Destination America. A vast majority of programming aired on Discovery is developed by producers outside the network. As a result, it is suggested that most shows should be contacted via network headquarters in Silver Spring, MD.
CABLE NETWORK

Deutsche Welle TV Washington Bureau 618001
Owner: Deutsche Welle
Editorial: 2000 M St NW, Ste 335, Washington, District Of Columbia 20036-3391 **Tel:** 1 202 785-5730.
Web site: http://www.dw-world.de
Profile: Deutsche Welle TV (DW-TV) is Germany's international satellite television service of news and information. DW-TV's Washington bureau produces segments of shows and occasionally an entire show, all of which are then broadcast from the headquaters in Germany.
CABLE NETWORK

Discovery Channel 457306
Owner: Discovery Communications, Inc.
Editorial: 1 Discovery Pl, Silver Spring, Maryland 20910-3354 **Tel:** 1 240 662-2000.
Web site: http://www.discovery.com
Profile: Discovery Channel is a widely distributed educational cable network in the United States, providing a wide array of original science and technology based programs, special and series.
CABLE NETWORK

Discovery Channel - Los Angeles Bureau 781794
Editorial: 10100 Santa Monica Blvd Ste 1500, Los Angeles, California 90067-4117 **Tel:** 1 310 551-1611.
CABLE NETWORK

Discovery Communications 34583
Owner: Discovery Communications, Inc.
Editorial: 1 Discovery Pl, Silver Spring, Maryland 20910-3354 **Tel:** 1 240 662-2000.
Web site: http://www.discovery.com
Profile: Family of networks providing a wide array of science and technology-based documentaries, specials, and series. Features original productions of a scientific and investigative nature, in addition to features on nature, wildlife, and human biology and history. ** A vast majority of programming aired on Discovery is developed by producers outside the network. As a result, it is suggested that most shows should be contacted via network headquarters in Silver Spring, MD. **
CABLE NETWORK

Discovery en Espanol 34739
Editorial: 6505 Blue Lagoon Dr, Ste 190, Miami, Florida 33126 **Tel:** 1 786 273-4700.
Web site: http://www.tudiscovery.com

Profile: Cable network offering quality programming in Spanish for the entire family, including science, technology, health, aviation, nature, history, culture, travel and exploration.
CABLE NETWORK

Discovery Familia 729924
Owner: Discovery Communications, Inc.
Editorial: 6505 Blue Lagoon Dr Ste 190, Miami, Florida 33126-6030 **Tel:** 1 786 273-4700.
Web site: http://www.discoveryfamilia.com/familia
Profile: Discovery Familia is the premiere Spanish-language network dedicated to bringing the best educational and entertaining, family-oriented programming to kids and families.
CABLE NETWORK

The Discovery Family 34722
Owner: Discovery Communications, Inc.
Editorial: 2950 N Hollywood Way Ste 100, Burbank, California 91505-1069 **Tel:** 1 818 531-3600.
Web site: http://kids.discovery.com
Profile: Discovery Family is a specialty cable channel that presents programs to help kids explore their world and satisfy their curiosities in an entertaining way. The target audience is children, ages 2 to 14. On October 10, 2010, Discovery Kids Channel relaunched as The Hub. As a joint venture of Discovery Communications and Hasbro, Inc., the network remains children's programming.
CABLE NETWORK

Discovery Life Channel 156433
Editorial: 1 Discovery Pl, Silver Spring, Maryland 20910-3354 **Tel:** 1 240 662-2000.
Web site: http://www.discoverylife.com
Profile: Discovery Life Channel is a network that embraces all of life's unplanned moments. Discovery Life brings viewers a kaleidoscope of human emotions and experiences through the true stories of ordinary people in extraordinary circumstances. From critical turning points to unexpected moments, Discovery Life explores how people tackle life's surprising twists and turns. On January 15, 2015, the network will rebranded to Discovery Life Channel from Discovery Fit & Health.
CABLE NETWORK

Disney Channel 34590
Editorial: 3800 W Alameda Ave Ste, Burbank, California 91505-4300 **Tel:** 1 818 569-7500.
Web site: http://disneychannel.disney.com
Profile: Family entertainment channel broadcasting original movies, specials, and children's entertainment programming culled from the vast video library of the Walt Disney Co. Programming is designed for kids and families. Disney Channel is a division of ABC Cable Networks Group, a subsidiary of The Walt Disney Company. It is currently in more than 80 million homes. Disney Channel isn't a news outlet for PR contacts to pitch.
CABLE NETWORK

Disney Junior 727023
Editorial: 3800 W Alameda Ave, Burbank, California 91505-4300 **Tel:** 1 818 5697500.
Web site: http://disney.go.com/junior/pre/index.html
Profile: Disney Junior is aimed at children ages 2 to 7 and features timeless characters and children's programming.
CABLE NETWORK

Disney XD 34725
Owner: Walt Disney Co.
Editorial: 3800 W Alameda Ave, Burbank, California 91505-4300 **Tel:** 1 818 569-7500.
Web site: http://disneyxd.disney.com/
Profile: Nationally-distributed cable network featuring the rich array of Disney animation archives from the 1930s to the 1990s. Network airs short features and series with classic Disney characters, in addition to animated Disney theatrical releases and classic character-themed programming. Disney rebranded Toon Disney television and online platforms in the U.S. to Disney XD on February 13, 2009. Disney XD includes a mix of live-action and animated programming for kids age 6 to 14, hyper-targeting boys and their quest for discovery, accomplishment, sports, adventure and humor.
CABLE NETWORK

DIY Network 62267
Owner: Scripps Networks, Inc.
Editorial: 9721 Sherrill Blvd, Knoxville, Tennessee 37932-3330 **Tel:** 1 865 694-2700.
Web site: http://www.diynetwork.com
Profile: DIY Network is the go-to destination for rip-up, knock-out home improvement television. DIY Network's programs and experts answer the most sought-after questions and offer creative projects for do-it-yourself enthusiasts. DIY Network's programming covers a broad range of categories, including home improvement and landscaping.
CABLE NETWORK

E! Entertainment Television 34786
Owner: NBC Universal
Editorial: 10 Universal City Plz, Universal City, California 91608-1002 **Tel:** 1 818 777-1000.
Email: etvteam@nbcuni.com
Web site: http://www.eonline.com
Profile: 24-hour network dedicated to the world of entertainment. The network offers compelling celebrity interviews, talk shows, news, docudramas, behind-the-scenes specials, comedy, movie previews and the most comprehensive coverage of the entertainment industry's awards shows.
CABLE NETWORK

E! Entertainment Television - New York Bureau 128812
Editorial: 5 Times Sq Fl 10, New York, New York 10036-6527 **Tel:** 1 212 852-5100.
Profile: The New York office for E! Entertainment Television.
CABLE NETWORK

E.W. Scripps Company 926669
Owner: E.W. Scripps Co.
Editorial: 312 Walnut St, Cincinnati, Ohio 45202-4024
Tel: 1 513 977-3000.
Web site: http://www.scripps.com
Profile: E.W. Scripps Company is a media enterprise driven to develop and expand its digital strategies while embracing its rich history in delivering quality journalism through television stations, newspapers. They produce national investigative stories for TV, print and online.
CABLE NETWORK

The Ecology Channel 34624
Owner: Ecology Communications Group, Inc.
Editorial: 9171 Victoria Dr, Ellicott City, Maryland 21042-2564 **Tel:** 1 410 465-0480.
Web site: http://www.ecology.com
Profile: Cable network focusing on the world of environmental and ecological development and preservation. Features news and informational programming related to trends, issues, and ideas in environmental processes and evolution.
CABLE NETWORK

El Rey Network 828196
Owner: El Netwarko Groupo
Editorial: 4900 Old Manor Rd, Austin, Texas 78723-4522
Email: info@elreynetwork.com
Web site: http://www.elreynetwork.com
Profile: El Rey Network is an entertainment network targeted towards English-speaking Latinos. Launched on March 11, 2014.
CABLE NETWORK

Enlace TBN 687908
Owner: Trinity Broadcasting Network
Editorial: 2823 W Irving Blvd, Irving, Texas 75061-4236 **Tel:** 1 469 499-0820.
Email: comments@tbn.org
Web site: http://www.enlace.org
Profile: Enlace TBN is a digital cable network for the Hispanic faith community. TBN Enlace is owned and operated by TBN, a nonprofit, nondenominational religious organization. TBN Enlace features a unique combination of inspirational programs from Latin America and the most popular programs from TBN.
CABLE NETWORK

ESPN 34759
Owner: Walt Disney Co.
Editorial: 935 Middle St, Bristol, Connecticut 06010-1000 **Tel:** 1 860 766-2000.
Web site: http://www.espn.com
Profile: This 24-hour sports programming network provides an extensive package of live and taped sporting events, including NFL football, NBA basketball, NASCAR, NCAA college football and basketball and Major League Baseball.
CABLE NETWORK

ESPN - New York Bureau 34804
Editorial: 77 W 66th St, Fl 21, New York, New York 10023 **Tel:** 1 212 916-9200.
CABLE NETWORK

ESPN Classic-The Classic Sports Network 34622
Editorial: 545 Middle St, Bristol, Connecticut 06010-8413 **Tel:** 1 860 766-2000.
Web site: http://www.espn.com
Profile: ESPN Classic focuses on the past glories of modern athletics and sport. The network features replays of classic ball games and championships, historical documentaries, interviews with sports heroes of yesterday, and collectible and merchandising information.
CABLE NETWORK

ESPN Deportes 151485
Owner: Walt Disney Co.
Editorial: 77 W 66th St, New York, New York 10023-6201 **Tel:** 1 860 766-2000.
Web site: http://espndeportes.espn.go.com/
Profile: This Spanish-language sports programming network provides an extensive Spanish-language package of live and taped sporting events, including NFL football, NHL hockey, NCAA college football and basketball, Major League Baseball, auto racing, boxing, and tennis. It also presents an extensive schedule of sports news programming throughout the day, in addition to special interviews with sports personalities and guest commentary about the sporting world.
CABLE NETWORK

ESPN2 34618
Owner: Walt Disney Co.
Editorial: 935 Middle St, Bristol, Connecticut 06010-1099 **Tel:** 1 860 766-2000.
Web site: http://espn.go.com
Profile: ESPN2 presents more than 4,800 live and/or original hours of sports programming annually featuring MLB, college football and basketball, and much more.
CABLE NETWORK

ESPNEWS 34672
Editorial: 935 Middle St, Bristol, Connecticut 6010
Tel: 1 860 766-2000.
Web site: http://sports.espn.go.com/espntv/espnNetwork?networkID=4
Profile: The only 24-hour sports news network, ESPNEWS features continuous news, highlights, scores, analysis and live press conferences. Since its inception in 1996, ESPNEWS has established itself as an immediate source of sports news and information, utilizing the vast resources of ESPN and its award-winning SportsCenter. ESPNEWS merges ESPN's on-air and online entities to present the ultimate interactive sports news outlet.
CABLE NETWORK

ESPNU 327887
Editorial: 11001 Rushmore Dr, Charlotte, North Carolina 28277-3434 **Tel:** 1 704 973-5000.
Web site: http://espn.go.com/espnu
Profile: Network devoted entirely to college sports. The network airs over 300 live collegiate sporting events throughout the year and features pregame, halftime, and postgame shows.
CABLE NETWORK

Everwell TV 578381
Owner: MediVista Media
Editorial: 1100 Spring St NW Ste 750, Atlanta, Georgia 30309-2859 **Tel:** 1 404 817-7767.
Email: contact@everwell.com
Web site: http://www.everwell.com
Profile: Everwell TV informs and entertains consumers with premier health video content in the waiting rooms of physicians.
CABLE NETWORK

EWTN Global Catholic Network 34657
Owner: Eternal Word Television Network Inc.
Editorial: 5817 Old Leeds Rd, Irondale, Alabama 35210-2164 **Tel:** 1 205 271-2900.
Email: viewer@ewtn.com
Web site: http://www.ewtn.com
Profile: A 24-hour national Catholic cable channel. Provides programming of a family-oriented nature through movies, regular series, documentaries, and talk shows. Includes coverage of daily Mass and prayer services across the country while furthering the teachings of the Catholic faith.
CABLE NETWORK

The Family Channel 519681
Owner: Luken Communications
Editorial: 225 E 8th St, Chattanooga, Tennessee 37402-2200 **Tel:** 1 423 468-5100.
Web site: http://www.famchannel.com
Profile: The Family Channel (formerly My Family TV previously owned by ValCom, Inc.) is an American general entertainment television network. It's programming consists of children programs, classics, entertainment, lifestyle, travel and outdoors, religious programming, talk shows and movies.
CABLE NETWORK

Feature Story News 77965
Owner: Marks(Simon)
Editorial: 1730 Rhode Island Ave NW, Washington, District Of Columbia 20036-3108 **Tel:** 1 202 296-9012.
Email: info@featurestory.com
Web site: http://featurestorynews.com
Profile: Feature Story News, the world's leading independent broadcast agency, offers a unique service in the news industry. The organization provides ready-to-air television and radio news material, tailored to individual on-air styles. Produced and edited to suit a program's on-air style, delivered by deadline, and complete with sign-off. Gives networks an international reach without the sky-high costs of opening and maintaining overseas bureaus.
CABLE NETWORK

Flix 734123
Owner: Showtime Networks Inc.
Editorial: 1633 Broadway Fl 7, New York, New York 10019-6708 **Tel:** 1 212 7081600.
Web site: http://www.sho.com/site/schedules/channel.do?channel=FLX
Profile: Flix is a premium television network owned by Showtime Networks Inc, a subsidiary of CBS Corporation, that features hit movies of the 80s, 90s and 00's. It was launched in 1992 and has the sister network channels of Showtime and The Movie Channel.
CABLE NETWORK

Food Network 34605
Owner: Scripps Networks, Inc.
Editorial: 75 9Th Ave Fl 2, New York, New York 10011-7028 **Tel:** 1 212 398-8836.
Web site: http://www.foodnetwork.com
Profile: Food Network is a 24-hour cable network dedicated to good food and good times. The network airs a variety of taped and live programs dealing with cooking, health, nutrition, and food. Shows emphasize unique recipes, cooking tips and techniques, and feature famous personalities in the cooking world.
CABLE NETWORK

Fort Worth Television 739418
Editorial: 401 W 2nd St, Fort Worth, Texas 76102-7302 **Tel:** 1 817 871-6014.
Email: fwtv@fortworthtexas.gov
Web site: http://www.fortworthgov.org/fwtv
Profile: Fort Worth TV, in partnership with the community, produces diverse and innovative programs for and about Fort Worth.
REGIONAL CABLE NETWORK

FOX Business Network 491507
Owner: News Corporation Ltd.
Editorial: 1211 Avenue of the Americas Fl 16, New York, New York 10036-8701 **Tel:** 1 212 601-7000.
Email: desk@foxbusiness.com
Web site: http://www.foxbusiness.com
Profile: FOX Business Network is a cable and satellite news channel offering in-depth and breaking business and financial news coverage. It launched October 15, 2007 to over 30 million subscribers.
CABLE NETWORK

FOX Business Network - Chicago Bureau 500275
Editorial: 20 S Wacker Dr, Chicago, Illinois 60606-7431 **Tel:** 1 312 494-0428.
Profile: FOX Business Network's Chicago bureau.
CABLE NETWORK

FOX Business Network - Los Angeles Bureau 506902
Editorial: 2044 Armacost Ave, Los Angeles, California 90025-6113 **Tel:** 1 310 571-2000.
Profile: FOX Business Network bureau in Los Angeles.
CABLE NETWORK

FOX Business Network - Washington Bureau 501887
Editorial: 400 N Capitol St NW Ste 550, Washington, District Of Columbia 20001-1502 **Tel:** 1 202 684-4000.
Profile: FOX Business Network bureau for Washington, D.C.
CABLE NETWORK

Fox Deportes 34772
Editorial: 1440 S Sepulveda Blvd, Los Angeles, California 90025-3458 **Tel:** 1 310 444-8100.
Web site: http://www.foxdeportes.com
Profile: Fox Deportes is the premier Spanish-language sports network in the United States. It delivers year round, high-profile quality sports programming that appeals most to the growing, diverse U.S. Hispanic market. The channel reaches more than 7 million cable and satellite households in the U.S. The network combines big event programming with game-day action positioning itself as "Hispanic America's Sports Network." On October 1, 2010 the network was renamed to Fox Deportes from Fox Sports en Espanol.
CABLE NETWORK

FOX News Channel 34764
Owner: News Corporation Ltd.
Editorial: 1211 Avenue of the Americas, New York, New York 10036-8701 **Tel:** 1 212 301-3000.
Email: desk@foxnews.com
Web site: http://www.foxnews.com
Profile: FOX News Channel is a cable network covering breaking news as well as political, entertainment and business news. The network offers live updates every 30 minutes, 24 hours a day. The network also features interviews with newsmakers.
CABLE NETWORK

FOX News Channel - Atlanta Bureau 62220
Editorial: 260 14th St NW Fl 1, Atlanta, Georgia 30318-5360 **Tel:** 1 404 685-2280.
CABLE NETWORK

FOX News Channel - Chicago Bureau 34811
Editorial: 55 W Wacker Dr Ste 500, Chicago, Illinois 60601-1791 **Tel:** 1 312 494-0428.
CABLE NETWORK

FOX News Channel - Dallas Bureau 75530
Editorial: 1201 Main St, Ste 2444, Dallas, Texas 75202-3916 **Tel:** 1 214 742-5005.
CABLE NETWORK

FOX News Channel - Denver Bureau 34814
Editorial: 100 E Speer Blvd, Ste 300, Denver, Colorado 80203-3437 **Tel:** 1 303 861-0460.
Email: fncdenver@gmail.com
CABLE NETWORK

FOX News Channel - Los Angeles Bureau 34812
Editorial: 2044 Armacost Ave, Los Angeles, California 90025-6113 **Tel:** 1 310 571-2000.
CABLE NETWORK

FOX News Channel - Miami Bureau 973940
Editorial: 1666 79th Street Cswy Ste 203, North Bay Village, Florida 33141-4134 **Tel:** 1 305 866-8007.
Email: miami@foxnews.com
CABLE NETWORK

FOX News Channel - San Francisco Bureau 34829
Editorial: 901 Battery St, Ste 210, San Francisco, California 94111 **Tel:** 1 415 951-8550.
CABLE NETWORK

FOX News Channel - Washington Bureau 34810
Editorial: 400 N Capitol St NW Ste 550, Washington, District Of Columbia 20001-1502 **Tel:** 1 202 824-6300.
Email: dc.desk@foxnews.com
CABLE NETWORK

FOX News Channel - Watertown Bureau 87141
Editorial: 50 Hunt St, Watertown, Massachusetts 02472-4625
CABLE NETWORK

FOX NewsEdge 34778
Owner: News Corporation Ltd.
Editorial: 1211 Avenue of the Americas Frnt 1, New York, New York 10036-8701 **Tel:** 1 212 301-3444.
Email: newsmanager@foxnews.com
Web site: http://www.foxnews.com
Profile: News service for the FOX Broadcasting Network, with bureaus around the country. News feeds may include material from the FNC/FOX News Channel.
CABLE NETWORK

FOX NewsEdge - Atlanta Bureau 231620
Editorial: 260 14th St NW, Fl 1, Atlanta, Georgia 30318-5360 **Tel:** 1 404 685-2280.
CABLE NETWORK

FOX NewsEdge - Dallas Bureau 70901
Editorial: 1201 Main St, Ste 2444, Dallas, Texas 75202-3916 **Tel:** 1 214 742-5735.
CABLE NETWORK

FOX NewsEdge - Denver Bureau 34827
Editorial: 999 18th St, Ste 1665, Denver, Colorado 80202 **Tel:** 1 303 861-0460.
CABLE NETWORK

FOX NewsEdge - Jerusalem Bureau 231658
Editorial: 206 Jaffa Road, Jerusalem 91131
CABLE NETWORK

FOX NewsEdge - Los Angeles Bureau 34824
Editorial: 2044 Armacost Ave, Los Angeles, California 90025-6113 **Tel:** 1 310 571-2000.
CABLE NETWORK

FOX NewsEdge - Paris Bureau 231659
Editorial: 10 Rue General Castlenau, Paris 75015
Tel: 33 147349529.
CABLE NETWORK

FOX NewsEdge - San Francisco Bureau 34831
Editorial: 901 Battery St, Ste 210, San Francisco, California 94111 **Tel:** 1 415 951-8550.
CABLE NETWORK

FOX NewsEdge - Washington Bureau 34825
Editorial: 400 N Capitol St NW, Ste 550, Washington, District Of Columbia 20001-1502 **Tel:** 1 202 824-6481.
CABLE NETWORK

FOX NewsEdge - West Newton Bureau 231621
Editorial: 1230 Washington St, West Newton, Massachusetts 02465-2146 **Tel:** 1 617 926-2986.
CABLE NETWORK

FOX Sports 1 34701
Owner: News Corporation Ltd
Editorial: 1220 W W T Harris Blvd, Charlotte, North Carolina 28262-8536 **Tel:** 1 704 501-5700.
Web site: http://www.foxsports.com/watch/foxsports1
Profile: FOX Sports 1 is a national, multi-sport network that will launch August 17, 2013. It features live college basketball, college football, Major League Baseball, NASCAR, soccer and UFC contests.
CABLE NETWORK

FOX Sports 2 150773
Owner: News Corporation Ltd.
Editorial: 1440 S Sepulveda Blvd, Los Angeles, California 90025-3458 **Tel:** 1 310 369-1000.
Web site: http://foxsports.com
Profile: FOX Sports 2 is a national, multi-sport network that will launch August 17, 2013. It features live college basketball, college football, Major League Baseball, NASCAR, soccer and UFC contests, including the weigh-ins and pre/post-fight coverage.
CABLE NETWORK

FOX Sports Arizona 34699
Owner: News Corporation Ltd.
Editorial: 455 N 3rd St Ste 290, Phoenix, Arizona 85004-2193 **Tel:** 1 602 257-9500.
Email: asktheasr@foxsports.net
Web site: http://www.foxsportsarizona.com
Profile: Arizona regional sports network offering coverage of the NHL's Phoenix Coyotes, MLB's Arizona Diamondbacks, PAC-10 football and basketball, University of Arizona, Arizona State University, Big 12 football, Conference USA football and Fox Sports News.
REGIONAL CABLE NETWORK

FOX Sports Florida 34775
Owner: Fox Broadcasting Company
Editorial: 500 E Broward Blvd Ste 1300, Fort Lauderdale, Florida 33394-3035 **Tel:** 1 954 975-3634.
Web site: http://www.foxsports.com/florida
Profile: Regional sports outlet serving over 6.1 million cable and satellite homes in Florida. Sports programs include live coverage of Orlando Magic and Miami Heat NBA basketball, and Tampa Bay Lightning NHL hockey. Network also broadcasts a wide variety of college athletics, including University of Florida, Florida State University, Acc and SEC events and also originates regional sports shows.
CABLE NETWORK

FOX Sports Midwest 34679
Owner: News Corporation Ltd.
Editorial: 333 S 18th St, Saint Louis, Missouri 63103-2256 **Tel:** 1 314 206-7000.
Email: midwest@foxsports.net
Web site: http://www.foxsportsmidwest.com
Profile: FOX Sports Midwest is a 24-hour cable television network dedicated to sports in the Midwest. The network emphasizes live game coverage of the St. Louis Cardinals baseball team, St. Louis Blues NHL hockey team, Kansas City Royals baseball and Indiana Pacers basketball. It also televises a significant number of Kansas State, Missouri, Nebraska and Missouri Valley conference college basketball games. The network shares staff and acts as the main headquarters for sister networks FOX Sports Indiana and FOX Sports Kansas City. Pitching for pregame shows for the St. Louis Cardinals, Kansas City Royals, St. Louis Blues and Indiana Pacers, should be relevant to those teams or their sports.
REGIONAL CABLE NETWORK

FOX Sports North 34632
Owner: News Corporation Ltd.
Editorial: 800 Lasalle Ave Ste 200, Minneapolis, Minnesota 55402-2010 **Tel:** 1 612 486-9500.
Email: communications@foxsports.net
Web site: http://www.foxsportsnorth.com
Profile: Serves outlets in Minnesota, Iowa, South Dakota, North Dakota, and Wisconsin. Focuses on live coverage of Minnesota Twins baseball, Minnesota Timberwolves NBA basketball, MLB Milwaukee Brewers, NBA Milwaukee Bucks, and NHL Minnesota Wild games. Also broadcasts University of Minnesota and University of Wisconsin athletic events.
REGIONAL CABLE NETWORK

FOX Sports Ohio 34780
Owner: News Corporation Ltd.
Editorial: 600 Vine St Ste 2204, Cincinnati, Ohio 45202-2491
Email: contactus-fso@foxsports.net
Web site: http://www.foxsportsohio.com
Profile: FOX Sports Ohio is a 24-hour cable television network dedicated to sports in Ohio. Viewers catch up-to-the-minute scores, statistics and video coverage of the day's Ohio sports action.
REGIONAL CABLE NETWORK

FOX Sports San Diego 795149
Owner: News Corporation Ltd.
Editorial: San Diego, California
Web site: http://www.foxsportssandiego.com
Profile: FOX Sports San Diego is a 24-hour cable television network dedicated to sports in the San Diego area. The network emphasizes live game coverage of the San Diego Padres. Coverage also includes the Los Angeles Clippers, Los Angeles Kings, Anaheim Ducks, and Chivas USA.
REGIONAL CABLE NETWORK

FOX Sports South 34610
Owner: News Corporation Ltd.
Editorial: 1175 Peachtree St NE Colon 100SQNE, Atlanta, Georgia 30361-3528 **Tel:** 1 404 230-7300.
Email: fssouth@foxsports.net
Web site: http://www.foxsportssouth.com
Profile: Regional sports outlet distributed to seven southern states. Spotlights coverage of the MLB Atlanta Braves, NBA Atlanta Hawks and NBA Charlotte Hornets games. In addition, the network airs NHL Carolina Hurricanes and Nashville Predators action. Includes collegiate programming from the ACC and SEC, daily NASCAR programming, professional soccer, PGA Tour golf, WTA and ATP Tour tennis, and outdoors programming.
REGIONAL CABLE NETWORK

FOX Sports West 34587
Owner: News Corporation Ltd.
Editorial: 10201 W Pico Blvd, Los Angeles, California 90064-2606 **Tel:** 1 213 743-7800.
Email: communications@foxsports.net
Web site: http://www.foxsports.com
Profile: Regional network serving households in Southern California, Arizona and Nevada. The network holds broadcast rights to the Los Angeles Lakers basketball games, in addition to Los Angeles Kings NHL hockey, Anaheim Angels professional baseball and a variety of collegiate sporting events.
REGIONAL CABLE NETWORK

Free Speech TV 34689
Owner: Free Speech TV
Editorial: 2900 Welton St Ste 300, Denver, Colorado 80205-3010 **Tel:** 1 303 442-8445.
Web site: http://www.freespeech.org
Profile: Free Speech TV provides a nationwide platform for voices traditionally absent from mainstream media. Working with activists and artists, FSTV uses television to expose social and environmental injustices - to help build community, to teach tolerance, to encourage personal creativity and stand for non-violent social action. FSTV is a media conduit to advance progressive social change. FSTV airs primarily social, political, cultural, and environmental documentaries, although some experimental and dramatic work is featured as well. FSTV acquires its programming from independent producers and distributors from all around the world.
CABLE NETWORK

Free State Studios 331060
Owner: Knology
Editorial: 644 New Hampshire St, Lawrence, Kansas 66044-2241 **Tel:** 1 785 832-6376.
Web site: http://freestatestudios.com/fss-homepage
Profile: Since the 1980s, Sunflower Broadband's Free State Studios (previously 6Productions) has been a pioneer in cable programming. The outlet has carved a niche with award-winning news, sports, weather and local programming that directly impacts the residents of Kansas with information they find nowhere else.
REGIONAL CABLE NETWORK

Freeform 34574
Editorial: 500 S Buena Vista St, Burbank, California 91521-0001 **Tel:** 1 818 560-1000.
Web site: http://freeform.go.com
Profile: Freeform offers fun, light-hearted programming with a twist for high school, college and young adults, which the network calls Becomers. Freeform represents the passion, fun, energy and new ideas that infuse young adulthood and millennials. The channel features original series and movies, major theatrical releases, and repurposed programming from the ABC Television Network. ABC Family does not accept any unsolicited pitches or story ideas. In January 2016, the network rebranded from ABC Family to Freeform, targeting younger viewers.
CABLE NETWORK

FSN Detroit 34716
Owner: News Corporation Ltd.
Editorial: 26555 Evergreen Rd, Southfield, Michigan 48076-4206 **Tel:** 1 248 226-9700.
Web site: http://www.foxsports.com/detroit
Profile: Network serving Michigan and parts of Indiana and Ohio. Broadcasts Detroit Tigers baseball games, Detroit Pistons NBA basketball and Detroit Red Wings NHL Hockey. Also covers University of Michigan and Michigan State University sports, as well as Big Ten Conference events.
REGIONAL CABLE NETWORK

FSN Florida 34634
Owner: News Corporation Ltd.
Editorial: 500 E Broward Blvd Ste 105, Fort Lauderdale, Florida 33394-3031 **Tel:** 1 954 375-3634.
Email: askus@foxsports.net
Web site: http://www.foxsportsflorida.com
Profile: FSN Florida is owned and managed by Fox Sports Networks, providing the very best in regional and local sports programming targeted to sports fans across Florida. FSN Florida's programming includes season-long coverage of MLB's Florida Marlins and Tampa Bay Devil Rays, the NHL's Florida Panthers and ACC athletics, including extensive men's basketball coverage. The network also airs original series and specials. FSN national programming also airs on FSN Florida, including Big 12 and Pac- 10 football and basketball as well as FSN's original shows.
REGIONAL CABLE NETWORK

FSN Prime Ticket 34678
Owner: News Corporation Ltd.
Editorial: 1150 S Olive St Ste 300, Los Angeles, California 90015-2278 **Tel:** 1 213 743-7800.
Web site: http://www.foxsports.com
Profile: Regional sports network serving Southern California. Outlet owns broadcast rights to Los Angeles Dodgers baseball, Anaheim Mighty Ducks NHL hockey and Los Angeles Clippers NBA basketball. The network also telecasts local college and high school athletics. The network was formerly known as FSN West 2.
REGIONAL CABLE NETWORK

FSN Southwest 34774
Owner: News Corporation Ltd.
Editorial: 100 E Royal Ln Ste 200, Irving, Texas 75039-4212 **Tel:** 1 972 868-1800.
Email: fssouthwest.feedback@fox.com
Web site: http://www.foxsports.com
Profile: Regional network serving Texas, Oklahoma, Arkansas and Louisiana. FSN Southwest provides live coverage of Texas Rangers major league baseball, NBA basketball with the Dallas Mavericks and San Antonio Spurs, and NHL hockey with the Dallas Stars. The network also airs collegiate and high school athletic contests.
REGIONAL CABLE NETWORK

FSN/FOX Sports Net 34765
Owner: News Corporation Ltd
Editorial: 10201 W Pico Blvd Ste 100-4350, Los Angeles, California 90064-2606 **Tel:** 1 310 369-6000.
Email: feedback@foxsports.com
Web site: http://www.foxsports.com
Profile: FSN is the national cable outlet for FOX Sports. The network provides a variety of sports news, information, and event programming via a combination of eleven owned and operated regional FOX Sports outlets and 10 affiliated regional sports cable networks located from coast-to-coast. The network holds telecast rights to numerous professional baseball, basketball, and hockey teams. FSN also airs an array of collegiate athletics, boxing, tennis, volleyball, and other sporting events.
CABLE NETWORK

Fuji Television 151525
Owner: Fujisankei Communications International, Inc.
Editorial: 150 E 52nd St, New York, New York 10022-6017 **Tel:** 1 212 753-8100.
Web site: http://www.fujisankei.com
Profile: Fuji Television gathers news for Fuji TV and Sankei Shimbun. It also produces, distributes, and acquires television programming, explores investment opportunities in film, music, publishing, and culture. Fuji also broadcasts Japanese-language television shows on American television stations and cable channels. Additionally, it strives to help American and European businesses target Japanese consumers.
CABLE NETWORK

Fuji Television - Los Angeles Bureau 848821
Editorial: 10100 Santa Monica Blvd, Los Angeles, California 90067-4003 **Tel:** 1 310 553-5828.
Email: info@fci-ny.com
Profile: Fuji Television gathers news for Fuji TV and Sankei Shimbun. It also produces, distributes, and acquires television programming, explores investment opportunities in film, music, publishing, and culture. Fuji also broadcasts Japanese-language television shows on American television stations and cable channels. Additionally, it strives to help American and European businesses target Japanese consumers
CABLE NETWORK

Fuji Television - Washington Bureau 151528
Editorial: 529 14th St NW Ste 330, Washington, District Of Columbia 20045-1301 **Tel:** 1 202 347-6070.
Web site: http://www.fujisankei.com
CABLE NETWORK

FUNimation 894348
Owner: Olympusat Media
Editorial: 560 Village Blvd, West Palm Beach, Florida 33409-1945 **Tel:** 1 561 684-5657.
Web site: http://www.funimation.tv/
Profile: The 24-hour network is devoted to providing Anime and cartoon. The network offers cable service in original, acquired and classic entertainment for youth and families.
CABLE NETWORK

Fuse 83022
Owner: SiTV Media
Editorial: 11 Penn Plz, New York, New York 10001-2006 **Tel:** 1 212 324-3450.
Email: inquiries@fuse.tv
Web site: http://www.fuse.tv
Profile: Fuse is the nation's only all-music, viewer-influenced television network, featuring music videos, exclusive artist interviews, live concerts and specials. Formerly known as MuchMusic USA, Fuse officially launched in May 2003.
CABLE NETWORK

Fusion 834717
Owner: Univision Communications Inc.
Editorial: 8551 NW 30th Ter, Doral, Florida 33122-1908
Email: tips@fusion.net
Web site: http://fusion.net
Profile: Fusion is a joint 24-hour English cable network operated by Univision Television Network. Editorial coverage focuses on the issues most relevant for a young, diverse and inclusive America, including the economy, entertainment, music, food, immigration, education, politics, health and wellness and more. The cable network launched on October 28, 2013.
CABLE NETWORK

FX 34758
Owner: News Corporation Ltd.
Editorial: 10201 W Pico Blvd Bldg 103, Los Angeles, California 90064-2606 **Tel:** 1 310 369-0949.
Email: user@fxnetworks.com
Web site: http://www.fxnetworks.com
Profile: FX, the flagship general entertainment basic cable network from Fox, is geared toward viewers with a young, savvy mindset. The diverse schedule includes a growing roster of distinctive original series and movies, a roster of acquired hit series, an established film library with box-office hits from 20th Century Fox and other major studios, with many basic cable television premieres. Marquee sports such as NASCAR and Major League Baseball are also featured.
CABLE NETWORK

FX Movie Channel 153125
Owner: News Corporation Ltd.
Editorial: 10201 W Pico Blvd, Los Angeles, California 90064-2606 **Tel:** 1 310 369-0949.
Web site: http://www.fxnetworks.com/fxm
Profile: FX Movie Channel, also known as FXM, features dramas, comedies and horror films, 24 hours a day. The network is distributed via cable and satellite around the world.
CABLE NETWORK

FYI Network 34737
Owner: A+E Networks
Editorial: 235 E 45th St, New York, New York 10017-3305 **Tel:** 1 212 210-1400.
Web site: http://www.fyi.tv
Profile: FYI, A Network for your Imagination, Innovation, and Inspiration. On July 8, 2014, the network was rebranded from bio to FYI Network. Bio. Online continues on under Say Media.
CABLE NETWORK

Galavision 34644
Owner: Univision Communications Inc.
Editorial: 9405 NW 41st St, Doral, Florida 33178-2301 **Tel:** 1 305 471-3900.
Web site: http://www.galavision.com
Profile: Round-the-clock basic cable channel serving the Hispanic-American community with family-oriented programming including kids shows, sports, movies, music and telenovelas.
CABLE NETWORK

GCN/Global Christian Network 539903
Editorial: 4440 Tuck Road, Loganville, Georgia 30052 **Tel:** 1 770 913-8036.
Email: info@gcntv.org
Web site: http://www.gcntv.org
Profile: GCN/Global Christian Network, also called The People Channel, delivers quality, innovative, multilingual television programs with Christian and family values to independent television stations, local networks, and home satellite and cable providers around the world. GCN aims to unite cultures and continents with the life-changing message of Jesus Christ through inspired and unique television that accompanies viewers in their daily lives. The network offers its audiences a diverse collage of colors, cultures, and faces presented through talk, magazines, music, history, news, comedy, entertainment, education, travel, life, youth, animations, teaching, worship, human interest and more.
CABLE NETWORK

Golf Channel 34626
Owner: NBC Universal
Editorial: 7580 Golf Channel Dr, Orlando, Florida 32819-8947 **Tel:** 1 407 345-4653.
Web site: http://www.golfchannel.com
Profile: 24-hour cable channel devoted to the world of golf. It features live coverage of men's, women's and senior tour events, educational instruction programs, travel-related shows and interviews and profiles of golf professionals.
CABLE NETWORK

Great American Country 34666
Owner: Scripps Networks, Inc.
Editorial: 49 Music Sq W Ste 301, Nashville, Tennessee 37203-3243 **Tel:** 1 865 560-3997.
Web site: http://www.gactv.com
Profile: Great American Country is America's main street for the widest variety of country music, its artists and the lifestyles they influence. In addition to country music videos, GAC features original programming, special music performances and live concerts, and is the exclusive television home of the Grand Ole Opry.
CABLE NETWORK

GSN 34625
Owner: Liberty Media Corporation
Editorial: 2150 Colorado Ave, Ste 100, Santa Monica, California 90404 **Tel:** 1 310 255-6800.
Email: community@gsn.com
Web site: http://www.gsn.com
Profile: GSN, the Network for Games, is the only U.S. television network dedicated to game-related programming and interactive game playing. The network features game shows, reality series, documentaries and casino games. As the industry leader in interactivity, GSN features over 133 hours per week of interactive programming, which allows viewers a chance to win prizes by playing along with GSN's televised games via gsn.com. Reaching 60 million Nielsen homes, GSN is distributed in the U.S. through all major cable systems and satellite providers. For further media information, visit GSN's press website at corp.gsn.com.
CABLE NETWORK

GTN Gateway Television News Network 417853
Owner: City of Black Jack, MO.
Editorial: 12500 Old Jamestown Rd, Black Jack, Missouri 63033-8509 **Tel:** 1 314 355-0400.
Web site: http://www.news20tv.com
Profile: GTN Gateway Television News Network is owned and operated by the City of Black Jack, MO. The channel is distributed through Charter Communications throughout St. Louis and parts of Illinois.
REGIONAL CABLE NETWORK

Hallmark Channel 34655
Owner: Crown Media Family Networks
Editorial: 12700 Ventura Blvd Ste 200, Studio City, California 91604-2469 **Tel:** 1 818 755-2400.
Web site: http://www.hallmarkchannel.com
Profile: The Hallmark Channel is a 24-hour television destination that provides a diverse slate of high-quality entertainment characterized by cinematic excellence and strong stories that are relevant to viewers and their lives. The network, launched in 2001, brings to audiences a brand with a 50-plus-year television legacy that resonates with viewers.
CABLE NETWORK

Hallmark Movies & Mysteries 734133
Owner: Crown Media Family Networks
Editorial: 12700 Ventura Blvd Ste 200, Studio City, California 91604-2469 **Tel:** 1 818 7552400.
Web site: http://www.hallmarkmoviechannel.com
Profile: Hallmark Movie Channel was launched in April 2008 and offers audiences an unparalleled family-friendly viewing experience. It is the fastest-growing cable TV network in 2009 and 2010 and now in 37 million homes, is a 24-hour digital cable network dedicated to bringing viewers original movies with a mix of classic theatrical films, presentations from the acclaimed Hallmark Hall of Fame library, Hallmark Channel Original Movies and special events.
CABLE NETWORK

HBO Family 152935
Owner: Time Warner Inc.
Editorial: 1100 Avenue of the Americas, New York, New York 10036-6712 **Tel:** 1 212 512-1000.
Email: family@hbo.com
Web site: http://www.hbo.com
Profile: Safe and commercial free, HBO Family programming is suitable for all the children in the family, whatever their ages. In the spirit of HBO, HBO Family offers high-quality, original programming that can't be found anywhere else.
CABLE NETWORK

HBO/Home Box Office 34783
Owner: Time Warner Inc.
Editorial: 1100 Avenue Of The Americas, New York, New York 10036 **Tel:** 1 212 512-1000.
Web site: http://www.hbo.com
Profile: Premium cable channel that features first-run theatrical motion pictures, original movies, investigative documentaries, drama and comedy series, concert specials, and live sporting events.
CABLE NETWORK

HBO/Home Box Office - Santa Monica Bureau 34845
Editorial: 2500 Broadway, Ste 400, Santa Monica, California 90404 **Tel:** 1 310 382-3200.
CABLE NETWORK

HETV 538272
Owner: Village of Hoffman Estates
Editorial: 1900 Hassell Rd, Hoffman Estates, Illinois 60169-6308 **Tel:** 1 847 781-2607.
Web site: http://www.hoffmanestates.com
REGIONAL CABLE NETWORK

HGTV 34627
Owner: Scripps Networks, Inc.
Editorial: 9721 Sherrill Blvd, Knoxville, Tennessee 37932-3330 **Tel:** 1 865 694-2700.
Web site: http://www.hgtv.com
Profile: Cable and Satellite Network with national distribution focusing on an array of home, lifestyle, decorating, gardening, hobbies and craft related topics. Broadcasts a potpourri of original and exclusive programming hosted by experts in these various fields. ** A vast majority of programming aired on HGTV is developed by producers outside the network. As a result, it is suggested that most shows should be contacted via network headquarters in Knoxville. ** Additionally, HGTV accepts ideas and information about product resources, potential guests, locations and events, and story ideas via their online resource directory at http://resourcedirectory.hgtv.com.
CABLE NETWORK

Hispanic Information & Television Network 231923
Editorial: 63 Flushing Ave Unit 211, Brooklyn, New York 11205-1072 **Tel:** 1 212 966-5660.
Email: programacion@hitn.org
Web site: http://www.hitn.tv
Profile: The Hispanic Information and Telecommunications Network Inc. was established in 1983 as a private non-profit organization to create a network of non-commercial telecommunications facilities to advance the educational, social, cultural, and economic aspirations of Hispanics.
CABLE NETWORK

History 34607
Owner: A+E Networks
Editorial: 235 E 45th St, New York, New York 10017-3305 **Tel:** 1 212 210-1400.
Web site: http://www.history.com
Profile: History broadcasts a range of documentaries, historical re-enactments, motion pictures, and mini-series dealing with significant figures, events, and inventions through the years.
CABLE NETWORK

History en Español 517400
Owner: A+E Networks
Editorial: 235 E 45th St Fl 8, New York, New York 10017-3305 **Tel:** 1 212 210-1400.
Web site: http://www.historyenespanol.com/espanol
Profile: History en Español is a 24-hour television network dedicated to the Spanish-speaking audience in the United States. It presents a wide range of Spanish-language programming that focuses on great dramatic moments and events as well as the pivotal figures in history. The network airs Spanish Language programming congruent with The History Channel's programming as well as content specifically related to Latin America.
CABLE NETWORK

HLN 34690
Owner: Time Warner Inc.
Editorial: 1 Cnn Ctr NW, Atlanta, Georgia 30303-2762 **Tel:** 1 404 827-1500.
Web site: http://www.cnn.com/specials/videos/hln
Profile: HLN provides viewers with the top stories in national and international news, current weather forecasts, consumer and financial updates, sports scores and highlights, as well as the latest in entertainment, fashion, health and more. Sectioned into four distinct dayparts, the content has been streamlined to focus on news that is most relevant and useful to their viewer's daily lives. In Session, truTV's daytime courtside programming, is produced by HLN.
CABLE NETWORK

ICN TV Network 882894
Owner: Beauty Media
Editorial: 9550 Flair Dr Ste 102, El Monte, California 91731-2917 **Tel:** 1 626 337-8889.
Web site: http://www.icntv.net
Profile: ICN TV Network, formally known as International Audio-Visual Communication Inc., was established in 1980. ICN has become the largest Chinese television media entity in the U.S.
CABLE NETWORK

IFC 34662
Owner: AMC Networks Inc.
Editorial: 11 Penn Plz, New York, New York 10001-2006 **Tel:** 1 917 542-6200.
Email: webmaster@ifc.com
Web site: http://www.ifc.com
Profile: Originally launched as Independent Film Channel, IFC airs first-run theatrical motion pictures produced by small and independent film companies and producers. Programming includes documentaries, animation, shorts, coverage of all major film festivals, cult classics, and exclusive originals.
CABLE NETWORK

INSP 34631
Owner: The Inspirational Networks, Inc.
Editorial: 3000 World Reach Dr, Indian Land, South Carolina 29707-6542 **Tel:** 1 803 578-1000.
Email: info@insp.com
Web site: http://www.insp.com
Profile: INSP is a 24-hour, daily network available to more than 70 million U.S. households via cable and satellite television. The network targets over 79 million Baby Boomers, 35 million of whom self-identify as "socially conservative". INSP features original and exclusive music programs and a wide variety of family friendly entertainment, including The Waltons, Little House on the Prairie, Brady Bunch, Happy Days and feature films. INSP is distributed to more than 2,800 cable systems and to DIRECTV and DISH Network.
CABLE NETWORK

Investigation Discovery 34720
Owner: Discovery Communications, Inc.
Editorial: 1 Discovery Pl, Silver Spring, Maryland 20910-3354 **Tel:** 1 240 662-3709.
Web site: http://investigation.discovery.com
Profile: Investigation Discovery brings viewers provocative, engaging and relevant documentary series and specials about the events and ideas shaping our times. The network has won multiple industry honors for its breakthrough programming, including three Emmys, and Overseas Press Club Award, three National Headliner Awards and a BANFF Rockie Award. In addition, the network has held films premiere at various film festivals, including the Sundance Film Festival, Tribeca Film Festival, San Francisco International Film Festival and the Tokyo Video Festival.
CABLE NETWORK

ION Life 617037
Owner: ION Media Networks
Editorial: 601 Clearwater Park Rd, West Palm Beach, Florida 33401-6233 **Tel:** 1 561 659-4122.
Web site: http://www.ionlife.com
Profile: ION Life is a digital television network that is carried by ION Television affiliates. The programming includes subjects pertaining to health and wellness, cooking, home decor, travel and fitness. ION Life is available via cable, satellite and telco carriage. The network launched on February 19. 2007.
CABLE NETWORK

Iran TV and Radio - New York Bureau 620804
Owner: Islamic Republic Of Iran Broadcasting (IRIB)
Editorial: 60 E 42nd St, Fl 30, New York, New York 10165-0059 **Tel:** 1 212 867-9220.
Email: englishradio@irib.ir
Web site: http://english.irib.ir
CABLE NETWORK

Al Jazeera English - Chicago Bureau 787024
Owner: Al Jazeera Network
Editorial: 875 N Michigan Ave, Chicago, Illinois 60611-1779 **Tel:** 1 202 496-4500.
Web site: http://www.aljazeera.com
Profile: Al Jazeera English is the 24-hour English-language news and current affairs channel headquartered in Doha, the capital of Qatar with broadcasting centers Kuala Lumpur, Malaysia; London and Washington, D.C. and supporting bureaus worldwide. Al Jazeera English is designed to be the English-language channel of reference for Middle Eastern events, balancing the current typical information flow by reporting from the developing world back to the west and from the southern to the northern hemisphere.
CABLE NETWORK

Al Jazeera English - New York Bureau 554711
Owner: Al Jazeera Network
Editorial: 405 E 42nd St Rm C-309, New York, New York 10017-3507 **Tel:** 1 212 317-8238.
Web site: http://www.aljazeera.com
Profile: Al Jazeera English is the 24-hour English-language news and current affairs channel headquartered in Doha, the capital of Qatar with broadcasting centers Kuala Lumpur, Malaysia; London and Washington, D.C. and supporting bureaus worldwide. Al Jazeera English is designed to be the English-language channel of reference for Middle Eastern events, balancing the current typical information flow by reporting from the developing world back to the west and from the southern to the northern hemisphere.
CABLE NETWORK

Al Jazeera English - Washington D.C. Bureau 551852
Owner: Al Jazeera Network
Editorial: 1627 K St NW, Washington, District Of Columbia 20006-1704 **Tel:** 1 202 689-3787.
Email: assignments@aljazeera.net
Web site: http://www.aljazeera.com
Profile: Al Jazeera English is the 24-hour English-language news and current affairs channel headquartered in Doha, the capital of Qatar with broadcasting centers Kuala Lumpur, Malaysia; London and Washington, D.C. and supporting bureaus worldwide. Al Jazeera English is designed to be the English-language channel of reference for Middle Eastern events, balancing the current typical information flow by reporting from the developing world back to the west and from the southern to the northern hemisphere.
CABLE NETWORK

Jewish Broadcasting Service 601949
Tel: 1 201 242-9460.
Email: mail@jbstv.org
Web site: http://jbstv.org
Profile: Formerly Shalom TV, Jewish Broadcasting Service is a mainstream Jewish cable television network covering the panorama of Jewish life. More than 34 million homes nationwide now have access to the free Jewish television service. Programs reflect and address the diversity and pluralism of the Jewish experience. The service does not represent any specific movement or organization in the Jewish community. Jewish Broadcasting Service is directed to every Jewish person with a sense of Jewish identity, and for members of the Jewish community seeking their roots.
CABLE NETWORK

The Jewish Channel 960256
Editorial: 520 8th Ave Fl 4, New York, New York 10018-4393 **Tel:** 1 212 643-9500.
Web site: http://tjctv.com
Profile: The Jewish Channel is a cable television channel available on a variety of cable providers with approximately 45,000 households subscribers. The Jewish Channel brings your culture home. Delivering hundreds of five-star movies, original news, cultural programming, and so much more, TJC gives you the opportunity to explore all that the Jewish world has to offer — from the comfort of your living room.
CABLE NETWORK

JTBC America 972816
Owner: Joins America Inc.
Editorial: 690 Wilshire Pl, Los Angeles, California 90005-3930 **Tel:** 1 213 368-2561.
Web site: http://www.jtbcamerica.com
Profile: Covers news and lifestyle topics pertaining to South Korea and of interest to Korean Americans.
CABLE NETWORK

Kansas Now 22 154273
Editorial: 1500 N West St, Wichita, Kansas 67203 **Tel:** 1 316 943-4221.
Email: news@kake.com
Web site: http://www.kake.com
Profile: Networks airs on Cox Cable systems throughout the state of Kansas and features a programming mixture of local news, weather and sports 24 hours a day. Uses the resources of KAKE-TV of Wichita and WIBW-TV of Topeka.
REGIONAL CABLE NETWORK

KCETLink 836683
Editorial: 2900 W Alameda Ave, Burbank, California 91505-4220 **Tel:** 1 747 201-5000.
Email: contact@kcet.org
Web site: http://www.kcet.org

Profile: KCETLink is the new national independent public transmedia organization formed by the merger between KCET and LInk Media.
REGIONAL CABLE NETWORK

LATV 410799
Owner: LATV LLC
Editorial: 2323 Corinth Ave, Los Angeles, California 90064 **Tel:** 1 310 943-5288.
Web site: http://www.latv.com
Profile: LATV is the nation's first bilingual music and entertainment network distributed via digital multicast. This network targets Hispanic teenagers and young adults. Programs are mainly focusing on music, lifestyle and entertainment.
CABLE NETWORK

Liberty Channel 155946
Editorial: 1971 University Blvd, Lynchburg, Virginia 24502 **Tel:** 1 800 332-1883.
Email: wtlu@liberty.edu
Web site: http://www.libertychannel.com
Profile: Liberty Channel is a satellite/cable network offering family-friendly television for every member of the American family, young to old. Liberty Channel is uplifting, inspirational and entertaining with a strong, conservative and moral foundation. The Liberty Channel provides viewers with a connection to America's most exciting university-Liberty University-in Lynchburg, VA.
CABLE NETWORK

Lifetime 34768
Owner: A+E Networks
Editorial: 685 3Rd Ave, New York, New York 10017-4024 **Tel:** 1 212 424-7000.
Web site: http://www.mylifetime.com
Profile: Lifetime is a national cable network dedicated to providing a wide variety of contemporary women's interest programming. This includes original movies, mini-series, celebrity close-ups, comedies, and lifestyle shows dealing with trends and issues of concern to women.
CABLE NETWORK

Lifetime - Los Angeles Bureau 76840
Owner: A+E Networks
Editorial: 2049 Century Park E, Ste 840, Los Angeles, California 90067-3110 **Tel:** 1 310 556-7500.
CABLE NETWORK

Lifetime Real Women 73603
Owner: A+E Networks
Editorial: 685 3Rd Ave, New York, New York 10017-4024 **Tel:** 1 212 424-7000.
Web site: http://www.lifetimetv.com
Profile: 24-hour channel relying on original series and movies based on true stories. All programming targets women and aims to provide entertainment that will engage and interest this group of viewers.
CABLE NETWORK

LMN 71135
Owner: A+E Networks
Editorial: 685 3rd Ave, New York, New York 10017-4024 **Tel:** 1 212 424-7000.
Web site: http://www.lmn.tv
Profile: The movies on LMN cover every dimension of a woman's life presented in a way that Lifetime Television viewers have come to know and value. Genres include drama, suspense, family, romance, issue-oriented, comedy and mystery.
CABLE NETWORK

Logo 331409
Owner: Viacom Inc.
Editorial: 1515 Broadway, New York, New York 10036-8901
Web site: http://www.logotv.com
Profile: This cable network is advertiser-supported and targets primarily gays and lesbians, ages 25 to 49. Logo provides a mix of original and acquired programming that is authentic, smart, inclusive and open-minded.
CABLE NETWORK

Manhattan Neighborhood Network/MNN 773283
Editorial: 537 W 59th St, New York, New York 10019-1006 **Tel:** 1 212 757-2670 312.
Email: info@mnn.org
Web site: http://www.mnn.org
Profile: Manhattan Neighborhood Network (MNN) is New York City's free, public access cable network.
REGIONAL CABLE NETWORK

MAVTV 824722
Owner: Lucas Oil Products Inc.
Editorial: 302 N Sheridan St, Corona, California 92880-2067 **Tel:** 1 877 475-1711.
Web site: http://www.mavtv.com
Profile: MAVTV was founded in 2002 by four former Showtime Networks executives and was originally geared towards a male dominated audience. In 2011, MAVTV was purchased by Lucas Oil Products, an automotive lubricant manufacturer with a history in television production. MAVTV is geared towards the modern American family and uses the tagline "American Real."
CABLE NETWORK

MCN/Metro Cable Network 363475
Editorial: 1229 2nd St NE, Minneapolis, Minnesota 55413-1129 **Tel:** 1 612 339-3221.
Email: gjacobson@mcn6.org
Web site: http://www.mcn6.org
Profile: Metro Cable Network (MCN) Channel Six, launched in October 1987, aims to provide residents of the Twin Cities with a broad base of regional interest programming.
REGIONAL CABLE NETWORK

MegaTV 605277
Owner: Spanish Broadcasting System Inc.
Editorial: 7007 NW 77th Ave, Miami, Florida 33166-2836 **Tel:** 1 305 644-4800.
Email: info@mega.tv
Web site: http://www.mega.tv
Profile: Spanish-language news, talk and entertainment network.
CABLE NETWORK

Mid-Atlantic Sports Network 484164
Owner: Baltimore Orioles, Washington Nationals
Editorial: 333 W Camden St, Baltimore, Maryland 21201-2496 **Tel:** 1 410 625-7100.
Web site: http://www.masnsports.com
Profile: Mid-Atlantic Sports Network (MASN) is a team-owned regional sports network that televises both Washington Nationals and Baltimore Orioles games in the mid-Atlantic region (Harrisburg, PA to Charlotte, NC). It is owned by the Baltimore Orioles and Washington Nationals baseball teams.
REGIONAL CABLE NETWORK

MLB Network 563196
Editorial: 40 Hartz Way, Secaucus, New Jersey 07094-2403 **Tel:** 1 201 520-6400.
Web site: http://www.mlb.com/network/
Profile: MLB Network airs live games, original programming, highlights, classic games, and coverage of baseball events.
CABLE NETWORK

Mnet 745480
Owner: CJ Corporation
Editorial: 11828 Teale St, Culver City, California 90230-6331 **Tel:** 1 310 313-5194.
Web site: http://www.mnetamerica.com
Profile: Mnet is the only 24/7 English-language television network in the U.S. devoted to Asian pop culture that serves all American viewers who love music and entertainment.
CABLE NETWORK

MSG Plus 34636
Owner: Cablevision
Editorial: 11 Penn Plz Frnt 3, New York, New York 10001-2021 **Tel:** 1 212 465-6000.
Web site: http://www.msgnetwork.com
Profile: MSG Plus is a cable television network distributed throughout the New York metropolitan area. Includes live coverage of New York Mets baseball, New York Islanders and New Jersey Devils professional hockey. The network changed its name from FSN New York to MSG Plus on March 10, 2008.
REGIONAL CABLE NETWORK

MSG/Madison Square Garden Network 34582
Editorial: 11 Penn Plz Frnt 3, New York, New York 10001-2021 **Tel:** 1 212 465-5926.
Email: info@msgnetworks.com
Web site: http://www.msgnetworks.com
Profile: The network serves the New York metropolitan area, New York state, northern New Jersey, Connecticut, and northeastern Pennsylvania. It provides live coverage of select New York-area professional sporting events, as well as exclusive programming from events at Madison Square Garden.
REGIONAL CABLE NETWORK

MSNBC 34763
Owner: NBC Universal
Editorial: 30 Rockefeller Plz Fl 3, New York, New York 10112-0015 **Tel:** 1 212 664-4444.
Email: planning@nbcuni.com
Web site: http://www.msnbc.com
Profile: Built on the worldwide resources of NBC, MSNBC defines news for the next generation with world class reporting and a full schedule of live news coverage, political analysis and award-winning documentary programming- 24 hours a day, seven days a week. MSNBC's companion, award-winning Web site, NBCNews.com, boasts the state-of-the art technology of Microsoft and the world-class reporting of NBC News. By developing programming simultaneously for cable and the Internet, MSNBC offers truly integrated television, interactive news and dynamic discussion of topical events.
CABLE NETWORK

MSNBC - Washington Bureau 34809
Owner: NBC Universal
Editorial: 4001 Nebraska Ave NW, Washington, District Of Columbia 20016-2733 **Tel:** 1 202 885-4800.
Web site: http://www.msnbc.com
Profile: Built on the worldwide resources of NBC, MSNBC defines news for the next generation with world class reporting and a full schedule of live news coverage, political analysis and award-winning documentary programming- 24 hours a day, seven days a week. MSNBC's companion, award-winning Web site, NBCNews.com, boasts the state-of-the art technology of Microsoft and the world-class reporting of NBC News. By developing programming simultaneously for cable and the Internet, MSNBC offers truly integrated television, interactive news and dynamic discussion of topical events.
CABLE NETWORK

MTV 34767
Owner: Viacom Inc.
Editorial: 345 Hudson St, New York, New York 10014-4502 **Tel:** 1 212 846-8000.
Web site: http://www.mtv.com
Profile: MTV is a 24-hour music video and entertainment channel that emphasizes the variety of styles and tastes in popular culture today. The network features news and interview programs with music stars and movie celebrities in addition to award shows, concerts, and special musical events.
CABLE NETWORK

MTV - Los Angeles Bureau 34815
Owner: Viacom Inc.
Editorial: 1575 N Gower St, Hollywood, California 90028-6487 **Tel:** 1 310 752-8000.
CABLE NETWORK

MTV Classic 63077
Owner: Viacom Inc.
Editorial: 1515 Broadway, New York, New York 10036-8901 **Tel:** 1 212 846-8000.
Web site: http://www.mtv.com/classic
Profile: MTV Classic is all about the best of MTV shows and music videos spanning from launch day back in 1981 through the early 2000s. Unplugged, Beavis and Butthead, Aeon Flux, Laguna Beach, Real World, Road Rules, and more.
CABLE NETWORK

MTV Latin America 624682
Owner: Viacom Inc.
Editorial: 1111 Lincoln Rd Fl 6, Miami Beach, Florida 33139-2402 **Tel:** 1 305 535-3700.
Web site: http://www.mtvla.com
Profile: MTV Latin America is the world's first 24-hour Spanish-language network specifically for young adults whose roots extend to both U.S. and Latin cultures.
CABLE NETWORK

MTV2 34671
Owner: Viacom Inc.
Editorial: 1515 Broadway, New York, New York 10036-8901 **Tel:** 1 212 846-8000.
Web site: http://www.mtv.com/mtv2
Profile: A spin-off of MTV, MTV2 provides a 24-hour video-intensive brand of music programming to cable outlets throughout the nation, with a playlist made up of a broad group of artists and genres of music. The network's target audience is young males, ages 12 to 24.
CABLE NETWORK

mtvU 61957
Owner: Viacom Inc.
Editorial: 770 Broadway, 10th Fl, New York, New York 10003 **Tel:** 1 212 654-7016.
Email: feedback@mtvu.com
Web site: http://www.mtvu.com
Profile: mtvU is dedicated to every aspect of college life, from music to news to student life and campus events. The channel is designed to reflect the fast pace of students' lifestyles, and to reach them everywhere they hang out, whether they're watching TV in their dorm rooms, surfing the Web, or walking across campus. mtvU takes a three-pronged approach to reaching students: on-air, online and on campus. With music at its heart, mtvU plays a diverse mix of music programming ranging from hip hop to rock to punk to reggae to dance, along with a constant focus on up-and-coming artists creating a buzz on campus.
CABLE NETWORK

Music Choice 739018
Owner: Music Choice
Editorial: 328 W 34th St, New York, New York 10001-2401 **Tel:** 1 646 459-3300.
Email: comments@musicchoice.com
Web site: http://www.musicchoice.com
Profile: With over 45 Music Channels to choose from, there's one for every music taste ? from today's hottest music to hits from the past. Our selection of Urban, Pop, Rock, Country, Christian, Kids, Classical and Oldies Channels offer hours of uninterrupted listening, along with fun artist facts. Available in 47 million households across the U.S., the Music Channels reach 44 million monthly viewers.
CABLE NETWORK

MUSL TV 733697
Editorial: 14141 Covello St Ste 10A, Van Nuys, California 91405-1448 **Tel:** 1 818 8495447.
Web site: http://www.musltv.com
Profile: MUSL TV (Muscle, Ultra-Sports and Lifestyle Network) is a 24/7 HD linear entertainment network fully devoted to all levels of fitness, training and competitive performance.
CABLE NETWORK

My Life 578454
Owner: National Cable Communications
Editorial: 405 Lexington Ave, Fl 6, New York, New York 10174-0699 **Tel:** 1 212 548-3300.
Web site: http://www.spotcable.com
Profile: My Life is a video-on-demand cable channel available to digital cable subscribers across the United States. An on demand channel allows viewers to pick what they watch, when they want to watch it. This channel features advertising-supported educational programming focusing on health and wellness. The channel should only be pitched regarding healthcare-related advertising.
CABLE NETWORK

Nat Geo Wild 491520
Owner: National Geographic Ventures & FOX Cable Networks
Editorial: 1145 17th St NW, Washington, District Of Columbia 20036-4707 **Tel:** 1 202 912-6500.
Email: newsdesk@nationalgeographic.com
Web site: http://channel.nationalgeographic.com/wild
Profile: Nat Geo Wild is a cable network that brings audiences extraordinary natural history programming and offers intimate encounters with nature's ferocious fighters and gentle creatures of land, sea and air.
CABLE NETWORK

National Geographic Channel 63244
Owner: National Geographic Ventures & FOX Cable Networks
Editorial: 1145 17th St NW, Washington, District Of Columbia 20036-4707 **Tel:** 1 202 912-6500.
Email: newsdesk@nationalgeographic.com
Web site: http://channel.nationalgeographic.com
Profile: National Geographic Channel is the critically acclaimed network for viewers who "Dare to Explore," providing info-rich entertainment that changes the way you see the world. A trusted source for over 100 years, National Geographic provides NGC with unique access to the most respected scientists, journalists and filmmakers, resulting in innovative and contemporary programming of unparalleled quality that pushes boundaries and takes you as far as you can go. NGC has carriage with all of the nation's major cable and satellite television providers, making it currently available to 67 million homes.
CABLE NETWORK

NBA TV 151106
Owner: Turner Sports Interactive, Inc.
Editorial: 450 Harmon Meadow Blvd, Secaucus, New Jersey 07094-3618 **Tel:** 1 201 865-1500.
Web site: http://www.nba.com/nba_tv
Profile: NBA TV, launched in 1999, is the ultimate source for everything basketball. NBA TV provides viewers behind-the-scenes access, authenticity and an insider's perspective. The network shows more than 100 NBA regular season and playoff games, WNBA games, D-League games, major international competitions and weekly Euroleague games.
CABLE NETWORK

NBC Everywhere 587364
Editorial: 30 Rockefeller Plz, New York, New York 10112-0015 **Tel:** 1 212 664-4444.
Web site: http://www.nbcstations.com/multi-market/capability/nbc-everywhere
Profile: NBC Everywhere reaches 1,000 gyms, 3,000 New York taxis, 8,000 schools, 1,005 grocery stores, 181 college campuses, as well as countless screens on commuter trains, arenas, and in Times Square.
REGIONAL CABLE NETWORK

NBC News Channel 34771
Owner: NBC Universal
Editorial: 925 Woodrdg Ctr Dr, Charlotte, North Carolina 28217-1986 **Tel:** 1 704 329-8700.
Profile: Syndicated news service of the NBC Television Network serving over 200 NBC affiliates throughout the United States. Provides video, reporting, and commentary on late-breaking news, business, sports, and features for use on local television broadcasts.
CABLE NETWORK

NBC News Channel - New York Bureau 34817
Editorial: 30 Rockefeller Plz Ste 724E, New York, New York 10112-0015 **Tel:** 1 212 664-7591.
CABLE NETWORK

NBC News Channel - Washington Bureau 34818
Editorial: 400 N Capitol St NW Ste 850, Washington, District Of Columbia 20001-1555 **Tel:** 1 202 783-2615.
CABLE NETWORK

NBC Sports Bay Area 34637
Owner: NBC Universal
Editorial: 370 3rd St, San Francisco, California 94107-1250 **Tel:** 1 415 296-8900.
Email: csnbayinfo@comcastsportsnet.com
Web site: http://www.csnbayarea.com
Profile: NBC Sports Bay Area provides more than 300 live events each year, including Bay Area college teams. Coverage includes the Oakland A's, San Francisco Giants, Golden State Warriors and San Jose Sharks.
REGIONAL CABLE NETWORK

NBC Sports California 441531
Owner: NBC Universal
Editorial: 360 3rd St Fl 2, San Francisco, California 94107-2154 **Tel:** 1 415 296-8900.
Email: csncainfo@comcastsportsnet.com
Web site: http://www.csnbayarea.com
Profile: NBC Sports California is home to viewers' favorite Northern California teams and other sports-related content, including the Sacramento Kings and Monarchs, Oakland Raiders, San Francisco 49ers, Cal State, San Jose State, UC Davis and many more. NBC Sports Bay Area and NBC Sports California are sister networks and share a Web site.
REGIONAL CABLE NETWORK

NBC Universo 77655
Owner: NBC Universal
Editorial: 10 Universal City Plz, Universal City, California 91608-1002
Web site: http://www.nbcuniverso.com
Profile: The network targets 18 to 34-year olds with a fresh, new and authentic programming line-up that includes music video programs, entertainment shows, young dramatic series, an eclectic blend of movies, game and comedy shows. The network aims to reflect an experience that is both Latin and uniquely American, with offerings that reflect common themes yet don't pander to stereotypes. It's committed to the development of original, domestic programming and is motivated cultural relevance more than language. NBC Universo reaches 2.8 million U.S. Hispanic households. It broadcasts to 18 of the top 20 U.S. Hispanic markets through cable, direct to home and low power television. On February 1, 2015, mun2 was rebranded to NBC Universo.
CABLE NETWORK

NBCSN 34639
Owner: NBC Universal
Editorial: 1701 John F Kennedy Blvd, Philadelphia, Pennsylvania 19103-2833 **Tel:** 1 203 356-7000.
Web site: http://www.nbcsports.com
Profile: NBCSN offers exclusive programming in all major sports categories including NFL, NHL, NBA, MLB, NCAA, Golf, Soccer, Olympics and more. The network is distributed via cable systems and satellite operators throughout the continental United States and Hawaii. On January 2, 2012, the network was rebranded from Versus.
CABLE NETWORK

NECN/New England Cable News 34596
Owner: NBC Universal
Editorial: 160 Wells Ave, Newton, Massachusetts 02459-3302 **Tel:** 1 617 630-5000.
Email: newsdesk@necn.com
Web site: http://www.necn.com
Profile: NECN is the largest regional cable news network in the country, serving over three million homes throughout New England and providing 24-hour access to breaking news, sports, weather and traffic. NECN serves all six New England states, including Rhode Island, where it is available on the Verizon FiOS network. The network broadcasts from its studios in Newton, MA and maintains bureaus in Manchester, NH; Hartford, CT; Worcester, MA; Portland, ME; and Burlington, VT.
REGIONAL CABLE NETWORK

NECN/New England Cable News - Manchester Bureau 231071
Editorial: 100 William Loeb Dr, Manchester, New Hampshire 3109 **Tel:** 1 603 668-1131.
CABLE NETWORK

NESN/New England Sports Network 34616
Owner: Boston Red Sox
Editorial: 480 Arsenal St Building #1, Watertown, Massachusetts 02472-2891 **Tel:** 1 617 536-9233.
Email: sports@nesn.com
Web site: http://www.nesn.com
Profile: Cable sports network distributed throughout New England. Provides live sports coverage of Boston Red Sox baseball and Boston Bruins NHL hockey. Also spotlights live collegiate sporting events and outdoor recreational sports. Provides programming in cooperation with ESPNews.
REGIONAL CABLE NETWORK

NET NY 602089
Editorial: 1712 10th Ave, Brooklyn, New York 11215-6215 **Tel:** 1 718 499-9705.
Web site: http://netny.tv
Profile: NET NY is a faith-centered network based in Brooklyn, NY. Broadcasts include news, entertainment, children's, and music, as well as religious programs. It serves the young and old, the churched and unchurched, and men and women from different social, ethnic and religious backgrounds, showing how they work together to make the world a better place. Network launched December 8, 2008.
CABLE NETWORK

New Tang Dynasty TV 552109
Editorial: 229 W 28th St, New York, New York 10001-5915 **Tel:** 1 212 736-8535.
Email: biz@ntdtv.com
Web site: http://english.ntdtv.com
Profile: New Tang Dynasty Television (NTDTV) is an independent, nonprofit television broadcaster established in 2001. Headquartered in New York City, NTDTV currently has reporters and correspondents in over 70 cities worldwide. The network has a partnership with the Epoch Times.
CABLE NETWORK

New Tang Dynasty TV - Bethesda Bureau 864473
Editorial: 10411 Motor City Dr Ste 750, Bethesda, Maryland 20817-1289
Profile: Provides news and entertainment in Mandarin and Cantonese to Chinese Canadians. New Tang Dynasty has a partnership with the Epoch Times.
CABLE NETWORK

New Tang Dynasty TV - Capital Federal Bureau 668009
Editorial: Coronel Diaz 1510, Piso 9, Capital Federal
Web site: http://spanish.ntdtv.com
Profile: Provides news and entertainment in Mandarin and Cantonese to Chinese Argentinians.
CABLE NETWORK

New Tang Dynasty TV - El Monte Bureau 928571
Editorial: 9550 Flair Dr Ste 313, El Monte, California 91731-2915 **Tel:** 1 626 593-2288.
Profile: Provides news and entertainment in Mandarin and Cantonese. New Tang Dynasty has a partnership with the Epoch Times.
CABLE NETWORK

New Tang Dynasty TV - Toronto Bureau 668008
Editorial: 420 Consumers Rd, Toronto, Ontario M2J 1P8 **Tel:** 1 416 787-1577.
Profile: Provides news and entertainment in Mandarin and Cantonese to Chinese Canadians.
CABLE NETWORK

News 12 Bronx 664047
Owner: Rainbow Media
Editorial: 930 Soundview Ave, Bronx, New York 10473-3704 **Tel:** 1 718 861-6800.
Email: news12bx@news12.com
Web site: http://bronx.news12.com
Profile: Cable news channel providing regional and local news, stories and events of interest to cable subscribers in Bronx, NY.
REGIONAL CABLE NETWORK

News 12 Brooklyn 771867
Owner: Rainbow Media
Editorial: 164 20th St, Brooklyn, New York 11232-1180 **Tel:** 1 718 861-6818.
Email: news12bkln@news12.com
Web site: http://brooklyn.news12.com
Profile: Available exclusively to Optimum Television and Time Warner subscribers, News 12 Brooklyn provides 24-hour access to local breaking news, traffic, weather, sports, and more.
REGIONAL CABLE NETWORK

News 12 Connecticut 34684
Owner: Rainbow Media
Editorial: 28 Cross St, Norwalk, Connecticut 06851-4632 **Tel:** 1 203 750-5600.
Email: news12ct@news12.com
Web site: http://connecticut.news12.com
Profile: 24-hour basic cable network providing local and regional news and information to cable systems across southwestern Connecticut.
REGIONAL CABLE NETWORK

News 12 Hudson Valley 827298
Owner: Rainbow Media
Editorial: 235 W Nyack Rd, West Nyack, New York 10994-1700 **Tel:** 1 845 624-8780.
Email: news12hv@news12.com
Web site: http://hudsonvalley.news12.com
Profile: News 12 Hudson Valley is a local cable news networks serving the Hudson Valley community.
REGIONAL CABLE NETWORK

News 12 Long Island 34649
Owner: Rainbow Media
Editorial: 1 Media Crossways, Woodbury, New York 11797-2062 **Tel:** 1 516 393-1390.
Email: news12li@news12.com
Web site: http://longisland.news12.com
Profile: Cable news channel providing regional and local news, stories and events of interest to cable subscribers in Nassau and Suffolk counties on Long Island.
REGIONAL CABLE NETWORK

News 12 New Jersey 34776
Owner: Rainbow Media
Editorial: 450 Raritan Center Pkwy Ste H, Edison, New Jersey 08837-3944 **Tel:** 1 732 346-3200.
Email: news12nj@news12.com
Web site: http://newjersey.news12.com
Profile: News 12 New Jersey offers news of importance to people of New Jersey, presented with perspective and depth. Regional news channel serving viewers in counties of central and northeastern New Jersey and the New York metropolitan area. Provides ongoing, around-the-clock coverage of breaking news and events in the region, in addition to public affairs, informational and lifestyle programming of local interest.
REGIONAL CABLE NETWORK

News 12 New Jersey - Trenton Bureau 34819
Editorial: CN021 125 W State St, Trenton, New Jersey 8625 **Tel:** 1 609 396-2381.
CABLE NETWORK

News 12 The Bronx 34731
Owner: Rainbow Media
Editorial: 930 Soundview Ave, Bronx, New York 10473-3704 **Tel:** 1 718 861-6800.
Email: news12bx@news12.com
Web site: http://www.news12.com
Profile: Regional news cable outlet serving the Bronx and Brooklyn boroughs of New York City. Provides news, sports, weather and information programming designed to cater to the local community.
REGIONAL CABLE NETWORK

News 12 Traffic & Weather 34751
Editorial: 111 Media Crossways Park Dr W, Woodbury, New York 11797-2002 **Tel:** 1 516 803-9000.
Web site: http://www.news12.com
Profile: The tri-state's first and only 24-hour local traffic, transit and weather channel, providing up-to-the-minute information for five different regions using cutting edge technology, links to national weather systems, and an extensive traffic camera network. Produced by the News 12 regional news services, News 12 Traffic & Weather is actually five separate services provided for five different regions: New York City, New Jersey, Connecticut, Westchester and Long Island.
REGIONAL CABLE NETWORK

News 12 Westchester 34654
Owner: Rainbow Media
Editorial: 6 Executive Plz, Yonkers, New York 10701-6832 **Tel:** 1 914 378-8916.
Email: news12wc@news12.com
Web site: http://westchester.news12.com
Profile: Cable all-news channel providing 24-hour coverage of breaking news, weather and sports around Westchester County and Hudson Valley in New York state.
REGIONAL CABLE NETWORK

News 13 34709
Owner: Charter Communications
Editorial: 20 N Orange Ave Ste 13, Orlando, Florida 32801-4603 **Tel:** 1 407 513-1300.
Email: newsdesk@mynews13.com
Web site: http://mynews13.com
Profile: 24-hour cable news channel covering nine counties in Central Florida and Orlando.
REGIONAL CABLE NETWORK

News 5 Now 457238
Owner: Evening Post Publishing Co.
Editorial: 2200 7th Ave, Pueblo, Colorado 81003-1821 **Tel:** 1 719 632-5030.
Web site: http://www.koaa.com
Profile: Colorado Springs, CO's local news and weather is available 24 hours a day, 7 days a week on News 5 Now. This channel can be seen on Comcast cable channel 9 in Colorado Springs, CO, Comcast digital cable channel 247 in Pueblo, CO, and streaming live at koaa.com. In addition to longer, local news cut-ins throughout the day.
REGIONAL CABLE NETWORK

News Channel 3 Anytime 70969
Editorial: 803 Channel 3 Dr, Wreg-Tv, Memphis, Tennessee 38103-4603 **Tel:** 1 901 543-2333.
Email: news@wreg.com
Web site: http://www.wreg.com
Profile: News Channel 3 Anytime is a regional cable news network provided as a joint venture service of Time Warner Communications and WREG-TV in Memphis. The network airs 24 hours a day, seven days a week, and provides the latest local news, weather and sports. The network is carried on Time Warner cable systems serving Memphis; Crittenden, AR; DeSoto, MS; Marshall, MS; Hardeman, TN; Haywood, TN; Shelby, TN; and Tipton, TN. Address mail to WREG-TV.
REGIONAL CABLE NETWORK

Newschannel 5+ 34747
Owner: The E.W. Scripps Co
Editorial: 474 James Robertson Pkwy, Nashville, Tennessee 37219-1212 **Tel:** 1 615 244-5000.
Email: plus@newschannel5.com
Web site: http://www.newschannel5.com
Profile: Newschannel 5+ is a regional cable network covering local news and information in 35 counties and 500,000 homes in the Nashville area. Programming consists of a blend of locally produced talk shows, encore performances of WTVF Newschannel 5 broadcasts and national and international news from The All News Channel.
REGIONAL CABLE NETWORK

NewsChannel 8 34715
Owner: Sinclair Broadcast Group, Inc.
Editorial: 1100 Wilson Blvd, Arlington, Virginia 22209-2249 **Tel:** 1 703 236-9552.
Web site: http://www.wjla.com/news/newschannel-8
Profile: Regional cable network serving as the Washington, D.C. metro area's 24-hour local news source. It provides community-based, solution-oriented news coverage to more than one million cable television homes in suburban Maryland, Northern Virginia and Washington, D.C. It differs from traditional TV news coverage because it allows 24-hour access to news and information in a non-sensationalized manner.
REGIONAL CABLE NETWORK

Newsmax TV 953399
Owner: Newsmax
Tel: 1 800 485-4350.
Web site: http://www.newsmaxtv.com
Profile: Offers news and commentary covering politics, health, entertainment, sports, and breaking news. Includes expert views and live programming from high-profile hosts and guests with a conservative lean.
CABLE NETWORK

News-Press 3 Now 538882
Editorial: 825 Edmond St, Saint Joseph, Missouri 64501-2737 **Tel:** 1 816 271-8500.
Web site: http://www.newspressnow.com
Profile: News-Press 3 Now is a regional cable network providing news to St. Joseph, MO and surrounding areas. Weather updates are available at the top and bottom of every hour, and three to four live newscasts are offered each day.
REGIONAL CABLE NETWORK

Newswatch Channel 15 34706
Owner: TEGNA Inc.
Editorial: 1024 N Rampart St, New Orleans, Louisiana 70116-2406 **Tel:** 1 504 529-4444.
Profile: 24-hour cable news channel serving New Orleans and surrounding regions and providing coverage of local news, weather, and sports. News programming provided in conjunction with WWL-TV New Orleans.
REGIONAL CABLE NETWORK

NFL Network 154604
Owner: NFL Enterprises, L.P.
Editorial: 10950 Washington Blvd, Culver City, California 90232-4026 **Tel:** 1 310 840-4635.
Web site: http://www.nfl.com/nflnetwork
Profile: NFL Network provides millions of football fans with a network to call their own. NFL Network takes 87 years of NFL history and combines it with the latest technology to bring television viewers sports entertainment at its highest level. NFL Network is a destination for all that happens around the league, on and off the field, during the season and throughout the offseason.
CABLE NETWORK

NHL Network 608352
Owner: National Hockey League
Editorial: 1185 Avenue of the Americas, New York, New York 10036-2601 **Tel:** 1 212 789-2000.
Email: nhlfoundation@nhl.com
Web site: http://www.nhl.com
Profile: NHL Network is the first 24-hour network dedicated to the National Hockey League, dedicated to comprehensive hockey coverage, both on and off the ice. The programming includes live games, daily highlight shows, up-to-the-minute hockey news and special events.
CABLE NETWORK

Nick Jr. 34732
Owner: Viacom Inc.
Editorial: 1515 Broadway, Fl 37, New York, New York 10036 **Tel:** 1 212 258-6000.
Email: press@nickjr.com
Web site: http://www.nickjr.com
Profile: Nick Jr. is the commercial-free, educational preschool network from Nickelodeon. Nick Jr. strives to be a place where preschoolers can engage with characters they love while building their imaginations, gaining key cognitive and social-emotional skills, and learning about the world around them. Through interactivity and rich story-telling informed by preschool educational experts, Nick Jr. helps kids learn early literacy, movement and exercise, basic math, science, music appreciation, art, language acquisition and social skills. Nick Jr. is targeted towards preschoolers ages 2 to 5 and their caregivers and currently reaches more than 56 million U.S. homes. On September 28, 2009, Noggin was rebranded to Nick Jr.
CABLE NETWORK

Nickelodeon 34577
Owner: Viacom Inc.
Editorial: 1515 Broadway, New York, New York 10036-8901 **Tel:** 1 212 258-7500.
Email: nickpressdepartment@nick.com
Web site: http://www.nick.com
Profile: Nickelodeon is the industry's leading producer of original programming for kids, the network offers a lineup of original animation, known as "Nicktoons," variety and game shows, as well as adventure shows. Nickelodeon is a division of Viacom Inc. Due the nature of programming at the network, there are NO opportunities for story or product pitches. Nickelodeon has requested that no contacts be listed.
CABLE NETWORK

Nickelodeon - Los Angeles Bureau 358054
Editorial: 1575 N Gower St, Hollywood, California 90028-6487 **Tel:** 1 310 752-8000.
Profile: Nickelodeon is the industry's leading producer of original programming for kids, the network offers an incredible lineup of original animation, known as "Nicktoons," variety and game shows, as well as adventure and news magazine shows. Nickelodeon is a division of Viacom Inc. Due the nature of programming at the network, there are NO opportunities for story or product pitches. Nickelodeon has requested that no contacts be listed.
CABLE NETWORK

Nippon Television - New York Bureau 621056
Owner: NTV International Corporation
Editorial: 645 5th Ave Rm 303, New York, New York 10022-5960 **Tel:** 1 212 660-6900.
Email: contact@ntvic.com
Web site: http://www.ntvic.com
CABLE NETWORK

One America News Network 874946
Owner: Herring Broadcasting, Inc.
Editorial: 4757 Morena Blvd, San Diego, California 92117-3462 **Tel:** 1 858 270-6900.
Email: info@oann.com
Web site: http://www.oann.com
Profile: The network provides unbiased, substantive national and international news 24/7.
CABLE NETWORK

United States of America

Orange Television Network
945547
Editorial: 215 University Pl Rm 278, Syracuse, New York 13210-2816 **Tel:** 1 315 443-6892.
Email: orangetv@syr.edu
Web site: http://orangetv.syr.edu
Profile: On the air since 2005, OTN is student produced TV and it's on the air 24/7 throughout the school year. We mean it when we say "Watch Yourself" because our student crews produce many of the comedy, sports, dance, music and artistic performances all over campus that have you as the star.
REGIONAL CABLE NETWORK

The Outdoor Channel 34674
Owner: Outdoor Channel Holdings Inc.
Editorial: 43445 Business Park Dr, Temecula, California 92590-3669 **Tel:** 1 951 699-6991.
Email: info@outdoorchannel.com
Web site: http://www.outdoorchannel.com
Profile: The Outdoor Channel is a nationally broadcast cable network featuring programming designed to educate and entertain outdoor enthusiasts of all ages. The channel promotes traditional outdoor activities that are a vital part of America's national heritage including fishing, hunting, bull riding, and shooting sports, with a focus on activities that families can enjoy in the great outdoors.
CABLE NETWORK

Outside Television Network
621210
Owner: Mariah Media, Inc.
Editorial: 33 Riverside Ave Fl 4, Westport, Connecticut 06880-4223 **Tel:** 1 203 221-9240.
Web site: http://www.outsidetelevision.com
Profile: Outside Television broadcasts in more than 110 prime destination-area markets around the country. Through its affiliated stations, it serves these local resorts by providing relevant local information combined with national entertainment. When visiting resort markets around the country, vacationers shows the best places to eat, what to do with the kids, where to shop, and how to get around.
CABLE NETWORK

Ovation - The Arts Network 34628
Owner: Hubbard Media Group
Editorial: 2850 Ocean Park Blvd Ste 225, Santa Monica, California 90405-6217 **Tel:** 1 310 430-7575.
Email: info@ovationtv.com
Web site: http://www.ovationtv.com
Profile: Ovation - the Arts Network is a cable television network featuring documentary and performance programs on the arts including theater, dance, opera, jazz, classical music, literature and the visual arts. The network presents tours of great museums and exhibitions, profiles of best-loved and up and coming artists; documentaries on musical styles and artistic movements; performances by preeminent musicians and orchestras, dance, theater and opera companies; behind-the-scenes coverage of important arts events and explorations into the arts of cultures around the world.
CABLE NETWORK

OWN: Oprah Winfrey Network
616305
Owner: Discovery Communications, Inc.
Editorial: 1041 N Formosa Ave, West Hollywood, California 90046-6703 **Tel:** 1 323 602-5500.
Web site: http://www.oprah.com/app/own-tv.html
Profile: OWN: Oprah Winfrey Show is the network of self-discovery, connecting people to each other and to their greatest potential. The programming includes a mix of nonfiction, short form programming, movies, documentaries and acquisitions. OWN is a joint venture between Oprah Winfrey and Discovery Communications launched on January 1, 2011.
CABLE NETWORK

Oxygen 34755
Owner: NBC Universal
Editorial: 75 9th Ave Fl 7, New York, New York 10011-7011 **Tel:** 1 212 651-5000.
Web site: http://www.oxygen.com
Profile: Oxygen is a cable network that focuses on true crime programming aimed towards women. The network re-branded to the crime network for women in summer 2017.
CABLE NETWORK

Pac-12 Network 822091
Owner: Pac-12 Media Enterprises
Editorial: 1350 Treat Blvd Ste 500, Walnut Creek, California 94597-8853 **Tel:** 1 925 932-4411.
Web site: http://pac-12.com
Profile: Pac-12 Network is a sports cable television network dedicated to the Pac-12 Conference.
CABLE NETWORK

Pacifica Community Television
560349
Owner: Pacifica Community Television
Editorial: 580 Crespi Dr Ste E, Pacifica, California 94044-3426 **Tel:** 1 650 355-8000.
Email: admin@PacificCoast.tv
Web site: http://pacificcoast.tv/
Profile: Pacifica Community Television provides public, educational, and government programming for viewers in the San Mateo County area.
REGIONAL CABLE NETWORK

PCN/Pennsylvania Cable Network 34686
Editorial: 401 Fallowfield Rd, Camp Hill, Pennsylvania 17011-4906 **Tel:** 1 717 730-6000.
Email: pcntv@pcntv.com
Web site: http://www.pcntv.com
Profile: Provides unedited live and same-day coverage of Pennsylvania House and Senate floor proceedings. Also televises committee hearings, press conferences, speeches and other public forums and events where the business of the state is debated, discussed and decided. Airs important business forums and meetings, tours museums and manufacturing facilities in the Commonwealth, and conducts weekly one-on-one interviews with prominent Pennsylvanians.
REGIONAL CABLE NETWORK

PCNC/Pittsburgh Cable News Channel 34659
Owner: Cox Media Group, Inc.
Editorial: 4145 Evergreen Rd, Pittsburgh, Pennsylvania 15214-1636 **Tel:** 1 412 237-1100.
Email: assignments@wpxi.com
Web site: http://www.wpxi.com/pcnc
Profile: PCNC/Pittsburgh Cable News Channel is a 24-hour all-news channel Cox Media Group, Inc. serving the Pittsburgh metropolitan area and western Pennsylvania. The network provides continuous live coverage of regional news, weather and sports. News and information programming is provided in conjunction with WPXI-TV Pittsburgh.
REGIONAL CABLE NETWORK

Peninsula TV 439799
Editorial: 610 Elm St Ste 211, San Carlos, California 94070-3070 **Tel:** 1 650 637-1936.
Web site: http://www.pentv.org
Profile: Peninsula TV premiered in June 1999 with a goal to provide area residents with a regional community cable television channel combining traditional governmental access with high quality original community programming.
REGIONAL CABLE NETWORK

Pierce County TV/PCTV 763507
Editorial: 4400 Steilacoom Blvd SW, Lakewood, Washington 98499-4002 **Tel:** 1 253 589-5878.
Email: pcrcc@co.pierce.wa.us
Web site: http://www.piercecountytv.org
Profile: Pierce County Television (PCTV) creates and manages government access programming for the cities, towns and unincorporated areas of Pierce County, WA. Programming consists of gavel-to-gavel meeting coverage, original news and magazine shows and other locally produced programs.
REGIONAL CABLE NETWORK

Pivot 882749
Owner: Participant Media
Editorial: 331 Foothill Rd Fl 3, Beverly Hills, California 90210-3669 **Tel:** 1 310 550-5100.
Email: press@pivot.tv
Web site: http://www.pivot.tv
Profile: Pivot is a television network from Participant Media — the people that brought you movies and documentaries like Lincoln, Food, Inc., and An Inconvenient Truth. Pivot delivers diverse talent and an entertaining mix of original and acquired programming. Content will range from a live nightly topical show to narrative films and documentaries, alongside original comedies and dramas. Available to more than 40 million subscribers at launch.
CABLE NETWORK

POP 81611
Owner: Lionsgate Entertainment Corp. & CBS Corp.
Editorial: 1800 N Highland Ave Fl 6, Los Angeles, California 90028-4521 **Tel:** 1 323 856-4000.
Email: press@tvgn.tv
Web site: http://poptv.com
Profile: Channel curates programming that celebrates being a fan of pop culture. POP is seen in more than 80 million homes nationwide. In January 2015, the network rebranded to the name POP. It had previously been known as TVGN, and before that TV Guide Network.
CABLE NETWORK

QVC 734272
Owner: Liberty Media Corporation
Editorial: 1200 Wilson Dr, West Chester, Pennsylvania 19380-4267 **Tel:** 1 484 7011000.
Web site: http://www.qvc.com
Profile: QVC is one of the largest multimedia retailers in the world. QVC provides its customers with thousands of contemporary beauty, fashion, jewelry and home products. Its programming is distributed to approximately 195 million homes worldwide.
CABLE NETWORK

ReelzChannel 468714
Owner: Hubbard Media Group
Editorial: 5650 University Blvd SE, Albuquerque, New Mexico 87106-9700 **Tel:** 1 505 212-8800.
Email: info@reelzchannel.com
Web site: http://www.reelzchannel.com
Profile: Dedicated to entertaining, informing, directing and connecting fans to everything movies. Original programming features movie reviews, celebrity interviews and behind-the-scenes clips.
CABLE NETWORK

ReelzChannel - Los Angeles Bureau 468722
Editorial: 1201 W 5th St Ste 345, Los Angeles, California 90017-2019 **Tel:** 1 213 534-3524.
CABLE NETWORK

ReelzChannel - New York Bureau 468723
Editorial: 122 E 42nd St Rm 1505, New York, New York 10168-1594 **Tel:** 1 212 697-2024.
CABLE NETWORK

Reuters Television 33056
Owner: Thomson Reuters
Editorial: 3 Times Sq, New York, New York 10036-6564 **Tel:** 1 646 223-4000.
Email: tvdne@thomsonreuters.com
Web site: http://www.reuters.com
Profile: Thomson Reuters is the world's largest news and television agency. It is a news production and broadcast services operation for local television stations and outlets. The network provides an array of national and international news, sports, business news, entertainment, and weather via a network of bureaus and satellites covering the globe.
CABLE NETWORK

Reuters Television - Los Angeles Bureau 33104
Editorial: 633 W 5th St Ste 2300, Los Angeles, California 90071-2049 **Tel:** 1 213 380-2014.
Web site: http://www.reuters.com
CABLE NETWORK

Reuters Television - Shanghai Bureau 854963
Editorial: AZIA Center #1233 Unit 4, Fl. 30, Lujiazui Ring Rd, Shanghai
CABLE NETWORK

Reuters Television - Singapore Bureau 887450
Editorial: 18 Science Park Drive, Singapore 118229
Tel: 1 65 67755088.
Email: rvn.asia@thomsonreuters.com
Profile: Reuters Television Singapore bureau.
CABLE NETWORK

Reuters Television - Washington Bureau 33103
Editorial: 1333 H St NW, Ste 500, Washington, District Of Columbia 20005-4707 **Tel:** 1 202 898-0056.
CABLE NETWORK

REVOLT TV 870482
Editorial: 1800 N Highland Ave Fl 6, Los Angeles, California 90028-4521
Email: contactus@revolt.tv
Web site: http://www.revolt.tv
Profile: REVOLT TV will deliver music content and be a destination for conversations around music, artists, and their creations. It will leverage the power of social media communication tools to fuel the live music dialog and influence music culture and content in real time for the video-centric generation.
CABLE NETWORK

RFD-TV 355281
Owner: Rural Media Group
Editorial: 49 Music Sq W Ste 301, Nashville, Tennessee 37203-3243 **Tel:** 1 615 227-9292.
Email: info@rfdtv.com
Web site: http://www.rfdtv.com
Profile: Launched in December 2000, RFD-TV is the nation's first 24-hour television network dedicated to serving the needs and interests of rural America and agriculture. The channel is produced and uplinked via satellite to all 50 states from Northstar Studios in Nashville, TN. The channel is carried by DISH Network, DIRECTV, Mediacom, and NCTC cable systems, with new cable systems adding the channel most everyday.
CABLE NETWORK

RLTV 418453
Editorial: 5525 Research Park Dr, Baltimore, Maryland 21228-4873 **Tel:** 1 410 402-9600.
Web site: http://www.rl.tv
Profile: RLTV is television for Americans 55 and older. The network informs viewers on topics including health, lifestyle, finance and politics and provides engaging stories about ordinary people who lead extraordinary lives.
CABLE NETWORK

RNN/Regional News Network
33071
Editorial: 800 Westchester Ave, Rye Brook, New York 10573-1354 **Tel:** 1 914 417-2700.
Email: newsdesk@fios1news.com
Web site: http://www.rnntv.com
Profile: Regional News Network covers the latest breaking regional news. Via news bureaus and studios in New York and Washington, D.C., RNN's broadcasting facilities attempt to offer both the latest technologies and prime locations.
REGIONAL CABLE NETWORK

RNN/Regional News Network - Kingston Bureau 74027
Editorial: 721 Broadway, Kingston, New York 12401-3449 **Tel:** 1 914 417-2709.
CABLE NETWORK

ROOT Sports Southwest 839316
Owner: DIRECTV Sports Networks, LLC
Editorial: 1201 San Jacinto St Ste 200, Houston, Texas 77002-6930
Web site: http://southwest.rootsports.com
Profile: The network covers sports in the U.S. Southwest Region: Arkansas, Louisiana, Eastern New Mexico, Oklahoma, and Texas.
REGIONAL CABLE NETWORK

ROOT Sports: Northwest Region 34617
Owner: DIRECTV Sports Networks, LLC
Editorial: 3626 156Th Ave Se, Bellevue, Washington 98006-1729 **Tel:** 1 425 641-0104.
Email: northwest@rootsports.com
Web site: http://northwest.rootsports.com
Profile: Distributed throughout Washington, Oregon, Idaho, Montana and Alaska. Programming emphasizes live broadcasts of Seattle Mariners baseball. Also provides coverage of events from the Pac-12, Big Sky and West Coast collegiate athletic conferences.
REGIONAL CABLE NETWORK

ROOT Sports: Pittsburgh Region 34615
Owner: DIRECTV Sports Networks, LLC
Editorial: 323 N Shore Dr Ste 200, Pittsburgh, Pennsylvania 15212-5320 **Tel:** 1 412 316-3800.
Web site: http://pittsburgh.rootsports.com
Profile: Network serving western Pennsylvania, West Virginia, western Maryland, southwestern New York, and parts of Ohio. Sports package includes live coverage of Pittsburgh Pirates baseball, Pittsburgh Penguins NHL hockey, and University of Pittsburgh and West Virginia University athletics.
REGIONAL CABLE NETWORK

ROOT Sports: Rocky Mountain Region 34773
Owner: DIRECTV Sports Networks, LLC
Editorial: 2399 Blake St Ste 130, Denver, Colorado 80205-2195 **Tel:** 1 720 898-2700.
Email: rockymountain@fsninsider.net
Web site: http://rockymountain.rootsports.com
Profile: Root Sports is the home of the Colorado Rockies, Utah Jazz, Mountain West Conference, Big Sky Conference and University of Denver. The network reaches 2.5 million households across nine states and delivers more than 350 live events each year- all of which are available in HD.
REGIONAL CABLE NETWORK

RT 619148
Owner: Autonomous Nonprofit Organization "TV-Novosti"
Editorial: 1325 G St NW, Washington, District Of Columbia 20005-3104
Email: rt-us@rttv.ru
Web site: https://www.rt.com
Profile: RT is a Russian-language television network broadcasting in Europe, North America and Israel, as well as in countries of the Commonwealth of Independent States. The network offers news and culture shows to the Russian-speaking diaspora.
CABLE NETWORK

RT America 944108
Editorial: 1325 G St NW, Washington, District Of Columbia 20005-3104 **Tel:** 1 202 942-7440.
Email: rt-us@rttv.ru
Web site: http://rt.com/usa
Profile: RT America is the US based arm of RT (Russia Today), a 24-hour English-language international broadcast news network headquartered in Moscow.
CABLE NETWORK

Science 34719
Owner: Discovery Communications, Inc.
Editorial: 8516 Georgia Ave, Silver Spring, Maryland 20910-3401 **Tel:** 1 240 662-2000.
Web site: http://www.sciencechannel.com
Profile: Specialty cable channel which uncovers the clues to the questions that have eluded us for centuries and reveal life's greatest mysteries and smallest wonders. Content is from the worlds of astronomy, physics, chemistry, earth science and related fields. ** A vast majority of programming aired on Discovery Science is developed by producers outside the network. As a result, it is suggested that most shows should be contacted via network headquarters in Silver Spring, MD. On June 8, 2011, Science Channel rebranded to Science.
CABLE NETWORK

Seattle Channel 786207
Editorial: 600 4th Ave Fl L1, Seattle, Washington 98104-1850
Email: contact@seattlechannel.org
Web site: http://www.seattlechannel.org
Profile: The Seattle Channel is a government access channel granted to the City of Seattle, and presents programs on cable television (channel 21 on Comcast and Millennium) and via the Internet to help citizens connect with their city. Programming includes series and special features highlighting the diverse civic and cultural landscape of the Seattle area.
REGIONAL CABLE NETWORK

The SEC Network 923359
Owner: Walt Disney Co.
Editorial: 11001 Rushmore Dr, Charlotte, North Carolina 28277-3434
Web site: http://secsports.go.com
Profile: The SEC Network is a joint venture between the Southeastern Conference and ESPN, which have created the multiplatform network which will launch August 14, 2014. The new network will televise 45 SEC football games, more than 100 men's basketball games, 60 women's basketball games, 75 baseball games, and events from across the SEC's 21 sports annually. Programming will also include in-depth

commentary and analysis in studio shows, daily news and information original content such as SEC Storied, spring football games, and more. Hundreds of additional live events from various sports will be offered exclusively on the digital platform.
CABLE NETWORK

Showtime Networks Inc. 34766
Owner: CBS Corporation
Editorial: 1633 Broadway, New York, New York 10019-6708 **Tel:** 1 212 708-1600.
Web site: http://www.sho.com
Profile: Showtime network provides a variety of movies and original programming. The network also markets and distributes sports and entertainment events for exhibition to subscribers on a pay-per-view basis through Showtime Event Television Pay Per View.
CABLE NETWORK

Showtime Networks Inc. - Los Angeles Bureau 34813
Editorial: 10880 Wilshire Blvd Ste 1600, Los Angeles, California 90024-4117 **Tel:** 1 310 234-5200.
CABLE NETWORK

Sinclair Broadcast Group 151524
Editorial: 10706 Beaver Dam Rd, Hunt Valley, Maryland 21030-2207 **Tel:** 1 410 568-1500.
Web site: http://www.sbgi.net
Profile: Sinclair Broadcast Group is a centralized news service located in Maryland which produces and distributes national and regional news, sports and weather to Sinclair owned and operated stations using current technology that allows repetitive efforts to be eliminated or reduced. This structure allows the local station to focus completely on reporting local news stories that affect the community.
CABLE NETWORK

SINO Television 541862
Owner: Multicultural Radio Broadcasting Inc.
Editorial: 27 William St #11F, New York, New York 10005-2701 **Tel:** 1 212 431-4300.
Web site: http://www.sinotv.us
Profile: SINO Television features 24 hours of Chinese language programming in New York, New Jersey and Connecticut. Programming includes news, sports, entertainment, financial reports drama, cooking shows, community programs and movies.
REGIONAL CABLE NETWORK

The Ski Channel 543933
Owner: Atonal Sports and Entertainment
Editorial: 881 Alma Real Dr, Pacific Palisades, California 90272-3731 **Tel:** 1 310 230-2050.
Email: info@theskichannel.com
Web site: http://www.theskichannel.com
Profile: The Ski Channel is an original ad supported network delivered via VOD, web, wireless and other means of distribution and the worlds first clearly defined Television 2.0 network. It is the only cable television network devoted to the wide variety of year round mountain activities such as skiing, snowboarding, hiking, biking, backpacking, climbing, etc, along with many off-slope activities. The Ski Channels' content includes a myriad of movies, events and episodic television shows and well as programming in news, weather, destination travel, equipment, instruction and real estate. The Ski Channel is distributed on Comcast, Time Warner Cable, DirecTV, DishNetwork, Verizon, Cox Communications, and several other cable providers.The network launched on December 25, 2008.
CABLE NETWORK

Sky Link TV 623085
Editorial: 500 Montebello Blvd, Rosemead, California 91770-4303 **Tel:** 1 323 888-0028.
Email: info@skylinktv.us
Web site: http://www.skylinktv.us
Profile: Sky Link TV is a 24-hour Mandarin Chinese general entertainment channel tailor-made for the Chinese audience in North America with a wide variety of programming. The program lineup includes top-rated, most popular Chinese and Korean dramas, immediate news from China and Taiwan, local-produced news that is customized for Chinese American audiences, popular political commentary programs, variety and talk shows from Taiwan and China.
CABLE NETWORK

Smile of a Child Network 377619
Owner: Trinity Broadcasting Network
Editorial: 2442 Michelle Dr, Tustin, California 92780
Tel: 1 714 832-2950.
Web site: http://www.smileofachild.org
Profile: Founded by the Trinity Broadcasting Network, Smile of a Child offers quality Christian children's programming 24 hours per day. It is available in 13 major markets via digital multi-casting. The programming both entertains as well as morally instructs children during their formative years by bringing the best moral and biblical teachings through fun and constructive television.
CABLE NETWORK

Smithsonian Channel 559115
Owner: SNI/SI Networks L.L.C.
Editorial: 1633 Broadway Fl 15, New York, New York 10019-6755 **Tel:** 1 212 708-1601.
Email: pressinquiries@smithsoniannetworks.com
Web site: http://www.smithsonianchannel.com
Profile: Smithsonian Channel showcases scientific, cultural and historical programming based largely upon the assets of the Smithsonian Institution, the world's largest museum complex. Smithsonian

Channel features original documentaries, short-subject explorations and innovative groundbreaking programs highlighting America's historical, cultural and scientific heritage.
CABLE NETWORK

Smithsonian Channel - Washington Bureau 771141
Editorial: 1225 19Th St Nw Ste 250, Washington, District Of Columbia 20036-2458 **Tel:** 1 202 261-1700.
CABLE NETWORK

SNY/SportsNet New York 441779
Owner: Comcast Corporation
Editorial: 4 World Trade Ctr Fl 50, New York, New York 10007-2366 **Tel:** 1 212 485-4800.
Email: sportsnetnewyork@sny.tv
Web site: https://www.sny.tv
Profile: SNY/SportsNet New York, which launched in spring 2006, is New York's regional sports network available to viewers in New York, Connecticut, most of New Jersey and northeastern Pennsylvania. The network's programming roster also includes classic sports programming, critically acclaimed original entertainment show, and exclusive interview and magazine programs.
REGIONAL CABLE NETWORK

Soldiers Radio and Television 473489
Owner: U.S. Army
Editorial: 2530 Crystal Dr Ste 100, Arlington, Virginia 22202-3934 **Tel:** 1 703 602-8009.
Email: dmajointdesk@dma.mil
Web site: http://www.army.mil/media/srtv
Profile: Produces radio and television programming that keeps both soldiers and the public informed on what's happening in the Army.
CABLE NETWORK

Sony Entertainment Television Asia 658756
Owner: Sony Entertainment Television Asia
Editorial: MSM North America Inc., 550 Madison Ave, New York, New York 10022 **Tel:** 1 212 833-7684.
Web site: http://www.setasia.tv
Profile: Features contemporary programming tailored to South Asian tastes and sensibilities. Reaching the upscale, economically active 18 to 49 year-old age group.
CABLE NETWORK

Spectrum News - Albany 88184
Owner: Charter Communications
Editorial: 104 Watervliet Avenue Ext, Albany, New York 12206-1628 **Tel:** 1 518 459-9999.
Email: albanynews@charter.com
Web site: http://www.twcnews.com/nys/capital-region.html
Profile: Regional cable news network providing unique news programming to more than 300,000 customers in and around Albany, Troy, Rensselaer, Saratoga, Glens Falls, Schenectady, Amsterdam and Gloversville/Johnstown, NY and Pittsfield and Athol, MA. Direct extensions for staff members correspond with the news department telephone line.
REGIONAL CABLE NETWORK

Spectrum News - Buffalo 584308
Owner: Charter Communications
Editorial: 355 Chicago St, Buffalo, New York 14204-2069 **Tel:** 1 716 558-8999.
Email: buffalo-news@charter.com
Web site: http://buffalo.twcnews.com
Profile: Time Warner Cable News - Buffalo (formerly YNN Buffalo) is a 24-hour news channel servicing the Buffalo, NY area.
REGIONAL CABLE NETWORK

Spectrum News - Central New York 154633
Owner: Charter Communications
Editorial: 815 Erie Blvd E, Syracuse, New York 13210-1016 **Tel:** 1 315 234-1000.
Email: yournews@charter.com
Web site: http://www.twcnews.com/nys/central-ny.html
Profile: Time Warner Cable News - Central New York (formerly YNN Central New York) is a regional, 24-hour news network covering central/upstate New York. The network is available to 560,000 Time Warner Cable subscribers from Northern Pennsylvania to the Canadian border. Based in Syracuse, NY, Time Warner Cable News Central New York operates seven regional newsrooms and produces three regional program feeds.
REGIONAL CABLE NETWORK

Spectrum News - Charlotte 759431
Owner: Charter Communications
Editorial: 316 E Morehead St Ste 100, Charlotte, North Carolina 28202-2313 **Tel:** 1 704 973-5800.
Email: cltnews@charter.com
Web site: http://www.twcnews.com/nc/charlotte.html
Profile: 24-hours a day, 7 days a week news network in North Carolina and broadcasts cover news in Mecklenburg, Gaston, Cleveland, Cabarrus, Iredell, Rowan, Stanly, Union, Anson and Richmond counties. The network has 1.3 million subscribers.
REGIONAL CABLE NETWORK

Spectrum News - Coastal North Carolina 939412
Owner: Charter Communications
Editorial: 2321 Scientific Park Dr, Wilmington, North Carolina 28405-1825 **Tel:** 1 866 963-9714.
Email: coastalncnews@charter.com
Web site: http://coastalnc.twcnews.com
Profile: Time Warner Cable News - Coastal Carolina is a 24-hour cable news channel dedicated to providing local news and information to viewers in the Wilmington, Newport and surrounding areas in North Carolina. There is an emphasis is on local news, with national news reports for one minute each half hour. Local weather forecasts air every 10 minutes.
REGIONAL CABLE NETWORK

Spectrum News - Greensboro 759437
Owner: Charter Communications
Editorial: 200 Centreport Dr Ste 2010, Greensboro, North Carolina 27409-9797 **Tel:** 1 336 856-9497.
Email: triadnews@charter.com
Web site: http://www.twcnews.com/nc/triad.html
Profile: Greensboro, NC office for Time Warner Cable News.
REGIONAL CABLE NETWORK

Spectrum News - Raleigh 81239
Owner: Charter Communications
Editorial: 2505 Atlantic Ave Ste 102, Raleigh, North Carolina 27604-1593 **Tel:** 1 919 882-4000.
Email: centralncnews@twcnews.com
Web site: http://www.twcnews.com/nc/triangle-sandhills.html
Profile: Time Warner Cable News - Raleigh is a 24-hour cable news channel dedicated to providing local news and information to viewers in the Raleigh, Durham/Chapel Hill, Down East, Sandhills/Fayetteville, Triad, Charlotte and surrounding areas in North Carolina. There is an emphasis is on local news, with national news reports for one minute each half hour. Local weather forecasts air every 10 minutes.
REGIONAL CABLE NETWORK

Spectrum News - Rochester 34670
Owner: Charter Communications
Editorial: 71 Mount Hope Ave, Rochester, New York 14620-1014 **Tel:** 1 585 756-2424.
Email: rochester@charter.com
Web site: http://www.twcnews.com/nys/rochester.html
Profile: Time Warner Cable News - Central New York (formerly YNN Rochester) is a 24-hour, independent, cable news network providing the greater Rochester, NY, area with up-to-the-minute news, weather, and sports. The news network follows the Time Warner tradition of the half-hour news wheel.
REGIONAL CABLE NETWORK

Spectrum News Austin 34754
Owner: Charter Communications
Editorial: 1708 Colorado St, Austin, Texas 78701-1209 **Tel:** 1 512 531-8000.
Email: txnewsdesk@charter.com
Web site: http://www.twcnews.com/tx/austin.html
Profile: Spectrum News Austin is a 24-hour regional cable news network serving Austin, TX, and the surrounding Central Texas area. Launched September 13, 1999, it is the fifth local news channel operated by Time Warner's regional cable companies. The network delivers community-oriented journalism on an around-the-clock basis, providing complete local coverage of news, weather, traffic, and sports as well as extended coverage of local breaking news events as they happen.
REGIONAL CABLE NETWORK

Spectrum News NY1 34597
Owner: Charter Communications
Editorial: 75 9th Ave Frnt 6, New York, New York 10011-7033 **Tel:** 1 212 379-3311.
Email: desk@ny1.com
Web site: http://www.ny1.com
Profile: Spectrum News NY1 is Charter Cable's 24-hour newschannel in New York City. On the air since September 8, 1992. The network covers the city's five boroughs including Manhattan, Bronx, Brooklyn, Queens and Staten Island. The network provides up-to-the-minute news, sports and weather, in addition to public affairs, business and sports-related talk programming.
REGIONAL CABLE NETWORK

Spectrum News San Antonio 940199
Owner: Charter Communications
Editorial: 1708 Colorado St, Austin, Texas 78701-1209 **Tel:** 1 512 531-8000.
Email: txnewsdesk@charter.com
Web site: http://www.twcnews.com/tx/san-antonio.html
Profile: Spectrum News San Antonio is a 24-hour, independent, cable news network providing the greater San Antonio, TX area with up-to-the-minute news, weather, and sports. The network offices are in Austin, but the content is local to San Antonio.
REGIONAL CABLE NETWORK

Spectrum Sports 546386
Owner: Charter Communications
Editorial: 7901 66th St N, Pinellas Park, Florida 33781-2106 **Tel:** 1 727 329-1947.
Email: commentssportsfl@charter.com
Web site: http://www.baynews9.com/Sports.html
Profile: Spectrum Sports offers 24-hour local sports programming for the Tampa Bay and Orlando markets. It features an array of local sporting events

including live high school and college games as well as in-depth coverage of college and professional teams throughout the state. The network provides over 5,500 hours of sports programming, produces over 1,000 studio shows, and features over 75 live high school sporting events per year. Spectrum Sportsis available on Digital Cable channel 47. It is also available on Digital Cable Ready TV channel 47.1.
REGIONAL CABLE NETWORK

Spike TV 34576
Owner: Viacom Inc.
Editorial: 345 Hudson St, New York, New York 10014-4502 **Tel:** 1 212 767-4001.
Web site: http://www.spike.com
Profile: Spike TV is dedicated to the things men want. The brand speaks to the bold, adventuresome side of men with action-packed entertainment, including a mix of comedy, blockbuster movies, sports, innovative originals and live events. It is available in 86 million homes and is a division of Viacom Inc. Spike TV will rebrand to The Paramount Network, with a tentative launch for 2018.
CABLE NETWORK

Spike TV - Los Angeles Bureau 350022
Editorial: 1575 N Gower St, Los Angeles, California 90028-6487 **Tel:** 1 310 407-1200.
CABLE NETWORK

Sportsman Channel 394603
Owner: InterMedia Partners VII L.P.
Editorial: 2855 S James Dr, Ste 101, New Berlin, Wisconsin 53151 **Tel:** 1 262 432-9100.
Email: sportsman@thesportsmanchannel.com
Web site: http://www.thesportsmanchannel.com
Profile: Launched in 2003, Sportsman Channel is the only television and digital media company fully devoted to the more than 82 million sportsmen in the United States, delivering entertaining and educational programming focused exclusively on hunting, shooting and fishing activities. Sportsman Channel is now available in HD, check with your local cable or satellite provider. In San Antonio, the Sportsman Channel is located on channel 267. Acquired by InterMedia Outdoors Holdings in 2006, Sportsman Channel reaches almost 27 million U.S. television households and is a part of the nation's largest multimedia company targeted exclusively to serving the information and entertainment needs of outdoors enthusiasts. The tagline of the network is "The Leader in Outdoor TV for the American Sportsman ." To learn more, visit www.thesportsmanchannel.com, follow on Twitter, @SPORTSMANchnl, or Fan on Facebook, www.facebook.com/sportsmanchannel Our strict programming guidelines serve the serious sportsman and do not allow for infomercials, motor sports, bull riding or any other variety outdoor programming.
CABLE NETWORK

SportsTime Ohio 513470
Owner: Paul Dolan
Editorial: 1333 Lakeside Ave E, Cleveland, Ohio 44114-1134 **Tel:** 1 216 344-7400.
Email: info@sportstimeohio.com
Web site: http://www.sportstimeohio.com
Profile: SportsTime Ohio, or STO, is the television home of the Cleveland Indians, Cleveland Browns, Horizon League and Ohio Athletic Conference basketball and OHSAA regular season games, playoffs and state championships as well as golf and sports talk programming. SportsTime Ohio is the sister network to Fox Sports Ohio, producing over 750 live sporting events and 4800 hours of live and original programming every year. Together, the two networks reach over five million households in Ohio, Kentucky, Indiana, Western Pennsylvania, western New York, and West Virginia.
REGIONAL CABLE NETWORK

Sprout 710966
Owner: NBC Universal
Tel: 1 877 768-8411.
Email: info@sproutonline.com
Web site: http://www.sproutonline.com
Profile: Sprout is the first 24-hour preschool destination available on TV, on demand and online for kids ages 2 to 5 and their parents and caregivers. The network will rebrand to Universal Kids on September 9, 2017.
CABLE NETWORK

Starz Encore 733945
Owner: Liberty Media Corp.
Editorial: 8900 Liberty Cir, Englewood, Colorado 80112-7057 **Tel:** 1 720 8527700.
Web site: http://www.starz.com
Profile: Starz Encore is a premium television channel featuring mainly older and recent blockbuster motion pictures. It launched in April 1991 and the channel's sister network is Starz.
CABLE NETWORK

Starz Entertainment 34620
Owner: Liberty Media Corp.
Editorial: 8900 Liberty Cir, Englewood, Colorado 80112-7057 **Tel:** 1 720 852-7700.
Web site: https://www.starz.com
Profile: Starz Entertainment is a premier movie service provider in the United States. It offers various movie channels, including the flagship Starz and Encore channels. Starz Entertainment also airs more than 1,000 movies per month across its pay television channels, including Starz On Demand, the only on-demand pay television subscription service available on cable, satellite and broadband platforms. The network also offers a suite of advanced video

offerings, including Starz! HD, Starz! Hi-Res, Sharper Movies HD, and Starz on Demand HD.
CABLE NETWORK

Starz InBlack 34697
Owner: Liberty Media Corp.
Editorial: 8900 Liberty Cir, Englewood, Colorado 80112-7057 **Tel:** 1 720 852-7700.
Web site: https://www.starz.com/schedule
Profile: Pay movie channel spotlighting the cinematic accomplishments of African-American filmmakers, and providing an audience for up-and-coming filmmakers. Programming includes exclusive first-run theatrical releases, recent popular titles, classic movies, independent films, films from Africa and the African Diaspora, and original productions 24 hours a day, seven days a week.
CABLE NETWORK

Sun Sports - Sunrise Bureau 34822
Editorial: 1550 Sawgrass Corporate Pkwy, Ste 350, Sunrise, Florida 33323-2822 **Tel:** 1 954 845-9994.
Web site: http://www.foxsportsflorida.com
Profile: Regional sports outlet serving over 6.1 million cable and satellite homes in Florida. Sports programs include live coverage of Orlando Magic and Miami Heat NBA basketball, and Tampa Bay Lightning NHL hockey. Network also broadcasts a wide variety of college athletics, including University of Florida, Florida State University, Acc and SEC events and also originates regional sports shows.
CABLE NETWORK

Suncoast News Network 34660
Owner: Citadel Communications, LLC
Editorial: 1741 Main St, Sarasota, Florida 34236-5812 **Tel:** 1 941 361-4600.
Email: news@snntv.com
Web site: http://www.snntv.com
Profile: Suncoast News Network is a 24-hour cable news network serving the Sarasota and Bradenton markets in Florida, in addition to surrounding counties. The network provides local and regional news, weather, and sports in partnership with the Sarasota Herald-Tribune daily newspaper.
REGIONAL CABLE NETWORK

SundanceTV 34664
Owner: AMC Networks Inc.
Editorial: 11 Penn Plz Fl 2, New York, New York 10001-2028 **Tel:** 1 212 324-8500.
Web site: http://www.sundance.tv
Profile: Under the creative direction of Robert Redford, Sundance is the television destination for independent-minded viewers seeking something different. Bold, uncompromising and irreverent, Sundance Channel offers audiences a diverse and engaging selection of films, documentaries and original programs, all uncut and commercial free.
CABLE NETWORK

The Surf Channel 882753
Editorial: 401 Wilshire Blvd Ste 230, Santa Monica, California 90401-1429 **Tel:** 1 310 260.6434.
Web site: http://www.thesurfchannel.com
Profile: The Surf Channel is an original, free, ad supported VOD television network delivered on cable, satellite and IPTV services, web and wireless.
CABLE NETWORK

Syfy 34787
Owner: NBC Universal
Editorial: 30 Rockefeller Plz, New York, New York 10112-0015 **Tel:** 1 212 664-4444.
Email: feedback@scifi.com
Web site: http://www.syfy.com
Profile: This network focuses on science fiction programming. It features made-for-television and theatrical films, themed specials, horror shows, and vintage science fiction television series like Knight Rider, The Twilight Zone and Star Trek.
CABLE NETWORK

Syfy - Universal City Bureau 34851
Editorial: 100 Universal City Plz, Bldg 1440, Universal City, California 91608 **Tel:** 1 818 777-6898.
CABLE NETWORK

TBN/Trinity Broadcasting Network 34578
Owner: Trinity Broadcasting Network
Editorial: 2442 Michelle Dr, Tustin, California 92780-7091 **Tel:** 1 714 832-2950.
Email: comments@tbn.org
Web site: http://www.tbn.org
Profile: Religious cable network with programming of a multi-denominational nature. TBN is the world's largest Christian television network. The network is distributed throughout America and around the world. TBN is seen on over 2,500 television stations, 17 satellites, the Internet and thousands of cable systems around the world. The network produces original Christian programs and gospel music concerts from Nashville and includes live coverage of major Christian events and informative talk shows with exciting guests.
CABLE NETWORK

TBS 34581
Owner: Time Warner Inc.
Editorial: 1010 Techwood Dr NW, Atlanta, Georgia 30318-5604 **Tel:** 1 404 827-1717.
Web site: http://www.tbs.com
Profile: TBS, a division of Turner Broadcasting System, Inc., bill itself as television's "Very Funny" network. It serves as home to such contemporary comedies as Sex and the City, Everybody Loves Raymond, Family Guy, Seinfeld and Friends. The network also features original comedy series programming, specials and special events, blockbuster movies and hosted movie showcases.
CABLE NETWORK

TBS - Los Angeles Bureau 586839
Editorial: 3500 W Olive Ave, Fl 15, Burbank, California 91505-4630 **Tel:** 1 818 977-5500.
CABLE NETWORK

TeenNick 510642
Owner: MTV Networks
Editorial: 1515 Broadway, New York, New York 10036-8901 **Tel:** 1 212 258-6000.
Web site: http://www.teennick.com
Profile: TeenNick is a 24 hour network for young adults featuring movies, original series, animated productions and general entertainment fare that focuses on the real life issues teens face every day. In addition to original programming, the network also airs hit series from Nickelodeon. In addition, Emmy winning Web site, www.The-N.com, provides fans with complete access to behind-the-scenes interviews, pictures and videos, plus a robust community of 2 million members who interact with message boards, user profiles and blogs. TeenNick is targeted towards teens between the ages of 13 and 16 and is currently available in over 56 million homes. On September 28, 2009, The N was rebranded to TeenNick.
CABLE NETWORK

The Tennis Channel 86388
Owner: Sinclair Broadcast Group, Inc.
Editorial: 2850 Ocean Park Blvd, Santa Monica, California 90405-2955 **Tel:** 1 310 314-9400.
Web site: http://tennischannel.com
Profile: The Tennis Channel serves up prestigious matches featuring today's most celebrated players. In addition to the major American tournaments such as the ATA and WTA, many other domestic tournaments and a wide array of international events are aired. In addition, World Team Tennis matches, scores of events from the Intercollegiate Tennis Association and top national junior events are shown along with a seasoning of other racket sports including squash, badminton, table tennis and paddle tennis. At the end of March 2016, Sinclair is expected to close as new owners of The Tennis Channel.
CABLE NETWORK

TheBlaze 896852
Owner: Mercury Radio Arts
Editorial: 6301 Riverside Dr, Irving, Texas 75039-3531
Web site: http://www.theblaze.com/tv
Profile: The network provides 24/7 news, opinion and entertainment programming from a libertarian conservative perspective.
CABLE NETWORK

Time Warner Cable Deportes 829406
Owner: Charter Communications
Email: twcdeportes@charter.com
Web site: http://twcdeportes.com
Profile: Time Warner Cable Deportes deliver the region's sports information with a year-round schedule of more than 120 live sports events as the exclusive local homes of the Los Angeles Lakers, LA Galaxy and Los Angeles Sparks.
REGIONAL CABLE NETWORK

Time Warner Cable Noticias 151697
Owner: Charter Communications
Editorial: 75 9th Ave Frnt 6, New York, New York 10011-7033 **Tel:** 1 212 379-3311.
Web site: http://www.ny1noticias.com
Profile: Spanish-language regional cable news channel serving the five boroughs of New York City. Provides up-to-the-minute news, sports and weather, in addition to public affairs, business and sports-related talk programming.
REGIONAL CABLE NETWORK

Time Warner Cable SportsChannel 897310
Owner: Charter Communications
Editorial: 6550 Winchester Ave, Kansas City, Missouri 64133-4660 **Tel:** 1 816 222-5530.
Email: sportschannelweb@charter.com
Web site: http://www.twcsportschannel.com/mo/kansascity
Profile: Time Warner Cable SportsChannel in Kansas City, formerly known as Metro Sports, is a regional sports network serving the Kansas City Metropolitan Area, Lawrence, Kansas, and the state of Nebraska. It launched on December 12, 1996.
REGIONAL CABLE NETWORK

TLC 34575
Owner: Discovery Communications, Inc.
Editorial: 8516 Georgia Ave, Silver Spring, Maryland 20910-3401 **Tel:** 1 240 662-2000.
Web site: http://producers.discovery.com
Profile: TLC is dedicated to high-quality, intelligent and relatable non-fiction entertainment that inspires, engages, informs and unites the audience in the spirit of life's possibilities. TLC intimately connects more than 94 million homes in North America. Programming includes a variety of documentaries, investigative reports and historic footage. A vast majority of programming aired on Discovery Science is developed by producers outside the network. As a result, it is suggested that most shows should be contacted via network headquarters in Silver Spring, MD.
CABLE NETWORK

TLC - Los Angeles Bureau 503938
Owner: Discovery Communications, Inc.
Editorial: 10100 Santa Monica Blvd, 1050, Los Angeles, California 90067-4003 **Tel:** 1 310 551-1611.
Web site: http://tlc.discovery.com
CABLE NETWORK

TMC/The Movie Channel 734126
Owner: Showtime Networks Inc.
Editorial: 1633 Broadway Fl 7, New York, New York 10019-6708 **Tel:** 1 212 7081600.
Web site: http://www.sho.com/site/tmc/home.do
Profile: TMC/The Movie Channel is a premium channel owned by Showtime Networks Inc., a subsidiary of CBS Corporation. The channel features mostly movies, as well as special behind the scenes features, softcore adult erotica and movie trivia. The channel launched in 1973 as Star Channel and was rebranded in 1979 to The Movie Channel. Sister networks include Showtime and Flix.
CABLE NETWORK

TNT/Turner Network Television 34779
Owner: Time Warner Inc.
Editorial: 1050 Techwood Dr NW, Atlanta, Georgia 30318-5604 **Tel:** 1 404 885-4339.
Web site: http://www.tnt.tv
Profile: Basic cable channel featuring movies, original series, original motion pictures, mini-series productions, off-net dramas and championship sports all supporting the network's brand as a destination for dramatic entertainment. TNT is available in high-definition.
CABLE NETWORK

Total Living Network 34736
Editorial: 2880 Vision Ct, Aurora, Illinois 60506 **Tel:** 1 630 801-3838.
Email: mail@tln.com
Web site: http://www.tln.com
Profile: Network providing a range of specialty programming dealing with health, fitness, spiritual and nutritional topics. TLN is a media provider offering entertaining and inspirational programming that offers practical information for today's lifestyles. TLN distributes programming through broadcast, cable, digital, satellite and the Internet.
CABLE NETWORK

Tr3s: MTV, Musica y Mas 602673
Owner: Viacom Inc.
Editorial: 1515 Broadway Fl 25, New York, New York 10036-8901 **Tel:** 1 212 846-8000.
Web site: http://www.tr3s.com
Profile: Tr3?s: MTV, Musica y Mas is in 7.4 million Hispanic TV households and 34 million total TV households, making it the most-widely distributed TV network dedicated to superserving today's bicultural Latino youth. Tr3?s: MTV, Musica y Mas programming is rooted in the fusion of American and Latino music, cultures, lifestyles and languages. Music programming is at the core of Tr3?s and the channel features hitmakers, emerging artists and new sounds that resonate with young U.S. Latinos. In addition to music programming, the Tr3?s programming slate also features lifestyle series, news, documentaries and other long-form programs that celebrate US Latino hybrid identity and culture.
CABLE NETWORK

Travel Channel 34584
Owner: Scripps Networks, Inc.
Editorial: 5425 Wisconsin Ave, Chevy Chase, Maryland 20815-3552 **Tel:** 1 301 244-7500.
Web site: http://www.travelchannel.com
Profile: Basic cable network devoted exclusively to travel entertainment capturing the fascination, freedom and fun of travel. Travel Channel delivers insightful stories about the world's most popular destinations and inspiring diversions. In 2016, the network will move to Knoxville, TN to join the other Scripps Networks. A spokesperson says current employees are being asked to move to Knoxville, though some may relocate to New York. Until details are finalized, company officials cannot say how many jobs will be created in Knoxville by the move.
CABLE NETWORK

Tribune Broadcasting Company 87774
Owner: Tribune Company
Editorial: 435 N Michigan Ave, Chicago, Illinois 60611-4066 **Tel:** 1 312 222-3342.
Web site: http://www.tribune.com
Profile: News service serving Tribune-owned television stations throughout the country. Tribune Broadcasting owns and operates 23 major-market television stations including the superstation WGN which can be viewed in more than 50 million homes outside of Chicago via cable and satellite services. Many of the Tribune stations are affiliates of CW Television Network, in which they have an investment. Tribune Broadcasting compiles stories and feeds to be distributed throughout the Tribune family of stations. Tribune Broadcasting is in the process of being sold to Sinclair Broadcast Group, and is expected to close at the end of 2017.
CABLE NETWORK

truTV 34594
Owner: Time Warner Inc.
Editorial: 1 Time Warner Ctr, New York, New York 10019-6038 **Tel:** 1 212 275-0700.
Web site: http://www.truTV.com
Profile: truTV is the home to comedy-driven reality programs and scripted series. It offers an innovative and entertaining look at the real world through authentic characters, humorous situations and engaging storytelling. The network was formerly known as Court TV, before re-branding to truTV which focused on original documentaries, series and specials, plus popular off-network series dealing with crime and investigation. The network made the shift to comedic programming in 2014.
CABLE NETWORK

TUFF TV 840763
Owner: TUFF TV Media Group, LLC
Editorial: 3340 Peachtree Rd NE, Atlanta, Georgia 30326-1023 **Tel:** 1 404 230-9600.
Email: info@tufftv.com
Web site: http://www.tufftv.com
Profile: TUFF TV is a digital broadcast network offering original programming targeted at men. The network launch in June 2009.
CABLE NETWORK

Turner Classic Movies 34619
Owner: Time Warner Inc.
Editorial: 1050 Techwood Dr NW, Atlanta, Georgia 30318-5604 **Tel:** 1 404 827-1700.
Web site: http://www.tcm.com
Profile: Airings of classic films from Hollywood's golden era. Commercial-free outlet with occasional themed marathons of individual actors, directors, and studios all culled from the vast film libraries of MGM and Warner Brothers.
CABLE NETWORK

TV Asia 621435
Editorial: 76 National Rd, Edison, New Jersey 08817-2809 **Tel:** 1 732 650-1100.
Email: info@tvasiausa.com
Web site: http://www.tvasiausa.com
Profile: TV Asia is a informational and entertainment channel for the South- Asian and Indian community in North America . The network is based on a wide range of programming from news, local community news and educational programs to dramas, music, movies, in-house programs.
CABLE NETWORK

TV Japan 504161
Owner: NHK Cosmomedia America, Inc.
Editorial: 100 Broadway Fl 15, New York, New York 10005-1983 **Tel:** 1 212 262-3377.
Email: tvjapan@tvjapan.net
Web site: http://nhkcosmomedia.com
Profile: TV Japan is a 24-hour Japanese-language television network offering news, drama, education, music and sports programming to the Japanese diaspora in the United States and Canada. Some of its programming comes from NHK, the Japanese public television network.
CABLE NETWORK

TV Japan - Santa Monica Bureau 618043
Editorial: 3130 Wilshire Blvd Ste 360, Santa Monica, California 90403-2367 **Tel:** 1 310 829-5575.
Web site: https://tvjapan.net
CABLE NETWORK

TV Land 34661
Owner: Viacom Inc.
Editorial: 345 Hudson St, New York, New York 10014-4502 **Tel:** 1 212 258-8000.
Email: postmaster@tvland.com
Web site: http://www.tvland.com
Profile: TV Land features programming from vintage and classic television series of yesterday. The network's eclectic program mixes popular dramas, sitcoms, westerns, retromercials and a television-preferential interstitial audience in mind.
CABLE NETWORK

TV One 156622
Owner: Urban One, Inc.
Editorial: 1010 Wayne Ave Ste 1000, Silver Spring, Maryland 20910-5668 **Tel:** 1 301 755-0400.
Web site: http://tvone.tv
Profile: Cable network targeting adult African American and urban viewers. The network includes a broad mix of original and existing programming from all the entertainment genres, including scripted and unscripted dramas, sitcoms, game shows, movies, plays and news magazines.
CABLE NETWORK

TV-2 KLBC 34745
Owner: Clark (Bruce & Lynn)
Editorial: 3100 Needles Hwy Ste 1700, Laughlin, Nevada 89029-0900 **Tel:** 1 702 298-2222.
Email: information@tv2klbc.com
Web site: http://www.tv2klbc.com
Profile: TV-2 KLBC is a cable origination station which serves 20,000 homes and over 10,000 hotel rooms throughout Laughlin, Nevada and Bullhead City, Arizona. TV-2 airs programming from the UPN Network as well as several syndicators from around the nation. TV-2 KLBC does NOT cover news related to the Las Vegas area.
REGIONAL CABLE NETWORK

TV5 MONDE USA 562147
Owner: TV5 MONDE
Editorial: 8733 W Sunset Blvd, West Hollywood, California 90069-2244 **Tel:** 1 800 737-0455.
Email: toutsavoir@tv5monde.org
Web site: http://www.tv5.org/usa
Profile: TV5 MONDE USA is a division of the French television station TV5 MONDE. The network offers programming in films, sports, news and documentaries. The network promotes programming from French-speaking countries including Canada, Belgium, Switzerland and France. All programming

originates in the central Paris offices. Story ideas and news tips should be sent to the main e-mail address.
CABLE NETWORK

TV8 Vail 768271
Owner: Vail Resorts Inc.
Editorial: 137 Benchmark Rd, Avon, Colorado 81620
Tel: 1 970 754-8888.
Email: tv8vail@vailresorts.com
Web site: http://www.tv8vail.com
Profile: TV8 Vail offers weather, news, events and all of the latest from the local community. It provides residents and visitors with an unequaled source of quality television entertainment and information about the area. The station is a leased access cable station carried on the Comcast Cable System from East Vail to Cordillera and on the Centry Link System in Eagle and Gypsum, Colorado.
REGIONAL CABLE NETWORK

TVG Network/Television Games Network 734457
Owner: Betfair
Editorial: 6701 Center Dr W Ste 160, Los Angeles, California 90045-1558 **Tel:** 1 310 2429400.
Email: pr@tvg.com
Web site: http://www.tvg.com
Profile: TVG Network is a specialty channel dedicated to horse racing. TVG Network is an interactive horse racing network that combines live, televised coverage from over 100 of the World's premier racetracks and allows viewers to make wagers from home: online, by phone, mobile phone and, where available, using a set-top remote control. In addition to live horse racing, TVG Network features professional race analysis, interviews, handicapping tips, feature stories on the superstars of horse racing, the horses, personalities and legends of racing other programming.
CABLE NETWORK

Univision Deportes Network 814534
Owner: Univision Communications Inc.
Editorial: 9405 NW 41st St, Doral, Florida 33178-2301
Tel: 1 305 471-3900.
Web site: http://www.univision.com/deportes
Profile: Univision Deportes Network is 24/7 all-sports network from Univision. The UDN difference is access to the top sports content such as the Liga Mexicana de Fútbol, Major League Soccer, CONCACAF Champions League, U.S. National Team, Mexican National Team, World Cup qualifiers and unmatched coverage leading up to World Cup 2014. The network launched in April 2012.
CABLE NETWORK

UP 475012
Owner: Humbard (Charles)
Editorial: 2077 Convention Center Concourse Ste 300, Atlanta, Georgia 30337-4210 **Tel:** 1 770 692-8890.
Web site: http://www.uptv.com
Profile: UP features uplifting music and entertainment, featuring music and inspiring stories the whole family will enjoy. UP is the only TV network with every program certified as family safe by the Parents Television Council. UP is found on DIRECTV channel 338 and DISH Network channel 188 nationally, and many local cable systems.On June 1, 2013, the network was rebranded from GMC to UP.
CABLE NETWORK

USA Network 34761
Owner: NBC Universal
Editorial: 30 Rockefeller Plz Fl 21, New York, New York 10112-0015 **Tel:** 1 212 664-4444.
Email: feedback@usanetwork.com
Web site: http://www.usanetwork.com
Profile: USA Network is basic cable television's leading provider of original series, feature movies, sporting events, off-net television shows, and blockbuster theatrical films. USA Network is a service of NBC Universal.
CABLE NETWORK

USA Network - Universal City Bureau 34806
Editorial: 100 Universal City Plz, Bldg 1440, Universal City, California 91608 **Tel:** 1 818 777-6898.
CABLE NETWORK

USArmenia TV 573657
Owner: USArmenia Worldwide
Editorial: 229 N Central Ave, Glendale, California 91203-3507 **Tel:** 1 818 955-9933.
Email: info@usatv.com
Web site: http://usatv.com/
Profile: USArmenia was established in May 2008 and features programming directly from Armenia and Los Angeles, CA. The programs will vary in content and style. The line-up includes, but is not limited to, reality shows, comedy programs, soap operas and news programs.
CABLE NETWORK

Velocity 825914
Owner: Discovery Communiations
Editorial: 1 Discovery Pl, Silver Spring, Maryland 20910-3354
Web site: http://velocity.discovery.com/videos
Profile: Velocity, an upscale male lifestyle network, features more than 400 premiere hours of new and returning series and specials showcasing the best of the automotive, sports and leisure, adventure, and travel genres. The cable network premiered in October 2011.
CABLE NETWORK

El Venezolano TV 963117
Owner: Grupo Editorial El Venezolano
Editorial: Miami, Florida
Email: info@elvenezolano.tv
Web site: http://elvenezolano.tv
Profile: El Venezolano airs entertainment programs, magazine shows and newscasts all of interest to the Venezuelan community in the United States.
REGIONAL CABLE NETWORK

Verizon FiOS1 News - Long Island 933261
Owner: Verizon Communications Inc.
Editorial: 800 Westchester Ave, Rye Brook, New York 10573-1354
Email: newsdesk@fios1news.com
Web site: http://www.fios1news.com/longisland
Profile: Verizon FiOS1 News is a local content channel that has everything a viewer wants to know about what's happening in the Long Island, NY area. The station features local weather forecasts, up to the minute traffic updates, as well as news, regional sports and feature stories.
REGIONAL CABLE NETWORK

Verizon FiOS1 News - New Jersey 933263
Owner: Verizon Communications Inc.
Editorial: 800 Westchester Ave, Rye Brook, New York 10573-1354 **Tel:** 1 914 417-2736.
Email: newsdesk@fios1news.com
Web site: http://www.fios1news.com/newjersey
Profile: Verizon FiOS1 - New Jersey is a local content channel that has everything a viewer wants to know about what's happening in Northern New Jersey. The station features local weather forecasts, up to the minute traffic updates, as well as news, regional sports and feature stories. The 24-hour network includes journalists using state of the art equipment including live streaming back packs which allow reporters to bring viewers live coverage from anywhere across the state. FiOS1's Mobile Journalists or MOJO's are also constantly on the beat providing the very latest news to our viewers.
REGIONAL CABLE NETWORK

VH1 34760
Owner: Viacom Inc.
Editorial: 1515 Broadway, New York, New York 10036-8901 **Tel:** 1 212 258-7800.
Web site: http://www.vh1.com
Profile: VH1 is a 24-hour cable network that connects viewers to today's hottest artists and music through series, specials, live events, exclusive online content, public affairs initiatives and other original programming.
CABLE NETWORK

VH1 - Los Angeles Bureau 34805
Editorial: 1575 N Gower St, Hollywood, California 90028-6487 **Tel:** 1 310 752-8000.
CABLE NETWORK

VICELAND 34738
Owner: Vice Media, Inc. & A+ E Networks
Editorial: 49 S 2nd St, Brooklyn, New York 11249-5119 **Tel:** 1 212 210-1400.
Web site: https://www.viceland.com
Profile: VICELAND is a culture and lifestyle network geared towards millennials and includes programming about society, music, technology, entertainment, and more. VICELAND is a partnership between Vice Media and the A&E Networks. H2 was replaced by VICELAND on February 29, 2016.
CABLE NETWORK

Voice of America Television Network 334255
Owner: Government-owned
Editorial: 330 Independence Ave SW, Washington, District Of Columbia 20237-0001 **Tel:** 1 202 203-4959.
Email: voanews@voanews.com
Web site: http://www.voanews.com
Profile: The Voice of America, which first went on the air in 1942, is a multimedia international broadcasting service funded by the U.S. government through the Broadcasting Board of Governors. VOA broadcasts more than 1,000 hours of news, information, educational, and cultural programming every week.
CABLE NETWORK

We TV 34629
Owner: AMC Networks Inc.
Editorial: 11 Penn Plz, New York, New York 10001-2006 **Tel:** 1 646 273-3500.
Web site: http://www.wetv.com
Profile: We TV offers compelling, entertaining stories that focus on key life stages of a modern woman, from getting married to having children and raising a family. Available in nearly 77 million homes, the network's original programming includes the critically acclaimed, viewer favorite The Locator (the network's most-watched series ever), the poignant, and often comical, real-life story of a family raising multiple toddlers, Raising Sextuplets, and a robust line-up of wedding series, including the hit show Bridezillas, Amazing Wedding Cakes and My Fair Wedding with David Tutera. WE tv is available in HD and WE tv On Demand is available in more than 30 million homes. The network launched in mid-January 2001.
CABLE NETWORK

The Weather Channel 34589
Owner: NBC Universal
Editorial: 300 Interstate North Pkwy SE, Atlanta, Georgia 30339-2403 **Tel:** 1 770 226-0000.
Web site: http://www.weather.com
Profile: 24-hour national weather news and information network. Features continuous, up-to-the-minute reports on weather conditions throughout the world, compelling weather-related feature specials, and regional, local, and national forecasts.
CABLE NETWORK

WGN America 79757
Owner: Tribune Broadcasting Co.
Editorial: 2501 W Bradley Pl, Chicago, Illinois 60618-4701 **Tel:** 1 773 528-2311.
Email: wgnamerica@tribunemedia.com
Web site: http://www.wgnamerica.com
Profile: Nationally-distributed cable television network which broadcasts a variety of programs consisting mainly of recent and classic off-network sitcoms, drama series and feature films. WGN America is in the process of being sold to Sinclair Broadcast Group, and is expected to close at the end of 2017.
CABLE NETWORK

WisconsinEye 489508
Editorial: 122 W Washington Ave, Ste 200, Madison, Wisconsin 53703 **Tel:** 1 608 316-6850.
Email: info@wiseye.org
Web site: http://www.wiseye.org
Profile: Statewide public affairs network with a mission to present an independent statewide view of community affairs and public policy discussion, beginning with nonpartisan, gavel-to-gavel coverage of state government in Madison. Focuses on local issues and civic activity that reflect the broad range of community and public life in Wisconsin.
REGIONAL CABLE NETWORK

The Word Network Television 721738
Owner: Adell Broadcasting
Editorial: 20733 W 10 Mile Rd, Southfield, Michigan 48075-1086 **Tel:** 1 248 357-4566.
Web site: http://www.thewordnetwork.org
Profile: The Word Network has established itself as a mainstream media broadcaster for African American ministries and gospel music. The Word Network offers value positive religious family programming embraced by millions of African Americans in urban and rural markets. The Word Network provides programming that is sensitive to, and touches the fabric of, the urban African American community.
CABLE NETWORK

Worship Network 34658
Owner: Christian Network Inc.(The)
Editorial: 320 Billingsly Ct, Franklin, Tennessee 37067-4706 **Tel:** 1 800 728-8723.
Web site: http://worship.net
Profile: The Worship Network is a national network that focuses on the Christian religion. Unique and uplifting television programming is featured, providing viewers with music, scripture, interactive fellowship and prayer. The format of the network emphasizes God-directed ministry rather than personality-driven television.
CABLE NETWORK

Xinhua News Agency - New York Bureau 727059
Editorial: 1540 Broadway, 44th Floor, New York, New York 10036-4039 **Tel:** 1 718 335-8388.
Web site: http://www.xinhuanet.com/english2010
CABLE NETWORK

YES Network 78734
Editorial: 805 3rd Ave Fl 30, New York, New York 10022-7533 **Tel:** 1 646 487-3600.
Email: info@yesnetwork.com
Web site: http://web.yesnetwork.com/index.jsp
Profile: The YES Network launched on March 19, 2002 as a 24-hour-a-day, 7-day-a-week premier sports and entertainment television network featuring the 27-time World Champion New York Yankees Major League Baseball team. The network is available to viewers in New York, Connecticut, and parts of New Jersey and Pennsylvania. YES broadcasts other professional and collegiate sports teams as well as classic sports footage. The schedule also includes original biography, interview and magazine programs.
REGIONAL CABLE NETWORK

Youtoo America 34579
Owner: Center Post Networks, LLC
Editorial: 6565 N MacArthur Blvd Ste 400, Irving, Texas 75039-2468 **Tel:** 1 214 444-7100.
Web site: http://youtooamerica.com
Profile: The nation's only full-time cable channel dedicated to providing lifestyle, entertainment, and information programming for the baby boomer generation. The network offers vintage sitcoms, dramas, music, entertainment and movies, as well as a variety of original series.
CABLE NETWORK

Z Living 858269
Owner: Asia TV USA Ltd
Editorial: Los Angeles, California
Web site: http://www.zliving.com
Profile: Z Living is a 24/7 TV network dedicated to empowering people in their pursuit of natural wellness. Z Living features engaging and entertaining lifestyle shows with an emphasis on healthy cooking, fitness, green living and eco-travel. The network was rebranded to Z Living from Veria Living in October 2014.
CABLE NETWORK

Uruguay

Television

Canal 10, Saeta TV 381475
Editorial: Lorenzo Carnelli 1234, Montevideo 11100
Tel: 598 2 4102120.
Email: subrayado@canal10.com.uy
Web site: http://www.canal10.com.uy
Profile: Primer canal de televisión abierta del país. Petenece a las familias De Feo y Fontaina dueños también de Radio Carve de Montevideo y Nuevotiempo (Mont.). Es el medio televisivo que produce la mayor cantidad de programas nacionales; periodísticos y de entetenimiento. Fecha de Aparición: 1957
TELEVISION NETWORK

Canal 4 Montecarlo TV 381474
Editorial: Paraguay 2253, Montevideo 11800
Tel: 598 2 9244444.
Email: secretarias@montecarlotv.com.uy
Web site: http://www.canal4.com.uy
Profile: Canal de televisión abierta perteneciente a la familia Romay Salvo que conforma un grupo que posee otros canales de televisión abierta (en el interior) y emisoras de radio. Pantalla orientada a la clase media y sectores populares. Tiene un acuerdo de programación con Telefé de Argentina. Fecha de Aparición: 22372
TELEVISION NETWORK

Televisión Nacional de Uruguay 381473
Editorial: Bvar. Artigas 2552, Montevideo 11600
Tel: 598 2 19595.
Email: contacto@tnu.com.uy
Web site: http://www.tnu.com.uy
Profile: Canal estatal de alcance nacional de alcance nacional a través de repetidoras, de escasa audiencia. Fecha de Aparición: 1965
TELEVISION NETWORK

Uzbekistan

Radio

Radio Grand 371233
Editorial: P.O. BOX 5655, ul Druzhby Narodovov 15, 1st floor, Tashkent 100043 **Tel:** 998 71 17 39 248.
Email: radio@grand.uz
Web site: http://www.grand.uz
Profile: CHR (Contemporary Hit Radio). 50% of the programmes are in Uzbek language and 50% are in Russian.
FM RADIO STATION

Television

Uzbek State TV 316393
Editorial: 69 Navoi St, Tashkent 100098
Tel: 998 71 13 38 106.
Email: info@mtrk.uz
Web site: http://www.mtrk.uz
TELEVISION STATION

Vanuatu

Radio

Radio Vanuatu 538708
Owner: Vanuatu Broadcasting & Television Corporation (VBTC)
Editorial: Port Vila, Vanuatu **Tel:** 678 22 999.
Web site: http://vbtc.com.vu
Profile: Radio station in Vanuatu covering local news.
RADIO NETWORK

Television

Television Blong Vanuatu 538718
Owner: Vanuatu Broadcasting & Television Corporation (VBTC)
Editorial: Port Vila, Vanuatu **Tel:** 678 22 999.
Web site: http://www.vanuatu2u.com/tv-vanuatu-television.html
Profile: Television Blong Vanuatu is the television channel in Vanuatu based in Port Vila. Launched in 1993 with the help of Radio France Overseas (RFO).
TELEVISION STATION

Venezuela

Venezuela

Radio

Radio Caracas Radio 290912
Owner: Empresas 1BC
Editorial: Avenida Jose Antonio Paez, Edificio RCR El Paraiso, Caracas **Tel:** 58 2124813590.
Email: rcrinformacion@rcr.com.ve
Web site: http://www.informercr.blogspot.com
Profile: Radio Caracas Radio is a Venezuelan radio network owned by Empresas 1BC. It broadcasts news from Caracas, Venezuela to regions and communities throughout the country. Presents also international news.
RADIO NETWORK

Television

Televen 316426
Editorial: Avenida Romulo Gallegos con 4 Transversal de Horizontes, Edificio Televen, Urbanizacion Boleita Norte, Caracas **Tel:** 58 212 280 00 11.
Email: pautasprensa@televen.com
Web site: http://www.televen.com
Profile: National television broadcasting news, entertainment, and sport programs.
TELEVISION NETWORK

Venevisión 316427
Editorial: Final Avenida La Salle Edificio Venevision, Colinas de los Caobos. Apartado 66774, Caracas **Tel:** 58 212 708 94 44.
Email: noticiero@venevision.com.ve
Web site: http://www.venevision.com.ve
Profile: Television network broadcasting news and producing original soap operas and series for the local and international market.
TELEVISION NETWORK

Vietnam

Radio

The Voice of Ho Chi Minh City's People 467716
Owner: Ho Chi Minh City People's Committee
Editorial: #3 Nguyen Dinh Chieu St, District 1, Ho Chi Minh City **Tel:** 84 8 38225933.
Email: radiohcm@hcm.vnn.vn
Web site: http://www.voh.com.vn
Profile: News, Music, etc.
AM RADIO STATION

Television

Hanoi TV and Radio 468356
Editorial: 3-5 Huynh Thuc Khang, Hanoi
Tel: 84 4 3835670.
Email: baodientu@hanoitv.vn
Web site: http://www.hanoitv.org.vn
Profile: Covers current events and news on television and radio outlets.
TELEVISION STATION

Ho Chi Minh City TV 468357
Editorial: 14 Dinh Tien Hoang St, Ho Chi Minh City
Tel: 84 8 38291667.
Email: web@htv.com.vn
Web site: http://www.htv.com.vn
Profile: Television coverage of all local news topics including music, movies, sports and game shows.
TELEVISION STATION

Yemen

Radio

Sana'a Radio 489435
Owner: Yemen General Corporation For Radio and TV
Editorial: PO Box 2371, Sana'a **Tel:** 967 1 282061.
Email: sanaaradio@yahoo.com

Profile: Sana'a Radio is a national radio station broadcasting Arabic entertainment, music, news, analysis and sports for 24-hours a day. The state-owned station broadcasts on 96.0 FM and MW 787. It originally launched in January 1946 but closed after two years, resuming in 1955. Between 1976 and 1990, broadcasting in northern Yemen was the responsibility of the Yemeni General Corporation for Radio and Television, while broadcasting in the south was controlled by the Radio and Television Authority. The two bodies merged upon the unification of Yemen in 1990 to form the General Corporation for Radio and Television, which operates under the Ministry of Information.
FM RADIO STATION

Television

Aden TV 492815
Owner: Yemen General Corporation For Radio and TV
Editorial: PO Box 1264, Tawahi, Aden
Tel: 967 2 202481.
Email: syednet2000@yahoo.com
Web site: http://www.tvaden.net
Profile: Aden TV is a state-owned terrestrial television station broadcasting news, drama serials, documentaries, religious shows, business programmes and public announcements. Previously called Yamania TV, the channel launched in 1964.
TELEVISION STATION

Yemen TV 411262
Owner: Yemen General Corporation For Radio and TV
Editorial: PO Box 1140, Sana'a **Tel:** 967 1 226466.
Email: info@yemen-tv.net
Web site: http://www.yemen-tv.net
Profile: Yemen TV is a state-owned television station broadcasting news, dramas, entertainment and documentaries. Most programmes are in Arabic, but also includes news broadcasts in English. The channel launched in 1975 and broadcasts terrestrially in Yemen and free-to-air on satellite.
TELEVISION STATION

Zambia

Radio

5fm 771894
Owner: AZoM.com Pty Ltd
Editorial: 9th Floor, Lotti House, Cairo Road, Lusaka
Tel: 260 211 221 515.
Email: 5fm@zamtel.zm
Web site: http://www.5fm.co.zm
Profile: Radio station focussing on local news and entertainment including health, technology, business, sports and world news.
RADIO NETWORK

Radio Maria 771895
Owner: AZoM.com Pty Ltd
Editorial: P.O. Box 510307, Chipata 10101
Tel: 260 21 6221154.
Email: director.zam@radiomaria.org
Web site: http://www.radiomaria.org/zambia
Profile: Radio station covering religion and society.
RADIO NETWORK

Zambia National Radio - ZNBC 771892
Owner: AZoM.com Pty Ltd
Editorial: Mass Media Complex, Alick Nkhata Road, Lusaka **Tel:** 260 211 251983.
Email: znbcnews@yahoo.com
Web site: http://www.znbc.co.zm
Profile: National radio station covering national and international news including health, business, entertainment and sports.
RADIO NETWORK

Television

Zambia National Television - ZNBC 771893
Owner: AZoM.com Pty Ltd
Editorial: Mass Media Complex, Alick Nkhata Road, Lusaka **Tel:** 260 211 251983.
Email: znbcnews@yahoo.com
Web site: http://www.znbc.co.zm
Profile: National television station covering national and international news including health, business, entertainment and sports.
TELEVISION STATION

Willings Volume 2
Section 4

Master Index

Section 4 Master Index

1/2 Formato - Agência de Fotografia, Lda.

Los Angeles Times - Sacramento Bureau

Bay News 9

The Carteret County News-Times

Section 4 Master Index

CHLS-FM

Delaware Gazette

Section 4 Master Index

IPS Agencia de Noticias

J

K

KBDI-TV

KEJS-FM

KLUZ-TV 751	KMGH2-TV 751	KMOX-AM 519	KMYO-FM 52
KLVE-FM 515	KMGH3-TV 751	KMOZ-AM 519	KMYS-TV 75
KLVF-FM 515	KMGH-TV 751	KMOZ-FM 519	KMYT-FM 52
KLVI-AM 515	KMGI-FM 517	KMPA-AM 519	KMYT-TV 75
KLVJ-FM 515	KMGJ-FM 517	KMPB-FM 519	KMYU-TV 75
KLVL-AM 515	KMGK-FM 517	KMPC-FM 519	KMYX-FM 52
KLVO-FM 515	KMGL-FM 517	KMPG-AM 519	KMYY-FM 52
KLVQ-AM 515	KMGM-FM 517	KMPH-AM 519	KMYZ-FM 52
KLVT-AM 515	KMGN-FM 517	KMPH-TV 751	KMZA-FM 52
KLVV-FM 515	KMGO-FM 517	KMPO-FM 519	KMZE-FM 52
KLWB-FM 515	KMGV-FM 517	KMPR-FM 519	KMZN-AM 52
KLWB-TV 751	KMGW-FM 517	KMPS-FM 519	KMZQ-AM 52
KLWN-AM 515	KMGX-FM 517	KMPT-AM 519	KMZQ-FM 52
KLXH-FM 515	KMGZ-FM 517	KMPX-TV 751	KMZU-FM 52
KLXI-FM 515	KMHA-FM 517	KMQA-FM 519	KMZZ-FM 52
KLXK-FM 515	KMHD-FM 517	KMRB-AM 519	KNAB-AM 52
KLXQ-FM 515	KMHK-FM 517	KMRC-AM 519	KNAB-FM 52
KLXR-AM 515	KMHL-AM 517	KMRF-AM 519	KNAF-AM 52
KLXS-FM 515	KMHM-FM 517	KMRJ-FM 519	KNAF-FM 52
KLXX-AM 515	KMHR-FM 517	KMRK-FM 519	KNAH-FM 52
KLYC-AM 515	KMHT-AM 517	KMRN-AM 519	KNAI-FM 52
KLYD-FM 515	KMHT-FM 517	KMRQ-FM 520	KNAM-AM 52
KLYK-FM 515	KMHX-FM 517	KMRR-FM 520	KNAS-FM 52
KLYQ-AM 515	KMIA-AM 517	KMRS-AM 520	KNAT2-TV 75
KLYR-AM 515	KMIC-AM 517	KMRV-AM 520	KNAT3-TV 75
KLYR-FM 515	KMID-TV 751	KMRX-FM 520	KNAT4-TV 75
KLYT-FM 515	KMIL-FM 517	KMRY-AM 520	KNAT5-TV 75
KLYV-FM 515	KMIN-AM 517	KMRZ-FM 520	KNAT-TV 75
KLYY-FM 515	KMIQ-FM 517	KMSA-FM 520	KNBA-FM 52
KLZA-FM 515	KMIR-TV 751	KMSB-TV 751	KNBB-FM 52
KLZ-AM 515	KMIS-AM 517	KMSD-AM 520	KNBC2-TV 75
KLZK-FM 515	KMIS-FM 517	KMSE-FM 520	KNBC4-TV 75
KLZS-AM 515	KMIT-FM 518	KMSO-FM 520	KNBC-TV 75
KLZT-FM 515	KMIX-FM 518	KMSP-TV 751	KNBJ-FM 52
KLZX-FM 515	KMIY-FM 518	KMSR-AM 520	KNBN-TV 75
KLZZ-FM 515	KMIZ2-TV 751	KMSS-TV 751	KNBR-AM 52
KMA-AM 515	KMIZ-TV 751	KMSW-FM 520	KNBT-FM 52
KMAD-FM 515	KMJ-AM 518	KMTA-AM 520	KNBX-FM 52
KMA-FM 516	KMJB-FM 518	KMTB-FM 520	KNBY-AM 52
KMAG-FM 516	KMJC-AM 518	KMTF-TV 751	KNBZ-FM 52
KMAJ-AM 516	KMJE-FM 518	KMTI-AM 520	KNCB-AM 52
KMAJ-FM 516	KMJ-FM 518	KMTK-FM 520	KNCB-FM 52
KMAK-FM 516	KMJI-FM 518	KMTL-AM 520	KNCI-FM 52
KMAL-AM 516	KMJJ-FM 518	KMTN-FM 520	KNCK-AM 52
KMAM-AM 516	KMJK-FM 518	KMTP2-TV 751	KNCK-FM 52
KMAN-AM 516	KMJM-AM 518	KMTP4-TV 751	KNCM-FM 52
KMAQ-AM 516	KMJM-FM 518	KMTP5-TV 751	KNCN-FM 52
KMAQ-FM 516	KMJO-FM 518	KMTP-TV 751	KNCO-AM 52
KMAR-FM 516	KMJQ-FM 518	KMTR-TV 751	KNCO-FM 52
KMAS-AM 516	KMJR-FM 518	KMTS-FM 520	KNCQ-FM 52
KMAT-FM 516	KMJV-FM 518	KMTT-AM 520	KNCR-AM 52
KMAV-FM 516	KMJX-FM 518	KMTV2-TV 751	KNCT-FM 52
KMAX-AM 516	KMKF-FM 518	KMTV-TV 752	KNCT-TV 75
KMAX-FM 516	KMKK-FM 518	KMTW-TV 752	KNCU-FM 52
KMAX-TV 751	KMKO-FM 518	KMTX-FM 520	KNCW-FM 52
KMBC2-TV 751	KMKS-FM 518	KMTY-FM 520	KNCY-AM 52
KMBC-TV 751	KMKT-FM 518	KMUC-FM 520	KNDA-FM 52
KMBI-AM 516	KMKX-FM 518	KMUD-FM 520	KNDC-AM 52
KMBI-FM 516	KMKY-AM 518	KMUN-FM 520	KNDD-FM 52
KMBL-AM 516	KMLA-FM 518	KMUV-TV 752	KNDE-FM 52
KMBQ-FM 516	KMLB-AM 518	KMUZ-FM 520	KNDI-AM 52
KMBR-FM 516	KMLE-FM 518	KMVA-FM 520	KNDK-AM 52
KMBX-AM 516	KMLK-FM 518	KMVE-FM 520	KNDK-FM 52
KMBY2-TV 751	KMLM-TV 751	KMVG-AM 520	KNDN-AM 52
KMBY-TV 751	KMLO-FM 518	KMVI-AM 520	KNDO-TV 75
KMBZ-AM 516	KMME-FM 518	KMVK-FM 520	KNDR-FM 52
KMBZ-FM 516	KMMG-FM 518	KMVL-AM 520	KNDY-AM 52
KMCD-AM 516	KMMJ-AM 518	KMV-LEHTI 80	KNDY-FM 52
KMCE-TV 751	KMMM-AM 518	KMVL-FM 520	KNDZ-FM 523
KMCH-FM 516	KMMO-AM 518	KMVN-FM 520	KNEA-AM 523
KMCI-TV 751	KMMO-FM 518	KMVP-AM 520	KNEB-AM 523
KMCK-FM 516	KMMQ-AM 518	KMVQ-FM 520	KNEB-FM 523
KMCM-FM 516	KMMR-FM 518	KMVR-FM 520	KNEC-FM 523
KMCN-FM 516	KMMS-AM 518	KMVT-TV 752	KNED-AM 523
KMCO-FM 516	KMMS-FM 518	KMVX-FM 520	KNEI-FM 523
KMCR-FM 516	KMMT-FM 518	KMWB-FM 520	KNEK-AM 523
KMCS-FM 516	KMMX-FM 519	KMWX-FM 521	KNEK-FM 523
KMCT-TV 751	KMMY-FM 519	KMWY-FM 521	KNEL-AM 523
KMCV-FM 516	KMMZ-FM 519	KMXA-AM 521	KNEL-FM 523
KMCX-FM 516	KMNA-FM 519	KMXA-FM 521	KNEM-AM 523
KMDL-FM 516	KMNB-FM 519	KMXB-FM 521	KNEN-FM 523
KMDO-AM 516	KMND-AM 519	KMXC-FM 521	KNEO-FM 523
KMDR2-FM 516	KMNS-AM 519	KMXE-FM 521	KNEP-TV 752
KMDX-FM 516	KMNT-FM 519	KMXF-FM 521	KNES-FM 523
KMDY-FM 516	KMNV-AM 519	KMXG-FM 521	KNET-AM 523
KMDZ-FM 516	KMNY-AM 519	KMXH-FM 521	KNEU-AM 523
KMED-AM 516	KMOC-FM 519	KMXI-FM 521	KNEV-FM 523
KMEG-TV 751	KMOD-FM 519	KMXJ-FM 521	KNEW-AM 523
KMEL-FM 517	KMOE-FM 519	KMXK-FM 521	KNEX-FM 523
KMEM-FM 517	KMOG-AM 519	KMXL-FM 521	KNEX-TV 752
KMER-AM 517	KMOH-TV 751	KMXN-FM 521	KNFL-AM 523
KMET-AM 517	KMOJ-FM 519	KMXO-AM 521	KNFM-FM 523
KMEX-TV 751	KMOK-FM 519	KMXP-FM 521	KNFO-FM 523
KMEZ-FM 517	KMOL-TV 751	KMXR-FM 521	KNFT-AM 523
KMFA-FM 517	KMOM-FM 519	KMXS-FM 521	KNFT-FM 523
KMFG-FM 517	KMON-AM 519	KMXT-FM 521	KNFX-FM 523
KMFR-AM 517	KMON-FM 519	KMXV-FM 521	KNGA-FM 523
KMFX-AM 517	KMOO-FM 519	KMXX-FM 521	KNGL-AM 523
KMFX-FM 517	KMOQ-FM 519	KMXY-FM 521	KNGN-AM 523
KMFY-FM 517	KMOT-TV 751	KMXZ-FM 521	KNGT-FM 523
KMGA-FM 517	KMOU-FM 519	KMYC-AM 521	KNHT-FM 523
KMGC-FM 517	KMOV2-TV 751	KMYI-FM 521	KNIA-AM 523
KMGE-FM 517	KMOV-TV 751	KMYK-FM 521	KNIC-TV 752

Koti-Lappi

KSDN-FM

KUTT-FM

KZAL-FM

Marshall County Tribune

O

Section 4 Master Index

Oriental Morning Post

Puntual

River Valley Newspapers

Section 4 Master Index

River Valley Times

Valdres Radio

Section 4 Master Index

Watertown Town Times

Section 4 Master Index

WCOG-AM

Section 4 Master Index

WEZQ-FM

WHRB-FM

WKJQ-AM

WMLQ-FM

Station	Page
WMLQ-FM	670
WMLR-AM	670
WMLS-FM	670
WMLT-AM	670
WMLU-FM	670
WMLV-FM	670
WMLW-TV	783
WMLX-FM	670
WMMA-FM	670
WMMB-AM	670
WMMC-FM	670
WMME-FM	670
WMMG-AM	670
WMMG-FM	670
WMMI-AM	670
WMMJ-FM	670
WMML-AM	670
WMMM-FM	670
WMMN-AM	670
WMMO-FM	670
WMMQ-FM	670
WMMR-FM	670
WMMS-FM	670
WMMT-FM	670
WMMV-AM	670
WMMW-AM	670
WMMX-FM	671
WMMY-FM	671
WMNA-FM	671
WMNC-AM	671
WMNC-FM	671
WMNF-FM	671
WMNI-AM	671
WMNI-FM	671
WMNP-FM	671
WMNR-FM	671
WMNV-FM	671
WMNX-FM	671
WMNZ-AM	671
WMOA-AM	671
WMOB-AM	671
WMOC-FM	671
WMOD-FM	671
WMOG-FM	671
WMOH-AM	671
WMOI-FM	671
WMOK-AM	671
WMOM-FM	671
WMON-AM	671
WMOO-FM	671
WMOP-AM	671
WMOQ-FM	671
WMOR2-TV	783
WMOR3-TV	784
WMOR-FM	671
WMOR-TV	784
WMOS-FM	671
WMOU-AM	671
WMOV-AM	671
WMOV-FM	671
WMOX-AM	671
WMOZ-FM	671
WMPB2-TV	784
WMPB3-TV	784
WMPB-TV	784
WMPC-AM	671
WMPI-FM	671
WMPL-AM	671
WMPM-AM	671
WMPO-AM	671
WMPR-FM	671
WMPS-AM	671
WMPV-TV	784
WMPW-AM	671
WMPX-AM	672
WMPZ-FM	672
WMQA-FM	672
WMQM-AM	672
WMQR-FM	672
WMQT-FM	672
WMQU-AM	672
WMQX-FM	672
WMQZ-FM	672
WMRC-AM	672
WMRD-AM	672
WMRE-AM	672
WMRF-FM	672
WMRI-AM	672
WMRK-FM	672
WMRN-AM	672
WMRN-FM	672
WMRQ2-FM	672
WMRQ-FM	672
WMRR-FM	672
WMRS-FM	672
WMRT-FM	672
WMRV-FM	672
WMRX-FM	672
WMRZ-FM	672
WMSA-AM	672
WMSG-AM	672
WMSI-FM	672
WMSJ-FM	672
WMSK-AM	672
WMSK-FM	672
WMSN-TV	784
WMSP-AM	672
WMSR-AM	672
WMST-AM	672
WMSU-FM	672
WMSX-FM	672
WMTA-AM	672
WMT-AM	672
WMTC-AM	672
WMTC-FM	673
WMTD-AM	673
WMTD-FM	673
WMTK-FM	673
WMTL-AM	673
WMTM-AM	673
WMTM-FM	673
WMTN-AM	673
WMTR-AM	673
WMTR-FM	673
WMTT-FM	673
WMTV-TV	784
WMTW-TV	784
WMTX-FM	673
WMTY-FM	673
WMUB-FM	673
WMUF-FM	673
WMUH-FM	673
WMUM-FM	673
WMUR2-TV	784
WMUR-TV	784
WMUS-FM	673
WMUV-FM	673
WMUZ-FM	673
WMVA-AM	673
WMVB-AM	673
WMVE-FM	673
WMVG-AM	673
WMVL-FM	673
WMVN-FM	673
WMVO-AM	673
WMVP-AM	673
WMVR-FM	673
WMVS-TV	784
WMVV-FM	673
WMVW-FM	673
WMWK-FM	673
WMWM-FM	673
WMWV-FM	673
WMWX-FM	673
WMXA-FM	673
WMXB-AM	673
WMXC-FM	673
WMXD-FM	673
WMXE-FM	673
WMXF-AM	674
WMXH-FM	674
WMXI-FM	674
WMXJ-FM	674
WMXL-FM	674
WMXM-FM	674
WMXN-FM	674
WMXO-FM	674
WMXQ-FM	674
WMXS-FM	674
WMXT-FM	674
WMXU-FM	674
WMXV-FM	674
WMXW-FM	674
WMXX-FM	674
WMXY-FM	674
WMXZ-FM	674
WMYA2-TV	784
WMYA-TV	784
WMYB-FM	674
WMYD2-TV	784
WMYD-TV	784
WMYF-AM	674
WMYG-TV	784
WMYI-FM	674
WMYJ-AM	674
WMYK-FM	674
WMYL-FM	674
WMYN-AM	674
WMYO-TV	784
WMYR-AM	674
WMYT3-TV	784
WMYT-TV	784
WMYV-TV	784
WMYX-FM	674
WMYY-FM	674
WMZK-FM	674
WMZQ-FM	674
WNAB-TV	784
WNAC2-TV	784
WNAC-TV	784
WNAE-AM	674
WNAH-AM	674
WNAM-AM	674
WNAP-AM	674
WNAT-AM	674
WNAU-AM	674
WNAV-AM	674
WNAW-AM	674
WNAX-AM	674
WNAX-FM	674
WNBB-FM	674
WNBC2-TV	784
WNBC4-TV	784
WNBC-TV	784
WNBF-AM	674
WNBH-AM	675
WNBL-FM	675
WNBM-FM	675
WNBP-AM	675
WNBS-AM	675
WNBT-AM	675
WNBT-FM	675
WNBU-FM	675
WNBW-TV	784
WNBY-AM	675
WNBY-FM	675
WNBZ-AM	675
WNCA-AM	675
WNCB-FM	675
WNCC-FM	675
WNCD-FM	675
WNCE-TV	784
WNCF-TV	784
WNCH-FM	675
WNCI-FM	675
WNCL-FM	675
WNCN2-TV	784
WNCN3-TV	784
WNCN-TV	784
WNCO-AM	675
WNCO-FM	675
WNCQ-FM	675
WNCR-TV	784
WNCS-FM	675
WNCT-AM	675
WNCT-FM	675
WNCT-TV	784
WNCV-FM	675
WNCW-FM	675
WNCX-FM	675
WNCY-FM	675
WNDA-TV	784
WNDB-AM	675
WNDD-FM	675
WNDE-AM	675
WNDH-FM	675
WNDI-AM	675
WNDI-FM	675
WNDN-FM	675
WNDR-AM	675
WNDT-FM	675
WNDU-TV	784
WNDV-FM	675
WNDY-TV	784
WNDZ-AM	675
WNEA-AM	675
WNEB-AM	676
WNED-FM	676
WNED-TV	785
WNEG-AM	676
WNEM-TV	785
WNEO2-TV	785
WNEO3-TV	785
WNEO4-TV	785
WNEO-TV	785
WNEP2-TV	785
WNEP-TV	785
WNER-AM	676
WNES-AM	676
WNET2-TV	785
WNET3-TV	785
WNET-TV	785
WNEU-TV	785
WNEV-FM	676
WNEW-FM	676
WNEX-AM	676
WNEZ-AM	676
WNFA-FM	676
WNFB-FM	676
WNFK-FM	676
WNFL-AM	676
WNFM-FM	676
WNFN-FM	676
WNFR-FM	676
WNFZ-FM	676
WNGA-FM	676
WNGC-FM	676
WNGE-FM	676
WNGH-FM	676
WNGL-AM	676
WNGN-FM	676
WNGO-AM	676
WNGU-FM	676
WNGY-FM	676
WNGZ-FM	676
WNHW-FM	676
WNIC-FM	676
WNIL-AM	676
WNIN-FM	676
WNIN-TV	785
WNIO-AM	676
WNIR-FM	676
WNIS-AM	676
WNIT-TV	785
WNIV-AM	676
WNIX-AM	676
WNJA-FM	676
WNJC-AM	676
WNJE-AM	676
WNJK-FM	676
WNJM-FM	676
WNJP-FM	676
WNJT-FM	677
WNJT-TV	785
WNJU-TV	785
WNJY-FM	677
WNKI-FM	677
WNKJ-FM	677
WNKO-FM	677
WNKR-FM	677
WNKS-FM	677
WNKT-FM	677
WNKX-FM	677
WNKY2-TV	785
WNKY-TV	785
WNLA-AM	677
WNLC-FM	677
WNLD-FM	677
WNLF-FM	677
WNLO-TV	785
WNLR-AM	677
WNLT-FM	677
WNMA-AM	677
WNMC-FM	677
WNML-AM	677
WNML-FM	677
WNMQ-FM	677
WNMT-AM	677
WNMX-FM	677
WNNC-AM	677
WNND-FM	677
WNNE-TV	785
WNNF-FM	677
WNNG-FM	677
WNNH-FM	677
WNNJ-FM	677
WNNK-FM	677
WNNL-FM	677
WNNO-FM	677
WNNP-FM	677
WNNR-AM	677
WNNS-FM	677
WNNT-FM	677
WNNW-AM	677
WNNW-FM	677
WNNX-FM	677
WNNZ-AM	677
WNOB-FM	677
WNOC-FM	678
WNOE-FM	678
WNOG-AM	678
WNOH-FM	678
WNOI-FM	678
WNOK-FM	678
WNOL-TV	785
WNOO-AM	678
WNOP-AM	678
WNOP-FM	678
WNOR-FM	678
WNOS-AM	678
WNOW-AM	678
WNOW-FM	678
WNOX-FM	678
WNPC-AM	678
WNPC-FM	678
WNPL-AM	678
WNPQ-FM	678
WNPR-FM	678
WNPT2-TV	785
WNPT-FM	678
WNPT-TV	785
WNPV-AM	678
WNPX-TV	785
WNPZ-AM	678
WNQM-AM	678
WNRG-AM	678
WNRG-FM	678
WNRI-AM	678
WNRJ-FM	678
WNRN-FM	678
WNRP-AM	678
WNRQ-FM	678
WNRW-FM	678
WNRZ-FM	678
WNS PUBLICATIONS	381
WNSH-FM	678
WNSL-FM	678
WNSN-FM	678
WNSP-FM	678
WNSR-AM	678
WNST-AM	678
WNSV-FM	678

Section 4 Master Index

WPHL2-TV

Call	Page	Call	Page	Call	Page	Call	Page
WPHL2-TV	787	WPRO-FM	688	WPXX2-TV	789	WQLZ-FM	692
WPHL-TV	787	WPRR-AM	688	WPXX3-TV	789	WQMF-FM	692
WPHM-AM	686	WPRS-AM	688	WPXX-TV	789	WQMG-FM	692
WPHN-FM	686	WPRS-FM	688	WPXY-FM	690	WQMJ-FM	692
WPHR-FM	686	WPRT-AM	688	WPXZ-FM	690	WQMP-FM	692
WPHT-AM	686	WPRT-FM	688	WPYA-FM	690	WQMT-FM	692
WPHZ-FM	686	WPRV-AM	688	WPYB-AM	690	WQMU-FM	692
WPIA-FM	686	WPRW-FM	688	WPYO-FM	690	WQMX-FM	692
WPIB-FM	686	WPRX-AM	688	WPYR-AM	690	WQMZ-FM	692
WPIC-AM	686	WPRY-AM	688	WPYX-FM	690	WQNA-FM	692
WPID-AM	686	WPRZ-FM	688	WPZE-FM	690	WQNC-FM	692
WPIE-AM	686	WPSD-TV	787	WPZR-FM	690	WQNO-AM	692
WPIG-FM	686	WPSF-FM	689	WPZS-FM	690	WQNQ-FM	692
WPIK-FM	686	WPSG-TV	787	WPZZ-FM	690	WQNR-FM	692
WPIL-FM	686	WPSK-FM	689	WQAD2-TV	789	WQNS-FM	692
WPIM-FM	686	WPSL-AM	689	WQAD3-TV	789	WQNT-AM	692
WPIN-AM	686	WPSN-AM	689	WQAD-TV	789	WQNU-FM	692
WPIN-FM	686	WPSO-AM	689	WQAH-FM	690	WQNY-FM	692
WPIO-FM	686	WPSP-AM	689	WQAK-FM	690	WQNZ-FM	692
WPIP-AM	687	WPST-FM	689	WQAL-FM	690	WQOK-FM	692
WPIR-FM	687	WPTA-TV	787	WQAM-AM	690	WQOL-FM	692
WPIT-AM	687	WPTB-AM	689	WQAW-TV	789	WQOM-AM	692
WPIX2-TV	787	WPTC-FM	689	WQBA-AM	690	WQON-FM	692
WPIX3-TV	787	WPTD-TV	788	WQBB-FM	690	WQOP-AM	692
WPIX-TV	787	WPTE-FM	689	WQBE-FM	690	WQOR-AM	692
WPJL-AM	687	WPTF-AM	689	WQBJ-FM	690	WQOW-TV	789
WPJM-AM	687	WPTH-FM	689	WQBK-FM	690	WQPC-FM	692
WPJS-AM	687	WPTI-FM	689	WQBN-AM	690	WQPO-FM	692
WPJX-AM	687	WPTJ-FM	689	WQBQ-AM	690	WQPW-FM	692
WPJY-FM	687	WPTK-AM	689	WQBR-FM	690	WQPX-TV	789
WPKE-AM	687	WPTL-AM	689	WQBT-FM	690	WQQB-FM	692
WPKF-FM	687	WPTM-FM	689	WQBU-FM	690	WQQK-FM	692
WPKG-FM	687	WPTN-AM	689	WQBX-FM	690	WQQL-FM	692
WPKL-FM	687	WPTO-TV	788	WQBZ-FM	690	WQQO-FM	692
WPKN-FM	687	WPTQ-FM	689	WQCB-FM	690	WQQQ-FM	693
WPKO-FM	687	WPTR-AM	689	WQCC-FM	690	WQQR-FM	693
WPKQ-FM	687	WPTV2-TV	788	WQCH-AM	690	WQQW-AM	693
WPKR-FM	687	WPTV-TV	788	WQCK-FM	690	WQQX-AM	693
WPKT-FM	687	WPTW-AM	689	WQCM-TV	690	WQRB-FM	693
WPKV-FM	687	WPTX-AM	689	WQCR-AM	690	WQRC-FM	693
WPKX-AM	687	WPTY-FM	689	WQCS-FM	690	WQRF-TV	789
WPKY-AM	687	WPTZ2-TV	788	WQCT-AM	690	WQRK-FM	693
WPKZ-AM	687	WPTZ-TV	788	WQCW-TV	789	WQRL-FM	693
WPLA-AM	687	WPUB-FM	689	WQCY-FM	690	WQRN-FM	693
WPLG2-TV	787	WPUL-AM	689	WQDC-FM	690	WQRS-FM	693
WPLG-TV	787	WPUP-FM	689	WQDK-FM	690	WQRV-FM	693
WPLJ-FM	687	WPUR-FM	689	WQDR-FM	690	WQRX-AM	693
WPLK-AM	687	WPUT-AM	689	WQDY-FM	690	WQSB-FM	693
WPLL-FM	687	WPVA-FM	689	WQED2-TV	789	WQSC-AM	693
WPLM-AM	687	WPVI2-TV	788	WQED3-TV	789	WQSE-AM	693
WPLM-FM	687	WPVI3-TV	788	WQED-FM	690	WQSH-FM	693
WPLN-AM	687	WPVI-TV	788	WQED-TV	789	WQSI-FM	693
WPLN-FM	687	WPVL-AM	689	WQEJ-FM	691	WQSL-FM	693
WPLO-AM	687	WPVL-FM	689	WQEL-FM	691	WQSM-FM	693
WPLR-FM	687	WPVM-FM	689	WQEN-FM	691	WQSO-FM	693
WPLV-AM	687	WPVN4-TV	788	WQEZ-FM	691	WQSR-FM	693
WPLW-FM	687	WPVQ-FM	689	WQFS-FM	691	WQSS-FM	693
WPLY-AM	687	WPWA-AM	689	WQFX-AM	691	WQST-FM	693
WPLZ-FM	687	WPWC-AM	689	WQFX-FM	691	WQTC-FM	693
WPMB-AM	687	WPWQ-FM	689	WQGA-FM	691	WQTE-FM	693
WPME-TV	787	WPWR-TV	788	WQGN-FM	691	WQTK-FM	693
WPMF-TV	787	WPWX-FM	689	WQGR-FM	691	WQTL-FM	693
WPMH-AM	687	WPWZ-FM	689	WQHH-FM	691	WQTT-AM	693
WPMI-TV	787	WPXA2-TV	788	WQHK-FM	691	WQTU-FM	693
WPMO-AM	687	WPXA3-TV	788	WQHL-AM	691	WQTV-TV	789
WPMT2-TV	787	WPXA4-TV	788	WQHL-FM	691	WQTW-AM	693
WPMT-TV	787	WPXA-TV	788	WQHQ-FM	691	WQTX-FM	693
WPMX-FM	687	WPXC2-TV	788	WQHR-FM	691	WQTY-FM	693
WPMZ-AM	688	WPXC3-TV	788	WQHS-TV	789	WQUA-FM	693
WPNA-AM	688	WPXC4-TV	788	WQHT-FM	691	WQUE-FM	693
WPNC-FM	688	WPXC-FM	689	WQHY-FM	691	WQUL-AM	693
WPNG-FM	688	WPXC-TV	788	WQHZ-FM	691	WQUS-FM	693
WPNH-AM	688	WPXE2-TV	788	WQIC-FM	691	WQUT-FM	693
WPNH-FM	688	WPXE3-TV	788	WQIK-FM	691	WQVE-FM	693
WPNN-AM	688	WPXE-TV	788	WQIL-FM	691	WQWK-AM	693
WPNT-TV	787	WPXH-TV	788	WQIO-FM	691	WQWV-FM	693
WPNW-AM	688	WPXI2-TV	788	WQJB-FM	691	WQXA-FM	693
WPNY-TV	787	WPXI-TV	788	WQJQ-FM	691	WQXB-FM	694
WPOC-FM	688	WPXJ-TV	788	WQKI-FM	691	WQXC-FM	694
WPOG-AM	688	WPXK-TV	788	WQKK-FM	691	WQXE-FM	694
WPOI-FM	688	WPXL-TV	788	WQKL-FM	691	WQXI-AM	694
WPOL-AM	688	WPXM2-TV	788	WQKQ-FM	691	WQXK-FM	694
WPOP-AM	688	WPXM3-TV	788	WQKR-AM	691	WQXL-AM	694
WPOR-FM	688	WPXM-TV	788	WQKS-FM	691	WQXM-AM	694
WPOS-FM	688	WPXN2-TV	788	WQKT-FM	691	WQXO-AM	694
WPOW-FM	688	WPXN3-TV	788	WQKX-FM	691	WQXQ-FM	694
WPPA-AM	688	WPXN4-TV	788	WQKY-FM	691	WQXR-FM	694
WPPB-FM	688	WPXN-FM	689	WQKZ-FM	691	WQXT-TV	789
WPPG-FM	688	WPXN-TV	788	WQLA-AM	691	WQXZ-FM	694
WPPI-FM	688	WPXP2-TV	788	WQLB-FM	691	WQYK-FM	694
WPPL-FM	688	WPXP3-TV	788	WQLC-FM	691	WQYX-FM	694
WPPN-FM	688	WPXP-TV	789	WQLF-FM	691	WQYZ-FM	694
WPPR-FM	688	WPXQ2-TV	789	WQLH-FM	691	WQZK-FM	694
WPPX-TV	787	WPXQ3-TV	789	WQLI-FM	692	WQZL-FM	694
WPPZ-FM	688	WPXQ4-TV	789	WQLJ-FM	692	WQZQ-AM	694
WPRB-FM	688	WPXQ-TV	789	WQLK-FM	692	WQZS-FM	694
WPRD-AM	688	WPXR-TV	789	WQLL-AM	692	WQZX-FM	694
WPRE-AM	688	WPXS-TV	789	WQLN-FM	692	WQZY-FM	694
WPRI-TV	787	WPXT-TV	789	WQLN-TV	789	WRAA-FM	694
WPRJ-FM	688	WPXV-TV	789	WQLR-AM	692	WRAB-AM	694
WPRK-FM	688	WPXW2-TV	789	WQLT-FM	692	WRAC-FM	694
WPRO-AM	688	WPXW3-TV	789	WQLV-FM	692	WRAD-AM	694
		WPXW-TV	789	WQLX-FM	692	WRAF-FM	694

WSDV-AM

WVKF-FM

Call sign	Page
WVKF-FM	718
WVKL-FM	718
WVKO-AM	718
WVKR-FM	719
WVKS-FM	719
WVKX-FM	719
WVLA-TV	796
WVLC-FM	719
WVLD-AM	719
WVLE-FM	719
WVLF-FM	719
WVLG-AM	719
WVLI-FM	719
WVLK-AM	719
WVLK-FM	719
WVLN-AM	719
WVLR-TV	796
WVLS-FM	719
WVLT-FM	719
WVLT-TV	796
WVLY-AM	719
WVLY-FM	719
WVLZ-AM	719
WVMD-FM	719
WVMJ-FM	719
WVMM-FM	719
WVMP-FM	719
WVMR-AM	719
WVMS-FM	719
WVMT-AM	719
WVMX-FM	719
WVNA-AM	719
WVNA-FM	719
WVNE-AM	719
WVNH-FM	719
WVNI-FM	719
WVNJ-AM	719
WVNL-FM	719
WVNN-AM	719
WVNN-FM	719
WVNO-FM	719
WVNR-AM	719
WVNS-TV	796
WVNT-AM	719
WVNU-FM	719
WVNV-FM	719
WVNW-FM	720
WVNY-TV	796
WVNZ-AM	720
WVOB-FM	720
WVOC-AM	720
WVOC-FM	720
WVOD-FM	720
WVOE-AM	720
WVOG-AM	720
WVOH-FM	720
WVOI-AM	720
WVOJ-AM	720
WVOK-AM	720
WVOK-FM	720
WVOL-AM	720
WVOM-FM	720
WVON-AM	720
WVOP-AM	720
WVOR-FM	720
WVOS-AM	720
WVOS-FM	720
WVOT-AM	720
WVOV-AM	720
WVOW-AM	720
WVOW-FM	720
WVOX-AM	720
WVPA-FM	720
WVPN-FM	720
WVPO-AM	720
WVPR-FM	720
WVPS-FM	720
WVPX2-TV	796
WVPX3-TV	796
WVPX-TV	796
WVQM-FM	720
WVRA-FM	720
WVRB-FM	720
WVRC-AM	720
WVRC-FM	720
WVRE-FM	720
WVRK-FM	720
WVRQ-AM	720
WVRQ-FM	720
WVRR-FM	720
WVRT-FM	721
WVRV-FM	721
WVRW-FM	721
WVRY-FM	721
WVRZ-FM	721
WVSA-AM	721
WVSC-FM	721
WVSG-AM	721
WVSL-AM	721
WVSM-AM	721
WVSP-FM	721
WVSR-FM	721
WVSZ-FM	721
WVTF-FM	721
WVTJ-AM	721
WVTK-FM	721
WVTL-AM	721
WVTM2-TV	796
WVTM-TV	796
WVTQ-FM	721
WVTS-AM	721
WVTT-FM	721
WVTV-TV	796
WVTX-TV	796
WVUE2-TV	796
WVUE-TV	796
WVUM-FM	721
WVUS-AM	721
WVUV-FM	388
WVVA-TV	796
WVVC-FM	721
WVVE-FM	721
WVVH-TV	796
WVVI-FM	721
WVVL-FM	721
WVVR-FM	721
WVVV-FM	721
WVWC-FM	721
WVXG-FM	721
WVXM-FM	721
WVXR-FM	721
WVXU-FM	721
WVXX-AM	721
WVYB-FM	721
WVYC-FM	721
WVYS-FM	721
WVZA-FM	721
WWAB-AM	721
WWAC-FM	721
WWAG-FM	721
WWAV-FM	722
WWAX-FM	722
WWAY-TV	796
WWBA-AM	722
WWBB-FM	722
WWBC-AM	722
WWBD-FM	722
WWBF-AM	722
WWBG-AM	722
WWBJ-AM	722
WWBL-FM	722
WWBN-FM	722
WWBR-FM	722
WWBT-TV	796
WWBU-FM	722
WWCA-AM	722
WWCB-AM	722
WWCD-FM	722
WWCH-AM	722
WWCI-TV	796
WWCK-AM	722
WWCK-FM	722
WWCL-AM	722
WWCN-FM	722
WWCO-AM	722
WWCP-TV	796
WWCS-AM	722
WWCT-FM	722
WWCW-TV	796
WWDB-AM	722
WWDC-FM	722
WWDJ-AM	722
WWDK-FM	722
WWDM-FM	722
WWDN-AM	722
WWDP-TV	796
WWDR-AM	722
WWDV-FM	722
WWDW-FM	722
WWDX-AM	722
WWEB-FM	722
WWEC-FM	722
WWEG-FM	722
WWEL-FM	722
WWET-FM	722
WWEV-FM	722
WWFD-AM	723
WWFE-AM	723
WWFF-FM	723
WWFG-FM	723
WWFM-FM	723
WWFN-FM	723
WWFW-FM	723
WWFX-FM	723
WWFY-FM	723
WWGB-AM	723
WWGE-AM	723
WWGF-FM	723
WWGK-AM	723
WWGM-FM	723
WWGO-FM	723
WWGP-AM	723
WWGR-FM	723
WWGY-FM	723
WWHB-TV	796
WWHG-FM	723
WWHM-AM	723
WWHN-AM	723
WWHO-TV	796
WWHP-FM	723
WWHQ-FM	723
WWHT-FM	723
WWHX-FM	723
WWIB-FM	723
WWIC-AM	723
WWIK-FM	723
WWIL-AM	723
WWIL-FM	723
WWIN-AM	723
WWIN-FM	723
WWIS-AM	723
WWIS-FM	723
WWIZ-FM	723
WWJ-AM	723
WWJB-AM	723
WWJC-AM	723
WWJD-FM	723
WWJK-FM	723
WWJM-FM	723
WWJO-FM	724
WWJ-TV	796
WWKA-FM	724
WWKB-AM	724
WWKC-FM	724
WWKF-AM	724
WWKI-FM	724
WWKL-FM	724
WWKR-FM	724
WWKT-FM	724
WWKU-AM	724
WWKX-FM	724
WWKY-FM	724
WWKZ-FM	724
WWL-AM	724
WWLB-FM	724
WWLD-FM	724
WWLF-FM	724
WWLG-FM	724
WWLI-FM	724
WWLL-FM	724
WWLP-TV	796
WWLR-FM	724
WWLS-FM	724
WWL-TV	796
WWLW-FM	724
WWLX-AM	724
WWLZ-AM	724
WWMB-TV	796
WWMC-AM	724
WWME2-TV	796
WWME-TV	796
WWMG-FM	724
WWMJ-FM	724
WWMK-AM	724
WWMP-FM	724
WWMS-FM	724
WWMT2-TV	796
WWMT-TV	796
WWMX-FM	724
WWNB-AM	724
WWNC-AM	724
WWNJ-FM	724
WWNL-AM	724
WWNN-AM	724
WWNQ-FM	724
WWNR-AM	724
WWNS-AM	724
WWNW-FM	724
WWNY-TV	796
WWOD-FM	725
WWOF-FM	725
WWOJ-FM	725
WWOL-AM	725
WWOR3-TV	796
WWOR-TV	796
WWOS-AM	725
WWOT-FM	725
WWOW-AM	725
WWOZ-FM	725
WWPA-AM	725
WWPC-FM	725
WWPG-FM	725
WWPN-FM	725
WWPR-AM	725
WWPR-FM	725
WWPW-FM	725
WWQM-FM	725
WWQQ-FM	725
WWRC-AM	725
WWRE-FM	725
WWRF-AM	725
WWRK-AM	725
WWRL-AM	725
WWRM-FM	725
WWRQ-FM	725
WWRR-FM	725
WWRS2-TV	797
WWRS3-TV	797
WWRS4-TV	797
WWRS5-TV	797
WWRS-TV	797
WWRU-AM	725
WWRV-AM	725
WWRW-FM	725
WWRZ-FM	725
WWSB-TV	797
WWSC-AM	725
WWSE-FM	725
WWSF-AM	725
WWSI-TV	797
WWSJ-AM	725
WWSK-FM	725
WWSL-FM	725
WWSM-AM	725
WWSN-FM	725
WWSR-FM	725
WWST-FM	725
WWSW-FM	725
WWTC-AM	725
WWTF-FM	726
WWTH-FM	726
WWTI-TV	797
WWTK-AM	726
WWTM-AM	726
WWTN-FM	726
WWTO2-TV	797
WWTO3-TV	797
WWTO4-TV	797
WWTO5-TV	797
WWTO-TV	797
WWTR-AM	726
WWTV-TV	797
WWTX-AM	726
WWUF-FM	726
WWUS-FM	726
WWUZ-FM	726
WWVA-AM	726
WWVO-FM	726
WWVR-FM	726
WWVT-AM	726
WWWA-FM	726
WWWC-AM	726
WWWE-AM	726
WWWH-FM	726
WWWI-AM	726
WWWI-FM	726
WWWK-FM	726
WWWL-AM	726
WWWQ-FM	726
WWWS-AM	726
WWWT-FM	726
WWWV-FM	726
WWWW-FM	726
WWWX-FM	726
WWWY-FM	726
WWWZ-FM	726
WWXL-AM	726
WWXM-FM	726
WWXT-FM	726
WWXX-FM	726
WWYC-AM	726
WWYL-FM	726
WWYN-FM	726
WWYO-AM	726
WWYY-FM	726
WWYZ-FM	726
WWZD-FM	727
WWZQ-AM	727
WWZW-FM	727
WWZY-FM	727
WXAJ-FM	727
WXAM-AM	727
WXAN-FM	727
WXAX-TV	797
WXBB-FM	727
WXBC-FM	727
WXBD-AM	727
WXBM-FM	727
WXBN-FM	727
WXBQ-FM	727
WXBW-FM	727
WXBX-FM	727
WXCC-FM	727
WXCE-AM	727
WXCH-FM	727
WXCL-FM	727
WXCM-FM	727
WXCO-AM	727
WXCR-FM	727
WXCV-FM	727
WXCW2-TV	797
WXCW-TV	727
WXCX-FM	727
WXCY-FM	727
WXDE-FM	727
WXDJ-FM	727
WXDX-FM	727
WXEF-FM	727
WXEL2-TV	797
WXEL3-TV	797
WXEL4-TV	797